# For Reference

**Not to be taken from this room**

# AMERICA AT THE POLLS

## 1960–2004

## JOHN F. KENNEDY TO GEORGE W. BUSH

## A HANDBOOK OF AMERICAN PRESIDENTIAL ELECTION STATISTICS

ALICE V. MCGILLIVRAY
RICHARD M. SCAMMON
RHODES COOK

11-6-2006
WW
$175

CQ Press

A Division of Congressional Quarterly Inc.

1255 22nd St. N.W., Suite 400

Washington, D.C. 20037

Phone: 202-729-1900; toll-free, 1-866-427-7737 (1-866-4CQ-PRESS)

Web: www.cqpress.com

∞ The paper used in this publication exceeds the requirements of the American National Standard for Information Sciences—Permanence of Paper for Printed Library Materials, ANSI Z39.48-1992.

Printed and bound in the United States of America

09  08  07  06  05     1  2  3  4  5

**Library of Congress Cataloging-in-Publication Data**

America at the polls: a handbook of American presidential election
    statistics / [compiled by] Alice V. McGillivray, Richard M. Scammon.
          p.   cm.
       The election returns for the 1920 to 1964 presidential contests
    were originally published in 1965 by the University of Pittsburgh Press.
       Contents: [v. 1] Harding to Eisenhower, 1920–1956—[v. 2]
    John F. Kennedy to George W. Bush, 1960–2004.
       ISBN 1-56802-058-9 [v. 1].—ISBN 1-56802-977-2—[v. 2]
       1. Presidents—United States—Election—Statistics. 2. Elections—
    United States—History—20th century—Statistics.  I. McGillivray,
    Alice V., 1934–1995. II. Scammon, Richard M., 1915–2001.
    JK524.A73    1994
    324.973'09'021—dc20                               94-30937

# CONTENTS

# INTRODUCTION

*America at the Polls* reports American electoral behavior in presidential elections beginning with the 1920 Republican landslide victory of Warren G. Harding and Calvin Coolidge over Democrats James M. Cox and Franklin D. Roosevelt. This reference work provides students of American politics and elections with the state-by-state, county-by-county details of each presidential contest in an easy-to-read format.

The first volume covers the ten presidential elections from the 1920 Harding victory to the 1956 landslide win of Republican Dwight D. Eisenhower. The second begins with the narrow victory of Democrat John F. Kennedy over Republican Richard M. Nixon in 1960 and ends with the 2004 reelection of George W. Bush to the White House.

Both volumes follow the same pattern of organization: a front section containing national summary tables of the state-by-state vote and electoral college vote for each of the elections; a chapter for each state beginning with a summary page that sets out the statewide vote and electoral college vote in the state; a county outline map; and the county-by-county details of each election. Each decennial census is carried with the appropriate voting data tables that include the Republican-Democratic-Other breakdown, pluralities, and percentages of total and major party votes for Republican and Democratic candidates.

In special cases, when a third party candidate received an appreciable vote, the statistics have been expanded to a four-column format and the plurality is calculated on a first-second party basis. In the volume covering 1920 to 1956, this four-column format will be found in the 1924 data in the eighteen states in the West and Midwest where the Progressive candidate, Robert M. La Follette, received over 17 percent of the statewide vote, and in the 1948 tables in the four southern states that were carried by States' Rights candidate Strom Thurmond. The four-column format also is used for the 1956 elections in South Carolina where an independent elector ticket ran second statewide and carried almost one-half of the counties, and in Mississippi where an independent ticket carried a number of counties and ran second in many others.

In the volume starting with the 1960 election, state tables reflect the 1968 county-by-county vote cast for the American Independent candidate, George C. Wallace, the 1992 and 1996 vote cast for Ross Perot, an independent candidate in 1992 and head of the Reform Party in 1996, and the 2000 vote cast for the Green Party headed by Ralph Nader. Special four-column tables are also included for the 1960 vote in Mississippi where the unpledged delegate ticket carried the state and for the 1964 election in Alabama where the Democratic elector candidates were unpledged.

In using these volumes, readers should give special attention to the Notes sections for each state. These notes give the composition of the "Other" vote and indicate any special circumstances of the state vote such as dual elector tickets, canvassing problems, and discrepancies or corrections in the canvassed returns. Creation of new counties also is noted, and the county-by-county tables carry all counties that voted in any election year covered in the volume. Therefore, voting data for any unit of a state will be in the same order for each election. The exception is Virginia, where only the counties and independent cities that voted in each election are carried.

Population data are not available for counties created between decennial censuses, except for 1995. In earlier elections, it should be noted that some states required a vote for each individual elector and the data presented are for the "highest elector," except in Michigan and New Jersey as indicated in the Notes sections for these states.

The final section details the votes cast in the presidential preference primaries by state and candidate with a chronological state-by-state summary table for each election year covered in the volume.

Except where indicated in the state Notes sections, the data compiled in *America at the Polls* have been taken from the official state canvass reports. For a few of the early elections in the 1920–1956 volume, these reports have been supplemented and interpreted by reference to the reports of the Clerk of the House of Representatives, files in the National Archives, various state publications, contemporary almanacs, and press material. The most important sources for interpretation of data for the early elections have been the Edgar Eugene Robinson volumes: *The Presidential Vote, 1896–1932,* and *They Voted for Roosevelt: The Presidential Vote, 1932–1944.* Although differences will be noted in the data published in *America at the Polls* and the figures used in these and other reference studies, the differences usually will be small and stem most often from varying interpretations of the available statistics.

The election returns for the 1920 to 1964 presidential contests contained in these volumes were originally published in 1965 in *America at the Polls.* That work, which is out of print, presented the returns in a more difficult to read format and did not include many enhancements that have been added to the new compilation. The current volumes include census data for each decade; additional columns of votes for prominent candidates outside the major parties, such as La Follette, Thurmond, Wallace, Perot, and Nader; county outline maps; and statewide summary vote tables. Perhaps most important for the user, all the tables for each of the elections are presented in the same format.

# UNITED STATES

## POPULAR VOTE FOR PRESIDENT 1920 TO 2004

| Year | Total Vote | Republican Vote | Republican Candidate | Democratic Vote | Democratic Candidate | Other Vote | Plurality | Percentage Total Vote Rep. | Total Vote Dem. | Major Vote Rep. | Major Vote Dem. |
|---|---|---|---|---|---|---|---|---|---|---|---|
| 2004 | 122,295,345 | 62,040,610 | Bush, George W. | 59,028,439 | Kerry, John | 1,226,296 | 3,012,171 R | 50.7% | 48.3% | 51.2% | 48.8% |
| 2000 | 105,396,627 | 50,455,156 | Bush, George W. | 50,992,335 | Gore, Al | 3,949,136 | 537,179 D | 47.9% | 48.4% | 49.7% | 50.3% |
| 1996 | 96,277,872 | 39,198,755 | Dole, Bob | 47,402,357 | Clinton, Bill | 9,676,760 | 8,203,602 D | 40.7% | 49.2% | 45.3% | 54.7% |
| 1992 | 104,425,014 | 39,103,882 | Bush, George | 44,909,326 | Clinton, Bill | 20,411,806 | 5,805,444 D | 37.4% | 43.0% | 46.5% | 53.5% |
| 1988 | 91,594,809 | 48,886,097 | Bush, George | 41,809,074 | Dukakis, Michael S. | 899,638 | 7,077,023 R | 53.4% | 45.6% | 53.9% | 46.1% |
| 1984 | 92,652,842 | 54,455,075 | Reagan, Ronald | 37,577,185 | Mondale, Walter F. | 620,582 | 16,877,890 R | 58.8% | 40.6% | 59.2% | 40.8% |
| 1980 | 86,515,221 | 43,904,153 | Reagan, Ronald | 35,483,883 | Carter, Jimmy | 7,127,185 | 8,420,270 R | 50.7% | 41.0% | 55.3% | 44.7% |
| 1976 | 81,555,889 | 39,147,793 | Ford, Gerald R. | 40,830,763 | Carter, Jimmy | 1,577,333 | 1,682,970 D | 48.0% | 50.1% | 48.9% | 51.1% |
| 1972 | 77,718,554 | 47,169,911 | Nixon, Richard M. | 29,170,383 | McGovern, George S. | 1,378,260 | 17,999,528 R | 60.7% | 37.5% | 61.8% | 38.2% |
| 1968 | 73,211,875 | 31,785,480 | Nixon, Richard M. | 31,275,166 | Humphrey, Hubert H. | 10,151,229 | 510,314 R | 43.4% | 42.7% | 50.4% | 49.6% |
| 1964 | 70,644,592 | 27,178,188 | Goldwater, Barry M. | 43,129,566 | Johnson, Lyndon B. | 336,838 | 15,951,378 D | 38.5% | 61.1% | 38.7% | 61.3% |
| 1960 | 68,838,219 | 34,108,157 | Nixon, Richard M. | 34,226,731 | Kennedy, John F. | 503,331 | 118,574 D | 49.5% | 49.7% | 49.9% | 50.1% |
| 1956 | 62,026,908 | 35,590,472 | Eisenhower, Dwight D. | 26,022,752 | Stevenson, Adlai E. | 413,684 | 9,567,720 R | 57.4% | 42.0% | 57.8% | 42.2% |
| 1952 | 61,550,918 | 33,936,234 | Eisenhower, Dwight D. | 27,314,992 | Stevenson, Adlai E. | 299,692 | 6,621,242 R | 55.1% | 44.4% | 55.4% | 44.6% |
| 1948 | 48,793,826 | 21,991,291 | Dewey, Thomas E. | 24,179,345 | Truman, Harry S. | 2,623,190 | 2,188,054 D | 45.1% | 49.6% | 47.6% | 52.4% |
| 1944 | 47,976,670 | 22,017,617 | Dewey, Thomas E. | 25,612,610 | Roosevelt, Franklin D. | 346,443 | 3,594,993 D | 45.9% | 53.4% | 46.2% | 53.8% |
| 1940 | 49,900,418 | 22,348,480 | Willkie, Wendell | 27,313,041 | Roosevelt, Franklin D. | 238,897 | 4,964,561 D | 44.8% | 54.7% | 45.0% | 55.0% |
| 1936 | 45,654,763 | 16,684,231 | Landon, Alfred M. | 27,757,333 | Roosevelt, Franklin D. | 1,213,199 | 11,073,102 D | 36.5% | 60.8% | 37.5% | 62.5% |
| 1932 | 39,758,759 | 15,760,684 | Hoover, Herbert C. | 22,829,501 | Roosevelt, Franklin D. | 1,168,574 | 7,068,817 D | 39.6% | 57.4% | 40.8% | 59.2% |
| 1928 | 36,805,951 | 21,437,277 | Hoover, Herbert C. | 15,007,698 | Smith, Alfred E. | 360,976 | 6,429,579 R | 58.2% | 40.8% | 58.8% | 41.2% |
| 1924 | 29,095,023 | 15,719,921 | Coolidge, Calvin | 8,386,704 | Davis, John W. | 4,988,398 | 7,333,217 R | 54.0% | 28.8% | 65.2% | 34.8% |
| 1920 | 26,768,613 | 16,153,115 | Harding, Warren G. | 9,133,092 | Cox, James M. | 1,482,406 | 7,020,023 R | 60.3% | 34.1% | 63.9% | 36.1% |

Note: For detail of other vote see note section included with each U.S. summary table that follows.

## ELECTORAL COLLEGE VOTE 1920 TO 2004

| Year | Total | Republican | Democratic | Other | |
|---|---|---|---|---|---|
| 2004 | 538 | 286 | 251 | 1 | EDWARDS |
| 2000 | 538 | 271 | 266 | 1 | (Blank) |
| 1996 | 538 | 159 | 379 | — | |
| 1992 | 538 | 168 | 370 | — | |
| 1988 | 538 | 426 | 111 | 1 | BENTSEN |
| 1984 | 538 | 525 | 13 | — | |
| 1980 | 538 | 489 | 49 | — | |
| 1976 | 538 | 240 | 297 | 1 | REAGAN |
| 1972 | 538 | 520 | 17 | 1 | LIBERTARIAN |
| 1968 | 538 | 301 | 191 | 46 | AIP |
| 1964 | 538 | 52 | 486 | — | |
| 1960 | 537 | 219 | 303 | 15 | BYRD |
| 1956 | 531 | 457 | 73 | 1 | JONES |
| 1952 | 531 | 442 | 89 | — | |
| 1948 | 531 | 189 | 303 | 39 | SR |
| 1944 | 531 | 99 | 432 | — | |
| 1940 | 531 | 82 | 449 | — | |
| 1936 | 531 | 8 | 523 | — | |
| 1932 | 531 | 59 | 472 | — | |
| 1928 | 531 | 444 | 87 | — | |
| 1924 | 531 | 382 | 136 | 13 | PROGRESSIVE |
| 1920 | 531 | 404 | 127 | — | |

# PRESIDENT 2004

In New York the Republican total includes votes for their candidate on the Conservative line and the Democratic total includes votes for their candidate on the Working Families line.

In Minnesota the Democratic candidate appears on the ballot as Democratic-Farmer-Labor; in North Dakota as Democratic-Nonpartisan League. In many states various third party candidates appeared on the ballot with variations of the party designations, were carried with entirely different party labels, or were listed as "Independent." The state notes sections list the party labels used by the third party candidates.

The candidates listed below include all who appeared on the ballot in at least one state. Write-in votes for third party candidates are credited to their total below.

| | |
|---|---|
| 62,040,610 | George W. Bush and Richard B. Cheney, *Republican* |
| 59,028,439 | John Kerry and John Edwards, *Democratic* |
| 465,650 | Ralph Nader and Peter Miguel Camejo, *Independent* |
| 397,265 | Michael Badnarik and Richard V. Campagna, *Libertarian* |
| 143,630 | Michael Peroutka and Chuck Baldwin, *Constitution* |
| 119,859 | David Cobb and Patricia LaMarche, *Green* |
| 27,607 | Leonard Peltier and Janice Jordan, *Peace and Freedom* |
| 10,837 | Walter F. Brown and Mary Alice Herbert, *Socialist* |
| 7,102 | James Harris and Margaret Trowe, *Socialist Workers* |
| 3,689 | Roger Calero and Arrin Hawkins, *Socialist Workers* |
| 2,387 | Thomas J. Harens and Jennifer A. Ryan, *Christian Freedom* |
| 1,944 | Gene Amondson and Leroy Pletten, *Concerns of People* |
| 1,861 | Bill Van Auken and Jim Lawrence, *Socialist Equality* |
| 1,646 | John Parker and Teresa Gutierrez, *Workers World* |
| 946 | Charles Jay and Marilyn Chambers Taylor, *Personal Choice* |
| 804 | Stanford E. "Andy" Andress and Irene M. Deasy, *Unaffiliated* |
| 140 | Earl F. Dodge and Howard F. Lydick, *Prohibition* |

In addition to the votes listed above, 37,241 scattered write-in votes were reported from various states, and 3,688 votes were cast for "None of these Candidates" in Nevada.

# UNITED STATES

## PRESIDENT 2004

| State | Electoral Vote Rep. | Electoral Vote Dem. | Electoral Vote Other | Total Vote | Republican | Democratic | Other | Rep.-Dem. Plurality | Percentage Total Vote Rep. | Percentage Total Vote Dem. | Percentage Major Vote Rep. | Percentage Major Vote Dem. |
|---|---|---|---|---|---|---|---|---|---|---|---|---|
| Alabama | 9 | | | 1,883,449 | 1,176,394 | 693,933 | 13,122 | 482,461 R | 62.5% | 36.8% | 62.9% | 37.1% |
| Alaska | 3 | | | 312,598 | 190,889 | 111,025 | 10,684 | 79,864 R | 61.1% | 35.5% | 63.2% | 36.8% |
| Arizona | 10 | | | 2,012,585 | 1,104,294 | 893,524 | 14,767 | 210,770 R | 54.9% | 44.4% | 55.3% | 44.7% |
| Arkansas | 6 | | | 1,054,945 | 572,898 | 469,953 | 12,094 | 102,945 R | 54.3% | 44.5% | 54.9% | 45.1% |
| California | | 55 | | 12,421,852 | 5,509,826 | 6,745,485 | 166,541 | 1,235,659 D | 44.4% | 54.3% | 45.0% | 55.0% |
| Colorado | 9 | | | 2,130,330 | 1,101,255 | 1,001,732 | 27,343 | 99,523 R | 51.7% | 47.0% | 52.4% | 47.6% |
| Connecticut | | 7 | | 1,578,769 | 693,826 | 857,488 | 27,455 | 163,662 D | 43.9% | 54.3% | 44.7% | 55.3% |
| Delaware | | 3 | | 375,190 | 171,660 | 200,152 | 3,378 | 28,492 D | 45.8% | 53.3% | 46.2% | 53.8% |
| Florida | 27 | | | 7,609,810 | 3,964,522 | 3,583,544 | 61,744 | 380,978 R | 52.1% | 47.1% | 52.5% | 47.5% |
| Georgia | 15 | | | 3,301,875 | 1,914,254 | 1,366,149 | 21,472 | 548,105 R | 58.0% | 41.4% | 58.4% | 41.6% |
| Hawaii | | 4 | | 429,013 | 194,191 | 231,708 | 3,114 | 37,517 D | 45.3% | 54.0% | 45.6% | 54.4% |
| Idaho | 4 | | | 598,447 | 409,235 | 181,098 | 8,114 | 228,137 R | 68.4% | 30.3% | 69.3% | 30.7% |
| Illinois | | 21 | | 5,274,322 | 2,345,946 | 2,891,550 | 36,826 | 545,604 D | 44.5% | 54.8% | 44.8% | 55.2% |
| Indiana | 11 | | | 2,468,002 | 1,479,438 | 969,011 | 19,553 | 510,427 R | 59.9% | 39.3% | 60.4% | 39.6% |
| Iowa | 7 | | | 1,506,908 | 751,957 | 741,898 | 13,053 | 10,059 R | 49.9% | 49.2% | 50.3% | 49.7% |
| Kansas | 6 | | | 1,187,756 | 736,456 | 434,993 | 16,307 | 301,463 R | 62.0% | 36.6% | 62.9% | 37.1% |
| Kentucky | 8 | | | 1,795,882 | 1,069,439 | 712,733 | 13,710 | 356,706 R | 59.5% | 39.7% | 60.0% | 40.0% |
| Louisiana | 9 | | | 1,943,106 | 1,102,169 | 820,299 | 20,638 | 281,870 R | 56.7% | 42.2% | 57.3% | 42.7% |
| Maine | | 4 | | 740,752 | 330,201 | 396,842 | 13,709 | 66,641 D | 44.6% | 53.6% | 45.4% | 54.6% |
| Maryland | | 10 | | 2,386,678 | 1,024,703 | 1,334,493 | 27,482 | 309,790 D | 42.9% | 55.9% | 43.4% | 56.6% |
| Massachusetts | | 12 | | 2,912,388 | 1,071,109 | 1,803,800 | 37,479 | 732,691 D | 36.8% | 61.9% | 37.3% | 62.7% |
| Michigan | | 17 | | 4,839,252 | 2,313,746 | 2,479,183 | 46,323 | 165,437 D | 47.8% | 51.2% | 48.3% | 51.7% |
| Minnesota | | 9 | 1 | 2,828,387 | 1,346,695 | 1,445,014 | 36,678 | 98,319 D | 47.6% | 51.1% | 48.2% | 51.8% |
| Mississippi | 6 | | | 1,152,145 | 684,981 | 458,094 | 9,070 | 226,887 R | 59.5% | 39.8% | 59.9% | 40.1% |
| Missouri | 11 | | | 2,731,364 | 1,455,713 | 1,259,171 | 16,480 | 196,542 R | 53.3% | 46.1% | 53.6% | 46.4% |
| Montana | 3 | | | 450,445 | 266,063 | 173,710 | 10,672 | 92,353 R | 59.1% | 38.6% | 60.5% | 39.5% |
| Nebraska | 5 | | | 778,186 | 512,814 | 254,328 | 11,044 | 258,486 R | 65.9% | 32.7% | 66.8% | 33.2% |
| Nevada | 5 | | | 829,587 | 418,690 | 397,190 | 13,707 | 21,500 R | 50.5% | 47.9% | 51.3% | 48.7% |
| New Hampshire | | 4 | | 677,738 | 331,237 | 340,511 | 5,990 | 9,274 D | 48.9% | 50.2% | 49.3% | 50.7% |
| New Jersey | | 15 | | 3,611,691 | 1,670,003 | 1,911,430 | 30,258 | 241,427 D | 46.2% | 52.9% | 46.6% | 53.4% |
| New Mexico | 5 | | | 756,304 | 376,930 | 370,942 | 8,432 | 5,988 R | 49.8% | 49.0% | 50.4% | 49.6% |
| New York | | 31 | | 7,391,036 | 2,962,567 | 4,314,280 | 114,189 | 1,351,713 D | 40.1% | 58.4% | 40.7% | 59.3% |
| North Carolina | 15 | | | 3,501,007 | 1,961,166 | 1,525,849 | 13,992 | 435,317 R | 56.0% | 43.6% | 56.2% | 43.8% |
| North Dakota | 3 | | | 312,833 | 196,651 | 111,052 | 5,130 | 85,599 R | 62.9% | 35.5% | 63.9% | 36.1% |
| Ohio | 20 | | | 5,627,908 | 2,859,768 | 2,741,167 | 26,973 | 118,601 R | 50.8% | 48.7% | 51.1% | 48.9% |
| Oklahoma | 7 | | | 1,463,758 | 959,792 | 503,966 | | 455,826 R | 65.6% | 34.4% | 65.6% | 34.4% |
| Oregon | | 7 | | 1,836,782 | 866,831 | 943,163 | 26,788 | 76,332 D | 47.2% | 51.3% | 47.9% | 52.1% |
| Pennsylvania | | 21 | | 5,769,590 | 2,793,847 | 2,938,095 | 37,648 | 144,248 D | 48.4% | 50.9% | 48.7% | 51.3% |
| Rhode Island | | 4 | | 437,134 | 169,046 | 259,760 | 8,328 | 90,714 D | 38.7% | 59.4% | 39.4% | 60.6% |
| South Carolina | 8 | | | 1,617,730 | 937,974 | 661,699 | 18,057 | 276,275 R | 58.0% | 40.9% | 58.6% | 41.4% |
| South Dakota | 3 | | | 388,215 | 232,584 | 149,244 | 6,387 | 83,340 R | 59.9% | 38.4% | 60.9% | 39.1% |
| Tennessee | 11 | | | 2,437,319 | 1,384,375 | 1,036,477 | 16,467 | 347,898 R | 56.8% | 42.5% | 57.2% | 42.8% |
| Texas | 34 | | | 7,410,765 | 4,526,917 | 2,832,704 | 51,144 | 1,694,213 R | 61.1% | 38.2% | 61.5% | 38.5% |
| Utah | 5 | | | 927,844 | 663,742 | 241,199 | 22,903 | 422,543 R | 71.5% | 26.0% | 73.3% | 26.7% |
| Vermont | | 3 | | 312,309 | 121,180 | 184,067 | 7,062 | 62,887 D | 38.8% | 58.9% | 39.7% | 60.3% |
| Virginia | 13 | | | 3,198,367 | 1,716,959 | 1,454,742 | 26,666 | 262,217 R | 53.7% | 45.5% | 54.1% | 45.9% |
| Washington | | 11 | | 2,859,084 | 1,304,894 | 1,510,201 | 43,989 | 205,307 D | 45.6% | 52.8% | 46.4% | 53.6% |
| West Virginia | 5 | | | 755,887 | 423,778 | 326,541 | 5,568 | 97,237 R | 56.1% | 43.2% | 56.5% | 43.5% |
| Wisconsin | | 10 | | 2,997,007 | 1,478,120 | 1,489,504 | 29,383 | 11,384 D | 49.3% | 49.7% | 49.8% | 50.2% |
| Wyoming | 3 | | | 243,428 | 167,629 | 70,776 | 5,023 | 96,853 R | 68.9% | 29.1% | 70.3% | 29.7% |
| District of Columbia | | 3 | | 227,586 | 21,256 | 202,970 | 3,360 | 181,714 D | 9.3% | 89.2% | 9.5% | 90.5% |
| Total | 286 | 251 | 1 | 122,295,345 | 62,040,610 | 59,028,439 | 1,226,296 | 3,012,171 R | 50.7% | 48.3% | 51.2% | 48.8% |

Note: A Democratic elector in Minnesota cast a vote for Edwards rather than Kerry.

# PRESIDENT 2000

In New York the Republican figures include Conservative and the Democratic figures include Liberal and Working Families.

In Minnesota the Democratic candidate appears on the ballot as Democratic-Farmer-Labor. In many states various non-major party candidates appeared on the ballot with variations of the party designations, were carried with entirely different party labels, or were listed as "Independent." The state Notes sections list the party labels used by the minor party candidates.

The candidates listed below include all who appeared on the ballot in at least one state. Write-in votes for minor party candidates are credited to their total below.

| | |
|---:|---|
| 50,455,156 | George W. Bush and Richard B. Cheney, *Republican* |
| 50,992,335 | Al Gore and Joseph I. Lieberman, *Democratic* |
| 2,882,738 | Ralph Nader and Winona La Duke, *Green* |
| 449,077 | Pat Buchanan and Ezola Foster, *Reform* |
| 384,429 | Harry Browne and Art Olivie, *Libertarian* |
| 98,020 | Howard Phillips and J. Curtis Frazier, *Constitution* |
| 83,525 | John Hagelin and Nat Goldhaber, *Natural Law* |
| 7,378 | James E. Harris, Jr. and Margaret Trowe, *Socialist Worker* |
| 5,775 | L. Neil Smith and Vin Suprynowicz, *Arizona Libertarian* |
| 5,602 | David McReynolds and Mary Cal Hollis, *Socialist* |
| 4,795 | Monica Moorehead and Gloria La Riva, *Workers World* |
| 1,606 | Cathy Gordon Brown and Sabrina R. Allen, *Independent* |
| 1,044 | Denny Lane and Dale Wilkinson, *Vermont Grassroots* |
| 535 | Randall Venson and Gene Kelly, *Independent* |
| 208 | Earl F. Dodge and W. Dean Watkins, *Prohibition* |
| 161 | Louie G. Youngkeit and Robert Leo Beck, *Unaffiliated* |

# UNITED STATES

## PRESIDENT 2000

| State | Electoral Vote Rep. | Dem. | Other | Total Vote | Republican | Democratic | Green (Nader) | Other | Rep.-Dem. Plurality | Percentage Rep. | Dem. | Green |
|---|---|---|---|---|---|---|---|---|---|---|---|---|
| Alabama | 9 | | | 1,666,272 | 941,173 | 692,611 | 18,323 | 14,165 | 248,562 R | 56.5% | 41.6% | 1.1% |
| Alaska | 3 | | | 285,560 | 167,398 | 79,004 | 28,747 | 10,411 | 88,394 R | 58.6% | 27.7% | 10.1% |
| Arizona | 8 | | | 1,532,016 | 781,652 | 685,341 | 45,645 | 19,378 | 96,311 R | 51.0% | 44.7% | 3.0% |
| Arkansas | 6 | | | 921,781 | 472,940 | 422,768 | 13,421 | 12,652 | 50,172 R | 51.3% | 45.9% | 1.5% |
| California | | 54 | | 10,965,856 | 4,567,429 | 5,861,203 | 418,707 | 118,517 | 1,293,774 D | 41.7% | 53.4% | 3.8% |
| Colorado | 8 | | | 1,741,368 | 883,748 | 738,227 | 91,434 | 27,959 | 145,521 R | 50.8% | 42.4% | 5.3% |
| Connecticut | | 8 | | 1,459,525 | 561,094 | 816,015 | 64,452 | 17,964 | 254,921 D | 38.4% | 55.9% | 4.4% |
| Delaware | | 3 | | 327,622 | 137,288 | 180,068 | 8,307 | 1,959 | 42,780 D | 41.9% | 55.0% | 2.5% |
| Florida | 25 | | | 5,963,110 | 2,912,790 | 2,912,253 | 97,488 | 40,579 | 537 R | 48.8% | 48.8% | 1.6% |
| Georgia | 13 | | | 2,596,645 | 1,419,720 | 1,116,230 | 13,273 | 47,422 | 303,490 R | 54.7% | 43.0% | 0.5% |
| Hawaii | | 4 | | 367,951 | 137,845 | 205,286 | 21,623 | 3,197 | 67,441 D | 37.5% | 55.8% | 5.9% |
| Idaho | 4 | | | 501,621 | 336,937 | 138,637 | 12,292 | 13,755 | 198,300 R | 67.2% | 27.6% | 2.5% |
| Illinois | | 22 | | 4,742,123 | 2,019,421 | 2,589,026 | 103,759 | 29,917 | 569,605 D | 42.6% | 54.6% | 2.2% |
| Indiana | 12 | | | 2,199,302 | 1,245,836 | 901,980 | 18,531 | 32,955 | 343,856 R | 56.6% | 41.0% | 0.8% |
| Iowa | | 7 | | 1,315,563 | 634,373 | 638,517 | 29,374 | 13,299 | 4,144 D | 48.2% | 48.5% | 2.2% |
| Kansas | 6 | | | 1,072,218 | 622,332 | 399,276 | 36,086 | 14,524 | 223,056 R | 58.0% | 37.2% | 3.4% |
| Kentucky | 8 | | | 1,544,187 | 872,492 | 638,898 | 23,192 | 9,605 | 233,594 R | 56.5% | 41.4% | 1.5% |
| Louisiana | 9 | | | 1,765,656 | 927,871 | 792,344 | 20,473 | 24,968 | 135,527 R | 52.6% | 44.9% | 1.2% |
| Maine | | 4 | | 651,817 | 286,616 | 319,951 | 37,127 | 8,123 | 33,335 D | 44.0% | 49.1% | 5.7% |
| Maryland | | 10 | | 2,020,480 | 813,797 | 1,140,782 | 53,768 | 12,133 | 326,985 D | 40.3% | 56.5% | 2.7% |
| Massachusetts | | 12 | | 2,702,984 | 878,502 | 1,616,487 | 173,564 | 34,431 | 737,985 D | 32.5% | 59.8% | 6.4% |
| Michigan | | 18 | | 4,232,711 | 1,953,139 | 2,170,418 | 84,165 | 24,989 | 217,279 D | 46.1% | 51.3% | 2.0% |
| Minnesota | | 10 | | 2,438,685 | 1,109,659 | 1,168,266 | 126,696 | 34,064 | 58,607 D | 45.5% | 47.9% | 5.2% |
| Mississippi | 7 | | | 994,184 | 572,844 | 404,614 | 8,122 | 8,604 | 168,230 R | 57.6% | 40.7% | 0.8% |
| Missouri | 11 | | | 2,359,892 | 1,189,924 | 1,111,138 | 38,515 | 20,315 | 78,786 R | 50.4% | 47.1% | 1.6% |
| Montana | 3 | | | 410,997 | 240,178 | 137,126 | 24,437 | 9,256 | 103,052 R | 58.4% | 33.4% | 5.9% |
| Nebraska | 5 | | | 697,019 | 433,862 | 231,780 | 24,540 | 6,837 | 202,082 R | 62.2% | 33.3% | 3.5% |
| Nevada | 4 | | | 608,970 | 301,575 | 279,978 | 15,008 | 12,409 | 21,597 R | 49.5% | 46.0% | 2.5% |
| New Hampshire | 4 | | | 569,081 | 273,559 | 266,348 | 22,198 | 6,976 | 7,211 R | 48.1% | 46.8% | 3.9% |
| New Jersey | | 15 | | 3,187,226 | 1,284,173 | 1,788,850 | 94,554 | 19,649 | 504,677 D | 40.3% | 56.1% | 3.0% |
| New Mexico | | 5 | | 598,605 | 286,417 | 286,783 | 21,251 | 4,154 | 366 D | 47.8% | 47.9% | 3.6% |
| New York | | 33 | | 6,821,999 | 2,403,374 | 4,107,697 | 244,030 | 66,898 | 1,704,323 D | 35.2% | 60.2% | 3.6% |
| North Carolina | 14 | | | 2,911,262 | 1,631,163 | 1,257,692 | — | 22,407 | 373,471 R | 56.0% | 43.2% | — |
| North Dakota | 3 | | | 288,256 | 174,852 | 95,284 | 9,486 | 8,634 | 79,568 R | 60.7% | 33.1% | 3.3% |
| Ohio | 21 | | | 4,701,998 | 2,350,363 | 2,183,628 | 117,799 | 50,208 | 166,735 R | 50.0% | 46.4% | 2.5% |
| Oklahoma | 8 | | | 1,234,229 | 744,337 | 474,276 | | 15,616 | 270,061 R | 60.3% | 38.4% | — |
| Oregon | | 7 | | 1,533,968 | 713,577 | 720,342 | 77,357 | 22,692 | 6,765 D | 46.5% | 47.0% | 5.0% |
| Pennsylvania | | 23 | | 4,913,119 | 2,281,127 | 2,485,967 | 103,392 | 42,633 | 204,840 D | 46.4% | 50.6% | 2.1% |
| Rhode Island | | 4 | | 409,047 | 130,555 | 249,508 | 25,052 | 3,932 | 118,953 D | 31.9% | 61.0% | 6.1% |
| South Carolina | 8 | | | 1,382,717 | 785,937 | 565,561 | 20,200 | 11,019 | 220,376 R | 56.8% | 40.9% | 1.5% |
| South Dakota | 3 | | | 316,269 | 190,700 | 118,804 | — | 6,765 | 71,896 R | 60.3% | 37.6% | — |
| Tennessee | 11 | | | 2,076,181 | 1,061,949 | 981,720 | 19,781 | 12,731 | 80,229 R | 51.1% | 47.3% | 1.0% |
| Texas | 32 | | | 6,407,637 | 3,799,639 | 2,433,746 | 137,994 | 36,258 | 1,365,893 R | 59.3% | 38.0% | 2.2% |
| Utah | 5 | | | 770,754 | 515,096 | 203,053 | 35,850 | 16,755 | 312,043 R | 66.8% | 26.3% | 4.7% |
| Vermont | | 3 | | 294,308 | 119,775 | 149,022 | 20,374 | 5,137 | 29,247 D | 40.7% | 50.6% | 6.9% |
| Virginia | 13 | | | 2,739,447 | 1,437,490 | 1,217,290 | 59,398 | 25,269 | 220,200 R | 52.5% | 44.4% | 2.2% |
| Washington | | 11 | | 2,487,433 | 1,108,864 | 1,247,652 | 103,002 | 27,915 | 138,788 D | 44.6% | 50.2% | 4.1% |
| West Virginia | 5 | | | 648,124 | 336,475 | 295,497 | 10,680 | 5,472 | 40,978 R | 51.9% | 45.6% | 1.6% |
| Wisconsin | | 11 | | 2,598,607 | 1,237,279 | 1,242,987 | 94,070 | 24,271 | 5,708 D | 47.6% | 47.8% | 3.6% |
| Wyoming | 3 | | | 218,351 | 147,947 | 60,481 | 4,625 | 5,298 | 87,466 R | 67.8% | 27.7% | 2.1% |
| District of Columbia | | 2 | 1 | 201,894 | 18,073 | 171,923 | 10,576 | 1,322 | 153,850 D | 9.0% | 85.2% | 5.2% |
| United States | 271 | 266 | 1 | 105,396,627 | 50,455,156 | 50,992,335 | 2,882,738 | 1,066,398 | 537,179 D | 47.9% | 48.4% | 2.7% |

# PRESIDENT 1996

In New York the Republican figures include Conservative, Freedom, and Right to Life votes and the Democratic figures include Liberal votes.

In Minnesota the Democratic candidate appears on the ballot as Democratic-Farmer-Labor. In many states various non-major party candidates appeared on the ballot with variations of the party designations, were carried with entirely different party labels or listed as "Independent". The state Note sections list the party labels used by the minor party candidates.

The candidates listed below include all those who appeared on the ballot in at least one state. Write-in votes for minor party candidates are credited to their total below.

| | |
|---:|---|
| 47,402,357 | Bill Clinton and Al Gore, *Democratic.* |
| 39,198,755 | Bob Dole and Jack Kemp, *Republican.* |
| 8,085,402 | Ross Perot and Pat Choate, *Reform.* |
| 685,040 | Ralph Nader and Winona LaDuke, *Green.* |
| 485,798 | Harry Browne and Jo Jorgensen, *Libertarian.* |
| 184,658 | Howard Phillips and Herbert W. Titus, *U.S. Taxpayers.* |
| 113,668 | John Hagelin and Mike Tompkins, *Natural Law.* |
| 29,083 | Monica Moorehead and Gloria La Riva, *Workers World.* |
| 25,332 | Marsha Feinland and Kate McClatchy, *Peace and Freedom.* |
| 8,930 | Charles Collins and Rosemary Giumarra, *Independent.* |
| 8,476 | James Harris and Laura Garza, *Socialist Workers.* |
| 5,378 | Dennis Peron and Arlin D. Troutt Jr., *Grassroots.* |
| 4,706 | Mary Cal Hollis and Eric Chester, *Socialist.* |
| 2,438 | Jerome White and Fred Mazelis, *Socialist Equality.* |
| 1,847 | Diane Beall Templin and Gary Van Horn, *American.* |
| 1,298 | Earl F. Dodge and Rachel B. Kelly, *Prohibition.* |
| 1,101 | A. Peter Crane and Connie Chandler, *Independent.* |
| 932 | Ralph Forbes and Pro-Life Anderson, *America First.* |
| 787 | John Birrenbach and George McMahon, *Independent Grassroots.* |
| 752 | Isabell Masters and Shirley Jean Masters, *Looking Back.* |
| 408 | Steve Michael and Ann Northrop, *Independent.* |

In addition to the votes listed above, 25,118 scattered write-in votes were reported from various states, and 5,608 votes were cast for "None of these Candidates" in Nevada.

# UNITED STATES

## PRESIDENT 1996

| State | Electoral Vote Rep. | Electoral Vote Dem. | Electoral Vote Other | Total Vote | Republican | Democratic | Reform | Other | Plurality | | Percentage Rep. | Percentage Dem. | Percentage Reform |
|---|---|---|---|---|---|---|---|---|---|---|---|---|---|
| Alabama | 9 | | | 1,534,349 | 769,044 | 662,165 | 92,149 | 10,991 | 106,879 | R | 50.1% | 43.2% | 6.0% |
| Alaska | 3 | | | 241,620 | 122,746 | 80,380 | 26,333 | 12,161 | 42,366 | R | 50.8% | 33.3% | 10.9% |
| Arizona | | 8 | | 1,404,405 | 622,073 | 653,288 | 112,072 | 16,972 | 31,215 | D | 44.3% | 46.5% | 8.0% |
| Arkansas | | 6 | | 884,262 | 325,416 | 475,171 | 69,884 | 13,791 | 149,755 | D | 36.8% | 53.7% | 7.9% |
| California | | 54 | | 10,019,484 | 3,828,380 | 5,119,835 | 697,847 | 373,422 | 1,291,455 | D | 38.2% | 51.1% | 7.0% |
| Colorado | 8 | | | 1,510,704 | 691,848 | 671,152 | 99,629 | 48,075 | 20,696 | R | 45.8% | 44.4% | 6.6% |
| Connecticut | | 8 | | 1,392,614 | 483,109 | 735,740 | 139,523 | 34,242 | 252,631 | D | 34.7% | 52.8% | 10.0% |
| Delaware | | 3 | | 271,084 | 99,062 | 140,355 | 28,719 | 2,948 | 41,293 | D | 36.5% | 51.8% | 10.6% |
| Florida | | 25 | | 5,303,794 | 2,244,536 | 2,546,870 | 483,870 | 28,518 | 302,334 | D | 42.3% | 48.0% | 9.1% |
| Georgia | 13 | | | 2,299,071 | 1,080,843 | 1,053,849 | 146,337 | 18,042 | 26,994 | R | 47.0% | 45.8% | 6.4% |
| Hawaii | | 4 | | 360,120 | 113,943 | 205,012 | 27,358 | 13,807 | 91,069 | D | 31.6% | 56.9% | 7.6% |
| Idaho | 4 | | | 491,719 | 256,595 | 165,443 | 62,518 | 7,163 | 91,152 | R | 52.2% | 33.6% | 12.7% |
| Illinois | | 22 | | 4,311,391 | 1,587,021 | 2,341,744 | 346,608 | 36,218 | 754,723 | D | 36.8% | 54.3% | 8.0% |
| Indiana | 12 | | | 2,135,842 | 1,006,693 | 887,424 | 224,299 | 17,426 | 119,269 | R | 47.1% | 41.5% | 10.5% |
| Iowa | | 7 | | 1,234,075 | 492,644 | 620,258 | 105,159 | 16,014 | 127,614 | D | 39.9% | 50.3% | 8.5% |
| Kansas | 6 | | | 1,074,300 | 583,245 | 387,659 | 92,639 | 10,757 | 195,586 | R | 54.3% | 36.1% | 8.6% |
| Kentucky | | 8 | | 1,388,708 | 623,283 | 636,614 | 120,396 | 8,415 | 13,331 | D | 44.9% | 45.8% | 8.7% |
| Louisiana | | 9 | | 1,783,959 | 712,586 | 927,837 | 123,293 | 20,243 | 215,251 | D | 39.9% | 52.0% | 6.9% |
| Maine | | 4 | | 605,897 | 186,378 | 312,788 | 85,970 | 20,761 | 126,410 | D | 30.8% | 51.6% | 14.2% |
| Maryland | | 10 | | 1,780,870 | 681,530 | 966,207 | 115,812 | 17,321 | 284,677 | D | 38.3% | 54.3% | 6.5% |
| Massachusetts | | 12 | | 2,556,785 | 718,107 | 1,571,763 | 227,217 | 39,698 | 853,656 | D | 28.1% | 61.5% | 8.9% |
| Michigan | | 18 | | 3,848,844 | 1,481,212 | 1,989,653 | 336,670 | 41,309 | 508,441 | D | 38.5% | 51.7% | 8.7% |
| Minnesota | | 10 | | 2,192,640 | 766,476 | 1,120,438 | 257,704 | 48,022 | 353,962 | D | 35.0% | 51.1% | 11.8% |
| Mississippi | 7 | | | 893,857 | 439,838 | 394,022 | 52,222 | 7,775 | 45,816 | R | 49.2% | 44.1% | 5.8% |
| Missouri | | 11 | | 2,158,065 | 890,016 | 1,025,935 | 217,188 | 24,926 | 135,919 | D | 41.2% | 47.5% | 10.1% |
| Montana | 3 | | | 407,261 | 179,652 | 167,922 | 55,229 | 4,458 | 11,730 | R | 44.1% | 41.2% | 13.6% |
| Nebraska | 5 | | | 677,415 | 363,467 | 236,761 | 71,278 | 5,909 | 126,706 | R | 53.7% | 35.0% | 10.5% |
| Nevada | | 4 | | 464,279 | 199,244 | 203,974 | 43,986 | 17,075 | 4,730 | D | 42.9% | 43.9% | 9.5% |
| New Hampshire | | 4 | | 499,175 | 196,532 | 246,214 | 48,390 | 8,039 | 49,682 | D | 39.4% | 49.3% | 9.7% |
| New Jersey | | 15 | | 3,075,807 | 1,103,078 | 1,652,329 | 262,134 | 58,266 | 549,251 | D | 35.9% | 53.7% | 8.5% |
| New Mexico | | 5 | | 556,074 | 232,751 | 273,495 | 32,257 | 17,571 | 40,744 | D | 41.9% | 49.2% | 5.8% |
| New York | | 33 | | 6,316,129 | 1,933,492 | 3,756,177 | 503,458 | 123,002 | 1,822,685 | D | 30.6% | 59.5% | 8.0% |
| North Carolina | 14 | | | 2,515,807 | 1,225,938 | 1,107,849 | 168,059 | 13,961 | 118,089 | R | 48.7% | 44.0% | 6.7% |
| North Dakota | 3 | | | 266,411 | 125,050 | 106,905 | 32,515 | 1,941 | 18,145 | R | 46.9% | 40.1% | 12.2% |
| Ohio | | 21 | | 4,534,434 | 1,859,883 | 2,148,222 | 483,207 | 43,122 | 288,339 | D | 41.0% | 47.4% | 10.7% |
| Oklahoma | 8 | | | 1,206,713 | 582,315 | 488,105 | 130,788 | 5,505 | 94,210 | R | 48.3% | 40.4% | 10.8% |
| Oregon | | 7 | | 1,377,760 | 538,152 | 649,641 | 121,221 | 68,746 | 111,489 | D | 39.1% | 47.2% | 8.8% |
| Pennsylvania | | 23 | | 4,506,118 | 1,801,169 | 2,215,819 | 430,984 | 58,146 | 414,650 | D | 40.0% | 49.2% | 9.6% |
| Rhode Island | | 4 | | 390,284 | 104,683 | 233,050 | 43,723 | 8,828 | 128,367 | D | 26.8% | 59.7% | 11.2% |
| South Carolina | 8 | | | 1,151,689 | 573,458 | 506,283 | 64,386 | 7,562 | 67,175 | R | 49.8% | 44.0% | 5.6% |
| South Dakota | 3 | | | 323,826 | 150,543 | 139,333 | 31,250 | 2,700 | 11,210 | R | 46.5% | 43.0% | 9.7% |
| Tennessee | | 11 | | 1,894,105 | 863,530 | 909,146 | 105,918 | 15,511 | 45,616 | D | 45.6% | 48.0% | 5.6% |
| Texas | 32 | | | 5,611,644 | 2,736,167 | 2,459,683 | 378,537 | 37,257 | 276,484 | R | 48.8% | 43.8% | 6.7% |
| Utah | 5 | | | 665,629 | 361,911 | 221,633 | 66,461 | 15,624 | 140,278 | R | 54.4% | 33.3% | 10.0% |
| Vermont | | 3 | | 258,449 | 80,352 | 137,894 | 31,024 | 9,179 | 57,542 | D | 31.1% | 53.4% | 12.0% |
| Virginia | 13 | | | 2,416,642 | 1,138,350 | 1,091,060 | 159,861 | 27,371 | 47,290 | R | 47.1% | 45.1% | 6.6% |
| Washington | | 11 | | 2,253,837 | 840,712 | 1,123,323 | 201,003 | 88,799 | 282,611 | D | 37.3% | 49.8% | 8.9% |
| West Virginia | | 5 | | 636,459 | 233,946 | 327,812 | 71,639 | 3,062 | 93,866 | D | 36.8% | 51.5% | 11.3% |
| Wisconsin | | 11 | | 2,196,169 | 845,029 | 1,071,971 | 227,339 | 51,830 | 226,942 | D | 38.5% | 48.8% | 10.4% |
| Wyoming | 3 | | | 211,571 | 105,388 | 77,934 | 25,928 | 2,321 | 27,454 | R | 49.8% | 36.8% | 12.3% |
| Dist. of Col. | | 3 | | 185,726 | 17,339 | 158,220 | 3,611 | 6,556 | 140,881 | D | 9.3% | 85.2% | 1.9% |
| United States | 159 | 379 | | 96,277,872 | 39,198,755 | 47,402,357 | 8,085,402 | 1,591,358 | 8,203,602 | D | 40.7% | 49.2% | 8.4% |

**PRESIDENT 1992**

In New York the Republican figures include Conservative and Right to Life votes and the Democratic figures include Liberal votes.

In many states, minor party candidates appeared on the ballot with variations of the party designations given below, were carried with entirely different party labels or listed as "Independent". In several states, minor party Vice-Presidential candidates were different from those listed below.

The candidates listed below include all those who appeared on the ballot in at least one state. Where identified by state authorities, write-in votes for minor party candidates are credited to their total.

44,909,326  Bill Clinton and Albert Gore, Jr., *Democratic.*
39,103,882  George Bush and J. Danforth Quayle, *Republican.*
19,741,657  Ross Perot and James Stockdale, *Independent.*
   291,627  Andre V. Marrou and Nancy Lord, *Libertarian.*
   107,014  James Gritz and Cyril Minett, *America First.*
    73,714  Lenora B. Fulani and Maria E. Munoz, *New Alliance.*
    43,434  Howard Phillips and Albion W. Knight, *Taxpayers.*
    39,179  John Hagelin and Mike Tompkins, *Natural Law.*
    27,961  Ron Daniels and Asiba Tupahache, *Peace and Feedom.*
    26,333  Lyndon H. LaRouche and James L. Bevel, *Economic Recovery.*
    23,096  James Warren and Willie Mae Reid, *Socialist Workers.*
     4,749  Drew Bradford and no Vice Presidential candidate, *Independent.*
     3,875  Jack Herer and Derrick P. Grimmer, *Grassroots.*
     3,057  J. Quinn Brisben and Barbara Garson, *Socialist.*
     3,050  Helen Halyard and Fred Mazelis, *Workers League.*
     2,199  John Yiamouyiannas and Allen C. McCone, *Take Back America.*
     1,149  Delbert L. Ehlers and Rick Wendt, *Independent.*
      961  Earl F. Dodge and George Ormsby, *Prohibition.*
      956  Jim Boren and Will Weidman, *Apathy.*
      405  Eugene A. Hem and Joanne Roland, *Third Party.*
      339  Isabell Masters and Walter Masters, *Looking Back.*
      292  Robert J. Smith and Doris Feimer, *American.*
      181  Gloria LaRiva and Larry Holmes, *Workers World.*

In addition, 14,041 scattered write-in votes were reported from various states and 2,537 votes were cast in Nevada for "None of these Candidates".

# UNITED STATES

## PRESIDENT 1992

| State | Electoral Vote Rep. | Dem. | Other | Total Vote | Republican | Democratic | Perot | Other | Plurality | Percentage Total Vote Rep. | Dem. | Perot |
|---|---|---|---|---|---|---|---|---|---|---|---|---|
| Alabama | 9 | | | 1,688,060 | 804,283 | 690,080 | 183,109 | 10,588 | 114,203 R | 47.6% | 40.9% | 10.8% |
| Alaska | 3 | | | 258,506 | 102,000 | 78,294 | 73,481 | 4,731 | 23,706 R | 39.5% | 30.3% | 28.4% |
| Arizona | 8 | | | 1,486,975 | 572,086 | 543,050 | 353,741 | 18,098 | 29,036 R | 38.5% | 36.5% | 23.8% |
| Arkansas | | 6 | | 950,653 | 337,324 | 505,823 | 99,132 | 8,374 | 168,499 D | 35.5% | 53.2% | 10.4% |
| California | | 54 | | 11,131,721 | 3,630,574 | 5,121,325 | 2,296,006 | 83,816 | 1,490,751 D | 32.6% | 46.0% | 20.6% |
| Colorado | | 8 | | 1,569,180 | 562,850 | 629,681 | 366,010 | 10,639 | 66,831 D | 35.9% | 40.1% | 23.3% |
| Connecticut | | 8 | | 1,616,332 | 578,313 | 682,318 | 348,771 | 6,930 | 104,005 D | 35.8% | 42.2% | 21.6% |
| Delaware | | 3 | | 289,735 | 102,313 | 126,054 | 59,213 | 2,155 | 23,741 D | 35.3% | 43.5% | 20.4% |
| Florida | 25 | | | 5,314,392 | 2,173,310 | 2,072,698 | 1,053,067 | 15,317 | 100,612 R | 40.9% | 39.0% | 19.8% |
| Georgia | | 13 | | 2,321,125 | 995,252 | 1,008,966 | 309,657 | 7,250 | 13,714 D | 42.9% | 43.5% | 13.3% |
| Hawaii | | 4 | | 372,842 | 136,822 | 179,310 | 53,003 | 3,707 | 42,488 D | 36.7% | 48.1% | 14.2% |
| Idaho | 4 | | | 482,142 | 202,645 | 137,013 | 130,395 | 12,089 | 65,632 R | 42.0% | 28.4% | 27.0% |
| Illinois | | 22 | | 5,050,157 | 1,734,096 | 2,453,350 | 840,515 | 22,196 | 719,254 D | 34.3% | 48.6% | 16.6% |
| Indiana | 12 | | | 2,305,871 | 989,375 | 848,420 | 455,934 | 12,142 | 140,955 R | 42.9% | 36.8% | 19.8% |
| Iowa | | 7 | | 1,354,607 | 504,891 | 586,353 | 253,468 | 9,895 | 81,462 D | 37.3% | 43.3% | 18.7% |
| Kansas | 6 | | | 1,157,335 | 449,951 | 390,434 | 312,358 | 4,592 | 59,517 R | 38.9% | 33.7% | 27.0% |
| Kentucky | | 8 | | 1,492,900 | 617,178 | 665,104 | 203,944 | 6,674 | 47,926 D | 41.3% | 44.6% | 13.7% |
| Louisiana | | 9 | | 1,790,017 | 733,386 | 815,971 | 211,478 | 29,182 | 82,585 D | 41.0% | 45.6% | 11.8% |
| Maine | | 4 | | 679,499 | 206,504 | 263,420 | 206,820 | 2,755 | 56,600 D | 30.4% | 38.8% | 30.4% |
| Maryland | | 12 | | 1,985,046 | 707,094 | 988,571 | 281,414 | 7,967 | 281,477 D | 35.6% | 49.8% | 14.2% |
| Massachusetts | | 10 | | 2,773,700 | 805,049 | 1,318,662 | 630,731 | 19,258 | 513,613 D | 29.0% | 47.5% | 22.7% |
| Michigan | | 18 | | 4,274,673 | 1,554,940 | 1,871,182 | 824,813 | 23,738 | 316,242 D | 36.4% | 43.8% | 19.3% |
| Minnesota | | 10 | | 2,347,948 | 747,841 | 1,020,997 | 562,506 | 16,604 | 273,156 D | 31.9% | 43.5% | 24.0% |
| Mississippi | 7 | | | 981,793 | 487,793 | 400,258 | 85,626 | 8,116 | 87,535 R | 49.7% | 40.8% | 8.7% |
| Missouri | | 11 | | 2,391,565 | 811,159 | 1,053,873 | 518,741 | 7,792 | 242,714 D | 33.9% | 44.1% | 21.7% |
| Montana | | 3 | | 410,611 | 144,207 | 154,507 | 107,225 | 4,672 | 10,300 D | 35.1% | 37.6% | 26.1% |
| Nebraska | 5 | | | 737,546 | 343,678 | 216,864 | 174,104 | 2,900 | 126,814 R | 46.6% | 29.4% | 23.6% |
| Nevada | | 4 | | 506,318 | 175,828 | 189,148 | 132,580 | 8,762 | 13,320 D | 34.7% | 37.4% | 26.2% |
| New Hampshire | | 4 | | 537,943 | 202,484 | 209,040 | 121,337 | 5,082 | 6,556 D | 37.6% | 38.9% | 22.6% |
| New Jersey | | 15 | | 3,343,594 | 1,356,865 | 1,436,206 | 521,829 | 28,694 | 79,341 D | 40.6% | 43.0% | 15.6% |
| New Mexico | | 5 | | 569,986 | 212,824 | 261,617 | 91,895 | 3,650 | 48,793 D | 37.3% | 45.9% | 16.1% |
| New York | | 33 | | 6,926,925 | 2,346,649 | 3,444,450 | 1,090,721 | 45,105 | 1,097,801 D | 33.9% | 49.7% | 15.7% |
| North Carolina | 14 | | | 2,611,850 | 1,134,661 | 1,114,042 | 357,864 | 5,283 | 20,619 R | 43.4% | 42.7% | 13.7% |
| North Dakota | 3 | | | 308,133 | 136,244 | 99,168 | 71,084 | 1,637 | 37,076 R | 44.2% | 32.2% | 23.1% |
| Ohio | | 21 | | 4,939,967 | 1,894,310 | 1,984,942 | 1,036,426 | 24,289 | 90,632 D | 38.3% | 40.2% | 21.0% |
| Oklahoma | 8 | | | 1,390,359 | 592,929 | 473,066 | 319,878 | 4,486 | 119,863 R | 42.6% | 34.0% | 23.0% |
| Oregon | | 7 | | 1,462,643 | 475,757 | 621,314 | 354,091 | 11,481 | 145,557 D | 32.5% | 42.5% | 24.2% |
| Pennsylvania | | 23 | | 4,959,810 | 1,791,841 | 2,239,164 | 902,667 | 26,138 | 447,323 D | 36.1% | 45.1% | 18.2% |
| Rhode Island | | 4 | | 453,477 | 131,601 | 213,299 | 105,045 | 3,532 | 81,698 D | 29.0% | 47.0% | 23.2% |
| South Carolina | 8 | | | 1,202,527 | 577,507 | 479,514 | 138,872 | 6,634 | 97,993 R | 48.0% | 39.9% | 11.5% |
| South Dakota | 3 | | | 336,254 | 136,718 | 124,888 | 73,295 | 1,353 | 11,830 R | 40.7% | 37.1% | 21.8% |
| Tennessee | | 11 | | 1,982,638 | 841,300 | 933,521 | 199,968 | 7,849 | 92,221 D | 42.4% | 47.1% | 10.1% |
| Texas | 32 | | | 6,154,018 | 2,496,071 | 2,281,815 | 1,354,781 | 21,351 | 214,256 R | 40.6% | 37.1% | 22.0% |
| Utah | 5 | | | 743,999 | 322,632 | 183,429 | 203,400 | 34,538 | 119,232 R | 43.4% | 24.7% | 27.3% |
| Vermont | | 3 | | 289,701 | 88,122 | 133,592 | 65,991 | 1,996 | 45,470 D | 30.4% | 46.1% | 22.8% |
| Virginia | 13 | | | 2,558,665 | 1,150,517 | 1,038,650 | 348,639 | 20,859 | 111,867 R | 45.0% | 40.6% | 13.6% |
| Washington | | 11 | | 2,288,230 | 731,234 | 993,037 | 541,780 | 22,179 | 261,803 D | 32.0% | 43.4% | 23.7% |
| West Virginia | | 5 | | 683,762 | 241,974 | 331,001 | 108,829 | 1,958 | 89,027 D | 35.4% | 48.4% | 15.9% |
| Wisconsin | | 11 | | 2,531,114 | 930,855 | 1,041,066 | 544,479 | 14,714 | 110,211 D | 36.8% | 41.1% | 21.5% |
| Wyoming | 3 | | | 200,598 | 79,347 | 68,160 | 51,263 | 1,828 | 11,187 R | 39.6% | 34.0% | 25.6% |
| Dist. of Col. | | 3 | | 227,572 | 20,698 | 192,619 | 9,681 | 4,574 | 171,921 D | 9.1% | 84.6% | 4.3% |
| United States | 168 | 370 | — | 104,425,014 | 39,103,882 | 44,909,326 | 19,741,657 | 670,149 | 5,805,444 D | 37.4% | 43.0% | 18.9% |

## PRESIDENT 1988

In West Virginia, one Democratic elector voted in the Electoral College for Lloyd Bentsen for President and Michael S. Dukakis for Vice-President.

In New York, the Republican figures include Conservative votes and the Democratic figures include Liberal votes.

In many states, minor party candidates appeared on the ballot with variations of the party designation given below, were listed as "Independent" or were carried with entirely different party labels. In several states, minor party Vice-Presidential candidates were different from those listed below.

The candidates listed below include all those who appeared on the ballot in at least one state. Republican, Democratic and New Alliance candidates appeared on the ballot in all fifty-one jurisdictions. The Libertarian nominees were on the ballot in all but four states. Where identified by state authorities, write-in votes for minor party candidates are credited to their total.

| | |
|---|---|
| 48,886,097 | George Bush and J. Danforth Quayle, *Republican*. |
| 41,809,074 | Michael S. Dukakis and Lloyd Bentsen, *Democratic*. |
| 432,179 | Ron Paul and Andre V. Marrou, *Libertarian*. |
| 217,219 | Lenora B. Fulani and Joyce Dattner, *New Alliance*. |
| 47,047 | David E. Duke and Floyd C. Parker, *Populist*. |
| 30,905 | Eugene J. McCarthy and Florence Rice, *Consumer*. |
| 27,818 | James C. Griffin and Charles J. Morsa, *American Independent*. |
| 25,562 | Lyndon H. LaRouche and Debra H. Freeman, *National Economic Recovery*. |
| 20,504 | William A. Marra and Joan Andrews, *Right to Life*. |
| 18,693 | Ed Winn and Barry Porster, *Workers World*. |
| 15,604 | James Warren and Kathleen Mickells, *Socialist Workers*. |
| 10,370 | Herbert Lewin and Vikki Murdock, *Peace and Freedom*. |
| 8,002 | Earl F. Dodge and George Ormsby, *Prohibition*. |
| 7,846 | Larry Holmes and Gloria LaRiva, *Workers World*. |
| 3,882 | Willa Kenoyer and Ron Ehrenreich, *Socialist*. |
| 3,475 | Delmar Dennis and Earl Jeppson, *American*. |
| 1,949 | Jack Herer and Dana Beal, *Grassroots*. |
| 372 | Louie G. Youngkeit with no Vice-Presidential candidate, *Independent*. |
| 236 | John G. Martin and Cleveland Sparrow, *Third World Assembly*. |

In addition, 21,041 scattered write-in votes were reported from various states and 6,934 votes were cast in Nevada for "None of these Candidates".

# UNITED STATES

## PRESIDENT 1988

| State | Electoral Vote Rep. | Dem. | Other | Total Vote | Republican | Democratic | Other | Plurality | Total Vote Rep. | Dem. | Major Vote Rep. | Dem. |
|---|---|---|---|---|---|---|---|---|---|---|---|---|
| Alabama | 9 | | | 1,378,476 | 815,576 | 549,506 | 13,394 | 266,070 R | 59.2% | 39.9% | 59.7% | 40.3% |
| Alaska | 3 | | | 200,116 | 119,251 | 72,584 | 8,281 | 46,667 R | 59.6% | 36.3% | 62.2% | 37.8% |
| Arizona | 7 | | | 1,171,873 | 702,541 | 454,029 | 15,303 | 248,512 R | 60.0% | 38.7% | 60.7% | 39.3% |
| Arkansas | 6 | | | 827,738 | 466,578 | 349,237 | 11,923 | 117,341 R | 56.4% | 42.2% | 57.2% | 42.8% |
| California | 47 | | | 9,887,065 | 5,054,917 | 4,702,233 | 129,915 | 352,684 R | 51.1% | 47.6% | 51.8% | 48.2% |
| Colorado | 8 | | | 1,372,394 | 728,177 | 621,453 | 22,764 | 106,724 R | 53.1% | 45.3% | 54.0% | 46.0% |
| Connecticut | 8 | | | 1,443,394 | 750,241 | 676,584 | 16,569 | 73,657 R | 52.0% | 46.9% | 52.6% | 47.4% |
| Delaware | 3 | | | 249,891 | 139,639 | 108,647 | 1,605 | 30,992 R | 55.9% | 43.5% | 56.2% | 43.8% |
| Florida | 21 | | | 4,302,313 | 2,618,885 | 1,656,701 | 26,727 | 962,184 R | 60.9% | 38.5% | 61.3% | 38.7% |
| Georgia | 12 | | | 1,809,672 | 1,081,331 | 714,792 | 13,549 | 366,539 R | 59.8% | 39.5% | 60.2% | 39.8% |
| Hawaii | | 4 | | 354,461 | 158,625 | 192,364 | 3,472 | 33,739 D | 44.8% | 54.3% | 45.2% | 54.8% |
| Idaho | 4 | | | 408,968 | 253,881 | 147,272 | 7,815 | 106,609 R | 62.1% | 36.0% | 63.3% | 36.7% |
| Illinois | 24 | | | 4,559,120 | 2,310,939 | 2,215,940 | 32,241 | 94,999 R | 50.7% | 48.6% | 51.0% | 49.0% |
| Indiana | 12 | | | 2,168,621 | 1,297,763 | 860,643 | 10,215 | 437,120 R | 59.8% | 39.7% | 60.1% | 39.9% |
| Iowa | | 8 | | 1,225,614 | 545,355 | 670,557 | 9,702 | 125,202 D | 44.5% | 54.7% | 44.9% | 55.1% |
| Kansas | 7 | | | 993,044 | 554,049 | 422,636 | 16,359 | 131,413 R | 55.8% | 42.6% | 56.7% | 43.3% |
| Kentucky | 9 | | | 1,322,517 | 734,281 | 580,368 | 7,868 | 153,913 R | 55.5% | 43.9% | 55.9% | 44.1% |
| Louisiana | 10 | | | 1,628,202 | 883,702 | 717,460 | 27,040 | 166,242 R | 54.3% | 44.1% | 55.2% | 44.8% |
| Maine | 4 | | | 555,035 | 307,131 | 243,569 | 4,335 | 63,562 R | 55.3% | 43.9% | 55.8% | 44.2% |
| Maryland | 10 | | | 1,714,358 | 876,167 | 826,304 | 11,887 | 49,863 R | 51.1% | 48.2% | 51.5% | 48.5% |
| Massachusetts | | 13 | | 2,632,805 | 1,194,635 | 1,401,415 | 36,755 | 206,780 D | 45.4% | 53.2% | 46.0% | 54.0% |
| Michigan | 20 | | | 3,669,163 | 1,965,486 | 1,675,783 | 27,894 | 289,703 R | 53.6% | 45.7% | 54.0% | 46.0% |
| Minnesota | | 10 | | 2,096,790 | 962,337 | 1,109,471 | 24,982 | 147,134 D | 45.9% | 52.9% | 46.4% | 53.6% |
| Mississippi | 7 | | | 931,527 | 557,890 | 363,921 | 9,716 | 193,969 R | 59.9% | 39.1% | 60.5% | 39.5% |
| Missouri | 11 | | | 2,093,713 | 1,084,953 | 1,001,619 | 7,141 | 83,334 R | 51.8% | 47.8% | 52.0% | 48.0% |
| Montana | 4 | | | 365,674 | 190,412 | 168,936 | 6,326 | 21,476 R | 52.1% | 46.2% | 53.0% | 47.0% |
| Nebraska | 5 | | | 661,465 | 397,956 | 259,235 | 4,274 | 138,721 R | 60.2% | 39.2% | 60.6% | 39.4% |
| Nevada | 4 | | | 350,067 | 206,040 | 132,738 | 11,289 | 73,302 R | 58.9% | 37.9% | 60.8% | 39.2% |
| New Hampshire | 4 | | | 451,074 | 281,537 | 163,696 | 5,841 | 117,841 R | 62.4% | 36.3% | 63.2% | 36.8% |
| New Jersey | 16 | | | 3,099,553 | 1,743,192 | 1,320,352 | 36,009 | 422,840 R | 56.2% | 42.6% | 56.9% | 43.1% |
| New Mexico | 5 | | | 521,287 | 270,341 | 244,497 | 6,449 | 25,844 R | 51.9% | 46.9% | 52.5% | 47.5% |
| New York | | 36 | | 6,485,683 | 3,081,871 | 3,347,882 | 55,930 | 266,011 D | 47.5% | 51.6% | 47.9% | 52.1% |
| North Carolina | 13 | | | 2,134,370 | 1,237,258 | 890,167 | 6,945 | 347,091 R | 58.0% | 41.7% | 58.2% | 41.8% |
| North Dakota | 3 | | | 297,261 | 166,559 | 127,739 | 2,963 | 38,820 R | 56.0% | 43.0% | 56.6% | 43.4% |
| Ohio | 23 | | | 4,393,699 | 2,416,549 | 1,939,629 | 37,521 | 476,920 R | 55.0% | 44.1% | 55.5% | 44.5% |
| Oklahoma | 8 | | | 1,171,036 | 678,367 | 483,423 | 9,246 | 194,944 R | 57.9% | 41.3% | 58.4% | 41.6% |
| Oregon | | 7 | | 1,201,694 | 560,126 | 616,206 | 25,362 | 56,080 D | 46.6% | 51.3% | 47.6% | 52.4% |
| Pennsylvania | 25 | | | 4,536,251 | 2,300,087 | 2,194,944 | 41,220 | 105,143 R | 50.7% | 48.4% | 51.2% | 48.8% |
| Rhode Island | | 4 | | 404,620 | 177,761 | 225,123 | 1,736 | 47,362 D | 43.9% | 55.6% | 44.1% | 55.9% |
| South Carolina | 8 | | | 986,009 | 606,443 | 370,554 | 9,012 | 235,889 R | 61.5% | 37.6% | 62.1% | 37.9% |
| South Dakota | 3 | | | 312,991 | 165,415 | 145,560 | 2,016 | 19,855 R | 52.8% | 46.5% | 53.2% | 46.8% |
| Tennessee | 11 | | | 1,636,250 | 947,233 | 679,794 | 9,223 | 267,439 R | 57.9% | 41.5% | 58.2% | 41.8% |
| Texas | 29 | | | 5,427,410 | 3,036,829 | 2,352,748 | 37,833 | 684,081 R | 56.0% | 43.3% | 56.3% | 43.7% |
| Utah | 5 | | | 647,008 | 428,442 | 207,343 | 11,223 | 221,099 R | 66.2% | 32.0% | 67.4% | 32.6% |
| Vermont | 3 | | | 243,328 | 124,331 | 115,775 | 3,222 | 8,556 R | 51.1% | 47.6% | 51.8% | 48.2% |
| Virginia | 12 | | | 2,191,609 | 1,309,162 | 859,799 | 22,648 | 449,363 R | 59.7% | 39.2% | 60.4% | 39.6% |
| Washington | | 10 | | 1,865,253 | 903,835 | 933,516 | 27,902 | 29,681 D | 48.5% | 50.0% | 49.2% | 50.8% |
| West Virginia | | 5 | 1 | 653,311 | 310,065 | 341,016 | 2,230 | 30,951 D | 47.5% | 52.2% | 47.6% | 52.4% |
| Wisconsin | | 11 | | 2,191,608 | 1,047,499 | 1,126,794 | 17,315 | 79,295 D | 47.8% | 51.4% | 48.2% | 51.8% |
| Wyoming | 3 | | | 176,551 | 106,867 | 67,113 | 2,571 | 39,754 R | 60.5% | 38.0% | 61.4% | 38.6% |
| Dist. of Col. | | 3 | | 192,877 | 27,590 | 159,407 | 5,880 | 131,817 D | 14.3% | 82.6% | 14.8% | 85.2% |
| United States | 426 | 111 | 1 | 91,594,809 | 48,886,097 | 41,809,074 | 899,638 | 7,077,023 R | 53.4% | 45.6% | 53.9% | 46.1% |

# PRESIDENT 1984

In New York the Republican figures include Conservative votes and the Democratic figures include Liberal votes.

In many states, minor party candidates appeared on the ballot with variations of the party designations given below, were listed as "Independent" or "Non-Party", or were carried with entirely different party lables. In Ohio and Rhode Island the Workers World candidate for President was Gavrielle Holmes. In several states, minor party Vice-Presidential candidates were different from those listed below.

The candidates listed below include all those who appeared on the ballot in at least one state. Where identified by state authorities, write-in votes for minor party candidates are credited to their total.

| | |
|---:|---|
| 54,455,075 | Ronald Reagan and George Bush, *Republican*. |
| 37,577,185 | Walter F. Mondale and Geraldine A. Ferraro, *Democratic*. |
| 228,314 | David Bergland and James A. Lewis, *Libertarian*. |
| 78,807 | Lyndon H. LaRouche and Billy M. Davis, *Independent*. |
| 72,200 | Sonia Johnson and Richard Walton, *Citizens*. |
| 66,336 | Bob Richards and Maureen Salaman, *Populist*. |
| 46,868 | Dennis L. Serrette and Nancy Ross, *Alliance*. |
| 36,386 | Gus Hall and Angela Davis, *Communist*. |
| 24,706 | Mel Mason and Matilde Zimmermann, *Socialist Workers*. |
| 17,985 | Larry Holmes and Gloria LaRiva, *Workers World*. |
| 13,161 | Delmar Dennis and Traves Brownlee, *American*. |
| 10,801 | Ed Winn and Helen Halyard, *Workers League*. |
| 4,242 | Earl F. Dodge and Warren C. Martin, *Prohibition*. |
| 1,486 | John B. Anderson and Grace Pierce, *National Unity*. |
| 892 | Gerald Baker and Ferris Alger, *Big Deal*. |
| 825 | Arthur J. Lowery and Raymond L. Garland, *United Soverign Citizens*. |

In addition, 13,623 scattered write-in votes were reported from various states and 3,950 votes were cast in Nevada for "None of these Candidates".

# UNITED STATES

## PRESIDENT 1984

| State | Electoral Vote Rep. | Electoral Vote Dem. | Electoral Vote Other | Total Vote | Republican | Democratic | Other | Plurality | Percentage Total Vote Rep. | Percentage Total Vote Dem. | Percentage Major Vote Rep. | Percentage Major Vote Dem. |
|---|---|---|---|---|---|---|---|---|---|---|---|---|
| Alabama | 9 | | | 1,441,713 | 872,849 | 551,899 | 16,965 | 320,950 R | 60.5% | 38.3% | 61.3% | 38.7% |
| Alaska | 3 | | | 207,605 | 138,377 | 62,007 | 7,221 | 76,370 R | 66.7% | 29.9% | 69.1% | 30.9% |
| Arizona | 7 | | | 1,025,897 | 681,416 | 333,854 | 10,627 | 347,562 R | 66.4% | 32.5% | 67.1% | 32.9% |
| Arkansas | 6 | | | 884,406 | 534,774 | 338,646 | 10,986 | 196,128 R | 60.5% | 38.3% | 61.2% | 38.8% |
| California | 47 | | | 9,505,423 | 5,467,009 | 3,922,519 | 115,895 | 1,544,490 R | 57.5% | 41.3% | 58.2% | 41.8% |
| Colorado | 8 | | | 1,295,380 | 821,817 | 454,975 | 18,588 | 366,842 R | 63.4% | 35.1% | 64.4% | 35.6% |
| Connecticut | 8 | | | 1,466,900 | 890,877 | 569,597 | 6,426 | 321,280 R | 60.7% | 38.8% | 61.0% | 39.0% |
| Delaware | 3 | | | 254,572 | 152,190 | 101,656 | 726 | 50,534 R | 59.8% | 39.9% | 60.0% | 40.0% |
| Florida | 21 | | | 4,180,051 | 2,730,350 | 1,448,816 | 885 | 1,281,534 R | 65.3% | 34.7% | 65.3% | 34.7% |
| Georgia | 12 | | | 1,776,120 | 1,068,722 | 706,628 | 770 | 362,094 R | 60.2% | 39.8% | 60.2% | 39.8% |
| Hawaii | 4 | | | 335,846 | 185,050 | 147,154 | 3,642 | 37,896 R | 55.1% | 43.8% | 55.7% | 44.3% |
| Idaho | 4 | | | 411,144 | 297,523 | 108,510 | 5,111 | 189,013 R | 72.4% | 26.4% | 73.3% | 26.7% |
| Illinois | 24 | | | 4,819,088 | 2,707,103 | 2,086,499 | 25,486 | 620,604 R | 56.2% | 43.3% | 56.5% | 43.5% |
| Indiana | 12 | | | 2,233,069 | 1,377,230 | 841,481 | 14,358 | 535,749 R | 61.7% | 37.7% | 62.1% | 37.9% |
| Iowa | 8 | | | 1,319,805 | 703,088 | 605,620 | 11,097 | 97,468 R | 53.3% | 45.9% | 53.7% | 46.3% |
| Kansas | 7 | | | 1,021,991 | 677,296 | 333,149 | 11,546 | 344,147 R | 66.3% | 32.6% | 67.0% | 33.0% |
| Kentucky | 9 | | | 1,369,345 | 821,702 | 539,539 | 8,104 | 282,163 R | 60.0% | 39.4% | 60.4% | 39.6% |
| Louisiana | 10 | | | 1,706,822 | 1,037,299 | 651,586 | 17,937 | 385,713 R | 60.8% | 38.2% | 61.4% | 38.6% |
| Maine | 4 | | | 553,144 | 336,500 | 214,515 | 2,129 | 121,985 R | 60.8% | 38.8% | 61.1% | 38.9% |
| Maryland | 10 | | | 1,675,873 | 879,918 | 787,935 | 8,020 | 91,983 R | 52.5% | 47.0% | 52.8% | 47.2% |
| Massachusetts | 13 | | | 2,559,453 | 1,310,936 | 1,239,606 | 8,911 | 71,330 R | 51.2% | 48.4% | 51.4% | 48.6% |
| Michigan | 20 | | | 3,801,658 | 2,251,571 | 1,529,638 | 20,449 | 721,933 R | 59.2% | 40.2% | 59.5% | 40.5% |
| Minnesota | | 10 | | 2,084,449 | 1,032,603 | 1,036,364 | 15,482 | 3,761 D | 49.5% | 49.7% | 49.9% | 50.1% |
| Mississippi | 7 | | | 941,104 | 582,377 | 352,192 | 6,535 | 230,185 R | 61.9% | 37.4% | 62.3% | 37.7% |
| Missouri | 11 | | | 2,122,783 | 1,274,188 | 848,583 | 12 | 425,605 R | 60.0% | 40.0% | 60.0% | 40.0% |
| Montana | 4 | | | 384,377 | 232,450 | 146,742 | 5,185 | 85,708 R | 60.5% | 38.2% | 61.3% | 38.7% |
| Nebraska | 5 | | | 652,090 | 460,054 | 187,866 | 4,170 | 272,188 R | 70.6% | 28.8% | 71.0% | 29.0% |
| Nevada | 4 | | | 286,667 | 188,770 | 91,655 | 6,242 | 97,115 R | 65.8% | 32.0% | 67.3% | 32.7% |
| New Hampshire | 4 | | | 389,066 | 267,051 | 120,395 | 1,620 | 146,656 R | 68.6% | 30.9% | 68.9% | 31.1% |
| New Jersey | 16 | | | 3,217,862 | 1,933,630 | 1,261,323 | 22,909 | 672,307 R | 60.1% | 39.2% | 60.5% | 39.5% |
| New Mexico | 5 | | | 514,370 | 307,101 | 201,769 | 5,500 | 105,332 R | 59.7% | 39.2% | 60.3% | 39.7% |
| New York | 36 | | | 6,806,810 | 3,664,763 | 3,119,609 | 22,438 | 545,154 R | 53.8% | 45.8% | 54.0% | 46.0% |
| North Carolina | 13 | | | 2,175,361 | 1,346,481 | 824,287 | 4,593 | 522,194 R | 61.9% | 37.9% | 62.0% | 38.0% |
| North Dakota | 3 | | | 308,971 | 200,336 | 104,429 | 4,206 | 95,907 R | 64.8% | 33.8% | 65.7% | 34.3% |
| Ohio | 23 | | | 4,547,619 | 2,678,560 | 1,825,440 | 43,619 | 853,120 R | 58.9% | 40.1% | 59.5% | 40.5% |
| Oklahoma | 8 | | | 1,255,676 | 861,530 | 385,080 | 9,066 | 476,450 R | 68.6% | 30.7% | 69.1% | 30.9% |
| Oregon | 7 | | | 1,226,527 | 685,700 | 536,479 | 4,348 | 149,221 R | 55.9% | 43.7% | 56.1% | 43.9% |
| Pennsylvania | 25 | | | 4,844,903 | 2,584,323 | 2,228,131 | 32,449 | 356,192 R | 53.3% | 46.0% | 53.7% | 46.3% |
| Rhode Island | 4 | | | 410,492 | 212,080 | 197,106 | 1,306 | 14,974 R | 51.7% | 48.0% | 51.8% | 48.2% |
| South Carolina | 8 | | | 968,529 | 615,539 | 344,459 | 8,531 | 271,080 R | 63.6% | 35.6% | 64.1% | 35.9% |
| South Dakota | 3 | | | 317,867 | 200,267 | 116,113 | 1,487 | 84,154 R | 63.0% | 36.5% | 63.3% | 36.7% |
| Tennessee | 11 | | | 1,711,994 | 990,212 | 711,714 | 10,068 | 278,498 R | 57.8% | 41.6% | 58.2% | 41.8% |
| Texas | 29 | | | 5,397,571 | 3,433,428 | 1,949,276 | 14,867 | 1,484,152 R | 63.6% | 36.1% | 63.8% | 36.2% |
| Utah | 5 | | | 629,656 | 469,105 | 155,369 | 5,182 | 313,736 R | 74.5% | 24.7% | 75.1% | 24.9% |
| Vermont | 3 | | | 234,561 | 135,865 | 95,730 | 2,966 | 40,135 R | 57.9% | 40.8% | 58.7% | 41.3% |
| Virginia | 12 | | | 2,146,635 | 1,337,078 | 796,250 | 13,307 | 540,828 R | 62.3% | 37.1% | 62.7% | 37.3% |
| Washington | 10 | | | 1,883,910 | 1,051,670 | 807,352 | 24,888 | 244,318 R | 55.8% | 42.9% | 56.6% | 43.4% |
| West Virginia | 6 | | | 735,742 | 405,483 | 328,125 | 2,134 | 77,358 R | 55.1% | 44.6% | 55.3% | 44.7% |
| Wisconsin | 11 | | | 2,211,689 | 1,198,584 | 995,740 | 17,365 | 202,844 R | 54.2% | 45.0% | 54.6% | 45.4% |
| Wyoming | 3 | | | 188,968 | 133,241 | 53,370 | 2,357 | 79,871 R | 70.5% | 28.2% | 71.4% | 28.6% |
| Dist. of Col. | | 3 | | 211,288 | 29,009 | 180,408 | 1,871 | 151,399 D | 13.7% | 85.4% | 13.9% | 86.1% |
| United States | 525 | 13 | — | 92,652,842 | 54,455,075 | 37,577,185 | 620,582 | 16,877,890 R | 58.8% | 40.6% | 59.2% | 40.8% |

# PRESIDENT 1980

In New York the Republican figures include Conservative votes. In many states, minor party candidates appeared on the ballot with variations of the party designations given below, were listed as "Independent" or were carried with entirely different party labels or with no party label at all. The Socialist Workers party nominee for President varied from state to state.

The candidates listed below include all those who appeared on the ballot in at least one state. Where identified by state authorities, write-in votes for minor party candidates are credited to their total.

| | |
|---|---|
| 43,904,153 | Ronald Reagan and George Bush, *Republican.* |
| 35,483,883 | Jimmy Carter and Walter F. Mondale, *Democratic.* |
| 5,720,060 | John B. Anderson and Patrick J. Lucey, *Independent.* |
| 921,299 | Edward E. Clark and David Koch, *Libertarian.* |
| 234,294 | Barry Commoner and LaDonna Harris, *Citizens.* |
| 45,023 | Gus Hall and Angela Davis, *Communist.* |
| 41,268 | John R. Rarick and Eileen M. Shearer, *American Independent.* |
| 38,737 | Clifton DeBerry and Matilde Zimmermann, *Socialist Workers.* |
| 32,327 | Ellen McCormack and Carroll Driscoll, *Right to Life.* |
| 18,116 | Maureen Smith and Elizabeth Barron, *Peace and Freedom.* |
| 13,300 | Deirdre Griswold and Larry Holmes, *Workers World.* |
| 7,212 | Benjamin C. Bubar and Earl F. Dodge, *Statesman.* |
| 6,898 | David McReynolds and Diane Drufenbrock, *Socialist* |
| 6,647 | Percy L. Greaves and Frank L. Varnum, *American.* |
| 6,272 | Andrew Pulley and Matilde Zimmerman, *Socialist Workers.* |
| 4,029 | Richard Congress and Matilde Zimmermann, *Socialist Workers.* |
| 3,694 | Kurt Lynen and Harry Kieve, *Middle Class.* |
| 1,718 | Bill Gahres and J. F. Loughlin, *Down With Lawyers.* |
| 1,555 | Frank W. Shelton and George E. Jackson, *American.* |
| 923 | Martin E. Wendelken and no Vice-Presidential candidate, *Independent.* |
| 296 | Harley McLain and Jewelie Goeller, *Natural Peoples.* |

In Minnesota 6,139 votes were cast for the American party electors without designated candidates for President or Vice President. In addition 13,185 scattered write-in votes were reported from various states and 4,193 votes were cast in Nevada for "None of these Candidates".

# UNITED STATES

## PRESIDENT 1980

| State | Electoral Vote Rep. | Electoral Vote Dem. | Electoral Vote Other | Total Vote | Republican | Democratic | Other | Plurality | Total Vote Rep. | Total Vote Dem. | Major Vote Rep. | Major Vote Dem. |
|---|---|---|---|---|---|---|---|---|---|---|---|---|
| Alabama | 9 | | | 1,341,929 | 654,192 | 636,730 | 51,007 | 17,462 R | 48.8% | 47.4% | 50.7% | 49.3% |
| Alaska | 3 | | | 158,445 | 86,112 | 41,842 | 30,491 | 44,270 R | 54.3% | 26.4% | 67.3% | 32.7% |
| Arizona | 6 | | | 873,945 | 529,688 | 246,843 | 97,414 | 282,845 R | 60.6% | 28.2% | 68.2% | 31.8% |
| Arkansas | 6 | | | 837,582 | 403,164 | 398,041 | 36,377 | 5,123 R | 48.1% | 47.5% | 50.3% | 49.7% |
| California | 45 | | | 8,587,063 | 4,524,858 | 3,083,661 | 978,544 | 1,441,197 R | 52.7% | 35.9% | 59.5% | 40.5% |
| Colorado | 7 | | | 1,184,415 | 652,264 | 367,973 | 164,178 | 284,291 R | 55.1% | 31.1% | 63.9% | 36.1% |
| Connecticut | 8 | | | 1,406,285 | 677,210 | 541,732 | 187,343 | 135,478 R | 48.2% | 38.5% | 55.6% | 44.4% |
| Delaware | 3 | | | 235,900 | 111,252 | 105,754 | 18,894 | 5,498 R | 47.2% | 44.8% | 51.3% | 48.7% |
| Florida | 17 | | | 3,686,930 | 2,046,951 | 1,419,475 | 220,504 | 627,476 R | 55.5% | 38.5% | 59.1% | 40.9% |
| Georgia | | 12 | | 1,596,695 | 654,168 | 890,733 | 51,794 | 236,565 D | 41.0% | 55.8% | 42.3% | 57.7% |
| Hawaii | | 4 | | 303,287 | 130,112 | 135,879 | 37,296 | 5,767 D | 42.9% | 44.8% | 48.9% | 51.1% |
| Idaho | 4 | | | 437,431 | 290,699 | 110,192 | 36,540 | 180,507 R | 66.5% | 25.2% | 72.5% | 27.5% |
| Illinois | 26 | | | 4,749,721 | 2,358,049 | 1,981,413 | 410,259 | 376,636 R | 49.6% | 41.7% | 54.3% | 45.7% |
| Indiana | 13 | | | 2,242,033 | 1,255,656 | 844,197 | 142,180 | 411,459 R | 56.0% | 37.7% | 59.8% | 40.2% |
| Iowa | 8 | | | 1,317,661 | 676,026 | 508,672 | 132,963 | 167,354 R | 51.3% | 38.6% | 57.1% | 42.9% |
| Kansas | 7 | | | 979,795 | 566,812 | 326,150 | 86,833 | 240,662 R | 57.9% | 33.3% | 63.5% | 36.5% |
| Kentucky | 9 | | | 1,294,627 | 635,274 | 616,417 | 42,936 | 18,857 R | 49.1% | 47.6% | 50.8% | 49.2% |
| Louisiana | 10 | | | 1,548,591 | 792,853 | 708,453 | 47,285 | 84,400 R | 51.2% | 45.7% | 52.8% | 47.2% |
| Maine | 4 | | | 523,011 | 238,522 | 220,974 | 63,515 | 17,548 R | 45.6% | 42.3% | 51.9% | 48.1% |
| Maryland | | 10 | | 1,540,496 | 680,606 | 726,161 | 133,729 | 45,555 D | 44.2% | 47.1% | 48.4% | 51.6% |
| Massachusetts | 14 | | | 2,524,298 | 1,057,631 | 1,053,802 | 412,865 | 3,829 R | 41.9% | 41.7% | 50.1% | 49.9% |
| Michigan | 21 | | | 3,909,725 | 1,915,225 | 1,661,532 | 332,968 | 253,693 R | 49.0% | 42.5% | 53.5% | 46.5% |
| Minnesota | | 10 | | 2,051,980 | 873,268 | 954,174 | 224,538 | 80,906 D | 42.6% | 46.5% | 47.8% | 52.2% |
| Mississippi | 7 | | | 892,620 | 441,089 | 429,281 | 22,250 | 11,808 R | 49.4% | 48.1% | 50.7% | 49.3% |
| Missouri | 12 | | | 2,099,824 | 1,074,181 | 931,182 | 94,461 | 142,999 R | 51.2% | 44.3% | 53.6% | 46.4% |
| Montana | 4 | | | 363,952 | 206,814 | 118,032 | 39,106 | 88,782 R | 56.8% | 32.4% | 63.7% | 36.3% |
| Nebraska | 5 | | | 640,854 | 419,937 | 166,851 | 54,066 | 253,086 R | 65.5% | 26.0% | 71.6% | 28.4% |
| Nevada | 3 | | | 247,885 | 155,017 | 66,666 | 26,202 | 88,351 R | 62.5% | 26.9% | 69.9% | 30.1% |
| New Hampshire | 4 | | | 383,990 | 221,705 | 108,864 | 53,421 | 112,841 R | 57.7% | 28.4% | 67.1% | 32.9% |
| New Jersey | 17 | | | 2,975,684 | 1,546,557 | 1,147,364 | 281,763 | 399,193 R | 52.0% | 38.6% | 57.4% | 42.6% |
| New Mexico | 4 | | | 456,971 | 250,779 | 167,826 | 38,366 | 82,953 R | 54.9% | 36.7% | 59.9% | 40.1% |
| New York | 41 | | | 6,201,959 | 2,893,831 | 2,728,372 | 579,756 | 165,459 R | 46.7% | 44.0% | 51.5% | 48.5% |
| North Carolina | 13 | | | 1,855,833 | 915,018 | 875,635 | 65,180 | 39,383 R | 49.3% | 47.2% | 51.1% | 48.9% |
| North Dakota | 3 | | | 301,545 | 193,695 | 79,189 | 28,661 | 114,506 R | 64.2% | 26.3% | 71.0% | 29.0% |
| Ohio | 25 | | | 4,283,603 | 2,206,545 | 1,752,414 | 324,644 | 454,131 R | 51.5% | 40.9% | 55.7% | 44.3% |
| Oklahoma | 8 | | | 1,149,708 | 695,570 | 402,026 | 52,112 | 293,544 R | 60.5% | 35.0% | 63.4% | 36.6% |
| Oregon | 6 | | | 1,181,516 | 571,044 | 456,890 | 153,582 | 114,154 R | 48.3% | 38.7% | 55.6% | 44.4% |
| Pennsylvania | 27 | | | 4,561,501 | 2,261,872 | 1,937,540 | 362,089 | 324,332 R | 49.6% | 42.5% | 53.9% | 46.1% |
| Rhode Island | | 4 | | 416,072 | 154,793 | 198,342 | 62,937 | 43,549 D | 37.2% | 47.7% | 43.8% | 56.2% |
| South Carolina | 8 | | | 894,071 | 441,841 | 430,385 | 21,845 | 11,456 R | 49.4% | 48.1% | 50.7% | 49.3% |
| South Dakota | 4 | | | 327,703 | 198,343 | 103,855 | 25,505 | 94,488 R | 60.5% | 31.7% | 65.6% | 34.4% |
| Tennessee | 10 | | | 1,617,616 | 787,761 | 783,051 | 46,804 | 4,710 R | 48.7% | 48.4% | 50.1% | 49.9% |
| Texas | 26 | | | 4,541,636 | 2,510,705 | 1,881,147 | 149,784 | 629,558 R | 55.3% | 41.4% | 57.2% | 42.8% |
| Utah | 4 | | | 604,222 | 439,687 | 124,266 | 40,269 | 315,421 R | 72.8% | 20.6% | 78.0% | 22.0% |
| Vermont | 3 | | | 213,299 | 94,628 | 81,952 | 36,719 | 12,676 R | 44.4% | 38.4% | 53.6% | 46.4% |
| Virginia | 12 | | | 1,866,032 | 989,609 | 752,174 | 124,249 | 237,435 R | 53.0% | 40.3% | 56.8% | 43.2% |
| Washington | 9 | | | 1,742,394 | 865,244 | 650,193 | 226,957 | 215,051 R | 49.7% | 37.3% | 57.1% | 42.9% |
| West Virginia | | 6 | | 737,715 | 334,206 | 367,462 | 36,047 | 33,256 D | 45.3% | 49.8% | 47.6% | 52.4% |
| Wisconsin | 11 | | | 2,273,221 | 1,088,845 | 981,584 | 202,792 | 107,261 R | 47.9% | 43.2% | 52.6% | 47.4% |
| Wyoming | 3 | | | 176,713 | 110,700 | 49,427 | 16,586 | 61,273 R | 62.6% | 28.0% | 69.1% | 30.9% |
| Dist. of Col. | | 3 | | 175,237 | 23,545 | 131,113 | 20,579 | 107,568 D | 13.4% | 74.8% | 15.2% | 84.8% |
| United States | 489 | 49 | — | 86,515,221 | 43,904,153 | 35,483,883 | 7,127,185 | 8,420,270 R | 50.7% | 41.0% | 55.3% | 44.7% |

## PRESIDENT 1976

In Washington, one Republican elector voted in the electoral College for Ronald Reagan for President and Robert Dole for Vice-President.

In New York the Republican figures include Conservative votes and the Democratic figures include Liberal votes. In Vermont the Democratic figures include votes cast on the Independent Vermonters party ticket.

In a number of states minor party candidates appeared on the ballot with variations of the party designations given below and in several cases with entirely different party names.

Eugene J. McCarthy appeared on the ballot with various party designations and with various Vice-Presidential candidates as running mates. In New Jersey Lester G. Maddox's Vice-Presidential candidate was Edmund O. Matzal.

The candidates listed below include all those who appeared on the ballot in at least one state. Where identified by state authorities, write-in votes for minor party candidates are credited to their total.

| | |
|---|---|
| 40,830,763 | Jimmy Carter and Walter F. Mondale, *Democratic.* |
| 39,147,793 | Gerald R. Ford and Robert Dole, *Republican.* |
| 756,691 | Eugene J. McCarthy and various Vice-Presidential candidates, *Independent.* |
| 173,011 | Roger L. MacBride and David D. Bergland, *Libertarian.* |
| 170,531 | Lester G. Maddox and William D. Dyke, *American Independent.* |
| 160,773 | Thomas J. Anderson and Rufus Shackelford, *American.* |
| 91,314 | Peter Camejo and Willie Mae Reid, *Socialist Workers.* |
| 58,992 | Gus Hall and Jarvis Tyner, *Communist.* |
| 49,024 | Margaret Wright and Benjamin Spock, *People's.* |
| 40,043 | Lyndon H. LaRouche and R. W. Evans, *United States Labor.* |
| 15,934 | Benjamin C. Bubar and Earl F. Dodge, *Prohibition.* |
| 9,616 | Julius Levin and Constance Blomen, *Socialist Labor.* |
| 6,038 | Frank P. Zeidler and J. Q. Brisben, *Socialist.* |
| 361 | Ernest L. Miller and Roy N. Eddy, *Restoration.* |
| 36 | Frank Taylor and Henry Swan, *United American.* |

In addition, 39,861 scattered write-in votes were reported from various states and 5,108 votes were cast in Nevada for "None of These Candidates".

# UNITED STATES

## PRESIDENT 1976

| State | Electoral Vote Rep. | Electoral Vote Dem. | Electoral Vote Other | Total Vote | Republican | Democratic | Other | Plurality | Percentage Total Vote Rep. | Total Vote Dem. | Major Vote Rep. | Major Vote Dem. |
|---|---|---|---|---|---|---|---|---|---|---|---|---|
| Alabama | | 9 | | 1,182,850 | 504,070 | 659,170 | 19,610 | 155,100 D | 42.6% | 55.7% | 43.3% | 56.7% |
| Alaska | 3 | | | 123,574 | 71,555 | 44,058 | 7,961 | 27,497 R | 57.9% | 35.7% | 61.9% | 38.1% |
| Arizona | 6 | | | 742,719 | 418,642 | 295,602 | 28,475 | 123,040 R | 56.4% | 39.8% | 58.6% | 41.4% |
| Arkansas | | 6 | | 767,535 | 267,903 | 498,604 | 1,028 | 230,701 D | 34.9% | 65.0% | 35.0% | 65.0% |
| California | 45 | | | 7,867,117 | 3,882,244 | 3,742,284 | 242,589 | 139,960 R | 49.3% | 47.6% | 50.9% | 49.1% |
| Colorado | 7 | | | 1,081,554 | 584,367 | 460,353 | 36,834 | 124,014 R | 54.0% | 42.6% | 55.9% | 44.1% |
| Connecticut | 8 | | | 1,381,526 | 719,261 | 647,895 | 14,370 | 71,366 R | 52.1% | 46.9% | 52.6% | 47.4% |
| Delaware | | 3 | | 235,834 | 109,831 | 122,596 | 3,407 | 12,765 D | 46.6% | 52.0% | 47.3% | 52.7% |
| Florida | | 17 | | 3,150,631 | 1,469,531 | 1,636,000 | 45,100 | 166,469 D | 46.6% | 51.9% | 47.3% | 52.7% |
| Georgia | | 12 | | 1,467,458 | 483,743 | 979,409 | 4,306 | 495,666 D | 33.0% | 66.7% | 33.1% | 66.9% |
| Hawaii | | 4 | | 291,301 | 140,003 | 147,375 | 3,923 | 7,372 D | 48.1% | 50.6% | 48.7% | 51.3% |
| Idaho | 4 | | | 344,071 | 204,151 | 126,549 | 13,371 | 77,602 R | 59.3% | 36.8% | 61.7% | 38.3% |
| Illinois | 26 | | | 4,718,914 | 2,364,269 | 2,271,295 | 83,350 | 92,974 R | 50.1% | 48.1% | 51.0% | 49.0% |
| Indiana | 13 | | | 2,220,362 | 1,183,958 | 1,014,714 | 21,690 | 169,244 R | 53.3% | 45.7% | 53.8% | 46.2% |
| Iowa | 8 | | | 1,279,306 | 632,863 | 619,931 | 26,512 | 12,932 R | 49.5% | 48.5% | 50.5% | 49.5% |
| Kansas | 7 | | | 957,845 | 502,752 | 430,421 | 24,672 | 72,331 R | 52.5% | 44.9% | 53.9% | 46.1% |
| Kentucky | | 9 | | 1,167,142 | 531,852 | 615,717 | 19,573 | 83,865 D | 45.6% | 52.8% | 46.3% | 53.7% |
| Louisiana | | 10 | | 1,278,439 | 587,446 | 661,365 | 29,628 | 73,919 D | 46.0% | 51.7% | 47.0% | 53.0% |
| Maine | 4 | | | 483,216 | 236,320 | 232,279 | 14,617 | 4,041 R | 48.9% | 48.1% | 50.4% | 49.6% |
| Maryland | | 10 | | 1,439,897 | 672,661 | 759,612 | 7,624 | 86,951 D | 46.7% | 52.8% | 47.0% | 53.0% |
| Massachusetts | | 14 | | 2,547,558 | 1,030,276 | 1,429,475 | 87,807 | 399,199 D | 40.4% | 56.1% | 41.9% | 58.1% |
| Michigan | 21 | | | 3,653,749 | 1,893,742 | 1,696,714 | 63,293 | 197,028 R | 51.8% | 46.4% | 52.7% | 47.3% |
| Minnesota | | 10 | | 1,949,931 | 819,395 | 1,070,440 | 60,096 | 251,045 D | 42.0% | 54.9% | 43.4% | 56.6% |
| Mississippi | | 7 | | 769,361 | 366,846 | 381,309 | 21,206 | 14,463 D | 47.7% | 49.6% | 49.0% | 51.0% |
| Missouri | | 12 | | 1,953,600 | 927,443 | 998,387 | 27,770 | 70,944 D | 47.5% | 51.1% | 48.2% | 51.8% |
| Montana | 4 | | | 328,734 | 173,703 | 149,259 | 5,772 | 24,444 R | 52.8% | 45.4% | 53.8% | 46.2% |
| Nebraska | 5 | | | 607,668 | 359,705 | 233,692 | 14,271 | 126,013 R | 59.2% | 38.5% | 60.6% | 39.4% |
| Nevada | 3 | | | 201,876 | 101,273 | 92,479 | 8,124 | 8,794 R | 50.2% | 45.8% | 52.3% | 47.7% |
| New Hampshire | 4 | | | 339,618 | 185,935 | 147,635 | 6,048 | 38,300 R | 54.7% | 43.5% | 55.7% | 44.3% |
| New Jersey | 17 | | | 3,014,472 | 1,509,688 | 1,444,653 | 60,131 | 65,035 R | 50.1% | 47.9% | 51.1% | 48.9% |
| New Mexico | 4 | | | 418,409 | 211,419 | 201,148 | 5,842 | 10,271 R | 50.5% | 48.1% | 51.2% | 48.8% |
| New York | | 41 | | 6,534,170 | 3,100,791 | 3,389,558 | 43,821 | 288,767 D | 47.5% | 51.9% | 47.8% | 52.2% |
| North Carolina | | 13 | | 1,678,914 | 741,960 | 927,365 | 9,589 | 185,405 D | 44.2% | 55.2% | 44.4% | 55.6% |
| North Dakota | 3 | | | 297,188 | 153,470 | 136,078 | 7,640 | 17,392 R | 51.6% | 45.8% | 53.0% | 47.0% |
| Ohio | | 25 | | 4,111,873 | 2,000,505 | 2,011,621 | 99,747 | 11,116 D | 48.7% | 48.9% | 49.9% | 50.1% |
| Oklahoma | 8 | | | 1,092,251 | 545,708 | 532,442 | 14,101 | 13,266 R | 50.0% | 48.7% | 50.6% | 49.4% |
| Oregon | 6 | | | 1,029,876 | 492,120 | 490,407 | 47,349 | 1,713 R | 47.8% | 47.6% | 50.1% | 49.9% |
| Pennsylvania | | 27 | | 4,620,787 | 2,205,604 | 2,328,677 | 86,506 | 123,073 D | 47.7% | 50.4% | 48.6% | 51.4% |
| Rhode Island | | 4 | | 411,170 | 181,249 | 227,636 | 2,285 | 46,387 D | 44.1% | 55.4% | 44.3% | 55.7% |
| South Carolina | | 8 | | 802,583 | 346,149 | 450,807 | 5,627 | 104,658 D | 43.1% | 56.2% | 43.4% | 56.6% |
| South Dakota | 4 | | | 300,678 | 151,505 | 147,068 | 2,105 | 4,437 R | 50.4% | 48.9% | 50.7% | 49.3% |
| Tennessee | | 10 | | 1,476,345 | 633,969 | 825,879 | 16,497 | 191,910 D | 42.9% | 55.9% | 43.4% | 56.6% |
| Texas | | 26 | | 4,071,884 | 1,953,300 | 2,082,319 | 36,265 | 129,019 D | 48.0% | 51.1% | 48.4% | 51.6% |
| Utah | 4 | | | 541,198 | 337,908 | 182,110 | 21,180 | 155,798 R | 62.4% | 33.6% | 65.0% | 35.0% |
| Vermont | 3 | | | 187,765 | 102,085 | 80,954 | 4,726 | 21,131 R | 54.4% | 43.1% | 55.8% | 44.2% |
| Virginia | 12 | | | 1,697,094 | 836,554 | 813,896 | 46,644 | 22,658 R | 49.3% | 48.0% | 50.7% | 49.3% |
| Washington | 8 | | 1 | 1,555,534 | 777,732 | 717,323 | 60,479 | 60,409 R | 50.0% | 46.1% | 52.0% | 48.0% |
| West Virginia | | 6 | | 750,964 | 314,760 | 435,914 | 290 | 121,154 D | 41.9% | 58.0% | 41.9% | 58.1% |
| Wisconsin | | 11 | | 2,104,175 | 1,004,987 | 1,040,232 | 58,956 | 35,245 D | 47.8% | 49.4% | 49.1% | 50.9% |
| Wyoming | 3 | | | 156,343 | 92,717 | 62,239 | 1,387 | 30,478 R | 59.3% | 39.8% | 59.8% | 40.2% |
| Dist. of Col. | | 3 | | 168,830 | 27,873 | 137,818 | 3,139 | 109,945 D | 16.5% | 81.6% | 16.8% | 83.2% |
| United States | 240 | 297 | 1 | 81,555,889 | 39,147,793 | 40,830,763 | 1,577,333 | 1,682,970 D | 48.0% | 50.1% | 48.9% | 51.1% |

# PRESIDENT 1972

In Virginia one Republican elector voted in the Electoral College for the Libertarian candidates for President and Vice-President.

In New York the Republican figures include Conservative votes and the Democratic figures include Liberal votes. In Alabama the Democratic figures include votes cast on the National Democratic Party of Alabama ticket and in South Carolina the Democratic figures include United Citizens Party votes.

In some states candidates appeared on the ballot under party names other than those used below. The Socialist Workers party vote listed below for Jenness and Pulley include votes cast for substitute candidates (Reed and DeBerry) or cast without named candidates in several states.

The Democratic Vice-Presidential candidate, Senator Thomas F. Eagleton, withdrew shortly after the party convention and R. Sargent Shriver was named by the Democratic National Committee as the party's candidate for Vice President.

The candidates listed below include all those who appeared on the ballot in at least one state. Where identified by state authorities, write-in votes for minor party candidates are credited to their total.

| | |
|---:|---|
| 47,169,911 | Richard M. Nixon and Spiro T. Agnew, *Republican*. |
| 29,170,383 | George S. McGovern and R. Sargent Shriver, *Democratic*. |
| 1,099,482 | John G. Schmitz and Thomas J. Anderson, *American*. |
| 78,756 | Benjamin Spock and Julius Hobson, *People's*. |
| 66,677 | Linda Jenness and Andrew Pulley, *Socialist Workers*. |
| 53,814 | Louis Fisher and Genevieve Gunderson, *Socialist Labor*. |
| 25,595 | Gus Hall and Jarvis Tyner, *Communist*. |
| 13,505 | E. Harold Munn and Marshall E. Uncapher, *Prohibition*. |
| 3,673 | John Hospers and Theodora Nathan, *Libertarian*. |
| 1,743 | John V. Mahalchik and Irving Homer, *America First*. |
| 220 | Gabriel Green and Daniel Fry, *Universal*. |

In addition, 34,795 scattered write-in votes were reported from various states.

Vice-President Agnew resigned in October 1973 and Representative Gerald R. Ford was nominated by President Nixon to fill the vacancy. This action was approved by the Senate in November and by the House of Representatives in December.

In August 1974 President Nixon resigned and was succeeded by Vice-President Ford. In the same month Nelson A. Rockefeller was nominated to be Vice-President and was confirmed by Congress in December 1974.

# UNITED STATES

## PRESIDENT 1972

| State | Electoral Vote Rep. | Electoral Vote Dem. | Electoral Vote Other | Total Vote | Republican | Democratic | Other | Plurality | Percentage Total Vote Rep. | Percentage Total Vote Dem. | Percentage Major Vote Rep. | Percentage Major Vote Dem. |
|---|---|---|---|---|---|---|---|---|---|---|---|---|
| Alabama | 9 | | | 1,006,111 | 728,701 | 256,923 | 20,487 | 471,778 R | 72.4% | 25.5% | 73.9% | 26.1% |
| Alaska | 3 | | | 95,219 | 55,349 | 32,967 | 6,903 | 22,382 R | 58.1% | 34.6% | 62.7% | 37.3% |
| Arizona | 6 | | | 622,926 | 402,812 | 198,540 | 21,574 | 204,272 R | 64.7% | 31.9% | 67.0% | 33.0% |
| Arkansas | 6 | | | 651,320 | 448,541 | 199,892 | 2,887 | 248,649 R | 68.9% | 30.7% | 69.2% | 30.8% |
| California | 45 | | | 8,367,862 | 4,602,096 | 3,475,847 | 289,919 | 1,126,249 R | 55.0% | 41.5% | 57.0% | 43.0% |
| Colorado | 7 | | | 953,884 | 597,189 | 329,980 | 26,715 | 267,209 R | 62.6% | 34.6% | 64.4% | 35.6% |
| Connecticut | 8 | | | 1,384,277 | 810,763 | 555,498 | 18,016 | 255,265 R | 58.6% | 40.1% | 59.3% | 40.7% |
| Delaware | 3 | | | 235,516 | 140,357 | 92,283 | 2,876 | 48,074 R | 59.6% | 39.2% | 60.3% | 39.7% |
| Florida | 17 | | | 2,583,283 | 1,857,759 | 718,117 | 7,407 | 1,139,642 R | 71.9% | 27.8% | 72.1% | 27.9% |
| Georgia | 12 | | | 1,174,772 | 881,496 | 289,529 | 3,747 | 591,967 R | 75.0% | 24.6% | 75.3% | 24.7% |
| Hawaii | 4 | | | 270,274 | 168,865 | 101,409 | | 67,456 R | 62.5% | 37.5% | 62.5% | 37.5% |
| Idaho | 4 | | | 310,379 | 199,384 | 80,826 | 30,169 | 118,558 R | 64.2% | 26.0% | 71.2% | 28.8% |
| Illinois | 26 | | | 4,723,236 | 2,788,179 | 1,913,472 | 21,585 | 874,707 R | 59.0% | 40.5% | 59.3% | 40.7% |
| Indiana | 13 | | | 2,125,529 | 1,405,154 | 708,568 | 11,807 | 696,586 R | 66.1% | 33.3% | 66.5% | 33.5% |
| Iowa | 8 | | | 1,225,944 | 706,207 | 496,206 | 23,531 | 210,001 R | 57.6% | 40.5% | 58.7% | 41.3% |
| Kansas | 7 | | | 916,095 | 619,812 | 270,287 | 25,996 | 349,525 R | 67.7% | 29.5% | 69.6% | 30.4% |
| Kentucky | 9 | | | 1,067,499 | 676,446 | 371,159 | 19,894 | 305,287 R | 63.4% | 34.8% | 64.6% | 35.4% |
| Louisiana | 10 | | | 1,051,491 | 686,852 | 298,142 | 66,497 | 388,710 R | 65.3% | 28.4% | 69.7% | 30.3% |
| Maine | 4 | | | 417,042 | 256,458 | 160,584 | | 95,874 R | 61.5% | 38.5% | 61.5% | 38.5% |
| Maryland | 10 | | | 1,353,812 | 829,305 | 505,781 | 18,726 | 323,524 R | 61.3% | 37.4% | 62.1% | 37.9% |
| Massachusetts | | 14 | | 2,458,756 | 1,112,078 | 1,332,540 | 14,138 | 220,462 D | 45.2% | 54.2% | 45.5% | 54.5% |
| Michigan | 21 | | | 3,489,727 | 1,961,721 | 1,459,435 | 68,571 | 502,286 R | 56.2% | 41.8% | 57.3% | 42.7% |
| Minnesota | 10 | | | 1,741,652 | 898,269 | 802,346 | 41,037 | 95,923 R | 51.6% | 46.1% | 52.8% | 47.2% |
| Mississippi | 7 | | | 645,963 | 505,125 | 126,782 | 14,056 | 378,343 R | 78.2% | 19.6% | 79.9% | 20.1% |
| Missouri | 12 | | | 1,855,803 | 1,153,852 | 697,147 | 4,804 | 456,705 R | 62.2% | 37.6% | 62.3% | 37.7% |
| Montana | 4 | | | 317,603 | 183,976 | 120,197 | 13,430 | 63,779 R | 57.9% | 37.8% | 60.5% | 39.5% |
| Nebraska | 5 | | | 576,289 | 406,298 | 169,991 | | 236,307 R | 70.5% | 29.5% | 70.5% | 29.5% |
| Nevada | 3 | | | 181,766 | 115,750 | 66,016 | | 49,734 R | 63.7% | 36.3% | 63.7% | 36.3% |
| New Hampshire | 4 | | | 334,055 | 213,724 | 116,435 | 3,896 | 97,289 R | 64.0% | 34.9% | 64.7% | 35.3% |
| New Jersey | 17 | | | 2,997,229 | 1,845,502 | 1,102,211 | 49,516 | 743,291 R | 61.6% | 36.8% | 62.6% | 37.4% |
| New Mexico | 4 | | | 386,241 | 235,606 | 141,084 | 9,551 | 94,522 R | 61.0% | 36.5% | 62.5% | 37.5% |
| New York | 41 | | | 7,165,919 | 4,192,778 | 2,951,084 | 22,057 | 1,241,694 R | 58.5% | 41.2% | 58.7% | 41.3% |
| North Carolina | 13 | | | 1,518,612 | 1,054,889 | 438,705 | 25,018 | 616,184 R | 69.5% | 28.9% | 70.6% | 29.4% |
| North Dakota | 3 | | | 280,514 | 174,109 | 100,384 | 6,021 | 73,725 R | 62.1% | 35.8% | 63.4% | 36.6% |
| Ohio | 25 | | | 4,094,787 | 2,441,827 | 1,558,889 | 94,071 | 882,938 R | 59.6% | 38.1% | 61.0% | 39.0% |
| Oklahoma | 8 | | | 1,029,900 | 759,025 | 247,147 | 23,728 | 511,878 R | 73.7% | 24.0% | 75.4% | 24.6% |
| Oregon | 6 | | | 927,946 | 486,686 | 392,760 | 48,500 | 93,926 R | 52.4% | 42.3% | 55.3% | 44.7% |
| Pennsylvania | 27 | | | 4,592,106 | 2,714,521 | 1,796,951 | 80,634 | 917,570 R | 59.1% | 39.1% | 60.2% | 39.8% |
| Rhode Island | 4 | | | 415,808 | 220,383 | 194,645 | 780 | 25,738 R | 53.0% | 46.8% | 53.1% | 46.9% |
| South Carolina | 8 | | | 673,960 | 477,044 | 186,824 | 10,092 | 290,220 R | 70.8% | 27.7% | 71.9% | 28.1% |
| South Dakota | 4 | | | 307,415 | 166,476 | 139,945 | 994 | 26,531 R | 54.2% | 45.5% | 54.3% | 45.7% |
| Tennessee | 10 | | | 1,201,182 | 813,147 | 357,293 | 30,742 | 455,854 R | 67.7% | 29.7% | 69.5% | 30.5% |
| Texas | 26 | | | 3,471,281 | 2,298,896 | 1,154,289 | 18,096 | 1,144,607 R | 66.2% | 33.3% | 66.6% | 33.4% |
| Utah | 4 | | | 478,476 | 323,643 | 126,284 | 28,549 | 197,359 R | 67.6% | 26.4% | 71.9% | 28.1% |
| Vermont | 3 | | | 186,947 | 117,149 | 68,174 | 1,624 | 48,975 R | 62.7% | 36.5% | 63.2% | 36.8% |
| Virginia | 11 | | 1 | 1,457,019 | 988,493 | 438,887 | 29,639 | 549,606 R | 67.8% | 30.1% | 69.3% | 30.7% |
| Washington | 9 | | | 1,470,847 | 837,135 | 568,334 | 65,378 | 268,801 R | 56.9% | 38.6% | 59.6% | 40.4% |
| West Virginia | 6 | | | 762,399 | 484,964 | 277,435 | | 207,529 R | 63.6% | 36.4% | 63.6% | 36.4% |
| Wisconsin | 11 | | | 1,852,890 | 989,430 | 810,174 | 53,286 | 179,256 R | 53.4% | 43.7% | 55.0% | 45.0% |
| Wyoming | 3 | | | 145,570 | 100,464 | 44,358 | 748 | 56,106 R | 69.0% | 30.5% | 69.4% | 30.6% |
| Dist. of Col. | | 3 | | 163,421 | 35,226 | 127,627 | 568 | 92,401 D | 21.6% | 78.1% | 21.6% | 78.4% |
| United States | 520 | 17 | 1 | 77,718,554 | 47,169,911 | 29,170,383 | 1,378,260 | 17,999,528 R | 60.7% | 37.5% | 61.8% | 38.2% |

## PRESIDENT 1968

In North Carolina one Republican elector voted in the Electoral College for the American Independent candidates for President and Vice-President.

In New York the Democratic figures include Liberal votes. In Alabama the Democratic vote is a combination of the votes cast for the Alabama Independent Democratic elector ticket and National Democratic Party of Alabama elector ticket. In some states candidates appeared on the ballot with variations of the party name used below. In some states the Vice-Presidential candidate of the American Independent party was listed as Marvin Griffin rather than Curtis E. LeMay.

The vote listed below for Eldridge Cleaver includes votes cast in California and Utah for the Peace and Freedom party where only the Vice Presidential candidate was on the ballot.

The candidates listed below include all those who appeared on the ballot in at least one state. Where identified by state authorities, write-in votes for minor party candidates are credited to their total.

| | |
|---|---|
| 31,785,480 | Richard M. Nixon and Spiro T. Agnew, *Republican*. |
| 31,275,166 | Hubert H. Humphrey and Edmund S. Muskie, *Democratic*. |
| 9,906,473 | George C. Wallace and Curtis E. LeMay, *American Independent*. |
| 52,588 | Henning A. Blomen and George S. Taylor, *Socialist Labor*. |
| 47,133 | Dick Gregory and various Vice-Presidential candidates, *Peace and Freedom*. |
| 41,388 | Fred Halstead and Paul Boutelle, *Socialist Workers*. |
| 36,563 | Eldridge Cleaver and various Vice-Presidential candidates, *Peace and Freedom*. |
| 25,552 | Eugene J. McCarthy and no Vice-Presidential candidate, *New Party*. |
| 15,123 | E. Harold Munn and Rolland E. Fisher, *Prohibition*. |
| 1,519 | Ventura Chavez and Adelicio Moya, *People's Constitutional*. |
| 1,075 | Charlene Mitchell and Michael Zagarell, *Communist*. |
| 142 | James Hensley and Roscoe B. MacKenna, *Universal*. |
| 34 | Richard K. Troxell and Merle Thayer, *Constitution*. |
| 17 | Kent M. Soeters and James P. Powers, *Berkeley Defense Group*. |

There were 12,430 votes cast in various states for elector tickets for which there were no formal Presidential or Vice-Presidential candidates. In addition, 11,192 scattered write-in votes were reported from various states.

# UNITED STATES

## PRESIDENT 1968

| State | Electoral Vote Rep. | Dem. | Other | Total Vote | Republican | Democratic | AIP | Other | Plurality | Percentage Total Vote Rep. | Dem. | AIP |
|---|---|---|---|---|---|---|---|---|---|---|---|---|
| Alabama | | | 10 | 1,049,922 | 146,923 | 196,579 | 691,425 | 14,995 | 494,846 A | 14.0% | 18.7% | 65.9% |
| Alaska | 3 | | | 83,035 | 37,600 | 35,411 | 10,024 | | 2,189 R | 45.3% | 42.6% | 12.1% |
| Arizona | 5 | | | 486,936 | 266,721 | 170,514 | 46,573 | 3,128 | 96,207 R | 54.8% | 35.0% | 9.6% |
| Arkansas | | | 6 | 619,969 | 190,759 | 188,228 | 240,982 | | 50,223 A | 30.8% | 30.4% | 38.9% |
| California | 40 | | | 7,251,587 | 3,467,664 | 3,244,318 | 487,270 | 52,335 | 223,346 R | 47.8% | 44.7% | 6.7% |
| Colorado | 6 | | | 811,199 | 409,345 | 335,174 | 60,813 | 5,867 | 74,171 R | 50.5% | 41.3% | 7.5% |
| Connecticut | | 8 | | 1,256,232 | 556,721 | 621,561 | 76,650 | 1,300 | 64,840 D | 44.3% | 49.5% | 6.1% |
| Delaware | 3 | | | 214,367 | 96,714 | 89,194 | 28,459 | | 7,520 R | 45.1% | 41.6% | 13.3% |
| Florida | 14 | | | 2,187,805 | 886,804 | 676,794 | 624,207 | | 210,010 R | 40.5% | 30.9% | 28.5% |
| Georgia | | | 12 | 1,250,266 | 380,111 | 334,440 | 535,550 | 165 | 155,439 A | 30.4% | 26.7% | 42.8% |
| Hawaii | | 4 | | 236,218 | 91,425 | 141,324 | 3,469 | | 49,899 D | 38.7% | 59.8% | 1.5% |
| Idaho | 4 | | | 291,183 | 165,369 | 89,273 | 36,541 | | 76,096 R | 56.8% | 30.7% | 12.5% |
| Illinois | 26 | | | 4,619,749 | 2,174,774 | 2,039,814 | 390,958 | 14,203 | 134,960 R | 47.1% | 44.2% | 8.5% |
| Indiana | 13 | | | 2,123,597 | 1,067,885 | 806,659 | 243,108 | 5,945 | 261,226 R | 50.3% | 38.0% | 11.4% |
| Iowa | 9 | | | 1,167,931 | 619,106 | 476,699 | 66,422 | 5,704 | 142,407 R | 53.0% | 40.8% | 5.7% |
| Kansas | 7 | | | 872,783 | 478,674 | 302,996 | 88,921 | 2,192 | 175,678 R | 54.8% | 34.7% | 10.2% |
| Kentucky | 9 | | | 1,055,893 | 462,411 | 397,541 | 193,098 | 2,843 | 64,870 R | 43.8% | 37.6% | 18.3% |
| Louisiana | | | 10 | 1,097,450 | 257,535 | 309,615 | 530,300 | | 220,685 A | 23.5% | 28.2% | 48.3% |
| Maine | | 4 | | 392,936 | 169,254 | 217,312 | 6,370 | | 48,058 D | 43.1% | 55.3% | 1.6% |
| Maryland | | 10 | | 1,235,039 | 517,995 | 538,310 | 178,734 | | 20,315 D | 41.9% | 43.6% | 14.5% |
| Massachusetts | | 14 | | 2,331,752 | 766,844 | 1,469,218 | 87,088 | 8,602 | 702,374 D | 32.9% | 63.0% | 3.7% |
| Michigan | | 21 | | 3,306,250 | 1,370,665 | 1,593,082 | 331,968 | 10,535 | 222,417 D | 41.5% | 48.2% | 10.0% |
| Minnesota | | 10 | | 1,588,506 | 658,643 | 857,738 | 68,931 | 3,194 | 199,095 D | 41.5% | 54.0% | 4.3% |
| Mississippi | | | 7 | 654,509 | 88,516 | 150,644 | 415,349 | | 264,705 A | 13.5% | 23.0% | 63.5% |
| Missouri | 12 | | | 1,809,502 | 811,932 | 791,444 | 206,126 | | 20,488 R | 44.9% | 43.7% | 11.4% |
| Montana | 4 | | | 274,404 | 138,835 | 114,117 | 20,015 | 1,437 | 24,718 R | 50.6% | 41.6% | 7.3% |
| Nebraska | 5 | | | 536,851 | 321,163 | 170,784 | 44,904 | | 150,379 R | 59.8% | 31.8% | 8.4% |
| Nevada | 3 | | | 154,218 | 73,188 | 60,598 | 20,432 | | 12,590 R | 47.5% | 39.3% | 13.2% |
| New Hampshire | 4 | | | 297,298 | 154,903 | 130,589 | 11,173 | 633 | 24,314 R | 52.1% | 43.9% | 3.8% |
| New Jersey | 17 | | | 2,875,395 | 1,325,467 | 1,264,206 | 262,187 | 23,535 | 61,261 R | 46.1% | 44.0% | 9.1% |
| New Mexico | 4 | | | 327,350 | 169,692 | 130,081 | 25,737 | 1,840 | 39,611 R | 51.8% | 39.7% | 7.9% |
| New York | | 43 | | 6,791,688 | 3,007,932 | 3,378,470 | 358,864 | 46,422 | 370,538 D | 44.3% | 49.7% | 5.3% |
| North Carolina | 12 | | 1 | 1,587,493 | 627,192 | 464,113 | 496,188 | | 131,004 R | 39.5% | 29.2% | 31.3% |
| North Dakota | 4 | | | 247,882 | 138,669 | 94,769 | 14,244 | 200 | 43,900 R | 55.9% | 38.2% | 5.7% |
| Ohio | 26 | | | 3,959,698 | 1,791,014 | 1,700,586 | 467,495 | 603 | 90,428 R | 45.2% | 42.9% | 11.8% |
| Oklahoma | 8 | | | 943,086 | 449,697 | 301,658 | 191,731 | | 148,039 R | 47.7% | 32.0% | 20.3% |
| Oregon | 6 | | | 819,622 | 408,433 | 358,866 | 49,683 | 2,640 | 49,567 R | 49.8% | 43.8% | 6.1% |
| Pennsylvania | | 29 | | 4,747,928 | 2,090,017 | 2,259,405 | 378,582 | 19,924 | 169,388 D | 44.0% | 47.6% | 8.0% |
| Rhode Island | | 4 | | 385,000 | 122,359 | 246,518 | 15,678 | 445 | 124,159 D | 31.8% | 64.0% | 4.1% |
| South Carolina | 8 | | | 666,978 | 254,062 | 197,486 | 215,430 | | 38,632 R | 38.1% | 29.6% | 32.3% |
| South Dakota | 4 | | | 281,264 | 149,841 | 118,023 | 13,400 | | 31,818 R | 53.3% | 42.0% | 4.8% |
| Tennessee | 11 | | | 1,248,617 | 472,592 | 351,233 | 424,792 | | 47,800 R | 37.8% | 28.1% | 34.0% |
| Texas | | 25 | | 3,079,216 | 1,227,844 | 1,266,804 | 584,269 | 299 | 38,960 D | 39.9% | 41.1% | 19.0% |
| Utah | 4 | | | 422,568 | 238,728 | 156,665 | 26,906 | 269 | 82,063 R | 56.5% | 37.1% | 6.4% |
| Vermont | 3 | | | 161,404 | 85,142 | 70,255 | 5,104 | 903 | 14,887 R | 52.8% | 43.5% | 3.2% |
| Virginia | 12 | | | 1,361,491 | 590,319 | 442,387 | 321,833 | 6,952 | 147,932 R | 43.4% | 32.5% | 23.6% |
| Washington | | 9 | | 1,304,281 | 588,510 | 616,037 | 96,990 | 2,744 | 27,527 D | 45.1% | 47.2% | 7.4% |
| West Virginia | | 7 | | 754,206 | 307,555 | 374,091 | 72,560 | | 66,536 D | 40.8% | 49.6% | 9.6% |
| Wisconsin | 12 | | | 1,691,538 | 809,997 | 748,804 | 127,835 | 4,902 | 61,193 R | 47.9% | 44.3% | 7.6% |
| Wyoming | 3 | | | 127,205 | 70,927 | 45,173 | 11,105 | | 25,754 R | 55.8% | 35.5% | 8.7% |
| Dist. of Col. | | 3 | | 170,578 | 31,012 | 139,566 | | | 108,554 D | 18.2% | 81.8% | |
| United States | 301 | 191 | 46 | 73,211,875 | 31,785,480 | 31,275,166 | 9,906,473 | 244,756 | 510,314 R | 43.4% | 42.7% | 13.5% |

## PRESIDENT 1964

In New York the Democratic figures include Liberal votes.

The candidates listed below include all those who appeared on the ballot in at least one state.

| | |
|---:|---|
| 43,129,566 | Lyndon B. Johnson and Hubert H. Humphrey, *Democratic*. |
| 27,178,188 | Barry M. Goldwater and William E. Miller, *Republican*. |
| 45,219 | Eric Hass and Henning A. Blomen, *Socialist Labor*. |
| 32,720 | Clifton DeBerry and Edward Shaw, *Socialist Workers*. |
| 23,267 | E. Harold Munn and Mark R. Shaw, *Prohibition*. |
| 6,953 | John Kasper and J. B. Stoner, *National States Rights*. |
| 5,060 | Joseph B. Lightburn and T. C. Billings, *Constitution*. |
| 19 | James Hensley and John O. Hopkins, *Universal*. |

In Alabama 210,732 votes were cast for an unpledged Democratic elector ticket. In addition, 12,868 scattered write-in votes were reported from various states.

# UNITED STATES

## PRESIDENT 1964

| State | Electoral Vote Rep. | Electoral Vote Dem. | Electoral Vote Other | Total Vote | Republican | Democratic | Other | Plurality | Percentage Total Vote Rep. | Percentage Total Vote Dem. | Percentage Major Vote Rep. | Percentage Major Vote Dem. |
|---|---|---|---|---|---|---|---|---|---|---|---|---|
| Alabama | 10 | | | 689,818 | 479,085 | | 210,733 | 268,353 R | 69.5% | | 100.0% | |
| Alaska | | 3 | | 67,259 | 22,930 | 44,329 | | 21,399 D | 34.1% | 65.9% | 34.1% | 65.9% |
| Arizona | 5 | | | 480,770 | 242,535 | 237,753 | 482 | 4,782 R | 50.4% | 49.5% | 50.5% | 49.5% |
| Arkansas | | 6 | | 560,426 | 243,264 | 314,197 | 2,965 | 70,933 D | 43.4% | 56.1% | 43.6% | 56.4% |
| California | | 40 | | 7,057,586 | 2,879,108 | 4,171,877 | 6,601 | 1,292,769 D | 40.8% | 59.1% | 40.8% | 59.2% |
| Colorado | | 6 | | 776,986 | 296,767 | 476,024 | 4,195 | 179,257 D | 38.2% | 61.3% | 38.4% | 61.6% |
| Connecticut | | 8 | | 1,218,578 | 390,996 | 826,269 | 1,313 | 435,273 D | 32.1% | 67.8% | 32.1% | 67.9% |
| Delaware | | 3 | | 201,320 | 78,078 | 122,704 | 538 | 44,626 D | 38.8% | 60.9% | 38.9% | 61.1% |
| Florida | | 14 | | 1,854,481 | 905,941 | 948,540 | | 42,599 D | 48.9% | 51.1% | 48.9% | 51.1% |
| Georgia | 12 | | | 1,139,335 | 616,584 | 522,556 | 195 | 94,028 R | 54.1% | 45.9% | 54.1% | 45.9% |
| Hawaii | | 4 | | 207,271 | 44,022 | 163,249 | | 119,227 D | 21.2% | 78.8% | 21.2% | 78.8% |
| Idaho | | 4 | | 292,477 | 143,557 | 148,920 | | 5,363 D | 49.1% | 50.9% | 49.1% | 50.9% |
| Illinois | | 26 | | 4,702,841 | 1,905,946 | 2,796,833 | 62 | 890,887 D | 40.5% | 59.5% | 40.5% | 59.5% |
| Indiana | | 13 | | 2,091,606 | 911,118 | 1,170,848 | 9,640 | 259,730 D | 43.6% | 56.0% | 43.8% | 56.2% |
| Iowa | | 9 | | 1,184,539 | 449,148 | 733,030 | 2,361 | 283,882 D | 37.9% | 61.9% | 38.0% | 62.0% |
| Kansas | | 7 | | 857,901 | 386,579 | 464,028 | 7,294 | 77,449 D | 45.1% | 54.1% | 45.4% | 54.6% |
| Kentucky | | 9 | | 1,046,105 | 372,977 | 669,659 | 3,469 | 296,682 D | 35.7% | 64.0% | 35.8% | 64.2% |
| Louisiana | 10 | | | 896,293 | 509,225 | 387,068 | | 122,157 R | 56.8% | 43.2% | 56.8% | 43.2% |
| Maine | | 4 | | 380,965 | 118,701 | 262,264 | | 143,563 D | 31.2% | 68.8% | 31.2% | 68.8% |
| Maryland | | 10 | | 1,116,457 | 385,495 | 730,912 | 50 | 345,417 D | 34.5% | 65.5% | 34.5% | 65.5% |
| Massachusetts | | 14 | | 2,344,798 | 549,727 | 1,786,422 | 8,649 | 1,236,695 D | 23.4% | 76.2% | 23.5% | 76.5% |
| Michigan | | 21 | | 3,203,102 | 1,060,152 | 2,136,615 | 6,335 | 1,076,463 D | 33.1% | 66.7% | 33.2% | 66.8% |
| Minnesota | | 10 | | 1,554,462 | 559,624 | 991,117 | 3,721 | 431,493 D | 36.0% | 63.8% | 36.1% | 63.9% |
| Mississippi | 7 | | | 409,146 | 356,528 | 52,618 | | 303,910 R | 87.1% | 12.9% | 87.1% | 12.9% |
| Missouri | | 12 | | 1,817,879 | 653,535 | 1,164,344 | | 510,809 D | 36.0% | 64.0% | 36.0% | 64.0% |
| Montana | | 4 | | 278,628 | 113,032 | 164,246 | 1,350 | 51,214 D | 40.6% | 58.9% | 40.8% | 59.2% |
| Nebraska | | 5 | | 584,154 | 276,847 | 307,307 | | 30,460 D | 47.4% | 52.6% | 47.4% | 52.6% |
| Nevada | | 3 | | 135,433 | 56,094 | 79,339 | | 23,245 D | 41.4% | 58.6% | 41.4% | 58.6% |
| New Hampshire | | 4 | | 288,093 | 104,029 | 184,064 | | 80,035 D | 36.1% | 63.9% | 36.1% | 63.9% |
| New Jersey | | 17 | | 2,847,663 | 964,174 | 1,868,231 | 15,258 | 904,057 D | 33.9% | 65.6% | 34.0% | 66.0% |
| New Mexico | | 4 | | 328,645 | 132,838 | 194,015 | 1,792 | 61,177 D | 40.4% | 59.0% | 40.6% | 59.4% |
| New York | | 43 | | 7,166,275 | 2,243,559 | 4,913,102 | 9,614 | 2,669,543 D | 31.3% | 68.6% | 31.3% | 68.7% |
| North Carolina | | 13 | | 1,424,983 | 624,844 | 800,139 | | 175,295 D | 43.8% | 56.2% | 43.8% | 56.2% |
| North Dakota | | 4 | | 258,389 | 108,207 | 149,784 | 398 | 41,577 D | 41.9% | 58.0% | 41.9% | 58.1% |
| Ohio | | 26 | | 3,969,196 | 1,470,865 | 2,498,331 | | 1,027,466 D | 37.1% | 62.9% | 37.1% | 62.9% |
| Oklahoma | | 8 | | 932,499 | 412,665 | 519,834 | | 107,169 D | 44.3% | 55.7% | 44.3% | 55.7% |
| Oregon | | 6 | | 786,305 | 282,779 | 501,017 | 2,509 | 218,238 D | 36.0% | 63.7% | 36.1% | 63.9% |
| Pennsylvania | | 29 | | 4,822,690 | 1,673,657 | 3,130,954 | 18,079 | 1,457,297 D | 34.7% | 64.9% | 34.8% | 65.2% |
| Rhode Island | | 4 | | 390,091 | 74,615 | 315,463 | 13 | 240,848 D | 19.1% | 80.9% | 19.1% | 80.9% |
| South Carolina | 8 | | | 524,779 | 309,048 | 215,723 | 8 | 93,325 R | 58.9% | 41.1% | 58.9% | 41.1% |
| South Dakota | | 4 | | 293,118 | 130,108 | 163,010 | | 32,902 D | 44.4% | 55.6% | 44.4% | 55.6% |
| Tennessee | | 11 | | 1,143,946 | 508,965 | 634,947 | 34 | 125,982 D | 44.5% | 55.5% | 44.5% | 55.5% |
| Texas | | 25 | | 2,626,811 | 958,566 | 1,663,185 | 5,060 | 704,619 D | 36.5% | 63.3% | 36.6% | 63.4% |
| Utah | | 4 | | 401,413 | 181,785 | 219,628 | | 37,843 D | 45.3% | 54.7% | 45.3% | 54.7% |
| Vermont | | 3 | | 163,089 | 54,942 | 108,127 | 20 | 53,185 D | 33.7% | 66.3% | 33.7% | 66.3% |
| Virginia | | 12 | | 1,042,267 | 481,334 | 558,038 | 2,895 | 76,704 D | 46.2% | 53.5% | 46.3% | 53.7% |
| Washington | | 9 | | 1,258,556 | 470,366 | 779,881 | 8,309 | 309,515 D | 37.4% | 62.0% | 37.6% | 62.4% |
| West Virginia | | 7 | | 792,040 | 253,953 | 538,087 | | 284,134 D | 32.1% | 67.9% | 32.1% | 67.9% |
| Wisconsin | | 12 | | 1,691,815 | 638,495 | 1,050,424 | 2,896 | 411,929 D | 37.7% | 62.1% | 37.8% | 62.2% |
| Wyoming | | 3 | | 142,716 | 61,998 | 80,718 | | 18,720 D | 43.4% | 56.6% | 43.4% | 56.6% |
| Dist. of Col. | | 3 | | 198,597 | 28,801 | 169,796 | | 140,995 D | 14.5% | 85.5% | 14.5% | 85.5% |
| United States | 52 | 486 | — | 70,644,592 | 27,178,188 | 43,129,566 | 336,838 | 15,951,378 D | 38.5% | 61.1% | 38.7% | 61.3% |

## PRESIDENT 1960

Senator Harry Flood Byrd received fifteen votes in the Electoral College; six of the eleven Democratic electors in Alabama, all eight of the unpledged Democratic electors in Mississippi and one of the eight Republican electors in Oklahoma voted for Senator Byrd for President. The Alabama and Mississippi electors also cast their fourteen votes for Senator Strom Thurmond for Vice-President; the single Oklahoma elector voted for Senator Barry M. Goldwater for Vice-President.

In New York the Democratic figures include Liberal votes.

The candidates listed below include all those who appeared on the ballot in at least one state.

| | |
|---|---|
| 34,226,731 | John F. Kennedy and Lyndon B. Johnson, *Democratic.* |
| 34,108,157 | Richard M. Nixon and Henry Cabot Lodge, *Republican.* |
| 47,522 | Eric Hass and Georgia Cozzini, *Socialist Labor.* |
| 46,203 | Rutherford L. Decker and E. Harold Munn, *Prohibition.* |
| 44,977 | Orval E. Faubus and John G. Crommelin, *National States Rights.* |
| 40,165 | Farrell Dobbs and Myra Tanner Weiss, *Socialist Workers.* |
| 18,162 | Charles L. Sullivan and Merritt B. Curtis, *Constitutional.* |
| 8,708 | J. Bracken Lee and Kent H. Courtney, *Conservative.* |
| 4,204 | C. Benton Coiner and Edward J. Silverman, Virginia Conservative. |
| 1,767 | Lar Daly and Merritt B. Curtis, Tax Cut. |
| 1,485 | Clennon King and Reginald Carter, Independent Afro-American. |
| 1,401 | Merritt B. Curtis and B. N. Miller, *Constitution.* |

In Louisiana 169,572 votes were cast for Independent electors; in Mississippi 116,248 votes were cast for an unpledged Democratic elector ticket; in Michigan 539 votes were cast for an Independent American ticket. In addition, 2,378 scattered write-in votes were reported from various states.

# UNITED STATES

## PRESIDENT 1960

| State | Electoral Vote Rep. | Dem. | Other | Total Vote | Republican | Democratic | Other | Plurality | Percentage Total Vote Rep. | Dem. | Major Vote Rep. | Dem. |
|---|---|---|---|---|---|---|---|---|---|---|---|---|
| Alabama | | 5 | 6 | 570,225 | 237,981 | 324,050 | 8,194 | 86,069 D | 41.7% | 56.8% | 42.3% | 57.7% |
| Alaska | 3 | | | 60,762 | 30,953 | 29,809 | | 1,144 R | 50.9% | 49.1% | 50.9% | 49.1% |
| Arizona | 4 | | | 398,491 | 221,241 | 176,781 | 469 | 44,460 R | 55.5% | 44.4% | 55.6% | 44.4% |
| Arkansas | | 8 | | 428,509 | 184,508 | 215,049 | 28,952 | 30,541 D | 43.1% | 50.2% | 46.2% | 53.8% |
| California | 32 | | | 6,506,578 | 3,259,722 | 3,224,099 | 22,757 | 35,623 R | 50.1% | 49.6% | 50.3% | 49.7% |
| Colorado | 6 | | | 736,236 | 402,242 | 330,629 | 3,365 | 71,613 R | 54.6% | 44.9% | 54.9% | 45.1% |
| Connecticut | | 8 | | 1,222,883 | 565,813 | 657,055 | 15 | 91,242 D | 46.3% | 53.7% | 46.3% | 53.7% |
| Delaware | | 3 | | 196,683 | 96,373 | 99,590 | 720 | 3,217 D | 49.0% | 50.6% | 49.2% | 50.8% |
| Florida | 10 | | | 1,544,176 | 795,476 | 748,700 | | 46,776 R | 51.5% | 48.5% | 51.5% | 48.5% |
| Georgia | | 12 | | 733,349 | 274,472 | 458,638 | 239 | 184,166 D | 37.4% | 62.5% | 37.4% | 62.6% |
| Hawaii | | 3 | | 184,705 | 92,295 | 92,410 | | 115 D | 50.0% | 50.0% | 50.0% | 50.0% |
| Idaho | 4 | | | 300,450 | 161,597 | 138,853 | | 22,744 R | 53.8% | 46.2% | 53.8% | 46.2% |
| Illinois | | 27 | | 4,757,409 | 2,368,988 | 2,377,846 | 10,575 | 8,858 D | 49.8% | 50.0% | 49.9% | 50.1% |
| Indiana | 13 | | | 2,135,360 | 1,175,120 | 952,358 | 7,882 | 222,762 R | 55.0% | 44.6% | 55.2% | 44.8% |
| Iowa | 10 | | | 1,273,810 | 722,381 | 550,565 | 864 | 171,816 R | 56.7% | 43.2% | 56.7% | 43.3% |
| Kansas | 8 | | | 928,825 | 561,474 | 363,213 | 4,138 | 198,261 R | 60.4% | 39.1% | 60.7% | 39.3% |
| Kentucky | 10 | | | 1,124,462 | 602,607 | 521,855 | | 80,752 R | 53.6% | 46.4% | 53.6% | 46.4% |
| Louisiana | | 10 | | 807,891 | 230,980 | 407,339 | 169,572 | 176,359 D | 28.6% | 50.4% | 36.2% | 63.8% |
| Maine | 5 | | | 421,767 | 240,608 | 181,159 | | 59,449 R | 57.0% | 43.0% | 57.0% | 43.0% |
| Maryland | | 9 | | 1,055,349 | 489,538 | 565,808 | 3 | 76,270 D | 46.4% | 53.6% | 46.4% | 53.6% |
| Massachusetts | | 16 | | 2,469,480 | 976,750 | 1,487,174 | 5,556 | 510,424 D | 39.6% | 60.2% | 39.6% | 60.4% |
| Michigan | | 20 | | 3,318,097 | 1,620,428 | 1,687,269 | 10,400 | 66,841 D | 48.8% | 50.9% | 49.0% | 51.0% |
| Minnesota | | 11 | | 1,541,887 | 757,915 | 779,933 | 4,039 | 22,018 D | 49.2% | 50.6% | 49.3% | 50.7% |
| Mississippi | | | 8 | 298,171 | 73,561 | 108,362 | 116,248 | 7,886 U | 24.7% | 36.3% | 40.4% | 59.6% |
| Missouri | | 13 | | 1,934,422 | 962,221 | 972,201 | | 9,980 D | 49.7% | 50.3% | 49.7% | 50.3% |
| Montana | 4 | | | 277,579 | 141,841 | 134,891 | 847 | 6,950 R | 51.1% | 48.6% | 51.3% | 48.7% |
| Nebraska | 6 | | | 613,095 | 380,553 | 232,542 | | 148,011 R | 62.1% | 37.9% | 62.1% | 37.9% |
| Nevada | | 3 | | 107,267 | 52,387 | 54,880 | | 2,493 D | 48.8% | 51.2% | 48.8% | 51.2% |
| New Hampshire | 4 | | | 295,761 | 157,989 | 137,772 | | 20,217 R | 53.4% | 46.6% | 53.4% | 46.6% |
| New Jersey | | 16 | | 2,773,111 | 1,363,324 | 1,385,415 | 24,372 | 22,091 D | 49.2% | 50.0% | 49.6% | 50.4% |
| New Mexico | | 4 | | 311,107 | 153,733 | 156,027 | 1,347 | 2,294 D | 49.4% | 50.2% | 49.6% | 50.4% |
| New York | | 45 | | 7,291,079 | 3,446,419 | 3,830,085 | 14,575 | 383,666 D | 47.3% | 52.5% | 47.4% | 52.6% |
| North Carolina | | 14 | | 1,368,556 | 655,420 | 713,136 | | 57,716 D | 47.9% | 52.1% | 47.9% | 52.1% |
| North Dakota | 4 | | | 278,431 | 154,310 | 123,963 | 158 | 30,347 R | 55.4% | 44.5% | 55.5% | 44.5% |
| Ohio | 25 | | | 4,161,859 | 2,217,611 | 1,944,248 | | 273,363 R | 53.3% | 46.7% | 53.3% | 46.7% |
| Oklahoma | 7 | | 1 | 903,150 | 533,039 | 370,111 | | 162,928 R | 59.0% | 41.0% | 59.0% | 41.0% |
| Oregon | 6 | | | 776,421 | 408,060 | 367,402 | 959 | 40,658 R | 52.6% | 47.3% | 52.6% | 47.4% |
| Pennsylvania | | 32 | | 5,006,541 | 2,439,956 | 2,556,282 | 10,303 | 116,326 D | 48.7% | 51.1% | 48.8% | 51.2% |
| Rhode Island | | 4 | | 405,535 | 147,502 | 258,032 | 1 | 110,530 D | 36.4% | 63.6% | 36.4% | 63.6% |
| South Carolina | | 8 | | 386,688 | 188,558 | 198,129 | 1 | 9,571 D | 48.8% | 51.2% | 48.8% | 51.2% |
| South Dakota | 4 | | | 306,487 | 178,417 | 128,070 | | 50,347 R | 58.2% | 41.8% | 58.2% | 41.8% |
| Tennessee | 11 | | | 1,051,792 | 556,577 | 481,453 | 13,762 | 75,124 R | 52.9% | 45.8% | 53.6% | 46.4% |
| Texas | | 24 | | 2,311,084 | 1,121,310 | 1,167,567 | 22,207 | 46,257 D | 48.5% | 50.5% | 49.0% | 51.0% |
| Utah | 4 | | | 374,709 | 205,361 | 169,248 | 100 | 36,113 R | 54.8% | 45.2% | 54.8% | 45.2% |
| Vermont | 3 | | | 167,324 | 98,131 | 69,186 | 7 | 28,945 R | 58.6% | 41.3% | 58.6% | 41.4% |
| Virginia | 12 | | | 771,449 | 404,521 | 362,327 | 4,601 | 42,194 R | 52.4% | 47.0% | 52.8% | 47.2% |
| Washington | 9 | | | 1,241,572 | 629,273 | 599,298 | 13,001 | 29,975 R | 50.7% | 48.3% | 51.2% | 48.8% |
| West Virginia | | 8 | | 837,781 | 395,995 | 441,786 | | 45,791 D | 47.3% | 52.7% | 47.3% | 52.7% |
| Wisconsin | 12 | | | 1,729,082 | 895,175 | 830,805 | 3,102 | 64,370 R | 51.8% | 48.0% | 51.9% | 48.1% |
| Wyoming | 3 | | | 140,782 | 77,451 | 63,331 | | 14,120 R | 55.0% | 45.0% | 55.0% | 45.0% |
| Dist. of Col. | | | | | | | | | | | | |
| United States | 219 | 303 | 15 | 68,838,219 | 34,108,157 | 34,226,731 | 503,331 | 118,574 D | 49.5% | 49.7% | 49.9% | 50.1% |

## PRESIDENT 1956

In Alabama, one of the eleven Democratic electors voted in the Electoral College for Walter B. Jones and Herman Talmadge rather than for the national Democratic candidates.

The Republican figures in Mississippi include votes cast for two elector tickets. In New York the Democratic figures include Liberal votes.

The candidates listed below include all those who appeared on the ballot in at least one state.

| | |
|---|---|
| 35,590,472 | Dwight D. Eisenhower and Richard M. Nixon, *Republican*. |
| 26,022,752 | Adlai E. Stevenson and Estes Kefauver, *Democratic*. |
| 111,178 | T. Coleman Andrews and Thomas H. Werdel, *States Rights*. |
| 44,450 | Eric Hass and Georgia Cozzini, *Socialist Labor*. |
| 41,937 | Enoch A. Holtwick and Edwin M. Cooper, *Prohibition*. |
| 7,797 | Farrell Dobbs and Myra Tanner Weiss, *Socialist Workers*. |
| 2,657 | Harry Flood Byrd and William E. Jenner, *States Rights*. |
| 2,126 | Darlington Hoopes and Samuel H. Friedman, *Socialist*. |
| 1,829 | Hanry B. Krajewski and Anne Marie Yezo, *American Third Party*. |
| 8 | Gerald L. K. Smith and Charles F. Robertson, *Christian Nationalist*. |

In Alabama 20,323 votes were cast for Independent electors; in Louisiana 44,520 votes were cast for Unpledged States Rights electors; in Mississippi 42,966 votes were cast for Independent electors and South Carolina 88,509 votes were cast for Independent electors. In addition, 5,384 scattered write-in votes were reported from various states.

# UNITED STATES

## PRESIDENT 1956

| State | Electoral Vote Rep. | Dem. | Other | Total Vote | Republican | Democratic | Other | Plurality | Total Vote Rep. | Dem. | Major Vote Rep. | Dem. |
|---|---|---|---|---|---|---|---|---|---|---|---|---|
| Alabama | | 10 | 1 | 496,861 | 195,694 | 280,844 | 20,323 | 85,150 D | 39.4% | 56.5% | 41.1% | 58.9% |
| Alaska | | | | | | | | | | | | |
| Arizona | 4 | | | 290,173 | 176,990 | 112,880 | 303 | 64,110 R | 61.0% | 38.9% | 61.1% | 38.9% |
| Arkansas | | 8 | | 406,572 | 186,287 | 213,277 | 7,008 | 26,990 D | 45.8% | 52.5% | 46.6% | 53.4% |
| California | 32 | | | 5,466,355 | 3,027,668 | 2,420,135 | 18,552 | 607,533 R | 55.4% | 44.3% | 55.6% | 44.4% |
| Colorado | 6 | | | 657,074 | 394,479 | 257,997 | 4,598 | 136,482 R | 60.0% | 39.3% | 60.5% | 39.5% |
| Connecticut | 8 | | | 1,117,121 | 711,837 | 405,079 | 205 | 306,758 R | 63.7% | 36.3% | 63.7% | 36.3% |
| Delaware | 3 | | | 177,988 | 98,057 | 79,421 | 510 | 18,636 R | 55.1% | 44.6% | 55.3% | 44.7% |
| Florida | 10 | | | 1,125,762 | 643,849 | 480,371 | 1,542 | 163,478 R | 57.2% | 42.7% | 57.3% | 42.7% |
| Georgia | | 12 | | 669,655 | 222,778 | 444,688 | 2,189 | 221,910 D | 33.3% | 66.4% | 33.4% | 66.6% |
| Hawaii | | | | | | | | | | | | |
| Idaho | 4 | | | 272,989 | 166,979 | 105,868 | 142 | 61,111 R | 61.2% | 38.8% | 61.2% | 38.8% |
| Illinois | 27 | | | 4,407,407 | 2,623,327 | 1,775,682 | 8,398 | 847,645 R | 59.5% | 40.3% | 59.6% | 40.4% |
| Indiana | 13 | | | 1,974,607 | 1,182,811 | 783,908 | 7,888 | 398,903 R | 59.9% | 39.7% | 60.1% | 39.9% |
| Iowa | 10 | | | 1,234,564 | 729,187 | 501,858 | 3,519 | 227,329 R | 59.1% | 40.7% | 59.2% | 40.8% |
| Kansas | 8 | | | 866,243 | 566,878 | 296,317 | 3,048 | 270,561 R | 65.4% | 34.2% | 65.7% | 34.3% |
| Kentucky | 10 | | | 1,053,805 | 572,192 | 476,453 | 5,160 | 95,739 R | 54.3% | 45.2% | 54.6% | 45.4% |
| Louisiana | 10 | | | 617,544 | 329,047 | 243,977 | 44,520 | 85,070 R | 53.3% | 39.5% | 57.4% | 42.6% |
| Maine | 5 | | | 351,706 | 249,238 | 102,468 | | 146,770 R | 70.9% | 29.1% | 70.9% | 29.1% |
| Maryland | 9 | | | 932,827 | 559,738 | 372,613 | 476 | 187,125 R | 60.0% | 39.9% | 60.0% | 40.0% |
| Massachusetts | 16 | | | 2,348,506 | 1,393,197 | 948,190 | 7,119 | 445,007 R | 59.3% | 40.4% | 59.5% | 40.5% |
| Michigan | 20 | | | 3,080,468 | 1,713,647 | 1,359,898 | 6,923 | 353,749 R | 55.6% | 44.1% | 55.8% | 44.2% |
| Minnesota | 11 | | | 1,340,005 | 719,302 | 617,525 | 3,178 | 101,777 R | 53.7% | 46.1% | 53.8% | 46.2% |
| Mississippi | | 8 | | 248,104 | 60,685 | 144,453 | 42,966 | 83,768 D | 24.5% | 58.2% | 29.6% | 70.4% |
| Missouri | | 13 | | 1,832,562 | 914,289 | 918,273 | | 3,984 D | 49.9% | 50.1% | 49.9% | 50.1% |
| Montana | 4 | | | 271,171 | 154,933 | 116,238 | | 38,695 R | 57.1% | 42.9% | 57.1% | 42.9% |
| Nebraska | 6 | | | 577,137 | 378,108 | 199,029 | | 179,079 R | 65.5% | 34.5% | 65.5% | 34.5% |
| Nevada | 3 | | | 96,689 | 56,049 | 40,640 | | 15,409 R | 58.0% | 42.0% | 58.0% | 42.0% |
| New Hampshire | 4 | | | 266,994 | 176,519 | 90,364 | 111 | 86,155 R | 66.1% | 33.8% | 66.1% | 33.9% |
| New Jersey | 16 | | | 2,484,312 | 1,606,942 | 850,337 | 27,033 | 756,605 R | 64.7% | 34.2% | 65.4% | 34.6% |
| New Mexico | 4 | | | 253,926 | 146,788 | 106,098 | 1,040 | 40,690 R | 57.8% | 41.8% | 58.0% | 42.0% |
| New York | 45 | | | 7,095,971 | 4,345,506 | 2,747,944 | 2,521 | 1,597,562 R | 61.2% | 38.7% | 61.3% | 38.7% |
| North Carolina | | 14 | | 1,165,592 | 575,062 | 590,530 | | 15,468 D | 49.3% | 50.7% | 49.3% | 50.7% |
| North Dakota | 4 | | | 253,991 | 156,766 | 96,742 | 483 | 60,024 R | 61.7% | 38.1% | 61.8% | 38.2% |
| Ohio | 25 | | | 3,702,265 | 2,262,610 | 1,439,655 | | 822,955 R | 61.1% | 38.9% | 61.1% | 38.9% |
| Oklahoma | 8 | | | 859,350 | 473,769 | 385,581 | | 88,188 R | 55.1% | 44.9% | 55.1% | 44.9% |
| Oregon | 6 | | | 736,132 | 406,393 | 329,204 | 535 | 77,189 R | 55.2% | 44.7% | 55.2% | 44.8% |
| Pennsylvania | 32 | | | 4,576,503 | 2,585,252 | 1,981,769 | 9,482 | 603,483 R | 56.5% | 43.3% | 56.6% | 43.4% |
| Rhode Island | 4 | | | 387,609 | 225,819 | 161,790 | | 64,029 R | 58.3% | 41.7% | 58.3% | 41.7% |
| South Carolina | | 8 | | 300,583 | 75,700 | 136,372 | 88,511 | 47,863 D | 25.2% | 45.4% | 35.7% | 64.3% |
| South Dakota | 4 | | | 293,857 | 171,569 | 122,288 | | 49,281 R | 58.4% | 41.6% | 58.4% | 41.6% |
| Tennessee | 11 | | | 939,404 | 462,288 | 456,507 | 20,609 | 5,781 R | 49.2% | 48.6% | 50.3% | 49.7% |
| Texas | 24 | | | 1,955,168 | 1,080,619 | 859,958 | 14,591 | 220,661 R | 55.3% | 44.0% | 55.7% | 44.3% |
| Utah | 4 | | | 333,995 | 215,631 | 118,364 | | 97,267 R | 64.6% | 35.4% | 64.6% | 35.4% |
| Vermont | 3 | | | 152,978 | 110,390 | 42,549 | 39 | 67,841 R | 72.2% | 27.8% | 72.2% | 27.8% |
| Virginia | 12 | | | 697,978 | 386,459 | 267,760 | 43,759 | 118,699 R | 55.4% | 38.4% | 59.1% | 40.9% |
| Washington | 9 | | | 1,150,889 | 620,430 | 523,002 | 7,457 | 97,428 R | 53.9% | 45.4% | 54.3% | 45.7% |
| West Virginia | 8 | | | 830,831 | 449,297 | 381,534 | | 67,763 R | 54.1% | 45.9% | 54.1% | 45.9% |
| Wisconsin | 12 | | | 1,550,558 | 954,844 | 586,768 | 8,946 | 368,076 R | 61.6% | 37.8% | 61.9% | 38.1% |
| Wyoming | 3 | | | 124,127 | 74,573 | 49,554 | | 25,019 R | 60.1% | 39.9% | 60.1% | 39.9% |
| Dist. of Col. | | | | | | | | | | | | |
| United States | 457 | 73 | 1 | 62,026,908 | 35,590,472 | 26,022,752 | 413,684 | 9,567,720 R | 57.4% | 42.0% | 57.8% | 42.2% |

# PRESIDENT 1952

Republican figures in South Carolina include votes cast for two elector tickets. In Mississippi the Republican total is the vote cast for an independent elector ticket pledged to vote for the nominees of the national Republican party. In New York the Democratic figures include Liberal votes.

Douglas MacArthur appeared on the ballot with various party designations and Vice-Presidential running mates.

The candidates listed below include all those who appeared on the ballot in at least one state.

|            |                                                                          |
|------------|--------------------------------------------------------------------------|
| 33,936,234 | Dwight D. Eisenhower and Richard M. Nixon, *Republican*.                 |
| 27,314,992 | Adlai E. Stevenson and John J. Sparkman, *Democratic*.                   |
| 140,023    | Vincent Hallinan and Charlotta Bass, *Progressive*.                      |
| 72,949     | Stuart Hamblen and Enoch A. Holtwick, *Prohibition*.                     |
| 30,267     | Eric Hass and Stephen Emery, *Socialist Labor*.                          |
| 20,203     | Darlington Hoopes and Samuel H. Friedman, *Socialist*.                   |
| 17,205     | Douglas MacArthur and Vivian Kellems, *Constitution*.                    |
| 10,312     | Farrell Dobbs and Myra Tanner Weiss, *Socialist Workers*.                |
| 4,203      | Hanry B. Krajewski and Frank Jenkins, *Poor Man's Party*.                |

In addition, 4,530 scattered write-in votes were reported from various states.

# UNITED STATES

## PRESIDENT 1952

| State | Electoral Vote Rep. | Dem. | Other | Total Vote | Republican | Democratic | Other | Plurality | Percentage Total Vote Rep. | Dem. | Major Vote Rep. | Dem. |
|---|---|---|---|---|---|---|---|---|---|---|---|---|
| Alabama | | 11 | | 426,120 | 149,231 | 275,075 | 1,814 | 125,844 D | 35.0% | 64.6% | 35.2% | 64.8% |
| Alaska | | | | | | | | | | | | |
| Arizona | 4 | | | 260,570 | 152,042 | 108,528 | | 43,514 R | 58.3% | 41.7% | 58.3% | 41.7% |
| Arkansas | | 8 | | 404,800 | 177,155 | 226,300 | 1,345 | 49,145 D | 43.8% | 55.9% | 43.9% | 56.1% |
| California | 32 | | | 5,141,849 | 2,897,310 | 2,197,548 | 46,991 | 699,762 R | 56.3% | 42.7% | 56.9% | 43.1% |
| Colorado | 6 | | | 630,103 | 379,782 | 245,504 | 4,817 | 134,278 R | 60.3% | 39.0% | 60.7% | 39.3% |
| Connecticut | 8 | | | 1,096,911 | 611,012 | 481,649 | 4,250 | 129,363 R | 55.7% | 43.9% | 55.9% | 44.1% |
| Delaware | 3 | | | 174,025 | 90,059 | 83,315 | 651 | 6,744 R | 51.8% | 47.9% | 51.9% | 48.1% |
| Florida | 10 | | | 989,337 | 544,036 | 444,950 | 351 | 99,086 R | 55.0% | 45.0% | 55.0% | 45.0% |
| Georgia | | 12 | | 655,785 | 198,961 | 456,823 | 1 | 257,862 D | 30.3% | 69.7% | 30.3% | 69.7% |
| Hawaii | | | | | | | | | | | | |
| Idaho | 4 | | | 276,254 | 180,707 | 95,081 | 466 | 85,626 R | 65.4% | 34.4% | 65.5% | 34.5% |
| Illinois | 27 | | | 4,481,058 | 2,457,327 | 2,013,920 | 9,811 | 443,407 R | 54.8% | 44.9% | 55.0% | 45.0% |
| Indiana | 13 | | | 1,955,049 | 1,136,259 | 801,530 | 17,260 | 334,729 R | 58.1% | 41.0% | 58.6% | 41.4% |
| Iowa | 10 | | | 1,268,773 | 808,906 | 451,513 | 8,354 | 357,393 R | 63.8% | 35.6% | 64.2% | 35.8% |
| Kansas | 8 | | | 896,166 | 616,302 | 273,296 | 6,568 | 343,006 R | 68.8% | 30.5% | 69.3% | 30.7% |
| Kentucky | | 10 | | 993,148 | 495,029 | 495,729 | 2,390 | 700 D | 49.8% | 49.9% | 50.0% | 50.0% |
| Louisiana | | 10 | | 651,952 | 306,925 | 345,027 | | 38,102 D | 47.1% | 52.9% | 47.1% | 52.9% |
| Maine | 5 | | | 351,786 | 232,353 | 118,806 | 627 | 113,547 R | 66.0% | 33.8% | 66.2% | 33.8% |
| Maryland | 9 | | | 902,074 | 499,424 | 395,337 | 7,313 | 104,087 R | 55.4% | 43.8% | 55.8% | 44.2% |
| Massachusetts | 16 | | | 2,383,398 | 1,292,325 | 1,083,525 | 7,548 | 208,800 R | 54.2% | 45.5% | 54.4% | 45.6% |
| Michigan | 20 | | | 2,798,592 | 1,551,529 | 1,230,657 | 16,406 | 320,872 R | 55.4% | 44.0% | 55.8% | 44.2% |
| Minnesota | 11 | | | 1,379,483 | 763,211 | 608,458 | 7,814 | 154,753 R | 55.3% | 44.1% | 55.6% | 44.4% |
| Mississippi | | 8 | | 285,532 | 112,966 | 172,566 | | 59,600 D | 39.6% | 60.4% | 39.6% | 60.4% |
| Missouri | 13 | | | 1,892,062 | 959,429 | 929,830 | 2,803 | 29,599 R | 50.7% | 49.1% | 50.8% | 49.2% |
| Montana | 4 | | | 265,037 | 157,394 | 106,213 | 1,430 | 51,181 R | 59.4% | 40.1% | 59.7% | 40.3% |
| Nebraska | 6 | | | 609,660 | 421,603 | 188,057 | | 233,546 R | 69.2% | 30.8% | 69.2% | 30.8% |
| Nevada | 3 | | | 82,190 | 50,502 | 31,688 | | 18,814 R | 61.4% | 38.6% | 61.4% | 38.6% |
| New Hampshire | 4 | | | 272,950 | 166,287 | 106,663 | | 59,624 R | 60.9% | 39.1% | 60.9% | 39.1% |
| New Jersey | 16 | | | 2,418,554 | 1,373,613 | 1,015,902 | 29,039 | 357,711 R | 56.8% | 42.0% | 57.5% | 42.5% |
| New Mexico | 4 | | | 238,608 | 132,170 | 105,661 | 777 | 26,509 R | 55.4% | 44.3% | 55.6% | 44.4% |
| New York | 45 | | | 7,128,239 | 3,952,813 | 3,104,601 | 70,825 | 848,212 R | 55.5% | 43.6% | 56.0% | 44.0% |
| North Carolina | | 14 | | 1,210,910 | 558,107 | 652,803 | | 94,696 D | 46.1% | 53.9% | 46.1% | 53.9% |
| North Dakota | 4 | | | 270,127 | 191,712 | 76,694 | 1,721 | 115,018 R | 71.0% | 28.4% | 71.4% | 28.6% |
| Ohio | 25 | | | 3,700,758 | 2,100,391 | 1,600,367 | | 500,024 R | 56.8% | 43.2% | 56.8% | 43.2% |
| Oklahoma | 8 | | | 948,984 | 518,045 | 430,939 | | 87,106 R | 54.6% | 45.4% | 54.6% | 45.4% |
| Oregon | 6 | | | 695,059 | 420,815 | 270,579 | 3,665 | 150,236 R | 60.5% | 38.9% | 60.9% | 39.1% |
| Pennsylvania | 32 | | | 4,580,969 | 2,415,789 | 2,146,269 | 18,911 | 269,520 R | 52.7% | 46.9% | 53.0% | 47.0% |
| Rhode Island | 4 | | | 414,498 | 210,935 | 203,293 | 270 | 7,642 R | 50.9% | 49.0% | 50.9% | 49.1% |
| South Carolina | | 8 | | 341,087 | 168,082 | 173,004 | 1 | 4,922 D | 49.3% | 50.7% | 49.3% | 50.7% |
| South Dakota | 4 | | | 294,283 | 203,857 | 90,426 | | 113,431 R | 69.3% | 30.7% | 69.3% | 30.7% |
| Tennessee | 11 | | | 892,553 | 446,147 | 443,710 | 2,696 | 2,437 R | 50.0% | 49.7% | 50.1% | 49.9% |
| Texas | 24 | | | 2,075,946 | 1,102,878 | 969,228 | 3,840 | 133,650 R | 53.1% | 46.7% | 53.2% | 46.8% |
| Utah | 4 | | | 329,554 | 194,190 | 135,364 | | 58,826 R | 58.9% | 41.1% | 58.9% | 41.1% |
| Vermont | 3 | | | 153,557 | 109,717 | 43,355 | 485 | 66,362 R | 71.5% | 28.2% | 71.7% | 28.3% |
| Virginia | 12 | | | 619,689 | 349,037 | 268,677 | 1,975 | 80,360 R | 56.3% | 43.4% | 56.5% | 43.5% |
| Washington | 9 | | | 1,102,708 | 599,107 | 492,845 | 10,756 | 106,262 R | 54.3% | 44.7% | 54.9% | 45.1% |
| West Virginia | | 8 | | 873,548 | 419,970 | 453,578 | | 33,608 D | 48.1% | 51.9% | 48.1% | 51.9% |
| Wisconsin | 12 | | | 1,607,370 | 979,744 | 622,175 | 5,451 | 357,569 R | 61.0% | 38.7% | 61.2% | 38.8% |
| Wyoming | 3 | | | 129,253 | 81,049 | 47,934 | 270 | 33,115 R | 62.7% | 37.1% | 62.8% | 37.2% |
| Dist. of Col. | | | | | | | | | | | | |
| United States | 442 | 89 | — | 61,550,918 | 33,936,234 | 27,314,992 | 299,692 | 6,621,242 R | 55.1% | 44.4% | 55.4% | 44.6% |

## PRESIDENT 1948

One of the twelve Democratic electors chosen in Tennessee cast his Electoral College vote for the States Rights nominees rather than for the national Democratic candidates.

In Alabama the Democratic electors were pledged to the States Rights candidates and there were no national Democratic electors on the ballot. The Republican figures in Mississippi include votes cast for two elector tickets. In New York the Democratic figures include Liberal votes.

The candidates listed below include all those who appeared on the ballot in at least one state.

24,179,345   Harry S. Truman and Alben W. Barkely, *Democratic.*
21,991,291   Thomas E. Dewey and Earl Warren, *Republican.*
 1,176,125   Strom Thurmond and Fielding L. Wright, *States Rights.*
 1,157,326   Henry A. Wallace and Glen H. Taylor, *Progressive.*
   139,572   Norman Thomas and Tucker P. Smith, *Socialist.*
   103,900   Claude A. Watson and Dale H. Learn, *Prohibition.*
    29,241   Edward A. Teicher and Stephen Emery, *Socialist Labor.*
    13,614   Farrell Dobbs and Grace Carlson, *Socialist Workers.*

In addition, 3,412 scattered write-in votes were reported from various states.

# UNITED STATES

## PRESIDENT 1948

| State | Electoral Vote Rep. | Electoral Vote Dem. | Electoral Vote Other | Total Vote | Republican | Democratic | Other | Plurality | Percentage Total Vote Rep. | Total Vote Dem. | Major Vote Rep. | Major Vote Dem. |
|---|---|---|---|---|---|---|---|---|---|---|---|---|
| Alabama | | | 11 | 214,980 | 40,930 | | 174,050 | 130,513 SR | 19.0% | | 100.0% | |
| Alaska | | | | | | | | | | | | |
| Arizona | | 4 | | 177,065 | 77,597 | 95,251 | 4,217 | 17,654 D | 43.8% | 53.8% | 44.9% | 55.1% |
| Arkansas | | 9 | | 242,475 | 50,959 | 149,659 | 41,857 | 98,700 D | 21.0% | 61.7% | 25.4% | 74.6% |
| California | | 25 | | 4,021,538 | 1,895,269 | 1,913,134 | 213,135 | 17,865 D | 47.1% | 47.6% | 49.8% | 50.2% |
| Colorado | | 6 | | 515,237 | 239,714 | 267,288 | 8,235 | 27,574 D | 46.5% | 51.9% | 47.3% | 52.7% |
| Connecticut | 8 | | | 883,518 | 437,754 | 423,297 | 22,467 | 14,457 R | 49.5% | 47.9% | 50.8% | 49.2% |
| Delaware | 3 | | | 139,073 | 69,588 | 67,813 | 1,672 | 1,775 R | 50.0% | 48.8% | 50.6% | 49.4% |
| Florida | | 8 | | 577,643 | 194,280 | 281,988 | 101,375 | 87,708 D | 33.6% | 48.8% | 40.8% | 59.2% |
| Georgia | | 12 | | 418,844 | 76,691 | 254,646 | 87,507 | 169,511 D | 18.3% | 60.8% | 23.1% | 76.9% |
| Hawaii | | | | | | | | | | | | |
| Idaho | | 4 | | 214,816 | 101,514 | 107,370 | 5,932 | 5,856 D | 47.3% | 50.0% | 48.6% | 51.4% |
| Illinois | | 28 | | 3,984,046 | 1,961,103 | 1,994,715 | 28,228 | 33,612 D | 49.2% | 50.1% | 49.6% | 50.4% |
| Indiana | 13 | | | 1,656,212 | 821,079 | 807,831 | 27,302 | 13,248 R | 49.6% | 48.8% | 50.4% | 49.6% |
| Iowa | | 10 | | 1,038,264 | 494,018 | 522,380 | 21,866 | 28,362 D | 47.6% | 50.3% | 48.6% | 51.4% |
| Kansas | 8 | | | 788,819 | 423,039 | 351,902 | 13,878 | 71,137 R | 53.6% | 44.6% | 54.6% | 45.4% |
| Kentucky | | 11 | | 822,658 | 341,210 | 466,756 | 14,692 | 125,546 D | 41.5% | 56.7% | 42.2% | 57.8% |
| Louisiana | | | 10 | 416,336 | 72,657 | 136,344 | 207,335 | 67,946 SR | 17.5% | 32.7% | 34.8% | 65.2% |
| Maine | 5 | | | 264,787 | 150,234 | 111,916 | 2,637 | 38,318 R | 56.7% | 42.3% | 57.3% | 42.7% |
| Maryland | 8 | | | 596,748 | 294,814 | 286,521 | 15,413 | 8,293 R | 49.4% | 48.0% | 50.7% | 49.3% |
| Massachusetts | | 16 | | 2,107,146 | 909,370 | 1,151,788 | 45,988 | 242,418 D | 43.2% | 54.7% | 44.1% | 55.9% |
| Michigan | 19 | | | 2,109,609 | 1,038,595 | 1,003,448 | 67,566 | 35,147 R | 49.2% | 47.6% | 50.9% | 49.1% |
| Minnesota | | 11 | | 1,212,226 | 483,617 | 692,966 | 35,643 | 209,349 D | 39.9% | 57.2% | 41.1% | 58.9% |
| Mississippi | | | 9 | 192,190 | 5,043 | 19,384 | 167,763 | 148,154 SR | 2.6% | 10.1% | 20.6% | 79.4% |
| Missouri | | 15 | | 1,578,628 | 655,039 | 917,315 | 6,274 | 262,276 D | 41.5% | 58.1% | 41.7% | 58.3% |
| Montana | | 4 | | 224,278 | 96,770 | 119,071 | 8,437 | 22,301 D | 43.1% | 53.1% | 44.8% | 55.2% |
| Nebraska | 6 | | | 488,940 | 264,774 | 224,165 | 1 | 40,609 R | 54.2% | 45.8% | 54.2% | 45.8% |
| Nevada | | 3 | | 62,117 | 29,357 | 31,291 | 1,469 | 1,934 D | 47.3% | 50.4% | 48.4% | 51.6% |
| New Hampshire | 4 | | | 231,440 | 121,299 | 107,995 | 2,146 | 13,304 R | 52.4% | 46.7% | 52.9% | 47.1% |
| New Jersey | 16 | | | 1,949,555 | 981,124 | 895,455 | 72,976 | 85,669 R | 50.3% | 45.9% | 52.3% | 47.7% |
| New Mexico | | 4 | | 187,063 | 80,303 | 105,464 | 1,296 | 25,161 D | 42.9% | 56.4% | 43.2% | 56.8% |
| New York | 47 | | | 6,177,337 | 2,841,163 | 2,780,204 | 555,970 | 60,959 R | 46.0% | 45.0% | 50.5% | 49.5% |
| North Carolina | | 14 | | 791,209 | 258,572 | 459,070 | 73,567 | 200,498 D | 32.7% | 58.0% | 36.0% | 64.0% |
| North Dakota | 4 | | | 220,716 | 115,139 | 95,812 | 9,765 | 19,327 R | 52.2% | 43.4% | 54.6% | 45.4% |
| Ohio | | 25 | | 2,936,071 | 1,445,684 | 1,452,791 | 37,596 | 7,107 D | 49.2% | 49.5% | 49.9% | 50.1% |
| Oklahoma | | 10 | | 721,599 | 268,817 | 452,782 | | 183,965 D | 37.3% | 62.7% | 37.3% | 62.7% |
| Oregon | 6 | | | 524,080 | 260,904 | 243,147 | 20,029 | 17,757 R | 49.8% | 46.4% | 51.8% | 48.2% |
| Pennsylvania | 35 | | | 3,735,348 | 1,902,197 | 1,752,426 | 80,725 | 149,771 R | 50.9% | 46.9% | 52.0% | 48.0% |
| Rhode Island | | 4 | | 327,702 | 135,787 | 188,736 | 3,179 | 52,949 D | 41.4% | 57.6% | 41.8% | 58.2% |
| South Carolina | | | 8 | 142,571 | 5,386 | 34,423 | 102,762 | 68,184 SR | 3.8% | 24.1% | 13.5% | 86.5% |
| South Dakota | 4 | | | 250,105 | 129,651 | 117,653 | 2,801 | 11,998 R | 51.8% | 47.0% | 52.4% | 47.6% |
| Tennessee | | 11 | 1 | 550,283 | 202,914 | 270,402 | 76,967 | 67,488 D | 36.9% | 49.1% | 42.9% | 57.1% |
| Texas | | 23 | | 1,249,577 | 303,467 | 824,235 | 121,875 | 520,768 D | 24.3% | 66.0% | 26.9% | 73.1% |
| Utah | | 4 | | 276,306 | 124,402 | 149,151 | 2,753 | 24,749 D | 45.0% | 54.0% | 45.5% | 54.5% |
| Vermont | 3 | | | 123,382 | 75,926 | 45,557 | 1,899 | 30,369 R | 61.5% | 36.9% | 62.5% | 37.5% |
| Virginia | | 11 | | 419,256 | 172,070 | 200,786 | 46,400 | 28,716 D | 41.0% | 47.9% | 46.1% | 53.9% |
| Washington | | 8 | | 905,058 | 386,314 | 476,165 | 42,579 | 89,851 D | 42.7% | 52.6% | 44.8% | 55.2% |
| West Virginia | | 8 | | 748,750 | 316,251 | 429,188 | 3,311 | 112,937 D | 42.2% | 57.3% | 42.4% | 57.6% |
| Wisconsin | | 12 | | 1,276,800 | 590,959 | 647,310 | 38,531 | 56,351 D | 46.3% | 50.7% | 47.7% | 52.3% |
| Wyoming | | 3 | | 101,425 | 47,947 | 52,354 | 1,124 | 4,407 D | 47.3% | 51.6% | 47.8% | 52.2% |
| Dist. of Col. | | | | | | | | | | | | |
| United States | 189 | 303 | 39 | 48,793,826 | 21,991,291 | 24,179,345 | 2,623,190 | 2,188,054 D | 45.1% | 49.6% | 47.6% | 52.4% |

## PRESIDENT 1944

The Republican figures in Georgia, Mississippi and South Carolina include votes cast for two elector tickets. The Democratic figures in Mississippi include votes cast for two elector tickets and the Democratic figures in New York include American Labor and Liberal votes.

In South Carolina an uncommitted Southern Democratic elector ticket ran in second place ahead of the Republican candidates.

The candidates listed below include all those who appeared on the ballot in at least one state.

| | |
|---|---|
| 25,612,610 | Franklin D. Roosevelt and Harry S. Truman, *Democratic*. |
| 22,017,617 | Thomas E. Dewey and John W. Bricker, *Republican*. |
| 79,003 | Norman Thomas and Darlington Hoopes, *Socialist*. |
| 74,779 | Claude A. Watson and Andrew Johnson, *Prohibition*. |
| 45,191 | Edward A. Teichert and Arla A. Albaugh, *Socialist Labor*. |
| 1,780 | Gerald L. K. Smith and Harry Romer, *America First*. |

In Texas 135,444 votes were cast for a Texas Regulars elector ticket and 7,799 votes were cast in South Carolina for an uncommitted Southern Democratic elector ticket. In addition, 2,447 scattered write-in votes were reported from various states.

# UNITED STATES

## PRESIDENT 1944

| State | Electoral Vote Rep. | Electoral Vote Dem. | Electoral Vote Other | Total Vote | Republican | Democratic | Other | Plurality | Percentage Total Vote Rep. | Percentage Total Vote Dem. | Percentage Major Vote Rep. | Percentage Major Vote Dem. |
|---|---|---|---|---|---|---|---|---|---|---|---|---|
| Alabama | | 11 | | 244,743 | 44,540 | 198,918 | 1,285 | 154,378 D | 18.2% | 81.3% | 18.3% | 81.7% |
| Alaska | | | | | | | | | | | | |
| Arizona | | 4 | | 137,634 | 56,287 | 80,926 | 421 | 24,639 D | 40.9% | 58.8% | 41.0% | 59.0% |
| Arkansas | | 9 | | 212,954 | 63,551 | 148,965 | 438 | 85,414 D | 29.8% | 70.0% | 29.9% | 70.1% |
| California | | 25 | | 3,520,875 | 1,512,965 | 1,988,564 | 19,346 | 475,599 D | 43.0% | 56.5% | 43.2% | 56.8% |
| Colorado | 6 | | | 505,039 | 268,731 | 234,331 | 1,977 | 34,400 R | 53.2% | 46.4% | 53.4% | 46.6% |
| Connecticut | | 8 | | 831,990 | 390,527 | 435,146 | 6,317 | 44,619 D | 46.9% | 52.3% | 47.3% | 52.7% |
| Delaware | | 3 | | 125,361 | 56,747 | 68,166 | 448 | 11,419 D | 45.3% | 54.4% | 45.4% | 54.6% |
| Florida | | 8 | | 482,803 | 143,215 | 339,377 | 211 | 196,162 D | 29.7% | 70.3% | 29.7% | 70.3% |
| Georgia | | 12 | | 328,129 | 59,900 | 268,187 | 42 | 208,287 D | 18.3% | 81.7% | 18.3% | 81.7% |
| Hawaii | | | | | | | | | | | | |
| Idaho | | 4 | | 208,321 | 100,137 | 107,399 | 785 | 7,262 D | 48.1% | 51.6% | 48.3% | 51.7% |
| Illinois | | 28 | | 4,036,061 | 1,939,314 | 2,079,479 | 17,268 | 140,165 D | 48.0% | 51.5% | 48.3% | 51.7% |
| Indiana | 13 | | | 1,672,091 | 875,891 | 781,403 | 14,797 | 94,488 R | 52.4% | 46.7% | 52.9% | 47.1% |
| Iowa | 10 | | | 1,052,599 | 547,267 | 499,876 | 5,456 | 47,391 R | 52.0% | 47.5% | 52.3% | 47.7% |
| Kansas | 8 | | | 733,776 | 442,096 | 287,458 | 4,222 | 154,638 R | 60.2% | 39.2% | 60.6% | 39.4% |
| Kentucky | | 11 | | 867,924 | 392,448 | 472,589 | 2,887 | 80,141 D | 45.2% | 54.5% | 45.4% | 54.6% |
| Louisiana | | 10 | | 349,383 | 67,750 | 281,564 | 69 | 213,814 D | 19.4% | 80.6% | 19.4% | 80.6% |
| Maine | 5 | | | 296,400 | 155,434 | 140,631 | 335 | 14,803 R | 52.4% | 47.4% | 52.5% | 47.5% |
| Maryland | | 8 | | 608,439 | 292,949 | 315,490 | | 22,541 D | 48.1% | 51.9% | 48.1% | 51.9% |
| Massachusetts | | 16 | | 1,960,665 | 921,350 | 1,035,296 | 4,019 | 113,946 D | 47.0% | 52.8% | 47.1% | 52.9% |
| Michigan | | 19 | | 2,205,223 | 1,084,423 | 1,106,899 | 13,901 | 22,476 D | 49.2% | 50.2% | 49.5% | 50.5% |
| Minnesota | | 11 | | 1,125,504 | 527,416 | 589,864 | 8,224 | 62,448 D | 46.9% | 52.4% | 47.2% | 52.8% |
| Mississippi | | 9 | | 180,234 | 11,613 | 168,621 | | 157,008 D | 6.4% | 93.6% | 6.4% | 93.6% |
| Missouri | | 15 | | 1,571,697 | 761,175 | 807,356 | 3,166 | 46,181 D | 48.4% | 51.4% | 48.5% | 51.5% |
| Montana | | 4 | | 207,355 | 93,163 | 112,556 | 1,636 | 19,393 D | 44.9% | 54.3% | 45.3% | 54.7% |
| Nebraska | 6 | | | 563,126 | 329,880 | 233,246 | | 96,634 R | 58.6% | 41.4% | 58.6% | 41.4% |
| Nevada | | 3 | | 54,234 | 24,611 | 29,623 | | 5,012 D | 45.4% | 54.6% | 45.4% | 54.6% |
| New Hampshire | | 4 | | 229,625 | 109,916 | 119,663 | 46 | 9,747 D | 47.9% | 52.1% | 47.9% | 52.1% |
| New Jersey | | 16 | | 1,963,761 | 961,335 | 987,874 | 14,552 | 26,539 D | 49.0% | 50.3% | 49.3% | 50.7% |
| New Mexico | | 4 | | 152,225 | 70,688 | 81,389 | 148 | 10,701 D | 46.4% | 53.5% | 46.5% | 53.5% |
| New York | | 47 | | 6,316,790 | 2,987,647 | 3,304,238 | 24,905 | 316,591 D | 47.3% | 52.3% | 47.5% | 52.5% |
| North Carolina | | 14 | | 790,554 | 263,155 | 527,399 | | 264,244 D | 33.3% | 66.7% | 33.3% | 66.7% |
| North Dakota | 4 | | | 220,182 | 118,535 | 100,144 | 1,503 | 18,391 R | 53.8% | 45.5% | 54.2% | 45.8% |
| Ohio | 25 | | | 3,153,056 | 1,582,293 | 1,570,763 | | 11,530 R | 50.2% | 49.8% | 50.2% | 49.8% |
| Oklahoma | | 10 | | 722,636 | 319,424 | 401,549 | 1,663 | 82,125 D | 44.2% | 55.6% | 44.3% | 55.7% |
| Oregon | | 6 | | 480,147 | 225,365 | 248,635 | 6,147 | 23,270 D | 46.9% | 51.8% | 47.5% | 52.5% |
| Pennsylvania | | 35 | | 3,794,793 | 1,835,054 | 1,940,479 | 19,260 | 105,425 D | 48.4% | 51.1% | 48.6% | 51.4% |
| Rhode Island | | 4 | | 299,276 | 123,487 | 175,356 | 433 | 51,869 D | 41.3% | 58.6% | 41.3% | 58.7% |
| South Carolina | | 8 | | 103,382 | 4,617 | 90,601 | 8,164 | 82,802 D | 4.5% | 87.6% | 4.8% | 95.2% |
| South Dakota | 4 | | | 232,076 | 135,365 | 96,711 | | 38,654 R | 58.3% | 41.7% | 58.3% | 41.7% |
| Tennessee | | 12 | | 510,692 | 200,311 | 308,707 | 1,674 | 108,396 D | 39.2% | 60.4% | 39.4% | 60.6% |
| Texas | | 23 | | 1,150,334 | 191,423 | 821,605 | 137,306 | 630,182 D | 16.6% | 71.4% | 18.9% | 81.1% |
| Utah | | 4 | | 248,319 | 97,891 | 150,088 | 340 | 52,197 D | 39.4% | 60.4% | 39.5% | 60.5% |
| Vermont | 3 | | | 125,361 | 71,527 | 53,820 | 14 | 17,707 R | 57.1% | 42.9% | 57.1% | 42.9% |
| Virginia | | 11 | | 388,485 | 145,243 | 242,276 | 966 | 97,033 D | 37.4% | 62.4% | 37.5% | 62.5% |
| Washington | | 8 | | 856,328 | 361,689 | 486,774 | 7,865 | 125,085 D | 42.2% | 56.8% | 42.6% | 57.4% |
| West Virginia | | 8 | | 715,596 | 322,819 | 392,777 | | 69,958 D | 45.1% | 54.9% | 45.1% | 54.9% |
| Wisconsin | 12 | | | 1,339,152 | 674,532 | 650,413 | 14,207 | 24,119 R | 50.4% | 48.6% | 50.9% | 49.1% |
| Wyoming | 3 | | | 101,340 | 51,921 | 49,419 | | 2,502 R | 51.2% | 48.8% | 51.2% | 48.8% |
| Dist. of Col. | | | | | | | | | | | | |
| United States | 99 | 432 | — | 47,976,670 | 22,017,617 | 25,612,610 | 346,443 | 3,594,993 D | 45.9% | 53.4% | 46.2% | 53.8% |

**PRESIDENT 1940**

The Republican figures in Connecticut, Georgia, Mississippi and South Carolina include votes cast for more than one elector ticket. In New York the Democratic figures include American Labor votes.

The candidates listed below include all those who appeared on the ballot in at least one state.

27,313,041   Franklin D. Roosevelt and Henry A. Wallace, *Democratic*.
22,348,480   Wendell Willkie and Charles L. McNary, *Republican*.
    116,410   Norman Thomas and Maynard C. Krueger, *Socialist*.
     58,708   Roger Babson and Edgar V. Moorman, *Prohibition*.
     46,259   Earl Browder and James W. Ford, *Communist*.
     14,892   John W. Aiken and Aaron M. Orange, *Socialist Labor*.
       545   Alfred Knutson with no Vice Presidential candidate, *Independent*.

In addition, 2,083 scattered write-in votes were reported from various states.

# UNITED STATES

## PRESIDENT 1940

| State | Electoral Vote Rep. | Electoral Vote Dem. | Electoral Vote Other | Total Vote | Republican | Democratic | Other | Plurality | % Total Vote Rep. | % Total Vote Dem. | % Major Vote Rep. | % Major Vote Dem. |
|---|---|---|---|---|---|---|---|---|---|---|---|---|
| Alabama | | 11 | | 294,219 | 42,184 | 250,726 | 1,309 | 208,542 D | 14.3% | 85.2% | 14.4% | 85.6% |
| Alaska | | | | | | | | | | | | |
| Arizona | | 3 | | 150,039 | 54,030 | 95,267 | 742 | 41,237 D | 36.0% | 63.5% | 36.2% | 63.8% |
| Arkansas | | 9 | | 200,429 | 42,122 | 157,213 | 1,094 | 115,091 D | 21.0% | 78.4% | 21.1% | 78.9% |
| California | | 22 | | 3,268,791 | 1,351,419 | 1,877,618 | 39,754 | 526,199 D | 41.3% | 57.4% | 41.9% | 58.1% |
| Colorado | 6 | | | 549,004 | 279,576 | 265,554 | 3,874 | 14,022 R | 50.9% | 48.4% | 51.3% | 48.7% |
| Connecticut | | 8 | | 781,502 | 361,819 | 417,621 | 2,062 | 55,802 D | 46.3% | 53.4% | 46.4% | 53.6% |
| Delaware | | 3 | | 136,374 | 61,440 | 74,599 | 335 | 13,159 D | 45.1% | 54.7% | 45.2% | 54.8% |
| Florida | | 7 | | 485,640 | 126,158 | 359,334 | 148 | 233,176 D | 26.0% | 74.0% | 26.0% | 74.0% |
| Georgia | | 12 | | 312,686 | 46,495 | 265,194 | 997 | 218,699 D | 14.9% | 84.8% | 14.9% | 85.1% |
| Hawaii | | | | | | | | | | | | |
| Idaho | | 4 | | 235,168 | 106,553 | 127,842 | 773 | 21,289 D | 45.3% | 54.4% | 45.5% | 54.5% |
| Illinois | | 29 | | 4,217,935 | 2,047,240 | 2,149,934 | 20,761 | 102,694 D | 48.5% | 51.0% | 48.8% | 51.2% |
| Indiana | 14 | | | 1,782,747 | 899,466 | 874,063 | 9,218 | 25,403 R | 50.5% | 49.0% | 50.7% | 49.3% |
| Iowa | 11 | | | 1,215,432 | 632,370 | 578,802 | 4,260 | 53,568 R | 52.0% | 47.6% | 52.2% | 47.8% |
| Kansas | 9 | | | 860,297 | 489,169 | 364,725 | 6,403 | 124,444 R | 56.9% | 42.4% | 57.3% | 42.7% |
| Kentucky | | 11 | | 970,163 | 410,384 | 557,322 | 2,457 | 146,938 D | 42.3% | 57.4% | 42.4% | 57.6% |
| Louisiana | | 10 | | 372,305 | 52,446 | 319,751 | 108 | 267,305 D | 14.1% | 85.9% | 14.1% | 85.9% |
| Maine | 5 | | | 320,840 | 163,951 | 156,478 | 411 | 7,473 R | 51.1% | 48.8% | 51.2% | 48.8% |
| Maryland | | 8 | | 660,104 | 269,534 | 384,546 | 6,024 | 115,012 D | 40.8% | 58.3% | 41.2% | 58.8% |
| Massachusetts | | 17 | | 2,026,993 | 939,700 | 1,076,522 | 10,771 | 136,822 D | 46.4% | 53.1% | 46.6% | 53.4% |
| Michigan | 19 | | | 2,085,929 | 1,039,917 | 1,032,991 | 13,021 | 6,926 R | 49.9% | 49.5% | 50.2% | 49.8% |
| Minnesota | | 11 | | 1,251,188 | 596,274 | 644,196 | 10,718 | 47,922 D | 47.7% | 51.5% | 48.1% | 51.9% |
| Mississippi | | 9 | | 175,824 | 7,364 | 168,267 | 193 | 160,903 D | 4.2% | 95.7% | 4.2% | 95.8% |
| Missouri | | 15 | | 1,833,729 | 871,009 | 958,476 | 4,244 | 87,467 D | 47.5% | 52.3% | 47.6% | 52.4% |
| Montana | | 4 | | 247,873 | 99,579 | 145,698 | 2,596 | 46,119 D | 40.2% | 58.8% | 40.6% | 59.4% |
| Nebraska | 7 | | | 615,878 | 352,201 | 263,677 | | 88,524 R | 57.2% | 42.8% | 57.2% | 42.8% |
| Nevada | | 3 | | 53,174 | 21,229 | 31,945 | | 10,716 D | 39.9% | 60.1% | 39.9% | 60.1% |
| New Hampshire | | 4 | | 235,419 | 110,127 | 125,292 | | 15,165 D | 46.8% | 53.2% | 46.8% | 53.2% |
| New Jersey | | 16 | | 1,972,552 | 945,475 | 1,016,808 | 10,269 | 71,333 D | 47.9% | 51.5% | 48.2% | 51.8% |
| New Mexico | | 3 | | 183,258 | 79,315 | 103,699 | 244 | 24,384 D | 43.3% | 56.6% | 43.3% | 56.7% |
| New York | | 47 | | 6,301,596 | 3,027,478 | 3,251,918 | 22,200 | 224,440 D | 48.0% | 51.6% | 48.2% | 51.8% |
| North Carolina | | 13 | | 822,648 | 213,633 | 609,015 | | 395,382 D | 26.0% | 74.0% | 26.0% | 74.0% |
| North Dakota | 4 | | | 280,775 | 154,590 | 124,036 | 2,149 | 30,554 R | 55.1% | 44.2% | 55.5% | 44.5% |
| Ohio | | 26 | | 3,319,912 | 1,586,773 | 1,733,139 | | 146,366 D | 47.8% | 52.2% | 47.8% | 52.2% |
| Oklahoma | | 11 | | 826,212 | 348,872 | 474,313 | 3,027 | 125,441 D | 42.2% | 57.4% | 42.4% | 57.6% |
| Oregon | | 5 | | 481,240 | 219,555 | 258,415 | 3,270 | 38,860 D | 45.6% | 53.7% | 45.9% | 54.1% |
| Pennsylvania | | 36 | | 4,078,714 | 1,889,848 | 2,171,035 | 17,831 | 281,187 D | 46.3% | 53.2% | 46.5% | 53.5% |
| Rhode Island | | 4 | | 321,152 | 138,654 | 182,181 | 317 | 43,527 D | 43.2% | 56.7% | 43.2% | 56.8% |
| South Carolina | | 8 | | 99,830 | 4,360 | 95,470 | | 91,110 D | 4.4% | 95.6% | 4.4% | 95.6% |
| South Dakota | 4 | | | 308,427 | 177,065 | 131,362 | | 45,703 R | 57.4% | 42.6% | 57.4% | 42.6% |
| Tennessee | | 11 | | 522,823 | 169,153 | 351,601 | 2,069 | 182,448 D | 32.4% | 67.3% | 32.5% | 67.5% |
| Texas | | 23 | | 1,124,437 | 212,692 | 909,974 | 1,771 | 697,282 D | 18.9% | 80.9% | 18.9% | 81.1% |
| Utah | | 4 | | 247,819 | 93,151 | 154,277 | 391 | 61,126 D | 37.6% | 62.3% | 37.6% | 62.4% |
| Vermont | 3 | | | 143,062 | 78,371 | 64,269 | 422 | 14,102 R | 54.8% | 44.9% | 54.9% | 45.1% |
| Virginia | | 11 | | 346,608 | 109,363 | 235,961 | 1,284 | 126,598 D | 31.6% | 68.1% | 31.7% | 68.3% |
| Washington | | 8 | | 793,833 | 322,123 | 462,145 | 9,565 | 140,022 D | 40.6% | 58.2% | 41.1% | 58.9% |
| West Virginia | | 8 | | 868,076 | 372,414 | 495,662 | | 123,248 D | 42.9% | 57.1% | 42.9% | 57.1% |
| Wisconsin | | 12 | | 1,405,522 | 679,206 | 704,821 | 21,495 | 25,615 D | 48.3% | 50.1% | 49.1% | 50.9% |
| Wyoming | | 3 | | 112,240 | 52,633 | 59,287 | 320 | 6,654 D | 46.9% | 52.8% | 47.0% | 53.0% |
| Dist. of Col. | | | | | | | | | | | | |
| United States | 82 | 449 | — | 49,900,418 | 22,348,480 | 27,313,041 | 238,897 | 4,964,561 D | 44.8% | 54.7% | 45.0% | 55.0% |

## PRESIDENT 1936

The Republican figures in Delaware, Mississippi, and South Carolina include votes cast for two elector tickets. In New York the Democratic figures include American Labor votes.

The candidates listed below include all those who appeared on the ballot in at least one state.

27,757,333   Franklin D. Roosevelt and John N. Garner, *Democratic*.
16,684,231   Alfred M. Landon and Frank Know, *Republican*.
    892,267   William Lemke and Thomas C. O'Brien, *Union*.
    187,833   Norman Thomas and George A. Nelson, *Socialist*.
     80,171   Earl Browder and James W. Ford, *Communist*.
     37,677   D. Leigh Colvin and Claude A. Watson, *Prohibition*.
     12,829   John W. Aiken and Emil F. Teichert, *Socialist Labor*.
      1,598   William Dudley Pelley and Willard W. Kemp, *Christian*.

In addition, 824 scattered write-in votes were reported from various states.

# UNITED STATES

## PRESIDENT 1936

| State | Electoral Vote Rep. | Electoral Vote Dem. | Electoral Vote Other | Total Vote | Republican | Democratic | Other | Plurality | Percentage Total Vote Rep. | Percentage Total Vote Dem. | Percentage Major Vote Rep. | Percentage Major Vote Dem. |
|---|---|---|---|---|---|---|---|---|---|---|---|---|
| Alabama | | 11 | | 275,744 | 35,358 | 238,196 | 2,190 | 202,838 D | 12.8% | 86.4% | 12.9% | 87.1% |
| Alaska | | | | | | | | | | | | |
| Arizona | | 3 | | 124,163 | 33,433 | 86,722 | 4,008 | 53,289 D | 26.9% | 69.8% | 27.8% | 72.2% |
| Arkansas | | 9 | | 179,431 | 32,049 | 146,765 | 617 | 114,716 D | 17.9% | 81.8% | 17.9% | 82.1% |
| California | | 22 | | 2,638,882 | 836,431 | 1,766,836 | 35,615 | 930,405 D | 31.7% | 67.0% | 32.1% | 67.9% |
| Colorado | | 6 | | 488,685 | 181,267 | 295,021 | 12,397 | 113,754 D | 37.1% | 60.4% | 38.1% | 61.9% |
| Connecticut | | 8 | | 690,723 | 278,685 | 382,129 | 29,909 | 103,444 D | 40.3% | 55.3% | 42.2% | 57.8% |
| Delaware | | 3 | | 127,603 | 57,236 | 69,702 | 665 | 12,466 D | 44.9% | 54.6% | 45.1% | 54.9% |
| Florida | | 7 | | 327,436 | 78,248 | 249,117 | 71 | 170,869 D | 23.9% | 76.1% | 23.9% | 76.1% |
| Georgia | | 12 | | 293,170 | 36,943 | 255,363 | 864 | 218,420 D | 12.6% | 87.1% | 12.6% | 87.4% |
| Hawaii | | | | | | | | | | | | |
| Idaho | | 4 | | 199,617 | 66,256 | 125,683 | 7,678 | 59,427 D | 33.2% | 63.0% | 34.5% | 65.5% |
| Illinois | | 29 | | 3,956,522 | 1,570,393 | 2,282,999 | 103,130 | 712,606 D | 39.7% | 57.7% | 40.8% | 59.2% |
| Indiana | | 14 | | 1,650,897 | 691,570 | 934,974 | 24,353 | 243,404 D | 41.9% | 56.6% | 42.5% | 57.5% |
| Iowa | | 11 | | 1,142,737 | 487,977 | 621,756 | 33,004 | 133,779 D | 42.7% | 54.4% | 44.0% | 56.0% |
| Kansas | | 9 | | 865,507 | 397,727 | 464,520 | 3,260 | 66,793 D | 46.0% | 53.7% | 46.1% | 53.9% |
| Kentucky | | 11 | | 926,214 | 369,702 | 541,944 | 14,568 | 172,242 D | 39.9% | 58.5% | 40.6% | 59.4% |
| Louisiana | | 10 | | 329,778 | 36,791 | 292,894 | 93 | 256,103 D | 11.2% | 88.8% | 11.2% | 88.8% |
| Maine | 5 | | | 304,240 | 168,823 | 126,333 | 9,084 | 42,490 R | 55.5% | 41.5% | 57.2% | 42.8% |
| Maryland | | 8 | | 624,896 | 231,435 | 389,612 | 3,849 | 158,177 D | 37.0% | 62.3% | 37.3% | 62.7% |
| Massachusetts | | 17 | | 1,840,357 | 768,613 | 942,716 | 129,028 | 174,103 D | 41.8% | 51.2% | 44.9% | 55.1% |
| Michigan | | 19 | | 1,805,098 | 699,733 | 1,016,794 | 88,571 | 317,061 D | 38.8% | 56.3% | 40.8% | 59.2% |
| Minnesota | | 11 | | 1,129,975 | 350,461 | 698,811 | 80,703 | 348,350 D | 31.0% | 61.8% | 33.4% | 66.6% |
| Mississippi | | 9 | | 162,142 | 4,467 | 157,333 | 342 | 152,866 D | 2.8% | 97.0% | 2.8% | 97.2% |
| Missouri | | 15 | | 1,828,635 | 697,891 | 1,111,043 | 19,701 | 413,152 D | 38.2% | 60.8% | 38.6% | 61.4% |
| Montana | | 4 | | 230,502 | 63,598 | 159,690 | 7,214 | 96,092 D | 27.6% | 69.3% | 28.5% | 71.5% |
| Nebraska | | 7 | | 608,023 | 247,731 | 347,445 | 12,847 | 99,714 D | 40.7% | 57.1% | 41.6% | 58.4% |
| Nevada | | 3 | | 43,848 | 11,923 | 31,925 | | 20,002 D | 27.2% | 72.8% | 27.2% | 72.8% |
| New Hampshire | | 4 | | 218,114 | 104,642 | 108,460 | 5,012 | 3,818 D | 48.0% | 49.7% | 49.1% | 50.9% |
| New Jersey | | 16 | | 1,820,437 | 720,322 | 1,083,850 | 16,265 | 363,528 D | 39.6% | 59.5% | 39.9% | 60.1% |
| New Mexico | | 3 | | 169,135 | 61,727 | 106,037 | 1,371 | 44,310 D | 36.5% | 62.7% | 36.8% | 63.2% |
| New York | | 47 | | 5,596,398 | 2,180,670 | 3,293,222 | 122,506 | 1,112,552 D | 39.0% | 58.8% | 39.8% | 60.2% |
| North Carolina | | 13 | | 839,475 | 223,294 | 616,141 | 40 | 392,847 D | 26.6% | 73.4% | 26.6% | 73.4% |
| North Dakota | | 4 | | 273,716 | 72,751 | 163,148 | 37,817 | 90,397 D | 26.6% | 59.6% | 30.8% | 69.2% |
| Ohio | | 26 | | 3,012,660 | 1,127,855 | 1,747,140 | 137,665 | 619,285 D | 37.4% | 58.0% | 39.2% | 60.8% |
| Oklahoma | | 11 | | 749,740 | 245,122 | 501,069 | 3,549 | 255,947 D | 32.7% | 66.8% | 32.8% | 67.2% |
| Oregon | | 5 | | 414,021 | 122,706 | 266,733 | 24,582 | 144,027 D | 29.6% | 64.4% | 31.5% | 68.5% |
| Pennsylvania | | 36 | | 4,138,105 | 1,690,300 | 2,353,788 | 94,017 | 663,488 D | 40.8% | 56.9% | 41.8% | 58.2% |
| Rhode Island | | 4 | | 310,278 | 125,031 | 164,338 | 20,909 | 39,307 D | 40.3% | 53.0% | 43.2% | 56.8% |
| South Carolina | | 8 | | 115,437 | 1,646 | 113,791 | | 112,145 D | 1.4% | 98.6% | 1.4% | 98.6% |
| South Dakota | | 4 | | 296,452 | 125,977 | 160,137 | 10,338 | 34,160 D | 42.5% | 54.0% | 44.0% | 56.0% |
| Tennessee | | 11 | | 477,086 | 147,055 | 328,083 | 1,948 | 181,028 D | 30.8% | 68.8% | 30.9% | 69.1% |
| Texas | | 23 | | 849,701 | 104,661 | 739,952 | 5,088 | 635,291 D | 12.3% | 87.1% | 12.4% | 87.6% |
| Utah | | 4 | | 216,679 | 64,555 | 150,248 | 1,876 | 85,693 D | 29.8% | 69.3% | 30.1% | 69.9% |
| Vermont | 3 | | | 143,689 | 81,023 | 62,124 | 542 | 18,899 R | 56.4% | 43.2% | 56.6% | 43.4% |
| Virginia | | 11 | | 334,590 | 98,336 | 234,980 | 1,274 | 136,644 D | 29.4% | 70.2% | 29.5% | 70.5% |
| Washington | | 8 | | 692,338 | 206,892 | 459,579 | 25,867 | 252,687 D | 29.9% | 66.4% | 31.0% | 69.0% |
| West Virginia | | 8 | | 829,945 | 325,358 | 502,582 | 2,005 | 177,224 D | 39.2% | 60.6% | 39.3% | 60.7% |
| Wisconsin | | 12 | | 1,258,560 | 380,828 | 802,984 | 74,748 | 422,156 D | 30.3% | 63.8% | 32.2% | 67.8% |
| Wyoming | | 3 | | 103,382 | 38,739 | 62,624 | 2,019 | 23,885 D | 37.5% | 60.6% | 38.2% | 61.8% |
| Dist. of Col. | | | | | | | | | | | | |
| United States | 8 | 523 | — | 45,654,763 | 16,684,231 | 27,757,333 | 1,213,199 | 11,073,102 D | 36.5% | 60.8% | 37.5% | 62.5% |

## PRESIDENT 1932

The Republican figures in Mississippi include votes cast for two elector tickets.

The candidates listed below include all those who appeared on the ballot in at least one state.

| | |
|---|---|
| 22,829,501 | Franklin D. Roosevelt and John N. Garner, *Democratic.* |
| 15,760,684 | Herbert C. Hoover and Charles Curtis, *Republican.* |
| 884,649 | Norman Thomas and James H. Maurer, *Socialist.* |
| 103,253 | William Z. Foster and James W. Ford, *Communist.* |
| 81,872 | William D. Upshaw and Frank S. Regan, *Prohibition.* |
| 53,247 | William H. Harvey and Frank Hemenway, *Liberty.* |
| 34,043 | Verne L. Reynolds and John W. Aiken, *Socialist Labor.* |
| 7,431 | Jacob S. Coxey and Julius J. Reiter, *Farmer-Labor.* |
| 1,645 | John Zahnd and Florence Garvin, *National.* |
| 740 | James R. Cox and Victor C. Tisdal, *Jobless.* |

In Texas, 157 votes were cast for a Jacksonian elector ticket; in Arizona 9 votes were cast for an Arizona Progressive Democratic elector ticket. In addition, 1,528 scattered write-in votes were reported from various states.

# UNITED STATES

## PRESIDENT 1932

| State | Electoral Vote | | | Total Vote | Republican | Democratic | Other | Plurality | Percentage | | | |
|---|---|---|---|---|---|---|---|---|---|---|---|---|
| | | | | | | | | | Total Vote | | Major Vote | |
| | Rep. | Dem. | Other | | | | | | Rep. | Dem. | Rep. | Dem. |
| Alabama | | 11 | | 245,303 | 34,675 | 207,910 | 2,718 | 173,235 D | 14.1% | 84.8% | 14.3% | 85.7% |
| Alaska | | | | | | | | | | | | |
| Arizona | | 3 | | 118,251 | 36,104 | 79,264 | 2,883 | 43,160 D | 30.5% | 67.0% | 31.3% | 68.7% |
| Arkansas | | 9 | | 216,569 | 27,465 | 186,829 | 2,275 | 159,364 D | 12.7% | 86.3% | 12.8% | 87.2% |
| California | | 22 | | 2,266,972 | 847,902 | 1,324,157 | 94,913 | 476,255 D | 37.4% | 58.4% | 39.0% | 61.0% |
| Colorado | | 6 | | 457,696 | 189,617 | 250,877 | 17,202 | 61,260 D | 41.4% | 54.8% | 43.0% | 57.0% |
| Connecticut | 8 | | | 594,183 | 288,420 | 281,632 | 24,131 | 6,788 R | 48.5% | 47.4% | 50.6% | 49.4% |
| Delaware | 3 | | | 112,901 | 57,073 | 54,319 | 1,509 | 2,754 R | 50.6% | 48.1% | 51.2% | 48.8% |
| Florida | | 7 | | 276,943 | 69,170 | 206,307 | 1,466 | 137,137 D | 25.0% | 74.5% | 25.1% | 74.9% |
| Georgia | | 12 | | 255,590 | 19,863 | 234,118 | 1,609 | 214,255 D | 7.8% | 91.6% | 7.8% | 92.2% |
| Hawaii | | | | | | | | | | | | |
| Idaho | | 4 | | 186,520 | 71,312 | 109,479 | 5,729 | 38,167 D | 38.2% | 58.7% | 39.4% | 60.6% |
| Illinois | | 29 | | 3,407,926 | 1,432,756 | 1,882,304 | 92,866 | 449,548 D | 42.0% | 55.2% | 43.2% | 56.8% |
| Indiana | | 14 | | 1,576,927 | 677,184 | 862,054 | 37,689 | 184,870 D | 42.9% | 54.7% | 44.0% | 56.0% |
| Iowa | | 11 | | 1,036,687 | 414,433 | 598,019 | 24,235 | 183,586 D | 40.0% | 57.7% | 40.9% | 59.1% |
| Kansas | | 9 | | 791,978 | 349,498 | 424,204 | 18,276 | 74,706 D | 44.1% | 53.6% | 45.2% | 54.8% |
| Kentucky | | 11 | | 983,059 | 394,716 | 580,574 | 7,769 | 185,858 D | 40.2% | 59.1% | 40.5% | 59.5% |
| Louisiana | | 10 | | 268,804 | 18,853 | 249,418 | 533 | 230,565 D | 7.0% | 92.8% | 7.0% | 93.0% |
| Maine | 5 | | | 298,444 | 166,631 | 128,907 | 2,906 | 37,724 R | 55.8% | 43.2% | 56.4% | 43.6% |
| Maryland | | 8 | | 511,054 | 184,184 | 314,314 | 12,556 | 130,130 D | 36.0% | 61.5% | 36.9% | 63.1% |
| Massachusetts | | 17 | | 1,580,114 | 736,959 | 800,148 | 43,007 | 63,189 D | 46.6% | 50.6% | 47.9% | 52.1% |
| Michigan | | 19 | | 1,664,765 | 739,894 | 871,700 | 53,171 | 131,806 D | 44.4% | 52.4% | 45.9% | 54.1% |
| Minnesota | | 11 | | 1,002,843 | 363,959 | 600,806 | 38,078 | 236,847 D | 36.3% | 59.9% | 37.7% | 62.3% |
| Mississippi | | 9 | | 146,034 | 5,180 | 140,168 | 686 | 134,988 D | 3.5% | 96.0% | 3.6% | 96.4% |
| Missouri | | 15 | | 1,609,894 | 564,713 | 1,025,406 | 19,775 | 460,693 D | 35.1% | 63.7% | 35.5% | 64.5% |
| Montana | | 4 | | 216,479 | 78,078 | 127,286 | 11,115 | 49,208 D | 36.1% | 58.8% | 38.0% | 62.0% |
| Nebraska | | 7 | | 570,135 | 201,177 | 359,082 | 9,876 | 157,905 D | 35.3% | 63.0% | 35.9% | 64.1% |
| Nevada | | 3 | | 41,430 | 12,674 | 28,756 | | 16,082 D | 30.6% | 69.4% | 30.6% | 69.4% |
| New Hampshire | 4 | | | 205,520 | 103,629 | 100,680 | 1,211 | 2,949 R | 50.4% | 49.0% | 50.7% | 49.3% |
| New Jersey | | 16 | | 1,630,063 | 775,684 | 806,630 | 47,749 | 30,946 D | 47.6% | 49.5% | 49.0% | 51.0% |
| New Mexico | | 3 | | 151,606 | 54,217 | 95,089 | 2,300 | 40,872 D | 35.8% | 62.7% | 36.3% | 63.7% |
| New York | | 47 | | 4,688,614 | 1,937,963 | 2,534,959 | 215,692 | 596,996 D | 41.3% | 54.1% | 43.3% | 56.7% |
| North Carolina | | 13 | | 711,498 | 208,344 | 497,566 | 5,588 | 289,222 D | 29.3% | 69.9% | 29.5% | 70.5% |
| North Dakota | | 4 | | 256,290 | 71,772 | 178,350 | 6,168 | 106,578 D | 28.0% | 69.6% | 28.7% | 71.3% |
| Ohio | | 26 | | 2,609,728 | 1,227,319 | 1,301,695 | 80,714 | 74,376 D | 47.0% | 49.9% | 48.5% | 51.5% |
| Oklahoma | | 11 | | 704,633 | 188,165 | 516,468 | | 328,303 D | 26.7% | 73.3% | 26.7% | 73.3% |
| Oregon | | 5 | | 368,751 | 136,019 | 213,871 | 18,861 | 77,852 D | 36.9% | 58.0% | 38.9% | 61.1% |
| Pennsylvania | 36 | | | 2,859,021 | 1,453,540 | 1,295,948 | 109,533 | 157,592 R | 50.8% | 45.3% | 52.9% | 47.1% |
| Rhode Island | | 4 | | 266,170 | 115,266 | 146,604 | 4,300 | 31,338 D | 43.3% | 55.1% | 44.0% | 56.0% |
| South Carolina | | 8 | | 104,407 | 1,978 | 102,347 | 82 | 100,369 D | 1.9% | 98.0% | 1.9% | 98.1% |
| South Dakota | | 4 | | 288,438 | 99,212 | 183,515 | 5,711 | 84,303 D | 34.4% | 63.6% | 35.1% | 64.9% |
| Tennessee | | 11 | | 390,273 | 126,752 | 259,473 | 4,048 | 132,721 D | 32.5% | 66.5% | 32.8% | 67.2% |
| Texas | | 23 | | 874,382 | 98,218 | 771,109 | 5,055 | 672,891 D | 11.2% | 88.2% | 11.3% | 88.7% |
| Utah | | 4 | | 206,578 | 84,795 | 116,750 | 5,033 | 31,955 D | 41.0% | 56.5% | 42.1% | 57.9% |
| Vermont | 3 | | | 136,980 | 78,984 | 56,266 | 1,730 | 22,718 R | 57.7% | 41.1% | 58.4% | 41.6% |
| Virginia | | 11 | | 297,942 | 89,637 | 203,979 | 4,326 | 114,342 D | 30.1% | 68.5% | 30.5% | 69.5% |
| Washington | | 8 | | 614,814 | 208,645 | 353,260 | 52,909 | 144,615 D | 33.9% | 57.5% | 37.1% | 62.9% |
| West Virginia | | 8 | | 743,774 | 330,731 | 405,124 | 7,919 | 74,393 D | 44.5% | 54.5% | 44.9% | 55.1% |
| Wisconsin | | 12 | | 1,114,814 | 347,741 | 707,410 | 59,663 | 359,669 D | 31.2% | 63.5% | 33.0% | 67.0% |
| Wyoming | | 3 | | 96,962 | 39,583 | 54,370 | 3,009 | 14,787 D | 40.8% | 56.1% | 42.1% | 57.9% |
| Dist. of Col. | | | | | | | | | | | | |
| United States | 59 | 472 | — | 39,758,759 | 15,760,684 | 22,829,501 | 1,168,574 | 7,068,817 D | 39.6% | 57.4% | 40.8% | 59.2% |

## PRESIDENT 1928

The Republican figures in Georgia, Mississippi, and South Carolina include votes cast for two or three elector tickets; in Pennsylvania the Communist total includes votes cast for two elector tickets.

The full list of candidates for President and Vice-President was:

21,437,277   Herbert C. Hoover and Charles Curtis, *Republican.*
15,007,698   Alfred E. Smith and Joseph T. Robinson, *Democratic.*
265,583   Norman Thomas and James H. Maurer, *Socialist.*
46,896   William Z. Foster and Benjamin Gitlow, *Communist*
21,586   Verne L. Reynolds and Jeremiah D. Crowley, *Socialist Labor.*
20,101   William F. Varney and James A. Edgerton, *Prohibition.*
6,390   Frank E. Webb and L. R. Tillman, *Farmer-Labor.*

In addition, 420 scattered write-in votes were reported from various states.

# UNITED STATES

## PRESIDENT 1928

| State | Electoral Vote Rep. | Electoral Vote Dem. | Electoral Vote Other | Total Vote | Republican | Democratic | Other | Plurality | Percentage Total Vote Rep. | Percentage Total Vote Dem. | Percentage Major Vote Rep. | Percentage Major Vote Dem. |
|---|---|---|---|---|---|---|---|---|---|---|---|---|
| Alabama | | 12 | | 248,981 | 120,725 | 127,796 | 460 | 7,071 D | 48.5% | 51.3% | 48.6% | 51.4% |
| Alaska | | | | | | | | | | | | |
| Arizona | 3 | | | 91,254 | 52,533 | 38,537 | 184 | 13,996 R | 57.6% | 42.2% | 57.7% | 42.3% |
| Arkansas | | 9 | | 197,726 | 77,784 | 119,196 | 746 | 41,412 D | 39.3% | 60.3% | 39.5% | 60.5% |
| California | 13 | | | 1,796,656 | 1,162,323 | 614,365 | 19,968 | 547,958 R | 64.7% | 34.2% | 65.4% | 34.6% |
| Colorado | 6 | | | 392,242 | 253,872 | 133,131 | 5,239 | 120,741 R | 64.7% | 33.9% | 65.6% | 34.4% |
| Connecticut | 7 | | | 553,118 | 296,641 | 252,085 | 4,392 | 44,556 R | 53.6% | 45.6% | 54.1% | 45.9% |
| Delaware | 3 | | | 104,602 | 68,860 | 35,354 | 388 | 33,506 R | 65.8% | 33.8% | 66.1% | 33.9% |
| Florida | 6 | | | 252,068 | 145,860 | 101,764 | 4,444 | 44,096 R | 57.9% | 40.4% | 58.9% | 41.1% |
| Georgia | | 14 | | 231,592 | 101,800 | 129,604 | 188 | 27,804 D | 44.0% | 56.0% | 44.0% | 56.0% |
| Hawaii | | | | | | | | | | | | |
| Idaho | 4 | | | 151,541 | 97,322 | 52,926 | 1,293 | 44,396 R | 64.2% | 34.9% | 64.8% | 35.2% |
| Illinois | 29 | | | 3,107,489 | 1,769,141 | 1,313,817 | 24,531 | 455,324 R | 56.9% | 42.3% | 57.4% | 42.6% |
| Indiana | 15 | | | 1,421,314 | 848,290 | 562,691 | 10,333 | 285,599 R | 59.7% | 39.6% | 60.1% | 39.9% |
| Iowa | 13 | | | 1,009,189 | 623,570 | 379,011 | 6,608 | 244,559 R | 61.8% | 37.6% | 62.2% | 37.8% |
| Kansas | 10 | | | 713,200 | 513,672 | 193,003 | 6,525 | 320,669 R | 72.0% | 27.1% | 72.7% | 27.3% |
| Kentucky | 13 | | | 940,521 | 558,064 | 381,070 | 1,387 | 176,994 R | 59.3% | 40.5% | 59.4% | 40.6% |
| Louisiana | | 10 | | 215,833 | 51,160 | 164,655 | 18 | 113,495 D | 23.7% | 76.3% | 23.7% | 76.3% |
| Maine | 6 | | | 262,170 | 179,923 | 81,179 | 1,068 | 98,744 R | 68.6% | 31.0% | 68.9% | 31.1% |
| Maryland | 8 | | | 528,348 | 301,479 | 223,626 | 3,243 | 77,853 R | 57.1% | 42.3% | 57.4% | 42.6% |
| Massachusetts | | 18 | | 1,577,823 | 775,566 | 792,758 | 9,499 | 17,192 D | 49.2% | 50.2% | 49.5% | 50.5% |
| Michigan | 15 | | | 1,372,082 | 965,396 | 396,762 | 9,924 | 568,634 R | 70.4% | 28.9% | 70.9% | 29.1% |
| Minnesota | 12 | | | 970,976 | 560,977 | 396,451 | 13,548 | 164,526 R | 57.8% | 40.8% | 58.6% | 41.4% |
| Mississippi | | 10 | | 151,568 | 27,030 | 124,538 | | 97,508 D | 17.8% | 82.2% | 17.8% | 82.2% |
| Missouri | 18 | | | 1,500,845 | 834,080 | 662,684 | 4,081 | 171,396 R | 55.6% | 44.2% | 55.7% | 44.3% |
| Montana | 4 | | | 194,108 | 113,300 | 78,578 | 2,230 | 34,722 R | 58.4% | 40.5% | 59.0% | 41.0% |
| Nebraska | 8 | | | 547,128 | 345,745 | 197,950 | 3,433 | 147,795 R | 63.2% | 36.2% | 63.6% | 36.4% |
| Nevada | 3 | | | 32,417 | 18,327 | 14,090 | | 4,237 R | 56.5% | 43.5% | 56.5% | 43.5% |
| New Hampshire | 4 | | | 196,757 | 115,404 | 80,715 | 638 | 34,689 R | 58.7% | 41.0% | 58.8% | 41.2% |
| New Jersey | 14 | | | 1,549,381 | 926,050 | 616,517 | 6,814 | 309,533 R | 59.8% | 39.8% | 60.0% | 40.0% |
| New Mexico | 3 | | | 118,077 | 69,708 | 48,211 | 158 | 21,497 R | 59.0% | 40.8% | 59.1% | 40.9% |
| New York | 45 | | | 4,405,626 | 2,193,344 | 2,089,863 | 122,419 | 103,481 R | 49.8% | 47.4% | 51.2% | 48.8% |
| North Carolina | 12 | | | 635,150 | 348,923 | 286,227 | | 62,696 R | 54.9% | 45.1% | 54.9% | 45.1% |
| North Dakota | 5 | | | 239,845 | 131,419 | 106,648 | 1,778 | 24,771 R | 54.8% | 44.5% | 55.2% | 44.8% |
| Ohio | 24 | | | 2,508,346 | 1,627,546 | 864,210 | 16,590 | 763,336 R | 64.9% | 34.5% | 65.3% | 34.7% |
| Oklahoma | 10 | | | 618,427 | 394,046 | 219,174 | 5,207 | 174,872 R | 63.7% | 35.4% | 64.3% | 35.7% |
| Oregon | 5 | | | 319,942 | 205,341 | 109,223 | 5,378 | 96,118 R | 64.2% | 34.1% | 65.3% | 34.7% |
| Pennsylvania | 38 | | | 3,150,612 | 2,055,382 | 1,067,586 | 27,644 | 987,796 R | 65.2% | 33.9% | 65.8% | 34.2% |
| Rhode Island | | 5 | | 237,194 | 117,522 | 118,973 | 699 | 1,451 D | 49.5% | 50.2% | 49.7% | 50.3% |
| South Carolina | | 9 | | 68,605 | 5,858 | 62,700 | 47 | 56,842 D | 8.5% | 91.4% | 8.5% | 91.5% |
| South Dakota | 5 | | | 261,857 | 157,603 | 102,660 | 1,594 | 54,943 R | 60.2% | 39.2% | 60.6% | 39.4% |
| Tennessee | 12 | | | 353,192 | 195,388 | 157,143 | 661 | 38,245 R | 55.3% | 44.5% | 55.4% | 44.6% |
| Texas | 20 | | | 717,733 | 372,324 | 344,542 | 867 | 27,782 R | 51.9% | 48.0% | 51.9% | 48.1% |
| Utah | 4 | | | 176,603 | 94,618 | 80,985 | 1,000 | 13,633 R | 53.6% | 45.9% | 53.9% | 46.1% |
| Vermont | 4 | | | 135,191 | 90,404 | 44,440 | 347 | 45,964 R | 66.9% | 32.9% | 67.0% | 33.0% |
| Virginia | 12 | | | 305,364 | 164,609 | 140,146 | 609 | 24,463 R | 53.9% | 45.9% | 54.0% | 46.0% |
| Washington | 7 | | | 500,840 | 335,844 | 156,772 | 8,224 | 179,072 R | 67.1% | 31.3% | 68.2% | 31.8% |
| West Virginia | 8 | | | 642,752 | 375,551 | 263,784 | 3,417 | 111,767 R | 58.4% | 41.0% | 58.7% | 41.3% |
| Wisconsin | 13 | | | 1,016,831 | 544,205 | 450,259 | 22,367 | 93,946 R | 53.5% | 44.3% | 54.7% | 45.3% |
| Wyoming | 3 | | | 82,835 | 52,748 | 29,299 | 788 | 23,449 R | 63.7% | 35.4% | 64.3% | 35.7% |
| Dist. of Col. | | | | | | | | | | | | |
| United States | 444 | 87 | — | 36,805,951 | 21,437,277 | 15,007,698 | 360,976 | 6,429,579 R | 58.2% | 40.8% | 58.8% | 41.2% |

# PRESIDENT 1924

The Progressive party carried Wisconsin and its thirteen Electoral College votes were cast for the Progressive nominees. The Progressive party candidates ran second in eleven other states in the Midwest and West and in several states the Progressive total includes votes cast for more than one elector ticket.

The candidates listed below include all those who appeared on the ballot in at least one state.

|  |  |
|---|---|
| 15,719,921 | Calvin Coolidge and Charles G. Dawes, *Republican.* |
| 8,386,704 | John W. Davis and Charles W. Bryan, *Democratic.* |
| 4,832,532 | Robert M. LaFollette and Burton K. Wheeler, *Progressive.* |
| 56,292 | Herman P. Faris and Marie Caroline Brehm, *Prohibition.* |
| 34,174 | Frank T. Johns and Verne L. Reynolds, *Socialist Labor.* |
| 33,360 | William Z. Foster and Benjamin Gitlow, *Communist.* |
| 24,340 | Gilbert O. Nations and Leander L. Pickett, *American.* |
| 2,948 | William J. Wallace and John C. Lincoln, *Commonwealth Land.* |

In addition, 4,752 scattered write-in votes were reported from various states.

# UNITED STATES

## PRESIDENT 1924

| State | Electoral Vote Rep. | Electoral Vote Dem. | Electoral Vote Other | Total Vote | Republican | Democratic | Progressive | Other | Plurality | | Percentage Rep. | Percentage Dem. | Percentage Prog. |
|---|---|---|---|---|---|---|---|---|---|---|---|---|---|
| Alabama | | 12 | | 164,563 | 42,823 | 113,138 | 8,040 | 562 | 70,315 | D | 26.0% | 68.8% | 4.9% |
| Alaska | | | | | | | | | | | | | |
| Arizona | 3 | | | 73,961 | 30,516 | 26,235 | 17,210 | | 4,281 | R | 41.3% | 35.5% | 23.3% |
| Arkansas | | 9 | | 138,540 | 40,583 | 84,790 | 13,167 | | 44,207 | D | 29.3% | 61.2% | 9.5% |
| California | 13 | | | 1,281,778 | 733,250 | 105,514 | 424,649 | 18,365 | 308,601 | R | 57.2% | 8.2% | 33.1% |
| Colorado | 6 | | | 342,261 | 195,171 | 75,238 | 69,946 | 1,906 | 119,933 | R | 57.0% | 22.0% | 20.4% |
| Connecticut | 7 | | | 400,396 | 246,322 | 110,184 | 42,416 | 1,474 | 136,138 | R | 61.5% | 27.5% | 10.6% |
| Delaware | 3 | | | 90,885 | 52,441 | 33,445 | 4,979 | 20 | 18,996 | R | 57.7% | 36.8% | 5.5% |
| Florida | | 6 | | 109,158 | 30,633 | 62,083 | 8,625 | 7,817 | 31,450 | D | 28.1% | 56.9% | 7.9% |
| Georgia | | 14 | | 166,635 | 30,300 | 123,262 | 12,687 | 386 | 92,962 | D | 18.2% | 74.0% | 7.6% |
| Hawaii | | | | | | | | | | | | | |
| Idaho | 4 | | | 147,690 | 69,791 | 23,951 | 53,948 | | 15,843 | R | 47.3% | 16.2% | 36.5% |
| Illinois | 29 | | | 2,470,067 | 1,453,321 | 576,975 | 432,027 | 7,744 | 876,346 | R | 58.8% | 23.4% | 17.5% |
| Indiana | 15 | | | 1,272,390 | 703,042 | 492,245 | 71,700 | 5,403 | 210,797 | R | 55.3% | 38.7% | 5.6% |
| Iowa | 13 | | | 976,770 | 537,458 | 160,382 | 274,448 | 4,482 | 263,010 | R | 55.0% | 16.4% | 28.1% |
| Kansas | 10 | | | 662,456 | 407,671 | 156,320 | 98,461 | 4 | 251,351 | R | 61.5% | 23.6% | 14.9% |
| Kentucky | 13 | | | 813,843 | 396,758 | 375,593 | 38,465 | 3,027 | 21,165 | R | 48.8% | 46.2% | 4.7% |
| Louisiana | | 10 | | 121,951 | 24,670 | 93,218 | | 4,063 | 68,548 | D | 20.2% | 76.4% | |
| Maine | 6 | | | 192,192 | 138,440 | 41,964 | 11,382 | 406 | 96,476 | R | 72.0% | 21.8% | 5.9% |
| Maryland | 8 | | | 358,630 | 162,414 | 148,072 | 47,157 | 987 | 14,342 | R | 45.3% | 41.3% | 13.1% |
| Massachusetts | 18 | | | 1,129,837 | 703,476 | 280,831 | 141,225 | 4,305 | 422,645 | R | 62.3% | 24.9% | 12.5% |
| Michigan | 15 | | | 1,160,419 | 874,631 | 152,359 | 122,014 | 11,415 | 722,272 | R | 75.4% | 13.1% | 10.5% |
| Minnesota | 12 | | | 822,146 | 420,759 | 55,913 | 339,192 | 6,282 | 81,567 | R | 51.2% | 6.8% | 41.3% |
| Mississippi | | 10 | | 112,442 | 8,494 | 100,474 | 3,474 | | 91,980 | D | 7.6% | 89.4% | 3.1% |
| Missouri | 18 | | | 1,310,095 | 648,488 | 574,962 | 83,996 | 2,649 | 73,526 | R | 49.5% | 43.9% | 6.4% |
| Montana | 4 | | | 174,425 | 74,138 | 33,805 | 66,124 | 358 | 8,014 | R | 42.5% | 19.4% | 37.9% |
| Nebraska | 8 | | | 463,559 | 218,985 | 137,299 | 105,681 | 1,594 | 81,686 | R | 47.2% | 29.6% | 22.8% |
| Nevada | 3 | | | 26,921 | 11,243 | 5,909 | 9,769 | | 1,474 | R | 41.8% | 21.9% | 36.3% |
| New Hampshire | 4 | | | 164,769 | 98,575 | 57,201 | 8,993 | | 41,374 | R | 59.8% | 34.7% | 5.5% |
| New Jersey | 14 | | | 1,088,054 | 676,277 | 298,043 | 109,028 | 4,706 | 378,234 | R | 62.2% | 27.4% | 10.0% |
| New Mexico | 3 | | | 112,830 | 54,745 | 48,542 | 9,543 | | 6,203 | R | 48.5% | 43.0% | 8.5% |
| New York | 45 | | | 3,263,939 | 1,820,058 | 950,796 | 474,913 | 18,172 | 869,262 | R | 55.8% | 29.1% | 14.6% |
| North Carolina | | 12 | | 481,608 | 190,754 | 284,190 | 6,651 | 13 | 93,436 | D | 39.6% | 59.0% | 1.4% |
| North Dakota | 5 | | | 199,081 | 94,931 | 13,858 | 89,922 | 370 | 5,009 | R | 47.7% | 7.0% | 45.2% |
| Ohio | 24 | | | 2,016,296 | 1,176,130 | 477,887 | 358,008 | 4,271 | 698,243 | R | 58.3% | 23.7% | 17.8% |
| Oklahoma | | 10 | | 527,828 | 225,756 | 255,798 | 46,274 | | 30,042 | D | 42.8% | 48.5% | 8.8% |
| Oregon | 5 | | | 279,488 | 142,579 | 67,589 | 68,403 | 917 | 74,176 | R | 51.0% | 24.2% | 24.5% |
| Pennsylvania | 38 | | | 2,144,850 | 1,401,481 | 409,192 | 307,567 | 26,610 | 992,289 | R | 65.3% | 19.1% | 14.3% |
| Rhode Island | 5 | | | 210,115 | 125,286 | 76,606 | 7,628 | 595 | 48,680 | R | 59.6% | 36.5% | 3.6% |
| South Carolina | | 9 | | 50,755 | 1,123 | 49,008 | 623 | 1 | 47,885 | D | 2.2% | 96.6% | 1.2% |
| South Dakota | 5 | | | 203,868 | 101,299 | 27,214 | 75,355 | | 25,944 | R | 49.7% | 13.3% | 37.0% |
| Tennessee | | 12 | | 301,030 | 130,831 | 159,339 | 10,666 | 194 | 28,508 | D | 43.5% | 52.9% | 3.5% |
| Texas | | 20 | | 657,054 | 130,794 | 483,381 | 42,879 | | 352,587 | D | 19.9% | 73.6% | 6.5% |
| Utah | 4 | | | 156,990 | 77,327 | 47,001 | 32,662 | | 30,326 | R | 49.3% | 29.9% | 20.8% |
| Vermont | 4 | | | 102,917 | 80,498 | 16,124 | 5,964 | 331 | 64,374 | R | 78.2% | 15.7% | 5.8% |
| Virginia | | 12 | | 223,603 | 73,328 | 139,717 | 10,369 | 189 | 66,389 | D | 32.8% | 62.5% | 4.6% |
| Washington | 7 | | | 421,549 | 220,224 | 42,842 | 150,727 | 7,756 | 69,497 | R | 52.2% | 10.2% | 35.8% |
| West Virginia | 8 | | | 583,662 | 288,635 | 257,232 | 36,723 | 1,072 | 31,403 | R | 49.5% | 44.1% | 6.3% |
| Wisconsin | | | 13 | 840,827 | 311,614 | 68,115 | 453,678 | 7,420 | 142,064 | P | 37.1% | 8.1% | 54.0% |
| Wyoming | 3 | | | 79,900 | 41,858 | 12,868 | 25,174 | | 16,684 | R | 52.4% | 16.1% | 31.5% |
| Dist. of Col. | | | | | | | | | | | | | |
| United States | 382 | 136 | 13 | 29,095,023 | 15,719,921 | 8,386,704 | 4,832,532 | 155,866 | 7,333,217 | R | 54.0% | 28.8% | 16.6% |

## PRESIDENT 1920

The Republican figures in South Carolina include votes cast for two elector tickets; the figures in Florida are the votes cast for the single elector candidate who ran on both the regular Republican ticket and the White Republican ticket. In Washington, the total vote for minor party candidates exceeded that for the Democratic candidates, but the Democratic total was greater than that for any one of the minor party nominees.

The candidates listed below include all those who appeared on the ballot in at least one state.

| | |
|---:|---|
| 16,153,115 | Warren G. Harding and Calvin Coolidge, *Republican*. |
| 9,133,092 | James M. Cox and Franklin D. Roosevelt, *Democratic*. |
| 915,490 | Eugene V. Debs and Seymour Stedman, *Socialist*. |
| 265,229 | Parley P. Christensen and Max S. Hayes, *Farmer-Labor*. |
| 189,339 | Aaron S. Watkins and D. Leigh Colvin, *Prohibition*. |
| 48,098 | James Ferguson and William J. Hough, *American*. |
| 30,594 | William W. Cox and August Gillhaus, *Socialist Labor*. |
| 5,833 | Robert C. Macauley and Richard C. Barnum, *Single Tax*. |

In Texas, 27,309 votes were cast for a Black-and-Tan Republican elector ticket. In addition, 514 scattered write-in votes were reported from various states.

# UNITED STATES

## PRESIDENT 1920

| State | Electoral Vote Rep. | Electoral Vote Dem. | Electoral Vote Other | Total Vote | Republican | Democratic | Other | Plurality | Percentage Total Vote Rep. | Percentage Total Vote Dem. | Percentage Major Vote Rep. | Percentage Major Vote Dem. |
|---|---|---|---|---|---|---|---|---|---|---|---|---|
| Alabama | | 12 | | 233,951 | 74,719 | 156,064 | 3,168 | 81,345 D | 31.9% | 66.7% | 32.4% | 67.6% |
| Alaska | | | | | | | | | | | | |
| Arizona | 3 | | | 66,803 | 37,016 | 29,546 | 241 | 7,470 R | 55.4% | 44.2% | 55.6% | 44.4% |
| Arkansas | | 9 | | 183,871 | 72,316 | 106,427 | 5,128 | 34,111 D | 39.3% | 57.9% | 40.5% | 59.5% |
| California | 13 | | | 943,463 | 624,992 | 229,191 | 89,280 | 395,801 R | 66.2% | 24.3% | 73.2% | 26.8% |
| Colorado | 6 | | | 292,053 | 173,248 | 104,936 | 13,869 | 68,312 R | 59.3% | 35.9% | 62.3% | 37.7% |
| Connecticut | 7 | | | 365,518 | 229,238 | 120,721 | 15,559 | 108,517 R | 62.7% | 33.0% | 65.5% | 34.5% |
| Delaware | 3 | | | 94,875 | 52,858 | 39,911 | 2,106 | 12,947 R | 55.7% | 42.1% | 57.0% | 43.0% |
| Florida | . | 6 | | 145,684 | 44,853 | 90,515 | 10,316 | 45,662 D | 30.8% | 62.1% | 33.1% | 66.9% |
| Georgia | | 14 | | 149,558 | 42,981 | 106,112 | 465 | 63,131 D | 28.7% | 71.0% | 28.8% | 71.2% |
| Hawaii | | | | | | | | | | | | |
| Idaho | 4 | | | 138,281 | 91,351 | 46,930 | | 44,421 R | 66.1% | 33.9% | 66.1% | 33.9% |
| Illinois | 29 | | | 2,094,714 | 1,420,480 | 534,395 | 139,839 | 886,085 R | 67.8% | 25.5% | 72.7% | 27.3% |
| Indiana | 15 | | | 1,262,974 | 696,370 | 511,364 | 55,240 | 185,006 R | 55.1% | 40.5% | 57.7% | 42.3% |
| Iowa | 13 | | | 894,959 | 634,674 | 227,804 | 32,481 | 406,870 R | 70.9% | 25.5% | 73.6% | 26.4% |
| Kansas | 10 | | | 570,243 | 369,268 | 185,464 | 15,511 | 183,804 R | 64.8% | 32.5% | 66.6% | 33.4% |
| Kentucky | | 13 | | 918,636 | 452,480 | 456,497 | 9,659 | 4,017 D | 49.3% | 49.7% | 49.8% | 50.2% |
| Louisiana | | 10 | | 126,397 | 38,539 | 87,519 | 339 | 48,980 D | 30.5% | 69.2% | 30.6% | 69.4% |
| Maine | 6 | | | 197,840 | 136,355 | 58,961 | 2,524 | 77,394 R | 68.9% | 29.8% | 69.8% | 30.2% |
| Maryland | 8 | | | 428,443 | 236,117 | 180,626 | 11,700 | 55,491 R | 55.1% | 42.2% | 56.7% | 43.3% |
| Massachusetts | 18 | | | 993,718 | 681,153 | 276,691 | 35,874 | 404,462 R | 68.5% | 27.8% | 71.1% | 28.9% |
| Michigan | 15 | | | 1,048,411 | 762,865 | 233,450 | 52,096 | 529,415 R | 72.8% | 22.3% | 76.6% | 23.4% |
| Minnesota | 12 | | | 735,838 | 519,421 | 142,994 | 73,423 | 376,427 R | 70.6% | 19.4% | 78.4% | 21.6% |
| Mississippi | | 10 | | 82,351 | 11,576 | 69,136 | 1,639 | 57,560 D | 14.1% | 84.0% | 14.3% | 85.7% |
| Missouri | 18 | | | 1,332,140 | 727,252 | 574,699 | 30,189 | 152,553 R | 54.6% | 43.1% | 55.9% | 44.1% |
| Montana | 4 | | | 179,006 | 109,430 | 57,372 | 12,204 | 52,058 R | 61.1% | 32.1% | 65.6% | 34.4% |
| Nebraska | 8 | | | 382,743 | 247,498 | 119,608 | 15,637 | 127,890 R | 64.7% | 31.3% | 67.4% | 32.6% |
| Nevada | 3 | | | 27,194 | 15,479 | 9,851 | 1,864 | 5,628 R | 56.9% | 36.2% | 61.1% | 38.9% |
| New Hampshire | 4 | | | 159,092 | 95,196 | 62,662 | 1,234 | 32,534 R | 59.8% | 39.4% | 60.3% | 39.7% |
| New Jersey | 14 | | | 910,251 | 615,333 | 258,761 | 36,157 | 356,572 R | 67.6% | 28.4% | 70.4% | 29.6% |
| New Mexico | 3 | | | 105,412 | 57,634 | 46,668 | 1,110 | 10,966 R | 54.7% | 44.3% | 55.3% | 44.7% |
| New York | 45 | | | 2,898,513 | 1,871,167 | 781,238 | 246,108 | 1,089,929 R | 64.6% | 27.0% | 70.5% | 29.5% |
| North Carolina | | 12 | | 538,649 | 232,819 | 305,367 | 463 | 72,548 D | 43.2% | 56.7% | 43.3% | 56.7% |
| North Dakota | 5 | | | 205,786 | 160,082 | 37,422 | 8,282 | 122,660 R | 77.8% | 18.2% | 81.1% | 18.9% |
| Ohio | 24 | | | 2,021,653 | 1,182,022 | 780,037 | 59,594 | 401,985 R | 58.5% | 38.6% | 60.2% | 39.8% |
| Oklahoma | 10 | | | 485,678 | 243,840 | 216,122 | 25,716 | 27,718 R | 50.2% | 44.5% | 53.0% | 47.0% |
| Oregon | 5 | | | 238,522 | 143,592 | 80,019 | 14,911 | 63,573 R | 60.2% | 33.5% | 64.2% | 35.8% |
| Pennsylvania | 38 | | | 1,851,248 | 1,218,215 | 503,202 | 129,831 | 715,013 R | 65.8% | 27.2% | 70.8% | 29.2% |
| Rhode Island | 5 | | | 167,981 | 107,463 | 55,062 | 5,456 | 52,401 R | 64.0% | 32.8% | 66.1% | 33.9% |
| South Carolina | | 9 | | 66,808 | 2,610 | 64,170 | 28 | 61,560 D | 3.9% | 96.1% | 3.9% | 96.1% |
| South Dakota | 5 | | | 182,237 | 110,692 | 35,938 | 35,607 | 74,754 R | 60.7% | 19.7% | 75.5% | 24.5% |
| Tennessee | 12 | | | 428,036 | 219,229 | 206,558 | 2,249 | 12,671 R | 51.2% | 48.3% | 51.5% | 48.5% |
| Texas | | 20 | | 486,109 | 114,658 | 287,920 | 83,531 | 173,262 D | 23.6% | 59.2% | 28.5% | 71.5% |
| Utah | 4 | | | 145,828 | 81,555 | 56,639 | 7,634 | 24,916 R | 55.9% | 38.8% | 59.0% | 41.0% |
| Vermont | 4 | | | 89,961 | 68,212 | 20,919 | 830 | 47,293 R | 75.8% | 23.3% | 76.5% | 23.5% |
| Virginia | | 12 | | 231,000 | 87,456 | 141,670 | 1,874 | 54,214 D | 37.9% | 61.3% | 38.2% | 61.8% |
| Washington | 7 | | | 398,715 | 223,137 | 84,298 | 91,280 | 138,839 R | 56.0% | 21.1% | 72.6% | 27.4% |
| West Virginia | 8 | | | 509,936 | 282,007 | 220,785 | 7,144 | 61,222 R | 55.3% | 43.3% | 56.1% | 43.9% |
| Wisconsin | 13 | | | 701,281 | 498,576 | 113,422 | 89,283 | 385,154 R | 71.1% | 16.2% | 81.5% | 18.5% |
| Wyoming | 3 | | | 56,253 | 35,091 | 17,429 | 3,733 | 17,662 R | 62.4% | 31.0% | 66.8% | 33.2% |
| Dist. of Col. | | | | | | | | | | | | |
| United States | 404 | 127 | — | 26,768,613 | 16,153,115 | 9,133,092 | 1,482,406 | 7,020,023 R | 60.3% | 34.1% | 63.9% | 36.1% |

# ALABAMA

## POPULAR VOTE FOR PRESIDENT 1920 TO 2004

| Year | Total Vote | Republican Vote | Candidate | Democratic Vote | Candidate | Other Vote | Plurality | Percentage Total Vote Rep. | Dem. | Major Vote Rep. | Dem. |
|------|-----------|-----------------|-----------|-----------------|-----------|-----------|-----------|----------------------------|------|-----------------|------|
| 2004 | 1,883,449 | 1,176,394 | Bush, George W. | 693,933 | Kerry, John | 13,122 | 482,461 R | 62.5% | 36.8% | 62.9% | 37.1% |
| 2000 ** | 1,666,272 | 941,173 | Bush, George W. | 692,611 | Gore, Al | 32,488 | 248,562 R | 56.5% | 41.6% | 57.6% | 42.4% |
| 1996 ** | 1,534,349 | 769,044 | Dole, Bob | 662,165 | Clinton, Bill | 103,140 | 106,879 R | 50.1% | 43.2% | 53.7% | 46.3% |
| 1992 ** | 1,688,060 | 804,283 | Bush, George | 690,080 | Clinton, Bill | 193,697 | 114,203 R | 47.6% | 40.9% | 53.8% | 46.2% |
| 1988 | 1,378,476 | 815,576 | Bush, George | 549,506 | Dukakis, Michael S. | 13,394 | 266,070 R | 59.2% | 39.9% | 59.7% | 40.3% |
| 1984 | 1,441,713 | 872,849 | Reagan, Ronald | 551,899 | Mondale, Walter F. | 16,965 | 320,950 R | 60.5% | 38.3% | 61.3% | 38.7% |
| 1980 ** | 1,341,929 | 654,192 | Reagan, Ronald | 636,730 | Carter, Jimmy | 51,007 | 17,462 R | 48.8% | 47.4% | 50.7% | 49.3% |
| 1976 | 1,182,850 | 504,070 | Ford, Gerald R. | 659,170 | Carter, Jimmy | 19,610 | 155,100 D | 42.6% | 55.7% | 43.3% | 56.7% |
| 1972 | 1,006,111 | 728,701 | Nixon, Richard M. | 256,923 | McGovern, George S. | 20,487 | 471,778 R | 72.4% | 25.5% | 73.9% | 26.1% |
| 1968 ** | 1,049,922 | 146,923 | Nixon, Richard M. | 196,579 | Humphrey, Hubert H. | 706,420 | 494,846 A | 14.0% | 18.7% | 42.8% | 57.2% |
| 1964 ** | 689,818 | 479,085 | Goldwater, Barry M. | | Johnson, Lyndon B. | 210,733 | 268,353 R | 69.5% | | 100.0% | |
| 1960 | 570,225 | 237,981 | Nixon, Richard M. | 324,050 | Kennedy, John F. | 8,194 | 86,069 D | 41.7% | 56.8% | 42.3% | 57.7% |
| 1956 | 496,861 | 195,694 | Eisenhower, Dwight D. | 280,844 | Stevenson, Adlai E. | 20,323 | 85,150 D | 39.4% | 56.5% | 41.1% | 58.9% |
| 1952 | 426,120 | 149,231 | Eisenhower, Dwight D. | 275,075 | Stevenson, Adlai E. | 1,814 | 125,844 D | 35.0% | 64.6% | 35.2% | 64.8% |
| 1948 ** | 214,980 | 40,930 | Dewey, Thomas E. | | Truman, Harry S. | 174,050 | 130,513 SR | 19.0% | | 100.0% | |
| 1944 | 244,743 | 44,540 | Dewey, Thomas E. | 198,918 | Roosevelt, Franklin D. | 1,285 | 154,378 D | 18.2% | 81.3% | 18.3% | 81.7% |
| 1940 | 294,219 | 42,184 | Willkie, Wendell | 250,726 | Roosevelt, Franklin D. | 1,309 | 208,542 D | 14.3% | 85.2% | 14.4% | 85.6% |
| 1936 | 275,744 | 35,358 | Landon, Alfred M. | 238,196 | Roosevelt, Franklin D. | 2,190 | 202,838 D | 12.8% | 86.4% | 12.9% | 87.1% |
| 1932 | 245,303 | 34,675 | Hoover, Herbert C. | 207,910 | Roosevelt, Franklin D. | 2,718 | 173,235 D | 14.1% | 84.8% | 14.3% | 85.7% |
| 1928 | 248,981 | 120,725 | Hoover, Herbert C. | 127,796 | Smith, Alfred E. | 460 | 7,071 D | 48.5% | 51.3% | 48.6% | 51.4% |
| 1924 | 164,563 | 42,823 | Coolidge, Calvin | 113,138 | Davis, John W. | 8,602 | 70,315 D | 26.0% | 68.8% | 27.5% | 72.5% |
| 1920 | 233,951 | 74,719 | Harding, Warren G. | 156,064 | Cox, James M. | 3,168 | 81,345 D | 31.9% | 66.7% | 32.4% | 67.6% |

In 2000 the other vote column includes 18,323 votes cast for Green (Nader). In 1996 the other vote column includes 92,149 votes cast for Perot. In 1992 the other vote column includes 183,109 votes cast for Perot. In 1980 the other column includes 16,481 votes for Independent (Anderson). In 1968 other vote was 691,425 American Independent (Wallace); 10,960 American Independent of Alabama; 4,022 Prohibition and 13 scattered. In 1964 and 1948 the national Democratic candidates were not represented on the ballot. In 1964 other vote was 210,732 Unpledged Democratic and 1 scattered. In 1948 other vote was 171,443 States Rights; 1,522 Progressive and 1,085 Prohibition.

## ELECTORAL COLLEGE VOTE 1920 TO 2004

| Year | Total | Republican | Democratic | Other |
|------|-------|------------|------------|-------|
| 2004 | 9 | 9 | | |
| 2000 | 9 | 9 | | |
| 1996 | 9 | 9 | | |
| 1992 | 9 | 9 | | |
| 1988 | 9 | 9 | | |
| 1984 | 9 | 9 | | |
| 1980 | 9 | 9 | | |
| 1976 | 9 | | 9 | |
| 1972 | 9 | 9 | | |
| 1968 | 10 | | | 10 AIP |
| 1964 | 10 | 10 | | |
| 1960 ** | 11 | | 5 | 6 BYRD |
| 1956 ** | 11 | | 10 | 1 JONES |
| 1952 | 11 | | 11 | |
| 1948 | 11 | | | 11 SR |
| 1944 | 11 | | 11 | |
| 1940 | 11 | | 11 | |
| 1936 | 11 | | 11 | |
| 1932 | 11 | | 11 | |
| 1928 | 12 | | 12 | |
| 1924 | 12 | | 12 | |
| 1920 | 12 | | 12 | |

In 1960 six of the eleven Democratic electors voted in the Electoral College for Harry Flood Byrd and Strom Thurmond rather than for the national Democratic candidates. In 1956 one of the eleven Democratic electors voted in the Electoral College for Walter B. Jones and Herman Talmadge rather than for the national Democratic candidates.

# ALABAMA

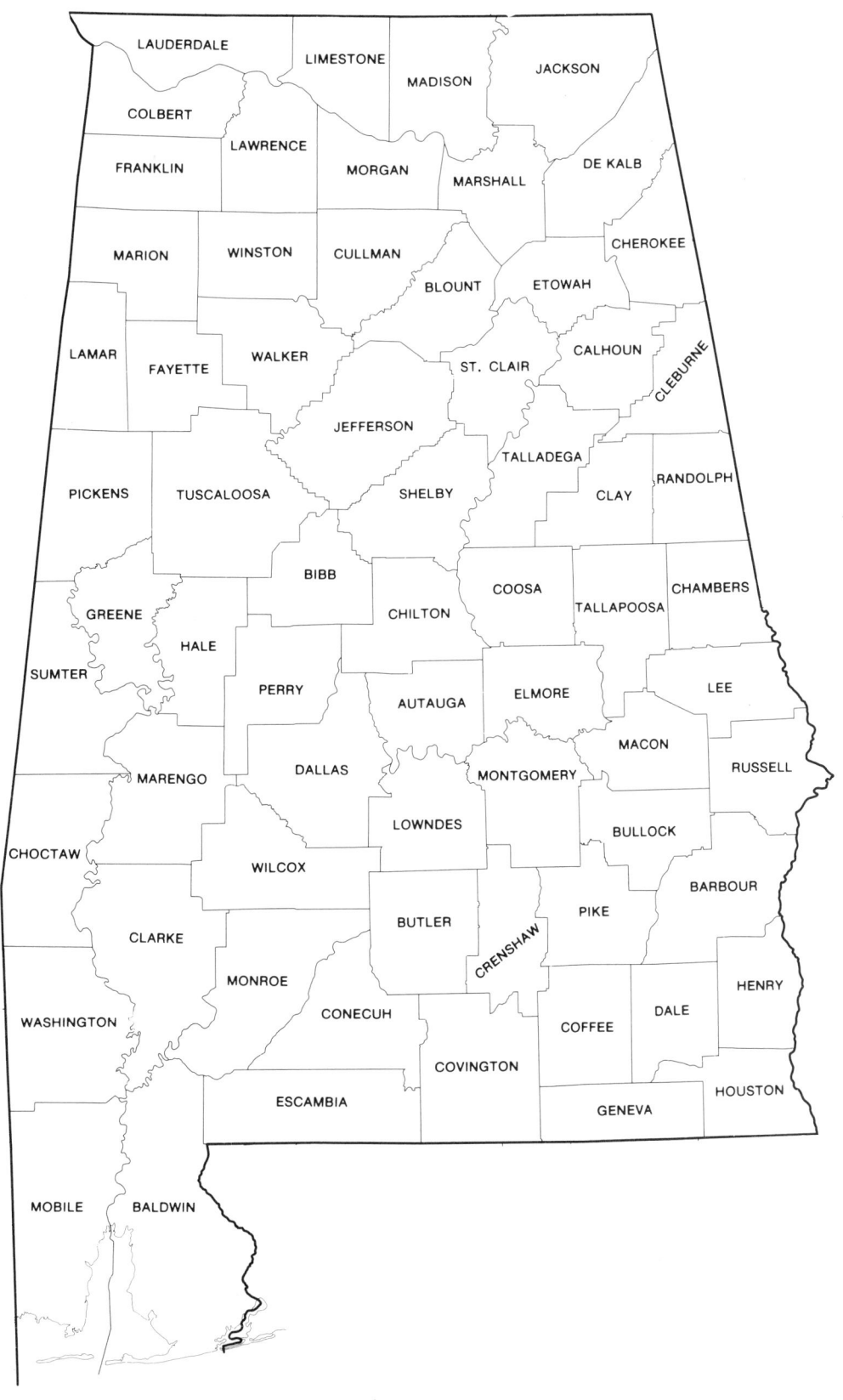

# ALABAMA

## PRESIDENT 2004

| 2000 Census Population | County | Total Vote | Republican | Democratic | Other | Rep.-Dem. Plurality | Percentage | | | |
|---|---|---|---|---|---|---|---|---|---|---|
| | | | | | | | Total Vote | | Major Vote | |
| | | | | | | | Rep. | Dem. | Rep. | Dem. |
| 43,671 | AUTAUGA | 20,081 | 15,196 | 4,758 | 127 | 10,438 R | 75.7% | 23.7% | 76.2% | 23.8% |
| 140,415 | BALDWIN | 69,320 | 52,971 | 15,599 | 750 | 37,372 R | 76.4% | 22.5% | 77.3% | 22.7% |
| 29,038 | BARBOUR | 10,777 | 5,899 | 4,832 | 46 | 1,067 R | 54.7% | 44.8% | 55.0% | 45.0% |
| 20,826 | BIBB | 7,600 | 5,472 | 2,089 | 39 | 3,383 R | 72.0% | 27.5% | 72.4% | 27.6% |
| 51,024 | BLOUNT | 21,504 | 17,386 | 3,938 | 180 | 13,448 R | 80.9% | 18.3% | 81.5% | 18.5% |
| 11,714 | BULLOCK | 4,717 | 1,494 | 3,210 | 13 | 1,716 D | 31.7% | 68.1% | 31.8% | 68.2% |
| 21,399 | BUTLER | 8,416 | 4,979 | 3,413 | 24 | 1,566 R | 59.2% | 40.6% | 59.3% | 40.7% |
| 112,249 | CALHOUN | 45,249 | 29,814 | 15,083 | 352 | 14,731 R | 65.9% | 33.3% | 66.4% | 33.6% |
| 36,583 | CHAMBERS | 13,032 | 7,622 | 5,347 | 63 | 2,275 R | 58.5% | 41.0% | 58.8% | 41.2% |
| 23,988 | CHEROKEE | 9,049 | 5,923 | 3,040 | 86 | 2,883 R | 65.5% | 33.6% | 66.1% | 33.9% |
| 39,593 | CHILTON | 16,693 | 12,829 | 3,778 | 86 | 9,051 R | 76.9% | 22.6% | 77.3% | 22.7% |
| 15,922 | CHOCTAW | 7,227 | 3,897 | 3,303 | 27 | 594 R | 53.9% | 45.7% | 54.1% | 45.9% |
| 27,867 | CLARKE | 11,394 | 6,730 | 4,627 | 37 | 2,103 R | 59.1% | 40.6% | 59.3% | 40.7% |
| 14,254 | CLAY | 6,576 | 4,624 | 1,893 | 59 | 2,731 R | 70.3% | 28.8% | 71.0% | 29.0% |
| 14,123 | CLEBURNE | 5,798 | 4,370 | 1,391 | 37 | 2,979 R | 75.4% | 24.0% | 75.9% | 24.1% |
| 43,615 | COFFEE | 17,616 | 13,019 | 4,480 | 117 | 8,539 R | 73.9% | 25.4% | 74.4% | 25.6% |
| 54,984 | COLBERT | 23,935 | 13,188 | 10,598 | 149 | 2,590 R | 55.1% | 44.3% | 55.4% | 44.6% |
| 14,089 | CONECUH | 6,021 | 3,271 | 2,719 | 31 | 552 R | 54.3% | 45.2% | 54.6% | 45.4% |
| 12,202 | COOSA | 5,001 | 2,905 | 2,055 | 41 | 850 R | 58.1% | 41.1% | 58.6% | 41.4% |
| 37,631 | COVINGTON | 14,627 | 11,119 | 3,423 | 85 | 7,696 R | 76.0% | 23.4% | 76.5% | 23.5% |
| 13,665 | CRENSHAW | 5,500 | 3,777 | 1,698 | 25 | 2,079 R | 68.7% | 30.9% | 69.0% | 31.0% |
| 77,483 | CULLMAN | 35,191 | 26,818 | 8,045 | 328 | 18,773 R | 76.2% | 22.9% | 76.9% | 23.1% |
| 49,129 | DALE | 18,231 | 13,621 | 4,484 | 126 | 9,137 R | 74.7% | 24.6% | 75.2% | 24.8% |
| 46,365 | DALLAS | 18,573 | 7,335 | 11,175 | 63 | 3,840 D | 39.5% | 60.2% | 39.6% | 60.4% |
| 64,452 | DE KALB | 24,169 | 16,904 | 7,092 | 173 | 9,812 R | 69.9% | 29.3% | 70.4% | 29.6% |
| 65,874 | ELMORE | 28,680 | 22,056 | 6,471 | 153 | 15,585 R | 76.9% | 22.6% | 77.3% | 22.7% |
| 38,440 | ESCAMBIA | 12,395 | 8,513 | 3,814 | 68 | 4,699 R | 68.7% | 30.8% | 69.1% | 30.9% |
| 103,459 | ETOWAH | 42,680 | 26,999 | 15,328 | 353 | 11,671 R | 63.3% | 35.9% | 63.8% | 36.2% |
| 18,495 | FAYETTE | 8,002 | 5,534 | 2,408 | 60 | 3,126 R | 69.2% | 30.1% | 69.7% | 30.3% |
| 31,223 | FRANKLIN | 12,269 | 7,690 | 4,514 | 65 | 3,176 R | 62.7% | 36.8% | 63.0% | 37.0% |
| 25,764 | GENEVA | 10,520 | 8,342 | 2,113 | 65 | 6,229 R | 79.3% | 20.1% | 79.8% | 20.2% |
| 9,974 | GREENE | 4,748 | 958 | 3,764 | 26 | 2,806 D | 20.2% | 79.3% | 20.3% | 79.7% |
| 17,185 | HALE | 7,945 | 3,281 | 4,631 | 33 | 1,350 D | 41.3% | 58.3% | 41.5% | 58.5% |
| 16,310 | HENRY | 7,361 | 4,881 | 2,452 | 28 | 2,429 R | 66.3% | 33.3% | 66.6% | 33.4% |
| 88,787 | HOUSTON | 36,201 | 26,874 | 9,144 | 183 | 17,730 R | 74.2% | 25.3% | 74.6% | 25.4% |
| 53,926 | JACKSON | 20,321 | 11,534 | 8,635 | 152 | 2,899 R | 56.8% | 42.5% | 57.2% | 42.8% |
| 662,047 | JEFFERSON | 292,967 | 158,680 | 132,286 | 2,001 | 26,394 R | 54.2% | 45.2% | 54.5% | 45.5% |
| 15,904 | LAMAR | 6,885 | 4,894 | 1,956 | 35 | 2,938 R | 71.1% | 28.4% | 71.4% | 28.6% |
| 87,966 | LAUDERDALE | 37,107 | 22,161 | 14,628 | 318 | 7,533 R | 59.7% | 39.4% | 60.2% | 39.8% |
| 34,803 | LAWRENCE | 14,001 | 7,730 | 6,155 | 116 | 1,575 R | 55.2% | 44.0% | 55.7% | 44.3% |
| 115,092 | LEE | 44,610 | 27,972 | 16,227 | 411 | 11,745 R | 62.7% | 36.4% | 63.3% | 36.7% |
| 65,676 | LIMESTONE | 29,073 | 19,702 | 9,126 | 245 | 10,576 R | 67.8% | 31.4% | 68.3% | 31.7% |
| 13,473 | LOWNDES | 6,021 | 1,786 | 4,233 | 2 | 2,447 D | 29.7% | 70.3% | 29.7% | 70.3% |
| 24,105 | MACON | 9,407 | 1,570 | 7,800 | 37 | 6,230 D | 16.7% | 82.9% | 16.8% | 83.2% |
| 276,700 | MADISON | 131,062 | 77,173 | 52,644 | 1,245 | 24,529 R | 58.9% | 40.2% | 59.4% | 40.6% |
| 22,539 | MARENGO | 10,322 | 5,255 | 5,037 | 30 | 218 R | 50.9% | 48.8% | 51.1% | 48.9% |
| 31,214 | MARION | 12,875 | 8,983 | 3,808 | 84 | 5,175 R | 69.8% | 29.6% | 70.2% | 29.8% |
| 82,231 | MARSHALL | 31,491 | 22,783 | 8,452 | 256 | 14,331 R | 72.3% | 26.8% | 72.9% | 27.1% |
| 399,843 | MOBILE | 156,771 | 92,014 | 63,732 | 1,025 | 28,282 R | 58.7% | 40.7% | 59.1% | 40.9% |
| 24,324 | MONROE | 9,534 | 5,831 | 3,666 | 37 | 2,165 R | 61.2% | 38.5% | 61.4% | 38.6% |
| 223,510 | MONTGOMERY | 89,650 | 44,097 | 45,160 | 393 | 1,063 D | 49.2% | 50.4% | 49.4% | 50.6% |
| 111,064 | MORGAN | 47,007 | 32,477 | 14,131 | 399 | 18,346 R | 69.1% | 30.1% | 69.7% | 30.3% |
| 11,861 | PERRY | 5,523 | 1,738 | 3,767 | 18 | 2,029 D | 31.5% | 68.2% | 31.6% | 68.4% |
| 20,949 | PICKENS | 9,132 | 5,170 | 3,915 | 47 | 1,255 R | 56.6% | 42.9% | 56.9% | 43.1% |
| 29,605 | PIKE | 11,883 | 7,483 | 4,334 | 66 | 3,149 R | 63.0% | 36.5% | 63.3% | 36.7% |
| 22,380 | RANDOLPH | 9,001 | 6,127 | 2,817 | 57 | 3,310 R | 68.1% | 31.3% | 68.5% | 31.5% |
| 49,756 | RUSSELL | 16,809 | 8,337 | 8,375 | 97 | 38 D | 49.6% | 49.8% | 49.9% | 50.1% |
| 64,742 | ST. CLAIR | 29,161 | 23,500 | 5,456 | 205 | 18,044 R | 80.6% | 18.7% | 81.2% | 18.8% |
| 143,293 | SHELBY | 78,906 | 63,435 | 14,850 | 621 | 48,585 R | 80.4% | 18.8% | 81.0% | 19.0% |
| 14,798 | SUMTER | 6,433 | 1,880 | 4,527 | 26 | 2,647 D | 29.2% | 70.4% | 29.3% | 70.7% |

# ALABAMA

## PRESIDENT 2004

| 2000 Census Population | County | Total Vote | Republican | Democratic | Other | Rep.-Dem. Plurality | Percentage | | | |
| --- | --- | --- | --- | --- | --- | --- | --- | --- | --- | --- |
| | | | | | | | Total Vote | | Major Vote | |
| | | | | | | | Rep. | Dem. | Rep. | Dem. |
| 80,321 | TALLADEGA | 29,898 | 18,331 | 11,374 | 193 | 6,957 R | 61.3% | 38.0% | 61.7% | 38.3% |
| 41,475 | TALLAPOOSA | 17,952 | 12,392 | 5,451 | 109 | 6,941 R | 69.0% | 30.4% | 69.5% | 30.5% |
| 164,875 | TUSCALOOSA | 69,830 | 42,877 | 26,447 | 506 | 16,430 R | 61.4% | 37.9% | 61.9% | 38.1% |
| 70,713 | WALKER | 28,367 | 19,167 | 9,016 | 184 | 10,151 R | 67.6% | 31.8% | 68.0% | 32.0% |
| 18,097 | WASHINGTON | 8,247 | 5,060 | 3,145 | 42 | 1,915 R | 61.4% | 38.1% | 61.7% | 38.3% |
| 13,183 | WILCOX | 5,682 | 1,834 | 3,838 | 10 | 2,004 D | 32.3% | 67.5% | 32.3% | 67.7% |
| 24,843 | WINSTON | 10,423 | 8,130 | 2,236 | 57 | 5,894 R | 78.0% | 21.5% | 78.4% | 21.6% |
| 4,447,100 | TOTAL | 1,883,449 | 1,176,394 | 693,933 | 13,122 | 482,461 R | 62.5% | 36.8% | 62.9% | 37.1% |

# ALABAMA

## PRESIDENT 2000

| 2000 Census Population | County | Total Vote | Republican | Democratic | Green (Nader) | Other | Rep.-Dem. Plurality | Percentage of Total Vote | | |
|---|---|---|---|---|---|---|---|---|---|---|
| | | | | | | | | Rep. | Dem. | Green |
| 43,671 | AUTAUGA | 17,208 | 11,993 | 4,942 | 160 | 113 | 7,051 R | 69.7% | 28.7% | 0.9% |
| 140,415 | BALDWIN | 56,480 | 40,872 | 13,997 | 1,033 | 578 | 26,875 R | 72.4% | 24.8% | 1.8% |
| 29,038 | BARBOUR | 4,116 | 1,860 | 2,197 | 20 | 39 | 337 D | 45.2% | 53.4% | 0.5% |
| 20,826 | BIBB | 7,101 | 4,273 | 2,710 | 52 | 66 | 1,563 R | 60.2% | 38.2% | 0.7% |
| 51,024 | BLOUNT | 17,973 | 12,667 | 4,977 | 154 | 175 | 7,690 R | 70.5% | 27.7% | 0.9% |
| 11,714 | BULLOCK | 4,904 | 1,433 | 3,395 | 24 | 52 | 1,962 D | 29.2% | 69.2% | 0.5% |
| 21,399 | BUTLER | 7,803 | 4,127 | 3,606 | 36 | 34 | 521 R | 52.9% | 46.2% | 0.5% |
| 112,249 | CALHOUN | 38,909 | 22,306 | 15,781 | 481 | 341 | 6,525 R | 57.3% | 40.6% | 1.2% |
| 36,583 | CHAMBERS | 11,834 | 6,037 | 5,616 | 95 | 86 | 421 R | 51.0% | 47.5% | 0.8% |
| 23,988 | CHEROKEE | 7,823 | 4,154 | 3,497 | 77 | 95 | 657 R | 53.1% | 44.7% | 1.0% |
| 39,593 | CHILTON | 15,092 | 10,066 | 4,806 | 92 | 128 | 5,260 R | 66.7% | 31.8% | 0.6% |
| 15,922 | CHOCTAW | 7,374 | 3,600 | 3,707 | 33 | 34 | 107 D | 48.8% | 50.3% | 0.4% |
| 27,867 | CLARKE | 10,752 | 5,988 | 4,679 | 33 | 52 | 1,309 R | 55.7% | 43.5% | 0.3% |
| 14,254 | CLAY | 5,883 | 3,719 | 2,045 | 52 | 67 | 1,674 R | 63.2% | 34.8% | 0.9% |
| 14,123 | CLEBURNE | 5,092 | 3,333 | 1,664 | 39 | 56 | 1,669 R | 65.5% | 32.7% | 0.8% |
| 43,615 | COFFEE | 15,434 | 9,938 | 5,220 | 155 | 121 | 4,718 R | 64.4% | 33.8% | 1.0% |
| 54,984 | COLBERT | 21,532 | 10,518 | 10,543 | 208 | 263 | 25 D | 48.8% | 49.0% | 1.0% |
| 14,089 | CONECUH | 5,551 | 2,699 | 2,783 | 35 | 34 | 84 D | 48.6% | 50.1% | 0.6% |
| 12,202 | COOSA | 4,567 | 2,382 | 2,104 | 34 | 47 | 278 R | 52.2% | 46.1% | 0.7% |
| 37,631 | COVINGTON | 13,613 | 8,961 | 4,440 | 123 | 89 | 4,521 R | 65.8% | 32.6% | 0.9% |
| 13,665 | CRENSHAW | 4,795 | 2,793 | 1,934 | 40 | 28 | 859 R | 58.2% | 40.3% | 0.8% |
| 77,483 | CULLMAN | 29,525 | 19,157 | 9,758 | 282 | 328 | 9,399 R | 64.9% | 33.0% | 1.0% |
| 49,129 | DALE | 15,806 | 10,593 | 4,906 | 188 | 119 | 5,687 R | 67.0% | 31.0% | 1.2% |
| 46,365 | DALLAS | 18,464 | 7,360 | 10,967 | 63 | 74 | 3,607 D | 39.9% | 59.4% | 0.3% |
| 64,452 | DE KALB | 20,285 | 12,827 | 7,056 | 175 | 227 | 5,771 R | 63.2% | 34.8% | 0.9% |
| 65,874 | ELMORE | 23,804 | 16,777 | 6,652 | 212 | 163 | 10,125 R | 70.5% | 27.9% | 0.9% |
| 38,440 | ESCAMBIA | 11,660 | 6,975 | 4,523 | 78 | 84 | 2,452 R | 59.8% | 38.8% | 0.7% |
| 103,459 | ETOWAH | 39,348 | 21,087 | 17,433 | 435 | 393 | 3,654 R | 53.6% | 44.3% | 1.1% |
| 18,495 | FAYETTE | 7,808 | 4,582 | 3,064 | 60 | 102 | 1,518 R | 58.7% | 39.2% | 0.8% |
| 31,223 | FRANKLIN | 11,103 | 6,119 | 4,793 | 72 | 119 | 1,326 R | 55.1% | 43.2% | 0.6% |
| 25,764 | GENEVA | 9,559 | 6,588 | 2,769 | 97 | 105 | 3,819 R | 68.9% | 29.0% | 1.0% |
| 9,974 | GREENE | 4,396 | 850 | 3,504 | 24 | 18 | 2,654 D | 19.3% | 79.7% | 0.5% |
| 17,185 | HALE | 7,731 | 2,984 | 4,652 | 43 | 52 | 1,668 D | 38.6% | 60.2% | 0.6% |
| 16,310 | HENRY | 6,932 | 4,054 | 2,782 | 48 | 48 | 1,272 R | 58.5% | 40.1% | 0.7% |
| 88,787 | HOUSTON | 32,057 | 22,150 | 9,412 | 257 | 238 | 12,738 R | 69.1% | 29.4% | 0.8% |
| 53,926 | JACKSON | 17,906 | 8,475 | 9,066 | 184 | 181 | 591 D | 47.3% | 50.6% | 1.0% |
| 662,047 | JEFFERSON | 273,763 | 138,491 | 129,889 | 3,393 | 1,990 | 8,602 R | 50.6% | 47.4% | 1.2% |
| 15,904 | LAMAR | 7,249 | 4,470 | 2,653 | 57 | 69 | 1,817 R | 61.7% | 36.6% | 0.8% |
| 87,966 | LAUDERDALE | 32,137 | 17,478 | 13,875 | 354 | 430 | 3,603 R | 54.4% | 43.2% | 1.1% |
| 34,803 | LAWRENCE | 12,185 | 5,671 | 6,296 | 63 | 155 | 625 D | 46.5% | 51.7% | 0.5% |
| 115,092 | LEE | 38,264 | 22,433 | 14,574 | 895 | 362 | 7,859 R | 58.6% | 38.1% | 2.3% |
| 65,676 | LIMESTONE | 23,634 | 14,204 | 8,992 | 193 | 245 | 5,212 R | 60.1% | 38.0% | 0.8% |
| 13,473 | LOWNDES | 6,243 | 1,638 | 4,557 | 18 | 30 | 2,919 D | 26.2% | 73.0% | 0.3% |
| 24,105 | MACON | 8,831 | 1,091 | 7,665 | 31 | 44 | 6,574 D | 12.4% | 86.8% | 0.4% |
| 276,700 | MADISON | 113,318 | 62,151 | 48,199 | 1,885 | 1,083 | 13,952 R | 54.8% | 42.5% | 1.7% |
| 22,539 | MARENGO | 9,608 | 4,690 | 4,841 | 40 | 37 | 151 D | 48.8% | 50.4% | 0.4% |
| 31,214 | MARION | 11,756 | 6,910 | 4,600 | 125 | 121 | 2,310 R | 58.8% | 39.1% | 1.1% |
| 82,231 | MARSHALL | 27,989 | 17,084 | 10,381 | 256 | 268 | 6,703 R | 61.0% | 37.1% | 0.9% |
| 399,843 | MOBILE | 139,745 | 78,162 | 58,640 | 1,585 | 1,358 | 19,522 R | 55.9% | 42.0% | 1.1% |
| 24,324 | MONROE | 8,951 | 5,153 | 3,741 | 25 | 32 | 1,412 R | 57.6% | 41.8% | 0.3% |
| 223,510 | MONTGOMERY | 80,328 | 38,827 | 40,371 | 677 | 453 | 1,544 D | 48.3% | 50.3% | 0.8% |
| 111,064 | MORGAN | 42,681 | 25,774 | 16,060 | 450 | 397 | 9,714 R | 60.4% | 37.6% | 1.1% |
| 11,861 | PERRY | 5,787 | 1,732 | 4,020 | 18 | 17 | 2,288 D | 29.9% | 69.5% | 0.3% |
| 20,949 | PICKENS | 8,540 | 4,306 | 4,143 | 39 | 52 | 163 R | 50.4% | 48.5% | 0.5% |
| 29,605 | PIKE | 10,544 | 6,058 | 4,357 | 75 | 54 | 1,701 R | 57.5% | 41.3% | 0.7% |
| 22,380 | RANDOLPH | 7,919 | 4,666 | 3,094 | 60 | 99 | 1,572 R | 58.9% | 39.1% | 0.8% |
| 49,756 | RUSSELL | 14,775 | 6,198 | 8,396 | 109 | 72 | 2,198 D | 41.9% | 56.8% | 0.7% |
| 64,742 | ST. CLAIR | 24,090 | 17,117 | 6,485 | 221 | 267 | 10,632 R | 71.1% | 26.9% | 0.9% |
| 143,293 | SHELBY | 62,128 | 47,651 | 13,183 | 812 | 482 | 34,468 R | 76.7% | 21.2% | 1.3% |
| 14,798 | SUMTER | 6,088 | 1,629 | 4,415 | 20 | 24 | 2,786 D | 26.8% | 72.5% | 0.3% |

# ALABAMA

## PRESIDENT 2000

| 2000 Census Population | County | Total Vote | Republican | Democratic | Green (Nader) | Other | Rep.-Dem. Plurality | Percentage of Total Vote | | |
|---|---|---|---|---|---|---|---|---|---|---|
| | | | | | | | | Rep. | Dem. | Green |
| 80,321 | TALLADEGA | 25,451 | 13,807 | 11,264 | 184 | 196 | 2,543 R | 54.2% | 44.3% | 0.7% |
| 41,475 | TALLAPOOSA | 16,253 | 9,805 | 6,183 | 153 | 112 | 3,622 R | 60.3% | 38.0% | 0.9% |
| 164,875 | TUSCALOOSA | 60,114 | 34,003 | 24,614 | 1,007 | 490 | 9,389 R | 56.6% | 40.9% | 1.7% |
| 70,713 | WALKER | 25,641 | 13,486 | 11,621 | 264 | 270 | 1,865 R | 52.6% | 45.3% | 1.0% |
| 18,097 | WASHINGTON | 7,596 | 4,117 | 3,386 | 26 | 67 | 731 R | 54.2% | 44.6% | 0.3% |
| 13,183 | WILCOX | 5,126 | 1,661 | 3,444 | 6 | 15 | 1,783 D | 32.4% | 67.2% | 0.1% |
| 24,843 | WINSTON | 9,318 | 6,413 | 2,692 | 88 | 125 | 3,721 R | 68.8% | 28.9% | 0.9% |
| 4,447,100 | TOTAL | 1,666,272 | 941,173 | 692,611 | 18,323 | 14,165 | 248,562 R | 56.5% | 41.6% | 1.1% |

# ALABAMA

## PRESIDENT 1996

| 1995 Census Pop. Est. | County | Total Vote | Republican | Democratic | Reform (Perot) | Other | Rep.-Dem. Plurality | Percentage of Total Vote | | |
|---|---|---|---|---|---|---|---|---|---|---|
| | | | | | | | | Rep. | Dem. | Reform |
| 39,381 | AUTAUGA | 15,422 | 9,509 | 5,015 | 813 | 85 | 4,494 R | 61.7% | 32.5% | 5.3% |
| 120,198 | BALDWIN | 47,119 | 29,487 | 12,776 | 4,520 | 336 | 16,711 R | 62.6% | 27.1% | 9.6% |
| 26,469 | BARBOUR | 8,953 | 3,627 | 4,787 | 515 | 24 | 1,160 D | 40.5% | 53.5% | 5.8% |
| 17,942 | BIBB | 6,301 | 3,037 | 2,775 | 455 | 34 | 262 R | 48.2% | 44.0% | 7.2% |
| 42,721 | BLOUNT | 15,327 | 9,056 | 5,061 | 985 | 225 | 3,995 R | 59.1% | 33.0% | 6.4% |
| 11,149 | BULLOCK | 4,384 | 1,154 | 3,078 | 111 | 41 | 1,924 D | 26.3% | 70.2% | 2.5% |
| 21,798 | BUTLER | 7,770 | 3,352 | 3,828 | 538 | 52 | 476 D | 43.1% | 49.3% | 6.9% |
| 117,263 | CALHOUN | 36,911 | 18,088 | 15,725 | 2,613 | 485 | 2,363 R | 49.0% | 42.6% | 7.1% |
| 37,262 | CHAMBERS | 11,097 | 4,707 | 5,515 | 812 | 63 | 808 D | 42.4% | 49.7% | 7.3% |
| 21,038 | CHEROKEE | 8,421 | 3,048 | 4,399 | 899 | 75 | 1,351 D | 36.2% | 52.2% | 10.7% |
| 34,912 | CHILTON | 14,278 | 7,910 | 5,354 | 929 | 85 | 2,556 R | 55.4% | 37.5% | 6.5% |
| 16,079 | CHOCTAW | 7,131 | 2,623 | 4,074 | 413 | 21 | 1,451 D | 36.8% | 57.1% | 5.8% |
| 27,993 | CLARKE | 10,118 | 4,785 | 4,831 | 478 | 24 | 46 D | 47.3% | 47.7% | 4.7% |
| 13,551 | CLAY | 5,568 | 2,694 | 2,306 | 538 | 30 | 388 R | 48.4% | 41.4% | 9.7% |
| 13,272 | CLEBURNE | 4,241 | 2,063 | 1,737 | 385 | 56 | 326 R | 48.6% | 41.0% | 9.1% |
| 42,359 | COFFEE | 14,159 | 7,805 | 5,168 | 1,042 | 144 | 2,637 R | 55.1% | 36.5% | 7.4% |
| 52,586 | COLBERT | 20,318 | 8,305 | 10,226 | 1,696 | 91 | 1,921 D | 40.9% | 50.3% | 8.3% |
| 14,022 | CONECUH | 5,461 | 2,093 | 2,903 | 445 | 20 | 810 D | 38.3% | 53.2% | 8.1% |
| 11,680 | COOSA | 4,131 | 1,721 | 2,121 | 262 | 27 | 400 D | 41.7% | 51.3% | 6.3% |
| 37,459 | COVINGTON | 11,913 | 6,035 | 4,543 | 1,098 | 237 | 1,492 R | 50.7% | 38.1% | 9.2% |
| 13,624 | CRENSHAW | 4,447 | 1,939 | 2,172 | 317 | 19 | 233 D | 43.6% | 48.8% | 7.1% |
| 72,489 | CULLMAN | 26,553 | 14,308 | 9,544 | 2,440 | 261 | 4,764 R | 53.9% | 35.9% | 9.2% |
| 50,001 | DALE | 14,330 | 8,288 | 4,732 | 1,216 | 94 | 3,556 R | 57.8% | 33.0% | 8.5% |
| 48,022 | DALLAS | 17,654 | 6,612 | 10,507 | 477 | 58 | 3,895 D | 37.5% | 59.5% | 2.7% |
| 57,271 | DE KALB | 18,143 | 9,823 | 6,544 | 1,609 | 167 | 3,279 R | 54.1% | 36.1% | 8.9% |
| 57,071 | ELMORE | 20,946 | 12,937 | 6,530 | 1,368 | 111 | 6,407 R | 61.8% | 31.2% | 6.5% |
| 36,541 | ESCAMBIA | 11,104 | 5,214 | 4,651 | 867 | 372 | 563 R | 47.0% | 41.9% | 7.8% |
| 100,259 | ETOWAH | 37,561 | 16,835 | 17,976 | 2,529 | 221 | 1,141 D | 44.8% | 47.9% | 6.7% |
| 18,019 | FAYETTE | 7,209 | 3,191 | 3,381 | 590 | 47 | 190 D | 44.3% | 46.9% | 8.2% |
| 29,313 | FRANKLIN | 10,482 | 4,449 | 5,028 | 966 | 39 | 579 D | 42.4% | 48.0% | 9.2% |
| 24,727 | GENEVA | 8,983 | 4,725 | 3,174 | 857 | 227 | 1,551 R | 52.6% | 35.3% | 9.5% |
| 10,076 | GREENE | 4,424 | 796 | 3,526 | 55 | 47 | 2,730 D | 18.0% | 79.7% | 1.2% |
| 16,212 | HALE | 5,473 | 1,893 | 3,372 | 190 | 18 | 1,479 D | 34.6% | 61.6% | 3.5% |
| 15,752 | HENRY | 6,637 | 3,082 | 3,019 | 515 | 21 | 63 R | 46.4% | 45.5% | 7.8% |
| 84,367 | HOUSTON | 28,063 | 17,476 | 8,791 | 1,653 | 143 | 8,685 R | 62.3% | 31.3% | 5.9% |
| 50,128 | JACKSON | 15,558 | 5,650 | 8,204 | 1,573 | 131 | 2,554 D | 36.3% | 52.7% | 10.1% |
| 657,827 | JEFFERSON | 260,906 | 130,980 | 120,208 | 7,997 | 1,721 | 10,772 R | 50.2% | 46.1% | 3.1% |
| 15,754 | LAMAR | 6,410 | 2,955 | 2,843 | 597 | 15 | 112 R | 46.1% | 44.4% | 9.3% |
| 83,598 | LAUDERDALE | 30,436 | 14,058 | 13,619 | 2,574 | 185 | 439 R | 46.2% | 44.7% | 8.5% |
| 32,803 | LAWRENCE | 10,143 | 3,893 | 5,254 | 964 | 32 | 1,361 D | 38.4% | 51.8% | 9.5% |
| 94,029 | LEE | 33,214 | 17,985 | 12,919 | 1,949 | 361 | 5,066 R | 54.1% | 38.9% | 5.9% |
| 59,344 | LIMESTONE | 20,682 | 10,862 | 8,045 | 1,659 | 116 | 2,817 R | 52.5% | 38.9% | 8.0% |
| 12,946 | LOWNDES | 5,441 | 1,369 | 3,970 | 72 | 30 | 2,601 D | 25.2% | 73.0% | 1.3% |
| 23,959 | MACON | 8,203 | 987 | 7,018 | 150 | 48 | 6,031 D | 12.0% | 85.6% | 1.8% |
| 258,340 | MADISON | 100,858 | 50,390 | 42,259 | 7,437 | 772 | 8,131 R | 50.0% | 41.9% | 7.4% |
| 23,662 | MARENGO | 9,294 | 4,013 | 4,899 | 337 | 45 | 886 D | 43.2% | 52.7% | 3.6% |
| 30,382 | MARION | 10,830 | 4,742 | 5,049 | 979 | 60 | 307 D | 43.8% | 46.6% | 9.0% |
| 78,195 | MARSHALL | 23,300 | 12,323 | 8,722 | 2,150 | 105 | 3,601 R | 52.9% | 37.4% | 9.2% |
| 397,413 | MOBILE | 130,103 | 66,775 | 54,749 | 7,555 | 1,024 | 12,026 R | 51.3% | 42.1% | 5.8% |
| 24,550 | MONROE | 8,698 | 4,382 | 3,815 | 486 | 15 | 567 R | 50.4% | 43.9% | 5.6% |
| 218,880 | MONTGOMERY | 78,744 | 37,784 | 38,382 | 2,036 | 542 | 598 D | 48.0% | 48.7% | 2.6% |
| 107,034 | MORGAN | 40,013 | 21,765 | 14,616 | 3,348 | 284 | 7,149 R | 54.4% | 36.5% | 8.4% |
| 12,708 | PERRY | 5,903 | 1,703 | 4,053 | 119 | 28 | 2,350 D | 28.8% | 68.7% | 2.0% |
| 20,956 | PICKENS | 7,773 | 3,322 | 4,018 | 403 | 30 | 696 D | 42.7% | 51.7% | 5.2% |
| 28,848 | PIKE | 10,341 | 5,281 | 4,514 | 503 | 43 | 767 R | 51.1% | 43.7% | 4.9% |
| 20,323 | RANDOLPH | 6,969 | 3,304 | 3,023 | 603 | 39 | 281 R | 47.4% | 43.4% | 8.7% |
| 51,436 | RUSSELL | 13,695 | 5,025 | 7,834 | 792 | 44 | 2,809 D | 36.7% | 57.2% | 5.8% |
| 57,713 | ST. CLAIR | 20,489 | 12,762 | 6,187 | 1,417 | 123 | 6,575 R | 62.3% | 30.2% | 6.9% |
| 123,500 | SHELBY | 50,773 | 37,090 | 11,280 | 2,035 | 368 | 25,810 R | 73.1% | 22.2% | 4.0% |
| 16,390 | SUMTER | 6,456 | 1,561 | 4,706 | 172 | 17 | 3,145 D | 24.2% | 72.9% | 2.7% |

# ALABAMA

## PRESIDENT 1996

| 1995 Census Pop. Est. | County | Total Vote | Republican | Democratic | Reform (Perot) | Other | Rep.-Dem. Plurality | Percentage of Total Vote | | |
|---|---|---|---|---|---|---|---|---|---|---|
| | | | | | | | | Rep. | Dem. | Reform |
| 76,737 | TALLADEGA | 22,778 | 10,931 | 10,385 | 1,335 | 127 | 546 R | 48.0% | 45.6% | 5.9% |
| 39,737 | TALLAPOOSA | 14,815 | 7,627 | 6,071 | 1,038 | 79 | 1,556 R | 51.5% | 41.0% | 7.0% |
| 158,732 | TUSCALOOSA | 54,382 | 27,939 | 23,067 | 3,048 | 328 | 4,872 R | 51.4% | 42.4% | 5.6% |
| 69,678 | WALKER | 24,939 | 9,837 | 12,929 | 2,012 | 161 | 3,092 D | 39.4% | 51.8% | 8.1% |
| 17,385 | WASHINGTON | 7,697 | 2,900 | 3,935 | 819 | 43 | 1,035 D | 37.7% | 51.1% | 10.6% |
| 13,628 | WILCOX | 4,847 | 1,454 | 3,303 | 71 | 19 | 1,849 D | 30.0% | 68.1% | 1.5% |
| 23,489 | WINSTON | 8,627 | 4,728 | 3,120 | 723 | 56 | 1,608 R | 54.8% | 36.2% | 8.4% |
| 4,252,982 | TOTAL | 1,534,349 | 769,044 | 662,165 | 92,149 | 10,991 | 106,879 R | 50.1% | 43.2% | 6.0% |

# ALABAMA

## PRESIDENT 1992

| 1990 Census Population | County | Total Vote | Republican | Democratic | Perot | Other | Plurality | Percentage Total Vote | | |
|---|---|---|---|---|---|---|---|---|---|---|
| | | | | | | | | Rep. | Dem. | Perot |
| 34,222 | AUTAUGA | 15,585 | 8,715 | 4,819 | 1,916 | 135 | 3,896 R | 55.9% | 30.9% | 12.3% |
| 98,280 | BALDWIN | 46,476 | 26,270 | 12,195 | 7,656 | 355 | 14,075 R | 56.5% | 26.2% | 16.5% |
| 25,417 | BARBOUR | 10,431 | 4,475 | 4,836 | 1,020 | 100 | 361 D | 42.9% | 46.4% | 9.8% |
| 16,576 | BIBB | 6,720 | 3,124 | 2,900 | 686 | 10 | 224 R | 46.5% | 43.2% | 10.2% |
| 39,248 | BLOUNT | 16,505 | 8,882 | 5,433 | 1,949 | 241 | 3,449 R | 53.8% | 32.9% | 11.8% |
| 11,042 | BULLOCK | 4,816 | 1,253 | 3,259 | 266 | 38 | 2,006 D | 26.0% | 67.7% | 5.5% |
| 21,892 | BUTLER | 8,478 | 3,494 | 4,021 | 867 | 96 | 527 D | 41.2% | 47.4% | 10.2% |
| 116,034 | CALHOUN | 42,800 | 20,623 | 16,453 | 4,717 | 1,007 | 4,170 R | 48.2% | 38.4% | 11.0% |
| 36,876 | CHAMBERS | 13,091 | 5,682 | 5,938 | 1,427 | 44 | 256 D | 43.4% | 45.4% | 10.9% |
| 19,543 | CHEROKEE | 7,876 | 2,745 | 4,222 | 846 | 63 | 1,477 D | 34.9% | 53.6% | 10.7% |
| 32,458 | CHILTON | 14,468 | 8,126 | 4,946 | 1,363 | 33 | 3,180 R | 56.2% | 34.2% | 9.4% |
| 16,018 | CHOCTAW | 7,560 | 3,069 | 3,941 | 489 | 61 | 872 D | 40.6% | 52.1% | 6.5% |
| 27,240 | CLARKE | 11,717 | 5,495 | 5,023 | 872 | 327 | 472 R | 46.9% | 42.9% | 7.4% |
| 13,252 | CLAY | 5,755 | 2,859 | 2,073 | 652 | 171 | 786 R | 49.7% | 36.0% | 11.3% |
| 12,730 | CLEBURNE | 5,237 | 2,425 | 2,144 | 630 | 38 | 281 R | 46.3% | 40.9% | 12.0% |
| 40,240 | COFFEE | 15,533 | 7,591 | 5,776 | 2,021 | 145 | 1,815 R | 48.9% | 37.2% | 13.0% |
| 51,666 | COLBERT | 22,439 | 8,073 | 12,206 | 2,098 | 62 | 4,133 D | 36.0% | 54.4% | 9.3% |
| 14,054 | CONECUH | 6,307 | 2,463 | 3,155 | 552 | 137 | 692 D | 39.1% | 50.0% | 8.8% |
| 11,063 | COOSA | 4,798 | 1,973 | 2,330 | 476 | 19 | 357 D | 41.1% | 48.6% | 9.9% |
| 36,478 | COVINGTON | 13,962 | 6,840 | 5,004 | 1,880 | 238 | 1,836 R | 49.0% | 35.8% | 13.5% |
| 13,635 | CRENSHAW | 5,290 | 2,339 | 2,404 | 485 | 62 | 65 D | 44.2% | 45.4% | 9.2% |
| 67,613 | CULLMAN | 29,043 | 14,411 | 10,451 | 4,113 | 68 | 3,960 R | 49.6% | 36.0% | 14.2% |
| 49,633 | DALE | 15,787 | 8,123 | 5,098 | 2,423 | 143 | 3,025 R | 51.5% | 32.3% | 15.3% |
| 48,130 | DALLAS | 19,604 | 7,394 | 11,053 | 1,110 | 47 | 3,659 D | 37.7% | 56.4% | 5.7% |
| 54,651 | DE KALB | 21,585 | 10,519 | 8,245 | 2,741 | 80 | 2,274 R | 48.7% | 38.2% | 12.7% |
| 49,210 | ELMORE | 20,388 | 11,356 | 6,223 | 2,765 | 44 | 5,133 R | 55.7% | 30.5% | 13.6% |
| 35,518 | ESCAMBIA | 12,824 | 5,955 | 4,809 | 1,616 | 444 | 1,146 R | 46.4% | 37.5% | 12.6% |
| 99,840 | ETOWAH | 42,451 | 17,467 | 20,558 | 4,277 | 149 | 3,091 D | 41.1% | 48.4% | 10.1% |
| 17,962 | FAYETTE | 8,470 | 3,604 | 3,830 | 1,012 | 24 | 226 D | 42.6% | 45.2% | 11.9% |
| 27,814 | FRANKLIN | 11,858 | 4,794 | 5,953 | 1,075 | 36 | 1,159 D | 40.4% | 50.2% | 9.1% |
| 23,647 | GENEVA | 9,867 | 4,843 | 3,622 | 1,323 | 79 | 1,221 R | 49.1% | 36.7% | 13.4% |
| 10,153 | GREENE | 4,881 | 805 | 3,865 | 194 | 17 | 3,060 D | 16.5% | 79.2% | 4.0% |
| 15,498 | HALE | 6,023 | 2,001 | 3,481 | 486 | 55 | 1,480 D | 33.2% | 57.8% | 8.1% |
| 15,374 | HENRY | 6,499 | 2,970 | 2,804 | 667 | 58 | 166 R | 45.7% | 43.1% | 10.3% |
| 81,331 | HOUSTON | 29,760 | 17,360 | 8,857 | 3,492 | 51 | 8,503 R | 58.3% | 29.8% | 11.7% |
| 47,796 | JACKSON | 18,916 | 5,711 | 10,628 | 2,462 | 115 | 4,917 D | 30.2% | 56.2% | 13.0% |
| 651,525 | JEFFERSON | 298,884 | 149,832 | 125,889 | 22,191 | 972 | 23,943 R | 50.1% | 42.1% | 7.4% |
| 15,715 | LAMAR | 6,898 | 3,262 | 2,849 | 763 | 24 | 413 R | 47.3% | 41.3% | 11.1% |
| 79,661 | LAUDERDALE | 33,756 | 13,728 | 15,936 | 4,009 | 83 | 2,208 D | 40.7% | 47.2% | 11.9% |
| 31,513 | LAWRENCE | 11,589 | 3,576 | 6,364 | 1,624 | 25 | 2,788 D | 30.9% | 54.9% | 14.0% |
| 87,146 | LEE | 35,490 | 16,885 | 13,770 | 4,572 | 263 | 3,115 R | 47.6% | 38.8% | 12.9% |
| 54,135 | LIMESTONE | 21,597 | 9,862 | 8,087 | 3,584 | 64 | 1,775 R | 45.7% | 37.4% | 16.6% |
| 12,658 | LOWNDES | 5,148 | 1,328 | 3,500 | 284 | 36 | 2,172 D | 25.8% | 68.0% | 5.5% |
| 24,928 | MACON | 8,762 | 1,134 | 7,253 | 283 | 92 | 6,119 D | 12.9% | 82.8% | 3.2% |
| 238,912 | MADISON | 107,834 | 51,444 | 38,974 | 16,989 | 427 | 12,470 R | 47.7% | 36.1% | 15.8% |
| 23,084 | MARENGO | 11,244 | 4,470 | 5,632 | 919 | 223 | 1,162 D | 39.8% | 50.1% | 8.2% |
| 29,830 | MARION | 13,270 | 5,692 | 6,167 | 1,389 | 22 | 475 D | 42.9% | 46.5% | 10.5% |
| 70,832 | MARSHALL | 26,717 | 12,249 | 10,421 | 3,795 | 252 | 1,828 R | 45.8% | 39.0% | 14.2% |
| 378,643 | MOBILE | 143,788 | 72,935 | 54,962 | 15,105 | 786 | 17,973 R | 50.7% | 38.2% | 10.5% |
| 23,968 | MONROE | 9,745 | 4,919 | 3,872 | 759 | 195 | 1,047 R | 50.5% | 39.7% | 7.8% |
| 209,085 | MONTGOMERY | 86,152 | 40,742 | 37,342 | 7,647 | 421 | 3,400 R | 47.3% | 43.3% | 8.9% |
| 100,043 | MORGAN | 43,978 | 21,073 | 15,091 | 7,683 | 131 | 5,982 R | 47.9% | 34.3% | 17.5% |
| 12,759 | PERRY | 5,813 | 1,829 | 3,712 | 213 | 59 | 1,883 D | 31.5% | 63.9% | 3.7% |
| 20,699 | PICKENS | 8,142 | 3,634 | 3,783 | 690 | 35 | 149 D | 44.6% | 46.5% | 8.5% |
| 27,595 | PIKE | 11,193 | 5,423 | 4,688 | 1,024 | 58 | 735 R | 48.4% | 41.9% | 9.1% |
| 19,881 | RANDOLPH | 8,152 | 3,813 | 3,318 | 919 | 102 | 495 R | 46.8% | 40.7% | 11.3% |
| 46,860 | RUSSELL | 15,689 | 5,587 | 8,647 | 1,360 | 95 | 3,060 D | 35.6% | 55.1% | 8.7% |
| 50,009 | ST. CLAIR | 21,624 | 12,447 | 6,517 | 2,614 | 46 | 5,930 R | 57.6% | 30.1% | 12.1% |
| 99,358 | SHELBY | 48,165 | 32,736 | 10,317 | 5,022 | 90 | 22,419 R | 68.0% | 21.4% | 10.4% |
| 16,174 | SUMTER | 7,025 | 1,807 | 4,810 | 388 | 20 | 3,003 D | 25.7% | 68.5% | 5.5% |

# ALABAMA

## PRESIDENT 1992

| 1990 Census Population | County | Total Vote | Republican | Democratic | Perot | Other | Plurality | Percentage Total Vote | | |
|---:|---|---:|---:|---:|---:|---:|---:|---:|---:|---:|
| | | | | | | | | Rep. | Dem. | Perot |
| 74,107 | TALLADEGA | 26,264 | 12,661 | 10,695 | 2,629 | 279 | 1,966 R | 48.2% | 40.7% | 10.0% |
| 38,826 | TALLAPOOSA | 15,456 | 8,140 | 5,703 | 1,562 | 51 | 2,437 R | 52.7% | 36.9% | 10.1% |
| 150,522 | TUSCALOOSA | 58,073 | 27,454 | 23,495 | 7,011 | 113 | 3,959 R | 47.3% | 40.5% | 12.1% |
| 67,670 | WALKER | 29,534 | 11,301 | 14,831 | 3,344 | 58 | 3,530 D | 38.3% | 50.2% | 11.3% |
| 16,694 | WASHINGTON | 8,162 | 3,270 | 4,046 | 829 | 17 | 776 D | 40.1% | 49.6% | 10.2% |
| 13,568 | WILCOX | 5,304 | 1,671 | 3,439 | 174 | 20 | 1,768 D | 31.5% | 64.8% | 3.3% |
| 22,053 | WINSTON | 10,089 | 5,550 | 3,415 | 1,110 | 14 | 2,135 R | 55.0% | 33.8% | 11.0% |
| 4,040,587 | TOTAL | 1,688,060 | 804,283 | 690,080 | 183,109 | 10,588 | 114,203 R | 47.6% | 40.9% | 10.8% |

# ALABAMA

## PRESIDENT 1988

| 1980 Census Population | County | Total Vote | Republican | Democratic | Other | Rep.-Dem. Plurality | Percentage | | | |
|---|---|---|---|---|---|---|---|---|---|---|
| | | | | | | | Total Vote | | Major Vote | |
| | | | | | | | Rep. | Dem. | Rep. | Dem. |
| 32,259 | AUTAUGA | 11,661 | 7,828 | 3,667 | 166 | 4,161 R | 67.1% | 31.4% | 68.1% | 31.9% |
| 78,556 | BALDWIN | 35,598 | 25,933 | 9,271 | 394 | 16,662 R | 72.8% | 26.0% | 73.7% | 26.3% |
| 24,756 | BARBOUR | 8,900 | 4,958 | 3,836 | 106 | 1,122 R | 55.7% | 43.1% | 56.4% | 43.6% |
| 15,723 | BIBB | 5,146 | 2,885 | 2,244 | 17 | 641 R | 56.1% | 43.6% | 56.2% | 43.8% |
| 36,459 | BLOUNT | 13,548 | 8,754 | 4,485 | 309 | 4,269 R | 64.6% | 33.1% | 66.1% | 33.9% |
| 10,596 | BULLOCK | 4,584 | 1,421 | 3,122 | 41 | 1,701 D | 31.0% | 68.1% | 31.3% | 68.7% |
| 21,680 | BUTLER | 7,460 | 3,923 | 3,465 | 72 | 458 R | 52.6% | 46.4% | 53.1% | 46.9% |
| 119,761 | CALHOUN | 33,970 | 19,806 | 12,451 | 1,713 | 7,355 R | 58.3% | 36.7% | 61.4% | 38.6% |
| 39,191 | CHAMBERS | 12,956 | 7,694 | 5,103 | 159 | 2,591 R | 59.4% | 39.4% | 60.1% | 39.9% |
| 18,760 | CHEROKEE | 6,101 | 2,868 | 3,176 | 57 | 308 D | 47.0% | 52.1% | 47.5% | 52.5% |
| 30,612 | CHILTON | 12,623 | 8,761 | 3,820 | 42 | 4,941 R | 69.4% | 30.3% | 69.6% | 30.4% |
| 16,839 | CHOCTAW | 7,131 | 3,629 | 3,491 | 11 | 138 R | 50.9% | 49.0% | 51.0% | 49.0% |
| 27,702 | CLARKE | 10,021 | 5,708 | 4,217 | 96 | 1,491 R | 57.0% | 42.1% | 57.5% | 42.5% |
| 13,703 | CLAY | 5,239 | 3,496 | 1,602 | 141 | 1,894 R | 66.7% | 30.6% | 68.6% | 31.4% |
| 12,595 | CLEBURNE | 4,491 | 3,071 | 1,383 | 37 | 1,688 R | 68.4% | 30.8% | 68.9% | 31.1% |
| 38,533 | COFFEE | 13,357 | 8,890 | 4,319 | 148 | 4,571 R | 66.6% | 32.3% | 67.3% | 32.7% |
| 54,519 | COLBERT | 18,409 | 7,775 | 10,397 | 237 | 2,622 D | 42.2% | 56.5% | 42.8% | 57.2% |
| 15,884 | CONECUH | 6,357 | 3,256 | 3,022 | 79 | 234 R | 51.2% | 47.5% | 51.9% | 48.1% |
| 11,377 | COOSA | 4,283 | 2,405 | 1,860 | 18 | 545 R | 56.2% | 43.4% | 56.4% | 43.6% |
| 36,850 | COVINGTON | 12,075 | 8,130 | 3,845 | 100 | 4,285 R | 67.3% | 31.8% | 67.9% | 32.1% |
| 14,110 | CRENSHAW | 4,478 | 2,617 | 1,836 | 25 | 781 R | 58.4% | 41.0% | 58.8% | 41.2% |
| 61,642 | CULLMAN | 23,197 | 14,351 | 8,517 | 329 | 5,834 R | 61.9% | 36.7% | 62.8% | 37.2% |
| 47,821 | DALE | 12,909 | 9,266 | 3,476 | 167 | 5,790 R | 71.8% | 26.9% | 72.7% | 27.3% |
| 53,981 | DALLAS | 17,423 | 7,630 | 9,660 | 133 | 2,030 D | 43.8% | 55.4% | 44.1% | 55.9% |
| 53,658 | DE KALB | 18,971 | 11,478 | 7,333 | 160 | 4,145 R | 60.5% | 38.7% | 61.0% | 39.0% |
| 43,390 | ELMORE | 15,540 | 10,852 | 4,501 | 187 | 6,351 R | 69.8% | 29.0% | 70.7% | 29.3% |
| 38,440 | ESCAMBIA | 10,954 | 6,807 | 4,020 | 127 | 2,787 R | 62.1% | 36.7% | 62.9% | 37.1% |
| 103,057 | ETOWAH | 35,891 | 17,828 | 17,762 | 301 | 66 R | 49.7% | 49.5% | 50.1% | 49.9% |
| 18,809 | FAYETTE | 7,557 | 4,338 | 3,186 | 33 | 1,152 R | 57.4% | 42.2% | 57.7% | 42.3% |
| 28,350 | FRANKLIN | 10,241 | 5,146 | 4,961 | 134 | 185 R | 50.2% | 48.4% | 50.9% | 49.1% |
| 24,253 | GENEVA | 8,472 | 5,703 | 2,685 | 84 | 3,018 R | 67.3% | 31.7% | 68.0% | 32.0% |
| 11,021 | GREENE | 4,377 | 1,048 | 3,295 | 34 | 2,247 D | 23.9% | 75.3% | 24.1% | 75.9% |
| 15,604 | HALE | 5,652 | 2,414 | 3,187 | 51 | 773 D | 42.7% | 56.4% | 43.1% | 56.9% |
| 15,302 | HENRY | 5,844 | 3,613 | 2,206 | 25 | 1,407 R | 61.8% | 37.7% | 62.1% | 37.9% |
| 74,632 | HOUSTON | 27,061 | 19,989 | 7,001 | 71 | 12,988 R | 73.9% | 25.9% | 74.1% | 25.9% |
| 51,407 | JACKSON | 13,671 | 6,090 | 7,418 | 163 | 1,328 D | 44.5% | 54.3% | 45.1% | 54.9% |
| 671,324 | JEFFERSON | 258,062 | 148,879 | 107,766 | 1,417 | 41,113 R | 57.7% | 41.8% | 58.0% | 42.0% |
| 16,453 | LAMAR | 5,499 | 3,214 | 2,274 | 11 | 940 R | 58.4% | 41.4% | 58.6% | 41.4% |
| 80,546 | LAUDERDALE | 26,190 | 12,942 | 12,862 | 386 | 80 R | 49.4% | 49.1% | 50.2% | 49.8% |
| 30,170 | LAWRENCE | 8,417 | 3,616 | 4,646 | 155 | 1,030 D | 43.0% | 55.2% | 43.8% | 56.2% |
| 76,283 | LEE | 26,685 | 17,180 | 9,078 | 427 | 8,102 R | 64.4% | 34.0% | 65.4% | 34.6% |
| 46,005 | LIMESTONE | 14,760 | 9,086 | 5,455 | 219 | 3,631 R | 61.6% | 37.0% | 62.5% | 37.5% |
| 13,253 | LOWNDES | 4,776 | 1,405 | 3,328 | 43 | 1,923 D | 29.4% | 69.7% | 29.7% | 70.3% |
| 26,829 | MACON | 7,756 | 1,304 | 6,351 | 101 | 5,047 D | 16.8% | 81.9% | 17.0% | 83.0% |
| 196,966 | MADISON | 79,894 | 53,575 | 25,800 | 519 | 27,775 R | 67.1% | 32.3% | 67.5% | 32.5% |
| 25,047 | MARENGO | 8,725 | 4,241 | 4,402 | 82 | 161 D | 48.6% | 50.5% | 49.1% | 50.9% |
| 30,041 | MARION | 10,497 | 5,955 | 4,505 | 37 | 1,450 R | 56.7% | 42.9% | 56.9% | 43.1% |
| 65,622 | MARSHALL | 19,947 | 12,148 | 7,357 | 442 | 4,791 R | 60.9% | 36.9% | 62.3% | 37.7% |
| 364,980 | MOBILE | 118,688 | 72,203 | 45,524 | 961 | 26,679 R | 60.8% | 38.4% | 61.3% | 38.7% |
| 22,651 | MONROE | 8,954 | 5,379 | 3,509 | 66 | 1,870 R | 60.1% | 39.2% | 60.5% | 39.5% |
| 197,038 | MONTGOMERY | 70,482 | 41,131 | 28,709 | 642 | 12,422 R | 58.4% | 40.7% | 58.9% | 41.1% |
| 90,231 | MORGAN | 29,407 | 18,679 | 10,594 | 134 | 8,085 R | 63.5% | 36.0% | 63.8% | 36.2% |
| 15,012 | PERRY | 5,758 | 2,107 | 3,574 | 77 | 1,467 D | 36.6% | 62.1% | 37.1% | 62.9% |
| 21,481 | PICKENS | 6,982 | 3,851 | 3,107 | 24 | 744 R | 55.2% | 44.5% | 55.3% | 44.7% |
| 28,050 | PIKE | 9,822 | 5,897 | 3,813 | 112 | 2,084 R | 60.0% | 38.8% | 60.7% | 39.3% |
| 20,075 | RANDOLPH | 7,224 | 4,625 | 2,462 | 137 | 2,163 R | 64.0% | 34.1% | 65.3% | 34.7% |
| 47,356 | RUSSELL | 13,087 | 6,333 | 6,589 | 165 | 256 D | 48.4% | 50.3% | 49.0% | 51.0% |
| 41,205 | ST. CLAIR | 14,997 | 10,604 | 4,335 | 58 | 6,269 R | 70.7% | 28.9% | 71.0% | 29.0% |
| 66,298 | SHELBY | 34,314 | 27,052 | 7,138 | 124 | 19,914 R | 78.8% | 20.8% | 79.1% | 20.9% |
| 16,908 | SUMTER | 6,635 | 2,212 | 4,390 | 33 | 2,178 D | 33.3% | 66.2% | 33.5% | 66.5% |

# ALABAMA

## PRESIDENT 1988

| 1980 Census Population | County | Total Vote | Republican | Democratic | Other | Rep.-Dem. Plurality | Percentage | | | |
|---|---|---|---|---|---|---|---|---|---|---|
| | | | | | | | Total Vote | | Major Vote | |
| | | | | | | | Rep. | Dem. | Rep. | Dem. |
| 73,826 | TALLADEGA | 21,507 | 12,973 | 8,291 | 243 | 4,682 R | 60.3% | 38.6% | 61.0% | 39.0% |
| 38,676 | TALLAPOOSA | 13,298 | 8,502 | 4,598 | 198 | 3,904 R | 63.9% | 34.6% | 64.9% | 35.1% |
| 137,541 | TUSCALOOSA | 45,758 | 27,396 | 18,166 | 196 | 9,230 R | 59.9% | 39.7% | 60.1% | 39.9% |
| 68,660 | WALKER | 22,700 | 11,011 | 11,338 | 351 | 327 D | 48.5% | 49.9% | 49.3% | 50.7% |
| 16,821 | WASHINGTON | 7,164 | 3,741 | 3,402 | 21 | 339 R | 52.2% | 47.5% | 52.4% | 47.6% |
| 14,755 | WILCOX | 5,118 | 1,739 | 3,369 | 10 | 1,630 D | 34.0% | 65.8% | 34.0% | 66.0% |
| 21,953 | WINSTON | 9,225 | 6,235 | 2,954 | 36 | 3,281 R | 67.6% | 32.0% | 67.9% | 32.1% |
| 3,893,888 | TOTAL | 1,378,476 | 815,576 | 549,506 | 13,394 | 266,070 R | 59.2% | 39.9% | 59.7% | 40.3% |

Ta

# ALABAMA

## PRESIDENT 1984

| 1980 Census Population | County | Total Vote | Republican | Democratic | Other | Rep.-Dem. Plurality | | Total Vote Rep. | Total Vote Dem. | Major Vote Rep. | Major Vote Dem. |
|---|---|---|---|---|---|---|---|---|---|---|---|
| 32,259 | AUTAUGA | 11,917 | 8,350 | 3,366 | 201 | 4,984 | R | 70.1% | 28.2% | 71.3% | 28.7% |
| 78,556 | BALDWIN | 33,045 | 24,964 | 7,272 | 809 | 17,692 | R | 75.5% | 22.0% | 77.4% | 22.6% |
| 24,756 | BARBOUR | 10,161 | 5,459 | 4,591 | 111 | 868 | R | 53.7% | 45.2% | 54.3% | 45.7% |
| 15,723 | BIBB | 5,687 | 3,487 | 2,167 | 33 | 1,320 | R | 61.3% | 38.1% | 61.7% | 38.3% |
| 36,459 | BLOUNT | 12,482 | 8,508 | 3,738 | 236 | 4,770 | R | 68.2% | 29.9% | 69.5% | 30.5% |
| 10,596 | BULLOCK | 5,299 | 1,697 | 3,537 | 65 | 1,840 | D | 32.0% | 66.7% | 32.4% | 67.6% |
| 21,680 | BUTLER | 8,709 | 4,941 | 3,641 | 127 | 1,300 | R | 56.7% | 41.8% | 57.6% | 42.4% |
| 119,761 | CALHOUN | 38,082 | 23,291 | 12,752 | 2,039 | 10,539 | R | 61.2% | 33.5% | 64.6% | 35.4% |
| 39,191 | CHAMBERS | 13,463 | 8,024 | 5,302 | 137 | 2,722 | R | 59.6% | 39.4% | 60.2% | 39.8% |
| 18,760 | CHEROKEE | 6,319 | 3,225 | 3,029 | 65 | 196 | R | 51.0% | 47.9% | 51.6% | 48.4% |
| 30,612 | CHILTON | 12,678 | 8,243 | 3,924 | 511 | 4,319 | R | 65.0% | 31.0% | 67.7% | 32.3% |
| 16,839 | CHOCTAW | 7,349 | 3,960 | 3,373 | 16 | 587 | R | 53.9% | 45.9% | 54.0% | 46.0% |
| 27,702 | CLARKE | 10,811 | 6,282 | 4,452 | 77 | 1,830 | R | 58.1% | 41.2% | 58.5% | 41.5% |
| 13,703 | CLAY | 5,033 | 3,432 | 1,456 | 145 | 1,976 | R | 68.2% | 28.9% | 70.2% | 29.8% |
| 12,595 | CLEBURNE | 4,623 | 3,259 | 1,238 | 126 | 2,021 | R | 70.5% | 26.8% | 72.5% | 27.5% |
| 38,533 | COFFEE | 15,118 | 10,558 | 4,370 | 190 | 6,188 | R | 69.8% | 28.9% | 70.7% | 29.3% |
| 54,519 | COLBERT | 21,032 | 9,530 | 11,008 | 494 | 1,478 | D | 45.3% | 52.3% | 46.4% | 53.6% |
| 15,884 | CONECUH | 6,336 | 3,538 | 2,737 | 61 | 801 | R | 55.8% | 43.2% | 56.4% | 43.6% |
| 11,377 | COOSA | 4,379 | 2,585 | 1,781 | 13 | 804 | R | 59.0% | 40.7% | 59.2% | 40.8% |
| 36,850 | COVINGTON | 13,883 | 9,944 | 3,812 | 127 | 6,132 | R | 71.6% | 27.5% | 72.3% | 27.7% |
| 14,110 | CRENSHAW | 5,272 | 3,261 | 1,904 | 107 | 1,357 | R | 61.9% | 36.1% | 63.1% | 36.9% |
| 61,642 | CULLMAN | 23,126 | 14,782 | 7,989 | 355 | 6,793 | R | 63.9% | 34.5% | 64.9% | 35.1% |
| 47,821 | DALE | 13,692 | 10,319 | 3,215 | 158 | 7,104 | R | 75.4% | 23.5% | 76.2% | 23.8% |
| 53,981 | DALLAS | 20,718 | 9,585 | 10,955 | 178 | 1,370 | D | 46.3% | 52.9% | 46.7% | 53.3% |
| 53,658 | DE KALB | 19,349 | 12,098 | 7,212 | 39 | 4,886 | R | 62.5% | 37.3% | 62.7% | 37.3% |
| 43,390 | ELMORE | 16,077 | 11,694 | 4,198 | 185 | 7,496 | R | 72.7% | 26.1% | 73.6% | 26.4% |
| 38,440 | ESCAMBIA | 12,724 | 8,694 | 3,853 | 177 | 4,841 | R | 68.3% | 30.3% | 69.3% | 30.7% |
| 103,057 | ETOWAH | 38,781 | 19,243 | 19,074 | 464 | 169 | R | 49.6% | 49.2% | 50.2% | 49.8% |
| 18,809 | FAYETTE | 7,201 | 4,654 | 2,533 | 14 | 2,121 | R | 64.6% | 35.2% | 64.8% | 35.2% |
| 28,350 | FRANKLIN | 10,027 | 5,304 | 4,601 | 122 | 703 | R | 52.9% | 45.9% | 53.5% | 46.5% |
| 24,253 | GENEVA | 9,011 | 6,308 | 2,330 | 373 | 3,978 | R | 70.0% | 25.9% | 73.0% | 27.0% |
| 11,021 | GREENE | 5,209 | 1,361 | 3,675 | 173 | 2,314 | D | 26.1% | 70.6% | 27.0% | 73.0% |
| 15,604 | HALE | 6,056 | 2,691 | 3,289 | 76 | 598 | D | 44.4% | 54.3% | 45.0% | 55.0% |
| 15,302 | HENRY | 6,236 | 3,952 | 2,231 | 53 | 1,721 | R | 63.4% | 35.8% | 63.9% | 36.1% |
| 74,632 | HOUSTON | 27,485 | 20,834 | 6,488 | 163 | 14,346 | R | 75.8% | 23.6% | 76.3% | 23.7% |
| 51,407 | JACKSON | 14,572 | 6,730 | 7,635 | 207 | 905 | D | 46.2% | 52.4% | 46.8% | 53.2% |
| 671,324 | JEFFERSON | 266,547 | 158,362 | 107,506 | 679 | 50,856 | R | 59.4% | 40.3% | 59.6% | 40.4% |
| 16,453 | LAMAR | 5,867 | 3,943 | 1,910 | 14 | 2,033 | R | 67.2% | 32.6% | 67.4% | 32.6% |
| 80,546 | LAUDERDALE | 28,659 | 15,354 | 12,907 | 398 | 2,447 | R | 53.6% | 45.0% | 54.3% | 45.7% |
| 30,170 | LAWRENCE | 9,494 | 4,466 | 4,866 | 162 | 400 | D | 47.0% | 51.3% | 47.9% | 52.1% |
| 76,283 | LEE | 26,161 | 16,757 | 9,077 | 327 | 7,680 | R | 64.1% | 34.7% | 64.9% | 35.1% |
| 46,005 | LIMESTONE | 14,010 | 8,423 | 5,410 | 177 | 3,013 | R | 60.1% | 38.6% | 60.9% | 39.1% |
| 13,253 | LOWNDES | 5,252 | 1,629 | 3,567 | 56 | 1,938 | D | 31.0% | 67.9% | 31.4% | 68.6% |
| 26,829 | MACON | 9,499 | 1,543 | 7,857 | 99 | 6,314 | D | 16.2% | 82.7% | 16.4% | 83.6% |
| 196,966 | MADISON | 78,142 | 50,428 | 26,889 | 825 | 23,539 | R | 64.5% | 34.4% | 65.2% | 34.8% |
| 25,047 | MARENGO | 10,213 | 5,261 | 4,811 | 141 | 450 | R | 51.5% | 47.1% | 52.2% | 47.8% |
| 30,041 | MARION | 10,713 | 6,771 | 3,918 | 24 | 2,853 | R | 63.2% | 36.6% | 63.3% | 36.7% |
| 65,622 | MARSHALL | 20,391 | 12,330 | 7,704 | 357 | 4,626 | R | 60.5% | 37.8% | 61.5% | 38.5% |
| 364,980 | MOBILE | 130,959 | 81,923 | 47,252 | 1,784 | 34,671 | R | 62.6% | 36.1% | 63.4% | 36.6% |
| 22,651 | MONROE | 9,756 | 5,917 | 3,725 | 114 | 2,192 | R | 60.6% | 38.2% | 61.4% | 38.6% |
| 197,038 | MONTGOMERY | 75,005 | 43,328 | 31,206 | 471 | 12,122 | R | 57.8% | 41.6% | 58.1% | 41.9% |
| 90,231 | MORGAN | 35,543 | 24,103 | 11,324 | 116 | 12,779 | R | 67.8% | 31.9% | 68.0% | 32.0% |
| 15,012 | PERRY | 6,408 | 2,600 | 3,731 | 77 | 1,131 | D | 40.6% | 58.2% | 41.1% | 58.9% |
| 21,481 | PICKENS | 8,296 | 4,685 | 3,586 | 25 | 1,099 | R | 56.5% | 43.2% | 56.6% | 43.4% |
| 28,050 | PIKE | 9,953 | 6,231 | 3,541 | 181 | 2,690 | R | 62.6% | 35.6% | 63.8% | 36.2% |
| 20,075 | RANDOLPH | 7,515 | 4,940 | 2,439 | 136 | 2,501 | R | 65.7% | 32.5% | 66.9% | 33.1% |
| 47,356 | RUSSELL | 14,452 | 6,654 | 7,610 | 188 | 956 | D | 46.0% | 52.7% | 46.6% | 53.4% |
| 41,205 | ST. CLAIR | 14,654 | 10,408 | 4,000 | 246 | 6,408 | R | 71.0% | 27.3% | 72.2% | 27.8% |
| 66,298 | SHELBY | 28,068 | 21,858 | 5,884 | 326 | 15,974 | R | 77.9% | 21.0% | 78.8% | 21.2% |
| 16,908 | SUMTER | 6,993 | 2,493 | 4,478 | 22 | 1,985 | D | 35.6% | 64.0% | 35.8% | 64.2% |

58

# ALABAMA

## PRESIDENT 1984

| 1980 Census Population | County | Total Vote | Republican | Democratic | Other | Rep.-Dem. Plurality | Percentage Total Vote Rep. | Dem. | Major Vote Rep. | Dem. |
|---|---|---|---|---|---|---|---|---|---|---|
| 73,826 | TALLADEGA | 23,020 | 14,067 | 8,490 | 463 | 5,577 R | 61.1% | 36.9% | 62.4% | 37.6% |
| 38,676 | TALLAPOOSA | 13,666 | 9,045 | 4,458 | 163 | 4,587 R | 66.2% | 32.6% | 67.0% | 33.0% |
| 137,541 | TUSCALOOSA | 44,739 | 28,075 | 16,066 | 598 | 12,009 R | 62.8% | 35.9% | 63.6% | 36.4% |
| 68,660 | WALKER | 23,753 | 12,852 | 10,591 | 310 | 2,261 R | 54.1% | 44.6% | 54.8% | 45.2% |
| 16,821 | WASHINGTON | 7,543 | 4,434 | 3,081 | 28 | 1,353 R | 58.8% | 40.8% | 59.0% | 41.0% |
| 14,755 | WILCOX | 5,022 | 2,337 | 2,663 | 22 | 326 D | 46.5% | 53.0% | 46.7% | 53.3% |
| 21,953 | WINSTON | 9,478 | 6,845 | 2,624 | 9 | 4,221 R | 72.2% | 27.7% | 72.3% | 27.7% |
| 3,893,888 | TOTAL | 1,441,713 | 872,849 | 551,899 | 16,965 | 320,950 R | 60.5% | 38.3% | 61.3% | 38.7% |

# ALABAMA

## PRESIDENT 1980

| 1980 Census Population | County | Total Vote | Republican | Democratic | Other | Rep.-Dem. Plurality | Percentage |||| 
|---|---|---|---|---|---|---|---|---|---|---|
| | | | | | | | Total Vote || Major Vote ||
| | | | | | | | Rep. | Dem. | Rep. | Dem. |
| 32,259 | AUTAUGA | 11,063 | 6,292 | 4,295 | 476 | 1,997 R | 56.9% | 38.8% | 59.4% | 40.6% |
| 78,556 | BALDWIN | 28,353 | 18,652 | 8,448 | 1,253 | 10,204 R | 65.8% | 29.8% | 68.8% | 31.2% |
| 24,756 | BARBOUR | 9,001 | 4,171 | 4,458 | 372 | 287 D | 46.3% | 49.5% | 48.3% | 51.7% |
| 15,723 | BIBB | 5,623 | 2,491 | 3,097 | 35 | 606 D | 44.3% | 55.1% | 44.6% | 55.4% |
| 36,459 | BLOUNT | 12,724 | 6,819 | 5,656 | 249 | 1,163 R | 53.6% | 44.5% | 54.7% | 45.3% |
| 10,596 | BULLOCK | 5,637 | 1,446 | 3,960 | 231 | 2,514 D | 25.7% | 70.3% | 26.7% | 73.3% |
| 21,680 | BUTLER | 8,368 | 3,810 | 4,156 | 402 | 346 D | 45.5% | 49.7% | 47.8% | 52.2% |
| 119,761 | CALHOUN | 35,541 | 17,475 | 17,017 | 1,049 | 458 R | 49.2% | 47.9% | 50.7% | 49.3% |
| 39,191 | CHAMBERS | 11,899 | 4,864 | 6,649 | 386 | 1,785 D | 40.9% | 55.9% | 42.2% | 57.8% |
| 18,760 | CHEROKEE | 6,438 | 2,482 | 3,764 | 192 | 1,282 D | 38.6% | 58.5% | 39.7% | 60.3% |
| 30,612 | CHILTON | 11,477 | 6,615 | 4,706 | 156 | 1,909 R | 57.6% | 41.0% | 58.4% | 41.6% |
| 16,839 | CHOCTAW | 6,580 | 2,859 | 3,680 | 41 | 821 D | 43.4% | 55.9% | 43.7% | 56.3% |
| 27,702 | CLARKE | 10,663 | 5,059 | 5,249 | 355 | 190 D | 47.4% | 49.2% | 49.1% | 50.9% |
| 13,703 | CLAY | 5,747 | 2,764 | 2,858 | 125 | 94 D | 48.1% | 49.7% | 49.2% | 50.8% |
| 12,595 | CLEBURNE | 4,526 | 2,389 | 2,050 | 87 | 339 R | 52.8% | 45.3% | 53.8% | 46.2% |
| 38,533 | COFFEE | 13,399 | 6,760 | 6,140 | 499 | 620 R | 50.5% | 45.8% | 52.4% | 47.6% |
| 54,519 | COLBERT | 20,013 | 6,619 | 12,550 | 844 | 5,931 D | 33.1% | 62.7% | 34.5% | 65.5% |
| 15,884 | CONECUH | 6,181 | 2,948 | 3,102 | 131 | 154 D | 47.7% | 50.2% | 48.7% | 51.3% |
| 11,377 | COOSA | 4,209 | 1,714 | 2,383 | 112 | 669 D | 40.7% | 56.6% | 41.8% | 58.2% |
| 36,850 | COVINGTON | 13,608 | 7,014 | 6,305 | 289 | 709 R | 51.5% | 46.3% | 52.7% | 47.3% |
| 14,110 | CRENSHAW | 5,256 | 2,478 | 2,704 | 74 | 226 D | 47.1% | 51.4% | 47.8% | 52.2% |
| 61,642 | CULLMAN | 22,240 | 10,212 | 11,525 | 503 | 1,313 D | 45.9% | 51.8% | 47.0% | 53.0% |
| 47,821 | DALE | 12,573 | 7,247 | 4,936 | 390 | 2,311 R | 57.6% | 39.3% | 59.5% | 40.5% |
| 53,981 | DALLAS | 18,147 | 7,647 | 9,770 | 730 | 2,123 D | 42.1% | 53.8% | 43.9% | 56.1% |
| 53,658 | DE KALB | 18,690 | 9,673 | 8,820 | 197 | 853 R | 51.8% | 47.2% | 52.3% | 47.7% |
| 43,390 | ELMORE | 15,190 | 8,688 | 5,947 | 555 | 2,741 R | 57.2% | 39.2% | 59.4% | 40.6% |
| 38,440 | ESCAMBIA | 12,053 | 6,513 | 5,148 | 392 | 1,365 R | 54.0% | 42.7% | 55.9% | 44.1% |
| 103,057 | ETOWAH | 37,806 | 16,177 | 20,790 | 839 | 4,613 D | 42.8% | 55.0% | 43.8% | 56.2% |
| 18,809 | FAYETTE | 6,789 | 3,315 | 3,389 | 85 | 74 D | 48.8% | 49.9% | 49.4% | 50.6% |
| 28,350 | FRANKLIN | 10,763 | 4,448 | 6,136 | 179 | 1,688 D | 41.3% | 57.0% | 42.0% | 58.0% |
| 24,253 | GENEVA | 9,628 | 4,747 | 4,703 | 178 | 44 R | 49.3% | 48.8% | 50.2% | 49.8% |
| 11,021 | GREENE | 4,538 | 1,034 | 3,474 | 30 | 2,440 D | 22.8% | 76.6% | 22.9% | 77.1% |
| 15,604 | HALE | 5,979 | 2,074 | 3,583 | 322 | 1,509 D | 34.7% | 59.9% | 36.7% | 63.3% |
| 15,302 | HENRY | 5,879 | 2,813 | 2,973 | 93 | 160 D | 47.8% | 50.6% | 48.6% | 51.4% |
| 74,632 | HOUSTON | 23,238 | 14,884 | 7,848 | 506 | 7,036 R | 64.1% | 33.8% | 65.5% | 34.5% |
| 51,407 | JACKSON | 14,203 | 4,897 | 8,776 | 530 | 3,879 D | 34.5% | 61.8% | 35.8% | 64.2% |
| 671,324 | JEFFERSON | 259,512 | 132,612 | 113,069 | 13,831 | 19,543 R | 51.1% | 43.6% | 54.0% | 46.0% |
| 16,453 | LAMAR | 6,186 | 2,778 | 3,366 | 42 | 588 D | 44.9% | 54.4% | 45.2% | 54.8% |
| 80,546 | LAUDERDALE | 27,243 | 10,467 | 15,379 | 1,397 | 4,912 D | 38.4% | 56.5% | 40.5% | 59.5% |
| 30,170 | LAWRENCE | 8,742 | 2,456 | 6,112 | 174 | 3,656 D | 28.1% | 69.9% | 28.7% | 71.3% |
| 76,283 | LEE | 21,972 | 10,982 | 9,606 | 1,384 | 1,376 R | 50.0% | 43.7% | 53.3% | 46.7% |
| 46,005 | LIMESTONE | 13,384 | 4,574 | 8,180 | 630 | 3,606 D | 34.2% | 61.1% | 35.9% | 64.1% |
| 13,253 | LOWNDES | 5,329 | 1,524 | 3,577 | 228 | 2,053 D | 28.6% | 67.1% | 29.9% | 70.1% |
| 26,829 | MACON | 8,774 | 1,259 | 7,028 | 487 | 5,769 D | 14.3% | 80.1% | 15.2% | 84.8% |
| 196,966 | MADISON | 65,072 | 30,604 | 30,469 | 3,999 | 135 R | 47.0% | 46.8% | 50.1% | 49.9% |
| 25,047 | MARENGO | 9,660 | 4,048 | 5,178 | 434 | 1,130 D | 41.9% | 53.6% | 43.9% | 56.1% |
| 30,041 | MARION | 10,738 | 5,182 | 5,450 | 106 | 268 D | 48.3% | 50.8% | 48.7% | 51.3% |
| 65,622 | MARSHALL | 19,933 | 8,159 | 10,854 | 920 | 2,695 D | 40.9% | 54.5% | 42.9% | 57.1% |
| 364,980 | MOBILE | 116,992 | 67,515 | 46,180 | 3,297 | 21,335 R | 57.7% | 39.5% | 59.4% | 40.6% |
| 22,651 | MONROE | 9,072 | 4,615 | 4,262 | 195 | 353 R | 50.9% | 47.0% | 52.0% | 48.0% |
| 197,038 | MONTGOMERY | 66,504 | 35,745 | 28,018 | 2,741 | 7,727 R | 53.7% | 42.1% | 56.1% | 43.9% |
| 90,231 | MORGAN | 29,271 | 13,214 | 14,703 | 1,354 | 1,489 D | 45.1% | 50.2% | 47.3% | 52.7% |
| 15,012 | PERRY | 6,522 | 2,262 | 4,208 | 52 | 1,946 D | 34.7% | 64.5% | 35.0% | 65.0% |
| 21,481 | PICKENS | 8,182 | 3,582 | 4,504 | 96 | 922 D | 43.8% | 55.0% | 44.3% | 55.7% |
| 28,050 | PIKE | 9,991 | 5,220 | 4,417 | 354 | 803 R | 52.2% | 44.2% | 54.2% | 45.8% |
| 20,075 | RANDOLPH | 7,094 | 3,279 | 3,378 | 437 | 99 D | 46.2% | 47.6% | 49.3% | 50.7% |
| 47,356 | RUSSELL | 13,500 | 4,485 | 8,123 | 892 | 3,638 D | 33.2% | 60.2% | 35.6% | 64.4% |
| 41,205 | ST. CLAIR | 13,654 | 7,768 | 5,236 | 650 | 2,532 R | 56.9% | 38.3% | 59.7% | 40.3% |
| 66,298 | SHELBY | 23,267 | 14,957 | 7,396 | 914 | 7,561 R | 64.3% | 31.8% | 66.9% | 33.1% |
| 16,908 | SUMTER | 7,199 | 2,104 | 5,015 | 80 | 2,911 D | 29.2% | 69.7% | 29.6% | 70.4% |

# ALABAMA

## PRESIDENT 1980

| 1980 Census Population | County | Total Vote | Republican | Democratic | Other | Rep.-Dem. Plurality | Percentage | | | |
|---|---|---|---|---|---|---|---|---|---|---|
| | | | | | | | Total Vote | | Major Vote | |
| | | | | | | | Rep. | Dem. | Rep. | Dem. |
| 73,826 | TALLADEGA | 20,641 | 9,902 | 10,159 | 580 | 257 D | 48.0% | 49.2% | 49.4% | 50.6% |
| 38,676 | TALLAPOOSA | 13,603 | 5,958 | 7,260 | 385 | 1,302 D | 43.8% | 53.4% | 45.1% | 54.9% |
| 137,541 | TUSCALOOSA | 40,720 | 19,750 | 19,103 | 1,867 | 647 R | 48.5% | 46.9% | 50.8% | 49.2% |
| 68,660 | WALKER | 22,828 | 8,795 | 13,616 | 417 | 4,821 D | 38.5% | 59.6% | 39.2% | 60.8% |
| 16,821 | WASHINGTON | 6,625 | 3,045 | 3,520 | 60 | 475 D | 46.0% | 53.1% | 46.4% | 53.6% |
| 14,755 | WILCOX | 7,261 | 2,280 | 4,951 | 30 | 2,671 D | 31.4% | 68.2% | 31.5% | 68.5% |
| 21,953 | WINSTON | 8,436 | 4,981 | 3,368 | 87 | 1,613 R | 59.0% | 39.9% | 59.7% | 40.3% |
| 3,893,888 | TOTAL | 1,341,929 | 654,192 | 636,730 | 51,007 | 17,462 R | 48.8% | 47.4% | 50.7% | 49.3% |

# ALABAMA

## PRESIDENT 1976

| 1970 Census Population | County | Total Vote | Republican | Democratic | Other | Rep.-Dem. Plurality | Percentage | | | |
|---|---|---|---|---|---|---|---|---|---|---|
| | | | | | | | Total Vote | | Major Vote | |
| | | | | | | | Rep. | Dem. | Rep. | Dem. |
| 24,460 | AUTAUGA | 9,338 | 4,512 | 4,640 | 186 | 128 D | 48.3% | 49.7% | 49.3% | 50.7% |
| 59,382 | BALDWIN | 22,967 | 13,256 | 9,191 | 520 | 4,065 R | 57.7% | 40.0% | 59.1% | 40.9% |
| 22,543 | BARBOUR | 8,690 | 3,758 | 4,730 | 202 | 972 D | 43.2% | 54.4% | 44.3% | 55.7% |
| 13,812 | BIBB | 4,474 | 1,591 | 2,850 | 33 | 1,259 D | 35.6% | 63.7% | 35.8% | 64.2% |
| 26,853 | BLOUNT | 10,978 | 4,233 | 6,645 | 100 | 2,412 D | 38.6% | 60.5% | 38.9% | 61.1% |
| 11,824 | BULLOCK | 5,092 | 1,482 | 3,536 | 74 | 2,054 D | 29.1% | 69.4% | 29.5% | 70.5% |
| 22,007 | BUTLER | 7,208 | 2,909 | 4,271 | 28 | 1,362 D | 40.4% | 59.3% | 40.5% | 59.5% |
| 103,092 | CALHOUN | 32,700 | 11,763 | 20,466 | 471 | 8,703 D | 36.0% | 62.6% | 36.5% | 63.5% |
| 36,356 | CHAMBERS | 11,848 | 5,488 | 6,164 | 196 | 676 D | 46.3% | 52.0% | 47.1% | 52.9% |
| 15,606 | CHEROKEE | 6,256 | 1,492 | 4,668 | 96 | 3,176 D | 23.8% | 74.6% | 24.2% | 75.8% |
| 25,180 | CHILTON | 10,385 | 4,725 | 5,550 | 110 | 825 D | 45.5% | 53.4% | 46.0% | 54.0% |
| 16,589 | CHOCTAW | 6,972 | 3,033 | 3,911 | 28 | 878 D | 43.5% | 56.1% | 43.7% | 56.3% |
| 26,724 | CLARKE | 9,006 | 4,126 | 4,737 | 143 | 611 D | 45.8% | 52.6% | 46.6% | 53.4% |
| 12,636 | CLAY | 4,858 | 1,883 | 2,946 | 29 | 1,063 D | 38.8% | 60.6% | 39.0% | 61.0% |
| 10,996 | CLEBURNE | 3,981 | 1,436 | 2,490 | 55 | 1,054 D | 36.1% | 62.5% | 36.6% | 63.4% |
| 34,872 | COFFEE | 12,651 | 4,683 | 7,844 | 124 | 3,161 D | 37.0% | 62.0% | 37.4% | 62.6% |
| 49,632 | COLBERT | 16,842 | 4,471 | 11,996 | 375 | 7,525 D | 26.5% | 71.2% | 27.2% | 72.8% |
| 15,645 | CONECUH | 4,980 | 1,812 | 3,086 | 82 | 1,274 D | 36.4% | 62.0% | 37.0% | 63.0% |
| 10,662 | COOSA | 3,766 | 1,196 | 2,533 | 37 | 1,337 D | 31.8% | 67.3% | 32.1% | 67.9% |
| 34,079 | COVINGTON | 12,224 | 4,977 | 7,081 | 166 | 2,104 D | 40.7% | 57.9% | 41.3% | 58.7% |
| 13,188 | CRENSHAW | 5,266 | 1,801 | 3,372 | 93 | 1,571 D | 34.2% | 64.0% | 34.8% | 65.2% |
| 52,445 | CULLMAN | 20,055 | 6,899 | 12,961 | 195 | 6,062 D | 34.4% | 64.6% | 34.7% | 65.3% |
| 52,938 | DALE | 11,531 | 4,996 | 6,346 | 189 | 1,350 D | 43.3% | 55.0% | 44.0% | 56.0% |
| 55,296 | DALLAS | 16,361 | 7,144 | 8,866 | 351 | 1,722 D | 43.7% | 54.2% | 44.6% | 55.4% |
| 41,981 | DE KALB | 16,437 | 6,597 | 9,759 | 81 | 3,162 D | 40.1% | 59.4% | 40.3% | 59.7% |
| 33,535 | ELMORE | 13,508 | 6,551 | 6,646 | 311 | 95 D | 48.5% | 49.2% | 49.6% | 50.4% |
| 34,906 | ESCAMBIA | 11,157 | 4,934 | 5,957 | 266 | 1,023 D | 44.2% | 53.4% | 45.3% | 54.7% |
| 94,144 | ETOWAH | 35,750 | 10,333 | 25,020 | 397 | 14,687 D | 28.9% | 70.0% | 29.2% | 70.8% |
| 16,252 | FAYETTE | 6,287 | 2,165 | 4,076 | 46 | 1,911 D | 34.4% | 64.8% | 34.7% | 65.3% |
| 23,933 | FRANKLIN | 9,721 | 3,345 | 6,279 | 97 | 2,934 D | 34.4% | 64.6% | 34.8% | 65.2% |
| 21,924 | GENEVA | 8,739 | 2,663 | 5,983 | 93 | 3,320 D | 30.5% | 68.5% | 30.8% | 69.2% |
| 10,650 | GREENE | 3,818 | 903 | 2,900 | 15 | 1,997 D | 23.7% | 76.0% | 23.7% | 76.3% |
| 15,888 | HALE | 5,394 | 2,034 | 3,236 | 124 | 1,202 D | 37.7% | 60.0% | 38.6% | 61.4% |
| 13,254 | HENRY | 5,234 | 2,052 | 3,144 | 38 | 1,092 D | 39.2% | 60.1% | 39.5% | 60.5% |
| 56,574 | HOUSTON | 19,738 | 10,672 | 8,787 | 279 | 1,885 R | 54.1% | 44.5% | 54.8% | 45.2% |
| 39,202 | JACKSON | 15,325 | 3,913 | 10,989 | 423 | 7,076 D | 25.5% | 71.7% | 26.3% | 73.7% |
| 644,991 | JEFFERSON | 217,090 | 113,590 | 99,531 | 3,969 | 14,059 R | 52.3% | 45.8% | 53.3% | 46.7% |
| 14,335 | LAMAR | 5,724 | 1,739 | 3,860 | 125 | 2,121 D | 30.4% | 67.4% | 31.1% | 68.9% |
| 68,111 | LAUDERDALE | 23,185 | 7,226 | 15,549 | 410 | 8,323 D | 31.2% | 67.1% | 31.7% | 68.3% |
| 27,281 | LAWRENCE | 8,284 | 1,415 | 6,810 | 59 | 5,395 D | 17.1% | 82.2% | 17.2% | 82.8% |
| 61,268 | LEE | 18,737 | 9,884 | 8,427 | 426 | 1,457 R | 52.8% | 45.0% | 54.0% | 46.0% |
| 41,699 | LIMESTONE | 12,000 | 2,997 | 8,803 | 200 | 5,806 D | 25.0% | 73.4% | 25.4% | 74.6% |
| 12,897 | LOWNDES | 5,462 | 1,621 | 3,732 | 109 | 2,111 D | 29.7% | 68.3% | 30.3% | 69.7% |
| 24,841 | MACON | 7,449 | 1,387 | 5,915 | 147 | 4,528 D | 18.6% | 79.4% | 19.0% | 81.0% |
| 186,540 | MADISON | 57,287 | 20,959 | 35,497 | 831 | 14,538 D | 36.6% | 62.0% | 37.1% | 62.9% |
| 23,819 | MARENGO | 8,755 | 3,841 | 4,731 | 183 | 890 D | 43.9% | 54.0% | 44.8% | 55.2% |
| 23,788 | MARION | 9,303 | 3,036 | 6,244 | 23 | 3,208 D | 32.6% | 67.1% | 32.7% | 67.3% |
| 54,211 | MARSHALL | 20,100 | 6,006 | 13,696 | 398 | 7,690 D | 29.9% | 68.1% | 30.5% | 69.5% |
| 317,308 | MOBILE | 105,876 | 53,835 | 50,264 | 1,777 | 3,571 R | 50.8% | 47.5% | 51.7% | 48.3% |
| 20,883 | MONROE | 7,263 | 3,476 | 3,669 | 118 | 193 D | 47.9% | 50.5% | 48.6% | 51.4% |
| 167,790 | MONTGOMERY | 54,733 | 29,360 | 24,641 | 732 | 4,719 R | 53.6% | 45.0% | 54.4% | 45.6% |
| 77,316 | MORGAN | 25,986 | 9,058 | 16,547 | 381 | 7,489 D | 34.9% | 63.7% | 35.4% | 64.6% |
| 15,388 | PERRY | 6,683 | 2,164 | 4,486 | 33 | 2,322 D | 32.4% | 67.1% | 32.5% | 67.5% |
| 20,326 | PICKENS | 6,786 | 2,969 | 3,776 | 41 | 807 D | 43.8% | 55.6% | 44.0% | 56.0% |
| 25,038 | PIKE | 9,889 | 4,363 | 5,387 | 139 | 1,024 D | 44.1% | 54.5% | 44.7% | 55.3% |
| 18,331 | RANDOLPH | 6,044 | 2,286 | 3,539 | 219 | 1,253 D | 37.8% | 58.6% | 39.2% | 60.8% |
| 45,394 | RUSSELL | 12,592 | 4,150 | 8,077 | 365 | 3,927 D | 33.0% | 64.1% | 33.9% | 66.1% |
| 27,956 | ST. CLAIR | 10,869 | 4,877 | 5,653 | 339 | 776 D | 44.9% | 52.0% | 46.3% | 53.7% |
| 38,037 | SHELBY | 16,629 | 9,035 | 7,197 | 397 | 1,838 R | 54.3% | 43.3% | 55.7% | 44.3% |
| 16,974 | SUMTER | 5,689 | 2,191 | 3,457 | 41 | 1,266 D | 38.5% | 60.8% | 38.8% | 61.2% |

# ALABAMA

## PRESIDENT 1976

| 1970 Census Population | County | Total Vote | Republican | Democratic | Other | Rep.-Dem. Plurality | Percentage | | | |
|---|---|---|---|---|---|---|---|---|---|---|
| | | | | | | | Total Vote | | Major Vote | |
| | | | | | | | Rep. | Dem. | Rep. | Dem. |
| 65,280 | TALLADEGA | 17,608 | 6,425 | 10,577 | 606 | 4,152 D | 36.5% | 60.1% | 37.8% | 62.2% |
| 33,840 | TALLAPOOSA | 13,163 | 5,237 | 7,614 | 312 | 2,377 D | 39.8% | 57.8% | 40.8% | 59.2% |
| 116,029 | TUSCALOOSA | 37,006 | 16,021 | 20,275 | 710 | 4,254 D | 43.3% | 54.8% | 44.1% | 55.9% |
| 56,246 | WALKER | 23,710 | 7,389 | 16,232 | 89 | 8,843 D | 31.2% | 68.5% | 31.3% | 68.7% |
| 16,241 | WASHINGTON | 5,670 | 2,171 | 3,471 | 28 | 1,300 D | 38.3% | 61.2% | 38.5% | 61.5% |
| 16,303 | WILCOX | 5,565 | 1,824 | 3,723 | 18 | 1,899 D | 32.8% | 66.9% | 32.9% | 67.1% |
| 16,654 | WINSTON | 7,868 | 3,710 | 4,134 | 24 | 424 D | 47.2% | 52.5% | 47.3% | 52.7% |
| 3,444,175 | TOTAL | 1,182,850 | 504,070 | 659,170 | 19,610 | 155,100 D | 42.6% | 55.7% | 43.3% | 56.7% |

# ALABAMA

## PRESIDENT 1972

| 1970 Census Population | County | Total Vote | Republican | Democratic | Other | Rep.-Dem. Plurality | Percentage Total Vote Rep. | Dem. | Major Vote Rep. | Dem. |
|---|---|---|---|---|---|---|---|---|---|---|
| 24,460 | AUTAUGA | 7,140 | 5,367 | 1,593 | 180 | 3,774 R | 75.2% | 22.3% | 77.1% | 22.9% |
| 59,382 | BALDWIN | 18,375 | 15,104 | 2,923 | 348 | 12,181 R | 82.2% | 15.9% | 83.8% | 16.2% |
| 22,543 | BARBOUR | 7,029 | 4,985 | 1,846 | 198 | 3,139 R | 70.9% | 26.3% | 73.0% | 27.0% |
| 13,812 | BIBB | 4,248 | 3,332 | 837 | 79 | 2,495 R | 78.4% | 19.7% | 79.9% | 20.1% |
| 26,853 | BLOUNT | 8,173 | 6,486 | 1,582 | 105 | 4,904 R | 79.4% | 19.4% | 80.4% | 19.6% |
| 11,824 | BULLOCK | 4,591 | 2,178 | 2,321 | 92 | 143 D | 47.4% | 50.6% | 48.4% | 51.6% |
| 22,007 | BUTLER | 6,128 | 4,685 | 1,401 | 42 | 3,284 R | 76.5% | 22.9% | 77.0% | 23.0% |
| 103,092 | CALHOUN | 26,471 | 20,364 | 5,832 | 275 | 14,532 R | 76.9% | 22.0% | 77.7% | 22.3% |
| 36,356 | CHAMBERS | 11,003 | 8,716 | 2,076 | 211 | 6,640 R | 79.2% | 18.9% | 80.8% | 19.2% |
| 15,606 | CHEROKEE | 4,422 | 3,179 | 1,182 | 61 | 1,997 R | 71.9% | 26.7% | 72.9% | 27.1% |
| 25,180 | CHILTON | 8,867 | 7,349 | 1,356 | 162 | 5,993 R | 82.9% | 15.3% | 84.4% | 15.6% |
| 16,589 | CHOCTAW | 5,030 | 3,055 | 1,934 | 41 | 1,121 R | 60.7% | 38.4% | 61.2% | 38.8% |
| 26,724 | CLARKE | 7,414 | 5,256 | 2,031 | 127 | 3,225 R | 70.9% | 27.4% | 72.1% | 27.9% |
| 12,636 | CLAY | 4,474 | 3,948 | 507 | 19 | 3,441 R | 88.2% | 11.3% | 88.6% | 11.4% |
| 10,996 | CLEBURNE | 4,014 | 3,420 | 581 | 13 | 2,839 R | 85.2% | 14.5% | 85.5% | 14.5% |
| 34,872 | COFFEE | 11,336 | 9,076 | 2,160 | 100 | 6,916 R | 80.1% | 19.1% | 80.8% | 19.2% |
| 49,632 | COLBERT | 16,564 | 11,215 | 4,811 | 538 | 6,404 R | 67.7% | 29.0% | 70.0% | 30.0% |
| 15,645 | CONECUH | 4,296 | 3,214 | 1,042 | 40 | 2,172 R | 74.8% | 24.3% | 75.5% | 24.5% |
| 10,662 | COOSA | 3,461 | 2,672 | 773 | 16 | 1,899 R | 77.2% | 22.3% | 77.6% | 22.4% |
| 34,079 | COVINGTON | 10,881 | 9,278 | 1,547 | 56 | 7,731 R | 85.3% | 14.2% | 85.7% | 14.3% |
| 13,188 | CRENSHAW | 4,294 | 3,129 | 1,085 | 80 | 2,044 R | 72.9% | 25.3% | 74.3% | 25.7% |
| 52,445 | CULLMAN | 18,091 | 14,390 | 3,571 | 130 | 10,819 R | 79.5% | 19.7% | 80.1% | 19.9% |
| 52,938 | DALE | 10,038 | 8,346 | 1,594 | 98 | 6,752 R | 83.1% | 15.9% | 84.0% | 16.0% |
| 55,296 | DALLAS | 14,280 | 8,644 | 5,427 | 209 | 3,217 R | 60.5% | 38.0% | 61.4% | 38.6% |
| 41,981 | DE KALB | 13,237 | 9,434 | 3,759 | 44 | 5,675 R | 71.3% | 28.4% | 71.5% | 28.5% |
| 33,535 | ELMORE | 10,590 | 8,461 | 1,891 | 238 | 6,570 R | 79.9% | 17.9% | 81.7% | 18.3% |
| 34,906 | ESCAMBIA | 9,591 | 7,883 | 1,598 | 110 | 6,285 R | 82.2% | 16.7% | 83.1% | 16.9% |
| 94,144 | ETOWAH | 28,581 | 20,851 | 7,372 | 358 | 13,479 R | 73.0% | 25.8% | 73.9% | 26.1% |
| 16,252 | FAYETTE | 5,094 | 4,240 | 836 | 18 | 3,404 R | 83.2% | 16.4% | 83.5% | 16.5% |
| 23,933 | FRANKLIN | 7,812 | 5,877 | 1,840 | 95 | 4,037 R | 75.2% | 23.6% | 76.2% | 23.8% |
| 21,924 | GENEVA | 6,938 | 5,851 | 1,049 | 38 | 4,802 R | 84.3% | 15.1% | 84.8% | 15.2% |
| 10,650 | GREENE | 4,735 | 1,404 | 3,235 | 96 | 1,831 D | 29.7% | 68.3% | 30.3% | 69.7% |
| 15,888 | HALE | 4,828 | 2,859 | 1,779 | 190 | 1,080 R | 59.2% | 36.8% | 61.6% | 38.4% |
| 13,254 | HENRY | 4,291 | 3,414 | 853 | 24 | 2,561 R | 79.6% | 19.9% | 80.0% | 20.0% |
| 56,574 | HOUSTON | 15,124 | 12,622 | 2,358 | 144 | 10,264 R | 83.5% | 15.6% | 84.3% | 15.7% |
| 39,202 | JACKSON | 9,410 | 6,202 | 2,985 | 223 | 3,217 R | 65.9% | 31.7% | 67.5% | 32.5% |
| 644,991 | JEFFERSON | 198,528 | 135,095 | 57,288 | 6,145 | 77,807 R | 68.0% | 28.9% | 70.2% | 29.8% |
| 14,335 | LAMAR | 4,075 | 3,283 | 766 | 26 | 2,517 R | 80.6% | 18.8% | 81.1% | 18.9% |
| 68,111 | LAUDERDALE | 20,108 | 14,410 | 5,112 | 586 | 9,298 R | 71.7% | 25.4% | 73.8% | 26.2% |
| 27,281 | LAWRENCE | 5,863 | 4,433 | 1,416 | 14 | 3,017 R | 75.6% | 24.2% | 75.8% | 24.2% |
| 61,268 | LEE | 15,441 | 11,571 | 3,622 | 248 | 7,949 R | 74.9% | 23.5% | 76.2% | 23.8% |
| 41,699 | LIMESTONE | 8,452 | 6,188 | 2,079 | 185 | 4,109 R | 73.2% | 24.6% | 74.9% | 25.1% |
| 12,897 | LOWNDES | 4,661 | 1,990 | 2,559 | 112 | 569 D | 42.7% | 54.9% | 43.7% | 56.3% |
| 24,841 | MACON | 5,845 | 1,931 | 3,636 | 278 | 1,705 D | 33.0% | 62.2% | 34.7% | 65.3% |
| 186,540 | MADISON | 52,984 | 38,899 | 13,108 | 977 | 25,791 R | 73.4% | 24.7% | 74.8% | 25.2% |
| 23,819 | MARENGO | 7,926 | 5,156 | 2,645 | 125 | 2,511 R | 65.1% | 33.4% | 66.1% | 33.9% |
| 23,788 | MARION | 6,942 | 5,927 | 986 | 29 | 4,941 R | 85.4% | 14.2% | 85.7% | 14.3% |
| 54,211 | MARSHALL | 16,238 | 12,090 | 3,894 | 254 | 8,196 R | 74.5% | 24.0% | 75.6% | 24.4% |
| 317,308 | MOBILE | 85,634 | 62,639 | 20,694 | 2,301 | 41,945 R | 73.1% | 24.2% | 75.2% | 24.8% |
| 20,883 | MONROE | 6,890 | 5,155 | 1,636 | 99 | 3,519 R | 74.8% | 23.7% | 75.9% | 24.1% |
| 167,790 | MONTGOMERY | 49,197 | 35,353 | 12,723 | 1,121 | 22,630 R | 71.9% | 25.9% | 73.5% | 26.5% |
| 77,306 | MORGAN | 23,553 | 18,100 | 5,004 | 449 | 13,096 R | 76.8% | 21.2% | 78.3% | 21.7% |
| 15,388 | PERRY | 5,699 | 2,800 | 2,718 | 181 | 82 R | 49.1% | 47.7% | 50.7% | 49.3% |
| 20,326 | PICKENS | 6,046 | 4,071 | 1,933 | 42 | 2,138 R | 67.3% | 32.0% | 67.8% | 32.2% |
| 25,038 | PIKE | 7,422 | 5,690 | 1,624 | 108 | 4,066 R | 76.7% | 21.9% | 77.8% | 22.2% |
| 18,331 | RANDOLPH | 5,892 | 4,427 | 1,330 | 135 | 3,097 R | 75.1% | 22.6% | 76.9% | 23.1% |
| 45,394 | RUSSELL | 9,043 | 6,034 | 2,644 | 365 | 3,390 R | 66.7% | 29.2% | 69.5% | 30.5% |
| 27,956 | ST. CLAIR | 8,710 | 6,952 | 1,538 | 220 | 5,414 R | 79.8% | 17.7% | 81.9% | 18.1% |
| 38,037 | SHELBY | 11,558 | 9,390 | 1,859 | 309 | 7,531 R | 81.2% | 16.1% | 83.5% | 16.5% |
| 16,974 | SUMTER | 5,461 | 2,686 | 2,737 | 38 | 51 D | 49.2% | 50.1% | 49.5% | 50.5% |

# ALABAMA

## PRESIDENT 1972

| 1970 Census Population | County | Total Vote | Republican | Democratic | Other | Rep.-Dem. Plurality | Percentage | | | |
|---|---|---|---|---|---|---|---|---|---|---|
| | | | | | | | Total Vote | | Major Vote | |
| | | | | | | | Rep. | Dem. | Rep. | Dem. |
| 65,280 | TALLADEGA | 17,455 | 12,763 | 4,567 | 125 | 8,196 R | 73.1% | 26.2% | 73.6% | 26.4% |
| 33,840 | TALLAPOOSA | 10,843 | 8,535 | 2,113 | 195 | 6,422 R | 78.7% | 19.5% | 80.2% | 19.8% |
| 116,029 | TUSCALOOSA | 30,179 | 21,172 | 8,272 | 735 | 12,900 R | 70.2% | 27.4% | 71.9% | 28.1% |
| 56,246 | WALKER | 18,507 | 14,581 | 3,724 | 202 | 10,857 R | 78.8% | 20.1% | 79.7% | 20.3% |
| 16,241 | WASHINGTON | 4,392 | 3,282 | 1,096 | 14 | 2,186 R | 74.7% | 25.0% | 75.0% | 25.0% |
| 16,303 | WILCOX | 5,945 | 2,641 | 3,254 | 50 | 613 D | 44.4% | 54.7% | 44.8% | 55.2% |
| 16,654 | WINSTON | 5,771 | 4,971 | 779 | 21 | 4,192 R | 86.1% | 13.5% | 86.5% | 13.5% |
| 3,444,165 | TOTAL | 1,006,111 | 728,701 | 256,923 | 20,487 | 471,778 R | 72.4% | 25.5% | 73.9% | 26.1% |

# ALABAMA

## PRESIDENT 1968

| 1960 Census Population | County | Total Vote | Republican | Democratic | AIP | Other | Plurality | Percentage Total Vote Rep. | Dem. | AIP |
|---|---|---|---|---|---|---|---|---|---|---|
| 18,739 | AUTAUGA | 7,782 | 606 | 1,553 | 5,523 | 100 | 3,970 A | 7.8% | 20.0% | 71.0% |
| 49,088 | BALDWIN | 18,404 | 2,154 | 1,821 | 14,167 | 262 | 12,013 A | 11.7% | 9.9% | 77.0% |
| 24,700 | BARBOUR | 7,946 | 386 | 1,898 | 5,491 | 171 | 3,593 A | 4.9% | 23.9% | 69.1% |
| 14,357 | BIBB | 4,673 | 263 | 652 | 3,746 | 12 | 3,094 A | 5.6% | 14.0% | 80.2% |
| 25,449 | BLOUNT | 9,086 | 2,013 | 331 | 6,536 | 206 | 4,523 A | 22.2% | 3.6% | 71.9% |
| 13,462 | BULLOCK | 4,347 | 190 | 1,964 | 2,161 | 32 | 197 A | 4.4% | 45.2% | 49.7% |
| 24,560 | BUTLER | 7,361 | 500 | 1,240 | 5,601 | 20 | 4,361 A | 6.8% | 16.8% | 76.1% |
| 95,878 | CALHOUN | 26,775 | 3,061 | 4,146 | 19,211 | 357 | 15,065 A | 11.4% | 15.5% | 71.7% |
| 37,828 | CHAMBERS | 10,636 | 1,082 | 1,358 | 7,885 | 311 | 6,527 A | 10.2% | 12.8% | 74.1% |
| 16,303 | CHEROKEE | 5,685 | 343 | 462 | 4,773 | 107 | 4,311 A | 6.0% | 8.1% | 84.0% |
| 25,693 | CHILTON | 8,902 | 1,602 | 566 | 6,611 | 123 | 5,009 A | 18.0% | 6.4% | 74.3% |
| 17,870 | CHOCTAW | 6,093 | 176 | 1,641 | 4,250 | 26 | 2,609 A | 2.9% | 26.9% | 69.8% |
| 25,738 | CLARKE | 8,626 | 488 | 1,717 | 6,168 | 253 | 4,451 A | 5.7% | 19.9% | 71.5% |
| 12,400 | CLAY | 5,044 | 706 | 256 | 4,048 | 34 | 3,342 A | 14.0% | 5.1% | 80.3% |
| 10,911 | CLEBURNE | 3,995 | 485 | 160 | 3,314 | 36 | 2,829 A | 12.1% | 4.0% | 83.0% |
| 30,583 | COFFEE | 10,766 | 682 | 1,071 | 8,885 | 128 | 7,814 A | 6.3% | 9.9% | 82.5% |
| 46,506 | COLBERT | 15,621 | 1,727 | 2,291 | 11,341 | 262 | 9,050 A | 11.1%. | 14.7% | 72.6% |
| 17,762 | CONECUH | 5,346 | 186 | 1,151 | 3,828 | 181 | 2,677 A | 3.5% | 21.5% | 71.6% |
| 10,726 | COOSA | 3,811 | 330 | 623 | 2,830 | 28 | 2,207 A | 8.7% | 16.3% | 74.3% |
| 35,631 | COVINGTON | 13,128 | 831 | 791 | 11,419 | 87 | 10,588 A | 6.3% | 6.0% | 87.0% |
| 14,909 | CRENSHAW | 5,480 | 209 | 726 | 4,513 | 32 | 3,787 A | 3.8% | 13.2% | 82.4% |
| 45,572 | CULLMAN | 17,265 | 4,964 | 1,115 | 11,063 | 123 | 6,099 A | 28.8% | 6.5% | 64.1% |
| 31,066 | DALE | 9,705 | 607 | 862 | 8,109 | 127 | 7,247 A | 6.3% | 8.9% | 83.6% |
| 56,667 | DALLAS | 16,636 | 1,246 | 6,516 | 8,798 | 76 | 2,282 A | 7.5% | 39.2% | 52.9% |
| 41,417 | DE KALB | 14,859 | 5,314 | 1,274 | 8,144 | 127 | 2,830 A | 35.8% | 8.6% | 54.8% |
| 30,524 | ELMORE | 11,812 | 801 | 1,745 | 9,038 | 228 | 7,293 A | 6.8% | 14.8% | 76.5% |
| 33,511 | ESCAMBIA | 10,765 | 680 | 1,492 | 8,474 | 119 | 6,982 A | 6.3% | 13.9% | 78.7% |
| 96,980 | ETOWAH | 31,186 | 4,351 | 4,613 | 21,416 | 806 | 16,803 A | 14.0% | 14.8% | 68.7% |
| 16,148 | FAYETTE | 6,238 | 827 | 676 | 4,683 | 52 | 3,856 A | 13.3% | 10.8% | 75.1% |
| 21,988 | FRANKLIN | 9,096 | 2,524 | 588 | 5,909 | 75 | 3,385 A | 27.7% | 6.5% | 65.0% |
| 22,310 | GENEVA | 8,581 | 284 | 380 | 7,871 | 46 | 7,491 A | 3.3% | 4.4% | 91.7% |
| 13,600 | GREENE | 3,969 | 180 | 2,229 | 1,555 | 5 | 674 D | 4.5% | 56.2% | 39.2% |
| 19,537 | HALE | 5,260 | 266 | 2,003 | 2,934 | 57 | 931 A | 5.1% | 38.1% | 55.8% |
| 15,286 | HENRY | 5,292 | 84 | 955 | 4,233 | 20 | 3,278 A | 1.6% | 18.0% | 80.0% |
| 50,718 | HOUSTON | 16,536 | 974 | 1,488 | 13,872 | 202 | 12,384 A | 5.9% | 9.0% | 83.9% |
| 36,681 | JACKSON | 10,908 | 1,191 | 1,022 | 8,504 | 191 | 7,313 A | 10.9% | 9.4% | 78.0% |
| 634,864 | JEFFERSON | 205,034 | 39,752 | 55,845 | 106,233 | 3,204 | 50,388 A | 19.4% | 27.2% | 51.8% |
| 14,271 | LAMAR | 5,925 | 364 | 302 | 5,229 | 30 | 4,865 A | 6.1% | 5.1% | 88.3% |
| 61,622 | LAUDERDALE | 18,883 | 2,952 | 2,166 | 13,467 | 298 | 10,515 A | 15.6% | 11.5% | 71.3% |
| 24,501 | LAWRENCE | 7,529 | 580 | 650 | 6,253 | 46 | 5,603 A | 7.7% | 8.6% | 83.1% |
| 49,754 | LEE | 13,136 | 2,366 | 2,803 | 7,721 | 246 | 4,918 A | 18.0% | 21.3% | 58.8% |
| 36,513 | LIMESTONE | 10,375 | 870 | 889 | 8,430 | 186 | 7,541 A | 8.4% | 8.6% | 81.3% |
| 15,417 | LOWNDES | 3,263 | 234 | 1,127 | 1,822 | 80 | 695 A | 7.2% | 34.5% | 55.8% |
| 26,717 | MACON | 6,381 | 257 | 4,450 | 1,619 | 55 | 2,831 D | 4.0% | 69.7% | 25.4% |
| 117,348 | MADISON | 51,953 | 13,213 | 8,004 | 29,823 | 913 | 16,610 A | 25.4% | 15.4% | 57.4% |
| 27,098 | MARENGO | 9,154 | 457 | 3,479 | 5,185 | 33 | 1,706 A | 5.0% | 38.0% | 56.6% |
| 21,837 | MARION | 8,403 | 1,492 | 365 | 6,415 | 131 | 4,923 A | 17.8% | 4.3% | 76.3% |
| 48,018 | MARSHALL | 16,680 | 2,725 | 955 | 12,742 | 258 | 10,017 A | 16.3% | 5.7% | 76.4% |
| 314,301 | MOBILE | 91,936 | 10,509 | 18,615 | 61,673 | 1,139 | 43,058 A | 11.4% | 20.2% | 67.1% |
| 22,372 | MONROE | 7,324 | 375 | 1,673 | 5,217 | 59 | 3,544 A | 5.1% | 22.8% | 71.2% |
| 169,210 | MONTGOMERY | 46,531 | 6,746 | 12,088 | 27,202 | 495 | 15,114 A | 14.5% | 26.0% | 58.5% |
| 60,454 | MORGAN | 22,277 | 3,043 | 1,878 | 16,841 | 515 | 13,798 A | 13.7% | 8.4% | 75.6% |
| 17,358 | PERRY | 5,553 | 308 | 2,457 | 2,768 | 20 | 311 A | 5.5% | 44.2% | 49.8% |
| 21,882 | PICKENS | 6,328 | 321 | 1,434 | 4,549 | 24 | 3,115 A | 5.1% | 22.7% | 71.9% |
| 25,987 | PIKE | 8,341 | 658 | 1,565 | 6,038 | 80 | 4,473 A | 7.9% | 18.8% | 72.4% |
| 19,477 | RANDOLPH | 6,804 | 839 | 666 | 5,103 | 196 | 4,264 A | 12.3% | 9.8% | 75.0% |
| 46,351 | RUSSELL | 11,245 | 704 | 2,707 | 7,584 | 250 | 4,877 A | 6.3% | 24.1% | 67.4% |
| 25,388 | ST. CLAIR | 9,697 | 1,635 | 869 | 7,050 | 143 | 5,415 A | 16.9% | 9.0% | 72.7% |
| 32,132 | SHELBY | 10,770 | 1,706 | 1,105 | 7,736 | 223 | 6,030 A | 15.8% | 10.3% | 71.8% |
| 20,041 | SUMTER | 4,807 | 303 | 2,336 | 2,158 | 10 | 178 D | 6.3% | 48.6% | 44.9% |

# ALABAMA

## PRESIDENT 1968

| 1960 Census Population | County | Total Vote | Republican | Democratic | AIP | Other | Plurality | Percentage Total Vote | | |
|---|---|---|---|---|---|---|---|---|---|---|
| | | | | | | | | Rep. | Dem. | AIP |
| 65,495 | TALLADEGA | 18,756 | 1,935 | 3,099 | 13,505 | 217 | 10,406 A | 10.3% | 16.5% | 72.0% |
| 35,007 | TALLAPOOSA | 11,821 | 1,205 | 1,331 | 9,043 | 242 | 7,712 A | 10.2% | 11.3% | 76.5% |
| 109,047 | TUSCALOOSA | 28,371 | 3,822 | 5,556 | 18,611 | 382 | 13,055 A | 13.5% | 19.6% | 65.6% |
| 54,211 | WALKER | 19,385 | 2,628 | 1,971 | 14,416 | 370 | 11,788 A | 13.6% | 10.2% | 74.4% |
| 15,372 | WASHINGTON | 5,683 | 200 | 902 | 4,545 | 36 | 3,643 A | 3.5% | 15.9% | 80.0% |
| 18,739 | WILCOX | 4,435 | 237 | 1,658 | 2,511 | 29 | 853 A | 5.3% | 37.4% | 56.6% |
| 14,858 | WINSTON | 5,527 | 2,174 | 258 | 3,032 | 63 | 858 A | 39.3% | 4.7% | 54.9% |
| 3,266,740 | TOTAL | 1,049,922 | 146,923 | 196,579 | 691,425 | 14,995 | 494,846 A | 14.0% | 18.7% | 65.9% |

# ALABAMA

## PRESIDENT 1964

| 1960 Census Population | County | Total Vote | Republican | Democratic | Unpledged | Other | Plurality | Percentage Total Vote | | |
|---|---|---|---|---|---|---|---|---|---|---|
| | | | | | | | | Rep. | Dem. | Unp. |
| 18,739 | AUTAUGA | 3,460 | 2,969 | | 490 | 1 | 2,479 R | 85.8% | | 14.2% |
| 49,088 | BALDWIN | 13,400 | 10,870 | | 2,530 | | 8,340 R | 81.1% | | 18.9% |
| 24,700 | BARBOUR | 4,831 | 3,853 | | 978 | | 2,875 R | 79.8% | | 20.2% |
| 14,357 | BIBB | 3,126 | 2,623 | | 503 | | 2,120 R | 83.9% | | 16.1% |
| 25,449 | BLOUNT | 6,869 | 4,442 | | 2,427 | | 2,015 R | 64.7% | | 35.3% |
| 13,462 | BULLOCK | 2,630 | 1,516 | | 1,114 | | 402 R | 57.6% | | 42.4% |
| 24,560 | BUTLER | 4,975 | 4,002 | | 973 | | 3,029 R | 80.4% | | 19.6% |
| 95,878 | CALHOUN | 16,845 | 10,635 | | 6,210 | | 4,425 R | 63.1% | | 36.9% |
| 37,828 | CHAMBERS | 7,187 | 4,630 | | 2,557 | | 2,073 R | 64.4% | | 35.6% |
| 16,303 | CHEROKEE | 3,809 | 1,893 | | 1,916 | | 23 U | 49.7% | | 50.3% |
| 25,693 | CHILTON | 6,847 | 5,202 | | 1,645 | | 3,557 R | 76.0% | | 24.0% |
| 17,870 | CHOCTAW | 2,910 | 2,497 | | 413 | | 2,084 R | 85.8% | | 14.2% |
| 25,738 | CLARKE | 5,384 | 4,460 | | 924 | | 3,536 R | 82.8% | | 17.2% |
| 12,400 | CLAY | 4,014 | 2,815 | | 1,199 | | 1,616 R | 70.1% | | 29.9% |
| 10,911 | CLEBURNE | 2,828 | 2,156 | | 672 | | 1,484 R | 76.2% | | 23.8% |
| 30,583 | COFFEE | 6,123 | 4,910 | | 1,213 | | 3,697 R | 80.2% | | 19.8% |
| 46,506 | COLBERT | 10,840 | 5,267 | | 5,573 | | 306 U | 48.6% | | 51.4% |
| 17,762 | CONECUH | 3,421 | 2,782 | | 639 | | 2,143 R | 81.3% | | 18.7% |
| 10,726 | COOSA | 2,718 | 1,978 | | 740 | | 1,238 R | 72.8% | | 27.2% |
| 35,631 | COVINGTON | 9,175 | 7,554 | | 1,621 | | 5,933 R | 82.3% | | 17.7% |
| 14,909 | CRENSHAW | 3,824 | 3,008 | | 816 | | 2,192 R | 78.7% | | 21.3% |
| 45,572 | CULLMAN | 12,262 | 7,152 | | 5,110 | | 2,042 R | 58.3% | | 41.7% |
| 31,066 | DALE | 5,933 | 4,970 | | 963 | | 4,007 R | 83.8% | | 16.2% |
| 56,667 | DALLAS | 6,607 | 5,888 | | 719 | | 5,169 R | 89.1% | | 10.9% |
| 41,417 | DE KALB | 11,694 | 6,746 | | 4,948 | | 1,798 R | 57.7% | | 42.3% |
| 30,524 | ELMORE | 7,596 | 6,363 | | 1,233 | | 5,130 R | 83.8% | | 16.2% |
| 33,511 | ESCAMBIA | 7,551 | 5,623 | | 1,928 | | 3,695 R | 74.5% | | 25.5% |
| 96,980 | ETOWAH | 21,833 | 12,894 | | 8,939 | | 3,955 R | 59.1% | | 40.9% |
| 16,148 | FAYETTE | 4,490 | 3,203 | | 1,287 | | 1,916 R | 71.3% | | 28.7% |
| 21,988 | FRANKLIN | 7,135 | 4,025 | | 3,110 | | 915 R | 56.4% | | 43.6% |
| 22,310 | GENEVA | 5,576 | 4,502 | | 1,074 | | 3,428 R | 80.7% | | 19.3% |
| 13,600 | GREENE | 1,711 | 1,124 | | 587 | | 537 R | 65.7% | | 34.3% |
| 19,537 | HALE | 2,446 | 1,898 | | 548 | | 1,350 R | 77.6% | | 22.4% |
| 15,286 | HENRY | 3,485 | 2,896 | | 589 | | 2,307 R | 83.1% | | 16.9% |
| 50,718 | HOUSTON | 11,774 | 10,353 | | 1,421 | | 8,932 R | 87.9% | | 12.1% |
| 36,681 | JACKSON | 5,875 | 2,730 | | 3,145 | | 415 U | 46.5% | | 53.5% |
| 634,864 | JEFFERSON | 138,838 | 100,756 | | 38,082 | | 62,674 R | 72.6% | | 27.4% |
| 14,271 | LAMAR | 3,775 | 2,734 | | 1,041 | | 1,693 R | 72.4% | | 27.6% |
| 61,622 | LAUDERDALE | 12,571 | 5,978 | | 6,593 | | 615 U | 47.6% | | 52.4% |
| 24,501 | LAWRENCE | 3,617 | 1,809 | | 1,808 | | 1 R | 50.0% | | 50.0% |
| 49,754 | LEE | 7,516 | 5,914 | | 1,602 | | 4,312 R | 78.7% | | 21.3% |
| 36,513 | LIMESTONE | 5,404 | 2,377 | | 3,027 | | 650 U | 44.0% | | 56.0% |
| 15,417 | LOWNDES | 1,858 | 1,548 | | 310 | | 1,238 R | 83.3% | | 16.7% |
| 26,717 | MACON | 4,831 | 1,858 | | 2,973 | | 1,115 U | 38.5% | | 61.5% |
| 117,348 | MADISON | 27,496 | 14,279 | | 13,217 | | 1,062 R | 51.9% | | 48.1% |
| 27,098 | MARENGO | 4,466 | 3,677 | | 789 | | 2,888 R | 82.3% | | 17.7% |
| 21,837 | MARION | 5,713 | 3,966 | | 1,747 | | 2,219 R | 69.4% | | 30.6% |
| 48,018 | MARSHALL | 10,140 | 5,712 | | 4,428 | | 1,284 R | 56.3% | | 43.7% |
| 314,301 | MOBILE | 69,981 | 49,493 | | 20,488 | | 29,005 R | 70.7% | | 29.3% |
| 22,372 | MONROE | 4,756 | 3,870 | | 886 | | 2,984 R | 81.4% | | 18.6% |
| 169,210 | MONTGOMERY | 30,497 | 23,015 | | 7,482 | | 15,533 R | 75.5% | | 24.5% |
| 60,454 | MORGAN | 12,381 | 7,013 | | 5,368 | | 1,645 R | 56.6% | | 43.4% |
| 17,358 | PERRY | 2,566 | 2,046 | | 520 | | 1,526 R | 79.7% | | 20.3% |
| 21,882 | PICKENS | 4,162 | 3,416 | | 746 | | 2,670 R | 82.1% | | 17.9% |
| 25,987 | PIKE | 5,176 | 4,373 | | 803 | | 3,570 R | 84.5% | | 15.5% |
| 19,477 | RANDOLPH | 4,991 | 3,127 | | 1,864 | | 1,263 R | 62.7% | | 37.3% |
| 46,351 | RUSSELL | 6,414 | 4,877 | | 1,537 | | 3,340 R | 76.0% | | 24.0% |
| 25,388 | ST. CLAIR | 6,802 | 4,813 | | 1,989 | | 2,824 R | 70.8% | | 29.2% |
| 32,132 | SHELBY | 7,980 | 6,037 | | 1,943 | | 4,094 R | 75.7% | | 24.3% |
| 20,041 | SUMTER | 2,058 | 1,653 | | 405 | | 1,248 R | 80.3% | | 19.7% |

# ALABAMA

## PRESIDENT 1964

| 1960 Census Population | County | Total Vote | Republican | Democratic | Unpledged | Other | Plurality | Percentage Total Vote | | |
|---|---|---|---|---|---|---|---|---|---|---|
| | | | | | | | | Rep. | Dem. | Unp. |
| 65,495 | TALLADEGA | 12,658 | 8,946 | | 3,712 | | 5,234 R | 70.7% | | 29.3% |
| 35,007 | TALLAPOOSA | 7,263 | 5,530 | | 1,733 | | 3,797 R | 76.1% | | 23.9% |
| 109,047 | TUSCALOOSA | 19,263 | 13,227 | | 6,036 | | 7,191 R | 68.7% | | 31.3% |
| 54,211 | WALKER | 14,692 | 8,582 | | 6,110 | | 2,472 R | 58.4% | | 41.6% |
| 15,372 | WASHINGTON | 3,994 | 2,803 | | 1,191 | | 1,612 R | 70.2% | | 29.8% |
| 18,739 | WILCOX | 1,946 | 1,789 | | 157 | | 1,632 R | 91.9% | | 8.1% |
| 14,858 | WINSTON | 4,829 | 3,438 | | 1,391 | | 2,047 R | 71.2% | | 28.8% |
| 3,266,740 | TOTAL | 689,818 | 479,085 | | 210,732 | 1 | 268,352 R | 69.5% | | 30.5% |

# ALABAMA

## PRESIDENT 1960

| 1960 Census Population | County | Total Vote | Republican | Democratic | Other | Rep.-Dem. Plurality | Percentage | | | |
|---|---|---|---|---|---|---|---|---|---|---|
| | | | | | | | Total Vote | | Major Vote | |
| | | | | | | | Rep. | Dem. | Rep. | Dem. |
| 18,739 | AUTAUGA | 2,651 | 1,149 | 1,413 | 89 | 264 D | 43.3% | 53.3% | 44.8% | 55.2% |
| 49,088 | BALDWIN | 10,728 | 4,812 | 5,729 | 187 | 917 D | 44.9% | 53.4% | 45.7% | 54.3% |
| 24,700 | BARBOUR | 3,493 | 1,166 | 2,290 | 37 | 1,124 D | 33.4% | 65.6% | 33.7% | 66.3% |
| 14,357 | BIBB | 2,757 | 1,052 | 1,701 | 4 | 649 D | 38.2% | 61.7% | 38.2% | 61.8% |
| 25,449 | BLOUNT | 5,990 | 2,557 | 3,414 | 19 | 857 D | 42.7% | 57.0% | 42.8% | 57.2% |
| 13,462 | BULLOCK | 1,256 | 412 | 838 | 6 | 426 D | 32.8% | 66.7% | 33.0% | 67.0% |
| 24,560 | BUTLER | 4,194 | 1,231 | 2,943 | 20 | 1,712 D | 29.4% | 70.2% | 29.5% | 70.5% |
| 95,878 | CALHOUN | 14,658 | 4,821 | 9,619 | 218 | 4,798 D | 32.9% | 65.6% | 33.4% | 66.6% |
| 37,828 | CHAMBERS | 7,154 | 1,865 | 5,172 | 117 | 3,307 D | 26.1% | 72.3% | 26.5% | 73.5% |
| 16,303 | CHEROKEE | 3,987 | 872 | 3,106 | 9 | 2,234 D | 21.9% | 77.9% | 21.9% | 78.1% |
| 25,693 | CHILTON | 5,041 | 3,201 | 1,821 | 19 | 1,380 R | 63.5% | 36.1% | 63.7% | 36.3% |
| 17,870 | CHOCTAW | 2,148 | 612 | 1,439 | 97 | 827 D | 28.5% | 67.0% | 29.8% | 70.2% |
| 25,738 | CLARKE | 4,259 | 2,016 | 2,151 | 92 | 135 D | 47.3% | 50.5% | 48.4% | 51.6% |
| 12,400 | CLAY | 3,311 | 1,548 | 1,740 | 23 | 192 D | 46.8% | 52.6% | 47.1% | 52.9% |
| 10,911 | CLEBURNE | 2,530 | 1,008 | 1,510 | 12 | 502 D | 39.8% | 59.7% | 40.0% | 60.0% |
| 30,583 | COFFEE | 5,884 | 1,381 | 4,480 | 23 | 3,099 D | 23.5% | 76.1% | 23.6% | 76.4% |
| 46,506 | COLBERT | 10,403 | 2,815 | 7,377 | 211 | 4,562 D | 27.1% | 70.9% | 27.6% | 72.4% |
| 17,762 | CONECUH | 2,667 | 650 | 1,917 | 100 | 1,267 D | 24.4% | 71.9% | 25.3% | 74.7% |
| 10,726 | COOSA | 2,584 | 1,073 | 1,492 | 19 | 419 D | 41.5% | 57.7% | 41.8% | 58.2% |
| 35,631 | COVINGTON | 7,775 | 2,047 | 5,686 | 42 | 3,639 D | 26.3% | 73.1% | 26.5% | 73.5% |
| 14,909 | CRENSHAW | 3,501 | 573 | 2,921 | 7 | 2,348 D | 16.4% | 83.4% | 16.4% | 83.6% |
| 45,572 | CULLMAN | 10,616 | 4,248 | 6,346 | 22 | 2,098 D | 40.0% | 59.8% | 40.1% | 59.9% |
| 31,066 | DALE | 4,351 | 1,634 | 2,663 | 54 | 1,029 D | 37.6% | 61.2% | 38.0% | 62.0% |
| 56,667 | DALLAS | 5,561 | 2,872 | 2,455 | 234 | 417 R | 51.6% | 44.1% | 53.9% | 46.1% |
| 41,417 | DE KALB | 11,464 | 5,585 | 5,849 | 30 | 264 D | 48.7% | 51.0% | 48.8% | 51.2% |
| 30,524 | ELMORE | 5,522 | 1,919 | 3,524 | 79 | 1,605 D | 34.8% | 63.8% | 35.3% | 64.7% |
| 33,511 | ESCAMBIA | 6,096 | 1,810 | 4,173 | 113 | 2,363 D | 29.7% | 68.5% | 30.3% | 69.7% |
| 96,980 | ETOWAH | 21,819 | 7,128 | 14,316 | 375 | 7,188 D | 32.7% | 65.6% | 33.2% | 66.8% |
| 16,148 | FAYETTE | 4,218 | 1,923 | 2,278 | 17 | 355 D | 45.6% | 54.0% | 45.8% | 54.2% |
| 21,988 | FRANKLIN | 7,551 | 4,069 | 3,443 | 39 | 626 R | 53.9% | 45.6% | 54.2% | 45.8% |
| 22,310 | GENEVA | 4,670 | 1,502 | 3,157 | 11 | 1,655 D | 32.2% | 67.6% | 32.2% | 67.8% |
| 13,600 | GREENE | 1,155 | 381 | 753 | 21 | 372 D | 33.0% | 65.2% | 33.6% | 66.4% |
| 19,537 | HALE | 2,123 | 741 | 1,369 | 13 | 628 D | 34.9% | 64.5% | 35.1% | 64.9% |
| 15,286 | HENRY | 2,745 | 588 | 2,140 | 17 | 1,552 D | 21.4% | 78.0% | 21.6% | 78.4% |
| 50,718 | HOUSTON | 8,100 | 4,055 | 3,960 | 85 | 95 R | 50.1% | 48.9% | 50.6% | 49.4% |
| 36,681 | JACKSON | 6,871 | 2,036 | 4,789 | 46 | 2,753 D | 29.6% | 69.7% | 29.8% | 70.2% |
| 634,864 | JEFFERSON | 106,758 | 60,004 | 44,681 | 2,073 | 15,323 R | 56.2% | 41.9% | 57.3% | 42.7% |
| 14,271 | LAMAR | 3,546 | 964 | 2,518 | 64 | 1,554 D | 27.2% | 71.0% | 27.7% | 72.3% |
| 61,622 | LAUDERDALE | 12,347 | 3,570 | 8,533 | 244 | 4,963 D | 28.9% | 69.1% | 29.5% | 70.5% |
| 24,501 | LAWRENCE | 4,315 | 1,365 | 2,937 | 13 | 1,572 D | 31.6% | 68.1% | 31.7% | 68.3% |
| 49,754 | LEE | 6,150 | 2,301 | 3,795 | 54 | 1,494 D | 37.4% | 61.7% | 37.7% | 62.3% |
| 36,513 | LIMESTONE | 5,279 | 991 | 4,277 | 11 | 3,286 D | 18.8% | 81.0% | 18.8% | 81.2% |
| 15,417 | LOWNDES | 1,329 | 432 | 884 | 13 | 452 D | 32.5% | 66.5% | 32.8% | 67.2% |
| 26,717 | MACON | 2,223 | 877 | 1,319 | 27 | 442 D | 39.5% | 59.3% | 39.9% | 60.1% |
| 117,348 | MADISON | 16,506 | 5,299 | 11,004 | 203 | 5,705 D | 32.1% | 66.7% | 32.5% | 67.5% |
| 27,098 | MARENGO | 3,300 | 1,235 | 1,915 | 150 | 680 D | 37.4% | 58.0% | 39.2% | 60.8% |
| 21,837 | MARION | 6,068 | 2,938 | 3,103 | 27 | 165 D | 48.4% | 51.1% | 48.6% | 51.4% |
| 48,018 | MARSHALL | 10,023 | 3,398 | 6,606 | 19 | 3,208 D | 33.9% | 65.9% | 34.0% | 66.0% |
| 314,301 | MOBILE | 55,267 | 24,608 | 29,221 | 1,438 | 4,613 D | 44.5% | 52.9% | 45.7% | 54.3% |
| 22,372 | MONROE | 3,306 | 989 | 2,279 | 38 | 1,290 D | 29.9% | 68.9% | 30.3% | 69.7% |
| 169,210 | MONTGOMERY | 22,311 | 11,778 | 10,159 | 374 | 1,619 R | 52.8% | 45.5% | 53.7% | 46.3% |
| 60,454 | MORGAN | 12,183 | 4,357 | 7,776 | 50 | 3,419 D | 35.8% | 63.8% | 35.9% | 64.1% |
| 17,358 | PERRY | 1,901 | 744 | 1,079 | 78 | 335 D | 39.1% | 56.8% | 40.8% | 59.2% |
| 21,882 | PICKENS | 3,250 | 1,277 | 1,926 | 47 | 649 D | 39.3% | 59.3% | 39.9% | 60.1% |
| 25,987 | PIKE | 4,534 | 1,006 | 3,503 | 25 | 2,497 D | 22.2% | 77.3% | 22.3% | 77.7% |
| 19,477 | RANDOLPH | 4,924 | 1,697 | 3,184 | 43 | 1,487 D | 34.5% | 64.7% | 34.8% | 65.2% |
| 46,351 | RUSSELL | 5,325 | 1,770 | 3,494 | 61 | 1,724 D | 33.2% | 65.6% | 33.6% | 66.4% |
| 25,388 | ST. CLAIR | 5,676 | 2,589 | 3,062 | 25 | 473 D | 45.6% | 53.9% | 45.8% | 54.2% |
| 32,132 | SHELBY | 6,470 | 3,157 | 3,252 | 61 | 95 D | 48.8% | 50.3% | 49.3% | 50.7% |
| 20,041 | SUMTER | 1,685 | 623 | 986 | 76 | 363 D | 37.0% | 58.5% | 38.7% | 61.3% |

# ALABAMA

## PRESIDENT 1960

| 1960 Census Population | County | Total Vote | Republican | Democratic | Other | Rep.-Dem. Plurality | Percentage | | | |
|---|---|---|---|---|---|---|---|---|---|---|
| | | | | | | | Total Vote | | Major Vote | |
| | | | | | | | Rep. | Dem. | Rep. | Dem. |
| 65,495 | TALLADEGA | 10,554 | 4,723 | 5,732 | 99 | 1,009 D | 44.8% | 54.3% | 45.2% | 54.8% |
| 35,007 | TALLAPOOSA | 7,692 | 2,150 | 5,494 | 48 | 3,344 D | 28.0% | 71.4% | 28.1% | 71.9% |
| 109,047 | TUSCALOOSA | 14,190 | 5,598 | 8,348 | 244 | 2,750 D | 39.5% | 58.8% | 40.1% | 59.9% |
| 54,211 | WALKER | 13,651 | 5,463 | 8,188 | | 2,725 D | 40.0% | 60.0% | 40.0% | 60.0% |
| 15,372 | WASHINGTON | 2,940 | 792 | 2,079 | 69 | 1,287 D | 26.9% | 70.7% | 27.6% | 72.4% |
| 18,739 | WILCOX | 1,581 | 513 | 1,061 | 7 | 548 D | 32.4% | 67.1% | 32.6% | 67.4% |
| 14,858 | WINSTON | 5,108 | 3,421 | 1,681 | 6 | 1,740 R | 67.0% | 32.9% | 67.1% | 32.9% |
| 3,266,740 | TOTAL | 570,225 | 237,981 | 324,050 | 8,194 | 86,069 D | 41.7% | 56.8% | 42.3% | 57.7% |

# ALABAMA

## ELECTION NOTES

**2004**  Other vote was 6,701 Independent (Ralph Nader); 3,529 Independent (Michael Badnarik); 1,994 Independent (Michael Peroutka); 898 scattered write-in.

**2000**  Other vote was 6,351 Independent (Buchanan); 5,893 Libertarian (Browne); 775 Independent (Phillips); 447 Independent (Hagelin); 699 scattered write-in. (Nader was also listed on the ballot as Independent.)

**1996**  Other vote was 5,290 Libertarian (Browne); 2,365 Independent (Phillips); 1,697 Natural Law (Hagelin); 1,123 scattered write-ins; 516 Independent (Harris).

**1992**  Other vote was 5,737 Marrou (Libertarian); 2,161 Fulani (Independent); 831 Warren (Independent); 641 LaRouche (Independent); 495 Hagelin (Independent); 723 scattered write-in. The Total of the other vote column includes the 723 write-in votes not available by county.

**1988**  Other vote was 8,460 Paul (Libertarian); 3,311 Fulani (Independent); 656 Warren (Independent); 461 Winn (Independent); 506 scattered write-in.

**1984**  Other vote was 9,504 Bergland (Libertarian); 4,671 Hall (Independent); 1,401 Richards (Independent); 730 Mason (Independent); 659 Serrette (Independent).

**1980**  Other vote was 16,481 Anderson (Independent); 15,010 Rarick (Conservative); 13,318 Clark (Libertarian); 1,743 Bubar (Statesman); 1,629 Hall (Communist); 1,303 DeBerry (Socialist Workers); 1,006 McReynolds (Socialist); 517 Commoner (Citizens).

**1976**  Other vote was 9,198 Maddox (Conservative); 6,669 Bubar (Prohibition); 1,954 Hall (Independent); 1,481 MacBride (Libertarian); 99 McCarthy (write-in); 70 Anderson (write-in); 1 Camejo (write-in); 1 LaRouche (write-in); 137 scattered write-in. The state-wide total for the other vote column includes these 308 write-in votes not reported by county.

**1972**  Other vote was 11,928 Schmitz (Conservative); 8,559 Munn (Prohibition). The Democratic candidate was also the nominee of the National Democratic Party of Alabama and 37,815 of his votes were received as the NDPA candidate. In Fayette county the votes for the Conservative and Prohibition candidates were omitted from the original canvass, but are included here.

**1968**  Other vote was 10,960 American Independent of Alabama (favorable to Wallace, but not recognized by him); 4,022 Munn (Prohibition); 13 scattered write-in. Of the six Presidential elector slates, the regular Democratic ticket was pledged to Wallace and two separate groups of electors were pledged to Humphrey. These two separate tickets were the Alabama Independent Democratic (142,435) and the National Democratic Party of Alabama (54,144) and the vote listed as Democratic for President in the county-by-county table is the combined vote of these two elector tickets.

**1964**  Other vote was 210,273 Unpledged Democratic; 1 scattered write-in.

**1960**  Other vote was 4,367 Faubus (National States Rights); 2,106 Decker (Prohibition); 1,485 King (Independent Afro-American); 236 scattered write-in. It should be noted that six of the eleven candidates on the Democratic elector list were "unpledged"—that is, they had been chosen without any advance commitment to support the Democratic national candidates. In the voting in the Electoral College in December 1960, these six voted for Senator Harry Flood Byrd for President.

# ALASKA

## POPULAR VOTE FOR PRESIDENT 1960 TO 2004

| Year | Total Vote | Republican | | Democratic | | Other Vote | Plurality | Percentage | | | |
|------|-----------|------|-----------|------|-----------|------------|-----------|------------|------|------------|------|
| | | | | | | | | Total Vote | | Major Vote | |
| | | Vote | Candidate | Vote | Candidate | | | Rep. | Dem. | Rep. | Dem. |
| 2004 | 312,598 | 190,889 | Bush, George W. | 111,025 | Kerry, John | 10,684 | 79,864 R | 61.1% | 35.5% | 63.2% | 36.8% |
| 2000 ** | 285,560 | 167,398 | Bush, George W. | 79,004 | Gore, Al | 39,158 | 88,394 R | 58.6% | 27.7% | 67.9% | 32.1% |
| 1996 ** | 241,620 | 122,746 | Dole, Bob | 80,380 | Clinton, Bill | 38,494 | 42,366 R | 50.8% | 33.3% | 60.4% | 39.6% |
| 1992 ** | 258,506 | 102,000 | Bush, George | 78,294 | Clinton, Bill | 78,212 | 23,706 R | 39.5% | 30.3% | 56.6% | 43.4% |
| 1988 | 200,116 | 119,251 | Bush, George | 72,584 | Dukakis, Michael S. | 8,281 | 46,667 R | 59.6% | 36.3% | 62.2% | 37.8% |
| 1984 | 207,605 | 138,377 | Reagan, Ronald | 62,007 | Mondale, Walter F. | 7,221 | 76,370 R | 66.7% | 29.9% | 69.1% | 30.9% |
| 1980 ** | 158,445 | 86,112 | Reagan, Ronald | 41,842 | Carter, Jimmy | 30,491 | 44,270 R | 54.3% | 26.4% | 67.3% | 32.7% |
| 1976 | 123,574 | 71,555 | Ford, Gerald R. | 44,058 | Carter, Jimmy | 7,961 | 27,497 R | 57.9% | 35.7% | 61.9% | 38.1% |
| 1972 | 95,219 | 55,349 | Nixon, Richard M. | 32,967 | McGovern, George S. | 6,903 | 22,382 R | 58.1% | 34.6% | 62.7% | 37.3% |
| 1968 | 83,035 | 37,600 | Nixon, Richard M. | 35,411 | Humphrey, Hubert H. | 10,024 | 2,189 R | 45.3% | 42.6% | 51.5% | 48.5% |
| 1964 | 67,259 | 22,930 | Goldwater, Barry M. | 44,329 | Johnson, Lyndon B. | | 21,399 D | 34.1% | 65.9% | 34.1% | 65.9% |
| 1960 | 60,762 | 30,953 | Nixon, Richard M. | 29,809 | Kennedy, John F. | | 1,144 R | 50.9% | 49.1% | 50.9% | 49.1% |

In 2000 the other vote column includes 28,747 votes cast for Green (Nader). In 1996 the other vote column includes 26,333 votes cast for Perot. In 1992 the other vote column includes 73,481 votes for Perot. In 1980 the other column includes 11,155 votes for Independent (Anderson). Alaska was formally admitted as a state in January 1959.

## ELECTORAL COLLEGE VOTE 1960 TO 2004

| Year | Total | Republican | Democratic | Other |
|------|-------|------------|------------|-------|
| 2004 | 3 | 3 | | |
| 2000 | 3 | 3 | | |
| 1996 | 3 | 3 | | |
| 1992 | 3 | 3 | | |
| 1988 | 3 | 3 | | |
| 1984 | 3 | 3 | | |
| 1980 | 3 | 3 | | |
| 1976 | 3 | 3 | | |
| 1972 | 3 | 3 | | |
| 1968 | 3 | 3 | | |
| 1964 | 3 | | 3 | |
| 1960 | 3 | 3 | | |

# ALASKA
## 2001–

40

39

Nome

9-11

Fairbanks

8

6

12

15

13-14

16

33

32

34

17-31

Anchorage

Bethel

38

37

36

35

5

4

3

Juneau

Sitka

2

Kodiak

1

Ketchikan

75

# ALASKA
## 1992–2000

76

# ALASKA

## 1984-1988

# ALASKA

## 1976-1980

# ALASKA

**1972**

# ALASKA

## 1964-1968

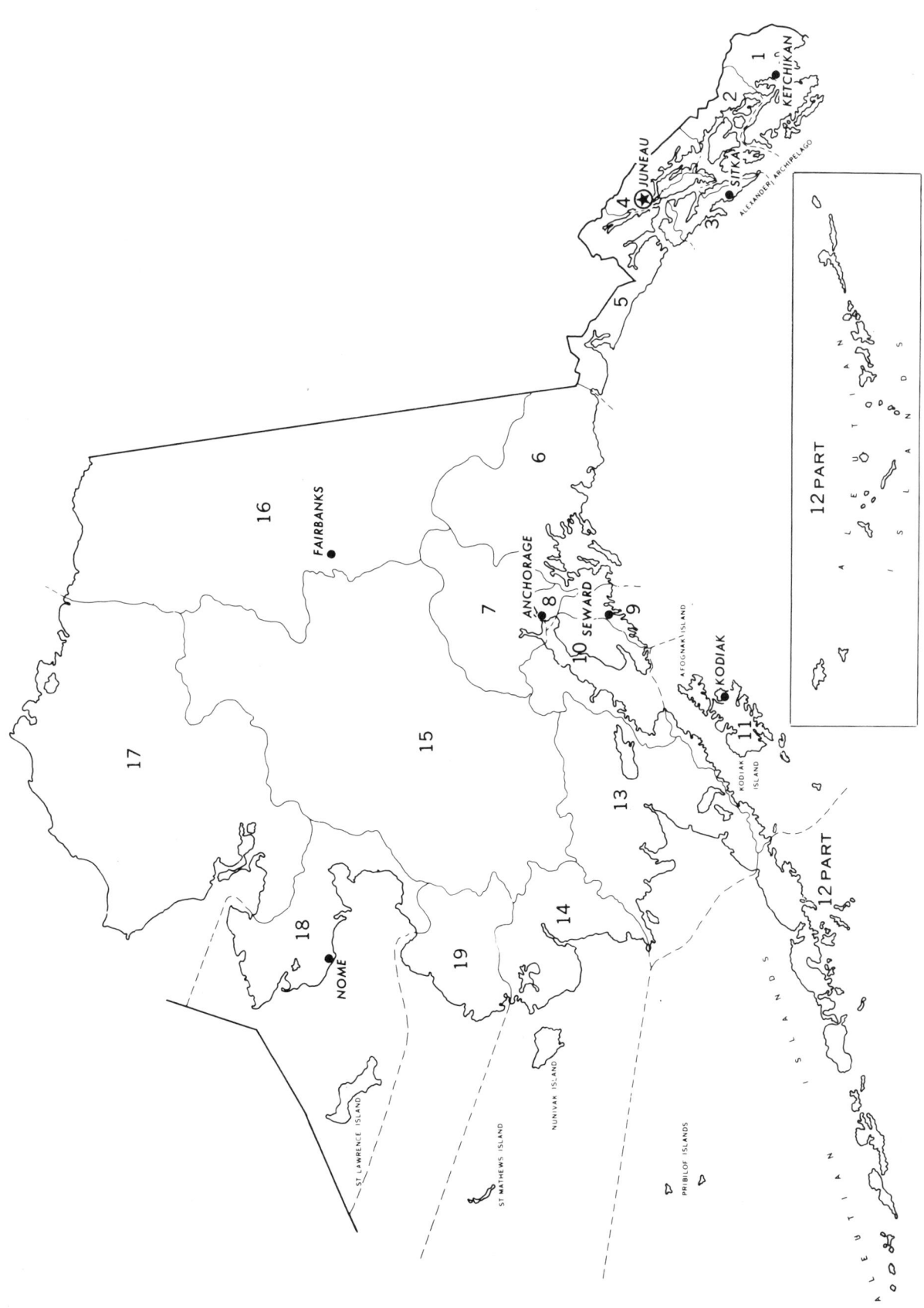

KETCHIKAN

1

2

SITKA

3

ALEXANDER ARCHIPELAGO

JUNEAU

4

5

6

FAIRBANKS

16

ANCHORAGE

7

8

SEWARD

9

10

AFOGNAK ISLAND

KODIAK

11

KODIAK ISLAND

12 PART

ALEUTIAN ISLANDS

15

13

14

17

18

NOME

19

ST LAWRENCE ISLAND

ST MATHEWS ISLAND

NUNIVAK ISLAND

PRIBILOF ISLANDS

12 PART

ALEUTIAN ISLANDS

80

# ALASKA

## 1960

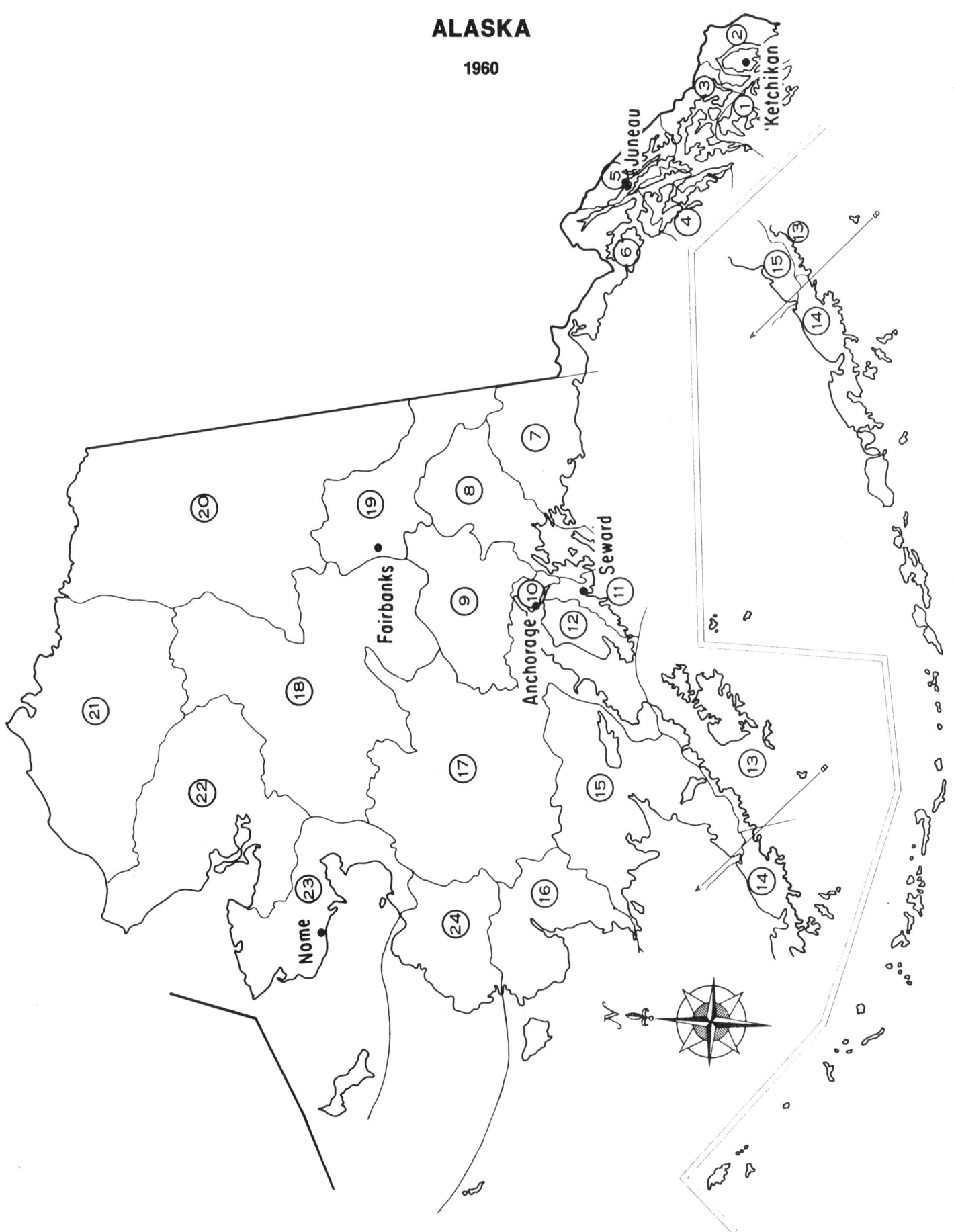

# ALASKA

## PRESIDENT 2004

| 2000 Census Population | District | Total Vote | Republican | Democratic | Other | Rep.-Dem. Plurality | Percentage | | | |
|---|---|---|---|---|---|---|---|---|---|---|
| | | | | | | | Total Vote | | Major Vote | |
| | | | | | | | Rep. | Dem. | Rep. | Dem. |
| 15,031 | DISTRICT 1 | 4,988 | 3,389 | 1,399 | 200 | 1,990 R | 67.9% | 28.0% | 70.8% | 29.2% |
| 14,991 | DISTRICT 2 | 5,878 | 3,214 | 2,403 | 261 | 811 R | 54.7% | 40.9% | 57.2% | 42.8% |
| 15,203 | DISTRICT 3 | 5,874 | 2,258 | 3,429 | 187 | 1,171 D | 38.4% | 58.4% | 39.7% | 60.3% |
| 15,508 | DISTRICT 4 | 5,811 | 3,263 | 2,353 | 195 | 910 R | 56.2% | 40.5% | 58.1% | 41.9% |
| 15,048 | DISTRICT 5 | 5,162 | 2,782 | 2,138 | 242 | 644 R | 53.9% | 41.4% | 56.5% | 43.5% |
| 14,905 | DISTRICT 6 | 4,792 | 2,892 | 1,685 | 215 | 1,207 R | 60.4% | 35.2% | 63.2% | 36.8% |
| 15,494 | DISTRICT 7 | 7,526 | 4,536 | 2,697 | 293 | 1,839 R | 60.3% | 35.8% | 62.7% | 37.3% |
| 15,552 | DISTRICT 8 | 7,116 | 3,547 | 3,251 | 318 | 296 R | 49.8% | 45.7% | 52.2% | 47.8% |
| 15,723 | DISTRICT 9 | 5,148 | 3,243 | 1,739 | 166 | 1,504 R | 63.0% | 33.8% | 65.1% | 34.9% |
| 15,599 | DISTRICT 10 | 4,045 | 2,693 | 1,236 | 116 | 1,457 R | 66.6% | 30.6% | 68.5% | 31.5% |
| 15,904 | DISTRICT 11 | 6,744 | 5,325 | 1,229 | 190 | 4,096 R | 79.0% | 18.2% | 81.2% | 18.8% |
| 16,303 | DISTRICT 12 | 5,352 | 3,926 | 1,262 | 164 | 2,664 R | 73.4% | 23.6% | 75.7% | 24.3% |
| 16,231 | DISTRICT 13 | 6,617 | 4,756 | 1,647 | 214 | 3,109 R | 71.9% | 24.9% | 74.3% | 25.7% |
| 16,119 | DISTRICT 14 | 6,240 | 4,734 | 1,338 | 168 | 3,396 R | 75.9% | 21.4% | 78.0% | 22.0% |
| 16,137 | DISTRICT 15 | 6,401 | 4,455 | 1,670 | 276 | 2,785 R | 69.6% | 26.1% | 72.7% | 27.3% |
| 16,104 | DISTRICT 16 | 7,125 | 5,133 | 1,779 | 213 | 3,354 R | 72.0% | 25.0% | 74.3% | 25.7% |
| 15,819 | DISTRICT 17 | 6,392 | 4,618 | 1,633 | 141 | 2,985 R | 72.2% | 25.5% | 73.9% | 26.1% |
| 15,639 | DISTRICT 18 | 3,189 | 2,231 | 902 | 56 | 1,329 R | 70.0% | 28.3% | 71.2% | 28.8% |
| 15,841 | DISTRICT 19 | 5,197 | 3,148 | 1,893 | 156 | 1,255 R | 60.6% | 36.4% | 62.4% | 37.6% |
| 15,837 | DISTRICT 20 | 3,540 | 1,999 | 1,377 | 164 | 622 R | 56.5% | 38.9% | 59.2% | 40.8% |
| 15,850 | DISTRICT 21 | 5,976 | 3,697 | 2,145 | 134 | 1,552 R | 61.9% | 35.9% | 63.3% | 36.7% |
| 15,831 | DISTRICT 22 | 4,533 | 2,369 | 2,003 | 161 | 366 R | 52.3% | 44.2% | 54.2% | 45.8% |
| 15,847 | DISTRICT 23 | 4,524 | 2,008 | 2,361 | 155 | 353 D | 44.4% | 52.2% | 46.0% | 54.0% |
| 15,812 | DISTRICT 24 | 4,884 | 2,847 | 1,886 | 151 | 961 R | 58.3% | 38.6% | 60.2% | 39.8% |
| 15,836 | DISTRICT 25 | 4,485 | 2,323 | 1,965 | 197 | 358 R | 51.8% | 43.8% | 54.2% | 45.8% |
| 15,823 | DISTRICT 26 | 6,023 | 2,981 | 2,864 | 178 | 117 R | 49.5% | 47.6% | 51.0% | 49.0% |
| 15,820 | DISTRICT 27 | 5,677 | 3,592 | 1,918 | 167 | 1,674 R | 63.3% | 33.8% | 65.2% | 34.8% |
| 15,839 | DISTRICT 28 | 6,358 | 4,183 | 2,019 | 156 | 2,164 R | 65.8% | 31.8% | 67.4% | 32.6% |
| 15,846 | DISTRICT 29 | 4,623 | 2,970 | 1,516 | 137 | 1,454 R | 64.2% | 32.8% | 66.2% | 33.8% |
| 15,839 | DISTRICT 30 | 6,113 | 3,945 | 2,031 | 137 | 1,914 R | 64.5% | 33.2% | 66.0% | 34.0% |
| 15,811 | DISTRICT 31 | 7,073 | 4,726 | 2,214 | 133 | 2,512 R | 66.8% | 31.3% | 68.1% | 31.9% |
| 15,329 | DISTRICT 32 | 7,832 | 4,560 | 3,063 | 209 | 1,497 R | 58.2% | 39.1% | 59.8% | 40.2% |
| 16,466 | DISTRICT 33 | 5,432 | 3,958 | 1,283 | 191 | 2,675 R | 72.9% | 23.6% | 75.5% | 24.5% |
| 16,409 | DISTRICT 34 | 5,680 | 4,304 | 1,164 | 212 | 3,140 R | 75.8% | 20.5% | 78.7% | 21.3% |
| 16,436 | DISTRICT 35 | 5,734 | 3,086 | 2,373 | 275 | 713 R | 53.8% | 41.4% | 56.5% | 43.5% |
| 14,928 | DISTRICT 36 | 4,460 | 2,840 | 1,452 | 168 | 1,388 R | 63.7% | 32.6% | 66.2% | 33.8% |
| 15,150 | DISTRICT 37 | 3,296 | 1,986 | 1,208 | 102 | 778 R | 60.3% | 36.7% | 62.2% | 37.8% |
| 14,921 | DISTRICT 38 | 3,688 | 1,792 | 1,723 | 173 | 69 R | 48.6% | 46.7% | 51.0% | 49.0% |
| 14,996 | DISTRICT 39 | 4,150 | 2,160 | 1,746 | 244 | 414 R | 52.0% | 42.1% | 55.3% | 44.7% |
| 15,155 | DISTRICT 40 | 4,243 | 2,391 | 1,680 | 172 | 711 R | 56.4% | 39.6% | 58.7% | 41.3% |
| 626,932 | Subtotal | 217,921 | 134,860 | 75,674 | 7,387 | 59,186 R | 61.9% | 34.7% | 64.1% | 35.9% |
| | Other Votes | 94,677 | 56,029 | 35,351 | 3,297 | 20,678 R | 59.2% | 37.3% | 61.3% | 38.7% |
| 626,932 | TOTAL | 312,598 | 190,889 | 111,025 | 10,684 | 79,864 R | 61.1% | 35.5% | 63.2% | 36.8% |

Note: There was not a complete presidential vote by state House district in 2004. The votes listed for each district were those cast by voters at the polls on election day. The line for "Other Votes" includes those cast in early voting or by absentee ballot.

# ALASKA

## PRESIDENT 2000

| 2000 Census Population | District | Total Vote | Republican | Democratic | Green (Nader) | Other | Rep.-Dem. Plurality | Percentage of Total Vote | | |
|---|---|---|---|---|---|---|---|---|---|---|
| | | | | | | | | Rep. | Dem. | Green |
| 14,199 | DISTRICT 1 | 6,656 | 4,681 | 1,284 | 475 | 216 | 3,397 R | 70.3% | 19.3% | 7.1% |
| 14,679 | DISTRICT 2 | 7,388 | 4,235 | 2,081 | 846 | 226 | 2,154 R | 57.3% | 28.2% | 11.5% |
| 15,201 | DISTRICT 3 | 8,225 | 3,135 | 3,693 | 1,161 | 236 | 558 D | 38.1% | 44.9% | 14.1% |
| 15,589 | DISTRICT 4 | 7,823 | 4,127 | 2,715 | 768 | 213 | 1,412 R | 52.8% | 34.7% | 9.8% |
| 13,286 | DISTRICT 5 | 6,437 | 3,545 | 1,931 | 751 | 210 | 1,614 R | 55.1% | 30.0% | 11.7% |
| 13,913 | DISTRICT 6 | 6,100 | 3,862 | 1,542 | 494 | 202 | 2,320 R | 63.3% | 25.3% | 8.1% |
| 16,904 | DISTRICT 7 | 8,677 | 4,868 | 1,893 | 1,563 | 353 | 2,975 R | 56.1% | 21.8% | 18.0% |
| 16,752 | DISTRICT 8 | 7,978 | 5,371 | 1,498 | 809 | 300 | 3,873 R | 67.3% | 18.8% | 10.1% |
| 15,810 | DISTRICT 9 | 6,800 | 4,789 | 1,203 | 478 | 330 | 3,586 R | 70.4% | 17.7% | 7.0% |
| 16,497 | DISTRICT 10 | 8,884 | 5,673 | 2,194 | 803 | 214 | 3,479 R | 63.9% | 24.7% | 9.0% |
| 14,906 | DISTRICT 11 | 6,980 | 3,960 | 2,043 | 743 | 234 | 1,917 R | 56.7% | 29.3% | 10.6% |
| 16,568 | DISTRICT 12 | 7,601 | 4,626 | 2,051 | 691 | 233 | 2,575 R | 60.9% | 27.0% | 9.1% |
| 15,204 | DISTRICT 13 | 7,973 | 3,853 | 2,661 | 1,230 | 229 | 1,192 R | 48.3% | 33.4% | 15.4% |
| 14,558 | DISTRICT 14 | 5,868 | 3,750 | 1,626 | 342 | 150 | 2,124 R | 63.9% | 27.7% | 5.8% |
| 15,359 | DISTRICT 15 | 5,870 | 2,453 | 2,106 | 1,068 | 243 | 347 R | 41.8% | 35.9% | 18.2% |
| 16,471 | DISTRICT 16 | 4,685 | 1,980 | 1,969 | 530 | 206 | 11 R | 42.3% | 42.0% | 11.3% |
| 20,153 | DISTRICT 17 | 7,704 | 4,564 | 2,230 | 641 | 269 | 2,334 R | 59.2% | 28.9% | 8.3% |
| 16,033 | DISTRICT 18 | 9,882 | 5,421 | 2,739 | 1,484 | 238 | 2,682 R | 54.9% | 27.7% | 15.0% |
| 18,537 | DISTRICT 19 | 7,951 | 4,619 | 2,350 | 728 | 254 | 2,269 R | 58.1% | 29.6% | 9.2% |
| 14,537 | DISTRICT 20 | 6,963 | 3,648 | 2,259 | 839 | 217 | 1,389 R | 52.4% | 32.4% | 12.0% |
| 15,618 | DISTRICT 21 | 6,629 | 3,263 | 2,309 | 810 | 247 | 954 R | 49.2% | 34.8% | 12.2% |
| 16,522 | DISTRICT 22 | 8,525 | 4,910 | 2,656 | 697 | 262 | 2,254 R | 57.6% | 31.2% | 8.2% |
| 12,433 | DISTRICT 23 | 4,630 | 2,961 | 1,282 | 283 | 104 | 1,679 R | 64.0% | 27.7% | 6.1% |
| 16,420 | DISTRICT 24 | 7,915 | 5,063 | 1,985 | 631 | 236 | 3,078 R | 64.0% | 25.1% | 8.0% |
| 15,700 | DISTRICT 25 | 8,201 | 5,489 | 1,697 | 743 | 272 | 3,792 R | 66.9% | 20.7% | 9.1% |
| 17,897 | DISTRICT 26 | 8,590 | 5,869 | 1,608 | 715 | 398 | 4,261 R | 68.3% | 18.7% | 8.3% |
| 21,751 | DISTRICT 27 | 10,438 | 6,714 | 2,199 | 1,014 | 511 | 4,515 R | 64.3% | 21.1% | 9.7% |
| 24,441 | DISTRICT 28 | 11,040 | 7,113 | 2,116 | 1,100 | 711 | 4,997 R | 64.4% | 19.2% | 10.0% |
| 15,911 | DISTRICT 29 | 8,823 | 4,054 | 2,806 | 1,628 | 335 | 1,248 R | 45.9% | 31.8% | 18.5% |
| 12,715 | DISTRICT 30 | 6,083 | 3,622 | 1,698 | 538 | 225 | 1,924 R | 59.5% | 27.9% | 8.8% |
| 13,638 | DISTRICT 31 | 5,965 | 3,326 | 1,831 | 535 | 273 | 1,495 R | 55.8% | 30.7% | 9.0% |
| 13,554 | DISTRICT 32 | 6,033 | 4,178 | 1,389 | 285 | 181 | 2,789 R | 69.3% | 23.0% | 4.7% |
| 15,314 | DISTRICT 33 | 8,712 | 5,804 | 1,765 | 789 | 354 | 4,039 R | 66.6% | 20.3% | 9.1% |
| 13,767 | DISTRICT 34 | 7,154 | 5,243 | 1,300 | 407 | 204 | 3,943 R | 73.3% | 18.2% | 5.7% |
| 12,769 | DISTRICT 35 | 6,382 | 4,278 | 1,208 | 588 | 308 | 3,070 R | 67.0% | 18.9% | 9.2% |
| 13,564 | DISTRICT 36 | 5,577 | 3,007 | 1,945 | 383 | 242 | 1,062 R | 53.9% | 34.9% | 6.9% |
| 15,453 | DISTRICT 37 | 5,028 | 2,725 | 1,821 | 255 | 227 | 904 R | 54.2% | 36.2% | 5.1% |
| 15,744 | DISTRICT 38 | 4,976 | 2,467 | 2,015 | 267 | 227 | 452 R | 49.6% | 40.5% | 5.4% |
| 17,322 | DISTRICT 39 | 5,188 | 2,321 | 2,282 | 383 | 202 | 39 R | 44.7% | 44.0% | 7.4% |
| 11,243 | DISTRICT 40 | 3,226 | 1,831 | 1,024 | 252 | 119 | 807 R | 56.8% | 31.7% | 7.8% |
| 626,932 | TOTAL | 285,560 | 167,398 | 79,004 | 28,747 | 10,411 | 88,394 R | 58.6% | 27.7% | 10.1% |

# ALASKA

## PRESIDENT 1996

| 1995 Census Pop. Est. | District | Total Vote | Republican | Democratic | Reform (Perot) | Other | Rep.-Dem. Plurality | Percentage of Total Vote | | |
|---|---|---|---|---|---|---|---|---|---|---|
| | | | | | | | | Rep. | Dem. | Reform |
| 14,908 | DISTRICT 1 | 6,667 | 4,209 | 1,480 | 696 | 282 | 2,729 R | 63.1% | 22.2% | 10.4% |
| 14,857 | DISTRICT 2 | 7,176 | 3,247 | 2,563 | 912 | 454 | 684 R | 45.2% | 35.7% | 12.7% |
| 14,702 | DISTRICT 3 | 7,790 | 2,671 | 3,724 | 654 | 741 | 1,053 D | 34.3% | 47.8% | 8.4% |
| 15,008 | DISTRICT 4 | 7,488 | 3,336 | 3,037 | 694 | 421 | 299 R | 44.6% | 40.6% | 9.3% |
| 14,643 | DISTRICT 5 | 5,925 | 2,564 | 2,148 | 826 | 387 | 416 R | 43.3% | 36.3% | 13.9% |
| 14,028 | DISTRICT 6 | 5,100 | 2,707 | 1,576 | 557 | 260 | 1,131 R | 53.1% | 30.9% | 10.9% |
| 15,688 | DISTRICT 7 | 7,214 | 3,517 | 2,177 | 907 | 613 | 1,340 R | 48.8% | 30.2% | 12.6% |
| 16,197 | DISTRICT 8 | 6,398 | 3,624 | 1,643 | 826 | 305 | 1,981 R | 56.6% | 25.7% | 12.9% |
| 14,650 | DISTRICT 9 | 5,733 | 3,459 | 1,334 | 727 | 213 | 2,125 R | 60.3% | 23.3% | 12.7% |
| 15,761 | DISTRICT 10 | 7,272 | 4,184 | 2,203 | 642 | 243 | 1,981 R | 57.5% | 30.3% | 8.8% |
| 15,943 | DISTRICT 11 | 5,877 | 3,073 | 1,946 | 603 | 255 | 1,127 R | 52.3% | 33.1% | 10.3% |
| 15,265 | DISTRICT 12 | 6,144 | 3,568 | 1,825 | 543 | 208 | 1,743 R | 58.1% | 29.7% | 8.8% |
| 15,642 | DISTRICT 13 | 7,038 | 3,270 | 2,780 | 608 | 380 | 490 R | 46.5% | 39.5% | 8.6% |
| 13,227 | DISTRICT 14 | 5,059 | 3,005 | 1,471 | 458 | 125 | 1,534 R | 59.4% | 29.1% | 9.1% |
| 15,762 | DISTRICT 15 | 5,039 | 1,974 | 2,178 | 552 | 335 | 204 D | 39.2% | 43.2% | 11.0% |
| 15,401 | DISTRICT 16 | 3,559 | 1,328 | 1,629 | 414 | 188 | 301 D | 37.3% | 45.8% | 11.6% |
| 16,948 | DISTRICT 17 | 5,989 | 3,284 | 1,868 | 633 | 204 | 1,416 R | 54.8% | 31.2% | 10.6% |
| 16,483 | DISTRICT 18 | 8,128 | 4,245 | 2,708 | 694 | 481 | 1,537 R | 52.2% | 33.3% | 8.5% |
| 17,462 | DISTRICT 19 | 6,068 | 3,159 | 2,014 | 636 | 259 | 1,145 R | 52.1% | 33.2% | 10.5% |
| 15,954 | DISTRICT 20 | 6,003 | 3,025 | 2,144 | 545 | 289 | 881 R | 50.4% | 35.7% | 9.1% |
| 15,825 | DISTRICT 21 | 5,624 | 2,553 | 2,228 | 557 | 286 | 325 R | 45.4% | 39.6% | 9.9% |
| 16,109 | DISTRICT 22 | 7,288 | 3,887 | 2,511 | 624 | 266 | 1,376 R | 53.3% | 34.5% | 8.6% |
| 11,963 | DISTRICT 23 | 3,685 | 2,127 | 1,071 | 388 | 99 | 1,056 R | 57.7% | 29.1% | 10.5% |
| 15,776 | DISTRICT 24 | 6,335 | 3,653 | 1,914 | 548 | 220 | 1,739 R | 57.7% | 30.2% | 8.7% |
| 16,057 | DISTRICT 25 | 6,643 | 4,099 | 1,629 | 691 | 224 | 2,470 R | 61.7% | 24.5% | 10.4% |
| 16,276 | DISTRICT 26 | 6,556 | 3,913 | 1,519 | 883 | 241 | 2,394 R | 59.7% | 23.2% | 13.5% |
| 18,590 | DISTRICT 27 | 7,749 | 4,384 | 1,887 | 1,122 | 356 | 2,497 R | 56.6% | 24.4% | 14.5% |
| 20,583 | DISTRICT 28 | 7,592 | 4,202 | 1,645 | 1,333 | 412 | 2,557 R | 55.3% | 21.7% | 17.6% |
| 14,334 | DISTRICT 29 | 7,510 | 3,012 | 3,023 | 658 | 817 | 11 D | 40.1% | 40.3% | 8.8% |
| 14,547 | DISTRICT 30 | 5,475 | 2,785 | 1,794 | 601 | 295 | 991 R | 50.9% | 32.8% | 11.0% |
| 13,565 | DISTRICT 31 | 5,557 | 2,721 | 1,903 | 684 | 249 | 818 R | 49.0% | 34.2% | 12.3% |
| 13,955 | DISTRICT 32 | 4,826 | 2,736 | 1,275 | 675 | 140 | 1,461 R | 56.7% | 26.4% | 14.0% |
| 14,503 | DISTRICT 33 | 7,112 | 4,089 | 1,852 | 759 | 412 | 2,237 R | 57.5% | 26.0% | 10.7% |
| 13,491 | DISTRICT 34 | 6,029 | 3,677 | 1,388 | 734 | 230 | 2,289 R | 61.0% | 23.0% | 12.2% |
| 13,350 | DISTRICT 35 | 5,687 | 3,016 | 1,447 | 875 | 349 | 1,569 R | 53.0% | 25.4% | 15.4% |
| 13,168 | DISTRICT 36 | 5,034 | 1,992 | 2,321 | 453 | 268 | 329 D | 39.6% | 46.1% | 9.0% |
| 14,558 | DISTRICT 37 | 4,575 | 1,835 | 2,134 | 456 | 150 | 299 D | 40.1% | 46.6% | 10.0% |
| 15,284 | DISTRICT 38 | 4,728 | 1,716 | 2,436 | 393 | 183 | 720 D | 36.3% | 51.5% | 8.3% |
| 16,280 | DISTRICT 39 | 4,938 | 1,618 | 2,692 | 404 | 224 | 1,074 D | 32.8% | 54.5% | 8.2% |
| 11,057 | DISTRICT 40 | 3,005 | 1,280 | 1,260 | 368 | 97 | 20 R | 42.6% | 41.9% | 12.2% |
| | FEDERAL ABSENTEE | 5 | 2 | 3 | | | 1 D | 40.0% | 60.0% | |
| 607,800 | TOTAL | 241,620 | 122,746 | 80,380 | 26,333 | 12,161 | 42,366 R | 50.8% | 33.3% | 10.9% |

# ALASKA

## PRESIDENT 1992

| 1990 Census Population | District | Total Vote | Republican | Democratic | Perot | Other | Plurality | Percentage Total Vote Rep. | Dem. | Perot |
|---|---|---|---|---|---|---|---|---|---|---|
| 13,985 | DISTRICT 1 | 6,760 | 2,495 | 2,055 | 2,120 | 90 | 375 R | 36.9% | 30.4% | 31.4% |
| 14,622 | DISTRICT 2 | 7,719 | 2,916 | 2,565 | 2,137 | 101 | 351 R | 37.8% | 33.2% | 27.7% |
| 13,595 | DISTRICT 3 | 8,042 | 2,447 | 4,064 | 1,424 | 107 | 1,617 D | 30.4% | 50.5% | 17.7% |
| 13,324 | DISTRICT 4 | 7,238 | 2,894 | 2,688 | 1,561 | 95 | 206 R | 40.0% | 37.1% | 21.6% |
| 13,483 | DISTRICT 5 | 5,742 | 1,844 | 2,095 | 1,684 | 119 | 251 D | 32.1% | 36.5% | 29.3% |
| 13,664 | DISTRICT 6 | 5,711 | 2,345 | 1,546 | 1,748 | 72 | 597 R | 41.1% | 27.1% | 30.6% |
| 13,941 | DISTRICT 7 | 6,704 | 2,173 | 2,088 | 2,244 | 199 | 71 P | 32.4% | 31.1% | 33.5% |
| 13,793 | DISTRICT 8 | 6,449 | 2,499 | 1,509 | 2,325 | 116 | 174 R | 38.8% | 23.4% | 36.1% |
| 13,810 | DISTRICT 9 | 6,414 | 2,349 | 1,540 | 2,368 | 157 | 19 P | 36.6% | 24.0% | 36.9% |
| 13,966 | DISTRICT 10 | 7,493 | 3,548 | 1,947 | 1,899 | 99 | 1,601 R | 47.4% | 26.0% | 25.3% |
| 13,981 | DISTRICT 11 | 6,920 | 2,730 | 2,009 | 2,081 | 100 | 649 R | 39.5% | 29.0% | 30.1% |
| 13,807 | DISTRICT 12 | 6,963 | 2,999 | 1,831 | 2,039 | 94 | 960 R | 43.1% | 26.3% | 29.3% |
| 13,876 | DISTRICT 13 | 7,989 | 2,963 | 3,001 | 1,907 | 118 | 38 D | 37.1% | 37.6% | 23.9% |
| 13,863 | DISTRICT 14 | 6,124 | 3,013 | 1,423 | 1,599 | 89 | 1,414 R | 49.2% | 23.2% | 26.1% |
| 13,859 | DISTRICT 15 | 5,941 | 1,842 | 2,389 | 1,591 | 119 | 547 D | 31.0% | 40.2% | 26.8% |
| 13,915 | DISTRICT 16 | 4,633 | 1,375 | 1,814 | 1,320 | 124 | 439 D | 29.7% | 39.2% | 28.5% |
| 13,964 | DISTRICT 17 | 6,423 | 2,623 | 1,749 | 1,958 | 93 | 665 R | 40.8% | 27.2% | 30.5% |
| 13,925 | DISTRICT 18 | 8,357 | 3,629 | 2,483 | 2,134 | 111 | 1,146 R | 43.4% | 29.7% | 25.5% |
| 13,919 | DISTRICT 19 | 6,419 | 2,539 | 1,931 | 1,840 | 109 | 608 R | 39.6% | 30.1% | 28.7% |
| 13,751 | DISTRICT 20 | 7,225 | 2,914 | 2,383 | 1,823 | 105 | 531 R | 40.3% | 33.0% | 25.2% |
| 13,928 | DISTRICT 21 | 6,632 | 2,437 | 2,386 | 1,693 | 116 | 51 R | 36.7% | 36.0% | 25.5% |
| 13,933 | DISTRICT 22 | 7,233 | 3,164 | 2,253 | 1,713 | 103 | 911 R | 43.7% | 31.1% | 23.7% |
| 13,898 | DISTRICT 23 | 4,550 | 2,127 | 1,139 | 1,217 | 67 | 910 R | 46.7% | 25.0% | 26.7% |
| 13,805 | DISTRICT 24 | 7,338 | 3,441 | 1,876 | 1,930 | 91 | 1,511 R | 46.9% | 25.6% | 26.3% |
| 13,934 | DISTRICT 25 | 6,927 | 3,197 | 1,513 | 2,122 | 95 | 1,075 R | 46.2% | 21.8% | 30.6% |
| 13,628 | DISTRICT 26 | 6,686 | 2,675 | 1,439 | 2,419 | 153 | 256 R | 40.0% | 21.5% | 36.2% |
| 13,970 | DISTRICT 27 | 6,970 | 2,757 | 1,625 | 2,401 | 187 | 356 R | 39.6% | 23.3% | 34.4% |
| 13,537 | DISTRICT 28 | 7,034 | 2,459 | 1,522 | 2,825 | 228 | 366 P | 35.0% | 21.6% | 40.2% |
| 13,257 | DISTRICT 29 | 7,623 | 2,205 | 3,216 | 2,026 | 176 | 1,011 D | 28.9% | 42.2% | 26.6% |
| 13,247 | DISTRICT 30 | 6,333 | 2,434 | 1,860 | 1,912 | 127 | 522 R | 38.4% | 29.4% | 30.2% |
| 13,390 | DISTRICT 31 | 6,340 | 2,223 | 1,969 | 1,992 | 156 | 231 R | 35.1% | 31.1% | 31.4% |
| 13,643 | DISTRICT 32 | 5,293 | 2,339 | 1,150 | 1,724 | 80 | 615 R | 44.2% | 21.7% | 32.6% |
| 13,226 | DISTRICT 33 | 7,252 | 3,100 | 1,712 | 2,278 | 162 | 822 R | 42.7% | 23.6% | 31.4% |
| 13,359 | DISTRICT 34 | 7,183 | 3,408 | 1,455 | 2,201 | 119 | 1,207 R | 47.4% | 20.3% | 30.6% |
| 13,215 | DISTRICT 35 | 6,415 | 2,525 | 1,572 | 2,139 | 179 | 386 R | 39.4% | 24.5% | 33.3% |
| 12,741 | DISTRICT 36 | 5,284 | 2,081 | 1,748 | 1,322 | 133 | 333 R | 39.4% | 33.1% | 25.0% |
| 13,346 | DISTRICT 37 | 4,543 | 1,689 | 1,822 | 925 | 107 | 133 D | 37.2% | 40.1% | 20.4% |
| 14,098 | DISTRICT 38 | 4,864 | 2,011 | 1,897 | 850 | 106 | 114 R | 41.3% | 39.0% | 17.5% |
| 13,858 | DISTRICT 39 | 4,516 | 1,777 | 1,797 | 860 | 82 | 20 D | 39.3% | 39.8% | 19.0% |
| 14,987 | DISTRICT 40 | 4,166 | 1,786 | 1,211 | 1,122 | 47 | 575 R | 42.9% | 29.1% | 26.9% |
| | FEDERAL ABSENTEE | 58 | 28 | 22 | 8 | | 6 R | 48.3% | 37.9% | 13.8% |
| 550,043 | TOTAL | 258,506 | 102,000 | 78,294 | 73,481 | 4,731 | 23,706 R | 39.5% | 30.3% | 28.4% |

# ALASKA

## PRESIDENT 1988

| 1980 Census Population | District | Total Vote | Republican | Democratic | Other | Rep.-Dem. Plurality | Percentage | | | |
|---|---|---|---|---|---|---|---|---|---|---|
| | | | | | | | Total Vote | | Major Vote | |
| | | | | | | | Rep. | Dem. | Rep. | Dem. |
| 17,940 | DISTRICT 1 | 8,010 | 4,564 | 3,167 | 279 | 1,397 R | 57.0% | 39.5% | 59.0% | 41.0% |
| 9,301 | DISTRICT 2 | 4,342 | 2,274 | 1,879 | 189 | 395 R | 52.4% | 43.3% | 54.8% | 45.2% |
| 9,266 | DISTRICT 3 | 4,355 | 2,313 | 1,884 | 158 | 429 R | 53.1% | 43.3% | 55.1% | 44.9% |
| 19,528 | DISTRICT 4 | 12,385 | 5,963 | 6,057 | 365 | 94 D | 48.1% | 48.9% | 49.6% | 50.4% |
| 19,068 | DISTRICT 5 | 11,372 | 6,874 | 3,696 | 802 | 3,178 R | 60.4% | 32.5% | 65.0% | 35.0% |
| 9,267 | DISTRICT 6 | 4,060 | 2,347 | 1,543 | 170 | 804 R | 57.8% | 38.0% | 60.3% | 39.7% |
| 8,853 | DISTRICT 7 | 6,186 | 3,806 | 2,088 | 292 | 1,718 R | 61.5% | 33.8% | 64.6% | 35.4% |
| 18,202 | DISTRICT 8 | 11,778 | 7,629 | 3,815 | 334 | 3,814 R | 64.8% | 32.4% | 66.7% | 33.3% |
| 18,005 | DISTRICT 9 | 11,195 | 6,876 | 3,980 | 339 | 2,896 R | 61.4% | 35.6% | 63.3% | 36.7% |
| 17,686 | DISTRICT 10 | 10,361 | 6,241 | 3,786 | 334 | 2,455 R | 60.2% | 36.5% | 62.2% | 37.8% |
| 17,958 | DISTRICT 11 | 6,022 | 3,189 | 2,590 | 243 | 599 R | 53.0% | 43.0% | 55.2% | 44.8% |
| 18,170 | DISTRICT 12 | 7,506 | 3,511 | 3,733 | 262 | 222 D | 46.8% | 49.7% | 48.5% | 51.5% |
| 18,907 | DISTRICT 13 | 7,877 | 4,968 | 2,643 | 266 | 2,325 R | 63.1% | 33.6% | 65.3% | 34.7% |
| 19,031 | DISTRICT 14 | 9,829 | 6,164 | 3,387 | 278 | 2,777 R | 62.7% | 34.5% | 64.5% | 35.5% |
| 18,561 | DISTRICT 15 | 13,085 | 8,949 | 3,726 | 410 | 5,223 R | 68.4% | 28.5% | 70.6% | 29.4% |
| 17,725 | DISTRICT 16 | 13,816 | 8,851 | 4,174 | 791 | 4,677 R | 64.1% | 30.2% | 68.0% | 32.0% |
| 9,112 | DISTRICT 17 | 4,681 | 3,093 | 1,302 | 286 | 1,791 R | 66.1% | 27.8% | 70.4% | 29.6% |
| 9,300 | DISTRICT 18 | 8,001 | 5,998 | 1,674 | 329 | 4,324 R | 75.0% | 20.9% | 78.2% | 21.8% |
| 8,934 | DISTRICT 19 | 7,689 | 4,485 | 2,737 | 467 | 1,748 R | 58.3% | 35.6% | 62.1% | 37.9% |
| 18,320 | DISTRICT 20 | 9,114 | 5,225 | 3,389 | 500 | 1,836 R | 57.3% | 37.2% | 60.7% | 39.3% |
| 9,247 | DISTRICT 21 | 6,282 | 3,127 | 2,816 | 339 | 311 R | 49.8% | 44.8% | 52.6% | 47.4% |
| 9,030 | DISTRICT 22 | 3,391 | 1,861 | 1,377 | 153 | 484 R | 54.9% | 40.6% | 57.5% | 42.5% |
| 9,388 | DISTRICT 23 | 3,413 | 1,898 | 1,390 | 125 | 508 R | 55.6% | 40.7% | 57.7% | 42.3% |
| 9,549 | DISTRICT 24 | 3,363 | 1,818 | 1,381 | 164 | 437 R | 54.1% | 41.1% | 56.8% | 43.2% |
| 9,698 | DISTRICT 25 | 3,145 | 1,611 | 1,430 | 104 | 181 R | 51.2% | 45.5% | 53.0% | 47.0% |
| 9,479 | DISTRICT 26 | 4,674 | 2,959 | 1,568 | 147 | 1,391 R | 63.3% | 33.5% | 65.4% | 34.6% |
| 9,592 | DISTRICT 27 | 4,184 | 2,657 | 1,372 | 155 | 1,285 R | 63.5% | 32.8% | 65.9% | 34.1% |
| 369,117 | TOTAL | 200,116 | 119,251 | 72,584 | 8,281 | 46,667 R | 59.6% | 36.3% | 62.2% | 37.8% |

86

# ALASKA

## PRESIDENT 1984

| 1980 Census Population | District | Total Vote | Republican | Democratic | Other | Rep.-Dem. Plurality | | Total Vote Rep. | Dem. | Major Vote Rep. | Dem. |
|---|---|---|---|---|---|---|---|---|---|---|---|
| 17,940 | DISTRICT 1 | 8,406 | 5,256 | 2,937 | 213 | 2,319 | R | 62.5% | 34.9% | 64.2% | 35.8% |
| 9,301 | DISTRICT 2 | 4,664 | 2,645 | 1,857 | 162 | 788 | R | 56.7% | 39.8% | 58.8% | 41.2% |
| 9,266 | DISTRICT 3 | 4,236 | 2,540 | 1,561 | 135 | 979 | R | 60.0% | 36.9% | 61.9% | 38.1% |
| 19,528 | DISTRICT 4 | 12,939 | 7,322 | 5,293 | 324 | 2,029 | R | 56.6% | 40.9% | 58.0% | 42.0% |
| 19,068 | DISTRICT 5 | 11,627 | 8,188 | 2,896 | 543 | 5,292 | R | 70.4% | 24.9% | 73.9% | 26.1% |
| 9,267 | DISTRICT 6 | 4,298 | 2,883 | 1,261 | 154 | 1,622 | R | 67.1% | 29.3% | 69.6% | 30.4% |
| 8,853 | DISTRICT 7 | 6,154 | 4,363 | 1,539 | 252 | 2,824 | R | 70.9% | 25.0% | 73.9% | 26.1% |
| 18,202 | DISTRICT 8 | 11,660 | 8,603 | 2,752 | 305 | 5,851 | R | 73.8% | 23.6% | 75.8% | 24.2% |
| 18,005 | DISTRICT 9 | 11,818 | 8,361 | 3,186 | 271 | 5,175 | R | 70.7% | 27.0% | 72.4% | 27.6% |
| 17,686 | DISTRICT 10 | 10,955 | 7,634 | 3,034 | 287 | 4,600 | R | 69.7% | 27.7% | 71.6% | 28.4% |
| 17,958 | DISTRICT 11 | 8,121 | 5,176 | 2,621 | 324 | 2,555 | R | 63.7% | 32.3% | 66.4% | 33.6% |
| 18,170 | DISTRICT 12 | 9,754 | 5,348 | 4,063 | 343 | 1,285 | R | 54.8% | 41.7% | 56.8% | 43.2% |
| 18,907 | DISTRICT 13 | 9,004 | 6,106 | 2,616 | 282 | 3,490 | R | 67.8% | 29.1% | 70.0% | 30.0% |
| 19,031 | DISTRICT 14 | 10,575 | 7,465 | 2,843 | 267 | 4,622 | R | 70.6% | 26.9% | 72.4% | 27.6% |
| 18,561 | DISTRICT 15 | 12,113 | 8,993 | 2,749 | 371 | 6,244 | R | 74.2% | 22.7% | 76.6% | 23.4% |
| 17,725 | DISTRICT 16 | 13,548 | 9,942 | 2,935 | 671 | 7,007 | R | 73.4% | 21.7% | 77.2% | 22.8% |
| 9,112 | DISTRICT 17 | 5,012 | 3,793 | 1,014 | 205 | 2,779 | R | 75.7% | 20.2% | 78.9% | 21.1% |
| 9,300 | DISTRICT 18 | 6,072 | 4,858 | 967 | 247 | 3,891 | R | 80.0% | 15.9% | 83.4% | 16.6% |
| 8,934 | DISTRICT 19 | 6,141 | 3,880 | 1,905 | 356 | 1,975 | R | 63.2% | 31.0% | 67.1% | 32.9% |
| 18,320 | DISTRICT 20 | 9,924 | 6,538 | 2,914 | 472 | 3,624 | R | 65.9% | 29.4% | 69.2% | 30.8% |
| 9,247 | DISTRICT 21 | 6,347 | 3,629 | 2,433 | 285 | 1,196 | R | 57.2% | 38.3% | 59.9% | 40.1% |
| 9,030 | DISTRICT 22 | 3,492 | 2,075 | 1,319 | 98 | 756 | R | 59.4% | 37.8% | 61.1% | 38.9% |
| 9,388 | DISTRICT 23 | 3,816 | 2,165 | 1,546 | 105 | 619 | R | 56.7% | 40.5% | 58.3% | 41.7% |
| 9,549 | DISTRICT 24 | 3,911 | 2,321 | 1,473 | 117 | 848 | R | 59.3% | 37.7% | 61.2% | 38.8% |
| 9,698 | DISTRICT 25 | 3,964 | 2,004 | 1,825 | 135 | 179 | R | 50.6% | 46.0% | 52.3% | 47.7% |
| 9,479 | DISTRICT 26 | 4,366 | 3,019 | 1,216 | 131 | 1,803 | R | 69.1% | 27.9% | 71.3% | 28.7% |
| 9,592 | DISTRICT 27 | 4,688 | 3,270 | 1,252 | 166 | 2,018 | R | 69.8% | 26.7% | 72.3% | 27.7% |
| 369,117 | TOTAL | 207,605 | 138,377 | 62,007 | 7,221 | 76,370 | R | 66.7% | 29.9% | 69.1% | 30.9% |

# ALASKA

## PRESIDENT 1980

| 1980 Census Population | District | Total Vote | Republican | Democratic | Other | Rep.-Dem. Plurality | Percentage | | | |
|---|---|---|---|---|---|---|---|---|---|---|
| | | | | | | | Total Vote | | Major Vote | |
| | | | | | | | Rep. | Dem. | Rep. | Dem. |
| 15,138 | DISTRICT 1 | 6,112 | 3,473 | 1,772 | 867 | 1,701 R | 56.8% | 29.0% | 66.2% | 33.8% |
| 7,804 | DISTRICT 2 | 3,368 | 1,612 | 1,256 | 500 | 356 R | 47.9% | 37.3% | 56.2% | 43.8% |
| 8,742 | DISTRICT 3 | 3,920 | 2,019 | 1,354 | 547 | 665 R | 51.5% | 34.5% | 59.9% | 40.1% |
| 22,143 | DISTRICT 4 | 11,489 | 5,345 | 3,899 | 2,245 | 1,446 R | 46.5% | 33.9% | 57.8% | 42.2% |
| 10,702 | DISTRICT 5 | 4,794 | 2,847 | 973 | 974 | 1,874 R | 59.4% | 20.3% | 74.5% | 25.5% |
| 17,739 | DISTRICT 6 | 8,176 | 5,008 | 1,316 | 1,852 | 3,692 R | 61.3% | 16.1% | 79.2% | 20.8% |
| 27,827 | DISTRICT 7 | 8,427 | 4,311 | 2,620 | 1,496 | 1,691 R | 51.2% | 31.1% | 62.2% | 37.8% |
| 40,976 | DISTRICT 8 | 12,605 | 7,432 | 2,860 | 2,313 | 4,572 R | 59.0% | 22.7% | 72.2% | 27.8% |
| 12,337 | DISTRICT 9 | 4,521 | 2,363 | 1,164 | 994 | 1,199 R | 52.3% | 25.7% | 67.0% | 33.0% |
| 28,385 | DISTRICT 10 | 12,388 | 7,659 | 2,778 | 1,951 | 4,881 R | 61.8% | 22.4% | 73.4% | 26.6% |
| 37,511 | DISTRICT 11 | 15,966 | 9,741 | 3,308 | 2,917 | 6,433 R | 61.0% | 20.7% | 74.6% | 25.4% |
| 25,981 | DISTRICT 12 | 12,009 | 7,450 | 2,456 | 2,103 | 4,994 R | 62.0% | 20.5% | 75.2% | 24.8% |
| 22,241 | DISTRICT 13 | 10,091 | 6,170 | 1,806 | 2,115 | 4,364 R | 61.1% | 17.9% | 77.4% | 22.6% |
| 8,757 | DISTRICT 14 | 2,983 | 1,473 | 844 | 666 | 629 R | 49.4% | 28.3% | 63.6% | 36.4% |
| 9,472 | DISTRICT 15 | 1,862 | 832 | 710 | 320 | 122 R | 44.7% | 38.1% | 54.0% | 46.0% |
| 6,830 | DISTRICT 16 | 2,286 | 869 | 1,083 | 334 | 214 D | 38.0% | 47.4% | 44.5% | 55.5% |
| 8,790 | DISTRICT 17 | 2,744 | 720 | 1,623 | 401 | 903 D | 26.2% | 59.1% | 30.7% | 69.3% |
| 8,322 | DISTRICT 18 | 2,386 | 769 | 1,327 | 290 | 558 D | 32.2% | 55.6% | 36.7% | 63.3% |
| 9,168 | DISTRICT 19 | 4,349 | 2,255 | 1,168 | 926 | 1,087 R | 51.9% | 26.9% | 65.9% | 34.1% |
| 55,756 | DISTRICT 20 | 22,999 | 11,673 | 5,310 | 6,016 | 6,363 R | 50.8% | 23.1% | 68.7% | 31.3% |
| 8,152 | DISTRICT 21 | 2,373 | 1,010 | 1,022 | 341 | 12 D | 42.6% | 43.1% | 49.7% | 50.3% |
| 7,708 | DISTRICT 22 | 2,597 | 1,081 | 1,193 | 323 | 112 D | 41.6% | 45.9% | 47.5% | 52.5% |
| 400,481 | TOTAL | 158,445 | 86,112 | 41,842 | 30,491 | 44,270 R | 54.3% | 26.4% | 67.3% | 32.7% |

# ALASKA

## PRESIDENT 1976

| 1970 Census Population | District | Total Vote | Republican | Democratic | Other | Rep.-Dem. Plurality | Percentage | | | |
|---|---|---|---|---|---|---|---|---|---|---|
| | | | | | | | Total Vote | | Major Vote | |
| | | | | | | | Rep. | Dem. | Rep. | Dem. |
| | DISTRICT 1 | 5,216 | 2,994 | 1,983 | 239 | 1,011 R | 57.4% | 38.0% | 60.2% | 39.8% |
| | DISTRICT 2 | 2,595 | 1,423 | 1,022 | 150 | 401 R | 54.8% | 39.4% | 58.2% | 41.8% |
| | DISTRICT 3 | 3,006 | 1,710 | 1,152 | 144 | 558 R | 56.9% | 38.3% | 59.7% | 40.3% |
| | DISTRICT 4 | 8,903 | 5,252 | 3,214 | 437 | 2,038 R | 59.0% | 36.1% | 62.0% | 38.0% |
| | DISTRICT 5 | 3,638 | 2,071 | 1,307 | 260 | 764 R | 56.9% | 35.9% | 61.3% | 38.7% |
| | DISTRICT 6 | 4,775 | 2,882 | 1,486 | 407 | 1,396 R | 60.4% | 31.1% | 66.0% | 34.0% |
| | DISTRICT 7 | 7,444 | 4,105 | 2,935 | 404 | 1,170 R | 55.1% | 39.4% | 58.3% | 41.7% |
| | DISTRICT 8 | 9,369 | 5,412 | 3,368 | 589 | 2,044 R | 57.8% | 35.9% | 61.6% | 38.4% |
| | DISTRICT 9 | 4,627 | 2,561 | 1,726 | 340 | 835 R | 55.3% | 37.3% | 59.7% | 40.3% |
| | DISTRICT 10 | 10,070 | 6,837 | 2,839 | 394 | 3,998 R | 67.9% | 28.2% | 70.7% | 29.3% |
| | DISTRICT 11 | 10,834 | 6,588 | 3,568 | 678 | 3,020 R | 60.8% | 32.9% | 64.9% | 35.1% |
| | DISTRICT 12 | 9,533 | 6,381 | 2,700 | 452 | 3,681 R | 66.9% | 28.3% | 70.3% | 29.7% |
| | DISTRICT 13 | 6,652 | 4,057 | 2,099 | 496 | 1,958 R | 61.0% | 31.6% | 65.9% | 34.1% |
| | DISTRICT 14 | 2,382 | 1,380 | 856 | 146 | 524 R | 57.9% | 35.9% | 61.7% | 38.3% |
| | DISTRICT 15 | 1,335 | 746 | 538 | 51 | 208 R | 55.9% | 40.3% | 58.1% | 41.9% |
| | DISTRICT 16 | 2,033 | 1,063 | 876 | 94 | 187 R | 52.3% | 43.1% | 54.8% | 45.2% |
| | DISTRICT 17 | 2,310 | 1,074 | 1,149 | 87 | 75 D | 46.5% | 49.7% | 48.3% | 51.7% |
| | DISTRICT 18 | 1,812 | 942 | 804 | 66 | 138 R | 52.0% | 44.4% | 54.0% | 46.0% |
| | DISTRICT 19 | 3,610 | 1,893 | 1,415 | 302 | 478 R | 52.4% | 39.2% | 57.2% | 42.8% |
| | DISTRICT 20 | 19,096 | 10,306 | 6,706 | 2,084 | 3,600 R | 54.0% | 35.1% | 60.6% | 39.4% |
| | DISTRICT 21 | 2,048 | 749 | 1,229 | 70 | 480 D | 36.6% | 60.0% | 37.9% | 62.1% |
| | DISTRICT 22 | 2,286 | 1,129 | 1,086 | 71 | 43 R | 49.4% | 47.5% | 51.0% | 49.0% |
| 302,173 | TOTAL | 123,574 | 71,555 | 44,058 | 7,961 | 27,497 R | 57.9% | 35.7% | 61.9% | 38.1% |

# ALASKA

## PRESIDENT 1972

| 1970 Census Population | District | Total Vote | Republican | Democratic | Other | Rep.-Dem. Plurality | Percentage | | | |
|---|---|---|---|---|---|---|---|---|---|---|
| | | | | | | | Total Vote | | Major Vote | |
| | | | | | | | Rep. | Dem. | Rep. | Dem. |
| 11,717 | DISTRICT 1 | 4,315 | 2,529 | 1,526 | 260 | 1,003 R | 58.6% | 35.4% | 62.4% | 37.6% |
| 7,522 | DISTRICT 2 | 2,490 | 1,386 | 967 | 137 | 419 R | 55.7% | 38.8% | 58.9% | 41.1% |
| 7,558 | DISTRICT 3 | 3,030 | 1,549 | 1,393 | 88 | 156 R | 51.1% | 46.0% | 52.7% | 47.3% |
| 15,768 | DISTRICT 4 | 7,457 | 4,277 | 2,968 | 212 | 1,309 R | 57.4% | 39.8% | 59.0% | 41.0% |
| 7,435 | DISTRICT 5 | 2,915 | 1,689 | 903 | 323 | 786 R | 57.9% | 31.0% | 65.2% | 34.8% |
| 7,670 | DISTRICT 6 | 3,636 | 2,384 | 849 | 403 | 1,535 R | 65.6% | 23.3% | 73.7% | 26.3% |
| 38,818 | DISTRICT 7 | 7,857 | 4,527 | 2,854 | 476 | 1,673 R | 57.6% | 36.3% | 61.3% | 38.7% |
| 23,102 | DISTRICT 8 | 8,402 | 5,275 | 2,454 | 673 | 2,821 R | 62.8% | 29.2% | 68.2% | 31.8% |
| 38,595 | DISTRICT 9 | 10,045 | 6,759 | 2,501 | 785 | 4,258 R | 67.3% | 24.9% | 73.0% | 27.0% |
| 23,310 | DISTRICT 10 | 10,632 | 6,882 | 2,854 | 896 | 4,028 R | 64.7% | 26.8% | 70.7% | 29.3% |
| 14,770 | DISTRICT 11 | 4,844 | 2,686 | 1,337 | 821 | 1,349 R | 55.5% | 27.6% | 66.8% | 33.2% |
| 7,568 | DISTRICT 12 | 1,900 | 1,117 | 727 | 56 | 390 R | 58.8% | 38.3% | 60.6% | 39.4% |
| 7,352 | DISTRICT 13 | 488 | 293 | 178 | 17 | 115 R | 60.0% | 36.5% | 62.2% | 37.8% |
| 7,361 | DISTRICT 14 | 1,956 | 1,042 | 843 | 71 | 199 R | 53.3% | 43.1% | 55.3% | 44.7% |
| 7,671 | DISTRICT 15 | 2,238 | 919 | 1,235 | 84 | 316 D | 41.1% | 55.2% | 42.7% | 57.3% |
| 7,635 | DISTRICT 16 | 2,004 | 902 | 1,004 | 98 | 102 D | 45.0% | 50.1% | 47.3% | 52.7% |
| 45,664 | DISTRICT 17 | 14,315 | 7,672 | 5,535 | 1,108 | 2,137 R | 53.6% | 38.7% | 58.1% | 41.9% |
| 7,419 | DISTRICT 18 | 2,038 | 1,202 | 640 | 196 | 562 R | 59.0% | 31.4% | 65.3% | 34.7% |
| 7,666 | DISTRICT 19 | 2,334 | 1,114 | 1,155 | 65 | 41 D | 47.7% | 49.5% | 49.1% | 50.9% |
| 7,660 | DISTRICT 20 | 2,323 | 1,145 | 1,044 | 134 | 101 R | 49.3% | 44.9% | 52.3% | 47.7% |
| 302,173 | TOTAL | 95,219 | 55,349 | 32,967 | 6,903 | 22,382 R | 58.1% | 34.6% | 62.7% | 37.3% |

# ALASKA

## PRESIDENT 1968

| 1960 Census Population | District | Total Vote | Republican | Democratic | AIP | Other | Plurality | Percentage Total Vote | | |
|---|---|---|---|---|---|---|---|---|---|---|
| | | | | | | | | Rep. | Dem. | AIP |
| | DISTRICT 1 | 4,539 | 2,151 | 1,871 | 517 | | 280 R | 47.4% | 41.2% | 11.4% |
| | DISTRICT 2 | 1,880 | 940 | 828 | 112 | | 112 R | 50.0% | 44.0% | 6.0% |
| | DISTRICT 3 | 2,497 | 1,110 | 1,236 | 151 | | 126 D | 44.5% | 49.5% | 6.0% |
| | DISTRICT 4 | 5,664 | 2,532 | 2,767 | 365 | | 235 D | 44.7% | 48.9% | 6.4% |
| | DISTRICT 5 | 1,372 | 590 | 646 | 136 | | 56 D | 43.0% | 47.1% | 9.9% |
| | DISTRICT 6 | 1,795 | 878 | 635 | 282 | | 243 R | 48.9% | 35.4% | 15.7% |
| | DISTRICT 7 | 2,318 | 1,075 | 893 | 350 | | 182 R | 46.4% | 38.5% | 15.1% |
| | DISTRICT 8 | 30,669 | 13,833 | 13,005 | 3,831 | | 828 R | 45.1% | 42.4% | 12.5% |
| | DISTRICT 9 | 908 | 371 | 449 | 88 | | 78 D | 40.9% | 49.4% | 9.7% |
| | DISTRICT 10 | 4,280 | 1,671 | 1,717 | 892 | | 46 D | 39.0% | 40.1% | 20.8% |
| | DISTRICT 11 | 2,095 | 986 | 862 | 247 | | 124 R | 47.1% | 41.1% | 11.8% |
| | DISTRICT 12 | 851 | 419 | 363 | 69 | | 56 R | 49.2% | 42.7% | 8.1% |
| | DISTRICT 13 | 1,244 | 591 | 553 | 100 | | 38 R | 47.5% | 44.5% | 8.0% |
| | DISTRICT 14 | 2,119 | 835 | 1,147 | 137 | | 312 D | 39.4% | 54.1% | 6.5% |
| | DISTRICT 15 | 2,117 | 964 | 848 | 305 | | 116 R | 45.5% | 40.1% | 14.4% |
| | DISTRICT 16 | 12,175 | 5,743 | 4,569 | 1,863 | | 1,174 R | 47.2% | 37.5% | 15.3% |
| | DISTRICT 17 | 1,845 | 785 | 962 | 98 | | 177 D | 42.5% | 52.1% | 5.3% |
| | DISTRICT 18 | 1,896 | 849 | 943 | 104 | | 94 D | 44.8% | 49.7% | 5.5% |
| | DISTRICT 19 | 897 | 274 | 559 | 64 | | 285 D | 30.5% | 62.3% | 7.1% |
| | NEW RESIDENT | 1,874 | 1,003 | 558 | 313 | | 445 R | 53.5% | 29.8% | 16.7% |
| 226,167 | TOTAL | 83,035 | 37,600 | 35,411 | 10,024 | | 2,189 R | 45.3% | 42.6% | 12.1% |

# ALASKA

## PRESIDENT 1964

| 1960 Census Population | District | Total Vote | Republican | Democratic | Other | Rep.-Dem. Plurality | Percentage | | | |
|---|---|---|---|---|---|---|---|---|---|---|
| | | | | | | | Total Vote | | Major Vote | |
| | | | | | | | Rep. | Dem. | Rep. | Dem. |
| | DISTRICT 1 | 4,595 | 1,554 | 3,041 | | 1,487 D | 33.8% | 66.2% | 33.8% | 66.2% |
| | DISTRICT 2 | 1,842 | 464 | 1,378 | | 914 D | 25.2% | 74.8% | 25.2% | 74.8% |
| | DISTRICT 3 | 2,396 | 651 | 1,745 | | 1,094 D | 27.2% | 72.8% | 27.2% | 72.8% |
| | DISTRICT 4 | 5,307 | 1,545 | 3,762 | | 2,217 D | 29.1% | 70.9% | 29.1% | 70.9% |
| | DISTRICT 5 | 1,306 | 250 | 1,056 | | 806 D | 19.1% | 80.9% | 19.1% | 80.9% |
| | DISTRICT 6 | 1,485 | 495 | 990 | | 495 D | 33.3% | 66.7% | 33.3% | 66.7% |
| | DISTRICT 7 | 2,205 | 963 | 1,242 | | 279 D | 43.7% | 56.3% | 43.7% | 56.3% |
| | DISTRICT 8 | 22,588 | 9,051 | 13,537 | | 4,486 D | 40.1% | 59.9% | 40.1% | 59.9% |
| | DISTRICT 9 | 938 | 264 | 674 | | 410 D | 28.1% | 71.9% | 28.1% | 71.9% |
| | DISTRICT 10 | 2,627 | 1,000 | 1,627 | | 627 D | 38.1% | 61.9% | 38.1% | 61.9% |
| | DISTRICT 11 | 1,582 | 399 | 1,183 | | 784 D | 25.2% | 74.8% | 25.2% | 74.8% |
| | DISTRICT 12 | 855 | 124 | 731 | | 607 D | 14.5% | 85.5% | 14.5% | 85.5% |
| | DISTRICT 13 | 1,198 | 267 | 931 | | 664 D | 22.3% | 77.7% | 22.3% | 77.7% |
| | DISTRICT 14 | 1,715 | 214 | 1,501 | | 1,287 D | 12.5% | 87.5% | 12.5% | 87.5% |
| | DISTRICT 15 | 1,966 | 600 | 1,366 | | 766 D | 30.5% | 69.5% | 30.5% | 69.5% |
| | DISTRICT 16 | 10,750 | 4,340 | 6,410 | | 2,070 D | 40.4% | 59.6% | 40.4% | 59.6% |
| | DISTRICT 17 | 1,401 | 252 | 1,149 | | 897 D | 18.0% | 82.0% | 18.0% | 82.0% |
| | DISTRICT 18 | 1,791 | 420 | 1,371 | | 951 D | 23.5% | 76.5% | 23.5% | 76.5% |
| | DISTRICT 19 | 712 | 77 | 635 | | 558 D | 10.8% | 89.2% | 10.8% | 89.2% |
| 226,167 | TOTAL | 67,259 | 22,930 | 44,329 | | 21,399 D | 34.1% | 65.9% | 34.1% | 65.9% |

# ALASKA

## PRESIDENT 1960

| 1960 Census Population | District | Total Vote | Republican | Democratic | Other | Rep.-Dem. Plurality | Percentage | | | |
|---|---|---|---|---|---|---|---|---|---|---|
| | | | | | | | Total Vote | | Major Vote | |
| | | | | | | | Rep. | Dem. | Rep. | Dem. |
| 1,772 | DISTRICT 1 | 358 | 147 | 211 | | 64 D | 41.1% | 58.9% | 41.1% | 58.9% |
| 10,070 | DISTRICT 2 | 3,650 | 1,898 | 1,752 | | 146 R | 52.0% | 48.0% | 52.0% | 48.0% |
| 4,181 | DISTRICT 3 | 1,439 | 760 | 679 | | 81 R | 52.8% | 47.2% | 52.8% | 47.2% |
| 6,690 | DISTRICT 4 | 2,116 | 984 | 1,132 | | 148 D | 46.5% | 53.5% | 46.5% | 53.5% |
| 9,745 | DISTRICT 5 | 3,950 | 2,031 | 1,919 | | 112 R | 51.4% | 48.6% | 51.4% | 48.6% |
| 2,945 | DISTRICT 6 | 1,099 | 461 | 638 | | 177 D | 41.9% | 58.1% | 41.9% | 58.1% |
| 1,759 | DISTRICT 7 | 542 | 267 | 275 | | 8 D | 49.3% | 50.7% | 49.3% | 50.7% |
| 2,844 | DISTRICT 8 | 722 | 337 | 385 | | 48 D | 46.7% | 53.3% | 46.7% | 53.3% |
| 5,188 | DISTRICT 9 | 2,008 | 1,045 | 963 | | 82 R | 52.0% | 48.0% | 52.0% | 48.0% |
| 82,833 | DISTRICT 10 | 19,708 | 10,537 | 9,171 | | 1,366 R | 53.5% | 46.5% | 53.5% | 46.5% |
| 2,956 | DISTRICT 11 | 1,154 | 539 | 615 | | 76 D | 46.7% | 53.3% | 46.7% | 53.3% |
| 6,097 | DISTRICT 12 | 1,952 | 907 | 1,045 | | 138 D | 46.5% | 53.5% | 46.5% | 53.5% |
| 7,174 | DISTRICT 13 | 1,356 | 555 | 801 | | 246 D | 40.9% | 59.1% | 40.9% | 59.1% |
| 6,011 | DISTRICT 14 | 563 | 161 | 402 | | 241 D | 28.6% | 71.4% | 28.6% | 71.4% |
| 4,024 | DISTRICT 15 | 817 | 304 | 513 | | 209 D | 37.2% | 62.8% | 37.2% | 62.8% |
| 5,537 | DISTRICT 16 | 724 | 523 | 201 | | 322 R | 72.2% | 27.8% | 72.2% | 27.8% |
| 2,301 | DISTRICT 17 | 536 | 295 | 241 | | 54 R | 55.0% | 45.0% | 55.0% | 45.0% |
| 4,097 | DISTRICT 18 | 861 | 367 | 494 | | 127 D | 42.6% | 57.4% | 42.6% | 57.4% |
| 43,412 | DISTRICT 19 | 8,664 | 4,229 | 4,435 | | 206 D | 48.8% | 51.2% | 48.8% | 51.2% |
| 1,619 | DISTRICT 20 | 434 | 178 | 256 | | 78 D | 41.0% | 59.0% | 41.0% | 59.0% |
| 2,133 | DISTRICT 21 | 429 | 186 | 243 | | 57 D | 43.4% | 56.6% | 43.4% | 56.6% |
| 3,560 | DISTRICT 22 | 840 | 547 | 293 | | 254 R | 65.1% | 34.9% | 65.1% | 34.9% |
| 6,091 | DISTRICT 23 | 1,693 | 941 | 752 | | 189 R | 55.6% | 44.4% | 55.6% | 44.4% |
| 3,128 | DISTRICT 24 | 265 | 90 | 175 | | 85 D | 34.0% | 66.0% | 34.0% | 66.0% |
| | ABSENTEE | 4,882 | 2,664 | 2,218 | | 446 R | 54.6% | 45.4% | 54.6% | 45.4% |
| 226,167 | TOTAL | 60,762 | 30,953 | 29,809 | | 1,144 R | 55.4% | 53.3% | 50.9% | 49.1% |

# ALASKA

Legislation to admit Alaska as the nation's 49th state was passed by Congress and signed by President Eisenhower in the summer of 1958. Primary elections and a referendum on statehood were held in August 1958 with Alaska voters approving statehood by a vote of 40,432 for statehood and 8,010 against. Alaska was formally admitted to statehood in January 1959.

Data for Alaska are carried by election districts. Included are election-district maps, with election years noted, so the user can relate data to geography. Population figures for these districts are not available except for the years 1960, 1972, 1980, 1984, 1992, and 2000.

## ELECTION NOTES

2004    Other vote was 5,069 Populist (Ralph Nader); 2,092 Alaskan Independence (Michael Peroutka); 1,675 Alaska Libertarian (Michael Badnarik); 1,058 Green (David Cobb); 790 scattered write-in.

2000    Other vote was 5,192 Reform (Buchanan); 2,636 Libertarian (Browne); 919 Natural Law (Hagelin); 596 Constitution (Phillips); 1,068 scattered write-in.

1996    Other vote was 7,597 Green (Nader); 2,276 Libertarian (Browne); 925 U.S. Taxpayers (Phillips); 729 Natural Law (Hagelin); 634 scattered write-ins.

1992    Other vote was 1,379 Gritz (America First); 1,378 Marrou (Libertarian); 469 LaRouche (Independents for Economic Recovery; 433 Hagelin (Natural Law); 377 Phillips (Taxpayers); 330 Fulani (New Alliance); 365 scattered write-in.

1988    Other vote was 5,484 Paul (Libertarian); 1,024 Fulani (New Alliance); 816 LaRouche (Democrats for Economic Recovery); 957 scattered write-in.

1984    Other vote was 6,378 Bergland (Libertarian); 843 scattered write-in.

1980    Other vote was 18,479 Clark (Libertarian); 11,155 Anderson (Independent); 857 scattered write-in. Clark, the Libertarian candidate, ran second in District 6.

1976    Other vote was 6,785 MacBride (Libertarian); 1,176 scattered write-in.

1972    Other vote was Schmitz (American Independent).

1968    Wallace on the ballot as Independent.

1964

1960

# ARIZONA

## POPULAR VOTE FOR PRESIDENT 1920 TO 2004

| Year | Total Vote | Republican | | Democratic | | Other Vote | Plurality | Percentage | | | |
|---|---|---|---|---|---|---|---|---|---|---|---|
| | | | | | | | | Total Vote | | Major Vote | |
| | | Vote | Candidate | Vote | Candidate | | | Rep. | Dem. | Rep. | Dem. |
| 2004 | 2,012,585 | 1,104,294 | Bush, George W. | 893,524 | Kerry, John | 14,767 | 210,770 R | 54.9% | 44.4% | 55.3% | 44.7% |
| 2000 ** | 1,532,016 | 781,652 | Bush, George W. | 685,341 | Gore, Al | 65,023 | 96,311 R | 51.0% | 44.7% | 53.3% | 46.7% |
| 1996 ** | 1,404,405 | 622,073 | Dole, Bob | 653,288 | Clinton, Bill | 129,044 | 31,215 D | 44.3% | 46.5% | 48.8% | 51.2% |
| 1992 ** | 1,486,975 | 572,086 | Bush, George | 543,050 | Clinton, Bill | 371,839 | 29,036 R | 38.5% | 36.5% | 51.3% | 48.7% |
| 1988 | 1,171,873 | 702,541 | Bush, George | 454,029 | Dukakis, Michael S. | 15,303 | 248,512 R | 60.0% | 38.7% | 60.7% | 39.3% |
| 1984 | 1,025,897 | 681,416 | Reagan, Ronald | 333,854 | Mondale, Walter F. | 10,627 | 347,562 R | 66.4% | 32.5% | 67.1% | 32.9% |
| 1980 ** | 873,945 | 529,688 | Reagan, Ronald | 246,843 | Carter, Jimmy | 97,414 | 282,845 R | 60.6% | 28.2% | 68.2% | 31.8% |
| 1976 | 742,719 | 418,642 | Ford, Gerald R. | 295,602 | Carter, Jimmy | 28,475 | 123,040 R | 56.4% | 39.8% | 58.6% | 41.4% |
| 1972 | 622,926 | 402,812 | Nixon, Richard M. | 198,540 | McGovern, George S. | 21,574 | 204,272 R | 64.7% | 31.9% | 67.0% | 33.0% |
| 1968 | 486,936 | 266,721 | Nixon, Richard M. | 170,514 | Humphrey, Hubert H. | 49,701 | 96,207 R | 54.8% | 35.0% | 61.0% | 39.0% |
| 1964 | 480,770 | 242,535 | Goldwater, Barry M. | 237,753 | Johnson, Lyndon B. | 482 | 4,782 R | 50.4% | 49.5% | 50.5% | 49.5% |
| 1960 | 398,491 | 221,241 | Nixon, Richard M. | 176,781 | Kennedy, John F. | 469 | 44,460 R | 55.5% | 44.4% | 55.6% | 44.4% |
| 1956 | 290,173 | 176,990 | Eisenhower, Dwight D. | 112,880 | Stevenson, Adlai E. | 303 | 64,110 R | 61.0% | 38.9% | 61.1% | 38.9% |
| 1952 | 260,570 | 152,042 | Eisenhower, Dwight D. | 108,528 | Stevenson, Adlai E. | | 43,514 R | 58.3% | 41.7% | 58.3% | 41.7% |
| 1948 | 177,065 | 77,597 | Dewey, Thomas E. | 95,251 | Truman, Harry S. | 4,217 | 17,654 D | 43.8% | 53.8% | 44.9% | 55.1% |
| 1944 | 137,634 | 56,287 | Dewey, Thomas E. | 80,926 | Roosevelt, Franklin D. | 421 | 24,639 D | 40.9% | 58.8% | 41.0% | 59.0% |
| 1940 | 150,039 | 54,030 | Willkie, Wendell | 95,267 | Roosevelt, Franklin D. | 742 | 41,237 D | 36.0% | 63.5% | 36.2% | 63.8% |
| 1936 | 124,163 | 33,433 | Landon, Alfred M. | 86,722 | Roosevelt, Franklin D. | 4,008 | 53,289 D | 26.9% | 69.8% | 27.8% | 72.2% |
| 1932 | 118,251 | 36,104 | Hoover, Herbert C. | 79,264 | Roosevelt, Franklin D. | 2,883 | 43,160 D | 30.5% | 67.0% | 31.3% | 68.7% |
| 1928 | 91,254 | 52,533 | Hoover, Herbert C. | 38,537 | Smith, Alfred E. | 184 | 13,996 R | 57.6% | 42.2% | 57.7% | 42.3% |
| 1924 | 73,961 | 30,516 | Coolidge, Calvin | 26,235 | Davis, John W. | 17,210 | 4,281 R | 41.3% | 35.5% | 53.8% | 46.2% |
| 1920 | 66,803 | 37,016 | Harding, Warren G. | 29,546 | Cox, James M. | 241 | 7,470 R | 55.4% | 44.2% | 55.6% | 44.4% |

In 2000 the other vote column includes 45,645 votes cast for Green (Nader). In 1996 the other vote column includes 112,072 votes cast for Perot. In 1992 the other vote column includes 353,741 votes cast for Perot. In 1980 the other column includes 76,952 votes for Independent (Anderson).

## ELECTORAL COLLEGE VOTE 1920 TO 2004

| Year | Total | Republican | Democratic | Other |
|---|---|---|---|---|
| 2004 | 10 | 10 | | |
| 2000 | 8 | 8 | | |
| 1996 | 8 | | 8 | |
| 1992 | 8 | 8 | | |
| 1988 | 7 | 7 | | |
| 1984 | 7 | 7 | | |
| 1980 | 6 | 6 | | |
| 1976 | 6 | 6 | | |
| 1972 | 6 | 6 | | |
| 1968 | 5 | 5 | | |
| 1964 | 5 | 5 | | |
| 1960 | 4 | 4 | | |
| 1956 | 4 | 4 | | |
| 1952 | 4 | 4 | | |
| 1948 | 4 | | 4 | |
| 1944 | 4 | | 4 | |
| 1940 | 3 | | 3 | |
| 1936 | 3 | | 3 | |
| 1932 | 3 | | 3 | |
| 1928 | 3 | 3 | | |
| 1924 | 3 | 3 | | |
| 1920 | 3 | 3 | | |

# ARIZONA

# ARIZONA

## PRESIDENT 2004

| 2000 Census Population | County | Total Vote | Republican | Democratic | Other | Rep.-Dem. Plurality | Percentage | | | |
|---|---|---|---|---|---|---|---|---|---|---|
| | | | | | | | Total Vote | | Major Vote | |
| | | | | | | | Rep. | Dem. | Rep. | Dem. |
| 69,423 | APACHE | 24,198 | 8,384 | 15,658 | 156 | 7,274 D | 34.6% | 64.7% | 34.9% | 65.1% |
| 117,755 | COCHISE | 44,483 | 26,556 | 17,514 | 413 | 9,042 R | 59.7% | 39.4% | 60.3% | 39.7% |
| 116,320 | COCONINO | 52,267 | 22,526 | 29,243 | 498 | 6,717 D | 43.1% | 55.9% | 43.5% | 56.5% |
| 51,335 | GILA | 20,843 | 12,343 | 8,314 | 186 | 4,029 R | 59.2% | 39.9% | 59.8% | 40.2% |
| 33,489 | GRAHAM | 10,720 | 7,467 | 3,185 | 68 | 4,282 R | 69.7% | 29.7% | 70.1% | 29.9% |
| 8,547 | GREENLEE | 3,067 | 1,899 | 1,146 | 22 | 753 R | 61.9% | 37.4% | 62.4% | 37.6% |
| 19,715 | LA PAZ | 5,055 | 3,158 | 1,849 | 48 | 1,309 R | 62.5% | 36.6% | 63.1% | 36.9% |
| 3,072,149 | MARICOPA | 1,192,751 | 679,455 | 504,849 | 8,447 | 174,606 R | 57.0% | 42.3% | 57.4% | 42.6% |
| 155,032 | MOHAVE | 57,807 | 36,794 | 20,503 | 510 | 16,291 R | 63.6% | 35.5% | 64.2% | 35.8% |
| 97,470 | NAVAJO | 32,343 | 17,277 | 14,815 | 251 | 2,462 R | 53.4% | 45.8% | 53.8% | 46.2% |
| 843,746 | PIMA | 366,907 | 171,109 | 193,128 | 2,670 | 22,019 D | 46.6% | 52.6% | 47.0% | 53.0% |
| 179,727 | PINAL | 64,622 | 37,006 | 27,252 | 364 | 9,754 R | 57.3% | 42.2% | 57.6% | 42.4% |
| 38,381 | SANTA CRUZ | 11,668 | 4,668 | 6,909 | 91 | 2,241 D | 40.0% | 59.2% | 40.3% | 59.7% |
| 167,517 | YAVAPAI | 87,389 | 53,468 | 33,127 | 794 | 20,341 R | 61.2% | 37.9% | 61.7% | 38.3% |
| 160,026 | YUMA | 38,465 | 22,184 | 16,032 | 249 | 6,152 R | 57.7% | 41.7% | 58.0% | 42.0% |
| 5,130,632 | TOTAL | 2,012,585 | 1,104,294 | 893,524 | 14,767 | 210,770 R | 54.9% | 44.4% | 55.3% | 44.7% |

# ARIZONA

## PRESIDENT 2000

| 2000 Census Population | County | Total Vote | Republican | Democratic | Green (Nader) | Other | Rep.-Dem. Plurality | Percentage of Total Vote | | |
|---|---|---|---|---|---|---|---|---|---|---|
| | | | | | | | | Rep. | Dem. | Green |
| 69,423 | APACHE | 19,433 | 5,947 | 13,025 | 245 | 216 | 7,078 D | 30.6% | 67.0% | 1.3% |
| 117,755 | COCHISE | 33,204 | 18,180 | 13,360 | 1,113 | 551 | 4,820 R | 54.8% | 40.2% | 3.4% |
| 116,320 | COCONINO | 40,883 | 17,562 | 20,280 | 2,478 | 563 | 2,718 D | 43.0% | 49.6% | 6.1% |
| 51,335 | GILA | 17,736 | 9,158 | 7,700 | 497 | 381 | 1,458 R | 51.6% | 43.4% | 2.8% |
| 33,489 | GRAHAM | 9,664 | 6,007 | 3,355 | 144 | 158 | 2,652 R | 62.2% | 34.7% | 1.5% |
| 8,547 | GREENLEE | 2,960 | 1,619 | 1,216 | 68 | 57 | 403 R | 54.7% | 41.1% | 2.3% |
| 19,715 | LA PAZ | 4,483 | 2,543 | 1,769 | 91 | 80 | 774 R | 56.7% | 39.5% | 2.0% |
| 3,072,149 | MARICOPA | 899,808 | 479,967 | 386,683 | 22,465 | 10,693 | 93,284 R | 53.3% | 43.0% | 2.5% |
| 155,032 | MOHAVE | 44,141 | 24,386 | 17,470 | 1,323 | 962 | 6,916 R | 55.2% | 39.6% | 3.0% |
| 97,470 | NAVAJO | 25,147 | 12,386 | 11,794 | 517 | 450 | 592 R | 49.3% | 46.9% | 2.1% |
| 843,746 | PIMA | 287,640 | 124,579 | 147,688 | 12,355 | 3,018 | 23,109 D | 43.3% | 51.3% | 4.3% |
| 179,727 | PINAL | 41,290 | 20,122 | 19,650 | 904 | 614 | 472 R | 48.7% | 47.6% | 2.2% |
| 38,381 | SANTA CRUZ | 8,893 | 3,344 | 5,233 | 217 | 99 | 1,889 D | 37.6% | 58.8% | 2.4% |
| 167,517 | YAVAPAI | 68,082 | 40,144 | 24,063 | 2,733 | 1,142 | 16,081 R | 59.0% | 35.3% | 4.0% |
| 160,026 | YUMA | 28,652 | 15,708 | 12,055 | 495 | 394 | 3,653 R | 54.8% | 42.1% | 1.7% |
| 5,130,632 | TOTAL | 1,532,016 | 781,652 | 685,341 | 45,645 | 19,378 | 96,311 R | 51.0% | 44.7% | 3.0% |

# ARIZONA

## PRESIDENT 1996

| 1995 Census Pop. Est. | County | Total Vote | Republican | Democratic | Reform (Perot) | Other | Rep.-Dem. Plurality | Percentage of Total Vote | | |
|---|---|---|---|---|---|---|---|---|---|---|
| | | | | | | | | Rep. | Dem. | Reform |
| 67,803 | APACHE | 18,684 | 4,761 | 12,394 | 1,296 | 233 | 7,633 D | 25.5% | 66.3% | 6.9% |
| 110,062 | COCHISE | 31,923 | 14,365 | 13,782 | 3,346 | 430 | 583 R | 45.0% | 43.2% | 10.5% |
| 110,498 | COCONINO | 38,522 | 13,638 | 20,475 | 3,666 | 743 | 6,837 D | 35.4% | 53.2% | 9.5% |
| 46,039 | GILA | 17,411 | 6,407 | 8,577 | 2,211 | 216 | 2,170 D | 36.8% | 49.3% | 12.7% |
| 29,589 | GRAHAM | 9,296 | 4,222 | 3,938 | 1,034 | 102 | 284 R | 45.4% | 42.4% | 11.1% |
| 9,232 | GREENLEE | 3,393 | 1,159 | 1,755 | 426 | 53 | 596 D | 34.2% | 51.7% | 12.6% |
| 14,310 | LA PAZ | 4,493 | 1,902 | 1,964 | 597 | 30 | 62 D | 42.3% | 43.7% | 13.3% |
| 2,432,372 | MARICOPA | 817,432 | 386,015 | 363,991 | 58,479 | 8,947 | 22,024 R | 47.2% | 44.5% | 7.2% |
| 121,602 | MOHAVE | 41,533 | 17,997 | 16,629 | 6,369 | 538 | 1,368 R | 43.3% | 40.0% | 15.3% |
| 89,253 | NAVAJO | 24,938 | 9,262 | 12,912 | 2,461 | 303 | 3,650 D | 37.1% | 51.8% | 9.9% |
| 752,428 | PIMA | 264,552 | 104,121 | 137,983 | 18,809 | 3,639 | 33,862 D | 39.4% | 52.2% | 7.1% |
| 131,210 | PINAL | 36,895 | 13,034 | 19,579 | 3,972 | 310 | 6,545 D | 35.3% | 53.1% | 10.8% |
| 36,078 | SANTA CRUZ | 8,167 | 2,256 | 5,241 | 600 | 70 | 2,985 D | 27.6% | 64.2% | 7.3% |
| 134,595 | YAVAPAI | 59,495 | 29,921 | 21,801 | 6,649 | 1,124 | 8,120 R | 50.3% | 36.6% | 11.2% |
| 132,869 | YUMA | 27,671 | 13,013 | 12,267 | 2,157 | 234 | 746 R | 47.0% | 44.3% | 7.8% |
| 4,217,940 | TOTAL | 1,404,405 | 622,073 | 653,288 | 112,072 | 16,972 | 31,215 D | 44.3% | 46.5% | 8.0% |

# ARIZONA

## PRESIDENT 1992

| 1990 Census Population | County | Total Vote | Republican | Democratic | Perot | Other | Plurality | Percentage Total Vote | | |
|---|---|---|---|---|---|---|---|---|---|---|
| | | | | | | | | Rep. | Dem. | Perot |
| 61,591 | APACHE | 18,258 | 4,588 | 11,218 | 1,979 | 473 | 6,630 D | 25.1% | 61.4% | 10.8% |
| 97,624 | COCHISE | 33,150 | 12,202 | 12,701 | 7,857 | 390 | 499 D | 36.8% | 38.3% | 23.7% |
| 96,591 | COCONINO | 42,618 | 13,769 | 18,888 | 9,363 | 598 | 5,119 D | 32.3% | 44.3% | 22.0% |
| 40,216 | GILA | 18,478 | 5,781 | 7,571 | 4,694 | 432 | 1,790 D | 31.3% | 41.0% | 25.4% |
| 26,554 | GRAHAM | 9,699 | 4,169 | 3,391 | 1,860 | 279 | 778 R | 43.0% | 35.0% | 19.2% |
| 8,008 | GREENLEE | 3,962 | 1,451 | 1,695 | 794 | 22 | 244 D | 36.6% | 42.8% | 20.0% |
| 13,844 | LA PAZ | 4,961 | 1,599 | 1,808 | 1,488 | 66 | 209 D | 32.2% | 36.4% | 30.0% |
| 2,122,101 | MARICOPA | 876,832 | 360,049 | 285,457 | 221,475 | 9,851 | 74,592 R | 41.1% | 32.6% | 25.3% |
| 93,497 | MOHAVE | 40,616 | 13,684 | 13,255 | 12,706 | 971 | 429 R | 33.7% | 32.6% | 31.3% |
| 77,658 | NAVAJO | 24,638 | 7,994 | 10,882 | 4,787 | 975 | 2,888 D | 32.4% | 44.2% | 19.4% |
| 666,880 | PIMA | 281,484 | 97,036 | 128,569 | 53,925 | 1,954 | 31,533 D | 34.5% | 45.7% | 19.2% |
| 116,379 | PINAL | 36,739 | 11,669 | 15,468 | 9,231 | 371 | 3,799 D | 31.8% | 42.1% | 25.1% |
| 29,676 | SANTA CRUZ | 8,080 | 3,024 | 3,512 | 1,447 | 97 | 488 D | 37.4% | 43.5% | 17.9% |
| 107,714 | YAVAPAI | 59,415 | 23,419 | 18,268 | 16,409 | 1,319 | 5,151 R | 39.4% | 30.7% | 27.6% |
| 106,895 | YUMA | 28,045 | 11,652 | 10,367 | 5,726 | 300 | 1,285 R | 41.5% | 37.0% | 20.4% |
| 3,665,228 | TOTAL | 1,486,975 | 572,086 | 543,050 | 353,741 | 18,098 | 29,036 R | 38.5% | 36.5% | 23.8% |

# ARIZONA

## PRESIDENT 1988

| 1980 Census Population | County | Total Vote | Republican | Democratic | Other | Rep.-Dem. Plurality | Percentage Total Vote Rep. | Dem. | Major Vote Rep. | Dem. |
|---|---|---|---|---|---|---|---|---|---|---|
| 52,108 | APACHE | 14,544 | 5,347 | 8,944 | 253 | 3,597 D | 36.8% | 61.5% | 37.4% | 62.6% |
| 85,686 | COCHISE | 28,050 | 15,815 | 11,812 | 423 | 4,003 R | 56.4% | 42.1% | 57.2% | 42.8% |
| 75,008 | COCONINO | 32,140 | 16,649 | 14,660 | 831 | 1,989 R | 51.8% | 45.6% | 53.2% | 46.8% |
| 37,080 | GILA | 15,299 | 7,861 | 7,147 | 291 | 714 R | 51.4% | 46.7% | 52.4% | 47.6% |
| 22,862 | GRAHAM | 8,652 | 5,120 | 3,407 | 125 | 1,713 R | 59.2% | 39.4% | 60.0% | 40.0% |
| 11,406 | GREENLEE | 3,302 | 1,526 | 1,733 | 43 | 207 D | 46.2% | 52.5% | 46.8% | 53.2% |
| 12,557 | LA PAZ | 4,376 | 2,562 | 1,746 | 68 | 816 R | 58.5% | 39.9% | 59.5% | 40.5% |
| 1,509,052 | MARICOPA | 681,518 | 442,337 | 230,952 | 8,229 | 211,385 R | 64.9% | 33.9% | 65.7% | 34.3% |
| 55,865 | MOHAVE | 28,286 | 17,651 | 10,197 | 438 | 7,454 R | 62.4% | 36.0% | 63.4% | 36.6% |
| 67,629 | NAVAJO | 19,677 | 10,393 | 9,023 | 261 | 1,370 R | 52.8% | 45.9% | 53.5% | 46.5% |
| 531,443 | PIMA | 234,473 | 117,899 | 113,824 | 2,750 | 4,075 R | 50.3% | 48.5% | 50.9% | 49.1% |
| 90,918 | PINAL | 29,180 | 14,966 | 13,850 | 364 | 1,116 R | 51.3% | 47.5% | 51.9% | 48.1% |
| 20,459 | SANTA CRUZ | 6,690 | 3,320 | 3,268 | 102 | 52 R | 49.6% | 48.8% | 50.4% | 49.6% |
| 68,145 | YAVAPAI | 43,206 | 27,842 | 14,514 | 850 | 13,328 R | 64.4% | 33.6% | 65.7% | 34.3% |
| 77,997 | YUMA | 22,480 | 13,253 | 8,952 | 275 | 4,301 R | 59.0% | 39.8% | 59.7% | 40.3% |
| 2,718,215 | TOTAL | 1,171,873 | 702,541 | 454,029 | 15,303 | 248,512 R | 60.0% | 38.7% | 60.7% | 39.3% |

# ARIZONA

## PRESIDENT 1984

| 1980 Census Population | County | Total Vote | Republican | Democratic | Other | Rep.-Dem. Plurality | Percentage Total Vote Rep. | Dem. | Major Vote Rep. | Dem. |
|---|---|---|---|---|---|---|---|---|---|---|
| 52,108 | APACHE | 13,032 | 5,638 | 7,277 | 117 | 1,639 D | 43.3% | 55.8% | 43.7% | 56.3% |
| 85,686 | COCHISE | 26,355 | 16,405 | 9,671 | 279 | 6,734 R | 62.2% | 36.7% | 62.9% | 37.1% |
| 75,008 | COCONINO | 29,735 | 17,581 | 11,528 | 626 | 6,053 R | 59.1% | 38.8% | 60.4% | 39.6% |
| 37,080 | GILA | 15,249 | 8,543 | 6,509 | 197 | 2,034 R | 56.0% | 42.7% | 56.8% | 43.2% |
| 22,862 | GRAHAM | 8,416 | 5,247 | 3,080 | 89 | 2,167 R | 62.3% | 36.6% | 63.0% | 37.0% |
| 11,406 | GREENLEE | 3,785 | 1,801 | 1,963 | 21 | 162 D | 47.6% | 51.9% | 47.8% | 52.2% |
| 12,557 | LA PAZ | 4,313 | 2,757 | 1,502 | 54 | 1,255 R | 63.9% | 34.8% | 64.7% | 35.3% |
| 1,509,052 | MARICOPA | 572,273 | 411,902 | 154,833 | 5,538 | 257,069 R | 72.0% | 27.1% | 72.7% | 27.3% |
| 55,865 | MOHAVE | 25,072 | 17,364 | 7,436 | 272 | 9,928 R | 69.3% | 29.7% | 70.0% | 30.0% |
| 67,629 | NAVAJO | 19,578 | 11,379 | 8,017 | 182 | 3,362 R | 58.1% | 40.9% | 58.7% | 41.3% |
| 531,443 | PIMA | 217,612 | 123,830 | 91,585 | 2,197 | 32,245 R | 56.9% | 42.1% | 57.5% | 42.5% |
| 90,918 | PINAL | 28,619 | 16,464 | 11,923 | 232 | 4,541 R | 57.5% | 41.7% | 58.0% | 42.0% |
| 20,459 | SANTA CRUZ | 6,389 | 3,855 | 2,463 | 71 | 1,392 R | 60.3% | 38.6% | 61.0% | 39.0% |
| 68,145 | YAVAPAI | 34,988 | 24,802 | 9,609 | 577 | 15,193 R | 70.9% | 27.5% | 72.1% | 27.9% |
| 77,997 | YUMA | 20,481 | 13,848 | 6,458 | 175 | 7,390 R | 67.6% | 31.5% | 68.2% | 31.8% |
| 2,718,215 | TOTAL | 1,025,897 | 681,416 | 333,854 | 10,627 | 347,562 R | 66.4% | 32.5% | 67.1% | 32.9% |

# ARIZONA

## PRESIDENT 1980

| 1980 Census Population | County | Total Vote | Republican | Democratic | Other | Rep.-Dem. Plurality | Percentage Total Vote Rep. | Dem. | Major Vote Rep. | Dem. |
|---|---|---|---|---|---|---|---|---|---|---|
| 52,108 | APACHE | 10,595 | 5,991 | 3,917 | 687 | 2,074 R | 56.5% | 37.0% | 60.5% | 39.5% |
| 85,686 | COCHISE | 22,445 | 13,351 | 7,028 | 2,066 | 6,323 R | 59.5% | 31.3% | 65.5% | 34.5% |
| 75,008 | COCONINO | 26,199 | 14,613 | 7,832 | 3,754 | 6,781 R | 55.8% | 29.9% | 65.1% | 34.9% |
| 37,080 | GILA | 13,399 | 7,405 | 5,068 | 926 | 2,337 R | 55.3% | 37.8% | 59.4% | 40.6% |
| 22,862 | GRAHAM | 7,961 | 4,765 | 2,801 | 395 | 1,964 R | 59.9% | 35.2% | 63.0% | 37.0% |
| 11,406 | GREENLEE | 3,782 | 1,537 | 2,043 | 202 | 506 D | 40.6% | 54.0% | 42.9% | 57.1% |
|  | LA PAZ | — | — | — | — | — | — | — | — | — |
| 1,509,052 | MARICOPA | 486,834 | 316,287 | 119,752 | 50,795 | 196,535 R | 65.0% | 24.6% | 72.5% | 27.5% |
| 55,865 | MOHAVE | 20,054 | 13,809 | 4,900 | 1,345 | 8,909 R | 68.9% | 24.4% | 73.8% | 26.2% |
| 67,629 | NAVAJO | 16,882 | 10,790 | 5,110 | 982 | 5,680 R | 63.9% | 30.3% | 67.9% | 32.1% |
| 531,443 | PIMA | 187,057 | 93,055 | 64,418 | 29,584 | 28,637 R | 49.7% | 34.4% | 59.1% | 40.9% |
| 90,918 | PINAL | 23,258 | 12,195 | 9,207 | 1,856 | 2,988 R | 52.4% | 39.6% | 57.0% | 43.0% |
| 20,459 | SANTA CRUZ | 5,340 | 2,674 | 2,089 | 577 | 585 R | 50.1% | 39.1% | 56.1% | 43.9% |
| 68,145 | YAVAPAI | 28,994 | 19,823 | 6,664 | 2,507 | 13,159 R | 68.4% | 23.0% | 74.8% | 25.2% |
| 90,554 | YUMA | 21,145 | 13,393 | 6,014 | 1,738 | 7,379 R | 63.3% | 28.4% | 69.0% | 31.0% |
| 2,718,215 | TOTAL | 873,945 | 529,688 | 246,843 | 97,414 | 282,845 R | 60.6% | 28.2% | 68.2% | 31.8% |

# ARIZONA

## PRESIDENT 1976

| 1970 Census Population | County | Total Vote | Republican | Democratic | Other | Rep.-Dem. Plurality | Percentage Total Vote Rep. | Dem. | Major Vote Rep. | Dem. |
|---|---|---|---|---|---|---|---|---|---|---|
| 32,304 | APACHE | 10,327 | 3,447 | 6,583 | 297 | 3,136 D | 33.4% | 63.7% | 34.4% | 65.6% |
| 61,910 | COCHISE | 19,883 | 9,921 | 9,281 | 681 | 640 R | 49.9% | 46.7% | 51.7% | 48.3% |
| 48,326 | COCONINO | 21,418 | 11,036 | 9,450 | 932 | 1,586 R | 51.5% | 44.1% | 53.9% | 46.1% |
| 29,255 | GILA | 11,962 | 5,136 | 6,440 | 386 | 1,304 D | 42.9% | 53.8% | 44.4% | 55.6% |
| 16,578 | GRAHAM | 6,958 | 3,659 | 3,050 | 249 | 609 R | 52.6% | 43.8% | 54.5% | 45.5% |
| 10,330 | GREENLEE | 4,247 | 1,532 | 2,601 | 114 | 1,069 D | 36.1% | 61.2% | 37.1% | 62.9% |
|  | LA PAZ | — | — | — | — | — | — | — | — | — |
| 968,487 | MARICOPA | 418,841 | 258,262 | 144,613 | 15,966 | 113,649 R | 61.7% | 34.5% | 64.1% | 35.9% |
| 25,857 | MOHAVE | 14,640 | 7,601 | 6,504 | 535 | 1,097 R | 51.9% | 44.4% | 53.9% | 46.1% |
| 47,559 | NAVAJO | 14,560 | 6,796 | 7,323 | 441 | 527 D | 46.7% | 50.3% | 48.1% | 51.9% |
| 351,667 | PIMA | 155,061 | 77,264 | 71,214 | 6,583 | 6,050 R | 49.8% | 45.9% | 52.0% | 48.0% |
| 68,579 | PINAL | 20,604 | 9,354 | 10,595 | 655 | 1,241 D | 45.4% | 51.4% | 46.9% | 53.1% |
| 13,966 | SANTA CRUZ | 4,738 | 2,312 | 2,265 | 161 | 47 R | 48.8% | 47.8% | 50.5% | 49.5% |
| 36,837 | YAVAPAI | 21,600 | 12,998 | 7,685 | 917 | 5,313 R | 60.2% | 35.6% | 62.8% | 37.2% |
| 60,827 | YUMA | 17,880 | 9,324 | 7,998 | 558 | 1,326 R | 52.1% | 44.7% | 53.8% | 46.2% |
| 1,772,482 | TOTAL | 742,719 | 418,642 | 295,602 | 28,475 | 123,040 R | 56.4% | 39.8% | 58.6% | 41.4% |

# ARIZONA

## PRESIDENT 1972

| 1970 Census Population | County | Total Vote | Republican | Democratic | Other | Rep.-Dem. Plurality | Percentage | | | |
|---|---|---|---|---|---|---|---|---|---|---|
| | | | | | | | Total Vote | | Major Vote | |
| | | | | | | | Rep. | Dem. | Rep. | Dem. |
| 32,304 | APACHE | 6,750 | 3,394 | 3,145 | 211 | 249 R | 50.3% | 46.6% | 51.9% | 48.1% |
| 61,910 | COCHISE | 18,299 | 11,706 | 6,023 | 570 | 5,683 R | 64.0% | 32.9% | 66.0% | 34.0% |
| 48,326 | COCONINO | 17,389 | 10,611 | 6,250 | 528 | 4,361 R | 61.0% | 35.9% | 62.9% | 37.1% |
| 29,255 | GILA | 10,372 | 5,673 | 4,295 | 404 | 1,378 R | 54.7% | 41.4% | 56.9% | 43.1% |
| 16,578 | GRAHAM | 5,943 | 3,575 | 1,863 | 505 | 1,712 R | 60.2% | 31.3% | 65.7% | 34.3% |
| 10,330 | GREENLEE | 3,858 | 1,758 | 2,013 | 87 | 255 D | 45.6% | 52.2% | 46.6% | 53.4% |
| | LA PAZ | — | — | — | — | — | — | — | — | — |
| 968,487 | MARICOPA | 353,000 | 244,593 | 95,135 | 13,272 | 149,458 R | 69.3% | 27.0% | 72.0% | 28.0% |
| 25,857 | MOHAVE | 9,801 | 6,755 | 2,588 | 458 | 4,167 R | 68.9% | 26.4% | 72.3% | 27.7% |
| 47,559 | NAVAJO | 11,572 | 6,999 | 4,003 | 570 | 2,996 R | 60.5% | 34.6% | 63.6% | 36.4% |
| 351,667 | PIMA | 131,997 | 73,154 | 56,223 | 2,620 | 16,931 R | 55.4% | 42.6% | 56.5% | 43.5% |
| 68,579 | PINAL | 17,559 | 10,584 | 6,404 | 571 | 4,180 R | 60.3% | 36.5% | 62.3% | 37.7% |
| 13,966 | SANTA CRUZ | 4,079 | 2,137 | 1,866 | 76 | 271 R | 52.4% | 45.7% | 53.4% | 46.6% |
| 36,837 | YAVAPAI | 17,201 | 12,277 | 3,977 | 947 | 8,300 R | 71.4% | 23.1% | 75.5% | 24.5% |
| 60,827 | YUMA | 15,106 | 9,596 | 4,755 | 755 | 4,841 R | 63.5% | 31.5% | 66.9% | 33.1% |
| 1,772,482 | TOTAL | 622,926 | 402,812 | 198,540 | 21,574 | 204,272 R | 64.7% | 31.9% | 67.0% | 33.0% |

# ARIZONA

## PRESIDENT 1968

| 1960 Census Population | County | Total Vote | Republican | Democratic | AIP | Other | Plurality | Percentage Total Vote | | |
|---|---|---|---|---|---|---|---|---|---|---|
| | | | | | | | | Rep. | Dem. | AIP |
| 30,438 | APACHE | 4,198 | 2,092 | 1,668 | 402 | 36 | 424 R | 49.8% | 39.7% | 9.6% |
| 55,039 | COCHISE | 16,711 | 7,619 | 6,597 | 2,393 | 102 | 1,022 R | 45.6% | 39.5% | 14.3% |
| 41,857 | COCONINO | 11,392 | 6,765 | 3,504 | 1,049 | 74 | 3,261 R | 59.4% | 30.8% | 9.2% |
| 25,745 | GILA | 9,706 | 3,610 | 4,831 | 1,222 | 43 | 1,221 D | 37.2% | 49.8% | 12.6% |
| 14,045 | GRAHAM | 4,929 | 2,327 | 1,726 | 859 | 17 | 601 R | 47.2% | 35.0% | 17.4% |
| 11,509 | GREENLEE | 3,751 | 1,026 | 2,434 | 276 | 15 | 1,408 D | 27.4% | 64.9% | 7.4% |
| | LA PAZ | — | — | — | — | — | — | — | — | — |
| 663,510 | MARICOPA | 274,651 | 162,262 | 86,204 | 24,941 | 1,244 | 76,058 R | 59.1% | 31.4% | 9.1% |
| 7,736 | MOHAVE | 6,212 | 3,208 | 2,109 | 883 | 12 | 1,099 R | 51.6% | 34.0% | 14.2% |
| 37,994 | NAVAJO | 9,012 | 4,596 | 2,930 | 1,438 | 48 | 1,666 R | 51.0% | 32.5% | 16.0% |
| 265,660 | PIMA | 97,766 | 49,479 | 39,786 | 7,221 | 1,280 | 9,693 R | 50.6% | 40.7% | 7.4% |
| 62,673 | PINAL | 16,246 | 6,883 | 7,409 | 1,869 | 85 | 526 D | 42.4% | 45.6% | 11.5% |
| 10,808 | SANTA CRUZ | 3,533 | 1,702 | 1,557 | 242 | 32 | 145 R | 48.2% | 44.1% | 6.8% |
| 28,912 | YAVAPAI | 14,196 | 8,296 | 3,989 | 1,837 | 74 | 4,307 R | 58.4% | 28.1% | 12.9% |
| 46,235 | YUMA | 14,633 | 6,856 | 5,770 | 1,941 | 66 | 1,086 R | 46.9% | 39.4% | 13.3% |
| 1,302,161 | TOTAL | 486,936 | 266,721 | 170,514 | 46,573 | 3,128 | 96,207 R | 54.8% | 35.0% | 9.6% |

# ARIZONA

## PRESIDENT 1964

| 1960 Census Population | County | Total Vote | Republican | Democratic | Other | Rep.-Dem. Plurality | Percentage Total Vote | | Major Vote | |
|---|---|---|---|---|---|---|---|---|---|---|
| | | | | | | | Rep. | Dem. | Rep. | Dem. |
| 30,438 | APACHE | 3,892 | 1,849 | 2,042 | 1 | 193 D | 47.5% | 52.5% | 47.5% | 52.5% |
| 55,039 | COCHISE | 16,697 | 7,644 | 9,045 | 8 | 1,401 D | 45.8% | 54.2% | 45.8% | 54.2% |
| 41,857 | COCONINO | 11,037 | 5,756 | 5,270 | 11 | 486 R | 52.2% | 47.7% | 52.2% | 47.8% |
| 25,745 | GILA | 10,537 | 3,713 | 6,821 | 3 | 3,108 D | 35.2% | 64.7% | 35.2% | 64.8% |
| 14,045 | GRAHAM | 5,438 | 2,655 | 2,783 | | 128 D | 48.8% | 51.2% | 48.8% | 51.2% |
| 11,509 | GREENLEE | 4,279 | 1,132 | 3,147 | | 2,015 D | 26.5% | 73.5% | 26.5% | 73.5% |
| | LA PAZ | — | — | — | — | — | | | | |
| 663,510 | MARICOPA | 265,326 | 143,114 | 122,042 | 170 | 21,072 R | 53.9% | 46.0% | 54.0% | 46.0% |
| 7,736 | MOHAVE | 4,339 | 2,091 | 2,243 | 5 | 152 D | 48.2% | 51.7% | 48.2% | 51.8% |
| 37,994 | NAVAJO | 9,649 | 4,870 | 4,770 | 9 | 100 R | 50.5% | 49.4% | 50.5% | 49.5% |
| 265,660 | PIMA | 101,278 | 46,955 | 54,120 | 203 | 7,165 D | 46.4% | 53.4% | 46.5% | 53.5% |
| 62,673 | PINAL | 16,872 | 6,956 | 9,911 | 5 | 2,955 D | 41.2% | 58.7% | 41.2% | 58.8% |
| 10,808 | SANTA CRUZ | 3,460 | 1,503 | 1,955 | 2 | 452 D | 43.4% | 56.5% | 43.5% | 56.5% |
| 28,912 | YAVAPAI | 13,556 | 7,749 | 5,747 | 60 | 2,002 R | 57.2% | 42.4% | 57.4% | 42.6% |
| 46,235 | YUMA | 14,410 | 6,548 | 7,857 | 5 | 1,309 D | 45.4% | 54.5% | 45.5% | 54.5% |
| 1,302,161 | TOTAL | 480,770 | 242,535 | 237,753 | 482 | 4,782 R | 50.4% | 49.5% | 50.5% | 49.5% |

# ARIZONA

## PRESIDENT 1960

| 1960 Census Population | County | Total Vote | Republican | Democratic | Other | Rep.-Dem. Plurality | Percentage Total Vote | | Major Vote | |
|---|---|---|---|---|---|---|---|---|---|---|
| | | | | | | | Rep. | Dem. | Rep. | Dem. |
| 30,438 | APACHE | 3,030 | 1,568 | 1,459 | 3 | 109 R | 51.7% | 48.2% | 51.8% | 48.2% |
| 55,039 | COCHISE | 15,007 | 7,572 | 7,419 | 16 | 153 R | 50.5% | 49.4% | 50.5% | 49.5% |
| 41,857 | COCONINO | 8,944 | 4,870 | 4,065 | 9 | 805 R | 54.4% | 45.4% | 54.5% | 45.5% |
| 25,745 | GILA | 9,065 | 3,806 | 5,251 | 8 | 1,445 D | 42.0% | 57.9% | 42.0% | 58.0% |
| 14,045 | GRAHAM | 4,583 | 2,491 | 2,091 | 1 | 400 R | 54.4% | 45.6% | 54.4% | 45.6% |
| 11,509 | GREENLEE | 4,386 | 1,313 | 3,069 | 4 | 1,756 D | 29.9% | 70.0% | 30.0% | 70.0% |
| | LA PAZ | — | — | — | — | — | | | | |
| 663,510 | MARICOPA | 214,059 | 127,090 | 86,834 | 135 | 40,256 R | 59.4% | 40.6% | 59.4% | 40.6% |
| 7,736 | MOHAVE | 2,952 | 1,641 | 1,303 | 8 | 338 R | 55.6% | 44.1% | 55.7% | 44.3% |
| 37,994 | NAVAJO | 7,151 | 4,090 | 3,052 | 9 | 1,038 R | 57.2% | 42.7% | 57.3% | 42.7% |
| 265,660 | PIMA | 89,144 | 46,734 | 42,171 | 239 | 4,563 R | 52.4% | 47.3% | 52.6% | 47.4% |
| 62,673 | PINAL | 13,684 | 6,441 | 7,232 | 11 | 791 D | 47.1% | 52.9% | 47.1% | 52.9% |
| 10,808 | SANTA CRUZ | 3,135 | 1,265 | 1,868 | 2 | 603 D | 40.4% | 59.6% | 40.4% | 59.6% |
| 28,912 | YAVAPAI | 11,147 | 6,813 | 4,325 | 9 | 2,488 R | 61.1% | 38.8% | 61.2% | 38.8% |
| 46,235 | YUMA | 12,204 | 5,547 | 6,642 | 15 | 1,095 D | 45.5% | 54.4% | 45.5% | 54.5% |
| 1,302,161 | TOTAL | 398,491 | 221,241 | 176,781 | 469 | 44,460 R | 55.5% | 44.4% | 55.6% | 44.4% |

# ARIZONA

LaPaz county was formed from the northern half of Yuma county after a vote on May 25, 1982 by the people of this region to form a new county. LaPaz became the fifteenth county in Arizona on January 1, 1983.

## ELECTION NOTES

**2004**  Other vote was 11,856 Libertarian (Michael Badnarik); 2,773 write-in (Ralph Nader); 138 write-in (David Cobb).

**2000**  Other vote was 12,373 Reform (Buchanan); 5,775 Libertarian (Smith); 1,120 Natural Law (Hagelin); 110 write-in (Phillips). (L. Neil Smith was the Libertarian candidate in Arizona, while Harry Browne was the party's standard-bearer elsewhere.)

**1996**  Other vote was 14,358 Libertarian (Browne); and write-ins as follows: 2,062 Nader; 347 Phillips; 153 Hagelin; 52 scattered.

**1992**  Other vote was 8,141 Gritz (Independent); 6,759 Marrou (Libertarian); 2,267 Hagelin (Natural Law); 923 Fulani (New Alliance); 8 LaRouche (write-in).

**1988**  Other vote was 13,351 Paul (Libertarian); 1,662 Fulani (New Alliance); 159 McCarthy (Independent write-in); 113 Duke (Populist write-in); 18 Dennis (American write-in). Early canvass gave the Dennis vote as 20.

**1984**  Other vote was 10,585 Bergland (Libertarian); 18 Johnson (write-in); 3 Winn (write-in); 21 scattered write-in.

**1980**  Other vote was 76,952 Anderson (Independent); 18,784 Clark (Libertarian); 1,100 DeBerry (Socialist Workers); 551 Commoner (write-in); 25 Hall (write-in); 2 Griswold (write-in).

**1976**  Other vote was 19,229 McCarthy (Independent); 7,647 MacBride (Libertarian); 928 Camejo (Socialist Workers); 564 Anderson (write-in); 85 Maddox (write-in); 22 Taylor (write-in).

**1972**  Other vote was 21,208 Schmitz (American Independent); 366 no Presidential candidate indicated (Socialist Workers). Socialist Workers votes in Pima and Yavapai counties are omitted in the data table due to a confusion in the structure of the ballot which permitted over-voting for individual Socialist Workers electors on many thousands of ballots. With the canvassed over-vote for individual electors in Pima and Yavapai counties included, the state-wide Socialist Workers vote would be 30,945.

**1968**  Wallace on the ballot as American Independent. Other vote was 2,751 McCarthy (New Party); 217 Cleaver (Peace and Freedom); 85 Halstead (Socialist Workers); 75 Blomen (Socialist Labor).

**1964**  Other vote was Hass (Socialist Labor).

**1960**  Other vote was Hass (Socialist Labor).

# ARKANSAS

## POPULAR VOTE FOR PRESIDENT 1920 TO 2004

| Year | Total Vote | Republican | | Democratic | | Other Vote | Plurality | Percentage | | | |
|------|-----------|-----------|-----------|-----------|-----------|-----------|-----------|-----------|-----------|-----------|-----------|
| | | | | | | | | Total Vote | | Major Vote | |
| | | Vote | Candidate | Vote | Candidate | | | Rep. | Dem. | Rep. | Dem. |
| 2004 | 1,054,945 | 572,898 | Bush, George W. | 469,953 | Kerry, John | 12,094 | 102,945 R | 54.3% | 44.5% | 54.9% | 45.1% |
| 2000 ** | 921,781 | 472,940 | Bush, George W. | 422,768 | Gore, Al | 26,073 | 50,172 R | 51.3% | 45.9% | 52.8% | 47.2% |
| 1996 ** | 884,262 | 325,416 | Dole, Bob | 475,171 | Clinton, Bill | 83,675 | 149,755 D | 36.8% | 53.7% | 40.6% | 59.4% |
| 1992 ** | 950,653 | 337,324 | Bush, George | 505,823 | Clinton, Bill | 107,506 | 168,499 D | 35.5% | 53.2% | 40.0% | 60.0% |
| 1988 | 827,738 | 466,578 | Bush, George | 349,237 | Dukakis, Michael S. | 11,923 | 117,341 R | 56.4% | 42.2% | 57.2% | 42.8% |
| 1984 | 884,406 | 534,774 | Reagan, Ronald | 338,646 | Mondale, Walter F. | 10,986 | 196,128 R | 60.5% | 38.3% | 61.2% | 38.8% |
| 1980 ** | 837,582 | 403,164 | Reagan, Ronald | 398,041 | Carter, Jimmy | 36,377 | 5,123 R | 48.1% | 47.5% | 50.3% | 49.7% |
| 1976 | 767,535 | 267,903 | Ford, Gerald R. | 498,604 | Carter, Jimmy | 1,028 | 230,701 D | 34.9% | 65.0% | 35.0% | 65.0% |
| 1972 | 651,320 | 448,541 | Nixon, Richard M. | 199,892 | McGovern, George S. | 2,887 | 248,649 R | 68.9% | 30.7% | 69.2% | 30.8% |
| 1968 ** | 619,969 | 190,759 | Nixon, Richard M. | 188,228 | Humphrey, Hubert H. | 240,982 | 50,223 A | 30.8% | 30.4% | 50.3% | 49.7% |
| 1964 | 560,426 | 243,264 | Goldwater, Barry M. | 314,197 | Johnson, Lyndon B. | 2,965 | 70,933 D | 43.4% | 56.1% | 43.6% | 56.4% |
| 1960 | 428,509 | 184,508 | Nixon, Richard M. | 215,049 | Kennedy, John F. | 28,952 | 30,541 D | 43.1% | 50.2% | 46.2% | 53.8% |
| 1956 | 406,572 | 186,287 | Eisenhower, Dwight D. | 213,277 | Stevenson, Adlai E. | 7,008 | 26,990 D | 45.8% | 52.5% | 46.6% | 53.4% |
| 1952 | 404,800 | 177,155 | Eisenhower, Dwight D. | 226,300 | Stevenson, Adlai E. | 1,345 | 49,145 D | 43.8% | 55.9% | 43.9% | 56.1% |
| 1948 ** | 242,475 | 50,959 | Dewey, Thomas E. | 149,659 | Truman, Harry S. | 41,857 | 98,700 D | 21.0% | 61.7% | 25.4% | 74.6% |
| 1944 | 212,954 | 63,551 | Dewey, Thomas E. | 148,965 | Roosevelt, Franklin D. | 438 | 85,414 D | 29.8% | 70.0% | 29.9% | 70.1% |
| 1940 | 200,429 | 42,122 | Willkie, Wendell | 157,213 | Roosevelt, Franklin D. | 1,094 | 115,091 D | 21.0% | 78.4% | 21.1% | 78.9% |
| 1936 | 179,431 | 32,049 | Landon, Alfred M. | 146,765 | Roosevelt, Franklin D. | 617 | 114,716 D | 17.9% | 81.8% | 17.9% | 82.1% |
| 1932 | 216,569 | 27,465 | Hoover, Herbert C. | 186,829 | Roosevelt, Franklin D. | 2,275 | 159,364 D | 12.7% | 86.3% | 12.8% | 87.2% |
| 1928 | 197,726 | 77,784 | Hoover, Herbert C. | 119,196 | Smith, Alfred E. | 746 | 41,412 D | 39.3% | 60.3% | 39.5% | 60.5% |
| 1924 | 138,540 | 40,583 | Coolidge, Calvin | 84,790 | Davis, John W. | 13,167 | 44,207 D | 29.3% | 61.2% | 32.4% | 67.6% |
| 1920 | 183,871 | 72,316 | Harding, Warren G. | 106,427 | Cox, James M. | 5,128 | 34,111 D | 39.3% | 57.9% | 40.5% | 59.5% |

In 2000 the other vote column includes 13,421 votes cast for Green (Nader). In 1996 the other vote column includes 69,884 votes cast for Perot. In 1992 the other vote column includes 99,132 votes cast for Perot. In 1980 the other column includes 22,468 votes for Independent (Anderson). In 1968 other vote was American (Wallace). In 1948 other vote was 40,068 States Rights; 1,037 Socialist; 751 Progressive and 1 Prohibition.

## ELECTORAL COLLEGE VOTE 1920 TO 2004

| Year | Total | Republican | Democratic | Other |
|------|-------|-----------|-----------|-------|
| 2004 | 6 | 6 | | |
| 2000 | 6 | 6 | | |
| 1996 | 6 | | 6 | |
| 1992 | 6 | | 6 | |
| 1988 | 6 | 6 | | |
| 1984 | 6 | 6 | | |
| 1980 | 6 | 6 | | |
| 1976 | 6 | | 6 | |
| 1972 | 6 | 6 | | |
| 1968 | 6 | | | 6 AIP |
| 1964 | 6 | | 6 | |
| 1960 | 8 | | 8 | |
| 1956 | 8 | | 8 | |
| 1952 | 8 | | 8 | |
| 1948 | 9 | | 9 | |
| 1944 | 9 | | 9 | |
| 1940 | 9 | | 9 | |
| 1936 | 9 | | 9 | |
| 1932 | 9 | | 9 | |
| 1928 | 9 | | 9 | |
| 1924 | 9 | | 9 | |
| 1920 | 9 | | 9 | |

104

# ARKANSAS

# ARKANSAS

## PRESIDENT 2004

| 2000 Census Population | County | Total Vote | Republican | Democratic | Other | Rep.-Dem. Plurality | Percentage | | | |
|---|---|---|---|---|---|---|---|---|---|---|
| | | | | | | | Total Vote | | Major Vote | |
| | | | | | | | Rep. | Dem. | Rep. | Dem. |
| 20,749 | ARKANSAS | 6,946 | 3,789 | 3,110 | 47 | 679 R | 54.5% | 44.8% | 54.9% | 45.1% |
| 24,209 | ASHLEY | 8,512 | 4,567 | 3,881 | 64 | 686 R | 53.7% | 45.6% | 54.1% | 45.9% |
| 38,386 | BAXTER | 18,530 | 11,128 | 7,129 | 273 | 3,999 R | 60.1% | 38.5% | 61.0% | 39.0% |
| 153,406 | BENTON | 68,121 | 46,571 | 20,756 | 794 | 25,815 R | 68.4% | 30.5% | 69.2% | 30.8% |
| 33,948 | BOONE | 14,777 | 9,793 | 4,640 | 344 | 5,153 R | 66.3% | 31.4% | 67.9% | 32.1% |
| 12,600 | BRADLEY | 4,249 | 2,011 | 2,206 | 32 | 195 D | 47.3% | 51.9% | 47.7% | 52.3% |
| 5,744 | CALHOUN | 2,299 | 1,340 | 939 | 20 | 401 R | 58.3% | 40.8% | 58.8% | 41.2% |
| 25,357 | CARROLL | 10,481 | 6,184 | 4,161 | 136 | 2,023 R | 59.0% | 39.7% | 59.8% | 40.2% |
| 14,117 | CHICOT | 4,757 | 1,725 | 2,993 | 39 | 1,268 D | 36.3% | 62.9% | 36.6% | 63.4% |
| 23,546 | CLARK | 9,211 | 4,144 | 4,990 | 77 | 846 D | 45.0% | 54.2% | 45.4% | 54.6% |
| 17,609 | CLAY | 6,096 | 2,759 | 3,264 | 73 | 505 D | 45.3% | 53.5% | 45.8% | 54.2% |
| 24,046 | CLEBURNE | 11,761 | 7,107 | 4,517 | 137 | 2,590 R | 60.4% | 38.4% | 61.1% | 38.9% |
| 8,571 | CLEVELAND | 3,496 | 2,009 | 1,450 | 37 | 559 R | 57.5% | 41.5% | 58.1% | 41.9% |
| 25,603 | COLUMBIA | 9,909 | 5,729 | 4,108 | 72 | 1,621 R | 57.8% | 41.5% | 58.2% | 41.8% |
| 20,336 | CONWAY | 8,084 | 4,009 | 3,982 | 93 | 27 R | 49.6% | 49.3% | 50.2% | 49.8% |
| 82,148 | CRAIGHEAD | 29,801 | 15,818 | 13,665 | 318 | 2,153 R | 53.1% | 45.9% | 53.7% | 46.3% |
| 53,247 | CRAWFORD | 20,401 | 13,391 | 6,764 | 246 | 6,627 R | 65.6% | 33.2% | 66.4% | 33.6% |
| 50,866 | CRITTENDEN | 15,300 | 6,930 | 8,277 | 93 | 1,347 D | 45.3% | 54.1% | 45.6% | 54.4% |
| 19,526 | CROSS | 7,074 | 3,864 | 3,135 | 75 | 729 R | 54.6% | 44.3% | 55.2% | 44.8% |
| 9,210 | DALLAS | 3,388 | 1,700 | 1,671 | 17 | 29 R | 50.2% | 49.3% | 50.4% | 49.6% |
| 15,341 | DESHA | 4,647 | 1,729 | 2,851 | 67 | 1,122 D | 37.2% | 61.4% | 37.8% | 62.2% |
| 18,723 | DREW | 6,249 | 3,262 | 2,952 | 35 | 310 R | 52.2% | 47.2% | 52.5% | 47.5% |
| 86,014 | FAULKNER | 36,686 | 21,514 | 14,538 | 634 | 6,976 R | 58.6% | 39.6% | 59.7% | 40.3% |
| 17,771 | FRANKLIN | 7,289 | 4,181 | 3,008 | 100 | 1,173 R | 57.4% | 41.3% | 58.2% | 41.8% |
| 11,642 | FULTON | 4,955 | 2,522 | 2,370 | 63 | 152 R | 50.9% | 47.8% | 51.6% | 48.4% |
| 88,068 | GARLAND | 40,154 | 21,734 | 18,040 | 380 | 3,694 R | 54.1% | 44.9% | 54.6% | 45.4% |
| 16,464 | GRANT | 6,770 | 4,205 | 2,524 | 41 | 1,681 R | 62.1% | 37.3% | 62.5% | 37.5% |
| 37,331 | GREENE | 13,955 | 7,237 | 6,564 | 154 | 673 R | 51.9% | 47.0% | 52.4% | 47.6% |
| 23,587 | HEMPSTEAD | 7,452 | 3,580 | 3,817 | 55 | 237 D | 48.0% | 51.2% | 48.4% | 51.6% |
| 30,353 | HOT SPRING | 12,065 | 5,960 | 5,901 | 204 | 59 R | 49.4% | 48.9% | 50.2% | 49.8% |
| 14,300 | HOWARD | 4,943 | 2,736 | 2,166 | 41 | 570 R | 55.4% | 43.8% | 55.8% | 44.2% |
| 34,233 | INDEPENDENCE | 13,011 | 7,430 | 5,443 | 138 | 1,987 R | 57.1% | 41.8% | 57.7% | 42.3% |
| 13,249 | IZARD | 5,493 | 2,833 | 2,586 | 74 | 247 R | 51.6% | 47.1% | 52.3% | 47.7% |
| 18,418 | JACKSON | 6,219 | 2,624 | 3,515 | 80 | 891 D | 42.2% | 56.5% | 42.7% | 57.3% |
| 84,278 | JEFFERSON | 30,493 | 10,218 | 19,675 | 600 | 9,457 D | 33.5% | 64.5% | 34.2% | 65.8% |
| 22,781 | JOHNSON | 8,044 | 4,311 | 3,622 | 111 | 689 R | 53.6% | 45.0% | 54.3% | 45.7% |
| 8,559 | LAFAYETTE | 3,191 | 1,604 | 1,567 | 20 | 37 R | 50.3% | 49.1% | 50.6% | 49.4% |
| 17,774 | LAWRENCE | 6,615 | 2,951 | 3,544 | 120 | 593 D | 44.6% | 53.6% | 45.4% | 54.6% |
| 12,580 | LEE | 4,080 | 1,492 | 2,548 | 40 | 1,056 D | 36.6% | 62.5% | 36.9% | 63.1% |
| 14,492 | LINCOLN | 4,109 | 1,921 | 2,149 | 39 | 228 D | 46.8% | 52.3% | 47.2% | 52.8% |
| 13,628 | LITTLE RIVER | 5,294 | 2,575 | 2,677 | 42 | 102 D | 48.6% | 50.6% | 49.0% | 51.0% |
| 22,486 | LOGAN | 8,551 | 5,076 | 3,361 | 114 | 1,715 R | 59.4% | 39.3% | 60.2% | 39.8% |
| 52,828 | LONOKE | 22,030 | 14,398 | 7,454 | 178 | 6,944 R | 65.4% | 33.8% | 65.9% | 34.1% |
| 14,243 | MADISON | 6,384 | 3,873 | 2,421 | 90 | 1,452 R | 60.7% | 37.9% | 61.5% | 38.5% |
| 16,140 | MARION | 6,867 | 4,127 | 2,602 | 138 | 1,525 R | 60.1% | 37.9% | 61.3% | 38.7% |
| 40,443 | MILLER | 14,678 | 8,448 | 6,139 | 91 | 2,309 R | 57.6% | 41.8% | 57.9% | 42.1% |
| 51,979 | MISSISSIPPI | 14,153 | 6,121 | 7,593 | 439 | 1,472 D | 43.2% | 53.6% | 44.6% | 55.4% |
| 10,254 | MONROE | 3,667 | 1,586 | 2,049 | 32 | 463 D | 43.3% | 55.9% | 43.6% | 56.4% |
| 9,245 | MONTGOMERY | 3,958 | 2,367 | 1,524 | 67 | 843 R | 59.8% | 38.5% | 60.8% | 39.2% |
| 9,955 | NEVADA | 3,477 | 1,752 | 1,694 | 31 | 58 R | 50.4% | 48.7% | 50.8% | 49.2% |
| 8,608 | NEWTON | 4,378 | 2,779 | 1,506 | 93 | 1,273 R | 63.5% | 34.4% | 64.9% | 35.1% |
| 28,790 | OUACHITA | 10,650 | 5,345 | 5,188 | 117 | 157 R | 50.2% | 48.7% | 50.7% | 49.3% |
| 10,209 | PERRY | 4,431 | 2,435 | 1,921 | 75 | 514 R | 55.0% | 43.4% | 55.9% | 44.1% |
| 26,445 | PHILLIPS | 8,868 | 3,161 | 5,642 | 65 | 2,481 D | 35.6% | 63.6% | 35.9% | 64.1% |
| 11,303 | PIKE | 3,367 | 2,013 | 1,310 | 44 | 703 R | 59.8% | 38.9% | 60.6% | 39.4% |
| 25,614 | POINSETT | 7,723 | 3,555 | 4,069 | 99 | 514 D | 46.0% | 52.7% | 46.6% | 53.4% |
| 20,229 | POLK | 7,799 | 5,192 | 2,473 | 134 | 2,719 R | 66.6% | 31.7% | 67.7% | 32.3% |
| 54,469 | POPE | 20,902 | 13,614 | 7,100 | 188 | 6,514 R | 65.1% | 34.0% | 65.7% | 34.3% |
| 9,539 | PRAIRIE | 3,624 | 2,030 | 1,562 | 32 | 468 R | 56.0% | 43.1% | 56.5% | 43.5% |
| 361,474 | PULASKI | 153,620 | 67,903 | 84,532 | 1,185 | 16,629 D | 44.2% | 55.0% | 44.5% | 55.5% |

# ARKANSAS

## PRESIDENT 2004

| 2000 Census Population | County | Total Vote | Republican | Democratic | Other | Rep.-Dem. Plurality | Percentage | | | |
|---|---|---|---|---|---|---|---|---|---|---|
| | | | | | | | Total Vote | | Major Vote | |
| | | | | | | | Rep. | Dem. | Rep. | Dem. |
| 18,195 | RANDOLPH | 6,667 | 3,158 | 3,412 | 97 | 254 D | 47.4% | 51.2% | 48.1% | 51.9% |
| 29,329 | ST. FRANCIS | 9,588 | 3,815 | 5,684 | 89 | 1,869 D | 39.8% | 59.3% | 40.2% | 59.8% |
| 83,529 | SALINE | 39,376 | 24,864 | 14,153 | 359 | 10,711 R | 63.1% | 35.9% | 63.7% | 36.3% |
| 10,996 | SCOTT | 4,038 | 2,514 | 1,473 | 51 | 1,041 R | 62.3% | 36.5% | 63.1% | 36.9% |
| 8,261 | SEARCY | 3,992 | 2,565 | 1,370 | 57 | 1,195 R | 64.3% | 34.3% | 65.2% | 34.8% |
| 115,071 | SEBASTIAN | 44,211 | 27,303 | 16,479 | 429 | 10,824 R | 61.8% | 37.3% | 62.4% | 37.6% |
| 15,757 | SEVIER | 4,601 | 2,516 | 2,035 | 50 | 481 R | 54.7% | 44.2% | 55.3% | 44.7% |
| 17,119 | SHARP | 7,470 | 4,097 | 3,265 | 108 | 832 R | 54.8% | 43.7% | 55.7% | 44.3% |
| 11,499 | STONE | 5,549 | 3,188 | 2,255 | 106 | 933 R | 57.5% | 40.6% | 58.6% | 41.4% |
| 45,629 | UNION | 17,832 | 10,502 | 7,071 | 259 | 3,431 R | 58.9% | 39.7% | 59.8% | 40.2% |
| 16,192 | VAN BUREN | 7,374 | 3,988 | 3,310 | 76 | 678 R | 54.1% | 44.9% | 54.6% | 45.4% |
| 157,715 | WASHINGTON | 64,103 | 35,726 | 27,597 | 780 | 8,129 R | 55.7% | 43.1% | 56.4% | 43.6% |
| 67,165 | WHITE | 26,425 | 17,001 | 9,129 | 295 | 7,872 R | 64.3% | 34.5% | 65.1% | 34.9% |
| 8,741 | WOODRUFF | 3,026 | 1,021 | 1,972 | 33 | 951 D | 33.7% | 65.2% | 34.1% | 65.9% |
| 21,139 | YELL | 6,659 | 3,678 | 2,913 | 68 | 765 R | 55.2% | 43.7% | 55.8% | 44.2% |
| 2,673,400 | TOTAL | 1,054,945 | 572,898 | 469,953 | 12,094 | 102,945 R | 54.3% | 44.5% | 54.9% | 45.1% |

# ARKANSAS

## PRESIDENT 2000

| 2000 Census Population | County | Total Vote | Republican | Democratic | Green (Nader) | Other | Rep.-Dem. Plurality | Percentage of Total Vote | | |
|---|---|---|---|---|---|---|---|---|---|---|
| | | | | | | | | Rep. | Dem. | Green |
| 20,749 | ARKANSAS | 6,372 | 3,353 | 2,877 | 65 | 77 | 476 R | 52.6% | 45.2% | 1.0% |
| 24,209 | ASHLEY | 8,271 | 3,876 | 4,253 | 61 | 81 | 377 D | 46.9% | 51.4% | 0.7% |
| 38,386 | BAXTER | 16,708 | 9,538 | 6,516 | 429 | 225 | 3,022 R | 57.1% | 39.0% | 2.6% |
| 153,406 | BENTON | 53,646 | 34,838 | 17,277 | 862 | 669 | 17,561 R | 64.9% | 32.2% | 1.6% |
| 33,948 | BOONE | 13,635 | 8,569 | 4,493 | 289 | 284 | 4,076 R | 62.8% | 33.0% | 2.1% |
| 12,600 | BRADLEY | 3,979 | 1,793 | 2,122 | 34 | 30 | 329 D | 45.1% | 53.3% | 0.9% |
| 5,744 | CALHOUN | 2,185 | 1,128 | 1,017 | 19 | 21 | 111 R | 51.6% | 46.5% | 0.9% |
| 25,357 | CARROLL | 9,590 | 5,556 | 3,595 | 301 | 138 | 1,961 R | 57.9% | 37.5% | 3.1% |
| 14,117 | CHICOT | 4,452 | 1,564 | 2,820 | 26 | 42 | 1,256 D | 35.1% | 63.3% | 0.6% |
| 23,546 | CLARK | 8,626 | 3,776 | 4,661 | 103 | 86 | 885 D | 43.8% | 54.0% | 1.2% |
| 17,609 | CLAY | 5,900 | 2,254 | 3,527 | 73 | 46 | 1,273 D | 38.2% | 59.8% | 1.2% |
| 24,046 | CLEBURNE | 10,207 | 5,730 | 4,120 | 183 | 174 | 1,610 R | 56.1% | 40.4% | 1.8% |
| 8,571 | CLEVELAND | 3,181 | 1,678 | 1,414 | 30 | 59 | 264 R | 52.8% | 44.5% | 0.9% |
| 25,603 | COLUMBIA | 9,307 | 5,018 | 4,003 | 70 | 216 | 1,015 R | 53.9% | 43.0% | 0.8% |
| 20,336 | CONWAY | 7,234 | 3,545 | 3,496 | 84 | 109 | 49 R | 49.0% | 48.3% | 1.2% |
| 82,148 | CRAIGHEAD | 25,157 | 12,158 | 12,376 | 409 | 214 | 218 D | 48.3% | 49.2% | 1.6% |
| 53,247 | CRAWFORD | 17,625 | 10,804 | 6,288 | 223 | 310 | 4,516 R | 61.3% | 35.7% | 1.3% |
| 50,866 | CRITTENDEN | 13,234 | 5,857 | 7,224 | 97 | 56 | 1,367 D | 44.3% | 54.6% | 0.7% |
| 19,526 | CROSS | 6,215 | 3,033 | 3,096 | 38 | 48 | 63 D | 48.8% | 49.8% | 0.6% |
| 9,210 | DALLAS | 3,325 | 1,571 | 1,710 | 21 | 23 | 139 D | 47.2% | 51.4% | 0.6% |
| 15,341 | DESHA | 4,495 | 1,603 | 2,776 | 38 | 78 | 1,173 D | 35.7% | 61.8% | 0.8% |
| 18,723 | DREW | 5,922 | 2,756 | 3,060 | 47 | 59 | 304 D | 46.5% | 51.7% | 0.8% |
| 86,014 | FAULKNER | 29,216 | 16,055 | 11,950 | 513 | 698 | 4,105 R | 55.0% | 40.9% | 1.8% |
| 17,771 | FRANKLIN | 6,140 | 3,277 | 2,674 | 100 | 89 | 603 R | 53.4% | 43.6% | 1.6% |
| 11,642 | FULTON | 4,108 | 2,036 | 1,976 | 51 | 45 | 60 R | 49.6% | 48.1% | 1.2% |
| 88,068 | GARLAND | 35,935 | 19,098 | 15,840 | 566 | 431 | 3,258 R | 53.1% | 44.1% | 1.6% |
| 16,464 | GRANT | 6,013 | 3,285 | 2,535 | 88 | 105 | 750 R | 54.6% | 42.2% | 1.5% |
| 37,331 | GREENE | 12,484 | 5,831 | 6,319 | 205 | 129 | 488 D | 46.7% | 50.6% | 1.6% |
| 23,587 | HEMPSTEAD | 7,289 | 3,257 | 3,937 | 50 | 45 | 680 D | 44.7% | 54.0% | 0.7% |
| 30,353 | HOT SPRING | 10,981 | 5,042 | 5,527 | 202 | 210 | 485 D | 45.9% | 50.3% | 1.8% |
| 14,300 | HOWARD | 4,459 | 2,326 | 2,063 | 50 | 20 | 263 R | 52.2% | 46.3% | 1.1% |
| 34,233 | INDEPENDENCE | 11,594 | 6,145 | 5,146 | 171 | 132 | 999 R | 53.0% | 44.4% | 1.5% |
| 13,249 | IZARD | 5,032 | 2,301 | 2,587 | 76 | 68 | 286 D | 45.7% | 51.4% | 1.5% |
| 18,418 | JACKSON | 6,072 | 2,280 | 3,651 | 77 | 64 | 1,371 D | 37.5% | 60.1% | 1.3% |
| 84,278 | JEFFERSON | 27,201 | 8,765 | 17,716 | 361 | 359 | 8,951 D | 32.2% | 65.1% | 1.3% |
| 22,781 | JOHNSON | 7,161 | 3,657 | 3,270 | 109 | 125 | 387 R | 51.1% | 45.7% | 1.5% |
| 8,559 | LAFAYETTE | 3,383 | 1,538 | 1,806 | 27 | 12 | 268 D | 45.5% | 53.4% | 0.8% |
| 17,774 | LAWRENCE | 6,040 | 2,626 | 3,255 | 87 | 72 | 629 D | 43.5% | 53.9% | 1.4% |
| 12,580 | LEE | 4,121 | 1,351 | 2,727 | 18 | 25 | 1,376 D | 32.8% | 66.2% | 0.4% |
| 14,492 | LINCOLN | 3,546 | 1,526 | 1,957 | 21 | 42 | 431 D | 43.0% | 55.2% | 0.6% |
| 13,628 | LITTLE RIVER | 5,263 | 2,283 | 2,883 | 50 | 47 | 600 D | 43.4% | 54.8% | 1.0% |
| 22,486 | LOGAN | 8,096 | 4,487 | 3,283 | 124 | 202 | 1,204 R | 55.4% | 40.6% | 1.5% |
| 52,828 | LONOKE | 17,943 | 10,606 | 6,851 | 237 | 249 | 3,755 R | 59.1% | 38.2% | 1.3% |
| 14,243 | MADISON | 5,628 | 3,387 | 2,055 | 88 | 98 | 1,332 R | 60.2% | 36.5% | 1.6% |
| 16,140 | MARION | 6,015 | 3,402 | 2,233 | 220 | 160 | 1,169 R | 56.6% | 37.1% | 3.7% |
| 40,443 | MILLER | 13,745 | 7,276 | 6,278 | 100 | 91 | 998 R | 52.9% | 45.7% | 0.7% |
| 51,979 | MISSISSIPPI | 12,586 | 5,199 | 7,107 | 110 | 170 | 1,908 D | 41.3% | 56.5% | 0.9% |
| 10,254 | MONROE | 3,293 | 1,329 | 1,910 | 29 | 25 | 581 D | 40.4% | 58.0% | 0.9% |
| 9,245 | MONTGOMERY | 3,739 | 2,128 | 1,438 | 101 | 72 | 690 R | 56.9% | 38.5% | 2.7% |
| 9,955 | NEVADA | 3,738 | 1,796 | 1,867 | 42 | 33 | 71 D | 48.0% | 49.9% | 1.1% |
| 8,608 | NEWTON | 3,927 | 2,529 | 1,205 | 112 | 81 | 1,324 R | 64.4% | 30.7% | 2.9% |
| 28,790 | OUACHITA | 10,395 | 4,739 | 5,464 | 100 | 92 | 725 D | 45.6% | 52.6% | 1.0% |
| 10,209 | PERRY | 4,007 | 2,114 | 1,648 | 61 | 184 | 466 R | 52.8% | 41.1% | 1.5% |
| 26,445 | PHILLIPS | 9,313 | 3,154 | 6,018 | 75 | 66 | 2,864 D | 33.9% | 64.6% | 0.8% |
| 11,303 | PIKE | 3,971 | 2,275 | 1,604 | 45 | 47 | 671 R | 57.3% | 40.4% | 1.1% |
| 25,614 | POINSETT | 7,235 | 2,988 | 4,102 | 87 | 58 | 1,114 D | 41.3% | 56.7% | 1.2% |
| 20,229 | POLK | 7,193 | 4,600 | 2,315 | 130 | 148 | 2,285 R | 64.0% | 32.2% | 1.8% |
| 54,469 | POPE | 18,422 | 11,244 | 6,669 | 259 | 250 | 4,575 R | 61.0% | 36.2% | 1.4% |
| 9,539 | PRAIRIE | 3,507 | 1,862 | 1,563 | 29 | 53 | 299 R | 53.1% | 44.6% | 0.8% |
| 361,474 | PULASKI | 127,151 | 55,866 | 68,320 | 1,756 | 1,209 | 12,454 D | 43.9% | 53.7% | 1.4% |

108

# ARKANSAS

## PRESIDENT 2000

| 2000 Census Population | County | Total Vote | Republican | Democratic | Green (Nader) | Other | Rep.-Dem. Plurality | Percentage of Total Vote | | |
|---|---|---|---|---|---|---|---|---|---|---|
| | | | | | | | | Rep. | Dem. | Green |
| 18,195 | RANDOLPH | 5,877 | 2,673 | 3,019 | 84 | 101 | 346 D | 45.5% | 51.4% | 1.4% |
| 29,329 | ST. FRANCIS | 8,496 | 3,414 | 4,986 | 42 | 54 | 1,572 D | 40.2% | 58.7% | 0.5% |
| 83,529 | SALINE | 32,391 | 18,617 | 12,700 | 533 | 541 | 5,917 R | 57.5% | 39.2% | 1.6% |
| 10,996 | SCOTT | 3,981 | 2,399 | 1,444 | 48 | 90 | 955 R | 60.3% | 36.3% | 1.2% |
| 8,261 | SEARCY | 4,058 | 2,610 | 1,229 | 83 | 136 | 1,381 R | 64.3% | 30.3% | 2.0% |
| 115,071 | SEBASTIAN | 40,159 | 23,483 | 15,555 | 503 | 618 | 7,928 R | 58.5% | 38.7% | 1.3% |
| 15,757 | SEVIER | 4,293 | 2,111 | 2,095 | 55 | 32 | 16 R | 49.2% | 48.8% | 1.3% |
| 17,119 | SHARP | 7,126 | 3,698 | 3,236 | 115 | 77 | 462 R | 51.9% | 45.4% | 1.6% |
| 11,499 | STONE | 4,860 | 2,623 | 2,043 | 98 | 96 | 580 R | 54.0% | 42.0% | 2.0% |
| 45,629 | UNION | 15,609 | 8,647 | 6,261 | 130 | 571 | 2,386 R | 55.4% | 40.1% | 0.8% |
| 16,192 | VAN BUREN | 6,984 | 3,485 | 3,202 | 153 | 144 | 283 R | 49.9% | 45.8% | 2.2% |
| 157,715 | WASHINGTON | 51,459 | 28,231 | 21,425 | 1,208 | 595 | 6,806 R | 54.9% | 41.6% | 2.3% |
| 67,165 | WHITE | 22,150 | 13,170 | 8,342 | 243 | 395 | 4,828 R | 59.5% | 37.7% | 1.1% |
| 8,741 | WOODRUFF | 2,651 | 898 | 1,699 | 19 | 35 | 801 D | 33.9% | 64.1% | 0.7% |
| 21,139 | YELL | 6,479 | 3,223 | 3,062 | 78 | 116 | 161 R | 49.7% | 47.3% | 1.2% |
| 2,673,400 | TOTAL | 921,781 | 472,940 | 422,768 | 13,421 | 12,652 | 50,172 R | 51.3% | 45.9% | 1.5% |

# ARKANSAS

## PRESIDENT 1996

| 1995 Census Pop. Est. | County | Total Vote | Republican | Democratic | Reform (Perot) | Other | Rep.-Dem. Plurality | Percentage of Total Vote | | |
|---|---|---|---|---|---|---|---|---|---|---|
| | | | | | | | | Rep. | Dem. | Reform |
| 21,032 | ARKANSAS | 6,698 | 1,910 | 4,220 | 463 | 105 | 2,310 D | 28.5% | 63.0% | 6.9% |
| 24,651 | ASHLEY | 8,281 | 2,428 | 5,011 | 704 | 138 | 2,583 D | 29.3% | 60.5% | 8.5% |
| 35,666 | BAXTER | 15,505 | 6,877 | 6,703 | 1,572 | 353 | 174 R | 44.4% | 43.2% | 10.1% |
| 120,932 | BENTON | 45,768 | 23,748 | 17,205 | 4,147 | 668 | 6,543 R | 51.9% | 37.6% | 9.1% |
| 31,364 | BOONE | 13,262 | 6,093 | 5,745 | 1,132 | 292 | 348 R | 45.9% | 43.3% | 8.5% |
| 11,650 | BRADLEY | 3,968 | 1,146 | 2,566 | 221 | 35 | 1,420 D | 28.9% | 64.7% | 5.6% |
| 5,801 | CALHOUN | 2,292 | 727 | 1,306 | 237 | 22 | 579 D | 31.7% | 57.0% | 10.3% |
| 21,933 | CARROLL | 8,823 | 3,957 | 3,689 | 986 | 191 | 268 R | 44.8% | 41.8% | 11.2% |
| 15,289 | CHICOT | 4,398 | 1,056 | 3,090 | 233 | 19 | 2,034 D | 24.0% | 70.3% | 5.3% |
| 22,101 | CLARK | 8,122 | 2,112 | 5,281 | 567 | 162 | 3,169 D | 26.0% | 65.0% | 7.0% |
| 17,601 | CLAY | 5,863 | 1,512 | 3,848 | 464 | 39 | 2,336 D | 25.8% | 65.6% | 7.9% |
| 21,865 | CLEBURNE | 9,464 | 3,807 | 4,475 | 1,021 | 161 | 668 D | 40.2% | 47.3% | 10.8% |
| 8,084 | CLEVELAND | 3,024 | 990 | 1,741 | 268 | 25 | 751 D | 32.7% | 57.6% | 8.9% |
| 25,670 | COLUMBIA | 8,982 | 3,376 | 4,730 | 678 | 198 | 1,354 D | 37.6% | 52.7% | 7.5% |
| 19,671 | CONWAY | 7,282 | 2,307 | 4,055 | 746 | 174 | 1,748 D | 31.7% | 55.7% | 10.2% |
| 74,794 | CRAIGHEAD | 24,582 | 9,210 | 13,284 | 1,778 | 310 | 4,074 D | 37.5% | 54.0% | 7.2% |
| 48,100 | CRAWFORD | 15,814 | 7,182 | 6,749 | 1,683 | 200 | 433 R | 45.4% | 42.7% | 10.6% |
| 49,889 | CRITTENDEN | 14,236 | 4,673 | 8,415 | 554 | 594 | 3,742 D | 32.8% | 59.1% | 3.9% |
| 19,370 | CROSS | 6,160 | 2,000 | 3,631 | 466 | 63 | 1,631 D | 32.5% | 58.9% | 7.6% |
| 9,493 | DALLAS | 3,435 | 1,041 | 2,118 | 236 | 40 | 1,077 D | 30.3% | 61.7% | 6.9% |
| 15,487 | DESHA | 4,553 | 978 | 3,230 | 247 | 98 | 2,252 D | 21.5% | 70.9% | 5.4% |
| 17,853 | DREW | 5,675 | 1,657 | 3,570 | 395 | 53 | 1,913 D | 29.2% | 62.9% | 7.0% |
| 71,758 | FAULKNER | 24,123 | 10,178 | 12,032 | 1,528 | 385 | 1,854 D | 42.2% | 49.9% | 6.3% |
| 16,122 | FRANKLIN | 6,188 | 2,246 | 3,269 | 626 | 47 | 1,023 D | 36.3% | 52.8% | 10.1% |
| 10,732 | FULTON | 4,223 | 1,351 | 2,361 | 455 | 56 | 1,010 D | 32.0% | 55.9% | 10.8% |
| 81,049 | GARLAND | 36,206 | 13,662 | 19,211 | 2,769 | 564 | 5,549 D | 37.7% | 53.1% | 7.6% |
| 15,022 | GRANT | 5,536 | 1,925 | 2,948 | 557 | 106 | 1,023 D | 34.8% | 53.3% | 10.1% |
| 34,620 | GREENE | 11,495 | 3,757 | 6,622 | 1,014 | 102 | 2,865 D | 32.7% | 57.6% | 8.8% |
| 22,194 | HEMPSTEAD | 7,551 | 2,021 | 4,983 | 501 | 46 | 2,962 D | 26.8% | 66.0% | 6.6% |
| 27,876 | HOT SPRING | 10,155 | 2,864 | 6,002 | 1,123 | 166 | 3,138 D | 28.2% | 59.1% | 11.1% |
| 13,655 | HOWARD | 4,632 | 1,478 | 2,741 | 369 | 44 | 1,263 D | 31.9% | 59.2% | 8.0% |
| 32,752 | INDEPENDENCE | 11,628 | 4,021 | 6,240 | 1,126 | 241 | 2,219 D | 34.6% | 53.7% | 9.7% |
| 12,619 | IZARD | 5,113 | 1,678 | 2,818 | 541 | 76 | 1,140 D | 32.8% | 55.1% | 10.6% |
| 18,622 | JACKSON | 6,500 | 1,525 | 4,304 | 611 | 60 | 2,779 D | 23.5% | 66.2% | 9.4% |
| 84,042 | JEFFERSON | 27,677 | 6,330 | 19,701 | 1,284 | 362 | 13,371 D | 22.9% | 71.2% | 4.6% |
| 20,508 | JOHNSON | 6,833 | 2,367 | 3,585 | 757 | 124 | 1,218 D | 34.6% | 52.5% | 11.1% |
| 9,213 | LAFAYETTE | 3,845 | 971 | 2,466 | 374 | 34 | 1,495 D | 25.3% | 64.1% | 9.7% |
| 17,468 | LAWRENCE | 6,141 | 1,823 | 3,652 | 609 | 57 | 1,829 D | 29.7% | 59.5% | 9.9% |
| 12,962 | LEE | 4,553 | 1,013 | 3,267 | 257 | 16 | 2,254 D | 22.2% | 71.8% | 5.6% |
| 14,119 | LINCOLN | 3,668 | 907 | 2,517 | 221 | 23 | 1,610 D | 24.7% | 68.6% | 6.0% |
| 13,413 | LITTLE RIVER | 5,112 | 1,409 | 3,183 | 480 | 40 | 1,774 D | 27.6% | 62.3% | 9.4% |
| 21,050 | LOGAN | 8,002 | 2,966 | 3,832 | 1,048 | 156 | 866 D | 37.1% | 47.9% | 13.1% |
| 45,966 | LONOKE | 16,056 | 6,414 | 8,049 | 1,369 | 224 | 1,635 D | 39.9% | 50.1% | 8.5% |
| 12,943 | MADISON | 5,355 | 2,303 | 2,504 | 461 | 87 | 201 D | 43.0% | 46.8% | 8.6% |
| 13,855 | MARION | 6,125 | 2,312 | 2,735 | 764 | 314 | 423 D | 37.7% | 44.7% | 12.5% |
| 39,082 | MILLER | 12,506 | 4,874 | 6,469 | 1,043 | 120 | 1,595 D | 39.0% | 51.7% | 8.3% |
| 50,811 | MISSISSIPPI | 13,347 | 3,919 | 8,301 | 1,016 | 111 | 4,382 D | 29.4% | 62.2% | 7.6% |
| 10,374 | MONROE | 3,458 | 973 | 2,247 | 202 | 36 | 1,274 D | 28.1% | 65.0% | 5.8% |
| 8,356 | MONTGOMERY | 3,460 | 1,137 | 1,830 | 427 | 66 | 693 D | 32.9% | 52.9% | 12.3% |
| 9,996 | NEVADA | 3,650 | 976 | 2,279 | 345 | 50 | 1,303 D | 26.7% | 62.4% | 9.5% |
| 7,989 | NEWTON | 4,154 | 1,927 | 1,631 | 498 | 98 | 296 R | 46.4% | 39.3% | 12.0% |
| 28,580 | OUACHITA | 10,609 | 3,136 | 6,635 | 733 | 105 | 3,499 D | 29.6% | 62.5% | 6.9% |
| 8,823 | PERRY | 3,482 | 1,143 | 1,873 | 395 | 71 | 730 D | 32.8% | 53.8% | 11.3% |
| 27,386 | PHILLIPS | 8,570 | 2,205 | 5,715 | 461 | 189 | 3,510 D | 25.7% | 66.7% | 5.4% |
| 10,332 | PIKE | 4,263 | 1,401 | 2,362 | 441 | 59 | 961 D | 32.9% | 55.4% | 10.3% |
| 24,640 | POINSETT | 7,427 | 2,034 | 4,686 | 647 | 60 | 2,652 D | 27.4% | 63.1% | 8.7% |
| 18,832 | POLK | 6,679 | 2,852 | 2,824 | 876 | 127 | 28 R | 42.7% | 42.3% | 13.1% |
| 51,181 | POPE | 18,840 | 8,243 | 8,433 | 1,891 | 273 | 190 D | 43.8% | 44.8% | 10.0% |
| 9,312 | PRAIRIE | 3,575 | 1,025 | 2,211 | 305 | 34 | 1,186 D | 28.7% | 61.8% | 8.5% |
| 352,240 | PULASKI | 127,733 | 44,780 | 75,084 | 6,014 | 1,855 | 30,304 D | 35.1% | 58.8% | 4.7% |

# ARKANSAS

## PRESIDENT 1996

| 1995 Census Pop. Est. | County | Total Vote | Republican | Democratic | Reform (Perot) | Other | Rep.-Dem. Plurality | Percentage of Total Vote | | |
|---|---|---|---|---|---|---|---|---|---|---|
| | | | | | | | | Rep. | Dem. | Reform |
| 17,430 | RANDOLPH | 5,633 | 1,789 | 3,213 | 561 | 70 | 1,424 D | 31.8% | 57.0% | 10.0% |
| 27,859 | ST. FRANCIS | 8,644 | 2,523 | 5,562 | 506 | 53 | 3,039 D | 29.2% | 64.3% | 5.9% |
| 73,604 | SALINE | 28,685 | 11,695 | 14,027 | 2,612 | 351 | 2,332 D | 40.8% | 48.9% | 9.1% |
| 10,628 | SCOTT | 4,297 | 1,426 | 2,259 | 513 | 99 | 833 D | 33.2% | 52.6% | 11.9% |
| 7,626 | SEARCY | 3,969 | 1,786 | 1,669 | 381 | 133 | 117 R | 45.0% | 42.1% | 9.6% |
| 104,402 | SEBASTIAN | 35,346 | 16,482 | 15,514 | 2,899 | 451 | 968 R | 46.6% | 43.9% | 8.2% |
| 14,501 | SEVIER | 4,425 | 1,379 | 2,553 | 446 | 47 | 1,174 D | 31.2% | 57.7% | 10.1% |
| 16,172 | SHARP | 6,970 | 2,635 | 3,573 | 687 | 75 | 938 D | 37.8% | 51.3% | 9.9% |
| 10,784 | STONE | 4,441 | 1,526 | 2,227 | 579 | 109 | 701 D | 34.4% | 50.1% | 13.0% |
| 46,191 | UNION | 15,940 | 6,053 | 8,373 | 1,073 | 441 | 2,320 D | 38.0% | 52.5% | 6.7% |
| 15,198 | VAN BUREN | 6,801 | 2,345 | 3,521 | 830 | 105 | 1,176 D | 34.5% | 51.8% | 12.2% |
| 131,708 | WASHINGTON | 43,967 | 19,476 | 20,419 | 3,133 | 939 | 943 D | 44.3% | 46.4% | 7.1% |
| 61,016 | WHITE | 20,991 | 8,659 | 10,204 | 1,828 | 300 | 1,545 D | 41.3% | 48.6% | 8.7% |
| 9,121 | WOODRUFF | 2,852 | 598 | 2,044 | 186 | 24 | 1,446 D | 21.0% | 71.7% | 6.5% |
| 18,739 | YELL | 6,644 | 2,111 | 3,749 | 714 | 70 | 1,638 D | 31.8% | 56.4% | 10.7% |
| 2,483,769 | TOTAL | 884,262 | 325,416 | 475,171 | 69,884 | 13,791 | 149,755 D | 36.8% | 53.7% | 7.9% |

# ARKANSAS

## PRESIDENT 1992

| 1990 Census Population | County | Total Vote | Republican | Democratic | Perot | Other | Plurality | Percentage Total Vote | | |
|---|---|---|---|---|---|---|---|---|---|---|
| | | | | | | | | Rep. | Dem. | Perot |
| 21,653 | ARKANSAS | 7,980 | 2,594 | 4,709 | 639 | 38 | 2,115 D | 32.5% | 59.0% | 8.0% |
| 24,319 | ASHLEY | 9,567 | 2,686 | 5,876 | 931 | 74 | 3,190 D | 28.1% | 61.4% | 9.7% |
| 31,186 | BAXTER | 15,732 | 5,640 | 6,991 | 2,938 | 163 | 1,351 D | 35.9% | 44.4% | 18.7% |
| 97,499 | BENTON | 43,279 | 21,126 | 15,774 | 6,128 | 251 | 5,352 R | 48.8% | 36.4% | 14.2% |
| 28,297 | BOONE | 14,437 | 6,094 | 6,128 | 2,079 | 136 | 34 D | 42.2% | 42.4% | 14.4% |
| 11,793 | BRADLEY | 4,837 | 1,482 | 2,954 | 391 | 10 | 1,472 D | 30.6% | 61.1% | 8.1% |
| 5,826 | CALHOUN | 2,702 | 1,047 | 1,389 | 257 | 9 | 342 D | 38.7% | 51.4% | 9.5% |
| 18,654 | CARROLL | 8,857 | 3,535 | 3,769 | 1,500 | 53 | 234 D | 39.9% | 42.6% | 16.9% |
| 15,713 | CHICOT | 5,099 | 1,242 | 3,504 | 347 | 6 | 2,262 D | 24.4% | 68.7% | 6.8% |
| 21,437 | CLARK | 8,922 | 2,403 | 5,767 | 714 | 38 | 3,364 D | 26.9% | 64.6% | 8.0% |
| 18,107 | CLAY | 7,080 | 1,647 | 4,848 | 568 | 17 | 3,201 D | 23.3% | 68.5% | 8.0% |
| 19,411 | CLEBURNE | 9,980 | 3,580 | 5,090 | 1,263 | 47 | 1,510 D | 35.9% | 51.0% | 12.7% |
| 7,781 | CLEVELAND | 3,378 | 1,127 | 1,893 | 337 | 21 | 766 D | 33.4% | 56.0% | 10.0% |
| 25,691 | COLUMBIA | 9,819 | 3,702 | 4,747 | 1,090 | 280 | 1,045 D | 37.7% | 48.3% | 11.1% |
| 19,151 | CONWAY | 8,481 | 2,719 | 4,898 | 803 | 61 | 2,179 D | 32.1% | 57.8% | 9.5% |
| 68,956 | CRAIGHEAD | 25,596 | 9,104 | 13,931 | 2,274 | 287 | 4,827 D | 35.6% | 54.4% | 8.9% |
| 42,493 | CRAWFORD | 16,165 | 6,882 | 6,656 | 2,442 | 185 | 226 R | 42.6% | 41.2% | 15.1% |
| 49,939 | CRITTENDEN | 17,108 | 5,910 | 9,683 | 848 | 667 | 3,773 D | 34.5% | 56.6% | 5.0% |
| 19,225 | CROSS | 6,986 | 2,303 | 4,058 | 602 | 23 | 1,755 D | 33.0% | 58.1% | 8.6% |
| 9,614 | DALLAS | 3,925 | 1,458 | 2,107 | 345 | 15 | 649 D | 37.1% | 53.7% | 8.8% |
| 16,798 | DESHA | 5,621 | 1,279 | 3,815 | 392 | 135 | 2,536 D | 22.8% | 67.9% | 7.0% |
| 17,369 | DREW | 6,298 | 1,938 | 3,748 | 596 | 16 | 1,810 D | 30.8% | 59.5% | 9.5% |
| 60,006 | FAULKNER | 25,215 | 9,491 | 13,000 | 2,437 | 287 | 3,509 D | 37.6% | 51.6% | 9.7% |
| 14,897 | FRANKLIN | 6,736 | 2,495 | 3,217 | 987 | 37 | 722 D | 37.0% | 47.8% | 14.7% |
| 10,037 | FULTON | 4,736 | 1,258 | 2,827 | 631 | 20 | 1,569 D | 26.6% | 59.7% | 13.3% |
| 73,397 | GARLAND | 35,995 | 12,886 | 18,811 | 3,475 | 823 | 5,925 D | 35.8% | 52.3% | 9.7% |
| 13,948 | GRANT | 6,198 | 2,272 | 3,190 | 702 | 34 | 918 D | 36.7% | 51.5% | 11.3% |
| 31,804 | GREENE | 12,322 | 3,510 | 7,541 | 1,213 | 58 | 4,031 D | 28.5% | 61.2% | 9.8% |
| 21,621 | HEMPSTEAD | 8,922 | 2,387 | 5,476 | 1,022 | 37 | 3,089 D | 26.8% | 61.4% | 11.5% |
| 26,115 | HOT SPRING | 10,616 | 3,036 | 6,308 | 1,209 | 63 | 3,272 D | 28.6% | 59.4% | 11.4% |
| 13,569 | HOWARD | 4,975 | 1,728 | 2,764 | 466 | 17 | 1,036 D | 34.7% | 55.6% | 9.4% |
| 31,192 | INDEPENDENCE | 12,840 | 4,232 | 7,083 | 1,444 | 81 | 2,851 D | 33.0% | 55.2% | 11.2% |
| 11,364 | IZARD | 5,588 | 1,532 | 3,419 | 606 | 31 | 1,887 D | 27.4% | 61.2% | 10.8% |
| 18,944 | JACKSON | 7,524 | 1,864 | 4,944 | 673 | 43 | 3,080 D | 24.8% | 65.7% | 8.9% |
| 85,487 | JEFFERSON | 31,692 | 7,525 | 21,819 | 2,067 | 281 | 14,294 D | 23.7% | 68.8% | 6.5% |
| 18,221 | JOHNSON | 7,578 | 2,563 | 3,951 | 1,013 | 51 | 1,388 D | 33.8% | 52.1% | 13.4% |
| 9,643 | LAFAYETTE | 3,979 | 1,188 | 2,273 | 504 | 14 | 1,085 D | 29.9% | 57.1% | 12.7% |
| 17,457 | LAWRENCE | 6,929 | 2,124 | 4,146 | 636 | 23 | 2,022 D | 30.7% | 59.8% | 9.2% |
| 13,053 | LEE | 5,066 | 1,293 | 3,436 | 308 | 29 | 2,143 D | 25.5% | 67.8% | 6.1% |
| 13,690 | LINCOLN | 4,347 | 1,142 | 2,805 | 390 | 10 | 1,663 D | 26.3% | 64.5% | 9.0% |
| 13,966 | LITTLE RIVER | 5,718 | 1,483 | 3,327 | 890 | 18 | 1,844 D | 25.9% | 58.2% | 15.6% |
| 20,557 | LOGAN | 8,687 | 3,408 | 3,995 | 1,220 | 64 | 587 D | 39.2% | 46.0% | 14.0% |
| 39,268 | LONOKE | 15,824 | 6,253 | 7,963 | 1,554 | 54 | 1,710 D | 39.5% | 50.3% | 9.8% |
| 11,618 | MADISON | 5,277 | 2,238 | 2,415 | 598 | 26 | 177 D | 42.4% | 45.8% | 11.3% |
| 12,001 | MARION | 6,245 | 2,023 | 2,757 | 1,327 | 138 | 734 D | 32.4% | 44.1% | 21.2% |
| 38,467 | MILLER | 14,623 | 5,273 | 7,050 | 2,249 | 51 | 1,777 D | 36.1% | 48.2% | 15.4% |
| 57,525 | MISSISSIPPI | 15,962 | 4,697 | 10,046 | 981 | 238 | 5,349 D | 29.4% | 62.9% | 6.1% |
| 11,333 | MONROE | 4,272 | 1,324 | 2,578 | 355 | 15 | 1,254 D | 31.0% | 60.3% | 8.3% |
| 7,841 | MONTGOMERY | 3,712 | 1,205 | 1,904 | 576 | 27 | 699 D | 32.5% | 51.3% | 15.5% |
| 10,101 | NEVADA | 3,948 | 1,217 | 2,242 | 455 | 34 | 1,025 D | 30.8% | 56.8% | 11.5% |
| 7,666 | NEWTON | 4,144 | 1,730 | 1,765 | 608 | 41 | 35 D | 41.7% | 42.6% | 14.7% |
| 30,574 | OUACHITA | 12,415 | 3,711 | 7,411 | 1,238 | 55 | 3,700 D | 29.9% | 59.7% | 10.0% |
| 7,969 | PERRY | 3,504 | 1,162 | 1,906 | 412 | 24 | 744 D | 33.2% | 54.4% | 11.8% |
| 28,838 | PHILLIPS | 9,837 | 2,695 | 6,456 | 634 | 52 | 3,761 D | 27.4% | 65.6% | 6.4% |
| 10,086 | PIKE | 4,232 | 1,577 | 2,168 | 472 | 15 | 591 D | 37.3% | 51.2% | 11.2% |
| 24,664 | POINSETT | 8,571 | 2,425 | 5,341 | 761 | 44 | 2,916 D | 28.3% | 62.3% | 8.9% |
| 17,347 | POLK | 7,217 | 2,757 | 3,162 | 1,225 | 73 | 405 D | 38.2% | 43.8% | 17.0% |
| 45,883 | POPE | 17,862 | 8,056 | 7,704 | 1,989 | 113 | 352 R | 45.1% | 43.1% | 11.1% |
| 9,518 | PRAIRIE | 3,956 | 1,154 | 2,366 | 434 | 2 | 1,212 D | 29.2% | 59.8% | 11.0% |
| 349,660 | PULASKI | 136,957 | 47,789 | 79,482 | 8,751 | 935 | 31,693 D | 34.9% | 58.0% | 6.4% |

# ARKANSAS

## PRESIDENT 1992

| 1990 Census Population | County | Total Vote | Republican | Democratic | Perot | Other | Plurality | Percentage Total Vote | | |
|---|---|---|---|---|---|---|---|---|---|---|
| | | | | | | | | Rep. | Dem. | Perot |
| 16,558 | RANDOLPH | 6,314 | 1,766 | 3,921 | 578 | 49 | 2,155 D | 28.0% | 62.1% | 9.2% |
| 28,497 | ST. FRANCIS | 10,635 | 3,289 | 6,548 | 766 | 32 | 3,259 D | 30.9% | 61.6% | 7.2% |
| 64,183 | SALINE | 25,661 | 10,105 | 12,671 | 2,751 | 134 | 2,566 D | 39.4% | 49.4% | 10.7% |
| 10,205 | SCOTT | 4,562 | 1,695 | 2,228 | 610 | 29 | 533 D | 37.2% | 48.8% | 13.4% |
| 7,841 | SEARCY | 3,984 | 1,772 | 1,679 | 503 | 30 | 93 R | 44.5% | 42.1% | 12.6% |
| 99,590 | SEBASTIAN | 39,659 | 16,817 | 16,570 | 6,023 | 249 | 247 R | 42.4% | 41.8% | 15.2% |
| 13,637 | SEVIER | 5,011 | 1,592 | 2,558 | 643 | 218 | 966 D | 31.8% | 51.0% | 12.8% |
| 14,109 | SHARP | 7,196 | 2,486 | 3,761 | 921 | 28 | 1,275 D | 34.5% | 52.3% | 12.8% |
| 9,775 | STONE | 5,039 | 1,672 | 2,622 | 697 | 48 | 950 D | 33.2% | 52.0% | 13.8% |
| 46,719 | UNION | 18,580 | 7,305 | 8,786 | 1,919 | 570 | 1,481 D | 39.3% | 47.3% | 10.3% |
| 14,008 | VAN BUREN | 7,361 | 2,612 | 3,819 | 888 | 42 | 1,207 D | 35.5% | 51.9% | 12.1% |
| 113,409 | WASHINGTON | 47,880 | 20,292 | 22,029 | 5,304 | 255 | 1,737 D | 42.4% | 46.0% | 11.1% |
| 54,676 | WHITE | 21,563 | 8,538 | 10,494 | 2,366 | 165 | 1,956 D | 39.6% | 48.7% | 11.0% |
| 9,520 | WOODRUFF | 3,495 | 676 | 2,589 | 227 | 3 | 1,913 D | 19.3% | 74.1% | 6.5% |
| 17,759 | YELL | 7,643 | 2,506 | 4,165 | 940 | 32 | 1,659 D | 32.8% | 54.5% | 12.3% |
| 2,350,725 | TOTAL | 950,653 | 337,324 | 505,823 | 99,132 | 8,374 | 168,499 D | 35.5% | 53.2% | 10.4% |

# ARKANSAS

## PRESIDENT 1988

| 1980 Census Population | County | Total Vote | Republican | Democratic | Other | Rep.-Dem. Plurality | Percentage Total Vote Rep. | Dem. | Major Vote Rep. | Dem. |
|---|---|---|---|---|---|---|---|---|---|---|
| 24,175 | ARKANSAS | 7,205 | 4,007 | 3,075 | 123 | 932 R | 55.6% | 42.7% | 56.6% | 43.4% |
| 26,538 | ASHLEY | 8,659 | 4,111 | 4,466 | 82 | 355 D | 47.5% | 51.6% | 47.9% | 52.1% |
| 27,409 | BAXTER | 13,597 | 8,614 | 4,808 | 175 | 3,806 R | 63.4% | 35.4% | 64.2% | 35.8% |
| 78,115 | BENTON | 34,110 | 24,295 | 9,399 | 416 | 14,896 R | 71.2% | 27.6% | 72.1% | 27.9% |
| 26,067 | BOONE | 11,816 | 7,567 | 3,998 | 251 | 3,569 R | 64.0% | 33.8% | 65.4% | 34.6% |
| 13,803 | BRADLEY | 4,269 | 2,089 | 2,167 | 13 | 78 D | 48.9% | 50.8% | 49.1% | 50.9% |
| 6,079 | CALHOUN | 2,344 | 1,316 | 1,024 | 4 | 292 R | 56.1% | 43.7% | 56.2% | 43.8% |
| 16,203 | CARROLL | 7,253 | 4,553 | 2,632 | 68 | 1,921 R | 62.8% | 36.3% | 63.4% | 36.6% |
| 17,793 | CHICOT | 4,346 | 1,901 | 2,426 | 19 | 525 D | 43.7% | 55.8% | 43.9% | 56.1% |
| 23,326 | CLARK | 8,130 | 3,389 | 4,675 | 66 | 1,286 D | 41.7% | 57.5% | 42.0% | 58.0% |
| 20,616 | CLAY | 6,240 | 2,766 | 3,442 | 32 | 676 D | 44.3% | 55.2% | 44.6% | 55.4% |
| 16,909 | CLEBURNE | 8,381 | 4,932 | 3,404 | 45 | 1,528 R | 58.8% | 40.6% | 59.2% | 40.8% |
| 7,868 | CLEVELAND | 2,881 | 1,462 | 1,404 | 15 | 58 R | 50.7% | 48.7% | 51.0% | 49.0% |
| 26,644 | COLUMBIA | 9,802 | 5,810 | 3,706 | 286 | 2,104 R | 59.3% | 37.8% | 61.1% | 38.9% |
| 19,505 | CONWAY | 8,239 | 4,066 | 4,134 | 39 | 68 D | 49.4% | 50.2% | 49.6% | 50.4% |
| 63,239 | CRAIGHEAD | 21,615 | 11,887 | 9,083 | 645 | 2,804 R | 55.0% | 42.0% | 56.7% | 43.3% |
| 36,892 | CRAWFORD | 12,832 | 9,092 | 3,582 | 158 | 5,510 R | 70.9% | 27.9% | 71.7% | 28.3% |
| 49,499 | CRITTENDEN | 14,384 | 7,441 | 6,702 | 241 | 739 R | 51.7% | 46.6% | 52.6% | 47.4% |
| 20,434 | CROSS | 6,212 | 3,186 | 2,989 | 37 | 197 R | 51.3% | 48.1% | 51.6% | 48.4% |
| 10,515 | DALLAS | 3,958 | 1,947 | 1,990 | 21 | 43 D | 49.2% | 50.3% | 49.5% | 50.5% |
| 19,760 | DESHA | 5,435 | 2,334 | 2,859 | 242 | 525 D | 42.9% | 52.6% | 44.9% | 55.1% |
| 17,910 | DREW | 5,620 | 2,995 | 2,578 | 47 | 417 R | 53.3% | 45.9% | 53.7% | 46.3% |
| 46,192 | FAULKNER | 18,279 | 10,678 | 7,302 | 299 | 3,376 R | 58.4% | 39.9% | 59.4% | 40.6% |
| 14,705 | FRANKLIN | 6,089 | 3,588 | 2,458 | 43 | 1,130 R | 58.9% | 40.4% | 59.3% | 40.7% |
| 9,975 | FULTON | 3,957 | 1,918 | 2,018 | 21 | 100 D | 48.5% | 51.0% | 48.7% | 51.3% |
| 70,531 | GARLAND | 31,642 | 19,281 | 11,406 | 955 | 7,875 R | 60.9% | 36.0% | 62.8% | 37.2% |
| 13,008 | GRANT | 4,904 | 2,717 | 2,142 | 45 | 575 R | 55.4% | 43.7% | 55.9% | 44.1% |
| 30,744 | GREENE | 10,310 | 5,161 | 5,065 | 84 | 96 R | 50.1% | 49.1% | 50.5% | 49.5% |
| 23,635 | HEMPSTEAD | 7,799 | 3,938 | 3,841 | 20 | 97 R | 50.5% | 49.2% | 50.6% | 49.4% |
| 26,819 | HOT SPRING | 9,405 | 4,181 | 5,090 | 134 | 909 D | 44.5% | 54.1% | 45.1% | 54.9% |
| 13,459 | HOWARD | 4,337 | 2,510 | 1,818 | 9 | 692 R | 57.9% | 41.9% | 58.0% | 42.0% |
| 30,147 | INDEPENDENCE | 11,208 | 6,637 | 4,523 | 48 | 2,114 R | 59.2% | 40.4% | 59.5% | 40.5% |
| 10,768 | IZARD | 5,517 | 2,824 | 2,652 | 41 | 172 R | 51.2% | 48.1% | 51.6% | 48.4% |
| 21,646 | JACKSON | 7,276 | 3,049 | 4,199 | 28 | 1,150 D | 41.9% | 57.7% | 42.1% | 57.9% |
| 90,718 | JEFFERSON | 29,752 | 12,520 | 16,664 | 568 | 4,144 D | 42.1% | 56.0% | 42.9% | 57.1% |
| 17,423 | JOHNSON | 6,941 | 4,046 | 2,818 | 77 | 1,228 R | 58.3% | 40.6% | 58.9% | 41.1% |
| 10,213 | LAFAYETTE | 3,800 | 1,860 | 1,915 | 25 | 55 D | 48.9% | 50.4% | 49.3% | 50.7% |
| 18,447 | LAWRENCE | 6,421 | 3,205 | 3,179 | 37 | 26 R | 49.9% | 49.5% | 50.2% | 49.8% |
| 15,539 | LEE | 4,812 | 1,863 | 2,878 | 71 | 1,015 D | 38.7% | 59.8% | 39.3% | 60.7% |
| 13,369 | LINCOLN | 3,794 | 1,557 | 2,204 | 33 | 647 D | 41.0% | 58.1% | 41.4% | 58.6% |
| 13,952 | LITTLE RIVER | 5,119 | 2,347 | 2,740 | 32 | 393 D | 45.8% | 53.5% | 46.1% | 53.9% |
| 20,144 | LOGAN | 3,504 | 2,203 | 1,254 | 47 | 949 R | 62.9% | 35.8% | 63.7% | 36.3% |
| 34,518 | LONOKE | 12,090 | 7,215 | 4,786 | 89 | 2,429 R | 59.7% | 39.6% | 60.1% | 39.9% |
| 11,373 | MADISON | 5,223 | 3,067 | 2,106 | 50 | 961 R | 58.7% | 40.3% | 59.3% | 40.7% |
| 11,334 | MARION | 5,178 | 2,993 | 2,033 | 152 | 960 R | 57.8% | 39.3% | 59.6% | 40.4% |
| 37,766 | MILLER | 12,629 | 7,110 | 5,437 | 82 | 1,673 R | 56.3% | 43.1% | 56.7% | 43.3% |
| 59,517 | MISSISSIPPI | 14,888 | 7,841 | 6,759 | 288 | 1,082 R | 52.7% | 45.4% | 53.7% | 46.3% |
| 14,052 | MONROE | 3,972 | 1,862 | 2,052 | 58 | 190 D | 46.9% | 51.7% | 47.6% | 52.4% |
| 7,771 | MONTGOMERY | 3,129 | 1,752 | 1,362 | 15 | 390 R | 56.0% | 43.5% | 56.3% | 43.7% |
| 11,097 | NEVADA | 3,459 | 1,714 | 1,732 | 13 | 18 D | 49.6% | 50.1% | 49.7% | 50.3% |
| 7,756 | NEWTON | 4,039 | 2,504 | 1,489 | 46 | 1,015 R | 62.0% | 36.9% | 62.7% | 37.3% |
| 30,541 | OUACHITA | 12,043 | 6,297 | 5,229 | 517 | 1,068 R | 52.3% | 43.4% | 54.6% | 45.4% |
| 7,266 | PERRY | 3,128 | 1,627 | 1,470 | 31 | 157 R | 52.0% | 47.0% | 52.5% | 47.5% |
| 34,772 | PHILLIPS | 9,861 | 3,892 | 5,580 | 389 | 1,688 D | 39.5% | 56.6% | 41.1% | 58.9% |
| 10,373 | PIKE | 3,797 | 2,105 | 1,681 | 11 | 424 R | 55.4% | 44.3% | 55.6% | 44.4% |
| 27,032 | POINSETT | 7,566 | 3,644 | 3,873 | 49 | 229 D | 48.2% | 51.2% | 48.5% | 51.5% |
| 17,007 | POLK | 6,595 | 4,099 | 2,390 | 106 | 1,709 R | 62.2% | 36.2% | 63.2% | 36.8% |
| 39,021 | POPE | 15,123 | 10,084 | 4,941 | 98 | 5,143 R | 66.7% | 32.7% | 67.1% | 32.9% |
| 10,140 | PRAIRIE | 3,656 | 1,947 | 1,688 | 21 | 259 R | 53.3% | 46.2% | 53.6% | 46.4% |
| 340,613 | PULASKI | 128,333 | 70,562 | 55,857 | 1,914 | 14,705 R | 55.0% | 43.5% | 55.8% | 44.2% |

114

# ARKANSAS

## PRESIDENT 1988

| 1980 Census Population | County | Total Vote | Republican | Democratic | Other | Rep.-Dem. Plurality | Percentage Total Vote Rep. | Dem. | Major Vote Rep. | Dem. |
|---|---|---|---|---|---|---|---|---|---|---|
| 16,834 | RANDOLPH | 5,418 | 2,560 | 2,781 | 77 | 221 D | 47.2% | 51.3% | 47.9% | 52.1% |
| 30,858 | ST. FRANCIS | 8,980 | 4,298 | 4,656 | 26 | 358 D | 47.9% | 51.8% | 48.0% | 52.0% |
| 53,161 | SALINE | 20,977 | 12,353 | 8,436 | 188 | 3,917 R | 58.9% | 40.2% | 59.4% | 40.6% |
| 9,685 | SCOTT | 4,262 | 2,507 | 1,707 | 48 | 800 R | 58.8% | 40.1% | 59.5% | 40.5% |
| 8,847 | SEARCY | 4,143 | 2,743 | 1,340 | 60 | 1,403 R | 66.2% | 32.3% | 67.2% | 32.8% |
| 95,172 | SEBASTIAN | 34,432 | 24,426 | 9,684 | 322 | 14,742 R | 70.9% | 28.1% | 71.6% | 28.4% |
| 14,060 | SEVIER | 4,327 | 2,254 | 2,037 | 36 | 217 R | 52.1% | 47.1% | 52.5% | 47.5% |
| 14,607 | SHARP | 6,612 | 3,623 | 2,955 | 34 | 668 R | 54.8% | 44.7% | 55.1% | 44.9% |
| 9,022 | STONE | 3,962 | 2,186 | 1,728 | 48 | 458 R | 55.2% | 43.6% | 55.9% | 44.1% |
| 48,573 | UNION | 17,256 | 10,581 | 5,931 | 744 | 4,650 R | 61.3% | 34.4% | 64.1% | 35.9% |
| 13,357 | VAN BUREN | 6,209 | 3,562 | 2,607 | 40 | 955 R | 57.4% | 42.0% | 57.7% | 42.3% |
| 100,494 | WASHINGTON | 36,658 | 23,601 | 12,557 | 500 | 11,044 R | 64.4% | 34.3% | 65.3% | 34.7% |
| 50,835 | WHITE | 18,234 | 11,094 | 6,957 | 183 | 4,137 R | 60.8% | 38.2% | 61.5% | 38.5% |
| 11,222 | WOODRUFF | 3,034 | 1,097 | 1,924 | 13 | 827 D | 36.2% | 63.4% | 36.3% | 63.7% |
| 17,026 | YELL | 6,331 | 3,535 | 2,763 | 33 | 772 R | 55.8% | 43.6% | 56.1% | 43.9% |
| 2,286,435 | TOTAL | 827,738 | 466,578 | 349,237 | 11,923 | 117,341 R | 56.4% | 42.2% | 57.2% | 42.8% |

# ARKANSAS

## PRESIDENT 1984

| 1980 Census Population | County | Total Vote | Republican | Democratic | Other | Rep.-Dem. Plurality | Percentage | | | |
|---|---|---|---|---|---|---|---|---|---|---|
| | | | | | | | Total Vote | | Major Vote | |
| | | | | | | | Rep. | Dem. | Rep. | Dem. |
| 24,175 | ARKANSAS | 8,008 | 4,804 | 3,153 | 51 | 1,651 R | 60.0% | 39.4% | 60.4% | 39.6% |
| 26,538 | ASHLEY | 9,089 | 5,675 | 3,373 | 41 | 2,302 R | 62.4% | 37.1% | 62.7% | 37.3% |
| 27,409 | BAXTER | 15,564 | 10,870 | 4,528 | 166 | 6,342 R | 69.8% | 29.1% | 70.6% | 29.4% |
| 78,115 | BENTON | 32,010 | 24,296 | 7,306 | 408 | 16,990 R | 75.9% | 22.8% | 76.9% | 23.1% |
| 26,067 | BOONE | 11,567 | 7,961 | 3,356 | 250 | 4,605 R | 68.8% | 29.0% | 70.3% | 29.7% |
| 13,803 | BRADLEY | 5,017 | 2,690 | 2,313 | 14 | 377 R | 53.6% | 46.1% | 53.8% | 46.2% |
| 6,079 | CALHOUN | 2,535 | 1,474 | 1,058 | 3 | 416 R | 58.1% | 41.7% | 58.2% | 41.8% |
| 16,203 | CARROLL | 7,390 | 5,041 | 2,263 | 86 | 2,778 R | 68.2% | 30.6% | 69.0% | 31.0% |
| 17,793 | CHICOT | 5,927 | 2,502 | 3,407 | 18 | 905 D | 42.2% | 57.5% | 42.3% | 57.7% |
| 23,326 | CLARK | 8,853 | 4,185 | 4,638 | 30 | 453 D | 47.3% | 52.4% | 47.4% | 52.6% |
| 20,616 | CLAY | 7,105 | 3,767 | 3,279 | 59 | 488 R | 53.0% | 46.2% | 53.5% | 46.5% |
| 16,909 | CLEBURNE | 9,008 | 5,769 | 3,172 | 67 | 2,597 R | 64.0% | 35.2% | 64.5% | 35.5% |
| 7,868 | CLEVELAND | 3,165 | 1,773 | 1,378 | 14 | 395 R | 56.0% | 43.5% | 56.3% | 43.7% |
| 26,644 | COLUMBIA | 10,285 | 6,526 | 3,680 | 79 | 2,846 R | 63.5% | 35.8% | 63.9% | 36.1% |
| 19,505 | CONWAY | 8,836 | 5,049 | 3,742 | 45 | 1,307 R | 57.1% | 42.3% | 57.4% | 42.6% |
| 63,239 | CRAIGHEAD | 22,343 | 14,047 | 8,035 | 261 | 6,012 R | 62.9% | 36.0% | 63.6% | 36.4% |
| 36,892 | CRAWFORD | 12,701 | 9,551 | 3,071 | 79 | 6,480 R | 75.2% | 24.2% | 75.7% | 24.3% |
| 49,499 | CRITTENDEN | 13,934 | 6,663 | 6,520 | 751 | 143 R | 47.8% | 46.8% | 50.5% | 49.5% |
| 20,434 | CROSS | 6,635 | 3,917 | 2,701 | 17 | 1,216 R | 59.0% | 40.7% | 59.2% | 40.8% |
| 10,515 | DALLAS | 4,472 | 2,361 | 2,035 | 76 | 326 R | 52.8% | 45.5% | 53.7% | 46.3% |
| 19,760 | DESHA | 5,878 | 2,696 | 2,918 | 264 | 222 D | 45.9% | 49.6% | 48.0% | 52.0% |
| 17,910 | DREW | 6,073 | 3,407 | 2,638 | 28 | 769 R | 56.1% | 43.4% | 56.4% | 43.6% |
| 46,192 | FAULKNER | 19,043 | 11,595 | 7,169 | 279 | 4,426 R | 60.9% | 37.6% | 61.8% | 38.2% |
| 14,705 | FRANKLIN | 6,843 | 4,382 | 2,399 | 62 | 1,983 R | 64.0% | 35.1% | 64.6% | 35.4% |
| 9,975 | FULTON | 4,223 | 2,329 | 1,864 | 30 | 465 R | 55.2% | 44.1% | 55.5% | 44.5% |
| 70,531 | GARLAND | 33,958 | 21,213 | 11,484 | 1,261 | 9,729 R | 62.5% | 33.8% | 64.9% | 35.1% |
| 13,008 | GRANT | 5,353 | 3,167 | 2,148 | 38 | 1,019 R | 59.2% | 40.1% | 59.6% | 40.4% |
| 30,744 | GREENE | 11,000 | 6,179 | 4,730 | 91 | 1,449 R | 56.2% | 43.0% | 56.6% | 43.4% |
| 23,635 | HEMPSTEAD | 8,268 | 4,904 | 3,327 | 37 | 1,577 R | 59.3% | 40.2% | 59.6% | 40.4% |
| 26,819 | HOT SPRING | 11,546 | 5,629 | 5,836 | 81 | 207 D | 48.8% | 50.5% | 49.1% | 50.9% |
| 13,459 | HOWARD | 4,832 | 3,079 | 1,746 | 7 | 1,333 R | 63.7% | 36.1% | 63.8% | 36.2% |
| 30,147 | INDEPENDENCE | 11,911 | 7,428 | 4,415 | 68 | 3,013 R | 62.4% | 37.1% | 62.7% | 37.3% |
| 10,768 | IZARD | 5,136 | 2,726 | 2,346 | 64 | 380 R | 53.1% | 45.7% | 53.7% | 46.3% |
| 21,646 | JACKSON | 7,981 | 3,901 | 4,038 | 42 | 137 D | 48.9% | 50.6% | 49.1% | 50.9% |
| 90,718 | JEFFERSON | 32,909 | 14,514 | 18,082 | 313 | 3,568 D | 44.1% | 54.9% | 44.5% | 55.5% |
| 17,423 | JOHNSON | 7,827 | 4,720 | 3,056 | 51 | 1,664 R | 60.3% | 39.0% | 60.7% | 39.3% |
| 10,213 | LAFAYETTE | 4,007 | 2,290 | 1,695 | 22 | 595 R | 57.1% | 42.3% | 57.5% | 42.5% |
| 18,447 | LAWRENCE | 6,676 | 4,039 | 2,594 | 43 | 1,445 R | 60.5% | 38.9% | 60.9% | 39.1% |
| 15,539 | LEE | 4,717 | 2,101 | 2,541 | 75 | 440 D | 44.5% | 53.9% | 45.3% | 54.7% |
| 13,369 | LINCOLN | 4,272 | 1,860 | 2,406 | 6 | 546 D | 43.5% | 56.3% | 43.6% | 56.4% |
| 13,952 | LITTLE RIVER | 5,295 | 3,155 | 2,090 | 50 | 1,065 R | 59.6% | 39.5% | 60.2% | 39.8% |
| 20,144 | LOGAN | 8,969 | 5,663 | 3,206 | 100 | 2,457 R | 63.1% | 35.7% | 63.9% | 36.1% |
| 34,518 | LONOKE | 13,142 | 8,425 | 4,636 | 81 | 3,789 R | 64.1% | 35.3% | 64.5% | 35.5% |
| 11,373 | MADISON | 5,703 | 3,516 | 2,133 | 54 | 1,383 R | 61.7% | 37.4% | 62.2% | 37.8% |
| 11,334 | MARION | 5,524 | 3,545 | 1,945 | 34 | 1,600 R | 64.2% | 35.2% | 64.6% | 35.4% |
| 37,766 | MILLER | 13,088 | 8,302 | 4,686 | 100 | 3,616 R | 63.4% | 35.8% | 63.9% | 36.1% |
| 59,517 | MISSISSIPPI | 17,766 | 10,180 | 7,548 | 38 | 2,632 R | 57.3% | 42.5% | 57.4% | 42.6% |
| 14,052 | MONROE | 4,971 | 2,508 | 2,413 | 50 | 95 R | 50.5% | 48.5% | 51.0% | 49.0% |
| 7,771 | MONTGOMERY | 3,757 | 2,221 | 1,497 | 39 | 724 R | 59.1% | 39.8% | 59.7% | 40.3% |
| 11,097 | NEVADA | 4,152 | 2,352 | 1,783 | 17 | 569 R | 56.6% | 42.9% | 56.9% | 43.1% |
| 7,756 | NEWTON | 4,173 | 2,749 | 1,414 | 10 | 1,335 R | 65.9% | 33.9% | 66.0% | 34.0% |
| 30,541 | OUACHITA | 13,089 | 6,700 | 5,858 | 531 | 842 R | 51.2% | 44.8% | 53.4% | 46.6% |
| 7,266 | PERRY | 3,480 | 2,047 | 1,404 | 29 | 643 R | 58.8% | 40.3% | 59.3% | 40.7% |
| 34,772 | PHILLIPS | 10,723 | 4,686 | 5,946 | 91 | 1,260 D | 43.7% | 55.5% | 44.1% | 55.9% |
| 10,373 | PIKE | 4,118 | 2,665 | 1,443 | 10 | 1,222 R | 64.7% | 35.0% | 64.9% | 35.1% |
| 27,032 | POINSETT | 9,587 | 5,622 | 3,906 | 59 | 1,716 R | 58.6% | 40.7% | 59.0% | 41.0% |
| 17,007 | POLK | 7,386 | 5,181 | 2,101 | 104 | 3,080 R | 70.1% | 28.4% | 71.1% | 28.9% |
| 39,021 | POPE | 15,855 | 10,667 | 5,082 | 106 | 5,585 R | 67.3% | 32.1% | 67.7% | 32.3% |
| 10,140 | PRAIRIE | 3,876 | 2,407 | 1,437 | 32 | 970 R | 62.1% | 37.1% | 62.6% | 37.4% |
| 340,613 | PULASKI | 133,418 | 77,651 | 54,237 | 1,530 | 23,414 R | 58.2% | 40.7% | 58.9% | 41.1% |

# ARKANSAS

## PRESIDENT 1984

| 1980 Census Population | County | Total Vote | Republican | Democratic | Other | Rep.-Dem. Plurality | | Percentage | | | |
|---|---|---|---|---|---|---|---|---|---|---|---|
| | | | | | | | | Total Vote | | Major Vote | |
| | | | | | | | | Rep. | Dem. | Rep. | Dem. |
| 16,834 | RANDOLPH | 5,733 | 3,188 | 2,507 | 38 | 681 | R | 55.6% | 43.7% | 56.0% | 44.0% |
| 30,858 | ST. FRANCIS | 10,322 | 5,378 | 4,866 | 78 | 512 | R | 52.1% | 47.1% | 52.5% | 47.5% |
| 53,161 | SALINE | 19,297 | 11,709 | 6,977 | 611 | 4,732 | R | 60.7% | 36.2% | 62.7% | 37.3% |
| 9,685 | SCOTT | 4,709 | 3,066 | 1,609 | 34 | 1,457 | R | 65.1% | 34.2% | 65.6% | 34.4% |
| 8,847 | SEARCY | 4,201 | 2,819 | 1,313 | 69 | 1,506 | R | 67.1% | 31.3% | 68.2% | 31.8% |
| 95,172 | SEBASTIAN | 36,817 | 27,595 | 8,688 | 534 | 18,907 | R | 75.0% | 23.6% | 76.1% | 23.9% |
| 14,060 | SEVIER | 5,271 | 3,302 | 1,942 | 27 | 1,360 | R | 62.6% | 36.8% | 63.0% | 37.0% |
| 14,607 | SHARP | 6,930 | 4,392 | 2,492 | 46 | 1,900 | R | 63.4% | 36.0% | 63.8% | 36.2% |
| 9,022 | STONE | 4,045 | 2,325 | 1,654 | 66 | 671 | R | 57.5% | 40.9% | 58.4% | 41.6% |
| 48,573 | UNION | 18,759 | 12,333 | 6,208 | 218 | 6,125 | R | 65.7% | 33.1% | 66.5% | 33.5% |
| 13,357 | VAN BUREN | 6,659 | 4,060 | 2,529 | 70 | 1,531 | R | 61.0% | 38.0% | 61.6% | 38.4% |
| 100,494 | WASHINGTON | 36,698 | 24,993 | 11,319 | 386 | 13,674 | R | 68.1% | 30.8% | 68.8% | 31.2% |
| 50,835 | WHITE | 19,435 | 12,566 | 6,603 | 266 | 5,963 | R | 64.7% | 34.0% | 65.6% | 34.4% |
| 11,222 | WOODRUFF | 3,759 | 1,675 | 2,055 | 29 | 380 | D | 44.6% | 54.7% | 44.9% | 55.1% |
| 17,026 | YELL | 6,802 | 4,051 | 2,679 | 72 | 1,372 | R | 59.6% | 39.4% | 60.2% | 39.8% |
| 2,286,435 | TOTAL | 884,406 | 534,774 | 338,646 | 10,986 | 196,128 | R | 60.5% | 38.3% | 61.2% | 38.8% |

# ARKANSAS

## PRESIDENT 1980

| 1980 Census Population | County | Total Vote | Republican | Democratic | Other | Rep.-Dem. Plurality | Total Vote Rep. | Total Vote Dem. | Major Vote Rep. | Major Vote Dem. |
|---|---|---|---|---|---|---|---|---|---|---|
| 24,175 | ARKANSAS | 7,985 | 3,409 | 4,303 | 273 | 894 D | 42.7% | 53.9% | 44.2% | 55.8% |
| 26,538 | ASHLEY | 8,748 | 3,960 | 4,552 | 236 | 592 D | 45.3% | 52.0% | 46.5% | 53.5% |
| 27,409 | BAXTER | 15,147 | 9,684 | 4,789 | 674 | 4,895 R | 63.9% | 31.6% | 66.9% | 33.1% |
| 78,115 | BENTON | 29,440 | 18,830 | 9,231 | 1,379 | 9,599 R | 64.0% | 31.4% | 67.1% | 32.9% |
| 26,067 | BOONE | 12,088 | 6,778 | 4,576 | 734 | 2,202 R | 56.1% | 37.9% | 59.7% | 40.3% |
| 13,803 | BRADLEY | 4,890 | 1,650 | 3,139 | 101 | 1,489 D | 33.7% | 64.2% | 34.5% | 65.5% |
| 6,079 | CALHOUN | 2,396 | 896 | 1,438 | 62 | 542 D | 37.4% | 60.0% | 38.4% | 61.6% |
| 16,203 | CARROLL | 7,728 | 4,273 | 2,977 | 478 | 1,296 R | 55.3% | 38.5% | 58.9% | 41.1% |
| 17,793 | CHICOT | 5,776 | 2,239 | 3,445 | 92 | 1,206 D | 38.8% | 59.6% | 39.4% | 60.6% |
| 23,326 | CLARK | 9,153 | 2,743 | 6,122 | 288 | 3,379 D | 30.0% | 66.9% | 30.9% | 69.1% |
| 20,616 | CLAY | 7,330 | 3,091 | 3,985 | 254 | 894 D | 42.2% | 54.4% | 43.7% | 56.3% |
| 16,909 | CLEBURNE | 8,355 | 4,042 | 4,021 | 292 | 21 R | 48.4% | 48.1% | 50.1% | 49.9% |
| 7,868 | CLEVELAND | 3,058 | 1,124 | 1,856 | 78 | 732 D | 36.8% | 60.7% | 37.7% | 62.3% |
| 26,644 | COLUMBIA | 9,967 | 5,259 | 4,445 | 263 | 814 R | 52.8% | 44.6% | 54.2% | 45.8% |
| 19,505 | CONWAY | 9,189 | 4,145 | 4,698 | 346 | 553 D | 45.1% | 51.1% | 46.9% | 53.1% |
| 63,239 | CRAIGHEAD | 21,456 | 11,010 | 9,231 | 1,215 | 1,779 R | 51.3% | 43.0% | 54.4% | 45.6% |
| 36,892 | CRAWFORD | 12,899 | 8,542 | 3,948 | 409 | 4,594 R | 66.2% | 30.6% | 68.4% | 31.6% |
| 49,499 | CRITTENDEN | 13,823 | 6,248 | 7,022 | 553 | 774 D | 45.2% | 50.8% | 47.1% | 52.9% |
| 20,434 | CROSS | 6,492 | 2,895 | 3,471 | 126 | 576 D | 44.6% | 53.5% | 45.5% | 54.5% |
| 10,515 | DALLAS | 4,539 | 1,596 | 2,838 | 105 | 1,242 D | 35.2% | 62.5% | 36.0% | 64.0% |
| 19,760 | DESHA | 6,037 | 2,057 | 3,748 | 232 | 1,691 D | 34.1% | 62.1% | 35.4% | 64.6% |
| 17,910 | DREW | 6,184 | 2,272 | 3,757 | 155 | 1,485 D | 36.7% | 60.8% | 37.7% | 62.3% |
| 46,192 | FAULKNER | 17,073 | 7,544 | 8,528 | 1,001 | 984 D | 44.2% | 50.0% | 46.9% | 53.1% |
| 14,705 | FRANKLIN | 6,426 | 3,448 | 2,716 | 262 | 732 R | 53.7% | 42.3% | 55.9% | 44.1% |
| 9,975 | FULTON | 4,257 | 2,101 | 2,037 | 119 | 64 R | 49.4% | 47.9% | 50.8% | 49.2% |
| 70,531 | GARLAND | 29,717 | 15,739 | 12,515 | 1,463 | 3,224 R | 53.0% | 42.1% | 55.7% | 44.3% |
| 13,008 | GRANT | 5,276 | 2,007 | 3,078 | 191 | 1,071 D | 38.0% | 58.3% | 39.5% | 60.5% |
| 30,744 | GREENE | 10,841 | 4,514 | 5,996 | 331 | 1,482 D | 41.6% | 55.3% | 42.9% | 57.1% |
| 23,635 | HEMPSTEAD | 8,628 | 3,852 | 4,671 | 105 | 819 D | 44.6% | 54.1% | 45.2% | 54.8% |
| 26,819 | HOT SPRINGS | 10,817 | 3,561 | 6,897 | 359 | 3,336 D | 32.9% | 63.8% | 34.1% | 65.9% |
| 13,459 | HOWARD | 5,064 | 2,386 | 2,564 | 114 | 178 D | 47.1% | 50.6% | 48.2% | 51.8% |
| 30,147 | INDEPENDENCE | 11,125 | 5,076 | 5,683 | 366 | 607 D | 45.6% | 51.1% | 47.2% | 52.8% |
| 10,768 | IZARD | 5,254 | 2,266 | 2,750 | 238 | 484 D | 43.1% | 52.3% | 45.2% | 54.8% |
| 21,646 | JACKSON | 8,081 | 3,191 | 4,651 | 239 | 1,460 D | 39.5% | 57.6% | 40.7% | 59.3% |
| 90,718 | JEFFERSON | 30,046 | 10,697 | 17,292 | 2,057 | 6,595 D | 35.6% | 57.6% | 38.2% | 61.8% |
| 17,423 | JOHNSON | 7,636 | 3,619 | 3,709 | 308 | 90 D | 47.4% | 48.6% | 49.4% | 50.6% |
| 10,213 | LAFAYETTE | 3,776 | 1,756 | 1,947 | 73 | 191 D | 46.5% | 51.6% | 47.4% | 52.6% |
| 18,447 | LAWRENCE | 6,963 | 3,245 | 3,547 | 171 | 302 D | 46.6% | 50.9% | 47.8% | 52.2% |
| 15,539 | LEE | 4,876 | 1,711 | 3,103 | 62 | 1,392 D | 35.1% | 63.6% | 35.5% | 64.5% |
| 13,369 | LINCOLN | 3,849 | 1,243 | 2,517 | 89 | 1,274 D | 32.3% | 65.4% | 33.1% | 66.9% |
| 13,952 | LITTLE RIVER | 5,024 | 2,272 | 2,631 | 121 | 359 D | 45.2% | 52.4% | 46.3% | 53.7% |
| 20,144 | LOGAN | 8,913 | 4,511 | 4,098 | 304 | 413 R | 50.6% | 46.0% | 52.4% | 47.6% |
| 34,518 | LONOKE | 11,585 | 5,619 | 5,605 | 361 | 14 R | 48.5% | 48.4% | 50.1% | 49.9% |
| 11,373 | MADISON | 5,835 | 3,180 | 2,434 | 221 | 746 R | 54.5% | 41.7% | 56.6% | 43.4% |
| 11,334 | MARION | 5,356 | 3,059 | 2,046 | 251 | 1,013 R | 57.1% | 38.2% | 59.9% | 40.1% |
| 37,766 | MILLER | 12,921 | 6,770 | 5,996 | 155 | 774 R | 52.4% | 46.4% | 53.0% | 47.0% |
| 59,517 | MISSISSIPPI | 16,417 | 7,170 | 8,908 | 339 | 1,738 D | 43.7% | 54.3% | 44.6% | 55.4% |
| 14,052 | MONROE | 4,829 | 2,027 | 2,686 | 116 | 659 D | 42.0% | 55.6% | 43.0% | 57.0% |
| 7,771 | MONTGOMERY | 3,612 | 1,585 | 1,878 | 149 | 293 D | 43.9% | 52.0% | 45.8% | 54.2% |
| 11,097 | NEVADA | 4,440 | 1,697 | 2,631 | 112 | 934 D | 38.2% | 59.3% | 39.2% | 60.8% |
| 7,756 | NEWTON | 4,033 | 2,423 | 1,436 | 174 | 987 R | 60.1% | 35.6% | 62.8% | 37.2% |
| 30,541 | OUACHITA | 12,208 | 4,329 | 7,152 | 727 | 2,823 D | 35.5% | 58.6% | 37.7% | 62.3% |
| 7,266 | PERRY | 3,186 | 1,459 | 1,606 | 121 | 147 D | 45.8% | 50.4% | 47.6% | 52.4% |
| 34,772 | PHILLIPS | 11,146 | 4,270 | 6,642 | 234 | 2,372 D | 38.3% | 59.6% | 39.1% | 60.9% |
| 10,373 | PIKE | 4,097 | 1,916 | 2,094 | 87 | 178 D | 46.8% | 51.1% | 47.8% | 52.2% |
| 27,032 | POINSETT | 9,180 | 4,040 | 4,894 | 246 | 854 D | 44.0% | 53.3% | 45.2% | 54.8% |
| 17,007 | POLK | 6,824 | 3,993 | 2,617 | 214 | 1,376 R | 58.5% | 38.3% | 60.4% | 39.6% |
| 39,021 | POPE | 14,230 | 7,217 | 6,364 | 649 | 853 R | 50.7% | 44.7% | 53.1% | 46.9% |
| 10,140 | PRAIRIE | 3,895 | 1,855 | 1,928 | 112 | 73 D | 47.6% | 49.5% | 49.0% | 51.0% |
| 340,613 | PULASKI | 112,937 | 52,125 | 54,839 | 5,973 | 2,714 D | 46.2% | 48.6% | 48.7% | 51.3% |

# ARKANSAS

## PRESIDENT 1980

| 1980 Census Population | County | Total Vote | Republican | Democratic | Other | Rep.-Dem. Plurality | Percentage | | | |
|---|---|---|---|---|---|---|---|---|---|---|
| | | | | | | | Total Vote | | Major Vote | |
| | | | | | | | Rep. | Dem. | Rep. | Dem. |
| 16,834 | RANDOLPH | 5,929 | 2,579 | 3,070 | 280 | 491 D | 43.5% | 51.8% | 45.7% | 54.3% |
| 30,858 | ST. FRANCIS | 10,487 | 4,485 | 5,816 | 186 | 1,331 D | 42.8% | 55.5% | 43.5% | 56.5% |
| 53,161 | SALINE | 19,555 | 8,330 | 10,368 | 857 | 2,038 D | 42.6% | 53.0% | 44.6% | 55.4% |
| 9,685 | SCOTT | 4,626 | 2,228 | 2,236 | 162 | 8 D | 48.2% | 48.3% | 49.9% | 50.1% |
| 8,847 | SEARCY | 4,183 | 2,459 | 1,536 | 188 | 923 R | 58.8% | 36.7% | 61.6% | 38.4% |
| 95,172 | SEBASTIAN | 36,879 | 23,403 | 10,141 | 3,335 | 13,262 R | 63.5% | 27.5% | 69.8% | 30.2% |
| 14,060 | SEVIER | 5,497 | 2,502 | 2,854 | 141 | 352 D | 45.5% | 51.9% | 46.7% | 53.3% |
| 14,607 | SHARP | 6,416 | 3,420 | 2,774 | 222 | 646 R | 53.3% | 43.2% | 55.2% | 44.8% |
| 9,022 | STONE | 3,975 | 1,793 | 1,968 | 214 | 175 D | 45.1% | 49.5% | 47.7% | 52.3% |
| 48,573 | UNION | 17,063 | 9,401 | 6,852 | 810 | 2,549 R | 55.1% | 40.2% | 57.8% | 42.2% |
| 13,357 | VAN BUREN | 6,292 | 3,090 | 2,968 | 234 | 122 R | 49.1% | 47.2% | 51.0% | 49.0% |
| 100,494 | WASHINGTON | 35,421 | 20,788 | 12,276 | 2,357 | 8,512 R | 58.7% | 34.7% | 62.9% | 37.1% |
| 50,835 | WHITE | 17,313 | 8,079 | 8,750 | 484 | 671 D | 46.7% | 50.5% | 48.0% | 52.0% |
| 11,222 | WOODRUFF | 3,756 | 1,204 | 2,452 | 100 | 1,248 D | 32.1% | 65.3% | 32.9% | 67.1% |
| 17,026 | YELL | 7,137 | 3,187 | 3,702 | 248 | 515 D | 44.7% | 51.9% | 46.3% | 53.7% |
| 2,286,435 | TOTAL | 837,582 | 403,164 | 398,041 | 36,377 | 5,123 R | 48.1% | 47.5% | 50.3% | 49.7% |

# ARKANSAS

## PRESIDENT 1976

| 1970 Census Population | County | Total Vote | Republican | Democratic | Other | Rep.-Dem. Plurality | Percentage Total Vote Rep. | Dem. | Major Vote Rep. | Dem. |
|---|---|---|---|---|---|---|---|---|---|---|
| 23,347 | ARKANSAS | 8,120 | 2,480 | 5,640 | | 3,160 D | 30.5% | 69.5% | 30.5% | 69.5% |
| 24,976 | ASHLEY | 8,354 | 3,092 | 5,253 | 9 | 2,161 D | 37.0% | 62.9% | 37.1% | 62.9% |
| 15,319 | BAXTER | 11,651 | 5,885 | 5,766 | | 119 R | 50.5% | 49.5% | 50.5% | 49.5% |
| 50,476 | BENTON | 24,017 | 12,670 | 11,289 | 58 | 1,381 R | 52.8% | 47.0% | 52.9% | 47.1% |
| 19,073 | BOONE | 9,347 | 3,959 | 5,388 | | 1,429 D | 42.4% | 57.6% | 42.4% | 57.6% |
| 12,778 | BRADLEY | 4,701 | 1,134 | 3,567 | | 2,433 D | 24.1% | 75.9% | 24.1% | 75.9% |
| 5,573 | CALHOUN | 2,514 | 495 | 2,014 | 5 | 1,519 D | 19.7% | 80.1% | 19.7% | 80.3% |
| 12,301 | CARROLL | 6,650 | 2,804 | 3,791 | 55 | 987 D | 42.2% | 57.0% | 42.5% | 57.5% |
| 18,164 | CHICOT | 5,495 | 1,621 | 3,868 | 6 | 2,247 D | 29.5% | 70.4% | 29.5% | 70.5% |
| 21,537 | CLARK | 8,479 | 1,816 | 6,641 | 22 | 4,825 D | 21.4% | 78.3% | 21.5% | 78.5% |
| 18,771 | CLAY | 7,557 | 1,893 | 5,664 | | 3,771 D | 25.0% | 75.0% | 25.0% | 75.0% |
| 10,349 | CLEBURNE | 7,731 | 1,992 | 5,726 | 13 | 3,734 D | 25.8% | 74.1% | 25.8% | 74.2% |
| 6,605 | CLEVELAND | 2,966 | 646 | 2,320 | | 1,674 D | 21.8% | 78.2% | 21.8% | 78.2% |
| 25,952 | COLUMBIA | 9,001 | 4,287 | 4,708 | 6 | 421 D | 47.6% | 52.3% | 47.7% | 52.3% |
| 16,805 | CONWAY | 8,629 | 2,177 | 6,443 | 9 | 4,266 D | 25.2% | 74.7% | 25.3% | 74.7% |
| 52,068 | CRAIGHEAD | 20,053 | 6,213 | 13,840 | | 7,627 D | 31.0% | 69.0% | 31.0% | 69.0% |
| 25,677 | CRAWFORD | 10,710 | 4,764 | 5,946 | | 1,182 D | 44.5% | 55.5% | 44.5% | 55.5% |
| 48,106 | CRITTENDEN | 13,465 | 5,202 | 8,249 | 14 | 3,047 D | 38.6% | 61.3% | 38.7% | 61.3% |
| 19,783 | CROSS | 6,137 | 1,909 | 4,198 | 30 | 2,289 D | 31.1% | 68.4% | 31.3% | 68.7% |
| 10,022 | DALLAS | 4,286 | 1,012 | 3,266 | 8 | 2,254 D | 23.6% | 76.2% | 23.7% | 76.3% |
| 18,761 | DESHA | 5,600 | 1,372 | 4,228 | | 2,856 D | 24.5% | 75.5% | 24.5% | 75.5% |
| 15,157 | DREW | 5,480 | 1,730 | 3,750 | | 2,020 D | 31.6% | 68.4% | 31.6% | 68.4% |
| 31,572 | FAULKNER | 15,343 | 3,904 | 11,423 | 16 | 7,519 D | 25.4% | 74.5% | 25.5% | 74.5% |
| 11,301 | FRANKLIN | 5,676 | 1,973 | 3,703 | | 1,730 D | 34.8% | 65.2% | 34.8% | 65.2% |
| 7,699 | FULTON | 3,715 | 1,038 | 2,670 | 7 | 1,632 D | 27.9% | 71.9% | 28.0% | 72.0% |
| 54,131 | GARLAND | 26,170 | 10,394 | 15,707 | 69 | 5,313 D | 39.7% | 60.0% | 39.8% | 60.2% |
| 9,711 | GRANT | 4,844 | 1,047 | 3,797 | | 2,750 D | 21.6% | 78.4% | 21.6% | 78.4% |
| 24,765 | GREENE | 10,192 | 2,690 | 7,495 | 7 | 4,805 D | 26.4% | 73.5% | 26.4% | 73.6% |
| 19,308 | HEMPSTEAD | 8,256 | 2,859 | 5,397 | | 2,538 D | 34.6% | 65.4% | 34.6% | 65.4% |
| 21,963 | HOT SPRINGS | 9,996 | 2,187 | 7,809 | | 5,622 D | 21.9% | 78.1% | 21.9% | 78.1% |
| 11,412 | HOWARD | 4,782 | 1,575 | 3,207 | | 1,632 D | 32.9% | 67.1% | 32.9% | 67.1% |
| 22,723 | INDEPENDENCE | 9,998 | 2,878 | 7,116 | 4 | 4,238 D | 28.8% | 71.2% | 28.8% | 71.2% |
| 7,381 | IZARD | 4,722 | 1,394 | 3,328 | | 1,934 D | 29.5% | 70.5% | 29.5% | 70.5% |
| 20,452 | JACKSON | 8,239 | 1,783 | 6,456 | | 4,673 D | 21.6% | 78.4% | 21.6% | 78.4% |
| 85,329 | JEFFERSON | 29,035 | 8,034 | 21,001 | | 12,967 D | 27.7% | 72.3% | 27.7% | 72.3% |
| 13,630 | JOHNSON | 7,217 | 2,173 | 5,044 | | 2,871 D | 30.1% | 69.9% | 30.1% | 69.9% |
| 10,018 | LAFAYETTE | 3,809 | 1,467 | 2,342 | | 875 D | 38.5% | 61.5% | 38.5% | 61.5% |
| 16,320 | LAWRENCE | 6,882 | 1,708 | 5,167 | 7 | 3,459 D | 24.8% | 75.1% | 24.8% | 75.2% |
| 18,884 | LEE | 5,038 | 1,574 | 3,463 | 1 | 1,889 D | 31.2% | 68.7% | 31.2% | 68.8% |
| 12,913 | LINCOLN | 3,744 | 699 | 3,045 | | 2,346 D | 18.7% | 81.3% | 18.7% | 81.3% |
| 11,194 | LITTLE RIVER | 4,573 | 1,431 | 3,142 | | 1,711 D | 31.3% | 68.7% | 31.3% | 68.7% |
| 16,789 | LOGAN | 8,294 | 2,909 | 5,313 | 72 | 2,404 D | 35.1% | 64.1% | 35.4% | 64.6% |
| 26,249 | LONOKE | 10,299 | 2,522 | 7,761 | 16 | 5,239 D | 24.5% | 75.4% | 24.5% | 75.5% |
| 9,453 | MADISON | 5,428 | 2,502 | 2,926 | | 424 D | 46.1% | 53.9% | 46.1% | 53.9% |
| 7,000 | MARION | 5,024 | 2,045 | 2,979 | | 934 D | 40.7% | 59.3% | 40.7% | 59.3% |
| 33,385 | MILLER | 11,580 | 4,737 | 6,821 | 22 | 2,084 D | 40.9% | 58.9% | 41.0% | 59.0% |
| 62,060 | MISSISSIPPI | 16,328 | 6,009 | 10,292 | 27 | 4,283 D | 36.8% | 63.0% | 36.9% | 63.1% |
| 15,657 | MONROE | 4,848 | 1,285 | 3,556 | 7 | 2,271 D | 26.5% | 73.3% | 26.5% | 73.5% |
| 5,821 | MONTGOMERY | 3,344 | 924 | 2,420 | | 1,496 D | 27.6% | 72.4% | 27.6% | 72.4% |
| 10,111 | NEVADA | 4,269 | 1,163 | 3,101 | 5 | 1,938 D | 27.2% | 72.6% | 27.3% | 72.7% |
| 5,844 | NEWTON | 3,481 | 1,641 | 1,840 | | 199 D | 47.1% | 52.9% | 47.1% | 52.9% |
| 30,896 | OUACHITA | 11,699 | 2,753 | 8,946 | | 6,193 D | 23.5% | 76.5% | 23.5% | 76.5% |
| 5,634 | PERRY | 3,142 | 832 | 2,310 | | 1,478 D | 26.5% | 73.5% | 26.5% | 73.5% |
| 40,046 | PHILLIPS | 11,117 | 3,342 | 7,774 | 1 | 4,432 D | 30.1% | 69.9% | 30.1% | 69.9% |
| 8,711 | PIKE | 4,066 | 1,234 | 2,822 | 10 | 1,588 D | 30.3% | 69.4% | 30.4% | 69.6% |
| 26,822 | POINSETT | 9,566 | 2,726 | 6,835 | 5 | 4,109 D | 28.5% | 71.5% | 28.5% | 71.5% |
| 13,297 | POLK | 5,966 | 2,432 | 3,505 | 29 | 1,073 D | 40.8% | 58.7% | 41.0% | 59.0% |
| 28,607 | POPE | 12,732 | 4,348 | 8,355 | 29 | 4,007 D | 34.2% | 65.6% | 34.2% | 65.8% |
| 10,249 | PRAIRIE | 3,649 | 813 | 2,836 | | 2,023 D | 22.3% | 77.7% | 22.3% | 77.7% |
| 287,189 | PULASKI | 101,475 | 37,690 | 63,541 | 244 | 25,851 D | 37.1% | 62.6% | 37.2% | 62.8% |

# ARKANSAS

## PRESIDENT 1976

| 1970 Census Population | County | Total Vote | Republican | Democratic | Other | Rep.-Dem. Plurality | Percentage Total Vote Rep. | Dem. | Major Vote Rep. | Dem. |
|---|---|---|---|---|---|---|---|---|---|---|
| 12,645 | RANDOLPH | 6,122 | 1,571 | 4,551 | | 2,980 D | 25.7% | 74.3% | 25.7% | 74.3% |
| 30,799 | ST. FRANCIS | 10,520 | 3,639 | 6,851 | 30 | 3,212 D | 34.6% | 65.1% | 34.7% | 65.3% |
| 36,107 | SALINE | 16,138 | 4,123 | 12,008 | 7 | 7,885 D | 25.5% | 74.4% | 25.6% | 74.4% |
| 8,207 | SCOTT | 4,314 | 1,427 | 2,880 | 7 | 1,453 D | 33.1% | 66.8% | 33.1% | 66.9% |
| 7,731 | SEARCY | 3,834 | 1,767 | 2,067 | | 300 D | 46.1% | 53.9% | 46.1% | 53.9% |
| 79,237 | SEBASTIAN | 33,397 | 17,665 | 15,698 | 34 | 1,967 R | 52.9% | 47.0% | 52.9% | 47.1% |
| 11,272 | SEVIER | 4,877 | 1,468 | 3,391 | 18 | 1,923 D | 30.1% | 69.5% | 30.2% | 69.8% |
| 8,233 | SHARP | 5,683 | 2,151 | 3,532 | | 1,381 D | 37.8% | 62.2% | 37.8% | 62.2% |
| 6,838 | STONE | 3,747 | 1,014 | 2,718 | 15 | 1,704 D | 27.1% | 72.5% | 27.2% | 72.8% |
| 45,428 | UNION | 16,182 | 7,918 | 8,257 | 7 | 339 D | 48.9% | 51.0% | 49.0% | 51.0% |
| 8,275 | VAN BUREN | 5,628 | 1,624 | 4,004 | | 2,380 D | 28.9% | 71.1% | 28.9% | 71.1% |
| 77,370 | WASHINGTON | 29,834 | 14,132 | 15,610 | 92 | 1,478 D | 47.4% | 52.3% | 47.5% | 52.5% |
| 39,253 | WHITE | 16,168 | 4,756 | 11,412 | | 6,656 D | 29.4% | 70.6% | 29.4% | 70.6% |
| 11,566 | WOODRUFF | 3,893 | 848 | 3,040 | 5 | 2,192 D | 21.8% | 78.1% | 21.8% | 78.2% |
| 14,208 | YELL | 7,717 | 1,932 | 5,785 | | 3,853 D | 25.0% | 75.0% | 25.0% | 75.0% |
| 1,923,295 | TOTAL | 767,535 | 267,903 | 498,604 | 1,028 | 230,701 D | 34.9% | 65.0% | 35.0% | 65.0% |

# ARKANSAS

## PRESIDENT 1972

| 1970 Census Population | County | Total Vote | Republican | Democratic | Other | Rep.-Dem. Plurality | Total Vote Rep. | Total Vote Dem. | Major Vote Rep. | Major Vote Dem. |
|---|---|---|---|---|---|---|---|---|---|---|
| 23,347 | ARKANSAS | 7,113 | 5,225 | 1,849 | 39 | 3,376 R | 73.5% | 26.0% | 73.9% | 26.1% |
| 24,976 | ASHLEY | 7,203 | 5,506 | 1,680 | 17 | 3,826 R | 76.4% | 23.3% | 76.6% | 23.4% |
| 15,319 | BAXTER | 9,431 | 6,754 | 2,677 | | 4,077 R | 71.6% | 28.4% | 71.6% | 28.4% |
| 50,476 | BENTON | 18,778 | 14,621 | 4,083 | 74 | 10,538 R | 77.9% | 21.7% | 78.2% | 21.8% |
| 19,073 | BOONE | 7,362 | 5,484 | 1,862 | 16 | 3,622 R | 74.5% | 25.3% | 74.7% | 25.3% |
| 12,778 | BRADLEY | 4,614 | 3,218 | 1,368 | 28 | 1,850 R | 69.7% | 29.6% | 70.2% | 29.8% |
| 5,573 | CALHOUN | 2,020 | 1,298 | 707 | 15 | 591 R | 64.3% | 35.0% | 64.7% | 35.3% |
| 12,301 | CARROLL | 5,086 | 3,565 | 1,401 | 120 | 2,164 R | 70.1% | 27.5% | 71.8% | 28.2% |
| 18,164 | CHICOT | 4,333 | 2,858 | 1,469 | 6 | 1,389 R | 66.0% | 33.9% | 66.1% | 33.9% |
| 21,537 | CLARK | 6,960 | 4,173 | 2,741 | 46 | 1,432 R | 60.0% | 39.4% | 60.4% | 39.6% |
| 18,771 | CLAY | 6,314 | 4,381 | 1,933 | | 2,448 R | 69.4% | 30.6% | 69.4% | 30.6% |
| 10,349 | CLEBURNE | 4,274 | 2,870 | 1,400 | 4 | 1,470 R | 67.2% | 32.8% | 67.2% | 32.8% |
| 6,605 | CLEVELAND | 2,571 | 1,837 | 734 | | 1,103 R | 71.5% | 28.5% | 71.5% | 28.5% |
| 25,952 | COLUMBIA | 8,023 | 5,801 | 2,193 | 29 | 3,608 R | 72.3% | 27.3% | 72.6% | 27.4% |
| 16,805 | CONWAY | 7,205 | 4,187 | 3,009 | 9 | 1,178 R | 58.1% | 41.8% | 58.2% | 41.8% |
| 52,068 | CRAIGHEAD | 17,155 | 11,312 | 5,843 | | 5,469 R | 65.9% | 34.1% | 65.9% | 34.1% |
| 25,677 | CRAWFORD | 8,566 | 6,974 | 1,520 | 72 | 5,454 R | 81.4% | 17.7% | 82.1% | 17.9% |
| 48,106 | CRITTENDEN | 11,217 | 7,971 | 3,246 | | 4,725 R | 71.1% | 28.9% | 71.1% | 28.9% |
| 19,783 | CROSS | 5,143 | 3,743 | 1,221 | 179 | 2,522 R | 72.8% | 23.7% | 75.4% | 24.6% |
| 10,022 | DALLAS | 3,554 | 2,152 | 1,402 | | 750 R | 60.6% | 39.4% | 60.6% | 39.4% |
| 18,761 | DESHA | 5,058 | 3,385 | 1,665 | 8 | 1,720 R | 66.9% | 32.9% | 67.0% | 33.0% |
| 15,157 | DREW | 8,285 | 6,124 | 2,161 | | 3,963 R | 73.9% | 26.1% | 73.9% | 26.1% |
| 31,572 | FAULKNER | 11,350 | 6,746 | 4,604 | | 2,142 R | 59.4% | 40.6% | 59.4% | 40.6% |
| 11,301 | FRANKLIN | 4,930 | 3,678 | 1,252 | | 2,426 R | 74.6% | 25.4% | 74.6% | 25.4% |
| 7,699 | FULTON | 2,990 | 2,030 | 960 | | 1,070 R | 67.9% | 32.1% | 67.9% | 32.1% |
| 54,131 | GARLAND | 21,112 | 15,602 | 5,207 | 303 | 10,395 R | 73.9% | 24.7% | 75.0% | 25.0% |
| 9,711 | GRANT | 3,581 | 2,414 | 1,147 | 20 | 1,267 R | 67.4% | 32.0% | 67.8% | 32.2% |
| 24,765 | GREENE | 8,391 | 6,128 | 2,263 | | 3,865 R | 73.0% | 27.0% | 73.0% | 27.0% |
| 19,308 | HEMPSTEAD | 7,010 | 4,963 | 2,047 | | 2,916 R | 70.8% | 29.2% | 70.8% | 29.2% |
| 21,963 | HOT SPRINGS | 8,333 | 5,378 | 2,872 | 83 | 2,506 R | 64.5% | 34.5% | 65.2% | 34.8% |
| 11,412 | HOWARD | 3,751 | 2,682 | 1,069 | | 1,613 R | 71.5% | 28.5% | 71.5% | 28.5% |
| 22,723 | INDEPENDENCE | 7,721 | 5,076 | 2,630 | 15 | 2,446 R | 65.7% | 34.1% | 65.9% | 34.1% |
| 7,381 | IZARD | 3,114 | 2,001 | 1,108 | 5 | 893 R | 64.3% | 35.6% | 64.4% | 35.6% |
| 20,452 | JACKSON | 6,288 | 4,196 | 2,092 | | 2,104 R | 66.7% | 33.3% | 66.7% | 33.3% |
| 85,329 | JEFFERSON | 27,260 | 16,888 | 10,346 | 26 | 6,542 R | 62.0% | 38.0% | 62.0% | 38.0% |
| 13,630 | JOHNSON | 6,152 | 4,107 | 2,045 | | 2,062 R | 66.8% | 33.2% | 66.8% | 33.2% |
| 10,018 | LAFAYETTE | 3,421 | 2,460 | 952 | 9 | 1,508 R | 71.9% | 27.8% | 72.1% | 27.9% |
| 16,320 | LAWRENCE | 5,732 | 3,981 | 1,751 | | 2,230 R | 69.5% | 30.5% | 69.5% | 30.5% |
| 18,884 | LEE | 5,481 | 3,540 | 1,907 | 34 | 1,633 R | 64.6% | 34.8% | 65.0% | 35.0% |
| 12,913 | LINCOLN | 3,433 | 2,318 | 1,115 | | 1,203 R | 67.5% | 32.5% | 67.5% | 32.5% |
| 11,194 | LITTLE RIVER | 3,641 | 2,550 | 1,091 | | 1,459 R | 70.0% | 30.0% | 70.0% | 30.0% |
| 16,789 | LOGAN | 6,950 | 4,964 | 1,956 | 30 | 3,008 R | 71.4% | 28.1% | 71.7% | 28.3% |
| 26,249 | LONOKE | 7,835 | 5,298 | 2,504 | 33 | 2,794 R | 67.6% | 32.0% | 67.9% | 32.1% |
| 9,453 | MADISON | 5,261 | 3,372 | 1,889 | | 1,483 R | 64.1% | 35.9% | 64.1% | 35.9% |
| 7,000 | MARION | 3,497 | 2,331 | 1,108 | 58 | 1,223 R | 66.7% | 31.7% | 67.8% | 32.2% |
| 33,385 | MILLER | 11,210 | 8,355 | 2,855 | | 5,500 R | 74.5% | 25.5% | 74.5% | 25.5% |
| 62,060 | MISSISSIPPI | 14,627 | 10,931 | 3,544 | 152 | 7,387 R | 74.7% | 24.2% | 75.5% | 24.5% |
| 15,657 | MONROE | 4,566 | 2,897 | 1,578 | 91 | 1,319 R | 63.4% | 34.6% | 64.7% | 35.3% |
| 5,821 | MONTGOMERY | 2,281 | 1,555 | 688 | 38 | 867 R | 68.2% | 30.2% | 69.3% | 30.7% |
| 10,111 | NEVADA | 3,692 | 2,513 | 1,179 | | 1,334 R | 68.1% | 31.9% | 68.1% | 31.9% |
| 5,844 | NEWTON | 2,755 | 1,924 | 831 | | 1,093 R | 69.8% | 30.2% | 69.8% | 30.2% |
| 30,896 | OUACHITA | 10,562 | 6,620 | 3,931 | 11 | 2,689 R | 62.7% | 37.2% | 62.7% | 37.3% |
| 5,634 | PERRY | 2,262 | 1,445 | 810 | 7 | 635 R | 63.9% | 35.8% | 64.1% | 35.9% |
| 40,046 | PHILLIPS | 10,586 | 6,235 | 4,283 | 68 | 1,952 R | 58.9% | 40.5% | 59.3% | 40.7% |
| 8,711 | PIKE | 3,143 | 2,316 | 798 | 29 | 1,518 R | 73.7% | 25.4% | 74.4% | 25.6% |
| 26,822 | POINSETT | 8,998 | 7,010 | 1,908 | 80 | 5,102 R | 77.9% | 21.2% | 78.6% | 21.4% |
| 13,297 | POLK | 4,823 | 3,609 | 1,120 | 94 | 2,489 R | 74.8% | 23.2% | 76.3% | 23.7% |
| 28,607 | POPE | 10,244 | 6,917 | 3,302 | 25 | 3,615 R | 67.5% | 32.2% | 67.7% | 32.3% |
| 10,249 | PRAIRIE | 3,059 | 2,186 | 873 | | 1,313 R | 71.5% | 28.5% | 71.5% | 28.5% |
| 287,189 | PULASKI | 91,468 | 57,576 | 33,611 | 281 | 23,965 R | 62.9% | 36.7% | 63.1% | 36.9% |

# ARKANSAS

## PRESIDENT 1972

| 1970 Census Population | County | Total Vote | Republican | Democratic | Other | Rep.-Dem. Plurality | Percentage | | | |
|---|---|---|---|---|---|---|---|---|---|---|
| | | | | | | | Total Vote | | Major Vote | |
| | | | | | | | Rep. | Dem. | Rep. | Dem. |
| 12,645 | RANDOLPH | 4,103 | 2,578 | 1,525 | | 1,053 R | 62.8% | 37.2% | 62.8% | 37.2% |
| 30,799 | ST. FRANCIS | 8,631 | 5,692 | 2,674 | 265 | 3,018 R | 65.9% | 31.0% | 68.0% | 32.0% |
| 36,107 | SALINE | 12,527 | 7,972 | 4,503 | 52 | 3,469 R | 63.6% | 35.9% | 63.9% | 36.1% |
| 8,207 | SCOTT | 3,195 | 2,424 | 771 | | 1,653 R | 75.9% | 24.1% | 75.9% | 24.1% |
| 7,731 | SEARCY | 4,016 | 3,163 | 853 | | 2,310 R | 78.8% | 21.2% | 78.8% | 21.2% |
| 79,237 | SEBASTIAN | 31,047 | 25,219 | 5,770 | 58 | 19,449 R | 81.2% | 18.6% | 81.4% | 18.6% |
| 11,272 | SEVIER | 3,613 | 2,526 | 1,048 | 39 | 1,478 R | 69.9% | 29.0% | 70.7% | 29.3% |
| 8,233 | SHARP | 3,840 | 2,677 | 1,154 | 9 | 1,523 R | 69.7% | 30.1% | 69.9% | 30.1% |
| 6,838 | STONE | 2,952 | 1,989 | 958 | 5 | 1,031 R | 67.4% | 32.5% | 67.5% | 32.5% |
| 45,428 | UNION | 15,543 | 11,925 | 3,531 | 87 | 8,394 R | 76.7% | 22.7% | 77.2% | 22.8% |
| 8,275 | VAN BUREN | 4,235 | 2,622 | 1,594 | 19 | 1,028 R | 61.9% | 37.6% | 62.2% | 37.8% |
| 77,370 | WASHINGTON | 24,701 | 17,523 | 7,108 | 70 | 10,415 R | 70.9% | 28.8% | 71.1% | 28.9% |
| 39,253 | WHITE | 12,941 | 8,701 | 4,161 | 79 | 4,540 R | 67.2% | 32.2% | 67.6% | 32.4% |
| 11,566 | WOODRUFF | 3,222 | 1,989 | 1,183 | 50 | 806 R | 61.7% | 36.7% | 62.7% | 37.3% |
| 14,208 | YELL | 4,979 | 3,310 | 1,669 | | 1,641 R | 66.5% | 33.5% | 66.5% | 33.5% |
| 1,923,295 | TOTAL | 651,320 | 448,541 | 199,892 | 2,887 | 248,649 R | 68.9% | 30.7% | 69.2% | 30.8% |

# ARKANSAS

## PRESIDENT 1968

| 1960 Census Population | County | Total Vote | Republican | Democratic | AIP | Other | Plurality | Percentage Total Vote Rep. | Dem. | AIP |
|---|---|---|---|---|---|---|---|---|---|---|
| 23,355 | ARKANSAS | 7,600 | 1,806 | 2,019 | 3,775 | | 1,756 A | 23.8% | 26.6% | 49.7% |
| 24,220 | ASHLEY | 7,906 | 1,470 | 2,035 | 4,401 | | 2,366 A | 18.6% | 25.7% | 55.7% |
| 9,943 | BAXTER | 6,866 | 3,401 | 1,952 | 1,513 | | 1,449 R | 49.5% | 28.4% | 22.0% |
| 36,272 | BENTON | 16,228 | 8,104 | 4,088 | 4,036 | | 4,016 R | 49.9% | 25.2% | 24.9% |
| 16,116 | BOONE | 7,425 | 3,349 | 1,907 | 2,169 | | 1,180 R | 45.1% | 25.7% | 29.2% |
| 14,029 | BRADLEY | 4,805 | 802 | 1,457 | 2,546 | | 1,089 A | 16.7% | 30.3% | 53.0% |
| 5,991 | CALHOUN | 2,190 | 287 | 688 | 1,215 | | 527 A | 13.1% | 31.4% | 55.5% |
| 11,284 | CARROLL | 5,068 | 2,596 | 1,298 | 1,174 | | 1,298 R | 51.2% | 25.6% | 23.2% |
| 18,990 | CHICOT | 5,647 | 865 | 2,595 | 2,187 | | 408 D | 15.3% | 46.0% | 38.7% |
| 20,950 | CLARK | 7,151 | 1,642 | 2,733 | 2,776 | | 43 A | 23.0% | 38.2% | 38.8% |
| 21,258 | CLAY | 6,358 | 2,410 | 1,663 | 2,285 | | 125 R | 37.9% | 26.2% | 35.9% |
| 9,059 | CLEBURNE | 4,160 | 1,301 | 1,202 | 1,657 | | 356 A | 31.3% | 28.9% | 39.8% |
| 6,944 | CLEVELAND | 2,470 | 312 | 407 | 1,751 | | 1,344 A | 12.6% | 16.5% | 70.9% |
| 26,400 | COLUMBIA | 8,246 | 1,916 | 2,487 | 3,843 | | 1,356 A | 23.2% | 30.2% | 46.6% |
| 15,430 | CONWAY | 6,491 | 1,973 | 2,560 | 1,958 | | 587 D | 30.4% | 39.4% | 30.2% |
| 47,303 | CRAIGHEAD | 15,527 | 5,047 | 3,738 | 6,742 | | 1,695 A | 32.5% | 24.1% | 43.4% |
| 21,318 | CRAWFORD | 7,218 | 2,723 | 1,578 | 2,917 | | 194 A | 37.7% | 21.9% | 40.4% |
| 47,564 | CRITTENDEN | 10,586 | 2,454 | 3,475 | 4,657 | | 1,182 A | 23.2% | 32.8% | 44.0% |
| 19,551 | CROSS | 5,704 | 1,093 | 1,555 | 3,056 | | 1,501 A | 19.2% | 27.3% | 53.6% |
| 10,522 | DALLAS | 3,647 | 672 | 1,253 | 1,722 | | 469 A | 18.4% | 34.4% | 47.2% |
| 20,770 | DESHA | 5,716 | 972 | 2,270 | 2,474 | | 204 A | 17.0% | 39.7% | 43.3% |
| 15,213 | DREW | 4,671 | 1,040 | 1,324 | 2,307 | | 983 A | 22.3% | 28.3% | 49.4% |
| 24,303 | FAULKNER | 10,922 | 2,791 | 3,756 | 4,375 | | 619 A | 25.6% | 34.4% | 40.1% |
| 10,213 | FRANKLIN | 4,593 | 1,333 | 1,149 | 2,111 | | 778 A | 29.0% | 25.0% | 46.0% |
| 6,657 | FULTON | 3,297 | 1,198 | 1,019 | 1,080 | | 118 R | 36.3% | 30.9% | 32.8% |
| 46,697 | GARLAND | 20,284 | 7,674 | 5,655 | 6,955 | | 719 R | 37.8% | 27.9% | 34.3% |
| 8,294 | GRANT | 3,673 | 627 | 852 | 2,194 | | 1,342 A | 17.1% | 23.2% | 59.7% |
| 25,198 | GREENE | 8,077 | 2,859 | 2,197 | 3,021 | | 162 A | 35.4% | 27.2% | 37.4% |
| 19,661 | HEMPSTEAD | 7,241 | 1,783 | 2,322 | 3,136 | | 814 A | 24.6% | 32.1% | 43.3% |
| 21,893 | HOT SPRINGS | 8,056 | 1,780 | 2,137 | 4,139 | | 2,002 A | 22.1% | 26.5% | 51.4% |
| 10,878 | HOWARD | 4,007 | 1,286 | 1,061 | 1,660 | | 374 A | 32.1% | 26.5% | 41.4% |
| 20,048 | INDEPENDENCE | 7,841 | 2,782 | 2,289 | 2,770 | | 12 R | 35.5% | 29.2% | 35.3% |
| 6,766 | IZARD | 2,988 | 931 | 948 | 1,109 | | 161 A | 31.2% | 31.7% | 37.1% |
| 22,843 | JACKSON | 6,932 | 1,356 | 2,051 | 3,525 | | 1,474 A | 19.6% | 29.6% | 50.9% |
| 81,373 | JEFFERSON | 24,038 | 4,860 | 9,125 | 10,053 | | 928 A | 20.2% | 38.0% | 41.8% |
| 12,421 | JOHNSON | 5,107 | 1,667 | 1,747 | 1,693 | | 54 D | 32.6% | 34.2% | 33.2% |
| 11,030 | LAFAYETTE | 3,584 | 672 | 1,208 | 1,704 | | 496 A | 18.8% | 33.7% | 47.5% |
| 17,267 | LAWRENCE | 6,214 | 1,788 | 1,613 | 2,813 | | 1,025 A | 28.8% | 26.0% | 45.3% |
| 21,001 | LEE | 4,876 | 834 | 2,135 | 1,907 | | 228 D | 17.1% | 43.8% | 39.1% |
| 14,447 | LINCOLN | 3,781 | 488 | 1,209 | 2,084 | | 875 A | 12.9% | 32.0% | 55.1% |
| 9,211 | LITTLE RIVER | 3,310 | 745 | 1,092 | 1,473 | | 381 A | 22.5% | 33.0% | 44.5% |
| 15,957 | LOGAN | 6,499 | 2,341 | 1,998 | 2,160 | | 181 R | 36.0% | 30.7% | 33.2% |
| 24,551 | LONOKE | 7,693 | 1,677 | 2,014 | 4,002 | | 1,988 A | 21.8% | 26.2% | 52.0% |
| 9,068 | MADISON | 4,922 | 2,320 | 1,574 | 1,028 | | 746 R | 47.1% | 32.0% | 20.9% |
| 6,041 | MARION | 3,252 | 1,385 | 990 | 877 | | 395 R | 42.6% | 30.4% | 27.0% |
| 31,686 | MILLER | 10,653 | 2,662 | 2,929 | 5,062 | | 2,133 A | 25.0% | 27.5% | 47.5% |
| 70,174 | MISSISSIPPI | 15,509 | 4,369 | 4,993 | 6,147 | | 1,154 A | 28.2% | 32.2% | 39.6% |
| 17,327 | MONROE | 4,993 | 804 | 1,783 | 2,406 | | 623 A | 16.1% | 35.7% | 48.2% |
| 5,370 | MONTGOMERY | 2,526 | 885 | 649 | 992 | | 107 A | 35.0% | 25.7% | 39.3% |
| 10,700 | NEVADA | 3,921 | 840 | 1,308 | 1,773 | | 465 A | 21.4% | 33.4% | 45.2% |
| 5,963 | NEWTON | 2,886 | 1,467 | 852 | 567 | | 615 R | 50.8% | 29.5% | 19.6% |
| 31,641 | OUACHITA | 11,843 | 2,209 | 4,603 | 5,031 | | 428 A | 18.7% | 38.9% | 42.5% |
| 4,927 | PERRY | 2,290 | 740 | 634 | 916 | | 176 A | 32.3% | 27.7% | 40.0% |
| 43,997 | PHILLIPS | 11,472 | 2,154 | 5,039 | 4,279 | | 760 D | 18.8% | 43.9% | 37.3% |
| 7,864 | PIKE | 3,295 | 1,104 | 656 | 1,535 | | 431 A | 33.5% | 19.9% | 46.6% |
| 30,834 | POINSETT | 7,886 | 2,140 | 1,672 | 4,074 | | 1,934 A | 27.1% | 21.2% | 51.7% |
| 11,981 | POLK | 5,196 | 2,094 | 1,290 | 1,812 | | 282 R | 40.3% | 24.8% | 34.9% |
| 21,177 | POPE | 8,666 | 3,319 | 2,578 | 2,769 | | 550 R | 38.3% | 29.7% | 32.0% |
| 10,515 | PRAIRIE | 3,582 | 693 | 875 | 2,014 | | 1,139 A | 19.3% | 24.4% | 56.2% |
| 242,980 | PULASKI | 80,150 | 26,709 | 27,597 | 25,844 | | 888 D | 33.3% | 34.4% | 32.2% |

# ARKANSAS

## PRESIDENT 1968

| 1960 Census Population | County | Total Vote | Republican | Democratic | AIP | Other | Plurality | Percentage Total Vote | | |
|---|---|---|---|---|---|---|---|---|---|---|
| | | | | | | | | Rep. | Dem. | AIP |
| 12,520 | RANDOLPH | 4,214 | 1,237 | 1,367 | 1,610 | | 243 A | 29.4% | 32.4% | 38.2% |
| 33,303 | ST. FRANCIS | 9,146 | 1,608 | 3,284 | 4,254 | | 970 A | 17.6% | 35.9% | 46.5% |
| 28,956 | SALINE | 11,294 | 2,614 | 3,111 | 5,569 | | 2,458 A | 23.1% | 27.5% | 49.3% |
| 7,297 | SCOTT | 3,400 | 1,162 | 1,000 | 1,238 | | 76 A | 34.2% | 29.4% | 36.4% |
| 8,124 | SEARCY | 3,359 | 1,909 | 724 | 726 | | 1,183 R | 56.8% | 21.6% | 21.6% |
| 66,685 | SEBASTIAN | 27,042 | 12,073 | 6,320 | 8,649 | | 3,424 R | 44.6% | 23.4% | 32.0% |
| 10,156 | SEVIER | 3,847 | 1,217 | 1,129 | 1,501 | | 284 A | 31.6% | 29.3% | 39.0% |
| 6,319 | SHARP | 3,460 | 1,136 | 1,025 | 1,299 | | 163 A | 32.8% | 29.6% | 37.5% |
| 6,294 | STONE | 2,664 | 987 | 698 | 979 | | 8 R | 37.0% | 26.2% | 36.7% |
| 49,518 | UNION | 17,198 | 4,919 | 4,426 | 7,853 | | 2,934 A | 28.6% | 25.7% | 45.7% |
| 7,228 | VAN BUREN | 3,698 | 1,325 | 1,149 | 1,224 | | 101 R | 35.8% | 31.1% | 33.1% |
| 55,797 | WASHINGTON | 21,863 | 10,640 | 6,131 | 5,092 | | 4,509 R | 48.7% | 28.0% | 23.3% |
| 32,745 | WHITE | 12,139 | 3,887 | 3,198 | 5,054 | | 1,167 A | 32.0% | 26.3% | 41.6% |
| 13,954 | WOODRUFF | 3,629 | 625 | 1,270 | 1,734 | | 464 A | 17.2% | 35.0% | 47.8% |
| 11,940 | YELL | 5,281 | 1,819 | 1,513 | 1,949 | | 130 A | 34.4% | 28.6% | 36.9% |
| 1,786,272 | TOTAL | 619,969 | 190,759 | 188,228 | 240,982 | | 50,223 A | 30.8% | 30.4% | 38.9% |

# ARKANSAS

## PRESIDENT 1964

| 1960 Census Population | County | Total Vote | Republican | Democratic | Other | Rep.-Dem. Plurality | Percentage Total Vote Rep. | Dem. | Major Vote Rep. | Dem. |
|---|---|---|---|---|---|---|---|---|---|---|
| 24,175 | ARKANSAS | 6,990 | 3,769 | 3,200 | 21 | 569 R | 53.9% | 45.8% | 54.1% | 45.9% |
| 26,538 | ASHLEY | 6,710 | 3,742 | 2,901 | 67 | 841 R | 55.8% | 43.2% | 56.3% | 43.7% |
| 27,409 | BAXTER | 4,891 | 1,986 | 2,900 | 5 | 914 D | 40.6% | 59.3% | 40.6% | 59.4% |
| 78,115 | BENTON | 11,662 | 5,977 | 5,655 | 30 | 322 R | 51.3% | 48.5% | 51.4% | 48.6% |
| 26,067 | BOONE | 6,646 | 2,857 | 3,770 | 19 | 913 D | 43.0% | 56.7% | 43.1% | 56.9% |
| 13,803 | BRADLEY | 4,102 | 1,852 | 2,229 | 21 | 377 D | 45.1% | 54.3% | 45.4% | 54.6% |
| 6,079 | CALHOUN | 2,322 | 889 | 1,409 | 24 | 520 D | 38.3% | 60.7% | 38.7% | 61.3% |
| 16,203 | CARROLL | 4,110 | 2,105 | 2,005 | | 100 R | 51.2% | 48.8% | 51.2% | 48.8% |
| 17,793 | CHICOT | 4,903 | 1,972 | 2,916 | 15 | 944 D | 40.2% | 59.5% | 40.3% | 59.7% |
| 23,326 | CLARK | 6,037 | 1,884 | 4,127 | 26 | 2,243 D | 31.2% | 68.4% | 31.3% | 68.7% |
| 20,616 | CLAY | 5,321 | 1,999 | 3,280 | 42 | 1,281 D | 37.6% | 61.6% | 37.9% | 62.1% |
| 16,909 | CLEBURNE | 3,875 | 1,221 | 2,645 | 9 | 1,424 D | 31.5% | 68.3% | 31.6% | 68.4% |
| 7,868 | CLEVELAND | 2,165 | 1,026 | 1,121 | 18 | 95 D | 47.4% | 51.8% | 47.8% | 52.2% |
| 26,644 | COLUMBIA | 7,533 | 4,009 | 3,485 | 39 | 524 R | 53.2% | 46.3% | 53.5% | 46.5% |
| 19,505 | CONWAY | 6,602 | 2,378 | 4,205 | 19 | 1,827 D | 36.0% | 63.7% | 36.1% | 63.9% |
| 63,239 | CRAIGHEAD | 13,541 | 5,163 | 8,334 | 44 | 3,171 D | 38.1% | 61.5% | 38.3% | 61.7% |
| 36,892 | CRAWFORD | 6,852 | 3,294 | 3,537 | 21 | 243 D | 48.1% | 51.6% | 48.2% | 51.8% |
| 49,499 | CRITTENDEN | 8,302 | 4,065 | 4,168 | 69 | 103 D | 49.0% | 50.2% | 49.4% | 50.6% |
| 20,434 | CROSS | 4,580 | 2,147 | 2,421 | 12 | 274 D | 46.9% | 52.9% | 47.0% | 53.0% |
| 10,515 | DALLAS | 3,447 | 1,625 | 1,779 | 43 | 154 D | 47.1% | 51.6% | 47.7% | 52.3% |
| 19,760 | DESHA | 5,236 | 1,930 | 3,294 | 12 | 1,364 D | 36.9% | 62.9% | 36.9% | 63.1% |
| 17,910 | DREW | 4,121 | 2,109 | 1,980 | 32 | 129 R | 51.2% | 48.0% | 51.6% | 48.4% |
| 46,192 | FAULKNER | 9,417 | 3,259 | 6,116 | 42 | 2,857 D | 34.6% | 64.9% | 34.8% | 65.2% |
| 14,705 | FRANKLIN | 4,298 | 1,580 | 2,685 | 33 | 1,105 D | 36.8% | 62.5% | 37.0% | 63.0% |
| 9,975 | FULTON | 2,557 | 846 | 1,704 | 7 | 858 D | 33.1% | 66.6% | 33.2% | 66.8% |
| 70,531 | GARLAND | 21,629 | 9,952 | 11,591 | 86 | 1,639 D | 46.0% | 53.6% | 46.2% | 53.8% |
| 13,008 | GRANT | 3,047 | 1,308 | 1,678 | 61 | 370 D | 42.9% | 55.1% | 43.8% | 56.2% |
| 30,744 | GREENE | 7,037 | 2,271 | 4,742 | 24 | 2,471 D | 32.3% | 67.4% | 32.4% | 67.6% |
| 23,635 | HEMPSTEAD | 5,891 | 2,493 | 3,355 | 43 | 862 D | 42.3% | 57.0% | 42.6% | 57.4% |
| 26,819 | HOT SPRING | 7,522 | 2,911 | 4,543 | 68 | 1,632 D | 38.7% | 60.4% | 39.1% | 60.9% |
| 13,459 | HOWARD | 3,063 | 1,649 | 1,320 | 94 | 329 R | 53.8% | 43.1% | 55.5% | 44.5% |
| 30,147 | INDEPENDENCE | 6,960 | 2,470 | 4,455 | 35 | 1,985 D | 35.5% | 64.0% | 35.7% | 64.3% |
| 10,768 | IZARD | 2,486 | 726 | 1,736 | 24 | 1,010 D | 29.2% | 69.8% | 29.5% | 70.5% |
| 21,646 | JACKSON | 6,828 | 2,141 | 4,651 | 36 | 2,510 D | 31.4% | 68.1% | 31.5% | 68.5% |
| 90,718 | JEFFERSON | 22,969 | 9,968 | 12,872 | 129 | 2,904 D | 43.4% | 56.0% | 43.6% | 56.4% |
| 17,423 | JOHNSON | 4,683 | 1,535 | 3,127 | 21 | 1,592 D | 32.8% | 66.8% | 32.9% | 67.1% |
| 10,213 | LAFAYETTE | 2,967 | 1,476 | 1,484 | 7 | 8 D | 49.7% | 50.0% | 49.9% | 50.1% |
| 18,447 | LAWRENCE | 5,538 | 2,013 | 3,498 | 27 | 1,485 D | 36.3% | 63.2% | 36.5% | 63.5% |
| 15,539 | LEE | 4,011 | 1,668 | 2,335 | 8 | 667 D | 41.6% | 58.2% | 41.7% | 58.3% |
| 13,369 | LINCOLN | 3,882 | 1,410 | 2,468 | 4 | 1,058 D | 36.3% | 63.6% | 36.4% | 63.6% |
| 13,952 | LITTLE RIVER | 3,194 | 1,141 | 2,040 | 13 | 899 D | 35.7% | 63.9% | 35.9% | 64.1% |
| 20,144 | LOGAN | 5,896 | 2,265 | 3,604 | 27 | 1,339 D | 38.4% | 61.1% | 38.6% | 61.4% |
| 34,518 | LONOKE | 7,477 | 3,636 | 3,818 | 23 | 182 D | 48.6% | 51.1% | 48.8% | 51.2% |
| 11,373 | MADISON | 4,726 | 1,997 | 2,715 | 14 | 718 D | 42.3% | 57.4% | 42.4% | 57.6% |
| 11,334 | MARION | 2,759 | 1,088 | 1,661 | 10 | 573 D | 39.4% | 60.2% | 39.6% | 60.4% |
| 37,766 | MILLER | 9,492 | 4,253 | 5,190 | 49 | 937 D | 44.8% | 54.7% | 45.0% | 55.0% |
| 59,517 | MISSISSIPPI | 14,911 | 6,213 | 8,678 | 20 | 2,465 D | 41.7% | 58.2% | 41.7% | 58.3% |
| 14,052 | MONROE | 4,237 | 1,968 | 2,258 | 11 | 290 D | 46.4% | 53.3% | 46.6% | 53.4% |
| 7,771 | MONTGOMERY | 2,202 | 832 | 1,358 | 12 | 526 D | 37.8% | 61.7% | 38.0% | 62.0% |
| 11,097 | NEVADA | 3,625 | 1,406 | 2,190 | 29 | 784 D | 38.8% | 60.4% | 39.1% | 60.9% |
| 7,756 | NEWTON | 2,769 | 1,357 | 1,374 | 38 | 17 D | 49.0% | 49.6% | 49.7% | 50.3% |
| 30,541 | OUACHITA | 10,698 | 3,572 | 7,056 | 70 | 3,484 D | 33.4% | 66.0% | 33.6% | 66.4% |
| 7,266 | PERRY | 2,387 | 1,048 | 1,320 | 19 | 272 D | 43.9% | 55.3% | 44.3% | 55.7% |
| 34,772 | PHILLIPS | 9,790 | 3,963 | 5,818 | 9 | 1,855 D | 40.5% | 59.4% | 40.5% | 59.5% |
| 10,373 | PIKE | 2,787 | 1,241 | 1,531 | 15 | 290 D | 44.5% | 54.9% | 44.8% | 55.2% |
| 27,032 | POINSETT | 8,679 | 3,031 | 5,635 | 13 | 2,604 D | 34.9% | 64.9% | 35.0% | 65.0% |
| 17,007 | POLK | 4,608 | 2,022 | 2,575 | 11 | 553 D | 43.9% | 55.9% | 44.0% | 56.0% |
| 39,021 | POPE | 7,780 | 2,651 | 4,972 | 157 | 2,321 D | 34.1% | 63.9% | 34.8% | 65.2% |
| 10,140 | PRAIRIE | 3,310 | 1,476 | 1,812 | 22 | 336 D | 44.6% | 54.7% | 44.9% | 55.1% |
| 340,613 | PULASKI | 79,289 | 38,312 | 40,535 | 442 | 2,223 D | 48.3% | 51.1% | 48.6% | 51.4% |

# ARKANSAS

## PRESIDENT 1964

| 1960 Census Population | County | Total Vote | Republican | Democratic | Other | Rep.-Dem. Plurality | Percentage | | | |
|---|---|---|---|---|---|---|---|---|---|---|
| | | | | | | | Total Vote | | Major Vote | |
| | | | | | | | Rep. | Dem. | Rep. | Dem. |
| 16,834 | RANDOLPH | 4,009 | 1,312 | 2,680 | 17 | 1,368 D | 32.7% | 66.8% | 32.9% | 67.1% |
| 30,858 | ST. FRANCIS | 7,038 | 3,377 | 3,651 | 10 | 274 D | 48.0% | 51.9% | 48.1% | 51.9% |
| 53,161 | SALINE | 9,313 | 3,628 | 5,605 | 80 | 1,977 D | 39.0% | 60.2% | 39.3% | 60.7% |
| 9,685 | SCOTT | 2,964 | 1,121 | 1,838 | 5 | 717 D | 37.8% | 62.0% | 37.9% | 62.1% |
| 8,847 | SEARCY | 3,163 | 1,649 | 1,508 | 6 | 141 R | 52.1% | 47.7% | 52.2% | 47.8% |
| 95,172 | SEBASTIAN | 23,493 | 13,110 | 10,299 | 84 | 2,811 R | 55.8% | 43.8% | 56.0% | 44.0% |
| 14,060 | SEVIER | 3,383 | 1,249 | 2,123 | 11 | 874 D | 36.9% | 62.8% | 37.0% | 63.0% |
| 14,607 | SHARP | 3,047 | 1,215 | 1,810 | 22 | 595 D | 39.9% | 59.4% | 40.2% | 59.8% |
| 9,022 | STONE | 2,340 | 942 | 1,374 | 24 | 432 D | 40.3% | 58.7% | 40.7% | 59.3% |
| 48,573 | UNION | 15,580 | 8,472 | 6,948 | 160 | 1,524 R | 54.4% | 44.6% | 54.9% | 45.1% |
| 13,357 | VAN BUREN | 3,352 | 1,270 | 2,054 | 28 | 784 D | 37.9% | 61.3% | 38.2% | 61.8% |
| 100,494 | WASHINGTON | 17,070 | 6,856 | 10,166 | 48 | 3,310 D | 40.2% | 59.6% | 40.3% | 59.7% |
| 50,835 | WHITE | 11,684 | 5,023 | 6,566 | 95 | 1,543 D | 43.0% | 56.2% | 43.3% | 56.7% |
| 11,222 | WOODRUFF | 3,693 | 1,366 | 2,307 | 20 | 941 D | 37.0% | 62.5% | 37.2% | 62.8% |
| 17,026 | YELL | 4,948 | 1,527 | 3,407 | 14 | 1,880 D | 30.9% | 68.9% | 30.9% | 69.1% |
| 2,286,435 | TOTAL | 560,426 | 243,264 | 314,197 | 2,965 | 70,933 D | 43.4% | 56.1% | 43.6% | 56.4% |

# ARKANSAS

## PRESIDENT 1960

| 1960 Census Population | County | Total Vote | Republican | Democratic | Other | Rep.-Dem. Plurality | Percentage | | | |
|---|---|---|---|---|---|---|---|---|---|---|
| | | | | | | | Total Vote | | Major Vote | |
| | | | | | | | Rep. | Dem. | Rep. | Dem. |
| 24,175 | ARKANSAS | 5,318 | 2,043 | 2,789 | 486 | 746 D | 38.4% | 52.4% | 42.3% | 57.7% |
| 26,538 | ASHLEY | 5,026 | 1,288 | 3,118 | 620 | 1,830 D | 25.6% | 62.0% | 29.2% | 70.8% |
| 27,409 | BAXTER | 3,879 | 2,108 | 1,694 | 77 | 414 R | 54.3% | 43.7% | 55.4% | 44.6% |
| 78,115 | BENTON | 11,590 | 7,832 | 3,619 | 139 | 4,213 R | 67.6% | 31.2% | 68.4% | 31.6% |
| 26,067 | BOONE | 6,233 | 3,388 | 2,774 | 71 | 614 R | 54.4% | 44.5% | 55.0% | 45.0% |
| 13,803 | BRADLEY | 4,210 | 873 | 2,960 | 377 | 2,087 D | 20.7% | 70.3% | 22.8% | 77.2% |
| 6,079 | CALHOUN | 1,598 | 295 | 1,151 | 152 | 856 D | 18.5% | 72.0% | 20.4% | 79.6% |
| 16,203 | CARROLL | 3,965 | 2,615 | 1,301 | 49 | 1,314 R | 66.0% | 32.8% | 66.8% | 33.2% |
| 17,793 | CHICOT | 3,051 | 979 | 1,803 | 269 | 824 D | 32.1% | 59.1% | 35.2% | 64.8% |
| 23,326 | CLARK | 5,083 | 1,357 | 3,295 | 431 | 1,938 D | 26.7% | 64.8% | 29.2% | 70.8% |
| 20,616 | CLAY | 4,568 | 2,543 | 1,908 | 117 | 635 R | 55.7% | 41.8% | 57.1% | 42.9% |
| 16,909 | CLEBURNE | 2,282 | 1,026 | 1,144 | 112 | 118 D | 45.0% | 50.1% | 47.3% | 52.7% |
| 7,868 | CLEVELAND | 1,715 | 290 | 1,216 | 209 | 926 D | 16.9% | 70.9% | 19.3% | 80.7% |
| 26,644 | COLUMBIA | 5,605 | 2,372 | 2,427 | 806 | 55 D | 42.3% | 43.3% | 49.4% | 50.6% |
| 19,505 | CONWAY | 4,796 | 1,685 | 2,900 | 211 | 1,215 D | 35.1% | 60.5% | 36.8% | 63.2% |
| 63,239 | CRAIGHEAD | 10,738 | 5,258 | 4,898 | 582 | 360 R | 49.0% | 45.6% | 51.8% | 48.2% |
| 36,892 | CRAWFORD | 5,907 | 3,373 | 2,430 | 104 | 943 R | 57.1% | 41.1% | 58.1% | 41.9% |
| 49,499 | CRITTENDEN | 5,128 | 2,234 | 2,679 | 215 | 445 D | 43.6% | 52.2% | 45.5% | 54.5% |
| 20,434 | CROSS | 3,615 | 1,287 | 2,088 | 240 | 801 D | 35.6% | 57.8% | 38.1% | 61.9% |
| 10,515 | DALLAS | 2,615 | 659 | 1,639 | 317 | 980 D | 25.2% | 62.7% | 28.7% | 71.3% |
| 19,760 | DESHA | 3,936 | 1,063 | 2,502 | 371 | 1,439 D | 27.0% | 63.6% | 29.8% | 70.2% |
| 17,910 | DREW | 3,372 | 889 | 2,107 | 376 | 1,218 D | 26.4% | 62.5% | 29.7% | 70.3% |
| 46,192 | FAULKNER | 6,609 | 2,426 | 3,820 | 363 | 1,394 D | 36.7% | 57.8% | 38.8% | 61.2% |
| 14,705 | FRANKLIN | 3,751 | 1,631 | 2,025 | 95 | 394 D | 43.5% | 54.0% | 44.6% | 55.4% |
| 9,975 | FULTON | 1,849 | 1,127 | 703 | 19 | 424 R | 61.0% | 38.0% | 61.6% | 38.4% |
| 70,531 | GARLAND | 13,944 | 7,204 | 6,333 | 407 | 871 R | 51.7% | 45.4% | 53.2% | 46.8% |
| 13,008 | GRANT | 2,269 | 563 | 1,394 | 312 | 831 D | 24.8% | 61.4% | 28.8% | 71.2% |
| 30,744 | GREENE | 5,569 | 2,658 | 2,774 | 137 | 116 D | 47.7% | 49.8% | 48.9% | 51.1% |
| 23,635 | HEMPSTEAD | 4,759 | 1,948 | 2,596 | 215 | 648 D | 40.9% | 54.5% | 42.9% | 57.1% |
| 26,819 | HOT SPRING | 5,854 | 1,732 | 3,454 | 668 | 1,722 D | 29.6% | 59.0% | 33.4% | 66.6% |
| 13,459 | HOWARD | 2,735 | 1,225 | 1,366 | 144 | 141 D | 44.8% | 49.9% | 47.3% | 52.7% |
| 30,147 | INDEPENDENCE | 5,289 | 2,639 | 2,487 | 163 | 152 R | 49.9% | 47.0% | 51.5% | 48.5% |
| 10,768 | IZARD | 2,248 | 808 | 1,340 | 100 | 532 D | 35.9% | 59.6% | 37.6% | 62.4% |
| 21,646 | JACKSON | 5,159 | 1,986 | 2,860 | 313 | 874 D | 38.5% | 55.4% | 41.0% | 59.0% |
| 90,718 | JEFFERSON | 15,235 | 4,839 | 8,442 | 1,954 | 3,603 D | 31.8% | 55.4% | 36.4% | 63.6% |
| 17,423 | JOHNSON | 3,523 | 1,490 | 1,938 | 95 | 448 D | 42.3% | 55.0% | 43.5% | 56.5% |
| 10,213 | LAFAYETTE | 2,325 | 713 | 1,286 | 326 | 573 D | 30.7% | 55.3% | 35.7% | 64.3% |
| 18,447 | LAWRENCE | 4,065 | 1,800 | 2,074 | 191 | 274 D | 44.3% | 51.0% | 46.5% | 53.5% |
| 15,539 | LEE | 2,701 | 1,034 | 1,409 | 258 | 375 D | 38.3% | 52.2% | 42.3% | 57.7% |
| 13,369 | LINCOLN | 2,646 | 626 | 1,780 | 240 | 1,154 D | 23.7% | 67.3% | 26.0% | 74.0% |
| 13,952 | LITTLE RIVER | 2,323 | 692 | 1,514 | 117 | 822 D | 29.8% | 65.2% | 31.4% | 68.6% |
| 20,144 | LOGAN | 4,764 | 2,014 | 2,636 | 114 | 622 D | 42.3% | 55.3% | 43.3% | 56.7% |
| 34,518 | LONOKE | 5,348 | 1,560 | 2,991 | 797 | 1,431 D | 29.2% | 55.9% | 34.3% | 65.7% |
| 11,373 | MADISON | 4,201 | 2,445 | 1,702 | 54 | 743 R | 58.2% | 40.5% | 59.0% | 41.0% |
| 11,334 | MARION | 2,008 | 1,016 | 968 | 24 | 48 R | 50.6% | 48.2% | 51.2% | 48.8% |
| 37,766 | MILLER | 8,117 | 3,113 | 4,550 | 454 | 1,437 D | 38.4% | 56.1% | 40.6% | 59.4% |
| 59,517 | MISSISSIPPI | 10,585 | 4,983 | 5,138 | 464 | 155 D | 47.1% | 48.5% | 49.2% | 50.8% |
| 14,052 | MONROE | 3,068 | 833 | 1,856 | 379 | 1,023 D | 27.2% | 60.5% | 31.0% | 69.0% |
| 7,771 | MONTGOMERY | 1,677 | 836 | 788 | 53 | 48 R | 49.9% | 47.0% | 51.5% | 48.5% |
| 11,097 | NEVADA | 2,751 | 937 | 1,605 | 209 | 668 D | 34.1% | 58.3% | 36.9% | 63.1% |
| 7,756 | NEWTON | 2,687 | 1,814 | 844 | 29 | 970 R | 67.5% | 31.4% | 68.2% | 31.8% |
| 30,541 | OUACHITA | 8,192 | 2,439 | 5,169 | 584 | 2,730 D | 29.8% | 63.1% | 32.1% | 67.9% |
| 7,266 | PERRY | 1,385 | 501 | 789 | 95 | 288 D | 36.2% | 57.0% | 38.8% | 61.2% |
| 34,772 | PHILLIPS | 6,677 | 2,168 | 4,105 | 404 | 1,937 D | 32.5% | 61.5% | 34.6% | 65.4% |
| 10,373 | PIKE | 2,102 | 1,013 | 997 | 92 | 16 R | 48.2% | 47.4% | 50.4% | 49.6% |
| 27,032 | POINSETT | 5,444 | 2,430 | 2,817 | 197 | 387 D | 44.6% | 51.7% | 46.3% | 53.7% |
| 17,007 | POLK | 3,632 | 1,882 | 1,635 | 115 | 247 R | 51.8% | 45.0% | 53.5% | 46.5% |
| 39,021 | POPE | 5,589 | 2,573 | 2,760 | 256 | 187 D | 46.0% | 49.4% | 48.2% | 51.8% |
| 10,140 | PRAIRIE | 2,636 | 734 | 1,680 | 222 | 946 D | 27.8% | 63.7% | 30.4% | 69.6% |
| 340,613 | PULASKI | 55,788 | 22,146 | 26,034 | 7,608 | 3,888 D | 39.7% | 46.7% | 46.0% | 54.0% |

# ARKANSAS

## PRESIDENT 1960

| 1960 Census Population | County | Total Vote | Republican | Democratic | Other | Rep.-Dem. Plurality | Percentage | | | |
|---|---|---|---|---|---|---|---|---|---|---|
| | | | | | | | Total Vote | | Major Vote | |
| | | | | | | | Rep. | Dem. | Rep. | Dem. |
| 16,834 | RANDOLPH | 3,278 | 1,620 | 1,556 | 102 | 64 R | 49.4% | 47.5% | 51.0% | 49.0% |
| 30,858 | ST. FRANCIS | 4,518 | 1,786 | 2,432 | 300 | 646 D | 39.5% | 53.8% | 42.3% | 57.7% |
| 53,161 | SALINE | 6,791 | 2,195 | 3,898 | 698 | 1,703 D | 32.3% | 57.4% | 36.0% | 64.0% |
| 9,685 | SCOTT | 2,264 | 1,137 | 1,116 | 11 | 21 R | 50.2% | 49.3% | 50.5% | 49.5% |
| 8,847 | SEARCY | 3,351 | 2,297 | 1,022 | 32 | 1,275 R | 68.5% | 30.5% | 69.2% | 30.8% |
| 95,172 | SEBASTIAN | 20,696 | 11,744 | 8,726 | 226 | 3,018 R | 56.7% | 42.2% | 57.4% | 42.6% |
| 14,060 | SEVIER | 2,835 | 1,141 | 1,580 | 114 | 439 D | 40.2% | 55.7% | 41.9% | 58.1% |
| 14,607 | SHARP | 1,786 | 911 | 807 | 68 | 104 R | 51.0% | 45.2% | 53.0% | 47.0% |
| 9,022 | STONE | 1,943 | 959 | 897 | 87 | 62 R | 49.4% | 46.2% | 51.7% | 48.3% |
| 48,573 | UNION | 13,565 | 5,631 | 6,500 | 1,434 | 869 D | 41.5% | 47.9% | 46.4% | 53.6% |
| 13,357 | VAN BUREN | 2,267 | 1,009 | 1,158 | 100 | 149 D | 44.5% | 51.1% | 46.6% | 53.4% |
| 100,494 | WASHINGTON | 15,679 | 10,088 | 5,391 | 200 | 4,697 R | 64.3% | 34.4% | 65.2% | 34.8% |
| 50,835 | WHITE | 9,834 | 3,985 | 5,244 | 605 | 1,259 D | 40.5% | 53.3% | 43.2% | 56.8% |
| 11,222 | WOODRUFF | 2,535 | 667 | 1,613 | 255 | 946 D | 26.3% | 63.6% | 29.3% | 70.7% |
| 17,026 | YELL | 3,433 | 1,303 | 2,008 | 122 | 705 D | 38.0% | 58.5% | 39.4% | 60.6% |
| 2,286,435 | TOTAL | 428,509 | 184,508 | 215,049 | 28,952 | 30,541 D | 43.1% | 50.2% | 46.2% | 53.8% |

# ARKANSAS

## ELECTION NOTES

**2004**     Other vote was 6,171 Populist Party of Arkansas (Ralph Nader); 2,352 Libertarian (Michael Badnarik); 2,083 Constitutional (Michael Peroutka); 1,488 Green Party of Arkansas (David Cobb).

**2000**     Other vote was 7,358 Reform (Buchanan); 2,781 Libertarian (Browne); 1,415 Constitutional (Phillips); 1,098 Natural Law (Hagelin).

**1996**     Other vote was 3,649 Green (Nader); 3,076 Libertarian (Browne); 2,065 U.S. Taxpayers (Phillips); 932 America First (R. Forbes); 823 Unaffiliated Independent Party (Collins); 749 Looking Back (Masters); 747 Workers World (Moorehead); 729 Natural Law (Hagelin); 538 Socialist (Hollis); 483 Prohibition (Dodge).

**1992**     Other vote was 1,437 Phillips (Taxpayers); 1,261 Marrou (Libertarian); 1,022 Fulani (New Alliance); 956 Boren (Apathy); 819 Gritz (America First); 764 Hagelin (Natural Law); 762 LaRouche (Justice, Industry, Agriculture); 554 Yiamouyiannis (Take Back America); 472 Dodge (Prohibition); 327 Masters (Looking Back).

**1988**     Other vote was 5,146 Duke (Independent); 3,297 Paul (Independent); 2,161 Fulani (Independent); 1,319 Dodge (Independent). The vote in Logan county appears to be low, but the official certified returns are presented in the table.

**1984**     Other vote was 2,221 Bergland (Libertarian); 1,890 LaRouche (Independent); 1,499 Hall (People Before Profits); 1,461 Richards (Populist); 1,291 Serrette (Independent Alliance); 960 Johnson (Citizen's Group); 842 Dodge (Prohibition); 822 Lowery (United Sovereign Citizens).

**1980**     Other vote was 22,468 Anderson (Anderson Coalition); 8,970 Clark (Libertarian); 2,345 Commoner (Citizens); 1,350 Bubar (Statesman); 1,244 Hall (People Before Profits).

**1976**     Other vote was 639 McCarthy (write-in); 389 Anderson (write-in).

**1972**     Other vote was Schmitz (write-in). Although the data indicate a possible discrepancy in both the Republican and Democratic vote in Drew county, the official state canvass figures are used here.

**1968**     Wallace on the ballot as American. Due to an undercount in Jefferson county, early unamended canvass gave the state-wide totals as 189,062 Republican; 184,901 Democratic; 235,627 American. The Democratic vote in Little River county was amended from 1,095.

**1964**     Other vote was Kasper (National States Rights).

**1960**     Other vote was Faubus (National States Rights).

# CALIFORNIA

## POPULAR VOTE FOR PRESIDENT 1920 TO 2004

| Year | Total Vote | Republican Vote | Republican Candidate | Democratic Vote | Democratic Candidate | Other Vote | Plurality | Percentage Total Vote Rep. | Dem. | Major Vote Rep. | Dem. |
|------|-----------|-----------------|---------------------|-----------------|---------------------|-----------|-----------|------|------|------|------|
| 2004 | 12,421,852 | 5,509,826 | Bush, George W. | 6,745,485 | Kerry, John | 166,541 | 1,235,659 D | 44.4% | 54.3% | 45.0% | 55.0% |
| 2000 ** | 10,965,856 | 4,567,429 | Bush, George W. | 5,861,203 | Gore, Al | 537,224 | 1,293,774 D | 41.7% | 53.4% | 43.8% | 56.2% |
| 1996 ** | 10,019,484 | 3,828,380 | Dole, Bob | 5,119,835 | Clinton, Bill | 1,071,269 | 1,291,455 D | 38.2% | 51.1% | 42.8% | 57.2% |
| 1992 ** | 11,131,721 | 3,630,574 | Bush, George | 5,121,325 | Clinton, Bill | 2,379,822 | 1,490,751 D | 32.6% | 46.0% | 41.5% | 58.5% |
| 1988 | 9,887,065 | 5,054,917 | Bush, George | 4,702,233 | Dukakis, Michael S. | 129,915 | 352,684 R | 51.1% | 47.6% | 51.8% | 48.2% |
| 1984 | 9,505,423 | 5,467,009 | Reagan, Ronald | 3,922,519 | Mondale, Walter F. | 115,895 | 1,544,490 R | 57.5% | 41.3% | 58.2% | 41.8% |
| 1980 ** | 8,587,063 | 4,524,858 | Reagan, Ronald | 3,083,661 | Carter, Jimmy | 978,544 | 1,441,197 R | 52.7% | 35.9% | 59.5% | 40.5% |
| 1976 | 7,867,117 | 3,882,244 | Ford, Gerald R. | 3,742,284 | Carter, Jimmy | 242,589 | 139,960 R | 49.3% | 47.6% | 50.9% | 49.1% |
| 1972 | 8,367,862 | 4,602,096 | Nixon, Richard M. | 3,475,847 | McGovern, George S. | 289,919 | 1,126,249 R | 55.0% | 41.5% | 57.0% | 43.0% |
| 1968 | 7,251,587 | 3,467,664 | Nixon, Richard M. | 3,244,318 | Humphrey, Hubert H. | 539,605 | 223,346 R | 47.8% | 44.7% | 51.7% | 48.3% |
| 1964 | 7,057,586 | 2,879,108 | Goldwater, Barry M. | 4,171,877 | Johnson, Lyndon B. | 6,601 | 1,292,769 D | 40.8% | 59.1% | 40.8% | 59.2% |
| 1960 | 6,506,578 | 3,259,722 | Nixon, Richard M. | 3,224,099 | Kennedy, John F. | 22,757 | 35,623 R | 50.1% | 49.6% | 50.3% | 49.7% |
| 1956 | 5,466,355 | 3,027,668 | Eisenhower, Dwight D. | 2,420,135 | Stevenson, Adlai E. | 18,552 | 607,533 R | 55.4% | 44.3% | 55.6% | 44.4% |
| 1952 | 5,141,849 | 2,897,310 | Eisenhower, Dwight D. | 2,197,548 | Stevenson, Adlai E. | 46,991 | 699,762 R | 56.3% | 42.7% | 56.9% | 43.1% |
| 1948 | 4,021,538 | 1,895,269 | Dewey, Thomas E. | 1,913,134 | Truman, Harry S. | 213,135 | 17,865 D | 47.1% | 47.6% | 49.8% | 50.2% |
| 1944 | 3,520,875 | 1,512,965 | Dewey, Thomas E. | 1,988,564 | Roosevelt, Franklin D. | 19,346 | 475,599 D | 43.0% | 56.5% | 43.2% | 56.8% |
| 1940 | 3,268,791 | 1,351,419 | Willkie, Wendell | 1,877,618 | Roosevelt, Franklin D. | 39,754 | 526,199 D | 41.3% | 57.4% | 41.9% | 58.1% |
| 1936 | 2,638,882 | 836,431 | Landon, Alfred M. | 1,766,836 | Roosevelt, Franklin D. | 35,615 | 930,405 D | 31.7% | 67.0% | 32.1% | 67.9% |
| 1932 | 2,266,972 | 847,902 | Hoover, Herbert C. | 1,324,157 | Roosevelt, Franklin D. | 94,913 | 476,255 D | 37.4% | 58.4% | 39.0% | 61.0% |
| 1928 | 1,796,656 | 1,162,323 | Hoover, Herbert C. | 614,365 | Smith, Alfred E. | 19,968 | 547,958 R | 64.7% | 34.2% | 65.4% | 34.6% |
| 1924 ** | 1,281,778 | 733,250 | Coolidge, Calvin | 105,514 | Davis, John W. | 443,014 | 308,601 R | 57.2% | 8.2% | 87.4% | 12.6% |
| 1920 | 943,463 | 624,992 | Harding, Warren G. | 229,191 | Cox, James M. | 89,280 | 395,801 R | 66.2% | 24.3% | 73.2% | 26.8% |

In 2000 the other vote column includes 418,707 votes cast for Green (Nader). In 1996 the other vote column includes 697,847 votes cast for Perot. In 1992 the other vote column includes 2,296,006 votes cast for Perot. In 1980 the other column includes 739,833 votes for Independent (Anderson). In 1924 the other vote was 424,649 Progressive and 18,365 Prohibition.

## ELECTORAL COLLEGE VOTE 1920 TO 2004

| Year | Total | Republican | Democratic | Other |
|------|-------|-----------|------------|-------|
| 2004 | 55 | | 55 | |
| 2000 | 54 | | 54 | |
| 1996 | 54 | | 54 | |
| 1992 | 54 | | 54 | |
| 1988 | 47 | 47 | | |
| 1984 | 47 | 47 | | |
| 1980 | 45 | 45 | | |
| 1976 | 45 | 45 | | |
| 1972 | 45 | 45 | | |
| 1968 | 40 | 40 | | |
| 1964 | 40 | | 40 | |
| 1960 | 32 | 32 | | |
| 1956 | 32 | 32 | | |
| 1952 | 32 | 32 | | |
| 1948 | 25 | | 25 | |
| 1944 | 25 | | 25 | |
| 1940 | 22 | | 22 | |
| 1936 | 22 | | 22 | |
| 1932 | 22 | | 22 | |
| 1928 | 13 | 13 | | |
| 1924 | 13 | 13 | | |
| 1920 | 13 | 13 | | |

# CALIFORNIA

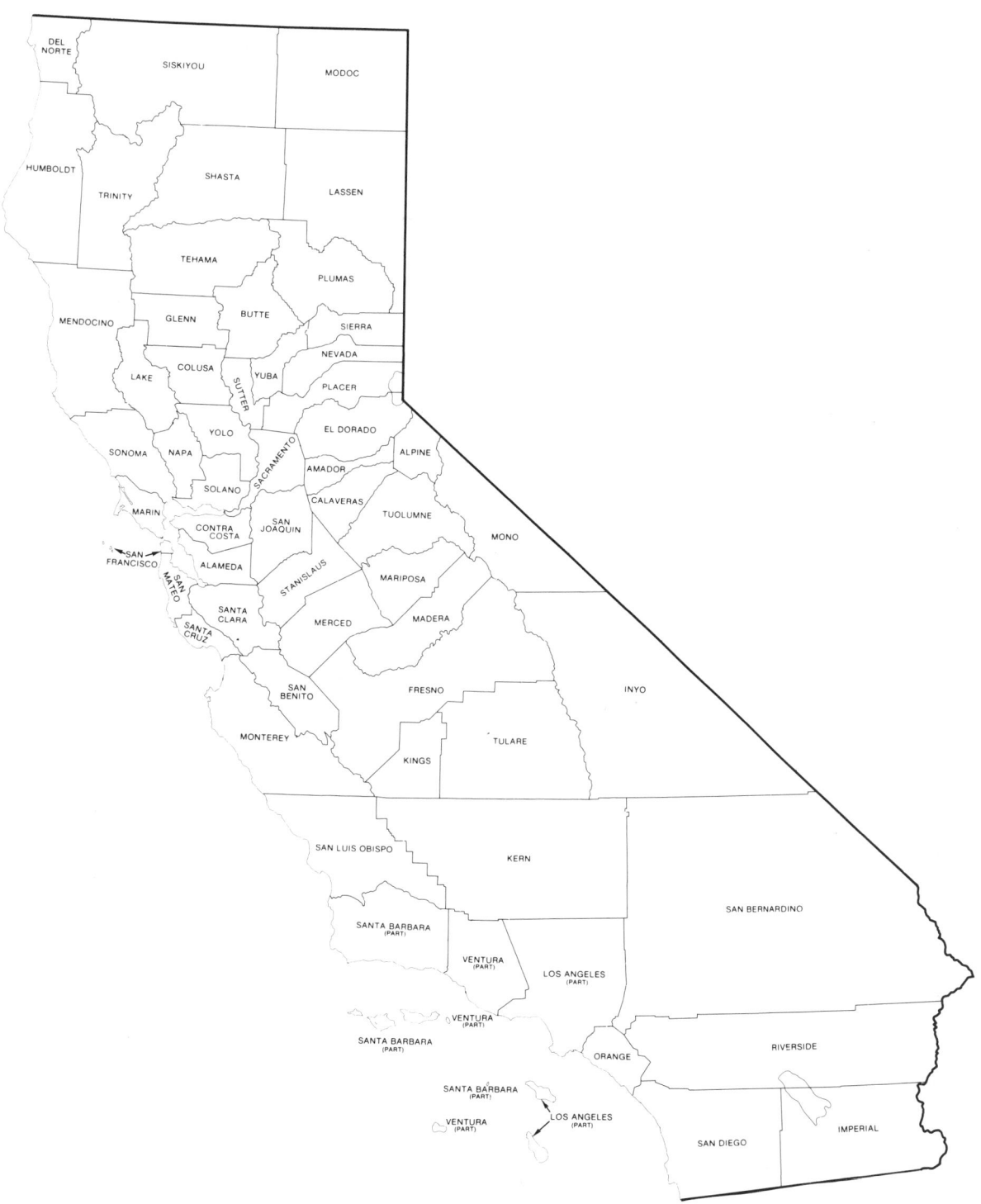

# CALIFORNIA

## PRESIDENT 2004

| 2000 Census Population | County | Total Vote | Republican | Democratic | Other | Rep.-Dem. Plurality | Percentage | | | |
|---|---|---|---|---|---|---|---|---|---|---|
| | | | | | | | Total Vote | | Major Vote | |
| | | | | | | | Rep. | Dem. | Rep. | Dem. |
| 1,443,741 | ALAMEDA | 562,090 | 130,911 | 422,585 | 8,594 | 291,674 D | 23.3% | 75.2% | 23.7% | 76.3% |
| 1,208 | ALPINE | 701 | 311 | 373 | 17 | 62 D | 44.4% | 53.2% | 45.5% | 54.5% |
| 35,100 | AMADOR | 17,891 | 11,107 | 6,541 | 243 | 4,566 R | 62.1% | 36.6% | 62.9% | 37.1% |
| 203,171 | BUTTE | 96,157 | 51,662 | 42,448 | 2,047 | 9,214 R | 53.7% | 44.1% | 54.9% | 45.1% |
| 40,554 | CALAVERAS | 22,343 | 13,601 | 8,286 | 456 | 5,315 R | 60.9% | 37.1% | 62.1% | 37.9% |
| 18,804 | COLUSA | 6,166 | 4,142 | 1,947 | 77 | 2,195 R | 67.2% | 31.6% | 68.0% | 32.0% |
| 948,816 | CONTRA COSTA | 413,028 | 150,608 | 257,254 | 5,166 | 106,646 D | 36.5% | 62.3% | 36.9% | 63.1% |
| 27,507 | DEL NORTE | 9,421 | 5,356 | 3,892 | 173 | 1,464 R | 56.9% | 41.3% | 57.9% | 42.1% |
| 156,299 | EL DORADO | 86,364 | 52,878 | 32,242 | 1,244 | 20,636 R | 61.2% | 37.3% | 62.1% | 37.9% |
| 799,407 | FRESNO | 247,463 | 141,988 | 103,154 | 2,321 | 38,834 R | 57.4% | 41.7% | 57.9% | 42.1% |
| 26,453 | GLENN | 9,454 | 6,308 | 2,995 | 151 | 3,313 R | 66.7% | 31.7% | 67.8% | 32.2% |
| 126,518 | HUMBOLDT | 65,886 | 25,714 | 37,988 | 2,184 | 12,274 D | 39.0% | 57.7% | 40.4% | 59.6% |
| 142,361 | IMPERIAL | 34,274 | 15,890 | 17,964 | 420 | 2,074 D | 46.4% | 52.4% | 46.9% | 53.1% |
| 17,945 | INYO | 8,616 | 5,091 | 3,350 | 175 | 1,741 R | 59.1% | 38.9% | 60.3% | 39.7% |
| 661,645 | KERN | 211,174 | 140,417 | 68,603 | 2,154 | 71,814 R | 66.5% | 32.5% | 67.2% | 32.8% |
| 129,461 | KINGS | 32,110 | 21,003 | 10,833 | 274 | 10,170 R | 65.4% | 33.7% | 66.0% | 34.0% |
| 58,309 | LAKE | 24,719 | 11,093 | 13,141 | 485 | 2,048 D | 44.9% | 53.2% | 45.8% | 54.2% |
| 33,828 | LASSEN | 11,450 | 8,126 | 3,158 | 166 | 4,968 R | 71.0% | 27.6% | 72.0% | 28.0% |
| 9,519,338 | LOS ANGELES | 3,023,280 | 1,076,225 | 1,907,736 | 39,319 | 831,511 D | 35.6% | 63.1% | 36.1% | 63.9% |
| 123,109 | MADERA | 38,850 | 24,871 | 13,481 | 498 | 11,390 R | 64.0% | 34.7% | 64.8% | 35.2% |
| 247,289 | MARIN | 135,325 | 34,378 | 99,070 | 1,877 | 64,692 D | 25.4% | 73.2% | 25.8% | 74.2% |
| 17,130 | MARIPOSA | 8,658 | 5,215 | 3,251 | 192 | 1,964 R | 60.2% | 37.5% | 61.6% | 38.4% |
| 86,265 | MENDOCINO | 38,429 | 12,955 | 24,385 | 1,089 | 11,430 D | 33.7% | 63.5% | 34.7% | 65.3% |
| 210,554 | MERCED | 57,960 | 32,773 | 24,491 | 696 | 8,282 R | 56.5% | 42.3% | 57.2% | 42.8% |
| 9,449 | MODOC | 4,467 | 3,235 | 1,149 | 83 | 2,086 R | 72.4% | 25.7% | 73.8% | 26.2% |
| 12,853 | MONO | 5,338 | 2,621 | 2,628 | 89 | 7 D | 49.1% | 49.2% | 49.9% | 50.1% |
| 401,762 | MONTEREY | 124,653 | 47,838 | 75,241 | 1,574 | 27,403 D | 38.4% | 60.4% | 38.9% | 61.1% |
| 124,279 | NAPA | 56,599 | 22,059 | 33,666 | 874 | 11,607 D | 39.0% | 59.5% | 39.6% | 60.4% |
| 92,033 | NEVADA | 53,920 | 28,790 | 24,220 | 910 | 4,570 R | 53.4% | 44.9% | 54.3% | 45.7% |
| 2,846,289 | ORANGE | 1,075,399 | 641,832 | 419,239 | 14,328 | 222,593 R | 59.7% | 39.0% | 60.5% | 39.5% |
| 248,399 | PLACER | 153,278 | 95,969 | 55,573 | 1,736 | 40,396 R | 62.6% | 36.3% | 63.3% | 36.7% |
| 20,824 | PLUMAS | 11,190 | 6,905 | 4,129 | 156 | 2,776 R | 61.7% | 36.9% | 62.6% | 37.4% |
| 1,545,387 | RIVERSIDE | 557,579 | 322,473 | 228,806 | 6,300 | 93,667 R | 57.8% | 41.0% | 58.5% | 41.5% |
| 1,223,499 | SACRAMENTO | 477,866 | 235,539 | 236,657 | 5,670 | 1,118 D | 49.3% | 49.5% | 49.9% | 50.1% |
| 53,234 | SAN BENITO | 18,725 | 8,698 | 9,851 | 176 | 1,153 D | 46.5% | 52.6% | 46.9% | 53.1% |
| 1,709,434 | SAN BERNARDINO | 523,276 | 289,306 | 227,789 | 6,181 | 61,517 R | 55.3% | 43.5% | 55.9% | 44.1% |
| 2,813,833 | SAN DIEGO | 1,136,344 | 596,033 | 526,437 | 13,874 | 69,596 R | 52.5% | 46.3% | 53.1% | 46.9% |
| 776,733 | SAN FRANCISCO | 357,465 | 54,355 | 296,772 | 6,338 | 242,417 D | 15.2% | 83.0% | 15.5% | 84.5% |
| 563,598 | SAN JOAQUIN | 189,864 | 100,978 | 87,012 | 1,874 | 13,966 R | 53.2% | 45.8% | 53.7% | 46.3% |
| 246,681 | SAN LUIS OBISPO | 129,050 | 67,995 | 58,742 | 2,313 | 9,253 R | 52.7% | 45.5% | 53.7% | 46.3% |
| 707,161 | SAN MATEO | 284,857 | 83,315 | 197,922 | 3,620 | 114,607 D | 29.2% | 69.5% | 29.6% | 70.4% |
| 399,347 | SANTA BARBARA | 169,861 | 76,806 | 90,314 | 2,741 | 13,508 D | 45.2% | 53.2% | 46.0% | 54.0% |
| 1,682,585 | SANTA CLARA | 603,816 | 209,094 | 386,100 | 8,622 | 177,006 D | 34.6% | 63.9% | 35.1% | 64.9% |
| 255,602 | SANTA CRUZ | 122,084 | 30,354 | 89,102 | 2,628 | 58,748 D | 24.9% | 73.0% | 25.4% | 74.6% |
| 163,256 | SHASTA | 77,731 | 52,249 | 24,339 | 1,143 | 27,910 R | 67.2% | 31.3% | 68.2% | 31.8% |
| 3,555 | SIERRA | 1,948 | 1,249 | 646 | 53 | 603 R | 64.1% | 33.2% | 65.9% | 34.1% |
| 44,301 | SISKIYOU | 20,899 | 12,673 | 7,880 | 346 | 4,793 R | 60.6% | 37.7% | 61.7% | 38.3% |
| 394,542 | SOLANO | 148,837 | 62,301 | 85,096 | 1,440 | 22,795 D | 41.9% | 57.2% | 42.3% | 57.7% |
| 458,614 | SONOMA | 220,690 | 68,204 | 148,261 | 4,225 | 80,057 D | 30.9% | 67.2% | 31.5% | 68.5% |
| 446,997 | STANISLAUS | 145,624 | 85,407 | 58,829 | 1,388 | 26,578 R | 58.6% | 40.4% | 59.2% | 40.8% |
| 78,930 | SUTTER | 30,145 | 20,254 | 9,602 | 289 | 10,652 R | 67.2% | 31.9% | 67.8% | 32.2% |
| 56,039 | TEHAMA | 23,444 | 15,572 | 7,504 | 368 | 8,068 R | 66.4% | 32.0% | 67.5% | 32.5% |
| 13,022 | TRINITY | 6,513 | 3,560 | 2,782 | 171 | 778 R | 54.7% | 42.7% | 56.1% | 43.9% |
| 368,021 | TULARE | 98,860 | 65,399 | 32,494 | 967 | 32,905 R | 66.2% | 32.9% | 66.8% | 33.2% |
| 54,501 | TUOLUMNE | 26,235 | 15,745 | 10,104 | 386 | 5,641 R | 60.0% | 38.5% | 60.9% | 39.1% |
| 753,197 | VENTURA | 313,193 | 160,314 | 148,859 | 4,020 | 11,455 R | 51.2% | 47.5% | 51.9% | 48.1% |
| 168,660 | YOLO | 72,269 | 28,005 | 42,885 | 1,379 | 14,880 D | 38.8% | 59.3% | 39.5% | 60.5% |
| 60,219 | YUBA | 18,024 | 12,076 | 5,687 | 261 | 6,389 R | 67.0% | 31.6% | 68.0% | 32.0% |
| 33,871,648 | TOTAL | 12,421,852 | 5,509,826 | 6,745,485 | 166,541 | 1,235,659 D | 44.4% | 54.3% | 45.0% | 55.0% |

# CALIFORNIA

## PRESIDENT 2000

| 2000 Census Population | County | Total Vote | Republican | Democratic | Green (Nader) | Other | Rep.-Dem. Plurality | Percentage of Total Vote | | |
|---|---|---|---|---|---|---|---|---|---|---|
| | | | | | | | | Rep. | Dem. | Green |
| 1,443,741 | ALAMEDA | 494,336 | 119,279 | 342,889 | 27,499 | 4,669 | 223,610 D | 24.1% | 69.4% | 5.6% |
| 1,208 | ALPINE | 586 | 281 | 265 | 25 | 15 | 16 R | 48.0% | 45.2% | 4.3% |
| 35,100 | AMADOR | 15,464 | 8,766 | 5,906 | 584 | 208 | 2,860 R | 56.7% | 38.2% | 3.8% |
| 203,171 | BUTTE | 83,721 | 45,584 | 31,338 | 5,727 | 1,072 | 14,246 R | 54.4% | 37.4% | 6.8% |
| 40,554 | CALAVERAS | 18,876 | 10,599 | 7,093 | 863 | 321 | 3,506 R | 56.2% | 37.6% | 4.6% |
| 18,804 | COLUSA | 5,590 | 3,629 | 1,745 | 151 | 65 | 1,884 R | 64.9% | 31.2% | 2.7% |
| 948,816 | CONTRA COSTA | 381,478 | 141,373 | 224,338 | 13,067 | 2,700 | 82,965 D | 37.1% | 58.8% | 3.4% |
| 27,507 | DEL NORTE | 8,294 | 4,526 | 3,117 | 485 | 166 | 1,409 R | 54.6% | 37.6% | 5.8% |
| 156,299 | EL DORADO | 72,136 | 42,045 | 26,220 | 3,013 | 858 | 15,825 R | 58.3% | 36.3% | 4.2% |
| 799,407 | FRESNO | 220,835 | 117,342 | 95,059 | 6,541 | 1,893 | 22,283 R | 53.1% | 43.0% | 3.0% |
| 26,453 | GLENN | 8,711 | 5,795 | 2,498 | 268 | 150 | 3,297 R | 66.5% | 28.7% | 3.1% |
| 126,518 | HUMBOLDT | 55,972 | 23,219 | 24,851 | 7,100 | 802 | 1,632 D | 41.5% | 44.4% | 12.7% |
| 142,361 | IMPERIAL | 28,937 | 12,524 | 15,489 | 608 | 316 | 2,965 D | 43.3% | 53.5% | 2.1% |
| 17,945 | INYO | 7,815 | 4,713 | 2,652 | 344 | 106 | 2,061 R | 60.3% | 33.9% | 4.4% |
| 661,645 | KERN | 182,308 | 110,663 | 66,003 | 3,474 | 2,168 | 44,660 R | 60.7% | 36.2% | 1.9% |
| 129,461 | KINGS | 28,335 | 16,377 | 11,041 | 567 | 350 | 5,336 R | 57.8% | 39.0% | 2.0% |
| 58,309 | LAKE | 20,919 | 8,699 | 10,717 | 1,265 | 238 | 2,018 D | 41.6% | 51.2% | 6.0% |
| 33,828 | LASSEN | 10,586 | 7,080 | 2,982 | 339 | 185 | 4,098 R | 66.9% | 28.2% | 3.2% |
| 9,519,338 | LOS ANGELES | 2,695,154 | 871,930 | 1,710,505 | 83,731 | 28,988 | 838,575 D | 32.4% | 63.5% | 3.1% |
| 123,109 | MADERA | 33,395 | 20,283 | 11,650 | 1,080 | 382 | 8,633 R | 60.7% | 34.9% | 3.2% |
| 247,289 | MARIN | 123,155 | 34,872 | 79,135 | 8,289 | 859 | 44,263 D | 28.3% | 64.3% | 6.7% |
| 17,130 | MARIPOSA | 8,074 | 4,727 | 2,816 | 379 | 152 | 1,911 R | 58.5% | 34.9% | 4.7% |
| 86,265 | MENDOCINO | 34,410 | 12,272 | 16,634 | 5,051 | 453 | 4,362 D | 35.7% | 48.3% | 14.7% |
| 210,554 | MERCED | 50,418 | 26,102 | 22,726 | 1,166 | 424 | 3,376 R | 51.8% | 45.1% | 2.3% |
| 9,449 | MODOC | 4,107 | 2,969 | 945 | 122 | 71 | 2,024 R | 72.3% | 23.0% | 3.0% |
| 12,853 | MONO | 4,371 | 2,296 | 1,788 | 230 | 57 | 508 R | 52.5% | 40.9% | 5.3% |
| 401,762 | MONTEREY | 117,534 | 43,761 | 67,618 | 5,059 | 1,096 | 23,857 D | 37.2% | 57.5% | 4.3% |
| 124,279 | NAPA | 51,724 | 20,633 | 28,097 | 2,471 | 523 | 7,464 D | 39.9% | 54.3% | 4.8% |
| 92,033 | NEVADA | 47,479 | 25,998 | 17,670 | 3,287 | 524 | 8,328 R | 54.8% | 37.2% | 6.9% |
| 2,846,289 | ORANGE | 970,905 | 541,299 | 391,819 | 26,833 | 10,954 | 149,480 R | 55.8% | 40.4% | 2.8% |
| 248,399 | PLACER | 117,799 | 69,835 | 42,449 | 4,449 | 1,066 | 27,386 R | 59.3% | 36.0% | 3.8% |
| 20,824 | PLUMAS | 10,401 | 6,343 | 3,458 | 456 | 144 | 2,885 R | 61.0% | 33.2% | 4.4% |
| 1,545,387 | RIVERSIDE | 451,127 | 231,955 | 202,576 | 11,678 | 4,918 | 29,379 R | 51.4% | 44.9% | 2.6% |
| 1,223,499 | SACRAMENTO | 431,550 | 195,619 | 212,792 | 17,659 | 5,480 | 17,173 D | 45.3% | 49.3% | 4.1% |
| 53,234 | SAN BENITO | 16,831 | 7,015 | 9,131 | 535 | 150 | 2,116 D | 41.7% | 54.3% | 3.2% |
| 1,709,434 | SAN BERNARDINO | 454,893 | 221,757 | 214,749 | 11,775 | 6,612 | 7,008 R | 48.7% | 47.2% | 2.6% |
| 2,813,833 | SAN DIEGO | 958,634 | 475,736 | 437,666 | 33,979 | 11,253 | 38,070 R | 49.6% | 45.7% | 3.5% |
| 776,733 | SAN FRANCISCO | 319,786 | 51,496 | 241,578 | 24,828 | 1,884 | 190,082 D | 16.1% | 75.5% | 7.8% |
| 563,598 | SAN JOAQUIN | 167,239 | 81,773 | 79,776 | 4,195 | 1,495 | 1,997 R | 48.9% | 47.7% | 2.5% |
| 246,681 | SAN LUIS OBISPO | 108,886 | 56,859 | 44,526 | 6,523 | 978 | 12,333 R | 52.2% | 40.9% | 6.0% |
| 707,161 | SAN MATEO | 259,399 | 80,296 | 166,757 | 10,433 | 1,913 | 86,461 D | 31.0% | 64.3% | 4.0% |
| 399,347 | SANTA BARBARA | 154,974 | 71,493 | 73,411 | 8,664 | 1,406 | 1,918 D | 46.1% | 47.4% | 5.6% |
| 1,682,585 | SANTA CLARA | 548,129 | 188,750 | 332,490 | 19,072 | 7,817 | 143,740 D | 34.4% | 60.7% | 3.5% |
| 255,602 | SANTA CRUZ | 108,350 | 29,627 | 66,618 | 10,844 | 1,261 | 36,991 D | 27.3% | 61.5% | 10.0% |
| 163,256 | SHASTA | 66,544 | 43,278 | 20,127 | 2,131 | 1,008 | 23,151 R | 65.0% | 30.2% | 3.2% |
| 3,555 | SIERRA | 1,847 | 1,172 | 540 | 86 | 49 | 632 R | 63.5% | 29.2% | 4.7% |
| 44,301 | SISKIYOU | 19,819 | 12,198 | 6,323 | 872 | 426 | 5,875 R | 61.5% | 31.9% | 4.4% |
| 394,542 | SOLANO | 131,735 | 51,604 | 75,116 | 3,869 | 1,146 | 23,512 D | 39.2% | 57.0% | 2.9% |
| 458,614 | SONOMA | 197,006 | 63,529 | 117,295 | 14,324 | 1,858 | 53,766 D | 32.2% | 59.5% | 7.3% |
| 446,997 | STANISLAUS | 128,267 | 67,188 | 56,448 | 3,398 | 1,233 | 10,740 R | 52.4% | 44.0% | 2.6% |
| 78,930 | SUTTER | 26,564 | 17,350 | 8,416 | 594 | 204 | 8,934 R | 65.3% | 31.7% | 2.2% |
| 56,039 | TEHAMA | 20,854 | 13,270 | 6,507 | 697 | 380 | 6,763 R | 63.6% | 31.2% | 3.3% |
| 13,022 | TRINITY | 5,797 | 3,340 | 1,932 | 396 | 129 | 1,408 R | 57.6% | 33.3% | 6.8% |
| 368,021 | TULARE | 89,818 | 54,070 | 33,006 | 1,834 | 908 | 21,064 R | 60.2% | 36.7% | 2.0% |
| 54,501 | TUOLUMNE | 23,727 | 13,172 | 9,359 | 949 | 247 | 3,813 R | 55.5% | 39.4% | 4.0% |
| 753,197 | VENTURA | 282,692 | 136,173 | 133,258 | 10,235 | 3,026 | 2,915 R | 48.2% | 47.1% | 3.6% |
| 168,660 | YOLO | 61,436 | 23,057 | 33,747 | 4,107 | 525 | 10,690 D | 37.5% | 54.9% | 6.7% |
| 60,219 | YUBA | 16,127 | 9,838 | 5,546 | 507 | 236 | 4,292 R | 61.0% | 34.4% | 3.1% |
| 33,871,648 | TOTAL | 10,965,856 | 4,567,429 | 5,861,203 | 418,707 | 118,517 | 1,293,774 D | 41.7% | 53.4% | 3.8% |

# CALIFORNIA

## PRESIDENT 1996

| 1995 Census Pop. Est. | County | Total Vote | Republican | Democratic | Reform (Perot) | Other | Rep.-Dem. Plurality | Percentage of Total Vote | | |
|---|---|---|---|---|---|---|---|---|---|---|
| | | | | | | | | Rep. | Dem. | Reform |
| 1,323,312 | ALAMEDA | 462,044 | 106,581 | 303,903 | 24,270 | 27,290 | 197,322 D | 23.1% | 65.8% | 5.3% |
| 1,229 | ALPINE | 614 | 264 | 258 | 63 | 29 | 6 R | 43.0% | 42.0% | 10.3% |
| 33,162 | AMADOR | 14,452 | 6,870 | 5,868 | 1,267 | 447 | 1,002 R | 47.5% | 40.6% | 8.8% |
| 192,880 | BUTTE | 79,550 | 38,961 | 30,651 | 6,393 | 3,545 | 8,310 R | 49.0% | 38.5% | 8.0% |
| 37,694 | CALAVERAS | 17,206 | 8,279 | 6,646 | 1,612 | 669 | 1,633 R | 48.1% | 38.6% | 9.4% |
| 17,596 | COLUSA | 5,612 | 3,047 | 2,054 | 404 | 107 | 993 R | 54.3% | 36.6% | 7.2% |
| 872,099 | CONTRA COSTA | 352,602 | 123,954 | 196,512 | 20,416 | 11,720 | 72,558 D | 35.2% | 55.7% | 5.8% |
| 26,956 | DEL NORTE | 8,889 | 3,670 | 3,652 | 1,225 | 342 | 18 R | 41.3% | 41.1% | 13.8% |
| 148,217 | EL DORADO | 63,196 | 32,759 | 22,957 | 5,077 | 2,403 | 9,802 R | 51.8% | 36.3% | 8.0% |
| 737,289 | FRESNO | 208,393 | 98,813 | 94,448 | 10,962 | 4,170 | 4,365 R | 47.4% | 45.3% | 5.3% |
| 26,028 | GLENN | 8,866 | 5,041 | 2,841 | 788 | 196 | 2,200 R | 56.9% | 32.0% | 8.9% |
| 122,747 | HUMBOLDT | 55,757 | 19,803 | 24,628 | 5,811 | 5,515 | 4,825 D | 35.5% | 44.2% | 10.4% |
| 138,072 | IMPERIAL | 26,400 | 9,705 | 14,591 | 1,778 | 326 | 4,886 D | 36.8% | 55.3% | 6.7% |
| 18,435 | INYO | 7,569 | 3,924 | 2,601 | 811 | 233 | 1,323 R | 51.8% | 34.4% | 10.7% |
| 617,528 | KERN | 171,391 | 92,151 | 62,658 | 13,452 | 3,130 | 29,493 R | 53.8% | 36.6% | 7.8% |
| 113,089 | KINGS | 25,815 | 12,368 | 11,254 | 1,745 | 448 | 1,114 R | 47.9% | 43.6% | 6.8% |
| 55,783 | LAKE | 21,335 | 7,458 | 10,432 | 2,539 | 906 | 2,974 D | 35.0% | 48.9% | 11.9% |
| 28,279 | LASSEN | 9,875 | 5,194 | 3,318 | 1,080 | 283 | 1,876 R | 52.6% | 33.6% | 10.9% |
| 9,138,789 | LOS ANGELES | 2,411,014 | 746,544 | 1,430,629 | 157,752 | 76,089 | 684,085 D | 31.0% | 59.3% | 6.5% |
| 107,004 | MADERA | 30,662 | 16,510 | 11,254 | 2,192 | 706 | 5,256 R | 53.8% | 36.7% | 7.1% |
| 233,883 | MARIN | 116,140 | 32,714 | 67,406 | 6,559 | 9,461 | 34,692 D | 28.2% | 58.0% | 5.6% |
| 15,772 | MARIPOSA | 7,949 | 3,976 | 2,920 | 729 | 324 | 1,056 R | 50.0% | 36.7% | 9.2% |
| 82,499 | MENDOCINO | 32,692 | 9,765 | 14,952 | 3,685 | 4,290 | 5,187 D | 29.9% | 45.7% | 11.3% |
| 194,407 | MERCED | 46,938 | 20,847 | 21,786 | 3,427 | 878 | 939 D | 44.4% | 46.4% | 7.3% |
| 9,559 | MODOC | 4,303 | 2,285 | 1,368 | 528 | 122 | 917 R | 53.1% | 31.8% | 12.3% |
| 10,433 | MONO | 4,091 | 1,882 | 1,580 | 447 | 182 | 302 R | 46.0% | 38.6% | 10.9% |
| 348,841 | MONTEREY | 108,558 | 39,794 | 57,700 | 7,240 | 3,824 | 17,906 D | 36.7% | 53.2% | 6.7% |
| 115,751 | NAPA | 48,319 | 17,439 | 24,588 | 4,254 | 2,038 | 7,149 D | 36.1% | 50.9% | 8.8% |
| 87,318 | NEVADA | 43,219 | 21,784 | 15,369 | 3,330 | 2,736 | 6,415 R | 50.4% | 35.6% | 7.7% |
| 2,563,971 | ORANGE | 864,576 | 446,717 | 327,485 | 66,195 | 24,179 | 119,232 R | 51.7% | 37.9% | 7.7% |
| 205,239 | PLACER | 94,427 | 49,808 | 34,981 | 6,542 | 3,096 | 14,827 R | 52.7% | 37.0% | 6.9% |
| 20,451 | PLUMAS | 9,750 | 4,905 | 3,540 | 919 | 386 | 1,365 R | 50.3% | 36.3% | 9.4% |
| 1,379,801 | RIVERSIDE | 391,613 | 178,611 | 168,579 | 35,481 | 8,942 | 10,032 R | 45.6% | 43.0% | 9.1% |
| 1,103,499 | SACRAMENTO | 407,414 | 166,049 | 203,019 | 23,856 | 14,490 | 36,970 D | 40.8% | 49.8% | 5.9% |
| 42,625 | SAN BENITO | 13,906 | 5,384 | 7,030 | 1,044 | 448 | 1,646 D | 38.7% | 50.6% | 7.5% |
| 1,569,586 | SAN BERNARDINO | 413,355 | 180,135 | 183,372 | 39,330 | 10,518 | 3,237 D | 43.6% | 44.4% | 9.5% |
| 2,644,132 | SAN DIEGO | 884,151 | 402,876 | 389,964 | 63,037 | 28,274 | 12,912 R | 45.6% | 44.1% | 7.1% |
| 730,570 | SAN FRANCISCO | 290,385 | 45,479 | 209,777 | 9,659 | 25,470 | 164,298 D | 15.7% | 72.2% | 3.3% |
| 523,969 | SAN JOAQUIN | 145,140 | 65,131 | 67,253 | 9,692 | 3,064 | 2,122 D | 44.9% | 46.3% | 6.7% |
| 226,071 | SAN LUIS OBISPO | 100,500 | 46,733 | 40,395 | 8,204 | 5,168 | 6,338 R | 46.5% | 40.2% | 8.2% |
| 681,362 | SAN MATEO | 251,532 | 73,508 | 152,304 | 15,047 | 10,673 | 78,796 D | 29.2% | 60.6% | 6.0% |
| 381,401 | SANTA BARBARA | 150,745 | 63,915 | 70,650 | 9,457 | 6,723 | 6,735 D | 42.4% | 46.9% | 6.3% |
| 1,565,253 | SANTA CLARA | 523,291 | 168,291 | 297,639 | 34,908 | 22,453 | 129,348 D | 32.2% | 56.9% | 6.7% |
| 236,669 | SANTA CRUZ | 103,062 | 27,766 | 58,250 | 6,555 | 10,491 | 30,484 D | 26.9% | 56.5% | 6.4% |
| 160,940 | SHASTA | 62,961 | 34,736 | 20,848 | 5,875 | 1,502 | 13,888 R | 55.2% | 33.1% | 9.3% |
| 3,399 | SIERRA | 1,707 | 877 | 573 | 170 | 87 | 304 R | 51.4% | 33.6% | 10.0% |
| 44,253 | SISKIYOU | 18,293 | 8,653 | 7,022 | 1,879 | 739 | 1,631 R | 47.3% | 38.4% | 10.3% |
| 366,134 | SOLANO | 117,279 | 40,742 | 64,644 | 8,682 | 3,211 | 23,902 D | 34.7% | 55.1% | 7.4% |
| 414,569 | SONOMA | 181,297 | 53,555 | 100,738 | 13,862 | 13,142 | 47,183 D | 29.5% | 55.6% | 7.6% |
| 410,870 | STANISLAUS | 117,007 | 52,403 | 53,738 | 8,360 | 2,506 | 1,335 D | 44.8% | 45.9% | 7.1% |
| 74,963 | SUTTER | 24,745 | 14,264 | 8,504 | 1,533 | 444 | 5,760 R | 57.6% | 34.4% | 6.2% |
| 53,798 | TEHAMA | 20,443 | 10,292 | 7,290 | 2,325 | 536 | 3,002 R | 50.3% | 35.7% | 11.4% |
| 13,429 | TRINITY | 5,893 | 2,530 | 2,203 | 856 | 304 | 327 R | 42.9% | 37.4% | 14.5% |
| 346,843 | TULARE | 85,846 | 46,272 | 32,669 | 5,106 | 1,799 | 13,603 R | 53.9% | 38.1% | 5.9% |
| 51,777 | TUOLUMNE | 21,972 | 10,386 | 8,950 | 1,925 | 711 | 1,436 R | 47.3% | 40.7% | 8.8% |
| 710,018 | VENTURA | 251,194 | 109,202 | 110,772 | 23,054 | 8,166 | 1,570 D | 43.5% | 44.1% | 9.2% |
| 147,769 | YOLO | 58,079 | 18,807 | 33,033 | 3,150 | 3,089 | 14,226 D | 32.4% | 56.9% | 5.4% |
| 61,141 | YUBA | 15,470 | 7,971 | 5,789 | 1,308 | 402 | 2,182 R | 51.5% | 37.4% | 8.5% |
| 31,589,153 | TOTAL | 10,019,484 | 3,828,380 | 5,119,835 | 697,847 | 373,422 | 1,291,455 D | 38.2% | 51.1% | 7.0% |

# CALIFORNIA

## PRESIDENT 1992

| 1990 Census Population | County | Total Vote | Republican | Democratic | Perot | Other | Plurality | Rep. | Dem. | Perot |
|---|---|---|---|---|---|---|---|---|---|---|
| 1,279,182 | ALAMEDA | 530,145 | 109,292 | 334,224 | 81,643 | 4,986 | 224,932 D | 20.6% | 63.0% | 15.4% |
| 1,113 | ALPINE | 631 | 222 | 215 | 186 | 8 | 7 R | 35.2% | 34.1% | 29.5% |
| 30,039 | AMADOR | 15,434 | 5,477 | 5,286 | 4,553 | 118 | 191 R | 35.5% | 34.2% | 29.5% |
| 182,120 | BUTTE | 85,014 | 31,608 | 32,489 | 20,231 | 686 | 881 D | 37.2% | 38.2% | 23.8% |
| 31,998 | CALAVERAS | 16,991 | 6,006 | 5,989 | 4,848 | 148 | 17 R | 35.3% | 35.2% | 28.5% |
| 16,275 | COLUSA | 5,635 | 2,589 | 1,798 | 1,206 | 42 | 791 R | 45.9% | 31.9% | 21.4% |
| 803,732 | CONTRA COSTA | 382,823 | 112,965 | 194,960 | 72,518 | 2,380 | 81,995 D | 29.5% | 50.9% | 18.9% |
| 23,460 | DEL NORTE | 9,353 | 3,083 | 3,639 | 2,575 | 56 | 556 D | 33.0% | 38.9% | 27.5% |
| 125,995 | EL DORADO | 64,887 | 25,906 | 21,012 | 17,503 | 466 | 4,894 R | 39.9% | 32.4% | 27.0% |
| 667,490 | FRESNO | 219,161 | 89,137 | 92,418 | 36,299 | 1,307 | 3,281 D | 40.7% | 42.2% | 16.6% |
| 24,798 | GLENN | 8,816 | 3,812 | 2,666 | 2,278 | 60 | 1,146 R | 43.2% | 30.2% | 25.8% |
| 119,118 | HUMBOLDT | 60,021 | 18,299 | 28,854 | 12,340 | 528 | 10,555 D | 30.5% | 48.1% | 20.6% |
| 109,303 | IMPERIAL | 25,318 | 9,759 | 11,109 | 4,247 | 203 | 1,350 D | 38.5% | 43.9% | 16.8% |
| 18,281 | INYO | 8,464 | 3,689 | 2,695 | 1,999 | 81 | 994 R | 43.6% | 31.8% | 23.6% |
| 543,477 | KERN | 179,263 | 80,762 | 60,510 | 36,891 | 1,100 | 20,252 R | 45.1% | 33.8% | 20.6% |
| 101,469 | KINGS | 25,651 | 10,673 | 9,982 | 4,899 | 97 | 691 R | 41.6% | 38.9% | 19.1% |
| 50,631 | LAKE | 23,213 | 6,678 | 10,548 | 5,797 | 190 | 3,870 D | 28.8% | 45.4% | 25.0% |
| 27,598 | LASSEN | 10,362 | 3,836 | 3,388 | 3,004 | 134 | 448 R | 37.0% | 32.7% | 29.0% |
| 8,863,164 | LOS ANGELES | 2,753,403 | 799,607 | 1,446,529 | 488,624 | 18,643 | 646,922 D | 29.0% | 52.5% | 17.7% |
| 88,090 | MADERA | 30,245 | 13,066 | 10,863 | 6,156 | 160 | 2,203 R | 43.2% | 35.9% | 20.4% |
| 230,096 | MARIN | 130,707 | 30,479 | 76,158 | 22,986 | 1,084 | 45,679 D | 23.3% | 58.3% | 17.6% |
| 14,302 | MARIPOSA | 8,287 | 2,982 | 3,023 | 2,211 | 71 | 41 D | 36.0% | 36.5% | 26.7% |
| 80,345 | MENDOCINO | 36,538 | 7,958 | 18,344 | 9,753 | 483 | 8,591 D | 21.8% | 50.2% | 26.7% |
| 178,403 | MERCED | 49,284 | 17,981 | 20,133 | 10,914 | 256 | 2,152 D | 36.5% | 40.9% | 22.1% |
| 9,678 | MODOC | 4,625 | 1,803 | 1,489 | 1,269 | 64 | 314 R | 39.0% | 32.2% | 27.4% |
| 9,956 | MONO | 4,355 | 1,570 | 1,489 | 1,248 | 48 | 81 R | 36.1% | 34.2% | 28.7% |
| 355,660 | MONTEREY | 116,689 | 36,461 | 54,861 | 24,472 | 895 | 18,400 D | 31.2% | 47.0% | 21.0% |
| 110,765 | NAPA | 53,455 | 15,662 | 24,215 | 13,150 | 428 | 8,553 D | 29.3% | 45.3% | 24.6% |
| 78,510 | NEVADA | 44,201 | 17,343 | 15,433 | 11,072 | 353 | 1,910 R | 39.2% | 34.9% | 25.0% |
| 2,410,556 | ORANGE | 972,549 | 426,613 | 306,930 | 232,394 | 6,612 | 119,683 R | 43.9% | 31.6% | 23.9% |
| 172,796 | PLACER | 91,366 | 38,298 | 30,783 | 21,741 | 544 | 7,515 R | 41.9% | 33.7% | 23.8% |
| 19,739 | PLUMAS | 9,949 | 3,599 | 3,742 | 2,551 | 57 | 143 D | 36.2% | 37.6% | 25.6% |
| 1,170,413 | RIVERSIDE | 430,275 | 159,457 | 166,241 | 102,233 | 2,344 | 6,784 D | 37.1% | 38.6% | 23.8% |
| 1,041,219 | SACRAMENTO | 453,512 | 160,366 | 197,540 | 91,412 | 4,194 | 37,174 D | 35.4% | 43.6% | 20.2% |
| 36,697 | SAN BENITO | 12,739 | 4,112 | 5,354 | 3,182 | 91 | 1,242 D | 32.3% | 42.0% | 25.0% |
| 1,418,380 | SAN BERNARDINO | 474,070 | 176,563 | 183,634 | 109,183 | 4,690 | 7,071 D | 37.2% | 38.7% | 23.0% |
| 2,498,016 | SAN DIEGO | 986,646 | 352,125 | 367,397 | 259,249 | 7,875 | 15,272 D | 35.7% | 37.2% | 26.3% |
| 723,959 | SAN FRANCISCO | 322,207 | 57,352 | 233,263 | 29,018 | 2,574 | 175,911 D | 17.8% | 72.4% | 9.0% |
| 480,628 | SAN JOAQUIN | 154,210 | 58,355 | 63,655 | 31,205 | 995 | 5,300 D | 37.8% | 41.3% | 20.2% |
| 217,162 | SAN LUIS OBISPO | 104,619 | 36,384 | 40,136 | 27,314 | 785 | 3,752 D | 34.8% | 38.4% | 26.1% |
| 649,623 | SAN MATEO | 276,508 | 75,080 | 149,232 | 50,465 | 1,731 | 74,152 D | 27.2% | 54.0% | 18.3% |
| 369,608 | SANTA BARBARA | 162,756 | 57,375 | 69,215 | 35,105 | 1,061 | 11,840 D | 35.3% | 42.5% | 21.6% |
| 1,497,577 | SANTA CLARA | 602,055 | 170,870 | 296,265 | 128,895 | 6,025 | 125,395 D | 28.4% | 49.2% | 21.4% |
| 229,734 | SANTA CRUZ | 113,992 | 24,916 | 66,183 | 21,615 | 1,278 | 41,267 D | 21.9% | 58.1% | 19.0% |
| 147,036 | SHASTA | 68,359 | 28,190 | 21,605 | 17,990 | 574 | 6,585 R | 41.2% | 31.6% | 26.3% |
| 3,318 | SIERRA | 1,875 | 691 | 653 | 519 | 12 | 38 R | 36.9% | 34.8% | 27.7% |
| 43,531 | SISKIYOU | 20,679 | 6,660 | 8,254 | 5,567 | 198 | 1,594 D | 32.2% | 39.9% | 26.9% |
| 340,421 | SOLANO | 132,111 | 38,883 | 64,320 | 27,851 | 1,057 | 25,437 D | 29.4% | 48.7% | 21.1% |
| 388,222 | SONOMA | 197,691 | 47,619 | 104,334 | 43,859 | 1,879 | 56,715 D | 24.1% | 52.8% | 22.2% |
| 370,522 | STANISLAUS | 128,005 | 47,275 | 52,415 | 27,651 | 664 | 5,140 D | 36.9% | 40.9% | 21.6% |
| 64,415 | SUTTER | 25,860 | 12,956 | 7,883 | 4,881 | 140 | 5,073 R | 50.1% | 30.5% | 18.9% |
| 49,625 | TEHAMA | 20,979 | 7,419 | 7,508 | 5,884 | 168 | 89 D | 35.4% | 35.8% | 28.0% |
| 13,063 | TRINITY | 6,029 | 1,886 | 1,967 | 2,092 | 84 | 125 P | 31.3% | 32.6% | 34.7% |
| 311,921 | TULARE | 88,553 | 40,482 | 31,188 | 16,430 | 453 | 9,294 R | 45.7% | 35.2% | 18.6% |
| 48,456 | TUOLUMNE | 24,178 | 8,525 | 9,216 | 6,294 | 143 | 691 D | 35.3% | 38.1% | 26.0% |
| 669,016 | VENTURA | 267,647 | 94,911 | 99,011 | 71,844 | 1,881 | 4,100 D | 35.5% | 37.0% | 26.8% |
| 141,092 | YOLO | 62,436 | 17,574 | 33,297 | 11,073 | 492 | 15,723 D | 28.1% | 53.3% | 17.7% |
| 58,228 | YUBA | 16,895 | 7,333 | 5,785 | 3,637 | 140 | 1,548 R | 43.4% | 34.2% | 21.5% |
| 29,760,021 | TOTAL | 11,131,721 | 3,630,574 | 5,121,325 | 2,296,006 | 83,816 | 1,490,751 D | 32.6% | 46.0% | 20.6% |

# CALIFORNIA

## PRESIDENT 1988

| 1980 Census Population | County | Total Vote | Republican | Democratic | Other | Rep.-Dem. Plurality | Percentage | | | |
|---|---|---|---|---|---|---|---|---|---|---|
| | | | | | | | Total Vote | | Major Vote | |
| | | | | | | | Rep. | Dem. | Rep. | Dem. |
| 1,105,379 | ALAMEDA | 478,998 | 162,815 | 310,283 | 5,900 | 147,468 D | 34.0% | 64.8% | 34.4% | 65.6% |
| 1,097 | ALPINE | 552 | 306 | 230 | 16 | 76 R | 55.4% | 41.7% | 57.1% | 42.9% |
| 19,314 | AMADOR | 12,338 | 6,893 | 5,197 | 248 | 1,696 R | 55.9% | 42.1% | 57.0% | 43.0% |
| 143,851 | BUTTE | 71,631 | 40,143 | 30,406 | 1,082 | 9,737 R | 56.0% | 42.4% | 56.9% | 43.1% |
| 20,710 | CALAVERAS | 13,574 | 7,640 | 5,674 | 260 | 1,966 R | 56.3% | 41.8% | 57.4% | 42.6% |
| 12,791 | COLUSA | 5,172 | 3,077 | 2,022 | 73 | 1,055 R | 59.5% | 39.1% | 60.3% | 39.7% |
| 656,380 | CONTRA COSTA | 331,511 | 158,652 | 169,411 | 3,448 | 10,759 D | 47.9% | 51.1% | 48.4% | 51.6% |
| 18,217 | DEL NORTE | 7,468 | 3,714 | 3,587 | 167 | 127 R | 49.7% | 48.0% | 50.9% | 49.1% |
| 85,812 | EL DORADO | 50,603 | 30,021 | 19,801 | 781 | 10,220 R | 59.3% | 39.1% | 60.3% | 39.7% |
| 514,621 | FRESNO | 189,870 | 94,835 | 92,635 | 2,400 | 2,200 R | 49.9% | 48.8% | 50.6% | 49.4% |
| 21,350 | GLENN | 7,966 | 4,944 | 2,894 | 128 | 2,050 R | 62.1% | 36.3% | 63.1% | 36.9% |
| 108,514 | HUMBOLDT | 52,146 | 21,460 | 29,781 | 905 | 8,321 D | 41.2% | 57.1% | 41.9% | 58.1% |
| 92,110 | IMPERIAL | 23,365 | 12,889 | 10,243 | 233 | 2,646 R | 55.2% | 43.8% | 55.7% | 44.3% |
| 17,895 | INYO | 7,837 | 5,042 | 2,653 | 142 | 2,389 R | 64.3% | 33.9% | 65.5% | 34.5% |
| 403,089 | KERN | 147,293 | 90,550 | 55,083 | 1,660 | 35,467 R | 61.5% | 37.4% | 62.2% | 37.8% |
| 73,738 | KINGS | 21,482 | 12,118 | 9,142 | 222 | 2,976 R | 56.4% | 42.6% | 57.0% | 43.0% |
| 36,366 | LAKE | 19,502 | 9,366 | 9,828 | 308 | 462 D | 48.0% | 50.4% | 48.8% | 51.2% |
| 21,661 | LASSEN | 8,802 | 5,157 | 3,446 | 199 | 1,711 R | 58.6% | 39.2% | 59.9% | 40.1% |
| 7,477,503 | LOS ANGELES | 2,644,671 | 1,239,716 | 1,372,352 | 32,603 | 132,636 D | 46.9% | 51.9% | 47.5% | 52.5% |
| 63,116 | MADERA | 24,281 | 13,255 | 10,642 | 384 | 2,613 R | 54.6% | 43.8% | 55.5% | 44.5% |
| 222,568 | MARIN | 117,920 | 46,855 | 69,394 | 1,671 | 22,539 D | 39.7% | 58.8% | 40.3% | 59.7% |
| 11,108 | MARIPOSA | 6,910 | 3,768 | 2,998 | 144 | 770 R | 54.5% | 43.4% | 55.7% | 44.3% |
| 66,738 | MENDOCINO | 30,947 | 12,979 | 17,152 | 816 | 4,173 D | 41.9% | 55.4% | 43.1% | 56.9% |
| 134,560 | MERCED | 42,414 | 21,717 | 20,105 | 592 | 1,612 R | 51.2% | 47.4% | 51.9% | 48.1% |
| 8,610 | MODOC | 4,017 | 2,518 | 1,416 | 83 | 1,102 R | 62.7% | 35.3% | 64.0% | 36.0% |
| 8,577 | MONO | 3,547 | 2,177 | 1,284 | 86 | 893 R | 61.4% | 36.2% | 62.9% | 37.1% |
| 290,444 | MONTEREY | 100,381 | 50,022 | 48,998 | 1,361 | 1,024 R | 49.8% | 48.8% | 50.5% | 49.5% |
| 99,199 | NAPA | 46,290 | 23,235 | 22,283 | 772 | 952 R | 50.2% | 48.1% | 51.0% | 49.0% |
| 51,645 | NEVADA | 37,023 | 21,383 | 14,980 | 660 | 6,403 R | 57.8% | 40.5% | 58.8% | 41.2% |
| 1,932,709 | ORANGE | 865,307 | 586,230 | 269,013 | 10,064 | 317,217 R | 67.7% | 31.1% | 68.5% | 31.5% |
| 117,247 | PLACER | 70,642 | 42,096 | 27,516 | 1,030 | 14,580 R | 59.6% | 39.0% | 60.5% | 39.5% |
| 17,340 | PLUMAS | 9,015 | 4,603 | 4,251 | 161 | 352 R | 51.1% | 47.2% | 52.0% | 48.0% |
| 663,166 | RIVERSIDE | 336,348 | 199,979 | 133,122 | 3,247 | 66,857 R | 59.5% | 39.6% | 60.0% | 40.0% |
| 783,381 | SACRAMENTO | 395,690 | 201,832 | 188,557 | 5,301 | 13,275 R | 51.0% | 47.7% | 51.7% | 48.3% |
| 25,005 | SAN BENITO | 10,308 | 5,578 | 4,559 | 171 | 1,019 R | 54.1% | 44.2% | 55.0% | 45.0% |
| 895,016 | SAN BERNARDINO | 392,008 | 235,167 | 151,118 | 5,723 | 84,049 R | 60.0% | 38.5% | 60.9% | 39.1% |
| 1,861,846 | SAN DIEGO | 869,195 | 523,143 | 333,264 | 12,788 | 189,879 R | 60.2% | 38.3% | 61.1% | 38.9% |
| 678,974 | SAN FRANCISCO | 277,394 | 72,503 | 201,887 | 3,004 | 129,384 D | 26.1% | 72.8% | 26.4% | 73.6% |
| 347,342 | SAN JOAQUIN | 138,453 | 75,309 | 61,699 | 1,445 | 13,610 R | 54.4% | 44.6% | 55.0% | 45.0% |
| 155,435 | SAN LUIS OBISPO | 83,467 | 46,613 | 35,667 | 1,187 | 10,946 R | 55.8% | 42.7% | 56.7% | 43.3% |
| 587,329 | SAN MATEO | 254,480 | 109,261 | 141,859 | 3,360 | 32,598 D | 42.9% | 55.7% | 43.5% | 56.5% |
| 298,694 | SANTA BARBARA | 142,940 | 77,524 | 63,586 | 1,830 | 13,938 R | 54.2% | 44.5% | 54.9% | 45.1% |
| 1,295,071 | SANTA CLARA | 541,528 | 254,442 | 277,810 | 9,276 | 23,368 D | 47.0% | 51.3% | 47.8% | 52.2% |
| 188,141 | SANTA CRUZ | 102,611 | 37,728 | 63,133 | 1,750 | 25,405 D | 36.8% | 61.5% | 37.4% | 62.6% |
| 115,715 | SHASTA | 54,585 | 32,402 | 21,171 | 1,012 | 11,231 R | 59.4% | 38.8% | 60.5% | 39.5% |
| 3,073 | SIERRA | 1,696 | 860 | 791 | 45 | 69 R | 50.7% | 46.6% | 52.1% | 47.9% |
| 39,732 | SISKIYOU | 17,797 | 9,056 | 8,365 | 376 | 691 R | 50.9% | 47.0% | 52.0% | 48.0% |
| 235,203 | SOLANO | 106,088 | 50,314 | 54,344 | 1,430 | 4,030 D | 47.4% | 51.2% | 48.1% | 51.9% |
| 299,681 | SONOMA | 161,583 | 67,725 | 91,262 | 2,596 | 23,537 D | 41.9% | 56.5% | 42.6% | 57.4% |
| 265,900 | STANISLAUS | 97,315 | 51,648 | 44,685 | 982 | 6,963 R | 53.1% | 45.9% | 53.6% | 46.4% |
| 52,246 | SUTTER | 20,898 | 14,100 | 6,557 | 241 | 7,543 R | 67.5% | 31.4% | 68.3% | 31.7% |
| 38,888 | TEHAMA | 17,434 | 9,854 | 7,213 | 367 | 2,641 R | 56.5% | 41.4% | 57.7% | 42.3% |
| 11,858 | TRINITY | 5,980 | 3,267 | 2,518 | 195 | 749 R | 54.6% | 42.1% | 56.5% | 43.5% |
| 245,738 | TULARE | 78,669 | 46,891 | 30,711 | 1,067 | 16,180 R | 59.6% | 39.0% | 60.4% | 39.6% |
| 33,928 | TUOLUMNE | 19,715 | 10,646 | 8,717 | 352 | 1,929 R | 54.0% | 44.2% | 55.0% | 45.0% |
| 529,174 | VENTURA | 239,473 | 147,604 | 89,065 | 2,804 | 58,539 R | 61.6% | 37.2% | 62.4% | 37.6% |
| 113,374 | YOLO | 53,372 | 22,358 | 30,429 | 585 | 8,071 D | 41.9% | 57.0% | 42.4% | 57.6% |
| 49,733 | YUBA | 14,563 | 8,937 | 5,444 | 182 | 3,493 R | 61.4% | 37.4% | 62.1% | 37.9% |
| 23,667,902 | TOTAL | 9,887,065 | 5,054,917 | 4,702,233 | 129,915 | 352,684 R | 51.1% | 47.6% | 51.8% | 48.2% |

# CALIFORNIA

## PRESIDENT 1984

| 1980 Census Population | County | Total Vote | Republican | Democratic | Other | Rep.-Dem. Plurality | | Total Vote Rep. | Dem. | Major Vote Rep. | Dem. |
|---|---|---|---|---|---|---|---|---|---|---|---|
| 1,105,379 | ALAMEDA | 480,874 | 192,408 | 282,041 | 6,425 | 89,633 | D | 40.0% | 58.7% | 40.6% | 59.4% |
| 1,097 | ALPINE | 466 | 264 | 194 | 8 | 70 | R | 56.7% | 41.6% | 57.6% | 42.4% |
| 19,314 | AMADOR | 11,363 | 6,986 | 4,188 | 189 | 2,798 | R | 61.5% | 36.9% | 62.5% | 37.5% |
| 143,851 | BUTTE | 71,964 | 45,381 | 25,421 | 1,162 | 19,960 | R | 63.1% | 35.3% | 64.1% | 35.9% |
| 20,710 | CALAVERAS | 11,877 | 7,632 | 4,081 | 164 | 3,551 | R | 64.3% | 34.4% | 65.2% | 34.8% |
| 12,791 | COLUSA | 5,188 | 3,388 | 1,725 | 75 | 1,663 | R | 65.3% | 33.2% | 66.3% | 33.7% |
| 656,380 | CONTRA COSTA | 316,318 | 172,331 | 140,994 | 2,993 | 31,337 | R | 54.5% | 44.6% | 55.0% | 45.0% |
| 18,217 | DEL NORTE | 6,841 | 3,996 | 2,696 | 149 | 1,300 | R | 58.4% | 39.4% | 59.7% | 40.3% |
| 85,812 | EL DORADO | 42,478 | 27,583 | 14,312 | 583 | 13,271 | R | 64.9% | 33.7% | 65.8% | 34.2% |
| 514,621 | FRESNO | 192,936 | 104,757 | 86,315 | 1,864 | 18,442 | R | 54.3% | 44.7% | 54.8% | 45.2% |
| 21,350 | GLENN | 8,632 | 6,020 | 2,488 | 124 | 3,532 | R | 69.7% | 28.8% | 70.8% | 29.2% |
| 108,514 | HUMBOLDT | 53,891 | 27,832 | 25,217 | 842 | 2,615 | R | 51.6% | 46.8% | 52.5% | 47.5% |
| 92,110 | IMPERIAL | 22,301 | 13,829 | 8,237 | 235 | 5,592 | R | 62.0% | 36.9% | 62.7% | 37.3% |
| 17,895 | INYO | 8,338 | 5,863 | 2,360 | 115 | 3,503 | R | 70.3% | 28.3% | 71.3% | 28.7% |
| 403,089 | KERN | 145,744 | 94,776 | 49,567 | 1,401 | 45,209 | R | 65.0% | 34.0% | 65.7% | 34.3% |
| 73,738 | KINGS | 20,848 | 13,364 | 7,324 | 160 | 6,040 | R | 64.1% | 35.1% | 64.6% | 35.4% |
| 36,366 | LAKE | 19,831 | 10,874 | 8,648 | 309 | 2,226 | R | 54.8% | 43.6% | 55.7% | 44.3% |
| 21,661 | LASSEN | 8,761 | 5,352 | 3,254 | 155 | 2,098 | R | 61.1% | 37.1% | 62.2% | 37.8% |
| 7,477,503 | LOS ANGELES | 2,612,914 | 1,424,113 | 1,158,912 | 29,889 | 265,201 | R | 54.5% | 44.4% | 55.1% | 44.9% |
| 63,116 | MADERA | 23,241 | 13,954 | 8,994 | 293 | 4,960 | R | 60.0% | 38.7% | 60.8% | 39.2% |
| 222,568 | MARIN | 116,050 | 56,887 | 57,533 | 1,630 | 646 | D | 49.0% | 49.6% | 49.7% | 50.3% |
| 11,108 | MARIPOSA | 6,518 | 3,989 | 2,399 | 130 | 1,590 | R | 61.2% | 36.8% | 62.4% | 37.6% |
| 66,738 | MENDOCINO | 31,422 | 16,369 | 14,407 | 646 | 1,962 | R | 52.1% | 45.9% | 53.2% | 46.8% |
| 134,560 | MERCED | 42,477 | 24,997 | 17,012 | 468 | 7,985 | R | 58.8% | 40.0% | 59.5% | 40.5% |
| 8,610 | MODOC | 4,310 | 2,995 | 1,219 | 96 | 1,776 | R | 69.5% | 28.3% | 71.1% | 28.9% |
| 8,577 | MONO | 3,677 | 2,659 | 962 | 56 | 1,697 | R | 72.3% | 26.2% | 73.4% | 26.6% |
| 290,444 | MONTEREY | 97,470 | 55,710 | 40,733 | 1,027 | 14,977 | R | 57.2% | 41.8% | 57.8% | 42.2% |
| 99,199 | NAPA | 45,561 | 26,322 | 18,599 | 640 | 7,723 | R | 57.8% | 40.8% | 58.6% | 41.4% |
| 51,645 | NEVADA | 31,768 | 19,809 | 11,198 | 761 | 8,611 | R | 62.4% | 35.2% | 63.9% | 36.1% |
| 1,932,709 | ORANGE | 850,077 | 635,013 | 206,272 | 8,792 | 428,741 | R | 74.7% | 24.3% | 75.5% | 24.5% |
| 117,247 | PLACER | 60,427 | 38,035 | 21,294 | 1,098 | 16,741 | R | 62.9% | 35.2% | 64.1% | 35.9% |
| 17,340 | PLUMAS | 9,228 | 5,224 | 3,837 | 167 | 1,387 | R | 56.6% | 41.6% | 57.7% | 42.3% |
| 663,166 | RIVERSIDE | 287,202 | 182,324 | 102,043 | 2,835 | 80,281 | R | 63.5% | 35.5% | 64.1% | 35.9% |
| 783,381 | SACRAMENTO | 368,841 | 204,922 | 159,128 | 4,791 | 45,794 | R | 55.6% | 43.1% | 56.3% | 43.7% |
| 25,005 | SAN BENITO | 9,380 | 5,695 | 3,554 | 131 | 2,141 | R | 60.7% | 37.9% | 61.6% | 38.4% |
| 895,016 | SAN BERNARDINO | 342,705 | 222,071 | 116,454 | 4,180 | 105,617 | R | 64.8% | 34.0% | 65.6% | 34.4% |
| 1,861,846 | SAN DIEGO | 769,267 | 502,344 | 257,029 | 9,894 | 245,315 | R | 65.3% | 33.4% | 66.2% | 33.8% |
| 678,974 | SAN FRANCISCO | 286,972 | 90,219 | 193,278 | 3,475 | 103,059 | D | 31.4% | 67.4% | 31.8% | 68.2% |
| 347,342 | SAN JOAQUIN | 137,213 | 81,795 | 53,846 | 1,572 | 27,949 | R | 59.6% | 39.2% | 60.3% | 39.7% |
| 155,435 | SAN LUIS OBISPO | 76,950 | 49,035 | 26,946 | 969 | 22,089 | R | 63.7% | 35.0% | 64.5% | 35.5% |
| 587,329 | SAN MATEO | 260,631 | 135,185 | 122,268 | 3,178 | 12,917 | R | 51.9% | 46.9% | 52.5% | 47.5% |
| 298,694 | SANTA BARBARA | 142,320 | 89,314 | 51,243 | 1,763 | 38,071 | R | 62.8% | 36.0% | 63.5% | 36.5% |
| 1,295,071 | SANTA CLARA | 526,639 | 288,638 | 229,865 | 8,136 | 58,773 | R | 54.8% | 43.6% | 55.7% | 44.3% |
| 188,141 | SANTA CRUZ | 92,147 | 41,652 | 49,091 | 1,404 | 7,439 | D | 45.2% | 53.3% | 45.9% | 54.1% |
| 115,715 | SHASTA | 53,127 | 33,041 | 19,298 | 788 | 13,743 | R | 62.2% | 36.3% | 63.1% | 36.9% |
| 3,073 | SIERRA | 1,896 | 1,078 | 781 | 37 | 297 | R | 56.9% | 41.2% | 58.0% | 42.0% |
| 39,732 | SISKIYOU | 18,101 | 10,544 | 7,130 | 427 | 3,414 | R | 58.3% | 39.4% | 59.7% | 40.3% |
| 235,203 | SOLANO | 94,798 | 51,678 | 41,982 | 1,138 | 9,696 | R | 54.5% | 44.3% | 55.2% | 44.8% |
| 299,681 | SONOMA | 149,657 | 76,447 | 71,295 | 1,915 | 5,152 | R | 51.1% | 47.6% | 51.7% | 48.3% |
| 265,900 | STANISLAUS | 93,985 | 55,665 | 37,459 | 861 | 18,206 | R | 59.2% | 39.9% | 59.8% | 40.2% |
| 52,246 | SUTTER | 20,323 | 14,477 | 5,535 | 311 | 8,942 | R | 71.2% | 27.2% | 72.3% | 27.7% |
| 38,888 | TEHAMA | 18,455 | 11,586 | 6,527 | 342 | 5,059 | R | 62.8% | 35.4% | 64.0% | 36.0% |
| 11,858 | TRINITY | 5,935 | 3,544 | 2,218 | 173 | 1,326 | R | 59.7% | 37.4% | 61.5% | 38.5% |
| 245,738 | TULARE | 79,943 | 51,066 | 28,065 | 812 | 23,001 | R | 63.9% | 35.1% | 64.5% | 35.5% |
| 33,928 | TUOLUMNE | 18,051 | 10,485 | 7,283 | 283 | 3,202 | R | 58.1% | 40.3% | 59.0% | 41.0% |
| 529,174 | VENTURA | 220,462 | 151,383 | 66,550 | 2,529 | 84,833 | R | 68.7% | 30.2% | 69.5% | 30.5% |
| 113,374 | YOLO | 50,853 | 24,329 | 25,879 | 645 | 1,550 | D | 47.8% | 50.9% | 48.5% | 51.5% |
| 49,733 | YUBA | 15,397 | 9,780 | 5,339 | 278 | 4,441 | R | 63.5% | 34.7% | 64.7% | 35.3% |
| 23,667,902 | TOTAL | 9,505,423 | 5,467,009 | 3,922,519 | 115,895 | 1,544,490 | R | 57.5% | 41.3% | 58.2% | 41.8% |

# CALIFORNIA

## PRESIDENT 1980

| 1980 Census Population | County | Total Vote | Republican | Democratic | Other | Rep.-Dem. Plurality | Percentage | | | |
|---|---|---|---|---|---|---|---|---|---|---|
| | | | | | | | Total Vote | | Major Vote | |
| | | | | | | | Rep. | Dem. | Rep. | Dem. |
| 1,105,379 | ALAMEDA | 417,617 | 158,531 | 201,720 | 57,366 | 43,189 D | 38.0% | 48.3% | 44.0% | 56.0% |
| 1,097 | ALPINE | 461 | 254 | 133 | 74 | 121 R | 55.1% | 28.9% | 65.6% | 34.4% |
| 19,314 | AMADOR | 9,670 | 5,401 | 3,191 | 1,078 | 2,210 R | 55.9% | 33.0% | 62.9% | 37.1% |
| 143,851 | BUTTE | 66,012 | 38,188 | 19,520 | 8,304 | 18,668 R | 57.9% | 29.6% | 66.2% | 33.8% |
| 20,710 | CALAVERAS | 10,275 | 6,054 | 3,076 | 1,145 | 2,978 R | 58.9% | 29.9% | 66.3% | 33.7% |
| 12,791 | COLUSA | 4,995 | 2,897 | 1,605 | 493 | 1,292 R | 58.0% | 32.1% | 64.3% | 35.7% |
| 656,380 | CONTRA COSTA | 287,545 | 144,112 | 107,398 | 36,035 | 36,714 R | 50.1% | 37.3% | 57.3% | 42.7% |
| 18,217 | DEL NORTE | 6,987 | 4,016 | 2,338 | 633 | 1,678 R | 57.5% | 33.5% | 63.2% | 36.8% |
| 85,812 | EL DORADO | 36,449 | 21,238 | 10,765 | 4,446 | 10,473 R | 58.3% | 29.5% | 66.4% | 33.6% |
| 514,621 | FRESNO | 161,386 | 82,515 | 65,254 | 13,617 | 17,261 R | 51.1% | 40.4% | 55.8% | 44.2% |
| 21,350 | GLENN | 8,312 | 5,386 | 2,227 | 699 | 3,159 R | 64.8% | 26.8% | 70.7% | 29.3% |
| 108,514 | HUMBOLDT | 48,712 | 24,047 | 17,133 | 7,532 | 6,914 R | 49.4% | 35.2% | 58.4% | 41.6% |
| 92,110 | IMPERIAL | 21,579 | 12,068 | 7,961 | 1,550 | 4,107 R | 55.9% | 36.9% | 60.3% | 39.7% |
| 17,895 | INYO | 8,027 | 5,201 | 2,080 | 746 | 3,121 R | 64.8% | 25.9% | 71.4% | 28.6% |
| 403,089 | KERN | 122,121 | 72,842 | 41,097 | 8,182 | 31,745 R | 59.6% | 33.7% | 63.9% | 36.1% |
| 73,738 | KINGS | 19,021 | 10,531 | 7,299 | 1,191 | 3,232 R | 55.4% | 38.4% | 59.1% | 40.9% |
| 36,366 | LAKE | 16,654 | 8,934 | 5,978 | 1,742 | 2,956 R | 53.6% | 35.9% | 59.9% | 40.1% |
| 21,661 | LASSEN | 8,198 | 4,464 | 2,941 | 793 | 1,523 R | 54.5% | 35.9% | 60.3% | 39.7% |
| 7,477,503 | LOS ANGELES | 2,440,185 | 1,224,533 | 979,830 | 235,822 | 244,703 R | 50.2% | 40.2% | 55.6% | 44.4% |
| 63,116 | MADERA | 19,780 | 10,599 | 7,783 | 1,398 | 2,816 R | 53.6% | 39.3% | 57.7% | 42.3% |
| 222,568 | MARIN | 108,507 | 49,678 | 39,231 | 19,598 | 10,447 R | 45.8% | 36.2% | 55.9% | 44.1% |
| 11,108 | MARIPOSA | 5,608 | 3,082 | 1,889 | 637 | 1,193 R | 55.0% | 33.7% | 62.0% | 38.0% |
| 66,738 | MENDOCINO | 28,224 | 12,432 | 10,784 | 5,008 | 1,648 R | 44.0% | 38.2% | 53.5% | 46.5% |
| 134,560 | MERCED | 36,996 | 18,043 | 15,886 | 3,067 | 2,157 R | 48.8% | 42.9% | 53.2% | 46.8% |
| 8,610 | MODOC | 4,000 | 2,579 | 1,046 | 375 | 1,533 R | 64.5% | 26.2% | 71.1% | 28.9% |
| 8,577 | MONO | 3,421 | 2,132 | 865 | 424 | 1,267 R | 62.3% | 25.3% | 71.1% | 28.9% |
| 290,444 | MONTEREY | 86,794 | 47,452 | 29,086 | 10,256 | 18,366 R | 54.7% | 33.5% | 62.0% | 38.0% |
| 99,199 | NAPA | 44,035 | 23,632 | 14,898 | 5,505 | 8,734 R | 53.7% | 33.8% | 61.3% | 38.7% |
| 51,645 | NEVADA | 26,261 | 15,207 | 7,605 | 3,449 | 7,602 R | 57.9% | 29.0% | 66.7% | 33.3% |
| 1,932,709 | ORANGE | 780,212 | 529,797 | 176,704 | 73,711 | 353,093 R | 67.9% | 22.6% | 75.0% | 25.0% |
| 117,247 | PLACER | 51,440 | 28,179 | 17,311 | 5,950 | 10,868 R | 54.8% | 33.7% | 61.9% | 38.1% |
| 17,340 | PLUMAS | 8,161 | 4,182 | 2,911 | 1,068 | 1,271 R | 51.2% | 35.7% | 59.0% | 41.0% |
| 663,166 | RIVERSIDE | 243,278 | 145,642 | 76,650 | 20,986 | 68,992 R | 59.9% | 31.5% | 65.5% | 34.5% |
| 783,381 | SACRAMENTO | 322,120 | 153,721 | 130,031 | 38,368 | 23,690 R | 47.7% | 40.4% | 54.2% | 45.8% |
| 25,005 | SAN BENITO | 7,602 | 4,054 | 2,749 | 799 | 1,305 R | 53.3% | 36.2% | 59.6% | 40.4% |
| 895,016 | SAN BERNARDINO | 289,812 | 172,957 | 91,790 | 25,065 | 81,167 R | 59.7% | 31.7% | 65.3% | 34.7% |
| 1,861,846 | SAN DIEGO | 716,866 | 435,910 | 195,410 | 85,546 | 240,500 R | 60.8% | 27.3% | 69.0% | 31.0% |
| 678,974 | SAN FRANCISCO | 254,028 | 80,967 | 133,184 | 39,877 | 52,217 D | 31.9% | 52.4% | 37.8% | 62.2% |
| 347,342 | SAN JOAQUIN | 116,863 | 64,718 | 41,551 | 10,594 | 23,167 R | 55.4% | 35.6% | 60.9% | 39.1% |
| 155,435 | SAN LUIS OBISPO | 69,527 | 38,631 | 20,508 | 10,388 | 18,123 R | 55.6% | 29.5% | 65.3% | 34.7% |
| 587,329 | SAN MATEO | 238,637 | 116,491 | 87,335 | 34,811 | 29,156 R | 48.8% | 36.6% | 57.2% | 42.8% |
| 298,694 | SANTA BARBARA | 128,995 | 69,629 | 40,650 | 18,716 | 28,979 R | 54.0% | 31.5% | 63.1% | 36.9% |
| 1,295,071 | SANTA CLARA | 477,003 | 229,048 | 166,995 | 80,960 | 62,053 R | 48.0% | 35.0% | 57.8% | 42.2% |
| 188,141 | SANTA CRUZ | 85,804 | 37,347 | 32,346 | 16,111 | 5,001 R | 43.5% | 37.7% | 53.6% | 46.4% |
| 115,715 | SHASTA | 47,418 | 27,547 | 15,364 | 4,507 | 12,183 R | 58.1% | 32.4% | 64.2% | 35.8% |
| 3,073 | SIERRA | 1,718 | 855 | 651 | 212 | 204 R | 49.8% | 37.9% | 56.8% | 43.2% |
| 39,732 | SISKIYOU | 16,738 | 9,331 | 5,664 | 1,743 | 3,667 R | 55.7% | 33.8% | 62.2% | 37.8% |
| 235,203 | SOLANO | 80,676 | 40,919 | 30,952 | 8,805 | 9,967 R | 50.7% | 38.4% | 56.9% | 43.1% |
| 299,681 | SONOMA | 125,985 | 60,722 | 45,596 | 19,667 | 15,126 R | 48.2% | 36.2% | 57.1% | 42.9% |
| 265,900 | STANISLAUS | 84,186 | 41,595 | 33,683 | 8,908 | 7,912 R | 49.4% | 40.0% | 55.3% | 44.7% |
| 52,246 | SUTTER | 18,557 | 11,778 | 5,103 | 1,676 | 6,675 R | 63.5% | 27.5% | 69.8% | 30.2% |
| 38,888 | TEHAMA | 15,457 | 9,140 | 4,832 | 1,485 | 4,308 R | 59.1% | 31.3% | 65.4% | 34.6% |
| 11,858 | TRINITY | 5,546 | 3,048 | 1,734 | 764 | 1,314 R | 55.0% | 31.3% | 63.7% | 36.3% |
| 245,738 | TULARE | 70,846 | 41,317 | 25,155 | 4,374 | 16,162 R | 58.3% | 35.5% | 62.2% | 37.8% |
| 33,928 | TUOLUMNE | 16,063 | 8,810 | 5,449 | 1,804 | 3,361 R | 54.8% | 33.9% | 61.8% | 38.2% |
| 529,174 | VENTURA | 190,650 | 114,930 | 56,311 | 19,409 | 58,619 R | 60.3% | 29.5% | 67.1% | 32.9% |
| 113,374 | YOLO | 49,690 | 19,603 | 21,527 | 8,560 | 1,924 D | 39.5% | 43.3% | 47.7% | 52.3% |
| 49,733 | YUBA | 14,111 | 7,942 | 4,896 | 1,273 | 3,046 R | 56.3% | 34.7% | 61.9% | 38.1% |
| 23,667,902 | TOTAL | 8,587,063 | 4,524,858 | 3,083,661 | 978,544 | 1,441,197 R | 52.7% | 35.9% | 59.5% | 40.5% |

# CALIFORNIA

## PRESIDENT 1976

| 1970 Census Population | County | Total Vote | Republican | Democratic | Other | Rep.-Dem. Plurality | Total Vote Rep. | Total Vote Dem. | Major Vote Rep. | Major Vote Dem. |
|---:|---|---:|---:|---:|---:|---:|---:|---:|---:|---:|
| 1,073,184 | ALAMEDA | 407,681 | 155,280 | 235,988 | 16,413 | 80,708 D | 38.1% | 57.9% | 39.7% | 60.3% |
| 484 | ALPINE | 447 | 225 | 189 | 33 | 36 R | 50.3% | 42.3% | 54.3% | 45.7% |
| 11,821 | AMADOR | 8,018 | 3,699 | 4,037 | 282 | 338 D | 46.1% | 50.3% | 47.8% | 52.2% |
| 101,969 | BUTTE | 54,854 | 28,400 | 24,203 | 2,251 | 4,197 R | 51.8% | 44.1% | 54.0% | 46.0% |
| 13,585 | CALAVERAS | 7,528 | 3,695 | 3,607 | 226 | 88 R | 49.1% | 47.9% | 50.6% | 49.4% |
| 12,430 | COLUSA | 5,182 | 2,733 | 2,340 | 109 | 393 R | 52.7% | 45.2% | 53.9% | 46.1% |
| 558,389 | CONTRA COSTA | 256,534 | 126,598 | 123,742 | 6,194 | 2,856 R | 49.3% | 48.2% | 50.6% | 49.4% |
| 14,580 | DEL NORTE | 5,478 | 2,481 | 2,789 | 208 | 308 D | 45.3% | 50.9% | 47.1% | 52.9% |
| 43,833 | EL DORADO | 26,154 | 12,472 | 12,763 | 919 | 291 D | 47.7% | 48.8% | 49.4% | 50.6% |
| 413,053 | FRESNO | 150,805 | 72,533 | 74,958 | 3,314 | 2,425 D | 48.1% | 49.7% | 49.2% | 50.8% |
| 17,521 | GLENN | 7,773 | 4,094 | 3,501 | 178 | 593 R | 52.7% | 45.0% | 53.9% | 46.1% |
| 99,692 | HUMBOLDT | 43,372 | 18,034 | 23,500 | 1,838 | 5,466 D | 41.6% | 54.2% | 43.4% | 56.6% |
| 74,492 | IMPERIAL | 21,262 | 10,618 | 10,244 | 400 | 374 R | 49.9% | 48.2% | 50.9% | 49.1% |
| 15,571 | INYO | 6,706 | 3,905 | 2,635 | 166 | 1,270 R | 58.2% | 39.3% | 59.7% | 40.3% |
| 329,162 | KERN | 110,961 | 58,023 | 50,567 | 2,371 | 7,456 R | 52.3% | 45.6% | 53.4% | 46.6% |
| 64,610 | KINGS | 16,642 | 8,263 | 8,061 | 318 | 202 R | 49.7% | 48.4% | 50.6% | 49.4% |
| 19,548 | LAKE | 12,285 | 5,462 | 6,374 | 449 | 912 D | 44.5% | 51.9% | 46.1% | 53.9% |
| 14,960 | LASSEN | 6,998 | 3,007 | 3,801 | 190 | 794 D | 43.0% | 54.3% | 44.2% | 55.8% |
| 7,032,075 | LOS ANGELES | 2,459,077 | 1,174,926 | 1,221,893 | 62,258 | 46,967 D | 47.8% | 49.7% | 49.0% | 51.0% |
| 41,519 | MADERA | 14,892 | 6,844 | 7,625 | 423 | 781 D | 46.0% | 51.2% | 47.3% | 52.7% |
| 206,038 | MARIN | 101,715 | 53,425 | 43,590 | 4,700 | 9,835 R | 52.5% | 42.9% | 55.1% | 44.9% |
| 6,015 | MARIPOSA | 4,317 | 2,012 | 2,093 | 212 | 81 D | 46.6% | 48.5% | 49.0% | 51.0% |
| 51,101 | MENDOCINO | 21,509 | 9,784 | 10,653 | 1,072 | 869 D | 45.5% | 49.5% | 47.9% | 52.1% |
| 104,629 | MERCED | 32,208 | 14,842 | 16,637 | 729 | 1,795 D | 46.1% | 51.7% | 47.1% | 52.9% |
| 7,469 | MODOC | 3,744 | 1,917 | 1,733 | 94 | 184 R | 51.2% | 46.3% | 52.5% | 47.5% |
| 4,016 | MONO | 2,721 | 1,600 | 1,025 | 96 | 575 R | 58.8% | 37.7% | 61.0% | 39.0% |
| 250,071 | MONTEREY | 80,153 | 40,896 | 36,849 | 2,408 | 4,047 R | 51.0% | 46.0% | 52.6% | 47.4% |
| 79,140 | NAPA | 40,205 | 20,839 | 18,048 | 1,318 | 2,791 R | 51.8% | 44.9% | 53.6% | 46.4% |
| 26,346 | NEVADA | 16,881 | 8,170 | 7,926 | 785 | 244 R | 48.4% | 47.0% | 50.8% | 49.2% |
| 1,420,386 | ORANGE | 657,433 | 408,632 | 232,246 | 16,555 | 176,386 R | 62.2% | 35.3% | 63.8% | 36.2% |
| 77,306 | PLACER | 40,311 | 18,154 | 21,026 | 1,131 | 2,872 D | 45.0% | 52.2% | 46.3% | 53.7% |
| 11,707 | PLUMAS | 6,563 | 2,884 | 3,429 | 250 | 545 D | 43.9% | 52.2% | 45.7% | 54.3% |
| 459,074 | RIVERSIDE | 198,558 | 97,774 | 96,228 | 4,556 | 1,546 R | 49.2% | 48.5% | 50.4% | 49.6% |
| 631,498 | SACRAMENTO | 275,876 | 123,110 | 144,203 | 8,563 | 21,093 D | 44.6% | 52.3% | 46.1% | 53.9% |
| 18,226 | SAN BENITO | 6,680 | 3,398 | 3,122 | 160 | 276 R | 50.9% | 46.7% | 52.1% | 47.9% |
| 684,072 | SAN BERNARDINO | 228,885 | 113,265 | 109,636 | 5,984 | 3,629 R | 49.5% | 47.9% | 50.8% | 49.2% |
| 1,357,854 | SAN DIEGO | 633,795 | 353,302 | 263,654 | 16,839 | 89,648 R | 55.7% | 41.6% | 57.3% | 42.7% |
| 715,674 | SAN FRANCISCO | 256,888 | 103,561 | 133,733 | 19,594 | 30,172 D | 40.3% | 52.1% | 43.6% | 56.4% |
| 290,208 | SAN JOAQUIN | 101,361 | 50,277 | 48,733 | 2,351 | 1,544 R | 49.6% | 48.1% | 50.8% | 49.2% |
| 105,690 | SAN LUIS OBISPO | 54,298 | 27,785 | 24,926 | 1,587 | 2,859 R | 51.2% | 45.9% | 52.7% | 47.3% |
| 556,234 | SAN MATEO | 231,741 | 117,338 | 102,896 | 11,507 | 14,442 R | 50.6% | 44.4% | 53.3% | 46.7% |
| 264,324 | SANTA BARBARA | 119,844 | 60,922 | 55,018 | 3,904 | 5,904 R | 50.8% | 45.9% | 52.5% | 47.5% |
| 1,064,714 | SANTA CLARA | 443,138 | 219,188 | 208,023 | 15,927 | 11,165 R | 49.5% | 46.9% | 51.3% | 48.7% |
| 123,790 | SANTA CRUZ | 73,969 | 31,872 | 37,772 | 4,325 | 5,900 D | 43.1% | 51.1% | 45.8% | 54.2% |
| 77,640 | SHASTA | 37,854 | 17,273 | 19,200 | 1,381 | 1,927 D | 45.6% | 50.7% | 47.4% | 52.6% |
| 2,365 | SIERRA | 1,576 | 680 | 841 | 55 | 161 D | 43.1% | 53.4% | 44.7% | 55.3% |
| 33,225 | SISKIYOU | 14,615 | 7,070 | 7,060 | 485 | 10 R | 48.4% | 48.3% | 50.0% | 50.0% |
| 169,941 | SOLANO | 61,644 | 26,136 | 33,682 | 1,826 | 7,546 D | 42.4% | 54.6% | 43.7% | 56.3% |
| 204,885 | SONOMA | 105,952 | 50,555 | 50,353 | 5,044 | 202 R | 47.7% | 47.5% | 50.1% | 49.9% |
| 194,506 | STANISLAUS | 73,465 | 32,937 | 38,448 | 2,080 | 5,511 D | 44.8% | 52.3% | 46.1% | 53.9% |
| 41,935 | SUTTER | 16,131 | 8,745 | 6,966 | 420 | 1,779 R | 54.2% | 43.2% | 55.7% | 44.3% |
| 29,517 | TEHAMA | 13,635 | 6,110 | 6,990 | 535 | 880 D | 44.8% | 51.3% | 46.6% | 53.4% |
| 7,615 | TRINITY | 4,356 | 1,989 | 2,172 | 195 | 183 D | 45.7% | 49.9% | 47.8% | 52.2% |
| 188,322 | TULARE | 58,441 | 31,864 | 25,551 | 1,026 | 6,313 R | 54.5% | 43.7% | 55.5% | 44.5% |
| 22,169 | TUOLUMNE | 13,003 | 6,104 | 6,492 | 407 | 388 D | 46.9% | 49.9% | 48.5% | 51.5% |
| 376,430 | VENTURA | 155,401 | 82,670 | 68,529 | 4,202 | 14,141 R | 53.2% | 44.1% | 54.7% | 45.3% |
| 91,788 | YOLO | 43,317 | 18,376 | 23,533 | 1,408 | 5,157 D | 42.4% | 54.3% | 43.8% | 56.2% |
| 44,736 | YUBA | 12,285 | 5,496 | 6,451 | 338 | 955 D | 44.7% | 52.5% | 46.0% | 54.0% |
| 19,953,134 | TOTAL | 7,867,117 | 3,882,244 | 3,742,284 | 242,589 | 139,960 R | 49.3% | 47.6% | 50.9% | 49.1% |

# CALIFORNIA

## PRESIDENT 1972

| 1970 Census Population | County | Total Vote | Republican | Democratic | Other | Rep.-Dem. Plurality | Percentage Total Vote Rep. | Dem. | Major Vote Rep. | Dem. |
|---|---|---|---|---|---|---|---|---|---|---|
| 1,073,184 | ALAMEDA | 471,195 | 201,862 | 259,254 | 10,079 | 57,392 D | 42.8% | 55.0% | 43.8% | 56.2% |
| 484 | ALPINE | 576 | 366 | 195 | 15 | 171 R | 63.5% | 33.9% | 65.2% | 34.8% |
| 11,821 | AMADOR | 6,616 | 3,533 | 2,705 | 378 | 828 R | 53.4% | 40.9% | 56.6% | 43.4% |
| 101,969 | BUTTE | 50,028 | 28,819 | 18,401 | 2,808 | 10,418 R | 57.6% | 36.8% | 61.0% | 39.0% |
| 13,585 | CALAVERAS | 6,779 | 4,119 | 2,268 | 392 | 1,851 R | 60.8% | 33.5% | 64.5% | 35.5% |
| 12,430 | COLUSA | 4,717 | 2,715 | 1,810 | 192 | 905 R | 57.6% | 38.4% | 60.0% | 40.0% |
| 558,389 | CONTRA COSTA | 256,884 | 139,044 | 111,718 | 6,122 | 27,326 R | 54.1% | 43.5% | 55.4% | 44.6% |
| 14,580 | DEL NORTE | 5,648 | 2,927 | 2,156 | 565 | 771 R | 51.8% | 38.2% | 57.6% | 42.4% |
| 43,833 | EL DORADO | 20,905 | 11,330 | 8,654 | 921 | 2,676 R | 54.2% | 41.4% | 56.7% | 43.3% |
| 413,053 | FRESNO | 156,719 | 79,051 | 72,682 | 4,986 | 6,369 R | 50.4% | 46.4% | 52.1% | 47.9% |
| 17,521 | GLENN | 7,743 | 4,569 | 2,681 | 493 | 1,888 R | 59.0% | 34.6% | 63.0% | 37.0% |
| 99,692 | HUMBOLDT | 45,763 | 22,345 | 21,132 | 2,286 | 1,213 R | 48.8% | 46.2% | 51.4% | 48.6% |
| 74,492 | IMPERIAL | 22,849 | 14,178 | 7,982 | 689 | 6,196 R | 62.1% | 34.9% | 64.0% | 36.0% |
| 15,571 | INYO | 7,159 | 4,873 | 2,006 | 280 | 2,867 R | 68.1% | 28.0% | 70.8% | 29.2% |
| 329,162 | KERN | 119,193 | 71,686 | 41,937 | 5,570 | 29,749 R | 60.1% | 35.2% | 63.1% | 36.9% |
| 64,610 | KINGS | 18,595 | 10,509 | 7,274 | 812 | 3,235 R | 56.5% | 39.1% | 59.1% | 40.9% |
| 19,548 | LAKE | 11,750 | 6,477 | 4,715 | 558 | 1,762 R | 55.1% | 40.1% | 57.9% | 42.1% |
| 14,960 | LASSEN | 7,122 | 3,618 | 3,134 | 370 | 484 R | 50.8% | 44.0% | 53.6% | 46.4% |
| 7,032,075 | LOS ANGELES | 2,830,370 | 1,549,717 | 1,189,977 | 90,676 | 359,740 R | 54.8% | 42.0% | 56.6% | 43.4% |
| 41,519 | MADERA | 14,892 | 7,835 | 6,580 | 477 | 1,255 R | 52.6% | 44.2% | 54.4% | 45.6% |
| 206,038 | MARIN | 103,883 | 54,123 | 47,414 | 2,346 | 6,709 R | 52.1% | 45.6% | 53.3% | 46.7% |
| 6,015 | MARIPOSA | 3,779 | 2,122 | 1,487 | 170 | 635 R | 56.2% | 39.3% | 58.8% | 41.2% |
| 51,101 | MENDOCINO | 21,814 | 11,128 | 9,435 | 1,251 | 1,693 R | 51.0% | 43.3% | 54.1% | 45.9% |
| 104,629 | MERCED | 32,648 | 17,737 | 13,914 | 997 | 3,823 R | 54.3% | 42.6% | 56.0% | 44.0% |
| 7,469 | MODOC | 3,565 | 2,085 | 1,271 | 209 | 814 R | 58.5% | 35.7% | 62.1% | 37.9% |
| 4,016 | MONO | 2,799 | 1,872 | 828 | 99 | 1,044 R | 66.9% | 29.6% | 69.3% | 30.7% |
| 250,071 | MONTEREY | 82,408 | 47,004 | 32,545 | 2,859 | 14,459 R | 57.0% | 39.5% | 59.1% | 40.9% |
| 79,140 | NAPA | 39,261 | 23,403 | 14,529 | 1,329 | 8,874 R | 59.6% | 37.0% | 61.7% | 38.3% |
| 26,346 | NEVADA | 14,638 | 8,004 | 5,693 | 941 | 2,311 R | 54.7% | 38.9% | 58.4% | 41.6% |
| 1,420,386 | ORANGE | 656,653 | 448,291 | 176,847 | 31,515 | 271,444 R | 68.3% | 26.9% | 71.7% | 28.3% |
| 77,306 | PLACER | 36,945 | 18,597 | 16,911 | 1,437 | 1,686 R | 50.3% | 45.8% | 52.4% | 47.6% |
| 11,707 | PLUMAS | 6,360 | 2,952 | 3,057 | 351 | 105 D | 46.4% | 48.1% | 49.1% | 50.9% |
| 459,074 | RIVERSIDE | 186,404 | 108,120 | 71,591 | 6,693 | 36,529 R | 58.0% | 38.4% | 60.2% | 39.8% |
| 631,498 | SACRAMENTO | 288,221 | 141,218 | 137,287 | 9,716 | 3,931 R | 49.0% | 47.6% | 50.7% | 49.3% |
| 18,226 | SAN BENITO | 6,881 | 3,961 | 2,582 | 338 | 1,379 R | 57.6% | 37.5% | 60.5% | 39.5% |
| 684,072 | SAN BERNARDINO | 242,256 | 144,689 | 85,986 | 11,581 | 58,703 R | 59.7% | 35.5% | 62.7% | 37.3% |
| 1,357,854 | SAN DIEGO | 601,137 | 371,627 | 206,455 | 23,055 | 165,172 R | 61.8% | 34.3% | 64.3% | 35.7% |
| 715,674 | SAN FRANCISCO | 304,770 | 127,461 | 170,882 | 6,427 | 43,421 D | 41.8% | 56.1% | 42.7% | 57.3% |
| 290,208 | SAN JOAQUIN | 111,469 | 61,646 | 44,062 | 5,761 | 17,584 R | 55.3% | 39.5% | 58.3% | 41.7% |
| 105,690 | SAN LUIS OBISPO | 51,033 | 28,566 | 20,779 | 1,688 | 7,787 R | 56.0% | 40.7% | 57.9% | 42.1% |
| 556,234 | SAN MATEO | 256,297 | 135,377 | 109,745 | 11,175 | 25,632 R | 52.8% | 42.8% | 55.2% | 44.8% |
| 264,324 | SANTA BARBARA | 121,541 | 67,075 | 50,609 | 3,857 | 16,466 R | 55.2% | 41.6% | 57.0% | 43.0% |
| 1,064,714 | SANTA CLARA | 457,293 | 237,334 | 208,506 | 11,453 | 28,828 R | 51.9% | 45.6% | 53.2% | 46.8% |
| 123,790 | SANTA CRUZ | 69,759 | 34,799 | 32,336 | 2,624 | 2,463 R | 49.9% | 46.4% | 51.8% | 48.2% |
| 77,640 | SHASTA | 35,603 | 16,618 | 17,214 | 1,771 | 596 D | 46.7% | 48.3% | 49.1% | 50.9% |
| 2,365 | SIERRA | 1,324 | 629 | 658 | 37 | 29 D | 47.5% | 49.7% | 48.9% | 51.1% |
| 33,225 | SISKIYOU | 14,696 | 7,563 | 6,434 | 699 | 1,129 R | 51.5% | 43.8% | 54.0% | 46.0% |
| 169,941 | SOLANO | 57,965 | 31,314 | 24,766 | 1,885 | 6,548 R | 54.0% | 42.7% | 55.8% | 44.2% |
| 204,885 | SONOMA | 105,434 | 57,697 | 43,746 | 3,991 | 13,951 R | 54.7% | 41.5% | 56.9% | 43.1% |
| 194,506 | STANISLAUS | 76,867 | 39,521 | 35,005 | 2,341 | 4,516 R | 51.4% | 45.5% | 53.0% | 47.0% |
| 41,935 | SUTTER | 16,372 | 10,224 | 5,409 | 739 | 4,815 R | 62.4% | 33.0% | 65.4% | 34.6% |
| 29,517 | TEHAMA | 12,424 | 6,054 | 5,175 | 1,195 | 879 R | 48.7% | 41.7% | 53.9% | 46.1% |
| 7,615 | TRINITY | 3,681 | 1,868 | 1,621 | 192 | 247 R | 50.7% | 44.0% | 53.5% | 46.5% |
| 188,322 | TULARE | 60,150 | 36,048 | 21,775 | 2,327 | 14,273 R | 59.9% | 36.2% | 62.3% | 37.7% |
| 22,169 | TUOLUMNE | 10,856 | 5,894 | 4,596 | 366 | 1,298 R | 54.3% | 42.3% | 56.2% | 43.8% |
| 376,430 | VENTURA | 150,805 | 95,310 | 49,307 | 6,188 | 46,003 R | 63.2% | 32.7% | 65.9% | 34.1% |
| 91,788 | YOLO | 42,738 | 17,969 | 23,694 | 1,075 | 5,725 D | 42.0% | 55.4% | 43.1% | 56.9% |
| 44,736 | YUBA | 11,630 | 6,623 | 4,435 | 572 | 2,188 R | 56.9% | 38.1% | 59.9% | 40.1% |
| 19,953,134 | TOTAL | 8,367,862 | 4,602,096 | 3,475,847 | 289,919 | 1,126,249 R | 55.0% | 41.5% | 57.0% | 43.0% |

# CALIFORNIA

## PRESIDENT 1968

| 1960 Census Population | County | Total Vote | Republican | Democratic | AIP | Other | Plurality | Percentage Total Vote | | |
|---|---|---|---|---|---|---|---|---|---|---|
| | | | | | | | | Rep. | Dem. | AIP |
| 905,670 | ALAMEDA | 407,349 | 153,285 | 219,545 | 28,426 | 6,093 | 66,260 D | 37.6% | 53.9% | 7.0% |
| 397 | ALPINE | 253 | 150 | 83 | 20 | | 67 R | 59.3% | 32.8% | 7.9% |
| 9,990 | AMADOR | 5,390 | 2,269 | 2,440 | 660 | 21 | 171 D | 42.1% | 45.3% | 12.2% |
| 62,030 | BUTTE | 39,211 | 22,225 | 12,887 | 3,891 | 208 | 9,338 R | 56.7% | 32.9% | 9.9% |
| 10,289 | CALAVERAS | 5,832 | 3,042 | 2,134 | 643 | 13 | 908 R | 52.2% | 36.6% | 11.0% |
| 12,075 | COLUSA | 4,577 | 2,361 | 1,858 | 344 | 14 | 503 R | 51.6% | 40.6% | 7.5% |
| 409,030 | CONTRA COSTA | 218,917 | 97,486 | 101,668 | 18,330 | 1,433 | 4,182 D | 44.5% | 46.4% | 8.4% |
| 17,771 | DEL NORTE | 5,168 | 2,387 | 2,236 | 495 | 50 | 151 R | 46.2% | 43.3% | 9.6% |
| 29,390 | EL DORADO | 15,241 | 7,468 | 6,054 | 1,676 | 43 | 1,414 R | 49.0% | 39.7% | 11.0% |
| 365,945 | FRESNO | 137,396 | 59,901 | 65,153 | 11,292 | 1,050 | 5,252 D | 43.6% | 47.4% | 8.2% |
| 17,245 | GLENN | 7,138 | 3,848 | 2,466 | 808 | 16 | 1,382 R | 53.9% | 34.5% | 11.3% |
| 104,892 | HUMBOLDT | 36,214 | 16,719 | 16,476 | 2,759 | 260 | 243 R | 46.2% | 45.5% | 7.6% |
| 72,105 | IMPERIAL | 20,446 | 10,818 | 7,481 | 2,100 | 47 | 3,337 R | 52.9% | 36.6% | 10.3% |
| 11,684 | INYO | 6,687 | 3,641 | 2,314 | 714 | 18 | 1,327 R | 54.4% | 34.6% | 10.7% |
| 291,984 | KERN | 115,832 | 53,990 | 49,284 | 12,309 | 249 | 4,706 R | 46.6% | 42.5% | 10.6% |
| 49,954 | KINGS | 18,101 | 7,796 | 8,643 | 1,640 | 22 | 847 D | 43.1% | 47.7% | 9.1% |
| 13,786 | LAKE | 9,111 | 4,464 | 3,777 | 838 | 32 | 687 R | 49.0% | 41.5% | 9.2% |
| 13,597 | LASSEN | 6,218 | 2,553 | 2,930 | 712 | 23 | 377 D | 41.1% | 47.1% | 11.5% |
| 6,038,771 | LOS ANGELES | 2,657,982 | 1,266,480 | 1,223,251 | 151,050 | 17,201 | 43,229 R | 47.6% | 46.0% | 5.7% |
| 60,468 | MADERA | 14,303 | 6,229 | 6,932 | 1,120 | 22 | 703 D | 43.6% | 48.5% | 7.8% |
| 146,820 | MARIN | 82,755 | 41,422 | 36,278 | 3,801 | 1,254 | 5,144 R | 50.1% | 43.8% | 4.6% |
| 5,064 | MARIPOSA | 2,997 | 1,496 | 1,187 | 302 | 12 | 309 R | 49.9% | 39.6% | 10.1% |
| 51,059 | MENDOCINO | 17,904 | 8,305 | 7,935 | 1,554 | 110 | 370 R | 46.4% | 44.3% | 8.7% |
| 90,446 | MERCED | 28,349 | 11,595 | 14,453 | 2,248 | 53 | 2,858 D | 40.9% | 51.0% | 7.9% |
| 8,308 | MODOC | 3,267 | 1,713 | 1,264 | 284 | 6 | 449 R | 52.4% | 38.7% | 8.7% |
| 2,213 | MONO | 1,758 | 1,130 | 465 | 156 | 7 | 665 R | 64.3% | 26.5% | 8.9% |
| 198,351 | MONTEREY | 67,124 | 33,670 | 28,261 | 4,800 | 393 | 5,409 R | 50.2% | 42.1% | 7.2% |
| 65,890 | NAPA | 32,612 | 14,270 | 14,762 | 3,476 | 104 | 492 D | 43.8% | 45.3% | 10.7% |
| 20,911 | NEVADA | 11,794 | 6,061 | 4,607 | 1,078 | 48 | 1,454 R | 51.4% | 39.1% | 9.1% |
| 703,925 | ORANGE | 498,707 | 314,905 | 148,869 | 33,034 | 1,899 | 166,036 R | 63.1% | 29.9% | 6.6% |
| 56,998 | PLACER | 29,144 | 12,427 | 14,050 | 2,574 | 93 | 1,623 D | 42.6% | 48.2% | 8.8% |
| 11,620 | PLUMAS | 5,611 | 2,097 | 2,961 | 529 | 24 | 864 D | 37.4% | 52.8% | 9.4% |
| 306,191 | RIVERSIDE | 157,670 | 83,414 | 61,146 | 12,432 | 678 | 22,268 R | 52.9% | 38.8% | 7.9% |
| 502,778 | SACRAMENTO | 233,246 | 97,177 | 118,769 | 16,269 | 1,031 | 21,592 D | 41.7% | 50.9% | 7.0% |
| 15,396 | SAN BENITO | 6,229 | 2,961 | 2,809 | 447 | 12 | 152 R | 47.5% | 45.1% | 7.2% |
| 503,591 | SAN BERNARDINO | 223,616 | 111,974 | 89,418 | 21,187 | 1,037 | 22,556 R | 50.1% | 40.0% | 9.5% |
| 1,033,011 | SAN DIEGO | 464,863 | 261,540 | 167,669 | 33,340 | 2,314 | 93,871 R | 56.3% | 36.1% | 7.2% |
| 742,855 | SAN FRANCISCO | 299,947 | 100,970 | 177,509 | 17,332 | 4,136 | 76,539 D | 33.7% | 59.2% | 5.8% |
| 249,989 | SAN JOAQUIN | 98,589 | 47,293 | 42,073 | 8,923 | 300 | 5,220 R | 48.0% | 42.7% | 9.1% |
| 81,044 | SAN LUIS OBISPO | 37,881 | 19,420 | 15,828 | 2,416 | 217 | 3,592 R | 51.3% | 41.8% | 6.4% |
| 444,387 | SAN MATEO | 225,668 | 98,654 | 106,519 | 14,720 | 5,775 | 7,865 D | 43.7% | 47.2% | 6.5% |
| 168,962 | SANTA BARBARA | 93,420 | 50,068 | 37,565 | 5,083 | 704 | 12,503 R | 53.6% | 40.2% | 5.4% |
| 642,315 | SANTA CLARA | 358,367 | 163,446 | 173,511 | 18,754 | 2,656 | 10,065 D | 45.6% | 48.4% | 5.2% |
| 84,219 | SANTA CRUZ | 49,944 | 25,365 | 20,492 | 3,465 | 622 | 4,873 R | 50.8% | 41.0% | 6.9% |
| 59,468 | SHASTA | 29,230 | 11,821 | 14,510 | 2,815 | 84 | 2,689 D | 40.4% | 49.6% | 9.6% |
| 2,247 | SIERRA | 1,193 | 548 | 559 | 85 | 1 | 11 D | 45.9% | 46.9% | 7.1% |
| 32,885 | SISKIYOU | 13,732 | 6,334 | 6,260 | 1,088 | 50 | 74 R | 46.1% | 45.6% | 7.9% |
| 134,597 | SOLANO | 50,952 | 17,683 | 27,271 | 5,810 | 188 | 9,588 D | 34.7% | 53.5% | 11.4% |
| 147,375 | SONOMA | 78,059 | 38,088 | 33,587 | 5,875 | 509 | 4,501 R | 48.8% | 43.0% | 7.5% |
| 157,294 | STANISLAUS | 65,063 | 29,573 | 31,316 | 3,973 | 201 | 1,743 D | 45.5% | 48.1% | 6.1% |
| 33,380 | SUTTER | 14,545 | 8,665 | 4,624 | 1,228 | 28 | 4,041 R | 59.6% | 31.8% | 8.4% |
| 25,305 | TEHAMA | 10,999 | 5,198 | 4,565 | 1,216 | 20 | 633 R | 47.3% | 41.5% | 11.1% |
| 9,706 | TRINITY | 3,307 | 1,426 | 1,433 | 432 | 16 | 7 D | 43.1% | 43.3% | 13.1% |
| 168,403 | TULARE | 56,189 | 29,314 | 22,180 | 4,580 | 115 | 7,134 R | 52.2% | 39.5% | 8.2% |
| 14,404 | TUOLUMNE | 9,119 | 4,330 | 3,913 | 865 | 11 | 417 R | 47.5% | 42.9% | 9.5% |
| 199,138 | VENTURA | 116,261 | 59,705 | 47,794 | 8,234 | 528 | 11,911 R | 51.4% | 41.1% | 7.1% |
| 65,727 | YOLO | 28,960 | 11,123 | 15,833 | 1,742 | 262 | 4,710 D | 38.4% | 54.7% | 6.0% |
| 33,859 | YUBA | 11,150 | 5,371 | 4,461 | 1,296 | 22 | 910 R | 48.2% | 40.0% | 11.6% |
| 15,717,204 | TOTAL | 7,251,587 | 3,467,664 | 3,244,318 | 487,270 | 52,335 | 223,346 R | 47.8% | 44.7% | 6.7% |

# CALIFORNIA

## PRESIDENT 1964

| 1960 Census Population | County | Total Vote | Republican | Democratic | Other | Rep.-Dem. Plurality | Percentage | | | |
|---|---|---|---|---|---|---|---|---|---|---|
| | | | | | | | Total Vote | | Major Vote | |
| | | | | | | | Rep. | Dem. | Rep. | Dem. |
| 905,670 | ALAMEDA | 427,340 | 142,998 | 283,833 | 509 | 140,835 D | 33.5% | 66.4% | 33.5% | 66.5% |
| 397 | ALPINE | 215 | 124 | 91 | | 33 R | 57.7% | 42.3% | 57.7% | 42.3% |
| 9,990 | AMADOR | 5,098 | 1,682 | 3,410 | 6 | 1,728 D | 33.0% | 66.9% | 33.0% | 67.0% |
| 62,030 | BUTTE | 40,419 | 19,574 | 20,831 | 14 | 1,257 D | 48.4% | 51.5% | 48.4% | 51.6% |
| 10,289 | CALAVERAS | 5,397 | 2,244 | 3,145 | 8 | 901 D | 41.6% | 58.3% | 41.6% | 58.4% |
| 12,075 | COLUSA | 4,606 | 1,811 | 2,790 | 5 | 979 D | 39.3% | 60.6% | 39.4% | 60.6% |
| 409,030 | CONTRA COSTA | 178,245 | 65,011 | 113,071 | 163 | 48,060 D | 36.5% | 63.4% | 36.5% | 63.5% |
| 17,771 | DEL NORTE | 5,727 | 2,075 | 3,652 | | 1,577 D | 36.2% | 63.8% | 36.2% | 63.8% |
| 29,390 | EL DORADO | 14,610 | 5,775 | 8,810 | 25 | 3,035 D | 39.5% | 60.3% | 39.6% | 60.4% |
| 365,945 | FRESNO | 136,308 | 46,792 | 89,375 | 141 | 42,583 D | 34.3% | 65.6% | 34.4% | 65.6% |
| 17,245 | GLENN | 7,290 | 3,351 | 3,937 | 2 | 586 D | 46.0% | 54.0% | 46.0% | 54.0% |
| 104,892 | HUMBOLDT | 38,499 | 12,909 | 25,515 | 75 | 12,606 D | 33.5% | 66.3% | 33.6% | 66.4% |
| 72,105 | IMPERIAL | 21,492 | 10,330 | 11,143 | 19 | 813 D | 48.1% | 51.8% | 48.1% | 51.9% |
| 11,684 | INYO | 5,915 | 2,751 | 3,161 | 3 | 410 D | 46.5% | 53.4% | 46.5% | 53.5% |
| 291,984 | KERN | 109,308 | 45,014 | 64,174 | 120 | 19,160 D | 41.2% | 58.7% | 41.2% | 58.8% |
| 49,954 | KINGS | 18,840 | 5,753 | 13,073 | 14 | 7,320 D | 30.5% | 69.4% | 30.6% | 69.4% |
| 13,786 | LAKE | 8,302 | 3,616 | 4,680 | 6 | 1,064 D | 43.6% | 56.4% | 43.6% | 56.4% |
| 13,597 | LASSEN | 6,201 | 2,124 | 4,072 | 5 | 1,948 D | 34.3% | 65.7% | 34.3% | 65.7% |
| 6,038,771 | LOS ANGELES | 2,730,918 | 1,161,067 | 1,568,300 | 1,551 | 407,233 D | 42.5% | 57.4% | 42.5% | 57.5% |
| 60,468 | MADERA | 13,862 | 4,461 | 9,391 | 10 | 4,930 D | 32.2% | 67.7% | 32.2% | 67.8% |
| 146,820 | MARIN | 75,364 | 28,682 | 46,462 | 220 | 17,780 D | 38.1% | 61.7% | 38.2% | 61.8% |
| 5,064 | MARIPOSA | 2,968 | 1,264 | 1,704 | | 440 D | 42.6% | 57.4% | 42.6% | 57.4% |
| 51,059 | MENDOCINO | 18,227 | 6,322 | 11,869 | 36 | 5,547 D | 34.7% | 65.1% | 34.8% | 65.2% |
| 90,446 | MERCED | 28,269 | 8,814 | 19,431 | 24 | 10,617 D | 31.2% | 68.7% | 31.2% | 68.8% |
| 8,308 | MODOC | 3,358 | 1,386 | 1,972 | | 586 D | 41.3% | 58.7% | 41.3% | 58.7% |
| 2,213 | MONO | 1,688 | 850 | 666 | | 184 R | 50.4% | 39.5% | 56.1% | 43.9% |
| 198,351 | MONTEREY | 64,735 | 24,579 | 40,093 | 172 | 15,514 D | 38.0% | 61.9% | 38.0% | 62.0% |
| 65,890 | NAPA | 31,169 | 11,567 | 19,580 | 63 | 8,013 D | 37.1% | 62.8% | 37.1% | 62.9% |
| 20,911 | NEVADA | 11,726 | 4,899 | 6,397 | 22 | 1,498 D | 41.8% | 54.6% | 43.4% | 56.6% |
| 703,925 | ORANGE | 400,766 | 224,196 | 176,539 | 430 | 47,657 R | 55.9% | 44.1% | 55.9% | 44.1% |
| 56,998 | PLACER | 27,653 | 9,389 | 18,256 | 31 | 8,867 D | 34.0% | 66.0% | 34.0% | 66.0% |
| 11,620 | PLUMAS | 5,800 | 1,686 | 4,019 | 8 | 2,333 D | 29.1% | 69.3% | 29.6% | 70.4% |
| 306,191 | RIVERSIDE | 142,025 | 61,165 | 80,528 | 95 | 19,363 D | 43.1% | 56.7% | 43.2% | 56.8% |
| 502,778 | SACRAMENTO | 227,553 | 77,871 | 149,668 | 332 | 71,797 D | 34.2% | 65.8% | 34.2% | 65.8% |
| 15,396 | SAN BENITO | 6,466 | 2,444 | 3,779 | 14 | 1,335 D | 37.8% | 58.4% | 39.3% | 60.7% |
| 503,591 | SAN BERNARDINO | 215,190 | 92,145 | 123,012 | 243 | 30,867 D | 42.8% | 57.2% | 42.8% | 57.2% |
| 1,033,011 | SAN DIEGO | 426,409 | 214,445 | 211,808 | 33 | 2,637 R | 50.3% | 49.7% | 50.3% | 49.7% |
| 742,855 | SAN FRANCISCO | 323,835 | 92,994 | 230,758 | 156 | 137,764 D | 28.7% | 71.3% | 28.7% | 71.3% |
| 249,989 | SAN JOAQUIN | 95,784 | 36,546 | 59,210 | 83 | 22,664 D | 38.2% | 61.8% | 38.2% | 61.8% |
| 81,044 | SAN LUIS OBISPO | 37,455 | 14,906 | 22,252 | 28 | 7,346 D | 39.8% | 59.4% | 40.1% | 59.9% |
| 444,387 | SAN MATEO | 218,979 | 77,916 | 140,978 | 297 | 63,062 D | 35.6% | 64.4% | 35.6% | 64.4% |
| 168,962 | SANTA BARBARA | 87,259 | 38,020 | 48,381 | 85 | 10,361 D | 43.6% | 55.4% | 44.0% | 56.0% |
| 642,315 | SANTA CLARA | 319,763 | 117,420 | 202,249 | 858 | 84,829 D | 36.7% | 63.2% | 36.7% | 63.3% |
| 84,219 | SANTA CRUZ | 45,580 | 18,836 | 26,714 | 94 | 7,878 D | 41.3% | 58.6% | 41.4% | 58.6% |
| 59,468 | SHASTA | 28,320 | 9,178 | 19,142 | 30 | 9,964 D | 32.4% | 67.6% | 32.4% | 67.6% |
| 2,247 | SIERRA | 1,264 | 413 | 828 | | 415 D | 32.7% | 65.5% | 33.3% | 66.7% |
| 32,885 | SISKIYOU | 14,359 | 5,186 | 9,126 | 23 | 3,940 D | 36.1% | 63.6% | 36.2% | 63.8% |
| 134,597 | SOLANO | 50,298 | 15,263 | 34,930 | 47 | 19,667 D | 30.3% | 69.4% | 30.4% | 69.6% |
| 147,375 | SONOMA | 72,108 | 27,677 | 44,354 | 105 | 16,677 D | 38.4% | 61.5% | 38.4% | 61.6% |
| 157,294 | STANISLAUS | 65,067 | 21,973 | 43,078 | 77 | 21,105 D | 33.8% | 66.2% | 33.8% | 66.2% |
| 33,380 | SUTTER | 14,038 | 7,241 | 6,787 | 16 | 454 R | 51.6% | 48.3% | 51.6% | 48.4% |
| 25,305 | TEHAMA | 11,469 | 4,529 | 6,928 | 10 | 2,399 D | 39.5% | 60.4% | 39.5% | 60.5% |
| 9,706 | TRINITY | 3,478 | 1,252 | 2,175 | 12 | 923 D | 36.0% | 62.5% | 36.5% | 63.5% |
| 168,403 | TULARE | 56,521 | 22,527 | 33,974 | 51 | 11,447 D | 39.9% | 60.1% | 39.9% | 60.1% |
| 14,404 | TUOLUMNE | 7,969 | 2,861 | 4,939 | 20 | 2,078 D | 35.9% | 62.0% | 36.7% | 63.3% |
| 199,138 | VENTURA | 98,101 | 40,264 | 57,805 | 169 | 17,541 D | 41.0% | 58.9% | 41.1% | 58.9% |
| 65,727 | YOLO | 26,251 | 7,976 | 18,266 | 32 | 10,290 D | 30.4% | 69.6% | 30.4% | 69.6% |
| 33,859 | YUBA | 11,730 | 4,964 | 6,766 | 9 | 1,802 D | 42.3% | 57.7% | 42.3% | 57.7% |
| 15,717,204 | TOTAL | 7,057,586 | 2,879,108 | 4,171,877 | 6,601 | 1,292,769 D | 40.8% | 59.1% | 40.8% | 59.2% |

# CALIFORNIA

## PRESIDENT 1960

| 1960 Census Population | County | Total Vote | Republican | Democratic | Other | Rep.-Dem. Plurality | Percentage Total Vote Rep. | Dem. | Major Vote Rep. | Dem. |
|---|---|---|---|---|---|---|---|---|---|---|
| 905,670 | ALAMEDA | 402,000 | 183,354 | 217,172 | 1,474 | 33,818 D | 45.6% | 54.0% | 45.8% | 54.2% |
| 397 | ALPINE | 172 | 132 | 40 | | 92 R | 76.7% | 23.3% | 76.7% | 23.3% |
| 9,990 | AMADOR | 4,887 | 2,175 | 2,690 | 22 | 515 D | 44.5% | 55.0% | 44.7% | 55.3% |
| 62,030 | BUTTE | 36,175 | 20,838 | 15,163 | 174 | 5,675 R | 57.6% | 41.9% | 57.9% | 42.1% |
| 10,289 | CALAVERAS | 5,361 | 2,820 | 2,509 | 32 | 311 R | 52.6% | 46.8% | 52.9% | 47.1% |
| 12,075 | COLUSA | 4,861 | 2,497 | 2,348 | 16 | 149 R | 51.4% | 48.3% | 51.5% | 48.5% |
| 409,030 | CONTRA COSTA | 177,123 | 82,922 | 93,622 | 579 | 10,700 D | 46.8% | 52.9% | 47.0% | 53.0% |
| 17,771 | DEL NORTE | 6,294 | 3,024 | 3,225 | 45 | 201 D | 48.0% | 51.2% | 48.4% | 51.6% |
| 29,390 | EL DORADO | 12,337 | 6,065 | 6,175 | 97 | 110 D | 49.2% | 50.1% | 49.6% | 50.4% |
| 365,945 | FRESNO | 130,702 | 57,930 | 72,164 | 608 | 14,234 D | 44.3% | 55.2% | 44.5% | 55.5% |
| 17,245 | GLENN | 7,356 | 3,911 | 3,410 | 35 | 501 R | 53.2% | 46.4% | 53.4% | 46.6% |
| 104,892 | HUMBOLDT | 38,691 | 18,074 | 20,391 | 226 | 2,317 D | 46.7% | 52.7% | 47.0% | 53.0% |
| 72,105 | IMPERIAL | 19,806 | 10,606 | 9,119 | 81 | 1,487 R | 53.5% | 46.0% | 53.8% | 46.2% |
| 11,684 | INYO | 5,420 | 2,962 | 2,443 | 15 | 519 R | 54.6% | 45.1% | 54.8% | 45.2% |
| 291,984 | KERN | 104,705 | 52,800 | 51,440 | 465 | 1,360 R | 50.4% | 49.1% | 50.7% | 49.3% |
| 49,954 | KINGS | 16,522 | 6,991 | 9,439 | 92 | 2,448 D | 42.3% | 57.1% | 42.6% | 57.4% |
| 13,786 | LAKE | 7,109 | 4,176 | 2,897 | 36 | 1,279 R | 58.7% | 40.8% | 59.0% | 41.0% |
| 13,597 | LASSEN | 5,877 | 2,365 | 3,472 | 40 | 1,107 D | 40.2% | 59.1% | 40.5% | 59.5% |
| 6,038,771 | LOS ANGELES | 2,634,499 | 1,302,661 | 1,323,818 | 8,020 | 21,157 D | 49.4% | 50.2% | 49.6% | 50.4% |
| 60,468 | MADERA | 14,057 | 5,869 | 8,126 | 62 | 2,257 D | 41.8% | 57.8% | 41.9% | 58.1% |
| 146,820 | MARIN | 65,665 | 37,620 | 27,888 | 157 | 9,732 R | 57.3% | 42.5% | 57.4% | 42.6% |
| 5,064 | MARIPOSA | 2,963 | 1,599 | 1,338 | 26 | 261 R | 54.0% | 45.2% | 54.4% | 45.6% |
| 51,059 | MENDOCINO | 18,871 | 9,301 | 9,476 | 94 | 175 D | 49.3% | 50.2% | 49.5% | 50.5% |
| 90,446 | MERCED | 27,646 | 11,990 | 15,545 | 111 | 3,555 D | 43.4% | 56.2% | 43.5% | 56.5% |
| 8,308 | MODOC | 3,550 | 1,839 | 1,691 | 20 | 148 R | 51.8% | 47.6% | 52.1% | 47.9% |
| 2,213 | MONO | 1,375 | 912 | 457 | 6 | 455 R | 66.3% | 33.2% | 66.6% | 33.4% |
| 198,351 | MONTEREY | 59,413 | 33,428 | 25,805 | 180 | 7,623 R | 56.3% | 43.4% | 56.4% | 43.6% |
| 65,890 | NAPA | 28,778 | 15,125 | 13,499 | 154 | 1,626 R | 52.6% | 46.9% | 52.8% | 47.2% |
| 20,911 | NEVADA | 10,141 | 5,419 | 4,633 | 89 | 786 R | 53.4% | 45.7% | 53.9% | 46.1% |
| 703,925 | ORANGE | 287,599 | 174,891 | 112,007 | 701 | 62,884 R | 60.8% | 38.9% | 61.0% | 39.0% |
| 56,998 | PLACER | 23,863 | 10,439 | 13,304 | 120 | 2,865 D | 43.7% | 55.8% | 44.0% | 56.0% |
| 11,620 | PLUMAS | 5,378 | 2,015 | 3,333 | 30 | 1,318 D | 37.5% | 62.0% | 37.7% | 62.3% |
| 306,191 | RIVERSIDE | 117,276 | 65,855 | 50,877 | 544 | 14,978 R | 56.2% | 43.4% | 56.4% | 43.6% |
| 502,778 | SACRAMENTO | 194,756 | 84,252 | 109,695 | 809 | 25,443 D | 43.3% | 56.3% | 43.4% | 56.6% |
| 15,396 | SAN BENITO | 5,945 | 3,056 | 2,876 | 13 | 180 R | 51.4% | 48.4% | 51.5% | 48.5% |
| 503,591 | SAN BERNARDINO | 191,313 | 99,481 | 90,888 | 944 | 8,593 R | 52.0% | 47.5% | 52.3% | 47.7% |
| 1,033,011 | SAN DIEGO | 395,421 | 223,056 | 171,259 | 1,106 | 51,797 R | 56.4% | 43.3% | 56.6% | 43.4% |
| 742,855 | SAN FRANCISCO | 342,219 | 143,001 | 197,734 | 1,484 | 54,733 D | 41.8% | 57.8% | 42.0% | 58.0% |
| 249,989 | SAN JOAQUIN | 91,657 | 48,441 | 42,855 | 361 | 5,586 R | 52.9% | 46.8% | 53.1% | 46.9% |
| 81,044 | SAN LUIS OBISPO | 33,055 | 17,862 | 14,975 | 218 | 2,887 R | 54.0% | 45.3% | 54.4% | 45.6% |
| 444,387 | SAN MATEO | 202,252 | 104,570 | 97,154 | 528 | 7,416 R | 51.7% | 48.0% | 51.8% | 48.2% |
| 168,962 | SANTA BARBARA | 68,402 | 38,805 | 29,409 | 188 | 9,396 R | 56.7% | 43.0% | 56.9% | 43.1% |
| 642,315 | SANTA CLARA | 250,092 | 131,735 | 117,667 | 690 | 14,068 R | 52.7% | 47.0% | 52.8% | 47.2% |
| 84,219 | SANTA CRUZ | 41,704 | 24,858 | 16,659 | 187 | 8,199 R | 59.6% | 39.9% | 59.9% | 40.1% |
| 59,468 | SHASTA | 24,301 | 9,462 | 14,691 | 148 | 5,229 D | 38.9% | 60.5% | 39.2% | 60.8% |
| 2,247 | SIERRA | 1,231 | 576 | 647 | 8 | 71 D | 46.8% | 52.6% | 47.1% | 52.9% |
| 32,885 | SISKIYOU | 14,620 | 6,279 | 8,245 | 96 | 1,966 D | 42.9% | 56.4% | 43.2% | 56.8% |
| 134,597 | SOLANO | 45,869 | 18,751 | 26,977 | 141 | 8,226 D | 40.9% | 58.8% | 41.0% | 59.0% |
| 147,375 | SONOMA | 64,032 | 34,641 | 29,147 | 244 | 5,494 R | 54.1% | 45.5% | 54.3% | 45.7% |
| 157,294 | STANISLAUS | 60,890 | 30,213 | 30,302 | 375 | 89 D | 49.6% | 49.8% | 49.9% | 50.1% |
| 33,380 | SUTTER | 11,954 | 7,520 | 4,379 | 55 | 3,141 R | 62.9% | 36.6% | 63.2% | 36.8% |
| 25,305 | TEHAMA | 11,052 | 5,522 | 5,483 | 47 | 39 R | 50.0% | 49.6% | 50.2% | 49.8% |
| 9,706 | TRINITY | 3,698 | 1,418 | 2,262 | 18 | 844 D | 38.3% | 61.2% | 38.5% | 61.5% |
| 168,403 | TULARE | 54,582 | 29,456 | 24,887 | 239 | 4,569 R | 54.0% | 45.6% | 54.2% | 45.8% |
| 14,404 | TUOLUMNE | 7,516 | 3,691 | 3,781 | 44 | 90 D | 49.1% | 50.3% | 49.4% | 50.6% |
| 199,138 | VENTURA | 70,723 | 35,074 | 35,334 | 315 | 260 D | 49.6% | 50.0% | 49.8% | 50.2% |
| 65,727 | YOLO | 22,589 | 10,104 | 12,395 | 90 | 2,291 D | 44.7% | 54.9% | 44.9% | 55.1% |
| 33,859 | YUBA | 10,233 | 5,293 | 4,882 | 58 | 411 R | 51.7% | 47.7% | 52.0% | 48.0% |
| 15,717,204 | TOTAL | 6,506,578 | 3,259,722 | 3,224,099 | 22,757 | 35,623 R | 50.1% | 49.6% | 50.3% | 49.7% |

# CALIFORNIA

## ELECTION NOTES

**2004**  Other vote was 50,165 Libertarian (Michael Badnarik); 40,771 Green (David Cobb); 27,607 Peace and Freedom (Leonard Peltier); 26,645 American Independent (Michael Peroutka); 21,213 write-in (Ralph Nader); 82 write-in (John Joseph Kennedy); 49 write-in (John Parker); 8 write-in (James Alexander-Pace); 1 write-in (Anthony Jabin).

**2000**  Other vote was 45,520 Libertarian (Browne); 44,987 Reform (Buchanan); 17,042 American Independent (Phillips); 10,934 Natural Law (Hagelin); 28 write-in (McReynolds); 6 write-in (Kenyon).

**1996**  Other vote was 237,016 Green (Nader); 73,600 Libertarian (Browne); 25,332 Peace and Freedom (Feinland); 21,202 American Independent (Phillips); 15,403 Natural Law (Hagelin); 869 scattered write-in.

**1992**  Other vote was 48,139 Marrou (Libertarian); 18,597 Daniels (Peace and Freedom); 12,711 Phillips (American Independent); 3,077 Gritz (write-in); 836 Hagelin (write-in); 180 LaRouche (write-in); 115 Warren (write-in); 12 Masters (write-in); 149 scattered write-in.

**1988**  Other vote was 70,105 Paul (Libertarian); 31,181 Fulani (Independent); 27,818 Griffin (American Independent); 483 Duke (write-in); 234 McCarthy (write-in); 58 Lewin (write-in); 11 Holmes (write-in) 25 scattered write-in.

**1984**  Other vote was 49,951 Bergland (Libertarian); 39,265 Richards (American Independent); 26,297 Johnson (Peace and Freedom); 16 Serrette (write-in); 366 scattered write-in.  The state-wide total for the other vote column includes these 382 write-in votes not reported by county.

**1980**  Other vote was 739,833 Anderson (Independent); 148,434 Clark (Libertarian); 61,063 Commoner (Independent); 18,116 Smith (Peace and Freedom); 9,856 Rarick (American Independent); 847 Hall (write-in); 231 Pulley (write-in); 87 Greaves (write-in); 36 Bubar (write-in); 15 Griswold (write-in); 26 scattered write-in. The state-wide total for the other vote column includes these 1,242 write-in votes not reported by county.

**1976**  Other vote was 58,412 McCarthy (write-in); 56,388 MacBride (Independent); 51,098 Maddox (American Independent); 41,731 Wright (Peace and Freedom); 17,259 Camejo (Independent); 12,766 Hall (Independent); 4,565 Anderson (write-in); 222 Levin (write-in); 34 Bubar (write-in); 26 Miller (write-in); 14 Taylor (write-in); 74 scattered write-in.

**1972**  Other vote was 232,554 Schmitz (American Independent); 55,167 Spock (Peace and Freedom); 980 Hospers (write-in); 574 Jenness (write-in); 373 Hall (write-in); 197 Fisher (write-in); 53 Munn (write-in); 21 Green (write-in).

**1968**  Wallace on the ballot as American Independent.  Other vote was 27,707 no Presidential candidate indicated but pledged to Peggy Terry for Vice-President (Peace and Freedom); 20,721 McCarthy (write-in); 3,230 Gregory (write-in); 341 Blomen (write-in); 260 Mitchell (write-in); 59 Munn (write-in); 17 Soeters (write-in).

**1964**  Other vote was 489 Hass (write-in); 378 DeBerry (write-in); 305 Munn (write-in); 19 Hensley (write-in); 5,410 scattered write-in.

**1960**  Other vote was 21,706 Decker (Prohibition); 1,051 Hass (write-in).

# COLORADO

## POPULAR VOTE FOR PRESIDENT 1920 TO 2004

| Year | Total Vote | Republican Vote | Republican Candidate | Democratic Vote | Democratic Candidate | Other Vote | Plurality | Percentage Total Vote Rep. | Total Vote Dem. | Major Vote Rep. | Major Vote Dem. |
|------|-----------|------|-----------|------|-----------|------|-----------|------|------|------|------|
| 2004 | 2,130,330 | 1,101,255 | Bush, George W. | 1,001,732 | Kerry, John | 27,343 | 99,523 R | 51.7% | 47.0% | 52.4% | 47.6% |
| 2000 ** | 1,741,368 | 883,748 | Bush, George W. | 738,227 | Gore, Al | 119,393 | 145,521 R | 50.8% | 42.4% | 54.5% | 45.5% |
| 1996 ** | 1,510,704 | 691,848 | Dole, Bob | 671,152 | Clinton, Bill | 147,704 | 20,696 R | 45.8% | 44.4% | 50.8% | 49.2% |
| 1992 ** | 1,569,180 | 562,850 | Bush, George | 629,681 | Clinton, Bill | 376,649 | 66,831 D | 35.9% | 40.1% | 47.2% | 52.8% |
| 1988 | 1,372,394 | 728,177 | Bush, George | 621,453 | Dukakis, Michael S. | 22,764 | 106,724 R | 53.1% | 45.3% | 54.0% | 46.0% |
| 1984 | 1,295,380 | 821,817 | Reagan, Ronald | 454,975 | Mondale, Walter F. | 18,588 | 366,842 R | 63.4% | 35.1% | 64.4% | 35.6% |
| 1980 ** | 1,184,415 | 652,264 | Reagan, Ronald | 367,973 | Carter, Jimmy | 164,178 | 284,291 R | 55.1% | 31.1% | 63.9% | 36.1% |
| 1976 | 1,081,554 | 584,367 | Ford, Gerald R. | 460,353 | Carter, Jimmy | 36,834 | 124,014 R | 54.0% | 42.6% | 55.9% | 44.1% |
| 1972 | 953,884 | 597,189 | Nixon, Richard M. | 329,980 | McGovern, George S. | 26,715 | 267,209 R | 62.6% | 34.6% | 64.4% | 35.6% |
| 1968 | 811,199 | 409,345 | Nixon, Richard M. | 335,174 | Humphrey, Hubert H. | 66,680 | 74,171 R | 50.5% | 41.3% | 55.0% | 45.0% |
| 1964 | 776,986 | 296,767 | Goldwater, Barry M. | 476,024 | Johnson, Lyndon B. | 4,195 | 179,257 D | 38.2% | 61.3% | 38.4% | 61.6% |
| 1960 | 736,236 | 402,242 | Nixon, Richard M. | 330,629 | Kennedy, John F. | 3,365 | 71,613 R | 54.6% | 44.9% | 54.9% | 45.1% |
| 1956 | 657,074 | 394,479 | Eisenhower, Dwight D. | 257,997 | Stevenson, Adlai E. | 4,598 | 136,482 R | 60.0% | 39.3% | 60.5% | 39.5% |
| 1952 | 630,103 | 379,782 | Eisenhower, Dwight D. | 245,504 | Stevenson, Adlai E. | 4,817 | 134,278 R | 60.3% | 39.0% | 60.7% | 39.3% |
| 1948 | 515,237 | 239,714 | Dewey, Thomas E. | 267,288 | Truman, Harry S. | 8,235 | 27,574 D | 46.5% | 51.9% | 47.3% | 52.7% |
| 1944 | 505,039 | 268,731 | Dewey, Thomas E. | 234,331 | Roosevelt, Franklin D. | 1,977 | 34,400 R | 53.2% | 46.4% | 53.4% | 46.6% |
| 1940 | 549,004 | 279,576 | Willkie, Wendell | 265,554 | Roosevelt, Franklin D. | 3,874 | 14,022 R | 50.9% | 48.4% | 51.3% | 48.7% |
| 1936 | 488,685 | 181,267 | Landon, Alfred M. | 295,021 | Roosevelt, Franklin D. | 12,397 | 113,754 D | 37.1% | 60.4% | 38.1% | 61.9% |
| 1932 | 457,696 | 189,617 | Hoover, Herbert C. | 250,877 | Roosevelt, Franklin D. | 17,202 | 61,260 D | 41.4% | 54.8% | 43.0% | 57.0% |
| 1928 | 392,242 | 253,872 | Hoover, Herbert C. | 133,131 | Smith, Alfred E. | 5,239 | 120,741 R | 64.7% | 33.9% | 65.6% | 34.4% |
| 1924 ** | 342,261 | 195,171 | Coolidge, Calvin | 75,238 | Davis, John W. | 71,852 | 119,933 R | 57.0% | 22.0% | 72.2% | 27.8% |
| 1920 | 292,053 | 173,248 | Harding, Warren G. | 104,936 | Cox, James M. | 13,869 | 68,312 R | 59.3% | 35.9% | 62.3% | 37.7% |

In 2000 the other vote column includes 91,434 votes cast for Green (Nader). In 1996 the other vote column includes 99,629 votes cast for Perot. In 1992 the other vote column includes 366,010 votes cast for Perot. In 1980 the other column includes 130,633 votes for Independent (Anderson). In 1924 other vote was 69,946 Progressive; 966 Prohibition; 562 Communist; and 378 Socialist Labor.

## ELECTORAL COLLEGE VOTE 1920 TO 2004

| Year | Total | Republican | Democratic | Other |
|------|-------|-----------|-----------|-------|
| 2004 | 9 | 9 | | |
| 2000 | 8 | 8 | | |
| 1996 | 8 | 8 | | |
| 1992 | 8 | | 8 | |
| 1988 | 8 | 8 | | |
| 1984 | 8 | 8 | | |
| 1980 | 7 | 7 | | |
| 1976 | 7 | 7 | | |
| 1972 | 7 | 7 | | |
| 1968 | 6 | 6 | | |
| 1964 | 6 | | 6 | |
| 1960 | 6 | 6 | | |
| 1956 | 6 | 6 | | |
| 1952 | 6 | 6 | | |
| 1948 | 6 | | 6 | |
| 1944 | 6 | 6 | | |
| 1940 | 6 | 6 | | |
| 1936 | 6 | | 6 | |
| 1932 | 6 | | 6 | |
| 1928 | 6 | 6 | | |
| 1924 | 6 | 6 | | |
| 1920 | 6 | 6 | | |

# COLORADO

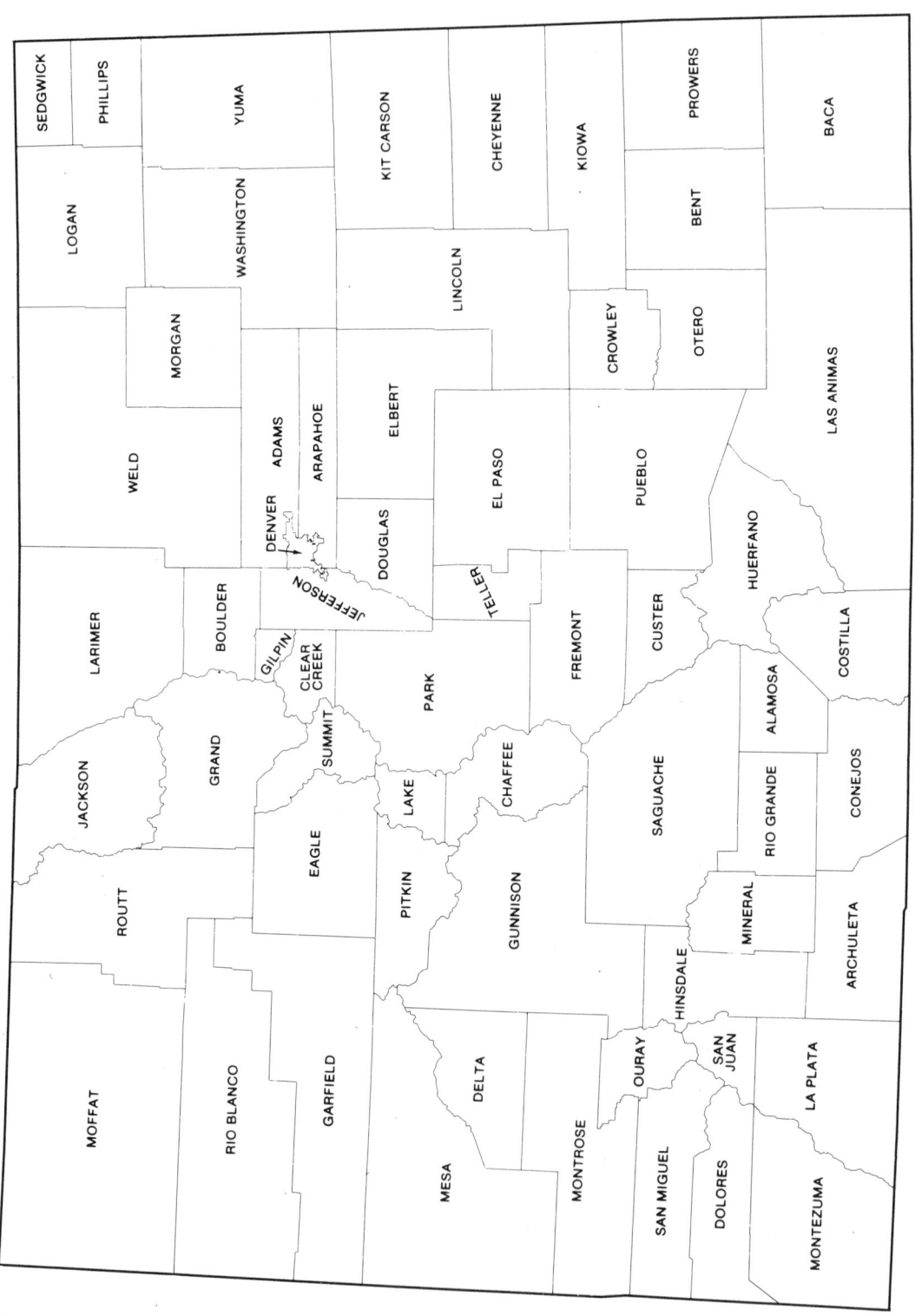

# COLORADO

## PRESIDENT 2004

| 2000 Census Population | County | Total Vote | Republican | Democratic | Other | Rep.-Dem. Plurality | Percentage | | | |
|---|---|---|---|---|---|---|---|---|---|---|
| | | | | | | | Total Vote | | Major Vote | |
| | | | | | | | Rep. | Dem. | Rep. | Dem. |
| 348,618 | ADAMS | 136,677 | 65,912 | 69,122 | 1,643 | 3,210 D | 48.2% | 50.6% | 48.8% | 51.2% |
| 14,966 | ALAMOSA | 6,279 | 3,179 | 3,017 | 83 | 162 R | 50.6% | 48.0% | 51.3% | 48.7% |
| 487,967 | ARAPAHOE | 232,365 | 119,475 | 110,262 | 2,628 | 9,213 R | 51.4% | 47.5% | 52.0% | 48.0% |
| 9,898 | ARCHULETA | 5,839 | 3,601 | 2,141 | 97 | 1,460 R | 61.7% | 36.7% | 62.7% | 37.3% |
| 4,517 | BACA | 2,186 | 1,680 | 483 | 23 | 1,197 R | 76.9% | 22.1% | 77.7% | 22.3% |
| 5,998 | BENT | 2,155 | 1,338 | 785 | 32 | 553 R | 62.1% | 36.4% | 63.0% | 37.0% |
| 269,814 | BOULDER | 159,259 | 51,586 | 105,564 | 2,109 | 53,978 D | 32.4% | 66.3% | 32.8% | 67.2% |
| 38,272 | BROOMFIELD* | 23,235 | 12,007 | 10,935 | 293 | 1,072 R | 51.7% | 47.1% | 52.3% | 47.7% |
| 16,242 | CHAFFEE | 8,770 | 4,875 | 3,766 | 129 | 1,109 R | 55.6% | 42.9% | 56.4% | 43.6% |
| 2,231 | CHEYENNE | 1,134 | 923 | 198 | 13 | 725 R | 81.4% | 17.5% | 82.3% | 17.7% |
| 9,322 | CLEAR CREEK | 5,613 | 2,522 | 2,989 | 102 | 467 D | 44.9% | 53.3% | 45.8% | 54.2% |
| 8,400 | CONEJOS | 3,803 | 1,864 | 1,894 | 45 | 30 D | 49.0% | 49.8% | 49.6% | 50.4% |
| 3,663 | COSTILLA | 1,760 | 566 | 1,170 | 24 | 604 D | 32.2% | 66.5% | 32.6% | 67.4% |
| 5,518 | CROWLEY | 1,493 | 1,006 | 478 | 9 | 528 R | 67.4% | 32.0% | 67.8% | 32.2% |
| 3,503 | CUSTER | 2,428 | 1,657 | 739 | 32 | 918 R | 68.2% | 30.4% | 69.2% | 30.8% |
| 27,834 | DELTA | 14,159 | 9,722 | 4,224 | 213 | 5,498 R | 68.7% | 29.8% | 69.7% | 30.3% |
| 554,636 | DENVER | 238,826 | 69,903 | 166,135 | 2,788 | 96,232 D | 29.3% | 69.6% | 29.6% | 70.4% |
| 1,844 | DOLORES | 1,146 | 785 | 333 | 28 | 452 R | 68.5% | 29.1% | 70.2% | 29.8% |
| 175,766 | DOUGLAS | 121,201 | 80,651 | 39,661 | 889 | 40,990 R | 66.5% | 32.7% | 67.0% | 33.0% |
| 41,659 | EAGLE | 18,511 | 8,533 | 9,744 | 234 | 1,211 D | 46.1% | 52.6% | 46.7% | 53.3% |
| 19,872 | ELBERT | 11,364 | 8,389 | 2,834 | 141 | 5,555 R | 73.8% | 24.9% | 74.7% | 25.3% |
| 516,929 | EL PASO | 241,788 | 161,361 | 77,648 | 2,779 | 83,713 R | 66.7% | 32.1% | 67.5% | 32.5% |
| 46,145 | FREMONT | 18,526 | 12,313 | 5,933 | 280 | 6,380 R | 66.5% | 32.0% | 67.5% | 32.5% |
| 43,791 | GARFIELD | 20,647 | 11,123 | 9,228 | 296 | 1,895 R | 53.9% | 44.7% | 54.7% | 45.3% |
| 4,757 | GILPIN | 3,196 | 1,329 | 1,807 | 60 | 478 D | 41.6% | 56.5% | 42.4% | 57.6% |
| 12,442 | GRAND | 7,609 | 4,260 | 3,243 | 106 | 1,017 R | 56.0% | 42.6% | 56.8% | 43.2% |
| 13,956 | GUNNISON | 8,420 | 3,479 | 4,782 | 159 | 1,303 D | 41.3% | 56.8% | 42.1% | 57.9% |
| 790 | HINSDALE | 602 | 355 | 236 | 11 | 119 R | 59.0% | 39.2% | 60.1% | 39.9% |
| 7,862 | HUERFANO | 3,402 | 1,700 | 1,663 | 39 | 37 R | 50.0% | 48.9% | 50.6% | 49.4% |
| 1,577 | JACKSON | 934 | 710 | 210 | 14 | 500 R | 76.0% | 22.5% | 77.2% | 22.8% |
| 525,507 | JEFFERSON | 271,568 | 140,644 | 126,558 | 4,366 | 14,086 R | 51.8% | 46.6% | 52.6% | 47.4% |
| 1,622 | KIOWA | 892 | 712 | 172 | 8 | 540 R | 79.8% | 19.3% | 80.5% | 19.5% |
| 8,011 | KIT CARSON | 3,502 | 2,721 | 729 | 52 | 1,992 R | 77.7% | 20.8% | 78.9% | 21.1% |
| 7,812 | LAKE | 2,949 | 1,261 | 1,623 | 65 | 362 D | 42.8% | 55.0% | 43.7% | 56.3% |
| 43,941 | LA PLATA | 25,513 | 11,704 | 13,409 | 400 | 1,705 D | 45.9% | 52.6% | 46.6% | 53.4% |
| 251,494 | LARIMER | 146,436 | 75,884 | 68,266 | 2,286 | 7,618 R | 51.8% | 46.6% | 52.6% | 47.4% |
| 15,207 | LAS ANIMAS | 6,592 | 3,196 | 3,300 | 96 | 104 D | 48.5% | 50.1% | 49.2% | 50.8% |
| 6,087 | LINCOLN | 2,337 | 1,819 | 503 | 15 | 1,316 R | 77.8% | 21.5% | 78.3% | 21.7% |
| 20,504 | LOGAN | 8,766 | 6,168 | 2,491 | 107 | 3,677 R | 70.4% | 28.4% | 71.2% | 28.8% |
| 116,255 | MESA | 61,885 | 41,539 | 19,564 | 782 | 21,975 R | 67.1% | 31.6% | 68.0% | 32.0% |
| 831 | MINERAL | 619 | 383 | 227 | 9 | 156 R | 61.9% | 36.7% | 62.8% | 37.2% |
| 13,184 | MOFFAT | 5,725 | 4,247 | 1,355 | 123 | 2,892 R | 74.2% | 23.7% | 75.8% | 24.2% |
| 23,830 | MONTEZUMA | 11,015 | 6,988 | 3,867 | 160 | 3,121 R | 63.4% | 35.1% | 64.4% | 35.6% |
| 33,432 | MONTROSE | 16,219 | 11,218 | 4,776 | 225 | 6,442 R | 69.2% | 29.4% | 70.1% | 29.9% |
| 27,171 | MORGAN | 9,936 | 6,787 | 3,039 | 110 | 3,748 R | 68.3% | 30.6% | 69.1% | 30.9% |
| 20,311 | OTERO | 8,180 | 4,947 | 3,164 | 69 | 1,783 R | 60.5% | 38.7% | 61.0% | 39.0% |
| 3,742 | OURAY | 2,721 | 1,402 | 1,278 | 41 | 124 R | 51.5% | 47.0% | 52.3% | 47.7% |
| 14,523 | PARK | 8,357 | 4,781 | 3,445 | 131 | 1,336 R | 57.2% | 41.2% | 58.1% | 41.9% |
| 4,480 | PHILLIPS | 2,325 | 1,717 | 582 | 26 | 1,135 R | 73.8% | 25.0% | 74.7% | 25.3% |
| 14,872 | PITKIN | 9,256 | 2,784 | 6,335 | 137 | 3,551 D | 30.1% | 68.4% | 30.5% | 69.5% |
| 14,483 | PROWERS | 4,745 | 3,392 | 1,308 | 45 | 2,084 R | 71.5% | 27.6% | 72.2% | 27.8% |
| 141,472 | PUEBLO | 67,187 | 31,117 | 35,369 | 701 | 4,252 D | 46.3% | 52.6% | 46.8% | 53.2% |
| 5,986 | RIO BLANCO | 3,003 | 2,403 | 566 | 34 | 1,837 R | 80.0% | 18.8% | 80.9% | 19.1% |
| 12,413 | RIO GRANDE | 5,526 | 3,448 | 2,006 | 72 | 1,442 R | 62.4% | 36.3% | 63.2% | 36.8% |
| 19,690 | ROUTT | 11,762 | 5,199 | 6,392 | 171 | 1,193 D | 44.2% | 54.3% | 44.9% | 55.1% |
| 5,917 | SAGUACHE | 2,803 | 1,163 | 1,594 | 46 | 431 D | 41.5% | 56.9% | 42.2% | 57.8% |
| 558 | SAN JUAN | 486 | 216 | 253 | 17 | 37 D | 44.4% | 52.1% | 46.1% | 53.9% |
| 6,594 | SAN MIGUEL | 4,019 | 1,079 | 2,876 | 64 | 1,797 D | 26.8% | 71.6% | 27.3% | 72.7% |
| 2,747 | SEDGWICK | 1,360 | 971 | 374 | 15 | 597 R | 71.4% | 27.5% | 72.2% | 27.8% |
| 23,548 | SUMMIT | 13,735 | 5,370 | 8,144 | 221 | 2,774 D | 39.1% | 59.3% | 39.7% | 60.3% |

# COLORADO

## PRESIDENT 2004

| 2000 Census Population | County | Total Vote | Republican | Democratic | Other | Rep.-Dem. Plurality | Percentage | | | |
|---|---|---|---|---|---|---|---|---|---|---|
| | | | | | | | Total Vote | | Major Vote | |
| | | | | | | | Rep. | Dem. | Rep. | Dem. |
| 20,555 | TELLER | 11,842 | 8,094 | 3,556 | 192 | 4,538 R | 68.3% | 30.0% | 69.5% | 30.5% |
| 4,926 | WASHINGTON | 2,530 | 2,050 | 455 | 25 | 1,595 R | 81.0% | 18.0% | 81.8% | 18.2% |
| 180,926 | WELD | 88,653 | 55,591 | 31,868 | 1,194 | 23,723 R | 62.7% | 35.9% | 63.6% | 36.4% |
| 9,841 | YUMA | 4,559 | 3,456 | 1,064 | 39 | 2,392 R | 75.8% | 23.3% | 76.5% | 23.5% |
| 4,301,261 | TOTAL | 2,130,330 | 1,101,255 | 1,001,732 | 27,343 | 99,523 R | 51.7% | 47.0% | 52.4% | 47.6% |

Note: Broomfield County was created effective 2001 out of portions of Adams, Boulder, Jefferson, and Weld counties. The population figures in this table have been adjusted for each county using 2000 census data.

# COLORADO

## PRESIDENT 2000

| 2000 Census Population | County | Total Vote | Republican | Democratic | Green (Nader) | Other | Rep.-Dem. Plurality | Percentage of Total Vote | | |
|---|---|---|---|---|---|---|---|---|---|---|
| | | | | | | | | Rep. | Dem. | Green |
| 363,857 | ADAMS | 107,852 | 47,561 | 54,132 | 4,165 | 1,994 | 6,571 D | 44.1% | 50.2% | 3.9% |
| 14,966 | ALAMOSA | 5,659 | 2,857 | 2,455 | 265 | 82 | 402 R | 50.5% | 43.4% | 4.7% |
| 487,967 | ARAPAHOE | 189,942 | 97,768 | 82,614 | 6,952 | 2,608 | 15,154 R | 51.5% | 43.5% | 3.7% |
| 9,898 | ARCHULETA | 4,758 | 2,988 | 1,432 | 265 | 73 | 1,556 R | 62.8% | 30.1% | 5.6% |
| 4,517 | BACA | 2,278 | 1,663 | 531 | 47 | 37 | 1,132 R | 73.0% | 23.3% | 2.1% |
| 5,998 | BENT | 1,963 | 1,096 | 783 | 44 | 40 | 313 R | 55.8% | 39.9% | 2.2% |
| 291,288 | BOULDER | 139,626 | 50,873 | 69,983 | 16,498 | 2,272 | 19,110 D | 36.4% | 50.1% | 11.8% |
| 16,242 | CHAFFEE | 7,610 | 4,300 | 2,768 | 459 | 83 | 1,532 R | 56.5% | 36.4% | 6.0% |
| 2,231 | CHEYENNE | 1,212 | 957 | 209 | 22 | 24 | 748 R | 79.0% | 17.2% | 1.8% |
| 9,322 | CLEAR CREEK | 4,924 | 2,247 | 2,188 | 354 | 135 | 59 R | 45.6% | 44.4% | 7.2% |
| 8,400 | CONEJOS | 3,671 | 1,772 | 1,749 | 79 | 71 | 23 R | 48.3% | 47.6% | 2.2% |
| 3,663 | COSTILLA | 1,648 | 504 | 1,054 | 71 | 19 | 550 D | 30.6% | 64.0% | 4.3% |
| 5,518 | CROWLEY | 1,445 | 855 | 511 | 28 | 51 | 344 R | 59.2% | 35.4% | 1.9% |
| 3,503 | CUSTER | 2,111 | 1,451 | 507 | 100 | 53 | 944 R | 68.7% | 24.0% | 4.7% |
| 27,834 | DELTA | 12,686 | 8,372 | 3,264 | 852 | 198 | 5,108 R | 66.0% | 25.7% | 6.7% |
| 554,636 | DENVER | 198,347 | 61,224 | 122,693 | 11,624 | 2,806 | 61,469 D | 30.9% | 61.9% | 5.9% |
| 1,844 | DOLORES | 1,134 | 741 | 293 | 73 | 27 | 448 R | 65.3% | 25.8% | 6.4% |
| 175,766 | DOUGLAS | 86,225 | 56,007 | 27,076 | 2,230 | 912 | 28,931 R | 65.0% | 31.4% | 2.6% |
| 41,659 | EAGLE | 15,188 | 7,165 | 6,772 | 1,045 | 206 | 393 R | 47.2% | 44.6% | 6.9% |
| 19,872 | ELBERT | 8,965 | 6,151 | 2,326 | 292 | 196 | 3,825 R | 68.6% | 25.9% | 3.3% |
| 516,929 | EL PASO | 200,757 | 128,294 | 61,799 | 7,116 | 3,548 | 66,495 R | 63.9% | 30.8% | 3.5% |
| 46,145 | FREMONT | 16,056 | 9,914 | 5,293 | 516 | 333 | 4,621 R | 61.7% | 33.0% | 3.2% |
| 43,791 | GARFIELD | 17,104 | 9,103 | 6,087 | 1,608 | 306 | 3,016 R | 53.2% | 35.6% | 9.4% |
| 4,757 | GILPIN | 2,465 | 1,006 | 1,099 | 276 | 84 | 93 D | 40.8% | 44.6% | 11.2% |
| 12,442 | GRAND | 6,353 | 3,570 | 2,308 | 366 | 109 | 1,262 R | 56.2% | 36.3% | 5.8% |
| 13,956 | GUNNISON | 7,236 | 3,128 | 3,059 | 927 | 122 | 69 R | 43.2% | 42.3% | 12.8% |
| 790 | HINSDALE | 566 | 316 | 188 | 51 | 11 | 128 R | 55.8% | 33.2% | 9.0% |
| 7,862 | HUERFANO | 3,174 | 1,466 | 1,495 | 169 | 44 | 29 D | 46.2% | 47.1% | 5.3% |
| 1,577 | JACKSON | 925 | 682 | 173 | 40 | 30 | 509 R | 73.7% | 18.7% | 4.3% |
| 527,056 | JEFFERSON | 235,491 | 120,138 | 100,970 | 10,336 | 4,047 | 19,168 R | 51.0% | 42.9% | 4.4% |
| 1,622 | KIOWA | 968 | 728 | 211 | 13 | 16 | 517 R | 75.2% | 21.8% | 1.3% |
| 8,011 | KIT CARSON | 3,458 | 2,542 | 809 | 58 | 49 | 1,733 R | 73.5% | 23.4% | 1.7% |
| 7,812 | LAKE | 2,628 | 1,056 | 1,296 | 213 | 63 | 240 D | 40.2% | 49.3% | 8.1% |
| 43,941 | LA PLATA | 20,490 | 9,993 | 7,864 | 2,378 | 255 | 2,129 R | 48.8% | 38.4% | 11.6% |
| 251,494 | LARIMER | 118,537 | 62,429 | 46,055 | 8,194 | 1,859 | 16,374 R | 52.7% | 38.9% | 6.9% |
| 15,207 | LAS ANIMAS | 6,094 | 2,569 | 3,243 | 199 | 83 | 674 D | 42.2% | 53.2% | 3.3% |
| 6,087 | LINCOLN | 2,199 | 1,630 | 510 | 27 | 32 | 1,120 R | 74.1% | 23.2% | 1.2% |
| 20,504 | LOGAN | 8,096 | 5,531 | 2,296 | 140 | 129 | 3,235 R | 68.3% | 28.4% | 1.7% |
| 116,255 | MESA | 51,054 | 32,396 | 15,465 | 2,235 | 958 | 16,931 R | 63.5% | 30.3% | 4.4% |
| 831 | MINERAL | 486 | 294 | 168 | 19 | 5 | 126 R | 60.5% | 34.6% | 3.9% |
| 13,184 | MOFFAT | 5,337 | 3,840 | 1,223 | 169 | 105 | 2,617 R | 72.0% | 22.9% | 3.2% |
| 23,830 | MONTEZUMA | 9,384 | 6,158 | 2,556 | 530 | 140 | 3,602 R | 65.6% | 27.2% | 5.6% |
| 33,432 | MONTROSE | 14,215 | 9,266 | 4,041 | 656 | 252 | 5,225 R | 65.2% | 28.4% | 4.6% |
| 27,171 | MORGAN | 8,998 | 5,722 | 2,885 | 211 | 180 | 2,837 R | 63.6% | 32.1% | 2.3% |
| 20,311 | OTERO | 7,312 | 4,082 | 2,963 | 138 | 129 | 1,119 R | 55.8% | 40.5% | 1.9% |
| 3,742 | OURAY | 2,233 | 1,279 | 705 | 224 | 25 | 574 R | 57.3% | 31.6% | 10.0% |
| 14,523 | PARK | 6,665 | 3,677 | 2,393 | 404 | 191 | 1,284 R | 55.2% | 35.9% | 6.1% |
| 4,480 | PHILLIPS | 2,223 | 1,576 | 564 | 48 | 35 | 1,012 R | 70.9% | 25.4% | 2.2% |
| 14,872 | PITKIN | 7,800 | 2,565 | 4,137 | 1,013 | 85 | 1,572 D | 32.9% | 53.0% | 13.0% |
| 14,483 | PROWERS | 4,524 | 3,026 | 1,361 | 79 | 58 | 1,665 R | 66.9% | 30.1% | 1.7% |
| 141,472 | PUEBLO | 53,946 | 22,827 | 28,888 | 1,520 | 711 | 6,061 D | 42.3% | 53.5% | 2.8% |
| 5,986 | RIO BLANCO | 2,855 | 2,185 | 543 | 85 | 42 | 1,642 R | 76.5% | 19.0% | 3.0% |
| 12,413 | RIO GRANDE | 5,075 | 3,111 | 1,707 | 179 | 78 | 1,404 R | 61.3% | 33.6% | 3.5% |
| 19,690 | ROUTT | 9,638 | 4,472 | 4,208 | 820 | 138 | 264 R | 46.4% | 43.7% | 8.5% |
| 5,917 | SAGUACHE | 2,529 | 1,078 | 1,145 | 261 | 45 | 67 D | 42.6% | 45.3% | 10.3% |
| 558 | SAN JUAN | 436 | 210 | 149 | 58 | 19 | 61 R | 48.2% | 34.2% | 13.3% |
| 6,594 | SAN MIGUEL | 3,255 | 1,043 | 1,598 | 560 | 54 | 555 D | 32.0% | 49.1% | 17.2% |
| 2,747 | SEDGWICK | 1,303 | 877 | 384 | 25 | 17 | 493 R | 67.3% | 29.5% | 1.9% |
| 23,548 | SUMMIT | 11,068 | 4,497 | 5,304 | 1,131 | 136 | 807 D | 40.6% | 47.9% | 10.2% |
| 20,555 | TELLER | 9,847 | 6,477 | 2,750 | 429 | 191 | 3,727 R | 65.8% | 27.9% | 4.4% |

# COLORADO

## PRESIDENT 2000

| 2000 Census Population | County | Total Vote | Republican | Democratic | Green (Nader) | Other | Rep.-Dem. Plurality | Percentage of Total Vote | | |
|---|---|---|---|---|---|---|---|---|---|---|
| | | | | | | | | Rep. | Dem. | Green |
| 4,926 | WASHINGTON | 2,445 | 1,878 | 477 | 50 | 40 | 1,401 R | 76.8% | 19.5% | 2.0% |
| 180,936 | WELD | 64,541 | 37,409 | 23,436 | 2,438 | 1,258 | 13,973 R | 58.0% | 36.3% | 3.8% |
| 9,841 | YUMA | 4,358 | 3,156 | 1,082 | 60 | 60 | 2,074 R | 72.4% | 24.8% | 1.4% |
| 4,301,261 | TOTAL | 1,741,368 | 883,748 | 738,227 | 91,434 | 27,959 | 145,521 R | 50.8% | 42.4% | 5.3% |

# COLORADO

## PRESIDENT 1996

| 1995 Census Pop. Est. | County | Total Vote | Republican | Democratic | Reform (Perot) | Other | Rep.-Dem. Plurality | Percentage of Total Vote | | |
|---|---|---|---|---|---|---|---|---|---|---|
| | | | | | | | | Rep. | Dem. | Reform |
| 303,297 | ADAMS | 94,214 | 36,666 | 48,314 | 7,206 | 2,028 | 11,648 D | 38.9% | 51.3% | 7.6% |
| 14,215 | ALAMOSA | 4,943 | 2,038 | 2,330 | 437 | 138 | 292 D | 41.2% | 47.1% | 8.8% |
| 449,103 | ARAPAHOE | 162,996 | 82,778 | 68,306 | 8,476 | 3,436 | 14,472 R | 50.8% | 41.9% | 5.2% |
| 7,100 | ARCHULETA | 3,437 | 1,963 | 997 | 360 | 117 | 966 R | 57.1% | 29.0% | 10.5% |
| 4,384 | BACA | 2,219 | 1,321 | 659 | 203 | 36 | 662 R | 59.5% | 29.7% | 9.1% |
| 5,518 | BENT | 2,199 | 917 | 1,046 | 209 | 27 | 129 D | 41.7% | 47.6% | 9.5% |
| 253,850 | BOULDER | 121,354 | 41,922 | 63,316 | 6,840 | 9,276 | 21,394 D | 34.5% | 52.2% | 5.6% |
| 14,413 | CHAFFEE | 6,515 | 3,052 | 2,768 | 538 | 157 | 284 R | 46.8% | 42.5% | 8.3% |
| 2,312 | CHEYENNE | 1,176 | 739 | 328 | 91 | 18 | 411 R | 62.8% | 27.9% | 7.7% |
| 8,745 | CLEAR CREEK | 4,160 | 1,746 | 1,863 | 365 | 186 | 117 D | 42.0% | 44.8% | 8.8% |
| 7,807 | CONEJOS | 3,186 | 1,149 | 1,726 | 245 | 66 | 577 D | 36.1% | 54.2% | 7.7% |
| 3,384 | COSTILLA | 1,641 | 333 | 1,168 | 112 | 28 | 835 D | 20.3% | 71.2% | 6.8% |
| 4,303 | CROWLEY | 1,371 | 680 | 559 | 114 | 18 | 121 R | 49.6% | 40.8% | 8.3% |
| 2,702 | CUSTER | 1,562 | 920 | 412 | 164 | 66 | 508 R | 58.9% | 26.4% | 10.5% |
| 25,077 | DELTA | 11,100 | 6,047 | 3,584 | 1,060 | 409 | 2,463 R | 54.5% | 32.3% | 9.5% |
| 494,462 | DENVER | 194,814 | 58,529 | 120,312 | 8,777 | 7,196 | 61,783 D | 30.0% | 61.8% | 4.5% |
| 1,588 | DOLORES | 807 | 417 | 276 | 95 | 19 | 141 R | 51.7% | 34.2% | 11.8% |
| 99,577 | DOUGLAS | 51,975 | 32,120 | 16,232 | 2,662 | 961 | 15,888 R | 61.8% | 31.2% | 5.1% |
| 28,844 | EAGLE | 11,341 | 4,637 | 5,094 | 1,193 | 417 | 457 D | 40.9% | 44.9% | 10.5% |
| 14,565 | ELBERT | 6,758 | 4,125 | 1,894 | 507 | 232 | 2,231 R | 61.0% | 28.0% | 7.5% |
| 465,800 | EL PASO | 173,441 | 102,403 | 55,822 | 11,175 | 4,041 | 46,581 R | 59.0% | 32.2% | 6.4% |
| 39,794 | FREMONT | 14,513 | 7,437 | 5,344 | 1,438 | 294 | 2,093 R | 51.2% | 36.8% | 9.9% |
| 35,338 | GARFIELD | 14,138 | 6,281 | 5,722 | 1,562 | 573 | 559 R | 44.4% | 40.5% | 11.0% |
| 3,576 | GILPIN | 1,789 | 682 | 799 | 184 | 124 | 117 D | 38.1% | 44.7% | 10.3% |
| 9,188 | GRAND | 4,890 | 2,264 | 2,012 | 473 | 141 | 252 R | 46.3% | 41.1% | 9.7% |
| 11,931 | GUNNISON | 6,021 | 2,230 | 2,812 | 570 | 409 | 582 D | 37.0% | 46.7% | 9.5% |
| 648 | HINSDALE | 547 | 289 | 185 | 56 | 17 | 104 R | 52.8% | 33.8% | 10.2% |
| 6,356 | HUERFANO | 2,776 | 996 | 1,483 | 210 | 87 | 487 D | 35.9% | 53.4% | 7.6% |
| 1,537 | JACKSON | 833 | 486 | 222 | 107 | 18 | 264 R | 58.3% | 26.7% | 12.8% |
| 484,869 | JEFFERSON | 209,723 | 101,517 | 89,494 | 12,967 | 5,745 | 12,023 R | 48.4% | 42.7% | 6.2% |
| 1,627 | KIOWA | 886 | 549 | 246 | 74 | 17 | 303 R | 62.0% | 27.8% | 8.4% |
| 7,301 | KIT CARSON | 3,432 | 2,068 | 1,073 | 235 | 56 | 995 R | 60.3% | 31.3% | 6.8% |
| 6,296 | LAKE | 2,450 | 728 | 1,338 | 274 | 110 | 610 D | 29.7% | 54.6% | 11.2% |
| 38,314 | LA PLATA | 17,321 | 8,057 | 6,509 | 1,403 | 1,352 | 1,548 R | 46.5% | 37.6% | 8.1% |
| 217,215 | LARIMER | 97,450 | 45,935 | 40,965 | 6,823 | 3,727 | 4,970 R | 47.1% | 42.0% | 7.0% |
| 14,268 | LAS ANIMAS | 6,042 | 1,905 | 3,611 | 427 | 99 | 1,706 D | 31.5% | 59.8% | 7.1% |
| 5,602 | LINCOLN | 2,203 | 1,272 | 729 | 164 | 38 | 543 R | 57.7% | 33.1% | 7.4% |
| 17,869 | LOGAN | 7,586 | 4,032 | 2,765 | 609 | 180 | 1,267 R | 53.2% | 36.4% | 8.0% |
| 106,548 | MESA | 46,612 | 24,761 | 17,114 | 3,707 | 1,030 | 7,647 R | 53.1% | 36.7% | 8.0% |
| 634 | MINERAL | 447 | 179 | 192 | 69 | 7 | 13 D | 40.0% | 43.0% | 15.4% |
| 12,136 | MOFFAT | 4,836 | 2,466 | 1,635 | 649 | 86 | 831 R | 51.0% | 33.8% | 13.4% |
| 21,591 | MONTEZUMA | 7,831 | 4,175 | 2,578 | 827 | 251 | 1,597 R | 53.3% | 32.9% | 10.6% |
| 28,829 | MONTROSE | 12,239 | 6,730 | 4,019 | 1,187 | 303 | 2,711 R | 55.0% | 32.8% | 9.7% |
| 23,729 | MORGAN | 8,707 | 4,557 | 3,347 | 687 | 116 | 1,210 R | 52.3% | 38.4% | 7.9% |
| 20,788 | OTERO | 7,437 | 3,356 | 3,386 | 581 | 114 | 30 D | 45.1% | 45.5% | 7.8% |
| 3,033 | OURAY | 1,794 | 984 | 569 | 167 | 74 | 415 R | 54.8% | 31.7% | 9.3% |
| 10,589 | PARK | 5,241 | 2,661 | 1,844 | 534 | 202 | 817 R | 50.8% | 35.2% | 10.2% |
| 4,309 | PHILLIPS | 2,185 | 1,284 | 706 | 156 | 39 | 578 R | 58.8% | 32.3% | 7.1% |
| 13,589 | PITKIN | 6,985 | 1,969 | 3,949 | 535 | 532 | 1,980 D | 28.2% | 56.5% | 7.7% |
| 13,591 | PROWERS | 4,652 | 2,504 | 1,745 | 342 | 61 | 759 R | 53.8% | 37.5% | 7.4% |
| 129,759 | PUEBLO | 50,301 | 17,402 | 28,791 | 3,374 | 734 | 11,389 D | 34.6% | 57.2% | 6.7% |
| 6,472 | RIO BLANCO | 2,715 | 1,697 | 731 | 243 | 44 | 966 R | 62.5% | 26.9% | 9.0% |
| 11,262 | RIO GRANDE | 4,301 | 2,129 | 1,720 | 379 | 73 | 409 R | 49.5% | 40.0% | 8.8% |
| 16,709 | ROUTT | 7,837 | 3,019 | 3,660 | 859 | 299 | 641 D | 38.5% | 46.7% | 11.0% |
| 5,514 | SAGUACHE | 1,952 | 712 | 969 | 160 | 111 | 257 D | 36.5% | 49.6% | 8.2% |
| 546 | SAN JUAN | 370 | 153 | 133 | 50 | 34 | 20 R | 41.4% | 35.9% | 13.5% |
| 4,929 | SAN MIGUEL | 2,743 | 773 | 1,535 | 231 | 204 | 762 D | 28.2% | 56.0% | 8.4% |
| 2,606 | SEDGWICK | 1,357 | 715 | 519 | 101 | 22 | 196 R | 52.7% | 38.2% | 7.4% |
| 17,204 | SUMMIT | 8,419 | 3,261 | 3,970 | 823 | 365 | 709 D | 38.7% | 47.2% | 9.8% |
| 17,478 | TELLER | 7,695 | 4,458 | 2,312 | 707 | 218 | 2,146 R | 57.9% | 30.0% | 9.2% |

152

# COLORADO

## PRESIDENT 1996

| 1995 Census Pop. Est. | County | Total Vote | Republican | Democratic | Reform (Perot) | Other | Rep.-Dem. Plurality | Percentage of Total Vote | | |
|---|---|---|---|---|---|---|---|---|---|---|
| | | | | | | | | Rep. | Dem. | Reform |
| 4,687 | WASHINGTON | 2,440 | 1,566 | 649 | 190 | 35 | 917 R | 64.2% | 26.6% | 7.8% |
| 148,014 | WELD | 53,390 | 26,518 | 21,325 | 4,347 | 1,200 | 5,193 R | 49.7% | 39.9% | 8.1% |
| 9,264 | YUMA | 4,409 | 2,589 | 1,439 | 319 | 62 | 1,150 R | 58.7% | 32.6% | 7.2% |
| 3,746,585 | TOTAL | 1,510,704 | 691,848 | 671,152 | 99,629 | 48,075 | 20,696 R | 45.8% | 44.4% | 6.6% |

# COLORADO

## PRESIDENT 1992

| 1990 Census Population | County | Total Vote | Republican | Democratic | Perot | Other | Plurality | Percentage Total Vote | | |
|---|---|---|---|---|---|---|---|---|---|---|
| | | | | | | | | Rep. | Dem. | Perot |
| 265,038 | ADAMS | 103,077 | 30,856 | 45,357 | 26,379 | 485 | 14,501 D | 29.9% | 44.0% | 25.6% |
| 13,617 | ALAMOSA | 4,617 | 1,572 | 1,928 | 1,089 | 28 | 356 D | 34.0% | 41.8% | 23.6% |
| 391,511 | ARAPAHOE | 183,935 | 72,221 | 66,607 | 44,363 | 744 | 5,614 R | 39.3% | 36.2% | 24.1% |
| 5,345 | ARCHULETA | 2,816 | 1,242 | 819 | 741 | 14 | 423 R | 44.1% | 29.1% | 26.3% |
| 4,556 | BACA | 2,622 | 1,240 | 726 | 647 | 9 | 514 R | 47.3% | 27.7% | 24.7% |
| 5,048 | BENT | 2,257 | 759 | 985 | 506 | 7 | 226 D | 33.6% | 43.6% | 22.4% |
| 225,339 | BOULDER | 126,771 | 33,553 | 64,567 | 27,762 | 889 | 31,014 D | 26.5% | 50.9% | 21.9% |
| 12,684 | CHAFFEE | 6,282 | 2,419 | 2,284 | 1,549 | 30 | 135 R | 38.5% | 36.4% | 24.7% |
| 2,397 | CHEYENNE | 1,212 | 615 | 301 | 292 | 4 | 314 R | 50.7% | 24.8% | 24.1% |
| 7,619 | CLEAR CREEK | 4,460 | 1,356 | 1,744 | 1,308 | 52 | 388 D | 30.4% | 39.1% | 29.3% |
| 7,453 | CONEJOS | 3,465 | 1,160 | 1,705 | 578 | 22 | 545 D | 33.5% | 49.2% | 16.7% |
| 3,190 | COSTILLA | 1,753 | 366 | 1,180 | 199 | 8 | 814 D | 20.9% | 67.3% | 11.4% |
| 3,946 | CROWLEY | 1,458 | 602 | 570 | 276 | 10 | 32 R | 41.3% | 39.1% | 18.9% |
| 1,926 | CUSTER | 1,375 | 651 | 343 | 368 | 13 | 283 R | 47.3% | 24.9% | 26.8% |
| 20,980 | DELTA | 10,494 | 4,359 | 3,424 | 2,627 | 84 | 935 R | 41.5% | 32.6% | 25.0% |
| 467,610 | DENVER | 217,919 | 55,418 | 121,961 | 37,298 | 3,242 | 66,543 D | 25.4% | 56.0% | 17.1% |
| 1,504 | DOLORES | 846 | 315 | 242 | 285 | 4 | 30 R | 37.2% | 28.6% | 33.7% |
| 60,391 | DOUGLAS | 40,060 | 18,592 | 9,991 | 11,329 | 148 | 7,263 R | 46.4% | 24.9% | 28.3% |
| 21,928 | EAGLE | 10,870 | 3,100 | 3,870 | 3,821 | 79 | 49 D | 28.5% | 35.6% | 35.2% |
| 9,646 | ELBERT | 5,045 | 2,205 | 1,237 | 1,567 | 36 | 638 D | 43.7% | 24.5% | 31.1% |
| 397,014 | EL PASO | 167,169 | 86,044 | 45,827 | 34,346 | 952 | 40,217 R | 51.5% | 27.4% | 20.5% |
| 32,273 | FREMONT | 15,131 | 5,961 | 5,356 | 3,709 | 105 | 605 R | 39.4% | 35.4% | 24.5% |
| 29,974 | GARFIELD | 13,976 | 4,404 | 5,082 | 4,408 | 82 | 674 D | 31.5% | 36.4% | 31.5% |
| 3,070 | GILPIN | 1,759 | 462 | 726 | 545 | 26 | 181 D | 26.3% | 41.3% | 31.0% |
| 7,966 | GRAND | 4,918 | 1,763 | 1,678 | 1,454 | 23 | 85 R | 35.8% | 34.1% | 29.6% |
| 10,273 | GUNNISON | 5,759 | 1,662 | 2,389 | 1,671 | 37 | 718 D | 28.9% | 41.5% | 29.0% |
| 467 | HINSDALE | 476 | 188 | 151 | 136 | 1 | 37 R | 39.5% | 31.7% | 28.6% |
| 6,009 | HUERFANO | 2,313 | 685 | 1,224 | 385 | 19 | 539 D | 29.6% | 52.9% | 16.6% |
| 1,605 | JACKSON | 966 | 422 | 216 | 326 | 2 | 96 R | 43.7% | 22.4% | 33.7% |
| 438,430 | JEFFERSON | 223,203 | 82,705 | 80,834 | 58,404 | 1,260 | 1,871 R | 37.1% | 36.2% | 26.2% |
| 1,688 | KIOWA | 1,030 | 472 | 290 | 267 | 1 | 182 R | 45.8% | 28.2% | 25.9% |
| 7,140 | KIT CARSON | 3,658 | 1,801 | 925 | 919 | 13 | 876 R | 49.2% | 25.3% | 25.1% |
| 6,007 | LAKE | 2,923 | 605 | 1,426 | 863 | 29 | 563 D | 20.7% | 48.8% | 29.5% |
| 32,284 | LA PLATA | 15,613 | 5,522 | 5,913 | 4,083 | 95 | 391 D | 35.4% | 37.9% | 26.2% |
| 186,136 | LARIMER | 99,660 | 35,995 | 38,232 | 24,879 | 554 | 2,237 D | 36.1% | 38.4% | 25.0% |
| 13,765 | LAS ANIMAS | 6,569 | 1,739 | 3,847 | 953 | 30 | 2,108 D | 26.5% | 58.6% | 14.5% |
| 4,529 | LINCOLN | 2,306 | 1,079 | 640 | 581 | 6 | 439 R | 46.8% | 27.8% | 25.2% |
| 17,567 | LOGAN | 8,345 | 3,420 | 2,718 | 2,184 | 23 | 702 R | 41.0% | 32.6% | 26.2% |
| 93,145 | MESA | 44,067 | 18,169 | 15,162 | 10,474 | 262 | 3,007 R | 41.2% | 34.4% | 23.8% |
| 558 | MINERAL | 449 | 159 | 171 | 117 | 2 | 12 D | 35.4% | 38.1% | 26.1% |
| 11,357 | MOFFAT | 5,095 | 1,809 | 1,386 | 1,875 | 25 | 66 P | 35.5% | 27.2% | 36.8% |
| 18,672 | MONTEZUMA | 7,638 | 3,124 | 2,270 | 2,205 | 39 | 854 R | 40.9% | 29.7% | 28.9% |
| 24,423 | MONTROSE | 11,723 | 4,847 | 3,713 | 3,093 | 70 | 1,134 R | 41.3% | 31.7% | 26.4% |
| 21,939 | MORGAN | 8,930 | 3,724 | 2,985 | 2,175 | 46 | 739 R | 41.7% | 33.4% | 24.4% |
| 20,185 | OTERO | 8,313 | 3,120 | 3,485 | 1,590 | 118 | 365 D | 37.5% | 41.9% | 19.1% |
| 2,295 | OURAY | 1,583 | 653 | 461 | 466 | 3 | 187 R | 41.3% | 29.1% | 29.4% |
| 7,174 | PARK | 4,276 | 1,530 | 1,307 | 1,396 | 43 | 134 R | 35.8% | 30.6% | 32.6% |
| 4,189 | PHILLIPS | 2,303 | 1,075 | 692 | 525 | 11 | 383 R | 46.7% | 30.0% | 22.8% |
| 12,661 | PITKIN | 7,469 | 1,686 | 3,820 | 1,907 | 56 | 1,913 D | 22.6% | 51.1% | 25.5% |
| 13,347 | PROWERS | 5,377 | 2,371 | 1,770 | 1,184 | 52 | 601 R | 44.1% | 32.9% | 22.0% |
| 123,051 | PUEBLO | 56,438 | 16,120 | 30,261 | 9,841 | 216 | 14,141 D | 28.6% | 53.6% | 17.4% |
| 5,972 | RIO BLANCO | 2,850 | 1,231 | 778 | 794 | 47 | 437 R | 43.2% | 27.3% | 27.9% |
| 10,770 | RIO GRANDE | 4,533 | 1,927 | 1,541 | 1,043 | 22 | 386 R | 42.5% | 34.0% | 23.0% |
| 14,088 | ROUTT | 8,161 | 2,358 | 3,188 | 2,564 | 51 | 624 D | 28.9% | 39.1% | 31.4% |
| 4,619 | SAGUACHE | 2,174 | 675 | 1,011 | 471 | 17 | 336 D | 31.0% | 46.5% | 21.7% |
| 745 | SAN JUAN | 453 | 118 | 147 | 183 | 5 | 36 P | 26.0% | 32.5% | 40.4% |
| 3,653 | SAN MIGUEL | 2,663 | 628 | 1,380 | 634 | 21 | 746 D | 23.6% | 51.8% | 23.8% |
| 2,690 | SEDGWICK | 1,146 | 447 | 397 | 295 | 7 | 50 R | 39.0% | 34.6% | 25.7% |
| 12,881 | SUMMIT | 8,370 | 2,256 | 3,344 | 2,715 | 55 | 629 D | 27.0% | 40.0% | 32.4% |
| 12,468 | TELLER | 6,914 | 3,050 | 1,873 | 1,927 | 64 | 1,123 R | 44.1% | 27.1% | 27.9% |

# COLORADO

## PRESIDENT 1992

| 1990 Census Population | County | Total Vote | Republican | Democratic | Perot | Other | Plurality | Percentage Total Vote | | |
|---|---|---|---|---|---|---|---|---|---|---|
| | | | | | | | | Rep. | Dem. | Perot |
| 4,812 | WASHINGTON | 2,613 | 1,266 | 660 | 671 | 16 | 595 R | 48.5% | 25.3% | 25.7% |
| 131,821 | WELD | 54,029 | 20,958 | 19,295 | 13,571 | 205 | 1,663 R | 38.8% | 35.7% | 25.1% |
| 8,954 | YUMA | 4,505 | 2,019 | 1,269 | 1,197 | 20 | 750 R | 44.8% | 28.2% | 26.6% |
| 3,294,394 | TOTAL | 1,569,180 | 562,850 | 629,681 | 366,010 | 10,639 | 66,831 D | 35.9% | 40.1% | 23.3% |

# COLORADO

## PRESIDENT 1988

| 1980 Census Population | County | Total Vote | Republican | Democratic | Other | Rep.-Dem. Plurality | Percentage | | | |
|---|---|---|---|---|---|---|---|---|---|---|
| | | | | | | | Total Vote | | Major Vote | |
| | | | | | | | Rep. | Dem. | Rep. | Dem. |
| 245,944 | ADAMS | 94,094 | 43,163 | 49,464 | 1,467 | 6,301 D | 45.9% | 52.6% | 46.6% | 53.4% |
| 11,799 | ALAMOSA | 4,780 | 2,567 | 2,146 | 67 | 421 R | 53.7% | 44.9% | 54.5% | 45.5% |
| 293,621 | ARAPAHOE | 159,245 | 95,926 | 61,113 | 2,206 | 34,813 R | 60.2% | 38.4% | 61.1% | 38.9% |
| 3,664 | ARCHULETA | 2,262 | 1,440 | 795 | 27 | 645 R | 63.7% | 35.1% | 64.4% | 35.6% |
| 5,419 | BACA | 2,556 | 1,670 | 851 | 35 | 819 R | 65.3% | 33.3% | 66.2% | 33.8% |
| 5,945 | BENT | 2,167 | 1,032 | 1,088 | 47 | 56 D | 47.6% | 50.2% | 48.7% | 51.3% |
| 189,625 | BOULDER | 107,223 | 48,174 | 57,265 | 1,784 | 9,091 D | 44.9% | 53.4% | 45.7% | 54.3% |
| 13,227 | CHAFFEE | 5,714 | 3,080 | 2,548 | 86 | 532 R | 53.9% | 44.6% | 54.7% | 45.3% |
| 2,153 | CHEYENNE | 1,186 | 760 | 399 | 27 | 361 R | 64.1% | 33.6% | 65.6% | 34.4% |
| 7,308 | CLEAR CREEK | 3,632 | 1,820 | 1,698 | 114 | 122 R | 50.1% | 46.8% | 51.7% | 48.3% |
| 7,794 | CONEJOS | 3,447 | 1,445 | 1,976 | 26 | 531 D | 41.9% | 57.3% | 42.2% | 57.8% |
| 3,071 | COSTILLA | 1,581 | 454 | 1,120 | 7 | 666 D | 28.7% | 70.8% | 28.8% | 71.2% |
| 2,988 | CROWLEY | 1,500 | 862 | 630 | 8 | 232 R | 57.5% | 42.0% | 57.8% | 42.2% |
| 1,528 | CUSTER | 1,084 | 753 | 310 | 21 | 443 R | 69.5% | 28.6% | 70.8% | 29.2% |
| 21,225 | DELTA | 9,144 | 5,449 | 3,521 | 174 | 1,928 R | 59.6% | 38.5% | 60.7% | 39.3% |
| 492,365 | DENVER | 209,430 | 77,753 | 127,173 | 4,504 | 49,420 D | 37.1% | 60.7% | 37.9% | 62.1% |
| 1,658 | DOLORES | 732 | 488 | 230 | 14 | 258 R | 66.7% | 31.4% | 68.0% | 32.0% |
| 25,153 | DOUGLAS | 24,350 | 17,035 | 6,931 | 384 | 10,104 R | 70.0% | 28.5% | 71.1% | 28.9% |
| 13,320 | EAGLE | 7,809 | 4,366 | 3,314 | 129 | 1,052 R | 55.9% | 42.4% | 56.8% | 43.2% |
| 6,850 | ELBERT | 4,448 | 2,805 | 1,566 | 77 | 1,239 R | 63.1% | 35.2% | 64.2% | 35.8% |
| 309,424 | EL PASO | 138,466 | 96,965 | 39,995 | 1,506 | 56,970 R | 70.0% | 28.9% | 70.8% | 29.2% |
| 28,676 | FREMONT | 13,088 | 7,623 | 5,278 | 187 | 2,345 R | 58.2% | 40.3% | 59.1% | 40.9% |
| 22,514 | GARFIELD | 11,114 | 6,358 | 4,620 | 136 | 1,738 R | 57.2% | 41.6% | 57.9% | 42.1% |
| 2,441 | GILPIN | 1,590 | 728 | 804 | 58 | 76 D | 45.8% | 50.6% | 47.5% | 52.5% |
| 7,475 | GRAND | 3,838 | 2,306 | 1,451 | 81 | 855 R | 60.1% | 37.8% | 61.4% | 38.6% |
| 10,689 | GUNNISON | 4,523 | 2,520 | 1,897 | 106 | 623 R | 55.7% | 41.9% | 57.1% | 42.9% |
| 408 | HINSDALE | 407 | 295 | 111 | 1 | 184 R | 72.5% | 27.3% | 72.7% | 27.3% |
| 6,440 | HUERFANO | 2,971 | 1,079 | 1,876 | 16 | 797 D | 36.3% | 63.1% | 36.5% | 63.5% |
| 1,863 | JACKSON | 891 | 584 | 294 | 13 | 290 R | 65.5% | 33.0% | 66.5% | 33.5% |
| 371,753 | JEFFERSON | 196,511 | 110,820 | 81,824 | 3,867 | 28,996 R | 56.4% | 41.6% | 57.5% | 42.5% |
| 1,936 | KIOWA | 1,053 | 645 | 398 | 10 | 247 R | 61.3% | 37.8% | 61.8% | 38.2% |
| 7,599 | KIT CARSON | 3,512 | 2,262 | 1,196 | 54 | 1,066 R | 64.4% | 34.1% | 65.4% | 34.6% |
| 8,830 | LAKE | 2,543 | 969 | 1,516 | 58 | 547 D | 38.1% | 59.6% | 39.0% | 61.0% |
| 27,424 | LA PLATA | 13,362 | 7,714 | 5,443 | 205 | 2,271 R | 57.7% | 40.7% | 58.6% | 41.4% |
| 149,184 | LARIMER | 83,066 | 45,967 | 35,703 | 1,396 | 10,264 R | 55.3% | 43.0% | 56.3% | 43.7% |
| 14,897 | LAS ANIMAS | 6,331 | 2,162 | 4,075 | 94 | 1,913 D | 34.1% | 64.4% | 34.7% | 65.3% |
| 4,663 | LINCOLN | 2,249 | 1,356 | 874 | 19 | 482 R | 60.3% | 38.9% | 60.8% | 39.2% |
| 19,800 | LOGAN | 7,975 | 4,485 | 3,382 | 108 | 1,103 R | 56.2% | 42.4% | 57.0% | 43.0% |
| 81,530 | MESA | 37,155 | 22,150 | 14,372 | 633 | 7,778 R | 59.6% | 38.7% | 60.6% | 39.4% |
| 804 | MINERAL | 394 | 217 | 174 | 3 | 43 R | 55.1% | 44.2% | 55.5% | 44.5% |
| 13,133 | MOFFAT | 4,519 | 2,757 | 1,634 | 128 | 1,123 R | 61.0% | 36.2% | 62.8% | 37.2% |
| 16,510 | MONTEZUMA | 6,551 | 4,208 | 2,233 | 110 | 1,975 R | 64.2% | 34.1% | 65.3% | 34.7% |
| 24,352 | MONTROSE | 9,993 | 6,012 | 3,748 | 233 | 2,264 R | 60.2% | 37.5% | 61.6% | 38.4% |
| 22,513 | MORGAN | 8,680 | 4,795 | 3,728 | 157 | 1,067 R | 55.2% | 42.9% | 56.3% | 43.7% |
| 22,567 | OTERO | 8,299 | 4,265 | 3,910 | 124 | 355 R | 51.4% | 47.1% | 52.2% | 47.8% |
| 1,925 | OURAY | 1,274 | 814 | 439 | 21 | 375 R | 63.9% | 34.5% | 65.0% | 35.0% |
| 5,333 | PARK | 3,357 | 1,909 | 1,343 | 105 | 566 R | 56.9% | 40.0% | 58.7% | 41.3% |
| 4,542 | PHILLIPS | 2,278 | 1,317 | 923 | 38 | 394 R | 57.8% | 40.5% | 58.8% | 41.2% |
| 10,338 | PITKIN | 6,326 | 2,801 | 3,420 | 105 | 619 D | 44.3% | 54.1% | 45.0% | 55.0% |
| 13,070 | PROWERS | 5,286 | 2,978 | 2,207 | 101 | 771 R | 56.3% | 41.8% | 57.4% | 42.6% |
| 125,972 | PUEBLO | 53,318 | 20,119 | 32,788 | 411 | 12,669 D | 37.7% | 61.5% | 38.0% | 62.0% |
| 6,255 | RIO BLANCO | 2,662 | 1,821 | 803 | 38 | 1,018 R | 68.4% | 30.2% | 69.4% | 30.6% |
| 10,511 | RIO GRANDE | 4,235 | 2,626 | 1,545 | 64 | 1,081 R | 62.0% | 36.5% | 63.0% | 37.0% |
| 13,404 | ROUTT | 6,319 | 3,264 | 2,922 | 133 | 342 R | 51.7% | 46.2% | 52.8% | 47.2% |
| 3,935 | SAGUACHE | 2,013 | 945 | 1,033 | 35 | 88 D | 46.9% | 51.3% | 47.8% | 52.2% |
| 833 | SAN JUAN | 417 | 210 | 192 | 15 | 18 R | 50.4% | 46.0% | 52.2% | 47.8% |
| 3,192 | SAN MIGUEL | 1,839 | 798 | 961 | 80 | 163 D | 43.4% | 52.3% | 45.4% | 54.6% |
| 3,266 | SEDGWICK | 1,545 | 921 | 611 | 13 | 310 R | 59.6% | 39.5% | 60.1% | 39.9% |
| 8,848 | SUMMIT | 5,624 | 2,893 | 2,595 | 136 | 298 R | 51.4% | 46.1% | 52.7% | 47.3% |
| 8,034 | TELLER | 5,500 | 3,760 | 1,656 | 84 | 2,104 R | 68.4% | 30.1% | 69.4% | 30.6% |

# COLORADO

## PRESIDENT 1988

| 1980 Census Population | County | Total Vote | Republican | Democratic | Other | Rep.-Dem. Plurality | Percentage | | | |
|---|---|---|---|---|---|---|---|---|---|---|
| | | | | | | | Total Vote | | Major Vote | |
| | | | | | | | Rep. | Dem. | Rep. | Dem. |
| 5,304 | WASHINGTON | 2,715 | 1,707 | 958 | 50 | 749 R | 62.9% | 35.3% | 64.1% | 35.9% |
| 123,438 | WELD | 47,807 | 26,497 | 20,548 | 762 | 5,949 R | 55.4% | 43.0% | 56.3% | 43.7% |
| 9,682 | YUMA | 4,414 | 2,513 | 1,835 | 66 | 678 R | 56.9% | 41.6% | 57.8% | 42.2% |
| 2,889,964 | TOTAL | 1,372,394 | 728,177 | 621,453 | 22,764 | 106,724 R | 53.1% | 45.3% | 54.0% | 46.0% |

# COLORADO

## PRESIDENT 1984

| 1980 Census Population | County | Total Vote | Republican | Democratic | Other | Rep.-Dem. Plurality | Percentage | | | |
|---|---|---|---|---|---|---|---|---|---|---|
| | | | | | | | Total Vote | | Major Vote | |
| | | | | | | | Rep. | Dem. | Rep. | Dem. |
| 245,944 | ADAMS | 91,511 | 55,092 | 35,285 | 1,134 | 19,807 R | 60.2% | 38.6% | 61.0% | 39.0% |
| 11,799 | ALAMOSA | 4,711 | 2,953 | 1,720 | 38 | 1,233 R | 62.7% | 36.5% | 63.2% | 36.8% |
| 293,621 | ARAPAHOE | 149,555 | 107,556 | 39,891 | 2,108 | 67,665 R | 71.9% | 26.7% | 72.9% | 27.1% |
| 3,664 | ARCHULETA | 2,163 | 1,557 | 584 | 22 | 973 R | 72.0% | 27.0% | 72.7% | 27.3% |
| 5,419 | BACA | 2,509 | 1,903 | 580 | 26 | 1,323 R | 75.8% | 23.1% | 76.6% | 23.4% |
| 5,945 | BENT | 2,199 | 1,314 | 859 | 26 | 455 R | 59.8% | 39.1% | 60.5% | 39.5% |
| 189,625 | BOULDER | 97,238 | 53,535 | 42,195 | 1,508 | 11,340 R | 55.1% | 43.4% | 55.9% | 44.1% |
| 13,227 | CHAFFEE | 5,550 | 3,680 | 1,779 | 91 | 1,901 R | 66.3% | 32.1% | 67.4% | 32.6% |
| 2,153 | CHEYENNE | 1,218 | 892 | 307 | 19 | 585 R | 73.2% | 25.2% | 74.4% | 25.6% |
| 7,308 | CLEAR CREEK | 3,292 | 2,151 | 1,089 | 52 | 1,062 R | 65.3% | 33.1% | 66.4% | 33.6% |
| 7,794 | CONEJOS | 3,247 | 1,669 | 1,553 | 25 | 116 R | 51.4% | 47.8% | 51.8% | 48.2% |
| 3,071 | COSTILLA | 1,631 | 621 | 997 | 13 | 376 D | 38.1% | 61.1% | 38.4% | 61.6% |
| 2,988 | CROWLEY | 1,527 | 993 | 517 | 17 | 476 R | 65.0% | 33.9% | 65.8% | 34.2% |
| 1,528 | CUSTER | 1,093 | 832 | 241 | 20 | 591 R | 76.1% | 22.0% | 77.5% | 22.5% |
| 21,225 | DELTA | 9,639 | 6,678 | 2,835 | 126 | 3,843 R | 69.3% | 29.4% | 70.2% | 29.8% |
| 492,365 | DENVER | 219,741 | 105,096 | 110,200 | 4,445 | 5,104 D | 47.8% | 50.1% | 48.8% | 51.2% |
| 1,658 | DOLORES | 850 | 667 | 173 | 10 | 494 R | 78.5% | 20.4% | 79.4% | 20.6% |
| 25,153 | DOUGLAS | 15,441 | 12,249 | 3,011 | 181 | 9,238 R | 79.3% | 19.5% | 80.3% | 19.7% |
| 13,320 | EAGLE | 6,633 | 4,500 | 2,032 | 101 | 2,468 R | 67.8% | 30.6% | 68.9% | 31.1% |
| 6,850 | ELBERT | 3,461 | 2,605 | 802 | 54 | 1,803 R | 75.3% | 23.2% | 76.5% | 23.5% |
| 309,424 | EL PASO | 117,773 | 88,377 | 28,185 | 1,211 | 60,192 R | 75.0% | 23.9% | 75.8% | 24.2% |
| 28,676 | FREMONT | 12,256 | 8,250 | 3,895 | 111 | 4,355 R | 67.3% | 31.8% | 67.9% | 32.1% |
| 22,514 | GARFIELD | 10,285 | 7,111 | 3,076 | 98 | 4,035 R | 69.1% | 29.9% | 69.8% | 30.2% |
| 2,441 | GILPIN | 1,571 | 896 | 634 | 41 | 262 R | 57.0% | 40.4% | 58.6% | 41.4% |
| 7,475 | GRAND | 3,940 | 2,865 | 1,017 | 58 | 1,848 R | 72.7% | 25.8% | 73.8% | 26.2% |
| 10,689 | GUNNISON | 4,606 | 3,100 | 1,424 | 82 | 1,676 R | 67.3% | 30.9% | 68.5% | 31.5% |
| 408 | HINSDALE | 414 | 310 | 98 | 6 | 212 R | 74.9% | 23.7% | 76.0% | 24.0% |
| 6,440 | HUERFANO | 3,224 | 1,581 | 1,602 | 41 | 21 D | 49.0% | 49.7% | 49.7% | 50.3% |
| 1,863 | JACKSON | 923 | 722 | 191 | 10 | 531 R | 78.2% | 20.7% | 79.1% | 20.9% |
| 371,753 | JEFFERSON | 180,628 | 124,496 | 53,700 | 2,432 | 70,796 R | 68.9% | 29.7% | 69.9% | 30.1% |
| 1,936 | KIOWA | 1,130 | 850 | 265 | 15 | 585 R | 75.2% | 23.5% | 76.2% | 23.8% |
| 7,599 | KIT CARSON | 3,584 | 2,762 | 778 | 44 | 1,984 R | 77.1% | 21.7% | 78.0% | 22.0% |
| 8,830 | LAKE | 2,747 | 1,364 | 1,324 | 59 | 40 R | 49.7% | 48.2% | 50.7% | 49.3% |
| 27,424 | LA PLATA | 12,918 | 8,719 | 4,040 | 159 | 4,679 R | 67.5% | 31.3% | 68.3% | 31.7% |
| 149,184 | LARIMER | 74,849 | 49,883 | 23,896 | 1,070 | 25,987 R | 66.6% | 31.9% | 67.6% | 32.4% |
| 14,897 | LAS ANIMAS | 6,742 | 2,992 | 3,670 | 80 | 678 D | 44.4% | 54.4% | 44.9% | 55.1% |
| 4,663 | LINCOLN | 2,278 | 1,661 | 587 | 30 | 1,074 R | 72.9% | 25.8% | 73.9% | 26.1% |
| 19,800 | LOGAN | 8,133 | 5,883 | 2,155 | 95 | 3,728 R | 72.3% | 26.5% | 73.2% | 26.8% |
| 81,530 | MESA | 34,074 | 23,736 | 9,938 | 400 | 13,798 R | 69.7% | 29.2% | 70.5% | 29.5% |
| 804 | MINERAL | 459 | 333 | 117 | 9 | 216 R | 72.5% | 25.5% | 74.0% | 26.0% |
| 13,133 | MOFFAT | 4,981 | 3,630 | 1,228 | 123 | 2,402 R | 72.9% | 24.7% | 74.7% | 25.3% |
| 16,510 | MONTEZUMA | 6,506 | 4,753 | 1,665 | 88 | 3,088 R | 73.1% | 25.6% | 74.1% | 25.9% |
| 24,352 | MONTROSE | 10,173 | 7,162 | 2,864 | 147 | 4,298 R | 70.4% | 28.2% | 71.4% | 28.6% |
| 22,513 | MORGAN | 8,556 | 6,097 | 2,331 | 128 | 3,766 R | 71.3% | 27.2% | 72.3% | 27.7% |
| 22,567 | OTERO | 8,615 | 5,373 | 3,005 | 237 | 2,368 R | 62.4% | 34.9% | 64.1% | 35.9% |
| 1,925 | OURAY | 1,290 | 914 | 366 | 10 | 548 R | 70.9% | 28.4% | 71.4% | 28.6% |
| 5,333 | PARK | 2,902 | 2,041 | 782 | 79 | 1,259 R | 70.3% | 26.9% | 72.3% | 27.7% |
| 4,542 | PHILLIPS | 2,367 | 1,689 | 651 | 27 | 1,038 R | 71.4% | 27.5% | 72.2% | 27.8% |
| 10,338 | PITKIN | 5,528 | 3,117 | 2,293 | 118 | 824 R | 56.4% | 41.5% | 57.6% | 42.4% |
| 13,070 | PROWERS | 5,095 | 3,501 | 1,467 | 127 | 2,034 R | 68.7% | 28.8% | 70.5% | 29.5% |
| 125,972 | PUEBLO | 52,200 | 24,634 | 27,126 | 440 | 2,492 D | 47.2% | 52.0% | 47.6% | 52.4% |
| 6,255 | RIO BLANCO | 2,637 | 2,131 | 484 | 22 | 1,647 R | 80.8% | 18.4% | 81.5% | 18.5% |
| 10,511 | RIO GRANDE | 4,262 | 3,122 | 1,104 | 36 | 2,018 R | 73.3% | 25.9% | 73.9% | 26.1% |
| 13,404 | ROUTT | 6,408 | 4,239 | 2,051 | 118 | 2,188 R | 66.2% | 32.0% | 67.4% | 32.6% |
| 3,935 | SAGUACHE | 2,084 | 1,201 | 867 | 16 | 334 R | 57.6% | 41.6% | 58.1% | 41.9% |
| 833 | SAN JUAN | 519 | 320 | 183 | 16 | 137 R | 61.7% | 35.3% | 63.6% | 36.4% |
| 3,192 | SAN MIGUEL | 1,521 | 833 | 654 | 34 | 179 R | 54.8% | 43.0% | 56.0% | 44.0% |
| 3,266 | SEDGWICK | 1,583 | 1,146 | 429 | 8 | 717 R | 72.4% | 27.1% | 72.8% | 27.2% |
| 8,848 | SUMMIT | 4,918 | 3,253 | 1,588 | 77 | 1,665 R | 66.1% | 32.3% | 67.2% | 32.8% |
| 8,034 | TELLER | 4,562 | 3,460 | 1,043 | 59 | 2,417 R | 75.8% | 22.9% | 76.8% | 23.2% |

# COLORADO

## PRESIDENT 1984

| 1980 Census Population | County | Total Vote | Republican | Democratic | Other | Rep.-Dem. Plurality | Percentage | | | |
|---|---|---|---|---|---|---|---|---|---|---|
| | | | | | | | Total Vote | | Major Vote | |
| | | | | | | | Rep. | Dem. | Rep. | Dem. |
| 5,304 | WASHINGTON | 2,684 | 2,080 | 568 | 36 | 1,512  R | 77.5% | 21.2% | 78.5% | 21.5% |
| 123,438 | WELD | 45,679 | 31,293 | 13,863 | 523 | 17,430  R | 68.5% | 30.3% | 69.3% | 30.7% |
| 9,682 | YUMA | 4,567 | 3,394 | 1,121 | 52 | 2,273  R | 74.3% | 24.5% | 75.2% | 24.8% |
| 2,889,964 | TOTAL | 1,295,380 | 821,817 | 454,975 | 18,588 | 366,842  R | 63.4% | 35.1% | 64.4% | 35.6% |

# COLORADO

## PRESIDENT 1980

| 1980 Census Population | County | Total Vote | Republican | Democratic | Other | Rep.-Dem. Plurality | Percentage | | | |
|---|---|---|---|---|---|---|---|---|---|---|
| | | | | | | | Total Vote | | Major Vote | |
| | | | | | | | Rep. | Dem. | Rep. | Dem. |
| 245,944 | ADAMS | 84,975 | 42,916 | 31,357 | 10,702 | 11,559 R | 50.5% | 36.9% | 57.8% | 42.2% |
| 11,799 | ALAMOSA | 4,828 | 2,601 | 1,821 | 406 | 780 R | 53.9% | 37.7% | 58.8% | 41.2% |
| 293,621 | ARAPAHOE | 127,980 | 79,594 | 30,148 | 18,238 | 49,446 R | 62.2% | 23.6% | 72.5% | 27.5% |
| 3,664 | ARCHULETA | 1,900 | 1,252 | 532 | 116 | 720 R | 65.9% | 28.0% | 70.2% | 29.8% |
| 5,419 | BACA | 2,692 | 1,999 | 551 | 142 | 1,448 R | 74.3% | 20.5% | 78.4% | 21.6% |
| 5,945 | BENT | 2,330 | 1,206 | 894 | 230 | 312 R | 51.8% | 38.4% | 57.4% | 42.6% |
| 189,625 | BOULDER | 87,069 | 40,698 | 28,422 | 17,949 | 12,276 R | 46.7% | 32.6% | 58.9% | 41.1% |
| 13,227 | CHAFFEE | 5,478 | 3,327 | 1,583 | 568 | 1,744 R | 60.7% | 28.9% | 67.8% | 32.2% |
| 2,153 | CHEYENNE | 1,239 | 816 | 322 | 101 | 494 R | 65.9% | 26.0% | 71.7% | 28.3% |
| 7,308 | CLEAR CREEK | 3,173 | 1,784 | 837 | 552 | 947 R | 56.2% | 26.4% | 68.1% | 31.9% |
| 7,794 | CONEJOS | 3,232 | 1,597 | 1,503 | 132 | 94 R | 49.4% | 46.5% | 51.5% | 48.5% |
| 3,071 | COSTILLA | 1,583 | 489 | 1,036 | 58 | 547 D | 30.9% | 65.4% | 32.1% | 67.9% |
| 2,988 | CROWLEY | 1,473 | 926 | 472 | 75 | 454 R | 62.9% | 32.0% | 66.2% | 33.8% |
| 1,528 | CUSTER | 1,010 | 674 | 231 | 105 | 443 R | 66.7% | 22.9% | 74.5% | 25.5% |
| 21,225 | DELTA | 9,227 | 6,179 | 2,348 | 700 | 3,831 R | 67.0% | 25.4% | 72.5% | 27.5% |
| 492,365 | DENVER | 209,508 | 88,398 | 85,903 | 35,207 | 2,495 R | 42.2% | 41.0% | 50.7% | 49.3% |
| 1,658 | DOLORES | 817 | 615 | 157 | 45 | 458 R | 75.3% | 19.2% | 79.7% | 20.3% |
| 25,153 | DOUGLAS | 11,596 | 8,126 | 2,108 | 1,362 | 6,018 R | 70.1% | 18.2% | 79.4% | 20.6% |
| 13,320 | EAGLE | 5,816 | 3,061 | 1,608 | 1,147 | 1,453 R | 52.6% | 27.6% | 65.6% | 34.4% |
| 6,850 | ELBERT | 3,122 | 2,107 | 698 | 317 | 1,409 R | 67.5% | 22.4% | 75.1% | 24.9% |
| 309,424 | EL PASO | 103,990 | 66,199 | 27,463 | 10,328 | 38,736 R | 63.7% | 26.4% | 70.7% | 29.3% |
| 28,676 | FREMONT | 12,113 | 7,162 | 3,952 | 999 | 3,210 R | 59.1% | 32.6% | 64.4% | 35.6% |
| 22,514 | GARFIELD | 9,325 | 5,416 | 2,639 | 1,270 | 2,777 R | 58.1% | 28.3% | 67.2% | 32.8% |
| 2,441 | GILPIN | 1,387 | 694 | 441 | 252 | 253 R | 50.0% | 31.8% | 61.1% | 38.9% |
| 7,475 | GRAND | 3,481 | 2,133 | 820 | 528 | 1,313 R | 61.3% | 23.6% | 72.2% | 27.8% |
| 10,689 | GUNNISON | 4,970 | 2,756 | 1,297 | 917 | 1,459 R | 55.5% | 26.1% | 68.0% | 32.0% |
| 408 | HINSDALE | 336 | 232 | 76 | 28 | 156 R | 69.0% | 22.6% | 75.3% | 24.7% |
| 6,440 | HUERFANO | 3,032 | 1,258 | 1,574 | 200 | 316 D | 41.5% | 51.9% | 44.4% | 55.6% |
| 1,863 | JACKSON | 1,059 | 673 | 283 | 103 | 390 R | 63.6% | 26.7% | 70.4% | 29.6% |
| 371,753 | JEFFERSON | 162,611 | 97,008 | 41,525 | 24,078 | 55,483 R | 59.7% | 25.5% | 70.0% | 30.0% |
| 1,936 | KIOWA | 1,159 | 754 | 331 | 74 | 423 R | 65.1% | 28.6% | 69.5% | 30.5% |
| 7,599 | KIT CARSON | 3,653 | 2,622 | 790 | 241 | 1,832 R | 71.8% | 21.6% | 76.8% | 23.2% |
| 8,830 | LAKE | 3,025 | 1,375 | 1,213 | 437 | 162 R | 45.5% | 40.1% | 53.1% | 46.9% |
| 27,424 | LA PLATA | 12,201 | 7,291 | 3,034 | 1,876 | 4,257 R | 59.8% | 24.9% | 70.6% | 29.4% |
| 149,184 | LARIMER | 64,129 | 36,240 | 17,072 | 10,817 | 19,168 R | 56.5% | 26.6% | 68.0% | 32.0% |
| 14,897 | LAS ANIMAS | 7,409 | 2,917 | 4,117 | 375 | 1,200 D | 39.4% | 55.6% | 41.5% | 58.5% |
| 4,663 | LINCOLN | 2,371 | 1,535 | 602 | 234 | 933 R | 64.7% | 25.4% | 71.8% | 28.2% |
| 19,800 | LOGAN | 8,293 | 5,238 | 2,332 | 723 | 2,906 R | 63.2% | 28.1% | 69.2% | 30.8% |
| 81,530 | MESA | 32,916 | 22,686 | 7,549 | 2,681 | 15,137 R | 68.9% | 22.9% | 75.0% | 25.0% |
| 804 | MINERAL | 450 | 271 | 125 | 54 | 146 R | 60.2% | 27.8% | 68.4% | 31.6% |
| 13,133 | MOFFAT | 4,925 | 3,344 | 1,079 | 502 | 2,265 R | 67.9% | 21.9% | 75.6% | 24.4% |
| 16,510 | MONTEZUMA | 6,006 | 4,120 | 1,467 | 419 | 2,653 R | 68.6% | 24.4% | 73.7% | 26.3% |
| 24,352 | MONTROSE | 9,800 | 6,685 | 2,232 | 883 | 4,453 R | 68.2% | 22.8% | 75.0% | 25.0% |
| 22,513 | MORGAN | 8,334 | 5,209 | 2,246 | 879 | 2,963 R | 62.5% | 26.9% | 69.9% | 30.1% |
| 22,567 | OTERO | 8,801 | 4,801 | 3,294 | 706 | 1,507 R | 54.6% | 37.4% | 59.3% | 40.7% |
| 1,925 | OURAY | 1,201 | 813 | 237 | 151 | 576 R | 67.7% | 19.7% | 77.4% | 22.6% |
| 5,333 | PARK | 2,735 | 1,623 | 674 | 438 | 949 R | 59.3% | 24.6% | 70.7% | 29.3% |
| 4,542 | PHILLIPS | 2,354 | 1,488 | 640 | 226 | 848 R | 63.2% | 27.2% | 69.9% | 30.1% |
| 10,338 | PITKIN | 5,417 | 2,153 | 1,760 | 1,504 | 393 R | 39.7% | 32.5% | 55.0% | 45.0% |
| 13,070 | PROWERS | 5,212 | 3,115 | 1,669 | 428 | 1,446 R | 59.8% | 32.0% | 65.1% | 34.9% |
| 125,972 | PUEBLO | 46,441 | 20,770 | 21,874 | 3,797 | 1,104 D | 44.7% | 47.1% | 48.7% | 51.3% |
| 6,255 | RIO BLANCO | 2,647 | 1,971 | 462 | 214 | 1,509 R | 74.5% | 17.5% | 81.0% | 19.0% |
| 10,511 | RIO GRANDE | 4,488 | 2,844 | 1,370 | 274 | 1,474 R | 63.4% | 30.5% | 67.5% | 32.5% |
| 13,404 | ROUTT | 6,702 | 3,574 | 1,944 | 1,184 | 1,630 R | 53.3% | 29.0% | 64.8% | 35.2% |
| 3,935 | SAGUACHE | 2,135 | 1,124 | 893 | 118 | 231 R | 52.6% | 41.8% | 55.7% | 44.3% |
| 833 | SAN JUAN | 549 | 268 | 146 | 135 | 122 R | 48.8% | 26.6% | 64.7% | 35.3% |
| 3,192 | SAN MIGUEL | 1,809 | 774 | 651 | 384 | 123 R | 42.8% | 36.0% | 54.3% | 45.7% |
| 3,266 | SEDGWICK | 1,708 | 1,151 | 438 | 119 | 713 R | 67.4% | 25.6% | 72.4% | 27.6% |
| 8,848 | SUMMIT | 4,355 | 2,027 | 1,285 | 1,043 | 742 R | 46.5% | 29.5% | 61.2% | 38.8% |
| 8,034 | TELLER | 3,707 | 2,457 | 802 | 448 | 1,655 R | 66.3% | 21.6% | 75.4% | 24.6% |

# COLORADO

## PRESIDENT 1980

| 1980 Census Population | County | Total Vote | Republican | Democratic | Other | Rep.-Dem. Plurality | Percentage | | | |
|---|---|---|---|---|---|---|---|---|---|---|
| | | | | | | | Total Vote | | Major Vote | |
| | | | | | | | Rep. | Dem. | Rep. | Dem. |
| 5,304 | WASHINGTON | 2,811 | 2,007 | 568 | 236 | 1,439 R | 71.4% | 20.2% | 77.9% | 22.1% |
| 123,438 | WELD | 40,646 | 23,901 | 11,433 | 5,312 | 12,468 R | 58.8% | 28.1% | 67.6% | 32.4% |
| 9,682 | YUMA | 4,674 | 3,220 | 1,043 | 411 | 2,177 R | 68.9% | 22.3% | 75.5% | 24.5% |
| 2,889,964 | TOTAL | 1,184,415 | 652,264 | 367,973 | 164,178 | 284,291 R | 55.1% | 31.1% | 63.9% | 36.1% |

# COLORADO

## PRESIDENT 1976

| 1970 Census Population | County | Total Vote | Republican | Democratic | Other | Rep.-Dem. Plurality | Percentage | | | |
|---|---|---|---|---|---|---|---|---|---|---|
| | | | | | | | Total Vote | | Major Vote | |
| | | | | | | | Rep. | Dem. | Rep. | Dem. |
| 185,789 | ADAMS | 78,127 | 35,392 | 40,551 | 2,184 | 5,159 D | 45.3% | 51.9% | 46.6% | 53.4% |
| 11,422 | ALAMOSA | 4,862 | 2,599 | 2,052 | 211 | 547 R | 53.5% | 42.2% | 55.9% | 44.1% |
| 162,142 | ARAPAHOE | 99,526 | 63,154 | 33,685 | 2,687 | 29,469 R | 63.5% | 33.8% | 65.2% | 34.8% |
| 2,733 | ARCHULETA | 1,432 | 768 | 632 | 32 | 136 R | 53.6% | 44.1% | 54.9% | 45.1% |
| 5,674 | BACA | 2,507 | 1,303 | 1,164 | 40 | 139 R | 52.0% | 46.4% | 52.8% | 47.2% |
| 6,493 | BENT | 2,480 | 1,156 | 1,268 | 56 | 112 D | 46.6% | 51.1% | 47.7% | 52.3% |
| 131,889 | BOULDER | 81,300 | 42,830 | 33,284 | 5,186 | 9,546 R | 52.7% | 40.9% | 56.3% | 43.7% |
| 10,162 | CHAFFEE | 5,162 | 2,925 | 2,064 | 173 | 861 R | 56.7% | 40.0% | 58.6% | 41.4% |
| 2,396 | CHEYENNE | 1,271 | 610 | 625 | 36 | 15 D | 48.0% | 49.2% | 49.4% | 50.6% |
| 4,819 | CLEAR CREEK | 2,669 | 1,477 | 1,069 | 123 | 408 R | 55.3% | 40.1% | 58.0% | 42.0% |
| 7,846 | CONEJOS | 3,194 | 1,426 | 1,698 | 70 | 272 D | 44.6% | 53.2% | 45.6% | 54.4% |
| 3,091 | COSTILLA | 1,454 | 392 | 1,033 | 29 | 641 D | 27.0% | 71.0% | 27.5% | 72.5% |
| 3,086 | CROWLEY | 1,519 | 834 | 667 | 18 | 167 R | 54.9% | 43.9% | 55.6% | 44.4% |
| 1,120 | CUSTER | 791 | 491 | 259 | 41 | 232 R | 62.1% | 32.7% | 65.5% | 34.5% |
| 15,286 | DELTA | 8,483 | 4,980 | 3,232 | 271 | 1,748 R | 58.7% | 38.1% | 60.6% | 39.4% |
| 514,678 | DENVER | 226,773 | 105,960 | 112,229 | 8,584 | 6,269 D | 46.7% | 49.5% | 48.6% | 51.4% |
| 1,641 | DOLORES | 752 | 343 | 374 | 35 | 31 D | 45.6% | 49.7% | 47.8% | 52.2% |
| 8,407 | DOUGLAS | 7,757 | 5,078 | 2,459 | 220 | 2,619 R | 65.5% | 31.7% | 67.4% | 32.6% |
| 7,498 | EAGLE | 4,618 | 2,963 | 1,502 | 153 | 1,461 R | 64.2% | 32.5% | 66.4% | 33.6% |
| 3,903 | ELBERT | 2,428 | 1,279 | 1,068 | 81 | 211 R | 52.7% | 44.0% | 54.5% | 45.5% |
| 235,972 | EL PASO | 86,168 | 50,929 | 32,911 | 2,328 | 18,018 R | 59.1% | 38.2% | 60.7% | 39.3% |
| 21,942 | FREMONT | 10,769 | 5,647 | 4,886 | 236 | 761 R | 52.4% | 45.4% | 53.6% | 46.4% |
| 14,821 | GARFIELD | 7,871 | 4,699 | 2,852 | 320 | 1,847 R | 59.7% | 36.2% | 62.2% | 37.8% |
| 1,272 | GILPIN | 1,095 | 451 | 563 | 81 | 112 D | 41.2% | 51.4% | 44.5% | 55.5% |
| 4,107 | GRAND | 2,760 | 1,703 | 910 | 147 | 793 R | 61.7% | 33.0% | 65.2% | 34.8% |
| 7,578 | GUNNISON | 4,150 | 2,568 | 1,250 | 332 | 1,318 R | 61.9% | 30.1% | 67.3% | 32.7% |
| 202 | HINSDALE | 284 | 189 | 83 | 12 | 106 R | 66.5% | 29.2% | 69.5% | 30.5% |
| 6,590 | HUERFANO | 3,165 | 1,182 | 1,932 | 51 | 750 D | 37.3% | 61.0% | 38.0% | 62.0% |
| 1,811 | JACKSON | 748 | 455 | 279 | 14 | 176 R | 60.8% | 37.3% | 62.0% | 38.0% |
| 233,031 | JEFFERSON | 144,102 | 87,080 | 52,782 | 4,240 | 34,298 R | 60.4% | 36.6% | 62.3% | 37.7% |
| 2,029 | KIOWA | 1,137 | 598 | 529 | 10 | 69 R | 52.6% | 46.5% | 53.1% | 46.9% |
| 7,530 | KIT CARSON | 3,621 | 1,888 | 1,647 | 86 | 241 R | 52.1% | 45.5% | 53.4% | 46.6% |
| 8,282 | LAKE | 3,279 | 1,575 | 1,549 | 155 | 26 R | 48.0% | 47.2% | 50.4% | 49.6% |
| 19,199 | LA PLATA | 10,573 | 6,228 | 3,843 | 502 | 2,385 R | 58.9% | 36.3% | 61.8% | 38.2% |
| 89,900 | LARIMER | 53,009 | 32,169 | 19,005 | . 1,835 | 13,164 R | 60.7% | 35.9% | 62.9% | 37.1% |
| 15,744 | LAS ANIMAS | 7,175 | 2,615 | 4,459 | 101 | 1,844 D | 36.4% | 62.1% | 37.0% | 63.0% |
| 4,836 | LINCOLN | 2,387 | 1,276 | 1,059 | 52 | 217 R | 53.5% | 44.4% | 54.6% | 45.4% |
| 18,852 | LOGAN | 7,988 | 4,256 | 3,543 | 189 | 713 R | 53.3% | 44.4% | 54.6% | 45.4% |
| 54,374 | MESA | 27,419 | 17,924 | 8,807 | 688 | 9,117 R | 65.4% | 32.1% | 67.1% | 32.9% |
| 786 | MINERAL | 423 | 235 | 167 | 21 | 68 R | 55.6% | 39.5% | 58.5% | 41.5% |
| 6,525 | MOFFAT | 3,775 | 2,099 | 1,451 | 225 | 648 R | 55.6% | 38.4% | 59.1% | 40.9% |
| 12,952 | MONTEZUMA | 5,190 | 3,002 | 1,993 | 195 | 1,009 R | 57.8% | 38.4% | 60.1% | 39.9% |
| 18,366 | MONTROSE | 8,300 | 4,838 | 3,164 | 298 | 1,674 R | 58.3% | 38.1% | 60.5% | 39.5% |
| 20,105 | MORGAN | 8,631 | 4,603 | 3,798 | 230 | 805 R | 53.3% | 44.0% | 54.8% | 45.2% |
| 23,523 | OTERO | 8,920 | 4,597 | 4,118 | 205 | 479 R | 51.5% | 46.2% | 52.7% | 47.3% |
| 1,546 | OURAY | 1,032 | 645 | 333 | 54 | 312 R | 62.5% | 32.3% | 66.0% | 34.0% |
| 2,185 | PARK | 1,872 | 1,034 | 741 | 97 | 293 R | 55.2% | 39.6% | 58.3% | 41.7% |
| 4,131 | PHILLIPS | 2,373 | 1,142 | 1,173 | 58 | 31 D | 48.1% | 49.4% | 49.3% | 50.7% |
| 6,185 | PITKIN | 5,512 | 2,955 | 2,194 | 363 | 761 R | 53.6% | 39.8% | 57.4% | 42.6% |
| 13,258 | PROWERS | 5,592 | 2,578 | 2,861 | 153 | 283 D | 46.1% | 51.2% | 47.4% | 52.6% |
| 118,238 | PUEBLO | 45,157 | 18,518 | 25,841 | 798 | 7,323 D | 41.0% | 57.2% | 41.7% | 58.3% |
| 4,842 | RIO BLANCO | 2,141 | 1,439 | 627 | 75 | 812 R | 67.2% | 29.3% | 69.7% | 30.3% |
| 10,494 | RIO GRANDE | 4,212 | 2,627 | 1,475 | 110 | 1,152 R | 62.4% | 35.0% | 64.0% | 36.0% |
| 6,592 | ROUTT | 5,213 | 2,822 | 2,130 | 261 | 692 R | 54.1% | 40.9% | 57.0% | 43.0% |
| 3,827 | SAGUACHE | 2,210 | 1,094 | 1,059 | 57 | 35 R | 49.5% | 47.9% | 50.8% | 49.2% |
| 831 | SAN JUAN | 411 | 221 | 167 | 23 | 54 R | 53.8% | 40.6% | 57.0% | 43.0% |
| 1,949 | SAN MIGUEL | 1,419 | 622 | 674 | 123 | 52 D | 43.8% | 47.5% | 48.0% | 52.0% |
| 3,405 | SEDGWICK | 1,700 | 902 | 773 | 25 | 129 R | 53.1% | 45.5% | 53.9% | 46.1% |
| 2,665 | SUMMIT | 3,142 | 1,826 | 1,087 | 229 | 739 R | 58.1% | 34.6% | 62.7% | 37.3% |
| 3,316 | TELLER | 2,521 | 1,410 | 986 | 125 | 424 R | 55.9% | 39.1% | 58.8% | 41.2% |

# COLORADO

## PRESIDENT 1976

| 1970 Census Population | County | Total Vote | Republican | Democratic | Other | Rep.-Dem. Plurality | Percentage | | | |
|---|---|---|---|---|---|---|---|---|---|---|
| | | | | | | | Total Vote | | Major Vote | |
| | | | | | | | Rep. | Dem. | Rep. | Dem. |
| 5,550 | WASHINGTON | 2,767 | 1,440 | 1,211 | 116 | 229 R | 52.0% | 43.8% | 54.3% | 45.7% |
| 89,297 | WELD | 39,732 | 21,976 | 16,501 | 1,255 | 5,475 R | 55.3% | 41.5% | 57.1% | 42.9% |
| 8,544 | YUMA | 4,504 | 2,350 | 2,025 | 129 | 325 R | 52.2% | 45.0% | 53.7% | 46.3% |
| 2,207,259 | TOTAL | 1,081,554 | 584,367 | 460,353 | 36,834 | 124,014 R | 54.0% | 42.6% | 55.9% | 44.1% |

# COLORADO

## PRESIDENT 1972

| 1970 Census Population | County | Total Vote | Republican | Democratic | Other | Rep.-Dem. Plurality | Percentage Total Vote Rep. | Dem. | Major Vote Rep. | Dem. |
|---:|---|---:|---:|---:|---:|---:|---:|---:|---:|---:|
| 185,789 | ADAMS | 66,412 | 40,372 | 24,170 | 1,870 | 16,202 R | 60.8% | 36.4% | 62.6% | 37.4% |
| 11,422 | ALAMOSA | 4,665 | 2,916 | 1,540 | 209 | 1,376 R | 62.5% | 33.0% | 65.4% | 34.6% |
| 162,142 | ARAPAHOE | 72,376 | 52,283 | 18,631 | 1,462 | 33,652 R | 72.2% | 25.7% | 73.7% | 26.3% |
| 2,733 | ARCHULETA | 940 | 606 | 300 | 34 | 306 R | 64.5% | 31.9% | 66.9% | 33.1% |
| 5,674 | BACA | 2,225 | 1,645 | 527 | 53 | 1,118 R | 73.9% | 23.7% | 75.7% | 24.3% |
| 6,493 | BENT | 2,372 | 1,525 | 787 | 60 | 738 R | 64.3% | 33.2% | 66.0% | 34.0% |
| 131,889 | BOULDER | 71,770 | 40,766 | 29,484 | 1,520 | 11,282 R | 56.8% | 41.1% | 58.0% | 42.0% |
| 10,162 | CHAFFEE | 4,291 | 2,859 | 1,354 | 78 | 1,505 R | 66.6% | 31.6% | 67.9% | 32.1% |
| 2,396 | CHEYENNE | 1,286 | 815 | 400 | 71 | 415 R | 63.4% | 31.1% | 67.1% | 32.9% |
| 4,819 | CLEAR CREEK | 2,502 | 1,557 | 815 | 130 | 742 R | 62.2% | 32.6% | 65.6% | 34.4% |
| 7,846 | CONEJOS | 2,987 | 1,658 | 1,140 | 189 | 518 R | 55.5% | 38.2% | 59.3% | 40.7% |
| 3,091 | COSTILLA | 1,428 | 602 | 744 | 82 | 142 D | 42.2% | 52.1% | 44.7% | 55.3% |
| 3,086 | CROWLEY | 1,548 | 1,094 | 414 | 40 | 680 R | 70.7% | 26.7% | 72.5% | 27.5% |
| 1,120 | CUSTER | 693 | 495 | 154 | 44 | 341 R | 71.4% | 22.2% | 76.3% | 23.7% |
| 15,286 | DELTA | 7,220 | 4,890 | 1,903 | 427 | 2,987 R | 67.7% | 26.4% | 72.0% | 28.0% |
| 514,678 | DENVER | 225,335 | 121,995 | 98,062 | 5,278 | 23,933 R | 54.1% | 43.5% | 55.4% | 44.6% |
| 1,641 | DOLORES | 694 | 498 | 166 | 30 | 332 R | 71.8% | 23.9% | 75.0% | 25.0% |
| 8,407 | DOUGLAS | 4,800 | 3,625 | 1,048 | 127 | 2,577 R | 75.5% | 21.8% | 77.6% | 22.4% |
| 7,498 | EAGLE | 3,301 | 1,920 | 1,306 | 75 | 614 R | 58.2% | 39.6% | 59.5% | 40.5% |
| 3,903 | ELBERT | 1,932 | 1,416 | 451 | 65 | 965 R | 73.3% | 23.3% | 75.8% | 24.2% |
| 235,972 | EL PASO | 77,985 | 53,892 | 21,234 | 2,859 | 32,658 R | 69.1% | 27.2% | 71.7% | 28.3% |
| 21,942 | FREMONT | 9,795 | 6,701 | 2,813 | 281 | 3,888 R | 68.4% | 28.7% | 70.4% | 29.6% |
| 14,821 | GARFIELD | 6,718 | 4,452 | 2,088 | 178 | 2,364 R | 66.3% | 31.1% | 68.1% | 31.9% |
| 1,272 | GILPIN | 905 | 516 | 362 | 27 | 154 R | 57.0% | 40.0% | 58.8% | 41.2% |
| 4,107 | GRAND | 2,461 | 1,721 | 685 | 55 | 1,036 R | 69.9% | 27.8% | 71.5% | 28.5% |
| 7,578 | GUNNISON | 3,508 | 2,231 | 1,187 | 90 | 1,044 R | 63.6% | 33.8% | 65.3% | 34.7% |
| 202 | HINSDALE | 222 | 172 | 44 | 6 | 128 R | 77.5% | 19.8% | 79.6% | 20.4% |
| 6,590 | HUERFANO | 3,027 | 1,620 | 1,341 | 66 | 279 R | 53.5% | 44.3% | 54.7% | 45.3% |
| 1,811 | JACKSON | 812 | 623 | 178 | 11 | 445 R | 76.7% | 21.9% | 77.8% | 22.2% |
| 233,031 | JEFFERSON | 114,597 | 80,082 | 31,555 | 2,960 | 48,527 R | 69.9% | 27.5% | 71.7% | 28.3% |
| 2,029 | KIOWA | 1,250 | 849 | 372 | 29 | 477 R | 67.9% | 29.8% | 69.5% | 30.5% |
| 7,530 | KIT CARSON | 3,267 | 2,316 | 824 | 127 | 1,492 R | 70.9% | 25.2% | 73.8% | 26.2% |
| 8,282 | LAKE | 2,899 | 1,556 | 1,263 | 80 | 293 R | 53.7% | 43.6% | 55.2% | 44.8% |
| 19,199 | LA PLATA | 9,144 | 5,691 | 2,830 | 623 | 2,861 R | 62.2% | 30.9% | 66.8% | 33.2% |
| 89,900 | LARIMER | 42,234 | 27,462 | 13,731 | 1,041 | 13,731 R | 65.0% | 32.5% | 66.7% | 33.3% |
| 15,744 | LAS ANIMAS | 6,957 | 3,659 | 3,222 | 76 | 437 R | 52.6% | 46.3% | 53.2% | 46.8% |
| 4,836 | LINCOLN | 2,396 | 1,678 | 685 | 33 | 993 R | 70.0% | 28.6% | 71.0% | 29.0% |
| 18,852 | LOGAN | 7,956 | 5,352 | 2,426 | 178 | 2,926 R | 67.3% | 30.5% | 68.8% | 31.2% |
| 54,374 | MESA | 22,613 | 15,527 | 6,358 | 728 | 9,169 R | 68.7% | 28.1% | 70.9% | 29.1% |
| 786 | MINERAL | 348 | 247 | 96 | 5 | 151 R | 71.0% | 27.6% | 72.0% | 28.0% |
| 6,525 | MOFFAT | 2,848 | 1,928 | 591 | 329 | 1,337 R | 67.7% | 20.8% | 76.5% | 23.5% |
| 12,952 | MONTEZUMA | 4,614 | 3,391 | 1,223 | | 2,168 R | 73.5% | 26.5% | 73.5% | 26.5% |
| 18,366 | MONTROSE | 7,059 | 4,571 | 1,870 | 618 | 2,701 R | 64.8% | 26.5% | 71.0% | 29.0% |
| 20,105 | MORGAN | 7,621 | 5,365 | 2,081 | 175 | 3,284 R | 70.4% | 27.3% | 72.1% | 27.9% |
| 23,523 | OTERO | 9,150 | 6,016 | 2,929 | 205 | 3,087 R | 65.7% | 32.0% | 67.3% | 32.7% |
| 1,546 | OURAY | 897 | 669 | 186 | 42 | 483 R | 74.6% | 20.7% | 78.2% | 21.8% |
| 2,185 | PARK | 1,424 | 1,001 | 386 | 37 | 615 R | 70.3% | 27.1% | 72.2% | 27.8% |
| 4,131 | PHILLIPS | 2,266 | 1,480 | 687 | 99 | 793 R | 65.3% | 30.3% | 68.3% | 31.7% |
| 6,185 | PITKIN | 4,674 | 2,064 | 2,531 | 79 | 467 D | 44.2% | 54.2% | 44.9% | 55.1% |
| 13,258 | PROWERS | 5,313 | 3,272 | 1,860 | 181 | 1,412 R | 61.6% | 35.0% | 63.8% | 36.2% |
| 118,238 | PUEBLO | 47,045 | 25,607 | 19,620 | 1,818 | 5,987 R | 54.4% | 41.7% | 56.6% | 43.4% |
| 4,842 | RIO BLANCO | 2,053 | 1,586 | 414 | 53 | 1,172 R | 77.3% | 20.2% | 79.3% | 20.7% |
| 10,494 | RIO GRANDE | 3,998 | 2,787 | 1,029 | 182 | 1,758 R | 69.7% | 25.7% | 73.0% | 27.0% |
| 6,592 | ROUTT | 4,431 | 2,629 | 1,613 | 189 | 1,016 R | 59.3% | 36.4% | 62.0% | 38.0% |
| 3,827 | SAGUACHE | 1,681 | 1,062 | 578 | 41 | 484 R | 63.2% | 34.4% | 64.8% | 35.2% |
| 831 | SAN JUAN | 408 | 238 | 140 | 30 | 98 R | 58.3% | 34.3% | 63.0% | 37.0% |
| 1,949 | SAN MIGUEL | 1,061 | 583 | 426 | 52 | 157 R | 54.9% | 40.2% | 57.8% | 42.2% |
| 3,405 | SEDGWICK | 1,664 | 1,129 | 485 | 50 | 644 R | 67.8% | 29.1% | 70.0% | 30.0% |
| 2,665 | SUMMIT | 1,833 | 1,082 | 707 | 44 | 375 R | 59.0% | 38.6% | 60.5% | 39.5% |
| 3,316 | TELLER | 2,044 | 1,440 | 535 | 69 | 905 R | 70.5% | 26.2% | 72.9% | 27.1% |

# COLORADO

## PRESIDENT 1972

| 1970 Census Population | County | Total Vote | Republican | Democratic | Other | Rep.-Dem. Plurality | Percentage | | | |
|---|---|---|---|---|---|---|---|---|---|---|
| | | | | | | | Total Vote | | Major Vote | |
| | | | | | | | Rep. | Dem. | Rep. | Dem. |
| 5,550 | WASHINGTON | 2,629 | 1,837 | 643 | 149 | 1,194 R | 69.9% | 24.5% | 74.1% | 25.9% |
| 89,297 | WELD | 37,255 | 24,695 | 11,690 | 870 | 13,005 R | 66.3% | 31.4% | 67.9% | 32.1% |
| 8,544 | YUMA | 4,045 | 2,873 | 1,066 | 106 | 1,807 R | 71.0% | 26.4% | 72.9% | 27.1% |
| 2,207,259 | TOTAL | 953,884 | 597,189 | 329,980 | 26,715 | 267,209 R | 62.6% | 34.6% | 64.4% | 35.6% |

# COLORADO

## PRESIDENT 1968

| 1960 Census Population | County | Total Vote | Republican | Democratic | AIP | Other | Plurality | Percentage Total Vote Rep. | Dem. | AIP |
|---|---|---|---|---|---|---|---|---|---|---|
| 120,296 | ADAMS | 55,493 | 24,343 | 25,111 | 5,702 | 337 | 768 D | 43.9% | 45.3% | 10.3% |
| 10,000 | ALAMOSA | 4,140 | 2,277 | 1,574 | 287 | 2 | 703 R | 55.0% | 38.0% | 6.9% |
| 113,426 | ARAPAHOE | 56,603 | 33,712 | 18,569 | 3,953 | 369 | 15,143 R | 59.6% | 32.8% | 7.0% |
| 2,629 | ARCHULETA | 979 | 486 | 409 | 83 | 1 | 77 R | 49.6% | 41.8% | 8.5% |
| 6,310 | BACA | 2,504 | 1,441 | 719 | 340 | 4 | 722 R | 57.5% | 28.7% | 13.6% |
| 7,419 | BENT | 2,591 | 1,228 | 1,126 | 231 | 6 | 102 R | 47.4% | 43.5% | 8.9% |
| 74,254 | BOULDER | 48,079 | 27,671 | 17,422 | 2,497 | 489 | 10,249 R | 57.6% | 36.2% | 5.2% |
| 8,298 | CHAFFEE | 4,155 | 2,121 | 1,667 | 358 | 9 | 454 R | 51.0% | 40.1% | 8.6% |
| 2,789 | CHEYENNE | 1,193 | 664 | 392 | 136 | 1 | 272 R | 55.7% | 32.9% | 11.4% |
| 2,793 | CLEAR CREEK | 1,918 | 1,011 | 719 | 183 | 5 | 292 R | 52.7% | 37.5% | 9.5% |
| 8,428 | CONEJOS | 2,981 | 1,361 | 1,492 | 117 | 11 | 131 D | 45.7% | 50.1% | 3.9% |
| 4,219 | COSTILLA | 1,482 | 477 | 933 | 32 | 40 | 456 D | 32.2% | 63.0% | 2.2% |
| 3,978 | CROWLEY | 1,540 | 775 | 565 | 196 | 4 | 210 R | 50.3% | 36.7% | 12.7% |
| 1,305 | CUSTER | 716 | 433 | 204 | 77 | 2 | 229 R | 60.5% | 28.5% | 10.8% |
| 15,602 | DELTA | 6,652 | 3,692 | 2,327 | 618 | 15 | 1,365 R | 55.5% | 35.0% | 9.3% |
| 493,887 | DENVER | 211,661 | 92,003 | 106,081 | 11,408 | 2,169 | 14,078 D | 43.5% | 50.1% | 5.4% |
| 2,196 | DOLORES | 741 | 392 | 217 | 131 | 1 | 175 R | 52.9% | 29.3% | 17.7% |
| 4,816 | DOUGLAS | 3,106 | 1,910 | 857 | 327 | 12 | 1,053 R | 61.5% | 27.6% | 10.5% |
| 4,677 | EAGLE | 2,136 | 1,049 | 927 | 160 | | 122 R | 49.1% | 43.4% | 7.5% |
| 3,708 | ELBERT | 1,713 | 1,043 | 484 | 185 | 1 | 559 R | 60.9% | 28.3% | 10.8% |
| 143,742 | EL PASO | 59,714 | 32,066 | 21,232 | 6,199 | 217 | 10,834 R | 53.7% | 35.6% | 10.4% |
| 20,196 | FREMONT | 9,189 | 4,908 | 3,292 | 967 | 22 | 1,616 R | 53.4% | 35.8% | 10.5% |
| 12,017 | GARFIELD | 6,056 | 3,157 | 2,273 | 607 | 19 | 884 R | 52.1% | 37.5% | 10.0% |
| 685 | GILPIN | 684 | 358 | 218 | 99 | 9 | 140 R | 52.3% | 31.9% | 14.5% |
| 3,557 | GRAND | 1,745 | 1,167 | 433 | 127 | 18 | 734 R | 66.9% | 24.8% | 7.3% |
| 5,477 | GUNNISON | 2,435 | 1,411 | 866 | 139 | 19 | 545 R | 57.9% | 35.6% | 5.7% |
| 208 | HINSDALE | 192 | 127 | 43 | 22 | | 84 R | 66.1% | 22.4% | 11.5% |
| 7,867 | HUERFANO | 3,228 | 1,133 | 1,934 | 150 | 11 | 801 D | 35.1% | 59.9% | 4.6% |
| 1,758 | JACKSON | 702 | 474 | 177 | 51 | | 297 R | 67.5% | 25.2% | 7.3% |
| 127,520 | JEFFERSON | 89,502 | 50,847 | 31,392 | 6,767 | 496 | 19,455 R | 56.8% | 35.1% | 7.6% |
| 2,425 | KIOWA | 1,224 | 689 | 423 | 112 | | 266 R | 56.3% | 34.6% | 9.2% |
| 6,957 | KIT CARSON | 3,242 | 1,977 | 1,026 | 232 | 7 | 951 R | 61.0% | 31.6% | 7.2% |
| 7,101 | LAKE | 2,887 | 1,025 | 1,550 | 287 | 25 | 525 D | 35.5% | 53.7% | 9.9% |
| 19,225 | LA PLATA | 7,483 | 4,269 | 2,523 | 673 | 18 | 1,746 R | 57.0% | 33.7% | 9.0% |
| 53,343 | LARIMER | 29,716 | 18,438 | 9,152 | 1,819 | 307 | 9,286 R | 62.0% | 30.8% | 6.1% |
| 19,983 | LAS ANIMAS | 7,510 | 2,499 | 4,602 | 388 | 21 | 2,103 D | 33.3% | 61.3% | 5.2% |
| 5,310 | LINCOLN | 2,465 | 1,407 | 809 | 247 | 2 | 598 R | 57.1% | 32.8% | 10.0% |
| 20,302 | LOGAN | 7,601 | 4,323 | 2,521 | 736 | 21 | 1,802 R | 56.9% | 33.2% | 9.7% |
| 50,715 | MESA | 21,671 | 10,745 | 8,775 | 2,076 | 75 | 1,970 R | 49.6% | 40.5% | 9.6% |
| 424 | MINERAL | 265 | 116 | 126 | 22 | 1 | 10 D | 43.8% | 47.5% | 8.3% |
| 7,061 | MOFFAT | 2,879 | 1,785 | 765 | 322 | 7 | 1,020 R | 62.0% | 26.6% | 11.2% |
| 14,024 | MONTEZUMA | 4,370 | 2,461 | 1,349 | 545 | 15 | 1,112 R | 56.3% | 30.9% | 12.5% |
| 18,286 | MONTROSE | 6,712 | 3,547 | 2,394 | 753 | 18 | 1,153 R | 52.8% | 35.7% | 11.2% |
| 21,192 | MORGAN | 7,512 | 4,598 | 2,310 | 593 | 11 | 2,288 R | 61.2% | 30.8% | 7.9% |
| 24,128 | OTERO | 9,445 | 4,690 | 3,891 | 723 | 141 | 799 R | 49.7% | 41.2% | 7.7% |
| 1,601 | OURAY | 775 | 401 | 250 | 120 | 4 | 151 R | 51.7% | 32.3% | 15.5% |
| 1,822 | PARK | 1,028 | 601 | 286 | 134 | 7 | 315 R | 58.5% | 27.8% | 13.0% |
| 4,440 | PHILLIPS | 2,177 | 1,237 | 723 | 211 | 6 | 514 R | 56.8% | 33.2% | 9.7% |
| 2,381 | PITKIN | 2,021 | 1,135 | 728 | 136 | 22 | 407 R | 56.2% | 36.0% | 6.7% |
| 13,296 | PROWERS | 5,589 | 2,741 | 2,329 | 503 | 16 | 412 R | 49.0% | 41.7% | 9.0% |
| 118,707 | PUEBLO | 48,306 | 16,646 | 27,215 | 3,823 | 622 | 10,569 D | 34.5% | 56.3% | 7.9% |
| 5,150 | RIO BLANCO | 2,003 | 1,294 | 502 | 204 | 3 | 792 R | 64.6% | 25.1% | 10.2% |
| 11,160 | RIO GRANDE | 4,188 | 2,442 | 1,562 | 182 | 2 | 880 R | 58.3% | 37.3% | 4.3% |
| 5,900 | ROUTT | 2,976 | 1,602 | 1,076 | 292 | 6 | 526 R | 53.8% | 36.2% | 9.8% |
| 4,473 | SAGUACHE | 1,571 | 824 | 648 | 97 | 2 | 176 R | 52.5% | 41.2% | 6.2% |
| 849 | SAN JUAN | 368 | 165 | 134 | 59 | 10 | 31 R | 44.8% | 36.4% | 16.0% |
| 2,944 | SAN MIGUEL | 797 | 422 | 311 | 60 | 4 | 111 R | 52.9% | 39.0% | 7.5% |
| 4,242 | SEDGWICK | 1,655 | 1,007 | 546 | 100 | 2 | 461 R | 60.8% | 33.0% | 6.0% |
| 2,073 | SUMMIT | 936 | 536 | 301 | 95 | 4 | 235 R | 57.3% | 32.2% | 10.1% |
| 2,495 | TELLER | 1,379 | 722 | 403 | 249 | 5 | 319 R | 52.4% | 29.2% | 18.1% |

# COLORADO

## PRESIDENT 1968

| 1960 Census Population | County | Total Vote | Republican | Democratic | AIP | Other | Plurality | Percentage Total Vote | | |
|---|---|---|---|---|---|---|---|---|---|---|
| | | | | | | | | Rep. | Dem. | AIP |
| 6,625 | WASHINGTON | 2,694 | 1,634 | 694 | 352 | 14 | 940 R | 60.7% | 25.8% | 13.1% |
| 72,344 | WELD | 29,886 | 17,101 | 10,420 | 2,189 | 176 | 6,681 R | 57.2% | 34.9% | 7.3% |
| 8,912 | YUMA | 4,038 | 2,529 | 1,175 | 330 | 4 | 1,354 R | 62.6% | 29.1% | 8.2% |
| 1,753,947 | TOTAL | 811,199 | 409,345 | 335,174 | 60,813 | 5,867 | 74,171 R | 50.5% | 41.3% | 7.5% |

# COLORADO

## PRESIDENT 1964

| 1960 Census Population | County | Total Vote | Republican | Democratic | Other | Rep.-Dem. Plurality | Percentage | | | |
|---|---|---|---|---|---|---|---|---|---|---|
| | | | | | | | Total Vote | | Major Vote | |
| | | | | | | | Rep. | Dem. | Rep. | Dem. |
| 120,296 | ADAMS | 51,454 | 15,652 | 35,498 | 304 | 19,846 D | 30.4% | 69.0% | 30.6% | 69.4% |
| 10,000 | ALAMOSA | 3,976 | 1,488 | 2,481 | 7 | 993 D | 37.4% | 62.4% | 37.5% | 62.5% |
| 113,426 | ARAPAHOE | 51,358 | 23,071 | 27,940 | 347 | 4,869 D | 44.9% | 54.4% | 45.2% | 54.8% |
| 2,629 | ARCHULETA | 1,008 | 370 | 632 | 6 | 262 D | 36.7% | 62.7% | 36.9% | 63.1% |
| 6,310 | BACA | 2,618 | 1,241 | 1,366 | 11 | 125 D | 47.4% | 52.2% | 47.6% | 52.4% |
| 7,419 | BENT | 2,696 | 937 | 1,737 | 22 | 800 D | 34.8% | 64.4% | 35.0% | 65.0% |
| 74,254 | BOULDER | 40,330 | 17,373 | 22,737 | 220 | 5,364 D | 43.1% | 56.4% | 43.3% | 56.7% |
| 8,298 | CHAFFEE | 3,951 | 1,476 | 2,463 | 12 | 987 D | 37.4% | 62.3% | 37.5% | 62.5% |
| 2,789 | CHEYENNE | 1,283 | 545 | 735 | 3 | 190 D | 42.5% | 57.3% | 42.6% | 57.4% |
| 2,793 | CLEAR CREEK | 1,767 | 676 | 1,086 | 5 | 410 D | 38.3% | 61.5% | 38.4% | 61.6% |
| 8,428 | CONEJOS | 3,076 | 1,031 | 2,033 | 12 | 1,002 D | 33.5% | 66.1% | 33.6% | 66.4% |
| 4,219 | COSTILLA | 1,589 | 299 | 1,284 | 6 | 985 D | 18.8% | 80.8% | 18.9% | 81.1% |
| 3,978 | CROWLEY | 1,663 | 690 | 967 | 6 | 277 D | 41.5% | 58.1% | 41.6% | 58.4% |
| 1,305 | CUSTER | 767 | 358 | 406 | 3 | 48 D | 46.7% | 52.9% | 46.9% | 53.1% |
| 15,602 | DELTA | 6,826 | 2,883 | 3,927 | 16 | 1,044 D | 42.2% | 57.5% | 42.3% | 57.7% |
| 493,887 | DENVER | 218,288 | 73,279 | 143,480 | 1,529 | 70,201 D | 33.6% | 65.7% | 33.8% | 66.2% |
| 2,196 | DOLORES | 818 | 322 | 496 | | 174 D | 39.4% | 60.6% | 39.4% | 60.6% |
| 4,816 | DOUGLAS | 2,791 | 1,336 | 1,442 | 13 | 106 D | 47.9% | 51.7% | 48.1% | 51.9% |
| 4,677 | EAGLE | 1,945 | 644 | 1,299 | 2 | 655 D | 33.1% | 66.8% | 33.1% | 66.9% |
| 3,708 | ELBERT | 1,785 | 924 | 857 | 4 | 67 R | 51.8% | 48.0% | 51.9% | 48.1% |
| 143,742 | EL PASO | 51,807 | 23,822 | 27,844 | 141 | 4,022 D | 46.0% | 53.7% | 46.1% | 53.9% |
| 20,196 | FREMONT | 9,088 | 3,875 | 5,181 | 32 | 1,306 D | 42.6% | 57.0% | 42.8% | 57.2% |
| 12,017 | GARFIELD | 5,488 | 2,282 | 3,196 | 10 | 914 D | 41.6% | 58.2% | 41.7% | 58.3% |
| 685 | GILPIN | 600 | 233 | 363 | 4 | 130 D | 38.8% | 60.5% | 39.1% | 60.9% |
| 3,557 | GRAND | 1,724 | 814 | 902 | 8 | 88 D | 47.2% | 52.3% | 47.4% | 52.6% |
| 5,477 | GUNNISON | 2,443 | 903 | 1,540 | | 637 D | 37.0% | 63.0% | 37.0% | 63.0% |
| 208 | HINSDALE | 201 | 107 | 94 | | 13 R | 53.2% | 46.8% | 53.2% | 46.8% |
| 7,867 | HUERFANO | 3,634 | 895 | 2,734 | 5 | 1,839 D | 24.6% | 75.2% | 24.7% | 75.3% |
| 1,758 | JACKSON | 741 | 354 | 384 | 3 | 30 D | 47.8% | 51.8% | 48.0% | 52.0% |
| 127,520 | JEFFERSON | 76,812 | 33,398 | 43,162 | 252 | 9,764 D | 43.5% | 56.2% | 43.6% | 56.4% |
| 2,425 | KIOWA | 1,280 | 579 | 701 | | 122 D | 45.2% | 54.8% | 45.2% | 54.8% |
| 6,957 | KIT CARSON | 3,233 | 1,316 | 1,906 | 11 | 590 D | 40.7% | 59.0% | 40.8% | 59.2% |
| 7,101 | LAKE | 3,051 | 681 | 2,362 | 8 | 1,681 D | 22.3% | 77.4% | 22.4% | 77.6% |
| 19,225 | LA PLATA | 8,007 | 3,550 | 4,442 | 15 | 892 D | 44.3% | 55.5% | 44.4% | 55.6% |
| 53,343 | LARIMER | 24,585 | 11,636 | 12,776 | 173 | 1,140 D | 47.3% | 52.0% | 47.7% | 52.3% |
| 19,983 | LAS ANIMAS | 8,453 | 1,833 | 6,591 | 29 | 4,758 D | 21.7% | 78.0% | 21.8% | 78.2% |
| 5,310 | LINCOLN | 2,439 | 1,104 | 1,327 | 8 | 223 D | 45.3% | 54.4% | 45.4% | 54.6% |
| 20,302 | LOGAN | 7,731 | 3,497 | 4,222 | 12 | 725 D | 45.2% | 54.6% | 45.3% | 54.7% |
| 50,715 | MESA | 21,082 | 8,317 | 12,716 | 49 | 4,399 D | 39.5% | 60.3% | 39.5% | 60.5% |
| 424 | MINERAL | 296 | 89 | 204 | 3 | 115 D | 30.1% | 68.9% | 30.4% | 69.6% |
| 7,061 | MOFFAT | 3,103 | 1,438 | 1,657 | 8 | 219 D | 46.3% | 53.4% | 46.5% | 53.5% |
| 14,024 | MONTEZUMA | 4,738 | 2,035 | 2,686 | 17 | 651 D | 43.0% | 56.7% | 43.1% | 56.9% |
| 18,286 | MONTROSE | 6,709 | 2,678 | 4,009 | 22 | 1,331 D | 39.9% | 59.8% | 40.0% | 60.0% |
| 21,192 | MORGAN | 7,520 | 3,228 | 4,271 | 21 | 1,043 D | 42.9% | 56.8% | 43.0% | 57.0% |
| 24,128 | OTERO | 9,636 | 3,605 | 5,999 | 32 | 2,394 D | 37.4% | 62.3% | 37.5% | 62.5% |
| 1,601 | OURAY | 820 | 358 | 456 | 6 | 98 D | 43.7% | 55.6% | 44.0% | 56.0% |
| 1,822 | PARK | 1,009 | 493 | 515 | 1 | 22 D | 48.9% | 51.0% | 48.9% | 51.1% |
| 4,440 | PHILLIPS | 2,260 | 1,012 | 1,243 | 5 | 231 D | 44.8% | 55.0% | 44.9% | 55.1% |
| 2,381 | PITKIN | 1,504 | 540 | 958 | 6 | 418 D | 35.9% | 63.7% | 36.0% | 64.0% |
| 13,296 | PROWERS | 5,822 | 2,044 | 3,759 | 19 | 1,715 D | 35.1% | 64.6% | 35.2% | 64.8% |
| 118,707 | PUEBLO | 48,536 | 13,103 | 34,933 | 500 | 21,830 D | 27.0% | 72.0% | 27.3% | 72.7% |
| 5,150 | RIO BLANCO | 2,152 | 1,015 | 1,134 | 3 | 119 D | 47.2% | 52.7% | 47.2% | 52.8% |
| 11,160 | RIO GRANDE | 3,867 | 1,699 | 2,161 | 7 | 462 D | 43.9% | 55.9% | 44.0% | 56.0% |
| 5,900 | ROUTT | 2,964 | 1,095 | 1,853 | 16 | 758 D | 36.9% | 62.5% | 37.1% | 62.9% |
| 4,473 | SAGUACHE | 1,725 | 622 | 1,099 | 4 | 477 D | 36.1% | 63.7% | 36.1% | 63.9% |
| 849 | SAN JUAN | 407 | 129 | 278 | | 149 D | 31.7% | 68.3% | 31.7% | 68.3% |
| 2,944 | SAN MIGUEL | 970 | 332 | 636 | 2 | 304 D | 34.2% | 65.6% | 34.3% | 65.7% |
| 4,242 | SEDGWICK | 1,839 | 895 | 942 | 2 | 47 D | 48.7% | 51.2% | 48.7% | 51.3% |
| 2,073 | SUMMIT | 828 | 344 | 483 | 1 | 139 D | 41.5% | 58.3% | 41.6% | 58.4% |
| 2,495 | TELLER | 1,264 | 577 | 685 | 2 | 108 D | 45.6% | 54.2% | 45.7% | 54.3% |

# COLORADO

## PRESIDENT 1964

| 1960 Census Population | County | Total Vote | Republican | Democratic | Other | Rep.-Dem. Plurality | Percentage | | | |
|---|---|---|---|---|---|---|---|---|---|---|
| | | | | | | | Total Vote | | Major Vote | |
| | | | | | | | Rep. | Dem. | Rep. | Dem. |
| 6,625 | WASHINGTON | 2,779 | 1,434 | 1,341 | 4 | 93 R | 51.6% | 48.3% | 51.7% | 48.3% |
| 72,344 | WELD | 29,679 | 12,204 | 17,268 | 207 | 5,064 D | 41.1% | 58.2% | 41.4% | 58.6% |
| 8,912 | YUMA | 4,171 | 2,007 | 2,145 | 19 | 138 D | 48.1% | 51.4% | 48.3% | 51.7% |
| 1,753,947 | TOTAL | 776,986 | 296,767 | 476,024 | 4,195 | 179,257 D | 38.2% | 61.3% | 38.4% | 61.6% |

# COLORADO

## PRESIDENT 1960

| 1960 Census Population | County | Total Vote | Republican | Democratic | Other | Rep.-Dem. Plurality | Percentage Total Vote Rep. | Dem. | Major Vote Rep. | Dem. |
|---|---|---|---|---|---|---|---|---|---|---|
| 120,296 | ADAMS | 39,798 | 18,452 | 21,168 | 178 | 2,716 D | 46.4% | 53.2% | 46.6% | 53.4% |
| 10,000 | ALAMOSA | 4,086 | 2,271 | 1,811 | 4 | 460 R | 55.6% | 44.3% | 55.6% | 44.4% |
| 113,426 | ARAPAHOE | 43,916 | 26,379 | 17,400 | 137 | 8,979 R | 60.1% | 39.6% | 60.3% | 39.7% |
| 2,629 | ARCHULETA | 1,057 | 489 | 567 | 1 | 78 D | 46.3% | 53.6% | 46.3% | 53.7% |
| 6,310 | BACA | 2,772 | 1,815 | 952 | 5 | 863 R | 65.5% | 34.3% | 65.6% | 34.4% |
| 7,419 | BENT | 2,904 | 1,671 | 1,228 | 5 | 443 R | 57.5% | 42.3% | 57.6% | 42.4% |
| 74,254 | BOULDER | 32,197 | 19,791 | 12,276 | 130 | 7,515 R | 61.5% | 38.1% | 61.7% | 38.3% |
| 8,298 | CHAFFEE | 4,016 | 2,094 | 1,918 | 4 | 176 R | 52.1% | 47.8% | 52.2% | 47.8% |
| 2,789 | CHEYENNE | 1,227 | 806 | 419 | 2 | 387 R | 65.7% | 34.1% | 65.8% | 34.2% |
| 2,793 | CLEAR CREEK | 1,652 | 964 | 688 | | 276 R | 58.4% | 41.6% | 58.4% | 41.6% |
| 8,428 | CONEJOS | 3,523 | 1,367 | 2,069 | 87 | 702 D | 38.8% | 58.7% | 39.8% | 60.2% |
| 4,219 | COSTILLA | 2,001 | 637 | 1,351 | 13 | 714 D | 31.8% | 67.5% | 32.0% | 68.0% |
| 3,978 | CROWLEY | 1,805 | 1,099 | 705 | 1 | 394 R | 60.9% | 39.1% | 60.9% | 39.1% |
| 1,305 | CUSTER | 823 | 509 | 314 | | 195 R | 61.8% | 38.2% | 61.8% | 38.2% |
| 15,602 | DELTA | 7,343 | 4,644 | 2,689 | 10 | 1,955 R | 63.2% | 36.6% | 63.3% | 36.7% |
| 493,887 | DENVER | 220,701 | 109,446 | 109,637 | 1,618 | 191 D | 49.6% | 49.7% | 50.0% | 50.0% |
| 2,196 | DOLORES | 862 | 476 | 386 | | 90 R | 55.2% | 44.8% | 55.2% | 44.8% |
| 4,816 | DOUGLAS | 2,313 | 1,490 | 823 | | 667 R | 64.4% | 35.6% | 64.4% | 35.6% |
| 4,677 | EAGLE | 1,871 | 989 | 880 | 2 | 109 R | 52.9% | 47.0% | 52.9% | 47.1% |
| 3,708 | ELBERT | 1,928 | 1,240 | 686 | 2 | 554 R | 64.3% | 35.6% | 64.4% | 35.6% |
| 143,742 | EL PASO | 48,704 | 31,625 | 17,018 | 61 | 14,607 R | 64.9% | 34.9% | 65.0% | 35.0% |
| 20,196 | FREMONT | 9,454 | 5,690 | 3,730 | 34 | 1,960 R | 60.2% | 39.5% | 60.4% | 39.6% |
| 12,017 | GARFIELD | 5,539 | 3,215 | 2,313 | 11 | 902 R | 58.0% | 41.8% | 58.2% | 41.8% |
| 685 | GILPIN | 538 | 315 | 223 | | 92 R | 58.6% | 41.4% | 58.6% | 41.4% |
| 3,557 | GRAND | 1,763 | 1,104 | 657 | 2 | 447 R | 62.6% | 37.3% | 62.7% | 37.3% |
| 5,477 | GUNNISON | 2,343 | 1,296 | 1,044 | 3 | 252 R | 55.3% | 44.6% | 55.4% | 44.6% |
| 208 | HINSDALE | 220 | 138 | 82 | | 56 R | 62.7% | 37.3% | 62.7% | 37.3% |
| 7,867 | HUERFANO | 4,053 | 1,367 | 2,673 | 13 | 1,306 D | 33.7% | 66.0% | 33.8% | 66.2% |
| 1,758 | JACKSON | 865 | 504 | 360 | 1 | 144 R | 58.3% | 41.6% | 58.3% | 41.7% |
| 127,520 | JEFFERSON | 57,204 | 34,105 | 22,962 | 137 | 11,143 R | 59.6% | 40.1% | 59.8% | 40.2% |
| 2,425 | KIOWA | 1,364 | 865 | 498 | 1 | 367 R | 63.4% | 36.5% | 63.5% | 36.5% |
| 6,957 | KIT CARSON | 3,361 | 2,248 | 1,103 | 10 | 1,145 R | 66.9% | 32.8% | 67.1% | 32.9% |
| 7,101 | LAKE | 2,803 | 954 | 1,842 | 7 | 888 D | 34.0% | 65.7% | 34.1% | 65.9% |
| 19,225 | LA PLATA | 8,111 | 4,772 | 3,329 | 10 | 1,443 R | 58.8% | 41.0% | 58.9% | 41.1% |
| 53,343 | LARIMER | 23,255 | 15,671 | 7,550 | 34 | 8,121 R | 67.4% | 32.5% | 67.5% | 32.5% |
| 19,983 | LAS ANIMAS | 9,722 | 2,989 | 6,704 | 29 | 3,715 D | 30.7% | 69.0% | 30.8% | 69.2% |
| 5,310 | LINCOLN | 2,542 | 1,498 | 1,041 | 3 | 457 R | 58.9% | 41.0% | 59.0% | 41.0% |
| 20,302 | LOGAN | 8,341 | 5,002 | 3,334 | 5 | 1,668 R | 60.0% | 40.0% | 60.0% | 40.0% |
| 50,715 | MESA | 22,132 | 13,015 | 9,072 | 45 | 3,943 R | 58.8% | 41.0% | 58.9% | 41.1% |
| 424 | MINERAL | 305 | 146 | 158 | 1 | 12 D | 47.9% | 51.8% | 48.0% | 52.0% |
| 7,061 | MOFFAT | 2,957 | 1,754 | 1,200 | 3 | 554 R | 59.3% | 40.6% | 59.4% | 40.6% |
| 14,024 | MONTEZUMA | 4,900 | 2,778 | 2,115 | 7 | 663 R | 56.7% | 43.2% | 56.8% | 43.2% |
| 18,286 | MONTROSE | 6,925 | 4,040 | 2,861 | 24 | 1,179 R | 58.3% | 41.3% | 58.5% | 41.5% |
| 21,192 | MORGAN | 8,259 | 5,092 | 3,151 | 16 | 1,941 R | 61.7% | 38.2% | 61.8% | 38.2% |
| 24,128 | OTERO | 10,229 | 6,015 | 4,199 | 15 | 1,816 R | 58.8% | 41.0% | 58.9% | 41.1% |
| 1,601 | OURAY | 940 | 508 | 432 | | 76 R | 54.0% | 46.0% | 54.0% | 46.0% |
| 1,822 | PARK | 1,082 | 642 | 438 | 2 | 204 R | 59.3% | 40.5% | 59.4% | 40.6% |
| 4,440 | PHILLIPS | 2,318 | 1,455 | 862 | 1 | 593 R | 62.8% | 37.2% | 62.8% | 37.2% |
| 2,381 | PITKIN | 1,167 | 679 | 488 | | 191 R | 58.2% | 41.8% | 58.2% | 41.8% |
| 13,296 | PROWERS | 6,030 | 3,567 | 2,457 | 6 | 1,110 R | 59.2% | 40.7% | 59.2% | 40.8% |
| 118,707 | PUEBLO | 48,582 | 20,579 | 27,421 | 582 | 6,842 D | 42.4% | 56.4% | 42.9% | 57.1% |
| 5,150 | RIO BLANCO | 2,188 | 1,391 | 794 | 3 | 597 R | 63.6% | 36.3% | 63.7% | 36.3% |
| 11,160 | RIO GRANDE | 4,312 | 2,524 | 1,782 | 6 | 742 R | 58.5% | 41.3% | 58.6% | 41.4% |
| 5,900 | ROUTT | 3,067 | 1,651 | 1,414 | 2 | 237 R | 53.8% | 46.1% | 53.9% | 46.1% |
| 4,473 | SAGUACHE | 1,949 | 956 | 984 | 9 | 28 D | 49.1% | 50.5% | 49.3% | 50.7% |
| 849 | SAN JUAN | 482 | 218 | 261 | 3 | 43 D | 45.2% | 54.1% | 45.5% | 54.5% |
| 2,944 | SAN MIGUEL | 1,139 | 525 | 612 | 2 | 87 D | 46.1% | 53.7% | 46.2% | 53.8% |
| 4,242 | SEDGWICK | 2,003 | 1,230 | 769 | 4 | 461 R | 61.4% | 38.4% | 61.5% | 38.5% |
| 2,073 | SUMMIT | 827 | 424 | 400 | 3 | 24 R | 51.3% | 48.4% | 51.5% | 48.5% |
| 2,495 | TELLER | 1,349 | 723 | 622 | 4 | 101 R | 53.6% | 46.1% | 53.8% | 46.2% |

# COLORADO

## PRESIDENT 1960

| 1960 Census Population | County | Total Vote | Republican | Democratic | Other | Rep.-Dem. Plurality | Percentage | | | |
|---|---|---|---|---|---|---|---|---|---|---|
| | | | | | | | Total Vote | | Major Vote | |
| | | | | | | | Rep. | Dem. | Rep. | Dem. |
| 6,625 | WASHINGTON | 3,022 | 1,979 | 1,039 | 4 | 940 R | 65.5% | 34.4% | 65.6% | 34.4% |
| 72,344 | WELD | 28,790 | 17,558 | 11,179 | 53 | 6,379 R | 61.0% | 38.8% | 61.1% | 38.9% |
| 8,912 | YUMA | 4,305 | 2,806 | 1,489 | 10 | 1,317 R | 65.2% | 34.6% | 65.3% | 34.7% |
| 1,753,947 | TOTAL | 736,236 | 402,242 | 330,629 | 3,365 | 71,613 R | 54.6% | 44.9% | 54.9% | 45.1% |

# COLORADO

## ELECTION NOTES

**2004** Other vote was 12,718 Colorado Reform (Ralph Nader); 7,664 Libertarian (Michael Badnarik); 2,562 American Constitution (Michael Peroutka); 1,591 Green (David Cobb); 804 Unaffiliated (Stanford E. "Andy" Andress); 700 write-in (John Joseph Kennedy); 378 Concerns of People (Gene Amondson); 329 Socialist Equality (Bill Van Auken); 241 Socialist Workers (James E. Harris); 216 Socialist (Walter F. Brown); 140 Prohibition (Earl F. Dodge).

**2000** Other vote was 12,799 Libertarian (Browne); 10,465 Unaffiliated/Freedom (Buchanan); 2,240 Natural Law (Hagelin); 1,319 American Constitution (Phillips); 712 Socialist (McReynolds); 216 Socialist Workers (Harris); 208 Prohibition (Dodge).

**1996** Other vote was 25,070 Green (Nader); 12,392 Libertarian (Browne); 2,813 American Constitution (Phillips); 2,809 Independent (Collins); 2,547 Natural Law (Hagelin); 669 Socialist (Hollis); 599 Workers World (Moorehead); 557 American (Templin); 375 Colorado Prohibition (Dodge); 244 Socialist Workers Campaign (Harris).

**1992** Other vote was 8,669 Marrou (Libertarian); 1,608 Fulani (New Alliance); 274 Gritz (write-in); 47 Hagelin (write-in); 21 Dodge (write-in); 20 LaRouche (write-in).

**1988** Other vote was 15,482 Paul (Libertarian); 4,604 Dodge (Prohibition); 2,539 Fulani (New Alliance); 139 Duke (write-in).

**1984** Other vote was 11,257 Bergland (Libertarian); 4,662 LaRouche (Independent); 978 Serrette (Independent Alliance); 810 Mason (Socialist Workers); 858 Dodge (Prohibition); 23 Johnson (write-in).

**1980** Other vote was 130,633 Anderson (National Unity Campaign); 25,744 Clark (Libertarian); 5,614 Commoner (Citizens); 1,180 Bubar (Statesman); 520 Pulley (Socialist Workers); 487 Hall (Communist).

**1976** Other vote was 26,107 McCarthy (Independent); 5,330 MacBride (Libertarian); 2,882 Bubar (Prohibition); 1,126 Camejo (Socialist Workers); 567 LaRouche (U.S. Labor); 403 Hall (Communist); 397 Anderson (write-in); 14 Levin (write-in); 6 Miller (write-in); 2 scattered write-in. Early unamended canvass gave the state-wide totals as 584,278 Republican; 460,801 Democratic; 26,047 Independent; 5,338 Libertarian; 2,886 Prohibition; 1,122 Socialist Workers; 565 U.S. Labor; 403 Communist. Listed write-in votes are from the original canvass. Amendments were made in the following counties: Boulder, Las Animas, Moffat, Montrose and Saguache.

**1972** Other vote was 17,269 Schmitz (American); 4,361 Fisher (Socialist Labor); 2,403 Spock (People's); 1,111 Hospers (Libertarian); 666 Jenness (Socialist Workers); 467 Munn (Prohibition); 432 Hall (Communist); 6 scattered write-in.

**1968** Wallace on the ballot as American Independent. Other vote was 3,016 Blomen (Socialist Labor); 1,393 Gregory (New Party); 275 Munn (Prohibition); 235 Halstead (Socialist Workers); 948 scattered write-in.

**1964** Other vote was 2,537 DeBerry (Socialist Workers); 1,356 Munn (Prohibition); 302 Hass (Socialist Labor).

**1960** Other vote was 2,803 Hass (Socialist Labor); 562 Dobbs (Socialist Workers). In an uncorrected canvass report the Dobbs vote in Summit county is given as ten (instead of none) and the state total as 572 (instead of 562).

# CONNECTICUT

## POPULAR VOTE FOR PRESIDENT 1920 TO 2004

| | | Republican | | Democratic | | Other | | Percentage | | | |
| | Total | | | | | | | Total Vote | | Major Vote | |
| Year | Vote | Vote | Candidate | Vote | Candidate | Vote | Plurality | Rep. | Dem. | Rep. | Dem. |
|---|---|---|---|---|---|---|---|---|---|---|---|
| 2004 | 1,578,769 | 693,826 | Bush, George W. | 857,488 | Kerry, John | 27,455 | 163,662 D | 43.9% | 54.3% | 44.7% | 55.3% |
| 2000** | 1,459,525 | 561,094 | Bush, George W. | 816,015 | Gore, Al | 82,416 | 254,921 D | 38.4% | 55.9% | 40.7% | 59.3% |
| 1996** | 1,392,614 | 483,109 | Dole, Bob | 735,740 | Clinton, Bill | 173,765 | 252,631 D | 34.7% | 52.8% | 39.6% | 60.4% |
| 1992** | 1,616,332 | 578,313 | Bush, George | 682,318 | Clinton, Bill | 355,701 | 104,005 D | 35.8% | 42.2% | 45.9% | 54.1% |
| 1988 | 1,443,394 | 750,241 | Bush, George | 676,584 | Dukakis, Michael S. | 16,569 | 73,657 R | 52.0% | 46.9% | 52.6% | 47.4% |
| 1984 | 1,466,900 | 890,877 | Reagan, Ronald | 569,597 | Mondale, Walter F. | 6,426 | 321,280 R | 60.7% | 38.8% | 61.0% | 39.0% |
| 1980** | 1,406,285 | 677,210 | Reagan, Ronald | 541,732 | Carter, Jimmy | 187,343 | 135,478 R | 48.2% | 38.5% | 55.6% | 44.4% |
| 1976 | 1,381,526 | 719,261 | Ford, Gerald R. | 647,895 | Carter, Jimmy | 14,370 | 71,366 R | 52.1% | 46.9% | 52.6% | 47.4% |
| 1972 | 1,384,277 | 810,763 | Nixon, Richard M. | 555,498 | McGovern, George S. | 18,016 | 255,265 R | 58.6% | 40.1% | 59.3% | 40.7% |
| 1968 | 1,256,232 | 556,721 | Nixon, Richard M. | 621,561 | Humphrey, Hubert H. | 77,950 | 64,840 D | 44.3% | 49.5% | 47.2% | 52.8% |
| 1964 | 1,218,578 | 390,996 | Goldwater, Barry M. | 826,269 | Johnson, Lyndon B. | 1,313 | 435,273 D | 32.1% | 67.8% | 32.1% | 67.9% |
| 1960 | 1,222,883 | 565,813 | Nixon, Richard M. | 657,055 | Kennedy, John F. | 15 | 91,242 D | 46.3% | 53.7% | 46.3% | 53.7% |
| 1956 | 1,117,121 | 711,837 | Eisenhower, Dwight D. | 405,079 | Stevenson, Adlai E. | 205 | 306,758 R | 63.7% | 36.3% | 63.7% | 36.3% |
| 1952 | 1,096,911 | 611,012 | Eisenhower, Dwight D. | 481,649 | Stevenson, Adlai E. | 4,250 | 129,363 R | 55.7% | 43.9% | 55.9% | 44.1% |
| 1948 | 883,518 | 437,754 | Dewey, Thomas E. | 423,297 | Truman, Harry S. | 22,467 | 14,457 R | 49.5% | 47.9% | 50.8% | 49.2% |
| 1944 | 831,990 | 390,527 | Dewey, Thomas E. | 435,146 | Roosevelt, Franklin D. | 6,317 | 44,619 D | 46.9% | 52.3% | 47.3% | 52.7% |
| 1940 | 781,502 | 361,819 | Willkie, Wendell | 417,621 | Roosevelt, Franklin D. | 2,062 | 55,802 D | 46.3% | 53.4% | 46.4% | 53.6% |
| 1936 | 690,723 | 278,685 | Landon, Alfred M. | 382,129 | Roosevelt, Franklin D. | 29,909 | 103,444 D | 40.3% | 55.3% | 42.2% | 57.8% |
| 1932 | 594,183 | 288,420 | Hoover, Herbert C. | 281,632 | Roosevelt, Franklin D. | 24,131 | 6,788 R | 48.5% | 47.4% | 50.6% | 49.4% |
| 1928 | 553,118 | 296,641 | Hoover, Herbert C. | 252,085 | Smith, Alfred E. | 4,392 | 44,556 R | 53.6% | 45.6% | 54.1% | 45.9% |
| 1924 | 400,396 | 246,322 | Coolidge, Calvin | 110,184 | Davis, John W. | 43,890 | 136,138 R | 61.5% | 27.5% | 69.1% | 30.9% |
| 1920 | 365,518 | 229,238 | Harding, Warren G. | 120,721 | Cox, James M. | 15,559 | 108,517 R | 62.7% | 33.0% | 65.5% | 34.5% |

In 2000 the other vote column includes 64,452 votes cast for Green (Nader). In 1996 the other vote column includes 139,523 votes cast for Perot. In 1992 the other vote column includes 348,771 votes cast for Perot. In 1980 the other column includes 171,807 votes for Independent (Anderson).

## ELECTORAL COLLEGE VOTE 1920 TO 2004

| Year | Total | Republican | Democratic | Other |
|---|---|---|---|---|
| 2004 | 7 | | 7 | |
| 2000 | 8 | | 8 | |
| 1996 | 8 | | 8 | |
| 1992 | 8 | | 8 | |
| 1988 | 8 | 8 | | |
| 1984 | 8 | 8 | | |
| 1980 | 8 | 8 | | |
| 1976 | 8 | 8 | | |
| 1972 | 8 | 8 | | |
| 1968 | 8 | | 8 | |
| 1964 | 8 | | 8 | |
| 1960 | 8 | | 8 | |
| 1956 | 8 | 8 | | |
| 1952 | 8 | 8 | | |
| 1948 | 8 | 8 | | |
| 1944 | 8 | | 8 | |
| 1940 | 8 | | 8 | |
| 1936 | 8 | | 8 | |
| 1932 | 8 | 8 | | |
| 1928 | 7 | 7 | | |
| 1924 | 7 | 7 | | |
| 1920 | 7 | 7 | | |

# CONNECTICUT

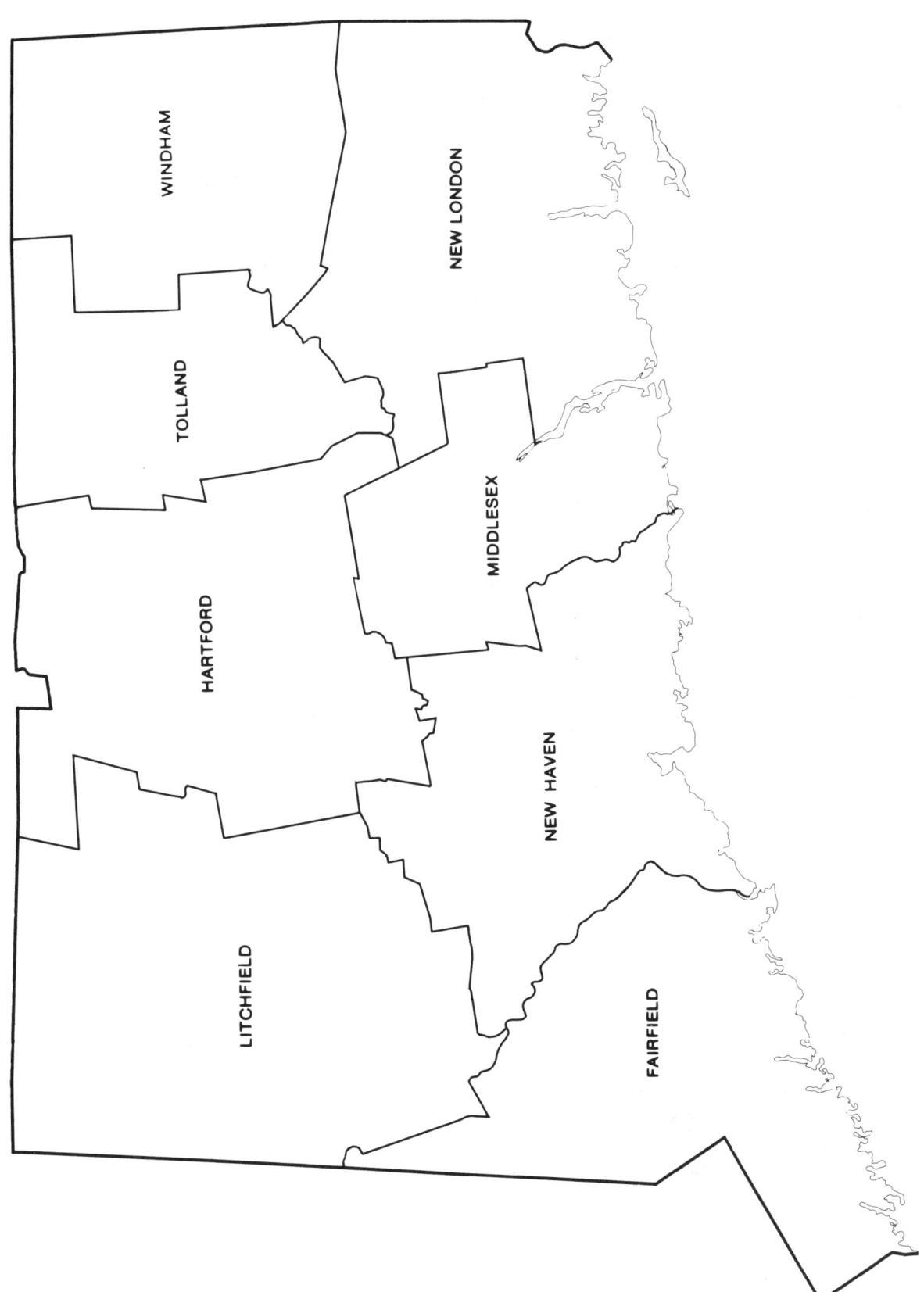

174

# CONNECTICUT

## PRESIDENT 2004

| 2000 Census Population | County | Total Vote | Republican | Democratic | Other | Rep.-Dem. Plurality | Total Vote Rep. | Dem. | Major Vote Rep. | Dem. |
|---|---|---|---|---|---|---|---|---|---|---|
| 882,567 | FAIRFIELD | 400,967 | 189,605 | 205,902 | 5,460 | 16,297 D | 47.3% | 51.4% | 47.9% | 52.1% |
| 857,183 | HARTFORD | 391,808 | 154,919 | 229,902 | 6,987 | 74,983 D | 39.5% | 58.7% | 40.3% | 59.7% |
| 182,193 | LITCHFIELD | 96,668 | 50,160 | 44,647 | 1,861 | 5,513 R | 51.9% | 46.2% | 52.9% | 47.1% |
| 155,071 | MIDDLESEX | 83,984 | 35,252 | 47,292 | 1,440 | 12,040 D | 42.0% | 56.3% | 42.7% | 57.3% |
| 824,008 | NEW HAVEN | 366,392 | 160,390 | 199,060 | 6,942 | 38,670 D | 43.8% | 54.3% | 44.6% | 55.4% |
| 259,088 | NEW LONDON | 118,360 | 49,931 | 66,062 | 2,367 | 16,131 D | 42.2% | 55.8% | 43.0% | 57.0% |
| 136,364 | TOLLAND | 71,729 | 31,245 | 39,146 | 1,338 | 7,901 D | 43.6% | 54.6% | 44.4% | 55.6% |
| 109,091 | WINDHAM | 48,861 | 22,324 | 25,477 | 1,060 | 3,153 D | 45.7% | 52.1% | 46.7% | 53.3% |
| 3,405,565 | TOTAL | 1,578,769 | 693,826 | 857,488 | 27,455 | 163,662 D | 43.9% | 54.3% | 44.7% | 55.3% |

# CONNECTICUT

## PRESIDENT 2000

| 2000 Census Population | County | Total Vote | Republican | Democratic | Green (Nader) | Other | Rep.-Dem. Plurality | Rep. | Dem. | Green |
|---|---|---|---|---|---|---|---|---|---|---|
| 882,567 | FAIRFIELD | 370,289 | 159,659 | 193,769 | 12,664 | 4,197 | 34,110 D | 43.1% | 52.3% | 3.4% |
| 857,183 | HARTFORD | 367,556 | 127,468 | 221,167 | 14,214 | 4,707 | 93,699 D | 34.7% | 60.2% | 3.9% |
| 182,193 | LITCHFIELD | 87,338 | 39,172 | 41,806 | 5,413 | 947 | 2,634 D | 44.9% | 47.9% | 6.2% |
| 155,071 | MIDDLESEX | 77,433 | 29,295 | 43,319 | 4,039 | 780 | 14,024 D | 37.8% | 55.9% | 5.2% |
| 824,008 | NEW HAVEN | 341,099 | 122,919 | 197,928 | 15,567 | 4,685 | 75,009 D | 36.0% | 58.0% | 4.6% |
| 259,088 | NEW LONDON | 109,147 | 41,168 | 60,449 | 6,218 | 1,312 | 19,281 D | 37.7% | 55.4% | 5.7% |
| 136,364 | TOLLAND | 62,700 | 24,705 | 33,554 | 3,711 | 730 | 8,849 D | 39.4% | 53.5% | 5.9% |
| 109,091 | WINDHAM | 43,963 | 16,708 | 24,023 | 2,626 | 606 | 7,315 D | 38.0% | 54.6% | 6.0% |
| 3,405,565 | TOTAL | 1,459,525 | 561,094 | 816,015 | 64,452 | 17,964 | 254,921 D | 38.4% | 55.9% | 4.4% |

# CONNECTICUT

## PRESIDENT 1996

| 1995 Census Pop. Est. | County | Total Vote | Republican | Democratic | Reform (Perot) | Other | Rep.-Dem. Plurality | Rep. | Dem. | Reform |
|---|---|---|---|---|---|---|---|---|---|---|
| 830,728 | FAIRFIELD | 352,228 | 144,632 | 172,337 | 27,328 | 7,931 | 27,705 D | 41.1% | 48.9% | 7.8% |
| 835,589 | HARTFORD | 356,842 | 111,566 | 203,549 | 33,685 | 8,042 | 91,983 D | 31.3% | 57.0% | 9.4% |
| 179,316 | LITCHFIELD | 81,398 | 31,645 | 37,375 | 9,646 | 2,732 | 5,730 D | 38.9% | 45.9% | 11.9% |
| 148,030 | MIDDLESEX | 71,788 | 22,960 | 37,695 | 9,136 | 1,997 | 14,735 D | 32.0% | 52.5% | 12.7% |
| 794,785 | NEW HAVEN | 325,891 | 106,636 | 178,323 | 33,454 | 7,478 | 71,687 D | 32.7% | 54.7% | 10.3% |
| 250,404 | NEW LONDON | 103,095 | 33,039 | 54,377 | 12,916 | 2,763 | 21,338 D | 32.0% | 52.7% | 12.5% |
| 131,604 | TOLLAND | 58,626 | 19,394 | 30,007 | 7,164 | 2,061 | 10,613 D | 33.1% | 51.2% | 12.2% |
| 104,206 | WINDHAM | 42,746 | 13,237 | 22,077 | 6,194 | 1,238 | 8,840 D | 31.0% | 51.6% | 14.5% |
| 3,274,662 | TOTAL | 1,392,614 | 483,109 | 735,740 | 139,523 | 34,242 | 252,631 D | 34.7% | 52.8% | 10.0% |

# CONNECTICUT

## PRESIDENT 1992

| 1990 Census Population | County | Total Vote | Republican | Democratic | Perot | Other | Plurality | Percentage Total Vote | | |
|---|---|---|---|---|---|---|---|---|---|---|
| | | | | | | | | Rep. | Dem. | Perot |
| 827,645 | FAIRFIELD | 409,410 | 175,158 | 160,202 | 72,532 | 1,518 | 14,956 R | 42.8% | 39.1% | 17.7% |
| 851,783 | HARTFORD | 414,804 | 132,591 | 195,495 | 85,005 | 1,713 | 62,904 D | 32.0% | 47.1% | 20.5% |
| 174,092 | LITCHFIELD | 93,213 | 34,492 | 33,686 | 24,639 | 396 | 806 R | 37.0% | 36.1% | 26.4% |
| 143,196 | MIDDLESEX | 81,027 | 24,646 | 34,707 | 21,306 | 368 | 10,061 D | 30.4% | 42.8% | 26.3% |
| 804,219 | NEW HAVEN | 385,132 | 141,264 | 161,374 | 80,817 | 1,677 | 20,110 D | 36.7% | 41.9% | 21.0% |
| 254,957 | NEW LONDON | 117,767 | 34,567 | 49,808 | 32,736 | 656 | 15,241 D | 29.4% | 42.3% | 27.8% |
| 128,699 | TOLLAND | 66,215 | 20,632 | 27,425 | 17,930 | 228 | 6,793 D | 31.2% | 41.4% | 27.1% |
| 102,525 | WINDHAM | 48,588 | 14,963 | 19,621 | 13,806 | 198 | 4,658 D | 30.8% | 40.4% | 28.4% |
| 3,287,116 | TOTAL | 1,616,332 | 578,313 | 682,318 | 348,771 | 6,930 | 104,005 D | 35.8% | 42.2% | 21.6% |

# CONNECTICUT

## PRESIDENT 1988

| 1980 Census Population | County | Total Vote | Republican | Democratic | Other | Rep.-Dem. Plurality | Percentage | | | |
|---|---|---|---|---|---|---|---|---|---|---|
| | | | | | | | Total Vote | | Major Vote | |
| | | | | | | | Rep. | Dem. | Rep. | Dem. |
| 807,143 | FAIRFIELD | 374,627 | 221,316 | 149,630 | 3,681 | 71,686 R | 59.1% | 39.9% | 59.7% | 40.3% |
| 807,766 | HARTFORD | 376,402 | 173,031 | 199,857 | 3,514 | 26,826 D | 46.0% | 53.1% | 46.4% | 53.6% |
| 156,769 | LITCHFIELD | 80,113 | 44,637 | 34,227 | 1,249 | 10,410 R | 55.7% | 42.7% | 56.6% | 43.4% |
| 129,017 | MIDDLESEX | 69,593 | 34,682 | 33,946 | 965 | 736 R | 49.8% | 48.8% | 50.5% | 49.5% |
| 761,337 | NEW HAVEN | 341,811 | 174,251 | 163,153 | 4,407 | 11,098 R | 51.0% | 47.7% | 51.6% | 48.4% |
| 238,409 | NEW LONDON | 103,011 | 52,681 | 48,882 | 1,448 | 3,799 R | 51.1% | 47.5% | 51.9% | 48.1% |
| 114,823 | TOLLAND | 55,926 | 28,375 | 26,884 | 667 | 1,491 R | 50.7% | 48.1% | 51.3% | 48.7% |
| 92,312 | WINDHAM | 41,904 | 21,268 | 20,005 | 631 | 1,263 R | 50.8% | 47.7% | 51.5% | 48.5% |
| 3,107,576 | TOTAL | 1,443,394 | 750,241 | 676,584 | 16,569 | 73,657 R | 52.0% | 46.9% | 52.6% | 47.4% |

# CONNECTICUT

## PRESIDENT 1984

| 1980 Census Population | County | Total Vote | Republican | Democratic | Other | Rep.-Dem. Plurality | Percentage | | | |
|---|---|---|---|---|---|---|---|---|---|---|
| | | | | | | | Total Vote | | Major Vote | |
| | | | | | | | Rep. | Dem. | Rep. | Dem. |
| 807,143 | FAIRFIELD | 391,179 | 257,319 | 132,253 | 1,607 | 125,066 R | 65.8% | 33.8% | 66.1% | 33.9% |
| 807,766 | HARTFORD | 378,405 | 208,210 | 168,609 | 1,586 | 39,601 R | 55.0% | 44.6% | 55.3% | 44.7% |
| 156,769 | LITCHFIELD | 79,416 | 52,583 | 26,564 | 269 | 26,019 R | 66.2% | 33.4% | 66.4% | 33.6% |
| 129,017 | MIDDLESEX | 66,722 | 39,580 | 26,915 | 227 | 12,665 R | 59.3% | 40.3% | 59.5% | 40.5% |
| 761,337 | NEW HAVEN | 354,712 | 212,166 | 140,945 | 1,601 | 71,221 R | 59.8% | 39.7% | 60.1% | 39.9% |
| 238,409 | NEW LONDON | 102,487 | 63,121 | 38,857 | 509 | 24,264 R | 61.6% | 37.9% | 61.9% | 38.1% |
| 114,823 | TOLLAND | 53,298 | 32,981 | 20,103 | 214 | 12,878 R | 61.9% | 37.7% | 62.1% | 37.9% |
| 92,312 | WINDHAM | 40,455 | 24,917 | 15,351 | 187 | 9,566 R | 61.6% | 37.9% | 61.9% | 38.1% |
| 3,107,576 | TOTAL | 1,466,900 | 890,877 | 569,597 | 6,426 | 321,280 R | 60.7% | 38.8% | 61.0% | 39.0% |

# CONNECTICUT

## PRESIDENT 1980

| 1980 Census Population | County | Total Vote | Republican | Democratic | Other | Rep.-Dem. Plurality | Percentage | | | |
|---|---|---|---|---|---|---|---|---|---|---|
| | | | | | | | Total Vote | | Major Vote | |
| | | | | | | | Rep. | Dem. | Rep. | Dem. |
| 807,143 | FAIRFIELD | 368,098 | 201,997 | 124,074 | 42,027 | 77,923 R | 54.9% | 33.7% | 61.9% | 38.1% |
| 807,766 | HARTFORD | 371,380 | 150,265 | 164,643 | 56,472 | 14,378 D | 40.5% | 44.3% | 47.7% | 52.3% |
| 156,769 | LITCHFIELD | 76,354 | 38,725 | 26,705 | 10,924 | 12,020 R | 50.7% | 35.0% | 59.2% | 40.8% |
| 129,017 | MIDDLESEX | 63,672 | 28,989 | 24,768 | 9,915 | 4,221 R | 45.5% | 38.9% | 53.9% | 46.1% |
| 761,337 | NEW HAVEN | 337,732 | 169,038 | 130,913 | 37,781 | 38,125 R | 50.1% | 38.8% | 56.4% | 43.6% |
| 238,409 | NEW LONDON | 98,448 | 47,217 | 36,628 | 14,603 | 10,589 R | 48.0% | 37.2% | 56.3% | 43.7% |
| 114,823 | TOLLAND | 50,346 | 22,127 | 18,557 | 9,662 | 3,570 R | 43.9% | 36.9% | 54.4% | 45.6% |
| 92,312 | WINDHAM | 39,419 | 18,852 | 15,444 | 5,123 | 3,408 R | 47.8% | 39.2% | 55.0% | 45.0% |
| 3,107,576 | TOTAL | 1,406,285 | 677,210 | 541,732 | 187,343 | 135,478 R | 48.2% | 38.5% | 55.6% | 44.4% |

# CONNECTICUT

## PRESIDENT 1976

| 1970 Census Population | County | Total Vote | Republican | Democratic | Other | Rep.-Dem. Plurality | Percentage | | | |
|---|---|---|---|---|---|---|---|---|---|---|
| | | | | | | | Total Vote | | Major Vote | |
| | | | | | | | Rep. | Dem. | Rep. | Dem. |
| 792,814 | FAIRFIELD | 360,224 | 209,458 | 148,353 | 2,413 | 61,105 R | 58.1% | 41.2% | 58.5% | 41.5% |
| 816,737 | HARTFORD | 368,494 | 175,064 | 191,257 | 2,173 | 16,193 D | 47.5% | 51.9% | 47.8% | 52.2% |
| 144,091 | LITCHFIELD | 73,583 | 40,705 | 32,419 | 459 | 8,286 R | 55.3% | 44.1% | 55.7% | 44.3% |
| 115,018 | MIDDLESEX | 60,550 | 31,115 | 29,097 | 338 | 2,018 R | 51.4% | 48.1% | 51.7% | 48.3% |
| 744,948 | NEW HAVEN | 334,189 | 174,342 | 157,402 | 2,445 | 16,940 R | 52.2% | 47.1% | 52.6% | 47.4% |
| 230,654 | NEW LONDON | 93,720 | 47,231 | 45,908 | 581 | 1,323 R | 50.4% | 49.0% | 50.7% | 49.3% |
| 103,440 | TOLLAND | 47,024 | 23,703 | 23,079 | 242 | 624 R | 50.4% | 49.1% | 50.7% | 49.3% |
| 84,515 | WINDHAM | 38,262 | 17,643 | 20,380 | 239 | 2,737 D | 46.1% | 53.3% | 46.4% | 53.6% |
| 3,032,217 | TOTAL | 1,381,526 | 719,261 | 647,895 | 14,370 | 71,366 R | 52.1% | 46.9% | 52.6% | 47.4% |

# CONNECTICUT

## PRESIDENT 1972

| 1970 Census Population | County | Total Vote | Republican | Democratic | Other | Rep.-Dem. Plurality | Percentage | | | |
|---|---|---|---|---|---|---|---|---|---|---|
| | | | | | | | Total Vote | | Major Vote | |
| | | | | | | | Rep. | Dem. | Rep. | Dem. |
| 792,814 | FAIRFIELD | 364,585 | 233,188 | 125,128 | 6,269 | 108,060 R | 64.0% | 34.3% | 65.1% | 34.9% |
| 816,737 | HARTFORD | 372,786 | 194,095 | 174,837 | 3,854 | 19,258 R | 52.1% | 46.9% | 52.6% | 47.4% |
| 144,091 | LITCHFIELD | 72,262 | 43,478 | 27,929 | 855 | 15,549 R | 60.2% | 38.6% | 60.9% | 39.1% |
| 115,018 | MIDDLESEX | 57,453 | 33,249 | 23,573 | 631 | 9,676 R | 57.9% | 41.0% | 58.5% | 41.5% |
| 744,948 | NEW HAVEN | 340,487 | 200,818 | 135,132 | 4,537 | 65,686 R | 59.0% | 39.7% | 59.8% | 40.2% |
| 230,654 | NEW LONDON | 92,352 | 58,516 | 32,935 | 901 | 25,581 R | 63.4% | 35.7% | 64.0% | 36.0% |
| 103,440 | TOLLAND | 45,728 | 25,798 | 19,505 | 425 | 6,293 R | 56.4% | 42.7% | 56.9% | 43.1% |
| 84,515 | WINDHAM | 38,624 | 21,621 | 16,459 | 544 | 5,162 R | 56.0% | 42.6% | 56.8% | 43.2% |
| 3,032,217 | TOTAL | 1,384,277 | 810,763 | 555,498 | 18,016 | 255,265 R | 58.6% | 40.1% | 59.3% | 40.7% |

# CONNECTICUT

## PRESIDENT 1968

| 1960 Census Population | County | Total Vote | Republican | Democratic | AIP | Other | Plurality | Percentage Total Vote | | |
|---|---|---|---|---|---|---|---|---|---|---|
| | | | | | | | | Rep. | Dem. | AIP |
| 653,589 | FAIRFIELD | 334,292 | 173,108 | 139,364 | 21,477 | 343 | 33,744 R | 51.8% | 41.7% | 6.4% |
| 689,555 | HARTFORD | 339,701 | 131,740 | 190,865 | 16,779 | 317 | 59,125 D | 38.8% | 56.2% | 4.9% |
| 119,856 | LITCHFIELD | 64,380 | 31,429 | 29,340 | 3,526 | 85 | 2,089 R | 48.8% | 45.6% | 5.5% |
| 88,865 | MIDDLESEX | 48,524 | 21,999 | 23,727 | 2,706 | 92 | 1,728 D | 45.3% | 48.9% | 5.6% |
| 660,315 | NEW HAVEN | 314,432 | 130,501 | 159,653 | 23,985 | 293 | 29,152 D | 41.5% | 50.8% | 7.6% |
| 185,745 | NEW LONDON | 83,574 | 37,116 | 41,507 | 4,879 | 72 | 4,391 D | 44.4% | 49.7% | 5.8% |
| 68,737 | TOLLAND | 36,655 | 16,666 | 18,007 | 1,918 | 64 | 1,341 D | 45.5% | 49.1% | 5.2% |
| 68,572 | WINDHAM | 34,674 | 14,162 | 19,098 | 1,380 | 34 | 4,936 D | 40.8% | 55.1% | 4.0% |
| 2,535,234 | TOTAL | 1,256,232 | 556,721 | 621,561 | 76,650 | 1,300 | 64,840 D | 44.3% | 49.5% | 6.1% |

# CONNECTICUT

## PRESIDENT 1964

| 1960 Census Population | County | Total Vote | Republican | Democratic | Other | Rep.-Dem. Plurality | Percentage | | | |
|---|---|---|---|---|---|---|---|---|---|---|
| | | | | | | | Total Vote | | Major Vote | |
| | | | | | | | Rep. | Dem. | Rep. | Dem. |
| 653,589 | FAIRFIELD | 320,619 | 125,576 | 194,782 | 261 | 69,206 D | 39.2% | 60.8% | 39.2% | 60.8% |
| 689,555 | HARTFORD | 329,504 | 88,811 | 240,071 | 622 | 151,260 D | 27.0% | 72.9% | 27.0% | 73.0% |
| 119,856 | LITCHFIELD | 61,068 | 20,834 | 40,172 | 62 | 19,338 D | 34.1% | 65.8% | 34.2% | 65.8% |
| 88,865 | MIDDLESEX | 45,285 | 14,697 | 30,517 | 71 | 15,820 D | 32.5% | 67.4% | 32.5% | 67.5% |
| 660,315 | NEW HAVEN | 316,570 | 97,656 | 218,743 | 171 | 121,087 D | 30.8% | 69.1% | 30.9% | 69.1% |
| 185,745 | NEW LONDON | 78,991 | 24,391 | 54,551 | 49 | 30,160 D | 30.9% | 69.1% | 30.9% | 69.1% |
| 68,737 | TOLLAND | 32,204 | 9,951 | 22,195 | 58 | 12,244 D | 30.9% | 68.9% | 31.0% | 69.0% |
| 68,572 | WINDHAM | 34,337 | 9,080 | 25,238 | 19 | 16,158 D | 26.4% | 73.5% | 26.5% | 73.5% |
| 2,535,234 | TOTAL | 1,218,578 | 390,996 | 826,269 | 1,313 | 435,273 D | 32.1% | 67.8% | 32.1% | 67.9% |

# CONNECTICUT

## PRESIDENT 1960

| 1960 Census Population | County | Total Vote | Republican | Democratic | Other | Rep.-Dem. Plurality | Percentage | | | |
|---|---|---|---|---|---|---|---|---|---|---|
| | | | | | | | Total Vote | | Major Vote | |
| | | | | | | | Rep. | Dem. | Rep. | Dem. |
| 653,589 | FAIRFIELD | 314,226 | 167,778 | 146,442 | 6 | 21,336 R | 53.4% | 46.6% | 53.4% | 46.6% |
| 689,555 | HARTFORD | 331,864 | 136,459 | 195,403 | 2 | 58,944 D | 41.1% | 58.9% | 41.1% | 58.9% |
| 119,856 | LITCHFIELD | 63,108 | 34,043 | 29,062 | 3 | 4,981 R | 53.9% | 46.1% | 53.9% | 46.1% |
| 88,865 | MIDDLESEX | 44,204 | 22,045 | 22,158 | 1 | 113 D | 49.9% | 50.1% | 49.9% | 50.1% |
| 660,315 | NEW HAVEN | 325,539 | 136,852 | 188,685 | 2 | 51,833 D | 42.0% | 58.0% | 42.0% | 58.0% |
| 185,745 | NEW LONDON | 78,696 | 38,070 | 40,625 | 1 | 2,555 D | 48.4% | 51.6% | 48.4% | 51.6% |
| 68,737 | TOLLAND | 29,961 | 15,386 | 14,575 | | 811 R | 51.4% | 48.6% | 51.4% | 48.6% |
| 68,572 | WINDHAM | 35,285 | 15,180 | 20,105 | | 4,925 D | 43.0% | 57.0% | 43.0% | 57.0% |
| 2,535,234 | TOTAL | 1,222,883 | 565,813 | 657,055 | 15 | 91,242 D | 46.3% | 53.7% | 46.3% | 53.7% |

# CONNECTICUT

## ELECTION NOTES

**2004**   Other vote was 12,969 Petitioning Candidate (Ralph Nader); 9,564 Green (David Cobb); 3,367 Libertarian (Michael Badnarik); 1,543 Concerned Citizens (Michael Peroutka); 12 write-in (Roger Calero).

**2000**   Other vote was 9,695 Concerned Citizens (Phillips); 4,731 Reform (Buchanan); 3,484 Libertarian (Browne); 40 write-in (Hagelin); 4 write-in (Harris); 4 write-in (Reicher); 3 write-in (Huber); 2 write-in (Strickland); 1 write-in (Pettway).

**1996**   Other vote was 24,321 Green (Nader); 5,788 Libertarian (Browne); 2,425 Concerned Citizens (Phillips); 1,703 Natural Law (Hagelin); 5 scattered write-in.

**1992**   Other vote was 5,391 Marrou (Libertarian); 1,363 Fulani (New Alliance); 75 Hagelin (write-in); 72 Gritz (write-in); 20 Phillips (write-in); 5 Warren (write-in) 4 LaRouche (write-in). The total for the other vote column includes the 176 write-in votes which were not available by county.

**1988**   Other vote was 14,071 Paul (Libertarian); 2,491 Fulani (New Alliance); 7 Marra (write-in). The total for the other vote column includes these 7 write-in votes which were not available by county.

**1984**   Other vote was 4,826 Hall (Communist); 1,374 Serrette (Connecticut Alliance); 204 Bergland (write-in); 14 Johnson (write-in); 8 scattered write-in. The state-wide total for the other vote column includes these 226 write-in votes not reported by county.

**1980**   Other vote was 171,807 Anderson (Anderson Coalition); 8,570 Clark (Libertarian); 6,130 Commoner (Citizens); 836 scattered write-in. The state-wide total for the other vote column includes the 836 write-in votes not reported by county.

**1976**   Other vote was 7,101 Maddox (George Wallace Party); 3,759 McCarthy (write-in); 1,789 LaRouche (U.S. Labor); 209 MacBride (write-in); 186 Hall (write-in); 155 Anderson (write-in); 42 Camejo (write-in); 5 Zeidler (write-in); 1 Levin (write-in); 1 Wright (write-in); 1,122 scattered write-in. The state-wide total for the other vote column includes these 5,480 write-in votes not reported by county.

**1972**   Other vote was 17,239 Schmitz (George Wallace Party); 777 scattered write-in.

**1968**   Wallace on the ballot as George Wallace party. Other vote was scattered write-in.

**1964**   Other vote was scattered write-in.

**1960**   Other vote was scattered write-in.

# DELAWARE

## POPULAR VOTE FOR PRESIDENT 1920 TO 2004

| Year | Total Vote | Republican | | Democratic | | Other Vote | Plurality | Percentage | | | |
| | | Vote | Candidate | Vote | Candidate | | | Total Vote | | Major Vote | |
| | | | | | | | | Rep. | Dem. | Rep. | Dem. |
|---|---|---|---|---|---|---|---|---|---|---|---|
| 2004 | 375,190 | 171,660 | Bush, George W. | 200,152 | Kerry, John | 3,378 | 28,492 D | 45.8% | 53.3% | 46.2% | 53.8% |
| 2000 ** | 327,622 | 137,288 | Bush, George W. | 180,068 | Gore, Al | 10,266 | 42,780 D | 41.9% | 55.0% | 43.3% | 56.7% |
| 1996 ** | 271,084 | 99,062 | Dole, Bob | 140,355 | Clinton, Bill | 31,667 | 41,293 D | 36.5% | 51.8% | 41.4% | 58.6% |
| 1992 ** | 289,735 | 102,313 | Bush, George | 126,054 | Clinton, Bill | 61,368 | 23,741 D | 35.3% | 43.5% | 44.8% | 55.2% |
| 1988 | 249,891 | 139,639 | Bush, George | 108,647 | Dukakis, Michael S. | 1,605 | 30,992 R | 55.9% | 43.5% | 56.2% | 43.8% |
| 1984 | 254,572 | 152,190 | Reagan, Ronald | 101,656 | Mondale, Walter F. | 726 | 50,534 R | 59.8% | 39.9% | 60.0% | 40.0% |
| 1980 ** | 235,900 | 111,252 | Reagan, Ronald | 105,754 | Carter, Jimmy | 18,894 | 5,498 R | 47.2% | 44.8% | 51.3% | 48.7% |
| 1976 | 235,834 | 109,831 | Ford, Gerald R. | 122,596 | Carter, Jimmy | 3,407 | 12,765 D | 46.6% | 52.0% | 47.3% | 52.7% |
| 1972 | 235,516 | 140,357 | Nixon, Richard M. | 92,283 | McGovern, George S. | 2,876 | 48,074 R | 59.6% | 39.2% | 60.3% | 39.7% |
| 1968 | 214,367 | 96,714 | Nixon, Richard M. | 89,194 | Humphrey, Hubert H. | 28,459 | 7,520 R | 45.1% | 41.6% | 52.0% | 48.0% |
| 1964 | 201,320 | 78,078 | Goldwater, Barry M. | 122,704 | Johnson, Lyndon B. | 538 | 44,626 D | 38.8% | 60.9% | 38.9% | 61.1% |
| 1960 | 196,683 | 96,373 | Nixon, Richard M. | 99,590 | Kennedy, John F. | 720 | 3,217 D | 49.0% | 50.6% | 49.2% | 50.8% |
| 1956 | 177,988 | 98,057 | Eisenhower, Dwight D. | 79,421 | Stevenson, Adlai E. | 510 | 18,636 R | 55.1% | 44.6% | 55.3% | 44.7% |
| 1952 | 174,025 | 90,059 | Eisenhower, Dwight D. | 83,315 | Stevenson, Adlai E. | 651 | 6,744 R | 51.8% | 47.9% | 51.9% | 48.1% |
| 1948 | 139,073 | 69,588 | Dewey, Thomas E. | 67,813 | Truman, Harry S. | 1,672 | 1,775 R | 50.0% | 48.8% | 50.6% | 49.4% |
| 1944 | 125,361 | 56,747 | Dewey, Thomas E. | 68,166 | Roosevelt, Franklin D. | 448 | 11,419 D | 45.3% | 54.4% | 45.4% | 54.6% |
| 1940 | 136,374 | 61,440 | Willkie, Wendell | 74,599 | Roosevelt, Franklin D. | 335 | 13,159 D | 45.1% | 54.7% | 45.2% | 54.8% |
| 1936 | 127,603 | 57,236 | Landon, Alfred M. | 69,702 | Roosevelt, Franklin D. | 665 | 12,466 D | 44.9% | 54.6% | 45.1% | 54.9% |
| 1932 | 112,901 | 57,073 | Hoover, Herbert C. | 54,319 | Roosevelt, Franklin D. | 1,509 | 2,754 R | 50.6% | 48.1% | 51.2% | 48.8% |
| 1928 | 104,602 | 68,860 | Hoover, Herbert C. | 35,354 | Smith, Alfred E. | 388 | 33,506 R | 65.8% | 33.8% | 66.1% | 33.9% |
| 1924 | 90,885 | 52,441 | Coolidge, Calvin | 33,445 | Davis, John W. | 4,999 | 18,996 R | 57.7% | 36.8% | 61.1% | 38.9% |
| 1920 | 94,875 | 52,858 | Harding, Warren G. | 39,911 | Cox, James M. | 2,106 | 12,947 R | 55.7% | 42.1% | 57.0% | 43.0% |

In 2000 the other vote column includes 8,307 votes cast for Green (Nader). In 1996 the other vote column includes 28,719 votes cast for Perot. In 1992 the other vote column includes 59,213 votes cast for Perot. In 1980 the other column includes 16,288 votes for Independent (Anderson).

## ELECTORAL COLLEGE VOTE 1920 TO 2004

| Year | Total | Republican | Democratic | Other |
|---|---|---|---|---|
| 2004 | 3 | | 3 | |
| 2000 | 3 | | 3 | |
| 1996 | 3 | | 3 | |
| 1992 | 3 | | 3 | |
| 1988 | 3 | 3 | | |
| 1984 | 3 | 3 | | |
| 1980 | 3 | 3 | | |
| 1976 | 3 | | 3 | |
| 1972 | 3 | 3 | | |
| 1968 | 3 | 3 | | |
| 1964 | 3 | | 3 | |
| 1960 | 3 | | 3 | |
| 1956 | 3 | 3 | | |
| 1952 | 3 | 3 | | |
| 1948 | 3 | 3 | | |
| 1944 | 3 | | 3 | |
| 1940 | 3 | | 3 | |
| 1936 | 3 | | 3 | |
| 1932 | 3 | 3 | | |
| 1928 | 3 | 3 | | |
| 1924 | 3 | 3 | | |
| 1920 | 3 | 3 | | |

# DELAWARE

NEW CASTLE

KENT

SUSSEX

# DELAWARE

## PRESIDENT 2004

| 2000 Census Population | County | Total Vote | Republican | Democratic | Other | Rep.-Dem. Plurality | Percentage | | | |
|---|---|---|---|---|---|---|---|---|---|---|
| | | | | | | | Total Vote | | Major Vote | |
| | | | | | | | Rep. | Dem. | Rep. | Dem. |
| 126,697 | KENT | 55,980 | 31,578 | 23,875 | 527 | 7,703 R | 56.4% | 42.6% | 56.9% | 43.1% |
| 500,265 | NEW CASTLE | 241,461 | 93,079 | 146,179 | 2,203 | 53,100 D | 38.5% | 60.5% | 38.9% | 61.1% |
| 156,638 | SUSSEX | 77,749 | 47,003 | 30,098 | 648 | 16,905 R | 60.5% | 38.7% | 61.0% | 39.0% |
| 783,600 | TOTAL | 375,190 | 171,660 | 200,152 | 3,378 | 28,492 D | 45.8% | 53.3% | 46.2% | 53.8% |

# DELAWARE

## PRESIDENT 2000

| 2000 Census Population | County | Total Vote | Republican | Democratic | Green (Nader) | Other | Rep.-Dem. Plurality | Percentage of Total Vote | | |
|---|---|---|---|---|---|---|---|---|---|---|
| | | | | | | | | Rep. | Dem. | Green |
| 126,697 | KENT | 48,264 | 24,081 | 22,790 | 1,082 | 311 | 1,291 R | 49.9% | 47.2% | 2.2% |
| 500,265 | NEW CASTLE | 213,059 | 78,587 | 127,539 | 5,767 | 1,166 | 48,952 D | 36.9% | 59.9% | 2.7% |
| 156,638 | SUSSEX | 66,299 | 34,620 | 29,739 | 1,458 | 482 | 4,881 R | 52.2% | 44.9% | 2.2% |
| 783,600 | TOTAL | 327,622 | 137,288 | 180,068 | 8,307 | 1,959 | 42,780 D | 41.9% | 55.0% | 2.5% |

# DELAWARE

## PRESIDENT 1996

| 1995 Census Pop. Est. | County | Total Vote | Republican | Democratic | Reform (Perot) | Other | Rep.-Dem. Plurality | Percentage of Total Vote | | |
|---|---|---|---|---|---|---|---|---|---|---|
| | | | | | | | | Rep. | Dem. | Reform |
| 121,725 | KENT | 39,252 | 15,932 | 18,327 | 4,705 | 288 | 2,395 D | 40.6% | 46.7% | 12.0% |
| 467,889 | NEW CASTLE | 179,546 | 60,943 | 98,837 | 17,748 | 2,018 | 37,894 D | 33.9% | 55.0% | 9.9% |
| 127,583 | SUSSEX | 52,012 | 22,187 | 23,191 | 6,266 | 368 | 1,004 D | 42.7% | 44.6% | 12.0% |
| 717,197 | TOTAL | 271,084 | 99,062 | 140,355 | 28,719 | 2,948 | 41,293 D | 36.5% | 51.8% | 10.6% |

Note: A total of 274 scattered write-in votes for president were included in the official statewide returns but were not broken down by county. They are included in the statewide total for Other.

# DELAWARE

## PRESIDENT 1992

| 1990 Census Population | County | Total Vote | Republican | Democratic | Perot | Other | Plurality | Percentage Total Vote | | |
|---|---|---|---|---|---|---|---|---|---|---|
| | | | | | | | | Rep. | Dem. | Perot |
| 110,993 | KENT | 40,255 | 15,562 | 15,364 | 8,916 | 413 | 198 R | 38.7% | 38.2% | 22.1% |
| 441,946 | NEW CASTLE | 196,904 | 66,311 | 91,516 | 37,581 | 1,496 | 25,205 D | 33.7% | 46.5% | 19.1% |
| 113,229 | SUSSEX | 52,576 | 20,440 | 19,174 | 12,716 | 246 | 1,266 R | 38.9% | 36.5% | 24.2% |
| 666,168 | TOTAL | 289,735 | 102,313 | 126,054 | 59,213 | 2,155 | 23,741 D | 35.3% | 43.5% | 20.4% |

# DELAWARE

## PRESIDENT 1988

| 1980 Census Population | County | Total Vote | Republican | Democratic | Other | Rep.-Dem. Plurality | Percentage | | | |
|---|---|---|---|---|---|---|---|---|---|---|
| | | | | | | | Total Vote | | Major Vote | |
| | | | | | | | Rep. | Dem. | Rep. | Dem. |
| 98,219 | KENT | 33,113 | 19,923 | 12,996 | 194 | 6,927 R | 60.2% | 39.2% | 60.5% | 39.5% |
| 398,115 | NEW CASTLE | 173,003 | 92,587 | 79,147 | 1,269 | 13,440 R | 53.5% | 45.7% | 53.9% | 46.1% |
| 98,004 | SUSSEX | 43,775 | 27,129 | 16,504 | 142 | 10,625 R | 62.0% | 37.7% | 62.2% | 37.8% |
| 594,338 | TOTAL | 249,891 | 139,639 | 108,647 | 1,605 | 30,992 R | 55.9% | 43.5% | 56.2% | 43.8% |

# DELAWARE

## PRESIDENT 1984

| 1980 Census Population | County | Total Vote | Republican | Democratic | Other | Rep.-Dem. Plurality | Percentage | | | |
|---|---|---|---|---|---|---|---|---|---|---|
| | | | | | | | Total Vote | | Major Vote | |
| | | | | | | | Rep. | Dem. | Rep. | Dem. |
| 98,219 | KENT | 33,403 | 21,531 | 11,789 | 83 | 9,742 R | 64.5% | 35.3% | 64.6% | 35.4% |
| 398,115 | NEW CASTLE | 179,077 | 102,322 | 76,238 | 517 | 26,084 R | 57.1% | 42.6% | 57.3% | 42.7% |
| 98,004 | SUSSEX | 42,092 | 28,337 | 13,629 | 126 | 14,708 R | 67.3% | 32.4% | 67.5% | 32.5% |
| 594,338 | TOTAL | 254,572 | 152,190 | 101,656 | 726 | 50,534 R | 59.8% | 39.9% | 60.0% | 40.0% |

# DELAWARE

## PRESIDENT 1980

| 1980 Census Population | County | Total Vote | Republican | Democratic | Other | Rep.-Dem. Plurality | Percentage | | | |
|---|---|---|---|---|---|---|---|---|---|---|
| | | | | | | | Total Vote | | Major Vote | |
| | | | | | | | Rep. | Dem. | Rep. | Dem. |
| 98,219 | KENT | 29,878 | 14,882 | 12,884 | 2,112 | 1,998 R | 49.8% | 43.1% | 53.6% | 46.4% |
| 398,115 | NEW CASTLE | 168,638 | 76,898 | 76,897 | 14,843 | 1 R | 45.6% | 45.6% | 50.0% | 50.0% |
| 98,004 | SUSSEX | 37,384 | 19,472 | 15,973 | 1,939 | 3,499 R | 52.1% | 42.7% | 54.9% | 45.1% |
| 594,338 | TOTAL | 235,900 | 111,252 | 105,754 | 18,894 | 5,498 R | 47.2% | 44.8% | 51.3% | 48.7% |

# DELAWARE

## PRESIDENT 1976

| 1970 Census Population | County | Total Vote | Republican | Democratic | Other | Rep.-Dem. Plurality | Percentage | | | |
|---|---|---|---|---|---|---|---|---|---|---|
| | | | | | | | Total Vote | | Major Vote | |
| | | | | | | | Rep. | Dem. | Rep. | Dem. |
| 81,892 | KENT | 29,428 | 12,604 | 16,523 | 301 | 3,919 D | 42.8% | 56.1% | 43.3% | 56.7% |
| 385,856 | NEW CASTLE | 170,338 | 80,074 | 87,521 | 2,743 | 7,447 D | 47.0% | 51.4% | 47.8% | 52.2% |
| 80,356 | SUSSEX | 36,068 | 17,153 | 18,552 | 363 | 1,399 D | 47.6% | 51.4% | 48.0% | 52.0% |
| 548,104 | TOTAL | 235,834 | 109,831 | 122,596 | 3,407 | 12,765 D | 46.6% | 52.0% | 47.3% | 52.7% |

# DELAWARE

## PRESIDENT 1972

| 1970 Census Population | County | Total Vote | Republican | Democratic | Other | Rep.-Dem. Plurality | Percentage | | | |
|---|---|---|---|---|---|---|---|---|---|---|
| | | | | | | | Total Vote | | Major Vote | |
| | | | | | | | Rep. | Dem. | Rep. | Dem. |
| 81,892 | KENT | 28,556 | 17,712 | 10,463 | 381 | 7,249 R | 62.0% | 36.6% | 62.9% | 37.1% |
| 385,856 | NEW CASTLE | 172,956 | 100,681 | 70,190 | 2,085 | 30,491 R | 58.2% | 40.6% | 58.9% | 41.1% |
| 80,356 | SUSSEX | 34,004 | 21,964 | 11,630 | 410 | 10,334 R | 64.6% | 34.2% | 65.4% | 34.6% |
| 548,104 | TOTAL | 235,516 | 140,357 | 92,283 | 2,876 | 48,074 R | 59.6% | 39.2% | 60.3% | 39.7% |

# DELAWARE

## PRESIDENT 1968

| 1960 Census Population | County | Total Vote | Republican | Democratic | AIP | Other | Plurality | Percentage Total Vote | | |
|---|---|---|---|---|---|---|---|---|---|---|
| | | | | | | | | Rep. | Dem. | AIP |
| 65,651 | KENT | 24,888 | 11,082 | 9,055 | 4,751 | | 2,027 R | 44.5% | 36.4% | 19.1% |
| 307,446 | NEW CASTLE | 156,413 | 70,014 | 68,468 | 17,931 | | 1,546 R | 44.8% | 43.8% | 11.5% |
| 73,195 | SUSSEX | 33,066 | 15,618 | 11,671 | 5,777 | | 3,947 R | 47.2% | 35.3% | 17.5% |
| 446,292 | TOTAL | 214,367 | 96,714 | 89,194 | 28,459 | | 7,520 R | 45.1% | 41.6% | 13.3% |

# DELAWARE

## PRESIDENT 1964

| 1960 Census Population | County | Total Vote | Republican | Democratic | Other | Rep.-Dem. Plurality | Percentage | | | |
|---|---|---|---|---|---|---|---|---|---|---|
| | | | | | | | Total Vote | | Major Vote | |
| | | | | | | | Rep. | Dem. | Rep. | Dem. |
| 65,651 | KENT | 22,054 | 9,006 | 12,981 | 67 | 3,975 D | 40.8% | 58.9% | 41.0% | 59.0% |
| 307,446 | NEW CASTLE | 146,893 | 54,767 | 91,752 | 374 | 36,985 D | 37.3% | 62.5% | 37.4% | 62.6% |
| 73,195 | SUSSEX | 32,373 | 14,305 | 17,971 | 97 | 3,666 D | 44.2% | 55.5% | 44.3% | 55.7% |
| 446,292 | TOTAL | 201,320 | 78,078 | 122,704 | 538 | 44,626 D | 38.8% | 60.9% | 38.9% | 61.1% |

# DELAWARE

## PRESIDENT 1960

| 1960 Census Population | County | Total Vote | Republican | Democratic | Other | Rep.-Dem. Plurality | Percentage | | | |
|---|---|---|---|---|---|---|---|---|---|---|
| | | | | | | | Total Vote | | Major Vote | |
| | | | | | | | Rep. | Dem. | Rep. | Dem. |
| 65,651 | KENT | 21,616 | 10,697 | 10,754 | 165 | 57 D | 49.5% | 49.8% | 49.9% | 50.1% |
| 307,446 | NEW CASTLE | 142,974 | 69,284 | 73,364 | 326 | 4,080 D | 48.5% | 51.3% | 48.6% | 51.4% |
| 73,195 | SUSSEX | 32,093 | 16,392 | 15,472 | 229 | 920 R | 51.1% | 48.2% | 51.4% | 48.6% |
| 446,292 | TOTAL | 196,683 | 96,373 | 99,590 | 720 | 3,217 D | 49.0% | 50.6% | 49.2% | 50.8% |

184

# DELAWARE

## ELECTION NOTES

**2004**  Other vote was 2,153 Independent Party of Delaware (Ralph Nader); 586 Libertarian (Michael Badnarik); 289 Constitution (Michael Peroutka); 250 Green (David Cobb); 100 Natural Law (Walter F. Brown).

**2000**  Other vote was 777 Reform (Buchanan); 774 Libertarian (Browne); 208 Constitution (Phillips); 107 Natural Law (Hagelin); 93 scattered write-in.

**1996**  Other vote was 2,052 Libertarian (Browne); 348 U.S. Taxpayer (Phillips); 274 Natural Law (Hagelin); 156 write-in (Nader); 118 scattered write-in.

**1992**  Other vote was 1,105 Fulani (New Alliance); 935 Marrou (Libertarian); 9 Gritz (write-in); 9 LaRouche (write-in); 6 Hagelin (write-in); 3 Warren (write-in); 2 Phillips (write-in); 86 scattered write-in.

**1988**  Other vote was 1,162 Paul (Libertarian); 443 Fulani (New Alliance).

**1984**  Other vote was 269 Dennis (American); 268 Bergland (Libertarian); 121 Johnson (Citizens); 68 Serrette (Independent).

**1980**  Other vote was 16,288 Anderson (Anderson Party); 1,974 Clark (Libertarian); 400 Greaves (American); 103 Commoner (write-in); 13 Hall (write-in); 6 Bubar (write-in); 4 Pulley (write-in); 3 Griswold (write-in); 2 McCormack (write-in); 101 scattered write-in.

**1976**  Other vote was 2,437 McCarthy (Non-Partisan); 645 Anderson (American); 136 LaRouche (U.S. Labor); 103 Bubar (Prohibition); 86 Levin (Socialist Labor). Early unamended canvass gave the vote in New Castle county as 80,023 Republican; 87,484 Democratic; 2,739 Other and the state-wide total vote as 109,780 Republican; 122,454 Democratic; 3,403 Other.

**1972**  Other vote was 2,638 Schmitz (American); 238 Munn (Prohibition).

**1968**  Wallace on the ballot as American.

**1964**  Other vote was 425 Munn (Prohibition); 113 Hass (Socialist Labor).

**1960**  Other vote was 354 Faubus (National States Rights); 284 Decker (Prohibition); 82 Hass (Socialist Labor).

# FLORIDA

## POPULAR VOTE FOR PRESIDENT 1920 TO 2004

| | | Republican | | Democratic | | Other | | | Percentage | | | |
| | Total | | | | | | | | Total Vote | | Major Vote | |
| Year | Vote | Vote | Candidate | Vote | Candidate | Vote | Plurality | | Rep. | Dem. | Rep. | Dem. |
|---|---|---|---|---|---|---|---|---|---|---|---|---|
| 2004 | 7,609,810 | 3,964,522 | Bush, George W. | 3,583,544 | Kerry, John | 61,744 | 380,978 R | | 52.1% | 47.1% | 52.5% | 47.5% |
| 2000 ** | 5,963,110 | 2,912,790 | Bush, George W. | 2,912,253 | Gore, Al | 138,067 | 537 R | | 48.8% | 48.8% | 50.0% | 50.0% |
| 1996 ** | 5,303,794 | 2,244,536 | Dole, Bob | 2,546,870 | Clinton, Bill | 512,388 | 302,334 D | | 42.3% | 48.0% | 46.8% | 53.2% |
| 1992 ** | 5,314,392 | 2,173,310 | Bush, George | 2,072,698 | Clinton, Bill | 1,068,384 | 100,612 R | | 40.9% | 39.0% | 51.2% | 48.8% |
| 1988 | 4,302,313 | 2,618,885 | Bush, George | 1,656,701 | Dukakis, Michael S. | 26,727 | 962,184 R | | 60.9% | 38.5% | 61.3% | 38.7% |
| 1984 | 4,180,051 | 2,730,350 | Reagan, Ronald | 1,448,816 | Mondale, Walter F. | 885 | 1,281,534 R | | 65.3% | 34.7% | 65.3% | 34.7% |
| 1980 ** | 3,686,930 | 2,046,951 | Reagan, Ronald | 1,419,475 | Carter, Jimmy | 220,504 | 627,476 R | | 55.5% | 38.5% | 59.1% | 40.9% |
| 1976 | 3,150,631 | 1,469,531 | Ford, Gerald R. | 1,636,000 | Carter, Jimmy | 45,100 | 166,469 D | | 46.6% | 51.9% | 47.3% | 52.7% |
| 1972 | 2,583,283 | 1,857,759 | Nixon, Richard M. | 718,117 | McGovern, George S. | 7,407 | 1,139,642 R | | 71.9% | 27.8% | 72.1% | 27.9% |
| 1968 ** | 2,187,805 | 886,804 | Nixon, Richard M. | 676,794 | Humphrey, Hubert H. | 624,207 | 210,010 R | | 40.5% | 30.9% | 56.7% | 43.3% |
| 1964 | 1,854,481 | 905,941 | Goldwater, Barry M. | 948,540 | Johnson, Lyndon B. | | 42,599 D | | 48.9% | 51.1% | 48.9% | 51.1% |
| 1960 | 1,544,176 | 795,476 | Nixon, Richard M. | 748,700 | Kennedy, John F. | | 46,776 R | | 51.5% | 48.5% | 51.5% | 48.5% |
| 1956 | 1,125,762 | 643,849 | Eisenhower, Dwight D. | 480,371 | Stevenson, Adlai E. | 1,542 | 163,478 R | | 57.2% | 42.7% | 57.3% | 42.7% |
| 1952 | 989,337 | 544,036 | Eisenhower, Dwight D. | 444,950 | Stevenson, Adlai E. | 351 | 99,086 R | | 55.0% | 45.0% | 55.0% | 45.0% |
| 1948 ** | 577,643 | 194,280 | Dewey, Thomas E. | 281,988 | Truman, Harry S. | 101,375 | 87,708 D | | 33.6% | 48.8% | 40.8% | 59.2% |
| 1944 | 482,803 | 143,215 | Dewey, Thomas E. | 339,377 | Roosevelt, Franklin D. | 211 | 196,162 D | | 29.7% | 70.3% | 29.7% | 70.3% |
| 1940 | 485,640 | 126,158 | Willkie, Wendell | 359,334 | Roosevelt, Franklin D. | 148 | 233,176 D | | 26.0% | 74.0% | 26.0% | 74.0% |
| 1936 | 327,436 | 78,248 | Landon, Alfred M. | 249,117 | Roosevelt, Franklin D. | 71 | 170,869 D | | 23.9% | 76.1% | 23.9% | 76.1% |
| 1932 | 276,943 | 69,170 | Hoover, Herbert C. | 206,307 | Roosevelt, Franklin D. | 1,466 | 137,137 D | | 25.0% | 74.5% | 25.1% | 74.9% |
| 1928 | 252,068 | 145,860 | Hoover, Herbert C. | 101,764 | Smith, Alfred E. | 4,444 | 44,096 R | | 57.9% | 40.4% | 58.9% | 41.1% |
| 1924 | 109,158 | 30,633 | Coolidge, Calvin | 62,083 | Davis, John W. | 16,442 | 31,450 D | | 28.1% | 56.9% | 33.0% | 67.0% |
| 1920 | 145,684 | 44,853 | Harding, Warren G. | 90,515 | Cox, James M. | 10,316 | 45,662 D | | 30.8% | 62.1% | 33.1% | 66.9% |

In 2000 the other vote column includes 97,488 votes cast for Green (Nader). In 1996 the other vote column includes 483,870 votes cast for Perot. In 1992 the other vote column includes 1,053,067 votes cast for Perot. In 1980 the other column includes 189,692 votes for Independent (Anderson). In 1968 other vote was George Wallace party. In 1948 the other vote was 89,755 States Rights and 11,620 Progressive.

## ELECTORAL COLLEGE VOTE 1920 TO 2004

| Year | Total | Republican | Democratic | Other |
|---|---|---|---|---|
| 2004 | 27 | 27 | | |
| 2000 | 25 | 25 | | |
| 1996 | 25 | | 25 | |
| 1992 | 25 | 25 | | |
| 1988 | 21 | 21 | | |
| 1984 | 21 | 21 | | |
| 1980 | 17 | 17 | | |
| 1976 | 17 | | 17 | |
| 1972 | 17 | 17 | | |
| 1968 | 14 | 14 | | |
| 1964 | 14 | | 14 | |
| 1960 | 10 | 10 | | |
| 1956 | 10 | 10 | | |
| 1952 | 10 | 10 | | |
| 1948 | 8 | | 8 | |
| 1944 | 8 | | 8 | |
| 1940 | 7 | | 7 | |
| 1936 | 7 | | 7 | |
| 1932 | 7 | | 7 | |
| 1928 | 6 | 6 | | |
| 1924 | 6 | | 6 | |
| 1920 | 6 | | 6 | |

# FLORIDA

# FLORIDA

## PRESIDENT 2004

| 2000 Census Population | County | Total Vote | Republican | Democratic | Other | Rep.-Dem. Plurality | Percentage Total Vote Rep. | Dem. | Major Vote Rep. | Dem. |
|---|---|---|---|---|---|---|---|---|---|---|
| 217,955 | ALACHUA | 111,328 | 47,762 | 62,504 | 1,062 | 14,742 D | 42.9% | 56.1% | 43.3% | 56.7% |
| 22,259 | BAKER | 9,955 | 7,738 | 2,180 | 37 | 5,558 R | 77.7% | 21.9% | 78.0% | 22.0% |
| 148,217 | BAY | 75,024 | 53,404 | 21,068 | 552 | 32,336 R | 71.2% | 28.1% | 71.7% | 28.3% |
| 26,088 | BRADFORD | 10,855 | 7,557 | 3,244 | 54 | 4,313 R | 69.6% | 29.9% | 70.0% | 30.0% |
| 476,230 | BREVARD | 265,462 | 153,068 | 110,309 | 2,085 | 42,759 R | 57.7% | 41.6% | 58.1% | 41.9% |
| 1,623,018 | BROWARD | 706,872 | 244,674 | 453,873 | 8,325 | 209,199 D | 34.6% | 64.2% | 35.0% | 65.0% |
| 13,017 | CALHOUN | 5,963 | 3,782 | 2,116 | 65 | 1,666 R | 63.4% | 35.5% | 64.1% | 35.9% |
| 141,627 | CHARLOTTE | 79,786 | 44,428 | 34,256 | 1,102 | 10,172 R | 55.7% | 42.9% | 56.5% | 43.5% |
| 118,085 | CITRUS | 69,467 | 39,500 | 29,277 | 690 | 10,223 R | 56.9% | 42.1% | 57.4% | 42.6% |
| 140,814 | CLAY | 81,495 | 62,078 | 18,971 | 446 | 43,107 R | 76.2% | 23.3% | 76.6% | 23.4% |
| 251,377 | COLLIER | 128,683 | 83,631 | 43,892 | 1,160 | 39,739 R | 65.0% | 34.1% | 65.6% | 34.4% |
| 56,513 | COLUMBIA | 24,991 | 16,758 | 8,031 | 202 | 8,727 R | 67.1% | 32.1% | 67.6% | 32.4% |
| 32,209 | DESOTO | 9,510 | 5,524 | 3,913 | 73 | 1,611 R | 58.1% | 41.1% | 58.5% | 41.5% |
| 13,827 | DIXIE | 6,442 | 4,434 | 1,960 | 48 | 2,474 R | 68.8% | 30.4% | 69.3% | 30.7% |
| 778,879 | DUVAL | 381,061 | 220,190 | 158,610 | 2,261 | 61,580 R | 57.8% | 41.6% | 58.1% | 41.9% |
| 294,410 | ESCAMBIA | 143,278 | 93,566 | 48,329 | 1,383 | 45,237 R | 65.3% | 33.7% | 65.9% | 34.1% |
| 49,832 | FLAGLER | 38,480 | 19,633 | 18,578 | 269 | 1,055 R | 51.0% | 48.3% | 51.4% | 48.6% |
| 11,057 | FRANKLIN | 5,931 | 3,472 | 2,401 | 58 | 1,071 R | 58.5% | 40.5% | 59.1% | 40.9% |
| 45,087 | GADSDEN | 20,984 | 6,253 | 14,629 | 102 | 8,376 D | 29.8% | 69.7% | 29.9% | 70.1% |
| 14,437 | GILCHRIST | 7,015 | 4,936 | 2,017 | 62 | 2,919 R | 70.4% | 28.8% | 71.0% | 29.0% |
| 10,576 | GLADES | 4,188 | 2,443 | 1,718 | 27 | 725 R | 58.3% | 41.0% | 58.7% | 41.3% |
| 13,332 | GULF | 7,277 | 4,805 | 2,407 | 65 | 2,398 R | 66.0% | 33.1% | 66.6% | 33.4% |
| 13,327 | HAMILTON | 5,079 | 2,792 | 2,260 | 27 | 532 R | 55.0% | 44.5% | 55.3% | 44.7% |
| 26,938 | HARDEE | 7,249 | 5,049 | 2,149 | 51 | 2,900 R | 69.7% | 29.6% | 70.1% | 29.9% |
| 36,210 | HENDRY | 9,775 | 5,757 | 3,960 | 58 | 1,797 R | 58.9% | 40.5% | 59.2% | 40.8% |
| 130,802 | HERNANDO | 80,547 | 42,635 | 37,187 | 725 | 5,448 R | 52.9% | 46.2% | 53.4% | 46.6% |
| 87,366 | HIGHLANDS | 41,496 | 25,878 | 15,347 | 271 | 10,531 R | 62.4% | 37.0% | 62.8% | 37.2% |
| 998,948 | HILLSBOROUGH | 463,222 | 245,576 | 214,132 | 3,514 | 31,444 R | 53.0% | 46.2% | 53.4% | 46.6% |
| 18,564 | HOLMES | 8,300 | 6,412 | 1,810 | 78 | 4,602 R | 77.3% | 21.8% | 78.0% | 22.0% |
| 112,947 | INDIAN RIVER | 61,414 | 36,938 | 23,956 | 520 | 12,982 R | 60.1% | 39.0% | 60.7% | 39.3% |
| 46,755 | JACKSON | 19,807 | 12,122 | 7,555 | 130 | 4,567 R | 61.2% | 38.1% | 61.6% | 38.4% |
| 12,902 | JEFFERSON | 7,478 | 3,298 | 4,135 | 45 | 837 D | 44.1% | 55.3% | 44.4% | 55.6% |
| 7,022 | LAFAYETTE | 3,325 | 2,460 | 845 | 20 | 1,615 R | 74.0% | 25.4% | 74.4% | 25.6% |
| 210,528 | LAKE | 123,950 | 74,389 | 48,221 | 1,340 | 26,168 R | 60.0% | 38.9% | 60.7% | 39.3% |
| 440,888 | LEE | 240,667 | 144,176 | 93,860 | 2,631 | 50,316 R | 59.9% | 39.0% | 60.6% | 39.4% |
| 239,452 | LEON | 136,379 | 51,615 | 83,873 | 891 | 32,258 D | 37.8% | 61.5% | 38.1% | 61.9% |
| 34,450 | LEVY | 16,652 | 10,410 | 6,074 | 168 | 4,336 R | 62.5% | 36.5% | 63.2% | 36.8% |
| 7,021 | LIBERTY | 3,021 | 1,927 | 1,070 | 24 | 857 R | 63.8% | 35.4% | 64.3% | 35.7% |
| 18,733 | MADISON | 8,304 | 4,191 | 4,050 | 63 | 141 R | 50.5% | 48.8% | 50.9% | 49.1% |
| 264,002 | MANATEE | 143,621 | 81,318 | 61,262 | 1,041 | 20,056 R | 56.6% | 42.7% | 57.0% | 43.0% |
| 258,916 | MARION | 139,677 | 81,283 | 57,271 | 1,123 | 24,012 R | 58.2% | 41.0% | 58.7% | 41.3% |
| 126,731 | MARTIN | 72,453 | 41,362 | 30,208 | 883 | 11,154 R | 57.1% | 41.7% | 57.8% | 42.2% |
| 2,253,362 | MIAMI-DADE | 774,726 | 361,095 | 409,732 | 3,899 | 48,637 D | 46.6% | 52.9% | 46.8% | 53.2% |
| 79,589 | MONROE | 39,535 | 19,467 | 19,654 | 414 | 187 D | 49.2% | 49.7% | 49.8% | 50.2% |
| 57,663 | NASSAU | 32,743 | 23,783 | 8,573 | 387 | 15,210 R | 72.6% | 26.2% | 73.5% | 26.5% |
| 170,498 | OKALOOSA | 89,756 | 69,693 | 19,368 | 695 | 50,325 R | 77.6% | 21.6% | 78.3% | 21.7% |
| 35,910 | OKEECHOBEE | 12,190 | 6,978 | 5,153 | 59 | 1,825 R | 57.2% | 42.3% | 57.5% | 42.5% |
| 896,344 | ORANGE | 388,044 | 192,539 | 193,354 | 2,151 | 815 D | 49.6% | 49.8% | 49.9% | 50.1% |
| 172,493 | OSCEOLA | 82,204 | 43,117 | 38,633 | 454 | 4,484 R | 52.5% | 47.0% | 52.7% | 47.3% |
| 1,131,184 | PALM BEACH | 544,622 | 212,688 | 328,687 | 3,247 | 115,999 D | 39.1% | 60.4% | 39.3% | 60.7% |
| 344,765 | PASCO | 190,916 | 103,230 | 84,749 | 2,937 | 18,481 R | 54.1% | 44.4% | 54.9% | 45.1% |
| 921,482 | PINELLAS | 455,357 | 225,686 | 225,460 | 4,211 | 226 R | 49.6% | 49.5% | 50.0% | 50.0% |
| 483,924 | POLK | 210,830 | 123,559 | 86,009 | 1,262 | 37,550 R | 58.6% | 40.8% | 59.0% | 41.0% |
| 70,423 | PUTNAM | 30,973 | 18,311 | 12,412 | 250 | 5,899 R | 59.1% | 40.1% | 59.6% | 40.4% |
| 123,135 | ST. JOHNS | 86,290 | 59,196 | 26,399 | 695 | 32,797 R | 68.6% | 30.6% | 69.2% | 30.8% |
| 192,695 | ST. LUCIE | 100,063 | 47,592 | 51,835 | 636 | 4,243 D | 47.6% | 51.8% | 47.9% | 52.1% |
| 117,743 | SANTA ROSA | 67,307 | 52,059 | 14,659 | 589 | 37,400 R | 77.3% | 21.8% | 78.0% | 22.0% |
| 325,957 | SARASOTA | 195,652 | 104,692 | 88,442 | 2,518 | 16,250 R | 53.5% | 45.2% | 54.2% | 45.8% |
| 365,196 | SEMINOLE | 186,195 | 108,172 | 76,971 | 1,052 | 31,201 R | 58.1% | 41.3% | 58.4% | 41.6% |
| 53,345 | SUMTER | 31,842 | 19,800 | 11,584 | 458 | 8,216 R | 62.2% | 36.4% | 63.1% | 36.9% |

# FLORIDA

## PRESIDENT 2004

| 2000 Census Population | County | Total Vote | Republican | Democratic | Other | Rep.-Dem. Plurality | Percentage | | | |
|---|---|---|---|---|---|---|---|---|---|---|
| | | | | | | | Total Vote | | Major Vote | |
| | | | | | | | Rep. | Dem. | Rep. | Dem. |
| 34,844 | SUWANNEE | 15,802 | 11,153 | 4,522 | 127 | 6,631 R | 70.6% | 28.6% | 71.2% | 28.8% |
| 19,256 | TAYLOR | 8,581 | 5,467 | 3,049 | 65 | 2,418 R | 63.7% | 35.5% | 64.2% | 35.8% |
| 13,442 | UNION | 4,675 | 3,396 | 1,251 | 28 | 2,145 R | 72.6% | 26.8% | 73.1% | 26.9% |
| 443,343 | VOLUSIA | 228,939 | 111,924 | 115,519 | 1,496 | 3,595 D | 48.9% | 50.5% | 49.2% | 50.8% |
| 22,863 | WAKULLA | 11,763 | 6,777 | 4,896 | 90 | 1,881 R | 57.6% | 41.6% | 58.1% | 41.9% |
| 40,601 | WALTON | 23,976 | 17,555 | 6,213 | 208 | 11,342 R | 73.2% | 25.9% | 73.9% | 26.1% |
| 20,973 | WASHINGTON | 10,366 | 7,369 | 2,912 | 85 | 4,457 R | 71.1% | 28.1% | 71.7% | 28.3% |
| 15,982,378 | TOTAL | 7,609,810 | 3,964,522 | 3,583,544 | 61,744 | 380,978 R | 52.1% | 47.1% | 52.5% | 47.5% |

# FLORIDA

## PRESIDENT 2000

| 2000 Census Population | County | Total Vote | Republican | Democratic | Green (Nader) | Other | Rep.-Dem. Plurality | Percentage of Total Vote | | |
|---|---|---|---|---|---|---|---|---|---|---|
| | | | | | | | | Rep. | Dem. | Green |
| 217,955 | ALACHUA | 85,729 | 34,124 | 47,365 | 3,226 | 1,014 | 13,241 D | 39.8% | 55.2% | 3.8% |
| 22,259 | BAKER | 8,154 | 5,610 | 2,392 | 53 | 99 | 3,218 R | 68.8% | 29.3% | 0.6% |
| 148,217 | BAY | 58,805 | 38,637 | 18,850 | 828 | 490 | 19,787 R | 65.7% | 32.1% | 1.4% |
| 26,088 | BRADFORD | 8,673 | 5,414 | 3,075 | 84 | 100 | 2,339 R | 62.4% | 35.5% | 1.0% |
| 476,230 | BREVARD | 218,395 | 115,185 | 97,318 | 4,470 | 1,422 | 17,867 R | 52.7% | 44.6% | 2.0% |
| 1,623,018 | BROWARD | 575,143 | 177,902 | 387,703 | 7,104 | 2,434 | 209,801 D | 30.9% | 67.4% | 1.2% |
| 13,017 | CALHOUN | 5,174 | 2,873 | 2,155 | 39 | 107 | 718 R | 55.5% | 41.7% | 0.8% |
| 141,627 | CHARLOTTE | 66,896 | 35,426 | 29,645 | 1,462 | 363 | 5,781 R | 53.0% | 44.3% | 2.2% |
| 118,085 | CITRUS | 57,204 | 29,767 | 25,525 | 1,379 | 533 | 4,242 R | 52.0% | 44.6% | 2.4% |
| 140,814 | CLAY | 57,353 | 41,736 | 14,632 | 562 | 423 | 27,104 R | 72.8% | 25.5% | 1.0% |
| 251,377 | COLLIER | 92,162 | 60,450 | 29,921 | 1,400 | 391 | 30,529 R | 65.6% | 32.5% | 1.5% |
| 56,513 | COLUMBIA | 18,508 | 10,964 | 7,047 | 258 | 239 | 3,917 R | 59.2% | 38.1% | 1.4% |
| 2,253,362 | DADE | 625,449 | 289,533 | 328,808 | 5,352 | 1,756 | 39,275 D | 46.3% | 52.6% | 0.9% |
| 32,209 | DESOTO | 7,811 | 4,256 | 3,320 | 157 | 78 | 936 R | 54.5% | 42.5% | 2.0% |
| 13,827 | DIXIE | 4,666 | 2,697 | 1,826 | 75 | 68 | 871 R | 57.8% | 39.1% | 1.6% |
| 778,879 | DUVAL | 264,636 | 152,098 | 107,864 | 2,757 | 1,917 | 44,234 R | 57.5% | 40.8% | 1.0% |
| 294,410 | ESCAMBIA | 116,648 | 73,017 | 40,943 | 1,727 | 961 | 32,074 R | 62.6% | 35.1% | 1.5% |
| 49,832 | FLAGLER | 27,111 | 12,613 | 13,897 | 435 | 166 | 1,284 D | 46.5% | 51.3% | 1.6% |
| 11,057 | FRANKLIN | 4,644 | 2,454 | 2,046 | 85 | 59 | 408 R | 52.8% | 44.1% | 1.8% |
| 45,087 | GADSDEN | 14,727 | 4,767 | 9,735 | 139 | 86 | 4,968 D | 32.4% | 66.1% | 0.9% |
| 14,437 | GILCHRIST | 5,395 | 3,300 | 1,910 | 97 | 88 | 1,390 R | 61.2% | 35.4% | 1.8% |
| 10,576 | GLADES | 3,365 | 1,841 | 1,442 | 56 | 26 | 399 R | 54.7% | 42.9% | 1.7% |
| 13,332 | GULF | 6,144 | 3,550 | 2,397 | 86 | 111 | 1,153 R | 57.8% | 39.0% | 1.4% |
| 13,327 | HAMILTON | 3,964 | 2,146 | 1,722 | 37 | 59 | 424 R | 54.1% | 43.4% | 0.9% |
| 26,938 | HARDEE | 6,233 | 3,765 | 2,339 | 75 | 54 | 1,426 R | 60.4% | 37.5% | 1.2% |
| 36,210 | HENDRY | 8,139 | 4,747 | 3,240 | 104 | 48 | 1,507 R | 58.3% | 39.8% | 1.3% |
| 130,802 | HERNANDO | 65,219 | 30,646 | 32,644 | 1,501 | 428 | 1,998 D | 47.0% | 50.1% | 2.3% |
| 87,366 | HIGHLANDS | 35,149 | 20,206 | 14,167 | 545 | 231 | 6,039 R | 57.5% | 40.3% | 1.6% |
| 998,948 | HILLSBOROUGH | 360,295 | 180,760 | 169,557 | 7,490 | 2,488 | 11,203 R | 50.2% | 47.1% | 2.1% |
| 18,564 | HOLMES | 7,395 | 5,011 | 2,177 | 94 | 113 | 2,834 R | 67.8% | 29.4% | 1.3% |
| 112,947 | INDIAN RIVER | 49,622 | 28,635 | 19,768 | 950 | 269 | 8,867 R | 57.7% | 39.8% | 1.9% |
| 46,755 | JACKSON | 16,300 | 9,138 | 6,868 | 138 | 156 | 2,270 R | 56.1% | 42.1% | 0.8% |
| 12,902 | JEFFERSON | 5,643 | 2,478 | 3,041 | 76 | 48 | 563 D | 43.9% | 53.9% | 1.3% |
| 7,022 | LAFAYETTE | 2,505 | 1,670 | 789 | 26 | 20 | 881 R | 66.7% | 31.5% | 1.0% |
| 210,528 | LAKE | 88,611 | 50,010 | 36,571 | 1,460 | 570 | 13,439 R | 56.4% | 41.3% | 1.6% |
| 440,888 | LEE | 184,377 | 106,141 | 73,560 | 3,587 | 1,089 | 32,581 R | 57.6% | 39.9% | 1.9% |
| 239,452 | LEON | 103,124 | 39,062 | 61,427 | 1,932 | 703 | 22,365 D | 37.9% | 59.6% | 1.9% |
| 34,450 | LEVY | 12,724 | 6,858 | 5,398 | 284 | 184 | 1,460 R | 53.9% | 42.4% | 2.2% |
| 7,021 | LIBERTY | 2,410 | 1,317 | 1,017 | 19 | 57 | 300 R | 54.6% | 42.2% | 0.8% |
| 18,733 | MADISON | 6,162 | 3,038 | 3,014 | 54 | 56 | 24 R | 49.3% | 48.9% | 0.9% |
| 264,002 | MANATEE | 110,221 | 57,952 | 49,177 | 2,491 | 601 | 8,775 R | 52.6% | 44.6% | 2.3% |
| 258,916 | MARION | 102,956 | 55,141 | 44,665 | 1,809 | 1,341 | 10,476 R | 53.6% | 43.4% | 1.8% |
| 126,731 | MARTIN | 62,013 | 33,970 | 26,620 | 1,118 | 305 | 7,350 R | 54.8% | 42.9% | 1.8% |
| 79,589 | MONROE | 33,887 | 16,059 | 16,483 | 1,090 | 255 | 424 D | 47.4% | 48.6% | 3.2% |
| 57,663 | NASSAU | 23,780 | 16,404 | 6,952 | 253 | 171 | 9,452 R | 69.0% | 29.2% | 1.1% |
| 170,498 | OKALOOSA | 70,680 | 52,093 | 16,948 | 985 | 654 | 35,145 R | 73.7% | 24.0% | 1.4% |
| 35,910 | OKEECHOBEE | 9,853 | 5,057 | 4,588 | 131 | 77 | 469 R | 51.3% | 46.6% | 1.3% |
| 896,344 | ORANGE | 280,125 | 134,517 | 140,220 | 3,879 | 1,509 | 5,703 D | 48.0% | 50.1% | 1.4% |
| 172,493 | OSCEOLA | 55,658 | 26,212 | 28,181 | 732 | 533 | 1,969 D | 47.1% | 50.6% | 1.3% |
| 1,131,184 | PALM BEACH | 433,186 | 152,951 | 269,732 | 5,565 | 4,938 | 116,781 D | 35.3% | 62.3% | 1.3% |
| 344,765 | PASCO | 142,731 | 68,582 | 69,564 | 3,393 | 1,192 | 982 D | 48.0% | 48.7% | 2.4% |
| 921,482 | PINELLAS | 398,472 | 184,825 | 200,630 | 10,022 | 2,995 | 15,805 D | 46.4% | 50.3% | 2.5% |
| 483,924 | POLK | 168,607 | 90,295 | 75,200 | 2,059 | 1,053 | 15,095 R | 53.6% | 44.6% | 1.2% |
| 70,423 | PUTNAM | 26,222 | 13,447 | 12,102 | 377 | 296 | 1,345 R | 51.3% | 46.2% | 1.4% |
| 123,135 | ST. JOHNS | 60,746 | 39,546 | 19,502 | 1,217 | 481 | 20,044 R | 65.1% | 32.1% | 2.0% |
| 192,695 | ST. LUCIE | 77,989 | 34,705 | 41,559 | 1,368 | 357 | 6,854 D | 44.5% | 53.3% | 1.8% |
| 117,743 | SANTA ROSA | 50,319 | 36,274 | 12,802 | 724 | 519 | 23,472 R | 72.1% | 25.4% | 1.4% |
| 325,957 | SARASOTA | 160,942 | 83,100 | 72,853 | 4,069 | 920 | 10,247 R | 51.6% | 45.3% | 2.5% |
| 365,196 | SEMINOLE | 137,634 | 75,677 | 59,174 | 1,946 | 837 | 16,503 R | 55.0% | 43.0% | 1.4% |
| 53,345 | SUMTER | 22,261 | 12,127 | 9,637 | 306 | 191 | 2,490 R | 54.5% | 43.3% | 1.4% |

# FLORIDA

## PRESIDENT 2000

| 2000 Census Population | County | Total Vote | Republican | Democratic | Green (Nader) | Other | Rep.-Dem. Plurality | Percentage of Total Vote | | |
|---|---|---|---|---|---|---|---|---|---|---|
| | | | | | | | | Rep. | Dem. | Green |
| 34,844 | SUWANNEE | 12,457 | 8,006 | 4,075 | 180 | 196 | 3,931 R | 64.3% | 32.7% | 1.4% |
| 19,256 | TAYLOR | 6,808 | 4,056 | 2,649 | 59 | 44 | 1,407 R | 59.6% | 38.9% | 0.9% |
| 13,442 | UNION | 3,826 | 2,332 | 1,407 | 33 | 54 | 925 R | 61.0% | 36.8% | 0.9% |
| 443,343 | VOLUSIA | 183,653 | 82,357 | 97,304 | 2,910 | 1,082 | 14,947 D | 44.8% | 53.0% | 1.6% |
| 22,863 | WAKULLA | 8,587 | 4,512 | 3,838 | 149 | 88 | 674 R | 52.5% | 44.7% | 1.7% |
| 40,601 | WALTON | 18,318 | 12,182 | 5,642 | 265 | 229 | 6,540 R | 66.5% | 30.8% | 1.4% |
| 20,973 | WASHINGTON | 8,025 | 4,994 | 2,798 | 93 | 140 | 2,196 R | 62.2% | 34.9% | 1.2% |
| | Federal Absentees | 2,490 | 1,575 | 836 | 62 | 17 | 739 R | 63.3% | 33.6% | 2.5% |
| 15,982,378 | TOTAL | 5,963,110 | 2,912,790 | 2,912,253 | 97,488 | 40,579 | 537 R | 48.8% | 48.8% | 1.6% |

# FLORIDA

## PRESIDENT 1996

| 1995 Census Pop. Est. | County | Total Vote | Republican | Democratic | Reform (Perot) | Other | Rep.-Dem. Plurality | Percentage of Total Vote | | |
|---|---|---|---|---|---|---|---|---|---|---|
| | | | | | | | | Rep. | Dem. | Reform |
| 196,106 | ALACHUA | 74,516 | 25,316 | 40,161 | 8,073 | 966 | 14,845 D | 34.0% | 53.9% | 10.8% |
| 20,153 | BAKER | 6,637 | 3,686 | 2,273 | 667 | 11 | 1,413 R | 55.5% | 34.2% | 10.0% |
| 142,690 | BAY | 51,694 | 28,365 | 17,068 | 5,926 | 335 | 11,297 R | 54.9% | 33.0% | 11.5% |
| 24,182 | BRADFORD | 8,248 | 4,039 | 3,356 | 819 | 34 | 683 R | 49.0% | 40.7% | 9.9% |
| 450,646 | BREVARD | 195,133 | 88,022 | 80,445 | 25,256 | 1,410 | 7,577 R | 45.1% | 41.2% | 12.9% |
| 1,412,165 | BROWARD | 505,098 | 142,870 | 320,779 | 38,967 | 2,482 | 177,909 D | 28.3% | 63.5% | 7.7% |
| 11,858 | CALHOUN | 4,158 | 1,717 | 1,794 | 630 | 17 | 77 D | 41.3% | 43.1% | 15.2% |
| 129,381 | CHARLOTTE | 63,027 | 27,847 | 27,121 | 7,783 | 276 | 726 R | 44.2% | 43.0% | 12.3% |
| 107,333 | CITRUS | 49,600 | 20,125 | 22,044 | 7,246 | 185 | 1,919 D | 40.6% | 44.4% | 14.6% |
| 124,431 | CLAY | 47,092 | 30,370 | 13,259 | 3,282 | 181 | 17,111 R | 64.5% | 28.2% | 7.0% |
| 181,381 | COLLIER | 72,517 | 42,593 | 23,185 | 6,320 | 419 | 19,408 R | 58.7% | 32.0% | 8.7% |
| 48,376 | COLUMBIA | 16,326 | 7,588 | 6,691 | 1,970 | 77 | 897 R | 46.5% | 41.0% | 12.1% |
| 2,031,336 | DADE | 553,782 | 209,740 | 317,555 | 24,729 | 1,758 | 107,815 D | 37.9% | 57.3% | 4.5% |
| 25,048 | DESOTO | 7,492 | 3,275 | 3,222 | 966 | 29 | 53 R | 43.7% | 43.0% | 12.9% |
| 12,159 | DIXIE | 3,800 | 1,399 | 1,734 | 653 | 14 | 335 D | 36.8% | 45.6% | 17.2% |
| 701,673 | DUVAL | 254,123 | 126,959 | 112,328 | 13,850 | 986 | 14,631 R | 50.0% | 44.2% | 5.5% |
| 273,804 | ESCAMBIA | 107,925 | 60,997 | 37,838 | 8,597 | 493 | 23,159 R | 56.5% | 35.1% | 8.0% |
| 40,643 | FLAGLER | 20,079 | 8,234 | 9,585 | 2,185 | 75 | 1,351 D | 41.0% | 47.7% | 10.9% |
| 10,301 | FRANKLIN | 4,570 | 1,563 | 2,096 | 878 | 33 | 533 D | 34.2% | 45.9% | 19.2% |
| 43,378 | GADSDEN | 14,199 | 3,817 | 9,407 | 938 | 37 | 5,590 D | 26.9% | 66.3% | 6.6% |
| 12,332 | GILCHRIST | 4,795 | 1,939 | 1,985 | 841 | 30 | 46 D | 40.4% | 41.4% | 17.5% |
| 7,665 | GLADES | 3,431 | 1,361 | 1,530 | 521 | 19 | 169 D | 39.7% | 44.6% | 15.2% |
| 13,390 | GULF | 5,992 | 2,430 | 2,480 | 1,054 | 28 | 50 D | 40.6% | 41.4% | 17.6% |
| 11,773 | HAMILTON | 3,673 | 1,520 | 1,735 | 406 | 12 | 215 D | 41.4% | 47.2% | 11.1% |
| 19,952 | HARDEE | 6,206 | 2,928 | 2,417 | 851 | 10 | 511 R | 47.2% | 38.9% | 13.7% |
| 28,114 | HENDRY | 8,899 | 3,855 | 3,885 | 1,135 | 24 | 30 D | 43.3% | 43.7% | 12.8% |
| 120,054 | HERNANDO | 58,066 | 22,046 | 28,524 | 7,272 | 224 | 6,478 D | 38.0% | 49.1% | 12.5% |
| 74,507 | HIGHLANDS | 33,714 | 15,617 | 14,250 | 3,739 | 108 | 1,367 R | 46.3% | 42.3% | 11.1% |
| 884,608 | HILLSBOROUGH | 308,271 | 136,656 | 144,266 | 25,156 | 2,193 | 7,610 D | 44.3% | 46.8% | 8.2% |
| 17,520 | HOLMES | 6,804 | 3,249 | 2,312 | 1,208 | 35 | 937 R | 47.8% | 34.0% | 17.8% |
| 97,144 | INDIAN RIVER | 43,972 | 22,714 | 16,375 | 4,637 | 246 | 6,339 R | 51.7% | 37.2% | 10.5% |
| 43,891 | JACKSON | 15,513 | 7,189 | 6,667 | 1,602 | 55 | 522 R | 46.3% | 43.0% | 10.3% |
| 12,950 | JEFFERSON | 4,809 | 1,851 | 2,544 | 393 | 21 | 693 D | 38.5% | 52.9% | 8.2% |
| 6,043 | LAFAYETTE | 2,322 | 1,166 | 829 | 316 | 11 | 337 R | 50.2% | 35.7% | 13.6% |
| 180,160 | LAKE | 73,923 | 35,097 | 29,752 | 8,815 | 259 | 5,345 R | 47.5% | 40.2% | 11.9% |
| 375,381 | LEE | 165,951 | 80,898 | 65,699 | 18,394 | 960 | 15,199 R | 48.7% | 39.6% | 11.1% |
| 213,917 | LEON | 91,717 | 33,930 | 50,072 | 6,673 | 1,042 | 16,142 D | 37.0% | 54.6% | 7.3% |
| 29,738 | LEVY | 11,065 | 4,299 | 4,938 | 1,774 | 54 | 639 D | 38.9% | 44.6% | 16.0% |
| 6,400 | LIBERTY | 2,164 | 913 | 868 | 376 | 7 | 45 R | 42.2% | 40.1% | 17.4% |
| 17,231 | MADISON | 5,587 | 2,195 | 2,794 | 578 | 20 | 599 D | 39.3% | 50.0% | 10.3% |
| 229,864 | MANATEE | 96,878 | 44,136 | 41,891 | 10,363 | 488 | 2,245 R | 45.6% | 43.2% | 10.7% |
| 226,678 | MARION | 90,171 | 41,409 | 37,045 | 11,341 | 376 | 4,364 R | 45.9% | 41.1% | 12.6% |
| 111,069 | MARTIN | 54,656 | 28,522 | 20,855 | 5,005 | 274 | 7,667 R | 52.2% | 38.2% | 9.2% |
| 81,850 | MONROE | 32,544 | 12,076 | 15,251 | 4,824 | 393 | 3,175 D | 37.1% | 46.9% | 14.8% |
| 50,767 | NASSAU | 21,167 | 12,141 | 7,277 | 1,657 | 92 | 4,864 R | 57.4% | 34.4% | 7.8% |
| 163,707 | OKALOOSA | 63,044 | 40,683 | 16,462 | 5,433 | 466 | 24,221 R | 64.5% | 26.1% | 8.6% |
| 30,222 | OKEECHOBEE | 9,941 | 3,418 | 4,826 | 1,666 | 31 | 1,408 D | 34.4% | 48.5% | 16.8% |
| 749,631 | ORANGE | 231,126 | 106,059 | 105,539 | 18,196 | 1,332 | 520 R | 45.9% | 45.7% | 7.9% |
| 130,771 | OSCEOLA | 46,491 | 18,337 | 21,874 | 6,092 | 188 | 3,537 D | 39.4% | 47.0% | 13.1% |
| 972,093 | PALM BEACH | 397,354 | 133,811 | 230,687 | 30,744 | 2,112 | 96,876 D | 33.7% | 58.1% | 7.7% |
| 304,938 | PASCO | 133,471 | 48,355 | 66,475 | 18,013 | 628 | 18,120 D | 36.2% | 49.8% | 13.5% |
| 870,884 | PINELLAS | 376,272 | 152,155 | 184,748 | 36,994 | 2,375 | 32,593 D | 40.4% | 49.1% | 9.8% |
| 436,701 | POLK | 150,173 | 67,962 | 66,747 | 14,993 | 471 | 1,215 R | 45.3% | 44.4% | 10.0% |
| 69,481 | PUTNAM | 25,152 | 9,786 | 12,010 | 3,272 | 84 | 2,224 D | 38.9% | 47.7% | 13.0% |
| 102,174 | ST. JOHNS | 48,549 | 27,318 | 16,716 | 4,205 | 310 | 10,602 R | 56.3% | 34.4% | 8.7% |
| 172,483 | ST. LUCIE | 73,906 | 28,899 | 36,169 | 8,483 | 355 | 7,270 D | 39.1% | 48.9% | 11.5% |
| 104,110 | SANTA ROSA | 42,410 | 26,301 | 10,936 | 4,961 | 212 | 15,365 R | 62.0% | 25.8% | 11.7% |
| 295,942 | SARASOTA | 148,986 | 69,213 | 63,665 | 14,941 | 1,167 | 5,548 R | 46.5% | 42.7% | 10.0% |
| 330,012 | SEMINOLE | 114,904 | 59,797 | 45,058 | 9,357 | 692 | 14,739 R | 52.0% | 39.2% | 8.1% |
| 34,788 | SUMTER | 15,400 | 5,960 | 7,017 | 2,375 | 48 | 1,057 D | 38.7% | 45.6% | 15.4% |

# FLORIDA

## PRESIDENT 1996

| 1995 Census Pop. Est. | County | Total Vote | Republican | Democratic | Reform (Perot) | Other | Rep.-Dem. Plurality | Percentage of Total Vote | | |
|---|---|---|---|---|---|---|---|---|---|---|
| | | | | | | | | Rep. | Dem. | Reform |
| 30,103 | SUWANNEE | 12,144 | 5,742 | 4,479 | 1,874 | 49 | 1,263 R | 47.3% | 36.9% | 15.4% |
| 17,445 | TAYLOR | 7,997 | 3,188 | 3,583 | 1,140 | 86 | 395 D | 39.9% | 44.8% | 14.3% |
| 12,433 | UNION | 3,462 | 1,636 | 1,388 | 425 | 13 | 248 R | 47.3% | 40.1% | 12.3% |
| 408,261 | VOLUSIA | 160,158 | 63,091 | 78,919 | 17,320 | 828 | 15,828 D | 39.4% | 49.3% | 10.8% |
| 17,111 | WAKULLA | 7,169 | 2,933 | 3,056 | 1,091 | 89 | 123 D | 40.9% | 42.6% | 15.2% |
| 33,615 | WALTON | 15,518 | 7,709 | 5,342 | 2,342 | 125 | 2,367 R | 49.7% | 34.4% | 15.1% |
| 18,623 | WASHINGTON | 7,861 | 3,524 | 2,992 | 1,287 | 58 | 532 R | 44.8% | 38.1% | 16.4% |
| 14,165,570 | TOTAL | 5,303,794 | 2,244,536 | 2,546,870 | 483,870 | 28,518 | 302,334 D | 42.3% | 48.0% | 9.1% |

# FLORIDA

## PRESIDENT 1992

| 1990 Census Population | County | Total Vote | Republican | Democratic | Perot | Other | Plurality | Percentage Total Vote | | |
|---|---|---|---|---|---|---|---|---|---|---|
| | | | | | | | | Rep. | Dem. | Perot |
| 181,596 | ALACHUA | 76,372 | 22,813 | 37,888 | 15,296 | 375 | 15,075 D | 29.9% | 49.6% | 20.0% |
| 18,486 | BAKER | 6,756 | 3,418 | 1,976 | 1,315 | 47 | 1,442 R | 50.6% | 29.2% | 19.5% |
| 126,994 | BAY | 45,689 | 22,842 | 12,846 | 9,712 | 289 | 9,996 R | 50.0% | 28.1% | 21.3% |
| 22,515 | BRADFORD | 8,341 | 3,672 | 3,041 | 1,574 | 54 | 631 R | 44.0% | 36.5% | 18.9% |
| 398,978 | BREVARD | 195,860 | 84,585 | 61,091 | 49,509 | 675 | 23,494 R | 43.2% | 31.2% | 25.3% |
| 1,255,488 | BROWARD | 533,050 | 164,832 | 276,361 | 90,937 | 920 | 111,529 D | 30.9% | 51.8% | 17.1% |
| 11,011 | CALHOUN | 4,579 | 1,721 | 1,665 | 1,176 | 17 | 56 R | 37.6% | 36.4% | 25.7% |
| 110,975 | CHARLOTTE | 62,064 | 24,311 | 22,907 | 14,720 | 126 | 1,404 R | 39.2% | 36.9% | 23.7% |
| 93,515 | CITRUS | 44,746 | 16,412 | 15,937 | 12,314 | 83 | 475 R | 36.7% | 35.6% | 27.5% |
| 105,986 | CLAY | 45,485 | 26,360 | 10,610 | 8,423 | 92 | 15,750 R | 58.0% | 23.3% | 18.5% |
| 152,099 | COLLIER | 71,944 | 38,448 | 18,796 | 14,518 | 182 | 19,652 R | 53.4% | 26.1% | 20.2% |
| 42,613 | COLUMBIA | 14,954 | 6,492 | 5,528 | 2,906 | 28 | 964 R | 43.4% | 37.0% | 19.4% |
| 1,937,094 | DADE | 544,843 | 235,313 | 254,609 | 54,003 | 918 | 19,296 D | 43.2% | 46.7% | 9.9% |
| 23,865 | DESOTO | 7,429 | 3,070 | 2,646 | 1,687 | 26 | 424 R | 41.3% | 35.6% | 22.7% |
| 10,585 | DIXIE | 4,373 | 1,401 | 1,855 | 1,094 | 23 | 454 D | 32.0% | 42.4% | 25.0% |
| 672,971 | DUVAL | 249,926 | 123,631 | 92,098 | 33,388 | 809 | 31,533 R | 49.5% | 36.9% | 13.4% |
| 262,798 | ESCAMBIA | 105,221 | 52,868 | 32,045 | 19,923 | 385 | 20,823 R | 50.2% | 30.5% | 18.9% |
| 28,701 | FLAGLER | 16,355 | 6,246 | 6,693 | 3,390 | 26 | 447 D | 38.2% | 40.9% | 20.7% |
| 8,967 | FRANKLIN | 4,380 | 1,664 | 1,535 | 1,144 | 37 | 129 R | 38.0% | 35.0% | 26.1% |
| 41,105 | GADSDEN | 14,394 | 3,975 | 8,486 | 1,871 | 62 | 4,511 D | 27.6% | 59.0% | 13.0% |
| 9,667 | GILCHRIST | 4,017 | 1,395 | 1,511 | 1,090 | 21 | 116 D | 34.7% | 37.6% | 27.1% |
| 7,591 | GLADES | 3,374 | 1,185 | 1,305 | 878 | 6 | 120 D | 35.1% | 38.7% | 26.0% |
| 11,504 | GULF | 5,854 | 2,651 | 1,938 | 1,245 | 20 | 713 R | 45.3% | 33.1% | 21.3% |
| 10,930 | HAMILTON | 3,725 | 1,402 | 1,622 | 695 | 6 | 220 D | 37.6% | 43.5% | 18.7% |
| 19,499 | HARDEE | 6,433 | 2,900 | 2,018 | 1,499 | 16 | 882 R | 45.1% | 31.4% | 23.3% |
| 25,773 | HENDRY | 8,016 | 3,279 | 2,691 | 2,032 | 14 | 588 R | 40.9% | 33.6% | 25.3% |
| 101,115 | HERNANDO | 49,086 | 17,902 | 19,174 | 11,848 | 162 | 1,272 D | 36.5% | 39.1% | 24.1% |
| 68,432 | HIGHLANDS | 32,391 | 14,499 | 11,237 | 6,593 | 62 | 3,262 R | 44.8% | 34.7% | 20.4% |
| 834,054 | HILLSBOROUGH | 310,502 | 130,643 | 115,282 | 63,054 | 1,523 | 15,361 R | 42.1% | 37.1% | 20.3% |
| 15,778 | HOLMES | 6,528 | 3,196 | 1,877 | 1,427 | 28 | 1,319 R | 49.0% | 28.8% | 21.9% |
| 90,208 | INDIAN RIVER | 43,962 | 19,140 | 12,360 | 12,375 | 87 | 6,765 R | 43.5% | 28.1% | 28.1% |
| 41,375 | JACKSON | 14,676 | 6,725 | 5,482 | 2,450 | 19 | 1,243 R | 45.8% | 37.4% | 16.7% |
| 11,296 | JEFFERSON | 4,678 | 1,506 | 2,271 | 895 | 6 | 765 D | 32.2% | 48.5% | 19.1% |
| 5,578 | LAFAYETTE | 2,525 | 1,039 | 867 | 612 | 7 | 172 R | 41.1% | 34.3% | 24.2% |
| 152,104 | LAKE | 69,787 | 30,825 | 23,200 | 15,614 | 148 | 7,625 R | 44.2% | 33.2% | 22.4% |
| 335,113 | LEE | 166,002 | 73,436 | 53,660 | 38,452 | 454 | 19,776 R | 44.2% | 32.3% | 23.2% |
| 192,493 | LEON | 97,294 | 31,983 | 47,791 | 17,212 | 308 | 15,808 D | 32.9% | 49.1% | 17.7% |
| 25,923 | LEVY | 10,936 | 3,796 | 4,330 | 2,784 | 26 | 534 D | 34.7% | 39.6% | 25.5% |
| 5,569 | LIBERTY | 2,576 | 1,126 | 820 | 617 | 13 | 306 R | 43.7% | 31.8% | 24.0% |
| 16,569 | MADISON | 5,838 | 2,007 | 2,648 | 1,174 | 9 | 641 D | 34.4% | 45.4% | 20.1% |
| 211,707 | MANATEE | 100,220 | 42,725 | 33,841 | 23,290 | 364 | 8,884 R | 42.6% | 33.8% | 23.2% |
| 194,833 | MARION | 86,989 | 35,442 | 30,829 | 20,529 | 189 | 4,613 R | 40.7% | 35.4% | 23.6% |
| 100,900 | MARTIN | 53,184 | 24,800 | 14,802 | 13,442 | 140 | 9,998 R | 46.6% | 27.8% | 25.3% |
| 78,024 | MONROE | 28,789 | 9,898 | 10,450 | 8,314 | 127 | 552 D | 34.4% | 36.3% | 28.9% |
| 43,941 | NASSAU | 18,174 | 9,367 | 5,503 | 3,255 | 49 | 3,864 R | 51.5% | 30.3% | 17.9% |
| 143,776 | OKALOOSA | 61,769 | 32,818 | 12,038 | 16,671 | 242 | 16,147 R | 53.1% | 19.5% | 27.0% |
| 29,627 | OKEECHOBEE | 9,370 | 3,298 | 3,418 | 2,647 | 7 | 120 D | 35.2% | 36.5% | 28.2% |
| 677,491 | ORANGE | 237,011 | 108,788 | 82,683 | 44,844 | 696 | 26,105 R | 45.9% | 34.9% | 18.9% |
| 107,728 | OSCEOLA | 45,267 | 19,143 | 15,010 | 11,021 | 93 | 4,133 R | 42.3% | 33.2% | 24.3% |
| 863,518 | PALM BEACH | 405,251 | 140,350 | 187,869 | 76,243 | 789 | 47,519 D | 34.6% | 46.4% | 18.8% |
| 281,131 | PASCO | 135,962 | 47,735 | 53,130 | 34,654 | 443 | 5,395 D | 35.1% | 39.1% | 25.5% |
| 851,659 | PINELLAS | 422,851 | 159,121 | 160,528 | 101,257 | 1,945 | 1,407 D | 37.6% | 38.0% | 23.9% |
| 405,382 | POLK | 145,900 | 65,963 | 51,450 | 28,204 | 283 | 14,513 R | 45.2% | 35.3% | 19.3% |
| 65,070 | PUTNAM | 25,661 | 8,910 | 10,709 | 5,979 | 63 | 1,799 D | 34.7% | 41.7% | 23.3% |
| 83,829 | ST. JOHNS | 39,986 | 20,188 | 12,291 | 7,400 | 107 | 7,897 R | 50.5% | 30.7% | 18.5% |
| 150,171 | ST. LUCIE | 68,233 | 24,400 | 23,876 | 19,817 | 140 | 524 R | 35.8% | 35.0% | 29.0% |
| 81,608 | SANTA ROSA | 32,777 | 17,339 | 6,556 | 8,788 | 94 | 8,551 R | 52.9% | 20.0% | 26.8% |
| 277,776 | SARASOTA | 156,352 | 66,855 | 54,552 | 34,289 | 656 | 12,303 R | 42.8% | 34.9% | 21.9% |
| 287,529 | SEMINOLE | 117,560 | 57,101 | 35,660 | 24,487 | 312 | 21,441 R | 48.6% | 30.3% | 20.8% |
| 31,577 | SUMTER | 12,329 | 4,366 | 5,027 | 2,901 | 35 | 661 D | 35.4% | 40.8% | 23.5% |

# FLORIDA

## PRESIDENT 1992

| 1990 Census Population | County | Total Vote | Republican | Democratic | Perot | Other | Plurality | Percentage Total Vote | | |
|---|---|---|---|---|---|---|---|---|---|---|
| | | | | | | | | Rep. | Dem. | Perot |
| 26,780 | SUWANNEE | 11,374 | 4,576 | 3,988 | 2,791 | 19 | 588 R | 40.2% | 35.1% | 24.5% |
| 17,111 | TAYLOR | 7,213 | 2,693 | 2,568 | 1,929 | 23 | 125 R | 37.3% | 35.6% | 26.7% |
| 10,252 | UNION | 3,571 | 1,546 | 1,248 | 770 | 7 | 298 R | 43.3% | 34.9% | 21.6% |
| 370,712 | VOLUSIA | 155,499 | 59,172 | 65,223 | 30,823 | 281 | 6,051 D | 38.1% | 41.9% | 19.8% |
| 14,202 | WAKULLA | 6,714 | 2,586 | 2,320 | 1,790 | 18 | 266 R | 38.5% | 34.6% | 26.7% |
| 27,760 | WALTON | 13,554 | 5,726 | 3,888 | 3,890 | 50 | 1,836 R | 42.2% | 28.7% | 28.7% |
| 16,919 | WASHINGTON | 7,871 | 3,695 | 2,544 | 1,596 | 36 | 1,151 R | 46.9% | 32.3% | 20.3% |
| 12,937,926 | TOTAL | 5,314,392 | 2,173,310 | 2,072,698 | 1,053,067 | 15,317 | 100,612 R | 40.9% | 39.0% | 19.8% |

# FLORIDA

## PRESIDENT 1988

| 1980 Census Population | County | Total Vote | Republican | Democratic | Other | Rep.-Dem. Plurality | Percentage Total Vote Rep. | Dem. | Major Vote Rep. | Dem. |
|---|---|---|---|---|---|---|---|---|---|---|
| 151,348 | ALACHUA | 60,213 | 30,153 | 29,396 | 664 | 757 R | 50.1% | 48.8% | 50.6% | 49.4% |
| 15,289 | BAKER | 4,781 | 3,418 | 1,355 | 8 | 2,063 R | 71.5% | 28.3% | 71.6% | 28.4% |
| 97,740 | BAY | 43,851 | 31,796 | 11,603 | 452 | 20,193 R | 72.5% | 26.5% | 73.3% | 26.7% |
| 20,023 | BRADFORD | 6,636 | 4,221 | 2,386 | 29 | 1,835 R | 63.6% | 36.0% | 63.9% | 36.1% |
| 272,959 | BREVARD | 149,159 | 104,854 | 43,004 | 1,301 | 61,850 R | 70.3% | 28.8% | 70.9% | 29.1% |
| 1,018,200 | BROWARD | 440,605 | 220,316 | 218,274 | 2,015 | 2,042 R | 50.0% | 49.5% | 50.2% | 49.8% |
| 9,294 | CALHOUN | 3,784 | 2,422 | 1,329 | 33 | 1,093 R | 64.0% | 35.1% | 64.6% | 35.4% |
| 58,460 | CHARLOTTE | 45,159 | 28,893 | 15,974 | 292 | 12,919 R | 64.0% | 35.4% | 64.4% | 35.6% |
| 54,703 | CITRUS | 33,474 | 21,072 | 12,184 | 218 | 8,888 R | 63.0% | 36.4% | 63.4% | 36.6% |
| 67,052 | CLAY | 33,837 | 25,942 | 7,773 | 122 | 18,169 R | 76.7% | 23.0% | 76.9% | 23.1% |
| 85,971 | COLLIER | 51,980 | 38,920 | 12,769 | 291 | 26,151 R | 74.9% | 24.6% | 75.3% | 24.7% |
| 35,399 | COLUMBIA | 11,916 | 7,761 | 4,073 | 82 | 3,688 R | 65.1% | 34.2% | 65.6% | 34.4% |
| 1,625,781 | DADE | 490,265 | 270,937 | 216,970 | 2,358 | 53,967 R | 55.3% | 44.3% | 55.5% | 44.5% |
| 19,039 | DESOTO | 6,464 | 4,243 | 2,181 | 40 | 2,062 R | 65.6% | 33.7% | 66.0% | 34.0% |
| 7,751 | DIXIE | 3,397 | 2,031 | 1,366 | | 665 R | 59.8% | 40.2% | 59.8% | 40.2% |
| 571,003 | DUVAL | 203,979 | 128,081 | 74,894 | 1,004 | 53,187 R | 62.8% | 36.7% | 63.1% | 36.9% |
| 233,794 | ESCAMBIA | 95,460 | 64,959 | 29,977 | 524 | 34,982 R | 68.0% | 31.4% | 68.4% | 31.6% |
| 10,913 | FLAGLER | 10,782 | 6,504 | 4,244 | 34 | 2,260 R | 60.3% | 39.4% | 60.5% | 39.5% |
| 7,661 | FRANKLIN | 3,269 | 1,913 | 1,283 | 73 | 630 R | 58.5% | 39.2% | 59.9% | 40.1% |
| 41,565 | GADSDEN | 12,577 | 5,992 | 6,372 | 213 | 380 D | 47.6% | 50.7% | 48.5% | 51.5% |
| 5,767 | GILCHRIST | 3,012 | 1,855 | 1,137 | 20 | 718 R | 61.6% | 37.7% | 62.0% | 38.0% |
| 5,992 | GLADES | 2,593 | 1,547 | 1,034 | 12 | 513 R | 59.7% | 39.9% | 59.9% | 40.1% |
| 10,658 | GULF | 4,872 | 3,042 | 1,688 | 142 | 1,354 R | 62.4% | 34.6% | 64.3% | 35.7% |
| 8,761 | HAMILTON | 3,396 | 2,062 | 1,318 | 16 | 744 R | 60.7% | 38.8% | 61.0% | 39.0% |
| 19,379 | HARDEE | 5,436 | 3,640 | 1,688 | 108 | 1,952 R | 67.0% | 31.1% | 68.3% | 31.7% |
| 18,599 | HENDRY | 6,035 | 3,965 | 2,036 | 34 | 1,929 R | 65.7% | 33.7% | 66.1% | 33.9% |
| 44,469 | HERNANDO | 36,863 | 21,195 | 15,437 | 231 | 5,758 R | 57.5% | 41.9% | 57.9% | 42.1% |
| 47,526 | HIGHLANDS | 24,941 | 16,723 | 8,091 | 127 | 8,632 R | 67.1% | 32.4% | 67.4% | 32.6% |
| 646,960 | HILLSBOROUGH | 250,716 | 150,151 | 99,014 | 1,551 | 51,137 R | 59.9% | 39.5% | 60.3% | 39.7% |
| 14,723 | HOLMES | 5,900 | 4,225 | 1,639 | 36 | 2,586 R | 71.6% | 27.8% | 72.0% | 28.0% |
| 59,896 | INDIAN RIVER | 35,333 | 24,630 | 10,451 | 252 | 14,179 R | 69.7% | 29.6% | 70.2% | 29.8% |
| 39,154 | JACKSON | 13,513 | 8,405 | 5,008 | 100 | 3,397 R | 62.2% | 37.1% | 62.7% | 37.3% |
| 10,703 | JEFFERSON | 4,398 | 2,326 | 2,055 | 17 | 271 R | 52.9% | 46.7% | 53.1% | 46.9% |
| 4,035 | LAFAYETTE | 2,185 | 1,451 | 722 | 12 | 729 R | 66.4% | 33.0% | 66.8% | 33.2% |
| 104,870 | LAKE | 54,572 | 37,327 | 16,766 | 479 | 20,561 R | 68.4% | 30.7% | 69.0% | 31.0% |
| 205,266 | LEE | 128,936 | 87,303 | 40,725 | 908 | 46,578 R | 67.7% | 31.6% | 68.2% | 31.8% |
| 148,655 | LEON | 70,158 | 36,055 | 33,472 | 631 | 2,583 R | 51.4% | 47.7% | 51.9% | 48.1% |
| 19,870 | LEVY | 8,791 | 5,253 | 3,434 | 104 | 1,819 R | 59.8% | 39.1% | 60.5% | 39.5% |
| 4,260 | LIBERTY | 2,177 | 1,421 | 709 | 47 | 712 R | 65.3% | 32.6% | 66.7% | 33.3% |
| 14,894 | MADISON | 4,529 | 2,563 | 1,951 | 15 | 612 R | 56.6% | 43.1% | 56.8% | 43.2% |
| 148,442 | MANATEE | 78,113 | 51,187 | 26,624 | 302 | 24,563 R | 65.5% | 34.1% | 65.8% | 34.2% |
| 122,488 | MARION | 62,520 | 41,501 | 20,685 | 334 | 20,816 R | 66.4% | 33.1% | 66.7% | 33.3% |
| 64,014 | MARTIN | 43,083 | 31,279 | 11,488 | 316 | 19,791 R | 72.6% | 26.7% | 73.1% | 26.9% |
| 63,188 | MONROE | 26,405 | 15,928 | 10,157 | 320 | 5,771 R | 60.3% | 38.5% | 61.1% | 38.9% |
| 32,894 | NASSAU | 12,575 | 8,374 | 4,143 | 58 | 4,231 R | 66.6% | 32.9% | 66.9% | 33.1% |
| 109,920 | OKALOOSA | 50,462 | 40,389 | 9,753 | 320 | 30,636 R | 80.0% | 19.3% | 80.5% | 19.5% |
| 20,264 | OKEECHOBEE | 7,791 | 4,736 | 3,007 | 48 | 1,729 R | 60.8% | 38.6% | 61.2% | 38.8% |
| 471,016 | ORANGE | 172,770 | 117,237 | 54,023 | 1,510 | 63,214 R | 67.9% | 31.3% | 68.5% | 31.5% |
| 49,287 | OSCEOLA | 31,381 | 21,355 | 9,812 | 214 | 11,543 R | 68.1% | 31.3% | 68.5% | 31.5% |
| 576,863 | PALM BEACH | 327,217 | 181,495 | 144,199 | 1,523 | 37,296 R | 55.5% | 44.1% | 55.7% | 44.3% |
| 193,643 | PASCO | 114,803 | 63,820 | 50,385 | 598 | 13,435 R | 55.6% | 43.9% | 55.9% | 44.1% |
| 728,531 | PINELLAS | 365,370 | 211,049 | 152,420 | 1,901 | 58,629 R | 57.8% | 41.7% | 58.1% | 41.9% |
| 321,652 | POLK | 116,040 | 77,104 | 38,249 | 687 | 38,855 R | 66.4% | 33.0% | 66.8% | 33.2% |
| 50,549 | PUTNAM | 20,307 | 11,624 | 8,575 | 108 | 3,049 R | 57.2% | 42.2% | 57.5% | 42.5% |
| 51,303 | ST. JOHNS | 27,347 | 19,189 | 8,002 | 156 | 11,187 R | 70.2% | 29.3% | 70.6% | 29.4% |
| 87,182 | ST. LUCIE | 50,004 | 32,258 | 17,431 | 315 | 14,827 R | 64.5% | 34.9% | 64.9% | 35.1% |
| 55,988 | SANTA ROSA | 24,424 | 19,021 | 5,259 | 144 | 13,762 R | 77.9% | 21.5% | 78.3% | 21.7% |
| 202,251 | SARASOTA | 127,483 | 84,649 | 42,125 | 709 | 42,524 R | 66.4% | 33.0% | 66.8% | 33.2% |
| 179,752 | SEMINOLE | 83,673 | 60,406 | 22,646 | 621 | 37,760 R | 72.2% | 27.1% | 72.7% | 27.3% |
| 24,272 | SUMTER | 9,896 | 5,936 | 3,900 | 60 | 2,036 R | 60.0% | 39.4% | 60.3% | 39.7% |

# FLORIDA

## PRESIDENT 1988

| 1980 Census Population | County | Total Vote | Republican | Democratic | Other | Rep.-Dem. Plurality | Percentage | | | |
|---|---|---|---|---|---|---|---|---|---|---|
| | | | | | | | Total Vote | | Major Vote | |
| | | | | | | | Rep. | Dem. | Rep. | Dem. |
| 22,287 | SUWANNEE | 9,122 | 5,863 | 3,129 | 130 | 2,734 R | 64.3% | 34.3% | 65.2% | 34.8% |
| 16,532 | TAYLOR | 5,875 | 4,057 | 1,763 | 55 | 2,294 R | 69.1% | 30.0% | 69.7% | 30.3% |
| 10,166 | UNION | 2,349 | 1,644 | 691 | 14 | 953 R | 70.0% | 29.4% | 70.4% | 29.6% |
| 258,762 | VOLUSIA | 131,182 | 74,195 | 55,469 | 1,518 | 18,726 R | 56.6% | 42.3% | 57.2% | 42.8% |
| 10,887 | WAKULLA | 4,805 | 3,158 | 1,605 | 42 | 1,553 R | 65.7% | 33.4% | 66.3% | 33.7% |
| 21,300 | WALTON | 10,808 | 7,490 | 3,235 | 83 | 4,255 R | 69.3% | 29.9% | 69.8% | 30.2% |
| 14,509 | WASHINGTON | 6,564 | 4,374 | 2,144 | 46 | 2,230 R | 66.6% | 32.7% | 67.1% | 32.9% |
| 9,746,324 | TOTAL | 4,302,313 | 2,618,885 | 1,656,701 | 26,727 | 962,184 R | 60.9% | 38.5% | 61.3% | 38.7% |

# FLORIDA

## PRESIDENT 1984

| 1980 Census Population | County | Total Vote | Republican | Democratic | Other | Rep.-Dem. Plurality | Percentage | | | |
|---|---|---|---|---|---|---|---|---|---|---|
| | | | | | | | Total Vote | | Major Vote | |
| | | | | | | | Rep. | Dem. | Rep. | Dem. |
| 151,348 | ALACHUA | 57,193 | 30,582 | 26,551 | 60 | 4,031 R | 53.5% | 46.4% | 53.5% | 46.5% |
| 15,289 | BAKER | 4,866 | 3,485 | 1,381 | | 2,104 R | 71.6% | 28.4% | 71.6% | 28.4% |
| 97,740 | BAY | 38,707 | 29,322 | 9,381 | 4 | 19,941 R | 75.8% | 24.2% | 75.8% | 24.2% |
| 20,023 | BRADFORD | 6,469 | 4,128 | 2,341 | | 1,787 R | 63.8% | 36.2% | 63.8% | 36.2% |
| 272,959 | BREVARD | 139,349 | 102,339 | 36,963 | 47 | 65,376 R | 73.4% | 26.5% | 73.5% | 26.5% |
| 1,018,200 | BROWARD | 449,077 | 254,501 | 194,542 | 34 | 59,959 R | 56.7% | 43.3% | 56.7% | 43.3% |
| 9,294 | CALHOUN | 3,806 | 2,493 | 1,312 | 1 | 1,181 R | 65.5% | 34.5% | 65.5% | 34.5% |
| 58,460 | CHARLOTTE | 38,769 | 27,464 | 11,303 | 2 | 16,161 R | 70.8% | 29.2% | 70.8% | 29.2% |
| 54,703 | CITRUS | 31,221 | 20,754 | 10,463 | 4 | 10,291 R | 66.5% | 33.5% | 66.5% | 33.5% |
| 67,052 | CLAY | 27,033 | 21,545 | 5,488 | | 16,057 R | 79.7% | 20.3% | 79.7% | 20.3% |
| 85,971 | COLLIER | 42,673 | 33,603 | 9,065 | 5 | 24,538 R | 78.7% | 21.2% | 78.8% | 21.2% |
| 35,399 | COLUMBIA | 13,068 | 8,807 | 4,261 | | 4,546 R | 67.4% | 32.6% | 67.4% | 32.6% |
| 1,625,781 | DADE | 548,044 | 324,216 | 223,793 | 35 | 100,423 R | 59.2% | 40.8% | 59.2% | 40.8% |
| 19,039 | DESOTO | 7,127 | 4,822 | 2,302 | 3 | 2,520 R | 67.7% | 32.3% | 67.7% | 32.3% |
| 7,751 | DIXIE | 3,428 | 2,204 | 1,224 | | 980 R | 64.3% | 35.7% | 64.3% | 35.7% |
| 571,003 | DUVAL | 206,132 | 128,653 | 77,459 | 20 | 51,194 R | 62.4% | 37.6% | 62.4% | 37.6% |
| 233,794 | ESCAMBIA | 93,458 | 66,638 | 26,798 | 22 | 39,840 R | 71.3% | 28.7% | 71.3% | 28.7% |
| 10,913 | FLAGLER | 7,907 | 4,907 | 2,999 | 1 | 1,908 R | 62.1% | 37.9% | 62.1% | 37.9% |
| 7,661 | FRANKLIN | 3,307 | 2,218 | 1,089 | | 1,129 R | 67.1% | 32.9% | 67.1% | 32.9% |
| 41,565 | GADSDEN | 13,206 | 5,805 | 7,399 | 2 | 1,594 D | 44.0% | 56.0% | 44.0% | 56.0% |
| 5,767 | GILCHRIST | 3,108 | 2,056 | 1,051 | 1 | 1,005 R | 66.2% | 33.8% | 66.2% | 33.8% |
| 5,992 | GLADES | 3,057 | 1,987 | 1,070 | | 917 R | 65.0% | 35.0% | 65.0% | 35.0% |
| 10,658 | GULF | 5,356 | 3,573 | 1,783 | | 1,790 R | 66.7% | 33.3% | 66.7% | 33.3% |
| 8,761 | HAMILTON | 3,322 | 1,921 | 1,401 | | 520 R | 57.8% | 42.2% | 57.8% | 42.2% |
| 19,379 | HARDEE | 5,493 | 3,957 | 1,536 | | 2,421 R | 72.0% | 28.0% | 72.0% | 28.0% |
| 18,599 | HENDRY | 6,542 | 4,524 | 2,018 | | 2,506 R | 69.2% | 30.8% | 69.2% | 30.8% |
| 44,469 | HERNANDO | 33,481 | 21,273 | 12,204 | 4 | 9,069 R | 63.5% | 36.5% | 63.5% | 36.5% |
| 47,526 | HIGHLANDS | 23,685 | 16,465 | 7,217 | 3 | 9,248 R | 69.5% | 30.5% | 69.5% | 30.5% |
| 646,960 | HILLSBOROUGH | 244,068 | 157,827 | 86,189 | 52 | 71,638 R | 64.7% | 35.3% | 64.7% | 35.3% |
| 14,723 | HOLMES | 5,778 | 4,547 | 1,231 | | 3,316 R | 78.7% | 21.3% | 78.7% | 21.3% |
| 59,896 | INDIAN RIVER | 32,425 | 23,694 | 8,731 | | 14,963 R | 73.1% | 26.9% | 73.1% | 26.9% |
| 39,154 | JACKSON | 14,042 | 9,086 | 4,956 | | 4,130 R | 64.7% | 35.3% | 64.7% | 35.3% |
| 10,703 | JEFFERSON | 4,300 | 2,244 | 2,055 | 1 | 189 R | 52.2% | 47.8% | 52.2% | 47.8% |
| 4,035 | LAFAYETTE | 2,375 | 1,513 | 862 | | 651 R | 63.7% | 36.3% | 63.7% | 36.3% |
| 104,870 | LAKE | 47,526 | 35,304 | 12,215 | 7 | 23,089 R | 74.3% | 25.7% | 74.3% | 25.7% |
| 205,266 | LEE | 115,047 | 85,006 | 30,011 | 30 | 54,995 R | 73.9% | 26.1% | 73.9% | 26.1% |
| 148,655 | LEON | 65,993 | 36,301 | 29,654 | 38 | 6,647 R | 55.0% | 44.9% | 55.0% | 45.0% |
| 19,870 | LEVY | 8,664 | 5,561 | 3,103 | | 2,458 R | 64.2% | 35.8% | 64.2% | 35.8% |
| 4,260 | LIBERTY | 2,058 | 1,409 | 649 | | 760 R | 68.5% | 31.5% | 68.5% | 31.5% |
| 14,894 | MADISON | 4,917 | 2,816 | 2,101 | | 715 R | 57.3% | 42.7% | 57.3% | 42.7% |
| 148,442 | MANATEE | 76,668 | 55,775 | 20,887 | 6 | 34,888 R | 72.7% | 27.2% | 72.8% | 27.2% |
| 122,488 | MARION | 54,023 | 37,796 | 16,221 | 6 | 21,575 R | 70.0% | 30.0% | 70.0% | 30.0% |
| 64,014 | MARTIN | 37,882 | 28,897 | 8,976 | 9 | 19,921 R | 76.3% | 23.7% | 76.3% | 23.7% |
| 63,188 | MONROE | 24,096 | 16,316 | 7,771 | 9 | 8,545 R | 67.7% | 32.3% | 67.7% | 32.3% |
| 32,894 | NASSAU | 11,517 | 8,033 | 3,483 | 1 | 4,550 R | 69.7% | 30.2% | 69.8% | 30.2% |
| 109,920 | OKALOOSA | 44,261 | 36,963 | 7,289 | 9 | 29,674 R | 83.5% | 16.5% | 83.5% | 16.5% |
| 20,264 | OKEECHOBEE | 6,673 | 4,447 | 2,226 | | 2,221 R | 66.6% | 33.4% | 66.6% | 33.4% |
| 471,016 | ORANGE | 170,909 | 122,007 | 48,737 | 165 | 73,270 R | 71.4% | 28.5% | 71.5% | 28.5% |
| 49,287 | OSCEOLA | 24,975 | 18,344 | 6,627 | 4 | 11,717 R | 73.4% | 26.5% | 73.5% | 26.5% |
| 576,863 | PALM BEACH | 302,855 | 186,755 | 116,071 | 29 | 70,684 R | 61.7% | 38.3% | 61.7% | 38.3% |
| 193,643 | PASCO | 107,578 | 66,609 | 40,961 | 8 | 25,648 R | 61.9% | 38.1% | 61.9% | 38.1% |
| 728,531 | PINELLAS | 369,145 | 240,535 | 128,547 | 63 | 111,988 R | 65.2% | 34.8% | 65.2% | 34.8% |
| 321,652 | POLK | 119,701 | 84,174 | 35,505 | 22 | 48,669 R | 70.3% | 29.7% | 70.3% | 29.7% |
| 50,549 | PUTNAM | 19,249 | 11,424 | 7,821 | 4 | 3,603 R | 59.3% | 40.6% | 59.4% | 40.6% |
| 51,303 | ST. JOHNS | 23,147 | 16,493 | 6,652 | 2 | 9,841 R | 71.3% | 28.7% | 71.3% | 28.7% |
| 87,182 | ST. LUCIE | 41,235 | 28,189 | 13,039 | 7 | 15,150 R | 68.4% | 31.6% | 68.4% | 31.6% |
| 55,988 | SANTA ROSA | 25,889 | 21,237 | 4,646 | 6 | 16,591 R | 82.0% | 17.9% | 82.0% | 18.0% |
| 202,251 | SARASOTA | 118,294 | 87,713 | 30,512 | 69 | 57,201 R | 74.1% | 25.8% | 74.2% | 25.8% |
| 179,752 | SEMINOLE | 74,071 | 56,229 | 17,789 | 53 | 38,440 R | 75.9% | 24.0% | 76.0% | 24.0% |
| 24,272 | SUMTER | 9,713 | 6,252 | 3,460 | 1 | 2,792 R | 64.4% | 35.6% | 64.4% | 35.6% |

# FLORIDA

## PRESIDENT 1984

| 1980 Census Population | County | Total Vote | Republican | Democratic | Other | Rep.-Dem. Plurality | Percentage | | | |
|---|---|---|---|---|---|---|---|---|---|---|
| | | | | | | | Total Vote | | Major Vote | |
| | | | | | | | Rep. | Dem. | Rep. | Dem. |
| 22,287 | SUWANNEE | 8,867 | 6,079 | 2,788 | | 3,291 R | 68.6% | 31.4% | 68.6% | 31.4% |
| 16,532 | TAYLOR | 5,758 | 4,030 | 1,728 | | 2,302 R | 70.0% | 30.0% | 70.0% | 30.0% |
| 10,166 | UNION | 2,567 | 1,804 | 761 | 2 | 1,043 R | 70.3% | 29.6% | 70.3% | 29.7% |
| 258,762 | VOLUSIA | 112,141 | 68,317 | 43,811 | 13 | 24,506 R | 60.9% | 39.1% | 60.9% | 39.1% |
| 10,887 | WAKULLA | 4,556 | 3,087 | 1,469 | | 1,618 R | 67.8% | 32.2% | 67.8% | 32.2% |
| 21,300 | WALTON | 9,617 | 7,117 | 2,500 | | 4,617 R | 74.0% | 26.0% | 74.0% | 26.0% |
| 14,509 | WASHINGTON | 6,520 | 4,603 | 1,916 | 1 | 2,687 R | 70.6% | 29.4% | 70.6% | 29.4% |
| | SPECIAL ABSENTEE | 2,067 | 1,575 | 472 | 20 | 1,103 R | 76.2% | 22.8% | 76.9% | 23.1% |
| 9,746,324 | TOTAL | 4,180,051 | 2,730,350 | 1,448,816 | 885 | 1,281,534 R | 65.3% | 34.7% | 65.3% | 34.7% |

# FLORIDA

## PRESIDENT 1980

| 1980 Census Population | County | Total Vote | Republican | Democratic | Other | Rep.-Dem. Plurality | Percentage | | | |
|---|---|---|---|---|---|---|---|---|---|---|
| | | | | | | | Total Vote | | Major Vote | |
| | | | | | | | Rep. | Dem. | Rep. | Dem. |
| 151,348 | ALACHUA | 51,355 | 19,804 | 26,849 | 4,702 | 7,045 D | 38.6% | 52.3% | 42.4% | 57.6% |
| 15,289 | BAKER | 4,976 | 2,283 | 2,611 | 82 | 328 D | 45.9% | 52.5% | 46.6% | 53.4% |
| 97,740 | BAY | 34,561 | 20,948 | 12,389 | 1,224 | 8,559 R | 60.6% | 35.8% | 62.8% | 37.2% |
| 20,023 | BRADFORD | 6,243 | 2,778 | 3,347 | 118 | 569 D | 44.5% | 53.6% | 45.4% | 54.6% |
| 272,959 | BREVARD | 115,636 | 69,460 | 39,007 | 7,169 | 30,453 R | 60.1% | 33.7% | 64.0% | 36.0% |
| 1,018,200 | BROWARD | 410,561 | 229,693 | 146,323 | 34,545 | 83,370 R | 55.9% | 35.6% | 61.1% | 38.9% |
| 9,294 | CALHOUN | 3,884 | 1,504 | 2,300 | 80 | 796 D | 38.7% | 59.2% | 39.5% | 60.5% |
| 58,460 | CHARLOTTE | 31,700 | 20,486 | 9,769 | 1,445 | 10,717 R | 64.6% | 30.8% | 67.7% | 32.3% |
| 54,703 | CITRUS | 24,430 | 14,286 | 9,162 | 982 | 5,124 R | 58.5% | 37.5% | 60.9% | 39.1% |
| 67,052 | CLAY | 24,122 | 15,643 | 7,630 | 849 | 8,013 R | 64.8% | 31.6% | 67.2% | 32.8% |
| 85,971 | COLLIER | 33,613 | 23,900 | 7,739 | 1,974 | 16,161 R | 71.1% | 23.0% | 75.5% | 24.5% |
| 35,399 | COLUMBIA | 11,648 | 5,643 | 5,680 | 325 | 37 D | 48.4% | 48.8% | 49.8% | 50.2% |
| 1,625,781 | DADE | 524,896 | 265,888 | 210,868 | 48,140 | 55,020 R | 50.7% | 40.2% | 55.8% | 44.2% |
| 19,039 | DESOTO | 6,285 | 3,356 | 2,713 | 216 | 643 R | 53.4% | 43.2% | 55.3% | 44.7% |
| 7,751 | DIXIE | 3,173 | 1,101 | 2,010 | 62 | 909 D | 34.7% | 63.3% | 35.4% | 64.6% |
| 571,003 | DUVAL | 195,545 | 98,664 | 90,466 | 6,415 | 8,198 R | 50.5% | 46.3% | 52.2% | 47.8% |
| 233,794 | ESCAMBIA | 88,559 | 51,794 | 33,513 | 3,252 | 18,281 R | 58.5% | 37.8% | 60.7% | 39.3% |
| 10,913 | FLAGLER | 5,600 | 2,895 | 2,503 | 202 | 392 R | 51.7% | 44.7% | 53.6% | 46.4% |
| 7,661 | FRANKLIN | 3,382 | 1,508 | 1,775 | 99 | 267 D | 44.6% | 52.5% | 45.9% | 54.1% |
| 41,565 | GADSDEN | 12,225 | 3,718 | 8,222 | 285 | 4,504 D | 30.4% | 67.3% | 31.1% | 68.9% |
| 5,767 | GILCHRIST | 2,793 | 1,093 | 1,627 | 73 | 534 D | 39.1% | 58.3% | 40.2% | 59.8% |
| 5,992 | GLADES | 2,389 | 1,098 | 1,203 | 88 | 105 D | 46.0% | 50.4% | 47.7% | 52.3% |
| 10,658 | GULF | 4,926 | 2,127 | 2,700 | 99 | 573 D | 43.2% | 54.8% | 44.1% | 55.9% |
| 8,761 | HAMILTON | 3,280 | 1,301 | 1,923 | 56 | 622 D | 39.7% | 58.6% | 40.4% | 59.6% |
| 19,379 | HARDEE | 5,332 | 2,603 | 2,599 | 130 | 4 R | 48.8% | 48.7% | 50.0% | 50.0% |
| 18,599 | HENDRY | 5,414 | 2,703 | 2,543 | 168 | 160 R | 49.9% | 47.0% | 51.5% | 48.5% |
| 44,469 | HERNANDO | 22,032 | 12,115 | 8,858 | 1,059 | 3,257 R | 55.0% | 40.2% | 57.8% | 42.2% |
| 47,526 | HIGHLANDS | 19,249 | 11,925 | 6,688 | 636 | 5,237 R | 62.0% | 34.7% | 64.1% | 35.9% |
| 646,960 | HILLSBOROUGH | 205,314 | 106,160 | 88,271 | 10,883 | 17,889 R | 51.7% | 43.0% | 54.6% | 45.4% |
| 14,723 | HOLMES | 6,137 | 3,221 | 2,767 | 149 | 454 R | 52.5% | 45.1% | 53.8% | 46.2% |
| 59,896 | INDIAN RIVER | 24,717 | 15,568 | 7,759 | 1,390 | 7,809 R | 63.0% | 31.4% | 66.7% | 33.3% |
| 39,154 | JACKSON | 14,181 | 6,348 | 7,567 | 266 | 1,219 D | 44.8% | 53.4% | 45.6% | 54.4% |
| 10,703 | JEFFERSON | 4,141 | 1,623 | 2,367 | 151 | 744 D | 39.2% | 57.2% | 40.7% | 59.3% |
| 4,035 | LAFAYETTE | 1,863 | 795 | 1,034 | 34 | 239 D | 42.7% | 55.5% | 43.5% | 56.5% |
| 104,870 | LAKE | 41,528 | 26,798 | 13,128 | 1,602 | 13,670 R | 64.5% | 31.6% | 67.1% | 32.9% |
| 205,266 | LEE | 94,613 | 61,033 | 28,125 | 5,455 | 32,908 R | 64.5% | 29.7% | 68.5% | 31.5% |
| 148,655 | LEON | 57,308 | 24,919 | 28,450 | 3,939 | 3,531 D | 43.5% | 49.6% | 46.7% | 53.3% |
| 19,870 | LEVY | 7,596 | 3,210 | 4,170 | 216 | 960 D | 42.3% | 54.9% | 43.5% | 56.5% |
| 4,260 | LIBERTY | 2,052 | 899 | 1,114 | 39 | 215 D | 43.8% | 54.3% | 44.7% | 55.3% |
| 14,894 | MADISON | 5,509 | 2,280 | 3,134 | 95 | 854 D | 41.4% | 56.9% | 42.1% | 57.9% |
| 148,442 | MANATEE | 65,576 | 40,535 | 21,679 | 3,362 | 18,856 R | 61.8% | 33.1% | 65.2% | 34.8% |
| 122,488 | MARION | 40,592 | 23,743 | 15,400 | 1,449 | 8,343 R | 58.5% | 37.9% | 60.7% | 39.3% |
| 64,014 | MARTIN | 30,154 | 20,521 | 8,087 | 1,546 | 12,434 R | 68.1% | 26.8% | 71.7% | 28.3% |
| 63,188 | MONROE | 21,806 | 11,644 | 7,920 | 2,242 | 3,724 R | 53.4% | 36.3% | 59.5% | 40.5% |
| 32,894 | NASSAU | 10,751 | 5,440 | 5,074 | 237 | 366 R | 50.6% | 47.2% | 51.7% | 48.3% |
| 109,920 | OKALOOSA | 40,323 | 28,072 | 10,845 | 1,406 | 17,227 R | 69.6% | 26.9% | 72.1% | 27.9% |
| 20,264 | OKEECHOBEE | 6,210 | 2,783 | 3,228 | 199 | 445 D | 44.8% | 52.0% | 46.3% | 53.7% |
| 471,016 | ORANGE | 143,201 | 87,454 | 48,767 | 6,980 | 38,687 R | 61.1% | 34.1% | 64.2% | 35.8% |
| 49,287 | OSCEOLA | 18,205 | 10,863 | 6,603 | 739 | 4,260 R | 59.7% | 36.3% | 62.2% | 37.8% |
| 576,863 | PALM BEACH | 252,930 | 143,639 | 91,991 | 17,300 | 51,648 R | 56.8% | 36.4% | 61.0% | 39.0% |
| 193,643 | PASCO | 88,445 | 50,120 | 34,054 | 4,271 | 16,066 R | 56.7% | 38.5% | 59.5% | 40.5% |
| 728,531 | PINELLAS | 345,003 | 185,728 | 138,428 | 20,847 | 47,300 R | 53.8% | 40.1% | 57.3% | 42.7% |
| 321,652 | POLK | 106,315 | 59,651 | 43,327 | 3,337 | 16,324 R | 56.1% | 40.8% | 57.9% | 42.1% |
| 50,549 | PUTNAM | 17,727 | 8,273 | 8,906 | 548 | 633 D | 46.7% | 50.2% | 48.2% | 51.8% |
| 51,303 | ST. JOHNS | 18,826 | 11,234 | 6,898 | 694 | 4,336 R | 59.7% | 36.6% | 62.0% | 38.0% |
| 87,182 | ST. LUCIE | 29,830 | 18,126 | 10,347 | 1,357 | 7,779 R | 60.8% | 34.7% | 63.7% | 36.3% |
| 55,988 | SANTA ROSA | 21,590 | 13,802 | 6,964 | 824 | 6,838 R | 63.9% | 32.3% | 66.5% | 33.5% |
| 202,251 | SARASOTA | 99,238 | 68,065 | 25,621 | 5,552 | 42,444 R | 68.6% | 25.8% | 72.7% | 27.3% |
| 179,752 | SEMINOLE | 60,439 | 39,989 | 17,443 | 3,007 | 22,546 R | 66.2% | 28.9% | 69.6% | 30.4% |
| 24,272 | SUMTER | 8,267 | 3,671 | 4,380 | 216 | 709 D | 44.4% | 53.0% | 45.6% | 54.4% |

# FLORIDA

## PRESIDENT 1980

| 1980 Census Population | County | Total Vote | Republican | Democratic | Other | Rep.-Dem. Plurality | Percentage | | | |
|---|---|---|---|---|---|---|---|---|---|---|
| | | | | | | | Total Vote | | Major Vote | |
| | | | | | | | Rep. | Dem. | Rep. | Dem. |
| 22,287 | SUWANNEE | 8,436 | 3,899 | 4,345 | 192 | 446 D | 46.2% | 51.5% | 47.3% | 52.7% |
| 16,532 | TAYLOR | 5,868 | 2,776 | 2,963 | 129 | 187 D | 47.3% | 50.5% | 48.4% | 51.6% |
| 10,166 | UNION | 2,423 | 1,123 | 1,237 | 63 | 114 D | 46.3% | 51.1% | 47.6% | 52.4% |
| 258,762 | VOLUSIA | 101,882 | 52,663 | 44,513 | 4,706 | 8,150 R | 51.7% | 43.7% | 54.2% | 45.8% |
| 10,887 | WAKULLA | 4,276 | 2,021 | 2,082 | 173 | 61 D | 47.3% | 48.7% | 49.3% | 50.7% |
| 21,300 | WALTON | 9,336 | 4,694 | 4,360 | 282 | 334 R | 50.3% | 46.7% | 51.8% | 48.2% |
| 14,509 | WASHINGTON | 6,513 | 3,251 | 3,110 | 152 | 141 R | 49.9% | 47.8% | 51.1% | 48.9% |
| 9,746,324 | TOTAL | 3,686,930 | 2,046,951 | 1,419,475 | 220,504 | 627,476 R | 55.5% | 38.5% | 59.1% | 40.9% |

# FLORIDA

## PRESIDENT 1976

| 1970 Census Population | County | Total Vote | Republican | Democratic | Other | Rep.-Dem. Plurality | Percentage Total Vote Rep. | Dem. | Major Vote Rep. | Dem. |
|---|---|---|---|---|---|---|---|---|---|---|
| 104,764 | ALACHUA | 44,578 | 15,546 | 27,895 | 1,137 | 12,349 D | 34.9% | 62.6% | 35.8% | 64.2% |
| 9,242 | BAKER | 4,195 | 1,058 | 2,985 | 152 | 1,927 D | 25.2% | 71.2% | 26.2% | 73.8% |
| 75,283 | BAY | 29,484 | 14,208 | 14,858 | 418 | 650 D | 48.2% | 50.4% | 48.9% | 51.1% |
| 14,625 | BRADFORD | 5,617 | 1,680 | 3,868 | 69 | 2,188 D | 29.9% | 68.9% | 30.3% | 69.7% |
| 230,006 | BREVARD | 92,364 | 44,470 | 46,421 | 1,473 | 1,951 D | 48.1% | 50.3% | 48.9% | 51.1% |
| 620,100 | BROWARD | 342,343 | 161,411 | 176,491 | 4,441 | 15,080 D | 47.1% | 51.6% | 47.8% | 52.2% |
| 7,624 | CALHOUN | 3,689 | 1,153 | 2,487 | 49 | 1,334 D | 31.3% | 67.4% | 31.7% | 68.3% |
| 27,559 | CHARLOTTE | 23,333 | 12,703 | 10,300 | 330 | 2,403 R | 54.4% | 44.1% | 55.2% | 44.8% |
| 19,196 | CITRUS | 17,707 | 7,973 | 9,438 | 296 | 1,465 D | 45.0% | 53.3% | 45.8% | 54.2% |
| 32,059 | CLAY | 17,148 | 8,468 | 8,410 | 270 | 58 R | 49.4% | 49.0% | 50.2% | 49.8% |
| 38,040 | COLLIER | 23,710 | 14,643 | 8,764 | 303 | 5,879 R | 61.8% | 37.0% | 62.6% | 37.4% |
| 25,250 | COLUMBIA | 10,766 | 3,947 | 6,683 | 136 | 2,736 D | 36.7% | 62.1% | 37.1% | 62.9% |
| 1,267,792 | DADE | 521,942 | 211,148 | 303,047 | 7,747 | 91,899 D | 40.5% | 58.1% | 41.1% | 58.9% |
| 13,060 | DESOTO | 4,822 | 2,000 | 2,715 | 107 | 715 D | 41.5% | 56.3% | 42.4% | 57.6% |
| 5,480 | DIXIE | 2,752 | 558 | 2,169 | 25 | 1,611 D | 20.3% | 78.8% | 20.5% | 79.5% |
| 528,865 | DUVAL | 182,561 | 74,997 | 105,912 | 1,652 | 30,915 D | 41.1% | 58.0% | 41.5% | 58.5% |
| 205,334 | ESCAMBIA | 80,715 | 41,471 | 38,279 | 965 | 3,192 R | 51.4% | 47.4% | 52.0% | 48.0% |
| 4,454 | FLAGLER | 3,373 | 1,262 | 2,086 | 25 | 824 D | 37.4% | 61.8% | 37.7% | 62.3% |
| 7,065 | FRANKLIN | 2,973 | 1,054 | 1,859 | 60 | 805 D | 35.5% | 62.5% | 36.2% | 63.8% |
| 39,184 | GADSDEN | 10,431 | 3,531 | 6,798 | 102 | 3,267 D | 33.9% | 65.2% | 34.2% | 65.8% |
| 3,551 | GILCHRIST | 2,354 | 528 | 1,807 | 19 | 1,279 D | 22.4% | 76.8% | 22.6% | 77.4% |
| 3,669 | GLADES | 1,965 | 624 | 1,311 | 30 | 687 D | 31.8% | 66.7% | 32.2% | 67.8% |
| 10,096 | GULF | 4,281 | 1,584 | 2,641 | 56 | 1,057 D | 37.0% | 61.7% | 37.5% | 62.5% |
| 7,787 | HAMILTON | 2,951 | 794 | 2,053 | 104 | 1,259 D | 26.9% | 69.6% | 27.9% | 72.1% |
| 14,889 | HARDEE | 5,107 | 2,189 | 2,670 | 248 | 481 D | 42.9% | 52.3% | 45.1% | 54.9% |
| 11,859 | HENDRY | 4,254 | 1,843 | 2,337 | 74 | 494 D | 43.3% | 54.9% | 44.1% | 55.9% |
| 17,004 | HERNANDO | 13,732 | 5,793 | 7,717 | 222 | 1,924 D | 42.2% | 56.2% | 42.9% | 57.1% |
| 29,507 | HIGHLANDS | 15,733 | 8,317 | 7,218 | 198 | 1,099 R | 52.9% | 45.9% | 53.5% | 46.5% |
| 490,265 | HILLSBOROUGH | 175,145 | 78,504 | 94,589 | 2,052 | 16,085 D | 44.8% | 54.0% | 45.4% | 54.6% |
| 10,720 | HOLMES | 5,180 | 1,850 | 3,256 | 74 | 1,406 D | 35.7% | 62.9% | 36.2% | 63.8% |
| 35,992 | INDIAN RIVER | 18,654 | 9,818 | 8,512 | 324 | 1,306 R | 52.6% | 45.6% | 53.6% | 46.4% |
| 34,434 | JACKSON | 12,652 | 4,795 | 7,687 | 170 | 2,892 D | 37.9% | 60.8% | 38.4% | 61.6% |
| 8,778 | JEFFERSON | 3,749 | 1,361 | 2,310 | 78 | 949 D | 36.3% | 61.6% | 37.1% | 62.9% |
| 2,892 | LAFAYETTE | 1,665 | 523 | 1,126 | 16 | 603 D | 31.4% | 67.6% | 31.7% | 68.3% |
| 69,305 | LAKE | 34,787 | 19,976 | 14,369 | 442 | 5,607 R | 57.4% | 41.3% | 58.2% | 41.8% |
| 105,216 | LEE | 69,789 | 38,038 | 30,567 | 1,184 | 7,471 R | 54.5% | 43.8% | 55.4% | 44.6% |
| 103,047 | LEON | 53,443 | 23,739 | 28,729 | 975 | 4,990 D | 44.4% | 53.8% | 45.2% | 54.8% |
| 12,756 | LEVY | 6,166 | 1,965 | 4,025 | 176 | 2,060 D | 31.9% | 65.3% | 32.8% | 67.2% |
| 3,379 | LIBERTY | 1,776 | 620 | 1,137 | 19 | 517 D | 34.9% | 64.0% | 35.3% | 64.7% |
| 13,481 | MADISON | 5,040 | 1,761 | 3,218 | 61 | 1,457 D | 34.9% | 63.8% | 35.4% | 64.6% |
| 97,115 | MANATEE | 54,360 | 29,300 | 24,342 | 718 | 4,958 R | 53.9% | 44.8% | 54.6% | 45.4% |
| 69,030 | MARION | 33,679 | 16,163 | 16,963 | 553 | 800 D | 48.0% | 50.4% | 48.8% | 51.2% |
| 28,035 | MARTIN | 20,756 | 11,682 | 8,785 | 289 | 2,897 R | 56.3% | 42.3% | 57.1% | 42.9% |
| 52,586 | MONROE | 19,757 | 8,232 | 11,079 | 446 | 2,847 D | 41.7% | 56.1% | 42.6% | 57.4% |
| 20,626 | NASSAU | 9,140 | 3,136 | 5,896 | 108 | 2,760 D | 34.3% | 64.5% | 34.7% | 65.3% |
| 88,187 | OKALOOSA | 33,295 | 18,598 | 14,210 | 487 | 4,388 R | 55.9% | 42.7% | 56.7% | 43.3% |
| 11,233 | OKEECHOBEE | 4,825 | 1,598 | 3,184 | 43 | 1,586 D | 33.1% | 66.0% | 33.4% | 66.6% |
| 344,311 | ORANGE | 130,437 | 70,451 | 58,442 | 1,544 | 12,009 R | 54.0% | 44.8% | 54.7% | 45.3% |
| 25,267 | OSCEOLA | 14,175 | 7,062 | 6,893 | 220 | 169 R | 49.8% | 48.6% | 50.6% | 49.4% |
| 348,753 | PALM BEACH | 198,657 | 98,236 | 96,705 | 3,716 | 1,531 R | 49.5% | 48.7% | 50.4% | 49.6% |
| 75,955 | PASCO | 62,747 | 28,306 | 33,710 | 731 | 5,404 D | 45.1% | 53.7% | 45.6% | 54.4% |
| 522,329 | PINELLAS | 295,569 | 150,003 | 141,879 | 3,687 | 8,124 R | 50.8% | 48.0% | 51.4% | 48.6% |
| 227,222 | POLK | 92,706 | 44,238 | 47,286 | 1,182 | 3,048 D | 47.7% | 51.0% | 48.3% | 51.7% |
| 36,290 | PUTNAM | 14,809 | 5,040 | 9,597 | 172 | 4,557 D | 34.0% | 64.8% | 34.4% | 65.6% |
| 30,727 | ST. JOHNS | 14,371 | 6,660 | 7,412 | 299 | 752 D | 46.3% | 51.6% | 47.3% | 52.7% |
| 50,836 | ST. LUCIE | 24,209 | 11,502 | 12,386 | 321 | 884 D | 47.5% | 51.2% | 48.1% | 51.9% |
| 37,741 | SANTA ROSA | 17,412 | 9,122 | 8,020 | 270 | 1,102 R | 52.4% | 46.1% | 53.2% | 46.8% |
| 120,413 | SARASOTA | 71,478 | 44,157 | 26,293 | 1,028 | 17,864 R | 61.8% | 36.8% | 62.7% | 37.3% |
| 83,692 | SEMINOLE | 46,813 | 26,655 | 19,609 | 549 | 7,046 R | 56.9% | 41.9% | 57.6% | 42.4% |
| 14,839 | SUMTER | 7,090 | 2,212 | 4,721 | 157 | 2,509 D | 31.2% | 66.6% | 31.9% | 68.1% |

# FLORIDA

## PRESIDENT 1976

| 1970 Census Population | County | Total Vote | Republican | Democratic | Other | Rep.-Dem. Plurality | Percentage | | | |
|---|---|---|---|---|---|---|---|---|---|---|
| | | | | | | | Total Vote | | Major Vote | |
| | | | | | | | Rep. | Dem. | Rep. | Dem. |
| 15,559 | SUWANNEE | 7,402 | 2,405 | 4,718 | 279 | 2,313 D | 32.5% | 63.7% | 33.8% | 66.2% |
| 13,641 | TAYLOR | 5,406 | 1,983 | 3,370 | 53 | 1,387 D | 36.7% | 62.3% | 37.0% | 63.0% |
| 8,112 | UNION | 2,040 | 544 | 1,480 | 16 | 936 D | 26.7% | 72.5% | 26.9% | 73.1% |
| 169,487 | VOLUSIA | 88,225 | 37,523 | 49,161 | 1,541 | 11,638 D | 42.5% | 55.7% | 43.3% | 56.7% |
| 6,308 | WAKULLA | 4,072 | 1,580 | 2,353 | 139 | 773 D | 38.8% | 57.8% | 40.2% | 59.8% |
| 16,087 | WALTON | 8,279 | 2,927 | 5,196 | 156 | 2,269 D | 35.4% | 62.8% | 36.0% | 64.0% |
| 11,453 | WASHINGTON | 5,996 | 2,313 | 3,566 | 117 | 1,253 D | 38.6% | 59.5% | 39.3% | 60.7% |
| 6,789,443 | TOTAL | 3,150,631 | 1,469,531 | 1,636,000 | 45,100 | 166,469 D | 46.6% | 51.9% | 47.3% | 52.7% |

# FLORIDA

## PRESIDENT 1972

| 1970 Census Population | County | Total Vote | Republican | Democratic | Other | Rep.-Dem. Plurality | Percentage | | | |
|---|---|---|---|---|---|---|---|---|---|---|
| | | | | | | | Total Vote | | Major Vote | |
| | | | | | | | Rep. | Dem. | Rep. | Dem. |
| 104,764 | ALACHUA | 39,861 | 22,536 | 17,245 | 80 | 5,291 R | 56.5% | 43.3% | 56.7% | 43.3% |
| 9,242 | BAKER | 2,323 | 1,943 | 379 | 1 | 1,564 R | 83.6% | 16.3% | 83.7% | 16.3% |
| 75,283 | BAY | 24,159 | 20,245 | 3,914 | | 16,331 R | 83.8% | 16.2% | 83.8% | 16.2% |
| 14,625 | BRADFORD | 4,957 | 3,652 | 1,217 | 88 | 2,435 R | 73.7% | 24.6% | 75.0% | 25.0% |
| 230,006 | BREVARD | 79,733 | 62,773 | 16,854 | 106 | 45,919 R | 78.7% | 21.1% | 78.8% | 21.2% |
| 620,100 | BROWARD | 271,409 | 196,528 | 74,127 | 754 | 122,401 R | 72.4% | 27.3% | 72.6% | 27.4% |
| 7,624 | CALHOUN | 2,533 | 2,069 | 461 | 3 | 1,608 R | 81.7% | 18.2% | 81.8% | 18.2% |
| 27,559 | CHARLOTTE | 16,817 | 12,888 | 3,874 | 55 | 9,014 R | 76.6% | 23.0% | 76.9% | 23.1% |
| 19,196 | CITRUS | 11,458 | 8,848 | 2,607 | 3 | 6,241 R | 77.2% | 22.8% | 77.2% | 22.8% |
| 32,059 | CLAY | 12,238 | 10,467 | 1,748 | 23 | 8,719 R | 85.5% | 14.3% | 85.7% | 14.3% |
| 38,040 | COLLIER | 16,744 | 13,501 | 3,201 | 42 | 10,300 R | 80.6% | 19.1% | 80.8% | 19.2% |
| 25,250 | COLUMBIA | 8,387 | 6,723 | 1,664 | | 5,059 R | 80.2% | 19.8% | 80.2% | 19.8% |
| 1,267,792 | DADE | 435,763 | 256,529 | 177,693 | 1,541 | 78,836 R | 58.9% | 40.8% | 59.1% | 40.9% |
| 13,060 | DESOTO | 3,813 | 2,958 | 852 | 3 | 2,106 R | 77.6% | 22.3% | 77.6% | 22.4% |
| 5,480 | DIXIE | 1,997 | 1,628 | 367 | 2 | 1,261 R | 81.5% | 18.4% | 81.6% | 18.4% |
| 528,865 | DUVAL | 169,204 | 122,154 | 46,530 | 520 | 75,624 R | 72.2% | 27.5% | 72.4% | 27.6% |
| 205,334 | ESCAMBIA | 70,464 | 56,071 | 14,078 | 315 | 41,993 R | 79.6% | 20.0% | 79.9% | 20.1% |
| 4,454 | FLAGLER | 1,902 | 1,409 | 493 | | 916 R | 74.1% | 25.9% | 74.1% | 25.9% |
| 7,065 | FRANKLIN | 2,772 | 2,277 | 490 | 5 | 1,787 R | 82.1% | 17.7% | 82.3% | 17.7% |
| 39,184 | GADSDEN | 9,826 | 5,995 | 3,829 | 2 | 2,166 R | 61.0% | 39.0% | 61.0% | 39.0% |
| 3,551 | GILCHRIST | 1,565 | 1,306 | 247 | 12 | 1,059 R | 83.5% | 15.8% | 84.1% | 15.9% |
| 3,669 | GLADES | 1,293 | 1,019 | 253 | 21 | 766 R | 78.8% | 19.6% | 80.1% | 19.9% |
| 10,096 | GULF | 3,346 | 2,628 | 713 | 5 | 1,915 R | 78.5% | 21.3% | 78.7% | 21.3% |
| 7,787 | HAMILTON | 2,374 | 1,741 | 626 | 7 | 1,115 R | 73.3% | 26.4% | 73.6% | 26.4% |
| 14,889 | HARDEE | 4,213 | 3,563 | 647 | 3 | 2,916 R | 84.6% | 15.4% | 84.6% | 15.4% |
| 11,859 | HENDRY | 3,504 | 2,763 | 739 | 2 | 2,024 R | 78.9% | 21.1% | 78.9% | 21.1% |
| 17,004 | HERNANDO | 8,409 | 6,296 | 2,110 | 3 | 4,186 R | 74.9% | 25.1% | 74.9% | 25.1% |
| 29,507 | HIGHLANDS | 12,133 | 9,645 | 2,458 | 30 | 7,187 R | 79.5% | 20.3% | 79.7% | 20.3% |
| 490,265 | HILLSBOROUGH | 152,510 | 106,956 | 45,305 | 249 | 61,651 R | 70.1% | 29.7% | 70.2% | 29.8% |
| 10,720 | HOLMES | 4,128 | 3,819 | 309 | | 3,510 R | 92.5% | 7.5% | 92.5% | 7.5% |
| 35,992 | INDIAN RIVER | 15,082 | 11,741 | 3,316 | 25 | 8,425 R | 77.8% | 22.0% | 78.0% | 22.0% |
| 34,434 | JACKSON | 11,132 | 8,904 | 2,220 | 8 | 6,684 R | 80.0% | 19.9% | 80.0% | 20.0% |
| 8,778 | JEFFERSON | 3,192 | 2,108 | 1,049 | 35 | 1,059 R | 66.0% | 32.9% | 66.8% | 33.2% |
| 2,892 | LAFAYETTE | 1,237 | 1,060 | 173 | 4 | 887 R | 85.7% | 14.0% | 86.0% | 14.0% |
| 69,305 | LAKE | 27,930 | 23,079 | 4,803 | 48 | 18,276 R | 82.6% | 17.2% | 82.8% | 17.2% |
| 105,216 | LEE | 46,235 | 36,738 | 9,404 | 93 | 27,334 R | 79.5% | 20.3% | 79.6% | 20.4% |
| 103,047 | LEON | 43,126 | 27,479 | 15,555 | 92 | 11,924 R | 63.7% | 36.1% | 63.9% | 36.1% |
| 12,756 | LEVY | 4,137 | 3,273 | 862 | 2 | 2,411 R | 79.1% | 20.8% | 79.2% | 20.8% |
| 3,379 | LIBERTY | 1,421 | 1,199 | 222 | | 977 R | 84.4% | 15.6% | 84.4% | 15.6% |
| 13,481 | MADISON | 4,438 | 3,236 | 1,187 | 15 | 2,049 R | 72.9% | 26.7% | 73.2% | 26.8% |
| 97,115 | MANATEE | 40,940 | 32,664 | 8,058 | 218 | 24,606 R | 79.8% | 19.7% | 80.2% | 19.8% |
| 69,030 | MARION | 24,948 | 19,505 | 5,397 | 46 | 14,108 R | 78.2% | 21.6% | 78.3% | 21.7% |
| 28,035 | MARTIN | 14,330 | 11,296 | 2,946 | 88 | 8,350 R | 78.8% | 20.6% | 79.3% | 20.7% |
| 52,586 | MONROE | 16,193 | 11,688 | 4,469 | 36 | 7,219 R | 72.2% | 27.6% | 72.3% | 27.7% |
| 20,626 | NASSAU | 6,392 | 5,078 | 1,293 | 21 | 3,785 R | 79.4% | 20.2% | 79.7% | 20.3% |
| 88,187 | OKALOOSA | 26,290 | 23,303 | 2,843 | 144 | 20,460 R | 88.6% | 10.8% | 89.1% | 10.9% |
| 11,233 | OKEECHOBEE | 3,203 | 2,581 | 621 | 1 | 1,960 R | 80.6% | 19.4% | 80.6% | 19.4% |
| 344,311 | ORANGE | 118,777 | 94,516 | 23,840 | 421 | 70,676 R | 79.6% | 20.1% | 79.9% | 20.1% |
| 25,267 | OSCEOLA | 11,237 | 9,320 | 1,875 | 42 | 7,445 R | 82.9% | 16.7% | 83.3% | 16.7% |
| 348,753 | PALM BEACH | 150,203 | 108,670 | 40,825 | 708 | 67,845 R | 72.3% | 27.2% | 72.7% | 27.3% |
| 75,955 | PASCO | 40,676 | 29,249 | 11,330 | 97 | 17,919 R | 71.9% | 27.9% | 72.1% | 27.9% |
| 522,329 | PINELLAS | 257,116 | 179,541 | 77,197 | 378 | 102,344 R | 69.8% | 30.0% | 69.9% | 30.1% |
| 227,222 | POLK | 77,460 | 60,748 | 16,419 | 293 | 44,329 R | 78.4% | 21.2% | 78.7% | 21.3% |
| 36,290 | PUTNAM | 11,716 | 8,741 | 2,901 | 74 | 5,840 R | 74.6% | 24.8% | 75.1% | 24.9% |
| 30,727 | ST. JOHNS | 11,511 | 8,919 | 2,549 | 43 | 6,370 R | 77.5% | 22.1% | 77.8% | 22.2% |
| 50,836 | ST. LUCIE | 18,910 | 14,258 | 4,593 | 59 | 9,665 R | 75.4% | 24.3% | 75.6% | 24.4% |
| 37,741 | SANTA ROSA | 14,245 | 12,669 | 1,491 | 85 | 11,178 R | 88.9% | 10.5% | 89.5% | 10.5% |
| 120,413 | SARASOTA | 61,210 | 48,939 | 12,235 | 36 | 36,704 R | 80.0% | 20.0% | 80.0% | 20.0% |
| 83,692 | SEMINOLE | 34,212 | 27,658 | 6,503 | 51 | 21,155 R | 80.8% | 19.0% | 81.0% | 19.0% |
| 14,839 | SUMTER | 4,817 | 3,695 | 1,107 | 15 | 2,588 R | 76.7% | 23.0% | 76.9% | 23.1% |

# FLORIDA

## PRESIDENT 1972

| 1970 Census Population | County | Total Vote | Republican | Democratic | Other | Rep.-Dem. Plurality | Percentage | | | |
|---|---|---|---|---|---|---|---|---|---|---|
| | | | | | | | Total Vote | | Major Vote | |
| | | | | | | | Rep. | Dem. | Rep. | Dem. |
| 15,559 | SUWANNEE | 5,491 | 4,435 | 1,027 | 29 | 3,408 R | 80.8% | 18.7% | 81.2% | 18.8% |
| 13,641 | TAYLOR | 4,863 | 4,109 | 754 | | 3,355 R | 84.5% | 15.5% | 84.5% | 15.5% |
| 8,112 | UNION | 1,567 | 1,314 | 253 | | 1,061 R | 83.9% | 16.1% | 83.9% | 16.1% |
| 169,487 | VOLUSIA | 74,583 | 52,656 | 21,637 | 290 | 31,019 R | 70.6% | 29.0% | 70.9% | 29.1% |
| 6,308 | WAKULLA | 3,007 | 2,466 | 539 | 2 | 1,927 R | 82.0% | 17.9% | 82.1% | 17.9% |
| 16,087 | WALTON | 7,235 | 6,217 | 988 | 30 | 5,229 R | 85.9% | 13.7% | 86.3% | 13.7% |
| 11,453 | WASHINGTON | 4,386 | 3,777 | 606 | 3 | 3,171 R | 86.1% | 13.8% | 86.2% | 13.8% |
| 6,789,443 | TOTAL | 2,583,283 | 1,857,759 | 718,117 | 7,407 | 1,139,642 R | 71.9% | 27.8% | 72.1% | 27.9% |

# FLORIDA

## PRESIDENT 1968

| 1960 Census Population | County | Total Vote | Republican | Democratic | AIP | Other | Plurality | Percentage Total Vote | | |
|---|---|---|---|---|---|---|---|---|---|---|
| | | | | | | | | Rep. | Dem. | AIP |
| 74,074 | ALACHUA | 28,426 | 9,670 | 10,060 | 8,696 | | 390 D | 34.0% | 35.4% | 30.6% |
| 7,363 | BAKER | 2,743 | 294 | 487 | 1,962 | | 1,475 A | 10.7% | 17.8% | 71.5% |
| 67,131 | BAY | 24,302 | 5,121 | 4,020 | 15,161 | | 10,040 A | 21.1% | 16.5% | 62.4% |
| 12,446 | BRADFORD | 4,731 | 718 | 1,173 | 2,840 | | 1,667 A | 15.2% | 24.8% | 60.0% |
| 111,435 | BREVARD | 77,314 | 37,124 | 18,281 | 21,909 | | 15,215 R | 48.0% | 23.6% | 28.3% |
| 333,946 | BROWARD | 194,727 | 106,122 | 56,613 | 31,992 | | 49,509 R | 54.5% | 29.1% | 16.4% |
| 7,422 | CALHOUN | 3,129 | 356 | 398 | 2,375 | | 1,977 A | 11.4% | 12.7% | 75.9% |
| 12,594 | CHARLOTTE | 11,973 | 6,056 | 3,647 | 2,270 | | 2,409 R | 50.6% | 30.5% | 19.0% |
| 9,268 | CITRUS | 7,148 | 2,767 | 1,775 | 2,606 | | 161 R | 38.7% | 24.8% | 36.5% |
| 19,535 | CLAY | 9,251 | 3,251 | 1,954 | 4,046 | | 795 A | 35.1% | 21.1% | 43.7% |
| 15,753 | COLLIER | 10,544 | 5,362 | 2,230 | 2,952 | | 2,410 R | 50.9% | 21.1% | 28.0% |
| 20,077 | COLUMBIA | 7,349 | 1,553 | 1,750 | 4,046 | | 2,296 A | 21.1% | 23.8% | 55.1% |
| 935,047 | DADE | 365,302 | 135,222 | 176,689 | 53,391 | | 41,467 D | 37.0% | 48.4% | 14.6% |
| 11,683 | DESOTO | 4,094 | 1,103 | 937 | 2,054 | | 951 A | 26.9% | 22.9% | 50.2% |
| 4,479 | DIXIE | 2,088 | 217 | 325 | 1,546 | | 1,221 A | 10.4% | 15.6% | 74.0% |
| 455,411 | DUVAL | 166,978 | 51,585 | 54,834 | 60,559 | | 5,725 A | 30.9% | 32.8% | 36.3% |
| 173,829 | ESCAMBIA | 68,370 | 15,089 | 16,281 | 37,000 | | 20,719 A | 22.1% | 23.8% | 54.1% |
| 4,566 | FLAGLER | 1,778 | 360 | 601 | 817 | | 216 A | 20.2% | 33.8% | 46.0% |
| 6,576 | FRANKLIN | 3,137 | 529 | 699 | 1,909 | | 1,210 A | 16.9% | 22.3% | 60.9% |
| 41,989 | GADSDEN | 9,057 | 1,337 | 3,274 | 4,446 | | 1,172 A | 14.8% | 36.1% | 49.1% |
| 2,868 | GILCHRIST | 1,510 | 183 | 208 | 1,119 | | 911 A | 12.1% | 13.8% | 74.1% |
| 2,950 | GLADES | 1,091 | 261 | 230 | 600 | | 339 A | 23.9% | 21.1% | 55.0% |
| 9,937 | GULF | 3,800 | 364 | 711 | 2,725 | | 2,014 A | 9.6% | 18.7% | 71.7% |
| 7,705 | HAMILTON | 2,731 | 337 | 820 | 1,574 | | 754 A | 12.3% | 30.0% | 57.6% |
| 12,370 | HARDEE | 4,510 | 1,278 | 703 | 2,529 | | 1,251 A | 28.3% | 15.6% | 56.1% |
| 8,119 | HENDRY | 3,329 | 900 | 791 | 1,638 | | 738 A | 27.0% | 23.8% | 49.2% |
| 11,205 | HERNANDO | 5,964 | 2,053 | 1,524 | 2,387 | | 334 A | 34.4% | 25.6% | 40.0% |
| 21,338 | HIGHLANDS | 10,617 | 4,560 | 2,582 | 3,475 | | 1,085 R | 42.9% | 24.3% | 32.7% |
| 397,788 | HILLSBOROUGH | 142,202 | 49,441 | 45,848 | 46,913 | | 2,528 R | 34.8% | 32.2% | 33.0% |
| 10,844 | HOLMES | 5,389 | 377 | 312 | 4,700 | | 4,323 A | 7.0% | 5.8% | 87.2% |
| 25,309 | INDIAN RIVER | 12,719 | 6,518 | 3,179 | 3,022 | | 3,339 R | 51.2% | 25.0% | 23.8% |
| 36,208 | JACKSON | 12,330 | 1,236 | 2,472 | 8,622 | | 6,150 A | 10.0% | 20.0% | 69.9% |
| 9,543 | JEFFERSON | 3,092 | 459 | 1,066 | 1,567 | | 501 A | 14.8% | 34.5% | 50.7% |
| 2,889 | LAFAYETTE | 1,477 | 137 | 215 | 1,125 | | 910 A | 9.3% | 14.6% | 76.2% |
| 57,383 | LAKE | 24,804 | 11,763 | 4,599 | 8,442 | | 3,321 R | 47.4% | 18.5% | 34.0% |
| 54,539 | LEE | 31,095 | 14,376 | 7,978 | 8,741 | | 5,635 R | 46.2% | 25.7% | 28.1% |
| 74,225 | LEON | 32,606 | 9,288 | 10,440 | 12,878 | | 2,438 A | 28.5% | 32.0% | 39.5% |
| 10,364 | LEVY | 3,961 | 745 | 767 | 2,449 | | 1,682 A | 18.8% | 19.4% | 61.8% |
| 3,138 | LIBERTY | 1,718 | 154 | 242 | 1,322 | | 1,080 A | 9.0% | 14.1% | 76.9% |
| 14,154 | MADISON | 4,735 | 654 | 1,378 | 2,703 | | 1,325 A | 13.8% | 29.1% | 57.1% |
| 69,168 | MANATEE | 34,747 | 18,247 | 8,286 | 8,214 | | 9,961 R | 52.5% | 23.8% | 23.6% |
| 51,616 | MARION | 22,866 | 7,468 | 5,798 | 9,600 | | 2,132 A | 32.7% | 25.4% | 42.0% |
| 16,932 | MARTIN | 10,230 | 5,179 | 2,580 | 2,471 | | 2,599 R | 50.6% | 25.2% | 24.2% |
| 47,921 | MONROE | 14,899 | 5,094 | 5,534 | 4,271 | | 440 D | 34.2% | 37.1% | 28.7% |
| 17,189 | NASSAU | 6,533 | 1,301 | 1,598 | 3,634 | | 2,036 A | 19.9% | 24.5% | 55.6% |
| 61,175 | OKALOOSA | 20,821 | 5,525 | 3,059 | 12,237 | | 6,712 A | 26.5% | 14.7% | 58.8% |
| 6,424 | OKEECHOBEE | 3,008 | 862 | 542 | 1,604 | | 742 A | 28.7% | 18.0% | 53.3% |
| 263,540 | ORANGE | 100,669 | 50,874 | 22,548 | 27,247 | | 23,627 R | 50.5% | 22.4% | 27.1% |
| 19,029 | OSCEOLA | 9,504 | 4,172 | 1,870 | 3,462 | | 710 R | 43.9% | 19.7% | 36.4% |
| 228,106 | PALM BEACH | 116,922 | 62,191 | 32,837 | 21,894 | | 29,354 R | 53.2% | 28.1% | 18.7% |
| 36,785 | PASCO | 23,001 | 9,743 | 6,292 | 6,966 | | 2,777 R | 42.4% | 27.4% | 30.3% |
| 374,665 | PINELLAS | 211,258 | 109,235 | 68,209 | 33,814 | | 41,026 R | 51.7% | 32.3% | 16.0% |
| 195,139 | POLK | 75,277 | 27,839 | 15,898 | 31,540 | | 3,701 A | 37.0% | 21.1% | 41.9% |
| 32,212 | PUTNAM | 11,025 | 2,955 | 2,920 | 5,150 | | 2,195 A | 26.8% | 26.5% | 46.7% |
| 30,034 | ST. JOHNS | 11,310 | 3,880 | 2,748 | 4,682 | | 802 A | 34.3% | 24.3% | 41.4% |
| 39,294 | ST. LUCIE | 16,923 | 7,281 | 5,232 | 4,410 | | 2,049 R | 43.0% | 30.9% | 26.1% |
| 29,547 | SANTA ROSA | 12,716 | 2,567 | 1,600 | 8,549 | | 5,982 A | 20.2% | 12.6% | 67.2% |
| 76,895 | SARASOTA | 47,328 | 30,160 | 10,127 | 7,041 | | 20,033 R | 63.7% | 21.4% | 14.9% |
| 54,947 | SEMINOLE | 24,216 | 10,821 | 6,120 | 7,275 | | 3,546 R | 44.7% | 25.3% | 30.0% |
| 11,869 | SUMTER | 5,066 | 910 | 1,277 | 2,879 | | 1,602 A | 18.0% | 25.2% | 56.8% |

# FLORIDA

## PRESIDENT 1968

| 1960 Census Population | County | Total Vote | Republican | Democratic | AIP | Other | Plurality | Percentage Total Vote | | |
|---|---|---|---|---|---|---|---|---|---|---|
| | | | | | | | | Rep. | Dem. | AIP |
| 14,961 | SUWANNEE | 5,982 | 845 | 1,182 | 3,955 | | 2,773 A | 14.1% | 19.8% | 66.1% |
| 13,168 | TAYLOR | 5,053 | 794 | 941 | 3,318 | | 2,377 A | 15.7% | 18.6% | 65.7% |
| 6,043 | UNION | 1,661 | 179 | 290 | 1,192 | | 902 A | 10.8% | 17.5% | 71.8% |
| 125,319 | VOLUSIA | 70,220 | 28,024 | 24,987 | 17,209 | | 3,037 R | 39.9% | 35.6% | 24.5% |
| 5,257 | WAKULLA | 2,355 | 247 | 440 | 1,668 | | 1,228 A | 10.5% | 18.7% | 70.8% |
| 15,576 | WALTON | 7,162 | 963 | 1,064 | 5,135 | | 4,071 A | 13.4% | 14.9% | 71.7% |
| 11,249 | WASHINGTON | 4,932 | 528 | 722 | 3,682 | | 2,960 A | 10.7% | 14.6% | 74.7% |
| 4,951,560 | TOTAL | 2,187,805 | 886,804 | 676,794 | 624,207 | | 210,010 R | 40.5% | 30.9% | 28.5% |

# FLORIDA

## PRESIDENT 1964

| 1960 Census Population | County | Total Vote | Republican | Democratic | Other | Rep.-Dem. Plurality | Percentage | | | |
|---|---|---|---|---|---|---|---|---|---|---|
| | | | | | | | Total Vote | | Major Vote | |
| | | | | | | | Rep. | Dem. | Rep. | Dem. |
| 74,074 | ALACHUA | 24,634 | 11,151 | 13,483 | | 2,332 D | 45.3% | 54.7% | 45.3% | 54.7% |
| 7,363 | BAKER | 2,258 | 1,121 | 1,137 | | 16 D | 49.6% | 50.4% | 49.6% | 50.4% |
| 67,131 | BAY | 20,695 | 12,849 | 7,846 | | 5,003 R | 62.1% | 37.9% | 62.1% | 37.9% |
| 12,446 | BRADFORD | 4,307 | 1,987 | 2,320 | | 333 D | 46.1% | 53.9% | 46.1% | 53.9% |
| 111,435 | BREVARD | 49,384 | 24,551 | 24,833 | | 282 D | 49.7% | 50.3% | 49.7% | 50.3% |
| 333,946 | BROWARD | 153,670 | 85,264 | 68,406 | | 16,858 R | 55.5% | 44.5% | 55.5% | 44.5% |
| 7,422 | CALHOUN | 2,773 | 1,793 | 980 | | 813 R | 64.7% | 35.3% | 64.7% | 35.3% |
| 12,594 | CHARLOTTE | 8,994 | 4,163 | 4,831 | | 668 D | 46.3% | 53.7% | 46.3% | 53.7% |
| 9,268 | CITRUS | 4,850 | 2,329 | 2,521 | | 192 D | 48.0% | 52.0% | 48.0% | 52.0% |
| 19,535 | CLAY | 6,919 | 3,805 | 3,114 | | 691 R | 55.0% | 45.0% | 55.0% | 45.0% |
| 15,753 | COLLIER | 6,458 | 3,581 | 2,877 | | 704 R | 55.5% | 44.5% | 55.5% | 44.5% |
| 20,077 | COLUMBIA | 7,394 | 4,145 | 3,249 | | 896 R | 56.1% | 43.9% | 56.1% | 43.9% |
| 935,047 | DADE | 326,421 | 117,480 | 208,941 | | 91,461 D | 36.0% | 64.0% | 36.0% | 64.0% |
| 11,683 | DESOTO | 3,763 | 1,986 | 1,777 | | 209 R | 52.8% | 47.2% | 52.8% | 47.2% |
| 4,479 | DIXIE | 1,831 | 908 | 923 | | 15 D | 49.6% | 50.4% | 49.6% | 50.4% |
| 455,411 | DUVAL | 160,481 | 81,116 | 79,365 | | 1,751 R | 50.5% | 49.5% | 50.5% | 49.5% |
| 173,829 | ESCAMBIA | 57,785 | 32,414 | 25,371 | | 7,043 R | 56.1% | 43.9% | 56.1% | 43.9% |
| 4,566 | FLAGLER | 1,658 | 718 | 940 | | 222 D | 43.3% | 56.7% | 43.3% | 56.7% |
| 6,576 | FRANKLIN | 2,785 | 1,419 | 1,366 | | 53 R | 51.0% | 49.0% | 51.0% | 49.0% |
| 41,989 | GADSDEN | 9,763 | 5,207 | 4,556 | | 651 R | 53.3% | 46.7% | 53.3% | 46.7% |
| 2,868 | GILCHRIST | 1,251 | 540 | 711 | | 171 D | 43.2% | 56.8% | 43.2% | 56.8% |
| 2,950 | GLADES | 982 | 541 | 441 | | 100 R | 55.1% | 44.9% | 55.1% | 44.9% |
| 9,937 | GULF | 3,660 | 2,001 | 1,659 | | 342 R | 54.7% | 45.3% | 54.7% | 45.3% |
| 7,705 | HAMILTON | 2,460 | 1,158 | 1,302 | | 144 D | 47.1% | 52.9% | 47.1% | 52.9% |
| 12,370 | HARDEE | 4,229 | 2,321 | 1,908 | | 413 R | 54.9% | 45.1% | 54.9% | 45.1% |
| 8,119 | HENDRY | 3,002 | 1,650 | 1,352 | | 298 R | 55.0% | 45.0% | 55.0% | 45.0% |
| 11,205 | HERNANDO | 4,657 | 2,337 | 2,320 | | 17 R | 50.2% | 49.8% | 50.2% | 49.8% |
| 21,338 | HIGHLANDS | 8,980 | 4,747 | 4,233 | | 514 R | 52.9% | 47.1% | 52.9% | 47.1% |
| 397,788 | HILLSBOROUGH | 121,905 | 50,616 | 71,289 | | 20,673 D | 41.5% | 58.5% | 41.5% | 58.5% |
| 10,844 | HOLMES | 4,418 | 3,225 | 1,193 | | 2,032 R | 73.0% | 27.0% | 73.0% | 27.0% |
| 25,309 | INDIAN RIVER | 11,313 | 6,191 | 5,122 | | 1,069 R | 54.7% | 45.3% | 54.7% | 45.3% |
| 36,208 | JACKSON | 11,450 | 7,064 | 4,386 | | 2,678 R | 61.7% | 38.3% | 61.7% | 38.3% |
| 9,543 | JEFFERSON | 3,188 | 1,684 | 1,504 | | 180 R | 52.8% | 47.2% | 52.8% | 47.2% |
| 2,889 | LAFAYETTE | 1,193 | 648 | 545 | | 103 R | 54.3% | 45.7% | 54.3% | 45.7% |
| 57,383 | LAKE | 20,670 | 12,897 | 7,773 | | 5,124 R | 62.4% | 37.6% | 62.4% | 37.6% |
| 54,539 | LEE | 23,090 | 12,886 | 10,204 | | 2,682 R | 55.8% | 44.2% | 55.8% | 44.2% |
| 74,225 | LEON | 26,108 | 15,181 | 10,927 | | 4,254 R | 58.1% | 41.9% | 58.1% | 41.9% |
| 10,364 | LEVY | 3,566 | 1,580 | 1,986 | | 406 D | 44.3% | 55.7% | 44.3% | 55.7% |
| 3,138 | LIBERTY | 1,287 | 910 | 377 | | 533 R | 70.7% | 29.3% | 70.7% | 29.3% |
| 14,154 | MADISON | 4,943 | 2,822 | 2,121 | | 701 R | 57.1% | 42.9% | 57.1% | 42.9% |
| 69,168 | MANATEE | 30,221 | 17,147 | 13,074 | | 4,073 R | 56.7% | 43.3% | 56.7% | 43.3% |
| 51,616 | MARION | 19,991 | 10,879 | 9,112 | | 1,767 R | 54.4% | 45.6% | 54.4% | 45.6% |
| 16,932 | MARTIN | 7,913 | 4,292 | 3,621 | | 671 R | 54.2% | 45.8% | 54.2% | 45.8% |
| 47,921 | MONROE | 13,778 | 4,842 | 8,936 | | 4,094 D | 35.1% | 64.9% | 35.1% | 64.9% |
| 17,189 | NASSAU | 5,915 | 3,134 | 2,781 | | 353 R | 53.0% | 47.0% | 53.0% | 47.0% |
| 61,175 | OKALOOSA | 17,851 | 9,961 | 7,890 | | 2,071 R | 55.8% | 44.2% | 55.8% | 44.2% |
| 6,424 | OKEECHOBEE | 2,332 | 1,316 | 1,016 | | 300 R | 56.4% | 43.6% | 56.4% | 43.6% |
| 263,540 | ORANGE | 87,132 | 48,884 | 38,248 | | 10,636 R | 56.1% | 43.9% | 56.1% | 43.9% |
| 19,029 | OSCEOLA | 8,047 | 4,516 | 3,531 | | 985 R | 56.1% | 43.9% | 56.1% | 43.9% |
| 228,106 | PALM BEACH | 93,450 | 49,614 | 43,836 | | 5,778 R | 53.1% | 46.9% | 53.1% | 46.9% |
| 36,785 | PASCO | 15,741 | 7,606 | 8,135 | | 529 D | 48.3% | 51.7% | 48.3% | 51.7% |
| 374,665 | PINELLAS | 178,795 | 80,414 | 98,381 | | 17,967 D | 45.0% | 55.0% | 45.0% | 55.0% |
| 195,139 | POLK | 65,261 | 35,906 | 29,355 | | 6,551 R | 55.0% | 45.0% | 55.0% | 45.0% |
| 32,212 | PUTNAM | 10,067 | 5,072 | 4,995 | | 77 R | 50.4% | 49.6% | 50.4% | 49.6% |
| 30,034 | ST. JOHNS | 11,807 | 7,450 | 4,357 | | 3,093 R | 63.1% | 36.9% | 63.1% | 36.9% |
| 39,294 | ST. LUCIE | 14,952 | 7,204 | 7,748 | | 544 D | 48.2% | 51.8% | 48.2% | 51.8% |
| 29,547 | SANTA ROSA | 9,553 | 5,983 | 3,570 | | 2,413 R | 62.6% | 37.4% | 62.6% | 37.4% |
| 76,895 | SARASOTA | 35,854 | 21,917 | 13,937 | | 7,980 R | 61.1% | 38.9% | 61.1% | 38.9% |
| 54,947 | SEMINOLE | 19,203 | 10,078 | 9,125 | | 953 R | 52.5% | 47.5% | 52.5% | 47.5% |
| 11,869 | SUMTER | 3,890 | 1,631 | 2,259 | | 628 D | 41.9% | 58.1% | 41.9% | 58.1% |

# FLORIDA

## PRESIDENT 1964

| 1960 Census Population | County | Total Vote | Republican | Democratic | Other | Rep.-Dem. Plurality | Percentage | | | |
|---|---|---|---|---|---|---|---|---|---|---|
| | | | | | | | Total Vote | | Major Vote | |
| | | | | | | | Rep. | Dem. | Rep. | Dem. |
| 14,961 | SUWANNEE | 5,395 | 3,002 | 2,393 | | 609 R | 55.6% | 44.4% | 55.6% | 44.4% |
| 13,168 | TAYLOR | 4,369 | 2,661 | 1,708 | | 953 R | 60.9% | 39.1% | 60.9% | 39.1% |
| 6,043 | UNION | 1,450 | 710 | 740 | | 30 D | 49.0% | 51.0% | 49.0% | 51.0% |
| 125,319 | VOLUSIA | 59,889 | 24,988 | 34,901 | | 9,913 D | 41.7% | 58.3% | 41.7% | 58.3% |
| 5,257 | WAKULLA | 2,023 | 1,270 | 753 | | 517 R | 62.8% | 37.2% | 62.8% | 37.2% |
| 15,576 | WALTON | 6,202 | 3,753 | 2,449 | | 1,304 R | 60.5% | 39.5% | 60.5% | 39.5% |
| 11,249 | WASHINGTON | 4,225 | 2,725 | 1,500 | | 1,225 R | 64.5% | 35.5% | 64.5% | 35.5% |
| 4,951,560 | TOTAL | 1,854,481 | 905,941 | 948,540 | | 42,599 D | 48.9% | 51.1% | 48.9% | 51.1% |

# FLORIDA

## PRESIDENT 1960

| 1960 Census Population | County | Total Vote | Republican | Democratic | Other | Rep.-Dem. Plurality | Percentage | | | |
|---|---|---|---|---|---|---|---|---|---|---|
| | | | | | | | Total Vote | | Major Vote | |
| | | | | | | | Rep. | Dem. | Rep. | Dem. |
| 74,074 | ALACHUA | 19,351 | 10,072 | 9,279 | | 793 R | 52.0% | 48.0% | 52.0% | 48.0% |
| 7,363 | BAKER | 1,867 | 398 | 1,469 | | 1,071 D | 21.3% | 78.7% | 21.3% | 78.7% |
| 67,131 | BAY | 16,014 | 5,435 | 10,579 | | 5,144 D | 33.9% | 66.1% | 33.9% | 66.1% |
| 12,446 | BRADFORD | 3,666 | 1,131 | 2,535 | | 1,404 D | 30.9% | 69.1% | 30.9% | 69.1% |
| 111,435 | BREVARD | 28,654 | 17,585 | 11,069 | | 6,516 R | 61.4% | 38.6% | 61.4% | 38.6% |
| 333,946 | BROWARD | 116,105 | 68,294 | 47,811 | | 20,483 R | 58.8% | 41.2% | 58.8% | 41.2% |
| 7,422 | CALHOUN | 2,228 | 634 | 1,594 | | 960 D | 28.5% | 71.5% | 28.5% | 71.5% |
| 12,594 | CHARLOTTE | 4,967 | 3,026 | 1,941 | | 1,085 R | 60.9% | 39.1% | 60.9% | 39.1% |
| 9,268 | CITRUS | 3,591 | 1,861 | 1,730 | | 131 R | 51.8% | 48.2% | 51.8% | 48.2% |
| 19,535 | CLAY | 5,243 | 2,515 | 2,728 | | 213 D | 48.0% | 52.0% | 48.0% | 52.0% |
| 15,753 | COLLIER | 4,458 | 2,708 | 1,750 | | 958 R | 60.7% | 39.3% | 60.7% | 39.3% |
| 20,077 | COLUMBIA | 5,789 | 2,094 | 3,695 | | 1,601 D | 36.2% | 63.8% | 36.2% | 63.8% |
| 935,047 | DADE | 317,620 | 134,506 | 183,114 | | 48,608 D | 42.3% | 57.7% | 42.3% | 57.7% |
| 11,683 | DESOTO | 3,367 | 1,687 | 1,680 | | 7 R | 50.1% | 49.9% | 50.1% | 49.9% |
| 4,479 | DIXIE | 1,368 | 392 | 976 | | 584 D | 28.7% | 71.3% | 28.7% | 71.3% |
| 455,411 | DUVAL | 129,164 | 59,073 | 70,091 | | 11,018 D | 45.7% | 54.3% | 45.7% | 54.3% |
| 173,829 | ESCAMBIA | 46,213 | 17,925 | 28,288 | | 10,363 D | 38.8% | 61.2% | 38.8% | 61.2% |
| 4,566 | FLAGLER | 1,359 | 426 | 933 | | 507 D | 31.3% | 68.7% | 31.3% | 68.7% |
| 6,576 | FRANKLIN | 2,258 | 764 | 1,494 | | 730 D | 33.8% | 66.2% | 33.8% | 66.2% |
| 41,989 | GADSDEN | 4,353 | 2,010 | 2,343 | | 333 D | 46.2% | 53.8% | 46.2% | 53.8% |
| 2,868 | GILCHRIST | 1,111 | 277 | 834 | | 557 D | 24.9% | 75.1% | 24.9% | 75.1% |
| 2,950 | GLADES | 708 | 314 | 394 | | 80 D | 44.4% | 55.6% | 44.4% | 55.6% |
| 9,937 | GULF | 3,005 | 657 | 2,348 | | 1,691 D | 21.9% | 78.1% | 21.9% | 78.1% |
| 7,705 | HAMILTON | 1,987 | 656 | 1,331 | | 675 D | 33.0% | 67.0% | 33.0% | 67.0% |
| 12,370 | HARDEE | 3,701 | 1,960 | 1,741 | | 219 R | 53.0% | 47.0% | 53.0% | 47.0% |
| 8,119 | HENDRY | 2,350 | 1,043 | 1,307 | | 264 D | 44.4% | 55.6% | 44.4% | 55.6% |
| 11,205 | HERNANDO | 3,769 | 1,809 | 1,960 | | 151 D | 48.0% | 52.0% | 48.0% | 52.0% |
| 21,338 | HIGHLANDS | 7,491 | 4,369 | 3,122 | | 1,247 R | 58.3% | 41.7% | 58.3% | 41.7% |
| 397,788 | HILLSBOROUGH | 111,127 | 48,887 | 62,240 | | 13,353 D | 44.0% | 56.0% | 44.0% | 56.0% |
| 10,844 | HOLMES | 3,605 | 1,235 | 2,370 | | 1,135 D | 34.3% | 65.7% | 34.3% | 65.7% |
| 25,309 | INDIAN RIVER | 7,626 | 4,656 | 2,970 | | 1,686 R | 61.1% | 38.9% | 61.1% | 38.9% |
| 36,208 | JACKSON | 8,845 | 2,851 | 5,994 | | 3,143 D | 32.2% | 67.8% | 32.2% | 67.8% |
| 9,543 | JEFFERSON | 1,729 | 600 | 1,129 | | 529 D | 34.7% | 65.3% | 34.7% | 65.3% |
| 2,889 | LAFAYETTE | 1,090 | 297 | 793 | | 496 D | 27.2% | 72.8% | 27.2% | 72.8% |
| 57,383 | LAKE | 17,915 | 12,979 | 4,936 | | 8,043 R | 72.4% | 27.6% | 72.4% | 27.6% |
| 54,539 | LEE | 15,851 | 10,357 | 5,494 | | 4,863 R | 65.3% | 34.7% | 65.3% | 34.7% |
| 74,225 | LEON | 19,512 | 9,079 | 10,433 | | 1,354 D | 46.5% | 53.5% | 46.5% | 53.5% |
| 10,364 | LEVY | 2,999 | 996 | 2,003 | | 1,007 D | 33.2% | 66.8% | 33.2% | 66.8% |
| 3,138 | LIBERTY | 1,105 | 243 | 862 | | 619 D | 22.0% | 78.0% | 22.0% | 78.0% |
| 14,154 | MADISON | 3,236 | 1,152 | 2,084 | | 932 D | 35.6% | 64.4% | 35.6% | 64.4% |
| 69,168 | MANATEE | 25,276 | 16,462 | 8,814 | | 7,648 R | 65.1% | 34.9% | 65.1% | 34.9% |
| 51,616 | MARION | 14,249 | 7,043 | 7,206 | | 163 D | 49.4% | 50.6% | 49.4% | 50.6% |
| 16,932 | MARTIN | 6,365 | 3,701 | 2,664 | | 1,037 R | 58.1% | 41.9% | 58.1% | 41.9% |
| 47,921 | MONROE | 10,388 | 3,416 | 6,972 | | 3,556 D | 32.9% | 67.1% | 32.9% | 67.1% |
| 17,189 | NASSAU | 4,948 | 1,666 | 3,282 | | 1,616 D | 33.7% | 66.3% | 33.7% | 66.3% |
| 61,175 | OKALOOSA | 12,948 | 4,685 | 8,263 | | 3,578 D | 36.2% | 63.8% | 36.2% | 63.8% |
| 6,424 | OKEECHOBEE | 1,756 | 631 | 1,125 | | 494 D | 35.9% | 64.1% | 35.9% | 64.1% |
| 263,540 | ORANGE | 67,973 | 48,244 | 19,729 | | 28,515 R | 71.0% | 29.0% | 71.0% | 29.0% |
| 19,029 | OSCEOLA | 6,869 | 4,691 | 2,178 | | 2,513 R | 68.3% | 31.7% | 68.3% | 31.7% |
| 228,106 | PALM BEACH | 75,208 | 45,337 | 29,871 | | 15,466 R | 60.3% | 39.7% | 60.3% | 39.7% |
| 36,785 | PASCO | 13,020 | 7,188 | 5,832 | | 1,356 R | 55.2% | 44.8% | 55.2% | 44.8% |
| 374,665 | PINELLAS | 159,833 | 101,779 | 58,054 | | 43,725 R | 63.7% | 36.3% | 63.7% | 36.3% |
| 195,139 | POLK | 55,164 | 31,618 | 23,546 | | 8,072 R | 57.3% | 42.7% | 57.3% | 42.7% |
| 32,212 | PUTNAM | 8,695 | 4,236 | 4,459 | | 223 D | 48.7% | 51.3% | 48.7% | 51.3% |
| 30,034 | ST. JOHNS | 9,708 | 4,125 | 5,583 | | 1,458 D | 42.5% | 57.5% | 42.5% | 57.5% |
| 39,294 | ST. LUCIE | 11,714 | 6,354 | 5,360 | | 994 R | 54.2% | 45.8% | 54.2% | 45.8% |
| 29,547 | SANTA ROSA | 7,737 | 2,777 | 4,960 | | 2,183 D | 35.9% | 64.1% | 35.9% | 64.1% |
| 76,895 | SARASOTA | 28,282 | 19,995 | 8,287 | | 11,708 R | 70.7% | 29.3% | 70.7% | 29.3% |
| 54,947 | SEMINOLE | 13,827 | 8,936 | 4,891 | | 4,045 R | 64.6% | 35.4% | 64.6% | 35.4% |
| 11,869 | SUMTER | 3,399 | 1,120 | 2,279 | | 1,159 D | 33.0% | 67.0% | 33.0% | 67.0% |

# FLORIDA

## PRESIDENT 1960

| 1960 Census Population | County | Total Vote | Republican | Democratic | Other | Rep.-Dem. Plurality | Percentage Total Vote Rep. | Dem. | Major Vote Rep. | Dem. |
|---|---|---|---|---|---|---|---|---|---|---|
| 14,961 | SUWANNEE | 4,325 | 1,536 | 2,789 | | 1,253 D | 35.5% | 64.5% | 35.5% | 64.5% |
| 13,168 | TAYLOR | 3,120 | 1,212 | 1,908 | | 696 D | 38.8% | 61.2% | 38.8% | 61.2% |
| 6,043 | UNION | 1,252 | 311 | 941 | | 630 D | 24.8% | 75.2% | 24.8% | 75.2% |
| 125,319 | VOLUSIA | 51,744 | 28,367 | 23,377 | | 4,990 R | 54.8% | 45.2% | 54.8% | 45.2% |
| 5,257 | WAKULLA | 1,525 | 379 | 1,146 | | 767 D | 24.9% | 75.1% | 24.9% | 75.1% |
| 15,576 | WALTON | 5,126 | 1,484 | 3,642 | | 2,158 D | 29.0% | 71.0% | 29.0% | 71.0% |
| 11,249 | WASHINGTON | 3,328 | 1,230 | 2,098 | | 868 D | 37.0% | 63.0% | 37.0% | 63.0% |
| 4,951,560 | TOTAL | 1,544,176 | 795,476 | 748,700 | | 46,776 R | 51.5% | 48.5% | 51.5% | 48.5% |

# FLORIDA

## ELECTION NOTES

**2004**   Other vote was 32,971 Reform (Ralph Nader); 11,996 Libertarian Party of Florida (Michael Badnarik); 6,626 Constitution Party of Florida (Michael Peroutka); 3,917 Green Party of Florida (David Cobb); 3,502 Socialist Party of Florida (Walter F. Brown); 2,732 Florida Socialist Workers (James Harris).

**2000**   Other vote was 17,484 Reform (Buchanan); 16,415 Libertarian (Browne); 2,281 Natural Law (Hagelin); 1,804 Workers World (Moorehead); 1,371 Constitution (Phillips); 622 Socialist (McReynolds); 562 Socialist Workers (Harris); 34 write-in (Chote); 6 write-in (McCarthy).

**1996**   Other vote was 23,965 Libertarian (Browne); 4,101 write-in (Nader); 418 write-in (Hagelin); 34 scattered write-in.

**1992**   Other vote was 15,079 Marrou (Libertarian); 214 Hagelin (write-in); 16 Brisben (write-in); 8 scattered write-in. County and statewide totals include the special federal absentee ballots which were counted separately and were not reported on earlier returns.

**1988**   Other vote was 19,796 Paul (Libertarian); 6,655 Fulani (New Alliance); 249 Duke (write-in); 14 Kenoyer (write-in); 13 scattered write-in. County and statewide totals include the special federal absentee ballots which were counted separately.

**1984**   Other vote was 754 Bergland (write-in); 58 Johnson (write-in); 34 Hall (write-in); 7 Mason (write-in); 32 scattered write-in. Special absentee votes listed at the end of the county-by-county table are ballots counted separately by court order.

**1980**   Other vote was 189,692 Anderson (Independent); 30,524 Clark (Libertarian); 123 Hall (write-in); 116 McReynolds (write-in); 41 DeBerry (write-in); 8 Griswold (write-in). County and state-wide totals include special absentee votes counted separately by court order.

**1976**   Other vote was 23,643 McCarthy (Independent); 21,325 Anderson (American); 103 MacBride (write-in); 19 Levin (write-in); 8 Zeidler (write-in); 2 Miller (write-in).

**1972**   Other vote was scattered write-in.

**1968**   Wallace on the ballot as George Wallace party.

**1964**

**1960**

# GEORGIA

## POPULAR VOTE FOR PRESIDENT 1920 TO 2004

| Year | Total Vote | Republican Vote | Republican Candidate | Democratic Vote | Democratic Candidate | Other Vote | Plurality | Percentage Total Vote Rep. | Percentage Total Vote Dem. | Percentage Major Vote Rep. | Percentage Major Vote Dem. |
|------|-----------|-----------|-----------|-----------|-----------|-----------|-----------|------|------|------|------|
| 2004 | 3,301,875 | 1,914,254 | Bush, George W. | 1,366,149 | Kerry, John | 21,472 | 548,105 R | 58.0% | 41.4% | 58.4% | 41.6% |
| 2000 ** | 2,596,645 | 1,419,720 | Bush, George W. | 1,116,230 | Gore, Al | 60,695 | 303,490 R | 54.7% | 43.0% | 56.0% | 44.0% |
| 1996 ** | 2,299,071 | 1,080,843 | Dole, Bob | 1,053,849 | Clinton, Bill | 164,379 | 26,994 R | 47.0% | 45.8% | 50.6% | 49.4% |
| 1992 ** | 2,321,125 | 995,252 | Bush, George | 1,008,966 | Clinton, Bill | 316,907 | 13,714 D | 42.9% | 43.5% | 49.7% | 50.3% |
| 1988 | 1,809,672 | 1,081,331 | Bush, George | 714,792 | Dukakis, Michael S. | 13,549 | 366,539 R | 59.8% | 39.5% | 60.2% | 39.8% |
| 1984 | 1,776,120 | 1,068,722 | Reagan, Ronald | 706,628 | Mondale, Walter F. | 770 | 362,094 R | 60.2% | 39.8% | 60.2% | 39.8% |
| 1980 ** | 1,596,695 | 654,168 | Reagan, Ronald | 890,733 | Carter, Jimmy | 51,794 | 236,565 D | 41.0% | 55.8% | 42.3% | 57.7% |
| 1976 | 1,467,458 | 483,743 | Ford, Gerald R. | 979,409 | Carter, Jimmy | 4,306 | 495,666 D | 33.0% | 66.7% | 33.1% | 66.9% |
| 1972 | 1,174,772 | 881,496 | Nixon, Richard M. | 289,529 | McGovern, George S. | 3,747 | 591,967 R | 75.0% | 24.6% | 75.3% | 24.7% |
| 1968 ** | 1,250,266 | 380,111 | Nixon, Richard M. | 334,440 | Humphrey, Hubert H. | 535,715 | 155,439 A | 30.4% | 26.7% | 53.2% | 46.8% |
| 1964 | 1,139,335 | 616,584 | Goldwater, Barry M. | 522,556 | Johnson, Lyndon B. | 195 | 94,028 R | 54.1% | 45.9% | 54.1% | 45.9% |
| 1960 | 733,349 | 274,472 | Nixon, Richard M. | 458,638 | Kennedy, John F. | 239 | 184,166 D | 37.4% | 62.5% | 37.4% | 62.6% |
| 1956 | 669,655 | 222,778 | Eisenhower, Dwight D. | 444,688 | Stevenson, Adlai E. | 2,189 | 221,910 D | 33.3% | 66.4% | 33.4% | 66.6% |
| 1952 | 655,785 | 198,961 | Eisenhower, Dwight D. | 456,823 | Stevenson, Adlai E. | 1 | 257,862 D | 30.3% | 69.7% | 30.3% | 69.7% |
| 1948 ** | 418,844 | 76,691 | Dewey, Thomas E. | 254,646 | Truman, Harry S. | 87,507 | 169,511 D | 18.3% | 60.8% | 23.1% | 76.9% |
| 1944 | 328,129 | 59,900 | Dewey, Thomas E. | 268,187 | Roosevelt, Franklin D. | 42 | 208,287 D | 18.3% | 81.7% | 18.3% | 81.7% |
| 1940 | 312,686 | 46,495 | Willkie, Wendell | 265,194 | Roosevelt, Franklin D. | 997 | 218,699 D | 14.9% | 84.8% | 14.9% | 85.1% |
| 1936 | 293,170 | 36,943 | Landon, Alfred M. | 255,363 | Roosevelt, Franklin D. | 864 | 218,420 D | 12.6% | 87.1% | 12.6% | 87.4% |
| 1932 | 255,590 | 19,863 | Hoover, Herbert C. | 234,118 | Roosevelt, Franklin D. | 1,609 | 214,255 D | 7.8% | 91.6% | 7.8% | 92.2% |
| 1928 | 231,592 | 101,800 | Hoover, Herbert C. | 129,604 | Smith, Alfred E. | 188 | 27,804 D | 44.0% | 56.0% | 44.0% | 56.0% |
| 1924 | 166,635 | 30,300 | Coolidge, Calvin | 123,262 | Davis, John W. | 13,073 | 92,962 D | 18.2% | 74.0% | 19.7% | 80.3% |
| 1920 | 149,558 | 42,981 | Harding, Warren G. | 106,112 | Cox, James M. | 465 | 63,131 D | 28.7% | 71.0% | 28.8% | 71.2% |

In 2000 the other vote column includes 13,273 votes cast for Green (Nader). In 1996 the other vote column includes 146,337 votes cast for Perot. In 1992 the other vote column includes 309,657 votes cast for Perot. In 1980 the other column includes 36,055 votes for Independent (Anderson). In 1968 other vote was 535,550 American (Wallace) and 165 scattered. In 1948 other vote was 85,135 States Rights; 1,636 Progressive; 732 Prohibition; 3 Socialist and 1 scattered

## ELECTORAL COLLEGE VOTE 1920 TO 2004

| Year | Total | Republican | Democratic | Other |
|------|-------|-----------|-----------|-------|
| 2004 | 15 | 15 | | |
| 2000 | 13 | 13 | | |
| 1996 | 13 | 13 | | |
| 1992 | 13 | | 13 | |
| 1988 | 12 | 12 | | |
| 1984 | 12 | 12 | | |
| 1980 | 12 | | 12 | |
| 1976 | 12 | | 12 | |
| 1972 | 12 | 12 | | |
| 1968 | 12 | | | 12 AIP |
| 1964 | 12 | 12 | | |
| 1960 | 12 | | 12 | |
| 1956 | 12 | | 12 | |
| 1952 | 12 | | 12 | |
| 1948 | 12 | | 12 | |
| 1944 | 12 | | 12 | |
| 1940 | 12 | | 12 | |
| 1936 | 12 | | 12 | |
| 1932 | 12 | | 12 | |
| 1928 | 14 | | 14 | |
| 1924 | 14 | | 14 | |
| 1920 | 14 | | 14 | |

# GEORGIA

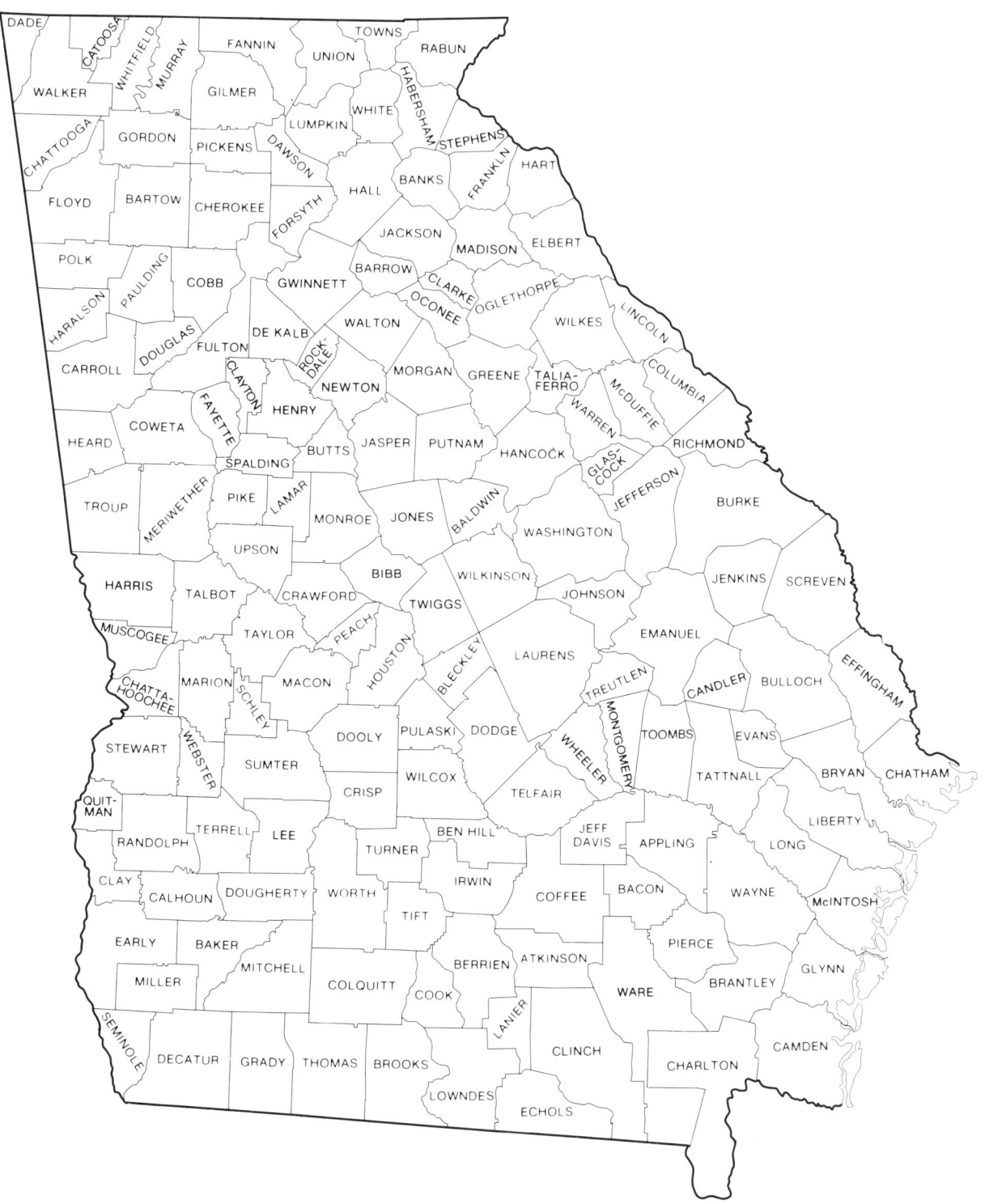

# GEORGIA

## PRESIDENT 2004

| 2000 Census Population | County | Total Vote | Republican | Democratic | Other | Rep.-Dem. Plurality | Percentage | | | |
|---|---|---|---|---|---|---|---|---|---|---|
| | | | | | | | Total Vote | | Major Vote | |
| | | | | | | | Rep. | Dem. | Rep. | Dem. |
| 17,419 | APPLING | 6,370 | 4,494 | 1,848 | 28 | 2,646 R | 70.5% | 29.0% | 70.9% | 29.1% |
| 7,609 | ATKINSON | 2,470 | 1,666 | 799 | 5 | 867 R | 67.4% | 32.3% | 67.6% | 32.4% |
| 10,103 | BACON | 3,792 | 2,853 | 930 | 9 | 1,923 R | 75.2% | 24.5% | 75.4% | 24.6% |
| 4,074 | BAKER | 1,764 | 821 | 936 | 7 | 115 D | 46.5% | 53.1% | 46.7% | 53.3% |
| 44,700 | BALDWIN | 14,560 | 7,709 | 6,775 | 76 | 934 R | 52.9% | 46.5% | 53.2% | 46.8% |
| 14,422 | BANKS | 5,592 | 4,410 | 1,149 | 33 | 3,261 R | 78.9% | 20.5% | 79.3% | 20.7% |
| 46,144 | BARROW | 17,744 | 13,520 | 4,095 | 129 | 9,425 R | 76.2% | 23.1% | 76.8% | 23.2% |
| 76,019 | BARTOW | 30,277 | 22,311 | 7,741 | 225 | 14,570 R | 73.7% | 25.6% | 74.2% | 25.8% |
| 17,484 | BEN HILL | 5,540 | 3,331 | 2,180 | 29 | 1,151 R | 60.1% | 39.4% | 60.4% | 39.6% |
| 16,235 | BERRIEN | 5,599 | 3,917 | 1,638 | 44 | 2,279 R | 70.0% | 29.3% | 70.5% | 29.5% |
| 153,887 | BIBB | 57,754 | 28,107 | 29,322 | 325 | 1,215 D | 48.7% | 50.8% | 48.9% | 51.1% |
| 11,666 | BLECKLEY | 4,468 | 3,167 | 1,281 | 20 | 1,886 R | 70.9% | 28.7% | 71.2% | 28.8% |
| 14,629 | BRANTLEY | 5,621 | 4,333 | 1,258 | 30 | 3,075 R | 77.1% | 22.4% | 77.5% | 22.5% |
| 16,450 | BROOKS | 5,116 | 2,912 | 2,193 | 11 | 719 R | 56.9% | 42.9% | 57.0% | 43.0% |
| 23,417 | BRYAN | 9,983 | 7,363 | 2,590 | 30 | 4,773 R | 73.8% | 25.9% | 74.0% | 26.0% |
| 55,983 | BULLOCH | 19,195 | 12,252 | 6,840 | 103 | 5,412 R | 63.8% | 35.6% | 64.2% | 35.8% |
| 22,243 | BURKE | 8,482 | 4,232 | 4,213 | 37 | 19 R | 49.9% | 49.7% | 50.1% | 49.9% |
| 19,522 | BUTTS | 7,735 | 5,119 | 2,572 | 44 | 2,547 R | 66.2% | 33.3% | 66.6% | 33.4% |
| 6,320 | CALHOUN | 2,019 | 890 | 1,119 | 10 | 229 D | 44.1% | 55.4% | 44.3% | 55.7% |
| 43,664 | CAMDEN | 14,175 | 9,488 | 4,637 | 50 | 4,851 R | 66.9% | 32.7% | 67.2% | 32.8% |
| 9,577 | CANDLER | 3,151 | 2,048 | 1,096 | 7 | 952 R | 65.0% | 34.8% | 65.1% | 34.9% |
| 87,268 | CARROLL | 35,317 | 24,837 | 10,224 | 256 | 14,613 R | 70.3% | 28.9% | 70.8% | 29.2% |
| 53,282 | CATOOSA | 22,328 | 16,406 | 5,807 | 115 | 10,599 R | 73.5% | 26.0% | 73.9% | 26.1% |
| 10,282 | CHARLTON | 3,387 | 2,311 | 1,064 | 12 | 1,247 R | 68.2% | 31.4% | 68.5% | 31.5% |
| 232,048 | CHATHAM | 91,607 | 45,484 | 45,630 | 493 | 146 D | 49.7% | 49.8% | 49.9% | 50.1% |
| 14,882 | CHATTAHOOCHEE | 1,689 | 905 | 773 | 11 | 132 R | 53.6% | 45.8% | 53.9% | 46.1% |
| 25,470 | CHATTOOGA | 7,853 | 4,992 | 2,809 | 52 | 2,183 R | 63.6% | 35.8% | 64.0% | 36.0% |
| 141,903 | CHEROKEE | 73,686 | 58,238 | 14,824 | 624 | 43,414 R | 79.0% | 20.1% | 79.7% | 20.3% |
| 101,489 | CLARKE | 37,388 | 15,052 | 21,718 | 618 | 6,666 D | 40.3% | 58.1% | 40.9% | 59.1% |
| 3,357 | CLAY | 1,309 | 509 | 798 | 2 | 289 D | 38.9% | 61.0% | 38.9% | 61.1% |
| 236,517 | CLAYTON | 79,600 | 23,106 | 56,113 | 381 | 33,007 D | 29.0% | 70.5% | 29.2% | 70.8% |
| 6,878 | CLINCH | 2,266 | 1,501 | 750 | 15 | 751 R | 66.2% | 33.1% | 66.7% | 33.3% |
| 607,751 | COBB | 279,866 | 173,467 | 103,955 | 2,444 | 69,512 R | 62.0% | 37.1% | 62.5% | 37.5% |
| 37,413 | COFFEE | 12,332 | 8,306 | 3,979 | 47 | 4,327 R | 67.4% | 32.3% | 67.6% | 32.4% |
| 42,053 | COLQUITT | 11,745 | 8,296 | 3,378 | 71 | 4,918 R | 70.6% | 28.8% | 71.1% | 28.9% |
| 89,288 | COLUMBIA | 47,170 | 35,549 | 11,442 | 179 | 24,107 R | 75.4% | 24.3% | 75.7% | 24.3% |
| 15,771 | COOK | 4,820 | 3,065 | 1,733 | 22 | 1,332 R | 63.6% | 36.0% | 63.9% | 36.1% |
| 89,215 | COWETA | 42,545 | 31,682 | 10,647 | 216 | 21,035 R | 74.5% | 25.0% | 74.8% | 25.2% |
| 12,495 | CRAWFORD | 4,406 | 2,830 | 1,552 | 24 | 1,278 R | 64.2% | 35.2% | 64.6% | 35.4% |
| 21,996 | CRISP | 6,251 | 3,865 | 2,357 | 29 | 1,508 R | 61.8% | 37.7% | 62.1% | 37.9% |
| 15,154 | DADE | 6,247 | 4,368 | 1,823 | 56 | 2,545 R | 69.9% | 29.2% | 70.6% | 29.4% |
| 15,999 | DAWSON | 8,117 | 6,649 | 1,407 | 61 | 5,242 R | 81.9% | 17.3% | 82.5% | 17.5% |
| 28,240 | DECATUR | 8,951 | 5,348 | 3,577 | 26 | 1,771 R | 59.7% | 40.0% | 59.9% | 40.1% |
| 665,865 | DEKALB | 276,509 | 73,570 | 200,787 | 2,152 | 127,217 D | 26.6% | 72.6% | 26.8% | 73.2% |
| 19,171 | DODGE | 6,995 | 4,584 | 2,384 | 27 | 2,200 R | 65.5% | 34.1% | 65.8% | 34.2% |
| 11,525 | DOOLY | 3,844 | 1,853 | 1,973 | 18 | 120 D | 48.2% | 51.3% | 48.4% | 51.6% |
| 96,065 | DOUGHERTY | 33,662 | 13,711 | 19,805 | 146 | 6,094 D | 40.7% | 58.8% | 40.9% | 59.1% |
| 92,174 | DOUGLAS | 42,104 | 25,846 | 15,997 | 261 | 9,849 R | 61.4% | 38.0% | 61.8% | 38.2% |
| 12,354 | EARLY | 4,213 | 2,495 | 1,701 | 17 | 794 R | 59.2% | 40.4% | 59.5% | 40.5% |
| 3,754 | ECHOLS | 991 | 757 | 231 | 3 | 526 R | 76.4% | 23.3% | 76.6% | 23.4% |
| 37,535 | EFFINGHAM | 16,167 | 12,503 | 3,613 | 51 | 8,890 R | 77.3% | 22.3% | 77.6% | 22.4% |
| 20,511 | ELBERT | 7,659 | 4,626 | 2,984 | 49 | 1,642 R | 60.4% | 39.0% | 60.8% | 39.2% |
| 21,837 | EMANUEL | 7,470 | 4,666 | 2,774 | 30 | 1,892 R | 62.5% | 37.1% | 62.7% | 37.3% |
| 10,495 | EVANS | 3,514 | 2,291 | 1,213 | 10 | 1,078 R | 65.2% | 34.5% | 65.4% | 34.6% |
| 19,798 | FANNIN | 9,666 | 6,862 | 2,727 | 77 | 4,135 R | 71.0% | 28.2% | 71.6% | 28.4% |
| 91,263 | FAYETTE | 52,587 | 37,346 | 14,887 | 354 | 22,459 R | 71.0% | 28.3% | 71.5% | 28.5% |
| 90,565 | FLOYD | 31,625 | 21,400 | 10,038 | 187 | 11,362 R | 67.7% | 31.7% | 68.1% | 31.9% |
| 98,407 | FORSYTH | 56,904 | 47,267 | 9,201 | 436 | 38,066 R | 83.1% | 16.2% | 83.7% | 16.3% |
| 20,285 | FRANKLIN | 7,502 | 5,218 | 2,245 | 39 | 2,973 R | 69.6% | 29.9% | 69.9% | 30.1% |
| 816,006 | FULTON | 336,407 | 134,372 | 199,436 | 2,599 | 65,064 D | 39.9% | 59.3% | 40.3% | 59.7% |

# GEORGIA

## PRESIDENT 2004

| 2000 Census Population | County | Total Vote | Republican | Democratic | Other | Rep.-Dem. Plurality | Percentage Total Vote Rep. | Dem. | Major Vote Rep. | Dem. |
|---|---|---|---|---|---|---|---|---|---|---|
| 23,456 | GILMER | 10,014 | 7,414 | 2,510 | 90 | 4,904 R | 74.0% | 25.1% | 74.7% | 25.3% |
| 2,556 | GLASCOCK | 1,269 | 1,016 | 250 | 3 | 766 R | 80.1% | 19.7% | 80.3% | 19.7% |
| 67,568 | GLYNN | 27,696 | 18,608 | 8,962 | 126 | 9,646 R | 67.2% | 32.4% | 67.5% | 32.5% |
| 44,104 | GORDON | 15,792 | 11,671 | 4,028 | 93 | 7,643 R | 73.9% | 25.5% | 74.3% | 25.7% |
| 23,659 | GRADY | 8,194 | 5,068 | 3,092 | 34 | 1,976 R | 61.9% | 37.7% | 62.1% | 37.9% |
| 14,406 | GREENE | 6,874 | 4,069 | 2,774 | 31 | 1,295 R | 59.2% | 40.4% | 59.5% | 40.5% |
| 588,448 | GWINNETT | 244,179 | 160,445 | 81,708 | 2,026 | 78,737 R | 65.7% | 33.5% | 66.3% | 33.7% |
| 35,902 | HABERSHAM | 13,269 | 10,434 | 2,750 | 85 | 7,684 R | 78.6% | 20.7% | 79.1% | 20.9% |
| 139,277 | HALL | 49,744 | 38,883 | 10,514 | 347 | 28,369 R | 78.2% | 21.1% | 78.7% | 21.3% |
| 10,076 | HANCOCK | 3,550 | 822 | 2,715 | 13 | 1,893 D | 23.2% | 76.5% | 23.2% | 76.8% |
| 25,690 | HARALSON | 10,193 | 7,703 | 2,434 | 56 | 5,269 R | 75.6% | 23.9% | 76.0% | 24.0% |
| 23,695 | HARRIS | 12,350 | 8,878 | 3,400 | 72 | 5,478 R | 71.9% | 27.5% | 72.3% | 27.7% |
| 22,997 | HART | 9,029 | 5,500 | 3,479 | 50 | 2,021 R | 60.9% | 38.5% | 61.3% | 38.7% |
| 11,012 | HEARD | 3,956 | 2,788 | 1,148 | 20 | 1,640 R | 70.5% | 29.0% | 70.8% | 29.2% |
| 119,341 | HENRY | 64,153 | 42,759 | 21,096 | 298 | 21,663 R | 66.7% | 32.9% | 67.0% | 33.0% |
| 110,765 | HOUSTON | 45,198 | 29,862 | 15,054 | 282 | 14,808 R | 66.1% | 33.3% | 66.5% | 33.5% |
| 9,931 | IRWIN | 3,414 | 2,347 | 1,051 | 16 | 1,296 R | 68.7% | 30.8% | 69.1% | 30.9% |
| 41,589 | JACKSON | 16,173 | 12,611 | 3,468 | 94 | 9,143 R | 78.0% | 21.4% | 78.4% | 21.6% |
| 11,426 | JASPER | 4,742 | 3,157 | 1,558 | 27 | 1,599 R | 66.6% | 32.9% | 67.0% | 33.0% |
| 12,684 | JEFF DAVIS | 4,845 | 3,549 | 1,277 | 19 | 2,272 R | 73.3% | 26.4% | 73.5% | 26.5% |
| 17,266 | JEFFERSON | 6,537 | 3,066 | 3,447 | 24 | 381 D | 46.9% | 52.7% | 47.1% | 52.9% |
| 8,575 | JENKINS | 3,404 | 1,898 | 1,494 | 12 | 404 R | 55.8% | 43.9% | 56.0% | 44.0% |
| 8,560 | JOHNSON | 3,553 | 2,279 | 1,263 | 11 | 1,016 R | 64.1% | 35.5% | 64.3% | 35.7% |
| 23,639 | JONES | 10,853 | 6,939 | 3,855 | 59 | 3,084 R | 63.9% | 35.5% | 64.3% | 35.7% |
| 15,912 | LAMAR | 6,498 | 4,027 | 2,432 | 39 | 1,595 R | 62.0% | 37.4% | 62.3% | 37.7% |
| 7,241 | LANIER | 2,587 | 1,641 | 931 | 15 | 710 R | 63.4% | 36.0% | 63.8% | 36.2% |
| 44,874 | LAURENS | 17,237 | 10,883 | 6,281 | 73 | 4,602 R | 63.1% | 36.4% | 63.4% | 36.6% |
| 24,757 | LEE | 10,421 | 8,201 | 2,182 | 38 | 6,019 R | 78.7% | 20.9% | 79.0% | 21.0% |
| 61,610 | LIBERTY | 12,805 | 6,131 | 6,619 | 55 | 488 D | 47.9% | 51.7% | 48.1% | 51.9% |
| 8,348 | LINCOLN | 3,657 | 2,309 | 1,337 | 11 | 972 R | 63.1% | 36.6% | 63.3% | 36.7% |
| 10,304 | LONG | 3,039 | 1,994 | 1,033 | 12 | 961 R | 65.6% | 34.0% | 65.9% | 34.1% |
| 92,115 | LOWNDES | 31,654 | 18,981 | 12,516 | 157 | 6,465 R | 60.0% | 39.5% | 60.3% | 39.7% |
| 21,016 | LUMPKIN | 8,886 | 6,690 | 2,091 | 105 | 4,599 R | 75.3% | 23.5% | 76.2% | 23.8% |
| 21,231 | MCDUFFIE | 7,773 | 4,846 | 2,899 | 28 | 1,947 R | 62.3% | 37.3% | 62.6% | 37.4% |
| 10,847 | MCINTOSH | 5,379 | 2,837 | 2,523 | 19 | 314 R | 52.7% | 46.9% | 52.9% | 47.1% |
| 14,074 | MACON | 4,777 | 1,851 | 2,906 | 20 | 1,055 D | 38.7% | 60.8% | 38.9% | 61.1% |
| 25,730 | MADISON | 9,843 | 7,254 | 2,527 | 62 | 4,727 R | 73.7% | 25.7% | 74.2% | 25.8% |
| 7,144 | MARION | 2,955 | 1,670 | 1,275 | 10 | 395 R | 56.5% | 43.1% | 56.7% | 43.3% |
| 22,534 | MERIWETHER | 8,155 | 4,402 | 3,709 | 44 | 693 R | 54.0% | 45.5% | 54.3% | 45.7% |
| 6,383 | MILLER | 2,442 | 1,694 | 736 | 12 | 958 R | 69.4% | 30.1% | 69.7% | 30.3% |
| 23,932 | MITCHELL | 7,267 | 3,885 | 3,360 | 22 | 525 R | 53.5% | 46.2% | 53.6% | 46.4% |
| 21,757 | MONROE | 9,789 | 6,522 | 3,216 | 51 | 3,306 R | 66.6% | 32.9% | 67.0% | 33.0% |
| 8,270 | MONTGOMERY | 3,169 | 2,150 | 1,007 | 12 | 1,143 R | 67.8% | 31.8% | 68.1% | 31.9% |
| 15,457 | MORGAN | 7,243 | 4,902 | 2,304 | 37 | 2,598 R | 67.7% | 31.8% | 68.0% | 32.0% |
| 36,506 | MURRAY | 10,689 | 7,745 | 2,899 | 45 | 4,846 R | 72.5% | 27.1% | 72.8% | 27.2% |
| 186,291 | MUSCOGEE | 64,006 | 30,850 | 32,867 | 289 | 2,017 D | 48.2% | 51.3% | 48.4% | 51.6% |
| 62,001 | NEWTON | 29,179 | 18,095 | 10,939 | 145 | 7,156 R | 62.0% | 37.5% | 62.3% | 37.7% |
| 26,225 | OCONEE | 14,182 | 10,276 | 3,789 | 117 | 6,487 R | 72.5% | 26.7% | 73.1% | 26.9% |
| 12,635 | OGLETHORPE | 5,631 | 3,688 | 1,899 | 44 | 1,789 R | 65.5% | 33.7% | 66.0% | 34.0% |
| 81,678 | PAULDING | 40,496 | 30,843 | 9,420 | 233 | 21,423 R | 76.2% | 23.3% | 76.6% | 23.4% |
| 23,668 | PEACH | 8,549 | 4,554 | 3,961 | 34 | 593 R | 53.3% | 46.3% | 53.5% | 46.5% |
| 22,983 | PICKENS | 10,630 | 8,115 | 2,444 | 71 | 5,671 R | 76.3% | 23.0% | 76.9% | 23.1% |
| 15,636 | PIERCE | 5,924 | 4,680 | 1,234 | 10 | 3,446 R | 79.0% | 20.8% | 79.1% | 20.9% |
| 13,688 | PIKE | 6,745 | 5,193 | 1,506 | 46 | 3,687 R | 77.0% | 22.3% | 77.5% | 22.5% |
| 38,127 | POLK | 12,414 | 8,467 | 3,868 | 79 | 4,599 R | 68.2% | 31.2% | 68.6% | 31.4% |
| 9,588 | PULASKI | 3,516 | 2,202 | 1,294 | 20 | 908 R | 62.6% | 36.8% | 63.0% | 37.0% |
| 18,812 | PUTNAM | 8,111 | 5,188 | 2,880 | 43 | 2,308 R | 64.0% | 35.5% | 64.3% | 35.7% |
| 2,598 | QUITMAN | 965 | 409 | 543 | 13 | 134 D | 42.4% | 56.3% | 43.0% | 57.0% |
| 15,050 | RABUN | 6,638 | 4,650 | 1,918 | 70 | 2,732 R | 70.1% | 28.9% | 70.8% | 29.2% |
| 7,791 | RANDOLPH | 3,047 | 1,418 | 1,612 | 17 | 194 D | 46.5% | 52.9% | 46.8% | 53.2% |

# GEORGIA

## PRESIDENT 2004

| 2000 Census Population | County | Total Vote | Republican | Democratic | Other | Rep.-Dem. Plurality | Percentage | | | |
|---|---|---|---|---|---|---|---|---|---|---|
| | | | | | | | Total Vote | | Major Vote | |
| | | | | | | | Rep. | Dem. | Rep. | Dem. |
| 199,775 | RICHMOND | 69,349 | 29,764 | 39,262 | 323 | 9,498 D | 42.9% | 56.6% | 43.1% | 56.9% |
| 70,111 | ROCKDALE | 31,181 | 18,856 | 12,136 | 189 | 6,720 R | 60.5% | 38.9% | 60.8% | 39.2% |
| 3,766 | SCHLEY | 1,530 | 1,063 | 464 | 3 | 599 R | 69.5% | 30.3% | 69.6% | 30.4% |
| 15,374 | SCREVEN | 5,923 | 3,360 | 2,534 | 29 | 826 R | 56.7% | 42.8% | 57.0% | 43.0% |
| 9,369 | SEMINOLE | 3,275 | 1,977 | 1,278 | 20 | 699 R | 60.4% | 39.0% | 60.7% | 39.3% |
| 58,417 | SPALDING | 21,026 | 13,461 | 7,460 | 105 | 6,001 R | 64.0% | 35.5% | 64.3% | 35.7% |
| 25,435 | STEPHENS | 9,670 | 6,904 | 2,714 | 52 | 4,190 R | 71.4% | 28.1% | 71.8% | 28.2% |
| 5,252 | STEWART | 2,031 | 797 | 1,220 | 14 | 423 D | 39.2% | 60.1% | 39.5% | 60.5% |
| 33,200 | SUMTER | 11,291 | 5,688 | 5,562 | 41 | 126 R | 50.4% | 49.3% | 50.6% | 49.4% |
| 6,498 | TALBOT | 2,945 | 1,103 | 1,830 | 12 | 727 D | 37.5% | 62.1% | 37.6% | 62.4% |
| 2,077 | TALIAFERRO | 951 | 335 | 612 | 4 | 277 D | 35.2% | 64.4% | 35.4% | 64.6% |
| 22,305 | TATTNALL | 6,463 | 4,657 | 1,787 | 19 | 2,870 R | 72.1% | 27.6% | 72.3% | 27.7% |
| 8,815 | TAYLOR | 3,381 | 1,912 | 1,458 | 11 | 454 R | 56.6% | 43.1% | 56.7% | 43.3% |
| 11,794 | TELFAIR | 3,775 | 2,171 | 1,590 | 14 | 581 R | 57.5% | 42.1% | 57.7% | 42.3% |
| 10,970 | TERRELL | 3,824 | 1,859 | 1,951 | 14 | 92 D | 48.6% | 51.0% | 48.8% | 51.2% |
| 42,737 | THOMAS | 15,707 | 9,659 | 5,997 | 51 | 3,662 R | 61.5% | 38.2% | 61.7% | 38.3% |
| 38,407 | TIFT | 12,529 | 8,619 | 3,864 | 46 | 4,755 R | 68.8% | 30.8% | 69.0% | 31.0% |
| 26,067 | TOOMBS | 8,814 | 6,196 | 2,567 | 51 | 3,629 R | 70.3% | 29.1% | 70.7% | 29.3% |
| 9,319 | TOWNS | 5,280 | 3,823 | 1,430 | 27 | 2,393 R | 72.4% | 27.1% | 72.8% | 27.2% |
| 6,854 | TREUTLEN | 2,758 | 1,691 | 1,052 | 15 | 639 R | 61.3% | 38.1% | 61.6% | 38.4% |
| 58,779 | TROUP | 21,927 | 14,183 | 7,630 | 114 | 6,553 R | 64.7% | 34.8% | 65.0% | 35.0% |
| 9,504 | TURNER | 2,964 | 1,815 | 1,135 | 14 | 680 R | 61.2% | 38.3% | 61.5% | 38.5% |
| 10,590 | TWIGGS | 4,365 | 2,112 | 2,220 | 33 | 108 D | 48.4% | 50.9% | 48.8% | 51.2% |
| 17,289 | UNION | 9,228 | 6,847 | 2,327 | 54 | 4,520 R | 74.2% | 25.2% | 74.6% | 25.4% |
| 27,597 | UPSON | 10,091 | 6,634 | 3,424 | 33 | 3,210 R | 65.7% | 33.9% | 66.0% | 34.0% |
| 61,053 | WALKER | 21,453 | 15,340 | 5,986 | 127 | 9,354 R | 71.5% | 27.9% | 71.9% | 28.1% |
| 60,687 | WALTON | 27,624 | 21,594 | 5,887 | 143 | 15,707 R | 78.2% | 21.3% | 78.6% | 21.4% |
| 35,483 | WARE | 11,281 | 7,790 | 3,449 | 42 | 4,341 R | 69.1% | 30.6% | 69.3% | 30.7% |
| 6,336 | WARREN | 2,489 | 1,121 | 1,360 | 8 | 239 D | 45.0% | 54.6% | 45.2% | 54.8% |
| 21,176 | WASHINGTON | 7,847 | 4,081 | 3,733 | 33 | 348 R | 52.0% | 47.6% | 52.2% | 47.8% |
| 26,565 | WAYNE | 9,555 | 6,819 | 2,683 | 53 | 4,136 R | 71.4% | 28.1% | 71.8% | 28.2% |
| 2,390 | WEBSTER | 1,008 | 485 | 515 | 8 | 30 D | 48.1% | 51.1% | 48.5% | 51.5% |
| 6,179 | WHEELER | 2,049 | 1,192 | 847 | 10 | 345 R | 58.2% | 41.3% | 58.5% | 41.5% |
| 19,944 | WHITE | 9,498 | 7,403 | 2,016 | 79 | 5,387 R | 77.9% | 21.2% | 78.6% | 21.4% |
| 83,525 | WHITFIELD | 26,378 | 19,297 | 6,933 | 148 | 12,364 R | 73.2% | 26.3% | 73.6% | 26.4% |
| 8,577 | WILCOX | 2,619 | 1,705 | 902 | 12 | 803 R | 65.1% | 34.4% | 65.4% | 34.6% |
| 10,687 | WILKES | 4,544 | 2,490 | 2,028 | 26 | 462 R | 54.8% | 44.6% | 55.1% | 44.9% |
| 10,220 | WILKINSON | 4,514 | 2,261 | 2,235 | 18 | 26 R | 50.1% | 49.5% | 50.3% | 49.7% |
| 21,967 | WORTH | 7,353 | 5,105 | 2,219 | 29 | 2,886 R | 69.4% | 30.2% | 69.7% | 30.3% |
| 8,186,453 | TOTAL | 3,301,875 | 1,914,254 | 1,366,149 | 21,472 | 548,105 R | 58.0% | 41.4% | 58.4% | 41.6% |

# GEORGIA

## PRESIDENT 2000

| 2000 Census Population | County | Total Vote | Republican | Democratic | Green (Nader) | Other | Rep.-Dem. Plurality | Percentage of Total Vote | | |
|---|---|---|---|---|---|---|---|---|---|---|
| | | | | | | | | Rep. | Dem. | Green |
| 17,419 | APPLING | 6,099 | 3,940 | 2,093 | 2 | 64 | 1,847 R | 64.6% | 34.3% | |
| 7,609 | ATKINSON | 2,071 | 1,228 | 821 | 1 | 21 | 407 R | 59.3% | 39.6% | |
| 10,103 | BACON | 2,995 | 2,010 | 956 | 2 | 27 | 1,054 R | 67.1% | 31.9% | 0.1% |
| 4,074 | BAKER | 1,519 | 615 | 893 | | 11 | 278 D | 40.5% | 58.8% | |
| 44,700 | BALDWIN | 12,126 | 6,041 | 5,893 | 22 | 170 | 148 R | 49.8% | 48.6% | 0.2% |
| 14,422 | BANKS | 4,533 | 3,202 | 1,220 | 14 | 97 | 1,982 R | 70.6% | 26.9% | 0.3% |
| 46,144 | BARROW | 12,102 | 7,925 | 3,657 | 61 | 459 | 4,268 R | 65.5% | 30.2% | 0.5% |
| 76,019 | BARTOW | 22,781 | 14,720 | 7,508 | 55 | 498 | 7,212 R | 64.6% | 33.0% | 0.2% |
| 17,484 | BEN HILL | 4,661 | 2,381 | 2,234 | | 46 | 147 R | 51.1% | 47.9% | |
| 16,235 | BERRIEN | 4,410 | 2,718 | 1,640 | | 52 | 1,078 R | 61.6% | 37.2% | |
| 153,887 | BIBB | 49,776 | 24,071 | 24,996 | 248 | 461 | 925 D | 48.4% | 50.2% | 0.5% |
| 11,666 | BLECKLEY | 3,749 | 2,436 | 1,273 | 1 | 39 | 1,163 R | 65.0% | 34.0% | |
| 14,629 | BRANTLEY | 4,566 | 3,118 | 1,372 | 5 | 71 | 1,746 R | 68.3% | 30.0% | 0.1% |
| 16,450 | BROOKS | 4,551 | 2,406 | 2,096 | 12 | 37 | 310 R | 52.9% | 46.1% | 0.3% |
| 23,417 | BRYAN | 7,059 | 4,835 | 2,172 | | 52 | 2,663 R | 68.5% | 30.8% | |
| 55,983 | BULLOCH | 14,782 | 8,990 | 5,561 | 137 | 94 | 3,429 R | 60.8% | 37.6% | 0.9% |
| 22,243 | BURKE | 7,135 | 3,381 | 3,720 | 7 | 27 | 339 D | 47.4% | 52.1% | 0.1% |
| 19,522 | BUTTS | 5,635 | 3,198 | 2,281 | 8 | 148 | 917 R | 56.8% | 40.5% | 0.1% |
| 6,320 | CALHOUN | 1,887 | 768 | 1,107 | | 12 | 339 D | 40.7% | 58.7% | |
| 43,664 | CAMDEN | 10,119 | 6,371 | 3,636 | 10 | 102 | 2,735 R | 63.0% | 35.9% | 0.1% |
| 9,577 | CANDLER | 2,722 | 1,643 | 1,053 | | 26 | 590 R | 60.4% | 38.7% | |
| 87,268 | CARROLL | 25,741 | 16,326 | 8,752 | 157 | 506 | 7,574 R | 63.4% | 34.0% | 0.6% |
| 53,282 | CATOOSA | 17,721 | 12,033 | 5,470 | 66 | 152 | 6,563 R | 67.9% | 30.9% | 0.4% |
| 10,282 | CHARLTON | 2,816 | 1,770 | 1,015 | 5 | 26 | 755 R | 62.9% | 36.0% | 0.2% |
| 232,048 | CHATHAM | 76,475 | 37,847 | 37,590 | 596 | 442 | 257 R | 49.5% | 49.2% | 0.8% |
| 14,882 | CHATTAHOOCHEE | 1,207 | 590 | 600 | 4 | 13 | 10 D | 48.9% | 49.7% | 0.3% |
| 25,470 | CHATTOOGA | 6,477 | 3,640 | 2,729 | 5 | 103 | 911 R | 56.2% | 42.1% | 0.1% |
| 141,903 | CHEROKEE | 52,348 | 38,033 | 12,295 | 306 | 1,714 | 25,738 R | 72.7% | 23.5% | 0.6% |
| 101,489 | CLARKE | 28,904 | 11,850 | 15,167 | 1,247 | 640 | 3,317 D | 41.0% | 52.5% | 4.3% |
| 3,357 | CLAY | 1,277 | 448 | 821 | | 8 | 373 D | 35.1% | 64.3% | |
| 236,517 | CLAYTON | 61,402 | 19,966 | 40,042 | 176 | 1,218 | 20,076 D | 32.5% | 65.2% | 0.3% |
| 6,878 | CLINCH | 1,929 | 1,091 | 816 | | 22 | 275 R | 56.6% | 42.3% | |
| 607,751 | COBB | 235,027 | 140,494 | 86,676 | 2,134 | 5,723 | 53,818 R | 59.8% | 36.9% | 0.9% |
| 37,413 | COFFEE | 9,430 | 5,756 | 3,593 | 8 | 73 | 2,163 R | 61.0% | 38.1% | 0.1% |
| 42,053 | COLQUITT | 9,972 | 6,589 | 3,297 | 5 | 81 | 3,292 R | 66.1% | 33.1% | 0.1% |
| 89,288 | COLUMBIA | 36,008 | 26,660 | 8,969 | 122 | 257 | 17,691 R | 74.0% | 24.9% | 0.3% |
| 15,771 | COOK | 3,944 | 2,279 | 1,639 | 3 | 23 | 640 R | 57.8% | 41.6% | 0.1% |
| 89,215 | COWETA | 31,226 | 21,327 | 9,056 | 133 | 710 | 12,271 R | 68.3% | 29.0% | 0.4% |
| 12,495 | CRAWFORD | 3,567 | 1,987 | 1,513 | 5 | 62 | 474 R | 55.7% | 42.4% | 0.1% |
| 21,996 | CRISP | 5,609 | 3,285 | 2,268 | 1 | 55 | 1,017 R | 58.6% | 40.4% | |
| 15,154 | DADE | 5,049 | 3,333 | 1,628 | 13 | 75 | 1,705 R | 66.0% | 32.2% | 0.3% |
| 15,999 | DAWSON | 5,898 | 4,210 | 1,458 | 28 | 202 | 2,752 R | 71.4% | 24.7% | 0.5% |
| 28,240 | DECATUR | 7,648 | 4,187 | 3,398 | 13 | 50 | 789 R | 54.7% | 44.4% | 0.2% |
| 665,865 | DE KALB | 219,980 | 58,807 | 154,509 | 1,930 | 4,734 | 95,702 D | 26.7% | 70.2% | 0.9% |
| 19,171 | DODGE | 5,877 | 3,472 | 2,326 | 1 | 78 | 1,146 R | 59.1% | 39.6% | |
| 11,525 | DOOLY | 3,520 | 1,588 | 1,901 | | 31 | 313 D | 45.1% | 54.0% | |
| 96,065 | DOUGHERTY | 29,064 | 12,248 | 16,650 | 68 | 98 | 4,402 D | 42.1% | 57.3% | 0.2% |
| 92,174 | DOUGLAS | 30,964 | 18,893 | 11,162 | 162 | 747 | 7,731 R | 61.0% | 36.0% | 0.5% |
| 12,354 | EARLY | 3,585 | 1,938 | 1,622 | 4 | 21 | 316 R | 54.1% | 45.2% | 0.1% |
| 3,754 | ECHOLS | 898 | 614 | 272 | | 12 | 342 R | 68.4% | 30.3% | |
| 37,535 | EFFINGHAM | 10,650 | 7,326 | 3,232 | 13 | 79 | 4,094 R | 68.8% | 30.3% | 0.1% |
| 20,511 | ELBERT | 5,853 | 3,262 | 2,527 | 14 | 50 | 735 R | 55.7% | 43.2% | 0.2% |
| 21,837 | EMANUEL | 6,263 | 3,343 | 2,835 | 1 | 84 | 508 R | 53.4% | 45.3% | |
| 10,495 | EVANS | 3,080 | 1,841 | 1,217 | 2 | 20 | 624 R | 59.8% | 39.5% | 0.1% |
| 19,798 | FANNIN | 8,390 | 5,463 | 2,736 | 33 | 158 | 2,727 R | 65.1% | 32.6% | 0.4% |
| 91,263 | FAYETTE | 42,449 | 29,338 | 11,912 | 259 | 940 | 17,426 R | 69.1% | 28.1% | 0.6% |
| 90,565 | FLOYD | 26,825 | 16,194 | 10,282 | | 349 | 5,912 R | 60.4% | 38.3% | |
| 98,407 | FORSYTH | 35,755 | 27,769 | 6,694 | 132 | 1,160 | 21,075 R | 77.7% | 18.7% | 0.4% |
| 20,285 | FRANKLIN | 5,762 | 3,659 | 2,040 | | 63 | 1,619 R | 63.5% | 35.4% | |
| 816,006 | FULTON | 263,212 | 104,870 | 152,039 | 1,264 | 5,039 | 47,169 D | 39.8% | 57.8% | 0.5% |

# GEORGIA

## PRESIDENT 2000

| 2000 Census Population | County | Total Vote | Republican | Democratic | Green (Nader) | Other | Rep.-Dem. Plurality | Percentage of Total Vote | | |
|---|---|---|---|---|---|---|---|---|---|---|
| | | | | | | | | Rep. | Dem. | Green |
| 23,456 | GILMER | 7,370 | 4,941 | 2,230 | 35 | 164 | 2,711 R | 67.0% | 30.3% | 0.5% |
| 2,556 | GLASCOCK | 1,020 | 763 | 249 | | 8 | 514 R | 74.8% | 24.4% | |
| 67,568 | GLYNN | 22,384 | 14,346 | 7,778 | 128 | 132 | 6,568 R | 64.1% | 34.7% | 0.6% |
| 44,104 | GORDON | 12,205 | 7,944 | 4,032 | 18 | 211 | 3,912 R | 65.1% | 33.0% | 0.1% |
| 23,659 | GRADY | 6,703 | 3,894 | 2,721 | 18 | 70 | 1,173 R | 58.1% | 40.6% | 0.3% |
| 14,406 | GREENE | 5,197 | 2,980 | 2,137 | 13 | 67 | 843 R | 57.3% | 41.1% | 0.3% |
| 588,448 | GWINNETT | 191,111 | 121,756 | 61,434 | 1,298 | 6,623 | 60,322 R | 63.7% | 32.1% | 0.7% |
| 35,902 | HABERSHAM | 9,691 | 6,964 | 2,530 | 36 | 161 | 4,434 R | 71.9% | 26.1% | 0.4% |
| 139,277 | HALL | 38,150 | 26,841 | 10,259 | 190 | 860 | 16,582 R | 70.4% | 26.9% | 0.5% |
| 10,076 | HANCOCK | 3,086 | 662 | 2,414 | 4 | 6 | 1,752 D | 21.5% | 78.2% | 0.1% |
| 25,690 | HARALSON | 8,167 | 5,153 | 2,869 | | 145 | 2,284 R | 63.1% | 35.1% | |
| 23,695 | HARRIS | 8,562 | 5,554 | 2,912 | 20 | 76 | 2,642 R | 64.9% | 34.0% | 0.2% |
| 22,997 | HART | 7,536 | 4,242 | 3,192 | 21 | 81 | 1,050 R | 56.3% | 42.4% | 0.3% |
| 11,012 | HEARD | 3,198 | 1,947 | 1,178 | 9 | 64 | 769 R | 60.9% | 36.8% | 0.3% |
| 119,341 | HENRY | 38,867 | 25,815 | 11,971 | 46 | 1,035 | 13,844 R | 66.4% | 30.8% | 0.1% |
| 110,765 | HOUSTON | 36,988 | 23,174 | 13,301 | 89 | 424 | 9,873 R | 62.7% | 36.0% | 0.2% |
| 9,931 | IRWIN | 2,852 | 1,720 | 1,105 | 3 | 24 | 615 R | 60.3% | 38.7% | 0.1% |
| 41,589 | JACKSON | 11,635 | 7,878 | 3,420 | 43 | 294 | 4,458 R | 67.7% | 29.4% | 0.4% |
| 11,426 | JASPER | 3,943 | 2,298 | 1,558 | 2 | 85 | 740 R | 58.3% | 39.5% | 0.1% |
| 12,684 | JEFF DAVIS | 4,221 | 2,797 | 1,379 | 2 | 43 | 1,418 R | 66.3% | 32.7% | |
| 17,266 | JEFFERSON | 5,566 | 2,559 | 2,973 | 2 | 32 | 414 D | 46.0% | 53.4% | |
| 8,575 | JENKINS | 2,593 | 1,317 | 1,250 | 5 | 21 | 67 R | 50.8% | 48.2% | 0.2% |
| 8,560 | JOHNSON | 2,883 | 1,797 | 1,065 | 1 | 20 | 732 R | 62.3% | 36.9% | |
| 23,639 | JONES | 8,068 | 4,850 | 3,102 | 24 | 92 | 1,748 R | 60.1% | 38.4% | 0.3% |
| 15,912 | LAMAR | 5,230 | 2,912 | 2,194 | 15 | 109 | 718 R | 55.7% | 42.0% | 0.3% |
| 7,241 | LANIER | 1,904 | 1,048 | 832 | 3 | 21 | 216 R | 55.0% | 43.7% | 0.2% |
| 44,874 | LAURENS | 14,036 | 8,133 | 5,724 | | 179 | 2,409 R | 57.9% | 40.8% | |
| 24,757 | LEE | 7,884 | 5,872 | 1,936 | 9 | 67 | 3,936 R | 74.5% | 24.6% | 0.1% |
| 61,610 | LIBERTY | 9,972 | 4,455 | 5,347 | 26 | 144 | 892 D | 44.7% | 53.6% | 0.3% |
| 8,348 | LINCOLN | 3,103 | 1,807 | 1,275 | | 21 | 532 R | 58.2% | 41.1% | |
| 10,304 | LONG | 2,314 | 1,320 | 975 | 1 | 18 | 345 R | 57.0% | 42.1% | |
| 92,115 | LOWNDES | 25,432 | 14,462 | 10,616 | 188 | 166 | 3,846 R | 56.9% | 41.7% | 0.7% |
| 21,016 | LUMPKIN | 6,750 | 4,427 | 2,121 | | 202 | 2,306 R | 65.6% | 31.4% | |
| 21,231 | MCDUFFIE | 6,550 | 3,926 | 2,580 | 6 | 38 | 1,346 R | 59.9% | 39.4% | 0.1% |
| 10,847 | MCINTOSH | 3,837 | 1,766 | 2,047 | 4 | 20 | 281 D | 46.0% | 53.3% | 0.1% |
| 14,074 | MACON | 4,355 | 1,566 | 2,757 | 3 | 29 | 1,191 D | 36.0% | 63.3% | 0.1% |
| 25,730 | MADISON | 7,993 | 5,529 | 2,285 | 44 | 135 | 3,244 R | 69.2% | 28.6% | 0.6% |
| 7,144 | MARION | 2,184 | 1,187 | 982 | | 15 | 205 R | 54.3% | 45.0% | |
| 22,534 | MERIWETHER | 6,709 | 3,162 | 3,441 | 13 | 93 | 279 D | 47.1% | 51.3% | 0.2% |
| 6,383 | MILLER | 2,150 | 1,349 | 783 | | 18 | 566 R | 62.7% | 36.4% | |
| 23,932 | MITCHELL | 5,799 | 2,790 | 2,971 | 5 | 33 | 181 D | 48.1% | 51.2% | 0.1% |
| 21,757 | MONROE | 7,541 | 4,561 | 2,839 | 18 | 123 | 1,722 R | 60.5% | 37.6% | 0.2% |
| 8,270 | MONTGOMERY | 2,509 | 1,465 | 1,013 | 8 | 23 | 452 R | 58.4% | 40.4% | 0.3% |
| 15,457 | MORGAN | 5,902 | 3,524 | 2,238 | 29 | 111 | 1,286 R | 59.7% | 37.9% | 0.5% |
| 36,506 | MURRAY | 8,372 | 5,539 | 2,684 | 10 | 139 | 2,855 R | 66.2% | 32.1% | 0.1% |
| 186,291 | MUSCOGEE | 52,163 | 23,479 | 28,193 | 243 | 248 | 4,714 D | 45.0% | 54.0% | 0.5% |
| 62,001 | NEWTON | 18,375 | 11,127 | 6,703 | 31 | 514 | 4,424 R | 60.6% | 36.5% | 0.2% |
| 26,225 | OCONEE | 11,168 | 7,611 | 3,184 | 148 | 225 | 4,427 R | 68.2% | 28.5% | 1.3% |
| 12,635 | OGLETHORPE | 4,385 | 2,706 | 1,519 | 69 | 91 | 1,187 R | 61.7% | 34.6% | 1.6% |
| 81,678 | PAULDING | 24,260 | 16,881 | 6,743 | 34 | 602 | 10,138 R | 69.6% | 27.8% | 0.1% |
| 23,668 | PEACH | 7,137 | 3,525 | 3,540 | 3 | 69 | 15 D | 49.4% | 49.6% | |
| 22,983 | PICKENS | 8,201 | 5,488 | 2,489 | 9 | 215 | 2,999 R | 66.9% | 30.3% | 0.1% |
| 15,636 | PIERCE | 4,681 | 3,348 | 1,300 | 2 | 31 | 2,048 R | 71.5% | 27.8% | |
| 13,688 | PIKE | 4,885 | 3,358 | 1,413 | 13 | 101 | 1,945 R | 68.7% | 28.9% | 0.3% |
| 38,127 | POLK | 10,116 | 5,841 | 4,112 | 26 | 137 | 1,729 R | 57.7% | 40.6% | 0.3% |
| 9,588 | PULASKI | 3,346 | 1,922 | 1,390 | 2 | 32 | 532 R | 57.4% | 41.5% | 0.1% |
| 18,812 | PUTNAM | 6,299 | 3,596 | 2,612 | 20 | 71 | 984 R | 57.1% | 41.5% | 0.3% |
| 2,598 | QUITMAN | 904 | 348 | 542 | | 14 | 194 D | 38.5% | 60.0% | |
| 15,050 | RABUN | 5,341 | 3,451 | 1,776 | 31 | 83 | 1,675 R | 64.6% | 33.3% | 0.6% |
| 7,791 | RANDOLPH | 2,569 | 1,174 | 1,381 | | 14 | 207 D | 45.7% | 53.8% | |

# GEORGIA

## PRESIDENT 2000

| 2000 Census Population | County | Total Vote | Republican | Democratic | Green (Nader) | Other | Rep.-Dem. Plurality | Percentage of Total Vote | | |
|---|---|---|---|---|---|---|---|---|---|---|
| | | | | | | | | Rep. | Dem. | Green |
| 199,775 | RICHMOND | 57,538 | 25,485 | 31,413 | 175 | 465 | 5,928 D | 44.3% | 54.6% | 0.3% |
| 70,111 | ROCKDALE | 24,490 | 15,440 | 8,295 | | 755 | 7,145 R | 63.0% | 33.9% | |
| 3,766 | SCHLEY | 1,176 | 706 | 460 | 1 | 9 | 246 R | 60.0% | 39.1% | 0.1% |
| 15,374 | SCREVEN | 4,719 | 2,461 | 2,233 | 3 | 22 | 228 R | 52.2% | 47.3% | 0.1% |
| 9,369 | SEMINOLE | 2,877 | 1,537 | 1,313 | | 27 | 224 R | 53.4% | 45.6% | |
| 58,417 | SPALDING | 15,391 | 9,271 | 5,831 | 8 | 281 | 3,440 R | 60.2% | 37.9% | 0.1% |
| 25,435 | STEPHENS | 8,376 | 5,370 | 2,869 | 9 | 128 | 2,501 R | 64.1% | 34.3% | 0.1% |
| 5,252 | STEWART | 1,954 | 675 | 1,267 | | 12 | 592 D | 34.5% | 64.8% | |
| 33,200 | SUMTER | 9,697 | 4,847 | 4,748 | 40 | 62 | 99 R | 50.0% | 49.0% | 0.4% |
| 6,498 | TALBOT | 2,531 | 844 | 1,662 | 3 | 22 | 818 D | 33.3% | 65.7% | 0.1% |
| 2,077 | TALIAFERRO | 832 | 271 | 556 | 2 | 3 | 285 D | 32.6% | 66.8% | 0.2% |
| 22,305 | TATTNALL | 5,610 | 3,597 | 1,963 | 1 | 49 | 1,634 R | 64.1% | 35.0% | |
| 8,815 | TAYLOR | 2,780 | 1,412 | 1,340 | 2 | 26 | 72 R | 50.8% | 48.2% | 0.1% |
| 11,794 | TELFAIR | 3,493 | 1,693 | 1,777 | 1 | 22 | 84 D | 48.5% | 50.9% | |
| 10,970 | TERRELL | 3,113 | 1,504 | 1,584 | 2 | 23 | 80 D | 48.3% | 50.9% | 0.1% |
| 42,737 | THOMAS | 12,058 | 7,093 | 4,862 | 40 | 63 | 2,231 R | 58.8% | 40.3% | 0.3% |
| 38,407 | TIFT | 10,328 | 6,678 | 3,547 | 22 | 81 | 3,131 R | 64.7% | 34.3% | 0.2% |
| 26,067 | TOOMBS | 7,210 | 4,487 | 2,643 | 13 | 67 | 1,844 R | 62.2% | 36.7% | 0.2% |
| 9,319 | TOWNS | 4,497 | 2,902 | 1,495 | 34 | 66 | 1,407 R | 64.5% | 33.2% | 0.8% |
| 6,854 | TREUTLEN | 1,963 | 1,062 | 879 | 3 | 19 | 183 R | 54.1% | 44.8% | 0.2% |
| 58,779 | TROUP | 17,804 | 11,198 | 6,379 | 80 | 147 | 4,819 R | 62.9% | 35.8% | 0.4% |
| 9,504 | TURNER | 2,456 | 1,258 | 1,169 | 2 | 27 | 89 R | 51.2% | 47.6% | 0.1% |
| 10,590 | TWIGGS | 3,615 | 1,570 | 1,977 | 4 | 64 | 407 D | 43.4% | 54.7% | 0.1% |
| 17,289 | UNION | 6,956 | 4,567 | 2,230 | 54 | 105 | 2,337 R | 65.7% | 32.1% | 0.8% |
| 27,597 | UPSON | 8,282 | 5,019 | 3,158 | 12 | 93 | 1,861 R | 60.6% | 38.1% | 0.1% |
| 61,053 | WALKER | 18,895 | 12,326 | 6,341 | | 228 | 5,985 R | 65.2% | 33.6% | |
| 60,687 | WALTON | 19,083 | 12,966 | 5,484 | 38 | 595 | 7,482 R | 67.9% | 28.7% | 0.2% |
| 35,483 | WARE | 9,628 | 6,099 | 3,480 | | 49 | 2,619 R | 63.3% | 36.1% | |
| 6,336 | WARREN | 2,145 | 933 | 1,196 | 2 | 14 | 263 D | 43.5% | 55.8% | 0.1% |
| 21,176 | WASHINGTON | 6,691 | 3,162 | 3,476 | 7 | 46 | 314 D | 47.3% | 52.0% | 0.1% |
| 26,565 | WAYNE | 8,004 | 5,219 | 2,736 | | 49 | 2,483 R | 65.2% | 34.2% | |
| 2,390 | WEBSTER | 909 | 359 | 541 | 1 | 8 | 182 D | 39.5% | 59.5% | 0.1% |
| 6,179 | WHEELER | 1,575 | 813 | 752 | 2 | 8 | 61 R | 51.6% | 47.7% | 0.1% |
| 19,944 | WHITE | 7,043 | 4,857 | 2,014 | 47 | 125 | 2,843 R | 69.0% | 28.6% | 0.7% |
| 83,525 | WHITFIELD | 23,302 | 15,852 | 7,034 | 131 | 285 | 8,818 R | 68.0% | 30.2% | 0.6% |
| 8,577 | WILCOX | 2,365 | 1,381 | 962 | | 22 | 419 R | 58.4% | 40.7% | |
| 10,687 | WILKES | 4,026 | 2,044 | 1,940 | 8 | 34 | 104 R | 50.8% | 48.2% | 0.2% |
| 10,220 | WILKINSON | 3,740 | 1,800 | 1,884 | 3 | 53 | 84 D | 48.1% | 50.4% | 0.1% |
| 21,967 | WORTH | 6,061 | 3,792 | 2,214 | 8 | 47 | 1,578 R | 62.6% | 36.5% | 0.1% |
| 8,186,453 | TOTAL | 2,596,645 | 1,419,720 | 1,116,230 | 13,273 | 47,422 | 303,490 R | 54.7% | 43.0% | 0.5% |

Note: The votes cast for Nader were write-ins. A blank indicates that he received no votes in that particular county.

# GEORGIA

## PRESIDENT 1996

| 1995 Census Pop. Est. | County | Total Vote | Republican | Democratic | Reform (Perot) | Other | Rep.-Dem. Plurality | | Percentage of Total Vote | | |
|---|---|---|---|---|---|---|---|---|---|---|---|
| | | | | | | | | | Rep. | Dem. | Reform |
| 16,359 | APPLING | 5,099 | 2,572 | 2,070 | 446 | 11 | 502 | R | 50.4% | 40.6% | 8.7% |
| 6,749 | ATKINSON | 1,826 | 784 | 823 | 215 | 4 | 39 | D | 42.9% | 45.1% | 11.8% |
| 10,438 | BACON | 3,357 | 1,580 | 1,360 | 402 | 15 | 220 | R | 47.1% | 40.5% | 12.0% |
| 3,766 | BAKER | 1,475 | 408 | 955 | 105 | 7 | 547 | D | 27.7% | 64.7% | 7.1% |
| 41,854 | BALDWIN | 11,205 | 4,570 | 5,740 | 849 | 46 | 1,170 | D | 40.8% | 51.2% | 7.6% |
| 11,616 | BANKS | 4,076 | 1,925 | 1,536 | 595 | 20 | 389 | R | 47.2% | 37.7% | 14.6% |
| 35,699 | BARROW | 10,346 | 5,342 | 3,928 | 942 | 134 | 1,414 | R | 51.6% | 38.0% | 9.1% |
| 63,732 | BARTOW | 18,025 | 9,250 | 6,853 | 1,770 | 152 | 2,397 | R | 51.3% | 38.0% | 9.8% |
| 17,258 | BEN HILL | 4,088 | 1,516 | 2,198 | 358 | 16 | 682 | D | 37.1% | 53.8% | 8.8% |
| 15,466 | BERRIEN | 4,549 | 1,950 | 2,066 | 525 | 8 | 116 | D | 42.9% | 45.4% | 11.5% |
| 155,066 | BIBB | 49,932 | 20,778 | 26,727 | 2,268 | 159 | 5,949 | D | 41.6% | 53.5% | 4.5% |
| 10,958 | BLECKLEY | 3,308 | 1,632 | 1,365 | 300 | 11 | 267 | R | 49.3% | 41.3% | 9.1% |
| 12,698 | BRANTLEY | 3,634 | 1,738 | 1,494 | 386 | 16 | 244 | R | 47.8% | 41.1% | 10.6% |
| 15,837 | BROOKS | 4,054 | 1,738 | 1,977 | 314 | 25 | 239 | D | 42.9% | 48.8% | 7.7% |
| 21,190 | BRYAN | 6,269 | 3,577 | 2,152 | 513 | 27 | 1,425 | R | 57.1% | 34.3% | 8.2% |
| 48,642 | BULLOCH | 13,041 | 6,646 | 5,396 | 939 | 60 | 1,250 | R | 51.0% | 41.4% | 7.2% |
| 21,742 | BURKE | 6,913 | 2,590 | 3,915 | 389 | 19 | 1,325 | D | 37.5% | 56.6% | 5.6% |
| 16,025 | BUTTS | 4,757 | 2,027 | 2,271 | 416 | 43 | 244 | D | 42.6% | 47.7% | 8.7% |
| 4,851 | CALHOUN | 1,868 | 541 | 1,217 | 106 | 4 | 676 | D | 29.0% | 65.1% | 5.7% |
| 40,714 | CAMDEN | 8,491 | 4,222 | 3,644 | 572 | 53 | 578 | R | 49.7% | 42.9% | 6.7% |
| 8,637 | CANDLER | 2,501 | 1,131 | 1,097 | 264 | 9 | 34 | R | 45.2% | 43.9% | 10.6% |
| 77,977 | CARROLL | 21,769 | 11,157 | 8,438 | 2,002 | 172 | 2,719 | R | 51.3% | 38.8% | 9.2% |
| 48,008 | CATOOSA | 14,746 | 8,237 | 5,185 | 1,257 | 67 | 3,052 | R | 55.9% | 35.2% | 8.5% |
| 9,296 | CHARLTON | 3,031 | 1,374 | 1,368 | 280 | 9 | 6 | R | 45.3% | 45.1% | 9.2% |
| 226,160 | CHATHAM | 71,278 | 31,987 | 35,781 | 3,028 | 482 | 3,794 | D | 44.9% | 50.2% | 4.2% |
| 15,871 | CHATTAHOOCHEE | 1,082 | 398 | 565 | 115 | 4 | 167 | D | 36.8% | 52.2% | 10.6% |
| 22,884 | CHATTOOGA | 6,326 | 2,513 | 3,003 | 796 | 14 | 490 | D | 39.7% | 47.5% | 12.6% |
| 114,751 | CHEROKEE | 38,677 | 24,527 | 10,802 | 2,872 | 476 | 13,725 | R | 63.4% | 27.9% | 7.4% |
| 90,207 | CLARKE | 27,349 | 10,504 | 15,206 | 1,201 | 438 | 4,702 | D | 38.4% | 55.6% | 4.4% |
| 3,473 | CLAY | 1,143 | 293 | 787 | 62 | 1 | 494 | D | 25.6% | 68.9% | 5.4% |
| 198,551 | CLAYTON | 55,243 | 20,625 | 30,687 | 3,494 | 437 | 10,062 | D | 37.3% | 55.5% | 6.3% |
| 6,438 | CLINCH | 1,952 | 789 | 973 | 182 | 8 | 184 | D | 40.4% | 49.8% | 9.3% |
| 525,453 | COBB | 200,589 | 114,188 | 73,750 | 10,438 | 2,213 | 40,438 | R | 56.9% | 36.8% | 5.2% |
| 32,697 | COFFEE | 8,075 | 3,934 | 3,407 | 711 | 23 | 527 | R | 48.7% | 42.2% | 8.8% |
| 38,072 | COLQUITT | 9,993 | 4,847 | 4,135 | 977 | 34 | 712 | R | 48.5% | 41.4% | 9.8% |
| 83,674 | COLUMBIA | 31,694 | 21,291 | 8,601 | 1,709 | 93 | 12,690 | R | 67.2% | 27.1% | 5.4% |
| 13,950 | COOK | 3,407 | 1,354 | 1,780 | 267 | 6 | 426 | D | 39.7% | 52.2% | 7.8% |
| 72,021 | COWETA | 22,981 | 13,058 | 7,794 | 1,949 | 180 | 5,264 | R | 56.8% | 33.9% | 8.5% |
| 10,166 | CRAWFORD | 3,103 | 1,290 | 1,534 | 270 | 9 | 244 | D | 41.6% | 49.4% | 8.7% |
| 20,716 | CRISP | 5,296 | 2,321 | 2,504 | 445 | 26 | 183 | D | 43.8% | 47.3% | 8.4% |
| 14,158 | DADE | 4,668 | 2,295 | 1,737 | 618 | 18 | 558 | R | 49.2% | 37.2% | 13.2% |
| 12,237 | DAWSON | 4,306 | 2,343 | 1,434 | 473 | 56 | 909 | R | 54.4% | 33.3% | 11.0% |
| 26,390 | DECATUR | 6,797 | 3,035 | 3,245 | 497 | 20 | 210 | D | 44.7% | 47.7% | 7.3% |
| 582,095 | DE KALB | 207,239 | 60,255 | 137,903 | 6,742 | 2,339 | 77,648 | D | 29.1% | 66.5% | 3.3% |
| 17,956 | DODGE | 5,781 | 2,478 | 2,696 | 587 | 20 | 218 | D | 42.9% | 46.6% | 10.2% |
| 10,314 | DOOLY | 3,160 | 990 | 1,951 | 207 | 12 | 961 | D | 31.3% | 61.7% | 6.6% |
| 97,511 | DOUGHERTY | 27,872 | 11,144 | 15,600 | 1,072 | 56 | 4,456 | D | 40.0% | 56.0% | 3.8% |
| 82,297 | DOUGLAS | 26,477 | 14,495 | 9,631 | 2,109 | 242 | 4,864 | R | 54.7% | 36.4% | 8.0% |
| 12,198 | EARLY | 3,273 | 1,374 | 1,648 | 246 | 5 | 274 | D | 42.0% | 50.4% | 7.5% |
| 2,325 | ECHOLS | 743 | 335 | 308 | 97 | 3 | 27 | R | 45.1% | 41.5% | 13.1% |
| 32,118 | EFFINGHAM | 8,848 | 5,022 | 3,031 | 769 | 26 | 1,991 | R | 56.8% | 34.3% | 8.7% |
| 19,173 | ELBERT | 5,857 | 2,393 | 2,900 | 552 | 12 | 507 | D | 40.9% | 49.5% | 9.4% |
| 20,954 | EMANUEL | 5,873 | 2,451 | 2,947 | 450 | 25 | 496 | D | 41.7% | 50.2% | 7.7% |
| 9,438 | EVANS | 2,538 | 1,206 | 1,117 | 204 | 11 | 89 | R | 47.5% | 44.0% | 8.0% |
| 17,480 | FANNIN | 6,931 | 3,373 | 2,741 | 782 | 35 | 632 | R | 48.7% | 39.5% | 11.3% |
| 78,879 | FAYETTE | 33,212 | 21,005 | 9,875 | 2,016 | 316 | 11,130 | R | 63.2% | 29.7% | 6.1% |
| 83,935 | FLOYD | 25,378 | 12,426 | 10,464 | 2,345 | 143 | 1,962 | R | 49.0% | 41.2% | 9.2% |
| 62,335 | FORSYTH | 23,171 | 15,013 | 5,957 | 1,889 | 312 | 9,056 | R | 64.8% | 25.7% | 8.2% |
| 17,701 | FRANKLIN | 5,399 | 2,364 | 2,338 | 665 | 32 | 26 | R | 43.8% | 43.3% | 12.3% |
| 700,689 | FULTON | 243,178 | 89,809 | 143,306 | 7,720 | 2,343 | 53,497 | D | 36.9% | 58.9% | 3.2% |

# GEORGIA

## PRESIDENT 1996

| 1995 Census Pop. Est. | County | Total Vote | Republican | Democratic | Reform (Perot) | Other | Rep.-Dem. Plurality | Percentage of Total Vote | | |
|---|---|---|---|---|---|---|---|---|---|---|
| | | | | | | | | Rep. | Dem. | Reform |
| 15,916 | GILMER | 6,366 | 3,121 | 2,464 | 725 | 56 | 657 R | 49.0% | 38.7% | 11.4% |
| 2,456 | GLASCOCK | 1,008 | 532 | 348 | 128 | | 184 R | 52.8% | 34.5% | 12.7% |
| 65,565 | GLYNN | 21,603 | 12,305 | 8,058 | 1,137 | 103 | 4,247 R | 57.0% | 37.3% | 5.3% |
| 38,442 | GORDON | 10,820 | 5,232 | 4,239 | 1,284 | 65 | 993 R | 48.4% | 39.2% | 11.9% |
| 21,312 | GRADY | 6,185 | 2,674 | 2,862 | 633 | 16 | 188 D | 43.2% | 46.3% | 10.2% |
| 12,781 | GREENE | 4,015 | 1,702 | 2,115 | 173 | 25 | 413 D | 42.4% | 52.7% | 4.3% |
| 457,058 | GWINNETT | 162,968 | 96,610 | 53,819 | 10,236 | 2,303 | 42,791 R | 59.3% | 33.0% | 6.3% |
| 30,146 | HABERSHAM | 9,110 | 4,730 | 3,170 | 1,149 | 61 | 1,560 R | 51.9% | 34.8% | 12.6% |
| 108,238 | HALL | 32,219 | 19,280 | 10,362 | 2,321 | 256 | 8,918 R | 59.8% | 32.2% | 7.2% |
| 9,100 | HANCOCK | 2,646 | 438 | 2,135 | 71 | 2 | 1,697 D | 16.6% | 80.7% | 2.7% |
| 23,378 | HARALSON | 6,953 | 3,260 | 2,850 | 808 | 35 | 410 R | 46.9% | 41.0% | 11.6% |
| 20,479 | HARRIS | 7,131 | 3,829 | 2,779 | 489 | 34 | 1,050 R | 53.7% | 39.0% | 6.9% |
| 20,848 | HART | 7,171 | 2,884 | 3,486 | 767 | 34 | 602 D | 40.2% | 48.6% | 10.7% |
| 9,573 | HEARD | 2,844 | 1,170 | 1,248 | 406 | 20 | 78 D | 41.1% | 43.9% | 14.3% |
| 84,553 | HENRY | 29,074 | 16,968 | 9,498 | 2,320 | 288 | 7,470 R | 58.4% | 32.7% | 8.0% |
| 99,647 | HOUSTON | 32,684 | 17,050 | 12,760 | 2,730 | 144 | 4,290 R | 52.2% | 39.0% | 8.4% |
| 8,725 | IRWIN | 2,540 | 1,085 | 1,225 | 224 | 6 | 140 D | 42.7% | 48.2% | 8.8% |
| 33,921 | JACKSON | 9,493 | 4,782 | 3,746 | 899 | 66 | 1,036 R | 50.4% | 39.5% | 9.5% |
| 9,168 | JASPER | 3,234 | 1,423 | 1,553 | 243 | 15 | 130 D | 44.0% | 48.0% | 7.5% |
| 12,366 | JEFF DAVIS | 3,816 | 1,796 | 1,576 | 428 | 16 | 220 R | 47.1% | 41.3% | 11.2% |
| 17,872 | JEFFERSON | 5,792 | 2,077 | 3,404 | 298 | 13 | 1,327 D | 35.9% | 58.8% | 5.1% |
| 8,658 | JENKINS | 2,463 | 955 | 1,336 | 166 | 6 | 381 D | 38.8% | 54.2% | 6.7% |
| 8,436 | JOHNSON | 2,255 | 815 | 1,194 | 242 | 4 | 379 D | 36.1% | 52.9% | 10.7% |
| 22,077 | JONES | 6,992 | 3,272 | 3,195 | 497 | 28 | 77 R | 46.8% | 45.7% | 7.1% |
| 13,797 | LAMAR | 4,545 | 1,988 | 2,125 | 409 | 23 | 137 D | 43.7% | 46.8% | 9.0% |
| 6,312 | LANIER | 1,502 | 519 | 818 | 160 | 5 | 299 D | 34.6% | 54.5% | 10.7% |
| 42,852 | LAURENS | 12,803 | 6,118 | 5,792 | 818 | 75 | 326 R | 47.8% | 45.2% | 6.4% |
| 19,922 | LEE | 6,513 | 3,983 | 2,005 | 506 | 19 | 1,978 R | 61.2% | 30.8% | 7.8% |
| 58,749 | LIBERTY | 8,129 | 3,042 | 4,462 | 580 | 45 | 1,420 D | 37.4% | 54.9% | 7.1% |
| 8,055 | LINCOLN | 2,939 | 1,391 | 1,334 | 208 | 6 | 57 R | 47.3% | 45.4% | 7.1% |
| 7,885 | LONG | 1,972 | 791 | 936 | 236 | 9 | 145 D | 40.1% | 47.5% | 12.0% |
| 82,952 | LOWNDES | 21,625 | 10,578 | 9,470 | 1,518 | 59 | 1,108 R | 48.9% | 43.8% | 7.0% |
| 16,822 | LUMPKIN | 5,169 | 2,576 | 1,949 | 588 | 56 | 627 R | 49.8% | 37.7% | 11.4% |
| 21,627 | MCDUFFIE | 6,385 | 3,254 | 2,725 | 395 | 11 | 529 R | 51.0% | 42.7% | 6.2% |
| 9,456 | MCINTOSH | 3,448 | 1,219 | 1,927 | 293 | 9 | 708 D | 35.4% | 55.9% | 8.5% |
| 13,249 | MACON | 3,791 | 1,006 | 2,618 | 159 | 8 | 1,612 D | 26.5% | 69.1% | 4.2% |
| 23,396 | MADISON | 7,477 | 3,992 | 2,571 | 868 | 46 | 1,421 R | 53.4% | 34.4% | 11.6% |
| 6,370 | MARION | 1,821 | 678 | 977 | 159 | 7 | 299 D | 37.2% | 53.7% | 8.7% |
| 23,041 | MERIWETHER | 6,253 | 2,259 | 3,492 | 480 | 22 | 1,233 D | 36.1% | 55.8% | 7.7% |
| 6,161 | MILLER | 1,996 | 847 | 909 | 235 | 5 | 62 D | 42.4% | 45.5% | 11.8% |
| 20,859 | MITCHELL | 5,587 | 2,033 | 3,165 | 372 | 17 | 1,132 D | 36.4% | 56.6% | 6.7% |
| 18,950 | MONROE | 6,348 | 3,054 | 2,768 | 488 | 38 | 286 R | 48.1% | 43.6% | 7.7% |
| 7,635 | MONTGOMERY | 2,686 | 1,163 | 1,233 | 284 | 6 | 70 D | 43.3% | 45.9% | 10.6% |
| 14,006 | MORGAN | 4,612 | 2,118 | 2,111 | 364 | 19 | 7 R | 45.9% | 45.8% | 7.9% |
| 30,032 | MURRAY | 7,124 | 3,289 | 2,861 | 938 | 36 | 428 R | 46.2% | 40.2% | 13.2% |
| 184,594 | MUSCOGEE | 46,248 | 19,360 | 24,867 | 1,891 | 130 | 5,507 D | 41.9% | 53.8% | 4.1% |
| 50,644 | NEWTON | 15,443 | 7,274 | 6,759 | 1,258 | 152 | 515 R | 47.1% | 43.8% | 8.1% |
| 21,190 | OCONEE | 8,813 | 5,116 | 2,992 | 615 | 90 | 2,124 R | 58.1% | 33.9% | 7.0% |
| 10,911 | OGLETHORPE | 3,805 | 1,826 | 1,570 | 369 | 40 | 256 R | 48.0% | 41.3% | 9.7% |
| 59,920 | PAULDING | 17,633 | 10,152 | 5,699 | 1,603 | 179 | 4,453 R | 57.6% | 32.3% | 9.1% |
| 22,906 | PEACH | 6,753 | 2,676 | 3,582 | 471 | 24 | 906 D | 39.6% | 53.0% | 7.0% |
| 16,881 | PICKENS | 6,566 | 3,041 | 2,693 | 783 | 49 | 348 R | 46.3% | 41.0% | 11.9% |
| 14,821 | PIERCE | 4,088 | 2,319 | 1,420 | 333 | 16 | 899 R | 56.7% | 34.7% | 8.1% |
| 11,441 | PIKE | 3,911 | 2,054 | 1,474 | 357 | 26 | 580 R | 52.5% | 37.7% | 9.1% |
| 34,771 | POLK | 9,550 | 4,130 | 4,298 | 1,076 | 46 | 168 D | 43.2% | 45.0% | 11.3% |
| 8,245 | PULASKI | 3,030 | 1,196 | 1,554 | 268 | 12 | 358 D | 39.5% | 51.3% | 8.8% |
| 15,991 | PUTNAM | 5,146 | 2,306 | 2,340 | 474 | 26 | 34 D | 44.8% | 45.5% | 9.2% |
| 2,420 | QUITMAN | 797 | 224 | 514 | 59 | | 290 D | 28.1% | 64.5% | 7.4% |
| 12,738 | RABUN | 4,767 | 2,213 | 1,943 | 585 | 26 | 270 R | 46.4% | 40.8% | 12.3% |
| 8,092 | RANDOLPH | 2,383 | 816 | 1,438 | 126 | 3 | 622 D | 34.2% | 60.3% | 5.3% |

# GEORGIA

## PRESIDENT 1996

| 1995 Census Pop. Est. | County | Total Vote | Republican | Democratic | Reform (Perot) | Other | Rep.-Dem. Plurality | Percentage of Total Vote | | |
|---|---|---|---|---|---|---|---|---|---|---|
| | | | | | | | | Rep. | Dem. | Reform |
| 195,508 | RICHMOND | 56,869 | 23,670 | 30,738 | 2,310 | 151 | 7,068 D | 41.6% | 54.1% | 4.1% |
| 64,448 | ROCKDALE | 22,696 | 13,006 | 7,656 | 1,750 | 284 | 5,350 R | 57.3% | 33.7% | 7.7% |
| 3,783 | SCHLEY | 1,170 | 470 | 576 | 123 | 1 | 106 D | 40.2% | 49.2% | 10.5% |
| 14,336 | SCREVEN | 4,219 | 1,862 | 2,087 | 263 | 7 | 225 D | 44.1% | 49.5% | 6.2% |
| 9,097 | SEMINOLE | 2,524 | 1,003 | 1,265 | 250 | 6 | 262 D | 39.7% | 50.1% | 9.9% |
| 57,306 | SPALDING | 14,536 | 7,376 | 6,017 | 1,059 | 84 | 1,359 R | 50.7% | 41.4% | 7.3% |
| 25,000 | STEPHENS | 7,979 | 3,890 | 3,072 | 979 | 38 | 818 R | 48.8% | 38.5% | 12.3% |
| 5,438 | STEWART | 2,218 | 525 | 1,537 | 152 | 4 | 1,012 D | 23.7% | 69.3% | 6.9% |
| 31,245 | SUMTER | 8,064 | 3,358 | 4,239 | 451 | 16 | 881 D | 41.6% | 52.6% | 5.6% |
| 6,741 | TALBOT | 2,346 | 652 | 1,579 | 111 | 4 | 927 D | 27.8% | 67.3% | 4.7% |
| 1,883 | TALIAFERRO | 886 | 235 | 615 | 36 | | 380 D | 26.5% | 69.4% | 4.1% |
| 18,588 | TATTNALL | 5,447 | 2,518 | 2,369 | 541 | 19 | 149 R | 46.2% | 43.5% | 9.9% |
| 8,048 | TAYLOR | 2,653 | 1,002 | 1,450 | 195 | 6 | 448 D | 37.8% | 54.7% | 7.4% |
| 11623 | TELFAIR | 3,332 | 1,143 | 1,856 | 322 | 11 | 713 D | 34.3% | 55.7% | 9.7% |
| 11,007 | TERRELL | 2,755 | 1,111 | 1,509 | 129 | 6 | 398 D | 40.3% | 54.8% | 4.7% |
| 41,419 | THOMAS | 11,519 | 5,649 | 5,183 | 667 | 20 | 466 R | 49.0% | 45.0% | 5.8% |
| 35,932 | TIFT | 10,577 | 5,613 | 4,198 | 728 | 38 | 1,415 R | 53.1% | 39.7% | 6.9% |
| 25,276 | TOOMBS | 7,038 | 3,646 | 2,763 | 602 | 27 | 883 R | 51.8% | 39.3% | 8.6% |
| 7,559 | TOWNS | 4,179 | 2,030 | 1,664 | 459 | 26 | 366 R | 48.6% | 39.8% | 11.0% |
| 5,943 | TREUTLEN | 1,759 | 723 | 912 | 122 | 2 | 189 D | 41.1% | 51.8% | 6.9% |
| 57,882 | TROUP | 15,837 | 8,716 | 5,940 | 1,090 | 91 | 2,776 R | 55.0% | 37.5% | 6.9% |
| 8,916 | TURNER | 2,455 | 924 | 1,272 | 246 | 13 | 348 D | 37.6% | 51.8% | 10.0% |
| 10,060 | TWIGGS | 3,110 | 958 | 1,927 | 210 | 15 | 969 D | 30.8% | 62.0% | 6.8% |
| 14,427 | UNION | 5,513 | 2,685 | 2,175 | 622 | 31 | 510 R | 48.7% | 39.5% | 11.3% |
| 26,961 | UPSON | 8,035 | 3,783 | 3,491 | 731 | 30 | 292 R | 47.1% | 43.4% | 9.1% |
| 60,654 | WALKER | 17,603 | 8,817 | 6,743 | 1,969 | 74 | 2,074 R | 50.1% | 38.3% | 11.2% |
| 46,694 | WALTON | 15,020 | 7,934 | 5,618 | 1,323 | 145 | 2,316 R | 52.8% | 37.4% | 8.8% |
| 35,589 | WARE | 9,580 | 4,746 | 4,171 | 636 | 27 | 575 R | 49.5% | 43.5% | 6.6% |
| 6,057 | WARREN | 2,052 | 735 | 1,230 | 83 | 4 | 495 D | 35.8% | 59.9% | 4.0% |
| 19,953 | WASHINGTON | 6,919 | 2,348 | 4,057 | 488 | 26 | 1,709 D | 33.9% | 58.6% | 7.1% |
| 24,818 | WAYNE | 7,126 | 3,709 | 2,734 | 665 | 18 | 975 R | 52.0% | 38.4% | 9.3% |
| 2,260 | WEBSTER | 823 | 235 | 529 | 59 | | 294 D | 28.6% | 64.3% | 7.2% |
| 4,830 | WHEELER | 1,357 | 460 | 751 | 141 | 5 | 291 D | 33.9% | 55.3% | 10.4% |
| 15,330 | WHITE | 5,420 | 2,959 | 1,864 | 556 | 41 | 1,095 R | 54.6% | 34.4% | 10.3% |
| 78,033 | WHITFIELD | 21,824 | 12,368 | 7,720 | 1,637 | 99 | 4,648 R | 56.7% | 35.4% | 7.5% |
| 7,100 | WILCOX | 2,122 | 882 | 1,067 | 171 | 2 | 185 D | 41.6% | 50.3% | 8.1% |
| 10,615 | WILKES | 3,586 | 1,417 | 1,971 | 184 | 14 | 554 D | 39.5% | 55.0% | 5.1% |
| 10,627 | WILKINSON | 3,909 | 1,332 | 2,278 | 287 | 12 | 946 D | 34.1% | 58.3% | 7.3% |
| 21,643 | WORTH | 5,725 | 2,752 | 2,300 | 521 | 152 | 452 R | 48.1% | 40.2% | 9.1% |
| 7,200,882 | TOTAL | 2,299,071 | 1,080,843 | 1,053,849 | 146,337 | 18,042 | 26,994 R | 47.0% | 45.8% | 6.4% |

# GEORGIA

## PRESIDENT 1992

| 1990 Census Population | County | Total Vote | Republican | Democratic | Perot | Other | Plurality | Percentage Total Vote | | |
|---:|---|---:|---:|---:|---:|---:|---:|---:|---:|---:|
| | | | | | | | | Rep. | Dem. | Perot |
| 15,744 | APPLING | 6,027 | 2,514 | 2,455 | 1,047 | 11 | 59 R | 41.7% | 40.7% | 17.4% |
| 6,213 | ATKINSON | 2,185 | 779 | 1,056 | 342 | 8 | 277 D | 35.7% | 48.3% | 15.7% |
| 9,566 | BACON | 3,335 | 1,301 | 1,423 | 604 | 7 | 122 D | 39.0% | 42.7% | 18.1% |
| 3,615 | BAKER | 1,468 | 391 | 864 | 210 | 3 | 473 D | 26.6% | 58.9% | 14.3% |
| 39,530 | BALDWIN | 11,788 | 4,262 | 5,813 | 1,679 | 34 | 1,551 D | 36.2% | 49.3% | 14.2% |
| 10,308 | BANKS | 3,671 | 1,551 | 1,530 | 583 | 7 | 21 R | 42.3% | 41.7% | 15.9% |
| 29,721 | BARROW | 9,982 | 4,328 | 3,991 | 1,633 | 30 | 337 R | 43.4% | 40.0% | 16.4% |
| 55,911 | BARTOW | 16,990 | 7,742 | 6,675 | 2,500 | 73 | 1,067 R | 45.6% | 39.3% | 14.7% |
| 16,245 | BEN HILL | 4,464 | 1,476 | 2,348 | 619 | 21 | 872 D | 33.1% | 52.6% | 13.9% |
| 14,153 | BERRIEN | 4,543 | 1,637 | 2,103 | 796 | 7 | 466 D | 36.0% | 46.3% | 17.5% |
| 149,967 | BIBB | 54,049 | 19,847 | 28,070 | 6,021 | 111 | 8,223 D | 36.7% | 51.9% | 11.1% |
| 10,430 | BLECKLEY | 3,956 | 1,570 | 1,710 | 662 | 14 | 140 D | 39.7% | 43.2% | 16.7% |
| 11,077 | BRANTLEY | 4,274 | 1,541 | 1,883 | 840 | 10 | 342 D | 36.1% | 44.1% | 19.7% |
| 15,398 | BROOKS | 4,315 | 1,779 | 1,895 | 630 | 11 | 116 D | 41.2% | 43.9% | 14.6% |
| 15,438 | BRYAN | 5,928 | 2,789 | 2,031 | 1,095 | 13 | 758 R | 47.0% | 34.3% | 18.5% |
| 43,125 | BULLOCH | 12,644 | 5,690 | 4,903 | 2,020 | 31 | 787 R | 45.0% | 38.8% | 16.0% |
| 20,579 | BURKE | 6,859 | 2,390 | 3,647 | 807 | 15 | 1,257 D | 34.8% | 53.2% | 11.8% |
| 15,326 | BUTTS | 4,851 | 1,768 | 2,448 | 619 | 16 | 680 D | 36.4% | 50.5% | 12.8% |
| 5,013 | CALHOUN | 2,018 | 464 | 1,301 | 248 | 5 | 837 D | 23.0% | 64.5% | 12.3% |
| 30,167 | CAMDEN | 7,572 | 3,517 | 2,952 | 1,077 | 26 | 565 R | 46.4% | 39.0% | 14.2% |
| 7,744 | CANDLER | 2,755 | 1,014 | 1,192 | 541 | 8 | 178 D | 36.8% | 43.3% | 19.6% |
| 71,422 | CARROLL | 22,586 | 10,750 | 8,404 | 3,358 | 74 | 2,346 R | 47.6% | 37.2% | 14.9% |
| 42,464 | CATOOSA | 14,731 | 7,599 | 4,817 | 2,290 | 25 | 2,782 R | 51.6% | 32.7% | 15.5% |
| 8,496 | CHARLTON | 2,892 | 1,333 | 1,127 | 427 | 5 | 206 R | 46.1% | 39.0% | 14.8% |
| 216,935 | CHATHAM | 72,069 | 31,925 | 31,533 | 8,269 | 342 | 392 R | 44.3% | 43.8% | 11.5% |
| 16,934 | CHATTAHOOCHEE | 1,198 | 413 | 604 | 177 | 4 | 191 D | 34.5% | 50.4% | 14.8% |
| 22,242 | CHATTOOGA | 6,404 | 2,439 | 2,976 | 965 | 24 | 537 D | 38.1% | 46.5% | 15.1% |
| 90,204 | CHEROKEE | 29,214 | 16,054 | 8,113 | 4,950 | 97 | 7,941 R | 55.0% | 27.8% | 16.9% |
| 87,594 | CLARKE | 28,998 | 10,459 | 15,403 | 2,987 | 149 | 4,944 D | 36.1% | 53.1% | 10.3% |
| 3,364 | CLAY | 1,197 | 264 | 778 | 155 | | 514 D | 22.1% | 65.0% | 12.9% |
| 182,052 | CLAYTON | 57,989 | 23,965 | 25,890 | 7,942 | 192 | 1,925 D | 41.3% | 44.6% | 13.7% |
| 6,160 | CLINCH | 1,837 | 790 | 759 | 286 | 2 | 31 R | 43.0% | 41.3% | 15.6% |
| 447,745 | COBB | 197,129 | 103,734 | 63,960 | 28,747 | 688 | 39,774 R | 52.6% | 32.4% | 14.6% |
| 29,592 | COFFEE | 8,339 | 3,778 | 3,275 | 1,256 | 30 | 503 R | 45.3% | 39.3% | 15.1% |
| 36,645 | COLQUITT | 10,276 | 4,680 | 3,891 | 1,682 | 23 | 789 R | 45.5% | 37.9% | 16.4% |
| 66,031 | COLUMBIA | 28,200 | 16,657 | 7,115 | 4,379 | 49 | 9,542 R | 59.1% | 25.2% | 15.5% |
| 13,456 | COOK | 3,605 | 1,318 | 1,731 | 537 | 19 | 413 D | 36.6% | 48.0% | 14.9% |
| 53,853 | COWETA | 20,552 | 9,814 | 7,093 | 3,587 | 58 | 2,721 R | 47.8% | 34.5% | 17.5% |
| 8,991 | CRAWFORD | 3,183 | 974 | 1,648 | 549 | 12 | 674 D | 30.6% | 51.8% | 17.2% |
| 20,011 | CRISP | 5,709 | 2,253 | 2,610 | 823 | 23 | 357 D | 39.5% | 45.7% | 14.4% |
| 13,147 | DADE | 4,804 | 2,191 | 1,782 | 823 | 8 | 409 R | 45.6% | 37.1% | 17.1% |
| 9,429 | DAWSON | 3,892 | 1,696 | 1,399 | 790 | 7 | 297 R | 43.6% | 35.9% | 20.3% |
| 25,511 | DECATUR | 7,419 | 3,142 | 3,198 | 1,068 | 11 | 56 D | 42.4% | 43.1% | 14.4% |
| 545,837 | DE KALB | 215,433 | 70,282 | 124,559 | 19,741 | 851 | 54,277 D | 32.6% | 57.8% | 9.2% |
| 17,607 | DODGE | 6,278 | 2,287 | 3,002 | 978 | 11 | 715 D | 36.4% | 47.8% | 15.6% |
| 9,901 | DOOLY | 3,387 | 1,034 | 1,993 | 350 | 10 | 959 D | 30.5% | 58.8% | 10.3% |
| 96,311 | DOUGHERTY | 30,931 | 12,455 | 15,236 | 3,178 | 62 | 2,781 D | 40.3% | 49.3% | 10.3% |
| 71,120 | DOUGLAS | 26,657 | 13,349 | 8,869 | 4,362 | 77 | 4,480 R | 50.1% | 33.3% | 16.4% |
| 11,854 | EARLY | 4,143 | 1,457 | 1,970 | 652 | 64 | 513 D | 35.2% | 47.6% | 15.7% |
| 2,334 | ECHOLS | 911 | 361 | 312 | 238 | | 49 R | 39.6% | 34.2% | 26.1% |
| 25,687 | EFFINGHAM | 7,963 | 3,814 | 2,690 | 1,443 | 16 | 1,124 R | 47.9% | 33.8% | 18.1% |
| 18,949 | ELBERT | 6,167 | 2,372 | 3,025 | 757 | 13 | 653 D | 38.5% | 49.1% | 12.3% |
| 20,546 | EMANUEL | 6,425 | 2,662 | 2,951 | 755 | 57 | 289 D | 41.4% | 45.9% | 11.8% |
| 8,724 | EVANS | 2,960 | 1,244 | 1,230 | 480 | 6 | 14 R | 42.0% | 41.6% | 16.2% |
| 15,992 | FANNIN | 7,195 | 3,255 | 2,902 | 1,028 | 10 | 353 R | 45.2% | 40.3% | 14.3% |
| 62,415 | FAYETTE | 31,687 | 17,576 | 8,430 | 5,598 | 83 | 9,146 R | 55.5% | 26.6% | 17.7% |
| 81,251 | FLOYD | 27,860 | 12,378 | 11,614 | 3,779 | 89 | 764 R | 44.4% | 41.7% | 13.6% |
| 44,083 | FORSYTH | 17,086 | 8,652 | 4,936 | 3,453 | 45 | 3,716 R | 50.6% | 28.9% | 20.2% |
| 16,650 | FRANKLIN | 5,923 | 2,391 | 2,505 | 1,014 | 13 | 114 D | 40.4% | 42.3% | 17.1% |
| 648,951 | FULTON | 257,406 | 85,451 | 147,459 | 23,578 | 918 | 62,008 D | 33.2% | 57.3% | 9.2% |

# GEORGIA

## PRESIDENT 1992

| 1990 Census Population | County | Total Vote | Republican | Democratic | Perot | Other | Plurality | Percentage Total Vote | | |
|---|---|---|---|---|---|---|---|---|---|---|
| | | | | | | | | Rep. | Dem. | Perot |
| 13,368 | GILMER | 5,888 | 2,661 | 2,311 | 879 | 37 | 350 R | 45.2% | 39.2% | 14.9% |
| 2,357 | GLASCOCK | 1,013 | 516 | 316 | 180 | 1 | 200 R | 50.9% | 31.2% | 17.8% |
| 62,496 | GLYNN | 22,932 | 11,242 | 8,581 | 3,053 | 56 | 2,661 R | 49.0% | 37.4% | 13.3% |
| 35,072 | GORDON | 11,213 | 5,265 | 4,103 | 1,818 | 27 | 1,162 R | 47.0% | 36.6% | 16.2% |
| 20,279 | GRADY | 6,033 | 2,370 | 2,520 | 1,126 | 17 | 150 D | 39.3% | 41.8% | 18.7% |
| 11,793 | GREENE | 4,058 | 1,307 | 2,259 | 483 | 9 | 952 D | 32.2% | 55.7% | 11.9% |
| 352,910 | GWINNETT | 150,576 | 81,822 | 44,253 | 23,926 | 575 | 37,569 R | 54.3% | 29.4% | 15.9% |
| 27,621 | HABERSHAM | 9,134 | 4,569 | 3,098 | 1,444 | 23 | 1,471 R | 50.0% | 33.9% | 15.8% |
| 95,428 | HALL | 32,433 | 16,108 | 11,214 | 5,043 | 68 | 4,894 R | 49.7% | 34.6% | 15.5% |
| 8,908 | HANCOCK | 3,157 | 506 | 2,461 | 189 | 1 | 1,955 D | 16.0% | 78.0% | 6.0% |
| 21,966 | HARALSON | 7,621 | 3,142 | 3,281 | 1,167 | 31 | 139 D | 41.2% | 43.1% | 15.3% |
| 17,788 | HARRIS | 6,960 | 3,316 | 2,679 | 954 | 11 | 637 R | 47.6% | 38.5% | 13.7% |
| 19,712 | HART | 7,609 | 2,607 | 3,614 | 1,376 | 12 | 1,007 D | 34.3% | 47.5% | 18.1% |
| 8,628 | HEARD | 3,273 | 1,190 | 1,456 | 617 | 10 | 266 D | 36.4% | 44.5% | 18.9% |
| 58,741 | HENRY | 24,284 | 12,634 | 7,817 | 3,769 | 64 | 4,817 R | 52.0% | 32.2% | 15.5% |
| 89,208 | HOUSTON | 32,748 | 14,119 | 12,270 | 6,263 | 96 | 1,849 R | 43.1% | 37.5% | 19.1% |
| 8,649 | IRWIN | 2,820 | 973 | 1,366 | 465 | 16 | 393 D | 34.5% | 48.4% | 16.5% |
| 30,005 | JACKSON | 9,165 | 3,976 | 3,792 | 1,381 | 16 | 184 R | 43.4% | 41.4% | 15.1% |
| 8,453 | JASPER | 3,023 | 1,153 | 1,485 | 373 | 12 | 332 D | 38.1% | 49.1% | 12.3% |
| 12,032 | JEFF DAVIS | 4,952 | 1,947 | 2,031 | 958 | 16 | 84 D | 39.3% | 41.0% | 19.3% |
| 17,408 | JEFFERSON | 5,989 | 2,077 | 3,220 | 685 | 7 | 1,143 D | 34.7% | 53.8% | 11.4% |
| 8,247 | JENKINS | 2,728 | 929 | 1,401 | 394 | 4 | 472 D | 34.1% | 51.4% | 14.4% |
| 8,329 | JOHNSON | 3,295 | 1,314 | 1,473 | 502 | 6 | 159 D | 39.9% | 44.7% | 15.2% |
| 20,739 | JONES | 7,279 | 2,770 | 3,338 | 1,159 | 12 | 568 D | 38.1% | 45.9% | 15.9% |
| 13,038 | LAMAR | 4,410 | 1,707 | 2,065 | 600 | 38 | 358 D | 38.7% | 46.8% | 13.6% |
| 5,531 | LANIER | 1,713 | 600 | 811 | 298 | 4 | 211 D | 35.0% | 47.3% | 17.4% |
| 39,988 | LAURENS | 14,059 | 6,146 | 6,184 | 1,602 | 127 | 38 D | 43.7% | 44.0% | 11.4% |
| 16,250 | LEE | 5,908 | 3,061 | 1,811 | 1,024 | 12 | 1,250 R | 51.8% | 30.7% | 17.3% |
| 52,745 | LIBERTY | 7,895 | 2,832 | 3,853 | 1,176 | 34 | 1,021 D | 35.9% | 48.8% | 14.9% |
| 7,442 | LINCOLN | 2,958 | 1,149 | 1,327 | 479 | 3 | 178 D | 38.8% | 44.9% | 16.2% |
| 6,202 | LONG | 1,957 | 719 | 874 | 355 | 9 | 155 D | 36.7% | 44.7% | 18.1% |
| 75,981 | LOWNDES | 22,192 | 10,276 | 9,019 | 2,864 | 33 | 1,257 R | 46.3% | 40.6% | 12.9% |
| 14,573 | LUMPKIN | 5,036 | 1,972 | 2,010 | 1,035 | 19 | 38 D | 39.2% | 39.9% | 20.6% |
| 20,119 | MCDUFFIE | 6,468 | 2,955 | 2,640 | 860 | 13 | 315 R | 45.7% | 40.8% | 13.3% |
| 8,634 | MCINTOSH | 3,517 | 1,027 | 1,925 | 550 | 15 | 898 D | 29.2% | 54.7% | 15.6% |
| 13,114 | MACON | 3,806 | 944 | 2,491 | 363 | 8 | 1,547 D | 24.8% | 65.4% | 9.5% |
| 21,050 | MADISON | 6,893 | 3,351 | 2,393 | 1,129 | 20 | 958 R | 48.6% | 34.7% | 16.4% |
| 5,590 | MARION | 2,056 | 711 | 1,145 | 198 | 2 | 434 D | 34.6% | 55.7% | 9.6% |
| 22,411 | MERIWETHER | 7,320 | 2,364 | 4,002 | 942 | 12 | 1,638 D | 32.3% | 54.7% | 12.9% |
| 6,280 | MILLER | 2,217 | 826 | 934 | 455 | 2 | 108 D | 37.3% | 42.1% | 20.5% |
| 20,275 | MITCHELL | 5,795 | 1,917 | 3,052 | 818 | 8 | 1,135 D | 33.1% | 52.7% | 14.1% |
| 17,113 | MONROE | 6,168 | 2,423 | 2,774 | 949 | 22 | 351 D | 39.3% | 45.0% | 15.4% |
| 7,163 | MONTGOMERY | 2,617 | 1,009 | 1,185 | 416 | 7 | 176 D | 38.6% | 45.3% | 15.9% |
| 12,883 | MORGAN | 4,455 | 1,797 | 2,057 | 596 | 5 | 260 D | 40.3% | 46.2% | 13.4% |
| 26,147 | MURRAY | 7,214 | 3,256 | 2,764 | 1,186 | 8 | 492 R | 45.1% | 38.3% | 16.4% |
| 179,278 | MUSCOGEE | 51,280 | 21,386 | 25,476 | 4,327 | 91 | 4,090 D | 41.7% | 49.7% | 8.4% |
| 41,808 | NEWTON | 13,659 | 5,804 | 5,811 | 1,998 | 46 | 7 D | 42.5% | 42.5% | 14.6% |
| 17,618 | OCONEE | 8,076 | 4,125 | 2,745 | 1,182 | 24 | 1,380 R | 51.1% | 34.0% | 14.6% |
| 9,763 | OGLETHORPE | 3,703 | 1,590 | 1,491 | 620 | 2 | 99 R | 42.9% | 40.3% | 16.7% |
| 41,611 | PAULDING | 15,088 | 7,180 | 5,212 | 2,654 | 42 | 1,968 R | 47.6% | 34.5% | 17.6% |
| 21,189 | PEACH | 6,973 | 2,327 | 3,677 | 947 | 22 | 1,350 D | 33.4% | 52.7% | 13.6% |
| 14,432 | PICKENS | 5,748 | 2,332 | 2,359 | 1,037 | 20 | 27 D | 40.6% | 41.0% | 18.0% |
| 13,328 | PIERCE | 4,472 | 1,899 | 1,852 | 708 | 13 | 47 R | 42.5% | 41.4% | 15.8% |
| 10,224 | PIKE | 4,104 | 1,822 | 1,651 | 623 | 8 | 171 R | 44.4% | 40.2% | 15.2% |
| 33,815 | POLK | 10,668 | 4,158 | 4,872 | 1,598 | 40 | 714 D | 39.0% | 45.7% | 15.0% |
| 8,108 | PULASKI | 3,451 | 1,075 | 1,756 | 614 | 6 | 681 D | 31.2% | 50.9% | 17.8% |
| 14,137 | PUTNAM | 4,694 | 1,756 | 2,149 | 775 | 14 | 393 D | 37.4% | 45.8% | 16.5% |
| 2,209 | QUITMAN | 922 | 284 | 523 | 113 | 2 | 239 D | 30.8% | 56.7% | 12.3% |
| 11,648 | RABUN | 4,622 | 1,902 | 1,878 | 825 | 17 | 24 R | 41.2% | 40.6% | 17.8% |
| 8,023 | RANDOLPH | 2,959 | 887 | 1,756 | 315 | 1 | 869 D | 30.0% | 59.3% | 10.6% |

# GEORGIA

## PRESIDENT 1992

| 1990 Census Population | County | Total Vote | Republican | Democratic | Perot | Other | Plurality | Percentage Total Vote | | |
|---|---|---|---|---|---|---|---|---|---|---|
| | | | | | | | | Rep. | Dem. | Perot |
| 189,719 | RICHMOND | 59,523 | 24,227 | 28,910 | 6,290 | 96 | 4,683 D | 40.7% | 48.6% | 10.6% |
| 54,091 | ROCKDALE | 22,690 | 11,945 | 7,003 | 3,664 | 78 | 4,942 R | 52.6% | 30.9% | 16.1% |
| 3,588 | SCHLEY | 1,296 | 511 | 601 | 180 | 4 | 90 D | 39.4% | 46.4% | 13.9% |
| 13,842 | SCREVEN | 4,366 | 1,705 | 1,940 | 709 | 12 | 235 D | 39.1% | 44.4% | 16.2% |
| 9,010 | SEMINOLE | 2,519 | 850 | 1,193 | 468 | 8 | 343 D | 33.7% | 47.4% | 18.6% |
| 54,457 | SPALDING | 15,734 | 7,262 | 6,392 | 2,044 | 36 | 870 R | 46.2% | 40.6% | 13.0% |
| 23,257 | STEPHENS | 8,493 | 4,047 | 2,976 | 1,448 | 22 | 1,071 R | 47.7% | 35.0% | 17.0% |
| 5,654 | STEWART | 2,909 | 1,186 | 1,540 | 175 | 8 | 354 D | 40.8% | 52.9% | 6.0% |
| 30,228 | SUMTER | 9,168 | 3,616 | 4,489 | 1,046 | 17 | 873 D | 39.4% | 49.0% | 11.4% |
| 6,524 | TALBOT | 2,682 | 671 | 1,768 | 238 | 5 | 1,097 D | 25.0% | 65.9% | 8.9% |
| 1,915 | TALIAFERRO | 1,106 | 269 | 755 | 80 | 2 | 486 D | 24.3% | 68.3% | 7.2% |
| 17,722 | TATTNALL | 5,942 | 2,566 | 2,360 | 996 | 20 | 206 R | 43.2% | 39.7% | 16.8% |
| 7,642 | TAYLOR | 2,872 | 1,078 | 1,508 | 281 | 5 | 430 D | 37.5% | 52.5% | 9.8% |
| 11,000 | TELFAIR | 4,192 | 1,324 | 2,238 | 613 | 17 | 914 D | 31.6% | 53.4% | 14.6% |
| 10,653 | TERRELL | 3,474 | 1,143 | 1,942 | 384 | 5 | 799 D | 32.9% | 55.9% | 11.1% |
| 38,986 | THOMAS | 11,948 | 5,500 | 4,841 | 1,591 | 16 | 659 R | 46.0% | 40.5% | 13.3% |
| 34,998 | TIFT | 9,569 | 4,485 | 3,930 | 1,139 | 15 | 555 R | 46.9% | 41.1% | 11.9% |
| 24,072 | TOOMBS | 7,490 | 3,609 | 2,648 | 1,210 | 23 | 961 R | 48.2% | 35.4% | 16.2% |
| 6,754 | TOWNS | 3,704 | 1,674 | 1,487 | 537 | 6 | 187 R | 45.2% | 40.1% | 14.5% |
| 5,994 | TREUTLEN | 2,344 | 898 | 1,116 | 318 | 12 | 218 D | 38.3% | 47.6% | 13.6% |
| 55,536 | TROUP | 17,039 | 8,118 | 6,412 | 2,488 | 21 | 1,706 R | 47.6% | 37.6% | 14.6% |
| 8,703 | TURNER | 3,024 | 936 | 1,669 | 370 | 49 | 733 D | 31.0% | 55.2% | 12.2% |
| 9,806 | TWIGGS | 3,392 | 853 | 2,097 | 432 | 10 | 1,244 D | 25.1% | 61.8% | 12.7% |
| 11,993 | UNION | 5,656 | 2,533 | 2,304 | 804 | 15 | 229 R | 44.8% | 40.7% | 14.2% |
| 26,300 | UPSON | 9,001 | 4,053 | 3,740 | 1,186 | 22 | 313 R | 45.0% | 41.6% | 13.2% |
| 58,340 | WALKER | 17,488 | 8,489 | 6,217 | 2,748 | 34 | 2,272 R | 48.5% | 35.6% | 15.7% |
| 38,586 | WALTON | 12,391 | 5,619 | 4,821 | 1,923 | 28 | 798 R | 45.3% | 38.9% | 15.5% |
| 35,471 | WARE | 10,424 | 4,573 | 4,573 | 1,263 | 15 | | 43.9% | 43.9% | 12.1% |
| 6,078 | WARREN | 2,175 | 751 | 1,239 | 180 | 5 | 488 D | 34.5% | 57.0% | 8.3% |
| 19,112 | WASHINGTON | 6,725 | 2,384 | 3,508 | 820 | 13 | 1,124 D | 35.4% | 52.2% | 12.2% |
| 22,356 | WAYNE | 7,552 | 3,381 | 3,052 | 1,107 | 12 | 329 R | 44.8% | 40.4% | 14.7% |
| 2,263 | WEBSTER | 911 | 208 | 600 | 103 | | 392 D | 22.8% | 65.9% | 11.3% |
| 4,903 | WHEELER | 1,699 | 601 | 880 | 214 | 4 | 279 D | 35.4% | 51.8% | 12.6% |
| 13,006 | WHITE | 5,229 | 2,477 | 1,756 | 981 | 15 | 721 R | 47.4% | 33.6% | 18.8% |
| 72,462 | WHITFIELD | 22,239 | 12,003 | 7,335 | 2,866 | 35 | 4,668 R | 54.0% | 33.0% | 12.9% |
| 7,008 | WILCOX | 2,723 | 916 | 1,365 | 433 | 9 | 449 D | 33.6% | 50.1% | 15.9% |
| 10,597 | WILKES | 3,962 | 1,535 | 1,955 | 464 | 8 | 420 D | 38.7% | 49.3% | 11.7% |
| 10,228 | WILKINSON | 4,072 | 1,232 | 2,286 | 520 | 34 | 1,054 D | 30.3% | 56.1% | 12.8% |
| 19,745 | WORTH | 5,837 | 2,344 | 2,578 | 905 | 10 | 234 D | 40.2% | 44.2% | 15.5% |
| 6,478,216 | TOTAL | 2,321,125 | 995,252 | 1,008,966 | 309,657 | 7,250 | 13,714 D | 42.9% | 43.5% | 13.3% |

# GEORGIA

## PRESIDENT 1988

| 1980 Census Population | County | Total Vote | Republican | Democratic | Other | Rep.-Dem. Plurality | Percentage Total Vote Rep. | Dem. | Major Vote Rep. | Dem. |
|---|---|---|---|---|---|---|---|---|---|---|
| 15,565 | APPLING | 4,859 | 3,000 | 1,837 | 22 | 1,163 R | 61.7% | 37.8% | 62.0% | 38.0% |
| 6,141 | ATKINSON | 2,025 | 1,126 | 887 | 12 | 239 R | 55.6% | 43.8% | 55.9% | 44.1% |
| 9,379 | BACON | 2,194 | 1,407 | 780 | 7 | 627 R | 64.1% | 35.6% | 64.3% | 35.7% |
| 3,808 | BAKER | 1,348 | 629 | 707 | 12 | 78 D | 46.7% | 52.4% | 47.1% | 52.9% |
| 34,686 | BALDWIN | 9,911 | 5,852 | 4,008 | 51 | 1,844 R | 59.0% | 40.4% | 59.4% | 40.6% |
| 8,702 | BANKS | 2,582 | 1,590 | 984 | 8 | 606 R | 61.6% | 38.1% | 61.8% | 38.2% |
| 21,354 | BARROW | 7,218 | 4,738 | 2,442 | 38 | 2,296 R | 65.6% | 33.8% | 66.0% | 34.0% |
| 40,760 | BARTOW | 13,044 | 8,039 | 4,884 | 121 | 3,155 R | 61.6% | 37.4% | 62.2% | 37.8% |
| 16,000 | BEN HILL | 3,918 | 2,005 | 1,867 | 46 | 138 R | 51.2% | 47.7% | 51.8% | 48.2% |
| 13,525 | BERRIEN | 3,420 | 2,030 | 1,381 | 9 | 649 R | 59.4% | 40.4% | 59.5% | 40.5% |
| 150,256 | BIBB | 44,396 | 22,179 | 22,084 | 133 | 95 R | 50.0% | 49.7% | 50.1% | 49.9% |
| 10,767 | BLECKLEY | 3,138 | 1,950 | 1,175 | 13 | 775 R | 62.1% | 37.4% | 62.4% | 37.6% |
| 8,701 | BRANTLEY | 3,007 | 1,539 | 1,450 | 18 | 89 R | 51.2% | 48.2% | 51.5% | 48.5% |
| 15,255 | BROOKS | 3,649 | 2,136 | 1,500 | 13 | 636 R | 58.5% | 41.1% | 58.7% | 41.3% |
| 10,175 | BRYAN | 4,235 | 2,802 | 1,423 | 10 | 1,379 R | 66.2% | 33.6% | 66.3% | 33.7% |
| 35,785 | BULLOCH | 9,794 | 6,354 | 3,417 | 23 | 2,937 R | 64.9% | 34.9% | 65.0% | 35.0% |
| 19,349 | BURKE | 5,872 | 2,988 | 2,861 | 23 | 127 R | 50.9% | 48.7% | 51.1% | 48.9% |
| 13,665 | BUTTS | 3,924 | 2,184 | 1,730 | 10 | 454 R | 55.7% | 44.1% | 55.8% | 44.2% |
| 5,717 | CALHOUN | 1,551 | 644 | 901 | 6 | 257 D | 41.5% | 58.1% | 41.7% | 58.3% |
| 13,371 | CAMDEN | 5,050 | 2,913 | 2,090 | 47 | 823 R | 57.7% | 41.4% | 58.2% | 41.8% |
| 7,518 | CANDLER | 2,144 | 1,261 | 877 | 6 | 384 R | 58.8% | 40.9% | 59.0% | 41.0% |
| 56,346 | CARROLL | 15,541 | 10,754 | 4,706 | 81 | 6,048 R | 69.2% | 30.3% | 69.6% | 30.4% |
| 36,991 | CATOOSA | 12,940 | 9,319 | 3,588 | 33 | 5,731 R | 72.0% | 27.7% | 72.2% | 27.8% |
| 7,343 | CHARLTON | 2,304 | 1,327 | 943 | 34 | 384 R | 57.6% | 40.9% | 58.5% | 41.5% |
| 202,226 | CHATHAM | 61,289 | 35,623 | 25,063 | 603 | 10,560 R | 58.1% | 40.9% | 58.7% | 41.3% |
| 21,732 | CHATTAHOOCHEE | 817 | 454 | 362 | 1 | 92 R | 55.6% | 44.3% | 55.6% | 44.4% |
| 21,856 | CHATTOOGA | 5,895 | 3,665 | 2,206 | 24 | 1,459 R | 62.2% | 37.4% | 62.4% | 37.6% |
| 51,699 | CHEROKEE | 19,088 | 14,593 | 4,378 | 117 | 10,215 R | 76.5% | 22.9% | 76.9% | 23.1% |
| 74,498 | CLARKE | 22,452 | 11,150 | 11,154 | 148 | 4 D | 49.7% | 49.7% | 50.0% | 50.0% |
| 3,553 | CLAY | 994 | 398 | 595 | 1 | 197 D | 40.0% | 59.9% | 40.1% | 59.9% |
| 150,357 | CLAYTON | 43,137 | 28,225 | 14,689 | 223 | 13,536 R | 65.4% | 34.1% | 65.8% | 34.2% |
| 6,660 | CLINCH | 1,465 | 863 | 594 | 8 | 269 R | 58.9% | 40.5% | 59.2% | 40.8% |
| 297,718 | COBB | 146,658 | 106,621 | 39,297 | 740 | 67,324 R | 72.7% | 26.8% | 73.1% | 26.9% |
| 26,894 | COFFEE | 6,822 | 4,019 | 2,777 | 26 | 1,242 R | 58.9% | 40.7% | 59.1% | 40.9% |
| 35,376 | COLQUITT | 8,691 | 5,653 | 2,998 | 40 | 2,655 R | 65.0% | 34.5% | 65.3% | 34.7% |
| 40,118 | COLUMBIA | 21,094 | 16,401 | 4,617 | 76 | 11,784 R | 77.8% | 21.9% | 78.0% | 22.0% |
| 13,490 | COOK | 2,792 | 1,555 | 1,226 | 11 | 329 R | 55.7% | 43.9% | 55.9% | 44.1% |
| 39,268 | COWETA | 13,929 | 9,668 | 4,212 | 49 | 5,456 R | 69.4% | 30.2% | 69.7% | 30.3% |
| 7,684 | CRAWFORD | 2,597 | 1,235 | 1,340 | 22 | 105 D | 47.6% | 51.6% | 48.0% | 52.0% |
| 19,489 | CRISP | 4,633 | 2,916 | 1,690 | 27 | 1,226 R | 62.9% | 36.5% | 63.3% | 36.7% |
| 12,318 | DADE | 3,671 | 2,539 | 1,120 | 12 | 1,419 R | 69.2% | 30.5% | 69.4% | 30.6% |
| 4,774 | DAWSON | 2,686 | 1,908 | 761 | 17 | 1,147 R | 71.0% | 28.3% | 71.5% | 28.5% |
| 25,495 | DECATUR | 6,241 | 3,866 | 2,348 | 27 | 1,518 R | 61.9% | 37.6% | 62.2% | 37.8% |
| 483,024 | DE KALB | 184,250 | 90,179 | 92,521 | 1,550 | 2,342 D | 48.9% | 50.2% | 49.4% | 50.6% |
| 16,955 | DODGE | 4,872 | 2,677 | 2,164 | 31 | 513 R | 54.9% | 44.4% | 55.3% | 44.7% |
| 10,826 | DOOLY | 3,021 | 1,386 | 1,613 | 22 | 227 D | 45.9% | 53.4% | 46.2% | 53.8% |
| 100,718 | DOUGHERTY | 30,517 | 15,520 | 12,579 | 2,418 | 2,941 R | 50.9% | 41.2% | 55.2% | 44.8% |
| 54,573 | DOUGLAS | 18,678 | 13,493 | 5,086 | 99 | 8,407 R | 72.2% | 27.2% | 72.6% | 27.4% |
| 13,158 | EARLY | 3,281 | 1,918 | 1,359 | 4 | 559 R | 58.5% | 41.4% | 58.5% | 41.5% |
| 2,297 | ECHOLS | 670 | 422 | 245 | 3 | 177 R | 63.0% | 36.6% | 63.3% | 36.7% |
| 18,327 | EFFINGHAM | 5,859 | 3,933 | 1,905 | 21 | 2,028 R | 67.1% | 32.5% | 67.4% | 32.6% |
| 18,758 | ELBERT | 4,925 | 2,796 | 2,118 | 11 | 678 R | 56.8% | 43.0% | 56.9% | 43.1% |
| 20,795 | EMANUEL | 5,988 | 3,530 | 2,387 | 71 | 1,143 R | 59.0% | 39.9% | 59.7% | 40.3% |
| 8,428 | EVANS | 2,753 | 1,707 | 1,023 | 23 | 684 R | 62.0% | 37.2% | 62.5% | 37.5% |
| 14,748 | FANNIN | 6,427 | 4,271 | 2,123 | 33 | 2,148 R | 66.5% | 33.0% | 66.8% | 33.2% |
| 29,043 | FAYETTE | 21,123 | 16,443 | 4,593 | 87 | 11,850 R | 77.8% | 21.7% | 78.2% | 21.8% |
| 79,800 | FLOYD | 23,386 | 14,697 | 8,548 | 141 | 6,149 R | 62.8% | 36.6% | 63.2% | 36.8% |
| 27,958 | FORSYTH | 10,344 | 7,947 | 2,347 | 50 | 5,600 R | 76.8% | 22.7% | 77.2% | 22.8% |
| 15,185 | FRANKLIN | 4,465 | 2,615 | 1,842 | 8 | 773 R | 58.6% | 41.3% | 58.7% | 41.3% |
| 589,904 | FULTON | 214,689 | 91,785 | 120,752 | 2,152 | 28,967 D | 42.8% | 56.2% | 43.2% | 56.8% |

# GEORGIA

## PRESIDENT 1988

| 1980 Census Population | County | Total Vote | Republican | Democratic | Other | Rep.-Dem. Plurality | Percentage | | | |
|---|---|---|---|---|---|---|---|---|---|---|
| | | | | | | | Total Vote | | Major Vote | |
| | | | | | | | Rep. | Dem. | Rep. | Dem. |
| 11,110 | GILMER | 4,746 | 3,353 | 1,363 | 30 | 1,990 R | 70.6% | 28.7% | 71.1% | 28.9% |
| 2,382 | GLASCOCK | 790 | 580 | 210 | | 370 R | 73.4% | 26.6% | 73.4% | 26.6% |
| 54,981 | GLYNN | 17,611 | 11,126 | 6,339 | 146 | 4,787 R | 63.2% | 36.0% | 63.7% | 36.3% |
| 30,070 | GORDON | 8,445 | 6,051 | 2,369 | 25 | 3,682 R | 71.7% | 28.1% | 71.9% | 28.1% |
| 19,845 | GRADY | 4,892 | 2,989 | 1,883 | 20 | 1,106 R | 61.1% | 38.5% | 61.4% | 38.6% |
| 11,391 | GREENE | 3,260 | 1,432 | 1,818 | 10 | 386 D | 43.9% | 55.8% | 44.1% | 55.9% |
| 166,903 | GWINNETT | 87,940 | 66,372 | 20,948 | 620 | 45,424 R | 75.5% | 23.8% | 76.0% | 24.0% |
| 25,020 | HABERSHAM | 7,014 | 4,871 | 2,114 | 29 | 2,757 R | 69.4% | 30.1% | 69.7% | 30.3% |
| 75,649 | HALL | 25,344 | 17,415 | 7,782 | 147 | 9,633 R | 68.7% | 30.7% | 69.1% | 30.9% |
| 9,466 | HANCOCK | 2,589 | 621 | 1,947 | 21 | 1,326 D | 24.0% | 75.2% | 24.2% | 75.8% |
| 18,422 | HARALSON | 6,950 | 4,529 | 2,404 | 17 | 2,125 R | 65.2% | 34.6% | 65.3% | 34.7% |
| 15,464 | HARRIS | 5,339 | 3,414 | 1,905 | 20 | 1,509 R | 63.9% | 35.7% | 64.2% | 35.8% |
| 18,585 | HART | 5,547 | 3,044 | 2,476 | 27 | 568 R | 54.9% | 44.6% | 55.1% | 44.9% |
| 6,520 | HEARD | 2,432 | 1,551 | 874 | 7 | 677 R | 63.8% | 35.9% | 64.0% | 36.0% |
| 36,309 | HENRY | 15,304 | 10,882 | 4,348 | 74 | 6,534 R | 71.1% | 28.4% | 71.5% | 28.5% |
| 77,605 | HOUSTON | 24,597 | 15,748 | 8,664 | 185 | 7,084 R | 64.0% | 35.2% | 64.5% | 35.5% |
| 8,988 | IRWIN | 2,151 | 1,226 | 918 | 7 | 308 R | 57.0% | 42.7% | 57.2% | 42.8% |
| 25,343 | JACKSON | 7,045 | 4,407 | 2,607 | 31 | 1,800 R | 62.6% | 37.0% | 62.8% | 37.2% |
| 7,553 | JASPER | 2,676 | 1,474 | 1,188 | 14 | 286 R | 55.1% | 44.4% | 55.4% | 44.6% |
| 11,473 | JEFF DAVIS | 3,305 | 2,050 | 1,242 | 13 | 808 R | 62.0% | 37.6% | 62.3% | 37.7% |
| 18,403 | JEFFERSON | 5,151 | 2,788 | 2,346 | 17 | 442 R | 54.1% | 45.5% | 54.3% | 45.7% |
| 8,841 | JENKINS | 2,248 | 1,288 | 953 | 7 | 335 R | 57.3% | 42.4% | 57.5% | 42.5% |
| 8,660 | JOHNSON | 2,494 | 1,567 | 927 | | 640 R | 62.8% | 37.2% | 62.8% | 37.2% |
| 16,579 | JONES | 6,302 | 3,618 | 2,662 | 22 | 956 R | 57.4% | 42.2% | 57.6% | 42.4% |
| 12,215 | LAMAR | 3,519 | 2,035 | 1,416 | 68 | 619 R | 57.8% | 40.2% | 59.0% | 41.0% |
| 5,654 | LANIER | 1,427 | 725 | 698 | 4 | 27 R | 50.8% | 48.9% | 50.9% | 49.1% |
| 36,990 | LAURENS | 11,970 | 6,929 | 4,879 | 162 | 2,050 R | 57.9% | 40.8% | 58.7% | 41.3% |
| 11,684 | LEE | 3,883 | 2,875 | 995 | 13 | 1,880 R | 74.0% | 25.6% | 74.3% | 25.7% |
| 37,583 | LIBERTY | 6,050 | 3,100 | 2,906 | 44 | 194 R | 51.2% | 48.0% | 51.6% | 48.4% |
| 6,716 | LINCOLN | 2,324 | 1,417 | 893 | 14 | 524 R | 61.0% | 38.4% | 61.3% | 38.7% |
| 4,524 | LONG | 1,551 | 858 | 681 | 12 | 177 R | 55.3% | 43.9% | 55.8% | 44.2% |
| 67,972 | LOWNDES | 17,333 | 10,855 | 6,427 | 51 | 4,428 R | 62.6% | 37.1% | 62.8% | 37.2% |
| 10,762 | LUMPKIN | 4,000 | 2,688 | 1,286 | 26 | 1,402 R | 67.2% | 32.2% | 67.6% | 32.4% |
| 18,546 | MCDUFFIE | 4,968 | 3,231 | 1,704 | 33 | 1,527 R | 65.0% | 34.3% | 65.5% | 34.5% |
| 8,046 | MCINTOSH | 2,824 | 1,273 | 1,527 | 24 | 254 D | 45.1% | 54.1% | 45.5% | 54.5% |
| 14,003 | MACON | 3,697 | 1,412 | 2,268 | 17 | 856 D | 38.2% | 61.3% | 38.4% | 61.6% |
| 17,747 | MADISON | 5,389 | 3,724 | 1,639 | 26 | 2,085 R | 69.1% | 30.4% | 69.4% | 30.6% |
| 5,297 | MARION | 1,652 | 804 | 844 | 4 | 40 D | 48.7% | 51.1% | 48.8% | 51.2% |
| 21,229 | MERIWETHER | 6,044 | 3,101 | 2,934 | 9 | 167 R | 51.3% | 48.5% | 51.4% | 48.6% |
| 7,038 | MILLER | 1,625 | 1,105 | 515 | 5 | 590 R | 68.0% | 31.7% | 68.2% | 31.8% |
| 21,114 | MITCHELL | 4,860 | 2,590 | 2,260 | 10 | 330 R | 53.3% | 46.5% | 53.4% | 46.6% |
| 14,610 | MONROE | 4,558 | 2,570 | 1,970 | 18 | 600 R | 56.4% | 43.2% | 56.6% | 43.4% |
| 7,011 | MONTGOMERY | 2,136 | 1,228 | 903 | 5 | 325 R | 57.5% | 42.3% | 57.6% | 42.4% |
| 11,572 | MORGAN | 3,628 | 2,108 | 1,508 | 12 | 600 R | 58.1% | 41.6% | 58.3% | 41.7% |
| 19,685 | MURRAY | 5,700 | 3,996 | 1,679 | 25 | 2,317 R | 70.1% | 29.5% | 70.4% | 29.6% |
| 170,108 | MUSCOGEE | 42,000 | 23,058 | 18,772 | 170 | 4,286 R | 54.9% | 44.7% | 55.1% | 44.9% |
| 34,489 | NEWTON | 8,969 | 5,809 | 3,111 | 49 | 2,698 R | 64.8% | 34.7% | 65.1% | 34.9% |
| 12,427 | OCONEE | 6,282 | 4,265 | 1,990 | 27 | 2,275 R | 67.9% | 31.7% | 68.2% | 31.8% |
| 8,929 | OGLETHORPE | 3,116 | 1,951 | 1,154 | 11 | 797 R | 62.6% | 37.0% | 62.8% | 37.2% |
| 26,110 | PAULDING | 10,091 | 7,329 | 2,717 | 45 | 4,612 R | 72.6% | 26.9% | 73.0% | 27.0% |
| 19,151 | PEACH | 5,796 | 2,782 | 2,972 | 42 | 190 D | 48.0% | 51.3% | 48.3% | 51.7% |
| 11,652 | PICKENS | 4,474 | 3,021 | 1,430 | 23 | 1,591 R | 67.5% | 32.0% | 67.9% | 32.1% |
| 11,897 | PIERCE | 3,509 | 1,947 | 1,558 | 4 | 389 R | 55.5% | 44.4% | 55.5% | 44.5% |
| 8,937 | PIKE | 3,274 | 2,074 | 1,176 | 24 | 898 R | 63.3% | 35.9% | 63.8% | 36.2% |
| 32,386 | POLK | 8,461 | 5,454 | 2,977 | 30 | 2,477 R | 64.5% | 35.2% | 64.7% | 35.3% |
| 8,950 | PULASKI | 2,888 | 1,400 | 1,476 | 12 | 76 D | 48.5% | 51.1% | 48.7% | 51.3% |
| 10,295 | PUTNAM | 3,656 | 2,111 | 1,532 | 13 | 579 R | 57.7% | 41.9% | 57.9% | 42.1% |
| 2,357 | QUITMAN | 738 | 296 | 436 | 6 | 140 D | 40.1% | 59.1% | 40.4% | 59.6% |
| 10,466 | RABUN | 3,608 | 2,278 | 1,301 | 29 | 977 R | 63.1% | 36.1% | 63.6% | 36.4% |
| 9,599 | RANDOLPH | 2,695 | 1,319 | 1,369 | 7 | 50 D | 48.9% | 50.8% | 49.1% | 50.9% |

# GEORGIA

## PRESIDENT 1988

| 1980 Census Population | County | Total Vote | Republican | Democratic | Other | Rep.-Dem. Plurality | Percentage Total Vote Rep. | Dem. | Major Vote Rep. | Dem. |
|---|---|---|---|---|---|---|---|---|---|---|
| 181,629 | RICHMOND | 48,258 | 27,566 | 20,489 | 203 | 7,077 R | 57.1% | 42.5% | 57.4% | 42.6% |
| 36,747 | ROCKDALE | 16,826 | 12,413 | 4,330 | 83 | 8,083 R | 73.8% | 25.7% | 74.1% | 25.9% |
| 3,433 | SCHLEY | 1,078 | 635 | 439 | 4 | 196 R | 58.9% | 40.7% | 59.1% | 40.9% |
| 14,043 | SCREVEN | 3,659 | 2,178 | 1,461 | 20 | 717 R | 59.5% | 39.9% | 59.9% | 40.1% |
| 9,057 | SEMINOLE | 2,645 | 1,469 | 1,171 | 5 | 298 R | 55.5% | 44.3% | 55.6% | 44.4% |
| 47,899 | SPALDING | 12,138 | 7,730 | 4,318 | 90 | 3,412 R | 63.7% | 35.6% | 64.2% | 35.8% |
| 21,763 | STEPHENS | 6,550 | 4,329 | 2,185 | 36 | 2,144 R | 66.1% | 33.4% | 66.5% | 33.5% |
| 5,896 | STEWART | 1,973 | 832 | 1,136 | 5 | 304 D | 42.2% | 57.6% | 42.3% | 57.7% |
| 29,360 | SUMTER | 7,668 | 4,289 | 3,332 | 47 | 957 R | 55.9% | 43.5% | 56.3% | 43.7% |
| 6,536 | TALBOT | 2,060 | 802 | 1,248 | 10 | 446 D | 38.9% | 60.6% | 39.1% | 60.9% |
| 2,032 | TALIAFERRO | 777 | 306 | 469 | 2 | 163 D | 39.4% | 60.4% | 39.5% | 60.5% |
| 18,134 | TATTNALL | 4,878 | 3,172 | 1,694 | 12 | 1,478 R | 65.0% | 34.7% | 65.2% | 34.8% |
| 7,902 | TAYLOR | 2,284 | 1,145 | 1,134 | 5 | 11 R | 50.1% | 49.6% | 50.2% | 49.8% |
| 11,445 | TELFAIR | 3,595 | 1,805 | 1,765 | 25 | 40 R | 50.2% | 49.1% | 50.6% | 49.4% |
| 12,017 | TERRELL | 2,905 | 1,517 | 1,383 | 5 | 134 R | 52.2% | 47.6% | 52.3% | 47.7% |
| 38,098 | THOMAS | 10,145 | 6,572 | 3,530 | 43 | 3,042 R | 64.8% | 34.8% | 65.1% | 34.9% |
| 32,862 | TIFT | 7,234 | 4,760 | 2,446 | 28 | 2,314 R | 65.8% | 33.8% | 66.1% | 33.9% |
| 22,592 | TOOMBS | 5,619 | 4,433 | 1,152 | 34 | 3,281 R | 78.9% | 20.5% | 79.4% | 20.6% |
| 5,638 | TOWNS | 2,738 | 1,783 | 942 | 13 | 841 R | 65.1% | 34.4% | 65.4% | 34.6% |
| 6,087 | TREUTLEN | 1,696 | 970 | 726 | | 244 R | 57.2% | 42.8% | 57.2% | 42.8% |
| 50,003 | TROUP | 14,089 | 9,484 | 4,562 | 43 | 4,922 R | 67.3% | 32.4% | 67.5% | 32.5% |
| 9,510 | TURNER | 2,597 | 1,312 | 1,122 | 163 | 190 R | 50.5% | 43.2% | 53.9% | 46.1% |
| 9,354 | TWIGGS | 3,005 | 1,261 | 1,730 | 14 | 469 D | 42.0% | 57.6% | 42.2% | 57.8% |
| 9,390 | UNION | 3,664 | 2,396 | 1,258 | 10 | 1,138 R | 65.4% | 34.3% | 65.6% | 34.4% |
| 25,998 | UPSON | 7,318 | 4,614 | 2,666 | 38 | 1,948 R | 63.1% | 36.4% | 63.4% | 36.6% |
| 56,470 | WALKER | 15,280 | 10,487 | 4,753 | 40 | 5,734 R | 68.6% | 31.1% | 68.8% | 31.2% |
| 31,211 | WALTON | 9,112 | 5,974 | 3,091 | 47 | 2,883 R | 65.6% | 33.9% | 65.9% | 34.1% |
| 37,180 | WARE | 9,163 | 4,819 | 4,292 | 52 | 527 R | 52.6% | 46.8% | 52.9% | 47.1% |
| 6,583 | WARREN | 2,003 | 897 | 1,091 | 15 | 194 D | 44.8% | 54.5% | 45.1% | 54.9% |
| 18,842 | WASHINGTON | 5,383 | 2,752 | 2,615 | 16 | 137 R | 51.1% | 48.6% | 51.3% | 48.7% |
| 20,750 | WAYNE | 5,766 | 3,340 | 2,417 | 9 | 923 R | 57.9% | 41.9% | 58.0% | 42.0% |
| 2,341 | WEBSTER | 790 | 361 | 427 | 2 | 66 D | 45.7% | 54.1% | 45.8% | 54.2% |
| 5,155 | WHEELER | 1,373 | 709 | 658 | 6 | 51 R | 51.6% | 47.9% | 51.9% | 48.1% |
| 10,120 | WHITE | 3,696 | 2,648 | 1,028 | 20 | 1,620 R | 71.6% | 27.8% | 72.0% | 28.0% |
| 65,789 | WHITFIELD | 17,451 | 12,761 | 4,618 | 72 | 8,143 R | 73.1% | 26.5% | 73.4% | 26.6% |
| 7,682 | WILCOX | 2,319 | 1,235 | 1,079 | 5 | 156 R | 53.3% | 46.5% | 53.4% | 46.6% |
| 10,951 | WILKES | 3,370 | 1,810 | 1,549 | 11 | 261 R | 53.7% | 46.0% | 53.9% | 46.1% |
| 10,368 | WILKINSON | 3,413 | 1,546 | 1,831 | 36 | 285 D | 45.3% | 53.6% | 45.8% | 54.2% |
| 18,064 | WORTH | 4,009 | 2,668 | 1,311 | 30 | 1,357 R | 66.6% | 32.7% | 67.1% | 32.9% |
| 5,463,105 | TOTAL | 1,809,672 | 1,081,331 | 714,792 | 13,549 | 366,539 R | 59.8% | 39.5% | 60.2% | 39.8% |

# GEORGIA

## PRESIDENT 1984

| 1980 Census Population | County | Total Vote | Republican | Democratic | Other | Rep.-Dem. Plurality | | Percentage | | | |
|---|---|---|---|---|---|---|---|---|---|---|---|
| | | | | | | | | Total Vote | | Major Vote | |
| | | | | | | | | Rep. | Dem. | Rep. | Dem. |
| 15,565 | APPLING | 4,887 | 2,929 | 1,958 | | 971 | R | 59.9% | 40.1% | 59.9% | 40.1% |
| 6,141 | ATKINSON | 1,845 | 944 | 901 | | 43 | R | 51.2% | 48.8% | 51.2% | 48.8% |
| 9,379 | BACON | 2,788 | 1,778 | 1,010 | | 768 | R | 63.8% | 36.2% | 63.8% | 36.2% |
| 3,808 | BAKER | 1,366 | 675 | 691 | | 16 | D | 49.4% | 50.6% | 49.4% | 50.6% |
| 34,686 | BALDWIN | 9,570 | 5,717 | 3,853 | | 1,864 | R | 59.7% | 40.3% | 59.7% | 40.3% |
| 8,702 | BANKS | 2,612 | 1,549 | 1,063 | | 486 | R | 59.3% | 40.7% | 59.3% | 40.7% |
| 21,354 | BARROW | 6,490 | 4,123 | 2,367 | | 1,756 | R | 63.5% | 36.5% | 63.5% | 36.5% |
| 40,760 | BARTOW | 11,884 | 7,104 | 4,780 | | 2,324 | R | 59.8% | 40.2% | 59.8% | 40.2% |
| 16,000 | BEN HILL | 4,172 | 2,313 | 1,859 | | 454 | R | 55.4% | 44.6% | 55.4% | 44.6% |
| 13,525 | BERRIEN | 4,065 | 2,395 | 1,670 | | 725 | R | 58.9% | 41.1% | 58.9% | 41.1% |
| 150,256 | BIBB | 50,597 | 24,170 | 26,427 | | 2,257 | D | 47.8% | 52.2% | 47.8% | 52.2% |
| 10,767 | BLECKLEY | 3,377 | 1,912 | 1,465 | | 447 | R | 56.6% | 43.4% | 56.6% | 43.4% |
| 8,701 | BRANTLEY | 3,196 | 1,679 | 1,517 | | 162 | R | 52.5% | 47.5% | 52.5% | 47.5% |
| 15,255 | BROOKS | 3,890 | 2,229 | 1,661 | | 568 | R | 57.3% | 42.7% | 57.3% | 42.7% |
| 10,175 | BRYAN | 3,663 | 2,265 | 1,398 | | 867 | R | 61.8% | 38.2% | 61.8% | 38.2% |
| 35,785 | BULLOCH | 9,761 | 6,117 | 3,644 | | 2,473 | R | 62.7% | 37.3% | 62.7% | 37.3% |
| 19,349 | BURKE | 6,264 | 3,137 | 3,127 | | 10 | R | 50.1% | 49.9% | 50.1% | 49.9% |
| 13,665 | BUTTS | 3,961 | 2,141 | 1,820 | | 321 | R | 54.1% | 45.9% | 54.1% | 45.9% |
| 5,717 | CALHOUN | 1,853 | 776 | 1,077 | | 301 | D | 41.9% | 58.1% | 41.9% | 58.1% |
| 13,371 | CAMDEN | 5,005 | 2,841 | 2,164 | | 677 | R | 56.8% | 43.2% | 56.8% | 43.2% |
| 7,518 | CANDLER | 2,511 | 1,497 | 1,014 | | 483 | R | 59.6% | 40.4% | 59.6% | 40.4% |
| 56,346 | CARROLL | 17,026 | 11,436 | 5,590 | | 5,846 | R | 67.2% | 32.8% | 67.2% | 32.8% |
| 36,991 | CATOOSA | 10,997 | 7,908 | 3,089 | | 4,819 | R | 71.9% | 28.1% | 71.9% | 28.1% |
| 7,343 | CHARLTON | 2,479 | 1,368 | 1,111 | | 257 | R | 55.2% | 44.8% | 55.2% | 44.8% |
| 202,226 | CHATHAM | 66,753 | 38,482 | 28,271 | | 10,211 | R | 57.6% | 42.4% | 57.6% | 42.4% |
| 21,732 | CHATTAHOOCHEE | 887 | 459 | 428 | | 31 | R | 51.7% | 48.3% | 51.7% | 48.3% |
| 21,856 | CHATTOOGA | 5,529 | 2,953 | 2,576 | | 377 | R | 53.4% | 46.6% | 53.4% | 46.6% |
| 51,699 | CHEROKEE | 14,645 | 11,146 | 3,499 | | 7,647 | R | 76.1% | 23.9% | 76.1% | 23.9% |
| 74,498 | CLARKE | 21,635 | 11,503 | 10,132 | | 1,371 | R | 53.2% | 46.8% | 53.2% | 46.8% |
| 3,553 | CLAY | 1,169 | 419 | 750 | | 331 | D | 35.8% | 64.2% | 35.8% | 64.2% |
| 150,357 | CLAYTON | 43,316 | 31,553 | 11,763 | | 19,790 | R | 72.8% | 27.2% | 72.8% | 27.2% |
| 6,660 | CLINCH | 1,487 | 862 | 625 | | 237 | R | 58.0% | 42.0% | 58.0% | 42.0% |
| 297,718 | COBB | 125,843 | 97,429 | 28,414 | | 69,015 | R | 77.4% | 22.6% | 77.4% | 22.6% |
| 26,894 | COFFEE | 6,833 | 4,200 | 2,633 | | 1,567 | R | 61.5% | 38.5% | 61.5% | 38.5% |
| 35,376 | COLQUITT | 9,023 | 5,815 | 3,208 | | 2,607 | R | 64.4% | 35.6% | 64.4% | 35.6% |
| 40,118 | COLUMBIA | 16,021 | 12,294 | 3,727 | | 8,567 | R | 76.7% | 23.3% | 76.7% | 23.3% |
| 13,490 | COOK | 3,370 | 1,860 | 1,510 | | 350 | R | 55.2% | 44.8% | 55.2% | 44.8% |
| 39,268 | COWETA | 11,631 | 7,981 | 3,650 | | 4,331 | R | 68.6% | 31.4% | 68.6% | 31.4% |
| 7,684 | CRAWFORD | 2,721 | 1,298 | 1,423 | | 125 | D | 47.7% | 52.3% | 47.7% | 52.3% |
| 19,489 | CRISP | 5,023 | 2,895 | 2,128 | | 767 | R | 57.6% | 42.4% | 57.6% | 42.4% |
| 12,318 | DADE | 3,900 | 2,750 | 1,150 | | 1,600 | R | 70.5% | 29.5% | 70.5% | 29.5% |
| 4,774 | DAWSON | 1,965 | 1,322 | 643 | | 679 | R | 67.3% | 32.7% | 67.3% | 32.7% |
| 25,495 | DECATUR | 6,790 | 4,134 | 2,656 | | 1,478 | R | 60.9% | 39.1% | 60.9% | 39.1% |
| 483,024 | DE KALB | 182,026 | 104,697 | 77,329 | | 27,368 | R | 57.5% | 42.5% | 57.5% | 42.5% |
| 16,955 | DODGE | 5,278 | 2,765 | 2,513 | | 252 | R | 52.4% | 47.6% | 52.4% | 47.6% |
| 10,826 | DOOLY | 3,161 | 1,435 | 1,726 | | 291 | D | 45.4% | 54.6% | 45.4% | 54.6% |
| 100,718 | DOUGHERTY | 29,824 | 16,920 | 12,904 | | 4,016 | R | 56.7% | 43.3% | 56.7% | 43.3% |
| 54,573 | DOUGLAS | 16,799 | 12,428 | 4,371 | | 8,057 | R | 74.0% | 26.0% | 74.0% | 26.0% |
| 13,158 | EARLY | 3,733 | 2,239 | 1,494 | | 745 | R | 60.0% | 40.0% | 60.0% | 40.0% |
| 2,297 | ECHOLS | 680 | 453 | 227 | | 226 | R | 66.6% | 33.4% | 66.6% | 33.4% |
| 18,327 | EFFINGHAM | 6,321 | 4,266 | 2,055 | | 2,211 | R | 67.5% | 32.5% | 67.5% | 32.5% |
| 18,758 | ELBERT | 6,036 | 3,366 | 2,670 | | 696 | R | 55.8% | 44.2% | 55.8% | 44.2% |
| 20,795 | EMANUEL | 6,378 | 3,920 | 2,458 | | 1,462 | R | 61.5% | 38.5% | 61.5% | 38.5% |
| 8,428 | EVANS | 2,794 | 1,601 | 1,193 | | 408 | R | 57.3% | 42.7% | 57.3% | 42.7% |
| 14,748 | FANNIN | 6,124 | 4,159 | 1,965 | | 2,194 | R | 67.9% | 32.1% | 67.9% | 32.1% |
| 29,043 | FAYETTE | 15,436 | 12,575 | 2,861 | | 9,714 | R | 81.5% | 18.5% | 81.5% | 18.5% |
| 79,800 | FLOYD | 24,310 | 15,437 | 8,873 | | 6,564 | R | 63.5% | 36.5% | 63.5% | 36.5% |
| 27,958 | FORSYTH | 9,116 | 6,841 | 2,275 | | 4,566 | R | 75.0% | 25.0% | 75.0% | 25.0% |
| 15,185 | FRANKLIN | 4,387 | 2,549 | 1,838 | | 711 | R | 58.1% | 41.9% | 58.1% | 41.9% |
| 589,904 | FULTON | 220,716 | 95,149 | 125,567 | | 30,418 | D | 43.1% | 56.9% | 43.1% | 56.9% |

# GEORGIA

## PRESIDENT 1984

| 1980 Census Population | County | Total Vote | Republican | Democratic | Other | Rep.-Dem. Plurality | | Percentage | | | |
|---|---|---|---|---|---|---|---|---|---|---|---|
| | | | | | | | | Total Vote | | Major Vote | |
| | | | | | | | | Rep. | Dem. | Rep. | Dem. |
| 11,110 | GILMER | 4,206 | 2,972 | 1,234 | | 1,738 | R | 70.7% | 29.3% | 70.7% | 29.3% |
| 2,382 | GLASCOCK | 1,144 | 827 | 317 | | 510 | R | 72.3% | 27.7% | 72.3% | 27.7% |
| 54,981 | GLYNN | 18,298 | 11,724 | 6,574 | | 5,150 | R | 64.1% | 35.9% | 64.1% | 35.9% |
| 30,070 | GORDON | 8,173 | 5,566 | 2,607 | | 2,959 | R | 68.1% | 31.9% | 68.1% | 31.9% |
| 19,845 | GRADY | 6,147 | 3,886 | 2,261 | | 1,625 | R | 63.2% | 36.8% | 63.2% | 36.8% |
| 11,391 | GREENE | 3,591 | 1,599 | 1,992 | | 393 | D | 44.5% | 55.5% | 44.5% | 55.5% |
| 166,903 | GWINNETT | 68,888 | 54,749 | 14,139 | | 40,610 | R | 79.5% | 20.5% | 79.5% | 20.5% |
| 25,020 | HABERSHAM | 6,772 | 4,647 | 2,125 | | 2,522 | R | 68.6% | 31.4% | 68.6% | 31.4% |
| 75,649 | HALL | 22,497 | 15,076 | 7,421 | | 7,655 | R | 67.0% | 33.0% | 67.0% | 33.0% |
| 9,466 | HANCOCK | 2,753 | 644 | 2,109 | | 1,465 | D | 23.4% | 76.6% | 23.4% | 76.6% |
| 18,422 | HARALSON | 5,883 | 3,945 | 1,938 | | 2,007 | R | 67.1% | 32.9% | 67.1% | 32.9% |
| 15,464 | HARRIS | 5,234 | 3,138 | 2,096 | | 1,042 | R | 60.0% | 40.0% | 60.0% | 40.0% |
| 18,585 | HART | 5,338 | 2,842 | 2,496 | | 346 | R | 53.2% | 46.8% | 53.2% | 46.8% |
| 6,520 | HEARD | 2,302 | 1,492 | 810 | | 682 | R | 64.8% | 35.2% | 64.8% | 35.2% |
| 36,309 | HENRY | 13,238 | 9,142 | 4,096 | | 5,046 | R | 69.1% | 30.9% | 69.1% | 30.9% |
| 77,605 | HOUSTON | 23,481 | 14,255 | 9,226 | | 5,029 | R | 60.7% | 39.3% | 60.7% | 39.3% |
| 8,988 | IRWIN | 2,235 | 1,330 | 905 | | 425 | R | 59.5% | 40.5% | 59.5% | 40.5% |
| 25,343 | JACKSON | 6,919 | 4,202 | 2,717 | | 1,485 | R | 60.7% | 39.3% | 60.7% | 39.3% |
| 7,553 | JASPER | 2,553 | 1,431 | 1,122 | | 309 | R | 56.1% | 43.9% | 56.1% | 43.9% |
| 11,473 | JEFF DAVIS | 3,613 | 2,233 | 1,380 | | 853 | R | 61.8% | 38.2% | 61.8% | 38.2% |
| 18,403 | JEFFERSON | 5,815 | 2,999 | 2,816 | | 183 | R | 51.6% | 48.4% | 51.6% | 48.4% |
| 8,841 | JENKINS | 2,507 | 1,399 | 1,108 | | 291 | R | 55.8% | 44.2% | 55.8% | 44.2% |
| 8,660 | JOHNSON | 2,932 | 1,733 | 1,199 | | 534 | R | 59.1% | 40.9% | 59.1% | 40.9% |
| 16,579 | JONES | 6,182 | 3,401 | 2,781 | | 620 | R | 55.0% | 45.0% | 55.0% | 45.0% |
| 12,215 | LAMAR | 3,803 | 2,198 | 1,605 | | 593 | R | 57.8% | 42.2% | 57.8% | 42.2% |
| 5,654 | LANIER | 1,593 | 852 | 741 | | 111 | R | 53.5% | 46.5% | 53.5% | 46.5% |
| 36,990 | LAURENS | 12,652 | 7,181 | 5,471 | | 1,710 | R | 56.8% | 43.2% | 56.8% | 43.2% |
| 11,684 | LEE | 4,256 | 2,972 | 1,284 | | 1,688 | R | 69.8% | 30.2% | 69.8% | 30.2% |
| 37,583 | LIBERTY | 6,032 | 3,229 | 2,803 | | 426 | R | 53.5% | 46.5% | 53.5% | 46.5% |
| 6,716 | LINCOLN | 2,472 | 1,357 | 1,115 | | 242 | R | 54.9% | 45.1% | 54.9% | 45.1% |
| 4,524 | LONG | 1,915 | 1,099 | 816 | | 283 | R | 57.4% | 42.6% | 57.4% | 42.6% |
| 67,972 | LOWNDES | 16,604 | 10,437 | 6,167 | | 4,270 | R | 62.9% | 37.1% | 62.9% | 37.1% |
| 10,762 | LUMPKIN | 3,101 | 1,991 | 1,110 | | 881 | R | 64.2% | 35.8% | 64.2% | 35.8% |
| 18,546 | MCDUFFIE | 5,290 | 3,284 | 2,006 | | 1,278 | R | 62.1% | 37.9% | 62.1% | 37.9% |
| 8,046 | MCINTOSH | 3,308 | 1,512 | 1,796 | | 284 | D | 45.7% | 54.3% | 45.7% | 54.3% |
| 14,003 | MACON | 4,036 | 1,515 | 2,521 | | 1,006 | D | 37.5% | 62.5% | 37.5% | 62.5% |
| 17,747 | MADISON | 5,458 | 3,768 | 1,690 | | 2,078 | R | 69.0% | 31.0% | 69.0% | 31.0% |
| 5,297 | MARION | 1,797 | 846 | 951 | | 105 | D | 47.1% | 52.9% | 47.1% | 52.9% |
| 21,229 | MERIWETHER | 6,059 | 3,195 | 2,864 | | 331 | R | 52.7% | 47.3% | 52.7% | 47.3% |
| 7,038 | MILLER | 1,874 | 1,348 | 526 | | 822 | R | 71.9% | 28.1% | 71.9% | 28.1% |
| 21,114 | MITCHELL | 5,528 | 2,737 | 2,791 | | 54 | D | 49.5% | 50.5% | 49.5% | 50.5% |
| 14,610 | MONROE | 4,609 | 2,420 | 2,189 | | 231 | R | 52.5% | 47.5% | 52.5% | 47.5% |
| 7,011 | MONTGOMERY | 2,315 | 1,365 | 950 | | 415 | R | 59.0% | 41.0% | 59.0% | 41.0% |
| 11,572 | MORGAN | 4,015 | 2,301 | 1,714 | | 587 | R | 57.3% | 42.7% | 57.3% | 42.7% |
| 19,685 | MURRAY | 5,170 | 3,521 | 1,649 | | 1,872 | R | 68.1% | 31.9% | 68.1% | 31.9% |
| 170,108 | MUSCOGEE | 44,651 | 23,816 | 20,835 | | 2,981 | R | 53.3% | 46.7% | 53.3% | 46.7% |
| 34,489 | NEWTON | 9,199 | 5,810 | 3,389 | | 2,421 | R | 63.2% | 36.8% | 63.2% | 36.8% |
| 12,427 | OCONEE | 4,938 | 3,471 | 1,467 | | 2,004 | R | 70.3% | 29.7% | 70.3% | 29.7% |
| 8,929 | OGLETHORPE | 3,360 | 2,122 | 1,238 | | 884 | R | 63.2% | 36.8% | 63.2% | 36.8% |
| 26,110 | PAULDING | 8,669 | 6,048 | 2,621 | | 3,427 | R | 69.8% | 30.2% | 69.8% | 30.2% |
| 19,151 | PEACH | 6,021 | 2,652 | 3,369 | | 717 | D | 44.0% | 56.0% | 44.0% | 56.0% |
| 11,652 | PICKENS | 4,130 | 2,801 | 1,329 | | 1,472 | R | 67.8% | 32.2% | 67.8% | 32.2% |
| 11,897 | PIERCE | 3,479 | 1,978 | 1,501 | | 477 | R | 56.9% | 43.1% | 56.9% | 43.1% |
| 8,937 | PIKE | 3,058 | 1,855 | 1,203 | | 652 | R | 60.7% | 39.3% | 60.7% | 39.3% |
| 32,386 | POLK | 8,697 | 5,435 | 3,262 | | 2,173 | R | 62.5% | 37.5% | 62.5% | 37.5% |
| 8,950 | PULASKI | 2,949 | 1,509 | 1,440 | | 69 | R | 51.2% | 48.8% | 51.2% | 48.8% |
| 10,295 | PUTNAM | 3,166 | 1,830 | 1,336 | | 494 | R | 57.8% | 42.2% | 57.8% | 42.2% |
| 2,357 | QUITMAN | 851 | 361 | 490 | | 129 | D | 42.4% | 57.6% | 42.4% | 57.6% |
| 10,466 | RABUN | 3,458 | 2,191 | 1,267 | | 924 | R | 63.4% | 36.6% | 63.4% | 36.6% |
| 9,599 | RANDOLPH | 3,032 | 1,578 | 1,454 | | 124 | R | 52.0% | 48.0% | 52.0% | 48.0% |

# GEORGIA

## PRESIDENT 1984

| 1980 Census Population | County | Total Vote | Republican | Democratic | Other | Rep.-Dem. Plurality | Percentage Total Vote Rep. | Dem. | Major Vote Rep. | Dem. |
|---|---|---|---|---|---|---|---|---|---|---|
| 181,629 | RICHMOND | 51,077 | 29,869 | 21,208 | | 8,661 R | 58.5% | 41.5% | 58.5% | 41.5% |
| 36,747 | ROCKDALE | 13,412 | 10,121 | 3,291 | | 6,830 R | 75.5% | 24.5% | 75.5% | 24.5% |
| 3,433 | SCHLEY | 1,017 | 614 | 403 | | 211 R | 60.4% | 39.6% | 60.4% | 39.6% |
| 14,043 | SCREVEN | 4,330 | 2,583 | 1,747 | | 836 R | 59.7% | 40.3% | 59.7% | 40.3% |
| 9,057 | SEMINOLE | 2,986 | 1,636 | 1,350 | | 286 R | 54.8% | 45.2% | 54.8% | 45.2% |
| 47,899 | SPALDING | 13,449 | 8,571 | 4,878 | | 3,693 R | 63.7% | 36.3% | 63.7% | 36.3% |
| 21,763 | STEPHENS | 6,329 | 4,057 | 2,272 | | 1,785 R | 64.1% | 35.9% | 64.1% | 35.9% |
| 5,896 | STEWART | 2,113 | 805 | 1,308 | | 503 D | 38.1% | 61.9% | 38.1% | 61.9% |
| 29,360 | SUMTER | 8,332 | 4,607 | 3,725 | | 882 R | 55.3% | 44.7% | 55.3% | 44.7% |
| 6,536 | TALBOT | 2,272 | 778 | 1,494 | | 716 D | 34.2% | 65.8% | 34.2% | 65.8% |
| 2,032 | TALIAFERRO | 868 | 318 | 550 | | 232 D | 36.6% | 63.4% | 36.6% | 63.4% |
| 18,134 | TATTNALL | 5,595 | 3,641 | 1,954 | | 1,687 R | 65.1% | 34.9% | 65.1% | 34.9% |
| 7,902 | TAYLOR | 2,632 | 1,292 | 1,340 | | 48 D | 49.1% | 50.9% | 49.1% | 50.9% |
| 11,445 | TELFAIR | 4,029 | 1,980 | 2,049 | | 69 D | 49.1% | 50.9% | 49.1% | 50.9% |
| 12,017 | TERRELL | 3,342 | 1,744 | 1,598 | | 146 R | 52.2% | 47.8% | 52.2% | 47.8% |
| 38,098 | THOMAS | 10,466 | 6,427 | 4,039 | | 2,388 R | 61.4% | 38.6% | 61.4% | 38.6% |
| 32,862 | TIFT | 7,165 | 4,429 | 2,736 | | 1,693 R | 61.8% | 38.2% | 61.8% | 38.2% |
| 22,592 | TOOMBS | 6,855 | 4,470 | 2,385 | | 2,085 R | 65.2% | 34.8% | 65.2% | 34.8% |
| 5,638 | TOWNS | 2,967 | 1,960 | 1,007 | | 953 R | 66.1% | 33.9% | 66.1% | 33.9% |
| 6,087 | TREUTLEN | 1,929 | 1,086 | 843 | | 243 R | 56.3% | 43.7% | 56.3% | 43.7% |
| 50,003 | TROUP | 14,612 | 9,340 | 5,272 | | 4,068 R | 63.9% | 36.1% | 63.9% | 36.1% |
| 9,510 | TURNER | 2,599 | 1,329 | 1,270 | | 59 R | 51.1% | 48.9% | 51.1% | 48.9% |
| 9,354 | TWIGGS | 2,898 | 1,143 | 1,755 | | 612 D | 39.4% | 60.6% | 39.4% | 60.6% |
| 9,390 | UNION | 3,026 | 1,914 | 1,112 | | 802 R | 63.3% | 36.7% | 63.3% | 36.7% |
| 25,998 | UPSON | 7,746 | 4,803 | 2,943 | | 1,860 R | 62.0% | 38.0% | 62.0% | 38.0% |
| 56,470 | WALKER | 15,734 | 10,734 | 5,000 | | 5,734 R | 68.2% | 31.8% | 68.2% | 31.8% |
| 31,211 | WALTON | 7,476 | 4,995 | 2,481 | | 2,514 R | 66.8% | 33.2% | 66.8% | 33.2% |
| 37,180 | WARE | 9,982 | 5,547 | 4,435 | | 1,112 R | 55.6% | 44.4% | 55.6% | 44.4% |
| 6,583 | WARREN | 2,345 | 1,087 | 1,258 | | 171 D | 46.4% | 53.6% | 46.4% | 53.6% |
| 18,842 | WASHINGTON | 5,921 | 2,887 | 3,034 | | 147 D | 48.8% | 51.2% | 48.8% | 51.2% |
| 20,750 | WAYNE | 6,132 | 3,698 | 2,434 | | 1,264 R | 60.3% | 39.7% | 60.3% | 39.7% |
| 2,341 | WEBSTER | 936 | 402 | 534 | | 132 D | 42.9% | 57.1% | 42.9% | 57.1% |
| 5,155 | WHEELER | 1,607 | 833 | 774 | | 59 R | 51.8% | 48.2% | 51.8% | 48.2% |
| 10,120 | WHITE | 3,459 | 2,369 | 1,090 | | 1,279 R | 68.5% | 31.5% | 68.5% | 31.5% |
| 65,789 | WHITFIELD | 17,241 | 11,957 | 5,284 | | 6,673 R | 69.4% | 30.6% | 69.4% | 30.6% |
| 7,682 | WILCOX | 2,430 | 1,218 | 1,212 | | 6 R | 50.1% | 49.9% | 50.1% | 49.9% |
| 10,951 | WILKES | 3,423 | 1,837 | 1,586 | | 251 R | 53.7% | 46.3% | 53.7% | 46.3% |
| 10,368 | WILKINSON | 3,858 | 1,756 | 2,102 | | 346 D | 45.5% | 54.5% | 45.5% | 54.5% |
| 18,064 | WORTH | 4,595 | 2,910 | 1,685 | | 1,225 R | 63.3% | 36.7% | 63.3% | 36.7% |
| 5,463,105 | TOTAL | 1,776,120 | 1,068,722 | 706,628 | 770 | 362,094 R | 60.2% | 39.8% | 60.2% | 39.8% |

# GEORGIA

## PRESIDENT 1980

| 1980 Census Population | County | Total Vote | Republican | Democratic | Other | Rep.-Dem. Plurality | Percentage Total Vote | | Major Vote | |
|---|---|---|---|---|---|---|---|---|---|---|
| | | | | | | | Rep. | Dem. | Rep. | Dem. |
| 15,565 | APPLING | 5,007 | 1,961 | 2,985 | 61 | 1,024 D | 39.2% | 59.6% | 39.6% | 60.4% |
| 6,141 | ATKINSON | 2,222 | 747 | 1,449 | 26 | 702 D | 33.6% | 65.2% | 34.0% | 66.0% |
| 9,379 | BACON | 3,106 | 1,427 | 1,622 | 57 | 195 D | 45.9% | 52.2% | 46.8% | 53.2% |
| 3,808 | BAKER | 1,564 | 510 | 1,035 | 19 | 525 D | 32.6% | 66.2% | 33.0% | 67.0% |
| 34,686 | BALDWIN | 8,326 | 3,639 | 4,368 | 319 | 729 D | 43.7% | 52.5% | 45.4% | 54.6% |
| 8,702 | BANKS | 2,868 | 746 | 2,091 | 31 | 1,345 D | 26.0% | 72.9% | 26.3% | 73.7% |
| 21,354 | BARROW | 6,309 | 2,284 | 3,876 | 149 | 1,592 D | 36.2% | 61.4% | 37.1% | 62.9% |
| 40,760 | BARTOW | 10,853 | 3,135 | 7,490 | 228 | 4,355 D | 28.9% | 69.0% | 29.5% | 70.5% |
| 16,000 | BEN HILL | 4,067 | 1,459 | 2,544 | 64 | 1,085 D | 35.9% | 62.6% | 36.4% | 63.6% |
| 13,525 | BERRIEN | 4,404 | 1,487 | 2,869 | 48 | 1,382 D | 33.8% | 65.1% | 34.1% | 65.9% |
| 150,256 | BIBB | 48,130 | 15,175 | 31,770 | 1,185 | 16,595 D | 31.5% | 66.0% | 32.3% | 67.7% |
| 10,767 | BLECKLEY | 3,440 | 1,261 | 2,014 | 165 | 753 D | 36.7% | 58.5% | 38.5% | 61.5% |
| 8,701 | BRANTLEY | 2,977 | 882 | 2,066 | 29 | 1,184 D | 29.6% | 69.4% | 29.9% | 70.1% |
| 15,255 | BROOKS | 3,827 | 1,546 | 2,230 | 51 | 684 D | 40.4% | 58.3% | 40.9% | 59.1% |
| 10,175 | BRYAN | 3,235 | 1,212 | 1,966 | 57 | 754 D | 37.5% | 60.8% | 38.1% | 61.9% |
| 35,785 | BULLOCH | 8,921 | 3,750 | 4,921 | 250 | 1,171 D | 42.0% | 55.2% | 43.2% | 56.8% |
| 19,349 | BURKE | 4,991 | 1,871 | 3,047 | 73 | 1,176 D | 37.5% | 61.0% | 38.0% | 62.0% |
| 13,665 | BUTTS | 3,845 | 1,210 | 2,574 | 61 | 1,364 D | 31.5% | 66.9% | 32.0% | 68.0% |
| 5,717 | CALHOUN | 2,087 | 652 | 1,414 | 21 | 762 D | 31.2% | 67.8% | 31.6% | 68.4% |
| 13,371 | CAMDEN | 4,443 | 1,439 | 2,924 | 80 | 1,485 D | 32.4% | 65.8% | 33.0% | 67.0% |
| 7,518 | CANDLER | 2,421 | 1,030 | 1,358 | 33 | 328 D | 42.5% | 56.1% | 43.1% | 56.9% |
| 56,346 | CARROLL | 14,475 | 5,815 | 8,202 | 458 | 2,387 D | 40.2% | 56.7% | 41.5% | 58.5% |
| 36,991 | CATOOSA | 11,059 | 5,962 | 4,921 | 176 | 1,041 R | 53.9% | 44.5% | 54.8% | 45.2% |
| 7,343 | CHARLTON | 2,286 | 779 | 1,469 | 38 | 690 D | 34.1% | 64.3% | 34.7% | 65.3% |
| 202,226 | CHATHAM | 56,781 | 26,499 | 28,413 | 1,869 | 1,914 D | 46.7% | 50.0% | 48.3% | 51.7% |
| 21,732 | CHATTAHOOCHEE | 752 | 256 | 476 | 20 | 220 D | 34.0% | 63.3% | 35.0% | 65.0% |
| 21,856 | CHATTOOGA | 6,330 | 1,946 | 4,279 | 105 | 2,333 D | 30.7% | 67.6% | 31.3% | 68.7% |
| 51,699 | CHEROKEE | 11,678 | 5,250 | 6,020 | 408 | 770 D | 45.0% | 51.5% | 46.6% | 53.4% |
| 74,498 | CLARKE | 19,899 | 8,094 | 10,519 | 1,286 | 2,425 D | 40.7% | 52.9% | 43.5% | 56.5% |
| 3,553 | CLAY | 1,241 | 316 | 909 | 16 | 593 D | 25.5% | 73.2% | 25.8% | 74.2% |
| 150,357 | CLAYTON | 38,051 | 19,160 | 17,540 | 1,351 | 1,620 R | 50.4% | 46.1% | 52.2% | 47.8% |
| 6,660 | CLINCH | 1,864 | 513 | 1,325 | 26 | 812 D | 27.5% | 71.1% | 27.9% | 72.1% |
| 297,718 | COBB | 95,816 | 51,977 | 39,157 | 4,682 | 12,820 R | 54.2% | 40.9% | 57.0% | 43.0% |
| 26,894 | COFFEE | 6,621 | 2,499 | 4,038 | 84 | 1,539 D | 37.7% | 61.0% | 38.2% | 61.8% |
| 35,376 | COLQUITT | 9,069 | 3,593 | 5,353 | 123 | 1,760 D | 39.6% | 59.0% | 40.2% | 59.8% |
| 40,118 | COLUMBIA | 11,938 | 6,293 | 5,335 | 310 | 958 R | 52.7% | 44.7% | 54.1% | 45.9% |
| 13,490 | COOK | 3,684 | 1,188 | 2,461 | 35 | 1,273 D | 32.2% | 66.8% | 32.6% | 67.4% |
| 39,268 | COWETA | 10,422 | 4,480 | 5,697 | 245 | 1,217 D | 43.0% | 54.7% | 44.0% | 56.0% |
| 7,684 | CRAWFORD | 2,375 | 642 | 1,673 | 60 | 1,031 D | 27.0% | 70.4% | 27.7% | 72.3% |
| 19,489 | CRISP | 5,347 | 1,861 | 3,403 | 83 | 1,542 D | 34.8% | 63.6% | 35.4% | 64.6% |
| 12,318 | DADE | 3,929 | 2,114 | 1,735 | 80 | 379 R | 53.8% | 44.2% | 54.9% | 45.1% |
| 4,774 | DAWSON | 1,837 | 729 | 1,072 | 36 | 343 D | 39.7% | 58.4% | 40.5% | 59.5% |
| 25,495 | DECATUR | 6,243 | 2,919 | 3,242 | 82 | 323 D | 46.8% | 51.9% | 47.4% | 52.6% |
| 483,024 | DE KALB | 167,405 | 74,904 | 82,743 | 9,758 | 7,839 D | 44.7% | 49.4% | 47.5% | 52.5% |
| 16,955 | DODGE | 6,453 | 1,719 | 4,635 | 99 | 2,916 D | 26.6% | 71.8% | 27.1% | 72.9% |
| 10,826 | DOOLY | 3,502 | 1,083 | 2,364 | 55 | 1,281 D | 30.9% | 67.5% | 31.4% | 68.6% |
| 100,718 | DOUGHERTY | 26,615 | 12,726 | 13,430 | 459 | 704 D | 47.8% | 50.5% | 48.7% | 51.3% |
| 54,573 | DOUGLAS | 14,238 | 6,945 | 6,807 | 486 | 138 R | 48.8% | 47.8% | 50.5% | 49.5% |
| 13,158 | EARLY | 3,682 | 1,538 | 2,110 | 34 | 572 D | 41.8% | 57.3% | 42.2% | 57.8% |
| 2,297 | ECHOLS | 783 | 259 | 515 | 9 | 256 D | 33.1% | 65.8% | 33.5% | 66.5% |
| 18,327 | EFFINGHAM | 5,377 | 2,528 | 2,783 | 66 | 255 D | 47.0% | 51.8% | 47.6% | 52.4% |
| 18,758 | ELBERT | 6,061 | 1,967 | 4,014 | 80 | 2,047 D | 32.5% | 66.2% | 32.9% | 67.1% |
| 20,795 | EMANUEL | 6,251 | 2,199 | 3,971 | 81 | 1,772 D | 35.2% | 63.5% | 35.6% | 64.4% |
| 8,428 | EVANS | 2,575 | 1,090 | 1,456 | 29 | 366 D | 42.3% | 56.5% | 42.8% | 57.2% |
| 14,748 | FANNIN | 5,829 | 3,196 | 2,526 | 107 | 670 R | 54.8% | 43.3% | 55.9% | 44.1% |
| 29,043 | FAYETTE | 10,549 | 6,351 | 3,798 | 400 | 2,553 R | 60.2% | 36.0% | 62.6% | 37.4% |
| 79,800 | FLOYD | 23,596 | 9,220 | 13,710 | 666 | 4,490 D | 39.1% | 58.1% | 40.2% | 59.8% |
| 27,958 | FORSYTH | 7,736 | 3,157 | 4,325 | 254 | 1,168 D | 40.8% | 55.9% | 42.2% | 57.8% |
| 15,185 | FRANKLIN | 4,960 | 1,387 | 3,528 | 45 | 2,141 D | 28.0% | 71.1% | 28.2% | 71.8% |
| 589,904 | FULTON | 192,723 | 64,909 | 118,748 | 9,066 | 53,839 D | 33.7% | 61.6% | 35.3% | 64.7% |

# GEORGIA

## PRESIDENT 1980

| 1980 Census Population | County | Total Vote | Republican | Democratic | Other | Rep.-Dem. Plurality | Percentage Total Vote Rep. | Dem. | Major Vote Rep. | Dem. |
|---|---|---|---|---|---|---|---|---|---|---|
| 11,110 | GILMER | 4,537 | 2,170 | 2,246 | 121 | 76 D | 47.8% | 49.5% | 49.1% | 50.9% |
| 2,382 | GLASCOCK | 1,138 | 510 | 614 | 14 | 104 D | 44.8% | 54.0% | 45.4% | 54.6% |
| 54,981 | GLYNN | 15,173 | 7,214 | 7,540 | 419 | 326 D | 47.5% | 49.7% | 48.9% | 51.1% |
| 30,070 | GORDON | 8,542 | 3,107 | 5,199 | 236 | 2,092 D | 36.4% | 60.9% | 37.4% | 62.6% |
| 19,845 | GRADY | 5,117 | 2,018 | 3,023 | 76 | 1,005 D | 39.4% | 59.1% | 40.0% | 60.0% |
| 11,391 | GREENE | 3,573 | 961 | 2,571 | 41 | 1,610 D | 26.9% | 72.0% | 27.2% | 72.8% |
| 166,903 | GWINNETT | 51,452 | 27,185 | 21,958 | 2,309 | 5,227 R | 52.8% | 42.7% | 55.3% | 44.7% |
| 25,020 | HABERSHAM | 6,781 | 2,224 | 4,394 | 163 | 2,170 D | 32.8% | 64.8% | 33.6% | 66.4% |
| 75,649 | HALL | 20,521 | 7,760 | 12,124 | 637 | 4,364 D | 37.8% | 59.1% | 39.0% | 61.0% |
| 9,466 | HANCOCK | 2,809 | 573 | 2,205 | 31 | 1,632 D | 20.4% | 78.5% | 20.6% | 79.4% |
| 18,422 | HARALSON | 5,960 | 2,229 | 3,606 | 125 | 1,377 D | 37.4% | 60.5% | 38.2% | 61.8% |
| 15,464 | HARRIS | 4,942 | 2,001 | 2,807 | 134 | 806 D | 40.5% | 56.8% | 41.6% | 58.4% |
| 18,585 | HART | 6,215 | 1,577 | 4,539 | 99 | 2,962 D | 25.4% | 73.0% | 25.8% | 74.2% |
| 6,520 | HEARD | 2,283 | 875 | 1,348 | 60 | 473 D | 38.3% | 59.0% | 39.4% | 60.6% |
| 36,309 | HENRY | 11,268 | 5,326 | 5,635 | 307 | 309 D | 47.3% | 50.0% | 48.6% | 51.4% |
| 77,605 | HOUSTON | 20,695 | 9,005 | 10,915 | 775 | 1,910 D | 43.5% | 52.7% | 45.2% | 54.8% |
| 8,988 | IRWIN | 2,632 | 1,056 | 1,555 | 21 | 499 D | 40.1% | 59.1% | 40.4% | 59.6% |
| 25,343 | JACKSON | 6,949 | 2,209 | 4,591 | 149 | 2,382 D | 31.8% | 66.1% | 32.5% | 67.5% |
| 7,553 | JASPER | 2,484 | 879 | 1,546 | 59 | 667 D | 35.4% | 62.2% | 36.2% | 63.8% |
| 11,473 | JEFF DAVIS | 3,311 | 1,191 | 2,059 | 61 | 868 D | 36.0% | 62.2% | 36.6% | 63.4% |
| 18,403 | JEFFERSON | 4,978 | 1,605 | 3,305 | 68 | 1,700 D | 32.2% | 66.4% | 32.7% | 67.3% |
| 8,841 | JENKINS | 2,493 | 824 | 1,632 | 37 | 808 D | 33.1% | 65.5% | 33.6% | 66.4% |
| 8,660 | JOHNSON | 3,029 | 1,123 | 1,854 | 52 | 731 D | 37.1% | 61.2% | 37.7% | 62.3% |
| 16,579 | JONES | 5,220 | 1,828 | 3,239 | 153 | 1,411 D | 35.0% | 62.0% | 36.1% | 63.9% |
| 12,215 | LAMAR | 3,828 | 1,298 | 2,453 | 77 | 1,155 D | 33.9% | 64.1% | 34.6% | 65.4% |
| 5,654 | LANIER | 1,604 | 470 | 1,116 | 18 | 646 D | 29.3% | 69.6% | 29.6% | 70.4% |
| 36,990 | LAURENS | 12,523 | 4,392 | 7,860 | 271 | 3,468 D | 35.1% | 62.8% | 35.8% | 64.2% |
| 11,684 | LEE | 3,661 | 1,942 | 1,670 | 49 | 272 R | 53.0% | 45.6% | 53.8% | 46.2% |
| 37,583 | LIBERTY | 4,683 | 1,507 | 3,099 | 77 | 1,592 D | 32.2% | 66.2% | 32.7% | 67.3% |
| 6,716 | LINCOLN | 2,440 | 806 | 1,617 | 17 | 811 D | 33.0% | 66.3% | 33.3% | 66.7% |
| 4,524 | LONG | 1,743 | 514 | 1,202 | 27 | 688 D | 29.5% | 69.0% | 30.0% | 70.0% |
| 67,972 | LOWNDES | 12,912 | 6,622 | 5,989 | 301 | 633 R | 51.3% | 46.4% | 52.5% | 47.5% |
| 10,762 | LUMPKIN | 3,085 | 1,024 | 1,951 | 110 | 927 D | 33.2% | 63.2% | 34.4% | 65.6% |
| 18,546 | MCDUFFIE | 4,683 | 1,928 | 2,667 | 88 | 739 D | 41.2% | 57.0% | 42.0% | 58.0% |
| 8,046 | MCINTOSH | 3,049 | 876 | 2,104 | 69 | 1,228 D | 28.7% | 69.0% | 29.4% | 70.6% |
| 14,003 | MACON | 3,979 | 894 | 3,025 | 60 | 2,131 D | 22.5% | 76.0% | 22.8% | 77.2% |
| 17,747 | MADISON | 5,401 | 2,330 | 2,980 | 91 | 650 D | 43.1% | 55.2% | 43.9% | 56.1% |
| 5,297 | MARION | 1,773 | 567 | 1,174 | 32 | 607 D | 32.0% | 66.2% | 32.6% | 67.4% |
| 21,229 | MERIWETHER | 5,805 | 1,838 | 3,876 | 91 | 2,038 D | 31.7% | 66.8% | 32.2% | 67.8% |
| 7,038 | MILLER | 2,053 | 900 | 1,127 | 26 | 227 D | 43.8% | 54.9% | 44.4% | 55.6% |
| 21,114 | MITCHELL | 5,856 | 2,231 | 3,566 | 59 | 1,335 D | 38.1% | 60.9% | 38.5% | 61.5% |
| 14,610 | MONROE | 3,860 | 1,242 | 2,542 | 76 | 1,300 D | 32.2% | 65.9% | 32.8% | 67.2% |
| 7,011 | MONTGOMERY | 2,640 | 948 | 1,663 | 29 | 715 D | 35.9% | 63.0% | 36.3% | 63.7% |
| 11,572 | MORGAN | 3,671 | 1,323 | 2,276 | 72 | 953 D | 36.0% | 62.0% | 36.8% | 63.2% |
| 19,685 | MURRAY | 4,701 | 1,538 | 3,094 | 69 | 1,556 D | 32.7% | 65.8% | 33.2% | 66.8% |
| 170,108 | MOSCOGEE | 39,566 | 15,203 | 23,272 | 1,091 | 8,069 D | 38.4% | 58.8% | 39.5% | 60.5% |
| 34,489 | NEWTON | 9,056 | 3,206 | 5,611 | 239 | 2,405 D | 35.4% | 62.0% | 36.4% | 63.6% |
| 12,427 | OCONEE | 4,367 | 2,065 | 2,141 | 161 | 76 D | 47.3% | 49.0% | 49.1% | 50.9% |
| 8,929 | OGLETHORPE | 2,856 | 1,187 | 1,611 | 58 | 424 D | 41.6% | 56.4% | 42.4% | 57.6% |
| 26,110 | PAULDING | 7,717 | 2,845 | 4,686 | 186 | 1,841 D | 36.9% | 60.7% | 37.8% | 62.2% |
| 19,151 | PEACH | 5,170 | 1,642 | 3,415 | 113 | 1,773 D | 31.8% | 66.1% | 32.5% | 67.5% |
| 11,652 | PICKENS | 4,077 | 1,612 | 2,358 | 107 | 746 D | 39.5% | 57.8% | 40.6% | 59.4% |
| 11,897 | PIERCE | 2,985 | 1,027 | 1,918 | 40 | 891 D | 34.4% | 64.3% | 34.9% | 65.1% |
| 8,937 | PIKE | 3,094 | 1,271 | 1,755 | 68 | 484 D | 41.1% | 56.7% | 42.0% | 58.0% |
| 32,386 | POLK | 8,562 | 2,949 | 5,421 | 192 | 2,472 D | 34.4% | 63.3% | 35.2% | 64.8% |
| 8,950 | PULASKI | 3,232 | 1,153 | 1,997 | 82 | 844 D | 35.7% | 61.8% | 36.6% | 63.4% |
| 10,295 | PUTNAM | 3,177 | 1,166 | 1,951 | 60 | 785 D | 36.7% | 61.4% | 37.4% | 62.6% |
| 2,357 | QUITMAN | 837 | 240 | 589 | 8 | 349 D | 28.7% | 70.4% | 29.0% | 71.0% |
| 10,466 | RABUN | 3,495 | 1,070 | 2,327 | 98 | 1,257 D | 30.6% | 66.6% | 31.5% | 68.5% |
| 9,599 | RANDOLPH | 2,743 | 879 | 1,861 | 3 | 982 D | 32.0% | 67.8% | 32.1% | 67.9% |

# GEORGIA

## PRESIDENT 1980

| 1980 Census Population | County | Total Vote | Republican | Democratic | Other | Rep.-Dem. Plurality | Percentage Total Vote Rep. | Dem. | Major Vote Rep. | Dem. |
|---|---|---|---|---|---|---|---|---|---|---|
| 181,629 | RICHMOND | 44,871 | 19,619 | 24,104 | 1,148 | 4,485 D | 43.7% | 53.7% | 44.9% | 55.1% |
| 36,747 | ROCKDALE | 10,067 | 5,300 | 4,395 | 372 | 905 R | 52.6% | 43.7% | 54.7% | 45.3% |
| 3,433 | SCHLEY | 1,085 | 453 | 613 | 19 | 160 D | 41.8% | 56.5% | 42.5% | 57.5% |
| 14,043 | SCREVEN | 3,664 | 1,490 | 2,117 | 57 | 627 D | 40.7% | 57.8% | 41.3% | 58.7% |
| 9,057 | SEMINOLE | 2,936 | 1,117 | 1,794 | 25 | 677 D | 38.0% | 61.1% | 38.4% | 61.6% |
| 47,899 | SPALDING | 12,331 | 4,809 | 7,176 | 346 | 2,367 D | 39.0% | 58.2% | 40.1% | 59.9% |
| 21,763 | STEPHENS | 6,692 | 2,045 | 4,529 | 118 | 2,484 D | 30.6% | 67.7% | 31.1% | 68.9% |
| 5,896 | STEWART | 2,087 | 611 | 1,440 | 36 | 829 D | 29.3% | 69.0% | 29.8% | 70.2% |
| 29,360 | SUMTER | 8,060 | 2,957 | 4,956 | 147 | 1,999 D | 36.7% | 61.5% | 37.4% | 62.6% |
| 6,536 | TALBOT | 2,243 | 572 | 1,635 | 36 | 1,063 D | 25.5% | 72.9% | 25.9% | 74.1% |
| 2,032 | TALIAFERRO | 954 | 270 | 670 | 14 | 400 D | 28.3% | 70.2% | 28.7% | 71.3% |
| 18,134 | TATTNALL | 5,002 | 2,082 | 2,864 | 56 | 782 D | 41.6% | 57.3% | 42.1% | 57.9% |
| 7,902 | TAYLOR | 2,698 | 815 | 1,845 | 38 | 1,030 D | 30.2% | 68.4% | 30.6% | 69.4% |
| 11,445 | TELFAIR | 3,941 | 1,173 | 2,700 | 68 | 1,527 D | 29.8% | 68.5% | 30.3% | 69.7% |
| 12,017 | TERRELL | 3,420 | 1,378 | 2,010 | 32 | 632 D | 40.3% | 58.8% | 40.7% | 59.3% |
| 38,098 | THOMAS | 10,161 | 4,294 | 5,695 | 172 | 1,401 D | 42.3% | 56.0% | 43.0% | 57.0% |
| 32,862 | TIFT | 8,022 | 3,280 | 4,572 | 170 | 1,292 D | 40.9% | 57.0% | 41.8% | 58.2% |
| 22,592 | TOOMBS | 6,197 | 2,835 | 3,255 | 107 | 420 D | 45.7% | 52.5% | 46.6% | 53.4% |
| 5,638 | TOWNS | 3,065 | 1,475 | 1,510 | 80 | 35 D | 48.1% | 49.3% | 49.4% | 50.6% |
| 6,087 | TREUTLEN | 2,004 | 668 | 1,307 | 29 | 639 D | 33.3% | 65.2% | 33.8% | 66.2% |
| 50,003 | TROUP | 13,429 | 5,398 | 7,716 | 315 | 2,318 D | 40.2% | 57.5% | 41.2% | 58.8% |
| 9,510 | TURNER | 2,921 | 898 | 1,990 | 33 | 1,092 D | 30.7% | 68.1% | 31.1% | 68.9% |
| 9,354 | TWIGGS | 2,980 | 747 | 2,213 | 20 | 1,466 D | 25.1% | 74.3% | 25.2% | 74.8% |
| 9,390 | UNION | 3,311 | 1,546 | 1,700 | 65 | 154 D | 46.7% | 51.3% | 47.6% | 52.4% |
| 25,998 | UPSON | 7,635 | 2,788 | 4,713 | 134 | 1,925 D | 36.5% | 61.7% | 37.2% | 62.8% |
| 56,470 | WALKER | 14,132 | 7,088 | 6,809 | 235 | 279 R | 50.2% | 48.2% | 51.0% | 49.0% |
| 31,211 | WALTON | 7,303 | 2,618 | 4,525 | 160 | 1,907 D | 35.8% | 62.0% | 36.7% | 63.3% |
| 37,180 | WARE | 10,137 | 3,715 | 6,307 | 115 | 2,592 D | 36.6% | 62.2% | 37.1% | 62.9% |
| 6,583 | WARREN | 2,321 | 779 | 1,517 | 25 | 738 D | 33.6% | 65.4% | 33.9% | 66.1% |
| 18,842 | WASHINGTON | 5,364 | 1,822 | 3,452 | 90 | 1,630 D | 34.0% | 64.4% | 34.5% | 65.5% |
| 20,750 | WAYNE | 6,157 | 2,213 | 3,843 | 101 | 1,630 D | 35.9% | 62.4% | 36.5% | 63.5% |
| 2,341 | WEBSTER | 940 | 312 | 608 | 20 | 296 D | 33.2% | 64.7% | 33.9% | 66.1% |
| 5,155 | WHEELER | 2,186 | 550 | 1,599 | 37 | 1,049 D | 25.2% | 73.1% | 25.6% | 74.4% |
| 10,120 | WHITE | 3,287 | 1,175 | 2,017 | 95 | 842 D | 35.7% | 61.4% | 36.8% | 63.2% |
| 65,789 | WHITFIELD | 16,439 | 6,404 | 9,691 | 344 | 3,287 D | 39.0% | 59.0% | 39.8% | 60.2% |
| 7,682 | WILCOX | 2,630 | 827 | 1,780 | 23 | 953 D | 31.4% | 67.7% | 31.7% | 68.3% |
| 10,951 | WILKES | 3,623 | 1,212 | 2,350 | 61 | 1,138 D | 33.5% | 64.9% | 34.0% | 66.0% |
| 10,368 | WILKINSON | 3,532 | 1,116 | 2,365 | 51 | 1,249 D | 31.6% | 67.0% | 32.1% | 67.9% |
| 18,064 | WORTH | 4,695 | 2,076 | 2,567 | 52 | 491 D | 44.2% | 54.7% | 44.7% | 55.3% |
| 5,463,105 | TOTAL | 1,596,695 | 654,168 | 890,733 | 51,794 | 236,565 D | 41.0% | 55.8% | 42.3% | 57.7% |

# GEORGIA

## PRESIDENT 1976

| 1970 Census Population | County | Total Vote | Republican | Democratic | Other | Rep.-Dem. Plurality | Total Vote Rep. | Dem. | Major Vote Rep. | Dem. |
|---|---|---|---|---|---|---|---|---|---|---|
| 12,726 | APPLING | 4,546 | 961 | 3,585 | | 2,624 D | 21.1% | 78.9% | 21.1% | 78.9% |
| 5,879 | ATKINSON | 1,907 | 347 | 1,560 | | 1,213 D | 18.2% | 81.8% | 18.2% | 81.8% |
| 8,233 | BACON | 2,989 | 594 | 2,395 | | 1,801 D | 19.9% | 80.1% | 19.9% | 80.1% |
| 3,875 | BAKER | 1,467 | 305 | 1,162 | | 857 D | 20.8% | 79.2% | 20.8% | 79.2% |
| 34,240 | BALDWIN | 8,286 | 3,612 | 4,674 | | 1,062 D | 43.6% | 56.4% | 43.6% | 56.4% |
| 6,833 | BANKS | 2,717 | 330 | 2,387 | | 2,057 D | 12.1% | 87.9% | 12.1% | 87.9% |
| 16,859 | BARROW | 6,120 | 1,364 | 4,756 | | 3,392 D | 22.3% | 77.7% | 22.3% | 77.7% |
| 32,663 | BARTOW | 10,042 | 1,876 | 8,166 | | 6,290 D | 18.7% | 81.3% | 18.7% | 81.3% |
| 13,171 | BEN HILL | 3,263 | 814 | 2,449 | | 1,635 D | 24.9% | 75.1% | 24.9% | 75.1% |
| 11,556 | BERRIEN | 3,949 | 555 | 3,394 | | 2,839 D | 14.1% | 85.9% | 14.1% | 85.9% |
| 143,418 | BIBB | 44,721 | 12,819 | 31,902 | | 19,083 D | 28.7% | 71.3% | 28.7% | 71.3% |
| 10,291 | BLECKLEY | 3,577 | 972 | 2,605 | | 1,633 D | 27.2% | 72.8% | 27.2% | 72.8% |
| 5,940 | BRANTLEY | 2,652 | 358 | 2,294 | | 1,936 D | 13.5% | 86.5% | 13.5% | 86.5% |
| 13,739 | BROOKS | 3,755 | 1,102 | 2,653 | | 1,551 D | 29.3% | 70.7% | 29.3% | 70.7% |
| 6,539 | BRYAN | 2,806 | 761 | 2,045 | | 1,284 D | 27.1% | 72.9% | 27.1% | 72.9% |
| 31,585 | BULLOCH | 8,355 | 3,156 | 5,199 | | 2,043 D | 37.8% | 62.2% | 37.8% | 62.2% |
| 18,255 | BURKE | 4,579 | 1,565 | 3,014 | | 1,449 D | 34.2% | 65.8% | 34.2% | 65.8% |
| 10,560 | BUTTS | 3,717 | 819 | 2,898 | | 2,079 D | 22.0% | 78.0% | 22.0% | 78.0% |
| 6,606 | CALHOUN | 1,830 | 436 | 1,394 | | 958 D | 23.8% | 76.2% | 23.8% | 76.2% |
| 11,334 | CAMDEN | 3,957 | 995 | 2,962 | | 1,967 D | 25.1% | 74.9% | 25.1% | 74.9% |
| 6,412 | CANDLER | 2,034 | 646 | 1,388 | | 742 D | 31.8% | 68.2% | 31.8% | 68.2% |
| 45,404 | CARROLL | 13,690 | 3,640 | 10,050 | | 6,410 D | 26.6% | 73.4% | 26.6% | 73.4% |
| 28,271 | CATOOSA | 9,819 | 3,799 | 6,020 | | 2,221 D | 38.7% | 61.3% | 38.7% | 61.3% |
| 5,680 | CHARLTON | 2,202 | 452 | 1,750 | | 1,298 D | 20.5% | 79.5% | 20.5% | 79.5% |
| 187,767 | CHATHAM | 56,235 | 24,160 | 32,075 | | 7,915 D | 43.0% | 57.0% | 43.0% | 57.0% |
| 25,813 | CHATTAHOOCHEE | 684 | 178 | 506 | | 328 D | 26.0% | 74.0% | 26.0% | 74.0% |
| 20,541 | CHATTOOGA | 5,773 | 1,087 | 4,686 | | 3,599 D | 18.8% | 81.2% | 18.8% | 81.2% |
| 31,059 | CHEROKEE | 9,148 | 2,609 | 6,539 | | 3,930 D | 28.5% | 71.5% | 28.5% | 71.5% |
| 65,177 | CLARKE | 17,952 | 6,610 | 11,342 | | 4,732 D | 36.8% | 63.2% | 36.8% | 63.2% |
| 3,636 | CLAY | 1,242 | 295 | 947 | | 652 D | 23.8% | 76.2% | 23.8% | 76.2% |
| 98,043 | CLAYTON | 34,337 | 12,905 | 21,432 | | 8,527 D | 37.6% | 62.4% | 37.6% | 62.4% |
| 6,405 | CLINCH | 1,797 | 383 | 1,414 | | 1,031 D | 21.3% | 78.7% | 21.3% | 78.7% |
| 196,793 | COBB | 79,326 | 34,324 | 45,002 | | 10,678 D | 43.3% | 56.7% | 43.3% | 56.7% |
| 22,828 | COFFEE | 6,018 | 1,417 | 4,601 | | 3,184 D | 23.5% | 76.5% | 23.5% | 76.5% |
| 32,200 | COLQUITT | 9,109 | 2,181 | 6,928 | | 4,747 D | 23.9% | 76.1% | 23.9% | 76.1% |
| 22,327 | COLUMBIA | 8,097 | 3,423 | 4,674 | | 1,251 D | 42.3% | 57.7% | 42.3% | 57.7% |
| 12,129 | COOK | 3,552 | 670 | 2,882 | | 2,212 D | 18.9% | 81.1% | 18.9% | 81.1% |
| 32,310 | COWETA | 9,239 | 3,044 | 6,195 | | 3,151 D | 32.9% | 67.1% | 32.9% | 67.1% |
| 5,748 | CRAWFORD | 2,220 | 378 | 1,842 | | 1,464 D | 17.0% | 83.0% | 17.0% | 83.0% |
| 18,087 | CRISP | 5,075 | 1,328 | 3,747 | | 2,419 D | 26.2% | 73.8% | 26.2% | 73.8% |
| 9,910 | DADE | 3,651 | 1,388 | 2,263 | | 875 D | 38.0% | 62.0% | 38.0% | 62.0% |
| 3,639 | DAWSON | 1,754 | 370 | 1,384 | | 1,014 D | 21.1% | 78.9% | 21.1% | 78.9% |
| 22,310 | DECATUR | 6,236 | 2,500 | 3,736 | | 1,236 D | 40.1% | 59.9% | 40.1% | 59.9% |
| 415,387 | DE KALB | 154,032 | 67,160 | 86,872 | | 19,712 D | 43.6% | 56.4% | 43.6% | 56.4% |
| 15,658 | DODGE | 6,115 | 848 | 5,267 | | 4,419 D | 13.9% | 86.1% | 13.9% | 86.1% |
| 10,404 | DOOLY | 3,096 | 655 | 2,441 | | 1,786 D | 21.2% | 78.8% | 21.2% | 78.8% |
| 89,639 | DOUGHERTY | 20,798 | 9,337 | 11,461 | | 2,124 D | 44.9% | 55.1% | 44.9% | 55.1% |
| 28,659 | DOUGLAS | 11,764 | 3,959 | 7,805 | | 3,846 D | 33.7% | 66.3% | 33.7% | 66.3% |
| 12,682 | EARLY | 3,562 | 1,157 | 2,405 | | 1,248 D | 32.5% | 67.5% | 32.5% | 67.5% |
| 1,924 | ECHOLS | 696 | 111 | 585 | | 474 D | 15.9% | 84.1% | 15.9% | 84.1% |
| 13,632 | EFFINGHAM | 4,560 | 1,654 | 2,906 | | 1,252 D | 36.3% | 63.7% | 36.3% | 63.7% |
| 17,262 | ELBERT | 5,691 | 961 | 4,730 | | 3,769 D | 16.9% | 83.1% | 16.9% | 83.1% |
| 18,189 | EMANUEL | 6,096 | 1,493 | 4,603 | | 3,110 D | 24.5% | 75.5% | 24.5% | 75.5% |
| 7,290 | EVANS | 2,377 | 746 | 1,631 | | 885 D | 31.4% | 68.6% | 31.4% | 68.6% |
| 13,357 | FANNIN | 6,048 | 2,646 | 3,402 | | 756 D | 43.8% | 56.3% | 43.8% | 56.3% |
| 11,364 | FAYETTE | 6,555 | 2,837 | 3,718 | | 881 D | 43.3% | 56.7% | 43.3% | 56.7% |
| 73,742 | FLOYD | 22,864 | 7,713 | 15,151 | | 7,438 D | 33.7% | 66.3% | 33.7% | 66.3% |
| 16,928 | FORSYTH | 6,136 | 1,443 | 4,693 | | 3,250 D | 23.5% | 76.5% | 23.5% | 76.5% |
| 12,784 | FRANKLIN | 4,879 | 687 | 4,192 | | 3,505 D | 14.1% | 85.9% | 14.1% | 85.9% |
| 607,592 | FULTON | 191,401 | 61,552 | 129,849 | | 68,297 D | 32.2% | 67.8% | 32.2% | 67.8% |

# GEORGIA

## PRESIDENT 1976

| 1970 Census Population | County | Total Vote | Republican | Democratic | Other | Rep.-Dem. Plurality | Total Vote Rep. | Total Vote Dem. | Major Vote Rep. | Major Vote Dem. |
|---|---|---|---|---|---|---|---|---|---|---|
| 8,956 | GILMER | 3,760 | 1,261 | 2,499 | | 1,238 D | 33.5% | 66.5% | 33.5% | 66.5% |
| 2,280 | GLASCOCK | 1,075 | 371 | 704 | | 333 D | 34.5% | 65.5% | 34.5% | 65.5% |
| 50,528 | GLYNN | 14,862 | 5,403 | 9,459 | | 4,056 D | 36.4% | 63.6% | 36.4% | 63.6% |
| 23,570 | GORDON | 7,750 | 1,698 | 6,052 | | 4,354 D | 21.9% | 78.1% | 21.9% | 78.1% |
| 17,826 | GRADY | 4,967 | 1,209 | 3,758 | | 2,549 D | 24.3% | 75.7% | 24.3% | 75.7% |
| 10,212 | GREENE | 3,186 | 652 | 2,534 | | 1,882 D | 20.5% | 79.5% | 20.5% | 79.5% |
| 72,349 | GWINNETT | 34,750 | 13,912 | 20,838 | | 6,926 D | 40.0% | 60.0% | 40.0% | 60.0% |
| 20,691 | HABERSHAM | 6,435 | 1,315 | 5,120 | | 3,805 D | 20.4% | 79.6% | 20.4% | 79.6% |
| 59,405 | HALL | 17,897 | 5,093 | 12,804 | | 7,711 D | 28.5% | 71.5% | 28.5% | 71.5% |
| 9,019 | HANCOCK | 2,768 | 651 | 2,117 | | 1,466 D | 23.5% | 76.5% | 23.5% | 76.5% |
| 15,927 | HARALSON | 5,851 | 1,301 | 4,550 | | 3,249 D | 22.2% | 77.8% | 22.2% | 77.8% |
| 11,520 | HARRIS | 4,405 | 1,544 | 2,861 | | 1,317 D | 35.1% | 64.9% | 35.1% | 64.9% |
| 15,814 | HART | 5,465 | 860 | 4,605 | | 3,745 D | 15.7% | 84.3% | 15.7% | 84.3% |
| 5,354 | HEARD | 2,026 | 433 | 1,593 | | 1,160 D | 21.4% | 78.6% | 21.4% | 78.6% |
| 23,724 | HENRY | 8,339 | 2,622 | 5,717 | | 3,095 D | 31.4% | 68.6% | 31.4% | 68.6% |
| 62,924 | HOUSTON | 18,568 | 5,404 | 13,164 | | 7,760 D | 29.1% | 70.9% | 29.1% | 70.9% |
| 8,036 | IRWIN | 2,573 | 561 | 2,012 | | 1,451 D | 21.8% | 78.2% | 21.8% | 78.2% |
| 21,093 | JACKSON | 7,170 | 1,239 | 5,931 | | 4,692 D | 17.3% | 82.7% | 17.3% | 82.7% |
| 5,760 | JASPER | 2,541 | 689 | 1,852 | | 1,163 D | 27.1% | 72.9% | 27.1% | 72.9% |
| 9,425 | JEFF DAVIS | 3,027 | 622 | 2,405 | | 1,783 D | 20.5% | 79.5% | 20.5% | 79.5% |
| 17,174 | JEFFERSON | 4,424 | 1,309 | 3,115 | | 1,806 D | 29.6% | 70.4% | 29.6% | 70.4% |
| 8,332 | JENKINS | 2,383 | 563 | 1,820 | | 1,257 D | 23.6% | 76.4% | 23.6% | 76.4% |
| 7,727 | JOHNSON | 2,908 | 698 | 2,210 | | 1,512 D | 24.0% | 76.0% | 24.0% | 76.0% |
| 12,218 | JONES | 4,788 | 1,317 | 3,471 | | 2,154 D | 27.5% | 72.5% | 27.5% | 72.5% |
| 10,688 | LAMAR | 3,632 | 847 | 2,785 | | 1,938 D | 23.3% | 76.7% | 23.3% | 76.7% |
| 5,031 | LANIER | 1,476 | 207 | 1,269 | | 1,062 D | 14.0% | 86.0% | 14.0% | 86.0% |
| 32,738 | LAURENS | 11,898 | 3,281 | 8,617 | | 5,336 D | 27.6% | 72.4% | 27.6% | 72.4% |
| 7,044 | LEE | 2,837 | 1,110 | 1,727 | | 617 D | 39.1% | 60.9% | 39.1% | 60.9% |
| 17,569 | LIBERTY | 4,307 | 979 | 3,328 | | 2,349 D | 22.7% | 77.3% | 22.7% | 77.3% |
| 5,895 | LINCOLN | 2,159 | 576 | 1,583 | | 1,007 D | 26.7% | 73.3% | 26.7% | 73.3% |
| 3,746 | LONG | 1,465 | 222 | 1,243 | | 1,021 D | 15.2% | 84.8% | 15.2% | 84.8% |
| 55,112 | LOWNDES | 13,342 | 4,512 | 8,830 | | 4,318 D | 33.8% | 66.2% | 33.8% | 66.2% |
| 8,728 | LUMPKIN | 2,848 | 547 | 2,301 | | 1,754 D | 19.2% | 80.8% | 19.2% | 80.8% |
| 15,276 | MCDUFFIE | 4,718 | 1,694 | 3,024 | | 1,330 D | 35.9% | 64.1% | 35.9% | 64.1% |
| 7,371 | MCINTOSH | 2,513 | 535 | 1,978 | | 1,443 D | 21.3% | 78.7% | 21.3% | 78.7% |
| 12,933 | MACON | 3,651 | 638 | 3,013 | | 2,375 D | 17.5% | 82.5% | 17.5% | 82.5% |
| 13,517 | MADISON | 4,482 | 1,115 | 3,367 | | 2,252 D | 24.9% | 75.1% | 24.9% | 75.1% |
| 5,099 | MARION | 1,605 | 291 | 1,314 | | 1,023 D | 18.1% | 81.9% | 18.1% | 81.9% |
| 19,461 | MERIWETHER | 6,280 | 1,450 | 4,830 | | 3,380 D | 23.1% | 76.9% | 23.1% | 76.9% |
| 6,397 | MILLER | 2,012 | 476 | 1,536 | | 1,060 D | 23.7% | 76.3% | 23.7% | 76.3% |
| 18,956 | MITCHELL | 6,067 | 1,572 | 4,495 | | 2,923 D | 25.9% | 74.1% | 25.9% | 74.1% |
| 10,991 | MONROE | 4,040 | 1,078 | 2,962 | | 1,884 D | 26.7% | 73.3% | 26.7% | 73.3% |
| 6,099 | MONTGOMERY | 2,236 | 626 | 1,610 | | 984 D | 28.0% | 72.0% | 28.0% | 72.0% |
| 9,904 | MORGAN | 3,178 | 904 | 2,274 | | 1,370 D | 28.4% | 71.6% | 28.4% | 71.6% |
| 12,986 | MURRAY | 4,400 | 889 | 3,511 | | 2,622 D | 20.2% | 79.8% | 20.2% | 79.8% |
| 167,377 | MUSCOGEE | 37,588 | 13,496 | 24,092 | | 10,596 D | 35.9% | 64.1% | 35.9% | 64.1% |
| 26,282 | NEWTON | 8,431 | 2,137 | 6,294 | | 4,157 D | 25.3% | 74.7% | 25.3% | 74.7% |
| 7,915 | OCONEE | 3,412 | 1,184 | 2,228 | | 1,044 D | 34.7% | 65.3% | 34.7% | 65.3% |
| 7,598 | OGLETHORPE | 2,665 | 811 | 1,854 | | 1,043 D | 30.4% | 69.6% | 30.4% | 69.6% |
| 17,520 | PAULDING | 6,852 | 1,432 | 5,420 | | 3,988 D | 20.9% | 79.1% | 20.9% | 79.1% |
| 15,990 | PEACH | 5,152 | 1,163 | 3,989 | | 2,826 D | 22.6% | 77.4% | 22.6% | 77.4% |
| 9,620 | PICKENS | 3,544 | 973 | 2,571 | | 1,598 D | 27.5% | 72.5% | 27.5% | 72.5% |
| 9,281 | PIERCE | 3,172 | 544 | 2,628 | | 2,084 D | 17.2% | 82.8% | 17.2% | 82.8% |
| 7,316 | PIKE | 2,679 | 776 | 1,903 | | 1,127 D | 29.0% | 71.0% | 29.0% | 71.0% |
| 29,656 | POLK | 8,059 | 1,944 | 6,115 | | 4,171 D | 24.1% | 75.9% | 24.1% | 75.9% |
| 8,066 | PULASKI | 2,803 | 485 | 2,318 | | 1,833 D | 17.3% | 82.7% | 17.3% | 82.7% |
| 8,394 | PUTNAM | 2,875 | 835 | 2,040 | | 1,205 D | 29.0% | 71.0% | 29.0% | 71.0% |
| 2,180 | QUITMAN | 990 | 313 | 677 | | 364 D | 31.6% | 68.4% | 31.6% | 68.4% |
| 8,327 | RABUN | 2,989 | 591 | 2,398 | | 1,807 D | 19.8% | 80.2% | 19.8% | 80.2% |
| 8,734 | RANDOLPH | 2,933 | 747 | 2,186 | | 1,439 D | 25.5% | 74.5% | 25.5% | 74.5% |

# GEORGIA

## PRESIDENT 1976

| 1970 Census Population | County | Total Vote | Republican | Democratic | Other | Rep.-Dem. Plurality | Percentage Total Vote Rep. | Dem. | Major Vote Rep. | Dem. |
|---|---|---|---|---|---|---|---|---|---|---|
| 162,437 | RICHMOND | 41,935 | 17,893 | 24,042 | | 6,149 D | 42.7% | 57.3% | 42.7% | 57.3% |
| 18,152 | ROCKDALE | 7,614 | 2,974 | 4,640 | | 1,666 D | 39.1% | 60.9% | 39.1% | 60.9% |
| 3,097 | SCHLEY | 1,051 | 268 | 783 | | 515 D | 25.5% | 74.5% | 25.5% | 74.5% |
| 12,591 | SCREVEN | 3,344 | 1,176 | 2,168 | | 992 D | 35.2% | 64.8% | 35.2% | 64.8% |
| 7,059 | SEMINOLE | 2,755 | 681 | 2,074 | | 1,393 D | 24.7% | 75.3% | 24.7% | 75.3% |
| 39,514 | SPALDING | 11,332 | 3,739 | 7,593 | | 3,854 D | 33.0% | 67.0% | 33.0% | 67.0% |
| 20,331 | STEPHENS | 6,900 | 1,340 | 5,560 | | 4,220 D | 19.4% | 80.6% | 19.4% | 80.6% |
| 6,511 | STEWART | 2,065 | 433 | 1,632 | | 1,199 D | 21.0% | 79.0% | 21.0% | 79.0% |
| 26,931 | SUMTER | 7,381 | 2,053 | 5,328 | | 3,275 D | 27.8% | 72.2% | 27.8% | 72.2% |
| 6,625 | TALBOT | 2,093 | 459 | 1,634 | | 1,175 D | 21.9% | 78.1% | 21.9% | 78.1% |
| 2,423 | TALIAFERRO | 984 | 236 | 748 | | 512 D | 24.0% | 76.0% | 24.0% | 76.0% |
| 16,557 | TATTNALL | 4,882 | 1,326 | 3,556 | | 2,230 D | 27.2% | 72.8% | 27.2% | 72.8% |
| 7,865 | TAYLOR | 2,466 | 504 | 1,962 | | 1,458 D | 20.4% | 79.6% | 20.4% | 79.6% |
| 11,381 | TELFAIR | 4,171 | 637 | 3,534 | | 2,897 D | 15.3% | 84.7% | 15.3% | 84.7% |
| 11,416 | TERRELL | 3,516 | 1,168 | 2,348 | | 1,180 D | 33.2% | 66.8% | 33.2% | 66.8% |
| 34,515 | THOMAS | 9,410 | 3,263 | 6,147 | | 2,884 D | 34.7% | 65.3% | 34.7% | 65.3% |
| 27,288 | TIFT | 7,347 | 2,162 | 5,185 | | 3,023 D | 29.4% | 70.6% | 29.4% | 70.6% |
| 19,151 | TOOMBS | 6,173 | 2,126 | 4,047 | | 1,921 D | 34.4% | 65.6% | 34.4% | 65.6% |
| 4,565 | TOWNS | 2,961 | 1,175 | 1,786 | | 611 D | 39.7% | 60.3% | 39.7% | 60.3% |
| 5,647 | TREUTLEN | 2,032 | 465 | 1,567 | | 1,102 D | 22.9% | 77.1% | 22.9% | 77.1% |
| 44,466 | TROUP | 12,121 | 4,422 | 7,699 | | 3,277 D | 36.5% | 63.5% | 36.5% | 63.5% |
| 8,790 | TURNER | 2,681 | 416 | 2,265 | | 1,849 D | 15.5% | 84.5% | 15.5% | 84.5% |
| 8,222 | TWIGGS | 3,028 | 513 | 2,515 | | 2,002 D | 16.9% | 83.1% | 16.9% | 83.1% |
| 6,811 | UNION | 3,949 | 1,154 | 2,795 | | 1,641 D | 29.2% | 70.8% | 29.2% | 70.8% |
| 23,505 | UPSON | 7,116 | 2,897 | 4,219 | | 1,322 D | 40.7% | 59.3% | 40.7% | 59.3% |
| 50,691 | WALKER | 12,814 | 4,807 | 8,007 | | 3,200 D | 37.5% | 62.5% | 37.5% | 62.5% |
| 23,404 | WALTON | 7,089 | 1,687 | 5,402 | | 3,715 D | 23.8% | 76.2% | 23.8% | 76.2% |
| 33,525 | WARE | 10,380 | 2,661 | 7,719 | | 5,058 D | 25.6% | 74.4% | 25.6% | 74.4% |
| 6,669 | WARREN | 2,055 | 720 | 1,335 | | 615 D | 35.0% | 65.0% | 35.0% | 65.0% |
| 17,480 | WASHINGTON | 5,522 | 1,657 | 3,865 | | 2,208 D | 30.0% | 70.0% | 30.0% | 70.0% |
| 17,858 | WAYNE | 5,988 | 1,499 | 4,489 | | 2,990 D | 25.0% | 75.0% | 25.0% | 75.0% |
| 2,362 | WEBSTER | 787 | 165 | 622 | | 457 D | 21.0% | 79.0% | 21.0% | 79.0% |
| 4,596 | WHEELER | 1,722 | 344 | 1,378 | | 1,034 D | 20.0% | 80.0% | 20.0% | 80.0% |
| 7,742 | WHITE | 2,750 | 625 | 2,125 | | 1,500 D | 22.7% | 77.3% | 22.7% | 77.3% |
| 55,108 | WHITFIELD | 14,973 | 4,498 | 10,475 | | 5,977 D | 30.0% | 70.0% | 30.0% | 70.0% |
| 6,998 | WILCOX | 2,499 | 346 | 2,153 | | 1,807 D | 13.8% | 86.2% | 13.8% | 86.2% |
| 10,184 | WILKES | 3,528 | 1,067 | 2,461 | | 1,394 D | 30.2% | 69.8% | 30.2% | 69.8% |
| 9,393 | WILKINSON | 3,489 | 837 | 2,652 | | 1,815 D | 24.0% | 76.0% | 24.0% | 76.0% |
| 14,770 | WORTH | 3,946 | 1,156 | 2,790 | | 1,634 D | 29.3% | 70.7% | 29.3% | 70.7% |
| 4,589,575 | TOTAL | 1,467,458 | 483,743 | 979,409 | 4,306 | 495,666 D | 33.0% | 66.7% | 33.1% | 66.9% |

# GEORGIA

## PRESIDENT 1972

| 1970 Census Population | County | Total Vote | Republican | Democratic | Other | Rep.-Dem. Plurality | Percentage Total Vote Rep. | Dem. | Major Vote Rep. | Dem. |
|---|---|---|---|---|---|---|---|---|---|---|
| 12,726 | APPLING | 3,267 | 2,755 | 512 | | 2,243 R | 84.3% | 15.7% | 84.3% | 15.7% |
| 5,879 | ATKINSON | 1,235 | 924 | 309 | 2 | 615 R | 74.8% | 25.0% | 74.9% | 25.1% |
| 8,233 | BACON | 1,963 | 1,771 | 192 | | 1,579 R | 90.2% | 9.8% | 90.2% | 9.8% |
| 3,875 | BAKER | 1,314 | 965 | 345 | 4 | 620 R | 73.4% | 26.3% | 73.7% | 26.3% |
| 34,240 | BALDWIN | 6,265 | 4,826 | 1,435 | 4 | 3,391 R | 77.0% | 22.9% | 77.1% | 22.9% |
| 6,833 | BANKS | 1,705 | 1,336 | 356 | 13 | 980 R | 78.4% | 20.9% | 79.0% | 21.0% |
| 16,859 | BARROW | 4,290 | 3,423 | 867 | | 2,556 R | 79.8% | 20.2% | 79.8% | 20.2% |
| 32,663 | BARTOW | 6,426 | 4,836 | 1,590 | | 3,246 R | 75.3% | 24.7% | 75.3% | 24.7% |
| 13,171 | BEN HILL | 2,828 | 2,104 | 703 | 21 | 1,401 R | 74.4% | 24.9% | 75.0% | 25.0% |
| 11,556 | BERRIEN | 2,680 | 2,285 | 371 | 24 | 1,914 R | 85.3% | 13.8% | 86.0% | 14.0% |
| 143,418 | BIBB | 37,838 | 27,402 | 10,201 | 235 | 17,201 R | 72.4% | 27.0% | 72.9% | 27.1% |
| 10,291 | BLECKLEY | 2,685 | 2,308 | 377 | | 1,931 R | 86.0% | 14.0% | 86.0% | 14.0% |
| 5,940 | BRANTLEY | 1,925 | 1,587 | 338 | | 1,249 R | 82.4% | 17.6% | 82.4% | 17.6% |
| 13,739 | BROOKS | 3,086 | 2,430 | 643 | 13 | 1,787 R | 78.7% | 20.8% | 79.1% | 20.9% |
| 6,539 | BRYAN | 1,672 | 1,409 | 263 | | 1,146 R | 84.3% | 15.7% | 84.3% | 15.7% |
| 31,585 | BULLOCH | 7,260 | 5,683 | 1,524 | 53 | 4,159 R | 78.3% | 21.0% | 78.9% | 21.1% |
| 18,255 | BURKE | 3,904 | 2,846 | 1,058 | | 1,788 R | 72.9% | 27.1% | 72.9% | 27.1% |
| 10,560 | BUTTS | 2,703 | 1,968 | 727 | 8 | 1,241 R | 72.8% | 26.9% | 73.0% | 27.0% |
| 6,606 | CALHOUN | 1,391 | 892 | 495 | 4 | 397 R | 64.1% | 35.6% | 64.3% | 35.7% |
| 11,334 | CAMDEN | 3,133 | 2,380 | 753 | | 1,627 R | 76.0% | 24.0% | 76.0% | 24.0% |
| 6,412 | CANDLER | 1,669 | 1,427 | 238 | 4 | 1,189 R | 85.5% | 14.3% | 85.7% | 14.3% |
| 45,404 | CARROLL | 10,454 | 8,296 | 2,158 | | 6,138 R | 79.4% | 20.6% | 79.4% | 20.6% |
| 28,271 | CATOOSA | 7,027 | 6,008 | 894 | 125 | 5,114 R | 85.5% | 12.7% | 87.0% | 13.0% |
| 5,680 | CHARLTON | 1,554 | 1,244 | 310 | | 934 R | 80.1% | 19.9% | 80.1% | 19.9% |
| 187,767 | CHATHAM | 53,674 | 38,079 | 15,566 | 29 | 22,513 R | 70.9% | 29.0% | 71.0% | 29.0% |
| 25,813 | CHATTAHOOCHEE | 468 | 345 | 121 | 2 | 224 R | 73.7% | 25.9% | 74.0% | 26.0% |
| 20,541 | CHATTOOGA | 4,145 | 3,188 | 923 | 34 | 2,265 R | 76.9% | 22.3% | 77.5% | 22.5% |
| 31,059 | CHEROKEE | 6,679 | 5,509 | 1,159 | 11 | 4,350 R | 82.5% | 17.4% | 82.6% | 17.4% |
| 65,177 | CLARKE | 17,555 | 11,465 | 6,090 | | 5,375 R | 65.3% | 34.7% | 65.3% | 34.7% |
| 3,636 | CLAY | 921 | 632 | 283 | 6 | 349 R | 68.6% | 30.7% | 69.1% | 30.9% |
| 98,043 | CLAYTON | 27,753 | 23,681 | 3,740 | 332 | 19,941 R | 85.3% | 13.5% | 86.4% | 13.6% |
| 6,405 | CLINCH | 1,366 | 1,127 | 239 | | 888 R | 82.5% | 17.5% | 82.5% | 17.5% |
| 196,793 | COBB | 52,002 | 43,977 | 7,688 | 337 | 36,289 R | 84.6% | 14.8% | 85.1% | 14.9% |
| 22,828 | COFFEE | 4,541 | 3,934 | 607 | | 3,327 R | 86.6% | 13.4% | 86.6% | 13.4% |
| 32,200 | COLQUITT | 7,834 | 6,900 | 930 | 4 | 5,970 R | 88.1% | 11.9% | 88.1% | 11.9% |
| 22,327 | COLUMBIA | 5,785 | 4,839 | 946 | | 3,893 R | 83.6% | 16.4% | 83.6% | 16.4% |
| 12,129 | COOK | 2,667 | 2,135 | 525 | 7 | 1,610 R | 80.1% | 19.7% | 80.3% | 19.7% |
| 32,310 | COWETA | 7,311 | 5,751 | 1,560 | | 4,191 R | 78.7% | 21.3% | 78.7% | 21.3% |
| 5,748 | CRAWFORD | 1,686 | 1,167 | 512 | 7 | 655 R | 69.2% | 30.4% | 69.5% | 30.5% |
| 18,087 | CRISP | 4,307 | 3,623 | 682 | 2 | 2,941 R | 84.1% | 15.8% | 84.2% | 15.8% |
| 9,910 | DADE | 2,268 | 2,110 | 148 | 10 | 1,962 R | 93.0% | 6.5% | 93.4% | 6.6% |
| 3,639 | DAWSON | 1,061 | 828 | 230 | 3 | 598 R | 78.0% | 21.7% | 78.3% | 21.7% |
| 22,310 | DECATUR | 5,504 | 4,292 | 1,196 | 16 | 3,096 R | 78.0% | 21.7% | 78.2% | 21.8% |
| 415,387 | DE KALB | 135,915 | 104,750 | 30,671 | 494 | 74,079 R | 77.1% | 22.6% | 77.4% | 22.6% |
| 15,658 | DODGE | 5,237 | 4,346 | 884 | 7 | 3,462 R | 83.0% | 16.9% | 83.1% | 16.9% |
| 10,404 | DOOLY | 2,494 | 1,904 | 590 | | 1,314 R | 76.3% | 23.7% | 76.3% | 23.7% |
| 89,639 | DOUGHERTY | 16,551 | 12,878 | 3,625 | 48 | 9,253 R | 77.8% | 21.9% | 78.0% | 22.0% |
| 28,659 | DOUGLAS | 7,633 | 6,610 | 982 | 41 | 5,628 R | 86.6% | 12.9% | 87.1% | 12.9% |
| 12,682 | EARLY | 2,912 | 2,396 | 513 | 3 | 1,883 R | 82.3% | 17.6% | 82.4% | 17.6% |
| 1,924 | ECHOLS | 472 | 404 | 68 | | 336 R | 85.6% | 14.4% | 85.6% | 14.4% |
| 13,632 | EFFINGHAM | 3,672 | 3,175 | 497 | | 2,678 R | 86.5% | 13.5% | 86.5% | 13.5% |
| 17,262 | ELBERT | 3,801 | 2,875 | 884 | 42 | 1,991 R | 75.6% | 23.3% | 76.5% | 23.5% |
| 18,189 | EMANUEL | 4,634 | 3,684 | 916 | 34 | 2,768 R | 79.5% | 19.8% | 80.1% | 19.9% |
| 7,290 | EVANS | 2,056 | 1,666 | 375 | 15 | 1,291 R | 81.0% | 18.2% | 81.6% | 18.4% |
| 13,357 | FANNIN | 4,732 | 3,783 | 949 | | 2,834 R | 79.9% | 20.1% | 79.9% | 20.1% |
| 11,364 | FAYETTE | 3,861 | 3,401 | 450 | 10 | 2,951 R | 88.1% | 11.7% | 88.3% | 11.7% |
| 73,742 | FLOYD | 18,922 | 15,485 | 3,372 | 65 | 12,113 R | 81.8% | 17.8% | 82.1% | 17.9% |
| 16,928 | FORSYTH | 3,536 | 2,968 | 549 | 19 | 2,419 R | 83.9% | 15.5% | 84.4% | 15.6% |
| 12,784 | FRANKLIN | 2,470 | 2,022 | 435 | 13 | 1,587 R | 81.9% | 17.6% | 82.3% | 17.7% |
| 607,592 | FULTON | 170,884 | 96,256 | 74,329 | 299 | 21,927 R | 56.3% | 43.5% | 56.4% | 43.6% |

# GEORGIA

## PRESIDENT 1972

| 1970 Census Population | County | Total Vote | Republican | Democratic | Other | Rep.-Dem. Plurality | Total Vote Rep. | Dem. | Major Vote Rep. | Dem. |
|---|---|---|---|---|---|---|---|---|---|---|
| 8,956 | GILMER | 3,497 | 2,729 | 768 | | 1,961 R | 78.0% | 22.0% | 78.0% | 22.0% |
| 2,280 | GLASCOCK | 619 | 578 | 41 | | 537 R | 93.4% | 6.6% | 93.4% | 6.6% |
| 50,528 | GLYNN | 12,474 | 9,443 | 3,002 | 29 | 6,441 R | 75.7% | 24.1% | 75.9% | 24.1% |
| 23,570 | GORDON | 5,228 | 4,344 | 870 | 14 | 3,474 R | 83.1% | 16.6% | 83.3% | 16.7% |
| 17,826 | GRADY | 4,608 | 3,732 | 874 | 2 | 2,858 R | 81.0% | 19.0% | 81.0% | 19.0% |
| 10,212 | GREENE | 2,612 | 1,679 | 919 | 14 | 760 R | 64.3% | 35.2% | 64.6% | 35.4% |
| 72,349 | GWINNETT | 21,177 | 18,181 | 2,896 | 100 | 15,285 R | 85.9% | 13.7% | 86.3% | 13.7% |
| 20,691 | HABERSHAM | 1,147 | 971 | 172 | 4 | 799 R | 84.7% | 15.0% | 85.0% | 15.0% |
| 59,405 | HALL | 13,134 | 10,686 | 2,440 | 8 | 8,246 R | 81.4% | 18.6% | 81.4% | 18.6% |
| 9,019 | HANCOCK | 3,104 | 1,595 | 1,502 | 7 | 93 R | 51.4% | 48.4% | 51.5% | 48.5% |
| 15,927 | HARALSON | 4,252 | 3,460 | 767 | 25 | 2,693 R | 81.4% | 18.0% | 81.9% | 18.1% |
| 11,520 | HARRIS | 3,324 | 2,617 | 701 | 6 | 1,916 R | 78.7% | 21.1% | 78.9% | 21.1% |
| 15,814 | HART | 3,136 | 2,308 | 784 | 44 | 1,524 R | 73.6% | 25.0% | 74.6% | 25.4% |
| 5,354 | HEARD | 1,530 | 1,239 | 276 | 15 | 963 R | 81.0% | 18.0% | 81.8% | 18.2% |
| 23,724 | HENRY | 6,622 | 5,155 | 1,460 | 7 | 3,695 R | 77.8% | 22.0% | 77.9% | 22.1% |
| 62,924 | HOUSTON | 16,170 | 13,576 | 2,556 | 38 | 11,020 R | 84.0% | 15.8% | 84.2% | 15.8% |
| 8,036 | IRWIN | 2,192 | 1,851 | 335 | 6 | 1,516 R | 84.4% | 15.3% | 84.7% | 15.3% |
| 21,093 | JACKSON | 5,218 | 4,124 | 1,055 | 39 | 3,069 R | 79.0% | 20.2% | 79.6% | 20.4% |
| 5,760 | JASPER | 1,752 | 1,289 | 463 | | 826 R | 73.6% | 26.4% | 73.6% | 26.4% |
| 9,425 | JEFF DAVIS | 2,159 | 1,857 | 302 | | 1,555 R | 86.0% | 14.0% | 86.0% | 14.0% |
| 17,174 | JEFFERSON | 3,987 | 2,777 | 1,184 | 26 | 1,593 R | 69.7% | 29.7% | 70.1% | 29.9% |
| 8,332 | JENKINS | 2,277 | 1,769 | 484 | 24 | 1,285 R | 77.7% | 21.3% | 78.5% | 21.5% |
| 7,727 | JOHNSON | 2,637 | 2,201 | 417 | 19 | 1,784 R | 83.5% | 15.8% | 84.1% | 15.9% |
| 12,218 | JONES | 3,368 | 2,483 | 861 | 24 | 1,622 R | 73.7% | 25.6% | 74.3% | 25.7% |
| 10,688 | LAMAR | 2,510 | 1,844 | 666 | | 1,178 R | 73.5% | 26.5% | 73.5% | 26.5% |
| 5,031 | LANIER | 1,046 | 850 | 193 | 3 | 657 R | 81.3% | 18.5% | 81.5% | 18.5% |
| 32,738 | LAURENS | 9,513 | 7,350 | 2,130 | 33 | 5,220 R | 77.3% | 22.4% | 77.5% | 22.5% |
| 7,044 | LEE | 1,853 | 1,441 | 390 | 22 | 1,051 R | 77.8% | 21.0% | 78.7% | 21.3% |
| 17,569 | LIBERTY | 3,556 | 2,337 | 1,217 | 2 | 1,120 R | 65.7% | 34.2% | 65.8% | 34.2% |
| 5,895 | LINCOLN | 1,586 | 1,246 | 340 | | 906 R | 78.6% | 21.4% | 78.6% | 21.4% |
| 3,746 | LONG | 1,000 | 764 | 236 | | 528 R | 76.4% | 23.6% | 76.4% | 23.6% |
| 55,112 | LOWNDES | 9,839 | 7,812 | 2,015 | 12 | 5,797 R | 79.4% | 20.5% | 79.5% | 20.5% |
| 8,728 | LUMPKIN | 1,869 | 1,477 | 385 | 7 | 1,092 R | 79.0% | 20.6% | 79.3% | 20.7% |
| 15,276 | MCDUFFIE | 3,988 | 2,990 | 996 | 2 | 1,994 R | 75.0% | 25.0% | 75.0% | 25.0% |
| 7,371 | MCINTOSH | 2,209 | 1,367 | 833 | 9 | 534 R | 61.9% | 37.7% | 62.1% | 37.9% |
| 12,933 | MACON | 2,842 | 2,005 | 837 | | 1,168 R | 70.5% | 29.5% | 70.5% | 29.5% |
| 13,517 | MADISON | 3,192 | 2,606 | 572 | 14 | 2,034 R | 81.6% | 17.9% | 82.0% | 18.0% |
| 5,099 | MARION | 1,016 | 850 | 164 | 2 | 686 R | 83.7% | 16.1% | 83.8% | 16.2% |
| 19,461 | MERIWETHER | 4,643 | 3,420 | 1,213 | 10 | 2,207 R | 73.7% | 26.1% | 73.8% | 26.2% |
| 6,397 | MILLER | 1,387 | 1,269 | 118 | | 1,151 R | 91.5% | 8.5% | 91.5% | 8.5% |
| 18,956 | MITCHELL | 3,537 | 2,400 | 1,120 | 17 | 1,280 R | 67.9% | 31.7% | 68.2% | 31.8% |
| 10,991 | MONROE | 2,977 | 2,181 | 789 | 7 | 1,392 R | 73.3% | 26.5% | 73.4% | 26.6% |
| 6,099 | MONTGOMERY | 1,707 | 1,370 | 337 | | 1,033 R | 80.3% | 19.7% | 80.3% | 19.7% |
| 9,904 | MORGAN | 2,693 | 2,007 | 668 | 18 | 1,339 R | 74.5% | 24.8% | 75.0% | 25.0% |
| 12,986 | MURRAY | 3,287 | 2,643 | 644 | | 1,999 R | 80.4% | 19.6% | 80.4% | 19.6% |
| 167,377 | MUSCOGEE | 36,739 | 28,449 | 8,234 | 56 | 20,215 R | 77.4% | 22.4% | 77.6% | 22.4% |
| 26,282 | NEWTON | 6,031 | 4,647 | 1,380 | 4 | 3,267 R | 77.1% | 22.9% | 77.1% | 22.9% |
| 7,915 | OCONEE | 2,505 | 2,029 | 464 | 12 | 1,565 R | 81.0% | 18.5% | 81.4% | 18.6% |
| 7,598 | OGLETHORPE | 2,059 | 1,712 | 326 | 21 | 1,386 R | 83.1% | 15.8% | 84.0% | 16.0% |
| 17,520 | PAULDING | 3,831 | 2,814 | 1,004 | 13 | 1,810 R | 73.5% | 26.2% | 73.7% | 26.3% |
| 15,990 | PEACH | 6,164 | 3,747 | 2,413 | 4 | 1,334 R | 60.8% | 39.1% | 60.8% | 39.2% |
| 9,620 | PICKENS | 2,621 | 2,101 | 520 | | 1,581 R | 80.2% | 19.8% | 80.2% | 19.8% |
| 9,281 | PIERCE | 2,256 | 1,982 | 269 | 5 | 1,713 R | 87.9% | 11.9% | 88.0% | 12.0% |
| 7,316 | PIKE | 1,864 | 1,432 | 423 | 9 | 1,009 R | 76.8% | 22.7% | 77.2% | 22.8% |
| 29,656 | POLK | 6,274 | 4,929 | 1,317 | 28 | 3,612 R | 78.6% | 21.0% | 78.9% | 21.1% |
| 8,066 | PULASKI | 2,412 | 1,966 | 444 | 2 | 1,522 R | 81.5% | 18.4% | 81.6% | 18.4% |
| 8,394 | PUTNAM | 2,567 | 1,963 | 604 | | 1,359 R | 76.5% | 23.5% | 76.5% | 23.5% |
| 2,180 | QUITMAN | 642 | 502 | 140 | | 362 R | 78.2% | 21.8% | 78.2% | 21.8% |
| 8,327 | RABUN | 1,855 | 1,477 | 366 | 12 | 1,111 R | 79.6% | 19.7% | 80.1% | 19.9% |
| 8,734 | RANDOLPH | 2,401 | 1,603 | 798 | | 805 R | 66.8% | 33.2% | 66.8% | 33.2% |

# GEORGIA

## PRESIDENT 1972

| 1970 Census Population | County | Total Vote | Republican | Democratic | Other | Rep.-Dem. Plurality | Percentage | | | |
|---|---|---|---|---|---|---|---|---|---|---|
| | | | | | | | Total Vote | | Major Vote | |
| | | | | | | | Rep. | Dem. | Rep. | Dem. |
| 162,437 | RICHMOND | 33,607 | 24,362 | 9,219 | 26 | 15,143 R | 72.5% | 27.4% | 72.5% | 27.5% |
| 18,152 | ROCKDALE | 4,376 | 3,560 | 791 | 25 | 2,769 R | 81.4% | 18.1% | 81.8% | 18.2% |
| 3,097 | SCHLEY | 858 | 694 | 162 | 2 | 532 R | 80.9% | 18.9% | 81.1% | 18.9% |
| 12,591 | SCREVEN | 2,977 | 2,402 | 575 | | 1,827 R | 80.7% | 19.3% | 80.7% | 19.3% |
| 7,059 | SEMINOLE | 2,227 | 1,851 | 376 | | 1,475 R | 83.1% | 16.9% | 83.1% | 16.9% |
| 39,514 | SPALDING | 8,898 | 7,183 | 1,702 | 13 | 5,481 R | 80.7% | 19.1% | 80.8% | 19.2% |
| 20,331 | STEPHENS | 4,649 | 3,773 | 871 | 5 | 2,902 R | 81.2% | 18.7% | 81.2% | 18.8% |
| 6,511 | STEWART | 1,375 | 1,020 | 353 | 2 | 667 R | 74.2% | 25.7% | 74.3% | 25.7% |
| 26,931 | SUMTER | 5,839 | 4,533 | 1,268 | 38 | 3,265 R | 77.6% | 21.7% | 78.1% | 21.9% |
| 6,625 | TALBOT | 1,500 | 990 | 508 | 2 | 482 R | 66.0% | 33.9% | 66.1% | 33.9% |
| 2,423 | TALIAFERRO | 957 | 585 | 372 | | 213 R | 61.1% | 38.9% | 61.1% | 38.9% |
| 16,557 | TATTNALL | 3,419 | 2,892 | 492 | 35 | 2,400 R | 84.6% | 14.4% | 85.5% | 14.5% |
| 7,865 | TAYLOR | 2,100 | 1,580 | 514 | 6 | 1,066 R | 75.2% | 24.5% | 75.5% | 24.5% |
| 11,381 | TELFAIR | 2,932 | 2,245 | 687 | | 1,558 R | 76.6% | 23.4% | 76.6% | 23.4% |
| 11,416 | TERRELL | 2,754 | 2,057 | 686 | 11 | 1,371 R | 74.7% | 24.9% | 75.0% | 25.0% |
| 34,515 | THOMAS | 8,839 | 6,668 | 2,171 | | 4,497 R | 75.4% | 24.6% | 75.4% | 24.6% |
| 27,288 | TIFT | 5,408 | 4,591 | 816 | 1 | 3,775 R | 84.9% | 15.1% | 84.9% | 15.1% |
| 19,151 | TOOMBS | 4,775 | 4,080 | 675 | 20 | 3,405 R | 85.4% | 14.1% | 85.8% | 14.2% |
| 4,565 | TOWNS | 1,979 | 1,573 | 404 | 2 | 1,169 R | 79.5% | 20.4% | 79.6% | 20.4% |
| 5,647 | TREUTLEN | 1,556 | 1,346 | 210 | | 1,136 R | 86.5% | 13.5% | 86.5% | 13.5% |
| 44,466 | TROUP | 10,429 | 8,350 | 2,056 | 23 | 6,294 R | 80.1% | 19.7% | 80.2% | 19.8% |
| 8,790 | TURNER | 2,565 | 2,120 | 437 | 8 | 1,683 R | 82.7% | 17.0% | 82.9% | 17.1% |
| 8,222 | TWIGGS | 2,488 | 1,363 | 1,113 | 12 | 250 R | 54.8% | 44.7% | 55.0% | 45.0% |
| 6,811 | UNION | 3,068 | 2,317 | 742 | 9 | 1,575 R | 75.5% | 24.2% | 75.7% | 24.3% |
| 23,505 | UPSON | 5,830 | 4,892 | 896 | 42 | 3,996 R | 83.9% | 15.4% | 84.5% | 15.5% |
| 50,691 | WALKER | 10,442 | 8,728 | 1,574 | 140 | 7,154 R | 83.6% | 15.1% | 84.7% | 15.3% |
| 23,404 | WALTON | 5,137 | 3,994 | 1,140 | 3 | 2,854 R | 77.7% | 22.2% | 77.8% | 22.2% |
| 33,525 | WARE | 8,303 | 6,578 | 1,724 | 1 | 4,854 R | 79.2% | 20.8% | 79.2% | 20.8% |
| 6,669 | WARREN | 1,654 | 1,175 | 475 | 4 | 700 R | 71.0% | 28.7% | 71.2% | 28.8% |
| 17,480 | WASHINGTON | 5,234 | 3,901 | 1,246 | 87 | 2,655 R | 74.5% | 23.8% | 75.8% | 24.2% |
| 17,858 | WAYNE | 4,410 | 3,677 | 733 | | 2,944 R | 83.4% | 16.6% | 83.4% | 16.6% |
| 2,362 | WEBSTER | 591 | 483 | 108 | | 375 R | 81.7% | 18.3% | 81.7% | 18.3% |
| 4,596 | WHEELER | 1,387 | 1,093 | 294 | | 799 R | 78.8% | 21.2% | 78.8% | 21.2% |
| 7,742 | WHITE | 1,893 | 1,537 | 343 | 13 | 1,194 R | 81.2% | 18.1% | 81.8% | 18.2% |
| 55,108 | WHITFIELD | 10,559 | 8,591 | 1,955 | 13 | 6,636 R | 81.4% | 18.5% | 81.5% | 18.5% |
| 6,998 | WILCOX | 2,180 | 1,863 | 315 | 2 | 1,548 R | 85.5% | 14.4% | 85.5% | 14.5% |
| 10,184 | WILKES | 2,841 | 2,195 | 646 | | 1,549 R | 77.3% | 22.7% | 77.3% | 22.7% |
| 9,393 | WILKINSON | 2,965 | 2,196 | 751 | 18 | 1,445 R | 74.1% | 25.3% | 74.5% | 25.5% |
| 14,770 | WORTH | 3,493 | 2,942 | 542 | 9 | 2,400 R | 84.2% | 15.5% | 84.4% | 15.6% |
| 4,589,575 | TOTAL | 1,174,772 | 881,496 | 289,529 | 3,747 | 591,967 R | 75.0% | 24.6% | 75.3% | 24.7% |

# GEORGIA

## PRESIDENT 1968

| 1960 Census Population | County | Total Vote | Republican | Democratic | AIP | Other | Plurality | Percentage Total Vote Rep. | Dem. | AIP |
|---|---|---|---|---|---|---|---|---|---|---|
| 13,246 | APPLING | 4,233 | 795 | 760 | 2,678 | | 1,883 A | 18.8% | 18.0% | 63.3% |
| 6,188 | ATKINSON | 2,528 | 288 | 686 | 1,554 | | 868 A | 11.4% | 27.1% | 61.5% |
| 8,359 | BACON | 2,800 | 586 | 279 | 1,935 | | 1,349 A | 20.9% | 10.0% | 69.1% |
| 4,543 | BAKER | 1,714 | 99 | 548 | 1,067 | | 519 A | 5.8% | 32.0% | 62.3% |
| 34,064 | BALDWIN | 7,111 | 2,318 | 2,109 | 2,678 | 6 | 360 A | 32.6% | 29.7% | 37.7% |
| 6,497 | BANKS | 2,128 | 398 | 296 | 1,434 | | 1,036 A | 18.7% | 13.9% | 67.4% |
| 14,485 | BARROW | 5,173 | 1,372 | 1,070 | 2,731 | | 1,359 A | 26.5% | 20.7% | 52.8% |
| 28,267 | BARTOW | 8,251 | 2,045 | 2,149 | 4,052 | 5 | 1,903 A | 24.8% | 26.0% | 49.1% |
| 13,633 | BEN HILL | 3,371 | 661 | 876 | 1,833 | 1 | 957 A | 19.6% | 26.0% | 54.4% |
| 12,038 | BERRIEN | 3,828 | 566 | 451 | 2,810 | 1 | 2,244 A | 14.8% | 11.8% | 73.4% |
| 141,249 | BIBB | 41,397 | 13,490 | 10,579 | 17,328 | | 3,838 A | 32.6% | 25.6% | 41.9% |
| 9,642 | BLECKLEY | 3,611 | 756 | 396 | 2,458 | 1 | 1,702 A | 20.9% | 11.0% | 68.1% |
| 5,891 | BRANTLEY | 2,263 | 237 | 317 | 1,709 | | 1,392 A | 10.5% | 14.0% | 75.5% |
| 15,292 | BROOKS | 3,780 | 589 | 787 | 2,404 | | 1,617 A | 15.6% | 20.8% | 63.6% |
| 6,226 | BRYAN | 2,369 | 381 | 560 | 1,428 | | 868 A | 16.1% | 23.6% | 60.3% |
| 24,263 | BULLOCH | 7,854 | 2,113 | 1,788 | 3,953 | | 1,840 A | 26.9% | 22.8% | 50.3% |
| 20,596 | BURKE | 4,894 | 1,416 | 1,676 | 1,802 | | 126 A | 28.9% | 34.2% | 36.8% |
| 8,976 | BUTTS | 3,033 | 584 | 959 | 1,490 | | 531 A | 19.3% | 31.6% | 49.1% |
| 7,341 | CALHOUN | 1,910 | 234 | 697 | 979 | | 282 A | 12.3% | 36.5% | 51.3% |
| 9,975 | CAMDEN | 3,885 | 751 | 1,146 | 1,988 | | 842 A | 19.3% | 29.5% | 51.2% |
| 6,672 | CANDLER | 2,763 | 552 | 587 | 1,624 | | 1,037 A | 20.0% | 21.2% | 58.8% |
| 36,451 | CARROLL | 11,970 | 3,135 | 2,326 | 6,509 | | 3,374 A | 26.2% | 19.4% | 54.4% |
| 21,101 | CATOOSA | 9,393 | 2,043 | 901 | 6,449 | | 4,406 A | 21.8% | 9.6% | 68.7% |
| 5,313 | CHARLTON | 1,944 | 332 | 455 | 1,157 | | 702 A | 17.1% | 23.4% | 59.5% |
| 188,299 | CHATHAM | 53,545 | 18,106 | 18,201 | 17,238 | | 95 D | 33.8% | 34.0% | 32.2% |
| 13,011 | CHATTAHOOCHEE | 521 | 70 | 148 | 303 | | 155 A | 13.4% | 28.4% | 58.2% |
| 19,954 | CHATTOOGA | 5,366 | 1,087 | 1,255 | 3,024 | | 1,769 A | 20.3% | 23.4% | 56.4% |
| 23,001 | CHEROKEE | 7,462 | 2,675 | 1,434 | 3,351 | 2 | 676 A | 35.8% | 19.2% | 44.9% |
| 45,363 | CLARKE | 14,808 | 5,800 | 5,543 | 3,452 | 13 | 257 R | 39.2% | 37.4% | 23.3% |
| 4,551 | CLAY | 1,258 | 133 | 516 | 608 | 1 | 92 A | 10.6% | 41.0% | 48.3% |
| 46,365 | CLAYTON | 23,438 | 8,256 | 3,510 | 11,665 | 7 | 3,409 A | 35.2% | 15.0% | 49.8% |
| 6,545 | CLINCH | 1,780 | 304 | 334 | 1,142 | | 808 A | 17.1% | 18.8% | 64.2% |
| 114,174 | COBB | 45,209 | 18,649 | 8,755 | 17,805 | | 844 R | 41.3% | 19.4% | 39.4% |
| 21,953 | COFFEE | 6,357 | 1,241 | 1,331 | 3,785 | | 2,454 A | 19.5% | 20.9% | 59.5% |
| 34,048 | COLQUITT | 9,326 | 1,882 | 1,119 | 6,325 | | 4,443 A | 20.2% | 12.0% | 67.8% |
| 13,423 | COLUMBIA | 4,748 | 1,636 | 905 | 2,207 | | 571 A | 34.5% | 19.1% | 46.5% |
| 11,822 | COOK | 3,564 | 521 | 603 | 2,438 | 2 | 1,835 A | 14.6% | 16.9% | 68.4% |
| 28,893 | COWETA | 7,437 | 2,442 | 1,204 | 3,791 | | 1,349 A | 32.8% | 16.2% | 51.0% |
| 5,816 | CRAWFORD | 1,621 | 246 | 489 | 886 | | 397 A | 15.2% | 30.2% | 54.7% |
| 17,768 | CRISP | 5,223 | 935 | 1,017 | 3,271 | | 2,254 A | 17.9% | 19.5% | 62.6% |
| 8,666 | DADE | 3,355 | 613 | 282 | 2,460 | | 1,847 A | 18.3% | 8.4% | 73.3% |
| 3,590 | DAWSON | 1,600 | 509 | 246 | 845 | | 336 A | 31.8% | 15.4% | 52.8% |
| 25,203 | DECATUR | 7,054 | 749 | 1,729 | 4,576 | | 2,847 A | 10.6% | 24.5% | 64.9% |
| 256,782 | DE KALB | 104,237 | 52,485 | 27,796 | 23,954 | 2 | 24,689 R | 50.4% | 26.7% | 23.0% |
| 16,483 | DODGE | 5,691 | 1,055 | 1,230 | 3,406 | | 2,176 A | 18.5% | 21.6% | 59.8% |
| 11,474 | DOOLY | 3,136 | 454 | 879 | 1,803 | | 924 A | 14.5% | 28.0% | 57.5% |
| 75,680 | DOUGHERTY | 18,762 | 5,611 | 3,831 | 9,317 | 3 | 3,706 A | 29.9% | 20.4% | 49.7% |
| 16,741 | DOUGLAS | 7,249 | 1,848 | 1,242 | 4,159 | | 2,311 A | 25.5% | 17.1% | 57.4% |
| 13,151 | EARLY | 3,909 | 327 | 785 | 2,797 | | 2,012 A | 8.4% | 20.1% | 71.6% |
| 1,876 | ECHOLS | 642 | 53 | 56 | 533 | | 477 A | 8.3% | 8.7% | 83.0% |
| 10,144 | EFFINGHAM | 3,965 | 769 | 635 | 2,561 | | 1,792 A | 19.4% | 16.0% | 64.6% |
| 17,835 | ELBERT | 5,382 | 914 | 1,216 | 3,252 | | 2,036 A | 17.0% | 22.6% | 60.4% |
| 17,815 | EMANUEL | 6,112 | 1,297 | 1,508 | 3,307 | | 1,799 A | 21.2% | 24.7% | 54.1% |
| 6,952 | EVANS | 2,510 | 543 | 492 | 1,475 | | 932 A | 21.6% | 19.6% | 58.8% |
| 13,620 | FANNIN | 5,892 | 3,475 | 1,229 | 1,188 | | 2,246 R | 59.0% | 20.9% | 20.2% |
| 8,199 | FAYETTE | 3,307 | 867 | 551 | 1,888 | 1 | 1,021 A | 26.2% | 16.7% | 57.1% |
| 69,130 | FLOYD | 21,512 | 7,470 | 4,036 | 10,001 | 5 | 2,531 A | 34.7% | 18.8% | 46.5% |
| 12,170 | FORSYTH | 4,433 | 1,389 | 647 | 2,397 | | 1,008 A | 31.3% | 14.6% | 54.1% |
| 13,274 | FRANKLIN | 4,173 | 716 | 766 | 2,691 | | 1,925 A | 17.2% | 18.4% | 64.5% |
| 556,326 | FULTON | 179,068 | 64,153 | 77,847 | 36,995 | 73 | 13,694 D | 35.8% | 43.5% | 20.7% |

# GEORGIA

## PRESIDENT 1968

| 1960 Census Population | County | Total Vote | Republican | Democratic | AIP | Other | Plurality | Percentage Total Vote Rep. | Dem. | AIP |
|---|---|---|---|---|---|---|---|---|---|---|
| 8,922 | GILMER | 4,023 | 2,074 | 690 | 1,259 | | 815 R | 51.6% | 17.2% | 31.3% |
| 2,672 | GLASCOCK | 965 | 185 | 47 | 733 | | 548 A | 19.2% | 4.9% | 76.0% |
| 41,954 | GLYNN | 12,317 | 3,725 | 3,247 | 5,341 | 4 | 1,616 A | 30.2% | 26.4% | 43.4% |
| 19,228 | GORDON | 6,053 | 1,815 | 1,161 | 3,077 | | 1,262 A | 30.0% | 19.2% | 50.8% |
| 18,015 | GRADY | 5,803 | 561 | 1,425 | 3,817 | | 2,392 A | 9.7% | 24.6% | 65.8% |
| 11,193 | GREENE | 3,510 | 652 | 1,635 | 1,223 | | 412 D | 18.6% | 46.6% | 34.8% |
| 43,541 | GWINNETT | 17,489 | 5,350 | 3,226 | 8,909 | 4 | 3,559 A | 30.6% | 18.4% | 50.9% |
| 18,116 | HABERSHAM | 5,689 | 1,611 | 1,070 | 3,008 | | 1,397 A | 28.3% | 18.8% | 52.9% |
| 49,739 | HALL | 13,643 | 4,923 | 3,174 | 5,546 | | 623 A | 36.1% | 23.3% | 40.7% |
| 9,979 | HANCOCK | 3,650 | 381 | 2,165 | 1,104 | | 1,061 D | 10.4% | 59.3% | 30.2% |
| 14,543 | HARALSON | 5,473 | 1,451 | 771 | 3,251 | | 1,800 A | 26.5% | 14.1% | 59.4% |
| 11,167 | HARRIS | 3,944 | 1,021 | 1,072 | 1,851 | | 779 A | 25.9% | 27.2% | 46.9% |
| 15,229 | HART | 4,774 | 586 | 979 | 3,208 | 1 | 2,229 A | 12.3% | 20.5% | 67.2% |
| 5,333 | HEARD | 1,812 | 303 | 356 | 1,153 | | 797 A | 16.7% | 19.6% | 63.6% |
| 17,619 | HENRY | 7,938 | 2,017 | 2,317 | 3,604 | | 1,287 A | 25.4% | 29.2% | 45.4% |
| 39,154 | HOUSTON | 14,457 | 4,285 | 2,831 | 7,339 | 2 | 3,054 A | 29.6% | 19.6% | 50.8% |
| 9,211 | IRWIN | 2,860 | 430 | 474 | 1,955 | 1 | 1,481 A | 15.0% | 16.6% | 68.4% |
| 18,499 | JACKSON | 6,149 | 1,139 | 1,537 | 3,473 | | 1,936 A | 18.5% | 25.0% | 56.5% |
| 6,135 | JASPER | 2,217 | 456 | 835 | 926 | | 91 A | 20.6% | 37.7% | 41.8% |
| 8,914 | JEFF DAVIS | 2,911 | 577 | 376 | 1,958 | | 1,381 A | 19.8% | 12.9% | 67.3% |
| 17,468 | JEFFERSON | 5,218 | 1,227 | 1,899 | 2,090 | 2 | 191 A | 23.5% | 36.4% | 40.1% |
| 9,148 | JENKINS | 2,527 | 574 | 704 | 1,249 | | 545 A | 22.7% | 27.9% | 49.4% |
| 8,048 | JOHNSON | 2,868 | 381 | 446 | 2,041 | | 1,595 A | 13.3% | 15.6% | 71.2% |
| 8,468 | JONES | 3,568 | 693 | 1,105 | 1,770 | | 665 A | 19.4% | 31.0% | 49.6% |
| 10,240 | LAMAR | 2,805 | 575 | 790 | 1,440 | | 650 A | 20.5% | 28.2% | 51.3% |
| 5,097 | LANIER | 1,542 | 241 | 277 | 1,024 | | 747 A | 15.6% | 18.0% | 66.4% |
| 32,313 | LAURENS | 12,838 | 2,738 | 3,451 | 6,649 | | 3,198 A | 21.3% | 26.9% | 51.8% |
| 6,204 | LEE | 2,264 | 389 | 673 | 1,201 | 1 | 528 A | 17.2% | 29.7% | 53.0% |
| 14,487 | LIBERTY | 3,529 | 592 | 1,572 | 1,365 | | 207 D | 16.8% | 44.5% | 38.7% |
| 5,906 | LINCOLN | 2,189 | 408 | 491 | 1,290 | | 799 A | 18.6% | 22.4% | 58.9% |
| 3,874 | LONG | 1,767 | 156 | 574 | 1,037 | | 463 A | 8.8% | 32.5% | 58.7% |
| 49,270 | LOWNDES | 11,154 | 3,073 | 2,402 | 5,679 | | 2,606 A | 27.6% | 21.5% | 50.9% |
| 7,241 | LUMPKIN | 2,131 | 687 | 396 | 1,048 | | 361 A | 32.2% | 18.6% | 49.2% |
| 12,627 | MCDUFFIE | 4,025 | 1,324 | 991 | 1,709 | 1 | 385 A | 32.9% | 24.6% | 42.5% |
| 6,364 | MCINTOSH | 2,099 | 315 | 943 | 841 | | 102 D | 15.0% | 44.9% | 40.1% |
| 13,170 | MACON | 3,111 | 598 | 954 | 1,559 | | 605 A | 19.2% | 30.7% | 50.1% |
| 11,246 | MADISON | 3,751 | 600 | 621 | 2,529 | 1 | 1,908 A | 16.0% | 16.6% | 67.4% |
| 5,477 | MARION | 1,282 | 186 | 247 | 849 | | 602 A | 14.5% | 19.3% | 66.2% |
| 19,756 | MERIWETHER | 5,451 | 1,120 | 1,760 | 2,571 | | 811 A | 20.5% | 32.3% | 47.2% |
| 6,908 | MILLER | 2,282 | 249 | 171 | 1,862 | | 1,613 A | 10.9% | 7.5% | 81.6% |
| 19,652 | MITCHELL | 5,634 | 731 | 1,255 | 3,647 | 1 | 2,392 A | 13.0% | 22.3% | 64.7% |
| 10,495 | MONROE | 3,220 | 770 | 1,028 | 1,422 | | 394 A | 23.9% | 31.9% | 44.2% |
| 6,284 | MONTGOMERY | 2,288 | 352 | 503 | 1,433 | | 930 A | 15.4% | 22.0% | 62.6% |
| 10,280 | MORGAN | 2,980 | 616 | 973 | 1,391 | | 418 A | 20.7% | 32.7% | 46.7% |
| 10,447 | MURRAY | 3,846 | 1,278 | 818 | 1,750 | | 472 A | 33.2% | 21.3% | 45.5% |
| 158,623 | MOSCOGEE | 34,590 | 11,193 | 7,591 | 15,804 | 2 | 4,611 A | 32.4% | 21.9% | 45.7% |
| 20,999 | NEWTON | 6,675 | 1,660 | 1,996 | 3,017 | 2 | 1,021 A | 24.9% | 29.9% | 45.2% |
| 6,304 | OCONEE | 2,532 | 713 | 414 | 1,405 | | 692 A | 28.2% | 16.4% | 55.5% |
| 7,926 | OGLETHORPE | 2,603 | 383 | 483 | 1,737 | | 1,254 A | 14.7% | 18.6% | 66.7% |
| 13,101 | PAULDING | 5,054 | 977 | 1,023 | 3,054 | | 2,031 A | 19.3% | 20.2% | 60.4% |
| 13,846 | PEACH | 3,904 | 904 | 1,362 | 1,638 | | 276 A | 23.2% | 34.9% | 42.0% |
| 8,903 | PICKENS | 3,728 | 1,659 | 677 | 1,392 | | 267 R | 44.5% | 18.2% | 37.3% |
| 9,678 | PIERCE | 3,230 | 579 | 507 | 2,144 | | 1,565 A | 17.9% | 15.7% | 66.4% |
| 7,138 | PIKE | 2,419 | 345 | 632 | 1,442 | | 810 A | 14.3% | 26.1% | 59.6% |
| 28,015 | POLK | 7,976 | 1,729 | 2,007 | 4,240 | | 2,233 A | 21.7% | 25.2% | 53.2% |
| 8,204 | PULASKI | 2,678 | 595 | 514 | 1,569 | | 974 A | 22.2% | 19.2% | 58.6% |
| 7,798 | PUTNAM | 2,743 | 594 | 972 | 1,177 | | 205 A | 21.7% | 35.4% | 42.9% |
| 2,432 | QUITMAN | 747 | 90 | 198 | 459 | | 261 A | 12.0% | 26.5% | 61.4% |
| 7,456 | RABUN | 2,679 | 680 | 590 | 1,407 | 2 | 727 A | 25.4% | 22.0% | 52.5% |
| 11,078 | RANDOLPH | 2,968 | 502 | 1,028 | 1,438 | | 410 A | 16.9% | 34.6% | 48.5% |

# GEORGIA

## PRESIDENT 1968

| 1960 Census Population | County | Total Vote | Republican | Democratic | AIP | Other | Plurality | Percentage Total Vote Rep. | Dem. | AIP |
|---|---|---|---|---|---|---|---|---|---|---|
| 135,601 | RICHMOND | 36,302 | 14,993 | 11,770 | 9,532 | 7 | 3,223 R | 41.3% | 32.4% | 26.3% |
| 10,572 | ROCKDALE | 4,623 | 1,195 | 1,213 | 2,215 | | 1,002 A | 25.8% | 26.2% | 47.9% |
| 3,256 | SCHLEY | 1,092 | 164 | 309 | 619 | | 310 A | 15.0% | 28.3% | 56.7% |
| 14,919 | SCREVEN | 4,157 | 916 | 1,411 | 1,830 | | 419 A | 22.0% | 33.9% | 44.0% |
| 6,802 | SEMINOLE | 2,493 | 201 | 369 | 1,922 | 1 | 1,553 A | 8.1% | 14.8% | 77.1% |
| 35,404 | SPALDING | 10,979 | 3,077 | 2,949 | 4,953 | | 1,876 A | 28.0% | 26.9% | 45.1% |
| 18,391 | STEPHENS | 5,132 | 1,295 | 1,035 | 2,802 | | 1,507 A | 25.2% | 20.2% | 54.6% |
| 7,371 | STEWART | 1,654 | 233 | 489 | 932 | | 443 A | 14.1% | 29.6% | 56.3% |
| 24,652 | SUMTER | 6,573 | 1,383 | 1,701 | 3,489 | | 1,788 A | 21.0% | 25.9% | 53.1% |
| 7,127 | TALBOT | 1,515 | 317 | 510 | 688 | | 178 A | 20.9% | 33.7% | 45.4% |
| 3,370 | TALIAFERRO | 1,418 | 232 | 678 | 508 | | 170 D | 16.4% | 47.8% | 35.8% |
| 15,837 | TATTNALL | 5,214 | 852 | 957 | 3,405 | | 2,448 A | 16.3% | 18.4% | 65.3% |
| 8,311 | TAYLOR | 2,710 | 393 | 691 | 1,626 | | 935 A | 14.5% | 25.5% | 60.0% |
| 11,715 | TELFAIR | 4,260 | 720 | 1,038 | 2,502 | | 1,464 A | 16.9% | 24.4% | 58.7% |
| 12,742 | TERRELL | 3,619 | 545 | 1,275 | 1,798 | 1 | 523 A | 15.1% | 35.2% | 49.7% |
| 34,319 | THOMAS | 9,885 | 2,261 | 2,583 | 5,039 | 2 | 2,456 A | 22.9% | 26.1% | 51.0% |
| 23,487 | TIFT | 6,821 | 1,692 | 1,187 | 3,942 | | 2,250 A | 24.8% | 17.4% | 57.8% |
| 16,837 | TOOMBS | 5,698 | 1,397 | 896 | 3,405 | | 2,008 A | 24.5% | 15.7% | 59.8% |
| 4,538 | TOWNS | 2,851 | 1,492 | 770 | 589 | | 722 R | 52.3% | 27.0% | 20.7% |
| 5,874 | TREUTLEN | 1,896 | 474 | 341 | 1,081 | | 607 A | 25.0% | 18.0% | 57.0% |
| 47,189 | TROUP | 12,367 | 3,239 | 2,896 | 6,232 | | 2,993 A | 26.2% | 23.4% | 50.4% |
| 8,439 | TURNER | 2,676 | 419 | 412 | 1,845 | | 1,426 A | 15.7% | 15.4% | 68.9% |
| 7,935 | TWIGGS | 2,315 | 336 | 812 | 1,167 | | 355 A | 14.5% | 35.1% | 50.4% |
| 6,510 | UNION | 3,101 | 1,221 | 974 | 906 | | 247 R | 39.4% | 31.4% | 29.2% |
| 23,800 | UPSON | 6,573 | 1,494 | 1,480 | 3,599 | | 2,105 A | 22.7% | 22.5% | 54.8% |
| 45,264 | WALKER | 14,321 | 3,664 | 1,930 | 8,725 | 2 | 5,061 A | 25.6% | 13.5% | 60.9% |
| 20,481 | WALTON | 6,998 | 1,399 | 1,552 | 4,047 | | 2,495 A | 20.0% | 22.2% | 57.8% |
| 34,219 | WARE | 10,197 | 2,047 | 2,255 | 5,895 | | 3,640 A | 20.1% | 22.1% | 57.8% |
| 7,360 | WARREN | 1,755 | 406 | 582 | 767 | | 185 A | 23.1% | 33.2% | 43.7% |
| 18,903 | WASHINGTON | 4,719 | 1,247 | 1,443 | 2,029 | | 586 A | 26.4% | 30.6% | 43.0% |
| 17,921 | WAYNE | 5,715 | 1,313 | 980 | 3,422 | | 2,109 A | 23.0% | 17.1% | 59.9% |
| 3,247 | WEBSTER | 713 | 72 | 147 | 494 | | 347 A | 10.1% | 20.6% | 69.3% |
| 5,342 | WHEELER | 1,673 | 251 | 488 | 934 | | 446 A | 15.0% | 29.2% | 55.8% |
| 6,935 | WHITE | 2,355 | 762 | 435 | 1,157 | 1 | 395 A | 32.4% | 18.5% | 49.1% |
| 42,109 | WHITFIELD | 11,508 | 4,828 | 2,723 | 3,954 | 3 | 874 R | 42.0% | 23.7% | 34.4% |
| 7,905 | WILCOX | 2,668 | 381 | 465 | 1,822 | | 1,357 A | 14.3% | 17.4% | 68.3% |
| 10,961 | WILKES | 3,535 | 873 | 953 | 1,709 | | 756 A | 24.7% | 27.0% | 48.3% |
| 9,250 | WILKINSON | 3,384 | 685 | 829 | 1,870 | | 1,041 A | 20.2% | 24.5% | 55.3% |
| 16,682 | WORTH | 4,372 | 603 | 719 | 3,049 | 1 | 2,330 A | 13.8% | 16.4% | 69.7% |
| 3,943,116 | TOTAL | 1,250,266 | 380,111 | 334,440 | 535,550 | 165 | 155,439 A | 30.4% | 26.7% | 42.8% |

# GEORGIA

## PRESIDENT 1964

| 1960 Census Population | County | Total Vote | Republican | Democratic | Other | Rep.-Dem. Plurality | Percentage Total Vote Rep. | Total Vote Dem. | Major Vote Rep. | Major Vote Dem. |
|---|---|---|---|---|---|---|---|---|---|---|
| 13,246 | APPLING | 4,159 | 2,597 | 1,562 | | 1,035 R | 62.4% | 37.6% | 62.4% | 37.6% |
| 6,188 | ATKINSON | 1,969 | 1,157 | 811 | 1 | 346 R | 58.8% | 41.2% | 58.8% | 41.2% |
| 8,359 | BACON | 3,315 | 2,136 | 1,179 | | 957 R | 64.4% | 35.6% | 64.4% | 35.6% |
| 4,543 | BAKER | 1,515 | 914 | 600 | 1 | 314 R | 60.3% | 39.6% | 60.4% | 39.6% |
| 34,064 | BALDWIN | 6,170 | 3,430 | 2,740 | | 690 R | 55.6% | 44.4% | 55.6% | 44.4% |
| 6,497 | BANKS | 1,806 | 548 | 1,258 | | 710 D | 30.3% | 69.7% | 30.3% | 69.7% |
| 14,485 | BARROW | 4,593 | 2,316 | 2,277 | | 39 R | 50.4% | 49.6% | 50.4% | 49.6% |
| 28,267 | BARTOW | 7,448 | 2,813 | 4,635 | | 1,822 D | 37.8% | 62.2% | 37.8% | 62.2% |
| 13,633 | BEN HILL | 3,613 | 2,089 | 1,523 | 1 | 566 R | 57.8% | 42.2% | 57.8% | 42.2% |
| 12,038 | BERRIEN | 6,731 | 4,073 | 2,658 | | 1,415 R | 60.5% | 39.5% | 60.5% | 39.5% |
| 141,249 | BIBB | 43,472 | 25,641 | 17,831 | | 7,810 R | 59.0% | 41.0% | 59.0% | 41.0% |
| 9,642 | BLECKLEY | 3,556 | 2,578 | 978 | | 1,600 R | 72.5% | 27.5% | 72.5% | 27.5% |
| 5,891 | BRANTLEY | 2,140 | 1,231 | 909 | | 322 R | 57.5% | 42.5% | 57.5% | 42.5% |
| 15,292 | BROOKS | 3,370 | 2,342 | 1,027 | 1 | 1,315 R | 69.5% | 30.5% | 69.5% | 30.5% |
| 6,226 | BRYAN | 2,290 | 1,433 | 857 | | 576 R | 62.6% | 37.4% | 62.6% | 37.4% |
| 24,263 | BULLOCH | 7,543 | 4,823 | 2,720 | | 2,103 R | 63.9% | 36.1% | 63.9% | 36.1% |
| 20,596 | BURKE | 4,242 | 3,034 | 1,208 | | 1,826 R | 71.5% | 28.5% | 71.5% | 28.5% |
| 8,976 | BUTTS | 2,795 | 1,261 | 1,534 | | 273 D | 45.1% | 54.9% | 45.1% | 54.9% |
| 7,341 | CALHOUN | 1,355 | 1,066 | 289 | | 777 R | 78.7% | 21.3% | 78.7% | 21.3% |
| 9,975 | CAMDEN | 3,495 | 1,802 | 1,693 | | 109 R | 51.6% | 48.4% | 51.6% | 48.4% |
| 6,672 | CANDLER | 2,505 | 1,710 | 795 | | 915 R | 68.3% | 31.7% | 68.3% | 31.7% |
| 36,451 | CARROLL | 9,780 | 4,984 | 4,794 | 2 | 190 R | 51.0% | 49.0% | 51.0% | 49.0% |
| 21,101 | CATOOSA | 7,071 | 4,143 | 2,922 | 6 | 1,221 R | 58.6% | 41.3% | 58.6% | 41.4% |
| 5,313 | CHARLTON | 1,753 | 1,179 | 574 | | 605 R | 67.3% | 32.7% | 67.3% | 32.7% |
| 188,299 | CHATHAM | 56,318 | 33,141 | 23,176 | 1 | 9,965 R | 58.8% | 41.2% | 58.8% | 41.2% |
| 13,011 | CHATTAHOOCHEE | 437 | 246 | 191 | | 55 R | 56.3% | 43.7% | 56.3% | 43.7% |
| 19,954 | CHATTOOGA | 5,465 | 1,476 | 3,986 | 3 | 2,510 D | 27.0% | 72.9% | 27.0% | 73.0% |
| 23,001 | CHEROKEE | 6,587 | 3,398 | 3,189 | | 209 R | 51.6% | 48.4% | 51.6% | 48.4% |
| 45,363 | CLARKE | 12,394 | 4,875 | 7,519 | | 2,644 D | 39.3% | 60.7% | 39.3% | 60.7% |
| 4,551 | CLAY | 906 | 544 | 360 | 2 | 184 R | 60.0% | 39.7% | 60.2% | 39.8% |
| 46,365 | CLAYTON | 16,367 | 10,488 | 5,869 | 10 | 4,619 R | 64.1% | 35.9% | 64.1% | 35.9% |
| 6,545 | CLINCH | 1,790 | 1,084 | 706 | | 378 R | 60.6% | 39.4% | 60.6% | 39.4% |
| 114,174 | COBB | 37,511 | 20,863 | 16,647 | 1 | 4,216 R | 55.6% | 44.4% | 55.6% | 44.4% |
| 21,953 | COFFEE | 7,111 | 4,392 | 2,719 | | 1,673 R | 61.8% | 38.2% | 61.8% | 38.2% |
| 34,048 | COLQUITT | 9,060 | 6,493 | 2,563 | 4 | 3,930 R | 71.7% | 28.3% | 71.7% | 28.3% |
| 13,423 | COLUMBIA | 4,003 | 2,575 | 1,428 | | 1,147 R | 64.3% | 35.7% | 64.3% | 35.7% |
| 11,822 | COOK | 3,395 | 2,058 | 1,337 | | 721 R | 60.6% | 39.4% | 60.6% | 39.4% |
| 28,893 | COWETA | 7,368 | 3,656 | 3,712 | | 56 D | 49.6% | 50.4% | 49.6% | 50.4% |
| 5,816 | CRAWFORD | 1,680 | 957 | 723 | | 234 R | 57.0% | 43.0% | 57.0% | 43.0% |
| 17,768 | CRISP | 5,093 | 3,337 | 1,756 | | 1,581 R | 65.5% | 34.5% | 65.5% | 34.5% |
| 8,666 | DADE | 2,608 | 1,378 | 1,227 | 3 | 151 R | 52.8% | 47.0% | 52.9% | 47.1% |
| 3,590 | DAWSON | 1,571 | 639 | 932 | | 293 D | 40.7% | 59.3% | 40.7% | 59.3% |
| 25,203 | DECATUR | 7,072 | 5,060 | 2,011 | 1 | 3,049 R | 71.5% | 28.4% | 71.6% | 28.4% |
| 256,782 | DE KALB | 86,602 | 49,448 | 37,154 | | 12,294 R | 57.1% | 42.9% | 57.1% | 42.9% |
| 16,483 | DODGE | 5,661 | 3,285 | 2,376 | | 909 R | 58.0% | 42.0% | 58.0% | 42.0% |
| 11,474 | DOOLY | 3,133 | 1,662 | 1,471 | | 191 R | 53.0% | 47.0% | 53.0% | 47.0% |
| 75,680 | DOUGHERTY | 18,024 | 12,776 | 5,248 | | 7,528 R | 70.9% | 29.1% | 70.9% | 29.1% |
| 16,741 | DOUGLAS | 5,816 | 3,315 | 2,501 | | 814 R | 57.0% | 43.0% | 57.0% | 43.0% |
| 13,151 | EARLY | 3,169 | 2,398 | 771 | | 1,627 R | 75.7% | 24.3% | 75.7% | 24.3% |
| 1,876 | ECHOLS | 583 | 399 | 184 | | 215 R | 68.4% | 31.6% | 68.4% | 31.6% |
| 10,144 | EFFINGHAM | 3,356 | 2,676 | 680 | | 1,996 R | 79.7% | 20.3% | 79.7% | 20.3% |
| 17,835 | ELBERT | 5,059 | 1,887 | 3,172 | | 1,285 D | 37.3% | 62.7% | 37.3% | 62.7% |
| 17,815 | EMANUEL | 5,590 | 3,311 | 2,279 | | 1,032 R | 59.2% | 40.8% | 59.2% | 40.8% |
| 6,952 | EVANS | 2,371 | 1,572 | 799 | | 773 R | 66.3% | 33.7% | 66.3% | 33.7% |
| 13,620 | FANNIN | 6,268 | 3,433 | 2,834 | 1 | 599 R | 54.8% | 45.2% | 54.8% | 45.2% |
| 8,199 | FAYETTE | 2,249 | 1,349 | 896 | 4 | 453 R | 60.0% | 39.8% | 60.1% | 39.9% |
| 69,130 | FLOYD | 18,636 | 9,849 | 8,750 | 37 | 1,099 R | 52.8% | 47.0% | 53.0% | 47.0% |
| 12,170 | FORSYTH | 3,154 | 1,471 | 1,682 | 1 | 211 D | 46.6% | 53.3% | 46.7% | 53.3% |
| 13,274 | FRANKLIN | 3,624 | 864 | 2,758 | 2 | 1,894 D | 23.8% | 76.1% | 23.9% | 76.1% |
| 556,326 | FULTON | 166,756 | 73,205 | 93,540 | 11 | 20,335 D | 43.9% | 56.1% | 43.9% | 56.1% |

# GEORGIA

## PRESIDENT 1964

| 1960 Census Population | County | Total Vote | Republican | Democratic | Other | Rep.-Dem. Plurality | Percentage Total Vote Rep. | Dem. | Major Vote Rep. | Dem. |
|---|---|---|---|---|---|---|---|---|---|---|
| 8,922 | GILMER | 4,326 | 2,167 | 2,159 | | 8 R | 50.1% | 49.9% | 50.1% | 49.9% |
| 2,672 | GLASCOCK | 970 | 836 | 134 | | 702 R | 86.2% | 13.8% | 86.2% | 13.8% |
| 41,954 | GLYNN | 13,057 | 7,341 | 5,712 | 4 | 1,629 R | 56.2% | 43.7% | 56.2% | 43.8% |
| 19,228 | GORDON | 5,577 | 2,317 | 3,260 | | 943 D | 41.5% | 58.5% | 41.5% | 58.5% |
| 18,015 | GRADY | 4,870 | 2,983 | 1,887 | | 1,096 R | 61.3% | 38.7% | 61.3% | 38.7% |
| 11,193 | GREENE | 3,791 | 1,093 | 2,698 | | 1,605 D | 28.8% | 71.2% | 28.8% | 71.2% |
| 43,541 | GWINNETT | 13,531 | 6,823 | 6,705 | 3 | 118 R | 50.4% | 49.6% | 50.4% | 49.6% |
| 18,116 | HABERSHAM | 5,009 | 1,595 | 3,412 | 2 | 1,817 D | 31.8% | 68.1% | 31.9% | 68.1% |
| 49,739 | HALL | 12,310 | 4,296 | 8,003 | 11 | 3,707 D | 34.9% | 65.0% | 34.9% | 65.1% |
| 9,979 | HANCOCK | 1,999 | 925 | 1,074 | | 149 D | 46.3% | 53.7% | 46.3% | 53.7% |
| 14,543 | HARALSON | 5,317 | 3,129 | 2,186 | 2 | 943 R | 58.8% | 41.1% | 58.9% | 41.1% |
| 11,167 | HARRIS | 3,106 | 2,166 | 940 | | 1,226 R | 69.7% | 30.3% | 69.7% | 30.3% |
| 15,229 | HART | 4,318 | 1,166 | 3,142 | 10 | 1,976 D | 27.0% | 72.8% | 27.1% | 72.9% |
| 5,333 | HEARD | 1,869 | 807 | 1,061 | 1 | 254 D | 43.2% | 56.8% | 43.2% | 56.8% |
| 17,619 | HENRY | 6,709 | 3,125 | 3,583 | 1 | 458 D | 46.6% | 53.4% | 46.6% | 53.4% |
| 39,154 | HOUSTON | 10,791 | 6,532 | 4,258 | 1 | 2,274 R | 60.5% | 39.5% | 60.5% | 39.5% |
| 9,211 | IRWIN | 2,757 | 2,017 | 740 | | 1,277 R | 73.2% | 26.8% | 73.2% | 26.8% |
| 18,499 | JACKSON | 5,617 | 1,664 | 3,953 | | 2,289 D | 29.6% | 70.4% | 29.6% | 70.4% |
| 6,135 | JASPER | 1,923 | 1,075 | 848 | | 227 R | 55.9% | 44.1% | 55.9% | 44.1% |
| 8,914 | JEFF DAVIS | 2,620 | 1,875 | 745 | | 1,130 R | 71.6% | 28.4% | 71.6% | 28.4% |
| 17,468 | JEFFERSON | 4,205 | 2,950 | 1,253 | 2 | 1,697 R | 70.2% | 29.8% | 70.2% | 29.8% |
| 9,148 | JENKINS | 2,417 | 1,509 | 908 | | 601 R | 62.4% | 37.6% | 62.4% | 37.6% |
| 8,048 | JOHNSON | 2,622 | 1,940 | 682 | | 1,258 R | 74.0% | 26.0% | 74.0% | 26.0% |
| 8,468 | JONES | 3,185 | 1,805 | 1,380 | | 425 R | 56.7% | 43.3% | 56.7% | 43.3% |
| 10,240 | LAMAR | 3,121 | 1,570 | 1,548 | 3 | 22 R | 50.3% | 49.6% | 50.4% | 49.6% |
| 5,097 | LANIER | 1,380 | 719 | 661 | | 58 R | 52.1% | 47.9% | 52.1% | 47.9% |
| 32,313 | LAURENS | 9,287 | 5,457 | 3,828 | 2 | 1,629 R | 58.8% | 41.2% | 58.8% | 41.2% |
| 6,204 | LEE | 1,285 | 1,041 | 244 | | 797 R | 81.0% | 19.0% | 81.0% | 19.0% |
| 14,487 | LIBERTY | 3,670 | 1,458 | 2,212 | | 754 D | 39.7% | 60.3% | 39.7% | 60.3% |
| 5,906 | LINCOLN | 1,296 | 943 | 353 | | 590 R | 72.8% | 27.2% | 72.8% | 27.2% |
| 3,874 | LONG | 1,582 | 246 | 1,336 | | 1,090 D | 15.5% | 84.5% | 15.5% | 84.5% |
| 49,270 | LOWNDES | 11,175 | 6,811 | 4,363 | 1 | 2,448 R | 60.9% | 39.0% | 61.0% | 39.0% |
| 7,241 | LUMPKIN | 2,045 | 855 | 1,189 | 1 | 334 D | 41.8% | 58.1% | 41.8% | 58.2% |
| 12,627 | MCDUFFIE | 3,781 | 2,657 | 1,124 | | 1,533 R | 70.3% | 29.7% | 70.3% | 29.7% |
| 6,364 | MCINTOSH | 1,988 | 795 | 1,193 | | 398 D | 40.0% | 60.0% | 40.0% | 60.0% |
| 13,170 | MACON | 2,799 | 1,723 | 1,076 | | 647 R | 61.6% | 38.4% | 61.6% | 38.4% |
| 11,246 | MADISON | 3,531 | 1,190 | 2,341 | | 1,151 D | 33.7% | 66.3% | 33.7% | 66.3% |
| 5,477 | MARION | 1,085 | 719 | 365 | 1 | 354 R | 66.3% | 33.6% | 66.3% | 33.7% |
| 19,756 | MERIWETHER | 4,674 | 2,250 | 2,423 | 1 | 173 D | 48.1% | 51.8% | 48.1% | 51.9% |
| 6,908 | MILLER | 1,932 | 1,658 | 274 | | 1,384 R | 85.8% | 14.2% | 85.8% | 14.2% |
| 19,652 | MITCHELL | 4,462 | 3,265 | 1,197 | | 2,068 R | 73.2% | 26.8% | 73.2% | 26.8% |
| 10,495 | MONROE | 3,244 | 1,665 | 1,578 | 1 | 87 R | 51.3% | 48.6% | 51.3% | 48.7% |
| 6,284 | MONTGOMERY | 2,287 | 1,409 | 878 | | 531 R | 61.6% | 38.4% | 61.6% | 38.4% |
| 10,280 | MORGAN | 3,139 | 1,485 | 1,654 | | 169 D | 47.3% | 52.7% | 47.3% | 52.7% |
| 10,447 | MURRAY | 3,495 | 1,064 | 2,426 | 5 | 1,362 D | 30.4% | 69.4% | 30.5% | 69.5% |
| 158,623 | MUSCOGEE | 33,474 | 21,025 | 12,446 | 3 | 8,579 R | 62.8% | 37.2% | 62.8% | 37.2% |
| 20,999 | NEWTON | 6,298 | 2,678 | 3,620 | | 942 D | 42.5% | 57.5% | 42.5% | 57.5% |
| 6,304 | OCONEE | 2,314 | 1,241 | 1,073 | | 168 R | 53.6% | 46.4% | 53.6% | 46.4% |
| 7,926 | OGLETHORPE | 1,990 | 1,126 | 864 | | 262 R | 56.6% | 43.4% | 56.6% | 43.4% |
| 13,101 | PAULDING | 4,427 | 1,914 | 2,513 | | 599 D | 43.2% | 56.8% | 43.2% | 56.8% |
| 13,846 | PEACH | 3,556 | 1,970 | 1,585 | 1 | 385 R | 55.4% | 44.6% | 55.4% | 44.6% |
| 8,903 | PICKENS | 3,885 | 1,955 | 1,930 | | 25 R | 50.3% | 49.7% | 50.3% | 49.7% |
| 9,678 | PIERCE | 2,963 | 1,981 | 982 | | 999 R | 66.9% | 33.1% | 66.9% | 33.1% |
| 7,138 | PIKE | 2,010 | 1,064 | 946 | | 118 R | 52.9% | 47.1% | 52.9% | 47.1% |
| 28,015 | POLK | 7,840 | 3,282 | 4,555 | 3 | 1,273 D | 41.9% | 58.1% | 41.9% | 58.1% |
| 8,204 | PULASKI | 2,726 | 1,768 | 953 | 5 | 815 R | 64.9% | 35.0% | 65.0% | 35.0% |
| 7,798 | PUTNAM | 2,214 | 1,196 | 1,018 | | 178 R | 54.0% | 46.0% | 54.0% | 46.0% |
| 2,432 | QUITMAN | 607 | 377 | 230 | | 147 R | 62.1% | 37.9% | 62.1% | 37.9% |
| 7,456 | RABUN | 2,347 | 551 | 1,796 | | 1,245 D | 23.5% | 76.5% | 23.5% | 76.5% |
| 11,078 | RANDOLPH | 2,621 | 1,656 | 962 | 3 | 694 R | 63.2% | 36.7% | 63.3% | 36.7% |

# GEORGIA

## PRESIDENT 1964

| 1960 Census Population | County | Total Vote | Republican | Democratic | Other | Rep.-Dem. Plurality | Total Vote Rep. | Total Vote Dem. | Major Vote Rep. | Major Vote Dem. |
|---|---|---|---|---|---|---|---|---|---|---|
| 135,601 | RICHMOND | 35,029 | 21,481 | 13,545 | 3 | 7,936 R | 61.3% | 38.7% | 61.3% | 38.7% |
| 10,572 | ROCKDALE | 3,475 | 1,503 | 1,972 | | 469 D | 43.3% | 56.7% | 43.3% | 56.7% |
| 3,256 | SCHLEY | 954 | 577 | 377 | | 200 R | 60.5% | 39.5% | 60.5% | 39.5% |
| 14,919 | SCREVEN | 3,706 | 2,260 | 1,446 | | 814 R | 61.0% | 39.0% | 61.0% | 39.0% |
| 6,802 | SEMINOLE | 1,721 | 1,294 | 427 | | 867 R | 75.2% | 24.8% | 75.2% | 24.8% |
| 35,404 | SPALDING | 10,229 | 4,763 | 5,466 | | 703 D | 46.6% | 53.4% | 46.6% | 53.4% |
| 18,391 | STEPHENS | 4,854 | 1,371 | 3,483 | | 2,112 D | 28.2% | 71.8% | 28.2% | 71.8% |
| 7,371 | STEWART | 1,413 | 1,037 | 373 | 3 | 664 R | 73.4% | 26.4% | 73.5% | 26.5% |
| 24,652 | SUMTER | 5,501 | 3,774 | 1,727 | | 2,047 R | 68.6% | 31.4% | 68.6% | 31.4% |
| 7,127 | TALBOT | 1,306 | 679 | 627 | | 52 R | 52.0% | 48.0% | 52.0% | 48.0% |
| 3,370 | TALIAFERRO | 965 | 337 | 628 | | 291 D | 34.9% | 65.1% | 34.9% | 65.1% |
| 15,837 | TATTNALL | 4,912 | 3,264 | 1,648 | | 1,616 R | 66.4% | 33.6% | 66.4% | 33.6% |
| 8,311 | TAYLOR | 2,470 | 1,372 | 1,097 | 1 | 275 R | 55.5% | 44.4% | 55.6% | 44.4% |
| 11,715 | TELFAIR | 3,786 | 1,914 | 1,872 | | 42 R | 50.6% | 49.4% | 50.6% | 49.4% |
| 12,742 | TERRELL | 2,490 | 1,921 | 569 | | 1,352 R | 77.1% | 22.9% | 77.1% | 22.9% |
| 34,319 | THOMAS | 9,563 | 6,306 | 3,257 | | 3,049 R | 65.9% | 34.1% | 65.9% | 34.1% |
| 23,487 | TIFT | 6,936 | 4,650 | 2,286 | | 2,364 R | 67.0% | 33.0% | 67.0% | 33.0% |
| 16,837 | TOOMBS | 5,228 | 3,543 | 1,685 | | 1,858 R | 67.8% | 32.2% | 67.8% | 32.2% |
| 4,538 | TOWNS | 2,432 | 1,140 | 1,289 | 3 | 149 D | 46.9% | 53.0% | 46.9% | 53.1% |
| 5,874 | TREUTLEN | 2,054 | 722 | 1,331 | 1 | 609 D | 35.2% | 64.8% | 35.2% | 64.8% |
| 47,189 | TROUP | 11,309 | 5,277 | 6,032 | | 755 D | 46.7% | 53.3% | 46.7% | 53.3% |
| 8,439 | TURNER | 2,391 | 1,672 | 719 | | 953 R | 69.9% | 30.1% | 69.9% | 30.1% |
| 7,935 | TWIGGS | 1,964 | 1,178 | 786 | | 392 R | 60.0% | 40.0% | 60.0% | 40.0% |
| 6,510 | UNION | 3,608 | 1,473 | 2,135 | | 662 D | 40.8% | 59.2% | 40.8% | 59.2% |
| 23,800 | UPSON | 6,384 | 3,103 | 3,275 | 6 | 172 D | 48.6% | 51.3% | 48.7% | 51.3% |
| 45,264 | WALKER | 11,401 | 5,939 | 5,454 | 8 | 485 R | 52.1% | 47.8% | 52.1% | 47.9% |
| 20,481 | WALTON | 5,226 | 2,874 | 2,350 | 2 | 524 R | 55.0% | 45.0% | 55.0% | 45.0% |
| 34,219 | WARE | 10,137 | 4,948 | 5,189 | | 241 D | 48.8% | 51.2% | 48.8% | 51.2% |
| 7,360 | WARREN | 1,454 | 1,070 | 384 | | 686 R | 73.6% | 26.4% | 73.6% | 26.4% |
| 18,903 | WASHINGTON | 4,127 | 2,296 | 1,830 | 1 | 466 R | 55.6% | 44.3% | 55.6% | 44.4% |
| 17,921 | WAYNE | 5,801 | 3,619 | 2,182 | | 1,437 R | 62.4% | 37.6% | 62.4% | 37.6% |
| 3,247 | WEBSTER | 601 | 457 | 144 | | 313 R | 76.0% | 24.0% | 76.0% | 24.0% |
| 5,342 | WHEELER | 1,829 | 849 | 980 | | 131 D | 46.4% | 53.6% | 46.4% | 53.6% |
| 6,935 | WHITE | 2,363 | 840 | 1,520 | 3 | 680 D | 35.5% | 64.3% | 35.6% | 64.4% |
| 42,109 | WHITFIELD | 11,880 | 4,546 | 7,330 | 4 | 2,784 D | 38.3% | 61.7% | 38.3% | 61.7% |
| 7,905 | WILCOX | 2,694 | 1,794 | 900 | | 894 R | 66.6% | 33.4% | 66.6% | 33.4% |
| 10,961 | WILKES | 3,089 | 1,652 | 1,437 | | 215 R | 53.5% | 46.5% | 53.5% | 46.5% |
| 9,250 | WILKINSON | 3,135 | 2,172 | 963 | | 1,209 R | 69.3% | 30.7% | 69.3% | 30.7% |
| 16,682 | WORTH | 4,019 | 3,157 | 862 | | 2,295 R | 78.6% | 21.4% | 78.6% | 21.4% |
| 3,943,116 | TOTAL | 1,139,335 | 616,584 | 522,556 | 195 | 94,028 R | 54.1% | 45.9% | 54.1% | 45.9% |

# GEORGIA

## PRESIDENT 1960

| 1960 Census Population | County | Total Vote | Republican | Democratic | Other | Rep.-Dem. Plurality | Percentage | | | |
|---|---|---|---|---|---|---|---|---|---|---|
| | | | | | | | Total Vote | | Major Vote | |
| | | | | | | | Rep. | Dem. | Rep. | Dem. |
| 13,246 | APPLING | 2,690 | 717 | 1,973 | | 1,256 D | 26.7% | 73.3% | 26.7% | 73.3% |
| 6,188 | ATKINSON | 1,537 | 239 | 1,298 | | 1,059 D | 15.5% | 84.5% | 15.5% | 84.5% |
| 8,359 | BACON | 1,747 | 579 | 1,168 | | 589 D | 33.1% | 66.9% | 33.1% | 66.9% |
| 4,543 | BAKER | 786 | 66 | 720 | | 654 D | 8.4% | 91.6% | 8.4% | 91.6% |
| 34,064 | BALDWIN | 3,526 | 1,264 | 2,262 | | 998 D | 35.8% | 64.2% | 35.8% | 64.2% |
| 6,497 | BANKS | 1,391 | 221 | 1,170 | | 949 D | 15.9% | 84.1% | 15.9% | 84.1% |
| 14,485 | BARROW | 3,336 | 577 | 2,759 | | 2,182 D | 17.3% | 82.7% | 17.3% | 82.7% |
| 28,267 | BARTOW | 4,837 | 1,292 | 3,545 | | 2,253 D | 26.7% | 73.3% | 26.7% | 73.3% |
| 13,633 | BEN HILL | 2,439 | 558 | 1,881 | | 1,323 D | 22.9% | 77.1% | 22.9% | 77.1% |
| 12,038 | BERRIEN | 3,155 | 368 | 2,787 | | 2,419 D | 11.7% | 88.3% | 11.7% | 88.3% |
| 141,249 | BIBB | 24,910 | 10,523 | 14,387 | | 3,864 D | 42.2% | 57.8% | 42.2% | 57.8% |
| 9,642 | BLECKLEY | 2,384 | 633 | 1,751 | | 1,118 D | 26.6% | 73.4% | 26.6% | 73.4% |
| 5,891 | BRANTLEY | 1,677 | 344 | 1,333 | | 989 D | 20.5% | 79.5% | 20.5% | 79.5% |
| 15,292 | BROOKS | 2,265 | 765 | 1,500 | | 735 D | 33.8% | 66.2% | 33.8% | 66.2% |
| 6,226 | BRYAN | 1,751 | 428 | 1,323 | | 895 D | 24.4% | 75.6% | 24.4% | 75.6% |
| 24,263 | BULLOCH | 4,879 | 1,506 | 3,373 | | 1,867 D | 30.9% | 69.1% | 30.9% | 69.1% |
| 20,596 | BURKE | 2,189 | 1,027 | 1,162 | | 135 D | 46.9% | 53.1% | 46.9% | 53.1% |
| 8,976 | BUTTS | 2,055 | 382 | 1,673 | | 1,291 D | 18.6% | 81.4% | 18.6% | 81.4% |
| 7,341 | CALHOUN | 934 | 131 | 803 | | 672 D | 14.0% | 86.0% | 14.0% | 86.0% |
| 9,975 | CAMDEN | 2,271 | 950 | 1,321 | | 371 D | 41.8% | 58.2% | 41.8% | 58.2% |
| 6,672 | CANDLER | 1,376 | 433 | 943 | | 510 D | 31.5% | 68.5% | 31.5% | 68.5% |
| 36,451 | CARROLL | 6,427 | 1,729 | 4,698 | | 2,969 D | 26.9% | 73.1% | 26.9% | 73.1% |
| 21,101 | CATOOSA | 4,188 | 2,074 | 2,114 | | 40 D | 49.5% | 50.5% | 49.5% | 50.5% |
| 5,313 | CHARLTON | 1,022 | 289 | 733 | | 444 D | 28.3% | 71.7% | 28.3% | 71.7% |
| 188,299 | CHATHAM | 34,175 | 17,935 | 16,240 | | 1,695 R | 52.5% | 47.5% | 52.5% | 47.5% |
| 13,011 | CHATTAHOOCHEE | 256 | 66 | 190 | | 124 D | 25.8% | 74.2% | 25.8% | 74.2% |
| 19,954 | CHATTOOGA | 5,282 | 1,596 | 3,686 | | 2,090 D | 30.2% | 69.8% | 30.2% | 69.8% |
| 23,001 | CHEROKEE | 5,418 | 2,341 | 3,077 | | 736 D | 43.2% | 56.8% | 43.2% | 56.8% |
| 45,363 | CLARKE | 7,062 | 2,250 | 4,812 | | 2,562 D | 31.9% | 68.1% | 31.9% | 68.1% |
| 4,551 | CLAY | 612 | 84 | 528 | | 444 D | 13.7% | 86.3% | 13.7% | 86.3% |
| 46,365 | CLAYTON | 8,845 | 2,953 | 5,892 | | 2,939 D | 33.4% | 66.6% | 33.4% | 66.6% |
| 6,545 | CLINCH | 1,295 | 397 | 898 | | 501 D | 30.7% | 69.3% | 30.7% | 69.3% |
| 114,174 | COBB | 21,146 | 8,240 | 12,906 | | 4,666 D | 39.0% | 61.0% | 39.0% | 61.0% |
| 21,953 | COFFEE | 4,363 | 987 | 3,376 | | 2,389 D | 22.6% | 77.4% | 22.6% | 77.4% |
| 34,048 | COLQUITT | 6,082 | 1,685 | 4,397 | | 2,712 D | 27.7% | 72.3% | 27.7% | 72.3% |
| 13,423 | COLUMBIA | 2,345 | 1,155 | 1,190 | | 35 D | 49.3% | 50.7% | 49.3% | 50.7% |
| 11,822 | COOK | 2,334 | 399 | 1,935 | | 1,536 D | 17.1% | 82.9% | 17.1% | 82.9% |
| 28,893 | COWETA | 5,014 | 1,159 | 3,855 | | 2,696 D | 23.1% | 76.9% | 23.1% | 76.9% |
| 5,816 | CRAWFORD | 1,000 | 203 | 797 | | 594 D | 20.3% | 79.7% | 20.3% | 79.7% |
| 17,768 | CRISP | 3,328 | 963 | 2,365 | | 1,402 D | 28.9% | 71.1% | 28.9% | 71.1% |
| 8,666 | DADE | 1,852 | 909 | 943 | | 34 D | 49.1% | 50.9% | 49.1% | 50.9% |
| 3,590 | DAWSON | 1,317 | 401 | 916 | | 515 D | 30.4% | 69.6% | 30.4% | 69.6% |
| 25,203 | DECATUR | 3,698 | 918 | 2,780 | | 1,862 D | 24.8% | 75.2% | 24.8% | 75.2% |
| 256,782 | DE KALB | 48,162 | 24,046 | 24,116 | | 70 D | 49.9% | 50.1% | 49.9% | 50.1% |
| 16,483 | DODGE | 4,764 | 1,134 | 3,630 | | 2,496 D | 23.8% | 76.2% | 23.8% | 76.2% |
| 11,474 | DOOLY | 1,953 | 220 | 1,733 | | 1,513 D | 11.3% | 88.7% | 11.3% | 88.7% |
| 75,680 | DOUGHERTY | 8,845 | 4,323 | 4,522 | | 199 D | 48.9% | 51.1% | 48.9% | 51.1% |
| 16,741 | DOUGLAS | 3,712 | 1,136 | 2,576 | | 1,440 D | 30.6% | 69.4% | 30.6% | 69.4% |
| 13,151 | EARLY | 2,158 | 254 | 1,904 | | 1,650 D | 11.8% | 88.2% | 11.8% | 88.2% |
| 1,876 | ECHOLS | 365 | 108 | 257 | | 149 D | 29.6% | 70.4% | 29.6% | 70.4% |
| 10,144 | EFFINGHAM | 1,765 | 885 | 880 | | 5 R | 50.1% | 49.9% | 50.1% | 49.9% |
| 17,835 | ELBERT | 4,281 | 609 | 3,672 | | 3,063 D | 14.2% | 85.8% | 14.2% | 85.8% |
| 17,815 | EMANUEL | 3,633 | 1,120 | 2,513 | | 1,393 D | 30.8% | 69.2% | 30.8% | 69.2% |
| 6,952 | EVANS | 1,636 | 567 | 1,069 | | 502 D | 34.7% | 65.3% | 34.7% | 65.3% |
| 13,620 | FANNIN | 4,601 | 3,022 | 1,579 | | 1,443 R | 65.7% | 34.3% | 65.7% | 34.3% |
| 8,199 | FAYETTE | 1,557 | 359 | 1,198 | | 839 D | 23.1% | 76.9% | 23.1% | 76.9% |
| 69,130 | FLOYD | 13,458 | 6,108 | 7,350 | | 1,242 D | 45.4% | 54.6% | 45.4% | 54.6% |
| 12,170 | FORSYTH | 3,150 | 841 | 2,309 | | 1,468 D | 26.7% | 73.3% | 26.7% | 73.3% |
| 13,274 | FRANKLIN | 3,517 | 308 | 3,209 | | 2,901 D | 8.8% | 91.2% | 8.8% | 91.2% |
| 556,326 | FULTON | 109,743 | 53,940 | 55,803 | | 1,863 D | 49.2% | 50.8% | 49.2% | 50.8% |

# GEORGIA

## PRESIDENT 1960

| 1960 Census Population | County | Total Vote | Republican | Democratic | Other | Rep.-Dem. Plurality | Percentage | | | |
|---|---|---|---|---|---|---|---|---|---|---|
| | | | | | | | Total Vote | | Major Vote | |
| | | | | | | | Rep. | Dem. | Rep. | Dem. |
| 8,922 | GILMER | 3,322 | 1,850 | 1,472 | | 378 R | 55.7% | 44.3% | 55.7% | 44.3% |
| 2,672 | GLASCOCK | 479 | 180 | 299 | | 119 D | 37.6% | 62.4% | 37.6% | 62.4% |
| 41,954 | GLYNN | 6,510 | 2,926 | 3,584 | | 658 D | 44.9% | 55.1% | 44.9% | 55.1% |
| 19,228 | GORDON | 3,301 | 1,148 | 2,153 | | 1,005 D | 34.8% | 65.2% | 34.8% | 65.2% |
| 18,015 | GRADY | 3,133 | 592 | 2,541 | | 1,949 D | 18.9% | 81.1% | 18.9% | 81.1% |
| 11,193 | GREENE | 2,307 | 328 | 1,979 | | 1,651 D | 14.2% | 85.8% | 14.2% | 85.8% |
| 43,541 | GWINNETT | 8,815 | 2,336 | 6,479 | | 4,143 D | 26.5% | 73.5% | 26.5% | 73.5% |
| 18,116 | HABERSHAM | 3,425 | 895 | 2,530 | | 1,635 D | 26.1% | 73.9% | 26.1% | 73.9% |
| 49,739 | HALL | 9,206 | 2,903 | 6,303 | | 3,400 D | 31.5% | 68.5% | 31.5% | 68.5% |
| 9,979 | HANCOCK | 1,066 | 286 | 780 | | 494 D | 26.8% | 73.2% | 26.8% | 73.2% |
| 14,543 | HARALSON | 4,652 | 1,869 | 2,783 | | 914 D | 40.2% | 59.8% | 40.2% | 59.8% |
| 11,167 | HARRIS | 2,097 | 735 | 1,362 | | 627 D | 35.1% | 64.9% | 35.1% | 64.9% |
| 15,229 | HART | 4,238 | 275 | 3,963 | | 3,688 D | 6.5% | 93.5% | 6.5% | 93.5% |
| 5,333 | HEARD | 1,405 | 181 | 1,224 | | 1,043 D | 12.9% | 87.1% | 12.9% | 87.1% |
| 17,619 | HENRY | 3,998 | 1,041 | 2,957 | | 1,916 D | 26.0% | 74.0% | 26.0% | 74.0% |
| 39,154 | HOUSTON | 5,790 | 1,757 | 4,033 | | 2,276 D | 30.3% | 69.7% | 30.3% | 69.7% |
| 9,211 | IRWIN | 1,977 | 352 | 1,625 | | 1,273 D | 17.8% | 82.2% | 17.8% | 82.2% |
| 18,499 | JACKSON | 4,125 | 472 | 3,653 | | 3,181 D | 11.4% | 88.6% | 11.4% | 88.6% |
| 6,135 | JASPER | 1,220 | 271 | 949 | | 678 D | 22.2% | 77.8% | 22.2% | 77.8% |
| 8,914 | JEFF DAVIS | 1,227 | 402 | 825 | | 423 D | 32.8% | 67.2% | 32.8% | 67.2% |
| 17,468 | JEFFERSON | 2,256 | 986 | 1,270 | | 284 D | 43.7% | 56.3% | 43.7% | 56.3% |
| 9,148 | JENKINS | 1,667 | 313 | 1,354 | | 1,041 D | 18.8% | 81.2% | 18.8% | 81.2% |
| 8,048 | JOHNSON | 1,786 | 488 | 1,298 | | 810 D | 27.3% | 72.7% | 27.3% | 72.7% |
| 8,468 | JONES | 1,904 | 489 | 1,415 | | 926 D | 25.7% | 74.3% | 25.7% | 74.3% |
| 10,240 | LAMAR | 1,842 | 479 | 1,363 | | 884 D | 26.0% | 74.0% | 26.0% | 74.0% |
| 5,097 | LANIER | 1,247 | 198 | 1,049 | | 851 D | 15.9% | 84.1% | 15.9% | 84.1% |
| 32,313 | LAURENS | 6,532 | 1,884 | 4,648 | | 2,764 D | 28.8% | 71.2% | 28.8% | 71.2% |
| 6,204 | LEE | 595 | 191 | 404 | | 213 D | 32.1% | 67.9% | 32.1% | 67.9% |
| 14,487 | LIBERTY | 2,519 | 929 | 1,590 | | 661 D | 36.9% | 63.1% | 36.9% | 63.1% |
| 5,906 | LINCOLN | 866 | 197 | 669 | | 472 D | 22.7% | 77.3% | 22.7% | 77.3% |
| 3,874 | LONG | 1,176 | 898 | 278 | | 620 R | 76.4% | 23.6% | 76.4% | 23.6% |
| 49,270 | LOWNDES | 6,513 | 2,908 | 3,605 | | 697 D | 44.6% | 55.4% | 44.6% | 55.4% |
| 7,241 | LUMPKIN | 1,370 | 495 | 875 | | 380 D | 36.1% | 63.9% | 36.1% | 63.9% |
| 12,627 | MCDUFFIE | 2,118 | 1,039 | 1,079 | | 40 D | 49.1% | 50.9% | 49.1% | 50.9% |
| 6,364 | MCINTOSH | 1,245 | 451 | 794 | | 343 D | 36.2% | 63.8% | 36.2% | 63.8% |
| 13,170 | MACON | 1,926 | 438 | 1,488 | | 1,050 D | 22.7% | 77.3% | 22.7% | 77.3% |
| 11,246 | MADISON | 2,623 | 205 | 2,418 | | 2,213 D | 7.8% | 92.2% | 7.8% | 92.2% |
| 5,477 | MARION | 799 | 154 | 645 | | 491 D | 19.3% | 80.7% | 19.3% | 80.7% |
| 19,756 | MERIWETHER | 3,806 | 706 | 3,100 | | 2,394 D | 18.5% | 81.5% | 18.5% | 81.5% |
| 6,908 | MILLER | 1,178 | 62 | 1,116 | | 1,054 D | 5.3% | 94.7% | 5.3% | 94.7% |
| 19,652 | MITCHELL | 3,694 | 430 | 3,264 | | 2,834 D | 11.6% | 88.4% | 11.6% | 88.4% |
| 10,495 | MONROE | 2,223 | 581 | 1,642 | | 1,061 D | 26.1% | 73.9% | 26.1% | 73.9% |
| 6,284 | MONTGOMERY | 1,832 | 381 | 1,451 | | 1,070 D | 20.8% | 79.2% | 20.8% | 79.2% |
| 10,280 | MORGAN | 1,861 | 373 | 1,488 | | 1,115 D | 20.0% | 80.0% | 20.0% | 80.0% |
| 10,447 | MURRAY | 2,801 | 925 | 1,876 | | 951 D | 33.0% | 67.0% | 33.0% | 67.0% |
| 158,623 | MUSCOGEE | 18,131 | 9,578 | 8,553 | | 1,025 R | 52.8% | 47.2% | 52.8% | 47.2% |
| 20,999 | NEWTON | 3,893 | 708 | 3,185 | | 2,477 D | 18.2% | 81.8% | 18.2% | 81.8% |
| 6,304 | OCONEE | 1,515 | 297 | 1,218 | | 921 D | 19.6% | 80.4% | 19.6% | 80.4% |
| 7,926 | OGLETHORPE | 1,548 | 142 | 1,406 | | 1,264 D | 9.2% | 90.8% | 9.2% | 90.8% |
| 13,101 | PAULDING | 3,208 | 812 | 2,396 | | 1,584 D | 25.3% | 74.7% | 25.3% | 74.7% |
| 13,846 | PEACH | 2,061 | 628 | 1,433 | | 805 D | 30.5% | 69.5% | 30.5% | 69.5% |
| 8,903 | PICKENS | 3,416 | 1,943 | 1,473 | | 470 R | 56.9% | 43.1% | 56.9% | 43.1% |
| 9,678 | PIERCE | 1,993 | 544 | 1,449 | | 905 D | 27.3% | 72.7% | 27.3% | 72.7% |
| 7,138 | PIKE | 1,283 | 255 | 1,028 | | 773 D | 19.9% | 80.1% | 19.9% | 80.1% |
| 28,015 | POLK | 6,097 | 1,746 | 4,351 | | 2,605 D | 28.6% | 71.4% | 28.6% | 71.4% |
| 8,204 | PULASKI | 1,490 | 334 | 1,156 | | 822 D | 22.4% | 77.6% | 22.4% | 77.6% |
| 7,798 | PUTNAM | 1,409 | 305 | 1,104 | | 799 D | 21.6% | 78.4% | 21.6% | 78.4% |
| 2,432 | QUITMAN | 455 | 67 | 388 | | 321 D | 14.7% | 85.3% | 14.7% | 85.3% |
| 7,456 | RABUN | 2,016 | 464 | 1,552 | | 1,088 D | 23.0% | 77.0% | 23.0% | 77.0% |
| 11,078 | RANDOLPH | 1,893 | 457 | 1,436 | | 979 D | 24.1% | 75.9% | 24.1% | 75.9% |

# GEORGIA

## PRESIDENT 1960

| 1960 Census Population | County | Total Vote | Republican | Democratic | Other | Rep.-Dem. Plurality | Percentage | | | |
|---|---|---|---|---|---|---|---|---|---|---|
| | | | | | | | Total Vote | | Major Vote | |
| | | | | | | | Rep. | Dem. | Rep. | Dem. |
| 135,601 | RICHMOND | 21,846 | 11,978 | 9,868 | | 2,110 R | 54.8% | 45.2% | 54.8% | 45.2% |
| 10,572 | ROCKDALE | 2,261 | 496 | 1,765 | | 1,269 D | 21.9% | 78.1% | 21.9% | 78.1% |
| 3,256 | SCHLEY | 605 | 138 | 467 | | 329 D | 22.8% | 77.2% | 22.8% | 77.2% |
| 14,919 | SCREVEN | 2,447 | 957 | 1,490 | | 533 D | 39.1% | 60.9% | 39.1% | 60.9% |
| 6,802 | SEMINOLE | 1,656 | 77 | 1,579 | | 1,502 D | 4.6% | 95.4% | 4.6% | 95.4% |
| 35,404 | SPALDING | 6,179 | 1,753 | 4,426 | | 2,673 D | 28.4% | 71.6% | 28.4% | 71.6% |
| 18,391 | STEPHENS | 3,902 | 815 | 3,087 | | 2,272 D | 20.9% | 79.1% | 20.9% | 79.1% |
| 7,371 | STEWART | 948 | 302 | 646 | | 344 D | 31.9% | 68.1% | 31.9% | 68.1% |
| 24,652 | SUMTER | 3,236 | 962 | 2,274 | | 1,312 D | 29.7% | 70.3% | 29.7% | 70.3% |
| 7,127 | TALBOT | 978 | 207 | 771 | | 564 D | 21.2% | 78.8% | 21.2% | 78.8% |
| 3,370 | TALIAFERRO | 803 | 148 | 655 | | 507 D | 18.4% | 81.6% | 18.4% | 81.6% |
| 15,837 | TATTNALL | 2,777 | 869 | 1,908 | | 1,039 D | 31.3% | 68.7% | 31.3% | 68.7% |
| 8,311 | TAYLOR | 1,566 | 365 | 1,201 | | 836 D | 23.3% | 76.7% | 23.3% | 76.7% |
| 11,715 | TELFAIR | 3,713 | 791 | 2,922 | | 2,131 D | 21.3% | 78.7% | 21.3% | 78.7% |
| 12,742 | TERRELL | 1,637 | 285 | 1,352 | | 1,067 D | 17.4% | 82.6% | 17.4% | 82.6% |
| 34,319 | THOMAS | 5,511 | 2,285 | 3,226 | | 941 D | 41.5% | 58.5% | 41.5% | 58.5% |
| 23,487 | TIFT | 4,387 | 1,423 | 2,964 | | 1,541 D | 32.4% | 67.6% | 32.4% | 67.6% |
| 16,837 | TOOMBS | 3,247 | 1,038 | 2,209 | | 1,171 D | 32.0% | 68.0% | 32.0% | 68.0% |
| 4,538 | TOWNS | 2,324 | 1,272 | 1,052 | | 220 R | 54.7% | 45.3% | 54.7% | 45.3% |
| 5,874 | TREUTLEN | 1,143 | 216 | 927 | | 711 D | 18.9% | 81.1% | 18.9% | 81.1% |
| 47,189 | TROUP | 8,553 | 2,808 | 5,745 | | 2,937 D | 32.8% | 67.2% | 32.8% | 67.2% |
| 8,439 | TURNER | 1,873 | 328 | 1,545 | | 1,217 D | 17.5% | 82.5% | 17.5% | 82.5% |
| 7,935 | TWIGGS | 1,108 | 263 | 845 | | 582 D | 23.7% | 76.3% | 23.7% | 76.3% |
| 6,510 | UNION | 2,722 | 1,537 | 1,185 | | 352 R | 56.5% | 43.5% | 56.5% | 43.5% |
| 23,800 | UPSON | 4,263 | 1,001 | 3,262 | | 2,261 D | 23.5% | 76.5% | 23.5% | 76.5% |
| 45,264 | WALKER | 8,593 | 4,027 | 4,566 | | 539 D | 46.9% | 53.1% | 46.9% | 53.1% |
| 20,481 | WALTON | 3,498 | 403 | 3,095 | | 2,692 D | 11.5% | 88.5% | 11.5% | 88.5% |
| 34,219 | WARE | 7,334 | 2,235 | 5,099 | | 2,864 D | 30.5% | 69.5% | 30.5% | 69.5% |
| 7,360 | WARREN | 846 | 375 | 471 | | 96 D | 44.3% | 55.7% | 44.3% | 55.7% |
| 18,903 | WASHINGTON | 2,960 | 956 | 2,004 | | 1,048 D | 32.3% | 67.7% | 32.3% | 67.7% |
| 17,921 | WAYNE | 4,246 | 1,384 | 2,862 | | 1,478 D | 32.6% | 67.4% | 32.6% | 67.4% |
| 3,247 | WEBSTER | 374 | 77 | 297 | | 220 D | 20.6% | 79.4% | 20.6% | 79.4% |
| 5,342 | WHEELER | 1,196 | 226 | 970 | | 744 D | 18.9% | 81.1% | 18.9% | 81.1% |
| 6,935 | WHITE | 2,446 | 662 | 1,784 | | 1,122 D | 27.1% | 72.9% | 27.1% | 72.9% |
| 42,109 | WHITFIELD | 7,752 | 4,148 | 3,604 | | 544 R | 53.5% | 46.5% | 53.5% | 46.5% |
| 7,905 | WILCOX | 2,020 | 306 | 1,714 | | 1,408 D | 15.1% | 84.9% | 15.1% | 84.9% |
| 10,961 | WILKES | 2,181 | 395 | 1,786 | | 1,391 D | 18.1% | 81.9% | 18.1% | 81.9% |
| 9,250 | WILKINSON | 1,955 | 631 | 1,324 | | 693 D | 32.3% | 67.7% | 32.3% | 67.7% |
| 16,682 | WORTH | 2,448 | 338 | 2,110 | | 1,772 D | 13.8% | 86.2% | 13.8% | 86.2% |
| 3,943,116 | TOTAL | 733,349 | 274,472 | 458,638 | 239 | 184,166 D | 37.4% | 62.5% | 37.4% | 62.6% |

# GEORGIA

## ELECTION NOTES

**2004**  Other vote was 18,387 Libertarian (Michael Badnarik); 2,231 write-in (Ralph Nader); 580 write-in (Michael Peroutka); 228 write-in (David Cobb); 26 write-in (Tom Tancredo); 8 write-in (John J. Kennedy); 7 write-in (David Byrne); 5 write-in (James Pace).

**2000**  Other vote was 36,332 Libertarian (Browne); 10,926 Independent (Buchanan); 140 write-in (Phillips); 11 write-in (Harris); 8 write-in (Strickland); 5 write-in (Schriner).

**1996**  Other vote was 17,870 Libertarian (Browne); 145 write-in (Phillips); 27 scattered write-in.

**1992**  Other vote was 7,110 Marrou (Libertarian); 78 Gritz (write-in); 44 Fulani (write-in); 9 Warren (write-in); 7 Phillips (write-in); 2 scattered write-in.

**1988**  Other vote was 8,435 Paul (Libertarian); 5,099 Fulani (New Alliance); 15 scattered write-in. The total of the other vote column includes these 15 write-in votes not available by county.

**1984**  Other vote was all write-in as follows: 152 Bergland; 95 Richards; 34 LaRouche; 10 Mason; 4 Dennis; 4 Johnson; 3 Anderson; 3 Lowrey; 2 Holmes; 2 Serrette; 1 Hall; 460 scattered write-in. The state-wide total for the other vote column is these 770 write-in votes not reported by county.

**1980**  Other vote was 36,055 Anderson (Independent); 15,627 Clark (Libertarian); 104 Commoner (write-in); 4 Pulley (write-in); 1 Griswold (write-in); 3 scattered write-in. The state-wide total for the other vote column includes these 112 write-in votes not reported by county. Early unamended canvass gave the Democratic state-wide total vote as 890,955.

**1976**  Other vote was all write-in as follows: 1,168 Anderson; 1,071 Maddox; 991 McCarthy; 175 MacBride; 43 Camejo; 3 Hall; 3 Miller; 2 Levin; 2 Zeidler; 1 LaRouche; 847 scattered write-in. The state-wide total for the other vote column is these 4,306 write-in votes not reported by county.

**1972**  Other vote was 812 Schmitz (write-in); 3 Fisher (write-in); 2,932 scattered write-in. Although the data indicate a possible discrepancy in the Republican vote in Mitchell county and in both the Republican and Democratic vote in Habersham county, the official state canvass figures are used in the table.

**1968**  Wallace on the ballot as American. Other vote was scattered write-in. The Democratic total vote is carried as certified by the state but the addition of the counties totals 334,438.

**1964**  Other vote was scattered write-in.

**1960**  Other vote was scattered write-in. The total in the other vote column represents the 239 scattered write-in votes not available by county.

# HAWAII

## POPULAR VOTE FOR PRESIDENT 1960 TO 2004

| Year | Total Vote | Republican Vote | Republican Candidate | Democratic Vote | Democratic Candidate | Other Vote | Plurality | Percentage Total Vote Rep. | Percentage Total Vote Dem. | Percentage Major Vote Rep. | Percentage Major Vote Dem. |
|------|-----------|-----------------|---------------------|-----------------|---------------------|-----------|-----------|------|------|------|------|
| 2004 | 429,013 | 194,191 | Bush, George W. | 231,708 | Kerry, John | 3,114 | 37,517 D | 45.3% | 54.0% | 45.6% | 54.4% |
| 2000** | 367,951 | 137,845 | Bush, George W. | 205,286 | Gore, Al | 24,820 | 67,441 D | 37.5% | 55.8% | 40.2% | 59.8% |
| 1996 ** | 360,120 | 113,943 | Dole, Bob | 205,012 | Clinton, Bill | 41,165 | 91,069 D | 31.6% | 56.9% | 35.7% | 64.3% |
| 1992 ** | 372,842 | 136,822 | Bush, George | 179,310 | Clinton, Bill | 56,710 | 42,488 D | 36.7% | 48.1% | 43.3% | 56.7% |
| 1988 | 354,461 | 158,625 | Bush, George | 192,364 | Dukakis, Michael S. | 3,472 | 33,739 D | 44.8% | 54.3% | 45.2% | 54.8% |
| 1984 | 335,846 | 185,050 | Reagan, Ronald | 147,154 | Mondale, Walter F. | 3,642 | 37,896 R | 55.1% | 43.8% | 55.7% | 44.3% |
| 1980 ** | 303,287 | 130,112 | Reagan, Ronald | 135,879 | Carter, Jimmy | 37,296 | 5,767 D | 42.9% | 44.8% | 48.9% | 51.1% |
| 1976 | 291,301 | 140,003 | Ford, Gerald R. | 147,375 | Carter, Jimmy | 3,923 | 7,372 D | 48.1% | 50.6% | 48.7% | 51.3% |
| 1972 | 270,274 | 168,865 | Nixon, Richard M. | 101,409 | McGovern, George S. | | 67,456 R | 62.5% | 37.5% | 62.5% | 37.5% |
| 1968 | 236,218 | 91,425 | Nixon, Richard M. | 141,324 | Humphrey, Hubert H. | 3,469 | 49,899 D | 38.7% | 59.8% | 39.3% | 60.7% |
| 1964 | 207,271 | 44,022 | Goldwater, Barry M. | 163,249 | Johnson, Lyndon B. | | 119,227 D | 21.2% | 78.8% | 21.2% | 78.8% |
| 1960 | 184,705 | 92,295 | Nixon, Richard M. | 92,410 | Kennedy, John F. | | 115 D | 50.0% | 50.0% | 50.0% | 50.0% |

In 2000 the other vote column includes 21,623 votes cast for Green (Nader). In 1996 the other vote column includes 27,358 votes cast for Perot. In 1992 the other vote column includes 53,003 votes cast for Perot. In 1980 the other column includes 32,021 votes for Independent (Anderson). Hawaii was formally admitted as a state in August 1959.

## ELECTORAL COLLEGE VOTE 1960 TO 2004

| Year | Total | Republican | Democratic | Other |
|------|-------|-----------|-----------|-------|
| 2004 | 4 | | 4 | |
| 2000 | 4 | | 4 | |
| 1996 | 4 | | 4 | |
| 1992 | 4 | | 4 | |
| 1988 | 4 | | 4 | |
| 1984 | 4 | 4 | | |
| 1980 | 4 | | 4 | |
| 1976 | 4 | | 4 | |
| 1972 | 4 | 4 | | |
| 1968 | 4 | | 4 | |
| 1964 | 4 | | 4 | |
| 1960 | 3 | | 3 | |

252

# HAWAII

PRINCIPAL ISLANDS

HAWAII COUNTY

HAWAII

MAUI

KALAWAO COUNTY

MAUI COUNTY

MOLOKAI

LANAI

KAHOOLAWE

HONOLULU COUNTY

OAHU

KAUAI

KAUAI COUNTY

NIIHAU

# HAWAII

## PRESIDENT 2004

| 2000 Census Population | County | Total Vote | Republican | Democratic | Other | Rep.-Dem. Plurality | Percentage | | | |
|---|---|---|---|---|---|---|---|---|---|---|
| | | | | | | | Total Vote | | Major Vote | |
| | | | | | | | Rep. | Dem. | Rep. | Dem. |
| 148,677 | HAWAII | 57,702 | 22,032 | 35,116 | 554 | 13,084 D | 38.2% | 60.9% | 38.6% | 61.4% |
| 876,156 | HONOLULU | 298,547 | 144,157 | 152,500 | 1,890 | 8,343 D | 48.3% | 51.1% | 48.6% | 51.4% |
| 58,463 | KAUAI | 24,876 | 9,740 | 14,916 | 220 | 5,176 D | 39.2% | 60.0% | 39.5% | 60.5% |
| 128,094 | MAUI | 47,430 | 18,187 | 28,803 | 440 | 10,616 D | 38.3% | 60.7% | 38.7% | 61.3% |
| | Overseas Ballots | 458 | 75 | 373 | 10 | 298 D | 16.4% | 81.4% | 16.7% | 83.3% |
| 1,211,537 | TOTAL | 429,013 | 194,191 | 231,708 | 3,114 | 37,517 D | 45.3% | 54.0% | 45.6% | 54.4% |

Note: The 2000 Census includes 147 people in Kalawao County; their votes are part of the Maui County returns.

# HAWAII

## PRESIDENT 2000

| 2000 Census Population | County | Total Vote | Republican | Democratic | Green (Nader) | Other | Rep.-Dem. Plurality | Percentage of Total Vote | | |
|---|---|---|---|---|---|---|---|---|---|---|
| | | | | | | | | Rep. | Dem. | Green |
| 148,677 | HAWAII | 50,860 | 17,050 | 28,670 | 4,604 | 536 | 11,620 D | 33.5% | 56.4% | 9.1% |
| 876,156 | HONOLULU | 255,990 | 101,310 | 139,618 | 13,037 | 2,025 | 38,308 D | 39.6% | 54.5% | 5.1% |
| 58,463 | KAUAI | 21,773 | 6,583 | 13,470 | 1,474 | 246 | 6,887 D | 30.2% | 61.9% | 6.8% |
| 128,094 | MAUI | 39,248 | 12,876 | 23,484 | 2,499 | 389 | 10,608 D | 32.8% | 59.8% | 6.4% |
| | OVERSEAS BALLOTS | 80 | 26 | 44 | 9 | 1 | 18 D | 32.5% | 55.0% | 11.3% |
| 1,211,537 | TOTAL | 367,951 | 137,845 | 205,286 | 21,623 | 3,197 | 67,441 D | 37.5% | 55.8% | 5.9% |

Note: The 2000 Census includes 147 people in Kalawao County; their votes are part of the Maui County results.

# HAWAII

## PRESIDENT 1996

| 1995 Census Pop. Est. | County | Total Vote | Republican | Democratic | Reform (Perot) | Other | Rep.-Dem. Plurality | Percentage of Total Vote | | |
|---|---|---|---|---|---|---|---|---|---|---|
| | | | | | | | | Rep. | Dem. | Reform |
| 137,531 | HAWAII | 48,977 | 13,516 | 27,262 | 5,137 | 3,062 | 13,746 D | 27.6% | 55.7% | 10.5% |
| 877,198 | HONOLULU | 255,181 | 85,748 | 143,755 | 17,388 | 8,290 | 58,007 D | 33.6% | 56.3% | 6.8% |
| 56,131 | KAUAI | 21,020 | 5,325 | 13,357 | 1,568 | 770 | 8,032 D | 25.3% | 63.5% | 7.5% |
| 115,864 | MAUI | 34,867 | 9,323 | 20,600 | 3,264 | 1,680 | 11,277 D | 26.7% | 59.1% | 9.4% |
| | OVERSEAS BALLOTS | 75 | 31 | 38 | 1 | 5 | 7 D | 41.3% | 50.7% | 1.3% |
| 1,186,815 | TOTAL | 360,120 | 113,943 | 205,012 | 27,358 | 13,807 | 91,069 D | 31.6% | 56.9% | 7.6% |

Note: 1995 population estimates for Hawaii include 91 people in Kalawao County, although no votes are recorded from there.

# HAWAII

## PRESIDENT 1992

| 1990 Census Population | County | Total Vote | Republican | Democratic | Perot | Other | Plurality | Percentage Total Vote | | |
|---|---|---|---|---|---|---|---|---|---|---|
| | | | | | | | | Rep. | Dem. | Perot |
| 120,317 | HAWAII | 50,916 | 15,460 | 25,725 | 8,889 | 842 | 10,265 D | 30.4% | 50.5% | 17.5% |
| 836,231 | HONOLULU | 265,841 | 103,937 | 123,908 | 35,728 | 2,268 | 19,971 D | 39.1% | 46.6% | 13.4% |
| 51,177 | KAUAI | 18,960 | 6,274 | 10,715 | 1,756 | 215 | 4,441 D | 33.1% | 56.5% | 9.3% |
| 100,504 | MAUI | 37,125 | 11,151 | 18,962 | 6,630 | 382 | 7,811 D | 30.0% | 51.1% | 17.9% |
| 1,108,229 | TOTAL | 372,842 | 136,822 | 179,310 | 53,003 | 3,707 | 42,488 D | 36.7% | 48.1% | 14.2% |

# HAWAII

## PRESIDENT 1988

| 1980 Census Population | County | Total Vote | Republican | Democratic | Other | Rep.-Dem. Plurality | Percentage | | | |
|---|---|---|---|---|---|---|---|---|---|---|
| | | | | | | | Total Vote | | Major Vote | |
| | | | | | | | Rep. | Dem. | Rep. | Dem. |
| 92,053 | HAWAII | 41,768 | 17,125 | 24,091 | 552 | 6,966 D | 41.0% | 57.7% | 41.5% | 58.5% |
| 762,565 | HONOLULU | 261,577 | 120,258 | 138,971 | 2,348 | 18,713 D | 46.0% | 53.1% | 46.4% | 53.6% |
| 39,082 | KAUAI | 20,266 | 8,298 | 11,770 | 198 | 3,472 D | 40.9% | 58.1% | 41.3% | 58.7% |
| 70,991 | MAUI | 30,850 | 12,944 | 17,532 | 374 | 4,588 D | 42.0% | 56.8% | 42.5% | 57.5% |
| 964,691 | TOTAL | 354,461 | 158,625 | 192,364 | 3,472 | 33,739 D | 44.8% | 54.3% | 45.2% | 54.8% |

# HAWAII

## PRESIDENT 1984

| 1980 Census Population | County | Total Vote | Republican | Democratic | Other | Rep.-Dem. Plurality | Percentage | | | |
|---|---|---|---|---|---|---|---|---|---|---|
| | | | | | | | Total Vote | | Major Vote | |
| | | | | | | | Rep. | Dem. | Rep. | Dem. |
| 92,053 | HAWAII | 39,143 | 20,707 | 17,866 | 570 | 2,841 R | 52.9% | 45.6% | 53.7% | 46.3% |
| 762,565 | HONOLULU | 250,132 | 140,258 | 107,404 | 2,470 | 32,854 R | 56.1% | 42.9% | 56.6% | 43.4% |
| 39,082 | KAUAI | 18,332 | 9,249 | 8,862 | 221 | 387 R | 50.5% | 48.3% | 51.1% | 48.9% |
| 70,991 | MAUI | 28,067 | 14,720 | 12,966 | 381 | 1,754 R | 52.4% | 46.2% | 53.2% | 46.8% |
| | SPECIAL BALLOTS | 172 | 116 | 56 | | 60 R | 67.4% | 32.6% | 67.4% | 32.6% |
| 964,691 | TOTAL | 335,846 | 185,050 | 147,154 | 3,642 | 37,896 R | 55.1% | 43.8% | 55.7% | 44.3% |

# HAWAII

## PRESIDENT 1980

| 1980 Census Population | County | Total Vote | Republican | Democratic | Other | Rep.-Dem. Plurality | Percentage Total Vote Rep. | Dem. | Major Vote Rep. | Dem. |
|---|---|---|---|---|---|---|---|---|---|---|
| 92,053 | HAWAII | 35,861 | 14,247 | 17,630 | 3,984 | 3,383 D | 39.7% | 49.2% | 44.7% | 55.3% |
| 762,565 | HONOLULU | 224,995 | 99,596 | 96,472 | 28,927 | 3,124 R | 44.3% | 42.9% | 50.8% | 49.2% |
| 39,082 | KAUAI | 16,621 | 5,883 | 9,081 | 1,657 | 3,198 D | 35.4% | 54.6% | 39.3% | 60.7% |
| 70,991 | MAUI | 25,751 | 10,359 | 12,674 | 2,718 | 2,315 D | 40.2% | 49.2% | 45.0% | 55.0% |
| | SPECIAL BALLOTS | 59 | 27 | 22 | 10 | 5 R | 45.8% | 37.3% | 55.1% | 44.9% |
| 964,691 | TOTAL | 303,287 | 130,112 | 135,879 | 37,296 | 5,767 D | 42.9% | 44.8% | 48.9% | 51.1% |

# HAWAII

## PRESIDENT 1976

| 1970 Census Population | County | Total Vote | Republican | Democratic | Other | Rep.-Dem. Plurality | Percentage Total Vote Rep. | Dem. | Major Vote Rep. | Dem. |
|---|---|---|---|---|---|---|---|---|---|---|
| 63,468 | HAWAII | 31,765 | 15,366 | 15,960 | 439 | 594 D | 48.4% | 50.2% | 49.1% | 50.9% |
| 630,528 | HONOLULU | 222,416 | 108,007 | 111,365 | 3,044 | 3,358 D | 48.6% | 50.1% | 49.2% | 50.8% |
| 29,761 | KAUAI | 14,522 | 6,278 | 8,105 | 139 | 1,827 D | 43.2% | 55.8% | 43.6% | 56.4% |
| 46,156 | MAUI | 22,538 | 10,318 | 11,921 | 299 | 1,603 D | 45.8% | 52.9% | 46.4% | 53.6% |
| | SPECIAL BALLOTS | 60 | 34 | 24 | 2 | 10 R | 56.7% | 40.0% | 58.6% | 41.4% |
| 769,913 | TOTAL | 291,301 | 140,003 | 147,375 | 3,923 | 7,372 D | 48.1% | 50.6% | 48.7% | 51.3% |

# HAWAII

## PRESIDENT 1972

| 1970 Census Population | County | Total Vote | Republican | Democratic | Other | Rep.-Dem. Plurality | Percentage Total Vote Rep. | Dem. | Major Vote Rep. | Dem. |
|---|---|---|---|---|---|---|---|---|---|---|
| 63,468 | HAWAII | 28,484 | 16,832 | 11,652 | | 5,180 R | 59.1% | 40.9% | 59.1% | 40.9% |
| 630,528 | HONOLULU | 209,801 | 132,844 | 76,957 | | 55,887 R | 63.3% | 36.7% | 63.3% | 36.7% |
| 29,761 | KAUAI | 12,972 | 7,571 | 5,401 | | 2,170 R | 58.4% | 41.6% | 58.4% | 41.6% |
| 46,156 | MAUI | 19,017 | 11,618 | 7,399 | | 4,219 R | 61.1% | 38.9% | 61.1% | 38.9% |
| 769,913 | TOTAL | 270,274 | 168,865 | 101,409 | | 67,456 R | 62.5% | 37.5% | 62.5% | 37.5% |

256

# HAWAII

## PRESIDENT 1968

| 1960 Census Population | County | Total Vote | Republican | Democratic | AIP | Other | Plurality | Percentage Total Vote Rep. | Dem. | AIP |
|---|---|---|---|---|---|---|---|---|---|---|
| 61,332 | HAWAII | 25,727 | 9,625 | 15,819 | 283 | | 6,194 D | 37.4% | 61.5% | 1.1% |
| 500,409 | HONOLULU | 182,194 | 71,259 | 108,141 | 2,794 | | 36,882 D | 39.1% | 59.4% | 1.5% |
| 28,176 | KAUAI | 11,346 | 4,140 | 7,051 | 155 | | 2,911 D | 36.5% | 62.1% | 1.4% |
| 42,855 | MAUI | 16,951 | 6,401 | 10,313 | 237 | | 3,912 D | 37.8% | 60.8% | 1.4% |
| 632,772 | TOTAL | 236,218 | 91,425 | 141,324 | 3,469 | | 49,899 D | 38.7% | 59.8% | 1.5% |

# HAWAII

## PRESIDENT 1964

| 1960 Census Population | County | Total Vote | Republican | Democratic | Other | Rep.-Dem. Plurality | Total Vote Rep. | Dem. | Major Vote Rep. | Dem. |
|---|---|---|---|---|---|---|---|---|---|---|
| 61,332 | HAWAII | 24,973 | 4,962 | 20,011 | | 15,049 D | 19.9% | 80.1% | 19.9% | 80.1% |
| 500,409 | HONOLULU | 155,395 | 33,536 | 121,859 | | 88,323 D | 21.6% | 78.4% | 21.6% | 78.4% |
| 28,176 | KAUAI | 10,684 | 1,971 | 8,713 | | 6,742 D | 18.4% | 81.6% | 18.4% | 81.6% |
| 42,855 | MAUI | 16,219 | 3,553 | 12,666 | | 9,113 D | 21.9% | 78.1% | 21.9% | 78.1% |
| 632,772 | TOTAL | 207,271 | 44,022 | 163,249 | | 119,227 D | 21.2% | 78.8% | 21.2% | 78.8% |

# HAWAII

## PRESIDENT 1960

| 1960 Census Population | County | Total Vote | Republican | Democratic | Other | Rep.-Dem. Plurality | Total Vote Rep. | Dem. | Major Vote Rep. | Dem. |
|---|---|---|---|---|---|---|---|---|---|---|
| 61,332 | HAWAII | 23,808 | 12,251 | 11,557 | | 694 R | 51.5% | 48.5% | 51.5% | 48.5% |
| 500,409 | HONOLULU | 134,456 | 65,541 | 68,915 | | 3,374 D | 48.7% | 51.3% | 48.7% | 51.3% |
| 28,176 | KAUAI | 10,291 | 5,655 | 4,636 | | 1,019 R | 55.0% | 45.0% | 55.0% | 45.0% |
| 42,855 | MAUI | 16,150 | 8,848 | 7,302 | | 1,546 R | 54.8% | 45.2% | 54.8% | 45.2% |
| 632,772 | TOTAL | 184,705 | 92,295 | 92,410 | | 115 D | 50.0% | 50.0% | 50.0% | 50.0% |

# HAWAII

Legislation to admit Hawaii as the nation's 50th state was passed by Congress and signed by President Eisenhower in March 1959. Primary elections and a referendum on statehood were held in June 1959 with Hawaii voters approving statehood by an overwhelming vote. Hawaii was formally admitted to statehood in August 1959. Kalawao county, an area of 14 square miles on Molokai Island, consists entirely of the Kalaupapa Hansen's disease settlement. The population and voting data for this settlement are included in the Maui county statistics.

## ELECTION NOTES

| | |
|---|---|
| 2004 | Other vote was 1,737 Green (David Cobb); 1,377 Libertarian (Michael Badnarik). |
| 2000 | Other vote was 1,477 Libertarian (Browne); 1,071 Reform (Buchanan); 343 Constitution (Phillips); 306 Natural Law (Hagelin). |
| 1996 | Other vote was 10,386 Green (Nader); 2,493 Libertarian (Browne); 570 Natural Law (Hagelin); 358 Taxpayers (Phillips). |
| 1992 | Other vote was 1,452 Gritz (Independent); 1,119 Marrou (Libertarian); 720 Fulani (National Alliance); 416 Hagelin (Natural Law). |
| 1988 | Other vote was 1,999 Paul (Libertarian); 1,003 Fulani (New Alliance); 470 LaRouche (National Economic Recovery). |
| 1984 | Other vote was 2,167 Bergland (Libertarian); 821 Hall (People Before Profits); 654 LaRouche (Hawaiians for LaRouche). Special ballots listed in the table are votes cast by new resident and overseas voters. |
| 1980 | Other vote was 32,021 Anderson (Independent); 3,269 Clark (Libertarian); 1,548 Commoner (Citizens); 458 Hall (Hawaii Hall Committee). Special ballots listed in the table are votes cast by new resident and overseas voters. |
| 1976 | Other vote was MacBride (Libertarian). Special ballots listed in the table are votes cast by new resident and overseas voters. |
| 1972 | |
| 1968 | Wallace on the ballot as American Independent. |
| 1964 | |
| 1960 | |

# IDAHO

## POPULAR VOTE FOR PRESIDENT 1920 TO 2004

| Year | Total Vote | Republican | | Democratic | | Other Vote | Plurality | Percentage | | | |
|---|---|---|---|---|---|---|---|---|---|---|---|
| | | | | | | | | Total Vote | | Major Vote | |
| | | Vote | Candidate | Vote | Candidate | | | Rep. | Dem. | Rep. | Dem. |
| 2004 | 598,447 | 409,235 | Bush, George W. | 181,098 | Kerry, John | 8,114 | 228,137 R | 68.4% | 30.3% | 69.3% | 30.7% |
| 2000 ** | 501,621 | 336,937 | Bush, George W. | 138,637 | Gore, Al | 26,047 | 198,300 R | 67.2% | 27.6% | 70.8% | 29.2% |
| 1996 ** | 491,719 | 256,595 | Dole, Bob | 165,443 | Clinton, Bill | 69,681 | 91,152 R | 52.2% | 33.6% | 60.8% | 39.2% |
| 1992 ** | 482,142 | 202,645 | Bush, George | 137,013 | Clinton, Bill | 142,484 | 65,632 R | 42.0% | 28.4% | 59.7% | 40.3% |
| 1988 | 408,968 | 253,881 | Bush, George | 147,272 | Dukakis, Michael S. | 7,815 | 106,609 R | 62.1% | 36.0% | 63.3% | 36.7% |
| 1984 | 411,144 | 297,523 | Reagan, Ronald | 108,510 | Mondale, Walter F. | 5,111 | 189,013 R | 72.4% | 26.4% | 73.3% | 26.7% |
| 1980** | 437,431 | 290,699 | Reagan, Ronald | 110,192 | Carter, Jimmy | 36,540 | 180,507 R | 66.5% | 25.2% | 72.5% | 27.5% |
| 1976 | 344,071 | 204,151 | Ford, Gerald R. | 126,549 | Carter, Jimmy | 13,371 | 77,602 R | 59.3% | 36.8% | 61.7% | 38.3% |
| 1972 | 310,379 | 199,384 | Nixon, Richard M. | 80,826 | McGovern, George S. | 30,169 | 118,558 R | 64.2% | 26.0% | 71.2% | 28.8% |
| 1968 | 291,183 | 165,369 | Nixon, Richard M. | 89,273 | Humphrey, Hubert H. | 36,541 | 76,096 R | 56.8% | 30.7% | 64.9% | 35.1% |
| 1964 | 292,477 | 143,557 | Goldwater, Barry M. | 148,920 | Johnson, Lyndon B. | | 5,363 D | 49.1% | 50.9% | 49.1% | 50.9% |
| 1960 | 300,450 | 161,597 | Nixon, Richard M. | 138,853 | Kennedy, John F. | | 22,744 R | 53.8% | 46.2% | 53.8% | 46.2% |
| 1956 | 272,989 | 166,979 | Eisenhower, Dwight D. | 105,868 | Stevenson, Adlai E. | 142 | 61,111 R | 61.2% | 38.8% | 61.2% | 38.8% |
| 1952 | 276,254 | 180,707 | Eisenhower, Dwight D. | 95,081 | Stevenson, Adlai E. | 466 | 85,626 R | 65.4% | 34.4% | 65.5% | 34.5% |
| 1948 | 214,816 | 101,514 | Dewey, Thomas E. | 107,370 | Truman, Harry S. | 5,932 | 5,856 D | 47.3% | 50.0% | 48.6% | 51.4% |
| 1944 | 208,321 | 100,137 | Dewey, Thomas E. | 107,399 | Roosevelt, Franklin D. | 785 | 7,262 D | 48.1% | 51.6% | 48.3% | 51.7% |
| 1940 | 235,168 | 106,553 | Willkie, Wendell | 127,842 | Roosevelt, Franklin D. | 773 | 21,289 D | 45.3% | 54.4% | 45.5% | 54.5% |
| 1936 | 199,617 | 66,256 | Landon, Alfred M. | 125,683 | Roosevelt, Franklin D. | 7,678 | 59,427 D | 33.2% | 63.0% | 34.5% | 65.5% |
| 1932 | 186,520 | 71,312 | Hoover, Herbert C. | 109,479 | Roosevelt, Franklin D. | 5,729 | 38,167 D | 38.2% | 58.7% | 39.4% | 60.6% |
| 1928 | 151,541 | 97,322 | Hoover, Herbert C. | 52,926 | Smith, Alfred E. | 1,293 | 44,396 R | 64.2% | 34.9% | 64.8% | 35.2% |
| 1924 ** | 147,690 | 69,791 | Coolidge, Calvin | 23,951 | Davis, John W. | 53,948 | 15,843 R | 47.3% | 16.2% | 74.5% | 25.5% |
| 1920 | 138,281 | 91,351 | Harding, Warren G. | 46,930 | Cox, James M. | | 44,421 R | 66.1% | 33.9% | 66.1% | 33.9% |

In 2000 the other vote column includes 12,292 votes cast for Green (Nader). In 1996 the other vote column includes 62,518 votes cast for Perot. In 1992 the other vote column includes 130,395 votes cast for Perot. In 1980 the other column includes 27,058 votes for Independent (Anderson). In 1924 the other vote was Progressive.

## ELECTORAL COLLEGE VOTE 1920 TO 2004

| Year | Total | Republican | Democratic | Other |
|---|---|---|---|---|
| 2004 | 4 | 4 | | |
| 2000 | 4 | 4 | | |
| 1996 | 4 | 4 | | |
| 1992 | 4 | 4 | | |
| 1988 | 4 | 4 | | |
| 1984 | 4 | 4 | | |
| 1980 | 4 | 4 | | |
| 1976 | 4 | 4 | | |
| 1972 | 4 | 4 | | |
| 1968 | 4 | 4 | | |
| 1964 | 4 | | 4 | |
| 1960 | 4 | 4 | | |
| 1956 | 4 | 4 | | |
| 1952 | 4 | 4 | | |
| 1948 | 4 | | 4 | |
| 1944 | 4 | | 4 | |
| 1940 | 4 | | 4 | |
| 1936 | 4 | | 4 | |
| 1932 | 4 | | 4 | |
| 1928 | 4 | 4 | | |
| 1924 | 4 | 4 | | |
| 1920 | 4 | 4 | | |

# IDAHO

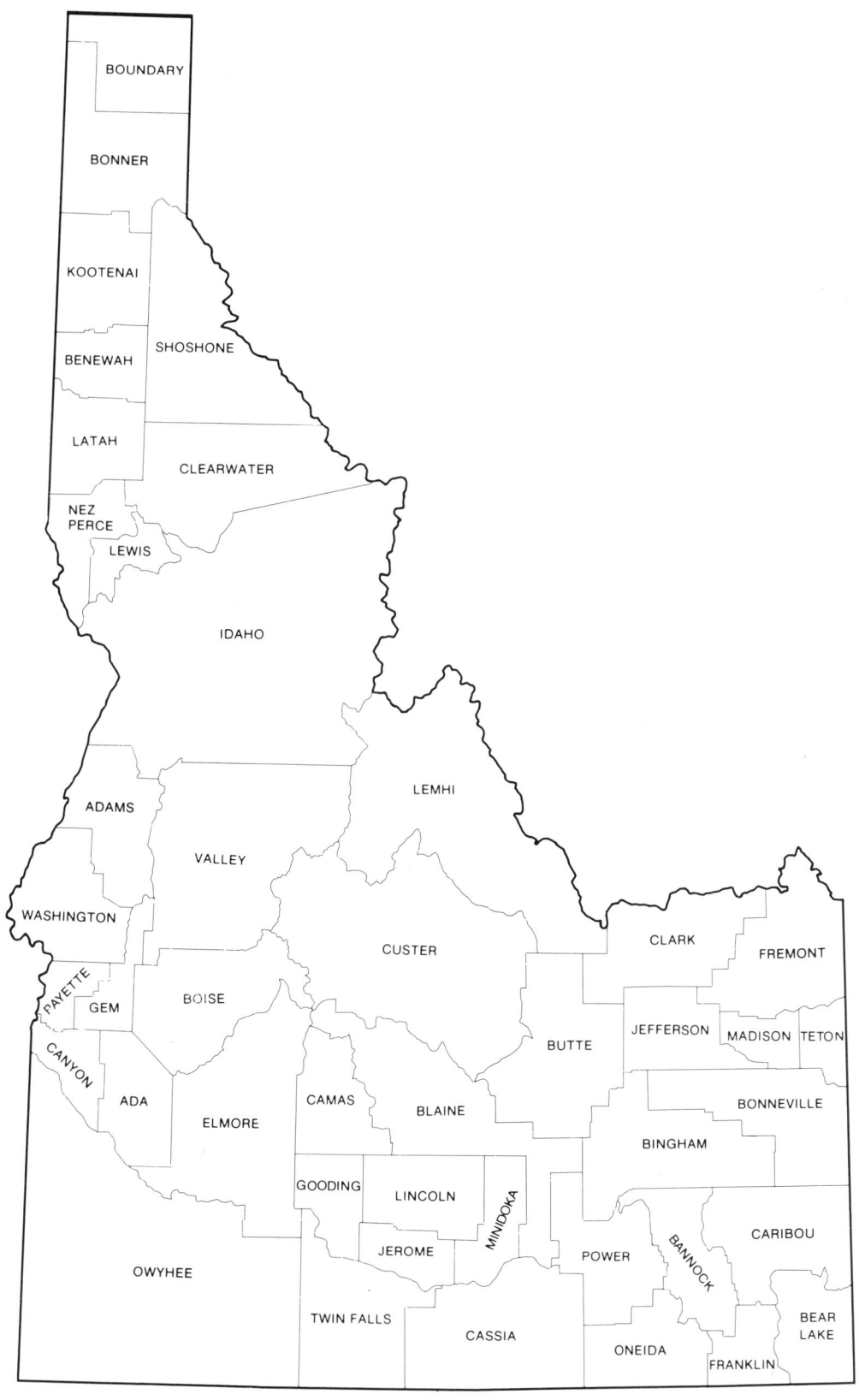

# IDAHO

## PRESIDENT 2004

| 2000 Census Population | County | Total Vote | Republican | Democratic | Other | Rep.-Dem. Plurality | Percentage | | | |
|---|---|---|---|---|---|---|---|---|---|---|
| | | | | | | | Total Vote | | Major Vote | |
| | | | | | | | Rep. | Dem. | Rep. | Dem. |
| 300,904 | ADA | 155,030 | 94,641 | 58,523 | 1,866 | 36,118 R | 61.0% | 37.7% | 61.8% | 38.2% |
| 3,476 | ADAMS | 2,063 | 1,468 | 555 | 40 | 913 R | 71.2% | 26.9% | 72.6% | 27.4% |
| 75,565 | BANNOCK | 34,844 | 21,479 | 12,903 | 462 | 8,576 R | 61.6% | 37.0% | 62.5% | 37.5% |
| 6,411 | BEAR LAKE | 3,040 | 2,506 | 494 | 40 | 2,012 R | 82.4% | 16.3% | 83.5% | 16.5% |
| 9,171 | BENEWAH | 4,050 | 2,823 | 1,148 | 79 | 1,675 R | 69.7% | 28.3% | 71.1% | 28.9% |
| 41,735 | BINGHAM | 16,565 | 12,734 | 3,605 | 226 | 9,129 R | 76.9% | 21.8% | 77.9% | 22.1% |
| 18,991 | BLAINE | 10,147 | 4,034 | 5,992 | 121 | 1,958 D | 39.8% | 59.1% | 40.2% | 59.8% |
| 6,670 | BOISE | 3,527 | 2,501 | 970 | 56 | 1,531 R | 70.9% | 27.5% | 72.1% | 27.9% |
| 36,835 | BONNER | 17,684 | 10,697 | 6,649 | 338 | 4,048 R | 60.5% | 37.6% | 61.7% | 38.3% |
| 82,522 | BONNEVILLE | 38,871 | 30,048 | 8,356 | 467 | 21,692 R | 77.3% | 21.5% | 78.2% | 21.8% |
| 9,871 | BOUNDARY | 4,379 | 3,012 | 1,268 | 99 | 1,744 R | 68.8% | 29.0% | 70.4% | 29.6% |
| 2,899 | BUTTE | 1,406 | 1,077 | 321 | 8 | 756 R | 76.6% | 22.8% | 77.0% | 23.0% |
| 991 | CAMAS | 595 | 450 | 139 | 6 | 311 R | 75.6% | 23.4% | 76.4% | 23.6% |
| 131,441 | CANYON | 55,698 | 41,599 | 13,415 | 684 | 28,184 R | 74.7% | 24.1% | 75.6% | 24.4% |
| 7,304 | CARIBOU | 3,281 | 2,753 | 491 | 37 | 2,262 R | 83.9% | 15.0% | 84.9% | 15.1% |
| 21,416 | CASSIA | 7,821 | 6,562 | 1,153 | 106 | 5,409 R | 83.9% | 14.7% | 85.1% | 14.9% |
| 1,022 | CLARK | 353 | 302 | 46 | 5 | 256 R | 85.6% | 13.0% | 86.8% | 13.2% |
| 8,930 | CLEARWATER | 4,034 | 2,839 | 1,117 | 78 | 1,722 R | 70.4% | 27.7% | 71.8% | 28.2% |
| 4,342 | CUSTER | 2,358 | 1,762 | 559 | 37 | 1,203 R | 74.7% | 23.7% | 75.9% | 24.1% |
| 29,130 | ELMORE | 8,061 | 6,011 | 1,959 | 91 | 4,052 R | 74.6% | 24.3% | 75.4% | 24.6% |
| 11,329 | FRANKLIN | 5,054 | 4,527 | 456 | 71 | 4,071 R | 89.6% | 9.0% | 90.8% | 9.2% |
| 11,819 | FREMONT | 5,769 | 4,965 | 741 | 63 | 4,224 R | 86.1% | 12.8% | 87.0% | 13.0% |
| 15,181 | GEM | 7,134 | 5,416 | 1,628 | 90 | 3,788 R | 75.9% | 22.8% | 76.9% | 23.1% |
| 14,155 | GOODING | 5,325 | 3,973 | 1,278 | 74 | 2,695 R | 74.6% | 24.0% | 75.7% | 24.3% |
| 15,511 | IDAHO | 7,970 | 6,017 | 1,689 | 264 | 4,328 R | 75.5% | 21.2% | 78.1% | 21.9% |
| 19,155 | JEFFERSON | 8,906 | 7,703 | 1,084 | 119 | 6,619 R | 86.5% | 12.2% | 87.7% | 12.3% |
| 18,342 | JEROME | 6,580 | 5,177 | 1,344 | 59 | 3,833 R | 78.7% | 20.4% | 79.4% | 20.6% |
| 108,685 | KOOTENAI | 54,603 | 36,173 | 17,584 | 846 | 18,589 R | 66.2% | 32.2% | 67.3% | 32.7% |
| 34,935 | LATAH | 17,553 | 8,686 | 8,430 | 437 | 256 R | 49.5% | 48.0% | 50.7% | 49.3% |
| 7,806 | LEMHI | 4,055 | 3,079 | 915 | 61 | 2,164 R | 75.9% | 22.6% | 77.1% | 22.9% |
| 3,747 | LEWIS | 1,820 | 1,359 | 440 | 21 | 919 R | 74.7% | 24.2% | 75.5% | 24.5% |
| 4,044 | LINCOLN | 1,876 | 1,388 | 466 | 22 | 922 R | 74.0% | 24.8% | 74.9% | 25.1% |
| 27,467 | MADISON | 11,637 | 10,693 | 826 | 118 | 9,867 R | 91.9% | 7.1% | 92.8% | 7.2% |
| 20,174 | MINIDOKA | 7,201 | 5,797 | 1,331 | 73 | 4,466 R | 80.5% | 18.5% | 81.3% | 18.7% |
| 37,410 | NEZ PERCE | 17,700 | 11,009 | 6,476 | 215 | 4,533 R | 62.2% | 36.6% | 63.0% | 37.0% |
| 4,125 | ONEIDA | 2,133 | 1,789 | 304 | 40 | 1,485 R | 83.9% | 14.3% | 85.5% | 14.5% |
| 10,644 | OWYHEE | 3,590 | 2,859 | 685 | 46 | 2,174 R | 79.6% | 19.1% | 80.7% | 19.3% |
| 20,578 | PAYETTE | 8,181 | 6,256 | 1,848 | 77 | 4,408 R | 76.5% | 22.6% | 77.2% | 22.8% |
| 7,538 | POWER | 2,958 | 2,105 | 829 | 24 | 1,276 R | 71.2% | 28.0% | 71.7% | 28.3% |
| 13,771 | SHOSHONE | 5,337 | 2,922 | 2,331 | 84 | 591 R | 54.7% | 43.7% | 55.6% | 44.4% |
| 5,999 | TETON | 3,690 | 2,235 | 1,416 | 39 | 819 R | 60.6% | 38.4% | 61.2% | 38.8% |
| 64,284 | TWIN FALLS | 26,435 | 19,672 | 6,458 | 305 | 13,214 R | 74.4% | 24.4% | 75.3% | 24.7% |
| 7,651 | VALLEY | 4,774 | 2,863 | 1,843 | 68 | 1,020 R | 60.0% | 38.6% | 60.8% | 39.2% |
| 9,977 | WASHINGTON | 4,359 | 3,274 | 1,033 | 52 | 2,241 R | 75.1% | 23.7% | 76.0% | 24.0% |
| 1,293,953 | TOTAL | 598,447 | 409,235 | 181,098 | 8,114 | 228,137 R | 68.4% | 30.3% | 69.3% | 30.7% |

# IDAHO

## PRESIDENT 2000

| 2000 Census Population | County | Total Vote | Republican | Democratic | Green (Nader) | Other | Rep.-Dem. Plurality | Percentage of Total Vote | | |
|---|---|---|---|---|---|---|---|---|---|---|
| | | | | | | | | Rep. | Dem. | Green |
| 300,904 | ADA | 123,485 | 75,050 | 40,650 | 4,846 | 2,939 | 34,400 R | 60.8% | 32.9% | 3.9% |
| 3,476 | ADAMS | 1,909 | 1,476 | 336 | 41 | 56 | 1,140 R | 77.3% | 17.6% | 2.1% |
| 75,565 | BANNOCK | 30,852 | 18,223 | 10,892 | 920 | 817 | 7,331 R | 59.1% | 35.3% | 3.0% |
| 6,411 | BEAR LAKE | 2,899 | 2,296 | 517 | 15 | 71 | 1,779 R | 79.2% | 17.8% | 0.5% |
| 9,171 | BENEWAH | 3,687 | 2,606 | 895 | 56 | 130 | 1,711 R | 70.7% | 24.3% | 1.5% |
| 41,735 | BINGHAM | 14,465 | 10,628 | 3,310 | 74 | 453 | 7,318 R | 73.5% | 22.9% | 0.5% |
| 18,991 | BLAINE | 7,938 | 3,528 | 3,748 | 428 | 234 | 220 D | 44.4% | 47.2% | 5.4% |
| 6,670 | BOISE | 3,055 | 2,019 | 745 | 123 | 168 | 1,274 R | 66.1% | 24.4% | 4.0% |
| 36,835 | BONNER | 14,537 | 8,945 | 4,318 | 893 | 381 | 4,627 R | 61.5% | 29.7% | 6.1% |
| 82,522 | BONNEVILLE | 33,556 | 24,988 | 7,235 | 363 | 970 | 17,753 R | 74.5% | 21.6% | 1.1% |
| 9,871 | BOUNDARY | 3,884 | 2,797 | 832 | 132 | 123 | 1,965 R | 72.0% | 21.4% | 3.4% |
| 2,899 | BUTTE | 1,460 | 1,054 | 354 | 5 | 47 | 700 R | 72.2% | 24.2% | 0.3% |
| 991 | CAMAS | 507 | 359 | 113 | 7 | 28 | 246 R | 70.8% | 22.3% | 1.4% |
| 131,441 | CANYON | 43,000 | 30,560 | 10,588 | 588 | 1,264 | 19,972 R | 71.1% | 24.6% | 1.4% |
| 7,304 | CARIBOU | 3,177 | 2,601 | 475 | 28 | 73 | 2,126 R | 81.9% | 15.0% | 0.9% |
| 21,416 | CASSIA | 7,279 | 5,983 | 1,087 | 20 | 189 | 4,896 R | 82.2% | 14.9% | 0.3% |
| 1,022 | CLARK | 382 | 311 | 63 | 1 | 7 | 248 R | 81.4% | 16.5% | 0.3% |
| 8,930 | CLEARWATER | 3,896 | 2,885 | 841 | 34 | 136 | 2,044 R | 74.1% | 21.6% | 0.9% |
| 4,342 | CUSTER | 2,330 | 1,794 | 416 | 44 | 76 | 1,378 R | 77.0% | 17.9% | 1.9% |
| 29,130 | ELMORE | 6,966 | 4,891 | 1,840 | 97 | 138 | 3,051 R | 70.2% | 26.4% | 1.4% |
| 11,329 | FRANKLIN | 4,243 | 3,594 | 513 | 19 | 117 | 3,081 R | 84.7% | 12.1% | 0.4% |
| 11,819 | FREMONT | 5,088 | 4,242 | 699 | 33 | 114 | 3,543 R | 83.4% | 13.7% | 0.6% |
| 15,181 | GEM | 5,983 | 4,376 | 1,346 | 45 | 216 | 3,030 R | 73.1% | 22.5% | 0.8% |
| 14,155 | GOODING | 5,026 | 3,502 | 1,282 | 55 | 187 | 2,220 R | 69.7% | 25.5% | 1.1% |
| 15,511 | IDAHO | 7,452 | 5,806 | 1,187 | 106 | 353 | 4,619 R | 77.9% | 15.9% | 1.4% |
| 19,155 | JEFFERSON | 7,836 | 6,480 | 1,100 | 25 | 231 | 5,380 R | 82.7% | 14.0% | 0.3% |
| 18,342 | JEROME | 6,007 | 4,418 | 1,360 | 24 | 205 | 3,058 R | 73.5% | 22.6% | 0.4% |
| 108,685 | KOOTENAI | 43,812 | 28,162 | 13,488 | 1,083 | 1,079 | 14,674 R | 64.3% | 30.8% | 2.5% |
| 34,935 | LATAH | 15,311 | 8,161 | 5,661 | 999 | 490 | 2,500 R | 53.3% | 37.0% | 6.5% |
| 7,806 | LEMHI | 3,641 | 2,859 | 660 | 12 | 110 | 2,199 R | 78.5% | 18.1% | 0.3% |
| 3,747 | LEWIS | 1,688 | 1,295 | 335 | 13 | 45 | 960 R | 76.7% | 19.8% | 0.8% |
| 4,044 | LINCOLN | 1,574 | 1,049 | 437 | 18 | 70 | 612 R | 66.6% | 27.8% | 1.1% |
| 27,467 | MADISON | 8,970 | 7,941 | 816 | 37 | 176 | 7,125 R | 88.5% | 9.1% | 0.4% |
| 20,174 | MINIDOKA | 6,518 | 4,907 | 1,344 | 30 | 237 | 3,563 R | 75.3% | 20.6% | 0.5% |
| 37,410 | NEZ PERCE | 16,021 | 10,577 | 4,995 | 141 | 308 | 5,582 R | 66.0% | 31.2% | 0.9% |
| 4,125 | ONEIDA | 1,798 | 1,426 | 307 | 8 | 57 | 1,119 R | 79.3% | 17.1% | 0.4% |
| 10,644 | OWYHEE | 3,188 | 2,450 | 623 | 22 | 93 | 1,827 R | 76.9% | 19.5% | 0.7% |
| 20,578 | PAYETTE | 6,858 | 4,961 | 1,643 | 80 | 174 | 3,318 R | 72.3% | 24.0% | 1.2% |
| 7,538 | POWER | 2,709 | 1,872 | 755 | 9 | 73 | 1,117 R | 69.1% | 27.9% | 0.3% |
| 13,771 | SHOSHONE | 5,385 | 2,879 | 2,225 | 92 | 189 | 654 R | 53.5% | 41.3% | 1.7% |
| 5,999 | TETON | 2,671 | 1,745 | 720 | 151 | 55 | 1,025 R | 65.3% | 27.0% | 5.7% |
| 64,284 | TWIN FALLS | 22,530 | 15,794 | 5,777 | 310 | 649 | 10,017 R | 70.1% | 25.6% | 1.4% |
| 7,651 | VALLEY | 3,978 | 2,548 | 1,129 | 201 | 100 | 1,419 R | 64.1% | 28.4% | 5.1% |
| 9,977 | WASHINGTON | 4,070 | 2,899 | 980 | 64 | 127 | 1,919 R | 71.2% | 24.1% | 1.6% |
| 1,293,953 | TOTAL | 501,621 | 336,937 | 138,637 | 12,292 | 13,755 | 198,300 R | 67.2% | 27.6% | 2.5% |

Note: The votes cast for Nader were write-ins.

# IDAHO

## PRESIDENT 1996

| 1995 Census Pop. Est. | County | Total Vote | Republican | Democratic | Reform (Perot) | Other | Rep.-Dem. Plurality | Percentage of Total Vote | | |
|---|---|---|---|---|---|---|---|---|---|---|
| | | | | | | | | Rep. | Dem. | Reform |
| 251,831 | ADA | 117,745 | 61,811 | 43,040 | 11,171 | 1,723 | 18,771 R | 52.5% | 36.6% | 9.5% |
| 3,877 | ADAMS | 1,949 | 1,053 | 537 | 311 | 48 | 516 R | 54.0% | 27.6% | 16.0% |
| 72,115 | BANNOCK | 31,377 | 14,058 | 12,806 | 4,158 | 355 | 1,252 R | 44.8% | 40.8% | 13.3% |
| 6,600 | BEAR LAKE | 2,808 | 1,583 | 805 | 396 | 24 | 778 R | 56.4% | 28.7% | 14.1% |
| 8,780 | BENEWAH | 3,919 | 1,667 | 1,488 | 701 | 63 | 179 R | 42.5% | 38.0% | 17.9% |
| 41,188 | BINGHAM | 14,881 | 8,391 | 4,304 | 2,021 | 165 | 4,087 R | 56.4% | 28.9% | 13.6% |
| 16,471 | BLAINE | 8,217 | 3,003 | 3,840 | 1,193 | 181 | 837 D | 36.5% | 46.7% | 14.5% |
| 4,768 | BOISE | 2,959 | 1,576 | 879 | 440 | 64 | 697 R | 53.3% | 29.7% | 14.9% |
| 33,080 | BONNER | 14,436 | 6,207 | 5,294 | 2,669 | 266 | 913 R | 43.0% | 36.7% | 18.5% |
| 79,531 | BONNEVILLE | 33,350 | 19,977 | 9,013 | 3,921 | 439 | 10,964 R | 59.9% | 27.0% | 11.8% |
| 9,548 | BOUNDARY | 3,870 | 1,937 | 1,194 | 626 | 113 | 743 R | 50.1% | 30.9% | 16.2% |
| 3,008 | BUTTE | 1,491 | 741 | 507 | 233 | 10 | 234 R | 49.7% | 34.0% | 15.6% |
| 848 | CAMAS | 544 | 283 | 156 | 95 | 10 | 127 R | 52.0% | 28.7% | 17.5% |
| 108,510 | CANYON | 40,329 | 23,988 | 11,800 | 3,956 | 585 | 12,188 R | 59.5% | 29.3% | 9.8% |
| 7,280 | CARIBOU | 3,120 | 1,740 | 841 | 501 | 38 | 899 R | 55.8% | 27.0% | 16.1% |
| 21,095 | CASSIA | 7,326 | 4,663 | 1,596 | 976 | 91 | 3,067 R | 63.7% | 21.8% | 13.3% |
| 822 | CLARK | 434 | 266 | 117 | 45 | 6 | 149 R | 61.3% | 27.0% | 10.4% |
| 9,115 | CLEARWATER | 3,883 | 1,658 | 1,507 | 650 | 68 | 151 R | 42.7% | 38.8% | 16.7% |
| 4,316 | CUSTER | 2,316 | 1,249 | 635 | 400 | 32 | 614 R | 53.9% | 27.4% | 17.3% |
| 23,181 | ELMORE | 6,904 | 3,668 | 2,324 | 845 | 67 | 1,344 R | 53.1% | 33.7% | 12.2% |
| 10,286 | FRANKLIN | 3,892 | 2,435 | 807 | 589 | 61 | 1,628 R | 62.6% | 20.7% | 15.1% |
| 11,532 | FREMONT | 4,835 | 3,042 | 1,114 | 630 | 49 | 1,928 R | 62.9% | 23.0% | 13.0% |
| 13,856 | GEM | 6,231 | 3,362 | 1,968 | 833 | 68 | 1,394 R | 54.0% | 31.6% | 13.4% |
| 12,980 | GOODING | 5,166 | 2,637 | 1,503 | 980 | 46 | 1,134 R | 51.0% | 29.1% | 19.0% |
| 14,789 | IDAHO | 7,101 | 3,871 | 1,979 | 1,083 | 168 | 1,892 R | 54.5% | 27.9% | 15.3% |
| 18,786 | JEFFERSON | 7,403 | 4,925 | 1,427 | 994 | 57 | 3,498 R | 66.5% | 19.3% | 13.4% |
| 17,017 | JEROME | 6,125 | 3,358 | 1,679 | 1,014 | 74 | 1,679 R | 54.8% | 27.4% | 16.6% |
| 91,678 | KOOTENAI | 39,186 | 18,740 | 13,627 | 6,083 | 736 | 5,113 R | 47.8% | 34.8% | 15.5% |
| 32,860 | LATAH | 16,290 | 6,311 | 7,741 | 1,828 | 410 | 1,430 D | 38.7% | 47.5% | 11.2% |
| 7,973 | LEMHI | 3,868 | 2,334 | 1,015 | 461 | 58 | 1,319 R | 60.3% | 26.2% | 11.9% |
| 3,937 | LEWIS | 1,880 | 861 | 674 | 316 | 29 | 187 R | 45.8% | 35.9% | 16.8% |
| 3,729 | LINCOLN | 1,562 | 744 | 478 | 319 | 21 | 266 R | 47.6% | 30.6% | 20.4% |
| 23,811 | MADISON | 7,728 | 5,706 | 1,216 | 744 | 62 | 4,490 R | 73.8% | 15.7% | 9.6% |
| 21,065 | MINIDOKA | 7,055 | 4,008 | 1,977 | 977 | 93 | 2,031 R | 56.8% | 28.0% | 13.8% |
| 36,549 | NEZ PERCE | 16,696 | 6,675 | 7,491 | 2,385 | 145 | 816 D | 40.0% | 44.9% | 14.3% |
| 3,843 | ONEIDA | 1,726 | 993 | 429 | 285 | 19 | 564 R | 57.5% | 24.9% | 16.5% |
| 9,520 | OWYHEE | 3,324 | 2,033 | 895 | 354 | 42 | 1,138 R | 61.2% | 26.9% | 10.6% |
| 19,532 | PAYETTE | 7,018 | 3,901 | 2,119 | 906 | 92 | 1,782 R | 55.6% | 30.2% | 12.9% |
| 7,986 | POWER | 2,936 | 1,501 | 1,070 | 344 | 21 | 431 R | 51.1% | 36.4% | 11.7% |
| 14,042 | SHOSHONE | 5,955 | 1,588 | 2,981 | 1,283 | 103 | 1,393 D | 26.7% | 50.1% | 21.5% |
| 4,706 | TETON | 2,488 | 1,251 | 866 | 326 | 45 | 385 R | 50.3% | 34.8% | 13.1% |
| 59,480 | TWIN FALLS | 22,896 | 12,393 | 6,826 | 3,383 | 294 | 5,567 R | 54.1% | 29.8% | 14.8% |
| 7,877 | VALLEY | 4,278 | 2,089 | 1,564 | 568 | 57 | 525 R | 48.8% | 36.6% | 13.3% |
| 9,463 | WASHINGTON | 4,222 | 2,318 | 1,314 | 525 | 65 | 1,004 R | 54.9% | 31.1% | 12.4% |
| 1,163,261 | TOTAL | 491,719 | 256,595 | 165,443 | 62,518 | 7,163 | 91,152 R | 52.2% | 33.6% | 12.7% |

# IDAHO

## PRESIDENT 1992

| 1990 Census Population | County | Total Vote | Republican | Democratic | Perot | Other | Plurality | Percentage Total Vote Rep. | Dem. | Perot |
|---|---|---|---|---|---|---|---|---|---|---|
| 205,775 | ADA | 110,166 | 49,000 | 31,941 | 28,192 | 1,033 | 17,059 R | 44.5% | 29.0% | 25.6% |
| 3,254 | ADAMS | 1,937 | 754 | 457 | 695 | 31 | 59 R | 38.9% | 23.6% | 35.9% |
| 66,026 | BANNOCK | 32,211 | 12,016 | 11,091 | 8,116 | 988 | 925 R | 37.3% | 34.4% | 25.2% |
| 6,084 | BEAR LAKE | 2,854 | 1,419 | 562 | 684 | 189 | 735 R | 49.7% | 19.7% | 24.0% |
| 7,937 | BENEWAH | 3,703 | 1,223 | 1,270 | 1,165 | 45 | 47 D | 33.0% | 34.3% | 31.5% |
| 37,583 | BINGHAM | 15,991 | 7,333 | 3,565 | 4,144 | 949 | 3,189 R | 45.9% | 22.3% | 25.9% |
| 13,552 | BLAINE | 8,022 | 2,243 | 2,865 | 2,831 | 83 | 34 D | 28.0% | 35.7% | 35.3% |
| 3,509 | BOISE | 2,320 | 912 | 623 | 754 | 31 | 158 R | 39.3% | 26.9% | 32.5% |
| 26,622 | BONNER | 13,821 | 3,937 | 4,995 | 4,645 | 244 | 350 D | 28.5% | 36.1% | 33.6% |
| 72,207 | BONNEVILLE | 35,376 | 16,557 | 7,014 | 10,241 | 1,564 | 6,316 R | 46.8% | 19.8% | 28.9% |
| 8,332 | BOUNDARY | 3,774 | 1,479 | 1,095 | 1,136 | 64 | 343 R | 39.2% | 29.0% | 30.1% |
| 2,918 | BUTTE | 1,503 | 602 | 433 | 392 | 76 | 169 R | 40.1% | 28.8% | 26.1% |
| 727 | CAMAS | 486 | 202 | 134 | 145 | 5 | 57 R | 41.6% | 27.6% | 29.8% |
| 90,076 | CANYON | 37,849 | 19,220 | 9,095 | 8,974 | 560 | 10,125 R | 50.8% | 24.0% | 23.7% |
| 6,963 | CARIBOU | 3,236 | 1,350 | 562 | 1,088 | 236 | 262 R | 41.7% | 17.4% | 33.6% |
| 19,532 | CASSIA | 7,622 | 4,052 | 1,351 | 1,785 | 434 | 2,267 R | 53.2% | 17.7% | 23.4% |
| 762 | CLARK | 423 | 195 | 95 | 119 | 14 | 76 R | 46.1% | 22.5% | 28.1% |
| 8,505 | CLEARWATER | 3,732 | 1,152 | 1,433 | 1,098 | 49 | 281 D | 30.9% | 38.4% | 29.4% |
| 4,133 | CUSTER | 2,164 | 829 | 564 | 729 | 42 | 100 R | 38.3% | 26.1% | 33.7% |
| 21,205 | ELMORE | 6,890 | 3,087 | 1,858 | 1,867 | 78 | 1,220 R | 44.8% | 27.0% | 27.1% |
| 9,232 | FRANKLIN | 4,050 | 2,115 | 524 | 890 | 521 | 1,225 R | 52.2% | 12.9% | 22.0% |
| 10,937 | FREMONT | 4,954 | 2,333 | 903 | 1,349 | 369 | 984 R | 47.1% | 18.2% | 27.2% |
| 11,844 | GEM | 5,723 | 2,455 | 1,609 | 1,555 | 104 | 846 R | 42.9% | 28.1% | 27.2% |
| 11,633 | GOODING | 5,564 | 2,178 | 1,530 | 1,591 | 265 | 587 R | 39.1% | 27.5% | 28.6% |
| 13,783 | IDAHO | 6,734 | 2,709 | 1,974 | 1,900 | 151 | 735 R | 40.2% | 29.3% | 28.2% |
| 16,543 | JEFFERSON | 7,116 | 3,471 | 978 | 2,164 | 503 | 1,307 R | 48.8% | 13.7% | 30.4% |
| 15,138 | JEROME | 6,720 | 2,972 | 1,739 | 1,768 | 241 | 1,204 R | 44.2% | 25.9% | 26.3% |
| 69,795 | KOOTENAI | 36,328 | 13,065 | 11,553 | 11,261 | 449 | 1,512 R | 36.0% | 31.8% | 31.0% |
| 30,617 | LATAH | 16,330 | 5,353 | 7,233 | 3,602 | 142 | 1,880 D | 32.8% | 44.3% | 22.1% |
| 6,899 | LEMHI | 3,821 | 1,540 | 996 | 1,175 | 110 | 365 R | 40.3% | 26.1% | 30.8% |
| 3,516 | LEWIS | 1,778 | 593 | 674 | 491 | 20 | 81 D | 33.4% | 37.9% | 27.6% |
| 3,308 | LINCOLN | 1,699 | 656 | 514 | 441 | 88 | 142 R | 38.6% | 30.3% | 26.0% |
| 23,674 | MADISON | 7,763 | 4,591 | 741 | 1,920 | 511 | 2,671 R | 59.1% | 9.5% | 24.7% |
| 19,361 | MINIDOKA | 7,417 | 3,304 | 1,815 | 1,875 | 423 | 1,429 R | 44.5% | 24.5% | 25.3% |
| 33,754 | NEZ PERCE | 16,974 | 5,431 | 7,069 | 4,363 | 111 | 1,638 D | 32.0% | 41.6% | 25.7% |
| 3,492 | ONEIDA | 1,866 | 713 | 351 | 590 | 212 | 123 R | 38.2% | 18.8% | 31.6% |
| 8,392 | OWYHEE | 3,072 | 1,469 | 686 | 862 | 55 | 607 R | 47.8% | 22.3% | 28.1% |
| 16,434 | PAYETTE | 6,745 | 2,895 | 1,656 | 2,055 | 139 | 840 R | 42.9% | 24.6% | 30.5% |
| 7,086 | POWER | 2,977 | 1,352 | 837 | 697 | 91 | 515 R | 45.4% | 28.1% | 23.4% |
| 13,931 | SHOSHONE | 6,548 | 1,441 | 3,182 | 1,878 | 47 | 1,304 D | 22.0% | 48.6% | 28.7% |
| 3,439 | TETON | 1,918 | 762 | 472 | 608 | 76 | 154 R | 39.7% | 24.6% | 31.7% |
| 53,580 | TWIN FALLS | 23,503 | 10,335 | 6,593 | 6,043 | 532 | 3,742 R | 44.0% | 28.1% | 25.7% |
| 6,109 | VALLEY | 4,153 | 1,548 | 1,259 | 1,313 | 33 | 235 R | 37.3% | 30.3% | 31.6% |
| 8,550 | WASHINGTON | 4,281 | 1,802 | 1,122 | 1,204 | 153 | 598 R | 42.1% | 26.2% | 28.1% |
| 1,006,749 | TOTAL | 482,142 | 202,645 | 137,013 | 130,395 | 12,089 | 65,632 R | 42.0% | 28.4% | 27.0% |

# IDAHO

## PRESIDENT 1988

| 1980 Census Population | County | Total Vote | Republican | Democratic | Other | Rep.-Dem. Plurality | Percentage | | | |
|---|---|---|---|---|---|---|---|---|---|---|
| | | | | | | | Total Vote | | Major Vote | |
| | | | | | | | Rep. | Dem. | Rep. | Dem. |
| 173,036 | ADA | 87,334 | 54,951 | 30,525 | 1,858 | 24,426 R | 62.9% | 35.0% | 64.3% | 35.7% |
| 3,347 | ADAMS | 1,799 | 1,107 | 643 | 49 | 464 R | 61.5% | 35.7% | 63.3% | 36.7% |
| 65,421 | BANNOCK | 28,601 | 14,986 | 13,074 | 541 | 1,912 R | 52.4% | 45.7% | 53.4% | 46.6% |
| 6,931 | BEAR LAKE | 2,980 | 2,084 | 867 | 29 | 1,217 R | 69.9% | 29.1% | 70.6% | 29.4% |
| 8,292 | BENEWAH | 3,238 | 1,650 | 1,518 | 70 | 132 R | 51.0% | 46.9% | 52.1% | 47.9% |
| 36,489 | BINGHAM | 14,705 | 10,131 | 4,346 | 228 | 5,785 R | 68.9% | 29.6% | 70.0% | 30.0% |
| 9,841 | BLAINE | 5,755 | 3,130 | 2,498 | 127 | 632 R | 54.4% | 43.4% | 55.6% | 44.4% |
| 2,999 | BOISE | 1,710 | 1,044 | 620 | 46 | 424 R | 61.1% | 36.3% | 62.7% | 37.3% |
| 24,163 | BONNER | 11,455 | 5,721 | 5,555 | 179 | 166 R | 49.9% | 48.5% | 50.7% | 49.3% |
| 65,980 | BONNEVILLE | 30,147 | 22,613 | 7,032 | 502 | 15,581 R | 75.0% | 23.3% | 76.3% | 23.7% |
| 7,289 | BOUNDARY | 3,202 | 1,800 | 1,336 | 66 | 464 R | 56.2% | 41.7% | 57.4% | 42.6% |
| 3,342 | BUTTE | 1,444 | 899 | 521 | 24 | 378 R | 62.3% | 36.1% | 63.3% | 36.7% |
| 818 | CAMAS | 437 | 288 | 136 | 13 | 152 R | 65.9% | 31.1% | 67.9% | 32.1% |
| 83,756 | CANYON | 32,396 | 21,426 | 10,207 | 763 | 11,219 R | 66.1% | 31.5% | 67.7% | 32.3% |
| 8,695 | CARIBOU | 3,144 | 2,239 | 867 | 38 | 1,372 R | 71.2% | 27.6% | 72.1% | 27.9% |
| 19,427 | CASSIA | 7,288 | 5,345 | 1,833 | 110 | 3,512 R | 73.3% | 25.2% | 74.5% | 25.5% |
| 798 | CLARK | 421 | 281 | 133 | 7 | 148 R | 66.7% | 31.6% | 67.9% | 32.1% |
| 10,390 | CLEARWATER | 3,617 | 1,659 | 1,861 | 97 | 202 D | 45.9% | 51.5% | 47.1% | 52.9% |
| 3,385 | CUSTER | 1,896 | 1,253 | 616 | 27 | 637 R | 66.1% | 32.5% | 67.0% | 33.0% |
| 21,565 | ELMORE | 5,919 | 3,756 | 2,078 | 85 | 1,678 R | 63.5% | 35.1% | 64.4% | 35.6% |
| 8,895 | FRANKLIN | 3,871 | 2,992 | 806 | 73 | 2,186 R | 77.3% | 20.8% | 78.8% | 21.2% |
| 10,813 | FREMONT | 4,652 | 3,401 | 1,178 | 73 | 2,223 R | 73.1% | 25.3% | 74.3% | 25.7% |
| 11,972 | GEM | 5,142 | 2,926 | 2,064 | 152 | 862 R | 56.9% | 40.1% | 58.6% | 41.4% |
| 11,874 | GOODING | 4,876 | 2,908 | 1,872 | 96 | 1,036 R | 59.6% | 38.4% | 60.8% | 39.2% |
| 14,769 | IDAHO | 5,871 | 3,541 | 2,198 | 132 | 1,343 R | 60.3% | 37.4% | 61.7% | 38.3% |
| 15,304 | JEFFERSON | 6,649 | 5,295 | 1,198 | 156 | 4,097 R | 79.6% | 18.0% | 81.5% | 18.5% |
| 14,840 | JEROME | 5,955 | 3,830 | 1,985 | 140 | 1,845 R | 64.3% | 33.3% | 65.9% | 34.1% |
| 59,770 | KOOTENAI | 27,130 | 15,093 | 11,621 | 416 | 3,472 R | 55.6% | 42.8% | 56.5% | 43.5% |
| 28,749 | LATAH | 13,136 | 6,367 | 6,544 | 225 | 177 D | 48.5% | 49.8% | 49.3% | 50.7% |
| 7,460 | LEMHI | 3,590 | 2,378 | 1,157 | 55 | 1,221 R | 66.2% | 32.2% | 67.3% | 32.7% |
| 4,118 | LEWIS | 1,612 | 786 | 807 | 19 | 21 D | 48.8% | 50.1% | 49.3% | 50.7% |
| 3,436 | LINCOLN | 1,525 | 918 | 574 | 33 | 344 R | 60.2% | 37.6% | 61.5% | 38.5% |
| 19,480 | MADISON | 7,302 | 6,197 | 1,009 | 96 | 5,188 R | 84.9% | 13.8% | 86.0% | 14.0% |
| 19,718 | MINIDOKA | 7,033 | 4,623 | 2,290 | 120 | 2,333 R | 65.7% | 32.6% | 66.9% | 33.1% |
| 33,220 | NEZ PERCE | 15,020 | 7,027 | 7,754 | 239 | 727 D | 46.8% | 51.6% | 47.5% | 52.5% |
| 3,258 | ONEIDA | 1,810 | 1,269 | 508 | 33 | 761 R | 70.1% | 28.1% | 71.4% | 28.6% |
| 8,272 | OWYHEE | 2,634 | 1,707 | 848 | 79 | 859 R | 64.8% | 32.2% | 66.8% | 33.2% |
| 15,722 | PAYETTE | 5,809 | 3,786 | 1,900 | 123 | 1,886 R | 65.2% | 32.7% | 66.6% | 33.4% |
| 6,844 | POWER | 2,981 | 1,838 | 1,095 | 48 | 743 R | 61.7% | 36.7% | 62.7% | 37.3% |
| 19,226 | SHOSHONE | 5,586 | 2,134 | 3,379 | 73 | 1,245 D | 38.2% | 60.5% | 38.7% | 61.3% |
| 2,897 | TETON | 1,527 | 982 | 531 | 14 | 451 R | 64.3% | 34.8% | 64.9% | 35.1% |
| 52,927 | TWIN FALLS | 20,734 | 13,243 | 7,078 | 413 | 6,165 R | 63.9% | 34.1% | 65.2% | 34.8% |
| 5,604 | VALLEY | 3,195 | 1,897 | 1,251 | 47 | 646 R | 59.4% | 39.2% | 60.3% | 39.7% |
| 8,803 | WASHINGTON | 3,840 | 2,380 | 1,359 | 101 | 1,021 R | 62.0% | 35.4% | 63.7% | 36.3% |
| 943,935 | TOTAL | 408,968 | 253,881 | 147,272 | 7,815 | 106,609 R | 62.1% | 36.0% | 63.3% | 36.7% |

# IDAHO

## PRESIDENT 1984

| 1980 Census Population | County | Total Vote | Republican | Democratic | Other | Rep.-Dem. Plurality | Percentage Total Vote Rep. | Dem. | Major Vote Rep. | Dem. |
|---|---|---|---|---|---|---|---|---|---|---|
| 173,036 | ADA | 82,924 | 60,036 | 21,760 | 1,128 | 38,276 R | 72.4% | 26.2% | 73.4% | 26.6% |
| 3,347 | ADAMS | 1,956 | 1,381 | 540 | 35 | 841 R | 70.6% | 27.6% | 71.9% | 28.1% |
| 65,421 | BANNOCK | 28,496 | 18,742 | 9,399 | 355 | 9,343 R | 65.8% | 33.0% | 66.6% | 33.4% |
| 6,931 | BEAR LAKE | 3,267 | 2,760 | 481 | 26 | 2,279 R | 84.5% | 14.7% | 85.2% | 14.8% |
| 8,292 | BENEWAH | 3,534 | 2,039 | 1,447 | 48 | 592 R | 57.7% | 40.9% | 58.5% | 41.5% |
| 36,489 | BINGHAM | 15,116 | 11,900 | 3,064 | 152 | 8,836 R | 78.7% | 20.3% | 79.5% | 20.5% |
| 9,841 | BLAINE | 5,657 | 3,603 | 1,971 | 83 | 1,632 R | 63.7% | 34.8% | 64.6% | 35.4% |
| 2,999 | BOISE | 1,721 | 1,249 | 436 | 36 | 813 R | 72.6% | 25.3% | 74.1% | 25.9% |
| 24,163 | BONNER | 11,699 | 6,889 | 4,628 | 182 | 2,261 R | 58.9% | 39.6% | 59.8% | 40.2% |
| 65,980 | BONNEVILLE | 29,490 | 24,392 | 4,877 | 221 | 19,515 R | 82.7% | 16.5% | 83.3% | 16.7% |
| 7,289 | BOUNDARY | 3,402 | 2,159 | 1,158 | 85 | 1,001 R | 63.5% | 34.0% | 65.1% | 34.9% |
| 3,342 | BUTTE | 1,685 | 1,245 | 429 | 11 | 816 R | 73.9% | 25.5% | 74.4% | 25.6% |
| 818 | CAMAS | 491 | 364 | 123 | 4 | 241 R | 74.1% | 25.1% | 74.7% | 25.3% |
| 83,756 | CANYON | 32,587 | 24,613 | 7,527 | 447 | 17,086 R | 75.5% | 23.1% | 76.6% | 23.4% |
| 8,695 | CARIBOU | 3,597 | 3,032 | 535 | 30 | 2,497 R | 84.3% | 14.9% | 85.0% | 15.0% |
| 19,427 | CASSIA | 7,597 | 6,503 | 1,036 | 58 | 5,467 R | 85.6% | 13.6% | 86.3% | 13.7% |
| 798 | CLARK | 415 | 353 | 59 | 3 | 294 R | 85.1% | 14.2% | 85.7% | 14.3% |
| 10,390 | CLEARWATER | 3,848 | 2,176 | 1,608 | 64 | 568 R | 56.5% | 41.8% | 57.5% | 42.5% |
| 3,385 | CUSTER | 2,144 | 1,653 | 461 | 30 | 1,192 R | 77.1% | 21.5% | 78.2% | 21.8% |
| 21,565 | ELMORE | 6,105 | 4,595 | 1,458 | 52 | 3,137 R | 75.3% | 23.9% | 75.9% | 24.1% |
| 8,895 | FRANKLIN | 3,742 | 3,261 | 439 | 42 | 2,822 R | 87.1% | 11.7% | 88.1% | 11.9% |
| 10,813 | FREMONT | 4,853 | 4,006 | 818 | 29 | 3,188 R | 82.5% | 16.9% | 83.0% | 17.0% |
| 11,972 | GEM | 5,350 | 3,644 | 1,607 | 99 | 2,037 R | 68.1% | 30.0% | 69.4% | 30.6% |
| 11,874 | GOODING | 5,119 | 3,819 | 1,247 | 53 | 2,572 R | 74.6% | 24.4% | 75.4% | 24.6% |
| 14,769 | IDAHO | 6,349 | 4,219 | 1,996 | 134 | 2,223 R | 66.5% | 31.4% | 67.9% | 32.1% |
| 15,304 | JEFFERSON | 6,563 | 5,770 | 743 | 50 | 5,027 R | 87.9% | 11.3% | 88.6% | 11.4% |
| 14,840 | JEROME | 6,259 | 4,913 | 1,284 | 62 | 3,629 R | 78.5% | 20.5% | 79.3% | 20.7% |
| 59,770 | KOOTENAI | 26,689 | 17,330 | 9,004 | 355 | 8,326 R | 64.9% | 33.7% | 65.8% | 34.2% |
| 28,749 | LATAH | 13,500 | 7,709 | 5,571 | 220 | 2,138 R | 57.1% | 41.3% | 58.0% | 42.0% |
| 7,460 | LEMHI | 3,708 | 2,810 | 852 | 46 | 1,958 R | 75.8% | 23.0% | 76.7% | 23.3% |
| 4,118 | LEWIS | 1,666 | 1,000 | 648 | 18 | 352 R | 60.0% | 38.9% | 60.7% | 39.3% |
| 3,436 | LINCOLN | 1,615 | 1,211 | 386 | 18 | 825 R | 75.0% | 23.9% | 75.8% | 24.2% |
| 19,480 | MADISON | 7,319 | 6,798 | 483 | 38 | 6,315 R | 92.9% | 6.6% | 93.4% | 6.6% |
| 19,718 | MINIDOKA | 7,420 | 5,938 | 1,398 | 84 | 4,540 R | 80.0% | 18.8% | 80.9% | 19.1% |
| 33,220 | NEZ PERCE | 14,330 | 8,153 | 5,981 | 196 | 2,172 R | 56.9% | 41.7% | 57.7% | 42.3% |
| 3,258 | ONEIDA | 1,898 | 1,528 | 360 | 10 | 1,168 R | 80.5% | 19.0% | 80.9% | 19.1% |
| 8,272 | OWYHEE | 2,755 | 2,141 | 574 | 40 | 1,567 R | 77.7% | 20.8% | 78.9% | 21.1% |
| 15,722 | PAYETTE | 6,121 | 4,605 | 1,410 | 106 | 3,195 R | 75.2% | 23.0% | 76.6% | 23.4% |
| 6,844 | POWER | 3,004 | 2,298 | 678 | 28 | 1,620 R | 76.5% | 22.6% | 77.2% | 22.8% |
| 19,226 | SHOSHONE | 6,284 | 3,156 | 3,033 | 95 | 123 R | 50.2% | 48.3% | 51.0% | 49.0% |
| 2,897 | TETON | 1,624 | 1,242 | 370 | 12 | 872 R | 76.5% | 22.8% | 77.0% | 23.0% |
| 52,927 | TWIN FALLS | 21,771 | 16,974 | 4,567 | 230 | 12,407 R | 78.0% | 21.0% | 78.8% | 21.2% |
| 5,604 | VALLEY | 3,286 | 2,299 | 945 | 42 | 1,354 R | 70.0% | 28.8% | 70.9% | 29.1% |
| 8,803 | WASHINGTON | 4,188 | 3,015 | 1,119 | 54 | 1,896 R | 72.0% | 26.7% | 72.9% | 27.1% |
| 943,935 | TOTAL | 411,144 | 297,523 | 108,510 | 5,111 | 189,013 R | 72.4% | 26.4% | 73.3% | 26.7% |

# IDAHO

## PRESIDENT 1980

| 1980 Census Population | County | Total Vote | Republican | Democratic | Other | Rep.-Dem. Plurality | Percentage | | | |
|---|---|---|---|---|---|---|---|---|---|---|
| | | | | | | | Total Vote | | Major Vote | |
| | | | | | | | Rep. | Dem. | Rep. | Dem. |
| 173,036 | ADA | 86,544 | 55,205 | 21,324 | 10,015 | 33,881 R | 63.8% | 24.6% | 72.1% | 27.9% |
| 3,347 | ADAMS | 1,897 | 1,189 | 590 | 118 | 599 R | 62.7% | 31.1% | 66.8% | 33.2% |
| 65,421 | BANNOCK | 29,859 | 18,477 | 8,639 | 2,743 | 9,838 R | 61.9% | 28.9% | 68.1% | 31.9% |
| 6,931 | BEAR LAKE | 3,567 | 2,941 | 508 | 118 | 2,433 R | 82.5% | 14.2% | 85.3% | 14.7% |
| 8,292 | BENEWAH | 3,846 | 2,111 | 1,361 | 374 | 750 R | 54.9% | 35.4% | 60.8% | 39.2% |
| 36,489 | BINGHAM | 15,487 | 11,781 | 2,933 | 773 | 8,848 R | 76.1% | 18.9% | 80.1% | 19.9% |
| 9,841 | BLAINE | 5,529 | 2,716 | 1,840 | 973 | 876 R | 49.1% | 33.3% | 59.6% | 40.4% |
| 2,999 | BOISE | 1,846 | 1,134 | 518 | 194 | 616 R | 61.4% | 28.1% | 68.6% | 31.4% |
| 24,163 | BONNER | 11,940 | 6,727 | 4,060 | 1,153 | 2,667 R | 56.3% | 34.0% | 62.4% | 37.6% |
| 65,980 | BONNEVILLE | 31,869 | 24,715 | 5,052 | 2,102 | 19,663 R | 77.6% | 15.9% | 83.0% | 17.0% |
| 7,289 | BOUNDARY | 3,513 | 2,088 | 1,087 | 338 | 1,001 R | 59.4% | 30.9% | 65.8% | 34.2% |
| 3,342 | BUTTE | 1,765 | 1,275 | 424 | 66 | 851 R | 72.2% | 24.0% | 75.0% | 25.0% |
| 818 | CAMAS | 530 | 360 | 145 | 25 | 215 R | 67.9% | 27.4% | 71.3% | 28.7% |
| 83,756 | CANYON | 36,016 | 24,375 | 9,172 | 2,469 | 15,203 R | 67.7% | 25.5% | 72.7% | 27.3% |
| 8,695 | CARIBOU | 3,892 | 3,234 | 481 | 177 | 2,753 R | 83.1% | 12.4% | 87.1% | 12.9% |
| 19,427 | CASSIA | 8,259 | 6,511 | 1,369 | 379 | 5,142 R | 78.8% | 16.6% | 82.6% | 17.4% |
| 798 | CLARK | 483 | 379 | 87 | 17 | 292 R | 78.5% | 18.0% | 81.3% | 18.7% |
| 10,390 | CLEARWATER | 4,314 | 2,178 | 1,699 | 437 | 479 R | 50.5% | 39.4% | 56.2% | 43.8% |
| 3,385 | CUSTER | 1,902 | 1,398 | 398 | 106 | 1,000 R | 73.5% | 20.9% | 77.8% | 22.2% |
| 21,565 | ELMORE | 6,157 | 3,994 | 1,760 | 403 | 2,234 R | 64.9% | 28.6% | 69.4% | 30.6% |
| 8,895 | FRANKLIN | 4,301 | 3,669 | 511 | 121 | 3,158 R | 85.3% | 11.9% | 87.8% | 12.2% |
| 10,813 | FREMONT | 5,253 | 4,167 | 926 | 160 | 3,241 R | 79.3% | 17.6% | 81.8% | 18.2% |
| 11,972 | GEM | 5,726 | 3,766 | 1,613 | 347 | 2,153 R | 65.8% | 28.2% | 70.0% | 30.0% |
| 11,874 | GOODING | 5,695 | 3,897 | 1,481 | 317 | 2,416 R | 68.4% | 26.0% | 72.5% | 27.5% |
| 14,769 | IDAHO | 7,073 | 4,425 | 2,078 | 570 | 2,347 R | 62.6% | 29.4% | 68.0% | 32.0% |
| 15,304 | JEFFERSON | 6,933 | 5,860 | 833 | 240 | 5,027 R | 84.5% | 12.0% | 87.6% | 12.4% |
| 14,840 | JEROME | 6,625 | 4,962 | 1,368 | 295 | 3,594 R | 74.9% | 20.6% | 78.4% | 21.6% |
| 59,770 | KOOTENAI | 26,912 | 17,022 | 7,521 | 2,369 | 9,501 R | 63.3% | 27.9% | 69.4% | 30.6% |
| 28,749 | LATAH | 14,892 | 6,967 | 5,037 | 2,888 | 1,930 R | 46.8% | 33.8% | 58.0% | 42.0% |
| 7,460 | LEMHI | 3,699 | 2,646 | 794 | 259 | 1,852 R | 71.5% | 21.5% | 76.9% | 23.1% |
| 4,118 | LEWIS | 2,053 | 1,088 | 774 | 191 | 314 R | 53.0% | 37.7% | 58.4% | 41.6% |
| 3,436 | LINCOLN | 1,872 | 1,294 | 462 | 116 | 832 R | 69.1% | 24.7% | 73.7% | 26.3% |
| 19,480 | MADISON | 7,414 | 6,555 | 728 | 131 | 5,827 R | 88.4% | 9.8% | 90.0% | 10.0% |
| 19,718 | MINIDOKA | 8,131 | 6,035 | 1,689 | 407 | 4,346 R | 74.2% | 20.8% | 78.1% | 21.9% |
| 33,220 | NEZ PERCE | 15,744 | 7,495 | 6,565 | 1,684 | 930 R | 47.6% | 41.7% | 53.3% | 46.7% |
| 3,258 | ONEIDA | 1,970 | 1,461 | 434 | 75 | 1,027 R | 74.2% | 22.0% | 77.1% | 22.9% |
| 8,272 | OWYHEE | 3,140 | 2,257 | 732 | 151 | 1,525 R | 71.9% | 23.3% | 75.5% | 24.5% |
| 15,722 | PAYETTE | 6,714 | 4,508 | 1,828 | 378 | 2,680 R | 67.1% | 27.2% | 71.1% | 28.9% |
| 6,844 | POWER | 3,143 | 2,235 | 727 | 181 | 1,508 R | 71.1% | 23.1% | 75.5% | 24.5% |
| 19,226 | SHOSHONE | 7,675 | 3,994 | 3,102 | 579 | 892 R | 52.0% | 40.4% | 56.3% | 43.7% |
| 2,897 | TETON | 1,686 | 1,227 | 360 | 99 | 867 R | 72.8% | 21.4% | 77.3% | 22.7% |
| 52,927 | TWIN FALLS | 23,708 | 17,425 | 4,835 | 1,448 | 12,590 R | 73.5% | 20.4% | 78.3% | 21.7% |
| 5,604 | VALLEY | 3,272 | 2,041 | 926 | 305 | 1,115 R | 62.4% | 28.3% | 68.8% | 31.2% |
| 8,803 | WASHINGTON | 4,585 | 2,915 | 1,421 | 249 | 1,494 R | 63.6% | 31.0% | 67.2% | 32.8% |
| 943,935 | TOTAL | 437,431 | 290,699 | 110,192 | 36,540 | 180,507 R | 66.5% | 25.2% | 72.5% | 27.5% |

# IDAHO

## PRESIDENT 1976

| 1970 Census Population | County | Total Vote | Republican | Democratic | Other | Rep.-Dem. Plurality | Percentage | | | |
|---|---|---|---|---|---|---|---|---|---|---|
| | | | | | | | Total Vote | | Major Vote | |
| | | | | | | | Rep. | Dem. | Rep. | Dem. |
| 112,230 | ADA | 64,530 | 41,135 | 21,125 | 2,270 | 20,010 R | 63.7% | 32.7% | 66.1% | 33.9% |
| 2,877 | ADAMS | 1,492 | 809 | 639 | 44 | 170 R | 54.2% | 42.8% | 55.9% | 44.1% |
| 52,200 | BANNOCK | 24,706 | 13,172 | 10,261 | 1,273 | 2,911 R | 53.3% | 41.5% | 56.2% | 43.8% |
| 5,801 | BEAR LAKE | 3,154 | 2,094 | 960 | 100 | 1,134 R | 66.4% | 30.4% | 68.6% | 31.4% |
| 6,230 | BENEWAH | 3,092 | 1,458 | 1,549 | 85 | 91 D | 47.2% | 50.1% | 48.5% | 51.5% |
| 29,167 | BINGHAM | 12,121 | 7,327 | 4,347 | 447 | 2,980 R | 60.4% | 35.9% | 62.8% | 37.2% |
| 5,749 | BLAINE | 3,966 | 2,176 | 1,604 | 186 | 572 R | 54.9% | 40.4% | 57.6% | 42.4% |
| 1,763 | BOISE | 1,167 | 684 | 433 | 50 | 251 R | 58.6% | 37.1% | 61.2% | 38.8% |
| 15,560 | BONNER | 8,897 | 4,549 | 4,065 | 283 | 484 R | 51.1% | 45.7% | 52.8% | 47.2% |
| 52,457 | BONNEVILLE | 24,018 | 15,793 | 7,230 | 995 | 8,563 R | 65.8% | 30.1% | 68.6% | 31.4% |
| 5,484 | BOUNDARY | 2,837 | 1,458 | 1,217 | 162 | 241 R | 51.4% | 42.9% | 54.5% | 45.5% |
| 2,925 | BUTTE | 1,491 | 751 | 663 | 77 | 88 R | 50.4% | 44.5% | 53.1% | 46.9% |
| 728 | CAMAS | 464 | 288 | 160 | 16 | 128 R | 62.1% | 34.5% | 64.3% | 35.7% |
| 61,288 | CANYON | 27,813 | 17,263 | 9,460 | 1,090 | 7,803 R | 62.1% | 34.0% | 64.6% | 35.4% |
| 6,534 | CARIBOU | 3,523 | 2,253 | 1,110 | 160 | 1,143 R | 64.0% | 31.5% | 67.0% | 33.0% |
| 17,017 | CASSIA | 6,909 | 4,575 | 1,881 | 453 | 2,694 R | 66.2% | 27.2% | 70.9% | 29.1% |
| 741 | CLARK | 524 | 334 | 169 | 21 | 165 R | 63.7% | 32.3% | 66.4% | 33.6% |
| 10,871 | CLEARWATER | 3,342 | 1,469 | 1,752 | 121 | 283 D | 44.0% | 52.4% | 45.6% | 54.4% |
| 2,967 | CUSTER | 1,421 | 850 | 516 | 55 | 334 R | 59.8% | 36.3% | 62.2% | 37.8% |
| 17,479 | ELMORE | 5,122 | 2,808 | 2,164 | 150 | 644 R | 54.8% | 42.2% | 56.5% | 43.5% |
| 7,373 | FRANKLIN | 4,080 | 2,720 | 1,157 | 203 | 1,563 R | 66.7% | 28.4% | 70.2% | 29.8% |
| 8,710 | FREMONT | 4,232 | 2,581 | 1,445 | 206 | 1,136 R | 61.0% | 34.1% | 64.1% | 35.9% |
| 9,387 | GEM | 4,605 | 2,401 | 1,978 | 226 | 423 R | 52.1% | 43.0% | 54.8% | 45.2% |
| 8,645 | GOODING | 5,035 | 2,909 | 1,923 | 203 | 986 R | 57.8% | 38.2% | 60.2% | 39.8% |
| 12,891 | IDAHO | 5,750 | 3,185 | 2,323 | 242 | 862 R | 55.4% | 40.4% | 57.8% | 42.2% |
| 11,740 | JEFFERSON | 5,593 | 3,599 | 1,745 | 249 | 1,854 R | 64.3% | 31.2% | 67.3% | 32.7% |
| 10,253 | JEROME | 5,192 | 3,188 | 1,800 | 204 | 1,388 R | 61.4% | 34.7% | 63.9% | 36.1% |
| 35,332 | KOOTENAI | 18,317 | 10,493 | 7,225 | 599 | 3,268 R | 57.3% | 39.4% | 59.2% | 40.8% |
| 24,891 | LATAH | 12,741 | 6,846 | 5,314 | 581 | 1,532 R | 53.7% | 41.7% | 56.3% | 43.7% |
| 5,566 | LEMHI | 3,052 | 1,685 | 1,159 | 208 | 526 R | 55.2% | 38.0% | 59.2% | 40.8% |
| 3,867 | LEWIS | 1,787 | 824 | 898 | 65 | 74 D | 46.1% | 50.3% | 47.9% | 52.1% |
| 3,057 | LINCOLN | 1,593 | 909 | 615 | 69 | 294 R | 57.1% | 38.6% | 59.6% | 40.4% |
| 13,452 | MADISON | 5,823 | 4,190 | 1,320 | 313 | 2,870 R | 72.0% | 22.7% | 76.0% | 24.0% |
| 15,731 | MINIDOKA | 6,378 | 3,600 | 2,441 | 337 | 1,159 R | 56.4% | 38.3% | 59.6% | 40.4% |
| 30,376 | NEZ PERCE | 12,819 | 6,151 | 6,324 | 344 | 173 D | 48.0% | 49.3% | 49.3% | 50.7% |
| 2,864 | ONEIDA | 1,755 | 1,065 | 637 | 53 | 428 R | 60.7% | 36.3% | 62.6% | 37.4% |
| 6,422 | OWYHEE | 2,649 | 1,519 | 1,054 | 76 | 465 R | 57.3% | 39.8% | 59.0% | 41.0% |
| 12,401 | PAYETTE | 5,463 | 3,115 | 2,195 | 153 | 920 R | 57.0% | 40.2% | 58.7% | 41.3% |
| 4,864 | POWER | 2,750 | 1,374 | 1,286 | 90 | 88 R | 50.0% | 46.8% | 51.7% | 48.3% |
| 19,718 | SHOSHONE | 6,909 | 3,570 | 3,216 | 123 | 354 R | 51.7% | 46.5% | 52.6% | 47.4% |
| 2,351 | TETON | 1,434 | 904 | 514 | 16 | 390 R | 63.0% | 35.8% | 63.8% | 36.2% |
| 41,807 | TWIN FALLS | 19,298 | 12,659 | 6,085 | 554 | 6,574 R | 65.6% | 31.5% | 67.5% | 32.5% |
| 3,609 | VALLEY | 2,366 | 1,374 | 897 | 95 | 477 R | 58.1% | 37.9% | 60.5% | 39.5% |
| 7,633 | WASHINGTON | 3,861 | 2,044 | 1,693 | 124 | 351 R | 52.9% | 43.8% | 54.7% | 45.3% |
| 713,008 | TOTAL | 344,071 | 204,151 | 126,549 | 13,371 | 77,602 R | 59.3% | 36.8% | 61.7% | 38.3% |

# IDAHO

## PRESIDENT 1972

| 1970 Census Population | County | Total Vote | Republican | Democratic | Other | Rep.-Dem. Plurality | Percentage Total Vote Rep. | Dem. | Major Vote Rep. | Dem. |
|---|---|---|---|---|---|---|---|---|---|---|
| 112,230 | ADA | 54,311 | 36,665 | 12,687 | 4,959 | 23,978 R | 67.5% | 23.4% | 74.3% | 25.7% |
| 2,877 | ADAMS | 1,421 | 963 | 293 | 165 | 670 R | 67.8% | 20.6% | 76.7% | 23.3% |
| 52,200 | BANNOCK | 22,191 | 12,856 | 7,840 | 1,495 | 5,016 R | 57.9% | 35.3% | 62.1% | 37.9% |
| 5,801 | BEAR LAKE | 3,185 | 2,213 | 716 | 256 | 1,497 R | 69.5% | 22.5% | 75.6% | 24.4% |
| 6,230 | BENEWAH | 2,690 | 1,494 | 1,062 | 134 | 432 R | 55.5% | 39.5% | 58.5% | 41.5% |
| 29,167 | BINGHAM | 10,705 | 6,886 | 2,476 | 1,343 | 4,410 R | 64.3% | 23.1% | 73.6% | 26.4% |
| 5,749 | BLAINE | 3,465 | 2,113 | 1,240 | 112 | 873 R | 61.0% | 35.8% | 63.0% | 37.0% |
| 1,763 | BOISE | 1,020 | 676 | 256 | 88 | 420 R | 66.3% | 25.1% | 72.5% | 27.5% |
| 15,560 | BONNER | 7,665 | 4,405 | 2,599 | 661 | 1,806 R | 57.5% | 33.9% | 62.9% | 37.1% |
| 52,457 | BONNEVILLE | 21,466 | 13,134 | 4,199 | 4,133 | 8,935 R | 61.2% | 19.6% | 75.8% | 24.2% |
| 5,484 | BOUNDARY | 2,678 | 1,587 | 860 | 231 | 727 R | 59.3% | 32.1% | 64.9% | 35.1% |
| 2,925 | BUTTE | 1,396 | 788 | 387 | 221 | 401 R | 56.4% | 27.7% | 67.1% | 32.9% |
| 728 | CAMAS | 463 | 344 | 95 | 24 | 249 R | 74.3% | 20.5% | 78.4% | 21.6% |
| 61,288 | CANYON | 26,857 | 18,383 | 5,630 | 2,844 | 12,753 R | 68.4% | 21.0% | 76.6% | 23.4% |
| 6,534 | CARIBOU | 2,958 | 2,069 | 614 | 275 | 1,455 R | 69.9% | 20.8% | 77.1% | 22.9% |
| 17,017 | CASSIA | 6,162 | 4,576 | 1,080 | 506 | 3,496 R | 74.3% | 17.5% | 80.9% | 19.1% |
| 741 | CLARK | 456 | 339 | 64 | 53 | 275 R | 74.3% | 14.0% | 84.1% | 15.9% |
| 10,871 | CLEARWATER | 3,138 | 1,590 | 1,412 | 136 | 178 R | 50.7% | 45.0% | 53.0% | 47.0% |
| 2,967 | CUSTER | 1,432 | 989 | 274 | 169 | 715 R | 69.1% | 19.1% | 78.3% | 21.7% |
| 17,479 | ELMORE | 4,625 | 3,078 | 1,153 | 394 | 1,925 R | 66.6% | 24.9% | 72.7% | 27.3% |
| 7,373 | FRANKLIN | 3,893 | 2,787 | 611 | 495 | 2,176 R | 71.6% | 15.7% | 82.0% | 18.0% |
| 8,710 | FREMONT | 4,270 | 2,621 | 819 | 830 | 1,802 R | 61.4% | 19.2% | 76.2% | 23.8% |
| 9,387 | GEM | 4,431 | 2,717 | 1,069 | 645 | 1,648 R | 61.3% | 24.1% | 71.8% | 28.2% |
| 8,645 | GOODING | 4,417 | 3,124 | 1,030 | 263 | 2,094 R | 70.7% | 23.3% | 75.2% | 24.8% |
| 12,891 | IDAHO | 5,201 | 3,235 | 1,622 | 344 | 1,613 R | 62.2% | 31.2% | 66.6% | 33.4% |
| 11,740 | JEFFERSON | 5,110 | 2,983 | 715 | 1,412 | 2,268 R | 58.4% | 14.0% | 80.7% | 19.3% |
| 10,253 | JEROME | 4,874 | 3,661 | 888 | 325 | 2,773 R | 75.1% | 18.2% | 80.5% | 19.5% |
| 35,332 | KOOTENAI | 16,238 | 9,958 | 5,162 | 1,118 | 4,796 R | 61.3% | 31.8% | 65.9% | 34.1% |
| 24,891 | LATAH | 10,918 | 6,043 | 4,548 | 327 | 1,495 R | 55.3% | 41.7% | 57.1% | 42.9% |
| 5,566 | LEMHI | 2,923 | 1,812 | 526 | 585 | 1,286 R | 62.0% | 18.0% | 77.5% | 22.5% |
| 3,867 | LEWIS | 1,687 | 961 | 635 | 91 | 326 R | 57.0% | 37.6% | 60.2% | 39.8% |
| 3,057 | LINCOLN | 1,506 | 1,120 | 313 | 73 | 807 R | 74.4% | 20.8% | 78.2% | 21.8% |
| 13,452 | MADISON | 5,216 | 3,606 | 710 | 900 | 2,896 R | 69.1% | 13.6% | 83.5% | 16.5% |
| 15,731 | MINIDOKA | 5,967 | 4,097 | 1,423 | 447 | 2,674 R | 68.7% | 23.8% | 74.2% | 25.8% |
| 30,376 | NEZ PERCE | 11,941 | 6,232 | 5,081 | 628 | 1,151 R | 52.2% | 42.6% | 55.1% | 44.9% |
| 2,864 | ONEIDA | 1,685 | 1,204 | 402 | 79 | 802 R | 71.5% | 23.9% | 75.0% | 25.0% |
| 6,422 | OWYHEE | 2,324 | 1,630 | 463 | 231 | 1,167 R | 70.1% | 19.9% | 77.9% | 22.1% |
| 12,401 | PAYETTE | 5,272 | 3,577 | 1,113 | 582 | 2,464 R | 67.8% | 21.1% | 76.3% | 23.7% |
| 4,864 | POWER | 2,180 | 1,405 | 625 | 150 | 780 R | 64.4% | 28.7% | 69.2% | 30.8% |
| 19,718 | SHOSHONE | 7,207 | 3,868 | 3,020 | 319 | 848 R | 53.7% | 41.9% | 56.2% | 43.8% |
| 2,351 | TETON | 1,359 | 932 | 298 | 129 | 634 R | 68.6% | 21.9% | 75.8% | 24.2% |
| 41,807 | TWIN FALLS | 17,673 | 13,075 | 3,344 | 1,254 | 9,731 R | 74.0% | 18.9% | 79.6% | 20.4% |
| 3,609 | VALLEY | 2,151 | 1,324 | 537 | 290 | 787 R | 61.6% | 25.0% | 71.1% | 28.9% |
| 7,633 | WASHINGTON | 3,652 | 2,264 | 935 | 453 | 1,329 R | 62.0% | 25.6% | 70.8% | 29.2% |
| 713,008 | TOTAL | 310,379 | 199,384 | 80,826 | 30,169 | 118,558 R | 64.2% | 26.0% | 71.2% | 28.8% |

# IDAHO

## PRESIDENT 1968

| 1960 Census Population | County | Total Vote | Republican | Democratic | AIP | Other | Plurality | Percentage Total Vote Rep. | Dem. | AIP |
|---|---|---|---|---|---|---|---|---|---|---|
| 93,460 | ADA | 47,881 | 30,185 | 11,529 | 6,167 | | 18,656 R | 63.0% | 24.1% | 12.9% |
| 2,978 | ADAMS | 1,431 | 844 | 360 | 227 | | 484 R | 59.0% | 25.2% | 15.9% |
| 49,342 | BANNOCK | 21,334 | 10,234 | 9,084 | 2,016 | | 1,150 R | 48.0% | 42.6% | 9.4% |
| 7,148 | BEAR LAKE | 3,101 | 1,866 | 1,058 | 177 | | 808 R | 60.2% | 34.1% | 5.7% |
| 6,036 | BENEWAH | 2,533 | 1,125 | 1,160 | 248 | | 35 D | 44.4% | 45.8% | 9.8% |
| 28,218 | BINGHAM | 10,765 | 6,484 | 2,988 | 1,293 | | 3,496 R | 60.2% | 27.8% | 12.0% |
| 4,598 | BLAINE | 2,484 | 1,337 | 815 | 332 | | 522 R | 53.8% | 32.8% | 13.4% |
| 1,646 | BOISE | 809 | 450 | 205 | 154 | | 245 R | 55.6% | 25.3% | 19.0% |
| 15,587 | BONNER | 7,082 | 3,240 | 3,063 | 779 | | 177 R | 45.7% | 43.3% | 11.0% |
| 46,906 | BONNEVILLE | 21,050 | 13,582 | 5,178 | 2,290 | | 8,404 R | 64.5% | 24.6% | 10.9% |
| 5,809 | BOUNDARY | 2,297 | 1,084 | 883 | 330 | | 201 R | 47.2% | 38.4% | 14.4% |
| 3,498 | BUTTE | 1,356 | 691 | 521 | 144 | | 170 R | 51.0% | 38.4% | 10.6% |
| 917 | CAMAS | 482 | 271 | 118 | 93 | | 153 R | 56.2% | 24.5% | 19.3% |
| 57,662 | CANYON | 23,898 | 14,995 | 5,717 | 3,186 | | 9,278 R | 62.7% | 23.9% | 13.3% |
| 5,976 | CARIBOU | 2,785 | 1,731 | 727 | 327 | | 1,004 R | 62.2% | 26.1% | 11.7% |
| 16,121 | CASSIA | 6,525 | 4,187 | 1,350 | 988 | | 2,837 R | 64.2% | 20.7% | 15.1% |
| 915 | CLARK | 407 | 271 | 87 | 49 | | 184 R | 66.6% | 21.4% | 12.0% |
| 8,548 | CLEARWATER | 3,468 | 1,287 | 1,838 | 343 | | 551 D | 37.1% | 53.0% | 9.9% |
| 2,996 | CUSTER | 1,423 | 711 | 385 | 327 | | 326 R | 50.0% | 27.1% | 23.0% |
| 16,719 | ELMORE | 3,769 | 1,908 | 1,230 | 631 | | 678 R | 50.6% | 32.6% | 16.7% |
| 8,457 | FRANKLIN | 3,795 | 2,509 | 831 | 455 | | 1,678 R | 66.1% | 21.9% | 12.0% |
| 8,679 | FREMONT | 3,925 | 2,297 | 961 | 667 | | 1,336 R | 58.5% | 24.5% | 17.0% |
| 9,127 | GEM | 3,997 | 2,314 | 1,183 | 500 | | 1,131 R | 57.9% | 29.6% | 12.5% |
| 9,544 | GOODING | 4,228 | 2,349 | 1,018 | 861 | | 1,331 R | 55.6% | 24.1% | 20.4% |
| 13,542 | IDAHO | 4,914 | 2,317 | 1,883 | 714 | | 434 R | 47.2% | 38.3% | 14.5% |
| 11,672 | JEFFERSON | 4,761 | 2,927 | 955 | 879 | | 1,972 R | 61.5% | 20.1% | 18.5% |
| 11,712 | JEROME | 4,602 | 2,785 | 976 | 841 | | 1,809 R | 60.5% | 21.2% | 18.3% |
| 29,556 | KOOTENAI | 14,771 | 7,092 | 6,207 | 1,472 | | 885 R | 48.0% | 42.0% | 10.0% |
| 21,170 | LATAH | 9,126 | 4,708 | 3,782 | 636 | | 926 R | 51.6% | 41.4% | 7.0% |
| 5,816 | LEMHI | 2,562 | 1,476 | 547 | 539 | | 929 R | 57.6% | 21.4% | 21.0% |
| 4,423 | LEWIS | 1,801 | 697 | 927 | 177 | | 230 D | 38.7% | 51.5% | 9.8% |
| 3,686 | LINCOLN | 1,545 | 972 | 350 | 223 | | 622 R | 62.9% | 22.7% | 14.4% |
| 9,417 | MADISON | 4,388 | 2,971 | 904 | 513 | | 2,067 R | 67.7% | 20.6% | 11.7% |
| 14,394 | MINIDOKA | 5,654 | 3,182 | 1,332 | 1,140 | | 1,850 R | 56.3% | 23.6% | 20.2% |
| 27,066 | NEZ PERCE | 12,579 | 5,019 | 6,502 | 1,058 | | 1,483 D | 39.9% | 51.7% | 8.4% |
| 3,603 | ONEIDA | 1,684 | 1,114 | 465 | 105 | | 649 R | 66.2% | 27.6% | 6.2% |
| 6,375 | OWYHEE | 2,323 | 1,385 | 562 | 376 | | 823 R | 59.6% | 24.2% | 16.2% |
| 12,363 | PAYETTE | 4,956 | 3,032 | 1,216 | 708 | | 1,816 R | 61.2% | 24.5% | 14.3% |
| 4,111 | POWER | 2,028 | 1,222 | 582 | 224 | | 640 R | 60.3% | 28.7% | 11.0% |
| 20,876 | SHOSHONE | 7,587 | 3,080 | 3,850 | 657 | | 770 D | 40.6% | 50.7% | 8.7% |
| 2,639 | TETON | 1,198 | 694 | 376 | 128 | | 318 R | 57.9% | 31.4% | 10.7% |
| 41,842 | TWIN FALLS | 18,373 | 11,564 | 4,001 | 2,808 | | 7,563 R | 62.9% | 21.8% | 15.3% |
| 3,663 | VALLEY | 2,002 | 1,160 | 534 | 308 | | 626 R | 57.9% | 26.7% | 15.4% |
| 8,378 | WASHINGTON | 3,504 | 2,020 | 1,033 | 451 | | 987 R | 57.6% | 29.5% | 12.9% |
| 667,191 | TOTAL | 291,183 | 165,369 | 89,273 | 36,541 | | 76,096 R | 56.8% | 30.7% | 12.5% |

# IDAHO

## PRESIDENT 1964

| 1960 Census Population | County | Total Vote | Republican | Democratic | Other | Rep.-Dem. Plurality | Percentage | | | |
|---|---|---|---|---|---|---|---|---|---|---|
| | | | | | | | Total Vote | | Major Vote | |
| | | | | | | | Rep. | Dem. | Rep. | Dem. |
| 93,460 | ADA | 45,043 | 25,404 | 19,639 | | 5,765 R | 56.4% | 43.6% | 56.4% | 43.6% |
| 2,978 | ADAMS | 1,439 | 689 | 750 | | 61 D | 47.9% | 52.1% | 47.9% | 52.1% |
| 49,342 | BANNOCK | 21,308 | 7,825 | 13,483 | | 5,658 D | 36.7% | 63.3% | 36.7% | 63.3% |
| 7,148 | BEAR LAKE | 3,266 | 1,409 | 1,857 | | 448 D | 43.1% | 56.9% | 43.1% | 56.9% |
| 6,036 | BENEWAH | 2,777 | 981 | 1,796 | | 815 D | 35.3% | 64.7% | 35.3% | 64.7% |
| 28,218 | BINGHAM | 10,595 | 5,364 | 5,231 | | 133 R | 50.6% | 49.4% | 50.6% | 49.4% |
| 4,598 | BLAINE | 2,454 | 1,161 | 1,293 | | 132 D | 47.3% | 52.7% | 47.3% | 52.7% |
| 1,646 | BOISE | 864 | 414 | 450 | | 36 D | 47.9% | 52.1% | 47.9% | 52.1% |
| 15,587 | BONNER | 7,303 | 2,975 | 4,328 | | 1,353 D | 40.7% | 59.3% | 40.7% | 59.3% |
| 46,906 | BONNEVILLE | 20,373 | 10,736 | 9,637 | | 1,099 R | 52.7% | 47.3% | 52.7% | 47.3% |
| 5,809 | BOUNDARY | 2,483 | 1,065 | 1,418 | | 353 D | 42.9% | 57.1% | 42.9% | 57.1% |
| 3,498 | BUTTE | 1,497 | 649 | 848 | | 199 D | 43.4% | 56.6% | 43.4% | 56.6% |
| 917 | CAMAS | 574 | 316 | 258 | | 58 R | 55.1% | 44.9% | 55.1% | 44.9% |
| 57,662 | CANYON | 24,067 | 13,466 | 10,601 | | 2,865 R | 56.0% | 44.0% | 56.0% | 44.0% |
| 5,976 | CARIBOU | 2,725 | 1,303 | 1,422 | | 119 D | 47.8% | 52.2% | 47.8% | 52.2% |
| 16,121 | CASSIA | 6,617 | 4,009 | 2,608 | | 1,401 R | 60.6% | 39.4% | 60.6% | 39.4% |
| 915 | CLARK | 448 | 262 | 186 | | 76 R | 58.5% | 41.5% | 58.5% | 41.5% |
| 8,548 | CLEARWATER | 3,213 | 767 | 2,446 | | 1,679 D | 23.9% | 76.1% | 23.9% | 76.1% |
| 2,996 | CUSTER | 1,434 | 720 | 714 | | 6 R | 50.2% | 49.8% | 50.2% | 49.8% |
| 16,719 | ELMORE | 4,167 | 1,857 | 2,310 | | 453 D | 44.6% | 55.4% | 44.6% | 55.4% |
| 8,457 | FRANKLIN | 3,983 | 2,400 | 1,583 | | 817 R | 60.3% | 39.7% | 60.3% | 39.7% |
| 8,679 | FREMONT | 3,915 | 1,945 | 1,970 | | 25 D | 49.7% | 50.3% | 49.7% | 50.3% |
| 9,127 | GEM | 4,307 | 1,979 | 2,328 | | 349 D | 45.9% | 54.1% | 45.9% | 54.1% |
| 9,544 | GOODING | 4,375 | 2,527 | 1,848 | | 679 R | 57.8% | 42.2% | 57.8% | 42.2% |
| 13,542 | IDAHO | 5,178 | 1,990 | 3,188 | | 1,198 D | 38.4% | 61.6% | 38.4% | 61.6% |
| 11,672 | JEFFERSON | 4,801 | 2,740 | 2,061 | | 679 R | 57.1% | 42.9% | 57.1% | 42.9% |
| 11,712 | JEROME | 4,941 | 3,113 | 1,828 | | 1,285 R | 63.0% | 37.0% | 63.0% | 37.0% |
| 29,556 | KOOTENAI | 14,311 | 6,096 | 8,215 | | 2,119 D | 42.6% | 57.4% | 42.6% | 57.4% |
| 21,170 | LATAH | 8,724 | 3,475 | 5,249 | | 1,774 D | 39.8% | 60.2% | 39.8% | 60.2% |
| 5,816 | LEMHI | 2,563 | 1,496 | 1,067 | | 429 R | 58.4% | 41.6% | 58.4% | 41.6% |
| 4,423 | LEWIS | 2,044 | 487 | 1,557 | | 1,070 D | 23.8% | 76.2% | 23.8% | 76.2% |
| 3,686 | LINCOLN | 1,586 | 969 | 617 | | 352 R | 61.1% | 38.9% | 61.1% | 38.9% |
| 9,417 | MADISON | 4,050 | 2,101 | 1,949 | | 152 R | 51.9% | 48.1% | 51.9% | 48.1% |
| 14,394 | MINIDOKA | 5,938 | 3,111 | 2,827 | | 284 R | 52.4% | 47.6% | 52.4% | 47.6% |
| 27,066 | NEZ PERCE | 13,157 | 3,912 | 9,245 | | 5,333 D | 29.7% | 70.3% | 29.7% | 70.3% |
| 3,603 | ONEIDA | 1,879 | 1,111 | 768 | | 343 R | 59.1% | 40.9% | 59.1% | 40.9% |
| 6,375 | OWYHEE | 2,384 | 1,216 | 1,168 | | 48 R | 51.0% | 49.0% | 51.0% | 49.0% |
| 12,363 | PAYETTE | 5,272 | 2,764 | 2,508 | | 256 R | 52.4% | 47.6% | 52.4% | 47.6% |
| 4,111 | POWER | 2,127 | 966 | 1,161 | | 195 D | 45.4% | 54.6% | 45.4% | 54.6% |
| 20,876 | SHOSHONE | 8,078 | 2,884 | 5,194 | | 2,310 D | 35.7% | 64.3% | 35.7% | 64.3% |
| 2,639 | TETON | 1,273 | 675 | 598 | | 77 R | 53.0% | 47.0% | 53.0% | 47.0% |
| 41,842 | TWIN FALLS | 19,156 | 11,518 | 7,638 | | 3,880 R | 60.1% | 39.9% | 60.1% | 39.9% |
| 3,663 | VALLEY | 2,106 | 980 | 1,126 | | 146 D | 46.5% | 53.5% | 46.5% | 53.5% |
| 8,378 | WASHINGTON | 3,682 | 1,730 | 1,952 | | 222 D | 47.0% | 53.0% | 47.0% | 53.0% |
| 667,191 | TOTAL | 292,477 | 143,557 | 148,920 | | 5,363 D | 49.1% | 50.9% | 49.1% | 50.9% |

# IDAHO

## PRESIDENT 1960

| 1960 Census Population | County | Total Vote | Republican | Democratic | Other | Rep.-Dem. Plurality | Percentage | | | |
|---|---|---|---|---|---|---|---|---|---|---|
| | | | | | | | Total Vote | | Major Vote | |
| | | | | | | | Rep. | Dem. | Rep. | Dem. |
| 93,460 | ADA | 44,720 | 27,703 | 17,017 | | 10,686 R | 61.9% | 38.1% | 61.9% | 38.1% |
| 2,978 | ADAMS | 1,523 | 799 | 724 | | 75 R | 52.5% | 47.5% | 52.5% | 47.5% |
| 49,342 | BANNOCK | 21,743 | 9,157 | 12,586 | | 3,429 D | 42.1% | 57.9% | 42.1% | 57.9% |
| 7,148 | BEAR LAKE | 3,526 | 1,963 | 1,563 | | 400 R | 55.7% | 44.3% | 55.7% | 44.3% |
| 6,036 | BENEWAH | 3,030 | 1,274 | 1,756 | | 482 D | 42.0% | 58.0% | 42.0% | 58.0% |
| 28,218 | BINGHAM | 10,777 | 5,934 | 4,843 | | 1,091 R | 55.1% | 44.9% | 55.1% | 44.9% |
| 4,598 | BLAINE | 2,468 | 1,216 | 1,252 | | 36 D | 49.3% | 50.7% | 49.3% | 50.7% |
| 1,646 | BOISE | 888 | 456 | 432 | | 24 R | 51.4% | 48.6% | 51.4% | 48.6% |
| 15,587 | BONNER | 7,639 | 3,575 | 4,064 | | 489 D | 46.8% | 53.2% | 46.8% | 53.2% |
| 46,906 | BONNEVILLE | 19,956 | 11,111 | 8,845 | | 2,266 R | 55.7% | 44.3% | 55.7% | 44.3% |
| 5,809 | BOUNDARY | 2,738 | 1,237 | 1,501 | | 264 D | 45.2% | 54.8% | 45.2% | 54.8% |
| 3,498 | BUTTE | 1,681 | 680 | 1,001 | | 321 D | 40.5% | 59.5% | 40.5% | 59.5% |
| 917 | CAMAS | 606 | 284 | 322 | | 38 D | 46.9% | 53.1% | 46.9% | 53.1% |
| 57,662 | CANYON | 25,546 | 15,865 | 9,681 | | 6,184 R | 62.1% | 37.9% | 62.1% | 37.9% |
| 5,976 | CARIBOU | 2,837 | 1,544 | 1,293 | | 251 R | 54.4% | 45.6% | 54.4% | 45.6% |
| 16,121 | CASSIA | 6,742 | 4,297 | 2,445 | | 1,852 R | 63.7% | 36.3% | 63.7% | 36.3% |
| 915 | CLARK | 459 | 283 | 176 | | 107 R | 61.7% | 38.3% | 61.7% | 38.3% |
| 8,548 | CLEARWATER | 3,600 | 1,193 | 2,407 | | 1,214 D | 33.1% | 66.9% | 33.1% | 66.9% |
| 2,996 | CUSTER | 1,489 | 651 | 838 | | 187 D | 43.7% | 56.3% | 43.7% | 56.3% |
| 16,719 | ELMORE | 4,666 | 2,226 | 2,440 | | 214 D | 47.7% | 52.3% | 47.7% | 52.3% |
| 8,457 | FRANKLIN | 3,985 | 2,633 | 1,352 | | 1,281 R | 66.1% | 33.9% | 66.1% | 33.9% |
| 8,679 | FREMONT | 4,117 | 2,230 | 1,887 | | 343 R | 54.2% | 45.8% | 54.2% | 45.8% |
| 9,127 | GEM | 4,404 | 2,428 | 1,976 | | 452 R | 55.1% | 44.9% | 55.1% | 44.9% |
| 9,544 | GOODING | 4,528 | 2,523 | 2,005 | | 518 R | 55.7% | 44.3% | 55.7% | 44.3% |
| 13,542 | IDAHO | 5,504 | 2,248 | 3,256 | | 1,008 D | 40.8% | 59.2% | 40.8% | 59.2% |
| 11,672 | JEFFERSON | 4,999 | 2,625 | 2,374 | | 251 R | 52.5% | 47.5% | 52.5% | 47.5% |
| 11,712 | JEROME | 5,182 | 3,031 | 2,151 | | 880 R | 58.5% | 41.5% | 58.5% | 41.5% |
| 29,556 | KOOTENAI | 14,448 | 6,704 | 7,744 | | 1,040 D | 46.4% | 53.6% | 46.4% | 53.6% |
| 21,170 | LATAH | 9,425 | 4,789 | 4,636 | | 153 R | 50.8% | 49.2% | 50.8% | 49.2% |
| 5,816 | LEMHI | 2,638 | 1,355 | 1,283 | | 72 R | 51.4% | 48.6% | 51.4% | 48.6% |
| 4,423 | LEWIS | 2,213 | 781 | 1,432 | | 651 D | 35.3% | 64.7% | 35.3% | 64.7% |
| 3,686 | LINCOLN | 1,753 | 970 | 783 | | 187 R | 55.3% | 44.7% | 55.3% | 44.7% |
| 9,417 | MADISON | 4,052 | 2,374 | 1,678 | | 696 R | 58.6% | 41.4% | 58.6% | 41.4% |
| 14,394 | MINIDOKA | 5,827 | 3,360 | 2,467 | | 893 R | 57.7% | 42.3% | 57.7% | 42.3% |
| 27,066 | NEZ PERCE | 13,147 | 5,203 | 7,944 | | 2,741 D | 39.6% | 60.4% | 39.6% | 60.4% |
| 3,603 | ONEIDA | 1,910 | 1,111 | 799 | | 312 R | 58.2% | 41.8% | 58.2% | 41.8% |
| 6,375 | OWYHEE | 2,629 | 1,500 | 1,129 | | 371 R | 57.1% | 42.9% | 57.1% | 42.9% |
| 12,363 | PAYETTE | 5,605 | 3,472 | 2,133 | | 1,339 R | 61.9% | 38.1% | 61.9% | 38.1% |
| 4,111 | POWER | 2,025 | 1,065 | 960 | | 105 R | 52.6% | 47.4% | 52.6% | 47.4% |
| 20,876 | SHOSHONE | 8,433 | 3,432 | 5,001 | | 1,569 D | 40.7% | 59.3% | 40.7% | 59.3% |
| 2,639 | TETON | 1,283 | 714 | 569 | | 145 R | 55.7% | 44.3% | 55.7% | 44.3% |
| 41,842 | TWIN FALLS | 19,584 | 12,171 | 7,413 | | 4,758 R | 62.1% | 37.9% | 62.1% | 37.9% |
| 3,663 | VALLEY | 2,095 | 1,179 | 916 | | 263 R | 56.3% | 43.7% | 56.3% | 43.7% |
| 8,378 | WASHINGTON | 4,030 | 2,251 | 1,779 | | 472 R | 55.9% | 44.1% | 55.9% | 44.1% |
| 667,191 | TOTAL | 300,450 | 161,597 | 138,853 | | 22,744 R | 53.8% | 46.2% | 53.8% | 46.2% |

# IDAHO

## ELECTION NOTES

**2004**    Other vote was 3,844 Libertarian (Michael Badnarik); 3,084 Constitution (Michael Peroutka); 1,115 write-in (Ralph Nader); 58 write-in (David Cobb); 9 write-in (John Joseph Kennedy); 3 write-in (Walter F. Brown); 1 write-in (Reverend Merepeace-msmere).

**2000**    Other vote was 7,615 Reform (Buchanan); 3,488 Libertarian (Browne); 1,469 Constitution (Phillips); 1,177 Natural Law (Hagelin); 4 write-in (Schriner); 1 write-in (Daigneau); 1 write-in (Msmere).

**1996**    Other vote was 3,325 Libertarian (Browne); 2,230 U.S. Taxpayers (Phillips); 1,600 Natural Law (Hagelin); 8 scattered write-in.

**1992**    Other vote was 10,281 Gritz (Independent); 1,167 Marrou (Libertarian); 613 Fulani (Independent); 24 Hagelin (write-in); 3 Brisben (write-in); 1 LaRouche (write-in). The total of the other vote column includes the 28 write-in votes not available by county.

**1988**    Other vote was 5,313 Paul (Libertarian); 2,502 Fulani (Independent).

**1984**    Other vote was 2,823 Bergland (Libertarian); 2,288 Richards (Populist).

**1980**    Other vote was 27,058 Anderson (Independent); 8,425 Clark (Libertarian); 1,057 Rarick (American).

**1976**    Other vote was 5,935 Maddox (American); 3,558 MacBride (Libertarian); 1,194 McCarthy (write-in); 739 LaRouche (U.S. Labor); 493 Anderson (write-in); 14 Camejo (write-in); 5 Hall (write-in); 2 Zeidler (write-in); 1 Wright (write-in); 1,430 scattered write-in. The write-in vote for McCarthy in Bannock county was amended from 82 to 74 which changed his state-wide total from 1,202 to the vote given above.

**1972**    Other vote was 28,869 Schmitz (American); 903 Spock (Peace and Freedom); 397 Jenness (Socialist Workers). In using the Republican-Democratic plurality figures, it should be noted that the American candidate ran second in Fremont, Jefferson, Lemhi and Madison counties.

**1968**    Wallace on the ballot as American Independent.

**1964**

**1960**

# ILLINOIS

## POPULAR VOTE FOR PRESIDENT 1920 TO 2004

| Year | Total Vote | Republican | | Democratic | | Other Vote | Plurality | Percentage | | | |
|---|---|---|---|---|---|---|---|---|---|---|---|
| | | | | | | | | Total Vote | | Major Vote | |
| | | Vote | Candidate | Vote | Candidate | | | Rep. | Dem. | Rep. | Dem. |
| 2004 | 5,274,322 | 2,345,946 | Bush, George W. | 2,891,550 | Kerry, John | 36,826 | 545,604 D | 44.5% | 54.8% | 44.8% | 55.2% |
| 2000 ** | 4,742,123 | 2,019,421 | Bush, George W. | 2,589,026 | Gore, Al | 133,676 | 569,605 D | 42.6% | 54.6% | 43.8% | 56.2% |
| 1996 ** | 4,311,391 | 1,587,021 | Dole, Bob | 2,341,744 | Clinton, Bill | 382,626 | 754,723 D | 36.8% | 54.3% | 40.4% | 59.6% |
| 1992 ** | 5,050,157 | 1,734,096 | Bush, George | 2,453,350 | Clinton, Bill | 862,711 | 719,254 D | 34.3% | 48.6% | 41.4% | 58.6% |
| 1988 | 4,559,120 | 2,310,939 | Bush, George | 2,215,940 | Dukakis, Michael S. | 32,241 | 94,999 R | 50.7% | 48.6% | 51.0% | 49.0% |
| 1984 | 4,819,088 | 2,707,103 | Reagan, Ronald | 2,086,499 | Mondale, Walter F. | 25,486 | 620,604 R | 56.2% | 43.3% | 56.5% | 43.5% |
| 1980 ** | 4,749,721 | 2,358,049 | Reagan, Ronald | 1,981,413 | Carter, Jimmy | 410,259 | 376,636 R | 49.6% | 41.7% | 54.3% | 45.7% |
| 1976 | 4,718,914 | 2,364,269 | Ford, Gerald R. | 2,271,295 | Carter, Jimmy | 83,350 | 92,974 R | 50.1% | 48.1% | 51.0% | 49.0% |
| 1972 | 4,723,236 | 2,788,179 | Nixon, Richard M. | 1,913,472 | McGovern, George S. | 21,585 | 874,707 R | 59.0% | 40.5% | 59.3% | 40.7% |
| 1968 | 4,619,749 | 2,174,774 | Nixon, Richard M. | 2,039,814 | Humphrey, Hubert H. | 405,161 | 134,960 R | 47.1% | 44.2% | 51.6% | 48.4% |
| 1964 | 4,702,841 | 1,905,946 | Goldwater, Barry M. | 2,796,833 | Johnson, Lyndon B. | 62 | 890,887 D | 40.5% | 59.5% | 40.5% | 59.5% |
| 1960 | 4,757,409 | 2,368,988 | Nixon, Richard M. | 2,377,846 | Kennedy, John F. | 10,575 | 8,858 D | 49.8% | 50.0% | 49.9% | 50.1% |
| 1956 | 4,407,407 | 2,623,327 | Eisenhower, Dwight D. | 1,775,682 | Stevenson, Adlai E. | 8,398 | 847,645 R | 59.5% | 40.3% | 59.6% | 40.4% |
| 1952 | 4,481,058 | 2,457,327 | Eisenhower, Dwight D. | 2,013,920 | Stevenson, Adlai E. | 9,811 | 443,407 R | 54.8% | 44.9% | 55.0% | 45.0% |
| 1948 | 3,984,046 | 1,961,103 | Dewey, Thomas E. | 1,994,715 | Truman, Harry S. | 28,228 | 33,612 D | 49.2% | 50.1% | 49.6% | 50.4% |
| 1944 | 4,036,061 | 1,939,314 | Dewey, Thomas E. | 2,079,479 | Roosevelt, Franklin D. | 17,268 | 140,165 D | 48.0% | 51.5% | 48.3% | 51.7% |
| 1940 | 4,217,935 | 2,047,240 | Willkie, Wendell | 2,149,934 | Roosevelt, Franklin D. | 20,761 | 102,694 D | 48.5% | 51.0% | 48.8% | 51.2% |
| 1936 | 3,956,522 | 1,570,393 | Landon, Alfred M. | 2,282,999 | Roosevelt, Franklin D. | 103,130 | 712,606 D | 39.7% | 57.7% | 40.8% | 59.2% |
| 1932 | 3,407,926 | 1,432,756 | Hoover, Herbert C. | 1,882,304 | Roosevelt, Franklin D. | 92,866 | 449,548 D | 42.0% | 55.2% | 43.2% | 56.8% |
| 1928 | 3,107,489 | 1,769,141 | Hoover, Herbert C. | 1,313,817 | Smith, Alfred E. | 24,531 | 455,324 R | 56.9% | 42.3% | 57.4% | 42.6% |
| 1924 ** | 2,470,067 | 1,453,321 | Coolidge, Calvin | 576,975 | Davis, John W. | 439,771 | 876,346 R | 58.8% | 23.4% | 71.6% | 28.4% |
| 1920 | 2,094,714 | 1,420,480 | Harding, Warren G. | 534,395 | Cox, James M. | 139,839 | 886,085 R | 67.8% | 25.5% | 72.7% | 27.3% |

In 2000 the other vote column includes 103,759 votes cast for Green (Nader). In 1996 the other vote column includes 346,408 votes cast for Perot. In 1992 the other vote column includes 840,515 votes cast for Perot. In 1980 the other column includes 346,754 votes for Independent (Anderson). In 1924 the other vote was 432,027 Progressive; 2,622 Communist; 2,367 Prohibition; 2,334 Socialist Labor; and 421 Commonwealth Land.

## ELECTORAL COLLEGE VOTE 1920 TO 2004

| Year | Total | Republican | Democratic | Other |
|---|---|---|---|---|
| 2004 | 21 | | 21 | |
| 2000 | 22 | | 22 | |
| 1996 | 22 | | 22 | |
| 1992 | 22 | | 22 | |
| 1988 | 24 | 24 | | |
| 1984 | 24 | 24 | | |
| 1980 | 26 | 26 | | |
| 1976 | 26 | 26 | | |
| 1972 | 26 | 26 | | |
| 1968 | 26 | 26 | | |
| 1964 | 26 | | 26 | |
| 1960 | 27 | | 27 | |
| 1956 | 27 | 27 | | |
| 1952 | 27 | 27 | | |
| 1948 | 28 | | 28 | |
| 1944 | 28 | | 28 | |
| 1940 | 29 | | 29 | |
| 1936 | 29 | | 29 | |
| 1932 | 29 | | 29 | |
| 1928 | 29 | 29 | | |
| 1924 | 29 | 29 | | |
| 1920 | 29 | 29 | | |

274

# ILLINOIS

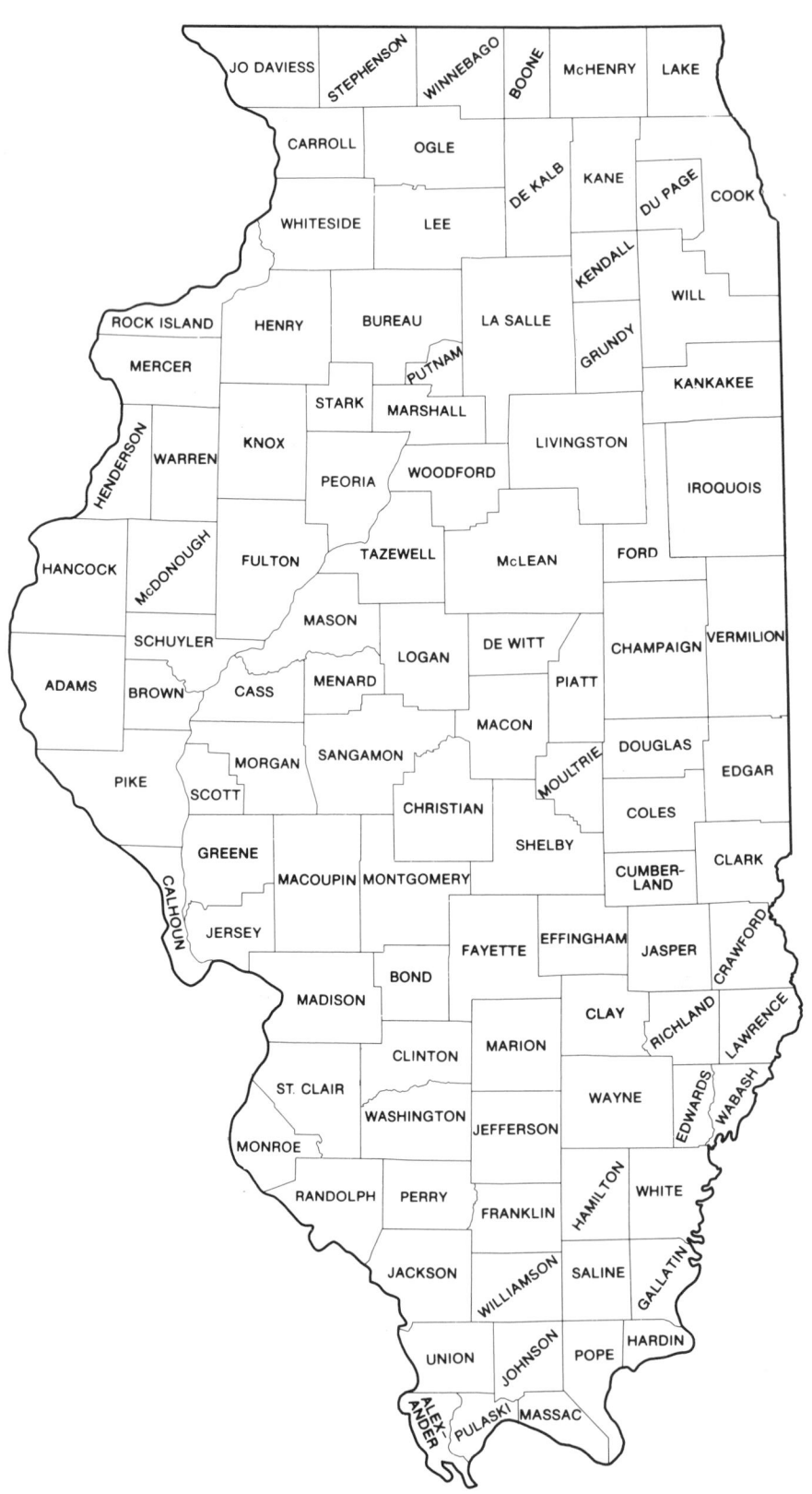

# ILLINOIS

## PRESIDENT 2004

| 2000 Census Population | County | Total Vote | Republican | Democratic | Other | Rep.-Dem. Plurality | Percentage | | | |
|---|---|---|---|---|---|---|---|---|---|---|
| | | | | | | | Total Vote | | Major Vote | |
| | | | | | | | Rep. | Dem. | Rep. | Dem. |
| 68,277 | ADAMS | 31,477 | 20,834 | 10,511 | 132 | 10,323 R | 66.2% | 33.4% | 66.5% | 33.5% |
| 9,590 | ALEXANDER | 3,873 | 1,831 | 2,016 | 26 | 185 D | 47.3% | 52.1% | 47.6% | 52.4% |
| 17,633 | BOND | 7,369 | 4,068 | 3,228 | 73 | 840 R | 55.2% | 43.8% | 55.8% | 44.2% |
| 41,786 | BOONE | 19,541 | 11,132 | 8,286 | 123 | 2,846 R | 57.0% | 42.4% | 57.3% | 42.7% |
| 6,950 | BROWN | 2,585 | 1,679 | 895 | 11 | 784 R | 65.0% | 34.6% | 65.2% | 34.8% |
| 35,503 | BUREAU | 17,902 | 9,822 | 7,961 | 119 | 1,861 R | 54.9% | 44.5% | 55.2% | 44.8% |
| 5,084 | CALHOUN | 2,706 | 1,317 | 1,367 | 22 | 50 D | 48.7% | 50.5% | 49.1% | 50.9% |
| 16,674 | CARROLL | 8,135 | 4,534 | 3,537 | 64 | 997 R | 55.7% | 43.5% | 56.2% | 43.8% |
| 13,695 | CASS | 5,700 | 3,163 | 2,492 | 45 | 671 R | 55.5% | 43.7% | 55.9% | 44.1% |
| 179,669 | CHAMPAIGN | 82,434 | 39,896 | 41,524 | 1,014 | 1,628 D | 48.4% | 50.4% | 49.0% | 51.0% |
| 35,372 | CHRISTIAN | 15,267 | 9,044 | 6,112 | 111 | 2,932 R | 59.2% | 40.0% | 59.7% | 40.3% |
| 17,008 | CLARK | 8,007 | 5,082 | 2,877 | 48 | 2,205 R | 63.5% | 35.9% | 63.9% | 36.1% |
| 14,560 | CLAY | 6,554 | 4,416 | 2,101 | 37 | 2,315 R | 67.4% | 32.1% | 67.8% | 32.2% |
| 35,535 | CLINTON | 17,131 | 10,219 | 6,797 | 115 | 3,422 R | 59.7% | 39.7% | 60.1% | 39.9% |
| 53,196 | COLES | 22,780 | 13,015 | 9,566 | 199 | 3,449 R | 57.1% | 42.0% | 57.6% | 42.4% |
| 5,376,741 | COOK | 2,049,434 | 597,405 | 1,439,724 | 12,305 | 842,319 D | 29.1% | 70.2% | 29.3% | 70.7% |
| 20,452 | CRAWFORD | 9,332 | 6,083 | 3,194 | 55 | 2,889 R | 65.2% | 34.2% | 65.6% | 34.4% |
| 11,253 | CUMBERLAND | 5,416 | 3,497 | 1,862 | 57 | 1,635 R | 64.6% | 34.4% | 65.3% | 34.7% |
| 88,969 | DE KALB | 40,768 | 21,095 | 19,263 | 410 | 1,832 R | 51.7% | 47.3% | 52.3% | 47.7% |
| 16,798 | DE WITT | 7,798 | 4,920 | 2,836 | 42 | 2,084 R | 63.1% | 36.4% | 63.4% | 36.6% |
| 19,922 | DOUGLAS | 8,540 | 5,702 | 2,767 | 71 | 2,935 R | 66.8% | 32.4% | 67.3% | 32.7% |
| 904,161 | DU PAGE | 402,446 | 218,902 | 180,097 | 3,447 | 38,805 R | 54.4% | 44.8% | 54.9% | 45.1% |
| 19,704 | EDGAR | 8,429 | 5,258 | 3,093 | 78 | 2,165 R | 62.4% | 36.7% | 63.0% | 37.0% |
| 6,971 | EDWARDS | 3,364 | 2,412 | 930 | 22 | 1,482 R | 71.7% | 27.6% | 72.2% | 27.8% |
| 34,264 | EFFINGHAM | 16,278 | 11,774 | 4,388 | 116 | 7,386 R | 72.3% | 27.0% | 72.8% | 27.2% |
| 21,802 | FAYETTE | 9,549 | 5,880 | 3,571 | 98 | 2,309 R | 61.6% | 37.4% | 62.2% | 37.8% |
| 14,241 | FORD | 6,479 | 4,511 | 1,912 | 56 | 2,599 R | 69.6% | 29.5% | 70.2% | 29.8% |
| 39,018 | FRANKLIN | 19,352 | 10,388 | 8,816 | 148 | 1,572 R | 53.7% | 45.6% | 54.1% | 45.9% |
| 38,250 | FULTON | 17,035 | 7,818 | 9,080 | 137 | 1,262 D | 45.9% | 53.3% | 46.3% | 53.7% |
| 6,445 | GALLATIN | 3,225 | 1,619 | 1,573 | 33 | 46 R | 50.2% | 48.8% | 50.7% | 49.3% |
| 14,761 | GREENE | 6,068 | 3,559 | 2,457 | 52 | 1,102 R | 58.7% | 40.5% | 59.2% | 40.8% |
| 37,535 | GRUNDY | 19,831 | 11,198 | 8,463 | 170 | 2,735 R | 56.5% | 42.7% | 57.0% | 43.0% |
| 8,621 | HAMILTON | 4,514 | 2,653 | 1,814 | 47 | 839 R | 58.8% | 40.2% | 59.4% | 40.6% |
| 20,121 | HANCOCK | 9,899 | 5,837 | 3,975 | 87 | 1,862 R | 59.0% | 40.2% | 59.5% | 40.5% |
| 4,800 | HARDIN | 2,437 | 1,501 | 923 | 13 | 578 R | 61.6% | 37.9% | 61.9% | 38.1% |
| 8,213 | HENDERSON | 4,153 | 1,857 | 2,269 | 27 | 412 D | 44.7% | 54.6% | 45.0% | 55.0% |
| 51,020 | HENRY | 25,241 | 13,212 | 11,877 | 152 | 1,335 R | 52.3% | 47.1% | 52.7% | 47.3% |
| 31,334 | IROQUOIS | 13,835 | 9,914 | 3,832 | 89 | 6,082 R | 71.7% | 27.7% | 72.1% | 27.9% |
| 59,612 | JACKSON | 25,826 | 11,190 | 14,300 | 336 | 3,110 D | 43.3% | 55.4% | 43.9% | 56.1% |
| 10,117 | JASPER | 5,336 | 3,529 | 1,781 | 26 | 1,748 R | 66.1% | 33.4% | 66.5% | 33.5% |
| 40,045 | JEFFERSON | 16,948 | 10,160 | 6,713 | 75 | 3,447 R | 59.9% | 39.6% | 60.2% | 39.8% |
| 21,668 | JERSEY | 10,137 | 5,435 | 4,597 | 105 | 838 R | 53.6% | 45.3% | 54.2% | 45.8% |
| 22,289 | JO DAVIESS | 11,584 | 6,174 | 5,311 | 99 | 863 R | 53.3% | 45.8% | 53.8% | 46.2% |
| 12,878 | JOHNSON | 5,865 | 3,997 | 1,813 | 55 | 2,184 R | 68.2% | 30.9% | 68.8% | 31.2% |
| 404,119 | KANE | 167,297 | 92,065 | 73,813 | 1,419 | 18,252 R | 55.0% | 44.1% | 55.5% | 44.5% |
| 103,833 | KANKAKEE | 45,036 | 24,739 | 20,003 | 294 | 4,736 R | 54.9% | 44.4% | 55.3% | 44.7% |
| 54,544 | KENDALL | 32,527 | 19,776 | 12,497 | 254 | 7,279 R | 60.8% | 38.4% | 61.3% | 38.7% |
| 55,836 | KNOX | 24,708 | 11,111 | 13,403 | 194 | 2,292 D | 45.0% | 54.2% | 45.3% | 54.7% |
| 644,356 | LAKE | 275,295 | 139,081 | 134,352 | 1,862 | 4,729 R | 50.5% | 48.8% | 50.9% | 49.1% |
| 111,509 | LA SALLE | 50,729 | 26,101 | 24,263 | 365 | 1,838 R | 51.5% | 47.8% | 51.8% | 48.2% |
| 15,452 | LAWRENCE | 6,729 | 4,162 | 2,518 | 49 | 1,644 R | 61.9% | 37.4% | 62.3% | 37.7% |
| 36,062 | LEE | 15,876 | 9,307 | 6,416 | 153 | 2,891 R | 58.6% | 40.4% | 59.2% | 40.8% |
| 39,678 | LIVINGSTON | 16,039 | 10,316 | 5,632 | 91 | 4,684 R | 64.3% | 35.1% | 64.7% | 35.3% |
| 31,183 | LOGAN | 13,467 | 9,112 | 4,273 | 82 | 4,839 R | 67.7% | 31.7% | 68.1% | 31.9% |
| 32,913 | MCDONOUGH | 14,929 | 7,656 | 7,119 | 154 | 537 R | 51.3% | 47.7% | 51.8% | 48.2% |
| 260,077 | MCHENRY | 127,948 | 76,412 | 50,330 | 1,206 | 26,082 R | 59.7% | 39.3% | 60.3% | 39.7% |
| 150,433 | MCLEAN | 71,620 | 41,276 | 29,877 | 467 | 11,399 R | 57.6% | 41.7% | 58.0% | 42.0% |
| 114,706 | MACON | 51,746 | 28,118 | 23,341 | 287 | 4,777 R | 54.3% | 45.1% | 54.6% | 45.4% |
| 49,019 | MACOUPIN | 22,785 | 11,413 | 11,193 | 179 | 220 R | 50.1% | 49.1% | 50.5% | 49.5% |
| 258,941 | MADISON | 123,678 | 59,384 | 63,399 | 895 | 4,015 D | 48.0% | 51.3% | 48.4% | 51.6% |

# ILLINOIS

## PRESIDENT 2004

| 2000 Census Population | County | Total Vote | Republican | Democratic | Other | Rep.-Dem. Plurality | Percentage | | | |
|---|---|---|---|---|---|---|---|---|---|---|
| | | | | | | | Total Vote | | Major Vote | |
| | | | | | | | Rep. | Dem. | Rep. | Dem. |
| 41,691 | MARION | 17,224 | 9,413 | 7,694 | 117 | 1,719 R | 54.7% | 44.7% | 55.0% | 45.0% |
| 13,180 | MARSHALL | 6,584 | 3,734 | 2,806 | 44 | 928 R | 56.7% | 42.6% | 57.1% | 42.9% |
| 16,038 | MASON | 7,183 | 3,907 | 3,215 | 61 | 692 R | 54.4% | 44.8% | 54.9% | 45.1% |
| 15,161 | MASSAC | 7,424 | 4,578 | 2,805 | 41 | 1,773 R | 61.7% | 37.8% | 62.0% | 38.0% |
| 12,486 | MENARD | 6,574 | 4,408 | 2,137 | 29 | 2,271 R | 67.1% | 32.5% | 67.3% | 32.7% |
| 16,957 | MERCER | 8,974 | 4,405 | 4,512 | 57 | 107 D | 49.1% | 50.3% | 49.4% | 50.6% |
| 27,619 | MONROE | 16,370 | 9,468 | 6,788 | 114 | 2,680 R | 57.8% | 41.5% | 58.2% | 41.8% |
| 30,652 | MONTGOMERY | 12,930 | 6,851 | 5,979 | 100 | 872 R | 53.0% | 46.2% | 53.4% | 46.6% |
| 36,616 | MORGAN | 15,180 | 9,392 | 5,650 | 138 | 3,742 R | 61.9% | 37.2% | 62.4% | 37.6% |
| 14,287 | MOULTRIE | 6,466 | 4,028 | 2,388 | 50 | 1,640 R | 62.3% | 36.9% | 62.8% | 37.2% |
| 51,032 | OGLE | 24,091 | 14,918 | 9,018 | 155 | 5,900 R | 61.9% | 37.4% | 62.3% | 37.7% |
| 183,433 | PEORIA | 82,771 | 41,051 | 41,121 | 599 | 70 D | 49.6% | 49.7% | 50.0% | 50.0% |
| 23,094 | PERRY | 10,425 | 5,589 | 4,770 | 66 | 819 R | 53.6% | 45.8% | 54.0% | 46.0% |
| 16,365 | PIATT | 8,586 | 5,392 | 3,124 | 70 | 2,268 R | 62.8% | 36.4% | 63.3% | 36.7% |
| 17,384 | PIKE | 7,980 | 5,032 | 2,849 | 99 | 2,183 R | 63.1% | 35.7% | 63.8% | 36.2% |
| 4,413 | POPE | 2,436 | 1,500 | 918 | 18 | 582 R | 61.6% | 37.7% | 62.0% | 38.0% |
| 7,348 | PULASKI | 3,108 | 1,720 | 1,372 | 16 | 348 R | 55.3% | 44.1% | 55.6% | 44.4% |
| 6,086 | PUTNAM | 3,352 | 1,623 | 1,704 | 25 | 81 D | 48.4% | 50.8% | 48.8% | 51.2% |
| 33,893 | RANDOLPH | 14,956 | 8,076 | 6,771 | 109 | 1,305 R | 54.0% | 45.3% | 54.4% | 45.6% |
| 16,149 | RICHLAND | 7,749 | 5,153 | 2,529 | 67 | 2,624 R | 66.5% | 32.6% | 67.1% | 32.9% |
| 149,374 | ROCK ISLAND | 69,972 | 29,663 | 39,880 | 429 | 10,217 D | 42.4% | 57.0% | 42.7% | 57.3% |
| 256,082 | ST. CLAIR | 113,189 | 50,203 | 62,410 | 576 | 12,207 D | 44.4% | 55.1% | 44.6% | 55.4% |
| 26,733 | SALINE | 11,814 | 7,057 | 4,697 | 60 | 2,360 R | 59.7% | 39.8% | 60.0% | 40.0% |
| 188,951 | SANGAMON | 95,375 | 55,904 | 38,630 | 841 | 17,274 R | 58.6% | 40.5% | 59.1% | 40.9% |
| 7,189 | SCHUYLER | 4,031 | 2,403 | 1,594 | 34 | 809 R | 59.6% | 39.5% | 60.1% | 39.9% |
| 5,537 | SCOTT | 2,636 | 1,696 | 927 | 13 | 769 R | 64.3% | 35.2% | 64.7% | 35.3% |
| 22,893 | SHELBY | 10,577 | 6,753 | 3,744 | 80 | 3,009 R | 63.8% | 35.4% | 64.3% | 35.7% |
| 6,332 | STARK | 3,061 | 1,841 | 1,189 | 31 | 652 R | 60.1% | 38.8% | 60.8% | 39.2% |
| 48,979 | STEPHENSON | 21,320 | 12,212 | 8,913 | 195 | 3,299 R | 57.3% | 41.8% | 57.8% | 42.2% |
| 128,485 | TAZEWELL | 62,338 | 36,058 | 25,814 | 466 | 10,244 R | 57.8% | 41.4% | 58.3% | 41.7% |
| 18,293 | UNION | 9,119 | 5,333 | 3,735 | 51 | 1,598 R | 58.5% | 41.0% | 58.8% | 41.2% |
| 83,919 | VERMILION | 33,714 | 18,731 | 14,726 | 257 | 4,005 R | 55.6% | 43.7% | 56.0% | 44.0% |
| 12,937 | WABASH | 6,006 | 4,212 | 1,752 | 42 | 2,460 R | 70.1% | 29.2% | 70.6% | 29.4% |
| 18,735 | WARREN | 8,457 | 4,474 | 3,938 | 45 | 536 R | 52.9% | 46.6% | 53.2% | 46.8% |
| 15,148 | WASHINGTON | 8,104 | 5,072 | 2,986 | 46 | 2,086 R | 62.6% | 36.8% | 62.9% | 37.1% |
| 17,151 | WAYNE | 8,287 | 6,102 | 2,139 | 46 | 3,963 R | 73.6% | 25.8% | 74.0% | 26.0% |
| 15,371 | WHITE | 8,301 | 5,180 | 3,071 | 50 | 2,109 R | 62.4% | 37.0% | 62.8% | 37.2% |
| 60,653 | WHITESIDE | 26,873 | 12,959 | 13,723 | 191 | 764 D | 48.2% | 51.1% | 48.6% | 51.4% |
| 502,266 | WILL | 249,609 | 130,728 | 117,172 | 1,709 | 13,556 R | 52.4% | 46.9% | 52.7% | 47.3% |
| 61,296 | WILLIAMSON | 29,960 | 18,086 | 11,685 | 189 | 6,401 R | 60.4% | 39.0% | 60.8% | 39.2% |
| 278,418 | WINNEBAGO | 121,425 | 60,782 | 59,740 | 903 | 1,042 R | 50.1% | 49.2% | 50.4% | 49.6% |
| 35,469 | WOODFORD | 18,802 | 12,698 | 6,005 | 99 | 6,693 R | 67.5% | 31.9% | 67.9% | 32.1% |
| 12,419,293 | TOTAL | 5,274,322 | 2,345,946 | 2,891,550 | 36,826 | 545,604 D | 44.5% | 54.8% | 44.8% | 55.2% |

# ILLINOIS

## PRESIDENT 2000

| 2000 Census Population | County | Total Vote | Republican | Democratic | Green (Nader) | Other | Rep.-Dem. Plurality | Percentage of Total Vote | | |
|---|---|---|---|---|---|---|---|---|---|---|
| | | | | | | | | Rep. | Dem. | Green |
| 68,277 | ADAMS | 30,109 | 17,331 | 12,197 | 371 | 210 | 5,134 R | 57.6% | 40.5% | 1.2% |
| 9,590 | ALEXANDER | 4,022 | 1,588 | 2,357 | 28 | 49 | 769 D | 39.5% | 58.6% | 0.7% |
| 17,633 | BOND | 7,032 | 3,804 | 3,060 | 113 | 55 | 744 R | 54.1% | 43.5% | 1.6% |
| 41,786 | BOONE | 15,523 | 8,617 | 6,481 | 325 | 100 | 2,136 R | 55.5% | 41.8% | 2.1% |
| 6,950 | BROWN | 2,660 | 1,529 | 1,077 | 29 | 25 | 452 R | 57.5% | 40.5% | 1.1% |
| 35,503 | BUREAU | 16,823 | 8,526 | 7,754 | 363 | 180 | 772 R | 50.7% | 46.1% | 2.2% |
| 5,084 | CALHOUN | 2,602 | 1,229 | 1,310 | 42 | 21 | 81 D | 47.2% | 50.3% | 1.6% |
| 16,674 | CARROLL | 7,177 | 3,835 | 3,113 | 154 | 75 | 722 R | 53.4% | 43.4% | 2.1% |
| 13,695 | CASS | 5,899 | 2,968 | 2,789 | 94 | 48 | 179 R | 50.3% | 47.3% | 1.6% |
| 179,669 | CHAMPAIGN | 74,285 | 34,645 | 35,515 | 3,543 | 582 | 870 D | 46.6% | 47.8% | 4.8% |
| 35,372 | CHRISTIAN | 14,771 | 7,537 | 6,799 | 269 | 166 | 738 R | 51.0% | 46.0% | 1.8% |
| 17,008 | CLARK | 7,512 | 4,398 | 2,932 | 126 | 56 | 1,466 R | 58.5% | 39.0% | 1.7% |
| 14,560 | CLAY | 6,135 | 3,789 | 2,212 | 78 | 56 | 1,577 R | 61.8% | 36.1% | 1.3% |
| 35,535 | CLINTON | 15,427 | 8,588 | 6,436 | 295 | 108 | 2,152 R | 55.7% | 41.7% | 1.9% |
| 53,196 | COLES | 20,093 | 10,495 | 8,904 | 507 | 187 | 1,591 R | 52.2% | 44.3% | 2.5% |
| 5,376,741 | COOK | 1,865,907 | 534,542 | 1,280,547 | 42,068 | 8,750 | 746,005 D | 28.6% | 68.6% | 2.3% |
| 20,452 | CRAWFORD | 8,500 | 4,974 | 3,333 | 118 | 75 | 1,641 R | 58.5% | 39.2% | 1.4% |
| 11,253 | CUMBERLAND | 4,975 | 2,964 | 1,870 | 72 | 69 | 1,094 R | 59.6% | 37.6% | 1.4% |
| 88,969 | DE KALB | 33,233 | 17,139 | 14,798 | 1,032 | 264 | 2,341 R | 51.6% | 44.5% | 3.1% |
| 16,798 | DE WITT | 7,051 | 3,968 | 2,870 | 133 | 80 | 1,098 R | 56.3% | 40.7% | 1.9% |
| 19,922 | DOUGLAS | 8,152 | 4,734 | 3,215 | 132 | 71 | 1,519 R | 58.1% | 39.4% | 1.6% |
| 904,161 | DU PAGE | 364,362 | 201,037 | 152,550 | 8,711 | 2,064 | 48,487 R | 55.2% | 41.9% | 2.4% |
| 19,704 | EDGAR | 8,232 | 4,833 | 3,216 | 113 | 70 | 1,617 R | 58.7% | 39.1% | 1.4% |
| 6,971 | EDWARDS | 3,260 | 2,212 | 978 | 42 | 28 | 1,234 R | 67.9% | 30.0% | 1.3% |
| 34,264 | EFFINGHAM | 14,485 | 9,855 | 4,225 | 213 | 192 | 5,630 R | 68.0% | 29.2% | 1.5% |
| 21,802 | FAYETTE | 9,338 | 5,200 | 3,886 | 122 | 130 | 1,314 R | 55.7% | 41.6% | 1.3% |
| 14,241 | FORD | 6,153 | 3,889 | 2,090 | 116 | 58 | 1,799 R | 63.2% | 34.0% | 1.9% |
| 39,018 | FRANKLIN | 19,212 | 8,490 | 10,201 | 347 | 174 | 1,711 D | 44.2% | 53.1% | 1.8% |
| 38,250 | FULTON | 16,277 | 6,936 | 8,940 | 276 | 125 | 2,004 D | 42.6% | 54.9% | 1.7% |
| 6,445 | GALLATIN | 3,558 | 1,591 | 1,878 | 40 | 49 | 287 D | 44.7% | 52.8% | 1.1% |
| 14,761 | GREENE | 5,767 | 3,129 | 2,490 | 93 | 55 | 639 R | 54.3% | 43.2% | 1.6% |
| 37,535 | GRUNDY | 16,584 | 8,709 | 7,516 | 257 | 102 | 1,193 R | 52.5% | 45.3% | 1.5% |
| 8,621 | HAMILTON | 4,587 | 2,519 | 1,943 | 75 | 50 | 576 R | 54.9% | 42.4% | 1.6% |
| 20,121 | HANCOCK | 9,691 | 5,134 | 4,256 | 161 | 140 | 878 R | 53.0% | 43.9% | 1.7% |
| 4,800 | HARDIN | 2,637 | 1,366 | 1,184 | 41 | 46 | 182 R | 51.8% | 44.9% | 1.6% |
| 8,213 | HENDERSON | 3,866 | 1,708 | 2,030 | 74 | 54 | 322 D | 44.2% | 52.5% | 1.9% |
| 51,020 | HENRY | 23,470 | 10,896 | 11,921 | 428 | 225 | 1,025 D | 46.4% | 50.8% | 1.8% |
| 31,334 | IROQUOIS | 13,424 | 8,685 | 4,397 | 229 | 113 | 4,288 R | 64.7% | 32.8% | 1.7% |
| 59,612 | JACKSON | 23,090 | 9,823 | 11,773 | 1,228 | 266 | 1,950 D | 42.5% | 51.0% | 5.3% |
| 10,117 | JASPER | 5,021 | 3,119 | 1,815 | 50 | 37 | 1,304 R | 62.1% | 36.1% | 1.0% |
| 40,045 | JEFFERSON | 15,360 | 8,362 | 6,685 | 211 | 102 | 1,677 R | 54.4% | 43.5% | 1.4% |
| 21,668 | JERSEY | 9,413 | 4,699 | 4,355 | 231 | 128 | 344 R | 49.9% | 46.3% | 2.5% |
| 22,289 | JO DAVIESS | 10,322 | 5,304 | 4,585 | 314 | 119 | 719 R | 51.4% | 44.4% | 3.0% |
| 12,878 | JOHNSON | 5,362 | 3,285 | 1,928 | 83 | 66 | 1,357 R | 61.3% | 36.0% | 1.5% |
| 404,119 | KANE | 141,405 | 76,996 | 60,127 | 3,274 | 1,008 | 16,869 R | 54.5% | 42.5% | 2.3% |
| 103,833 | KANKAKEE | 40,183 | 20,049 | 19,180 | 713 | 241 | 869 R | 49.9% | 47.7% | 1.8% |
| 54,544 | KENDALL | 22,769 | 13,688 | 8,444 | 481 | 156 | 5,244 R | 60.1% | 37.1% | 2.1% |
| 55,836 | KNOX | 23,174 | 9,912 | 12,572 | 455 | 235 | 2,660 D | 42.8% | 54.3% | 2.0% |
| 644,356 | LAKE | 242,164 | 120,988 | 115,058 | 4,843 | 1,275 | 5,930 R | 50.0% | 47.5% | 2.0% |
| 111,509 | LA SALLE | 46,007 | 21,276 | 23,355 | 992 | 384 | 2,079 D | 46.2% | 50.8% | 2.2% |
| 15,452 | LAWRENCE | 6,578 | 3,594 | 2,822 | 101 | 61 | 772 R | 54.6% | 42.9% | 1.5% |
| 36,062 | LEE | 14,620 | 8,069 | 6,111 | 320 | 120 | 1,958 R | 55.2% | 41.8% | 2.2% |
| 39,678 | LIVINGSTON | 15,421 | 9,187 | 5,829 | 285 | 120 | 3,358 R | 59.6% | 37.8% | 1.8% |
| 31,183 | LOGAN | 13,065 | 8,141 | 4,600 | 208 | 116 | 3,541 R | 62.3% | 35.2% | 1.6% |
| 32,913 | MCDONOUGH | 13,012 | 6,465 | 6,080 | 364 | 103 | 385 R | 49.7% | 46.7% | 2.8% |
| 260,077 | MCHENRY | 106,185 | 62,112 | 40,698 | 2,751 | 624 | 21,414 R | 58.5% | 38.3% | 2.6% |
| 150,433 | MCLEAN | 60,898 | 34,008 | 24,936 | 1,546 | 408 | 9,072 R | 55.8% | 40.9% | 2.5% |
| 114,706 | MACON | 49,499 | 23,830 | 24,262 | 982 | 425 | 432 D | 48.1% | 49.0% | 2.0% |
| 49,019 | MACOUPIN | 21,389 | 9,749 | 11,015 | 426 | 199 | 1,266 D | 45.6% | 51.5% | 2.0% |
| 258,941 | MADISON | 111,104 | 48,821 | 59,077 | 2,359 | 847 | 10,256 D | 43.9% | 53.2% | 2.1% |

# ILLINOIS

## PRESIDENT 2000

| 2000 Census Population | County | Total Vote | Republican | Democratic | Green (Nader) | Other | Rep.-Dem. Plurality | Percentage of Total Vote | | |
|---|---|---|---|---|---|---|---|---|---|---|
| | | | | | | | | Rep. | Dem. | Green |
| 41,691 | MARION | 16,663 | 8,240 | 8,068 | 238 | 117 | 172 R | 49.5% | 48.4% | 1.4% |
| 13,180 | MARSHALL | 5,907 | 3,145 | 2,570 | 134 | 58 | 575 R | 53.2% | 43.5% | 2.3% |
| 16,038 | MASON | 6,772 | 3,411 | 3,192 | 117 | 52 | 219 R | 50.4% | 47.1% | 1.7% |
| 15,161 | MASSAC | 6,744 | 3,676 | 2,912 | 83 | 73 | 764 R | 54.5% | 43.2% | 1.2% |
| 12,486 | MENARD | 6,202 | 3,862 | 2,164 | 135 | 41 | 1,698 R | 62.3% | 34.9% | 2.2% |
| 16,957 | MERCER | 8,318 | 3,688 | 4,400 | 156 | 74 | 712 D | 44.3% | 52.9% | 1.9% |
| 27,619 | MONROE | 13,796 | 7,632 | 5,797 | 262 | 105 | 1,835 R | 55.3% | 42.0% | 1.9% |
| 30,652 | MONTGOMERY | 13,093 | 6,226 | 6,542 | 191 | 134 | 316 D | 47.6% | 50.0% | 1.5% |
| 36,616 | MORGAN | 14,334 | 8,058 | 5,899 | 253 | 124 | 2,159 R | 56.2% | 41.2% | 1.8% |
| 14,287 | MOULTRIE | 5,725 | 3,058 | 2,529 | 78 | 60 | 529 R | 53.4% | 44.2% | 1.4% |
| 51,032 | OGLE | 20,601 | 12,325 | 7,673 | 467 | 136 | 4,652 R | 59.8% | 37.2% | 2.3% |
| 183,433 | PEORIA | 76,812 | 36,398 | 38,604 | 1,332 | 478 | 2,206 D | 47.4% | 50.3% | 1.7% |
| 23,094 | PERRY | 9,942 | 4,802 | 4,862 | 173 | 105 | 60 D | 48.3% | 48.9% | 1.7% |
| 16,365 | PIATT | 8,385 | 4,619 | 3,488 | 217 | 61 | 1,131 R | 55.1% | 41.6% | 2.6% |
| 17,384 | PIKE | 8,112 | 4,706 | 3,198 | 115 | 93 | 1,508 R | 58.0% | 39.4% | 1.4% |
| 4,413 | POPE | 2,330 | 1,346 | 927 | 31 | 26 | 419 R | 57.8% | 39.8% | 1.3% |
| 7,348 | PULASKI | 3,016 | 1,430 | 1,518 | 31 | 37 | 88 D | 47.4% | 50.3% | 1.0% |
| 6,086 | PUTNAM | 3,179 | 1,437 | 1,657 | 58 | 27 | 220 D | 45.2% | 52.1% | 1.8% |
| 33,893 | RANDOLPH | 14,287 | 7,127 | 6,794 | 229 | 137 | 333 R | 49.9% | 47.6% | 1.6% |
| 16,149 | RICHLAND | 7,428 | 4,718 | 2,491 | 134 | 85 | 2,227 R | 63.5% | 33.5% | 1.8% |
| 149,374 | ROCK ISLAND | 65,095 | 25,194 | 37,957 | 1,364 | 580 | 12,763 D | 38.7% | 58.3% | 2.1% |
| 256,082 | ST. CLAIR | 100,393 | 42,299 | 55,961 | 1,569 | 564 | 13,662 D | 42.1% | 55.7% | 1.6% |
| 26,733 | SALINE | 11,650 | 5,933 | 5,427 | 181 | 109 | 506 R | 50.9% | 46.6% | 1.6% |
| 188,951 | SANGAMON | 91,485 | 50,374 | 38,414 | 2,001 | 696 | 11,960 R | 55.1% | 42.0% | 2.2% |
| 7,189 | SCHUYLER | 3,772 | 2,077 | 1,587 | 72 | 36 | 490 R | 55.1% | 42.1% | 1.9% |
| 5,537 | SCOTT | 2,469 | 1,458 | 954 | 31 | 26 | 504 R | 59.1% | 38.6% | 1.3% |
| 22,893 | SHELBY | 10,163 | 5,851 | 4,018 | 162 | 132 | 1,833 R | 57.6% | 39.5% | 1.6% |
| 6,332 | STARK | 2,989 | 1,694 | 1,211 | 55 | 29 | 483 R | 56.7% | 40.5% | 1.8% |
| 48,979 | STEPHENSON | 19,378 | 10,715 | 8,062 | 476 | 125 | 2,653 R | 55.3% | 41.6% | 2.5% |
| 128,485 | TAZEWELL | 58,348 | 31,537 | 25,379 | 1,022 | 410 | 6,158 R | 54.0% | 43.5% | 1.8% |
| 18,293 | UNION | 8,660 | 4,397 | 3,982 | 189 | 92 | 415 R | 50.8% | 46.0% | 2.2% |
| 83,919 | VERMILION | 32,100 | 15,783 | 15,406 | 605 | 306 | 377 R | 49.2% | 48.0% | 1.9% |
| 12,937 | WABASH | 5,508 | 3,406 | 1,987 | 75 | 40 | 1,419 R | 61.8% | 36.1% | 1.4% |
| 18,735 | WARREN | 7,631 | 3,899 | 3,524 | 130 | 78 | 375 R | 51.1% | 46.2% | 1.7% |
| 15,148 | WASHINGTON | 7,138 | 4,353 | 2,638 | 96 | 51 | 1,715 R | 61.0% | 37.0% | 1.3% |
| 17,151 | WAYNE | 7,693 | 5,347 | 2,209 | 77 | 60 | 3,138 R | 69.5% | 28.7% | 1.0% |
| 15,371 | WHITE | 7,637 | 4,521 | 2,958 | 113 | 45 | 1,563 R | 59.2% | 38.7% | 1.5% |
| 60,653 | WHITESIDE | 24,837 | 11,252 | 12,886 | 515 | 184 | 1,634 D | 45.3% | 51.9% | 2.1% |
| 502,266 | WILL | 191,670 | 95,828 | 90,902 | 3,769 | 1,171 | 4,926 R | 50.0% | 47.4% | 2.0% |
| 61,296 | WILLIAMSON | 26,939 | 14,012 | 12,192 | 476 | 259 | 1,820 R | 52.0% | 45.3% | 1.8% |
| 278,418 | WINNEBAGO | 109,297 | 53,816 | 51,981 | 2,637 | 863 | 1,835 R | 49.2% | 47.6% | 2.4% |
| 35,469 | WOODFORD | 16,793 | 10,905 | 5,529 | 263 | 96 | 5,376 R | 64.9% | 32.9% | 1.6% |
| 12,419,293 | TOTAL | 4,742,123 | 2,019,421 | 2,589,026 | 103,759 | 29,917 | 569,605 D | 42.6% | 54.6% | 2.2% |

# ILLINOIS

## PRESIDENT 1996

| 1995 Census Pop. Est. | County | Total Vote | Republican | Democratic | Reform (Perot) | Other | Rep.-Dem. Plurality | Percentage of Total Vote | | |
|---|---|---|---|---|---|---|---|---|---|---|
| | | | | | | | | Rep. | Dem. | Reform |
| 68,043 | ADAMS | 28,411 | 13,836 | 11,336 | 3,069 | 170 | 2,500 R | 48.7% | 39.9% | 10.8% |
| 10,180 | ALEXANDER | 4,304 | 1,212 | 2,753 | 321 | 18 | 1,541 D | 28.2% | 64.0% | 7.5% |
| 15,738 | BOND | 6,970 | 3,018 | 3,213 | 685 | 54 | 195 D | 43.3% | 46.1% | 9.8% |
| 36,180 | BOONE | 13,009 | 6,181 | 5,345 | 1,377 | 106 | 836 R | 47.5% | 41.1% | 10.6% |
| 6,247 | BROWN | 2,297 | 1,053 | 997 | 237 | 10 | 56 R | 45.8% | 43.4% | 10.3% |
| 36,049 | BUREAU | 16,073 | 6,528 | 7,651 | 1,798 | 96 | 1,123 D | 40.6% | 47.6% | 11.2% |
| 4,948 | CALHOUN | 3,013 | 941 | 1,676 | 363 | 33 | 735 D | 31.2% | 55.6% | 12.0% |
| 16,872 | CARROLL | 6,799 | 3,029 | 2,926 | 792 | 52 | 103 R | 44.6% | 43.0% | 11.6% |
| 13,330 | CASS | 5,667 | 2,214 | 2,834 | 589 | 30 | 620 D | 39.1% | 50.0% | 10.4% |
| 169,096 | CHAMPAIGN | 66,429 | 28,232 | 32,454 | 4,806 | 937 | 4,222 D | 42.5% | 48.9% | 7.2% |
| 34,920 | CHRISTIAN | 14,837 | 5,563 | 7,431 | 1,727 | 116 | 1,868 D | 37.5% | 50.1% | 11.6% |
| 16,284 | CLARK | 7,220 | 3,409 | 2,995 | 781 | 35 | 414 R | 47.2% | 41.5% | 10.8% |
| 14,435 | CLAY | 6,228 | 2,703 | 2,750 | 719 | 56 | 47 D | 43.4% | 44.2% | 11.5% |
| 35,285 | CLINTON | 13,844 | 6,065 | 6,104 | 1,580 | 95 | 39 D | 43.8% | 44.1% | 11.4% |
| 52,357 | COLES | 19,298 | 8,038 | 8,950 | 2,137 | 173 | 912 D | 41.7% | 46.4% | 11.1% |
| 5,136,877 | COOK | 1,726,666 | 461,557 | 1,153,289 | 96,633 | 15,187 | 691,732 D | 26.7% | 66.8% | 5.6% |
| 19,911 | CRAWFORD | 8,693 | 3,965 | 3,627 | 1,057 | 44 | 338 R | 45.6% | 41.7% | 12.2% |
| 11,110 | CUMBERLAND | 4,469 | 2,002 | 1,776 | 657 | 34 | 226 R | 44.8% | 39.7% | 14.7% |
| 83,441 | DE KALB | 28,527 | 12,380 | 12,715 | 3,009 | 423 | 335 D | 43.4% | 44.6% | 10.5% |
| 16,824 | DE WITT | 6,589 | 2,978 | 2,878 | 694 | 39 | 100 R | 45.2% | 43.7% | 10.5% |
| 19,799 | DOUGLAS | 7,013 | 3,272 | 2,955 | 740 | 46 | 317 R | 46.7% | 42.1% | 10.6% |
| 853,458 | DU PAGE | 324,486 | 164,630 | 129,709 | 27,419 | 2,728 | 34,921 R | 50.7% | 40.0% | 8.4% |
| 19,984 | EDGAR | 8,302 | 3,746 | 3,552 | 935 | 69 | 194 R | 45.1% | 42.8% | 11.3% |
| 7,262 | EDWARDS | 3,103 | 1,613 | 1,089 | 384 | 17 | 524 R | 52.0% | 35.1% | 12.4% |
| 33,009 | EFFINGHAM | 14,204 | 7,696 | 4,825 | 1,555 | 128 | 2,871 R | 54.2% | 34.0% | 10.9% |
| 21,235 | FAYETTE | 8,792 | 3,881 | 3,887 | 964 | 60 | 6 D | 44.1% | 44.2% | 11.0% |
| 14,127 | FORD | 5,770 | 3,077 | 2,065 | 590 | 38 | 1,012 R | 53.3% | 35.8% | 10.2% |
| 40,809 | FRANKLIN | 17,358 | 5,354 | 9,814 | 2,096 | 94 | 4,460 D | 30.8% | 56.5% | 12.1% |
| 38,788 | FULTON | 15,706 | 5,155 | 8,857 | 1,610 | 84 | 3,702 D | 32.8% | 56.4% | 10.3% |
| 6,779 | GALLATIN | 3,513 | 856 | 2,113 | 527 | 17 | 1,257 D | 24.4% | 60.1% | 15.0% |
| 15,643 | GREENE | 5,934 | 2,245 | 2,734 | 903 | 52 | 489 D | 37.8% | 46.1% | 15.2% |
| 35,159 | GRUNDY | 14,902 | 6,177 | 6,759 | 1,860 | 106 | 582 D | 41.5% | 45.4% | 12.5% |
| 8,525 | HAMILTON | 4,509 | 1,677 | 2,242 | 560 | 30 | 565 D | 37.2% | 49.7% | 12.4% |
| 21,292 | HANCOCK | 9,178 | 3,961 | 4,001 | 1,148 | 68 | 40 D | 43.2% | 43.6% | 12.5% |
| 5,184 | HARDIN | 2,617 | 790 | 1,323 | 485 | 19 | 533 D | 30.2% | 50.6% | 18.5% |
| 8,432 | HENDERSON | 3,619 | 1,233 | 1,953 | 408 | 25 | 720 D | 34.1% | 54.0% | 11.3% |
| 51,719 | HENRY | 21,897 | 8,393 | 11,201 | 2,194 | 109 | 2,808 D | 38.3% | 51.2% | 10.0% |
| 31,411 | IROQUOIS | 12,737 | 6,564 | 4,559 | 1,522 | 92 | 2,005 R | 51.5% | 35.8% | 11.9% |
| 61,502 | JACKSON | 22,011 | 7,422 | 12,214 | 2,082 | 293 | 4,792 D | 33.7% | 55.5% | 9.5% |
| 10,591 | JASPER | 4,951 | 2,234 | 2,038 | 641 | 38 | 196 R | 45.1% | 41.2% | 12.9% |
| 38,998 | JEFFERSON | 14,981 | 5,937 | 7,263 | 1,647 | 134 | 1,326 D | 39.6% | 48.5% | 11.0% |
| 21,188 | JERSEY | 8,766 | 3,211 | 4,275 | 1,186 | 94 | 1,064 D | 36.6% | 48.8% | 13.5% |
| 21,931 | JO DAVIESS | 9,306 | 3,915 | 4,171 | 1,131 | 89 | 256 D | 42.1% | 44.8% | 12.2% |
| 12,426 | JOHNSON | 4,930 | 2,241 | 2,009 | 640 | 40 | 232 R | 45.5% | 40.8% | 13.0% |
| 359,950 | KANE | 114,693 | 54,375 | 47,902 | 11,270 | 1,146 | 6,473 R | 47.4% | 41.8% | 9.8% |
| 102,046 | KANKAKEE | 35,241 | 14,595 | 16,820 | 3,574 | 252 | 2,225 D | 41.4% | 47.7% | 10.1% |
| 45,398 | KENDALL | 17,672 | 8,958 | 6,499 | 2,055 | 160 | 2,459 R | 50.7% | 36.8% | 11.6% |
| 56,070 | KNOX | 22,548 | 7,822 | 12,487 | 2,096 | 143 | 4,665 D | 34.7% | 55.4% | 9.3% |
| 572,431 | LAKE | 204,764 | 93,149 | 93,315 | 16,640 | 1,660 | 166 D | 45.5% | 45.6% | 8.1% |
| 109,955 | LA SALLE | 42,491 | 15,299 | 21,643 | 5,259 | 290 | 6,344 D | 36.0% | 50.9% | 12.4% |
| 15,918 | LAWRENCE | 6,392 | 2,568 | 2,871 | 916 | 37 | 303 D | 40.2% | 44.9% | 14.3% |
| 35,798 | LEE | 14,182 | 6,677 | 5,895 | 1,520 | 90 | 782 R | 47.1% | 41.6% | 10.7% |
| 40,404 | LIVINGSTON | 14,788 | 7,653 | 5,641 | 1,409 | 85 | 2,012 R | 51.8% | 38.1% | 9.5% |
| 31,267 | LOGAN | 12,345 | 6,518 | 4,618 | 1,141 | 68 | 1,900 R | 52.8% | 37.4% | 9.2% |
| 35,519 | MCDONOUGH | 12,035 | 5,049 | 5,632 | 1,217 | 137 | 583 D | 42.0% | 46.8% | 10.1% |
| 224,677 | MCHENRY | 83,256 | 41,136 | 31,240 | 10,082 | 798 | 9,896 R | 49.4% | 37.5% | 12.1% |
| 139,274 | MCLEAN | 53,435 | 26,428 | 22,708 | 3,816 | 483 | 3,720 R | 49.5% | 42.5% | 7.1% |
| 116,414 | MACON | 47,235 | 18,161 | 24,256 | 4,540 | 278 | 6,095 D | 38.4% | 51.4% | 9.6% |
| 48,729 | MACOUPIN | 21,075 | 7,235 | 11,107 | 2,532 | 201 | 3,872 D | 34.3% | 52.7% | 12.0% |
| 256,458 | MADISON | 100,573 | 35,758 | 53,568 | 10,121 | 1,126 | 17,810 D | 35.6% | 53.3% | 10.1% |

# ILLINOIS

## PRESIDENT 1996

| 1995 Census Pop. Est. | County | Total Vote | Republican | Democratic | Reform (Perot) | Other | Rep.-Dem. Plurality | Percentage of Total Vote | | |
|---|---|---|---|---|---|---|---|---|---|---|
| | | | | | | | | Rep. | Dem. | Reform |
| 41,997 | MARION | 15,763 | 5,999 | 7,792 | 1,825 | 147 | 1,793 D | 38.1% | 49.4% | 11.6% |
| 12,791 | MARSHALL | 5,714 | 2,453 | 2,640 | 586 | 35 | 187 D | 42.9% | 46.2% | 10.3% |
| 16,691 | MASON | 6,444 | 2,430 | 3,385 | 600 | 29 | 955 D | 37.7% | 52.5% | 9.3% |
| 15,370 | MASSAC | 6,058 | 2,507 | 2,841 | 675 | 35 | 334 D | 41.4% | 46.9% | 11.1% |
| 12,284 | MENARD | 5,868 | 3,106 | 2,204 | 534 | 24 | 902 R | 52.9% | 37.6% | 9.1% |
| 17,444 | MERCER | 7,897 | 2,688 | 4,278 | 889 | 42 | 1,590 D | 34.0% | 54.2% | 11.3% |
| 24,719 | MONROE | 11,535 | 5,350 | 4,798 | 1,276 | 111 | 552 R | 46.4% | 41.6% | 11.1% |
| 30,994 | MONTGOMERY | 12,631 | 4,770 | 6,338 | 1,436 | 87 | 1,568 D | 37.8% | 50.2% | 11.4% |
| 36,171 | MORGAN | 14,238 | 6,352 | 6,150 | 1,633 | 103 | 202 R | 44.6% | 43.2% | 11.5% |
| 14,168 | MOULTRIE | 5,451 | 2,199 | 2,629 | 596 | 27 | 430 D | 40.3% | 48.2% | 10.9% |
| 49,406 | OGLE | 18,335 | 9,558 | 6,765 | 1,876 | 136 | 2,793 R | 52.1% | 36.9% | 10.2% |
| 183,377 | PEORIA | 74,102 | 30,990 | 37,383 | 5,220 | 509 | 6,393 D | 41.8% | 50.4% | 7.0% |
| 21,295 | PERRY | 9,921 | 3,237 | 5,347 | 1,262 | 75 | 2,110 D | 32.6% | 53.9% | 12.7% |
| 16,158 | PIATT | 7,412 | 3,265 | 3,274 | 818 | 55 | 9 D | 44.1% | 44.2% | 11.0% |
| 17,338 | PIKE | 7,952 | 3,225 | 3,604 | 1,039 | 84 | 379 D | 40.6% | 45.3% | 13.1% |
| 4,691 | POPE | 2,054 | 850 | 915 | 277 | 12 | 65 D | 41.4% | 44.5% | 13.5% |
| 7,464 | PULASKI | 2,814 | 1,036 | 1,524 | 235 | 19 | 488 D | 36.8% | 54.2% | 8.4% |
| 5,718 | PUTNAM | 2,764 | 987 | 1,425 | 322 | 30 | 438 D | 35.7% | 51.6% | 11.6% |
| 34,296 | RANDOLPH | 14,647 | 5,422 | 7,419 | 1,698 | 108 | 1,997 D | 37.0% | 50.7% | 11.6% |
| 16,788 | RICHLAND | 6,815 | 3,137 | 2,679 | 927 | 72 | 458 R | 46.0% | 39.3% | 13.6% |
| 149,830 | ROCK ISLAND | 60,955 | 20,626 | 34,822 | 5,135 | 372 | 14,196 D | 33.8% | 57.1% | 8.4% |
| 265,424 | ST. CLAIR | 94,429 | 33,066 | 53,405 | 7,027 | 931 | 20,339 D | 35.0% | 56.6% | 7.4% |
| 26,521 | SALINE | 11,665 | 3,693 | 6,156 | 1,752 | 64 | 2,463 D | 31.7% | 52.8% | 15.0% |
| 184,731 | SANGAMON | 88,105 | 42,174 | 38,902 | 6,446 | 583 | 3,272 R | 47.9% | 44.2% | 7.3% |
| 7,798 | SCHUYLER | 3,749 | 1,597 | 1,636 | 483 | 33 | 39 D | 42.6% | 43.6% | 12.9% |
| 5,629 | SCOTT | 2,538 | 1,112 | 1,012 | 396 | 18 | 100 R | 43.8% | 39.9% | 15.6% |
| 22,561 | SHELBY | 9,788 | 4,215 | 4,249 | 1,262 | 62 | 34 D | 43.1% | 43.4% | 12.9% |
| 6,396 | STARK | 2,864 | 1,278 | 1,262 | 312 | 12 | 16 R | 44.6% | 44.1% | 10.9% |
| 48,844 | STEPHENSON | 18,125 | 8,871 | 7,145 | 1,940 | 169 | 1,726 R | 48.9% | 39.4% | 10.7% |
| 127,602 | TAZEWELL | 53,678 | 24,395 | 24,139 | 4,814 | 330 | 256 R | 45.4% | 45.0% | 9.0% |
| 18,114 | UNION | 8,282 | 3,147 | 4,252 | 832 | 51 | 1,105 D | 38.0% | 51.3% | 10.0% |
| 86,541 | VERMILION | 31,329 | 12,015 | 15,525 | 3,577 | 212 | 3,510 D | 38.4% | 49.6% | 11.4% |
| 12,929 | WABASH | 5,274 | 2,381 | 2,177 | 683 | 33 | 204 R | 45.1% | 41.3% | 13.0% |
| 18,816 | WARREN | 7,250 | 2,974 | 3,500 | 742 | 34 | 526 D | 41.0% | 48.3% | 10.2% |
| 15,238 | WASHINGTON | 6,927 | 3,339 | 2,744 | 790 | 54 | 595 R | 48.2% | 39.6% | 11.4% |
| 17,208 | WAYNE | 8,140 | 4,029 | 3,054 | 999 | 58 | 975 R | 49.5% | 37.5% | 12.3% |
| 15,903 | WHITE | 7,352 | 2,878 | 3,553 | 888 | 33 | 675 D | 39.1% | 48.3% | 12.1% |
| 60,352 | WHITESIDE | 23,344 | 8,859 | 11,913 | 2,436 | 136 | 3,054 D | 37.9% | 51.0% | 10.4% |
| 413,379 | WILL | 148,304 | 62,506 | 69,354 | 15,485 | 959 | 6,848 D | 42.1% | 46.8% | 10.4% |
| 59,750 | WILLIAMSON | 25,272 | 9,734 | 12,510 | 2,877 | 151 | 2,776 D | 38.5% | 49.5% | 11.4% |
| 264,952 | WINNEBAGO | 99,910 | 44,479 | 46,264 | 8,192 | 975 | 1,785 D | 44.5% | 46.3% | 8.2% |
| 34,576 | WOODFORD | 15,043 | 8,527 | 5,270 | 1,170 | 76 | 3,257 R | 56.7% | 35.0% | 7.8% |
| 11,829,940 | TOTAL | 4,311,391 | 1,587,021 | 2,341,744 | 346,408 | 36,218 | 754,723 D | 36.8% | 54.3% | 8.0% |

# ILLINOIS

## PRESIDENT 1992

| 1990 Census Population | County | Total Vote | Republican | Democratic | Perot | Other | Plurality | Percentage Total Vote Rep. | Dem. | Perot |
|---|---|---|---|---|---|---|---|---|---|---|
| 66,090 | ADAMS | 31,579 | 13,529 | 11,748 | 6,157 | 145 | 1,781 R | 42.8% | 37.2% | 19.5% |
| 10,626 | ALEXANDER | 4,362 | 1,301 | 2,566 | 474 | 21 | 1,265 D | 29.8% | 58.8% | 10.9% |
| 14,991 | BOND | 7,548 | 2,715 | 3,428 | 1,373 | 32 | 713 D | 36.0% | 45.4% | 18.2% |
| 30,806 | BOONE | 13,627 | 5,589 | 5,114 | 2,880 | 44 | 475 R | 41.0% | 37.5% | 21.1% |
| 5,836 | BROWN | 2,689 | 1,029 | 1,146 | 504 | 10 | 117 D | 38.3% | 42.6% | 18.7% |
| 35,688 | BUREAU | 17,907 | 6,836 | 7,551 | 3,465 | 55 | 715 D | 38.2% | 42.2% | 19.3% |
| 5,322 | CALHOUN | 2,803 | 745 | 1,519 | 532 | 7 | 774 D | 26.6% | 54.2% | 19.0% |
| 16,805 | CARROLL | 7,679 | 3,297 | 2,854 | 1,502 | 26 | 443 R | 42.9% | 37.2% | 19.6% |
| 13,437 | CASS | 6,447 | 2,162 | 3,200 | 1,072 | 13 | 1,038 D | 33.5% | 49.6% | 16.6% |
| 173,025 | CHAMPAIGN | 76,092 | 27,096 | 35,003 | 13,571 | 422 | 7,907 D | 35.6% | 46.0% | 17.8% |
| 34,418 | CHRISTIAN | 17,590 | 5,087 | 9,042 | 3,401 | 60 | 3,955 D | 28.9% | 51.4% | 19.3% |
| 15,921 | CLARK | 7,979 | 3,175 | 3,338 | 1,450 | 16 | 163 D | 39.8% | 41.8% | 18.2% |
| 14,460 | CLAY | 6,652 | 2,471 | 2,962 | 1,193 | 26 | 491 D | 37.1% | 44.5% | 17.9% |
| 33,944 | CLINTON | 15,822 | 5,771 | 6,686 | 3,315 | 50 | 915 D | 36.5% | 42.3% | 21.0% |
| 51,644 | COLES | 22,300 | 8,098 | 9,402 | 4,707 | 93 | 1,304 D | 36.3% | 42.2% | 21.1% |
| 5,105,067 | COOK | 2,146,655 | 605,300 | 1,249,533 | 281,999 | 9,823 | 644,233 D | 28.2% | 58.2% | 13.1% |
| 19,464 | CRAWFORD | 9,671 | 3,606 | 3,964 | 2,062 | 39 | 358 D | 37.3% | 41.0% | 21.3% |
| 10,670 | CUMBERLAND | 5,202 | 1,860 | 2,111 | 1,209 | 22 | 251 D | 35.8% | 40.6% | 23.2% |
| 77,932 | DE KALB | 34,232 | 12,655 | 13,744 | 7,680 | 153 | 1,089 D | 37.0% | 40.1% | 22.4% |
| 16,516 | DE WITT | 7,759 | 3,164 | 3,009 | 1,543 | 43 | 155 R | 40.8% | 38.8% | 19.9% |
| 19,464 | DOUGLAS | 8,276 | 3,309 | 3,341 | 1,600 | 26 | 32 D | 40.0% | 40.4% | 19.3% |
| 781,666 | DU PAGE | 370,987 | 178,271 | 114,564 | 76,839 | 1,313 | 63,707 R | 48.1% | 30.9% | 20.7% |
| 19,595 | EDGAR | 9,776 | 3,790 | 4,014 | 1,930 | 42 | 224 D | 38.8% | 41.1% | 19.7% |
| 7,440 | EDWARDS | 3,552 | 1,601 | 1,299 | 634 | 18 | 302 R | 45.1% | 36.6% | 17.8% |
| 31,704 | EFFINGHAM | 14,981 | 6,329 | 5,221 | 3,354 | 77 | 1,108 R | 42.2% | 34.9% | 22.4% |
| 20,893 | FAYETTE | 10,118 | 3,508 | 4,833 | 1,730 | 47 | 1,325 D | 34.7% | 47.8% | 17.1% |
| 14,275 | FORD | 6,481 | 3,046 | 2,175 | 1,222 | 38 | 871 R | 47.0% | 33.6% | 18.9% |
| 40,319 | FRANKLIN | 21,481 | 5,504 | 12,744 | 3,180 | 53 | 7,240 D | 25.6% | 59.3% | 14.8% |
| 38,080 | FULTON | 17,701 | 5,062 | 9,725 | 2,874 | 40 | 4,663 D | 28.6% | 54.9% | 16.2% |
| 6,909 | GALLATIN | 3,944 | 990 | 2,371 | 568 | 15 | 1,381 D | 25.1% | 60.1% | 14.4% |
| 15,317 | GREENE | 7,032 | 2,391 | 3,164 | 1,461 | 16 | 773 D | 34.0% | 45.0% | 20.8% |
| 32,337 | GRUNDY | 16,265 | 6,346 | 6,122 | 3,724 | 73 | 224 R | 39.0% | 37.6% | 22.9% |
| 8,499 | HAMILTON | 4,974 | 1,521 | 2,582 | 862 | 9 | 1,061 D | 30.6% | 51.9% | 17.3% |
| 21,373 | HANCOCK | 10,069 | 3,714 | 4,213 | 2,091 | 51 | 499 D | 36.9% | 41.8% | 20.8% |
| 5,189 | HARDIN | 3,173 | 985 | 1,665 | 515 | 8 | 680 D | 31.0% | 52.5% | 16.2% |
| 8,096 | HENDERSON | 4,048 | 1,310 | 2,013 | 715 | 10 | 703 D | 32.4% | 49.7% | 17.7% |
| 51,159 | HENRY | 24,371 | 8,989 | 11,077 | 4,231 | 74 | 2,088 D | 36.9% | 45.5% | 17.4% |
| 30,787 | IROQUOIS | 14,530 | 6,948 | 4,440 | 3,073 | 69 | 2,508 R | 47.8% | 30.6% | 21.1% |
| 61,067 | JACKSON | 24,434 | 6,899 | 13,373 | 3,995 | 167 | 6,474 D | 28.2% | 54.7% | 16.4% |
| 10,609 | JASPER | 5,480 | 1,996 | 2,284 | 1,160 | 40 | 288 D | 36.4% | 41.7% | 21.2% |
| 37,020 | JEFFERSON | 17,597 | 5,497 | 8,665 | 3,403 | 32 | 3,168 D | 31.2% | 49.2% | 19.3% |
| 20,539 | JERSEY | 10,093 | 2,933 | 4,749 | 2,363 | 48 | 1,816 D | 29.1% | 47.1% | 23.4% |
| 21,821 | JO DAVIESS | 10,454 | 4,249 | 4,044 | 2,102 | 59 | 205 R | 40.6% | 38.7% | 20.1% |
| 11,347 | JOHNSON | 5,391 | 2,124 | 2,299 | 944 | 24 | 175 D | 39.4% | 42.6% | 17.5% |
| 317,471 | KANE | 127,938 | 55,684 | 44,568 | 27,179 | 507 | 11,116 R | 43.5% | 34.8% | 21.2% |
| 96,255 | KANKAKEE | 40,071 | 15,411 | 17,229 | 7,264 | 167 | 1,818 D | 38.5% | 43.0% | 18.1% |
| 39,413 | KENDALL | 18,406 | 8,521 | 5,423 | 4,394 | 68 | 3,098 R | 46.3% | 29.5% | 23.9% |
| 56,393 | KNOX | 25,296 | 8,331 | 12,524 | 4,357 | 84 | 4,193 D | 32.9% | 49.5% | 17.2% |
| 516,418 | LAKE | 223,987 | 99,000 | 81,693 | 42,384 | 910 | 17,307 R | 44.2% | 36.5% | 18.9% |
| 106,913 | LA SALLE | 49,931 | 16,078 | 23,276 | 10,434 | 143 | 7,198 D | 32.2% | 46.6% | 20.9% |
| 15,972 | LAWRENCE | 7,488 | 2,681 | 3,270 | 1,498 | 39 | 589 D | 35.8% | 43.7% | 20.0% |
| 34,392 | LEE | 15,417 | 6,652 | 5,530 | 3,191 | 44 | 1,122 R | 43.1% | 35.9% | 20.7% |
| 39,301 | LIVINGSTON | 17,098 | 8,004 | 6,007 | 3,029 | 58 | 1,997 R | 46.8% | 35.1% | 17.7% |
| 30,798 | LOGAN | 14,195 | 6,567 | 5,169 | 2,420 | 39 | 1,398 R | 46.3% | 36.4% | 17.0% |
| 35,244 | MCDONOUGH | 13,922 | 5,297 | 5,814 | 2,770 | 41 | 517 D | 38.0% | 41.8% | 19.9% |
| 183,241 | MCHENRY | 88,294 | 41,356 | 24,783 | 21,817 | 338 | 16,573 R | 46.8% | 28.1% | 24.7% |
| 129,180 | MCLEAN | 59,285 | 25,726 | 23,090 | 10,282 | 187 | 2,636 R | 43.4% | 38.9% | 17.3% |
| 117,206 | MACON | 55,580 | 18,684 | 27,449 | 9,236 | 211 | 8,765 D | 33.6% | 49.4% | 16.6% |
| 47,679 | MACOUPIN | 23,661 | 6,518 | 12,050 | 5,018 | 75 | 5,532 D | 27.5% | 50.9% | 21.2% |
| 249,238 | MADISON | 114,095 | 32,167 | 58,484 | 23,110 | 334 | 26,317 D | 28.2% | 51.3% | 20.3% |

# ILLINOIS

## PRESIDENT 1992

| 1990 Census Population | County | Total Vote | Republican | Democratic | Perot | Other | Plurality | Percentage Total Vote | | |
|---|---|---|---|---|---|---|---|---|---|---|
| | | | | | | | | Rep. | Dem. | Perot |
| 41,561 | MARION | 18,883 | 5,764 | 9,669 | 3,407 | 43 | 3,905 D | 30.5% | 51.2% | 18.0% |
| 12,846 | MARSHALL | 6,496 | 2,491 | 2,819 | 1,169 | 17 | 328 D | 38.3% | 43.4% | 18.0% |
| 16,269 | MASON | 7,702 | 2,473 | 3,969 | 1,245 | 15 | 1,496 D | 32.1% | 51.5% | 16.2% |
| 14,752 | MASSAC | 7,056 | 2,754 | 3,347 | 892 | 63 | 593 D | 39.0% | 47.4% | 12.6% |
| 11,164 | MENARD | 6,299 | 2,834 | 2,264 | 1,179 | 22 | 570 R | 45.0% | 35.9% | 18.7% |
| 17,290 | MERCER | 8,540 | 2,983 | 3,990 | 1,535 | 32 | 1,007 D | 34.9% | 46.7% | 18.0% |
| 22,422 | MONROE | 12,542 | 4,807 | 4,894 | 2,813 | 28 | 87 D | 38.3% | 39.0% | 22.4% |
| 30,728 | MONTGOMERY | 14,837 | 4,407 | 7,424 | 2,956 | 50 | 3,017 D | 29.7% | 50.0% | 19.9% |
| 36,397 | MORGAN | 16,297 | 6,566 | 6,351 | 3,317 | 63 | 215 R | 40.3% | 39.0% | 20.4% |
| 13,930 | MOULTRIE | 6,465 | 2,065 | 3,056 | 1,322 | 22 | 991 D | 31.9% | 47.3% | 20.4% |
| 45,957 | OGLE | 20,109 | 9,008 | 6,512 | 4,455 | 134 | 2,496 R | 44.8% | 32.4% | 22.2% |
| 182,827 | PEORIA | 81,328 | 30,718 | 38,099 | 12,195 | 316 | 7,381 D | 37.8% | 46.8% | 15.0% |
| 21,412 | PERRY | 11,086 | 3,105 | 6,009 | 1,955 | 17 | 2,904 D | 28.0% | 54.2% | 17.6% |
| 15,548 | PIATT | 8,447 | 3,076 | 3,520 | 1,822 | 29 | 444 D | 36.4% | 41.7% | 21.6% |
| 17,577 | PIKE | 9,037 | 3,342 | 4,016 | 1,643 | 36 | 674 D | 37.0% | 44.4% | 18.2% |
| 4,373 | POPE | 2,411 | 951 | 1,063 | 391 | 6 | 112 D | 39.4% | 44.1% | 16.2% |
| 7,523 | PULASKI | 3,549 | 1,169 | 1,987 | 379 | 14 | 818 D | 32.9% | 56.0% | 10.7% |
| 5,730 | PUTNAM | 3,308 | 969 | 1,574 | 752 | 13 | 605 D | 29.3% | 47.6% | 22.7% |
| 34,583 | RANDOLPH | 16,565 | 4,899 | 8,529 | 3,092 | 45 | 3,630 D | 29.6% | 51.5% | 18.7% |
| 16,545 | RICHLAND | 8,061 | 3,053 | 3,286 | 1,689 | 33 | 233 D | 37.9% | 40.8% | 21.0% |
| 148,723 | ROCK ISLAND | 72,039 | 23,212 | 37,412 | 10,416 | 999 | 14,200 D | 32.2% | 51.9% | 14.5% |
| 262,852 | ST. CLAIR | 107,541 | 31,951 | 57,625 | 17,592 | 373 | 25,674 D | 29.7% | 53.6% | 16.4% |
| 26,551 | SALINE | 13,254 | 3,667 | 7,258 | 2,302 | 27 | 3,591 D | 27.7% | 54.8% | 17.4% |
| 178,386 | SANGAMON | 96,860 | 39,641 | 40,052 | 16,861 | 306 | 411 D | 40.9% | 41.4% | 17.4% |
| 7,498 | SCHUYLER | 3,995 | 1,512 | 1,650 | 815 | 18 | 138 D | 37.8% | 41.3% | 20.4% |
| 5,644 | SCOTT | 2,783 | 1,132 | 1,057 | 588 | 6 | 75 R | 40.7% | 38.0% | 21.1% |
| 22,261 | SHELBY | 11,175 | 3,631 | 5,101 | 2,401 | 42 | 1,470 D | 32.5% | 45.6% | 21.5% |
| 6,534 | STARK | 3,351 | 1,384 | 1,336 | 625 | 6 | 48 R | 41.3% | 39.9% | 18.7% |
| 48,052 | STEPHENSON | 21,656 | 9,005 | 7,899 | 4,677 | 75 | 1,106 R | 41.6% | 36.5% | 21.6% |
| 123,692 | TAZEWELL | 59,994 | 23,469 | 26,428 | 9,927 | 170 | 2,959 D | 39.1% | 44.1% | 16.5% |
| 17,619 | UNION | 9,083 | 3,003 | 4,681 | 1,373 | 26 | 1,678 D | 33.1% | 51.5% | 15.1% |
| 88,257 | VERMILION | 38,461 | 11,703 | 18,383 | 8,162 | 213 | 6,680 D | 30.4% | 47.8% | 21.2% |
| 13,111 | WABASH | 6,240 | 2,485 | 2,436 | 1,302 | 17 | 49 R | 39.8% | 39.0% | 20.9% |
| 19,181 | WARREN | 8,446 | 3,325 | 3,661 | 1,436 | 24 | 336 D | 39.4% | 43.3% | 17.0% |
| 14,965 | WASHINGTON | 7,555 | 3,003 | 2,986 | 1,542 | 24 | 17 R | 39.7% | 39.5% | 20.4% |
| 17,241 | WAYNE | 8,872 | 3,809 | 3,332 | 1,702 | 29 | 477 R | 42.9% | 37.6% | 19.2% |
| 16,522 | WHITE | 8,811 | 3,057 | 4,308 | 1,428 | 18 | 1,251 D | 34.7% | 48.9% | 16.2% |
| 60,186 | WHITESIDE | 27,153 | 10,146 | 12,329 | 4,589 | 89 | 2,183 D | 37.4% | 45.4% | 16.9% |
| 357,313 | WILL | 152,123 | 58,337 | 59,633 | 32,788 | 1,365 | 1,296 D | 38.3% | 39.2% | 21.6% |
| 57,733 | WILLIAMSON | 28,760 | 9,462 | 14,361 | 4,779 | 158 | 4,899 D | 32.9% | 49.9% | 16.6% |
| 252,913 | WINNEBAGO | 112,215 | 42,221 | 48,298 | 21,227 | 469 | 6,077 D | 37.6% | 43.0% | 18.9% |
| 32,653 | WOODFORD | 16,305 | 8,032 | 5,490 | 2,733 | 50 | 2,542 R | 49.3% | 33.7% | 16.8% |
| 11,430,602 | TOTAL | 5,050,157 | 1,734,096 | 2,453,350 | 840,515 | 22,196 | 719,254 D | 34.3% | 48.6% | 16.6% |

# ILLINOIS

## PRESIDENT 1988

| 1980 Census Population | County | Total Vote | Republican | Democratic | Other | Rep.-Dem. Plurality | Percentage | | | |
|---|---|---|---|---|---|---|---|---|---|---|
| | | | | | | | Total Vote | | Major Vote | |
| | | | | | | | Rep. | Dem. | Rep. | Dem. |
| 71,622 | ADAMS | 29,710 | 15,831 | 13,768 | 111 | 2,063 R | 53.3% | 46.3% | 53.5% | 46.5% |
| 12,264 | ALEXANDER | 4,663 | 1,954 | 2,693 | 16 | 739 D | 41.9% | 57.8% | 42.0% | 58.0% |
| 16,224 | BOND | 7,105 | 3,608 | 3,459 | 38 | 149 R | 50.8% | 48.7% | 51.1% | 48.9% |
| 28,630 | BOONE | 11,222 | 6,923 | 4,234 | 65 | 2,689 R | 61.7% | 37.7% | 62.1% | 37.9% |
| 5,411 | BROWN | 2,646 | 1,373 | 1,267 | 6 | 106 R | 51.9% | 47.9% | 52.0% | 48.0% |
| 39,114 | BUREAU | 16,351 | 8,896 | 7,354 | 101 | 1,542 R | 54.4% | 45.0% | 54.7% | 45.3% |
| 5,867 | CALHOUN | 2,790 | 1,238 | 1,544 | 8 | 306 D | 44.4% | 55.3% | 44.5% | 55.5% |
| 18,779 | CARROLL | 7,512 | 4,464 | 2,990 | 58 | 1,474 R | 59.4% | 39.8% | 59.9% | 40.1% |
| 15,084 | CASS | 6,267 | 2,916 | 3,316 | 35 | 400 D | 46.5% | 52.9% | 46.8% | 53.2% |
| 168,392 | CHAMPAIGN | 63,499 | 33,247 | 29,733 | 519 | 3,514 R | 52.4% | 46.8% | 52.8% | 47.2% |
| 36,446 | CHRISTIAN | 15,436 | 7,040 | 8,295 | 101 | 1,255 D | 45.6% | 53.7% | 45.9% | 54.1% |
| 16,913 | CLARK | 7,811 | 4,508 | 3,275 | 28 | 1,233 R | 57.7% | 41.9% | 57.9% | 42.1% |
| 15,283 | CLAY | 6,279 | 3,494 | 2,761 | 24 | 733 R | 55.6% | 44.0% | 55.9% | 44.1% |
| 32,617 | CLINTON | 13,680 | 7,681 | 5,935 | 64 | 1,746 R | 56.1% | 43.4% | 56.4% | 43.6% |
| 52,260 | COLES | 19,504 | 11,043 | 8,327 | 134 | 2,716 R | 56.6% | 42.7% | 57.0% | 43.0% |
| 5,253,655 | COOK | 2,026,144 | 878,582 | 1,129,973 | 17,589 | 251,391 D | 43.4% | 55.8% | 43.7% | 56.3% |
| 20,818 | CRAWFORD | 8,571 | 4,951 | 3,555 | 65 | 1,396 R | 57.8% | 41.5% | 58.2% | 41.8% |
| 11,062 | CUMBERLAND | 4,600 | 2,667 | 1,904 | 29 | 763 R | 58.0% | 41.4% | 58.3% | 41.7% |
| 74,624 | DE KALB | 29,190 | 17,182 | 11,811 | 197 | 5,371 R | 58.9% | 40.5% | 59.3% | 40.7% |
| 18,108 | DE WITT | 6,645 | 3,942 | 2,660 | 43 | 1,282 R | 59.3% | 40.0% | 59.7% | 40.3% |
| 19,774 | DOUGLAS | 7,598 | 4,378 | 3,184 | 36 | 1,194 R | 57.6% | 41.9% | 57.9% | 42.1% |
| 658,835 | DU PAGE | 314,054 | 217,907 | 94,285 | 1,862 | 123,622 R | 69.4% | 30.0% | 69.8% | 30.2% |
| 21,725 | EDGAR | 9,459 | 5,538 | 3,880 | 41 | 1,658 R | 58.5% | 41.0% | 58.8% | 41.2% |
| 7,961 | EDWARDS | 3,450 | 2,212 | 1,218 | 20 | 994 R | 64.1% | 35.3% | 64.5% | 35.5% |
| 30,944 | EFFINGHAM | 13,066 | 8,431 | 4,553 | 82 | 3,878 R | 64.5% | 34.8% | 64.9% | 35.1% |
| 22,167 | FAYETTE | 10,118 | 5,452 | 4,632 | 34 | 820 R | 53.9% | 45.8% | 54.1% | 45.9% |
| 15,265 | FORD | 6,145 | 4,059 | 2,026 | 60 | 2,033 R | 66.1% | 33.0% | 66.7% | 33.3% |
| 43,201 | FRANKLIN | 18,783 | 7,677 | 11,023 | 83 | 3,346 D | 40.9% | 58.7% | 41.1% | 58.9% |
| 43,687 | FULTON | 16,108 | 6,999 | 9,046 | 63 | 2,047 D | 43.5% | 56.2% | 43.6% | 56.4% |
| 7,590 | GALLATIN | 4,063 | 1,580 | 2,455 | 28 | 875 D | 38.9% | 60.4% | 39.2% | 60.8% |
| 16,661 | GREENE | 6,203 | 3,136 | 3,020 | 47 | 116 R | 50.6% | 48.7% | 50.9% | 49.1% |
| 30,582 | GRUNDY | 14,361 | 8,743 | 5,525 | 93 | 3,218 R | 60.9% | 38.5% | 61.3% | 38.7% |
| 9,172 | HAMILTON | 5,256 | 2,622 | 2,618 | 16 | 4 R | 49.9% | 49.8% | 50.0% | 50.0% |
| 23,877 | HANCOCK | 9,378 | 4,568 | 4,740 | 70 | 172 D | 48.7% | 50.5% | 49.1% | 50.9% |
| 5,383 | HARDIN | 2,824 | 1,504 | 1,308 | 12 | 196 R | 53.3% | 46.3% | 53.5% | 46.5% |
| 9,114 | HENDERSON | 3,821 | 1,726 | 2,085 | 10 | 359 D | 45.2% | 54.6% | 45.3% | 54.7% |
| 57,968 | HENRY | 23,048 | 11,358 | 11,594 | 96 | 236 D | 49.3% | 50.3% | 49.5% | 50.5% |
| 32,976 | IROQUOIS | 13,886 | 9,596 | 4,221 | 69 | 5,375 R | 69.1% | 30.4% | 69.5% | 30.5% |
| 61,522 | JACKSON | 21,185 | 9,687 | 11,334 | 164 | 1,647 D | 45.7% | 53.5% | 46.1% | 53.9% |
| 11,318 | JASPER | 5,189 | 3,024 | 2,135 | 30 | 889 R | 58.3% | 41.1% | 58.6% | 41.4% |
| 36,552 | JEFFERSON | 15,426 | 7,624 | 7,729 | 73 | 105 D | 49.4% | 50.1% | 49.7% | 50.3% |
| 20,538 | JERSEY | 8,752 | 4,343 | 4,376 | 33 | 33 D | 49.6% | 50.0% | 49.8% | 50.2% |
| 23,520 | JO DAVIESS | 9,137 | 4,923 | 4,141 | 73 | 782 R | 53.9% | 45.3% | 54.3% | 45.7% |
| 9,624 | JOHNSON | 4,692 | 2,797 | 1,872 | 23 | 925 R | 59.6% | 39.9% | 59.9% | 40.1% |
| 278,405 | KANE | 103,412 | 66,283 | 36,366 | 763 | 29,917 R | 64.1% | 35.2% | 64.6% | 35.4% |
| 102,926 | KANKAKEE | 35,755 | 20,316 | 15,147 | 292 | 5,169 R | 56.8% | 42.4% | 57.3% | 42.7% |
| 37,202 | KENDALL | 15,084 | 10,653 | 4,347 | 84 | 6,306 R | 70.6% | 28.8% | 71.0% | 29.0% |
| 61,607 | KNOX | 23,700 | 10,842 | 12,752 | 106 | 1,910 D | 45.7% | 53.8% | 46.0% | 54.0% |
| 440,372 | LAKE | 179,633 | 114,115 | 64,327 | 1,191 | 49,788 R | 63.5% | 35.8% | 64.0% | 36.0% |
| 112,033 | LA SALLE | 44,650 | 22,166 | 22,271 | 213 | 105 D | 49.6% | 49.9% | 49.9% | 50.1% |
| 17,807 | LAWRENCE | 6,823 | 3,655 | 3,140 | 28 | 515 R | 53.6% | 46.0% | 53.8% | 46.2% |
| 36,328 | LEE | 13,596 | 8,903 | 4,608 | 85 | 4,295 R | 65.5% | 33.9% | 65.9% | 34.1% |
| 41,381 | LIVINGSTON | 15,405 | 10,324 | 5,009 | 72 | 5,315 R | 67.0% | 32.5% | 67.3% | 32.7% |
| 31,802 | LOGAN | 13,286 | 8,490 | 4,727 | 69 | 3,763 R | 63.9% | 35.6% | 64.2% | 35.8% |
| 37,467 | MCDONOUGH | 12,493 | 7,173 | 5,247 | 73 | 1,926 R | 57.4% | 42.0% | 57.8% | 42.2% |
| 147,897 | MCHENRY | 65,499 | 46,135 | 18,919 | 445 | 27,216 R | 70.4% | 28.9% | 70.9% | 29.1% |
| 119,149 | MCLEAN | 49,511 | 30,572 | 18,659 | 280 | 11,913 R | 61.7% | 37.7% | 62.1% | 37.9% |
| 131,375 | MACON | 49,489 | 23,862 | 25,364 | 263 | 1,502 D | 48.2% | 51.3% | 48.5% | 51.5% |
| 49,384 | MACOUPIN | 21,669 | 9,362 | 12,195 | 112 | 2,833 D | 43.2% | 56.3% | 43.4% | 56.6% |
| 247,691 | MADISON | 99,695 | 44,907 | 54,175 | 613 | 9,268 D | 45.0% | 54.3% | 45.3% | 54.7% |

# ILLINOIS

## PRESIDENT 1988

| 1980 Census Population | County | Total Vote | Republican | Democratic | Other | Rep.-Dem. Plurality | Percentage Total Vote Rep. | Dem. | Major Vote Rep. | Dem. |
|---|---|---|---|---|---|---|---|---|---|---|
| 43,523 | MARION | 17,373 | 8,695 | 8,592 | 86 | 103 R | 50.0% | 49.5% | 50.3% | 49.7% |
| 14,479 | MARSHALL | 6,367 | 3,588 | 2,742 | 37 | 846 R | 56.4% | 43.1% | 56.7% | 43.3% |
| 19,492 | MASON | 6,855 | 3,424 | 3,406 | 25 | 18 R | 49.9% | 49.7% | 50.1% | 49.9% |
| 14,990 | MASSAC | 6,763 | 3,507 | 3,227 | 29 | 280 R | 51.9% | 47.7% | 52.1% | 47.9% |
| 11,700 | MENARD | 5,705 | 3,560 | 2,103 | 42 | 1,457 R | 62.4% | 36.9% | 62.9% | 37.1% |
| 19,286 | MERCER | 7,929 | 3,683 | 4,204 | 42 | 521 D | 46.4% | 53.0% | 46.7% | 53.3% |
| 20,117 | MONROE | 10,851 | 6,275 | 4,529 | 47 | 1,746 R | 57.8% | 41.7% | 58.1% | 41.9% |
| 31,686 | MONTGOMERY | 13,759 | 6,388 | 7,293 | 78 | 905 D | 46.4% | 53.0% | 46.7% | 53.3% |
| 37,502 | MORGAN | 14,886 | 8,808 | 6,032 | 46 | 2,776 R | 59.2% | 40.5% | 59.4% | 40.6% |
| 14,546 | MOULTRIE | 6,212 | 3,167 | 3,013 | 32 | 154 R | 51.0% | 48.5% | 51.2% | 48.8% |
| 46,338 | OGLE | 17,394 | 11,644 | 5,641 | 109 | 6,003 R | 66.9% | 32.4% | 67.4% | 32.6% |
| 200,466 | PEORIA | 73,230 | 37,605 | 35,253 | 372 | 2,352 R | 51.4% | 48.1% | 51.6% | 48.4% |
| 21,714 | PERRY | 9,781 | 4,576 | 5,167 | 38 | 591 D | 46.8% | 52.8% | 47.0% | 53.0% |
| 16,581 | PIATT | 7,277 | 4,137 | 3,099 | 41 | 1,038 R | 56.9% | 42.6% | 57.2% | 42.8% |
| 18,896 | PIKE | 8,599 | 3,965 | 4,614 | 20 | 649 D | 46.1% | 53.7% | 46.2% | 53.8% |
| 4,404 | POPE | 2,208 | 1,202 | 996 | 10 | 206 R | 54.4% | 45.1% | 54.7% | 45.3% |
| 8,840 | PULASKI | 3,478 | 1,666 | 1,793 | 19 | 127 D | 47.9% | 51.6% | 48.2% | 51.8% |
| 6,085 | PUTNAM | 3,139 | 1,516 | 1,601 | 22 | 85 D | 48.3% | 51.0% | 48.6% | 51.4% |
| 35,652 | RANDOLPH | 15,318 | 7,396 | 7,844 | 78 | 448 D | 48.3% | 51.2% | 48.5% | 51.5% |
| 17,587 | RICHLAND | 7,153 | 4,264 | 2,863 | 26 | 1,401 R | 59.6% | 40.0% | 59.8% | 40.2% |
| 165,968 | ROCK ISLAND | 67,901 | 27,412 | 40,174 | 315 | 12,762 D | 40.4% | 59.2% | 40.6% | 59.4% |
| 267,531 | ST. CLAIR | 97,313 | 41,439 | 55,465 | 409 | 14,026 D | 42.6% | 57.0% | 42.8% | 57.2% |
| 28,448 | SALINE | 12,521 | 5,798 | 6,676 | 47 | 878 D | 46.3% | 53.3% | 46.5% | 53.5% |
| 176,089 | SANGAMON | 88,403 | 50,175 | 37,729 | 499 | 12,446 R | 56.8% | 42.7% | 57.1% | 42.9% |
| 8,365 | SCHUYLER | 4,066 | 2,178 | 1,866 | 22 | 312 R | 53.6% | 45.9% | 53.9% | 46.1% |
| 6,142 | SCOTT | 2,790 | 1,535 | 1,243 | 12 | 292 R | 55.0% | 44.6% | 55.3% | 44.7% |
| 23,923 | SHELBY | 10,078 | 5,370 | 4,650 | 58 | 720 R | 53.3% | 46.1% | 53.6% | 46.4% |
| 7,389 | STARK | 3,153 | 1,841 | 1,274 | 38 | 567 R | 58.4% | 40.4% | 59.1% | 40.9% |
| 49,536 | STEPHENSON | 18,945 | 11,342 | 7,460 | 143 | 3,882 R | 59.9% | 39.4% | 60.3% | 39.7% |
| 132,078 | TAZEWELL | 53,727 | 28,861 | 24,603 | 263 | 4,258 R | 53.7% | 45.8% | 54.0% | 46.0% |
| 17,765 | UNION | 8,479 | 4,244 | 4,197 | 38 | 47 R | 50.1% | 49.5% | 50.3% | 49.7% |
| 95,222 | VERMILION | 35,067 | 16,943 | 17,918 | 206 | 975 D | 48.3% | 51.1% | 48.6% | 51.4% |
| 13,713 | WABASH | 5,726 | 3,453 | 2,241 | 32 | 1,212 R | 60.3% | 39.1% | 60.6% | 39.4% |
| 21,943 | WARREN | 8,254 | 4,584 | 3,617 | 53 | 967 R | 55.5% | 43.8% | 55.9% | 44.1% |
| 15,472 | WASHINGTON | 6,874 | 4,127 | 2,689 | 58 | 1,438 R | 60.0% | 39.1% | 60.5% | 39.5% |
| 18,059 | WAYNE | 8,660 | 5,481 | 3,135 | 44 | 2,346 R | 63.3% | 36.2% | 63.6% | 36.4% |
| 17,864 | WHITE | 8,531 | 4,354 | 4,144 | 33 | 210 R | 51.0% | 48.6% | 51.2% | 48.8% |
| 65,970 | WHITESIDE | 24,462 | 12,978 | 11,328 | 156 | 1,650 R | 53.1% | 46.3% | 53.4% | 46.6% |
| 324,460 | WILL | 123,731 | 73,129 | 49,816 | 786 | 23,313 R | 59.1% | 40.3% | 59.5% | 40.5% |
| 56,538 | WILLIAMSON | 25,130 | 12,274 | 12,712 | 144 | 438 D | 48.8% | 50.6% | 49.1% | 50.9% |
| 250,884 | WINNEBAGO | 101,550 | 55,699 | 45,280 | 571 | 10,419 R | 54.8% | 44.6% | 55.2% | 44.8% |
| 33,320 | WOODFORD | 14,155 | 9,474 | 4,604 | 77 | 4,870 R | 66.9% | 32.5% | 67.3% | 32.7% |
| 11,426,518 | TOTAL | 4,559,120 | 2,310,939 | 2,215,940 | 32,241 | 94,999 R | 50.7% | 48.6% | 51.0% | 49.0% |

# ILLINOIS

## PRESIDENT 1984

| 1980 Census Population | County | Total Vote | Republican | Democratic | Other | Rep.-Dem. Plurality | Percentage Total Vote Rep. | Dem. | Major Vote Rep. | Dem. |
|---|---|---|---|---|---|---|---|---|---|---|
| 71,622 | ADAMS | 30,649 | 20,225 | 10,336 | 88 | 9,889 R | 66.0% | 33.7% | 66.2% | 33.8% |
| 12,264 | ALEXANDER | 5,467 | 2,574 | 2,872 | 21 | 298 D | 47.1% | 52.5% | 47.3% | 52.7% |
| 16,224 | BOND | 7,131 | 4,240 | 2,870 | 21 | 1,370 R | 59.5% | 40.2% | 59.6% | 40.4% |
| 28,630 | BOONE | 11,306 | 7,536 | 3,717 | 53 | 3,819 R | 66.7% | 32.9% | 67.0% | 33.0% |
| 5,411 | BROWN | 2,446 | 1,478 | 959 | 9 | 519 R | 60.4% | 39.2% | 60.6% | 39.4% |
| 39,114 | BUREAU | 18,765 | 11,741 | 6,925 | 99 | 4,816 R | 62.6% | 36.9% | 62.9% | 37.1% |
| 5,867 | CALHOUN | 3,107 | 1,648 | 1,443 | 16 | 205 R | 53.0% | 46.4% | 53.3% | 46.7% |
| 18,779 | CARROLL | 7,658 | 5,237 | 2,398 | 23 | 2,839 R | 68.4% | 31.3% | 68.6% | 31.4% |
| 15,084 | CASS | 6,399 | 3,435 | 2,937 | 27 | 498 R | 53.7% | 45.9% | 53.9% | 46.1% |
| 168,392 | CHAMPAIGN | 66,925 | 39,224 | 27,266 | 435 | 11,958 R | 58.6% | 40.7% | 59.0% | 41.0% |
| 36,446 | CHRISTIAN | 16,152 | 8,534 | 7,541 | 77 | 993 R | 52.8% | 46.7% | 53.1% | 46.9% |
| 16,913 | CLARK | 8,382 | 5,318 | 3,032 | 32 | 2,286 R | 63.4% | 36.2% | 63.7% | 36.3% |
| 15,283 | CLAY | 7,104 | 4,562 | 2,524 | 18 | 2,038 R | 64.2% | 35.5% | 64.4% | 35.6% |
| 32,617 | CLINTON | 13,899 | 9,233 | 4,628 | 38 | 4,605 R | 66.4% | 33.3% | 66.6% | 33.4% |
| 52,260 | COLES | 21,295 | 14,044 | 7,156 | 95 | 6,888 R | 65.9% | 33.6% | 66.2% | 33.8% |
| 5,253,655 | COOK | 2,180,735 | 1,055,558 | 1,112,641 | 12,536 | 57,083 D | 48.4% | 51.0% | 48.7% | 51.3% |
| 20,818 | CRAWFORD | 9,424 | 6,261 | 3,130 | 33 | 3,131 R | 66.4% | 33.2% | 66.7% | 33.3% |
| 11,062 | CUMBERLAND | 4,762 | 3,002 | 1,733 | 27 | 1,269 R | 63.0% | 36.4% | 63.4% | 36.6% |
| 74,624 | DE KALB | 31,465 | 20,294 | 10,942 | 229 | 9,352 R | 64.5% | 34.8% | 65.0% | 35.0% |
| 18,108 | DE WITT | 6,915 | 4,534 | 2,352 | 29 | 2,182 R | 65.6% | 34.0% | 65.8% | 34.2% |
| 19,774 | DOUGLAS | 8,604 | 5,691 | 2,886 | 27 | 2,805 R | 66.1% | 33.5% | 66.4% | 33.6% |
| 658,835 | DU PAGE | 300,215 | 227,141 | 71,430 | 1,644 | 155,711 R | 75.7% | 23.8% | 76.1% | 23.9% |
| 21,725 | EDGAR | 10,099 | 6,821 | 3,241 | 37 | 3,580 R | 67.5% | 32.1% | 67.8% | 32.2% |
| 7,961 | EDWARDS | 3,845 | 2,778 | 1,057 | 10 | 1,721 R | 72.2% | 27.5% | 72.4% | 27.6% |
| 30,944 | EFFINGHAM | 13,504 | 9,617 | 3,841 | 46 | 5,776 R | 71.2% | 28.4% | 71.5% | 28.5% |
| 22,167 | FAYETTE | 10,473 | 6,607 | 3,844 | 22 | 2,763 R | 63.1% | 36.7% | 63.2% | 36.8% |
| 15,265 | FORD | 6,663 | 4,871 | 1,763 | 29 | 3,108 R | 73.1% | 26.5% | 73.4% | 26.6% |
| 43,201 | FRANKLIN | 20,377 | 9,656 | 10,667 | 54 | 1,011 D | 47.4% | 52.3% | 47.5% | 52.5% |
| 43,687 | FULTON | 18,377 | 9,147 | 9,131 | 99 | 16 R | 49.8% | 49.7% | 50.0% | 50.0% |
| 7,590 | GALLATIN | 4,112 | 1,939 | 2,164 | 9 | 225 D | 47.2% | 52.6% | 47.3% | 52.7% |
| 16,661 | GREENE | 6,655 | 4,057 | 2,563 | 35 | 1,494 R | 61.0% | 38.5% | 61.3% | 38.7% |
| 30,582 | GRUNDY | 14,325 | 9,595 | 4,671 | 59 | 4,924 R | 67.0% | 32.6% | 67.3% | 32.7% |
| 9,172 | HAMILTON | 5,346 | 3,074 | 2,251 | 21 | 823 R | 57.5% | 42.1% | 57.7% | 42.3% |
| 23,877 | HANCOCK | 10,001 | 6,251 | 3,713 | 37 | 2,538 R | 62.5% | 37.1% | 62.7% | 37.3% |
| 5,383 | HARDIN | 2,899 | 1,689 | 1,205 | 5 | 484 R | 58.3% | 41.6% | 58.4% | 41.6% |
| 9,114 | HENDERSON | 4,278 | 2,289 | 1,969 | 20 | 320 R | 53.5% | 46.0% | 53.8% | 46.2% |
| 57,968 | HENRY | 25,262 | 14,504 | 10,679 | 79 | 3,825 R | 57.4% | 42.3% | 57.6% | 42.4% |
| 32,976 | IROQUOIS | 14,685 | 11,327 | 3,300 | 58 | 8,027 R | 77.1% | 22.5% | 77.4% | 22.6% |
| 61,522 | JACKSON | 25,896 | 13,609 | 12,105 | 182 | 1,504 R | 52.6% | 46.7% | 52.9% | 47.1% |
| 11,318 | JASPER | 5,454 | 3,673 | 1,750 | 31 | 1,923 R | 67.3% | 32.1% | 67.7% | 32.3% |
| 36,552 | JEFFERSON | 16,885 | 9,642 | 7,200 | 43 | 2,442 R | 57.1% | 42.6% | 57.2% | 42.8% |
| 20,538 | JERSEY | 8,934 | 5,146 | 3,762 | 26 | 1,384 R | 57.6% | 42.1% | 57.8% | 42.2% |
| 23,520 | JO DAVIESS | 9,302 | 5,877 | 3,348 | 77 | 2,529 R | 63.2% | 36.0% | 63.7% | 36.3% |
| 9,624 | JOHNSON | 5,083 | 3,424 | 1,647 | 12 | 1,777 R | 67.4% | 32.4% | 67.5% | 32.5% |
| 278,405 | KANE | 105,159 | 72,655 | 31,875 | 629 | 40,780 R | 69.1% | 30.3% | 69.5% | 30.5% |
| 102,926 | KANKAKEE | 39,665 | 23,807 | 15,246 | 612 | 8,561 R | 60.0% | 38.4% | 61.0% | 39.0% |
| 37,202 | KENDALL | 14,730 | 10,872 | 3,789 | 69 | 7,083 R | 73.8% | 25.7% | 74.2% | 25.8% |
| 61,607 | KNOX | 27,122 | 14,974 | 12,027 | 121 | 2,947 R | 55.2% | 44.3% | 55.5% | 44.5% |
| 440,372 | LAKE | 173,224 | 118,401 | 53,947 | 876 | 64,454 R | 68.4% | 31.1% | 68.7% | 31.3% |
| 112,033 | LA SALLE | 48,139 | 27,388 | 20,532 | 219 | 6,856 R | 56.9% | 42.7% | 57.2% | 42.8% |
| 17,807 | LAWRENCE | 7,638 | 4,686 | 2,924 | 28 | 1,762 R | 61.4% | 38.3% | 61.6% | 38.4% |
| 36,328 | LEE | 15,155 | 11,178 | 3,919 | 58 | 7,259 R | 73.8% | 25.9% | 74.0% | 26.0% |
| 41,381 | LIVINGSTON | 16,919 | 12,291 | 4,567 | 61 | 7,724 R | 72.6% | 27.0% | 72.9% | 27.1% |
| 31,802 | LOGAN | 14,046 | 9,932 | 4,052 | 62 | 5,880 R | 70.7% | 28.8% | 71.0% | 29.0% |
| 37,467 | MCDONOUGH | 14,001 | 9,383 | 4,561 | 57 | 4,822 R | 67.0% | 32.6% | 67.3% | 32.7% |
| 147,897 | MCHENRY | 62,042 | 47,282 | 14,420 | 340 | 32,862 R | 76.2% | 23.2% | 76.6% | 23.4% |
| 119,149 | MCLEAN | 48,349 | 32,221 | 15,880 | 248 | 16,341 R | 66.6% | 32.8% | 67.0% | 33.0% |
| 131,375 | MACON | 56,112 | 30,457 | 25,463 | 192 | 4,994 R | 54.3% | 45.4% | 54.5% | 45.5% |
| 49,384 | MACOUPIN | 22,953 | 12,282 | 10,602 | 69 | 1,680 R | 53.5% | 46.2% | 53.7% | 46.3% |
| 247,691 | MADISON | 105,713 | 57,021 | 48,352 | 340 | 8,669 R | 53.9% | 45.7% | 54.1% | 45.9% |

# ILLINOIS

## PRESIDENT 1984

| 1980 Census Population | County | Total Vote | Republican | Democratic | Other | Rep.-Dem. Plurality | | Percentage | | | |
|---|---|---|---|---|---|---|---|---|---|---|---|
| | | | | | | | | Total Vote | | Major Vote | |
| | | | | | | | | Rep. | Dem. | Rep. | Dem. |
| 43,523 | MARION | 18,945 | 11,300 | 7,599 | 46 | 3,701 | R | 59.6% | 40.1% | 59.8% | 40.2% |
| 14,479 | MARSHALL | 6,493 | 4,060 | 2,386 | 47 | 1,674 | R | 62.5% | 36.7% | 63.0% | 37.0% |
| 19,492 | MASON | 7,486 | 4,109 | 3,354 | 23 | 755 | R | 54.9% | 44.8% | 55.1% | 44.9% |
| 14,990 | MASSAC | 7,049 | 3,827 | 3,194 | 28 | 633 | R | 54.3% | 45.3% | 54.5% | 45.5% |
| 11,700 | MENARD | 5,766 | 3,925 | 1,826 | 15 | 2,099 | R | 68.1% | 31.7% | 68.2% | 31.8% |
| 19,286 | MERCER | 8,927 | 4,907 | 3,982 | 38 | 925 | R | 55.0% | 44.6% | 55.2% | 44.8% |
| 20,117 | MONROE | 10,217 | 6,936 | 3,256 | 25 | 3,680 | R | 67.9% | 31.9% | 68.1% | 31.9% |
| 31,686 | MONTGOMERY | 14,605 | 8,191 | 6,360 | 54 | 1,831 | R | 56.1% | 43.5% | 56.3% | 43.7% |
| 37,502 | MORGAN | 16,097 | 10,683 | 5,361 | 53 | 5,322 | R | 66.4% | 33.3% | 66.6% | 33.4% |
| 14,546 | MOULTRIE | 6,072 | 3,593 | 2,458 | 21 | 1,135 | R | 59.2% | 40.5% | 59.4% | 40.6% |
| 46,338 | OGLE | 18,396 | 13,503 | 4,803 | 90 | 8,700 | R | 73.4% | 26.1% | 73.8% | 26.2% |
| 200,466 | PEORIA | 82,899 | 45,607 | 36,830 | 462 | 8,777 | R | 55.0% | 44.4% | 55.3% | 44.7% |
| 21,714 | PERRY | 10,472 | 5,852 | 4,584 | 36 | 1,268 | R | 55.9% | 43.8% | 56.1% | 43.9% |
| 16,581 | PIATT | 7,879 | 5,000 | 2,840 | 39 | 2,160 | R | 63.5% | 36.0% | 63.8% | 36.2% |
| 18,896 | PIKE | 9,285 | 5,295 | 3,965 | 25 | 1,330 | R | 57.0% | 42.7% | 57.2% | 42.8% |
| 4,404 | POPE | 2,492 | 1,545 | 940 | 7 | 605 | R | 62.0% | 37.7% | 62.2% | 37.8% |
| 8,840 | PULASKI | 3,664 | 1,923 | 1,724 | 17 | 199 | R | 52.5% | 47.1% | 52.7% | 47.3% |
| 6,085 | PUTNAM | 3,413 | 1,912 | 1,487 | 14 | 425 | R | 56.0% | 43.6% | 56.3% | 43.7% |
| 35,652 | RANDOLPH | 15,829 | 9,415 | 6,355 | 59 | 3,060 | R | 59.5% | 40.1% | 59.7% | 40.3% |
| 17,587 | RICHLAND | 7,874 | 5,665 | 2,182 | 27 | 3,483 | R | 71.9% | 27.7% | 72.2% | 27.8% |
| 165,968 | ROCK ISLAND | 75,672 | 35,121 | 40,208 | 343 | 5,087 | D | 46.4% | 53.1% | 46.6% | 53.4% |
| 267,531 | ST. CLAIR | 104,148 | 51,046 | 52,294 | 808 | 1,248 | D | 49.0% | 50.2% | 49.4% | 50.6% |
| 28,448 | SALINE | 13,251 | 7,176 | 6,038 | 37 | 1,138 | R | 54.2% | 45.6% | 54.3% | 45.7% |
| 176,089 | SANGAMON | 88,523 | 54,086 | 34,059 | 378 | 20,027 | R | 61.1% | 38.5% | 61.4% | 38.6% |
| 8,365 | SCHUYLER | 4,061 | 2,515 | 1,533 | 13 | 982 | R | 61.9% | 37.7% | 62.1% | 37.9% |
| 6,142 | SCOTT | 2,935 | 1,976 | 943 | 16 | 1,033 | R | 67.3% | 32.1% | 67.7% | 32.3% |
| 23,923 | SHELBY | 10,730 | 6,372 | 4,317 | 41 | 2,055 | R | 59.4% | 40.2% | 59.6% | 40.4% |
| 7,389 | STARK | 3,318 | 2,228 | 1,072 | 18 | 1,156 | R | 67.1% | 32.3% | 67.5% | 32.5% |
| 49,536 | STEPHENSON | 21,131 | 14,237 | 6,723 | 171 | 7,514 | R | 67.4% | 31.8% | 67.9% | 32.1% |
| 132,078 | TAZEWELL | 57,115 | 33,782 | 23,095 | 238 | 10,687 | R | 59.1% | 40.4% | 59.4% | 40.6% |
| 17,765 | UNION | 8,564 | 4,721 | 3,815 | 28 | 906 | R | 55.1% | 44.5% | 55.3% | 44.7% |
| 95,222 | VERMILION | 39,611 | 22,932 | 16,530 | 149 | 6,402 | R | 57.9% | 41.7% | 58.1% | 41.9% |
| 13,713 | WABASH | 5,453 | 3,639 | 1,795 | 19 | 1,844 | R | 66.7% | 32.9% | 67.0% | 33.0% |
| 21,943 | WARREN | 9,193 | 5,846 | 3,318 | 29 | 2,528 | R | 63.6% | 36.1% | 63.8% | 36.2% |
| 15,472 | WASHINGTON | 7,516 | 5,129 | 2,363 | 24 | 2,766 | R | 68.2% | 31.4% | 68.5% | 31.5% |
| 18,059 | WAYNE | 8,951 | 6,298 | 2,621 | 32 | 3,677 | R | 70.4% | 29.3% | 70.6% | 29.4% |
| 17,864 | WHITE | 8,983 | 5,500 | 3,457 | 26 | 2,043 | R | 61.2% | 38.5% | 61.4% | 38.6% |
| 65,970 | WHITESIDE | 28,096 | 16,743 | 11,226 | 127 | 5,517 | R | 59.6% | 40.0% | 59.9% | 40.1% |
| 324,460 | WILL | 124,397 | 78,684 | 45,193 | 520 | 33,491 | R | 63.3% | 36.3% | 63.5% | 36.5% |
| 56,538 | WILLIAMSON | 26,630 | 14,930 | 11,614 | 86 | 3,316 | R | 56.1% | 43.6% | 56.2% | 43.8% |
| 250,884 | WINNEBAGO | 109,451 | 64,203 | 44,629 | 619 | 19,574 | R | 58.7% | 40.8% | 59.0% | 41.0% |
| 33,320 | WOODFORD | 15,272 | 10,758 | 4,425 | 89 | 6,333 | R | 70.4% | 29.0% | 70.9% | 29.1% |
| 11,426,518 | TOTAL | 4,819,088 | 2,707,103 | 2,086,499 | 25,486 | 620,604 | R | 56.2% | 43.3% | 56.5% | 43.5% |

# ILLINOIS

## PRESIDENT 1980

| 1980 Census Population | County | Total Vote | Republican | Democratic | Other | Rep.-Dem. Plurality | Percentage Total Vote Rep. | Dem. | Major Vote Rep. | Dem. |
|---|---|---|---|---|---|---|---|---|---|---|
| 71,622 | ADAMS | 31,917 | 19,842 | 10,606 | 1,469 | 9,236 R | 62.2% | 33.2% | 65.2% | 34.8% |
| 12,264 | ALEXANDER | 5,678 | 2,650 | 2,925 | 103 | 275 D | 46.7% | 51.5% | 47.5% | 52.5% |
| 16,224 | BOND | 7,532 | 4,398 | 2,834 | 300 | 1,564 R | 58.4% | 37.6% | 60.8% | 39.2% |
| 28,630 | BOONE | 11,614 | 6,697 | 3,175 | 1,742 | 3,522 R | 57.7% | 27.3% | 67.8% | 32.2% |
| 5,411 | BROWN | 2,692 | 1,660 | 950 | 82 | 710 R | 61.7% | 35.3% | 63.6% | 36.4% |
| 39,114 | BUREAU | 18,587 | 11,484 | 5,753 | 1,350 | 5,731 R | 61.8% | 31.0% | 66.6% | 33.4% |
| 5,867 | CALHOUN | 2,895 | 1,591 | 1,208 | 96 | 383 R | 55.0% | 41.7% | 56.8% | 43.2% |
| 18,779 | CARROLL | 8,023 | 5,084 | 2,154 | 785 | 2,930 R | 63.4% | 26.8% | 70.2% | 29.8% |
| 15,084 | CASS | 6,770 | 3,965 | 2,543 | 262 | 1,422 R | 58.6% | 37.6% | 60.9% | 39.1% |
| 168,392 | CHAMPAIGN | 65,360 | 33,329 | 21,017 | 11,014 | 12,312 R | 51.0% | 32.2% | 61.3% | 38.7% |
| 36,446 | CHRISTIAN | 16,036 | 8,770 | 6,625 | 641 | 2,145 R | 54.7% | 41.3% | 57.0% | 43.0% |
| 16,913 | CLARK | 8,666 | 5,476 | 2,855 | 335 | 2,621 R | 63.2% | 32.9% | 65.7% | 34.3% |
| 15,283 | CLAY | 7,266 | 4,447 | 2,587 | 232 | 1,860 R | 61.2% | 35.6% | 63.2% | 36.8% |
| 32,617 | CLINTON | 13,593 | 8,500 | 4,470 | 623 | 4,030 R | 62.5% | 32.9% | 65.5% | 34.5% |
| 52,260 | COLES | 20,671 | 11,994 | 6,743 | 1,934 | 5,251 R | 58.0% | 32.6% | 64.0% | 36.0% |
| 5,253,655 | COOK | 2,163,097 | 856,574 | 1,124,584 | 181,939 | 268,010 D | 39.6% | 52.0% | 43.2% | 56.8% |
| 20,818 | CRAWFORD | 9,710 | 5,894 | 3,372 | 444 | 2,522 R | 60.7% | 34.7% | 63.6% | 36.4% |
| 11,062 | CUMBERLAND | 5,289 | 3,159 | 1,892 | 238 | 1,267 R | 59.7% | 35.8% | 62.5% | 37.5% |
| 74,624 | DE KALB | 30,365 | 16,370 | 8,913 | 5,082 | 7,457 R | 53.9% | 29.4% | 64.7% | 35.3% |
| 18,108 | DE WITT | 7,344 | 4,648 | 2,262 | 434 | 2,386 R | 63.3% | 30.8% | 67.3% | 32.7% |
| 19,774 | DOUGLAS | 8,294 | 5,330 | 2,564 | 400 | 2,766 R | 64.3% | 30.9% | 67.5% | 32.5% |
| 658,835 | DU PAGE | 284,749 | 182,308 | 68,991 | 33,450 | 113,317 R | 64.0% | 24.2% | 72.5% | 27.5% |
| 21,725 | EDGAR | 10,515 | 6,639 | 3,394 | 482 | 3,245 R | 63.1% | 32.3% | 66.2% | 33.8% |
| 7,961 | EDWARDS | 3,751 | 2,556 | 1,041 | 154 | 1,515 R | 68.1% | 27.8% | 71.1% | 28.9% |
| 30,944 | EFFINGHAM | 13,808 | 9,104 | 4,229 | 475 | 4,875 R | 65.9% | 30.6% | 68.3% | 31.7% |
| 22,167 | FAYETTE | 10,408 | 6,523 | 3,614 | 271 | 2,909 R | 62.7% | 34.7% | 64.3% | 35.7% |
| 15,265 | FORD | 7,214 | 5,024 | 1,803 | 387 | 3,221 R | 69.6% | 25.0% | 73.6% | 26.4% |
| 43,201 | FRANKLIN | 19,856 | 9,731 | 9,425 | 700 | 306 R | 49.0% | 47.5% | 50.8% | 49.2% |
| 43,687 | FULTON | 18,957 | 10,316 | 7,481 | 1,160 | 2,835 R | 54.4% | 39.5% | 58.0% | 42.0% |
| 7,590 | GALLATIN | 3,466 | 1,700 | 1,678 | 88 | 22 R | 49.0% | 48.4% | 50.3% | 49.7% |
| 16,661 | GREENE | 7,120 | 4,224 | 2,607 | 289 | 1,617 R | 59.3% | 36.6% | 61.8% | 38.2% |
| 30,582 | GRUNDY | 13,204 | 8,397 | 3,970 | 837 | 4,427 R | 63.6% | 30.1% | 67.9% | 32.1% |
| 9,172 | HAMILTON | 5,456 | 3,254 | 1,990 | 212 | 1,264 R | 59.6% | 36.5% | 62.1% | 37.9% |
| 23,877 | HANCOCK | 10,585 | 6,597 | 3,522 | 466 | 3,075 R | 62.3% | 33.3% | 65.2% | 34.8% |
| 5,383 | HARDIN | 3,114 | 1,721 | 1,314 | 79 | 407 R | 55.3% | 42.2% | 56.7% | 43.3% |
| 9,114 | HENDERSON | 4,246 | 2,443 | 1,609 | 194 | 834 R | 57.5% | 37.9% | 60.3% | 39.7% |
| 57,968 | HENRY | 24,206 | 14,506 | 7,977 | 1,723 | 6,529 R | 59.9% | 33.0% | 64.5% | 35.5% |
| 32,976 | IROQUOIS | 15,327 | 11,247 | 3,362 | 718 | 7,885 R | 73.4% | 21.9% | 77.0% | 23.0% |
| 61,522 | JACKSON | 23,829 | 10,505 | 10,291 | 3,033 | 214 R | 44.1% | 43.2% | 50.5% | 49.5% |
| 11,318 | JASPER | 5,612 | 3,548 | 1,846 | 218 | 1,702 R | 63.2% | 32.9% | 65.8% | 34.2% |
| 36,552 | JEFFERSON | 16,340 | 8,972 | 6,761 | 607 | 2,211 R | 54.9% | 41.4% | 57.0% | 43.0% |
| 20,538 | JERSEY | 8,985 | 5,266 | 3,324 | 395 | 1,942 R | 58.6% | 37.0% | 61.3% | 38.7% |
| 23,520 | JO DAVIESS | 8,971 | 5,186 | 2,678 | 1,107 | 2,508 R | 57.8% | 29.9% | 65.9% | 34.1% |
| 9,624 | JOHNSON | 4,888 | 3,201 | 1,586 | 101 | 1,615 R | 65.5% | 32.4% | 66.9% | 33.1% |
| 278,405 | KANE | 103,784 | 64,106 | 29,015 | 10,663 | 35,091 R | 61.8% | 28.0% | 68.8% | 31.2% |
| 102,926 | KANKAKEE | 40,873 | 23,810 | 14,626 | 2,437 | 9,184 R | 58.3% | 35.8% | 61.9% | 38.1% |
| 37,202 | KENDALL | 14,327 | 10,028 | 3,143 | 1,156 | 6,885 R | 70.0% | 21.9% | 76.1% | 23.9% |
| 61,607 | KNOX | 26,198 | 14,907 | 8,749 | 2,542 | 6,158 R | 56.9% | 33.4% | 63.0% | 37.0% |
| 440,372 | LAKE | 164,853 | 96,350 | 48,287 | 20,216 | 48,063 R | 58.4% | 29.3% | 66.6% | 33.4% |
| 112,033 | LA SALLE | 47,835 | 27,323 | 16,818 | 3,694 | 10,505 R | 57.1% | 35.2% | 61.9% | 38.1% |
| 17,807 | LAWRENCE | 7,856 | 4,453 | 3,030 | 373 | 1,423 R | 56.7% | 38.6% | 59.5% | 40.5% |
| 36,328 | LEE | 15,438 | 11,373 | 3,170 | 895 | 8,203 R | 73.7% | 20.5% | 78.2% | 21.8% |
| 41,381 | LIVINGSTON | 16,823 | 11,544 | 4,111 | 1,168 | 7,433 R | 68.6% | 24.4% | 73.7% | 26.3% |
| 31,802 | LOGAN | 14,366 | 9,681 | 3,916 | 769 | 5,765 R | 67.4% | 27.3% | 71.2% | 28.8% |
| 37,467 | MCDONOUGH | 14,589 | 8,995 | 4,093 | 1,501 | 4,902 R | 61.7% | 28.1% | 68.7% | 31.3% |
| 147,897 | MCHENRY | 61,655 | 40,045 | 14,540 | 7,070 | 25,505 R | 65.0% | 23.6% | 73.4% | 26.6% |
| 119,149 | MCLEAN | 49,232 | 30,096 | 13,587 | 5,549 | 16,509 R | 61.1% | 27.6% | 68.9% | 31.1% |
| 131,375 | MACON | 53,956 | 28,298 | 22,325 | 3,333 | 5,973 R | 52.4% | 41.4% | 55.9% | 44.1% |
| 49,384 | MACOUPIN | 22,354 | 12,131 | 9,116 | 1,107 | 3,015 R | 54.3% | 40.8% | 57.1% | 42.9% |
| 247,691 | MADISON | 100,124 | 51,160 | 43,860 | 5,104 | 7,300 R | 51.1% | 43.8% | 53.8% | 46.2% |

# ILLINOIS

## PRESIDENT 1980

| 1980 Census Population | County | Total Vote | Republican | Democratic | Other | Rep.-Dem. Plurality | Percentage | | | |
|---|---|---|---|---|---|---|---|---|---|---|
| | | | | | | | Total Vote | | Major Vote | |
| | | | | | | | Rep. | Dem. | Rep. | Dem. |
| 43,523 | MARION | 18,678 | 10,969 | 6,990 | 719 | 3,979 R | 58.7% | 37.4% | 61.1% | 38.9% |
| 14,479 | MARSHALL | 6,711 | 4,349 | 1,903 | 459 | 2,446 R | 64.8% | 28.4% | 69.6% | 30.4% |
| 19,492 | MASON | 7,693 | 4,644 | 2,680 | 369 | 1,964 R | 60.4% | 34.8% | 63.4% | 36.6% |
| 14,990 | MASSAC | 7,272 | 4,284 | 2,821 | 167 | 1,463 R | 58.9% | 38.8% | 60.3% | 39.7% |
| 11,700 | MENARD | 5,534 | 3,622 | 1,589 | 323 | 2,033 R | 65.4% | 28.7% | 69.5% | 30.5% |
| 19,286 | MERCER | 9,156 | 5,144 | 3,361 | 651 | 1,783 R | 56.2% | 36.7% | 60.5% | 39.5% |
| 20,117 | MONROE | 9,924 | 6,315 | 3,121 | 488 | 3,194 R | 63.6% | 31.4% | 66.9% | 33.1% |
| 31,686 | MONTGOMERY | 15,415 | 8,947 | 5,721 | 747 | 3,226 R | 58.0% | 37.1% | 61.0% | 39.0% |
| 37,502 | MORGAN | 16,997 | 10,406 | 5,483 | 1,108 | 4,923 R | 61.2% | 32.3% | 65.5% | 34.5% |
| 14,546 | MOULTRIE | 6,161 | 3,495 | 2,332 | 334 | 1,163 R | 56.7% | 37.9% | 60.0% | 40.0% |
| 46,338 | OGLE | 18,871 | 12,533 | 4,067 | 2,271 | 8,466 R | 66.4% | 21.6% | 75.5% | 24.5% |
| 200,466 | PEORIA | 83,510 | 47,815 | 28,276 | 7,419 | 19,539 R | 57.3% | 33.9% | 62.8% | 37.2% |
| 21,714 | PERRY | 10,610 | 5,888 | 4,337 | 385 | 1,551 R | 55.5% | 40.9% | 57.6% | 42.4% |
| 16,581 | PIATT | 7,818 | 4,867 | 2,421 | 530 | 2,446 R | 62.3% | 31.0% | 66.8% | 33.2% |
| 18,896 | PIKE | 9,361 | 5,301 | 3,695 | 365 | 1,606 R | 56.6% | 39.5% | 58.9% | 41.1% |
| 4,404 | POPE | 2,455 | 1,501 | 880 | 74 | 621 R | 61.1% | 35.8% | 63.0% | 37.0% |
| 8,840 | PULASKI | 4,099 | 2,083 | 1,955 | 61 | 128 R | 50.8% | 47.7% | 51.6% | 48.4% |
| 6,085 | PUTNAM | 3,414 | 1,959 | 1,158 | 297 | 801 R | 57.4% | 33.9% | 62.8% | 37.2% |
| 35,652 | RANDOLPH | 15,494 | 8,810 | 6,052 | 632 | 2,758 R | 56.9% | 39.1% | 59.3% | 40.7% |
| 17,587 | RICHLAND | 8,126 | 5,241 | 2,463 | 422 | 2,778 R | 64.5% | 30.3% | 68.0% | 32.0% |
| 165,968 | ROCK ISLAND | 71,775 | 34,788 | 30,045 | 6,942 | 4,743 R | 48.5% | 41.9% | 53.7% | 46.3% |
| 267,531 | ST. CLAIR | 100,673 | 46,063 | 50,046 | 4,564 | 3,983 D | 45.8% | 49.7% | 47.9% | 52.1% |
| 28,448 | SALINE | 13,265 | 7,157 | 5,683 | 425 | 1,474 R | 54.0% | 42.8% | 55.7% | 44.3% |
| 176,089 | SANGAMON | 85,200 | 49,372 | 29,354 | 6,474 | 20,018 R | 57.9% | 34.5% | 62.7% | 37.3% |
| 8,365 | SCHUYLER | 4,460 | 2,799 | 1,445 | 216 | 1,354 R | 62.8% | 32.4% | 66.0% | 34.0% |
| 6,142 | SCOTT | 3,042 | 1,990 | 941 | 111 | 1,049 R | 65.4% | 30.9% | 67.9% | 32.1% |
| 23,923 | SHELBY | 10,894 | 6,441 | 3,988 | 465 | 2,453 R | 59.1% | 36.6% | 61.8% | 38.2% |
| 7,389 | STARK | 3,380 | 2,358 | 806 | 216 | 1,552 R | 69.8% | 23.8% | 74.5% | 25.5% |
| 49,536 | STEPHENSON | 20,388 | 10,779 | 6,195 | 3,414 | 4,584 R | 52.9% | 30.4% | 63.5% | 36.5% |
| 132,078 | TAZEWELL | 56,462 | 35,481 | 16,924 | 4,057 | 18,557 R | 62.8% | 30.0% | 67.7% | 32.3% |
| 17,765 | UNION | 8,441 | 4,289 | 3,781 | 371 | 508 R | 50.8% | 44.8% | 53.1% | 46.9% |
| 95,222 | VERMILION | 39,567 | 22,579 | 14,498 | 2,490 | 8,081 R | 57.1% | 36.6% | 60.9% | 39.1% |
| 13,713 | WABASH | 5,837 | 3,571 | 1,975 | 291 | 1,596 R | 61.2% | 33.8% | 64.4% | 35.6% |
| 21,943 | WARREN | 9,071 | 5,667 | 2,756 | 648 | 2,911 R | 62.5% | 30.4% | 67.3% | 32.7% |
| 15,472 | WASHINGTON | 7,762 | 5,354 | 2,158 | 250 | 3,196 R | 69.0% | 27.8% | 71.3% | 28.7% |
| 18,059 | WAYNE | 9,557 | 6,013 | 3,258 | 286 | 2,755 R | 62.9% | 34.1% | 64.9% | 35.1% |
| 17,864 | WHITE | 9,072 | 5,279 | 3,463 | 330 | 1,816 R | 58.2% | 38.2% | 60.4% | 39.6% |
| 65,970 | WHITESIDE | 26,064 | 17,389 | 7,191 | 1,484 | 10,198 R | 66.7% | 27.6% | 70.7% | 29.3% |
| 324,460 | WILL | 120,658 | 69,310 | 41,975 | 9,373 | 27,335 R | 57.4% | 34.8% | 62.3% | 37.7% |
| 56,538 | WILLIAMSON | 26,228 | 14,451 | 10,779 | 998 | 3,672 R | 55.1% | 41.1% | 57.3% | 42.7% |
| 250,884 | WINNEBAGO | 105,089 | 48,825 | 32,384 | 23,880 | 16,441 R | 46.5% | 30.8% | 60.1% | 39.9% |
| 33,320 | WOODFORD | 15,268 | 10,791 | 3,552 | 925 | 7,239 R | 70.7% | 23.3% | 75.2% | 24.8% |
| 11,426,518 | TOTAL | 4,749,721 | 2,358,049 | 1,981,413 | 410,259 | 376,636 R | 49.6% | 41.7% | 54.3% | 45.7% |

# ILLINOIS

## PRESIDENT 1976

| 1970 Census Population | County | Total Vote | Republican | Democratic | Other | Rep.-Dem. Plurality | Percentage | | | |
|---|---|---|---|---|---|---|---|---|---|---|
| | | | | | | | Total Vote | | Major Vote | |
| | | | | | | | Rep. | Dem. | Rep. | Dem. |
| 70,861 | ADAMS | 30,485 | 18,189 | 11,926 | 370 | 6,263 R | 59.7% | 39.1% | 60.4% | 39.6% |
| 12,015 | ALEXANDER | 5,658 | 2,349 | 3,246 | 63 | 897 D | 41.5% | 57.4% | 42.0% | 58.0% |
| 14,012 | BOND | 7,478 | 3,716 | 3,682 | 80 | 34 R | 49.7% | 49.2% | 50.2% | 49.8% |
| 25,440 | BOONE | 11,082 | 6,470 | 4,458 | 154 | 2,012 R | 58.4% | 40.2% | 59.2% | 40.8% |
| 5,586 | BROWN | 3,103 | 1,519 | 1,533 | 51 | 14 D | 49.0% | 49.4% | 49.8% | 50.2% |
| 38,541 | BUREAU | 18,648 | 10,854 | 7,566 | 228 | 3,288 R | 58.2% | 40.6% | 58.9% | 41.1% |
| 5,675 | CALHOUN | 2,943 | 1,364 | 1,549 | 30 | 185 D | 46.3% | 52.6% | 46.8% | 53.2% |
| 19,276 | CARROLL | 8,526 | 5,059 | 3,372 | 95 | 1,687 R | 59.3% | 39.5% | 60.0% | 40.0% |
| 14,219 | CASS | 7,144 | 3,524 | 3,589 | 31 | 65 D | 49.3% | 50.2% | 49.5% | 50.5% |
| 163,281 | CHAMPAIGN | 63,107 | 34,546 | 26,858 | 1,703 | 7,688 R | 54.7% | 42.6% | 56.3% | 43.7% |
| 35,948 | CHRISTIAN | 16,960 | 7,445 | 9,306 | 209 | 1,861 D | 43.9% | 54.9% | 44.4% | 55.6% |
| 16,216 | CLARK | 8,622 | 4,506 | 4,071 | 45 | 435 R | 52.3% | 47.2% | 52.5% | 47.5% |
| 14,735 | CLAY | 7,729 | 3,860 | 3,837 | 32 | 23 R | 49.9% | 49.6% | 50.1% | 49.9% |
| 28,315 | CLINTON | 13,671 | 7,245 | 6,275 | 151 | 970 R | 53.0% | 45.9% | 53.6% | 46.4% |
| 47,815 | COLES | 20,162 | 11,021 | 8,639 | 502 | 2,382 R | 54.7% | 42.8% | 56.1% | 43.9% |
| 5,492,369 | COOK | 2,209,581 | 987,498 | 1,180,814 | 41,269 | 193,316 D | 44.7% | 53.4% | 45.5% | 54.5% |
| 19,824 | CRAWFORD | 10,622 | 5,522 | 5,007 | 93 | 515 R | 52.0% | 47.1% | 52.4% | 47.6% |
| 9,772 | CUMBERLAND | 5,344 | 2,518 | 2,752 | 74 | 234 D | 47.1% | 51.5% | 47.8% | 52.2% |
| 71,654 | DE KALB | 30,728 | 18,193 | 11,535 | 1,000 | 6,658 R | 59.2% | 37.5% | 61.2% | 38.8% |
| 16,975 | DE WITT | 7,666 | 4,137 | 3,477 | 52 | 660 R | 54.0% | 45.4% | 54.3% | 45.7% |
| 18,997 | DOUGLAS | 8,522 | 4,635 | 3,826 | 61 | 809 R | 54.4% | 44.9% | 54.8% | 45.2% |
| 491,882 | DU PAGE | 254,547 | 175,055 | 72,137 | 7,355 | 102,918 R | 68.8% | 28.3% | 70.8% | 29.2% |
| 21,591 | EDGAR | 11,021 | 5,842 | 5,058 | 121 | 784 R | 53.0% | 45.9% | 53.6% | 46.4% |
| 7,090 | EDWARDS | 4,066 | 2,379 | 1,648 | 39 | 731 R | 58.5% | 40.5% | 59.1% | 40.9% |
| 24,608 | EFFINGHAM | 13,391 | 7,194 | 5,952 | 245 | 1,242 R | 53.7% | 44.4% | 54.7% | 45.3% |
| 20,752 | FAYETTE | 10,255 | 5,059 | 5,128 | 68 | 69 D | 49.3% | 50.0% | 49.7% | 50.3% |
| 16,382 | FORD | 7,553 | 4,801 | 2,690 | 62 | 2,111 R | 63.6% | 35.6% | 64.1% | 35.9% |
| 38,329 | FRANKLIN | 20,324 | 7,420 | 12,818 | 86 | 5,398 D | 36.5% | 63.1% | 36.7% | 63.3% |
| 41,890 | FULTON | 19,090 | 9,588 | 9,314 | 188 | 274 R | 50.2% | 48.8% | 50.7% | 49.3% |
| 7,418 | GALLATIN | 4,123 | 1,499 | 2,611 | 13 | 1,112 D | 36.4% | 63.3% | 36.5% | 63.5% |
| 17,014 | GREENE | 7,827 | 3,706 | 4,057 | 64 | 351 D | 47.3% | 51.8% | 47.7% | 52.3% |
| 26,535 | GRUNDY | 13,201 | 7,581 | 5,534 | 86 | 2,047 R | 57.4% | 41.9% | 57.8% | 42.2% |
| 8,665 | HAMILTON | 5,498 | 2,433 | 3,036 | 29 | 603 D | 44.3% | 55.2% | 44.5% | 55.5% |
| 23,645 | HANCOCK | 10,881 | 6,043 | 4,730 | 108 | 1,313 R | 55.5% | 43.5% | 56.1% | 43.9% |
| 4,914 | HARDIN | 3,017 | 1,393 | 1,602 | 22 | 209 D | 46.2% | 53.1% | 46.5% | 53.5% |
| 8,451 | HENDERSON | 4,407 | 2,210 | 2,152 | 45 | 58 R | 50.1% | 48.8% | 50.7% | 49.3% |
| 53,217 | HENRY | 22,934 | 12,849 | 9,822 | 263 | 3,027 R | 56.0% | 42.8% | 56.7% | 43.3% |
| 33,532 | IROQUOIS | 15,481 | 10,129 | 5,167 | 185 | 4,962 R | 65.4% | 33.4% | 66.2% | 33.8% |
| 55,008 | JACKSON | 24,122 | 10,152 | 12,940 | 1,030 | 2,788 D | 42.1% | 53.6% | 44.0% | 56.0% |
| 10,741 | JASPER | 5,650 | 2,794 | 2,772 | 84 | 22 R | 49.5% | 49.1% | 50.2% | 49.8% |
| 31,446 | JEFFERSON | 16,520 | 7,422 | 8,989 | 109 | 1,567 D | 44.9% | 54.4% | 45.2% | 54.8% |
| 18,492 | JERSEY | 8,983 | 4,273 | 4,625 | 85 | 352 D | 47.6% | 51.5% | 48.0% | 52.0% |
| 21,766 | JO DAVIESS | 9,628 | 5,478 | 3,979 | 171 | 1,499 R | 56.9% | 41.3% | 57.9% | 42.1% |
| 7,550 | JOHNSON | 4,628 | 2,417 | 2,182 | 29 | 235 R | 52.2% | 47.1% | 52.6% | 47.4% |
| 251,005 | KANE | 95,374 | 59,275 | 34,057 | 2,042 | 25,218 R | 62.2% | 35.7% | 63.5% | 36.5% |
| 97,250 | KANKAKEE | 42,108 | 23,003 | 18,394 | 711 | 4,609 R | 54.6% | 43.7% | 55.6% | 44.4% |
| 26,374 | KENDALL | 13,349 | 9,011 | 4,202 | 136 | 4,809 R | 67.5% | 31.5% | 68.2% | 31.8% |
| 61,280 | KNOX | 25,967 | 14,123 | 11,525 | 319 | 2,598 R | 54.4% | 44.4% | 55.1% | 44.9% |
| 382,638 | LAKE | 153,204 | 92,231 | 57,741 | 3,232 | 34,490 R | 60.2% | 37.7% | 61.5% | 38.5% |
| 111,409 | LA SALLE | 48,865 | 25,114 | 23,105 | 646 | 2,009 R | 51.4% | 47.3% | 52.1% | 47.9% |
| 17,522 | LAWRENCE | 8,442 | 4,345 | 4,044 | 53 | 301 R | 51.5% | 47.9% | 51.8% | 48.2% |
| 37,947 | LEE | 15,076 | 8,674 | 6,076 | 326 | 2,598 R | 57.5% | 40.3% | 58.8% | 41.2% |
| 40,690 | LIVINGSTON | 15,640 | 10,097 | 5,174 | 369 | 4,923 R | 64.6% | 33.1% | 66.1% | 33.9% |
| 33,538 | LOGAN | 14,386 | 8,623 | 5,686 | 77 | 2,937 R | 59.9% | 39.5% | 60.3% | 39.7% |
| 36,653 | MCDONOUGH | 15,534 | 9,683 | 5,464 | 387 | 4,219 R | 62.3% | 35.2% | 63.9% | 36.1% |
| 111,555 | MCHENRY | 54,989 | 37,115 | 16,799 | 1,075 | 20,316 R | 67.5% | 30.5% | 68.8% | 31.2% |
| 104,389 | MCLEAN | 45,879 | 28,493 | 16,601 | 785 | 11,892 R | 62.1% | 36.2% | 63.2% | 36.8% |
| 125,010 | MACON | 53,599 | 24,893 | 28,243 | 463 | 3,350 D | 46.4% | 52.7% | 46.8% | 53.2% |
| 44,557 | MACOUPIN | 22,486 | 10,242 | 11,910 | 334 | 1,668 D | 45.5% | 53.0% | 46.2% | 53.8% |
| 250,934 | MADISON | 101,998 | 44,183 | 56,457 | 1,358 | 12,274 D | 43.3% | 55.4% | 43.9% | 56.1% |

# ILLINOIS

## PRESIDENT 1976

| 1970 Census Population | County | Total Vote | Republican | Democratic | Other | Rep.-Dem. Plurality | Percentage | | | |
|---|---|---|---|---|---|---|---|---|---|---|
| | | | | | | | Total Vote | | Major Vote | |
| | | | | | | | Rep. | Dem. | Rep. | Dem. |
| 38,986 | MARION | 18,720 | 8,729 | 9,834 | 157 | 1,105 D | 46.6% | 52.5% | 47.0% | 53.0% |
| 13,302 | MARSHALL | 6,662 | 4,017 | 2,570 | 75 | 1,447 R | 60.3% | 38.6% | 61.0% | 39.0% |
| 16,161 | MASON | 7,849 | 3,847 | 3,947 | 55 | 100 D | 49.0% | 50.3% | 49.4% | 50.6% |
| 13,889 | MASSAC | 6,937 | 3,226 | 3,666 | 45 | 440 D | 46.5% | 52.8% | 46.8% | 53.2% |
| 9,685 | MENARD | 5,479 | 3,137 | 2,301 | 41 | 836 R | 57.3% | 42.0% | 57.7% | 42.3% |
| 17,294 | MERCER | 8,982 | 4,816 | 4,090 | 76 | 726 R | 53.6% | 45.5% | 54.1% | 45.9% |
| 18,831 | MONROE | 9,716 | 5,602 | 3,984 | 130 | 1,618 R | 57.7% | 41.0% | 58.4% | 41.6% |
| 30,260 | MONTGOMERY | 15,848 | 7,379 | 8,322 | 147 | 943 D | 46.6% | 52.5% | 47.0% | 53.0% |
| 36,174 | MORGAN | 16,489 | 8,885 | 7,403 | 201 | 1,482 R | 53.9% | 44.9% | 54.5% | 45.5% |
| 13,263 | MOULTRIE | 6,169 | 2,803 | 3,332 | 34 | 529 D | 45.4% | 54.0% | 45.7% | 54.3% |
| 42,867 | OGLE | 17,797 | 11,073 | 6,463 | 261 | 4,610 R | 62.2% | 36.3% | 63.1% | 36.9% |
| 195,318 | PEORIA | 82,123 | 46,526 | 34,606 | 991 | 11,920 R | 56.7% | 42.1% | 57.3% | 42.7% |
| 19,757 | PERRY | 11,395 | 5,286 | 5,976 | 133 | 690 D | 46.4% | 52.4% | 46.9% | 53.1% |
| 15,509 | PIATT | 8,020 | 4,442 | 3,509 | 69 | 933 R | 55.4% | 43.8% | 55.9% | 44.1% |
| 19,185 | PIKE | 10,110 | 4,975 | 5,006 | 129 | 31 D | 49.2% | 49.5% | 49.8% | 50.2% |
| 3,857 | POPE | 2,275 | 1,187 | 1,070 | 18 | 117 R | 52.2% | 47.0% | 52.6% | 47.4% |
| 8,741 | PULASKI | 4,345 | 1,836 | 2,489 | 20 | 653 D | 42.3% | 57.3% | 42.5% | 57.5% |
| 5,007 | PUTNAM | 2,959 | 1,572 | 1,344 | 43 | 228 R | 53.1% | 45.4% | 53.9% | 46.1% |
| 31,379 | RANDOLPH | 17,038 | 8,190 | 8,693 | 155 | 503 D | 48.1% | 51.0% | 48.5% | 51.5% |
| 16,829 | RICHLAND | 8,057 | 4,434 | 3,485 | 138 | 949 R | 55.0% | 43.3% | 56.0% | 44.0% |
| 166,734 | ROCK ISLAND | 71,261 | 34,007 | 35,994 | 1,260 | 1,987 D | 47.7% | 50.5% | 48.6% | 51.4% |
| 285,176 | ST. CLAIR | 101,065 | 40,333 | 59,177 | 1,555 | 18,844 D | 39.9% | 58.6% | 40.5% | 59.5% |
| 25,721 | SALINE | 13,493 | 5,970 | 7,472 | 51 | 1,502 D | 44.2% | 55.4% | 44.4% | 55.6% |
| 161,335 | SANGAMON | 82,910 | 43,309 | 38,017 | 1,584 | 5,292 R | 52.2% | 45.9% | 53.3% | 46.7% |
| 8,135 | SCHUYLER | 4,669 | 2,635 | 2,014 | 20 | 621 R | 56.4% | 43.1% | 56.7% | 43.3% |
| 6,096 | SCOTT | 3,232 | 1,789 | 1,424 | 19 | 365 R | 55.4% | 44.1% | 55.7% | 44.3% |
| 22,589 | SHELBY | 11,493 | 5,234 | 6,172 | 87 | 938 D | 45.5% | 53.7% | 45.9% | 54.1% |
| 7,510 | STARK | 3,459 | 2,191 | 1,146 | 122 | 1,045 R | 63.3% | 33.1% | 65.7% | 34.3% |
| 48,861 | STEPHENSON | 19,137 | 11,678 | 7,192 | 267 | 4,486 R | 61.0% | 37.6% | 61.9% | 38.1% |
| 118,649 | TAZEWELL | 52,503 | 28,951 | 22,821 | 731 | 6,130 R | 55.1% | 43.5% | 55.9% | 44.1% |
| 16,071 | UNION | 8,578 | 3,531 | 5,003 | 44 | 1,472 D | 41.2% | 58.3% | 41.4% | 58.6% |
| 97,047 | VERMILION | 38,546 | 19,751 | 18,438 | 357 | 1,313 R | 51.2% | 47.8% | 51.7% | 48.3% |
| 12,841 | WABASH | 6,227 | 3,388 | 2,781 | 58 | 607 R | 54.4% | 44.7% | 54.9% | 45.1% |
| 21,595 | WARREN | 9,826 | 5,822 | 3,808 | 196 | 2,014 R | 59.3% | 38.8% | 60.5% | 39.5% |
| 13,780 | WASHINGTON | 7,843 | 4,485 | 3,222 | 136 | 1,263 R | 57.2% | 41.1% | 58.2% | 41.8% |
| 17,004 | WAYNE | 9,581 | 5,211 | 4,303 | 67 | 908 R | 54.4% | 44.9% | 54.8% | 45.2% |
| 17,312 | WHITE | 9,933 | 4,600 | 5,306 | 27 | 706 D | 46.3% | 53.4% | 46.4% | 53.6% |
| 62,877 | WHITESIDE | 25,854 | 14,308 | 11,255 | 291 | 3,053 R | 55.3% | 43.5% | 56.0% | 44.0% |
| 249,498 | WILL | 114,695 | 61,784 | 51,103 | 1,808 | 10,681 R | 53.9% | 44.6% | 54.7% | 45.3% |
| 49,021 | WILLIAMSON | 24,553 | 10,703 | 13,600 | 250 | 2,897 D | 43.6% | 55.4% | 44.0% | 56.0% |
| 246,623 | WINNEBAGO | 97,360 | 52,736 | 42,399 | 2,225 | 10,337 R | 54.2% | 43.5% | 55.4% | 44.6% |
| 28,012 | WOODFORD | 13,902 | 8,899 | 4,819 | 184 | 4,080 R | 64.0% | 34.7% | 64.9% | 35.1% |
| 11,113,976 | TOTAL | 4,718,914 | 2,364,269 | 2,271,295 | 83,350 | 92,974 R | 50.1% | 48.1% | 51.0% | 49.0% |

# ILLINOIS

## PRESIDENT 1972

| 1970 Census Population | County | Total Vote | Republican | Democratic | Other | Rep.-Dem. Plurality | Total Vote Rep. | Total Vote Dem. | Major Vote Rep. | Major Vote Dem. |
|---|---|---|---|---|---|---|---|---|---|---|
| 70,861 | ADAMS | 29,846 | 20,731 | 9,055 | 60 | 11,676 R | 69.5% | 30.3% | 69.6% | 30.4% |
| 12,015 | ALEXANDER | 6,209 | 3,669 | 2,482 | 58 | 1,187 R | 59.1% | 40.0% | 59.6% | 40.4% |
| 14,012 | BOND | 7,183 | 4,475 | 2,704 | 4 | 1,771 R | 62.3% | 37.6% | 62.3% | 37.7% |
| 25,440 | BOONE | 10,165 | 7,003 | 3,131 | 31 | 3,872 R | 68.9% | 30.8% | 69.1% | 30.9% |
| 5,586 | BROWN | 3,022 | 1,780 | 1,203 | 39 | 577 R | 58.9% | 39.8% | 59.7% | 40.3% |
| 38,541 | BUREAU | 18,952 | 12,786 | 6,133 | 33 | 6,653 R | 67.5% | 32.4% | 67.6% | 32.4% |
| 5,675 | CALHOUN | 3,017 | 1,705 | 1,299 | 13 | 406 R | 56.5% | 43.1% | 56.8% | 43.2% |
| 19,276 | CARROLL | 8,631 | 6,041 | 2,571 | 19 | 3,470 R | 70.0% | 29.8% | 70.1% | 29.9% |
| 14,219 | CASS | 7,219 | 4,414 | 2,803 | 2 | 1,611 R | 61.1% | 38.8% | 61.2% | 38.8% |
| 163,281 | CHAMPAIGN | 58,679 | 33,700 | 24,743 | 236 | 8,957 R | 57.4% | 42.2% | 57.7% | 42.3% |
| 35,948 | CHRISTIAN | 17,675 | 10,072 | 7,556 | 47 | 2,516 R | 57.0% | 42.7% | 57.1% | 42.9% |
| 16,216 | CLARK | 8,680 | 5,706 | 2,965 | 9 | 2,741 R | 65.7% | 34.2% | 65.8% | 34.2% |
| 14,735 | CLAY | 8,138 | 5,283 | 2,844 | 11 | 2,439 R | 64.9% | 34.9% | 65.0% | 35.0% |
| 28,315 | CLINTON | 12,712 | 7,931 | 4,756 | 25 | 3,175 R | 62.4% | 37.4% | 62.5% | 37.5% |
| 47,815 | COLES | 21,751 | 13,681 | 7,988 | 82 | 5,693 R | 62.9% | 36.7% | 63.1% | 36.9% |
| 5,492,369 | COOK | 2,311,037 | 1,234,307 | 1,063,268 | 13,462 | 171,039 R | 53.4% | 46.0% | 53.7% | 46.3% |
| 19,824 | CRAWFORD | 10,055 | 6,568 | 3,477 | 10 | 3,091 R | 65.3% | 34.6% | 65.4% | 34.6% |
| 9,772 | CUMBERLAND | 5,358 | 3,257 | 2,083 | 18 | 1,174 R | 60.8% | 38.9% | 61.0% | 39.0% |
| 71,654 | DE KALB | 31,384 | 18,910 | 12,375 | 99 | 6,535 R | 60.3% | 39.4% | 60.4% | 39.6% |
| 16,975 | DE WITT | 7,705 | 5,025 | 2,672 | 8 | 2,353 R | 65.2% | 34.7% | 65.3% | 34.7% |
| 18,997 | DOUGLAS | 8,506 | 5,840 | 2,656 | 10 | 3,184 R | 68.7% | 31.2% | 68.7% | 31.3% |
| 491,882 | DU PAGE | 229,739 | 172,341 | 57,043 | 355 | 115,298 R | 75.0% | 24.8% | 75.1% | 24.9% |
| 21,591 | EDGAR | 11,116 | 7,195 | 3,889 | 32 | 3,306 R | 64.7% | 35.0% | 64.9% | 35.1% |
| 7,090 | EDWARDS | 4,081 | 3,017 | 1,055 | 9 | 1,962 R | 73.9% | 25.9% | 74.1% | 25.9% |
| 24,608 | EFFINGHAM | 13,193 | 8,752 | 4,431 | 10 | 4,321 R | 66.3% | 33.6% | 66.4% | 33.6% |
| 20,752 | FAYETTE | 10,768 | 6,574 | 4,192 | 2 | 2,382 R | 61.1% | 38.9% | 61.1% | 38.9% |
| 16,382 | FORD | 7,591 | 5,656 | 1,934 | 1 | 3,722 R | 74.5% | 25.5% | 74.5% | 25.5% |
| 38,329 | FRANKLIN | 18,729 | 10,121 | 8,545 | 63 | 1,576 R | 54.0% | 45.6% | 54.2% | 45.8% |
| 41,890 | FULTON | 19,949 | 12,328 | 7,529 | 92 | 4,799 R | 61.8% | 37.7% | 62.1% | 37.9% |
| 7,418 | GALLATIN | 4,001 | 2,148 | 1,844 | 9 | 304 R | 53.7% | 46.1% | 53.8% | 46.2% |
| 17,014 | GREENE | 7,521 | 4,673 | 2,824 | 24 | 1,849 R | 62.1% | 37.5% | 62.3% | 37.7% |
| 26,535 | GRUNDY | 12,341 | 8,725 | 3,584 | 32 | 5,141 R | 70.7% | 29.0% | 70.9% | 29.1% |
| 8,665 | HAMILTON | 5,299 | 3,282 | 2,006 | 11 | 1,276 R | 61.9% | 37.9% | 62.1% | 37.9% |
| 23,645 | HANCOCK | 11,129 | 7,519 | 3,592 | 18 | 3,927 R | 67.6% | 32.3% | 67.7% | 32.3% |
| 4,914 | HARDIN | 3,062 | 1,915 | 1,140 | 7 | 775 R | 62.5% | 37.2% | 62.7% | 37.3% |
| 8,451 | HENDERSON | 4,436 | 2,689 | 1,744 | 3 | 945 R | 60.6% | 39.3% | 60.7% | 39.3% |
| 53,217 | HENRY | 23,185 | 14,796 | 8,368 | 21 | 6,428 R | 63.8% | 36.1% | 63.9% | 36.1% |
| 33,532 | IROQUOIS | 15,784 | 11,995 | 3,723 | 66 | 8,272 R | 76.0% | 23.6% | 76.3% | 23.7% |
| 55,008 | JACKSON | 25,594 | 12,393 | 13,146 | 55 | 753 D | 48.4% | 51.4% | 48.5% | 51.5% |
| 10,741 | JASPER | 5,657 | 3,461 | 2,114 | 82 | 1,347 R | 61.2% | 37.4% | 62.1% | 37.9% |
| 31,446 | JEFFERSON | 15,905 | 9,448 | 6,396 | 61 | 3,052 R | 59.4% | 40.2% | 59.6% | 40.4% |
| 18,492 | JERSEY | 8,507 | 5,164 | 3,317 | 26 | 1,847 R | 60.7% | 39.0% | 60.9% | 39.1% |
| 21,766 | JO DAVIESS | 9,097 | 5,763 | 3,318 | 16 | 2,445 R | 63.4% | 36.5% | 63.5% | 36.5% |
| 7,550 | JOHNSON | 4,123 | 2,826 | 1,293 | 4 | 1,533 R | 68.5% | 31.4% | 68.6% | 31.4% |
| 251,005 | KANE | 92,377 | 64,546 | 27,525 | 306 | 37,021 R | 69.9% | 29.8% | 70.1% | 29.9% |
| 97,250 | KANKAKEE | 40,373 | 26,866 | 13,434 | 73 | 13,432 R | 66.5% | 33.3% | 66.7% | 33.3% |
| 26,374 | KENDALL | 11,917 | 9,373 | 2,525 | 19 | 6,848 R | 78.7% | 21.2% | 78.8% | 21.2% |
| 61,280 | KNOX | 26,766 | 17,315 | 9,333 | 118 | 7,982 R | 64.7% | 34.9% | 65.0% | 35.0% |
| 382,638 | LAKE | 139,812 | 92,052 | 47,416 | 344 | 44,636 R | 65.8% | 33.9% | 66.0% | 34.0% |
| 111,409 | LA SALLE | 52,687 | 31,190 | 21,405 | 92 | 9,785 R | 59.2% | 40.6% | 59.3% | 40.7% |
| 17,522 | LAWRENCE | 8,181 | 5,347 | 2,818 | 16 | 2,529 R | 65.4% | 34.4% | 65.5% | 34.5% |
| 37,947 | LEE | 15,489 | 10,636 | 4,788 | 65 | 5,848 R | 68.7% | 30.9% | 69.0% | 31.0% |
| 40,690 | LIVINGSTON | 18,339 | 13,217 | 5,110 | 12 | 8,107 R | 72.1% | 27.9% | 72.1% | 27.9% |
| 33,538 | LOGAN | 14,692 | 10,277 | 4,395 | 20 | 5,882 R | 69.9% | 29.9% | 70.0% | 30.0% |
| 36,653 | MCDONOUGH | 15,738 | 10,573 | 5,143 | 22 | 5,430 R | 67.2% | 32.7% | 67.3% | 32.7% |
| 111,555 | MCHENRY | 48,312 | 36,114 | 12,090 | 108 | 24,024 R | 74.8% | 25.0% | 74.9% | 25.1% |
| 104,389 | MCLEAN | 45,955 | 31,060 | 14,824 | 71 | 16,236 R | 67.6% | 32.3% | 67.7% | 32.3% |
| 125,010 | MACON | 50,029 | 29,596 | 20,296 | 137 | 9,300 R | 59.2% | 40.6% | 59.3% | 40.7% |
| 44,557 | MACOUPIN | 23,407 | 13,583 | 9,662 | 162 | 3,921 R | 58.0% | 41.3% | 58.4% | 41.6% |
| 250,934 | MADISON | 99,116 | 55,385 | 43,289 | 442 | 12,096 R | 55.9% | 43.7% | 56.1% | 43.9% |

# ILLINOIS

## PRESIDENT 1972

| 1970 Census Population | County | Total Vote | Republican | Democratic | Other | Rep.-Dem. Plurality | Percentage | | | |
|---|---|---|---|---|---|---|---|---|---|---|
| | | | | | | | Total Vote | | Major Vote | |
| | | | | | | | Rep. | Dem. | Rep. | Dem. |
| 38,986 | MARION | 17,754 | 10,755 | 6,968 | 31 | 3,787 R | 60.6% | 39.2% | 60.7% | 39.3% |
| 13,302 | MARSHALL | 6,602 | 4,452 | 2,141 | 9 | 2,311 R | 67.4% | 32.4% | 67.5% | 32.5% |
| 16,161 | MASON | 7,810 | 4,897 | 2,901 | 12 | 1,996 R | 62.7% | 37.1% | 62.8% | 37.2% |
| 13,889 | MASSAC | 6,162 | 4,313 | 1,831 | 18 | 2,482 R | 70.0% | 29.7% | 70.2% | 29.8% |
| 9,685 | MENARD | 5,263 | 3,657 | 1,587 | 19 | 2,070 R | 69.5% | 30.2% | 69.7% | 30.3% |
| 17,294 | MERCER | 8,940 | 5,452 | 3,477 | 11 | 1,975 R | 61.0% | 38.9% | 61.1% | 38.9% |
| 18,831 | MONROE | 9,466 | 6,479 | 2,958 | 29 | 3,521 R | 68.4% | 31.2% | 68.7% | 31.3% |
| 30,260 | MONTGOMERY | 15,913 | 9,025 | 6,858 | 30 | 2,167 R | 56.7% | 43.1% | 56.8% | 43.2% |
| 36,174 | MORGAN | 16,789 | 11,103 | 5,674 | 12 | 5,429 R | 66.1% | 33.8% | 66.2% | 33.8% |
| 13,263 | MOULTRIE | 5,507 | 3,143 | 2,350 | 14 | 793 R | 57.1% | 42.7% | 57.2% | 42.8% |
| 42,867 | OGLE | 18,290 | 13,512 | 4,743 | 35 | 8,769 R | 73.9% | 25.9% | 74.0% | 26.0% |
| 195,318 | PEORIA | 78,032 | 50,324 | 27,264 | 444 | 23,060 R | 64.5% | 34.9% | 64.9% | 35.1% |
| 19,757 | PERRY | 11,064 | 6,968 | 4,084 | 12 | 2,884 R | 63.0% | 36.9% | 63.0% | 37.0% |
| 15,509 | PIATT | 7,468 | 5,057 | 2,394 | 17 | 2,663 R | 67.7% | 32.1% | 67.9% | 32.1% |
| 19,185 | PIKE | 9,863 | 5,940 | 3,883 | 40 | 2,057 R | 60.2% | 39.4% | 60.5% | 39.5% |
| 3,857 | POPE | 2,218 | 1,440 | 773 | 5 | 667 R | 64.9% | 34.9% | 65.1% | 34.9% |
| 8,741 | PULASKI | 4,193 | 2,485 | 1,683 | 25 | 802 R | 59.3% | 40.1% | 59.6% | 40.4% |
| 5,007 | PUTNAM | 2,787 | 1,665 | 1,112 | 10 | 553 R | 59.7% | 39.9% | 60.0% | 40.0% |
| 31,379 | RANDOLPH | 16,215 | 9,761 | 6,440 | 14 | 3,321 R | 60.2% | 39.7% | 60.2% | 39.8% |
| 16,829 | RICHLAND | 8,125 | 5,558 | 2,553 | 14 | 3,005 R | 68.4% | 31.4% | 68.5% | 31.5% |
| 166,734 | ROCK ISLAND | 70,330 | 37,548 | 32,529 | 253 | 5,019 R | 53.4% | 46.3% | 53.6% | 46.4% |
| 285,176 | ST. CLAIR | 98,097 | 50,519 | 46,636 | 942 | 3,883 R | 51.5% | 47.5% | 52.0% | 48.0% |
| 25,721 | SALINE | 12,918 | 7,660 | 5,226 | 32 | 2,434 R | 59.3% | 40.5% | 59.4% | 40.6% |
| 161,335 | SANGAMON | 77,075 | 50,458 | 25,720 | 897 | 24,738 R | 65.5% | 33.4% | 66.2% | 33.8% |
| 8,135 | SCHUYLER | 4,534 | 2,994 | 1,534 | 6 | 1,460 R | 66.0% | 33.8% | 66.1% | 33.9% |
| 6,096 | SCOTT | 3,376 | 2,228 | 1,145 | 3 | 1,083 R | 66.0% | 33.9% | 66.1% | 33.9% |
| 22,589 | SHELBY | 11,626 | 7,217 | 4,389 | 20 | 2,828 R | 62.1% | 37.8% | 62.2% | 37.8% |
| 7,510 | STARK | 3,540 | 2,529 | 993 | 18 | 1,536 R | 71.4% | 28.1% | 71.8% | 28.2% |
| 48,861 | STEPHENSON | 20,019 | 13,584 | 6,404 | 31 | 7,180 R | 67.9% | 32.0% | 68.0% | 32.0% |
| 118,649 | TAZEWELL | 47,613 | 31,937 | 15,576 | 100 | 16,361 R | 67.1% | 32.7% | 67.2% | 32.8% |
| 16,071 | UNION | 8,480 | 5,034 | 3,428 | 18 | 1,606 R | 59.4% | 40.4% | 59.5% | 40.5% |
| 97,047 | VERMILION | 39,425 | 24,863 | 14,413 | 149 | 10,450 R | 63.1% | 36.6% | 63.3% | 36.7% |
| 12,841 | WABASH | 6,306 | 4,310 | 1,985 | 11 | 2,325 R | 68.3% | 31.5% | 68.5% | 31.5% |
| 21,595 | WARREN | 10,008 | 7,021 | 2,969 | 18 | 4,052 R | 70.2% | 29.7% | 70.3% | 29.7% |
| 13,780 | WASHINGTON | 7,522 | 5,179 | 2,327 | 16 | 2,852 R | 68.9% | 30.9% | 69.0% | 31.0% |
| 17,004 | WAYNE | 9,175 | 6,400 | 2,763 | 12 | 3,637 R | 69.8% | 30.1% | 69.8% | 30.2% |
| 17,312 | WHITE | 9,746 | 6,052 | 3,678 | 16 | 2,374 R | 62.1% | 37.7% | 62.2% | 37.8% |
| 62,877 | WHITESIDE | 25,301 | 17,305 | 7,909 | 87 | 9,396 R | 68.4% | 31.3% | 68.6% | 31.4% |
| 249,498 | WILL | 99,218 | 65,155 | 33,633 | 430 | 31,522 R | 65.7% | 33.9% | 66.0% | 34.0% |
| 49,021 | WILLIAMSON | 23,329 | 14,101 | 9,202 | 26 | 4,899 R | 60.4% | 39.4% | 60.5% | 39.5% |
| 246,623 | WINNEBAGO | 94,013 | 57,682 | 35,937 | 394 | 21,745 R | 61.4% | 38.2% | 61.6% | 38.4% |
| 28,012 | WOODFORD | 13,203 | 9,622 | 3,558 | 23 | 6,064 R | 72.9% | 26.9% | 73.0% | 27.0% |
| 11,113,976 | TOTAL | 4,723,236 | 2,788,179 | 1,913,472 | 21,585 | 874,707 R | 59.0% | 40.5% | 59.3% | 40.7% |

# ILLINOIS

## PRESIDENT 1968

| 1960 Census Population | County | Total Vote | Republican | Democratic | AIP | Other | Plurality | Percentage Total Vote Rep. | Dem. | AIP |
|---|---|---|---|---|---|---|---|---|---|---|
| 68,467 | ADAMS | 32,108 | 17,444 | 11,521 | 3,115 | 28 | 5,923 R | 54.3% | 35.9% | 9.7% |
| 16,061 | ALEXANDER | 6,934 | 2,540 | 2,929 | 1,443 | 22 | 389 D | 36.6% | 42.2% | 20.8% |
| 14,060 | BOND | 6,953 | 3,674 | 2,516 | 758 | 5 | 1,158 R | 52.8% | 36.2% | 10.9% |
| 20,326 | BOONE | 9,533 | 5,936 | 2,801 | 783 | 13 | 3,135 R | 62.3% | 29.4% | 8.2% |
| 6,210 | BROWN | 3,163 | 1,629 | 1,265 | 247 | 22 | 364 R | 51.5% | 40.0% | 7.8% |
| 37,594 | BUREAU | 18,703 | 11,216 | 6,304 | 1,171 | 12 | 4,912 R | 60.0% | 33.7% | 6.3% |
| 5,933 | CALHOUN | 3,139 | 1,542 | 1,329 | 266 | 2 | 213 R | 49.1% | 42.3% | 8.5% |
| 19,507 | CARROLL | 8,282 | 5,275 | 2,558 | 440 | 9 | 2,717 R | 63.7% | 30.9% | 5.3% |
| 14,539 | CASS | 7,139 | 3,411 | 3,302 | 424 | 2 | 109 R | 47.8% | 46.3% | 5.9% |
| 132,436 | CHAMPAIGN | 48,648 | 26,027 | 18,425 | 3,857 | 339 | 7,602 R | 53.5% | 37.9% | 7.9% |
| 37,207 | CHRISTIAN | 17,694 | 7,486 | 8,465 | 1,730 | 13 | 979 D | 42.3% | 47.8% | 9.8% |
| 16,546 | CLARK | 8,575 | 4,809 | 2,813 | 949 | 4 | 1,996 R | 56.1% | 32.8% | 11.1% |
| 15,815 | CLAY | 7,986 | 4,429 | 2,878 | 672 | 7 | 1,551 R | 55.5% | 36.0% | 8.4% |
| 24,029 | CLINTON | 12,199 | 6,561 | 4,453 | 1,180 | 5 | 2,108 R | 53.8% | 36.5% | 9.7% |
| 42,860 | COLES | 19,766 | 10,449 | 7,337 | 1,973 | 7 | 3,112 R | 52.9% | 37.1% | 10.0% |
| 5,129,725 | COOK | 2,336,538 | 960,493 | 1,181,316 | 186,921 | 7,808 | 220,823 D | 41.1% | 50.6% | 8.0% |
| 20,751 | CRAWFORD | 10,098 | 5,870 | 3,383 | 840 | 5 | 2,487 R | 58.1% | 33.5% | 8.3% |
| 9,936 | CUMBERLAND | 5,028 | 2,671 | 1,828 | 512 | 17 | 843 R | 53.1% | 36.4% | 10.2% |
| 51,714 | DE KALB | 22,999 | 14,535 | 6,974 | 1,238 | 252 | 7,561 R | 63.2% | 30.3% | 5.4% |
| 17,253 | DE WITT | 7,834 | 4,247 | 2,823 | 759 | 5 | 1,424 R | 54.2% | 36.0% | 9.7% |
| 19,243 | DOUGLAS | 8,537 | 5,058 | 2,824 | 651 | 4 | 2,234 R | 59.2% | 33.1% | 7.6% |
| 313,459 | DU PAGE | 187,496 | 124,893 | 48,492 | 13,814 | 297 | 76,401 R | 66.6% | 25.9% | 7.4% |
| 22,550 | EDGAR | 11,151 | 6,281 | 3,565 | 1,292 | 13 | 2,716 R | 56.3% | 32.0% | 11.6% |
| 7,940 | EDWARDS | 4,135 | 2,633 | 1,095 | 403 | 4 | 1,538 R | 63.7% | 26.5% | 9.7% |
| 23,107 | EFFINGHAM | 11,972 | 6,698 | 4,496 | 777 | 1 | 2,202 R | 55.9% | 37.6% | 6.5% |
| 21,946 | FAYETTE | 10,403 | 5,449 | 4,011 | 939 | 4 | 1,438 R | 52.4% | 38.6% | 9.0% |
| 16,606 | FORD | 8,004 | 5,233 | 2,216 | 550 | 5 | 3,017 R | 65.4% | 27.7% | 6.9% |
| 39,281 | FRANKLIN | 21,074 | 9,036 | 10,095 | 1,930 | 13 | 1,059 D | 42.9% | 47.9% | 9.2% |
| 41,954 | FULTON | 20,509 | 9,582 | 9,622 | 1,234 | 71 | 40 D | 46.7% | 46.9% | 6.0% |
| 7,638 | GALLATIN | 4,190 | 1,802 | 1,980 | 404 | 4 | 178 D | 43.0% | 47.3% | 9.6% |
| 17,460 | GREENE | 7,708 | 3,944 | 3,094 | 660 | 10 | 850 R | 51.2% | 40.1% | 8.6% |
| 22,350 | GRUNDY | 11,105 | 6,607 | 3,407 | 1,085 | 6 | 3,200 R | 59.5% | 30.7% | 9.8% |
| 10,010 | HAMILTON | 5,513 | 2,912 | 1,951 | 643 | 7 | 961 R | 52.8% | 35.4% | 11.7% |
| 24,574 | HANCOCK | 11,397 | 6,866 | 3,720 | 806 | 5 | 3,146 R | 60.2% | 32.6% | 7.1% |
| 5,879 | HARDIN | 2,883 | 1,492 | 1,199 | 187 | 5 | 293 R | 51.8% | 41.6% | 6.5% |
| 8,237 | HENDERSON | 4,148 | 2,224 | 1,635 | 288 | 1 | 589 R | 53.6% | 39.4% | 6.9% |
| 49,317 | HENRY | 22,731 | 12,524 | 8,455 | 1,725 | 27 | 4,069 R | 55.1% | 37.2% | 7.6% |
| 33,562 | IROQUOIS | 16,033 | 10,885 | 3,897 | 1,225 | 26 | 6,988 R | 67.9% | 24.3% | 7.6% |
| 42,151 | JACKSON | 19,657 | 9,134 | 8,856 | 1,645 | 22 | 278 R | 46.5% | 45.1% | 8.4% |
| 11,346 | JASPER | 5,686 | 2,944 | 2,012 | 728 | 2 | 932 R | 51.8% | 35.4% | 12.8% |
| 32,315 | JEFFERSON | 15,467 | 7,367 | 6,476 | 1,612 | 12 | 891 R | 47.6% | 41.9% | 10.4% |
| 17,023 | JERSEY | 8,130 | 3,806 | 3,350 | 971 | 3 | 456 R | 46.8% | 41.2% | 11.9% |
| 21,821 | JO DAVIESS | 9,408 | 5,563 | 3,228 | 607 | 10 | 2,335 R | 59.1% | 34.3% | 6.5% |
| 6,928 | JOHNSON | 3,975 | 2,406 | 1,143 | 421 | 5 | 1,263 R | 60.5% | 28.8% | 10.6% |
| 208,246 | KANE | 87,420 | 54,144 | 26,609 | 6,340 | 327 | 27,535 R | 61.9% | 30.4% | 7.3% |
| 92,063 | KANKAKEE | 38,250 | 20,025 | 14,460 | 3,735 | 30 | 5,565 R | 52.4% | 37.8% | 9.8% |
| 17,540 | KENDALL | 10,198 | 7,184 | 2,228 | 780 | 6 | 4,956 R | 70.4% | 21.8% | 7.6% |
| 61,280 | KNOX | 26,396 | 14,216 | 9,707 | 2,394 | 79 | 4,509 R | 53.9% | 36.8% | 9.1% |
| 293,656 | LAKE | 121,903 | 68,999 | 43,409 | 8,738 | 757 | 25,590 R | 56.6% | 35.6% | 7.2% |
| 110,800 | LA SALLE | 51,610 | 26,054 | 22,940 | 2,590 | 26 | 3,114 R | 50.5% | 44.4% | 5.0% |
| 18,540 | LAWRENCE | 8,946 | 4,883 | 3,075 | 972 | 16 | 1,808 R | 54.6% | 34.4% | 10.9% |
| 38,749 | LEE | 15,255 | 9,598 | 4,727 | 925 | 5 | 4,871 R | 62.9% | 31.0% | 6.1% |
| 40,341 | LIVINGSTON | 18,160 | 11,963 | 5,234 | 950 | 13 | 6,729 R | 65.9% | 28.8% | 5.2% |
| 33,656 | LOGAN | 14,289 | 8,638 | 4,552 | 1,083 | 16 | 4,086 R | 60.5% | 31.9% | 7.6% |
| 28,928 | MCDONOUGH | 12,924 | 8,496 | 3,785 | 628 | 15 | 4,711 R | 65.7% | 29.3% | 4.9% |
| 84,210 | MCHENRY | 41,185 | 27,245 | 10,896 | 2,701 | 343 | 16,349 R | 66.2% | 26.5% | 6.6% |
| 83,877 | MCLEAN | 37,630 | 22,284 | 12,779 | 2,351 | 216 | 9,505 R | 59.2% | 34.0% | 6.2% |
| 118,257 | MACON | 49,741 | 21,027 | 23,369 | 5,163 | 182 | 2,342 D | 42.3% | 47.0% | 10.4% |
| 43,524 | MACOUPIN | 23,368 | 10,262 | 10,750 | 2,325 | 31 | 488 D | 43.9% | 46.0% | 9.9% |
| 224,689 | MADISON | 101,129 | 39,622 | 46,384 | 14,987 | 136 | 6,762 D | 39.2% | 45.9% | 14.8% |

# ILLINOIS

## PRESIDENT 1968

| 1960 Census Population | County | Total Vote | Republican | Democratic | AIP | Other | Plurality | Percentage Total Vote Rep. | Dem. | AIP |
|---|---|---|---|---|---|---|---|---|---|---|
| 39,349 | MARION | 17,649 | 8,134 | 7,737 | 1,680 | 98 | 397 R | 46.1% | 43.8% | 9.5% |
| 13,334 | MARSHALL | 6,677 | 3,897 | 2,455 | 313 | 12 | 1,442 R | 58.4% | 36.8% | 4.7% |
| 15,193 | MASON | 7,853 | 3,899 | 3,365 | 572 | 17 | 534 R | 49.6% | 42.8% | 7.3% |
| 14,341 | MASSAC | 6,446 | 3,578 | 1,934 | 926 | 8 | 1,644 R | 55.5% | 30.0% | 14.4% |
| 9,248 | MENARD | 4,995 | 2,980 | 1,640 | 372 | 3 | 1,340 R | 59.7% | 32.8% | 7.4% |
| 17,149 | MERCER | 8,600 | 4,844 | 3,143 | 607 | 6 | 1,701 R | 56.3% | 36.5% | 7.1% |
| 15,507 | MONROE | 9,167 | 5,086 | 2,822 | 1,253 | 6 | 2,264 R | 55.5% | 30.8% | 13.7% |
| 31,244 | MONTGOMERY | 16,339 | 7,547 | 7,318 | 1,468 | 6 | 229 R | 46.2% | 44.8% | 9.0% |
| 36,571 | MORGAN | 16,327 | 8,902 | 6,281 | 1,137 | 7 | 2,621 R | 54.5% | 38.5% | 7.0% |
| 13,635 | MOULTRIE | 6,127 | 3,094 | 2,447 | 571 | 15 | 647 R | 50.5% | 39.9% | 9.3% |
| 38,106 | OGLE | 17,641 | 12,168 | 4,399 | 1,060 | 14 | 7,769 R | 69.0% | 24.9% | 6.0% |
| 189,044 | PEORIA | 74,105 | 37,021 | 30,937 | 5,648 | 499 | 6,084 R | 50.0% | 41.7% | 7.6% |
| 19,184 | PERRY | 10,983 | 5,384 | 4,449 | 1,144 | 6 | 935 R | 49.0% | 40.5% | 10.4% |
| 14,960 | PIATT | 7,059 | 3,973 | 2,447 | 636 | 3 | 1,526 R | 56.3% | 34.7% | 9.0% |
| 20,552 | PIKE | 9,939 | 5,035 | 4,191 | 697 | 16 | 844 R | 50.7% | 42.2% | 7.0% |
| 4,061 | POPE | 2,268 | 1,307 | 732 | 226 | 3 | 575 R | 57.6% | 32.3% | 10.0% |
| 10,490 | PULASKI | 4,632 | 1,741 | 2,076 | 815 |  | 335 D | 37.6% | 44.8% | 17.6% |
| 4,570 | PUTNAM | 2,505 | 1,351 | 988 | 162 | 4 | 363 R | 53.9% | 39.4% | 6.5% |
| 29,988 | RANDOLPH | 15,250 | 7,681 | 5,953 | 1,607 | 9 | 1,728 R | 50.4% | 39.0% | 10.5% |
| 16,299 | RICHLAND | 8,137 | 4,781 | 2,495 | 853 | 8 | 2,286 R | 58.8% | 30.7% | 10.5% |
| 150,991 | ROCK ISLAND | 70,140 | 30,404 | 34,506 | 5,054 | 176 | 4,102 D | 43.3% | 49.2% | 7.2% |
| 262,509 | ST. CLAIR | 100,874 | 34,442 | 50,726 | 15,260 | 446 | 16,284 D | 34.1% | 50.3% | 15.1% |
| 26,227 | SALINE | 13,849 | 6,913 | 5,985 | 939 | 12 | 928 R | 49.9% | 43.2% | 6.8% |
| 146,539 | SANGAMON | 72,996 | 36,510 | 29,542 | 6,586 | 358 | 6,968 R | 50.0% | 40.5% | 9.0% |
| 8,746 | SCHUYLER | 4,600 | 2,760 | 1,475 | 346 | 19 | 1,285 R | 60.0% | 32.1% | 7.5% |
| 6,377 | SCOTT | 3,548 | 1,971 | 1,252 | 325 |  | 719 R | 55.6% | 35.3% | 9.2% |
| 23,404 | SHELBY | 11,137 | 5,487 | 4,528 | 1,115 | 7 | 959 R | 49.3% | 40.7% | 10.0% |
| 8,152 | STARK | 3,665 | 2,292 | 1,128 | 239 | 6 | 1,164 R | 62.5% | 30.8% | 6.5% |
| 46,207 | STEPHENSON | 19,928 | 11,821 | 7,040 | 1,050 | 17 | 4,781 R | 59.3% | 35.3% | 5.3% |
| 99,789 | TAZEWELL | 48,422 | 22,971 | 20,712 | 4,711 | 28 | 2,259 R | 47.4% | 42.8% | 9.7% |
| 17,645 | UNION | 8,372 | 3,889 | 3,603 | 871 | 9 | 286 R | 46.5% | 43.0% | 10.4% |
| 96,176 | VERMILION | 43,424 | 21,391 | 16,238 | 5,726 | 69 | 5,153 R | 49.3% | 37.4% | 13.2% |
| 14,047 | WABASH | 6,392 | 3,529 | 2,244 | 614 | 5 | 1,285 R | 55.2% | 35.1% | 9.6% |
| 21,587 | WARREN | 9,795 | 5,877 | 3,085 | 824 | 9 | 2,792 R | 60.0% | 31.5% | 8.4% |
| 13,569 | WASHINGTON | 7,569 | 4,793 | 2,093 | 671 | 12 | 2,700 R | 63.3% | 27.7% | 8.9% |
| 19,008 | WAYNE | 9,284 | 5,532 | 2,993 | 745 | 14 | 2,539 R | 59.6% | 32.2% | 8.0% |
| 19,373 | WHITE | 9,952 | 5,351 | 3,837 | 761 | 3 | 1,514 R | 53.8% | 38.6% | 7.6% |
| 59,887 | WHITESIDE | 24,534 | 15,177 | 8,132 | 1,179 | 46 | 7,045 R | 61.9% | 33.1% | 4.8% |
| 191,617 | WILL | 88,460 | 43,630 | 31,576 | 12,595 | 659 | 12,054 R | 49.3% | 35.7% | 14.2% |
| 46,117 | WILLIAMSON | 23,588 | 11,886 | 9,660 | 2,031 | 11 | 2,226 R | 50.4% | 41.0% | 8.6% |
| 209,765 | WINNEBAGO | 90,739 | 47,646 | 36,702 | 6,176 | 215 | 10,944 R | 52.5% | 40.4% | 6.8% |
| 24,579 | WOODFORD | 12,747 | 7,876 | 4,005 | 856 | 10 | 3,871 R | 61.8% | 31.4% | 6.7% |
| 10,081,158 | TOTAL | 4,619,749 | 2,174,774 | 2,039,814 | 390,958 | 14,203 | 134,960 R | 47.1% | 44.2% | 8.5% |

# ILLINOIS

## PRESIDENT 1964

| 1960 Census Population | County | Total Vote | Republican | Democratic | Other | Rep.-Dem. Plurality | Percentage |  |  |  |
|---|---|---|---|---|---|---|---|---|---|---|
|  |  |  |  |  |  |  | Total Vote |  | Major Vote |  |
|  |  |  |  |  |  |  | Rep. | Dem. | Rep. | Dem. |
| 68,467 | ADAMS | 32,314 | 13,993 | 18,321 |  | 4,328 D | 43.3% | 56.7% | 43.3% | 56.7% |
| 16,061 | ALEXANDER | 7,658 | 2,895 | 4,763 |  | 1,868 D | 37.8% | 62.2% | 37.8% | 62.2% |
| 14,060 | BOND | 6,873 | 3,058 | 3,815 |  | 757 D | 44.5% | 55.5% | 44.5% | 55.5% |
| 20,326 | BOONE | 8,747 | 5,053 | 3,694 |  | 1,359 R | 57.8% | 42.2% | 57.8% | 42.2% |
| 6,210 | BROWN | 3,438 | 1,355 | 2,083 |  | 728 D | 39.4% | 60.6% | 39.4% | 60.6% |
| 37,594 | BUREAU | 18,638 | 9,552 | 9,086 |  | 466 R | 51.3% | 48.7% | 51.3% | 48.7% |
| 5,933 | CALHOUN | 3,093 | 1,288 | 1,805 |  | 517 D | 41.6% | 58.4% | 41.6% | 58.4% |
| 19,507 | CARROLL | 8,549 | 4,487 | 4,062 |  | 425 D | 52.5% | 47.5% | 52.5% | 47.5% |
| 14,539 | CASS | 7,260 | 2,836 | 4,424 |  | 1,588 D | 39.1% | 60.9% | 39.1% | 60.9% |
| 132,436 | CHAMPAIGN | 47,802 | 22,010 | 25,792 |  | 3,782 D | 46.0% | 54.0% | 46.0% | 54.0% |
| 37,207 | CHRISTIAN | 18,051 | 6,153 | 11,898 |  | 5,745 D | 34.1% | 65.9% | 34.1% | 65.9% |
| 16,546 | CLARK | 8,867 | 4,403 | 4,464 |  | 61 D | 49.7% | 50.3% | 49.7% | 50.3% |
| 15,815 | CLAY | 8,216 | 3,665 | 4,551 |  | 886 D | 44.6% | 55.4% | 44.6% | 55.4% |
| 24,029 | CLINTON | 12,031 | 4,692 | 7,339 |  | 2,647 D | 39.0% | 61.0% | 39.0% | 61.0% |
| 42,860 | COLES | 20,255 | 8,878 | 11,377 |  | 2,499 D | 43.8% | 56.2% | 43.8% | 56.2% |
| 5,129,725 | COOK | 2,432,899 | 895,718 | 1,537,181 |  | 641,463 D | 36.8% | 63.2% | 36.8% | 63.2% |
| 20,751 | CRAWFORD | 10,458 | 4,834 | 5,624 |  | 790 D | 46.2% | 53.8% | 46.2% | 53.8% |
| 9,936 | CUMBERLAND | 5,307 | 2,251 | 3,056 |  | 805 D | 42.4% | 57.6% | 42.4% | 57.6% |
| 51,714 | DE KALB | 22,049 | 11,791 | 10,257 | 1 | 1,534 R | 53.5% | 46.5% | 53.5% | 46.5% |
| 17,253 | DE WITT | 7,976 | 3,605 | 4,371 |  | 766 D | 45.2% | 54.8% | 45.2% | 54.8% |
| 19,243 | DOUGLAS | 8,918 | 4,223 | 4,695 |  | 472 D | 47.4% | 52.6% | 47.4% | 52.6% |
| 313,459 | DU PAGE | 165,100 | 98,871 | 66,229 |  | 32,642 R | 59.9% | 40.1% | 59.9% | 40.1% |
| 22,550 | EDGAR | 11,793 | 5,827 | 5,966 |  | 139 D | 49.4% | 50.6% | 49.4% | 50.6% |
| 7,940 | EDWARDS | 4,253 | 2,262 | 1,991 |  | 271 R | 53.2% | 46.8% | 53.2% | 46.8% |
| 23,107 | EFFINGHAM | 11,826 | 5,044 | 6,782 |  | 1,738 D | 42.7% | 57.3% | 42.7% | 57.3% |
| 21,946 | FAYETTE | 10,787 | 4,492 | 6,295 |  | 1,803 D | 41.6% | 58.4% | 41.6% | 58.4% |
| 16,606 | FORD | 8,077 | 4,650 | 3,427 |  | 1,223 R | 57.6% | 42.4% | 57.6% | 42.4% |
| 39,281 | FRANKLIN | 21,201 | 7,620 | 13,581 |  | 5,961 D | 35.9% | 64.1% | 35.9% | 64.1% |
| 41,954 | FULTON | 20,815 | 7,785 | 13,030 |  | 5,245 D | 37.4% | 62.6% | 37.4% | 62.6% |
| 7,638 | GALLATIN | 4,239 | 1,394 | 2,845 |  | 1,451 D | 32.9% | 67.1% | 32.9% | 67.1% |
| 17,460 | GREENE | 7,909 | 3,128 | 4,781 |  | 1,653 D | 39.5% | 60.5% | 39.5% | 60.5% |
| 22,350 | GRUNDY | 10,768 | 5,522 | 5,246 |  | 276 R | 51.3% | 48.7% | 51.3% | 48.7% |
| 10,010 | HAMILTON | 5,694 | 2,561 | 3,133 |  | 572 D | 45.0% | 55.0% | 45.0% | 55.0% |
| 24,574 | HANCOCK | 11,756 | 5,557 | 6,199 |  | 642 D | 47.3% | 52.7% | 47.3% | 52.7% |
| 5,879 | HARDIN | 2,963 | 1,324 | 1,639 |  | 315 D | 44.7% | 55.3% | 44.7% | 55.3% |
| 8,237 | HENDERSON | 4,134 | 1,863 | 2,271 |  | 408 D | 45.1% | 54.9% | 45.1% | 54.9% |
| 49,317 | HENRY | 22,729 | 10,644 | 12,085 |  | 1,441 D | 46.8% | 53.2% | 46.8% | 53.2% |
| 33,562 | IROQUOIS | 16,452 | 9,423 | 7,029 |  | 2,394 R | 57.3% | 42.7% | 57.3% | 42.7% |
| 42,151 | JACKSON | 19,178 | 7,013 | 12,165 |  | 5,152 D | 36.6% | 63.4% | 36.6% | 63.4% |
| 11,346 | JASPER | 6,020 | 2,614 | 3,406 |  | 792 D | 43.4% | 56.6% | 43.4% | 56.6% |
| 32,315 | JEFFERSON | 15,901 | 6,248 | 9,653 |  | 3,405 D | 39.3% | 60.7% | 39.3% | 60.7% |
| 17,023 | JERSEY | 6,977 | 3,041 | 3,936 |  | 895 D | 43.6% | 56.4% | 43.6% | 56.4% |
| 21,821 | JO DAVIESS | 9,425 | 4,607 | 4,818 |  | 211 D | 48.9% | 51.1% | 48.9% | 51.1% |
| 6,928 | JOHNSON | 3,987 | 2,217 | 1,770 |  | 447 R | 55.6% | 44.4% | 55.6% | 44.4% |
| 208,246 | KANE | 87,094 | 46,391 | 40,703 |  | 5,688 R | 53.3% | 46.7% | 53.3% | 46.7% |
| 92,063 | KANKAKEE | 36,874 | 16,082 | 20,792 |  | 4,710 D | 43.6% | 56.4% | 43.6% | 56.4% |
| 17,540 | KENDALL | 9,140 | 5,710 | 3,430 |  | 2,280 R | 62.5% | 37.5% | 62.5% | 37.5% |
| 61,280 | KNOX | 27,850 | 12,850 | 15,000 |  | 2,150 D | 46.1% | 53.9% | 46.1% | 53.9% |
| 293,656 | LAKE | 121,667 | 58,840 | 62,785 | 42 | 3,945 D | 48.4% | 51.6% | 48.4% | 51.6% |
| 110,800 | LA SALLE | 52,139 | 21,216 | 30,923 |  | 9,707 D | 40.7% | 59.3% | 40.7% | 59.3% |
| 18,540 | LAWRENCE | 9,312 | 4,176 | 5,136 |  | 960 D | 44.8% | 55.2% | 44.8% | 55.2% |
| 38,749 | LEE | 15,760 | 8,445 | 7,315 |  | 1,130 R | 53.6% | 46.4% | 53.6% | 46.4% |
| 40,341 | LIVINGSTON | 18,715 | 10,239 | 8,476 |  | 1,763 R | 54.7% | 45.3% | 54.7% | 45.3% |
| 33,656 | LOGAN | 14,517 | 6,805 | 7,712 |  | 907 D | 46.9% | 53.1% | 46.9% | 53.1% |
| 28,928 | MCDONOUGH | 13,051 | 6,907 | 6,144 |  | 763 R | 52.9% | 47.1% | 52.9% | 47.1% |
| 84,210 | MCHENRY | 40,517 | 22,503 | 18,014 |  | 4,489 R | 55.5% | 44.5% | 55.5% | 44.5% |
| 83,877 | MCLEAN | 38,670 | 19,120 | 19,550 |  | 430 D | 49.4% | 50.6% | 49.4% | 50.6% |
| 118,257 | MACON | 53,002 | 17,957 | 35,045 |  | 17,088 D | 33.9% | 66.1% | 33.9% | 66.1% |
| 43,524 | MACOUPIN | 23,657 | 8,430 | 15,227 |  | 6,797 D | 35.6% | 64.4% | 35.6% | 64.4% |
| 224,689 | MADISON | 95,124 | 30,009 | 65,115 |  | 35,106 D | 31.5% | 68.5% | 31.5% | 68.5% |

# ILLINOIS

## PRESIDENT 1964

| 1960 Census Population | County | Total Vote | Republican | Democratic | Other | Rep.-Dem. Plurality | Percentage | | | |
|---|---|---|---|---|---|---|---|---|---|---|
| | | | | | | | Total Vote | | Major Vote | |
| | | | | | | | Rep. | Dem. | Rep. | Dem. |
| 39,349 | MARION | 19,423 | 7,060 | 12,363 | | 5,303 D | 36.3% | 63.7% | 36.3% | 63.7% |
| 13,334 | MARSHALL | 6,770 | 3,209 | 3,561 | | 352 D | 47.4% | 52.6% | 47.4% | 52.6% |
| 15,193 | MASON | 7,690 | 2,833 | 4,857 | | 2,024 D | 36.8% | 63.2% | 36.8% | 63.2% |
| 14,341 | MASSAC | 6,474 | 3,078 | 3,396 | | 318 D | 47.5% | 52.5% | 47.5% | 52.5% |
| 9,248 | MENARD | 4,813 | 2,322 | 2,491 | | 169 D | 48.2% | 51.8% | 48.2% | 51.8% |
| 17,149 | MERCER | 8,630 | 4,220 | 4,410 | | 190 D | 48.9% | 51.1% | 48.9% | 51.1% |
| 15,507 | MONROE | 8,541 | 3,936 | 4,605 | | 669 D | 46.1% | 53.9% | 46.1% | 53.9% |
| 31,244 | MONTGOMERY | 17,006 | 6,425 | 10,581 | | 4,156 D | 37.8% | 62.2% | 37.8% | 62.2% |
| 36,571 | MORGAN | 16,475 | 7,240 | 9,235 | | 1,995 D | 43.9% | 56.1% | 43.9% | 56.1% |
| 13,635 | MOULTRIE | 6,226 | 2,493 | 3,733 | | 1,240 D | 40.0% | 60.0% | 40.0% | 60.0% |
| 38,106 | OGLE | 17,347 | 10,430 | 6,917 | | 3,513 R | 60.1% | 39.9% | 60.1% | 39.9% |
| 189,044 | PEORIA | 80,687 | 33,327 | 47,360 | | 14,033 D | 41.3% | 58.7% | 41.3% | 58.7% |
| 19,184 | PERRY | 10,926 | 4,287 | 6,639 | | 2,352 D | 39.2% | 60.8% | 39.2% | 60.8% |
| 14,960 | PIATT | 7,038 | 3,141 | 3,897 | | 756 D | 44.6% | 55.4% | 44.6% | 55.4% |
| 20,552 | PIKE | 10,689 | 4,113 | 6,576 | | 2,463 D | 38.5% | 61.5% | 38.5% | 61.5% |
| 4,061 | POPE | 2,446 | 1,329 | 1,117 | | 212 R | 54.3% | 45.7% | 54.3% | 45.7% |
| 10,490 | PULASKI | 5,048 | 1,716 | 3,332 | | 1,616 D | 34.0% | 66.0% | 34.0% | 66.0% |
| 4,570 | PUTNAM | 2,490 | 1,131 | 1,359 | | 228 D | 45.4% | 54.6% | 45.4% | 54.6% |
| 29,988 | RANDOLPH | 15,002 | 5,803 | 9,199 | | 3,396 D | 38.7% | 61.3% | 38.7% | 61.3% |
| 16,299 | RICHLAND | 8,140 | 3,901 | 4,239 | | 338 D | 47.9% | 52.1% | 47.9% | 52.1% |
| 150,991 | ROCK ISLAND | 65,473 | 23,714 | 41,759 | | 18,045 D | 36.2% | 63.8% | 36.2% | 63.8% |
| 262,509 | ST. CLAIR | 102,231 | 28,226 | 74,005 | | 45,779 D | 27.6% | 72.4% | 27.6% | 72.4% |
| 26,227 | SALINE | 14,028 | 5,691 | 8,337 | | 2,646 D | 40.6% | 59.4% | 40.6% | 59.4% |
| 146,539 | SANGAMON | 76,166 | 33,077 | 43,073 | 16 | 9,996 D | 43.4% | 56.6% | 43.4% | 56.6% |
| 8,746 | SCHUYLER | 4,921 | 2,417 | 2,504 | | 87 D | 49.1% | 50.9% | 49.1% | 50.9% |
| 6,377 | SCOTT | 3,579 | 1,627 | 1,952 | | 325 D | 45.5% | 54.5% | 45.5% | 54.5% |
| 23,404 | SHELBY | 11,369 | 4,281 | 7,088 | | 2,807 D | 37.7% | 62.3% | 37.7% | 62.3% |
| 8,152 | STARK | 3,893 | 2,117 | 1,776 | | 341 R | 54.4% | 45.6% | 54.4% | 45.6% |
| 46,207 | STEPHENSON | 20,106 | 9,252 | 10,854 | | 1,602 D | 46.0% | 54.0% | 46.0% | 54.0% |
| 99,789 | TAZEWELL | 45,731 | 17,170 | 28,561 | | 11,391 D | 37.5% | 62.5% | 37.5% | 62.5% |
| 17,645 | UNION | 8,350 | 3,142 | 5,208 | | 2,066 D | 37.6% | 62.4% | 37.6% | 62.4% |
| 96,176 | VERMILION | 44,271 | 19,506 | 24,765 | | 5,259 D | 44.1% | 55.9% | 44.1% | 55.9% |
| 14,047 | WABASH | 6,626 | 2,905 | 3,721 | | 816 D | 43.8% | 56.2% | 43.8% | 56.2% |
| 21,587 | WARREN | 9,931 | 5,258 | 4,670 | 3 | 588 R | 52.9% | 47.0% | 53.0% | 47.0% |
| 13,569 | WASHINGTON | 7,510 | 3,840 | 3,670 | | 170 R | 51.1% | 48.9% | 51.1% | 48.9% |
| 19,008 | WAYNE | 9,943 | 4,745 | 5,198 | | 453 D | 47.7% | 52.3% | 47.7% | 52.3% |
| 19,373 | WHITE | 9,963 | 4,000 | 5,963 | | 1,963 D | 40.1% | 59.9% | 40.1% | 59.9% |
| 59,887 | WHITESIDE | 25,476 | 12,940 | 12,536 | | 404 R | 50.8% | 49.2% | 50.8% | 49.2% |
| 191,617 | WILL | 88,282 | 38,619 | 49,663 | | 11,044 D | 43.7% | 56.3% | 43.7% | 56.3% |
| 46,117 | WILLIAMSON | 23,743 | 9,130 | 14,613 | | 5,483 D | 38.5% | 61.5% | 38.5% | 61.5% |
| 209,765 | WINNEBAGO | 88,754 | 39,920 | 48,834 | | 8,914 D | 45.0% | 55.0% | 45.0% | 55.0% |
| 24,579 | WOODFORD | 12,162 | 6,248 | 5,914 | | 334 R | 51.4% | 48.6% | 51.4% | 48.6% |
| 10,081,158 | TOTAL | 4,702,841 | 1,905,946 | 2,796,833 | 62 | 890,887 D | 40.5% | 59.5% | 40.5% | 59.5% |

# ILLINOIS

## PRESIDENT 1960

| 1960 Census Population | County | Total Vote | Republican | Democratic | Other | Rep.-Dem. Plurality | Percentage | | | |
|---|---|---|---|---|---|---|---|---|---|---|
| | | | | | | | Total Vote | | Major Vote | |
| | | | | | | | Rep. | Dem. | Rep. | Dem. |
| 68,467 | ADAMS | 33,529 | 18,674 | 14,827 | 28 | 3,847 R | 55.7% | 44.2% | 55.7% | 44.3% |
| 16,061 | ALEXANDER | 8,638 | 4,143 | 4,477 | 18 | 334 D | 48.0% | 51.8% | 48.1% | 51.9% |
| 14,060 | BOND | 7,162 | 4,297 | 2,856 | 9 | 1,441 R | 60.0% | 39.9% | 60.1% | 39.9% |
| 20,326 | BOONE | 9,162 | 6,552 | 2,605 | 5 | 3,947 R | 71.5% | 28.4% | 71.6% | 28.4% |
| 6,210 | BROWN | 3,740 | 1,889 | 1,849 | 2 | 40 R | 50.5% | 49.4% | 50.5% | 49.5% |
| 37,594 | BUREAU | 20,407 | 12,597 | 7,786 | 24 | 4,811 R | 61.7% | 38.2% | 61.8% | 38.2% |
| 5,933 | CALHOUN | 3,267 | 1,654 | 1,608 | 5 | 46 R | 50.6% | 49.2% | 50.7% | 49.3% |
| 19,507 | CARROLL | 9,418 | 6,282 | 3,097 | 39 | 3,185 R | 66.7% | 32.9% | 67.0% | 33.0% |
| 14,539 | CASS | 7,715 | 4,015 | 3,692 | 8 | 323 R | 52.0% | 47.9% | 52.1% | 47.9% |
| 132,436 | CHAMPAIGN | 45,441 | 27,793 | 17,115 | 533 | 10,678 R | 61.2% | 37.7% | 61.9% | 38.1% |
| 37,207 | CHRISTIAN | 19,485 | 9,263 | 10,207 | 15 | 944 D | 47.5% | 52.4% | 47.6% | 52.4% |
| 16,546 | CLARK | 9,273 | 5,319 | 3,949 | 5 | 1,370 R | 57.4% | 42.6% | 57.4% | 42.6% |
| 15,815 | CLAY | 8,538 | 5,134 | 3,394 | 10 | 1,740 R | 60.1% | 39.8% | 60.2% | 39.8% |
| 24,029 | CLINTON | 11,903 | 5,709 | 6,188 | 6 | 479 D | 48.0% | 52.0% | 48.0% | 52.0% |
| 42,860 | COLES | 20,814 | 12,166 | 8,629 | 19 | 3,537 R | 58.5% | 41.5% | 58.5% | 41.5% |
| 5,129,725 | COOK | 2,445,269 | 1,059,607 | 1,378,343 | 7,319 | 318,736 D | 43.3% | 56.4% | 43.5% | 56.5% |
| 20,751 | CRAWFORD | 11,058 | 6,809 | 4,245 | 4 | 2,564 R | 61.6% | 38.4% | 61.6% | 38.4% |
| 9,936 | CUMBERLAND | 5,500 | 3,020 | 2,475 | 5 | 545 R | 54.9% | 45.0% | 55.0% | 45.0% |
| 51,714 | DE KALB | 22,388 | 15,586 | 6,783 | 19 | 8,803 R | 69.6% | 30.3% | 69.7% | 30.3% |
| 17,253 | DE WITT | 8,689 | 5,074 | 3,607 | 8 | 1,467 R | 58.4% | 41.5% | 58.4% | 41.6% |
| 19,243 | DOUGLAS | 9,299 | 5,761 | 3,532 | 6 | 2,229 R | 62.0% | 38.0% | 62.0% | 38.0% |
| 313,459 | DU PAGE | 145,445 | 101,014 | 44,263 | 168 | 56,751 R | 69.5% | 30.4% | 69.5% | 30.5% |
| 22,550 | EDGAR | 12,376 | 7,348 | 5,024 | 4 | 2,324 R | 59.4% | 40.6% | 59.4% | 40.6% |
| 7,940 | EDWARDS | 4,745 | 3,291 | 1,446 | 8 | 1,845 R | 69.4% | 30.5% | 69.5% | 30.5% |
| 23,107 | EFFINGHAM | 12,092 | 6,410 | 5,676 | 6 | 734 R | 53.0% | 46.9% | 53.0% | 47.0% |
| 21,946 | FAYETTE | 11,504 | 6,586 | 4,907 | 11 | 1,679 R | 57.2% | 42.7% | 57.3% | 42.7% |
| 16,606 | FORD | 8,478 | 5,779 | 2,698 | 1 | 3,081 R | 68.2% | 31.8% | 68.2% | 31.8% |
| 39,281 | FRANKLIN | 23,266 | 11,861 | 11,368 | 37 | 493 R | 51.0% | 48.9% | 51.1% | 48.9% |
| 41,954 | FULTON | 22,251 | 11,999 | 10,194 | 58 | 1,805 R | 53.9% | 45.8% | 54.1% | 45.9% |
| 7,638 | GALLATIN | 4,570 | 2,179 | 2,386 | 5 | 207 D | 47.7% | 52.2% | 47.7% | 52.3% |
| 17,460 | GREENE | 8,344 | 4,487 | 3,847 | 10 | 640 R | 53.8% | 46.1% | 53.8% | 46.2% |
| 22,350 | GRUNDY | 11,228 | 6,948 | 4,276 | 4 | 2,672 R | 61.9% | 38.1% | 61.9% | 38.1% |
| 10,010 | HAMILTON | 6,454 | 3,804 | 2,639 | 11 | 1,165 R | 58.9% | 40.9% | 59.0% | 41.0% |
| 24,574 | HANCOCK | 12,990 | 8,036 | 4,947 | 7 | 3,089 R | 61.9% | 38.1% | 61.9% | 38.1% |
| 5,879 | HARDIN | 3,413 | 1,944 | 1,465 | 4 | 479 R | 57.0% | 42.9% | 57.0% | 43.0% |
| 8,237 | HENDERSON | 4,273 | 2,572 | 1,697 | 4 | 875 R | 60.2% | 39.7% | 60.2% | 39.8% |
| 49,317 | HENRY | 24,690 | 14,297 | 10,372 | 21 | 3,925 R | 57.9% | 42.0% | 58.0% | 42.0% |
| 33,562 | IROQUOIS | 17,213 | 11,376 | 5,821 | 16 | 5,555 R | 66.1% | 33.8% | 66.2% | 33.8% |
| 42,151 | JACKSON | 19,112 | 10,568 | 8,527 | 17 | 2,041 R | 55.3% | 44.6% | 55.3% | 44.7% |
| 11,346 | JASPER | 6,421 | 3,393 | 3,027 | 1 | 366 R | 52.8% | 47.1% | 52.9% | 47.1% |
| 32,315 | JEFFERSON | 17,625 | 9,841 | 7,784 | | 2,057 R | 55.8% | 44.2% | 55.8% | 44.2% |
| 17,023 | JERSEY | 8,343 | 4,247 | 4,087 | 9 | 160 R | 50.9% | 49.0% | 51.0% | 49.0% |
| 21,821 | JO DAVIESS | 10,417 | 6,111 | 4,293 | 13 | 1,818 R | 58.7% | 41.2% | 58.7% | 41.3% |
| 6,928 | JOHNSON | 4,197 | 2,778 | 1,413 | 6 | 1,365 R | 66.2% | 33.7% | 66.3% | 33.7% |
| 208,246 | KANE | 86,761 | 55,389 | 31,279 | 93 | 24,110 R | 63.8% | 36.1% | 63.9% | 36.1% |
| 92,063 | KANKAKEE | 37,452 | 20,311 | 17,115 | 26 | 3,196 R | 54.2% | 45.7% | 54.3% | 45.7% |
| 17,540 | KENDALL | 8,228 | 5,975 | 2,242 | 11 | 3,733 R | 72.6% | 27.2% | 72.7% | 27.3% |
| 61,280 | KNOX | 29,850 | 17,938 | 11,889 | 23 | 6,049 R | 60.1% | 39.8% | 60.1% | 39.9% |
| 293,656 | LAKE | 114,899 | 67,809 | 46,941 | 149 | 20,868 R | 59.0% | 40.9% | 59.1% | 40.9% |
| 110,800 | LA SALLE | 55,125 | 27,552 | 27,532 | 41 | 20 R | 50.0% | 49.9% | 50.0% | 50.0% |
| 18,540 | LAWRENCE | 9,800 | 6,120 | 3,667 | 13 | 2,453 R | 62.4% | 37.4% | 62.5% | 37.5% |
| 38,749 | LEE | 16,739 | 10,835 | 5,896 | 8 | 4,939 R | 64.7% | 35.2% | 64.8% | 35.2% |
| 40,341 | LIVINGSTON | 19,783 | 13,139 | 6,642 | 2 | 6,497 R | 66.4% | 33.6% | 66.4% | 33.6% |
| 33,656 | LOGAN | 15,090 | 9,383 | 5,691 | 16 | 3,692 R | 62.2% | 37.7% | 62.2% | 37.8% |
| 28,928 | MCDONOUGH | 13,893 | 9,363 | 4,520 | 10 | 4,843 R | 67.4% | 32.5% | 67.4% | 32.6% |
| 84,210 | MCHENRY | 38,508 | 25,787 | 12,659 | 62 | 13,128 R | 67.0% | 32.9% | 67.1% | 32.9% |
| 83,877 | MCLEAN | 38,761 | 24,758 | 13,971 | 32 | 10,787 R | 63.9% | 36.0% | 63.9% | 36.1% |
| 118,257 | MACON | 53,288 | 27,151 | 26,029 | 108 | 1,122 R | 51.0% | 48.8% | 51.1% | 48.9% |
| 43,524 | MACOUPIN | 24,896 | 11,731 | 13,120 | 45 | 1,389 D | 47.1% | 52.7% | 47.2% | 52.8% |
| 224,689 | MADISON | 97,904 | 42,984 | 54,787 | 133 | 11,803 D | 43.9% | 56.0% | 44.0% | 56.0% |

# ILLINOIS

## PRESIDENT 1960

| 1960 Census Population | County | Total Vote | Republican | Democratic | Other | Rep.-Dem. Plurality | Percentage | | | |
|---|---|---|---|---|---|---|---|---|---|---|
| | | | | | | | Total Vote | | Major Vote | |
| | | | | | | | Rep. | Dem. | Rep. | Dem. |
| 39,349 | MARION | 20,250 | 11,121 | 9,116 | 13 | 2,005 R | 54.9% | 45.0% | 55.0% | 45.0% |
| 13,334 | MARSHALL | 7,138 | 4,150 | 2,981 | 7 | 1,169 R | 58.1% | 41.8% | 58.2% | 41.8% |
| 15,193 | MASON | 8,180 | 4,337 | 3,824 | 19 | 513 R | 53.0% | 46.7% | 53.1% | 46.9% |
| 14,341 | MASSAC | 7,171 | 4,521 | 2,644 | 6 | 1,877 R | 63.0% | 36.9% | 63.1% | 36.9% |
| 9,248 | MENARD | 5,193 | 3,120 | 2,068 | 5 | 1,052 R | 60.1% | 39.8% | 60.1% | 39.9% |
| 17,149 | MERCER | 9,061 | 5,582 | 3,476 | 3 | 2,106 R | 61.6% | 38.4% | 61.6% | 38.4% |
| 15,507 | MONROE | 8,133 | 4,731 | 3,398 | 4 | 1,333 R | 58.2% | 41.8% | 58.2% | 41.8% |
| 31,244 | MONTGOMERY | 18,007 | 9,178 | 8,815 | 14 | 363 R | 51.0% | 49.0% | 51.0% | 49.0% |
| 36,571 | MORGAN | 17,062 | 9,791 | 7,259 | 12 | 2,532 R | 57.4% | 42.5% | 57.4% | 42.6% |
| 13,635 | MOULTRIE | 6,831 | 3,752 | 3,079 | | 673 R | 54.9% | 45.1% | 54.9% | 45.1% |
| 38,106 | OGLE | 18,025 | 13,226 | 4,792 | 7 | 8,434 R | 73.4% | 26.6% | 73.4% | 26.6% |
| 189,044 | PEORIA | 84,676 | 45,529 | 39,061 | 86 | 6,468 R | 53.8% | 46.1% | 53.8% | 46.2% |
| 19,184 | PERRY | 11,672 | 6,708 | 4,958 | 6 | 1,750 R | 57.5% | 42.5% | 57.5% | 42.5% |
| 14,960 | PIATT | 7,399 | 4,506 | 2,889 | 4 | 1,617 R | 60.9% | 39.0% | 60.9% | 39.1% |
| 20,552 | PIKE | 11,436 | 5,965 | 5,461 | 10 | 504 R | 52.2% | 47.8% | 52.2% | 47.8% |
| 4,061 | POPE | 2,665 | 1,689 | 971 | 5 | 718 R | 63.4% | 36.4% | 63.5% | 36.5% |
| 10,490 | PULASKI | 4,961 | 2,621 | 2,322 | 18 | 299 R | 52.8% | 46.8% | 53.0% | 47.0% |
| 4,570 | PUTNAM | 2,619 | 1,457 | 1,160 | 2 | 297 R | 55.6% | 44.3% | 55.7% | 44.3% |
| 29,988 | RANDOLPH | 15,347 | 7,988 | 7,344 | 15 | 644 R | 52.0% | 47.9% | 52.1% | 47.9% |
| 16,299 | RICHLAND | 8,353 | 5,329 | 3,015 | 9 | 2,314 R | 63.8% | 36.1% | 63.9% | 36.1% |
| 150,991 | ROCK ISLAND | 66,454 | 32,534 | 33,812 | 108 | 1,278 D | 49.0% | 50.9% | 49.0% | 51.0% |
| 262,509 | ST. CLAIR | 109,751 | 42,046 | 67,367 | 338 | 25,321 D | 38.3% | 61.4% | 38.4% | 61.6% |
| 26,227 | SALINE | 15,707 | 8,853 | 6,835 | 19 | 2,018 R | 56.4% | 43.5% | 56.4% | 43.6% |
| 146,539 | SANGAMON | 77,335 | 41,483 | 35,793 | 59 | 5,690 R | 53.6% | 46.3% | 53.7% | 46.3% |
| 8,746 | SCHUYLER | 5,164 | 3,047 | 2,115 | 2 | 932 R | 59.0% | 41.0% | 59.0% | 41.0% |
| 6,377 | SCOTT | 3,814 | 2,267 | 1,543 | 4 | 724 R | 59.4% | 40.5% | 59.5% | 40.5% |
| 23,404 | SHELBY | 12,603 | 6,872 | 5,720 | 11 | 1,152 R | 54.5% | 45.4% | 54.6% | 45.4% |
| 8,152 | STARK | 4,314 | 2,925 | 1,383 | 6 | 1,542 R | 67.8% | 32.1% | 67.9% | 32.1% |
| 46,207 | STEPHENSON | 21,995 | 13,872 | 8,055 | 68 | 5,817 R | 63.1% | 36.6% | 63.3% | 36.7% |
| 99,789 | TAZEWELL | 44,526 | 23,967 | 20,521 | 38 | 3,446 R | 53.8% | 46.1% | 53.9% | 46.1% |
| 17,645 | UNION | 8,763 | 4,432 | 4,321 | 10 | 111 R | 50.6% | 49.3% | 50.6% | 49.4% |
| 96,176 | VERMILION | 46,342 | 26,571 | 19,702 | 69 | 6,869 R | 57.3% | 42.5% | 57.4% | 42.6% |
| 14,047 | WABASH | 7,278 | 4,261 | 3,013 | 4 | 1,248 R | 58.5% | 41.4% | 58.6% | 41.4% |
| 21,587 | WARREN | 11,066 | 7,221 | 3,835 | 10 | 3,386 R | 65.3% | 34.7% | 65.3% | 34.7% |
| 13,569 | WASHINGTON | 8,157 | 5,053 | 3,093 | 11 | 1,960 R | 61.9% | 37.9% | 62.0% | 38.0% |
| 19,008 | WAYNE | 10,615 | 6,652 | 3,954 | 9 | 2,698 R | 62.7% | 37.2% | 62.7% | 37.3% |
| 19,373 | WHITE | 10,577 | 5,810 | 4,756 | 11 | 1,054 R | 54.9% | 45.0% | 55.0% | 45.0% |
| 59,887 | WHITESIDE | 26,592 | 17,434 | 9,112 | 46 | 8,322 R | 65.6% | 34.3% | 65.7% | 34.3% |
| 191,617 | WILL | 83,712 | 42,575 | 41,056 | 81 | 1,519 R | 50.9% | 49.0% | 50.9% | 49.1% |
| 46,117 | WILLIAMSON | 25,096 | 13,732 | 11,335 | 29 | 2,397 R | 54.7% | 45.2% | 54.8% | 45.2% |
| 209,765 | WINNEBAGO | 89,741 | 49,541 | 40,090 | 110 | 9,451 R | 55.2% | 44.7% | 55.3% | 44.7% |
| 24,579 | WOODFORD | 12,509 | 8,101 | 4,401 | 7 | 3,700 R | 64.8% | 35.2% | 64.8% | 35.2% |
| 10,081,158 | TOTAL | 4,757,409 | 2,368,988 | 2,377,846 | 10,575 | 8,858 D | 49.8% | 50.0% | 49.9% | 50.1% |

# ILLINOIS

## ELECTION NOTES

**2004**  Other vote was 32,442 Libertarian (Michael Badnarik); 3,571 write-in (Ralph Nader); 440 write-in (Michael Peroutka); 241 write-in (David Cobb); 115 write-in (Peter M. Camejo); 4 write-in (Lawson Bone); 4 write-in (Ernest Virag); 3 write-in (John Joseph Kennedy); 2 write-in (David Cook); 1 write-in (Margaret Trowe); 1 write-in (Joann Breivogel); 1 write-in (John Kennedy); 1 write-in (Robert M. Christensen). The Nader write-in vote included 2,357 votes cast for the Nader-Camejo ticket and 1,214 votes for Nader alone.

**2000**  Other vote was 16,106 Independent (Buchanan); 11,623 Libertarian (Browne); 2,127 Reform (Hagelin); 57 write-in (Phillips); 4 write-in (McReynolds).

**1996**  Other vote was 22,548 Libertarian (Browne); 7,606 U.S. Taxpayers (Phillips); 4,606 Natural Law (Hagelin); 1,447 write-in (Nader); 11 scattered write-in.

**1992**  Other vote was 9,218 Marrou (Libertarian); 5,267 Fulani (New Alliance); 3,577 Gritz (Populist); 2,751 Hagelin (Natural Law); 1,361 Warren (Socialist Workers); 22 scattered write-in.

**1988**  Other vote was 14,944 Paul (Libertarian); 10,276 Fulani (Solidarity); 7,021 Winn (Independent).

**1984**  Other vote was 10,086 Bergland (Libertarian); 4,672 Hall (Communist); 2,716 Johnson (Citizens); 2,632 Winn (Independent); 2,386 Serrette (Independent); 2,132 Mason (Socialist Workers); 862 scattered write-in.

**1980**  Other vote was 346,754 Anderson (Independent); 38,939 Clark (Libertarian); 10,692 Commoner (Citizens); 9,711 Hall (Communist); 2,257 Griswold (Workers World); 1,302 DeBerry (Socialist Workers); 604 scattered write-in.

**1976**  Other vote was 55,939 McCarthy (Independent); 9,250 Hall (Communist); 8,057 MacBride (Libertarian); 3,615 Camejo (Socialist Workers); 2,422 Levin (Socialist Labor); 2,018 LaRouche (U.S. Labor); 387 Anderson (write-in); 1,662 scattered write-in. In the final printed return - "The Official Vote" - the Schuyler county Republican vote was carried incorrectly as 22,635 and the Republican total state-wide vote as 2,384,269.

**1972**  Other vote was 12,344 Fisher (Socialist Labor); 4,541 Hall (Communist); 2,471 Schmitz (American); 2,229 scattered write-in.

**1968**  Wallace on the ballot as Independent. Other vote was 13,878 Blomen (Socialist Labor); 325 scattered write-in.

**1964**  Other vote was scattered write-in.

**1960**  Other vote was 10,560 Hass (Socialist Labor); 15 scattered write-in.

# INDIANA

## POPULAR VOTE FOR PRESIDENT 1920 TO 2004

| Year | Total Vote | Republican | | Democratic | | Other Vote | Plurality | Percentage | | | |
|---|---|---|---|---|---|---|---|---|---|---|---|
| | | | | | | | | Total Vote | | Major Vote | |
| | | Vote | Candidate | Vote | Candidate | | | Rep. | Dem. | Rep. | Dem. |
| 2004 | 2,468,002 | 1,479,438 | Bush, George W. | 969,011 | Kerry, John | 19,553 | 510,427 R | 59.9% | 39.3% | 60.4% | 39.6% |
| 2000 ** | 2,199,302 | 1,245,836 | Bush, George W. | 901,980 | Gore, Al | 51,486 | 343,856 R | 56.6% | 41.0% | 58.0% | 42.0% |
| 1996 ** | 2,135,842 | 1,006,693 | Dole, Bob | 887,424 | Clinton, Bill | 241,725 | 119,269 R | 47.1% | 41.5% | 53.1% | 46.9% |
| 1992 ** | 2,305,871 | 989,375 | Bush, George | 848,420 | Clinton, Bill | 468,076 | 140,955 R | 42.9% | 36.8% | 53.8% | 46.2% |
| 1988 | 2,168,621 | 1,297,763 | Bush, George | 860,643 | Dukakis, Michael S. | 10,215 | 437,120 R | 59.8% | 39.7% | 60.1% | 39.9% |
| 1984 | 2,233,069 | 1,377,230 | Reagan, Ronald | 841,481 | Mondale, Walter F. | 14,358 | 535,749 R | 61.7% | 37.7% | 62.1% | 37.9% |
| 1980** | 2,242,033 | 1,255,656 | Reagan, Ronald | 844,197 | Carter, Jimmy | 142,180 | 411,459 R | 56.0% | 37.7% | 59.8% | 40.2% |
| 1976 | 2,220,362 | 1,183,958 | Ford, Gerald R. | 1,014,714 | Carter, Jimmy | 21,690 | 169,244 R | 53.3% | 45.7% | 53.8% | 46.2% |
| 1972 | 2,125,529 | 1,405,154 | Nixon, Richard M. | 708,568 | McGovern, George S. | 11,807 | 696,586 R | 66.1% | 33.3% | 66.5% | 33.5% |
| 1968 | 2,123,597 | 1,067,885 | Nixon, Richard M. | 806,659 | Humphrey, Hubert H. | 249,053 | 261,226 R | 50.3% | 38.0% | 57.0% | 43.0% |
| 1964 | 2,091,606 | 911,118 | Goldwater, Barry M. | 1,170,848 | Johnson, Lyndon B. | 9,640 | 259,730 D | 43.6% | 56.0% | 43.8% | 56.2% |
| 1960 | 2,135,360 | 1,175,120 | Nixon, Richard M. | 952,358 | Kennedy, John F. | 7,882 | 222,762 R | 55.0% | 44.6% | 55.2% | 44.8% |
| 1956 | 1,974,607 | 1,182,811 | Eisenhower, Dwight D. | 783,908 | Stevenson, Adlai E. | 7,888 | 398,903 R | 59.9% | 39.7% | 60.1% | 39.9% |
| 1952 | 1,955,049 | 1,136,259 | Eisenhower, Dwight D. | 801,530 | Stevenson, Adlai E. | 17,260 | 334,729 R | 58.1% | 41.0% | 58.6% | 41.4% |
| 1948 | 1,656,212 | 821,079 | Dewey, Thomas E. | 807,831 | Truman, Harry S. | 27,302 | 13,248 R | 49.6% | 48.8% | 50.4% | 49.6% |
| 1944 | 1,672,091 | 875,891 | Dewey, Thomas E. | 781,403 | Roosevelt, Franklin D. | 14,797 | 94,488 R | 52.4% | 46.7% | 52.9% | 47.1% |
| 1940 | 1,782,747 | 899,466 | Willkie, Wendell | 874,063 | Roosevelt, Franklin D. | 9,218 | 25,403 R | 50.5% | 49.0% | 50.7% | 49.3% |
| 1936 | 1,650,897 | 691,570 | Landon, Alfred M. | 934,974 | Roosevelt, Franklin D. | 24,353 | 243,404 D | 41.9% | 56.6% | 42.5% | 57.5% |
| 1932 | 1,576,927 | 677,184 | Hoover, Herbert C. | 862,054 | Roosevelt, Franklin D. | 37,689 | 184,870 D | 42.9% | 54.7% | 44.0% | 56.0% |
| 1928 | 1,421,314 | 848,290 | Hoover, Herbert C. | 562,691 | Smith, Alfred E. | 10,333 | 285,599 R | 59.7% | 39.6% | 60.1% | 39.9% |
| 1924 | 1,272,390 | 703,042 | Coolidge, Calvin | 492,245 | Davis, John W. | 77,103 | 210,797 R | 55.3% | 38.7% | 58.8% | 41.2% |
| 1920 | 1,262,974 | 696,370 | Harding, Warren G. | 511,364 | Cox, James M. | 55,240 | 185,006 R | 55.1% | 40.5% | 57.7% | 42.3% |

In 2000 the other vote column includes 18,531 votes cast for Green (Nader). In 1996 the other vote column includes 224,299 votes cast for Perot. In 1992 the other vote column includes 455,934 votes cast for Perot. In 1980 the other column includes 111,639 votes for Independent (Anderson).

## ELECTORAL COLLEGE VOTE 1920 TO 2004

| Year | Total | Republican | Democratic | Other |
|---|---|---|---|---|
| 2004 | 11 | 11 | | |
| 2000 | 12 | 12 | | |
| 1996 | 12 | 12 | | |
| 1992 | 12 | 12 | | |
| 1988 | 12 | 12 | | |
| 1984 | 12 | 12 | | |
| 1980 | 13 | 13 | | |
| 1976 | 13 | 13 | | |
| 1972 | 13 | 13 | | |
| 1968 | 13 | 13 | | |
| 1964 | 13 | | 13 | |
| 1960 | 13 | 13 | | |
| 1956 | 13 | 13 | | |
| 1952 | 13 | 13 | | |
| 1948 | 13 | 13 | | |
| 1944 | 13 | 13 | | |
| 1940 | 14 | 14 | | |
| 1936 | 14 | | 14 | |
| 1932 | 14 | | 14 | |
| 1928 | 15 | 15 | | |
| 1924 | 15 | 15 | | |
| 1920 | 15 | 15 | | |

# INDIANA

# INDIANA

## PRESIDENT 2004

| 2000 Census Population | County | Total Vote | Republican | Democratic | Other | Rep.-Dem. Plurality | | Percentage | | | |
|---|---|---|---|---|---|---|---|---|---|---|---|
| | | | | | | | | Total Vote | | Major Vote | |
| | | | | | | | | Rep. | Dem. | Rep. | Dem. |
| 33,625 | ADAMS | 13,340 | 9,734 | 3,512 | 94 | 6,222 | R | 73.0% | 26.3% | 73.5% | 26.5% |
| 331,849 | ALLEN | 129,609 | 82,013 | 46,710 | 886 | 35,303 | R | 63.3% | 36.0% | 63.7% | 36.3% |
| 71,435 | BARTHOLOMEW | 28,515 | 19,093 | 9,191 | 231 | 9,902 | R | 67.0% | 32.2% | 67.5% | 32.5% |
| 9,421 | BENTON | 3,992 | 2,797 | 1,135 | 60 | 1,662 | R | 70.1% | 28.4% | 71.1% | 28.9% |
| 14,048 | BLACKFORD | 5,380 | 3,447 | 1,903 | 30 | 1,544 | R | 64.1% | 35.4% | 64.4% | 35.6% |
| 46,107 | BOONE | 22,898 | 17,055 | 5,636 | 207 | 11,419 | R | 74.5% | 24.6% | 75.2% | 24.8% |
| 14,957 | BROWN | 7,330 | 4,512 | 2,730 | 88 | 1,782 | R | 61.6% | 37.2% | 62.3% | 37.7% |
| 20,165 | CARROLL | 8,638 | 5,868 | 2,689 | 81 | 3,179 | R | 67.9% | 31.1% | 68.6% | 31.4% |
| 40,930 | CASS | 13,931 | 9,480 | 4,315 | 136 | 5,165 | R | 68.0% | 31.0% | 68.7% | 31.3% |
| 96,472 | CLARK | 42,337 | 24,495 | 17,648 | 194 | 6,847 | R | 57.9% | 41.7% | 58.1% | 41.9% |
| 26,556 | CLAY | 10,783 | 7,361 | 3,333 | 89 | 4,028 | R | 68.3% | 30.9% | 68.8% | 31.2% |
| 33,866 | CLINTON | 11,877 | 8,471 | 3,335 | 71 | 5,136 | R | 71.3% | 28.1% | 71.8% | 28.2% |
| 10,743 | CRAWFORD | 4,574 | 2,609 | 1,932 | 33 | 677 | R | 57.0% | 42.2% | 57.5% | 42.5% |
| 29,820 | DAVIESS | 10,599 | 7,936 | 2,573 | 90 | 5,363 | R | 74.9% | 24.3% | 75.5% | 24.5% |
| 46,109 | DEARBORN | 20,969 | 14,231 | 6,596 | 142 | 7,635 | R | 67.9% | 31.5% | 68.3% | 31.7% |
| 24,555 | DECATUR | 10,199 | 7,499 | 2,621 | 79 | 4,878 | R | 73.5% | 25.7% | 74.1% | 25.9% |
| 40,285 | DE KALB | 15,403 | 10,468 | 4,810 | 125 | 5,658 | R | 68.0% | 31.2% | 68.5% | 31.5% |
| 118,769 | DELAWARE | 47,939 | 27,064 | 20,436 | 439 | 6,628 | R | 56.5% | 42.6% | 57.0% | 43.0% |
| 39,674 | DUBOIS | 17,066 | 11,726 | 5,210 | 130 | 6,516 | R | 68.7% | 30.5% | 69.2% | 30.8% |
| 182,791 | ELKHART | 61,380 | 42,967 | 17,966 | 447 | 25,001 | R | 70.0% | 29.3% | 70.5% | 29.5% |
| 25,588 | FAYETTE | 9,468 | 5,761 | 3,626 | 81 | 2,135 | R | 60.8% | 38.3% | 61.4% | 38.6% |
| 70,823 | FLOYD | 33,890 | 19,877 | 13,857 | 156 | 6,020 | R | 58.7% | 40.9% | 58.9% | 41.1% |
| 17,954 | FOUNTAIN | 7,804 | 5,260 | 2,477 | 67 | 2,783 | R | 67.4% | 31.7% | 68.0% | 32.0% |
| 22,151 | FRANKLIN | 9,992 | 6,977 | 2,925 | 90 | 4,052 | R | 69.8% | 29.3% | 70.5% | 29.5% |
| 20,511 | FULTON | 8,703 | 6,027 | 2,607 | 69 | 3,420 | R | 69.3% | 30.0% | 69.8% | 30.2% |
| 32,500 | GIBSON | 14,614 | 9,133 | 5,378 | 103 | 3,755 | R | 62.5% | 36.8% | 62.9% | 37.1% |
| 73,403 | GRANT | 27,460 | 18,769 | 8,509 | 182 | 10,260 | R | 68.4% | 31.0% | 68.8% | 31.2% |
| 33,157 | GREENE | 13,352 | 8,609 | 4,606 | 137 | 4,003 | R | 64.5% | 34.5% | 65.1% | 34.9% |
| 182,740 | HAMILTON | 104,906 | 77,887 | 26,388 | 631 | 51,499 | R | 74.2% | 25.2% | 74.7% | 25.3% |
| 55,391 | HANCOCK | 27,867 | 20,771 | 6,912 | 184 | 13,859 | R | 74.5% | 24.8% | 75.0% | 25.0% |
| 34,325 | HARRISON | 17,310 | 11,015 | 6,171 | 124 | 4,844 | R | 63.6% | 35.6% | 64.1% | 35.9% |
| 104,093 | HENDRICKS | 52,302 | 38,430 | 13,548 | 324 | 24,882 | R | 73.5% | 25.9% | 73.9% | 26.1% |
| 48,508 | HENRY | 20,504 | 13,137 | 7,176 | 191 | 5,961 | R | 64.1% | 35.0% | 64.7% | 35.3% |
| 84,964 | HOWARD | 37,021 | 23,714 | 12,998 | 309 | 10,716 | R | 64.1% | 35.1% | 64.6% | 35.4% |
| 38,075 | HUNTINGTON | 15,627 | 11,617 | 3,877 | 133 | 7,740 | R | 74.3% | 24.8% | 75.0% | 25.0% |
| 41,335 | JACKSON | 16,309 | 11,083 | 5,092 | 134 | 5,991 | R | 68.0% | 31.2% | 68.5% | 31.5% |
| 30,043 | JASPER | 11,844 | 8,056 | 3,678 | 110 | 4,378 | R | 68.0% | 31.1% | 68.7% | 31.3% |
| 21,806 | JAY | 8,232 | 5,427 | 2,740 | 65 | 2,687 | R | 65.9% | 33.3% | 66.5% | 33.5% |
| 31,705 | JEFFERSON | 12,971 | 7,763 | 5,117 | 91 | 2,646 | R | 59.8% | 39.4% | 60.3% | 39.7% |
| 27,554 | JENNINGS | 10,517 | 6,864 | 3,538 | 115 | 3,326 | R | 65.3% | 33.6% | 66.0% | 34.0% |
| 115,209 | JOHNSON | 51,255 | 37,765 | 13,109 | 381 | 24,656 | R | 73.7% | 25.6% | 74.2% | 25.8% |
| 39,256 | KNOX | 15,746 | 9,990 | 5,649 | 107 | 4,341 | R | 63.4% | 35.9% | 63.9% | 36.1% |
| 74,057 | KOSCIUSKO | 28,360 | 22,136 | 5,977 | 247 | 16,159 | R | 78.1% | 21.1% | 78.7% | 21.3% |
| 34,909 | LAGRANGE | 9,003 | 6,430 | 2,523 | 50 | 3,907 | R | 71.4% | 28.0% | 71.8% | 28.2% |
| 484,564 | LAKE | 188,022 | 71,903 | 114,743 | 1,376 | 42,840 | D | 38.2% | 61.0% | 38.5% | 61.5% |
| 110,106 | LA PORTE | 42,606 | 20,916 | 21,114 | 576 | 198 | D | 49.1% | 49.6% | 49.8% | 50.2% |
| 45,922 | LAWRENCE | 17,698 | 12,207 | 5,346 | 145 | 6,861 | R | 69.0% | 30.2% | 69.5% | 30.5% |
| 133,358 | MADISON | 54,855 | 32,526 | 21,882 | 447 | 10,644 | R | 59.3% | 39.9% | 59.8% | 40.2% |
| 860,454 | MARION | 320,838 | 156,072 | 162,249 | 2,517 | 6,177 | D | 48.6% | 50.6% | 49.0% | 51.0% |
| 45,128 | MARSHALL | 17,814 | 12,074 | 5,593 | 147 | 6,481 | R | 67.8% | 31.4% | 68.3% | 31.7% |
| 10,369 | MARTIN | 4,996 | 3,414 | 1,522 | 60 | 1,892 | R | 68.3% | 30.5% | 69.2% | 30.8% |
| 36,082 | MIAMI | 13,628 | 9,600 | 3,886 | 142 | 5,714 | R | 70.4% | 28.5% | 71.2% | 28.8% |
| 120,563 | MONROE | 50,467 | 22,834 | 26,965 | 668 | 4,131 | D | 45.2% | 53.4% | 45.9% | 54.1% |
| 37,629 | MONTGOMERY | 14,548 | 10,901 | 3,536 | 111 | 7,365 | R | 74.9% | 24.3% | 75.5% | 24.5% |
| 66,689 | MORGAN | 26,029 | 19,197 | 6,650 | 182 | 12,547 | R | 73.8% | 25.5% | 74.3% | 25.7% |
| 14,566 | NEWTON | 5,848 | 3,757 | 2,032 | 59 | 1,725 | R | 64.2% | 34.7% | 64.9% | 35.1% |
| 46,275 | NOBLE | 15,679 | 10,859 | 4,703 | 117 | 6,156 | R | 69.3% | 30.0% | 69.8% | 30.2% |
| 5,623 | OHIO | 2,958 | 1,796 | 1,139 | 23 | 657 | R | 60.7% | 38.5% | 61.2% | 38.8% |
| 19,306 | ORANGE | 8,652 | 5,683 | 2,885 | 84 | 2,798 | R | 65.7% | 33.3% | 66.3% | 33.7% |
| 21,786 | OWEN | 7,604 | 5,000 | 2,536 | 68 | 2,464 | R | 65.8% | 33.4% | 66.3% | 33.7% |

# INDIANA

## PRESIDENT 2004

| 2000 Census Population | County | Total Vote | Republican | Democratic | Other | Rep.-Dem. Plurality | | Percentage | | | |
|---|---|---|---|---|---|---|---|---|---|---|---|
| | | | | | | | | Total Vote | | Major Vote | |
| | | | | | | | | Rep. | Dem. | Rep. | Dem. |
| 17,241 | PARKE | 6,971 | 4,550 | 2,362 | 59 | 2,188 | R | 65.3% | 33.9% | 65.8% | 34.2% |
| 18,899 | PERRY | 8,315 | 4,137 | 4,131 | 47 | 6 | R | 49.8% | 49.7% | 50.0% | 50.0% |
| 12,837 | PIKE | 6,212 | 3,745 | 2,418 | 49 | 1,327 | R | 60.3% | 38.9% | 60.8% | 39.2% |
| 146,798 | PORTER | 64,873 | 34,794 | 29,388 | 691 | 5,406 | R | 53.6% | 45.3% | 54.2% | 45.8% |
| 27,061 | POSEY | 11,986 | 7,833 | 4,085 | 68 | 3,748 | R | 65.4% | 34.1% | 65.7% | 34.3% |
| 13,755 | PULASKI | 5,614 | 3,797 | 1,750 | 67 | 2,047 | R | 67.6% | 31.2% | 68.5% | 31.5% |
| 36,019 | PUTNAM | 13,136 | 8,908 | 4,103 | 125 | 4,805 | R | 67.8% | 31.2% | 68.5% | 31.5% |
| 27,401 | RANDOLPH | 11,092 | 7,172 | 3,812 | 108 | 3,360 | R | 64.7% | 34.4% | 65.3% | 34.7% |
| 26,523 | RIPLEY | 11,834 | 8,224 | 3,510 | 100 | 4,714 | R | 69.5% | 29.7% | 70.1% | 29.9% |
| 18,261 | RUSH | 7,421 | 5,363 | 2,000 | 58 | 3,363 | R | 72.3% | 27.0% | 72.8% | 27.2% |
| 265,559 | ST. JOSEPH | 108,619 | 55,254 | 52,637 | 728 | 2,617 | R | 50.9% | 48.5% | 51.2% | 48.8% |
| 22,960 | SCOTT | 8,677 | 4,793 | 3,822 | 62 | 971 | R | 55.2% | 44.0% | 55.6% | 44.4% |
| 43,445 | SHELBY | 16,027 | 11,397 | 4,519 | 111 | 6,878 | R | 71.1% | 28.2% | 71.6% | 28.4% |
| 20,391 | SPENCER | 9,924 | 5,934 | 3,920 | 70 | 2,014 | R | 59.8% | 39.5% | 60.2% | 39.8% |
| 23,556 | STARKE | 8,937 | 4,846 | 3,987 | 104 | 859 | R | 54.2% | 44.6% | 54.9% | 45.1% |
| 33,214 | STEUBEN | 12,905 | 8,433 | 4,345 | 127 | 4,088 | R | 65.3% | 33.7% | 66.0% | 34.0% |
| 21,751 | SULLIVAN | 8,394 | 4,999 | 3,341 | 54 | 1,658 | R | 59.6% | 39.8% | 59.9% | 40.1% |
| 9,065 | SWITZERLAND | 3,671 | 2,161 | 1,479 | 31 | 682 | R | 58.9% | 40.3% | 59.4% | 40.6% |
| 148,955 | TIPPECANOE | 52,360 | 30,897 | 20,818 | 645 | 10,079 | R | 59.0% | 39.8% | 59.7% | 40.3% |
| 16,577 | TIPTON | 7,892 | 5,628 | 2,203 | 61 | 3,425 | R | 71.3% | 27.9% | 71.9% | 28.1% |
| 7,349 | UNION | 3,344 | 2,266 | 1,045 | 33 | 1,221 | R | 67.8% | 31.3% | 68.4% | 31.6% |
| 171,922 | VANDERBURGH | 70,654 | 41,463 | 28,767 | 424 | 12,696 | R | 58.7% | 40.7% | 59.0% | 41.0% |
| 16,788 | VERMILLION | 7,017 | 3,536 | 3,424 | 57 | 112 | R | 50.4% | 48.8% | 50.8% | 49.2% |
| 105,848 | VIGO | 39,744 | 20,988 | 18,426 | 330 | 2,562 | R | 52.8% | 46.4% | 53.3% | 46.7% |
| 34,960 | WABASH | 13,602 | 9,607 | 3,920 | 75 | 5,687 | R | 70.6% | 28.8% | 71.0% | 29.0% |
| 8,419 | WARREN | 3,960 | 2,565 | 1,356 | 39 | 1,209 | R | 64.8% | 34.2% | 65.4% | 34.6% |
| 52,383 | WARRICK | 26,025 | 16,930 | 8,980 | 115 | 7,950 | R | 65.1% | 34.5% | 65.3% | 34.7% |
| 27,223 | WASHINGTON | 10,880 | 6,915 | 3,879 | 86 | 3,036 | R | 63.6% | 35.7% | 64.1% | 35.9% |
| 71,097 | WAYNE | 27,657 | 16,586 | 10,775 | 296 | 5,811 | R | 60.0% | 39.0% | 60.6% | 39.4% |
| 27,600 | WELLS | 12,354 | 9,168 | 3,112 | 74 | 6,056 | R | 74.2% | 25.2% | 74.7% | 25.3% |
| 25,267 | WHITE | 10,366 | 6,974 | 3,277 | 115 | 3,697 | R | 67.3% | 31.6% | 68.0% | 32.0% |
| 30,707 | WHITLEY | 13,481 | 9,512 | 3,880 | 89 | 5,632 | R | 70.6% | 28.8% | 71.0% | 29.0% |
| 6,080,485 | TOTAL | 2,468,002 | 1,479,438 | 969,011 | 19,553 | 510,427 | R | 59.9% | 39.3% | 60.4% | 39.6% |

# INDIANA

## PRESIDENT 2000

| 2000 Census Population | County | Total Vote | Republican | Democratic | Green (Nader) | Other | Rep.-Dem. Plurality | Percentage of Total Vote | | |
|---|---|---|---|---|---|---|---|---|---|---|
| | | | | | | | | Rep. | Dem. | Green |
| 33,625 | ADAMS | 12,590 | 8,555 | 3,775 | 45 | 215 | 4,780 R | 68.0% | 30.0% | 0.4% |
| 331,849 | ALLEN | 114,320 | 70,426 | 41,636 | 556 | 1,702 | 28,790 R | 61.6% | 36.4% | 0.5% |
| 71,435 | BARTHOLOMEW | 25,769 | 16,200 | 9,015 | 181 | 373 | 7,185 R | 62.9% | 35.0% | 0.7% |
| 9,421 | BENTON | 3,874 | 2,441 | 1,328 | 20 | 85 | 1,113 R | 63.0% | 34.3% | 0.5% |
| 14,048 | BLACKFORD | 4,893 | 2,699 | 2,103 | 18 | 73 | 596 R | 55.2% | 43.0% | 0.4% |
| 46,107 | BOONE | 18,396 | 13,161 | 4,763 | 196 | 276 | 8,398 R | 71.5% | 25.9% | 1.1% |
| 14,957 | BROWN | 6,817 | 3,871 | 2,608 | 210 | 128 | 1,263 R | 56.8% | 38.3% | 3.1% |
| 20,165 | CARROLL | 8,268 | 5,102 | 2,965 | 87 | 114 | 2,137 R | 61.7% | 35.9% | 1.1% |
| 40,930 | CASS | 15,106 | 9,305 | 5,412 | | 389 | 3,893 R | 61.6% | 35.8% | |
| 96,472 | CLARK | 37,336 | 19,417 | 17,360 | 212 | 347 | 2,057 R | 52.0% | 46.5% | 0.6% |
| 26,556 | CLAY | 10,158 | 6,393 | 3,605 | 19 | 141 | 2,788 R | 62.9% | 35.5% | 0.2% |
| 33,866 | CLINTON | 10,991 | 7,141 | 3,643 | 40 | 167 | 3,498 R | 65.0% | 33.1% | 0.4% |
| 10,743 | CRAWFORD | 4,209 | 2,327 | 1,817 | 17 | 48 | 510 R | 55.3% | 43.2% | 0.4% |
| 29,820 | DAVIESS | 9,761 | 6,872 | 2,697 | 49 | 143 | 4,175 R | 70.4% | 27.6% | 0.5% |
| 46,109 | DEARBORN | 17,650 | 11,452 | 6,020 | | 178 | 5,432 R | 64.9% | 34.1% | |
| 24,555 | DECATUR | 9,171 | 6,115 | 2,889 | 11 | 156 | 3,226 R | 66.7% | 31.5% | 0.1% |
| 40,285 | DE KALB | 13,785 | 8,701 | 4,776 | 71 | 237 | 3,925 R | 63.1% | 34.6% | 0.5% |
| 118,769 | DELAWARE | 44,147 | 22,105 | 20,876 | 386 | 780 | 1,229 R | 50.1% | 47.3% | 0.9% |
| 39,674 | DUBOIS | 15,504 | 10,134 | 5,090 | 42 | 238 | 5,044 R | 65.4% | 32.8% | 0.3% |
| 182,791 | ELKHART | 54,482 | 36,756 | 16,402 | 642 | 682 | 20,354 R | 67.5% | 30.1% | 1.2% |
| 25,588 | FAYETTE | 8,647 | 5,060 | 3,415 | 31 | 141 | 1,645 R | 58.5% | 39.5% | 0.4% |
| 70,823 | FLOYD | 30,030 | 16,486 | 13,209 | 52 | 283 | 3,277 R | 54.9% | 44.0% | 0.2% |
| 17,954 | FOUNTAIN | 7,281 | 4,408 | 2,717 | 18 | 138 | 1,691 R | 60.5% | 37.3% | 0.2% |
| 22,151 | FRANKLIN | 8,339 | 5,587 | 2,591 | 25 | 136 | 2,996 R | 67.0% | 31.1% | 0.3% |
| 20,511 | FULTON | 8,327 | 5,218 | 2,960 | 37 | 112 | 2,258 R | 62.7% | 35.5% | 0.4% |
| 32,500 | GIBSON | 13,772 | 7,734 | 5,802 | 77 | 159 | 1,932 R | 56.2% | 42.1% | 0.6% |
| 73,403 | GRANT | 26,386 | 16,153 | 9,712 | 84 | 437 | 6,441 R | 61.2% | 36.8% | 0.3% |
| 33,157 | GREENE | 12,619 | 7,452 | 4,898 | 57 | 212 | 2,554 R | 59.1% | 38.8% | 0.5% |
| 182,740 | HAMILTON | 75,926 | 56,372 | 18,002 | 669 | 883 | 38,370 R | 74.2% | 23.7% | 0.9% |
| 55,391 | HANCOCK | 22,950 | 15,943 | 6,503 | 126 | 378 | 9,440 R | 69.5% | 28.3% | 0.5% |
| 34,325 | HARRISON | 14,896 | 8,711 | 5,870 | 101 | 214 | 2,841 R | 58.5% | 39.4% | 0.7% |
| 104,093 | HENDRICKS | 40,221 | 28,651 | 10,786 | 164 | 620 | 17,865 R | 71.2% | 26.8% | 0.4% |
| 48,508 | HENRY | 18,315 | 10,321 | 7,647 | 9 | 338 | 2,674 R | 56.4% | 41.8% | |
| 84,964 | HOWARD | 34,095 | 20,331 | 12,899 | 343 | 522 | 7,432 R | 59.6% | 37.8% | 1.0% |
| 38,075 | HUNTINGTON | 14,620 | 10,113 | 4,119 | 162 | 226 | 5,994 R | 69.2% | 28.2% | 1.1% |
| 41,335 | JACKSON | 14,602 | 9,054 | 5,330 | 27 | 191 | 3,724 R | 62.0% | 36.5% | 0.2% |
| 30,043 | JASPER | 11,167 | 7,212 | 3,744 | 71 | 140 | 3,468 R | 64.6% | 33.5% | 0.6% |
| 21,806 | JAY | 8,030 | 4,687 | 3,167 | 15 | 161 | 1,520 R | 58.4% | 39.4% | 0.2% |
| 31,705 | JEFFERSON | 11,931 | 6,582 | 5,117 | 84 | 148 | 1,465 R | 55.2% | 42.9% | 0.7% |
| 27,554 | JENNINGS | 9,494 | 5,732 | 3,549 | 47 | 166 | 2,183 R | 60.4% | 37.4% | 0.5% |
| 115,209 | JOHNSON | 42,284 | 29,404 | 11,952 | 178 | 750 | 17,452 R | 69.5% | 28.3% | 0.4% |
| 39,256 | KNOX | 15,054 | 8,485 | 6,300 | 76 | 193 | 2,185 R | 56.4% | 41.8% | 0.5% |
| 74,057 | KOSCIUSKO | 25,284 | 19,040 | 5,785 | 92 | 367 | 13,255 R | 75.3% | 22.9% | 0.4% |
| 34,909 | LAGRANGE | 8,333 | 5,437 | 2,733 | 51 | 112 | 2,704 R | 65.2% | 32.8% | 0.6% |
| 484,564 | LAKE | 175,994 | 63,389 | 109,078 | 1,659 | 1,868 | 45,689 D | 36.0% | 62.0% | 0.9% |
| 110,106 | LA PORTE | 39,747 | 18,994 | 19,736 | 413 | 604 | 742 D | 47.8% | 49.7% | 1.0% |
| 45,922 | LAWRENCE | 16,142 | 10,677 | 5,071 | 101 | 293 | 5,606 R | 66.1% | 31.4% | 0.6% |
| 133,358 | MADISON | 52,216 | 27,956 | 23,403 | | 857 | 4,553 R | 53.5% | 44.8% | |
| 860,454 | MARION | 279,903 | 137,810 | 134,189 | 2,967 | 4,937 | 3,621 R | 49.2% | 47.9% | 1.1% |
| 45,128 | MARSHALL | 16,150 | 10,266 | 5,541 | 109 | 234 | 4,725 R | 63.6% | 34.3% | 0.7% |
| 10,369 | MARTIN | 4,609 | 3,008 | 1,518 | 14 | 69 | 1,490 R | 65.3% | 32.9% | 0.3% |
| 36,082 | MIAMI | 12,928 | 8,401 | 4,155 | 44 | 328 | 4,246 R | 65.0% | 32.1% | 0.3% |
| 120,563 | MONROE | 40,220 | 19,147 | 17,523 | 2,991 | 559 | 1,624 R | 47.6% | 43.6% | 7.4% |
| 37,629 | MONTGOMERY | 13,101 | 8,891 | 3,899 | 132 | 179 | 4,992 R | 67.9% | 29.8% | 1.0% |
| 66,689 | MORGAN | 22,036 | 15,286 | 6,228 | 151 | 371 | 9,058 R | 69.4% | 28.3% | 0.7% |
| 14,566 | NEWTON | 5,510 | 3,250 | 2,101 | 28 | 131 | 1,149 R | 59.0% | 38.1% | 0.5% |
| 46,275 | NOBLE | 14,216 | 9,103 | 4,822 | 66 | 225 | 4,281 R | 64.0% | 33.9% | 0.5% |
| 5,623 | OHIO | 2,492 | 1,515 | 951 | 6 | 20 | 564 R | 60.8% | 38.2% | 0.2% |
| 19,306 | ORANGE | 7,458 | 4,687 | 2,601 | 46 | 124 | 2,086 R | 62.8% | 34.9% | 0.6% |
| 21,786 | OWEN | 6,503 | 4,019 | 2,253 | 85 | 146 | 1,766 R | 61.8% | 34.6% | 1.3% |

# INDIANA

## PRESIDENT 2000

| 2000 Census Population | County | Total Vote | Republican | Democratic | Green (Nader) | Other | Rep.-Dem. Plurality | Percentage of Total Vote | | |
|---|---|---|---|---|---|---|---|---|---|---|
| | | | | | | | | Rep. | Dem. | Green |
| 17,241 | PARKE | 6,447 | 3,841 | 2,481 | 20 | 105 | 1,360 R | 59.6% | 38.5% | 0.3% |
| 18,899 | PERRY | 7,387 | 3,461 | 3,823 | 26 | 77 | 362 D | 46.9% | 51.8% | 0.4% |
| 12,837 | PIKE | 6,302 | 3,566 | 2,605 | 3 | 128 | 961 R | 56.6% | 41.3% | |
| 146,798 | PORTER | 59,378 | 31,157 | 26,790 | 592 | 839 | 4,367 R | 52.5% | 45.1% | 1.0% |
| 27,061 | POSEY | 11,110 | 6,498 | 4,430 | 52 | 130 | 2,068 R | 58.5% | 39.9% | 0.5% |
| 13,755 | PULASKI | 5,518 | 3,497 | 1,919 | 17 | 85 | 1,578 R | 63.4% | 34.8% | 0.3% |
| 36,019 | PUTNAM | 11,871 | 7,352 | 4,123 | 144 | 252 | 3,229 R | 61.9% | 34.7% | 1.2% |
| 27,401 | RANDOLPH | 10,132 | 6,020 | 3,906 | 20 | 186 | 2,114 R | 59.4% | 38.6% | 0.2% |
| 26,523 | RIPLEY | 10,675 | 6,988 | 3,498 | 23 | 166 | 3,490 R | 65.5% | 32.8% | 0.2% |
| 18,261 | RUSH | 7,284 | 4,749 | 2,370 | 21 | 144 | 2,379 R | 65.2% | 32.5% | 0.3% |
| 265,559 | ST. JOSEPH | 97,474 | 47,581 | 47,703 | 905 | 1,285 | 122 D | 48.8% | 48.9% | 0.9% |
| 22,960 | SCOTT | 7,846 | 3,761 | 3,915 | 40 | 130 | 154 D | 47.9% | 49.9% | 0.5% |
| 43,445 | SHELBY | 15,310 | 9,590 | 5,374 | 71 | 275 | 4,216 R | 62.6% | 35.1% | 0.5% |
| 20,391 | SPENCER | 8,987 | 5,096 | 3,752 | 42 | 97 | 1,344 R | 56.7% | 41.7% | 0.5% |
| 23,556 | STARKE | 8,701 | 4,349 | 4,136 | 27 | 189 | 213 R | 50.0% | 47.5% | 0.3% |
| 33,214 | STEUBEN | 11,277 | 6,953 | 4,103 | 40 | 181 | 2,850 R | 61.7% | 36.4% | 0.4% |
| 21,751 | SULLIVAN | 8,262 | 4,319 | 3,833 | 4 | 106 | 486 R | 52.3% | 46.4% | |
| 9,065 | SWITZERLAND | 3,239 | 1,831 | 1,336 | 15 | 57 | 495 R | 56.5% | 41.2% | 0.5% |
| 148,955 | TIPPECANOE | 46,295 | 26,106 | 18,220 | 1,054 | 915 | 7,886 R | 56.4% | 39.4% | 2.3% |
| 16,577 | TIPTON | 7,316 | 4,784 | 2,392 | 6 | 134 | 2,392 R | 65.4% | 32.7% | 0.1% |
| 7,349 | UNION | 2,828 | 1,838 | 927 | 11 | 52 | 911 R | 65.0% | 32.8% | 0.4% |
| 171,922 | VANDERBURGH | 66,221 | 35,846 | 29,222 | 381 | 772 | 6,624 R | 54.1% | 44.1% | 0.6% |
| 16,788 | VERMILLION | 6,633 | 3,130 | 3,370 | 13 | 120 | 240 D | 47.2% | 50.8% | 0.2% |
| 105,848 | VIGO | 36,228 | 18,021 | 17,570 | 158 | 479 | 451 R | 49.7% | 48.5% | 0.4% |
| 34,960 | WABASH | 12,883 | 8,321 | 4,277 | 125 | 160 | 4,044 R | 64.6% | 33.2% | 1.0% |
| 8,419 | WARREN | 3,768 | 2,218 | 1,471 | 21 | 58 | 747 R | 58.9% | 39.0% | 0.6% |
| 52,383 | WARRICK | 22,309 | 13,205 | 8,749 | 105 | 250 | 4,456 R | 59.2% | 39.2% | 0.5% |
| 27,223 | WASHINGTON | 9,801 | 5,868 | 3,675 | 52 | 206 | 2,193 R | 59.9% | 37.5% | 0.5% |
| 71,097 | WAYNE | 25,151 | 14,273 | 10,273 | 209 | 396 | 4,000 R | 56.7% | 40.8% | 0.8% |
| 27,600 | WELLS | 11,281 | 7,755 | 3,319 | 30 | 177 | 4,436 R | 68.7% | 29.4% | 0.3% |
| 25,267 | WHITE | 9,904 | 6,037 | 3,655 | 39 | 173 | 2,382 R | 61.0% | 36.9% | 0.4% |
| 30,707 | WHITLEY | 12,432 | 8,080 | 4,107 | 30 | 215 | 3,973 R | 65.0% | 33.0% | 0.2% |
| 6,080,485 | TOTAL | 2,199,302 | 1,245,836 | 901,980 | 18,531 | 32,955 | 343,856 R | 56.6% | 41.0% | 0.8% |

Note: The votes cast for Nader were write-ins. A blank indicates that he received no votes in that particular county. The vote totals for each candidate listed above are as certified, although the county totals for Nader add to 18,506 and the county totals for the "Other" vote adds to 32,983.

# INDIANA

## PRESIDENT 1996

| 1995 Census Pop. Est. | County | Total Vote | Republican | Democratic | Reform (Perot) | Other | Rep.-Dem. Plurality | Percentage of Total Vote | | |
|---|---|---|---|---|---|---|---|---|---|---|
| | | | | | | | | Rep. | Dem. | Reform |
| 32,311 | ADAMS | 12,637 | 6,960 | 4,247 | 1,346 | 84 | 2,713 R | 55.1% | 33.6% | 10.7% |
| 308,503 | ALLEN | 110,645 | 59,255 | 41,450 | 8,808 | 1,132 | 17,805 R | 53.6% | 37.5% | 8.0% |
| 68,065 | BARTHOLOMEW | 25,558 | 13,188 | 9,301 | 2,815 | 254 | 3,887 R | 51.6% | 36.4% | 11.0% |
| 9,703 | BENTON | 3,900 | 1,947 | 1,311 | 609 | 33 | 636 R | 49.9% | 33.6% | 15.6% |
| 14,162 | BLACKFORD | 5,130 | 2,070 | 2,335 | 681 | 44 | 265 D | 40.4% | 45.5% | 13.3% |
| 41,813 | BOONE | 17,596 | 11,338 | 4,625 | 1,498 | 135 | 6,713 R | 64.4% | 26.3% | 8.5% |
| 15,098 | BROWN | 6,309 | 2,988 | 2,413 | 802 | 106 | 575 R | 47.4% | 38.2% | 12.7% |
| 19,505 | CARROLL | 8,031 | 4,062 | 2,747 | 1,171 | 51 | 1,315 R | 50.6% | 34.2% | 14.6% |
| 38,584 | CASS | 15,641 | 8,020 | 5,419 | 2,029 | 173 | 2,601 R | 51.3% | 34.6% | 13.0% |
| 91,826 | CLARK | 35,916 | 14,396 | 17,799 | 3,578 | 143 | 3,403 D | 40.1% | 49.6% | 10.0% |
| 26,306 | CLAY | 9,915 | 4,858 | 3,605 | 1,406 | 46 | 1,253 R | 49.0% | 36.4% | 14.2% |
| 32,594 | CLINTON | 11,571 | 6,156 | 3,949 | 1,355 | 111 | 2,207 R | 53.2% | 34.1% | 11.7% |
| 10,442 | CRAWFORD | 4,810 | 1,759 | 2,324 | 700 | 27 | 565 D | 36.6% | 48.3% | 14.6% |
| 28,603 | DAVIESS | 9,815 | 5,531 | 3,230 | 994 | 60 | 2,301 R | 56.4% | 32.9% | 10.1% |
| 44,367 | DEARBORN | 16,439 | 8,318 | 6,269 | 1,731 | 121 | 2,049 R | 50.6% | 38.1% | 10.5% |
| 24,998 | DECATUR | 9,409 | 4,782 | 3,190 | 1,389 | 48 | 1,592 R | 50.8% | 33.9% | 14.8% |
| 37,955 | DE KALB | 13,339 | 6,851 | 4,840 | 1,534 | 114 | 2,011 R | 51.4% | 36.3% | 11.5% |
| 118,577 | DELAWARE | 44,863 | 18,126 | 20,385 | 6,042 | 310 | 2,259 D | 40.4% | 45.4% | 13.5% |
| 38,732 | DUBOIS | 15,250 | 6,840 | 6,499 | 1,777 | 134 | 341 R | 44.9% | 42.6% | 11.7% |
| 166,994 | ELKHART | 50,850 | 28,770 | 16,598 | 5,133 | 349 | 12,172 R | 56.6% | 32.6% | 10.1% |
| 26,430 | FAYETTE | 9,120 | 4,091 | 3,822 | 1,137 | 70 | 269 R | 44.9% | 41.9% | 12.5% |
| 70,058 | FLOYD | 29,072 | 12,473 | 13,814 | 2,609 | 176 | 1,341 D | 42.9% | 47.5% | 9.0% |
| 18,060 | FOUNTAIN | 7,374 | 3,984 | 2,327 | 1,033 | 30 | 1,657 R | 54.0% | 31.6% | 14.0% |
| 20,957 | FRANKLIN | 7,975 | 4,167 | 2,808 | 943 | 57 | 1,359 R | 52.3% | 35.2% | 11.8% |
| 19,922 | FULTON | 8,070 | 3,934 | 2,956 | 1,143 | 37 | 978 R | 48.7% | 36.6% | 14.2% |
| 32,165 | GIBSON | 13,528 | 5,392 | 6,488 | 1,585 | 63 | 1,096 D | 39.9% | 48.0% | 11.7% |
| 73,720 | GRANT | 26,478 | 13,443 | 9,818 | 3,008 | 209 | 3,625 R | 50.8% | 37.1% | 11.4% |
| 32,696 | GREENE | 12,862 | 5,746 | 5,277 | 1,690 | 149 | 469 R | 44.7% | 41.0% | 13.1% |
| 140,650 | HAMILTON | 61,619 | 42,792 | 14,153 | 4,234 | 440 | 28,639 R | 69.4% | 23.0% | 6.9% |
| 50,768 | HANCOCK | 21,428 | 12,907 | 6,123 | 2,258 | 140 | 6,784 R | 60.2% | 28.6% | 10.5% |
| 32,594 | HARRISON | 13,885 | 6,073 | 5,900 | 1,839 | 73 | 173 R | 43.7% | 42.5% | 13.2% |
| 86,620 | HENDRICKS | 35,303 | 22,293 | 9,392 | 3,405 | 213 | 12,901 R | 63.1% | 26.6% | 9.6% |
| 49,275 | HENRY | 18,691 | 8,537 | 7,667 | 2,381 | 106 | 870 R | 45.7% | 41.0% | 12.7% |
| 83,763 | HOWARD | 33,205 | 16,771 | 11,999 | 4,172 | 263 | 4,772 R | 50.5% | 36.1% | 12.6% |
| 36,807 | HUNTINGTON | 14,076 | 8,275 | 4,287 | 1,400 | 114 | 3,988 R | 58.8% | 30.5% | 9.9% |
| 40,403 | JACKSON | 12,675 | 5,883 | 5,150 | 1,590 | 52 | 733 R | 46.4% | 40.6% | 12.5% |
| 27,895 | JASPER | 10,077 | 5,173 | 3,554 | 1,271 | 79 | 1,619 R | 51.3% | 35.3% | 12.6% |
| 21,901 | JAY | 8,017 | 3,584 | 3,356 | 1,022 | 55 | 228 R | 44.7% | 41.9% | 12.7% |
| 30,813 | JEFFERSON | 11,785 | 4,827 | 5,441 | 1,438 | 79 | 614 D | 41.0% | 46.2% | 12.2% |
| 26,168 | JENNINGS | 10,420 | 4,461 | 4,223 | 1,629 | 107 | 238 R | 42.8% | 40.5% | 15.6% |
| 101,690 | JOHNSON | 39,259 | 23,733 | 11,278 | 3,975 | 273 | 12,455 R | 60.5% | 28.7% | 10.1% |
| 40,194 | KNOX | 15,532 | 6,395 | 7,003 | 2,022 | 112 | 608 D | 41.2% | 45.1% | 13.0% |
| 69,210 | KOSCIUSKO | 23,945 | 15,084 | 6,166 | 2,531 | 164 | 8,918 R | 63.0% | 25.8% | 10.6% |
| 31,653 | LAGRANGE | 7,740 | 4,033 | 2,704 | 949 | 54 | 1,329 R | 52.1% | 34.9% | 12.3% |
| 482,672 | LAKE | 163,860 | 47,873 | 100,198 | 15,051 | 738 | 52,325 D | 29.2% | 61.1% | 9.2% |
| 110,384 | LA PORTE | 39,377 | 14,106 | 19,879 | 5,133 | 259 | 5,773 D | 35.8% | 50.5% | 13.0% |
| 45,097 | LAWRENCE | 16,009 | 8,107 | 5,703 | 2,063 | 136 | 2,404 R | 50.6% | 35.6% | 12.9% |
| 132,796 | MADISON | 53,720 | 23,151 | 23,772 | 6,447 | 350 | 621 D | 43.1% | 44.3% | 12.0% |
| 817,604 | MARION | 282,214 | 133,329 | 124,448 | 21,358 | 3,079 | 8,881 R | 47.2% | 44.1% | 7.6% |
| 44,879 | MARSHALL | 15,440 | 8,158 | 5,486 | 1,698 | 98 | 2,672 R | 52.8% | 35.5% | 11.0% |
| 10,545 | MARTIN | 4,720 | 2,281 | 1,848 | 485 | 106 | 433 R | 48.3% | 39.2% | 10.3% |
| 32,611 | MIAMI | 12,760 | 6,719 | 4,260 | 1,657 | 124 | 2,459 R | 52.7% | 33.4% | 13.0% |
| 115,208 | MONROE | 39,609 | 16,744 | 18,531 | 3,179 | 1,155 | 1,787 D | 42.3% | 46.8% | 8.0% |
| 36,090 | MONTGOMERY | 13,397 | 7,705 | 3,825 | 1,766 | 101 | 3,880 R | 57.5% | 28.6% | 13.2% |
| 62,115 | MORGAN | 21,596 | 12,872 | 5,812 | 2,755 | 157 | 7,060 R | 59.6% | 26.9% | 12.8% |
| 14,413 | NEWTON | 4,810 | 2,075 | 1,897 | 801 | 37 | 178 R | 43.1% | 39.4% | 16.7% |
| 40,884 | NOBLE | 13,519 | 6,782 | 5,101 | 1,521 | 115 | 1,681 R | 50.2% | 37.7% | 11.3% |
| 5,395 | OHIO | 2,474 | 1,098 | 1,083 | 281 | 12 | 15 R | 44.4% | 43.8% | 11.4% |
| 19,011 | ORANGE | 7,343 | 3,355 | 3,016 | 938 | 34 | 339 R | 45.7% | 41.1% | 12.8% |
| 19,663 | OWEN | 6,266 | 3,056 | 2,244 | 874 | 92 | 812 R | 48.8% | 35.8% | 13.9% |

# INDIANA

## PRESIDENT 1996

| 1995 Census Pop. Est. | County | Total Vote | Republican | Democratic | Reform (Perot) | Other | Rep.-Dem. Plurality | Percentage of Total Vote | | |
|---|---|---|---|---|---|---|---|---|---|---|
| | | | | | | | | Rep. | Dem. | Reform |
| 16,094 | PARKE | 6,619 | 3,151 | 2,453 | 981 | 34 | 698 R | 47.6% | 37.1% | 14.8% |
| 19,129 | PERRY | 7,930 | 2,554 | 4,427 | 913 | 36 | 1,873 D | 32.2% | 55.8% | 11.5% |
| 12,610 | PIKE | 5,872 | 2,174 | 2,780 | 884 | 34 | 606 D | 37.0% | 47.3% | 15.1% |
| 140,487 | PORTER | 54,601 | 22,931 | 24,044 | 7,169 | 457 | 1,113 D | 42.0% | 44.0% | 13.1% |
| 26,493 | POSEY | 10,954 | 4,638 | 4,965 | 1,304 | 47 | 327 D | 42.3% | 45.3% | 11.9% |
| 12,960 | PULASKI | 5,391 | 2,693 | 2,010 | 634 | 54 | 683 R | 50.0% | 37.3% | 11.8% |
| 32,939 | PUTNAM | 11,616 | 5,958 | 3,962 | 1,619 | 77 | 1,996 R | 51.3% | 34.1% | 13.9% |
| 27,377 | RANDOLPH | 10,420 | 4,708 | 4,087 | 1,557 | 68 | 621 R | 45.2% | 39.2% | 14.9% |
| 26,829 | RIPLEY | 10,676 | 5,303 | 4,097 | 1,216 | 60 | 1,206 R | 49.7% | 38.4% | 11.4% |
| 18,456 | RUSH | 7,428 | 3,827 | 2,578 | 973 | 50 | 1,249 R | 51.5% | 34.7% | 13.1% |
| 258,083 | ST. JOSEPH | 93,188 | 38,281 | 45,704 | 8,379 | 824 | 7,423 D | 41.1% | 49.0% | 9.0% |
| 22,568 | SCOTT | 7,207 | 2,620 | 3,798 | 760 | 29 | 1,178 D | 36.4% | 52.7% | 10.5% |
| 42,809 | SHELBY | 15,142 | 7,778 | 5,374 | 1,874 | 116 | 2,404 R | 51.4% | 35.5% | 12.4% |
| 20,374 | SPENCER | 8,620 | 3,770 | 4,058 | 739 | 53 | 288 D | 43.7% | 47.1% | 8.6% |
| 22,620 | STARKE | 8,150 | 3,108 | 3,854 | 1,096 | 92 | 746 D | 38.1% | 47.3% | 13.4% |
| 30,060 | STEUBEN | 11,130 | 5,513 | 4,124 | 1,390 | 103 | 1,389 R | 49.5% | 37.1% | 12.5% |
| 19,879 | SULLIVAN | 8,642 | 3,207 | 4,076 | 1,178 | 181 | 869 D | 37.1% | 47.2% | 13.6% |
| 8,222 | SWITZERLAND | 3,187 | 1,266 | 1,496 | 403 | 22 | 230 D | 39.7% | 46.9% | 12.6% |
| 135,285 | TIPPECANOE | 45,586 | 22,556 | 17,232 | 5,394 | 404 | 5,324 R | 49.5% | 37.8% | 11.8% |
| 16,463 | TIPTON | 7,385 | 3,980 | 2,478 | 861 | 66 | 1,502 R | 53.9% | 33.6% | 11.7% |
| 7,292 | UNION | 2,730 | 1,334 | 1,019 | 364 | 13 | 315 R | 48.9% | 37.3% | 13.3% |
| 168,065 | VANDERBURGH | 65,961 | 28,509 | 30,934 | 6,132 | 386 | 2,425 D | 43.2% | 46.9% | 9.3% |
| 16,841 | VERMILLION | 6,653 | 2,334 | 3,251 | 1,029 | 39 | 917 D | 35.1% | 48.9% | 15.5% |
| 106,622 | VIGO | 38,499 | 15,751 | 17,974 | 4,508 | 266 | 2,223 D | 40.9% | 46.7% | 11.7% |
| 34,896 | WABASH | 12,996 | 6,990 | 4,577 | 1,294 | 135 | 2,413 R | 53.8% | 35.2% | 10.0% |
| 8,394 | WARREN | 3,647 | 1,678 | 1,394 | 560 | 15 | 284 R | 46.0% | 38.2% | 15.4% |
| 49,380 | WARRICK | 21,109 | 9,221 | 9,285 | 2,471 | 132 | 64 D | 43.7% | 44.0% | 11.7% |
| 26,088 | WASHINGTON | 9,211 | 4,066 | 3,819 | 1,264 | 62 | 247 R | 44.1% | 41.5% | 13.7% |
| 72,802 | WAYNE | 25,801 | 12,188 | 10,905 | 2,525 | 183 | 1,283 R | 47.2% | 42.3% | 9.8% |
| 26,506 | WELLS | 11,294 | 6,322 | 3,752 | 1,157 | 63 | 2,570 R | 56.0% | 33.2% | 10.2% |
| 24,505 | WHITE | 9,698 | 4,642 | 3,396 | 1,610 | 50 | 1,246 R | 47.9% | 35.0% | 16.6% |
| 29,426 | WHITLEY | 11,625 | 5,965 | 4,176 | 1,392 | 92 | 1,789 R | 51.3% | 35.9% | 12.0% |
| 5,803,471 | TOTAL | 2,135,842 | 1,006,693 | 887,424 | 224,299 | 17,426 | 119,269 R | 47.1% | 41.5% | 10.5% |

# INDIANA

## PRESIDENT 1992

| 1990 Census Population | County | Total Vote | Republican | Democratic | Perot | Other | Plurality | Percentage Total Vote | | |
|---|---|---|---|---|---|---|---|---|---|---|
| | | | | | | | | Rep. | Dem. | Perot |
| 31,095 | ADAMS | 12,708 | 6,078 | 3,708 | 2,865 | 57 | 2,370 R | 47.8% | 29.2% | 22.5% |
| 300,836 | ALLEN | 121,577 | 55,003 | 39,629 | 25,809 | 1,136 | 15,374 R | 45.2% | 32.6% | 21.2% |
| 63,657 | BARTHOLOMEW | 27,440 | 13,146 | 8,284 | 5,882 | 128 | 4,862 R | 47.9% | 30.2% | 21.4% |
| 9,441 | BENTON | 4,323 | 2,030 | 1,221 | 1,056 | 16 | 809 R | 47.0% | 28.2% | 24.4% |
| 14,067 | BLACKFORD | 5,778 | 2,347 | 2,088 | 1,319 | 24 | 259 R | 40.6% | 36.1% | 22.8% |
| 38,147 | BOONE | 17,358 | 9,485 | 3,982 | 3,826 | 65 | 5,503 R | 54.6% | 22.9% | 22.0% |
| 14,080 | BROWN | 6,325 | 2,633 | 2,029 | 1,635 | 28 | 604 R | 41.6% | 32.1% | 25.8% |
| 18,809 | CARROLL | 8,562 | 3,800 | 2,561 | 2,173 | 28 | 1,239 R | 44.4% | 29.9% | 25.4% |
| 38,413 | CASS | 16,237 | 7,421 | 4,757 | 3,944 | 115 | 2,664 R | 45.7% | 29.3% | 24.3% |
| 87,777 | CLARK | 36,694 | 13,333 | 17,460 | 5,653 | 248 | 4,127 D | 36.3% | 47.6% | 15.4% |
| 24,705 | CLAY | 10,164 | 4,696 | 3,306 | 2,134 | 28 | 1,390 R | 46.2% | 32.5% | 21.0% |
| 30,974 | CLINTON | 12,224 | 6,141 | 3,490 | 2,535 | 58 | 2,651 R | 50.2% | 28.6% | 20.7% |
| 9,914 | CRAWFORD | 4,994 | 1,903 | 2,260 | 819 | 12 | 357 D | 38.1% | 45.3% | 16.4% |
| 27,533 | DAVIESS | 10,520 | 5,591 | 3,201 | 1,695 | 33 | 2,390 R | 53.1% | 30.4% | 16.1% |
| 38,835 | DEARBORN | 15,567 | 6,974 | 5,116 | 3,384 | 93 | 1,858 R | 44.8% | 32.9% | 21.7% |
| 23,645 | DECATUR | 10,291 | 5,195 | 2,774 | 2,299 | 23 | 2,421 R | 50.5% | 27.0% | 22.3% |
| 35,324 | DE KALB | 15,022 | 6,682 | 4,652 | 3,554 | 134 | 2,030 R | 44.5% | 31.0% | 23.7% |
| 119,659 | DELAWARE | 50,721 | 20,473 | 19,556 | 10,453 | 239 | 917 R | 40.4% | 38.6% | 20.6% |
| 36,616 | DUBOIS | 15,989 | 6,785 | 5,878 | 3,195 | 131 | 907 R | 42.4% | 36.8% | 20.0% |
| 156,198 | ELKHART | 52,184 | 27,920 | 14,660 | 9,450 | 154 | 13,260 R | 53.5% | 28.1% | 18.1% |
| 26,015 | FAYETTE | 10,710 | 4,376 | 3,969 | 2,299 | 66 | 407 R | 40.9% | 37.1% | 21.5% |
| 64,404 | FLOYD | 29,651 | 11,932 | 13,166 | 4,421 | 132 | 1,234 D | 40.2% | 44.4% | 14.9% |
| 17,808 | FOUNTAIN | 8,410 | 3,391 | 2,829 | 2,162 | 28 | 562 R | 40.3% | 33.6% | 25.7% |
| 19,580 | FRANKLIN | 8,167 | 3,831 | 2,456 | 1,858 | 22 | 1,375 R | 46.9% | 30.1% | 22.8% |
| 18,840 | FULTON | 8,527 | 3,982 | 2,552 | 1,963 | 30 | 1,430 R | 46.7% | 29.9% | 23.0% |
| 31,913 | GIBSON | 14,800 | 5,172 | 6,909 | 2,680 | 39 | 1,737 D | 34.9% | 46.7% | 18.1% |
| 74,169 | GRANT | 28,738 | 13,806 | 9,211 | 5,597 | 124 | 4,595 R | 48.0% | 32.1% | 19.5% |
| 30,410 | GREENE | 13,608 | 5,410 | 5,431 | 2,610 | 157 | 21 D | 39.8% | 39.9% | 19.2% |
| 108,936 | HAMILTON | 55,434 | 34,622 | 10,215 | 10,365 | 232 | 24,257 R | 62.5% | 18.4% | 18.7% |
| 45,527 | HANCOCK | 20,639 | 11,072 | 4,752 | 4,752 | 63 | 6,320 R | 53.6% | 23.0% | 23.0% |
| 29,890 | HARRISON | 13,671 | 5,403 | 5,768 | 2,469 | 31 | 365 D | 39.5% | 42.2% | 18.1% |
| 75,717 | HENDRICKS | 33,136 | 18,373 | 7,071 | 7,519 | 173 | 10,854 R | 55.4% | 21.3% | 22.7% |
| 48,139 | HENRY | 19,989 | 8,720 | 6,794 | 4,416 | 59 | 1,926 R | 43.6% | 34.0% | 22.1% |
| 80,827 | HOWARD | 34,340 | 15,306 | 10,288 | 8,575 | 171 | 5,018 R | 44.6% | 30.0% | 25.0% |
| 35,427 | HUNTINGTON | 16,013 | 9,093 | 3,855 | 2,967 | 98 | 5,238 R | 56.8% | 24.1% | 18.5% |
| 37,730 | JACKSON | 16,170 | 7,246 | 5,663 | 3,148 | 113 | 1,583 R | 44.8% | 35.0% | 19.5% |
| 24,960 | JASPER | 9,890 | 4,809 | 3,033 | 2,019 | 29 | 1,776 R | 48.6% | 30.7% | 20.4% |
| 21,512 | JAY | 8,836 | 3,609 | 3,208 | 1,994 | 25 | 401 R | 40.8% | 36.3% | 22.6% |
| 29,797 | JEFFERSON | 13,191 | 4,937 | 5,510 | 2,565 | 179 | 573 D | 37.4% | 41.8% | 19.4% |
| 23,661 | JENNINGS | 10,295 | 4,392 | 3,471 | 2,370 | 62 | 921 R | 42.7% | 33.7% | 23.0% |
| 88,109 | JOHNSON | 37,438 | 20,353 | 8,712 | 8,246 | 127 | 11,641 R | 54.4% | 23.3% | 22.0% |
| 39,884 | KNOX | 17,284 | 6,683 | 6,718 | 3,719 | 164 | 35 D | 38.7% | 38.9% | 21.5% |
| 65,294 | KOSCIUSKO | 24,683 | 14,179 | 5,307 | 5,115 | 82 | 8,872 R | 57.4% | 21.5% | 20.7% |
| 29,477 | LAGRANGE | 7,444 | 3,584 | 2,093 | 1,736 | 31 | 1,491 R | 48.1% | 28.1% | 23.3% |
| 475,594 | LAKE | 186,298 | 53,867 | 102,778 | 28,635 | 1,018 | 48,911 D | 28.9% | 55.2% | 15.4% |
| 107,066 | LA PORTE | 42,463 | 14,962 | 17,717 | 9,641 | 143 | 2,755 D | 35.2% | 41.7% | 22.7% |
| 42,836 | LAWRENCE | 16,781 | 7,712 | 5,557 | 3,452 | 60 | 2,155 R | 46.0% | 33.1% | 20.6% |
| 130,669 | MADISON | 59,058 | 23,479 | 22,276 | 13,100 | 203 | 1,203 R | 39.8% | 37.7% | 22.2% |
| 797,159 | MARION | 323,790 | 141,369 | 122,234 | 57,878 | 2,309 | 19,135 R | 43.7% | 37.8% | 17.9% |
| 42,182 | MARSHALL | 16,567 | 8,048 | 4,912 | 3,522 | 85 | 3,136 R | 48.6% | 29.6% | 21.3% |
| 10,369 | MARTIN | 5,438 | 2,523 | 2,018 | 883 | 14 | 505 R | 46.4% | 37.1% | 16.2% |
| 36,897 | MIAMI | 13,918 | 6,416 | 3,967 | 3,428 | 107 | 2,449 R | 46.1% | 28.5% | 24.6% |
| 108,978 | MONROE | 43,587 | 16,661 | 19,712 | 6,943 | 271 | 3,051 D | 38.2% | 45.2% | 15.9% |
| 34,436 | MONTGOMERY | 14,564 | 7,602 | 3,371 | 3,511 | 80 | 4,091 R | 52.2% | 23.1% | 24.1% |
| 55,920 | MORGAN | 21,107 | 10,939 | 4,690 | 5,375 | 103 | 5,564 R | 51.8% | 22.2% | 25.5% |
| 13,551 | NEWTON | 5,344 | 2,295 | 1,757 | 1,274 | 18 | 538 R | 42.9% | 32.9% | 23.8% |
| 37,877 | NOBLE | 13,713 | 5,883 | 4,411 | 3,328 | 91 | 1,472 R | 42.9% | 32.2% | 24.3% |
| 5,315 | OHIO | 2,514 | 1,009 | 970 | 527 | 8 | 39 R | 40.1% | 38.6% | 21.0% |
| 18,409 | ORANGE | 8,015 | 3,738 | 2,948 | 1,296 | 33 | 790 R | 46.6% | 36.8% | 16.2% |
| 17,281 | OWEN | 6,555 | 2,753 | 2,207 | 1,563 | 32 | 546 R | 42.0% | 33.7% | 23.8% |

# INDIANA

## PRESIDENT 1992

| 1990 Census Population | County | Total Vote | Republican | Democratic | Perot | Other | Plurality | Percentage Total Vote | | |
|---|---|---|---|---|---|---|---|---|---|---|
| | | | | | | | | Rep. | Dem. | Perot |
| 15,410 | PARKE | 7,099 | 2,953 | 2,429 | 1,696 | 21 | 524 R | 41.6% | 34.2% | 23.9% |
| 19,107 | PERRY | 9,382 | 2,973 | 4,829 | 1,560 | 20 | 1,856 D | 31.7% | 51.5% | 16.6% |
| 12,509 | PIKE | 6,371 | 2,156 | 2,960 | 1,238 | 17 | 804 D | 33.8% | 46.5% | 19.4% |
| 128,932 | PORTER | 57,067 | 22,644 | 21,022 | 13,096 | 305 | 1,622 R | 39.7% | 36.8% | 22.9% |
| 25,968 | POSEY | 11,453 | 4,435 | 4,632 | 2,357 | 29 | 197 D | 38.7% | 40.4% | 20.6% |
| 12,643 | PULASKI | 5,916 | 2,712 | 1,950 | 1,214 | 40 | 762 R | 45.8% | 33.0% | 20.5% |
| 30,315 | PUTNAM | 12,048 | 5,341 | 3,487 | 3,174 | 46 | 1,854 R | 44.3% | 28.9% | 26.3% |
| 27,148 | RANDOLPH | 11,784 | 4,937 | 3,870 | 2,939 | 38 | 1,067 R | 41.9% | 32.8% | 24.9% |
| 24,616 | RIPLEY | 10,937 | 5,033 | 3,480 | 2,406 | 18 | 1,553 R | 46.0% | 31.8% | 22.0% |
| 18,129 | RUSH | 8,008 | 3,873 | 2,168 | 1,948 | 19 | 1,705 R | 48.4% | 27.1% | 24.3% |
| 247,052 | ST. JOSEPH | 104,465 | 38,934 | 46,203 | 18,828 | 500 | 7,269 D | 37.3% | 44.2% | 18.0% |
| 20,991 | SCOTT | 7,859 | 2,649 | 4,085 | 1,092 | 33 | 1,436 D | 33.7% | 52.0% | 13.9% |
| 40,307 | SHELBY | 16,211 | 8,075 | 4,560 | 3,521 | 55 | 3,515 R | 49.8% | 28.1% | 21.7% |
| 19,490 | SPENCER | 9,579 | 3,789 | 4,301 | 1,464 | 25 | 512 D | 39.6% | 44.9% | 15.3% |
| 22,747 | STARKE | 8,758 | 3,100 | 3,695 | 1,885 | 78 | 595 D | 35.4% | 42.2% | 21.5% |
| 27,446 | STEUBEN | 11,469 | 4,868 | 3,630 | 2,896 | 75 | 1,238 R | 42.4% | 31.7% | 25.3% |
| 18,993 | SULLIVAN | 9,168 | 3,052 | 4,211 | 1,857 | 48 | 1,159 D | 33.3% | 45.9% | 20.3% |
| 7,738 | SWITZERLAND | 3,388 | 1,211 | 1,535 | 636 | 6 | 324 D | 35.7% | 45.3% | 18.8% |
| 130,598 | TIPPECANOE | 50,334 | 23,050 | 17,343 | 9,684 | 257 | 5,707 R | 45.8% | 34.5% | 19.2% |
| 16,119 | TIPTON | 7,883 | 3,906 | 2,125 | 1,816 | 36 | 1,781 R | 49.5% | 27.0% | 23.0% |
| 6,976 | UNION | 2,968 | 1,394 | 898 | 664 | 12 | 496 R | 47.0% | 30.3% | 22.4% |
| 165,058 | VANDERBURGH | 76,840 | 30,271 | 33,799 | 12,513 | 257 | 3,528 D | 39.4% | 44.0% | 16.3% |
| 16,773 | VERMILLION | 7,832 | 2,360 | 3,652 | 1,794 | 26 | 1,292 D | 30.1% | 46.6% | 22.9% |
| 106,107 | VIGO | 42,161 | 15,834 | 18,050 | 8,141 | 136 | 2,216 D | 37.6% | 42.8% | 19.3% |
| 35,069 | WABASH | 15,101 | 7,062 | 4,518 | 3,424 | 97 | 2,544 R | 46.8% | 29.9% | 22.7% |
| 8,176 | WARREN | 4,003 | 1,601 | 1,367 | 1,020 | 15 | 234 R | 40.0% | 34.1% | 25.5% |
| 44,920 | WARRICK | 20,614 | 8,087 | 8,612 | 3,862 | 53 | 525 D | 39.2% | 41.8% | 18.7% |
| 23,717 | WASHINGTON | 10,057 | 4,043 | 4,092 | 1,846 | 76 | 49 D | 40.2% | 40.7% | 18.4% |
| 71,951 | WAYNE | 27,346 | 12,221 | 9,960 | 5,095 | 70 | 2,261 R | 44.7% | 36.4% | 18.6% |
| 25,948 | WELLS | 12,039 | 5,799 | 3,282 | 2,890 | 68 | 2,517 R | 48.2% | 27.3% | 24.0% |
| 23,265 | WHITE | 10,221 | 4,622 | 2,988 | 2,582 | 29 | 1,634 R | 45.2% | 29.2% | 25.3% |
| 27,651 | WHITLEY | 12,056 | 5,217 | 3,569 | 3,195 | 75 | 1,648 R | 43.3% | 29.6% | 26.5% |
| 5,544,159 | TOTAL | 2,305,871 | 989,375 | 848,420 | 455,934 | 12,142 | 140,955 R | 42.9% | 36.8% | 19.8% |

# INDIANA

## PRESIDENT 1988

| 1980 Census Population | County | Total Vote | Republican | Democratic | Other | Rep.-Dem. Plurality | Percentage Total Vote Rep. | Total Vote Dem. | Major Vote Rep. | Major Vote Dem. |
|---|---|---|---|---|---|---|---|---|---|---|
| 29,619 | ADAMS | 11,997 | 8,137 | 3,811 | 49 | 4,326 R | 67.8% | 31.8% | 68.1% | 31.9% |
| 294,335 | ALLEN | 114,935 | 74,638 | 39,238 | 1,059 | 35,400 R | 64.9% | 34.1% | 65.5% | 34.5% |
| 65,088 | BARTHOLOMEW | 26,291 | 17,364 | 8,804 | 123 | 8,560 R | 66.0% | 33.5% | 66.4% | 33.6% |
| 10,218 | BENTON | 4,069 | 2,698 | 1,349 | 22 | 1,349 R | 66.3% | 33.2% | 66.7% | 33.3% |
| 15,570 | BLACKFORD | 5,608 | 3,336 | 2,253 | 19 | 1,083 R | 59.5% | 40.2% | 59.7% | 40.3% |
| 36,446 | BOONE | 15,806 | 11,608 | 4,168 | 30 | 7,440 R | 73.4% | 26.4% | 73.6% | 26.4% |
| 12,377 | BROWN | 5,501 | 3,348 | 2,115 | 38 | 1,233 R | 60.9% | 38.4% | 61.3% | 38.7% |
| 19,722 | CARROLL | 7,964 | 4,981 | 2,952 | 31 | 2,029 R | 62.5% | 37.1% | 62.8% | 37.2% |
| 40,936 | CASS | 16,851 | 10,970 | 5,784 | 97 | 5,186 R | 65.1% | 34.3% | 65.5% | 34.5% |
| 88,838 | CLARK | 31,192 | 16,544 | 14,528 | 120 | 2,016 R | 53.0% | 46.6% | 53.2% | 46.8% |
| 24,862 | CLAY | 9,629 | 5,852 | 3,724 | 53 | 2,128 R | 60.8% | 38.7% | 61.1% | 38.9% |
| 31,545 | CLINTON | 13,021 | 8,570 | 4,412 | 39 | 4,158 R | 65.8% | 33.9% | 66.0% | 34.0% |
| 9,820 | CRAWFORD | 4,596 | 2,532 | 2,036 | 28 | 496 R | 55.1% | 44.3% | 55.4% | 44.6% |
| 27,836 | DAVIESS | 10,294 | 6,768 | 3,483 | 43 | 3,285 R | 65.7% | 33.8% | 66.0% | 34.0% |
| 34,291 | DEARBORN | 13,309 | 8,195 | 5,066 | 48 | 3,129 R | 61.6% | 38.1% | 61.8% | 38.2% |
| 23,841 | DECATUR | 9,272 | 6,245 | 2,979 | 48 | 3,266 R | 67.4% | 32.1% | 67.7% | 32.3% |
| 33,606 | DE KALB | 13,716 | 9,018 | 4,657 | 41 | 4,361 R | 65.7% | 34.0% | 65.9% | 34.1% |
| 128,587 | DELAWARE | 48,112 | 27,348 | 20,548 | 216 | 6,800 R | 56.8% | 42.7% | 57.1% | 42.9% |
| 34,238 | DUBOIS | 16,048 | 9,995 | 5,954 | 99 | 4,041 R | 62.3% | 37.1% | 62.7% | 37.3% |
| 137,330 | ELKHART | 48,200 | 33,793 | 14,236 | 171 | 19,557 R | 70.1% | 29.5% | 70.4% | 29.6% |
| 28,272 | FAYETTE | 10,108 | 5,949 | 4,118 | 41 | 1,831 R | 58.9% | 40.7% | 59.1% | 40.9% |
| 61,169 | FLOYD | 25,393 | 14,291 | 11,024 | 78 | 3,267 R | 56.3% | 43.4% | 56.5% | 43.5% |
| 19,033 | FOUNTAIN | 8,441 | 5,113 | 3,279 | 49 | 1,834 R | 60.6% | 38.8% | 60.9% | 39.1% |
| 19,612 | FRANKLIN | 7,271 | 4,777 | 2,472 | 22 | 2,305 R | 65.7% | 34.0% | 65.9% | 34.1% |
| 19,335 | FULTON | 8,051 | 5,234 | 2,788 | 29 | 2,446 R | 65.0% | 34.6% | 65.2% | 34.8% |
| 33,156 | GIBSON | 14,684 | 7,610 | 7,031 | 43 | 579 R | 51.8% | 47.9% | 52.0% | 48.0% |
| 80,934 | GRANT | 29,371 | 18,441 | 10,799 | 131 | 7,642 R | 62.8% | 36.8% | 63.1% | 36.9% |
| 30,416 | GREENE | 13,746 | 7,689 | 5,979 | 78 | 1,710 R | 55.9% | 43.5% | 56.3% | 43.7% |
| 82,027 | HAMILTON | 45,615 | 36,654 | 8,853 | 108 | 27,801 R | 80.4% | 19.4% | 80.5% | 19.5% |
| 43,939 | HANCOCK | 18,780 | 13,374 | 5,355 | 51 | 8,019 R | 71.2% | 28.5% | 71.4% | 28.6% |
| 27,276 | HARRISON | 11,661 | 6,702 | 4,933 | 26 | 1,769 R | 57.5% | 42.3% | 57.6% | 42.4% |
| 69,804 | HENDRICKS | 29,803 | 22,090 | 7,643 | 70 | 14,447 R | 74.1% | 25.6% | 74.3% | 25.7% |
| 53,336 | HENRY | 19,116 | 11,280 | 7,779 | 57 | 3,501 R | 59.0% | 40.7% | 59.2% | 40.8% |
| 86,896 | HOWARD | 31,620 | 19,971 | 11,518 | 131 | 8,453 R | 63.2% | 36.4% | 63.4% | 36.6% |
| 35,596 | HUNTINGTON | 15,594 | 11,675 | 3,873 | 46 | 7,802 R | 74.9% | 24.8% | 75.1% | 24.9% |
| 36,523 | JACKSON | 15,088 | 9,470 | 5,550 | 68 | 3,920 R | 62.8% | 36.8% | 63.0% | 37.0% |
| 26,138 | JASPER | 9,292 | 6,009 | 3,237 | 46 | 2,772 R | 64.7% | 34.8% | 65.0% | 35.0% |
| 23,239 | JAY | 8,620 | 5,363 | 3,212 | 45 | 2,151 R | 62.2% | 37.3% | 62.5% | 37.5% |
| 30,419 | JEFFERSON | 12,268 | 6,949 | 5,221 | 98 | 1,728 R | 56.6% | 42.6% | 57.1% | 42.9% |
| 22,854 | JENNINGS | 9,348 | 5,636 | 3,667 | 45 | 1,969 R | 60.3% | 39.2% | 60.6% | 39.4% |
| 77,240 | JOHNSON | 33,778 | 24,654 | 9,001 | 123 | 15,653 R | 73.0% | 26.6% | 73.3% | 26.7% |
| 41,838 | KNOX | 16,881 | 9,813 | 7,006 | 62 | 2,807 R | 58.1% | 41.5% | 58.3% | 41.7% |
| 59,555 | KOSCIUSKO | 23,163 | 17,761 | 5,321 | 81 | 12,440 R | 76.7% | 23.0% | 76.9% | 23.1% |
| 25,550 | LAGRANGE | 6,546 | 4,495 | 2,029 | 22 | 2,466 R | 68.7% | 31.0% | 68.9% | 31.1% |
| 522,965 | LAKE | 185,735 | 79,929 | 105,026 | 780 | 25,097 D | 43.0% | 56.5% | 43.2% | 56.8% |
| 108,632 | LA PORTE | 38,285 | 20,537 | 17,585 | 163 | 2,952 R | 53.6% | 45.9% | 53.9% | 46.1% |
| 42,472 | LAWRENCE | 16,599 | 10,742 | 5,787 | 70 | 4,955 R | 64.7% | 34.9% | 65.0% | 35.0% |
| 139,336 | MADISON | 57,241 | 32,596 | 24,443 | 202 | 8,153 R | 56.9% | 42.7% | 57.1% | 42.9% |
| 765,233 | MARION | 315,095 | 184,519 | 128,627 | 1,949 | 55,892 R | 58.6% | 40.8% | 58.9% | 41.1% |
| 39,155 | MARSHALL | 16,038 | 10,490 | 5,488 | 60 | 5,002 R | 65.4% | 34.2% | 65.7% | 34.3% |
| 11,001 | MARTIN | 5,219 | 3,066 | 2,132 | 21 | 934 R | 58.7% | 40.9% | 59.0% | 41.0% |
| 39,820 | MIAMI | 13,236 | 8,533 | 4,613 | 90 | 3,920 R | 64.5% | 34.9% | 64.9% | 35.1% |
| 98,785 | MONROE | 37,038 | 20,756 | 15,855 | 427 | 4,901 R | 56.0% | 42.8% | 56.7% | 43.3% |
| 35,501 | MONTGOMERY | 14,472 | 10,793 | 3,623 | 56 | 7,170 R | 74.6% | 25.0% | 74.9% | 25.1% |
| 51,999 | MORGAN | 19,736 | 14,284 | 5,375 | 77 | 8,909 R | 72.4% | 27.2% | 72.7% | 27.3% |
| 14,844 | NEWTON | 5,035 | 3,274 | 1,744 | 17 | 1,530 R | 65.0% | 34.6% | 65.2% | 34.8% |
| 35,443 | NOBLE | 12,089 | 7,889 | 4,143 | 57 | 3,746 R | 65.3% | 34.3% | 65.6% | 34.4% |
| 5,114 | OHIO | 2,531 | 1,412 | 1,113 | 6 | 299 R | 55.8% | 44.0% | 55.9% | 44.1% |
| 18,677 | ORANGE | 8,015 | 5,245 | 2,739 | 31 | 2,506 R | 65.4% | 34.2% | 65.7% | 34.3% |
| 15,841 | OWEN | 6,363 | 3,837 | 2,484 | 42 | 1,353 R | 60.3% | 39.0% | 60.7% | 39.3% |

# INDIANA

## PRESIDENT 1988

| 1980 Census Population | County | Total Vote | Republican | Democratic | Other | Rep.-Dem. Plurality | Percentage | | | |
|---|---|---|---|---|---|---|---|---|---|---|
| | | | | | | | Total Vote | | Major Vote | |
| | | | | | | | Rep. | Dem. | Rep. | Dem. |
| 16,372 | PARKE | 7,053 | 4,458 | 2,563 | 32 | 1,895 R | 63.2% | 36.3% | 63.5% | 36.5% |
| 19,346 | PERRY | 9,580 | 4,720 | 4,804 | 56 | 84 D | 49.3% | 50.1% | 49.6% | 50.4% |
| 13,465 | PIKE | 6,371 | 3,294 | 3,037 | 40 | 257 R | 51.7% | 47.7% | 52.0% | 48.0% |
| 119,816 | PORTER | 49,345 | 29,790 | 19,390 | 165 | 10,400 R | 60.4% | 39.3% | 60.6% | 39.4% |
| 26,414 | POSEY | 10,490 | 5,987 | 4,468 | 35 | 1,519 R | 57.1% | 42.6% | 57.3% | 42.7% |
| 13,258 | PULASKI | 5,917 | 3,677 | 2,213 | 27 | 1,464 R | 62.1% | 37.4% | 62.4% | 37.6% |
| 29,163 | PUTNAM | 11,021 | 7,119 | 3,850 | 52 | 3,269 R | 64.6% | 34.9% | 64.9% | 35.1% |
| 29,997 | RANDOLPH | 10,908 | 6,856 | 3,990 | 62 | 2,866 R | 62.9% | 36.6% | 63.2% | 36.8% |
| 24,398 | RIPLEY | 10,051 | 6,414 | 3,605 | 32 | 2,809 R | 63.8% | 35.9% | 64.0% | 36.0% |
| 19,604 | RUSH | 7,583 | 5,112 | 2,451 | 20 | 2,661 R | 67.4% | 32.3% | 67.6% | 32.4% |
| 241,617 | ST. JOSEPH | 97,864 | 49,481 | 48,056 | 327 | 1,425 R | 50.6% | 49.1% | 50.7% | 49.3% |
| 20,422 | SCOTT | 6,854 | 3,455 | 3,378 | 21 | 77 R | 50.4% | 49.3% | 50.6% | 49.4% |
| 39,887 | SHELBY | 15,621 | 10,176 | 5,382 | 63 | 4,794 R | 65.1% | 34.5% | 65.4% | 34.6% |
| 19,361 | SPENCER | 9,055 | 4,964 | 4,061 | 30 | 903 R | 54.8% | 44.8% | 55.0% | 45.0% |
| 21,997 | STARKE | 8,606 | 4,458 | 4,104 | 44 | 354 R | 51.8% | 47.7% | 52.1% | 47.9% |
| 24,694 | STEUBEN | 10,000 | 6,855 | 3,114 | 31 | 3,741 R | 68.6% | 31.1% | 68.8% | 31.2% |
| 21,107 | SULLIVAN | 8,597 | 4,246 | 4,320 | 31 | 74 D | 49.4% | 50.3% | 49.6% | 50.4% |
| 7,153 | SWITZERLAND | 3,059 | 1,572 | 1,479 | 8 | 93 R | 51.4% | 48.3% | 51.5% | 48.5% |
| 121,702 | TIPPECANOE | 44,364 | 27,897 | 16,256 | 211 | 11,641 R | 62.9% | 36.6% | 63.2% | 36.8% |
| 16,819 | TIPTON | 7,666 | 5,148 | 2,485 | 33 | 2,663 R | 67.2% | 32.4% | 67.4% | 32.6% |
| 6,860 | UNION | 2,770 | 1,814 | 946 | 10 | 868 R | 65.5% | 34.2% | 65.7% | 34.3% |
| 167,515 | VANDERBURGH | 70,453 | 38,928 | 31,270 | 255 | 7,658 R | 55.3% | 44.4% | 55.5% | 44.5% |
| 18,229 | VERMILLION | 7,772 | 3,674 | 4,044 | 54 | 370 D | 47.3% | 52.0% | 47.6% | 52.4% |
| 112,385 | VIGO | 41,293 | 21,929 | 19,192 | 172 | 2,737 R | 53.1% | 46.5% | 53.3% | 46.7% |
| 36,640 | WABASH | 13,384 | 9,153 | 4,168 | 63 | 4,985 R | 68.4% | 31.1% | 68.7% | 31.3% |
| 8,976 | WARREN | 3,799 | 2,243 | 1,542 | 14 | 701 R | 59.0% | 40.6% | 59.3% | 40.7% |
| 41,474 | WARRICK | 18,564 | 10,504 | 7,999 | 61 | 2,505 R | 56.6% | 43.1% | 56.8% | 43.2% |
| 21,932 | WASHINGTON | 8,416 | 4,998 | 3,370 | 48 | 1,628 R | 59.4% | 40.0% | 59.7% | 40.3% |
| 76,058 | WAYNE | 26,702 | 16,388 | 10,209 | 105 | 6,179 R | 61.4% | 38.2% | 61.6% | 38.4% |
| 25,401 | WELLS | 11,188 | 7,712 | 3,437 | 39 | 4,275 R | 68.9% | 30.7% | 69.2% | 30.8% |
| 23,867 | WHITE | 9,513 | 6,220 | 3,256 | 37 | 2,964 R | 65.4% | 34.2% | 65.6% | 34.4% |
| 26,215 | WHITLEY | 11,386 | 7,679 | 3,642 | 65 | 4,037 R | 67.4% | 32.0% | 67.8% | 32.2% |
| 5,490,224 | TOTAL | 2,168,621 | 1,297,763 | 860,643 | 10,215 | 437,120 R | 59.8% | 39.7% | 60.1% | 39.9% |

# INDIANA

## PRESIDENT 1984

| 1980 Census Population | County | Total Vote | Republican | Democratic | Other | Rep.-Dem. Plurality | Percentage | | | |
|---|---|---|---|---|---|---|---|---|---|---|
| | | | | | | | Total Vote | | Major Vote | |
| | | | | | | | Rep. | Dem. | Rep. | Dem. |
| 29,619 | ADAMS | 11,952 | 7,958 | 3,923 | 71 | 4,035 R | 66.6% | 32.8% | 67.0% | 33.0% |
| 294,335 | ALLEN | 114,975 | 75,505 | 38,462 | 1,008 | 37,043 R | 65.7% | 33.5% | 66.3% | 33.7% |
| 65,088 | BARTHOLOMEW | 26,970 | 18,704 | 8,075 | 191 | 10,629 R | 69.4% | 29.9% | 69.8% | 30.2% |
| 10,218 | BENTON | 4,662 | 3,281 | 1,357 | 24 | 1,924 R | 70.4% | 29.1% | 70.7% | 29.3% |
| 15,570 | BLACKFORD | 6,230 | 3,787 | 2,395 | 48 | 1,392 R | 60.8% | 38.4% | 61.3% | 38.7% |
| 36,446 | BOONE | 15,850 | 11,790 | 3,982 | 78 | 7,808 R | 74.4% | 25.1% | 74.8% | 25.2% |
| 12,377 | BROWN | 6,198 | 3,517 | 2,657 | 24 | 860 R | 56.7% | 42.9% | 57.0% | 43.0% |
| 19,722 | CARROLL | 8,364 | 5,528 | 2,774 | 62 | 2,754 R | 66.1% | 33.2% | 66.6% | 33.4% |
| 40,936 | CASS | 17,971 | 12,355 | 5,521 | 95 | 6,834 R | 68.7% | 30.7% | 69.1% | 30.9% |
| 88,838 | CLARK | 33,785 | 19,419 | 14,138 | 228 | 5,281 R | 57.5% | 41.8% | 57.9% | 42.1% |
| 24,862 | CLAY | 10,725 | 6,957 | 3,707 | 61 | 3,250 R | 64.9% | 34.6% | 65.2% | 34.8% |
| 31,545 | CLINTON | 13,363 | 8,969 | 4,329 | 65 | 4,640 R | 67.1% | 32.4% | 67.4% | 32.6% |
| 9,820 | CRAWFORD | 4,910 | 2,633 | 2,256 | 21 | 377 R | 53.6% | 45.9% | 53.9% | 46.1% |
| 27,836 | DAVIESS | 11,311 | 7,721 | 3,545 | 45 | 4,176 R | 68.3% | 31.3% | 68.5% | 31.5% |
| 34,291 | DEARBORN | 14,132 | 9,149 | 4,920 | 63 | 4,229 R | 64.7% | 34.8% | 65.0% | 35.0% |
| 23,841 | DECATUR | 9,363 | 6,551 | 2,766 | 46 | 3,785 R | 70.0% | 29.5% | 70.3% | 29.7% |
| 33,606 | DE KALB | 13,528 | 8,769 | 4,617 | 142 | 4,152 R | 64.8% | 34.1% | 65.5% | 34.5% |
| 128,587 | DELAWARE | 50,171 | 30,092 | 19,791 | 288 | 10,301 R | 60.0% | 39.4% | 60.3% | 39.7% |
| 34,238 | DUBOIS | 14,962 | 9,391 | 5,423 | 148 | 3,968 R | 62.8% | 36.2% | 63.4% | 36.6% |
| 137,330 | ELKHART | 48,097 | 34,621 | 13,240 | 236 | 21,381 R | 72.0% | 27.5% | 72.3% | 27.7% |
| 28,272 | FAYETTE | 11,346 | 7,142 | 4,122 | 82 | 3,020 R | 62.9% | 36.3% | 63.4% | 36.6% |
| 61,169 | FLOYD | 26,279 | 15,466 | 10,616 | 197 | 4,850 R | 58.9% | 40.4% | 59.3% | 40.7% |
| 19,033 | FOUNTAIN | 8,397 | 5,450 | 2,897 | 50 | 2,553 R | 64.9% | 34.5% | 65.3% | 34.7% |
| 19,612 | FRANKLIN | 7,472 | 5,202 | 2,225 | 45 | 2,977 R | 69.6% | 29.8% | 70.0% | 30.0% |
| 19,335 | FULTON | 8,635 | 6,057 | 2,527 | 51 | 3,530 R | 70.1% | 29.3% | 70.6% | 29.4% |
| 33,156 | GIBSON | 15,777 | 8,618 | 7,082 | 77 | 1,536 R | 54.6% | 44.9% | 54.9% | 45.1% |
| 80,934 | GRANT | 30,673 | 20,482 | 9,986 | 205 | 10,496 R | 66.8% | 32.6% | 67.2% | 32.8% |
| 30,416 | GREENE | 13,898 | 8,438 | 5,267 | 193 | 3,171 R | 60.7% | 37.9% | 61.6% | 38.4% |
| 82,027 | HAMILTON | 36,761 | 30,254 | 6,364 | 143 | 23,890 R | 82.3% | 17.3% | 82.6% | 17.4% |
| 43,939 | HANCOCK | 17,504 | 12,880 | 4,550 | 74 | 8,330 R | 73.6% | 26.0% | 73.9% | 26.1% |
| 27,276 | HARRISON | 11,969 | 7,255 | 4,634 | 80 | 2,621 R | 60.6% | 38.7% | 61.0% | 39.0% |
| 69,804 | HENDRICKS | 28,135 | 21,307 | 6,659 | 169 | 14,648 R | 75.7% | 23.7% | 76.2% | 23.8% |
| 53,336 | HENRY | 19,062 | 11,926 | 7,064 | 72 | 4,862 R | 62.6% | 37.1% | 62.8% | 37.2% |
| 86,896 | HOWARD | 33,046 | 22,386 | 10,458 | 202 | 11,928 R | 67.7% | 31.6% | 68.2% | 31.8% |
| 35,596 | HUNTINGTON | 15,487 | 10,805 | 4,598 | 84 | 6,207 R | 69.8% | 29.7% | 70.1% | 29.9% |
| 36,523 | JACKSON | 15,234 | 9,879 | 5,163 | 192 | 4,716 R | 64.8% | 33.9% | 65.7% | 34.3% |
| 26,138 | JASPER | 9,444 | 6,537 | 2,821 | 86 | 3,716 R | 69.2% | 29.9% | 69.9% | 30.1% |
| 23,239 | JAY | 9,207 | 5,975 | 3,174 | 58 | 2,801 R | 64.9% | 34.5% | 65.3% | 34.7% |
| 30,419 | JEFFERSON | 12,639 | 7,482 | 4,952 | 205 | 2,530 R | 59.2% | 39.2% | 60.2% | 39.8% |
| 22,854 | JENNINGS | 9,707 | 6,356 | 3,264 | 87 | 3,092 R | 65.5% | 33.6% | 66.1% | 33.9% |
| 77,240 | JOHNSON | 31,368 | 23,482 | 7,715 | 171 | 15,767 R | 74.9% | 24.6% | 75.3% | 24.7% |
| 41,838 | KNOX | 17,459 | 10,872 | 6,417 | 170 | 4,455 R | 62.3% | 36.8% | 62.9% | 37.1% |
| 59,555 | KOSCIUSKO | 22,547 | 17,560 | 4,877 | 110 | 12,683 R | 77.9% | 21.6% | 78.3% | 21.7% |
| 25,550 | LAGRANGE | 6,692 | 4,772 | 1,884 | 36 | 2,888 R | 71.3% | 28.2% | 71.7% | 28.3% |
| 522,965 | LAKE | 214,143 | 94,870 | 117,984 | 1,289 | 23,114 D | 44.3% | 55.1% | 44.6% | 55.4% |
| 108,632 | LA PORTE | 39,567 | 23,346 | 15,904 | 317 | 7,442 R | 59.0% | 40.2% | 59.5% | 40.5% |
| 42,472 | LAWRENCE | 17,150 | 11,440 | 5,608 | 102 | 5,832 R | 66.7% | 32.7% | 67.1% | 32.9% |
| 139,336 | MADISON | 59,014 | 36,510 | 22,254 | 250 | 14,256 R | 61.9% | 37.7% | 62.1% | 37.9% |
| 765,233 | MARION | 317,148 | 184,880 | 130,185 | 2,083 | 54,695 R | 58.3% | 41.0% | 58.7% | 41.3% |
| 39,155 | MARSHALL | 16,144 | 11,100 | 4,931 | 113 | 6,169 R | 68.8% | 30.5% | 69.2% | 30.8% |
| 11,001 | MARTIN | 5,332 | 3,363 | 1,937 | 32 | 1,426 R | 63.1% | 36.3% | 63.5% | 36.5% |
| 39,820 | MIAMI | 13,892 | 9,551 | 4,224 | 117 | 5,327 R | 68.8% | 30.4% | 69.3% | 30.7% |
| 98,785 | MONROE | 36,826 | 21,772 | 14,719 | 335 | 7,053 R | 59.1% | 40.0% | 59.7% | 40.3% |
| 35,501 | MONTGOMERY | 14,834 | 11,119 | 3,626 | 89 | 7,493 R | 75.0% | 24.4% | 75.4% | 24.6% |
| 51,999 | MORGAN | 19,607 | 14,884 | 4,627 | 96 | 10,257 R | 75.9% | 23.6% | 76.3% | 23.7% |
| 14,844 | NEWTON | 5,194 | 3,560 | 1,596 | 38 | 1,964 R | 68.5% | 30.7% | 69.0% | 31.0% |
| 35,443 | NOBLE | 12,867 | 8,459 | 4,237 | 171 | 4,222 R | 65.7% | 32.9% | 66.6% | 33.4% |
| 5,114 | OHIO | 2,577 | 1,503 | 1,068 | 6 | 435 R | 58.3% | 41.4% | 58.5% | 41.5% |
| 18,677 | ORANGE | 8,515 | 5,909 | 2,571 | 35 | 3,338 R | 69.4% | 30.2% | 69.7% | 30.3% |
| 15,841 | OWEN | 6,323 | 4,204 | 2,082 | 37 | 2,122 R | 66.5% | 32.9% | 66.9% | 33.1% |

INDIANA

PRESIDENT 1984

1980 Census Population	County	Total Vote	Republican	Democratic	Other	Rep.-Dem. Plurality	Percentage Total Vote Rep.	Percentage Total Vote Dem.	Percentage Major Vote Rep.	Percentage Major Vote Dem.
16,372	PARKE	7,294	5,052	2,205	37	2,847 R	69.3%	30.2%	69.6%	30.4%
19,346	PERRY	9,588	4,785	4,760	43	25 R	49.9%	49.6%	50.1%	49.9%
13,465	PIKE	6,963	3,689	3,231	43	458 R	53.0%	46.4%	53.3%	46.7%
119,816	PORTER	50,682	32,505	17,862	315	14,643 R	64.1%	35.2%	64.5%	35.5%
26,414	POSEY	10,957	6,472	4,452	33	2,020 R	59.1%	40.6%	59.2%	40.8%
13,258	PULASKI	6,226	4,167	2,008	51	2,159 R	66.9%	32.3%	67.5%	32.5%
29,163	PUTNAM	11,272	7,820	3,392	60	4,428 R	69.4%	30.1%	69.7%	30.3%
29,997	RANDOLPH	11,671	7,793	3,805	73	3,988 R	66.8%	32.6%	67.2%	32.8%
24,398	RIPLEY	10,506	7,143	3,336	27	3,807 R	68.0%	31.8%	68.2%	31.8%
19,604	RUSH	7,771	5,429	2,307	35	3,122 R	69.9%	29.7%	70.2%	29.8%
241,617	ST. JOSEPH	102,493	54,404	47,513	576	6,891 R	53.1%	46.4%	53.4%	46.6%
20,422	SCOTT	7,588	4,110	3,460	18	650 R	54.2%	45.6%	54.3%	45.7%
39,887	SHELBY	16,522	11,056	5,357	109	5,699 R	66.9%	32.4%	67.4%	32.6%
19,361	SPENCER	9,846	5,816	4,005	25	1,811 R	59.1%	40.7%	59.2%	40.8%
21,997	STARKE	8,889	5,104	3,674	111	1,430 R	57.4%	41.3%	58.1%	41.9%
24,694	STEUBEN	8,921	6,424	2,441	56	3,983 R	72.0%	27.4%	72.5%	27.5%
21,107	SULLIVAN	8,813	4,771	4,006	36	765 R	54.1%	45.5%	54.4%	45.6%
7,153	SWITZERLAND	3,347	1,857	1,484	6	373 R	55.5%	44.3%	55.6%	44.4%
121,702	TIPPECANOE	45,876	29,706	15,789	381	13,917 R	64.8%	34.4%	65.3%	34.7%
16,819	TIPTON	8,069	5,687	2,328	54	3,359 R	70.5%	28.9%	71.0%	29.0%
6,860	UNION	2,800	1,970	816	14	1,154 R	70.4%	29.1%	70.7%	29.3%
167,515	VANDERBURGH	72,330	40,994	31,049	287	9,945 R	56.7%	42.9%	56.9%	43.1%
18,229	VERMILLION	8,154	4,428	3,666	60	762 R	54.3%	45.0%	54.7%	45.3%
112,385	VIGO	44,973	26,259	18,429	285	7,830 R	58.4%	41.0%	58.8%	41.2%
36,640	WABASH	14,028	9,862	4,077	89	5,785 R	70.3%	29.1%	70.8%	29.2%
8,976	WARREN	3,862	2,525	1,309	28	1,216 R	65.4%	33.9%	65.9%	34.1%
41,474	WARRICK	16,637	10,202	6,345	90	3,857 R	61.3%	38.1%	61.7%	38.3%
21,932	WASHINGTON	9,380	5,874	3,334	172	2,540 R	62.6%	35.5%	63.8%	36.2%
76,058	WAYNE	29,251	18,955	10,173	123	8,782 R	64.8%	34.8%	65.1%	34.9%
25,401	WELLS	10,920	7,579	3,274	67	4,305 R	69.4%	30.0%	69.8%	30.2%
23,867	WHITE	10,499	7,279	3,157	63	4,122 R	69.3%	30.1%	69.7%	30.3%
26,215	WHITLEY	11,551	7,763	3,690	98	4,073 R	67.2%	31.9%	67.8%	32.2%
5,490,224	TOTAL	2,233,069	1,377,230	841,481	14,358	535,749 R	61.7%	37.7%	62.1%	37.9%

# INDIANA

## PRESIDENT 1980

| 1980 Census Population | County | Total Vote | Republican | Democratic | Other | Rep.-Dem. Plurality | Percentage | | | |
|---|---|---|---|---|---|---|---|---|---|---|
| | | | | | | | Total Vote | | Major Vote | |
| | | | | | | | Rep. | Dem. | Rep. | Dem. |
| 29,619 | ADAMS | 11,978 | 6,368 | 4,673 | 937 | 1,695 R | 53.2% | 39.0% | 57.7% | 42.3% |
| 294,335 | ALLEN | 118,898 | 68,524 | 37,765 | 12,609 | 30,759 R | 57.6% | 31.8% | 64.5% | 35.5% |
| 65,088 | BARTHOLOMEW | 26,974 | 15,801 | 9,260 | 1,913 | 6,541 R | 58.6% | 34.3% | 63.1% | 36.9% |
| 10,218 | BENTON | 4,963 | 3,189 | 1,520 | 254 | 1,669 R | 64.3% | 30.6% | 67.7% | 32.3% |
| 15,570 | BLACKFORD | 5,962 | 3,168 | 2,431 | 363 | 737 R | 53.1% | 40.8% | 56.6% | 43.4% |
| 36,446 | BOONE | 15,859 | 10,484 | 4,535 | 840 | 5,949 R | 66.1% | 28.6% | 69.8% | 30.2% |
| 12,377 | BROWN | 5,291 | 2,884 | 2,014 | 393 | 870 R | 54.5% | 38.1% | 58.9% | 41.1% |
| 19,722 | CARROLL | 8,699 | 5,262 | 2,966 | 471 | 2,296 R | 60.5% | 34.1% | 64.0% | 36.0% |
| 40,936 | CASS | 18,274 | 11,500 | 5,838 | 936 | 5,662 R | 62.9% | 31.9% | 66.3% | 33.7% |
| 88,838 | CLARK | 31,181 | 15,508 | 14,137 | 1,536 | 1,371 R | 49.7% | 45.3% | 52.3% | 47.7% |
| 24,862 | CLAY | 11,812 | 6,980 | 4,363 | 469 | 2,617 R | 59.1% | 36.9% | 61.5% | 38.5% |
| 31,545 | CLINTON | 13,962 | 8,158 | 5,258 | 546 | 2,900 R | 58.4% | 37.7% | 60.8% | 39.2% |
| 9,820 | CRAWFORD | 4,864 | 2,554 | 2,130 | 180 | 424 R | 52.5% | 43.8% | 54.5% | 45.5% |
| 27,836 | DAVIESS | 11,532 | 7,022 | 4,057 | 453 | 2,965 R | 60.9% | 35.2% | 63.4% | 36.6% |
| 34,291 | DEARBORN | 13,249 | 7,467 | 5,135 | 647 | 2,332 R | 56.4% | 38.8% | 59.3% | 40.7% |
| 23,841 | DECATUR | 9,951 | 5,819 | 3,646 | 486 | 2,173 R | 58.5% | 36.6% | 61.5% | 38.5% |
| 33,606 | DE KALB | 13,950 | 7,886 | 4,911 | 1,153 | 2,975 R | 56.5% | 35.2% | 61.6% | 38.4% |
| 128,587 | DELAWARE | 52,647 | 28,342 | 20,923 | 3,382 | 7,419 R | 53.8% | 39.7% | 57.5% | 42.5% |
| 34,238 | DUBOIS | 14,276 | 6,775 | 6,700 | 801 | 75 R | 47.5% | 46.9% | 50.3% | 49.7% |
| 137,330 | ELKHART | 48,994 | 30,081 | 14,883 | 4,030 | 15,198 R | 61.4% | 30.4% | 66.9% | 33.1% |
| 28,272 | FAYETTE | 10,732 | 6,004 | 4,304 | 424 | 1,700 R | 55.9% | 40.1% | 58.2% | 41.8% |
| 61,169 | FLOYD | 25,467 | 12,456 | 11,543 | 1,468 | 913 R | 48.9% | 45.3% | 51.9% | 48.1% |
| 19,033 | FOUNTAIN | 8,506 | 5,289 | 2,845 | 372 | 2,444 R | 62.2% | 33.4% | 65.0% | 35.0% |
| 19,612 | FRANKLIN | 7,701 | 4,551 | 2,834 | 316 | 1,717 R | 59.1% | 36.8% | 61.6% | 38.4% |
| 19,335 | FULTON | 8,728 | 5,458 | 2,788 | 482 | 2,670 R | 62.5% | 31.9% | 66.2% | 33.8% |
| 33,156 | GIBSON | 15,189 | 7,643 | 6,834 | 712 | 809 R | 50.3% | 45.0% | 52.8% | 47.2% |
| 80,934 | GRANT | 30,909 | 19,078 | 10,390 | 1,441 | 8,688 R | 61.7% | 33.6% | 64.7% | 35.3% |
| 30,416 | GREENE | 14,098 | 7,452 | 6,027 | 619 | 1,425 R | 52.9% | 42.8% | 55.3% | 44.7% |
| 82,027 | HAMILTON | 35,327 | 26,218 | 7,036 | 2,073 | 19,182 R | 74.2% | 19.9% | 78.8% | 21.2% |
| 43,939 | HANCOCK | 18,138 | 12,093 | 5,124 | 921 | 6,969 R | 66.7% | 28.3% | 70.2% | 29.8% |
| 27,276 | HARRISON | 11,594 | 6,287 | 4,865 | 442 | 1,422 R | 54.2% | 42.0% | 56.4% | 43.6% |
| 69,804 | HENDRICKS | 28,117 | 19,366 | 7,412 | 1,339 | 11,954 R | 68.9% | 26.4% | 72.3% | 27.7% |
| 53,336 | HENRY | 21,196 | 12,724 | 7,626 | 846 | 5,098 R | 60.0% | 36.0% | 62.5% | 37.5% |
| 86,896 | HOWARD | 35,910 | 21,272 | 12,916 | 1,722 | 8,356 R | 59.2% | 36.0% | 62.2% | 37.8% |
| 35,596 | HUNTINGTON | 15,937 | 9,497 | 5,415 | 1,025 | 4,082 R | 59.6% | 34.0% | 63.7% | 36.3% |
| 36,523 | JACKSON | 15,942 | 8,903 | 6,425 | 614 | 2,478 R | 55.8% | 40.3% | 58.1% | 41.9% |
| 26,138 | JASPER | 9,276 | 6,316 | 2,544 | 416 | 3,772 R | 68.1% | 27.4% | 71.3% | 28.7% |
| 23,239 | JAY | 9,217 | 5,351 | 3,256 | 610 | 2,095 R | 58.1% | 35.3% | 62.2% | 37.8% |
| 30,419 | JEFFERSON | 13,087 | 6,831 | 5,496 | 760 | 1,335 R | 52.2% | 42.0% | 55.4% | 44.6% |
| 22,854 | JENNINGS | 9,822 | 5,498 | 3,931 | 393 | 1,567 R | 56.0% | 40.0% | 58.3% | 41.7% |
| 77,240 | JOHNSON | 30,174 | 20,018 | 8,445 | 1,711 | 11,573 R | 66.3% | 28.0% | 70.3% | 29.7% |
| 41,838 | KNOX | 18,822 | 10,083 | 7,829 | 910 | 2,254 R | 53.6% | 41.6% | 56.3% | 43.7% |
| 59,555 | KOSCIUSKO | 22,730 | 15,633 | 5,684 | 1,413 | 9,949 R | 68.8% | 25.0% | 73.3% | 26.7% |
| 25,550 | LAGRANGE | 6,815 | 4,259 | 2,095 | 461 | 2,164 R | 62.5% | 30.7% | 67.0% | 33.0% |
| 522,965 | LAKE | 207,339 | 95,408 | 101,145 | 10,786 | 5,737 D | 46.0% | 48.8% | 48.5% | 51.5% |
| 108,632 | LA PORTE | 40,538 | 22,424 | 15,387 | 2,727 | 7,037 R | 55.3% | 38.0% | 59.3% | 40.7% |
| 42,472 | LAWRENCE | 17,296 | 10,846 | 5,826 | 624 | 5,020 R | 62.7% | 33.7% | 65.1% | 34.9% |
| 139,336 | MADISON | 62,092 | 35,582 | 23,554 | 2,956 | 12,028 R | 57.3% | 37.9% | 60.2% | 39.8% |
| 765,233 | MARION | 314,269 | 168,680 | 126,103 | 19,486 | 42,577 R | 53.7% | 40.1% | 57.2% | 42.8% |
| 39,155 | MARSHALL | 16,411 | 10,209 | 5,113 | 1,089 | 5,096 R | 62.2% | 31.2% | 66.6% | 33.4% |
| 11,001 | MARTIN | 5,779 | 3,082 | 2,479 | 218 | 603 R | 53.3% | 42.9% | 55.4% | 44.6% |
| 39,820 | MIAMI | 14,304 | 8,672 | 4,927 | 705 | 3,745 R | 60.6% | 34.4% | 63.8% | 36.2% |
| 98,785 | MONROE | 36,894 | 18,233 | 13,316 | 5,345 | 4,917 R | 49.4% | 36.1% | 57.8% | 42.2% |
| 35,501 | MONTGOMERY | 14,917 | 9,936 | 4,158 | 823 | 5,778 R | 66.6% | 27.9% | 70.5% | 29.5% |
| 51,999 | MORGAN | 19,438 | 13,321 | 5,439 | 678 | 7,882 R | 68.5% | 28.0% | 71.0% | 29.0% |
| 14,844 | NEWTON | 5,763 | 3,850 | 1,649 | 264 | 2,201 R | 66.8% | 28.6% | 70.0% | 30.0% |
| 35,443 | NOBLE | 13,282 | 7,624 | 4,721 | 937 | 2,903 R | 57.4% | 35.5% | 61.8% | 38.2% |
| 5,114 | OHIO | 2,420 | 1,264 | 1,074 | 82 | 190 R | 52.2% | 44.4% | 54.1% | 45.9% |
| 18,677 | ORANGE | 8,558 | 5,073 | 3,228 | 257 | 1,845 R | 59.3% | 37.7% | 61.1% | 38.9% |
| 15,841 | OWEN | 6,212 | 3,632 | 2,325 | 255 | 1,307 R | 58.5% | 37.4% | 61.0% | 39.0% |

# INDIANA

## PRESIDENT 1980

| 1980 Census Population | County | Total Vote | Republican | Democratic | Other | Rep.-Dem. Plurality | Percentage Total Vote Rep. | Dem. | Major Vote Rep. | Dem. |
|---|---|---|---|---|---|---|---|---|---|---|
| 16,372 | PARKE | 7,315 | 4,595 | 2,432 | 288 | 2,163 R | 62.8% | 33.2% | 65.4% | 34.6% |
| 19,346 | PERRY | 9,468 | 4,350 | 4,540 | 578 | 190 D | 45.9% | 48.0% | 48.9% | 51.1% |
| 13,465 | PIKE | 6,952 | 3,343 | 3,346 | 263 | 3 D | 48.1% | 48.1% | 50.0% | 50.0% |
| 119,816 | PORTER | 46,816 | 30,055 | 12,869 | 3,892 | 17,186 R | 64.2% | 27.5% | 70.0% | 30.0% |
| 26,414 | POSEY | 11,354 | 6,096 | 4,465 | 793 | 1,631 R | 53.7% | 39.3% | 57.7% | 42.3% |
| 13,258 | PULASKI | 6,310 | 3,916 | 2,092 | 302 | 1,824 R | 62.1% | 33.2% | 65.2% | 34.8% |
| 29,163 | PUTNAM | 11,748 | 7,090 | 3,996 | 662 | 3,094 R | 60.4% | 34.0% | 64.0% | 36.0% |
| 29,997 | RANDOLPH | 12,390 | 7,762 | 4,025 | 603 | 3,737 R | 62.6% | 32.5% | 65.9% | 34.1% |
| 24,398 | RIPLEY | 10,233 | 5,770 | 4,022 | 441 | 1,748 R | 56.4% | 39.3% | 58.9% | 41.1% |
| 19,604 | RUSH | 7,511 | 4,829 | 2,388 | 294 | 2,441 R | 64.3% | 31.8% | 66.9% | 33.1% |
| 241,617 | ST. JOSEPH | 103,114 | 50,607 | 44,218 | 8,289 | 6,389 R | 49.1% | 42.9% | 53.4% | 46.6% |
| 20,422 | SCOTT | 7,329 | 3,432 | 3,694 | 203 | 262 D | 46.8% | 50.4% | 48.2% | 51.8% |
| 39,887 | SHELBY | 17,150 | 10,496 | 5,861 | 793 | 4,635 R | 61.2% | 34.2% | 64.2% | 35.8% |
| 19,361 | SPENCER | 9,705 | 5,284 | 4,153 | 268 | 1,131 R | 54.4% | 42.8% | 56.0% | 44.0% |
| 21,997 | STARKE | 9,110 | 5,035 | 3,615 | 460 | 1,420 R | 55.3% | 39.7% | 58.2% | 41.8% |
| 24,694 | STEUBEN | 9,008 | 5,670 | 2,606 | 732 | 3,064 R | 62.9% | 28.9% | 68.5% | 31.5% |
| 21,107 | SULLIVAN | 9,103 | 4,465 | 4,335 | 303 | 130 R | 49.0% | 47.6% | 50.7% | 49.3% |
| 7,153 | SWITZERLAND | 3,360 | 1,584 | 1,704 | 72 | 120 D | 47.1% | 50.7% | 48.2% | 51.8% |
| 121,702 | TIPPECANOE | 48,470 | 27,589 | 14,636 | 6,245 | 12,953 R | 56.9% | 30.2% | 65.3% | 34.7% |
| 16,819 | TIPTON | 8,071 | 5,150 | 2,547 | 374 | 2,603 R | 63.8% | 31.6% | 66.9% | 33.1% |
| 6,860 | UNION | 2,780 | 1,766 | 898 | 116 | 868 R | 63.5% | 32.3% | 66.3% | 33.7% |
| 167,515 | VANDERBURGH | 70,982 | 36,248 | 29,930 | 4,804 | 6,318 R | 51.1% | 42.2% | 54.8% | 45.2% |
| 18,229 | VERMILLION | 8,400 | 4,195 | 3,793 | 412 | 402 R | 49.9% | 45.2% | 52.5% | 47.5% |
| 112,385 | VIGO | 46,527 | 24,133 | 19,261 | 3,133 | 4,872 R | 51.9% | 41.4% | 55.6% | 44.4% |
| 36,640 | WABASH | 14,368 | 8,738 | 4,620 | 1,010 | 4,118 R | 60.8% | 32.2% | 65.4% | 34.6% |
| 8,976 | WARREN | 4,157 | 2,665 | 1,287 | 205 | 1,378 R | 64.1% | 31.0% | 67.4% | 32.6% |
| 41,474 | WARRICK | 16,570 | 8,681 | 6,845 | 1,044 | 1,836 R | 52.4% | 41.3% | 55.9% | 44.1% |
| 21,932 | WASHINGTON | 9,297 | 5,234 | 3,663 | 400 | 1,571 R | 56.3% | 39.4% | 58.8% | 41.2% |
| 76,058 | WAYNE | 28,052 | 16,981 | 9,599 | 1,472 | 7,382 R | 60.5% | 34.2% | 63.9% | 36.1% |
| 25,401 | WELLS | 10,445 | 5,864 | 3,760 | 821 | 2,104 R | 56.1% | 36.0% | 60.9% | 39.1% |
| 23,867 | WHITE | 10,855 | 6,999 | 3,247 | 609 | 3,752 R | 64.5% | 29.9% | 68.3% | 31.7% |
| 26,215 | WHITLEY | 12,821 | 7,146 | 4,497 | 1,178 | 2,649 R | 55.7% | 35.1% | 61.4% | 38.6% |
| 5,490,224 | TOTAL | 2,242,033 | 1,255,656 | 844,197 | 142,180 | 411,459 R | 56.0% | 37.7% | 59.8% | 40.2% |

# INDIANA

## PRESIDENT 1976

| 1970 Census Population | County | Total Vote | Republican | Democratic | Other | Rep.-Dem. Plurality | Percentage | | | |
|---|---|---|---|---|---|---|---|---|---|---|
| | | | | | | | Total Vote | | Major Vote | |
| | | | | | | | Rep. | Dem. | Rep. | Dem. |
| 26,871 | ADAMS | 11,306 | 6,280 | 4,908 | 118 | 1,372 R | 55.5% | 43.4% | 56.1% | 43.9% |
| 280,455 | ALLEN | 117,769 | 71,321 | 44,744 | 1,704 | 26,577 R | 60.6% | 38.0% | 61.4% | 38.6% |
| 57,022 | BARTHOLOMEW | 26,187 | 14,771 | 11,203 | 213 | 3,568 R | 56.4% | 42.8% | 56.9% | 43.1% |
| 11,262 | BENTON | 5,234 | 3,093 | 2,071 | 70 | 1,022 R | 59.1% | 39.6% | 59.9% | 40.1% |
| 15,888 | BLACKFORD | 6,120 | 2,886 | 3,174 | 60 | 288 D | 47.2% | 51.9% | 47.6% | 52.4% |
| 30,870 | BOONE | 14,986 | 9,214 | 5,686 | 86 | 3,528 R | 61.5% | 37.9% | 61.8% | 38.2% |
| 9,057 | BROWN | 4,904 | 2,466 | 2,381 | 57 | 85 R | 50.3% | 48.6% | 50.9% | 49.1% |
| 17,734 | CARROLL | 8,493 | 4,797 | 3,606 | 90 | 1,191 R | 56.5% | 42.5% | 57.1% | 42.9% |
| 40,456 | CASS | 18,231 | 10,342 | 7,610 | 279 | 2,732 R | 56.7% | 41.7% | 57.6% | 42.4% |
| 75,876 | CLARK | 29,731 | 12,732 | 16,670 | 329 | 3,938 D | 42.8% | 56.1% | 43.3% | 56.7% |
| 23,933 | CLAY | 11,265 | 5,674 | 5,433 | 158 | 241 R | 50.4% | 48.2% | 51.1% | 48.9% |
| 30,547 | CLINTON | 14,963 | 8,199 | 6,662 | 102 | 1,537 R | 54.8% | 44.5% | 55.2% | 44.8% |
| 8,033 | CRAWFORD | 4,948 | 2,181 | 2,721 | 46 | 540 D | 44.1% | 55.0% | 44.5% | 55.5% |
| 26,602 | DAVIESS | 11,838 | 6,829 | 4,952 | 57 | 1,877 R | 57.7% | 41.8% | 58.0% | 42.0% |
| 29,430 | DEARBORN | 12,595 | 6,176 | 6,348 | 71 | 172 D | 49.0% | 50.4% | 49.3% | 50.7% |
| 22,738 | DECATUR | 9,985 | 5,555 | 4,365 | 65 | 1,190 R | 55.6% | 43.7% | 56.0% | 44.0% |
| 30,837 | DE KALB | 14,246 | 7,860 | 6,151 | 235 | 1,709 R | 55.2% | 43.2% | 56.1% | 43.9% |
| 129,219 | DELAWARE | 52,087 | 26,417 | 25,151 | 519 | 1,266 R | 50.7% | 48.3% | 51.2% | 48.8% |
| 30,934 | DUBOIS | 13,884 | 6,383 | 7,385 | 116 | 1,002 D | 46.0% | 53.2% | 46.4% | 53.6% |
| 126,529 | ELKHART | 45,429 | 27,291 | 17,581 | 557 | 9,710 R | 60.1% | 38.7% | 60.8% | 39.2% |
| 26,216 | FAYETTE | 11,288 | 5,704 | 5,519 | 65 | 185 R | 50.5% | 48.9% | 50.8% | 49.2% |
| 55,622 | FLOYD | 24,255 | 11,259 | 12,744 | 252 | 1,485 D | 46.4% | 52.5% | 46.9% | 53.1% |
| 18,257 | FOUNTAIN | 9,052 | 4,903 | 4,089 | 60 | 814 R | 54.2% | 45.2% | 54.5% | 45.5% |
| 16,943 | FRANKLIN | 6,845 | 3,557 | 3,234 | 54 | 323 R | 52.0% | 47.2% | 52.4% | 47.6% |
| 16,984 | FULTON | 8,703 | 5,083 | 3,488 | 132 | 1,595 R | 58.4% | 40.1% | 59.3% | 40.7% |
| 30,444 | GIBSON | 15,599 | 7,105 | 8,430 | 64 | 1,325 D | 45.5% | 54.0% | 45.7% | 54.3% |
| 83,955 | GRANT | 30,554 | 16,847 | 13,468 | 239 | 3,379 R | 55.1% | 44.1% | 55.6% | 44.4% |
| 26,894 | GREENE | 13,843 | 6,442 | 7,263 | 138 | 821 D | 46.5% | 52.5% | 47.0% | 53.0% |
| 54,532 | HAMILTON | 29,958 | 21,828 | 7,857 | 273 | 13,971 R | 72.9% | 26.2% | 73.5% | 26.5% |
| 35,096 | HANCOCK | 16,427 | 10,072 | 6,191 | 164 | 3,881 R | 61.3% | 37.7% | 61.9% | 38.1% |
| 20,423 | HARRISON | 10,699 | 4,911 | 5,685 | 103 | 774 D | 45.9% | 53.1% | 46.3% | 53.7% |
| 53,974 | HENDRICKS | 26,104 | 16,725 | 9,066 | 313 | 7,659 R | 64.1% | 34.7% | 64.8% | 35.2% |
| 52,603 | HENRY | 21,848 | 11,620 | 10,137 | 91 | 1,483 R | 53.2% | 46.4% | 53.4% | 46.6% |
| 83,198 | HOWARD | 34,653 | 19,571 | 14,815 | 267 | 4,756 R | 56.5% | 42.8% | 56.9% | 43.1% |
| 34,970 | HUNTINGTON | 15,890 | 9,182 | 6,515 | 193 | 2,667 R | 57.8% | 41.0% | 58.5% | 41.5% |
| 33,187 | JACKSON | 15,358 | 7,615 | 7,610 | 133 | 5 R | 49.6% | 49.6% | 50.0% | 50.0% |
| 20,429 | JASPER | 8,884 | 5,398 | 3,286 | 200 | 2,112 R | 60.8% | 37.0% | 62.2% | 37.8% |
| 23,575 | JAY | 8,817 | 4,606 | 4,124 | 87 | 482 R | 52.2% | 46.8% | 52.8% | 47.2% |
| 27,006 | JEFFERSON | 11,873 | 5,573 | 6,139 | 161 | 566 D | 46.9% | 51.7% | 47.6% | 52.4% |
| 19,454 | JENNINGS | 9,012 | 4,505 | 4,430 | 77 | 75 R | 50.0% | 49.2% | 50.4% | 49.6% |
| 61,138 | JOHNSON | 26,749 | 16,414 | 10,075 | 260 | 6,339 R | 61.4% | 37.7% | 62.0% | 38.0% |
| 41,546 | KNOX | 18,860 | 9,100 | 9,612 | 148 | 512 D | 48.3% | 51.0% | 48.6% | 51.4% |
| 48,127 | KOSCIUSKO | 22,124 | 14,505 | 7,328 | 291 | 7,177 R | 65.6% | 33.1% | 66.4% | 33.6% |
| 20,890 | LAGRANGE | 6,772 | 3,876 | 2,835 | 61 | 1,041 R | 57.2% | 41.9% | 57.8% | 42.2% |
| 546,253 | LAKE | 212,741 | 90,119 | 120,700 | 1,922 | 30,581 D | 42.4% | 56.7% | 42.7% | 57.3% |
| 105,342 | LA PORTE | 40,655 | 21,989 | 18,217 | 449 | 3,772 R | 54.1% | 44.8% | 54.7% | 45.3% |
| 38,038 | LAWRENCE | 17,440 | 9,278 | 7,908 | 254 | 1,370 R | 53.2% | 45.3% | 54.0% | 46.0% |
| 138,451 | MADISON | 62,820 | 32,437 | 29,811 | 572 | 2,626 R | 51.6% | 47.5% | 52.1% | 47.9% |
| 792,299 | MARION | 325,576 | 177,767 | 145,274 | 2,535 | 32,493 R | 54.6% | 44.6% | 55.0% | 45.0% |
| 34,986 | MARSHALL | 16,408 | 9,707 | 6,424 | 277 | 3,283 R | 59.2% | 39.2% | 60.2% | 39.8% |
| 10,969 | MARTIN | 5,565 | 2,702 | 2,827 | 36 | 125 D | 48.6% | 50.8% | 48.9% | 51.1% |
| 39,246 | MIAMI | 14,665 | 8,263 | 6,257 | 145 | 2,006 R | 56.3% | 42.7% | 56.9% | 43.1% |
| 84,849 | MONROE | 36,182 | 18,938 | 16,609 | 635 | 2,329 R | 52.3% | 45.9% | 53.3% | 46.7% |
| 33,930 | MONTGOMERY | 14,977 | 9,509 | 5,320 | 148 | 4,189 R | 63.5% | 35.5% | 64.1% | 35.9% |
| 44,176 | MORGAN | 18,427 | 10,983 | 7,181 | 263 | 3,802 R | 59.6% | 39.0% | 60.5% | 39.5% |
| 11,606 | NEWTON | 5,483 | 3,204 | 2,236 | 43 | 968 R | 58.4% | 40.8% | 58.9% | 41.1% |
| 31,382 | NOBLE | 13,013 | 6,885 | 5,875 | 253 | 1,010 R | 52.9% | 45.1% | 54.0% | 46.0% |
| 4,289 | OHIO | 2,337 | 1,027 | 1,300 | 10 | 273 D | 43.9% | 55.6% | 44.1% | 55.9% |
| 16,968 | ORANGE | 8,476 | 4,399 | 4,031 | 46 | 368 R | 51.9% | 47.6% | 52.2% | 47.8% |
| 12,163 | OWEN | 6,055 | 2,896 | 3,103 | 56 | 207 D | 47.8% | 51.2% | 48.3% | 51.7% |

# INDIANA

## PRESIDENT 1976

| 1970 Census Population | County | Total Vote | Republican | Democratic | Other | Rep.-Dem. Plurality | Percentage | | | |
|---|---|---|---|---|---|---|---|---|---|---|
| | | | | | | | Total Vote | | Major Vote | |
| | | | | | | | Rep. | Dem. | Rep. | Dem. |
| 14,600 | PARKE | 7,144 | 3,929 | 3,158 | 57 | 771 R | 55.0% | 44.2% | 55.4% | 44.6% |
| 19,075 | PERRY | 9,746 | 4,088 | 5,620 | 38 | 1,532 D | 41.9% | 57.7% | 42.1% | 57.9% |
| 12,281 | PIKE | 7,101 | 3,138 | 3,938 | 25 | 800 D | 44.2% | 55.5% | 44.3% | 55.7% |
| 87,114 | PORTER | 42,658 | 25,489 | 16,468 | 701 | 9,021 R | 59.8% | 38.6% | 60.8% | 39.2% |
| 21,740 | POSEY | 10,488 | 5,136 | 5,298 | 54 | 162 D | 49.0% | 50.5% | 49.2% | 50.8% |
| 12,534 | PULASKI | 6,615 | 3,586 | 2,813 | 216 | 773 R | 54.2% | 42.5% | 56.0% | 44.0% |
| 26,932 | PUTNAM | 11,297 | 6,063 | 5,116 | 118 | 947 R | 53.7% | 45.3% | 54.2% | 45.8% |
| 28,915 | RANDOLPH | 12,320 | 6,891 | 5,330 | 99 | 1,561 R | 55.9% | 43.3% | 56.4% | 43.6% |
| 21,138 | RIPLEY | 10,157 | 5,293 | 4,792 | 72 | 501 R | 52.1% | 47.2% | 52.5% | 47.5% |
| 20,352 | RUSH | 7,830 | 4,723 | 3,052 | 55 | 1,671 R | 60.3% | 39.0% | 60.7% | 39.3% |
| 245,045 | ST. JOSEPH | 100,324 | 50,358 | 49,156 | 810 | 1,202 R | 50.2% | 49.0% | 50.6% | 49.4% |
| 17,144 | SCOTT | 6,966 | 2,657 | 4,229 | 80 | 1,572 D | 38.1% | 60.7% | 38.6% | 61.4% |
| 37,797 | SHELBY | 16,150 | 8,918 | 7,098 | 134 | 1,820 R | 55.2% | 44.0% | 55.7% | 44.3% |
| 17,134 | SPENCER | 8,990 | 4,166 | 4,796 | 28 | 630 D | 46.3% | 53.3% | 46.5% | 53.5% |
| 19,280 | STARKE | 9,241 | 4,354 | 4,753 | 134 | 399 D | 47.1% | 51.4% | 47.8% | 52.2% |
| 20,159 | STEUBEN | 8,575 | 5,079 | 3,323 | 173 | 1,756 R | 59.2% | 38.8% | 60.4% | 39.6% |
| 19,889 | SULLIVAN | 9,006 | 3,747 | 5,198 | 61 | 1,451 D | 41.6% | 57.7% | 41.9% | 58.1% |
| 6,306 | SWITZERLAND | 3,491 | 1,329 | 2,150 | 12 | 821 D | 38.1% | 61.6% | 38.2% | 61.8% |
| 109,378 | TIPPECANOE | 47,587 | 29,186 | 17,850 | 551 | 11,336 R | 61.3% | 37.5% | 62.1% | 37.9% |
| 16,650 | TIPTON | 8,328 | 4,776 | 3,428 | 124 | 1,348 R | 57.3% | 41.2% | 58.2% | 41.8% |
| 6,582 | UNION | 2,800 | 1,631 | 1,160 | 9 | 471 R | 58.3% | 41.4% | 58.4% | 41.6% |
| 168,772 | VANDERBURGH | 73,211 | 37,975 | 34,911 | 325 | 3,064 R | 51.9% | 47.7% | 52.1% | 47.9% |
| 16,793 | VERMILLION | 8,538 | 3,674 | 4,791 | 73 | 1,117 D | 43.0% | 56.1% | 43.4% | 56.6% |
| 114,528 | VIGO | 48,610 | 23,555 | 24,684 | 371 | 1,129 D | 48.5% | 50.8% | 48.8% | 51.2% |
| 35,553 | WABASH | 14,340 | 8,534 | 5,704 | 102 | 2,830 R | 59.5% | 39.8% | 59.9% | 40.1% |
| 8,705 | WARREN | 4,312 | 2,377 | 1,906 | 29 | 471 R | 55.1% | 44.2% | 55.5% | 44.5% |
| 27,972 | WARRICK | 15,096 | 7,200 | 7,804 | 92 | 604 D | 47.7% | 51.7% | 48.0% | 52.0% |
| 19,278 | WASHINGTON | 8,318 | 3,794 | 4,409 | 115 | 615 D | 45.6% | 53.0% | 46.3% | 53.7% |
| 79,109 | WAYNE | 29,191 | 16,697 | 12,306 | 188 | 4,391 R | 57.2% | 42.2% | 57.6% | 42.4% |
| 23,821 | WELLS | 9,934 | 5,596 | 4,250 | 88 | 1,346 R | 56.3% | 42.8% | 56.8% | 43.2% |
| 20,995 | WHITE | 10,369 | 6,287 | 3,963 | 119 | 2,324 R | 60.6% | 38.2% | 61.3% | 38.7% |
| 23,395 | WHITLEY | 12,441 | 6,761 | 5,445 | 235 | 1,316 R | 54.3% | 43.8% | 55.4% | 44.6% |
| 5,193,669 | TOTAL | 2,220,362 | 1,183,958 | 1,014,714 | 21,690 | 169,244 R | 53.3% | 45.7% | 53.8% | 46.2% |

# INDIANA

## PRESIDENT 1972

| 1970 Census Population | County | Total Vote | Republican | Democratic | Other | Rep.-Dem. Plurality | Percentage | | | |
|---|---|---|---|---|---|---|---|---|---|---|
| | | | | | | | Total Vote | | Major Vote | |
| | | | | | | | Rep. | Dem. | Rep. | Dem. |
| 26,871 | ADAMS | 11,572 | 7,549 | 3,971 | 52 | 3,578 R | 65.2% | 34.3% | 65.5% | 34.5% |
| 280,455 | ALLEN | 116,199 | 76,924 | 38,621 | 654 | 38,303 R | 66.2% | 33.2% | 66.6% | 33.4% |
| 57,022 | BARTHOLOMEW | 24,502 | 17,365 | 6,974 | 163 | 10,391 R | 70.9% | 28.5% | 71.3% | 28.7% |
| 11,262 | BENTON | 5,289 | 3,703 | 1,566 | 20 | 2,137 R | 70.0% | 29.6% | 70.3% | 29.7% |
| 15,888 | BLACKFORD | 6,219 | 3,876 | 2,311 | 32 | 1,565 R | 62.3% | 37.2% | 62.6% | 37.4% |
| 30,870 | BOONE | 13,147 | 9,874 | 3,235 | 38 | 6,639 R | 75.1% | 24.6% | 75.3% | 24.7% |
| 9,057 | BROWN | 4,207 | 2,737 | 1,443 | 27 | 1,294 R | 65.1% | 34.3% | 65.5% | 34.5% |
| 17,734 | CARROLL | 8,137 | 5,885 | 2,214 | 38 | 3,671 R | 72.3% | 27.2% | 72.7% | 27.3% |
| 40,456 | CASS | 18,176 | 12,681 | 5,317 | 178 | 7,364 R | 69.8% | 29.3% | 70.5% | 29.5% |
| 75,876 | CLARK | 27,113 | 16,111 | 10,838 | 164 | 5,273 R | 59.4% | 40.0% | 59.8% | 40.2% |
| 23,933 | CLAY | 10,937 | 7,146 | 3,742 | 49 | 3,404 R | 65.3% | 34.2% | 65.6% | 34.4% |
| 30,547 | CLINTON | 14,187 | 9,849 | 4,283 | 55 | 5,566 R | 69.4% | 30.2% | 69.7% | 30.3% |
| 8,033 | CRAWFORD | 4,449 | 2,623 | 1,801 | 25 | 822 R | 59.0% | 40.5% | 59.3% | 40.7% |
| 26,602 | DAVIESS | 12,071 | 8,490 | 3,538 | 43 | 4,952 R | 70.3% | 29.3% | 70.6% | 29.4% |
| 29,430 | DEARBORN | 11,885 | 7,689 | 4,137 | 59 | 3,552 R | 64.7% | 34.8% | 65.0% | 35.0% |
| 22,738 | DECATUR | 9,822 | 6,761 | 2,994 | 67 | 3,767 R | 68.8% | 30.5% | 69.3% | 30.7% |
| 30,837 | DE KALB | 13,297 | 8,834 | 4,354 | 109 | 4,480 R | 66.4% | 32.7% | 67.0% | 33.0% |
| 129,219 | DELAWARE | 50,567 | 32,468 | 17,936 | 163 | 14,532 R | 64.2% | 35.5% | 64.4% | 35.6% |
| 30,934 | DUBOIS | 13,179 | 6,637 | 6,365 | 177 | 272 R | 50.4% | 48.3% | 51.0% | 49.0% |
| 126,529 | ELKHART | 43,941 | 31,009 | 12,659 | 273 | 18,350 R | 70.6% | 28.8% | 71.0% | 29.0% |
| 26,216 | FAYETTE | 10,829 | 7,273 | 3,519 | 37 | 3,754 R | 67.2% | 32.5% | 67.4% | 32.6% |
| 55,622 | FLOYD | 22,636 | 13,198 | 9,243 | 195 | 3,955 R | 58.3% | 40.8% | 58.8% | 41.2% |
| 18,257 | FOUNTAIN | 9,003 | 5,979 | 2,977 | 47 | 3,002 R | 66.4% | 33.1% | 66.8% | 33.2% |
| 16,943 | FRANKLIN | 6,479 | 4,324 | 2,131 | 24 | 2,193 R | 66.7% | 32.9% | 67.0% | 33.0% |
| 16,984 | FULTON | 8,358 | 6,170 | 2,150 | 38 | 4,020 R | 73.8% | 25.7% | 74.2% | 25.8% |
| 30,444 | GIBSON | 14,819 | 9,115 | 5,633 | 71 | 3,482 R | 61.5% | 38.0% | 61.8% | 38.2% |
| 83,955 | GRANT | 28,958 | 20,969 | 7,912 | 77 | 13,057 R | 72.4% | 27.3% | 72.6% | 27.4% |
| 26,894 | GREENE | 13,045 | 8,453 | 4,450 | 142 | 4,003 R | 64.8% | 34.1% | 65.5% | 34.5% |
| 54,532 | HAMILTON | 24,470 | 20,247 | 4,151 | 72 | 16,096 R | 82.7% | 17.0% | 83.0% | 17.0% |
| 35,096 | HANCOCK | 14,150 | 11,019 | 3,069 | 62 | 7,950 R | 77.9% | 21.7% | 78.2% | 21.8% |
| 20,423 | HARRISON | 9,888 | 5,910 | 3,927 | 51 | 1,983 R | 59.8% | 39.7% | 60.1% | 39.9% |
| 53,974 | HENDRICKS | 22,153 | 17,699 | 4,384 | 70 | 13,315 R | 79.9% | 19.8% | 80.1% | 19.9% |
| 52,603 | HENRY | 20,208 | 14,538 | 5,610 | 60 | 8,928 R | 71.9% | 27.8% | 72.2% | 27.8% |
| 83,198 | HOWARD | 31,341 | 23,089 | 8,083 | 169 | 15,006 R | 73.7% | 25.8% | 74.1% | 25.9% |
| 34,970 | HUNTINGTON | 15,855 | 10,858 | 4,908 | 89 | 5,950 R | 68.5% | 31.0% | 68.9% | 31.1% |
| 33,187 | JACKSON | 14,689 | 9,546 | 4,984 | 159 | 4,562 R | 65.0% | 33.9% | 65.7% | 34.3% |
| 20,429 | JASPER | 8,357 | 6,369 | 1,920 | 68 | 4,449 R | 76.2% | 23.0% | 76.8% | 23.2% |
| 23,575 | JAY | 9,484 | 6,090 | 3,349 | 45 | 2,741 R | 64.2% | 35.3% | 64.5% | 35.5% |
| 27,006 | JEFFERSON | 11,103 | 6,722 | 4,267 | 114 | 2,455 R | 60.5% | 38.4% | 61.2% | 38.8% |
| 19,454 | JENNINGS | 8,157 | 5,156 | 2,903 | 98 | 2,253 R | 63.2% | 35.6% | 64.0% | 36.0% |
| 61,138 | JOHNSON | 22,724 | 17,537 | 5,067 | 120 | 12,470 R | 77.2% | 22.3% | 77.6% | 22.4% |
| 41,546 | KNOX | 18,196 | 11,940 | 6,089 | 167 | 5,851 R | 65.6% | 33.5% | 66.2% | 33.8% |
| 48,127 | KOSCIUSKO | 20,545 | 16,216 | 4,233 | 96 | 11,983 R | 78.9% | 20.6% | 79.3% | 20.7% |
| 20,890 | LAGRANGE | 5,839 | 4,152 | 1,658 | 29 | 2,494 R | 71.1% | 28.4% | 71.5% | 28.5% |
| 546,253 | LAKE | 205,342 | 115,480 | 88,510 | 1,352 | 26,970 R | 56.2% | 43.1% | 56.6% | 43.4% |
| 105,342 | LA PORTE | 39,776 | 26,243 | 13,222 | 311 | 13,021 R | 66.0% | 33.2% | 66.5% | 33.5% |
| 38,038 | LAWRENCE | 15,284 | 10,936 | 4,278 | 70 | 6,658 R | 71.6% | 28.0% | 71.9% | 28.1% |
| 138,451 | MADISON | 60,134 | 39,036 | 20,921 | 177 | 18,115 R | 64.9% | 34.8% | 65.1% | 34.9% |
| 792,299 | MARION | 309,766 | 206,065 | 102,166 | 1,535 | 103,899 R | 66.5% | 33.0% | 66.9% | 33.1% |
| 34,986 | MARSHALL | 16,308 | 11,908 | 4,349 | 51 | 7,559 R | 73.0% | 26.7% | 73.2% | 26.8% |
| 10,969 | MARTIN | 5,509 | 3,470 | 2,021 | 18 | 1,449 R | 63.0% | 36.7% | 63.2% | 36.8% |
| 39,246 | MIAMI | 13,450 | 9,477 | 3,889 | 84 | 5,588 R | 70.5% | 28.9% | 70.9% | 29.1% |
| 84,849 | MONROE | 35,596 | 19,953 | 15,241 | 402 | 4,712 R | 56.1% | 42.8% | 56.7% | 43.3% |
| 33,930 | MONTGOMERY | 14,471 | 10,997 | 3,431 | 43 | 7,566 R | 76.0% | 23.7% | 76.2% | 23.8% |
| 44,176 | MORGAN | 15,435 | 11,980 | 3,390 | 65 | 8,590 R | 77.6% | 22.0% | 77.9% | 22.1% |
| 11,606 | NEWTON | 5,028 | 3,771 | 1,252 | 5 | 2,519 R | 75.0% | 24.9% | 75.1% | 24.9% |
| 31,382 | NOBLE | 12,226 | 7,916 | 4,250 | 60 | 3,666 R | 64.7% | 34.8% | 65.1% | 34.9% |
| 4,289 | OHIO | 2,299 | 1,368 | 922 | 9 | 446 R | 59.5% | 40.1% | 59.7% | 40.3% |
| 16,968 | ORANGE | 8,674 | 5,715 | 2,932 | 27 | 2,783 R | 65.9% | 33.8% | 66.1% | 33.9% |
| 12,163 | OWEN | 5,626 | 3,896 | 1,708 | 22 | 2,188 R | 69.2% | 30.4% | 69.5% | 30.5% |

# INDIANA

## PRESIDENT 1972

| 1970 Census Population | County | Total Vote | Republican | Democratic | Other | Rep.-Dem. Plurality | Percentage | | | |
|---|---|---|---|---|---|---|---|---|---|---|
| | | | | | | | Total Vote | | Major Vote | |
| | | | | | | | Rep. | Dem. | Rep. | Dem. |
| 14,600 | PARKE | 7,250 | 5,014 | 2,207 | 29 | 2,807 R | 69.2% | 30.4% | 69.4% | 30.6% |
| 19,075 | PERRY | 9,510 | 5,204 | 4,277 | 29 | 927 R | 54.7% | 45.0% | 54.9% | 45.1% |
| 12,281 | PIKE | 6,939 | 4,252 | 2,648 | 39 | 1,604 R | 61.3% | 38.2% | 61.6% | 38.4% |
| 87,114 | PORTER | 36,030 | 26,877 | 8,943 | 210 | 17,934 R | 74.6% | 24.8% | 75.0% | 25.0% |
| 21,740 | POSEY | 10,378 | 6,771 | 3,586 | 21 | 3,185 R | 65.2% | 34.6% | 65.4% | 34.6% |
| 12,534 | PULASKI | 6,146 | 4,243 | 1,863 | 40 | 2,380 R | 69.0% | 30.3% | 69.5% | 30.5% |
| 26,932 | PUTNAM | 11,243 | 7,879 | 3,339 | 25 | 4,540 R | 70.1% | 29.7% | 70.2% | 29.8% |
| 28,915 | RANDOLPH | 12,232 | 8,754 | 3,409 | 69 | 5,345 R | 71.6% | 27.9% | 72.0% | 28.0% |
| 21,138 | RIPLEY | 10,231 | 6,594 | 3,601 | 36 | 2,993 R | 64.5% | 35.2% | 64.7% | 35.3% |
| 20,352 | RUSH | 7,752 | 5,965 | 1,764 | 23 | 4,201 R | 76.9% | 22.8% | 77.2% | 22.8% |
| 245,045 | ST. JOSEPH | 107,039 | 64,808 | 41,629 | 602 | 23,179 R | 60.5% | 38.9% | 60.9% | 39.1% |
| 17,144 | SCOTT | 6,391 | 3,564 | 2,785 | 42 | 779 R | 55.8% | 43.6% | 56.1% | 43.9% |
| 37,797 | SHELBY | 14,900 | 10,794 | 4,028 | 78 | 6,766 R | 72.4% | 27.0% | 72.8% | 27.2% |
| 17,134 | SPENCER | 9,415 | 5,518 | 3,867 | 30 | 1,651 R | 58.6% | 41.1% | 58.8% | 41.2% |
| 19,280 | STARKE | 8,567 | 5,520 | 2,994 | 53 | 2,526 R | 64.4% | 34.9% | 64.8% | 35.2% |
| 20,159 | STEUBEN | 8,075 | 5,636 | 2,401 | 38 | 3,235 R | 69.8% | 29.7% | 70.1% | 29.9% |
| 19,889 | SULLIVAN | 9,001 | 5,338 | 3,624 | 39 | 1,714 R | 59.3% | 40.3% | 59.6% | 40.4% |
| 6,306 | SWITZERLAND | 3,497 | 1,872 | 1,612 | 13 | 260 R | 53.5% | 46.1% | 53.7% | 46.3% |
| 109,378 | TIPPECANOE | 46,366 | 31,565 | 14,598 | 203 | 16,967 R | 68.1% | 31.5% | 68.4% | 31.6% |
| 16,650 | TIPTON | 7,808 | 5,674 | 2,095 | 39 | 3,579 R | 72.7% | 26.8% | 73.0% | 27.0% |
| 6,582 | UNION | 2,818 | 2,043 | 765 | 10 | 1,278 R | 72.5% | 27.1% | 72.8% | 27.2% |
| 168,772 | VANDERBURGH | 71,437 | 48,806 | 22,163 | 468 | 26,643 R | 68.3% | 31.0% | 68.8% | 31.2% |
| 16,793 | VERMILLION | 8,323 | 4,764 | 3,515 | 44 | 1,249 R | 57.2% | 42.2% | 57.5% | 42.5% |
| 114,528 | VIGO | 48,957 | 29,730 | 18,898 | 329 | 10,832 R | 60.7% | 38.6% | 61.1% | 38.9% |
| 35,553 | WABASH | 14,659 | 10,011 | 4,601 | 47 | 5,410 R | 68.3% | 31.4% | 68.5% | 31.5% |
| 8,705 | WARREN | 3,925 | 2,746 | 1,164 | 15 | 1,582 R | 70.0% | 29.7% | 70.2% | 29.8% |
| 27,972 | WARRICK | 12,941 | 8,520 | 4,296 | 125 | 4,224 R | 65.8% | 33.2% | 66.5% | 33.5% |
| 19,278 | WASHINGTON | 7,922 | 4,758 | 3,086 | 78 | 1,672 R | 60.1% | 39.0% | 60.7% | 39.3% |
| 79,109 | WAYNE | 29,361 | 21,610 | 7,655 | 96 | 13,955 R | 73.6% | 26.1% | 73.8% | 26.2% |
| 23,821 | WELLS | 9,769 | 6,425 | 3,244 | 100 | 3,181 R | 65.8% | 33.2% | 66.4% | 33.6% |
| 20,995 | WHITE | 10,137 | 7,419 | 2,675 | 43 | 4,744 R | 73.2% | 26.4% | 73.5% | 26.5% |
| 23,395 | WHITLEY | 11,404 | 7,489 | 3,838 | 77 | 3,651 R | 65.7% | 33.7% | 66.1% | 33.9% |
| 5,193,669 | TOTAL | 2,125,529 | 1,405,154 | 708,568 | 11,807 | 696,586 R | 66.1% | 33.3% | 66.5% | 33.5% |

# INDIANA

## PRESIDENT 1968

| 1960 Census Population | County | Total Vote | Republican | Democratic | AIP | Other | Plurality | Percentage Total Vote Rep. | Dem. | AIP |
|---|---|---|---|---|---|---|---|---|---|---|
| 24,643 | ADAMS | 11,259 | 5,774 | 4,667 | 762 | 56 | 1,107 R | 51.3% | 41.5% | 6.8% |
| 232,196 | ALLEN | 108,954 | 59,211 | 40,411 | 9,121 | 211 | 18,800 R | 54.3% | 37.1% | 8.4% |
| 48,198 | BARTHOLOMEW | 24,424 | 13,628 | 8,268 | 2,438 | 90 | 5,360 R | 55.8% | 33.9% | 10.0% |
| 11,912 | BENTON | 5,586 | 3,326 | 1,854 | 400 | 6 | 1,472 R | 59.5% | 33.2% | 7.2% |
| 14,792 | BLACKFORD | 6,504 | 3,052 | 2,898 | 534 | 20 | 154 R | 46.9% | 44.6% | 8.2% |
| 27,543 | BOONE | 13,407 | 7,905 | 4,118 | 1,346 | 38 | 3,787 R | 59.0% | 30.7% | 10.0% |
| 7,024 | BROWN | 3,807 | 1,881 | 1,327 | 587 | 12 | 554 R | 49.4% | 34.9% | 15.4% |
| 16,934 | CARROLL | 8,535 | 4,796 | 2,816 | 918 | 5 | 1,980 R | 56.2% | 33.0% | 10.8% |
| 40,931 | CASS | 18,318 | 9,441 | 7,142 | 1,678 | 57 | 2,299 R | 51.5% | 39.0% | 9.2% |
| 62,795 | CLARK | 26,886 | 10,305 | 11,493 | 4,982 | 106 | 1,188 D | 38.3% | 42.7% | 18.5% |
| 24,207 | CLAY | 11,298 | 5,743 | 3,956 | 1,569 | 30 | 1,787 R | 50.8% | 35.0% | 13.9% |
| 30,765 | CLINTON | 14,707 | 7,929 | 5,714 | 1,033 | 31 | 2,215 R | 53.9% | 38.9% | 7.0% |
| 8,379 | CRAWFORD | 4,280 | 2,132 | 1,536 | 589 | 23 | 596 R | 49.8% | 35.9% | 13.8% |
| 26,636 | DAVIESS | 12,393 | 7,036 | 4,071 | 1,274 | 12 | 2,965 R | 56.8% | 32.8% | 10.3% |
| 28,674 | DEARBORN | 12,760 | 6,208 | 4,842 | 1,704 | 6 | 1,366 R | 48.7% | 37.9% | 13.4% |
| 20,019 | DECATUR | 9,833 | 5,474 | 3,602 | 731 | 26 | 1,872 R | 55.7% | 36.6% | 7.4% |
| 28,271 | DE KALB | 13,438 | 7,650 | 4,790 | 931 | 67 | 2,860 R | 56.9% | 35.6% | 6.9% |
| 110,938 | DELAWARE | 49,523 | 23,554 | 19,532 | 6,349 | 88 | 4,022 R | 47.6% | 39.4% | 12.8% |
| 27,463 | DUBOIS | 13,563 | 5,865 | 6,725 | 958 | 15 | 860 D | 43.2% | 49.6% | 7.1% |
| 106,790 | ELKHART | 42,289 | 24,484 | 14,222 | 3,440 | 143 | 10,262 R | 57.9% | 33.6% | 8.1% |
| 24,454 | FAYETTE | 11,266 | 5,286 | 4,549 | 1,413 | 18 | 737 R | 46.9% | 40.4% | 12.5% |
| 51,397 | FLOYD | 23,701 | 9,714 | 10,671 | 3,266 | 50 | 957 D | 41.0% | 45.0% | 13.8% |
| 18,706 | FOUNTAIN | 9,637 | 5,110 | 3,237 | 1,280 | 10 | 1,873 R | 53.0% | 33.6% | 13.3% |
| 17,015 | FRANKLIN | 6,634 | 3,468 | 2,386 | 775 | 5 | 1,082 R | 52.3% | 36.0% | 11.7% |
| 16,957 | FULTON | 8,474 | 5,145 | 2,561 | 757 | 11 | 2,584 R | 60.7% | 30.2% | 8.9% |
| 29,949 | GIBSON | 15,957 | 7,645 | 6,777 | 1,497 | 38 | 868 R | 47.9% | 42.5% | 9.4% |
| 75,741 | GRANT | 30,826 | 16,170 | 10,938 | 3,602 | 116 | 5,232 R | 52.5% | 35.5% | 11.7% |
| 26,327 | GREENE | 13,491 | 6,525 | 5,493 | 1,419 | 54 | 1,032 R | 48.4% | 40.7% | 10.5% |
| 40,132 | HAMILTON | 21,069 | 14,250 | 4,586 | 2,202 | 31 | 9,664 R | 67.6% | 21.8% | 10.5% |
| 26,665 | HANCOCK | 13,366 | 7,516 | 3,902 | 1,896 | 52 | 3,614 R | 56.2% | 29.2% | 14.2% |
| 19,207 | HARRISON | 9,731 | 4,410 | 3,725 | 1,557 | 39 | 685 R | 45.3% | 38.3% | 16.0% |
| 40,896 | HENDRICKS | 21,032 | 12,597 | 5,155 | 3,231 | 49 | 7,442 R | 59.9% | 24.5% | 15.4% |
| 48,899 | HENRY | 22,097 | 11,626 | 8,045 | 2,366 | 60 | 3,581 R | 52.6% | 36.4% | 10.7% |
| 69,509 | HOWARD | 31,566 | 15,905 | 11,026 | 4,507 | 128 | 4,879 R | 50.4% | 34.9% | 14.3% |
| 33,814 | HUNTINGTON | 16,523 | 9,002 | 6,238 | 1,250 | 33 | 2,764 R | 54.5% | 37.8% | 7.6% |
| 30,556 | JACKSON | 14,821 | 7,710 | 5,140 | 1,891 | 80 | 2,570 R | 52.0% | 34.7% | 12.8% |
| 18,842 | JASPER | 8,252 | 4,996 | 2,201 | 1,003 | 52 | 2,795 R | 60.5% | 26.7% | 12.2% |
| 22,572 | JAY | 10,705 | 5,460 | 4,290 | 918 | 37 | 1,170 R | 51.0% | 40.1% | 8.6% |
| 24,061 | JEFFERSON | 11,623 | 5,731 | 4,635 | 1,196 | 61 | 1,096 R | 49.3% | 39.9% | 10.3% |
| 17,267 | JENNINGS | 8,640 | 4,416 | 2,996 | 1,214 | 14 | 1,420 R | 51.1% | 34.7% | 14.1% |
| 43,704 | JOHNSON | 21,111 | 12,089 | 5,946 | 3,021 | 55 | 6,143 R | 57.3% | 28.2% | 14.3% |
| 41,561 | KNOX | 17,818 | 8,369 | 7,297 | 2,053 | 99 | 1,072 R | 47.0% | 41.0% | 11.5% |
| 40,373 | KOSCIUSKO | 19,744 | 12,633 | 5,342 | 1,700 | 69 | 7,291 R | 64.0% | 27.1% | 8.6% |
| 17,380 | LAGRANGE | 5,408 | 3,328 | 1,691 | 380 | 9 | 1,637 R | 61.5% | 31.3% | 7.0% |
| 513,269 | LAKE | 213,574 | 77,911 | 99,897 | 35,099 | 667 | 21,986 D | 36.5% | 46.8% | 16.4% |
| 95,111 | LA PORTE | 40,783 | 20,295 | 15,780 | 4,587 | 121 | 4,515 R | 49.8% | 38.7% | 11.2% |
| 36,564 | LAWRENCE | 16,248 | 8,830 | 5,349 | 1,995 | 74 | 3,481 R | 54.3% | 32.9% | 12.3% |
| 125,819 | MADISON | 59,368 | 28,726 | 23,886 | 6,613 | 143 | 4,840 R | 48.4% | 40.2% | 11.1% |
| 697,567 | MARION | 310,922 | 162,503 | 115,715 | 32,043 | 661 | 46,788 R | 52.3% | 37.2% | 10.3% |
| 32,443 | MARSHALL | 16,394 | 9,290 | 5,385 | 1,685 | 34 | 3,905 R | 56.7% | 32.8% | 10.3% |
| 10,608 | MARTIN | 5,435 | 2,512 | 2,315 | 604 | 4 | 197 R | 46.2% | 42.6% | 11.1% |
| 38,000 | MIAMI | 13,655 | 7,295 | 5,019 | 1,294 | 47 | 2,276 R | 53.4% | 36.8% | 9.5% |
| 59,225 | MONROE | 27,080 | 13,752 | 10,789 | 2,361 | 178 | 2,963 R | 50.8% | 39.8% | 8.7% |
| 32,089 | MONTGOMERY | 15,175 | 9,085 | 4,752 | 1,309 | 29 | 4,333 R | 59.9% | 31.3% | 8.6% |
| 33,875 | MORGAN | 16,130 | 8,944 | 4,042 | 3,122 | 22 | 4,902 R | 55.4% | 25.1% | 19.4% |
| 11,502 | NEWTON | 5,093 | 3,145 | 1,453 | 483 | 12 | 1,692 R | 61.8% | 28.5% | 9.5% |
| 28,162 | NOBLE | 13,046 | 6,699 | 5,075 | 1,253 | 19 | 1,624 R | 51.3% | 38.9% | 9.6% |
| 4,165 | OHIO | 2,287 | 1,053 | 991 | 243 | | 62 R | 46.0% | 43.3% | 10.6% |
| 16,877 | ORANGE | 8,512 | 4,666 | 2,918 | 915 | 13 | 1,748 R | 54.8% | 34.3% | 10.7% |
| 11,400 | OWEN | 5,618 | 2,898 | 1,932 | 776 | 12 | 966 R | 51.6% | 34.4% | 13.8% |

# INDIANA

## PRESIDENT 1968

| 1960 Census Population | County | Total Vote | Republican | Democratic | AIP | Other | Plurality | Percentage Total Vote Rep. | Dem. | AIP |
|---|---|---|---|---|---|---|---|---|---|---|
| 14,804 | PARKE | 7,124 | 3,738 | 2,472 | 907 | 7 | 1,266 R | 52.5% | 34.7% | 12.7% |
| 17,232 | PERRY | 9,108 | 4,211 | 4,343 | 547 | 7 | 132 D | 46.2% | 47.7% | 6.0% |
| 12,797 | PIKE | 6,802 | 3,087 | 2,953 | 745 | 17 | 134 R | 45.4% | 43.4% | 11.0% |
| 60,279 | PORTER | 32,582 | 17,328 | 8,914 | 6,126 | 214 | 8,414 R | 53.2% | 27.4% | 18.8% |
| 19,214 | POSEY | 10,150 | 5,045 | 3,889 | 1,204 | 12 | 1,156 R | 49.7% | 38.3% | 11.9% |
| 12,837 | PULASKI | 6,133 | 3,361 | 2,071 | 681 | 20 | 1,290 R | 54.8% | 33.8% | 11.1% |
| 24,927 | PUTNAM | 11,410 | 5,873 | 3,692 | 1,826 | 19 | 2,181 R | 51.5% | 32.4% | 16.0% |
| 28,434 | RANDOLPH | 12,667 | 7,238 | 3,962 | 1,431 | 36 | 3,276 R | 57.1% | 31.3% | 11.3% |
| 20,641 | RIPLEY | 10,399 | 5,389 | 3,787 | 1,215 | 8 | 1,602 R | 51.8% | 36.4% | 11.7% |
| 20,393 | RUSH | 8,421 | 5,004 | 2,636 | 761 | 20 | 2,368 R | 59.4% | 31.3% | 9.0% |
| 238,614 | ST. JOSEPH | 106,864 | 47,114 | 47,414 | 11,948 | 388 | 300 D | 44.1% | 44.4% | 11.2% |
| 14,643 | SCOTT | 6,267 | 2,671 | 2,796 | 784 | 16 | 125 D | 42.6% | 44.6% | 12.5% |
| 34,093 | SHELBY | 16,226 | 8,574 | 5,417 | 2,205 | 30 | 3,157 R | 52.8% | 33.4% | 13.6% |
| 16,074 | SPENCER | 8,993 | 4,603 | 3,767 | 612 | 11 | 836 R | 51.2% | 41.9% | 6.8% |
| 17,911 | STARKE | 8,365 | 4,011 | 3,208 | 1,097 | 49 | 803 R | 47.9% | 38.4% | 13.1% |
| 17,184 | STEUBEN | 7,618 | 4,762 | 2,268 | 577 | 11 | 2,494 R | 62.5% | 29.8% | 7.6% |
| 21,721 | SULLIVAN | 9,874 | 4,266 | 4,453 | 1,135 | 20 | 187 D | 43.2% | 45.1% | 11.5% |
| 7,092 | SWITZERLAND | 3,438 | 1,515 | 1,466 | 452 | 5 | 49 R | 44.1% | 42.6% | 13.1% |
| 89,122 | TIPPECANOE | 40,968 | 24,352 | 14,528 | 2,000 | 88 | 9,824 R | 59.4% | 35.5% | 4.9% |
| 15,856 | TIPTON | 7,802 | 4,270 | 2,646 | 861 | 25 | 1,624 R | 54.7% | 33.9% | 11.0% |
| 6,457 | UNION | 3,019 | 1,691 | 920 | 404 | 4 | 771 R | 56.0% | 30.5% | 13.4% |
| 165,794 | VANDERBURGH | 77,577 | 38,231 | 31,326 | 7,737 | 283 | 6,905 R | 49.3% | 40.4% | 10.0% |
| 17,683 | VERMILLION | 8,637 | 3,607 | 3,845 | 1,175 | 10 | 238 D | 41.8% | 44.5% | 13.6% |
| 108,458 | VIGO | 46,664 | 20,814 | 20,328 | 5,386 | 136 | 486 R | 44.6% | 43.6% | 11.5% |
| 32,605 | WABASH | 14,101 | 8,611 | 4,598 | 836 | 56 | 4,013 R | 61.1% | 32.6% | 5.9% |
| 8,545 | WARREN | 4,342 | 2,475 | 1,375 | 483 | 9 | 1,100 R | 57.0% | 31.7% | 11.1% |
| 23,577 | WARRICK | 12,081 | 5,742 | 4,784 | 1,503 | 52 | 958 R | 47.5% | 39.6% | 12.4% |
| 17,819 | WASHINGTON | 8,004 | 3,891 | 2,936 | 1,143 | 34 | 955 R | 48.6% | 36.7% | 14.3% |
| 74,039 | WAYNE | 32,308 | 17,335 | 10,686 | 4,240 | 47 | 6,649 R | 53.7% | 33.1% | 13.1% |
| 21,220 | WELLS | 10,101 | 5,361 | 3,827 | 882 | 31 | 1,534 R | 53.1% | 37.9% | 8.7% |
| 19,709 | WHITE | 10,305 | 5,932 | 3,395 | 965 | 13 | 2,537 R | 57.6% | 32.9% | 9.4% |
| 20,954 | WHITLEY | 10,671 | 5,684 | 3,848 | 1,120 | 19 | 1,836 R | 53.3% | 36.1% | 10.5% |
| 4,662,498 | TOTAL | 2,123,597 | 1,067,885 | 806,659 | 243,108 | 5,945 | 261,226 R | 50.3% | 38.0% | 11.4% |

# INDIANA

## PRESIDENT 1964

| 1960 Census Population | County | Total Vote | Republican | Democratic | Other | Rep.-Dem. Plurality | Percentage Total Vote Rep. | Dem. | Major Vote Rep. | Dem. |
|---|---|---|---|---|---|---|---|---|---|---|
| 24,643 | ADAMS | 10,973 | 4,230 | 6,637 | 106 | 2,407 D | 38.5% | 60.5% | 38.9% | 61.1% |
| 232,196 | ALLEN | 100,353 | 49,284 | 50,706 | 363 | 1,422 D | 49.1% | 50.5% | 49.3% | 50.7% |
| 48,198 | BARTHOLOMEW | 24,090 | 11,026 | 12,940 | 124 | 1,914 D | 45.8% | 53.7% | 46.0% | 54.0% |
| 11,912 | BENTON | 5,831 | 2,886 | 2,940 | 5 | 54 D | 49.5% | 50.4% | 49.5% | 50.5% |
| 14,792 | BLACKFORD | 6,829 | 2,552 | 4,210 | 67 | 1,658 D | 37.4% | 61.6% | 37.7% | 62.3% |
| 27,543 | BOONE | 14,181 | 7,419 | 6,716 | 46 | 703 R | 52.3% | 47.4% | 52.5% | 47.5% |
| 7,024 | BROWN | 3,544 | 1,390 | 2,135 | 19 | 745 D | 39.2% | 60.2% | 39.4% | 60.6% |
| 16,934 | CARROLL | 8,714 | 3,896 | 4,789 | 29 | 893 D | 44.7% | 55.0% | 44.9% | 55.1% |
| 40,931 | CASS | 18,978 | 7,735 | 11,148 | 95 | 3,413 D | 40.8% | 58.7% | 41.0% | 59.0% |
| 62,795 | CLARK | 25,156 | 7,701 | 17,330 | 125 | 9,629 D | 30.6% | 68.9% | 30.8% | 69.2% |
| 24,207 | CLAY | 12,026 | 5,412 | 6,528 | 86 | 1,116 D | 45.0% | 54.3% | 45.3% | 54.7% |
| 30,765 | CLINTON | 15,582 | 7,157 | 8,353 | 72 | 1,196 D | 45.9% | 53.6% | 46.1% | 53.9% |
| 8,379 | CRAWFORD | 4,380 | 1,828 | 2,514 | 38 | 686 D | 41.7% | 57.4% | 42.1% | 57.9% |
| 26,636 | DAVIESS | 12,895 | 6,319 | 6,528 | 48 | 209 D | 49.0% | 50.6% | 49.2% | 50.8% |
| 28,674 | DEARBORN | 13,198 | 5,473 | 7,699 | 26 | 2,226 D | 41.5% | 58.3% | 41.6% | 58.4% |
| 20,019 | DECATUR | 10,315 | 4,702 | 5,564 | 49 | 862 D | 45.6% | 53.9% | 45.8% | 54.2% |
| 28,271 | DE KALB | 13,889 | 6,210 | 7,559 | 120 | 1,349 D | 44.7% | 54.4% | 45.1% | 54.9% |
| 110,938 | DELAWARE | 48,678 | 20,022 | 28,469 | 187 | 8,447 D | 41.1% | 58.5% | 41.3% | 58.7% |
| 27,463 | DUBOIS | 13,939 | 3,800 | 10,114 | 25 | 6,314 D | 27.3% | 72.6% | 27.3% | 72.7% |
| 106,790 | ELKHART | 41,914 | 19,870 | 21,679 | 365 | 1,809 D | 47.4% | 51.7% | 47.8% | 52.2% |
| 24,454 | FAYETTE | 11,393 | 4,637 | 6,713 | 43 | 2,076 D | 40.7% | 58.9% | 40.9% | 59.1% |
| 51,397 | FLOYD | 23,638 | 7,834 | 15,656 | 148 | 7,822 D | 33.1% | 66.2% | 33.4% | 66.6% |
| 18,706 | FOUNTAIN | 10,278 | 4,666 | 5,574 | 38 | 908 D | 45.4% | 54.2% | 45.6% | 54.4% |
| 17,015 | FRANKLIN | 6,995 | 2,956 | 4,021 | 18 | 1,065 D | 42.3% | 57.5% | 42.4% | 57.6% |
| 16,957 | FULTON | 8,818 | 4,410 | 4,374 | 34 | 36 R | 50.0% | 49.6% | 50.2% | 49.8% |
| 29,949 | GIBSON | 16,458 | 5,865 | 10,507 | 86 | 4,642 D | 35.6% | 63.8% | 35.8% | 64.2% |
| 75,741 | GRANT | 32,494 | 14,688 | 17,574 | 232 | 2,886 D | 45.2% | 54.1% | 45.5% | 54.5% |
| 26,327 | GREENE | 14,570 | 5,919 | 8,574 | 77 | 2,655 D | 40.6% | 58.8% | 40.8% | 59.2% |
| 40,132 | HAMILTON | 19,681 | 12,060 | 7,553 | 68 | 4,507 R | 61.3% | 38.4% | 61.5% | 38.5% |
| 26,665 | HANCOCK | 12,993 | 6,370 | 6,573 | 50 | 203 D | 49.0% | 50.6% | 49.2% | 50.8% |
| 19,207 | HARRISON | 9,708 | 3,671 | 5,949 | 88 | 2,278 D | 37.8% | 61.3% | 38.2% | 61.8% |
| 40,896 | HENDRICKS | 20,405 | 11,497 | 8,857 | 51 | 2,640 R | 56.3% | 43.4% | 56.5% | 43.5% |
| 48,899 | HENRY | 22,697 | 10,184 | 12,374 | 139 | 2,190 D | 44.9% | 54.5% | 45.1% | 54.9% |
| 69,509 | HOWARD | 30,941 | 12,897 | 17,809 | 235 | 4,912 D | 41.7% | 57.6% | 42.0% | 58.0% |
| 33,814 | HUNTINGTON | 16,844 | 7,438 | 9,308 | 98 | 1,870 D | 44.2% | 55.3% | 44.4% | 55.6% |
| 30,556 | JACKSON | 14,971 | 6,285 | 8,572 | 114 | 2,287 D | 42.0% | 57.3% | 42.3% | 57.7% |
| 18,842 | JASPER | 8,516 | 4,497 | 3,995 | 24 | 502 R | 52.8% | 46.9% | 53.0% | 47.0% |
| 22,572 | JAY | 11,318 | 4,439 | 6,781 | 98 | 2,342 D | 39.2% | 59.9% | 39.6% | 60.4% |
| 24,061 | JEFFERSON | 11,586 | 4,808 | 6,694 | 84 | 1,886 D | 41.5% | 57.8% | 41.8% | 58.2% |
| 17,267 | JENNINGS | 7,811 | 3,469 | 4,307 | 35 | 838 D | 44.4% | 55.1% | 44.6% | 55.4% |
| 43,704 | JOHNSON | 20,663 | 10,472 | 10,099 | 92 | 373 R | 50.7% | 48.9% | 50.9% | 49.1% |
| 41,561 | KNOX | 20,411 | 7,612 | 12,678 | 121 | 5,066 D | 37.3% | 62.1% | 37.5% | 62.5% |
| 40,373 | KOSCIUSKO | 19,388 | 10,488 | 8,759 | 141 | 1,729 R | 54.1% | 45.2% | 54.5% | 45.5% |
| 17,380 | LAGRANGE | 5,640 | 2,785 | 2,818 | 37 | 33 D | 49.4% | 50.0% | 49.7% | 50.3% |
| 513,269 | LAKE | 209,523 | 73,722 | 134,978 | 823 | 61,256 D | 35.2% | 64.4% | 35.3% | 64.7% |
| 95,111 | LA PORTE | 38,594 | 16,270 | 22,220 | 104 | 5,950 D | 42.2% | 57.6% | 42.3% | 57.7% |
| 36,564 | LAWRENCE | 16,956 | 8,186 | 8,677 | 93 | 491 D | 48.3% | 51.2% | 48.5% | 51.5% |
| 125,819 | MADISON | 57,729 | 24,171 | 33,325 | 233 | 9,154 D | 41.9% | 57.7% | 42.0% | 58.0% |
| 697,567 | MARION | 296,381 | 143,015 | 152,418 | 948 | 9,403 D | 48.3% | 51.4% | 48.4% | 51.6% |
| 32,443 | MARSHALL | 16,415 | 7,895 | 8,397 | 123 | 502 D | 48.1% | 51.2% | 48.5% | 51.5% |
| 10,608 | MARTIN | 5,146 | 2,000 | 3,137 | 9 | 1,137 D | 38.9% | 61.0% | 38.9% | 61.1% |
| 38,000 | MIAMI | 14,060 | 6,270 | 7,667 | 123 | 1,397 D | 44.6% | 54.5% | 45.0% | 55.0% |
| 59,225 | MONROE | 22,372 | 10,309 | 11,918 | 145 | 1,609 D | 46.1% | 53.3% | 46.4% | 53.6% |
| 32,089 | MONTGOMERY | 15,930 | 7,823 | 8,042 | 65 | 219 D | 49.1% | 50.5% | 49.3% | 50.7% |
| 33,875 | MORGAN | 15,428 | 8,347 | 7,011 | 70 | 1,336 R | 54.1% | 45.4% | 54.3% | 45.7% |
| 11,502 | NEWTON | 5,340 | 2,780 | 2,547 | 13 | 233 R | 52.1% | 47.7% | 52.2% | 47.8% |
| 28,162 | NOBLE | 13,363 | 5,682 | 7,621 | 60 | 1,939 D | 42.5% | 57.0% | 42.7% | 57.3% |
| 4,165 | OHIO | 2,308 | 905 | 1,397 | 6 | 492 D | 39.2% | 60.5% | 39.3% | 60.7% |
| 16,877 | ORANGE | 8,710 | 4,187 | 4,490 | 33 | 303 D | 48.1% | 51.5% | 48.3% | 51.7% |
| 11,400 | OWEN | 6,160 | 2,788 | 3,339 | 33 | 551 D | 45.3% | 54.2% | 45.5% | 54.5% |

# INDIANA

## PRESIDENT 1964

| 1960 Census Population | County | Total Vote | Republican | Democratic | Other | Rep.-Dem. Plurality | Percentage | | | |
|---|---|---|---|---|---|---|---|---|---|---|
| | | | | | | | Total Vote | | Major Vote | |
| | | | | | | | Rep. | Dem. | Rep. | Dem. |
| 14,804 | PARKE | 7,621 | 3,570 | 4,034 | 17 | 464 D | 46.8% | 52.9% | 46.9% | 53.1% |
| 17,232 | PERRY | 9,341 | 3,090 | 6,226 | 25 | 3,136 D | 33.1% | 66.7% | 33.2% | 66.8% |
| 12,797 | PIKE | 7,272 | 2,703 | 4,519 | 50 | 1,816 D | 37.2% | 62.1% | 37.4% | 62.6% |
| 60,279 | PORTER | 27,607 | 14,480 | 12,975 | 152 | 1,505 R | 52.5% | 47.0% | 52.7% | 47.3% |
| 19,214 | POSEY | 9,770 | 3,573 | 6,164 | 33 | 2,591 D | 36.6% | 63.1% | 36.7% | 63.3% |
| 12,837 | PULASKI | 6,634 | 3,202 | 3,408 | 24 | 206 D | 48.3% | 51.4% | 48.4% | 51.6% |
| 24,927 | PUTNAM | 11,630 | 5,331 | 6,275 | 24 | 944 D | 45.8% | 54.0% | 45.9% | 54.1% |
| 28,434 | RANDOLPH | 13,506 | 6,551 | 6,804 | 151 | 253 D | 48.5% | 50.4% | 49.1% | 50.9% |
| 20,641 | RIPLEY | 10,552 | 4,587 | 5,933 | 32 | 1,346 D | 43.5% | 56.2% | 43.6% | 56.4% |
| 20,393 | RUSH | 9,025 | 4,507 | 4,450 | 68 | 57 R | 49.9% | 49.3% | 50.3% | 49.7% |
| 238,614 | ST. JOSEPH | 106,346 | 39,872 | 65,844 | 630 | 25,972 D | 37.5% | 61.9% | 37.7% | 62.3% |
| 14,643 | SCOTT | 6,203 | 1,992 | 4,205 | 6 | 2,213 D | 32.1% | 67.8% | 32.1% | 67.9% |
| 34,093 | SHELBY | 16,455 | 7,310 | 9,078 | 67 | 1,768 D | 44.4% | 55.2% | 44.6% | 55.4% |
| 16,074 | SPENCER | 8,834 | 3,980 | 4,834 | 20 | 854 D | 45.1% | 54.7% | 45.2% | 54.8% |
| 17,911 | STARKE | 8,321 | 3,466 | 4,838 | 17 | 1,372 D | 41.7% | 58.1% | 41.7% | 58.3% |
| 17,184 | STEUBEN | 8,105 | 4,075 | 3,999 | 31 | 76 R | 50.3% | 49.3% | 50.5% | 49.5% |
| 21,721 | SULLIVAN | 11,260 | 3,867 | 7,351 | 42 | 3,484 D | 34.3% | 65.3% | 34.5% | 65.5% |
| 7,092 | SWITZERLAND | 3,640 | 1,390 | 2,231 | 19 | 841 D | 38.2% | 61.3% | 38.4% | 61.6% |
| 89,122 | TIPPECANOE | 39,372 | 19,036 | 20,257 | 79 | 1,221 D | 48.3% | 51.5% | 48.4% | 51.6% |
| 15,856 | TIPTON | 8,316 | 3,863 | 4,410 | 43 | 547 D | 46.5% | 53.0% | 46.7% | 53.3% |
| 6,457 | UNION | 3,005 | 1,531 | 1,463 | 11 | 68 R | 50.9% | 48.7% | 51.1% | 48.9% |
| 165,794 | VANDERBURGH | 73,407 | 27,231 | 45,796 | 380 | 18,565 D | 37.1% | 62.4% | 37.3% | 62.7% |
| 17,683 | VERMILLION | 9,382 | 3,397 | 5,957 | 28 | 2,560 D | 36.2% | 63.5% | 36.3% | 63.7% |
| 108,458 | VIGO | 46,751 | 19,001 | 27,606 | 144 | 8,605 D | 40.6% | 59.0% | 40.8% | 59.2% |
| 32,605 | WABASH | 14,535 | 6,905 | 7,485 | 145 | 580 D | 47.5% | 51.5% | 48.0% | 52.0% |
| 8,545 | WARREN | 4,425 | 2,154 | 2,261 | 10 | 107 D | 48.7% | 51.1% | 48.8% | 51.2% |
| 23,577 | WARRICK | 11,640 | 4,376 | 7,222 | 42 | 2,846 D | 37.6% | 62.0% | 37.7% | 62.3% |
| 17,819 | WASHINGTON | 8,573 | 3,598 | 4,943 | 32 | 1,345 D | 42.0% | 57.7% | 42.1% | 57.9% |
| 74,039 | WAYNE | 30,724 | 15,342 | 15,269 | 113 | 73 R | 49.9% | 49.7% | 50.1% | 49.9% |
| 21,220 | WELLS | 10,055 | 4,018 | 5,945 | 92 | 1,927 D | 40.0% | 59.1% | 40.3% | 59.7% |
| 19,709 | WHITE | 10,455 | 5,015 | 5,407 | 33 | 392 D | 48.0% | 51.7% | 48.1% | 51.9% |
| 20,954 | WHITLEY | 10,747 | 4,896 | 5,798 | 53 | 902 D | 45.6% | 53.9% | 45.8% | 54.2% |
| 4,662,498 | TOTAL | 2,091,606 | 911,118 | 1,170,848 | 9,640 | 259,730 D | 43.6% | 56.0% | 43.8% | 56.2% |

# INDIANA

## PRESIDENT 1960

| 1960 Census Population | County | Total Vote | Republican | Democratic | Other | Rep.-Dem. Plurality | Percentage Total Vote Rep. | Dem. | Major Vote Rep. | Dem. |
|---|---|---|---|---|---|---|---|---|---|---|
| 24,643 | ADAMS | 11,409 | 6,972 | 4,338 | 99 | 2,634 R | 61.1% | 38.0% | 61.6% | 38.4% |
| 232,196 | ALLEN | 99,618 | 60,103 | 39,235 | 280 | 20,868 R | 60.3% | 39.4% | 60.5% | 39.5% |
| 48,198 | BARTHOLOMEW | 23,026 | 13,606 | 9,290 | 130 | 4,316 R | 59.1% | 40.3% | 59.4% | 40.6% |
| 11,912 | BENTON | 6,032 | 3,626 | 2,399 | 7 | 1,227 R | 60.1% | 39.8% | 60.2% | 39.8% |
| 14,792 | BLACKFORD | 7,009 | 3,738 | 3,228 | 43 | 510 R | 53.3% | 46.1% | 53.7% | 46.3% |
| 27,543 | BOONE | 14,416 | 8,979 | 5,377 | 60 | 3,602 R | 62.3% | 37.3% | 62.5% | 37.5% |
| 7,024 | BROWN | 3,244 | 1,679 | 1,533 | 32 | 146 R | 51.8% | 47.3% | 52.3% | 47.7% |
| 16,934 | CARROLL | 8,744 | 5,411 | 3,299 | 34 | 2,112 R | 61.9% | 37.7% | 62.1% | 37.9% |
| 40,931 | CASS | 19,577 | 11,392 | 8,091 | 94 | 3,301 R | 58.2% | 41.3% | 58.5% | 41.5% |
| 62,795 | CLARK | 27,304 | 12,803 | 14,431 | 70 | 1,628 D | 46.9% | 52.9% | 47.0% | 53.0% |
| 24,207 | CLAY | 12,834 | 7,434 | 5,342 | 58 | 2,092 R | 57.9% | 41.6% | 58.2% | 41.8% |
| 30,765 | CLINTON | 16,217 | 9,620 | 6,533 | 64 | 3,087 R | 59.3% | 40.3% | 59.6% | 40.4% |
| 8,379 | CRAWFORD | 5,255 | 2,915 | 2,305 | 35 | 610 R | 55.5% | 43.9% | 55.8% | 44.2% |
| 26,636 | DAVIESS | 13,763 | 8,285 | 5,433 | 45 | 2,852 R | 60.2% | 39.5% | 60.4% | 39.6% |
| 28,674 | DEARBORN | 13,854 | 7,619 | 6,216 | 19 | 1,403 R | 55.0% | 44.9% | 55.1% | 44.9% |
| 20,019 | DECATUR | 10,370 | 6,240 | 4,080 | 50 | 2,160 R | 60.2% | 39.3% | 60.5% | 39.5% |
| 28,271 | DE KALB | 14,295 | 8,957 | 5,277 | 61 | 3,680 R | 62.7% | 36.9% | 62.9% | 37.1% |
| 110,938 | DELAWARE | 49,610 | 26,167 | 23,266 | 177 | 2,901 R | 52.7% | 46.9% | 52.9% | 47.1% |
| 27,463 | DUBOIS | 13,353 | 5,117 | 8,214 | 22 | 3,097 D | 38.3% | 61.5% | 38.4% | 61.6% |
| 106,790 | ELKHART | 44,693 | 28,056 | 16,264 | 373 | 11,792 R | 62.8% | 36.4% | 63.3% | 36.7% |
| 24,454 | FAYETTE | 12,023 | 6,729 | 5,246 | 48 | 1,483 R | 56.0% | 43.6% | 56.2% | 43.8% |
| 51,397 | FLOYD | 24,037 | 11,629 | 12,346 | 62 | 717 D | 48.4% | 51.4% | 48.5% | 51.5% |
| 18,706 | FOUNTAIN | 10,429 | 6,123 | 4,277 | 29 | 1,846 R | 58.7% | 41.0% | 58.9% | 41.1% |
| 17,015 | FRANKLIN | 7,645 | 4,108 | 3,523 | 14 | 585 R | 53.7% | 46.1% | 53.8% | 46.2% |
| 16,957 | FULTON | 9,133 | 6,038 | 3,047 | 48 | 2,991 R | 66.1% | 33.4% | 66.5% | 33.5% |
| 29,949 | GIBSON | 16,399 | 8,838 | 7,479 | 82 | 1,359 R | 53.9% | 45.6% | 54.2% | 45.8% |
| 75,741 | GRANT | 32,841 | 19,021 | 13,642 | 178 | 5,379 R | 57.9% | 41.5% | 58.2% | 41.8% |
| 26,327 | GREENE | 15,239 | 8,810 | 6,325 | 104 | 2,485 R | 57.8% | 41.5% | 58.2% | 41.8% |
| 40,132 | HAMILTON | 18,984 | 13,409 | 5,511 | 64 | 7,898 R | 70.6% | 29.0% | 70.9% | 29.1% |
| 26,665 | HANCOCK | 12,528 | 7,543 | 4,930 | 55 | 2,613 R | 60.2% | 39.4% | 60.5% | 39.5% |
| 19,207 | HARRISON | 9,989 | 5,374 | 4,566 | 49 | 808 R | 53.8% | 45.7% | 54.1% | 45.9% |
| 40,896 | HENDRICKS | 19,066 | 12,490 | 6,481 | 95 | 6,009 R | 65.5% | 34.0% | 65.8% | 34.2% |
| 48,899 | HENRY | 23,530 | 13,752 | 9,629 | 149 | 4,123 R | 58.4% | 40.9% | 58.8% | 41.2% |
| 69,509 | HOWARD | 31,502 | 17,938 | 13,415 | 149 | 4,523 R | 56.9% | 42.6% | 57.2% | 42.8% |
| 33,814 | HUNTINGTON | 17,930 | 10,658 | 7,163 | 109 | 3,495 R | 59.4% | 39.9% | 59.8% | 40.2% |
| 30,556 | JACKSON | 14,861 | 8,213 | 6,582 | 66 | 1,631 R | 55.3% | 44.3% | 55.5% | 44.5% |
| 18,842 | JASPER | 8,339 | 5,364 | 2,959 | 16 | 2,405 R | 64.3% | 35.5% | 64.4% | 35.6% |
| 22,572 | JAY | 11,492 | 6,519 | 4,899 | 74 | 1,620 R | 56.7% | 42.6% | 57.1% | 42.9% |
| 24,061 | JEFFERSON | 11,492 | 6,333 | 5,119 | 40 | 1,214 R | 55.1% | 44.5% | 55.3% | 44.7% |
| 17,267 | JENNINGS | 7,908 | 4,478 | 3,403 | 27 | 1,075 R | 56.6% | 43.0% | 56.8% | 43.2% |
| 43,704 | JOHNSON | 19,919 | 12,426 | 7,400 | 93 | 5,026 R | 62.4% | 37.2% | 62.7% | 37.3% |
| 41,561 | KNOX | 21,516 | 11,490 | 9,918 | 108 | 1,572 R | 53.4% | 46.1% | 53.7% | 46.3% |
| 40,373 | KOSCIUSKO | 19,591 | 13,539 | 5,839 | 213 | 7,700 R | 69.1% | 29.8% | 69.9% | 30.1% |
| 17,380 | LAGRANGE | 6,422 | 4,433 | 1,965 | 24 | 2,468 R | 69.0% | 30.6% | 69.3% | 30.7% |
| 513,269 | LAKE | 211,358 | 78,278 | 132,554 | 526 | 54,276 D | 37.0% | 62.7% | 37.1% | 62.9% |
| 95,111 | LA PORTE | 43,140 | 22,738 | 20,317 | 85 | 2,421 R | 52.7% | 47.1% | 52.8% | 47.2% |
| 36,564 | LAWRENCE | 18,182 | 11,119 | 6,977 | 86 | 4,142 R | 61.2% | 38.4% | 61.4% | 38.6% |
| 125,819 | MADISON | 59,445 | 31,098 | 28,154 | 193 | 2,944 R | 52.3% | 47.4% | 52.5% | 47.5% |
| 697,567 | MARION | 288,206 | 166,202 | 121,336 | 668 | 44,866 R | 57.7% | 42.1% | 57.8% | 42.2% |
| 32,443 | MARSHALL | 16,744 | 10,460 | 6,210 | 74 | 4,250 R | 62.5% | 37.1% | 62.7% | 37.3% |
| 10,608 | MARTIN | 5,346 | 2,756 | 2,585 | 5 | 171 R | 51.6% | 48.4% | 51.6% | 48.4% |
| 38,000 | MIAMI | 15,131 | 8,844 | 6,191 | 96 | 2,653 R | 58.4% | 40.9% | 58.8% | 41.2% |
| 59,225 | MONROE | 22,184 | 14,513 | 7,535 | 136 | 6,978 R | 65.4% | 34.0% | 65.8% | 34.2% |
| 32,089 | MONTGOMERY | 16,511 | 10,957 | 5,477 | 77 | 5,480 R | 66.4% | 33.2% | 66.7% | 33.3% |
| 33,875 | MORGAN | 14,860 | 9,416 | 5,375 | 69 | 4,041 R | 63.4% | 36.2% | 63.7% | 36.3% |
| 11,502 | NEWTON | 5,401 | 3,517 | 1,870 | 14 | 1,647 R | 65.1% | 34.6% | 65.3% | 34.7% |
| 28,162 | NOBLE | 13,387 | 8,069 | 5,264 | 54 | 2,805 R | 60.3% | 39.3% | 60.5% | 39.5% |
| 4,165 | OHIO | 2,336 | 1,314 | 1,015 | 7 | 299 R | 56.3% | 43.5% | 56.4% | 43.6% |
| 16,877 | ORANGE | 9,442 | 5,589 | 3,818 | 35 | 1,771 R | 59.2% | 40.4% | 59.4% | 40.6% |
| 11,400 | OWEN | 6,128 | 3,700 | 2,379 | 49 | 1,321 R | 60.4% | 38.8% | 60.9% | 39.1% |

# INDIANA

## PRESIDENT 1960

| 1960 Census Population | County | Total Vote | Republican | Democratic | Other | Rep.-Dem. Plurality | Percentage Total Vote Rep. | Dem. | Major Vote Rep. | Dem. |
|---|---|---|---|---|---|---|---|---|---|---|
| 14,804 | PARKE | 8,046 | 4,662 | 3,361 | 23 | 1,301 R | 57.9% | 41.8% | 58.1% | 41.9% |
| 17,232 | PERRY | 9,308 | 4,372 | 4,920 | 16 | 548 D | 47.0% | 52.9% | 47.1% | 52.9% |
| 12,797 | PIKE | 7,716 | 4,606 | 3,046 | 64 | 1,560 R | 59.7% | 39.5% | 60.2% | 39.8% |
| 60,279 | PORTER | 26,474 | 15,666 | 10,733 | 75 | 4,933 R | 59.2% | 40.5% | 59.3% | 40.7% |
| 19,214 | POSEY | 9,857 | 5,369 | 4,457 | 31 | 912 R | 54.5% | 45.2% | 54.6% | 45.4% |
| 12,837 | PULASKI | 6,771 | 3,905 | 2,746 | 120 | 1,159 R | 57.7% | 40.6% | 58.7% | 41.3% |
| 24,927 | PUTNAM | 11,423 | 6,583 | 4,798 | 42 | 1,785 R | 57.6% | 42.0% | 57.8% | 42.2% |
| 28,434 | RANDOLPH | 14,677 | 9,528 | 5,035 | 114 | 4,493 R | 64.9% | 34.3% | 65.4% | 34.6% |
| 20,641 | RIPLEY | 10,818 | 6,053 | 4,730 | 35 | 1,323 R | 56.0% | 43.7% | 56.1% | 43.9% |
| 20,393 | RUSH | 9,782 | 6,215 | 3,516 | 51 | 2,699 R | 63.5% | 35.9% | 63.9% | 36.1% |
| 238,614 | ST. JOSEPH | 117,499 | 53,621 | 63,553 | 325 | 9,932 D | 45.6% | 54.1% | 45.8% | 54.2% |
| 14,643 | SCOTT | 6,301 | 3,213 | 3,064 | 24 | 149 R | 51.0% | 48.6% | 51.2% | 48.8% |
| 34,093 | SHELBY | 16,602 | 9,421 | 7,111 | 70 | 2,310 R | 56.7% | 42.8% | 57.0% | 43.0% |
| 16,074 | SPENCER | 9,373 | 5,050 | 4,303 | 20 | 747 R | 53.9% | 45.9% | 54.0% | 46.0% |
| 17,911 | STARKE | 8,619 | 4,592 | 3,995 | 32 | 597 R | 53.3% | 46.4% | 53.5% | 46.5% |
| 17,184 | STEUBEN | 8,079 | 5,464 | 2,588 | 27 | 2,876 R | 67.6% | 32.0% | 67.9% | 32.1% |
| 21,721 | SULLIVAN | 12,060 | 6,012 | 5,975 | 73 | 37 R | 49.9% | 49.5% | 50.2% | 49.8% |
| 7,092 | SWITZERLAND | 3,905 | 1,929 | 1,955 | 21 | 26 D | 49.4% | 50.1% | 49.7% | 50.3% |
| 89,122 | TIPPECANOE | 38,668 | 24,572 | 14,041 | 55 | 10,531 R | 63.5% | 36.3% | 63.6% | 36.4% |
| 15,856 | TIPTON | 8,223 | 4,924 | 3,299 |  | 1,625 R | 59.9% | 40.1% | 59.9% | 40.1% |
| 6,457 | UNION | 3,275 | 2,087 | 1,180 | 8 | 907 R | 63.7% | 36.0% | 63.9% | 36.1% |
| 165,794 | VANDERBURGH | 77,635 | 41,068 | 36,330 | 237 | 4,738 R | 52.9% | 46.8% | 53.1% | 46.9% |
| 17,683 | VERMILLION | 10,227 | 4,798 | 5,391 | 38 | 593 D | 46.9% | 52.7% | 47.1% | 52.9% |
| 108,458 | VIGO | 50,178 | 24,940 | 25,105 | 133 | 165 D | 49.7% | 50.0% | 49.8% | 50.2% |
| 32,605 | WABASH | 15,297 | 10,420 | 4,788 | 89 | 5,632 R | 68.1% | 31.3% | 68.5% | 31.5% |
| 8,545 | WARREN | 4,464 | 2,870 | 1,574 | 20 | 1,296 R | 64.3% | 35.3% | 64.6% | 35.4% |
| 23,577 | WARRICK | 11,554 | 6,482 | 5,042 | 30 | 1,440 R | 56.1% | 43.6% | 56.2% | 43.8% |
| 17,819 | WASHINGTON | 8,913 | 5,057 | 3,821 | 35 | 1,236 R | 56.7% | 42.9% | 57.0% | 43.0% |
| 74,039 | WAYNE | 32,580 | 19,764 | 12,721 | 95 | 7,043 R | 60.7% | 39.0% | 60.8% | 39.2% |
| 21,220 | WELLS | 10,242 | 6,034 | 4,128 | 80 | 1,906 R | 58.9% | 40.3% | 59.4% | 40.6% |
| 19,709 | WHITE | 10,612 | 6,678 | 3,914 | 20 | 2,764 R | 62.9% | 36.9% | 63.0% | 37.0% |
| 20,954 | WHITLEY | 10,943 | 6,621 | 4,266 | 56 | 2,355 R | 60.5% | 39.0% | 60.8% | 39.2% |
| 4,662,498 | TOTAL | 2,135,360 | 1,175,120 | 952,358 | 7,882 | 222,762 R | 55.0% | 44.6% | 55.2% | 44.8% |

326

# INDIANA

## ELECTION NOTES

**2004**    Other vote was 18,058 Libertarian (Michael Badnarik); 1,328 write-in (Ralph Nader); 102 write-in (David Cobb); 37 write-in (John Joseph Kennedy); 22 write-in (Walter F. Brown); 6 write-in (Lawson Mitchell Bone).

**2000**    Other vote was 16,959 Independent (Buchanan); 15,530 Libertarian (Browne); 167 Natural Law write-in (Hagelin); 200 Constitution write-in (Phillips); 43 Independent write-in (McReynolds); 24 Independent write-in (Schriner); 15 Independent write-in (Judd); 8 Republican write-in (Birchler); 5 Veterans Industrial Party write-in (Easton); 4 Independent write-in (Strickland). In Indiana, write-in candidates can be designated by party or as Independent. Nader was a Green Party write-in.

**1996**    Other vote was 15,632 Libertarian (Browne); 1,121 write-in (Nader); 453 write-in (Phillips); 120 write-in (Hagelin); 100 scattered write-in.

**1992**    Other vote was 7,936 Marrou (Libertarian); 2,583 Fulani (New Alliance); 1,467 Gritz (write-in); 126 Hagelin (write-in); 16 Brisben (write-in); 14 LaRouche (write-in).

**1988**    Other vote was Fulani (New Alliance).

**1984**    Other vote was 7,617 Dennis (American); 6,741 Bergland (Libertarian).

**1980**    Other vote was 111,639 Anderson (Independent); 19,627 Clark (Libertarian); 4,852 Commoner (Citizens); 4,750 Greaves (American); 702 Hall (Communist); 610 DeBerry (Socialist Workers).

**1976**    Other vote was 14,048 Anderson (American); 5,695 Camejo (Socialist Workers); 1,947 LaRouche (U.S. Labor). Early unamended canvass gave the total state-wide Republican vote as 1,185,958.

**1972**    Other vote was 5,575 Reed (Socialist Workers); 4,544 Spock (Peace and Freedom); 1,688 Fisher (Socialist Labor).

**1968**    Wallace on the ballot as George C. Wallace party. Other vote was 4,616 Munn (Prohibition); 1,293 Halstead (Socialist Workers); 36 Gregory (write-in).

**1964**    Other vote was 8,266 Munn (Prohibition); 1,374 Hass (Socialist Labor).

**1960**    Other vote was 6,746 Decker (Prohibition); 1,136 Hass (Socialist Labor).

# IOWA

## POPULAR VOTE FOR PRESIDENT 1920 TO 2004

| Year | Total Vote | Republican Vote | Republican Candidate | Democratic Vote | Democratic Candidate | Other Vote | Plurality | Percentage Total Vote Rep. | Dem. | Major Vote Rep. | Dem. |
|---|---|---|---|---|---|---|---|---|---|---|---|
| 2004 | 1,506,908 | 751,957 | Bush, George W. | 741,898 | Kerry, John | 13,053 | 10,059 R | 49.9% | 49.2% | 50.3% | 49.7% |
| 2000** | 1,315,563 | 634,373 | Bush, George W. | 638,517 | Gore, Al | 42,673 | 4,144 D | 48.2% | 48.5% | 49.8% | 50.2% |
| 1996 ** | 1,234,075 | 492,644 | Dole, Bob | 620,258 | Clinton, Bill | 121,173 | 127,614 D | 39.9% | 50.3% | 44.3% | 55.7% |
| 1992 ** | 1,354,607 | 504,891 | Bush, George | 586,353 | Clinton, Bill | 263,363 | 81,462 D | 37.3% | 43.3% | 46.3% | 53.7% |
| 1988 | 1,225,614 | 545,355 | Bush, George | 670,557 | Dukakis, Michael S. | 9,702 | 125,202 D | 44.5% | 54.7% | 44.9% | 55.1% |
| 1984 | 1,319,805 | 703,088 | Reagan, Ronald | 605,620 | Mondale, Walter F. | 11,097 | 97,468 R | 53.3% | 45.9% | 53.7% | 46.3% |
| 1980** | 1,317,661 | 676,026 | Reagan, Ronald | 508,672 | Carter, Jimmy | 132,963 | 167,354 R | 51.3% | 38.6% | 57.1% | 42.9% |
| 1976 | 1,279,306 | 632,863 | Ford, Gerald R. | 619,931 | Carter, Jimmy | 26,512 | 12,932 R | 49.5% | 48.5% | 50.5% | 49.5% |
| 1972 | 1,225,944 | 706,207 | Nixon, Richard M. | 496,206 | McGovern, George S. | 23,531 | 210,001 R | 57.6% | 40.5% | 58.7% | 41.3% |
| 1968 | 1,167,931 | 619,106 | Nixon, Richard M. | 476,699 | Humphrey, Hubert H. | 72,126 | 142,407 R | 53.0% | 40.8% | 56.5% | 43.5% |
| 1964 | 1,184,539 | 449,148 | Goldwater, Barry M. | 733,030 | Johnson, Lyndon B. | 2,361 | 283,882 D | 37.9% | 61.9% | 38.0% | 62.0% |
| 1960 | 1,273,810 | 722,381 | Nixon, Richard M. | 550,565 | Kennedy, John F. | 864 | 171,816 R | 56.7% | 43.2% | 56.7% | 43.3% |
| 1956 | 1,234,564 | 729,187 | Eisenhower, Dwight D. | 501,858 | Stevenson, Adlai E. | 3,519 | 227,329 R | 59.1% | 40.7% | 59.2% | 40.8% |
| 1952 | 1,268,773 | 808,906 | Eisenhower, Dwight D. | 451,513 | Stevenson, Adlai E. | 8,354 | 357,393 R | 63.8% | 35.6% | 64.2% | 35.8% |
| 1948 | 1,038,264 | 494,018 | Dewey, Thomas E. | 522,380 | Truman, Harry S. | 21,866 | 28,362 D | 47.6% | 50.3% | 48.6% | 51.4% |
| 1944 | 1,052,599 | 547,267 | Dewey, Thomas E. | 499,876 | Roosevelt, Franklin D. | 5,456 | 47,391 R | 52.0% | 47.5% | 52.3% | 47.7% |
| 1940 | 1,215,432 | 632,370 | Willkie, Wendell | 578,802 | Roosevelt, Franklin D. | 4,260 | 53,568 R | 52.0% | 47.6% | 52.2% | 47.8% |
| 1936 | 1,142,737 | 487,977 | Landon, Alfred M. | 621,756 | Roosevelt, Franklin D. | 33,004 | 133,779 D | 42.7% | 54.4% | 44.0% | 56.0% |
| 1932 | 1,036,687 | 414,433 | Hoover, Herbert C. | 598,019 | Roosevelt, Franklin D. | 24,235 | 183,586 D | 40.0% | 57.7% | 40.9% | 59.1% |
| 1928 | 1,009,189 | 623,570 | Hoover, Herbert C. | 379,011 | Smith, Alfred E. | 6,608 | 244,559 R | 61.8% | 37.6% | 62.2% | 37.8% |
| 1924 ** | 976,770 | 537,458 | Coolidge, Calvin | 160,382 | Davis, John W. | 278,930 | 263,010 R | 55.0% | 16.4% | 77.0% | 23.0% |
| 1920 | 894,959 | 634,674 | Harding, Warren G. | 227,804 | Cox, James M. | 32,481 | 406,870 R | 70.9% | 25.5% | 73.6% | 26.4% |

In 2000 the other vote column includes 29,374 votes cast for Green (Nader). In 1996 the other vote column includes 105,159 votes cast for Perot. In 1992 the other vote column includes 253,468 votes cast for Perot. In 1980 the other column includes 115,633 votes for Independent (Anderson). In 1924 the other vote was 274,448 Progressive; 4,037 Communist; and 445 scattered.

## ELECTORAL COLLEGE VOTE 1920 TO 2004

| Year | Total | Republican | Democratic | Other |
|---|---|---|---|---|
| 2004 | 7 | 7 | | |
| 2000 | 7 | | 7 | |
| 1996 | 7 | | 7 | |
| 1992 | 7 | | 7 | |
| 1988 | 8 | | 8 | |
| 1984 | 8 | 8 | | |
| 1980 | 8 | 8 | | |
| 1976 | 8 | 8 | | |
| 1972 | 8 | 8 | | |
| 1968 | 9 | 9 | | |
| 1964 | 9 | | 9 | |
| 1960 | 10 | 10 | | |
| 1956 | 10 | 10 | | |
| 1952 | 10 | 10 | | |
| 1948 | 10 | | 10 | |
| 1944 | 10 | 10 | | |
| 1940 | 11 | 11 | | |
| 1936 | 11 | | 11 | |
| 1932 | 11 | | 11 | |
| 1928 | 13 | 13 | | |
| 1924 | 13 | 13 | | |
| 1920 | 13 | 13 | | |

# IOWA

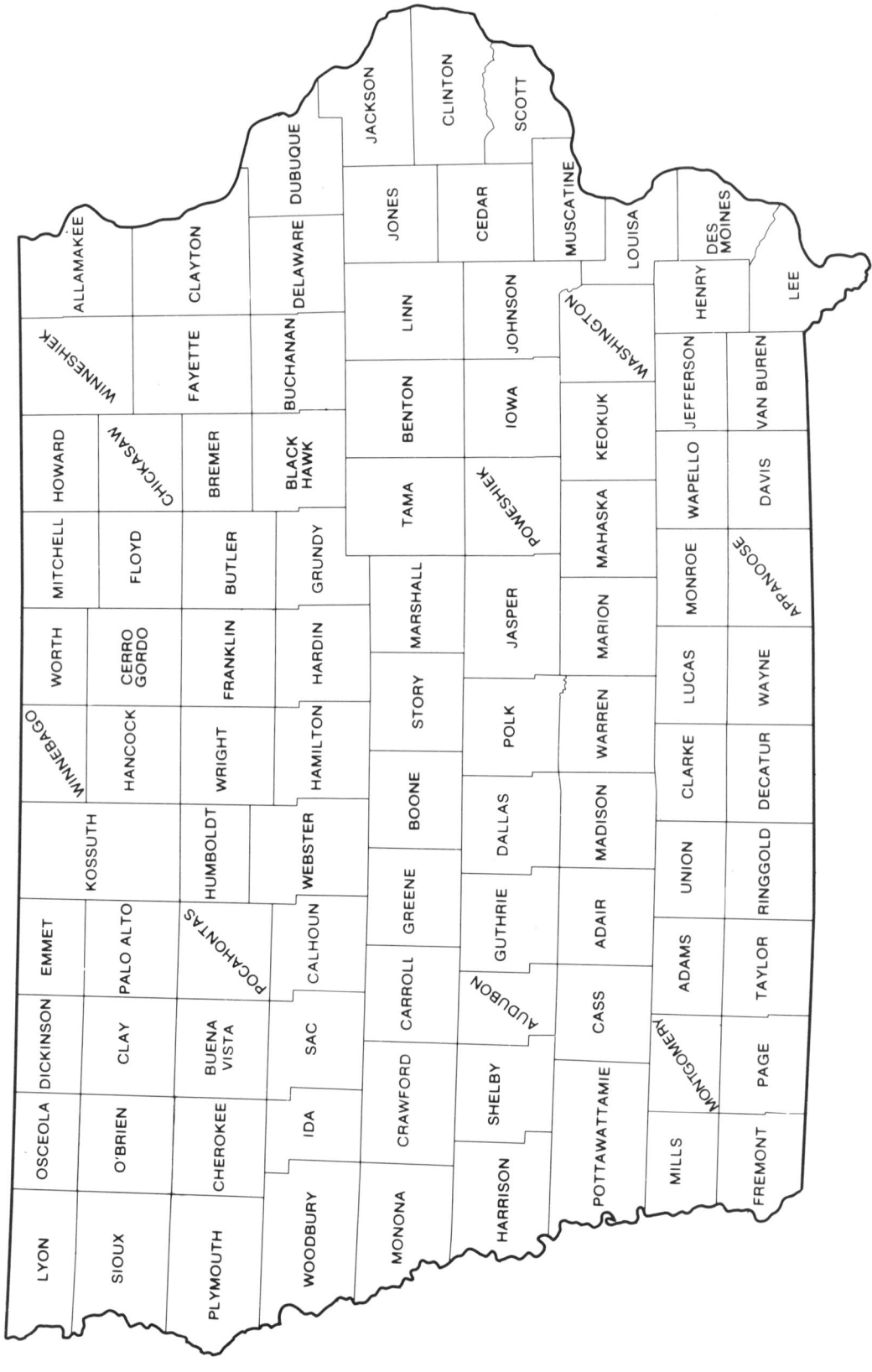

# IOWA

## PRESIDENT 2004

| 2000 Census Population | County | Total Vote | Republican | Democratic | Other | Rep.-Dem. Plurality | Percentage | | | |
|---|---|---|---|---|---|---|---|---|---|---|
| | | | | | | | Total Vote | | Major Vote | |
| | | | | | | | Rep. | Dem. | Rep. | Dem. |
| 8,243 | ADAIR | 4,278 | 2,402 | 1,844 | 32 | 558 R | 56.1% | 43.1% | 56.6% | 43.4% |
| 4,482 | ADAMS | 2,325 | 1,317 | 977 | 31 | 340 R | 56.6% | 42.0% | 57.4% | 42.6% |
| 14,675 | ALLAMAKEE | 7,062 | 3,530 | 3,449 | 83 | 81 R | 50.0% | 48.8% | 50.6% | 49.4% |
| 13,721 | APPANOOSE | 6,450 | 3,340 | 3,063 | 47 | 277 R | 51.8% | 47.5% | 52.2% | 47.8% |
| 6,830 | AUDUBON | 3,592 | 1,958 | 1,608 | 26 | 350 R | 54.5% | 44.8% | 54.9% | 45.1% |
| 25,308 | BENTON | 13,501 | 6,658 | 6,747 | 96 | 89 D | 49.3% | 50.0% | 49.7% | 50.3% |
| 128,012 | BLACK HAWK | 63,907 | 28,046 | 35,392 | 469 | 7,346 D | 43.9% | 55.4% | 44.2% | 55.8% |
| 26,224 | BOONE | 14,009 | 6,870 | 7,027 | 112 | 157 D | 49.0% | 50.2% | 49.4% | 50.6% |
| 23,325 | BREMER | 12,779 | 6,665 | 6,025 | 89 | 640 R | 52.2% | 47.1% | 52.5% | 47.5% |
| 21,093 | BUCHANAN | 10,475 | 4,797 | 5,608 | 70 | 811 D | 45.8% | 53.5% | 46.1% | 53.9% |
| 20,411 | BUENA VISTA | 8,490 | 4,887 | 3,520 | 83 | 1,367 R | 57.6% | 41.5% | 58.1% | 41.9% |
| 15,305 | BUTLER | 7,475 | 4,417 | 3,001 | 57 | 1,416 R | 59.1% | 40.1% | 59.5% | 40.5% |
| 11,115 | CALHOUN | 5,542 | 3,255 | 2,243 | 44 | 1,012 R | 58.7% | 40.5% | 59.2% | 40.8% |
| 21,421 | CARROLL | 10,524 | 5,762 | 4,689 | 73 | 1,073 R | 54.8% | 44.6% | 55.1% | 44.9% |
| 14,684 | CASS | 7,543 | 4,796 | 2,679 | 68 | 2,117 R | 63.6% | 35.5% | 64.2% | 35.8% |
| 18,187 | CEDAR | 9,694 | 4,869 | 4,747 | 78 | 122 R | 50.2% | 49.0% | 50.6% | 49.4% |
| 46,447 | CERRO GORDO | 24,516 | 10,960 | 13,372 | 184 | 2,412 D | 44.7% | 54.5% | 45.0% | 55.0% |
| 13,035 | CHEROKEE | 6,796 | 3,758 | 2,988 | 50 | 770 R | 55.3% | 44.0% | 55.7% | 44.3% |
| 13,095 | CHICKASAW | 6,806 | 3,040 | 3,708 | 58 | 668 D | 44.7% | 54.5% | 45.1% | 54.9% |
| 9,133 | CLARKE | 4,566 | 2,200 | 2,323 | 43 | 123 D | 48.2% | 50.9% | 48.6% | 51.4% |
| 17,372 | CLAY | 8,588 | 4,898 | 3,547 | 143 | 1,351 R | 57.0% | 41.3% | 58.0% | 42.0% |
| 18,678 | CLAYTON | 9,168 | 4,312 | 4,736 | 120 | 424 D | 47.0% | 51.7% | 47.7% | 52.3% |
| 50,149 | CLINTON | 24,684 | 10,666 | 13,813 | 205 | 3,147 D | 43.2% | 56.0% | 43.6% | 56.4% |
| 16,942 | CRAWFORD | 7,242 | 3,955 | 3,220 | 67 | 735 R | 54.6% | 44.5% | 55.1% | 44.9% |
| 40,750 | DALLAS | 26,293 | 15,183 | 10,917 | 193 | 4,266 R | 57.7% | 41.5% | 58.2% | 41.8% |
| 8,541 | DAVIS | 3,918 | 2,148 | 1,731 | 39 | 417 R | 54.8% | 44.2% | 55.4% | 44.6% |
| 8,689 | DECATUR | 4,011 | 2,088 | 1,859 | 64 | 229 R | 52.1% | 46.3% | 52.9% | 47.1% |
| 18,404 | DELAWARE | 9,200 | 4,908 | 4,227 | 65 | 681 R | 53.3% | 45.9% | 53.7% | 46.3% |
| 42,351 | DES MOINES | 20,874 | 8,221 | 12,456 | 197 | 4,235 D | 39.4% | 59.7% | 39.8% | 60.2% |
| 16,424 | DICKINSON | 9,553 | 5,337 | 4,140 | 76 | 1,197 R | 55.9% | 43.3% | 56.3% | 43.7% |
| 89,143 | DUBUQUE | 47,043 | 20,100 | 26,561 | 382 | 6,461 D | 42.7% | 56.5% | 43.1% | 56.9% |
| 11,027 | EMMET | 5,156 | 2,697 | 2,405 | 54 | 292 R | 52.3% | 46.6% | 52.9% | 47.1% |
| 22,008 | FAYETTE | 10,392 | 5,128 | 5,185 | 79 | 57 D | 49.3% | 49.9% | 49.7% | 50.3% |
| 16,900 | FLOYD | 8,167 | 3,745 | 4,349 | 73 | 604 D | 45.9% | 53.3% | 46.3% | 53.7% |
| 10,704 | FRANKLIN | 5,521 | 3,128 | 2,340 | 53 | 788 R | 56.7% | 42.4% | 57.2% | 42.8% |
| 8,010 | FREMONT | 3,911 | 2,362 | 1,510 | 39 | 852 R | 60.4% | 38.6% | 61.0% | 39.0% |
| 10,366 | GREENE | 5,113 | 2,618 | 2,459 | 36 | 159 R | 51.2% | 48.1% | 51.6% | 48.4% |
| 12,369 | GRUNDY | 6,849 | 4,429 | 2,386 | 34 | 2,043 R | 64.7% | 34.8% | 65.0% | 35.0% |
| 11,353 | GUTHRIE | 5,994 | 3,325 | 2,614 | 55 | 711 R | 55.5% | 43.6% | 56.0% | 44.0% |
| 16,438 | HAMILTON | 8,335 | 4,367 | 3,895 | 73 | 472 R | 52.4% | 46.7% | 52.9% | 47.1% |
| 12,100 | HANCOCK | 5,905 | 3,368 | 2,484 | 53 | 884 R | 57.0% | 42.1% | 57.6% | 42.4% |
| 18,812 | HARDIN | 8,949 | 4,875 | 4,015 | 59 | 860 R | 54.5% | 44.9% | 54.8% | 45.2% |
| 15,666 | HARRISON | 7,680 | 4,680 | 2,906 | 94 | 1,774 R | 60.9% | 37.8% | 61.7% | 38.3% |
| 20,336 | HENRY | 9,457 | 5,220 | 4,127 | 110 | 1,093 R | 55.2% | 43.6% | 55.8% | 44.2% |
| 9,932 | HOWARD | 4,697 | 2,028 | 2,614 | 55 | 586 D | 43.2% | 55.7% | 43.7% | 56.3% |
| 10,381 | HUMBOLDT | 5,350 | 3,162 | 2,146 | 42 | 1,016 R | 59.1% | 40.1% | 59.6% | 40.4% |
| 7,837 | IDA | 3,774 | 2,342 | 1,415 | 17 | 927 R | 62.1% | 37.5% | 62.3% | 37.7% |
| 15,671 | IOWA | 8,454 | 4,544 | 3,841 | 69 | 703 R | 53.7% | 45.4% | 54.2% | 45.8% |
| 20,296 | JACKSON | 10,011 | 4,242 | 5,656 | 113 | 1,414 D | 42.4% | 56.5% | 42.9% | 57.1% |
| 37,213 | JASPER | 20,062 | 9,462 | 10,430 | 170 | 968 D | 47.2% | 52.0% | 47.6% | 52.4% |
| 16,181 | JEFFERSON | 8,281 | 3,648 | 4,490 | 143 | 842 D | 44.1% | 54.2% | 44.8% | 55.2% |
| 111,006 | JOHNSON | 65,373 | 22,715 | 41,847 | 811 | 19,132 D | 34.7% | 64.0% | 35.2% | 64.8% |
| 20,221 | JONES | 9,978 | 4,834 | 5,054 | 90 | 220 D | 48.4% | 50.7% | 48.9% | 51.1% |
| 11,400 | KEOKUK | 5,480 | 3,119 | 2,294 | 67 | 825 R | 56.9% | 41.9% | 57.6% | 42.4% |
| 17,163 | KOSSUTH | 9,258 | 5,042 | 4,132 | 84 | 910 R | 54.5% | 44.6% | 55.0% | 45.0% |
| 38,052 | LEE | 17,858 | 7,472 | 10,152 | 234 | 2,680 D | 41.8% | 56.8% | 42.4% | 57.6% |
| 191,701 | LINN | 110,740 | 49,442 | 60,442 | 856 | 11,000 D | 44.6% | 54.6% | 45.0% | 55.0% |
| 12,183 | LOUISA | 4,916 | 2,572 | 2,297 | 47 | 275 R | 52.3% | 46.7% | 52.8% | 47.2% |
| 9,422 | LUCAS | 4,571 | 2,543 | 1,987 | 41 | 556 R | 55.6% | 43.5% | 56.1% | 43.9% |
| 11,763 | LYON | 6,101 | 4,751 | 1,303 | 47 | 3,448 R | 77.9% | 21.4% | 78.5% | 21.5% |

# IOWA

## PRESIDENT 2004

| 2000 Census Population | County | Total Vote | Republican | Democratic | Other | Rep.-Dem. Plurality | Percentage Total Vote Rep. | Dem. | Major Vote Rep. | Dem. |
|---|---|---|---|---|---|---|---|---|---|---|
| 14,019 | MADISON | 8,004 | 4,538 | 3,380 | 86 | 1,158 R | 56.7% | 42.2% | 57.3% | 42.7% |
| 22,335 | MAHASKA | 10,728 | 6,858 | 3,790 | 80 | 3,068 R | 63.9% | 35.3% | 64.4% | 35.6% |
| 32,052 | MARION | 16,696 | 9,990 | 6,574 | 132 | 3,416 R | 59.8% | 39.4% | 60.3% | 39.7% |
| 39,311 | MARSHALL | 19,164 | 9,557 | 9,443 | 164 | 114 R | 49.9% | 49.3% | 50.3% | 49.7% |
| 14,547 | MILLS | 6,940 | 4,556 | 2,308 | 76 | 2,248 R | 65.6% | 33.3% | 66.4% | 33.6% |
| 10,874 | MITCHELL | 5,480 | 2,646 | 2,785 | 49 | 139 D | 48.3% | 50.8% | 48.7% | 51.3% |
| 10,020 | MONONA | 5,018 | 2,575 | 2,397 | 46 | 178 R | 51.3% | 47.8% | 51.8% | 48.2% |
| 8,016 | MONROE | 3,963 | 2,067 | 1,855 | 41 | 212 R | 52.2% | 46.8% | 52.7% | 47.3% |
| 11,771 | MONTGOMERY | 5,556 | 3,601 | 1,899 | 56 | 1,702 R | 64.8% | 34.2% | 65.5% | 34.5% |
| 41,722 | MUSCATINE | 18,717 | 9,020 | 9,542 | 155 | 522 D | 48.2% | 51.0% | 48.6% | 51.4% |
| 15,102 | O'BRIEN | 7,731 | 5,328 | 2,330 | 73 | 2,998 R | 68.9% | 30.1% | 69.6% | 30.4% |
| 7,003 | OSCEOLA | 3,266 | 2,295 | 934 | 37 | 1,361 R | 70.3% | 28.6% | 71.1% | 28.9% |
| 16,976 | PAGE | 7,513 | 5,243 | 2,211 | 59 | 3,032 R | 69.8% | 29.4% | 70.3% | 29.7% |
| 10,147 | PALO ALTO | 5,191 | 2,674 | 2,482 | 35 | 192 R | 51.5% | 47.8% | 51.9% | 48.1% |
| 24,849 | PLYMOUTH | 12,222 | 7,810 | 4,278 | 134 | 3,532 R | 63.9% | 35.0% | 64.6% | 35.4% |
| 8,662 | POCAHONTAS | 4,313 | 2,441 | 1,822 | 50 | 619 R | 56.6% | 42.2% | 57.3% | 42.7% |
| 374,601 | POLK | 202,618 | 95,828 | 105,218 | 1,572 | 9,390 D | 47.3% | 51.9% | 47.7% | 52.3% |
| 87,704 | POTTAWATTAMIE | 41,820 | 24,558 | 16,906 | 356 | 7,652 R | 58.7% | 40.4% | 59.2% | 40.8% |
| 18,815 | POWESHIEK | 10,091 | 4,965 | 5,043 | 83 | 78 D | 49.2% | 50.0% | 49.6% | 50.4% |
| 5,469 | RINGGOLD | 2,778 | 1,466 | 1,286 | 26 | 180 R | 52.8% | 46.3% | 53.3% | 46.7% |
| 11,529 | SAC | 5,374 | 3,128 | 2,215 | 31 | 913 R | 58.2% | 41.2% | 58.5% | 41.5% |
| 158,668 | SCOTT | 82,722 | 39,958 | 42,122 | 642 | 2,164 D | 48.3% | 50.9% | 48.7% | 51.3% |
| 13,173 | SHELBY | 6,670 | 4,256 | 2,355 | 59 | 1,901 R | 63.8% | 35.3% | 64.4% | 35.6% |
| 31,589 | SIOUX | 16,570 | 14,229 | 2,259 | 82 | 11,970 R | 85.9% | 13.6% | 86.3% | 13.7% |
| 79,981 | STORY | 44,652 | 20,819 | 23,296 | 537 | 2,477 D | 46.6% | 52.2% | 47.2% | 52.8% |
| 18,103 | TAMA | 9,001 | 4,456 | 4,487 | 58 | 31 D | 49.5% | 49.9% | 49.8% | 50.2% |
| 6,958 | TAYLOR | 3,190 | 1,908 | 1,252 | 30 | 656 R | 59.8% | 39.2% | 60.4% | 39.6% |
| 12,309 | UNION | 5,978 | 3,165 | 2,747 | 66 | 418 R | 52.9% | 46.0% | 53.5% | 46.5% |
| 7,809 | VAN BUREN | 3,836 | 2,211 | 1,568 | 57 | 643 R | 57.6% | 40.9% | 58.5% | 41.5% |
| 36,051 | WAPELLO | 16,707 | 7,403 | 9,125 | 179 | 1,722 D | 44.3% | 54.6% | 44.8% | 55.2% |
| 40,671 | WARREN | 23,053 | 12,160 | 10,730 | 163 | 1,430 R | 52.7% | 46.5% | 53.1% | 46.9% |
| 20,670 | WASHINGTON | 10,688 | 5,977 | 4,595 | 116 | 1,382 R | 55.9% | 43.0% | 56.5% | 43.5% |
| 6,730 | WAYNE | 3,133 | 1,733 | 1,379 | 21 | 354 R | 55.3% | 44.0% | 55.7% | 44.3% |
| 40,235 | WEBSTER | 18,631 | 8,959 | 9,561 | 111 | 602 D | 48.1% | 51.3% | 48.4% | 51.6% |
| 11,723 | WINNEBAGO | 5,952 | 3,175 | 2,707 | 70 | 468 R | 53.3% | 45.5% | 54.0% | 46.0% |
| 21,310 | WINNESHIEK | 10,784 | 5,324 | 5,354 | 106 | 30 D | 49.4% | 49.6% | 49.9% | 50.1% |
| 103,877 | WOODBURY | 44,195 | 22,451 | 21,455 | 289 | 996 R | 50.8% | 48.5% | 51.1% | 48.9% |
| 7,909 | WORTH | 4,123 | 1,795 | 2,286 | 42 | 491 D | 43.5% | 55.4% | 44.0% | 56.0% |
| 14,334 | WRIGHT | 6,603 | 3,631 | 2,930 | 42 | 701 R | 55.0% | 44.4% | 55.3% | 44.7% |
| 2,926,324 | TOTAL | 1,506,908 | 751,957 | 741,898 | 13,053 | 10,059 R | 49.9% | 49.2% | 50.3% | 49.7% |

# IOWA

## PRESIDENT 2000

| 2000 Census Population | County | Total Vote | Republican | Democratic | Green (Nader) | Other | Rep.-Dem. Plurality | Percentage of Total Vote Rep. | Dem. | Green |
|---|---|---|---|---|---|---|---|---|---|---|
| 8,243 | ADAIR | 4,123 | 2,275 | 1,753 | 66 | 29 | 522 R | 55.2% | 42.5% | 1.6% |
| 4,482 | ADAMS | 2,145 | 1,170 | 897 | 51 | 27 | 273 R | 54.5% | 41.8% | 2.4% |
| 14,675 | ALLAMAKEE | 6,462 | 3,277 | 2,883 | 199 | 103 | 394 R | 50.7% | 44.6% | 3.1% |
| 13,721 | APPANOOSE | 5,704 | 2,992 | 2,560 | 105 | 47 | 432 R | 52.5% | 44.9% | 1.8% |
| 6,830 | AUDUBON | 3,784 | 1,909 | 1,780 | 56 | 39 | 129 R | 50.4% | 47.0% | 1.5% |
| 25,308 | BENTON | 11,766 | 5,468 | 5,915 | 231 | 152 | 447 D | 46.5% | 50.3% | 2.0% |
| 128,012 | BLACK HAWK | 55,085 | 23,468 | 30,112 | 1,132 | 373 | 6,644 D | 42.6% | 54.7% | 2.1% |
| 26,224 | BOONE | 12,249 | 5,625 | 6,270 | 252 | 102 | 645 D | 45.9% | 51.2% | 2.1% |
| 23,325 | BREMER | 11,175 | 5,675 | 5,169 | 260 | 71 | 506 R | 50.8% | 46.3% | 2.3% |
| 21,093 | BUCHANAN | 9,410 | 4,092 | 5,045 | 171 | 102 | 953 D | 43.5% | 53.6% | 1.8% |
| 20,411 | BUENA VISTA | 7,977 | 4,354 | 3,297 | 227 | 99 | 1,057 R | 54.6% | 41.3% | 2.8% |
| 15,305 | BUTLER | 6,724 | 3,837 | 2,735 | 113 | 39 | 1,102 R | 57.1% | 40.7% | 1.7% |
| 11,115 | CALHOUN | 5,041 | 2,776 | 2,132 | 93 | 40 | 644 R | 55.1% | 42.3% | 1.8% |
| 21,421 | CARROLL | 9,568 | 4,879 | 4,463 | 146 | 80 | 416 R | 51.0% | 46.6% | 1.5% |
| 14,684 | CASS | 6,880 | 4,206 | 2,481 | 147 | 46 | 1,725 R | 61.1% | 36.1% | 2.1% |
| 18,187 | CEDAR | 8,344 | 4,031 | 4,033 | 212 | 68 | 2 D | 48.3% | 48.3% | 2.5% |
| 46,447 | CERRO GORDO | 22,162 | 9,397 | 12,185 | 408 | 172 | 2,788 D | 42.4% | 55.0% | 1.8% |
| 13,035 | CHEROKEE | 6,592 | 3,463 | 2,845 | 160 | 124 | 618 R | 52.5% | 43.2% | 2.4% |
| 13,095 | CHICKASAW | 6,584 | 2,936 | 3,435 | 145 | 68 | 499 D | 44.6% | 52.2% | 2.2% |
| 9,133 | CLARKE | 4,176 | 1,984 | 2,081 | 75 | 36 | 97 D | 47.5% | 49.8% | 1.8% |
| 17,372 | CLAY | 7,578 | 3,992 | 3,294 | 166 | 126 | 698 R | 52.7% | 43.5% | 2.2% |
| 18,678 | CLAYTON | 8,571 | 4,034 | 4,238 | 206 | 93 | 204 D | 47.1% | 49.4% | 2.4% |
| 50,149 | CLINTON | 22,180 | 9,229 | 12,276 | 471 | 204 | 3,047 D | 41.6% | 55.3% | 2.1% |
| 16,942 | CRAWFORD | 6,555 | 3,482 | 2,838 | 146 | 89 | 644 R | 53.1% | 43.3% | 2.2% |
| 40,750 | DALLAS | 19,330 | 10,306 | 8,561 | 320 | 143 | 1,745 R | 53.3% | 44.3% | 1.7% |
| 8,541 | DAVIS | 3,758 | 1,956 | 1,691 | 67 | 44 | 265 R | 52.0% | 45.0% | 1.8% |
| 8,689 | DECATUR | 3,709 | 1,903 | 1,674 | 94 | 38 | 229 R | 51.3% | 45.1% | 2.5% |
| 18,404 | DELAWARE | 8,349 | 4,273 | 3,808 | 161 | 107 | 465 R | 51.2% | 45.6% | 1.9% |
| 42,351 | DES MOINES | 19,365 | 7,385 | 11,351 | 409 | 220 | 3,966 D | 38.1% | 58.6% | 2.1% |
| 16,424 | DICKINSON | 8,121 | 4,225 | 3,660 | 169 | 67 | 565 R | 52.0% | 45.1% | 2.1% |
| 89,143 | DUBUQUE | 40,323 | 16,462 | 22,341 | 987 | 533 | 5,879 D | 40.8% | 55.4% | 2.4% |
| 11,027 | EMMET | 4,630 | 2,331 | 2,165 | 98 | 36 | 166 R | 50.3% | 46.8% | 2.1% |
| 22,008 | FAYETTE | 9,621 | 4,747 | 4,640 | 174 | 60 | 107 R | 49.3% | 48.2% | 1.8% |
| 16,900 | FLOYD | 7,238 | 3,191 | 3,830 | 154 | 63 | 639 D | 44.1% | 52.9% | 2.1% |
| 10,704 | FRANKLIN | 4,938 | 2,657 | 2,122 | 110 | 49 | 535 R | 53.8% | 43.0% | 2.2% |
| 8,010 | FREMONT | 3,616 | 2,069 | 1,459 | 63 | 25 | 610 R | 57.2% | 40.3% | 1.7% |
| 10,366 | GREENE | 4,719 | 2,282 | 2,301 | 106 | 30 | 19 D | 48.4% | 48.8% | 2.2% |
| 12,369 | GRUNDY | 6,111 | 3,851 | 2,139 | 70 | 51 | 1,712 R | 63.0% | 35.0% | 1.1% |
| 11,353 | GUTHRIE | 5,469 | 2,840 | 2,493 | 86 | 50 | 347 R | 51.9% | 45.6% | 1.6% |
| 16,438 | HAMILTON | 7,574 | 3,968 | 3,407 | 141 | 58 | 561 R | 52.4% | 45.0% | 1.9% |
| 12,100 | HANCOCK | 5,438 | 2,988 | 2,281 | 123 | 46 | 707 R | 54.9% | 41.9% | 2.3% |
| 18,812 | HARDIN | 8,435 | 4,486 | 3,734 | 141 | 74 | 752 R | 53.2% | 44.3% | 1.7% |
| 15,666 | HARRISON | 6,543 | 3,802 | 2,551 | 126 | 64 | 1,251 R | 58.1% | 39.0% | 1.9% |
| 20,336 | HENRY | 8,671 | 4,476 | 3,907 | 183 | 105 | 569 R | 51.6% | 45.1% | 2.1% |
| 9,932 | HOWARD | 4,491 | 1,922 | 2,426 | 100 | 43 | 504 D | 42.8% | 54.0% | 2.2% |
| 10,381 | HUMBOLDT | 4,940 | 2,846 | 1,949 | 100 | 45 | 897 R | 57.6% | 39.5% | 2.0% |
| 7,837 | IDA | 3,491 | 1,968 | 1,411 | 58 | 54 | 557 R | 56.4% | 40.4% | 1.7% |
| 15,671 | IOWA | 7,413 | 3,894 | 3,230 | 188 | 101 | 664 R | 52.5% | 43.6% | 2.5% |
| 20,296 | JACKSON | 9,032 | 3,769 | 4,945 | 227 | 91 | 1,176 D | 41.7% | 54.7% | 2.5% |
| 37,213 | JASPER | 17,835 | 8,729 | 8,699 | 267 | 140 | 30 R | 48.9% | 48.8% | 1.5% |
| 16,181 | JEFFERSON | 7,548 | 3,248 | 2,863 | 206 | 1,231 | 385 R | 43.0% | 37.9% | 2.7% |
| 111,006 | JOHNSON | 52,769 | 17,899 | 31,174 | 3,248 | 448 | 13,275 D | 33.9% | 59.1% | 6.2% |
| 20,221 | JONES | 9,143 | 4,201 | 4,690 | 195 | 57 | 489 D | 45.9% | 51.3% | 2.1% |
| 11,400 | KEOKUK | 4,947 | 2,571 | 2,181 | 99 | 96 | 390 R | 52.0% | 44.1% | 2.0% |
| 17,163 | KOSSUTH | 8,878 | 4,612 | 3,960 | 206 | 100 | 652 R | 51.9% | 44.6% | 2.3% |
| 38,052 | LEE | 16,572 | 6,339 | 9,632 | 325 | 276 | 3,293 D | 38.3% | 58.1% | 2.0% |
| 191,701 | LINN | 92,064 | 40,417 | 48,897 | 2,106 | 644 | 8,480 D | 43.9% | 53.1% | 2.3% |
| 12,183 | LOUISA | 4,637 | 2,207 | 2,294 | 85 | 51 | 87 D | 47.6% | 49.5% | 1.8% |
| 9,422 | LUCAS | 4,303 | 2,262 | 1,934 | 65 | 42 | 328 R | 52.6% | 44.9% | 1.5% |
| 11,763 | LYON | 5,342 | 3,918 | 1,313 | 68 | 43 | 2,605 R | 73.3% | 24.6% | 1.3% |

# IOWA

## PRESIDENT 2000

| 2000 Census Population | County | Total Vote | Republican | Democratic | Green (Nader) | Other | Rep.-Dem. Plurality | Percentage of Total Vote | | |
|---|---|---|---|---|---|---|---|---|---|---|
| | | | | | | | | Rep. | Dem. | Green |
| 14,019 | MADISON | 6,969 | 3,662 | 3,093 | 128 | 86 | 569 R | 52.5% | 44.4% | 1.8% |
| 22,335 | MAHASKA | 9,543 | 5,971 | 3,370 | 143 | 59 | 2,601 R | 62.6% | 35.3% | 1.5% |
| 32,052 | MARION | 14,408 | 8,358 | 5,741 | 208 | 101 | 2,617 R | 58.0% | 39.8% | 1.4% |
| 39,311 | MARSHALL | 17,624 | 8,785 | 8,322 | 340 | 177 | 463 R | 49.8% | 47.2% | 1.9% |
| 14,547 | MILLS | 5,915 | 3,684 | 2,039 | 126 | 66 | 1,645 R | 62.3% | 34.5% | 2.1% |
| 10,874 | MITCHELL | 5,162 | 2,388 | 2,650 | 87 | 37 | 262 D | 46.3% | 51.3% | 1.7% |
| 10,020 | MONONA | 4,560 | 2,304 | 2,086 | 93 | 77 | 218 R | 50.5% | 45.7% | 2.0% |
| 8,016 | MONROE | 3,647 | 1,858 | 1,699 | 54 | 36 | 159 R | 50.9% | 46.6% | 1.5% |
| 11,771 | MONTGOMERY | 5,394 | 3,417 | 1,838 | 85 | 54 | 1,579 R | 63.3% | 34.1% | 1.6% |
| 41,722 | MUSCATINE | 16,076 | 7,483 | 8,058 | 371 | 164 | 575 D | 46.5% | 50.1% | 2.3% |
| 15,102 | O'BRIEN | 7,044 | 4,674 | 2,170 | 108 | 92 | 2,504 R | 66.4% | 30.8% | 1.5% |
| 7,003 | OSCEOLA | 3,063 | 2,064 | 913 | 56 | 30 | 1,151 R | 67.4% | 29.8% | 1.8% |
| 16,976 | PAGE | 7,059 | 4,588 | 2,293 | 125 | 53 | 2,295 R | 65.0% | 32.5% | 1.8% |
| 10,147 | PALO ALTO | 4,823 | 2,341 | 2,326 | 81 | 75 | 15 R | 48.5% | 48.2% | 1.7% |
| 24,849 | PLYMOUTH | 10,118 | 6,189 | 3,499 | 198 | 232 | 2,690 R | 61.2% | 34.6% | 2.0% |
| 8,662 | POCAHONTAS | 4,141 | 2,242 | 1,736 | 78 | 85 | 506 R | 54.1% | 41.9% | 1.9% |
| 374,601 | POLK | 174,167 | 79,927 | 89,715 | 3,366 | 1,159 | 9,788 D | 45.9% | 51.5% | 1.9% |
| 87,704 | POTTAWATTAMIE | 34,467 | 18,783 | 14,726 | 690 | 268 | 4,057 R | 54.5% | 42.7% | 2.0% |
| 18,815 | POWESHIEK | 8,980 | 4,396 | 4,222 | 287 | 75 | 174 R | 49.0% | 47.0% | 3.2% |
| 5,469 | RINGGOLD | 2,692 | 1,369 | 1,246 | 47 | 30 | 123 R | 50.9% | 46.3% | 1.7% |
| 11,529 | SAC | 5,033 | 2,776 | 2,099 | 97 | 61 | 677 R | 55.2% | 41.7% | 1.9% |
| 158,668 | SCOTT | 70,568 | 32,801 | 35,857 | 1,386 | 524 | 3,056 D | 46.5% | 50.8% | 2.0% |
| 13,173 | SHELBY | 6,009 | 3,655 | 2,179 | 113 | 62 | 1,476 R | 60.8% | 36.3% | 1.9% |
| 31,589 | SIOUX | 14,692 | 12,241 | 2,148 | 156 | 147 | 10,093 R | 83.3% | 14.6% | 1.1% |
| 79,981 | STORY | 35,364 | 16,228 | 17,478 | 1,317 | 341 | 1,250 D | 45.9% | 49.4% | 3.7% |
| 18,103 | TAMA | 8,315 | 4,034 | 4,045 | 160 | 76 | 11 D | 48.5% | 48.6% | 1.9% |
| 6,958 | TAYLOR | 3,096 | 1,770 | 1,247 | 46 | 33 | 523 R | 57.2% | 40.3% | 1.5% |
| 12,309 | UNION | 5,740 | 3,003 | 2,540 | 108 | 89 | 463 R | 52.3% | 44.3% | 1.9% |
| 7,809 | VAN BUREN | 3,561 | 2,016 | 1,440 | 51 | 54 | 576 R | 56.6% | 40.4% | 1.4% |
| 36,051 | WAPELLO | 15,139 | 6,313 | 8,355 | 317 | 154 | 2,042 D | 41.7% | 55.2% | 2.1% |
| 40,671 | WARREN | 19,653 | 9,621 | 9,521 | 371 | 140 | 100 R | 49.0% | 48.4% | 1.9% |
| 20,670 | WASHINGTON | 9,094 | 4,827 | 3,932 | 245 | 90 | 895 R | 53.1% | 43.2% | 2.7% |
| 6,730 | WAYNE | 3,021 | 1,666 | 1,300 | 31 | 24 | 366 R | 55.1% | 43.0% | 1.0% |
| 40,235 | WEBSTER | 17,048 | 8,172 | 8,479 | 282 | 115 | 307 D | 47.9% | 49.7% | 1.7% |
| 11,723 | WINNEBAGO | 5,527 | 2,662 | 2,691 | 115 | 59 | 29 D | 48.2% | 48.7% | 2.1% |
| 21,310 | WINNESHIEK | 9,417 | 4,647 | 4,339 | 343 | 88 | 308 R | 49.3% | 46.1% | 3.6% |
| 103,877 | WOODBURY | 37,896 | 18,864 | 17,691 | 804 | 537 | 1,173 R | 49.8% | 46.7% | 2.1% |
| 7,909 | WORTH | 4,004 | 1,659 | 2,208 | 91 | 46 | 549 D | 41.4% | 55.1% | 2.3% |
| 14,334 | WRIGHT | 6,336 | 3,384 | 2,796 | 107 | 49 | 588 R | 53.4% | 44.1% | 1.7% |
| 2,926,324 | TOTAL | 1,315,563 | 634,373 | 638,517 | 29,374 | 13,299 | 4,144 D | 48.2% | 48.5% | 2.2% |

# IOWA

## PRESIDENT 1996

| 1995 Census Pop. Est. | County | Total Vote | Republican | Democratic | Reform (Perot) | Other | Rep.-Dem. Plurality | Percentage of Total Vote | | |
|---|---|---|---|---|---|---|---|---|---|---|
| | | | | | | | | Rep. | Dem. | Reform |
| 8,286 | ADAIR | 3,935 | 1,655 | 1,802 | 458 | 20 | 147 D | 42.1% | 45.8% | 11.6% |
| 4,500 | ADAMS | 2,326 | 920 | 1,070 | 320 | 16 | 150 D | 39.6% | 46.0% | 13.8% |
| 14,079 | ALLAMAKEE | 5,781 | 2,457 | 2,551 | 680 | 93 | 94 D | 42.5% | 44.1% | 11.8% |
| 13,674 | APPANOOSE | 5,592 | 2,233 | 2,747 | 554 | 58 | 514 D | 39.9% | 49.1% | 9.9% |
| 6,875 | AUDUBON | 3,488 | 1,314 | 1,827 | 314 | 33 | 513 D | 37.7% | 52.4% | 9.0% |
| 24,137 | BENTON | 10,279 | 3,835 | 5,546 | 846 | 52 | 1,711 D | 37.3% | 54.0% | 8.2% |
| 123,077 | BLACK HAWK | 53,109 | 19,322 | 29,651 | 3,623 | 513 | 10,329 D | 36.4% | 55.8% | 6.8% |
| 25,502 | BOONE | 11,835 | 4,293 | 6,446 | 987 | 109 | 2,153 D | 36.3% | 54.5% | 8.3% |
| 23,218 | BREMER | 10,172 | 4,213 | 5,023 | 862 | 74 | 810 D | 41.4% | 49.4% | 8.5% |
| 21,294 | BUCHANAN | 8,951 | 3,043 | 4,997 | 836 | 75 | 1,954 D | 34.0% | 55.8% | 9.3% |
| 20,065 | BUENA VISTA | 7,965 | 3,636 | 3,420 | 831 | 78 | 216 R | 45.6% | 42.9% | 10.4% |
| 15,745 | BUTLER | 6,631 | 3,036 | 3,061 | 489 | 45 | 25 D | 45.8% | 46.2% | 7.4% |
| 11,430 | CALHOUN | 4,779 | 2,077 | 2,193 | 462 | 47 | 116 D | 43.5% | 45.9% | 9.7% |
| 21,603 | CARROLL | 8,790 | 3,392 | 4,333 | 998 | 67 | 941 D | 38.6% | 49.3% | 11.4% |
| 15,047 | CASS | 6,865 | 3,384 | 2,616 | 809 | 56 | 768 R | 49.3% | 38.1% | 11.8% |
| 17,682 | CEDAR | 7,676 | 2,966 | 3,856 | 756 | 98 | 890 D | 38.6% | 50.2% | 9.8% |
| 46,633 | CERRO GORDO | 21,227 | 7,427 | 11,943 | 1,689 | 168 | 4,516 D | 35.0% | 56.3% | 8.0% |
| 13,591 | CHEROKEE | 6,370 | 2,629 | 2,853 | 834 | 54 | 224 D | 41.3% | 44.8% | 13.1% |
| 13,429 | CHICKASAW | 6,360 | 2,191 | 3,355 | 759 | 55 | 1,164 D | 34.4% | 52.8% | 11.9% |
| 8,136 | CLARKE | 3,923 | 1,401 | 2,053 | 440 | 29 | 652 D | 35.7% | 52.3% | 11.2% |
| 17,412 | CLAY | 7,655 | 3,129 | 3,659 | 802 | 65 | 530 D | 40.9% | 47.8% | 10.5% |
| 18,833 | CLAYTON | 8,194 | 2,944 | 4,284 | 912 | 54 | 1,340 D | 35.9% | 52.3% | 11.1% |
| 50,889 | CLINTON | 21,595 | 7,624 | 11,481 | 2,300 | 190 | 3,857 D | 35.3% | 53.2% | 10.7% |
| 16,461 | CRAWFORD | 6,715 | 2,686 | 3,140 | 847 | 42 | 454 D | 40.0% | 46.8% | 12.6% |
| 32,947 | DALLAS | 16,010 | 6,647 | 8,017 | 1,198 | 148 | 1,370 D | 41.5% | 50.1% | 7.5% |
| 8,539 | DAVIS | 3,759 | 1,445 | 1,894 | 382 | 38 | 449 D | 38.4% | 50.4% | 10.2% |
| 8,177 | DECATUR | 3,623 | 1,287 | 1,846 | 452 | 38 | 559 D | 35.5% | 51.0% | 12.5% |
| 18,394 | DELAWARE | 7,497 | 3,065 | 3,704 | 679 | 49 | 639 D | 40.9% | 49.4% | 9.1% |
| 42,679 | DES MOINES | 18,574 | 5,778 | 10,761 | 1,792 | 243 | 4,983 D | 31.1% | 57.9% | 9.6% |
| 15,664 | DICKINSON | 7,646 | 3,129 | 3,562 | 901 | 54 | 433 D | 40.9% | 46.6% | 11.8% |
| 88,566 | DUBUQUE | 38,051 | 13,391 | 20,839 | 3,304 | 517 | 7,448 D | 35.2% | 54.8% | 8.7% |
| 11,153 | EMMET | 4,411 | 1,641 | 2,270 | 470 | 30 | 629 D | 37.2% | 51.5% | 10.7% |
| 21,799 | FAYETTE | 9,624 | 3,848 | 4,832 | 890 | 54 | 984 D | 40.0% | 50.2% | 9.2% |
| 16,603 | FLOYD | 6,887 | 2,379 | 3,769 | 689 | 50 | 1,390 D | 34.5% | 54.7% | 10.0% |
| 11,106 | FRANKLIN | 4,733 | 2,054 | 2,232 | 417 | 30 | 178 D | 43.4% | 47.2% | 8.8% |
| 8,097 | FREMONT | 3,562 | 1,576 | 1,481 | 480 | 25 | 95 R | 44.2% | 41.6% | 13.5% |
| 10,080 | GREENE | 4,799 | 1,861 | 2,519 | 396 | 23 | 658 D | 38.8% | 52.5% | 8.3% |
| 12,303 | GRUNDY | 5,687 | 2,928 | 2,322 | 401 | 36 | 606 R | 51.5% | 40.8% | 7.1% |
| 11,406 | GUTHRIE | 5,140 | 2,034 | 2,552 | 515 | 39 | 518 D | 39.6% | 49.6% | 10.0% |
| 16,193 | HAMILTON | 7,277 | 3,109 | 3,455 | 661 | 52 | 346 D | 42.7% | 47.5% | 9.1% |
| 12,184 | HANCOCK | 5,309 | 2,353 | 2,399 | 529 | 28 | 46 D | 44.3% | 45.2% | 10.0% |
| 18,685 | HARDIN | 8,324 | 3,505 | 4,053 | 713 | 53 | 548 D | 42.1% | 48.7% | 8.6% |
| 15,115 | HARRISON | 6,527 | 3,070 | 2,576 | 820 | 61 | 494 R | 47.0% | 39.5% | 12.6% |
| 19,826 | HENRY | 8,275 | 3,478 | 3,798 | 914 | 85 | 320 D | 42.0% | 45.9% | 11.0% |
| 9,887 | HOWARD | 4,405 | 1,528 | 2,303 | 555 | 19 | 775 D | 34.7% | 52.3% | 12.6% |
| 10,284 | HUMBOLDT | 4,933 | 2,236 | 2,080 | 590 | 27 | 156 R | 45.3% | 42.2% | 12.0% |
| 8,193 | IDA | 3,732 | 1,684 | 1,589 | 436 | 23 | 95 R | 45.1% | 42.6% | 11.7% |
| 15,193 | IOWA | 7,035 | 3,042 | 3,354 | 575 | 64 | 312 D | 43.2% | 47.7% | 8.2% |
| 20,120 | JACKSON | 8,461 | 2,827 | 4,609 | 936 | 89 | 1,782 D | 33.4% | 54.5% | 11.1% |
| 35,163 | JASPER | 16,585 | 6,414 | 8,776 | 1,263 | 132 | 2,362 D | 38.7% | 52.9% | 7.6% |
| 16,829 | JEFFERSON | 7,397 | 2,541 | 2,597 | 571 | 1,688 | 56 D | 34.4% | 35.1% | 7.7% |
| 101,291 | JOHNSON | 45,732 | 13,402 | 27,888 | 2,313 | 2,129 | 14,486 D | 29.3% | 61.0% | 5.1% |
| 20,273 | JONES | 8,581 | 3,083 | 4,668 | 765 | 65 | 1,585 D | 35.9% | 54.4% | 8.9% |
| 11,564 | KEOKUK | 5,101 | 2,080 | 2,545 | 432 | 44 | 465 D | 40.8% | 49.9% | 8.5% |
| 18,147 | KOSSUTH | 8,505 | 3,477 | 4,031 | 932 | 65 | 554 D | 40.9% | 47.4% | 11.0% |
| 39,130 | LEE | 15,662 | 4,932 | 8,831 | 1,734 | 165 | 3,899 D | 31.5% | 56.4% | 11.1% |
| 178,559 | LINN | 83,035 | 30,958 | 45,497 | 5,607 | 973 | 14,539 D | 37.3% | 54.8% | 6.8% |
| 11,793 | LOUISA | 4,275 | 1,565 | 2,081 | 590 | 39 | 516 D | 36.6% | 48.7% | 13.8% |
| 9,015 | LUCAS | 4,209 | 1,586 | 2,168 | 433 | 22 | 582 D | 37.7% | 51.5% | 10.3% |
| 11,890 | LYON | 5,352 | 3,396 | 1,489 | 422 | 45 | 1,907 R | 63.5% | 27.8% | 7.9% |

334

# IOWA

## PRESIDENT 1996

| 1995 Census Pop. Est. | County | Total Vote | Republican | Democratic | Reform (Perot) | Other | Rep.-Dem. Plurality | Percentage of Total Vote | | |
|---|---|---|---|---|---|---|---|---|---|---|
| | | | | | | | | Rep. | Dem. | Reform |
| 13,490 | MADISON | 6,327 | 2,550 | 3,070 | 654 | 53 | 520 D | 40.3% | 48.5% | 10.3% |
| 21,927 | MAHASKA | 8,941 | 4,473 | 3,737 | 656 | 75 | 736 R | 50.0% | 41.8% | 7.3% |
| 31,102 | MARION | 13,052 | 6,100 | 5,978 | 871 | 103 | 122 R | 46.7% | 45.8% | 6.7% |
| 38,627 | MARSHALL | 17,324 | 7,017 | 8,669 | 1,455 | 183 | 1,652 D | 40.5% | 50.0% | 8.4% |
| 13,802 | MILLS | 5,772 | 2,958 | 2,068 | 683 | 63 | 890 R | 51.2% | 35.8% | 11.8% |
| 11,129 | MITCHELL | 5,071 | 1,877 | 2,596 | 563 | 35 | 719 D | 37.0% | 51.2% | 11.1% |
| 9,968 | MONONA | 4,238 | 1,674 | 1,952 | 580 | 32 | 278 D | 39.5% | 46.1% | 13.7% |
| 8,177 | MONROE | 3,513 | 1,272 | 1,884 | 329 | 28 | 612 D | 36.2% | 53.6% | 9.4% |
| 11,939 | MONTGOMERY | 5,198 | 2,583 | 1,912 | 663 | 40 | 671 R | 49.7% | 36.8% | 12.8% |
| 41,435 | MUSCATINE | 15,386 | 5,858 | 7,674 | 1,705 | 149 | 1,816 D | 38.1% | 49.9% | 11.1% |
| 15,349 | O'BRIEN | 6,735 | 3,877 | 2,236 | 578 | 44 | 1,641 R | 57.6% | 33.2% | 8.6% |
| 7,077 | OSCEOLA | 3,051 | 1,736 | 1,010 | 274 | 31 | 726 R | 56.9% | 33.1% | 9.0% |
| 16,676 | PAGE | 7,043 | 4,032 | 2,220 | 753 | 38 | 1,812 R | 57.2% | 31.5% | 10.7% |
| 10,200 | PALO ALTO | 4,703 | 1,817 | 2,371 | 477 | 38 | 554 D | 38.6% | 50.4% | 10.1% |
| 24,220 | PLYMOUTH | 9,956 | 5,117 | 3,745 | 997 | 97 | 1,372 R | 51.4% | 37.6% | 10.0% |
| 9,119 | POCAHONTAS | 4,215 | 1,707 | 1,981 | 478 | 49 | 274 D | 40.5% | 47.0% | 11.3% |
| 349,560 | POLK | 156,106 | 60,884 | 83,877 | 9,516 | 1,829 | 22,993 D | 39.0% | 53.7% | 6.1% |
| 83,701 | POTTAWATTAMIE | 32,821 | 15,648 | 13,276 | 3,534 | 363 | 2,372 R | 47.7% | 40.4% | 10.8% |
| 19,014 | POWESHIEK | 8,214 | 3,221 | 4,183 | 681 | 129 | 962 D | 39.2% | 50.9% | 8.3% |
| 5,373 | RINGGOLD | 2,740 | 967 | 1,439 | 310 | 24 | 472 D | 35.3% | 52.5% | 11.3% |
| 12,087 | SAC | 4,997 | 2,209 | 2,170 | 579 | 39 | 39 R | 44.2% | 43.4% | 11.6% |
| 156,694 | SCOTT | 65,202 | 26,751 | 32,694 | 4,991 | 766 | 5,943 D | 41.0% | 50.1% | 7.7% |
| 13,089 | SHELBY | 5,941 | 3,056 | 2,176 | 652 | 57 | 880 R | 51.4% | 36.6% | 11.0% |
| 31,398 | SIOUX | 14,110 | 10,864 | 2,392 | 718 | 136 | 8,472 R | 77.0% | 17.0% | 5.1% |
| 74,638 | STORY | 32,695 | 12,468 | 17,234 | 2,091 | 902 | 4,766 D | 38.1% | 52.7% | 6.4% |
| 17,878 | TAMA | 7,752 | 2,986 | 3,994 | 713 | 59 | 1,008 D | 38.5% | 51.5% | 9.2% |
| 7,152 | TAYLOR | 3,276 | 1,419 | 1,458 | 379 | 20 | 39 D | 43.3% | 44.5% | 11.6% |
| 12,416 | UNION | 5,657 | 2,156 | 2,787 | 660 | 54 | 631 D | 38.1% | 49.3% | 11.7% |
| 7,767 | VAN BUREN | 3,375 | 1,460 | 1,536 | 347 | 32 | 76 D | 43.3% | 45.5% | 10.3% |
| 35,770 | WAPELLO | 14,770 | 4,828 | 8,437 | 1,376 | 129 | 3,609 D | 32.7% | 57.1% | 9.3% |
| 38,940 | WARREN | 17,472 | 6,905 | 9,120 | 1,267 | 180 | 2,215 D | 39.5% | 52.2% | 7.3% |
| 20,508 | WASHINGTON | 8,173 | 3,600 | 3,828 | 636 | 109 | 228 D | 44.0% | 46.8% | 7.8% |
| 6,866 | WAYNE | 3,267 | 1,295 | 1,650 | 310 | 12 | 355 D | 39.6% | 50.5% | 9.5% |
| 39,206 | WEBSTER | 16,328 | 6,275 | 8,380 | 1,580 | 93 | 2,105 D | 38.4% | 51.3% | 9.7% |
| 11,900 | WINNEBAGO | 5,521 | 2,211 | 2,679 | 590 | 41 | 468 D | 40.0% | 48.5% | 10.7% |
| 21,058 | WINNESHIEK | 8,770 | 3,532 | 4,122 | 973 | 143 | 590 D | 40.3% | 47.0% | 11.1% |
| 101,827 | WOODBURY | 37,464 | 16,368 | 17,224 | 3,436 | 436 | 856 D | 43.7% | 46.0% | 9.2% |
| 7,926 | WORTH | 4,012 | 1,284 | 2,293 | 403 | 32 | 1,009 D | 32.0% | 57.2% | 10.0% |
| 14,314 | WRIGHT | 5,959 | 2,473 | 2,912 | 536 | 38 | 439 D | 41.5% | 48.9% | 9.0% |
| 2,841,764 | TOTAL | 1,234,075 | 492,644 | 620,258 | 105,159 | 16,014 | 127,614 D | 39.9% | 50.3% | 8.5% |

# IOWA

## PRESIDENT 1992

| 1990 Census Population | County | Total Vote | Republican | Democratic | Perot | Other | Plurality | Percentage Total Vote Rep. | Dem. | Perot |
|---|---|---|---|---|---|---|---|---|---|---|
| 8,409 | ADAIR | 4,194 | 1,713 | 1,655 | 814 | 12 | 58 R | 40.8% | 39.5% | 19.4% |
| 4,866 | ADAMS | 2,596 | 863 | 1,034 | 679 | 20 | 171 D | 33.2% | 39.8% | 26.2% |
| 13,855 | ALLAMAKEE | 6,679 | 2,627 | 2,362 | 1,543 | 147 | 265 R | 39.3% | 35.4% | 23.1% |
| 13,743 | APPANOOSE | 6,373 | 2,346 | 2,810 | 1,161 | 56 | 464 D | 36.8% | 44.1% | 18.2% |
| 7,334 | AUDUBON | 3,873 | 1,373 | 1,589 | 887 | 24 | 216 D | 35.5% | 41.0% | 22.9% |
| 22,429 | BENTON | 10,439 | 3,469 | 4,467 | 2,454 | 49 | 998 D | 33.2% | 42.8% | 23.5% |
| 123,798 | BLACK HAWK | 61,550 | 21,398 | 29,584 | 10,182 | 386 | 8,186 D | 34.8% | 48.1% | 16.5% |
| 25,186 | BOONE | 12,219 | 4,148 | 5,913 | 2,070 | 88 | 1,765 D | 33.9% | 48.4% | 16.9% |
| 22,813 | BREMER | 11,714 | 4,482 | 4,774 | 2,338 | 120 | 292 D | 38.3% | 40.8% | 20.0% |
| 20,844 | BUCHANAN | 9,654 | 3,313 | 4,166 | 2,126 | 49 | 853 D | 34.3% | 43.2% | 22.0% |
| 19,965 | BUENA VISTA | 9,257 | 3,863 | 3,374 | 1,955 | 65 | 489 R | 41.7% | 36.4% | 21.1% |
| 15,731 | BUTLER | 7,137 | 3,209 | 2,548 | 1,333 | 47 | 661 R | 45.0% | 35.7% | 18.7% |
| 11,508 | CALHOUN | 5,274 | 2,169 | 2,140 | 946 | 19 | 29 R | 41.1% | 40.6% | 17.9% |
| 21,423 | CARROLL | 9,475 | 3,439 | 3,800 | 2,192 | 44 | 361 D | 36.3% | 40.1% | 23.1% |
| 15,128 | CASS | 7,058 | 3,176 | 2,231 | 1,608 | 43 | 945 R | 45.0% | 31.6% | 22.8% |
| 17,381 | CEDAR | 8,240 | 2,965 | 3,296 | 1,945 | 34 | 331 D | 36.0% | 40.0% | 23.6% |
| 46,733 | CERRO GORDO | 24,293 | 8,250 | 11,415 | 4,498 | 130 | 3,165 D | 34.0% | 47.0% | 18.5% |
| 14,098 | CHEROKEE | 6,893 | 2,768 | 2,590 | 1,503 | 32 | 178 R | 40.2% | 37.6% | 21.8% |
| 13,295 | CHICKASAW | 6,640 | 2,129 | 2,913 | 1,566 | 32 | 784 D | 32.1% | 43.9% | 23.6% |
| 8,287 | CLARKE | 4,260 | 1,417 | 1,921 | 899 | 23 | 504 D | 33.3% | 45.1% | 21.1% |
| 17,585 | CLAY | 8,380 | 3,011 | 3,346 | 1,964 | 59 | 335 D | 35.9% | 39.9% | 23.4% |
| 19,054 | CLAYTON | 9,190 | 3,044 | 3,742 | 2,309 | 95 | 698 D | 33.1% | 40.7% | 25.1% |
| 51,040 | CLINTON | 24,960 | 8,746 | 11,683 | 4,414 | 117 | 2,937 D | 35.0% | 46.8% | 17.7% |
| 16,775 | CRAWFORD | 7,672 | 2,693 | 3,004 | 1,905 | 70 | 311 D | 35.1% | 39.2% | 24.8% |
| 29,755 | DALLAS | 14,861 | 5,587 | 6,554 | 2,665 | 55 | 967 D | 37.6% | 44.1% | 17.9% |
| 8,312 | DAVIS | 4,041 | 1,344 | 1,962 | 718 | 17 | 618 D | 33.3% | 48.6% | 17.8% |
| 8,338 | DECATUR | 3,986 | 1,316 | 1,866 | 786 | 18 | 550 D | 33.0% | 46.8% | 19.7% |
| 18,035 | DELAWARE | 8,492 | 3,195 | 3,093 | 2,144 | 60 | 102 R | 37.6% | 36.4% | 25.2% |
| 42,614 | DES MOINES | 21,190 | 6,378 | 11,309 | 3,386 | 117 | 4,931 D | 30.1% | 53.4% | 16.0% |
| 14,909 | DICKINSON | 8,304 | 3,196 | 3,106 | 1,974 | 28 | 90 R | 38.5% | 37.4% | 23.8% |
| 86,403 | DUBUQUE | 42,968 | 14,007 | 20,539 | 8,208 | 214 | 6,532 D | 32.6% | 47.8% | 19.1% |
| 11,569 | EMMET | 5,032 | 1,749 | 2,239 | 1,010 | 34 | 490 D | 34.8% | 44.5% | 20.1% |
| 21,843 | FAYETTE | 10,861 | 3,879 | 4,412 | 2,493 | 77 | 533 D | 35.7% | 40.6% | 23.0% |
| 17,058 | FLOYD | 7,750 | 2,404 | 3,688 | 1,611 | 47 | 1,284 D | 31.0% | 47.6% | 20.8% |
| 11,364 | FRANKLIN | 5,266 | 2,137 | 2,049 | 1,045 | 35 | 88 R | 40.6% | 38.9% | 19.8% |
| 8,226 | FREMONT | 3,911 | 1,459 | 1,422 | 1,003 | 27 | 37 R | 37.3% | 36.4% | 25.6% |
| 10,045 | GREENE | 5,353 | 1,952 | 2,422 | 956 | 23 | 470 D | 36.5% | 45.2% | 17.9% |
| 12,029 | GRUNDY | 6,156 | 3,160 | 1,895 | 1,069 | 32 | 1,265 R | 51.3% | 30.8% | 17.4% |
| 10,935 | GUTHRIE | 5,453 | 1,962 | 2,234 | 1,216 | 41 | 272 D | 36.0% | 41.0% | 22.3% |
| 16,071 | HAMILTON | 7,681 | 3,031 | 3,262 | 1,348 | 40 | 231 D | 39.5% | 42.5% | 17.5% |
| 12,638 | HANCOCK | 5,806 | 2,428 | 2,175 | 1,170 | 33 | 253 R | 41.8% | 37.5% | 20.2% |
| 19,094 | HARDIN | 8,979 | 3,590 | 3,792 | 1,547 | 50 | 202 D | 40.0% | 42.2% | 17.2% |
| 14,730 | HARRISON | 6,868 | 2,763 | 2,349 | 1,691 | 65 | 414 R | 40.2% | 34.2% | 24.6% |
| 19,226 | HENRY | 8,628 | 3,435 | 3,544 | 1,522 | 127 | 109 D | 39.8% | 41.1% | 17.6% |
| 9,809 | HOWARD | 4,862 | 1,516 | 2,099 | 1,193 | 54 | 583 D | 31.2% | 43.2% | 24.5% |
| 10,756 | HUMBOLDT | 5,185 | 2,299 | 1,765 | 1,093 | 28 | 534 R | 44.3% | 34.0% | 21.1% |
| 8,365 | IDA | 4,239 | 1,714 | 1,449 | 1,061 | 15 | 265 R | 40.4% | 34.2% | 25.0% |
| 14,630 | IOWA | 6,965 | 2,656 | 2,560 | 1,709 | 40 | 96 R | 38.1% | 36.8% | 24.5% |
| 19,950 | JACKSON | 9,305 | 2,673 | 4,421 | 2,096 | 115 | 1,748 D | 28.7% | 47.5% | 22.5% |
| 34,795 | JASPER | 18,012 | 6,866 | 8,120 | 2,972 | 54 | 1,254 D | 38.1% | 45.1% | 16.5% |
| 16,310 | JEFFERSON | 8,341 | 2,541 | 2,562 | 1,241 | 1,997 | 21 D | 30.5% | 30.7% | 14.9% |
| 96,119 | JOHNSON | 51,774 | 14,041 | 28,656 | 8,625 | 452 | 14,615 D | 27.1% | 55.3% | 16.7% |
| 19,444 | JONES | 8,900 | 3,071 | 3,508 | 2,306 | 15 | 437 D | 34.5% | 39.4% | 25.9% |
| 11,624 | KEOKUK | 5,577 | 1,981 | 2,329 | 1,238 | 29 | 348 D | 35.5% | 41.8% | 22.2% |
| 18,591 | KOSSUTH | 9,059 | 3,464 | 3,660 | 1,906 | 29 | 196 D | 38.2% | 40.4% | 21.0% |
| 38,687 | LEE | 17,152 | 4,777 | 9,366 | 2,920 | 89 | 4,589 D | 27.9% | 54.6% | 17.0% |
| 168,767 | LINN | 88,885 | 30,215 | 38,567 | 19,643 | 460 | 8,352 D | 34.0% | 43.4% | 22.1% |
| 11,592 | LOUISA | 4,844 | 1,691 | 2,091 | 1,044 | 18 | 400 D | 34.9% | 43.2% | 21.6% |
| 9,070 | LUCAS | 4,674 | 1,734 | 2,072 | 848 | 20 | 338 D | 37.1% | 44.3% | 18.1% |
| 11,952 | LYON | 5,726 | 3,272 | 1,331 | 1,068 | 55 | 1,941 R | 57.1% | 23.2% | 18.7% |

# IOWA

## PRESIDENT 1992

| 1990 Census Population | County | Total Vote | Republican | Democratic | Perot | Other | Plurality | Percentage Total Vote | | |
|---|---|---|---|---|---|---|---|---|---|---|
| | | | | | | | | Rep. | Dem. | Perot |
| 12,483 | MADISON | 6,149 | 2,421 | 2,525 | 1,168 | 35 | 104 D | 39.4% | 41.1% | 19.0% |
| 21,522 | MAHASKA | 10,247 | 4,953 | 3,714 | 1,508 | 72 | 1,239 R | 48.3% | 36.2% | 14.7% |
| 30,001 | MARION | 13,533 | 6,062 | 5,531 | 1,896 | 44 | 531 R | 44.8% | 40.9% | 14.0% |
| 38,276 | MARSHALL | 18,289 | 6,784 | 8,303 | 3,100 | 102 | 1,519 D | 37.1% | 45.4% | 17.0% |
| 13,202 | MILLS | 6,166 | 2,699 | 1,798 | 1,638 | 31 | 901 R | 43.8% | 29.2% | 26.6% |
| 10,928 | MITCHELL | 5,347 | 1,933 | 2,177 | 1,199 | 38 | 244 D | 36.2% | 40.7% | 22.4% |
| 10,034 | MONONA | 4,849 | 1,660 | 1,939 | 1,231 | 19 | 279 D | 34.2% | 40.0% | 25.4% |
| 8,114 | MONROE | 3,782 | 1,323 | 1,829 | 612 | 18 | 506 D | 35.0% | 48.4% | 16.2% |
| 12,076 | MONTGOMERY | 5,369 | 2,404 | 1,599 | 1,341 | 25 | 805 R | 44.8% | 29.8% | 25.0% |
| 39,907 | MUSCATINE | 16,864 | 6,087 | 7,089 | 3,583 | 105 | 1,002 D | 36.1% | 42.0% | 21.2% |
| 15,444 | O'BRIEN | 7,578 | 3,869 | 2,122 | 1,557 | 30 | 1,747 R | 51.1% | 28.0% | 20.5% |
| 7,267 | OSCEOLA | 3,600 | 1,756 | 990 | 813 | 41 | 766 R | 48.8% | 27.5% | 22.6% |
| 16,870 | PAGE | 7,310 | 3,670 | 1,951 | 1,669 | 20 | 1,719 R | 50.2% | 26.7% | 22.8% |
| 10,669 | PALO ALTO | 5,379 | 1,789 | 2,374 | 1,186 | 30 | 585 D | 33.3% | 44.1% | 22.0% |
| 23,388 | PLYMOUTH | 10,484 | 5,196 | 3,171 | 2,039 | 78 | 2,025 R | 49.6% | 30.2% | 19.4% |
| 9,525 | POCAHONTAS | 4,669 | 1,743 | 1,919 | 942 | 65 | 176 D | 37.3% | 41.1% | 20.2% |
| 327,140 | POLK | 167,258 | 63,708 | 78,585 | 24,155 | 810 | 14,877 D | 38.1% | 47.0% | 14.4% |
| 82,628 | POTTAWATTAMIE | 37,115 | 15,671 | 13,228 | 8,035 | 181 | 2,443 R | 42.2% | 35.6% | 21.6% |
| 19,033 | POWESHIEK | 9,047 | 3,245 | 4,056 | 1,680 | 66 | 811 D | 35.9% | 44.8% | 18.6% |
| 5,420 | RINGGOLD | 2,869 | 967 | 1,341 | 551 | 10 | 374 D | 33.7% | 46.7% | 19.2% |
| 12,324 | SAC | 5,215 | 2,138 | 1,896 | 1,157 | 24 | 242 R | 41.0% | 36.4% | 22.2% |
| 150,979 | SCOTT | 74,662 | 28,844 | 33,765 | 11,423 | 630 | 4,921 D | 38.6% | 45.2% | 15.3% |
| 13,230 | SHELBY | 6,544 | 2,809 | 2,094 | 1,614 | 27 | 715 R | 42.9% | 32.0% | 24.7% |
| 29,903 | SIOUX | 14,730 | 10,637 | 2,226 | 1,771 | 96 | 8,411 R | 72.2% | 15.1% | 12.0% |
| 74,252 | STORY | 36,311 | 12,702 | 17,118 | 6,275 | 216 | 4,416 D | 35.0% | 47.1% | 17.3% |
| 17,419 | TAMA | 8,330 | 2,948 | 3,573 | 1,748 | 61 | 625 D | 35.4% | 42.9% | 21.0% |
| 7,114 | TAYLOR | 3,551 | 1,200 | 1,430 | 910 | 11 | 230 D | 33.8% | 40.3% | 25.6% |
| 12,750 | UNION | 6,102 | 2,224 | 2,565 | 1,280 | 33 | 341 D | 36.4% | 42.0% | 21.0% |
| 7,676 | VAN BUREN | 3,710 | 1,418 | 1,464 | 811 | 17 | 46 D | 38.2% | 39.5% | 21.9% |
| 35,687 | WAPELLO | 16,083 | 4,852 | 8,670 | 2,513 | 48 | 3,818 D | 30.2% | 53.9% | 15.6% |
| 36,033 | WARREN | 19,157 | 7,242 | 8,612 | 3,217 | 86 | 1,370 D | 37.8% | 45.0% | 16.8% |
| 19,612 | WASHINGTON | 9,018 | 3,576 | 3,384 | 1,994 | 64 | 192 R | 39.7% | 37.5% | 22.1% |
| 7,067 | WAYNE | 3,584 | 1,299 | 1,632 | 642 | 11 | 333 D | 36.2% | 45.5% | 17.9% |
| 40,342 | WEBSTER | 18,921 | 6,992 | 8,562 | 3,272 | 95 | 1,570 D | 37.0% | 45.3% | 17.3% |
| 12,122 | WINNEBAGO | 6,078 | 2,407 | 2,322 | 1,329 | 20 | 85 R | 39.6% | 38.2% | 21.9% |
| 20,847 | WINNESHIEK | 9,624 | 3,331 | 3,791 | 2,416 | 86 | 460 D | 34.6% | 39.4% | 25.1% |
| 98,276 | WOODBURY | 42,864 | 18,148 | 17,398 | 7,182 | 136 | 750 R | 42.3% | 40.6% | 16.8% |
| 7,991 | WORTH | 4,448 | 1,382 | 2,009 | 1,044 | 13 | 627 D | 31.1% | 45.2% | 23.5% |
| 14,269 | WRIGHT | 6,665 | 2,708 | 2,776 | 1,151 | 30 | 68 D | 40.6% | 41.7% | 17.3% |
| 2,776,755 | TOTAL | 1,354,607 | 504,891 | 586,353 | 253,468 | 9,895 | 81,462 D | 37.3% | 43.3% | 18.7% |

# IOWA

## PRESIDENT 1988

| 1980 Census Population | County | Total Vote | Republican | Democratic | Other | Rep.-Dem. Plurality | Percentage Total Vote Rep. | Dem. | Major Vote Rep. | Dem. |
|---|---|---|---|---|---|---|---|---|---|---|
| 9,509 | ADAIR | 4,123 | 1,833 | 2,261 | 29 | 428 D | 44.5% | 54.8% | 44.8% | 55.2% |
| 5,731 | ADAMS | 2,380 | 1,080 | 1,283 | 17 | 203 D | 45.4% | 53.9% | 45.7% | 54.3% |
| 15,108 | ALLAMAKEE | 5,995 | 3,186 | 2,768 | 41 | 418 R | 53.1% | 46.2% | 53.5% | 46.5% |
| 15,511 | APPANOOSE | 6,088 | 2,779 | 3,209 | 100 | 430 D | 45.6% | 52.7% | 46.4% | 53.6% |
| 8,559 | AUDUBON | 3,371 | 1,478 | 1,863 | 30 | 385 D | 43.8% | 55.3% | 44.2% | 55.8% |
| 23,649 | BENTON | 9,977 | 4,011 | 5,873 | 93 | 1,862 D | 40.2% | 58.9% | 40.6% | 59.4% |
| 137,961 | BLACK HAWK | 56,171 | 24,112 | 31,657 | 402 | 7,545 D | 42.9% | 56.4% | 43.2% | 56.8% |
| 26,184 | BOONE | 11,686 | 4,381 | 7,232 | 73 | 2,851 D | 37.5% | 61.9% | 37.7% | 62.3% |
| 24,820 | BREMER | 10,099 | 5,079 | 4,961 | 59 | 118 R | 50.3% | 49.1% | 50.6% | 49.4% |
| 22,900 | BUCHANAN | 8,321 | 3,495 | 4,778 | 48 | 1,283 D | 42.0% | 57.4% | 42.2% | 57.8% |
| 20,774 | BUENA VISTA | 8,825 | 4,170 | 4,580 | 75 | 410 D | 47.3% | 51.9% | 47.7% | 52.3% |
| 17,668 | BUTLER | 6,146 | 3,523 | 2,593 | 30 | 930 R | 57.3% | 42.2% | 57.6% | 42.4% |
| 13,542 | CALHOUN | 5,505 | 2,474 | 2,990 | 41 | 516 D | 44.9% | 54.3% | 45.3% | 54.7% |
| 22,951 | CARROLL | 9,273 | 3,701 | 5,437 | 135 | 1,736 D | 39.9% | 58.6% | 40.5% | 59.5% |
| 16,932 | CASS | 6,968 | 3,962 | 2,934 | 72 | 1,028 R | 56.9% | 42.1% | 57.5% | 42.5% |
| 18,635 | CEDAR | 7,479 | 3,373 | 4,032 | 74 | 659 D | 45.1% | 53.9% | 45.6% | 54.4% |
| 48,458 | CERRO GORDO | 22,365 | 9,358 | 12,857 | 150 | 3,499 D | 41.8% | 57.5% | 42.1% | 57.9% |
| 16,238 | CHEROKEE | 6,855 | 3,218 | 3,574 | 63 | 356 D | 46.9% | 52.1% | 47.4% | 52.6% |
| 15,437 | CHICKASAW | 6,136 | 2,549 | 3,530 | 57 | 981 D | 41.5% | 57.5% | 41.9% | 58.1% |
| 8,612 | CLARKE | 3,934 | 1,631 | 2,262 | 41 | 631 D | 41.5% | 57.5% | 41.9% | 58.1% |
| 19,576 | CLAY | 7,870 | 3,641 | 4,173 | 56 | 532 D | 46.3% | 53.0% | 46.6% | 53.4% |
| 21,098 | CLAYTON | 8,242 | 3,839 | 4,320 | 83 | 481 D | 46.6% | 52.4% | 47.1% | 52.9% |
| 57,122 | CLINTON | 23,002 | 10,243 | 12,549 | 210 | 2,306 D | 44.5% | 54.6% | 44.9% | 55.1% |
| 18,935 | CRAWFORD | 7,311 | 3,375 | 3,868 | 68 | 493 D | 46.2% | 52.9% | 46.6% | 53.4% |
| 29,513 | DALLAS | 12,419 | 4,858 | 7,501 | 60 | 2,643 D | 39.1% | 60.4% | 39.3% | 60.7% |
| 9,104 | DAVIS | 3,849 | 1,563 | 2,246 | 40 | 683 D | 40.6% | 58.4% | 41.0% | 59.0% |
| 9,794 | DECATUR | 3,627 | 1,406 | 2,192 | 29 | 786 D | 38.8% | 60.4% | 39.1% | 60.9% |
| 18,933 | DELAWARE | 7,432 | 3,425 | 3,947 | 60 | 522 D | 46.1% | 53.1% | 46.5% | 53.5% |
| 46,203 | DES MOINES | 19,374 | 7,652 | 11,593 | 129 | 3,941 D | 39.5% | 59.8% | 39.8% | 60.2% |
| 15,629 | DICKINSON | 7,101 | 3,678 | 3,342 | 81 | 336 R | 51.8% | 47.1% | 52.4% | 47.6% |
| 93,745 | DUBUQUE | 38,547 | 14,530 | 23,797 | 220 | 9,267 D | 37.7% | 61.7% | 37.9% | 62.1% |
| 13,336 | EMMET | 4,977 | 2,173 | 2,778 | 26 | 605 D | 43.7% | 55.8% | 43.9% | 56.1% |
| 25,488 | FAYETTE | 10,287 | 4,921 | 5,304 | 62 | 383 D | 47.8% | 51.6% | 48.1% | 51.9% |
| 19,597 | FLOYD | 7,733 | 3,266 | 4,377 | 90 | 1,111 D | 42.2% | 56.6% | 42.7% | 57.3% |
| 13,036 | FRANKLIN | 4,951 | 2,320 | 2,594 | 37 | 274 D | 46.9% | 52.4% | 47.2% | 52.8% |
| 9,401 | FREMONT | 3,527 | 1,946 | 1,547 | 34 | 399 R | 55.2% | 43.9% | 55.7% | 44.3% |
| 12,119 | GREENE | 5,164 | 2,091 | 3,011 | 62 | 920 D | 40.5% | 58.3% | 41.0% | 59.0% |
| 14,366 | GRUNDY | 5,682 | 3,433 | 2,211 | 38 | 1,222 R | 60.4% | 38.9% | 60.8% | 39.2% |
| 11,983 | GUTHRIE | 4,983 | 2,005 | 2,910 | 68 | 905 D | 40.2% | 58.4% | 40.8% | 59.2% |
| 17,862 | HAMILTON | 7,494 | 3,277 | 4,156 | 61 | 879 D | 43.7% | 55.5% | 44.1% | 55.9% |
| 13,833 | HANCOCK | 5,593 | 2,731 | 2,831 | 31 | 100 D | 48.8% | 50.6% | 49.1% | 50.9% |
| 21,776 | HARDIN | 9,001 | 3,856 | 5,088 | 57 | 1,232 D | 42.8% | 56.5% | 43.1% | 56.9% |
| 16,348 | HARRISON | 6,027 | 3,108 | 2,883 | 36 | 225 R | 51.6% | 47.8% | 51.9% | 48.1% |
| 18,890 | HENRY | 7,758 | 3,951 | 3,754 | 53 | 197 R | 50.9% | 48.4% | 51.3% | 48.7% |
| 11,114 | HOWARD | 4,325 | 1,970 | 2,330 | 25 | 360 D | 45.5% | 53.9% | 45.8% | 54.2% |
| 12,246 | HUMBOLDT | 5,357 | 2,594 | 2,713 | 50 | 119 D | 48.4% | 50.6% | 48.9% | 51.1% |
| 8,908 | IDA | 3,779 | 1,951 | 1,787 | 41 | 164 R | 51.6% | 47.3% | 52.2% | 47.8% |
| 15,429 | IOWA | 6,685 | 3,247 | 3,338 | 100 | 91 D | 48.6% | 49.9% | 49.3% | 50.7% |
| 22,503 | JACKSON | 8,233 | 3,237 | 4,864 | 132 | 1,627 D | 39.3% | 59.1% | 40.0% | 60.0% |
| 36,425 | JASPER | 15,733 | 6,703 | 8,940 | 90 | 2,237 D | 42.6% | 56.8% | 42.8% | 57.2% |
| 16,316 | JEFFERSON | 7,296 | 3,614 | 3,594 | 88 | 20 R | 49.5% | 49.3% | 50.1% | 49.9% |
| 81,717 | JOHNSON | 44,647 | 15,453 | 28,759 | 435 | 13,306 D | 34.6% | 64.4% | 35.0% | 65.0% |
| 20,401 | JONES | 8,185 | 3,496 | 4,641 | 48 | 1,145 D | 42.7% | 56.7% | 43.0% | 57.0% |
| 12,921 | KEOKUK | 5,230 | 2,278 | 2,899 | 53 | 621 D | 43.6% | 55.4% | 44.0% | 56.0% |
| 21,891 | KOSSUTH | 9,107 | 3,938 | 5,088 | 81 | 1,150 D | 43.2% | 55.9% | 43.6% | 56.4% |
| 43,106 | LEE | 17,290 | 6,228 | 10,911 | 151 | 4,683 D | 36.0% | 63.1% | 36.3% | 63.7% |
| 169,775 | LINN | 76,718 | 33,129 | 42,993 | 596 | 9,864 D | 43.2% | 56.0% | 43.5% | 56.5% |
| 12,055 | LOUISA | 4,380 | 2,060 | 2,268 | 52 | 208 D | 47.0% | 51.8% | 47.6% | 52.4% |
| 10,313 | LUCAS | 4,243 | 1,776 | 2,454 | 13 | 678 D | 41.9% | 57.8% | 42.0% | 58.0% |
| 12,896 | LYON | 5,264 | 3,517 | 1,706 | 41 | 1,811 R | 66.8% | 32.4% | 67.3% | 32.7% |

# IOWA

## PRESIDENT 1988

| 1980 Census Population | County | Total Vote | Republican | Democratic | Other | Rep.-Dem. Plurality | Percentage Total Vote Rep. | Dem. | Major Vote Rep. | Dem. |
|---|---|---|---|---|---|---|---|---|---|---|
| 12,597 | MADISON | 5,862 | 2,410 | 3,421 | 31 | 1,011 D | 41.1% | 58.4% | 41.3% | 58.7% |
| 22,867 | MAHASKA | 9,320 | 4,798 | 4,451 | 71 | 347 R | 51.5% | 47.8% | 51.9% | 48.1% |
| 29,669 | MARION | 12,954 | 5,914 | 6,922 | 118 | 1,008 D | 45.7% | 53.4% | 46.1% | 53.9% |
| 41,652 | MARSHALL | 17,549 | 7,657 | 9,760 | 132 | 2,103 D | 43.6% | 55.6% | 44.0% | 56.0% |
| 13,406 | MILLS | 5,369 | 3,212 | 2,092 | 65 | 1,120 R | 59.8% | 39.0% | 60.6% | 39.4% |
| 12,329 | MITCHELL | 5,251 | 2,338 | 2,870 | 43 | 532 D | 44.5% | 54.7% | 44.9% | 55.1% |
| 11,692 | MONONA | 4,491 | 2,068 | 2,408 | 15 | 340 D | 46.0% | 53.6% | 46.2% | 53.8% |
| 9,209 | MONROE | 3,667 | 1,313 | 2,338 | 16 | 1,025 D | 35.8% | 63.8% | 36.0% | 64.0% |
| 13,413 | MONTGOMERY | 5,100 | 3,166 | 1,898 | 36 | 1,268 R | 62.1% | 37.2% | 62.5% | 37.5% |
| 40,436 | MUSCATINE | 14,102 | 6,904 | 7,059 | 139 | 155 D | 49.0% | 50.1% | 49.4% | 50.6% |
| 16,972 | O'BRIEN | 7,072 | 4,241 | 2,768 | 63 | 1,473 R | 60.0% | 39.1% | 60.5% | 39.5% |
| 8,371 | OSCEOLA | 3,264 | 1,951 | 1,277 | 36 | 674 R | 59.8% | 39.1% | 60.4% | 39.6% |
| 19,063 | PAGE | 6,803 | 4,583 | 2,185 | 35 | 2,398 R | 67.4% | 32.1% | 67.7% | 32.3% |
| 12,721 | PALO ALTO | 5,463 | 2,041 | 3,377 | 45 | 1,336 D | 37.4% | 61.8% | 37.7% | 62.3% |
| 24,743 | PLYMOUTH | 9,607 | 5,316 | 4,220 | 71 | 1,096 R | 55.3% | 43.9% | 55.7% | 44.3% |
| 11,369 | POCAHONTAS | 4,652 | 1,871 | 2,722 | 59 | 851 D | 40.2% | 58.5% | 40.7% | 59.3% |
| 303,170 | POLK | 143,144 | 57,854 | 84,476 | 814 | 26,622 D | 40.4% | 59.0% | 40.6% | 59.4% |
| 86,561 | POTTAWATTAMIE | 32,405 | 17,193 | 14,958 | 254 | 2,235 R | 53.1% | 4C.2% | 53.5% | 46.5% |
| 19,306 | POWESHIEK | 8,625 | 3,683 | 4,876 | 66 | 1,193 D | 42.7% | 56.5% | 43.0% | 57.0% |
| 6,112 | RINGGOLD | 2,731 | 1,110 | 1,609 | 12 | 499 D | 40.6% | 58.9% | 40.8% | 59.2% |
| 14,118 | SAC | 5,077 | 2,411 | 2,613 | 53 | 202 D | 47.5% | 51.5% | 48.0% | 52.0% |
| 160,022 | SCOTT | 66,035 | 31,025 | 34,415 | 595 | 3,390 D | 47.0% | 52.1% | 47.4% | 52.6% |
| 15,043 | SHELBY | 5,860 | 3,019 | 2,806 | 35 | 213 R | 51.5% | 47.9% | 51.8% | 48.2% |
| 30,813 | SIOUX | 13,288 | 10,270 | 2,923 | 95 | 7,347 R | 77.3% | 22.0% | 77.8% | 22.2% |
| 72,326 | STORY | 33,105 | 13,782 | 19,051 | 272 | 5,269 D | 41.6% | 57.5% | 42.0% | 58.0% |
| 19,533 | TAMA | 8,012 | 3,362 | 4,584 | 66 | 1,222 D | 42.0% | 57.2% | 42.3% | 57.7% |
| 8,353 | TAYLOR | 3,332 | 1,647 | 1,671 | 14 | 24 D | 49.4% | 50.2% | 49.6% | 50.4% |
| 13,858 | UNION | 6,041 | 2,751 | 3,236 | 54 | 485 D | 45.5% | 53.6% | 45.9% | 54.1% |
| 8,626 | VAN BUREN | 3,334 | 1,692 | 1,612 | 30 | 80 R | 50.7% | 48.4% | 51.2% | 48.8% |
| 40,241 | WAPELLO | 15,673 | 5,350 | 10,177 | 146 | 4,827 D | 34.1% | 64.9% | 34.5% | 65.5% |
| 34,878 | WARREN | 16,131 | 6,424 | 9,627 | 80 | 3,203 D | 39.8% | 59.7% | 40.0% | 60.0% |
| 20,141 | WASHINGTON | 7,616 | 3,741 | 3,776 | 99 | 35 D | 49.1% | 49.6% | 49.8% | 50.2% |
| 8,199 | WAYNE | 3,477 | 1,467 | 1,988 | 22 | 521 D | 42.2% | 57.2% | 42.5% | 57.5% |
| 45,953 | WEBSTER | 17,393 | 6,926 | 10,267 | 200 | 3,341 D | 39.8% | 59.0% | 40.3% | 59.7% |
| 13,010 | WINNEBAGO | 5,703 | 2,863 | 2,804 | 36 | 59 R | 50.2% | 49.2% | 50.5% | 49.5% |
| 21,876 | WINNESHIEK | 8,725 | 4,194 | 4,443 | 88 | 249 D | 48.1% | 50.9% | 48.6% | 51.4% |
| 100,884 | WOODBURY | 39,225 | 18,790 | 20,153 | 282 | 1,363 D | 47.9% | 51.4% | 48.3% | 51.7% |
| 9,075 | WORTH | 3,982 | 1,488 | 2,440 | 54 | 952 D | 37.4% | 61.3% | 37.9% | 62.1% |
| 16,319 | WRIGHT | 6,054 | 2,658 | 3,353 | 43 | 695 D | 43.9% | 55.4% | 44.2% | 55.8% |
| 2,913,808 | TOTAL | 1,225,614 | 545,355 | 670,557 | 9,702 | 125,202 D | 44.5% | 54.7% | 44.9% | 55.1% |

# IOWA

## PRESIDENT 1984

| 1980 Census Population | County | Total Vote | Republican | Democratic | Other | Rep.-Dem. Plurality | Percentage | | | |
|---|---|---|---|---|---|---|---|---|---|---|
| | | | | | | | Total Vote | | Major Vote | |
| | | | | | | | Rep. | Dem. | Rep. | Dem. |
| 9,509 | ADAIR | 4,619 | 2,615 | 1,979 | 25 | 636 R | 56.6% | 42.8% | 56.9% | 43.1% |
| 5,731 | ADAMS | 2,960 | 1,706 | 1,221 | 33 | 485 R | 57.6% | 41.3% | 58.3% | 41.7% |
| 15,108 | ALLAMAKEE | 6,354 | 3,997 | 2,282 | 75 | 1,715 R | 62.9% | 35.9% | 63.7% | 36.3% |
| 15,511 | APPANOOSE | 6,759 | 3,412 | 3,289 | 58 | 123 R | 50.5% | 48.7% | 50.9% | 49.1% |
| 8,559 | AUDUBON | 4,195 | 2,306 | 1,854 | 35 | 452 R | 55.0% | 44.2% | 55.4% | 44.6% |
| 23,649 | BENTON | 10,678 | 5,566 | 4,993 | 119 | 573 R | 52.1% | 46.8% | 52.7% | 47.3% |
| 137,961 | BLACK HAWK | 64,233 | 32,262 | 31,467 | 504 | 795 R | 50.2% | 49.0% | 50.6% | 49.4% |
| 26,184 | BOONE | 12,277 | 5,746 | 6,485 | 46 | 739 D | 46.8% | 52.8% | 47.0% | 53.0% |
| 24,820 | BREMER | 11,055 | 6,895 | 4,084 | 76 | 2,811 R | 62.4% | 36.9% | 62.8% | 37.2% |
| 22,900 | BUCHANAN | 9,152 | 4,965 | 4,129 | 58 | 836 R | 54.3% | 45.1% | 54.6% | 45.4% |
| 20,774 | BUENA VISTA | 9,405 | 5,193 | 4,109 | 103 | 1,084 R | 55.2% | 43.7% | 55.8% | 44.2% |
| 17,668 | BUTLER | 6,924 | 4,570 | 2,323 | 31 | 2,247 R | 66.0% | 33.5% | 66.3% | 33.7% |
| 13,542 | CALHOUN | 5,898 | 3,311 | 2,541 | 46 | 770 R | 56.1% | 43.1% | 56.6% | 43.4% |
| 22,951 | CARROLL | 10,077 | 5,021 | 4,960 | 96 | 61 R | 49.8% | 49.2% | 50.3% | 49.7% |
| 16,932 | CASS | 7,531 | 5,053 | 2,417 | 61 | 2,636 R | 67.1% | 32.1% | 67.6% | 32.4% |
| 18,635 | CEDAR | 7,748 | 4,617 | 3,086 | 45 | 1,531 R | 59.6% | 39.8% | 59.9% | 40.1% |
| 48,458 | CERRO GORDO | 22,950 | 11,214 | 11,570 | 166 | 356 D | 48.9% | 50.4% | 49.2% | 50.8% |
| 16,238 | CHEROKEE | 7,470 | 4,046 | 3,349 | 75 | 697 R | 54.2% | 44.8% | 54.7% | 45.3% |
| 15,437 | CHICKASAW | 6,917 | 3,661 | 3,186 | 70 | 475 R | 52.9% | 46.1% | 53.5% | 46.5% |
| 8,612 | CLARKE | 4,321 | 2,262 | 2,030 | 29 | 232 R | 52.3% | 47.0% | 52.7% | 47.3% |
| 19,576 | CLAY | 8,316 | 4,450 | 3,774 | 92 | 676 R | 53.5% | 45.4% | 54.1% | 45.9% |
| 21,098 | CLAYTON | 8,553 | 5,029 | 3,446 | 78 | 1,583 R | 58.8% | 40.3% | 59.3% | 40.7% |
| 57,122 | CLINTON | 25,404 | 13,914 | 11,240 | 250 | 2,674 R | 54.8% | 44.2% | 55.3% | 44.7% |
| 18,935 | CRAWFORD | 8,053 | 4,552 | 3,396 | 105 | 1,156 R | 56.5% | 42.2% | 57.3% | 42.7% |
| 29,513 | DALLAS | 12,707 | 6,080 | 6,564 | 63 | 484 D | 47.8% | 51.7% | 48.1% | 51.9% |
| 9,104 | DAVIS | 4,182 | 1,956 | 2,187 | 39 | 231 D | 46.8% | 52.3% | 47.2% | 52.8% |
| 9,794 | DECATUR | 4,242 | 2,104 | 2,098 | 40 | 6 R | 49.6% | 49.5% | 50.1% | 49.9% |
| 18,933 | DELAWARE | 8,001 | 4,769 | 3,158 | 74 | 1,611 R | 59.6% | 39.5% | 60.2% | 39.8% |
| 46,203 | DES MOINES | 20,850 | 9,559 | 11,173 | 118 | 1,614 D | 45.8% | 53.6% | 46.1% | 53.9% |
| 15,629 | DICKINSON | 7,170 | 4,064 | 3,025 | 81 | 1,039 R | 56.7% | 42.2% | 57.3% | 42.7% |
| 93,745 | DUBUQUE | 41,491 | 19,239 | 21,876 | 376 | 2,637 D | 46.4% | 52.7% | 46.8% | 53.2% |
| 13,336 | EMMET | 5,725 | 2,946 | 2,746 | 33 | 200 R | 51.5% | 48.0% | 51.8% | 48.2% |
| 25,488 | FAYETTE | 11,302 | 6,505 | 4,677 | 120 | 1,828 R | 57.6% | 41.4% | 58.2% | 41.8% |
| 19,597 | FLOYD | 8,553 | 4,341 | 4,154 | 58 | 187 R | 50.8% | 48.6% | 51.1% | 48.9% |
| 13,036 | FRANKLIN | 5,545 | 3,129 | 2,349 | 67 | 780 R | 56.4% | 42.4% | 57.1% | 42.9% |
| 9,401 | FREMONT | 4,147 | 2,686 | 1,426 | 35 | 1,260 R | 64.8% | 34.4% | 65.3% | 34.7% |
| 12,119 | GREENE | 5,554 | 2,579 | 2,831 | 144 | 252 D | 46.4% | 51.0% | 47.7% | 52.3% |
| 14,366 | GRUNDY | 6,518 | 4,527 | 1,915 | 76 | 2,612 R | 69.5% | 29.4% | 70.3% | 29.7% |
| 11,983 | GUTHRIE | 5,363 | 2,783 | 2,517 | 63 | 266 R | 51.9% | 46.9% | 52.5% | 47.5% |
| 17,862 | HAMILTON | 7,695 | 4,279 | 3,330 | 86 | 949 R | 55.6% | 43.3% | 56.2% | 43.8% |
| 13,833 | HANCOCK | 5,938 | 3,362 | 2,539 | 37 | 823 R | 56.6% | 42.8% | 57.0% | 43.0% |
| 21,776 | HARDIN | 9,732 | 5,195 | 4,477 | 60 | 718 R | 53.4% | 46.0% | 53.7% | 46.3% |
| 16,348 | HARRISON | 6,882 | 4,352 | 2,495 | 35 | 1,857 R | 63.2% | 36.3% | 63.6% | 36.4% |
| 18,890 | HENRY | 7,955 | 4,516 | 3,377 | 62 | 1,139 R | 56.8% | 42.5% | 57.2% | 42.8% |
| 11,114 | HOWARD | 4,898 | 2,718 | 2,135 | 45 | 583 R | 55.5% | 43.6% | 56.0% | 44.0% |
| 12,246 | HUMBOLDT | 5,863 | 3,396 | 2,406 | 61 | 990 R | 57.9% | 41.0% | 58.5% | 41.5% |
| 8,908 | IDA | 4,202 | 2,618 | 1,559 | 25 | 1,059 R | 62.3% | 37.1% | 62.7% | 37.3% |
| 15,429 | IOWA | 7,251 | 4,352 | 2,815 | 84 | 1,537 R | 60.0% | 38.8% | 60.7% | 39.3% |
| 22,503 | JACKSON | 9,340 | 4,811 | 4,400 | 129 | 411 R | 51.5% | 47.1% | 52.2% | 47.8% |
| 36,425 | JASPER | 16,699 | 8,576 | 8,023 | 100 | 553 R | 51.4% | 48.0% | 51.7% | 48.3% |
| 16,316 | JEFFERSON | 7,725 | 4,727 | 2,961 | 37 | 1,766 R | 61.2% | 38.3% | 61.5% | 38.5% |
| 81,717 | JOHNSON | 45,044 | 18,677 | 26,000 | 367 | 7,323 D | 41.5% | 57.7% | 41.8% | 58.2% |
| 20,401 | JONES | 8,791 | 4,907 | 3,825 | 59 | 1,082 R | 55.8% | 43.5% | 56.2% | 43.8% |
| 12,921 | KEOKUK | 5,656 | 2,913 | 2,649 | 94 | 264 R | 51.5% | 46.8% | 52.4% | 47.6% |
| 21,891 | KOSSUTH | 9,814 | 4,872 | 4,838 | 104 | 34 R | 49.6% | 49.3% | 50.2% | 49.8% |
| 43,106 | LEE | 17,809 | 8,756 | 8,912 | 141 | 156 D | 49.2% | 50.0% | 49.6% | 50.4% |
| 169,775 | LINN | 80,315 | 41,061 | 38,528 | 726 | 2,533 R | 51.1% | 48.0% | 51.6% | 48.4% |
| 12,055 | LOUISA | 4,573 | 2,623 | 1,927 | 23 | 696 R | 57.4% | 42.1% | 57.6% | 42.4% |
| 10,313 | LUCAS | 5,085 | 2,630 | 2,422 | 33 | 208 R | 51.7% | 47.6% | 52.1% | 47.9% |
| 12,896 | LYON | 5,642 | 4,178 | 1,401 | 63 | 2,777 R | 74.1% | 24.8% | 74.9% | 25.1% |

# IOWA

## PRESIDENT 1984

| 1980 Census Population | County | Total Vote | Republican | Democratic | Other | Rep.-Dem. Plurality | | Percentage | | | |
|---|---|---|---|---|---|---|---|---|---|---|---|
| | | | | | | | | Total Vote | | Major Vote | |
| | | | | | | | | Rep. | Dem. | Rep. | Dem. |
| 12,597 | MADISON | 6,261 | 3,168 | 3,067 | 26 | 101 | R | 50.6% | 49.0% | 50.8% | 49.2% |
| 22,867 | MAHASKA | 10,293 | 6,086 | 4,107 | 100 | 1,979 | R | 59.1% | 39.9% | 59.7% | 40.3% |
| 29,669 | MARION | 13,634 | 7,259 | 6,313 | 62 | 946 | R | 53.2% | 46.3% | 53.5% | 46.5% |
| 41,652 | MARSHALL | 19,840 | 10,839 | 8,809 | 192 | 2,030 | R | 54.6% | 44.4% | 55.2% | 44.8% |
| 13,406 | MILLS | 5,486 | 3,994 | 1,434 | 58 | 2,560 | R | 72.8% | 26.1% | 73.6% | 26.4% |
| 12,329 | MITCHELL | 5,743 | 3,144 | 2,531 | 68 | 613 | R | 54.7% | 44.1% | 55.4% | 44.6% |
| 11,692 | MONONA | 4,959 | 2,746 | 2,159 | 54 | 587 | R | 55.4% | 43.5% | 56.0% | 44.0% |
| 9,209 | MONROE | 4,291 | 1,927 | 2,342 | 22 | 415 | D | 44.9% | 54.6% | 45.1% | 54.9% |
| 13,413 | MONTGOMERY | 5,930 | 4,224 | 1,661 | 45 | 2,563 | R | 71.2% | 28.0% | 71.8% | 28.2% |
| 40,436 | MUSCATINE | 15,168 | 9,069 | 5,986 | 113 | 3,083 | R | 59.8% | 39.5% | 60.2% | 39.8% |
| 16,972 | O'BRIEN | 7,569 | 5,008 | 2,479 | 82 | 2,529 | R | 66.2% | 32.8% | 66.9% | 33.1% |
| 8,371 | OSCEOLA | 3,463 | 2,285 | 1,146 | 32 | 1,139 | R | 66.0% | 33.1% | 66.6% | 33.4% |
| 19,063 | PAGE | 7,828 | 5,876 | 1,914 | 38 | 3,962 | R | 75.1% | 24.5% | 75.4% | 24.6% |
| 12,721 | PALO ALTO | 5,810 | 2,715 | 3,018 | 77 | 303 | D | 46.7% | 51.9% | 47.4% | 52.6% |
| 24,743 | PLYMOUTH | 10,027 | 6,482 | 3,464 | 81 | 3,018 | R | 64.6% | 34.5% | 65.2% | 34.8% |
| 11,369 | POCAHONTAS | 5,188 | 2,627 | 2,481 | 80 | 146 | R | 50.6% | 47.8% | 51.4% | 48.6% |
| 303,170 | POLK | 147,848 | 71,413 | 75,413 | 1,022 | 4,000 | D | 48.3% | 51.0% | 48.6% | 51.4% |
| 86,561 | POTTAWATTAMIE | 34,112 | 21,527 | 12,329 | 256 | 9,198 | R | 63.1% | 36.1% | 63.6% | 36.4% |
| 19,306 | POWESHIEK | 8,889 | 4,715 | 4,103 | 71 | 612 | R | 53.0% | 46.2% | 53.5% | 46.5% |
| 6,112 | RINGGOLD | 3,117 | 1,512 | 1,593 | 12 | 81 | D | 48.5% | 51.1% | 48.7% | 51.3% |
| 14,118 | SAC | 5,729 | 3,298 | 2,363 | 68 | 935 | R | 57.6% | 41.2% | 58.3% | 41.7% |
| 160,022 | SCOTT | 71,212 | 38,034 | 32,550 | 628 | 5,484 | R | 53.4% | 45.7% | 53.9% | 46.1% |
| 15,043 | SHELBY | 6,537 | 4,200 | 2,291 | 46 | 1,909 | R | 64.2% | 35.0% | 64.7% | 35.3% |
| 30,813 | SIOUX | 14,293 | 11,665 | 2,585 | 43 | 9,080 | R | 81.6% | 18.1% | 81.9% | 18.1% |
| 72,326 | STORY | 38,410 | 19,804 | 18,277 | 329 | 1,527 | R | 51.6% | 47.6% | 52.0% | 48.0% |
| 19,533 | TAMA | 8,990 | 4,882 | 4,061 | 47 | 821 | R | 54.3% | 45.2% | 54.6% | 45.4% |
| 8,353 | TAYLOR | 4,022 | 2,496 | 1,499 | 27 | 997 | R | 62.1% | 37.3% | 62.5% | 37.5% |
| 13,858 | UNION | 6,576 | 3,583 | 2,875 | 118 | 708 | R | 54.5% | 43.7% | 55.5% | 44.5% |
| 8,626 | VAN BUREN | 3,769 | 2,138 | 1,606 | 25 | 532 | R | 56.7% | 42.6% | 57.1% | 42.9% |
| 40,241 | WAPELLO | 17,800 | 7,098 | 10,545 | 157 | 3,447 | D | 39.9% | 59.2% | 40.2% | 59.8% |
| 34,878 | WARREN | 16,570 | 8,277 | 8,171 | 122 | 106 | R | 50.0% | 49.3% | 50.3% | 49.7% |
| 20,141 | WASHINGTON | 7,770 | 4,613 | 3,079 | 78 | 1,534 | R | 59.4% | 39.6% | 60.0% | 40.0% |
| 8,199 | WAYNE | 4,021 | 2,061 | 1,927 | 33 | 134 | R | 51.3% | 47.9% | 51.7% | 48.3% |
| 45,953 | WEBSTER | 19,802 | 9,619 | 9,930 | 253 | 311 | D | 48.6% | 50.1% | 49.2% | 50.8% |
| 13,010 | WINNEBAGO | 6,314 | 3,616 | 2,669 | 29 | 947 | R | 57.3% | 42.3% | 57.5% | 42.5% |
| 21,876 | WINNESHIEK | 9,105 | 5,277 | 3,724 | 104 | 1,553 | R | 58.0% | 40.9% | 58.6% | 41.4% |
| 100,884 | WOODBURY | 42,350 | 23,002 | 18,951 | 397 | 4,051 | R | 54.3% | 44.7% | 54.8% | 45.2% |
| 9,075 | WORTH | 4,266 | 1,985 | 2,263 | 18 | 278 | D | 46.5% | 53.0% | 46.7% | 53.3% |
| 16,319 | WRIGHT | 6,705 | 3,675 | 2,980 | 50 | 695 | R | 54.8% | 44.4% | 55.2% | 44.8% |
| 2,913,808 | TOTAL | 1,319,805 | 703,088 | 605,620 | 11,097 | 97,468 | R | 53.3% | 45.9% | 53.7% | 46.3% |

# IOWA

## PRESIDENT 1980

| 1980 Census Population | County | Total Vote | Republican | Democratic | Other | Rep.-Dem. Plurality | Percentage Total Vote Rep. | Dem. | Major Vote Rep. | Dem. |
|---|---|---|---|---|---|---|---|---|---|---|
| 9,509 | ADAIR | 4,689 | 2,821 | 1,454 | 414 | 1,367 R | 60.2% | 31.0% | 66.0% | 34.0% |
| 5,731 | ADAMS | 2,984 | 1,779 | 940 | 265 | 839 R | 59.6% | 31.5% | 65.4% | 34.6% |
| 15,108 | ALLAMAKEE | 6,586 | 4,000 | 2,170 | 416 | 1,830 R | 60.7% | 32.9% | 64.8% | 35.2% |
| 15,511 | APPANOOSE | 6,728 | 3,544 | 2,769 | 415 | 775 R | 52.7% | 41.2% | 56.1% | 43.9% |
| 8,559 | AUDUBON | 4,353 | 2,523 | 1,546 | 284 | 977 R | 58.0% | 35.5% | 62.0% | 38.0% |
| 23,649 | BENTON | 10,635 | 5,329 | 4,223 | 1,083 | 1,106 R | 50.1% | 39.7% | 55.8% | 44.2% |
| 137,961 | BLACK HAWK | 63,722 | 29,627 | 27,443 | 6,652 | 2,184 R | 46.5% | 43.1% | 51.9% | 48.1% |
| 26,184 | BOONE | 12,087 | 5,732 | 5,126 | 1,229 | 606 R | 47.4% | 42.4% | 52.8% | 47.2% |
| 24,820 | BREMER | 11,318 | 6,706 | 3,527 | 1,085 | 3,179 R | 59.3% | 31.2% | 65.5% | 34.5% |
| 22,900 | BUCHANAN | 9,422 | 5,041 | 3,605 | 776 | 1,436 R | 53.5% | 38.3% | 58.3% | 41.7% |
| 20,774 | BUENA VISTA | 9,676 | 5,272 | 3,468 | 936 | 1,804 R | 54.5% | 35.8% | 60.3% | 39.7% |
| 17,668 | BUTLER | 7,177 | 4,730 | 1,990 | 457 | 2,740 R | 65.9% | 27.7% | 70.4% | 29.6% |
| 13,542 | CALHOUN | 6,328 | 3,633 | 2,150 | 545 | 1,483 R | 57.4% | 34.0% | 62.8% | 37.2% |
| 22,951 | CARROLL | 9,737 | 5,017 | 3,885 | 835 | 1,132 R | 51.5% | 39.9% | 56.4% | 43.6% |
| 16,932 | CASS | 8,126 | 5,391 | 2,176 | 559 | 3,215 R | 66.3% | 26.8% | 71.2% | 28.8% |
| 18,635 | CEDAR | 7,797 | 4,398 | 2,589 | 810 | 1,809 R | 56.4% | 33.2% | 62.9% | 37.1% |
| 48,458 | CERRO GORDO | 22,828 | 11,189 | 9,363 | 2,276 | 1,826 R | 49.0% | 41.0% | 54.4% | 45.6% |
| 16,238 | CHEROKEE | 7,500 | 4,087 | 2,719 | 694 | 1,368 R | 54.5% | 36.3% | 60.0% | 40.0% |
| 15,437 | CHICKASAW | 7,433 | 3,929 | 2,935 | 569 | 994 R | 52.9% | 39.5% | 57.2% | 42.8% |
| 8,612 | CLARKE | 4,404 | 2,417 | 1,614 | 373 | 803 R | 54.9% | 36.6% | 60.0% | 40.0% |
| 19,576 | CLAY | 8,764 | 4,479 | 3,179 | 1,106 | 1,300 R | 51.1% | 36.3% | 58.5% | 41.5% |
| 21,098 | CLAYTON | 9,206 | 5,115 | 3,297 | 794 | 1,818 R | 55.6% | 35.8% | 60.8% | 39.2% |
| 57,122 | CLINTON | 25,211 | 13,025 | 9,698 | 2,488 | 3,327 R | 51.7% | 38.5% | 57.3% | 42.7% |
| 18,935 | CRAWFORD | 8,002 | 4,883 | 2,500 | 619 | 2,383 R | 61.0% | 31.2% | 66.1% | 33.9% |
| 29,513 | DALLAS | 12,964 | 6,296 | 5,310 | 1,358 | 986 R | 48.6% | 41.0% | 54.2% | 45.8% |
| 9,104 | DAVIS | 3,930 | 2,003 | 1,689 | 238 | 314 R | 51.0% | 43.0% | 54.3% | 45.7% |
| 9,794 | DECATUR | 4,640 | 2,212 | 2,048 | 380 | 164 R | 47.7% | 44.1% | 51.9% | 48.1% |
| 18,933 | DELAWARE | 7,794 | 4,316 | 2,671 | 807 | 1,645 R | 55.4% | 34.3% | 61.8% | 38.2% |
| 46,203 | DES MOINES | 20,417 | 9,158 | 9,977 | 1,282 | 819 D | 44.9% | 48.9% | 47.9% | 52.1% |
| 15,629 | DICKINSON | 7,442 | 4,028 | 2,620 | 794 | 1,408 R | 54.1% | 35.2% | 60.6% | 39.4% |
| 93,745 | DUBUQUE | 41,539 | 18,649 | 18,689 | 4,201 | 40 D | 44.9% | 45.0% | 49.9% | 50.1% |
| 13,336 | EMMET | 5,724 | 3,062 | 2,153 | 509 | 909 R | 53.5% | 37.6% | 58.7% | 41.3% |
| 25,488 | FAYETTE | 11,523 | 6,374 | 4,377 | 772 | 1,997 R | 55.3% | 38.0% | 59.3% | 40.7% |
| 19,597 | FLOYD | 9,118 | 4,665 | 3,634 | 819 | 1,031 R | 51.2% | 39.9% | 56.2% | 43.8% |
| 13,036 | FRANKLIN | 5,682 | 3,290 | 1,920 | 472 | 1,370 R | 57.9% | 33.8% | 63.1% | 36.9% |
| 9,401 | FREMONT | 4,131 | 2,693 | 1,203 | 235 | 1,490 R | 65.2% | 29.1% | 69.1% | 30.9% |
| 12,119 | GREENE | 5,939 | 3,154 | 2,210 | 575 | 944 R | 53.1% | 37.2% | 58.8% | 41.2% |
| 14,366 | GRUNDY | 7,026 | 4,644 | 1,869 | 513 | 2,775 R | 66.1% | 26.6% | 71.3% | 28.7% |
| 11,983 | GUTHRIE | 5,514 | 3,214 | 1,866 | 434 | 1,348 R | 58.3% | 33.8% | 63.3% | 36.7% |
| 17,862 | HAMILTON | 8,266 | 4,745 | 2,741 | 780 | 2,004 R | 57.4% | 33.2% | 63.4% | 36.6% |
| 13,833 | HANCOCK | 6,092 | 3,681 | 1,918 | 493 | 1,763 R | 60.4% | 31.5% | 65.7% | 34.3% |
| 21,776 | HARDIN | 9,920 | 5,329 | 3,757 | 834 | 1,572 R | 53.7% | 37.9% | 58.7% | 41.3% |
| 16,348 | HARRISON | 7,053 | 4,502 | 2,152 | 399 | 2,350 R | 63.8% | 30.5% | 67.7% | 32.3% |
| 18,890 | HENRY | 8,462 | 4,430 | 3,317 | 715 | 1,113 R | 52.4% | 39.2% | 57.2% | 42.8% |
| 11,114 | HOWARD | 5,576 | 2,975 | 2,214 | 387 | 761 R | 53.4% | 39.7% | 57.3% | 42.7% |
| 12,246 | HUMBOLDT | 5,899 | 3,575 | 1,840 | 484 | 1,735 R | 60.6% | 31.2% | 66.0% | 34.0% |
| 8,908 | IDA | 4,354 | 2,825 | 1,235 | 294 | 1,590 R | 64.9% | 28.4% | 69.6% | 30.4% |
| 15,429 | IOWA | 7,522 | 4,153 | 2,606 | 763 | 1,547 R | 55.2% | 34.6% | 61.4% | 38.6% |
| 22,503 | JACKSON | 8,754 | 4,479 | 3,518 | 757 | 961 R | 51.2% | 40.2% | 56.0% | 44.0% |
| 36,425 | JASPER | 16,966 | 8,286 | 7,258 | 1,422 | 1,028 R | 48.8% | 42.8% | 53.3% | 46.7% |
| 16,316 | JEFFERSON | 7,299 | 4,099 | 2,577 | 623 | 1,522 R | 56.2% | 35.3% | 61.4% | 38.6% |
| 81,717 | JOHNSON | 42,997 | 13,642 | 20,122 | 9,233 | 6,480 D | 31.7% | 46.8% | 40.4% | 59.6% |
| 20,401 | JONES | 8,913 | 4,506 | 3,521 | 886 | 985 R | 50.6% | 39.5% | 56.1% | 43.9% |
| 12,921 | KEOKUK | 5,975 | 3,145 | 2,390 | 440 | 755 R | 52.6% | 40.0% | 56.8% | 43.2% |
| 21,891 | KOSSUTH | 10,262 | 5,568 | 3,810 | 884 | 1,758 R | 54.3% | 37.1% | 59.4% | 40.6% |
| 43,106 | LEE | 18,265 | 8,793 | 8,204 | 1,268 | 589 R | 48.1% | 44.9% | 51.7% | 48.3% |
| 169,775 | LINN | 78,224 | 36,254 | 31,950 | 10,020 | 4,304 R | 46.3% | 40.8% | 53.2% | 46.8% |
| 12,055 | LOUISA | 4,584 | 2,530 | 1,700 | 354 | 830 R | 55.2% | 37.1% | 59.8% | 40.2% |
| 10,313 | LUCAS | 4,929 | 2,593 | 1,989 | 347 | 604 R | 52.6% | 40.4% | 56.6% | 43.4% |
| 12,896 | LYON | 6,208 | 4,349 | 1,431 | 428 | 2,918 R | 70.1% | 23.1% | 75.2% | 24.8% |

# IOWA

## PRESIDENT 1980

| 1980 Census Population | County | Total Vote | Republican | Democratic | Other | Rep.-Dem. Plurality | Percentage | | | |
|---|---|---|---|---|---|---|---|---|---|---|
| | | | | | | | Total Vote | | Major Vote | |
| | | | | | | | Rep. | Dem. | Rep. | Dem. |
| 12,597 | MADISON | 6,411 | 3,320 | 2,496 | 595 | 824 R | 51.8% | 38.9% | 57.1% | 42.9% |
| 22,867 | MAHASKA | 10,363 | 5,650 | 3,968 | 745 | 1,682 R | 54.5% | 38.3% | 58.7% | 41.3% |
| 29,669 | MARION | 13,518 | 6,665 | 5,490 | 1,363 | 1,175 R | 49.3% | 40.6% | 54.8% | 45.2% |
| 41,652 | MARSHALL | 19,626 | 10,707 | 7,114 | 1,805 | 3,593 R | 54.6% | 36.2% | 60.1% | 39.9% |
| 13,406 | MILLS | 5,183 | 3,581 | 1,244 | 358 | 2,337 R | 69.1% | 24.0% | 74.2% | 25.8% |
| 12,329 | MITCHELL | 5,864 | 3,401 | 2,040 | 423 | 1,361 R | 58.0% | 34.8% | 62.5% | 37.5% |
| 11,692 | MONONA | 5,284 | 3,268 | 1,660 | 356 | 1,608 R | 61.8% | 31.4% | 66.3% | 33.7% |
| 9,209 | MONROE | 4,117 | 2,003 | 1,866 | 248 | 137 R | 48.7% | 45.3% | 51.8% | 48.2% |
| 13,413 | MONTGOMERY | 6,054 | 4,115 | 1,556 | 383 | 2,559 R | 68.0% | 25.7% | 72.6% | 27.4% |
| 40,436 | MUSCATINE | 15,145 | 7,829 | 5,597 | 1,719 | 2,232 R | 51.7% | 37.0% | 58.3% | 41.7% |
| 16,972 | O'BRIEN | 7,761 | 4,937 | 2,210 | 614 | 2,727 R | 63.6% | 28.5% | 69.1% | 30.9% |
| 8,371 | OSCEOLA | 3,486 | 2,177 | 1,051 | 258 | 1,126 R | 62.4% | 30.1% | 67.4% | 32.6% |
| 19,063 | PAGE | 7,810 | 5,618 | 1,772 | 420 | 3,846 R | 71.9% | 22.7% | 76.0% | 24.0% |
| 12,721 | PALO ALTO | 5,968 | 3,025 | 2,463 | 480 | 562 R | 50.7% | 41.3% | 55.1% | 44.9% |
| 24,743 | PLYMOUTH | 10,346 | 6,515 | 2,965 | 866 | 3,550 R | 63.0% | 28.7% | 68.7% | 31.3% |
| 11,369 | POCAHONTAS | 5,686 | 3,194 | 1,959 | 533 | 1,235 R | 56.2% | 34.5% | 62.0% | 38.0% |
| 303,170 | POLK | 143,758 | 64,156 | 61,984 | 17,618 | 2,172 R | 44.6% | 43.1% | 50.9% | 49.1% |
| 86,561 | POTTAWATTAMIE | 33,170 | 20,222 | 10,709 | 2,239 | 9,513 R | 61.0% | 32.3% | 65.4% | 34.6% |
| 19,306 | POWESHIEK | 9,102 | 4,598 | 3,529 | 975 | 1,069 R | 50.5% | 38.8% | 56.6% | 43.4% |
| 6,112 | RINGGOLD | 3,251 | 1,884 | 1,150 | 217 | 734 R | 58.0% | 35.4% | 62.1% | 37.9% |
| 14,118 | SAC | 6,264 | 3,725 | 1,976 | 563 | 1,749 R | 59.5% | 31.5% | 65.3% | 34.7% |
| 160,022 | SCOTT | 67,926 | 34,701 | 26,391 | 6,834 | 8,310 R | 51.1% | 38.9% | 56.8% | 43.2% |
| 15,043 | SHELBY | 6,477 | 4,147 | 1,892 | 438 | 2,255 R | 64.0% | 29.2% | 68.7% | 31.3% |
| 30,813 | SIOUX | 14,167 | 10,768 | 2,698 | 701 | 8,070 R | 76.0% | 19.0% | 80.0% | 20.0% |
| 72,326 | STORY | 37,371 | 15,829 | 13,529 | 8,013 | 2,300 R | 42.4% | 36.2% | 53.9% | 46.1% |
| 19,533 | TAMA | 8,602 | 4,840 | 3,049 | 713 | 1,791 R | 56.3% | 35.4% | 61.4% | 38.6% |
| 8,353 | TAYLOR | 4,213 | 2,715 | 1,226 | 272 | 1,489 R | 64.4% | 29.1% | 68.9% | 31.1% |
| 13,858 | UNION | 5,979 | 3,372 | 2,182 | 425 | 1,190 R | 56.4% | 36.5% | 60.7% | 39.3% |
| 8,626 | VAN BUREN | 3,680 | 2,142 | 1,311 | 227 | 831 R | 58.2% | 35.6% | 62.0% | 38.0% |
| 40,241 | WAPELLO | 17,668 | 7,475 | 8,923 | 1,270 | 1,448 D | 42.3% | 50.5% | 45.6% | 54.4% |
| 34,878 | WARREN | 15,519 | 7,360 | 6,610 | 1,549 | 750 R | 47.4% | 42.6% | 52.7% | 47.3% |
| 20,141 | WASHINGTON | 7,627 | 3,967 | 2,877 | 783 | 1,090 R | 52.0% | 37.7% | 58.0% | 42.0% |
| 8,199 | WAYNE | 4,104 | 2,221 | 1,627 | 256 | 594 R | 54.1% | 39.6% | 57.7% | 42.3% |
| 45,953 | WEBSTER | 21,030 | 10,438 | 9,001 | 1,591 | 1,437 R | 49.6% | 42.8% | 53.7% | 46.3% |
| 13,010 | WINNEBAGO | 6,479 | 3,808 | 2,208 | 463 | 1,600 R | 58.8% | 34.1% | 63.3% | 36.7% |
| 21,876 | WINNESHIEK | 9,304 | 5,033 | 3,201 | 1,070 | 1,832 R | 54.1% | 34.4% | 61.1% | 38.9% |
| 100,884 | WOODBURY | 43,275 | 23,553 | 15,930 | 3,792 | 7,623 R | 54.4% | 36.8% | 59.7% | 40.3% |
| 9,075 | WORTH | 4,310 | 2,247 | 1,721 | 342 | 526 R | 52.1% | 39.9% | 56.6% | 43.4% |
| 16,319 | WRIGHT | 7,147 | 3,936 | 2,645 | 566 | 1,291 R | 55.1% | 37.0% | 59.8% | 40.2% |
| 2,913,808 | TOTAL | 1,317,661 | 676,026 | 508,672 | 132,963 | 167,354 R | 51.3% | 38.6% | 57.1% | 42.9% |

# IOWA

## PRESIDENT 1976

| 1970 Census Population | County | Total Vote | Republican | Democratic | Other | Rep.-Dem. Plurality | Percentage Total Vote Rep. | Dem. | Major Vote Rep. | Dem. |
|---|---|---|---|---|---|---|---|---|---|---|
| 9,487 | ADAIR | 4,722 | 2,326 | 2,294 | 102 | 32 R | 49.3% | 48.6% | 50.3% | 49.7% |
| 6,322 | ADAMS | 2,937 | 1,388 | 1,507 | 42 | 119 D | 47.3% | 51.3% | 47.9% | 52.1% |
| 14,968 | ALLAMAKEE | 6,303 | 3,648 | 2,568 | 87 | 1,080 R | 57.9% | 40.7% | 58.7% | 41.3% |
| 15,007 | APPANOOSE | 6,558 | 3,036 | 3,424 | 98 | 388 D | 46.3% | 52.2% | 47.0% | 53.0% |
| 9,595 | AUDUBON | 4,133 | 1,978 | 2,104 | 51 | 126 D | 47.9% | 50.9% | 48.5% | 51.5% |
| 22,885 | BENTON | 10,703 | 5,014 | 5,514 | 175 | 500 D | 46.8% | 51.5% | 47.6% | 52.4% |
| 132,916 | BLACK HAWK | 61,715 | 30,994 | 29,508 | 1,213 | 1,486 R | 50.2% | 47.8% | 51.2% | 48.8% |
| 26,470 | BOONE | 12,263 | 5,413 | 6,595 | 255 | 1,182 D | 44.1% | 53.8% | 45.1% | 54.9% |
| 22,737 | BREMER | 10,685 | 6,252 | 4,203 | 230 | 2,049 R | 58.5% | 39.3% | 59.8% | 40.2% |
| 21,746 | BUCHANAN | 9,223 | 4,794 | 4,258 | 171 | 536 R | 52.0% | 46.2% | 53.0% | 47.0% |
| 20,693 | BUENA VISTA | 9,567 | 5,126 | 4,227 | 214 | 899 R | 53.6% | 44.2% | 54.8% | 45.2% |
| 16,953 | BUTLER | 6,808 | 4,207 | 2,503 | 98 | 1,704 R | 61.8% | 36.8% | 62.7% | 37.3% |
| 14,287 | CALHOUN | 6,300 | 3,215 | 3,001 | 84 | 214 R | 51.0% | 47.6% | 51.7% | 48.3% |
| 22,912 | CARROLL | 9,608 | 4,094 | 5,333 | 181 | 1,239 D | 42.6% | 55.5% | 43.4% | 56.6% |
| 17,007 | CASS | 7,549 | 4,589 | 2,866 | 94 | 1,723 R | 60.8% | 38.0% | 61.6% | 38.4% |
| 17,655 | CEDAR | 7,822 | 4,308 | 3,354 | 160 | 954 R | 55.1% | 42.9% | 56.2% | 43.8% |
| 49,335 | CERRO GORDO | 22,196 | 10,604 | 11,189 | 403 | 585 D | 47.8% | 50.4% | 48.7% | 51.3% |
| 17,269 | CHEROKEE | 7,478 | 3,993 | 3,358 | 127 | 635 R | 53.4% | 44.9% | 54.3% | 45.7% |
| 14,969 | CHICKASAW | 6,988 | 3,432 | 3,503 | 53 | 71 D | 49.1% | 50.1% | 49.5% | 50.5% |
| 7,581 | CLARKE | 4,149 | 1,737 | 2,333 | 79 | 596 D | 41.9% | 56.2% | 42.7% | 57.3% |
| 18,464 | CLAY | 8,500 | 4,548 | 3,776 | 176 | 772 R | 53.5% | 44.4% | 54.6% | 45.4% |
| 20,606 | CLAYTON | 8,807 | 4,826 | 3,804 | 177 | 1,022 R | 54.8% | 43.2% | 55.9% | 44.1% |
| 56,749 | CLINTON | 24,534 | 12,401 | 11,746 | 387 | 655 R | 50.5% | 47.9% | 51.4% | 48.6% |
| 19,116 | CRAWFORD | 7,948 | 3,879 | 3,903 | 166 | 24 D | 48.8% | 49.1% | 49.8% | 50.2% |
| 26,085 | DALLAS | 12,247 | 5,308 | 6,722 | 217 | 1,414 D | 43.3% | 54.9% | 44.1% | 55.9% |
| 8,207 | DAVIS | 4,129 | 1,631 | 2,426 | 72 | 795 D | 39.5% | 58.8% | 40.2% | 59.8% |
| 9,737 | DECATUR | 4,707 | 1,932 | 2,698 | 77 | 766 D | 41.0% | 57.3% | 41.7% | 58.3% |
| 18,770 | DELAWARE | 7,481 | 4,161 | 3,168 | 152 | 993 R | 55.6% | 42.3% | 56.8% | 43.2% |
| 46,982 | DES MOINES | 20,536 | 9,023 | 11,268 | 245 | 2,245 D | 43.9% | 54.9% | 44.5% | 55.5% |
| 12,565 | DICKINSON | 7,010 | 3,795 | 3,074 | 141 | 721 R | 54.1% | 43.9% | 55.2% | 44.8% |
| 90,609 | DUBUQUE | 39,049 | 17,459 | 20,548 | 1,042 | 3,089 D | 44.7% | 52.6% | 45.9% | 54.1% |
| 14,009 | EMMET | 5,687 | 2,872 | 2,720 | 95 | 152 R | 50.5% | 47.8% | 51.4% | 48.6% |
| 26,898 | FAYETTE | 12,102 | 6,618 | 5,220 | 264 | 1,398 R | 54.7% | 43.1% | 55.9% | 44.1% |
| 19,860 | FLOYD | 9,178 | 4,361 | 4,646 | 171 | 285 D | 47.5% | 50.6% | 48.4% | 51.6% |
| 13,255 | FRANKLIN | 5,843 | 3,056 | 2,682 | 105 | 374 R | 52.3% | 45.9% | 53.3% | 46.7% |
| 9,282 | FREMONT | 4,176 | 2,163 | 1,964 | 49 | 199 R | 51.8% | 47.0% | 52.4% | 47.6% |
| 12,716 | GREENE | 5,989 | 2,811 | 3,094 | 84 | 283 D | 46.9% | 51.7% | 47.6% | 52.4% |
| 14,119 | GRUNDY | 6,660 | 4,173 | 2,410 | 77 | 1,763 R | 62.7% | 36.2% | 63.4% | 36.6% |
| 12,243 | GUTHRIE | 5,641 | 2,644 | 2,873 | 124 | 229 D | 46.9% | 50.9% | 47.9% | 52.1% |
| 18,383 | HAMILTON | 8,025 | 3,932 | 3,953 | 140 | 21 D | 49.0% | 49.3% | 49.9% | 50.1% |
| 13,330 | HANCOCK | 6,187 | 3,127 | 2,975 | 85 | 152 R | 50.5% | 48.1% | 51.2% | 48.8% |
| 22,248 | HARDIN | 9,328 | 4,682 | 4,479 | 167 | 203 R | 50.2% | 48.0% | 51.1% | 48.9% |
| 16,240 | HARRISON | 6,790 | 3,489 | 3,228 | 73 | 261 R | 51.4% | 47.5% | 51.9% | 48.1% |
| 18,114 | HENRY | 7,887 | 3,848 | 3,882 | 157 | 34 D | 48.8% | 49.2% | 49.8% | 50.2% |
| 11,442 | HOWARD | 5,616 | 2,618 | 2,917 | 81 | 299 D | 46.6% | 51.9% | 47.3% | 52.7% |
| 12,519 | HUMBOLDT | 5,841 | 3,075 | 2,677 | 89 | 398 R | 52.6% | 45.8% | 53.5% | 46.5% |
| 9,190 | IDA | 4,555 | 2,590 | 1,868 | 97 | 722 R | 56.9% | 41.0% | 58.1% | 41.9% |
| 15,419 | IOWA | 7,411 | 3,926 | 3,367 | 118 | 559 R | 53.0% | 45.4% | 53.8% | 46.2% |
| 20,839 | JACKSON | 8,886 | 4,221 | 4,467 | 198 | 246 D | 47.5% | 50.3% | 48.6% | 51.4% |
| 35,425 | JASPER | 16,786 | 7,728 | 8,783 | 275 | 1,055 D | 46.0% | 52.3% | 46.8% | 53.2% |
| 15,774 | JEFFERSON | 7,244 | 3,746 | 3,377 | 121 | 369 R | 51.7% | 46.6% | 52.6% | 47.4% |
| 72,127 | JOHNSON | 38,710 | 16,090 | 20,208 | 2,412 | 4,118 D | 41.6% | 52.2% | 44.3% | 55.7% |
| 19,868 | JONES | 8,831 | 4,463 | 4,245 | 123 | 218 R | 50.5% | 48.1% | 51.3% | 48.7% |
| 13,943 | KEOKUK | 6,504 | 2,920 | 3,482 | 102 | 562 D | 44.9% | 53.5% | 45.6% | 54.4% |
| 22,937 | KOSSUTH | 10,046 | 4,653 | 5,190 | 203 | 537 D | 46.3% | 51.7% | 47.3% | 52.7% |
| 42,996 | LEE | 17,465 | 8,195 | 9,017 | 253 | 822 D | 46.9% | 51.6% | 47.6% | 52.4% |
| 163,213 | LINN | 76,397 | 36,513 | 38,252 | 1,632 | 1,739 D | 47.8% | 50.1% | 48.8% | 51.2% |
| 10,682 | LOUISA | 4,441 | 2,284 | 2,089 | 68 | 195 R | 51.4% | 47.0% | 52.2% | 47.8% |
| 10,163 | LUCAS | 4,894 | 2,071 | 2,733 | 90 | 662 D | 42.3% | 55.8% | 43.1% | 56.9% |
| 13,340 | LYON | 5,554 | 3,558 | 1,870 | 126 | 1,688 R | 64.1% | 33.7% | 65.5% | 34.5% |

# IOWA

## PRESIDENT 1976

| 1970 Census Population | County | Total Vote | Republican | Democratic | Other | Rep.-Dem. Plurality | Percentage | | | |
|---|---|---|---|---|---|---|---|---|---|---|
| | | | | | | | Total Vote | | Major Vote | |
| | | | | | | | Rep. | Dem. | Rep. | Dem. |
| 11,558 | MADISON | 5,910 | 2,681 | 3,109 | 120 | 428 D | 45.4% | 52.6% | 46.3% | 53.7% |
| 22,177 | MAHASKA | 10,251 | 5,267 | 4,838 | 146 | 429 R | 51.4% | 47.2% | 52.1% | 47.9% |
| 26,352 | MARION | 11,857 | 5,429 | 6,226 | 202 | 797 D | 45.8% | 52.5% | 46.6% | 53.4% |
| 41,076 | MARSHALL | 18,630 | 9,562 | 8,695 | 373 | 867 R | 51.3% | 46.7% | 52.4% | 47.6% |
| 11,832 | MILLS | 4,710 | 2,722 | 1,908 | 80 | 814 R | 57.8% | 40.5% | 58.8% | 41.2% |
| 13,108 | MITCHELL | 5,892 | 2,887 | 2,906 | 99 | 19 D | 49.0% | 49.3% | 49.8% | 50.2% |
| 12,069 | MONONA | 5,370 | 2,636 | 2,661 | 73 | 25 D | 49.1% | 49.6% | 49.8% | 50.2% |
| 9,357 | MONROE | 3,996 | 1,581 | 2,360 | 55 | 779 D | 39.6% | 59.1% | 40.1% | 59.9% |
| 12,781 | MONTGOMERY | 5,974 | 3,673 | 2,229 | 72 | 1,444 R | 61.5% | 37.3% | 62.2% | 37.8% |
| 37,181 | MUSCATINE | 14,496 | 7,697 | 6,567 | 232 | 1,130 R | 53.1% | 45.3% | 54.0% | 46.0% |
| 17,522 | O'BRIEN | 7,506 | 4,643 | 2,732 | 131 | 1,911 R | 61.9% | 36.4% | 63.0% | 37.0% |
| 8,555 | OSCEOLA | 3,341 | 1,955 | 1,309 | 77 | 646 R | 58.5% | 39.2% | 59.9% | 40.1% |
| 18,507 | PAGE | 8,335 | 5,343 | 2,865 | 127 | 2,478 R | 64.1% | 34.4% | 65.1% | 34.9% |
| 13,289 | PALO ALTO | 5,904 | 2,623 | 3,182 | 99 | 559 D | 44.4% | 53.9% | 45.2% | 54.8% |
| 24,312 | PLYMOUTH | 10,016 | 5,590 | 4,284 | 142 | 1,306 R | 55.8% | 42.8% | 56.6% | 43.4% |
| 12,729 | POCAHONTAS | 5,889 | 2,700 | 3,055 | 134 | 355 D | 45.8% | 51.9% | 46.9% | 53.1% |
| 286,101 | POLK | 137,763 | 62,316 | 71,917 | 3,530 | 9,601 D | 45.2% | 52.2% | 46.4% | 53.6% |
| 86,991 | POTTAWATTAMIE | 32,519 | 17,264 | 14,754 | 501 | 2,510 R | 53.1% | 45.4% | 53.9% | 46.1% |
| 18,803 | POWESHIEK | 8,735 | 4,194 | 4,360 | 181 | 166 D | 48.0% | 49.9% | 49.0% | 51.0% |
| 6,373 | RINGGOLD | 3,336 | 1,543 | 1,739 | 54 | 196 D | 46.3% | 52.1% | 47.0% | 53.0% |
| 15,573 | SAC | 6,493 | 3,347 | 2,996 | 150 | 351 R | 51.5% | 46.1% | 52.8% | 47.2% |
| 142,687 | SCOTT | 65,940 | 35,021 | 29,771 | 1,148 | 5,250 R | 53.1% | 45.1% | 54.1% | 45.9% |
| 15,528 | SHELBY | 6,261 | 3,301 | 2,851 | 109 | 450 R | 52.7% | 45.5% | 53.7% | 46.3% |
| 27,996 | SIOUX | 12,935 | 9,448 | 3,322 | 165 | 6,126 R | 73.0% | 25.7% | 74.0% | 26.0% |
| 62,783 | STORY | 35,476 | 18,394 | 15,717 | 1,365 | 2,677 R | 51.8% | 44.3% | 53.9% | 46.1% |
| 20,147 | TAMA | 9,107 | 4,379 | 4,580 | 148 | 201 D | 48.1% | 50.3% | 48.9% | 51.1% |
| 8,790 | TAYLOR | 4,054 | 2,059 | 1,947 | 48 | 112 R | 50.8% | 48.0% | 51.4% | 48.6% |
| 13,557 | UNION | 5,948 | 2,873 | 2,955 | 120 | 82 D | 48.3% | 49.7% | 49.3% | 50.7% |
| 8,643 | VAN BUREN | 3,671 | 1,804 | 1,807 | 60 | 3 D | 49.1% | 49.2% | 50.0% | 50.0% |
| 42,149 | WAPELLO | 17,268 | 6,786 | 10,249 | 233 | 3,463 D | 39.3% | 59.4% | 39.8% | 60.2% |
| 27,432 | WARREN | 14,108 | 6,099 | 7,653 | 356 | 1,554 D | 43.2% | 54.2% | 44.3% | 55.7% |
| 18,967 | WASHINGTON | 7,807 | 4,218 | 3,448 | 141 | 770 R | 54.0% | 44.2% | 55.0% | 45.0% |
| 8,405 | WAYNE | 3,995 | 1,781 | 2,145 | 69 | 364 D | 44.6% | 53.7% | 45.4% | 54.6% |
| 48,391 | WEBSTER | 19,995 | 9,068 | 10,543 | 384 | 1,475 D | 45.4% | 52.7% | 46.2% | 53.8% |
| 12,990 | WINNEBAGO | 6,346 | 3,315 | 2,950 | 81 | 365 R | 52.2% | 46.5% | 52.9% | 47.1% |
| 21,758 | WINNESHIEK | 9,149 | 4,765 | 4,158 | 226 | 607 R | 52.1% | 45.4% | 53.4% | 46.6% |
| 103,052 | WOODBURY | 43,287 | 22,853 | 19,664 | 770 | 3,189 R | 52.8% | 45.4% | 53.8% | 46.2% |
| 8,968 | WORTH | 4,425 | 1,964 | 2,399 | 62 | 435 D | 44.4% | 54.2% | 45.0% | 55.0% |
| 17,294 | WRIGHT | 7,282 | 3,544 | 3,637 | 101 | 93 D | 48.7% | 49.9% | 49.4% | 50.6% |
| 2,825,041 | TOTAL | 1,279,306 | 632,863 | 619,931 | 26,512 | 12,932 R | 49.5% | 48.5% | 50.5% | 49.5% |

# IOWA

## PRESIDENT 1972

| 1970 Census Population | County | Total Vote | Republican | Democratic | Other | Rep.-Dem. Plurality | Percentage | | | |
|---|---|---|---|---|---|---|---|---|---|---|
| | | | | | | | Total Vote | | Major Vote | |
| | | | | | | | Rep. | Dem. | Rep. | Dem. |
| 9,487 | ADAIR | 4,782 | 3,041 | 1,642 | 99 | 1,399 R | 63.6% | 34.3% | 64.9% | 35.1% |
| 6,322 | ADAMS | 3,045 | 1,814 | 1,161 | 70 | 653 R | 59.6% | 38.1% | 61.0% | 39.0% |
| 14,968 | ALLAMAKEE | 6,562 | 4,150 | 2,271 | 141 | 1,879 R | 63.2% | 34.6% | 64.6% | 35.4% |
| 15,007 | APPANOOSE | 6,747 | 4,321 | 2,283 | 143 | 2,038 R | 64.0% | 33.8% | 65.4% | 34.6% |
| 9,595 | AUDUBON | 4,082 | 2,515 | 1,533 | 34 | 982 R | 61.6% | 37.6% | 62.1% | 37.9% |
| 22,885 | BENTON | 9,749 | 5,273 | 4,282 | 194 | 991 R | 54.1% | 43.9% | 55.2% | 44.8% |
| 132,916 | BLACK HAWK | 53,782 | 30,929 | 21,721 | 1,132 | 9,208 R | 57.5% | 40.4% | 58.7% | 41.3% |
| 26,470 | BOONE | 11,551 | 6,271 | 5,057 | 223 | 1,214 R | 54.3% | 43.8% | 55.4% | 44.6% |
| 22,737 | BREMER | 9,611 | 6,333 | 3,122 | 156 | 3,211 R | 65.9% | 32.5% | 67.0% | 33.0% |
| 21,746 | BUCHANAN | 9,048 | 5,277 | 3,609 | 162 | 1,668 R | 58.3% | 39.9% | 59.4% | 40.6% |
| 20,693 | BUENA VISTA | 9,281 | 5,685 | 3,460 | 136 | 2,225 R | 61.3% | 37.3% | 62.2% | 37.8% |
| 16,953 | BUTLER | 6,426 | 4,615 | 1,682 | 129 | 2,933 R | 71.8% | 26.2% | 73.3% | 26.7% |
| 14,287 | CALHOUN | 6,368 | 3,821 | 2,446 | 101 | 1,375 R | 60.0% | 38.4% | 61.0% | 39.0% |
| 22,912 | CARROLL | 9,285 | 4,415 | 4,608 | 262 | 193 D | 47.5% | 49.6% | 48.9% | 51.1% |
| 17,007 | CASS | 7,263 | 5,234 | 1,923 | 106 | 3,311 R | 72.1% | 26.5% | 73.1% | 26.9% |
| 17,655 | CEDAR | 7,023 | 4,452 | 2,465 | 106 | 1,987 R | 63.4% | 35.1% | 64.4% | 35.6% |
| 49,335 | CERRO GORDO | 21,693 | 11,856 | 9,460 | 377 | 2,396 R | 54.7% | 43.6% | 55.6% | 44.4% |
| 17,269 | CHEROKEE | 7,594 | 4,726 | 2,780 | 88 | 1,946 R | 62.2% | 36.6% | 63.0% | 37.0% |
| 14,969 | CHICKASAW | 7,030 | 3,836 | 3,134 | 60 | 702 R | 54.6% | 44.6% | 55.0% | 45.0% |
| 7,581 | CLARKE | 3,901 | 2,214 | 1,590 | 97 | 624 R | 56.8% | 40.8% | 58.2% | 41.8% |
| 18,464 | CLAY | 7,696 | 4,564 | 2,887 | 245 | 1,677 R | 59.3% | 37.5% | 61.3% | 38.7% |
| 20,606 | CLAYTON | 9,048 | 5,447 | 3,366 | 235 | 2,081 R | 60.2% | 37.2% | 61.8% | 38.2% |
| 56,749 | CLINTON | 22,964 | 12,768 | 9,895 | 301 | 2,873 R | 55.6% | 43.1% | 56.3% | 43.7% |
| 19,116 | CRAWFORD | 7,667 | 4,493 | 3,018 | 156 | 1,475 R | 58.6% | 39.4% | 59.8% | 40.2% |
| 26,085 | DALLAS | 11,436 | 6,143 | 5,085 | 208 | 1,058 R | 53.7% | 44.5% | 54.7% | 45.3% |
| 8,207 | DAVIS | 4,188 | 2,287 | 1,806 | 95 | 481 R | 54.6% | 43.1% | 55.9% | 44.1% |
| 9,737 | DECATUR | 4,593 | 2,638 | 1,880 | 75 | 758 R | 57.4% | 40.9% | 58.4% | 41.6% |
| 18,770 | DELAWARE | 7,920 | 4,848 | 2,944 | 128 | 1,904 R | 61.2% | 37.2% | 62.2% | 37.8% |
| 46,982 | DES MOINES | 19,358 | 10,216 | 8,869 | 273 | 1,347 R | 52.8% | 45.8% | 53.5% | 46.5% |
| 12,565 | DICKINSON | 6,381 | 3,739 | 2,373 | 269 | 1,366 R | 58.6% | 37.2% | 61.2% | 38.8% |
| 90,609 | DUBUQUE | 36,521 | 17,272 | 18,417 | 832 | 1,145 D | 47.3% | 50.4% | 48.4% | 51.6% |
| 14,009 | EMMET | 5,461 | 3,436 | 1,970 | 55 | 1,466 R | 62.9% | 36.1% | 63.6% | 36.4% |
| 26,898 | FAYETTE | 11,940 | 7,263 | 4,413 | 264 | 2,850 R | 60.8% | 37.0% | 62.2% | 37.8% |
| 19,860 | FLOYD | 8,192 | 4,726 | 3,338 | 128 | 1,388 R | 57.7% | 40.7% | 58.6% | 41.4% |
| 13,255 | FRANKLIN | 5,786 | 3,643 | 1,986 | 157 | 1,657 R | 63.0% | 34.3% | 64.7% | 35.3% |
| 9,282 | FREMONT | 3,907 | 2,642 | 1,210 | 55 | 1,432 R | 67.6% | 31.0% | 68.6% | 31.4% |
| 12,716 | GREENE | 5,680 | 3,371 | 2,152 | 157 | 1,219 R | 59.3% | 37.9% | 61.0% | 39.0% |
| 14,119 | GRUNDY | 6,625 | 4,706 | 1,844 | 75 | 2,862 R | 71.0% | 27.8% | 71.8% | 28.2% |
| 12,243 | GUTHRIE | 6,022 | 3,655 | 2,258 | 109 | 1,397 R | 60.7% | 37.5% | 61.8% | 38.2% |
| 18,383 | HAMILTON | 7,890 | 4,803 | 2,913 | 174 | 1,890 R | 60.9% | 36.9% | 62.2% | 37.8% |
| 13,330 | HANCOCK | 6,129 | 3,706 | 2,349 | 74 | 1,357 R | 60.5% | 38.3% | 61.2% | 38.8% |
| 22,248 | HARDIN | 9,556 | 5,869 | 3,516 | 171 | 2,353 R | 61.4% | 36.8% | 62.5% | 37.5% |
| 16,240 | HARRISON | 7,171 | 4,721 | 2,369 | 81 | 2,352 R | 65.8% | 33.0% | 66.6% | 33.4% |
| 18,114 | HENRY | 7,884 | 5,066 | 2,721 | 97 | 2,345 R | 64.3% | 34.5% | 65.1% | 34.9% |
| 11,442 | HOWARD | 5,481 | 2,980 | 2,439 | 62 | 541 R | 54.4% | 44.5% | 55.0% | 45.0% |
| 12,519 | HUMBOLDT | 5,792 | 3,622 | 2,062 | 108 | 1,560 R | 62.5% | 35.6% | 63.7% | 36.3% |
| 9,190 | IDA | 4,359 | 2,819 | 1,490 | 50 | 1,329 R | 64.7% | 34.2% | 65.4% | 34.6% |
| 15,419 | IOWA | 6,964 | 4,202 | 2,578 | 184 | 1,624 R | 60.3% | 37.0% | 62.0% | 38.0% |
| 20,839 | JACKSON | 8,924 | 4,975 | 3,704 | 245 | 1,271 R | 55.7% | 41.5% | 57.3% | 42.7% |
| 35,425 | JASPER | 16,513 | 9,133 | 7,007 | 373 | 2,126 R | 55.3% | 42.4% | 56.6% | 43.4% |
| 15,774 | JEFFERSON | 7,139 | 4,628 | 2,362 | 149 | 2,266 R | 64.8% | 33.1% | 66.2% | 33.8% |
| 72,127 | JOHNSON | 36,236 | 14,823 | 20,922 | 491 | 6,099 D | 40.9% | 57.7% | 41.5% | 58.5% |
| 19,868 | JONES | 8,521 | 4,962 | 3,468 | 91 | 1,494 R | 58.2% | 40.7% | 58.9% | 41.1% |
| 13,943 | KEOKUK | 6,565 | 3,831 | 2,619 | 115 | 1,212 R | 58.4% | 39.9% | 59.4% | 40.6% |
| 22,937 | KOSSUTH | 10,358 | 5,841 | 4,393 | 124 | 1,448 R | 56.4% | 42.4% | 57.1% | 42.9% |
| 42,996 | LEE | 17,618 | 9,748 | 7,510 | 360 | 2,238 R | 55.3% | 42.6% | 56.5% | 43.5% |
| 163,213 | LINN | 69,160 | 36,503 | 31,370 | 1,287 | 5,133 R | 52.8% | 45.4% | 53.8% | 46.2% |
| 10,682 | LOUISA | 4,577 | 2,806 | 1,707 | 64 | 1,099 R | 61.3% | 37.3% | 62.2% | 37.8% |
| 10,163 | LUCAS | 4,690 | 2,851 | 1,759 | 80 | 1,092 R | 60.8% | 37.5% | 61.8% | 38.2% |
| 13,340 | LYON | 5,252 | 3,788 | 1,407 | 57 | 2,381 R | 72.1% | 26.8% | 72.9% | 27.1% |

# IOWA

## PRESIDENT 1972

| 1970 Census Population | County | Total Vote | Republican | Democratic | Other | Rep.-Dem. Plurality | Percentage | | | |
|---|---|---|---|---|---|---|---|---|---|---|
| | | | | | | | Total Vote | | Major Vote | |
| | | | | | | | Rep. | Dem. | Rep. | Dem. |
| 11,558 | MADISON | 5,864 | 3,480 | 2,234 | 150 | 1,246 R | 59.3% | 38.1% | 60.9% | 39.1% |
| 22,177 | MAHASKA | 9,988 | 6,374 | 3,382 | 232 | 2,992 R | 63.8% | 33.9% | 65.3% | 34.7% |
| 26,352 | MARION | 11,531 | 6,583 | 4,643 | 305 | 1,940 R | 57.1% | 40.3% | 58.6% | 41.4% |
| 41,076 | MARSHALL | 17,744 | 10,798 | 6,618 | 328 | 4,180 R | 60.9% | 37.3% | 62.0% | 38.0% |
| 11,832 | MILLS | 4,712 | 3,531 | 1,060 | 121 | 2,471 R | 74.9% | 22.5% | 76.9% | 23.1% |
| 13,108 | MITCHELL | 5,911 | 3,395 | 2,449 | 67 | 946 R | 57.4% | 41.4% | 58.1% | 41.9% |
| 12,069 | MONONA | 5,495 | 3,237 | 2,189 | 69 | 1,048 R | 58.9% | 39.8% | 59.7% | 40.3% |
| 9,357 | MONROE | 4,155 | 2,357 | 1,736 | 62 | 621 R | 56.7% | 41.8% | 57.6% | 42.4% |
| 12,781 | MONTGOMERY | 6,041 | 4,391 | 1,559 | 91 | 2,832 R | 72.7% | 25.8% | 73.8% | 26.2% |
| 37,181 | MUSCATINE | 13,642 | 8,436 | 4,917 | 289 | 3,519 R | 61.8% | 36.0% | 63.2% | 36.8% |
| 17,522 | O'BRIEN | 7,491 | 5,159 | 2,224 | 108 | 2,935 R | 68.9% | 29.7% | 69.9% | 30.1% |
| 8,555 | OSCEOLA | 3,616 | 2,262 | 1,317 | 37 | 945 R | 62.6% | 36.4% | 63.2% | 36.8% |
| 18,507 | PAGE | 8,112 | 6,200 | 1,790 | 122 | 4,410 R | 76.4% | 22.1% | 77.6% | 22.4% |
| 13,289 | PALO ALTO | 6,066 | 3,141 | 2,845 | 80 | 296 R | 51.8% | 46.9% | 52.5% | 47.5% |
| 24,312 | PLYMOUTH | 10,466 | 6,339 | 4,033 | 94 | 2,306 R | 60.6% | 38.5% | 61.1% | 38.9% |
| 12,729 | POCAHONTAS | 5,487 | 3,138 | 2,241 | 108 | 897 R | 57.2% | 40.8% | 58.3% | 41.7% |
| 286,101 | POLK | 132,659 | 70,245 | 59,169 | 3,245 | 11,076 R | 53.0% | 44.6% | 54.3% | 45.7% |
| 86,991 | POTTAWATTAMIE | 28,450 | 19,722 | 8,074 | 654 | 11,648 R | 69.3% | 28.4% | 71.0% | 29.0% |
| 18,803 | POWESHIEK | 8,648 | 4,785 | 3,718 | 145 | 1,067 R | 55.3% | 43.0% | 56.3% | 43.7% |
| 6,373 | RINGGOLD | 3,303 | 2,264 | 1,003 | 36 | 1,261 R | 68.5% | 30.4% | 69.3% | 30.7% |
| 15,573 | SAC | 6,541 | 4,017 | 2,452 | 72 | 1,565 R | 61.4% | 37.5% | 62.1% | 37.9% |
| 142,687 | SCOTT | 59,455 | 34,135 | 23,810 | 1,510 | 10,325 R | 57.4% | 40.0% | 58.9% | 41.1% |
| 15,528 | SHELBY | 6,439 | 4,052 | 2,259 | 128 | 1,793 R | 62.9% | 35.1% | 64.2% | 35.8% |
| 27,996 | SIOUX | 13,697 | 10,721 | 2,867 | 109 | 7,854 R | 78.3% | 20.9% | 78.9% | 21.1% |
| 62,783 | STORY | 31,025 | 16,617 | 13,972 | 436 | 2,645 R | 53.6% | 45.0% | 54.3% | 45.7% |
| 20,147 | TAMA | 8,880 | 5,058 | 3,693 | 129 | 1,365 R | 57.0% | 41.6% | 57.8% | 42.2% |
| 8,790 | TAYLOR | 4,336 | 3,042 | 1,247 | 47 | 1,795 R | 70.2% | 28.8% | 70.9% | 29.1% |
| 13,557 | UNION | 5,977 | 3,734 | 2,112 | 131 | 1,622 R | 62.5% | 35.3% | 63.9% | 36.1% |
| 8,643 | VAN BUREN | 3,596 | 2,272 | 1,268 | 56 | 1,004 R | 63.2% | 35.3% | 64.2% | 35.8% |
| 42,149 | WAPELLO | 18,171 | 9,301 | 8,348 | 522 | 953 R | 51.2% | 45.9% | 52.7% | 47.3% |
| 27,432 | WARREN | 12,804 | 7,332 | 5,143 | 329 | 2,189 R | 57.3% | 40.2% | 58.8% | 41.2% |
| 18,967 | WASHINGTON | 8,089 | 5,187 | 2,784 | 118 | 2,403 R | 64.1% | 34.4% | 65.1% | 34.9% |
| 8,405 | WAYNE | 4,324 | 2,681 | 1,574 | 69 | 1,107 R | 62.0% | 36.4% | 63.0% | 37.0% |
| 48,391 | WEBSTER | 19,893 | 11,133 | 8,358 | 402 | 2,775 R | 56.0% | 42.0% | 57.1% | 42.9% |
| 12,990 | WINNEBAGO | 6,669 | 4,300 | 2,324 | 45 | 1,976 R | 64.5% | 34.8% | 64.9% | 35.1% |
| 21,758 | WINNESHIEK | 10,452 | 5,877 | 4,401 | 174 | 1,476 R | 56.2% | 42.1% | 57.2% | 42.8% |
| 103,052 | WOODBURY | 41,430 | 23,757 | 16,974 | 699 | 6,783 R | 57.3% | 41.0% | 58.3% | 41.7% |
| 8,968 | WORTH | 4,636 | 2,564 | 2,034 | 38 | 530 R | 55.3% | 43.9% | 55.8% | 44.2% |
| 17,294 | WRIGHT | 7,162 | 4,278 | 2,780 | 104 | 1,498 R | 59.7% | 38.8% | 60.6% | 39.4% |
| 2,825,041 | TOTAL | 1,225,944 | 706,207 | 496,206 | 23,531 | 210,001 R | 57.6% | 40.5% | 58.7% | 41.3% |

# IOWA

## PRESIDENT 1968

| 1960 Census Population | County | Total Vote | Republican | Democratic | AIP | Other | Plurality | Percentage Total Vote Rep. | Dem. | AIP |
|---|---|---|---|---|---|---|---|---|---|---|
| 10,893 | ADAIR | 4,586 | 2,789 | 1,559 | 234 | 4 | 1,230 R | 60.8% | 34.0% | 5.1% |
| 7,468 | ADAMS | 3,128 | 1,868 | 993 | 260 | 7 | 875 R | 59.7% | 31.7% | 8.3% |
| 15,982 | ALLAMAKEE | 7,110 | 4,449 | 2,245 | 407 | 9 | 2,204 R | 62.6% | 31.6% | 5.7% |
| 16,015 | APPANOOSE | 7,053 | 3,497 | 3,005 | 540 | 11 | 492 R | 49.6% | 42.6% | 7.7% |
| 10,919 | AUDUBON | 4,504 | 2,592 | 1,710 | 198 | 4 | 882 R | 57.5% | 38.0% | 4.4% |
| 23,422 | BENTON | 9,635 | 5,016 | 3,944 | 602 | 73 | 1,072 R | 52.1% | 40.9% | 6.2% |
| 122,482 | BLACK HAWK | 49,554 | 25,594 | 21,097 | 2,621 | 242 | 4,497 R | 51.6% | 42.6% | 5.3% |
| 28,037 | BOONE | 11,096 | 5,260 | 5,219 | 562 | 55 | 41 R | 47.4% | 47.0% | 5.1% |
| 21,108 | BREMER | 8,523 | 5,604 | 2,481 | 423 | 15 | 3,123 R | 65.8% | 29.1% | 5.0% |
| 22,293 | BUCHANAN | 8,674 | 4,541 | 3,670 | 454 | 9 | 871 R | 52.4% | 42.3% | 5.2% |
| 21,189 | BUENA VISTA | 9,050 | 5,599 | 3,051 | 386 | 14 | 2,548 R | 61.9% | 33.7% | 4.3% |
| 17,467 | BUTLER | 6,589 | 4,651 | 1,673 | 252 | 13 | 2,978 R | 70.6% | 25.4% | 3.8% |
| 15,923 | CALHOUN | 6,458 | 3,715 | 2,361 | 335 | 47 | 1,354 R | 57.5% | 36.6% | 5.2% |
| 23,431 | CARROLL | 9,202 | 3,927 | 4,809 | 412 | 54 | 882 D | 42.7% | 52.3% | 4.5% |
| 17,919 | CASS | 7,761 | 5,223 | 2,136 | 369 | 33 | 3,087 R | 67.3% | 27.5% | 4.8% |
| 17,791 | CEDAR | 7,614 | 4,494 | 2,675 | 438 | 7 | 1,819 R | 59.0% | 35.1% | 5.8% |
| 49,894 | CERRO GORDO | 20,310 | 10,661 | 8,554 | 1,036 | 59 | 2,107 R | 52.5% | 42.1% | 5.1% |
| 18,598 | CHEROKEE | 7,496 | 4,436 | 2,705 | 340 | 15 | 1,731 R | 59.2% | 36.1% | 4.5% |
| 15,034 | CHICKASAW | 6,764 | 3,510 | 2,966 | 286 | 2 | 544 R | 51.9% | 43.8% | 4.2% |
| 8,222 | CLARKE | 4,000 | 2,059 | 1,655 | 286 | | 404 R | 51.5% | 41.4% | 7.1% |
| 18,504 | CLAY | 7,628 | 4,325 | 2,840 | 369 | 94 | 1,485 R | 56.7% | 37.2% | 4.8% |
| 21,962 | CLAYTON | 8,878 | 5,132 | 3,168 | 541 | 37 | 1,964 R | 57.8% | 35.7% | 6.1% |
| 55,060 | CLINTON | 22,175 | 11,513 | 9,515 | 1,059 | 88 | 1,998 R | 51.9% | 42.9% | 4.8% |
| 18,569 | CRAWFORD | 7,744 | 4,287 | 2,851 | 539 | 67 | 1,436 R | 55.4% | 36.8% | 7.0% |
| 24,123 | DALLAS | 11,287 | 5,549 | 5,062 | 640 | 36 | 487 R | 49.2% | 44.8% | 5.7% |
| 9,199 | DAVIS | 4,278 | 2,016 | 1,904 | 355 | 3 | 112 R | 47.1% | 44.5% | 8.3% |
| 10,539 | DECATUR | 4,588 | 2,261 | 2,057 | 262 | 8 | 204 R | 49.3% | 44.8% | 5.7% |
| 18,483 | DELAWARE | 7,829 | 4,650 | 2,760 | 412 | 7 | 1,890 R | 59.4% | 35.3% | 5.3% |
| 44,605 | DES MOINES | 19,979 | 8,452 | 10,164 | 1,318 | 45 | 1,712 D | 42.3% | 50.9% | 6.6% |
| 12,574 | DICKINSON | 6,151 | 3,472 | 2,286 | 281 | 112 | 1,186 R | 56.4% | 37.2% | 4.6% |
| 80,048 | DUBUQUE | 34,863 | 14,197 | 18,664 | 1,701 | 301 | 4,467 D | 40.7% | 53.5% | 4.9% |
| 14,871 | EMMET | 5,847 | 3,444 | 2,163 | 230 | 10 | 1,281 R | 58.9% | 37.0% | 3.9% |
| 28,581 | FAYETTE | 11,687 | 6,935 | 4,098 | 636 | 18 | 2,837 R | 59.3% | 35.1% | 5.4% |
| 21,102 | FLOYD | 8,178 | 4,792 | 2,971 | 390 | 25 | 1,821 R | 58.6% | 36.3% | 4.8% |
| 15,472 | FRANKLIN | 5,677 | 3,604 | 1,777 | 240 | 56 | 1,827 R | 63.5% | 31.3% | 4.2% |
| 10,282 | FREMONT | 4,270 | 2,385 | 1,484 | 396 | 5 | 901 R | 55.9% | 34.8% | 9.3% |
| 14,379 | GREENE | 5,736 | 3,208 | 2,208 | 269 | 51 | 1,000 R | 55.9% | 38.5% | 4.7% |
| 14,132 | GRUNDY | 6,840 | 4,866 | 1,675 | 290 | 9 | 3,191 R | 71.1% | 24.5% | 4.2% |
| 13,607 | GUTHRIE | 5,751 | 3,346 | 2,063 | 335 | 7 | 1,283 R | 58.2% | 35.9% | 5.8% |
| 20,032 | HAMILTON | 8,001 | 4,607 | 3,058 | 301 | 35 | 1,549 R | 57.6% | 38.2% | 3.8% |
| 14,604 | HANCOCK | 5,949 | 3,544 | 2,131 | 249 | 25 | 1,413 R | 59.6% | 35.8% | 4.2% |
| 22,533 | HARDIN | 9,134 | 5,308 | 3,227 | 407 | 192 | 2,081 R | 58.1% | 35.3% | 4.5% |
| 17,600 | HARRISON | 6,825 | 3,867 | 2,410 | 540 | 8 | 1,457 R | 56.7% | 35.3% | 7.9% |
| 18,187 | HENRY | 7,659 | 4,613 | 2,532 | 503 | 11 | 2,081 R | 60.2% | 33.1% | 6.6% |
| 12,734 | HOWARD | 5,827 | 3,141 | 2,420 | 253 | 13 | 721 R | 53.9% | 41.5% | 4.3% |
| 13,156 | HUMBOLDT | 5,410 | 3,239 | 1,940 | 217 | 14 | 1,299 R | 59.9% | 35.9% | 4.0% |
| 10,269 | IDA | 4,425 | 2,753 | 1,463 | 208 | 1 | 1,290 R | 62.2% | 33.1% | 4.7% |
| 16,396 | IOWA | 7,111 | 4,133 | 2,586 | 367 | 25 | 1,547 R | 58.1% | 36.4% | 5.2% |
| 20,754 | JACKSON | 8,553 | 4,535 | 3,413 | 489 | 116 | 1,122 R | 53.0% | 39.9% | 5.7% |
| 35,282 | JASPER | 15,255 | 7,901 | 6,556 | 742 | 56 | 1,345 R | 51.8% | 43.0% | 4.9% |
| 15,818 | JEFFERSON | 6,939 | 4,130 | 2,411 | 377 | 21 | 1,719 R | 59.5% | 34.7% | 5.4% |
| 53,663 | JOHNSON | 25,944 | 11,384 | 13,541 | 736 | 283 | 2,157 D | 43.9% | 52.2% | 2.8% |
| 20,693 | JONES | 8,412 | 4,513 | 3,415 | 475 | 9 | 1,098 R | 53.6% | 40.6% | 5.6% |
| 15,492 | KEOKUK | 6,737 | 3,588 | 2,807 | 332 | 10 | 781 R | 53.3% | 41.7% | 4.9% |
| 25,314 | KOSSUTH | 10,089 | 5,350 | 4,392 | 310 | 37 | 958 R | 53.0% | 43.5% | 3.1% |
| 44,207 | LEE | 18,036 | 8,883 | 8,076 | 1,052 | 25 | 807 R | 49.3% | 44.8% | 5.8% |
| 136,899 | LINN | 64,430 | 30,918 | 29,898 | 3,182 | 432 | 1,020 R | 48.0% | 46.4% | 4.9% |
| 10,290 | LOUISA | 4,484 | 2,529 | 1,632 | 323 | | 897 R | 56.4% | 36.4% | 7.2% |
| 10,923 | LUCAS | 4,782 | 2,543 | 1,942 | 290 | 7 | 601 R | 53.2% | 40.6% | 6.1% |
| 14,468 | LYON | 5,754 | 4,195 | 1,403 | 151 | 5 | 2,792 R | 72.9% | 24.4% | 2.6% |

# IOWA

## PRESIDENT 1968

| 1960 Census Population | County | Total Vote | Republican | Democratic | AIP | Other | Plurality | Percentage Total Vote | | |
|---:|---|---:|---:|---:|---:|---:|---:|---:|---:|---:|
| | | | | | | | | Rep. | Dem. | AIP |
| 12,295 | MADISON | 5,679 | 3,151 | 2,192 | 327 | 9 | 959 R | 55.5% | 38.6% | 5.8% |
| 23,602 | MAHASKA | 9,970 | 5,670 | 3,721 | 420 | 159 | 1,949 R | 56.9% | 37.3% | 4.2% |
| 25,886 | MARION | 11,062 | 5,791 | 4,618 | 597 | 56 | 1,173 R | 52.4% | 41.7% | 5.4% |
| 37,984 | MARSHALL | 16,686 | 9,402 | 6,362 | 819 | 103 | 3,040 R | 56.3% | 38.1% | 4.9% |
| 13,050 | MILLS | 4,672 | 2,916 | 1,216 | 532 | 8 | 1,700 R | 62.4% | 26.0% | 11.4% |
| 14,043 | MITCHELL | 5,830 | 3,533 | 2,103 | 192 | 2 | 1,430 R | 60.6% | 36.1% | 3.3% |
| 13,916 | MONONA | 5,610 | 2,980 | 2,184 | 437 | 9 | 796 R | 53.1% | 38.9% | 7.8% |
| 10,463 | MONROE | 4,705 | 2,143 | 2,240 | 312 | 10 | 97 D | 45.5% | 47.6% | 6.6% |
| 14,467 | MONTGOMERY | 6,481 | 4,155 | 1,892 | 425 | 9 | 2,263 R | 64.1% | 29.2% | 6.6% |
| 33,840 | MUSCATINE | 12,874 | 7,361 | 4,726 | 643 | 144 | 2,635 R | 57.2% | 36.7% | 5.0% |
| 18,840 | O'BRIEN | 8,068 | 5,594 | 2,146 | 322 | 6 | 3,448 R | 69.3% | 26.6% | 4.0% |
| 10,064 | OSCEOLA | 4,102 | 2,516 | 1,420 | 164 | 2 | 1,096 R | 61.3% | 34.6% | 4.0% |
| 21,023 | PAGE | 8,679 | 5,907 | 2,128 | 634 | 10 | 3,779 R | 68.1% | 24.5% | 7.3% |
| 14,736 | PALO ALTO | 6,223 | 3,114 | 2,874 | 234 | 1 | 240 R | 50.0% | 46.2% | 3.8% |
| 23,906 | PLYMOUTH | 10,037 | 6,236 | 3,234 | 557 | 10 | 3,002 R | 62.1% | 32.2% | 5.5% |
| 14,234 | POCAHONTAS | 5,594 | 2,940 | 2,364 | 254 | 36 | 576 R | 52.6% | 42.3% | 4.5% |
| 266,315 | POLK | 114,784 | 51,814 | 52,731 | 9,524 | 715 | 917 D | 45.1% | 45.9% | 8.3% |
| 83,102 | POTTAWATTAMIE | 28,399 | 16,038 | 9,495 | 2,758 | 108 | 6,543 R | 56.5% | 33.4% | 9.7% |
| 19,300 | POWESHIEK | 8,112 | 4,470 | 3,250 | 367 | 25 | 1,220 R | 55.1% | 40.1% | 4.5% |
| 7,910 | RINGGOLD | 3,481 | 1,986 | 1,237 | 256 | 2 | 749 R | 57.1% | 35.5% | 7.4% |
| 17,007 | SAC | 6,676 | 4,182 | 2,207 | 280 | 7 | 1,975 R | 62.6% | 33.1% | 4.2% |
| 119,067 | SCOTT | 55,018 | 25,783 | 24,596 | 4,133 | 506 | 1,187 R | 46.9% | 44.7% | 7.5% |
| 15,825 | SHELBY | 6,626 | 3,886 | 2,365 | 330 | 45 | 1,521 R | 58.6% | 35.7% | 5.0% |
| 26,375 | SIOUX | 12,507 | 10,010 | 2,181 | 315 | 1 | 7,829 R | 80.0% | 17.4% | 2.5% |
| 49,327 | STORY | 23,675 | 13,327 | 9,456 | 772 | 120 | 3,871 R | 56.3% | 39.9% | 3.3% |
| 21,413 | TAMA | 9,253 | 4,955 | 3,767 | 494 | 37 | 1,188 R | 53.6% | 40.7% | 5.3% |
| 10,288 | TAYLOR | 4,636 | 2,765 | 1,501 | 368 | 2 | 1,264 R | 59.6% | 32.4% | 7.9% |
| 13,712 | UNION | 5,898 | 3,365 | 2,137 | 374 | 22 | 1,228 R | 57.1% | 36.2% | 6.3% |
| 9,778 | VAN BUREN | 3,869 | 2,294 | 1,331 | 237 | 7 | 963 R | 59.3% | 34.4% | 6.1% |
| 46,126 | WAPELLO | 18,647 | 7,825 | 9,375 | 1,355 | 92 | 1,550 D | 42.0% | 50.3% | 7.3% |
| 20,829 | WARREN | 11,171 | 5,619 | 4,613 | 919 | 20 | 1,006 R | 50.3% | 41.3% | 8.2% |
| 19,406 | WASHINGTON | 7,943 | 4,899 | 2,679 | 349 | 16 | 2,220 R | 61.7% | 33.7% | 4.4% |
| 9,800 | WAYNE | 4,573 | 2,553 | 1,723 | 283 | 14 | 830 R | 55.8% | 37.7% | 6.2% |
| 47,810 | WEBSTER | 19,097 | 9,349 | 8,572 | 1,026 | 150 | 777 R | 49.0% | 44.9% | 5.4% |
| 13,099 | WINNEBAGO | 5,954 | 3,543 | 2,163 | 246 | 2 | 1,380 R | 59.5% | 36.3% | 4.1% |
| 21,651 | WINNESHIEK | 9,319 | 5,600 | 3,364 | 344 | 11 | 2,236 R | 60.1% | 36.1% | 3.7% |
| 107,849 | WOODBURY | 41,803 | 21,159 | 18,281 | 2,153 | 210 | 2,878 R | 50.6% | 43.7% | 5.2% |
| 10,259 | WORTH | 4,420 | 2,383 | 1,815 | 214 | 8 | 568 R | 53.9% | 41.1% | 4.8% |
| 19,447 | WRIGHT | 7,549 | 4,299 | 2,969 | 248 | 33 | 1,330 R | 56.9% | 39.3% | 3.3% |
| 2,757,537 | TOTAL | 1,167,931 | 619,106 | 476,699 | 66,422 | 5,704 | 142,407 R | 53.0% | 40.8% | 5.7% |

# IOWA

## PRESIDENT 1964

| 1960 Census Population | County | Total Vote | Republican | Democratic | Other | Rep.-Dem. Plurality | Percentage Total Vote Rep. | Dem. | Major Vote Rep. | Dem. |
|---|---|---|---|---|---|---|---|---|---|---|
| 10,893 | ADAIR | 4,812 | 1,953 | 2,851 | 8 | 898 D | 40.6% | 59.2% | 40.7% | 59.3% |
| 7,468 | ADAMS | 3,263 | 1,321 | 1,941 | 1 | 620 D | 40.5% | 59.5% | 40.5% | 59.5% |
| 15,982 | ALLAMAKEE | 7,200 | 3,691 | 3,504 | 5 | 187 R | 51.3% | 48.7% | 51.3% | 48.7% |
| 16,015 | APPANOOSE | 7,856 | 2,872 | 4,960 | 24 | 2,088 D | 36.6% | 63.1% | 36.7% | 63.3% |
| 10,919 | AUDUBON | 4,885 | 1,871 | 3,011 | 3 | 1,140 D | 38.3% | 61.6% | 38.3% | 61.7% |
| 23,422 | BENTON | 10,084 | 3,453 | 6,614 | 17 | 3,161 D | 34.2% | 65.6% | 34.3% | 65.7% |
| 122,482 | BLACK HAWK | 50,516 | 19,744 | 30,716 | 56 | 10,972 D | 39.1% | 60.8% | 39.1% | 60.9% |
| 28,037 | BOONE | 11,335 | 3,543 | 7,699 | 93 | 4,156 D | 31.3% | 67.9% | 31.5% | 68.5% |
| 21,108 | BREMER | 8,939 | 3,880 | 5,045 | 14 | 1,165 D | 43.4% | 56.4% | 43.5% | 56.5% |
| 22,293 | BUCHANAN | 8,823 | 3,187 | 5,621 | 15 | 2,434 D | 36.1% | 63.7% | 36.2% | 63.8% |
| 21,189 | BUENA VISTA | 8,997 | 3,747 | 5,245 | 5 | 1,498 D | 41.6% | 58.3% | 41.7% | 58.3% |
| 17,467 | BUTLER | 6,832 | 3,462 | 3,370 | | 92 R | 50.7% | 49.3% | 50.7% | 49.3% |
| 15,923 | CALHOUN | 6,837 | 2,422 | 4,407 | 8 | 1,985 D | 35.4% | 64.5% | 35.5% | 64.5% |
| 23,431 | CARROLL | 10,207 | 2,387 | 7,807 | 13 | 5,420 D | 23.4% | 76.5% | 23.4% | 76.6% |
| 17,919 | CASS | 8,198 | 4,182 | 4,006 | 10 | 176 R | 51.0% | 48.9% | 51.1% | 48.9% |
| 17,791 | CEDAR | 7,735 | 3,106 | 4,617 | 12 | 1,511 D | 40.2% | 59.7% | 40.2% | 59.8% |
| 49,894 | CERRO GORDO | 21,071 | 7,884 | 13,156 | 31 | 5,272 D | 37.4% | 62.4% | 37.5% | 62.5% |
| 18,598 | CHEROKEE | 7,525 | 3,180 | 4,336 | 9 | 1,156 D | 42.3% | 57.6% | 42.3% | 57.7% |
| 15,034 | CHICKASAW | 7,182 | 2,632 | 4,545 | 5 | 1,913 D | 36.6% | 63.3% | 36.7% | 63.3% |
| 8,222 | CLARKE | 4,212 | 1,546 | 2,659 | 7 | 1,113 D | 36.7% | 63.1% | 36.8% | 63.2% |
| 18,504 | CLAY | 7,749 | 2,999 | 4,631 | 119 | 1,632 D | 38.7% | 59.8% | 39.3% | 60.7% |
| 21,962 | CLAYTON | 9,550 | 3,923 | 5,624 | 3 | 1,701 D | 41.1% | 58.9% | 41.1% | 58.9% |
| 55,060 | CLINTON | 22,533 | 8,219 | 14,267 | 47 | 6,048 D | 36.5% | 63.3% | 36.6% | 63.4% |
| 18,569 | CRAWFORD | 8,037 | 2,999 | 5,024 | 14 | 2,025 D | 37.3% | 62.5% | 37.4% | 62.6% |
| 24,123 | DALLAS | 11,262 | 3,763 | 7,447 | 52 | 3,684 D | 33.4% | 66.1% | 33.6% | 66.4% |
| 9,199 | DAVIS | 4,402 | 1,424 | 2,966 | 12 | 1,542 D | 32.3% | 67.4% | 32.4% | 67.6% |
| 10,539 | DECATUR | 4,885 | 1,542 | 3,331 | 12 | 1,789 D | 31.6% | 68.2% | 31.6% | 68.4% |
| 18,483 | DELAWARE | 8,065 | 3,427 | 4,623 | 15 | 1,196 D | 42.5% | 57.3% | 42.6% | 57.4% |
| 44,605 | DES MOINES | 19,762 | 5,830 | 13,894 | 38 | 8,064 D | 29.5% | 70.3% | 29.6% | 70.4% |
| 12,574 | DICKINSON | 5,938 | 2,443 | 3,490 | 5 | 1,047 D | 41.1% | 58.8% | 41.2% | 58.8% |
| 80,048 | DUBUQUE | 33,823 | 10,104 | 23,695 | 24 | 13,591 D | 29.9% | 70.1% | 29.9% | 70.1% |
| 14,871 | EMMET | 6,103 | 2,611 | 3,487 | 5 | 876 D | 42.8% | 57.1% | 42.8% | 57.2% |
| 28,581 | FAYETTE | 12,482 | 5,567 | 6,900 | 15 | 1,333 D | 44.6% | 55.3% | 44.7% | 55.3% |
| 21,102 | FLOYD | 9,043 | 3,721 | 5,317 | 5 | 1,596 D | 41.1% | 58.8% | 41.2% | 58.8% |
| 15,472 | FRANKLIN | 6,061 | 2,452 | 3,582 | 27 | 1,130 D | 40.5% | 59.1% | 40.6% | 59.4% |
| 10,282 | FREMONT | 4,761 | 2,044 | 2,703 | 14 | 659 D | 42.9% | 56.8% | 43.1% | 56.9% |
| 14,379 | GREENE | 5,986 | 2,141 | 3,828 | 17 | 1,687 D | 35.8% | 63.9% | 35.9% | 64.1% |
| 14,132 | GRUNDY | 6,808 | 3,215 | 3,582 | 11 | 367 D | 47.2% | 52.6% | 47.3% | 52.7% |
| 13,607 | GUTHRIE | 6,146 | 2,169 | 3,962 | 15 | 1,793 D | 35.3% | 64.5% | 35.4% | 64.6% |
| 20,032 | HAMILTON | 8,332 | 3,127 | 5,195 | 10 | 2,068 D | 37.5% | 62.3% | 37.6% | 62.4% |
| 14,604 | HANCOCK | 6,133 | 2,269 | 3,857 | 7 | 1,588 D | 37.0% | 62.9% | 37.0% | 63.0% |
| 22,533 | HARDIN | 9,304 | 3,828 | 5,459 | 17 | 1,631 D | 41.1% | 58.7% | 41.2% | 58.8% |
| 17,600 | HARRISON | 7,787 | 3,203 | 4,575 | 9 | 1,372 D | 41.1% | 58.8% | 41.2% | 58.8% |
| 18,187 | HENRY | 7,482 | 3,247 | 4,223 | 12 | 976 D | 43.4% | 56.4% | 43.5% | 56.5% |
| 12,734 | HOWARD | 6,211 | 2,360 | 3,841 | 10 | 1,481 D | 38.0% | 61.8% | 38.1% | 61.9% |
| 13,156 | HUMBOLDT | 5,630 | 2,250 | 3,376 | 4 | 1,126 D | 40.0% | 60.0% | 40.0% | 60.0% |
| 10,269 | IDA | 4,884 | 1,977 | 2,905 | 2 | 928 D | 40.5% | 59.5% | 40.5% | 59.5% |
| 16,396 | IOWA | 7,102 | 2,828 | 4,261 | 13 | 1,433 D | 39.8% | 60.0% | 39.9% | 60.1% |
| 20,754 | JACKSON | 8,205 | 3,066 | 5,130 | 9 | 2,064 D | 37.4% | 62.5% | 37.4% | 62.6% |
| 35,282 | JASPER | 15,561 | 5,321 | 10,216 | 24 | 4,895 D | 34.2% | 65.7% | 34.2% | 65.8% |
| 15,818 | JEFFERSON | 6,916 | 2,755 | 4,135 | 26 | 1,380 D | 39.8% | 59.8% | 40.0% | 60.0% |
| 53,663 | JOHNSON | 21,618 | 6,860 | 14,717 | 41 | 7,857 D | 31.7% | 68.1% | 31.8% | 68.2% |
| 20,693 | JONES | 8,672 | 3,154 | 5,511 | 7 | 2,357 D | 36.4% | 63.5% | 36.4% | 63.6% |
| 15,492 | KEOKUK | 7,404 | 2,597 | 4,790 | 17 | 2,193 D | 35.1% | 64.7% | 35.2% | 64.8% |
| 25,314 | KOSSUTH | 10,674 | 3,776 | 6,893 | 5 | 3,117 D | 35.4% | 64.6% | 35.4% | 64.6% |
| 44,207 | LEE | 18,582 | 6,321 | 12,244 | 17 | 5,923 D | 34.0% | 65.9% | 34.0% | 66.0% |
| 136,899 | LINN | 62,029 | 21,845 | 40,106 | 78 | 18,261 D | 35.2% | 64.7% | 35.3% | 64.7% |
| 10,290 | LOUISA | 4,481 | 1,845 | 2,624 | 12 | 779 D | 41.2% | 58.6% | 41.3% | 58.7% |
| 10,923 | LUCAS | 5,260 | 1,935 | 3,310 | 15 | 1,375 D | 36.8% | 62.9% | 36.9% | 63.1% |
| 14,468 | LYON | 5,935 | 3,185 | 2,747 | 3 | 438 R | 53.7% | 46.3% | 53.7% | 46.3% |

# IOWA

## PRESIDENT 1964

| 1960 Census Population | County | Total Vote | Republican | Democratic | Other | Rep.-Dem. Plurality | Percentage | | | |
|---|---|---|---|---|---|---|---|---|---|---|
| | | | | | | | Total Vote | | Major Vote | |
| | | | | | | | Rep. | Dem. | Rep. | Dem. |
| 12,295 | MADISON | 5,780 | 2,250 | 3,518 | 12 | 1,268 D | 38.9% | 60.9% | 39.0% | 61.0% |
| 23,602 | MAHASKA | 10,205 | 3,787 | 6,396 | 22 | 2,609 D | 37.1% | 62.7% | 37.2% | 62.8% |
| 25,886 | MARION | 11,842 | 3,903 | 7,911 | 28 | 4,008 D | 33.0% | 66.8% | 33.0% | 67.0% |
| 37,984 | MARSHALL | 16,176 | 6,323 | 9,815 | 38 | 3,492 D | 39.1% | 60.7% | 39.2% | 60.8% |
| 13,050 | MILLS | 4,889 | 2,424 | 2,463 | 2 | 39 D | 49.6% | 50.4% | 49.6% | 50.4% |
| 14,043 | MITCHELL | 6,373 | 2,489 | 3,868 | 16 | 1,379 D | 39.1% | 60.7% | 39.2% | 60.8% |
| 13,916 | MONONA | 6,187 | 2,208 | 3,971 | 8 | 1,763 D | 35.7% | 64.2% | 35.7% | 64.3% |
| 10,463 | MONROE | 4,791 | 1,588 | 3,186 | 17 | 1,598 D | 33.1% | 66.5% | 33.3% | 66.7% |
| 14,467 | MONTGOMERY | 6,601 | 3,101 | 3,489 | 11 | 388 D | 47.0% | 52.9% | 47.1% | 52.9% |
| 33,840 | MUSCATINE | 13,577 | 5,547 | 8,020 | 10 | 2,473 D | 40.9% | 59.1% | 40.9% | 59.1% |
| 18,840 | O'BRIEN | 8,637 | 4,336 | 4,295 | 6 | 41 R | 50.2% | 49.7% | 50.2% | 49.8% |
| 10,064 | OSCEOLA | 4,301 | 1,798 | 2,498 | 5 | 700 D | 41.8% | 58.1% | 41.9% | 58.1% |
| 21,023 | PAGE | 9,209 | 4,775 | 4,402 | 32 | 373 R | 51.9% | 47.8% | 52.0% | 48.0% |
| 14,736 | PALO ALTO | 6,647 | 2,206 | 4,441 | | 2,235 D | 33.2% | 66.8% | 33.2% | 66.8% |
| 23,906 | PLYMOUTH | 10,613 | 4,920 | 5,691 | 2 | 771 D | 46.4% | 53.6% | 46.4% | 53.6% |
| 14,234 | POCAHONTAS | 6,072 | 2,079 | 3,988 | 5 | 1,909 D | 34.2% | 65.7% | 34.3% | 65.7% |
| 266,315 | POLK | 111,953 | 37,280 | 74,194 | 479 | 36,914 D | 33.3% | 66.3% | 33.4% | 66.6% |
| 83,102 | POTTAWATTAMIE | 31,799 | 14,208 | 17,569 | 22 | 3,361 D | 44.7% | 55.3% | 44.7% | 55.3% |
| 19,300 | POWESHIEK | 8,334 | 3,109 | 5,213 | 12 | 2,104 D | 37.3% | 62.6% | 37.4% | 62.6% |
| 7,910 | RINGGOLD | 3,840 | 1,571 | 2,260 | 9 | 689 D | 40.9% | 58.9% | 41.0% | 59.0% |
| 17,007 | SAC | 7,302 | 2,937 | 4,358 | 7 | 1,421 D | 40.2% | 59.7% | 40.3% | 59.7% |
| 119,067 | SCOTT | 51,098 | 19,488 | 31,526 | 84 | 12,038 D | 38.1% | 61.7% | 38.2% | 61.8% |
| 15,825 | SHELBY | 7,137 | 2,928 | 4,148 | 61 | 1,220 D | 41.0% | 58.1% | 41.4% | 58.6% |
| 26,375 | SIOUX | 12,323 | 8,078 | 4,233 | 12 | 3,845 R | 65.6% | 34.4% | 65.6% | 34.4% |
| 49,327 | STORY | 20,610 | 8,188 | 12,329 | 93 | 4,141 D | 39.7% | 59.8% | 39.9% | 60.1% |
| 21,413 | TAMA | 9,608 | 3,543 | 6,057 | 8 | 2,514 D | 36.9% | 63.0% | 36.9% | 63.1% |
| 10,288 | TAYLOR | 4,942 | 2,162 | 2,780 | | 618 D | 43.7% | 56.3% | 43.7% | 56.3% |
| 13,712 | UNION | 6,263 | 2,502 | 3,751 | 10 | 1,249 D | 39.9% | 59.9% | 40.0% | 60.0% |
| 9,778 | VAN BUREN | 4,257 | 1,700 | 2,555 | 2 | 855 D | 39.9% | 60.0% | 40.0% | 60.0% |
| 46,126 | WAPELLO | 19,546 | 5,524 | 13,971 | 51 | 8,447 D | 28.3% | 71.5% | 28.3% | 71.7% |
| 20,829 | WARREN | 10,351 | 3,679 | 6,639 | 33 | 2,960 D | 35.5% | 64.1% | 35.7% | 64.3% |
| 19,406 | WASHINGTON | 7,919 | 3,315 | 4,587 | 17 | 1,272 D | 41.9% | 57.9% | 42.0% | 58.0% |
| 9,800 | WAYNE | 5,062 | 1,994 | 3,062 | 6 | 1,068 D | 39.4% | 60.5% | 39.4% | 60.6% |
| 47,810 | WEBSTER | 19,635 | 6,576 | 13,005 | 54 | 6,429 D | 33.5% | 66.2% | 33.6% | 66.4% |
| 13,099 | WINNEBAGO | 6,017 | 2,331 | 3,677 | 9 | 1,346 D | 38.7% | 61.1% | 38.8% | 61.2% |
| 21,651 | WINNESHIEK | 9,759 | 3,941 | 5,811 | 7 | 1,870 D | 40.4% | 59.5% | 40.4% | 59.6% |
| 107,849 | WOODBURY | 44,218 | 17,347 | 26,841 | 30 | 9,494 D | 39.2% | 60.7% | 39.3% | 60.7% |
| 10,259 | WORTH | 4,723 | 1,777 | 2,936 | 10 | 1,159 D | 37.6% | 62.2% | 37.7% | 62.3% |
| 19,447 | WRIGHT | 7,836 | 2,831 | 4,998 | 7 | 2,167 D | 36.1% | 63.8% | 36.2% | 63.8% |
| 2,757,537 | TOTAL | 1,184,539 | 449,148 | 733,030 | 2,361 | 283,882 D | 37.9% | 61.9% | 38.0% | 62.0% |

# IOWA

## PRESIDENT 1960

| 1960 Census Population | County | Total Vote | Republican | Democratic | Other | Rep.-Dem. Plurality | Percentage Total Vote Rep. | Dem. | Major Vote Rep. | Dem. |
|---|---|---|---|---|---|---|---|---|---|---|
| 10,893 | ADAIR | 5,630 | 3,383 | 2,245 | 2 | 1,138 R | 60.1% | 39.9% | 60.1% | 39.9% |
| 7,468 | ADAMS | 3,828 | 2,185 | 1,643 | | 542 R | 57.1% | 42.9% | 57.1% | 42.9% |
| 15,982 | ALLAMAKEE | 7,916 | 4,970 | 2,933 | 13 | 2,037 R | 62.8% | 37.1% | 62.9% | 37.1% |
| 16,015 | APPANOOSE | 8,480 | 5,040 | 3,422 | 18 | 1,618 R | 59.4% | 40.4% | 59.6% | 40.4% |
| 10,919 | AUDUBON | 5,532 | 2,935 | 2,595 | 2 | 340 R | 53.1% | 46.9% | 53.1% | 46.9% |
| 23,422 | BENTON | 10,601 | 5,972 | 4,620 | 9 | 1,352 R | 56.3% | 43.6% | 56.4% | 43.6% |
| 122,482 | BLACK HAWK | 52,551 | 28,435 | 24,078 | 38 | 4,357 R | 54.1% | 45.8% | 54.1% | 45.9% |
| 28,037 | BOONE | 12,527 | 6,761 | 5,759 | 7 | 1,002 R | 54.0% | 46.0% | 54.0% | 46.0% |
| 21,108 | BREMER | 9,742 | 6,504 | 3,234 | 4 | 3,270 R | 66.8% | 33.2% | 66.8% | 33.2% |
| 22,293 | BUCHANAN | 9,433 | 5,179 | 4,251 | 3 | 928 R | 54.9% | 45.1% | 54.9% | 45.1% |
| 21,189 | BUENA VISTA | 9,996 | 6,351 | 3,637 | 8 | 2,714 R | 63.5% | 36.4% | 63.6% | 36.4% |
| 17,467 | BUTLER | 7,616 | 5,345 | 2,268 | 3 | 3,077 R | 70.2% | 29.8% | 70.2% | 29.8% |
| 15,923 | CALHOUN | 7,615 | 4,485 | 3,123 | 7 | 1,362 R | 58.9% | 41.0% | 59.0% | 41.0% |
| 23,431 | CARROLL | 11,721 | 4,648 | 7,064 | 9 | 2,416 D | 39.7% | 60.3% | 39.7% | 60.3% |
| 17,919 | CASS | 9,354 | 6,290 | 3,059 | 5 | 3,231 R | 67.2% | 32.7% | 67.3% | 32.7% |
| 17,791 | CEDAR | 8,425 | 5,217 | 3,203 | 5 | 2,014 R | 61.9% | 38.0% | 62.0% | 38.0% |
| 49,894 | CERRO GORDO | 22,889 | 12,830 | 10,044 | 15 | 2,786 R | 56.1% | 43.9% | 56.1% | 43.9% |
| 18,598 | CHEROKEE | 8,106 | 4,791 | 3,309 | 6 | 1,482 R | 59.1% | 40.8% | 59.1% | 40.9% |
| 15,034 | CHICKASAW | 7,889 | 3,822 | 4,063 | 4 | 241 D | 48.4% | 51.5% | 48.5% | 51.5% |
| 8,222 | CLARKE | 4,550 | 2,631 | 1,906 | 13 | 725 R | 57.8% | 41.9% | 58.0% | 42.0% |
| 18,504 | CLAY | 8,604 | 5,165 | 3,437 | 2 | 1,728 R | 60.0% | 39.9% | 60.0% | 40.0% |
| 21,962 | CLAYTON | 11,057 | 6,441 | 4,612 | 4 | 1,829 R | 58.3% | 41.7% | 58.3% | 41.7% |
| 55,060 | CLINTON | 24,330 | 13,797 | 10,508 | 25 | 3,289 R | 56.7% | 43.2% | 56.8% | 43.2% |
| 18,569 | CRAWFORD | 8,518 | 4,791 | 3,720 | 7 | 1,071 R | 56.2% | 43.7% | 56.3% | 43.7% |
| 24,123 | DALLAS | 12,176 | 6,566 | 5,597 | 13 | 969 R | 53.9% | 46.0% | 54.0% | 46.0% |
| 9,199 | DAVIS | 4,949 | 2,641 | 2,303 | 5 | 338 R | 53.4% | 46.5% | 53.4% | 46.6% |
| 10,539 | DECATUR | 5,457 | 3,039 | 2,411 | 7 | 628 R | 55.7% | 44.2% | 55.8% | 44.2% |
| 18,483 | DELAWARE | 8,703 | 5,015 | 3,688 | | 1,327 R | 57.6% | 42.4% | 57.6% | 42.4% |
| 44,605 | DES MOINES | 20,591 | 10,678 | 9,872 | 41 | 806 R | 51.9% | 47.9% | 52.0% | 48.0% |
| 12,574 | DICKINSON | 6,273 | 3,575 | 2,696 | 2 | 879 R | 57.0% | 43.0% | 57.0% | 43.0% |
| 80,048 | DUBUQUE | 34,766 | 12,740 | 22,007 | 19 | 9,267 D | 36.6% | 63.3% | 36.7% | 63.3% |
| 14,871 | EMMET | 6,853 | 4,284 | 2,563 | 6 | 1,721 R | 62.5% | 37.4% | 62.6% | 37.4% |
| 28,581 | FAYETTE | 13,611 | 8,330 | 5,256 | 25 | 3,074 R | 61.2% | 38.6% | 61.3% | 38.7% |
| 21,102 | FLOYD | 9,746 | 5,774 | 3,970 | 2 | 1,804 R | 59.2% | 40.7% | 59.3% | 40.7% |
| 15,472 | FRANKLIN | 6,996 | 4,514 | 2,476 | 6 | 2,038 R | 64.5% | 35.4% | 64.6% | 35.4% |
| 10,282 | FREMONT | 5,336 | 3,027 | 2,307 | 2 | 720 R | 56.7% | 43.2% | 56.7% | 43.3% |
| 14,379 | GREENE | 6,954 | 4,063 | 2,879 | 12 | 1,184 R | 58.4% | 41.4% | 58.5% | 41.5% |
| 14,132 | GRUNDY | 7,166 | 4,989 | 2,174 | 3 | 2,815 R | 69.6% | 30.3% | 69.6% | 30.4% |
| 13,607 | GUTHRIE | 6,949 | 4,046 | 2,896 | 7 | 1,150 R | 58.2% | 41.7% | 58.3% | 41.7% |
| 20,032 | HAMILTON | 9,174 | 5,265 | 3,905 | 4 | 1,360 R | 57.4% | 42.6% | 57.4% | 42.6% |
| 14,604 | HANCOCK | 6,937 | 4,179 | 2,757 | 1 | 1,422 R | 60.2% | 39.7% | 60.3% | 39.7% |
| 22,533 | HARDIN | 10,330 | 6,438 | 3,888 | 4 | 2,550 R | 62.3% | 37.6% | 62.3% | 37.7% |
| 17,600 | HARRISON | 8,562 | 4,940 | 3,613 | 9 | 1,327 R | 57.7% | 42.2% | 57.8% | 42.2% |
| 18,187 | HENRY | 8,377 | 5,531 | 2,839 | 7 | 2,692 R | 66.0% | 33.9% | 66.1% | 33.9% |
| 12,734 | HOWARD | 6,784 | 3,378 | 3,406 | | 28 D | 49.8% | 50.2% | 49.8% | 50.2% |
| 13,156 | HUMBOLDT | 6,243 | 3,537 | 2,706 | | 831 R | 56.7% | 43.3% | 56.7% | 43.3% |
| 10,269 | IDA | 5,241 | 3,290 | 1,949 | 2 | 1,341 R | 62.8% | 37.2% | 62.8% | 37.2% |
| 16,396 | IOWA | 7,790 | 4,944 | 2,828 | 18 | 2,116 R | 63.5% | 36.3% | 63.6% | 36.4% |
| 20,754 | JACKSON | 9,434 | 5,084 | 4,345 | 5 | 739 R | 53.9% | 46.1% | 53.9% | 46.1% |
| 35,282 | JASPER | 16,585 | 9,332 | 7,242 | 11 | 2,090 R | 56.3% | 43.7% | 56.3% | 43.7% |
| 15,818 | JEFFERSON | 7,722 | 4,942 | 2,780 | | 2,162 R | 64.0% | 36.0% | 64.0% | 36.0% |
| 53,663 | JOHNSON | 21,508 | 10,927 | 10,563 | 18 | 364 R | 50.8% | 49.1% | 50.8% | 49.2% |
| 20,693 | JONES | 9,469 | 5,541 | 3,924 | 4 | 1,617 R | 58.5% | 41.4% | 58.5% | 41.5% |
| 15,492 | KEOKUK | 8,115 | 4,697 | 3,408 | 10 | 1,289 R | 57.9% | 42.0% | 58.0% | 42.0% |
| 25,314 | KOSSUTH | 12,084 | 6,278 | 5,806 | | 472 R | 52.0% | 48.0% | 52.0% | 48.0% |
| 44,207 | LEE | 20,701 | 10,765 | 9,936 | | 829 R | 52.0% | 48.0% | 52.0% | 48.0% |
| 136,899 | LINN | 61,839 | 34,200 | 27,614 | 25 | 6,586 R | 55.3% | 44.7% | 55.3% | 44.7% |
| 10,290 | LOUISA | 5,004 | 3,036 | 1,966 | 2 | 1,070 R | 60.7% | 39.3% | 60.7% | 39.3% |
| 10,923 | LUCAS | 5,865 | 3,512 | 2,344 | 9 | 1,168 R | 59.9% | 40.0% | 60.0% | 40.0% |
| 14,468 | LYON | 6,676 | 4,917 | 1,752 | 7 | 3,165 R | 73.7% | 26.2% | 73.7% | 26.3% |

# IOWA

## PRESIDENT 1960

| 1960 Census Population | County | Total Vote | Republican | Democratic | Other | Rep.-Dem. Plurality | Percentage Total Vote Rep. | Total Vote Dem. | Major Vote Rep. | Major Vote Dem. |
|---|---|---|---|---|---|---|---|---|---|---|
| 12,295 | MADISON | 6,529 | 3,804 | 2,722 | 3 | 1,082 R | 58.3% | 41.7% | 58.3% | 41.7% |
| 23,602 | MAHASKA | 10,901 | 7,129 | 3,746 | 26 | 3,383 R | 65.4% | 34.4% | 65.6% | 34.4% |
| 25,886 | MARION | 12,008 | 7,444 | 4,547 | 17 | 2,897 R | 62.0% | 37.9% | 62.1% | 37.9% |
| 37,984 | MARSHALL | 17,042 | 10,265 | 6,761 | 16 | 3,504 R | 60.2% | 39.7% | 60.3% | 39.7% |
| 13,050 | MILLS | 5,256 | 3,436 | 1,820 | | 1,616 R | 65.4% | 34.6% | 65.4% | 34.6% |
| 14,043 | MITCHELL | 6,798 | 3,915 | 2,873 | 10 | 1,042 R | 57.6% | 42.3% | 57.7% | 42.3% |
| 13,916 | MONONA | 7,070 | 3,863 | 3,207 | | 656 R | 54.6% | 45.4% | 54.6% | 45.4% |
| 10,463 | MONROE | 5,391 | 2,922 | 2,459 | 10 | 463 R | 54.2% | 45.6% | 54.3% | 45.7% |
| 14,467 | MONTGOMERY | 7,630 | 4,974 | 2,655 | 1 | 2,319 R | 65.2% | 34.8% | 65.2% | 34.8% |
| 33,840 | MUSCATINE | 14,698 | 8,555 | 6,135 | 8 | 2,420 R | 58.2% | 41.7% | 58.2% | 41.8% |
| 18,840 | O'BRIEN | 9,480 | 6,509 | 2,967 | 4 | 3,542 R | 68.7% | 31.3% | 68.7% | 31.3% |
| 10,064 | OSCEOLA | 4,782 | 2,965 | 1,814 | 3 | 1,151 R | 62.0% | 37.9% | 62.0% | 38.0% |
| 21,023 | PAGE | 10,172 | 7,089 | 3,075 | 8 | 4,014 R | 69.7% | 30.2% | 69.7% | 30.3% |
| 14,736 | PALO ALTO | 7,249 | 3,551 | 3,695 | 3 | 144 D | 49.0% | 51.0% | 49.0% | 51.0% |
| 23,906 | PLYMOUTH | 11,103 | 6,432 | 4,671 | | 1,761 R | 57.9% | 42.1% | 57.9% | 42.1% |
| 14,234 | POCAHONTAS | 6,859 | 3,445 | 3,408 | 6 | 37 R | 50.2% | 49.7% | 50.3% | 49.7% |
| 266,315 | POLK | 119,234 | 64,077 | 55,091 | 66 | 8,986 R | 53.7% | 46.2% | 53.8% | 46.2% |
| 83,102 | POTTAWATTAMIE | 33,261 | 19,223 | 14,025 | 13 | 5,198 R | 57.8% | 42.2% | 57.8% | 42.2% |
| 19,300 | POWESHIEK | 8,904 | 5,232 | 3,671 | 1 | 1,561 R | 58.8% | 41.2% | 58.8% | 41.2% |
| 7,910 | RINGGOLD | 4,321 | 2,538 | 1,781 | 2 | 757 R | 58.7% | 41.2% | 58.8% | 41.2% |
| 17,007 | SAC | 7,904 | 4,850 | 3,054 | | 1,796 R | 61.4% | 38.6% | 61.4% | 38.6% |
| 119,067 | SCOTT | 50,671 | 27,617 | 23,004 | 50 | 4,613 R | 54.5% | 45.4% | 54.6% | 45.4% |
| 15,825 | SHELBY | 7,644 | 4,210 | 3,427 | 7 | 783 R | 55.1% | 44.8% | 55.1% | 44.9% |
| 26,375 | SIOUX | 12,934 | 10,284 | 2,643 | 7 | 7,641 R | 79.5% | 20.4% | 79.6% | 20.4% |
| 49,327 | STORY | 21,004 | 13,708 | 7,281 | 15 | 6,427 R | 65.3% | 34.7% | 65.3% | 34.7% |
| 21,413 | TAMA | 10,486 | 5,535 | 4,950 | 1 | 585 R | 52.8% | 47.2% | 52.8% | 47.2% |
| 10,288 | TAYLOR | 5,581 | 3,452 | 2,126 | 3 | 1,326 R | 61.9% | 38.1% | 61.9% | 38.1% |
| 13,712 | UNION | 7,142 | 4,417 | 2,720 | 5 | 1,697 R | 61.8% | 38.1% | 61.9% | 38.1% |
| 9,778 | VAN BUREN | 4,894 | 3,129 | 1,760 | 5 | 1,369 R | 63.9% | 36.0% | 64.0% | 36.0% |
| 46,126 | WAPELLO | 22,167 | 11,036 | 11,116 | 15 | 80 D | 49.8% | 50.1% | 49.8% | 50.2% |
| 20,829 | WARREN | 10,149 | 6,013 | 4,136 | | 1,877 R | 59.2% | 40.8% | 59.2% | 40.8% |
| 19,406 | WASHINGTON | 9,089 | 5,861 | 3,222 | 6 | 2,639 R | 64.5% | 35.4% | 64.5% | 35.5% |
| 9,800 | WAYNE | 5,715 | 3,401 | 2,307 | 7 | 1,094 R | 59.5% | 40.4% | 59.6% | 40.4% |
| 47,810 | WEBSTER | 21,435 | 10,741 | 10,680 | 14 | 61 R | 50.1% | 49.8% | 50.1% | 49.9% |
| 13,099 | WINNEBAGO | 6,549 | 4,082 | 2,463 | 4 | 1,619 R | 62.3% | 37.6% | 62.4% | 37.6% |
| 21,651 | WINNESHIEK | 10,530 | 5,737 | 4,786 | 7 | 951 R | 54.5% | 45.5% | 54.5% | 45.5% |
| 107,849 | WOODBURY | 48,744 | 26,832 | 21,906 | 6 | 4,926 R | 55.0% | 44.9% | 55.1% | 44.9% |
| 10,259 | WORTH | 5,048 | 2,740 | 2,303 | 5 | 437 R | 54.3% | 45.6% | 54.3% | 45.7% |
| 19,447 | WRIGHT | 9,560 | 5,386 | 4,159 | 15 | 1,227 R | 56.3% | 43.5% | 56.4% | 43.6% |
| 2,757,537 | TOTAL | 1,273,810 | 722,381 | 550,565 | 864 | 171,816 R | 56.7% | 43.2% | 56.7% | 43.3% |

# IOWA

## ELECTION NOTES

2004    Other vote was 5,973 Nominated by Petition (Ralph Nader); 2,992 Libertarian (Michael Badnarik); 1,304 Constitution (Michael Peroutka); 1,141 Iowa Green (David Cobb); 373 Socialist Workers (James Harris); 176 Nominated by Petition (Bill Van Auken); 1,094 scattered write-in.

2000    Other vote was 5,731 Reform (Buchanan); 3,209 Libertarian (Browne); 2,281 Nominated by Petition (Hagelin); 613 Constitution (Phillips); 190 Socialist Workers (Harris); 107 Socialist (McReynolds); 1,168 scattered write-in.

1996    Other vote was 6,550 Green (Nader); 3,349 Natural Law (Hagelin); 2,315 Libertarian (Browne); 2,229 U.S. Taxpayers (Phillips); 331 Socialist Workers (Harris); 1,240 scattered write-in.

1992    Other vote was 3,079 Hagelin (Natural Law); 1,177 Gritz (America First); 1,149 Ehlers (Independent); 1,076 Marrou (Libertarian); 669 Herer (Grassroots); 604 Yiamouyiannis (Independent); 480 Phillips (Taxpayers); 273 Warren (Socialist Workers); 238 LaRouche (Economic Recovery); 212 Daniels (Campaign for a New Tomorrow); 197 Fulani (New Alliance); 741 scattered write-in.

1988    Other vote was 3,526 LaRouche (by petition); 2,494 Paul (Libertarian); 755 Duke (Patriotic); 540 Fulani (New Alliance); 334 Kenoyer (Socialist); 235 Winn (Workers League); 205 Warren (Socialist Workers); 1,613 scattered write-in.

1984    Other vote was 6,248 LaRouche (by petition); 1,844 Bergland (Libertarian); 892 Baker (Big Deal); 463 Serrette (by petition); 313 Mason (Socialist Workers); 286 Hall (Communist); 1,051 scattered write-in.

1980    Other vote was 115,633 Anderson (by petition); 13,123 Clark (Libertarian); 2,273 Commoner (Citizens); 534 McReynolds (Socialist); 298 Hall (Communist); 244 DeBerry (Socialist Workers); 189 Greaves (American); 150 Bubar (Statesman); 519 scattered write-in.

1976    Other vote was 20,051 McCarthy (Independent); 3,040 Anderson (American); 1,452 MacBride (Libertarian); 554 Hall (Communist); 267 Camejo (Socialist Workers); 241 LaRouche (U.S. Labor); 234 Zeidler (Socialist); 167 Levin (Socialist Labor); 506 scattered write-in.

1972    Other vote was 22,056 Schmitz (American Independent); 488 Jenness (Socialist Workers); 272 Hall (Communist); 199 Green (Universal); 195 Fisher (Socialist Labor); 321 scattered write-in.

1968    Wallace on the ballot as American Independent. Other vote was 3,377 Halstead (Socialist Workers); 1,332 Cleaver (Peace and Freedom); 362 Munn (Prohibition); 241 Blomen (Socialist Labor); 142 Hensley (Universal); 250 scattered write-in.

1964    Other vote was 1,902 Munn (Prohibition); 182 Hass (Socialist Labor); 159 DeBerry (Socialist Workers); 118 scattered write-in.

1960    Other vote was 634 Dobbs (Socialist Workers); 230 Hass (Socialist Labor).

# KANSAS

## POPULAR VOTE FOR PRESIDENT 1920 TO 2004

| Year | Total Vote | Republican Vote | Republican Candidate | Democratic Vote | Democratic Candidate | Other Vote | Plurality | Percentage Total Vote Rep. | Dem. | Major Vote Rep. | Dem. |
|------|-----------|-----------------|----------------------|-----------------|----------------------|-----------|-----------|------|------|------|------|
| 2004 | 1,187,756 | 736,456 | Bush, George W. | 434,993 | Kerry, John | 16,307 | 301,463 R | 62.0% | 36.6% | 62.9% | 37.1% |
| 2000** | 1,072,218 | 622,332 | Bush, George W. | 399,276 | Gore, Al | 50,610 | 223,056 R | 58.0% | 37.2% | 60.9% | 39.1% |
| 1996 ** | 1,074,300 | 583,245 | Dole, Bob | 387,659 | Clinton, Bill | 103,396 | 195,586 R | 54.3% | 36.1% | 60.1% | 39.9% |
| 1992 ** | 1,157,335 | 449,951 | Bush, George | 390,434 | Clinton, Bill | 316,950 | 59,517 R | 38.9% | 33.7% | 53.5% | 46.5% |
| 1988 | 993,044 | 554,049 | Bush, George | 422,636 | Dukakis, Michael S. | 16,359 | 131,413 R | 55.8% | 42.6% | 56.7% | 43.3% |
| 1984 | 1,021,991 | 677,296 | Reagan, Ronald | 333,149 | Mondale, Walter F. | 11,546 | 344,147 R | 66.3% | 32.6% | 67.0% | 33.0% |
| 1980 ** | 979,795 | 566,812 | Reagan, Ronald | 326,150 | Carter, Jimmy | 86,833 | 240,662 R | 57.9% | 33.3% | 63.5% | 36.5% |
| 1976 | 957,845 | 502,752 | Ford, Gerald R. | 430,421 | Carter, Jimmy | 24,672 | 72,331 R | 52.5% | 44.9% | 53.9% | 46.1% |
| 1972 | 916,095 | 619,812 | Nixon, Richard M. | 270,287 | McGovern, George S. | 25,996 | 349,525 R | 67.7% | 29.5% | 69.6% | 30.4% |
| 1968 | 872,783 | 478,674 | Nixon, Richard M. | 302,996 | Humphrey, Hubert H. | 91,113 | 175,678 R | 54.8% | 34.7% | 61.2% | 38.8% |
| 1964 | 857,901 | 386,579 | Goldwater, Barry M. | 464,028 | Johnson, Lyndon B. | 7,294 | 77,449 D | 45.1% | 54.1% | 45.4% | 54.6% |
| 1960 | 928,825 | 561,474 | Nixon, Richard M. | 363,213 | Kennedy, John F. | 4,138 | 198,261 R | 60.4% | 39.1% | 60.7% | 39.3% |
| 1956 | 866,243 | 566,878 | Eisenhower, Dwight D. | 296,317 | Stevenson, Adlai E. | 3,048 | 270,561 R | 65.4% | 34.2% | 65.7% | 34.3% |
| 1952 | 896,166 | 616,302 | Eisenhower, Dwight D. | 273,296 | Stevenson, Adlai E. | 6,568 | 343,006 R | 68.8% | 30.5% | 69.3% | 30.7% |
| 1948 | 788,819 | 423,039 | Dewey, Thomas E. | 351,902 | Truman, Harry S. | 13,878 | 71,137 R | 53.6% | 44.6% | 54.6% | 45.4% |
| 1944 | 733,776 | 442,096 | Dewey, Thomas E. | 287,458 | Roosevelt, Franklin D. | 4,222 | 154,638 R | 60.2% | 39.2% | 60.6% | 39.4% |
| 1940 | 860,297 | 489,169 | Willkie, Wendell | 364,725 | Roosevelt, Franklin D. | 6,403 | 124,444 R | 56.9% | 42.4% | 57.3% | 42.7% |
| 1936 | 865,507 | 397,727 | Landon, Alfred M. | 464,520 | Roosevelt, Franklin D. | 3,260 | 66,793 D | 46.0% | 53.7% | 46.1% | 53.9% |
| 1932 | 791,978 | 349,498 | Hoover, Herbert C. | 424,204 | Roosevelt, Franklin D. | 18,276 | 74,706 D | 44.1% | 53.6% | 45.2% | 54.8% |
| 1928 | 713,200 | 513,672 | Hoover, Herbert C. | 193,003 | Smith, Alfred E. | 6,525 | 320,669 R | 72.0% | 27.1% | 72.7% | 27.3% |
| 1924 ** | 662,456 | 407,671 | Coolidge, Calvin | 156,320 | Davis, John W. | 98,465 | 251,351 R | 61.5% | 23.6% | 72.3% | 27.7% |
| 1920 | 570,243 | 369,268 | Harding, Warren G. | 185,464 | Cox, James M. | 15,511 | 183,804 R | 64.8% | 32.5% | 66.6% | 33.4% |

In 2000 the other vote column includes 36,086 votes cast for Green (Nader). In 1996 the other vote column includes 92,639 votes cast for Perot. In 1992 the other vote column includes 312,358 votes cast for Perot. In 1980 the other column includes 68,231 votes for Independent (Anderson). In 1924 the other vote was 98,461 Progressive and 4 scattered.

## ELECTORAL COLLEGE VOTE 1920 TO 2004

| Year | Total | Republican | Democratic | Other |
|------|-------|------------|------------|-------|
| 2004 | 6 | 6 | | |
| 2000 | 6 | 6 | | |
| 1996 | 6 | 6 | | |
| 1992 | 6 | 6 | | |
| 1988 | 7 | 7 | | |
| 1984 | 7 | 7 | | |
| 1980 | 7 | 7 | | |
| 1976 | 7 | 7 | | |
| 1972 | 7 | 7 | | |
| 1968 | 7 | 7 | | |
| 1964 | 7 | | 7 | |
| 1960 | 8 | 8 | | |
| 1956 | 8 | 8 | | |
| 1952 | 8 | 8 | | |
| 1948 | 8 | 8 | | |
| 1944 | 8 | 8 | | |
| 1940 | 9 | 9 | | |
| 1936 | 9 | | 9 | |
| 1932 | 9 | | 9 | |
| 1928 | 10 | 10 | | |
| 1924 | 10 | 10 | | |
| 1920 | 10 | 10 | | |

# KANSAS

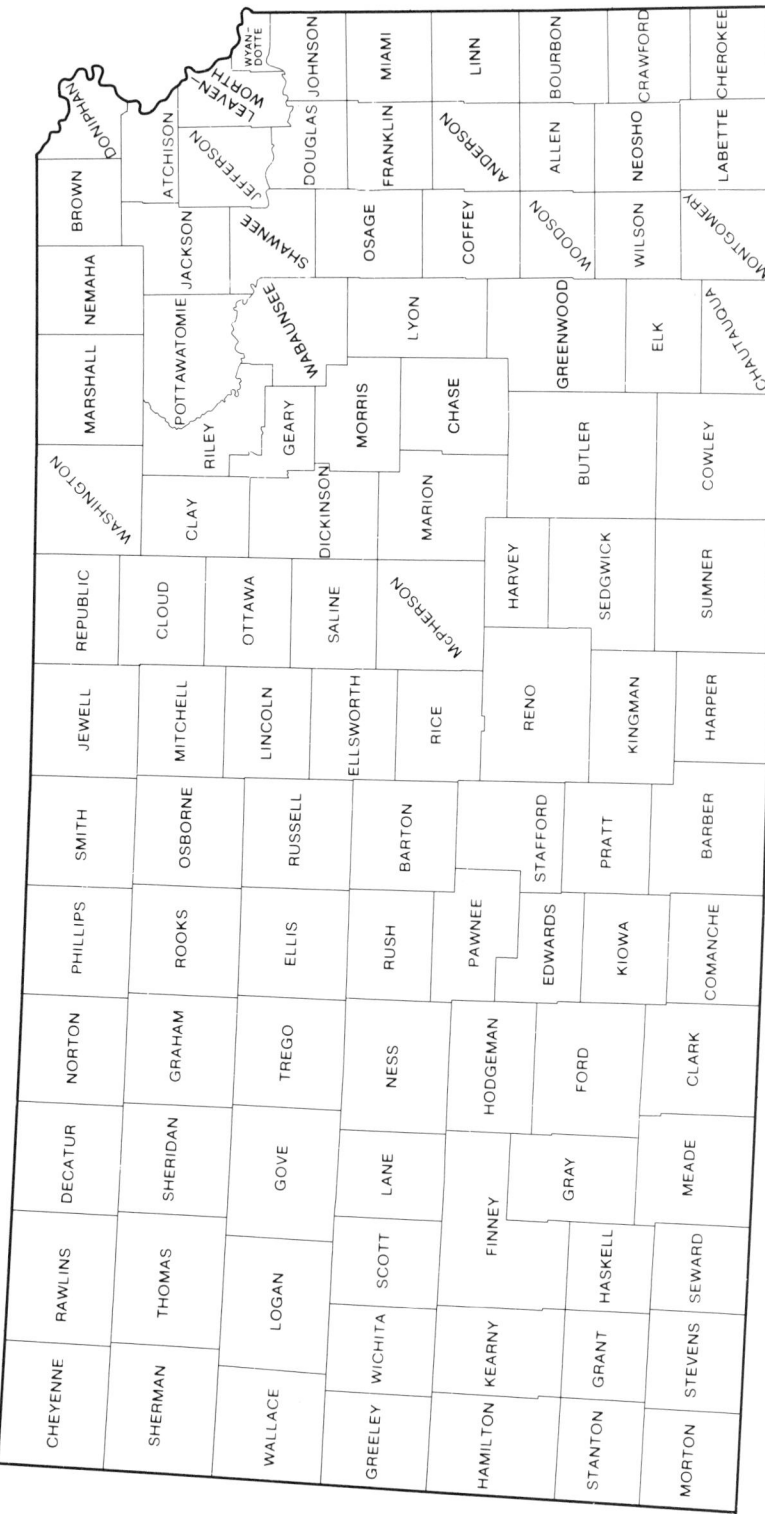

# KANSAS

## PRESIDENT 2004

| 2000 Census Population | County | Total Vote | Republican | Democratic | Other | Rep.-Dem. Plurality | Percentage | | | |
|---|---|---|---|---|---|---|---|---|---|---|
| | | | | | | | Total Vote | | Major Vote | |
| | | | | | | | Rep. | Dem. | Rep. | Dem. |
| 14,385 | ALLEN | 5,873 | 3,867 | 1,922 | 84 | 1,945 R | 65.8% | 32.7% | 66.8% | 33.2% |
| 8,110 | ANDERSON | 3,863 | 2,500 | 1,295 | 68 | 1,205 R | 64.7% | 33.5% | 65.9% | 34.1% |
| 16,774 | ATCHISON | 7,118 | 3,880 | 3,120 | 118 | 760 R | 54.5% | 43.8% | 55.4% | 44.6% |
| 5,307 | BARBER | 2,403 | 1,782 | 588 | 33 | 1,194 R | 74.2% | 24.5% | 75.2% | 24.8% |
| 28,205 | BARTON | 11,706 | 8,666 | 2,874 | 166 | 5,792 R | 74.0% | 24.6% | 75.1% | 24.9% |
| 15,379 | BOURBON | 6,686 | 4,372 | 2,216 | 98 | 2,156 R | 65.4% | 33.1% | 66.4% | 33.6% |
| 10,724 | BROWN | 4,418 | 3,092 | 1,268 | 58 | 1,824 R | 70.0% | 28.7% | 70.9% | 29.1% |
| 59,482 | BUTLER | 26,280 | 18,438 | 7,495 | 347 | 10,943 R | 70.2% | 28.5% | 71.1% | 28.9% |
| 3,030 | CHASE | 1,501 | 1,055 | 418 | 28 | 637 R | 70.3% | 27.8% | 71.6% | 28.4% |
| 4,359 | CHAUTAUQUA | 1,960 | 1,529 | 404 | 27 | 1,125 R | 78.0% | 20.6% | 79.1% | 20.9% |
| 22,605 | CHEROKEE | 9,913 | 6,083 | 3,726 | 104 | 2,357 R | 61.4% | 37.6% | 62.0% | 38.0% |
| 3,165 | CHEYENNE | 1,692 | 1,353 | 320 | 19 | 1,033 R | 80.0% | 18.9% | 80.9% | 19.1% |
| 2,390 | CLARK | 1,291 | 1,014 | 257 | 20 | 757 R | 78.5% | 19.9% | 79.8% | 20.2% |
| 8,822 | CLAY | 4,010 | 3,174 | 793 | 43 | 2,381 R | 79.2% | 19.8% | 80.0% | 20.0% |
| 10,268 | CLOUD | 4,503 | 3,221 | 1,210 | 72 | 2,011 R | 71.5% | 26.9% | 72.7% | 27.3% |
| 8,865 | COFFEY | 4,408 | 3,259 | 1,093 | 56 | 2,166 R | 73.9% | 24.8% | 74.9% | 25.1% |
| 1,967 | COMANCHE | 981 | 770 | 200 | 11 | 570 R | 78.5% | 20.4% | 79.4% | 20.6% |
| 36,291 | COWLEY | 14,447 | 9,407 | 4,818 | 222 | 4,589 R | 65.1% | 33.3% | 66.1% | 33.9% |
| 38,242 | CRAWFORD | 16,527 | 8,626 | 7,617 | 284 | 1,009 R | 52.2% | 46.1% | 53.1% | 46.9% |
| 3,472 | DECATUR | 1,740 | 1,355 | 355 | 30 | 1,000 R | 77.9% | 20.4% | 79.2% | 20.8% |
| 19,344 | DICKINSON | 8,791 | 6,295 | 2,364 | 132 | 3,931 R | 71.6% | 26.9% | 72.7% | 27.3% |
| 8,249 | DONIPHAN | 3,603 | 2,491 | 1,065 | 47 | 1,426 R | 69.1% | 29.6% | 70.1% | 29.9% |
| 99,962 | DOUGLAS | 50,111 | 20,544 | 28,634 | 933 | 8,090 D | 41.0% | 57.1% | 41.8% | 58.2% |
| 3,449 | EDWARDS | 1,496 | 1,084 | 386 | 26 | 698 R | 72.5% | 25.8% | 73.7% | 26.3% |
| 3,261 | ELK | 1,515 | 1,119 | 369 | 27 | 750 R | 73.9% | 24.4% | 75.2% | 24.8% |
| 27,507 | ELLIS | 12,187 | 7,891 | 4,033 | 263 | 3,858 R | 64.7% | 33.1% | 66.2% | 33.8% |
| 6,525 | ELLSWORTH | 3,102 | 2,259 | 801 | 42 | 1,458 R | 72.8% | 25.8% | 73.8% | 26.2% |
| 40,523 | FINNEY | 9,933 | 7,479 | 2,351 | 103 | 5,128 R | 75.3% | 23.7% | 76.1% | 23.9% |
| 32,458 | FORD | 9,016 | 6,632 | 2,286 | 98 | 4,346 R | 73.6% | 25.4% | 74.4% | 25.6% |
| 24,784 | FRANKLIN | 11,476 | 7,391 | 3,921 | 164 | 3,470 R | 64.4% | 34.2% | 65.3% | 34.7% |
| 27,947 | GEARY | 7,328 | 4,703 | 2,531 | 94 | 2,172 R | 64.2% | 34.5% | 65.0% | 35.0% |
| 3,068 | GOVE | 1,467 | 1,196 | 247 | 24 | 949 R | 81.5% | 16.8% | 82.9% | 17.1% |
| 2,946 | GRAHAM | 1,440 | 1,082 | 334 | 24 | 748 R | 75.1% | 23.2% | 76.4% | 23.6% |
| 7,909 | GRANT | 2,758 | 2,169 | 561 | 28 | 1,608 R | 78.6% | 20.3% | 79.5% | 20.5% |
| 5,904 | GRAY | 2,245 | 1,816 | 408 | 21 | 1,408 R | 80.9% | 18.2% | 81.7% | 18.3% |
| 1,534 | GREELEY | 735 | 584 | 138 | 13 | 446 R | 79.5% | 18.8% | 80.9% | 19.1% |
| 7,673 | GREENWOOD | 3,244 | 2,282 | 911 | 51 | 1,371 R | 70.3% | 28.1% | 71.5% | 28.5% |
| 2,670 | HAMILTON | 1,130 | 888 | 229 | 13 | 659 R | 78.6% | 20.3% | 79.5% | 20.5% |
| 6,536 | HARPER | 2,930 | 2,154 | 727 | 49 | 1,427 R | 73.5% | 24.8% | 74.8% | 25.2% |
| 32,869 | HARVEY | 15,110 | 9,534 | 5,331 | 245 | 4,203 R | 63.1% | 35.3% | 64.1% | 35.9% |
| 4,307 | HASKELL | 1,599 | 1,356 | 227 | 16 | 1,129 R | 84.8% | 14.2% | 85.7% | 14.3% |
| 2,085 | HODGEMAN | 1,183 | 953 | 223 | 7 | 730 R | 80.6% | 18.9% | 81.0% | 19.0% |
| 12,657 | JACKSON | 5,888 | 3,730 | 2,064 | 94 | 1,666 R | 63.3% | 35.1% | 64.4% | 35.6% |
| 18,426 | JEFFERSON | 8,793 | 5,408 | 3,253 | 132 | 2,155 R | 61.5% | 37.0% | 62.4% | 37.6% |
| 3,791 | JEWELL | 1,915 | 1,495 | 385 | 35 | 1,110 R | 78.1% | 20.1% | 79.5% | 20.5% |
| 451,086 | JOHNSON | 258,687 | 158,103 | 97,866 | 2,718 | 60,237 R | 61.1% | 37.8% | 61.8% | 38.2% |
| 4,531 | KEARNY | 1,455 | 1,177 | 272 | 6 | 905 R | 80.9% | 18.7% | 81.2% | 18.8% |
| 8,673 | KINGMAN | 3,764 | 2,801 | 904 | 59 | 1,897 R | 74.4% | 24.0% | 75.6% | 24.4% |
| 3,278 | KIOWA | 1,565 | 1,275 | 256 | 34 | 1,019 R | 81.5% | 16.4% | 83.3% | 16.7% |
| 22,835 | LABETTE | 9,139 | 5,400 | 3,615 | 124 | 1,785 R | 59.1% | 39.6% | 59.9% | 40.1% |
| 2,155 | LANE | 1,014 | 823 | 181 | 10 | 642 R | 81.2% | 17.9% | 82.0% | 18.0% |
| 68,691 | LEAVENWORTH | 27,331 | 15,949 | 11,039 | 343 | 4,910 R | 58.4% | 40.4% | 59.1% | 40.9% |
| 3,578 | LINCOLN | 1,800 | 1,368 | 391 | 41 | 977 R | 76.0% | 21.7% | 77.8% | 22.2% |
| 9,570 | LINN | 4,741 | 3,048 | 1,631 | 62 | 1,417 R | 64.3% | 34.4% | 65.1% | 34.9% |
| 3,046 | LOGAN | 1,523 | 1,255 | 248 | 20 | 1,007 R | 82.4% | 16.3% | 83.5% | 16.5% |
| 35,935 | LYON | 13,440 | 7,951 | 5,234 | 255 | 2,717 R | 59.2% | 38.9% | 60.3% | 39.7% |
| 29,554 | MCPHERSON | 13,367 | 9,595 | 3,589 | 183 | 6,006 R | 71.8% | 26.8% | 72.8% | 27.2% |
| 13,361 | MARION | 6,159 | 4,516 | 1,536 | 107 | 2,980 R | 73.3% | 24.9% | 74.6% | 25.4% |
| 10,965 | MARSHALL | 5,108 | 3,261 | 1,789 | 58 | 1,472 R | 63.8% | 35.0% | 64.6% | 35.4% |
| 4,631 | MEADE | 2,121 | 1,748 | 356 | 17 | 1,392 R | 82.4% | 16.8% | 83.1% | 16.9% |

# KANSAS

## PRESIDENT 2004

| 2000 Census Population | County | Total Vote | Republican | Democratic | Other | Rep.-Dem. Plurality | Percentage | | | |
|---|---|---|---|---|---|---|---|---|---|---|
| | | | | | | | Total Vote | | Major Vote | |
| | | | | | | | Rep. | Dem. | Rep. | Dem. |
| 28,351 | MIAMI | 14,016 | 9,013 | 4,838 | 165 | 4,175 R | 64.3% | 34.5% | 65.1% | 34.9% |
| 6,932 | MITCHELL | 3,349 | 2,609 | 693 | 47 | 1,916 R | 77.9% | 20.7% | 79.0% | 21.0% |
| 36,252 | MONTGOMERY | 14,116 | 9,598 | 4,338 | 180 | 5,260 R | 68.0% | 30.7% | 68.9% | 31.1% |
| 6,104 | MORRIS | 2,936 | 1,961 | 931 | 44 | 1,030 R | 66.8% | 31.7% | 67.8% | 32.2% |
| 3,496 | MORTON | 1,576 | 1,287 | 276 | 13 | 1,011 R | 81.7% | 17.5% | 82.3% | 17.7% |
| 10,717 | NEMAHA | 5,463 | 4,027 | 1,355 | 81 | 2,672 R | 73.7% | 24.8% | 74.8% | 25.2% |
| 16,997 | NEOSHO | 7,231 | 4,705 | 2,424 | 102 | 2,281 R | 65.1% | 33.5% | 66.0% | 34.0% |
| 3,454 | NESS | 1,818 | 1,407 | 382 | 29 | 1,025 R | 77.4% | 21.0% | 78.6% | 21.4% |
| 5,953 | NORTON | 2,599 | 2,092 | 473 | 34 | 1,619 R | 80.5% | 18.2% | 81.6% | 18.4% |
| 16,712 | OSAGE | 7,463 | 4,800 | 2,537 | 126 | 2,263 R | 64.3% | 34.0% | 65.4% | 34.6% |
| 4,452 | OSBORNE | 2,075 | 1,587 | 454 | 34 | 1,133 R | 76.5% | 21.9% | 77.8% | 22.2% |
| 6,163 | OTTAWA | 2,971 | 2,333 | 595 | 43 | 1,738 R | 78.5% | 20.0% | 79.7% | 20.3% |
| 7,233 | PAWNEE | 2,988 | 2,172 | 773 | 43 | 1,399 R | 72.7% | 25.9% | 73.8% | 26.2% |
| 6,001 | PHILLIPS | 2,847 | 2,256 | 557 | 34 | 1,699 R | 79.2% | 19.6% | 80.2% | 19.8% |
| 18,209 | POTTAWATOMIE | 8,823 | 6,326 | 2,176 | 321 | 4,150 R | 71.7% | 24.7% | 74.4% | 25.6% |
| 9,647 | PRATT | 4,384 | 3,121 | 1,200 | 63 | 1,921 R | 71.2% | 27.4% | 72.2% | 27.8% |
| 2,966 | RAWLINS | 1,720 | 1,414 | 289 | 17 | 1,125 R | 82.2% | 16.8% | 83.0% | 17.0% |
| 64,790 | RENO | 27,324 | 17,748 | 9,114 | 462 | 8,634 R | 65.0% | 33.4% | 66.1% | 33.9% |
| 5,835 | REPUBLIC | 2,889 | 2,238 | 607 | 44 | 1,631 R | 77.5% | 21.0% | 78.7% | 21.3% |
| 10,761 | RICE | 4,376 | 3,182 | 1,130 | 64 | 2,052 R | 72.7% | 25.8% | 73.8% | 26.2% |
| 62,843 | RILEY | 20,911 | 12,672 | 7,908 | 331 | 4,764 R | 60.6% | 37.8% | 61.6% | 38.4% |
| 5,685 | ROOKS | 2,710 | 2,121 | 534 | 55 | 1,587 R | 78.3% | 19.7% | 79.9% | 20.1% |
| 3,551 | RUSH | 1,789 | 1,226 | 517 | 46 | 709 R | 68.5% | 28.9% | 70.3% | 29.7% |
| 7,370 | RUSSELL | 3,525 | 2,671 | 810 | 44 | 1,861 R | 75.8% | 23.0% | 76.7% | 23.3% |
| 53,597 | SALINE | 23,041 | 15,111 | 7,524 | 406 | 7,587 R | 65.6% | 32.7% | 66.8% | 33.2% |
| 5,120 | SCOTT | 2,299 | 1,924 | 347 | 28 | 1,577 R | 83.7% | 15.1% | 84.7% | 15.3% |
| 452,869 | SEDGWICK | 177,679 | 110,381 | 64,839 | 2,459 | 45,542 R | 62.1% | 36.5% | 63.0% | 37.0% |
| 22,510 | SEWARD | 5,439 | 4,272 | 1,122 | 45 | 3,150 R | 78.5% | 20.6% | 79.2% | 20.8% |
| 169,871 | SHAWNEE | 81,577 | 44,188 | 36,264 | 1,125 | 7,924 R | 54.2% | 44.5% | 54.9% | 45.1% |
| 2,813 | SHERIDAN | 1,406 | 1,144 | 239 | 23 | 905 R | 81.4% | 17.0% | 82.7% | 17.3% |
| 6,760 | SHERMAN | 2,762 | 2,088 | 632 | 42 | 1,456 R | 75.6% | 22.9% | 76.8% | 23.2% |
| 4,536 | SMITH | 2,370 | 1,803 | 540 | 27 | 1,263 R | 76.1% | 22.8% | 77.0% | 23.0% |
| 4,789 | STAFFORD | 2,186 | 1,649 | 506 | 31 | 1,143 R | 75.4% | 23.1% | 76.5% | 23.5% |
| 2,406 | STANTON | 966 | 796 | 165 | 5 | 631 R | 82.4% | 17.1% | 82.8% | 17.2% |
| 5,463 | STEVENS | 2,265 | 1,936 | 310 | 19 | 1,626 R | 85.5% | 13.7% | 86.2% | 13.8% |
| 25,946 | SUMNER | 10,488 | 7,092 | 3,217 | 179 | 3,875 R | 67.6% | 30.7% | 68.8% | 31.2% |
| 8,180 | THOMAS | 3,870 | 3,007 | 816 | 47 | 2,191 R | 77.7% | 21.1% | 78.7% | 21.3% |
| 3,319 | TREGO | 1,686 | 1,225 | 434 | 27 | 791 R | 72.7% | 25.7% | 73.8% | 26.2% |
| 6,885 | WABAUNSEE | 3,604 | 2,531 | 1,001 | 72 | 1,530 R | 70.2% | 27.8% | 71.7% | 28.3% |
| 1,749 | WALLACE | 876 | 742 | 112 | 22 | 630 R | 84.7% | 12.8% | 86.9% | 13.1% |
| 6,483 | WASHINGTON | 3,190 | 2,498 | 643 | 49 | 1,855 R | 78.3% | 20.2% | 79.5% | 20.5% |
| 2,531 | WICHITA | 1,062 | 869 | 183 | 10 | 686 R | 81.8% | 17.2% | 82.6% | 17.4% |
| 10,332 | WILSON | 4,398 | 3,263 | 1,060 | 75 | 2,203 R | 74.2% | 24.1% | 75.5% | 24.5% |
| 3,788 | WOODSON | 1,763 | 1,204 | 530 | 29 | 674 R | 68.3% | 30.1% | 69.4% | 30.6% |
| 157,882 | WYANDOTTE | 53,401 | 17,919 | 34,923 | 559 | 17,004 D | 33.6% | 65.4% | 33.9% | 66.1% |
| 2,688,418 | TOTAL | 1,187,756 | 736,456 | 434,993 | 16,307 | 301,463 R | 62.0% | 36.6% | 62.9% | 37.1% |

# KANSAS

## PRESIDENT 2000

| 2000 Census Population | County | Total Vote | Republican | Democratic | Green (Nader) | Other | Rep.-Dem. Plurality | Percentage of Total Vote | | |
|---|---|---|---|---|---|---|---|---|---|---|
| | | | | | | | | Rep. | Dem. | Green |
| 14,385 | ALLEN | 5,766 | 3,379 | 2,132 | 164 | 91 | 1,247 R | 58.6% | 37.0% | 2.8% |
| 8,110 | ANDERSON | 3,478 | 1,984 | 1,327 | 94 | 73 | 657 R | 57.0% | 38.2% | 2.7% |
| 16,774 | ATCHISON | 6,900 | 3,378 | 3,171 | 233 | 118 | 207 R | 49.0% | 46.0% | 3.4% |
| 5,307 | BARBER | 2,498 | 1,755 | 637 | 73 | 33 | 1,118 R | 70.3% | 25.5% | 2.9% |
| 28,205 | BARTON | 10,955 | 7,302 | 3,238 | 251 | 164 | 4,064 R | 66.7% | 29.6% | 2.3% |
| 15,379 | BOURBON | 6,308 | 3,852 | 2,211 | 159 | 86 | 1,641 R | 61.1% | 35.1% | 2.5% |
| 10,724 | BROWN | 4,691 | 2,985 | 1,512 | 120 | 74 | 1,473 R | 63.6% | 32.2% | 2.6% |
| 59,482 | BUTLER | 21,002 | 13,377 | 6,755 | 497 | 373 | 6,622 R | 63.7% | 32.2% | 2.4% |
| 3,030 | CHASE | 1,317 | 848 | 391 | 56 | 22 | 457 R | 64.4% | 29.7% | 4.3% |
| 4,359 | CHAUTAUQUA | 1,880 | 1,347 | 443 | 36 | 54 | 904 R | 71.6% | 23.6% | 1.9% |
| 22,605 | CHEROKEE | 9,130 | 5,014 | 3,783 | 225 | 108 | 1,231 R | 54.9% | 41.4% | 2.5% |
| 3,165 | CHEYENNE | 1,727 | 1,312 | 350 | 47 | 18 | 962 R | 76.0% | 20.3% | 2.7% |
| 2,390 | CLARK | 1,261 | 926 | 292 | 34 | 9 | 634 R | 73.4% | 23.2% | 2.7% |
| 8,822 | CLAY | 4,088 | 2,998 | 951 | 93 | 46 | 2,047 R | 73.3% | 23.3% | 2.3% |
| 10,268 | CLOUD | 4,503 | 2,918 | 1,314 | 210 | 61 | 1,604 R | 64.8% | 29.2% | 4.7% |
| 8,865 | COFFEY | 4,040 | 2,700 | 1,196 | 96 | 48 | 1,504 R | 66.8% | 29.6% | 2.4% |
| 1,967 | COMANCHE | 1,006 | 760 | 211 | 18 | 17 | 549 R | 75.5% | 21.0% | 1.8% |
| 36,291 | COWLEY | 14,210 | 8,080 | 5,535 | 416 | 179 | 2,545 R | 56.9% | 39.0% | 2.9% |
| 38,242 | CRAWFORD | 15,034 | 7,160 | 7,076 | 630 | 168 | 84 R | 47.6% | 47.1% | 4.2% |
| 3,472 | DECATUR | 1,759 | 1,255 | 424 | 51 | 29 | 831 R | 71.3% | 24.1% | 2.9% |
| 19,344 | DICKINSON | 8,092 | 5,243 | 2,413 | 322 | 114 | 2,830 R | 64.8% | 29.8% | 4.0% |
| 8,249 | DONIPHAN | 3,649 | 2,350 | 1,134 | 90 | 75 | 1,216 R | 64.4% | 31.1% | 2.5% |
| 99,962 | DOUGLAS | 39,838 | 17,062 | 18,249 | 4,031 | 496 | 1,187 D | 42.8% | 45.8% | 10.1% |
| 3,449 | EDWARDS | 1,563 | 1,062 | 447 | 33 | 21 | 615 R | 67.9% | 28.6% | 2.1% |
| 3,261 | ELK | 1,550 | 1,080 | 402 | 34 | 34 | 678 R | 69.7% | 25.9% | 2.2% |
| 27,507 | ELLIS | 11,160 | 6,516 | 3,926 | 543 | 175 | 2,590 R | 58.4% | 35.2% | 4.9% |
| 6,525 | ELLSWORTH | 2,839 | 1,845 | 825 | 130 | 39 | 1,020 R | 65.0% | 29.1% | 4.6% |
| 40,523 | FINNEY | 9,150 | 6,442 | 2,431 | 182 | 95 | 4,011 R | 70.4% | 26.6% | 2.0% |
| 32,458 | FORD | 8,917 | 6,050 | 2,566 | 200 | 101 | 3,484 R | 67.8% | 28.8% | 2.2% |
| 24,784 | FRANKLIN | 9,658 | 5,925 | 3,321 | 306 | 106 | 2,604 R | 61.3% | 34.4% | 3.2% |
| 27,947 | GEARY | 6,866 | 3,977 | 2,660 | 158 | 71 | 1,317 R | 57.9% | 38.7% | 2.3% |
| 3,068 | GOVE | 1,495 | 1,122 | 296 | 44 | 33 | 826 R | 75.1% | 19.8% | 2.9% |
| 2,946 | GRAHAM | 1,474 | 1,058 | 346 | 47 | 23 | 712 R | 71.8% | 23.5% | 3.2% |
| 7,909 | GRANT | 2,856 | 2,126 | 683 | 39 | 8 | 1,443 R | 74.4% | 23.9% | 1.4% |
| 5,904 | GRAY | 2,160 | 1,631 | 482 | 27 | 20 | 1,149 R | 75.5% | 22.3% | 1.3% |
| 1,534 | GREELEY | 803 | 628 | 143 | 24 | 8 | 485 R | 78.2% | 17.8% | 3.0% |
| 7,673 | GREENWOOD | 3,561 | 2,392 | 1,027 | 81 | 61 | 1,365 R | 67.2% | 28.8% | 2.3% |
| 2,670 | HAMILTON | 1,192 | 901 | 264 | 15 | 12 | 637 R | 75.6% | 22.1% | 1.3% |
| 6,536 | HARPER | 3,055 | 2,076 | 869 | 75 | 35 | 1,207 R | 68.0% | 28.4% | 2.5% |
| 32,869 | HARVEY | 13,684 | 8,271 | 4,591 | 651 | 171 | 3,680 R | 60.4% | 33.6% | 4.8% |
| 4,307 | HASKELL | 1,616 | 1,323 | 263 | 16 | 14 | 1,060 R | 81.9% | 16.3% | 1.0% |
| 2,085 | HODGEMAN | 1,088 | 835 | 217 | 21 | 15 | 618 R | 76.7% | 19.9% | 1.9% |
| 12,657 | JACKSON | 5,250 | 3,001 | 1,990 | 123 | 136 | 1,011 R | 57.2% | 37.9% | 2.3% |
| 18,426 | JEFFERSON | 7,877 | 4,423 | 3,000 | 321 | 133 | 1,423 R | 56.2% | 38.1% | 4.1% |
| 3,791 | JEWELL | 1,877 | 1,400 | 380 | 57 | 40 | 1,020 R | 74.6% | 20.2% | 3.0% |
| 451,086 | JOHNSON | 217,536 | 129,965 | 79,118 | 6,493 | 1,960 | 50,847 R | 59.7% | 36.4% | 3.0% |
| 4,531 | KEARNY | 1,437 | 1,084 | 320 | 16 | 17 | 764 R | 75.4% | 22.3% | 1.1% |
| 8,673 | KINGMAN | 3,808 | 2,672 | 991 | 86 | 59 | 1,681 R | 70.2% | 26.0% | 2.3% |
| 3,278 | KIOWA | 1,608 | 1,262 | 294 | 34 | 18 | 968 R | 78.5% | 18.3% | 2.1% |
| 22,835 | LABETTE | 8,538 | 4,475 | 3,745 | 230 | 88 | 730 R | 52.4% | 43.9% | 2.7% |
| 2,155 | LANE | 1,133 | 846 | 252 | 23 | 12 | 594 R | 74.7% | 22.2% | 2.0% |
| 68,691 | LEAVENWORTH | 23,271 | 12,583 | 9,733 | 679 | 276 | 2,850 R | 54.1% | 41.8% | 2.9% |
| 3,578 | LINCOLN | 1,890 | 1,295 | 469 | 98 | 28 | 826 R | 68.5% | 24.8% | 5.2% |
| 9,570 | LINN | 4,259 | 2,513 | 1,587 | 91 | 68 | 926 R | 59.0% | 37.3% | 2.1% |
| 3,046 | LOGAN | 1,397 | 1,088 | 231 | 49 | 29 | 857 R | 77.9% | 16.5% | 3.5% |
| 35,935 | LYON | 12,455 | 6,652 | 5,190 | 417 | 196 | 1,462 R | 53.4% | 41.7% | 3.3% |
| 29,554 | MCPHERSON | 12,461 | 8,501 | 3,272 | 534 | 154 | 5,229 R | 68.2% | 26.3% | 4.3% |
| 13,361 | MARION | 5,903 | 4,156 | 1,475 | 189 | 83 | 2,681 R | 70.4% | 25.0% | 3.2% |
| 10,965 | MARSHALL | 5,115 | 3,066 | 1,831 | 134 | 84 | 1,235 R | 59.9% | 35.8% | 2.6% |
| 4,631 | MEADE | 2,053 | 1,604 | 400 | 33 | 16 | 1,204 R | 78.1% | 19.5% | 1.6% |

# KANSAS

## PRESIDENT 2000

| 2000 Census Population | County | Total Vote | Republican | Democratic | Green (Nader) | Other | Rep.-Dem. Plurality | Percentage of Total Vote | | |
|---|---|---|---|---|---|---|---|---|---|---|
| | | | | | | | | Rep. | Dem. | Green |
| 28,351 | MIAMI | 11,607 | 6,611 | 4,554 | 294 | 148 | 2,057 R | 57.0% | 39.2% | 2.5% |
| 6,932 | MITCHELL | 3,266 | 2,350 | 751 | 115 | 50 | 1,599 R | 72.0% | 23.0% | 3.5% |
| 36,252 | MONTGOMERY | 13,745 | 8,496 | 4,770 | 269 | 210 | 3,726 R | 61.8% | 34.7% | 2.0% |
| 6,104 | MORRIS | 2,641 | 1,599 | 882 | 104 | 56 | 717 R | 60.5% | 33.4% | 3.9% |
| 3,496 | MORTON | 1,557 | 1,203 | 321 | 19 | 14 | 882 R | 77.3% | 20.6% | 1.2% |
| 10,717 | NEMAHA | 5,290 | 3,578 | 1,494 | 102 | 116 | 2,084 R | 67.6% | 28.2% | 1.9% |
| 16,997 | NEOSHO | 6,886 | 4,014 | 2,588 | 194 | 90 | 1,426 R | 58.3% | 37.6% | 2.8% |
| 3,454 | NESS | 1,876 | 1,420 | 383 | 49 | 24 | 1,037 R | 75.7% | 20.4% | 2.6% |
| 5,953 | NORTON | 2,451 | 1,744 | 598 | 65 | 44 | 1,146 R | 71.2% | 24.4% | 2.7% |
| 16,712 | OSAGE | 6,613 | 3,770 | 2,530 | 171 | 142 | 1,240 R | 57.0% | 38.3% | 2.6% |
| 4,452 | OSBORNE | 2,030 | 1,432 | 484 | 74 | 40 | 948 R | 70.5% | 23.8% | 3.6% |
| 6,163 | OTTAWA | 2,791 | 1,977 | 631 | 145 | 38 | 1,346 R | 70.8% | 22.6% | 5.2% |
| 7,233 | PAWNEE | 2,940 | 1,850 | 968 | 93 | 29 | 882 R | 62.9% | 32.9% | 3.2% |
| 6,001 | PHILLIPS | 2,792 | 2,057 | 611 | 85 | 39 | 1,446 R | 73.7% | 21.9% | 3.0% |
| 18,209 | POTTAWATOMIE | 7,731 | 4,985 | 2,037 | 252 | 457 | 2,948 R | 64.5% | 26.3% | 3.3% |
| 9,647 | PRATT | 4,416 | 2,885 | 1,314 | 149 | 68 | 1,571 R | 65.3% | 29.8% | 3.4% |
| 2,966 | RAWLINS | 1,740 | 1,349 | 306 | 49 | 36 | 1,043 R | 77.5% | 17.6% | 2.8% |
| 64,790 | RENO | 25,430 | 15,179 | 9,025 | 877 | 349 | 6,154 R | 59.7% | 35.5% | 3.4% |
| 5,835 | REPUBLIC | 2,985 | 2,239 | 604 | 103 | 39 | 1,635 R | 75.0% | 20.2% | 3.5% |
| 10,761 | RICE | 4,520 | 2,903 | 1,422 | 128 | 67 | 1,481 R | 64.2% | 31.5% | 2.8% |
| 62,843 | RILEY | 18,253 | 10,672 | 6,188 | 1,171 | 222 | 4,484 R | 58.5% | 33.9% | 6.4% |
| 5,685 | ROOKS | 2,775 | 2,016 | 597 | 105 | 57 | 1,419 R | 72.6% | 21.5% | 3.8% |
| 3,551 | RUSH | 1,854 | 1,235 | 505 | 82 | 32 | 730 R | 66.6% | 27.2% | 4.4% |
| 7,370 | RUSSELL | 3,482 | 2,434 | 886 | 121 | 41 | 1,548 R | 69.9% | 25.4% | 3.5% |
| 53,597 | SALINE | 21,527 | 12,412 | 7,487 | 1,367 | 261 | 4,925 R | 57.7% | 34.8% | 6.4% |
| 5,120 | SCOTT | 2,303 | 1,811 | 418 | 52 | 22 | 1,393 R | 78.6% | 18.2% | 2.3% |
| 452,869 | SEDGWICK | 163,417 | 93,724 | 62,561 | 4,669 | 2,463 | 31,163 R | 57.4% | 38.3% | 2.9% |
| 22,510 | SEWARD | 5,096 | 3,869 | 1,126 | 60 | 41 | 2,743 R | 75.9% | 22.1% | 1.2% |
| 169,871 | SHAWNEE | 74,373 | 35,894 | 34,818 | 2,529 | 1,132 | 1,076 R | 48.3% | 46.8% | 3.4% |
| 2,813 | SHERIDAN | 1,489 | 1,132 | 281 | 55 | 21 | 851 R | 76.0% | 18.9% | 3.7% |
| 6,760 | SHERMAN | 2,682 | 1,894 | 681 | 60 | 47 | 1,213 R | 70.6% | 25.4% | 2.2% |
| 4,536 | SMITH | 2,184 | 1,534 | 534 | 79 | 37 | 1,000 R | 70.2% | 24.5% | 3.6% |
| 4,789 | STAFFORD | 2,200 | 1,546 | 567 | 54 | 33 | 979 R | 70.3% | 25.8% | 2.5% |
| 2,406 | STANTON | 1,029 | 785 | 215 | 16 | 13 | 570 R | 76.3% | 20.9% | 1.6% |
| 5,463 | STEVENS | 2,111 | 1,714 | 345 | 34 | 18 | 1,369 R | 81.2% | 16.3% | 1.6% |
| 25,946 | SUMNER | 10,232 | 6,176 | 3,549 | 306 | 201 | 2,627 R | 60.4% | 34.7% | 3.0% |
| 8,180 | THOMAS | 3,780 | 2,822 | 807 | 93 | 58 | 2,015 R | 74.7% | 21.3% | 2.5% |
| 3,319 | TREGO | 1,837 | 1,220 | 516 | 69 | 32 | 704 R | 66.4% | 28.1% | 3.8% |
| 6,885 | WABAUNSEE | 3,420 | 2,182 | 1,025 | 96 | 117 | 1,157 R | 63.8% | 30.0% | 2.8% |
| 1,749 | WALLACE | 861 | 737 | 103 | 14 | 7 | 634 R | 85.6% | 12.0% | 1.6% |
| 6,483 | WASHINGTON | 3,267 | 2,446 | 687 | 77 | 57 | 1,759 R | 74.9% | 21.0% | 2.4% |
| 2,531 | WICHITA | 1,090 | 859 | 207 | 15 | 9 | 652 R | 78.8% | 19.0% | 1.4% |
| 10,332 | WILSON | 4,095 | 2,748 | 1,186 | 100 | 61 | 1,562 R | 67.1% | 29.0% | 2.4% |
| 3,788 | WOODSON | 1,595 | 974 | 521 | 59 | 41 | 453 R | 61.1% | 32.7% | 3.7% |
| 157,882 | WYANDOTTE | 48,272 | 14,024 | 32,411 | 1,287 | 550 | 18,387 D | 29.1% | 67.1% | 2.7% |
| 2,688,418 | TOTAL | 1,072,218 | 622,332 | 399,276 | 36,086 | 14,524 | 223,056 R | 58.0% | 37.2% | 3.4% |

# KANSAS

## PRESIDENT 1996

| 1995 Census Pop. Est. | County | Total Vote | Republican | Democratic | Reform (Perot) | Other | Rep.-Dem. Plurality | Percentage of Total Vote | | |
|---|---|---|---|---|---|---|---|---|---|---|
| | | | | | | | | Rep. | Dem. | Reform |
| 14,739 | ALLEN | 5,943 | 2,797 | 2,299 | 793 | 54 | 498 R | 47.1% | 38.7% | 13.3% |
| 8,000 | ANDERSON | 3,506 | 1,636 | 1,367 | 449 | 54 | 269 R | 46.7% | 39.0% | 12.8% |
| 16,258 | ATCHISON | 6,538 | 2,828 | 2,926 | 727 | 57 | 98 D | 43.3% | 44.8% | 11.1% |
| 5,603 | BARBER | 2,729 | 1,696 | 730 | 279 | 24 | 966 R | 62.1% | 26.7% | 10.2% |
| 28,614 | BARTON | 12,099 | 7,855 | 3,121 | 1,004 | 119 | 4,734 R | 64.9% | 25.8% | 8.3% |
| 15,013 | BOURBON | 6,614 | 3,318 | 2,491 | 760 | 45 | 827 R | 50.2% | 37.7% | 11.5% |
| 11,075 | BROWN | 4,751 | 2,688 | 1,529 | 497 | 37 | 1,159 R | 56.6% | 32.2% | 10.5% |
| 57,746 | BUTLER | 23,816 | 13,979 | 7,294 | 2,274 | 269 | 6,685 R | 58.7% | 30.6% | 9.5% |
| 2,885 | CHASE | 1,550 | 778 | 496 | 259 | 17 | 282 R | 50.2% | 32.0% | 16.7% |
| 4,439 | CHAUTAUQUA | 1,960 | 1,142 | 568 | 222 | 28 | 574 R | 58.3% | 29.0% | 11.3% |
| 22,437 | CHEROKEE | 9,043 | 4,138 | 3,771 | 1,072 | 62 | 367 R | 45.8% | 41.7% | 11.9% |
| 3,230 | CHEYENNE | 1,812 | 1,211 | 422 | 174 | 5 | 789 R | 66.8% | 23.3% | 9.6% |
| 2,379 | CLARK | 1,315 | 855 | 334 | 109 | 17 | 521 R | 65.0% | 25.4% | 8.3% |
| 9,317 | CLAY | 4,177 | 2,793 | 963 | 389 | 32 | 1,830 R | 66.9% | 23.1% | 9.3% |
| 10,488 | CLOUD | 5,018 | 2,743 | 1,615 | 609 | 51 | 1,128 R | 54.7% | 32.2% | 12.1% |
| 8,691 | COFFEY | 4,090 | 2,369 | 1,118 | 572 | 31 | 1,251 R | 57.9% | 27.3% | 14.0% |
| 2,099 | COMANCHE | 1,127 | 691 | 298 | 133 | 5 | 393 R | 61.3% | 26.4% | 11.8% |
| 37,107 | COWLEY | 15,499 | 7,872 | 5,588 | 1,904 | 135 | 2,284 R | 50.8% | 36.1% | 12.3% |
| 36,488 | CRAWFORD | 15,880 | 6,447 | 7,504 | 1,785 | 144 | 1,057 D | 40.6% | 47.3% | 11.2% |
| 3,547 | DECATUR | 1,844 | 1,255 | 417 | 156 | 16 | 838 R | 68.1% | 22.6% | 8.5% |
| 19,911 | DICKINSON | 8,548 | 5,174 | 2,423 | 888 | 63 | 2,751 R | 60.5% | 28.3% | 10.4% |
| 7,608 | DONIPHAN | 3,054 | 1,962 | 1,050 | | 42 | 912 R | 64.2% | 34.4% | |
| 88,206 | DOUGLAS | 37,800 | 16,116 | 18,116 | 2,630 | 938 | 2,000 D | 42.6% | 47.9% | 7.0% |
| 3,564 | EDWARDS | 1,815 | 1,088 | 539 | 180 | 8 | 549 R | 59.9% | 29.7% | 9.9% |
| 3,356 | ELK | 1,643 | 933 | 488 | 206 | 16 | 445 R | 56.8% | 29.7% | 12.5% |
| 26,145 | ELLIS | 11,952 | 6,809 | 4,142 | 894 | 107 | 2,667 R | 57.0% | 34.7% | 7.5% |
| 6,445 | ELLSWORTH | 3,240 | 2,078 | 899 | 245 | 18 | 1,179 R | 64.1% | 27.7% | 7.6% |
| 34,913 | FINNEY | 9,457 | 6,188 | 2,420 | 805 | 44 | 3,768 R | 65.4% | 25.6% | 8.5% |
| 28,909 | FORD | 9,267 | 5,681 | 2,628 | 914 | 44 | 3,053 R | 61.3% | 28.4% | 9.9% |
| 23,164 | FRANKLIN | 9,835 | 5,007 | 3,552 | 1,184 | 92 | 1,455 R | 50.9% | 36.1% | 12.0% |
| 29,638 | GEARY | 6,790 | 3,686 | 2,444 | 618 | 42 | 1,242 R | 54.3% | 36.0% | 9.1% |
| 3,091 | GOVE | 1,623 | 1,123 | 351 | 141 | 8 | 772 R | 69.2% | 21.6% | 8.7% |
| 3,336 | GRAHAM | 1,626 | 1,031 | 432 | 152 | 11 | 599 R | 63.4% | 26.6% | 9.3% |
| 7,837 | GRANT | 2,664 | 1,772 | 633 | 250 | 9 | 1,139 R | 66.5% | 23.8% | 9.4% |
| 5,367 | GRAY | 2,037 | 1,457 | 404 | 164 | 12 | 1,053 R | 71.5% | 19.8% | 8.1% |
| 1,834 | GREELEY | 788 | 567 | 161 | 47 | 13 | 406 R | 72.0% | 20.4% | 6.0% |
| 8,032 | GREENWOOD | 3,635 | 1,932 | 1,108 | 552 | 43 | 824 R | 53.1% | 30.5% | 15.2% |
| 2,343 | HAMILTON | 1,249 | 811 | 342 | 84 | 12 | 469 R | 64.9% | 27.4% | 6.7% |
| 6,651 | HARPER | 3,159 | 1,941 | 836 | 355 | 27 | 1,105 R | 61.4% | 26.5% | 11.2% |
| 31,145 | HARVEY | 14,504 | 8,382 | 4,918 | 1,023 | 181 | 3,464 R | 57.8% | 33.9% | 7.1% |
| 4,027 | HASKELL | 1,554 | 1,143 | 304 | 96 | 11 | 839 R | 73.6% | 19.6% | 6.2% |
| 2,268 | HODGEMAN | 1,164 | 808 | 251 | 99 | 6 | 557 R | 69.4% | 21.6% | 8.5% |
| 11,809 | JACKSON | 5,460 | 2,682 | 1,983 | 735 | 60 | 699 R | 49.1% | 36.3% | 13.5% |
| 17,133 | JEFFERSON | 7,668 | 3,781 | 2,757 | 1,030 | 100 | 1,024 R | 49.3% | 36.0% | 13.4% |
| 3,952 | JEWELL | 1,991 | 1,374 | 417 | 188 | 12 | 957 R | 69.0% | 20.9% | 9.4% |
| 401,054 | JOHNSON | 190,894 | 110,368 | 68,129 | 10,425 | 1,972 | 42,239 R | 57.8% | 35.7% | 5.5% |
| 4,182 | KEARNY | 1,486 | 1,041 | 335 | 106 | 4 | 706 R | 70.1% | 22.5% | 7.1% |
| 8,566 | KINGMAN | 4,113 | 2,659 | 1,006 | 409 | 39 | 1,653 R | 64.6% | 24.5% | 9.9% |
| 3,605 | KIOWA | 1,781 | 1,264 | 331 | 170 | 16 | 933 R | 71.0% | 18.6% | 9.5% |
| 22,862 | LABETTE | 9,380 | 4,283 | 3,931 | 1,091 | 75 | 352 R | 45.7% | 41.9% | 11.6% |
| 2,275 | LANE | 1,224 | 865 | 271 | 86 | 2 | 594 R | 70.7% | 22.1% | 7.0% |
| 69,323 | LEAVENWORTH | 22,500 | 10,778 | 9,098 | 2,419 | 205 | 1,680 R | 47.9% | 40.4% | 10.8% |
| 3,431 | LINCOLN | 2,128 | 1,372 | 528 | 212 | 16 | 844 R | 64.5% | 24.8% | 10.0% |
| 8,698 | LINN | 4,235 | 2,077 | 1,590 | 535 | 33 | 487 R | 49.0% | 37.5% | 12.6% |
| 3,178 | LOGAN | 1,572 | 1,155 | 296 | 112 | 9 | 859 R | 73.5% | 18.8% | 7.1% |
| 34,650 | LYON | 13,221 | 6,612 | 4,884 | 1,584 | 141 | 1,728 R | 50.0% | 36.9% | 12.0% |
| 27,267 | MCPHERSON | 12,883 | 8,142 | 3,536 | 1,115 | 90 | 4,606 R | 63.2% | 27.4% | 8.7% |
| 12,961 | MARION | 6,389 | 4,173 | 1,673 | 492 | 51 | 2,500 R | 65.3% | 26.2% | 7.7% |
| 11,261 | MARSHALL | 5,500 | 2,811 | 1,932 | 713 | 44 | 879 R | 51.1% | 35.1% | 13.0% |
| 4,355 | MEADE | 2,059 | 1,443 | 426 | 173 | 17 | 1,017 R | 70.1% | 20.7% | 8.4% |

# KANSAS

## PRESIDENT 1996

| 1995 Census Pop. Est. | County | Total Vote | Republican | Democratic | Reform (Perot) | Other | Rep.-Dem. Plurality | Percentage of Total Vote | | |
|---|---|---|---|---|---|---|---|---|---|---|
| | | | | | | | | Rep. | Dem. | Reform |
| 25,187 | MIAMI | 10,955 | 5,256 | 4,237 | 1,339 | 123 | 1,019 R | 48.0% | 38.7% | 12.2% |
| 7,092 | MITCHELL | 3,544 | 2,435 | 833 | 246 | 30 | 1,602 R | 68.7% | 23.5% | 6.9% |
| 37,694 | MONTGOMERY | 14,365 | 7,428 | 5,269 | 1,528 | 140 | 2,159 R | 51.7% | 36.7% | 10.6% |
| 6,327 | MORRIS | 2,989 | 1,553 | 965 | 451 | 20 | 588 R | 52.0% | 32.3% | 15.1% |
| 3,303 | MORTON | 1,581 | 1,073 | 376 | 124 | 8 | 697 R | 67.9% | 23.8% | 7.8% |
| 10,443 | NEMAHA | 5,375 | 3,014 | 1,648 | 676 | 37 | 1,366 R | 56.1% | 30.7% | 12.6% |
| 16,994 | NEOSHO | 6,897 | 3,409 | 2,527 | 907 | 54 | 882 R | 49.4% | 36.6% | 13.2% |
| 3,752 | NESS | 1,960 | 1,336 | 428 | 186 | 10 | 908 R | 68.2% | 21.8% | 9.5% |
| 5,735 | NORTON | 2,731 | 1,814 | 640 | 265 | 12 | 1,174 R | 66.4% | 23.4% | 9.7% |
| 16,729 | OSAGE | 7,146 | 3,487 | 2,502 | 1,101 | 56 | 985 R | 48.8% | 35.0% | 15.4% |
| 4,696 | OSBORNE | 2,392 | 1,582 | 608 | 191 | 11 | 974 R | 66.1% | 25.4% | 8.0% |
| 5,749 | OTTAWA | 2,890 | 1,846 | 752 | 261 | 31 | 1,094 R | 63.9% | 26.0% | 9.0% |
| 7,615 | PAWNEE | 3,154 | 1,927 | 932 | 275 | 20 | 995 R | 61.1% | 29.5% | 8.7% |
| 6,270 | PHILLIPS | 3,024 | 2,005 | 758 | 242 | 19 | 1,247 R | 66.3% | 25.1% | 8.0% |
| 17,548 | POTTAWATOMIE | 7,744 | 4,504 | 1,997 | 1,035 | 208 | 2,507 R | 58.2% | 25.8% | 13.4% |
| 9,696 | PRATT | 4,401 | 2,591 | 1,367 | 408 | 35 | 1,224 R | 58.9% | 31.1% | 9.3% |
| 3,234 | RAWLINS | 1,888 | 1,393 | 335 | 146 | 14 | 1,058 R | 73.8% | 17.7% | 7.7% |
| 63,263 | RENO | 26,300 | 14,275 | 9,108 | 2,661 | 256 | 5,167 R | 54.3% | 34.6% | 10.1% |
| 6,215 | REPUBLIC | 3,263 | 2,283 | 688 | 268 | 24 | 1,595 R | 70.0% | 21.1% | 8.2% |
| 10,086 | RICE | 4,789 | 2,842 | 1,434 | 482 | 31 | 1,408 R | 59.3% | 29.9% | 10.1% |
| 69,784 | RILEY | 19,607 | 11,113 | 6,746 | 1,478 | 270 | 4,367 R | 56.7% | 34.4% | 7.5% |
| 5,884 | ROOKS | 2,787 | 1,864 | 650 | 251 | 22 | 1,214 R | 66.9% | 23.3% | 9.0% |
| 3,541 | RUSH | 1,989 | 1,239 | 547 | 185 | 18 | 692 R | 62.3% | 27.5% | 9.3% |
| 7,701 | RUSSELL | 4,238 | 3,347 | 705 | 164 | 22 | 2,642 R | 79.0% | 16.6% | 3.9% |
| 51,831 | SALINE | 22,541 | 12,475 | 7,728 | 2,192 | 146 | 4,747 R | 55.3% | 34.3% | 9.7% |
| 5,074 | SCOTT | 2,384 | 1,750 | 458 | 160 | 16 | 1,292 R | 73.4% | 19.2% | 6.7% |
| 419,333 | SEDGWICK | 166,599 | 93,397 | 59,643 | 11,875 | 1,684 | 33,754 R | 56.1% | 35.8% | 7.1% |
| 19,370 | SEWARD | 5,573 | 3,812 | 1,309 | 396 | 56 | 2,503 R | 68.4% | 23.5% | 7.1% |
| 165,062 | SHAWNEE | 75,663 | 34,845 | 32,803 | 7,304 | 711 | 2,042 R | 46.1% | 43.4% | 9.7% |
| 2,824 | SHERIDAN | 1,420 | 1,053 | 264 | 95 | 8 | 789 R | 74.2% | 18.6% | 6.7% |
| 6,706 | SHERMAN | 3,084 | 2,110 | 736 | 220 | 18 | 1,374 R | 68.4% | 23.9% | 7.1% |
| 4,782 | SMITH | 2,490 | 1,628 | 638 | 213 | 11 | 990 R | 65.4% | 25.6% | 8.6% |
| 5,193 | STAFFORD | 2,545 | 1,604 | 651 | 276 | 14 | 953 R | 63.0% | 25.6% | 10.8% |
| 2,331 | STANTON | 882 | 628 | 189 | 60 | 5 | 439 R | 71.2% | 21.4% | 6.8% |
| 5,257 | STEVENS | 2,184 | 1,548 | 405 | 213 | 18 | 1,143 R | 70.9% | 18.5% | 9.8% |
| 26,519 | SUMNER | 10,977 | 5,952 | 3,638 | 1,260 | 127 | 2,314 R | 54.2% | 33.1% | 11.5% |
| 8,331 | THOMAS | 3,907 | 2,725 | 866 | 295 | 21 | 1,859 R | 69.7% | 22.2% | 7.6% |
| 3,449 | TREGO | 1,972 | 1,205 | 548 | 209 | 10 | 657 R | 61.1% | 27.8% | 10.6% |
| 6,603 | WABAUNSEE | 3,384 | 1,884 | 966 | 479 | 55 | 918 R | 55.7% | 28.5% | 14.2% |
| 1,798 | WALLACE | 968 | 738 | 160 | 65 | 5 | 578 R | 76.2% | 16.5% | 6.7% |
| 6,833 | WASHINGTON | 3,557 | 2,397 | 804 | 326 | 30 | 1,593 R | 67.4% | 22.6% | 9.2% |
| 2,841 | WICHITA | 1,119 | 796 | 239 | 80 | 4 | 557 R | 71.1% | 21.4% | 7.1% |
| 10,321 | WILSON | 4,357 | 2,458 | 1,297 | 562 | 40 | 1,161 R | 56.4% | 29.8% | 12.9% |
| 3,999 | WOODSON | 1,832 | 953 | 598 | 269 | 12 | 355 R | 52.0% | 32.6% | 14.7% |
| 153,826 | WYANDOTTE | 49,654 | 14,011 | 31,252 | 3,931 | 460 | 17,241 D | 28.2% | 62.9% | 7.9% |
| 2,565,328 | TOTAL | 1,074,300 | 583,245 | 387,659 | 92,639 | 10,757 | 195,586 R | 54.3% | 36.1% | 8.6% |

# KANSAS

## PRESIDENT 1992

| 1990 Census Population | County | Total Vote | Republican | Democratic | Perot | Other | Plurality | Percentage Total Vote | | |
|---|---|---|---|---|---|---|---|---|---|---|
| | | | | | | | | Rep. | Dem. | Perot |
| 14,638 | ALLEN | 6,430 | 2,351 | 2,312 | 1,746 | 21 | 39 R | 36.6% | 36.0% | 27.2% |
| 7,803 | ANDERSON | 3,687 | 1,218 | 1,178 | 1,282 | 9 | 64 P | 33.0% | 32.0% | 34.8% |
| 16,932 | ATCHISON | 7,533 | 2,521 | 2,959 | 2,020 | 33 | 438 D | 33.5% | 39.3% | 26.8% |
| 5,874 | BARBER | 2,881 | 1,225 | 759 | 893 | 4 | 332 R | 42.5% | 26.3% | 31.0% |
| 29,382 | BARTON | 13,582 | 5,113 | 3,846 | 4,574 | 49 | 539 R | 37.6% | 28.3% | 33.7% |
| 14,966 | BOURBON | 7,162 | 2,876 | 2,509 | 1,763 | 14 | 367 R | 40.2% | 35.0% | 24.6% |
| 11,128 | BROWN | 5,294 | 2,203 | 1,476 | 1,603 | 12 | 600 R | 41.6% | 27.9% | 30.3% |
| 50,580 | BUTLER | 23,629 | 9,166 | 7,029 | 7,355 | 79 | 1,811 R | 38.8% | 29.7% | 31.1% |
| 3,021 | CHASE | 1,685 | 610 | 470 | 600 | 5 | 10 R | 36.2% | 27.9% | 35.6% |
| 4,407 | CHAUTAUQUA | 2,073 | 853 | 598 | 607 | 15 | 246 R | 41.1% | 28.8% | 29.3% |
| 21,374 | CHEROKEE | 9,757 | 3,589 | 4,083 | 2,067 | 18 | 494 D | 36.8% | 41.8% | 21.2% |
| 3,243 | CHEYENNE | 1,755 | 863 | 407 | 477 | 8 | 386 R | 49.2% | 23.2% | 27.2% |
| 2,418 | CLARK | 1,315 | 676 | 293 | 341 | 5 | 335 R | 51.4% | 22.3% | 25.9% |
| 9,158 | CLAY | 4,590 | 2,198 | 947 | 1,434 | 11 | 764 R | 47.9% | 20.6% | 31.2% |
| 11,023 | CLOUD | 5,448 | 2,131 | 1,720 | 1,578 | 19 | 411 R | 39.1% | 31.6% | 29.0% |
| 8,404 | COFFEY | 4,300 | 1,824 | 1,021 | 1,443 | 12 | 381 R | 42.4% | 23.7% | 33.6% |
| 2,313 | COMANCHE | 1,285 | 636 | 325 | 324 | | 311 R | 49.5% | 25.3% | 25.2% |
| 36,915 | COWLEY | 15,784 | 5,422 | 5,405 | 4,911 | 46 | 17 R | 34.4% | 34.2% | 31.1% |
| 35,568 | CRAWFORD | 16,591 | 5,468 | 7,366 | 3,706 | 51 | 1,898 D | 33.0% | 44.4% | 22.3% |
| 4,021 | DECATUR | 2,089 | 940 | 576 | 565 | 8 | 364 R | 45.0% | 27.6% | 27.0% |
| 18,958 | DICKINSON | 9,222 | 3,851 | 2,518 | 2,833 | 20 | 1,018 R | 41.8% | 27.3% | 30.7% |
| 8,134 | DONIPHAN | 3,976 | 1,579 | 1,177 | 1,200 | 20 | 379 R | 39.7% | 29.6% | 30.2% |
| 81,798 | DOUGLAS | 42,265 | 12,949 | 19,439 | 9,630 | 247 | 6,490 D | 30.6% | 46.0% | 22.8% |
| 3,787 | EDWARDS | 1,925 | 769 | 567 | 584 | 5 | 185 R | 39.9% | 29.5% | 30.3% |
| 3,327 | ELK | 1,742 | 748 | 485 | 503 | 6 | 245 R | 42.9% | 27.8% | 28.9% |
| 26,004 | ELLIS | 12,453 | 3,985 | 4,544 | 3,887 | 37 | 559 D | 32.0% | 36.5% | 31.2% |
| 6,586 | ELLSWORTH | 3,239 | 1,197 | 1,010 | 1,020 | 12 | 177 R | 37.0% | 31.2% | 31.5% |
| 33,070 | FINNEY | 10,933 | 5,278 | 2,612 | 3,011 | 32 | 2,267 R | 48.3% | 23.9% | 27.5% |
| 27,463 | FORD | 10,358 | 4,342 | 2,635 | 3,341 | 40 | 1,001 R | 41.9% | 25.4% | 32.3% |
| 21,994 | FRANKLIN | 9,883 | 3,699 | 2,968 | 3,184 | 32 | 515 R | 37.4% | 30.0% | 32.2% |
| 30,453 | GEARY | 7,556 | 2,928 | 2,559 | 2,057 | 12 | 369 R | 38.8% | 33.9% | 27.2% |
| 3,231 | GOVE | 1,706 | 792 | 379 | 532 | 3 | 260 R | 46.4% | 22.2% | 31.2% |
| 3,543 | GRAHAM | 1,912 | 752 | 554 | 603 | 3 | 149 R | 39.3% | 29.0% | 31.5% |
| 7,159 | GRANT | 3,019 | 1,561 | 619 | 835 | 4 | 726 R | 51.7% | 20.5% | 27.7% |
| 5,396 | GRAY | 2,173 | 1,039 | 443 | 686 | 5 | 353 R | 47.8% | 20.4% | 31.6% |
| 1,774 | GREELEY | 873 | 504 | 191 | 175 | 3 | 313 R | 57.7% | 21.9% | 20.0% |
| 7,847 | GREENWOOD | 3,853 | 1,411 | 1,262 | 1,167 | 13 | 149 R | 36.6% | 32.8% | 30.3% |
| 2,388 | HAMILTON | 1,378 | 716 | 386 | 271 | 5 | 330 R | 52.0% | 28.0% | 19.7% |
| 7,124 | HARPER | 3,378 | 1,371 | 845 | 1,151 | 11 | 220 R | 40.6% | 25.0% | 34.1% |
| 31,028 | HARVEY | 15,012 | 6,259 | 5,047 | 3,653 | 53 | 1,212 R | 41.7% | 33.6% | 24.3% |
| 3,886 | HASKELL | 1,826 | 1,023 | 336 | 462 | 5 | 561 R | 56.0% | 18.4% | 25.3% |
| 2,177 | HODGEMAN | 1,229 | 625 | 258 | 343 | 3 | 282 R | 50.9% | 21.0% | 27.9% |
| 11,525 | JACKSON | 5,552 | 1,970 | 1,639 | 1,927 | 16 | 43 R | 35.5% | 29.5% | 34.7% |
| 15,905 | JEFFERSON | 7,781 | 2,569 | 2,538 | 2,642 | 32 | 73 P | 33.0% | 32.6% | 34.0% |
| 4,251 | JEWELL | 2,300 | 1,050 | 546 | 698 | 6 | 352 R | 45.7% | 23.7% | 30.3% |
| 355,054 | JOHNSON | 194,924 | 85,418 | 59,573 | 49,136 | 797 | 25,845 R | 43.8% | 30.6% | 25.2% |
| 4,027 | KEARNY | 1,709 | 943 | 384 | 376 | 6 | 559 R | 55.2% | 22.5% | 22.0% |
| 8,292 | KINGMAN | 4,163 | 1,680 | 1,100 | 1,370 | 13 | 310 R | 40.4% | 26.4% | 32.9% |
| 3,660 | KIOWA | 1,891 | 1,057 | 355 | 475 | 4 | 582 R | 55.9% | 18.8% | 25.1% |
| 23,693 | LABETTE | 10,177 | 3,368 | 4,196 | 2,577 | 36 | 828 D | 33.1% | 41.2% | 25.3% |
| 2,375 | LANE | 1,299 | 674 | 265 | 356 | 4 | 318 R | 51.9% | 20.4% | 27.4% |
| 64,371 | LEAVENWORTH | 23,177 | 7,738 | 8,077 | 7,306 | 56 | 339 D | 33.4% | 34.8% | 31.5% |
| 3,653 | LINCOLN | 2,172 | 893 | 612 | 657 | 10 | 236 R | 41.1% | 28.2% | 30.2% |
| 8,254 | LINN | 4,134 | 1,413 | 1,353 | 1,358 | 10 | 55 R | 34.2% | 32.7% | 32.8% |
| 3,081 | LOGAN | 1,709 | 905 | 355 | 446 | 3 | 459 R | 53.0% | 20.8% | 26.1% |
| 34,732 | LYON | 14,656 | 5,090 | 4,811 | 4,717 | 38 | 279 R | 34.7% | 32.8% | 32.2% |
| 27,268 | MCPHERSON | 12,991 | 5,745 | 3,645 | 3,561 | 40 | 2,100 R | 44.2% | 28.1% | 27.4% |
| 12,888 | MARION | 6,351 | 3,142 | 1,627 | 1,557 | 25 | 1,515 R | 49.5% | 25.6% | 24.5% |
| 11,705 | MARSHALL | 5,858 | 2,030 | 2,022 | 1,786 | 20 | 8 R | 34.7% | 34.5% | 30.5% |
| 4,247 | MEADE | 2,164 | 1,135 | 430 | 592 | 7 | 543 R | 52.4% | 19.9% | 27.4% |

# KANSAS

## PRESIDENT 1992

| 1990 Census Population | County | Total Vote | Republican | Democratic | Perot | Other | Plurality | Percentage Total Vote | | |
|---|---|---|---|---|---|---|---|---|---|---|
| | | | | | | | | Rep. | Dem. | Perot |
| 23,466 | MIAMI | 11,096 | 3,528 | 3,835 | 3,701 | 32 | 134 D | 31.8% | 34.6% | 33.4% |
| 7,203 | MITCHELL | 3,650 | 1,601 | 938 | 1,098 | 13 | 503 R | 43.9% | 25.7% | 30.1% |
| 38,816 | MONTGOMERY | 15,912 | 6,848 | 5,453 | 3,570 | 41 | 1,395 R | 43.0% | 34.3% | 22.4% |
| 6,198 | MORRIS | 3,111 | 1,071 | 957 | 1,071 | 12 | | 34.4% | 30.8% | 34.4% |
| 3,480 | MORTON | 1,670 | 915 | 398 | 350 | 7 | 517 R | 54.8% | 23.8% | 21.0% |
| 10,446 | NEMAHA | 5,619 | 2,220 | 1,580 | 1,804 | 15 | 416 R | 39.5% | 28.1% | 32.1% |
| 17,035 | NEOSHO | 7,893 | 2,926 | 2,799 | 2,136 | 32 | 127 R | 37.1% | 35.5% | 27.1% |
| 4,033 | NESS | 2,218 | 967 | 565 | 678 | 8 | 289 R | 43.6% | 25.5% | 30.6% |
| 5,947 | NORTON | 3,068 | 1,469 | 779 | 815 | 5 | 654 R | 47.9% | 25.4% | 26.6% |
| 15,248 | OSAGE | 7,421 | 2,561 | 2,297 | 2,532 | 31 | 29 R | 34.5% | 31.0% | 34.1% |
| 4,867 | OSBORNE | 2,607 | 1,003 | 779 | 819 | 6 | 184 R | 38.5% | 29.9% | 31.4% |
| 5,634 | OTTAWA | 2,820 | 1,284 | 764 | 762 | 10 | 520 R | 45.5% | 27.1% | 27.0% |
| 7,555 | PAWNEE | 3,585 | 1,357 | 1,118 | 1,097 | 13 | 239 R | 37.9% | 31.2% | 30.6% |
| 6,590 | PHILLIPS | 3,388 | 1,579 | 843 | 955 | 11 | 624 R | 46.6% | 24.9% | 28.2% |
| 16,128 | POTTAWATOMIE | 8,016 | 3,106 | 2,099 | 2,759 | 52 | 347 R | 38.7% | 26.2% | 34.4% |
| 9,702 | PRATT | 4,786 | 1,779 | 1,466 | 1,528 | 13 | 251 R | 37.2% | 30.6% | 31.9% |
| 3,404 | RAWLINS | 1,935 | 1,023 | 393 | 517 | 2 | 506 R | 52.9% | 20.3% | 26.7% |
| 62,389 | RENO | 28,379 | 11,377 | 9,257 | 7,636 | 109 | 2,120 R | 40.1% | 32.6% | 26.9% |
| 6,482 | REPUBLIC | 3,806 | 1,767 | 939 | 1,084 | 16 | 683 R | 46.4% | 24.7% | 28.5% |
| 10,610 | RICE | 5,271 | 2,158 | 1,555 | 1,543 | 15 | 603 R | 40.9% | 29.5% | 29.3% |
| 67,139 | RILEY | 21,797 | 8,394 | 7,933 | 5,387 | 83 | 461 R | 38.5% | 36.4% | 24.7% |
| 6,039 | ROOKS | 3,090 | 1,249 | 771 | 1,063 | 7 | 186 R | 40.4% | 25.0% | 34.4% |
| 3,842 | RUSH | 2,118 | 756 | 689 | 665 | 8 | 67 R | 35.7% | 32.5% | 31.4% |
| 7,835 | RUSSELL | 4,015 | 1,434 | 1,178 | 1,395 | 8 | 39 R | 35.7% | 29.3% | 34.7% |
| 49,301 | SALINE | 23,623 | 8,565 | 7,890 | 7,108 | 60 | 675 R | 36.3% | 33.4% | 30.1% |
| 5,289 | SCOTT | 2,535 | 1,426 | 480 | 621 | 8 | 805 R | 56.3% | 18.9% | 24.5% |
| 403,662 | SEDGWICK | 186,574 | 75,577 | 62,670 | 47,238 | 1,089 | 12,907 R | 40.5% | 33.6% | 25.3% |
| 18,743 | SEWARD | 6,806 | 3,477 | 1,488 | 1,818 | 23 | 1,659 R | 51.1% | 21.9% | 26.7% |
| 160,976 | SHAWNEE | 82,294 | 29,344 | 31,972 | 20,653 | 325 | 2,628 D | 35.7% | 38.9% | 25.1% |
| 3,043 | SHERIDAN | 1,636 | 739 | 347 | 546 | 4 | 193 R | 45.2% | 21.2% | 33.4% |
| 6,926 | SHERMAN | 3,278 | 1,630 | 810 | 828 | 10 | 802 R | 49.7% | 24.7% | 25.3% |
| 5,078 | SMITH | 2,852 | 1,236 | 789 | 816 | 11 | 420 R | 43.3% | 27.7% | 28.6% |
| 5,365 | STAFFORD | 2,760 | 1,064 | 777 | 910 | 9 | 154 R | 38.6% | 28.2% | 33.0% |
| 2,333 | STANTON | 998 | 556 | 224 | 214 | 4 | 332 R | 55.7% | 22.4% | 21.4% |
| 5,048 | STEVENS | 2,477 | 1,408 | 390 | 674 | 5 | 734 R | 56.8% | 15.7% | 27.2% |
| 25,841 | SUMNER | 11,589 | 4,087 | 3,564 | 3,887 | 51 | 200 R | 35.3% | 30.8% | 33.5% |
| 8,258 | THOMAS | 3,923 | 1,849 | 932 | 1,129 | 13 | 720 R | 47.1% | 23.8% | 28.8% |
| 3,694 | TREGO | 1,912 | 727 | 608 | 574 | 3 | 119 R | 38.0% | 31.8% | 30.0% |
| 6,603 | WABAUNSEE | 3,386 | 1,254 | 851 | 1,258 | 23 | 4 P | 37.0% | 25.1% | 37.2% |
| 1,821 | WALLACE | 1,066 | 679 | 164 | 219 | 4 | 460 R | 63.7% | 15.4% | 20.5% |
| 7,073 | WASHINGTON | 3,702 | 1,740 | 893 | 1,054 | 15 | 686 R | 47.0% | 24.1% | 28.5% |
| 2,758 | WICHITA | 1,230 | 681 | 241 | 303 | 5 | 378 R | 55.4% | 19.6% | 24.6% |
| 10,289 | WILSON | 4,635 | 1,925 | 1,331 | 1,365 | 14 | 560 R | 41.5% | 28.7% | 29.4% |
| 4,116 | WOODSON | 1,866 | 662 | 590 | 604 | 10 | 58 R | 35.5% | 31.6% | 32.4% |
| 161,993 | WYANDOTTE | 61,133 | 12,872 | 34,397 | 13,620 | 244 | 20,777 D | 21.1% | 56.3% | 22.3% |
| 2,477,574 | TOTAL | 1,157,335 | 449,951 | 390,434 | 312,358 | 4,592 | 59,517 R | 38.9% | 33.7% | 27.0% |

364

# KANSAS

## PRESIDENT 1988

| 1980 Census Population | County | Total Vote | Republican | Democratic | Other | Rep.-Dem. Plurality | Percentage Total Vote Rep. | Dem. | Major Vote Rep. | Dem. |
|---|---|---|---|---|---|---|---|---|---|---|
| 15,654 | ALLEN | 5,898 | 3,429 | 2,392 | 77 | 1,037 R | 58.1% | 40.6% | 58.9% | 41.1% |
| 8,749 | ANDERSON | 3,283 | 1,781 | 1,466 | 36 | 315 R | 54.2% | 44.7% | 54.9% | 45.1% |
| 18,397 | ATCHISON | 6,614 | 3,243 | 3,177 | 194 | 66 R | 49.0% | 48.0% | 50.5% | 49.5% |
| 6,548 | BARBER | 2,706 | 1,539 | 1,118 | 49 | 421 R | 56.9% | 41.3% | 57.9% | 42.1% |
| 31,343 | BARTON | 13,075 | 7,741 | 5,024 | 310 | 2,717 R | 59.2% | 38.4% | 60.6% | 39.4% |
| 15,969 | BOURBON | 6,332 | 3,660 | 2,623 | 49 | 1,037 R | 57.8% | 41.4% | 58.3% | 41.7% |
| 11,955 | BROWN | 4,812 | 3,059 | 1,719 | 34 | 1,340 R | 63.6% | 35.7% | 64.0% | 36.0% |
| 44,782 | BUTLER | 19,056 | 10,976 | 7,690 | 390 | 3,286 R | 57.6% | 40.4% | 58.8% | 41.2% |
| 3,309 | CHASE | 1,458 | 884 | 538 | 36 | 346 R | 60.6% | 36.9% | 62.2% | 37.8% |
| 5,016 | CHAUTAUQUA | 1,934 | 1,247 | 661 | 26 | 586 R | 64.5% | 34.2% | 65.4% | 34.6% |
| 22,304 | CHEROKEE | 8,402 | 4,281 | 4,069 | 52 | 212 R | 51.0% | 48.4% | 51.3% | 48.7% |
| 3,678 | CHEYENNE | 1,743 | 1,105 | 594 | 44 | 511 R | 63.4% | 34.1% | 65.0% | 35.0% |
| 2,599 | CLARK | 1,315 | 876 | 409 | 30 | 467 R | 66.6% | 31.1% | 68.2% | 31.8% |
| 9,802 | CLAY | 4,157 | 2,997 | 1,112 | 48 | 1,885 R | 72.1% | 26.8% | 72.9% | 27.1% |
| 12,494 | CLOUD | 5,128 | 3,043 | 2,022 | 63 | 1,021 R | 59.3% | 39.4% | 60.1% | 39.9% |
| 9,370 | COFFEY | 3,870 | 2,581 | 1,246 | 43 | 1,335 R | 66.7% | 32.2% | 67.4% | 32.6% |
| 2,554 | COMANCHE | 1,123 | 738 | 375 | 10 | 363 R | 65.7% | 33.4% | 66.3% | 33.7% |
| 36,824 | COWLEY | 14,286 | 7,778 | 6,186 | 322 | 1,592 R | 54.4% | 43.3% | 55.7% | 44.3% |
| 37,916 | CRAWFORD | 14,850 | 6,940 | 7,783 | 127 | 843 D | 46.7% | 52.4% | 47.1% | 52.9% |
| 4,509 | DECATUR | 2,148 | 1,291 | 793 | 64 | 498 R | 60.1% | 36.9% | 61.9% | 38.1% |
| 20,175 | DICKINSON | 8,092 | 5,121 | 2,870 | 101 | 2,251 R | 63.3% | 35.5% | 64.1% | 35.9% |
| 9,268 | DONIPHAN | 3,514 | 2,162 | 1,312 | 40 | 850 R | 61.5% | 37.3% | 62.2% | 37.8% |
| 67,640 | DOUGLAS | 32,361 | 16,149 | 15,752 | 460 | 397 R | 49.9% | 48.7% | 50.6% | 49.4% |
| 4,271 | EDWARDS | 1,843 | 993 | 792 | 58 | 201 R | 53.9% | 43.0% | 55.6% | 44.4% |
| 3,918 | ELK | 1,706 | 1,075 | 608 | 23 | 467 R | 63.0% | 35.6% | 63.9% | 36.1% |
| 26,098 | ELLIS | 10,672 | 5,194 | 5,289 | 189 | 95 D | 48.7% | 49.6% | 49.5% | 50.5% |
| 6,640 | ELLSWORTH | 3,000 | 1,711 | 1,219 | 70 | 492 R | 57.0% | 40.6% | 58.4% | 41.6% |
| 23,825 | FINNEY | 8,947 | 5,381 | 3,408 | 158 | 1,973 R | 60.1% | 38.1% | 61.2% | 38.8% |
| 24,315 | FORD | 9,697 | 5,685 | 3,817 | 195 | 1,868 R | 58.6% | 39.4% | 59.8% | 40.2% |
| 22,062 | FRANKLIN | 8,465 | 4,777 | 3,592 | 96 | 1,185 R | 56.4% | 42.4% | 57.1% | 42.9% |
| 29,852 | GEARY | 6,573 | 3,782 | 2,721 | 70 | 1,061 R | 57.5% | 41.4% | 58.2% | 41.8% |
| 3,726 | GOVE | 1,684 | 966 | 663 | 55 | 303 R | 57.4% | 39.4% | 59.3% | 40.7% |
| 3,995 | GRAHAM | 1,868 | 1,139 | 702 | 27 | 437 R | 61.0% | 37.6% | 61.9% | 38.1% |
| 6,977 | GRANT | 2,597 | 1,654 | 907 | 36 | 747 R | 63.7% | 34.9% | 64.6% | 35.4% |
| 5,138 | GRAY | 1,917 | 1,180 | 696 | 41 | 484 R | 61.6% | 36.3% | 62.9% | 37.1% |
| 1,845 | GREELEY | 853 | 506 | 317 | 30 | 189 R | 59.3% | 37.2% | 61.5% | 38.5% |
| 8,764 | GREENWOOD | 3,716 | 2,217 | 1,421 | 78 | 796 R | 59.7% | 38.2% | 60.9% | 39.1% |
| 2,514 | HAMILTON | 1,335 | 801 | 517 | 17 | 284 R | 60.0% | 38.7% | 60.8% | 39.2% |
| 7,778 | HARPER | 3,268 | 1,941 | 1,235 | 92 | 706 R | 59.4% | 37.8% | 61.1% | 38.9% |
| 30,531 | HARVEY | 12,711 | 6,893 | 5,503 | 315 | 1,390 R | 54.2% | 43.3% | 55.6% | 44.4% |
| 3,814 | HASKELL | 1,430 | 964 | 427 | 39 | 537 R | 67.4% | 29.9% | 69.3% | 30.7% |
| 2,269 | HODGEMAN | 1,212 | 732 | 439 | 41 | 293 R | 60.4% | 36.2% | 62.5% | 37.5% |
| 11,644 | JACKSON | 5,075 | 2,759 | 2,261 | 55 | 498 R | 54.4% | 44.6% | 55.0% | 45.0% |
| 15,207 | JEFFERSON | 6,492 | 3,605 | 2,810 | 77 | 795 R | 55.5% | 43.3% | 56.2% | 43.8% |
| 5,241 | JEWELL | 2,274 | 1,546 | 684 | 44 | 862 R | 68.0% | 30.1% | 69.3% | 30.7% |
| 270,269 | JOHNSON | 152,199 | 95,591 | 55,183 | 1,425 | 40,408 R | 62.8% | 36.3% | 63.4% | 36.6% |
| 3,435 | KEARNY | 1,625 | 1,073 | 524 | 28 | 549 R | 66.0% | 32.2% | 67.2% | 32.8% |
| 8,960 | KINGMAN | 3,754 | 2,205 | 1,420 | 129 | 785 R | 58.7% | 37.8% | 60.8% | 39.2% |
| 4,046 | KIOWA | 1,795 | 1,276 | 485 | 34 | 791 R | 71.1% | 27.0% | 72.5% | 27.5% |
| 25,682 | LABETTE | 9,684 | 5,125 | 4,433 | 126 | 692 R | 52.9% | 45.8% | 53.6% | 46.4% |
| 2,472 | LANE | 1,250 | 768 | 450 | 32 | 318 R | 61.4% | 36.0% | 63.1% | 36.9% |
| 54,809 | LEAVENWORTH | 18,870 | 9,913 | 8,797 | 160 | 1,116 R | 52.5% | 46.6% | 53.0% | 47.0% |
| 4,145 | LINCOLN | 2,060 | 1,229 | 796 | 35 | 433 R | 59.7% | 38.6% | 60.7% | 39.3% |
| 8,234 | LINN | 3,691 | 2,163 | 1,497 | 31 | 666 R | 58.6% | 40.6% | 59.1% | 40.9% |
| 3,478 | LOGAN | 1,535 | 988 | 503 | 44 | 485 R | 64.4% | 32.8% | 66.3% | 33.7% |
| 35,108 | LYON | 12,334 | 6,820 | 5,314 | 200 | 1,506 R | 55.3% | 43.1% | 56.2% | 43.8% |
| 26,855 | MCPHERSON | 11,164 | 6,563 | 4,354 | 247 | 2,209 R | 58.8% | 39.0% | 60.1% | 39.9% |
| 13,522 | MARION | 5,850 | 3,685 | 2,024 | 141 | 1,661 R | 63.0% | 34.6% | 64.5% | 35.5% |
| 12,787 | MARSHALL | 5,790 | 3,140 | 2,560 | 90 | 580 R | 54.2% | 44.2% | 55.1% | 44.9% |
| 4,788 | MEADE | 2,028 | 1,322 | 664 | 42 | 658 R | 65.2% | 32.7% | 66.6% | 33.4% |

# KANSAS

## PRESIDENT 1988

| 1980 Census Population | County | Total Vote | Republican | Democratic | Other | Rep.-Dem. Plurality | Percentage | | | |
|---|---|---|---|---|---|---|---|---|---|---|
| | | | | | | | Total Vote | | Major Vote | |
| | | | | | | | Rep. | Dem. | Rep. | Dem. |
| 21,618 | MIAMI | 9,306 | 4,807 | 4,427 | 72 | 380 R | 51.7% | 47.6% | 52.1% | 47.9% |
| 8,117 | MITCHELL | 3,462 | 2,257 | 1,145 | 60 | 1,112 R | 65.2% | 33.1% | 66.3% | 33.7% |
| 42,281 | MONTGOMERY | 14,628 | 9,067 | 5,429 | 132 | 3,638 R | 62.0% | 37.1% | 62.5% | 37.5% |
| 6,419 | MORRIS | 2,894 | 1,682 | 1,165 | 47 | 517 R | 58.1% | 40.3% | 59.1% | 40.9% |
| 3,454 | MORTON | 1,669 | 1,074 | 569 | 26 | 505 R | 64.3% | 34.1% | 65.4% | 34.6% |
| 11,211 | NEMAHA | 5,182 | 2,849 | 2,261 | 72 | 588 R | 55.0% | 43.6% | 55.8% | 44.2% |
| 18,967 | NEOSHO | 7,222 | 3,739 | 3,402 | 81 | 337 R | 51.8% | 47.1% | 52.4% | 47.6% |
| 4,498 | NESS | 2,174 | 1,230 | 887 | 57 | 343 R | 56.6% | 40.8% | 58.1% | 41.9% |
| 6,689 | NORTON | 2,847 | 1,923 | 855 | 69 | 1,068 R | 67.5% | 30.0% | 69.2% | 30.8% |
| 15,319 | OSAGE | 6,435 | 3,496 | 2,840 | 99 | 656 R | 54.3% | 44.1% | 55.2% | 44.8% |
| 5,959 | OSBORNE | 2,544 | 1,541 | 943 | 60 | 598 R | 60.6% | 37.1% | 62.0% | 38.0% |
| 5,971 | OTTAWA | 2,834 | 1,836 | 953 | 45 | 883 R | 64.8% | 33.6% | 65.8% | 34.2% |
| 8,065 | PAWNEE | 3,373 | 1,825 | 1,474 | 74 | 351 R | 54.1% | 43.7% | 55.3% | 44.7% |
| 7,406 | PHILLIPS | 3,315 | 2,316 | 960 | 39 | 1,356 R | 69.9% | 29.0% | 70.7% | 29.3% |
| 14,782 | POTTAWATOMIE | 6,549 | 3,897 | 2,544 | 108 | 1,353 R | 59.5% | 38.8% | 60.5% | 39.5% |
| 10,275 | PRATT | 4,245 | 2,505 | 1,651 | 89 | 854 R | 59.0% | 38.9% | 60.3% | 39.7% |
| 4,105 | RAWLINS | 1,983 | 1,318 | 612 | 53 | 706 R | 66.5% | 30.9% | 68.3% | 31.7% |
| 64,983 | RENO | 24,954 | 12,753 | 11,545 | 656 | 1,208 R | 51.1% | 46.3% | 52.5% | 47.5% |
| 7,569 | REPUBLIC | 3,462 | 2,346 | 1,069 | 47 | 1,277 R | 67.8% | 30.9% | 68.7% | 31.3% |
| 11,900 | RICE | 4,645 | 2,503 | 2,033 | 109 | 470 R | 53.9% | 43.8% | 55.2% | 44.8% |
| 63,505 | RILEY | 17,007 | 9,507 | 7,283 | 217 | 2,224 R | 55.9% | 42.8% | 56.6% | 43.4% |
| 7,006 | ROOKS | 3,007 | 1,938 | 1,012 | 57 | 926 R | 64.4% | 33.7% | 65.7% | 34.3% |
| 4,516 | RUSH | 2,153 | 1,045 | 1,020 | 88 | 25 R | 48.5% | 47.4% | 50.6% | 49.4% |
| 8,868 | RUSSELL | 3,926 | 2,403 | 1,448 | 75 | 955 R | 61.2% | 36.9% | 62.4% | 37.6% |
| 48,905 | SALINE | 19,618 | 11,371 | 7,998 | 249 | 3,373 R | 58.0% | 40.8% | 58.7% | 41.3% |
| 5,782 | SCOTT | 2,375 | 1,590 | 717 | 68 | 873 R | 66.9% | 30.2% | 68.9% | 31.1% |
| 366,531 | SEDGWICK | 155,745 | 86,124 | 65,618 | 4,003 | 20,506 R | 55.3% | 42.1% | 56.8% | 43.2% |
| 17,071 | SEWARD | 5,797 | 4,089 | 1,655 | 53 | 2,434 R | 70.5% | 28.5% | 71.2% | 28.8% |
| 154,916 | SHAWNEE | 70,197 | 35,489 | 33,940 | 768 | 1,549 R | 50.6% | 48.3% | 51.1% | 48.9% |
| 3,544 | SHERIDAN | 1,556 | 901 | 600 | 55 | 301 R | 57.9% | 38.6% | 60.0% | 40.0% |
| 7,759 | SHERMAN | 3,065 | 1,929 | 1,082 | 54 | 847 R | 62.9% | 35.3% | 64.1% | 35.9% |
| 5,947 | SMITH | 2,988 | 1,951 | 1,004 | 33 | 947 R | 65.3% | 33.6% | 66.0% | 34.0% |
| 5,694 | STAFFORD | 2,738 | 1,532 | 1,121 | 85 | 411 R | 56.0% | 40.9% | 57.7% | 42.3% |
| 2,339 | STANTON | 950 | 592 | 310 | 48 | 282 R | 62.3% | 32.6% | 65.6% | 34.4% |
| 4,736 | STEVENS | 2,307 | 1,642 | 612 | 53 | 1,030 R | 71.2% | 26.5% | 72.8% | 27.2% |
| 24,928 | SUMNER | 10,042 | 5,394 | 4,417 | 231 | 977 R | 53.7% | 44.0% | 55.0% | 45.0% |
| 8,451 | THOMAS | 3,870 | 2,342 | 1,408 | 120 | 934 R | 60.5% | 36.4% | 62.5% | 37.5% |
| 4,165 | TREGO | 1,831 | 979 | 795 | 57 | 184 R | 53.5% | 43.4% | 55.2% | 44.8% |
| 6,867 | WABAUNSEE | 2,967 | 1,737 | 1,166 | 64 | 571 R | 58.5% | 39.3% | 59.8% | 40.2% |
| 2,045 | WALLACE | 941 | 655 | 257 | 29 | 398 R | 69.6% | 27.3% | 71.8% | 28.2% |
| 8,543 | WASHINGTON | 3,380 | 2,269 | 1,063 | 48 | 1,206 R | 67.1% | 31.4% | 68.1% | 31.9% |
| 3,041 | WICHITA | 1,148 | 721 | 399 | 28 | 322 R | 62.8% | 34.8% | 64.4% | 35.6% |
| 12,128 | WILSON | 4,346 | 2,743 | 1,545 | 58 | 1,198 R | 63.1% | 35.5% | 64.0% | 36.0% |
| 4,600 | WOODSON | 1,847 | 1,062 | 761 | 24 | 301 R | 57.5% | 41.2% | 58.3% | 41.7% |
| 172,335 | WYANDOTTE | 58,399 | 19,097 | 38,678 | 624 | 19,581 D | 32.7% | 66.2% | 33.1% | 66.9% |
| 2,363,679 | TOTAL | 993,044 | 554,049 | 422,636 | 16,359 | 131,413 R | 55.8% | 42.6% | 56.7% | 43.3% |

# KANSAS

## PRESIDENT 1984

| 1980 Census Population | County | Total Vote | Republican | Democratic | Other | Rep.-Dem. Plurality | Percentage Total Vote Rep. | Dem. | Major Vote Rep. | Dem. |
|---|---|---|---|---|---|---|---|---|---|---|
| 15,654 | ALLEN | 6,117 | 4,267 | 1,778 | 72 | 2,489 R | 69.8% | 29.1% | 70.6% | 29.4% |
| 8,749 | ANDERSON | 3,667 | 2,462 | 1,155 | 50 | 1,307 R | 67.1% | 31.5% | 68.1% | 31.9% |
| 18,397 | ATCHISON | 7,255 | 4,537 | 2,641 | 77 | 1,896 R | 62.5% | 36.4% | 63.2% | 36.8% |
| 6,548 | BARBER | 2,940 | 2,112 | 806 | 22 | 1,306 R | 71.8% | 27.4% | 72.4% | 27.6% |
| 31,343 | BARTON | 13,538 | 10,232 | 3,111 | 195 | 7,121 R | 75.6% | 23.0% | 76.7% | 23.3% |
| 15,969 | BOURBON | 7,102 | 4,858 | 2,175 | 69 | 2,683 R | 68.4% | 30.6% | 69.1% | 30.9% |
| 11,955 | BROWN | 5,264 | 3,894 | 1,303 | 67 | 2,591 R | 74.0% | 24.8% | 74.9% | 25.1% |
| 44,782 | BUTLER | 19,564 | 12,976 | 6,371 | 217 | 6,605 R | 66.3% | 32.6% | 67.1% | 32.9% |
| 3,309 | CHASE | 1,570 | 1,162 | 393 | 15 | 769 R | 74.0% | 25.0% | 74.7% | 25.3% |
| 5,016 | CHAUTAUQUA | 2,205 | 1,688 | 497 | 20 | 1,191 R | 76.6% | 22.5% | 77.3% | 22.7% |
| 22,304 | CHEROKEE | 9,553 | 5,801 | 3,663 | 89 | 2,138 R | 60.7% | 38.3% | 61.3% | 38.7% |
| 3,678 | CHEYENNE | 1,824 | 1,442 | 356 | 26 | 1,086 R | 79.1% | 19.5% | 80.2% | 19.8% |
| 2,599 | CLARK | 1,426 | 1,075 | 324 | 27 | 751 R | 75.4% | 22.7% | 76.8% | 23.2% |
| 9,802 | CLAY | 4,519 | 3,559 | 919 | 41 | 2,640 R | 78.8% | 20.3% | 79.5% | 20.5% |
| 12,494 | CLOUD | 5,811 | 3,860 | 1,880 | 71 | 1,980 R | 66.4% | 32.4% | 67.2% | 32.8% |
| 9,370 | COFFEY | 4,139 | 3,063 | 1,037 | 39 | 2,026 R | 74.0% | 25.1% | 74.7% | 25.3% |
| 2,554 | COMANCHE | 1,293 | 993 | 285 | 15 | 708 R | 76.8% | 22.0% | 77.7% | 22.3% |
| 36,824 | COWLEY | 15,399 | 10,008 | 5,193 | 198 | 4,815 R | 65.0% | 33.7% | 65.8% | 34.2% |
| 37,916 | CRAWFORD | 16,381 | 9,518 | 6,722 | 141 | 2,796 R | 58.1% | 41.0% | 58.6% | 41.4% |
| 4,509 | DECATUR | 2,265 | 1,770 | 467 | 28 | 1,303 R | 78.1% | 20.6% | 79.1% | 20.9% |
| 20,175 | DICKINSON | 8,771 | 6,487 | 2,168 | 116 | 4,319 R | 74.0% | 24.7% | 75.0% | 25.0% |
| 9,268 | DONIPHAN | 3,820 | 2,818 | 962 | 40 | 1,856 R | 73.8% | 25.2% | 74.6% | 25.4% |
| 67,640 | DOUGLAS | 32,233 | 18,975 | 12,880 | 378 | 6,095 R | 58.9% | 40.0% | 59.6% | 40.4% |
| 4,271 | EDWARDS | 2,002 | 1,352 | 606 | 44 | 746 R | 67.5% | 30.3% | 69.1% | 30.9% |
| 3,918 | ELK | 1,785 | 1,301 | 452 | 32 | 849 R | 72.9% | 25.3% | 74.2% | 25.8% |
| 26,098 | ELLIS | 11,099 | 7,509 | 3,457 | 133 | 4,052 R | 67.7% | 31.1% | 68.5% | 31.5% |
| 6,640 | ELLSWORTH | 3,298 | 2,353 | 905 | 40 | 1,448 R | 71.3% | 27.4% | 72.2% | 27.8% |
| 23,825 | FINNEY | 9,494 | 6,938 | 2,458 | 98 | 4,480 R | 73.1% | 25.9% | 73.8% | 26.2% |
| 24,315 | FORD | 9,947 | 6,935 | 2,914 | 98 | 4,021 R | 69.7% | 29.3% | 70.4% | 29.6% |
| 22,062 | FRANKLIN | 8,899 | 6,284 | 2,523 | 92 | 3,761 R | 70.6% | 28.4% | 71.4% | 28.6% |
| 29,852 | GEARY | 6,821 | 4,464 | 2,296 | 61 | 2,168 R | 65.4% | 33.7% | 66.0% | 34.0% |
| 3,726 | GOVE | 1,784 | 1,310 | 426 | 48 | 884 R | 73.4% | 23.9% | 75.5% | 24.5% |
| 3,995 | GRAHAM | 1,923 | 1,423 | 480 | 20 | 943 R | 74.0% | 25.0% | 74.8% | 25.2% |
| 6,977 | GRANT | 2,679 | 2,043 | 615 | 21 | 1,428 R | 76.3% | 23.0% | 76.9% | 23.1% |
| 5,138 | GRAY | 2,126 | 1,580 | 514 | 32 | 1,066 R | 74.3% | 24.2% | 75.5% | 24.5% |
| 1,845 | GREELEY | 954 | 699 | 227 | 28 | 472 R | 73.3% | 23.8% | 75.5% | 24.5% |
| 8,764 | GREENWOOD | 4,118 | 2,901 | 1,173 | 44 | 1,728 R | 70.4% | 28.5% | 71.2% | 28.8% |
| 2,514 | HAMILTON | 1,468 | 1,037 | 408 | 23 | 629 R | 70.6% | 27.8% | 71.8% | 28.2% |
| 7,778 | HARPER | 3,449 | 2,521 | 893 | 35 | 1,628 R | 73.1% | 25.9% | 73.8% | 26.2% |
| 30,531 | HARVEY | 13,280 | 8,507 | 4,599 | 174 | 3,908 R | 64.1% | 34.6% | 64.9% | 35.1% |
| 3,814 | HASKELL | 1,452 | 1,152 | 283 | 17 | 869 R | 79.3% | 19.5% | 80.3% | 19.7% |
| 2,269 | HODGEMAN | 1,266 | 939 | 306 | 21 | 633 R | 74.2% | 24.2% | 75.4% | 24.6% |
| 11,644 | JACKSON | 5,179 | 3,466 | 1,667 | 46 | 1,799 R | 66.9% | 32.2% | 67.5% | 32.5% |
| 15,207 | JEFFERSON | 6,563 | 4,524 | 1,990 | 49 | 2,534 R | 68.9% | 30.3% | 69.5% | 30.5% |
| 5,241 | JEWELL | 2,604 | 1,992 | 583 | 29 | 1,409 R | 76.5% | 22.4% | 77.4% | 22.6% |
| 270,269 | JOHNSON | 140,882 | 101,987 | 38,019 | 876 | 63,968 R | 72.4% | 27.0% | 72.8% | 27.2% |
| 3,435 | KEARNY | 1,548 | 1,214 | 321 | 13 | 893 R | 78.4% | 20.7% | 79.1% | 20.9% |
| 8,960 | KINGMAN | 3,923 | 2,826 | 1,047 | 50 | 1,779 R | 72.0% | 26.7% | 73.0% | 27.0% |
| 4,046 | KIOWA | 1,933 | 1,537 | 361 | 35 | 1,176 R | 79.5% | 18.7% | 81.0% | 19.0% |
| 25,682 | LABETTE | 10,260 | 6,542 | 3,631 | 87 | 2,911 R | 63.8% | 35.4% | 64.3% | 35.7% |
| 2,472 | LANE | 1,306 | 1,008 | 282 | 16 | 726 R | 77.2% | 21.6% | 78.1% | 21.9% |
| 54,809 | LEAVENWORTH | 17,970 | 11,194 | 6,604 | 172 | 4,590 R | 62.3% | 36.8% | 62.9% | 37.1% |
| 4,145 | LINCOLN | 2,293 | 1,723 | 551 | 19 | 1,172 R | 75.1% | 24.0% | 75.8% | 24.2% |
| 8,234 | LINN | 3,974 | 2,795 | 1,152 | 27 | 1,643 R | 70.3% | 29.0% | 70.8% | 29.2% |
| 3,478 | LOGAN | 1,603 | 1,235 | 331 | 37 | 904 R | 77.0% | 20.6% | 78.9% | 21.1% |
| 35,108 | LYON | 14,121 | 9,796 | 4,188 | 137 | 5,608 R | 69.4% | 29.7% | 70.1% | 29.9% |
| 26,855 | MCPHERSON | 12,004 | 8,630 | 3,185 | 189 | 5,445 R | 71.9% | 26.5% | 73.0% | 27.0% |
| 13,522 | MARION | 6,116 | 4,407 | 1,632 | 77 | 2,775 R | 72.1% | 26.7% | 73.0% | 27.0% |
| 12,787 | MARSHALL | 5,983 | 4,098 | 1,813 | 72 | 2,285 R | 68.5% | 30.3% | 69.3% | 30.7% |
| 4,788 | MEADE | 2,338 | 1,804 | 491 | 43 | 1,313 R | 77.2% | 21.0% | 78.6% | 21.4% |

# KANSAS

## PRESIDENT 1984

| 1980 Census Population | County | Total Vote | Republican | Democratic | Other | Rep.-Dem. Plurality | Percentage | | | |
|---|---|---|---|---|---|---|---|---|---|---|
| | | | | | | | Total Vote | | Major Vote | |
| | | | | | | | Rep. | Dem. | Rep. | Dem. |
| 21,618 | MIAMI | 9,036 | 5,877 | 3,076 | 83 | 2,801 R | 65.0% | 34.0% | 65.6% | 34.4% |
| 8,117 | MITCHELL | 3,996 | 3,036 | 919 | 41 | 2,117 R | 76.0% | 23.0% | 76.8% | 23.2% |
| 42,281 | MONTGOMERY | 17,127 | 12,023 | 4,933 | 171 | 7,090 R | 70.2% | 28.8% | 70.9% | 29.1% |
| 6,419 | MORRIS | 3,103 | 2,240 | 820 | 43 | 1,420 R | 72.2% | 26.4% | 73.2% | 26.8% |
| 3,454 | MORTON | 1,874 | 1,533 | 322 | 19 | 1,211 R | 81.8% | 17.2% | 82.6% | 17.4% |
| 11,211 | NEMAHA | 5,485 | 3,653 | 1,761 | 71 | 1,892 R | 66.6% | 32.1% | 67.5% | 32.5% |
| 18,967 | NEOSHO | 7,749 | 4,968 | 2,679 | 102 | 2,289 R | 64.1% | 34.6% | 65.0% | 35.0% |
| 4,498 | NESS | 2,362 | 1,779 | 540 | 43 | 1,239 R | 75.3% | 22.9% | 76.7% | 23.3% |
| 6,689 | NORTON | 3,176 | 2,515 | 611 | 50 | 1,904 R | 79.2% | 19.2% | 80.5% | 19.5% |
| 15,319 | OSAGE | 6,443 | 4,288 | 2,072 | 83 | 2,216 R | 66.6% | 32.2% | 67.4% | 32.6% |
| 5,959 | OSBORNE | 2,909 | 2,171 | 686 | 52 | 1,485 R | 74.6% | 23.6% | 76.0% | 24.0% |
| 5,971 | OTTAWA | 3,096 | 2,345 | 699 | 52 | 1,646 R | 75.7% | 22.6% | 77.0% | 23.0% |
| 8,065 | PAWNEE | 3,730 | 2,570 | 1,092 | 68 | 1,478 R | 68.9% | 29.3% | 70.2% | 29.8% |
| 7,406 | PHILLIPS | 3,477 | 2,813 | 626 | 38 | 2,187 R | 80.9% | 18.0% | 81.8% | 18.2% |
| 14,782 | POTTAWATOMIE | 6,468 | 4,598 | 1,798 | 72 | 2,800 R | 71.1% | 27.8% | 71.9% | 28.1% |
| 10,275 | PRATT | 4,549 | 3,244 | 1,255 | 50 | 1,989 R | 71.3% | 27.6% | 72.1% | 27.9% |
| 4,105 | RAWLINS | 2,082 | 1,625 | 412 | 45 | 1,213 R | 78.0% | 19.8% | 79.8% | 20.2% |
| 64,983 | RENO | 26,159 | 16,568 | 9,229 | 362 | 7,339 R | 63.3% | 35.3% | 64.2% | 35.8% |
| 7,569 | REPUBLIC | 3,934 | 3,009 | 887 | 38 | 2,122 R | 76.5% | 22.5% | 77.2% | 22.8% |
| 11,900 | RICE | 5,239 | 3,598 | 1,559 | 82 | 2,039 R | 68.7% | 29.8% | 69.8% | 30.2% |
| 63,505 | RILEY | 17,458 | 11,308 | 5,975 | 175 | 5,333 R | 64.8% | 34.2% | 65.4% | 34.6% |
| 7,006 | ROOKS | 3,349 | 2,604 | 699 | 46 | 1,905 R | 77.8% | 20.9% | 78.8% | 21.2% |
| 4,516 | RUSH | 2,530 | 1,758 | 718 | 54 | 1,040 R | 69.5% | 28.4% | 71.0% | 29.0% |
| 8,868 | RUSSELL | 4,771 | 3,673 | 1,055 | 43 | 2,618 R | 77.0% | 22.1% | 77.7% | 22.3% |
| 48,905 | SALINE | 21,961 | 15,244 | 6,526 | 191 | 8,718 R | 69.4% | 29.7% | 70.0% | 30.0% |
| 5,782 | SCOTT | 2,486 | 2,017 | 427 | 42 | 1,590 R | 81.1% | 17.2% | 82.5% | 17.5% |
| 366,531 | SEDGWICK | 153,315 | 95,874 | 55,263 | 2,178 | 40,611 R | 62.5% | 36.0% | 63.4% | 36.6% |
| 17,071 | SEWARD | 6,484 | 5,222 | 1,198 | 64 | 4,024 R | 80.5% | 18.5% | 81.3% | 18.7% |
| 154,916 | SHAWNEE | 70,589 | 43,465 | 26,338 | 786 | 17,127 R | 61.6% | 37.3% | 62.3% | 37.7% |
| 3,544 | SHERIDAN | 1,725 | 1,274 | 419 | 32 | 855 R | 73.9% | 24.3% | 75.3% | 24.7% |
| 7,759 | SHERMAN | 3,463 | 2,702 | 714 | 47 | 1,988 R | 78.0% | 20.6% | 79.1% | 20.9% |
| 5,947 | SMITH | 3,079 | 2,332 | 684 | 63 | 1,648 R | 75.7% | 22.2% | 77.3% | 22.7% |
| 5,694 | STAFFORD | 2,958 | 2,062 | 844 | 52 | 1,218 R | 69.7% | 28.5% | 71.0% | 29.0% |
| 2,339 | STANTON | 1,022 | 783 | 205 | 34 | 578 R | 76.6% | 20.1% | 79.3% | 20.7% |
| 4,736 | STEVENS | 2,271 | 1,863 | 386 | 22 | 1,477 R | 82.0% | 17.0% | 82.8% | 17.2% |
| 24,928 | SUMNER | 10,793 | 6,942 | 3,708 | 143 | 3,234 R | 64.3% | 34.4% | 65.2% | 34.8% |
| 8,451 | THOMAS | 4,051 | 3,107 | 887 | 57 | 2,220 R | 76.7% | 21.9% | 77.8% | 22.2% |
| 4,165 | TREGO | 2,118 | 1,491 | 598 | 29 | 893 R | 70.4% | 28.2% | 71.4% | 28.6% |
| 6,867 | WABAUNSEE | 3,130 | 2,276 | 805 | 49 | 1,471 R | 72.7% | 25.7% | 73.9% | 26.1% |
| 2,045 | WALLACE | 1,010 | 838 | 152 | 20 | 686 R | 83.0% | 15.0% | 84.6% | 15.4% |
| 8,543 | WASHINGTON | 3,936 | 2,979 | 889 | 68 | 2,090 R | 75.7% | 22.6% | 77.0% | 23.0% |
| 3,041 | WICHITA | 1,161 | 916 | 232 | 13 | 684 R | 78.9% | 20.0% | 79.8% | 20.2% |
| 12,128 | WILSON | 5,071 | 3,663 | 1,344 | 64 | 2,319 R | 72.2% | 26.5% | 73.2% | 26.8% |
| 4,600 | WOODSON | 2,030 | 1,408 | 596 | 26 | 812 R | 69.4% | 29.4% | 70.3% | 29.7% |
| 172,335 | WYANDOTTE | 64,136 | 27,459 | 36,042 | 635 | 8,583 D | 42.8% | 56.2% | 43.2% | 56.8% |
| 2,363,679 | TOTAL | 1,021,991 | 677,296 | 333,149 | 11,546 | 344,147 R | 66.3% | 32.6% | 67.0% | 33.0% |

# KANSAS

## PRESIDENT 1980

| 1980 Census Population | County | Total Vote | Republican | Democratic | Other | Rep.-Dem. Plurality | Percentage Total Vote Rep. | Dem. | Major Vote Rep. | Dem. |
|---|---|---|---|---|---|---|---|---|---|---|
| 15,654 | ALLEN | 6,317 | 3,811 | 2,009 | 497 | 1,802 R | 60.3% | 31.8% | 65.5% | 34.5% |
| 8,749 | ANDERSON | 3,773 | 2,363 | 1,170 | 240 | 1,193 R | 62.6% | 31.0% | 66.9% | 33.1% |
| 18,397 | ATCHISON | 7,581 | 4,084 | 3,063 | 434 | 1,021 R | 53.9% | 40.4% | 57.1% | 42.9% |
| 6,548 | BARBER | 2,994 | 1,872 | 914 | 208 | 958 R | 62.5% | 30.5% | 67.2% | 32.8% |
| 31,343 | BARTON | 13,852 | 9,147 | 3,663 | 1,042 | 5,484 R | 66.0% | 26.4% | 71.4% | 28.6% |
| 15,969 | BOURBON | 7,199 | 4,263 | 2,605 | 331 | 1,658 R | 59.2% | 36.2% | 62.1% | 37.9% |
| 11,955 | BROWN | 5,322 | 3,598 | 1,370 | 354 | 2,228 R | 67.6% | 25.7% | 72.4% | 27.6% |
| 44,782 | BUTLER | 18,453 | 10,210 | 6,875 | 1,368 | 3,335 R | 55.3% | 37.3% | 59.8% | 40.2% |
| 3,309 | CHASE | 1,603 | 1,073 | 413 | 117 | 660 R | 66.9% | 25.8% | 72.2% | 27.8% |
| 5,016 | CHAUTAUQUA | 2,187 | 1,566 | 543 | 78 | 1,023 R | 71.6% | 24.8% | 74.3% | 25.7% |
| 22,304 | CHEROKEE | 9,662 | 5,296 | 3,969 | 397 | 1,327 R | 54.8% | 41.1% | 57.2% | 42.8% |
| 3,678 | CHEYENNE | 1,800 | 1,330 | 358 | 112 | 972 R | 73.9% | 19.9% | 78.8% | 21.2% |
| 2,599 | CLARK | 1,417 | 901 | 430 | 86 | 471 R | 63.6% | 30.3% | 67.7% | 32.3% |
| 9,802 | CLAY | 4,667 | 3,449 | 932 | 286 | 2,517 R | 73.9% | 20.0% | 78.7% | 21.3% |
| 12,494 | CLOUD | 5,817 | 3,581 | 1,793 | 443 | 1,788 R | 61.6% | 30.8% | 66.6% | 33.4% |
| 9,370 | COFFEY | 3,602 | 2,491 | 938 | 173 | 1,553 R | 69.2% | 26.0% | 72.6% | 27.4% |
| 2,554 | COMANCHE | 1,340 | 877 | 393 | 70 | 484 R | 65.4% | 29.3% | 69.1% | 30.9% |
| 36,824 | COWLEY | 15,312 | 8,749 | 5,474 | 1,089 | 3,275 R | 57.1% | 35.7% | 61.5% | 38.5% |
| 37,916 | CRAWFORD | 16,855 | 8,058 | 7,658 | 1,139 | 400 R | 47.8% | 45.4% | 51.3% | 48.7% |
| 4,509 | DECATUR | 2,250 | 1,642 | 443 | 165 | 1,199 R | 73.0% | 19.7% | 78.8% | 21.2% |
| 20,175 | DICKINSON | 8,359 | 5,654 | 2,108 | 597 | 3,546 R | 67.6% | 25.2% | 72.8% | 27.2% |
| 9,268 | DONIPHAN | 3,719 | 2,523 | 1,001 | 195 | 1,522 R | 67.8% | 26.9% | 71.6% | 28.4% |
| 67,640 | DOUGLAS | 28,784 | 14,106 | 9,360 | 5,318 | 4,746 R | 49.0% | 32.5% | 60.1% | 39.9% |
| 4,271 | EDWARDS | 2,204 | 1,409 | 616 | 179 | 793 R | 63.9% | 27.9% | 69.6% | 30.4% |
| 3,918 | ELK | 1,837 | 1,280 | 482 | 75 | 798 R | 69.7% | 26.2% | 72.6% | 27.4% |
| 26,098 | ELLIS | 10,724 | 5,634 | 3,940 | 1,150 | 1,694 R | 52.5% | 36.7% | 58.8% | 41.2% |
| 6,640 | ELLSWORTH | 3,270 | 2,155 | 886 | 229 | 1,269 R | 65.9% | 27.1% | 70.9% | 29.1% |
| 23,825 | FINNEY | 8,246 | 4,831 | 2,689 | 726 | 2,142 R | 58.6% | 32.6% | 64.2% | 35.8% |
| 24,315 | FORD | 9,661 | 5,686 | 3,194 | 781 | 2,492 R | 58.9% | 33.1% | 64.0% | 36.0% |
| 22,062 | FRANKLIN | 8,808 | 5,525 | 2,726 | 557 | 2,799 R | 62.7% | 30.9% | 67.0% | 33.0% |
| 29,852 | GEARY | 6,304 | 3,534 | 2,357 | 413 | 1,177 R | 56.1% | 37.4% | 60.0% | 40.0% |
| 3,726 | GOVE | 1,776 | 1,263 | 396 | 117 | 867 R | 71.1% | 22.3% | 76.1% | 23.9% |
| 3,995 | GRAHAM | 2,045 | 1,450 | 473 | 122 | 977 R | 70.9% | 23.1% | 75.4% | 24.6% |
| 6,977 | GRANT | 2,592 | 1,711 | 683 | 198 | 1,028 R | 66.0% | 26.4% | 71.5% | 28.5% |
| 5,138 | GRAY | 2,057 | 1,310 | 583 | 164 | 727 R | 63.7% | 28.3% | 69.2% | 30.8% |
| 1,845 | GREELEY | 947 | 600 | 235 | 112 | 365 R | 63.4% | 24.8% | 71.9% | 28.1% |
| 8,764 | GREENWOOD | 4,155 | 2,685 | 1,241 | 229 | 1,444 R | 64.6% | 29.9% | 68.4% | 31.6% |
| 2,514 | HAMILTON | 1,375 | 889 | 402 | 84 | 487 R | 64.7% | 29.2% | 68.9% | 31.1% |
| 7,778 | HARPER | 3,512 | 2,254 | 990 | 268 | 1,264 R | 64.2% | 28.2% | 69.5% | 30.5% |
| 30,531 | HARVEY | 12,912 | 7,045 | 4,173 | 1,694 | 2,872 R | 54.6% | 32.3% | 62.8% | 37.2% |
| 3,814 | HASKELL | 1,499 | 1,014 | 374 | 111 | 640 R | 67.6% | 24.9% | 73.1% | 26.9% |
| 2,269 | HODGEMAN | 1,256 | 831 | 339 | 86 | 492 R | 66.2% | 27.0% | 71.0% | 29.0% |
| 11,644 | JACKSON | 5,070 | 3,211 | 1,537 | 322 | 1,674 R | 63.3% | 30.3% | 67.6% | 32.4% |
| 15,207 | JEFFERSON | 6,263 | 4,046 | 1,776 | 441 | 2,270 R | 64.6% | 28.4% | 69.5% | 30.5% |
| 5,241 | JEWELL | 2,849 | 2,074 | 578 | 197 | 1,496 R | 72.8% | 20.3% | 78.2% | 21.8% |
| 270,269 | JOHNSON | 123,983 | 78,048 | 33,210 | 12,725 | 44,838 R | 63.0% | 26.8% | 70.2% | 29.8% |
| 3,435 | KEARNY | 1,392 | 924 | 375 | 93 | 549 R | 66.4% | 26.9% | 71.1% | 28.9% |
| 8,960 | KINGMAN | 4,102 | 2,610 | 1,133 | 359 | 1,477 R | 63.6% | 27.6% | 69.7% | 30.3% |
| 4,046 | KIOWA | 1,986 | 1,433 | 438 | 115 | 995 R | 72.2% | 22.1% | 76.6% | 23.4% |
| 25,682 | LABETTE | 9,921 | 5,244 | 3,947 | 730 | 1,297 R | 52.9% | 39.8% | 57.1% | 42.9% |
| 2,472 | LANE | 1,368 | 924 | 321 | 123 | 603 R | 67.5% | 23.5% | 74.2% | 25.8% |
| 54,809 | LEAVENWORTH | 16,656 | 9,157 | 6,354 | 1,145 | 2,803 R | 55.0% | 38.1% | 59.0% | 41.0% |
| 4,145 | LINCOLN | 2,335 | 1,685 | 528 | 122 | 1,157 R | 72.2% | 22.6% | 76.1% | 23.9% |
| 8,234 | LINN | 3,710 | 2,407 | 1,157 | 146 | 1,250 R | 64.9% | 31.2% | 67.5% | 32.5% |
| 3,478 | LOGAN | 1,730 | 1,261 | 358 | 111 | 903 R | 72.9% | 20.7% | 77.9% | 22.1% |
| 35,108 | LYON | 14,551 | 8,431 | 4,680 | 1,440 | 3,751 R | 57.9% | 32.2% | 64.3% | 35.7% |
| 26,855 | MCPHERSON | 11,631 | 6,843 | 3,340 | 1,448 | 3,503 R | 58.8% | 28.7% | 67.2% | 32.8% |
| 13,522 | MARION | 6,150 | 3,960 | 1,569 | 621 | 2,391 R | 64.4% | 25.5% | 71.6% | 28.4% |
| 12,787 | MARSHALL | 6,097 | 4,127 | 1,555 | 415 | 2,572 R | 67.7% | 25.5% | 72.6% | 27.4% |
| 4,788 | MEADE | 2,258 | 1,618 | 482 | 158 | 1,136 R | 71.7% | 21.3% | 77.0% | 23.0% |

# KANSAS

## PRESIDENT 1980

| 1980 Census Population | County | Total Vote | Republican | Democratic | Other | Rep.-Dem. Plurality | Percentage | | | |
|---|---|---|---|---|---|---|---|---|---|---|
| | | | | | | | Total Vote | | Major Vote | |
| | | | | | | | Rep. | Dem. | Rep. | Dem. |
| 21,618 | MIAMI | 8,301 | 4,740 | 3,071 | 490 | 1,669 R | 57.1% | 37.0% | 60.7% | 39.3% |
| 8,117 | MITCHELL | 3,953 | 2,821 | 876 | 256 | 1,945 R | 71.4% | 22.2% | 76.3% | 23.7% |
| 42,281 | MONTGOMERY | 16,915 | 10,856 | 5,282 | 777 | 5,574 R | 64.2% | 31.2% | 67.3% | 32.7% |
| 6,419 | MORRIS | 2,949 | 1,933 | 810 | 206 | 1,123 R | 65.5% | 27.5% | 70.5% | 29.5% |
| 3,454 | MORTON | 1,662 | 1,157 | 414 | 91 | 743 R | 69.6% | 24.9% | 73.6% | 26.4% |
| 11,211 | NEMAHA | 5,456 | 3,546 | 1,600 | 310 | 1,946 R | 65.0% | 29.3% | 68.9% | 31.1% |
| 18,967 | NEOSHO | 8,077 | 4,613 | 2,923 | 541 | 1,690 R | 57.1% | 36.2% | 61.2% | 38.8% |
| 4,498 | NESS | 2,455 | 1,657 | 616 | 182 | 1,041 R | 67.5% | 25.1% | 72.9% | 27.1% |
| 6,689 | NORTON | 3,477 | 2,625 | 666 | 186 | 1,959 R | 75.5% | 19.2% | 79.8% | 20.2% |
| 15,319 | OSAGE | 6,324 | 3,817 | 2,088 | 419 | 1,729 R | 60.4% | 33.0% | 64.6% | 35.4% |
| 5,959 | OSBORNE | 2,984 | 2,188 | 620 | 176 | 1,568 R | 73.3% | 20.8% | 77.9% | 22.1% |
| 5,971 | OTTAWA | 2,947 | 2,118 | 630 | 199 | 1,488 R | 71.9% | 21.4% | 77.1% | 22.9% |
| 8,065 | PAWNEE | 3,691 | 2,170 | 1,184 | 337 | 986 R | 58.8% | 32.1% | 64.7% | 35.3% |
| 7,406 | PHILLIPS | 3,667 | 2,731 | 748 | 188 | 1,983 R | 74.5% | 20.4% | 78.5% | 21.5% |
| 14,782 | POTTAWATOMIE | 6,144 | 3,895 | 1,724 | 525 | 2,171 R | 63.4% | 28.1% | 69.3% | 30.7% |
| 10,275 | PRATT | 4,683 | 2,866 | 1,369 | 448 | 1,497 R | 61.2% | 29.2% | 67.7% | 32.3% |
| 4,105 | RAWLINS | 2,076 | 1,524 | 427 | 125 | 1,097 R | 73.4% | 20.6% | 78.1% | 21.9% |
| 64,983 | RENO | 26,121 | 13,804 | 9,615 | 2,702 | 4,189 R | 52.8% | 36.8% | 58.9% | 41.1% |
| 7,569 | REPUBLIC | 4,120 | 3,031 | 850 | 239 | 2,181 R | 73.6% | 20.6% | 78.1% | 21.9% |
| 11,900 | RICE | 5,568 | 3,211 | 1,847 | 510 | 1,364 R | 57.7% | 33.2% | 63.5% | 36.5% |
| 63,505 | RILEY | 16,818 | 8,904 | 5,224 | 2,690 | 3,680 R | 52.9% | 31.1% | 63.0% | 37.0% |
| 7,006 | ROOKS | 3,187 | 2,275 | 725 | 187 | 1,550 R | 71.4% | 22.7% | 75.8% | 24.2% |
| 4,516 | RUSH | 2,572 | 1,840 | 557 | 175 | 1,283 R | 71.5% | 21.7% | 76.8% | 23.2% |
| 8,868 | RUSSELL | 4,437 | 3,241 | 910 | 286 | 2,331 R | 73.0% | 20.5% | 78.1% | 21.9% |
| 48,905 | SALINE | 21,169 | 12,758 | 6,382 | 2,029 | 6,376 R | 60.3% | 30.1% | 66.7% | 33.3% |
| 5,782 | SCOTT | 2,418 | 1,829 | 456 | 133 | 1,373 R | 75.6% | 18.9% | 80.0% | 20.0% |
| 366,531 | SEDGWICK | 145,431 | 75,317 | 55,105 | 15,009 | 20,212 R | 51.8% | 37.9% | 57.7% | 42.3% |
| 17,071 | SEWARD | 6,191 | 4,385 | 1,460 | 346 | 2,925 R | 70.8% | 23.6% | 75.0% | 25.0% |
| 154,916 | SHAWNEE | 67,776 | 36,290 | 24,852 | 6,634 | 11,438 R | 53.5% | 36.7% | 59.4% | 40.6% |
| 3,544 | SHERIDAN | 1,693 | 1,202 | 391 | 100 | 811 R | 71.0% | 23.1% | 75.5% | 24.5% |
| 7,759 | SHERMAN | 3,362 | 2,315 | 779 | 268 | 1,536 R | 68.9% | 23.2% | 74.8% | 25.2% |
| 5,947 | SMITH | 3,368 | 2,415 | 719 | 234 | 1,696 R | 71.7% | 21.3% | 77.1% | 22.9% |
| 5,694 | STAFFORD | 2,976 | 1,865 | 872 | 239 | 993 R | 62.7% | 29.3% | 68.1% | 31.9% |
| 2,339 | STANTON | 992 | 672 | 231 | 89 | 441 R | 67.7% | 23.3% | 74.4% | 25.6% |
| 4,736 | STEVENS | 2,085 | 1,502 | 478 | 105 | 1,024 R | 72.0% | 22.9% | 75.9% | 24.1% |
| 24,928 | SUMNER | 10,496 | 6,038 | 3,761 | 697 | 2,277 R | 57.5% | 35.8% | 61.6% | 38.4% |
| 8,451 | THOMAS | 4,202 | 2,789 | 1,045 | 368 | 1,744 R | 66.4% | 24.9% | 72.7% | 27.3% |
| 4,165 | TREGO | 2,048 | 1,340 | 523 | 185 | 817 R | 65.4% | 25.5% | 71.9% | 28.1% |
| 6,867 | WABAUNSEE | 3,317 | 2,255 | 853 | 209 | 1,402 R | 68.0% | 25.7% | 72.6% | 27.4% |
| 2,045 | WALLACE | 1,036 | 811 | 167 | 58 | 644 R | 78.3% | 16.1% | 82.9% | 17.1% |
| 8,543 | WASHINGTON | 4,083 | 3,058 | 784 | 241 | 2,274 R | 74.9% | 19.2% | 79.6% | 20.4% |
| 3,041 | WICHITA | 1,258 | 880 | 303 | 75 | 577 R | 70.0% | 24.1% | 74.4% | 25.6% |
| 12,128 | WILSON | 4,801 | 3,328 | 1,205 | 268 | 2,123 R | 69.3% | 25.1% | 73.4% | 26.6% |
| 4,600 | WOODSON | 2,189 | 1,435 | 646 | 108 | 789 R | 65.6% | 29.5% | 69.0% | 31.0% |
| 172,335 | WYANDOTTE | 60,223 | 23,012 | 32,763 | 4,448 | 9,751 D | 38.2% | 54.4% | 41.3% | 58.7% |
| 2,363,679 | TOTAL | 979,795 | 566,812 | 326,150 | 86,833 | 240,662 R | 57.9% | 33.3% | 63.5% | 36.5% |

# KANSAS

## PRESIDENT 1976

| 1970 Census Population | County | Total Vote | Republican | Democratic | Other | Rep.-Dem. Plurality | Total Vote Rep. | Total Vote Dem. | Major Vote Rep. | Major Vote Dem. |
|---|---|---|---|---|---|---|---|---|---|---|
| 15,043 | ALLEN | 6,141 | 3,269 | 2,746 | 126 | 523 R | 53.2% | 44.7% | 54.3% | 45.7% |
| 8,501 | ANDERSON | 3,844 | 1,872 | 1,886 | 86 | 14 D | 48.7% | 49.1% | 49.8% | 50.2% |
| 19,165 | ATCHISON | 8,344 | 4,030 | 4,108 | 206 | 78 D | 48.3% | 49.2% | 49.5% | 50.5% |
| 7,016 | BARBER | 3,109 | 1,568 | 1,494 | 47 | 74 R | 50.4% | 48.1% | 51.2% | 48.8% |
| 30,663 | BARTON | 13,142 | 7,311 | 5,497 | 334 | 1,814 R | 55.6% | 41.8% | 57.1% | 42.9% |
| 15,215 | BOURBON | 6,929 | 3,589 | 3,237 | 103 | 352 R | 51.8% | 46.7% | 52.6% | 47.4% |
| 11,685 | BROWN | 5,245 | 3,407 | 1,745 | 93 | 1,662 R | 65.0% | 33.3% | 66.1% | 33.9% |
| 38,658 | BUTLER | 17,316 | 8,390 | 8,540 | 386 | 150 D | 48.5% | 49.3% | 49.6% | 50.4% |
| 3,408 | CHASE | 1,601 | 922 | 643 | 36 | 279 R | 57.6% | 40.2% | 58.9% | 41.1% |
| 4,642 | CHAUTAUQUA | 2,078 | 1,159 | 866 | 53 | 293 R | 55.8% | 41.7% | 57.2% | 42.8% |
| 21,549 | CHEROKEE | 9,218 | 3,957 | 5,154 | 107 | 1,197 D | 42.9% | 55.9% | 43.4% | 56.6% |
| 4,256 | CHEYENNE | 1,805 | 1,008 | 758 | 39 | 250 R | 55.8% | 42.0% | 57.1% | 42.9% |
| 2,896 | CLARK | 1,469 | 761 | 680 | 28 | 81 R | 51.8% | 46.3% | 52.8% | 47.2% |
| 9,890 | CLAY | 4,832 | 3,085 | 1,610 | 137 | 1,475 R | 63.8% | 33.3% | 65.7% | 34.3% |
| 13,466 | CLOUD | 6,061 | 2,954 | 2,976 | 131 | 22 D | 48.7% | 49.1% | 49.8% | 50.2% |
| 7,397 | COFFEY | 3,783 | 2,145 | 1,549 | 89 | 596 R | 56.7% | 40.9% | 58.1% | 41.9% |
| 2,702 | COMANCHE | 1,364 | 719 | 630 | 15 | 89 R | 52.7% | 46.2% | 53.3% | 46.7% |
| 35,012 | COWLEY | 14,931 | 7,513 | 7,095 | 323 | 418 R | 50.3% | 47.5% | 51.4% | 48.6% |
| 37,850 | CRAWFORD | 16,504 | 7,225 | 9,021 | 258 | 1,796 D | 43.8% | 54.7% | 44.5% | 55.5% |
| 4,988 | DECATUR | 2,336 | 1,232 | 1,011 | 93 | 221 R | 52.7% | 43.3% | 54.9% | 45.1% |
| 19,993 | DICKINSON | 8,617 | 4,759 | 3,672 | 186 | 1,087 R | 55.2% | 42.6% | 56.4% | 43.6% |
| 9,107 | DONIPHAN | 3,969 | 2,469 | 1,428 | 72 | 1,041 R | 62.2% | 36.0% | 63.4% | 36.6% |
| 57,932 | DOUGLAS | 27,842 | 14,277 | 11,922 | 1,643 | 2,355 R | 51.3% | 42.8% | 54.5% | 45.5% |
| 4,581 | EDWARDS | 2,357 | 1,001 | 1,304 | 52 | 303 D | 42.5% | 55.3% | 43.4% | 56.6% |
| 3,858 | ELK | 1,982 | 1,087 | 865 | 30 | 222 R | 54.8% | 43.6% | 55.7% | 44.3% |
| 24,730 | ELLIS | 11,240 | 4,719 | 6,280 | 241 | 1,561 D | 42.0% | 55.9% | 42.9% | 57.1% |
| 6,146 | ELLSWORTH | 3,246 | 1,618 | 1,573 | 55 | 45 R | 49.8% | 48.5% | 50.7% | 49.3% |
| 19,029 | FINNEY | 7,667 | 3,711 | 3,813 | 143 | 102 D | 48.4% | 49.7% | 49.3% | 50.7% |
| 22,587 | FORD | 9,827 | 4,679 | 4,934 | 214 | 255 D | 47.6% | 50.2% | 48.7% | 51.3% |
| 20,007 | FRANKLIN | 8,578 | 4,760 | 3,607 | 211 | 1,153 R | 55.5% | 42.0% | 56.9% | 43.1% |
| 28,111 | GEARY | 6,196 | 3,230 | 2,843 | 123 | 387 R | 52.1% | 45.9% | 53.2% | 46.8% |
| 3,940 | GOVE | 1,757 | 860 | 848 | 49 | 12 R | 48.9% | 48.3% | 50.4% | 49.6% |
| 4,751 | GRAHAM | 2,088 | 1,112 | 936 | 40 | 176 R | 53.3% | 44.8% | 54.3% | 45.7% |
| 5,961 | GRANT | 2,422 | 1,226 | 1,151 | 45 | 75 R | 50.6% | 47.5% | 51.6% | 48.4% |
| 4,516 | GRAY | 1,989 | 837 | 1,111 | 41 | 274 D | 42.1% | 55.9% | 43.0% | 57.0% |
| 1,819 | GREELEY | 896 | 389 | 479 | 28 | 90 D | 43.4% | 53.5% | 44.8% | 55.2% |
| 9,141 | GREENWOOD | 4,144 | 2,319 | 1,737 | 88 | 582 R | 56.0% | 41.9% | 57.2% | 42.8% |
| 2,747 | HAMILTON | 1,343 | 560 | 746 | 37 | 186 D | 41.7% | 55.5% | 42.9% | 57.1% |
| 7,871 | HARPER | 3,554 | 1,777 | 1,681 | 96 | 96 R | 50.0% | 47.3% | 51.4% | 48.6% |
| 27,236 | HARVEY | 12,987 | 6,624 | 6,003 | 360 | 621 R | 51.0% | 46.2% | 52.5% | 47.5% |
| 3,672 | HASKELL | 1,464 | 761 | 676 | 27 | 85 R | 52.0% | 46.2% | 53.0% | 47.0% |
| 2,662 | HODGEMAN | 1,315 | 576 | 697 | 42 | 121 D | 43.8% | 53.0% | 45.2% | 54.8% |
| 10,342 | JACKSON | 4,968 | 2,725 | 2,129 | 114 | 596 R | 54.9% | 42.9% | 56.1% | 43.9% |
| 11,945 | JEFFERSON | 5,851 | 3,225 | 2,470 | 156 | 755 R | 55.1% | 42.2% | 56.6% | 43.4% |
| 6,099 | JEWELL | 2,770 | 1,592 | 1,111 | 67 | 481 R | 57.5% | 40.1% | 58.9% | 41.1% |
| 220,073 | JOHNSON | 114,142 | 75,798 | 35,605 | 2,739 | 40,193 R | 66.4% | 31.2% | 68.0% | 32.0% |
| 3,047 | KEARNY | 1,377 | 674 | 658 | 45 | 16 R | 48.9% | 47.8% | 50.6% | 49.4% |
| 8,886 | KINGMAN | 4,093 | 1,839 | 2,142 | 112 | 303 D | 44.9% | 52.3% | 46.2% | 53.8% |
| 4,088 | KIOWA | 1,984 | 1,180 | 764 | 40 | 416 R | 59.5% | 38.5% | 60.7% | 39.3% |
| 25,775 | LABETTE | 10,177 | 4,640 | 5,294 | 243 | 654 D | 45.6% | 52.0% | 46.7% | 53.3% |
| 2,707 | LANE | 1,331 | 651 | 646 | 34 | 5 R | 48.9% | 48.5% | 50.2% | 49.8% |
| 53,340 | LEAVENWORTH | 16,778 | 8,407 | 8,022 | 349 | 385 R | 50.1% | 47.8% | 51.2% | 48.8% |
| 4,582 | LINCOLN | 2,247 | 1,225 | 985 | 37 | 240 R | 54.5% | 43.8% | 55.4% | 44.6% |
| 7,770 | LINN | 3,602 | 1,873 | 1,681 | 48 | 192 R | 52.0% | 46.7% | 52.7% | 47.3% |
| 3,814 | LOGAN | 1,697 | 957 | 694 | 46 | 263 R | 56.4% | 40.9% | 58.0% | 42.0% |
| 32,071 | LYON | 13,428 | 7,062 | 5,634 | 732 | 1,428 R | 52.6% | 42.0% | 55.6% | 44.4% |
| 24,778 | MCPHERSON | 11,860 | 6,187 | 5,366 | 307 | 821 R | 52.2% | 45.2% | 53.6% | 46.4% |
| 13,935 | MARION | 6,140 | 3,519 | 2,483 | 138 | 1,036 R | 57.3% | 40.4% | 58.6% | 41.4% |
| 13,139 | MARSHALL | 6,360 | 3,226 | 3,004 | 130 | 222 R | 50.7% | 47.2% | 51.8% | 48.2% |
| 4,912 | MEADE | 2,152 | 1,109 | 983 | 60 | 126 R | 51.5% | 45.7% | 53.0% | 47.0% |

# KANSAS

## PRESIDENT 1976

| 1970 Census Population | County | Total Vote | Republican | Democratic | Other | Rep.-Dem. Plurality | Percentage Total Vote Rep. | Dem. | Major Vote Rep. | Dem. |
|---|---|---|---|---|---|---|---|---|---|---|
| 19,254 | MIAMI | 8,216 | 3,999 | 4,000 | 217 | 1 D | 48.7% | 48.7% | 50.0% | 50.0% |
| 8,010 | MITCHELL | 3,880 | 2,095 | 1,700 | 85 | 395 R | 54.0% | 43.8% | 55.2% | 44.8% |
| 39,949 | MONTGOMERY | 16,391 | 8,864 | 7,157 | 370 | 1,707 R | 54.1% | 43.7% | 55.3% | 44.7% |
| 6,432 | MORRIS | 3,102 | 1,698 | 1,337 | 67 | 361 R | 54.7% | 43.1% | 55.9% | 44.1% |
| 3,576 | MORTON | 1,509 | 738 | 735 | 36 | 3 R | 48.9% | 48.7% | 50.1% | 49.9% |
| 11,825 | NEMAHA | 5,441 | 2,759 | 2,586 | 96 | 173 R | 50.7% | 47.5% | 51.6% | 48.4% |
| 18,812 | NEOSHO | 8,024 | 4,038 | 3,842 | 144 | 196 R | 50.3% | 47.9% | 51.2% | 48.8% |
| 4,791 | NESS | 2,184 | 1,016 | 1,106 | 62 | 90 D | 46.5% | 50.6% | 47.9% | 52.1% |
| 7,279 | NORTON | 3,635 | 2,201 | 1,337 | 97 | 864 R | 60.6% | 36.8% | 62.2% | 37.8% |
| 13,352 | OSAGE | 5,828 | 2,945 | 2,755 | 128 | 190 R | 50.5% | 47.3% | 51.7% | 48.3% |
| 6,416 | OSBORNE | 2,840 | 1,574 | 1,190 | 76 | 384 R | 55.4% | 41.9% | 56.9% | 43.1% |
| 6,183 | OTTAWA | 3,082 | 1,629 | 1,393 | 60 | 236 R | 52.9% | 45.2% | 53.9% | 46.1% |
| 8,484 | PAWNEE | 3,751 | 1,692 | 1,959 | 100 | 267 D | 45.1% | 52.2% | 46.3% | 53.7% |
| 7,888 | PHILLIPS | 3,675 | 2,317 | 1,264 | 94 | 1,053 R | 63.0% | 34.4% | 64.7% | 35.3% |
| 11,755 | POTTAWATOMIE | 5,897 | 3,483 | 2,316 | 98 | 1,167 R | 59.1% | 39.3% | 60.1% | 39.9% |
| 10,056 | PRATT | 4,850 | 2,427 | 2,307 | 116 | 120 R | 50.0% | 47.6% | 51.3% | 48.7% |
| 4,393 | RAWLINS | 2,131 | 1,148 | 903 | 80 | 245 R | 53.9% | 42.4% | 56.0% | 44.0% |
| 60,765 | RENO | 26,512 | 11,212 | 14,620 | 680 | 3,408 D | 42.3% | 55.1% | 43.4% | 56.6% |
| 8,498 | REPUBLIC | 3,994 | 2,294 | 1,617 | 83 | 677 R | 57.4% | 40.5% | 58.7% | 41.3% |
| 12,320 | RICE | 5,765 | 2,584 | 3,056 | 125 | 472 D | 44.8% | 53.0% | 45.8% | 54.2% |
| 56,788 | RILEY | 16,568 | 9,518 | 6,540 | 510 | 2,978 R | 57.4% | 39.5% | 59.3% | 40.7% |
| 7,628 | ROOKS | 3,137 | 1,664 | 1,412 | 61 | 252 R | 53.0% | 45.0% | 54.1% | 45.9% |
| 5,117 | RUSH | 2,581 | 1,170 | 1,359 | 52 | 189 D | 45.3% | 52.7% | 46.3% | 53.7% |
| 9,428 | RUSSELL | 4,669 | 3,165 | 1,453 | 51 | 1,712 R | 67.8% | 31.1% | 68.5% | 31.5% |
| 46,592 | SALINE | 20,107 | 11,218 | 8,476 | 413 | 2,742 R | 55.8% | 42.2% | 57.0% | 43.0% |
| 5,606 | SCOTT | 2,183 | 1,195 | 919 | 69 | 276 R | 54.7% | 42.1% | 56.5% | 43.5% |
| 350,694 | SEDGWICK | 137,629 | 69,828 | 63,989 | 3,812 | 5,839 R | 50.7% | 46.5% | 52.2% | 47.8% |
| 15,744 | SEWARD | 5,615 | 3,604 | 1,907 | 104 | 1,697 R | 64.2% | 34.0% | 65.4% | 34.6% |
| 155,322 | SHAWNEE | 67,370 | 37,101 | 28,578 | 1,691 | 8,523 R | 55.1% | 42.4% | 56.5% | 43.5% |
| 3,859 | SHERIDAN | 1,705 | 838 | 793 | 74 | 45 R | 49.1% | 46.5% | 51.4% | 48.6% |
| 7,792 | SHERMAN | 3,332 | 1,671 | 1,573 | 88 | 98 R | 50.2% | 47.2% | 51.5% | 48.5% |
| 6,757 | SMITH | 3,436 | 2,009 | 1,333 | 94 | 676 R | 58.5% | 38.8% | 60.1% | 39.9% |
| 5,943 | STAFFORD | 3,162 | 1,430 | 1,659 | 73 | 229 D | 45.2% | 52.5% | 46.3% | 53.7% |
| 2,287 | STANTON | 1,040 | 510 | 489 | 41 | 21 R | 49.0% | 47.0% | 51.1% | 48.9% |
| 4,198 | STEVENS | 2,205 | 1,262 | 901 | 42 | 361 R | 57.2% | 40.9% | 58.3% | 41.7% |
| 23,553 | SUMNER | 10,340 | 4,645 | 5,385 | 310 | 740 D | 44.9% | 52.1% | 46.3% | 53.7% |
| 7,501 | THOMAS | 4,164 | 2,246 | 1,802 | 116 | 444 R | 53.9% | 43.3% | 55.5% | 44.5% |
| 4,436 | TREGO | 2,068 | 1,025 | 1,003 | 40 | 22 R | 49.6% | 48.5% | 50.5% | 49.5% |
| 6,397 | WABAUNSEE | 3,336 | 1,921 | 1,354 | 61 | 567 R | 57.6% | 40.6% | 58.7% | 41.3% |
| 2,215 | WALLACE | 1,137 | 600 | 486 | 51 | 114 R | 52.8% | 42.7% | 55.2% | 44.8% |
| 9,249 | WASHINGTON | 4,213 | 2,543 | 1,564 | 106 | 979 R | 60.4% | 37.1% | 61.9% | 38.1% |
| 3,274 | WICHITA | 1,238 | 593 | 614 | 31 | 21 D | 47.9% | 49.6% | 49.1% | 50.9% |
| 11,317 | WILSON | 4,818 | 2,682 | 2,047 | 89 | 635 R | 55.7% | 42.5% | 56.7% | 43.3% |
| 4,789 | WOODSON | 2,041 | 1,104 | 904 | 33 | 200 R | 54.1% | 44.3% | 55.0% | 45.0% |
| 186,845 | WYANDOTTE | 62,555 | 23,141 | 37,478 | 1,936 | 14,337 D | 37.0% | 59.9% | 38.2% | 61.8% |
| 2,249,071 | TOTAL | 957,845 | 502,752 | 430,421 | 24,672 | 72,331 R | 52.5% | 44.9% | 53.9% | 46.1% |

# KANSAS

## PRESIDENT 1972

| 1970 Census Population | County | Total Vote | Republican | Democratic | Other | Rep.-Dem. Plurality | Percentage | | | |
|---|---|---|---|---|---|---|---|---|---|---|
| | | | | | | | Total Vote | | Major Vote | |
| | | | | | | | Rep. | Dem. | Rep. | Dem. |
| 15,043 | ALLEN | 5,669 | 3,938 | 1,610 | 121 | 2,328 R | 69.5% | 28.4% | 71.0% | 29.0% |
| 8,501 | ANDERSON | 3,836 | 2,718 | 1,035 | 83 | 1,683 R | 70.9% | 27.0% | 72.4% | 27.6% |
| 19,165 | ATCHISON | 8,066 | 5,471 | 2,404 | 191 | 3,067 R | 67.8% | 29.8% | 69.5% | 30.5% |
| 7,016 | BARBER | 3,108 | 2,308 | 727 | 73 | 1,581 R | 74.3% | 23.4% | 76.0% | 24.0% |
| 30,663 | BARTON | 12,312 | 8,479 | 3,481 | 352 | 4,998 R | 68.9% | 28.3% | 70.9% | 29.1% |
| 15,215 | BOURBON | 6,814 | 4,776 | 1,912 | 126 | 2,864 R | 70.1% | 28.1% | 71.4% | 28.6% |
| 11,685 | BROWN | 5,466 | 4,314 | 1,038 | 114 | 3,276 R | 78.9% | 19.0% | 80.6% | 19.4% |
| 38,658 | BUTLER | 16,389 | 11,045 | 4,669 | 675 | 6,376 R | 67.4% | 28.5% | 70.3% | 29.7% |
| 3,408 | CHASE | 1,557 | 1,184 | 315 | 58 | 869 R | 76.0% | 20.2% | 79.0% | 21.0% |
| 4,642 | CHAUTAUQUA | 1,982 | 1,546 | 378 | 58 | 1,168 R | 78.0% | 19.1% | 80.4% | 19.6% |
| 21,549 | CHEROKEE | 8,980 | 6,019 | 2,806 | 155 | 3,213 R | 67.0% | 31.2% | 68.2% | 31.8% |
| 4,256 | CHEYENNE | 1,907 | 1,440 | 399 | 68 | 1,041 R | 75.5% | 20.9% | 78.3% | 21.7% |
| 2,896 | CLARK | 1,502 | 1,142 | 311 | 49 | 831 R | 76.0% | 20.7% | 78.6% | 21.4% |
| 9,890 | CLAY | 4,542 | 3,562 | 887 | 93 | 2,675 R | 78.4% | 19.5% | 80.1% | 19.9% |
| 13,466 | CLOUD | 5,773 | 3,832 | 1,806 | 135 | 2,026 R | 66.4% | 31.3% | 68.0% | 32.0% |
| 7,397 | COFFEY | 3,523 | 2,667 | 782 | 74 | 1,885 R | 75.7% | 22.2% | 77.3% | 22.7% |
| 2,702 | COMANCHE | 1,363 | 1,052 | 281 | 30 | 771 R | 77.2% | 20.6% | 78.9% | 21.1% |
| 35,012 | COWLEY | 14,653 | 10,332 | 3,592 | 729 | 6,740 R | 70.5% | 24.5% | 74.2% | 25.8% |
| 37,850 | CRAWFORD | 16,637 | 9,652 | 6,683 | 302 | 2,969 R | 58.0% | 40.2% | 59.1% | 40.9% |
| 4,988 | DECATUR | 2,431 | 1,707 | 616 | 108 | 1,091 R | 70.2% | 25.3% | 73.5% | 26.5% |
| 19,993 | DICKINSON | 8,647 | 6,515 | 1,957 | 175 | 4,558 R | 75.3% | 22.6% | 76.9% | 23.1% |
| 9,107 | DONIPHAN | 3,643 | 2,856 | 690 | 97 | 2,166 R | 78.4% | 18.9% | 80.5% | 19.5% |
| 57,932 | DOUGLAS | 27,527 | 15,316 | 11,646 | 565 | 3,670 R | 55.6% | 42.3% | 56.8% | 43.2% |
| 4,581 | EDWARDS | 2,377 | 1,534 | .757 | 86 | 777 R | 64.5% | 31.8% | 67.0% | 33.0% |
| 3,858 | ELK | 2,002 | 1,522 | 428 | 52 | 1,094 R | 76.0% | 21.4% | 78.1% | 21.9% |
| 24,730 | ELLIS | 9,813 | 5,463 | 4,113 | 237 | 1,350 R | 55.7% | 41.9% | 57.0% | 43.0% |
| 6,146 | ELLSWORTH | 3,201 | 2,087 | 1,028 | 86 | 1,059 R | 65.2% | 32.1% | 67.0% | 33.0% |
| 19,029 | FINNEY | 6,602 | 4,335 | 2,062 | 205 | 2,273 R | 65.7% | 31.2% | 67.8% | 32.2% |
| 22,587 | FORD | 9,285 | 6,232 | 2,804 | 249 | 3,428 R | 67.1% | 30.2% | 69.0% | 31.0% |
| 20,007 | FRANKLIN | 8,267 | 6,011 | 2,056 | 200 | 3,955 R | 72.7% | 24.9% | 74.5% | 25.5% |
| 28,111 | GEARY | 6,140 | 4,299 | 1,708 | 133 | 2,591 R | 70.0% | 27.8% | 71.6% | 28.4% |
| 3,940 | GOVE | 1,755 | 1,226 | 466 | 63 | 760 R | 69.9% | 26.6% | 72.5% | 27.5% |
| 4,751 | GRAHAM | 1,964 | 1,440 | 488 | 36 | 952 R | 73.3% | 24.8% | 74.7% | 25.3% |
| 5,961 | GRANT | 2,007 | 1,469 | 476 | 62 | 993 R | 73.2% | 23.7% | 75.5% | 24.5% |
| 4,516 | GRAY | 1,786 | 1,235 | 511 | 40 | 724 R | 69.1% | 28.6% | 70.7% | 29.3% |
| 1,819 | GREELEY | 933 | 639 | 212 | 82 | 427 R | 68.5% | 22.7% | 75.1% | 24.9% |
| 9,141 | GREENWOOD | 4,238 | 3,157 | 951 | 130 | 2,206 R | 74.5% | 22.4% | 76.9% | 23.1% |
| 2,747 | HAMILTON | 1,399 | 941 | 394 | 64 | 547 R | 67.3% | 28.2% | 70.5% | 29.5% |
| 7,871 | HARPER | 3,471 | 2,628 | 729 | 114 | 1,899 R | 75.7% | 21.0% | 78.3% | 21.7% |
| 27,236 | HARVEY | 12,327 | 8,287 | 3,555 | 485 | 4,732 R | 67.2% | 28.8% | 70.0% | 30.0% |
| 3,672 | HASKELL | 1,448 | 1,036 | 383 | 29 | 653 R | 71.5% | 26.5% | 73.0% | 27.0% |
| 2,662 | HODGEMAN | 1,247 | 853 | 331 | 63 | 522 R | 68.4% | 26.5% | 72.0% | 28.0% |
| 10,342 | JACKSON | 4,672 | 3,363 | 1,191 | 118 | 2,172 R | 72.0% | 25.5% | 73.8% | 26.2% |
| 11,945 | JEFFERSON | 5,061 | 3,679 | 1,237 | 145 | 2,442 R | 72.7% | 24.4% | 74.8% | 25.2% |
| 6,099 | JEWELL | 3,028 | 2,242 | 716 | 70 | 1,526 R | 74.0% | 23.6% | 75.8% | 24.2% |
| 220,073 | JOHNSON | 102,727 | 76,161 | 24,324 | 2,242 | 51,837 R | 74.1% | 23.7% | 75.8% | 24.2% |
| 3,047 | KEARNY | 1,236 | 876 | 325 | 35 | 551 R | 70.9% | 26.3% | 72.9% | 27.1% |
| 8,886 | KINGMAN | 4,000 | 2,756 | 1,107 | 137 | 1,649 R | 68.9% | 27.7% | 71.3% | 28.7% |
| 4,088 | KIOWA | 2,042 | 1,559 | 406 | 77 | 1,153 R | 76.3% | 19.9% | 79.3% | 20.7% |
| 25,775 | LABETTE | 9,881 | 6,399 | 3,210 | 272 | 3,189 R | 64.8% | 32.5% | 66.6% | 33.4% |
| 2,707 | LANE | 1,288 | 943 | 294 | 51 | 649 R | 73.2% | 22.8% | 76.2% | 23.8% |
| 53,340 | LEAVENWORTH | 15,897 | 10,762 | 4,727 | 408 | 6,035 R | 67.7% | 29.7% | 69.5% | 30.5% |
| 4,582 | LINCOLN | 2,182 | 1,649 | 476 | 57 | 1,173 R | 75.6% | 21.8% | 77.6% | 22.4% |
| 7,770 | LINN | 3,532 | 2,593 | 876 | 63 | 1,717 R | 73.4% | 24.8% | 74.7% | 25.3% |
| 3,814 | LOGAN | 1,663 | 1,164 | 428 | 71 | 736 R | 70.0% | 25.7% | 73.1% | 26.9% |
| 32,071 | LYON | 13,143 | 9,157 | 3,720 | 266 | 5,437 R | 69.7% | 28.3% | 71.1% | 28.9% |
| 24,778 | MCPHERSON | 10,569 | 7,457 | 2,858 | 254 | 4,599 R | 70.6% | 27.0% | 72.3% | 27.7% |
| 13,935 | MARION | 6,059 | 4,373 | 1,478 | 208 | 2,895 R | 72.2% | 24.4% | 74.7% | 25.3% |
| 13,139 | MARSHALL | 6,098 | 4,127 | 1,823 | 148 | 2,304 R | 67.7% | 29.9% | 69.4% | 30.6% |
| 4,912 | MEADE | 2,296 | 1,712 | 526 | 58 | 1,186 R | 74.6% | 22.9% | 76.5% | 23.5% |

# KANSAS

## PRESIDENT 1972

| 1970 Census Population | County | Total Vote | Republican | Democratic | Other | Rep.-Dem. Plurality | Percentage Total Vote Rep. | Dem. | Major Vote Rep. | Dem. |
|---|---|---|---|---|---|---|---|---|---|---|
| 19,254 | MIAMI | 7,581 | 5,234 | 2,140 | 207 | 3,094 R | 69.0% | 28.2% | 71.0% | 29.0% |
| 8,010 | MITCHELL | 3,953 | 2,830 | 1,030 | 93 | 1,800 R | 71.6% | 26.1% | 73.3% | 26.7% |
| 39,949 | MONTGOMERY | 15,907 | 11,717 | 3,685 | 505 | 8,032 R | 73.7% | 23.2% | 76.1% | 23.9% |
| 6,432 | MORRIS | 3,246 | 2,471 | 704 | 71 | 1,767 R | 76.1% | 21.7% | 77.8% | 22.2% |
| 3,576 | MORTON | 1,603 | 1,165 | 363 | 75 | 802 R | 72.7% | 22.6% | 76.2% | 23.8% |
| 11,825 | NEMAHA | 5,342 | 3,422 | 1,777 | 143 | 1,645 R | 64.1% | 33.3% | 65.8% | 34.2% |
| 18,812 | NEOSHO | 7,738 | 5,034 | 2,559 | 145 | 2,475 R | 65.1% | 33.1% | 66.3% | 33.7% |
| 4,791 | NESS | 2,251 | 1,539 | 652 | 60 | 887 R | 68.4% | 29.0% | 70.2% | 29.8% |
| 7,279 | NORTON | 3,546 | 2,688 | 776 | 82 | 1,912 R | 75.8% | 21.9% | 77.6% | 22.4% |
| 13,352 | OSAGE | 5,728 | 4,073 | 1,522 | 133 | 2,551 R | 71.1% | 26.6% | 72.8% | 27.2% |
| 6,416 | OSBORNE | 2,972 | 2,182 | 724 | 66 | 1,458 R | 73.4% | 24.4% | 75.1% | 24.9% |
| 6,183 | OTTAWA | 2,831 | 2,065 | 705 | 61 | 1,360 R | 72.9% | 24.9% | 74.5% | 25.5% |
| 8,484 | PAWNEE | 3,600 | 2,370 | 1,110 | 120 | 1,260 R | 65.8% | 30.8% | 68.1% | 31.9% |
| 7,888 | PHILLIPS | 3,833 | 2,919 | 827 | 87 | 2,092 R | 76.2% | 21.6% | 77.9% | 22.1% |
| 11,755 | POTTAWATOMIE | 5,369 | 3,947 | 1,298 | 124 | 2,649 R | 73.5% | 24.2% | 75.3% | 24.7% |
| 10,056 | PRATT | 4,569 | 3,253 | 1,214 | 102 | 2,039 R | 71.2% | 26.6% | 72.8% | 27.2% |
| 4,393 | RAWLINS | 2,204 | 1,553 | 560 | 91 | 993 R | 70.5% | 25.4% | 73.5% | 26.5% |
| 60,765 | RENO | 24,628 | 15,714 | 8,183 | 731 | 7,531 R | 63.8% | 33.2% | 65.8% | 34.2% |
| 8,498 | REPUBLIC | 4,068 | 2,921 | 1,059 | 88 | 1,862 R | 71.8% | 26.0% | 73.4% | 26.6% |
| 12,320 | RICE | 5,803 | 3,843 | 1,825 | 135 | 2,018 R | 66.2% | 31.4% | 67.8% | 32.2% |
| 56,788 | RILEY | 16,809 | 11,120 | 5,333 | 356 | 5,787 R | 66.2% | 31.7% | 67.6% | 32.4% |
| 7,628 | ROOKS | 3,425 | 2,457 | 904 | 64 | 1,553 R | 71.7% | 26.4% | 73.1% | 26.9% |
| 5,117 | RUSH | 2,512 | 1,639 | 806 | 67 | 833 R | 65.2% | 32.1% | 67.0% | 33.0% |
| 9,428 | RUSSELL | 4,292 | 3,168 | 1,011 | 113 | 2,157 R | 73.8% | 23.6% | 75.8% | 24.2% |
| 46,592 | SALINE | 18,319 | 12,592 | 5,406 | 321 | 7,186 R | 68.7% | 29.5% | 70.0% | 30.0% |
| 5,606 | SCOTT | 2,082 | 1,547 | 449 | 86 | 1,098 R | 74.3% | 21.6% | 77.5% | 22.5% |
| 350,694 | SEDGWICK | 127,701 | 83,949 | 39,220 | 4,532 | 44,729 R | 65.7% | 30.7% | 68.2% | 31.8% |
| 15,744 | SEWARD | 5,003 | 3,866 | 989 | 148 | 2,877 R | 77.3% | 19.8% | 79.6% | 20.4% |
| 155,322 | SHAWNEE | 65,506 | 43,727 | 20,383 | 1,396 | 23,344 R | 66.8% | 31.1% | 68.2% | 31.8% |
| 3,859 | SHERIDAN | 1,761 | 1,134 | 552 | 75 | 582 R | 64.4% | 31.3% | 67.3% | 32.7% |
| 7,792 | SHERMAN | 3,182 | 2,225 | 785 | 172 | 1,440 R | 69.9% | 24.7% | 73.9% | 26.1% |
| 6,757 | SMITH | 3,501 | 2,600 | 818 | 83 | 1,782 R | 74.3% | 23.4% | 76.1% | 23.9% |
| 5,943 | STAFFORD | 3,127 | 2,200 | 844 | 83 | 1,356 R | 70.4% | 27.0% | 72.3% | 27.7% |
| 2,287 | STANTON | 1,054 | 754 | 259 | 41 | 495 R | 71.5% | 24.6% | 74.4% | 25.6% |
| 4,198 | STEVENS | 1,869 | 1,392 | 408 | 69 | 984 R | 74.5% | 21.8% | 77.3% | 22.7% |
| 23,553 | SUMNER | 10,195 | 6,941 | 2,685 | 569 | 4,256 R | 68.1% | 26.3% | 72.1% | 27.9% |
| 7,501 | THOMAS | 3,396 | 2,300 | 943 | 153 | 1,357 R | 67.7% | 27.8% | 70.9% | 29.1% |
| 4,436 | TREGO | 2,046 | 1,369 | 621 | 56 | 748 R | 66.9% | 30.4% | 68.8% | 31.2% |
| 6,397 | WABAUNSEE | 3,203 | 2,461 | 662 | 80 | 1,799 R | 76.8% | 20.7% | 78.8% | 21.2% |
| 2,215 | WALLACE | 1,068 | 782 | 214 | 72 | 568 R | 73.2% | 20.0% | 78.5% | 21.5% |
| 9,249 | WASHINGTON | 4,394 | 3,301 | 996 | 97 | 2,305 R | 75.1% | 22.7% | 76.8% | 23.2% |
| 3,274 | WICHITA | 1,136 | 794 | 288 | 54 | 506 R | 69.9% | 25.4% | 73.4% | 26.6% |
| 11,317 | WILSON | 4,770 | 3,568 | 1,043 | 159 | 2,525 R | 74.8% | 21.9% | 77.4% | 22.6% |
| 4,789 | WOODSON | 2,193 | 1,592 | 550 | 51 | 1,042 R | 72.6% | 25.1% | 74.3% | 25.7% |
| 186,845 | WYANDOTTE | 64,816 | 34,157 | 28,206 | 2,453 | 5,951 R | 52.7% | 43.5% | 54.8% | 45.2% |
| 2,249,071 | TOTAL | 916,095 | 619,812 | 270,287 | 25,996 | 349,525 R | 67.7% | 29.5% | 69.6% | 30.4% |

# KANSAS

## PRESIDENT 1968

| 1960 Census Population | County | Total Vote | Republican | Democratic | AIP | Other | Plurality | Percentage Total Vote Rep. | Dem. | AIP |
|---|---|---|---|---|---|---|---|---|---|---|
| 16,369 | ALLEN | 5,900 | 3,520 | 1,875 | 492 | 13 | 1,645 R | 59.7% | 31.8% | 8.3% |
| 9,035 | ANDERSON | 3,814 | 2,168 | 1,242 | 397 | 7 | 926 R | 56.8% | 32.6% | 10.4% |
| 20,898 | ATCHISON | 7,922 | 3,644 | 3,379 | 888 | 11 | 265 R | 46.0% | 42.7% | 11.2% |
| 8,713 | BARBER | 3,341 | 2,023 | 1,027 | 283 | 8 | 996 R | 60.6% | 30.7% | 8.5% |
| 32,368 | BARTON | 12,208 | 6,700 | 4,464 | 1,017 | 27 | 2,236 R | 54.9% | 36.6% | 8.3% |
| 16,090 | BOURBON | 7,004 | 3,983 | 2,241 | 769 | 11 | 1,742 R | 56.9% | 32.0% | 11.0% |
| 13,229 | BROWN | 5,420 | 3,748 | 1,199 | 463 | 10 | 2,549 R | 69.2% | 22.1% | 8.5% |
| 38,395 | BUTLER | 15,541 | 7,893 | 5,952 | 1,671 | 25 | 1,941 R | 50.8% | 38.3% | 10.8% |
| 3,921 | CHASE | 1,658 | 1,038 | 462 | 154 | 4 | 576 R | 62.6% | 27.9% | 9.3% |
| 5,956 | CHAUTAUQUA | 2,346 | 1,537 | 478 | 329 | 2 | 1,059 R | 65.5% | 20.4% | 14.0% |
| 22,279 | CHEROKEE | 8,872 | 4,211 | 3,597 | 1,054 | 10 | 614 R | 47.5% | 40.5% | 11.9% |
| 4,708 | CHEYENNE | 2,014 | 1,423 | 412 | 174 | 5 | 1,011 R | 70.7% | 20.5% | 8.6% |
| 3,396 | CLARK | 1,579 | 920 | 446 | 210 | 3 | 474 R | 58.3% | 28.2% | 13.3% |
| 10,675 | CLAY | 4,635 | 3,335 | 926 | 357 | 17 | 2,409 R | 72.0% | 20.0% | 7.7% |
| 14,407 | CLOUD | 5,843 | 3,282 | 2,132 | 412 | 17 | 1,150 R | 56.2% | 36.5% | 7.1% |
| 8,403 | COFFEY | 3,525 | 2,223 | 933 | 367 | 2 | 1,290 R | 63.1% | 26.5% | 10.4% |
| 3,271 | COMANCHE | 1,446 | 906 | 451 | 85 | 4 | 455 R | 62.7% | 31.2% | 5.9% |
| 37,861 | COWLEY | 14,861 | 8,070 | 5,014 | 1,751 | 26 | 3,056 R | 54.3% | 33.7% | 11.8% |
| 37,032 | CRAWFORD | 16,213 | 7,344 | 7,191 | 1,653 | 25 | 153 R | 45.3% | 44.4% | 10.2% |
| 5,778 | DECATUR | 2,516 | 1,654 | 652 | 206 | 4 | 1,002 R | 65.7% | 25.9% | 8.2% |
| 21,572 | DICKINSON | 8,666 | 5,574 | 2,399 | 675 | 18 | 3,175 R | 64.3% | 27.7% | 7.8% |
| 9,574 | DONIPHAN | 3,794 | 2,402 | 958 | 425 | 9 | 1,444 R | 63.3% | 25.3% | 11.2% |
| 43,720 | DOUGLAS | 19,583 | 10,533 | 6,936 | 2,080 | 34 | 3,597 R | 53.8% | 35.4% | 10.6% |
| 5,118 | EDWARDS | 2,264 | 1,243 | 832 | 182 | 7 | 411 R | 54.9% | 36.7% | 8.0% |
| 5,048 | ELK | 2,053 | 1,327 | 503 | 216 | 7 | 824 R | 64.6% | 24.5% | 10.5% |
| 21,270 | ELLIS | 8,441 | 3,944 | 3,809 | 671 | 17 | 135 R | 46.7% | 45.1% | 7.9% |
| 7,677 | ELLSWORTH | 3,087 | 1,776 | 1,060 | 246 | 5 | 716 R | 57.5% | 34.3% | 8.0% |
| 16,093 | FINNEY | 6,323 | 3,295 | 2,521 | 496 | 11 | 774 R | 52.1% | 39.9% | 7.8% |
| 20,938 | FORD | 8,797 | 4,645 | 3,191 | 935 | 26 | 1,454 R | 52.8% | 36.3% | 10.6% |
| 19,548 | FRANKLIN | 8,239 | 4,875 | 2,524 | 825 | 15 | 2,351 R | 59.2% | 30.6% | 10.0% |
| 28,779 | GEARY | 5,827 | 2,954 | 2,228 | 625 | 20 | 726 R | 50.7% | 38.2% | 10.7% |
| 4,107 | GOVE | 1,724 | 1,018 | 538 | 164 | 4 | 480 R | 59.0% | 31.2% | 9.5% |
| 5,586 | GRAHAM | 2,154 | 1,308 | 597 | 243 | 6 | 711 R | 60.7% | 27.7% | 11.3% |
| 5,269 | GRANT | 1,961 | 1,121 | 618 | 217 | 5 | 503 R | 57.2% | 31.5% | 11.1% |
| 4,380 | GRAY | 1,723 | 952 | 612 | 151 | 8 | 340 R | 55.3% | 35.5% | 8.8% |
| 2,087 | GREELEY | 777 | 465 | 227 | 82 | 3 | 238 R | 59.8% | 29.2% | 10.6% |
| 11,253 | GREENWOOD | 4,451 | 2,937 | 1,122 | 381 | 11 | 1,815 R | 66.0% | 25.2% | 8.6% |
| 3,144 | HAMILTON | 1,335 | 751 | 410 | 170 | 4 | 341 R | 56.3% | 30.7% | 12.7% |
| 9,541 | HARPER | 3,674 | 2,351 | 1,015 | 297 | 11 | 1,336 R | 64.0% | 27.6% | 8.1% |
| 25,865 | HARVEY | 10,841 | 6,682 | 3,351 | 780 | 28 | 3,331 R | 61.6% | 30.9% | 7.2% |
| 2,990 | HASKELL | 1,407 | 762 | 476 | 167 | 2 | 286 R | 54.2% | 33.8% | 11.9% |
| 3,115 | HODGEMAN | 1,277 | 756 | 387 | 130 | 4 | 369 R | 59.2% | 30.3% | 10.2% |
| 10,309 | JACKSON | 4,411 | 2,678 | 1,225 | 501 | 7 | 1,453 R | 60.7% | 27.8% | 11.4% |
| 11,252 | JEFFERSON | 4,915 | 2,781 | 1,355 | 774 | 5 | 1,426 R | 56.6% | 27.6% | 15.7% |
| 7,217 | JEWELL | 3,282 | 2,172 | 842 | 252 | 16 | 1,330 R | 66.2% | 25.7% | 7.7% |
| 143,792 | JOHNSON | 87,912 | 55,060 | 26,034 | 6,635 | 183 | 29,026 R | 62.6% | 29.6% | 7.5% |
| 3,108 | KEARNY | 1,243 | 721 | 423 | 95 | 4 | 298 R | 58.0% | 34.0% | 7.6% |
| 9,958 | KINGMAN | 3,845 | 2,318 | 1,201 | 319 | 7 | 1,117 R | 60.3% | 31.2% | 8.3% |
| 4,626 | KIOWA | 2,094 | 1,484 | 481 | 123 | 6 | 1,003 R | 70.9% | 23.0% | 5.9% |
| 26,805 | LABETTE | 10,750 | 5,503 | 3,974 | 1,251 | 22 | 1,529 R | 51.2% | 37.0% | 11.6% |
| 3,060 | LANE | 1,288 | 781 | 385 | 118 | 4 | 396 R | 60.6% | 29.9% | 9.2% |
| 48,524 | LEAVENWORTH | 14,645 | 7,081 | 5,546 | 2,000 | 18 | 1,535 R | 48.4% | 37.9% | 13.7% |
| 5,556 | LINCOLN | 2,525 | 1,721 | 583 | 217 | 4 | 1,138 R | 68.2% | 23.1% | 8.6% |
| 8,274 | LINN | 3,565 | 2,250 | 893 | 419 | 3 | 1,357 R | 63.1% | 25.0% | 11.8% |
| 4,036 | LOGAN | 1,756 | 1,120 | 411 | 221 | 4 | 709 R | 63.8% | 23.4% | 12.6% |
| 26,928 | LYON | 11,446 | 6,558 | 4,020 | 847 | 21 | 2,538 R | 57.3% | 35.1% | 7.4% |
| 24,285 | MCPHERSON | 9,880 | 6,420 | 2,893 | 543 | 24 | 3,527 R | 65.0% | 29.3% | 5.5% |
| 15,143 | MARION | 6,092 | 4,287 | 1,494 | 304 | 7 | 2,793 R | 70.4% | 24.5% | 5.0% |
| 15,598 | MARSHALL | 6,517 | 3,835 | 1,949 | 731 | 2 | 1,886 R | 58.8% | 29.9% | 11.2% |
| 5,505 | MEADE | 2,281 | 1,511 | 572 | 196 | 2 | 939 R | 66.2% | 25.1% | 8.6% |

# KANSAS

## PRESIDENT 1968

| 1960 Census Population | County | Total Vote | Republican | Democratic | AIP | Other | Plurality | Percentage Total Vote Rep. | Dem. | AIP |
|---|---|---|---|---|---|---|---|---|---|---|
| 19,884 | MIAMI | 7,386 | 3,614 | 2,739 | 1,023 | 10 | 875 R | 48.9% | 37.1% | 13.9% |
| 8,866 | MITCHELL | 3,861 | 2,428 | 1,144 | 283 | 6 | 1,284 R | 62.9% | 29.6% | 7.3% |
| 45,007 | MONTGOMERY | 17,386 | 9,697 | 5,210 | 2,456 | 23 | 4,487 R | 55.8% | 30.0% | 14.1% |
| 7,392 | MORRIS | 3,230 | 1,938 | 976 | 313 | 3 | 962 R | 60.0% | 30.2% | 9.7% |
| 3,354 | MORTON | 1,509 | 770 | 475 | 262 | 2 | 295 R | 51.0% | 31.5% | 17.4% |
| 12,897 | NEMAHA | 5,560 | 3,003 | 1,925 | 628 | 4 | 1,078 R | 54.0% | 34.6% | 11.3% |
| 19,455 | NEOSHO | 7,464 | 3,950 | 2,725 | 784 | 5 | 1,225 R | 52.9% | 36.5% | 10.5% |
| 5,470 | NESS | 2,322 | 1,352 | 767 | 192 | 11 | 585 R | 58.2% | 33.0% | 8.3% |
| 8,035 | NORTON | 3,586 | 2,543 | 841 | 193 | 9 | 1,702 R | 70.9% | 23.5% | 5.4% |
| 12,886 | OSAGE | 5,622 | 3,157 | 1,664 | 792 | 9 | 1,493 R | 56.2% | 29.6% | 14.1% |
| 7,506 | OSBORNE | 3,170 | 2,073 | 793 | 301 | 3 | 1,280 R | 65.4% | 25.0% | 9.5% |
| 6,779 | OTTAWA | 2,777 | 1,740 | 777 | 253 | 7 | 963 R | 62.7% | 28.0% | 9.1% |
| 10,254 | PAWNEE | 3,759 | 2,037 | 1,416 | 300 | 6 | 621 R | 54.2% | 37.7% | 8.0% |
| 8,709 | PHILLIPS | 3,759 | 2,567 | 844 | 340 | 8 | 1,723 R | 68.3% | 22.5% | 9.0% |
| 11,957 | POTTAWATOMIE | 5,130 | 3,267 | 1,368 | 490 | 5 | 1,899 R | 63.7% | 26.7% | 9.6% |
| 12,122 | PRATT | 4,611 | 2,670 | 1,490 | 435 | 16 | 1,180 R | 57.9% | 32.3% | 9.4% |
| 5,279 | RAWLINS | 2,182 | 1,438 | 553 | 153 | 38 | 885 R | 65.9% | 25.3% | 7.0% |
| 59,055 | RENO | 23,474 | 11,804 | 9,872 | 1,710 | 88 | 1,932 R | 50.3% | 42.1% | 7.3% |
| 9,768 | REPUBLIC | 4,288 | 2,841 | 1,187 | 240 | 20 | 1,654 R | 66.3% | 27.7% | 5.6% |
| 13,909 | RICE | 5,586 | 3,141 | 2,049 | 386 | 10 | 1,092 R | 56.2% | 36.7% | 6.9% |
| 41,914 | RILEY | 13,345 | 8,296 | 4,258 | 772 | 19 | 4,038 R | 62.2% | 31.9% | 5.8% |
| 9,734 | ROOKS | 3,574 | 2,252 | 1,012 | 307 | 3 | 1,240 R | 63.0% | 28.3% | 8.6% |
| 6,160 | RUSH | 2,560 | 1,471 | 864 | 217 | 8 | 607 R | 57.5% | 33.8% | 8.5% |
| 11,348 | RUSSELL | 4,739 | 3,177 | 1,261 | 290 | 11 | 1,916 R | 67.0% | 26.6% | 6.1% |
| 54,715 | SALINE | 16,822 | 9,324 | 6,286 | 1,169 | 43 | 3,038 R | 55.4% | 37.4% | 6.9% |
| 5,228 | SCOTT | 2,074 | 1,374 | 500 | 193 | 7 | 874 R | 66.2% | 24.1% | 9.3% |
| 343,231 | SEDGWICK | 117,469 | 60,853 | 44,041 | 12,255 | 320 | 16,812 R | 51.8% | 37.5% | 10.4% |
| 15,930 | SEWARD | 4,918 | 3,065 | 1,291 | 550 | 12 | 1,774 R | 62.3% | 26.3% | 11.2% |
| 141,286 | SHAWNEE | 59,850 | 31,140 | 21,735 | 6,817 | 158 | 9,405 R | 52.0% | 36.3% | 11.4% |
| 4,267 | SHERIDAN | 1,717 | 1,002 | 563 | 144 | 8 | 439 R | 58.4% | 32.8% | 8.4% |
| 6,682 | SHERMAN | 3,134 | 1,803 | 954 | 368 | 9 | 849 R | 57.5% | 30.4% | 11.7% |
| 7,776 | SMITH | 3,790 | 2,558 | 939 | 279 | 14 | 1,619 R | 67.5% | 24.8% | 7.4% |
| 7,451 | STAFFORD | 3,320 | 1,851 | 1,205 | 253 | 11 | 646 R | 55.8% | 36.3% | 7.6% |
| 2,108 | STANTON | 909 | 541 | 288 | 78 | 2 | 253 R | 59.5% | 31.7% | 8.6% |
| 4,400 | STEVENS | 1,982 | 1,157 | 528 | 296 | 1 | 629 R | 58.4% | 26.6% | 14.9% |
| 25,316 | SUMNER | 10,320 | 5,622 | 3,562 | 1,116 | 20 | 2,060 R | 54.5% | 34.5% | 10.8% |
| 7,358 | THOMAS | 3,295 | 1,971 | 1,074 | 241 | 9 | 897 R | 59.8% | 32.6% | 7.3% |
| 5,473 | TREGO | 2,064 | 1,211 | 623 | 226 | 4 | 588 R | 58.7% | 30.2% | 10.9% |
| 6,648 | WABAUNSEE | 3,084 | 1,979 | 695 | 402 | 8 | 1,284 R | 64.2% | 22.5% | 13.0% |
| 2,069 | WALLACE | 988 | 608 | 235 | 144 | 1 | 373 R | 61.5% | 23.8% | 14.6% |
| 10,739 | WASHINGTON | 4,652 | 3,177 | 1,131 | 332 | 12 | 2,046 R | 68.3% | 24.3% | 7.1% |
| 2,765 | WICHITA | 1,254 | 757 | 364 | 130 | 3 | 393 R | 60.4% | 29.0% | 10.4% |
| 13,077 | WILSON | 5,272 | 3,340 | 1,276 | 640 | 16 | 2,064 R | 63.4% | 24.2% | 12.1% |
| 5,423 | WOODSON | 2,315 | 1,450 | 639 | 222 | 4 | 811 R | 62.6% | 27.6% | 9.6% |
| 185,495 | WYANDOTTE | 69,171 | 23,091 | 34,189 | 11,510 | 381 | 11,098 D | 33.4% | 49.4% | 16.6% |
| 2,178,611 | TOTAL | 872,783 | 478,674 | 302,996 | 88,921 | 2,192 | 175,678 R | 54.8% | 34.7% | 10.2% |

# KANSAS

## PRESIDENT 1964

| 1960 Census Population | County | Total Vote | Republican | Democratic | Other | Rep.-Dem. Plurality | Percentage Total Vote Rep. | Dem. | Major Vote Rep. | Dem. |
|---|---|---|---|---|---|---|---|---|---|---|
| 16,369 | ALLEN | 6,252 | 2,841 | 3,369 | 42 | 528 D | 45.4% | 53.9% | 45.7% | 54.3% |
| 9,035 | ANDERSON | 3,780 | 1,692 | 2,058 | 30 | 366 D | 44.8% | 54.4% | 45.1% | 54.9% |
| 20,898 | ATCHISON | 8,229 | 3,147 | 5,037 | 45 | 1,890 D | 38.2% | 61.2% | 38.5% | 61.5% |
| 8,713 | BARBER | 3,624 | 1,758 | 1,845 | 21 | 87 D | 48.5% | 50.9% | 48.8% | 51.2% |
| 32,368 | BARTON | 12,221 | 4,826 | 7,340 | 55 | 2,514 D | 39.5% | 60.1% | 39.7% | 60.3% |
| 16,090 | BOURBON | 7,323 | 3,290 | 3,980 | 53 | 690 D | 44.9% | 54.3% | 45.3% | 54.7% |
| 13,229 | BROWN | 5,636 | 3,213 | 2,386 | 37 | 827 R | 57.0% | 42.3% | 57.4% | 42.6% |
| 38,395 | BUTLER | 15,532 | 6,364 | 9,061 | 107 | 2,697 D | 41.0% | 58.3% | 41.3% | 58.7% |
| 3,921 | CHASE | 1,793 | 902 | 886 | 5 | 16 R | 50.3% | 49.4% | 50.4% | 49.6% |
| 5,956 | CHAUTAUQUA | 2,640 | 1,463 | 1,163 | 14 | 300 R | 55.4% | 44.1% | 55.7% | 44.3% |
| 22,279 | CHEROKEE | 9,497 | 3,730 | 5,720 | 47 | 1,990 D | 39.3% | 60.2% | 39.5% | 60.5% |
| 4,708 | CHEYENNE | 2,040 | 1,147 | 886 | 7 | 261 R | 56.2% | 43.4% | 56.4% | 43.6% |
| 3,396 | CLARK | 1,665 | 777 | 881 | 7 | 104 D | 46.7% | 52.9% | 46.9% | 53.1% |
| 10,675 | CLAY | 4,873 | 3,030 | 1,806 | 37 | 1,224 R | 62.2% | 37.1% | 62.7% | 37.3% |
| 14,407 | CLOUD | 6,043 | 2,680 | 3,314 | 49 | 634 D | 44.3% | 54.8% | 44.7% | 55.3% |
| 8,403 | COFFEY | 3,606 | 1,998 | 1,594 | 14 | 404 R | 55.4% | 44.2% | 55.6% | 44.4% |
| 3,271 | COMANCHE | 1,524 | 694 | 818 | 12 | 124 D | 45.5% | 53.7% | 45.9% | 54.1% |
| 37,861 | COWLEY | 14,797 | 7,092 | 7,591 | 114 | 499 D | 47.9% | 51.3% | 48.3% | 51.7% |
| 37,032 | CRAWFORD | 16,644 | 6,286 | 10,282 | 76 | 3,996 D | 37.8% | 61.8% | 37.9% | 62.1% |
| 5,778 | DECATUR | 2,712 | 1,382 | 1,314 | 16 | 68 R | 51.0% | 48.5% | 51.3% | 48.7% |
| 21,572 | DICKINSON | 8,847 | 4,704 | 4,070 | 73 | 634 R | 53.2% | 46.0% | 53.6% | 46.4% |
| 9,574 | DONIPHAN | 3,824 | 1,952 | 1,856 | 16 | 96 R | 51.0% | 48.5% | 51.3% | 48.7% |
| 43,720 | DOUGLAS | 17,353 | 7,825 | 9,416 | 112 | 1,591 D | 45.1% | 54.3% | 45.4% | 54.6% |
| 5,118 | EDWARDS | 2,377 | 932 | 1,427 | 18 | 495 D | 39.2% | 60.0% | 39.5% | 60.5% |
| 5,048 | ELK | 2,273 | 1,267 | 994 | 12 | 273 R | 55.7% | 43.7% | 56.0% | 44.0% |
| 21,270 | ELLIS | 8,020 | 2,440 | 5,553 | 27 | 3,113 D | 30.4% | 69.2% | 30.5% | 69.5% |
| 7,677 | ELLSWORTH | 3,537 | 1,406 | 2,118 | 13 | 712 D | 39.8% | 59.9% | 39.9% | 60.1% |
| 16,093 | FINNEY | 5,883 | 2,201 | 3,639 | 43 | 1,438 D | 37.4% | 61.9% | 37.7% | 62.3% |
| 20,938 | FORD | 8,761 | 3,481 | 5,221 | 59 | 1,740 D | 39.7% | 59.6% | 40.0% | 60.0% |
| 19,548 | FRANKLIN | 8,221 | 3,725 | 4,410 | 86 | 685 D | 45.3% | 53.6% | 45.8% | 54.2% |
| 28,779 | GEARY | 5,745 | 2,259 | 3,419 | 67 | 1,160 D | 39.3% | 59.5% | 39.8% | 60.2% |
| 4,107 | GOVE | 1,813 | 774 | 1,022 | 17 | 248 D | 42.7% | 56.4% | 43.1% | 56.9% |
| 5,586 | GRAHAM | 2,408 | 1,194 | 1,193 | 21 | 1 R | 49.6% | 49.5% | 50.0% | 50.0% |
| 5,269 | GRANT | 1,775 | 727 | 1,023 | 25 | 296 D | 41.0% | 57.6% | 41.5% | 58.5% |
| 4,380 | GRAY | 1,793 | 643 | 1,136 | 14 | 493 D | 35.9% | 63.4% | 36.1% | 63.9% |
| 2,087 | GREELEY | 866 | 388 | 469 | 9 | 81 D | 44.8% | 54.2% | 45.3% | 54.7% |
| 11,253 | GREENWOOD | 4,801 | 2,717 | 2,048 | 36 | 669 R | 56.6% | 42.7% | 57.0% | 43.0% |
| 3,144 | HAMILTON | 1,421 | 685 | 726 | 10 | 41 D | 48.2% | 51.1% | 48.5% | 51.5% |
| 9,541 | HARPER | 3,810 | 1,969 | 1,813 | 28 | 156 R | 51.7% | 47.6% | 52.1% | 47.9% |
| 25,865 | HARVEY | 10,415 | 4,979 | 5,306 | 130 | 327 D | 47.8% | 50.9% | 48.4% | 51.6% |
| 2,990 | HASKELL | 1,409 | 570 | 820 | 19 | 250 D | 40.5% | 58.2% | 41.0% | 59.0% |
| 3,115 | HODGEMAN | 1,434 | 607 | 821 | 6 | 214 D | 42.3% | 57.3% | 42.5% | 57.5% |
| 10,309 | JACKSON | 4,336 | 2,334 | 1,971 | 31 | 363 R | 53.8% | 45.5% | 54.2% | 45.8% |
| 11,252 | JEFFERSON | 4,485 | 2,380 | 2,066 | 39 | 314 R | 53.1% | 46.1% | 53.5% | 46.5% |
| 7,217 | JEWELL | 3,535 | 1,895 | 1,601 | 39 | 294 R | 53.6% | 45.3% | 54.2% | 45.8% |
| 143,792 | JOHNSON | 69,179 | 37,672 | 31,213 | 294 | 6,459 R | 54.5% | 45.1% | 54.7% | 45.3% |
| 3,108 | KEARNY | 1,315 | 563 | 737 | 15 | 174 D | 42.8% | 56.0% | 43.3% | 56.7% |
| 9,958 | KINGMAN | 4,175 | 1,917 | 2,226 | 32 | 309 D | 45.9% | 53.3% | 46.3% | 53.7% |
| 4,626 | KIOWA | 2,130 | 1,135 | 970 | 25 | 165 R | 53.3% | 45.5% | 53.9% | 46.1% |
| 26,805 | LABETTE | 11,062 | 4,761 | 6,208 | 93 | 1,447 D | 43.0% | 56.1% | 43.4% | 56.6% |
| 3,060 | LANE | 1,370 | 586 | 773 | 11 | 187 D | 42.8% | 56.4% | 43.1% | 56.9% |
| 48,524 | LEAVENWORTH | 13,089 | 5,544 | 7,479 | 66 | 1,935 D | 42.4% | 57.1% | 42.6% | 57.4% |
| 5,556 | LINCOLN | 2,703 | 1,373 | 1,316 | 14 | 57 R | 50.8% | 48.7% | 51.1% | 48.9% |
| 8,274 | LINN | 3,679 | 1,939 | 1,725 | 15 | 214 R | 52.7% | 46.9% | 52.9% | 47.1% |
| 4,036 | LOGAN | 1,941 | 967 | 957 | 17 | 10 R | 49.8% | 49.3% | 50.3% | 49.7% |
| 26,928 | LYON | 11,462 | 5,184 | 6,197 | 81 | 1,013 D | 45.2% | 54.1% | 45.5% | 54.5% |
| 24,285 | MCPHERSON | 9,826 | 4,483 | 5,173 | 170 | 690 D | 45.6% | 52.6% | 46.4% | 53.6% |
| 15,143 | MARION | 6,341 | 3,481 | 2,792 | 68 | 689 R | 54.9% | 44.0% | 55.5% | 44.5% |
| 15,598 | MARSHALL | 6,822 | 3,432 | 3,334 | 56 | 98 R | 50.3% | 48.9% | 50.7% | 49.3% |
| 5,505 | MEADE | 2,492 | 1,290 | 1,179 | 23 | 111 R | 51.8% | 47.3% | 52.2% | 47.8% |

# KANSAS

## PRESIDENT 1964

| 1960 Census Population | County | Total Vote | Republican | Democratic | Other | Rep.-Dem. Plurality | Percentage Total Vote | | Major Vote | |
|---|---|---|---|---|---|---|---|---|---|---|
| | | | | | | | Rep. | Dem. | Rep. | Dem. |
| 19,884 | MIAMI | 7,570 | 2,907 | 4,620 | 43 | 1,713 D | 38.4% | 61.0% | 38.6% | 61.4% |
| 8,866 | MITCHELL | 3,880 | 1,951 | 1,898 | 31 | 53 R | 50.3% | 48.9% | 50.7% | 49.3% |
| 45,007 | MONTGOMERY | 17,416 | 8,437 | 8,853 | 126 | 416 D | 48.4% | 50.8% | 48.8% | 51.2% |
| 7,392 | MORRIS | 3,323 | 1,683 | 1,605 | 35 | 78 R | 50.6% | 48.3% | 51.2% | 48.8% |
| 3,354 | MORTON | 1,561 | 609 | 938 | 14 | 329 D | 39.0% | 60.1% | 39.4% | 60.6% |
| 12,897 | NEMAHA | 5,683 | 2,391 | 3,260 | 32 | 869 D | 42.1% | 57.4% | 42.3% | 57.7% |
| 19,455 | NEOSHO | 8,296 | 3,458 | 4,795 | 43 | 1,337 D | 41.7% | 57.8% | 41.9% | 58.1% |
| 5,470 | NESS | 2,615 | 1,034 | 1,562 | 19 | 528 D | 39.5% | 59.7% | 39.8% | 60.2% |
| 8,035 | NORTON | 3,736 | 2,245 | 1,449 | 42 | 796 R | 60.1% | 38.8% | 60.8% | 39.2% |
| 12,886 | OSAGE | 5,460 | 2,681 | 2,737 | 42 | 56 D | 49.1% | 50.1% | 49.5% | 50.5% |
| 7,506 | OSBORNE | 3,401 | 1,700 | 1,659 | 42 | 41 R | 50.0% | 48.8% | 50.6% | 49.4% |
| 6,779 | OTTAWA | 3,052 | 1,491 | 1,535 | 26 | 44 D | 48.9% | 50.3% | 49.3% | 50.7% |
| 10,254 | PAWNEE | 4,074 | 1,468 | 2,577 | 29 | 1,109 D | 36.0% | 63.3% | 36.3% | 63.7% |
| 8,709 | PHILLIPS | 4,000 | 2,164 | 1,804 | 32 | 360 R | 54.1% | 45.1% | 54.5% | 45.5% |
| 11,957 | POTTAWATOMIE | 5,070 | 2,606 | 2,432 | 32 | 174 R | 51.4% | 48.0% | 51.7% | 48.3% |
| 12,122 | PRATT | 5,129 | 2,493 | 2,594 | 42 | 101 D | 48.6% | 50.6% | 49.0% | 51.0% |
| 5,279 | RAWLINS | 2,261 | 1,292 | 959 | 10 | 333 R | 57.1% | 42.4% | 57.4% | 42.6% |
| 59,055 | RENO | 23,973 | 8,829 | 14,936 | 208 | 6,107 D | 36.8% | 62.3% | 37.2% | 62.8% |
| 9,768 | REPUBLIC | 4,674 | 2,414 | 2,222 | 38 | 192 R | 51.6% | 47.5% | 52.1% | 47.9% |
| 13,909 | RICE | 6,098 | 2,390 | 3,665 | 43 | 1,275 D | 39.2% | 60.1% | 39.5% | 60.5% |
| 41,914 | RILEY | 12,137 | 6,396 | 5,597 | 144 | 799 R | 52.7% | 46.1% | 53.3% | 46.7% |
| 9,734 | ROOKS | 3,924 | 1,985 | 1,923 | 16 | 62 R | 50.6% | 49.0% | 50.8% | 49.2% |
| 6,160 | RUSH | 2,901 | 1,098 | 1,778 | 25 | 680 D | 37.8% | 61.3% | 38.2% | 61.8% |
| 11,348 | RUSSELL | 4,977 | 2,435 | 2,505 | 37 | 70 D | 48.9% | 50.3% | 49.3% | 50.7% |
| 54,715 | SALINE | 16,357 | 6,533 | 9,725 | 99 | 3,192 D | 39.9% | 59.5% | 40.2% | 59.8% |
| 5,228 | SCOTT | 2,177 | 1,143 | 1,016 | 18 | 127 R | 52.5% | 46.7% | 52.9% | 47.1% |
| 343,231 | SEDGWICK | 120,181 | 52,592 | 66,372 | 1,217 | 13,780 D | 43.8% | 55.2% | 44.2% | 55.8% |
| 15,930 | SEWARD | 5,462 | 2,910 | 2,520 | 32 | 390 R | 53.3% | 46.1% | 53.6% | 46.4% |
| 141,286 | SHAWNEE | 56,625 | 25,736 | 30,626 | 263 | 4,890 D | 45.4% | 54.1% | 45.7% | 54.3% |
| 4,267 | SHERIDAN | 1,847 | 808 | 1,028 | 11 | 220 D | 43.7% | 55.7% | 44.0% | 56.0% |
| 6,682 | SHERMAN | 3,010 | 1,463 | 1,522 | 25 | 59 D | 48.6% | 50.6% | 49.0% | 51.0% |
| 7,776 | SMITH | 3,871 | 2,026 | 1,809 | 36 | 217 R | 52.3% | 46.7% | 52.8% | 47.2% |
| 7,451 | STAFFORD | 3,641 | 1,516 | 2,087 | 38 | 571 D | 41.6% | 57.3% | 42.1% | 57.9% |
| 2,108 | STANTON | 970 | 459 | 500 | 11 | 41 D | 47.3% | 51.5% | 47.9% | 52.1% |
| 4,400 | STEVENS | 2,020 | 992 | 1,006 | 22 | 14 D | 49.1% | 49.8% | 49.6% | 50.4% |
| 25,316 | SUMNER | 10,450 | 4,760 | 5,574 | 116 | 814 D | 45.6% | 53.3% | 46.1% | 53.9% |
| 7,358 | THOMAS | 3,348 | 1,528 | 1,793 | 27 | 265 D | 45.6% | 53.6% | 46.0% | 54.0% |
| 5,473 | TREGO | 2,162 | 974 | 1,177 | 11 | 203 D | 45.1% | 54.4% | 45.3% | 54.7% |
| 6,648 | WABAUNSEE | 3,152 | 1,839 | 1,287 | 26 | 552 R | 58.3% | 40.8% | 58.8% | 41.2% |
| 2,069 | WALLACE | 1,018 | 516 | 496 | 6 | 20 R | 50.7% | 48.7% | 51.0% | 49.0% |
| 10,739 | WASHINGTON | 4,705 | 2,654 | 2,015 | 36 | 639 R | 56.4% | 42.8% | 56.8% | 43.2% |
| 2,765 | WICHITA | 1,197 | 529 | 662 | 6 | 133 D | 44.2% | 55.3% | 44.4% | 55.6% |
| 13,077 | WILSON | 5,556 | 2,919 | 2,592 | 45 | 327 R | 52.5% | 46.7% | 53.0% | 47.0% |
| 5,423 | WOODSON | 2,431 | 1,279 | 1,128 | 24 | 151 R | 52.6% | 46.4% | 53.1% | 46.9% |
| 185,495 | WYANDOTTE | 65,351 | 20,553 | 43,442 | 1,356 | 22,889 D | 31.5% | 66.5% | 32.1% | 67.9% |
| 2,178,611 | TOTAL | 857,901 | 386,579 | 464,028 | 7,294 | 77,449 D | 45.1% | 54.1% | 45.4% | 54.6% |

# KANSAS

## PRESIDENT 1960

| 1960 Census Population | County | Total Vote | Republican | Democratic | Other | Rep.-Dem. Plurality | Percentage Total Vote Rep. | Dem. | Major Vote Rep. | Dem. |
|---|---|---|---|---|---|---|---|---|---|---|
| 16,369 | ALLEN | 7,508 | 4,947 | 2,540 | 21 | 2,407 R | 65.9% | 33.8% | 66.1% | 33.9% |
| 9,035 | ANDERSON | 4,274 | 2,665 | 1,589 | 20 | 1,076 R | 62.4% | 37.2% | 62.6% | 37.4% |
| 20,898 | ATCHISON | 9,160 | 4,793 | 4,336 | 31 | 457 R | 52.3% | 47.3% | 52.5% | 47.5% |
| 8,713 | BARBER | 4,066 | 2,703 | 1,347 | 16 | 1,356 R | 66.5% | 33.1% | 66.7% | 33.3% |
| 32,368 | BARTON | 13,665 | 7,599 | 6,036 | 30 | 1,563 R | 55.6% | 44.2% | 55.7% | 44.3% |
| 16,090 | BOURBON | 8,031 | 5,062 | 2,928 | 41 | 2,134 R | 63.0% | 36.5% | 63.4% | 36.6% |
| 13,229 | BROWN | 6,515 | 4,707 | 1,773 | 35 | 2,934 R | 72.2% | 27.2% | 72.6% | 27.4% |
| 38,395 | BUTLER | 17,232 | 10,059 | 7,112 | 61 | 2,947 R | 58.4% | 41.3% | 58.6% | 41.4% |
| 3,921 | CHASE | 1,992 | 1,276 | 708 | 8 | 568 R | 64.1% | 35.5% | 64.3% | 35.7% |
| 5,956 | CHAUTAUQUA | 3,062 | 2,160 | 885 | 17 | 1,275 R | 70.5% | 28.9% | 70.9% | 29.1% |
| 22,279 | CHEROKEE | 10,192 | 5,753 | 4,366 | 73 | 1,387 R | 56.4% | 42.8% | 56.9% | 43.1% |
| 4,708 | CHEYENNE | 2,271 | 1,622 | 636 | 13 | 986 R | 71.4% | 28.0% | 71.8% | 28.2% |
| 3,396 | CLARK | 1,830 | 1,286 | 538 | 6 | 748 R | 70.3% | 29.4% | 70.5% | 29.5% |
| 10,675 | CLAY | 5,226 | 3,937 | 1,246 | 43 | 2,691 R | 75.3% | 23.8% | 76.0% | 24.0% |
| 14,407 | CLOUD | 6,677 | 4,045 | 2,607 | 25 | 1,438 R | 60.6% | 39.0% | 60.8% | 39.2% |
| 8,403 | COFFEY | 4,197 | 2,925 | 1,263 | 9 | 1,662 R | 69.7% | 30.1% | 69.8% | 30.2% |
| 3,271 | COMANCHE | 1,652 | 1,187 | 460 | 5 | 727 R | 71.9% | 27.8% | 72.1% | 27.9% |
| 37,861 | COWLEY | 16,580 | 10,276 | 6,205 | 99 | 4,071 R | 62.0% | 37.4% | 62.4% | 37.6% |
| 37,032 | CRAWFORD | 17,777 | 9,383 | 8,325 | 69 | 1,058 R | 52.8% | 46.8% | 53.0% | 47.0% |
| 5,778 | DECATUR | 2,892 | 1,846 | 1,038 | 8 | 808 R | 63.8% | 35.9% | 64.0% | 36.0% |
| 21,572 | DICKINSON | 10,055 | 6,956 | 3,054 | 45 | 3,902 R | 69.2% | 30.4% | 69.5% | 30.5% |
| 9,574 | DONIPHAN | 4,277 | 2,882 | 1,383 | 12 | 1,499 R | 67.4% | 32.3% | 67.6% | 32.4% |
| 43,720 | DOUGLAS | 17,065 | 11,337 | 5,690 | 38 | 5,647 R | 66.4% | 33.3% | 66.6% | 33.4% |
| 5,118 | EDWARDS | 2,584 | 1,588 | 986 | 10 | 602 R | 61.5% | 38.2% | 61.7% | 38.3% |
| 5,048 | ELK | 2,673 | 1,830 | 823 | 20 | 1,007 R | 68.5% | 30.8% | 69.0% | 31.0% |
| 21,270 | ELLIS | 8,977 | 3,156 | 5,815 | 6 | 2,659 D | 35.2% | 64.8% | 35.2% | 64.8% |
| 7,677 | ELLSWORTH | 3,687 | 2,189 | 1,488 | 10 | 701 R | 59.4% | 40.4% | 59.5% | 40.5% |
| 16,093 | FINNEY | 6,240 | 3,720 | 2,490 | 30 | 1,230 R | 59.6% | 39.9% | 59.9% | 40.1% |
| 20,938 | FORD | 9,017 | 5,200 | 3,792 | 25 | 1,408 R | 57.7% | 42.1% | 57.8% | 42.2% |
| 19,548 | FRANKLIN | 9,029 | 6,158 | 2,824 | 47 | 3,334 R | 68.2% | 31.3% | 68.6% | 31.4% |
| 28,779 | GEARY | 6,183 | 3,789 | 2,365 | 29 | 1,424 R | 61.3% | 38.3% | 61.6% | 38.4% |
| 4,107 | GOVE | 1,907 | 1,065 | 828 | 14 | 237 R | 55.8% | 43.4% | 56.3% | 43.7% |
| 5,586 | GRAHAM | 2,497 | 1,572 | 918 | 7 | 654 R | 63.0% | 36.8% | 63.1% | 36.9% |
| 5,269 | GRANT | 1,942 | 1,235 | 702 | 5 | 533 R | 63.6% | 36.1% | 63.8% | 36.2% |
| 4,380 | GRAY | 1,899 | 1,150 | 744 | 5 | 406 R | 60.6% | 39.2% | 60.7% | 39.3% |
| 2,087 | GREELEY | 914 | 645 | 262 | 7 | 383 R | 70.6% | 28.7% | 71.1% | 28.9% |
| 11,253 | GREENWOOD | 5,571 | 3,758 | 1,804 | 9 | 1,954 R | 67.5% | 32.4% | 67.6% | 32.4% |
| 3,144 | HAMILTON | 1,481 | 885 | 591 | 5 | 294 R | 59.8% | 39.9% | 60.0% | 40.0% |
| 9,541 | HARPER | 4,622 | 3,158 | 1,439 | 25 | 1,719 R | 68.3% | 31.1% | 68.7% | 31.3% |
| 25,865 | HARVEY | 11,404 | 7,798 | 3,537 | 69 | 4,261 R | 68.4% | 31.0% | 68.8% | 31.2% |
| 2,990 | HASKELL | 1,328 | 853 | 471 | 4 | 382 R | 64.2% | 35.5% | 64.4% | 35.6% |
| 3,115 | HODGEMAN | 1,507 | 926 | 570 | 11 | 356 R | 61.4% | 37.8% | 61.9% | 38.1% |
| 10,309 | JACKSON | 4,861 | 3,279 | 1,567 | 15 | 1,712 R | 67.5% | 32.2% | 67.7% | 32.3% |
| 11,252 | JEFFERSON | 5,101 | 3,353 | 1,739 | 9 | 1,614 R | 65.7% | 34.1% | 65.8% | 34.2% |
| 7,217 | JEWELL | 4,033 | 2,914 | 1,095 | 24 | 1,819 R | 72.3% | 27.2% | 72.7% | 27.3% |
| 143,792 | JOHNSON | 65,033 | 43,026 | 21,914 | 93 | 21,112 R | 66.2% | 33.7% | 66.3% | 33.7% |
| 3,108 | KEARNY | 1,362 | 846 | 513 | 3 | 333 R | 62.1% | 37.7% | 62.3% | 37.7% |
| 9,958 | KINGMAN | 4,662 | 2,904 | 1,735 | 23 | 1,169 R | 62.3% | 37.2% | 62.6% | 37.4% |
| 4,626 | KIOWA | 2,229 | 1,662 | 555 | 12 | 1,107 R | 74.6% | 24.9% | 75.0% | 25.0% |
| 26,805 | LABETTE | 12,807 | 7,491 | 5,248 | 68 | 2,243 R | 58.5% | 41.0% | 58.8% | 41.2% |
| 3,060 | LANE | 1,379 | 902 | 462 | 15 | 440 R | 65.4% | 33.5% | 66.1% | 33.9% |
| 48,524 | LEAVENWORTH | 14,832 | 7,870 | 6,926 | 36 | 944 R | 53.1% | 46.7% | 53.2% | 46.8% |
| 5,556 | LINCOLN | 2,884 | 2,052 | 822 | 10 | 1,230 R | 71.2% | 28.5% | 71.4% | 28.6% |
| 8,274 | LINN | 4,024 | 2,824 | 1,176 | 24 | 1,648 R | 70.2% | 29.2% | 70.6% | 29.4% |
| 4,036 | LOGAN | 1,906 | 1,243 | 651 | 12 | 592 R | 65.2% | 34.2% | 65.6% | 34.4% |
| 26,928 | LYON | 12,266 | 7,470 | 4,755 | 41 | 2,715 R | 60.9% | 38.8% | 61.1% | 38.9% |
| 24,285 | MCPHERSON | 10,759 | 7,920 | 2,774 | 65 | 5,146 R | 73.6% | 25.8% | 74.1% | 25.9% |
| 15,143 | MARION | 7,172 | 5,250 | 1,904 | 18 | 3,346 R | 73.2% | 26.5% | 73.4% | 26.6% |
| 15,598 | MARSHALL | 7,891 | 4,932 | 2,931 | 28 | 2,001 R | 62.5% | 37.1% | 62.7% | 37.3% |
| 5,505 | MEADE | 2,591 | 1,826 | 754 | 11 | 1,072 R | 70.5% | 29.1% | 70.8% | 29.2% |

# KANSAS

## PRESIDENT 1960

| 1960 Census Population | County | Total Vote | Republican | Democratic | Other | Rep.-Dem. Plurality | Percentage | | | |
|---|---|---|---|---|---|---|---|---|---|---|
| | | | | | | | Total Vote | | Major Vote | |
| | | | | | | | Rep. | Dem. | Rep. | Dem. |
| 19,884 | MIAMI | 8,396 | 4,857 | 3,505 | 34 | 1,352 R | 57.8% | 41.7% | 58.1% | 41.9% |
| 8,866 | MITCHELL | 4,497 | 2,779 | 1,692 | 26 | 1,087 R | 61.8% | 37.6% | 62.2% | 37.8% |
| 45,007 | MONTGOMERY | 20,638 | 12,536 | 7,938 | 164 | 4,598 R | 60.7% | 38.5% | 61.2% | 38.8% |
| 7,392 | MORRIS | 3,580 | 2,413 | 1,148 | 19 | 1,265 R | 67.4% | 32.1% | 67.8% | 32.2% |
| 3,354 | MORTON | 1,513 | 918 | 586 | 9 | 332 R | 60.7% | 38.7% | 61.0% | 39.0% |
| 12,897 | NEMAHA | 6,267 | 3,360 | 2,884 | 23 | 476 R | 53.6% | 46.0% | 53.8% | 46.2% |
| 19,455 | NEOSHO | 9,371 | 5,877 | 3,451 | 43 | 2,426 R | 62.7% | 36.8% | 63.0% | 37.0% |
| 5,470 | NESS | 2,655 | 1,683 | 960 | 12 | 723 R | 63.4% | 36.2% | 63.7% | 36.3% |
| 8,035 | NORTON | 4,089 | 2,781 | 1,300 | 8 | 1,481 R | 68.0% | 31.8% | 68.1% | 31.9% |
| 12,886 | OSAGE | 6,061 | 3,880 | 2,150 | 31 | 1,730 R | 64.0% | 35.5% | 64.3% | 35.7% |
| 7,506 | OSBORNE | 3,903 | 2,731 | 1,152 | 20 | 1,579 R | 70.0% | 29.5% | 70.3% | 29.7% |
| 6,779 | OTTAWA | 3,278 | 2,190 | 1,072 | 16 | 1,118 R | 66.8% | 32.7% | 67.1% | 32.9% |
| 10,254 | PAWNEE | 4,489 | 2,618 | 1,853 | 18 | 765 R | 58.3% | 41.3% | 58.6% | 41.4% |
| 8,709 | PHILLIPS | 4,145 | 3,123 | 1,004 | 18 | 2,119 R | 75.3% | 24.2% | 75.7% | 24.3% |
| 11,957 | POTTAWATOMIE | 5,804 | 3,666 | 2,125 | 13 | 1,541 R | 63.2% | 36.6% | 63.3% | 36.7% |
| 12,122 | PRATT | 5,506 | 3,501 | 1,968 | 37 | 1,533 R | 63.6% | 35.7% | 64.0% | 36.0% |
| 5,279 | RAWLINS | 2,527 | 1,560 | 951 | 16 | 609 R | 61.7% | 37.6% | 62.1% | 37.9% |
| 59,055 | RENO | 24,339 | 14,655 | 9,557 | 127 | 5,098 R | 60.2% | 39.3% | 60.5% | 39.5% |
| 9,768 | REPUBLIC | 5,117 | 3,358 | 1,724 | 35 | 1,634 R | 65.6% | 33.7% | 66.1% | 33.9% |
| 13,909 | RICE | 6,680 | 4,329 | 2,328 | 23 | 2,001 R | 64.8% | 34.9% | 65.0% | 35.0% |
| 41,914 | RILEY | 12,600 | 9,068 | 3,482 | 50 | 5,586 R | 72.0% | 27.6% | 72.3% | 27.7% |
| 9,734 | ROOKS | 4,490 | 2,840 | 1,639 | 11 | 1,201 R | 63.3% | 36.5% | 63.4% | 36.6% |
| 6,160 | RUSH | 3,097 | 1,668 | 1,418 | 11 | 250 R | 53.9% | 45.8% | 54.1% | 45.9% |
| 11,348 | RUSSELL | 5,501 | 3,607 | 1,870 | 24 | 1,737 R | 65.6% | 34.0% | 65.9% | 34.1% |
| 54,715 | SALINE | 17,568 | 11,023 | 6,495 | 50 | 4,528 R | 62.7% | 37.0% | 62.9% | 37.1% |
| 5,228 | SCOTT | 2,124 | 1,514 | 598 | 12 | 916 R | 71.3% | 28.2% | 71.7% | 28.3% |
| 343,231 | SEDGWICK | 133,084 | 73,501 | 58,887 | 696 | 14,614 R | 55.2% | 44.2% | 55.5% | 44.5% |
| 15,930 | SEWARD | 5,642 | 3,974 | 1,654 | 14 | 2,320 R | 70.4% | 29.3% | 70.6% | 29.4% |
| 141,286 | SHAWNEE | 55,749 | 33,803 | 21,799 | 147 | 12,004 R | 60.6% | 39.1% | 60.8% | 39.2% |
| 4,267 | SHERIDAN | 2,016 | 1,047 | 954 | 15 | 93 R | 51.9% | 47.3% | 52.3% | 47.7% |
| 6,682 | SHERMAN | 3,119 | 2,030 | 1,074 | 15 | 956 R | 65.1% | 34.4% | 65.4% | 34.6% |
| 7,776 | SMITH | 4,192 | 3,013 | 1,157 | 22 | 1,856 R | 71.9% | 27.6% | 72.3% | 27.7% |
| 7,451 | STAFFORD | 3,862 | 2,531 | 1,305 | 26 | 1,226 R | 65.5% | 33.8% | 66.0% | 34.0% |
| 2,108 | STANTON | 954 | 627 | 323 | 4 | 304 R | 65.7% | 33.9% | 66.0% | 34.0% |
| 4,400 | STEVENS | 2,044 | 1,405 | 630 | 9 | 775 R | 68.7% | 30.8% | 69.0% | 31.0% |
| 25,316 | SUMNER | 11,736 | 7,219 | 4,462 | 55 | 2,757 R | 61.5% | 38.0% | 61.8% | 38.2% |
| 7,358 | THOMAS | 3,384 | 2,081 | 1,285 | 18 | 796 R | 61.5% | 38.0% | 61.8% | 38.2% |
| 5,473 | TREGO | 2,309 | 1,426 | 875 | 8 | 551 R | 61.8% | 37.9% | 62.0% | 38.0% |
| 6,648 | WABAUNSEE | 3,331 | 2,351 | 969 | 11 | 1,382 R | 70.6% | 29.1% | 70.8% | 29.2% |
| 2,069 | WALLACE | 1,066 | 727 | 339 | | 388 R | 68.2% | 31.8% | 68.2% | 31.8% |
| 10,739 | WASHINGTON | 5,444 | 3,707 | 1,706 | 31 | 2,001 R | 68.1% | 31.3% | 68.5% | 31.5% |
| 2,765 | WICHITA | 1,262 | 702 | 554 | 6 | 148 R | 55.6% | 43.9% | 55.9% | 44.1% |
| 13,077 | WILSON | 6,394 | 4,333 | 2,034 | 27 | 2,299 R | 67.8% | 31.8% | 68.1% | 31.9% |
| 5,423 | WOODSON | 2,751 | 1,853 | 888 | 10 | 965 R | 67.4% | 32.3% | 67.6% | 32.4% |
| 185,495 | WYANDOTTE | 76,801 | 34,764 | 41,433 | 604 | 6,669 D | 45.3% | 53.9% | 45.6% | 54.4% |
| 2,178,611 | TOTAL | 928,825 | 561,474 | 363,213 | 4,138 | 198,261 R | 60.4% | 39.1% | 60.7% | 39.3% |

# KANSAS

## ELECTION NOTES

**2004**  Other vote was 9,348 Reform (Ralph Nader); 4,013 Libertarian (Michael Badnarik); 2,899 Independent (Michael Peroutka); 33 write-in (David Cobb); 5 write-in (John Joseph Kennedy); 5 write-in (Bill Van Auken); 4 write-in (Walter F. Brown).

**2000**  Other vote was 7,370 Reform (Buchanan); 4,525 Libertarian (Browne); 1,375 Independent (Hagelin); 1,254 Constitution (Phillips). Nader was listed on the ballot as an Independent.

**1996**  Other vote was 4,557 Libertarian (Browne); 3,519 Independent (Phillips); 1,655 Independent (Hagelin); 914 write-in (Nader); 112 scattered write-in.

**1992**  Other vote was 4,314 Marrou (Libertarian); 79 Gritz (write-in); 77 Hagelin (write-in); 55 Phillips (write-in); 10 Fulani (write-in); 57 scattered write-in.

**1988**  Other vote was 12,553 Paul (Independent); 3,806 Fulani (Independent).

**1984**  Other vote was 3,564 Richards (Conservative); 3,329 Bergland (Libertarian); 2,544 Serrette (Independent); 2,109 Dodge (Prohibition).

**1980**  Other vote was 68,231 Anderson (Independent); 14,470 Clark (Independent); 1,555 Shelton (American); 967 Hall (Independent); 821 Bubar (Statesman); 789 Rarick (Conservative).

**1976**  Other vote was 13,185 McCarthy (Independent); 4,724 Anderson (American); 3,242 MacBride (Independent); 2,118 Maddox (Conservative); 1,403 Bubar (Prohibition).

**1972**  Other vote was 21,808 Schmitz (Conservative); 4,188 Munn (Prohibition).

**1968**  Wallace on the ballot as Conservative. Other vote was Munn (Prohibition).

**1964**  Other vote was 5,393 Munn (Prohibition); 1,901 Hass (Socialist Labor).

**1960**  Other vote was Decker (Prohibition).

# KENTUCKY

## POPULAR VOTE FOR PRESIDENT 1920 TO 2004

| Year | Total Vote | Republican Vote | Republican Candidate | Democratic Vote | Democratic Candidate | Other Vote | Plurality | Percentage Total Vote Rep. | Percentage Total Vote Dem. | Percentage Major Vote Rep. | Percentage Major Vote Dem. |
|------|-----------|-----------------|----------------------|-----------------|----------------------|------------|-----------|------|------|------|------|
| 2004 | 1,795,882 | 1,069,439 | Bush, George W. | 712,733 | Kerry, John | 13,710 | 356,706 R | 59.5% | 39.7% | 60.0% | 40.0% |
| 2000** | 1,544,187 | 872,492 | Bush, George W. | 638,898 | Gore, Al | 32,797 | 233,594 R | 56.5% | 41.4% | 57.7% | 42.3% |
| 1996 ** | 1,388,708 | 623,283 | Dole, Bob | 636,614 | Clinton, Bill | 128,811 | 13,331 D | 44.9% | 45.8% | 49.5% | 50.5% |
| 1992 ** | 1,492,900 | 617,178 | Bush, George | 665,104 | Clinton, Bill | 210,618 | 47,926 D | 41.3% | 44.6% | 48.1% | 51.9% |
| 1988 | 1,322,517 | 734,281 | Bush, George | 580,368 | Dukakis, Michael S. | 7,868 | 153,913 R | 55.5% | 43.9% | 55.9% | 44.1% |
| 1984 | 1,369,345 | 821,702 | Reagan, Ronald | 539,539 | Mondale, Walter F. | 8,104 | 282,163 R | 60.0% | 39.4% | 60.4% | 39.6% |
| 1980 ** | 1,294,627 | 635,274 | Reagan, Ronald | 616,417 | Carter, Jimmy | 42,936 | 18,857 R | 49.1% | 47.6% | 50.8% | 49.2% |
| 1976 | 1,167,142 | 531,852 | Ford, Gerald R. | 615,717 | Carter, Jimmy | 19,573 | 83,865 D | 45.6% | 52.8% | 46.3% | 53.7% |
| 1972 | 1,067,499 | 676,446 | Nixon, Richard M. | 371,159 | McGovern, George S. | 19,894 | 305,287 R | 63.4% | 34.8% | 64.6% | 35.4% |
| 1968 | 1,055,893 | 462,411 | Nixon, Richard M. | 397,541 | Humphrey, Hubert H. | 195,941 | 64,870 R | 43.8% | 37.6% | 53.8% | 46.2% |
| 1964 | 1,046,105 | 372,977 | Goldwater, Barry M. | 669,659 | Johnson, Lyndon B. | 3,469 | 296,682 D | 35.7% | 64.0% | 35.8% | 64.2% |
| 1960 | 1,124,462 | 602,607 | Nixon, Richard M. | 521,855 | Kennedy, John F. | | 80,752 R | 53.6% | 46.4% | 53.6% | 46.4% |
| 1956 | 1,053,805 | 572,192 | Eisenhower, Dwight D. | 476,453 | Stevenson, Adlai E. | 5,160 | 95,739 R | 54.3% | 45.2% | 54.6% | 45.4% |
| 1952 | 993,148 | 495,029 | Eisenhower, Dwight D. | 495,729 | Stevenson, Adlai E. | 2,390 | 700 D | 49.8% | 49.9% | 50.0% | 50.0% |
| 1948 | 822,658 | 341,210 | Dewey, Thomas E. | 466,756 | Truman, Harry S. | 14,692 | 125,546 D | 41.5% | 56.7% | 42.2% | 57.8% |
| 1944 | 867,924 | 392,448 | Dewey, Thomas E. | 472,589 | Roosevelt, Franklin D. | 2,887 | 80,141 D | 45.2% | 54.5% | 45.4% | 54.6% |
| 1940 | 970,163 | 410,384 | Willkie, Wendell | 557,322 | Roosevelt, Franklin D. | 2,457 | 146,938 D | 42.3% | 57.4% | 42.4% | 57.6% |
| 1936 | 926,214 | 369,702 | Landon, Alfred M. | 541,944 | Roosevelt, Franklin D. | 14,568 | 172,242 D | 39.9% | 58.5% | 40.6% | 59.4% |
| 1932 | 983,059 | 394,716 | Hoover, Herbert C. | 580,574 | Roosevelt, Franklin D. | 7,769 | 185,858 D | 40.2% | 59.1% | 40.5% | 59.5% |
| 1928 | 940,521 | 558,064 | Hoover, Herbert C. | 381,070 | Smith, Alfred E. | 1,387 | 176,994 R | 59.3% | 40.5% | 59.4% | 40.6% |
| 1924 | 813,843 | 396,758 | Coolidge, Calvin | 375,593 | Davis, John W. | 41,492 | 21,165 R | 48.8% | 46.2% | 51.4% | 48.6% |
| 1920 | 918,636 | 452,480 | Harding, Warren G. | 456,497 | Cox, James M. | 9,659 | 4,017 D | 49.3% | 49.7% | 49.8% | 50.2% |

In 2000 the other vote column includes 23,192 votes cast for Green (Nader). In 1996 the other vote column includes 120,396 votes cast for Perot. In 1992 the other vote column includes 203,944 votes cast for Perot. In 1980 the other column includes 31,127 votes for Independent (Anderson).

## ELECTORAL COLLEGE VOTE 1920 TO 2004

| Year | Total | Republican | Democratic | Other |
|------|-------|------------|------------|-------|
| 2004 | 8 | 8 | | |
| 2000 | 8 | 8 | | |
| 1996 | 8 | | 8 | |
| 1992 | 8 | | 8 | |
| 1988 | 9 | 9 | | |
| 1984 | 9 | 9 | | |
| 1980 | 9 | 9 | | |
| 1976 | 9 | | 9 | |
| 1972 | 9 | 9 | | |
| 1968 | 9 | 9 | | |
| 1964 | 9 | | 9 | |
| 1960 | 10 | 10 | | |
| 1956 | 10 | 10 | | |
| 1952 | 10 | | 10 | |
| 1948 | 11 | | 11 | |
| 1944 | 11 | | 11 | |
| 1940 | 11 | | 11 | |
| 1936 | 11 | | 11 | |
| 1932 | 11 | | 11 | |
| 1928 | 13 | 13 | | |
| 1924 | 13 | 13 | | |
| 1920 | 13 | | 13 | |

# KENTUCKY

# KENTUCKY

## PRESIDENT 2004

| 2000 Census Population | County | Total Vote | Republican | Democratic | Other | Rep.-Dem. Plurality | Percentage | | | |
|---|---|---|---|---|---|---|---|---|---|---|
| | | | | | | | Total Vote | | Major Vote | |
| | | | | | | | Rep. | Dem. | Rep. | Dem. |
| 17,244 | ADAIR | 7,447 | 5,628 | 1,764 | 55 | 3,864 R | 75.6% | 23.7% | 76.1% | 23.9% |
| 17,800 | ALLEN | 7,163 | 5,202 | 1,923 | 38 | 3,279 R | 72.6% | 26.8% | 73.0% | 27.0% |
| 19,111 | ANDERSON | 9,591 | 6,363 | 3,141 | 87 | 3,222 R | 66.3% | 32.7% | 67.0% | 33.0% |
| 8,286 | BALLARD | 4,177 | 2,389 | 1,759 | 29 | 630 R | 57.2% | 42.1% | 57.6% | 42.4% |
| 38,033 | BARREN | 16,140 | 10,822 | 5,216 | 102 | 5,606 R | 67.1% | 32.3% | 67.5% | 32.5% |
| 11,085 | BATH | 4,919 | 2,269 | 2,608 | 42 | 339 D | 46.1% | 53.0% | 46.5% | 53.5% |
| 30,060 | BELL | 11,002 | 6,722 | 4,210 | 70 | 2,512 R | 61.1% | 38.3% | 61.5% | 38.5% |
| 85,991 | BOONE | 45,082 | 32,329 | 12,391 | 362 | 19,938 R | 71.7% | 27.5% | 72.3% | 27.7% |
| 19,360 | BOURBON | 8,217 | 4,953 | 3,198 | 66 | 1,755 R | 60.3% | 38.9% | 60.8% | 39.2% |
| 49,752 | BOYD | 21,780 | 11,501 | 10,132 | 147 | 1,369 R | 52.8% | 46.5% | 53.2% | 46.8% |
| 27,697 | BOYLE | 12,490 | 7,764 | 4,646 | 80 | 3,118 R | 62.2% | 37.2% | 62.6% | 37.4% |
| 8,279 | BRACKEN | 3,610 | 2,363 | 1,213 | 34 | 1,150 R | 65.5% | 33.6% | 66.1% | 33.9% |
| 16,100 | BREATHITT | 5,944 | 2,542 | 3,327 | 75 | 785 D | 42.8% | 56.0% | 43.3% | 56.7% |
| 18,648 | BRECKINRIDGE | 8,520 | 5,580 | 2,884 | 56 | 2,696 R | 65.5% | 33.8% | 65.9% | 34.1% |
| 61,236 | BULLITT | 28,627 | 19,433 | 9,043 | 151 | 10,390 R | 67.9% | 31.6% | 68.2% | 31.8% |
| 13,010 | BUTLER | 5,578 | 4,109 | 1,436 | 33 | 2,673 R | 73.7% | 25.7% | 74.1% | 25.9% |
| 13,060 | CALDWELL | 6,349 | 4,066 | 2,245 | 38 | 1,821 R | 64.0% | 35.4% | 64.4% | 35.6% |
| 34,177 | CALLOWAY | 15,145 | 9,293 | 5,728 | 124 | 3,565 R | 61.4% | 37.8% | 61.9% | 38.1% |
| 88,616 | CAMPBELL | 40,178 | 25,540 | 14,253 | 385 | 11,287 R | 63.6% | 35.5% | 64.2% | 35.8% |
| 5,351 | CARLISLE | 2,845 | 1,734 | 1,102 | 9 | 632 R | 60.9% | 38.7% | 61.1% | 38.9% |
| 10,155 | CARROLL | 3,897 | 2,175 | 1,688 | 34 | 487 R | 55.8% | 43.3% | 56.3% | 43.7% |
| 26,889 | CARTER | 11,117 | 5,422 | 5,577 | 118 | 155 D | 48.8% | 50.2% | 49.3% | 50.7% |
| 15,447 | CASEY | 6,321 | 5,109 | 1,174 | 38 | 3,935 R | 80.8% | 18.6% | 81.3% | 18.7% |
| 72,265 | CHRISTIAN | 21,015 | 13,935 | 6,970 | 110 | 6,965 R | 66.3% | 33.2% | 66.7% | 33.3% |
| 33,144 | CLARK | 15,317 | 9,540 | 5,661 | 116 | 3,879 R | 62.3% | 37.0% | 62.8% | 37.2% |
| 24,556 | CLAY | 7,687 | 5,726 | 1,901 | 60 | 3,825 R | 74.5% | 24.7% | 75.1% | 24.9% |
| 9,634 | CLINTON | 4,352 | 3,369 | 952 | 31 | 2,417 R | 77.4% | 21.9% | 78.0% | 22.0% |
| 9,384 | CRITTENDEN | 4,190 | 2,726 | 1,438 | 26 | 1,288 R | 65.1% | 34.3% | 65.5% | 34.5% |
| 7,147 | CUMBERLAND | 3,239 | 2,356 | 848 | 35 | 1,508 R | 72.7% | 26.2% | 73.5% | 26.5% |
| 91,545 | DAVIESS | 41,483 | 25,372 | 15,788 | 323 | 9,584 R | 61.2% | 38.1% | 61.6% | 38.4% |
| 11,644 | EDMONSON | 5,481 | 3,595 | 1,856 | 30 | 1,739 R | 65.6% | 33.9% | 66.0% | 34.0% |
| 6,748 | ELLIOTT | 2,957 | 871 | 2,064 | 22 | 1,193 D | 29.5% | 69.8% | 29.7% | 70.3% |
| 15,307 | ESTILL | 5,575 | 3,633 | 1,907 | 35 | 1,726 R | 65.2% | 34.2% | 65.6% | 34.4% |
| 260,512 | FAYETTE | 125,584 | 66,406 | 57,994 | 1,184 | 8,412 R | 52.9% | 46.2% | 53.4% | 46.6% |
| 13,792 | FLEMING | 6,203 | 3,749 | 2,406 | 48 | 1,343 R | 60.4% | 38.8% | 60.9% | 39.1% |
| 42,441 | FLOYD | 17,885 | 6,612 | 11,132 | 141 | 4,520 D | 37.0% | 62.2% | 37.3% | 62.7% |
| 47,687 | FRANKLIN | 24,134 | 12,281 | 11,620 | 233 | 661 R | 50.9% | 48.1% | 51.4% | 48.6% |
| 7,752 | FULTON | 2,890 | 1,527 | 1,340 | 23 | 187 R | 52.8% | 46.4% | 53.3% | 46.7% |
| 7,870 | GALLATIN | 3,073 | 1,869 | 1,188 | 16 | 681 R | 60.8% | 38.7% | 61.1% | 38.9% |
| 14,792 | GARRARD | 6,658 | 4,784 | 1,841 | 33 | 2,943 R | 71.9% | 27.7% | 72.2% | 27.8% |
| 22,384 | GRANT | 8,824 | 5,951 | 2,818 | 55 | 3,133 R | 67.4% | 31.9% | 67.9% | 32.1% |
| 37,028 | GRAVES | 16,231 | 9,903 | 6,206 | 122 | 3,697 R | 61.0% | 38.2% | 61.5% | 38.5% |
| 24,053 | GRAYSON | 10,143 | 7,170 | 2,905 | 68 | 4,265 R | 70.7% | 28.6% | 71.2% | 28.8% |
| 11,518 | GREEN | 5,206 | 3,866 | 1,312 | 28 | 2,554 R | 74.3% | 25.2% | 74.7% | 25.3% |
| 36,891 | GREENUP | 16,435 | 8,696 | 7,630 | 109 | 1,066 R | 52.9% | 46.4% | 53.3% | 46.7% |
| 8,392 | HANCOCK | 4,029 | 2,286 | 1,709 | 34 | 577 R | 56.7% | 42.4% | 57.2% | 42.8% |
| 94,174 | HARDIN | 36,441 | 24,627 | 11,507 | 307 | 13,120 R | 67.6% | 31.6% | 68.2% | 31.8% |
| 33,202 | HARLAN | 11,070 | 6,659 | 4,332 | 79 | 2,327 R | 60.2% | 39.1% | 60.6% | 39.4% |
| 17,983 | HARRISON | 7,731 | 4,855 | 2,807 | 69 | 2,048 R | 62.8% | 36.3% | 63.4% | 36.6% |
| 17,445 | HART | 6,784 | 4,269 | 2,470 | 45 | 1,799 R | 62.9% | 36.4% | 63.3% | 36.7% |
| 44,829 | HENDERSON | 18,701 | 10,467 | 8,101 | 133 | 2,366 R | 56.0% | 43.3% | 56.4% | 43.6% |
| 15,060 | HENRY | 6,499 | 4,094 | 2,366 | 39 | 1,728 R | 63.0% | 36.4% | 63.4% | 36.6% |
| 5,262 | HICKMAN | 2,342 | 1,395 | 926 | 21 | 469 R | 59.6% | 39.5% | 60.1% | 39.9% |
| 46,519 | HOPKINS | 18,843 | 12,314 | 6,420 | 109 | 5,894 R | 65.4% | 34.1% | 65.7% | 34.3% |
| 13,495 | JACKSON | 5,178 | 4,369 | 769 | 40 | 3,600 R | 84.4% | 14.9% | 85.0% | 15.0% |
| 693,604 | JEFFERSON | 337,351 | 164,566 | 170,158 | 2,627 | 5,592 D | 48.8% | 50.4% | 49.2% | 50.8% |
| 39,041 | JESSAMINE | 18,580 | 12,972 | 5,476 | 132 | 7,496 R | 69.8% | 29.5% | 70.3% | 29.7% |
| 23,445 | JOHNSON | 9,304 | 5,940 | 3,288 | 76 | 2,652 R | 63.8% | 35.3% | 64.4% | 35.6% |
| 151,464 | KENTON | 67,124 | 43,664 | 22,834 | 626 | 20,830 R | 65.0% | 34.0% | 65.7% | 34.3% |
| 17,649 | KNOTT | 7,394 | 2,648 | 4,685 | 61 | 2,037 D | 35.8% | 63.4% | 36.1% | 63.9% |

# KENTUCKY

## PRESIDENT 2004

| 2000 Census Population | County | Total Vote | Republican | Democratic | Other | Rep.-Dem. Plurality | Percentage Total Vote Rep. | Dem. | Major Vote Rep. | Dem. |
|---|---|---|---|---|---|---|---|---|---|---|
| 31,795 | KNOX | 12,028 | 8,108 | 3,822 | 98 | 4,286 R | 67.4% | 31.8% | 68.0% | 32.0% |
| 13,373 | LARUE | 5,968 | 4,111 | 1,823 | 34 | 2,288 R | 68.9% | 30.5% | 69.3% | 30.7% |
| 52,715 | LAUREL | 22,264 | 16,819 | 5,297 | 148 | 11,522 R | 75.5% | 23.8% | 76.0% | 24.0% |
| 15,569 | LAWRENCE | 6,513 | 3,755 | 2,705 | 53 | 1,050 R | 57.7% | 41.5% | 58.1% | 41.9% |
| 7,916 | LEE | 2,920 | 2,018 | 878 | 24 | 1,140 R | 69.1% | 30.1% | 69.7% | 30.3% |
| 12,401 | LESLIE | 4,964 | 3,661 | 1,266 | 37 | 2,395 R | 73.8% | 25.5% | 74.3% | 25.7% |
| 25,277 | LETCHER | 9,065 | 4,801 | 4,192 | 72 | 609 R | 53.0% | 46.2% | 53.4% | 46.6% |
| 14,092 | LEWIS | 5,484 | 3,778 | 1,667 | 39 | 2,111 R | 68.9% | 30.4% | 69.4% | 30.6% |
| 23,361 | LINCOLN | 8,863 | 5,996 | 2,796 | 71 | 3,200 R | 67.7% | 31.5% | 68.2% | 31.8% |
| 9,804 | LIVINGSTON | 4,706 | 2,675 | 2,007 | 24 | 668 R | 56.8% | 42.6% | 57.1% | 42.9% |
| 26,573 | LOGAN | 10,644 | 6,815 | 3,768 | 61 | 3,047 R | 64.0% | 35.4% | 64.4% | 35.6% |
| 8,080 | LYON | 3,925 | 2,132 | 1,769 | 24 | 363 R | 54.3% | 45.1% | 54.7% | 45.3% |
| 65,514 | MCCRACKEN | 29,797 | 18,218 | 11,361 | 218 | 6,857 R | 61.1% | 38.1% | 61.6% | 38.4% |
| 17,080 | MCCREARY | 5,693 | 4,121 | 1,530 | 42 | 2,591 R | 72.4% | 26.9% | 72.9% | 27.1% |
| 9,938 | MCLEAN | 4,435 | 2,584 | 1,823 | 28 | 761 R | 58.3% | 41.1% | 58.6% | 41.4% |
| 70,872 | MADISON | 30,707 | 18,922 | 11,525 | 260 | 7,397 R | 61.6% | 37.5% | 62.1% | 37.9% |
| 13,332 | MAGOFFIN | 5,718 | 2,836 | 2,843 | 39 | 7 D | 49.6% | 49.7% | 49.9% | 50.1% |
| 18,212 | MARION | 7,354 | 3,905 | 3,399 | 50 | 506 R | 53.1% | 46.2% | 53.5% | 46.5% |
| 30,125 | MARSHALL | 15,521 | 9,049 | 6,383 | 89 | 2,666 R | 58.3% | 41.1% | 58.6% | 41.4% |
| 12,578 | MARTIN | 4,539 | 2,996 | 1,504 | 39 | 1,492 R | 66.0% | 33.1% | 66.6% | 33.4% |
| 16,800 | MASON | 7,079 | 4,381 | 2,644 | 54 | 1,737 R | 61.9% | 37.3% | 62.4% | 37.6% |
| 26,349 | MEADE | 10,951 | 7,152 | 3,724 | 75 | 3,428 R | 65.3% | 34.0% | 65.8% | 34.2% |
| 6,556 | MENIFEE | 2,528 | 1,215 | 1,284 | 29 | 69 D | 48.1% | 50.8% | 48.6% | 51.4% |
| 20,817 | MERCER | 10,028 | 6,745 | 3,224 | 59 | 3,521 R | 67.3% | 32.1% | 67.7% | 32.3% |
| 10,037 | METCALFE | 4,157 | 2,645 | 1,472 | 40 | 1,173 R | 63.6% | 35.4% | 64.2% | 35.8% |
| 11,756 | MONROE | 5,843 | 4,657 | 1,158 | 28 | 3,499 R | 79.7% | 19.8% | 80.1% | 19.9% |
| 22,554 | MONTGOMERY | 10,230 | 5,647 | 4,506 | 77 | 1,141 R | 55.2% | 44.0% | 55.6% | 44.4% |
| 13,948 | MORGAN | 5,272 | 2,682 | 2,532 | 58 | 150 R | 50.9% | 48.0% | 51.4% | 48.6% |
| 31,839 | MUHLENBERG | 13,479 | 6,749 | 6,636 | 94 | 113 R | 50.1% | 49.2% | 50.4% | 49.6% |
| 37,477 | NELSON | 16,844 | 10,161 | 6,524 | 159 | 3,637 R | 60.3% | 38.7% | 60.9% | 39.1% |
| 6,813 | NICHOLAS | 3,059 | 1,700 | 1,332 | 27 | 368 R | 55.6% | 43.5% | 56.1% | 43.9% |
| 22,916 | OHIO | 10,028 | 6,311 | 3,627 | 90 | 2,684 R | 62.9% | 36.2% | 63.5% | 36.5% |
| 46,178 | OLDHAM | 27,132 | 18,801 | 8,080 | 251 | 10,721 R | 69.3% | 29.8% | 69.9% | 30.1% |
| 10,547 | OWEN | 4,741 | 3,084 | 1,615 | 42 | 1,469 R | 65.0% | 34.1% | 65.6% | 34.4% |
| 4,858 | OWSLEY | 1,999 | 1,558 | 430 | 11 | 1,128 R | 77.9% | 21.5% | 78.4% | 21.6% |
| 14,390 | PENDLETON | 6,025 | 4,045 | 1,940 | 40 | 2,105 R | 67.1% | 32.2% | 67.6% | 32.4% |
| 29,390 | PERRY | 11,655 | 6,187 | 5,400 | 68 | 787 R | 53.1% | 46.3% | 53.4% | 46.6% |
| 68,736 | PIKE | 26,770 | 12,611 | 14,002 | 157 | 1,391 D | 47.1% | 52.3% | 47.4% | 52.6% |
| 13,237 | POWELL | 4,960 | 2,687 | 2,249 | 24 | 438 R | 54.2% | 45.3% | 54.4% | 45.6% |
| 56,217 | PULASKI | 25,516 | 19,535 | 5,829 | 152 | 13,706 R | 76.6% | 22.8% | 77.0% | 23.0% |
| 2,266 | ROBERTSON | 1,090 | 670 | 413 | 7 | 257 R | 61.5% | 37.9% | 61.9% | 38.1% |
| 16,582 | ROCKCASTLE | 6,166 | 4,804 | 1,320 | 42 | 3,484 R | 77.9% | 21.4% | 78.4% | 21.6% |
| 22,094 | ROWAN | 8,706 | 4,063 | 4,556 | 87 | 493 D | 46.7% | 52.3% | 47.1% | 52.9% |
| 16,315 | RUSSELL | 7,821 | 6,009 | 1,772 | 40 | 4,237 R | 76.8% | 22.7% | 77.2% | 22.8% |
| 33,061 | SCOTT | 17,051 | 10,600 | 6,325 | 126 | 4,275 R | 62.2% | 37.1% | 62.6% | 37.4% |
| 33,337 | SHELBY | 16,314 | 10,909 | 5,277 | 128 | 5,632 R | 66.9% | 32.3% | 67.4% | 32.6% |
| 16,405 | SIMPSON | 7,043 | 4,273 | 2,730 | 40 | 1,543 R | 60.7% | 38.8% | 61.0% | 39.0% |
| 11,766 | SPENCER | 6,822 | 4,816 | 1,970 | 36 | 2,846 R | 70.6% | 28.9% | 71.0% | 29.0% |
| 22,927 | TAYLOR | 10,295 | 7,247 | 2,979 | 69 | 4,268 R | 70.4% | 28.9% | 70.9% | 29.1% |
| 11,971 | TODD | 4,754 | 3,242 | 1,491 | 21 | 1,751 R | 68.2% | 31.4% | 68.5% | 31.5% |
| 12,597 | TRIGG | 6,111 | 4,023 | 2,046 | 42 | 1,977 R | 65.8% | 33.5% | 66.3% | 33.7% |
| 8,125 | TRIMBLE | 3,790 | 2,332 | 1,428 | 30 | 904 R | 61.5% | 37.7% | 62.0% | 38.0% |
| 15,637 | UNION | 5,977 | 3,534 | 2,398 | 45 | 1,136 R | 59.1% | 40.1% | 59.6% | 40.4% |
| 92,522 | WARREN | 39,712 | 25,100 | 14,326 | 286 | 10,774 R | 63.2% | 36.1% | 63.7% | 36.3% |
| 10,916 | WASHINGTON | 5,236 | 3,479 | 1,724 | 33 | 1,755 R | 66.4% | 32.9% | 66.9% | 33.1% |
| 19,923 | WAYNE | 7,685 | 5,027 | 2,616 | 42 | 2,411 R | 65.4% | 34.0% | 65.8% | 34.2% |
| 14,120 | WEBSTER | 5,547 | 3,207 | 2,304 | 36 | 903 R | 57.8% | 41.5% | 58.2% | 41.8% |
| 35,865 | WHITLEY | 13,629 | 9,559 | 3,985 | 85 | 5,574 R | 70.1% | 29.2% | 70.6% | 29.4% |
| 7,065 | WOLFE | 3,155 | 1,385 | 1,744 | 26 | 359 D | 43.9% | 55.3% | 44.3% | 55.7% |
| 23,208 | WOODFORD | 11,502 | 6,937 | 4,480 | 85 | 2,457 R | 60.3% | 38.9% | 60.8% | 39.2% |
| 4,041,769 | TOTAL | 1,795,882 | 1,069,439 | 712,733 | 13,710 | 356,706 R | 59.5% | 39.7% | 60.0% | 40.0% |

# KENTUCKY

## PRESIDENT 2000

| 2000 Census Population | County | Total Vote | Republican | Democratic | Green (Nader) | Other | Rep.-Dem. Plurality | Percentage of Total Vote | | |
|---|---|---|---|---|---|---|---|---|---|---|
| | | | | | | | | Rep. | Dem. | Green |
| 17,244 | ADAIR | 7,328 | 5,460 | 1,779 | 48 | 41 | 3,681 R | 74.5% | 24.3% | 0.7% |
| 17,800 | ALLEN | 6,429 | 4,415 | 1,950 | 31 | 33 | 2,465 R | 68.7% | 30.3% | 0.5% |
| 19,111 | ANDERSON | 7,967 | 4,909 | 2,902 | 120 | 36 | 2,007 R | 61.6% | 36.4% | 1.5% |
| 8,286 | BALLARD | 3,770 | 1,824 | 1,880 | 23 | 43 | 56 D | 48.4% | 49.9% | 0.6% |
| 38,033 | BARREN | 13,844 | 8,741 | 4,930 | 108 | 65 | 3,811 R | 63.1% | 35.6% | 0.8% |
| 11,085 | BATH | 4,473 | 2,303 | 2,087 | 49 | 34 | 216 R | 51.5% | 46.7% | 1.1% |
| 30,060 | BELL | 10,611 | 5,585 | 4,787 | 102 | 137 | 798 R | 52.6% | 45.1% | 1.0% |
| 85,991 | BOONE | 31,984 | 22,016 | 9,248 | 485 | 235 | 12,768 R | 68.8% | 28.9% | 1.5% |
| 19,360 | BOURBON | 7,102 | 3,881 | 3,048 | 126 | 47 | 833 R | 54.6% | 42.9% | 1.8% |
| 49,752 | BOYD | 19,182 | 9,247 | 9,541 | 274 | 120 | 294 D | 48.2% | 49.7% | 1.4% |
| 27,697 | BOYLE | 10,326 | 6,126 | 3,963 | 177 | 60 | 2,163 R | 59.3% | 38.4% | 1.7% |
| 8,279 | BRACKEN | 3,019 | 2,065 | 888 | 37 | 29 | 1,177 R | 68.4% | 29.4% | 1.2% |
| 16,100 | BREATHITT | 5,073 | 2,084 | 2,902 | 57 | 30 | 818 D | 41.1% | 57.2% | 1.1% |
| 18,648 | BRECKINRIDGE | 7,453 | 4,763 | 2,595 | 48 | 47 | 2,168 R | 63.9% | 34.8% | 0.6% |
| 61,236 | BULLITT | 22,701 | 14,054 | 8,195 | 270 | 182 | 5,859 R | 61.9% | 36.1% | 1.2% |
| 13,010 | BUTLER | 5,010 | 3,654 | 1,299 | 27 | 30 | 2,355 R | 72.9% | 25.9% | 0.5% |
| 13,060 | CALDWELL | 5,482 | 3,161 | 2,223 | 54 | 44 | 938 R | 57.7% | 40.6% | 1.0% |
| 34,177 | CALLOWAY | 13,673 | 7,705 | 5,635 | 236 | 97 | 2,070 R | 56.4% | 41.2% | 1.7% |
| 88,616 | CAMPBELL | 33,829 | 20,789 | 12,040 | 720 | 280 | 8,749 R | 61.5% | 35.6% | 2.1% |
| 5,351 | CARLISLE | 2,593 | 1,405 | 1,149 | 14 | 25 | 256 R | 54.2% | 44.3% | 0.5% |
| 10,155 | CARROLL | 3,499 | 1,818 | 1,601 | 57 | 23 | 217 R | 52.0% | 45.8% | 1.6% |
| 26,889 | CARTER | 8,959 | 4,617 | 4,182 | 97 | 63 | 435 R | 51.5% | 46.7% | 1.1% |
| 15,447 | CASEY | 5,469 | 4,284 | 1,122 | 36 | 27 | 3,162 R | 78.3% | 20.5% | 0.7% |
| 72,265 | CHRISTIAN | 17,773 | 10,787 | 6,778 | 137 | 71 | 4,009 R | 60.7% | 38.1% | 0.8% |
| 33,144 | CLARK | 12,473 | 7,297 | 4,918 | 191 | 67 | 2,379 R | 58.5% | 39.4% | 1.5% |
| 24,556 | CLAY | 6,719 | 4,926 | 1,723 | 28 | 42 | 3,203 R | 73.3% | 25.6% | 0.4% |
| 9,634 | CLINTON | 4,305 | 3,224 | 1,032 | 24 | 25 | 2,192 R | 74.9% | 24.0% | 0.6% |
| 9,384 | CRITTENDEN | 4,154 | 2,469 | 1,610 | 41 | 34 | 859 R | 59.4% | 38.8% | 1.0% |
| 7,147 | CUMBERLAND | 3,006 | 2,220 | 736 | 22 | 28 | 1,484 R | 73.9% | 24.5% | 0.7% |
| 91,545 | DAVIESS | 36,240 | 21,361 | 14,126 | 506 | 247 | 7,235 R | 58.9% | 39.0% | 1.4% |
| 11,644 | EDMONSON | 4,995 | 3,250 | 1,710 | 17 | 18 | 1,540 R | 65.1% | 34.2% | 0.3% |
| 6,748 | ELLIOTT | 2,381 | 827 | 1,525 | 19 | 10 | 698 D | 34.7% | 64.0% | 0.8% |
| 15,307 | ESTILL | 4,710 | 3,033 | 1,591 | 51 | 35 | 1,442 R | 64.4% | 33.8% | 1.1% |
| 260,512 | FAYETTE | 105,477 | 54,495 | 47,277 | 3,052 | 653 | 7,218 R | 51.7% | 44.8% | 2.9% |
| 13,792 | FLEMING | 5,179 | 3,282 | 1,813 | 43 | 41 | 1,469 R | 63.4% | 35.0% | 0.8% |
| 42,441 | FLOYD | 15,394 | 5,068 | 10,088 | 129 | 109 | 5,020 D | 32.9% | 65.5% | 0.8% |
| 47,687 | FRANKLIN | 21,654 | 10,209 | 10,853 | 449 | 143 | 644 D | 47.1% | 50.1% | 2.1% |
| 7,752 | FULTON | 2,788 | 1,293 | 1,452 | 20 | 23 | 159 D | 46.4% | 52.1% | 0.7% |
| 7,870 | GALLATIN | 2,459 | 1,345 | 1,049 | 38 | 27 | 296 R | 54.7% | 42.7% | 1.5% |
| 14,792 | GARRARD | 5,823 | 4,043 | 1,713 | 43 | 24 | 2,330 R | 69.4% | 29.4% | 0.7% |
| 22,384 | GRANT | 7,103 | 4,405 | 2,568 | 90 | 40 | 1,837 R | 62.0% | 36.2% | 1.3% |
| 37,028 | GRAVES | 14,235 | 7,849 | 6,097 | 131 | 158 | 1,752 R | 55.1% | 42.8% | 0.9% |
| 24,053 | GRAYSON | 8,554 | 5,843 | 2,604 | 58 | 49 | 3,239 R | 68.3% | 30.4% | 0.7% |
| 11,518 | GREEN | 4,756 | 3,615 | 1,085 | 31 | 25 | 2,530 R | 76.0% | 22.8% | 0.7% |
| 36,891 | GREENUP | 14,663 | 7,233 | 7,164 | 178 | 88 | 69 R | 49.3% | 48.9% | 1.2% |
| 8,392 | HANCOCK | 3,610 | 2,032 | 1,508 | 49 | 21 | 524 R | 56.3% | 41.8% | 1.4% |
| 94,174 | HARDIN | 30,690 | 18,964 | 11,095 | 437 | 194 | 7,869 R | 61.8% | 36.2% | 1.4% |
| 33,202 | HARLAN | 10,535 | 4,980 | 5,365 | 110 | 80 | 385 D | 47.3% | 50.9% | 1.0% |
| 17,983 | HARRISON | 6,611 | 3,793 | 2,658 | 114 | 46 | 1,135 R | 57.4% | 40.2% | 1.7% |
| 17,445 | HART | 6,019 | 3,725 | 2,201 | 53 | 40 | 1,524 R | 61.9% | 36.6% | 0.9% |
| 44,829 | HENDERSON | 16,039 | 7,698 | 8,054 | 217 | 70 | 356 D | 48.0% | 50.2% | 1.4% |
| 15,060 | HENRY | 5,473 | 3,244 | 2,117 | 73 | 39 | 1,127 R | 59.3% | 38.7% | 1.3% |
| 5,262 | HICKMAN | 2,124 | 1,151 | 940 | 18 | 15 | 211 R | 54.2% | 44.3% | 0.8% |
| 46,519 | HOPKINS | 16,489 | 9,490 | 6,734 | 160 | 105 | 2,756 R | 57.6% | 40.8% | 1.0% |
| 13,495 | JACKSON | 4,855 | 4,079 | 701 | 45 | 30 | 3,378 R | 84.0% | 14.4% | 0.9% |
| 693,604 | JEFFERSON | 302,362 | 145,052 | 149,901 | 5,935 | 1,474 | 4,849 D | 48.0% | 49.6% | 2.0% |
| 39,041 | JESSAMINE | 15,061 | 10,074 | 4,633 | 266 | 88 | 5,441 R | 66.9% | 30.8% | 1.8% |
| 23,445 | JOHNSON | 8,180 | 4,783 | 3,251 | 85 | 61 | 1,532 R | 58.5% | 39.7% | 1.0% |
| 151,464 | KENTON | 56,249 | 35,363 | 19,100 | 1,293 | 493 | 16,263 R | 62.9% | 34.0% | 2.3% |
| 17,649 | KNOTT | 6,458 | 2,029 | 4,349 | 42 | 38 | 2,320 D | 31.4% | 67.3% | 0.7% |

# KENTUCKY

## PRESIDENT 2000

| 2000 Census Population | County | Total Vote | Republican | Democratic | Green (Nader) | Other | Rep.-Dem. Plurality | Percentage of Total Vote | | |
|---|---|---|---|---|---|---|---|---|---|---|
| | | | | | | | | Rep. | Dem. | Green |
| 31,795 | KNOX | 9,910 | 6,058 | 3,690 | 83 | 79 | 2,368 R | 61.1% | 37.2% | 0.8% |
| 13,373 | LARUE | 5,179 | 3,384 | 1,727 | 41 | 27 | 1,657 R | 65.3% | 33.3% | 0.8% |
| 52,715 | LAUREL | 18,120 | 13,029 | 4,856 | 138 | 97 | 8,173 R | 71.9% | 26.8% | 0.8% |
| 15,569 | LAWRENCE | 5,307 | 2,969 | 2,258 | 47 | 33 | 711 R | 55.9% | 42.5% | 0.9% |
| 7,916 | LEE | 2,764 | 1,893 | 836 | 17 | 18 | 1,057 R | 68.5% | 30.2% | 0.6% |
| 12,401 | LESLIE | 4,434 | 3,159 | 1,210 | 28 | 37 | 1,949 R | 71.2% | 27.3% | 0.6% |
| 25,277 | LETCHER | 8,985 | 4,092 | 4,698 | 127 | 68 | 606 D | 45.5% | 52.3% | 1.4% |
| 14,092 | LEWIS | 4,568 | 3,217 | 1,293 | 39 | 19 | 1,924 R | 70.4% | 28.3% | 0.9% |
| 23,361 | LINCOLN | 7,597 | 4,795 | 2,678 | 71 | 53 | 2,117 R | 63.1% | 35.3% | 0.9% |
| 9,804 | LIVINGSTON | 4,230 | 2,118 | 2,022 | 43 | 47 | 96 R | 50.1% | 47.8% | 1.0% |
| 26,573 | LOGAN | 9,332 | 5,344 | 3,885 | 61 | 42 | 1,459 R | 57.3% | 41.6% | 0.7% |
| 8,080 | LYON | 3,420 | 1,688 | 1,680 | 30 | 22 | 8 R | 49.4% | 49.1% | 0.9% |
| 65,514 | MCCRACKEN | 26,689 | 14,745 | 11,412 | 302 | 230 | 3,333 R | 55.2% | 42.8% | 1.1% |
| 17,080 | MCCREARY | 4,799 | 3,321 | 1,418 | 38 | 22 | 1,903 R | 69.2% | 29.5% | 0.8% |
| 9,938 | MCLEAN | 4,022 | 2,219 | 1,747 | 44 | 12 | 472 R | 55.2% | 43.4% | 1.1% |
| 70,872 | MADISON | 23,666 | 13,682 | 9,309 | 525 | 150 | 4,373 R | 57.8% | 39.3% | 2.2% |
| 13,332 | MAGOFFIN | 5,453 | 2,785 | 2,603 | 23 | 42 | 182 R | 51.1% | 47.7% | 0.4% |
| 18,212 | MARION | 6,176 | 3,259 | 2,778 | 93 | 46 | 481 R | 52.8% | 45.0% | 1.5% |
| 30,125 | MARSHALL | 13,761 | 7,294 | 6,203 | 140 | 124 | 1,091 R | 53.0% | 45.1% | 1.0% |
| 12,578 | MARTIN | 4,456 | 2,667 | 1,714 | 36 | 39 | 953 R | 59.9% | 38.5% | 0.8% |
| 16,800 | MASON | 5,873 | 3,572 | 2,178 | 88 | 35 | 1,394 R | 60.8% | 37.1% | 1.5% |
| 26,349 | MEADE | 9,071 | 5,319 | 3,596 | 104 | 52 | 1,723 R | 58.6% | 39.6% | 1.1% |
| 6,556 | MENIFEE | 2,249 | 1,170 | 1,038 | 19 | 22 | 132 R | 52.0% | 46.2% | 0.8% |
| 20,817 | MERCER | 8,632 | 5,362 | 3,092 | 129 | 49 | 2,270 R | 62.1% | 35.8% | 1.5% |
| 10,037 | METCALFE | 3,849 | 2,476 | 1,318 | 41 | 14 | 1,158 R | 64.3% | 34.2% | 1.1% |
| 11,756 | MONROE | 5,569 | 4,377 | 1,158 | 15 | 19 | 3,219 R | 78.6% | 20.8% | 0.3% |
| 22,554 | MONTGOMERY | 8,519 | 4,534 | 3,833 | 87 | 65 | 701 R | 53.2% | 45.0% | 1.0% |
| 13,948 | MORGAN | 4,240 | 2,295 | 1,875 | 44 | 26 | 420 R | 54.1% | 44.2% | 1.0% |
| 31,839 | MUHLENBERG | 11,956 | 5,518 | 6,295 | 87 | 56 | 777 D | 46.2% | 52.7% | 0.7% |
| 37,477 | NELSON | 13,488 | 7,714 | 5,481 | 212 | 81 | 2,233 R | 57.2% | 40.6% | 1.6% |
| 6,813 | NICHOLAS | 2,673 | 1,613 | 994 | 42 | 24 | 619 R | 60.3% | 37.2% | 1.6% |
| 22,916 | OHIO | 8,882 | 5,413 | 3,303 | 103 | 63 | 2,110 R | 60.9% | 37.2% | 1.2% |
| 46,178 | OLDHAM | 20,268 | 13,580 | 6,236 | 349 | 103 | 7,344 R | 67.0% | 30.8% | 1.7% |
| 10,547 | OWEN | 4,070 | 2,582 | 1,394 | 68 | 26 | 1,188 R | 63.4% | 34.3% | 1.7% |
| 4,858 | OWSLEY | 1,826 | 1,466 | 339 | 10 | 11 | 1,127 R | 80.3% | 18.6% | 0.5% |
| 14,390 | PENDLETON | 4,803 | 3,044 | 1,670 | 57 | 32 | 1,374 R | 63.4% | 34.8% | 1.2% |
| 29,390 | PERRY | 11,000 | 5,300 | 5,514 | 103 | 83 | 214 D | 48.2% | 50.1% | 0.9% |
| 68,736 | PIKE | 24,935 | 11,005 | 13,611 | 169 | 150 | 2,606 D | 44.1% | 54.6% | 0.7% |
| 13,237 | POWELL | 4,362 | 2,258 | 2,008 | 63 | 33 | 250 R | 51.8% | 46.0% | 1.4% |
| 56,217 | PULASKI | 21,541 | 15,845 | 5,415 | 178 | 103 | 10,430 R | 73.6% | 25.1% | 0.8% |
| 2,266 | ROBERTSON | 998 | 630 | 341 | 24 | 3 | 289 R | 63.1% | 34.2% | 2.4% |
| 16,582 | ROCKCASTLE | 5,247 | 3,992 | 1,174 | 45 | 36 | 2,818 R | 76.1% | 22.4% | 0.9% |
| 22,094 | ROWAN | 7,226 | 3,546 | 3,505 | 136 | 39 | 41 R | 49.1% | 48.5% | 1.9% |
| 16,315 | RUSSELL | 7,074 | 5,268 | 1,710 | 54 | 42 | 3,558 R | 74.5% | 24.2% | 0.8% |
| 33,061 | SCOTT | 13,786 | 7,952 | 5,472 | 272 | 90 | 2,480 R | 57.7% | 39.7% | 2.0% |
| 33,337 | SHELBY | 12,738 | 8,068 | 4,435 | 179 | 56 | 3,633 R | 63.3% | 34.8% | 1.4% |
| 16,405 | SIMPSON | 5,824 | 3,169 | 2,583 | 38 | 34 | 586 R | 54.4% | 44.4% | 0.7% |
| 11,766 | SPENCER | 4,772 | 3,150 | 1,554 | 35 | 33 | 1,596 R | 66.0% | 32.6% | 0.7% |
| 22,927 | TAYLOR | 9,051 | 6,151 | 2,790 | 70 | 40 | 3,361 R | 68.0% | 30.8% | 0.8% |
| 11,971 | TODD | 4,187 | 2,646 | 1,496 | 14 | 31 | 1,150 R | 63.2% | 35.7% | 0.3% |
| 12,597 | TRIGG | 5,344 | 3,130 | 2,110 | 69 | 35 | 1,020 R | 58.6% | 39.5% | 1.3% |
| 8,125 | TRIMBLE | 3,081 | 1,837 | 1,181 | 37 | 26 | 656 R | 59.6% | 38.3% | 1.2% |
| 15,637 | UNION | 5,368 | 2,749 | 2,547 | 54 | 18 | 202 R | 51.2% | 47.4% | 1.0% |
| 92,522 | WARREN | 32,975 | 20,235 | 12,180 | 407 | 153 | 8,055 R | 61.4% | 36.9% | 1.2% |
| 10,916 | WASHINGTON | 4,588 | 3,044 | 1,458 | 59 | 27 | 1,586 R | 66.3% | 31.8% | 1.3% |
| 19,923 | WAYNE | 6,474 | 4,069 | 2,312 | 45 | 48 | 1,757 R | 62.9% | 35.7% | 0.7% |
| 14,120 | WEBSTER | 5,072 | 2,599 | 2,388 | 52 | 33 | 211 R | 51.2% | 47.1% | 1.0% |
| 35,865 | WHITLEY | 11,774 | 7,502 | 4,101 | 107 | 64 | 3,401 R | 63.7% | 34.8% | 0.9% |
| 7,065 | WOLFE | 2,425 | 1,267 | 1,136 | 11 | 11 | 131 R | 52.2% | 46.8% | 0.5% |
| 23,208 | WOODFORD | 10,137 | 5,890 | 3,995 | 199 | 53 | 1,895 R | 58.1% | 39.4% | 2.0% |
| 4,041,769 | TOTAL | 1,544,187 | 872,492 | 638,898 | 23,192 | 9,605 | 233,594 R | 56.5% | 41.4% | 1.5% |

# KENTUCKY

## PRESIDENT 1996

| 1995 Census Pop. Est. | County | Total Vote | Republican | Democratic | Reform (Perot) | Other | Rep.-Dem. Plurality | Percentage of Total Vote | | |
|---|---|---|---|---|---|---|---|---|---|---|
| | | | | | | | | Rep. | Dem. | Reform |
| 16,292 | ADAIR | 6,538 | 3,876 | 1,821 | 790 | 51 | 2,055 R | 59.3% | 27.9% | 12.1% |
| 15,706 | ALLEN | 5,230 | 3,032 | 1,781 | 393 | 24 | 1,251 R | 58.0% | 34.1% | 7.5% |
| 17,152 | ANDERSON | 6,653 | 2,972 | 2,898 | 751 | 32 | 74 R | 44.7% | 43.6% | 11.3% |
| 8,232 | BALLARD | 3,742 | 1,064 | 2,255 | 411 | 12 | 1,191 D | 28.4% | 60.3% | 11.0% |
| 35,768 | BARREN | 11,844 | 5,700 | 5,044 | 1,065 | 35 | 656 R | 48.1% | 42.6% | 9.0% |
| 10,159 | BATH | 3,570 | 1,229 | 1,886 | 428 | 27 | 657 D | 34.4% | 52.8% | 12.0% |
| 30,490 | BELL | 10,008 | 3,917 | 5,058 | 940 | 93 | 1,141 D | 39.1% | 50.5% | 9.4% |
| 70,097 | BOONE | 25,607 | 15,085 | 8,379 | 1,900 | 243 | 6,706 R | 58.9% | 32.7% | 7.4% |
| 19,257 | BOURBON | 6,258 | 2,592 | 3,030 | 603 | 33 | 438 D | 41.4% | 48.4% | 9.6% |
| 50,613 | BOYD | 18,893 | 7,054 | 9,668 | 2,070 | 101 | 2,614 D | 37.3% | 51.2% | 11.0% |
| 26,699 | BOYLE | 8,782 | 4,157 | 3,877 | 709 | 39 | 280 R | 47.3% | 44.1% | 8.1% |
| 8,209 | BRACKEN | 2,720 | 1,371 | 1,055 | 271 | 23 | 316 R | 50.4% | 38.8% | 10.0% |
| 15,539 | BREATHITT | 4,578 | 1,058 | 3,106 | 397 | 17 | 2,048 D | 23.1% | 67.8% | 8.7% |
| 16,722 | BRECKINRIDGE | 6,797 | 3,151 | 2,956 | 670 | 20 | 195 R | 46.4% | 43.5% | 9.9% |
| 56,127 | BULLITT | 18,395 | 8,697 | 7,651 | 1,973 | 74 | 1,046 R | 47.3% | 41.6% | 10.7% |
| 11,634 | BUTLER | 4,149 | 2,531 | 1,260 | 348 | 10 | 1,271 R | 61.0% | 30.4% | 8.4% |
| 13,207 | CALDWELL | 5,155 | 2,067 | 2,434 | 637 | 17 | 367 D | 40.1% | 47.2% | 12.4% |
| 32,506 | CALLOWAY | 11,566 | 4,989 | 5,281 | 1,223 | 73 | 292 D | 43.1% | 45.7% | 10.6% |
| 87,111 | CAMPBELL | 31,216 | 16,640 | 11,957 | 2,312 | 307 | 4,683 R | 53.3% | 38.3% | 7.4% |
| 5,443 | CARLISLE | 2,427 | 816 | 1,355 | 245 | 11 | 539 D | 33.6% | 55.8% | 10.1% |
| 9,668 | CARROLL | 3,237 | 1,170 | 1,689 | 351 | 27 | 519 D | 36.1% | 52.2% | 10.8% |
| 26,172 | CARTER | 7,771 | 3,240 | 3,728 | 781 | 22 | 488 D | 41.7% | 48.0% | 10.1% |
| 14,508 | CASEY | 4,873 | 3,187 | 1,106 | 525 | 55 | 2,081 R | 65.4% | 22.7% | 10.8% |
| 65,666 | CHRISTIAN | 16,260 | 8,285 | 6,843 | 1,064 | 68 | 1,442 R | 51.0% | 42.1% | 6.5% |
| 30,822 | CLARK | 10,896 | 4,739 | 4,987 | 1,095 | 75 | 248 D | 43.5% | 45.8% | 10.0% |
| 22,835 | CLAY | 6,401 | 3,716 | 2,135 | 478 | 72 | 1,581 R | 58.1% | 33.4% | 7.5% |
| 9,309 | CLINTON | 3,976 | 2,521 | 1,072 | 350 | 33 | 1,449 R | 63.4% | 27.0% | 8.8% |
| 9,470 | CRITTENDEN | 3,404 | 1,509 | 1,480 | 400 | 15 | 29 R | 44.3% | 43.5% | 11.8% |
| 6,957 | CUMBERLAND | 2,662 | 1,654 | 753 | 227 | 28 | 901 R | 62.1% | 28.3% | 8.5% |
| 90,662 | DAVIESS | 34,930 | 15,844 | 15,366 | 3,344 | 376 | 478 R | 45.4% | 44.0% | 9.6% |
| 10,758 | EDMONSON | 4,519 | 2,619 | 1,595 | 298 | 7 | 1,024 R | 58.0% | 35.3% | 6.6% |
| 6,543 | ELLIOTT | 2,015 | 421 | 1,298 | 284 | 12 | 877 D | 20.9% | 64.4% | 14.1% |
| 15,646 | ESTILL | 4,450 | 2,220 | 1,724 | 479 | 27 | 496 R | 49.9% | 38.7% | 10.8% |
| 238,885 | FAYETTE | 92,664 | 42,930 | 43,632 | 5,345 | 757 | 702 D | 46.3% | 47.1% | 5.8% |
| 13,054 | FLEMING | 4,764 | 2,313 | 1,913 | 522 | 16 | 400 R | 48.6% | 40.2% | 11.0% |
| 44,100 | FLOYD | 14,384 | 3,139 | 9,655 | 1,518 | 72 | 6,516 D | 21.8% | 67.1% | 10.6% |
| 46,136 | FRANKLIN | 20,367 | 7,132 | 11,251 | 1,873 | 111 | 4,119 D | 35.0% | 55.2% | 9.2% |
| 7,317 | FULTON | 2,710 | 863 | 1,614 | 223 | 10 | 751 D | 31.8% | 59.6% | 8.2% |
| 6,175 | GALLATIN | 2,346 | 838 | 1,189 | 299 | 20 | 351 D | 35.7% | 50.7% | 12.7% |
| 12,994 | GARRARD | 4,371 | 2,540 | 1,486 | 337 | 8 | 1,054 R | 58.1% | 34.0% | 7.7% |
| 18,763 | GRANT | 5,937 | 2,697 | 2,541 | 661 | 38 | 156 R | 45.4% | 42.8% | 11.1% |
| 35,139 | GRAVES | 13,803 | 5,130 | 6,991 | 1,596 | 86 | 1,861 D | 37.2% | 50.6% | 11.6% |
| 22,744 | GRAYSON | 7,722 | 4,249 | 2,716 | 677 | 80 | 1,533 R | 55.0% | 35.2% | 8.8% |
| 10,416 | GREEN | 4,540 | 2,763 | 1,285 | 475 | 17 | 1,478 R | 60.9% | 28.3% | 10.5% |
| 36,992 | GREENUP | 13,956 | 5,370 | 6,883 | 1,627 | 76 | 1,513 D | 38.5% | 49.3% | 11.7% |
| 8,483 | HANCOCK | 3,339 | 1,356 | 1,547 | 418 | 18 | 191 D | 40.6% | 46.3% | 12.5% |
| 90,345 | HARDIN | 26,617 | 12,642 | 11,031 | 2,815 | 129 | 1,611 R | 47.5% | 41.4% | 10.6% |
| 36,237 | HARLAN | 10,127 | 3,337 | 5,874 | 884 | 32 | 2,537 D | 33.0% | 58.0% | 8.7% |
| 16,978 | HARRISON | 6,204 | 2,433 | 2,934 | 801 | 36 | 501 D | 39.2% | 47.3% | 12.9% |
| 16,209 | HART | 5,758 | 2,701 | 2,527 | 501 | 29 | 174 R | 46.9% | 43.9% | 8.7% |
| 44,431 | HENDERSON | 14,806 | 5,092 | 8,051 | 1,556 | 107 | 2,959 D | 34.4% | 54.4% | 10.5% |
| 14,208 | HENRY | 5,010 | 2,110 | 2,324 | 564 | 12 | 214 D | 42.1% | 46.4% | 11.3% |
| 5,346 | HICKMAN | 2,173 | 695 | 1,220 | 247 | 11 | 525 D | 32.0% | 56.1% | 11.4% |
| 46,640 | HOPKINS | 15,190 | 6,363 | 7,239 | 1,512 | 76 | 876 D | 41.9% | 47.7% | 10.0% |
| 12,702 | JACKSON | 4,351 | 3,045 | 960 | 299 | 47 | 2,085 R | 70.0% | 22.1% | 6.9% |
| 672,918 | JEFFERSON | 279,913 | 114,860 | 144,207 | 19,413 | 1,433 | 29,347 D | 41.0% | 51.5% | 6.9% |
| 34,218 | JESSAMINE | 12,210 | 6,686 | 4,428 | 1,040 | 56 | 2,258 R | 54.8% | 36.3% | 8.5% |
| 24,063 | JOHNSON | 7,664 | 3,262 | 3,348 | 1,010 | 44 | 86 D | 42.6% | 43.7% | 13.2% |
| 145,474 | KENTON | 52,180 | 28,579 | 19,407 | 3,680 | 514 | 9,172 R | 54.8% | 37.2% | 7.1% |
| 18,414 | KNOTT | 6,607 | 1,201 | 4,842 | 517 | 47 | 3,641 D | 18.2% | 73.3% | 7.8% |

# KENTUCKY

## PRESIDENT 1996

| 1995 Census Pop. Est. | County | Total Vote | Republican | Democratic | Reform (Perot) | Other | Rep.-Dem. Plurality | Percentage of Total Vote | | |
|---|---|---|---|---|---|---|---|---|---|---|
| | | | | | | | | Rep. | Dem. | Reform |
| 31,371 | KNOX | 9,095 | 4,502 | 3,736 | 811 | 46 | 766 R | 49.5% | 41.1% | 8.9% |
| 12,641 | LARUE | 4,658 | 2,140 | 2,040 | 469 | 9 | 100 R | 45.9% | 43.8% | 10.1% |
| 48,076 | LAUREL | 15,090 | 9,454 | 4,306 | 1,211 | 119 | 5,148 R | 62.7% | 28.5% | 8.0% |
| 15,339 | LAWRENCE | 4,503 | 1,812 | 2,195 | 481 | 15 | 383 D | 40.2% | 48.7% | 10.7% |
| 7,858 | LEE | 2,522 | 1,302 | 1,023 | 181 | 16 | 279 R | 51.6% | 40.6% | 7.2% |
| 13,616 | LESLIE | 4,090 | 2,296 | 1,466 | 304 | 24 | 830 R | 56.1% | 35.8% | 7.4% |
| 26,957 | LETCHER | 7,226 | 2,222 | 4,160 | 782 | 62 | 1,938 D | 30.8% | 57.6% | 10.8% |
| 13,365 | LEWIS | 4,370 | 2,365 | 1,415 | 561 | 29 | 950 R | 54.1% | 32.4% | 12.8% |
| 21,485 | LINCOLN | 6,111 | 3,006 | 2,550 | 526 | 29 | 456 R | 49.2% | 41.7% | 8.6% |
| 9,365 | LIVINGSTON | 3,968 | 1,258 | 2,228 | 449 | 33 | 970 D | 31.7% | 56.1% | 11.3% |
| 25,774 | LOGAN | 8,807 | 3,888 | 4,181 | 704 | 34 | 293 D | 44.1% | 47.5% | 8.0% |
| 7,752 | LYON | 2,936 | 999 | 1,641 | 284 | 12 | 642 D | 34.0% | 55.9% | 9.7% |
| 64,577 | MCCRACKEN | 25,287 | 10,221 | 12,670 | 2,268 | 128 | 2,449 D | 40.4% | 50.1% | 9.0% |
| 16,612 | MCCREARY | 4,795 | 2,527 | 1,710 | 488 | 70 | 817 R | 52.7% | 35.7% | 10.2% |
| 9,705 | MCLEAN | 3,595 | 1,368 | 1,834 | 385 | 8 | 466 D | 38.1% | 51.0% | 10.7% |
| 63,112 | MADISON | 19,102 | 9,212 | 8,142 | 1,613 | 135 | 1,070 R | 48.2% | 42.6% | 8.4% |
| 13,743 | MAGOFFIN | 4,045 | 1,434 | 2,249 | 337 | 25 | 815 D | 35.5% | 55.6% | 8.3% |
| 16,755 | MARION | 5,710 | 2,013 | 2,922 | 757 | 18 | 909 D | 35.3% | 51.2% | 13.3% |
| 29,329 | MARSHALL | 12,078 | 4,579 | 6,054 | 1,391 | 54 | 1,475 D | 37.9% | 50.1% | 11.5% |
| 12,897 | MARTIN | 3,845 | 1,612 | 1,807 | 401 | 25 | 195 D | 41.9% | 47.0% | 10.4% |
| 17,214 | MASON | 5,539 | 2,588 | 2,444 | 484 | 23 | 144 R | 46.7% | 44.1% | 8.7% |
| 27,371 | MEADE | 7,449 | 2,855 | 3,653 | 912 | 29 | 798 D | 38.3% | 49.0% | 12.2% |
| 5,387 | MENIFEE | 1,781 | 608 | 979 | 179 | 15 | 371 D | 34.1% | 55.0% | 10.1% |
| 20,045 | MERCER | 7,282 | 3,264 | 3,179 | 738 | 101 | 85 R | 44.8% | 43.7% | 10.1% |
| 9,318 | METCALFE | 3,377 | 1,651 | 1,349 | 355 | 22 | 302 R | 48.9% | 39.9% | 10.5% |
| 11,677 | MONROE | 4,851 | 3,300 | 1,114 | 415 | 22 | 2,186 R | 68.0% | 23.0% | 8.6% |
| 20,582 | MONTGOMERY | 6,796 | 2,681 | 3,372 | 705 | 38 | 691 D | 39.4% | 49.6% | 10.4% |
| 13,344 | MORGAN | 3,695 | 1,439 | 1,843 | 380 | 33 | 404 D | 38.9% | 49.9% | 10.3% |
| 31,709 | MUHLENBERG | 11,386 | 3,569 | 6,564 | 1,218 | 35 | 2,995 D | 31.3% | 57.6% | 10.7% |
| 33,422 | NELSON | 11,159 | 4,645 | 5,392 | 1,067 | 55 | 747 D | 41.6% | 48.3% | 9.6% |
| 6,999 | NICHOLAS | 2,311 | 950 | 1,092 | 265 | 4 | 142 D | 41.1% | 47.3% | 11.5% |
| 21,555 | OHIO | 8,072 | 3,475 | 3,487 | 1,076 | 34 | 12 D | 43.1% | 43.2% | 13.3% |
| 41,011 | OLDHAM | 18,301 | 10,477 | 6,202 | 1,521 | 101 | 4,275 R | 57.2% | 33.9% | 8.3% |
| 9,589 | OWEN | 3,796 | 1,709 | 1,603 | 454 | 30 | 106 R | 45.0% | 42.2% | 12.0% |
| 5,384 | OWSLEY | 1,728 | 920 | 647 | 153 | 8 | 273 R | 53.2% | 37.4% | 8.9% |
| 13,461 | PENDLETON | 4,612 | 2,177 | 1,926 | 462 | 47 | 251 R | 47.2% | 41.8% | 10.0% |
| 31,286 | PERRY | 10,323 | 3,382 | 6,015 | 894 | 32 | 2,633 D | 32.8% | 58.3% | 8.7% |
| 73,710 | PIKE | 23,495 | 7,160 | 14,126 | 2,148 | 61 | 6,966 D | 30.5% | 60.1% | 9.1% |
| 12,211 | POWELL | 4,239 | 1,526 | 2,156 | 523 | 34 | 630 D | 36.0% | 50.9% | 12.3% |
| 54,570 | PULASKI | 18,829 | 11,945 | 5,340 | 1,420 | 124 | 6,605 R | 63.4% | 28.4% | 7.5% |
| 2,226 | ROBERTSON | 850 | 368 | 360 | 117 | 5 | 8 R | 43.3% | 42.4% | 13.8% |
| 15,417 | ROCKCASTLE | 4,650 | 3,106 | 1,160 | 338 | 46 | 1,946 R | 66.8% | 24.9% | 7.3% |
| 21,541 | ROWAN | 6,304 | 2,309 | 3,215 | 724 | 56 | 906 D | 36.6% | 51.0% | 11.5% |
| 15,856 | RUSSELL | 6,456 | 4,017 | 1,582 | 837 | 20 | 2,435 R | 62.2% | 24.5% | 13.0% |
| 27,813 | SCOTT | 9,615 | 4,349 | 4,258 | 977 | 31 | 91 R | 45.2% | 44.3% | 10.2% |
| 27,696 | SHELBY | 10,761 | 5,307 | 4,629 | 780 | 45 | 678 R | 49.3% | 43.0% | 7.2% |
| 16,084 | SIMPSON | 5,358 | 2,186 | 2,749 | 401 | 22 | 563 D | 40.8% | 51.3% | 7.5% |
| 8,178 | SPENCER | 3,368 | 1,614 | 1,404 | 341 | 9 | 210 R | 47.9% | 41.7% | 10.1% |
| 22,677 | TAYLOR | 8,335 | 4,573 | 2,897 | 829 | 36 | 1,676 R | 54.9% | 34.8% | 9.9% |
| 11,182 | TODD | 4,118 | 1,912 | 1,744 | 424 | 38 | 168 R | 46.4% | 42.4% | 10.3% |
| 11,497 | TRIGG | 4,474 | 1,975 | 2,087 | 394 | 18 | 112 D | 44.1% | 46.6% | 8.8% |
| 6,912 | TRIMBLE | 2,568 | 999 | 1,245 | 308 | 16 | 246 D | 38.9% | 48.5% | 12.0% |
| 16,499 | UNION | 5,084 | 1,554 | 2,913 | 598 | 19 | 1,359 D | 30.6% | 57.3% | 11.8% |
| 84,448 | WARREN | 29,406 | 15,784 | 11,642 | 1,835 | 145 | 4,142 R | 53.7% | 39.6% | 6.2% |
| 10,704 | WASHINGTON | 4,161 | 2,116 | 1,639 | 383 | 23 | 477 R | 50.9% | 39.4% | 9.2% |
| 18,411 | WAYNE | 6,055 | 3,122 | 2,422 | 481 | 30 | 700 R | 51.6% | 40.0% | 7.9% |
| 13,469 | WEBSTER | 5,102 | 1,568 | 2,852 | 660 | 22 | 1,284 D | 30.7% | 55.9% | 12.9% |
| 35,216 | WHITLEY | 10,680 | 5,402 | 4,174 | 1,027 | 77 | 1,228 R | 50.6% | 39.1% | 9.6% |
| 7,230 | WOLFE | 2,297 | 772 | 1,297 | 202 | 26 | 525 D | 33.6% | 56.5% | 8.8% |
| 21,629 | WOODFORD | 8,977 | 4,270 | 3,910 | 746 | 51 | 360 R | 47.6% | 43.6% | 8.3% |
| 3,860,219 | TOTAL | 1,388,708 | 623,283 | 636,614 | 120,396 | 8,415 | 13,331 D | 44.9% | 45.8% | 8.7% |

# KENTUCKY

## PRESIDENT 1992

| 1990 Census Population | County | Total Vote | Republican | Democratic | Perot | Other | Plurality | Percentage Total Vote Rep. | Dem. | Perot |
|---|---|---|---|---|---|---|---|---|---|---|
| 15,360 | ADAIR | 6,424 | 3,740 | 2,044 | 617 | 23 | 1,696 R | 58.2% | 31.8% | 9.6% |
| 14,628 | ALLEN | 5,415 | 2,747 | 2,040 | 606 | 22 | 707 R | 50.7% | 37.7% | 11.2% |
| 14,571 | ANDERSON | 6,472 | 2,731 | 2,491 | 1,219 | 31 | 240 R | 42.2% | 38.5% | 18.8% |
| 7,902 | BALLARD | 3,880 | 1,108 | 2,268 | 500 | 4 | 1,160 D | 28.6% | 58.5% | 12.9% |
| 34,001 | BARREN | 12,973 | 5,467 | 5,688 | 1,778 | 40 | 221 D | 42.1% | 43.8% | 13.7% |
| 9,692 | BATH | 4,204 | 1,259 | 2,229 | 694 | 22 | 970 D | 29.9% | 53.0% | 16.5% |
| 31,506 | BELL | 11,575 | 4,501 | 5,745 | 1,193 | 136 | 1,244 D | 38.9% | 49.6% | 10.3% |
| 57,589 | BOONE | 23,575 | 12,306 | 6,514 | 4,676 | 79 | 5,792 R | 52.2% | 27.6% | 19.8% |
| 19,236 | BOURBON | 6,920 | 2,707 | 2,895 | 1,290 | 28 | 188 D | 39.1% | 41.8% | 18.6% |
| 51,150 | BOYD | 21,147 | 7,387 | 10,496 | 3,195 | 69 | 3,109 D | 34.9% | 49.6% | 15.1% |
| 25,641 | BOYLE | 9,278 | 4,019 | 3,894 | 1,335 | 30 | 125 R | 43.3% | 42.0% | 14.4% |
| 7,766 | BRACKEN | 2,932 | 1,162 | 1,259 | 500 | 11 | 97 D | 39.6% | 42.9% | 17.1% |
| 15,703 | BREATHITT | 5,336 | 1,303 | 3,496 | 515 | 22 | 2,193 D | 24.4% | 65.5% | 9.7% |
| 16,312 | BRECKINRIDGE | 7,013 | 2,941 | 3,113 | 945 | 14 | 172 D | 41.9% | 44.4% | 13.5% |
| 47,567 | BULLITT | 18,969 | 7,745 | 7,830 | 3,333 | 61 | 85 D | 40.8% | 41.3% | 17.6% |
| 11,245 | BUTLER | 4,806 | 2,729 | 1,468 | 596 | 13 | 1,261 R | 56.8% | 30.5% | 12.4% |
| 13,232 | CALDWELL | 5,651 | 1,966 | 3,000 | 670 | 15 | 1,034 D | 34.8% | 53.1% | 11.9% |
| 30,735 | CALLOWAY | 12,740 | 4,654 | 6,181 | 1,853 | 52 | 1,527 D | 36.5% | 48.5% | 14.5% |
| 83,866 | CAMPBELL | 32,840 | 16,382 | 10,673 | 5,659 | 126 | 5,709 R | 49.9% | 32.5% | 17.2% |
| 5,238 | CARLISLE | 2,545 | 844 | 1,383 | 309 | 9 | 539 D | 33.2% | 54.3% | 12.1% |
| 9,292 | CARROLL | 3,746 | 1,046 | 2,119 | 566 | 15 | 1,073 D | 27.9% | 56.6% | 15.1% |
| 24,340 | CARTER | 8,560 | 3,305 | 4,224 | 989 | 42 | 919 D | 38.6% | 49.3% | 11.6% |
| 14,211 | CASEY | 5,302 | 3,317 | 1,409 | 542 | 34 | 1,908 R | 62.6% | 26.6% | 10.2% |
| 68,941 | CHRISTIAN | 16,288 | 7,737 | 6,709 | 1,789 | 53 | 1,028 R | 47.5% | 41.2% | 11.0% |
| 29,496 | CLARK | 11,517 | 4,625 | 4,892 | 1,955 | 45 | 267 D | 40.2% | 42.5% | 17.0% |
| 21,746 | CLAY | 7,427 | 4,747 | 2,012 | 648 | 20 | 2,735 R | 63.9% | 27.1% | 8.7% |
| 9,135 | CLINTON | 4,436 | 2,830 | 1,241 | 348 | 17 | 1,589 R | 63.8% | 28.0% | 7.8% |
| 9,196 | CRITTENDEN | 3,820 | 1,576 | 1,740 | 495 | 9 | 164 D | 41.3% | 45.5% | 13.0% |
| 6,784 | CUMBERLAND | 3,061 | 1,866 | 917 | 268 | 10 | 949 R | 61.0% | 30.0% | 8.8% |
| 87,189 | DAVIESS | 36,929 | 14,936 | 16,592 | 5,112 | 289 | 1,656 D | 40.4% | 44.9% | 13.8% |
| 10,357 | EDMONSON | 4,585 | 2,486 | 1,653 | 438 | 8 | 833 R | 54.2% | 36.1% | 9.6% |
| 6,455 | ELLIOTT | 2,525 | 444 | 1,796 | 273 | 12 | 1,352 D | 17.6% | 71.1% | 10.8% |
| 14,614 | ESTILL | 5,039 | 2,453 | 1,837 | 736 | 13 | 616 R | 48.7% | 36.5% | 14.6% |
| 225,366 | FAYETTE | 95,534 | 41,908 | 38,306 | 14,215 | 1,105 | 3,602 R | 43.9% | 40.1% | 14.9% |
| 12,292 | FLEMING | 5,135 | 2,045 | 2,257 | 815 | 18 | 212 D | 39.8% | 44.0% | 15.9% |
| 43,586 | FLOYD | 18,674 | 3,540 | 13,351 | 1,723 | 60 | 9,811 D | 19.0% | 71.5% | 9.2% |
| 43,781 | FRANKLIN | 21,031 | 7,591 | 9,896 | 3,340 | 204 | 2,305 D | 36.1% | 47.1% | 15.9% |
| 8,271 | FULTON | 3,204 | 1,073 | 1,813 | 306 | 12 | 740 D | 33.5% | 56.6% | 9.6% |
| 5,393 | GALLATIN | 2,329 | 699 | 1,171 | 445 | 14 | 472 D | 30.0% | 50.3% | 19.1% |
| 11,579 | GARRARD | 4,797 | 2,359 | 1,730 | 697 | 11 | 629 R | 49.2% | 36.1% | 14.5% |
| 15,737 | GRANT | 5,395 | 2,128 | 2,097 | 1,149 | 21 | 31 R | 39.4% | 38.9% | 21.3% |
| 33,550 | GRAVES | 15,341 | 5,311 | 8,001 | 1,943 | 86 | 2,690 D | 34.6% | 52.2% | 12.7% |
| 21,050 | GRAYSON | 8,507 | 4,533 | 2,909 | 993 | 72 | 1,624 R | 53.3% | 34.2% | 11.7% |
| 10,371 | GREEN | 4,986 | 2,709 | 1,760 | 500 | 17 | 949 R | 54.3% | 35.3% | 10.0% |
| 36,742 | GREENUP | 14,414 | 4,975 | 7,214 | 2,188 | 37 | 2,239 D | 34.5% | 50.0% | 15.2% |
| 7,864 | HANCOCK | 3,605 | 1,261 | 1,714 | 551 | 79 | 453 D | 35.0% | 47.5% | 15.3% |
| 89,240 | HARDIN | 25,958 | 12,299 | 9,417 | 4,026 | 216 | 2,882 R | 47.4% | 36.3% | 15.5% |
| 36,574 | HARLAN | 12,203 | 3,970 | 6,796 | 1,391 | 46 | 2,826 D | 32.5% | 55.7% | 11.4% |
| 16,248 | HARRISON | 6,189 | 2,148 | 2,795 | 1,225 | 21 | 647 D | 34.7% | 45.2% | 19.8% |
| 14,890 | HART | 5,858 | 2,401 | 2,852 | 579 | 26 | 451 D | 41.0% | 48.7% | 9.9% |
| 43,044 | HENDERSON | 16,126 | 5,125 | 8,270 | 2,678 | 53 | 3,145 D | 31.8% | 51.3% | 16.6% |
| 12,823 | HENRY | 5,219 | 1,640 | 2,838 | 720 | 21 | 1,198 D | 31.4% | 54.4% | 13.8% |
| 5,566 | HICKMAN | 2,457 | 861 | 1,296 | 294 | 6 | 435 D | 35.0% | 52.7% | 12.0% |
| 46,126 | HOPKINS | 17,531 | 6,032 | 8,881 | 2,565 | 53 | 2,849 D | 34.4% | 50.7% | 14.6% |
| 11,955 | JACKSON | 4,533 | 3,398 | 776 | 341 | 18 | 2,622 R | 75.0% | 17.1% | 7.5% |
| 664,937 | JEFFERSON | 309,793 | 116,566 | 152,728 | 39,822 | 677 | 36,162 D | 37.6% | 49.3% | 12.9% |
| 30,508 | JESSAMINE | 12,339 | 6,474 | 3,764 | 2,059 | 42 | 2,710 R | 52.5% | 30.5% | 16.7% |
| 23,248 | JOHNSON | 8,436 | 3,614 | 3,669 | 1,118 | 35 | 55 D | 42.8% | 43.5% | 13.3% |
| 142,031 | KENTON | 53,135 | 27,261 | 16,344 | 9,336 | 194 | 10,917 R | 51.3% | 30.8% | 17.6% |
| 17,906 | KNOTT | 7,328 | 1,243 | 5,500 | 560 | 25 | 4,257 D | 17.0% | 75.1% | 7.6% |

# KENTUCKY

## PRESIDENT 1992

| 1990 Census Population | County | Total Vote | Republican | Democratic | Perot | Other | Plurality | Percentage Total Vote | | |
|---|---|---|---|---|---|---|---|---|---|---|
| | | | | | | | | Rep. | Dem. | Perot |
| 29,676 | KNOX | 9,825 | 5,011 | 3,787 | 972 | 55 | 1,224 R | 51.0% | 38.5% | 9.9% |
| 11,679 | LARUE | 4,930 | 2,154 | 2,190 | 582 | 4 | 36 D | 43.7% | 44.4% | 11.8% |
| 43,438 | LAUREL | 15,050 | 8,583 | 4,560 | 1,859 | 48 | 4,023 R | 57.0% | 30.3% | 12.4% |
| 13,998 | LAWRENCE | 5,057 | 2,084 | 2,400 | 557 | 16 | 316 D | 41.2% | 47.5% | 11.0% |
| 7,422 | LEE | 3,158 | 1,617 | 1,170 | 356 | 15 | 447 R | 51.2% | 37.0% | 11.3% |
| 13,642 | LESLIE | 4,936 | 2,879 | 1,591 | 450 | 16 | 1,288 R | 58.3% | 32.2% | 9.1% |
| 27,000 | LETCHER | 10,090 | 3,011 | 5,817 | 1,206 | 56 | 2,806 D | 29.8% | 57.7% | 12.0% |
| 13,029 | LEWIS | 4,904 | 2,493 | 1,713 | 673 | 25 | 780 R | 50.8% | 34.9% | 13.7% |
| 20,045 | LINCOLN | 5,946 | 2,624 | 2,532 | 762 | 28 | 92 R | 44.1% | 42.6% | 12.8% |
| 9,062 | LIVINGSTON | 4,312 | 1,339 | 2,386 | 578 | 9 | 1,047 D | 31.1% | 55.3% | 13.4% |
| 24,416 | LOGAN | 8,849 | 3,710 | 4,064 | 1,043 | 32 | 354 D | 41.9% | 45.9% | 11.8% |
| 6,624 | LYON | 2,703 | 820 | 1,583 | 293 | 7 | 763 D | 30.3% | 58.6% | 10.8% |
| 62,879 | MCCRACKEN | 27,153 | 10,657 | 13,341 | 3,077 | 78 | 2,684 D | 39.2% | 49.1% | 11.3% |
| 15,603 | MCCREARY | 6,210 | 3,588 | 1,934 | 624 | 64 | 1,654 R | 57.8% | 31.1% | 10.0% |
| 9,628 | MCLEAN | 4,129 | 1,355 | 2,223 | 529 | 22 | 868 D | 32.8% | 53.8% | 12.8% |
| 57,508 | MADISON | 19,841 | 8,719 | 8,005 | 3,038 | 79 | 714 R | 43.9% | 40.3% | 15.3% |
| 13,077 | MAGOFFIN | 5,711 | 1,992 | 3,261 | 440 | 18 | 1,269 D | 34.9% | 57.1% | 7.7% |
| 16,499 | MARION | 6,324 | 2,091 | 3,403 | 805 | 25 | 1,312 D | 33.1% | 53.8% | 12.7% |
| 27,205 | MARSHALL | 12,749 | 4,368 | 6,576 | 1,773 | 32 | 2,208 D | 34.3% | 51.6% | 13.9% |
| 12,526 | MARTIN | 4,095 | 1,961 | 1,715 | 393 | 26 | 246 R | 47.9% | 41.9% | 9.6% |
| 16,666 | MASON | 6,029 | 2,432 | 2,657 | 916 | 24 | 225 D | 40.3% | 44.1% | 15.2% |
| 24,170 | MEADE | 7,365 | 2,641 | 3,387 | 1,298 | 39 | 746 D | 35.9% | 46.0% | 17.6% |
| 5,092 | MENIFEE | 2,145 | 557 | 1,311 | 254 | 23 | 754 D | 26.0% | 61.1% | 11.8% |
| 19,148 | MERCER | 7,653 | 3,211 | 3,010 | 1,298 | 134 | 201 R | 42.0% | 39.3% | 17.0% |
| 8,963 | METCALFE | 3,813 | 1,683 | 1,703 | 409 | 18 | 20 D | 44.1% | 44.7% | 10.7% |
| 11,401 | MONROE | 5,803 | 3,776 | 1,515 | 480 | 32 | 2,261 R | 65.1% | 26.1% | 8.3% |
| 19,561 | MONTGOMERY | 7,611 | 2,590 | 3,686 | 1,308 | 27 | 1,096 D | 34.0% | 48.4% | 17.2% |
| 11,648 | MORGAN | 4,411 | 1,239 | 2,655 | 498 | 19 | 1,416 D | 28.1% | 60.2% | 11.3% |
| 31,318 | MUHLENBERG | 13,114 | 3,551 | 7,901 | 1,624 | 38 | 4,350 D | 27.1% | 60.2% | 12.4% |
| 29,710 | NELSON | 11,672 | 4,495 | 5,437 | 1,638 | 102 | 942 D | 38.5% | 46.6% | 14.0% |
| 6,725 | NICHOLAS | 2,789 | 894 | 1,341 | 513 | 41 | 447 D | 32.1% | 48.1% | 18.4% |
| 21,105 | OHIO | 8,865 | 3,385 | 4,022 | 1,423 | 35 | 637 D | 38.2% | 45.4% | 16.1% |
| 33,263 | OLDHAM | 16,639 | 8,263 | 5,457 | 2,855 | 64 | 2,806 R | 49.7% | 32.8% | 17.2% |
| 9,035 | OWEN | 3,569 | 1,108 | 1,830 | 613 | 18 | 722 D | 31.0% | 51.3% | 17.2% |
| 5,036 | OWSLEY | 2,342 | 1,437 | 678 | 209 | 18 | 759 R | 61.4% | 28.9% | 8.9% |
| 12,036 | PENDLETON | 4,669 | 1,810 | 1,740 | 1,086 | 33 | 70 R | 38.8% | 37.3% | 23.3% |
| 30,283 | PERRY | 12,103 | 4,128 | 6,619 | 1,308 | 48 | 2,491 D | 34.1% | 54.7% | 10.8% |
| 72,583 | PIKE | 28,082 | 8,212 | 17,358 | 2,444 | 68 | 9,146 D | 29.2% | 61.8% | 8.7% |
| 11,686 | POWELL | 5,041 | 1,809 | 2,323 | 874 | 35 | 514 D | 35.9% | 46.1% | 17.3% |
| 49,489 | PULASKI | 19,414 | 11,423 | 5,465 | 2,449 | 77 | 5,958 R | 58.8% | 28.1% | 12.6% |
| 2,124 | ROBERTSON | 945 | 329 | 439 | 170 | 7 | 110 D | 34.8% | 46.5% | 18.0% |
| 14,803 | ROCKCASTLE | 4,897 | 3,287 | 1,144 | 446 | 20 | 2,143 R | 67.1% | 23.4% | 9.1% |
| 20,353 | ROWAN | 7,274 | 2,469 | 3,558 | 1,212 | 35 | 1,089 D | 33.9% | 48.9% | 16.7% |
| 14,716 | RUSSELL | 7,285 | 4,641 | 1,950 | 673 | 21 | 2,691 R | 63.7% | 26.8% | 9.2% |
| 23,867 | SCOTT | 9,273 | 3,810 | 3,639 | 1,800 | 24 | 171 R | 41.1% | 39.2% | 19.4% |
| 24,824 | SHELBY | 10,445 | 4,550 | 4,398 | 1,451 | 46 | 152 R | 43.6% | 42.1% | 13.9% |
| 15,145 | SIMPSON | 5,840 | 2,280 | 2,834 | 708 | 18 | 554 D | 39.0% | 48.5% | 12.1% |
| 6,801 | SPENCER | 3,167 | 1,305 | 1,383 | 466 | 13 | 78 D | 41.2% | 43.7% | 14.7% |
| 21,146 | TAYLOR | 8,920 | 4,319 | 3,518 | 1,044 | 39 | 801 R | 48.4% | 39.4% | 11.7% |
| 10,940 | TODD | 4,202 | 1,691 | 1,858 | 612 | 41 | 167 D | 40.2% | 44.2% | 14.6% |
| 10,361 | TRIGG | 4,855 | 1,820 | 2,438 | 573 | 24 | 618 D | 37.5% | 50.2% | 11.8% |
| 6,090 | TRIMBLE | 2,631 | 789 | 1,413 | 413 | 16 | 624 D | 30.0% | 53.7% | 15.7% |
| 16,557 | UNION | 5,739 | 1,605 | 3,325 | 794 | 15 | 1,720 D | 28.0% | 57.9% | 13.8% |
| 76,673 | WARREN | 29,896 | 14,748 | 11,529 | 3,533 | 86 | 3,219 R | 49.3% | 38.6% | 11.8% |
| 10,441 | WASHINGTON | 4,695 | 2,098 | 2,008 | 542 | 47 | 90 R | 44.7% | 42.8% | 11.5% |
| 17,468 | WAYNE | 6,507 | 3,412 | 2,516 | 560 | 19 | 896 R | 52.4% | 38.7% | 8.6% |
| 13,955 | WEBSTER | 5,665 | 1,408 | 3,380 | 854 | 23 | 1,972 D | 24.9% | 59.7% | 15.1% |
| 33,326 | WHITLEY | 12,167 | 5,998 | 4,600 | 1,533 | 36 | 1,398 R | 49.3% | 37.8% | 12.6% |
| 6,503 | WOLFE | 2,684 | 697 | 1,674 | 297 | 16 | 977 D | 26.0% | 62.4% | 11.1% |
| 19,955 | WOODFORD | 8,725 | 3,992 | 3,161 | 1,535 | 37 | 831 R | 45.8% | 36.2% | 17.6% |
| 3,685,296 | TOTAL | 1,492,900 | 617,178 | 665,104 | 203,944 | 6,674 | 47,926 D | 41.3% | 44.6% | 13.7% |

# KENTUCKY
## PRESIDENT 1988

| 1980 Census Population | County | Total Vote | Republican | Democratic | Other | Rep.-Dem. Plurality | Percentage Total Vote Rep. | Dem. | Major Vote Rep. | Dem. |
|---|---|---|---|---|---|---|---|---|---|---|
| 15,233 | ADAIR | 6,113 | 4,346 | 1,723 | 44 | 2,623 R | 71.1% | 28.2% | 71.6% | 28.4% |
| 14,128 | ALLEN | 4,923 | 3,342 | 1,573 | 8 | 1,769 R | 67.9% | 32.0% | 68.0% | 32.0% |
| 12,567 | ANDERSON | 5,450 | 3,225 | 2,176 | 49 | 1,049 R | 59.2% | 39.9% | 59.7% | 40.3% |
| 8,798 | BALLARD | 3,629 | 1,460 | 2,162 | 7 | 702 D | 40.2% | 59.6% | 40.3% | 59.7% |
| 34,009 | BARREN | 11,506 | 6,653 | 4,799 | 54 | 1,854 R | 57.8% | 41.7% | 58.1% | 41.9% |
| 10,025 | BATH | 3,724 | 1,614 | 2,099 | 11 | 485 D | 43.3% | 56.4% | 43.5% | 56.5% |
| 34,330 | BELL | 11,193 | 5,759 | 5,182 | 252 | 577 R | 51.5% | 46.3% | 52.6% | 47.4% |
| 45,842 | BOONE | 18,157 | 12,667 | 5,382 | 108 | 7,285 R | 69.8% | 29.6% | 70.2% | 29.8% |
| 19,405 | BOURBON | 6,175 | 3,308 | 2,793 | 74 | 515 R | 53.6% | 45.2% | 54.2% | 45.8% |
| 55,513 | BOYD | 18,988 | 9,379 | 9,552 | 57 | 173 D | 49.4% | 50.3% | 49.5% | 50.5% |
| 25,066 | BOYLE | 8,354 | 4,746 | 3,575 | 33 | 1,171 R | 56.8% | 42.8% | 57.0% | 43.0% |
| 7,738 | BRACKEN | 2,824 | 1,630 | 1,176 | 18 | 454 R | 57.7% | 41.6% | 58.1% | 41.9% |
| 17,004 | BREATHITT | 5,580 | 2,149 | 3,387 | 44 | 1,238 D | 38.5% | 60.7% | 38.8% | 61.2% |
| 16,861 | BRECKINRIDGE | 6,623 | 3,841 | 2,765 | 17 | 1,076 R | 58.0% | 41.7% | 58.1% | 41.9% |
| 43,346 | BULLITT | 15,013 | 8,859 | 6,005 | 149 | 2,854 R | 59.0% | 40.0% | 59.6% | 40.4% |
| 11,064 | BUTLER | 4,539 | 3,278 | 1,245 | 16 | 2,033 R | 72.2% | 27.4% | 72.5% | 27.5% |
| 13,473 | CALDWELL | 5,577 | 2,952 | 2,564 | 61 | 388 R | 52.9% | 46.0% | 53.5% | 46.5% |
| 30,031 | CALLOWAY | 11,546 | 6,225 | 5,287 | 34 | 938 R | 53.9% | 45.8% | 54.1% | 45.9% |
| 83,317 | CAMPBELL | 29,104 | 19,387 | 9,553 | 164 | 9,834 R | 66.6% | 32.8% | 67.0% | 33.0% |
| 5,487 | CARLISLE | 2,564 | 1,104 | 1,428 | 32 | 324 D | 43.1% | 55.7% | 43.6% | 56.4% |
| 9,270 | CARROLL | 3,636 | 1,702 | 1,913 | 21 | 211 D | 46.8% | 52.6% | 47.1% | 52.9% |
| 25,060 | CARTER | 8,944 | 4,325 | 4,570 | 49 | 245 D | 48.4% | 51.1% | 48.6% | 51.4% |
| 14,818 | CASEY | 5,117 | 3,857 | 1,216 | 44 | 2,641 R | 75.4% | 23.8% | 76.0% | 24.0% |
| 66,878 | CHRISTIAN | 15,008 | 9,250 | 5,704 | 54 | 3,546 R | 61.6% | 38.0% | 61.9% | 38.1% |
| 28,322 | CLARK | 9,622 | 5,329 | 4,252 | 41 | 1,077 R | 55.4% | 44.2% | 55.6% | 44.4% |
| 22,752 | CLAY | 5,884 | 4,156 | 1,709 | 19 | 2,447 R | 70.6% | 29.0% | 70.9% | 29.1% |
| 9,321 | CLINTON | 4,175 | 3,248 | 899 | 28 | 2,349 R | 77.8% | 21.5% | 78.3% | 21.7% |
| 9,207 | CRITTENDEN | 3,666 | 2,211 | 1,443 | 12 | 768 R | 60.3% | 39.4% | 60.5% | 39.5% |
| 7,289 | CUMBERLAND | 2,995 | 2,231 | 753 | 11 | 1,478 R | 74.5% | 25.1% | 74.8% | 25.2% |
| 85,949 | DAVIESS | 32,445 | 17,356 | 14,815 | 274 | 2,541 R | 53.5% | 45.7% | 53.9% | 46.1% |
| 9,962 | EDMONSON | 3,828 | 2,555 | 1,243 | 30 | 1,312 R | 66.7% | 32.5% | 67.3% | 32.7% |
| 6,908 | ELLIOTT | 2,357 | 550 | 1,797 | 10 | 1,247 D | 23.3% | 76.2% | 23.4% | 76.6% |
| 14,495 | ESTILL | 4,794 | 3,077 | 1,692 | 25 | 1,385 R | 64.2% | 35.3% | 64.5% | 35.5% |
| 204,165 | FAYETTE | 81,525 | 48,065 | 32,554 | 906 | 15,511 R | 59.0% | 39.9% | 59.6% | 40.4% |
| 12,323 | FLEMING | 4,522 | 2,409 | 2,086 | 27 | 323 R | 53.3% | 46.1% | 53.6% | 46.4% |
| 48,764 | FLOYD | 17,764 | 5,296 | 12,327 | 141 | 7,031 D | 29.8% | 69.4% | 30.1% | 69.9% |
| 41,830 | FRANKLIN | 19,271 | 9,805 | 9,271 | 195 | 534 R | 50.9% | 48.1% | 51.4% | 48.6% |
| 8,971 | FULTON | 3,016 | 1,474 | 1,531 | 11 | 57 D | 48.9% | 50.8% | 49.1% | 50.9% |
| 4,842 | GALLATIN | 1,952 | 881 | 1,060 | 11 | 179 D | 45.1% | 54.3% | 45.4% | 54.6% |
| 10,853 | GARRARD | 4,455 | 2,681 | 1,710 | 64 | 971 R | 60.2% | 38.4% | 61.1% | 38.9% |
| 13,308 | GRANT | 4,801 | 2,835 | 1,896 | 70 | 939 R | 59.1% | 39.5% | 59.9% | 40.1% |
| 34,049 | GRAVES | 13,545 | 6,274 | 7,153 | 118 | 879 D | 46.3% | 52.8% | 46.7% | 53.3% |
| 20,854 | GRAYSON | 7,842 | 5,186 | 2,575 | 81 | 2,611 R | 66.1% | 32.8% | 66.8% | 33.2% |
| 11,043 | GREEN | 4,751 | 3,139 | 1,595 | 17 | 1,544 R | 66.1% | 33.6% | 66.3% | 33.7% |
| 39,132 | GREENUP | 13,558 | 6,559 | 6,956 | 43 | 397 D | 48.4% | 51.3% | 48.5% | 51.5% |
| 7,742 | HANCOCK | 3,243 | 1,733 | 1,478 | 32 | 255 R | 53.4% | 45.6% | 54.0% | 46.0% |
| 88,917 | HARDIN | 20,599 | 13,240 | 7,262 | 97 | 5,978 R | 64.3% | 35.3% | 64.6% | 35.4% |
| 41,889 | HARLAN | 12,576 | 5,166 | 7,341 | 69 | 2,175 D | 41.1% | 58.4% | 41.3% | 58.7% |
| 15,166 | HARRISON | 5,753 | 2,983 | 2,748 | 22 | 235 R | 51.9% | 47.8% | 52.1% | 47.9% |
| 15,402 | HART | 5,468 | 2,927 | 2,519 | 22 | 408 R | 53.5% | 46.1% | 53.7% | 46.3% |
| 40,849 | HENDERSON | 14,620 | 6,911 | 7,648 | 61 | 737 D | 47.3% | 52.3% | 47.5% | 52.5% |
| 12,740 | HENRY | 4,866 | 2,286 | 2,544 | 36 | 258 D | 47.0% | 52.3% | 47.3% | 52.7% |
| 6,065 | HICKMAN | 2,315 | 1,142 | 1,158 | 15 | 16 D | 49.3% | 50.0% | 49.7% | 50.3% |
| 46,174 | HOPKINS | 15,505 | 7,979 | 7,453 | 73 | 526 R | 51.5% | 48.1% | 51.7% | 48.3% |
| 11,996 | JACKSON | 4,610 | 3,926 | 678 | 6 | 3,248 R | 85.2% | 14.7% | 85.3% | 14.7% |
| 685,004 | JEFFERSON | 268,629 | 139,711 | 127,936 | 982 | 11,775 R | 52.0% | 47.6% | 52.2% | 47.8% |
| 26,146 | JESSAMINE | 10,116 | 7,057 | 2,955 | 104 | 4,102 R | 69.8% | 29.2% | 70.5% | 29.5% |
| 24,432 | JOHNSON | 8,211 | 4,619 | 3,538 | 54 | 1,081 R | 56.3% | 43.1% | 56.6% | 43.4% |
| 137,058 | KENTON | 45,793 | 30,738 | 14,838 | 217 | 15,900 R | 67.1% | 32.4% | 67.4% | 32.6% |
| 17,940 | KNOTT | 6,926 | 1,691 | 5,185 | 50 | 3,494 D | 24.4% | 74.9% | 24.6% | 75.4% |

# KENTUCKY

## PRESIDENT 1988

| 1980 Census Population | County | Total Vote | Republican | Democratic | Other | Rep.-Dem. Plurality | Percentage Total Vote Rep. | Dem. | Major Vote Rep. | Dem. |
|---|---|---|---|---|---|---|---|---|---|---|
| 30,239 | KNOX | 7,882 | 4,903 | 2,919 | 60 | 1,984 R | 62.2% | 37.0% | 62.7% | 37.3% |
| 11,922 | LARUE | 4,423 | 2,590 | 1,822 | 11 | 768 R | 58.6% | 41.2% | 58.7% | 41.3% |
| 38,982 | LAUREL | 12,994 | 9,296 | 3,620 | 78 | 5,676 R | 71.5% | 27.9% | 72.0% | 28.0% |
| 14,121 | LAWRENCE | 4,508 | 2,294 | 2,198 | 16 | 96 R | 50.9% | 48.8% | 51.1% | 48.9% |
| 7,754 | LEE | 2,590 | 1,588 | 984 | 18 | 604 R | 61.3% | 38.0% | 61.7% | 38.3% |
| 14,882 | LESLIE | 4,409 | 3,280 | 1,105 | 24 | 2,175 R | 74.4% | 25.1% | 74.8% | 25.2% |
| 30,687 | LETCHER | 8,344 | 3,601 | 4,697 | 46 | 1,096 D | 43.2% | 56.3% | 43.4% | 56.6% |
| 14,545 | LEWIS | 4,696 | 3,108 | 1,568 | 20 | 1,540 R | 66.2% | 33.4% | 66.5% | 33.5% |
| 19,053 | LINCOLN | 6,232 | 3,530 | 2,677 | 25 | 853 R | 56.6% | 43.0% | 56.9% | 43.1% |
| 9,219 | LIVINGSTON | 3,909 | 1,834 | 2,052 | 23 | 218 D | 46.9% | 52.5% | 47.2% | 52.8% |
| 24,138 | LOGAN | 7,705 | 4,295 | 3,379 | 31 | 916 R | 55.7% | 43.9% | 56.0% | 44.0% |
| 6,490 | LYON | 2,422 | 1,077 | 1,337 | 8 | 260 D | 44.5% | 55.2% | 44.6% | 55.4% |
| 61,310 | MCCRACKEN | 24,643 | 12,160 | 12,208 | 275 | 48 D | 49.3% | 49.5% | 49.9% | 50.1% |
| 15,634 | MCCREARY | 5,193 | 3,477 | 1,644 | 72 | 1,833 R | 67.0% | 31.7% | 67.9% | 32.1% |
| 10,090 | MCLEAN | 4,111 | 1,829 | 2,269 | 13 | 440 D | 44.5% | 55.2% | 44.6% | 55.4% |
| 53,352 | MADISON | 16,766 | 9,958 | 6,672 | 136 | 3,286 R | 59.4% | 39.8% | 59.9% | 40.1% |
| 13,515 | MAGOFFIN | 5,080 | 2,158 | 2,895 | 27 | 737 D | 42.5% | 57.0% | 42.7% | 57.3% |
| 17,910 | MARION | 5,673 | 2,500 | 3,152 | 21 | 652 D | 44.1% | 55.6% | 44.2% | 55.8% |
| 25,637 | MARSHALL | 11,171 | 5,256 | 5,888 | 27 | 632 D | 47.1% | 52.7% | 47.2% | 52.8% |
| 13,925 | MARTIN | 4,196 | 2,587 | 1,581 | 28 | 1,006 R | 61.7% | 37.7% | 62.1% | 37.9% |
| 17,765 | MASON | 5,895 | 3,158 | 2,721 | 16 | 437 R | 53.6% | 46.2% | 53.7% | 46.3% |
| 22,854 | MEADE | 6,545 | 3,441 | 3,079 | 25 | 362 R | 52.6% | 47.0% | 52.8% | 47.2% |
| 5,117 | MENIFEE | 1,788 | 670 | 1,096 | 22 | 426 D | 37.5% | 61.3% | 37.9% | 62.1% |
| 19,011 | MERCER | 6,843 | 3,904 | 2,832 | 107 | 1,072 R | 57.1% | 41.4% | 58.0% | 42.0% |
| 9,484 | METCALFE | 3,915 | 2,179 | 1,705 | 31 | 474 R | 55.7% | 43.6% | 56.1% | 43.9% |
| 12,353 | MONROE | 5,266 | 4,214 | 1,025 | 27 | 3,189 R | 80.0% | 19.5% | 80.4% | 19.6% |
| 20,046 | MONTGOMERY | 6,537 | 3,435 | 3,082 | 20 | 353 R | 52.5% | 47.1% | 52.7% | 47.3% |
| 12,103 | MORGAN | 3,817 | 1,452 | 2,329 | 36 | 877 D | 38.0% | 61.0% | 38.4% | 61.6% |
| 32,238 | MUHLENBERG | 12,322 | 5,369 | 6,912 | 41 | 1,543 D | 43.6% | 56.1% | 43.7% | 56.3% |
| 27,584 | NELSON | 10,179 | 5,283 | 4,788 | 108 | 495 R | 51.9% | 47.0% | 52.5% | 47.5% |
| 7,157 | NICHOLAS | 2,559 | 1,271 | 1,242 | 46 | 29 R | 49.7% | 48.5% | 50.6% | 49.4% |
| 21,765 | OHIO | 8,545 | 4,910 | 3,612 | 23 | 1,298 R | 57.5% | 42.3% | 57.6% | 42.4% |
| 27,795 | OLDHAM | 12,792 | 8,716 | 4,025 | 51 | 4,691 R | 68.1% | 31.5% | 68.4% | 31.6% |
| 8,924 | OWEN | 3,311 | 1,468 | 1,823 | 20 | 355 D | 44.3% | 55.1% | 44.6% | 55.4% |
| 5,709 | OWSLEY | 1,613 | 1,266 | 345 | 2 | 921 R | 78.5% | 21.4% | 78.6% | 21.4% |
| 10,989 | PENDLETON | 4,091 | 2,487 | 1,576 | 28 | 911 R | 60.8% | 38.5% | 61.2% | 38.8% |
| 33,763 | PERRY | 10,772 | 5,154 | 5,557 | 61 | 403 D | 47.8% | 51.6% | 48.1% | 51.9% |
| 81,123 | PIKE | 26,416 | 9,976 | 16,339 | 101 | 6,363 D | 37.8% | 61.9% | 37.9% | 62.1% |
| 11,101 | POWELL | 4,258 | 2,128 | 2,113 | 17 | 15 R | 50.0% | 49.6% | 50.2% | 49.8% |
| 45,803 | PULASKI | 18,342 | 13,482 | 4,788 | 72 | 8,694 R | 73.5% | 26.1% | 73.8% | 26.2% |
| 2,265 | ROBERTSON | 1,035 | 511 | 515 | 9 | 4 D | 49.4% | 49.8% | 49.8% | 50.2% |
| 13,973 | ROCKCASTLE | 4,948 | 3,880 | 1,041 | 27 | 2,839 R | 78.4% | 21.0% | 78.8% | 21.2% |
| 19,049 | ROWAN | 6,077 | 3,093 | 2,968 | 16 | 125 R | 50.9% | 48.8% | 51.0% | 49.0% |
| 13,708 | RUSSELL | 5,777 | 4,292 | 1,455 | 30 | 2,837 R | 74.3% | 25.2% | 74.7% | 25.3% |
| 21,813 | SCOTT | 7,908 | 4,482 | 3,380 | 46 | 1,102 R | 56.7% | 42.7% | 57.0% | 43.0% |
| 23,328 | SHELBY | 8,871 | 4,998 | 3,834 | 39 | 1,164 R | 56.3% | 43.2% | 56.6% | 43.4% |
| 14,673 | SIMPSON | 4,859 | 2,699 | 2,138 | 22 | 561 R | 55.5% | 44.0% | 55.8% | 44.2% |
| 5,929 | SPENCER | 2,505 | 1,368 | 1,121 | 16 | 247 R | 54.6% | 44.8% | 55.0% | 45.0% |
| 21,178 | TAYLOR | 8,280 | 5,362 | 2,879 | 39 | 2,483 R | 64.8% | 34.8% | 65.1% | 34.9% |
| 11,874 | TODD | 3,958 | 2,282 | 1,632 | 44 | 650 R | 57.7% | 41.2% | 58.3% | 41.7% |
| 9,384 | TRIGG | 4,434 | 2,427 | 1,991 | 16 | 436 R | 54.7% | 44.9% | 54.9% | 45.1% |
| 6,253 | TRIMBLE | 2,440 | 1,083 | 1,342 | 15 | 259 D | 44.4% | 55.0% | 44.7% | 55.3% |
| 17,821 | UNION | 5,628 | 2,292 | 3,316 | 20 | 1,024 D | 40.7% | 58.9% | 40.9% | 59.1% |
| 71,828 | WARREN | 26,484 | 16,703 | 9,684 | 97 | 7,019 R | 63.1% | 36.6% | 63.3% | 36.7% |
| 10,764 | WASHINGTON | 4,454 | 2,445 | 1,950 | 59 | 495 R | 54.9% | 43.8% | 55.6% | 44.4% |
| 17,022 | WAYNE | 5,747 | 3,672 | 2,057 | 18 | 1,615 R | 63.9% | 35.8% | 64.1% | 35.9% |
| 14,832 | WEBSTER | 5,202 | 2,159 | 3,019 | 24 | 860 D | 41.5% | 58.0% | 41.7% | 58.3% |
| 33,396 | WHITLEY | 11,188 | 7,337 | 3,794 | 57 | 3,543 R | 65.6% | 33.9% | 65.9% | 34.1% |
| 6,698 | WOLFE | 2,480 | 916 | 1,516 | 48 | 600 D | 36.9% | 61.1% | 37.7% | 62.3% |
| 17,778 | WOODFORD | 7,204 | 4,512 | 2,653 | 39 | 1,859 R | 62.6% | 36.8% | 63.0% | 37.0% |
| 3,660,777 | TOTAL | 1,322,517 | 734,281 | 580,368 | 7,868 | 153,913 R | 55.5% | 43.9% | 55.9% | 44.1% |

# KENTUCKY

## PRESIDENT 1984

| 1980 Census Population | County | Total Vote | Republican | Democratic | Other | Rep.-Dem. Plurality | Percentage Total Vote Rep. | Dem. | Major Vote Rep. | Dem. |
|---|---|---|---|---|---|---|---|---|---|---|
| 15,233 | ADAIR | 6,344 | 4,500 | 1,812 | 32 | 2,688 R | 70.9% | 28.6% | 71.3% | 28.7% |
| 14,128 | ALLEN | 4,963 | 3,427 | 1,521 | 15 | 1,906 R | 69.1% | 30.6% | 69.3% | 30.7% |
| 12,567 | ANDERSON | 5,185 | 3,425 | 1,717 | 43 | 1,708 R | 66.1% | 33.1% | 66.6% | 33.4% |
| 8,798 | BALLARD | 3,685 | 1,663 | 2,002 | 20 | 339 D | 45.1% | 54.3% | 45.4% | 54.6% |
| 34,009 | BARREN | 12,277 | 7,717 | 4,503 | 57 | 3,214 R | 62.9% | 36.7% | 63.2% | 36.8% |
| 10,025 | BATH | 3,820 | 2,020 | 1,781 | 19 | 239 R | 52.9% | 46.6% | 53.1% | 46.9% |
| 34,330 | BELL | 12,961 | 7,249 | 5,490 | 222 | 1,759 R | 55.9% | 42.4% | 56.9% | 43.1% |
| 45,842 | BOONE | 17,649 | 12,690 | 4,853 | 106 | 7,837 R | 71.9% | 27.5% | 72.3% | 27.7% |
| 19,405 | BOURBON | 6,553 | 3,836 | 2,649 | 68 | 1,187 R | 58.5% | 40.4% | 59.2% | 40.8% |
| 55,513 | BOYD | 20,621 | 10,925 | 9,601 | 95 | 1,324 R | 53.0% | 46.6% | 53.2% | 46.8% |
| 25,066 | BOYLE | 9,076 | 5,675 | 3,378 | 23 | 2,297 R | 62.5% | 37.2% | 62.7% | 37.3% |
| 7,738 | BRACKEN | 2,976 | 1,812 | 1,136 | 28 | 676 R | 60.9% | 38.2% | 61.5% | 38.5% |
| 17,004 | BREATHITT | 6,309 | 2,855 | 3,435 | 19 | 580 D | 45.3% | 54.4% | 45.4% | 54.6% |
| 16,861 | BRECKINRIDGE | 7,132 | 4,432 | 2,669 | 31 | 1,763 R | 62.1% | 37.4% | 62.4% | 37.6% |
| 43,346 | BULLITT | 14,676 | 9,556 | 5,005 | 115 | 4,551 R | 65.1% | 34.1% | 65.6% | 34.4% |
| 11,064 | BUTLER | 4,191 | 3,121 | 1,055 | 15 | 2,066 R | 74.5% | 25.2% | 74.7% | 25.3% |
| 13,473 | CALDWELL | 5,653 | 3,162 | 2,427 | 64 | 735 R | 55.9% | 42.9% | 56.6% | 43.4% |
| 30,031 | CALLOWAY | 11,515 | 6,442 | 5,028 | 45 | 1,414 R | 55.9% | 43.7% | 56.2% | 43.8% |
| 83,317 | CAMPBELL | 30,679 | 21,473 | 9,068 | 138 | 12,405 R | 70.0% | 29.6% | 70.3% | 29.7% |
| 5,487 | CARLISLE | 2,608 | 1,308 | 1,277 | 23 | 31 R | 50.2% | 49.0% | 50.6% | 49.4% |
| 9,270 | CARROLL | 3,400 | 1,824 | 1,564 | 12 | 260 R | 53.6% | 46.0% | 53.8% | 46.2% |
| 25,060 | CARTER | 8,675 | 4,656 | 3,985 | 34 | 671 R | 53.7% | 45.9% | 53.9% | 46.1% |
| 14,818 | CASEY | 5,513 | 4,356 | 1,122 | 35 | 3,234 R | 79.0% | 20.4% | 79.5% | 20.5% |
| 66,878 | CHRISTIAN | 16,209 | 10,708 | 5,432 | 69 | 5,276 R | 66.1% | 33.5% | 66.3% | 33.7% |
| 28,322 | CLARK | 9,757 | 6,130 | 3,595 | 32 | 2,535 R | 62.8% | 36.8% | 63.0% | 37.0% |
| 22,752 | CLAY | 6,426 | 4,772 | 1,634 | 20 | 3,138 R | 74.3% | 25.4% | 74.5% | 25.5% |
| 9,321 | CLINTON | 4,322 | 3,459 | 838 | 25 | 2,621 R | 80.0% | 19.4% | 80.5% | 19.5% |
| 9,207 | CRITTENDEN | 3,663 | 2,167 | 1,483 | 13 | 684 R | 59.2% | 40.5% | 59.4% | 40.6% |
| 7,289 | CUMBERLAND | 3,509 | 2,729 | 766 | 14 | 1,963 R | 77.8% | 21.8% | 78.1% | 21.9% |
| 85,949 | DAVIESS | 33,086 | 19,495 | 13,347 | 244 | 6,148 R | 58.9% | 40.3% | 59.4% | 40.6% |
| 9,962 | EDMONSON | 4,224 | 3,001 | 1,200 | 23 | 1,801 R | 71.0% | 28.4% | 71.4% | 28.6% |
| 6,908 | ELLIOTT | 2,294 | 601 | 1,683 | 10 | 1,082 D | 26.2% | 73.4% | 26.3% | 73.7% |
| 14,495 | ESTILL | 5,122 | 3,512 | 1,593 | 17 | 1,919 R | 68.6% | 31.1% | 68.8% | 31.2% |
| 204,165 | FAYETTE | 81,746 | 51,993 | 28,961 | 792 | 23,032 R | 63.6% | 35.4% | 64.2% | 35.8% |
| 12,323 | FLEMING | 4,459 | 2,824 | 1,616 | 19 | 1,208 R | 63.3% | 36.2% | 63.6% | 36.4% |
| 48,764 | FLOYD | 15,543 | 5,218 | 10,259 | 66 | 5,041 D | 33.6% | 66.0% | 33.7% | 66.3% |
| 41,830 | FRANKLIN | 19,024 | 11,057 | 7,790 | 177 | 3,267 R | 58.1% | 40.9% | 58.7% | 41.3% |
| 8,971 | FULTON | 3,330 | 1,780 | 1,534 | 16 | 246 R | 53.5% | 46.1% | 53.7% | 46.3% |
| 4,842 | GALLATIN | 2,093 | 1,042 | 1,042 | 9 | | 49.8% | 49.8% | 50.0% | 50.0% |
| 10,853 | GARRARD | 4,885 | 3,284 | 1,566 | 35 | 1,718 R | 67.2% | 32.1% | 67.7% | 32.3% |
| 13,308 | GRANT | 4,620 | 2,840 | 1,685 | 95 | 1,155 R | 61.5% | 36.5% | 62.8% | 37.2% |
| 34,049 | GRAVES | 14,170 | 7,287 | 6,759 | 124 | 528 R | 51.4% | 47.7% | 51.9% | 48.1% |
| 20,854 | GRAYSON | 7,777 | 5,524 | 2,200 | 53 | 3,324 R | 71.0% | 28.3% | 71.5% | 28.5% |
| 11,043 | GREEN | 4,838 | 3,210 | 1,611 | 17 | 1,599 R | 66.3% | 33.3% | 66.6% | 33.4% |
| 39,132 | GREENUP | 14,462 | 7,451 | 6,923 | 88 | 528 R | 51.5% | 47.9% | 51.8% | 48.2% |
| 7,742 | HANCOCK | 3,301 | 1,967 | 1,287 | 47 | 680 R | 59.6% | 39.0% | 60.4% | 39.6% |
| 88,917 | HARDIN | 20,771 | 14,293 | 6,329 | 149 | 7,964 R | 68.8% | 30.5% | 69.3% | 30.7% |
| 41,889 | HARLAN | 14,762 | 6,959 | 7,663 | 140 | 704 D | 47.1% | 51.9% | 47.6% | 52.4% |
| 15,166 | HARRISON | 5,890 | 3,467 | 2,405 | 18 | 1,062 R | 58.9% | 40.8% | 59.0% | 41.0% |
| 15,402 | HART | 5,372 | 3,065 | 2,278 | 29 | 787 R | 57.1% | 42.4% | 57.4% | 42.6% |
| 40,849 | HENDERSON | 14,242 | 7,389 | 6,795 | 58 | 594 R | 51.9% | 47.7% | 52.1% | 47.9% |
| 12,740 | HENRY | 5,110 | 2,802 | 2,279 | 29 | 523 R | 54.8% | 44.6% | 55.1% | 44.9% |
| 6,065 | HICKMAN | 2,437 | 1,380 | 1,049 | 8 | 331 R | 56.6% | 43.0% | 56.8% | 43.2% |
| 46,174 | HOPKINS | 16,166 | 9,368 | 6,743 | 55 | 2,625 R | 57.9% | 41.7% | 58.1% | 41.9% |
| 11,996 | JACKSON | 4,413 | 3,856 | 542 | 15 | 3,314 R | 87.4% | 12.3% | 87.7% | 12.3% |
| 685,004 | JEFFERSON | 290,750 | 167,640 | 122,133 | 977 | 45,507 R | 57.7% | 42.0% | 57.9% | 42.1% |
| 26,146 | JESSAMINE | 9,556 | 7,081 | 2,379 | 96 | 4,702 R | 74.1% | 24.9% | 74.9% | 25.1% |
| 24,432 | JOHNSON | 8,349 | 5,225 | 3,078 | 46 | 2,147 R | 62.6% | 36.9% | 62.9% | 37.1% |
| 137,058 | KENTON | 49,245 | 34,304 | 14,642 | 299 | 19,662 R | 69.7% | 29.7% | 70.1% | 29.9% |
| 17,940 | KNOTT | 6,248 | 1,728 | 4,487 | 33 | 2,759 D | 27.7% | 71.8% | 27.8% | 72.2% |

# KENTUCKY

## PRESIDENT 1984

| 1980 Census Population | County | Total Vote | Republican | Democratic | Other | Rep.-Dem. Plurality | | Percentage Total Vote Rep. | Dem. | Major Vote Rep. | Dem. |
|---|---|---|---|---|---|---|---|---|---|---|---|
| 30,239 | KNOX | 8,699 | 5,730 | 2,932 | 37 | 2,798 | R | 65.9% | 33.7% | 66.2% | 33.8% |
| 11,922 | LARUE | 4,400 | 2,873 | 1,514 | 13 | 1,359 | R | 65.3% | 34.4% | 65.5% | 34.5% |
| 38,982 | LAUREL | 12,929 | 9,621 | 3,267 | 41 | 6,354 | R | 74.4% | 25.3% | 74.7% | 25.3% |
| 14,121 | LAWRENCE | 4,959 | 2,713 | 2,223 | 23 | 490 | R | 54.7% | 44.8% | 55.0% | 45.0% |
| 7,754 | LEE | 2,640 | 1,862 | 768 | 10 | 1,094 | R | 70.5% | 29.1% | 70.8% | 29.2% |
| 14,882 | LESLIE | 4,475 | 3,385 | 1,075 | 15 | 2,310 | R | 75.6% | 24.0% | 75.9% | 24.1% |
| 30,687 | LETCHER | 8,830 | 4,073 | 4,707 | 50 | 634 | D | 46.1% | 53.3% | 46.4% | 53.6% |
| 14,545 | LEWIS | 4,947 | 3,445 | 1,484 | 18 | 1,961 | R | 69.6% | 30.0% | 69.9% | 30.1% |
| 19,053 | LINCOLN | 6,522 | 3,996 | 2,498 | 28 | 1,498 | R | 61.3% | 38.3% | 61.5% | 38.5% |
| 9,219 | LIVINGSTON | 3,891 | 1,866 | 2,007 | 18 | 141 | D | 48.0% | 51.6% | 48.2% | 51.8% |
| 24,138 | LOGAN | 8,310 | 4,889 | 3,347 | 74 | 1,542 | R | 58.8% | 40.3% | 59.4% | 40.6% |
| 6,490 | LYON | 2,255 | 969 | 1,272 | 14 | 303 | D | 43.0% | 56.4% | 43.2% | 56.8% |
| 61,310 | MCCRACKEN | 25,765 | 12,903 | 12,535 | 327 | 368 | R | 50.1% | 48.7% | 50.7% | 49.3% |
| 15,634 | MCCREARY | 5,707 | 4,028 | 1,609 | 70 | 2,419 | R | 70.6% | 28.2% | 71.5% | 28.5% |
| 10,090 | MCLEAN | 3,882 | 1,942 | 1,917 | 23 | 25 | R | 50.0% | 49.4% | 50.3% | 49.7% |
| 53,352 | MADISON | 17,926 | 11,309 | 6,509 | 108 | 4,800 | R | 63.1% | 36.3% | 63.5% | 36.5% |
| 13,515 | MAGOFFIN | 5,298 | 2,343 | 2,942 | 13 | 599 | D | 44.2% | 55.5% | 44.3% | 55.7% |
| 17,910 | MARION | 6,159 | 3,305 | 2,835 | 19 | 470 | R | 53.7% | 46.0% | 53.8% | 46.2% |
| 25,637 | MARSHALL | 10,917 | 5,152 | 5,725 | 40 | 573 | D | 47.2% | 52.4% | 47.4% | 52.6% |
| 13,925 | MARTIN | 4,770 | 3,248 | 1,471 | 51 | 1,777 | R | 68.1% | 30.8% | 68.8% | 31.2% |
| 17,765 | MASON | 5,446 | 2,751 | 2,663 | 32 | 88 | R | 50.5% | 48.9% | 50.8% | 49.2% |
| 22,854 | MEADE | 6,347 | 3,820 | 2,503 | 24 | 1,317 | R | 60.2% | 39.4% | 60.4% | 39.6% |
| 5,117 | MENIFEE | 1,770 | 785 | 956 | 29 | 171 | D | 44.4% | 54.0% | 45.1% | 54.9% |
| 19,011 | MERCER | 7,189 | 4,592 | 2,516 | 81 | 2,076 | R | 63.9% | 35.0% | 64.6% | 35.4% |
| 9,484 | METCALFE | 3,944 | 2,349 | 1,575 | 20 | 774 | R | 59.6% | 39.9% | 59.9% | 40.1% |
| 12,353 | MONROE | 5,753 | 4,670 | 1,052 | 31 | 3,618 | R | 81.2% | 18.3% | 81.6% | 18.4% |
| 20,046 | MONTGOMERY | 6,377 | 3,864 | 2,490 | 23 | 1,374 | R | 60.6% | 39.0% | 60.8% | 39.2% |
| 12,103 | MORGAN | 4,330 | 1,834 | 2,481 | 15 | 647 | D | 42.4% | 57.3% | 42.5% | 57.5% |
| 32,238 | MUHLENBERG | 12,277 | 6,094 | 6,157 | 26 | 63 | D | 49.6% | 50.2% | 49.7% | 50.3% |
| 27,584 | NELSON | 10,319 | 6,044 | 4,199 | 76 | 1,845 | R | 58.6% | 40.7% | 59.0% | 41.0% |
| 7,157 | NICHOLAS | 2,675 | 1,535 | 1,107 | 33 | 428 | R | 57.4% | 41.4% | 58.1% | 41.9% |
| 21,765 | OHIO | 8,417 | 5,119 | 3,253 | 45 | 1,866 | R | 60.8% | 38.6% | 61.1% | 38.9% |
| 27,795 | OLDHAM | 10,991 | 8,112 | 2,857 | 22 | 5,255 | R | 73.8% | 26.0% | 74.0% | 26.0% |
| 8,924 | OWEN | 3,408 | 1,778 | 1,612 | 18 | 166 | R | 52.2% | 47.3% | 52.4% | 47.6% |
| 5,709 | OWSLEY | 1,851 | 1,466 | 375 | 10 | 1,091 | R | 79.2% | 20.3% | 79.6% | 20.4% |
| 10,989 | PENDLETON | 4,340 | 2,767 | 1,529 | 44 | 1,238 | R | 63.8% | 35.2% | 64.4% | 35.6% |
| 33,763 | PERRY | 10,537 | 5,218 | 5,258 | 61 | 40 | D | 49.5% | 49.9% | 49.8% | 50.2% |
| 81,123 | PIKE | 27,812 | 11,869 | 15,817 | 126 | 3,948 | D | 42.7% | 56.9% | 42.9% | 57.1% |
| 11,101 | POWELL | 3,857 | 2,269 | 1,575 | 13 | 694 | R | 58.8% | 40.8% | 59.0% | 41.0% |
| 45,803 | PULASKI | 18,893 | 14,434 | 4,384 | 75 | 10,050 | R | 76.4% | 23.2% | 76.7% | 23.3% |
| 2,265 | ROBERTSON | 1,043 | 567 | 467 | 9 | 100 | R | 54.4% | 44.8% | 54.8% | 45.2% |
| 13,973 | ROCKCASTLE | 5,428 | 4,328 | 1,089 | 11 | 3,239 | R | 79.7% | 20.1% | 79.9% | 20.1% |
| 19,049 | ROWAN | 6,470 | 3,698 | 2,748 | 24 | 950 | R | 57.2% | 42.5% | 57.4% | 42.6% |
| 13,708 | RUSSELL | 5,954 | 4,476 | 1,448 | 30 | 3,028 | R | 75.2% | 24.3% | 75.6% | 24.4% |
| 21,813 | SCOTT | 7,144 | 4,461 | 2,606 | 77 | 1,855 | R | 62.4% | 36.5% | 63.1% | 36.9% |
| 23,328 | SHELBY | 8,739 | 5,390 | 3,326 | 23 | 2,064 | R | 61.7% | 38.1% | 61.8% | 38.2% |
| 14,673 | SIMPSON | 5,236 | 3,073 | 2,140 | 23 | 933 | R | 58.7% | 40.9% | 58.9% | 41.1% |
| 5,929 | SPENCER | 2,372 | 1,456 | 910 | 6 | 546 | R | 61.4% | 38.4% | 61.5% | 38.5% |
| 21,178 | TAYLOR | 9,245 | 5,932 | 3,286 | 27 | 2,646 | R | 64.2% | 35.5% | 64.4% | 35.6% |
| 11,874 | TODD | 4,280 | 2,364 | 1,505 | 411 | 859 | R | 55.2% | 35.2% | 61.1% | 38.9% |
| 9,384 | TRIGG | 4,436 | 2,512 | 1,905 | 19 | 607 | R | 56.6% | 42.9% | 56.9% | 43.1% |
| 6,253 | TRIMBLE | 2,490 | 1,389 | 1,088 | 13 | 301 | R | 55.8% | 43.7% | 56.1% | 43.9% |
| 17,821 | UNION | 5,637 | 2,524 | 3,090 | 23 | 566 | D | 44.8% | 54.8% | 45.0% | 55.0% |
| 71,828 | WARREN | 24,178 | 16,167 | 7,937 | 74 | 8,230 | R | 66.9% | 32.8% | 67.1% | 32.9% |
| 10,764 | WASHINGTON | 4,655 | 2,804 | 1,786 | 65 | 1,018 | R | 60.2% | 38.4% | 61.1% | 38.9% |
| 17,022 | WAYNE | 6,691 | 4,449 | 2,227 | 15 | 2,222 | R | 66.5% | 33.3% | 66.6% | 33.4% |
| 14,832 | WEBSTER | 5,580 | 2,504 | 3,042 | 34 | 538 | D | 44.9% | 54.5% | 45.1% | 54.9% |
| 33,396 | WHITLEY | 11,516 | 7,851 | 3,575 | 90 | 4,276 | R | 68.2% | 31.0% | 68.7% | 31.3% |
| 6,698 | WOLFE | 2,693 | 1,257 | 1,394 | 42 | 137 | D | 46.7% | 51.8% | 47.4% | 52.6% |
| 17,778 | WOODFORD | 7,112 | 4,746 | 2,290 | 76 | 2,456 | R | 66.7% | 32.2% | 67.5% | 32.5% |
| 3,660,777 | TOTAL | 1,369,345 | 821,702 | 539,539 | 8,104 | 282,163 | R | 60.0% | 39.4% | 60.4% | 39.6% |

# KENTUCKY

## PRESIDENT 1980

| 1980 Census Population | County | Total Vote | Republican | Democratic | Other | Rep.-Dem. Plurality | Percentage |||| 
|---|---|---|---|---|---|---|---|---|---|---|
| | | | | | | | Total Vote || Major Vote ||
| | | | | | | | Rep. | Dem. | Rep. | Dem. |
| 15,233 | ADAIR | 6,418 | 4,051 | 2,285 | 82 | 1,766 R | 63.1% | 35.6% | 63.9% | 36.1% |
| 14,128 | ALLEN | 5,278 | 3,186 | 2,010 | 82 | 1,176 R | 60.4% | 38.1% | 61.3% | 38.7% |
| 12,567 | ANDERSON | 4,764 | 2,052 | 2,567 | 145 | 515 D | 43.1% | 53.9% | 44.4% | 55.6% |
| 8,798 | BALLARD | 3,826 | 1,190 | 2,583 | 53 | 1,393 D | 31.1% | 67.5% | 31.5% | 68.5% |
| 34,009 | BARREN | 11,933 | 6,405 | 5,285 | 243 | 1,120 R | 53.7% | 44.3% | 54.8% | 45.2% |
| 10,025 | BATH | 3,698 | 1,463 | 2,174 | 61 | 711 D | 39.6% | 58.8% | 40.2% | 59.8% |
| 34,330 | BELL | 12,088 | 5,433 | 6,362 | 293 | 929 D | 44.9% | 52.6% | 46.1% | 53.9% |
| 45,842 | BOONE | 14,148 | 8,263 | 5,374 | 511 | 2,889 R | 58.4% | 38.0% | 60.6% | 39.4% |
| 19,405 | BOURBON | 6,346 | 2,475 | 3,641 | 230 | 1,166 D | 39.0% | 57.4% | 40.5% | 59.5% |
| 55,513 | BOYD | 21,695 | 10,367 | 10,702 | 626 | 335 D | 47.8% | 49.3% | 49.2% | 50.8% |
| 25,066 | BOYLE | 8,574 | 3,848 | 4,429 | 297 | 581 D | 44.9% | 51.7% | 46.5% | 53.5% |
| 7,738 | BRACKEN | 2,644 | 1,154 | 1,420 | 70 | 266 D | 43.6% | 53.7% | 44.8% | 55.2% |
| 17,004 | BREATHITT | 5,532 | 1,532 | 3,916 | 84 | 2,384 D | 27.7% | 70.8% | 28.1% | 71.9% |
| 16,861 | BRECKINRIDGE | 6,891 | 3,629 | 3,163 | 99 | 466 R | 52.7% | 45.9% | 53.4% | 46.6% |
| 43,346 | BULLITT | 12,576 | 6,364 | 5,884 | 328 | 480 R | 50.6% | 46.8% | 52.0% | 48.0% |
| 11,064 | BUTLER | 4,450 | 3,129 | 1,274 | 47 | 1,855 R | 70.3% | 28.6% | 71.1% | 28.9% |
| 13,473 | CALDWELL | 5,645 | 2,609 | 2,924 | 112 | 315 D | 46.2% | 51.8% | 47.2% | 52.8% |
| 30,031 | CALLOWAY | 11,964 | 4,498 | 6,809 | 657 | 2,311 D | 37.6% | 56.9% | 39.8% | 60.2% |
| 83,317 | CAMPBELL | 29,208 | 16,743 | 11,059 | 1,406 | 5,684 R | 57.3% | 37.9% | 60.2% | 39.8% |
| 5,487 | CARLISLE | 2,545 | 975 | 1,542 | 28 | 567 D | 38.3% | 60.6% | 38.7% | 61.3% |
| 9,270 | CARROLL | 3,328 | 1,076 | 2,127 | 125 | 1,051 D | 32.3% | 63.9% | 33.6% | 66.4% |
| 25,060 | CARTER | 7,839 | 3,934 | 3,782 | 123 | 152 R | 50.2% | 48.2% | 51.0% | 49.0% |
| 14,818 | CASEY | 5,632 | 4,239 | 1,298 | 95 | 2,941 R | 75.3% | 23.0% | 76.6% | 23.4% |
| 66,878 | CHRISTIAN | 15,512 | 8,209 | 7,048 | 255 | 1,161 R | 52.9% | 45.4% | 53.8% | 46.2% |
| 28,322 | CLARK | 9,685 | 4,302 | 5,071 | 312 | 769 D | 44.4% | 52.4% | 45.9% | 54.1% |
| 22,752 | CLAY | 6,778 | 4,594 | 2,121 | 63 | 2,473 R | 67.8% | 31.3% | 68.4% | 31.6% |
| 9,321 | CLINTON | 4,590 | 3,539 | 1,000 | 51 | 2,539 R | 77.1% | 21.8% | 78.0% | 22.0% |
| 9,207 | CRITTENDEN | 3,771 | 2,219 | 1,508 | 44 | 711 R | 58.8% | 40.0% | 59.5% | 40.5% |
| 7,289 | CUMBERLAND | 3,081 | 2,216 | 821 | 44 | 1,395 R | 71.9% | 26.6% | 73.0% | 27.0% |
| 85,949 | DAVIESS | 30,717 | 14,643 | 14,902 | 1,172 | 259 D | 47.7% | 48.5% | 49.6% | 50.4% |
| 9,962 | EDMONSON | 4,233 | 2,913 | 1,252 | 68 | 1,661 R | 68.8% | 29.6% | 69.9% | 30.1% |
| 6,908 | ELLIOTT | 2,241 | 551 | 1,668 | 22 | 1,117 D | 24.6% | 74.4% | 24.8% | 75.2% |
| 14,495 | ESTILL | 4,861 | 2,818 | 1,965 | 78 | 853 R | 58.0% | 40.4% | 58.9% | 41.1% |
| 204,165 | FAYETTE | 71,817 | 35,349 | 30,511 | 5,957 | 4,838 R | 49.2% | 42.5% | 53.7% | 46.3% |
| 12,323 | FLEMING | 4,315 | 2,189 | 2,051 | 75 | 138 R | 50.7% | 47.5% | 51.6% | 48.4% |
| 48,764 | FLOYD | 15,385 | 4,179 | 10,975 | 231 | 6,796 D | 27.2% | 71.3% | 27.6% | 72.4% |
| 41,830 | FRANKLIN | 18,530 | 6,455 | 11,193 | 882 | 4,738 D | 34.8% | 60.4% | 36.6% | 63.4% |
| 8,971 | FULTON | 3,547 | 1,462 | 2,016 | 69 | 554 D | 41.2% | 56.8% | 42.0% | 58.0% |
| 4,842 | GALLATIN | 1,704 | 684 | 988 | 32 | 304 D | 40.1% | 58.0% | 40.9% | 59.1% |
| 10,853 | GARRARD | 4,480 | 2,585 | 1,774 | 121 | 811 R | 57.7% | 39.6% | 59.3% | 40.7% |
| 13,308 | GRANT | 4,183 | 1,779 | 2,272 | 132 | 493 D | 42.5% | 54.3% | 43.9% | 56.1% |
| 34,049 | GRAVES | 13,816 | 6,556 | 6,999 | 261 | 443 D | 47.5% | 50.7% | 48.4% | 51.6% |
| 20,854 | GRAYSON | 8,076 | 5,084 | 2,788 | 204 | 2,296 R | 63.0% | 34.5% | 64.6% | 35.4% |
| 11,043 | GREEN | 4,587 | 2,775 | 1,758 | 54 | 1,017 R | 60.5% | 38.3% | 61.2% | 38.8% |
| 39,132 | GREENUP | 14,275 | 6,857 | 7,126 | 292 | 269 D | 48.0% | 49.9% | 49.0% | 51.0% |
| 7,742 | HANCOCK | 3,004 | 1,367 | 1,530 | 107 | 163 D | 45.5% | 50.9% | 47.2% | 52.8% |
| 88,917 | HARDIN | 18,738 | 9,779 | 8,339 | 620 | 1,440 R | 52.2% | 44.5% | 54.0% | 46.0% |
| 41,889 | HARLAN | 14,457 | 5,460 | 8,798 | 199 | 3,338 D | 37.8% | 60.9% | 38.3% | 61.7% |
| 15,166 | HARRISON | 5,645 | 2,184 | 3,319 | 142 | 1,135 D | 38.7% | 58.8% | 39.7% | 60.3% |
| 15,402 | HART | 6,204 | 3,129 | 3,005 | 70 | 124 R | 50.4% | 48.4% | 51.0% | 49.0% |
| 40,849 | HENDERSON | 13,659 | 5,074 | 8,082 | 503 | 3,008 D | 37.1% | 59.2% | 38.6% | 61.4% |
| 12,740 | HENRY | 4,810 | 1,723 | 2,999 | 88 | 1,276 D | 35.8% | 62.3% | 36.5% | 63.5% |
| 6,065 | HICKMAN | 2,668 | 1,143 | 1,456 | 69 | 313 D | 42.8% | 54.6% | 44.0% | 56.0% |
| 46,174 | HOPKINS | 15,355 | 6,238 | 8,810 | 307 | 2,572 D | 40.6% | 57.4% | 41.5% | 58.5% |
| 11,996 | JACKSON | 4,123 | 3,379 | 702 | 42 | 2,677 R | 82.0% | 17.0% | 82.8% | 17.2% |
| 685,004 | JEFFERSON | 265,286 | 127,254 | 125,844 | 12,188 | 1,410 R | 48.0% | 47.4% | 50.3% | 49.7% |
| 26,146 | JESSAMINE | 8,530 | 4,809 | 3,310 | 411 | 1,499 R | 56.4% | 38.8% | 59.2% | 40.8% |
| 24,432 | JOHNSON | 8,329 | 5,039 | 3,142 | 148 | 1,897 R | 60.5% | 37.7% | 61.6% | 38.4% |
| 137,058 | KENTON | 46,232 | 25,965 | 17,907 | 2,360 | 8,058 R | 56.2% | 38.7% | 59.2% | 40.8% |
| 17,940 | KNOTT | 7,065 | 1,602 | 5,405 | 58 | 3,803 D | 22.7% | 76.5% | 22.9% | 77.1% |

# KENTUCKY

## PRESIDENT 1980

| 1980 Census Population | County | Total Vote | Republican | Democratic | Other | Rep.-Dem. Plurality | Percentage Total Vote Rep. | Total Vote Dem. | Major Vote Rep. | Major Vote Dem. |
|---:|---|---:|---:|---:|---:|---:|---:|---:|---:|---:|
| 30,239 | KNOX | 9,240 | 5,539 | 3,543 | 158 | 1,996 R | 59.9% | 38.3% | 61.0% | 39.0% |
| 11,922 | LARUE | 4,249 | 2,000 | 2,183 | 66 | 183 D | 47.1% | 51.4% | 47.8% | 52.2% |
| 38,982 | LAUREL | 12,997 | 8,868 | 3,969 | 160 | 4,899 R | 68.2% | 30.5% | 69.1% | 30.9% |
| 14,121 | LAWRENCE | 4,980 | 2,564 | 2,362 | 54 | 202 R | 51.5% | 47.4% | 52.1% | 47.9% |
| 7,754 | LEE | 2,726 | 1,650 | 1,017 | 59 | 633 R | 60.5% | 37.3% | 61.9% | 38.1% |
| 14,882 | LESLIE | 4,921 | 3,536 | 1,327 | 58 | 2,209 R | 71.9% | 27.0% | 72.7% | 27.3% |
| 30,687 | LETCHER | 7,818 | 3,426 | 4,280 | 112 | 854 D | 43.8% | 54.7% | 44.5% | 55.5% |
| 14,545 | LEWIS | 4,393 | 2,802 | 1,543 | 48 | 1,259 R | 63.8% | 35.1% | 64.5% | 35.5% |
| 19,053 | LINCOLN | 6,105 | 3,034 | 2,991 | 80 | 43 R | 49.7% | 49.0% | 50.4% | 49.6% |
| 9,219 | LIVINGSTON | 4,008 | 1,670 | 2,287 | 51 | 617 D | 41.7% | 57.1% | 42.2% | 57.8% |
| 24,138 | LOGAN | 7,781 | 3,366 | 4,264 | 151 | 898 D | 43.3% | 54.8% | 44.1% | 55.9% |
| 6,490 | LYON | 2,527 | 968 | 1,496 | 63 | 528 D | 38.3% | 59.2% | 39.3% | 60.7% |
| 61,310 | MCCRACKEN | 24,325 | 10,281 | 13,365 | 679 | 3,084 D | 42.3% | 54.9% | 43.5% | 56.5% |
| 15,634 | MCCREARY | 5,312 | 3,786 | 1,377 | 149 | 2,409 R | 71.3% | 25.9% | 73.3% | 26.7% |
| 10,090 | MCLEAN | 3,710 | 1,497 | 2,147 | 66 | 650 D | 40.4% | 57.9% | 41.1% | 58.9% |
| 53,352 | MADISON | 17,671 | 8,437 | 8,208 | 1,026 | 229 R | 47.7% | 46.4% | 50.7% | 49.3% |
| 13,515 | MAGOFFIN | 5,297 | 2,265 | 2,986 | 46 | 721 D | 42.8% | 56.4% | 43.1% | 56.9% |
| 17,910 | MARION | 5,816 | 2,126 | 3,577 | 113 | 1,451 D | 36.6% | 61.5% | 37.3% | 62.7% |
| 25,637 | MARSHALL | 10,779 | 4,403 | 6,231 | 145 | 1,828 D | 40.8% | 57.8% | 41.4% | 58.6% |
| 13,925 | MARTIN | 4,430 | 2,793 | 1,567 | 70 | 1,226 R | 63.0% | 35.4% | 64.1% | 35.9% |
| 17,765 | MASON | 6,287 | 2,926 | 3,181 | 180 | 255 D | 46.5% | 50.6% | 47.9% | 52.1% |
| 22,854 | MEADE | 6,059 | 2,740 | 3,205 | 114 | 465 D | 45.2% | 52.9% | 46.1% | 53.9% |
| 5,117 | MENIFEE | 1,543 | 547 | 966 | 30 | 419 D | 35.5% | 62.6% | 36.2% | 63.8% |
| 19,011 | MERCER | 6,970 | 3,275 | 3,528 | 167 | 253 D | 47.0% | 50.6% | 48.1% | 51.9% |
| 9,484 | METCALFE | 3,707 | 2,013 | 1,628 | 66 | 385 R | 54.3% | 43.9% | 55.3% | 44.7% |
| 12,353 | MONROE | 5,813 | 4,592 | 1,156 | 65 | 3,436 R | 79.0% | 19.9% | 79.9% | 20.1% |
| 20,046 | MONTGOMERY | 6,418 | 2,869 | 3,391 | 158 | 522 D | 44.7% | 52.8% | 45.8% | 54.2% |
| 12,103 | MORGAN | 4,199 | 1,450 | 2,698 | 51 | 1,248 D | 34.5% | 64.3% | 35.0% | 65.0% |
| 32,238 | MUHLENBERG | 11,706 | 4,893 | 6,616 | 197 | 1,723 D | 41.8% | 56.5% | 42.5% | 57.5% |
| 27,584 | NELSON | 9,114 | 3,349 | 5,514 | 251 | 2,165 D | 36.7% | 60.5% | 37.8% | 62.2% |
| 7,157 | NICHOLAS | 2,351 | 915 | 1,349 | 87 | 434 D | 38.9% | 57.4% | 40.4% | 59.6% |
| 21,765 | OHIO | 8,921 | 5,272 | 3,486 | 163 | 1,786 R | 59.1% | 39.1% | 60.2% | 39.8% |
| 27,795 | OLDHAM | 9,510 | 5,586 | 3,487 | 437 | 2,099 R | 58.7% | 36.7% | 61.6% | 38.4% |
| 8,924 | OWEN | 3,344 | 944 | 2,323 | 77 | 1,379 D | 28.2% | 69.5% | 28.9% | 71.1% |
| 5,709 | OWSLEY | 1,699 | 1,250 | 437 | 12 | 813 R | 73.6% | 25.7% | 74.1% | 25.9% |
| 10,989 | PENDLETON | 3,866 | 1,757 | 1,992 | 117 | 235 D | 45.4% | 51.5% | 46.9% | 53.1% |
| 33,763 | PERRY | 10,367 | 4,226 | 6,031 | 110 | 1,805 D | 40.8% | 58.2% | 41.2% | 58.8% |
| 81,123 | PIKE | 25,720 | 10,550 | 14,878 | 292 | 4,328 D | 41.0% | 57.8% | 41.5% | 58.5% |
| 11,101 | POWELL | 3,767 | 1,716 | 2,006 | 45 | 290 D | 45.6% | 53.3% | 46.1% | 53.9% |
| 45,803 | PULASKI | 19,919 | 12,970 | 6,570 | 379 | 6,400 R | 65.1% | 33.0% | 66.4% | 33.6% |
| 2,265 | ROBERTSON | 999 | 416 | 562 | 21 | 146 D | 41.6% | 56.3% | 42.5% | 57.5% |
| 13,973 | ROCKCASTLE | 4,947 | 3,543 | 1,345 | 59 | 2,198 R | 71.6% | 27.2% | 72.5% | 27.5% |
| 19,049 | ROWAN | 5,987 | 2,758 | 2,975 | 254 | 217 D | 46.1% | 49.7% | 48.1% | 51.9% |
| 13,708 | RUSSELL | 5,540 | 3,804 | 1,693 | 43 | 2,111 R | 68.7% | 30.6% | 69.2% | 30.8% |
| 21,813 | SCOTT | 6,667 | 2,868 | 3,531 | 268 | 663 D | 43.0% | 53.0% | 44.8% | 55.2% |
| 23,328 | SHELBY | 8,108 | 3,423 | 4,429 | 256 | 1,006 D | 42.2% | 54.6% | 43.6% | 56.4% |
| 14,673 | SIMPSON | 4,819 | 2,020 | 2,713 | 86 | 693 D | 41.9% | 56.3% | 42.7% | 57.3% |
| 5,929 | SPENCER | 2,200 | 935 | 1,216 | 49 | 281 D | 42.5% | 55.3% | 43.5% | 56.5% |
| 21,178 | TAYLOR | 7,768 | 4,243 | 3,400 | 125 | 843 R | 54.6% | 43.8% | 55.5% | 44.5% |
| 11,874 | TODD | 3,981 | 1,945 | 1,956 | 80 | 11 D | 48.9% | 49.1% | 49.9% | 50.1% |
| 9,384 | TRIGG | 4,605 | 1,913 | 2,619 | 73 | 706 D | 41.5% | 56.9% | 42.2% | 57.8% |
| 6,253 | TRIMBLE | 2,392 | 824 | 1,478 | 90 | 654 D | 34.4% | 61.8% | 35.8% | 64.2% |
| 17,821 | UNION | 5,437 | 1,847 | 3,479 | 111 | 1,632 D | 34.0% | 64.0% | 34.7% | 65.3% |
| 71,828 | WARREN | 22,604 | 12,184 | 9,643 | 777 | 2,541 R | 53.9% | 42.7% | 55.8% | 44.2% |
| 10,764 | WASHINGTON | 4,249 | 2,008 | 2,147 | 94 | 139 D | 47.3% | 50.5% | 48.3% | 51.7% |
| 17,022 | WAYNE | 6,716 | 3,972 | 2,673 | 71 | 1,299 R | 59.1% | 39.8% | 59.8% | 40.2% |
| 14,832 | WEBSTER | 5,535 | 1,939 | 3,506 | 90 | 1,567 D | 35.0% | 63.3% | 35.6% | 64.4% |
| 33,396 | WHITLEY | 11,077 | 7,007 | 3,889 | 181 | 3,118 R | 63.3% | 35.1% | 64.3% | 35.7% |
| 6,698 | WOLFE | 2,805 | 951 | 1,814 | 40 | 863 D | 33.9% | 64.7% | 34.4% | 65.6% |
| 17,778 | WOODFORD | 6,515 | 3,105 | 3,122 | 288 | 17 D | 47.7% | 47.9% | 49.9% | 50.1% |
| 3,660,777 | TOTAL | 1,294,627 | 635,274 | 616,417 | 42,936 | 18,857 R | 49.1% | 47.6% | 50.8% | 49.2% |

# KENTUCKY

## PRESIDENT 1976

| 1970 Census Population | County | Total Vote | Republican | Democratic | Other | Rep.-Dem. Plurality | Percentage Total Vote Rep. | Dem. | Major Vote Rep. | Dem. |
|---|---|---|---|---|---|---|---|---|---|---|
| 13,037 | ADAIR | 5,634 | 3,201 | 2,366 | 67 | 835 R | 56.8% | 42.0% | 57.5% | 42.5% |
| 12,598 | ALLEN | 4,778 | 2,508 | 2,231 | 39 | 277 R | 52.5% | 46.7% | 52.9% | 47.1% |
| 9,358 | ANDERSON | 4,132 | 1,682 | 2,388 | 62 | 706 D | 40.7% | 57.8% | 41.3% | 58.7% |
| 8,276 | BALLARD | 3,693 | 649 | 2,794 | 250 | 2,145 D | 17.6% | 75.7% | 18.8% | 81.2% |
| 28,677 | BARREN | 9,771 | 3,797 | 5,878 | 96 | 2,081 D | 38.9% | 60.2% | 39.2% | 60.8% |
| 9,235 | BATH | 3,071 | 938 | 2,113 | 20 | 1,175 D | 30.5% | 68.8% | 30.7% | 69.3% |
| 31,087 | BELL | 10,483 | 5,035 | 5,284 | 164 | 249 D | 48.0% | 50.4% | 48.8% | 51.2% |
| 32,812 | BOONE | 11,385 | 5,602 | 5,602 | 181 | | 49.2% | 49.2% | 50.0% | 50.0% |
| 18,476 | BOURBON | 5,904 | 2,260 | 3,504 | 140 | 1,244 D | 38.3% | 59.3% | 39.2% | 60.8% |
| 52,376 | BOYD | 20,459 | 9,106 | 11,150 | 203 | 2,044 D | 44.5% | 54.5% | 45.0% | 55.0% |
| 21,090 | BOYLE | 7,703 | 3,511 | 4,095 | 97 | 584 D | 45.6% | 53.2% | 46.2% | 53.8% |
| 7,227 | BRACKEN | 2,495 | 879 | 1,577 | 39 | 698 D | 35.2% | 63.2% | 35.8% | 64.2% |
| 14,221 | BREATHITT | 4,576 | 1,014 | 3,544 | 18 | 2,530 D | 22.2% | 77.4% | 22.2% | 77.8% |
| 14,789 | BRECKINRIDGE | 6,111 | 2,698 | 3,347 | 66 | 649 D | 44.1% | 54.8% | 44.6% | 55.4% |
| 26,090 | BULLITT | 9,477 | 3,639 | 5,623 | 215 | 1,984 D | 38.4% | 59.3% | 39.3% | 60.7% |
| 9,723 | BUTLER | 3,981 | 2,363 | 1,588 | 30 | 775 R | 59.4% | 39.9% | 59.8% | 40.2% |
| 13,179 | CALDWELL | 4,899 | 1,808 | 3,016 | 75 | 1,208 D | 36.9% | 61.6% | 37.5% | 62.5% |
| 27,692 | CALLOWAY | 11,507 | 3,171 | 8,141 | 195 | 4,970 D | 27.6% | 70.7% | 28.0% | 72.0% |
| 88,561 | CAMPBELL | 28,821 | 15,798 | 12,423 | 600 | 3,375 R | 54.8% | 43.1% | 56.0% | 44.0% |
| 5,354 | CARLISLE | 2,456 | 435 | 1,985 | 36 | 1,550 D | 17.7% | 80.8% | 18.0% | 82.0% |
| 8,523 | CARROLL | 3,099 | 815 | 2,251 | 33 | 1,436 D | 26.3% | 72.6% | 26.6% | 73.4% |
| 19,850 | CARTER | 7,133 | 3,185 | 3,915 | 33 | 730 D | 44.7% | 54.9% | 44.9% | 55.1% |
| 12,930 | CASEY | 5,032 | 3,379 | 1,602 | 51 | 1,777 R | 67.2% | 31.8% | 67.8% | 32.2% |
| 56,224 | CHRISTIAN | 12,914 | 4,964 | 7,845 | 105 | 2,881 D | 38.4% | 60.7% | 38.8% | 61.2% |
| 24,090 | CLARK | 7,768 | 3,114 | 4,575 | 79 | 1,461 D | 40.1% | 58.9% | 40.5% | 59.5% |
| 18,481 | CLAY | 5,336 | 3,652 | 1,674 | 10 | 1,978 R | 68.4% | 31.4% | 68.6% | 31.4% |
| 8,174 | CLINTON | 3,389 | 2,354 | 987 | 48 | 1,367 R | 69.5% | 29.1% | 70.5% | 29.5% |
| 8,493 | CRITTENDEN | 3,352 | 1,596 | 1,715 | 41 | 119 D | 47.6% | 51.2% | 48.2% | 51.8% |
| 6,850 | CUMBERLAND | 2,527 | 1,653 | 853 | 21 | 800 R | 65.4% | 33.8% | 66.0% | 34.0% |
| 79,486 | DAVIESS | 27,454 | 12,826 | 14,114 | 514 | 1,288 D | 46.7% | 51.4% | 47.6% | 52.4% |
| 8,751 | EDMONSON | 3,411 | 1,976 | 1,418 | 17 | 558 R | 57.9% | 41.6% | 58.2% | 41.8% |
| 5,933 | ELLIOTT | 2,461 | 455 | 1,987 | 19 | 1,532 D | 18.5% | 80.7% | 18.6% | 81.4% |
| 12,752 | ESTILL | 4,314 | 2,250 | 2,034 | 30 | 216 R | 52.2% | 47.1% | 52.5% | 47.5% |
| 174,323 | FAYETTE | 64,989 | 35,170 | 28,012 | 1,807 | 7,158 R | 54.1% | 43.1% | 55.7% | 44.3% |
| 11,366 | FLEMING | 3,983 | 1,647 | 2,317 | 19 | 670 D | 41.4% | 58.2% | 41.5% | 58.5% |
| 35,889 | FLOYD | 13,333 | 3,108 | 10,151 | 74 | 7,043 D | 23.3% | 76.1% | 23.4% | 76.6% |
| 34,481 | FRANKLIN | 16,441 | 5,536 | 10,475 | 430 | 4,939 D | 33.7% | 63.7% | 34.6% | 65.4% |
| 10,183 | FULTON | 3,470 | 1,060 | 2,370 | 40 | 1,310 D | 30.5% | 68.3% | 30.9% | 69.1% |
| 4,134 | GALLATIN | 1,623 | 436 | 1,164 | 23 | 728 D | 26.9% | 71.7% | 27.3% | 72.8% |
| 9,457 | GARRARD | 3,988 | 2,045 | 1,887 | 56 | 158 R | 51.3% | 47.3% | 52.0% | 48.0% |
| 9,999 | GRANT | 3,634 | 1,212 | 2,336 | 86 | 1,124 D | 33.4% | 64.3% | 34.2% | 65.8% |
| 30,939 | GRAVES | 12,420 | 3,195 | 8,982 | 243 | 5,787 D | 25.7% | 72.3% | 26.2% | 73.8% |
| 16,445 | GRAYSON | 6,790 | 3,658 | 3,064 | 68 | 594 R | 53.9% | 45.1% | 54.4% | 45.6% |
| 10,350 | GREEN | 4,519 | 2,397 | 2,085 | 37 | 312 R | 53.0% | 46.1% | 53.5% | 46.5% |
| 33,192 | GREENUP | 12,013 | 5,062 | 6,880 | 71 | 1,818 D | 42.1% | 57.3% | 42.4% | 57.6% |
| 7,080 | HANCOCK | 2,747 | 1,124 | 1,562 | 61 | 438 D | 40.9% | 56.9% | 41.8% | 58.2% |
| 78,421 | HARDIN | 15,185 | 6,965 | 7,977 | 243 | 1,012 D | 45.9% | 52.5% | 46.6% | 53.4% |
| 37,370 | HARLAN | 12,006 | 4,624 | 7,300 | 82 | 2,676 D | 38.5% | 60.8% | 38.8% | 61.2% |
| 14,158 | HARRISON | 5,551 | 1,911 | 3,582 | 58 | 1,671 D | 34.4% | 64.5% | 34.8% | 65.2% |
| 13,980 | HART | 5,244 | 2,013 | 3,189 | 42 | 1,176 D | 38.4% | 60.8% | 38.7% | 61.3% |
| 36,031 | HENDERSON | 12,118 | 4,053 | 7,916 | 149 | 3,863 D | 33.4% | 65.3% | 33.9% | 66.1% |
| 10,910 | HENRY | 4,220 | 1,192 | 2,985 | 43 | 1,793 D | 28.2% | 70.7% | 28.5% | 71.5% |
| 6,264 | HICKMAN | 2,716 | 585 | 2,035 | 96 | 1,450 D | 21.5% | 74.9% | 22.3% | 77.7% |
| 38,167 | HOPKINS | 12,990 | 5,115 | 7,749 | 126 | 2,634 D | 39.4% | 59.7% | 39.8% | 60.2% |
| 10,005 | JACKSON | 3,466 | 2,766 | 680 | 20 | 2,086 R | 79.8% | 19.6% | 80.3% | 19.7% |
| 695,055 | JEFFERSON | 259,445 | 130,262 | 122,731 | 6,452 | 7,531 R | 50.2% | 47.3% | 51.5% | 48.5% |
| 17,430 | JESSAMINE | 6,004 | 3,081 | 2,795 | 128 | 286 R | 51.3% | 46.6% | 52.4% | 47.6% |
| 17,539 | JOHNSON | 8,635 | 4,891 | 3,683 | 61 | 1,208 R | 56.6% | 42.7% | 57.0% | 43.0% |
| 129,440 | KENTON | 41,680 | 22,087 | 18,833 | 760 | 3,254 R | 53.0% | 45.2% | 54.0% | 46.0% |
| 14,698 | KNOTT | 5,779 | 962 | 4,762 | 55 | 3,800 D | 16.6% | 82.4% | 16.8% | 83.2% |

# KENTUCKY

## PRESIDENT 1976

| 1970 Census Population | County | Total Vote | Republican | Democratic | Other | Rep.-Dem. Plurality | Percentage | | | |
|---|---|---|---|---|---|---|---|---|---|---|
| | | | | | | | Total Vote | | Major Vote | |
| | | | | | | | Rep. | Dem. | Rep. | Dem. |
| 23,689 | KNOX | 8,661 | 4,931 | 3,642 | 88 | 1,289 R | 56.9% | 42.1% | 57.5% | 42.5% |
| 10,672 | LARUE | 3,655 | 1,409 | 2,207 | 39 | 798 D | 38.5% | 60.4% | 39.0% | 61.0% |
| 27,386 | LAUREL | 10,073 | 6,186 | 3,813 | 74 | 2,373 R | 61.4% | 37.9% | 61.9% | 38.1% |
| 10,726 | LAWRENCE | 4,283 | 1,838 | 2,402 | 43 | 564 D | 42.9% | 56.1% | 43.3% | 56.7% |
| 6,587 | LEE | 2,563 | 1,449 | 1,091 | 23 | 358 R | 56.5% | 42.6% | 57.0% | 43.0% |
| 11,623 | LESLIE | 5,271 | 3,770 | 1,478 | 23 | 2,292 R | 71.5% | 28.0% | 71.8% | 28.2% |
| 23,165 | LETCHER | 7,748 | 3,122 | 4,590 | 36 | 1,468 D | 40.3% | 59.2% | 40.5% | 59.5% |
| 12,355 | LEWIS | 4,332 | 2,383 | 1,929 | 20 | 454 R | 55.0% | 44.5% | 55.3% | 44.7% |
| 16,663 | LINCOLN | 5,925 | 2,694 | 3,198 | 33 | 504 D | 45.5% | 54.0% | 45.7% | 54.3% |
| 7,596 | LIVINGSTON | 3,415 | 878 | 2,497 | 40 | 1,619 D | 25.7% | 73.1% | 26.0% | 74.0% |
| 21,793 | LOGAN | 7,389 | 2,430 | 4,850 | 109 | 2,420 D | 32.9% | 65.6% | 33.4% | 66.6% |
| 5,562 | LYON | 2,221 | 585 | 1,606 | 30 | 1,021 D | 26.3% | 72.3% | 26.7% | 73.3% |
| 58,281 | MCCRACKEN | 22,687 | 6,997 | 14,956 | 734 | 7,959 D | 30.8% | 65.9% | 31.9% | 68.1% |
| 12,548 | MCCREARY | 5,142 | 3,272 | 1,827 | 43 | 1,445 R | 63.6% | 35.5% | 64.2% | 35.8% |
| 9,062 | MCLEAN | 3,593 | 1,212 | 2,346 | 35 | 1,134 D | 33.7% | 65.3% | 34.1% | 65.9% |
| 42,730 | MADISON | 14,114 | 6,581 | 7,299 | 234 | 718 D | 46.6% | 51.7% | 47.4% | 52.6% |
| 10,443 | MAGOFFIN | 4,263 | 1,793 | 2,451 | 19 | 658 D | 42.1% | 57.5% | 42.2% | 57.8% |
| 16,714 | MARION | 5,322 | 1,723 | 3,520 | 79 | 1,797 D | 32.4% | 66.1% | 32.9% | 67.1% |
| 20,381 | MARSHALL | 9,614 | 2,578 | 6,906 | 130 | 4,328 D | 26.8% | 71.8% | 27.2% | 72.8% |
| 9,377 | MARTIN | 3,413 | 2,120 | 1,267 | 26 | 853 R | 62.1% | 37.1% | 62.6% | 37.4% |
| 17,273 | MASON | 6,004 | 2,529 | 3,397 | 78 | 868 D | 42.1% | 56.6% | 42.7% | 57.3% |
| 18,796 | MEADE | 4,868 | 1,755 | 3,030 | 83 | 1,275 D | 36.1% | 62.2% | 36.7% | 63.3% |
| 4,050 | MENIFEE | 1,356 | 304 | 1,041 | 11 | 737 D | 22.4% | 76.8% | 22.6% | 77.4% |
| 15,960 | MERCER | 5,991 | 2,451 | 3,411 | 129 | 960 D | 40.9% | 56.9% | 41.8% | 58.2% |
| 8,177 | METCALFE | 3,266 | 1,356 | 1,877 | 33 | 521 D | 41.5% | 57.5% | 41.9% | 58.1% |
| 11,642 | MONROE | 4,795 | 3,352 | 1,412 | 31 | 1,940 R | 69.9% | 29.4% | 70.4% | 29.6% |
| 15,364 | MONTGOMERY | 5,234 | 2,032 | 3,141 | 61 | 1,109 D | 38.8% | 60.0% | 39.3% | 60.7% |
| 10,019 | MORGAN | 3,897 | 973 | 2,897 | 27 | 1,924 D | 25.0% | 74.3% | 25.1% | 74.9% |
| 27,537 | MUHLENBERG | 11,449 | 4,292 | 7,058 | 99 | 2,766 D | 37.5% | 61.6% | 37.8% | 62.2% |
| 23,477 | NELSON | 7,504 | 2,804 | 4,454 | 246 | 1,650 D | 37.4% | 59.4% | 38.6% | 61.4% |
| 6,508 | NICHOLAS | 2,378 | 738 | 1,582 | 58 | 844 D | 31.0% | 66.5% | 31.8% | 68.2% |
| 18,790 | OHIO | 7,337 | 3,764 | 3,508 | 65 | 256 R | 51.3% | 47.8% | 51.8% | 48.2% |
| 14,687 | OLDHAM | 6,631 | 3,695 | 2,819 | 117 | 876 R | 55.7% | 42.5% | 56.7% | 43.3% |
| 7,470 | OWEN | 3,051 | 676 | 2,332 | 43 | 1,656 D | 22.2% | 76.4% | 22.5% | 77.5% |
| 5,023 | OWSLEY | 1,367 | 1,053 | 305 | 9 | 748 R | 77.0% | 22.3% | 77.5% | 22.5% |
| 9,949 | PENDLETON | 3,427 | 1,230 | 2,147 | 50 | 917 D | 35.9% | 62.6% | 36.4% | 63.6% |
| 26,259 | PERRY | 10,116 | 4,434 | 5,633 | 49 | 1,199 D | 43.8% | 55.7% | 44.0% | 56.0% |
| 61,059 | PIKE | 23,691 | 9,178 | 14,320 | 193 | 5,142 D | 38.7% | 60.4% | 39.1% | 60.9% |
| 7,704 | POWELL | 3,029 | 1,148 | 1,859 | 22 | 711 D | 37.9% | 61.4% | 38.2% | 61.8% |
| 35,234 | PULASKI | 15,083 | 9,226 | 5,752 | 105 | 3,474 R | 61.2% | 38.1% | 61.6% | 38.4% |
| 2,163 | ROBERTSON | 828 | 275 | 546 | 7 | 271 D | 33.2% | 65.9% | 33.5% | 66.5% |
| 12,305 | ROCKCASTLE | 4,013 | 2,583 | 1,408 | 22 | 1,175 R | 64.4% | 35.1% | 64.7% | 35.3% |
| 17,010 | ROWAN | 5,868 | 2,244 | 3,541 | 83 | 1,297 D | 38.2% | 60.3% | 38.8% | 61.2% |
| 10,542 | RUSSELL | 4,732 | 2,882 | 1,803 | 47 | 1,079 R | 60.9% | 38.1% | 61.5% | 38.5% |
| 17,948 | SCOTT | 5,638 | 2,408 | 3,118 | 112 | 710 D | 42.7% | 55.3% | 43.6% | 56.4% |
| 18,999 | SHELBY | 6,847 | 2,916 | 3,841 | 90 | 925 D | 42.6% | 56.1% | 43.2% | 56.8% |
| 13,054 | SIMPSON | 4,299 | 1,481 | 2,782 | 36 | 1,301 D | 34.4% | 64.7% | 34.7% | 65.3% |
| 5,488 | SPENCER | 1,983 | 742 | 1,209 | 32 | 467 D | 37.4% | 61.0% | 38.0% | 62.0% |
| 17,138 | TAYLOR | 6,866 | 3,337 | 3,456 | 73 | 119 D | 48.6% | 50.3% | 49.1% | 50.9% |
| 10,823 | TODD | 3,597 | 1,095 | 2,436 | 66 | 1,341 D | 30.4% | 67.7% | 31.0% | 69.0% |
| 8,620 | TRIGG | 3,745 | 991 | 2,727 | 27 | 1,736 D | 26.5% | 72.8% | 26.7% | 73.3% |
| 5,349 | TRIMBLE | 2,113 | 517 | 1,568 | 28 | 1,051 D | 24.5% | 74.2% | 24.8% | 75.2% |
| 15,882 | UNION | 5,312 | 1,716 | 3,540 | 56 | 1,824 D | 32.3% | 66.6% | 32.6% | 67.4% |
| 57,432 | WARREN | 19,291 | 9,439 | 9,657 | 195 | 218 D | 48.9% | 50.1% | 49.4% | 50.6% |
| 10,728 | WASHINGTON | 4,235 | 1,765 | 2,376 | 94 | 611 D | 41.7% | 56.1% | 42.6% | 57.4% |
| 14,268 | WAYNE | 5,817 | 3,243 | 2,537 | 37 | 706 R | 55.8% | 43.6% | 56.1% | 43.9% |
| 13,282 | WEBSTER | 4,970 | 1,402 | 3,523 | 45 | 2,121 D | 28.2% | 70.9% | 28.5% | 71.5% |
| 24,145 | WHITLEY | 10,392 | 6,100 | 4,212 | 80 | 1,888 R | 58.7% | 40.5% | 59.2% | 40.8% |
| 5,669 | WOLFE | 2,458 | 659 | 1,777 | 22 | 1,118 D | 26.8% | 72.3% | 27.1% | 72.9% |
| 14,434 | WOODFORD | 5,465 | 2,646 | 2,689 | 130 | 43 D | 48.4% | 49.2% | 49.6% | 50.4% |
| 3,219,311 | TOTAL | 1,167,142 | 531,852 | 615,717 | 19,573 | 83,865 D | 45.6% | 52.8% | 46.3% | 53.7% |

# KENTUCKY

## PRESIDENT 1972

| 1970 Census Population | County | Total Vote | Republican | Democratic | Other | Rep.-Dem. Plurality | Percentage | | | |
|---|---|---|---|---|---|---|---|---|---|---|
| | | | | | | | Total Vote | | Major Vote | |
| | | | | | | | Rep. | Dem. | Rep. | Dem. |
| 13,037 | ADAIR | 5,531 | 3,859 | 1,610 | 62 | 2,249 R | 69.8% | 29.1% | 70.6% | 29.4% |
| 12,598 | ALLEN | 4,332 | 3,025 | 1,259 | 48 | 1,766 R | 69.8% | 29.1% | 70.6% | 29.4% |
| 9,358 | ANDERSON | 3,670 | 2,298 | 1,302 | 70 | 996 R | 62.6% | 35.5% | 63.8% | 36.2% |
| 8,276 | BALLARD | 3,089 | 1,542 | 1,411 | 136 | 131 R | 49.9% | 45.7% | 52.2% | 47.8% |
| 28,677 | BARREN | 9,696 | 6,070 | 3,384 | 242 | 2,686 R | 62.6% | 34.9% | 64.2% | 35.8% |
| 9,235 | BATH | 3,282 | 1,919 | 1,347 | 16 | 572 R | 58.5% | 41.0% | 58.8% | 41.2% |
| 31,087 | BELL | 9,867 | 6,518 | 3,219 | 130 | 3,299 R | 66.1% | 32.6% | 66.9% | 33.1% |
| 32,812 | BOONE | 10,280 | 7,355 | 2,595 | 330 | 4,760 R | 71.5% | 25.2% | 73.9% | 26.1% |
| 18,476 | BOURBON | 5,127 | 3,180 | 1,860 | 87 | 1,320 R | 62.0% | 36.3% | 63.1% | 36.9% |
| 52,376 | BOYD | 19,437 | 12,812 | 6,434 | 191 | 6,378 R | 65.9% | 33.1% | 66.6% | 33.4% |
| 21,090 | BOYLE | 6,781 | 4,317 | 2,395 | 69 | 1,922 R | 63.7% | 35.3% | 64.3% | 35.7% |
| 7,227 | BRACKEN | 2,532 | 1,628 | 873 | 31 | 755 R | 64.3% | 34.5% | 65.1% | 34.9% |
| 14,221 | BREATHITT | 4,541 | 1,846 | 2,677 | 18 | 831 D | 40.7% | 59.0% | 40.8% | 59.2% |
| 14,789 | BRECKINRIDGE | 5,563 | 3,574 | 1,921 | 68 | 1,653 R | 64.2% | 34.5% | 65.0% | 35.0% |
| 26,090 | BULLITT | 7,553 | 4,517 | 2,827 | 209 | 1,690 R | 59.8% | 37.4% | 61.5% | 38.5% |
| 9,723 | BUTLER | 3,818 | 2,941 | 835 | 42 | 2,106 R | 77.0% | 21.9% | 77.9% | 22.1% |
| 13,179 | CALDWELL | 4,451 | 2,952 | 1,345 | 154 | 1,607 R | 66.3% | 30.2% | 68.7% | 31.3% |
| 27,692 | CALLOWAY | 8,732 | 5,167 | 3,468 | 97 | 1,699 R | 59.2% | 39.7% | 59.8% | 40.2% |
| 88,561 | CAMPBELL | 29,445 | 20,025 | 8,585 | 835 | 11,440 R | 68.0% | 29.2% | 70.0% | 30.0% |
| 5,354 | CARLISLE | 2,097 | 1,169 | 872 | 56 | 297 R | 55.7% | 41.6% | 57.3% | 42.7% |
| 8,523 | CARROLL | 2,574 | 1,228 | 1,308 | 38 | 80 D | 47.7% | 50.8% | 48.4% | 51.6% |
| 19,850 | CARTER | 6,727 | 4,082 | 2,591 | 54 | 1,491 R | 60.7% | 38.5% | 61.2% | 38.8% |
| 12,930 | CASEY | 4,728 | 3,727 | 913 | 88 | 2,814 R | 78.8% | 19.3% | 80.3% | 19.7% |
| 56,224 | CHRISTIAN | 11,705 | 7,414 | 4,063 | 228 | 3,351 R | 63.3% | 34.7% | 64.6% | 35.4% |
| 24,090 | CLARK | 6,585 | 4,506 | 2,020 | 59 | 2,486 R | 68.4% | 30.7% | 69.0% | 31.0% |
| 18,481 | CLAY | 5,781 | 4,046 | 1,709 | 26 | 2,337 R | 70.0% | 29.6% | 70.3% | 29.7% |
| 8,174 | CLINTON | 3,307 | 2,632 | 659 | 16 | 1,973 R | 79.6% | 19.9% | 80.0% | 20.0% |
| 8,493 | CRITTENDEN | 3,143 | 2,248 | 859 | 36 | 1,389 R | 71.5% | 27.3% | 72.4% | 27.6% |
| 6,850 | CUMBERLAND | 3,002 | 2,294 | 686 | 22 | 1,608 R | 76.4% | 22.9% | 77.0% | 23.0% |
| 79,486 | DAVIESS | 26,256 | 17,234 | 8,168 | 854 | 9,066 R | 65.6% | 31.1% | 67.8% | 32.2% |
| 8,751 | EDMONSON | 3,074 | 2,327 | 722 | 25 | 1,605 R | 75.7% | 23.5% | 76.3% | 23.7% |
| 5,933 | ELLIOTT | 2,297 | 782 | 1,499 | 16 | 717 D | 34.0% | 65.3% | 34.3% | 65.7% |
| 12,752 | ESTILL | 4,399 | 3,054 | 1,322 | 23 | 1,732 R | 69.4% | 30.1% | 69.8% | 30.2% |
| 174,323 | FAYETTE | 63,666 | 42,362 | 19,828 | 1,476 | 22,534 R | 66.5% | 31.1% | 68.1% | 31.9% |
| 11,366 | FLEMING | 3,982 | 2,484 | 1,455 | 43 | 1,029 R | 62.4% | 36.5% | 63.1% | 36.9% |
| 35,889 | FLOYD | 13,800 | 6,099 | 7,544 | 157 | 1,445 D | 44.2% | 54.7% | 44.7% | 55.3% |
| 34,481 | FRANKLIN | 13,679 | 7,781 | 5,601 | 297 | 2,180 R | 56.9% | 40.9% | 58.1% | 41.9% |
| 10,183 | FULTON | 2,947 | 1,807 | 1,024 | 116 | 783 R | 61.3% | 34.7% | 63.8% | 36.2% |
| 4,134 | GALLATIN | 1,347 | 719 | 612 | 16 | 107 R | 53.4% | 45.4% | 54.0% | 46.0% |
| 9,457 | GARRARD | 4,657 | 3,143 | 1,441 | 73 | 1,702 R | 67.5% | 30.9% | 68.6% | 31.4% |
| 9,999 | GRANT | 3,258 | 2,086 | 1,054 | 118 | 1,032 R | 64.0% | 32.4% | 66.4% | 33.6% |
| 30,939 | GRAVES | 10,100 | 6,098 | 3,701 | 301 | 2,397 R | 60.4% | 36.6% | 62.2% | 37.8% |
| 16,445 | GRAYSON | 6,111 | 4,155 | 1,839 | 117 | 2,316 R | 68.0% | 30.1% | 69.3% | 30.7% |
| 10,350 | GREEN | 4,003 | 2,755 | 1,209 | 39 | 1,546 R | 68.8% | 30.2% | 69.5% | 30.5% |
| 33,192 | GREENUP | 11,437 | 6,828 | 4,491 | 118 | 2,337 R | 59.7% | 39.3% | 60.3% | 39.7% |
| 7,080 | HANCOCK | 2,450 | 1,583 | 791 | 76 | 792 R | 64.6% | 32.3% | 66.7% | 33.3% |
| 78,421 | HARDIN | 13,256 | 8,740 | 4,060 | 456 | 4,680 R | 65.9% | 30.6% | 68.3% | 31.7% |
| 37,370 | HARLAN | 10,985 | 6,527 | 4,349 | 109 | 2,178 R | 59.4% | 39.6% | 60.0% | 40.0% |
| 14,158 | HARRISON | 4,576 | 2,732 | 1,780 | 64 | 952 R | 59.7% | 38.9% | 60.5% | 39.5% |
| 13,980 | HART | 5,939 | 3,582 | 2,307 | 50 | 1,275 R | 60.3% | 38.8% | 60.8% | 39.2% |
| 36,031 | HENDERSON | 10,269 | 6,231 | 3,889 | 149 | 2,342 R | 60.7% | 37.9% | 61.6% | 38.4% |
| 10,910 | HENRY | 3,656 | 1,919 | 1,688 | 49 | 231 R | 52.5% | 46.2% | 53.2% | 46.8% |
| 6,264 | HICKMAN | 2,524 | 1,430 | 976 | 118 | 454 R | 56.7% | 38.7% | 59.4% | 40.6% |
| 38,167 | HOPKINS | 10,388 | 7,133 | 3,129 | 126 | 4,004 R | 68.7% | 30.1% | 69.5% | 30.5% |
| 10,005 | JACKSON | 5,753 | 5,303 | 436 | 14 | 4,867 R | 92.2% | 7.6% | 92.4% | 7.6% |
| 695,055 | JEFFERSON | 235,764 | 142,436 | 88,143 | 5,185 | 54,293 R | 60.4% | 37.4% | 61.8% | 38.2% |
| 17,430 | JESSAMINE | 5,238 | 3,819 | 1,269 | 150 | 2,550 R | 72.9% | 24.2% | 75.1% | 24.9% |
| 17,539 | JOHNSON | 6,792 | 4,907 | 1,840 | 45 | 3,067 R | 72.2% | 27.1% | 72.7% | 27.3% |
| 129,440 | KENTON | 42,121 | 28,076 | 12,872 | 1,173 | 15,204 R | 66.7% | 30.6% | 68.6% | 31.4% |
| 14,698 | KNOTT | 4,287 | 1,479 | 2,774 | 34 | 1,295 D | 34.5% | 64.7% | 34.8% | 65.2% |

# KENTUCKY

## PRESIDENT 1972

| 1970 Census Population | County | Total Vote | Republican | Democratic | Other | Rep.-Dem. Plurality | Percentage Total Vote Rep. | Dem. | Major Vote Rep. | Dem. |
|---|---|---|---|---|---|---|---|---|---|---|
| 23,689 | KNOX | 6,879 | 5,017 | 1,805 | 57 | 3,212 R | 72.9% | 26.2% | 73.5% | 26.5% |
| 10,672 | LARUE | 3,980 | 2,449 | 1,483 | 48 | 966 R | 61.5% | 37.3% | 62.3% | 37.7% |
| 27,386 | LAUREL | 9,620 | 7,276 | 2,274 | 70 | 5,002 R | 75.6% | 23.6% | 76.2% | 23.8% |
| 10,726 | LAWRENCE | 3,955 | 2,392 | 1,529 | 34 | 863 R | 60.5% | 38.7% | 61.0% | 39.0% |
| 6,587 | LEE | 2,388 | 1,629 | 744 | 15 | 885 R | 68.2% | 31.2% | 68.6% | 31.4% |
| 11,623 | LESLIE | 4,236 | 3,299 | 913 | 24 | 2,386 R | 77.9% | 21.6% | 78.3% | 21.7% |
| 23,165 | LETCHER | 7,197 | 4,213 | 2,908 | 76 | 1,305 R | 58.5% | 40.4% | 59.2% | 40.8% |
| 12,355 | LEWIS | 4,365 | 3,124 | 1,200 | 41 | 1,924 R | 71.6% | 27.5% | 72.2% | 27.8% |
| 16,663 | LINCOLN | 5,571 | 3,623 | 1,882 | 66 | 1,741 R | 65.0% | 33.8% | 65.8% | 34.2% |
| 7,596 | LIVINGSTON | 2,790 | 1,673 | 1,065 | 52 | 608 R | 60.0% | 38.2% | 61.1% | 38.9% |
| 21,793 | LOGAN | 6,175 | 3,573 | 2,459 | 143 | 1,114 R | 57.9% | 39.8% | 59.2% | 40.8% |
| 5,562 | LYON | 1,760 | 1,030 | 687 | 43 | 343 R | 58.5% | 39.0% | 60.0% | 40.0% |
| 58,281 | MCCRACKEN | 19,518 | 11,260 | 7,567 | 691 | 3,693 R | 57.7% | 38.8% | 59.8% | 40.2% |
| 12,548 | MCCREARY | 3,976 | 3,203 | 684 | 89 | 2,519 R | 80.6% | 17.2% | 82.4% | 17.6% |
| 9,062 | MCLEAN | 3,530 | 2,298 | 1,191 | 41 | 1,107 R | 65.1% | 33.7% | 65.9% | 34.1% |
| 42,730 | MADISON | 13,199 | 8,659 | 4,328 | 212 | 4,331 R | 65.6% | 32.8% | 66.7% | 33.3% |
| 10,443 | MAGOFFIN | 4,281 | 2,243 | 2,024 | 14 | 219 R | 52.4% | 47.3% | 52.6% | 47.4% |
| 16,714 | MARION | 4,765 | 2,370 | 2,351 | 44 | 19 R | 49.7% | 49.3% | 50.2% | 49.8% |
| 20,381 | MARSHALL | 7,252 | 4,290 | 2,806 | 156 | 1,484 R | 59.2% | 38.7% | 60.5% | 39.5% |
| 9,377 | MARTIN | 3,204 | 2,495 | 661 | 48 | 1,834 R | 77.9% | 20.6% | 79.1% | 20.9% |
| 17,273 | MASON | 6,037 | 3,529 | 2,459 | 49 | 1,070 R | 58.5% | 40.7% | 58.9% | 41.1% |
| 18,796 | MEADE | 4,090 | 2,492 | 1,541 | 57 | 951 R | 60.9% | 37.7% | 61.8% | 38.2% |
| 4,050 | MENIFEE | 1,358 | 596 | 732 | 30 | 136 D | 43.9% | 53.9% | 44.9% | 55.1% |
| 15,960 | MERCER | 5,410 | 3,575 | 1,707 | 128 | 1,868 R | 66.1% | 31.6% | 67.7% | 32.3% |
| 8,177 | METCALFE | 3,238 | 1,896 | 1,308 | 34 | 588 R | 58.6% | 40.4% | 59.2% | 40.8% |
| 11,642 | MONROE | 4,566 | 3,770 | 768 | 28 | 3,002 R | 82.6% | 16.8% | 83.1% | 16.9% |
| 15,364 | MONTGOMERY | 4,579 | 2,868 | 1,657 | 54 | 1,211 R | 62.6% | 36.2% | 63.4% | 36.6% |
| 10,019 | MORGAN | 3,369 | 1,535 | 1,815 | 19 | 280 D | 45.6% | 53.9% | 45.8% | 54.2% |
| 27,537 | MUHLENBERG | 8,978 | 5,596 | 3,246 | 136 | 2,350 R | 62.3% | 36.2% | 63.3% | 36.7% |
| 23,477 | NELSON | 6,528 | 3,495 | 2,828 | 205 | 667 R | 53.5% | 43.3% | 55.3% | 44.7% |
| 6,508 | NICHOLAS | 1,914 | 1,076 | 804 | 34 | 272 R | 56.2% | 42.0% | 57.2% | 42.8% |
| 18,790 | OHIO | 3,334 | 2,392 | 906 | 36 | 1,486 R | 71.7% | 27.2% | 72.5% | 27.5% |
| 14,687 | OLDHAM | 4,472 | 3,041 | 1,311 | 120 | 1,730 R | 68.0% | 29.3% | 69.9% | 30.1% |
| 7,470 | OWEN | 2,651 | 1,456 | 1,161 | 34 | 295 R | 54.9% | 43.8% | 55.6% | 44.4% |
| 5,023 | OWSLEY | 1,587 | 1,328 | 251 | 8 | 1,077 R | 83.7% | 15.8% | 84.1% | 15.9% |
| 9,949 | PENDLETON | 2,922 | 1,966 | 909 | 47 | 1,057 R | 67.3% | 31.1% | 68.4% | 31.6% |
| 26,259 | PERRY | 9,050 | 5,373 | 3,601 | 76 | 1,772 R | 59.4% | 39.8% | 59.9% | 40.1% |
| 61,059 | PIKE | 22,200 | 12,535 | 9,513 | 152 | 3,022 R | 56.5% | 42.9% | 56.9% | 43.1% |
| 7,704 | POWELL | 3,024 | 1,766 | 1,230 | 28 | 536 R | 58.4% | 40.7% | 58.9% | 41.1% |
| 35,234 | PULASKI | 13,770 | 10,602 | 3,080 | 88 | 7,522 R | 77.0% | 22.4% | 77.5% | 22.5% |
| 2,163 | ROBERTSON | 894 | 456 | 421 | 17 | 35 R | 51.0% | 47.1% | 52.0% | 48.0% |
| 12,305 | ROCKCASTLE | 4,446 | 3,437 | 968 | 41 | 2,469 R | 77.3% | 21.8% | 78.0% | 22.0% |
| 17,010 | ROWAN | 5,458 | 3,245 | 2,169 | 44 | 1,076 R | 59.5% | 39.7% | 59.9% | 40.1% |
| 10,542 | RUSSELL | 5,220 | 3,992 | 1,169 | 59 | 2,823 R | 76.5% | 22.4% | 77.3% | 22.7% |
| 17,948 | SCOTT | 5,026 | 3,255 | 1,642 | 129 | 1,613 R | 64.8% | 32.7% | 66.5% | 33.5% |
| 18,999 | SHELBY | 6,065 | 3,893 | 2,074 | 98 | 1,819 R | 64.2% | 34.2% | 65.2% | 34.8% |
| 13,054 | SIMPSON | 3,652 | 2,285 | 1,325 | 42 | 960 R | 62.6% | 36.3% | 63.3% | 36.7% |
| 5,488 | SPENCER | 1,629 | 1,120 | 481 | 28 | 639 R | 68.8% | 29.5% | 70.0% | 30.0% |
| 17,138 | TAYLOR | 5,952 | 4,035 | 1,859 | 58 | 2,176 R | 67.8% | 31.2% | 68.5% | 31.5% |
| 10,823 | TODD | 3,315 | 1,964 | 1,222 | 129 | 742 R | 59.2% | 36.9% | 61.6% | 38.4% |
| 8,620 | TRIGG | 3,337 | 1,767 | 1,514 | 56 | 253 R | 53.0% | 45.4% | 53.9% | 46.1% |
| 5,349 | TRIMBLE | 1,712 | 935 | 757 | 20 | 178 R | 54.6% | 44.2% | 55.3% | 44.7% |
| 15,882 | UNION | 4,604 | 2,701 | 1,855 | 48 | 846 R | 58.7% | 40.3% | 59.3% | 40.7% |
| 57,432 | WARREN | 18,691 | 12,481 | 5,934 | 276 | 6,547 R | 66.8% | 31.7% | 67.8% | 32.2% |
| 10,728 | WASHINGTON | 4,051 | 2,378 | 1,552 | 121 | 826 R | 58.7% | 38.3% | 60.5% | 39.5% |
| 14,268 | WAYNE | 5,420 | 3,514 | 1,853 | 53 | 1,661 R | 64.8% | 34.2% | 65.5% | 34.5% |
| 13,282 | WEBSTER | 4,162 | 2,396 | 1,712 | 54 | 684 R | 57.6% | 41.1% | 58.3% | 41.7% |
| 24,145 | WHITLEY | 9,062 | 6,788 | 2,199 | 75 | 4,589 R | 74.9% | 24.3% | 75.5% | 24.5% |
| 5,669 | WOLFE | 1,917 | 936 | 957 | 24 | 21 D | 48.8% | 49.9% | 49.4% | 50.6% |
| 14,434 | WOODFORD | 4,781 | 3,363 | 1,268 | 150 | 2,095 R | 70.3% | 26.5% | 72.6% | 27.4% |
| 3,219,311 | TOTAL | 1,067,499 | 676,446 | 371,159 | 19,894 | 305,287 R | 63.4% | 34.8% | 64.6% | 35.4% |

# KENTUCKY

## PRESIDENT 1968

| 1960 Census Population | County | Total Vote | Republican | Democratic | AIP | Other | Plurality | Percentage Total Vote Rep. | Dem. | AIP |
|---:|---|---:|---:|---:|---:|---:|---:|---:|---:|---:|
| 14,699 | ADAIR | 5,450 | 3,239 | 1,362 | 844 | 5 | 1,877 R | 59.4% | 25.0% | 15.5% |
| 12,269 | ALLEN | 4,790 | 2,952 | 927 | 905 | 6 | 2,025 R | 61.6% | 19.4% | 18.9% |
| 8,618 | ANDERSON | 3,596 | 1,594 | 1,334 | 657 | 11 | 260 R | 44.3% | 37.1% | 18.3% |
| 8,291 | BALLARD | 3,444 | 564 | 1,632 | 1,197 | 51 | 435 D | 16.4% | 47.4% | 34.8% |
| 28,303 | BARREN | 9,826 | 4,209 | 3,464 | 2,140 | 13 | 745 R | 42.8% | 35.3% | 21.8% |
| 9,114 | BATH | 3,331 | 1,277 | 1,394 | 658 | 2 | 117 D | 38.3% | 41.8% | 19.8% |
| 35,336 | BELL | 10,275 | 4,905 | 4,138 | 1,204 | 28 | 767 R | 47.7% | 40.3% | 11.7% |
| 21,940 | BOONE | 9,051 | 4,081 | 2,725 | 2,240 | 5 | 1,356 R | 45.1% | 30.1% | 24.7% |
| 18,178 | BOURBON | 5,460 | 1,848 | 2,566 | 1,023 | 23 | 718 D | 33.8% | 47.0% | 18.7% |
| 52,163 | BOYD | 19,001 | 8,632 | 7,914 | 2,443 | 12 | 718 R | 45.4% | 41.7% | 12.9% |
| 21,257 | BOYLE | 6,738 | 2,715 | 2,663 | 1,356 | 4 | 52 R | 40.3% | 39.5% | 20.1% |
| 7,422 | BRACKEN | 2,732 | 1,115 | 1,067 | 548 | 2 | 48 R | 40.8% | 39.1% | 20.1% |
| 15,490 | BREATHITT | 4,678 | 1,361 | 2,954 | 361 | 2 | 1,593 D | 29.1% | 63.1% | 7.7% |
| 14,734 | BRECKINRIDGE | 5,873 | 2,779 | 2,024 | 1,067 | 3 | 755 R | 47.3% | 34.5% | 18.2% |
| 15,726 | BULLITT | 6,310 | 1,965 | 2,135 | 2,180 | 30 | 45 A | 31.1% | 33.8% | 34.5% |
| 9,586 | BUTLER | 3,967 | 2,637 | 691 | 634 | 5 | 1,946 R | 66.5% | 17.4% | 16.0% |
| 13,073 | CALDWELL | 5,065 | 2,139 | 1,439 | 1,426 | 61 | 700 R | 42.2% | 28.4% | 28.2% |
| 20,972 | CALLOWAY | 8,682 | 2,672 | 3,854 | 2,150 | 6 | 1,182 D | 30.8% | 44.4% | 24.8% |
| 86,803 | CAMPBELL | 28,203 | 13,681 | 9,747 | 4,750 | 25 | 3,934 R | 48.5% | 34.6% | 16.8% |
| 5,608 | CARLISLE | 2,438 | 479 | 1,144 | 807 | 8 | 337 D | 19.6% | 46.9% | 33.1% |
| 7,978 | CARROLL | 3,152 | 868 | 1,765 | 514 | 5 | 897 D | 27.5% | 56.0% | 16.3% |
| 20,817 | CARTER | 6,511 | 3,234 | 2,344 | 926 | 7 | 890 R | 49.7% | 36.0% | 14.2% |
| 14,327 | CASEY | 5,235 | 3,698 | 879 | 649 | 9 | 2,819 R | 70.6% | 16.8% | 12.4% |
| 56,904 | CHRISTIAN | 12,614 | 3,788 | 4,281 | 4,527 | 18 | 246 A | 30.0% | 33.9% | 35.9% |
| 21,075 | CLARK | 6,808 | 2,698 | 2,385 | 1,722 | 3 | 313 R | 39.6% | 35.0% | 25.3% |
| 20,748 | CLAY | 6,204 | 4,663 | 1,213 | 327 | 1 | 3,450 R | 75.2% | 19.6% | 5.3% |
| 8,886 | CLINTON | 3,425 | 2,572 | 568 | 280 | 5 | 2,004 R | 75.1% | 16.6% | 8.2% |
| 8,648 | CRITTENDEN | 3,533 | 1,942 | 838 | 748 | 5 | 1,104 R | 55.0% | 23.7% | 21.2% |
| 7,835 | CUMBERLAND | 3,120 | 2,116 | 646 | 355 | 3 | 1,470 R | 67.8% | 20.7% | 11.4% |
| 70,588 | DAVIESS | 25,142 | 10,111 | 9,947 | 5,015 | 69 | 164 R | 40.2% | 39.6% | 19.9% |
| 8,085 | EDMONSON | 3,484 | 2,280 | 679 | 516 | 9 | 1,601 R | 65.4% | 19.5% | 14.8% |
| 6,330 | ELLIOTT | 2,186 | 515 | 1,387 | 280 | 4 | 872 D | 23.6% | 63.4% | 12.8% |
| 12,466 | ESTILL | 4,174 | 2,236 | 1,261 | 675 | 2 | 975 R | 53.6% | 30.2% | 16.2% |
| 131,906 | FAYETTE | 50,373 | 24,948 | 16,902 | 8,354 | 169 | 8,046 R | 49.5% | 33.6% | 16.6% |
| 10,890 | FLEMING | 4,167 | 2,220 | 1,406 | 535 | 6 | 814 R | 53.3% | 33.7% | 12.8% |
| 41,642 | FLOYD | 13,043 | 3,550 | 8,333 | 1,150 | 10 | 4,783 D | 27.2% | 63.9% | 8.8% |
| 29,421 | FRANKLIN | 13,165 | 4,057 | 6,396 | 2,655 | 57 | 2,339 D | 30.8% | 48.6% | 20.2% |
| 11,256 | FULTON | 3,818 | 1,079 | 1,204 | 1,526 | 9 | 322 A | 28.3% | 31.5% | 40.0% |
| 3,867 | GALLATIN | 1,407 | 413 | 685 | 304 | 5 | 272 D | 29.4% | 48.7% | 21.6% |
| 9,747 | GARRARD | 3,927 | 2,205 | 1,000 | 675 | 47 | 1,205 R | 56.1% | 25.5% | 17.2% |
| 9,489 | GRANT | 3,522 | 1,386 | 1,169 | 941 | 26 | 217 R | 39.4% | 33.2% | 26.7% |
| 30,021 | GRAVES | 12,213 | 3,239 | 5,103 | 3,829 | 42 | 1,274 D | 26.5% | 41.8% | 31.4% |
| 15,834 | GRAYSON | 5,885 | 3,598 | 1,595 | 657 | 35 | 2,003 R | 61.1% | 27.1% | 11.2% |
| 11,249 | GREEN | 4,170 | 2,448 | 1,003 | 712 | 7 | 1,445 R | 58.7% | 24.1% | 17.1% |
| 29,238 | GREENUP | 10,755 | 4,698 | 4,689 | 1,365 | 3 | 9 R | 43.7% | 43.6% | 12.7% |
| 5,330 | HANCOCK | 2,347 | 1,049 | 867 | 419 | 12 | 182 R | 44.7% | 36.9% | 17.9% |
| 67,789 | HARDIN | 12,737 | 5,329 | 4,470 | 2,845 | 93 | 859 R | 41.8% | 35.1% | 22.3% |
| 51,107 | HARLAN | 13,077 | 4,572 | 6,389 | 2,099 | 17 | 1,817 D | 35.0% | 48.9% | 16.1% |
| 13,704 | HARRISON | 4,850 | 1,637 | 2,373 | 839 | 1 | 736 D | 33.8% | 48.9% | 17.3% |
| 14,119 | HART | 5,484 | 2,817 | 1,658 | 1,002 | 7 | 1,159 R | 51.4% | 30.2% | 18.3% |
| 33,519 | HENDERSON | 10,726 | 3,512 | 5,062 | 2,132 | 20 | 1,550 D | 32.7% | 47.2% | 19.9% |
| 10,987 | HENRY | 3,967 | 1,271 | 1,978 | 711 | 7 | 707 D | 32.0% | 49.9% | 17.9% |
| 6,747 | HICKMAN | 2,686 | 623 | 880 | 1,154 | 29 | 274 A | 23.2% | 32.8% | 43.0% |
| 38,458 | HOPKINS | 11,869 | 3,791 | 4,391 | 3,668 | 19 | 600 D | 31.9% | 37.0% | 30.9% |
| 10,677 | JACKSON | 3,684 | 3,098 | 304 | 279 | 3 | 2,794 R | 84.1% | 8.3% | 7.6% |
| 610,947 | JEFFERSON | 222,657 | 95,942 | 90,242 | 35,561 | 912 | 5,700 R | 43.1% | 40.5% | 16.0% |
| 13,625 | JESSAMINE | 5,143 | 2,338 | 1,334 | 1,440 | 31 | 898 R | 45.5% | 25.9% | 28.0% |
| 19,748 | JOHNSON | 6,536 | 4,046 | 2,142 | 344 | 4 | 1,904 R | 61.9% | 32.8% | 5.3% |
| 120,700 | KENTON | 39,557 | 17,263 | 14,656 | 7,612 | 26 | 2,607 R | 43.6% | 37.1% | 19.2% |
| 17,362 | KNOTT | 4,867 | 1,098 | 3,335 | 428 | 6 | 2,237 D | 22.6% | 68.5% | 8.8% |

# KENTUCKY

## PRESIDENT 1968

| 1960 Census Population | County | Total Vote | Republican | Democratic | AIP | Other | Plurality | Percentage Total Vote Rep. | Dem. | AIP |
|---:|---|---:|---:|---:|---:|---:|---:|---:|---:|---:|
| 25,258 | KNOX | 7,595 | 4,388 | 2,244 | 944 | 19 | 2,144 R | 57.8% | 29.5% | 12.4% |
| 10,346 | LARUE | 3,897 | 1,862 | 1,251 | 776 | 8 | 611 R | 47.8% | 32.1% | 19.9% |
| 24,901 | LAUREL | 9,251 | 6,251 | 1,756 | 1,236 | 8 | 4,495 R | 67.6% | 19.0% | 13.4% |
| 12,134 | LAWRENCE | 4,249 | 1,946 | 1,825 | 476 | 2 | 121 R | 45.8% | 43.0% | 11.2% |
| 7,420 | LEE | 2,298 | 1,339 | 674 | 285 | | 665 R | 58.3% | 29.3% | 12.4% |
| 10,941 | LESLIE | 3,679 | 2,615 | 828 | 236 | | 1,787 R | 71.1% | 22.5% | 6.4% |
| 30,102 | LETCHER | 7,667 | 3,243 | 3,499 | 920 | 5 | 256 D | 42.3% | 45.6% | 12.0% |
| 13,115 | LEWIS | 4,257 | 2,760 | 1,017 | 472 | 8 | 1,743 R | 64.8% | 23.9% | 11.1% |
| 16,503 | LINCOLN | 5,461 | 2,591 | 1,736 | 1,129 | 5 | 855 R | 47.4% | 31.8% | 20.7% |
| 7,029 | LIVINGSTON | 3,307 | 1,079 | 1,272 | 953 | 3 | 193 D | 32.6% | 38.5% | 28.8% |
| 20,896 | LOGAN | 8,687 | 3,402 | 3,339 | 1,881 | 65 | 63 R | 39.2% | 38.4% | 21.7% |
| 5,924 | LYON | 1,938 | 579 | 719 | 619 | 21 | 100 D | 29.9% | 37.1% | 31.9% |
| 57,306 | MCCRACKEN | 21,544 | 5,887 | 9,741 | 5,810 | 106 | 3,854 D | 27.3% | 45.2% | 27.0% |
| 12,463 | MCCREARY | 3,949 | 2,670 | 759 | 479 | 41 | 1,911 R | 67.6% | 19.2% | 12.1% |
| 9,355 | MCLEAN | 3,840 | 1,372 | 1,373 | 1,084 | 11 | 1 D | 35.7% | 35.8% | 28.2% |
| 33,482 | MADISON | 11,878 | 5,325 | 3,884 | 2,558 | 111 | 1,441 R | 44.8% | 32.7% | 21.5% |
| 11,156 | MAGOFFIN | 4,123 | 1,967 | 1,927 | 229 | | 40 R | 47.7% | 46.7% | 5.6% |
| 16,887 | MARION | 4,906 | 1,620 | 2,436 | 849 | 1 | 816 D | 33.0% | 49.7% | 17.3% |
| 16,736 | MARSHALL | 7,921 | 2,432 | 3,301 | 2,183 | 5 | 869 D | 30.7% | 41.7% | 27.6% |
| 10,201 | MARTIN | 2,840 | 1,943 | 759 | 136 | 2 | 1,184 R | 68.4% | 26.7% | 4.8% |
| 18,454 | MASON | 6,570 | 2,661 | 2,772 | 1,131 | 6 | 111 D | 40.5% | 42.2% | 17.2% |
| 18,938 | MEADE | 4,200 | 1,385 | 1,926 | 886 | 3 | 541 D | 33.0% | 45.9% | 21.1% |
| 4,276 | MENIFEE | 1,317 | 509 | 554 | 247 | 7 | 45 D | 38.6% | 42.1% | 18.8% |
| 14,596 | MERCER | 5,646 | 2,432 | 1,950 | 1,227 | 37 | 482 R | 43.1% | 34.5% | 21.7% |
| 8,367 | METCALFE | 3,046 | 1,566 | 1,001 | 469 | 10 | 565 R | 51.4% | 32.9% | 15.4% |
| 11,799 | MONROE | 5,372 | 4,086 | 693 | 590 | 3 | 3,393 R | 76.1% | 12.9% | 11.0% |
| 13,461 | MONTGOMERY | 4,508 | 2,113 | 1,408 | 980 | 7 | 705 R | 46.9% | 31.2% | 21.7% |
| 11,056 | MORGAN | 3,961 | 1,341 | 2,222 | 398 | | 881 D | 33.9% | 56.1% | 10.0% |
| 27,791 | MUHLENBERG | 9,750 | 3,853 | 3,688 | 2,198 | 11 | 165 R | 39.5% | 37.8% | 22.5% |
| 22,168 | NELSON | 6,916 | 2,373 | 3,420 | 1,104 | 19 | 1,047 D | 34.3% | 49.5% | 16.0% |
| 6,677 | NICHOLAS | 2,062 | 725 | 911 | 413 | 13 | 186 D | 35.2% | 44.2% | 20.0% |
| 17,725 | OHIO | 6,470 | 3,504 | 1,695 | 1,263 | 8 | 1,809 R | 54.2% | 26.2% | 19.5% |
| 13,388 | OLDHAM | 3,993 | 1,655 | 1,399 | 937 | 2 | 256 R | 41.4% | 35.0% | 23.5% |
| 8,237 | OWEN | 3,134 | 827 | 1,608 | 697 | 2 | 781 D | 26.4% | 51.3% | 22.2% |
| 5,369 | OWSLEY | 1,877 | 1,417 | 303 | 157 | | 1,114 R | 75.5% | 16.1% | 8.4% |
| 9,968 | PENDLETON | 3,533 | 1,614 | 1,156 | 760 | 3 | 458 R | 45.7% | 32.7% | 21.5% |
| 34,961 | PERRY | 9,541 | 3,993 | 4,562 | 983 | 3 | 569 D | 41.9% | 47.8% | 10.3% |
| 68,264 | PIKE | 22,526 | 8,911 | 11,663 | 1,933 | 19 | 2,752 D | 39.6% | 51.8% | 8.6% |
| 6,674 | POWELL | 2,718 | 1,157 | 934 | 625 | 2 | 223 R | 42.6% | 34.4% | 23.0% |
| 34,403 | PULASKI | 12,901 | 8,290 | 2,823 | 1,780 | 8 | 5,467 R | 64.3% | 21.9% | 13.8% |
| 2,443 | ROBERTSON | 1,011 | 416 | 406 | 186 | 3 | 10 R | 41.1% | 40.2% | 18.4% |
| 12,334 | ROCKCASTLE | 4,588 | 3,072 | 868 | 644 | 4 | 2,204 R | 67.0% | 18.9% | 14.0% |
| 12,808 | ROWAN | 4,459 | 2,017 | 1,898 | 541 | 3 | 119 R | 45.2% | 42.6% | 12.1% |
| 11,076 | RUSSELL | 4,721 | 3,035 | 961 | 718 | 7 | 2,074 R | 64.3% | 20.4% | 15.2% |
| 15,376 | SCOTT | 4,984 | 1,748 | 1,961 | 1,242 | 33 | 213 D | 35.1% | 39.3% | 24.9% |
| 18,493 | SHELBY | 6,054 | 2,287 | 2,579 | 1,185 | 3 | 292 D | 37.8% | 42.6% | 19.6% |
| 11,548 | SIMPSON | 4,339 | 1,435 | 1,505 | 1,390 | 9 | 70 D | 33.1% | 34.7% | 32.0% |
| 5,680 | SPENCER | 1,750 | 733 | 564 | 448 | 5 | 169 R | 41.9% | 32.2% | 25.6% |
| 16,285 | TAYLOR | 5,959 | 3,032 | 1,367 | 1,554 | 6 | 1,478 R | 50.9% | 22.9% | 26.1% |
| 11,364 | TODD | 4,479 | 1,433 | 1,082 | 1,932 | 32 | 499 A | 32.0% | 24.2% | 43.1% |
| 8,870 | TRIGG | 3,621 | 1,100 | 1,330 | 1,180 | 11 | 150 D | 30.4% | 36.7% | 32.6% |
| 5,102 | TRIMBLE | 1,967 | 511 | 1,045 | 406 | 5 | 534 D | 26.0% | 53.1% | 20.6% |
| 14,537 | UNION | 5,794 | 1,371 | 2,616 | 1,804 | 3 | 812 D | 23.7% | 45.2% | 31.1% |
| 45,491 | WARREN | 17,665 | 8,084 | 5,200 | 4,365 | 16 | 2,884 R | 45.8% | 29.4% | 24.7% |
| 11,168 | WASHINGTON | 4,019 | 1,863 | 1,675 | 472 | 9 | 188 R | 46.4% | 41.7% | 11.7% |
| 14,700 | WAYNE | 5,002 | 3,055 | 1,467 | 475 | 5 | 1,588 R | 61.1% | 29.3% | 9.5% |
| 14,244 | WEBSTER | 4,905 | 1,446 | 2,114 | 1,337 | 8 | 668 D | 29.5% | 43.1% | 27.3% |
| 25,815 | WHITLEY | 9,439 | 5,639 | 2,134 | 1,650 | 16 | 3,505 R | 59.7% | 22.6% | 17.5% |
| 6,534 | WOLFE | 2,207 | 758 | 1,162 | 282 | 5 | 404 D | 34.3% | 52.7% | 12.8% |
| 11,913 | WOODFORD | 4,472 | 1,901 | 1,646 | 894 | 31 | 255 R | 42.5% | 36.8% | 20.0% |
| 3,038,156 | TOTAL | 1,055,893 | 462,411 | 397,541 | 193,098 | 2,843 | 64,870 R | 43.8% | 37.6% | 18.3% |

# KENTUCKY

## PRESIDENT 1964

| 1960 Census Population | County | Total Vote | Republican | Democratic | Other | Rep.-Dem. Plurality | Percentage | | | |
|---|---|---|---|---|---|---|---|---|---|---|
| | | | | | | | Total Vote | | Major Vote | |
| | | | | | | | Rep. | Dem. | Rep. | Dem. |
| 14,699 | ADAIR | 5,927 | 3,052 | 2,854 | 21 | 198 R | 51.5% | 48.2% | 51.7% | 48.3% |
| 12,269 | ALLEN | 4,342 | 2,309 | 2,023 | 10 | 286 R | 53.2% | 46.6% | 53.3% | 46.7% |
| 8,618 | ANDERSON | 3,586 | 1,085 | 2,491 | 10 | 1,406 D | 30.3% | 69.5% | 30.3% | 69.7% |
| 8,291 | BALLARD | 3,409 | 519 | 2,867 | 23 | 2,348 D | 15.2% | 84.1% | 15.3% | 84.7% |
| 28,303 | BARREN | 9,380 | 2,936 | 6,420 | 24 | 3,484 D | 31.3% | 68.4% | 31.4% | 68.6% |
| 9,114 | BATH | 3,587 | 1,009 | 2,571 | 7 | 1,562 D | 28.1% | 71.7% | 28.2% | 71.8% |
| 35,336 | BELL | 11,227 | 4,185 | 6,979 | 63 | 2,794 D | 37.3% | 62.2% | 37.5% | 62.5% |
| 21,940 | BOONE | 8,522 | 3,430 | 5,077 | 15 | 1,647 D | 40.2% | 59.6% | 40.3% | 59.7% |
| 18,178 | BOURBON | 5,316 | 1,222 | 4,068 | 26 | 2,846 D | 23.0% | 76.5% | 23.1% | 76.9% |
| 52,163 | BOYD | 18,437 | 6,941 | 11,436 | 60 | 4,495 D | 37.6% | 62.0% | 37.8% | 62.2% |
| 21,257 | BOYLE | 6,962 | 1,972 | 4,976 | 14 | 3,004 D | 28.3% | 71.5% | 28.4% | 71.6% |
| 7,422 | BRACKEN | 2,819 | 861 | 1,958 | | 1,097 D | 30.5% | 69.5% | 30.5% | 69.5% |
| 15,490 | BREATHITT | 5,383 | 669 | 4,714 | | 4,045 D | 12.4% | 87.6% | 12.4% | 87.6% |
| 14,734 | BRECKINRIDGE | 5,911 | 2,167 | 3,733 | 11 | 1,566 D | 36.7% | 63.2% | 36.7% | 63.3% |
| 15,726 | BULLITT | 5,330 | 1,417 | 3,900 | 13 | 2,483 D | 26.6% | 73.2% | 26.7% | 73.3% |
| 9,586 | BUTLER | 3,992 | 2,429 | 1,555 | 8 | 874 R | 60.8% | 39.0% | 61.0% | 39.0% |
| 13,073 | CALDWELL | 4,598 | 1,738 | 2,831 | 29 | 1,093 D | 37.8% | 61.6% | 38.0% | 62.0% |
| 20,972 | CALLOWAY | 8,886 | 1,576 | 7,290 | 20 | 5,714 D | 17.7% | 82.0% | 17.8% | 82.2% |
| 86,803 | CAMPBELL | 28,264 | 12,209 | 16,012 | 43 | 3,803 D | 43.2% | 56.7% | 43.3% | 56.7% |
| 5,608 | CARLISLE | 1,853 | 282 | 1,565 | 6 | 1,283 D | 15.2% | 84.5% | 15.3% | 84.7% |
| 7,978 | CARROLL | 3,105 | 491 | 2,592 | 22 | 2,101 D | 15.8% | 83.5% | 15.9% | 84.1% |
| 20,817 | CARTER | 6,987 | 2,821 | 4,136 | 30 | 1,315 D | 40.4% | 59.2% | 40.5% | 59.5% |
| 14,327 | CASEY | 5,356 | 3,457 | 1,875 | 24 | 1,582 R | 64.5% | 35.0% | 64.8% | 35.2% |
| 56,904 | CHRISTIAN | 12,630 | 3,882 | 8,727 | 21 | 4,845 D | 30.7% | 69.1% | 30.8% | 69.2% |
| 21,075 | CLARK | 6,237 | 2,019 | 4,205 | 13 | 2,186 D | 32.4% | 67.4% | 32.4% | 67.6% |
| 20,748 | CLAY | 6,343 | 3,223 | 3,098 | 22 | 125 R | 50.8% | 48.8% | 51.0% | 49.0% |
| 8,886 | CLINTON | 3,369 | 2,351 | 994 | 24 | 1,357 R | 69.8% | 29.5% | 70.3% | 29.7% |
| 8,648 | CRITTENDEN | 3,497 | 1,863 | 1,627 | 7 | 236 R | 53.3% | 46.5% | 53.4% | 46.6% |
| 7,835 | CUMBERLAND | 3,164 | 1,794 | 1,348 | 22 | 446 R | 56.7% | 42.6% | 57.1% | 42.9% |
| 70,588 | DAVIESS | 23,755 | 8,350 | 15,253 | 152 | 6,903 D | 35.2% | 64.2% | 35.4% | 64.6% |
| 8,085 | EDMONSON | 2,647 | 1,603 | 1,022 | 22 | 581 R | 60.6% | 38.6% | 61.1% | 38.9% |
| 6,330 | ELLIOTT | 2,351 | 323 | 2,026 | 2 | 1,703 D | 13.7% | 86.2% | 13.8% | 86.2% |
| 12,466 | ESTILL | 4,102 | 1,996 | 2,105 | 1 | 109 D | 48.7% | 51.3% | 48.7% | 51.3% |
| 131,906 | FAYETTE | 44,192 | 18,739 | 25,317 | 136 | 6,578 D | 42.4% | 57.3% | 42.5% | 57.5% |
| 10,890 | FLEMING | 4,352 | 1,668 | 2,678 | 6 | 1,010 D | 38.3% | 61.5% | 38.4% | 61.6% |
| 41,642 | FLOYD | 14,041 | 2,352 | 11,644 | 45 | 9,292 D | 16.8% | 82.9% | 16.8% | 83.2% |
| 29,421 | FRANKLIN | 12,494 | 2,320 | 10,130 | 44 | 7,810 D | 18.6% | 81.1% | 18.6% | 81.4% |
| 11,256 | FULTON | 3,672 | 1,169 | 2,493 | 10 | 1,324 D | 31.8% | 67.9% | 31.9% | 68.1% |
| 3,867 | GALLATIN | 1,517 | 267 | 1,246 | 4 | 979 D | 17.6% | 82.1% | 17.6% | 82.4% |
| 9,747 | GARRARD | 3,935 | 1,828 | 2,092 | 15 | 264 D | 46.5% | 53.2% | 46.6% | 53.4% |
| 9,489 | GRANT | 3,545 | 1,068 | 2,461 | 16 | 1,393 D | 30.1% | 69.4% | 30.3% | 69.7% |
| 30,021 | GRAVES | 12,390 | 2,389 | 9,958 | 43 | 7,569 D | 19.3% | 80.4% | 19.3% | 80.7% |
| 15,834 | GRAYSON | 5,894 | 2,974 | 2,920 | | 54 R | 50.5% | 49.5% | 50.5% | 49.5% |
| 11,249 | GREEN | 4,286 | 2,110 | 2,160 | 16 | 50 D | 49.2% | 50.4% | 49.4% | 50.6% |
| 29,238 | GREENUP | 10,764 | 4,045 | 6,680 | 39 | 2,635 D | 37.6% | 62.1% | 37.7% | 62.3% |
| 5,330 | HANCOCK | 2,190 | 756 | 1,423 | 11 | 667 D | 34.5% | 65.0% | 34.7% | 65.3% |
| 67,789 | HARDIN | 11,264 | 3,744 | 7,460 | 60 | 3,716 D | 33.2% | 66.2% | 33.4% | 66.6% |
| 51,107 | HARLAN | 13,428 | 4,025 | 9,394 | 9 | 5,369 D | 30.0% | 70.0% | 30.0% | 70.0% |
| 13,704 | HARRISON | 5,246 | 1,054 | 4,179 | 13 | 3,125 D | 20.1% | 79.7% | 20.1% | 79.9% |
| 14,119 | HART | 5,295 | 1,961 | 3,313 | 21 | 1,352 D | 37.0% | 62.6% | 37.2% | 62.8% |
| 33,519 | HENDERSON | 10,785 | 2,734 | 8,022 | 29 | 5,288 D | 25.4% | 74.4% | 25.4% | 74.6% |
| 10,987 | HENRY | 4,363 | 838 | 3,521 | 4 | 2,683 D | 19.2% | 80.7% | 19.2% | 80.8% |
| 6,747 | HICKMAN | 2,774 | 613 | 2,149 | 12 | 1,536 D | 22.1% | 77.5% | 22.2% | 77.8% |
| 38,458 | HOPKINS | 11,297 | 3,328 | 7,954 | 15 | 4,626 D | 29.5% | 70.4% | 29.5% | 70.5% |
| 10,677 | JACKSON | 3,597 | 2,654 | 920 | 23 | 1,734 R | 73.8% | 25.6% | 74.3% | 25.7% |
| 610,947 | JEFFERSON | 227,823 | 80,951 | 146,023 | 849 | 65,072 D | 35.5% | 64.1% | 35.7% | 64.3% |
| 13,625 | JESSAMINE | 6,205 | 3,075 | 3,053 | 77 | 22 R | 49.6% | 49.2% | 50.2% | 49.8% |
| 19,748 | JOHNSON | 4,482 | 1,968 | 2,485 | 29 | 517 D | 43.9% | 55.4% | 44.2% | 55.8% |
| 120,700 | KENTON | 38,795 | 15,630 | 23,103 | 62 | 7,473 D | 40.3% | 59.6% | 40.4% | 59.6% |
| 17,362 | KNOTT | 5,230 | 482 | 4,739 | 9 | 4,257 D | 9.2% | 90.6% | 9.2% | 90.8% |

# KENTUCKY

## PRESIDENT 1964

| 1960 Census Population | County | Total Vote | Republican | Democratic | Other | Rep.-Dem. Plurality | Percentage Total Vote Rep. | Total Vote Dem. | Major Vote Rep. | Major Vote Dem. |
|---|---|---|---|---|---|---|---|---|---|---|
| 25,258 | KNOX | 7,770 | 3,583 | 4,150 | 37 | 567 D | 46.1% | 53.4% | 46.3% | 53.7% |
| 10,346 | LARUE | 3,957 | 1,195 | 2,742 | 20 | 1,547 D | 30.2% | 69.3% | 30.4% | 69.6% |
| 24,901 | LAUREL | 8,665 | 5,008 | 3,633 | 24 | 1,375 R | 57.8% | 41.9% | 58.0% | 42.0% |
| 12,134 | LAWRENCE | 4,455 | 1,745 | 2,703 | 7 | 958 D | 39.2% | 60.7% | 39.2% | 60.8% |
| 7,420 | LEE | 2,543 | 1,162 | 1,376 | 5 | 214 D | 45.7% | 54.1% | 45.8% | 54.2% |
| 10,941 | LESLIE | 3,774 | 1,971 | 1,795 | 8 | 176 R | 52.2% | 47.6% | 52.3% | 47.7% |
| 30,102 | LETCHER | 8,063 | 2,632 | 5,420 | 11 | 2,788 D | 32.6% | 67.2% | 32.7% | 67.3% |
| 13,115 | LEWIS | 4,294 | 2,230 | 2,047 | 17 | 183 R | 51.9% | 47.7% | 52.1% | 47.9% |
| 16,503 | LINCOLN | 5,277 | 1,958 | 3,307 | 12 | 1,349 D | 37.1% | 62.7% | 37.2% | 62.8% |
| 7,029 | LIVINGSTON | 2,979 | 821 | 2,147 | 11 | 1,326 D | 27.6% | 72.1% | 27.7% | 72.3% |
| 20,896 | LOGAN | 8,494 | 2,232 | 6,234 | 28 | 4,002 D | 26.3% | 73.4% | 26.4% | 73.6% |
| 5,924 | LYON | 2,006 | 583 | 1,412 | 11 | 829 D | 29.1% | 70.4% | 29.2% | 70.8% |
| 57,306 | MCCRACKEN | 20,808 | 4,543 | 16,178 | 87 | 11,635 D | 21.8% | 77.7% | 21.9% | 78.1% |
| 12,463 | MCCREARY | 3,683 | 2,230 | 1,428 | 25 | 802 R | 60.5% | 38.8% | 61.0% | 39.0% |
| 9,355 | MCLEAN | 3,755 | 1,173 | 2,576 | 6 | 1,403 D | 31.2% | 68.6% | 31.3% | 68.7% |
| 33,482 | MADISON | 11,200 | 4,266 | 6,877 | 57 | 2,611 D | 38.1% | 61.4% | 38.3% | 61.7% |
| 11,156 | MAGOFFIN | 3,853 | 1,327 | 2,498 | 28 | 1,171 D | 34.4% | 64.8% | 34.7% | 65.3% |
| 16,887 | MARION | 5,344 | 1,074 | 4,265 | 5 | 3,191 D | 20.1% | 79.8% | 20.1% | 79.9% |
| 16,736 | MARSHALL | 7,668 | 1,679 | 5,968 | 21 | 4,289 D | 21.9% | 77.8% | 22.0% | 78.0% |
| 10,201 | MARTIN | 3,306 | 1,567 | 1,694 | 45 | 127 D | 47.4% | 51.2% | 48.1% | 51.9% |
| 18,454 | MASON | 6,952 | 2,437 | 4,502 | 13 | 2,065 D | 35.1% | 64.8% | 35.1% | 64.9% |
| 18,938 | MEADE | 4,136 | 1,055 | 3,076 | 5 | 2,021 D | 25.5% | 74.4% | 25.5% | 74.5% |
| 4,276 | MENIFEE | 1,401 | 318 | 1,076 | 7 | 758 D | 22.7% | 76.8% | 22.8% | 77.2% |
| 14,596 | MERCER | 5,317 | 1,732 | 3,564 | 21 | 1,832 D | 32.6% | 67.0% | 32.7% | 67.3% |
| 8,367 | METCALFE | 3,252 | 1,277 | 1,967 | 8 | 690 D | 39.3% | 60.5% | 39.4% | 60.6% |
| 11,799 | MONROE | 5,010 | 3,293 | 1,713 | 4 | 1,580 R | 65.7% | 34.2% | 65.8% | 34.2% |
| 13,461 | MONTGOMERY | 4,583 | 1,540 | 3,039 | 4 | 1,499 D | 33.6% | 66.3% | 33.6% | 66.4% |
| 11,056 | MORGAN | 3,887 | 546 | 3,293 | 48 | 2,747 D | 14.0% | 84.7% | 14.2% | 85.8% |
| 27,791 | MUHLENBERG | 9,741 | 3,300 | 6,421 | 20 | 3,121 D | 33.9% | 65.9% | 33.9% | 66.1% |
| 22,168 | NELSON | 7,296 | 1,683 | 5,586 | 27 | 3,903 D | 23.1% | 76.6% | 23.2% | 76.8% |
| 6,677 | NICHOLAS | 2,378 | 621 | 1,742 | 15 | 1,121 D | 26.1% | 73.3% | 26.3% | 73.7% |
| 17,725 | OHIO | 6,287 | 2,979 | 3,303 | 5 | 324 D | 47.4% | 52.5% | 47.4% | 52.6% |
| 13,388 | OLDHAM | 3,884 | 1,256 | 2,622 | 6 | 1,366 D | 32.3% | 67.5% | 32.4% | 67.6% |
| 8,237 | OWEN | 3,389 | 405 | 2,980 | 4 | 2,575 D | 12.0% | 87.9% | 12.0% | 88.0% |
| 5,369 | OWSLEY | 1,744 | 1,167 | 571 | 6 | 596 R | 66.9% | 32.7% | 67.1% | 32.9% |
| 9,968 | PENDLETON | 3,815 | 1,313 | 2,495 | 7 | 1,182 D | 34.4% | 65.4% | 34.5% | 65.5% |
| 34,961 | PERRY | 9,947 | 3,211 | 6,728 | 8 | 3,517 D | 32.3% | 67.6% | 32.3% | 67.7% |
| 68,264 | PIKE | 21,253 | 7,078 | 14,140 | 35 | 7,062 D | 33.3% | 66.5% | 33.4% | 66.6% |
| 6,674 | POWELL | 2,625 | 993 | 1,622 | 10 | 629 D | 37.8% | 61.8% | 38.0% | 62.0% |
| 34,403 | PULASKI | 13,278 | 7,383 | 5,840 | 55 | 1,543 R | 55.6% | 44.0% | 55.8% | 44.2% |
| 2,443 | ROBERTSON | 1,119 | 383 | 734 | 2 | 351 D | 34.2% | 65.6% | 34.3% | 65.7% |
| 12,334 | ROCKCASTLE | 4,476 | 2,829 | 1,631 | 16 | 1,198 R | 63.2% | 36.4% | 63.4% | 36.6% |
| 12,808 | ROWAN | 4,396 | 1,554 | 2,824 | 18 | 1,270 D | 35.4% | 64.2% | 35.5% | 64.5% |
| 11,076 | RUSSELL | 4,273 | 2,521 | 1,729 | 23 | 792 R | 59.0% | 40.5% | 59.3% | 40.7% |
| 15,376 | SCOTT | 4,639 | 1,330 | 3,289 | 20 | 1,959 D | 28.7% | 70.9% | 28.8% | 71.2% |
| 18,493 | SHELBY | 6,333 | 1,384 | 4,933 | 16 | 3,549 D | 21.9% | 77.9% | 21.9% | 78.1% |
| 11,548 | SIMPSON | 4,144 | 967 | 3,168 | 9 | 2,201 D | 23.3% | 76.4% | 23.4% | 76.6% |
| 5,680 | SPENCER | 1,954 | 525 | 1,422 | 7 | 897 D | 26.9% | 72.8% | 27.0% | 73.0% |
| 16,285 | TAYLOR | 5,709 | 2,594 | 3,082 | 33 | 488 D | 45.4% | 54.0% | 45.7% | 54.3% |
| 11,364 | TODD | 4,091 | 1,339 | 2,738 | 14 | 1,399 D | 32.7% | 66.9% | 32.8% | 67.2% |
| 8,870 | TRIGG | 3,714 | 912 | 2,790 | 12 | 1,878 D | 24.6% | 75.1% | 24.6% | 75.4% |
| 5,102 | TRIMBLE | 2,178 | 292 | 1,881 | 5 | 1,589 D | 13.4% | 86.4% | 13.4% | 86.6% |
| 14,537 | UNION | 5,181 | 1,220 | 3,934 | 27 | 2,714 D | 23.5% | 75.9% | 23.7% | 76.3% |
| 45,491 | WARREN | 15,831 | 5,915 | 9,887 | 29 | 3,972 D | 37.4% | 62.5% | 37.4% | 62.6% |
| 11,168 | WASHINGTON | 4,351 | 1,561 | 2,790 | | 1,229 D | 35.9% | 64.1% | 35.9% | 64.1% |
| 14,700 | WAYNE | 5,144 | 2,389 | 2,737 | 18 | 348 D | 46.4% | 53.2% | 46.6% | 53.4% |
| 14,244 | WEBSTER | 4,964 | 1,217 | 3,741 | 6 | 2,524 D | 24.5% | 75.4% | 24.5% | 75.5% |
| 25,815 | WHITLEY | 9,599 | 4,779 | 4,782 | 38 | 3 D | 49.8% | 49.8% | 50.0% | 50.0% |
| 6,534 | WOLFE | 2,597 | 562 | 2,018 | 17 | 1,456 D | 21.6% | 77.7% | 21.8% | 78.2% |
| 11,913 | WOODFORD | 4,213 | 1,215 | 2,974 | 24 | 1,759 D | 28.8% | 70.6% | 29.0% | 71.0% |
| 3,038,156 | TOTAL | 1,046,105 | 372,977 | 669,659 | 3,469 | 296,682 D | 35.7% | 64.0% | 35.8% | 64.2% |

# KENTUCKY

## PRESIDENT 1960

| 1960 Census Population | County | Total Vote | Republican | Democratic | Other | Rep.-Dem. Plurality | Percentage | | | |
|---|---|---|---|---|---|---|---|---|---|---|
| | | | | | | | Total Vote | | Major Vote | |
| | | | | | | | Rep. | Dem. | Rep. | Dem. |
| 14,699 | ADAIR | 6,890 | 4,621 | 2,269 | | 2,352 R | 67.1% | 32.9% | 67.1% | 32.9% |
| 12,269 | ALLEN | 5,073 | 3,410 | 1,663 | | 1,747 R | 67.2% | 32.8% | 67.2% | 32.8% |
| 8,618 | ANDERSON | 4,071 | 2,033 | 2,038 | | 5 D | 49.9% | 50.1% | 49.9% | 50.1% |
| 8,291 | BALLARD | 3,867 | 1,121 | 2,746 | | 1,625 D | 29.0% | 71.0% | 29.0% | 71.0% |
| 28,303 | BARREN | 10,133 | 5,187 | 4,946 | | 241 R | 51.2% | 48.8% | 51.2% | 48.8% |
| 9,114 | BATH | 3,954 | 1,888 | 2,066 | | 178 D | 47.7% | 52.3% | 47.7% | 52.3% |
| 35,336 | BELL | 11,986 | 6,805 | 5,181 | | 1,624 R | 56.8% | 43.2% | 56.8% | 43.2% |
| 21,940 | BOONE | 7,800 | 4,835 | 2,965 | | 1,870 R | 62.0% | 38.0% | 62.0% | 38.0% |
| 18,178 | BOURBON | 5,535 | 2,379 | 3,156 | | 777 D | 43.0% | 57.0% | 43.0% | 57.0% |
| 52,163 | BOYD | 20,399 | 11,305 | 9,094 | | 2,211 R | 55.4% | 44.6% | 55.4% | 44.6% |
| 21,257 | BOYLE | 6,932 | 3,624 | 3,308 | | 316 R | 52.3% | 47.7% | 52.3% | 47.7% |
| 7,422 | BRACKEN | 3,328 | 2,002 | 1,326 | | 676 R | 60.2% | 39.8% | 60.2% | 39.8% |
| 15,490 | BREATHITT | 5,303 | 1,996 | 3,307 | | 1,311 D | 37.6% | 62.4% | 37.6% | 62.4% |
| 14,734 | BRECKINRIDGE | 7,115 | 3,979 | 3,136 | | 843 R | 55.9% | 44.1% | 55.9% | 44.1% |
| 15,726 | BULLITT | 5,120 | 2,683 | 2,437 | | 246 R | 52.4% | 47.6% | 52.4% | 47.6% |
| 9,586 | BUTLER | 4,648 | 3,656 | 992 | | 2,664 R | 78.7% | 21.3% | 78.7% | 21.3% |
| 13,073 | CALDWELL | 5,579 | 3,442 | 2,137 | | 1,305 R | 61.7% | 38.3% | 61.7% | 38.3% |
| 20,972 | CALLOWAY | 8,049 | 3,356 | 4,693 | | 1,337 D | 41.7% | 58.3% | 41.7% | 58.3% |
| 86,803 | CAMPBELL | 32,078 | 17,388 | 14,690 | | 2,698 R | 54.2% | 45.8% | 54.2% | 45.8% |
| 5,608 | CARLISLE | 2,748 | 978 | 1,770 | | 792 D | 35.6% | 64.4% | 35.6% | 64.4% |
| 7,978 | CARROLL | 3,360 | 1,135 | 2,225 | | 1,090 D | 33.8% | 66.2% | 33.8% | 66.2% |
| 20,817 | CARTER | 8,435 | 4,956 | 3,479 | | 1,477 R | 58.8% | 41.2% | 58.8% | 41.2% |
| 14,327 | CASEY | 6,224 | 4,811 | 1,413 | | 3,398 R | 77.3% | 22.7% | 77.3% | 22.7% |
| 56,904 | CHRISTIAN | 12,125 | 5,251 | 6,874 | | 1,623 D | 43.3% | 56.7% | 43.3% | 56.7% |
| 21,075 | CLARK | 6,341 | 3,317 | 3,024 | | 293 R | 52.3% | 47.7% | 52.3% | 47.7% |
| 20,748 | CLAY | 6,303 | 4,922 | 1,381 | | 3,541 R | 78.1% | 21.9% | 78.1% | 21.9% |
| 8,886 | CLINTON | 4,190 | 3,524 | 666 | | 2,858 R | 84.1% | 15.9% | 84.1% | 15.9% |
| 8,648 | CRITTENDEN | 4,089 | 2,770 | 1,319 | | 1,451 R | 67.7% | 32.3% | 67.7% | 32.3% |
| 7,835 | CUMBERLAND | 3,537 | 2,697 | 840 | | 1,857 R | 76.3% | 23.7% | 76.3% | 23.7% |
| 70,588 | DAVIESS | 23,231 | 13,385 | 9,846 | | 3,539 R | 57.6% | 42.4% | 57.6% | 42.4% |
| 8,085 | EDMONSON | 3,960 | 2,884 | 1,076 | | 1,808 R | 72.8% | 27.2% | 72.8% | 27.2% |
| 6,330 | ELLIOTT | 2,523 | 789 | 1,734 | | 945 D | 31.3% | 68.7% | 31.3% | 68.7% |
| 12,466 | ESTILL | 4,993 | 3,238 | 1,755 | | 1,483 R | 64.9% | 35.1% | 64.9% | 35.1% |
| 131,906 | FAYETTE | 41,647 | 25,169 | 16,478 | | 8,691 R | 60.4% | 39.6% | 60.4% | 39.6% |
| 10,890 | FLEMING | 4,993 | 2,777 | 2,216 | | 561 R | 55.6% | 44.4% | 55.6% | 44.4% |
| 41,642 | FLOYD | 14,886 | 5,010 | 9,876 | | 4,866 D | 33.7% | 66.3% | 33.7% | 66.3% |
| 29,421 | FRANKLIN | 11,794 | 4,742 | 7,052 | | 2,310 D | 40.2% | 59.8% | 40.2% | 59.8% |
| 11,256 | FULTON | 4,275 | 1,567 | 2,708 | | 1,141 D | 36.7% | 63.3% | 36.7% | 63.3% |
| 3,867 | GALLATIN | 1,784 | 756 | 1,028 | | 272 D | 42.4% | 57.6% | 42.4% | 57.6% |
| 9,747 | GARRARD | 4,539 | 2,759 | 1,780 | | 979 R | 60.8% | 39.2% | 60.8% | 39.2% |
| 9,489 | GRANT | 4,062 | 2,163 | 1,899 | | 264 R | 53.2% | 46.8% | 53.2% | 46.8% |
| 30,021 | GRAVES | 12,543 | 4,854 | 7,689 | | 2,835 D | 38.7% | 61.3% | 38.7% | 61.3% |
| 15,834 | GRAYSON | 7,162 | 4,807 | 2,355 | | 2,452 R | 67.1% | 32.9% | 67.1% | 32.9% |
| 11,249 | GREEN | 5,186 | 3,606 | 1,580 | | 2,026 R | 69.5% | 30.5% | 69.5% | 30.5% |
| 29,238 | GREENUP | 11,346 | 6,101 | 5,245 | | 856 R | 53.8% | 46.2% | 53.8% | 46.2% |
| 5,330 | HANCOCK | 2,506 | 1,488 | 1,018 | | 470 R | 59.4% | 40.6% | 59.4% | 40.6% |
| 67,789 | HARDIN | 11,332 | 6,191 | 5,141 | | 1,050 R | 54.6% | 45.4% | 54.6% | 45.4% |
| 51,107 | HARLAN | 16,696 | 7,485 | 9,211 | | 1,726 D | 44.8% | 55.2% | 44.8% | 55.2% |
| 13,704 | HARRISON | 5,787 | 2,306 | 3,481 | | 1,175 D | 39.8% | 60.2% | 39.8% | 60.2% |
| 14,119 | HART | 6,739 | 3,610 | 3,129 | | 481 R | 53.6% | 46.4% | 53.6% | 46.4% |
| 33,519 | HENDERSON | 10,867 | 5,302 | 5,565 | | 263 D | 48.8% | 51.2% | 48.8% | 51.2% |
| 10,987 | HENRY | 4,683 | 1,714 | 2,969 | | 1,255 D | 36.6% | 63.4% | 36.6% | 63.4% |
| 6,747 | HICKMAN | 3,144 | 968 | 2,176 | | 1,208 D | 30.8% | 69.2% | 30.8% | 69.2% |
| 38,458 | HOPKINS | 12,010 | 5,574 | 6,436 | | 862 D | 46.4% | 53.6% | 46.4% | 53.6% |
| 10,677 | JACKSON | 4,342 | 3,923 | 419 | | 3,504 R | 90.4% | 9.6% | 90.4% | 9.6% |
| 610,947 | JEFFERSON | 235,755 | 118,575 | 117,180 | | 1,395 R | 50.3% | 49.7% | 50.3% | 49.7% |
| 13,625 | JESSAMINE | 4,809 | 2,787 | 2,022 | | 765 R | 58.0% | 42.0% | 58.0% | 42.0% |
| 19,748 | JOHNSON | 7,939 | 5,317 | 2,622 | | 2,695 R | 67.0% | 33.0% | 67.0% | 33.0% |
| 120,700 | KENTON | 41,323 | 21,857 | 19,466 | | 2,391 R | 52.9% | 47.1% | 52.9% | 47.1% |
| 17,362 | KNOTT | 5,369 | 1,412 | 3,957 | | 2,545 D | 26.3% | 73.7% | 26.3% | 73.7% |

# KENTUCKY

## PRESIDENT 1960

| 1960 Census Population | County | Total Vote | Republican | Democratic | Other | Rep.-Dem. Plurality | Percentage Total Vote Rep. | Dem. | Major Vote Rep. | Dem. |
|---|---|---|---|---|---|---|---|---|---|---|
| 25,258 | KNOX | 8,770 | 5,814 | 2,956 | | 2,858 R | 66.3% | 33.7% | 66.3% | 33.7% |
| 10,346 | LARUE | 4,381 | 2,668 | 1,713 | | 955 R | 60.9% | 39.1% | 60.9% | 39.1% |
| 24,901 | LAUREL | 9,794 | 7,485 | 2,309 | | 5,176 R | 76.4% | 23.6% | 76.4% | 23.6% |
| 12,134 | LAWRENCE | 5,540 | 3,030 | 2,510 | | 520 R | 54.7% | 45.3% | 54.7% | 45.3% |
| 7,420 | LEE | 2,970 | 2,012 | 958 | | 1,054 R | 67.7% | 32.3% | 67.7% | 32.3% |
| 10,941 | LESLIE | 4,689 | 3,894 | 795 | | 3,099 R | 83.0% | 17.0% | 83.0% | 17.0% |
| 30,102 | LETCHER | 8,666 | 4,408 | 4,258 | | 150 R | 50.9% | 49.1% | 50.9% | 49.1% |
| 13,115 | LEWIS | 5,498 | 3,816 | 1,682 | | 2,134 R | 69.4% | 30.6% | 69.4% | 30.6% |
| 16,503 | LINCOLN | 6,128 | 3,747 | 2,381 | | 1,366 R | 61.1% | 38.9% | 61.1% | 38.9% |
| 7,029 | LIVINGSTON | 3,157 | 1,639 | 1,518 | | 121 R | 51.9% | 48.1% | 51.9% | 48.1% |
| 20,896 | LOGAN | 8,836 | 4,117 | 4,719 | | 602 D | 46.6% | 53.4% | 46.6% | 53.4% |
| 5,924 | LYON | 2,403 | 1,024 | 1,379 | | 355 D | 42.6% | 57.4% | 42.6% | 57.4% |
| 57,306 | MCCRACKEN | 22,228 | 9,689 | 12,539 | | 2,850 D | 43.6% | 56.4% | 43.6% | 56.4% |
| 12,463 | MCCREARY | 4,595 | 3,671 | 924 | | 2,747 R | 79.9% | 20.1% | 79.9% | 20.1% |
| 9,355 | MCLEAN | 3,985 | 2,269 | 1,716 | | 553 R | 56.9% | 43.1% | 56.9% | 43.1% |
| 33,482 | MADISON | 12,313 | 6,692 | 5,621 | | 1,071 R | 54.3% | 45.7% | 54.3% | 45.7% |
| 11,156 | MAGOFFIN | 5,207 | 2,736 | 2,471 | | 265 R | 52.5% | 47.5% | 52.5% | 47.5% |
| 16,887 | MARION | 6,495 | 2,203 | 4,292 | | 2,089 D | 33.9% | 66.1% | 33.9% | 66.1% |
| 16,736 | MARSHALL | 6,872 | 3,388 | 3,484 | | 96 D | 49.3% | 50.7% | 49.3% | 50.7% |
| 10,201 | MARTIN | 3,925 | 2,809 | 1,116 | | 1,693 R | 71.6% | 28.4% | 71.6% | 28.4% |
| 18,454 | MASON | 7,487 | 4,334 | 3,153 | | 1,181 R | 57.9% | 42.1% | 57.9% | 42.1% |
| 18,938 | MEADE | 4,211 | 1,826 | 2,385 | | 559 D | 43.4% | 56.6% | 43.4% | 56.6% |
| 4,276 | MENIFEE | 1,806 | 817 | 989 | | 172 D | 45.2% | 54.8% | 45.2% | 54.8% |
| 14,596 | MERCER | 6,282 | 3,569 | 2,713 | | 856 R | 56.8% | 43.2% | 56.8% | 43.2% |
| 8,367 | METCALFE | 3,699 | 2,146 | 1,553 | | 593 R | 58.0% | 42.0% | 58.0% | 42.0% |
| 11,799 | MONROE | 5,307 | 4,337 | 970 | | 3,367 R | 81.7% | 18.3% | 81.7% | 18.3% |
| 13,461 | MONTGOMERY | 5,080 | 2,451 | 2,629 | | 178 D | 48.2% | 51.8% | 48.2% | 51.8% |
| 11,056 | MORGAN | 4,628 | 1,718 | 2,910 | | 1,192 D | 37.1% | 62.9% | 37.1% | 62.9% |
| 27,791 | MUHLENBERG | 10,395 | 5,968 | 4,427 | | 1,541 R | 57.4% | 42.6% | 57.4% | 42.6% |
| 22,168 | NELSON | 7,734 | 3,021 | 4,713 | | 1,692 D | 39.1% | 60.9% | 39.1% | 60.9% |
| 6,677 | NICHOLAS | 2,513 | 1,058 | 1,455 | | 397 D | 42.1% | 57.9% | 42.1% | 57.9% |
| 17,725 | OHIO | 7,650 | 5,230 | 2,420 | | 2,810 R | 68.4% | 31.6% | 68.4% | 31.6% |
| 13,388 | OLDHAM | 4,181 | 2,221 | 1,960 | | 261 R | 53.1% | 46.9% | 53.1% | 46.9% |
| 8,237 | OWEN | 3,658 | 1,212 | 2,446 | | 1,234 D | 33.1% | 66.9% | 33.1% | 66.9% |
| 5,369 | OWSLEY | 2,515 | 2,169 | 346 | | 1,823 R | 86.2% | 13.8% | 86.2% | 13.8% |
| 9,968 | PENDLETON | 3,884 | 2,387 | 1,497 | | 890 R | 61.5% | 38.5% | 61.5% | 38.5% |
| 34,961 | PERRY | 10,725 | 5,754 | 4,971 | | 783 R | 53.7% | 46.3% | 53.7% | 46.3% |
| 68,264 | PIKE | 22,995 | 9,956 | 13,039 | | 3,083 D | 43.3% | 56.7% | 43.3% | 56.7% |
| 6,674 | POWELL | 2,630 | 1,508 | 1,122 | | 386 R | 57.3% | 42.7% | 57.3% | 42.7% |
| 34,403 | PULASKI | 14,996 | 11,899 | 3,097 | | 8,802 R | 79.3% | 20.7% | 79.3% | 20.7% |
| 2,443 | ROBERTSON | 1,246 | 594 | 652 | | 58 D | 47.7% | 52.3% | 47.7% | 52.3% |
| 12,334 | ROCKCASTLE | 5,123 | 3,982 | 1,141 | | 2,841 R | 77.7% | 22.3% | 77.7% | 22.3% |
| 12,808 | ROWAN | 4,970 | 2,558 | 2,412 | | 146 R | 51.5% | 48.5% | 51.5% | 48.5% |
| 11,076 | RUSSELL | 4,866 | 3,636 | 1,230 | | 2,406 R | 74.7% | 25.3% | 74.7% | 25.3% |
| 15,376 | SCOTT | 4,798 | 2,200 | 2,598 | | 398 D | 45.9% | 54.1% | 45.9% | 54.1% |
| 18,493 | SHELBY | 6,756 | 2,934 | 3,822 | | 888 D | 43.4% | 56.6% | 43.4% | 56.6% |
| 11,548 | SIMPSON | 4,569 | 1,927 | 2,642 | | 715 D | 42.2% | 57.8% | 42.2% | 57.8% |
| 5,680 | SPENCER | 2,182 | 1,134 | 1,048 | | 86 R | 52.0% | 48.0% | 52.0% | 48.0% |
| 16,285 | TAYLOR | 6,855 | 4,669 | 2,186 | | 2,483 R | 68.1% | 31.9% | 68.1% | 31.9% |
| 11,364 | TODD | 4,673 | 1,846 | 2,827 | | 981 D | 39.5% | 60.5% | 39.5% | 60.5% |
| 8,870 | TRIGG | 3,911 | 1,500 | 2,411 | | 911 D | 38.4% | 61.6% | 38.4% | 61.6% |
| 5,102 | TRIMBLE | 2,330 | 743 | 1,587 | | 844 D | 31.9% | 68.1% | 31.9% | 68.1% |
| 14,537 | UNION | 5,246 | 1,789 | 3,457 | | 1,668 D | 34.1% | 65.9% | 34.1% | 65.9% |
| 45,491 | WARREN | 16,531 | 9,074 | 7,457 | | 1,617 R | 54.9% | 45.1% | 54.9% | 45.1% |
| 11,168 | WASHINGTON | 5,023 | 2,632 | 2,391 | | 241 R | 52.4% | 47.6% | 52.4% | 47.6% |
| 14,700 | WAYNE | 5,937 | 3,973 | 1,964 | | 2,009 R | 66.9% | 33.1% | 66.9% | 33.1% |
| 14,244 | WEBSTER | 5,677 | 2,498 | 3,179 | | 681 D | 44.0% | 56.0% | 44.0% | 56.0% |
| 25,815 | WHITLEY | 10,514 | 7,553 | 2,961 | | 4,592 R | 71.8% | 28.2% | 71.8% | 28.2% |
| 6,534 | WOLFE | 2,813 | 1,259 | 1,554 | | 295 D | 44.8% | 55.2% | 44.8% | 55.2% |
| 11,913 | WOODFORD | 4,177 | 2,227 | 1,950 | | 277 R | 53.3% | 46.7% | 53.3% | 46.7% |
| 3,038,156 | TOTAL | 1,124,462 | 602,607 | 521,855 | | 80,752 R | 53.6% | 46.4% | 53.6% | 46.4% |

# KENTUCKY

## ELECTION NOTES

**2004**  Other vote was 8,856 Independent (Ralph Nader); 2,619 Libertarian (Michael Badnarik); 2,213 Constitution (Michael Peroutka); 13 write-in (Walter F. Brown); 9 write-in (John Joseph Kennedy).

**2000**  Other vote was 4,173 Reform (Buchanan); 2,896 Libertarian (Browne); 1,533 Natural Law (Hagelin); 923 Constitution (Phillips); 80 write-in (Strickland).

**1996**  Other vote was 4,009 Libertarian (Browne); 2,204 Taxpayers (Phillips); 1,493 Natural Law (Hagelin); 701 write-in (Nader); 8 scattered write-in.

**1992**  Other vote was 4,513 Marrou (Libertarian); 989 Phillips (Taxpayers); 695 Hagelin (Natural Law); 430 Fulani (New Alliance); 47 Gritz (write-in).

**1988**  Other vote was 4,494 Duke (Populist); 2,118 Paul (Libertarian); 1,256 Fulani (New Alliance).

**1984**  Other vote was 3,129 Mason (Socialist Workers); 1,776 LaRouche (Independent); 1,479 Anderson (National Unity); 599 Johnson (Citizens); 428 Dennis (American); 365 Serrette (Independent Alliance); 328 Hall (Communist).

**1980**  Other vote was 31,127 Anderson (Anderson Coalition); 5,531 Clark (Libertarian); 4,233 McCormack (Respect for Life); 1,304 Commoner (Citizens); 393 Pulley (Socialist Workers); 348 Hall (Communist). Early unamended canvass gave the Democratic state-wide total vote as 617,417.

**1976**  Other vote was 8,308 Anderson (American); 6,837 McCarthy (Independent); 2,328 Maddox (American Independent); 814 MacBride (Libertarian); 510 LaRouche (U.S. Labor); 426 Hall (Communist); 350 Camejo (Socialist Workers).

**1972**  Other vote was 17,627 Schmitz (American); 1,118 Spock (People's); 685 Jenness (Socialist Workers); 464 Hall (Communist). Although the data indicate a possible discrepancy in the Republican vote in Jackson county, the official state canvass figures are used here. Although the data indicate a possible undercount in the vote in Ohio county, the official state canvass figures are used here.

**1968**  Wallace on the ballot as American. Other vote was Halstead (Socialist Workers). Early unamended canvass gave the Hart county Democratic vote as 1,657.

**1964**  Other vote was Kasper (National States Rights).

**1960**

# LOUISIANA

## POPULAR VOTE FOR PRESIDENT 1920 TO 2004

| Year | Total Vote | Republican Vote | Candidate | Democratic Vote | Candidate | Other Vote | Plurality | Percentage Total Vote Rep. | Dem. | Major Vote Rep. | Dem. |
|---|---|---|---|---|---|---|---|---|---|---|---|
| 2004 | 1,943,106 | 1,102,169 | Bush, George W. | 820,299 | Kerry, John | 20,638 | 281,870 R | 56.7% | 42.2% | 57.3% | 42.7% |
| 2000** | 1,765,656 | 927,871 | Bush, George W. | 792,344 | Gore, Al | 45,441 | 135,527 R | 52.6% | 44.9% | 53.9% | 46.1% |
| 1996 ** | 1,783,959 | 712,586 | Dole, Bob | 927,837 | Clinton, Bill | 143,536 | 215,251 D | 39.9% | 52.0% | 43.4% | 56.6% |
| 1992 ** | 1,790,017 | 733,386 | Bush, George | 815,971 | Clinton, Bill | 240,660 | 82,585 D | 41.0% | 45.6% | 47.3% | 52.7% |
| 1988 | 1,628,202 | 883,702 | Bush, George | 717,460 | Dukakis, Michael S. | 27,040 | 166,242 R | 54.3% | 44.1% | 55.2% | 44.8% |
| 1984 | 1,706,822 | 1,037,299 | Reagan, Ronald | 651,586 | Mondale, Walter F. | 17,937 | 385,713 R | 60.8% | 38.2% | 61.4% | 38.6% |
| 1980** | 1,548,591 | 792,853 | Reagan, Ronald | 708,453 | Carter, Jimmy | 47,285 | 84,400 R | 51.2% | 45.7% | 52.8% | 47.2% |
| 1976 | 1,278,439 | 587,446 | Ford, Gerald R. | 661,365 | Carter, Jimmy | 29,628 | 73,919 D | 46.0% | 51.7% | 47.0% | 53.0% |
| 1972 | 1,051,491 | 686,852 | Nixon, Richard M. | 298,142 | McGovern, George S. | 66,497 | 388,710 R | 65.3% | 28.4% | 69.7% | 30.3% |
| 1968 ** | 1,097,450 | 257,535 | Nixon, Richard M. | 309,615 | Humphrey, Hubert H. | 530,300 | 220,685 A | 23.5% | 28.2% | 45.4% | 54.6% |
| 1964 | 896,293 | 509,225 | Goldwater, Barry M. | 387,068 | Johnson, Lyndon B. | | 122,157 R | 56.8% | 43.2% | 56.8% | 43.2% |
| 1960 | 807,891 | 230,980 | Nixon, Richard M. | 407,339 | Kennedy, John F. | 169,572 | 176,359 D | 28.6% | 50.4% | 36.2% | 63.8% |
| 1956 | 617,544 | 329,047 | Eisenhower, Dwight D. | 243,977 | Stevenson, Adlai E. | 44,520 | 85,070 R | 53.3% | 39.5% | 57.4% | 42.6% |
| 1952 | 651,952 | 306,925 | Eisenhower, Dwight D. | 345,027 | Stevenson, Adlai E. | | 38,102 D | 47.1% | 52.9% | 47.1% | 52.9% |
| 1948 ** | 416,336 | 72,657 | Dewey, Thomas E. | 136,344 | Truman, Harry S. | 207,335 | 67,946 SR | 17.5% | 32.7% | 34.8% | 65.2% |
| 1944 | 349,383 | 67,750 | Dewey, Thomas E. | 281,564 | Roosevelt, Franklin D. | 69 | 213,814 D | 19.4% | 80.6% | 19.4% | 80.6% |
| 1940 | 372,305 | 52,446 | Willkie, Wendell | 319,751 | Roosevelt, Franklin D. | 108 | 267,305 D | 14.1% | 85.9% | 14.1% | 85.9% |
| 1936 | 329,778 | 36,791 | Landon, Alfred M. | 292,894 | Roosevelt, Franklin D. | 93 | 256,103 D | 11.2% | 88.8% | 11.2% | 88.8% |
| 1932 | 268,804 | 18,853 | Hoover, Herbert C. | 249,418 | Roosevelt, Franklin D. | 533 | 230,565 D | 7.0% | 92.8% | 7.0% | 93.0% |
| 1928 | 215,833 | 51,160 | Hoover, Herbert C. | 164,655 | Smith, Alfred E. | 18 | 113,495 D | 23.7% | 76.3% | 23.7% | 76.3% |
| 1924 | 121,951 | 24,670 | Coolidge, Calvin | 93,218 | Davis, John W. | 4,063 | 68,548 D | 20.2% | 76.4% | 20.9% | 79.1% |
| 1920 | 126,397 | 38,539 | Harding, Warren G. | 87,519 | Cox, James M. | 339 | 48,980 D | 30.5% | 69.2% | 30.6% | 69.4% |

In 2000 the other vote column includes 20,473 votes cast for Green (Nader). In 1996 the other vote column includes 123,293 votes cast for Perot. In 1992 the other vote column includes 211,478 votes cast for Perot. In 1980 the other column includes 26,345 votes for Independent (Anderson). In 1968 other vote was American (Wallace). In 1948 other vote was 204,290 States Rights; 3,035 Progressive and 10 scattered.

## ELECTORAL COLLEGE VOTE 1920 TO 2004

| Year | Total | Republican | Democratic | Other |
|---|---|---|---|---|
| 2004 | 9 | 9 | | |
| 2000 | 9 | 9 | | |
| 1996 | 9 | | 9 | |
| 1992 | 9 | | 9 | |
| 1988 | 10 | 10 | | |
| 1984 | 10 | 10 | | |
| 1980 | 10 | 10 | | |
| 1976 | 10 | | 10 | |
| 1972 | 10 | 10 | | |
| 1968 | 10 | | | 10 AIP |
| 1964 | 10 | 10 | | |
| 1960 | 10 | | 10 | |
| 1956 | 10 | 10 | | |
| 1952 | 10 | | 10 | |
| 1948 | 10 | | | 10 SR |
| 1944 | 10 | | 10 | |
| 1940 | 10 | | 10 | |
| 1936 | 10 | | 10 | |
| 1932 | 10 | | 10 | |
| 1928 | 10 | | 10 | |
| 1924 | 10 | | 10 | |
| 1920 | 10 | | 10 | |

# LOUISIANA

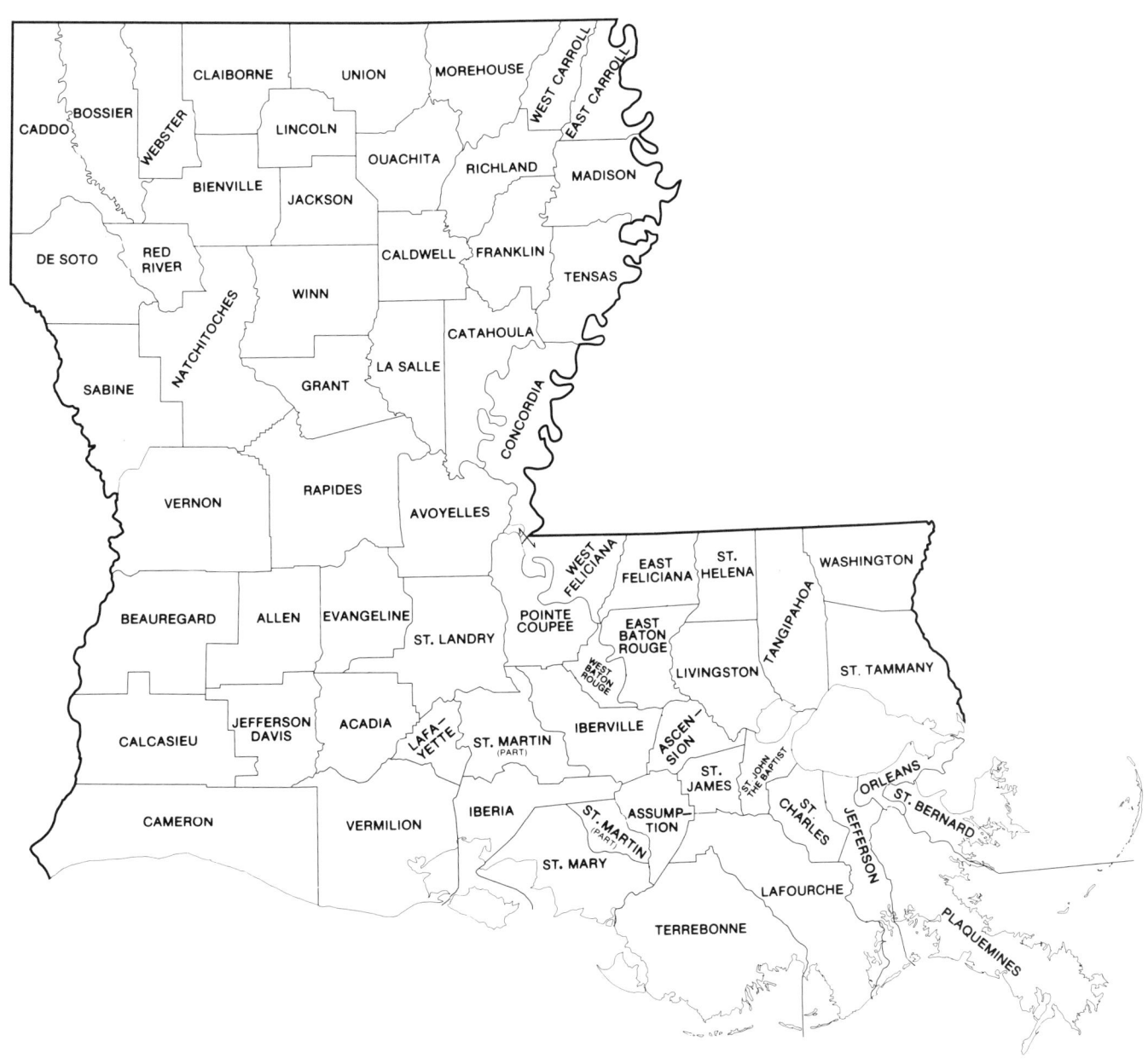

# LOUISIANA

## PRESIDENT 2004

| 2000 Census Population | Parish | Total Vote | Republican | Democratic | Other | Rep.-Dem. Plurality | Total Vote Rep. | Total Vote Dem. | Major Vote Rep. | Major Vote Dem. |
|---|---|---|---|---|---|---|---|---|---|---|
| 58,861 | ACADIA | 25,230 | 16,083 | 8,937 | 210 | 7,146 R | 63.7% | 35.4% | 64.3% | 35.7% |
| 25,440 | ALLEN | 9,124 | 5,140 | 3,791 | 193 | 1,349 R | 56.3% | 41.5% | 57.6% | 42.4% |
| 76,627 | ASCENSION | 39,100 | 24,661 | 13,955 | 484 | 10,706 R | 63.1% | 35.7% | 63.9% | 36.1% |
| 23,388 | ASSUMPTION | 10,735 | 4,966 | 5,585 | 184 | 619 D | 46.3% | 52.0% | 47.1% | 52.9% |
| 41,481 | AVOYELLES | 15,525 | 8,302 | 6,976 | 247 | 1,326 R | 53.5% | 44.9% | 54.3% | 45.7% |
| 32,986 | BEAUREGARD | 13,281 | 9,470 | 3,666 | 145 | 5,804 R | 71.3% | 27.6% | 72.1% | 27.9% |
| 15,752 | BIENVILLE | 7,157 | 3,612 | 3,399 | 146 | 213 R | 50.5% | 47.5% | 51.5% | 48.5% |
| 98,310 | BOSSIER | 42,705 | 30,040 | 12,317 | 348 | 17,723 R | 70.3% | 28.8% | 70.9% | 29.1% |
| 252,161 | CADDO | 106,595 | 54,292 | 51,739 | 564 | 2,553 R | 50.9% | 48.5% | 51.2% | 48.8% |
| 183,577 | CALCASIEU | 79,698 | 46,075 | 32,864 | 759 | 13,211 R | 57.8% | 41.2% | 58.4% | 41.6% |
| 10,560 | CALDWELL | 4,752 | 3,308 | 1,384 | 60 | 1,924 R | 69.6% | 29.1% | 70.5% | 29.5% |
| 9,991 | CAMERON | 4,640 | 3,190 | 1,367 | 83 | 1,823 R | 68.8% | 29.5% | 70.0% | 30.0% |
| 10,920 | CATAHOULA | 4,954 | 3,219 | 1,673 | 62 | 1,546 R | 65.0% | 33.8% | 65.8% | 34.2% |
| 16,851 | CLAIBORNE | 6,630 | 3,704 | 2,854 | 72 | 850 R | 55.9% | 43.0% | 56.5% | 43.5% |
| 20,247 | CONCORDIA | 8,980 | 5,427 | 3,446 | 107 | 1,981 R | 60.4% | 38.4% | 61.2% | 38.8% |
| 25,494 | DE SOTO | 11,336 | 6,211 | 5,026 | 99 | 1,185 R | 54.8% | 44.3% | 55.3% | 44.7% |
| 412,852 | EAST BATON ROUGE | 183,642 | 99,943 | 82,298 | 1,401 | 17,645 R | 54.4% | 44.8% | 54.8% | 45.2% |
| 9,421 | EAST CARROLL | 3,395 | 1,357 | 1,980 | 58 | 623 D | 40.0% | 58.3% | 40.7% | 59.3% |
| 21,360 | EAST FELICIANA | 9,201 | 5,021 | 4,091 | 89 | 930 R | 54.6% | 44.5% | 55.1% | 44.9% |
| 35,434 | EVANGELINE | 13,979 | 7,949 | 5,757 | 273 | 2,192 R | 56.9% | 41.2% | 58.0% | 42.0% |
| 21,263 | FRANKLIN | 9,103 | 6,141 | 2,828 | 134 | 3,313 R | 67.5% | 31.1% | 68.5% | 31.5% |
| 18,698 | GRANT | 7,991 | 5,911 | 1,977 | 103 | 3,934 R | 74.0% | 24.7% | 74.9% | 25.1% |
| 73,266 | IBERIA | 32,273 | 19,420 | 12,426 | 427 | 6,994 R | 60.2% | 38.5% | 61.0% | 39.0% |
| 33,320 | IBERVILLE | 14,827 | 6,333 | 8,259 | 235 | 1,926 D | 42.7% | 55.7% | 43.4% | 56.6% |
| 15,397 | JACKSON | 7,647 | 5,038 | 2,525 | 84 | 2,513 R | 65.9% | 33.0% | 66.6% | 33.4% |
| 455,466 | JEFFERSON | 191,663 | 117,882 | 72,136 | 1,645 | 45,746 R | 61.5% | 37.6% | 62.0% | 38.0% |
| 31,435 | JEFFERSON DAVIS | 13,007 | 8,055 | 4,745 | 207 | 3,310 R | 61.9% | 36.5% | 62.9% | 37.1% |
| 190,503 | LAFAYETTE | 89,923 | 57,732 | 31,210 | 981 | 26,522 R | 64.2% | 34.7% | 64.9% | 35.1% |
| 89,974 | LAFOURCHE | 37,864 | 22,734 | 14,417 | 713 | 8,317 R | 60.0% | 38.1% | 61.2% | 38.8% |
| 14,282 | LA SALLE | 6,238 | 5,015 | 1,155 | 68 | 3,860 R | 80.4% | 18.5% | 81.3% | 18.7% |
| 42,509 | LINCOLN | 18,218 | 10,791 | 7,242 | 185 | 3,549 R | 59.2% | 39.8% | 59.8% | 40.2% |
| 91,814 | LIVINGSTON | 44,253 | 33,976 | 9,895 | 382 | 24,081 R | 76.8% | 22.4% | 77.4% | 22.6% |
| 13,728 | MADISON | 4,673 | 2,291 | 2,334 | 48 | 43 D | 49.0% | 49.9% | 49.5% | 50.5% |
| 31,021 | MOREHOUSE | 12,971 | 7,471 | 5,336 | 164 | 2,135 R | 57.6% | 41.1% | 58.3% | 41.7% |
| 39,080 | NATCHITOCHES | 16,966 | 9,261 | 7,398 | 307 | 1,863 R | 54.6% | 43.6% | 55.6% | 44.4% |
| 484,674 | ORLEANS | 197,103 | 42,847 | 152,610 | 1,646 | 109,763 D | 21.7% | 77.4% | 21.9% | 78.1% |
| 147,250 | OUACHITA | 64,444 | 41,750 | 22,016 | 678 | 19,734 R | 64.8% | 34.2% | 65.5% | 34.5% |
| 26,757 | PLAQUEMINES | 12,153 | 7,866 | 4,181 | 106 | 3,685 R | 64.7% | 34.4% | 65.3% | 34.7% |
| 22,763 | POINTE COUPEE | 11,271 | 5,429 | 5,712 | 130 | 283 D | 48.2% | 50.7% | 48.7% | 51.3% |
| 126,337 | RAPIDES | 54,069 | 34,492 | 18,904 | 673 | 15,588 R | 63.8% | 35.0% | 64.6% | 35.4% |
| 9,622 | RED RIVER | 4,717 | 2,507 | 2,140 | 70 | 367 R | 53.1% | 45.4% | 53.9% | 46.1% |
| 20,981 | RICHLAND | 8,665 | 5,471 | 3,082 | 112 | 2,389 R | 63.1% | 35.6% | 64.0% | 36.0% |
| 23,459 | SABINE | 9,576 | 6,711 | 2,743 | 122 | 3,968 R | 70.1% | 28.6% | 71.0% | 29.0% |
| 67,229 | ST. BERNARD | 29,838 | 19,597 | 9,956 | 285 | 9,641 R | 65.7% | 33.4% | 66.3% | 33.7% |
| 48,072 | ST. CHARLES | 23,837 | 14,747 | 8,856 | 234 | 5,891 R | 61.9% | 37.2% | 62.5% | 37.5% |
| 10,525 | ST. HELENA | 5,508 | 2,235 | 3,173 | 100 | 938 D | 40.6% | 57.6% | 41.3% | 58.7% |
| 21,216 | ST. JAMES | 11,108 | 4,545 | 6,407 | 156 | 1,862 D | 40.9% | 57.7% | 41.5% | 58.5% |
| 43,044 | ST. JOHN THE BAPTIST | 19,617 | 9,039 | 10,305 | 273 | 1,266 D | 46.1% | 52.5% | 46.7% | 53.3% |
| 87,700 | ST. LANDRY | 36,760 | 18,315 | 18,166 | 279 | 149 R | 49.8% | 49.4% | 50.2% | 49.8% |
| 48,583 | ST. MARTIN | 22,824 | 12,095 | 10,321 | 408 | 1,774 R | 53.0% | 45.2% | 54.0% | 46.0% |
| 53,500 | ST. MARY | 22,694 | 12,877 | 9,547 | 270 | 3,330 R | 56.7% | 42.1% | 57.4% | 42.6% |
| 191,268 | ST. TAMMANY | 100,592 | 75,139 | 24,665 | 788 | 50,474 R | 74.7% | 24.5% | 75.3% | 24.7% |
| 100,588 | TANGIPAHOA | 42,135 | 26,181 | 15,345 | 609 | 10,836 R | 62.1% | 36.4% | 63.0% | 37.0% |
| 6,618 | TENSAS | 2,963 | 1,453 | 1,469 | 41 | 16 D | 49.0% | 49.6% | 49.7% | 50.3% |
| 104,503 | TERREBONNE | 40,574 | 26,358 | 13,684 | 532 | 12,674 R | 65.0% | 33.7% | 65.8% | 34.2% |
| 22,803 | UNION | 10,718 | 7,457 | 3,089 | 172 | 4,368 R | 69.6% | 28.8% | 70.7% | 29.3% |
| 53,807 | VERMILION | 24,552 | 15,069 | 9,085 | 398 | 5,984 R | 61.4% | 37.0% | 62.4% | 37.6% |
| 52,531 | VERNON | 15,229 | 11,032 | 4,035 | 162 | 6,997 R | 72.4% | 26.5% | 73.2% | 26.8% |
| 43,926 | WASHINGTON | 17,841 | 11,006 | 6,554 | 281 | 4,452 R | 61.7% | 36.7% | 62.7% | 37.3% |
| 41,831 | WEBSTER | 18,449 | 11,070 | 6,833 | 546 | 4,237 R | 60.0% | 37.0% | 61.8% | 38.2% |

# LOUISIANA

## PRESIDENT 2004

| 2000 Census Population | Parish | Total Vote | Republican | Democratic | Other | Rep.-Dem. Plurality | Percentage | | | |
|---|---|---|---|---|---|---|---|---|---|---|
| | | | | | | | Total Vote | | Major Vote | |
| | | | | | | | Rep. | Dem. | Rep. | Dem. |
| 21,601 | WEST BATON ROUGE | 10,835 | 5,822 | 4,932 | 81 | 890 R | 53.7% | 45.5% | 54.1% | 45.9% |
| 12,314 | WEST CARROLL | 5,033 | 3,740 | 1,231 | 62 | 2,509 R | 74.3% | 24.5% | 75.2% | 24.8% |
| 15,111 | WEST FELICIANA | 5,218 | 2,932 | 2,214 | 72 | 718 R | 56.2% | 42.4% | 57.0% | 43.0% |
| 16,894 | WINN | 6,507 | 4,366 | 2,056 | 85 | 2,310 R | 67.1% | 31.6% | 68.0% | 32.0% |
| 4,468,976 | TOTAL | 1,943,106 | 1,102,169 | 820,299 | 20,638 | 281,870 R | 56.7% | 42.2% | 57.3% | 42.7% |

# LOUISIANA

## PRESIDENT 2000

| 2000 Census Population | Parish | Total Vote | Republican | Democratic | Green (Nader) | Other | Rep.-Dem. Plurality | Percentage of Total Vote | | |
|---|---|---|---|---|---|---|---|---|---|---|
| | | | | | | | | Rep. | Dem. | Green |
| 58,861 | ACADIA | 23,238 | 13,814 | 8,892 | 227 | 305 | 4,922 R | 59.4% | 38.3% | 1.0% |
| 25,440 | ALLEN | 8,292 | 4,035 | 3,914 | 115 | 228 | 121 R | 48.7% | 47.2% | 1.4% |
| 76,627 | ASCENSION | 30,844 | 16,818 | 13,385 | 340 | 301 | 3,433 R | 54.5% | 43.4% | 1.1% |
| 23,388 | ASSUMPTION | 10,053 | 4,388 | 5,222 | 119 | 324 | 834 D | 43.6% | 51.9% | 1.2% |
| 41,481 | AVOYELLES | 14,653 | 7,329 | 6,701 | 170 | 453 | 628 R | 50.0% | 45.7% | 1.2% |
| 32,986 | BEAUREGARD | 12,205 | 7,862 | 3,958 | 155 | 230 | 3,904 R | 64.4% | 32.4% | 1.3% |
| 15,752 | BIENVILLE | 7,006 | 3,269 | 3,413 | 50 | 274 | 144 D | 46.7% | 48.7% | 0.7% |
| 98,310 | BOSSIER | 35,915 | 23,224 | 11,933 | 295 | 463 | 11,291 R | 64.7% | 33.2% | 0.8% |
| 252,161 | CADDO | 95,639 | 46,807 | 47,530 | 734 | 568 | 723 D | 48.9% | 49.7% | 0.8% |
| 183,577 | CALCASIEU | 73,636 | 38,086 | 33,919 | 895 | 736 | 4,167 R | 51.7% | 46.1% | 1.2% |
| 10,560 | CALDWELL | 4,328 | 2,817 | 1,359 | 37 | 115 | 1,458 R | 65.1% | 31.4% | 0.9% |
| 9,991 | CAMERON | 4,183 | 2,593 | 1,435 | 46 | 109 | 1,158 R | 62.0% | 34.3% | 1.1% |
| 10,920 | CATAHOULA | 4,765 | 2,912 | 1,718 | 28 | 107 | 1,194 R | 61.1% | 36.1% | 0.6% |
| 16,851 | CLAIBORNE | 6,281 | 3,384 | 2,721 | 35 | 141 | 663 R | 53.9% | 43.3% | 0.6% |
| 20,247 | CONCORDIA | 8,499 | 4,627 | 3,569 | 54 | 249 | 1,058 R | 54.4% | 42.0% | 0.6% |
| 25,494 | DE SOTO | 10,596 | 5,260 | 5,036 | 67 | 233 | 224 R | 49.6% | 47.5% | 0.6% |
| 412,852 | EAST BATON ROUGE | 168,989 | 89,128 | 76,516 | 2,105 | 1,240 | 12,612 R | 52.7% | 45.3% | 1.2% |
| 9,421 | EAST CARROLL | 3,245 | 1,280 | 1,876 | 16 | 73 | 596 D | 39.4% | 57.8% | 0.5% |
| 21,360 | EAST FELICIANA | 8,099 | 4,051 | 3,870 | 60 | 118 | 181 R | 50.0% | 47.8% | 0.7% |
| 35,434 | EVANGELINE | 13,612 | 7,290 | 5,763 | 140 | 419 | 1,527 R | 53.6% | 42.3% | 1.0% |
| 21,263 | FRANKLIN | 8,356 | 5,363 | 2,792 | 51 | 150 | 2,571 R | 64.2% | 33.4% | 0.6% |
| 18,698 | GRANT | 7,055 | 4,784 | 2,099 | 57 | 115 | 2,685 R | 67.8% | 29.8% | 0.8% |
| 73,266 | IBERIA | 30,020 | 17,236 | 11,762 | 365 | 657 | 5,474 R | 57.4% | 39.2% | 1.2% |
| 33,320 | IBERVILLE | 14,503 | 5,573 | 8,355 | 175 | 400 | 2,782 D | 38.4% | 57.6% | 1.2% |
| 15,397 | JACKSON | 7,106 | 4,347 | 2,582 | 53 | 124 | 1,765 R | 61.2% | 36.3% | 0.7% |
| 455,466 | JEFFERSON | 179,151 | 105,003 | 70,411 | 2,293 | 1,444 | 34,592 R | 58.6% | 39.3% | 1.3% |
| 31,435 | JEFFERSON DAVIS | 12,546 | 6,945 | 5,162 | 143 | 296 | 1,783 R | 55.4% | 41.1% | 1.1% |
| 190,503 | LAFAYETTE | 78,293 | 48,491 | 27,190 | 1,510 | 1,102 | 21,301 R | 61.9% | 34.7% | 1.9% |
| 89,974 | LAFOURCHE | 34,449 | 18,575 | 14,627 | 424 | 823 | 3,948 R | 53.9% | 42.5% | 1.2% |
| 14,282 | LA SALLE | 6,108 | 4,564 | 1,397 | 57 | 90 | 3,167 R | 74.7% | 22.9% | 0.9% |
| 42,509 | LINCOLN | 16,551 | 9,246 | 6,851 | 124 | 330 | 2,395 R | 55.9% | 41.4% | 0.7% |
| 91,814 | LIVINGSTON | 36,865 | 24,889 | 11,008 | 384 | 584 | 13,881 R | 67.5% | 29.9% | 1.0% |
| 13,728 | MADISON | 4,743 | 2,127 | 2,489 | 37 | 90 | 362 D | 44.8% | 52.5% | 0.8% |
| 31,021 | MOREHOUSE | 12,321 | 6,641 | 5,289 | 103 | 288 | 1,352 R | 53.9% | 42.9% | 0.8% |
| 39,080 | NATCHITOCHES | 14,857 | 7,332 | 6,924 | 109 | 492 | 408 R | 49.4% | 46.6% | 0.7% |
| 484,674 | ORLEANS | 181,221 | 39,404 | 137,630 | 3,025 | 1,162 | 98,226 D | 21.7% | 75.9% | 1.7% |
| 147,250 | OUACHITA | 58,211 | 35,107 | 21,457 | 529 | 1,118 | 13,650 R | 60.3% | 36.9% | 0.9% |
| 26,757 | PLAQUEMINES | 10,931 | 6,302 | 4,425 | 104 | 100 | 1,877 R | 57.7% | 40.5% | 1.0% |
| 22,763 | POINTE COUPEE | 10,832 | 4,710 | 5,813 | 108 | 201 | 1,103 D | 43.5% | 53.7% | 1.0% |
| 126,337 | RAPIDES | 49,024 | 28,831 | 18,898 | 446 | 849 | 9,933 R | 58.8% | 38.5% | 0.9% |
| 9,622 | RED RIVER | 4,522 | 2,200 | 2,177 | 35 | 110 | 23 R | 48.7% | 48.1% | 0.8% |
| 20,981 | RICHLAND | 8,485 | 4,895 | 3,282 | 51 | 257 | 1,613 R | 57.7% | 38.7% | 0.6% |
| 23,459 | SABINE | 8,862 | 5,754 | 2,846 | 81 | 181 | 2,908 R | 64.9% | 32.1% | 0.9% |
| 67,229 | ST. BERNARD | 28,621 | 16,255 | 11,682 | 397 | 287 | 4,573 R | 56.8% | 40.8% | 1.4% |
| 48,072 | ST. CHARLES | 21,510 | 11,981 | 8,918 | 215 | 396 | 3,063 R | 55.7% | 41.5% | 1.0% |
| 10,525 | ST. HELENA | 5,254 | 1,965 | 3,059 | 65 | 165 | 1,094 D | 37.4% | 58.2% | 1.2% |
| 21,216 | ST. JAMES | 10,705 | 3,813 | 6,523 | 61 | 308 | 2,710 D | 35.6% | 60.9% | 0.6% |
| 43,044 | ST. JOHN THE BAPTIST | 17,713 | 7,423 | 9,745 | 164 | 381 | 2,322 D | 41.9% | 55.0% | 0.9% |
| 87,700 | ST. LANDRY | 34,151 | 15,449 | 18,067 | 225 | 410 | 2,618 D | 45.2% | 52.9% | 0.7% |
| 48,583 | ST. MARTIN | 20,778 | 9,961 | 9,853 | 268 | 696 | 108 R | 47.9% | 47.4% | 1.3% |
| 53,500 | ST. MARY | 21,810 | 11,325 | 9,851 | 214 | 420 | 1,474 R | 51.9% | 45.2% | 1.0% |
| 191,268 | ST. TAMMANY | 83,737 | 59,193 | 22,722 | 1,199 | 623 | 36,471 R | 70.7% | 27.1% | 1.4% |
| 100,588 | TANGIPAHOA | 37,155 | 20,421 | 15,843 | 405 | 486 | 4,578 R | 55.0% | 42.6% | 1.1% |
| 6,618 | TENSAS | 3,010 | 1,330 | 1,580 | 20 | 80 | 250 D | 44.2% | 52.5% | 0.7% |
| 104,503 | TERREBONNE | 36,675 | 21,314 | 14,414 | 310 | 637 | 6,900 R | 58.1% | 39.3% | 0.8% |
| 22,803 | UNION | 9,343 | 5,772 | 3,205 | 66 | 300 | 2,567 R | 61.8% | 34.3% | 0.7% |
| 53,807 | VERMILION | 22,235 | 12,495 | 8,704 | 307 | 729 | 3,791 R | 56.2% | 39.1% | 1.4% |
| 52,531 | VERNON | 13,827 | 8,794 | 4,655 | 151 | 227 | 4,139 R | 63.6% | 33.7% | 1.1% |
| 43,926 | WASHINGTON | 16,887 | 8,983 | 7,399 | 126 | 379 | 1,584 R | 53.2% | 43.8% | 0.7% |
| 41,831 | WEBSTER | 17,090 | 9,420 | 7,197 | 120 | 353 | 2,223 R | 55.1% | 42.1% | 0.7% |

# LOUISIANA

## PRESIDENT 2000

| 2000 Census Population | Parish | Total Vote | Republican | Democratic | Green (Nader) | Other | Rep.-Dem. Plurality | Percentage of Total Vote | | |
|---|---|---|---|---|---|---|---|---|---|---|
| | | | | | | | | Rep. | Dem. | Green |
| 21,601 | WEST BATON ROUGE | 10,169 | 4,924 | 5,058 | 69 | 118 | 134 D | 48.4% | 49.7% | 0.7% |
| 12,314 | WEST CARROLL | 4,675 | 3,220 | 1,319 | 25 | 111 | 1,901 R | 68.9% | 28.2% | 0.5% |
| 15,111 | WEST FELICIANA | 4,860 | 2,512 | 2,187 | 62 | 99 | 325 R | 51.7% | 45.0% | 1.3% |
| 16,894 | WINN | 6,361 | 4,028 | 2,167 | 52 | 114 | 1,861 R | 63.3% | 34.1% | 0.8% |
| 4,468,976 | TOTAL | 1,765,656 | 927,871 | 792,344 | 20,473 | 24,968 | 135,527 R | 52.6% | 44.9% | 1.2% |

# LOUISIANA

## PRESIDENT 1996

| 1995 Census Pop. Est. | Parish | Total Vote | Republican | Democratic | Reform (Perot) | Other | Rep.-Dem. Plurality | Percentage of Total Vote | | |
|---|---|---|---|---|---|---|---|---|---|---|
| | | | | | | | | Rep. | Dem. | Reform |
| 57,380 | ACADIA | 23,927 | 9,246 | 12,300 | 2,234 | 147 | 3,054 D | 38.6% | 51.4% | 9.3% |
| 23,615 | ALLEN | 8,844 | 2,589 | 4,930 | 1,187 | 138 | 2,341 D | 29.3% | 55.7% | 13.4% |
| 65,847 | ASCENSION | 29,400 | 10,885 | 15,263 | 3,027 | 225 | 4,378 D | 37.0% | 51.9% | 10.3% |
| 22,859 | ASSUMPTION | 10,212 | 2,698 | 6,416 | 904 | 194 | 3,718 D | 26.4% | 62.8% | 8.9% |
| 40,115 | AVOYELLES | 16,410 | 4,433 | 9,689 | 1,937 | 351 | 5,256 D | 27.0% | 59.0% | 11.8% |
| 31,788 | BEAUREGARD | 12,499 | 5,526 | 4,925 | 1,834 | 214 | 601 R | 44.2% | 39.4% | 14.7% |
| 15,812 | BIENVILLE | 7,384 | 2,402 | 4,335 | 457 | 190 | 1,933 D | 32.5% | 58.7% | 6.2% |
| 90,886 | BOSSIER | 35,382 | 16,852 | 15,504 | 2,660 | 366 | 1,348 R | 47.6% | 43.8% | 7.5% |
| 246,697 | CADDO | 99,379 | 38,445 | 55,543 | 4,821 | 570 | 17,098 D | 38.7% | 55.9% | 4.9% |
| 175,868 | CALCASIEU | 73,661 | 26,494 | 38,238 | 8,281 | 648 | 11,744 D | 36.0% | 51.9% | 11.2% |
| 10,198 | CALDWELL | 4,559 | 1,842 | 2,117 | 514 | 86 | 275 D | 40.4% | 46.4% | 11.3% |
| 8,801 | CAMERON | 4,148 | 1,365 | 2,103 | 594 | 86 | 738 D | 32.9% | 50.7% | 14.3% |
| 11,175 | CATAHOULA | 5,166 | 1,770 | 2,692 | 615 | 89 | 922 D | 34.3% | 52.1% | 11.9% |
| 17,261 | CLAIBORNE | 6,739 | 2,500 | 3,609 | 530 | 100 | 1,109 D | 37.1% | 53.6% | 7.9% |
| 21,055 | CONCORDIA | 8,715 | 3,134 | 4,565 | 855 | 161 | 1,431 D | 36.0% | 52.4% | 9.8% |
| 25,174 | DE SOTO | 10,520 | 3,526 | 6,221 | 646 | 127 | 2,695 D | 33.5% | 59.1% | 6.1% |
| 397,364 | EAST BATON ROUGE | 170,647 | 77,811 | 83,493 | 7,990 | 1,353 | 5,682 D | 45.6% | 48.9% | 4.7% |
| 9,506 | EAST CARROLL | 3,411 | 1,008 | 2,149 | 186 | 68 | 1,141 D | 29.6% | 63.0% | 5.5% |
| 20,554 | EAST FELICIANA | 8,401 | 2,949 | 4,714 | 660 | 78 | 1,765 D | 35.1% | 56.1% | 7.9% |
| 33,843 | EVANGELINE | 14,854 | 5,278 | 7,847 | 1,447 | 282 | 2,569 D | 35.5% | 52.8% | 9.7% |
| 22,270 | FRANKLIN | 9,000 | 3,961 | 4,076 | 814 | 149 | 115 D | 44.0% | 45.3% | 9.0% |
| 18,270 | GRANT | 7,292 | 3,117 | 2,980 | 1,055 | 140 | 137 R | 42.7% | 40.9% | 14.5% |
| 71,291 | IBERIA | 29,965 | 12,014 | 15,087 | 2,448 | 416 | 3,073 D | 40.1% | 50.3% | 8.2% |
| 31,073 | IBERVILLE | 14,879 | 4,031 | 9,553 | 1,076 | 219 | 5,522 D | 27.1% | 64.2% | 7.2% |
| 15,722 | JACKSON | 7,067 | 3,030 | 3,368 | 571 | 98 | 338 D | 42.9% | 47.7% | 8.1% |
| 457,333 | JEFFERSON | 184,466 | 92,820 | 80,407 | 9,667 | 1,572 | 12,413 R | 50.3% | 43.6% | 5.2% |
| 31,725 | JEFFERSON DAVIS | 12,943 | 4,311 | 6,897 | 1,543 | 192 | 2,586 D | 33.3% | 53.3% | 11.9% |
| 179,689 | LAFAYETTE | 74,468 | 36,419 | 32,504 | 4,631 | 914 | 3,915 R | 48.9% | 43.6% | 6.2% |
| 87,577 | LAFOURCHE | 34,596 | 12,105 | 18,810 | 2,984 | 697 | 6,705 D | 35.0% | 54.4% | 8.6% |
| 13,894 | LA SALLE | 6,506 | 2,925 | 2,543 | 947 | 91 | 382 R | 45.0% | 39.1% | 14.6% |
| 43,140 | LINCOLN | 15,855 | 6,973 | 7,903 | 761 | 218 | 930 D | 44.0% | 49.8% | 4.8% |
| 80,572 | LIVINGSTON | 34,095 | 16,159 | 13,276 | 4,150 | 510 | 2,883 R | 47.4% | 38.9% | 12.2% |
| 12,688 | MADISON | 5,065 | 1,591 | 3,085 | 315 | 74 | 1,494 D | 31.4% | 60.9% | 6.2% |
| 32,052 | MOREHOUSE | 12,493 | 5,193 | 6,160 | 963 | 177 | 967 D | 41.6% | 49.3% | 7.7% |
| 37,861 | NATCHITOCHES | 15,170 | 5,471 | 8,296 | 1,053 | 350 | 2,825 D | 36.1% | 54.7% | 6.9% |
| 481,913 | ORLEANS | 189,911 | 39,576 | 144,720 | 3,805 | 1,810 | 105,144 D | 20.8% | 76.2% | 2.0% |
| 146,826 | OUACHITA | 57,594 | 28,559 | 24,525 | 3,586 | 924 | 4,034 R | 49.6% | 42.6% | 6.2% |
| 25,693 | PLAQUEMINES | 10,797 | 4,493 | 5,348 | 856 | 100 | 855 D | 41.6% | 49.5% | 7.9% |
| 23,265 | POINTE COUPEE | 11,332 | 3,545 | 6,835 | 845 | 107 | 3,290 D | 31.3% | 60.3% | 7.5% |
| 127,167 | RAPIDES | 49,931 | 21,548 | 23,004 | 4,670 | 709 | 1,456 D | 43.2% | 46.1% | 9.4% |
| 9,430 | RED RIVER | 4,296 | 1,344 | 2,641 | 268 | 43 | 1,297 D | 31.3% | 61.5% | 6.2% |
| 20,763 | RICHLAND | 8,710 | 3,765 | 4,143 | 645 | 157 | 378 D | 43.2% | 47.6% | 7.4% |
| 23,659 | SABINE | 9,007 | 3,543 | 4,263 | 1,043 | 158 | 720 D | 39.3% | 47.3% | 11.6% |
| 67,297 | ST. BERNARD | 30,892 | 13,549 | 14,312 | 2,664 | 367 | 763 D | 43.9% | 46.3% | 8.6% |
| 46,515 | ST. CHARLES | 21,393 | 9,316 | 10,612 | 1,307 | 158 | 1,296 D | 43.5% | 49.6% | 6.1% |
| 9,817 | ST. HELENA | 5,608 | 1,455 | 3,692 | 417 | 44 | 2,237 D | 25.9% | 65.8% | 7.4% |
| 21,038 | ST. JAMES | 10,743 | 2,832 | 7,247 | 608 | 56 | 4,415 D | 26.4% | 67.5% | 5.7% |
| 42,092 | ST. JOHN THE BAPTIST | 17,051 | 6,025 | 9,937 | 966 | 123 | 3,912 D | 35.3% | 58.3% | 5.7% |
| 82,791 | ST. LANDRY | 35,453 | 12,273 | 20,636 | 2,311 | 233 | 8,363 D | 34.6% | 58.2% | 6.5% |
| 45,997 | ST. MARTIN | 20,736 | 6,296 | 12,492 | 1,607 | 341 | 6,196 D | 30.4% | 60.2% | 7.7% |
| 57,443 | ST. MARY | 22,569 | 8,018 | 12,402 | 1,850 | 299 | 4,384 D | 35.5% | 55.0% | 8.2% |
| 173,413 | ST. TAMMANY | 74,526 | 44,761 | 24,281 | 4,741 | 743 | 20,480 R | 60.1% | 32.6% | 6.4% |
| 93,229 | TANGIPAHOA | 37,591 | 15,517 | 18,617 | 3,144 | 313 | 3,100 D | 41.3% | 49.5% | 8.4% |
| 6,899 | TENSAS | 3,099 | 1,000 | 1,882 | 176 | 41 | 882 D | 32.3% | 60.7% | 5.7% |
| 101,180 | TERREBONNE | 36,361 | 13,944 | 18,550 | 3,359 | 508 | 4,606 D | 38.3% | 51.0% | 9.2% |
| 21,541 | UNION | 9,543 | 4,418 | 4,260 | 696 | 169 | 158 R | 46.3% | 44.6% | 7.3% |
| 50,746 | VERMILION | 22,661 | 7,653 | 12,609 | 1,954 | 445 | 4,956 D | 33.8% | 55.6% | 8.6% |
| 55,260 | VERNON | 13,966 | 5,449 | 6,195 | 2,068 | 254 | 746 D | 39.0% | 44.4% | 14.8% |
| 43,154 | WASHINGTON | 18,023 | 6,642 | 9,603 | 1,643 | 135 | 2,961 D | 36.9% | 53.3% | 9.1% |
| 42,195 | WEBSTER | 17,517 | 6,153 | 9,688 | 1,324 | 352 | 3,535 D | 35.1% | 55.3% | 7.6% |

# LOUISIANA

## PRESIDENT 1996

| 1995 Census Pop. Est. | Parish | Total Vote | Republican | Democratic | Reform (Perot) | Other | Rep.-Dem. Plurality | Percentage of Total Vote | | |
|---|---|---|---|---|---|---|---|---|---|---|
| | | | | | | | | Rep. | Dem. | Reform |
| 20,211 | WEST BATON ROUGE | 9,798 | 3,254 | 5,697 | 799 | 48 | 2,443 D | 33.2% | 58.1% | 8.2% |
| 12,138 | WEST CARROLL | 4,764 | 2,366 | 1,853 | 461 | 84 | 513 R | 49.7% | 38.9% | 9.7% |
| 12,679 | WEST FELICIANA | 4,506 | 1,616 | 2,416 | 388 | 86 | 800 D | 35.9% | 53.6% | 8.6% |
| 17,028 | WINN | 7,463 | 2,803 | 3,779 | 735 | 146 | 976 D | 37.6% | 50.6% | 9.8% |
| 4,342,334 | TOTAL | 1,783,959 | 712,586 | 927,837 | 123,293 | 20,243 | 215,251 D | 39.9% | 52.0% | 6.9% |

# LOUISIANA

## PRESIDENT 1992

| 1990 Census Population | Parish | Total Vote | Republican | Democratic | Perot | Other | Plurality | Percentage Total Vote Rep. | Dem. | Perot |
|---|---|---|---|---|---|---|---|---|---|---|
| 55,882 | ACADIA | 24,568 | 9,017 | 12,276 | 3,145 | 130 | 3,259 D | 36.7% | 50.0% | 12.8% |
| 21,226 | ALLEN | 10,017 | 3,069 | 5,626 | 1,245 | 77 | 2,557 D | 30.6% | 56.2% | 12.4% |
| 58,214 | ASCENSION | 27,748 | 10,275 | 13,036 | 4,295 | 142 | 2,761 D | 37.0% | 47.0% | 15.5% |
| 22,753 | ASSUMPTION | 10,453 | 2,928 | 5,639 | 1,358 | 528 | 2,711 D | 28.0% | 53.9% | 13.0% |
| 39,159 | AVOYELLES | 16,549 | 4,851 | 8,696 | 2,139 | 863 | 3,845 D | 29.3% | 52.5% | 12.9% |
| 30,083 | BEAUREGARD | 12,551 | 5,119 | 5,037 | 2,103 | 292 | 82 R | 40.8% | 40.1% | 16.8% |
| 15,979 | BIENVILLE | 7,432 | 2,412 | 3,899 | 832 | 289 | 1,487 D | 32.5% | 52.5% | 11.2% |
| 86,088 | BOSSIER | 32,801 | 15,628 | 11,313 | 4,863 | 997 | 4,315 R | 47.6% | 34.5% | 14.8% |
| 248,253 | CADDO | 102,678 | 42,665 | 47,733 | 11,830 | 450 | 5,068 D | 41.6% | 46.5% | 11.5% |
| 168,134 | CALCASIEU | 69,862 | 24,847 | 33,570 | 10,980 | 465 | 8,723 D | 35.6% | 48.1% | 15.7% |
| 9,810 | CALDWELL | 4,684 | 1,752 | 2,061 | 653 | 218 | 309 D | 37.4% | 44.0% | 13.9% |
| 9,260 | CAMERON | 4,338 | 1,329 | 1,985 | 995 | 29 | 656 D | 30.6% | 45.8% | 22.9% |
| 11,065 | CATAHOULA | 5,471 | 1,976 | 2,570 | 773 | 152 | 594 D | 36.1% | 47.0% | 14.1% |
| 17,405 | CLAIBORNE | 6,996 | 2,599 | 3,263 | 926 | 208 | 664 D | 37.1% | 46.6% | 13.2% |
| 20,828 | CONCORDIA | 9,148 | 3,223 | 4,283 | 1,317 | 325 | 1,060 D | 35.2% | 46.8% | 14.4% |
| 25,346 | DE SOTO | 11,021 | 3,643 | 5,671 | 1,358 | 349 | 2,028 D | 33.1% | 51.5% | 12.3% |
| 380,105 | EAST BATON ROUGE | 166,691 | 81,072 | 68,622 | 16,102 | 895 | 12,450 R | 48.6% | 41.2% | 9.7% |
| 9,709 | EAST CARROLL | 3,375 | 1,142 | 1,835 | 283 | 115 | 693 D | 33.8% | 54.4% | 8.4% |
| 19,211 | EAST FELICIANA | 7,895 | 2,813 | 4,093 | 932 | 57 | 1,280 D | 35.6% | 51.8% | 11.8% |
| 33,274 | EVANGELINE | 16,376 | 5,147 | 8,564 | 2,124 | 541 | 3,417 D | 31.4% | 52.3% | 13.0% |
| 22,387 | FRANKLIN | 9,653 | 3,889 | 4,127 | 1,311 | 326 | 238 D | 40.3% | 42.8% | 13.6% |
| 17,526 | GRANT | 7,878 | 3,214 | 3,122 | 1,174 | 368 | 92 R | 40.8% | 39.6% | 14.9% |
| 68,297 | IBERIA | 30,530 | 11,905 | 13,040 | 4,337 | 1,248 | 1,135 D | 39.0% | 42.7% | 14.2% |
| 31,049 | IBERVILLE | 15,594 | 5,211 | 8,218 | 1,543 | 622 | 3,007 D | 33.4% | 52.7% | 9.9% |
| 15,705 | JACKSON | 7,566 | 3,072 | 3,370 | 882 | 242 | 298 D | 40.6% | 44.5% | 11.7% |
| 448,306 | JEFFERSON | 187,038 | 100,493 | 64,302 | 21,278 | 965 | 36,191 R | 53.7% | 34.4% | 11.4% |
| 30,722 | JEFFERSON DAVIS | 13,838 | 4,513 | 7,022 | 2,221 | 82 | 2,509 D | 32.6% | 50.7% | 16.1% |
| 164,762 | LAFAYETTE | 71,762 | 32,406 | 28,583 | 9,124 | 1,649 | 3,823 R | 45.2% | 39.8% | 12.7% |
| 85,860 | LAFOURCHE | 35,645 | 12,744 | 16,182 | 5,077 | 1,642 | 3,438 D | 35.8% | 45.4% | 14.2% |
| 13,662 | LA SALLE | 6,723 | 3,068 | 2,389 | 993 | 273 | 679 R | 45.6% | 35.5% | 14.8% |
| 41,745 | LINCOLN | 16,561 | 7,220 | 7,205 | 1,751 | 385 | 15 R | 43.6% | 43.5% | 10.6% |
| 70,526 | LIVINGSTON | 31,421 | 14,808 | 11,499 | 4,971 | 143 | 3,309 R | 47.1% | 36.6% | 15.8% |
| 12,463 | MADISON | 5,106 | 1,702 | 2,773 | 469 | 162 | 1,071 D | 33.3% | 54.3% | 9.2% |
| 31,938 | MOREHOUSE | 13,463 | 5,364 | 6,013 | 1,727 | 359 | 649 D | 39.8% | 44.7% | 12.8% |
| 36,689 | NATCHITOCHES | 14,779 | 5,694 | 6,974 | 1,606 | 505 | 1,280 D | 38.5% | 47.2% | 10.9% |
| 496,938 | ORLEANS | 197,349 | 52,019 | 133,261 | 10,889 | 1,180 | 81,242 D | 26.4% | 67.5% | 5.5% |
| 142,191 | OUACHITA | 56,502 | 27,600 | 20,835 | 6,612 | 1,455 | 6,765 R | 48.8% | 36.9% | 11.7% |
| 25,575 | PLAQUEMINES | 11,257 | 5,018 | 4,467 | 1,729 | 43 | 551 R | 44.6% | 39.7% | 15.4% |
| 22,540 | POINTE COUPEE | 11,322 | 3,563 | 6,512 | 1,157 | 90 | 2,949 D | 31.5% | 57.5% | 10.2% |
| 131,556 | RAPIDES | 51,882 | 22,783 | 20,873 | 6,599 | 1,627 | 1,910 R | 43.9% | 40.2% | 12.7% |
| 9,387 | RED RIVER | 4,680 | 1,649 | 2,360 | 566 | 105 | 711 D | 35.2% | 50.4% | 12.1% |
| 20,629 | RICHLAND | 8,903 | 3,808 | 3,706 | 1,054 | 335 | 102 R | 42.8% | 41.6% | 11.8% |
| 22,646 | SABINE | 9,348 | 3,586 | 4,173 | 1,219 | 370 | 587 D | 38.4% | 44.6% | 13.0% |
| 66,631 | ST. BERNARD | 32,938 | 16,131 | 12,305 | 4,308 | 194 | 3,826 R | 49.0% | 37.4% | 13.1% |
| 42,437 | ST. CHARLES | 20,877 | 9,158 | 8,810 | 2,593 | 316 | 348 R | 43.9% | 42.2% | 12.4% |
| 9,874 | ST. HELENA | 5,618 | 1,515 | 3,416 | 589 | 98 | 1,901 D | 27.0% | 60.8% | 10.5% |
| 20,879 | ST. JAMES | 11,186 | 3,339 | 6,609 | 993 | 245 | 3,270 D | 29.8% | 59.1% | 8.9% |
| 39,996 | ST. JOHN THE BAPTIST | 17,851 | 6,730 | 8,977 | 1,922 | 222 | 2,247 D | 37.7% | 50.3% | 10.8% |
| 80,331 | ST. LANDRY | 36,815 | 11,882 | 20,383 | 4,266 | 284 | 8,501 D | 32.3% | 55.4% | 11.6% |
| 43,978 | ST. MARTIN | 20,426 | 5,909 | 11,252 | 2,573 | 692 | 5,343 D | 28.9% | 55.1% | 12.6% |
| 58,086 | ST. MARY | 23,440 | 8,792 | 10,648 | 3,257 | 743 | 1,856 D | 37.5% | 45.4% | 13.9% |
| 144,508 | ST. TAMMANY | 66,921 | 37,839 | 19,735 | 9,005 | 342 | 18,104 R | 56.5% | 29.5% | 13.5% |
| 85,709 | TANGIPAHOA | 34,245 | 14,128 | 15,194 | 4,612 | 311 | 1,066 D | 41.3% | 44.4% | 13.5% |
| 7,103 | TENSAS | 3,266 | 1,153 | 1,666 | 353 | 94 | 513 D | 35.3% | 51.0% | 10.8% |
| 96,982 | TERREBONNE | 34,664 | 14,662 | 13,325 | 5,505 | 1,172 | 1,337 R | 42.3% | 38.4% | 15.9% |
| 20,690 | UNION | 10,069 | 4,434 | 4,005 | 1,209 | 421 | 429 R | 44.0% | 39.8% | 12.0% |
| 50,055 | VERMILION | 23,444 | 7,062 | 12,324 | 3,127 | 931 | 5,262 D | 30.1% | 52.6% | 13.3% |
| 61,961 | VERNON | 14,767 | 5,912 | 6,005 | 2,313 | 537 | 93 D | 40.0% | 40.7% | 15.7% |
| 43,185 | WASHINGTON | 18,753 | 7,227 | 9,095 | 2,303 | 128 | 1,868 D | 38.5% | 48.5% | 12.3% |
| 41,989 | WEBSTER | 18,264 | 6,640 | 8,380 | 2,629 | 615 | 1,740 D | 36.4% | 45.9% | 14.4% |

# LOUISIANA

## PRESIDENT 1992

| 1990 Census Population | Parish | Total Vote | Republican | Democratic | Perot | Other | Plurality | Percentage Total Vote | | |
|---|---|---|---|---|---|---|---|---|---|---|
| | | | | | | | | Rep. | Dem. | Perot |
| 19,419 | WEST BATON ROUGE | 9,976 | 3,522 | 5,131 | 1,249 | 74 | 1,609 D | 35.3% | 51.4% | 12.5% |
| 12,093 | WEST CARROLL | 5,120 | 2,082 | 2,068 | 771 | 199 | 14 R | 40.7% | 40.4% | 15.1% |
| 12,915 | WEST FELICIANA | 4,374 | 1,501 | 2,328 | 516 | 29 | 827 D | 34.3% | 53.2% | 11.8% |
| 16,269 | WINN | 7,549 | 2,932 | 3,537 | 843 | 237 | 605 D | 38.8% | 46.9% | 11.2% |
| 4,219,973 | TOTAL | 1,790,017 | 733,386 | 815,971 | 211,478 | 29,182 | 82,585 D | 41.0% | 45.6% | 11.8% |

# LOUISIANA

## PRESIDENT 1988

| 1980 Census Population | Parish | Total Vote | Republican | Democratic | Other | Rep.-Dem. Plurality | Percentage Total Vote Rep. | Total Vote Dem. | Major Vote Rep. | Major Vote Dem. |
|---|---|---|---|---|---|---|---|---|---|---|
| 56,427 | ACADIA | 23,110 | 11,319 | 11,510 | 281 | 191 D | 49.0% | 49.8% | 49.6% | 50.4% |
| 21,390 | ALLEN | 8,989 | 3,674 | 5,204 | 111 | 1,530 D | 40.9% | 57.9% | 41.4% | 58.6% |
| 50,068 | ASCENSION | 23,240 | 10,726 | 12,147 | 367 | 1,421 D | 46.2% | 52.3% | 46.9% | 53.1% |
| 22,084 | ASSUMPTION | 9,995 | 4,017 | 5,610 | 368 | 1,593 D | 40.2% | 56.1% | 41.7% | 58.3% |
| 41,393 | AVOYELLES | 15,600 | 7,659 | 7,353 | 588 | 306 R | 49.1% | 47.1% | 51.0% | 49.0% |
| 29,692 | BEAUREGARD | 11,284 | 6,466 | 4,704 | 114 | 1,762 R | 57.3% | 41.7% | 57.9% | 42.1% |
| 16,387 | BIENVILLE | 7,537 | 3,680 | 3,705 | 152 | 25 D | 48.8% | 49.2% | 49.8% | 50.2% |
| 80,721 | BOSSIER | 30,085 | 20,807 | 9,035 | 243 | 11,772 R | 69.2% | 30.0% | 69.7% | 30.3% |
| 252,358 | CADDO | 94,402 | 54,498 | 39,204 | 700 | 15,294 R | 57.7% | 41.5% | 58.2% | 41.8% |
| 167,223 | CALCASIEU | 64,100 | 29,649 | 33,932 | 519 | 4,283 D | 46.3% | 52.9% | 46.6% | 53.4% |
| 10,761 | CALDWELL | 4,559 | 2,997 | 1,423 | 139 | 1,574 R | 65.7% | 31.2% | 67.8% | 32.2% |
| 9,336 | CAMERON | 4,070 | 1,775 | 2,257 | 38 | 482 D | 43.6% | 55.5% | 44.0% | 56.0% |
| 12,287 | CATAHOULA | 4,950 | 2,862 | 1,916 | 172 | 946 R | 57.8% | 38.7% | 59.9% | 40.1% |
| 17,095 | CLAIBORNE | 7,007 | 3,756 | 3,158 | 93 | 598 R | 53.6% | 45.1% | 54.3% | 45.7% |
| 22,981 | CONCORDIA | 8,761 | 5,037 | 3,461 | 263 | 1,576 R | 57.5% | 39.5% | 59.3% | 40.7% |
| 25,727 | DE SOTO | 10,516 | 5,022 | 5,366 | 128 | 344 D | 47.8% | 51.0% | 48.3% | 51.7% |
| 366,191 | EAST BATON ROUGE | 147,584 | 86,791 | 59,270 | 1,523 | 27,521 R | 58.8% | 40.2% | 59.4% | 40.6% |
| 11,772 | EAST CARROLL | 3,460 | 1,536 | 1,809 | 115 | 273 D | 44.4% | 52.3% | 45.9% | 54.1% |
| 19,015 | EAST FELICIANA | 7,349 | 3,527 | 3,659 | 163 | 132 D | 48.0% | 49.8% | 49.1% | 50.9% |
| 33,343 | EVANGELINE | 15,400 | 7,437 | 7,693 | 270 | 256 D | 48.3% | 50.0% | 49.2% | 50.8% |
| 24,141 | FRANKLIN | 8,876 | 5,520 | 3,043 | 313 | 2,477 R | 62.2% | 34.3% | 64.5% | 35.5% |
| 16,703 | GRANT | 7,245 | 4,402 | 2,628 | 215 | 1,774 R | 60.8% | 36.3% | 62.6% | 37.4% |
| 63,752 | IBERIA | 28,331 | 15,438 | 12,166 | 727 | 3,272 R | 54.5% | 42.9% | 55.9% | 44.1% |
| 32,159 | IBERVILLE | 14,836 | 5,855 | 8,678 | 303 | 2,823 D | 39.5% | 58.5% | 40.3% | 59.7% |
| 17,321 | JACKSON | 7,249 | 4,251 | 2,842 | 156 | 1,409 R | 58.6% | 39.2% | 59.9% | 40.1% |
| 454,592 | JEFFERSON | 166,370 | 110,942 | 53,035 | 2,393 | 57,907 R | 66.7% | 31.9% | 67.7% | 32.3% |
| 32,168 | JEFFERSON DAVIS | 12,791 | 5,851 | 6,799 | 141 | 948 D | 45.7% | 53.2% | 46.3% | 53.7% |
| 150,017 | LAFAYETTE | 61,658 | 36,648 | 24,133 | 877 | 12,515 R | 59.4% | 39.1% | 60.3% | 39.7% |
| 82,483 | LAFOURCHE | 32,179 | 16,152 | 15,013 | 1,014 | 1,139 R | 50.2% | 46.7% | 51.8% | 48.2% |
| 17,004 | LA SALLE | 6,359 | 4,559 | 1,622 | 178 | 2,937 R | 71.7% | 25.5% | 73.8% | 26.2% |
| 39,763 | LINCOLN | 14,657 | 8,853 | 5,427 | 377 | 3,426 R | 60.4% | 37.0% | 62.0% | 38.0% |
| 58,806 | LIVINGSTON | 25,743 | 15,779 | 9,659 | 305 | 6,120 R | 61.3% | 37.5% | 62.0% | 38.0% |
| 15,975 | MADISON | 4,911 | 2,334 | 2,416 | 161 | 82 D | 47.5% | 49.2% | 49.1% | 50.9% |
| 34,803 | MOREHOUSE | 12,140 | 7,335 | 4,496 | 309 | 2,839 R | 60.4% | 37.0% | 62.0% | 38.0% |
| 39,863 | NATCHITOCHES | 13,733 | 7,224 | 6,151 | 358 | 1,073 R | 52.6% | 44.8% | 54.0% | 46.0% |
| 557,515 | ORLEANS | 183,800 | 64,763 | 116,851 | 2,186 | 52,088 D | 35.2% | 63.6% | 35.7% | 64.3% |
| 139,241 | OUACHITA | 50,292 | 33,858 | 15,429 | 1,005 | 18,429 R | 67.3% | 30.7% | 68.7% | 31.3% |
| 26,049 | PLAQUEMINES | 10,293 | 6,084 | 3,997 | 212 | 2,087 R | 59.1% | 38.8% | 60.4% | 39.6% |
| 24,045 | POINTE COUPEE | 10,930 | 4,333 | 6,308 | 289 | 1,975 D | 39.6% | 57.7% | 40.7% | 59.3% |
| 135,282 | RAPIDES | 48,891 | 29,977 | 17,928 | 986 | 12,049 R | 61.3% | 36.7% | 62.6% | 37.4% |
| 10,433 | RED RIVER | 4,586 | 2,266 | 2,254 | 66 | 12 R | 49.4% | 49.1% | 50.1% | 49.9% |
| 22,187 | RICHLAND | 8,315 | 5,226 | 2,833 | 256 | 2,393 R | 62.9% | 34.1% | 64.8% | 35.2% |
| 25,280 | SABINE | 8,541 | 4,767 | 3,532 | 242 | 1,235 R | 55.8% | 41.4% | 57.4% | 42.6% |
| 64,097 | ST. BERNARD | 31,736 | 19,609 | 11,406 | 721 | 8,203 R | 61.8% | 35.9% | 63.2% | 36.8% |
| 37,259 | ST. CHARLES | 17,995 | 9,685 | 7,973 | 337 | 1,712 R | 53.8% | 44.3% | 54.8% | 45.2% |
| 9,827 | ST. HELENA | 5,153 | 2,006 | 3,013 | 134 | 1,007 D | 38.9% | 58.5% | 40.0% | 60.0% |
| 21,495 | ST. JAMES | 10,719 | 3,799 | 6,707 | 213 | 2,908 D | 35.4% | 62.6% | 36.2% | 63.8% |
| 31,924 | ST. JOHN THE BAPTIST | 16,219 | 7,464 | 8,366 | 389 | 902 D | 46.0% | 51.6% | 47.2% | 52.8% |
| 84,128 | ST. LANDRY | 35,457 | 15,790 | 19,091 | 576 | 3,301 D | 44.5% | 53.8% | 45.3% | 54.7% |
| 40,214 | ST. MARTIN | 18,129 | 7,541 | 10,148 | 440 | 2,607 D | 41.6% | 56.0% | 42.6% | 57.4% |
| 64,253 | ST. MARY | 22,318 | 11,540 | 10,364 | 414 | 1,176 R | 51.7% | 46.4% | 52.7% | 47.3% |
| 110,869 | ST. TAMMANY | 54,823 | 38,334 | 15,638 | 851 | 22,696 R | 69.9% | 28.5% | 71.0% | 29.0% |
| 80,698 | TANGIPAHOA | 30,688 | 16,669 | 13,527 | 492 | 3,142 R | 54.3% | 44.1% | 55.2% | 44.8% |
| 8,525 | TENSAS | 3,290 | 1,645 | 1,556 | 89 | 89 R | 50.0% | 47.3% | 51.4% | 48.6% |
| 94,393 | TERREBONNE | 32,212 | 18,745 | 12,686 | 781 | 6,059 R | 58.2% | 39.4% | 59.6% | 40.4% |
| 21,167 | UNION | 9,369 | 5,900 | 3,210 | 259 | 2,690 R | 63.0% | 34.3% | 64.8% | 35.2% |
| 48,458 | VERMILION | 21,966 | 9,224 | 12,180 | 562 | 2,956 D | 42.0% | 55.4% | 43.1% | 56.9% |
| 53,475 | VERNON | 12,761 | 7,453 | 4,998 | 310 | 2,455 R | 58.4% | 39.2% | 59.9% | 40.1% |
| 44,207 | WASHINGTON | 18,094 | 9,374 | 8,369 | 351 | 1,005 R | 51.8% | 46.3% | 52.8% | 47.2% |
| 43,631 | WEBSTER | 17,805 | 10,204 | 7,434 | 167 | 2,770 R | 57.3% | 41.8% | 57.9% | 42.1% |

# LOUISIANA

## PRESIDENT 1988

| 1980 Census Population | Parish | Total Vote | Republican | Democratic | Other | Rep.-Dem. Plurality | Percentage | | | |
|---|---|---|---|---|---|---|---|---|---|---|
| | | | | | | | Total Vote | | Major Vote | |
| | | | | | | | Rep. | Dem. | Rep. | Dem. |
| 19,086 | WEST BATON ROUGE | 8,801 | 3,972 | 4,686 | 143 | 714 D | 45.1% | 53.2% | 45.9% | 54.1% |
| 12,922 | WEST CARROLL | 4,797 | 3,077 | 1,607 | 113 | 1,470 R | 64.1% | 33.5% | 65.7% | 34.3% |
| 12,186 | WEST FELICIANA | 4,089 | 1,854 | 2,146 | 89 | 292 D | 45.3% | 52.5% | 46.4% | 53.7% |
| 17,253 | WINN | 7,057 | 4,165 | 2,699 | 193 | 1,466 R | 59.0% | 38.2% | 60.7% | 39.3% |
| 4,205,900 | TOTAL | 1,628,202 | 883,702 | 717,460 | 27,040 | 166,242 R | 54.3% | 44.1% | 55.2% | 44.8% |

# LOUISIANA

## PRESIDENT 1984

| 1980 Census Population | Parish | Total Vote | Republican | Democratic | Other | Rep.-Dem. Plurality | | Percentage | | | |
|---|---|---|---|---|---|---|---|---|---|---|---|
| | | | | | | | | Total Vote | | Major Vote | |
| | | | | | | | | Rep. | Dem. | Rep. | Dem. |
| 56,427 | ACADIA | 24,602 | 14,906 | 9,262 | 434 | 5,644 | R | 60.6% | 37.6% | 61.7% | 38.3% |
| 21,390 | ALLEN | 9,382 | 4,474 | 4,842 | 66 | 368 | D | 47.7% | 51.6% | 48.0% | 52.0% |
| 50,068 | ASCENSION | 23,170 | 11,945 | 11,048 | 177 | 897 | R | 51.6% | 47.7% | 52.0% | 48.0% |
| 22,084 | ASSUMPTION | 10,363 | 5,433 | 4,660 | 270 | 773 | R | 52.4% | 45.0% | 53.8% | 46.2% |
| 41,393 | AVOYELLES | 16,673 | 9,402 | 6,808 | 463 | 2,594 | R | 56.4% | 40.8% | 58.0% | 42.0% |
| 29,692 | BEAUREGARD | 11,648 | 7,353 | 4,199 | 96 | 3,154 | R | 63.1% | 36.0% | 63.7% | 36.3% |
| 16,387 | BIENVILLE | 8,226 | 4,587 | 3,530 | 109 | 1,057 | R | 55.8% | 42.9% | 56.5% | 43.5% |
| 80,721 | BOSSIER | 29,782 | 22,638 | 7,006 | 138 | 15,632 | R | 76.0% | 23.5% | 76.4% | 23.6% |
| 252,358 | CADDO | 99,601 | 63,429 | 35,727 | 445 | 27,702 | R | 63.7% | 35.9% | 64.0% | 36.0% |
| 167,223 | CALCASIEU | 69,210 | 35,566 | 33,214 | 430 | 2,352 | R | 51.4% | 48.0% | 51.7% | 48.3% |
| 10,761 | CALDWELL | 4,819 | 3,341 | 1,348 | 130 | 1,993 | R | 69.3% | 28.0% | 71.3% | 28.7% |
| 9,336 | CAMERON | 3,906 | 2,265 | 1,608 | 33 | 657 | R | 58.0% | 41.2% | 58.5% | 41.5% |
| 12,287 | CATAHOULA | 5,391 | 3,640 | 1,649 | 102 | 1,991 | R | 67.5% | 30.6% | 68.8% | 31.2% |
| 17,095 | CLAIBORNE | 7,214 | 4,349 | 2,788 | 77 | 1,561 | R | 60.3% | 38.6% | 60.9% | 39.1% |
| 22,981 | CONCORDIA | 9,692 | 6,177 | 3,332 | 183 | 2,845 | R | 63.7% | 34.4% | 65.0% | 35.0% |
| 25,727 | DE SOTO | 10,739 | 5,989 | 4,642 | 108 | 1,347 | R | 55.8% | 43.2% | 56.3% | 43.7% |
| 366,191 | EAST BATON ROUGE | 153,268 | 95,704 | 56,673 | 891 | 39,031 | R | 62.4% | 37.0% | 62.8% | 37.2% |
| 11,772 | EAST CARROLL | 4,132 | 1,974 | 2,089 | 69 | 115 | D | 47.8% | 50.6% | 48.6% | 51.4% |
| 19,015 | EAST FELICIANA | 8,401 | 4,166 | 4,122 | 113 | 44 | R | 49.6% | 49.1% | 50.3% | 49.7% |
| 33,343 | EVANGELINE | 15,844 | 8,680 | 6,981 | 183 | 1,699 | R | 54.8% | 44.1% | 55.4% | 44.6% |
| 24,141 | FRANKLIN | 9,894 | 6,708 | 2,937 | 249 | 3,771 | R | 67.8% | 29.7% | 69.5% | 30.5% |
| 16,703 | GRANT | 8,097 | 5,334 | 2,588 | 175 | 2,746 | R | 65.9% | 32.0% | 67.3% | 32.7% |
| 63,752 | IBERIA | 28,526 | 17,727 | 10,170 | 629 | 7,557 | R | 62.1% | 35.7% | 63.5% | 36.5% |
| 32,159 | IBERVILLE | 15,159 | 6,455 | 8,587 | 117 | 2,132 | D | 42.6% | 56.6% | 42.9% | 57.1% |
| 17,321 | JACKSON | 7,761 | 5,034 | 2,568 | 159 | 2,466 | R | 64.9% | 33.1% | 66.2% | 33.8% |
| 454,592 | JEFFERSON | 166,023 | 123,997 | 41,183 | 843 | 82,814 | R | 74.7% | 24.8% | 75.1% | 24.9% |
| 32,168 | JEFFERSON DAVIS | 14,464 | 8,296 | 5,962 | 206 | 2,334 | R | 57.4% | 41.2% | 58.2% | 41.8% |
| 150,017 | LAFAYETTE | 64,458 | 44,344 | 19,265 | 849 | 25,079 | R | 68.8% | 29.9% | 69.7% | 30.3% |
| 82,483 | LAFOURCHE | 32,005 | 20,930 | 10,186 | 889 | 10,744 | R | 65.4% | 31.8% | 67.3% | 32.7% |
| 17,004 | LA SALLE | 6,875 | 5,404 | 1,318 | 153 | 4,086 | R | 78.6% | 19.2% | 80.4% | 19.6% |
| 39,763 | LINCOLN | 14,701 | 9,087 | 5,432 | 182 | 3,655 | R | 61.8% | 36.9% | 62.6% | 37.4% |
| 58,806 | LIVINGSTON | 26,576 | 17,465 | 8,913 | 198 | 8,552 | R | 65.7% | 33.5% | 66.2% | 33.8% |
| 15,975 | MADISON | 5,864 | 2,849 | 2,906 | 109 | 57 | D | 48.6% | 49.6% | 49.5% | 50.5% |
| 34,803 | MOREHOUSE | 13,685 | 8,585 | 4,829 | 271 | 3,756 | R | 62.7% | 35.3% | 64.0% | 36.0% |
| 39,863 | NATCHITOCHES | 14,978 | 8,836 | 5,806 | 336 | 3,030 | R | 59.0% | 38.8% | 60.3% | 39.7% |
| 557,515 | ORLEANS | 206,956 | 86,316 | 119,478 | 1,162 | 33,162 | D | 41.7% | 57.7% | 41.9% | 58.1% |
| 139,241 | OUACHITA | 53,574 | 37,270 | 15,525 | 779 | 21,745 | R | 69.6% | 29.0% | 70.6% | 29.4% |
| 26,049 | PLAQUEMINES | 10,977 | 7,655 | 3,261 | 61 | 4,394 | R | 69.7% | 29.7% | 70.1% | 29.9% |
| 24,045 | POINTE COUPEE | 12,287 | 5,477 | 6,732 | 78 | 1,255 | D | 44.6% | 54.8% | 44.9% | 55.1% |
| 135,282 | RAPIDES | 49,963 | 32,879 | 16,121 | 963 | 16,758 | R | 65.8% | 32.3% | 67.1% | 32.9% |
| 10,433 | RED RIVER | 5,067 | 3,060 | 1,958 | 49 | 1,102 | R | 60.4% | 38.6% | 61.0% | 39.0% |
| 22,187 | RICHLAND | 9,083 | 5,980 | 2,918 | 185 | 3,062 | R | 65.8% | 32.1% | 67.2% | 32.8% |
| 25,280 | SABINE | 9,500 | 6,295 | 2,980 | 225 | 3,315 | R | 66.3% | 31.4% | 67.9% | 32.1% |
| 64,097 | ST. BERNARD | 32,657 | 24,428 | 8,076 | 153 | 16,352 | R | 74.8% | 24.7% | 75.2% | 24.8% |
| 37,259 | ST. CHARLES | 17,082 | 10,185 | 6,784 | 113 | 3,401 | R | 59.6% | 39.7% | 60.0% | 40.0% |
| 9,827 | ST. HELENA | 5,435 | 2,366 | 2,956 | 113 | 590 | D | 43.5% | 54.4% | 44.5% | 55.5% |
| 21,495 | ST. JAMES | 10,735 | 4,627 | 5,989 | 119 | 1,362 | D | 43.1% | 55.8% | 43.6% | 56.4% |
| 31,924 | ST. JOHN THE BAPTIST | 16,851 | 9,093 | 7,646 | 112 | 1,447 | R | 54.0% | 45.4% | 54.3% | 45.7% |
| 84,128 | ST. LANDRY | 37,223 | 19,055 | 17,950 | 218 | 1,105 | R | 51.2% | 48.2% | 51.5% | 48.5% |
| 40,214 | ST. MARTIN | 18,591 | 9,698 | 8,589 | 304 | 1,109 | R | 52.2% | 46.2% | 53.0% | 47.0% |
| 64,253 | ST. MARY | 24,974 | 15,275 | 9,411 | 288 | 5,864 | R | 61.2% | 37.7% | 61.9% | 38.1% |
| 110,869 | ST. TAMMANY | 50,775 | 38,664 | 11,719 | 392 | 26,945 | R | 76.1% | 23.1% | 76.7% | 23.3% |
| 80,698 | TANGIPAHOA | 32,579 | 19,580 | 12,799 | 200 | 6,781 | R | 60.1% | 39.3% | 60.5% | 39.5% |
| 8,525 | TENSAS | 3,655 | 1,956 | 1,628 | 71 | 328 | R | 53.5% | 44.5% | 54.6% | 45.4% |
| 94,393 | TERREBONNE | 34,089 | 23,696 | 9,640 | 753 | 14,056 | R | 69.5% | 28.3% | 71.1% | 28.9% |
| 21,167 | UNION | 9,723 | 6,585 | 2,916 | 222 | 3,669 | R | 67.7% | 30.0% | 69.3% | 30.7% |
| 48,458 | VERMILION | 22,378 | 12,721 | 9,033 | 624 | 3,688 | R | 56.8% | 40.4% | 58.5% | 41.5% |
| 53,475 | VERNON | 13,369 | 9,035 | 4,076 | 258 | 4,959 | R | 67.6% | 30.5% | 68.9% | 31.1% |
| 44,207 | WASHINGTON | 18,988 | 11,185 | 7,680 | 123 | 3,505 | R | 58.9% | 40.4% | 59.3% | 40.7% |
| 43,631 | WEBSTER | 18,677 | 12,055 | 6,509 | 113 | 5,546 | R | 64.5% | 34.9% | 64.9% | 35.1% |

# LOUISIANA

## PRESIDENT 1984

| 1980 Census Population | Parish | Total Vote | Republican | Democratic | Other | Rep.-Dem. Plurality | Percentage | | | |
|---|---|---|---|---|---|---|---|---|---|---|
| | | | | | | | Total Vote | | Major Vote | |
| | | | | | | | Rep. | Dem. | Rep. | Dem. |
| 19,086 | WEST BATON ROUGE | 8,883 | 4,189 | 4,631 | 63 | 442 D | 47.2% | 52.1% | 47.5% | 52.5% |
| 12,922 | WEST CARROLL | 5,469 | 3,874 | 1,474 | 121 | 2,400 R | 70.8% | 27.0% | 72.4% | 27.6% |
| 12,186 | WEST FELICIANA | 4,426 | 2,097 | 2,296 | 33 | 199 D | 47.4% | 51.9% | 47.7% | 52.3% |
| 17,253 | WINN | 7,727 | 4,934 | 2,633 | 160 | 2,301 R | 63.9% | 34.1% | 65.2% | 34.8% |
| 4,205,900 | TOTAL | 1,706,822 | 1,037,299 | 651,586 | 17,937 | 385,713 R | 60.8% | 38.2% | 61.4% | 38.6% |

# LOUISIANA

## PRESIDENT 1980

| 1980 Census Population | Parish | Total Vote | Republican | Democratic | Other | Rep.-Dem. Plurality | Percentage | | | |
|---|---|---|---|---|---|---|---|---|---|---|
| | | | | | | | Total Vote | | Major Vote | |
| | | | | | | | Rep. | Dem. | Rep. | Dem. |
| 56,427 | ACADIA | 22,100 | 11,533 | 9,948 | 619 | 1,585 R | 52.2% | 45.0% | 53.7% | 46.3% |
| 21,390 | ALLEN | 9,564 | 3,328 | 6,057 | 179 | 2,729 D | 34.8% | 63.3% | 35.5% | 64.5% |
| 50,068 | ASCENSION | 20,200 | 7,238 | 12,381 | 581 | 5,143 D | 35.8% | 61.3% | 36.9% | 63.1% |
| 22,084 | ASSUMPTION | 9,073 | 4,001 | 4,679 | 393 | 678 D | 44.1% | 51.6% | 46.1% | 53.9% |
| 41,393 | AVOYELLES | 16,071 | 8,216 | 7,174 | 681 | 1,042 R | 51.1% | 44.6% | 53.4% | 46.6% |
| 29,692 | BEAUREGARD | 11,059 | 5,250 | 5,556 | 253 | 306 D | 47.5% | 50.2% | 48.6% | 51.4% |
| 16,387 | BIENVILLE | 7,770 | 3,508 | 4,123 | 139 | 615 D | 45.1% | 53.1% | 46.0% | 54.0% |
| 80,721 | BOSSIER | 26,339 | 16,515 | 9,377 | 447 | 7,138 R | 62.7% | 35.6% | 63.8% | 36.2% |
| 252,358 | CADDO | 89,184 | 51,202 | 36,422 | 1,560 | 14,780 R | 57.4% | 40.8% | 58.4% | 41.6% |
| 167,223 | CALCASIEU | 64,859 | 27,600 | 35,446 | 1,813 | 7,846 D | 42.6% | 54.7% | 43.8% | 56.2% |
| 10,761 | CALDWELL | 4,581 | 2,653 | 1,786 | 142 | 867 R | 57.9% | 39.0% | 59.8% | 40.2% |
| 9,336 | CAMERON | 3,798 | 1,449 | 2,221 | 128 | 772 D | 38.2% | 58.5% | 39.5% | 60.5% |
| 12,287 | CATAHOULA | 5,531 | 2,942 | 2,414 | 175 | 528 R | 53.2% | 43.6% | 54.9% | 45.1% |
| 17,095 | CLAIBORNE | 7,074 | 3,538 | 3,443 | 93 | 95 R | 50.0% | 48.7% | 50.7% | 49.3% |
| 22,981 | CONCORDIA | 9,102 | 4,933 | 3,956 | 213 | 977 R | 54.2% | 43.5% | 55.5% | 44.5% |
| 25,727 | DE SOTO | 10,327 | 4,349 | 5,861 | 117 | 1,512 D | 42.1% | 56.8% | 42.6% | 57.4% |
| 366,191 | EAST BATON ROUGE | 133,168 | 71,063 | 57,442 | 4,663 | 13,621 R | 53.4% | 43.1% | 55.3% | 44.7% |
| 11,772 | EAST CARROLL | 4,231 | 1,867 | 2,283 | 81 | 416 D | 44.1% | 54.0% | 45.0% | 55.0% |
| 19,015 | EAST FELICIANA | 6,873 | 2,650 | 4,033 | 190 | 1,383 D | 38.6% | 58.7% | 39.7% | 60.3% |
| 33,343 | EVANGELINE | 14,461 | 7,412 | 6,722 | 327 | 690 R | 51.3% | 46.5% | 52.4% | 47.6% |
| 24,141 | FRANKLIN | 9,748 | 5,301 | 4,177 | 270 | 1,124 R | 54.4% | 42.8% | 55.9% | 44.1% |
| 16,703 | GRANT | 7,148 | 3,611 | 3,290 | 247 | 321 R | 50.5% | 46.0% | 52.3% | 47.7% |
| 63,752 | IBERIA | 25,028 | 14,273 | 9,681 | 1,074 | 4,592 R | 57.0% | 38.7% | 59.6% | 40.4% |
| 32,159 | IBERVILLE | 14,135 | 4,463 | 9,361 | 311 | 4,898 D | 31.6% | 66.2% | 32.3% | 67.7% |
| 17,321 | JACKSON | 7,730 | 3,923 | 3,609 | 198 | 314 R | 50.8% | 46.7% | 52.1% | 47.9% |
| 454,592 | JEFFERSON | 155,111 | 99,403 | 50,870 | 4,838 | 48,533 R | 64.1% | 32.8% | 66.1% | 33.9% |
| 32,168 | JEFFERSON DAVIS | 12,127 | 5,667 | 6,140 | 320 | 473 D | 46.7% | 50.6% | 48.0% | 52.0% |
| 150,017 | LAFAYETTE | 53,526 | 31,429 | 19,694 | 2,403 | 11,735 R | 58.7% | 36.8% | 61.5% | 38.5% |
| 82,483 | LAFOURCHE | 30,818 | 14,951 | 14,222 | 1,645 | 729 R | 48.5% | 46.1% | 51.2% | 48.8% |
| 17,004 | LA SALLE | 6,634 | 3,792 | 2,665 | 177 | 1,127 R | 57.2% | 40.2% | 58.7% | 41.3% |
| 39,763 | LINCOLN | 13,470 | 7,515 | 5,598 | 357 | 1,917 R | 55.8% | 41.6% | 57.3% | 42.7% |
| 58,806 | LIVINGSTON | 22,609 | 10,666 | 11,319 | 624 | 653 D | 47.2% | 50.1% | 48.5% | 51.5% |
| 15,975 | MADISON | 5,928 | 2,531 | 3,264 | 133 | 733 D | 42.7% | 55.1% | 43.7% | 56.3% |
| 34,803 | MOREHOUSE | 12,397 | 7,254 | 4,856 | 287 | 2,398 R | 58.5% | 39.2% | 59.9% | 40.1% |
| 39,863 | NATCHITOCHES | 14,189 | 6,668 | 7,102 | 419 | 434 D | 47.0% | 50.1% | 48.4% | 51.6% |
| 557,515 | ORLEANS | 187,904 | 74,302 | 106,858 | 6,744 | 32,556 D | 39.5% | 56.9% | 41.0% | 59.0% |
| 139,241 | OUACHITA | 47,314 | 29,799 | 16,306 | 1,209 | 13,493 R | 63.0% | 34.5% | 64.6% | 35.4% |
| 26,049 | PLAQUEMINES | 10,079 | 5,489 | 4,318 | 272 | 1,171 R | 54.5% | 42.8% | 56.0% | 44.0% |
| 24,045 | POINTE COUPEE | 10,263 | 3,667 | 6,395 | 201 | 2,728 D | 35.7% | 62.3% | 36.4% | 63.6% |
| 135,282 | RAPIDES | 46,302 | 25,576 | 19,436 | 1,290 | 6,140 R | 55.2% | 42.0% | 56.8% | 43.2% |
| 10,433 | RED RIVER | 4,986 | 2,147 | 2,776 | 63 | 629 D | 43.1% | 55.7% | 43.6% | 56.4% |
| 22,187 | RICHLAND | 8,744 | 4,772 | 3,745 | 227 | 1,027 R | 54.6% | 42.8% | 56.0% | 44.0% |
| 25,280 | SABINE | 9,585 | 4,265 | 5,100 | 220 | 835 D | 44.5% | 53.2% | 45.5% | 54.5% |
| 64,097 | ST. BERNARD | 32,065 | 19,410 | 11,367 | 1,288 | 8,043 R | 60.5% | 35.4% | 63.1% | 36.9% |
| 37,259 | ST. CHARLES | 15,123 | 6,779 | 7,898 | 446 | 1,119 D | 44.8% | 52.2% | 46.2% | 53.8% |
| 9,827 | ST. HELENA | 4,852 | 1,531 | 3,183 | 138 | 1,652 D | 31.6% | 65.6% | 32.5% | 67.5% |
| 21,495 | ST. JAMES | 9,824 | 3,429 | 6,206 | 189 | 2,777 D | 34.9% | 63.2% | 35.6% | 64.4% |
| 31,924 | ST. JOHN THE BAPTIST | 13,861 | 5,819 | 7,647 | 395 | 1,828 D | 42.0% | 55.2% | 43.2% | 56.8% |
| 84,128 | ST. LANDRY | 32,678 | 14,940 | 17,125 | 613 | 2,185 D | 45.7% | 52.4% | 46.6% | 53.4% |
| 40,214 | ST. MARTIN | 15,040 | 6,701 | 7,760 | 579 | 1,059 D | 44.6% | 51.6% | 46.3% | 53.7% |
| 64,253 | ST. MARY | 21,606 | 10,378 | 10,506 | 722 | 128 D | 48.0% | 48.6% | 49.7% | 50.3% |
| 110,869 | ST. TAMMANY | 42,698 | 27,214 | 14,161 | 1,323 | 13,053 R | 63.7% | 33.2% | 65.8% | 34.2% |
| 80,698 | TANGIPAHOA | 31,342 | 15,187 | 15,272 | 883 | 85 D | 48.5% | 48.7% | 49.9% | 50.1% |
| 8,525 | TENSAS | 3,785 | 1,645 | 2,046 | 94 | 401 D | 43.5% | 54.1% | 44.6% | 55.4% |
| 94,393 | TERREBONNE | 28,681 | 16,644 | 10,804 | 1,233 | 5,840 R | 58.0% | 37.7% | 60.6% | 39.4% |
| 21,167 | UNION | 9,198 | 5,130 | 3,841 | 227 | 1,289 R | 55.8% | 41.8% | 57.2% | 42.8% |
| 48,458 | VERMILION | 21,409 | 10,481 | 9,743 | 1,185 | 738 R | 49.0% | 45.5% | 51.8% | 48.2% |
| 53,475 | VERNON | 13,436 | 5,869 | 7,198 | 369 | 1,329 D | 43.7% | 53.6% | 44.9% | 55.1% |
| 44,207 | WASHINGTON | 19,472 | 8,681 | 10,413 | 378 | 1,732 D | 44.6% | 53.5% | 45.5% | 54.5% |
| 43,631 | WEBSTER | 17,647 | 8,865 | 8,568 | 214 | 297 R | 50.2% | 48.6% | 50.9% | 49.1% |

# LOUISIANA

## PRESIDENT 1980

| 1980 Census Population | Parish | Total Vote | Republican | Democratic | Other | Rep.-Dem. Plurality | Percentage | | | |
|---|---|---|---|---|---|---|---|---|---|---|
| | | | | | | | Total Vote | | Major Vote | |
| | | | | | | | Rep. | Dem. | Rep. | Dem. |
| 19,086 | WEST BATON ROUGE | 7,753 | 2,828 | 4,739 | 186 | 1,911 D | 36.5% | 61.1% | 37.4% | 62.6% |
| 12,922 | WEST CARROLL | 5,712 | 3,430 | 2,118 | 164 | 1,312 R | 60.0% | 37.1% | 61.8% | 38.2% |
| 12,186 | WEST FELICIANA | 3,722 | 1,237 | 2,341 | 144 | 1,104 D | 33.2% | 62.9% | 34.6% | 65.4% |
| 17,253 | WINN | 7,547 | 3,944 | 3,411 | 192 | 533 R | 52.3% | 45.2% | 53.6% | 46.4% |
| 4,205,900 | TOTAL | 1,548,591 | 792,853 | 708,453 | 47,285 | 84,400 R | 51.2% | 45.7% | 52.8% | 47.2% |

# LOUISIANA

## PRESIDENT 1976

| 1970 Census Population | Parish | Total Vote | Republican | Democratic | Other | Rep.-Dem. Plurality | Percentage Total Vote Rep. | Dem. | Major Vote Rep. | Dem. |
|---|---|---|---|---|---|---|---|---|---|---|
| 52,109 | ACADIA | 17,648 | 6,296 | 10,814 | 538 | 4,518 D | 35.7% | 61.3% | 36.8% | 63.2% |
| 20,794 | ALLEN | 7,673 | 2,080 | 5,373 | 220 | 3,293 D | 27.1% | 70.0% | 27.9% | 72.1% |
| 37,086 | ASCENSION | 13,978 | 4,435 | 9,100 | 443 | 4,665 D | 31.7% | 65.1% | 32.8% | 67.2% |
| 19,654 | ASSUMPTION | 7,711 | 3,117 | 4,401 | 193 | 1,284 D | 40.4% | 57.1% | 41.5% | 58.5% |
| 37,751 | AVOYELLES | 13,315 | 4,574 | 8,104 | 637 | 3,530 D | 34.4% | 60.9% | 36.1% | 63.9% |
| 22,888 | BEAUREGARD | 8,786 | 3,196 | 5,322 | 268 | 2,126 D | 36.4% | 60.6% | 37.5% | 62.5% |
| 16,024 | BIENVILLE | 6,011 | 2,499 | 3,402 | 110 | 903 D | 41.6% | 56.6% | 42.3% | 57.7% |
| 63,703 | BOSSIER | 20,487 | 12,132 | 8,062 | 293 | 4,070 R | 59.2% | 39.4% | 60.1% | 39.9% |
| 230,184 | CADDO | 74,340 | 42,627 | 30,593 | 1,120 | 12,034 R | 57.3% | 41.2% | 58.2% | 41.8% |
| 145,415 | CALCASIEU | 52,595 | 17,485 | 33,980 | 1,130 | 16,495 D | 33.2% | 64.6% | 34.0% | 66.0% |
| 9,354 | CALDWELL | 3,806 | 1,890 | 1,830 | 86 | 60 R | 49.7% | 48.1% | 50.8% | 49.2% |
| 8,194 | CAMERON | 3,338 | 819 | 2,432 | 87 | 1,613 D | 24.5% | 72.9% | 25.2% | 74.8% |
| 11,769 | CATAHOULA | 4,767 | 2,086 | 2,547 | 134 | 461 D | 43.8% | 53.4% | 45.0% | 55.0% |
| 17,024 | CLAIBORNE | 6,207 | 3,216 | 2,891 | 100 | 325 R | 51.8% | 46.6% | 52.7% | 47.3% |
| 22,578 | CONCORDIA | 7,912 | 3,849 | 3,892 | 171 | 43 D | 48.6% | 49.2% | 49.7% | 50.3% |
| 22,764 | DE SOTO | 8,348 | 3,601 | 4,630 | 117 | 1,029 D | 43.1% | 55.5% | 43.7% | 56.3% |
| 285,167 | EAST BATON ROUGE | 103,807 | 51,655 | 49,956 | 2,196 | 1,699 D | 49.8% | 48.1% | 50.8% | 49.2% |
| 12,884 | EAST CARROLL | 4,158 | 1,681 | 2,367 | 110 | 686 D | 40.4% | 56.9% | 41.5% | 58.5% |
| 17,657 | EAST FELICIANA | 5,323 | 1,668 | 3,485 | 170 | 1,817 D | 31.3% | 65.5% | 32.4% | 67.6% |
| 31,932 | EVANGELINE | 11,558 | 3,715 | 7,578 | 265 | 3,863 D | 32.1% | 65.6% | 32.9% | 67.1% |
| 23,946 | FRANKLIN | 7,991 | 3,947 | 3,824 | 220 | 123 R | 49.4% | 47.9% | 50.8% | 49.2% |
| 13,671 | GRANT | 6,136 | 2,280 | 3,670 | 186 | 1,390 D | 37.2% | 59.8% | 38.3% | 61.7% |
| 57,397 | IBERIA | 20,753 | 10,392 | 9,984 | 377 | 408 R | 50.1% | 48.1% | 51.0% | 49.0% |
| 30,746 | IBERVILLE | 11,389 | 3,822 | 7,254 | 313 | 3,432 D | 33.6% | 63.7% | 34.5% | 65.5% |
| 15,963 | JACKSON | 7,060 | 3,310 | 3,605 | 145 | 295 D | 46.9% | 51.1% | 47.9% | 52.1% |
| 338,229 | JEFFERSON | 127,560 | 71,787 | 53,257 | 2,516 | 18,530 R | 56.3% | 41.8% | 57.4% | 42.6% |
| 29,554 | JEFFERSON DAVIS | 10,278 | 3,603 | 6,376 | 299 | 2,773 D | 35.1% | 62.0% | 36.1% | 63.9% |
| 111,745 | LAFAYETTE | 43,699 | 22,805 | 19,918 | 976 | 2,887 R | 52.2% | 45.6% | 53.4% | 46.6% |
| 68,941 | LAFOURCHE | 26,266 | 11,434 | 14,131 | 701 | 2,697 D | 43.5% | 53.8% | 44.7% | 55.3% |
| 13,295 | LA SALLE | 6,310 | 3,161 | 2,961 | 188 | 200 R | 50.1% | 46.9% | 51.6% | 48.4% |
| 33,800 | LINCOLN | 11,969 | 6,828 | 4,971 | 170 | 1,857 R | 57.0% | 41.5% | 57.9% | 42.1% |
| 36,511 | LIVINGSTON | 15,895 | 5,555 | 9,875 | 465 | 4,320 D | 34.9% | 62.1% | 36.0% | 64.0% |
| 15,065 | MADISON | 7,128 | 2,096 | 4,933 | 99 | 2,837 D | 29.4% | 69.2% | 29.8% | 70.2% |
| 32,463 | MOREHOUSE | 9,692 | 5,418 | 4,017 | 257 | 1,401 R | 55.9% | 41.4% | 57.4% | 42.6% |
| 35,219 | NATCHITOCHES | 12,417 | 5,248 | 6,692 | 477 | 1,444 D | 42.3% | 53.9% | 44.0% | 56.0% |
| 593,471 | ORLEANS | 168,304 | 70,925 | 93,130 | 4,249 | 22,205 D | 42.1% | 55.3% | 43.2% | 56.8% |
| 115,387 | OUACHITA | 40,451 | 24,082 | 15,738 | 631 | 8,344 R | 59.5% | 38.9% | 60.5% | 39.5% |
| 25,225 | PLAQUEMINES | 8,855 | 6,052 | 2,614 | 189 | 3,438 R | 68.3% | 29.5% | 69.8% | 30.2% |
| 22,002 | POINTE COUPEE | 7,876 | 2,567 | 5,147 | 162 | 2,580 D | 32.6% | 65.4% | 33.3% | 66.7% |
| 118,078 | RAPIDES | 39,264 | 17,766 | 20,851 | 647 | 3,085 D | 45.2% | 53.1% | 46.0% | 54.0% |
| 9,226 | RED RIVER | 3,707 | 1,728 | 1,906 | 73 | 178 D | 46.6% | 51.4% | 47.6% | 52.4% |
| 21,774 | RICHLAND | 7,270 | 3,630 | 3,495 | 145 | 135 R | 49.9% | 48.1% | 50.9% | 49.1% |
| 18,638 | SABINE | 8,351 | 3,531 | 4,555 | 265 | 1,024 D | 42.3% | 54.5% | 43.7% | 56.3% |
| 51,185 | ST. BERNARD | 26,508 | 12,707 | 12,969 | 832 | 262 D | 47.9% | 48.9% | 49.5% | 50.5% |
| 29,550 | ST. CHARLES | 11,505 | 4,270 | 6,872 | 363 | 2,602 D | 37.1% | 59.7% | 38.3% | 61.7% |
| 9,937 | ST. HELENA | 3,788 | 1,046 | 2,622 | 120 | 1,576 D | 27.6% | 69.2% | 28.5% | 71.5% |
| 19,733 | ST. JAMES | 7,466 | 2,751 | 4,531 | 184 | 1,780 D | 36.8% | 60.7% | 37.8% | 62.2% |
| 23,813 | ST. JOHN THE BAPTIST | 9,609 | 3,597 | 5,700 | 312 | 2,103 D | 37.4% | 59.3% | 38.7% | 61.3% |
| 80,364 | ST. LANDRY | 26,243 | 9,956 | 15,613 | 674 | 5,657 D | 37.9% | 59.5% | 38.9% | 61.1% |
| 32,453 | ST. MARTIN | 12,433 | 4,112 | 7,992 | 329 | 3,880 D | 33.1% | 64.3% | 34.0% | 66.0% |
| 60,752 | ST. MARY | 18,708 | 8,919 | 9,401 | 388 | 482 D | 47.7% | 50.3% | 48.7% | 51.3% |
| 63,585 | ST. TAMMANY | 31,399 | 15,822 | 14,691 | 886 | 1,131 R | 50.4% | 46.8% | 51.9% | 48.1% |
| 65,875 | TANGIPAHOA | 24,311 | 9,242 | 14,432 | 637 | 5,190 D | 38.0% | 59.4% | 39.0% | 61.0% |
| 9,732 | TENSAS | 3,677 | 1,553 | 2,081 | 43 | 528 D | 42.2% | 56.6% | 42.7% | 57.3% |
| 76,049 | TERREBONNE | 24,282 | 12,895 | 10,627 | 760 | 2,268 R | 53.1% | 43.8% | 54.8% | 45.2% |
| 18,447 | UNION | 7,905 | 4,139 | 3,600 | 166 | 539 R | 52.4% | 45.5% | 53.5% | 46.5% |
| 43,071 | VERMILION | 17,850 | 6,133 | 11,246 | 471 | 5,113 D | 34.4% | 63.0% | 35.3% | 64.7% |
| 53,794 | VERNON | 10,465 | 3,970 | 6,202 | 293 | 2,232 D | 37.9% | 59.3% | 39.0% | 61.0% |
| 41,987 | WASHINGTON | 16,073 | 5,677 | 10,000 | 396 | 4,323 D | 35.3% | 62.2% | 36.2% | 63.8% |
| 39,939 | WEBSTER | 15,017 | 7,550 | 7,286 | 181 | 264 R | 50.3% | 48.5% | 50.9% | 49.1% |

# LOUISIANA

## PRESIDENT 1976

| 1970 Census Population | Parish | Total Vote | Republican | Democratic | Other | Rep.-Dem. Plurality | Percentage | | | |
|---|---|---|---|---|---|---|---|---|---|---|
| | | | | | | | Total Vote | | Major Vote | |
| | | | | | | | Rep. | Dem. | Rep. | Dem. |
| 16,864 | WEST BATON ROUGE | 5,884 | 1,913 | 3,809 | 162 | 1,896 D | 32.5% | 64.7% | 33.4% | 66.6% |
| 13,028 | WEST CARROLL | 5,112 | 2,407 | 2,595 | 110 | 188 D | 47.1% | 50.8% | 48.1% | 51.9% |
| 11,376 | WEST FELICIANA | 2,926 | 990 | 1,890 | 46 | 900 D | 33.8% | 64.6% | 34.4% | 65.6% |
| 16,369 | WINN | 6,889 | 3,209 | 3,543 | 137 | 334 D | 46.6% | 51.4% | 47.5% | 52.5% |
| 3,643,180 | TOTAL | 1,278,439 | 587,446 | 661,365 | 29,628 | 73,919 D | 46.0% | 51.7% | 47.0% | 53.0% |

# LOUISIANA

## PRESIDENT 1972

| 1970 Census Population | Parish | Total Vote | Republican | Democratic | Other | Rep.-Dem. Plurality | Total Vote Rep. | Total Vote Dem. | Major Vote Rep. | Major Vote Dem. |
|---|---|---|---|---|---|---|---|---|---|---|
| 52,109 | ACADIA | 15,194 | 9,698 | 4,406 | 1,090 | 5,292 R | 63.8% | 29.0% | 68.8% | 31.2% |
| 20,794 | ALLEN | 6,028 | 3,581 | 2,029 | 418 | 1,552 R | 59.4% | 33.7% | 63.8% | 36.2% |
| 37,086 | ASCENSION | 9,521 | 5,187 | 3,324 | 1,010 | 1,863 R | 54.5% | 34.9% | 60.9% | 39.1% |
| 19,654 | ASSUMPTION | 6,365 | 3,751 | 2,065 | 549 | 1,686 R | 58.9% | 32.4% | 64.5% | 35.5% |
| 37,751 | AVOYELLES | 10,778 | 6,225 | 3,395 | 1,158 | 2,830 R | 57.8% | 31.5% | 64.7% | 35.3% |
| 22,888 | BEAUREGARD | 7,139 | 4,955 | 1,728 | 456 | 3,227 R | 69.4% | 24.2% | 74.1% | 25.9% |
| 16,024 | BIENVILLE | 5,737 | 3,384 | 1,890 | 463 | 1,494 R | 59.0% | 32.9% | 64.2% | 35.8% |
| 63,703 | BOSSIER | 16,350 | 12,856 | 2,914 | 580 | 9,942 R | 78.6% | 17.8% | 81.5% | 18.5% |
| 230,184 | CADDO | 65,867 | 47,215 | 15,649 | 3,003 | 31,566 R | 71.7% | 23.8% | 75.1% | 24.9% |
| 145,415 | CALCASIEU | 42,925 | 24,778 | 15,330 | 2,817 | 9,448 R | 57.7% | 35.7% | 61.8% | 38.2% |
| 9,354 | CALDWELL | 2,995 | 2,306 | 508 | 181 | 1,798 R | 77.0% | 17.0% | 81.9% | 18.1% |
| 8,194 | CAMERON | 2,284 | 1,391 | 739 | 154 | 652 R | 60.9% | 32.4% | 65.3% | 34.7% |
| 11,769 | CATAHOULA | 3,668 | 2,683 | 823 | 162 | 1,860 R | 73.1% | 22.4% | 76.5% | 23.5% |
| 17,024 | CLAIBORNE | 5,356 | 3,432 | 1,551 | 373 | 1,881 R | 64.1% | 29.0% | 68.9% | 31.1% |
| 22,578 | CONCORDIA | 7,023 | 4,521 | 2,142 | 360 | 2,379 R | 64.4% | 30.5% | 67.9% | 32.1% |
| 22,764 | DE SOTO | 7,153 | 4,017 | 2,596 | 540 | 1,421 R | 56.2% | 36.3% | 60.7% | 39.3% |
| 285,167 | EAST BATON ROUGE | 80,542 | 52,648 | 23,617 | 4,277 | 29,031 R | 65.4% | 29.3% | 69.0% | 31.0% |
| 12,884 | EAST CARROLL | 3,587 | 1,736 | 1,661 | 190 | 75 R | 48.4% | 46.3% | 51.1% | 48.9% |
| 17,657 | EAST FELICIANA | 4,067 | 1,992 | 1,603 | 472 | 389 R | 49.0% | 39.4% | 55.4% | 44.6% |
| 31,932 | EVANGELINE | 9,201 | 5,523 | 2,919 | 759 | 2,604 R | 60.0% | 31.7% | 65.4% | 34.6% |
| 23,946 | FRANKLIN | 6,734 | 4,967 | 1,272 | 495 | 3,695 R | 73.8% | 18.9% | 79.6% | 20.4% |
| 13,671 | GRANT | 4,739 | 3,626 | 859 | 254 | 2,767 R | 76.5% | 18.1% | 80.8% | 19.2% |
| 57,397 | IBERIA | 17,940 | 11,812 | 5,143 | 985 | 6,669 R | 65.8% | 28.7% | 69.7% | 30.3% |
| 30,746 | IBERVILLE | 8,466 | 3,972 | 3,650 | 844 | 322 R | 46.9% | 43.1% | 52.1% | 47.9% |
| 15,963 | JACKSON | 5,935 | 4,152 | 1,477 | 306 | 2,675 R | 70.0% | 24.9% | 73.8% | 26.2% |
| 338,229 | JEFFERSON | 101,841 | 75,348 | 20,981 | 5,512 | 54,367 R | 74.0% | 20.6% | 78.2% | 21.8% |
| 29,554 | JEFFERSON DAVIS | 8,949 | 5,903 | 2,551 | 495 | 3,352 R | 66.0% | 28.5% | 69.8% | 30.2% |
| 111,745 | LAFAYETTE | 33,198 | 22,939 | 8,740 | 1,519 | 14,199 R | 69.1% | 26.3% | 72.4% | 27.6% |
| 68,941 | LAFOURCHE | 20,737 | 13,936 | 5,713 | 1,088 | 8,223 R | 67.2% | 27.5% | 70.9% | 29.1% |
| 13,295 | LA SALLE | 4,733 | 3,858 | 651 | 224 | 3,207 R | 81.5% | 13.8% | 85.6% | 14.4% |
| 33,800 | LINCOLN | 9,741 | 6,736 | 2,589 | 416 | 4,147 R | 69.2% | 26.6% | 72.2% | 27.8% |
| 36,511 | LIVINGSTON | 10,253 | 7,481 | 1,898 | 874 | 5,583 R | 73.0% | 18.5% | 79.8% | 20.2% |
| 15,065 | MADISON | 4,917 | 2,420 | 2,249 | 248 | 171 R | 49.2% | 45.7% | 51.8% | 48.2% |
| 32,463 | MOREHOUSE | 8,620 | 5,770 | 2,355 | 495 | 3,415 R | 66.9% | 27.3% | 71.0% | 29.0% |
| 35,219 | NATCHITOCHES | 10,803 | 6,994 | 3,180 | 629 | 3,814 R | 64.7% | 29.4% | 68.7% | 31.3% |
| 593,471 | ORLEANS | 161,446 | 88,075 | 60,790 | 12,581 | 27,285 R | 54.6% | 37.7% | 59.2% | 40.8% |
| 115,387 | OUACHITA | 33,263 | 24,860 | 6,920 | 1,483 | 17,940 R | 74.7% | 20.8% | 78.2% | 21.8% |
| 25,225 | PLAQUEMINES | 7,941 | 6,595 | 990 | 356 | 5,605 R | 83.0% | 12.5% | 86.9% | 13.1% |
| 22,002 | POINTE COUPEE | 6,853 | 3,192 | 3,133 | 528 | 59 R | 46.6% | 45.7% | 50.5% | 49.5% |
| 118,078 | RAPIDES | 32,011 | 22,306 | 8,422 | 1,283 | 13,884 R | 69.7% | 26.3% | 72.6% | 27.4% |
| 9,226 | RED RIVER | 3,404 | 2,245 | 957 | 202 | 1,288 R | 66.0% | 28.1% | 70.1% | 29.9% |
| 21,774 | RICHLAND | 6,079 | 4,304 | 1,335 | 440 | 2,969 R | 70.8% | 22.0% | 76.3% | 23.7% |
| 18,638 | SABINE | 6,680 | 4,935 | 1,332 | 413 | 3,603 R | 73.9% | 19.9% | 78.7% | 21.3% |
| 51,185 | ST. BERNARD | 19,563 | 15,198 | 3,189 | 1,176 | 12,009 R | 77.7% | 16.3% | 82.7% | 17.3% |
| 29,550 | ST. CHARLES | 9,052 | 5,469 | 2,788 | 795 | 2,681 R | 60.4% | 30.8% | 66.2% | 33.8% |
| 9,937 | ST. HELENA | 2,781 | 1,446 | 943 | 392 | 503 R | 52.0% | 33.9% | 60.5% | 39.5% |
| 19,733 | ST. JAMES | 6,291 | 3,112 | 2,633 | 546 | 479 R | 49.5% | 41.9% | 54.2% | 45.8% |
| 23,813 | ST. JOHN THE BAPTIST | 7,086 | 3,525 | 2,815 | 746 | 710 R | 49.7% | 39.7% | 55.6% | 44.4% |
| 80,364 | ST. LANDRY | 21,945 | 12,510 | 7,421 | 2,014 | 5,089 R | 57.0% | 33.8% | 62.8% | 37.2% |
| 32,453 | ST. MARTIN | 10,221 | 6,337 | 3,202 | 682 | 3,135 R | 62.0% | 31.3% | 66.4% | 33.6% |
| 60,752 | ST. MARY | 16,243 | 11,117 | 4,435 | 691 | 6,682 R | 68.4% | 27.3% | 71.5% | 28.5% |
| 63,585 | ST. TAMMANY | 20,825 | 15,438 | 3,949 | 1,438 | 11,489 R | 74.1% | 19.0% | 79.6% | 20.4% |
| 65,875 | TANGIPAHOA | 18,457 | 11,607 | 5,227 | 1,623 | 6,380 R | 62.9% | 28.3% | 68.9% | 31.1% |
| 9,732 | TENSAS | 3,426 | 1,729 | 1,568 | 129 | 161 R | 50.5% | 45.8% | 52.4% | 47.6% |
| 76,049 | TERREBONNE | 19,182 | 13,753 | 4,415 | 1,014 | 9,338 R | 71.7% | 23.0% | 75.7% | 24.3% |
| 18,447 | UNION | 6,157 | 4,322 | 1,465 | 370 | 2,857 R | 70.2% | 23.8% | 74.7% | 25.3% |
| 43,071 | VERMILION | 13,420 | 8,909 | 3,876 | 635 | 5,033 R | 66.4% | 28.9% | 69.7% | 30.3% |
| 53,794 | VERNON | 8,020 | 6,225 | 1,345 | 450 | 4,880 R | 77.6% | 16.8% | 82.2% | 17.8% |
| 41,987 | WASHINGTON | 12,196 | 8,162 | 2,947 | 1,087 | 5,215 R | 66.9% | 24.2% | 73.5% | 26.5% |
| 39,939 | WEBSTER | 12,349 | 8,829 | 2,859 | 661 | 5,970 R | 71.5% | 23.2% | 75.5% | 24.5% |

# LOUISIANA

## PRESIDENT 1972

| 1970 Census Population | Parish | Total Vote | Republican | Democratic | Other | Rep.-Dem. Plurality | Percentage | | | |
|---|---|---|---|---|---|---|---|---|---|---|
| | | | | | | | Total Vote | | Major Vote | |
| | | | | | | | Rep. | Dem. | Rep. | Dem. |
| 16,864 | WEST BATON ROUGE | 4,942 | 2,626 | 1,849 | 467 | 777 R | 53.1% | 37.4% | 58.7% | 41.3% |
| 13,028 | WEST CARROLL | 3,880 | 2,997 | 571 | 312 | 2,426 R | 77.2% | 14.7% | 84.0% | 16.0% |
| 11,376 | WEST FELICIANA | 2,376 | 1,001 | 1,079 | 296 | 78 D | 42.1% | 45.4% | 48.1% | 51.9% |
| 16,369 | WINN | 6,016 | 4,235 | 1,490 | 291 | 2,745 R | 70.4% | 24.8% | 74.0% | 26.0% |
| 3,643,180 | TOTAL | 1,051,491 | 686,852 | 298,142 | 66,497 | 388,710 R | 65.3% | 28.4% | 69.7% | 30.3% |

# LOUISIANA

## PRESIDENT 1968

| 1960 Census Population | Parish | Total Vote | Republican | Democratic | AIP | Other | Plurality | Percentage Total Vote Rep. | Dem. | AIP |
|---|---|---|---|---|---|---|---|---|---|---|
| 49,931 | ACADIA | 16,991 | 3,178 | 4,098 | 9,715 | | 5,617 A | 18.7% | 24.1% | 57.2% |
| 19,867 | ALLEN | 7,259 | 1,004 | 2,026 | 4,229 | | 2,203 A | 13.8% | 27.9% | 58.3% |
| 27,927 | ASCENSION | 10,545 | 1,338 | 3,203 | 6,004 | | 2,801 A | 12.7% | 30.4% | 56.9% |
| 17,991 | ASSUMPTION | 6,205 | 1,222 | 2,085 | 2,898 | | 813 A | 19.7% | 33.6% | 46.7% |
| 37,606 | AVOYELLES | 12,192 | 2,459 | 2,973 | 6,760 | | 3,787 A | 20.2% | 24.4% | 55.4% |
| 19,191 | BEAUREGARD | 7,232 | 1,615 | 1,569 | 4,048 | | 2,433 A | 22.3% | 21.7% | 56.0% |
| 16,726 | BIENVILLE | 6,175 | 941 | 1,768 | 3,466 | | 1,698 A | 15.2% | 28.6% | 56.1% |
| 57,622 | BOSSIER | 15,776 | 3,745 | 2,782 | 9,249 | | 5,504 A | 23.7% | 17.6% | 58.6% |
| 223,859 | CADDO | 67,362 | 21,224 | 17,675 | 28,463 | | 7,239 A | 31.5% | 26.2% | 42.3% |
| 145,475 | CALCASIEU | 44,363 | 9,520 | 14,593 | 20,250 | | 5,657 A | 21.5% | 32.9% | 45.6% |
| 9,004 | CALDWELL | 3,715 | 490 | 973 | 2,252 | | 1,279 A | 13.2% | 26.2% | 60.6% |
| 6,909 | CAMERON | 2,593 | 405 | 533 | 1,655 | | 1,122 A | 15.6% | 20.6% | 63.8% |
| 11,421 | CATAHOULA | 4,201 | 755 | 769 | 2,677 | | 1,908 A | 18.0% | 18.3% | 63.7% |
| 19,407 | CLAIBORNE | 5,973 | 1,117 | 1,545 | 3,311 | | 1,766 A | 18.7% | 25.9% | 55.4% |
| 20,467 | CONCORDIA | 7,499 | 974 | 1,983 | 4,542 | | 2,559 A | 13.0% | 26.4% | 60.6% |
| 24,248 | DE SOTO | 8,564 | 974 | 3,400 | 4,190 | | 790 A | 11.4% | 39.7% | 48.9% |
| 230,058 | EAST BATON ROUGE | 78,681 | 21,661 | 21,770 | 35,250 | | 13,480 A | 27.5% | 27.7% | 44.8% |
| 14,433 | EAST CARROLL | 4,218 | 586 | 1,926 | 1,706 | | 220 D | 13.9% | 45.7% | 40.4% |
| 20,198 | EAST FELICIANA | 4,091 | 457 | 1,409 | 2,225 | | 816 A | 11.2% | 34.4% | 54.4% |
| 31,639 | EVANGELINE | 11,558 | 1,549 | 2,647 | 7,362 | | 4,715 A | 13.4% | 22.9% | 63.7% |
| 26,088 | FRANKLIN | 7,127 | 1,052 | 681 | 5,394 | | 4,342 A | 14.8% | 9.6% | 75.7% |
| 13,330 | GRANT | 5,515 | 1,113 | 932 | 3,470 | | 2,357 A | 20.2% | 16.9% | 62.9% |
| 51,657 | IBERIA | 19,029 | 5,448 | 5,510 | 8,071 | | 2,561 A | 28.6% | 29.0% | 42.4% |
| 29,939 | IBERVILLE | 9,787 | 1,413 | 4,084 | 4,290 | | 206 A | 14.4% | 41.7% | 43.8% |
| 15,828 | JACKSON | 6,570 | 1,104 | 1,525 | 3,941 | | 2,416 A | 16.8% | 23.2% | 60.0% |
| 208,769 | JEFFERSON | 91,573 | 29,478 | 20,193 | 41,902 | | 12,424 A | 32.2% | 22.1% | 45.8% |
| 29,825 | JEFFERSON DAVIS | 9,751 | 2,213 | 2,641 | 4,897 | | 2,256 A | 22.7% | 27.1% | 50.2% |
| 84,656 | LAFAYETTE | 30,375 | 10,669 | 7,983 | 11,723 | | 1,054 A | 35.1% | 26.3% | 38.6% |
| 55,381 | LAFOURCHE | 21,223 | 4,797 | 5,516 | 10,910 | | 5,394 A | 22.6% | 26.0% | 51.4% |
| 13,011 | LA SALLE | 5,846 | 1,258 | 710 | 3,878 | | 2,620 A | 21.5% | 12.1% | 66.3% |
| 28,535 | LINCOLN | 8,877 | 2,643 | 2,009 | 4,225 | | 1,582 A | 29.8% | 22.6% | 47.6% |
| 26,974 | LIVINGSTON | 12,254 | 947 | 1,400 | 9,907 | | 8,507 A | 7.7% | 11.4% | 80.8% |
| 16,444 | MADISON | 5,688 | 649 | 2,659 | 2,380 | | 279 D | 11.4% | 46.7% | 41.8% |
| 33,709 | MOREHOUSE | 8,942 | 1,772 | 1,793 | 5,377 | | 3,584 A | 19.8% | 20.1% | 60.1% |
| 35,653 | NATCHITOCHES | 11,802 | 2,352 | 3,945 | 5,505 | | 1,560 A | 19.9% | 33.4% | 46.6% |
| 627,525 | ORLEANS | 178,668 | 47,728 | 72,451 | 58,489 | | 13,962 D | 26.7% | 40.6% | 32.7% |
| 101,663 | OUACHITA | 31,704 | 10,089 | 6,470 | 15,145 | | 5,056 A | 31.8% | 20.4% | 47.8% |
| 22,545 | PLAQUEMINES | 8,542 | 968 | 1,144 | 6,430 | | 5,286 A | 11.3% | 13.4% | 75.3% |
| 22,488 | POINTE COUPEE | 7,497 | 850 | 3,139 | 3,508 | | 369 A | 11.3% | 41.9% | 46.8% |
| 111,351 | RAPIDES | 35,231 | 10,199 | 8,793 | 16,239 | | 6,040 A | 28.9% | 25.0% | 46.1% |
| 9,978 | RED RIVER | 3,771 | 380 | 914 | 2,477 | | 1,563 A | 10.1% | 24.2% | 65.7% |
| 23,824 | RICHLAND | 6,463 | 1,031 | 1,017 | 4,415 | | 3,384 A | 16.0% | 15.7% | 68.3% |
| 18,564 | SABINE | 6,810 | 1,125 | 1,159 | 4,526 | | 3,367 A | 16.5% | 17.0% | 66.5% |
| 32,186 | ST. BERNARD | 19,027 | 3,486 | 2,485 | 13,056 | | 9,570 A | 18.3% | 13.1% | 68.6% |
| 21,219 | ST. CHARLES | 9,128 | 1,675 | 3,070 | 4,383 | | 1,313 A | 18.4% | 33.6% | 48.0% |
| 9,162 | ST. HELENA | 3,370 | 219 | 1,351 | 1,800 | | 449 A | 6.5% | 40.1% | 53.4% |
| 18,369 | ST. JAMES | 6,530 | 778 | 2,987 | 2,765 | | 222 D | 11.9% | 45.7% | 42.3% |
| 18,439 | ST. JOHN THE BAPTIST | 7,431 | 940 | 3,245 | 3,246 | | 1 A | 12.6% | 43.7% | 43.7% |
| 81,493 | ST. LANDRY | 25,242 | 3,508 | 9,075 | 12,659 | | 3,584 A | 13.9% | 36.0% | 50.2% |
| 29,063 | ST. MARTIN | 9,705 | 1,625 | 3,321 | 4,759 | | 1,438 A | 16.7% | 34.2% | 49.0% |
| 48,833 | ST. MARY | 16,659 | 4,586 | 5,312 | 6,761 | | 1,449 A | 27.5% | 31.9% | 40.6% |
| 38,643 | ST. TAMMANY | 20,761 | 4,846 | 4,445 | 11,470 | | 6,624 A | 23.3% | 21.4% | 55.2% |
| 59,434 | TANGIPAHOA | 20,978 | 2,907 | 4,983 | 13,088 | | 8,105 A | 13.9% | 23.8% | 62.4% |
| 11,796 | TENSAS | 2,638 | 503 | 845 | 1,290 | | 445 A | 19.1% | 32.0% | 48.9% |
| 60,771 | TERREBONNE | 18,677 | 5,214 | 4,627 | 8,836 | | 3,622 A | 27.9% | 24.8% | 47.3% |
| 17,624 | UNION | 6,746 | 1,113 | 1,336 | 4,297 | | 2,961 A | 16.5% | 19.8% | 63.7% |
| 38,855 | VERMILION | 15,208 | 3,278 | 3,806 | 8,124 | | 4,318 A | 21.6% | 25.0% | 53.4% |
| 18,301 | VERNON | 8,606 | 1,574 | 1,496 | 5,536 | | 3,962 A | 18.3% | 17.4% | 64.3% |
| 44,015 | WASHINGTON | 15,718 | 1,695 | 3,021 | 11,002 | | 7,981 A | 10.8% | 19.2% | 70.0% |
| 39,701 | WEBSTER | 14,013 | 2,496 | 2,871 | 8,646 | | 5,775 A | 17.8% | 20.5% | 61.7% |

# LOUISIANA

## PRESIDENT 1968

| 1960 Census Population | Parish | Total Vote | Republican | Democratic | AIP | Other | Plurality | Percentage Total Vote | | |
|---|---|---|---|---|---|---|---|---|---|---|
| | | | | | | | | Rep. | Dem. | AIP |
| 14,796 | WEST BATON ROUGE | 5,254 | 669 | 2,016 | 2,569 | | 553 A | 12.7% | 38.4% | 48.9% |
| 14,177 | WEST CARROLL | 4,554 | 585 | 395 | 3,574 | | 2,989 A | 12.8% | 8.7% | 78.5% |
| 12,395 | WEST FELICIANA | 2,672 | 296 | 1,303 | 1,073 | | 230 D | 11.1% | 48.8% | 40.2% |
| 16,034 | WINN | 6,295 | 1,050 | 1,230 | 4,015 | | 2,785 A | 16.7% | 19.5% | 63.8% |
| 3,257,022 | TOTAL | 1,097,450 | 257,535 | 309,615 | 530,300 | | 220,685 A | 23.5% | 28.2% | 48.3% |

# LOUISIANA

## PRESIDENT 1964

| 1960 Census Population | Parish | Total Vote | Republican | Democratic | Other | Rep.-Dem. Plurality | Percentage Total Vote Rep. | Dem. | Major Vote Rep. | Dem. |
|---|---|---|---|---|---|---|---|---|---|---|
| 49,931 | ACADIA | 16,169 | 6,706 | 9,463 | | 2,757 D | 41.5% | 58.5% | 41.5% | 58.5% |
| 19,867 | ALLEN | 6,491 | 2,704 | 3,787 | | 1,083 D | 41.7% | 58.3% | 41.7% | 58.3% |
| 27,927 | ASCENSION | 8,076 | 3,197 | 4,879 | | 1,682 D | 39.6% | 60.4% | 39.6% | 60.4% |
| 17,991 | ASSUMPTION | 5,168 | 2,112 | 3,056 | | 944 D | 40.9% | 59.1% | 40.9% | 59.1% |
| 37,606 | AVOYELLES | 9,976 | 4,874 | 5,102 | | 228 D | 48.9% | 51.1% | 48.9% | 51.1% |
| 19,191 | BEAUREGARD | 6,398 | 3,349 | 3,049 | | 300 R | 52.3% | 47.7% | 52.3% | 47.7% |
| 16,726 | BIENVILLE | 4,595 | 3,740 | 855 | | 2,885 R | 81.4% | 18.6% | 81.4% | 18.6% |
| 57,622 | BOSSIER | 11,759 | 9,822 | 1,937 | | 7,885 R | 83.5% | 16.5% | 83.5% | 16.5% |
| 223,859 | CADDO | 52,355 | 42,197 | 10,158 | | 32,039 R | 80.6% | 19.4% | 80.6% | 19.4% |
| 145,475 | CALCASIEU | 40,331 | 17,046 | 23,285 | | 6,239 D | 42.3% | 57.7% | 42.3% | 57.7% |
| 9,004 | CALDWELL | 3,143 | 2,534 | 609 | | 1,925 R | 80.6% | 19.4% | 80.6% | 19.4% |
| 6,909 | CAMERON | 2,447 | 871 | 1,576 | | 705 D | 35.6% | 64.4% | 35.6% | 64.4% |
| 11,421 | CATAHOULA | 2,947 | 2,387 | 560 | | 1,827 R | 81.0% | 19.0% | 81.0% | 19.0% |
| 19,407 | CLAIBORNE | 4,399 | 3,917 | 482 | | 3,435 R | 89.0% | 11.0% | 89.0% | 11.0% |
| 20,467 | CONCORDIA | 4,831 | 4,022 | 809 | | 3,213 R | 83.3% | 16.7% | 83.3% | 16.7% |
| 24,248 | DE SOTO | 5,208 | 3,954 | 1,254 | | 2,700 R | 75.9% | 24.1% | 75.9% | 24.1% |
| 230,058 | EAST BATON ROUGE | 63,116 | 36,964 | 26,152 | | 10,812 R | 58.6% | 41.4% | 58.6% | 41.4% |
| 14,433 | EAST CARROLL | 1,749 | 1,486 | 263 | | 1,223 R | 85.0% | 15.0% | 85.0% | 15.0% |
| 20,198 | EAST FELICIANA | 2,386 | 1,900 | 486 | | 1,414 R | 79.6% | 20.4% | 79.6% | 20.4% |
| 31,639 | EVANGELINE | 10,138 | 3,975 | 6,163 | | 2,188 D | 39.2% | 60.8% | 39.2% | 60.8% |
| 26,088 | FRANKLIN | 6,229 | 5,470 | 759 | | 4,711 R | 87.8% | 12.2% | 87.8% | 12.2% |
| 13,330 | GRANT | 4,746 | 3,292 | 1,454 | | 1,838 R | 69.4% | 30.6% | 69.4% | 30.6% |
| 51,657 | IBERIA | 16,337 | 8,196 | 8,141 | | 55 R | 50.2% | 49.8% | 50.2% | 49.8% |
| 29,939 | IBERVILLE | 7,877 | 3,432 | 4,445 | | 1,013 D | 43.6% | 56.4% | 43.6% | 56.4% |
| 15,828 | JACKSON | 6,073 | 4,521 | 1,552 | | 2,969 R | 74.4% | 25.6% | 74.4% | 25.6% |
| 208,769 | JEFFERSON | 68,965 | 37,161 | 31,804 | | 5,357 R | 53.9% | 46.1% | 53.9% | 46.1% |
| 29,825 | JEFFERSON DAVIS | 8,639 | 3,673 | 4,966 | | 1,293 D | 42.5% | 57.5% | 42.5% | 57.5% |
| 84,656 | LAFAYETTE | 26,885 | 12,398 | 14,487 | | 2,089 D | 46.1% | 53.9% | 46.1% | 53.9% |
| 55,381 | LAFOURCHE | 18,209 | 6,164 | 12,045 | | 5,881 D | 33.9% | 66.1% | 33.9% | 66.1% |
| 13,011 | LA SALLE | 5,183 | 4,319 | 864 | | 3,455 R | 83.3% | 16.7% | 83.3% | 16.7% |
| 28,535 | LINCOLN | 7,480 | 5,766 | 1,714 | | 4,052 R | 77.1% | 22.9% | 77.1% | 22.9% |
| 26,974 | LIVINGSTON | 9,017 | 5,508 | 3,509 | | 1,999 R | 61.1% | 38.9% | 61.1% | 38.9% |
| 16,444 | MADISON | 2,478 | 2,061 | 417 | | 1,644 R | 83.2% | 16.8% | 83.2% | 16.8% |
| 33,709 | MOREHOUSE | 7,113 | 6,222 | 891 | | 5,331 R | 87.5% | 12.5% | 87.5% | 12.5% |
| 35,653 | NATCHITOCHES | 8,500 | 5,525 | 2,975 | | 2,550 R | 65.0% | 35.0% | 65.0% | 35.0% |
| 627,525 | ORLEANS | 163,094 | 81,049 | 82,045 | | 996 D | 49.7% | 50.3% | 49.7% | 50.3% |
| 101,663 | OUACHITA | 25,198 | 21,024 | 4,174 | | 16,850 R | 83.4% | 16.6% | 83.4% | 16.6% |
| 22,545 | PLAQUEMINES | 5,679 | 4,904 | 775 | | 4,129 R | 86.4% | 13.6% | 86.4% | 13.6% |
| 22,488 | POINTE COUPEE | 4,574 | 2,327 | 2,247 | | 80 R | 50.9% | 49.1% | 50.9% | 49.1% |
| 111,351 | RAPIDES | 28,114 | 18,122 | 9,992 | | 8,130 R | 64.5% | 35.5% | 64.5% | 35.5% |
| 9,978 | RED RIVER | 2,569 | 2,235 | 334 | | 1,901 R | 87.0% | 13.0% | 87.0% | 13.0% |
| 23,824 | RICHLAND | 5,245 | 4,498 | 747 | | 3,751 R | 85.8% | 14.2% | 85.8% | 14.2% |
| 18,564 | SABINE | 6,246 | 4,165 | 2,081 | | 2,084 R | 66.7% | 33.3% | 66.7% | 33.3% |
| 32,186 | ST. BERNARD | 14,230 | 8,055 | 6,175 | | 1,880 R | 56.6% | 43.4% | 56.6% | 43.4% |
| 21,219 | ST. CHARLES | 7,800 | 2,715 | 5,085 | | 2,370 D | 34.8% | 65.2% | 34.8% | 65.2% |
| 9,162 | ST. HELENA | 2,025 | 1,319 | 706 | | 613 R | 65.1% | 34.9% | 65.1% | 34.9% |
| 18,369 | ST. JAMES | 5,681 | 1,467 | 4,214 | | 2,747 D | 25.8% | 74.2% | 25.8% | 74.2% |
| 18,439 | ST. JOHN THE BAPTIST | 5,652 | 1,694 | 3,958 | | 2,264 D | 30.0% | 70.0% | 30.0% | 70.0% |
| 81,493 | ST. LANDRY | 22,727 | 10,920 | 11,807 | | 887 D | 48.0% | 52.0% | 48.0% | 52.0% |
| 29,063 | ST. MARTIN | 7,468 | 2,793 | 4,675 | | 1,882 D | 37.4% | 62.6% | 37.4% | 62.6% |
| 48,833 | ST. MARY | 12,857 | 5,530 | 7,327 | | 1,797 D | 43.0% | 57.0% | 43.0% | 57.0% |
| 38,643 | ST. TAMMANY | 14,577 | 7,883 | 6,694 | | 1,189 R | 54.1% | 45.9% | 54.1% | 45.9% |
| 59,434 | TANGIPAHOA | 16,841 | 9,732 | 7,109 | | 2,623 R | 57.8% | 42.2% | 57.8% | 42.2% |
| 11,796 | TENSAS | 1,847 | 1,655 | 192 | | 1,463 R | 89.6% | 10.4% | 89.6% | 10.4% |
| 60,771 | TERREBONNE | 15,306 | 6,729 | 8,577 | | 1,848 D | 44.0% | 56.0% | 44.0% | 56.0% |
| 17,624 | UNION | 5,689 | 4,534 | 1,155 | | 3,379 R | 79.7% | 20.3% | 79.7% | 20.3% |
| 38,855 | VERMILION | 14,188 | 4,984 | 9,204 | | 4,220 D | 35.1% | 64.9% | 35.1% | 64.9% |
| 18,301 | VERNON | 7,260 | 3,696 | 3,564 | | 132 R | 50.9% | 49.1% | 50.9% | 49.1% |
| 44,015 | WASHINGTON | 12,263 | 7,438 | 4,825 | | 2,613 R | 60.7% | 39.3% | 60.7% | 39.3% |
| 39,701 | WEBSTER | 9,932 | 8,177 | 1,755 | | 6,422 R | 82.3% | 17.7% | 82.3% | 17.7% |

# LOUISIANA

## PRESIDENT 1964

| 1960 Census Population | Parish | Total Vote | Republican | Democratic | Other | Rep.-Dem. Plurality | Percentage | | | |
|---|---|---|---|---|---|---|---|---|---|---|
| | | | | | | | Total Vote | | Major Vote | |
| | | | | | | | Rep. | Dem. | Rep. | Dem. |
| 14,796 | WEST BATON ROUGE | 3,727 | 1,835 | 1,892 | | 57 D | 49.2% | 50.8% | 49.2% | 50.8% |
| 14,177 | WEST CARROLL | 3,412 | 3,017 | 395 | | 2,622 R | 88.4% | 11.6% | 88.4% | 11.6% |
| 12,395 | WEST FELICIANA | 1,120 | 897 | 223 | | 674 R | 80.1% | 19.9% | 80.1% | 19.9% |
| 16,034 | WINN | 5,559 | 4,366 | 1,193 | | 3,173 R | 78.5% | 21.5% | 78.5% | 21.5% |
| 3,257,022 | TOTAL | 896,293 | 509,225 | 387,068 | | 122,157 R | 56.8% | 43.2% | 56.8% | 43.2% |

# LOUISIANA

## PRESIDENT 1960

| 1980 Census Population | Parish | Total Vote | Republican | Democratic | Other | Rep.-Dem. Plurality | Percentage Total Vote Rep. | Dem. | Major Vote Rep. | Dem. |
|---|---|---|---|---|---|---|---|---|---|---|
| 49,931 | ACADIA | 15,084 | 2,616 | 11,440 | 1,028 | 8,824 D | 17.3% | 75.8% | 18.6% | 81.4% |
| 19,867 | ALLEN | 6,215 | 1,676 | 3,719 | 820 | 2,043 D | 27.0% | 59.8% | 31.1% | 68.9% |
| 27,927 | ASCENSION | 7,610 | 1,012 | 5,689 | 909 | 4,677 D | 13.3% | 74.8% | 15.1% | 84.9% |
| 17,991 | ASSUMPTION | 4,211 | 766 | 3,019 | 426 | 2,253 D | 18.2% | 71.7% | 20.2% | 79.8% |
| 37,606 | AVOYELLES | 10,035 | 1,270 | 7,625 | 1,140 | 6,355 D | 12.7% | 76.0% | 14.3% | 85.7% |
| 19,191 | BEAUREGARD | 5,965 | 2,432 | 2,903 | 630 | 471 D | 40.8% | 48.7% | 45.6% | 54.4% |
| 16,726 | BIENVILLE | 3,548 | 1,230 | 625 | 1,693 | 605 R | 34.7% | 17.6% | 66.3% | 33.7% |
| 57,622 | BOSSIER | 8,720 | 3,429 | 2,198 | 3,093 | 1,231 R | 39.3% | 25.2% | 60.9% | 39.1% |
| 223,859 | CADDO | 46,301 | 25,139 | 11,481 | 9,681 | 13,658 R | 54.3% | 24.8% | 68.6% | 31.4% |
| 145,475 | CALCASIEU | 37,627 | 10,243 | 24,233 | 3,151 | 13,990 D | 27.2% | 64.4% | 29.7% | 70.3% |
| 9,004 | CALDWELL | 2,041 | 716 | 694 | 631 | 22 R | 35.1% | 34.0% | 50.8% | 49.2% |
| 6,909 | CAMERON | 2,340 | 322 | 1,944 | 74 | 1,622 D | 13.8% | 83.1% | 14.2% | 85.8% |
| 11,421 | CATAHOULA | 2,132 | 971 | 558 | 603 | 413 R | 45.5% | 26.2% | 63.5% | 36.5% |
| 19,407 | CLAIBORNE | 3,854 | 1,336 | 489 | 2,029 | 847 R | 34.7% | 12.7% | 73.2% | 26.8% |
| 20,467 | CONCORDIA | 3,331 | 1,009 | 768 | 1,554 | 241 R | 30.3% | 23.1% | 56.8% | 43.2% |
| 24,248 | DE SOTO | 4,439 | 1,603 | 1,183 | 1,653 | 420 R | 36.1% | 26.7% | 57.5% | 42.5% |
| 230,058 | EAST BATON ROUGE | 56,435 | 17,749 | 26,326 | 12,360 | 8,577 D | 31.5% | 46.6% | 40.3% | 59.7% |
| 14,433 | EAST CARROLL | 1,524 | 448 | 364 | 712 | 84 R | 29.4% | 23.9% | 55.2% | 44.8% |
| 20,198 | EAST FELICIANA | 1,927 | 313 | 475 | 1,139 | 162 D | 16.2% | 24.6% | 39.7% | 60.3% |
| 31,639 | EVANGELINE | 9,764 | 1,105 | 7,865 | 794 | 6,760 D | 11.3% | 80.6% | 12.3% | 87.7% |
| 26,088 | FRANKLIN | 4,039 | 1,336 | 1,213 | 1,490 | 123 R | 33.1% | 30.0% | 52.4% | 47.6% |
| 13,330 | GRANT | 3,882 | 1,254 | 1,219 | 1,409 | 35 R | 32.3% | 31.4% | 50.7% | 49.3% |
| 51,657 | IBERIA | 15,470 | 3,551 | 9,235 | 2,684 | 5,684 D | 23.0% | 59.7% | 27.8% | 72.2% |
| 29,939 | IBERVILLE | 6,309 | 1,000 | 4,558 | 751 | 3,558 D | 15.9% | 72.2% | 18.0% | 82.0% |
| 15,828 | JACKSON | 4,100 | 1,799 | 1,398 | 903 | 401 R | 43.9% | 34.1% | 56.3% | 43.7% |
| 208,769 | JEFFERSON | 62,638 | 17,215 | 32,119 | 13,304 | 14,904 D | 27.5% | 51.3% | 34.9% | 65.1% |
| 29,825 | JEFFERSON DAVIS | 8,712 | 2,251 | 5,904 | 557 | 3,653 D | 25.8% | 67.8% | 27.6% | 72.4% |
| 84,656 | LAFAYETTE | 22,684 | 6,047 | 14,132 | 2,505 | 8,085 D | 26.7% | 62.3% | 30.0% | 70.0% |
| 55,381 | LAFOURCHE | 16,055 | 2,930 | 12,244 | 881 | 9,314 D | 18.2% | 76.3% | 19.3% | 80.7% |
| 13,011 | LA SALLE | 3,842 | 2,123 | 843 | 876 | 1,280 R | 55.3% | 21.9% | 71.6% | 28.4% |
| 28,535 | LINCOLN | 5,109 | 2,766 | 1,051 | 1,292 | 1,715 R | 54.1% | 20.6% | 72.5% | 27.5% |
| 26,974 | LIVINGSTON | 6,628 | 954 | 2,881 | 2,793 | 1,927 D | 14.4% | 43.5% | 24.9% | 75.1% |
| 16,444 | MADISON | 1,888 | 629 | 235 | 1,024 | 394 R | 33.3% | 12.4% | 72.8% | 27.2% |
| 33,709 | MOREHOUSE | 4,780 | 2,551 | 1,085 | 1,144 | 1,466 R | 53.4% | 22.7% | 70.2% | 29.8% |
| 35,653 | NATCHITOCHES | 7,060 | 2,562 | 2,781 | 1,717 | 219 D | 36.3% | 39.4% | 48.0% | 52.0% |
| 627,525 | ORLEANS | 175,767 | 47,111 | 87,242 | 41,414 | 40,131 D | 26.8% | 49.6% | 35.1% | 64.9% |
| 101,663 | OUACHITA | 19,291 | 10,525 | 5,202 | 3,564 | 5,323 R | 54.6% | 27.0% | 66.9% | 33.1% |
| 22,545 | PLAQUEMINES | 5,146 | 712 | 1,087 | 3,347 | 375 D | 13.8% | 21.1% | 39.6% | 60.4% |
| 22,488 | POINTE COUPEE | 4,112 | 674 | 2,953 | 485 | 2,279 D | 16.4% | 71.8% | 18.6% | 81.4% |
| 111,351 | RAPIDES | 23,782 | 8,155 | 9,651 | 5,976 | 1,496 D | 34.3% | 40.6% | 45.8% | 54.2% |
| 9,978 | RED RIVER | 1,917 | 406 | 377 | 1,134 | 29 R | 21.2% | 19.7% | 51.9% | 48.1% |
| 23,824 | RICHLAND | 3,869 | 1,378 | 996 | 1,495 | 382 R | 35.6% | 25.7% | 58.0% | 42.0% |
| 18,564 | SABINE | 5,889 | 2,419 | 2,412 | 1,058 | 7 R | 41.1% | 41.0% | 50.1% | 49.9% |
| 32,186 | ST. BERNARD | 10,949 | 1,431 | 4,660 | 4,858 | 3,229 D | 13.1% | 42.6% | 23.5% | 76.5% |
| 21,219 | ST. CHARLES | 6,602 | 1,377 | 4,708 | 517 | 3,331 D | 20.9% | 71.3% | 22.6% | 77.4% |
| 9,162 | ST. HELENA | 1,809 | 296 | 678 | 835 | 382 D | 16.4% | 37.5% | 30.4% | 69.6% |
| 18,369 | ST. JAMES | 5,314 | 620 | 4,362 | 332 | 3,742 D | 11.7% | 82.1% | 12.4% | 87.6% |
| 18,439 | ST. JOHN THE BAPTIST | 4,720 | 488 | 3,782 | 450 | 3,294 D | 10.3% | 80.1% | 11.4% | 88.6% |
| 81,493 | ST. LANDRY | 20,262 | 3,083 | 14,625 | 2,554 | 11,542 D | 15.2% | 72.2% | 17.4% | 82.6% |
| 29,063 | ST. MARTIN | 7,063 | 858 | 5,506 | 699 | 4,648 D | 12.1% | 78.0% | 13.5% | 86.5% |
| 48,833 | ST. MARY | 10,832 | 2,992 | 6,671 | 1,169 | 3,679 D | 27.6% | 61.6% | 31.0% | 69.0% |
| 38,643 | ST. TAMMANY | 11,063 | 2,850 | 5,179 | 3,034 | 2,329 D | 25.8% | 46.8% | 35.5% | 64.5% |
| 59,434 | TANGIPAHOA | 14,351 | 3,285 | 6,648 | 4,418 | 3,363 D | 22.9% | 46.3% | 33.1% | 66.9% |
| 11,796 | TENSAS | 1,208 | 510 | 247 | 451 | 263 R | 42.2% | 20.4% | 67.4% | 32.6% |
| 60,771 | TERREBONNE | 13,210 | 3,126 | 8,992 | 1,092 | 5,866 D | 23.7% | 68.1% | 25.8% | 74.2% |
| 17,624 | UNION | 4,063 | 2,017 | 1,034 | 1,012 | 983 R | 49.6% | 25.4% | 66.1% | 33.9% |
| 38,855 | VERMILION | 14,595 | 2,170 | 11,257 | 1,168 | 9,087 D | 14.9% | 77.1% | 16.2% | 83.8% |
| 18,301 | VERNON | 6,160 | 1,991 | 3,145 | 1,024 | 1,154 D | 32.3% | 51.1% | 38.8% | 61.2% |
| 44,015 | WASHINGTON | 11,400 | 1,847 | 5,678 | 3,875 | 3,831 D | 16.2% | 49.8% | 24.5% | 75.5% |
| 39,701 | WEBSTER | 7,667 | 3,139 | 1,273 | 3,255 | 1,866 R | 40.9% | 16.6% | 71.1% | 28.9% |

# LOUISIANA

## PRESIDENT 1960

| 1980 Census Population | Parish | Total Vote | Republican | Democratic | Other | Rep.-Dem. Plurality | Percentage | | | |
|---|---|---|---|---|---|---|---|---|---|---|
| | | | | | | | Total Vote | | Major Vote | |
| | | | | | | | Rep. | Dem. | Rep. | Dem. |
| 14,796 | WEST BATON ROUGE | 3,141 | 390 | 2,315 | 436 | 1,925 D | 12.4% | 73.7% | 14.4% | 85.6% |
| 14,177 | WEST CARROLL | 2,423 | 742 | 784 | 897 | 42 D | 30.6% | 32.4% | 48.6% | 51.4% |
| 12,395 | WEST FELICIANA | 891 | 196 | 271 | 424 | 75 D | 22.0% | 30.4% | 42.0% | 58.0% |
| 16,034 | WINN | 4,096 | 1,839 | 1,108 | 1,149 | 731 R | 44.9% | 27.1% | 62.4% | 37.6% |
| 3,257,022 | TOTAL | 807,891 | 230,980 | 407,339 | 169,572 | 176,359 D | 28.6% | 50.4% | 36.2% | 63.8% |

# LOUISIANA

## ELECTION NOTES

**2004**  Other vote was 7,032 The Better Life (Ralph Nader); 5,203 Constitution (Michael Peroutka); 2,781 Libertarian (Michael Badnarik); 1,795 Protecting Working Families (Walter Brown); 1,566 Prohibition (Gene Amondson); 1,276 Louisiana Green (David Cobb); 985 Socialist Workers (James Harris).

**2000**  Other vote was 14,356 Reform (Buchanan); 5,483 Constitution (Phillips); 2,951 Libertarian (Browne); 1,103 Socialist Workers (Harris); 1,075 Natural Law (Hagelin).

**1996**  Other vote was 7,499 Libertarian (Browne); 4,719 Liberty, Ecology, Community (Nader); 3,366 Taxpayers (Phillips); 2,981 Natural Law (Hagelin); 1,678 Workers World (Moorehead).

**1992**  Other vote was 18,545 Gritz (America First); 3,155 Marrou (Libertarian); 1,663 Daniels (Equal Justice & Opportunity); 1,552 Phillips (Taxpayers); 1,434 Fulani (More Perfect Democracy); 1,136 La Rouche (Justice, Liberty, Agriculture); 889 Hagelin (Natural Law); 808 Yiamonyiannis (Independent).

**1988**  Other vote was 18,612 Duke (Populist); 4,115 Paul (Libertarian); 2,355 Fulani (New Alliance); 1,958 LaRouche (National Economic Recovery).

**1984**  Other vote was 9,502 Johnson (Citizens); 3,552 LaRouche (Independent); 1,876 Bergland (Libertarian); 1,310 Richards (Populist); 1,164 Mason (Socialist Workers); 533 Serrette (New Alliance).

**1980**  Other vote was 26,345 Anderson (Independent); 10,333 Rarick (American Independent); 8,240 Clark (Libertarian); 1,584 Commoner (Citizens); 783 DeBerry (Socialist Workers).

**1976**  Other vote was 10,058 Maddox (American); 7,417 Hall (Communist); 6,588 McCarthy (Independent); 3,325 MacBride (Libertarian); 2,240 Camejo (Socialist Workers). Although the data indicate a possible discrepancy in the Democratic vote in Madison county, the official state canvass figures are used here.

**1972**  Other vote was 52,099 Schmitz (American); 14,398 no Presidential candidate indicated (Socialist Workers).

**1968**  Wallace on the ballot as American.

**1964**

**1960**  Other vote was cast for an unpledged Independent elector slate. The other vote column contains only the votes cast for this unpledged Independent elector slate and it should be noted, in using the Republican-Democratic plurality figures, that the Independent electors carried a number of parishes and were second in others.

# MAINE

## POPULAR VOTE FOR PRESIDENT 1920 TO 2004

| Year | Total Vote | Republican | | Democratic | | Other Vote | Plurality | Percentage | | | |
|------|-----------|------------|-----------|------------|-----------|-----------|-----------|-----------|-----------|-----------|-----------|
| | | | | | | | | Total Vote | | Major Vote | |
| | | Vote | Candidate | Vote | Candidate | | | Rep. | Dem. | Rep. | Dem. |
| 2004 | 740,752 | 330,201 | Bush, George W. | 396,842 | Kerry, John | 13,709 | 66,641 D | 44.6% | 53.6% | 45.4% | 54.6% |
| 2000** | 651,817 | 286,616 | Bush, George W. | 319,951 | Gore, Al | 45,250 | 33,335 D | 44.0% | 49.1% | 47.3% | 52.7% |
| 1996 ** | 605,897 | 186,378 | Dole, Bob | 312,788 | Clinton, Bill | 106,731 | 126,410 D | 30.8% | 51.6% | 37.3% | 62.7% |
| 1992 ** | 679,499 | 206,504 | Bush, George | 263,420 | Clinton, Bill | 209,575 | 56,600 D | 30.4% | 38.8% | 43.9% | 56.1% |
| 1988 | 555,035 | 307,131 | Bush, George | 243,569 | Dukakis, Michael S. | 4,335 | 63,562 R | 55.3% | 43.9% | 55.8% | 44.2% |
| 1984 | 553,144 | 336,500 | Reagan, Ronald | 214,515 | Mondale, Walter F. | 2,129 | 121,985 R | 60.8% | 38.8% | 61.1% | 38.9% |
| 1980** | 523,011 | 238,522 | Reagan, Ronald | 220,974 | Carter, Jimmy | 63,515 | 17,548 R | 45.6% | 42.3% | 51.9% | 48.1% |
| 1976 | 483,216 | 236,320 | Ford, Gerald R. | 232,279 | Carter, Jimmy | 14,617 | 4,041 R | 48.9% | 48.1% | 50.4% | 49.6% |
| 1972 | 417,042 | 256,458 | Nixon, Richard M. | 160,584 | McGovern, George S. | | 95,874 R | 61.5% | 38.5% | 61.5% | 38.5% |
| 1968 | 392,936 | 169,254 | Nixon, Richard M. | 217,312 | Humphrey, Hubert H. | 6,370 | 48,058 D | 43.1% | 55.3% | 43.8% | 56.2% |
| 1964 | 380,965 | 118,701 | Goldwater, Barry M. | 262,264 | Johnson, Lyndon B. | | 143,563 D | 31.2% | 68.8% | 31.2% | 68.8% |
| 1960 | 421,767 | 240,608 | Nixon, Richard M. | 181,159 | Kennedy, John F. | | 59,449 R | 57.0% | 43.0% | 57.0% | 43.0% |
| 1956 | 351,706 | 249,238 | Eisenhower, Dwight D. | 102,468 | Stevenson, Adlai E. | | 146,770 R | 70.9% | 29.1% | 70.9% | 29.1% |
| 1952 | 351,786 | 232,353 | Eisenhower, Dwight D. | 118,806 | Stevenson, Adlai E. | 627 | 113,547 R | 66.0% | 33.8% | 66.2% | 33.8% |
| 1948 | 264,787 | 150,234 | Dewey, Thomas E. | 111,916 | Truman, Harry S. | 2,637 | 38,318 R | 56.7% | 42.3% | 57.3% | 42.7% |
| 1944 | 296,400 | 155,434 | Dewey, Thomas E. | 140,631 | Roosevelt, Franklin D. | 335 | 14,803 R | 52.4% | 47.4% | 52.5% | 47.5% |
| 1940 | 320,840 | 163,951 | Willkie, Wendell | 156,478 | Roosevelt, Franklin D. | 411 | 7,473 R | 51.1% | 48.8% | 51.2% | 48.8% |
| 1936 | 304,240 | 168,823 | Landon, Alfred M. | 126,333 | Roosevelt, Franklin D. | 9,084 | 42,490 R | 55.5% | 41.5% | 57.2% | 42.8% |
| 1932 | 298,444 | 166,631 | Hoover, Herbert C. | 128,907 | Roosevelt, Franklin D. | 2,906 | 37,724 R | 55.8% | 43.2% | 56.4% | 43.6% |
| 1928 | 262,170 | 179,923 | Hoover, Herbert C. | 81,179 | Smith, Alfred E. | 1,068 | 98,744 R | 68.6% | 31.0% | 68.9% | 31.1% |
| 1924 | 192,192 | 138,440 | Coolidge, Calvin | 41,964 | Davis, John W. | 11,788 | 96,476 R | 72.0% | 21.8% | 76.7% | 23.3% |
| 1920 | 197,840 | 136,355 | Harding, Warren G. | 58,961 | Cox, James M. | 2,524 | 77,394 R | 68.9% | 29.8% | 69.8% | 30.2% |

In 2000 the other vote column includes 37,127 votes cast for Green (Nader). In 1996 the other vote column includes 85,970 votes cast for Perot. In 1992 the other vote column includes 206,820 votes cast for Perot who came in second statewide. In 1980 the other column includes 53,327 votes for Independent (Anderson).

## ELECTORAL COLLEGE VOTE 1920 TO 2004

| Year | Total | Republican | Democratic | Other |
|------|-------|------------|------------|-------|
| 2004 | 4 | | 4 | |
| 2000 | 4 | | 4 | |
| 1996 | 4 | | 4 | |
| 1992 | 4 | | 4 | |
| 1988 | 4 | 4 | | |
| 1984 | 4 | 4 | | |
| 1980 | 4 | 4 | | |
| 1976 | 4 | 4 | | |
| 1972 | 4 | 4 | | |
| 1968 | 4 | | 4 | |
| 1964 | 4 | | 4 | |
| 1960 | 5 | 5 | | |
| 1956 | 5 | 5 | | |
| 1952 | 5 | 5 | | |
| 1948 | 5 | 5 | | |
| 1944 | 5 | 5 | | |
| 1940 | 5 | 5 | | |
| 1936 | 5 | 5 | | |
| 1932 | 5 | 5 | | |
| 1928 | 6 | 6 | | |
| 1924 | 6 | 6 | | |
| 1920 | 6 | 6 | | |

436

# MAINE

AROOSTOOK

PISCATAQUIS

SOMERSET

FRANKLIN

PENOBSCOT

WASHINGTON

OXFORD

HANCOCK

WALDO

ANDROSCOGGIN

KENNEBEC

SAGADAHOC

LINCOLN

KNOX

CUMBERLAND

YORK

# MAINE

## PRESIDENT 2004

| 2000 Census Population | County | Total Vote | Republican | Democratic | Other | Rep.-Dem. Plurality | Percentage | | | |
|---|---|---|---|---|---|---|---|---|---|---|
| | | | | | | | Total Vote | | Major Vote | |
| | | | | | | | Rep. | Dem. | Rep. | Dem. |
| 103,793 | ANDROSCOGGIN | 56,067 | 24,519 | 30,503 | 1,045 | 5,984 D | 43.7% | 54.4% | 44.6% | 55.4% |
| 73,938 | AROOSTOOK | 37,733 | 17,564 | 19,569 | 600 | 2,005 D | 46.5% | 51.9% | 47.3% | 52.7% |
| 265,612 | CUMBERLAND | 162,962 | 65,384 | 94,846 | 2,732 | 29,462 D | 40.1% | 58.2% | 40.8% | 59.2% |
| 29,467 | FRANKLIN | 17,257 | 7,378 | 9,465 | 414 | 2,087 D | 42.8% | 54.8% | 43.8% | 56.2% |
| 51,791 | HANCOCK | 33,122 | 14,405 | 18,048 | 669 | 3,643 D | 43.5% | 54.5% | 44.4% | 55.6% |
| 117,114 | KENNEBEC | 66,772 | 29,761 | 35,616 | 1,395 | 5,855 D | 44.6% | 53.3% | 45.5% | 54.5% |
| 39,618 | KNOX | 23,247 | 10,103 | 12,690 | 454 | 2,587 D | 43.5% | 54.6% | 44.3% | 55.7% |
| 33,616 | LINCOLN | 22,142 | 10,370 | 11,351 | 421 | 981 D | 46.8% | 51.3% | 47.7% | 52.3% |
| 54,755 | OXFORD | 31,546 | 14,196 | 16,618 | 732 | 2,422 D | 45.0% | 52.7% | 46.1% | 53.9% |
| 144,919 | PENOBSCOT | 82,112 | 40,318 | 40,417 | 1,377 | 99 D | 49.1% | 49.2% | 49.9% | 50.1% |
| 17,235 | PISCATAQUIS | 9,940 | 5,299 | 4,409 | 232 | 890 R | 53.3% | 44.4% | 54.6% | 45.4% |
| 35,214 | SAGADAHOC | 21,079 | 9,497 | 11,107 | 475 | 1,610 D | 45.1% | 52.7% | 46.1% | 53.9% |
| 50,888 | SOMERSET | 27,108 | 12,953 | 13,555 | 600 | 602 D | 47.8% | 50.0% | 48.9% | 51.1% |
| 36,280 | WALDO | 22,322 | 10,309 | 11,555 | 458 | 1,246 D | 46.2% | 51.8% | 47.2% | 52.8% |
| 33,941 | WASHINGTON | 17,310 | 8,619 | 8,391 | 300 | 228 R | 49.8% | 48.5% | 50.7% | 49.3% |
| 186,742 | YORK | 110,033 | 49,526 | 58,702 | 1,805 | 9,176 D | 45.0% | 53.3% | 45.8% | 54.2% |
| 1,274,923 | TOTAL | 740,752 | 330,201 | 396,842 | 13,709 | 66,641 D | 44.6% | 53.6% | 45.4% | 54.6% |

# MAINE

## PRESIDENT 2000

| 2000 Census Population | County | Total Vote | Republican | Democratic | Green (Nader) | Other | Rep.-Dem. Plurality | Percentage of Total Vote | | |
|---|---|---|---|---|---|---|---|---|---|---|
| | | | | | | | | Rep. | Dem. | Green |
| 103,793 | ANDROSCOGGIN | 49,245 | 19,948 | 26,251 | 2,388 | 658 | 6,303 D | 40.5% | 53.3% | 4.8% |
| 73,938 | AROOSTOOK | 35,143 | 16,555 | 17,196 | 1,055 | 337 | 641 D | 47.1% | 48.9% | 3.0% |
| 265,612 | CUMBERLAND | 142,620 | 58,543 | 74,203 | 8,576 | 1,298 | 15,660 D | 41.0% | 52.0% | 6.0% |
| 29,467 | FRANKLIN | 15,448 | 6,459 | 7,593 | 1,115 | 281 | 1,134 D | 41.8% | 49.2% | 7.2% |
| 51,791 | HANCOCK | 28,574 | 12,732 | 12,983 | 2,513 | 346 | 251 D | 44.6% | 45.4% | 8.8% |
| 117,114 | KENNEBEC | 58,907 | 23,967 | 31,198 | 2,955 | 787 | 7,231 D | 40.7% | 53.0% | 5.0% |
| 39,618 | KNOX | 20,501 | 8,968 | 9,453 | 1,810 | 270 | 485 D | 43.7% | 46.1% | 8.8% |
| 33,616 | LINCOLN | 19,671 | 9,457 | 8,634 | 1,323 | 257 | 823 R | 48.1% | 43.9% | 6.7% |
| 54,755 | OXFORD | 27,493 | 11,835 | 13,649 | 1,509 | 500 | 1,814 D | 43.0% | 49.6% | 5.5% |
| 144,919 | PENOBSCOT | 73,206 | 35,620 | 32,868 | 3,772 | 946 | 2,752 R | 48.7% | 44.9% | 5.2% |
| 17,235 | PISCATAQUIS | 9,256 | 4,845 | 3,745 | 471 | 195 | 1,100 R | 52.3% | 40.5% | 5.1% |
| 35,214 | SAGADAHOC | 18,406 | 8,052 | 8,844 | 1,278 | 232 | 792 D | 43.7% | 48.0% | 6.9% |
| 50,888 | SOMERSET | 23,951 | 10,684 | 11,538 | 1,239 | 490 | 854 D | 44.6% | 48.2% | 5.2% |
| 36,280 | WALDO | 19,138 | 8,689 | 8,477 | 1,690 | 282 | 212 R | 45.4% | 44.3% | 8.8% |
| 33,941 | WASHINGTON | 15,708 | 7,958 | 6,701 | 802 | 247 | 1,257 R | 50.7% | 42.7% | 5.1% |
| 186,742 | YORK | 94,550 | 42,304 | 46,618 | 4,631 | 997 | 4,314 D | 44.7% | 49.3% | 4.9% |
| 1,274,923 | TOTAL | 651,817 | 286,616 | 319,951 | 37,127 | 8,123 | 33,335 D | 44.0% | 49.1% | 5.7% |

# MAINE

## PRESIDENT 1996

| 1995 Census Pop. Est. | County | Total Vote | Republican | Democratic | Reform (Perot) | Other | Rep.-Dem. Plurality | Percentage of Total Vote | | |
|---|---|---|---|---|---|---|---|---|---|---|
| | | | | | | | | Rep. | Dem. | Reform |
| 103,751 | ANDROSCOGGIN | 46,731 | 12,053 | 26,428 | 7,079 | 1,171 | 14,375 D | 25.8% | 56.6% | 15.1% |
| 78,633 | AROOSTOOK | 34,792 | 10,400 | 18,022 | 5,747 | 623 | 7,622 D | 29.9% | 51.8% | 16.5% |
| 248,526 | CUMBERLAND | 129,610 | 42,620 | 69,496 | 12,696 | 4,798 | 26,876 D | 32.9% | 53.6% | 9.8% |
| 29,511 | FRANKLIN | 14,596 | 3,757 | 7,759 | 2,567 | 513 | 4,002 D | 25.7% | 53.2% | 17.6% |
| 49,272 | HANCOCK | 26,448 | 8,345 | 12,256 | 4,094 | 1,753 | 3,911 D | 31.6% | 46.3% | 15.5% |
| 117,000 | KENNEBEC | 55,654 | 15,403 | 30,257 | 8,281 | 1,713 | 14,854 D | 27.7% | 54.4% | 14.9% |
| 37,372 | KNOX | 18,883 | 6,192 | 8,839 | 2,780 | 1,072 | 2,647 D | 32.8% | 46.8% | 14.7% |
| 31,334 | LINCOLN | 18,173 | 6,372 | 8,130 | 2,923 | 748 | 1,758 D | 35.1% | 44.7% | 16.1% |
| 53,440 | OXFORD | 26,091 | 7,238 | 13,580 | 4,589 | 684 | 6,342 D | 27.7% | 52.0% | 17.6% |
| 145,905 | PENOBSCOT | 70,517 | 22,885 | 35,961 | 9,673 | 1,998 | 13,076 D | 32.5% | 51.0% | 13.7% |
| 18,486 | PISCATAQUIS | 8,920 | 2,815 | 4,343 | 1,524 | 238 | 1,528 D | 31.6% | 48.7% | 17.1% |
| 33,959 | SAGADAHOC | 16,924 | 5,346 | 8,417 | 2,451 | 710 | 3,071 D | 31.6% | 49.7% | 14.5% |
| 51,346 | SOMERSET | 23,111 | 6,247 | 11,773 | 4,449 | 642 | 5,526 D | 27.0% | 50.9% | 19.3% |
| 35,707 | WALDO | 17,279 | 5,318 | 8,012 | 2,816 | 1,133 | 2,694 D | 30.8% | 46.4% | 16.3% |
| 36,156 | WASHINGTON | 15,189 | 4,793 | 7,198 | 2,721 | 477 | 2,405 D | 31.6% | 47.4% | 17.9% |
| 170,984 | YORK | 82,979 | 26,594 | 42,317 | 11,580 | 2,488 | 15,723 D | 32.0% | 51.0% | 14.0% |
| 1,241,382 | TOTAL | 605,897 | 186,378 | 312,788 | 85,970 | 20,761 | 126,410 D | 30.8% | 51.6% | 14.2% |

# MAINE

## PRESIDENT 1992

| 1990 Census Population | County | Total Vote | Republican | Democratic | Perot | Other | Plurality | Percentage Total Vote | | |
|---|---|---|---|---|---|---|---|---|---|---|
| | | | | | | | | Rep. | Dem. | Perot |
| 105,259 | ANDROSCOGGIN | 55,144 | 14,174 | 22,247 | 18,518 | 205 | 3,729 D | 25.7% | 40.3% | 33.6% |
| 86,936 | AROOSTOOK | 38,585 | 12,409 | 15,682 | 10,376 | 118 | 3,273 D | 32.2% | 40.6% | 26.9% |
| 243,135 | CUMBERLAND | 141,522 | 45,752 | 60,781 | 34,443 | 546 | 15,029 D | 32.3% | 42.9% | 24.3% |
| 29,008 | FRANKLIN | 16,523 | 4,608 | 6,739 | 5,115 | 61 | 1,624 D | 27.9% | 40.8% | 31.0% |
| 46,948 | HANCOCK | 28,805 | 8,657 | 10,126 | 9,865 | 157 | 261 D | 30.1% | 35.2% | 34.2% |
| 115,904 | KENNEBEC | 63,921 | 17,135 | 25,125 | 21,436 | 225 | 3,689 D | 26.8% | 39.3% | 33.5% |
| 36,310 | KNOX | 20,338 | 6,310 | 7,631 | 6,303 | 94 | 1,321 D | 31.0% | 37.5% | 31.0% |
| 30,357 | LINCOLN | 19,036 | 6,405 | 6,714 | 5,808 | 109 | 309 D | 33.6% | 35.3% | 30.5% |
| 52,602 | OXFORD | 29,356 | 8,194 | 11,202 | 9,815 | 145 | 1,387 D | 27.9% | 38.2% | 33.4% |
| 146,601 | PENOBSCOT | 80,444 | 24,218 | 29,485 | 26,437 | 304 | 3,048 D | 30.1% | 36.7% | 32.9% |
| 18,653 | PISCATAQUIS | 10,031 | 2,970 | 3,323 | 3,688 | 50 | 365 P | 29.6% | 33.1% | 36.8% |
| 33,535 | SAGADAHOC | 18,513 | 5,917 | 6,828 | 5,705 | 63 | 911 D | 32.0% | 36.9% | 30.8% |
| 49,767 | SOMERSET | 26,424 | 6,780 | 9,274 | 10,293 | 77 | 1,019 P | 25.7% | 35.1% | 39.0% |
| 33,018 | WALDO | 18,529 | 5,241 | 6,472 | 6,702 | 114 | 230 P | 28.3% | 34.9% | 36.2% |
| 35,308 | WASHINGTON | 17,765 | 5,493 | 6,284 | 5,894 | 94 | 390 D | 30.9% | 35.4% | 33.2% |
| 164,587 | YORK | 94,563 | 32,241 | 35,507 | 26,422 | 393 | 3,266 D | 34.1% | 37.5% | 27.9% |
| 1,227,928 | TOTAL | 679,499 | 206,504 | 263,420 | 206,820 | 2,755 | 56,600 D | 30.4% | 38.8% | 30.4% |

# MAINE

## PRESIDENT 1988

| 1980 Census Population | County | Total Vote | Republican | Democratic | Other | Rep.-Dem. Plurality | Percentage | | | |
|---|---|---|---|---|---|---|---|---|---|---|
| | | | | | | | Total Vote | | Major Vote | |
| | | | | | | | Rep. | Dem. | Rep. | Dem. |
| 99,657 | ANDROSCOGGIN | 44,585 | 23,061 | 21,165 | 359 | 1,896 R | 51.7% | 47.5% | 52.1% | 47.9% |
| 91,331 | AROOSTOOK | 32,246 | 17,213 | 14,850 | 183 | 2,363 R | 53.4% | 46.1% | 53.7% | 46.3% |
| 215,789 | CUMBERLAND | 119,075 | 63,028 | 55,220 | 827 | 7,808 R | 52.9% | 46.4% | 53.3% | 46.7% |
| 27,098 | FRANKLIN | 13,256 | 7,180 | 5,960 | 116 | 1,220 R | 54.2% | 45.0% | 54.6% | 45.4% |
| 41,781 | HANCOCK | 23,107 | 12,957 | 9,929 | 221 | 3,028 R | 56.1% | 43.0% | 56.6% | 43.4% |
| 109,889 | KENNEBEC | 51,745 | 27,734 | 23,578 | 433 | 4,156 R | 53.6% | 45.6% | 54.0% | 46.0% |
| 32,941 | KNOX | 17,650 | 10,156 | 7,343 | 151 | 2,813 R | 57.5% | 41.6% | 58.0% | 42.0% |
| 25,691 | LINCOLN | 15,920 | 9,837 | 5,939 | 144 | 3,898 R | 61.8% | 37.3% | 62.4% | 37.6% |
| 48,968 | OXFORD | 24,266 | 13,568 | 10,523 | 175 | 3,045 R | 55.9% | 43.4% | 56.3% | 43.7% |
| 137,015 | PENOBSCOT | 63,754 | 34,912 | 28,429 | 413 | 6,483 R | 54.8% | 44.6% | 55.1% | 44.9% |
| 17,634 | PISCATAQUIS | 8,217 | 4,788 | 3,323 | 106 | 1,465 R | 58.3% | 40.4% | 59.0% | 41.0% |
| 28,795 | SAGADAHOC | 15,158 | 8,825 | 6,212 | 121 | 2,613 R | 58.2% | 41.0% | 58.7% | 41.3% |
| 45,028 | SOMERSET | 20,201 | 11,430 | 8,603 | 168 | 2,827 R | 56.6% | 42.6% | 57.1% | 42.9% |
| 28,414 | WALDO | 14,778 | 8,236 | 6,402 | 140 | 1,834 R | 55.7% | 43.3% | 56.3% | 43.7% |
| 34,963 | WASHINGTON | 13,828 | 7,872 | 5,831 | 125 | 2,041 R | 56.9% | 42.2% | 57.4% | 42.6% |
| 139,666 | YORK | 77,249 | 46,334 | 30,262 | 653 | 16,072 R | 60.0% | 39.2% | 60.5% | 39.5% |
| 1,124,660 | TOTAL | 555,035 | 307,131 | 243,569 | 4,335 | 63,562 R | 55.3% | 43.9% | 55.8% | 44.2% |

# MAINE

## PRESIDENT 1984

| 1980 Census Population | County | Total Vote | Republican | Democratic | Other | Rep.-Dem. Plurality | Percentage | | | |
|---|---|---|---|---|---|---|---|---|---|---|
| | | | | | | | Total Vote | | Major Vote | |
| | | | | | | | Rep. | Dem. | Rep. | Dem. |
| 99,657 | ANDROSCOGGIN | 47,000 | 26,904 | 19,885 | 211 | 7,019 R | 57.2% | 42.3% | 57.5% | 42.5% |
| 91,331 | AROOSTOOK | 34,338 | 21,837 | 12,348 | 153 | 9,489 R | 63.6% | 36.0% | 63.9% | 36.1% |
| 215,789 | CUMBERLAND | 116,026 | 65,842 | 49,894 | 290 | 15,948 R | 56.7% | 43.0% | 56.9% | 43.1% |
| 27,098 | FRANKLIN | 13,349 | 8,330 | 4,954 | 65 | 3,376 R | 62.4% | 37.1% | 62.7% | 37.3% |
| 41,781 | HANCOCK | 22,511 | 14,660 | 7,764 | 87 | 6,896 R | 65.1% | 34.5% | 65.4% | 34.6% |
| 109,889 | KENNEBEC | 53,191 | 31,753 | 21,183 | 255 | 10,570 R | 59.7% | 39.8% | 60.0% | 40.0% |
| 32,941 | KNOX | 17,401 | 11,311 | 6,024 | 66 | 5,287 R | 65.0% | 34.6% | 65.2% | 34.8% |
| 25,691 | LINCOLN | 15,236 | 10,312 | 4,869 | 55 | 5,443 R | 67.7% | 32.0% | 67.9% | 32.1% |
| 48,968 | OXFORD | 23,948 | 15,408 | 8,430 | 110 | 6,978 R | 64.3% | 35.2% | 64.6% | 35.4% |
| 137,015 | PENOBSCOT | 65,054 | 40,403 | 24,445 | 206 | 15,958 R | 62.1% | 37.6% | 62.3% | 37.7% |
| 17,634 | PISCATAQUIS | 8,482 | 5,427 | 3,016 | 39 | 2,411 R | 64.0% | 35.6% | 64.3% | 35.7% |
| 28,795 | SAGADAHOC | 14,520 | 9,222 | 5,208 | 90 | 4,014 R | 63.5% | 35.9% | 63.9% | 36.1% |
| 45,028 | SOMERSET | 20,771 | 13,010 | 7,657 | 104 | 5,353 R | 62.6% | 36.9% | 63.0% | 37.0% |
| 28,414 | WALDO | 14,166 | 8,814 | 5,289 | 63 | 3,525 R | 62.2% | 37.3% | 62.5% | 37.5% |
| 34,963 | WASHINGTON | 15,081 | 9,713 | 5,308 | 60 | 4,405 R | 64.4% | 35.2% | 64.7% | 35.3% |
| 139,666 | YORK | 72,070 | 43,554 | 28,241 | 275 | 15,313 R | 60.4% | 39.2% | 60.7% | 39.3% |
| 1,124,660 | TOTAL | 553,144 | 336,500 | 214,515 | 2,129 | 121,985 R | 60.8% | 38.8% | 61.1% | 38.9% |

# MAINE

## PRESIDENT 1980

| 1980 Census Population | County | Total Vote | Republican | Democratic | Other | Rep.-Dem. Plurality | Percentage | | | |
|---|---|---|---|---|---|---|---|---|---|---|
| | | | | | | | Total Vote | | Major Vote | |
| | | | | | | | Rep. | Dem. | Rep. | Dem. |
| 99,657 | ANDROSCOGGIN | 46,080 | 18,399 | 22,715 | 4,966 | 4,316 D | 39.9% | 49.3% | 44.8% | 55.2% |
| 91,331 | AROOSTOOK | 33,846 | 16,343 | 14,492 | 3,011 | 1,851 R | 48.3% | 42.8% | 53.0% | 47.0% |
| 215,789 | CUMBERLAND | 107,461 | 45,820 | 47,337 | 14,304 | 1,517 D | 42.6% | 44.1% | 49.2% | 50.8% |
| 27,098 | FRANKLIN | 12,128 | 5,680 | 4,979 | 1,469 | 701 R | 46.8% | 41.1% | 53.3% | 46.7% |
| 41,781 | HANCOCK | 21,334 | 11,435 | 7,027 | 2,872 | 4,408 R | 53.6% | 32.9% | 61.9% | 38.1% |
| 109,889 | KENNEBEC | 49,077 | 21,517 | 20,943 | 6,617 | 574 R | 43.8% | 42.7% | 50.7% | 49.3% |
| 32,941 | KNOX | 15,581 | 7,631 | 5,732 | 2,218 | 1,899 R | 49.0% | 36.8% | 57.1% | 42.9% |
| 25,691 | LINCOLN | 14,259 | 7,434 | 4,776 | 2,049 | 2,658 R | 52.1% | 33.5% | 60.9% | 39.1% |
| 48,968 | OXFORD | 23,474 | 11,041 | 9,914 | 2,519 | 1,127 R | 47.0% | 42.2% | 52.7% | 47.3% |
| 137,015 | PENOBSCOT | 62,793 | 28,869 | 26,519 | 7,405 | 2,350 R | 46.0% | 42.2% | 52.1% | 47.9% |
| 17,634 | PISCATAQUIS | 8,555 | 4,015 | 3,550 | 990 | 465 R | 46.9% | 41.5% | 53.1% | 46.9% |
| 28,795 | SAGADAHOC | 13,145 | 5,946 | 5,663 | 1,536 | 283 R | 45.2% | 43.1% | 51.2% | 48.8% |
| 45,028 | SOMERSET | 19,513 | 9,286 | 8,115 | 2,112 | 1,171 R | 47.6% | 41.6% | 53.4% | 46.6% |
| 28,414 | WALDO | 13,140 | 6,514 | 4,883 | 1,743 | 1,631 R | 49.6% | 37.2% | 57.2% | 42.8% |
| 34,963 | WASHINGTON | 14,788 | 7,180 | 6,050 | 1,558 | 1,130 R | 48.6% | 40.9% | 54.3% | 45.7% |
| 139,666 | YORK | 67,837 | 31,412 | 28,279 | 8,146 | 3,133 R | 46.3% | 41.7% | 52.6% | 47.4% |
| 1,124,660 | TOTAL | 523,011 | 238,522 | 220,974 | 63,515 | 17,548 R | 45.6% | 42.3% | 51.9% | 48.1% |

# MAINE

## PRESIDENT 1976

| 1970 Census Population | County | Total Vote | Republican | Democratic | Other | Rep.-Dem. Plurality | Percentage | | | |
|---|---|---|---|---|---|---|---|---|---|---|
| | | | | | | | Total Vote | | Major Vote | |
| | | | | | | | Rep. | Dem. | Rep. | Dem. |
| 91,279 | ANDROSCOGGIN | 43,665 | 16,330 | 26,484 | 851 | 10,154 D | 37.4% | 60.7% | 38.1% | 61.9% |
| 94,078 | AROOSTOOK | 32,051 | 15,550 | 15,484 | 1,017 | 66 R | 48.5% | 48.3% | 50.1% | 49.9% |
| 192,528 | CUMBERLAND | 98,626 | 48,959 | 47,007 | 2,660 | 1,952 R | 49.6% | 47.7% | 51.0% | 49.0% |
| 22,444 | FRANKLIN | 11,384 | 5,799 | 5,140 | 445 | 659 R | 50.9% | 45.2% | 53.0% | 47.0% |
| 34,590 | HANCOCK | 19,647 | 12,064 | 6,725 | 858 | 5,339 R | 61.4% | 34.2% | 64.2% | 35.8% |
| 95,247 | KENNEBEC | 47,412 | 22,534 | 23,473 | 1,405 | 939 D | 47.5% | 49.5% | 49.0% | 51.0% |
| 29,013 | KNOX | 14,786 | 8,315 | 5,922 | 549 | 2,393 R | 56.2% | 40.1% | 58.4% | 41.6% |
| 20,537 | LINCOLN | 12,797 | 7,554 | 4,818 | 425 | 2,736 R | 59.0% | 37.6% | 61.1% | 38.9% |
| 43,457 | OXFORD | 21,516 | 10,551 | 10,340 | 625 | 211 R | 49.0% | 48.1% | 50.5% | 49.5% |
| 125,393 | PENOBSCOT | 55,613 | 29,016 | 24,672 | 1,925 | 4,344 R | 52.2% | 44.4% | 54.0% | 46.0% |
| 16,285 | PISCATAQUIS | 8,090 | 4,084 | 3,727 | 279 | 357 R | 50.5% | 46.1% | 52.3% | 47.7% |
| 23,452 | SAGADAHOC | 11,876 | 5,988 | 5,529 | 359 | 459 R | 50.4% | 46.6% | 52.0% | 48.0% |
| 40,597 | SOMERSET | 18,966 | 8,868 | 9,465 | 633 | 597 D | 46.8% | 49.9% | 48.4% | 51.6% |
| 23,328 | WALDO | 11,633 | 6,289 | 4,853 | 491 | 1,436 R | 54.1% | 41.7% | 56.4% | 43.6% |
| 29,859 | WASHINGTON | 14,235 | 7,039 | 6,644 | 552 | 395 R | 49.4% | 46.7% | 51.4% | 48.6% |
| 111,576 | YORK | 60,919 | 27,380 | 31,996 | 1,543 | 4,616 D | 44.9% | 52.5% | 46.1% | 53.9% |
| 993,663 | TOTAL | 483,216 | 236,320 | 232,279 | 14,617 | 4,041 R | 48.9% | 48.1% | 50.4% | 49.6% |

# MAINE

## PRESIDENT 1972

| 1970 Census Population | County | Total Vote | Republican | Democratic | Other | Rep.-Dem. Plurality | Percentage | | | |
| | | | | | | | Total Vote | | Major Vote | |
| | | | | | | | Rep. | Dem. | Rep. | Dem. |
|---|---|---|---|---|---|---|---|---|---|---|
| 91,279 | ANDROSCOGGIN | 38,915 | 19,406 | 19,509 | | 103 D | 49.9% | 50.1% | 49.9% | 50.1% |
| 94,078 | AROOSTOOK | 30,525 | 19,051 | 11,474 | | 7,577 R | 62.4% | 37.6% | 62.4% | 37.6% |
| 192,528 | CUMBERLAND | 84,594 | 51,268 | 33,326 | | 17,942 R | 60.6% | 39.4% | 60.6% | 39.4% |
| 22,444 | FRANKLIN | 8,946 | 5,958 | 2,988 | | 2,970 R | 66.6% | 33.4% | 66.6% | 33.4% |
| 34,590 | HANCOCK | 16,080 | 11,889 | 4,191 | | 7,698 R | 73.9% | 26.1% | 73.9% | 26.1% |
| 95,247 | KENNEBEC | 40,996 | 24,617 | 16,379 | | 8,238 R | 60.0% | 40.0% | 60.0% | 40.0% |
| 29,013 | KNOX | 12,079 | 8,478 | 3,601 | | 4,877 R | 70.2% | 29.8% | 70.2% | 29.8% |
| 20,537 | LINCOLN | 10,483 | 7,580 | 2,903 | | 4,677 R | 72.3% | 27.7% | 72.3% | 27.7% |
| 43,457 | OXFORD | 18,775 | 12,114 | 6,661 | | 5,453 R | 64.5% | 35.5% | 64.5% | 35.5% |
| 125,393 | PENOBSCOT | 48,738 | 30,186 | 18,552 | | 11,634 R | 61.9% | 38.1% | 61.9% | 38.1% |
| 16,285 | PISCATAQUIS | 7,135 | 4,617 | 2,518 | | 2,099 R | 64.7% | 35.3% | 64.7% | 35.3% |
| 23,452 | SAGADAHOC | 9,877 | 6,463 | 3,414 | | 3,049 R | 65.4% | 34.6% | 65.4% | 34.6% |
| 40,597 | SOMERSET | 16,000 | 10,079 | 5,921 | | 4,158 R | 63.0% | 37.0% | 63.0% | 37.0% |
| 23,328 | WALDO | 9,421 | 6,480 | 2,941 | | 3,539 R | 68.8% | 31.2% | 68.8% | 31.2% |
| 29,859 | WASHINGTON | 11,562 | 7,820 | 3,742 | | 4,078 R | 67.6% | 32.4% | 67.6% | 32.4% |
| 111,576 | YORK | 52,916 | 30,452 | 22,464 | | 7,988 R | 57.5% | 42.5% | 57.5% | 42.5% |
| 993,663 | TOTAL | 417,042 | 256,458 | 160,584 | | 95,874 R | 61.5% | 38.5% | 61.5% | 38.5% |

# MAINE

## PRESIDENT 1968

| 1960 Census Population | County | Total Vote | Republican | Democratic | AIP | Other | Plurality | Percentage Total Vote | | |
| | | | | | | | | Rep. | Dem. | AIP |
|---|---|---|---|---|---|---|---|---|---|---|
| 86,312 | ANDROSCOGGIN | 37,752 | 10,390 | 26,820 | 542 | | 16,430 D | 27.5% | 71.0% | 1.4% |
| 106,064 | AROOSTOOK | 29,236 | 13,919 | 15,044 | 273 | | 1,125 D | 47.6% | 51.5% | 0.9% |
| 182,751 | CUMBERLAND | 78,048 | 32,275 | 44,697 | 1,076 | | 12,422 D | 41.4% | 57.3% | 1.4% |
| 20,069 | FRANKLIN | 8,596 | 4,127 | 4,307 | 162 | | 180 D | 48.0% | 50.1% | 1.9% |
| 32,293 | HANCOCK | 14,185 | 8,929 | 4,979 | 277 | | 3,950 R | 62.9% | 35.1% | 2.0% |
| 89,150 | KENNEBEC | 38,292 | 16,009 | 21,752 | 531 | | 5,743 D | 41.8% | 56.8% | 1.4% |
| 28,575 | KNOX | 11,918 | 6,585 | 5,119 | 214 | | 1,466 R | 55.3% | 43.0% | 1.8% |
| 18,497 | LINCOLN | 9,261 | 5,659 | 3,380 | 222 | | 2,279 R | 61.1% | 36.5% | 2.4% |
| 44,345 | OXFORD | 19,275 | 8,030 | 10,870 | 375 | | 2,840 D | 41.7% | 56.4% | 1.9% |
| 126,346 | PENOBSCOT | 44,999 | 20,011 | 24,327 | 661 | | 4,316 D | 44.5% | 54.1% | 1.5% |
| 17,379 | PISCATAQUIS | 6,918 | 3,199 | 3,561 | 158 | | 362 D | 46.2% | 51.5% | 2.3% |
| 22,793 | SAGADAHOC | 9,888 | 4,126 | 5,553 | 209 | | 1,427 D | 41.7% | 56.2% | 2.1% |
| 39,749 | SOMERSET | 15,356 | 6,720 | 8,312 | 324 | | 1,592 D | 43.8% | 54.1% | 2.1% |
| 22,632 | WALDO | 8,580 | 4,821 | 3,525 | 234 | | 1,296 R | 56.2% | 41.1% | 2.7% |
| 32,908 | WASHINGTON | 11,980 | 5,523 | 6,249 | 208 | | 726 D | 46.1% | 52.2% | 1.7% |
| 99,402 | YORK | 48,652 | 18,931 | 28,817 | 904 | | 9,886 D | 38.9% | 59.2% | 1.9% |
| 969,265 | TOTAL | 392,936 | 169,254 | 217,312 | 6,370 | | 48,058 D | 43.1% | 55.3% | 1.6% |

# MAINE

## PRESIDENT 1964

| 1960 Census Population | County | Total Vote | Republican | Democratic | Other | Rep.-Dem. Plurality | Percentage | | | |
|---|---|---|---|---|---|---|---|---|---|---|
| | | | | | | | Total Vote | | Major Vote | |
| | | | | | | | Rep. | Dem. | Rep. | Dem. |
| 86,312 | ANDROSCOGGIN | 37,521 | 7,441 | 30,080 | | 22,639 D | 19.8% | 80.2% | 19.8% | 80.2% |
| 106,064 | AROOSTOOK | 27,546 | 9,994 | 17,552 | | 7,558 D | 36.3% | 63.7% | 36.3% | 63.7% |
| 182,751 | CUMBERLAND | 73,209 | 22,365 | 50,844 | | 28,479 D | 30.5% | 69.5% | 30.5% | 69.5% |
| 20,069 | FRANKLIN | 8,671 | 2,887 | 5,784 | | 2,897 D | 33.3% | 66.7% | 33.3% | 66.7% |
| 32,293 | HANCOCK | 13,719 | 6,304 | 7,415 | | 1,111 D | 46.0% | 54.0% | 46.0% | 54.0% |
| 89,150 | KENNEBEC | 36,120 | 11,307 | 24,813 | | 13,506 D | 31.3% | 68.7% | 31.3% | 68.7% |
| 28,575 | KNOX | 11,426 | 4,404 | 7,022 | | 2,618 D | 38.5% | 61.5% | 38.5% | 61.5% |
| 18,497 | LINCOLN | 9,083 | 3,984 | 5,099 | | 1,115 D | 43.9% | 56.1% | 43.9% | 56.1% |
| 44,345 | OXFORD | 18,956 | 5,340 | 13,616 | | 8,276 D | 28.2% | 71.8% | 28.2% | 71.8% |
| 126,346 | PENOBSCOT | 43,215 | 14,449 | 28,766 | | 14,317 D | 33.4% | 66.6% | 33.4% | 66.6% |
| 17,379 | PISCATAQUIS | 7,254 | 2,473 | 4,781 | | 2,308 D | 34.1% | 65.9% | 34.1% | 65.9% |
| 22,793 | SAGADAHOC | 9,739 | 2,733 | 7,006 | | 4,273 D | 28.1% | 71.9% | 28.1% | 71.9% |
| 39,749 | SOMERSET | 15,235 | 4,541 | 10,694 | | 6,153 D | 29.8% | 70.2% | 29.8% | 70.2% |
| 22,632 | WALDO | 8,721 | 3,324 | 5,397 | | 2,073 D | 38.1% | 61.9% | 38.1% | 61.9% |
| 32,908 | WASHINGTON | 13,128 | 3,816 | 9,312 | | 5,496 D | 29.1% | 70.9% | 29.1% | 70.9% |
| 99,402 | YORK | 47,422 | 13,339 | 34,083 | | 20,744 D | 28.1% | 71.9% | 28.1% | 71.9% |
| 969,265 | TOTAL | 380,965 | 118,701 | 262,264 | | 143,563 D | 31.2% | 68.8% | 31.2% | 68.8% |

# MAINE

## PRESIDENT 1960

| 1960 Census Population | County | Total Vote | Republican | Democratic | Other | Rep.-Dem. Plurality | Percentage | | | |
|---|---|---|---|---|---|---|---|---|---|---|
| | | | | | | | Total Vote | | Major Vote | |
| | | | | | | | Rep. | Dem. | Rep. | Dem. |
| 86,312 | ANDROSCOGGIN | 40,751 | 14,654 | 26,097 | | 11,443 D | 36.0% | 64.0% | 36.0% | 64.0% |
| 106,064 | AROOSTOOK | 33,497 | 18,698 | 14,799 | | 3,899 R | 55.8% | 44.2% | 55.8% | 44.2% |
| 182,751 | CUMBERLAND | 80,824 | 47,271 | 33,553 | | 13,718 R | 58.5% | 41.5% | 58.5% | 41.5% |
| 20,069 | FRANKLIN | 9,440 | 6,136 | 3,304 | | 2,832 R | 65.0% | 35.0% | 65.0% | 35.0% |
| 32,293 | HANCOCK | 15,482 | 12,119 | 3,363 | | 8,756 R | 78.3% | 21.7% | 78.3% | 21.7% |
| 89,150 | KENNEBEC | 39,951 | 21,699 | 18,252 | | 3,447 R | 54.3% | 45.7% | 54.3% | 45.7% |
| 28,575 | KNOX | 12,899 | 9,083 | 3,816 | | 5,267 R | 70.4% | 29.6% | 70.4% | 29.6% |
| 18,497 | LINCOLN | 9,899 | 7,562 | 2,337 | | 5,225 R | 76.4% | 23.6% | 76.4% | 23.6% |
| 44,345 | OXFORD | 20,666 | 11,715 | 8,951 | | 2,764 R | 56.7% | 43.3% | 56.7% | 43.3% |
| 126,346 | PENOBSCOT | 47,634 | 28,459 | 19,175 | | 9,284 R | 59.7% | 40.3% | 59.7% | 40.3% |
| 17,379 | PISCATAQUIS | 7,818 | 4,959 | 2,859 | | 2,100 R | 63.4% | 36.6% | 63.4% | 36.6% |
| 22,793 | SAGADAHOC | 10,351 | 6,386 | 3,965 | | 2,421 R | 61.7% | 38.3% | 61.7% | 38.3% |
| 39,749 | SOMERSET | 17,098 | 10,142 | 6,956 | | 3,186 R | 59.3% | 40.7% | 59.3% | 40.7% |
| 22,632 | WALDO | 9,689 | 6,844 | 2,845 | | 3,999 R | 70.6% | 29.4% | 70.6% | 29.4% |
| 32,908 | WASHINGTON | 13,834 | 9,118 | 4,716 | | 4,402 R | 65.9% | 34.1% | 65.9% | 34.1% |
| 99,402 | YORK | 51,934 | 25,763 | 26,171 | | 408 D | 49.6% | 50.4% | 49.6% | 50.4% |
| 969,265 | TOTAL | 421,767 | 240,608 | 181,159 | | 59,449 R | 57.0% | 43.0% | 57.0% | 43.0% |

# MAINE

## ELECTION NOTES

**2004**  Other vote was 8,069 The Better Life (Ralph Nader); 2,936 Green Independent (David Cobb); 1,965 Libertarian (Michael Badnarik); 735 Constitution (Michael Peroutka); 4 write-in (Bill Van Auken).

**2000**  Other vote was 4,443 Reform (Buchanan); 3,074 Libertarian (Browne); 579 Constitution (Phillips); 27 write-in (Hagelin). The official returns listed the Hagelin vote as "Other."

**1996**  Other vote was 15,279 Green (Nader); 2,996 Libertarian (Browne); 1,517 Taxpayers (Phillips); 825 Natural Law (Hagelin); 144 scattered write-in.

**1992**  Other vote was 1,681 Marrou (Libertarian); 519 Fulani (New Alliance); 464 Phillips (Taxpayers); 91 scattered write-in.

**1988**  Other vote was 2,700 Paul (Libertarian); 1,405 Fulani (New Alliance); 230 scattered write-in.

**1984**  Other vote was 1,292 Hall (Independent); 755 Serrette (Independent); 82 scattered write-in.

**1980**  Other vote was 53,327 Anderson (Independent); 5,119 Clark (Libertarian); 4,394 Commoner (Citizens); 591 Hall (Communist); 84 scattered write-in.

**1976**  Other vote was 10,874 McCarthy (Independent); 3,495 Bubar (Prohibition); 28 Anderson (write-in); 14 Hall (write-in); 11 MacBride (write-in); 8 Maddox (write-in); 1 Camejo (write-in); 1 Levin (write-in); 185 scattered write-in.

**1972**

**1968**  Wallace on the ballot as George C. Wallace party.

**1964**

**1960**

# MARYLAND

## POPULAR VOTE FOR PRESIDENT 1920 TO 2004

| Year | Total Vote | Republican | | Democratic | | Other Vote | Plurality | Percentage | | | |
|------|-----------|------------|-----------|------------|-----------|------------|-----------|------------|------|------------|------|
| | | | | | | | | Total Vote | | Major Vote | |
| | | Vote | Candidate | Vote | Candidate | | | Rep. | Dem. | Rep. | Dem. |
| 2004 | 2,386,678 | 1,024,703 | Bush, George W. | 1,334,493 | Kerry, John | 27,482 | 309,790 D | 42.9% | 55.9% | 43.4% | 56.6% |
| 2000** | 2,020,480 | 813,797 | Bush, George W. | 1,140,782 | Gore, Al | 65,901 | 326,985 D | 40.3% | 56.5% | 41.6% | 58.4% |
| 1996 ** | 1,780,870 | 681,530 | Dole, Bob | 966,207 | Clinton, Bill | 133,133 | 284,677 D | 38.3% | 54.3% | 41.4% | 58.6% |
| 1992 ** | 1,985,046 | 707,094 | Bush, George | 988,571 | Clinton, Bill | 289,381 | 281,477 D | 35.6% | 49.8% | 41.7% | 58.3% |
| 1988 | 1,714,358 | 876,167 | Bush, George | 826,304 | Dukakis, Michael S. | 11,887 | 49,863 R | 51.1% | 48.2% | 51.5% | 48.5% |
| 1984 | 1,675,873 | 879,918 | Reagan, Ronald | 787,935 | Mondale, Walter F. | 8,020 | 91,983 R | 52.5% | 47.0% | 52.8% | 47.2% |
| 1980 ** | 1,540,496 | 680,606 | Reagan, Ronald | 726,161 | Carter, Jimmy | 133,729 | 45,555 D | 44.2% | 47.1% | 48.4% | 51.6% |
| 1976 | 1,439,897 | 672,661 | Ford, Gerald R. | 759,612 | Carter, Jimmy | 7,624 | 86,951 D | 46.7% | 52.8% | 47.0% | 53.0% |
| 1972 | 1,353,812 | 829,305 | Nixon, Richard M. | 505,781 | McGovern, George S. | 18,726 | 323,524 R | 61.3% | 37.4% | 62.1% | 37.9% |
| 1968 | 1,235,039 | 517,995 | Nixon, Richard M. | 538,310 | Humphrey, Hubert H. | 178,734 | 20,315 D | 41.9% | 43.6% | 49.0% | 51.0% |
| 1964 | 1,116,457 | 385,495 | Goldwater, Barry M. | 730,912 | Johnson, Lyndon B. | 50 | 345,417 D | 34.5% | 65.5% | 34.5% | 65.5% |
| 1960 | 1,055,349 | 489,538 | Nixon, Richard M. | 565,808 | Kennedy, John F. | 3 | 76,270 D | 46.4% | 53.6% | 46.4% | 53.6% |
| 1956 | 932,827 | 559,738 | Eisenhower, Dwight D. | 372,613 | Stevenson, Adlai E. | 476 | 187,125 R | 60.0% | 39.9% | 60.0% | 40.0% |
| 1952 | 902,074 | 499,424 | Eisenhower, Dwight D. | 395,337 | Stevenson, Adlai E. | 7,313 | 104,087 R | 55.4% | 43.8% | 55.8% | 44.2% |
| 1948 | 596,748 | 294,814 | Dewey, Thomas E. | 286,521 | Truman, Harry S. | 15,413 | 8,293 R | 49.4% | 48.0% | 50.7% | 49.3% |
| 1944 | 608,439 | 292,949 | Dewey, Thomas E. | 315,490 | Roosevelt, Franklin D. | | 22,541 D | 48.1% | 51.9% | 48.1% | 51.9% |
| 1940 | 660,104 | 269,534 | Willkie, Wendell | 384,546 | Roosevelt, Franklin D. | 6,024 | 115,012 D | 40.8% | 58.3% | 41.2% | 58.8% |
| 1936 | 624,896 | 231,435 | Landon, Alfred M. | 389,612 | Roosevelt, Franklin D. | 3,849 | 158,177 D | 37.0% | 62.3% | 37.3% | 62.7% |
| 1932 | 511,054 | 184,184 | Hoover, Herbert C. | 314,314 | Roosevelt, Franklin D. | 12,556 | 130,130 D | 36.0% | 61.5% | 36.9% | 63.1% |
| 1928 | 528,348 | 301,479 | Hoover, Herbert C. | 223,626 | Smith, Alfred E. | 3,243 | 77,853 R | 57.1% | 42.3% | 57.4% | 42.6% |
| 1924 | 358,630 | 162,414 | Coolidge, Calvin | 148,072 | Davis, John W. | 48,144 | 14,342 R | 45.3% | 41.3% | 52.3% | 47.7% |
| 1920 | 428,443 | 236,117 | Harding, Warren G. | 180,626 | Cox, James M. | 11,700 | 55,491 R | 55.1% | 42.2% | 56.7% | 43.3% |

In 2000 the other vote column includes 53,768 votes cast for Green (Nader). In 1996 the other vote column includes 115,812 votes cast for Perot. In 1992 the other vote column includes 281,414 votes cast for Perot. In 1980 the other column includes 119,537 votes for Independent (Anderson).

## ELECTORAL COLLEGE VOTE 1920 TO 2004

| Year | Total | Republican | Democratic | Other |
|------|-------|------------|------------|-------|
| 2004 | 10 | | 10 | |
| 2000 | 10 | | 10 | |
| 1996 | 10 | | 10 | |
| 1992 | 10 | | 10 | |
| 1988 | 10 | 10 | | |
| 1984 | 10 | 10 | | |
| 1980 | 10 | | 10 | |
| 1976 | 10 | | 10 | |
| 1972 | 10 | 10 | | |
| 1968 | 10 | | 10 | |
| 1964 | 10 | | 10 | |
| 1960 | 9 | | 9 | |
| 1956 | 9 | 9 | | |
| 1952 | 9 | 9 | | |
| 1948 | 8 | 8 | | |
| 1944 | 8 | | 8 | |
| 1940 | 8 | | 8 | |
| 1936 | 8 | | 8 | |
| 1932 | 8 | | 8 | |
| 1928 | 8 | 8 | | |
| 1924 | 8 | 8 | | |
| 1920 | 8 | 8 | | |

# MARYLAND

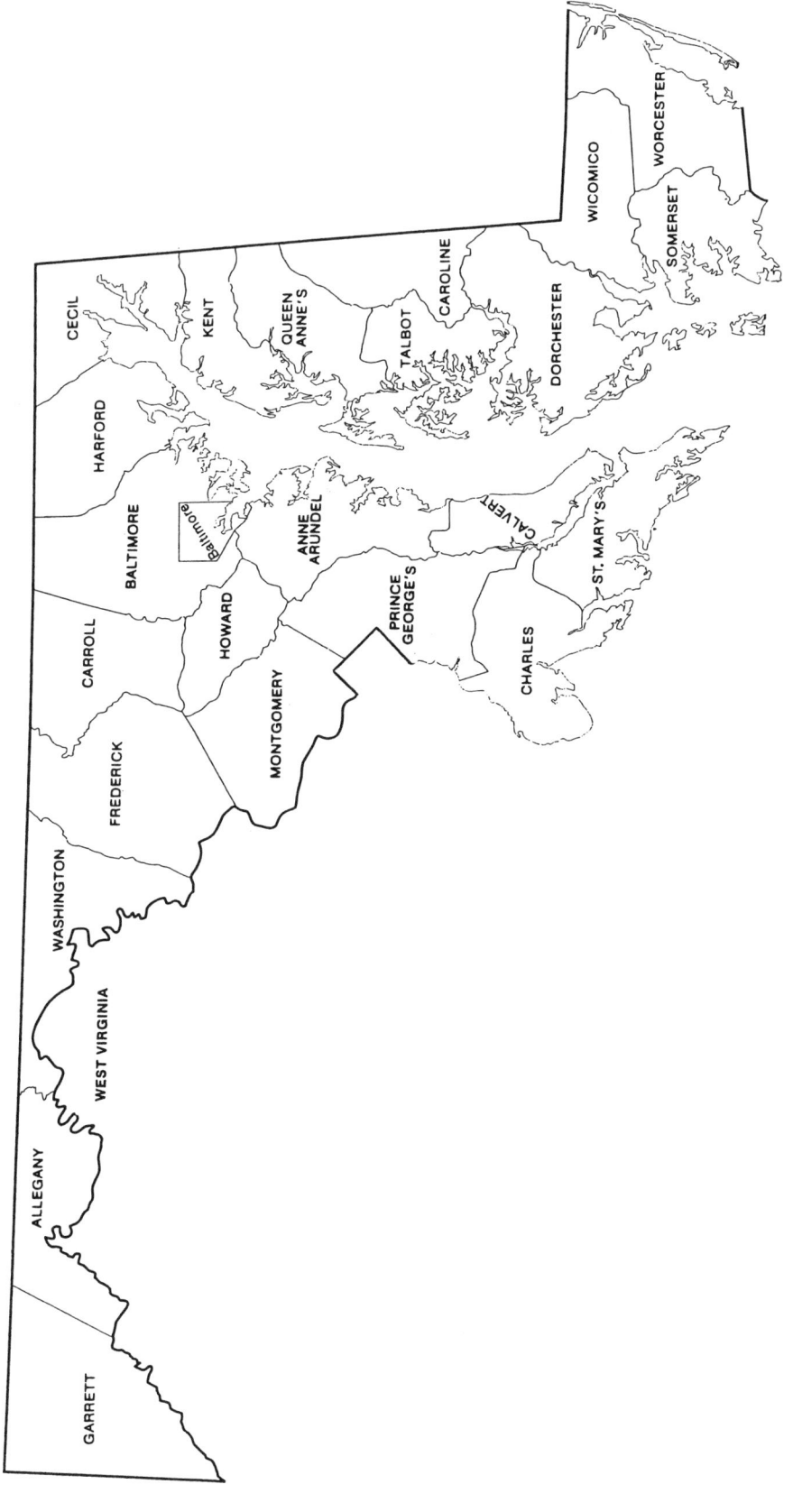

# MARYLAND

## PRESIDENT 2004

| 2000 Census Population | County | Total Vote | Republican | Democratic | Other | Rep.-Dem. Plurality | Percentage | | | |
|---|---|---|---|---|---|---|---|---|---|---|
| | | | | | | | Total Vote | | Major Vote | |
| | | | | | | | Rep. | Dem. | Rep. | Dem. |
| 74,930 | ALLEGANY | 29,855 | 18,980 | 10,576 | 299 | 8,404 R | 63.6% | 35.4% | 64.2% | 35.8% |
| 489,656 | ANNE ARUNDEL | 239,667 | 133,231 | 103,324 | 3,112 | 29,907 R | 55.6% | 43.1% | 56.3% | 43.7% |
| 651,154 | BALTIMORE CITY | 213,563 | 36,230 | 175,022 | 2,311 | 138,792 D | 17.0% | 82.0% | 17.2% | 82.8% |
| 754,292 | BALTIMORE COUNTY | 353,479 | 166,051 | 182,474 | 4,954 | 16,423 D | 47.0% | 51.6% | 47.6% | 52.4% |
| 74,563 | CALVERT | 39,351 | 23,017 | 15,967 | 367 | 7,050 R | 58.5% | 40.6% | 59.0% | 41.0% |
| 29,772 | CAROLINE | 11,356 | 7,396 | 3,810 | 150 | 3,586 R | 65.1% | 33.6% | 66.0% | 34.0% |
| 150,897 | CARROLL | 79,349 | 55,275 | 22,974 | 1,100 | 32,301 R | 69.7% | 29.0% | 70.6% | 29.4% |
| 85,951 | CECIL | 37,674 | 22,556 | 14,680 | 438 | 7,876 R | 59.9% | 39.0% | 60.6% | 39.4% |
| 120,546 | CHARLES | 58,241 | 28,442 | 29,354 | 445 | 912 D | 48.8% | 50.4% | 49.2% | 50.8% |
| 30,674 | DORCHESTER | 13,339 | 7,801 | 5,411 | 127 | 2,390 R | 58.5% | 40.6% | 59.0% | 41.0% |
| 195,277 | FREDERICK | 100,594 | 59,934 | 39,503 | 1,157 | 20,431 R | 59.6% | 39.3% | 60.3% | 39.7% |
| 29,846 | GARRETT | 12,484 | 9,085 | 3,291 | 108 | 5,794 R | 72.8% | 26.4% | 73.4% | 26.6% |
| 218,590 | HARFORD | 112,728 | 71,565 | 39,685 | 1,478 | 31,880 R | 63.5% | 35.2% | 64.3% | 35.7% |
| 247,842 | HOWARD | 133,810 | 59,724 | 72,257 | 1,829 | 12,533 D | 44.6% | 54.0% | 45.3% | 54.7% |
| 19,197 | KENT | 9,285 | 4,900 | 4,278 | 107 | 622 R | 52.8% | 46.1% | 53.4% | 46.6% |
| 873,341 | MONTGOMERY | 415,225 | 136,334 | 273,936 | 4,955 | 137,602 D | 32.8% | 66.0% | 33.2% | 66.8% |
| 801,515 | PRINCE GEORGES | 318,474 | 55,532 | 260,532 | 2,410 | 205,000 D | 17.4% | 81.8% | 17.6% | 82.4% |
| 40,563 | QUEEN ANNES | 21,794 | 14,489 | 7,070 | 235 | 7,419 R | 66.5% | 32.4% | 67.2% | 32.8% |
| 86,211 | ST. MARYS | 37,916 | 23,725 | 13,776 | 415 | 9,949 R | 62.6% | 36.3% | 63.3% | 36.7% |
| 24,747 | SOMERSET | 8,994 | 4,884 | 4,034 | 76 | 850 R | 54.3% | 44.9% | 54.8% | 45.2% |
| 33,812 | TALBOT | 18,864 | 11,288 | 7,367 | 209 | 3,921 R | 59.8% | 39.1% | 60.5% | 39.5% |
| 131,923 | WASHINGTON | 57,904 | 36,917 | 20,387 | 600 | 16,530 R | 63.8% | 35.2% | 64.4% | 35.6% |
| 84,644 | WICOMICO | 37,503 | 21,998 | 15,137 | 368 | 6,861 R | 58.7% | 40.4% | 59.2% | 40.8% |
| 46,543 | WORCESTER | 25,229 | 15,349 | 9,648 | 232 | 5,701 R | 60.8% | 38.2% | 61.4% | 38.6% |
| 5,296,486 | TOTAL | 2,386,678 | 1,024,703 | 1,334,493 | 27,482 | 309,790 D | 42.9% | 55.9% | 43.4% | 56.6% |

# MARYLAND

## PRESIDENT 2000

| 2000 Census Pop. Est. | County | Total Vote | Republican | Democratic | Green (Nader) | Other | Rep.-Dem. Plurality | Percentage of Total Vote | | |
|---|---|---|---|---|---|---|---|---|---|---|
| | | | | | | | | Rep. | Dem. | Green |
| 74,930 | ALLEGANY | 26,371 | 14,656 | 10,894 | 610 | 211 | 3,762 R | 55.6% | 41.3% | 2.3% |
| 489,656 | ANNE ARUNDEL | 200,657 | 104,209 | 89,624 | 5,493 | 1,331 | 14,585 R | 51.9% | 44.7% | 2.7% |
| 651,154 | BALTIMORE CITY | 192,404 | 27,150 | 158,765 | 5,512 | 977 | 131,615 D | 14.1% | 82.5% | 2.9% |
| 754,292 | BALTIMORE COUNTY | 304,084 | 133,033 | 160,635 | 8,544 | 1,872 | 27,602 D | 43.7% | 52.8% | 2.8% |
| 74,563 | CALVERT | 29,806 | 16,004 | 12,986 | 660 | 156 | 3,018 R | 53.7% | 43.6% | 2.2% |
| 29,772 | CAROLINE | 8,952 | 5,300 | 3,396 | 198 | 58 | 1,904 R | 59.2% | 37.9% | 2.2% |
| 150,897 | CARROLL | 64,027 | 41,742 | 20,146 | 1,681 | 458 | 21,596 R | 65.2% | 31.5% | 2.6% |
| 85,951 | CECIL | 28,876 | 15,494 | 12,327 | 794 | 261 | 3,167 R | 53.7% | 42.7% | 2.7% |
| 120,546 | CHARLES | 44,592 | 21,768 | 21,873 | 755 | 196 | 105 D | 48.8% | 49.1% | 1.7% |
| 30,674 | DORCHESTER | 11,392 | 5,847 | 5,232 | 222 | 91 | 615 R | 51.3% | 45.9% | 1.9% |
| 195,277 | FREDERICK | 78,661 | 45,350 | 30,725 | 2,052 | 534 | 14,625 R | 57.7% | 39.1% | 2.6% |
| 29,846 | GARRETT | 10,655 | 7,514 | 2,872 | 203 | 66 | 4,642 R | 70.5% | 27.0% | 1.9% |
| 218,590 | HARFORD | 91,424 | 52,862 | 35,665 | 2,298 | 599 | 17,197 R | 57.8% | 39.0% | 2.5% |
| 247,842 | HOWARD | 112,779 | 49,809 | 58,556 | 3,643 | 771 | 8,747 D | 44.2% | 51.9% | 3.2% |
| 19,197 | KENT | 8,085 | 4,155 | 3,627 | 270 | 33 | 528 R | 51.4% | 44.9% | 3.3% |
| 873,341 | MONTGOMERY | 371,688 | 124,580 | 232,453 | 12,485 | 2,170 | 107,873 D | 33.5% | 62.5% | 3.4% |
| 801,515 | PRINCE GEORGES | 266,909 | 49,987 | 211,119 | 4,497 | 1,306 | 161,132 D | 18.7% | 79.1% | 1.7% |
| 40,563 | QUEEN ANNES | 16,761 | 9,970 | 6,257 | 446 | 88 | 3,713 R | 59.5% | 37.3% | 2.7% |
| 86,211 | ST. MARYS | 29,501 | 16,856 | 11,912 | 568 | 165 | 4,944 R | 57.1% | 40.4% | 1.9% |
| 24,747 | SOMERSET | 7,604 | 3,609 | 3,785 | 142 | 68 | 176 D | 47.5% | 49.8% | 1.9% |
| 33,812 | TALBOT | 15,234 | 8,874 | 5,854 | 424 | 82 | 3,020 R | 58.3% | 38.4% | 2.8% |
| 131,923 | WASHINGTON | 47,470 | 27,948 | 18,221 | 1,027 | 274 | 9,727 R | 58.9% | 38.4% | 2.2% |
| 84,644 | WICOMICO | 31,795 | 16,338 | 14,469 | 762 | 226 | 1,869 R | 51.4% | 45.5% | 2.4% |
| 46,543 | WORCESTER | 20,753 | 10,742 | 9,389 | 482 | 140 | 1,353 R | 51.8% | 45.2% | 2.3% |
| 5,296,486 | TOTAL | 2,020,480 | 813,797 | 1,140,782 | 53,768 | 12,133 | 326,985 D | 40.3% | 56.5% | 2.7% |

448

# MARYLAND

## PRESIDENT 1996

| 1995 Census Pop. Est. | County | Total Vote | Republican | Democratic | Reform (Perot) | Other | Rep.-Dem. Plurality | Percentage of Total Vote | | |
|---|---|---|---|---|---|---|---|---|---|---|
| | | | | | | | | Rep. | Dem. | Reform |
| 73,954 | ALLEGANY | 26,002 | 12,136 | 11,025 | 2,652 | 189 | 1,111 R | 46.7% | 42.4% | 10.2% |
| 461,807 | ANNE ARUNDEL | 171,685 | 83,574 | 72,147 | 14,287 | 1,677 | 11,427 R | 48.7% | 42.0% | 8.3% |
| 691,131 | BALTIMORE CITY | 183,323 | 28,467 | 145,441 | 7,473 | 1,942 | 116,974 D | 15.5% | 79.3% | 4.1% |
| 715,360 | BALTIMORE COUNTY | 269,968 | 114,449 | 132,599 | 20,393 | 2,527 | 18,150 D | 42.4% | 49.1% | 7.6% |
| 64,598 | CALVERT | 23,566 | 11,509 | 10,008 | 1,932 | 117 | 1,501 R | 48.8% | 42.5% | 8.2% |
| 29,072 | CAROLINE | 8,177 | 3,874 | 3,251 | 947 | 105 | 623 R | 47.4% | 39.8% | 11.6% |
| 140,203 | CARROLL | 52,997 | 30,316 | 17,122 | 4,873 | 686 | 13,194 R | 57.2% | 32.3% | 9.2% |
| 78,174 | CECIL | 24,460 | 10,885 | 10,144 | 3,124 | 307 | 741 R | 44.5% | 41.5% | 12.8% |
| 111,633 | CHARLES | 35,823 | 17,432 | 15,890 | 2,333 | 168 | 1,542 R | 48.7% | 44.4% | 6.5% |
| 30,170 | DORCHESTER | 10,054 | 4,337 | 4,613 | 1,008 | 96 | 276 D | 43.1% | 45.9% | 10.0% |
| 175,399 | FREDERICK | 65,303 | 34,494 | 25,081 | 4,989 | 739 | 9,413 R | 52.8% | 38.4% | 7.6% |
| 29,461 | GARRETT | 9,786 | 5,400 | 3,121 | 1,200 | 65 | 2,279 R | 55.2% | 31.9% | 12.3% |
| 205,367 | HARFORD | 78,191 | 39,686 | 29,779 | 7,939 | 787 | 9,907 R | 50.8% | 38.1% | 10.2% |
| 219,125 | HOWARD | 95,508 | 40,849 | 47,569 | 6,011 | 1,079 | 6,720 D | 42.8% | 49.8% | 6.3% |
| 18,736 | KENT | 6,998 | 3,055 | 3,207 | 676 | 60 | 152 D | 43.7% | 45.8% | 9.7% |
| 809,569 | MONTGOMERY | 334,897 | 117,730 | 198,807 | 14,450 | 3,910 | 81,077 D | 35.2% | 59.4% | 4.3% |
| 767,413 | PRINCE GEORGES | 240,302 | 52,697 | 176,612 | 9,153 | 1,840 | 123,915 D | 21.9% | 73.5% | 3.8% |
| 36,992 | QUEEN ANNES | 13,639 | 7,147 | 5,054 | 1,312 | 126 | 2,093 R | 52.4% | 37.1% | 9.6% |
| 81,037 | ST. MARYS | 23,808 | 11,835 | 9,988 | 1,827 | 158 | 1,847 R | 49.7% | 42.0% | 7.7% |
| 24,431 | SOMERSET | 7,169 | 2,919 | 3,557 | 613 | 80 | 638 D | 40.7% | 49.6% | 8.6% |
| 32,405 | TALBOT | 12,855 | 6,997 | 4,821 | 914 | 123 | 2,176 R | 54.4% | 37.5% | 7.1% |
| 127,199 | WASHINGTON | 42,142 | 21,434 | 16,481 | 3,934 | 293 | 4,953 R | 50.9% | 39.1% | 9.3% |
| 79,256 | WICOMICO | 27,286 | 12,687 | 12,303 | 2,160 | 136 | 384 R | 46.5% | 45.1% | 7.9% |
| 39,946 | WORCESTER | 16,931 | 7,621 | 7,587 | 1,612 | 111 | 34 R | 45.0% | 44.8% | 9.5% |
| 5,042,438 | TOTAL | 1,780,870 | 681,530 | 966,207 | 115,812 | 17,321 | 284,677 D | 38.3% | 54.3% | 6.5% |

# MARYLAND

## PRESIDENT 1992

| 1990 Census Population | County | Total Vote | Republican | Democratic | Perot | Other | Plurality | Percentage Total Vote | | |
|---|---|---|---|---|---|---|---|---|---|---|
| | | | | | | | | Rep. | Dem. | Perot |
| 74,946 | ALLEGANY | 30,595 | 13,862 | 11,501 | 5,081 | 151 | 2,361 R | 45.3% | 37.6% | 16.6% |
| 427,239 | ANNE ARUNDEL | 185,634 | 81,467 | 68,629 | 35,191 | 347 | 12,838 R | 43.9% | 37.0% | 19.0% |
| 736,014 | BALTIMORE CITY | 245,091 | 40,725 | 185,753 | 17,381 | 1,232 | 145,028 D | 16.6% | 75.8% | 7.1% |
| 692,134 | BALTIMORE COUNTY | 323,220 | 126,728 | 143,498 | 51,757 | 1,237 | 16,770 D | 39.2% | 44.4% | 16.0% |
| 51,372 | CALVERT | 23,249 | 10,026 | 8,619 | 4,499 | 105 | 1,407 R | 43.1% | 37.1% | 19.4% |
| 27,035 | CAROLINE | 8,459 | 3,856 | 2,822 | 1,729 | 52 | 1,034 R | 45.6% | 33.4% | 20.4% |
| 123,372 | CARROLL | 54,930 | 28,405 | 15,447 | 10,965 | 113 | 12,958 R | 51.7% | 28.1% | 20.0% |
| 71,347 | CECIL | 27,319 | 10,784 | 10,232 | 6,115 | 188 | 552 R | 39.5% | 37.5% | 22.4% |
| 101,154 | CHARLES | 38,454 | 17,293 | 14,498 | 6,501 | 162 | 2,795 R | 45.0% | 37.7% | 16.9% |
| 30,236 | DORCHESTER | 10,957 | 4,934 | 3,933 | 2,010 | 80 | 1,001 R | 45.0% | 35.9% | 18.3% |
| 150,208 | FREDERICK | 64,691 | 31,290 | 21,848 | 11,373 | 180 | 9,442 R | 48.4% | 33.8% | 17.6% |
| 28,138 | GARRETT | 10,580 | 5,714 | 2,856 | 1,987 | 23 | 2,858 R | 54.0% | 27.0% | 18.8% |
| 182,132 | HARFORD | 80,687 | 36,350 | 27,164 | 17,002 | 171 | 9,186 R | 45.1% | 33.7% | 21.1% |
| 187,328 | HOWARD | 99,798 | 38,594 | 44,763 | 16,182 | 259 | 6,169 D | 38.7% | 44.9% | 16.2% |
| 17,842 | KENT | 7,628 | 3,094 | 3,093 | 1,411 | 30 | 1 R | 40.6% | 40.5% | 18.5% |
| 757,027 | MONTGOMERY | 362,613 | 119,705 | 199,757 | 41,971 | 1,180 | 80,052 D | 33.0% | 55.1% | 11.6% |
| 729,268 | PRINCE GEORGES | 256,859 | 62,955 | 168,691 | 23,355 | 1,858 | 105,736 D | 24.5% | 65.7% | 9.1% |
| 33,953 | QUEEN ANNES | 14,514 | 6,829 | 4,668 | 2,958 | 59 | 2,161 R | 47.1% | 32.2% | 20.4% |
| 75,974 | ST. MARYS | 25,085 | 11,485 | 8,931 | 4,550 | 119 | 2,554 R | 45.8% | 35.6% | 18.1% |
| 23,440 | SOMERSET | 7,936 | 3,450 | 3,210 | 1,230 | 46 | 240 R | 43.5% | 40.4% | 15.5% |
| 30,549 | TALBOT | 13,708 | 6,774 | 4,642 | 2,233 | 59 | 2,132 R | 49.4% | 33.9% | 16.3% |
| 121,393 | WASHINGTON | 46,208 | 21,977 | 16,495 | 7,537 | 199 | 5,482 R | 47.6% | 35.7% | 16.3% |
| 74,339 | WICOMICO | 30,272 | 13,560 | 11,481 | 5,140 | 91 | 2,079 R | 44.8% | 37.9% | 17.0% |
| 35,028 | WORCESTER | 16,559 | 7,237 | 6,040 | 3,256 | 26 | 1,197 R | 43.7% | 36.5% | 19.7% |
| 4,781,468 | TOTAL | 1,985,046 | 707,094 | 988,571 | 281,414 | 7,967 | 281,477 D | 35.6% | 49.8% | 14.2% |

# MARYLAND

## PRESIDENT 1988

| 1980 Census Population | County | Total Vote | Republican | Democratic | Other | Rep.-Dem. Plurality | Percentage | | | |
|---|---|---|---|---|---|---|---|---|---|---|
| | | | | | | | Total Vote | | Major Vote | |
| | | | | | | | Rep. | Dem. | Rep. | Dem. |
| 80,548 | ALLEGANY | 29,503 | 17,462 | 11,844 | 197 | 5,618 R | 59.2% | 40.1% | 59.6% | 40.4% |
| 370,775 | ANNE ARUNDEL | 155,101 | 98,540 | 55,440 | 1,121 | 43,100 R | 63.5% | 35.7% | 64.0% | 36.0% |
| 786,775 | BALTIMORE CITY | 232,367 | 59,089 | 170,813 | 2,465 | 111,724 D | 25.4% | 73.5% | 25.7% | 74.3% |
| 655,615 | BALTIMORE COUNTY | 287,295 | 163,881 | 121,570 | 1,844 | 42,311 R | 57.0% | 42.3% | 57.4% | 42.6% |
| 34,638 | CALVERT | 17,397 | 10,956 | 6,376 | 65 | 4,580 R | 63.0% | 36.6% | 63.2% | 36.8% |
| 23,143 | CAROLINE | 7,123 | 4,661 | 2,440 | 22 | 2,221 R | 65.4% | 34.3% | 65.6% | 34.4% |
| 96,356 | CARROLL | 43,747 | 31,224 | 12,368 | 155 | 18,856 R | 71.4% | 28.3% | 71.6% | 28.4% |
| 60,430 | CECIL | 21,155 | 13,224 | 7,807 | 124 | 5,417 R | 62.5% | 36.9% | 62.9% | 37.1% |
| 72,751 | CHARLES | 32,764 | 20,828 | 11,823 | 113 | 9,005 R | 63.6% | 36.1% | 63.8% | 36.2% |
| 30,623 | DORCHESTER | 10,140 | 6,343 | 3,709 | 88 | 2,634 R | 62.6% | 36.6% | 63.1% | 36.9% |
| 114,792 | FREDERICK | 49,867 | 32,575 | 17,061 | 231 | 15,514 R | 65.3% | 34.2% | 65.6% | 34.4% |
| 26,498 | GARRETT | 9,282 | 6,665 | 2,557 | 60 | 4,108 R | 71.8% | 27.5% | 72.3% | 27.7% |
| 145,930 | HARFORD | 58,566 | 38,493 | 19,803 | 270 | 18,690 R | 65.7% | 33.8% | 66.0% | 34.0% |
| 118,572 | HOWARD | 78,530 | 44,153 | 34,007 | 370 | 10,146 R | 56.2% | 43.3% | 56.5% | 43.5% |
| 16,695 | KENT | 6,732 | 3,761 | 2,925 | 46 | 836 R | 55.9% | 43.4% | 56.3% | 43.7% |
| 579,053 | MONTGOMERY | 320,896 | 154,191 | 165,187 | 1,518 | 10,996 D | 48.1% | 51.5% | 48.3% | 51.7% |
| 665,071 | PRINCE GEORGES | 222,881 | 86,545 | 133,816 | 2,520 | 47,271 D | 38.8% | 60.0% | 39.3% | 60.7% |
| 25,508 | QUEEN ANNES | 11,703 | 7,803 | 3,857 | 43 | 3,946 R | 66.7% | 33.0% | 66.9% | 33.1% |
| 59,895 | ST. MARYS | 20,290 | 12,767 | 7,434 | 89 | 5,333 R | 62.9% | 36.6% | 63.2% | 36.8% |
| 19,188 | SOMERSET | 7,165 | 4,222 | 2,911 | 32 | 1,311 R | 58.9% | 40.6% | 59.2% | 40.8% |
| 25,604 | TALBOT | 12,199 | 8,170 | 3,948 | 81 | 4,222 R | 67.0% | 32.4% | 67.4% | 32.6% |
| 113,086 | WASHINGTON | 40,638 | 25,912 | 14,408 | 318 | 11,504 R | 63.8% | 35.5% | 64.3% | 35.7% |
| 64,540 | WICOMICO | 25,755 | 16,272 | 9,413 | 70 | 6,859 R | 63.2% | 36.5% | 63.4% | 36.6% |
| 30,889 | WORCESTER | 13,262 | 8,430 | 4,787 | 45 | 3,643 R | 63.6% | 36.1% | 63.8% | 36.2% |
| 4,216,975 | TOTAL | 1,714,358 | 876,167 | 826,304 | 11,887 | 49,863 R | 51.1% | 48.2% | 51.5% | 48.5% |

# MARYLAND

## PRESIDENT 1984

| 1980 Census Population | County | Total Vote | Republican | Democratic | Other | Rep.-Dem. Plurality | | Percentage Total Vote | | Major Vote | |
|---|---|---|---|---|---|---|---|---|---|---|---|
| | | | | | | | | Rep. | Dem. | Rep. | Dem. |
| 80,548 | ALLEGANY | 31,223 | 19,763 | 11,143 | 317 | 8,620 | R | 63.3% | 35.7% | 63.9% | 36.1% |
| 370,775 | ANNE ARUNDEL | 142,591 | 94,171 | 47,565 | 855 | 46,606 | R | 66.0% | 33.4% | 66.4% | 33.6% |
| 786,775 | BALTIMORE CITY | 284,163 | 80,120 | 202,277 | 1,766 | 122,157 | D | 28.2% | 71.2% | 28.4% | 71.6% |
| 655,615 | BALTIMORE COUNTY | 280,428 | 171,929 | 106,908 | 1,591 | 65,021 | R | 61.3% | 38.1% | 61.7% | 38.3% |
| 34,638 | CALVERT | 13,840 | 8,303 | 5,455 | 82 | 2,848 | R | 60.0% | 39.4% | 60.4% | 39.6% |
| 23,143 | CAROLINE | 7,099 | 4,876 | 2,198 | 25 | 2,678 | R | 68.7% | 31.0% | 68.9% | 31.1% |
| 96,356 | CARROLL | 36,199 | 27,230 | 8,898 | 71 | 18,332 | R | 75.2% | 24.6% | 75.4% | 24.6% |
| 60,430 | CECIL | 19,885 | 13,111 | 6,681 | 93 | 6,430 | R | 65.9% | 33.6% | 66.2% | 33.8% |
| 72,751 | CHARLES | 26,460 | 16,132 | 10,264 | 64 | 5,868 | R | 61.0% | 38.8% | 61.1% | 38.9% |
| 30,623 | DORCHESTER | 9,981 | 6,699 | 3,160 | 122 | 3,539 | R | 67.1% | 31.7% | 67.9% | 32.1% |
| 114,792 | FREDERICK | 43,113 | 29,606 | 13,411 | 96 | 16,195 | R | 68.7% | 31.1% | 68.8% | 31.2% |
| 26,498 | GARRETT | 9,477 | 7,042 | 2,386 | 49 | 4,656 | R | 74.3% | 25.2% | 74.7% | 25.3% |
| 145,930 | HARFORD | 54,642 | 37,382 | 17,133 | 127 | 20,249 | R | 68.4% | 31.4% | 68.6% | 31.4% |
| 118,572 | HOWARD | 61,688 | 35,641 | 25,713 | 334 | 9,928 | R | 57.8% | 41.7% | 58.1% | 41.9% |
| 16,695 | KENT | 6,323 | 3,897 | 2,390 | 36 | 1,507 | R | 61.6% | 37.8% | 62.0% | 38.0% |
| 579,053 | MONTGOMERY | 293,870 | 146,924 | 146,036 | 910 | 888 | R | 50.0% | 49.7% | 50.2% | 49.8% |
| 665,071 | PRINCE GEORGES | 232,220 | 95,121 | 136,063 | 1,036 | 40,942 | D | 41.0% | 58.6% | 41.1% | 58.9% |
| 25,508 | QUEEN ANNES | 9,763 | 6,784 | 2,938 | 41 | 3,846 | R | 69.5% | 30.1% | 69.8% | 30.2% |
| 59,895 | ST. MARYS | 17,670 | 11,201 | 6,420 | 49 | 4,781 | R | 63.4% | 36.3% | 63.6% | 36.4% |
| 19,188 | SOMERSET | 6,970 | 4,508 | 2,439 | 23 | 2,069 | R | 64.7% | 35.0% | 64.9% | 35.1% |
| 25,604 | TALBOT | 11,256 | 8,028 | 3,198 | 30 | 4,830 | R | 71.3% | 28.4% | 71.5% | 28.5% |
| 113,086 | WASHINGTON | 40,666 | 27,118 | 13,329 | 219 | 13,789 | R | 66.7% | 32.8% | 67.0% | 33.0% |
| 64,540 | WICOMICO | 24,332 | 16,124 | 8,160 | 48 | 7,964 | R | 66.3% | 33.5% | 66.4% | 33.6% |
| 30,889 | WORCESTER | 12,014 | 8,208 | 3,770 | 36 | 4,438 | R | 68.3% | 31.4% | 68.5% | 31.5% |
| 4,216,975 | TOTAL | 1,675,873 | 879,918 | 787,935 | 8,020 | 91,983 | R | 52.5% | 47.0% | 52.8% | 47.2% |

# MARYLAND

## PRESIDENT 1980

| 1980 Census Population | County | Total Vote | Republican | Democratic | Other | Rep.-Dem. Plurality | Percentage | | | |
|---|---|---|---|---|---|---|---|---|---|---|
| | | | | | | | Total Vote | | Major Vote | |
| | | | | | | | Rep. | Dem. | Rep. | Dem. |
| 80,548 | ALLEGANY | 31,484 | 17,512 | 12,167 | 1,805 | 5,345 R | 55.6% | 38.6% | 59.0% | 41.0% |
| 370,775 | ANNE ARUNDEL | 131,632 | 69,443 | 50,780 | 11,409 | 18,663 R | 52.8% | 38.6% | 57.8% | 42.2% |
| 786,775 | BALTIMORE CITY | 264,775 | 57,902 | 191,911 | 14,962 | 134,009 D | 21.9% | 72.5% | 23.2% | 76.8% |
| 655,615 | BALTIMORE COUNTY | 279,917 | 132,490 | 121,280 | 26,147 | 11,210 R | 47.3% | 43.3% | 52.2% | 47.8% |
| 34,638 | CALVERT | 10,870 | 5,440 | 4,745 | 685 | 695 R | 50.0% | 43.7% | 53.4% | 46.6% |
| 23,143 | CAROLINE | 6,765 | 3,582 | 2,833 | 350 | 749 R | 52.9% | 41.9% | 55.8% | 44.2% |
| 96,356 | CARROLL | 32,940 | 19,859 | 10,393 | 2,688 | 9,466 R | 60.3% | 31.6% | 65.6% | 34.4% |
| 60,430 | CECIL | 18,846 | 9,673 | 7,937 | 1,236 | 1,736 R | 51.3% | 42.1% | 54.9% | 45.1% |
| 72,751 | CHARLES | 22,020 | 11,807 | 8,887 | 1,326 | 2,920 R | 53.6% | 40.4% | 57.1% | 42.9% |
| 30,623 | DORCHESTER | 10,550 | 5,160 | 4,908 | 482 | 252 R | 48.9% | 46.5% | 51.3% | 48.7% |
| 114,792 | FREDERICK | 39,130 | 22,033 | 13,629 | 3,468 | 8,404 R | 56.3% | 34.8% | 61.8% | 38.2% |
| 26,498 | GARRETT | 8,545 | 5,475 | 2,708 | 362 | 2,767 R | 64.1% | 31.7% | 66.9% | 33.1% |
| 145,930 | HARFORD | 50,941 | 26,713 | 20,042 | 4,186 | 6,671 R | 52.4% | 39.3% | 57.1% | 42.9% |
| 118,572 | HOWARD | 51,599 | 24,272 | 20,702 | 6,625 | 3,570 R | 47.0% | 40.1% | 54.0% | 46.0% |
| 16,695 | KENT | 6,304 | 2,889 | 2,986 | 429 | 97 D | 45.8% | 47.4% | 49.2% | 50.8% |
| 579,053 | MONTGOMERY | 266,151 | 125,515 | 105,822 | 34,814 | 19,693 R | 47.2% | 39.8% | 54.3% | 45.7% |
| 665,071 | PRINCE GEORGES | 193,987 | 78,977 | 98,757 | 16,253 | 19,780 D | 40.7% | 50.9% | 44.4% | 55.6% |
| 25,508 | QUEEN ANNES | 9,112 | 4,749 | 3,820 | 543 | 929 R | 52.1% | 41.9% | 55.4% | 44.6% |
| 59,895 | ST. MARYS | 16,056 | 8,267 | 6,773 | 1,016 | 1,494 R | 51.5% | 42.2% | 55.0% | 45.0% |
| 19,188 | SOMERSET | 6,937 | 3,312 | 3,342 | 283 | 30 D | 47.7% | 48.2% | 49.8% | 50.2% |
| 25,604 | TALBOT | 10,711 | 6,044 | 3,995 | 672 | 2,049 R | 56.4% | 37.3% | 60.2% | 39.8% |
| 113,086 | WASHINGTON | 39,083 | 22,901 | 14,118 | 2,064 | 8,783 R | 58.6% | 36.1% | 61.9% | 38.1% |
| 64,540 | WICOMICO | 21,905 | 11,229 | 9,431 | 1,245 | 1,798 R | 51.3% | 43.1% | 54.4% | 45.6% |
| 30,889 | WORCESTER | 10,236 | 5,362 | 4,195 | 679 | 1,167 R | 52.4% | 41.0% | 56.1% | 43.9% |
| 4,216,975 | TOTAL | 1,540,496 | 680,606 | 726,161 | 133,729 | 45,555 D | 44.2% | 47.1% | 48.4% | 51.6% |

# MARYLAND

## PRESIDENT 1976

| 1970 Census Population | County | Total Vote | Republican | Democratic | Other | Rep.-Dem. Plurality | Percentage Total Vote Rep. | Dem. | Major Vote Rep. | Dem. |
|---|---|---|---|---|---|---|---|---|---|---|
| 84,044 | ALLEGANY | 31,496 | 15,435 | 15,967 | 94 | 532 D | 49.0% | 50.7% | 49.2% | 50.8% |
| 297,539 | ANNE ARUNDEL | 116,100 | 61,353 | 54,351 | 396 | 7,002 R | 52.8% | 46.8% | 53.0% | 47.0% |
| 905,759 | BALTIMORE CITY | 261,832 | 81,762 | 178,593 | 1,477 | 96,831 D | 31.2% | 68.2% | 31.4% | 68.6% |
| 621,077 | BALTIMORE COUNTY | 262,866 | 143,293 | 118,505 | 1,068 | 24,788 R | 54.5% | 45.1% | 54.7% | 45.3% |
| 20,682 | CALVERT | 8,074 | 3,439 | 4,626 | 9 | 1,187 D | 42.6% | 57.3% | 42.6% | 57.4% |
| 19,781 | CAROLINE | 6,140 | 3,114 | 3,017 | 9 | 97 R | 50.7% | 49.1% | 50.8% | 49.2% |
| 69,006 | CARROLL | 25,684 | 15,661 | 9,940 | 83 | 5,721 R | 61.0% | 38.7% | 61.2% | 38.8% |
| 53,291 | CECIL | 16,811 | 7,833 | 8,950 | 28 | 1,117 D | 46.6% | 53.2% | 46.7% | 53.3% |
| 47,678 | CHARLES | 17,343 | 7,792 | 9,525 | 26 | 1,733 D | 44.9% | 54.9% | 45.0% | 55.0% |
| 29,405 | DORCHESTER | 9,301 | 4,768 | 4,528 | 5 | 240 R | 51.3% | 48.7% | 51.3% | 48.7% |
| 84,927 | FREDERICK | 32,704 | 17,941 | 14,542 | 221 | 3,399 R | 54.9% | 44.5% | 55.2% | 44.8% |
| 21,476 | GARRETT | 8,000 | 4,640 | 3,332 | 28 | 1,308 R | 58.0% | 41.7% | 58.2% | 41.8% |
| 115,378 | HARFORD | 44,227 | 24,309 | 19,890 | 28 | 4,419 R | 55.0% | 45.0% | 55.0% | 45.0% |
| 61,911 | HOWARD | 42,007 | 21,200 | 20,533 | 274 | 667 R | 50.5% | 48.9% | 50.8% | 49.2% |
| 16,146 | KENT | 6,041 | 2,821 | 3,211 | 9 | 390 D | 46.7% | 53.2% | 46.8% | 53.2% |
| 522,809 | MONTGOMERY | 256,177 | 122,674 | 131,098 | 2,405 | 8,424 D | 47.9% | 51.2% | 48.3% | 51.7% |
| 660,567 | PRINCE GEORGES | 193,966 | 81,027 | 111,743 | 1,196 | 30,716 D | 41.8% | 57.6% | 42.0% | 58.0% |
| 18,422 | QUEEN ANNES | 6,966 | 3,479 | 3,457 | 30 | 22 R | 49.9% | 49.6% | 50.2% | 49.8% |
| 47,388 | ST. MARYS | 12,905 | 5,640 | 7,227 | 38 | 1,587 D | 43.7% | 56.0% | 43.8% | 56.2% |
| 18,924 | SOMERSET | 6,727 | 3,254 | 3,472 | 1 | 218 D | 48.4% | 51.6% | 48.4% | 51.6% |
| 23,682 | TALBOT | 9,590 | 5,848 | 3,715 | 27 | 2,133 R | 61.0% | 38.7% | 61.2% | 38.8% |
| 103,829 | WASHINGTON | 36,233 | 20,194 | 15,902 | 137 | 4,292 R | 55.7% | 43.9% | 55.9% | 44.1% |
| 54,236 | WICOMICO | 19,977 | 10,537 | 9,412 | 28 | 1,125 R | 52.7% | 47.1% | 52.8% | 47.2% |
| 24,442 | WORCESTER | 8,730 | 4,647 | 4,076 | 7 | 571 R | 53.2% | 46.7% | 53.3% | 46.7% |
| 3,922,399 | TOTAL | 1,439,897 | 672,661 | 759,612 | 7,624 | 86,951 D | 46.7% | 52.8% | 47.0% | 53.0% |

# MARYLAND

## PRESIDENT 1972

| 1970 Census Population | County | Total Vote | Republican | Democratic | Other | Rep.-Dem. Plurality | Percentage | | | |
| --- | --- | --- | --- | --- | --- | --- | --- | --- | --- | --- |
| | | | | | | | Total Vote | | Major Vote | |
| | | | | | | | Rep. | Dem. | Rep. | Dem. |
| 84,044 | ALLEGANY | 32,048 | 20,687 | 10,808 | 553 | 9,879 R | 64.6% | 33.7% | 65.7% | 34.3% |
| 297,539 | ANNE ARUNDEL | 99,239 | 71,707 | 26,082 | 1,450 | 45,625 R | 72.3% | 26.3% | 73.3% | 26.7% |
| 905,759 | BALTIMORE CITY | 264,652 | 119,486 | 141,323 | 3,843 | 21,837 D | 45.1% | 53.4% | 45.8% | 54.2% |
| 621,077 | BALTIMORE COUNTY | 250,224 | 175,897 | 70,309 | 4,018 | 105,588 R | 70.3% | 28.1% | 71.4% | 28.6% |
| 20,682 | CALVERT | 6,344 | 4,024 | 2,232 | 88 | 1,792 R | 63.4% | 35.2% | 64.3% | 35.7% |
| 19,781 | CAROLINE | 5,948 | 4,325 | 1,567 | 56 | 2,758 R | 72.7% | 26.3% | 73.4% | 26.6% |
| 69,006 | CARROLL | 21,808 | 16,847 | 4,408 | 553 | 12,439 R | 77.3% | 20.2% | 79.3% | 20.7% |
| 53,291 | CECIL | 15,191 | 10,759 | 4,113 | 319 | 6,646 R | 70.8% | 27.1% | 72.3% | 27.7% |
| 47,678 | CHARLES | 14,353 | 9,665 | 4,502 | 186 | 5,163 R | 67.3% | 31.4% | 68.2% | 31.8% |
| 29,405 | DORCHESTER | 9,149 | 6,859 | 2,136 | 154 | 4,723 R | 75.0% | 23.3% | 76.3% | 23.7% |
| 84,927 | FREDERICK | 28,651 | 19,907 | 8,235 | 509 | 11,672 R | 69.5% | 28.7% | 70.7% | 29.3% |
| 21,476 | GARRETT | 7,154 | 5,480 | 1,510 | 164 | 3,970 R | 76.6% | 21.1% | 78.4% | 21.6% |
| 115,378 | HARFORD | 34,366 | 25,141 | 8,737 | 488 | 16,404 R | 73.2% | 25.4% | 74.2% | 25.8% |
| 61,911 | HOWARD | 30,316 | 19,265 | 10,668 | 383 | 8,597 R | 63.5% | 35.2% | 64.4% | 35.6% |
| 16,146 | KENT | 6,271 | 4,036 | 2,168 | 67 | 1,868 R | 64.4% | 34.6% | 65.1% | 34.9% |
| 522,809 | MONTGOMERY | 235,557 | 133,090 | 100,228 | 2,239 | 32,862 R | 56.5% | 42.5% | 57.0% | 43.0% |
| 660,567 | PRINCE GEORGES | 198,410 | 116,166 | 79,914 | 2,330 | 36,252 R | 58.5% | 40.3% | 59.2% | 40.8% |
| 18,422 | QUEEN ANNES | 6,217 | 4,380 | 1,712 | 125 | 2,668 R | 70.5% | 27.5% | 71.9% | 28.1% |
| 47,388 | ST. MARYS | 11,382 | 7,689 | 3,571 | 122 | 4,118 R | 67.6% | 31.4% | 68.3% | 31.7% |
| 18,924 | SOMERSET | 6,449 | 4,342 | 2,036 | 71 | 2,306 R | 67.3% | 31.6% | 68.1% | 31.9% |
| 23,682 | TALBOT | 8,859 | 6,620 | 2,181 | 58 | 4,439 R | 74.7% | 24.6% | 75.2% | 24.8% |
| 103,829 | WASHINGTON | 34,985 | 24,234 | 10,039 | 712 | 14,195 R | 69.3% | 28.7% | 70.7% | 29.3% |
| 54,236 | WICOMICO | 18,815 | 13,115 | 5,510 | 190 | 7,605 R | 69.7% | 29.3% | 70.4% | 29.6% |
| 24,442 | WORCESTER | 7,424 | 5,584 | 1,792 | 48 | 3,792 R | 75.2% | 24.1% | 75.7% | 24.3% |
| 3,922,399 | TOTAL | 1,353,812 | 829,305 | 505,781 | 18,726 | 323,524 R | 61.3% | 37.4% | 62.1% | 37.9% |

# MARYLAND

## PRESIDENT 1968

| 1960 Census Population | County | Total Vote | Republican | Democratic | AIP | Other | Plurality | Percentage Total Vote | | |
|---:|---|---:|---:|---:|---:|---|---:|---:|---:|---:|
| | | | | | | | | Rep. | Dem. | AIP |
| 84,169 | ALLEGANY | 31,910 | 13,561 | 13,227 | 5,122 | | 334 R | 42.5% | 41.5% | 16.1% |
| 206,634 | ANNE ARUNDEL | 77,625 | 36,557 | 25,381 | 15,687 | | 11,176 R | 47.1% | 32.7% | 20.2% |
| 492,428 | BALTIMORE CITY | 219,011 | 108,930 | 80,798 | 29,283 | | 28,132 R | 49.7% | 36.9% | 13.4% |
| 939,024 | BALTIMORE COUNTY | 289,884 | 80,146 | 178,450 | 31,288 | | 98,304 D | 27.6% | 61.6% | 10.8% |
| 15,826 | CALVERT | 5,449 | 1,946 | 2,032 | 1,471 | | 86 D | 35.7% | 37.3% | 27.0% |
| 19,462 | CAROLINE | 6,231 | 3,120 | 1,697 | 1,414 | | 1,423 R | 50.1% | 27.2% | 22.7% |
| 52,785 | CARROLL | 19,631 | 11,888 | 4,658 | 3,085 | | 7,230 R | 60.6% | 23.7% | 15.7% |
| 48,408 | CECIL | 14,214 | 6,462 | 4,517 | 3,235 | | 1,945 R | 45.5% | 31.8% | 22.8% |
| 32,572 | CHARLES | 12,065 | 4,645 | 4,247 | 3,173 | | 398 R | 38.5% | 35.2% | 26.3% |
| 29,666 | DORCHESTER | 10,114 | 4,183 | 2,714 | 3,217 | | 966 R | 41.4% | 26.8% | 31.8% |
| 71,930 | FREDERICK | 26,313 | 13,649 | 8,316 | 4,348 | | 5,333 R | 51.9% | 31.6% | 16.5% |
| 20,420 | GARRETT | 6,772 | 4,021 | 1,933 | 818 | | 2,088 R | 59.4% | 28.5% | 12.1% |
| 76,722 | HARFORD | 30,691 | 15,799 | 9,914 | 4,978 | | 5,885 R | 51.5% | 32.3% | 16.2% |
| 36,152 | HOWARD | 18,505 | 9,957 | 5,752 | 2,796 | | 4,205 R | 53.8% | 31.1% | 15.1% |
| 15,481 | KENT | 6,335 | 2,946 | 2,243 | 1,146 | | 703 R | 46.5% | 35.4% | 18.1% |
| 340,928 | MONTGOMERY | 191,403 | 84,651 | 92,026 | 14,726 | | 7,375 D | 44.2% | 48.1% | 7.7% |
| 357,395 | PRINCE GEORGES | 177,660 | 73,269 | 71,524 | 32,867 | | 1,745 R | 41.2% | 40.3% | 18.5% |
| 16,569 | QUEEN ANNES | 6,155 | 2,888 | 1,969 | 1,298 | | 919 R | 46.9% | 32.0% | 21.1% |
| 38,915 | ST. MARYS | 9,175 | 3,348 | 3,280 | 2,547 | | 68 R | 36.5% | 35.7% | 27.8% |
| 19,623 | SOMERSET | 7,047 | 2,829 | 2,319 | 1,899 | | 510 R | 40.1% | 32.9% | 26.9% |
| 21,578 | TALBOT | 8,883 | 4,902 | 2,609 | 1,372 | | 2,293 R | 55.2% | 29.4% | 15.4% |
| 91,219 | WASHINGTON | 34,053 | 16,050 | 11,266 | 6,737 | | 4,784 R | 47.1% | 33.1% | 19.8% |
| 49,050 | WICOMICO | 18,455 | 8,707 | 5,392 | 4,356 | | 3,315 R | 47.2% | 29.2% | 23.6% |
| 23,733 | WORCESTER | 7,458 | 3,541 | 2,046 | 1,871 | | 1,495 R | 47.5% | 27.4% | 25.1% |
| 3,100,689 | TOTAL | 1,235,039 | 517,995 | 538,310 | 178,734 | | 20,315 D | 41.9% | 43.6% | 14.5% |

# MARYLAND

## PRESIDENT 1964

| 1960 Census Population | County | Total Vote | Republican | Democratic | Other | Rep.-Dem. Plurality | Percentage | | | |
|---|---|---|---|---|---|---|---|---|---|---|
| | | | | | | | Total Vote | | Major Vote | |
| | | | | | | | Rep. | Dem. | Rep. | Dem. |
| 84,169 | ALLEGANY | 32,809 | 12,384 | 20,425 | | 8,041 D | 37.7% | 62.3% | 37.7% | 62.3% |
| 206,634 | ANNE ARUNDEL | 64,706 | 26,725 | 37,981 | | 11,256 D | 41.3% | 58.7% | 41.3% | 58.7% |
| 939,024 | BALTIMORE CITY | 316,805 | 76,089 | 240,716 | | 164,627 D | 24.0% | 76.0% | 24.0% | 76.0% |
| 492,428 | BALTIMORE COUNTY | 195,073 | 77,870 | 117,153 | 50 | 39,283 D | 39.9% | 60.1% | 39.9% | 60.1% |
| 15,826 | CALVERT | 5,100 | 1,765 | 3,335 | | 1,570 D | 34.6% | 65.4% | 34.6% | 65.4% |
| 19,462 | CAROLINE | 6,406 | 2,696 | 3,710 | | 1,014 D | 42.1% | 57.9% | 42.1% | 57.9% |
| 52,785 | CARROLL | 16,783 | 8,332 | 8,451 | | 119 D | 49.6% | 50.4% | 49.6% | 50.4% |
| 48,408 | CECIL | 13,184 | 5,330 | 7,854 | | 2,524 D | 40.4% | 59.6% | 40.4% | 59.6% |
| 32,572 | CHARLES | 10,001 | 3,455 | 6,546 | | 3,091 D | 34.5% | 65.5% | 34.5% | 65.5% |
| 29,666 | DORCHESTER | 9,891 | 5,327 | 4,564 | | 763 R | 53.9% | 46.1% | 53.9% | 46.1% |
| 71,930 | FREDERICK | 23,812 | 9,264 | 14,548 | | 5,284 D | 38.9% | 61.1% | 38.9% | 61.1% |
| 20,420 | GARRETT | 7,139 | 3,624 | 3,515 | | 109 R | 50.8% | 49.2% | 50.8% | 49.2% |
| 76,722 | HARFORD | 23,518 | 9,968 | 13,550 | | 3,582 D | 42.4% | 57.6% | 42.4% | 57.6% |
| 36,152 | HOWARD | 15,018 | 6,833 | 8,185 | | 1,352 D | 45.5% | 54.5% | 45.5% | 54.5% |
| 15,481 | KENT | 6,121 | 2,008 | 4,113 | | 2,105 D | 32.8% | 67.2% | 32.8% | 67.2% |
| 340,928 | MONTGOMERY | 155,667 | 52,554 | 103,113 | | 50,559 D | 33.8% | 66.2% | 33.8% | 66.2% |
| 357,395 | PRINCE GEORGES | 128,219 | 46,413 | 81,806 | | 35,393 D | 36.2% | 63.8% | 36.2% | 63.8% |
| 16,569 | QUEEN ANNES | 6,007 | 1,955 | 4,052 | | 2,097 D | 32.5% | 67.5% | 32.5% | 67.5% |
| 38,915 | ST. MARYS | 8,709 | 2,878 | 5,831 | | 2,953 D | 33.0% | 67.0% | 33.0% | 67.0% |
| 19,623 | SOMERSET | 7,682 | 3,155 | 4,527 | | 1,372 D | 41.1% | 58.9% | 41.1% | 58.9% |
| 21,578 | TALBOT | 8,364 | 3,693 | 4,671 | | 978 D | 44.2% | 55.8% | 44.2% | 55.8% |
| 91,219 | WASHINGTON | 32,614 | 12,756 | 19,858 | | 7,102 D | 39.1% | 60.9% | 39.1% | 60.9% |
| 49,050 | WICOMICO | 16,143 | 7,448 | 8,695 | | 1,247 D | 46.1% | 53.9% | 46.1% | 53.9% |
| 23,733 | WORCESTER | 6,686 | 2,973 | 3,713 | | 740 D | 44.5% | 55.5% | 44.5% | 55.5% |
| 3,100,689 | TOTAL | 1,116,457 | 385,495 | 730,912 | 50 | 345,417 D | 34.5% | 65.5% | 34.5% | 65.5% |

# MARYLAND

## PRESIDENT 1960

| 1960 Census Population | County | Total Vote | Republican | Democratic | Other | Rep.-Dem. Plurality | Percentage | | | |
| --- | --- | --- | --- | --- | --- | --- | --- | --- | --- | --- |
| | | | | | | | Total Vote | | Major Vote | |
| | | | | | | | Rep. | Dem. | Rep. | Dem. |
| 84,169 | ALLEGANY | 34,190 | 20,489 | 13,701 | | 6,788 R | 59.9% | 40.1% | 59.9% | 40.1% |
| 206,634 | ANNE ARUNDEL | 56,658 | 30,595 | 26,063 | | 4,532 R | 54.0% | 46.0% | 54.0% | 46.0% |
| 939,024 | BALTIMORE CITY | 317,457 | 114,705 | 202,752 | | 88,047 D | 36.1% | 63.9% | 36.1% | 63.9% |
| 492,428 | BALTIMORE COUNTY | 190,423 | 96,027 | 94,396 | | 1,631 R | 50.4% | 49.6% | 50.4% | 49.6% |
| 15,826 | CALVERT | 4,708 | 2,173 | 2,535 | | 362 D | 46.2% | 53.8% | 46.2% | 53.8% |
| 19,462 | CAROLINE | 7,079 | 3,698 | 3,381 | | 317 R | 52.2% | 47.8% | 52.2% | 47.8% |
| 52,785 | CARROLL | 17,208 | 11,445 | 5,763 | | 5,682 R | 66.5% | 33.5% | 66.5% | 33.5% |
| 48,408 | CECIL | 13,433 | 7,368 | 6,065 | | 1,303 R | 54.8% | 45.2% | 54.8% | 45.2% |
| 32,572 | CHARLES | 10,042 | 4,560 | 5,482 | | 922 D | 45.4% | 54.6% | 45.4% | 54.6% |
| 29,666 | DORCHESTER | 9,590 | 4,626 | 4,964 | | 338 D | 48.2% | 51.8% | 48.2% | 51.8% |
| 71,930 | FREDERICK | 23,319 | 13,408 | 9,910 | 1 | 3,498 R | 57.5% | 42.5% | 57.5% | 42.5% |
| 20,420 | GARRETT | 7,414 | 5,057 | 2,357 | | 2,700 R | 68.2% | 31.8% | 68.2% | 31.8% |
| 76,722 | HARFORD | 21,383 | 12,090 | 9,293 | | 2,797 R | 56.5% | 43.5% | 56.5% | 43.5% |
| 36,152 | HOWARD | 12,465 | 7,051 | 5,412 | 2 | 1,639 R | 56.6% | 43.4% | 56.6% | 43.4% |
| 15,481 | KENT | 6,343 | 3,264 | 3,079 | | 185 R | 51.5% | 48.5% | 51.5% | 48.5% |
| 340,928 | MONTGOMERY | 128,704 | 62,679 | 66,025 | | 3,346 D | 48.7% | 51.3% | 48.7% | 51.3% |
| 357,395 | PRINCE GEORGES | 106,830 | 44,817 | 62,013 | | 17,196 D | 42.0% | 58.0% | 42.0% | 58.0% |
| 16,569 | QUEEN ANNES | 6,032 | 2,906 | 3,126 | | 220 D | 48.2% | 51.8% | 48.2% | 51.8% |
| 38,915 | ST. MARYS | 8,832 | 3,080 | 5,752 | | 2,672 D | 34.9% | 65.1% | 34.9% | 65.1% |
| 19,623 | SOMERSET | 7,978 | 4,030 | 3,948 | | 82 R | 50.5% | 49.5% | 50.5% | 49.5% |
| 21,578 | TALBOT | 8,457 | 4,995 | 3,462 | | 1,533 R | 59.1% | 40.9% | 59.1% | 40.9% |
| 91,219 | WASHINGTON | 33,460 | 17,828 | 15,632 | | 2,196 R | 53.3% | 46.7% | 53.3% | 46.7% |
| 49,050 | WICOMICO | 16,021 | 8,671 | 7,350 | | 1,321 R | 54.1% | 45.9% | 54.1% | 45.9% |
| 23,733 | WORCESTER | 7,323 | 3,976 | 3,347 | | 629 R | 54.3% | 45.7% | 54.3% | 45.7% |
| 3,100,689 | TOTAL | 1,055,349 | 489,538 | 565,808 | 3 | 76,270 D | 46.4% | 53.6% | 46.4% | 53.6% |

# MARYLAND

## ELECTION NOTES

**2004**    Other vote was 11,854 Populist (Ralph Nader); 6,094 Libertarian (Michael Badnarik); 3,632 Green (David Cobb); 3,421 Constitution (Michael Peroutka); 27 write-in (Joe Schriner); 7 write-in (John Joseph Kennedy); 4 write-in (Theodis "Ted" Brown Sr.); 2 write-in (Lawson Bone); 1 write-in (Robert A. Boyle II); 2,440 scattered write-in.

**2000**    Other vote was 5,310 Libertarian (Browne); 4,248 Reform (Buchanan); 919 Constitution (Phillips); 176 write-in (Hagelin); 3 write-in (Miller); 3 write-in (Officewala); 3 write-in (Schriner); 2 write-in (Crawford); 2 write-in (Peters); 1 write-in/Democratic (Brown); 1 write-in (Easton); 1 write-in (LaBelle); 1 write-in (Pearlman); 1 write-in (Strickland); 1,462 scattered write-in. Write-in candidates could indicate a party affiliation.

**1996**    Other vote was 8,765 Libertarian (Browne); 3,402 Taxpayers (Phillips); 2,606 write-in (Nader); 2,517 Natural Law (Hagelin); 31 scattered write-in.

**1992**    Other vote was 4,715 Marrou (Libertarian); 2,786 Fulani (New Alliance); 191 Hagelin (write-in); 167 Daniels (write-in); 41 Gritz (write-in); 25 Warren (write-in); 22 Phillips (write-in); 18 LaRouche (write-in); 2 scattered write-in.

**1988**    Other vote was 6,748 Paul (Libertarian); 5,115 Fulani (New Alliance); 24 scattered write-in.

**1984**    Other vote was 5,721 Bergland (Libertarian); 898 Hall (Communist); 745 Holmes (Workers); 656 Serrette (Alliance).

**1980**    Other vote was 119,537 Anderson (Independent); 14,192 Clark (Libertarian).

**1976**    Other vote was 4,541 McCarthy (write-in); 321 Anderson (write-in); 261 Camejo (write-in); 255 MacBride (write-in); 171 Maddox (write-in); 68 Hall (write-in); 21 LaRouche (write-in); 16 Zeidler (write-in); 8 Miller (write-in); 8 Wright (write-in); 7 Levin (write-in); 2 Bubar (write-in); 1,945 scattered write-in.

**1972**    Other vote was Schmitz (American).

**1968**    Wallace on the ballot as American.

**1964**    Other vote was scattered write-in.

**1960**    Other vote was scattered write-in.

# MASSACHUSETTS

## POPULAR VOTE FOR PRESIDENT 1920 TO 2004

| Year | Total Vote | Republican | | Democratic | | Other Vote | Plurality | Percentage | | | |
|------|------|------|------|------|------|------|------|------|------|------|------|
| | | Vote | Candidate | Vote | Candidate | | | Total Vote | | Major Vote | |
| | | | | | | | | Rep. | Dem. | Rep. | Dem. |
| 2004 | 2,912,388 | 1,071,109 | Bush, George W. | 1,803,800 | Kerry, John | 37,479 | 732,691 D | 36.8% | 61.9% | 37.3% | 62.7% |
| 2000** | 2,702,984 | 878,502 | Bush, George W. | 1,616,487 | Gore, Al | 207,995 | 737,985 D | 32.5% | 59.8% | 35.2% | 64.8% |
| 1996 ** | 2,556,785 | 718,107 | Dole, Bob | 1,571,763 | Clinton, Bill | 266,915 | 853,656 D | 28.1% | 61.5% | 31.4% | 68.6% |
| 1992 ** | 2,773,700 | 805,049 | Bush, George | 1,318,662 | Clinton, Bill | 649,989 | 513,613 D | 29.0% | 47.5% | 37.9% | 62.1% |
| 1988 | 2,632,805 | 1,194,635 | Bush, George | 1,401,415 | Dukakis, Michael S. | 36,755 | 206,780 D | 45.4% | 53.2% | 46.0% | 54.0% |
| 1984 | 2,559,453 | 1,310,936 | Reagan, Ronald | 1,239,606 | Mondale, Walter F. | 8,911 | 71,330 R | 51.2% | 48.4% | 51.4% | 48.6% |
| 1980** | 2,524,298 | 1,057,631 | Reagan, Ronald | 1,053,802 | Carter, Jimmy | 412,865 | 3,829 R | 41.9% | 41.7% | 50.1% | 49.9% |
| 1976 | 2,547,558 | 1,030,276 | Ford, Gerald R. | 1,429,475 | Carter, Jimmy | 87,807 | 399,199 D | 40.4% | 56.1% | 41.9% | 58.1% |
| 1972 | 2,458,756 | 1,112,078 | Nixon, Richard M. | 1,332,540 | McGovern, George S. | 14,138 | 220,462 D | 45.2% | 54.2% | 45.5% | 54.5% |
| 1968 | 2,331,752 | 766,844 | Nixon, Richard M. | 1,469,218 | Humphrey, Hubert H. | 95,690 | 702,374 D | 32.9% | 63.0% | 34.3% | 65.7% |
| 1964 | 2,344,798 | 549,727 | Goldwater, Barry M. | 1,786,422 | Johnson, Lyndon B. | 8,649 | 1,236,695 D | 23.4% | 76.2% | 23.5% | 76.5% |
| 1960 | 2,469,480 | 976,750 | Nixon, Richard M. | 1,487,174 | Kennedy, John F. | 5,556 | 510,424 D | 39.6% | 60.2% | 39.6% | 60.4% |
| 1956 | 2,348,506 | 1,393,197 | Eisenhower, Dwight D. | 948,190 | Stevenson, Adlai E. | 7,119 | 445,007 R | 59.3% | 40.4% | 59.5% | 40.5% |
| 1952 | 2,383,398 | 1,292,325 | Eisenhower, Dwight D. | 1,083,525 | Stevenson, Adlai E. | 7,548 | 208,800 R | 54.2% | 45.5% | 54.4% | 45.6% |
| 1948 | 2,107,146 | 909,370 | Dewey, Thomas E. | 1,151,788 | Truman, Harry S. | 45,988 | 242,418 D | 43.2% | 54.7% | 44.1% | 55.9% |
| 1944 | 1,960,665 | 921,350 | Dewey, Thomas E. | 1,035,296 | Roosevelt, Franklin D. | 4,019 | 113,946 D | 47.0% | 52.8% | 47.1% | 52.9% |
| 1940 | 2,026,993 | 939,700 | Willkie, Wendell | 1,076,522 | Roosevelt, Franklin D. | 10,771 | 136,822 D | 46.4% | 53.1% | 46.6% | 53.4% |
| 1936 | 1,840,357 | 768,613 | Landon, Alfred M. | 942,716 | Roosevelt, Franklin D. | 129,028 | 174,103 D | 41.8% | 51.2% | 44.9% | 55.1% |
| 1932 | 1,580,114 | 736,959 | Hoover, Herbert C. | 800,148 | Roosevelt, Franklin D. | 43,007 | 63,189 D | 46.6% | 50.6% | 47.9% | 52.1% |
| 1928 | 1,577,823 | 775,566 | Hoover, Herbert C. | 792,758 | Smith, Alfred E. | 9,499 | 17,192 D | 49.2% | 50.2% | 49.5% | 50.5% |
| 1924 | 1,129,837 | 703,476 | Coolidge, Calvin | 280,831 | Davis, John W. | 145,530 | 422,645 R | 62.3% | 24.9% | 71.5% | 28.5% |
| 1920 | 993,718 | 681,153 | Harding, Warren G. | 276,691 | Cox, James M. | 35,874 | 404,462 R | 68.5% | 27.8% | 71.1% | 28.9% |

In 2000 the other vote column includes 173,564 votes cast for Green (Nader). In 1996 the other vote column includes 227,217 votes cast for Perot. In 1992 the other vote column includes 630,731 votes cast for Perot. In 1980 the other column includes 382,539 votes for Independent (Anderson).

## ELECTORAL COLLEGE VOTE 1920 TO 2004

| Year | Total | Republican | Democratic | Other |
|------|------|------|------|------|
| 2004 | 12 | | 12 | |
| 2000 | 12 | | 12 | |
| 1996 | 12 | | 12 | |
| 1992 | 12 | | 12 | |
| 1988 | 13 | | 13 | |
| 1984 | 13 | 13 | | |
| 1980 | 14 | 14 | | |
| 1976 | 14 | | 14 | |
| 1972 | 14 | | 14 | |
| 1968 | 14 | | 14 | |
| 1964 | 14 | | 14 | |
| 1960 | 16 | | 16 | |
| 1956 | 16 | 16 | | |
| 1952 | 16 | 16 | | |
| 1948 | 16 | | 16 | |
| 1944 | 16 | | 16 | |
| 1940 | 17 | | 17 | |
| 1936 | 17 | | 17 | |
| 1932 | 17 | | 17 | |
| 1928 | 18 | | 18 | |
| 1924 | 18 | 18 | | |
| 1920 | 18 | 18 | | |

# MASSACHUSETTS

# MASSACHUSETTS

## PRESIDENT 2004

| 2000 Census Population | County | Total Vote | Republican | Democratic | Other | Rep.-Dem. Plurality | Percentage | | | |
|---|---|---|---|---|---|---|---|---|---|---|
| | | | | | | | Total Vote | | Major Vote | |
| | | | | | | | Rep. | Dem. | Rep. | Dem. |
| 222,230 | BARNSTABLE | 132,148 | 58,527 | 72,156 | 1,465 | 13,629 D | 44.3% | 54.6% | 44.8% | 55.2% |
| 134,953 | BERKSHIRE | 65,291 | 16,806 | 47,743 | 742 | 30,937 D | 25.7% | 73.1% | 26.0% | 74.0% |
| 534,678 | BRISTOL | 232,878 | 82,524 | 147,854 | 2,500 | 65,330 D | 35.4% | 63.5% | 35.8% | 64.2% |
| 14,987 | DUKES | 9,997 | 2,602 | 7,265 | 130 | 4,663 D | 26.0% | 72.7% | 26.4% | 73.6% |
| 723,419 | ESSEX | 333,233 | 135,114 | 194,068 | 4,051 | 58,954 D | 40.5% | 58.2% | 41.0% | 59.0% |
| 71,535 | FRANKLIN | 37,381 | 11,058 | 25,550 | 773 | 14,492 D | 29.6% | 68.4% | 30.2% | 69.8% |
| 456,228 | HAMPDEN | 186,639 | 70,925 | 113,710 | 2,004 | 42,785 D | 38.0% | 60.9% | 38.4% | 61.6% |
| 152,251 | HAMPSHIRE | 74,422 | 21,315 | 51,680 | 1,427 | 30,365 D | 28.6% | 69.4% | 29.2% | 70.8% |
| 1,465,396 | MIDDLESEX | 688,960 | 237,815 | 440,862 | 10,283 | 203,047 D | 34.5% | 64.0% | 35.0% | 65.0% |
| 9,520 | NANTUCKET | 5,724 | 2,040 | 3,608 | 76 | 1,568 D | 35.6% | 63.0% | 36.1% | 63.9% |
| 650,308 | NORFOLK | 331,137 | 127,763 | 199,392 | 3,982 | 71,629 D | 38.6% | 60.2% | 39.1% | 60.9% |
| 472,822 | PLYMOUTH | 233,297 | 105,603 | 125,178 | 2,516 | 19,575 D | 45.3% | 53.7% | 45.8% | 54.2% |
| 689,807 | SUFFOLK | 240,645 | 54,923 | 182,592 | 3,130 | 127,669 D | 22.8% | 75.9% | 23.1% | 76.9% |
| 750,963 | WORCESTER | 340,636 | 144,094 | 192,142 | 4,400 | 48,048 D | 42.3% | 56.4% | 42.9% | 57.1% |
| 6,349,097 | TOTAL | 2,912,388 | 1,071,109 | 1,803,800 | 37,479 | 732,691 D | 36.8% | 61.9% | 37.3% | 62.7% |

# MASSACHUSETTS

## PRESIDENT 2000

| 2000 Census Population | County | Total Vote | Republican | Democratic | Green (Nader) | Other | Rep.-Dem. Plurality | Percentage of Total Vote | | |
|---|---|---|---|---|---|---|---|---|---|---|
| | | | | | | | | Rep. | Dem. | Green |
| 222,230 | BARNSTABLE | 121,086 | 49,686 | 62,363 | 7,976 | 1,061 | 12,677 D | 41.0% | 51.5% | 6.6% |
| 134,953 | BERKSHIRE | 59,411 | 15,805 | 37,934 | 4,472 | 1,200 | 22,129 D | 26.6% | 63.9% | 7.5% |
| 534,678 | BRISTOL | 211,337 | 62,848 | 136,325 | 9,554 | 2,610 | 73,477 D | 29.7% | 64.5% | 4.5% |
| 14,987 | DUKES | 8,856 | 2,315 | 5,474 | 983 | 84 | 3,159 D | 26.1% | 61.8% | 11.1% |
| 723,419 | ESSEX | 310,333 | 110,010 | 178,400 | 17,955 | 3,968 | 68,390 D | 35.4% | 57.5% | 5.8% |
| 71,535 | FRANKLIN | 33,366 | 10,176 | 17,945 | 4,627 | 618 | 7,769 D | 30.5% | 53.8% | 13.9% |
| 456,228 | HAMPDEN | 172,093 | 59,558 | 100,103 | 10,326 | 2,106 | 40,545 D | 34.6% | 58.2% | 6.0% |
| 152,251 | HAMPSHIRE | 68,626 | 19,202 | 38,543 | 10,010 | 871 | 19,341 D | 28.0% | 56.2% | 14.6% |
| 1,465,396 | MIDDLESEX | 657,048 | 198,914 | 404,043 | 45,529 | 8,562 | 205,129 D | 30.3% | 61.5% | 6.9% |
| 9,520 | NANTUCKET | 4,926 | 1,624 | 2,874 | 378 | 50 | 1,250 D | 33.0% | 58.3% | 7.7% |
| 650,308 | NORFOLK | 317,177 | 107,033 | 188,450 | 17,505 | 4,189 | 81,417 D | 33.7% | 59.4% | 5.5% |
| 472,822 | PLYMOUTH | 211,577 | 82,751 | 115,376 | 11,021 | 2,429 | 32,625 D | 39.1% | 54.5% | 5.2% |
| 689,807 | SUFFOLK | 217,000 | 44,441 | 154,888 | 15,051 | 2,620 | 110,447 D | 20.5% | 71.4% | 6.9% |
| 750,963 | WORCESTER | 310,148 | 114,139 | 173,769 | 18,177 | 4,063 | 59,630 D | 36.8% | 56.0% | 5.9% |
| 6,349,097 | TOTAL | 2,702,984 | 878,502 | 1,616,487 | 173,564 | 34,431 | 737,985 D | 32.5% | 59.8% | 6.4% |

# MASSACHUSETTS

## PRESIDENT 1996

| 1995 Census Pop. Est. | County | Total Vote | Republican | Democratic | Reform (Perot) | Other | Rep.-Dem. Plurality | Percentage of Total Vote | | |
|---|---|---|---|---|---|---|---|---|---|---|
| | | | | | | | | Rep. | Dem. | Reform |
| 199,804 | BARNSTABLE | 110,737 | 40,144 | 59,223 | 9,889 | 1,481 | 19,079 D | 36.3% | 53.5% | 8.9% |
| 135,743 | BERKSHIRE | 60,774 | 13,055 | 39,338 | 7,569 | 812 | 26,283 D | 21.5% | 64.7% | 12.5% |
| 512,637 | BRISTOL | 198,213 | 47,164 | 127,725 | 21,438 | 1,886 | 80,561 D | 23.8% | 64.4% | 10.8% |
| 12,808 | DUKES | 7,702 | 1,739 | 5,137 | 657 | 169 | 3,398 D | 22.6% | 66.7% | 8.5% |
| 683,723 | ESSEX | 291,442 | 89,120 | 171,021 | 27,068 | 4,233 | 81,901 D | 30.6% | 58.7% | 9.3% |
| 70,903 | FRANKLIN | 32,742 | 8,055 | 19,728 | 3,848 | 1,111 | 11,673 D | 24.6% | 60.3% | 11.8% |
| 443,463 | HAMPDEN | 172,239 | 48,513 | 105,050 | 16,942 | 1,734 | 56,537 D | 28.2% | 61.0% | 9.8% |
| 149,124 | HAMPSHIRE | 65,309 | 14,787 | 41,844 | 6,589 | 2,089 | 27,057 D | 22.6% | 64.1% | 10.1% |
| 1,408,450 | MIDDLESEX | 627,977 | 169,926 | 398,190 | 48,112 | 11,749 | 228,264 D | 27.1% | 63.4% | 7.7% |
| 7,153 | NANTUCKET | 4,159 | 1,222 | 2,453 | 400 | 84 | 1,231 D | 29.4% | 59.0% | 9.6% |
| 635,578 | NORFOLK | 300,471 | 92,982 | 180,504 | 22,949 | 4,036 | 87,522 D | 30.9% | 60.1% | 7.6% |
| 454,151 | PLYMOUTH | 194,011 | 64,626 | 106,072 | 20,808 | 2,505 | 41,446 D | 33.3% | 54.7% | 10.7% |
| 641,155 | SUFFOLK | 199,392 | 39,753 | 145,586 | 10,980 | 3,073 | 105,833 D | 19.9% | 73.0% | 5.5% |
| 718,858 | WORCESTER | 291,617 | 87,021 | 169,892 | 29,968 | 4,736 | 82,871 D | 29.8% | 58.3% | 10.3% |
| 6,073,550 | TOTAL | 2,556,785 | 718,107 | 1,571,763 | 227,217 | 39,698 | 853,656 D | 28.1% | 61.5% | 8.9% |

# MASSACHUSETTS

## PRESIDENT 1992

| 1990 Census Population | County | Total Vote | Republican | Democratic | Perot | Other | Plurality | Percentage Total Vote | | |
|---|---|---|---|---|---|---|---|---|---|---|
| | | | | | | | | Rep. | Dem. | Perot |
| 186,605 | BARNSTABLE | 108,997 | 33,916 | 46,641 | 27,727 | 713 | 12,725 D | 31.1% | 42.8% | 25.4% |
| 139,352 | BERKSHIRE | 67,746 | 14,726 | 36,857 | 15,799 | 364 | 21,058 D | 21.7% | 54.4% | 23.3% |
| 506,325 | BRISTOL | 211,754 | 52,370 | 102,406 | 55,845 | 1,133 | 46,561 D | 24.7% | 48.4% | 26.4% |
| 11,639 | DUKES | 7,888 | 1,827 | 4,292 | 1,714 | 55 | 2,465 D | 23.2% | 54.4% | 21.7% |
| 670,080 | ESSEX | 322,328 | 102,212 | 140,593 | 77,459 | 2,064 | 38,381 D | 31.7% | 43.6% | 24.0% |
| 70,092 | FRANKLIN | 35,827 | 8,691 | 17,246 | 9,596 | 294 | 7,650 D | 24.3% | 48.1% | 26.8% |
| 456,310 | HAMPDEN | 188,265 | 54,621 | 86,026 | 46,678 | 940 | 31,405 D | 29.0% | 45.7% | 24.8% |
| 146,568 | HAMPSHIRE | 70,071 | 15,694 | 37,879 | 15,705 | 793 | 22,174 D | 22.4% | 54.1% | 22.4% |
| 1,398,468 | MIDDLESEX | 689,453 | 193,703 | 343,994 | 146,831 | 4,925 | 150,291 D | 28.1% | 49.9% | 21.3% |
| 6,012 | NANTUCKET | 4,216 | 1,158 | 2,037 | 989 | 32 | 879 D | 27.5% | 48.3% | 23.5% |
| 616,087 | NORFOLK | 324,390 | 103,255 | 150,488 | 67,537 | 3,110 | 47,233 D | 31.8% | 46.4% | 20.8% |
| 435,276 | PLYMOUTH | 207,710 | 69,514 | 79,160 | 57,886 | 1,150 | 9,646 D | 33.5% | 38.1% | 27.9% |
| 663,906 | SUFFOLK | 219,273 | 51,378 | 132,921 | 32,914 | 2,060 | 81,543 D | 23.4% | 60.6% | 15.0% |
| 709,705 | WORCESTER | 315,782 | 101,984 | 138,122 | 74,051 | 1,625 | 36,138 D | 32.3% | 43.7% | 23.5% |
| 6,016,425 | TOTAL | 2,773,700 | 805,049 | 1,318,662 | 630,731 | 19,258 | 513,613 D | 29.0% | 47.5% | 22.7% |

# MASSACHUSETTS

## PRESIDENT 1988

| 1980 Census Population | County | Total Vote | Republican | Democratic | Other | Rep.-Dem. Plurality | Percentage Total Vote Rep. | Dem. | Major Vote Rep. | Dem. |
|---|---|---|---|---|---|---|---|---|---|---|
| 147,925 | BARNSTABLE | 99,872 | 49,676 | 48,747 | 1,449 | 929 R | 49.7% | 48.8% | 50.5% | 49.5% |
| 145,110 | BERKSHIRE | 62,859 | 24,116 | 38,217 | 526 | 14,101 D | 38.4% | 60.8% | 38.7% | 61.3% |
| 474,641 | BRISTOL | 193,530 | 83,797 | 107,854 | 1,879 | 24,057 D | 43.3% | 55.7% | 43.7% | 56.3% |
| 8,942 | DUKES | 7,025 | 2,441 | 4,495 | 89 | 2,054 D | 34.7% | 64.0% | 35.2% | 64.8% |
| 633,632 | ESSEX | 305,500 | 148,614 | 151,816 | 5,070 | 3,202 D | 48.6% | 49.7% | 49.5% | 50.5% |
| 64,317 | FRANKLIN | 33,123 | 13,475 | 19,310 | 338 | 5,835 D | 40.7% | 58.3% | 41.1% | 58.9% |
| 443,018 | HAMPDEN | 173,420 | 74,872 | 97,332 | 1,216 | 22,460 D | 43.2% | 56.1% | 43.5% | 56.5% |
| 138,813 | HAMPSHIRE | 64,915 | 24,331 | 39,834 | 750 | 15,503 D | 37.5% | 61.4% | 37.9% | 62.1% |
| 1,367,034 | MIDDLESEX | 662,628 | 290,352 | 361,563 | 10,713 | 71,211 D | 43.8% | 54.6% | 44.5% | 55.5% |
| 5,087 | NANTUCKET | 3,731 | 1,469 | 2,209 | 53 | 740 D | 39.4% | 59.2% | 39.9% | 60.1% |
| 606,587 | NORFOLK | 315,056 | 150,306 | 160,289 | 4,461 | 9,983 D | 47.7% | 50.9% | 48.4% | 51.6% |
| 405,437 | PLYMOUTH | 193,480 | 105,684 | 84,587 | 3,209 | 21,097 R | 54.6% | 43.7% | 55.5% | 44.5% |
| 650,142 | SUFFOLK | 224,410 | 77,137 | 143,677 | 3,596 | 66,540 D | 34.4% | 64.0% | 34.9% | 65.1% |
| 646,352 | WORCESTER | 293,256 | 148,365 | 141,485 | 3,406 | 6,880 R | 50.6% | 48.2% | 51.2% | 48.8% |
| 5,737,037 | TOTAL | 2,632,805 | 1,194,635 | 1,401,415 | 36,755 | 206,780 D | 45.4% | 53.2% | 46.0% | 54.0% |

# MASSACHUSETTS

## PRESIDENT 1984

| 1980 Census Population | County | Total Vote | Republican | Democratic | Other | Rep.-Dem. Plurality | Percentage Total Vote Rep. | Dem. | Major Vote Rep. | Dem. |
|---|---|---|---|---|---|---|---|---|---|---|
| 147,925 | BARNSTABLE | 89,951 | 51,261 | 38,369 | 321 | 12,892 R | 57.0% | 42.7% | 57.2% | 42.8% |
| 145,110 | BERKSHIRE | 63,785 | 33,712 | 29,745 | 328 | 3,967 R | 52.9% | 46.6% | 53.1% | 46.9% |
| 474,641 | BRISTOL | 188,039 | 93,232 | 94,010 | 797 | 778 D | 49.6% | 50.0% | 49.8% | 50.2% |
| 8,942 | DUKES | 6,125 | 2,788 | 3,313 | 24 | 525 D | 45.5% | 54.1% | 45.7% | 54.3% |
| 633,632 | ESSEX | 295,656 | 162,152 | 132,353 | 1,151 | 29,799 R | 54.8% | 44.8% | 55.1% | 44.9% |
| 64,317 | FRANKLIN | 31,533 | 15,883 | 15,502 | 148 | 381 R | 50.4% | 49.2% | 50.6% | 49.4% |
| 443,018 | HAMPDEN | 174,971 | 89,330 | 84,985 | 656 | 4,345 R | 51.1% | 48.6% | 51.2% | 48.8% |
| 138,813 | HAMPSHIRE | 63,942 | 28,111 | 35,597 | 234 | 7,486 D | 44.0% | 55.7% | 44.1% | 55.9% |
| 1,367,034 | MIDDLESEX | 646,754 | 319,604 | 325,065 | 2,085 | 5,461 D | 49.4% | 50.3% | 49.6% | 50.4% |
| 5,087 | NANTUCKET | 3,170 | 1,697 | 1,456 | 17 | 241 R | 53.5% | 45.9% | 53.8% | 46.2% |
| 606,587 | NORFOLK | 299,319 | 160,313 | 138,222 | 784 | 22,091 R | 53.6% | 46.2% | 53.7% | 46.3% |
| 405,437 | PLYMOUTH | 174,771 | 105,230 | 68,923 | 618 | 36,307 R | 60.2% | 39.4% | 60.4% | 39.6% |
| 650,142 | SUFFOLK | 244,997 | 91,563 | 152,568 | 866 | 61,005 D | 37.4% | 62.3% | 37.5% | 62.5% |
| 646,352 | WORCESTER | 276,440 | 156,060 | 119,498 | 882 | 36,562 R | 56.5% | 43.2% | 56.6% | 43.4% |
| 5,737,037 | TOTAL | 2,559,453 | 1,310,936 | 1,239,606 | 8,911 | 71,330 R | 51.2% | 48.4% | 51.4% | 48.6% |

# MASSACHUSETTS

## PRESIDENT 1980

| 1980 Census Population | County | Total Vote | Republican | Democratic | Other | Rep.-Dem. Plurality | Percentage | | | |
|---|---|---|---|---|---|---|---|---|---|---|
| | | | | | | | Total Vote | | Major Vote | |
| | | | | | | | Rep. | Dem. | Rep. | Dem. |
| 147,925 | BARNSTABLE | 82,273 | 41,493 | 23,952 | 16,828 | 17,541 R | 50.4% | 29.1% | 63.4% | 36.6% |
| 145,110 | BERKSHIRE | 68,031 | 27,063 | 29,458 | 11,510 | 2,395 D | 39.8% | 43.3% | 47.9% | 52.1% |
| 474,641 | BRISTOL | 188,605 | 77,545 | 83,460 | 27,600 | 5,915 D | 41.1% | 44.3% | 48.2% | 51.8% |
| 8,942 | DUKES | 5,397 | 1,809 | 2,370 | 1,218 | 561 D | 33.5% | 43.9% | 43.3% | 56.7% |
| 633,632 | ESSEX | 297,533 | 130,252 | 116,173 | 51,108 | 14,079 R | 43.8% | 39.0% | 52.9% | 47.1% |
| 64,317 | FRANKLIN | 30,122 | 12,528 | 11,830 | 5,764 | 698 R | 41.6% | 39.3% | 51.4% | 48.6% |
| 443,018 | HAMPDEN | 179,720 | 72,528 | 80,369 | 26,823 | 7,841 D | 40.4% | 44.7% | 47.4% | 52.6% |
| 138,813 | HAMPSHIRE | 60,355 | 21,117 | 27,611 | 11,627 | 6,494 D | 35.0% | 45.7% | 43.3% | 56.7% |
| 1,367,034 | MIDDLESEX | 637,679 | 256,999 | 270,751 | 109,929 | 13,752 D | 40.3% | 42.5% | 48.7% | 51.3% |
| 5,087 | NANTUCKET | 2,838 | 1,149 | 1,040 | 649 | 109 R | 40.5% | 36.6% | 52.5% | 47.5% |
| 606,587 | NORFOLK | 303,729 | 136,184 | 117,274 | 50,271 | 18,910 R | 44.8% | 38.6% | 53.7% | 46.3% |
| 405,437 | PLYMOUTH | 173,248 | 85,593 | 58,772 | 28,883 | 26,821 R | 49.4% | 33.9% | 59.3% | 40.7% |
| 650,142 | SUFFOLK | 216,207 | 73,271 | 113,416 | 29,520 | 40,145 D | 33.9% | 52.5% | 39.2% | 60.8% |
| 646,352 | WORCESTER | 278,561 | 120,100 | 117,326 | 41,135 | 2,774 R | 43.1% | 42.1% | 50.6% | 49.4% |
| 5,737,037 | TOTAL | 2,524,298 | 1,057,631 | 1,053,802 | 412,865 | 3,829 R | 41.9% | 41.7% | 50.1% | 49.9% |

# MASSACHUSETTS

## PRESIDENT 1976

| 1970 Census Population | County | Total Vote | Republican | Democratic | Other | Rep.-Dem. Plurality | Percentage | | | |
|---|---|---|---|---|---|---|---|---|---|---|
| | | | | | | | Total Vote | | Major Vote | |
| | | | | | | | Rep. | Dem. | Rep. | Dem. |
| 96,656 | BARNSTABLE | 73,117 | 39,295 | 31,268 | 2,554 | 8,027 R | 53.7% | 42.8% | 55.7% | 44.3% |
| 149,402 | BERKSHIRE | 68,871 | 27,462 | 39,337 | 2,072 | 11,875 D | 39.9% | 57.1% | 41.1% | 58.9% |
| 444,301 | BRISTOL | 191,771 | 69,957 | 116,318 | 5,496 | 46,361 D | 36.5% | 60.7% | 37.6% | 62.4% |
| 6,117 | DUKES | 5,135 | 2,365 | 2,513 | 257 | 148 D | 46.1% | 48.9% | 48.5% | 51.5% |
| 637,887 | ESSEX | 301,444 | 125,538 | 165,710 | 10,196 | 40,172 D | 41.6% | 55.0% | 43.1% | 56.9% |
| 59,210 | FRANKLIN | 31,181 | 14,837 | 14,985 | 1,359 | 148 D | 47.6% | 48.1% | 49.8% | 50.2% |
| 459,050 | HAMPDEN | 185,290 | 70,008 | 110,028 | 5,254 | 40,020 D | 37.8% | 59.4% | 38.9% | 61.1% |
| 123,981 | HAMPSHIRE | 60,075 | 22,219 | 34,947 | 2,909 | 12,728 D | 37.0% | 58.2% | 38.9% | 61.1% |
| 1,397,268 | MIDDLESEX | 643,382 | 260,044 | 359,919 | 23,419 | 99,875 D | 40.4% | 55.9% | 41.9% | 58.1% |
| 3,774 | NANTUCKET | 2,626 | 1,399 | 1,115 | 112 | 284 R | 53.3% | 42.5% | 55.6% | 44.4% |
| 605,051 | NORFOLK | 302,616 | 136,628 | 155,342 | 10,646 | 18,714 D | 45.1% | 51.3% | 46.8% | 53.2% |
| 333,314 | PLYMOUTH | 164,433 | 74,684 | 83,663 | 6,086 | 8,979 D | 45.4% | 50.9% | 47.2% | 52.8% |
| 735,190 | SUFFOLK | 232,372 | 80,623 | 142,010 | 9,739 | 61,387 D | 34.7% | 61.1% | 36.2% | 63.8% |
| 637,969 | WORCESTER | 285,245 | 105,217 | 172,320 | 7,708 | 67,103 D | 36.9% | 60.4% | 37.9% | 62.1% |
| 5,689,170 | TOTAL | 2,547,558 | 1,030,276 | 1,429,475 | 87,807 | 399,199 D | 40.4% | 56.1% | 41.9% | 58.1% |

# MASSACHUSETTS

## PRESIDENT 1972

| 1970 Census Population | County | Total Vote | Republican | Democratic | Other | Rep.-Dem. Plurality | Percentage | | | |
|---|---|---|---|---|---|---|---|---|---|---|
| | | | | | | | Total Vote | | Major Vote | |
| | | | | | | | Rep. | Dem. | Rep. | Dem. |
| 96,656 | BARNSTABLE | 59,442 | 36,340 | 22,636 | 466 | 13,704 R | 61.1% | 38.1% | 61.6% | 38.4% |
| 149,402 | BERKSHIRE | 66,284 | 30,380 | 35,391 | 513 | 5,011 D | 45.8% | 53.4% | 46.2% | 53.8% |
| 444,301 | BRISTOL | 188,768 | 84,390 | 103,163 | 1,215 | 18,773 D | 44.7% | 54.7% | 45.0% | 55.0% |
| 6,117 | DUKES | 4,336 | 2,312 | 2,001 | 23 | 311 R | 53.3% | 46.1% | 53.6% | 46.4% |
| 637,887 | ESSEX | 297,084 | 138,040 | 157,324 | 1,720 | 19,284 D | 46.5% | 53.0% | 46.7% | 53.3% |
| 59,210 | FRANKLIN | 28,263 | 16,088 | 11,968 | 207 | 4,120 R | 56.9% | 42.3% | 57.3% | 42.7% |
| 459,050 | HAMPDEN | 182,133 | 86,164 | 94,945 | 1,024 | 8,781 D | 47.3% | 52.1% | 47.6% | 52.4% |
| 123,981 | HAMPSHIRE | 53,654 | 24,529 | 28,572 | 553 | 4,043 D | 45.7% | 53.3% | 46.2% | 53.8% |
| 1,397,268 | MIDDLESEX | 617,651 | 269,064 | 345,343 | 3,244 | 76,279 D | 43.6% | 55.9% | 43.8% | 56.2% |
| 3,774 | NANTUCKET | 2,380 | 1,418 | 952 | 10 | 466 R | 59.6% | 40.0% | 59.8% | 40.2% |
| 605,051 | NORFOLK | 286,749 | 134,459 | 150,732 | 1,558 | 16,273 D | 46.9% | 52.6% | 47.1% | 52.9% |
| 333,314 | PLYMOUTH | 146,064 | 76,062 | 69,124 | 878 | 6,938 R | 52.1% | 47.3% | 52.4% | 47.6% |
| 735,190 | SUFFOLK | 252,821 | 85,272 | 166,250 | 1,299 | 80,978 D | 33.7% | 65.8% | 33.9% | 66.1% |
| 637,969 | WORCESTER | 273,127 | 127,560 | 144,139 | 1,428 | 16,579 D | 46.7% | 52.8% | 46.9% | 53.1% |
| 5,689,170 | TOTAL | 2,458,756 | 1,112,078 | 1,332,540 | 14,138 | 220,462 D | 45.2% | 54.2% | 45.5% | 54.5% |

# MASSACHUSETTS

## PRESIDENT 1968

| 1960 Census Population | County | Total Vote | Republican | Democratic | AIP | Other | Plurality | Percentage Total Vote | | |
|---|---|---|---|---|---|---|---|---|---|---|
| | | | | | | | | Rep. | Dem. | AIP |
| 70,286 | BARNSTABLE | 42,162 | 24,296 | 16,546 | 1,242 | 78 | 7,750 R | 57.6% | 39.2% | 2.9% |
| 142,135 | BERKSHIRE | 64,465 | 23,078 | 38,497 | 2,593 | 297 | 15,419 D | 35.8% | 59.7% | 4.0% |
| 398,488 | BRISTOL | 183,569 | 56,672 | 119,439 | 6,999 | 459 | 62,767 D | 30.9% | 65.1% | 3.8% |
| 5,829 | DUKES | 3,196 | 1,576 | 1,540 | 75 | 5 | 36 R | 49.3% | 48.2% | 2.3% |
| 568,831 | ESSEX | 281,685 | 99,721 | 171,901 | 9,236 | 827 | 72,180 D | 35.4% | 61.0% | 3.3% |
| 54,864 | FRANKLIN | 25,386 | 12,345 | 12,072 | 893 | 76 | 273 R | 48.6% | 47.6% | 3.5% |
| 429,353 | HAMPDEN | 178,150 | 55,783 | 111,376 | 9,846 | 1,145 | 55,593 D | 31.3% | 62.5% | 5.5% |
| 103,229 | HAMPSHIRE | 45,412 | 16,270 | 26,666 | 2,314 | 162 | 10,396 D | 35.8% | 58.7% | 5.1% |
| 1,238,742 | MIDDLESEX | 577,596 | 188,304 | 370,310 | 16,561 | 2,421 | 182,006 D | 32.6% | 64.1% | 2.9% |
| 3,559 | NANTUCKET | 1,792 | 991 | 744 | 52 | 5 | 247 R | 55.3% | 41.5% | 2.9% |
| 510,256 | NORFOLK | 266,206 | 95,858 | 160,513 | 9,080 | 755 | 64,655 D | 36.0% | 60.3% | 3.4% |
| 248,449 | PLYMOUTH | 127,977 | 54,644 | 67,771 | 5,342 | 220 | 13,127 D | 42.7% | 53.0% | 4.2% |
| 791,329 | SUFFOLK | 268,977 | 48,952 | 203,406 | 15,121 | 1,498 | 154,454 D | 18.2% | 75.6% | 5.6% |
| 583,228 | WORCESTER | 265,179 | 88,354 | 168,437 | 7,734 | 654 | 80,083 D | 33.3% | 63.5% | 2.9% |
| 5,148,578 | TOTAL | 2,331,752 | 766,844 | 1,469,218 | 87,088 | 8,602 | 702,374 D | 32.9% | 63.0% | 3.7% |

# MASSACHUSETTS

## PRESIDENT 1964

| | | | | | | | Percentage | | | |
| | | | | | | | Total Vote | | Major Vote | |
| 1960 Census Population | County | Total Vote | Republican | Democratic | Other | Rep.-Dem. Plurality | Rep. | Dem. | Rep. | Dem. |
|---|---|---|---|---|---|---|---|---|---|---|
| 70,286 | BARNSTABLE | 35,355 | 15,133 | 20,101 | 121 | 4,968 D | 42.8% | 56.9% | 42.9% | 57.1% |
| 142,135 | BERKSHIRE | 64,331 | 15,160 | 48,839 | 332 | 33,679 D | 23.6% | 75.9% | 23.7% | 76.3% |
| 398,488 | BRISTOL | 186,636 | 39,230 | 146,885 | 521 | 107,655 D | 21.0% | 78.7% | 21.1% | 78.9% |
| 5,829 | DUKES | 3,214 | 1,015 | 2,187 | 12 | 1,172 D | 31.6% | 68.0% | 31.7% | 68.3% |
| 568,831 | ESSEX | 282,945 | 71,653 | 210,135 | 1,157 | 138,482 D | 25.3% | 74.3% | 25.4% | 74.6% |
| 54,864 | FRANKLIN | 25,624 | 8,344 | 17,106 | 174 | 8,762 D | 32.6% | 66.8% | 32.8% | 67.2% |
| 429,353 | HAMPDEN | 178,219 | 44,299 | 133,085 | 835 | 88,786 D | 24.9% | 74.7% | 25.0% | 75.0% |
| 103,229 | HAMPSHIRE | 43,645 | 11,385 | 32,058 | 202 | 20,673 D | 26.1% | 73.5% | 26.2% | 73.8% |
| 1,238,742 | MIDDLESEX | 576,810 | 134,729 | 439,790 | 2,291 | 305,061 D | 23.4% | 76.2% | 23.5% | 76.5% |
| 3,559 | NANTUCKET | 1,787 | 587 | 1,197 | 3 | 610 D | 32.8% | 67.0% | 32.9% | 67.1% |
| 510,256 | NORFOLK | 256,012 | 68,612 | 186,488 | 912 | 117,876 D | 26.8% | 72.8% | 26.9% | 73.1% |
| 248,449 | PLYMOUTH | 120,335 | 37,941 | 82,007 | 387 | 44,066 D | 31.5% | 68.1% | 31.6% | 68.4% |
| 791,329 | SUFFOLK | 298,254 | 40,251 | 257,161 | 842 | 216,910 D | 13.5% | 86.2% | 13.5% | 86.5% |
| 583,228 | WORCESTER | 271,631 | 61,388 | 209,383 | 860 | 147,995 D | 22.6% | 77.1% | 22.7% | 77.3% |
| 5,148,578 | TOTAL | 2,344,798 | 549,727 | 1,786,422 | 8,649 | 1,236,695 D | 23.4% | 76.2% | 23.5% | 76.5% |

# MASSACHUSETTS

## PRESIDENT 1960

| | | | | | | | Percentage | | | |
| | | | | | | | Total Vote | | Major Vote | |
| 1960 Census Population | County | Total Vote | Republican | Democratic | Other | Rep.-Dem. Plurality | Rep. | Dem. | Rep. | Dem. |
|---|---|---|---|---|---|---|---|---|---|---|
| 70,286 | BARNSTABLE | 33,372 | 20,900 | 12,423 | 49 | 8,477 R | 62.6% | 37.2% | 62.7% | 37.3% |
| 142,135 | BERKSHIRE | 68,629 | 27,335 | 41,132 | 162 | 13,797 D | 39.8% | 59.9% | 39.9% | 60.1% |
| 398,488 | BRISTOL | 194,722 | 64,290 | 130,049 | 383 | 65,759 D | 33.0% | 66.8% | 33.1% | 66.9% |
| 5,829 | DUKES | 3,286 | 1,998 | 1,282 | 6 | 716 R | 60.8% | 39.0% | 60.9% | 39.1% |
| 568,831 | ESSEX | 295,081 | 126,599 | 167,875 | 607 | 41,276 D | 42.9% | 56.9% | 43.0% | 57.0% |
| 54,864 | FRANKLIN | 28,011 | 15,682 | 12,282 | 47 | 3,400 R | 56.0% | 43.8% | 56.1% | 43.9% |
| 429,353 | HAMPDEN | 193,828 | 72,054 | 121,061 | 713 | 49,007 D | 37.2% | 62.5% | 37.3% | 62.7% |
| 103,229 | HAMPSHIRE | 45,096 | 19,346 | 25,667 | 83 | 6,321 D | 42.9% | 56.9% | 43.0% | 57.0% |
| 1,238,742 | MIDDLESEX | 603,516 | 246,126 | 356,130 | 1,260 | 110,004 D | 40.8% | 59.0% | 40.9% | 59.1% |
| 3,559 | NANTUCKET | 1,919 | 1,219 | 698 | 2 | 521 R | 63.5% | 36.4% | 63.6% | 36.4% |
| 510,256 | NORFOLK | 257,721 | 121,744 | 135,474 | 503 | 13,730 D | 47.2% | 52.6% | 47.3% | 52.7% |
| 248,449 | PLYMOUTH | 118,349 | 60,977 | 57,175 | 197 | 3,802 R | 51.5% | 48.3% | 51.6% | 48.4% |
| 791,329 | SUFFOLK | 339,617 | 85,750 | 252,823 | 1,044 | 167,073 D | 25.2% | 74.4% | 25.3% | 74.7% |
| 583,228 | WORCESTER | 286,333 | 112,730 | 173,103 | 500 | 60,373 D | 39.4% | 60.5% | 39.4% | 60.6% |
| 5,148,578 | TOTAL | 2,469,480 | 976,750 | 1,487,174 | 5,556 | 510,424 D | 39.6% | 60.2% | 39.6% | 60.4% |

# MASSACHUSETTS

## ELECTION NOTES

**2004**    Other vote was 15,022 Libertarian (Michael Badnarik); 10,623 Green-Rainbow (David Cobb); 4,806 write-in (Ralph Nader); 7,028 scattered write-in.

**2000**    Other vote was 16,366 Libertarian (Browne); 11,149 Reform (Buchanan); 2,884 Independent (Hagelin); 42 write-in (McReynolds); 3,990 scattered write-in.

**1996**    Other vote was 20,426 Libertarian (Browne); 5,184 Natural Law (Hagelin); 4,565 write-in (Nader); 3,277 Workers World (Moorehead); 6,246 scattered write-in.

**1992**    Other vote was 9,024 Marrou (Libertarian); 3,172 Fulani (New Alliance); 2,218 Phillips (Independent Voters); 1,812 Hagelin (Natural Law); 1,027 LaRouche (LaRouche for President); 13 Brisben (write-in); 2 Dodge (write-in); 1,990 scattered write-in. The data presented in the table are from Public Document 43, "Massachusetts Elections 1992" which vary slightly from earlier returns.

**1988**    Other vote was 24,251 Paul (Libertarian); 9,561 Fulani (New Alliance); 18 Dodge (write-in); 15 Kenoyer (write-in); 2,910 scattered write-in.

**1984**    Other vote was 7,998 Serrette (Independent Alliance); 18 Johnson (write-in); 3 Dodge (write-in); 892 scattered write-in.

**1980**    Other vote was 382,539 Anderson (Anderson Coalition); 22,038 Clark (Libertarian); 3,735 DeBerry (Socialist Workers); 2,056 Commoner (write-in); 62 McReynolds (write-in); 34 Bubar (write-in); 19 Griswold (write-in); 2,382 scattered write-in. Early unamended canvass gave the Republican state-wide total vote as 1,056,223 and the Socialist Workers state-wide total vote as 5,143.

**1976**    Other vote was 65,637 McCarthy (Independent); 8,138 Camejo (Socialist Workers); 7,555 Anderson (American); 4,922 LaRouche (U.S. Labor); 135 MacBride (write-in); 33 Wright (write-in); 19 Levin (write-in); 14 Bubar (write-in); 1,354 scattered write-in.

**1972**    Other vote was 10,600 Jenness (Socialist Workers); 2,877 Schmitz (write-in); 129 Fisher (write-in); 101 Spock (write-in); 46 Hall (write-in); 43 Hospers (write-in); 342 scattered write-in.

**1968**    Wallace on the ballot as Independent. Other vote was 6,180 Blomen (Socialist Labor); 2,369 Munn (Prohibition); 53 scattered write-in.

**1964**    Other vote was 4,755 Hass (Socialist Labor); 3,735 Munn (Prohibition); 159 scattered write-in.

**1960**    Other vote was 3,892 Hass (Socialist Labor); 1,633 Decker (Prohibition); 31 scattered.

# MICHIGAN

## POPULAR VOTE FOR PRESIDENT 1920 TO 2004

| Year | Total Vote | Republican | | Democratic | | Other Vote | Plurality | Percentage | | | |
|------|-----------|------|-----------|------|-----------|------|-----------|------------|------|-----------|------|
| | | | | | | | | Total Vote | | Major Vote | |
| | | Vote | Candidate | Vote | Candidate | | | Rep. | Dem. | Rep. | Dem. |
| 2004 | 4,839,252 | 2,313,746 | Bush, George W. | 2,479,183 | Kerry, John | 46,323 | 165,437 D | 47.8% | 51.2% | 48.3% | 51.7% |
| 2000 ** | 4,232,711 | 1,953,139 | Bush, George W. | 2,170,418 | Gore, Al | 109,154 | 217,279 D | 46.1% | 51.3% | 47.4% | 52.6% |
| 1996 ** | 3,848,844 | 1,481,212 | Dole, Bob | 1,989,653 | Clinton, Bill | 377,979 | 508,441 D | 38.5% | 51.7% | 42.7% | 57.3% |
| 1992 ** | 4,274,673 | 1,554,940 | Bush, George | 1,871,182 | Clinton, Bill | 848,551 | 316,242 D | 36.4% | 43.8% | 45.4% | 54.6% |
| 1988 | 3,669,163 | 1,965,486 | Bush, George | 1,675,783 | Dukakis, Michael S. | 27,894 | 289,703 R | 53.6% | 45.7% | 54.0% | 46.0% |
| 1984 | 3,801,658 | 2,251,571 | Reagan, Ronald | 1,529,638 | Mondale, Walter F. | 20,449 | 721,933 R | 59.2% | 40.2% | 59.5% | 40.5% |
| 1980 ** | 3,909,725 | 1,915,225 | Reagan, Ronald | 1,661,532 | Carter, Jimmy | 332,968 | 253,693 R | 49.0% | 42.5% | 53.5% | 46.5% |
| 1976 | 3,653,749 | 1,893,742 | Ford, Gerald R. | 1,696,714 | Carter, Jimmy | 63,293 | 197,028 R | 51.8% | 46.4% | 52.7% | 47.3% |
| 1972 | 3,489,727 | 1,961,721 | Nixon, Richard M. | 1,459,435 | McGovern, George S. | 68,571 | 502,286 R | 56.2% | 41.8% | 57.3% | 42.7% |
| 1968 | 3,306,250 | 1,370,665 | Nixon, Richard M. | 1,593,082 | Humphrey, Hubert H. | 342,503 | 222,417 D | 41.5% | 48.2% | 46.2% | 53.8% |
| 1964 | 3,203,102 | 1,060,152 | Goldwater, Barry M. | 2,136,615 | Johnson, Lyndon B. | 6,335 | 1,076,463 D | 33.1% | 66.7% | 33.2% | 66.8% |
| 1960 | 3,318,097 | 1,620,428 | Nixon, Richard M. | 1,687,269 | Kennedy, John F. | 10,400 | 66,841 D | 48.8% | 50.9% | 49.0% | 51.0% |
| 1956 | 3,080,468 | 1,713,647 | Eisenhower, Dwight D. | 1,359,898 | Stevenson, Adlai E. | 6,923 | 353,749 R | 55.6% | 44.1% | 55.8% | 44.2% |
| 1952 | 2,798,592 | 1,551,529 | Eisenhower, Dwight D. | 1,230,657 | Stevenson, Adlai E. | 16,406 | 320,872 R | 55.4% | 44.0% | 55.8% | 44.2% |
| 1948 | 2,109,609 | 1,038,595 | Dewey, Thomas E. | 1,003,448 | Truman, Harry S. | 67,566 | 35,147 R | 49.2% | 47.6% | 50.9% | 49.1% |
| 1944 | 2,205,223 | 1,084,423 | Dewey, Thomas E. | 1,106,899 | Roosevelt, Franklin D. | 13,901 | 22,476 D | 49.2% | 50.2% | 49.5% | 50.5% |
| 1940 | 2,085,929 | 1,039,917 | Willkie, Wendell | 1,032,991 | Roosevelt, Franklin D. | 13,021 | 6,926 R | 49.9% | 49.5% | 50.2% | 49.8% |
| 1936 | 1,805,098 | 699,733 | Landon, Alfred M. | 1,016,794 | Roosevelt, Franklin D. | 88,571 | 317,061 D | 38.8% | 56.3% | 40.8% | 59.2% |
| 1932 | 1,664,765 | 739,894 | Hoover, Herbert C. | 871,700 | Roosevelt, Franklin D. | 53,171 | 131,806 D | 44.4% | 52.4% | 45.9% | 54.1% |
| 1928 | 1,372,082 | 965,396 | Hoover, Herbert C. | 396,762 | Smith, Alfred E. | 9,924 | 568,634 R | 70.4% | 28.9% | 70.9% | 29.1% |
| 1924 ** | 1,160,419 | 874,631 | Coolidge, Calvin | 152,359 | Davis, John W. | 133,429 | 722,272 R | 75.4% | 13.1% | 85.2% | 14.8% |
| 1920 | 1,048,411 | 762,865 | Harding, Warren G. | 233,450 | Cox, James M. | 52,096 | 529,415 R | 72.8% | 22.3% | 76.6% | 23.4% |

In 2000 the other vote column includes 84,165 votes cast for Green (Nader). In 1996 the other vote column includes 336,670 votes cast for Perot. In 1992 the other vote column includes 824,813 votes cast for Perot. In 1980 the other column includes 275,223 votes for Independent (Anderson). In 1924 the other vote was 122,014 Progressive; 6,085 Prohibition; and 5,330 Socialist Labor.

## ELECTORAL COLLEGE VOTE 1920 TO 2004

| Year | Total | Republican | Democratic | Other |
|------|-------|-----------|-----------|-------|
| 2004 | 17 | | 17 | |
| 2000 | 18 | | 18 | |
| 1996 | 18 | | 18 | |
| 1992 | 18 | | 18 | |
| 1988 | 20 | 20 | | |
| 1984 | 20 | 20 | | |
| 1980 | 21 | 21 | | |
| 1976 | 21 | 21 | | |
| 1972 | 21 | 21 | | |
| 1968 | 21 | | 21 | |
| 1964 | 21 | | 21 | |
| 1960 | 20 | | 20 | |
| 1956 | 20 | 20 | | |
| 1952 | 20 | 20 | | |
| 1948 | 19 | 19 | | |
| 1944 | 19 | | 19 | |
| 1940 | 19 | 19 | | |
| 1936 | 19 | | 19 | |
| 1932 | 19 | | 19 | |
| 1928 | 15 | 15 | | |
| 1924 | 15 | 15 | | |
| 1920 | 15 | 15 | | |

# MICHIGAN

# MICHIGAN

## PRESIDENT 2004

| 2000 Census Population | County | Total Vote | Republican | Democratic | Other | Rep.-Dem. Plurality | Percentage Total Vote Rep. | Dem. | Major Vote Rep. | Dem. |
|---|---|---|---|---|---|---|---|---|---|---|
| 11,719 | ALCONA | 6,531 | 3,592 | 2,871 | 68 | 721 R | 55.0% | 44.0% | 55.6% | 44.4% |
| 9,862 | ALGER | 4,765 | 2,318 | 2,395 | 52 | 77 D | 48.6% | 50.3% | 49.2% | 50.8% |
| 105,665 | ALLEGAN | 53,907 | 34,022 | 19,355 | 530 | 14,667 R | 63.1% | 35.9% | 63.7% | 36.3% |
| 31,314 | ALPENA | 15,211 | 7,665 | 7,407 | 139 | 258 R | 50.4% | 48.7% | 50.9% | 49.1% |
| 23,110 | ANTRIM | 13,619 | 8,379 | 5,072 | 168 | 3,307 R | 61.5% | 37.2% | 62.3% | 37.7% |
| 17,269 | ARENAC | 8,216 | 4,071 | 4,076 | 69 | 5 D | 49.5% | 49.6% | 50.0% | 50.0% |
| 8,746 | BARAGA | 3,684 | 1,977 | 1,660 | 47 | 317 R | 53.7% | 45.1% | 54.4% | 45.6% |
| 56,755 | BARRY | 30,272 | 18,638 | 11,312 | 322 | 7,326 R | 61.6% | 37.4% | 62.2% | 37.8% |
| 110,157 | BAY | 57,059 | 25,448 | 31,049 | 562 | 5,601 D | 44.6% | 54.4% | 45.0% | 55.0% |
| 15,998 | BENZIE | 9,778 | 5,284 | 4,383 | 111 | 901 R | 54.0% | 44.8% | 54.7% | 45.3% |
| 162,453 | BERRIEN | 74,671 | 41,076 | 32,846 | 749 | 8,230 R | 55.0% | 44.0% | 55.6% | 44.4% |
| 45,787 | BRANCH | 17,967 | 10,784 | 7,004 | 179 | 3,780 R | 60.0% | 39.0% | 60.6% | 39.4% |
| 137,985 | CALHOUN | 62,667 | 32,093 | 29,891 | 683 | 2,202 R | 51.2% | 47.7% | 51.8% | 48.2% |
| 51,104 | CASS | 22,697 | 12,964 | 9,537 | 196 | 3,427 R | 57.1% | 42.0% | 57.6% | 42.4% |
| 26,090 | CHARLEVOIX | 14,139 | 8,214 | 5,729 | 196 | 2,485 R | 58.1% | 40.5% | 58.9% | 41.1% |
| 26,448 | CHEBOYGAN | 13,887 | 7,798 | 5,941 | 148 | 1,857 R | 56.2% | 42.8% | 56.8% | 43.2% |
| 38,543 | CHIPPEWA | 16,488 | 9,122 | 7,203 | 163 | 1,919 R | 55.3% | 43.7% | 55.9% | 44.1% |
| 31,252 | CLARE | 14,226 | 7,088 | 6,984 | 154 | 104 R | 49.8% | 49.1% | 50.4% | 49.6% |
| 64,753 | CLINTON | 37,807 | 21,989 | 15,483 | 335 | 6,506 R | 58.2% | 41.0% | 58.7% | 41.3% |
| 14,273 | CRAWFORD | 7,235 | 4,017 | 3,126 | 92 | 891 R | 55.5% | 43.2% | 56.2% | 43.8% |
| 38,520 | DELTA | 19,238 | 9,680 | 9,381 | 177 | 299 R | 50.3% | 48.8% | 50.8% | 49.2% |
| 27,472 | DICKINSON | 13,549 | 7,734 | 5,650 | 165 | 2,084 R | 57.1% | 41.7% | 57.8% | 42.2% |
| 103,655 | EATON | 55,755 | 29,781 | 25,411 | 563 | 4,370 R | 53.4% | 45.6% | 54.0% | 46.0% |
| 31,437 | EMMET | 17,372 | 10,332 | 6,846 | 194 | 3,486 R | 59.5% | 39.4% | 60.1% | 39.9% |
| 436,141 | GENESEE | 213,775 | 83,870 | 128,334 | 1,571 | 44,464 D | 39.2% | 60.0% | 39.5% | 60.5% |
| 26,023 | GLADWIN | 13,227 | 6,770 | 6,343 | 114 | 427 R | 51.2% | 48.0% | 51.6% | 48.4% |
| 17,370 | GOGEBIC | 8,452 | 3,935 | 4,421 | 96 | 486 D | 46.6% | 52.3% | 47.1% | 52.9% |
| 77,654 | GRAND TRAVERSE | 46,191 | 27,446 | 18,256 | 489 | 9,190 R | 59.4% | 39.5% | 60.1% | 39.9% |
| 42,285 | GRATIOT | 17,379 | 9,834 | 7,377 | 168 | 2,457 R | 56.6% | 42.4% | 57.1% | 42.9% |
| 46,527 | HILLSDALE | 20,216 | 12,804 | 7,123 | 289 | 5,681 R | 63.3% | 35.2% | 64.3% | 35.7% |
| 36,016 | HOUGHTON | 15,851 | 8,889 | 6,731 | 231 | 2,158 R | 56.1% | 42.5% | 56.9% | 43.1% |
| 36,079 | HURON | 17,466 | 9,671 | 7,629 | 166 | 2,042 R | 55.4% | 43.7% | 55.9% | 44.1% |
| 279,320 | INGHAM | 133,053 | 54,734 | 76,877 | 1,442 | 22,143 D | 41.1% | 57.8% | 41.6% | 58.4% |
| 61,518 | IONIA | 27,618 | 16,621 | 10,647 | 350 | 5,974 R | 60.2% | 38.6% | 61.0% | 39.0% |
| 27,339 | IOSCO | 14,006 | 7,301 | 6,557 | 148 | 744 R | 52.1% | 46.8% | 52.7% | 47.3% |
| 13,138 | IRON | 6,511 | 3,224 | 3,215 | 72 | 9 R | 49.5% | 49.4% | 50.1% | 49.9% |
| 63,351 | ISABELLA | 24,390 | 11,754 | 12,334 | 302 | 580 D | 48.2% | 50.6% | 48.8% | 51.2% |
| 158,422 | JACKSON | 71,795 | 40,029 | 31,025 | 741 | 9,004 R | 55.8% | 43.2% | 56.3% | 43.7% |
| 238,603 | KALAMAZOO | 119,783 | 57,147 | 61,462 | 1,174 | 4,315 D | 47.7% | 51.3% | 48.2% | 51.8% |
| 16,571 | KALKASKA | 8,380 | 5,084 | 3,189 | 107 | 1,895 R | 60.7% | 38.1% | 61.5% | 38.5% |
| 574,335 | KENT | 290,891 | 171,201 | 116,909 | 2,781 | 54,292 R | 58.9% | 40.2% | 59.4% | 40.6% |
| 2,301 | KEWEENAW | 1,439 | 781 | 630 | 28 | 151 R | 54.3% | 43.8% | 55.4% | 44.6% |
| 11,333 | LAKE | 5,246 | 2,503 | 2,675 | 68 | 172 D | 47.7% | 51.0% | 48.3% | 51.7% |
| 87,904 | LAPEER | 44,147 | 25,556 | 18,086 | 505 | 7,470 R | 57.9% | 41.0% | 58.6% | 41.4% |
| 21,119 | LEELANAU | 13,917 | 7,733 | 6,048 | 136 | 1,685 R | 55.6% | 43.5% | 56.1% | 43.9% |
| 98,890 | LENAWEE | 47,012 | 25,675 | 20,787 | 550 | 4,888 R | 54.6% | 44.2% | 55.3% | 44.7% |
| 156,951 | LIVINGSTON | 93,742 | 58,860 | 33,991 | 891 | 24,869 R | 62.8% | 36.3% | 63.4% | 36.6% |
| 7,024 | LUCE | 2,829 | 1,749 | 1,045 | 35 | 704 R | 61.8% | 36.9% | 62.6% | 37.4% |
| 11,943 | MACKINAC | 6,599 | 3,706 | 2,819 | 74 | 887 R | 56.2% | 42.7% | 56.8% | 43.2% |
| 788,149 | MACOMB | 402,410 | 202,166 | 196,160 | 4,084 | 6,006 R | 50.2% | 48.7% | 50.8% | 49.2% |
| 24,527 | MANISTEE | 12,740 | 6,295 | 6,272 | 173 | 23 R | 49.4% | 49.2% | 50.1% | 49.9% |
| 64,634 | MARQUETTE | 32,488 | 14,690 | 17,412 | 386 | 2,722 D | 45.2% | 53.6% | 45.8% | 54.2% |
| 28,274 | MASON | 14,611 | 8,124 | 6,333 | 154 | 1,791 R | 55.6% | 43.3% | 56.2% | 43.8% |
| 40,553 | MECOSTA | 17,581 | 9,710 | 7,730 | 141 | 1,980 R | 55.2% | 44.0% | 55.7% | 44.3% |
| 25,326 | MENOMINEE | 11,419 | 5,942 | 5,326 | 151 | 616 R | 52.0% | 46.6% | 52.7% | 47.3% |
| 82,874 | MIDLAND | 43,275 | 24,369 | 18,355 | 551 | 6,014 R | 56.3% | 42.4% | 57.0% | 43.0% |
| 14,478 | MISSAUKEE | 7,421 | 5,055 | 2,319 | 47 | 2,736 R | 68.1% | 31.2% | 68.6% | 31.4% |
| 145,945 | MONROE | 74,132 | 37,470 | 36,089 | 573 | 1,381 R | 50.5% | 48.7% | 50.9% | 49.1% |
| 61,266 | MONTCALM | 26,734 | 14,968 | 11,471 | 295 | 3,497 R | 56.0% | 42.9% | 56.6% | 43.4% |
| 10,315 | MONTMORENCY | 5,563 | 3,300 | 2,196 | 67 | 1,104 R | 59.3% | 39.5% | 60.0% | 40.0% |

# MICHIGAN

## PRESIDENT 2004

| 2000 Census Population | County | Total Vote | Republican | Democratic | Other | Rep.-Dem. Plurality | Percentage | | | |
|---|---|---|---|---|---|---|---|---|---|---|
| | | | | | | | Total Vote | | Major Vote | |
| | | | | | | | Rep. | Dem. | Rep. | Dem. |
| 170,200 | MUSKEGON | 80,313 | 35,302 | 44,282 | 729 | 8,980 D | 44.0% | 55.1% | 44.4% | 55.6% |
| 47,874 | NEWAYGO | 22,873 | 13,608 | 9,057 | 208 | 4,551 R | 59.5% | 39.6% | 60.0% | 40.0% |
| 1,194,156 | OAKLAND | 641,977 | 316,633 | 319,387 | 5,957 | 2,754 D | 49.3% | 49.8% | 49.8% | 50.2% |
| 26,873 | OCEANA | 12,297 | 6,677 | 5,441 | 179 | 1,236 R | 54.3% | 44.2% | 55.1% | 44.9% |
| 21,645 | OGEMAW | 10,796 | 5,454 | 5,215 | 127 | 239 R | 50.5% | 48.3% | 51.1% | 48.9% |
| 7,818 | ONTONAGON | 4,192 | 2,262 | 1,863 | 67 | 399 R | 54.0% | 44.4% | 54.8% | 45.2% |
| 23,197 | OSCEOLA | 11,188 | 6,599 | 4,467 | 122 | 2,132 R | 59.0% | 39.9% | 59.6% | 40.4% |
| 9,418 | OSCODA | 4,409 | 2,570 | 1,792 | 47 | 778 R | 58.3% | 40.6% | 58.9% | 41.1% |
| 23,301 | OTSEGO | 12,307 | 7,470 | 4,674 | 163 | 2,796 R | 60.7% | 38.0% | 61.5% | 38.5% |
| 238,314 | OTTAWA | 128,643 | 92,048 | 35,552 | 1,043 | 56,496 R | 71.6% | 27.6% | 72.1% | 27.9% |
| 14,411 | PRESQUE ISLE | 7,516 | 3,982 | 3,432 | 102 | 550 R | 53.0% | 45.7% | 53.7% | 46.3% |
| 25,469 | ROSCOMMON | 14,359 | 7,364 | 6,810 | 185 | 554 R | 51.3% | 47.4% | 52.0% | 48.0% |
| 210,039 | SAGINAW | 102,852 | 47,165 | 54,887 | 800 | 7,722 D | 45.9% | 53.4% | 46.2% | 53.8% |
| 164,235 | ST. CLAIR | 79,743 | 42,740 | 36,174 | 829 | 6,566 R | 53.6% | 45.4% | 54.2% | 45.8% |
| 62,422 | ST. JOSEPH | 25,239 | 15,340 | 9,648 | 251 | 5,692 R | 60.8% | 38.2% | 61.4% | 38.6% |
| 44,547 | SANILAC | 20,763 | 12,632 | 7,883 | 248 | 4,749 R | 60.8% | 38.0% | 61.6% | 38.4% |
| 8,903 | SCHOOLCRAFT | 4,441 | 2,267 | 2,137 | 37 | 130 R | 51.0% | 48.1% | 51.5% | 48.5% |
| 71,687 | SHIAWASSEE | 36,651 | 19,407 | 16,881 | 363 | 2,526 R | 53.0% | 46.1% | 53.5% | 46.5% |
| 58,266 | TUSCOLA | 28,338 | 15,389 | 12,631 | 318 | 2,758 R | 54.3% | 44.6% | 54.9% | 45.1% |
| 76,263 | VAN BUREN | 34,174 | 17,634 | 16,151 | 389 | 1,483 R | 51.6% | 47.3% | 52.2% | 47.8% |
| 322,895 | WASHTENAW | 173,264 | 61,455 | 109,953 | 1,856 | 48,498 D | 35.5% | 63.5% | 35.9% | 64.1% |
| 2,061,162 | WAYNE | 864,728 | 257,750 | 600,047 | 6,931 | 342,297 D | 29.8% | 69.4% | 30.0% | 70.0% |
| 30,484 | WEXFORD | 15,160 | 8,966 | 6,034 | 160 | 2,932 R | 59.1% | 39.8% | 59.8% | 40.2% |
| 9,938,444 | TOTAL | 4,839,252 | 2,313,746 | 2,479,183 | 46,323 | 165,437 D | 47.8% | 51.2% | 48.3% | 51.7% |

# MICHIGAN

## PRESIDENT 2000

| 2000 Census Population | County | Total Vote | Republican | Democratic | Green (Nader) | Other | Rep.-Dem. Plurality | Percentage of Total Vote Rep. | Dem. | Green |
|---|---|---|---|---|---|---|---|---|---|---|
| 11,719 | ALCONA | 5,997 | 3,152 | 2,696 | 124 | 25 | 456 R | 52.6% | 45.0% | 2.1% |
| 9,862 | ALGER | 4,366 | 2,142 | 2,071 | 126 | 27 | 71 R | 49.1% | 47.4% | 2.9% |
| 105,665 | ALLEGAN | 44,891 | 28,197 | 15,495 | 930 | 269 | 12,702 R | 62.8% | 34.5% | 2.1% |
| 31,314 | ALPENA | 14,132 | 6,769 | 7,053 | 262 | 48 | 284 D | 47.9% | 49.9% | 1.9% |
| 23,110 | ANTRIM | 11,507 | 6,780 | 4,329 | 312 | 86 | 2,451 R | 58.9% | 37.6% | 2.7% |
| 17,269 | ARENAC | 7,267 | 3,421 | 3,685 | 117 | 44 | 264 D | 47.1% | 50.7% | 1.6% |
| 8,746 | BARAGA | 3,393 | 1,836 | 1,400 | 141 | 16 | 436 R | 54.1% | 41.3% | 4.2% |
| 56,755 | BARRY | 26,244 | 15,716 | 9,769 | 612 | 147 | 5,947 R | 59.9% | 37.2% | 2.3% |
| 110,157 | BAY | 51,636 | 22,150 | 28,251 | 972 | 263 | 6,101 D | 42.9% | 54.7% | 1.9% |
| 15,998 | BENZIE | 8,072 | 4,172 | 3,546 | 312 | 42 | 626 R | 51.7% | 43.9% | 3.9% |
| 162,453 | BERRIEN | 65,241 | 35,689 | 28,152 | 1,154 | 246 | 7,537 R | 54.7% | 43.2% | 1.8% |
| 45,787 | BRANCH | 15,783 | 8,743 | 6,691 | 279 | 70 | 2,052 R | 55.4% | 42.4% | 1.8% |
| 137,985 | CALHOUN | 55,080 | 26,291 | 27,312 | 1,176 | 301 | 1,021 D | 47.7% | 49.6% | 2.1% |
| 51,104 | CASS | 19,825 | 10,545 | 8,808 | 371 | 101 | 1,737 R | 53.2% | 44.4% | 1.9% |
| 26,090 | CHARLEVOIX | 12,487 | 7,018 | 4,958 | 424 | 87 | 2,060 R | 56.2% | 39.7% | 3.4% |
| 26,448 | CHEBOYGAN | 12,617 | 6,815 | 5,484 | 257 | 61 | 1,331 R | 54.0% | 43.5% | 2.0% |
| 38,543 | CHIPPEWA | 14,354 | 7,526 | 6,370 | 361 | 97 | 1,156 R | 52.4% | 44.4% | 2.5% |
| 31,252 | CLARE | 12,607 | 5,937 | 6,287 | 262 | 121 | 350 D | 47.1% | 49.9% | 2.1% |
| 64,753 | CLINTON | 32,199 | 18,054 | 13,394 | 602 | 149 | 4,660 R | 56.1% | 41.6% | 1.9% |
| 14,273 | CRAWFORD | 6,364 | 3,345 | 2,790 | 176 | 53 | 555 R | 52.6% | 43.8% | 2.8% |
| 38,520 | DELTA | 17,316 | 8,871 | 7,970 | 390 | 85 | 901 R | 51.2% | 46.0% | 2.3% |
| 27,472 | DICKINSON | 12,832 | 6,932 | 5,533 | 301 | 66 | 1,399 R | 54.0% | 43.1% | 2.3% |
| 103,655 | EATON | 49,272 | 24,803 | 23,211 | 989 | 269 | 1,592 R | 50.3% | 47.1% | 2.0% |
| 31,437 | EMMET | 14,711 | 8,602 | 5,451 | 534 | 124 | 3,151 R | 58.5% | 37.1% | 3.6% |
| 436,141 | GENESEE | 190,865 | 66,641 | 119,833 | 3,623 | 768 | 53,192 D | 34.9% | 62.8% | 1.9% |
| 26,023 | GLADWIN | 11,629 | 5,743 | 5,573 | 227 | 86 | 170 R | 49.4% | 47.9% | 2.0% |
| 17,370 | GOGEBIC | 8,339 | 3,929 | 4,066 | 285 | 59 | 137 D | 47.1% | 48.8% | 3.4% |
| 77,654 | GRAND TRAVERSE | 38,229 | 22,358 | 14,371 | 1,263 | 237 | 7,987 R | 58.5% | 37.6% | 3.3% |
| 42,285 | GRATIOT | 15,179 | 8,312 | 6,538 | 265 | 64 | 1,774 R | 54.8% | 43.1% | 1.7% |
| 46,527 | HILLSDALE | 17,473 | 10,483 | 6,495 | 363 | 132 | 3,988 R | 60.0% | 37.2% | 2.1% |
| 36,016 | HOUGHTON | 14,216 | 7,895 | 5,688 | 518 | 115 | 2,207 R | 55.5% | 40.0% | 3.6% |
| 36,079 | HURON | 16,095 | 8,911 | 6,899 | 230 | 55 | 2,012 R | 55.4% | 42.9% | 1.4% |
| 279,320 | INGHAM | 120,595 | 47,314 | 69,231 | 3,290 | 760 | 21,917 D | 39.2% | 57.4% | 2.7% |
| 61,518 | IONIA | 23,970 | 13,915 | 9,481 | 423 | 151 | 4,434 R | 58.1% | 39.6% | 1.8% |
| 27,339 | IOSCO | 13,222 | 6,345 | 6,505 | 308 | 64 | 160 D | 48.0% | 49.2% | 2.3% |
| 13,138 | IRON | 6,188 | 2,967 | 3,014 | 160 | 47 | 47 D | 47.9% | 48.7% | 2.6% |
| 63,351 | ISABELLA | 21,069 | 10,053 | 10,228 | 666 | 122 | 175 D | 47.7% | 48.5% | 3.2% |
| 158,422 | JACKSON | 61,946 | 32,066 | 28,160 | 1,329 | 391 | 3,906 R | 51.8% | 45.5% | 2.1% |
| 238,603 | KALAMAZOO | 100,656 | 48,254 | 48,807 | 3,086 | 509 | 553 D | 47.9% | 48.5% | 3.1% |
| 16,571 | KALKASKA | 6,849 | 3,842 | 2,774 | 173 | 60 | 1,068 R | 56.1% | 40.5% | 2.5% |
| 574,335 | KENT | 250,318 | 148,602 | 95,442 | 5,019 | 1,255 | 53,160 R | 59.4% | 38.1% | 2.0% |
| 2,301 | KEWEENAW | 1,343 | 740 | 540 | 53 | 10 | 200 R | 55.1% | 40.2% | 3.9% |
| 11,333 | LAKE | 4,693 | 1,961 | 2,584 | 110 | 38 | 623 D | 41.8% | 55.1% | 2.3% |
| 87,904 | LAPEER | 37,234 | 20,351 | 15,749 | 794 | 340 | 4,602 R | 54.7% | 42.3% | 2.1% |
| 21,119 | LEELANAU | 12,009 | 6,840 | 4,635 | 456 | 78 | 2,205 R | 57.0% | 38.6% | 3.8% |
| 98,890 | LENAWEE | 40,093 | 20,681 | 18,365 | 760 | 287 | 2,316 R | 51.6% | 45.8% | 1.9% |
| 156,951 | LIVINGSTON | 75,475 | 44,637 | 28,780 | 1,498 | 560 | 15,857 R | 59.1% | 38.1% | 2.0% |
| 7,024 | LUCE | 2,536 | 1,480 | 956 | 74 | 26 | 524 R | 58.4% | 37.7% | 2.9% |
| 11,943 | MACKINAC | 5,970 | 3,272 | 2,533 | 136 | 29 | 739 R | 54.8% | 42.4% | 2.3% |
| 788,149 | MACOMB | 345,559 | 164,265 | 172,625 | 6,145 | 2,524 | 8,360 D | 47.5% | 50.0% | 1.8% |
| 24,527 | MANISTEE | 11,428 | 5,401 | 5,639 | 320 | 68 | 238 D | 47.3% | 49.3% | 2.8% |
| 64,634 | MARQUETTE | 29,179 | 12,577 | 15,503 | 936 | 163 | 2,926 D | 43.1% | 53.1% | 3.2% |
| 28,274 | MASON | 13,016 | 7,066 | 5,579 | 301 | 70 | 1,487 R | 54.3% | 42.9% | 2.3% |
| 40,553 | MECOSTA | 14,754 | 8,072 | 6,300 | 325 | 57 | 1,772 R | 54.7% | 42.7% | 2.2% |
| 25,326 | MENOMINEE | 10,434 | 5,529 | 4,597 | 269 | 39 | 932 R | 53.0% | 44.1% | 2.6% |
| 82,874 | MIDLAND | 38,888 | 21,887 | 15,959 | 794 | 248 | 5,928 R | 56.3% | 41.0% | 2.0% |
| 14,478 | MISSAUKEE | 6,496 | 4,274 | 2,062 | 123 | 37 | 2,212 R | 65.8% | 31.7% | 1.9% |
| 145,945 | MONROE | 61,795 | 28,940 | 31,555 | 996 | 304 | 2,615 D | 46.8% | 51.1% | 1.6% |
| 61,266 | MONTCALM | 22,904 | 12,696 | 9,627 | 483 | 98 | 3,069 R | 55.4% | 42.0% | 2.1% |
| 10,315 | MONTMORENCY | 5,009 | 2,750 | 2,139 | 92 | 28 | 611 R | 54.9% | 42.7% | 1.8% |

# MICHIGAN

## PRESIDENT 2000

| 2000 Census Population | County | Total Vote | Republican | Democratic | Green (Nader) | Other | Rep.-Dem. Plurality | Percentage of Total Vote | | |
|---|---|---|---|---|---|---|---|---|---|---|
| | | | | | | | | Rep. | Dem. | Green |
| 170,200 | MUSKEGON | 69,270 | 30,028 | 37,865 | 1,131 | 246 | 7,837 D | 43.3% | 54.7% | 1.6% |
| 47,874 | NEWAYGO | 19,557 | 11,399 | 7,677 | 361 | 120 | 3,722 R | 58.3% | 39.3% | 1.8% |
| 1,194,156 | OAKLAND | 570,265 | 274,319 | 281,201 | 10,382 | 4,363 | 6,882 D | 48.1% | 49.3% | 1.8% |
| 26,873 | OCEANA | 10,772 | 5,913 | 4,597 | 211 | 51 | 1,316 R | 54.9% | 42.7% | 2.0% |
| 21,645 | OGEMAW | 9,855 | 4,706 | 4,896 | 191 | 62 | 190 D | 47.8% | 49.7% | 1.9% |
| 7,818 | ONTONAGON | 4,151 | 2,472 | 1,514 | 135 | 30 | 958 R | 59.6% | 36.5% | 3.3% |
| 23,197 | OSCEOLA | 9,930 | 5,680 | 4,006 | 186 | 58 | 1,674 R | 57.2% | 40.3% | 1.9% |
| 9,418 | OSCODA | 3,992 | 2,207 | 1,677 | 88 | 20 | 530 R | 55.3% | 42.0% | 2.2% |
| 23,301 | OTSEGO | 10,505 | 6,108 | 4,034 | 315 | 48 | 2,074 R | 58.1% | 38.4% | 3.0% |
| 238,314 | OTTAWA | 110,599 | 78,703 | 29,600 | 1,866 | 430 | 49,103 R | 71.2% | 26.8% | 1.7% |
| 14,411 | PRESQUE ISLE | 7,080 | 3,660 | 3,242 | 136 | 42 | 418 R | 51.7% | 45.8% | 1.9% |
| 25,469 | ROSCOMMON | 12,928 | 6,190 | 6,433 | 256 | 49 | 243 D | 47.9% | 49.8% | 2.0% |
| 210,039 | SAGINAW | 93,756 | 41,152 | 50,825 | 1,418 | 361 | 9,673 D | 43.9% | 54.2% | 1.5% |
| 164,235 | ST. CLAIR | 68,516 | 33,571 | 33,002 | 1,341 | 602 | 569 R | 49.0% | 48.2% | 2.0% |
| 62,422 | ST. JOSEPH | 22,024 | 12,906 | 8,574 | 434 | 110 | 4,332 R | 58.6% | 38.9% | 2.0% |
| 44,547 | SANILAC | 18,566 | 10,966 | 7,153 | 320 | 127 | 3,813 R | 59.1% | 38.5% | 1.7% |
| 8,903 | SCHOOLCRAFT | 4,198 | 2,088 | 2,036 | 56 | 18 | 52 R | 49.7% | 48.5% | 1.3% |
| 71,687 | SHIAWASSEE | 32,218 | 15,816 | 15,520 | 639 | 243 | 296 R | 49.1% | 48.2% | 2.0% |
| 58,266 | TUSCOLA | 24,652 | 13,213 | 10,845 | 454 | 140 | 2,368 R | 53.6% | 44.0% | 1.8% |
| 76,263 | VAN BUREN | 29,482 | 14,792 | 13,796 | 686 | 208 | 996 R | 50.2% | 46.8% | 2.3% |
| 322,895 | WASHTENAW | 144,940 | 52,459 | 86,647 | 4,843 | 991 | 34,188 D | 36.2% | 59.8% | 3.3% |
| 2,061,162 | WAYNE | 768,627 | 223,021 | 530,414 | 11,287 | 3,905 | 307,393 D | 29.0% | 69.0% | 1.5% |
| 30,484 | WEXFORD | 12,982 | 7,215 | 5,326 | 352 | 89 | 1,889 R | 55.6% | 41.0% | 2.7% |
| 9,938,444 | TOTAL | 4,232,711 | 1,953,139 | 2,170,418 | 84,165 | 24,989 | 217,279 D | 46.1% | 51.3% | 2.0% |

# MICHIGAN

## PRESIDENT 1996

| 1995 Census Pop. Est. | County | Total Vote | Republican | Democratic | Reform (Perot) | Other | Rep.-Dem. Plurality | Percentage of Total Vote | | |
|---|---|---|---|---|---|---|---|---|---|---|
| | | | | | | | | Rep. | Dem. | Reform |
| 10,587 | ALCONA | 5,555 | 2,227 | 2,619 | 669 | 40 | 392 D | 40.1% | 47.1% | 12.0% |
| 9,846 | ALGER | 4,231 | 1,429 | 2,229 | 537 | 36 | 800 D | 33.8% | 52.7% | 12.7% |
| 97,692 | ALLEGAN | 38,790 | 20,859 | 14,361 | 3,269 | 301 | 6,498 R | 53.8% | 37.0% | 8.4% |
| 30,841 | ALPENA | 13,492 | 4,525 | 7,114 | 1,730 | 123 | 2,589 D | 33.5% | 52.7% | 12.8% |
| 20,257 | ANTRIM | 10,098 | 4,630 | 4,226 | 1,129 | 113 | 404 R | 45.9% | 41.8% | 11.2% |
| 16,151 | ARENAC | 6,591 | 2,247 | 3,472 | 844 | 28 | 1,225 D | 34.1% | 52.7% | 12.8% |
| 8,493 | BARAGA | 3,294 | 1,209 | 1,601 | 460 | 24 | 392 D | 36.7% | 48.6% | 14.0% |
| 52,643 | BARRY | 23,120 | 11,139 | 9,467 | 2,282 | 232 | 1,672 R | 48.2% | 40.9% | 9.9% |
| 111,529 | BAY | 49,603 | 16,038 | 27,835 | 5,410 | 320 | 11,797 D | 32.3% | 56.1% | 10.9% |
| 13,660 | BENZIE | 6,785 | 2,856 | 3,081 | 763 | 85 | 225 D | 42.1% | 45.4% | 11.2% |
| 162,623 | BERRIEN | 59,295 | 28,254 | 24,614 | 5,958 | 469 | 3,640 R | 47.6% | 41.5% | 10.0% |
| 42,738 | BRANCH | 14,805 | 6,321 | 6,567 | 1,779 | 138 | 246 D | 42.7% | 44.4% | 12.0% |
| 140,689 | CALHOUN | 52,443 | 20,953 | 26,287 | 4,765 | 438 | 5,334 D | 40.0% | 50.1% | 9.1% |
| 49,603 | CASS | 17,980 | 7,373 | 8,207 | 2,241 | 159 | 834 D | 41.0% | 45.6% | 12.5% |
| 23,052 | CHARLEVOIX | 10,996 | 4,864 | 4,689 | 1,303 | 140 | 175 R | 44.2% | 42.6% | 11.8% |
| 22,854 | CHEBOYGAN | 10,833 | 4,244 | 5,018 | 1,462 | 109 | 774 D | 39.2% | 46.3% | 13.5% |
| 36,859 | CHIPPEWA | 13,259 | 5,137 | 6,532 | 1,453 | 137 | 1,395 D | 38.7% | 49.3% | 11.0% |
| 28,078 | CLARE | 11,683 | 3,742 | 6,311 | 1,531 | 99 | 2,569 D | 32.0% | 54.0% | 13.1% |
| 61,657 | CLINTON | 28,601 | 13,694 | 11,945 | 2,698 | 264 | 1,749 R | 47.9% | 41.8% | 9.4% |
| 13,523 | CRAWFORD | 5,721 | 2,157 | 2,666 | 840 | 58 | 509 D | 37.7% | 46.6% | 14.7% |
| 38,655 | DELTA | 16,150 | 5,925 | 8,561 | 1,543 | 121 | 2,636 D | 36.7% | 53.0% | 9.6% |
| 27,176 | DICKINSON | 11,591 | 4,408 | 5,614 | 1,478 | 91 | 1,206 D | 38.0% | 48.4% | 12.8% |
| 98,087 | EATON | 44,666 | 20,092 | 19,781 | 4,378 | 415 | 311 R | 45.0% | 44.3% | 9.8% |
| 27,352 | EMMET | 12,580 | 6,002 | 4,892 | 1,512 | 174 | 1,110 R | 47.7% | 38.9% | 12.0% |
| 436,381 | GENESEE | 174,056 | 49,332 | 106,065 | 17,671 | 988 | 56,733 D | 28.3% | 60.9% | 10.2% |
| 24,304 | GLADWIN | 10,692 | 3,670 | 5,494 | 1,466 | 62 | 1,824 D | 34.3% | 51.4% | 13.7% |
| 17,894 | GOGEBIC | 8,186 | 2,769 | 4,436 | 917 | 64 | 1,667 D | 33.8% | 54.2% | 11.2% |
| 70,869 | GRAND TRAVERSE | 33,329 | 16,355 | 12,987 | 3,527 | 460 | 3,368 R | 49.1% | 39.0% | 10.6% |
| 39,973 | GRATIOT | 14,875 | 6,214 | 6,793 | 1,762 | 106 | 579 D | 41.8% | 45.7% | 11.8% |
| 45,224 | HILLSDALE | 16,366 | 7,947 | 5,955 | 2,262 | 202 | 1,992 R | 48.6% | 36.4% | 13.8% |
| 36,140 | HOUGHTON | 13,671 | 5,941 | 5,957 | 1,584 | 189 | 16 D | 43.5% | 43.6% | 11.6% |
| 35,224 | HURON | 14,855 | 6,126 | 6,827 | 1,811 | 91 | 701 D | 41.2% | 46.0% | 12.2% |
| 277,889 | INGHAM | 116,815 | 43,096 | 63,584 | 8,640 | 1,495 | 20,488 D | 36.9% | 54.4% | 7.4% |
| 59,846 | IONIA | 21,452 | 9,574 | 9,261 | 2,354 | 263 | 313 R | 44.6% | 43.2% | 11.0% |
| 24,482 | IOSCO | 12,424 | 4,410 | 6,240 | 1,710 | 64 | 1,830 D | 35.5% | 50.2% | 13.8% |
| 13,177 | IRON | 6,059 | 2,014 | 3,232 | 755 | 58 | 1,218 D | 33.2% | 53.3% | 12.5% |
| 56,213 | ISABELLA | 19,342 | 7,460 | 9,635 | 2,069 | 178 | 2,175 D | 38.6% | 49.8% | 10.7% |
| 154,010 | JACKSON | 56,256 | 24,987 | 24,633 | 5,968 | 668 | 354 R | 44.4% | 43.8% | 10.6% |
| 227,973 | KALAMAZOO | 93,135 | 40,703 | 45,644 | 5,867 | 921 | 4,941 D | 43.7% | 49.0% | 6.3% |
| 14,696 | KALKASKA | 6,095 | 2,455 | 2,666 | 922 | 52 | 211 D | 40.3% | 43.7% | 15.1% |
| 525,355 | KENT | 223,379 | 121,335 | 85,912 | 14,120 | 2,012 | 35,423 R | 54.3% | 38.5% | 6.3% |
| 1,967 | KEWEENAW | 1,242 | 491 | 572 | 169 | 10 | 81 D | 39.5% | 46.1% | 13.6% |
| 9,664 | LAKE | 4,394 | 1,213 | 2,606 | 552 | 23 | 1,393 D | 27.6% | 59.3% | 12.6% |
| 83,854 | LAPEER | 32,841 | 13,369 | 14,308 | 4,793 | 371 | 939 D | 40.7% | 43.6% | 14.6% |
| 18,502 | LEELANAU | 10,237 | 5,155 | 4,019 | 924 | 139 | 1,136 R | 50.4% | 39.3% | 9.0% |
| 96,706 | LENAWEE | 35,619 | 14,168 | 16,924 | 4,167 | 360 | 2,756 D | 39.8% | 47.5% | 11.7% |
| 133,601 | LIVINGSTON | 60,242 | 30,598 | 22,517 | 6,337 | 790 | 8,081 R | 50.8% | 37.4% | 10.5% |
| 5,599 | LUCE | 2,459 | 964 | 1,107 | 366 | 22 | 143 D | 39.2% | 45.0% | 14.9% |
| 10,978 | MACKINAC | 5,762 | 2,281 | 2,700 | 742 | 39 | 419 D | 39.6% | 46.9% | 12.9% |
| 733,607 | MACOMB | 306,028 | 120,616 | 151,430 | 29,859 | 4,123 | 30,814 D | 39.4% | 49.5% | 9.8% |
| 22,915 | MANISTEE | 10,539 | 3,807 | 5,383 | 1,230 | 119 | 1,576 D | 36.1% | 51.1% | 11.7% |
| 65,442 | MARQUETTE | 26,758 | 8,805 | 15,168 | 2,492 | 293 | 6,363 D | 32.9% | 56.7% | 9.3% |
| 27,487 | MASON | 12,251 | 5,066 | 5,597 | 1,525 | 63 | 531 D | 41.4% | 45.7% | 12.4% |
| 37,725 | MECOSTA | 13,124 | 5,289 | 6,370 | 1,373 | 92 | 1,081 D | 40.3% | 48.5% | 10.5% |
| 24,569 | MENOMINEE | 10,184 | 4,038 | 4,880 | 1,205 | 61 | 842 D | 39.7% | 47.9% | 11.8% |
| 79,748 | MIDLAND | 35,967 | 16,547 | 15,177 | 3,964 | 279 | 1,370 R | 46.0% | 42.2% | 11.0% |
| 13,522 | MISSAUKEE | 6,025 | 3,012 | 2,256 | 719 | 38 | 756 R | 50.0% | 37.4% | 11.9% |
| 139,550 | MONROE | 52,529 | 19,678 | 26,072 | 6,315 | 464 | 6,394 D | 37.5% | 49.6% | 12.0% |
| 57,866 | MONTCALM | 21,446 | 8,679 | 10,053 | 2,530 | 184 | 1,374 D | 40.5% | 46.9% | 11.8% |
| 9,683 | MONTMORENCY | 4,592 | 1,760 | 2,120 | 682 | 30 | 360 D | 38.3% | 46.2% | 14.9% |

# MICHIGAN

## PRESIDENT 1996

| 1995 Census Pop. Est. | County | Total Vote | Republican | Democratic | Reform (Perot) | Other | Rep.-Dem. Plurality | Percentage of Total Vote | | |
|---|---|---|---|---|---|---|---|---|---|---|
| | | | | | | | | Rep. | Dem. | Reform |
| 164,459 | MUSKEGON | 63,438 | 21,873 | 35,328 | 5,794 | 443 | 13,455 D | 34.5% | 55.7% | 9.1% |
| 43,587 | NEWAYGO | 17,651 | 7,868 | 7,614 | 2,047 | 122 | 254 R | 44.6% | 43.1% | 11.6% |
| 1,153,461 | OAKLAND | 505,642 | 219,855 | 241,884 | 36,709 | 7,194 | 22,029 D | 43.5% | 47.8% | 7.3% |
| 23,875 | OCEANA | 9,742 | 3,947 | 4,419 | 1,286 | 90 | 472 D | 40.5% | 45.4% | 13.2% |
| 20,559 | OGEMAW | 9,064 | 2,904 | 4,725 | 1,369 | 66 | 1,821 D | 32.0% | 52.1% | 15.1% |
| 8,639 | ONTONAGON | 4,247 | 1,523 | 2,080 | 604 | 40 | 557 D | 35.9% | 49.0% | 14.2% |
| 21,756 | OSCEOLA | 9,090 | 3,855 | 4,085 | 1,068 | 82 | 230 D | 42.4% | 44.9% | 11.7% |
| 8,682 | OSCODA | 3,725 | 1,545 | 1,652 | 503 | 25 | 107 D | 41.5% | 44.3% | 13.5% |
| 20,762 | OTSEGO | 8,320 | 3,638 | 3,351 | 1,280 | 51 | 287 R | 43.7% | 40.3% | 15.4% |
| 210,389 | OTTAWA | 95,416 | 61,436 | 27,024 | 6,275 | 681 | 34,412 R | 64.4% | 28.3% | 6.6% |
| 14,242 | PRESQUE ISLE | 6,892 | 2,463 | 3,449 | 932 | 48 | 986 D | 35.7% | 50.0% | 13.5% |
| 22,593 | ROSCOMMON | 11,834 | 4,135 | 6,092 | 1,539 | 68 | 1,957 D | 34.9% | 51.5% | 13.0% |
| 212,295 | SAGINAW | 87,794 | 31,577 | 47,579 | 8,081 | 557 | 16,002 D | 36.0% | 54.2% | 9.2% |
| 154,231 | ST. CLAIR | 60,118 | 22,495 | 28,881 | 8,134 | 608 | 6,386 D | 37.4% | 48.0% | 13.5% |
| 60,684 | ST. JOSEPH | 20,794 | 9,764 | 8,529 | 2,319 | 182 | 1,235 R | 47.0% | 41.0% | 11.2% |
| 42,203 | SANILAC | 17,314 | 7,821 | 7,092 | 2,265 | 136 | 729 R | 45.2% | 41.0% | 13.1% |
| 8,700 | SCHOOLCRAFT | 3,871 | 1,200 | 2,187 | 460 | 24 | 987 D | 31.0% | 56.5% | 11.9% |
| 72,079 | SHIAWASSEE | 30,375 | 11,714 | 14,662 | 3,703 | 296 | 2,948 D | 38.6% | 48.3% | 12.2% |
| 57,491 | TUSCOLA | 22,641 | 9,154 | 10,314 | 3,013 | 160 | 1,160 D | 40.4% | 45.6% | 13.3% |
| 74,591 | VAN BUREN | 27,975 | 11,347 | 13,355 | 2,946 | 327 | 2,008 D | 40.6% | 47.7% | 10.5% |
| 292,609 | WASHTENAW | 124,028 | 40,097 | 73,106 | 8,020 | 2,805 | 33,009 D | 32.3% | 58.9% | 6.5% |
| 2,055,500 | WAYNE | 731,597 | 175,886 | 504,466 | 43,554 | 7,691 | 328,580 D | 24.0% | 69.0% | 6.0% |
| 28,686 | WEXFORD | 11,888 | 4,866 | 5,510 | 1,386 | 126 | 644 D | 40.9% | 46.3% | 11.7% |
| 9,549,353 | TOTAL | 3,848,844 | 1,481,212 | 1,989,653 | 336,670 | 41,309 | 508,441 D | 38.5% | 51.7% | 8.7% |

# MICHIGAN

## PRESIDENT 1992

| 1990 Census Population | County | Total Vote | Republican | Democratic | Perot | Other | Plurality | Percentage Total Vote Rep. | Dem. | Perot |
|---|---|---|---|---|---|---|---|---|---|---|
| 10,145 | ALCONA | 5,779 | 2,247 | 2,383 | 1,117 | 32 | 136 D | 38.9% | 41.2% | 19.3% |
| 8,972 | ALGER | 4,570 | 1,471 | 2,144 | 941 | 14 | 673 D | 32.2% | 46.9% | 20.6% |
| 90,509 | ALLEGAN | 40,835 | 19,077 | 12,823 | 8,742 | 193 | 6,254 R | 46.7% | 31.4% | 21.4% |
| 30,605 | ALPENA | 15,069 | 4,878 | 6,894 | 3,236 | 61 | 2,016 D | 32.4% | 45.7% | 21.5% |
| 18,185 | ANTRIM | 9,991 | 3,984 | 3,431 | 2,528 | 48 | 553 R | 39.9% | 34.3% | 25.3% |
| 14,931 | ARENAC | 7,206 | 2,330 | 3,244 | 1,608 | 24 | 914 D | 32.3% | 45.0% | 22.3% |
| 7,954 | BARAGA | 3,630 | 1,160 | 1,695 | 754 | 21 | 535 D | 32.0% | 46.7% | 20.8% |
| 50,057 | BARRY | 24,599 | 9,489 | 8,652 | 6,303 | 155 | 837 R | 38.6% | 35.2% | 25.6% |
| 111,723 | BAY | 54,355 | 16,383 | 26,492 | 11,258 | 222 | 10,109 D | 30.1% | 48.7% | 20.7% |
| 12,200 | BENZIE | 6,852 | 2,438 | 2,715 | 1,657 | 42 | 277 D | 35.6% | 39.6% | 24.2% |
| 161,378 | BERRIEN | 69,615 | 29,252 | 25,840 | 14,056 | 467 | 3,412 R | 42.0% | 37.1% | 20.2% |
| 41,502 | BRANCH | 16,593 | 5,976 | 5,850 | 4,683 | 84 | 126 R | 36.0% | 35.3% | 28.2% |
| 135,982 | CALHOUN | 58,702 | 19,791 | 25,542 | 13,058 | 311 | 5,751 D | 33.7% | 43.5% | 22.2% |
| 49,477 | CASS | 20,283 | 7,391 | 8,047 | 4,756 | 89 | 656 D | 36.4% | 39.7% | 23.4% |
| 21,468 | CHARLEVOIX | 11,525 | 4,017 | 4,063 | 3,360 | 85 | 46 D | 34.9% | 35.3% | 29.2% |
| 21,398 | CHEBOYGAN | 10,864 | 3,864 | 4,459 | 2,495 | 46 | 595 D | 35.6% | 41.0% | 23.0% |
| 34,604 | CHIPPEWA | 13,647 | 5,462 | 5,434 | 2,706 | 45 | 28 R | 40.0% | 39.8% | 19.8% |
| 24,952 | CLARE | 12,163 | 3,916 | 5,346 | 2,812 | 89 | 1,430 D | 32.2% | 44.0% | 23.1% |
| 57,883 | CLINTON | 30,339 | 12,216 | 10,116 | 7,877 | 130 | 2,100 R | 40.3% | 33.3% | 26.0% |
| 12,260 | CRAWFORD | 5,925 | 2,193 | 2,252 | 1,442 | 38 | 59 D | 37.0% | 38.0% | 24.3% |
| 37,780 | DELTA | 17,962 | 6,027 | 8,387 | 3,485 | 63 | 2,360 D | 33.6% | 46.7% | 19.4% |
| 26,831 | DICKINSON | 13,031 | 4,273 | 5,689 | 3,022 | 47 | 1,416 D | 32.8% | 43.7% | 23.2% |
| 92,879 | EATON | 47,883 | 18,669 | 16,752 | 12,208 | 254 | 1,917 R | 39.0% | 35.0% | 25.5% |
| 25,040 | EMMET | 13,232 | 5,312 | 4,245 | 3,576 | 99 | 1,067 R | 40.1% | 32.1% | 27.0% |
| 430,459 | GENESEE | 199,998 | 47,834 | 105,156 | 46,259 | 749 | 57,322 D | 23.9% | 52.6% | 23.1% |
| 21,896 | GLADWIN | 10,776 | 3,616 | 4,457 | 2,649 | 54 | 841 D | 33.6% | 41.4% | 24.6% |
| 18,052 | GOGEBIC | 9,225 | 2,838 | 4,792 | 1,543 | 52 | 1,954 D | 30.8% | 51.9% | 16.7% |
| 64,273 | GRAND TRAVERSE | 34,461 | 13,629 | 11,148 | 9,495 | 189 | 2,481 R | 39.5% | 32.3% | 27.6% |
| 38,982 | GRATIOT | 15,879 | 6,280 | 5,678 | 3,866 | 55 | 602 R | 39.5% | 35.8% | 24.3% |
| 43,431 | HILLSDALE | 17,891 | 7,579 | 5,244 | 4,968 | 100 | 2,335 R | 42.4% | 29.3% | 27.8% |
| 35,446 | HOUGHTON | 15,173 | 5,575 | 6,558 | 2,945 | 95 | 983 D | 36.7% | 43.2% | 19.4% |
| 34,951 | HURON | 16,632 | 6,491 | 6,023 | 4,064 | 54 | 468 R | 39.0% | 36.2% | 24.4% |
| 281,912 | INGHAM | 133,792 | 43,926 | 61,596 | 27,683 | 587 | 17,670 D | 32.8% | 46.0% | 20.7% |
| 57,024 | IONIA | 23,822 | 9,135 | 8,370 | 6,211 | 106 | 765 R | 38.3% | 35.1% | 26.1% |
| 30,209 | IOSCO | 13,492 | 4,912 | 5,369 | 3,131 | 80 | 457 D | 36.4% | 39.8% | 23.2% |
| 13,175 | IRON | 7,000 | 1,971 | 3,648 | 1,344 | 37 | 1,677 D | 28.2% | 52.1% | 19.2% |
| 54,624 | ISABELLA | 22,037 | 7,706 | 8,784 | 5,434 | 113 | 1,078 D | 35.0% | 39.9% | 24.7% |
| 149,756 | JACKSON | 64,644 | 25,424 | 23,686 | 15,194 | 340 | 1,738 R | 39.3% | 36.6% | 23.5% |
| 223,411 | KALAMAZOO | 103,858 | 38,035 | 43,568 | 21,666 | 589 | 5,533 D | 36.6% | 41.9% | 20.9% |
| 13,497 | KALKASKA | 6,426 | 2,173 | 2,297 | 1,915 | 41 | 124 D | 33.8% | 35.7% | 29.8% |
| 500,631 | KENT | 242,553 | 115,285 | 82,305 | 43,707 | 1,256 | 32,980 R | 47.5% | 33.9% | 18.0% |
| 1,701 | KEWEENAW | 1,173 | 378 | 582 | 212 | 1 | 204 D | 32.2% | 49.6% | 18.1% |
| 8,583 | LAKE | 4,546 | 1,194 | 2,351 | 981 | 20 | 1,157 D | 26.3% | 51.7% | 21.6% |
| 74,768 | LAPEER | 35,084 | 12,326 | 11,982 | 10,541 | 235 | 344 R | 35.1% | 34.2% | 30.0% |
| 16,527 | LEELANAU | 10,187 | 3,993 | 3,445 | 2,685 | 64 | 548 R | 39.2% | 33.8% | 26.4% |
| 91,476 | LENAWEE | 39,365 | 14,297 | 15,399 | 9,517 | 152 | 1,102 D | 36.3% | 39.1% | 24.2% |
| 115,645 | LIVINGSTON | 61,735 | 27,539 | 17,851 | 15,971 | 374 | 9,688 R | 44.6% | 28.9% | 25.9% |
| 5,763 | LUCE | 2,603 | 958 | 972 | 660 | 13 | 14 D | 36.8% | 37.3% | 25.4% |
| 10,674 | MACKINAC | 5,977 | 2,278 | 2,293 | 1,379 | 27 | 15 D | 38.1% | 38.4% | 23.1% |
| 717,400 | MACOMB | 349,238 | 147,795 | 130,732 | 67,954 | 2,757 | 17,063 R | 42.3% | 37.4% | 19.5% |
| 21,265 | MANISTEE | 11,651 | 3,491 | 5,193 | 2,923 | 44 | 1,702 D | 30.0% | 44.6% | 25.1% |
| 70,887 | MARQUETTE | 31,629 | 9,665 | 16,038 | 5,768 | 158 | 6,373 D | 30.6% | 50.7% | 18.2% |
| 25,537 | MASON | 13,082 | 5,102 | 4,829 | 3,096 | 55 | 273 R | 39.0% | 36.9% | 23.7% |
| 37,308 | MECOSTA | 15,835 | 6,047 | 6,097 | 3,612 | 79 | 50 D | 38.2% | 38.5% | 22.8% |
| 24,920 | MENOMINEE | 11,082 | 3,995 | 4,559 | 2,487 | 41 | 564 D | 36.0% | 41.1% | 22.4% |
| 75,651 | MIDLAND | 38,624 | 16,149 | 13,382 | 8,945 | 148 | 2,767 R | 41.8% | 34.6% | 23.2% |
| 12,147 | MISSAUKEE | 6,058 | 2,829 | 1,893 | 1,306 | 30 | 936 R | 46.7% | 31.2% | 21.6% |
| 133,600 | MONROE | 59,031 | 20,250 | 24,957 | 13,551 | 273 | 4,707 D | 34.3% | 42.3% | 23.0% |
| 53,059 | MONTCALM | 22,780 | 8,420 | 8,730 | 5,504 | 126 | 310 D | 37.0% | 38.3% | 24.2% |
| 8,936 | MONTMORENCY | 4,791 | 1,794 | 1,903 | 1,077 | 17 | 109 D | 37.4% | 39.7% | 22.5% |

# MICHIGAN

## PRESIDENT 1992

| 1990 Census Population | County | Total Vote | Republican | Democratic | Perot | Other | Plurality | Percentage Total Vote | | |
|---|---|---|---|---|---|---|---|---|---|---|
| | | | | | | | | Rep. | Dem. | Perot |
| 158,983 | MUSKEGON | 71,948 | 23,769 | 32,515 | 15,268 | 396 | 8,746 D | 33.0% | 45.2% | 21.2% |
| 38,202 | NEWAYGO | 17,916 | 7,333 | 6,455 | 4,056 | 72 | 878 R | 40.9% | 36.0% | 22.6% |
| 1,083,592 | OAKLAND | 555,760 | 242,160 | 214,733 | 94,911 | 3,956 | 27,427 R | 43.6% | 38.6% | 17.1% |
| 22,454 | OCEANA | 10,557 | 3,944 | 3,846 | 2,713 | 54 | 98 R | 37.4% | 36.4% | 25.7% |
| 18,681 | OGEMAW | 9,126 | 2,936 | 4,016 | 2,122 | 52 | 1,080 D | 32.2% | 44.0% | 23.3% |
| 8,854 | ONTONAGON | 4,745 | 1,463 | 2,451 | 805 | 26 | 988 D | 30.8% | 51.7% | 17.0% |
| 20,146 | OSCEOLA | 9,376 | 3,606 | 3,529 | 2,199 | 42 | 77 R | 38.5% | 37.6% | 23.5% |
| 7,842 | OSCODA | 3,831 | 1,583 | 1,471 | 755 | 22 | 112 R | 41.3% | 38.4% | 19.7% |
| 17,957 | OTSEGO | 9,207 | 3,393 | 3,129 | 2,635 | 50 | 264 R | 36.9% | 34.0% | 28.6% |
| 187,768 | OTTAWA | 96,211 | 56,862 | 22,180 | 16,855 | 314 | 34,682 R | 59.1% | 23.1% | 17.5% |
| 13,743 | PRESQUE ISLE | 7,345 | 2,398 | 3,308 | 1,612 | 27 | 910 D | 32.6% | 45.0% | 21.9% |
| 19,776 | ROSCOMMON | 12,007 | 4,170 | 5,243 | 2,551 | 43 | 1,073 D | 34.7% | 43.7% | 21.2% |
| 211,946 | SAGINAW | 96,905 | 32,103 | 43,819 | 20,523 | 460 | 11,716 D | 33.1% | 45.2% | 21.2% |
| 145,607 | ST. CLAIR | 66,832 | 24,508 | 23,385 | 18,523 | 416 | 1,123 R | 36.7% | 35.0% | 27.7% |
| 58,913 | ST. JOSEPH | 23,971 | 9,836 | 7,817 | 6,209 | 109 | 2,019 R | 41.0% | 32.6% | 25.9% |
| 39,928 | SANILAC | 18,758 | 7,891 | 5,868 | 4,894 | 105 | 2,023 R | 42.1% | 31.3% | 26.1% |
| 8,302 | SCHOOLCRAFT | 4,129 | 1,253 | 2,139 | 721 | 16 | 886 D | 30.3% | 51.8% | 17.5% |
| 69,770 | SHIAWASSEE | 32,360 | 10,930 | 12,629 | 8,632 | 169 | 1,699 D | 33.8% | 39.0% | 26.7% |
| 55,498 | TUSCOLA | 24,666 | 8,636 | 9,138 | 6,765 | 127 | 502 D | 35.0% | 37.0% | 27.4% |
| 70,060 | VAN BUREN | 30,237 | 10,357 | 12,466 | 7,255 | 159 | 2,109 D | 34.3% | 41.2% | 24.0% |
| 282,937 | WASHTENAW | 137,466 | 41,386 | 73,325 | 21,889 | 866 | 31,939 D | 30.1% | 53.3% | 15.9% |
| 2,111,687 | WAYNE | 841,965 | 227,002 | 508,464 | 102,074 | 4,425 | 281,462 D | 27.0% | 60.4% | 12.1% |
| 26,360 | WEXFORD | 12,575 | 4,696 | 4,894 | 2,923 | 62 | 198 D | 37.3% | 38.9% | 23.2% |
| 9,295,297 | TOTAL | 4,274,673 | 1,554,940 | 1,871,182 | 824,813 | 23,738 | 316,242 D | 36.4% | 43.8% | 19.3% |

# MICHIGAN

## PRESIDENT 1988

| 1980 Census Population | County | Total Vote | Republican | Democratic | Other | Rep.-Dem. Plurality | Percentage Total Vote Rep. | Dem. | Major Vote Rep. | Dem. |
|---:|---|---:|---:|---:|---:|---:|---:|---:|---:|---:|
| 9,740 | ALCONA | 4,905 | 2,966 | 1,918 | 21 | 1,048 R | 60.5% | 39.1% | 60.7% | 39.3% |
| 9,225 | ALGER | 4,059 | 1,830 | 2,210 | 19 | 380 D | 45.1% | 54.4% | 45.3% | 54.7% |
| 81,555 | ALLEGAN | 33,188 | 22,163 | 10,785 | 240 | 11,378 R | 66.8% | 32.5% | 67.3% | 32.7% |
| 32,315 | ALPENA | 13,054 | 6,664 | 6,341 | 49 | 323 R | 51.0% | 48.6% | 51.2% | 48.8% |
| 16,194 | ANTRIM | 8,444 | 5,231 | 3,159 | 54 | 2,072 R | 61.9% | 37.4% | 62.3% | 37.7% |
| 14,706 | ARENAC | 6,300 | 3,064 | 3,211 | 25 | 147 D | 48.6% | 51.0% | 48.8% | 51.2% |
| 8,484 | BARAGA | 3,404 | 1,630 | 1,753 | 21 | 123 D | 47.9% | 51.5% | 48.2% | 51.8% |
| 45,781 | BARRY | 20,681 | 12,546 | 7,983 | 152 | 4,563 R | 60.7% | 38.6% | 61.1% | 38.9% |
| 119,881 | BAY | 49,152 | 20,710 | 28,225 | 217 | 7,515 D | 42.1% | 57.4% | 42.3% | 57.7% |
| 11,205 | BENZIE | 5,732 | 3,240 | 2,437 | 55 | 803 R | 56.5% | 42.5% | 57.1% | 42.9% |
| 171,276 | BERRIEN | 60,183 | 37,799 | 21,948 | 436 | 15,851 R | 62.8% | 36.5% | 63.3% | 36.7% |
| 40,188 | BRANCH | 14,531 | 9,225 | 5,231 | 75 | 3,994 R | 63.5% | 36.0% | 63.8% | 36.2% |
| 141,557 | CALHOUN | 49,787 | 26,771 | 22,717 | 299 | 4,054 R | 53.8% | 45.6% | 54.1% | 45.9% |
| 49,499 | CASS | 17,756 | 10,229 | 7,444 | 83 | 2,785 R | 57.6% | 41.9% | 57.9% | 42.1% |
| 19,907 | CHARLEVOIX | 9,762 | 5,802 | 3,875 | 85 | 1,927 R | 59.4% | 39.7% | 60.0% | 40.0% |
| 20,649 | CHEBOYGAN | 9,380 | 5,395 | 3,943 | 42 | 1,452 R | 57.5% | 42.0% | 57.8% | 42.2% |
| 29,029 | CHIPPEWA | 12,068 | 6,786 | 5,222 | 60 | 1,564 R | 56.2% | 43.3% | 56.5% | 43.5% |
| 23,822 | CLARE | 10,448 | 5,661 | 4,710 | 77 | 951 R | 54.2% | 45.1% | 54.6% | 45.4% |
| 55,893 | CLINTON | 24,837 | 15,497 | 9,225 | 115 | 6,272 R | 62.4% | 37.1% | 62.7% | 37.3% |
| 9,465 | CRAWFORD | 4,973 | 3,097 | 1,825 | 51 | 1,272 R | 62.3% | 36.7% | 62.9% | 37.1% |
| 38,947 | DELTA | 16,065 | 7,114 | 8,891 | 60 | 1,777 D | 44.3% | 55.3% | 44.4% | 55.6% |
| 25,341 | DICKINSON | 12,343 | 6,158 | 6,129 | 56 | 29 R | 49.9% | 49.7% | 50.1% | 49.9% |
| 88,337 | EATON | 39,806 | 24,193 | 15,322 | 291 | 8,871 R | 60.8% | 38.5% | 61.2% | 38.8% |
| 22,992 | EMMET | 11,386 | 7,105 | 4,170 | 111 | 2,935 R | 62.4% | 36.6% | 63.0% | 37.0% |
| 450,449 | GENESEE | 176,859 | 70,922 | 104,880 | 1,057 | 33,958 D | 40.1% | 59.3% | 40.3% | 59.7% |
| 19,957 | GLADWIN | 8,986 | 4,746 | 4,164 | 76 | 582 R | 52.8% | 46.3% | 53.3% | 46.7% |
| 19,686 | GOGEBIC | 8,691 | 3,509 | 5,151 | 31 | 1,642 D | 40.4% | 59.3% | 40.5% | 59.5% |
| 54,899 | GRAND TRAVERSE | 27,525 | 17,191 | 10,098 | 236 | 7,093 R | 62.5% | 36.7% | 63.0% | 37.0% |
| 40,448 | GRATIOT | 14,230 | 8,447 | 5,719 | 64 | 2,728 R | 59.4% | 40.2% | 59.6% | 40.4% |
| 42,071 | HILLSDALE | 15,479 | 10,571 | 4,763 | 145 | 5,808 R | 68.3% | 30.8% | 68.9% | 31.1% |
| 37,872 | HOUGHTON | 13,694 | 7,098 | 6,510 | 86 | 588 R | 51.8% | 47.5% | 52.2% | 47.8% |
| 36,459 | HURON | 15,214 | 9,419 | 5,714 | 81 | 3,705 R | 61.9% | 37.6% | 62.2% | 37.8% |
| 275,520 | INGHAM | 115,435 | 58,363 | 55,984 | 1,088 | 2,379 R | 50.6% | 48.5% | 51.0% | 49.0% |
| 51,815 | IONIA | 20,369 | 12,028 | 8,160 | 181 | 3,868 R | 59.1% | 40.1% | 59.6% | 40.4% |
| 28,349 | IOSCO | 12,225 | 7,234 | 4,929 | 62 | 2,305 R | 59.2% | 40.3% | 59.5% | 40.5% |
| 13,635 | IRON | 6,674 | 2,866 | 3,774 | 34 | 908 D | 42.9% | 56.5% | 43.2% | 56.8% |
| 54,110 | ISABELLA | 18,482 | 10,362 | 7,960 | 160 | 2,402 R | 56.1% | 43.1% | 56.6% | 43.4% |
| 151,495 | JACKSON | 56,127 | 33,885 | 21,865 | 377 | 12,020 R | 60.4% | 39.0% | 60.8% | 39.2% |
| 212,378 | KALAMAZOO | 90,235 | 50,205 | 39,457 | 573 | 10,748 R | 55.6% | 43.7% | 56.0% | 44.0% |
| 10,952 | KALKASKA | 5,504 | 3,369 | 2,092 | 43 | 1,277 R | 61.2% | 38.0% | 61.7% | 38.3% |
| 444,506 | KENT | 206,842 | 131,910 | 73,467 | 1,465 | 58,443 R | 63.8% | 35.5% | 64.2% | 35.8% |
| 1,963 | KEWEENAW | 1,170 | 536 | 631 | 3 | 95 D | 45.8% | 53.9% | 45.9% | 54.1% |
| 7,711 | LAKE | 3,698 | 1,713 | 1,958 | 27 | 245 D | 46.3% | 52.9% | 46.7% | 53.3% |
| 70,038 | LAPEER | 27,697 | 16,670 | 10,736 | 291 | 5,934 R | 60.2% | 38.8% | 60.8% | 39.2% |
| 14,007 | LEELANAU | 8,619 | 5,215 | 3,331 | 73 | 1,884 R | 60.5% | 38.6% | 61.0% | 39.0% |
| 89,948 | LENAWEE | 33,048 | 19,115 | 13,690 | 243 | 5,425 R | 57.8% | 41.4% | 58.3% | 41.7% |
| 100,289 | LIVINGSTON | 45,546 | 31,331 | 13,749 | 466 | 17,582 R | 68.8% | 30.2% | 69.5% | 30.5% |
| 6,659 | LUCE | 2,417 | 1,528 | 864 | 25 | 664 R | 63.2% | 35.7% | 63.9% | 36.1% |
| 10,178 | MACKINAC | 5,242 | 3,127 | 2,093 | 22 | 1,034 R | 59.7% | 39.9% | 59.9% | 40.1% |
| 694,600 | MACOMB | 291,116 | 175,632 | 112,856 | 2,628 | 62,776 R | 60.3% | 38.8% | 60.9% | 39.1% |
| 23,019 | MANISTEE | 10,209 | 5,368 | 4,765 | 76 | 603 R | 52.6% | 46.7% | 53.0% | 47.0% |
| 74,101 | MARQUETTE | 27,267 | 11,704 | 15,418 | 145 | 3,714 D | 42.9% | 56.5% | 43.2% | 56.8% |
| 26,365 | MASON | 11,413 | 6,800 | 4,531 | 82 | 2,269 R | 59.6% | 39.7% | 60.0% | 40.0% |
| 36,961 | MECOSTA | 12,981 | 8,181 | 4,736 | 64 | 3,445 R | 63.0% | 36.5% | 63.3% | 36.7% |
| 26,201 | MENOMINEE | 10,406 | 5,440 | 4,918 | 48 | 522 R | 52.3% | 47.3% | 52.5% | 47.5% |
| 73,578 | MIDLAND | 33,817 | 19,994 | 13,452 | 371 | 6,542 R | 59.1% | 39.8% | 59.8% | 40.2% |
| 10,009 | MISSAUKEE | 5,224 | 3,566 | 1,621 | 37 | 1,945 R | 68.3% | 31.0% | 68.7% | 31.3% |
| 134,659 | MONROE | 48,324 | 26,189 | 21,847 | 288 | 4,342 R | 54.2% | 45.2% | 54.5% | 45.5% |
| 47,555 | MONTCALM | 18,754 | 10,963 | 7,664 | 127 | 3,299 R | 58.5% | 40.9% | 58.9% | 41.1% |
| 7,492 | MONTMORENCY | 4,100 | 2,514 | 1,563 | 23 | 951 R | 61.3% | 38.1% | 61.7% | 38.3% |

# MICHIGAN

## PRESIDENT 1988

| 1980 Census Population | County | Total Vote | Republican | Democratic | Other | Rep.-Dem. Plurality | Percentage | | | |
|---|---|---|---|---|---|---|---|---|---|---|
| | | | | | | | Total Vote | | Major Vote | |
| | | | | | | | Rep. | Dem. | Rep. | Dem. |
| 157,589 | MUSKEGON | 62,907 | 33,567 | 28,977 | 363 | 4,590 R | 53.4% | 46.1% | 53.7% | 46.3% |
| 34,917 | NEWAYGO | 15,385 | 9,896 | 5,389 | 100 | 4,507 R | 64.3% | 35.0% | 64.7% | 35.3% |
| 1,011,793 | OAKLAND | 462,488 | 283,359 | 174,745 | 4,384 | 108,614 R | 61.3% | 37.8% | 61.9% | 38.1% |
| 22,002 | OCEANA | 9,114 | 5,693 | 3,356 | 65 | 2,337 R | 62.5% | 36.8% | 62.9% | 37.1% |
| 16,436 | OGEMAW | 8,150 | 4,091 | 4,012 | 47 | 79 R | 50.2% | 49.2% | 50.5% | 49.5% |
| 9,861 | ONTONAGON | 4,562 | 2,023 | 2,517 | 22 | 494 D | 44.3% | 55.2% | 44.6% | 55.4% |
| 18,928 | OSCEOLA | 8,121 | 5,218 | 2,860 | 43 | 2,358 R | 64.3% | 35.2% | 64.6% | 35.4% |
| 6,858 | OSCODA | 3,167 | 1,972 | 1,170 | 25 | 802 R | 62.3% | 36.9% | 62.8% | 37.2% |
| 14,993 | OTSEGO | 7,298 | 4,620 | 2,635 | 43 | 1,985 R | 63.3% | 36.1% | 63.7% | 36.3% |
| 157,174 | OTTAWA | 80,729 | 61,515 | 18,769 | 445 | 42,746 R | 76.2% | 23.2% | 76.6% | 23.4% |
| 14,267 | PRESQUE ISLE | 6,679 | 3,614 | 3,025 | 40 | 589 R | 54.1% | 45.3% | 54.4% | 45.6% |
| 16,374 | ROSCOMMON | 10,303 | 5,866 | 4,394 | 43 | 1,472 R | 56.9% | 42.6% | 57.2% | 42.8% |
| 228,059 | SAGINAW | 88,566 | 42,401 | 45,616 | 549 | 3,215 D | 47.9% | 51.5% | 48.2% | 51.8% |
| 138,802 | ST. CLAIR | 53,658 | 32,336 | 20,909 | 413 | 11,427 R | 60.3% | 39.0% | 60.7% | 39.3% |
| 56,083 | ST. JOSEPH | 20,196 | 13,084 | 7,017 | 95 | 6,067 R | 64.8% | 34.7% | 65.1% | 34.9% |
| 40,789 | SANILAC | 16,207 | 10,653 | 5,445 | 109 | 5,208 R | 65.7% | 33.6% | 66.2% | 33.8% |
| 8,575 | SCHOOLCRAFT | 3,886 | 1,802 | 2,071 | 13 | 269 D | 46.4% | 53.3% | 46.5% | 53.5% |
| 71,140 | SHIAWASSEE | 28,748 | 15,506 | 13,056 | 186 | 2,450 R | 53.9% | 45.4% | 54.3% | 45.7% |
| 56,961 | TUSCOLA | 21,254 | 12,093 | 9,060 | 101 | 3,033 R | 56.9% | 42.6% | 57.2% | 42.8% |
| 66,814 | VAN BUREN | 25,400 | 14,522 | 10,668 | 210 | 3,854 R | 57.2% | 42.0% | 57.6% | 42.4% |
| 264,748 | WASHTENAW | 117,920 | 55,029 | 61,799 | 1,092 | 6,770 D | 46.7% | 52.4% | 47.1% | 52.9% |
| 2,337,891 | WAYNE | 748,156 | 291,996 | 450,222 | 5,938 | 158,226 D | 39.0% | 60.2% | 39.3% | 60.7% |
| 25,102 | WEXFORD | 10,406 | 6,043 | 4,287 | 76 | 1,756 R | 58.1% | 41.2% | 58.5% | 41.5% |
| 9,262,078 | TOTAL | 3,669,163 | 1,965,486 | 1,675,783 | 27,894 | 289,703 R | 53.6% | 45.7% | 54.0% | 46.0% |

# MICHIGAN

## PRESIDENT 1984

| 1980 Census Population | County | Total Vote | Republican | Democratic | Other | Rep.-Dem. Plurality | Percentage Total Vote Rep. | Percentage Total Vote Dem. | Percentage Major Vote Rep. | Percentage Major Vote Dem. |
|---|---|---|---|---|---|---|---|---|---|---|
| 9,740 | ALCONA | 4,853 | 3,223 | 1,616 | 14 | 1,607 R | 66.4% | 33.3% | 66.6% | 33.4% |
| 9,225 | ALGER | 4,208 | 2,175 | 2,018 | 15 | 157 R | 51.7% | 48.0% | 51.9% | 48.1% |
| 81,555 | ALLEGAN | 32,338 | 23,762 | 8,389 | 187 | 15,373 R | 73.5% | 25.9% | 73.9% | 26.1% |
| 32,315 | ALPENA | 13,397 | 8,212 | 5,136 | 49 | 3,076 R | 61.3% | 38.3% | 61.5% | 38.5% |
| 16,194 | ANTRIM | 8,277 | 5,726 | 2,507 | 44 | 3,219 R | 69.2% | 30.3% | 69.5% | 30.5% |
| 14,706 | ARENAC | 5,941 | 3,483 | 2,436 | 22 | 1,047 R | 58.6% | 41.0% | 58.8% | 41.2% |
| 8,484 | BARAGA | 3,792 | 1,965 | 1,818 | 9 | 147 R | 51.8% | 47.9% | 51.9% | 48.1% |
| 45,781 | BARRY | 20,265 | 14,245 | 5,898 | 122 | 8,347 R | 70.3% | 29.1% | 70.7% | 29.3% |
| 119,881 | BAY | 49,030 | 26,198 | 22,597 | 235 | 3,601 R | 53.4% | 46.1% | 53.7% | 46.3% |
| 11,205 | BENZIE | 5,502 | 3,590 | 1,866 | 46 | 1,724 R | 65.2% | 33.9% | 65.8% | 34.2% |
| 171,276 | BERRIEN | 64,824 | 43,160 | 21,228 | 436 | 21,932 R | 66.6% | 32.7% | 67.0% | 33.0% |
| 40,188 | BRANCH | 14,945 | 11,004 | 3,860 | 81 | 7,144 R | 73.6% | 25.8% | 74.0% | 26.0% |
| 141,557 | CALHOUN | 55,067 | 34,470 | 20,313 | 284 | 14,157 R | 62.6% | 36.9% | 62.9% | 37.1% |
| 49,499 | CASS | 18,394 | 11,647 | 6,634 | 113 | 5,013 R | 63.3% | 36.1% | 63.7% | 36.3% |
| 19,907 | CHARLEVOIX | 9,595 | 6,355 | 3,175 | 65 | 3,180 R | 66.2% | 33.1% | 66.7% | 33.3% |
| 20,649 | CHEBOYGAN | 9,452 | 6,053 | 3,358 | 41 | 2,695 R | 64.0% | 35.5% | 64.3% | 35.7% |
| 29,029 | CHIPPEWA | 12,757 | 8,135 | 4,575 | 47 | 3,560 R | 63.8% | 35.9% | 64.0% | 36.0% |
| 23,822 | CLARE | 10,412 | 6,587 | 3,764 | 61 | 2,823 R | 63.3% | 36.2% | 63.6% | 36.4% |
| 55,893 | CLINTON | 23,726 | 17,387 | 6,226 | 113 | 11,161 R | 73.3% | 26.2% | 73.6% | 26.4% |
| 9,465 | CRAWFORD | 4,896 | 3,303 | 1,558 | 35 | 1,745 R | 67.5% | 31.8% | 67.9% | 32.1% |
| 38,947 | DELTA | 16,942 | 8,952 | 7,934 | 56 | 1,018 R | 52.8% | 46.8% | 53.0% | 47.0% |
| 25,341 | DICKINSON | 12,530 | 6,880 | 5,614 | 36 | 1,266 R | 54.9% | 44.8% | 55.1% | 44.9% |
| 88,337 | EATON | 38,199 | 27,720 | 10,290 | 189 | 17,430 R | 72.6% | 26.9% | 72.9% | 27.1% |
| 22,992 | EMMET | 11,080 | 7,760 | 3,254 | 66 | 4,506 R | 70.0% | 29.4% | 70.5% | 29.5% |
| 450,449 | GENESEE | 183,387 | 92,943 | 89,491 | 953 | 3,452 R | 50.7% | 48.8% | 50.9% | 49.1% |
| 19,957 | GLADWIN | 8,844 | 5,401 | 3,368 | 75 | 2,033 R | 61.1% | 38.1% | 61.6% | 38.4% |
| 19,686 | GOGEBIC | 9,581 | 4,006 | 5,554 | 21 | 1,548 D | 41.8% | 58.0% | 41.9% | 58.1% |
| 54,899 | GRAND TRAVERSE | 25,464 | 18,036 | 7,271 | 157 | 10,765 R | 70.8% | 28.6% | 71.3% | 28.7% |
| 40,448 | GRATIOT | 14,506 | 10,456 | 4,000 | 50 | 6,456 R | 72.1% | 27.6% | 72.3% | 27.7% |
| 42,071 | HILLSDALE | 15,768 | 12,063 | 3,616 | 89 | 8,447 R | 76.5% | 22.9% | 76.9% | 23.1% |
| 37,872 | HOUGHTON | 15,141 | 8,652 | 6,434 | 55 | 2,218 R | 57.1% | 42.5% | 57.4% | 42.6% |
| 36,459 | HURON | 15,091 | 11,073 | 3,966 | 52 | 7,107 R | 73.4% | 26.3% | 73.6% | 26.4% |
| 275,520 | INGHAM | 116,083 | 68,753 | 46,411 | 919 | 22,342 R | 59.2% | 40.0% | 59.7% | 40.3% |
| 51,815 | IONIA | 20,035 | 14,162 | 5,735 | 138 | 8,427 R | 70.7% | 28.6% | 71.2% | 28.8% |
| 28,349 | IOSCO | 11,804 | 7,907 | 3,850 | 47 | 4,057 R | 67.0% | 32.6% | 67.3% | 32.7% |
| 13,635 | IRON | 7,056 | 3,468 | 3,559 | 29 | 91 D | 49.1% | 50.4% | 49.4% | 50.6% |
| 54,110 | ISABELLA | 18,793 | 12,215 | 6,435 | 143 | 5,780 R | 65.0% | 34.2% | 65.5% | 34.5% |
| 151,495 | JACKSON | 58,785 | 40,133 | 18,340 | 312 | 21,793 R | 68.3% | 31.2% | 68.6% | 31.4% |
| 212,378 | KALAMAZOO | 91,388 | 58,327 | 32,460 | 601 | 25,867 R | 63.8% | 35.5% | 64.2% | 35.8% |
| 10,952 | KALKASKA | 5,239 | 3,623 | 1,595 | 21 | 2,028 R | 69.2% | 30.4% | 69.4% | 30.6% |
| 444,506 | KENT | 205,020 | 137,417 | 66,238 | 1,365 | 71,179 R | 67.0% | 32.3% | 67.5% | 32.5% |
| 1,963 | KEWEENAW | 1,227 | 599 | 628 | | 29 D | 48.8% | 51.2% | 48.8% | 51.2% |
| 7,711 | LAKE | 4,003 | 2,125 | 1,845 | 33 | 280 R | 53.1% | 46.1% | 53.5% | 46.5% |
| 70,038 | LAPEER | 27,200 | 19,222 | 7,800 | 178 | 11,422 R | 70.7% | 28.7% | 71.1% | 28.9% |
| 14,007 | LEELANAU | 7,921 | 5,356 | 2,498 | 67 | 2,858 R | 67.6% | 31.5% | 68.2% | 31.8% |
| 89,948 | LENAWEE | 33,597 | 22,409 | 11,012 | 176 | 11,397 R | 66.7% | 32.8% | 67.1% | 32.9% |
| 100,289 | LIVINGSTON | 42,812 | 31,846 | 10,720 | 246 | 21,126 R | 74.4% | 25.0% | 74.8% | 25.2% |
| 6,659 | LUCE | 2,561 | 1,715 | 833 | 13 | 882 R | 67.0% | 32.5% | 67.3% | 32.7% |
| 10,178 | MACKINAC | 5,593 | 3,627 | 1,949 | 17 | 1,678 R | 64.8% | 34.8% | 65.0% | 35.0% |
| 694,600 | MACOMB | 293,525 | 194,300 | 97,816 | 1,409 | 96,484 R | 66.2% | 33.3% | 66.5% | 33.5% |
| 23,019 | MANISTEE | 10,298 | 6,328 | 3,917 | 53 | 2,411 R | 61.4% | 38.0% | 61.8% | 38.2% |
| 74,101 | MARQUETTE | 28,402 | 14,196 | 14,074 | 132 | 122 R | 50.0% | 49.6% | 50.2% | 49.8% |
| 26,365 | MASON | 12,092 | 8,202 | 3,803 | 87 | 4,399 R | 67.8% | 31.5% | 68.3% | 31.7% |
| 36,961 | MECOSTA | 13,142 | 9,023 | 4,048 | 71 | 4,975 R | 68.7% | 30.8% | 69.0% | 31.0% |
| 26,201 | MENOMINEE | 11,089 | 6,618 | 4,425 | 46 | 2,193 R | 59.7% | 39.9% | 59.9% | 40.1% |
| 73,578 | MIDLAND | 32,552 | 21,521 | 10,769 | 262 | 10,752 R | 66.1% | 33.1% | 66.6% | 33.4% |
| 10,009 | MISSAUKEE | 5,256 | 3,970 | 1,256 | 30 | 2,714 R | 75.5% | 23.9% | 76.0% | 24.0% |
| 134,659 | MONROE | 49,287 | 29,419 | 19,617 | 251 | 9,802 R | 59.7% | 39.8% | 60.0% | 40.0% |
| 47,555 | MONTCALM | 18,689 | 13,109 | 5,491 | 89 | 7,618 R | 70.1% | 29.4% | 70.5% | 29.5% |
| 7,492 | MONTMORENCY | 4,313 | 2,913 | 1,387 | 13 | 1,526 R | 67.5% | 32.2% | 67.7% | 32.3% |

# MICHIGAN

## PRESIDENT 1984

| 1980 Census Population | County | Total Vote | Republican | Democratic | Other | Rep.-Dem. Plurality | Percentage | | | |
|---|---|---|---|---|---|---|---|---|---|---|
| | | | | | | | Total Vote | | Major Vote | |
| | | | | | | | Rep. | Dem. | Rep. | Dem. |
| 157,589 | MUSKEGON | 64,863 | 39,355 | 25,247 | 261 | 14,108 R | 60.7% | 38.9% | 60.9% | 39.1% |
| 34,917 | NEWAYGO | 15,205 | 10,636 | 4,496 | 73 | 6,140 R | 70.0% | 29.6% | 70.3% | 29.7% |
| 1,011,793 | OAKLAND | 458,800 | 306,050 | 150,286 | 2,464 | 155,764 R | 66.7% | 32.8% | 67.1% | 32.9% |
| 22,002 | OCEANA | 9,325 | 6,405 | 2,865 | 55 | 3,540 R | 68.7% | 30.7% | 69.1% | 30.9% |
| 16,436 | OGEMAW | 8,060 | 4,901 | 3,132 | 27 | 1,769 R | 60.8% | 38.9% | 61.0% | 39.0% |
| 9,861 | ONTONAGON | 4,836 | 2,464 | 2,350 | 22 | 114 R | 51.0% | 48.6% | 51.2% | 48.8% |
| 18,928 | OSCEOLA | 8,090 | 5,923 | 2,127 | 40 | 3,796 R | 73.2% | 26.3% | 73.6% | 26.4% |
| 6,858 | OSCODA | 3,209 | 2,239 | 951 | 19 | 1,288 R | 69.8% | 29.6% | 70.2% | 29.8% |
| 14,993 | OTSEGO | 6,795 | 4,639 | 2,117 | 39 | 2,522 R | 68.3% | 31.2% | 68.7% | 31.3% |
| 157,174 | OTTAWA | 75,468 | 60,142 | 15,000 | 326 | 45,142 R | 79.7% | 19.9% | 80.0% | 20.0% |
| 14,267 | PRESQUE ISLE | 6,724 | 4,207 | 2,481 | 36 | 1,726 R | 62.6% | 36.9% | 62.9% | 37.1% |
| 16,374 | ROSCOMMON | 9,823 | 6,419 | 3,359 | 45 | 3,060 R | 65.3% | 34.2% | 65.6% | 34.4% |
| 228,059 | SAGINAW | 90,416 | 51,495 | 38,420 | 501 | 13,075 R | 57.0% | 42.5% | 57.3% | 42.7% |
| 138,802 | ST. CLAIR | 53,399 | 36,114 | 16,998 | 287 | 19,116 R | 67.6% | 31.8% | 68.0% | 32.0% |
| 56,083 | ST. JOSEPH | 21,296 | 15,405 | 5,795 | 96 | 9,610 R | 72.3% | 27.2% | 72.7% | 27.3% |
| 40,789 | SANILAC | 16,810 | 12,627 | 4,126 | 57 | 8,501 R | 75.1% | 24.5% | 75.4% | 24.6% |
| 8,575 | SCHOOLCRAFT | 4,077 | 2,139 | 1,920 | 18 | 219 R | 52.5% | 47.1% | 52.7% | 47.3% |
| 71,140 | SHIAWASSEE | 28,431 | 18,756 | 9,514 | 161 | 9,242 R | 66.0% | 33.5% | 66.3% | 33.7% |
| 56,961 | TUSCOLA | 20,993 | 14,698 | 6,212 | 83 | 8,486 R | 70.0% | 29.6% | 70.3% | 29.7% |
| 66,814 | VAN BUREN | 25,445 | 16,426 | 8,853 | 166 | 7,573 R | 64.6% | 34.8% | 65.0% | 35.0% |
| 264,748 | WASHTENAW | 114,569 | 58,736 | 55,084 | 749 | 3,652 R | 51.3% | 48.1% | 51.6% | 48.4% |
| 2,337,891 | WAYNE | 868,343 | 367,391 | 496,632 | 4,320 | 129,241 D | 42.3% | 57.2% | 42.5% | 57.5% |
| 25,102 | WEXFORD | 10,715 | 7,279 | 3,398 | 38 | 3,881 R | 67.9% | 31.7% | 68.2% | 31.8% |
| 9,262,078 | TOTAL | 3,801,658 | 2,251,571 | 1,529,638 | 20,449 | 721,933 R | 59.2% | 40.2% | 59.5% | 40.5% |

# MICHIGAN

## PRESIDENT 1980

| 1980 Census Population | County | Total Vote | Republican | Democratic | Other | Rep.-Dem. Plurality | Percentage | | | |
|---|---|---|---|---|---|---|---|---|---|---|
| | | | | | | | Total Vote | | Major Vote | |
| | | | | | | | Rep. | Dem. | Rep. | Dem. |
| 9,740 | ALCONA | 5,062 | 2,905 | 1,857 | 300 | 1,048 R | 57.4% | 36.7% | 61.0% | 39.0% |
| 9,225 | ALGER | 4,647 | 2,059 | 2,242 | 346 | 183 D | 44.3% | 48.2% | 47.9% | 52.1% |
| 81,555 | ALLEGAN | 33,031 | 20,560 | 9,877 | 2,594 | 10,683 R | 62.2% | 29.9% | 67.5% | 32.5% |
| 32,315 | ALPENA | 13,832 | 6,901 | 5,834 | 1,097 | 1,067 R | 49.9% | 42.2% | 54.2% | 45.8% |
| 16,194 | ANTRIM | 8,364 | 4,706 | 2,909 | 749 | 1,797 R | 56.3% | 34.8% | 61.8% | 38.2% |
| 14,706 | ARENAC | 6,431 | 3,436 | 2,547 | 448 | 889 R | 53.4% | 39.6% | 57.4% | 42.6% |
| 8,484 | BARAGA | 3,921 | 2,046 | 1,609 | 266 | 437 R | 52.2% | 41.0% | 56.0% | 44.0% |
| 45,781 | BARRY | 20,654 | 12,006 | 6,857 | 1,791 | 5,149 R | 58.1% | 33.2% | 63.6% | 36.4% |
| 119,881 | BAY | 54,592 | 25,331 | 24,517 | 4,744 | 814 R | 46.4% | 44.9% | 50.8% | 49.2% |
| 11,205 | BENZIE | 5,498 | 3,054 | 1,842 | 602 | 1,212 R | 55.5% | 33.5% | 62.4% | 37.6% |
| 171,276 | BERRIEN | 67,978 | 41,458 | 22,152 | 4,368 | 19,306 R | 61.0% | 32.6% | 65.2% | 34.8% |
| 40,188 | BRANCH | 16,230 | 10,224 | 4,635 | 1,371 | 5,589 R | 63.0% | 28.6% | 68.8% | 31.2% |
| 141,557 | CALHOUN | 59,176 | 30,912 | 23,022 | 5,242 | 7,890 R | 52.2% | 38.9% | 57.3% | 42.7% |
| 49,499 | CASS | 19,735 | 11,206 | 7,058 | 1,471 | 4,148 R | 56.8% | 35.8% | 61.4% | 38.6% |
| 19,907 | CHARLEVOIX | 9,796 | 5,053 | 3,741 | 1,002 | 1,312 R | 51.6% | 38.2% | 57.5% | 42.5% |
| 20,649 | CHEBOYGAN | 9,954 | 5,221 | 3,938 | 795 | 1,283 R | 52.5% | 39.6% | 57.0% | 43.0% |
| 29,029 | CHIPPEWA | 13,494 | 7,059 | 5,268 | 1,167 | 1,791 R | 52.3% | 39.0% | 57.3% | 42.7% |
| 23,822 | CLARE | 10,718 | 5,719 | 4,164 | 835 | 1,555 R | 53.4% | 38.9% | 57.9% | 42.1% |
| 55,893 | CLINTON | 24,691 | 14,968 | 7,539 | 2,184 | 7,429 R | 60.6% | 30.5% | 66.5% | 33.5% |
| 9,465 | CRAWFORD | 4,964 | 2,652 | 1,826 | 486 | 826 R | 53.4% | 36.8% | 59.2% | 40.8% |
| 38,947 | DELTA | 17,692 | 8,146 | 8,475 | 1,071 | 329 D | 46.0% | 47.9% | 49.0% | 51.0% |
| 25,341 | DICKINSON | 13,077 | 6,614 | 5,694 | 769 | 920 R | 50.6% | 43.5% | 53.7% | 46.3% |
| 88,337 | EATON | 39,977 | 22,927 | 12,742 | 4,308 | 10,185 R | 57.4% | 31.9% | 64.3% | 35.7% |
| 22,992 | EMMET | 11,006 | 5,930 | 3,724 | 1,352 | 2,206 R | 53.9% | 33.8% | 61.4% | 38.6% |
| 450,449 | GENESEE | 183,900 | 78,572 | 90,393 | 14,935 | 11,821 D | 42.7% | 49.2% | 46.5% | 53.5% |
| 19,957 | GLADWIN | 8,825 | 4,509 | 3,733 | 583 | 776 R | 51.1% | 42.3% | 54.7% | 45.3% |
| 19,686 | GOGEBIC | 10,252 | 4,388 | 5,254 | 610 | 866 D | 42.8% | 51.2% | 45.5% | 54.5% |
| 54,899 | GRAND TRAVERSE | 24,706 | 14,484 | 7,150 | 3,072 | 7,334 R | 58.6% | 28.9% | 67.0% | 33.0% |
| 40,448 | GRATIOT | 15,670 | 9,294 | 4,916 | 1,460 | 4,378 R | 59.3% | 31.4% | 65.4% | 34.6% |
| 42,071 | HILLSDALE | 16,501 | 10,951 | 4,375 | 1,175 | 6,576 R | 66.4% | 26.5% | 71.5% | 28.5% |
| 37,872 | HOUGHTON | 16,534 | 7,926 | 6,858 | 1,750 | 1,068 R | 47.9% | 41.5% | 53.6% | 46.4% |
| 36,459 | HURON | 16,167 | 10,553 | 4,434 | 1,180 | 6,119 R | 65.3% | 27.4% | 70.4% | 29.6% |
| 275,520 | INGHAM | 125,631 | 56,777 | 48,278 | 20,576 | 8,499 R | 45.2% | 38.4% | 54.0% | 46.0% |
| 51,815 | IONIA | 20,982 | 12,040 | 7,039 | 1,903 | 5,001 R | 57.4% | 33.5% | 63.1% | 36.9% |
| 28,349 | IOSCO | 11,815 | 6,680 | 4,255 | 880 | 2,425 R | 56.5% | 36.0% | 61.1% | 38.9% |
| 13,635 | IRON | 7,732 | 3,507 | 3,742 | 483 | 235 D | 45.4% | 48.4% | 48.4% | 51.6% |
| 54,110 | ISABELLA | 20,715 | 10,407 | 7,293 | 3,015 | 3,114 R | 50.2% | 35.2% | 58.8% | 41.2% |
| 151,495 | JACKSON | 62,580 | 33,749 | 23,685 | 5,146 | 10,064 R | 53.9% | 37.8% | 58.8% | 41.2% |
| 212,378 | KALAMAZOO | 95,617 | 48,669 | 34,528 | 12,420 | 14,141 R | 50.9% | 36.1% | 58.5% | 41.5% |
| 10,952 | KALKASKA | 4,966 | 2,802 | 1,807 | 357 | 995 R | 56.4% | 36.4% | 60.8% | 39.2% |
| 444,506 | KENT | 206,290 | 112,604 | 72,790 | 20,896 | 39,814 R | 54.6% | 35.3% | 60.7% | 39.3% |
| 1,963 | KEWEENAW | 1,260 | 583 | 570 | 107 | 13 R | 46.3% | 45.2% | 50.6% | 49.4% |
| 7,711 | LAKE | 4,003 | 1,730 | 2,041 | 232 | 311 D | 43.2% | 51.0% | 45.9% | 54.1% |
| 70,038 | LAPEER | 28,069 | 15,996 | 9,671 | 2,402 | 6,325 R | 57.0% | 34.5% | 62.3% | 37.7% |
| 14,007 | LEELANAU | 7,935 | 4,585 | 2,348 | 1,002 | 2,237 R | 57.8% | 29.6% | 66.1% | 33.9% |
| 89,948 | LENAWEE | 36,085 | 20,366 | 12,935 | 2,784 | 7,431 R | 56.4% | 35.8% | 61.2% | 38.8% |
| 100,289 | LIVINGSTON | 41,570 | 25,012 | 12,626 | 3,932 | 12,386 R | 60.2% | 30.4% | 66.5% | 33.5% |
| 6,659 | LUCE | 2,882 | 1,659 | 992 | 231 | 667 R | 57.6% | 34.4% | 62.6% | 37.4% |
| 10,178 | MACKINAC | 5,784 | 3,021 | 2,262 | 501 | 759 R | 52.2% | 39.1% | 57.2% | 42.8% |
| 694,600 | MACOMB | 297,119 | 154,155 | 120,125 | 22,839 | 34,030 R | 51.9% | 40.4% | 56.2% | 43.8% |
| 23,019 | MANISTEE | 10,702 | 5,662 | 4,164 | 876 | 1,498 R | 52.9% | 38.9% | 57.6% | 42.4% |
| 74,101 | MARQUETTE | 29,479 | 13,181 | 13,312 | 2,986 | 131 D | 44.7% | 45.2% | 49.8% | 50.2% |
| 26,365 | MASON | 12,276 | 7,137 | 4,134 | 1,005 | 3,003 R | 58.1% | 33.7% | 63.3% | 36.7% |
| 36,961 | MECOSTA | 14,528 | 7,754 | 5,228 | 1,546 | 2,526 R | 53.4% | 36.0% | 59.7% | 40.3% |
| 26,201 | MENOMINEE | 11,749 | 6,170 | 4,962 | 617 | 1,208 R | 52.5% | 42.2% | 55.4% | 44.6% |
| 73,578 | MIDLAND | 33,610 | 17,828 | 12,019 | 3,763 | 5,809 R | 53.0% | 35.8% | 59.7% | 40.3% |
| 10,009 | MISSAUKEE | 5,075 | 3,221 | 1,563 | 291 | 1,658 R | 63.5% | 30.8% | 67.3% | 32.7% |
| 134,659 | MONROE | 49,964 | 25,612 | 20,578 | 3,774 | 5,034 R | 51.3% | 41.2% | 55.4% | 44.6% |
| 47,555 | MONTCALM | 19,150 | 10,822 | 6,706 | 1,622 | 4,116 R | 56.5% | 35.0% | 61.7% | 38.3% |
| 7,492 | MONTMORENCY | 4,308 | 2,400 | 1,654 | 254 | 746 R | 55.7% | 38.4% | 59.2% | 40.8% |

# MICHIGAN

## PRESIDENT 1980

| 1980 Census Population | County | Total Vote | Republican | Democratic | Other | Rep.-Dem. Plurality | Percentage | | | |
|---|---|---|---|---|---|---|---|---|---|---|
| | | | | | | | Total Vote | | Major Vote | |
| | | | | | | | Rep. | Dem. | Rep. | Dem. |
| 157,589 | MUSKEGON | 67,954 | 36,512 | 26,645 | 4,797 | 9,867 R | 53.7% | 39.2% | 57.8% | 42.2% |
| 34,917 | NEWAYGO | 15,223 | 8,918 | 5,236 | 1,069 | 3,682 R | 58.6% | 34.4% | 63.0% | 37.0% |
| 1,011,793 | OAKLAND | 463,328 | 253,211 | 164,869 | 45,248 | 88,342 R | 54.7% | 35.6% | 60.6% | 39.4% |
| 22,002 | OCEANA | 9,564 | 5,465 | 3,386 | 713 | 2,079 R | 57.1% | 35.4% | 61.7% | 38.3% |
| 16,436 | OGEMAW | 8,128 | 4,169 | 3,426 | 533 | 743 R | 51.3% | 42.2% | 54.9% | 45.1% |
| 9,861 | ONTONAGON | 5,248 | 2,569 | 2,375 | 304 | 194 R | 49.0% | 45.3% | 52.0% | 48.0% |
| 18,928 | OSCEOLA | 8,164 | 4,902 | 2,650 | 612 | 2,252 R | 60.0% | 32.5% | 64.9% | 35.1% |
| 6,858 | OSCODA | 3,466 | 1,915 | 1,325 | 226 | 590 R | 55.3% | 38.2% | 59.1% | 40.9% |
| 14,993 | OTSEGO | 7,023 | 3,771 | 2,666 | 586 | 1,105 R | 53.7% | 38.0% | 58.6% | 41.4% |
| 157,174 | OTTAWA | 75,484 | 51,217 | 18,435 | 5,832 | 32,782 R | 67.9% | 24.4% | 73.5% | 26.5% |
| 14,267 | PRESQUE ISLE | 6,912 | 3,486 | 2,952 | 474 | 534 R | 50.4% | 42.7% | 54.1% | 45.9% |
| 16,374 | ROSCOMMON | 9,659 | 5,280 | 3,763 | 616 | 1,517 R | 54.7% | 39.0% | 58.4% | 41.6% |
| 228,059 | SAGINAW | 93,800 | 45,233 | 41,650 | 6,917 | 3,583 R | 48.2% | 44.4% | 52.1% | 47.9% |
| 138,802 | ST. CLAIR | 55,778 | 31,021 | 20,410 | 4,347 | 10,611 R | 55.6% | 36.6% | 60.3% | 39.7% |
| 56,083 | ST. JOSEPH | 21,570 | 13,631 | 6,318 | 1,621 | 7,313 R | 63.2% | 29.3% | 68.3% | 31.7% |
| 40,789 | SANILAC | 18,117 | 12,158 | 4,898 | 1,061 | 7,260 R | 67.1% | 27.0% | 71.3% | 28.7% |
| 8,575 | SCHOOLCRAFT | 4,374 | 2,097 | 1,964 | 313 | 133 R | 47.9% | 44.9% | 51.6% | 48.4% |
| 71,140 | SHIAWASSEE | 30,470 | 15,756 | 11,985 | 2,729 | 3,771 R | 51.7% | 39.3% | 56.8% | 43.2% |
| 56,961 | TUSCOLA | 22,505 | 13,306 | 7,632 | 1,567 | 5,674 R | 59.1% | 33.9% | 63.5% | 36.5% |
| 66,814 | VAN BUREN | 25,824 | 14,451 | 9,248 | 2,125 | 5,203 R | 56.0% | 35.8% | 61.0% | 39.0% |
| 264,748 | WASHTENAW | 116,179 | 48,699 | 51,013 | 16,467 | 2,314 D | 41.9% | 43.9% | 48.8% | 51.2% |
| 2,337,891 | WAYNE | 890,844 | 315,532 | 522,024 | 53,288 | 206,492 D | 35.4% | 58.6% | 37.7% | 62.3% |
| 25,102 | WEXFORD | 11,160 | 6,027 | 4,173 | 960 | 1,854 R | 54.0% | 37.4% | 59.1% | 40.9% |
| 9,262,078 | TOTAL | 3,909,725 | 1,915,225 | 1,661,532 | 332,968 | 253,693 R | 49.0% | 42.5% | 53.5% | 46.5% |

484

# MICHIGAN

## PRESIDENT 1976

| 1970 Census Population | County | Total Vote | Republican | Democratic | Other | Rep.-Dem. Plurality | Percentage Total Vote Rep. | Dem. | Major Vote Rep. | Dem. |
|---|---|---|---|---|---|---|---|---|---|---|
| 7,113 | ALCONA | 4,403 | 2,328 | 2,038 | 37 | 290 R | 52.9% | 46.3% | 53.3% | 46.7% |
| 8,568 | ALGER | 4,161 | 1,722 | 2,379 | 60 | 657 D | 41.4% | 57.2% | 42.0% | 58.0% |
| 66,575 | ALLEGAN | 29,471 | 19,330 | 9,794 | 347 | 9,536 R | 65.6% | 33.2% | 66.4% | 33.6% |
| 30,708 | ALPENA | 12,866 | 6,380 | 6,310 | 176 | 70 R | 49.6% | 49.0% | 50.3% | 49.7% |
| 12,612 | ANTRIM | 7,518 | 4,369 | 3,032 | 117 | 1,337 R | 58.1% | 40.3% | 59.0% | 41.0% |
| 11,149 | ARENAC | 5,423 | 2,687 | 2,695 | 41 | 8 D | 49.5% | 49.7% | 49.9% | 50.1% |
| 7,789 | BARAGA | 3,614 | 1,788 | 1,778 | 48 | 10 R | 49.5% | 49.2% | 50.1% | 49.9% |
| 38,166 | BARRY | 18,388 | 11,178 | 6,967 | 243 | 4,211 R | 60.8% | 37.9% | 61.6% | 38.4% |
| 117,339 | BAY | 49,689 | 23,174 | 25,958 | 557 | 2,784 D | 46.6% | 52.2% | 47.2% | 52.8% |
| 8,593 | BENZIE | 5,038 | 3,085 | 1,891 | 62 | 1,194 R | 61.2% | 37.5% | 62.0% | 38.0% |
| 163,875 | BERRIEN | 66,798 | 40,835 | 25,163 | 800 | 15,672 R | 61.1% | 37.7% | 61.9% | 38.1% |
| 37,906 | BRANCH | 14,802 | 8,251 | 6,301 | 250 | 1,950 R | 55.7% | 42.6% | 56.7% | 43.3% |
| 141,963 | CALHOUN | 56,520 | 30,390 | 25,229 | 901 | 5,161 R | 53.8% | 44.6% | 54.6% | 45.4% |
| 43,312 | CASS | 17,939 | 9,893 | 7,843 | 203 | 2,050 R | 55.1% | 43.7% | 55.8% | 44.2% |
| 16,541 | CHARLEVOIX | 9,258 | 5,145 | 3,953 | 160 | 1,192 R | 55.6% | 42.7% | 56.6% | 43.4% |
| 16,573 | CHEBOYGAN | 8,878 | 4,894 | 3,880 | 104 | 1,014 R | 55.1% | 43.7% | 55.8% | 44.2% |
| 32,412 | CHIPPEWA | 13,175 | 7,025 | 6,022 | 128 | 1,003 R | 53.3% | 45.7% | 53.8% | 46.2% |
| 16,695 | CLARE | 9,126 | 4,879 | 4,153 | 94 | 726 R | 53.5% | 45.5% | 54.0% | 46.0% |
| 48,492 | CLINTON | 21,353 | 13,475 | 7,549 | 329 | 5,926 R | 63.1% | 35.4% | 64.1% | 35.9% |
| 6,482 | CRAWFORD | 4,303 | 2,359 | 1,889 | 55 | 470 R | 54.8% | 43.9% | 55.5% | 44.5% |
| 35,924 | DELTA | 17,033 | 7,809 | 9,027 | 197 | 1,218 D | 45.8% | 53.0% | 46.4% | 53.6% |
| 23,753 | DICKINSON | 12,177 | 5,922 | 6,134 | 121 | 212 D | 48.6% | 50.4% | 49.1% | 50.9% |
| 68,892 | EATON | 34,750 | 22,120 | 12,083 | 547 | 10,037 R | 63.7% | 34.8% | 64.7% | 35.3% |
| 18,331 | EMMET | 10,104 | 5,910 | 4,013 | 181 | 1,897 R | 58.5% | 39.7% | 59.6% | 40.4% |
| 444,341 | GENESEE | 171,438 | 80,004 | 88,967 | 2,467 | 8,963 D | 46.7% | 51.9% | 47.3% | 52.7% |
| 13,471 | GLADWIN | 7,567 | 3,794 | 3,719 | 54 | 75 R | 50.1% | 49.1% | 50.5% | 49.5% |
| 20,676 | GOGEBIC | 10,392 | 3,953 | 6,341 | 98 | 2,388 D | 38.0% | 61.0% | 38.4% | 61.6% |
| 39,175 | GRAND TRAVERSE | 21,150 | 13,505 | 7,263 | 382 | 6,242 R | 63.9% | 34.3% | 65.0% | 35.0% |
| 39,246 | GRATIOT | 15,118 | 9,526 | 5,429 | 163 | 4,097 R | 63.0% | 35.9% | 63.7% | 36.3% |
| 37,171 | HILLSDALE | 14,955 | 9,307 | 5,427 | 221 | 3,880 R | 62.2% | 36.3% | 63.2% | 36.8% |
| 34,652 | HOUGHTON | 15,600 | 8,049 | 7,352 | 199 | 697 R | 51.6% | 47.1% | 52.3% | 47.7% |
| 34,083 | HURON | 15,176 | 9,297 | 5,721 | 158 | 3,576 R | 61.3% | 37.7% | 61.9% | 38.1% |
| 261,039 | INGHAM | 119,327 | 66,729 | 47,890 | 4,708 | 18,839 R | 55.9% | 40.1% | 58.2% | 41.8% |
| 45,848 | IONIA | 18,791 | 11,737 | 6,820 | 234 | 4,917 R | 62.5% | 36.3% | 63.2% | 36.8% |
| 24,905 | IOSCO | 10,498 | 5,500 | 4,875 | 123 | 625 R | 52.4% | 46.4% | 53.0% | 47.0% |
| 13,813 | IRON | 7,718 | 3,224 | 4,401 | 93 | 1,177 D | 41.8% | 57.0% | 42.3% | 57.7% |
| 44,594 | ISABELLA | 18,345 | 10,577 | 7,281 | 487 | 3,296 R | 57.7% | 39.7% | 59.2% | 40.8% |
| 143,274 | JACKSON | 58,457 | 32,873 | 24,726 | 858 | 8,147 R | 56.2% | 42.3% | 57.1% | 42.9% |
| 201,550 | KALAMAZOO | 87,085 | 51,462 | 33,411 | 2,212 | 18,051 R | 59.1% | 38.4% | 60.6% | 39.4% |
| 5,272 | KALKASKA | 4,291 | 2,280 | 1,957 | 54 | 323 R | 53.1% | 45.6% | 53.8% | 46.2% |
| 411,044 | KENT | 188,633 | 126,805 | 59,000 | 2,828 | 67,805 R | 67.2% | 31.3% | 68.2% | 31.8% |
| 2,264 | KEWEENAW | 1,271 | 606 | 658 | 7 | 52 D | 47.7% | 51.8% | 47.9% | 52.1% |
| 5,661 | LAKE | 3,808 | 1,598 | 2,179 | 31 | 581 D | 42.0% | 57.2% | 42.3% | 57.7% |
| 52,317 | LAPEER | 22,215 | 12,349 | 9,503 | 363 | 2,846 R | 55.6% | 42.8% | 56.5% | 43.5% |
| 10,872 | LEELANAU | 6,803 | 4,240 | 2,437 | 126 | 1,803 R | 62.3% | 35.8% | 63.5% | 36.5% |
| 81,609 | LENAWEE | 33,435 | 18,397 | 14,610 | 428 | 3,787 R | 55.0% | 43.7% | 55.7% | 44.3% |
| 58,967 | LIVINGSTON | 32,486 | 19,437 | 12,415 | 634 | 7,022 R | 59.8% | 38.2% | 61.0% | 39.0% |
| 6,789 | LUCE | 2,495 | 1,379 | 1,099 | 17 | 280 R | 55.3% | 44.0% | 55.6% | 44.4% |
| 9,660 | MACKINAC | 5,627 | 3,107 | 2,452 | 68 | 655 R | 55.2% | 43.6% | 55.9% | 44.1% |
| 625,309 | MACOMB | 258,603 | 132,499 | 121,176 | 4,928 | 11,323 R | 51.2% | 46.9% | 52.2% | 47.8% |
| 20,094 | MANISTEE | 10,134 | 5,532 | 4,479 | 123 | 1,053 R | 54.6% | 44.2% | 55.3% | 44.7% |
| 64,686 | MARQUETTE | 26,315 | 12,984 | 12,837 | 494 | 147 R | 49.3% | 48.8% | 50.3% | 49.7% |
| 22,612 | MASON | 11,516 | 6,812 | 4,541 | 163 | 2,271 R | 59.2% | 39.4% | 60.0% | 40.0% |
| 27,992 | MECOSTA | 12,221 | 7,287 | 4,725 | 209 | 2,562 R | 59.6% | 38.7% | 60.7% | 39.3% |
| 24,587 | MENOMINEE | 11,357 | 5,633 | 5,596 | 128 | 37 R | 49.6% | 49.3% | 50.2% | 49.8% |
| 63,769 | MIDLAND | 30,101 | 17,631 | 11,959 | 511 | 5,672 R | 58.6% | 39.7% | 59.6% | 40.4% |
| 7,126 | MISSAUKEE | 4,681 | 2,943 | 1,688 | 50 | 1,255 R | 62.9% | 36.1% | 63.5% | 36.5% |
| 118,479 | MONROE | 44,597 | 20,676 | 23,290 | 631 | 2,614 D | 46.4% | 52.2% | 47.0% | 53.0% |
| 39,660 | MONTCALM | 17,294 | 10,439 | 6,684 | 171 | 3,755 R | 60.4% | 38.6% | 61.0% | 39.0% |
| 5,247 | MONTMORENCY | 3,617 | 1,882 | 1,684 | 51 | 198 R | 52.0% | 46.6% | 52.8% | 47.2% |

# MICHIGAN

## PRESIDENT 1976

| 1970 Census Population | County | Total Vote | Republican | Democratic | Other | Rep.-Dem. Plurality | Percentage | | | |
|---|---|---|---|---|---|---|---|---|---|---|
| | | | | | | | Total Vote | | Major Vote | |
| | | | | | | | Rep. | Dem. | Rep. | Dem. |
| 157,426 | MUSKEGON | 63,407 | 35,548 | 27,013 | 846 | 8,535 R | 56.1% | 42.6% | 56.8% | 43.2% |
| 27,992 | NEWAYGO | 14,050 | 8,258 | 5,622 | 170 | 2,636 R | 58.8% | 40.0% | 59.5% | 40.5% |
| 907,871 | OAKLAND | 416,205 | 244,271 | 164,266 | 7,668 | 80,005 R | 58.7% | 39.5% | 59.8% | 40.2% |
| 17,984 | OCEANA | 8,798 | 5,236 | 3,427 | 135 | 1,809 R | 59.5% | 39.0% | 60.4% | 39.6% |
| 11,903 | OGEMAW | 6,824 | 3,212 | 3,545 | 67 | 333 D | 47.1% | 51.9% | 47.5% | 52.5% |
| 10,548 | ONTONAGON | 5,607 | 2,462 | 3,104 | 41 | 642 D | 43.9% | 55.4% | 44.2% | 55.8% |
| 14,838 | OSCEOLA | 7,178 | 4,467 | 2,603 | 108 | 1,864 R | 62.2% | 36.3% | 63.2% | 36.8% |
| 4,726 | OSCODA | 2,677 | 1,541 | 1,108 | 28 | 433 R | 57.6% | 41.4% | 58.2% | 41.8% |
| 10,422 | OTSEGO | 5,952 | 3,155 | 2,724 | 73 | 431 R | 53.0% | 45.8% | 53.7% | 46.3% |
| 128,181 | OTTAWA | 66,370 | 49,196 | 16,381 | 793 | 32,815 R | 74.1% | 24.7% | 75.0% | 25.0% |
| 12,836 | PRESQUE ISLE | 6,948 | 3,545 | 3,334 | 69 | 211 R | 51.0% | 48.0% | 51.5% | 48.5% |
| 9,892 | ROSCOMMON | 8,401 | 4,608 | 3,691 | 102 | 917 R | 54.9% | 43.9% | 55.5% | 44.5% |
| 219,743 | SAGINAW | 84,071 | 46,765 | 36,280 | 1,026 | 10,485 R | 55.6% | 43.2% | 56.3% | 43.7% |
| 120,175 | ST. CLAIR | 49,889 | 26,311 | 22,734 | 844 | 3,577 R | 52.7% | 45.6% | 53.6% | 46.4% |
| 47,392 | ST. JOSEPH | 19,295 | 11,784 | 7,306 | 205 | 4,478 R | 61.1% | 37.9% | 61.7% | 38.3% |
| 34,889 | SANILAC | 16,856 | 10,597 | 6,042 | 217 | 4,555 R | 62.9% | 35.8% | 63.7% | 36.3% |
| 8,226 | SCHOOLCRAFT | 4,154 | 1,933 | 2,158 | 63 | 225 D | 46.5% | 51.9% | 47.3% | 52.7% |
| 63,075 | SHIAWASSEE | 27,721 | 15,113 | 12,202 | 406 | 2,911 R | 54.5% | 44.0% | 55.3% | 44.7% |
| 48,603 | TUSCOLA | 20,144 | 12,059 | 7,932 | 153 | 4,127 R | 59.9% | 39.4% | 60.3% | 39.7% |
| 56,173 | VAN BUREN | 24,302 | 13,615 | 10,366 | 321 | 3,249 R | 56.0% | 42.7% | 56.8% | 43.2% |
| 234,103 | WASHTENAW | 111,689 | 56,807 | 50,917 | 3,965 | 5,890 R | 50.9% | 45.6% | 52.7% | 47.3% |
| 2,666,751 | WAYNE | 912,990 | 348,588 | 548,767 | 15,635 | 200,179 D | 38.2% | 60.1% | 38.8% | 61.2% |
| 19,717 | WEXFORD | 10,317 | 5,670 | 4,519 | 128 | 1,151 R | 55.0% | 43.8% | 55.6% | 44.4% |
| 8,875,083 | TOTAL | 3,653,749 | 1,893,742 | 1,696,714 | 63,293 | 197,028 R | 51.8% | 46.4% | 52.7% | 47.3% |

# MICHIGAN

## PRESIDENT 1972

| 1970 Census Population | County | Total Vote | Republican | Democratic | Other | Rep.-Dem. Plurality | Percentage Total Vote Rep. | Dem. | Major Vote Rep. | Dem. |
|---|---|---|---|---|---|---|---|---|---|---|
| 7,113 | ALCONA | 3,693 | 2,434 | 1,195 | 64 | 1,239 R | 65.9% | 32.4% | 67.1% | 32.9% |
| 8,568 | ALGER | 3,878 | 2,035 | 1,803 | 40 | 232 R | 52.5% | 46.5% | 53.0% | 47.0% |
| 66,575 | ALLEGAN | 26,873 | 18,407 | 7,883 | 583 | 10,524 R | 68.5% | 29.3% | 70.0% | 30.0% |
| 30,708 | ALPENA | 11,831 | 6,513 | 5,104 | 214 | 1,409 R | 55.1% | 43.1% | 56.1% | 43.9% |
| 12,612 | ANTRIM | 6,280 | 4,068 | 2,000 | 212 | 2,068 R | 64.8% | 31.8% | 67.0% | 33.0% |
| 11,149 | ARENAC | 4,506 | 2,588 | 1,829 | 89 | 759 R | 57.4% | 40.6% | 58.6% | 41.4% |
| 7,789 | BARAGA | 3,468 | 1,905 | 1,517 | 46 | 388 R | 54.9% | 43.7% | 55.7% | 44.3% |
| 38,166 | BARRY | 16,229 | 10,393 | 5,484 | 352 | 4,909 R | 64.0% | 33.8% | 65.5% | 34.5% |
| 117,339 | BAY | 46,118 | 23,094 | 21,712 | 1,312 | 1,382 R | 50.1% | 47.1% | 51.5% | 48.5% |
| 8,593 | BENZIE | 4,054 | 2,686 | 1,310 | 58 | 1,376 R | 66.3% | 32.3% | 67.2% | 32.8% |
| 163,875 | BERRIEN | 63,051 | 43,047 | 18,597 | 1,407 | 24,450 R | 68.3% | 29.5% | 69.8% | 30.2% |
| 37,906 | BRANCH | 13,521 | 8,388 | 4,887 | 246 | 3,501 R | 62.0% | 36.1% | 63.2% | 36.8% |
| 141,963 | CALHOUN | 55,828 | 32,531 | 22,154 | 1,143 | 10,377 R | 58.3% | 39.7% | 59.5% | 40.5% |
| 43,312 | CASS | 15,679 | 10,398 | 4,982 | 299 | 5,416 R | 66.3% | 31.8% | 67.6% | 32.4% |
| 16,541 | CHARLEVOIX | 7,658 | 4,522 | 2,831 | 305 | 1,691 R | 59.0% | 37.0% | 61.5% | 38.5% |
| 16,573 | CHEBOYGAN | 7,662 | 4,529 | 2,985 | 148 | 1,544 R | 59.1% | 39.0% | 60.3% | 39.7% |
| 32,412 | CHIPPEWA | 11,906 | 7,028 | 4,744 | 134 | 2,284 R | 59.0% | 39.8% | 59.7% | 40.3% |
| 16,695 | CLARE | 6,986 | 4,402 | 2,434 | 150 | 1,968 R | 63.0% | 34.8% | 64.4% | 35.6% |
| 48,492 | CLINTON | 19,648 | 13,438 | 5,870 | 340 | 7,568 R | 68.4% | 29.9% | 69.6% | 30.4% |
| 6,482 | CRAWFORD | 3,151 | 1,953 | 1,143 | 55 | 810 R | 62.0% | 36.3% | 63.1% | 36.9% |
| 35,924 | DELTA | 15,886 | 7,647 | 8,003 | 236 | 356 D | 48.1% | 50.4% | 48.9% | 51.1% |
| 23,753 | DICKINSON | 11,715 | 5,989 | 5,339 | 387 | 650 R | 51.1% | 45.6% | 52.9% | 47.1% |
| 68,892 | EATON | 29,811 | 20,413 | 8,986 | 412 | 11,427 R | 68.5% | 30.1% | 69.4% | 30.6% |
| 18,331 | EMMET | 8,541 | 5,288 | 3,081 | 172 | 2,207 R | 61.9% | 36.1% | 63.2% | 36.8% |
| 444,341 | GENESEE | 162,449 | 85,747 | 73,896 | 2,806 | 11,851 R | 52.8% | 45.5% | 53.7% | 46.3% |
| 13,471 | GLADWIN | 5,625 | 3,484 | 2,016 | 125 | 1,468 R | 61.9% | 35.8% | 63.3% | 36.7% |
| 20,676 | GOGEBIC | 10,776 | 5,631 | 4,984 | 161 | 647 R | 52.3% | 46.3% | 53.0% | 47.0% |
| 39,175 | GRAND TRAVERSE | 17,621 | 11,421 | 5,810 | 390 | 5,611 R | 64.8% | 33.0% | 66.3% | 33.7% |
| 39,246 | GRATIOT | 14,478 | 9,904 | 4,370 | 204 | 5,534 R | 68.4% | 30.2% | 69.4% | 30.6% |
| 37,171 | HILLSDALE | 13,484 | 9,261 | 3,942 | 281 | 5,319 R | 68.7% | 29.2% | 70.1% | 29.9% |
| 34,652 | HOUGHTON | 15,590 | 9,053 | 6,402 | 135 | 2,651 R | 58.1% | 41.1% | 58.6% | 41.4% |
| 34,083 | HURON | 14,595 | 9,832 | 4,456 | 307 | 5,376 R | 67.4% | 30.5% | 68.8% | 31.2% |
| 261,039 | INGHAM | 118,182 | 63,376 | 53,458 | 1,348 | 9,918 R | 53.6% | 45.2% | 54.2% | 45.8% |
| 45,848 | IONIA | 17,412 | 10,898 | 6,240 | 274 | 4,658 R | 62.6% | 35.8% | 63.6% | 36.4% |
| 24,905 | IOSCO | 8,971 | 5,750 | 3,065 | 156 | 2,685 R | 64.1% | 34.2% | 65.2% | 34.8% |
| 13,813 | IRON | 7,376 | 3,630 | 3,512 | 234 | 118 R | 49.2% | 47.6% | 50.8% | 49.2% |
| 44,594 | ISABELLA | 17,443 | 9,682 | 7,446 | 315 | 2,236 R | 55.5% | 42.7% | 56.5% | 43.5% |
| 143,274 | JACKSON | 54,891 | 34,220 | 19,350 | 1,321 | 14,870 R | 62.3% | 35.3% | 63.9% | 36.1% |
| 201,550 | KALAMAZOO | 85,710 | 50,405 | 33,324 | 1,981 | 17,081 R | 58.8% | 38.9% | 60.2% | 39.8% |
| 5,272 | KALKASKA | 2,881 | 1,855 | 924 | 102 | 931 R | 64.4% | 32.1% | 66.8% | 33.2% |
| 411,044 | KENT | 175,441 | 104,041 | 67,587 | 3,813 | 36,454 R | 59.3% | 38.5% | 60.6% | 39.4% |
| 2,264 | KEWEENAW | 1,182 | 715 | 456 | 11 | 259 R | 60.5% | 38.6% | 61.1% | 38.9% |
| 5,661 | LAKE | 3,129 | 1,532 | 1,548 | 49 | 16 D | 49.0% | 49.5% | 49.7% | 50.3% |
| 52,317 | LAPEER | 17,585 | 11,615 | 5,531 | 439 | 6,084 R | 66.1% | 31.5% | 67.7% | 32.3% |
| 10,872 | LEELANAU | 5,786 | 3,809 | 1,855 | 122 | 1,954 R | 65.8% | 32.1% | 67.2% | 32.8% |
| 81,609 | LENAWEE | 30,647 | 19,125 | 11,018 | 504 | 8,107 R | 62.4% | 36.0% | 63.4% | 36.6% |
| 58,967 | LIVINGSTON | 25,210 | 16,856 | 7,634 | 720 | 9,222 R | 66.9% | 30.3% | 68.8% | 31.2% |
| 6,789 | LUCE | 2,487 | 1,579 | 862 | 46 | 717 R | 63.5% | 34.7% | 64.7% | 35.3% |
| 9,660 | MACKINAC | 5,102 | 3,096 | 1,937 | 69 | 1,159 R | 60.7% | 38.0% | 61.5% | 38.5% |
| 625,309 | MACOMB | 235,746 | 147,777 | 82,346 | 5,623 | 65,431 R | 62.7% | 34.9% | 64.2% | 35.8% |
| 20,094 | MANISTEE | 8,863 | 5,070 | 3,625 | 168 | 1,445 R | 57.2% | 40.9% | 58.3% | 41.7% |
| 64,686 | MARQUETTE | 25,157 | 13,249 | 11,555 | 353 | 1,694 R | 52.7% | 45.9% | 53.4% | 46.6% |
| 22,612 | MASON | 10,703 | 6,811 | 3,697 | 195 | 3,114 R | 63.6% | 34.5% | 64.8% | 35.2% |
| 27,992 | MECOSTA | 11,134 | 7,158 | 3,799 | 177 | 3,359 R | 64.3% | 34.1% | 65.3% | 34.7% |
| 24,587 | MENOMINEE | 10,980 | 6,060 | 4,657 | 263 | 1,403 R | 55.2% | 42.4% | 56.5% | 43.5% |
| 63,769 | MIDLAND | 26,825 | 16,473 | 9,504 | 848 | 6,969 R | 61.4% | 35.4% | 63.4% | 36.6% |
| 7,126 | MISSAUKEE | 3,685 | 2,647 | 924 | 114 | 1,723 R | 71.8% | 25.1% | 74.1% | 25.9% |
| 118,479 | MONROE | 42,465 | 23,263 | 17,726 | 1,476 | 5,537 R | 54.8% | 41.7% | 56.8% | 43.2% |
| 39,660 | MONTCALM | 15,477 | 9,591 | 5,602 | 284 | 3,989 R | 62.0% | 36.2% | 63.1% | 36.9% |
| 5,247 | MONTMORENCY | 2,788 | 1,798 | 914 | 76 | 884 R | 64.5% | 32.8% | 66.3% | 33.7% |

# MICHIGAN

## PRESIDENT 1972

| 1970 Census Population | County | Total Vote | Republican | Democratic | Other | Rep.-Dem. Plurality | Percentage | | | |
|---|---|---|---|---|---|---|---|---|---|---|
| | | | | | | | Total Vote | | Major Vote | |
| | | | | | | | Rep. | Dem. | Rep. | Dem. |
| 157,426 | MUSKEGON | 61,109 | 36,428 | 22,804 | 1,877 | 13,624 R | 59.6% | 37.3% | 61.5% | 38.5% |
| 27,992 | NEWAYGO | 12,565 | 8,245 | 3,978 | 342 | 4,267 R | 65.6% | 31.7% | 67.5% | 32.5% |
| 907,871 | OAKLAND | 378,640 | 241,613 | 129,400 | 7,627 | 112,213 R | 63.8% | 34.2% | 65.1% | 34.9% |
| 17,984 | OCEANA | 7,775 | 4,992 | 2,525 | 258 | 2,467 R | 64.2% | 32.5% | 66.4% | 33.6% |
| 11,903 | OGEMAW | 5,541 | 3,367 | 2,056 | 118 | 1,311 R | 60.8% | 37.1% | 62.1% | 37.9% |
| 10,548 | ONTONAGON | 5,286 | 3,040 | 2,140 | 106 | 900 R | 57.5% | 40.5% | 58.7% | 41.3% |
| 14,838 | OSCEOLA | 6,345 | 4,441 | 1,706 | 198 | 2,735 R | 70.0% | 26.9% | 72.2% | 27.8% |
| 4,726 | OSCODA | 2,309 | 1,561 | 678 | 70 | 883 R | 67.6% | 29.4% | 69.7% | 30.3% |
| 10,422 | OTSEGO | 4,838 | 2,854 | 1,912 | 72 | 942 R | 59.0% | 39.5% | 59.9% | 40.1% |
| 128,181 | OTTAWA | 58,559 | 42,169 | 15,119 | 1,271 | 27,050 R | 72.0% | 25.8% | 73.6% | 26.4% |
| 12,836 | PRESQUE ISLE | 5,997 | 3,372 | 2,440 | 185 | 932 R | 56.2% | 40.7% | 58.0% | 42.0% |
| 9,892 | ROSCOMMON | 6,445 | 4,136 | 2,187 | 122 | 1,949 R | 64.2% | 33.9% | 65.4% | 34.6% |
| 219,743 | SAGINAW | 78,521 | 47,920 | 29,424 | 1,177 | 18,496 R | 61.0% | 37.5% | 62.0% | 38.0% |
| 120,175 | ST. CLAIR | 45,159 | 28,471 | 15,712 | 976 | 12,759 R | 63.0% | 34.8% | 64.4% | 35.6% |
| 47,392 | ST. JOSEPH | 17,988 | 12,438 | 5,119 | 431 | 7,319 R | 69.1% | 28.5% | 70.8% | 29.2% |
| 34,889 | SANILAC | 15,124 | 11,031 | 3,780 | 313 | 7,251 R | 72.9% | 25.0% | 74.5% | 25.5% |
| 8,226 | SCHOOLCRAFT | 4,123 | 2,310 | 1,759 | 54 | 551 R | 56.0% | 42.7% | 56.8% | 43.2% |
| 63,075 | SHIAWASSEE | 25,136 | 15,489 | 8,932 | 715 | 6,557 R | 61.6% | 35.5% | 63.4% | 36.6% |
| 48,603 | TUSCOLA | 17,947 | 12,198 | 5,449 | 300 | 6,749 R | 68.0% | 30.4% | 69.1% | 30.9% |
| 56,173 | VAN BUREN | 21,520 | 13,903 | 7,159 | 458 | 6,744 R | 64.6% | 33.3% | 66.0% | 34.0% |
| 234,103 | WASHTENAW | 107,575 | 50,535 | 55,350 | 1,690 | 4,815 D | 47.0% | 51.5% | 47.7% | 52.3% |
| 2,666,751 | WAYNE | 966,877 | 435,877 | 514,913 | 16,087 | 79,036 D | 45.1% | 53.3% | 45.8% | 54.2% |
| 19,717 | WEXFORD | 8,499 | 5,221 | 3,048 | 230 | 2,173 R | 61.4% | 35.9% | 63.1% | 36.9% |
| 8,875,083 | TOTAL | 3,489,727 | 1,961,721 | 1,459,435 | 68,571 | 502,286 R | 56.2% | 41.8% | 57.3% | 42.7% |

# MICHIGAN

## PRESIDENT 1968

| 1960 Census Population | County | Total Vote | Republican | Democratic | AIP | Other | Plurality | Percentage Total Vote Rep. | Dem. | AIP |
|---|---|---|---|---|---|---|---|---|---|---|
| 6,352 | ALCONA | 3,152 | 1,852 | 958 | 338 | 4 | 894 R | 58.8% | 30.4% | 10.7% |
| 9,250 | ALGER | 3,512 | 1,406 | 1,927 | 173 | 6 | 521 D | 40.0% | 54.9% | 4.9% |
| 57,729 | ALLEGAN | 24,483 | 14,769 | 7,276 | 2,389 | 49 | 7,493 R | 60.3% | 29.7% | 9.8% |
| 28,556 | ALPENA | 11,261 | 5,717 | 4,788 | 747 | 9 | 929 R | 50.8% | 42.5% | 6.6% |
| 10,373 | ANTRIM | 5,068 | 3,002 | 1,690 | 374 | 2 | 1,312 R | 59.2% | 33.3% | 7.4% |
| 9,860 | ARENAC | 3,989 | 2,089 | 1,573 | 324 | 3 | 516 R | 52.4% | 39.4% | 8.1% |
| 7,151 | BARAGA | 3,318 | 1,508 | 1,680 | 116 | 14 | 172 D | 45.4% | 50.6% | 3.5% |
| 31,738 | BARRY | 15,400 | 8,492 | 5,206 | 1,674 | 28 | 3,286 R | 55.1% | 33.8% | 10.9% |
| 107,042 | BAY | 42,567 | 18,779 | 21,410 | 2,291 | 87 | 2,631 D | 44.1% | 50.3% | 5.4% |
| 7,834 | BENZIE | 3,510 | 2,138 | 1,147 | 219 | 6 | 991 R | 60.9% | 32.7% | 6.2% |
| 149,865 | BERRIEN | 62,916 | 32,136 | 21,266 | 9,333 | 181 | 10,870 R | 51.1% | 33.8% | 14.8% |
| 34,903 | BRANCH | 12,654 | 7,071 | 4,518 | 1,037 | 28 | 2,553 R | 55.9% | 35.7% | 8.2% |
| 138,858 | CALHOUN | 54,960 | 26,181 | 22,633 | 5,944 | 202 | 3,548 R | 47.6% | 41.2% | 10.8% |
| 36,932 | CASS | 14,906 | 6,996 | 5,616 | 2,257 | 37 | 1,380 R | 46.9% | 37.7% | 15.1% |
| 13,421 | CHARLEVOIX | 6,703 | 3,696 | 2,446 | 556 | 5 | 1,250 R | 55.1% | 36.5% | 8.3% |
| 14,550 | CHEBOYGAN | 6,899 | 3,422 | 2,840 | 634 | 3 | 582 R | 49.6% | 41.2% | 9.2% |
| 32,655 | CHIPPEWA | 10,297 | 5,359 | 4,132 | 793 | 13 | 1,227 R | 52.0% | 40.1% | 7.7% |
| 11,647 | CLARE | 5,831 | 3,315 | 1,909 | 602 | 5 | 1,406 R | 56.9% | 32.7% | 10.3% |
| 37,969 | CLINTON | 16,585 | 9,416 | 5,548 | 1,591 | 30 | 3,868 R | 56.8% | 33.5% | 9.6% |
| 4,971 | CRAWFORD | 2,300 | 1,266 | 845 | 187 | 2 | 421 R | 55.0% | 36.7% | 8.1% |
| 34,298 | DELTA | 14,364 | 5,829 | 7,821 | 700 | 14 | 1,992 D | 40.6% | 54.4% | 4.9% |
| 23,917 | DICKINSON | 11,194 | 4,920 | 5,726 | 533 | 15 | 806 D | 44.0% | 51.2% | 4.8% |
| 49,684 | EATON | 24,826 | 14,184 | 8,347 | 2,252 | 43 | 5,837 R | 57.1% | 33.6% | 9.1% |
| 15,904 | EMMET | 7,488 | 4,405 | 2,624 | 446 | 13 | 1,781 R | 58.8% | 35.0% | 6.0% |
| 374,313 | GENESEE | 164,013 | 63,948 | 75,174 | 24,539 | 352 | 11,226 D | 39.0% | 45.8% | 15.0% |
| 10,769 | GLADWIN | 5,022 | 2,840 | 1,668 | 511 | 3 | 1,172 R | 56.6% | 33.2% | 10.2% |
| 24,370 | GOGEBIC | 10,426 | 4,140 | 5,839 | 434 | 13 | 1,699 D | 39.7% | 56.0% | 4.2% |
| 33,490 | GRAND TRAVERSE | 14,567 | 8,960 | 4,741 | 843 | 23 | 4,219 R | 61.5% | 32.5% | 5.8% |
| 37,012 | GRATIOT | 13,408 | 8,404 | 4,040 | 949 | 15 | 4,364 R | 62.7% | 30.1% | 7.1% |
| 34,742 | HILLSDALE | 13,444 | 8,506 | 3,803 | 1,107 | 28 | 4,703 R | 63.3% | 28.3% | 8.2% |
| 35,654 | HOUGHTON | 14,143 | 6,639 | 6,988 | 473 | 43 | 349 D | 46.9% | 49.4% | 3.3% |
| 34,006 | HURON | 13,552 | 8,743 | 3,607 | 1,178 | 24 | 5,136 R | 64.5% | 26.6% | 8.7% |
| 211,296 | INGHAM | 90,953 | 46,805 | 37,362 | 6,432 | 354 | 9,443 R | 51.5% | 41.1% | 7.1% |
| 43,132 | IONIA | 15,968 | 8,625 | 6,055 | 1,261 | 27 | 2,570 R | 54.0% | 37.9% | 7.9% |
| 16,505 | IOSCO | 7,340 | 4,068 | 2,533 | 736 | 3 | 1,535 R | 55.4% | 34.5% | 10.0% |
| 17,184 | IRON | 7,772 | 3,292 | 4,130 | 340 | 10 | 838 D | 42.4% | 53.1% | 4.4% |
| 35,348 | ISABELLA | 12,396 | 7,111 | 4,450 | 808 | 27 | 2,661 R | 57.4% | 35.9% | 6.5% |
| 131,994 | JACKSON | 51,857 | 27,828 | 18,205 | 5,689 | 135 | 9,623 R | 53.7% | 35.1% | 11.0% |
| 169,712 | KALAMAZOO | 73,832 | 39,796 | 26,437 | 7,398 | 201 | 13,359 R | 53.9% | 35.8% | 10.0% |
| 4,382 | KALKASKA | 2,233 | 1,190 | 753 | 288 | 2 | 437 R | 53.3% | 33.7% | 12.9% |
| 363,187 | KENT | 159,850 | 85,810 | 61,891 | 11,584 | 565 | 23,919 R | 53.7% | 38.7% | 7.2% |
| 2,417 | KEWEENAW | 1,194 | 525 | 602 | 65 | 2 | 77 D | 44.0% | 50.4% | 5.4% |
| 5,338 | LAKE | 2,798 | 1,094 | 1,482 | 220 | 2 | 388 D | 39.1% | 53.0% | 7.9% |
| 41,926 | LAPEER | 16,163 | 8,866 | 5,199 | 2,081 | 17 | 3,667 R | 54.9% | 32.2% | 12.9% |
| 9,321 | LEELANAU | 4,659 | 2,798 | 1,562 | 292 | 7 | 1,236 R | 60.1% | 33.5% | 6.3% |
| 77,789 | LENAWEE | 29,147 | 16,280 | 10,552 | 2,197 | 118 | 5,728 R | 55.9% | 36.2% | 7.5% |
| 38,233 | LIVINGSTON | 19,670 | 10,034 | 7,052 | 2,543 | 41 | 2,982 R | 51.0% | 35.9% | 12.9% |
| 7,827 | LUCE | 2,316 | 1,351 | 855 | 109 | 1 | 496 R | 58.3% | 36.9% | 4.7% |
| 10,853 | MACKINAC | 4,577 | 2,507 | 1,751 | 317 | 2 | 756 R | 54.8% | 38.3% | 6.9% |
| 405,804 | MACOMB | 207,577 | 63,139 | 114,552 | 29,239 | 647 | 51,413 D | 30.4% | 55.2% | 14.1% |
| 19,042 | MANISTEE | 8,306 | 4,007 | 3,671 | 614 | 14 | 336 R | 48.2% | 44.2% | 7.4% |
| 56,154 | MARQUETTE | 20,995 | 8,960 | 11,199 | 802 | 34 | 2,239 D | 42.7% | 53.3% | 3.8% |
| 21,929 | MASON | 9,831 | 5,311 | 3,660 | 854 | 6 | 1,651 R | 54.0% | 37.2% | 8.7% |
| 21,051 | MECOSTA | 8,426 | 5,053 | 2,738 | 625 | 10 | 2,315 R | 60.0% | 32.5% | 7.4% |
| 24,685 | MENOMINEE | 10,108 | 4,599 | 4,877 | 620 | 12 | 278 D | 45.5% | 48.2% | 6.1% |
| 51,450 | MIDLAND | 23,658 | 14,329 | 7,428 | 1,849 | 52 | 6,901 R | 60.6% | 31.4% | 7.8% |
| 6,784 | MISSAUKEE | 3,191 | 2,161 | 736 | 292 | 2 | 1,425 R | 67.7% | 23.1% | 9.2% |
| 101,120 | MONROE | 39,572 | 15,685 | 18,921 | 4,873 | 93 | 3,236 D | 39.6% | 47.8% | 12.3% |
| 35,795 | MONTCALM | 14,902 | 8,329 | 5,303 | 1,244 | 26 | 3,026 R | 55.9% | 35.6% | 8.3% |
| 4,424 | MONTMORENCY | 2,351 | 1,279 | 810 | 260 | 2 | 469 R | 54.4% | 34.5% | 11.1% |

# MICHIGAN

## PRESIDENT 1968

| 1960 Census Population | County | Total Vote | Republican | Democratic | AIP | Other | Plurality | Percentage Total Vote | | |
|---|---|---|---|---|---|---|---|---|---|---|
| | | | | | | | | Rep. | Dem. | AIP |
| 149,943 | MUSKEGON | 58,683 | 28,233 | 24,492 | 5,808 | 150 | 3,741 R | 48.1% | 41.7% | 9.9% |
| 24,160 | NEWAYGO | 11,048 | 6,626 | 3,369 | 1,042 | 11 | 3,257 R | 60.0% | 30.5% | 9.4% |
| 690,259 | OAKLAND | 345,458 | 156,538 | 154,630 | 33,024 | 1,266 | 1,908 R | 45.3% | 44.8% | 9.6% |
| 16,547 | OCEANA | 6,957 | 3,911 | 2,152 | 876 | 18 | 1,759 R | 56.2% | 30.9% | 12.6% |
| 9,680 | OGEMAW | 4,630 | 2,526 | 1,647 | 454 | 3 | 879 R | 54.6% | 35.6% | 9.8% |
| 10,584 | ONTONAGON | 5,009 | 2,290 | 2,462 | 252 | 5 | 172 D | 45.7% | 49.2% | 5.0% |
| 13,595 | OSCEOLA | 5,810 | 3,705 | 1,509 | 583 | 13 | 2,196 R | 63.8% | 26.0% | 10.0% |
| 3,447 | OSCODA | 1,844 | 1,124 | 563 | 157 | | 561 R | 61.0% | 30.5% | 8.5% |
| 7,545 | OTSEGO | 3,793 | 1,871 | 1,661 | 259 | 2 | 210 R | 49.3% | 43.8% | 6.8% |
| 98,719 | OTTAWA | 49,342 | 33,356 | 12,431 | 3,460 | 95 | 20,925 R | 67.6% | 25.2% | 7.0% |
| 13,117 | PRESQUE ISLE | 5,251 | 2,565 | 2,300 | 385 | 1 | 265 R | 48.8% | 43.8% | 7.3% |
| 7,200 | ROSCOMMON | 4,713 | 2,635 | 1,639 | 431 | 8 | 996 R | 55.9% | 34.8% | 9.1% |
| 190,752 | SAGINAW | 77,423 | 38,070 | 32,266 | 6,906 | 181 | 5,804 R | 49.2% | 41.7% | 8.9% |
| 107,201 | ST. CLAIR | 42,669 | 21,084 | 16,251 | 5,261 | 73 | 4,833 R | 49.4% | 38.1% | 12.3% |
| 42,332 | ST. JOSEPH | 17,645 | 10,445 | 5,413 | 1,759 | 28 | 5,032 R | 59.2% | 30.7% | 10.0% |
| 32,314 | SANILAC | 14,168 | 9,273 | 3,193 | 1,692 | 10 | 6,080 R | 65.5% | 22.5% | 11.9% |
| 8,953 | SCHOOLCRAFT | 3,844 | 1,745 | 1,869 | 227 | 3 | 124 D | 45.4% | 48.6% | 5.9% |
| 53,446 | SHIAWASSEE | 22,532 | 11,465 | 8,619 | 2,377 | 71 | 2,846 R | 50.9% | 38.3% | 10.5% |
| 43,305 | TUSCOLA | 16,610 | 10,205 | 4,698 | 1,682 | 25 | 5,507 R | 61.4% | 28.3% | 10.1% |
| 48,395 | VAN BUREN | 20,607 | 10,676 | 7,304 | 2,560 | 67 | 3,372 R | 51.8% | 35.4% | 12.4% |
| 172,440 | WASHTENAW | 77,814 | 36,432 | 33,073 | 7,456 | 853 | 3,359 R | 46.8% | 42.5% | 9.6% |
| 2,666,297 | WAYNE | 1,034,260 | 270,566 | 654,157 | 105,606 | 3,931 | 383,591 D | 26.2% | 63.2% | 10.2% |
| 18,466 | WEXFORD | 7,740 | 4,364 | 2,832 | 535 | 9 | 1,532 R | 56.4% | 36.6% | 6.9% |
| 7,823,194 | TOTAL | 3,306,250 | 1,370,665 | 1,593,082 | 331,968 | 10,535 | 222,417 D | 41.5% | 48.2% | 10.0% |

# MICHIGAN

## PRESIDENT 1964

| 1960 Census Population | County | Total Vote | Republican | Democratic | Other | Rep.-Dem. Plurality | Percentage Total Vote Rep. | Dem. | Major Vote Rep. | Dem. |
|---:|---|---:|---:|---:|---:|---:|---:|---:|---:|---:|
| 6,352 | ALCONA | 2,815 | 1,199 | 1,611 | 5 | 412 D | 42.6% | 57.2% | 42.7% | 57.3% |
| 9,250 | ALGER | 3,755 | 1,010 | 2,743 | 2 | 1,733 D | 26.9% | 73.0% | 26.9% | 73.1% |
| 57,729 | ALLEGAN | 23,194 | 11,223 | 11,934 | 37 | 711 D | 48.4% | 51.5% | 48.5% | 51.5% |
| 28,556 | ALPENA | 11,472 | 3,954 | 7,508 | 10 | 3,554 D | 34.5% | 65.4% | 34.5% | 65.5% |
| 10,373 | ANTRIM | 4,863 | 2,172 | 2,684 | 7 | 512 D | 44.7% | 55.2% | 44.7% | 55.3% |
| 9,860 | ARENAC | 3,852 | 1,413 | 2,436 | 3 | 1,023 D | 36.7% | 63.2% | 36.7% | 63.3% |
| 7,151 | BARAGA | 3,736 | 1,160 | 2,568 | 8 | 1,408 D | 31.0% | 68.7% | 31.1% | 68.9% |
| 31,738 | BARRY | 13,650 | 5,509 | 8,102 | 39 | 2,593 D | 40.4% | 59.4% | 40.5% | 59.5% |
| 107,042 | BAY | 41,706 | 11,896 | 29,754 | 56 | 17,858 D | 28.5% | 71.3% | 28.6% | 71.4% |
| 7,834 | BENZIE | 3,662 | 1,674 | 1,983 | 5 | 309 D | 45.7% | 54.2% | 45.8% | 54.2% |
| 149,865 | BERRIEN | 60,162 | 26,387 | 33,653 | 122 | 7,266 D | 43.9% | 55.9% | 43.9% | 56.1% |
| 34,903 | BRANCH | 13,034 | 5,110 | 7,858 | 66 | 2,748 D | 39.2% | 60.3% | 39.4% | 60.6% |
| 138,858 | CALHOUN | 52,025 | 18,987 | 32,939 | 99 | 13,952 D | 36.5% | 63.3% | 36.6% | 63.4% |
| 36,932 | CASS | 14,742 | 5,925 | 8,789 | 28 | 2,864 D | 40.2% | 59.6% | 40.3% | 59.7% |
| 13,421 | CHARLEVOIX | 6,428 | 2,664 | 3,757 | 7 | 1,093 D | 41.4% | 58.4% | 41.5% | 58.5% |
| 14,550 | CHEBOYGAN | 6,381 | 2,342 | 4,028 | 11 | 1,686 D | 36.7% | 63.1% | 36.8% | 63.2% |
| 32,655 | CHIPPEWA | 10,658 | 4,098 | 6,537 | 23 | 2,439 D | 38.4% | 61.3% | 38.5% | 61.5% |
| 11,647 | CLARE | 5,197 | 2,258 | 2,927 | 12 | 669 D | 43.4% | 56.3% | 43.5% | 56.5% |
| 37,969 | CLINTON | 14,837 | 5,891 | 8,932 | 14 | 3,041 D | 39.7% | 60.2% | 39.7% | 60.3% |
| 4,971 | CRAWFORD | 2,160 | 696 | 1,464 | | 768 D | 32.2% | 67.8% | 32.2% | 67.8% |
| 34,298 | DELTA | 14,507 | 4,434 | 10,046 | 27 | 5,612 D | 30.6% | 69.2% | 30.6% | 69.4% |
| 23,917 | DICKINSON | 11,297 | 3,365 | 7,921 | 11 | 4,556 D | 29.8% | 70.1% | 29.8% | 70.2% |
| 49,684 | EATON | 21,555 | 8,919 | 12,590 | 46 | 3,671 D | 41.4% | 58.4% | 41.5% | 58.5% |
| 15,904 | EMMET | 6,937 | 2,731 | 4,197 | 9 | 1,466 D | 39.4% | 60.5% | 39.4% | 60.6% |
| 374,313 | GENESEE | 148,878 | 48,311 | 100,346 | 221 | 52,035 D | 32.5% | 67.4% | 32.5% | 67.5% |
| 10,769 | GLADWIN | 4,683 | 1,941 | 2,725 | 17 | 784 D | 41.4% | 58.2% | 41.6% | 58.4% |
| 24,370 | GOGEBIC | 11,319 | 3,350 | 7,945 | 24 | 4,595 D | 29.6% | 70.2% | 29.7% | 70.3% |
| 33,490 | GRAND TRAVERSE | 13,693 | 6,198 | 7,475 | 20 | 1,277 D | 45.3% | 54.6% | 45.3% | 54.7% |
| 37,012 | GRATIOT | 12,778 | 5,369 | 7,383 | 26 | 2,014 D | 42.0% | 57.8% | 42.1% | 57.9% |
| 34,742 | HILLSDALE | 13,090 | 6,420 | 6,564 | 106 | 144 D | 49.0% | 50.1% | 49.4% | 50.6% |
| 35,654 | HOUGHTON | 14,791 | 5,024 | 9,761 | 6 | 4,737 D | 34.0% | 66.0% | 34.0% | 66.0% |
| 34,006 | HURON | 13,626 | 6,263 | 7,349 | 14 | 1,086 D | 46.0% | 53.9% | 46.0% | 54.0% |
| 211,296 | INGHAM | 86,829 | 32,965 | 53,685 | 179 | 20,720 D | 38.0% | 61.8% | 38.0% | 62.0% |
| 43,132 | IONIA | 16,113 | 5,698 | 10,362 | 53 | 4,664 D | 35.4% | 64.3% | 35.5% | 64.5% |
| 16,505 | IOSCO | 7,044 | 2,704 | 4,336 | 4 | 1,632 D | 38.4% | 61.6% | 38.4% | 61.6% |
| 17,184 | IRON | 8,423 | 2,399 | 6,011 | 13 | 3,612 D | 28.5% | 71.4% | 28.5% | 71.5% |
| 35,348 | ISABELLA | 11,727 | 4,672 | 7,040 | 15 | 2,368 D | 39.8% | 60.0% | 39.9% | 60.1% |
| 131,994 | JACKSON | 49,247 | 20,940 | 28,219 | 88 | 7,279 D | 42.5% | 57.3% | 42.6% | 57.4% |
| 169,712 | KALAMAZOO | 68,104 | 27,100 | 40,789 | 215 | 13,689 D | 39.8% | 59.9% | 39.9% | 60.1% |
| 4,382 | KALKASKA | 2,084 | 861 | 1,220 | 3 | 359 D | 41.3% | 58.5% | 41.4% | 58.6% |
| 363,187 | KENT | 153,959 | 66,830 | 86,860 | 269 | 20,030 D | 43.4% | 56.4% | 43.5% | 56.5% |
| 2,417 | KEWEENAW | 1,235 | 374 | 860 | 1 | 486 D | 30.3% | 69.6% | 30.3% | 69.7% |
| 5,338 | LAKE | 2,770 | 791 | 1,978 | 1 | 1,187 D | 28.6% | 71.4% | 28.6% | 71.4% |
| 41,926 | LAPEER | 14,624 | 6,012 | 8,595 | 17 | 2,583 D | 41.1% | 58.8% | 41.2% | 58.8% |
| 9,321 | LEELANAU | 4,451 | 2,074 | 2,369 | 8 | 295 D | 46.6% | 53.2% | 46.7% | 53.3% |
| 77,789 | LENAWEE | 28,260 | 11,385 | 16,815 | 60 | 5,430 D | 40.3% | 59.5% | 40.4% | 59.6% |
| 38,233 | LIVINGSTON | 16,441 | 6,723 | 9,698 | 20 | 2,975 D | 40.9% | 59.0% | 40.9% | 59.1% |
| 7,827 | LUCE | 2,331 | 871 | 1,459 | 1 | 588 D | 37.4% | 62.6% | 37.4% | 62.6% |
| 10,853 | MACKINAC | 4,717 | 1,967 | 2,748 | 2 | 781 D | 41.7% | 58.3% | 41.7% | 58.3% |
| 405,804 | MACOMB | 176,521 | 44,684 | 131,450 | 387 | 86,766 D | 25.3% | 74.5% | 25.4% | 74.6% |
| 19,042 | MANISTEE | 8,444 | 2,918 | 5,520 | 6 | 2,602 D | 34.6% | 65.4% | 34.6% | 65.4% |
| 56,154 | MARQUETTE | 20,696 | 6,615 | 14,045 | 36 | 7,430 D | 32.0% | 67.9% | 32.0% | 68.0% |
| 21,929 | MASON | 9,846 | 3,842 | 5,993 | 11 | 2,151 D | 39.0% | 60.9% | 39.1% | 60.9% |
| 21,051 | MECOSTA | 7,677 | 3,454 | 4,214 | 9 | 760 D | 45.0% | 54.9% | 45.0% | 55.0% |
| 24,685 | MENOMINEE | 10,682 | 3,545 | 7,119 | 18 | 3,574 D | 33.2% | 66.6% | 33.2% | 66.8% |
| 51,450 | MIDLAND | 21,655 | 9,020 | 12,587 | 48 | 3,567 D | 41.7% | 58.1% | 41.7% | 58.3% |
| 6,784 | MISSAUKEE | 3,075 | 1,786 | 1,288 | 1 | 498 R | 58.1% | 41.9% | 58.1% | 41.9% |
| 101,120 | MONROE | 38,111 | 11,499 | 26,528 | 84 | 15,029 D | 30.2% | 69.6% | 30.2% | 69.8% |
| 35,795 | MONTCALM | 14,177 | 5,181 | 8,970 | 26 | 3,789 D | 36.5% | 63.3% | 36.6% | 63.4% |
| 4,424 | MONTMORENCY | 2,236 | 863 | 1,369 | 4 | 506 D | 38.6% | 61.2% | 38.7% | 61.3% |

# MICHIGAN

## PRESIDENT 1964

| 1960 Census Population | County | Total Vote | Republican | Democratic | Other | Rep.-Dem. Plurality | Percentage | | | |
|---|---|---|---|---|---|---|---|---|---|---|
| | | | | | | | Total Vote | | Major Vote | |
| | | | | | | | Rep. | Dem. | Rep. | Dem. |
| 149,943 | MUSKEGON | 59,034 | 22,146 | 36,769 | 119 | 14,623 D | 37.5% | 62.3% | 37.6% | 62.4% |
| 24,160 | NEWAYGO | 10,399 | 4,931 | 5,457 | 11 | 526 D | 47.4% | 52.5% | 47.5% | 52.5% |
| 690,259 | OAKLAND | 297,508 | 114,025 | 182,797 | 686 | 68,772 D | 38.3% | 61.4% | 38.4% | 61.6% |
| 16,547 | OCEANA | 6,743 | 2,958 | 3,773 | 12 | 815 D | 43.9% | 56.0% | 43.9% | 56.1% |
| 9,680 | OGEMAW | 4,425 | 1,609 | 2,812 | 4 | 1,203 D | 36.4% | 63.5% | 36.4% | 63.6% |
| 10,584 | ONTONAGON | 5,150 | 1,658 | 3,485 | 7 | 1,827 D | 32.2% | 67.7% | 32.2% | 67.8% |
| 13,595 | OSCEOLA | 5,690 | 2,779 | 2,891 | 20 | 112 D | 48.8% | 50.8% | 49.0% | 51.0% |
| 3,447 | OSCODA | 1,721 | 784 | 930 | 7 | 146 D | 45.6% | 54.0% | 45.7% | 54.3% |
| 7,545 | OTSEGO | 3,462 | 1,214 | 2,245 | 3 | 1,031 D | 35.1% | 64.8% | 35.1% | 64.9% |
| 98,719 | OTTAWA | 44,735 | 24,512 | 20,151 | 72 | 4,361 R | 54.8% | 45.0% | 54.9% | 45.1% |
| 13,117 | PRESQUE ISLE | 5,337 | 1,770 | 3,565 | 2 | 1,795 D | 33.2% | 66.8% | 33.2% | 66.8% |
| 7,200 | ROSCOMMON | 4,074 | 1,722 | 2,345 | 7 | 623 D | 42.3% | 57.6% | 42.3% | 57.7% |
| 190,752 | SAGINAW | 73,582 | 28,146 | 45,309 | 127 | 17,163 D | 38.3% | 61.6% | 38.3% | 61.7% |
| 107,201 | ST. CLAIR | 41,735 | 17,011 | 24,662 | 62 | 7,651 D | 40.8% | 59.1% | 40.8% | 59.2% |
| 42,332 | ST. JOSEPH | 16,623 | 7,307 | 9,284 | 32 | 1,977 D | 44.0% | 55.9% | 44.0% | 56.0% |
| 32,314 | SANILAC | 13,874 | 7,590 | 6,266 | 18 | 1,324 R | 54.7% | 45.2% | 54.8% | 45.2% |
| 8,953 | SCHOOLCRAFT | 4,076 | 1,397 | 2,675 | 4 | 1,278 D | 34.3% | 65.6% | 34.3% | 65.7% |
| 53,446 | SHIAWASSEE | 21,503 | 7,786 | 13,676 | 41 | 5,890 D | 36.2% | 63.6% | 36.3% | 63.7% |
| 43,305 | TUSCOLA | 16,905 | 7,509 | 9,374 | 22 | 1,865 D | 44.4% | 55.5% | 44.5% | 55.5% |
| 48,395 | VAN BUREN | 19,504 | 8,120 | 11,336 | 48 | 3,216 D | 41.6% | 58.1% | 41.7% | 58.3% |
| 172,440 | WASHTENAW | 67,890 | 25,595 | 42,089 | 206 | 16,494 D | 37.7% | 62.0% | 37.8% | 62.2% |
| 2,666,297 | WAYNE | 1,094,724 | 260,901 | 831,674 | 2,149 | 570,773 D | 23.8% | 76.0% | 23.9% | 76.1% |
| 18,466 | WEXFORD | 7,446 | 3,016 | 4,414 | 16 | 1,398 D | 40.5% | 59.3% | 40.6% | 59.4% |
| 7,823,194 | TOTAL | 3,203,102 | 1,060,152 | 2,136,615 | 6,335 | 1,076,463 D | 33.1% | 66.7% | 33.2% | 66.8% |

# MICHIGAN

## PRESIDENT 1960

| 1960 Census Population | County | Total Vote | Republican | Democratic | Other | Rep.-Dem. Plurality | Percentage Total Vote Rep. | Percentage Total Vote Dem. | Percentage Major Vote Rep. | Percentage Major Vote Dem. |
|---|---|---|---|---|---|---|---|---|---|---|
| 6,352 | ALCONA | 3,099 | 2,053 | 1,038 | 8 | 1,015 R | 66.2% | 33.5% | 66.4% | 33.6% |
| 9,250 | ALGER | 3,990 | 1,663 | 2,321 | 6 | 658 D | 41.7% | 58.2% | 41.7% | 58.3% |
| 57,729 | ALLEGAN | 23,472 | 16,660 | 6,752 | 60 | 9,908 R | 71.0% | 28.8% | 71.2% | 28.8% |
| 28,556 | ALPENA | 11,653 | 6,573 | 5,071 | 9 | 1,502 R | 56.4% | 43.5% | 56.4% | 43.6% |
| 10,373 | ANTRIM | 5,052 | 3,398 | 1,647 | 7 | 1,751 R | 67.3% | 32.6% | 67.4% | 32.6% |
| 9,860 | ARENAC | 4,250 | 2,352 | 1,888 | 10 | 464 R | 55.3% | 44.4% | 55.5% | 44.5% |
| 7,151 | BARAGA | 3,836 | 1,861 | 1,964 | 11 | 103 D | 48.5% | 51.2% | 48.7% | 51.3% |
| 31,738 | BARRY | 13,767 | 9,298 | 4,406 | 63 | 4,892 R | 67.5% | 32.0% | 67.8% | 32.2% |
| 107,042 | BAY | 44,011 | 20,909 | 22,998 | 104 | 2,089 D | 47.5% | 52.3% | 47.6% | 52.4% |
| 7,834 | BENZIE | 3,795 | 2,484 | 1,306 | 5 | 1,178 R | 65.5% | 34.4% | 65.5% | 34.5% |
| 149,865 | BERRIEN | 61,506 | 37,425 | 23,837 | 244 | 13,588 R | 60.8% | 38.8% | 61.1% | 38.9% |
| 34,903 | BRANCH | 13,587 | 8,752 | 4,759 | 76 | 3,993 R | 64.4% | 35.0% | 64.8% | 35.2% |
| 138,858 | CALHOUN | 55,793 | 32,080 | 23,511 | 202 | 8,569 R | 57.5% | 42.1% | 57.7% | 42.3% |
| 36,932 | CASS | 15,117 | 8,585 | 6,468 | 64 | 2,117 R | 56.8% | 42.8% | 57.0% | 43.0% |
| 13,421 | CHARLEVOIX | 6,419 | 3,987 | 2,422 | 10 | 1,565 R | 62.1% | 37.7% | 62.2% | 37.8% |
| 14,550 | CHEBOYGAN | 6,796 | 3,817 | 2,977 | 2 | 840 R | 56.2% | 43.8% | 56.2% | 43.8% |
| 32,655 | CHIPPEWA | 11,751 | 6,490 | 5,239 | 22 | 1,251 R | 55.2% | 44.6% | 55.3% | 44.7% |
| 11,647 | CLARE | 5,130 | 3,616 | 1,507 | 7 | 2,109 R | 70.5% | 29.4% | 70.6% | 29.4% |
| 37,969 | CLINTON | 15,072 | 10,227 | 4,822 | 23 | 5,405 R | 67.9% | 32.0% | 68.0% | 32.0% |
| 4,971 | CRAWFORD | 2,251 | 1,464 | 783 | 4 | 681 R | 65.0% | 34.8% | 65.2% | 34.8% |
| 34,298 | DELTA | 14,413 | 6,460 | 7,924 | 29 | 1,464 D | 44.8% | 55.0% | 44.9% | 55.1% |
| 23,917 | DICKINSON | 11,995 | 5,336 | 6,645 | 14 | 1,309 D | 44.5% | 55.4% | 44.5% | 55.5% |
| 49,684 | EATON | 21,149 | 14,163 | 6,912 | 74 | 7,251 R | 67.0% | 32.7% | 67.2% | 32.8% |
| 15,904 | EMMET | 7,198 | 4,574 | 2,602 | 22 | 1,972 R | 63.5% | 36.1% | 63.7% | 36.3% |
| 374,313 | GENESEE | 147,457 | 74,940 | 72,059 | 458 | 2,881 R | 50.8% | 48.9% | 51.0% | 49.0% |
| 10,769 | GLADWIN | 4,712 | 3,282 | 1,424 | 6 | 1,858 R | 69.7% | 30.2% | 69.7% | 30.3% |
| 24,370 | GOGEBIC | 12,659 | 5,429 | 7,200 | 30 | 1,771 D | 42.9% | 56.9% | 43.0% | 57.0% |
| 33,490 | GRAND TRAVERSE | 13,540 | 8,618 | 4,886 | 36 | 3,732 R | 63.6% | 36.1% | 63.8% | 36.2% |
| 37,012 | GRATIOT | 13,734 | 9,854 | 3,859 | 21 | 5,995 R | 71.7% | 28.1% | 71.9% | 28.1% |
| 34,742 | HILLSDALE | 14,340 | 10,208 | 4,069 | 63 | 6,139 R | 71.2% | 28.4% | 71.5% | 28.5% |
| 35,654 | HOUGHTON | 15,822 | 7,767 | 8,021 | 34 | 254 D | 49.1% | 50.7% | 49.2% | 50.8% |
| 34,006 | HURON | 15,386 | 9,592 | 5,775 | 19 | 3,817 R | 62.3% | 37.5% | 62.4% | 37.6% |
| 211,296 | INGHAM | 86,907 | 54,655 | 32,043 | 209 | 22,612 R | 62.9% | 36.9% | 63.0% | 37.0% |
| 43,132 | IONIA | 16,834 | 10,405 | 6,377 | 52 | 4,028 R | 61.8% | 37.9% | 62.0% | 38.0% |
| 16,505 | IOSCO | 6,866 | 4,308 | 2,549 | 9 | 1,759 R | 62.7% | 37.1% | 62.8% | 37.2% |
| 17,184 | IRON | 9,165 | 3,919 | 5,232 | 14 | 1,313 D | 42.8% | 57.1% | 42.8% | 57.2% |
| 35,348 | ISABELLA | 12,335 | 7,880 | 4,431 | 24 | 3,449 R | 63.9% | 35.9% | 64.0% | 36.0% |
| 131,994 | JACKSON | 55,779 | 34,660 | 20,995 | 124 | 13,665 R | 62.1% | 37.6% | 62.3% | 37.7% |
| 169,712 | KALAMAZOO | 67,434 | 42,800 | 24,286 | 348 | 18,514 R | 63.5% | 36.0% | 63.8% | 36.2% |
| 4,382 | KALKASKA | 2,039 | 1,341 | 693 | 5 | 648 R | 65.8% | 34.0% | 65.9% | 34.1% |
| 363,187 | KENT | 157,296 | 95,477 | 61,313 | 506 | 34,164 R | 60.7% | 39.0% | 60.9% | 39.1% |
| 2,417 | KEWEENAW | 1,343 | 684 | 655 | 4 | 29 R | 50.9% | 48.8% | 51.1% | 48.9% |
| 5,338 | LAKE | 2,757 | 1,441 | 1,313 | 3 | 128 R | 52.3% | 47.6% | 52.3% | 47.7% |
| 41,926 | LAPEER | 15,567 | 10,450 | 5,099 | 18 | 5,351 R | 67.1% | 32.8% | 67.2% | 32.8% |
| 9,321 | LEELANAU | 4,546 | 2,730 | 1,810 | 6 | 920 R | 60.1% | 39.8% | 60.1% | 39.9% |
| 77,789 | LENAWEE | 30,719 | 19,859 | 10,785 | 75 | 9,074 R | 64.6% | 35.1% | 64.8% | 35.2% |
| 38,233 | LIVINGSTON | 15,987 | 10,340 | 5,608 | 39 | 4,732 R | 64.7% | 35.1% | 64.8% | 35.2% |
| 7,827 | LUCE | 2,362 | 1,534 | 828 | | 706 R | 64.9% | 35.1% | 64.9% | 35.1% |
| 10,853 | MACKINAC | 5,117 | 3,064 | 2,042 | 11 | 1,022 R | 59.9% | 39.9% | 60.0% | 40.0% |
| 405,804 | MACOMB | 168,195 | 61,989 | 105,681 | 525 | 43,692 D | 36.9% | 62.8% | 37.0% | 63.0% |
| 19,042 | MANISTEE | 8,999 | 4,867 | 4,122 | 10 | 745 R | 54.1% | 45.8% | 54.1% | 45.9% |
| 56,154 | MARQUETTE | 21,917 | 10,690 | 11,177 | 50 | 487 D | 48.8% | 51.0% | 48.9% | 51.1% |
| 21,929 | MASON | 10,326 | 6,011 | 4,305 | 10 | 1,706 R | 58.2% | 41.7% | 58.3% | 41.7% |
| 21,051 | MECOSTA | 7,703 | 5,306 | 2,380 | 17 | 2,926 R | 68.9% | 30.9% | 69.0% | 31.0% |
| 24,685 | MENOMINEE | 10,938 | 5,064 | 5,857 | 17 | 793 D | 46.3% | 53.5% | 46.4% | 53.6% |
| 51,450 | MIDLAND | 21,071 | 14,235 | 6,815 | 21 | 7,420 R | 67.6% | 32.3% | 67.6% | 32.4% |
| 6,784 | MISSAUKEE | 3,171 | 2,531 | 627 | 13 | 1,904 R | 79.8% | 19.8% | 80.1% | 19.9% |
| 101,120 | MONROE | 38,423 | 18,607 | 19,684 | 132 | 1,077 D | 48.4% | 51.2% | 48.6% | 51.4% |
| 35,795 | MONTCALM | 14,892 | 10,085 | 4,767 | 40 | 5,318 R | 67.7% | 32.0% | 67.9% | 32.1% |
| 4,424 | MONTMORENCY | 2,433 | 1,565 | 866 | 2 | 699 R | 64.3% | 35.6% | 64.4% | 35.6% |

# MICHIGAN

## PRESIDENT 1960

| 1960 Census Population | County | Total Vote | Republican | Democratic | Other | Rep.-Dem. Plurality | Percentage | | | |
|---|---|---|---|---|---|---|---|---|---|---|
| | | | | | | | Total Vote | | Major Vote | |
| | | | | | | | Rep. | Dem. | Rep. | Dem. |
| 149,943 | MUSKEGON | 61,661 | 32,667 | 28,755 | 239 | 3,912 R | 53.0% | 46.6% | 53.2% | 46.8% |
| 24,160 | NEWAYGO | 10,872 | 7,453 | 3,404 | 15 | 4,049 R | 68.6% | 31.3% | 68.6% | 31.4% |
| 690,259 | OAKLAND | 298,562 | 162,026 | 135,531 | 1,005 | 26,495 R | 54.3% | 45.4% | 54.5% | 45.5% |
| 16,547 | OCEANA | 7,082 | 4,418 | 2,651 | 13 | 1,767 R | 62.4% | 37.4% | 62.5% | 37.5% |
| 9,680 | OGEMAW | 4,542 | 2,664 | 1,867 | 11 | 797 R | 58.7% | 41.1% | 58.8% | 41.2% |
| 10,584 | ONTONAGON | 5,175 | 2,620 | 2,553 | 2 | 67 R | 50.6% | 49.3% | 50.6% | 49.4% |
| 13,595 | OSCEOLA | 5,865 | 4,477 | 1,378 | 10 | 3,099 R | 76.3% | 23.5% | 76.5% | 23.5% |
| 3,447 | OSCODA | 1,634 | 1,174 | 458 | 2 | 716 R | 71.8% | 28.0% | 71.9% | 28.1% |
| 7,545 | OTSEGO | 3,469 | 1,944 | 1,521 | 4 | 423 R | 56.0% | 43.8% | 56.1% | 43.9% |
| 98,719 | OTTAWA | 43,423 | 32,678 | 10,617 | 128 | 22,061 R | 75.3% | 24.5% | 75.5% | 24.5% |
| 13,117 | PRESQUE ISLE | 5,602 | 2,950 | 2,649 | 3 | 301 R | 52.7% | 47.3% | 52.7% | 47.3% |
| 7,200 | ROSCOMMON | 3,962 | 2,731 | 1,226 | 5 | 1,505 R | 68.9% | 30.9% | 69.0% | 31.0% |
| 190,752 | SAGINAW | 74,272 | 41,351 | 32,715 | 206 | 8,636 R | 55.7% | 44.0% | 55.8% | 44.2% |
| 107,201 | ST. CLAIR | 45,774 | 27,366 | 18,332 | 76 | 9,034 R | 59.8% | 40.0% | 59.9% | 40.1% |
| 42,332 | ST. JOSEPH | 17,847 | 12,337 | 5,445 | 65 | 6,892 R | 69.1% | 30.5% | 69.4% | 30.6% |
| 32,314 | SANILAC | 15,185 | 11,005 | 4,153 | 27 | 6,852 R | 72.5% | 27.3% | 72.6% | 27.4% |
| 8,953 | SCHOOLCRAFT | 4,298 | 2,183 | 2,107 | 8 | 76 R | 50.8% | 49.0% | 50.9% | 49.1% |
| 53,446 | SHIAWASSEE | 22,604 | 13,757 | 8,773 | 74 | 4,984 R | 60.9% | 38.8% | 61.1% | 38.9% |
| 43,305 | TUSCOLA | 17,308 | 11,931 | 5,357 | 20 | 6,574 R | 68.9% | 31.0% | 69.0% | 31.0% |
| 48,395 | VAN BUREN | 20,096 | 12,903 | 7,082 | 111 | 5,821 R | 64.2% | 35.2% | 64.6% | 35.4% |
| 172,440 | WASHTENAW | 64,986 | 39,632 | 25,129 | 225 | 14,503 R | 61.0% | 38.7% | 61.2% | 38.8% |
| 2,666,297 | WAYNE | 1,171,909 | 394,485 | 773,327 | 4,097 | 378,842 D | 33.7% | 66.0% | 33.8% | 66.2% |
| 18,466 | WEXFORD | 8,096 | 5,262 | 2,807 | 27 | 2,455 R | 65.0% | 34.7% | 65.2% | 34.8% |
| 7,823,194 | TOTAL | 3,318,097 | 1,620,428 | 1,687,269 | 10,400 | 66,841 D | 48.8% | 50.9% | 49.0% | 51.0% |

# MICHIGAN

## ELECTION NOTES

**2004**   Other vote was 24,035 No Party Affiliation (Ralph Nader); 10,552 Libertarian (Michael Badnarik); 5,325 Green (David Cobb); 4,980 U.S. Taxpayers (Michael Peroutka); 1,431 Natural Law (Walter F. Brown).

**2000**   Other vote was 16,711 Libertarian (Browne); 3,791 U.S. Taxpayers (Phillips); 2,426 Natural Law (Hagelin); 2,061 write-in (Buchanan). Official state returns listed Buchanan with 1,851 votes, but later totals from Wayne County increased his vote there from 14 to 224, an increase of 210 votes.

**1996**   Other vote was 27,670 Libertarian (Browne); 4,254 Natural Law (Hagelin); 3,153 Workers World (Moorehead); 2,322 write-in (Nader); 1,554 Socialist Equality (White); 539 write-in (Phillips); 1,817 scattered write-in.

**1992**   Other vote was 10,175 Marrou (Libertarian); 8,263 Phillips (Tisch Independent Citizens); 2,954 Hagelin (Natural Law); 1,432 Halyard (Workers League); 168 Gritz (write-in); 21 Fulani (write-in); 14 LaRouche (write-in); 711 scattered write-in.

**1988**   Other vote was 18,336 Paul (Libertarian); 2,513 Fulani (Independent); 2,497 McCarthy (Independent); 1,958 Winn (Workers League); 819 Warren (Independent); 804 Holmes (Independent); 60 Duke (write-in); 5 Dodge (write-in); 902 scattered write-in.

**1984**   Other vote was 10,055 Bergland (Libertarian); 3,862 LaRouche (Independent); 1,416 Holmes (Workers World); 1,191 Johnson (Independent); 1,049 Mason (Socialist Workers); 1,048 Hall (Communist); 665 Serrette (Independent); 561 Winn (Workers League); 602 scattered write-in.

**1980**   Other vote was 275,223 Anderson (Anderson Coalition); 41,597 Clark (Libertarian); 11,930 Commoner (Citizens); 3,262 Hall (Independent); 30 Griswold (write-in); 21 Greaves (write-in); 9 Bubar (write-in); 5 Rarick (write-in); 891 scattered write-in.

**1976**   Other vote was 47,905 McCarthy (Independent); 5,406 MacBride (Libertarian); 3,504 Wright (Human Rights); 1,804 Camejo (Socialist Workers); 1,366 LaRouche (U.S. Labor); 1,148 Levin (Socialist Labor); 2,160 scattered write-in.

**1972**   Other vote was 63,321 Schmitz (American Independent); 2,437 Fisher (Socialist Labor); 1,603 Jenness (Socialist Workers); 1,210 Hall (Communist).

**1968**   Wallace on the ballot as American Independent. Other vote was 4,585 Cleaver (New Politics); 4,099 Halstead (Socialist Workers); 1,762 Blomen (Socialist Labor); 60 Munn (write-in); 29 scattered write-in.

**1964**   Other vote was 3,817 DeBerry (Socialist Workers); 1,704 Hass (Socialist Labor); 669 Munn (Prohibition); 145 scattered write-in.

**1960**   Other vote was 4,347 Dobbs (Socialist Workers); 2,029 Decker (Prohibition); 1,767 Daly (Tax Cut); 1,718 Hass (Socialist Labor); 539 unpledged Independent American ticket.

# MINNESOTA

## POPULAR VOTE FOR PRESIDENT 1920 TO 2004

| Year | Total Vote | Republican Vote | Republican Candidate | Democratic Vote | Democratic Candidate | Other Vote | Plurality | Percentage Total Vote Rep. | Percentage Total Vote Dem. | Percentage Major Vote Rep. | Percentage Major Vote Dem. |
|------|-----------|-----------------|---------------------|-----------------|---------------------|-----------|-----------|-----------|-----------|-----------|-----------|
| 2004 | 2,828,387 | 1,346,695 | Bush, George W. | 1,445,014 | Kerry, John | 36,678 | 98,319 D | 47.6% | 51.1% | 48.2% | 51.8% |
| 2000 ** | 2,438,685 | 1,109,659 | Bush, George W. | 1,168,266 | Gore, Al | 160,760 | 58,607 D | 45.5% | 47.9% | 48.7% | 51.3% |
| 1996 ** | 2,192,640 | 766,476 | Dole, Bob | 1,120,438 | Clinton, Bill | 305,726 | 353,962 D | 35.0% | 51.1% | 40.6% | 59.4% |
| 1992 ** | 2,347,948 | 747,841 | Bush, George | 1,020,997 | Clinton, Bill | 579,110 | 273,156 D | 31.9% | 43.5% | 42.3% | 57.7% |
| 1988 | 2,096,790 | 962,337 | Bush, George | 1,109,471 | Dukakis, Michael S. | 24,982 | 147,134 D | 45.9% | 52.9% | 46.4% | 53.6% |
| 1984 | 2,084,449 | 1,032,603 | Reagan, Ronald | 1,036,364 | Mondale, Walter F. | 15,482 | 3,761 D | 49.5% | 49.7% | 49.9% | 50.1% |
| 1980** | 2,051,980 | 873,268 | Reagan, Ronald | 954,174 | Carter, Jimmy | 224,538 | 80,906 D | 42.6% | 46.5% | 47.8% | 52.2% |
| 1976 | 1,949,931 | 819,395 | Ford, Gerald R. | 1,070,440 | Carter, Jimmy | 60,096 | 251,045 D | 42.0% | 54.9% | 43.4% | 56.6% |
| 1972 | 1,741,652 | 898,269 | Nixon, Richard M. | 802,346 | McGovern, George S. | 41,037 | 95,923 R | 51.6% | 46.1% | 52.8% | 47.2% |
| 1968 | 1,588,506 | 658,643 | Nixon, Richard M. | 857,738 | Humphrey, Hubert H. | 72,125 | 199,095 D | 41.5% | 54.0% | 43.4% | 56.6% |
| 1964 | 1,554,462 | 559,624 | Goldwater, Barry M. | 991,117 | Johnson, Lyndon B. | 3,721 | 431,493 D | 36.0% | 63.8% | 36.1% | 63.9% |
| 1960 | 1,541,887 | 757,915 | Nixon, Richard M. | 779,933 | Kennedy, John F. | 4,039 | 22,018 D | 49.2% | 50.6% | 49.3% | 50.7% |
| 1956 | 1,340,005 | 719,302 | Eisenhower, Dwight D. | 617,525 | Stevenson, Adlai E. | 3,178 | 101,777 R | 53.7% | 46.1% | 53.8% | 46.2% |
| 1952 | 1,379,483 | 763,211 | Eisenhower, Dwight D. | 608,458 | Stevenson, Adlai E. | 7,814 | 154,753 R | 55.3% | 44.1% | 55.6% | 44.4% |
| 1948 | 1,212,226 | 483,617 | Dewey, Thomas E. | 692,966 | Truman, Harry S. | 35,643 | 209,349 D | 39.9% | 57.2% | 41.1% | 58.9% |
| 1944 | 1,125,504 | 527,416 | Dewey, Thomas E. | 589,864 | Roosevelt, Franklin D. | 8,224 | 62,448 D | 46.9% | 52.4% | 47.2% | 52.8% |
| 1940 | 1,251,188 | 596,274 | Willkie, Wendell | 644,196 | Roosevelt, Franklin D. | 10,718 | 47,922 D | 47.7% | 51.5% | 48.1% | 51.9% |
| 1936 | 1,129,975 | 350,461 | Landon, Alfred M. | 698,811 | Roosevelt, Franklin D. | 80,703 | 348,350 D | 31.0% | 61.8% | 33.4% | 66.6% |
| 1932 | 1,002,843 | 363,959 | Hoover, Herbert C. | 600,806 | Roosevelt, Franklin D. | 38,078 | 236,847 D | 36.3% | 59.9% | 37.7% | 62.3% |
| 1928 | 970,976 | 560,977 | Hoover, Herbert C. | 396,451 | Smith, Alfred E. | 13,548 | 164,526 R | 57.8% | 40.8% | 58.6% | 41.4% |
| 1924 ** | 822,146 | 420,759 | Coolidge, Calvin | 55,913 | Davis, John W. | 345,474 | 81,567 R | 51.2% | 6.8% | 88.3% | 11.7% |
| 1920 | 735,838 | 519,421 | Harding, Warren G. | 142,994 | Cox, James M. | 73,423 | 376,427 R | 70.6% | 19.4% | 78.4% | 21.6% |

In 2000 the other vote column includes 126,696 votes cast for Green (Nader). In 1996 the other vote column includes 257,704 votes cast for Perot. In 1992 the other vote column includes 562,506 votes cast for Perot. In 1980 the other column includes 174,990 votes for Independent (Anderson). In 1924 the other vote was 339,192 Progressive; 4,427 Communist; and 1,855 Socialist Labor.

## ELECTORAL COLLEGE VOTE 1920 TO 2004

| Year | Total | Republican | Democratic | Other |
|------|-------|-----------|-----------|-------|
| 2004* | 10 | | 9 | 1 |
| 2000 | 10 | | 10 | |
| 1996 | 10 | | 10 | |
| 1992 | 10 | | 10 | |
| 1988 | 10 | | 10 | |
| 1984 | 10 | | 10 | |
| 1980 | 10 | | 10 | |
| 1976 | 10 | | 10 | |
| 1972 | 10 | 10 | | |
| 1968 | 10 | | 10 | |
| 1964 | 10 | | 10 | |
| 1960 | 11 | | 11 | |
| 1956 | 11 | 11 | | |
| 1952 | 11 | 11 | | |
| 1948 | 11 | | 11 | |
| 1944 | 11 | | 11 | |
| 1940 | 11 | | 11 | |
| 1936 | 11 | | 11 | |
| 1932 | 11 | | 11 | |
| 1928 | 12 | 12 | | |
| 1924 | 12 | 12 | | |
| 1920 | 12 | 12 | | |

*In 2004 a Democratic elector in Minnesota cast a vote for Edwards rather than Kerry.

# MINNESOTA

# MINNESOTA

## PRESIDENT 2004

| 2000 Census Population | County | Total Vote | Republican | Democratic | Other | Rep.-Dem. Plurality | Percentage | | | |
|---|---|---|---|---|---|---|---|---|---|---|
| | | | | | | | Total Vote | | Major Vote | |
| | | | | | | | Rep. | Dem. | Rep. | Dem. |
| 15,301 | AITKIN | 9,452 | 4,768 | 4,539 | 145 | 229 R | 50.4% | 48.0% | 51.2% | 48.8% |
| 298,084 | ANOKA | 174,066 | 91,853 | 80,226 | 1,987 | 11,627 R | 52.8% | 46.1% | 53.4% | 46.6% |
| 30,000 | BECKER | 16,801 | 9,795 | 6,756 | 250 | 3,039 R | 58.3% | 40.2% | 59.2% | 40.8% |
| 39,650 | BELTRAMI | 21,131 | 10,237 | 10,592 | 302 | 355 D | 48.4% | 50.1% | 49.1% | 50.9% |
| 34,226 | BENTON | 18,384 | 10,043 | 8,059 | 282 | 1,984 R | 54.6% | 43.8% | 55.5% | 44.5% |
| 5,820 | BIG STONE | 3,067 | 1,483 | 1,536 | 48 | 53 D | 48.4% | 50.1% | 49.1% | 50.9% |
| 55,941 | BLUE EARTH | 33,119 | 15,737 | 16,865 | 517 | 1,128 D | 47.5% | 50.9% | 48.3% | 51.7% |
| 26,911 | BROWN | 13,778 | 8,395 | 5,158 | 225 | 3,237 R | 60.9% | 37.4% | 61.9% | 38.1% |
| 31,671 | CARLTON | 18,334 | 6,642 | 11,462 | 230 | 4,820 D | 36.2% | 62.5% | 36.7% | 63.3% |
| 70,205 | CARVER | 45,411 | 28,510 | 16,456 | 445 | 12,054 R | 62.8% | 36.2% | 63.4% | 36.6% |
| 27,150 | CASS | 15,910 | 8,875 | 6,835 | 200 | 2,040 R | 55.8% | 43.0% | 56.5% | 43.5% |
| 13,088 | CHIPPEWA | 6,606 | 3,089 | 3,424 | 93 | 335 D | 46.8% | 51.8% | 47.4% | 52.6% |
| 41,101 | CHISAGO | 28,260 | 15,705 | 12,219 | 336 | 3,486 R | 55.6% | 43.2% | 56.2% | 43.8% |
| 51,229 | CLAY | 27,737 | 14,365 | 12,989 | 383 | 1,376 R | 51.8% | 46.8% | 52.5% | 47.5% |
| 8,423 | CLEARWATER | 4,361 | 2,438 | 1,871 | 52 | 567 R | 55.9% | 42.9% | 56.6% | 43.4% |
| 5,168 | COOK | 3,303 | 1,489 | 1,733 | 81 | 244 D | 45.1% | 52.5% | 46.2% | 53.8% |
| 12,167 | COTTONWOOD | 6,369 | 3,557 | 2,726 | 86 | 831 R | 55.8% | 42.8% | 56.6% | 43.4% |
| 55,099 | CROW WING | 33,545 | 19,106 | 14,005 | 434 | 5,101 R | 57.0% | 41.7% | 57.7% | 42.3% |
| 355,904 | DAKOTA | 215,846 | 108,959 | 104,635 | 2,252 | 4,324 R | 50.5% | 48.5% | 51.0% | 49.0% |
| 17,731 | DODGE | 9,868 | 5,593 | 4,117 | 158 | 1,476 R | 56.7% | 41.7% | 57.6% | 42.4% |
| 32,821 | DOUGLAS | 20,309 | 11,793 | 8,219 | 297 | 3,574 R | 58.1% | 40.5% | 58.9% | 41.1% |
| 16,181 | FARIBAULT | 8,681 | 4,794 | 3,767 | 120 | 1,027 R | 55.2% | 43.4% | 56.0% | 44.0% |
| 21,122 | FILLMORE | 11,698 | 5,694 | 5,825 | 179 | 131 D | 48.7% | 49.8% | 49.4% | 50.6% |
| 32,584 | FREEBORN | 17,666 | 7,681 | 9,733 | 252 | 2,052 D | 43.5% | 55.1% | 44.1% | 55.9% |
| 44,127 | GOODHUE | 25,608 | 13,134 | 12,103 | 371 | 1,031 R | 51.3% | 47.3% | 52.0% | 48.0% |
| 6,289 | GRANT | 3,819 | 1,893 | 1,856 | 70 | 37 R | 49.6% | 48.6% | 50.5% | 49.5% |
| 1,116,200 | HENNEPIN | 646,981 | 255,133 | 383,841 | 8,007 | 128,708 D | 39.4% | 59.3% | 39.9% | 60.1% |
| 19,718 | HOUSTON | 11,082 | 5,631 | 5,276 | 175 | 355 R | 50.8% | 47.6% | 51.6% | 48.4% |
| 18,376 | HUBBARD | 11,340 | 6,444 | 4,741 | 155 | 1,703 R | 56.8% | 41.8% | 57.6% | 42.4% |
| 31,287 | ISANTI | 19,313 | 11,190 | 7,883 | 240 | 3,307 R | 57.9% | 40.8% | 58.7% | 41.3% |
| 43,992 | ITASCA | 24,367 | 10,705 | 13,290 | 372 | 2,585 D | 43.9% | 54.5% | 44.6% | 55.4% |
| 11,268 | JACKSON | 5,779 | 3,024 | 2,652 | 103 | 372 R | 52.3% | 45.9% | 53.3% | 46.7% |
| 14,996 | KANABEC | 8,248 | 4,527 | 3,592 | 129 | 935 R | 54.9% | 43.5% | 55.8% | 44.2% |
| 41,203 | KANDIYOHI | 21,349 | 11,704 | 9,337 | 308 | 2,367 R | 54.8% | 43.7% | 55.6% | 44.4% |
| 5,285 | KITTSON | 2,682 | 1,307 | 1,333 | 42 | 26 D | 48.7% | 49.7% | 49.5% | 50.5% |
| 14,355 | KOOCHICHING | 7,309 | 3,539 | 3,662 | 108 | 123 D | 48.4% | 50.1% | 49.1% | 50.9% |
| 8,067 | LAC QUI PARLE | 4,541 | 2,093 | 2,390 | 58 | 297 D | 46.1% | 52.6% | 46.7% | 53.3% |
| 11,058 | LAKE | 7,071 | 2,769 | 4,212 | 90 | 1,443 D | 39.2% | 59.6% | 39.7% | 60.3% |
| 4,522 | LAKE OF THE WOODS | 2,400 | 1,428 | 921 | 51 | 507 R | 59.5% | 38.4% | 60.8% | 39.2% |
| 25,426 | LE SUEUR | 14,424 | 7,746 | 6,466 | 212 | 1,280 R | 53.7% | 44.8% | 54.5% | 45.5% |
| 6,429 | LINCOLN | 3,342 | 1,736 | 1,558 | 48 | 178 R | 51.9% | 46.6% | 52.7% | 47.3% |
| 25,425 | LYON | 12,673 | 7,203 | 5,292 | 178 | 1,911 R | 56.8% | 41.8% | 57.6% | 42.4% |
| 34,898 | MCLEOD | 18,412 | 11,407 | 6,712 | 293 | 4,695 R | 62.0% | 36.5% | 63.0% | 37.0% |
| 5,190 | MAHNOMEN | 2,508 | 1,132 | 1,339 | 37 | 207 D | 45.1% | 53.4% | 45.8% | 54.2% |
| 10,155 | MARSHALL | 5,562 | 3,187 | 2,308 | 67 | 879 R | 57.3% | 41.5% | 58.0% | 42.0% |
| 21,802 | MARTIN | 11,047 | 6,311 | 4,590 | 146 | 1,721 R | 57.1% | 41.5% | 57.9% | 42.1% |
| 22,644 | MEEKER | 12,334 | 6,854 | 5,292 | 188 | 1,562 R | 55.6% | 42.9% | 56.4% | 43.6% |
| 22,330 | MILLE LACS | 13,065 | 7,194 | 5,677 | 194 | 1,517 R | 55.1% | 43.5% | 55.9% | 44.1% |
| 31,712 | MORRISON | 16,758 | 9,698 | 6,794 | 266 | 2,904 R | 57.9% | 40.5% | 58.8% | 41.2% |
| 38,603 | MOWER | 20,222 | 7,591 | 12,334 | 297 | 4,743 D | 37.5% | 61.0% | 38.1% | 61.9% |
| 9,165 | MURRAY | 4,998 | 2,719 | 2,218 | 61 | 501 R | 54.4% | 44.4% | 55.1% | 44.9% |
| 29,771 | NICOLLET | 17,741 | 8,689 | 8,797 | 255 | 108 D | 49.0% | 49.6% | 49.7% | 50.3% |
| 20,832 | NOBLES | 9,204 | 5,159 | 3,898 | 147 | 1,261 R | 56.1% | 42.4% | 57.0% | 43.0% |
| 7,442 | NORMAN | 3,810 | 1,794 | 1,954 | 62 | 160 D | 47.1% | 51.3% | 47.9% | 52.1% |
| 124,277 | OLMSTED | 71,575 | 37,371 | 33,285 | 919 | 4,086 R | 52.2% | 46.5% | 52.9% | 47.1% |
| 57,159 | OTTER TAIL | 32,178 | 19,734 | 12,038 | 406 | 7,696 R | 61.3% | 37.4% | 62.1% | 37.9% |
| 13,584 | PENNINGTON | 7,017 | 3,767 | 3,117 | 133 | 650 R | 53.7% | 44.4% | 54.7% | 45.3% |
| 26,530 | PINE | 14,518 | 7,033 | 7,228 | 257 | 195 D | 48.4% | 49.8% | 49.3% | 50.7% |
| 9,895 | PIPESTONE | 5,032 | 3,066 | 1,900 | 66 | 1,166 R | 60.9% | 37.8% | 61.7% | 38.3% |
| 31,369 | POLK | 15,668 | 8,724 | 6,729 | 215 | 1,995 R | 55.7% | 42.9% | 56.5% | 43.5% |

# MINNESOTA

## PRESIDENT 2004

| 2000 Census Population | County | Total Vote | Republican | Democratic | Other | Rep.-Dem. Plurality | | Percentage | | | |
|---|---|---|---|---|---|---|---|---|---|---|---|
| | | | | | | | | Total Vote | | Major Vote | |
| | | | | | | | | Rep. | Dem. | Rep. | Dem. |
| 11,236 | POPE | 6,700 | 3,303 | 3,301 | 96 | 2 | R | 49.3% | 49.3% | 50.0% | 50.0% |
| 511,035 | RAMSEY | 272,577 | 97,096 | 171,846 | 3,635 | 74,750 | D | 35.6% | 63.0% | 36.1% | 63.9% |
| 4,299 | RED LAKE | 2,177 | 1,164 | 963 | 50 | 201 | R | 53.5% | 44.2% | 54.7% | 45.3% |
| 16,815 | REDWOOD | 8,139 | 4,898 | 3,104 | 137 | 1,794 | R | 60.2% | 38.1% | 61.2% | 38.8% |
| 17,154 | RENVILLE | 8,349 | 4,430 | 3,787 | 132 | 643 | R | 53.1% | 45.4% | 53.9% | 46.1% |
| 56,665 | RICE | 30,745 | 13,881 | 16,425 | 439 | 2,544 | D | 45.1% | 53.4% | 45.8% | 54.2% |
| 9,721 | ROCK | 5,191 | 3,111 | 2,000 | 80 | 1,111 | R | 59.9% | 38.5% | 60.9% | 39.1% |
| 16,338 | ROSEAU | 7,911 | 5,355 | 2,442 | 114 | 2,913 | R | 67.7% | 30.9% | 68.7% | 31.3% |
| 200,528 | ST. LOUIS | 119,565 | 40,112 | 77,958 | 1,495 | 37,846 | D | 33.5% | 65.2% | 34.0% | 66.0% |
| 89,498 | SCOTT | 60,639 | 36,055 | 23,958 | 626 | 12,097 | R | 59.5% | 39.5% | 60.1% | 39.9% |
| 64,417 | SHERBURNE | 41,454 | 25,182 | 15,816 | 456 | 9,366 | R | 60.7% | 38.2% | 61.4% | 38.6% |
| 15,356 | SIBLEY | 7,949 | 4,669 | 3,109 | 171 | 1,560 | R | 58.7% | 39.1% | 60.0% | 40.0% |
| 133,166 | STEARNS | 75,577 | 41,726 | 32,659 | 1,192 | 9,067 | R | 55.2% | 43.2% | 56.1% | 43.9% |
| 33,680 | STEELE | 18,695 | 10,389 | 7,994 | 312 | 2,395 | R | 55.6% | 42.8% | 56.5% | 43.5% |
| 10,053 | STEVENS | 5,949 | 3,030 | 2,821 | 98 | 209 | R | 50.9% | 47.4% | 51.8% | 48.2% |
| 11,956 | SWIFT | 5,735 | 2,481 | 3,165 | 89 | 684 | D | 43.3% | 55.2% | 43.9% | 56.1% |
| 24,426 | TODD | 12,214 | 6,945 | 5,034 | 235 | 1,911 | R | 56.9% | 41.2% | 58.0% | 42.0% |
| 4,134 | TRAVERSE | 2,141 | 1,076 | 1,026 | 39 | 50 | R | 50.3% | 47.9% | 51.2% | 48.8% |
| 21,610 | WABASHA | 11,835 | 6,120 | 5,548 | 167 | 572 | R | 51.7% | 46.9% | 52.5% | 47.5% |
| 13,713 | WADENA | 7,093 | 4,214 | 2,791 | 88 | 1,423 | R | 59.4% | 39.3% | 60.2% | 39.8% |
| 19,526 | WASECA | 9,800 | 5,457 | 4,179 | 164 | 1,278 | R | 55.7% | 42.6% | 56.6% | 43.4% |
| 201,130 | WASHINGTON | 128,449 | 65,751 | 61,395 | 1,303 | 4,356 | R | 51.2% | 47.8% | 51.7% | 48.3% |
| 11,876 | WATONWAN | 5,583 | 2,970 | 2,514 | 99 | 456 | R | 53.2% | 45.0% | 54.2% | 45.8% |
| 7,138 | WILKIN | 3,527 | 2,303 | 1,169 | 55 | 1,134 | R | 65.3% | 33.1% | 66.3% | 33.7% |
| 49,985 | WINONA | 27,422 | 12,686 | 14,231 | 505 | 1,545 | D | 46.3% | 51.9% | 47.1% | 52.9% |
| 89,986 | WRIGHT | 59,534 | 36,176 | 22,618 | 740 | 13,558 | R | 60.8% | 38.0% | 61.5% | 38.5% |
| 11,080 | YELLOW MEDICINE | 5,758 | 2,878 | 2,799 | 81 | 79 | R | 50.0% | 48.6% | 50.7% | 49.3% |
| 4,919,479 | TOTAL | 2,828,387 | 1,346,695 | 1,445,014 | 36,678 | 98,319 | D | 47.6% | 51.1% | 48.2% | 51.8% |

# MINNESOTA

## PRESIDENT 2000

| 2000 Census Population | County | Total Vote | Republican | Democratic | Green (Nader) | Other | Rep.-Dem. Plurality | Percentage of Total Vote | | |
|---|---|---|---|---|---|---|---|---|---|---|
| | | | | | | | | Rep. | Dem. | Green |
| 15,301 | AITKIN | 8,260 | 3,755 | 3,830 | 403 | 272 | 75 D | 45.5% | 46.4% | 4.9% |
| 298,084 | ANOKA | 145,619 | 69,256 | 68,008 | 6,616 | 1,739 | 1,248 R | 47.6% | 46.7% | 4.5% |
| 30,000 | BECKER | 14,333 | 8,152 | 5,253 | 591 | 337 | 2,899 R | 56.9% | 36.6% | 4.1% |
| 39,650 | BELTRAMI | 17,217 | 8,346 | 7,301 | 1,269 | 301 | 1,045 R | 48.5% | 42.4% | 7.4% |
| 34,226 | BENTON | 14,908 | 7,663 | 6,009 | 862 | 374 | 1,654 R | 51.4% | 40.3% | 5.8% |
| 5,820 | BIG STONE | 2,980 | 1,370 | 1,430 | 109 | 71 | 60 D | 46.0% | 48.0% | 3.7% |
| 55,941 | BLUE EARTH | 27,402 | 12,942 | 12,329 | 1,761 | 370 | 613 R | 47.2% | 45.0% | 6.4% |
| 26,911 | BROWN | 12,834 | 7,370 | 4,650 | 561 | 253 | 2,720 R | 57.4% | 36.2% | 4.4% |
| 31,671 | CARLTON | 15,081 | 5,578 | 8,620 | 634 | 249 | 3,042 D | 37.0% | 57.2% | 4.2% |
| 70,205 | CARVER | 35,021 | 20,790 | 12,462 | 1,381 | 388 | 8,328 R | 59.4% | 35.6% | 3.9% |
| 27,150 | CASS | 13,593 | 7,134 | 5,534 | 663 | 262 | 1,600 R | 52.5% | 40.7% | 4.9% |
| 13,088 | CHIPPEWA | 6,352 | 2,977 | 2,952 | 268 | 155 | 25 R | 46.9% | 46.5% | 4.2% |
| 41,101 | CHISAGO | 21,987 | 10,937 | 9,593 | 1,116 | 341 | 1,344 R | 49.7% | 43.6% | 5.1% |
| 51,229 | CLAY | 23,358 | 11,712 | 10,128 | 963 | 555 | 1,584 R | 50.1% | 43.4% | 4.1% |
| 8,423 | CLEARWATER | 3,824 | 2,137 | 1,466 | 134 | 87 | 671 R | 55.9% | 38.3% | 3.5% |
| 5,168 | COOK | 2,820 | 1,295 | 1,171 | 290 | 64 | 124 R | 45.9% | 41.5% | 10.3% |
| 12,167 | COTTONWOOD | 6,181 | 3,369 | 2,503 | 208 | 101 | 866 R | 54.5% | 40.5% | 3.4% |
| 55,099 | CROW WING | 28,128 | 15,035 | 11,255 | 1,314 | 524 | 3,780 R | 53.5% | 40.0% | 4.7% |
| 355,904 | DAKOTA | 182,249 | 87,250 | 85,446 | 7,799 | 1,754 | 1,804 R | 47.9% | 46.9% | 4.3% |
| 17,731 | DODGE | 8,050 | 4,213 | 3,370 | 327 | 140 | 843 R | 52.3% | 41.9% | 4.1% |
| 32,821 | DOUGLAS | 17,205 | 9,811 | 6,352 | 746 | 296 | 3,459 R | 57.0% | 36.9% | 4.3% |
| 16,181 | FARIBAULT | 8,424 | 4,336 | 3,624 | 309 | 155 | 712 R | 51.5% | 43.0% | 3.7% |
| 21,122 | FILLMORE | 10,223 | 4,646 | 5,020 | 409 | 148 | 374 D | 45.4% | 49.1% | 4.0% |
| 32,584 | FREEBORN | 16,139 | 6,843 | 8,514 | 555 | 227 | 1,671 D | 42.4% | 52.8% | 3.4% |
| 44,127 | GOODHUE | 22,257 | 10,852 | 9,981 | 1,093 | 331 | 871 R | 48.8% | 44.8% | 4.9% |
| 6,289 | GRANT | 3,624 | 1,804 | 1,507 | 214 | 99 | 297 R | 49.8% | 41.6% | 5.9% |
| 1,116,200 | HENNEPIN | 573,846 | 225,657 | 307,599 | 35,584 | 5,006 | 81,942 D | 39.3% | 53.6% | 6.2% |
| 19,718 | HOUSTON | 10,167 | 5,077 | 4,502 | 421 | 167 | 575 R | 49.9% | 44.3% | 4.1% |
| 18,376 | HUBBARD | 9,613 | 5,307 | 3,632 | 484 | 190 | 1,675 R | 55.2% | 37.8% | 5.0% |
| 31,287 | ISANTI | 14,929 | 7,668 | 6,247 | 753 | 261 | 1,421 R | 51.4% | 41.8% | 5.0% |
| 43,992 | ITASCA | 21,714 | 9,545 | 10,583 | 1,137 | 449 | 1,038 D | 44.0% | 48.7% | 5.2% |
| 11,268 | JACKSON | 5,438 | 2,773 | 2,364 | 194 | 107 | 409 R | 51.0% | 43.5% | 3.6% |
| 14,996 | KANABEC | 6,811 | 3,480 | 2,831 | 344 | 156 | 649 R | 51.1% | 41.6% | 5.1% |
| 41,203 | KANDIYOHI | 19,285 | 10,026 | 8,220 | 734 | 305 | 1,806 R | 52.0% | 42.6% | 3.8% |
| 5,285 | KITTSON | 2,637 | 1,353 | 1,107 | 68 | 109 | 246 R | 51.3% | 42.0% | 2.6% |
| 14,355 | KOOCHICHING | 6,879 | 3,523 | 2,903 | 302 | 151 | 620 R | 51.2% | 42.2% | 4.4% |
| 8,067 | LAC QUI PARLE | 4,453 | 1,941 | 2,244 | 160 | 108 | 303 D | 43.6% | 50.4% | 3.6% |
| 11,058 | LAKE | 6,563 | 2,465 | 3,579 | 426 | 93 | 1,114 D | 37.6% | 54.5% | 6.5% |
| 4,522 | LAKE OF THE WOODS | 2,187 | 1,216 | 848 | 74 | 49 | 368 R | 55.6% | 38.8% | 3.4% |
| 25,426 | LE SUEUR | 12,331 | 6,138 | 5,361 | 603 | 229 | 777 R | 49.8% | 43.5% | 4.9% |
| 6,429 | LINCOLN | 3,284 | 1,513 | 1,590 | 105 | 76 | 77 D | 46.1% | 48.4% | 3.2% |
| 25,425 | LYON | 11,489 | 6,087 | 4,737 | 460 | 205 | 1,350 R | 53.0% | 41.2% | 4.0% |
| 34,898 | MCLEOD | 15,394 | 8,782 | 5,609 | 681 | 322 | 3,173 R | 57.0% | 36.4% | 4.4% |
| 5,190 | MAHNOMEN | 2,224 | 1,122 | 921 | 96 | 85 | 201 R | 50.4% | 41.4% | 4.3% |
| 10,155 | MARSHALL | 5,199 | 2,912 | 1,910 | 160 | 217 | 1,002 R | 56.0% | 36.7% | 3.1% |
| 21,802 | MARTIN | 10,371 | 5,686 | 4,166 | 376 | 143 | 1,520 R | 54.8% | 40.2% | 3.6% |
| 22,644 | MEEKER | 10,672 | 5,520 | 4,402 | 517 | 233 | 1,118 R | 51.7% | 41.2% | 4.8% |
| 22,330 | MILLE LACS | 10,253 | 5,223 | 4,376 | 448 | 206 | 847 R | 50.9% | 42.7% | 4.4% |
| 31,712 | MORRISON | 14,677 | 8,197 | 5,274 | 633 | 573 | 2,923 R | 55.8% | 35.9% | 4.3% |
| 38,603 | MOWER | 18,480 | 6,873 | 10,693 | 678 | 236 | 3,820 D | 37.2% | 57.9% | 3.7% |
| 9,165 | MURRAY | 4,753 | 2,407 | 2,093 | 149 | 104 | 314 R | 50.6% | 44.0% | 3.1% |
| 29,771 | NICOLLET | 15,327 | 7,221 | 7,041 | 842 | 223 | 180 R | 47.1% | 45.9% | 5.5% |
| 20,832 | NOBLES | 8,872 | 4,766 | 3,760 | 238 | 108 | 1,006 R | 53.7% | 42.4% | 2.7% |
| 7,442 | NORMAN | 3,641 | 1,808 | 1,575 | 123 | 135 | 233 R | 49.7% | 43.3% | 3.4% |
| 124,277 | OLMSTED | 59,392 | 30,641 | 25,822 | 2,198 | 731 | 4,819 R | 51.6% | 43.5% | 3.7% |
| 57,159 | OTTER TAIL | 28,511 | 16,963 | 9,844 | 1,120 | 584 | 7,119 R | 59.5% | 34.5% | 3.9% |
| 13,584 | PENNINGTON | 6,320 | 3,380 | 2,458 | 255 | 227 | 922 R | 53.5% | 38.9% | 4.0% |
| 26,530 | PINE | 13,068 | 5,854 | 6,148 | 734 | 332 | 294 D | 44.8% | 47.0% | 5.6% |
| 9,895 | PIPESTONE | 4,894 | 2,693 | 1,970 | 140 | 91 | 723 R | 55.0% | 40.3% | 2.9% |
| 31,369 | POLK | 14,140 | 7,609 | 5,764 | 369 | 398 | 1,845 R | 53.8% | 40.8% | 2.6% |

# MINNESOTA

## PRESIDENT 2000

| 2000 Census Population | County | Total Vote | Republican | Democratic | Green (Nader) | Other | Rep.-Dem. Plurality | Percentage of Total Vote | | |
|---|---|---|---|---|---|---|---|---|---|---|
| | | | | | | | | Rep. | Dem. | Green |
| 11,236 | POPE | 5,987 | 2,808 | 2,771 | 264 | 144 | 37 R | 46.9% | 46.3% | 4.4% |
| 511,035 | RAMSEY | 244,278 | 87,669 | 138,470 | 15,522 | 2,617 | 50,801 D | 35.9% | 56.7% | 6.4% |
| 4,299 | RED LAKE | 2,090 | 1,090 | 830 | 68 | 102 | 260 R | 52.2% | 39.7% | 3.3% |
| 16,815 | REDWOOD | 7,748 | 4,589 | 2,681 | 314 | 164 | 1,908 R | 59.2% | 34.6% | 4.1% |
| 17,154 | RENVILLE | 8,122 | 4,036 | 3,533 | 355 | 198 | 503 R | 49.7% | 43.5% | 4.4% |
| 56,665 | RICE | 26,021 | 10,876 | 13,140 | 1,639 | 366 | 2,264 D | 41.8% | 50.5% | 6.3% |
| 9,721 | ROCK | 5,010 | 2,772 | 2,081 | 116 | 41 | 691 R | 55.3% | 41.5% | 2.3% |
| 16,338 | ROSEAU | 7,166 | 4,695 | 2,128 | 176 | 167 | 2,567 R | 65.5% | 29.7% | 2.5% |
| 200,528 | ST. LOUIS | 107,464 | 35,420 | 64,237 | 6,290 | 1,517 | 28,817 D | 33.0% | 59.8% | 5.9% |
| 89,498 | SCOTT | 43,793 | 23,954 | 17,503 | 1,829 | 507 | 6,451 R | 54.7% | 40.0% | 4.2% |
| 64,417 | SHERBURNE | 30,835 | 16,813 | 12,109 | 1,501 | 412 | 4,704 R | 54.5% | 39.3% | 4.9% |
| 15,356 | SIBLEY | 7,335 | 4,087 | 2,687 | 361 | 200 | 1,400 R | 55.7% | 36.6% | 4.9% |
| 133,166 | STEARNS | 62,476 | 32,402 | 24,800 | 3,820 | 1,454 | 7,602 R | 51.9% | 39.7% | 6.1% |
| 33,680 | STEELE | 16,066 | 8,223 | 6,900 | 697 | 246 | 1,323 R | 51.2% | 42.9% | 4.3% |
| 10,053 | STEVENS | 5,752 | 2,831 | 2,434 | 393 | 94 | 397 R | 49.2% | 42.3% | 6.8% |
| 11,956 | SWIFT | 5,437 | 2,376 | 2,698 | 218 | 145 | 322 D | 43.7% | 49.6% | 4.0% |
| 24,426 | TODD | 11,092 | 6,031 | 4,132 | 485 | 444 | 1,899 R | 54.4% | 37.3% | 4.4% |
| 4,134 | TRAVERSE | 2,106 | 1,074 | 884 | 86 | 62 | 190 R | 51.0% | 42.0% | 4.1% |
| 21,610 | WABASHA | 10,531 | 5,245 | 4,522 | 571 | 193 | 723 R | 49.8% | 42.9% | 5.4% |
| 13,713 | WADENA | 6,382 | 3,733 | 2,251 | 253 | 145 | 1,482 R | 58.5% | 35.3% | 4.0% |
| 19,526 | WASECA | 8,864 | 4,608 | 3,694 | 398 | 164 | 914 R | 52.0% | 41.7% | 4.5% |
| 201,130 | WASHINGTON | 107,009 | 51,502 | 49,637 | 4,891 | 979 | 1,865 R | 48.1% | 46.4% | 4.6% |
| 11,876 | WATONWAN | 5,134 | 2,562 | 2,258 | 212 | 102 | 304 R | 49.9% | 44.0% | 4.1% |
| 7,138 | WILKIN | 3,305 | 2,032 | 1,046 | 77 | 150 | 986 R | 61.5% | 31.6% | 2.3% |
| 49,985 | WINONA | 23,918 | 10,773 | 11,069 | 1,750 | 326 | 296 D | 45.0% | 46.3% | 7.3% |
| 89,986 | WRIGHT | 43,366 | 23,861 | 16,762 | 1,977 | 766 | 7,099 R | 55.0% | 38.7% | 4.6% |
| 11,080 | YELLOW MEDICINE | 5,515 | 2,598 | 2,528 | 232 | 157 | 70 R | 47.1% | 45.8% | 4.2% |
| 4,919,479 | TOTAL | 2,438,685 | 1,109,659 | 1,168,266 | 126,696 | 34,064 | 58,607 D | 45.5% | 47.9% | 5.2% |

# MINNESOTA

## PRESIDENT 1996

| 1995 Census Pop. Est. | County | Total Vote | Republican | Democratic | Reform (Perot) | Other | Rep.-Dem. Plurality | Percentage of Total Vote | | |
|---|---|---|---|---|---|---|---|---|---|---|
| | | | | | | | | Rep. | Dem. | Reform |
| 13,444 | AITKIN | 7,404 | 2,327 | 3,810 | 1,155 | 112 | 1,483 D | 31.4% | 51.5% | 15.6% |
| 275,760 | ANOKA | 124,022 | 41,745 | 63,756 | 16,448 | 2,073 | 22,011 D | 33.7% | 51.4% | 13.3% |
| 29,119 | BECKER | 13,374 | 5,461 | 5,911 | 1,813 | 189 | 450 D | 40.8% | 44.2% | 13.6% |
| 37,932 | BELTRAMI | 15,848 | 5,806 | 8,006 | 1,635 | 401 | 2,200 D | 36.6% | 50.5% | 10.3% |
| 32,950 | BENTON | 13,233 | 4,835 | 6,006 | 2,133 | 259 | 1,171 D | 36.5% | 45.4% | 16.1% |
| 5,898 | BIG STONE | 3,001 | 990 | 1,619 | 368 | 24 | 629 D | 33.0% | 53.9% | 12.3% |
| 54,134 | BLUE EARTH | 25,261 | 9,082 | 12,420 | 3,324 | 435 | 3,338 D | 36.0% | 49.2% | 13.2% |
| 27,128 | BROWN | 12,359 | 5,580 | 4,864 | 1,786 | 129 | 716 R | 45.1% | 39.4% | 14.5% |
| 30,421 | CARLTON | 13,915 | 4,034 | 8,052 | 1,591 | 238 | 4,018 D | 29.0% | 57.9% | 11.4% |
| 59,220 | CARVER | 28,168 | 12,380 | 11,554 | 3,781 | 453 | 826 R | 44.0% | 41.0% | 13.4% |
| 24,738 | CASS | 12,029 | 4,791 | 5,437 | 1,620 | 181 | 646 D | 39.8% | 45.2% | 13.5% |
| 13,114 | CHIPPEWA | 6,124 | 2,119 | 3,178 | 782 | 45 | 1,059 D | 34.6% | 51.9% | 12.8% |
| 37,024 | CHISAGO | 17,733 | 5,984 | 8,611 | 2,812 | 326 | 2,627 D | 33.7% | 48.6% | 15.9% |
| 52,178 | CLAY | 21,319 | 8,764 | 10,476 | 1,733 | 346 | 1,712 D | 41.1% | 49.1% | 8.1% |
| 8,366 | CLEARWATER | 3,514 | 1,423 | 1,578 | 471 | 42 | 155 D | 40.5% | 44.9% | 13.4% |
| 4,479 | COOK | 2,529 | 1,010 | 1,169 | 246 | 104 | 159 D | 39.9% | 46.2% | 9.7% |
| 12,371 | COTTONWOOD | 6,172 | 2,633 | 2,737 | 741 | 61 | 104 D | 42.7% | 44.3% | 12.0% |
| 49,779 | CROW WING | 24,963 | 10,095 | 11,156 | 3,423 | 289 | 1,061 D | 40.4% | 44.7% | 13.7% |
| 316,466 | DAKOTA | 154,266 | 57,244 | 77,297 | 17,095 | 2,630 | 20,053 D | 37.1% | 50.1% | 11.1% |
| 16,701 | DODGE | 7,435 | 2,888 | 3,233 | 1,223 | 91 | 345 D | 38.8% | 43.5% | 16.4% |
| 30,397 | DOUGLAS | 15,464 | 6,747 | 6,450 | 2,093 | 174 | 297 R | 43.6% | 41.7% | 13.5% |
| 16,434 | FARIBAULT | 8,262 | 3,272 | 3,817 | 1,103 | 70 | 545 D | 39.6% | 46.2% | 13.4% |
| 20,751 | FILLMORE | 9,861 | 3,466 | 4,732 | 1,575 | 88 | 1,266 D | 35.1% | 48.0% | 16.0% |
| 31,934 | FREEBORN | 15,988 | 5,166 | 8,458 | 2,226 | 138 | 3,292 D | 32.3% | 52.9% | 13.9% |
| 42,297 | GOODHUE | 20,318 | 7,293 | 9,931 | 2,806 | 288 | 2,638 D | 35.9% | 48.9% | 13.8% |
| 6,221 | GRANT | 3,562 | 1,284 | 1,806 | 434 | 38 | 522 D | 36.0% | 50.7% | 12.2% |
| 1,053,467 | HENNEPIN | 524,306 | 173,887 | 285,126 | 47,663 | 17,630 | 111,239 D | 33.2% | 54.4% | 9.1% |
| 19,296 | HOUSTON | 9,450 | 3,674 | 4,153 | 1,439 | 184 | 479 D | 38.9% | 43.9% | 15.2% |
| 16,116 | HUBBARD | 8,711 | 3,593 | 3,802 | 1,141 | 175 | 209 D | 41.2% | 43.6% | 13.1% |
| 28,286 | ISANTI | 12,955 | 4,450 | 6,041 | 2,242 | 222 | 1,591 D | 34.3% | 46.6% | 17.3% |
| 43,047 | ITASCA | 20,473 | 6,506 | 10,706 | 2,889 | 372 | 4,200 D | 31.8% | 52.3% | 14.1% |
| 11,777 | JACKSON | 5,839 | 2,153 | 2,727 | 908 | 51 | 574 D | 36.9% | 46.7% | 15.6% |
| 13,580 | KANABEC | 5,948 | 1,924 | 2,927 | 996 | 101 | 1,003 D | 32.3% | 49.2% | 16.7% |
| 40,793 | KANDIYOHI | 18,532 | 7,119 | 9,009 | 2,229 | 175 | 1,890 D | 38.4% | 48.6% | 12.0% |
| 5,459 | KITTSON | 2,749 | 1,055 | 1,394 | 270 | 30 | 339 D | 38.4% | 50.7% | 9.8% |
| 15,983 | KOOCHICHING | 6,730 | 2,080 | 3,472 | 1,098 | 80 | 1,392 D | 30.9% | 51.6% | 16.3% |
| 8,398 | LAC QUI PARLE | 4,465 | 1,447 | 2,420 | 561 | 37 | 973 D | 32.4% | 54.2% | 12.6% |
| 10,570 | LAKE | 6,029 | 1,684 | 3,388 | 752 | 205 | 1,704 D | 27.9% | 56.2% | 12.5% |
| 4,491 | LAKE OF THE WOODS | 2,011 | 814 | 888 | 287 | 22 | 74 D | 40.5% | 44.2% | 14.3% |
| 24,361 | LE SUEUR | 11,209 | 3,902 | 5,457 | 1,699 | 151 | 1,555 D | 34.8% | 48.7% | 15.2% |
| 6,697 | LINCOLN | 3,378 | 1,199 | 1,641 | 504 | 34 | 442 D | 35.5% | 48.6% | 14.9% |
| 24,995 | LYON | 11,477 | 4,932 | 5,062 | 1,351 | 132 | 130 D | 43.0% | 44.1% | 11.8% |
| 33,254 | MCLEOD | 14,063 | 5,474 | 6,027 | 2,402 | 160 | 553 D | 38.9% | 42.9% | 17.1% |
| 5,145 | MAHNOMEN | 2,209 | 877 | 1,026 | 270 | 36 | 149 D | 39.7% | 46.4% | 12.2% |
| 10,596 | MARSHALL | 5,154 | 2,068 | 2,333 | 710 | 43 | 265 D | 40.1% | 45.3% | 13.8% |
| 22,493 | MARTIN | 10,517 | 4,303 | 4,718 | 1,405 | 91 | 415 D | 40.9% | 44.9% | 13.4% |
| 21,293 | MEEKER | 9,639 | 3,428 | 4,531 | 1,571 | 109 | 1,103 D | 35.6% | 47.0% | 16.3% |
| 20,083 | MILLE LACS | 8,875 | 2,948 | 4,336 | 1,467 | 124 | 1,388 D | 33.2% | 48.9% | 16.5% |
| 30,178 | MORRISON | 13,288 | 5,054 | 5,728 | 2,310 | 196 | 674 D | 38.0% | 43.1% | 17.4% |
| 37,312 | MOWER | 18,063 | 4,994 | 10,413 | 2,464 | 192 | 5,419 D | 27.6% | 57.6% | 13.6% |
| 9,511 | MURRAY | 4,869 | 1,907 | 2,173 | 753 | 36 | 266 D | 39.2% | 44.6% | 15.5% |
| 29,722 | NICOLLET | 13,842 | 5,057 | 6,772 | 1,737 | 276 | 1,715 D | 36.5% | 48.9% | 12.5% |
| 20,166 | NOBLES | 9,061 | 3,769 | 4,106 | 1,132 | 54 | 337 D | 41.6% | 45.3% | 12.5% |
| 7,724 | NORMAN | 3,722 | 1,392 | 1,875 | 425 | 30 | 483 D | 37.4% | 50.4% | 11.4% |
| 112,619 | OLMSTED | 52,044 | 22,860 | 22,857 | 5,640 | 687 | 3 R | 43.9% | 43.9% | 10.8% |
| 53,207 | OTTER TAIL | 25,850 | 11,808 | 10,519 | 3,191 | 332 | 1,289 R | 45.7% | 40.7% | 12.3% |
| 13,372 | PENNINGTON | 5,915 | 2,129 | 2,814 | 910 | 62 | 685 D | 36.0% | 47.6% | 15.4% |
| 22,878 | PINE | 10,308 | 3,080 | 5,432 | 1,597 | 199 | 2,352 D | 29.9% | 52.7% | 15.5% |
| 10,339 | PIPESTONE | 4,722 | 2,096 | 1,999 | 599 | 28 | 97 R | 44.4% | 42.3% | 12.7% |
| 32,692 | POLK | 13,587 | 5,563 | 6,369 | 1,502 | 153 | 806 D | 40.9% | 46.9% | 11.1% |

# MINNESOTA

## PRESIDENT 1996

| 1995 Census Pop. Est. | County | Total Vote | Republican | Democratic | Reform (Perot) | Other | Rep.-Dem. Plurality | Percentage of Total Vote | | |
|---|---|---|---|---|---|---|---|---|---|---|
| | | | | | | | | Rep. | Dem. | Reform |
| 10,940 | POPE | 5,529 | 1,992 | 2,803 | 665 | 69 | 811 D | 36.0% | 50.7% | 12.0% |
| 482,115 | RAMSEY | 228,213 | 66,954 | 133,878 | 20,351 | 7,030 | 66,924 D | 29.3% | 58.7% | 8.9% |
| 4,418 | RED LAKE | 2,106 | 695 | 1,053 | 334 | 24 | 358 D | 33.0% | 50.0% | 15.9% |
| 16,947 | REDWOOD | 7,851 | 3,700 | 2,997 | 1,053 | 101 | 703 R | 47.1% | 38.2% | 13.4% |
| 17,280 | RENVILLE | 8,238 | 2,887 | 3,956 | 1,311 | 84 | 1,069 D | 35.0% | 48.0% | 15.9% |
| 51,931 | RICE | 23,320 | 7,016 | 12,821 | 2,872 | 611 | 5,805 D | 30.1% | 55.0% | 12.3% |
| 9,837 | ROCK | 4,904 | 2,169 | 2,142 | 554 | 39 | 27 R | 44.2% | 43.7% | 11.3% |
| 15,997 | ROSEAU | 6,909 | 2,988 | 2,759 | 1,081 | 81 | 229 R | 43.2% | 39.9% | 15.6% |
| 197,144 | ST. LOUIS | 100,196 | 25,553 | 60,736 | 11,308 | 2,599 | 35,183 D | 25.5% | 60.6% | 11.3% |
| 69,916 | SCOTT | 32,847 | 12,734 | 14,657 | 4,886 | 570 | 1,923 D | 38.8% | 44.6% | 14.9% |
| 52,861 | SHERBURNE | 23,275 | 8,699 | 10,551 | 3,665 | 360 | 1,852 D | 37.4% | 45.3% | 15.7% |
| 14,720 | SIBLEY | 6,647 | 2,590 | 2,769 | 1,226 | 62 | 179 D | 39.0% | 41.7% | 18.4% |
| 125,852 | STEARNS | 55,045 | 21,474 | 24,238 | 8,150 | 1,183 | 2,764 D | 39.0% | 44.0% | 14.8% |
| 31,503 | STEELE | 14,964 | 5,617 | 6,974 | 2,197 | 176 | 1,357 D | 37.5% | 46.6% | 14.7% |
| 10,416 | STEVENS | 5,455 | 2,141 | 2,741 | 467 | 106 | 600 D | 39.2% | 50.2% | 8.6% |
| 10,784 | SWIFT | 5,330 | 1,541 | 3,054 | 690 | 45 | 1,513 D | 28.9% | 57.3% | 12.9% |
| 23,994 | TODD | 10,701 | 4,078 | 4,520 | 1,958 | 145 | 442 D | 38.1% | 42.2% | 18.3% |
| 4,290 | TRAVERSE | 2,229 | 775 | 1,135 | 295 | 24 | 360 D | 34.8% | 50.9% | 13.2% |
| 20,502 | WABASHA | 9,573 | 3,452 | 4,523 | 1,474 | 124 | 1,071 D | 36.1% | 47.2% | 15.4% |
| 13,173 | WADENA | 6,040 | 2,696 | 2,480 | 801 | 63 | 216 R | 44.6% | 41.1% | 13.3% |
| 18,002 | WASECA | 8,472 | 3,171 | 3,819 | 1,385 | 97 | 648 D | 37.4% | 45.1% | 16.3% |
| 179,824 | WASHINGTON | 88,057 | 31,219 | 45,119 | 10,106 | 1,613 | 13,900 D | 35.5% | 51.2% | 11.5% |
| 11,616 | WATONWAN | 5,291 | 1,997 | 2,534 | 711 | 49 | 537 D | 37.7% | 47.9% | 13.4% |
| 7,404 | WILKIN | 3,220 | 1,508 | 1,319 | 358 | 35 | 189 R | 46.8% | 41.0% | 11.1% |
| 48,558 | WINONA | 21,616 | 7,955 | 10,272 | 2,907 | 482 | 2,317 D | 36.8% | 47.5% | 13.4% |
| 78,623 | WRIGHT | 34,874 | 13,224 | 15,542 | 5,550 | 558 | 2,318 D | 37.9% | 44.6% | 15.9% |
| 11,745 | YELLOW MEDICINE | 5,624 | 2,006 | 2,741 | 818 | 59 | 735 D | 35.7% | 48.7% | 14.5% |
| 4,609,548 | TOTAL | 2,192,640 | 766,476 | 1,120,438 | 257,704 | 48,022 | 353,962 D | 35.0% | 51.1% | 11.8% |

# MINNESOTA

## PRESIDENT 1992

| 1990 Census Population | County | Total Vote | Republican | Democratic | Perot | Other | Plurality | Percentage Total Vote | | |
|---|---|---|---|---|---|---|---|---|---|---|
| | | | | | | | | Rep. | Dem. | Perot |
| 12,425 | AITKIN | 7,559 | 2,151 | 3,400 | 1,951 | 57 | 1,249 D | 28.5% | 45.0% | 25.8% |
| 243,641 | ANOKA | 130,020 | 39,458 | 54,621 | 35,140 | 801 | 15,163 D | 30.3% | 42.0% | 27.0% |
| 27,881 | BECKER | 13,702 | 5,430 | 4,958 | 3,238 | 76 | 472 R | 39.6% | 36.2% | 23.6% |
| 34,384 | BELTRAMI | 15,987 | 5,204 | 7,210 | 3,473 | 100 | 2,006 D | 32.6% | 45.1% | 21.7% |
| 30,185 | BENTON | 14,371 | 5,053 | 5,156 | 4,048 | 114 | 103 D | 35.2% | 35.9% | 28.2% |
| 6,285 | BIG STONE | 3,420 | 1,052 | 1,610 | 740 | 18 | 558 D | 30.8% | 47.1% | 21.6% |
| 54,044 | BLUE EARTH | 27,847 | 8,813 | 11,531 | 7,299 | 204 | 2,718 D | 31.6% | 41.4% | 26.2% |
| 26,984 | BROWN | 13,621 | 5,390 | 4,278 | 3,845 | 108 | 1,112 R | 39.6% | 31.4% | 28.2% |
| 29,259 | CARLTON | 14,747 | 3,922 | 7,736 | 3,005 | 84 | 3,814 D | 26.6% | 52.5% | 20.4% |
| 47,915 | CARVER | 26,604 | 10,201 | 8,349 | 7,942 | 112 | 1,852 R | 38.3% | 31.4% | 29.9% |
| 21,791 | CASS | 12,197 | 4,276 | 4,901 | 2,939 | 81 | 625 D | 35.1% | 40.2% | 24.1% |
| 13,228 | CHIPPEWA | 6,617 | 2,143 | 2,929 | 1,505 | 40 | 786 D | 32.4% | 44.3% | 22.7% |
| 30,521 | CHISAGO | 17,119 | 4,813 | 7,077 | 5,098 | 131 | 1,979 D | 28.1% | 41.3% | 29.8% |
| 50,422 | CLAY | 23,478 | 9,666 | 9,845 | 3,835 | 132 | 179 D | 41.2% | 41.9% | 16.3% |
| 8,309 | CLEARWATER | 3,758 | 1,315 | 1,587 | 841 | 15 | 272 D | 35.0% | 42.2% | 22.4% |
| 3,868 | COOK | 2,618 | 878 | 1,005 | 704 | 31 | 127 D | 33.5% | 38.4% | 26.9% |
| 12,694 | COTTONWOOD | 6,651 | 2,481 | 2,382 | 1,749 | 39 | 99 R | 37.3% | 35.8% | 26.3% |
| 44,249 | CROW WING | 24,539 | 9,112 | 8,896 | 6,367 | 164 | 216 R | 37.1% | 36.3% | 25.9% |
| 275,227 | DAKOTA | 157,080 | 52,312 | 63,660 | 40,244 | 864 | 11,348 D | 33.3% | 40.5% | 25.6% |
| 15,731 | DODGE | 7,972 | 3,049 | 2,620 | 2,231 | 72 | 429 R | 38.2% | 32.9% | 28.0% |
| 28,674 | DOUGLAS | 15,859 | 6,356 | 5,252 | 4,138 | 113 | 1,104 R | 40.1% | 33.1% | 26.1% |
| 16,937 | FARIBAULT | 9,146 | 3,439 | 3,339 | 2,322 | 46 | 100 R | 37.6% | 36.5% | 25.4% |
| 20,777 | FILLMORE | 10,658 | 3,583 | 3,977 | 3,011 | 87 | 394 D | 33.6% | 37.3% | 28.3% |
| 33,060 | FREEBORN | 17,813 | 5,089 | 7,759 | 4,878 | 87 | 2,670 D | 28.6% | 43.6% | 27.4% |
| 40,690 | GOODHUE | 21,250 | 7,321 | 7,916 | 5,790 | 223 | 595 D | 34.5% | 37.3% | 27.2% |
| 6,246 | GRANT | 3,666 | 1,201 | 1,561 | 885 | 19 | 360 D | 32.8% | 42.6% | 24.1% |
| 1,032,431 | HENNEPIN | 586,619 | 179,581 | 278,648 | 123,659 | 4,731 | 99,067 D | 30.6% | 47.5% | 21.1% |
| 18,497 | HOUSTON | 10,451 | 3,853 | 3,744 | 2,697 | 157 | 109 R | 36.9% | 35.8% | 25.8% |
| 14,939 | HUBBARD | 8,589 | 3,227 | 3,362 | 1,949 | 51 | 135 D | 37.6% | 39.1% | 22.7% |
| 25,921 | ISANTI | 13,366 | 3,988 | 5,386 | 3,898 | 94 | 1,398 D | 29.8% | 40.3% | 29.2% |
| 40,863 | ITASCA | 20,838 | 5,952 | 9,621 | 5,147 | 118 | 3,669 D | 28.6% | 46.2% | 24.7% |
| 11,677 | JACKSON | 6,252 | 1,824 | 2,481 | 1,918 | 29 | 563 D | 29.2% | 39.7% | 30.7% |
| 12,802 | KANABEC | 6,288 | 1,876 | 2,532 | 1,836 | 44 | 656 D | 29.8% | 40.3% | 29.2% |
| 38,761 | KANDIYOHI | 19,656 | 6,784 | 7,914 | 4,869 | 89 | 1,130 D | 34.5% | 40.3% | 24.8% |
| 5,767 | KITTSON | 2,984 | 1,098 | 1,307 | 558 | 21 | 209 D | 36.8% | 43.8% | 18.7% |
| 16,299 | KOOCHICHING | 7,465 | 1,954 | 3,474 | 1,993 | 44 | 1,481 D | 26.2% | 46.5% | 26.7% |
| 8,924 | LAC QUI PARLE | 4,968 | 1,435 | 2,342 | 1,163 | 28 | 907 D | 28.9% | 47.1% | 23.4% |
| 10,415 | LAKE | 6,357 | 1,465 | 3,415 | 1,437 | 40 | 1,950 D | 23.0% | 53.7% | 22.6% |
| 4,076 | LAKE OF THE WOODS | 2,198 | 762 | 794 | 629 | 13 | 32 D | 34.7% | 36.1% | 28.6% |
| 23,239 | LE SUEUR | 11,954 | 3,858 | 4,662 | 3,363 | 71 | 804 D | 32.3% | 39.0% | 28.1% |
| 6,890 | LINCOLN | 3,636 | 1,084 | 1,555 | 967 | 30 | 471 D | 29.8% | 42.8% | 26.6% |
| 24,789 | LYON | 12,324 | 4,591 | 4,481 | 3,180 | 72 | 110 R | 37.3% | 36.4% | 25.8% |
| 32,030 | MCLEOD | 15,347 | 5,422 | 4,919 | 4,933 | 73 | 489 R | 35.3% | 32.1% | 32.1% |
| 5,044 | MAHNOMEN | 2,389 | 854 | 1,035 | 483 | 17 | 181 D | 35.7% | 43.3% | 20.2% |
| 10,993 | MARSHALL | 5,803 | 2,136 | 2,309 | 1,306 | 52 | 173 D | 36.8% | 39.8% | 22.5% |
| 22,914 | MARTIN | 11,609 | 4,438 | 4,019 | 3,089 | 63 | 419 R | 38.2% | 34.6% | 26.6% |
| 20,846 | MEEKER | 10,540 | 3,497 | 3,861 | 3,120 | 62 | 364 D | 33.2% | 36.6% | 29.6% |
| 18,670 | MILLE LACS | 9,154 | 2,814 | 3,648 | 2,615 | 77 | 834 D | 30.7% | 39.9% | 28.6% |
| 29,604 | MORRISON | 14,442 | 5,038 | 5,588 | 3,710 | 106 | 550 D | 34.9% | 38.7% | 25.7% |
| 37,385 | MOWER | 20,210 | 5,147 | 9,935 | 5,001 | 127 | 4,788 D | 25.5% | 49.2% | 24.7% |
| 9,660 | MURRAY | 5,213 | 1,609 | 1,993 | 1,588 | 23 | 384 D | 30.9% | 38.2% | 30.5% |
| 28,076 | NICOLLET | 15,039 | 5,091 | 6,055 | 3,799 | 94 | 964 D | 33.9% | 40.3% | 25.3% |
| 20,098 | NOBLES | 9,930 | 3,548 | 3,756 | 2,586 | 40 | 208 D | 35.7% | 37.8% | 26.0% |
| 7,975 | NORMAN | 4,121 | 1,541 | 1,784 | 776 | 20 | 243 D | 37.4% | 43.3% | 18.8% |
| 106,470 | OLMSTED | 56,662 | 23,404 | 19,039 | 13,806 | 413 | 4,365 R | 41.3% | 33.6% | 24.4% |
| 50,714 | OTTER TAIL | 26,670 | 11,074 | 9,176 | 6,274 | 146 | 1,898 R | 41.5% | 34.4% | 23.5% |
| 13,306 | PENNINGTON | 6,359 | 2,155 | 2,578 | 1,598 | 28 | 423 D | 33.9% | 40.5% | 25.1% |
| 21,264 | PINE | 10,813 | 2,841 | 4,929 | 2,952 | 91 | 1,977 D | 26.3% | 45.6% | 27.3% |
| 10,491 | PIPESTONE | 5,170 | 1,953 | 1,773 | 1,429 | 15 | 180 R | 37.8% | 34.3% | 27.6% |
| 32,498 | POLK | 14,934 | 5,817 | 5,850 | 3,176 | 91 | 33 D | 39.0% | 39.2% | 21.3% |

# MINNESOTA

## PRESIDENT 1992

| 1990 Census Population | County | Total Vote | Republican | Democratic | Perot | Other | Plurality | Percentage Total Vote | | |
|---|---|---|---|---|---|---|---|---|---|---|
| | | | | | | | | Rep. | Dem. | Perot |
| 10,745 | POPE | 5,970 | 1,886 | 2,619 | 1,390 | 75 | 733 D | 31.6% | 43.9% | 23.3% |
| 485,765 | RAMSEY | 251,915 | 68,206 | 130,932 | 50,757 | 2,020 | 62,726 D | 27.1% | 52.0% | 20.1% |
| 4,525 | RED LAKE | 2,201 | 691 | 1,020 | 472 | 18 | 329 D | 31.4% | 46.3% | 21.4% |
| 17,254 | REDWOOD | 8,913 | 3,408 | 2,740 | 2,710 | 55 | 668 R | 38.2% | 30.7% | 30.4% |
| 17,673 | RENVILLE | 8,920 | 2,852 | 3,414 | 2,598 | 56 | 562 D | 32.0% | 38.3% | 29.1% |
| 49,183 | RICE | 24,113 | 7,015 | 10,908 | 6,057 | 133 | 3,893 D | 29.1% | 45.2% | 25.1% |
| 9,806 | ROCK | 5,338 | 2,065 | 2,006 | 1,244 | 23 | 59 R | 38.7% | 37.6% | 23.3% |
| 15,026 | ROSEAU | 7,269 | 2,785 | 2,346 | 2,099 | 39 | 439 R | 38.3% | 32.3% | 28.9% |
| 198,213 | ST. LOUIS | 108,815 | 24,579 | 61,813 | 21,714 | 709 | 37,234 D | 22.6% | 56.8% | 20.0% |
| 57,846 | SCOTT | 32,216 | 10,936 | 11,225 | 9,881 | 174 | 289 D | 33.9% | 34.8% | 30.7% |
| 41,945 | SHERBURNE | 21,841 | 7,339 | 7,843 | 6,534 | 125 | 504 D | 33.6% | 35.9% | 29.9% |
| 14,366 | SIBLEY | 7,185 | 2,315 | 2,421 | 2,407 | 42 | 14 D | 32.2% | 33.7% | 33.5% |
| 118,791 | STEARNS | 59,340 | 22,502 | 21,451 | 14,834 | 553 | 1,051 R | 37.9% | 36.1% | 25.0% |
| 30,729 | STEELE | 15,789 | 5,964 | 5,152 | 4,542 | 131 | 812 R | 37.8% | 32.6% | 28.8% |
| 10,634 | STEVENS | 5,816 | 2,229 | 2,466 | 1,086 | 35 | 237 D | 38.3% | 42.4% | 18.7% |
| 10,724 | SWIFT | 5,991 | 1,603 | 2,980 | 1,359 | 49 | 1,377 D | 26.8% | 49.7% | 22.7% |
| 23,363 | TODD | 11,104 | 3,990 | 4,059 | 2,976 | 79 | 69 D | 35.9% | 36.6% | 26.8% |
| 4,463 | TRAVERSE | 2,484 | 841 | 1,053 | 582 | 8 | 212 D | 33.9% | 42.4% | 23.4% |
| 19,744 | WABASHA | 10,217 | 3,397 | 3,736 | 3,012 | 72 | 339 D | 33.2% | 36.6% | 29.5% |
| 13,154 | WADENA | 6,398 | 2,492 | 2,340 | 1,535 | 31 | 152 R | 38.9% | 36.6% | 24.0% |
| 18,079 | WASECA | 9,006 | 3,118 | 3,146 | 2,621 | 121 | 28 D | 34.6% | 34.9% | 29.1% |
| 145,896 | WASHINGTON | 85,499 | 26,568 | 35,820 | 22,585 | 526 | 9,252 D | 31.1% | 41.9% | 26.4% |
| 11,682 | WATONWAN | 5,578 | 1,871 | 2,100 | 1,574 | 33 | 229 D | 33.5% | 37.6% | 28.2% |
| 7,516 | WILKIN | 3,510 | 1,626 | 1,122 | 748 | 14 | 504 R | 46.3% | 32.0% | 21.3% |
| 47,828 | WINONA | 24,518 | 8,585 | 9,707 | 5,993 | 233 | 1,122 D | 35.0% | 39.6% | 24.4% |
| 68,710 | WRIGHT | 35,160 | 11,650 | 12,465 | 10,829 | 216 | 815 D | 33.1% | 35.5% | 30.8% |
| 11,684 | YELLOW MEDICINE | 6,193 | 1,909 | 2,593 | 1,645 | 46 | 684 D | 30.8% | 41.9% | 26.6% |
| 4,375,099 | TOTAL | 2,347,948 | 747,841 | 1,020,997 | 562,506 | 16,604 | 273,156 D | 31.9% | 43.5% | 24.0% |

# MINNESOTA

## PRESIDENT 1988

| 1980 Census Population | County | Total Vote | Republican | Democratic | Other | Rep.-Dem. Plurality | Percentage Total Vote Rep. | Dem. | Major Vote Rep. | Dem. |
|---|---|---|---|---|---|---|---|---|---|---|
| 13,404 | AITKIN | 6,955 | 3,011 | 3,863 | 81 | 852 D | 43.3% | 55.5% | 43.8% | 56.2% |
| 195,998 | ANOKA | 105,931 | 46,853 | 57,953 | 1,125 | 11,100 D | 44.2% | 54.7% | 44.7% | 55.3% |
| 29,336 | BECKER | 12,672 | 6,738 | 5,787 | 147 | 951 R | 53.2% | 45.7% | 53.8% | 46.2% |
| 30,982 | BELTRAMI | 14,402 | 6,652 | 7,566 | 184 | 914 D | 46.2% | 52.5% | 46.8% | 53.2% |
| 25,187 | BENTON | 12,070 | 6,060 | 5,861 | 149 | 199 R | 50.2% | 48.6% | 50.8% | 49.2% |
| 7,716 | BIG STONE | 3,526 | 1,469 | 2,026 | 31 | 557 D | 41.7% | 57.5% | 42.0% | 58.0% |
| 52,314 | BLUE EARTH | 24,570 | 11,959 | 12,375 | 236 | 416 D | 48.7% | 50.4% | 49.1% | 50.9% |
| 28,645 | BROWN | 12,200 | 6,898 | 5,109 | 193 | 1,789 R | 56.5% | 41.9% | 57.4% | 42.6% |
| 29,936 | CARLTON | 13,579 | 4,626 | 8,790 | 163 | 4,164 D | 34.1% | 64.7% | 34.5% | 65.5% |
| 37,046 | CARVER | 21,262 | 12,560 | 8,439 | 263 | 4,121 R | 59.1% | 39.7% | 59.8% | 40.2% |
| 21,050 | CASS | 11,141 | 5,895 | 5,127 | 119 | 768 R | 52.9% | 46.0% | 53.5% | 46.5% |
| 14,941 | CHIPPEWA | 6,514 | 3,190 | 3,238 | 86 | 48 D | 49.0% | 49.7% | 49.6% | 50.4% |
| 25,717 | CHISAGO | 14,196 | 6,163 | 7,875 | 158 | 1,712 D | 43.4% | 55.5% | 43.9% | 56.1% |
| 49,327 | CLAY | 21,715 | 10,380 | 11,186 | 149 | 806 D | 47.8% | 51.5% | 48.1% | 51.9% |
| 8,761 | CLEARWATER | 3,569 | 1,763 | 1,769 | 37 | 6 D | 49.4% | 49.6% | 49.9% | 50.1% |
| 4,092 | COOK | 2,189 | 1,078 | 1,080 | 31 | 2 D | 49.2% | 49.3% | 50.0% | 50.0% |
| 14,854 | COTTONWOOD | 6,560 | 3,390 | 3,095 | 75 | 295 R | 51.7% | 47.2% | 52.3% | 47.7% |
| 41,722 | CROW WING | 20,929 | 11,017 | 9,674 | 238 | 1,343 R | 52.6% | 46.2% | 53.2% | 46.8% |
| 194,279 | DAKOTA | 124,773 | 61,606 | 61,942 | 1,225 | 336 D | 49.4% | 49.6% | 49.9% | 50.1% |
| 14,773 | DODGE | 6,854 | 3,848 | 2,925 | 81 | 923 R | 56.1% | 42.7% | 56.8% | 43.2% |
| 27,839 | DOUGLAS | 13,858 | 7,898 | 5,803 | 157 | 2,095 R | 57.0% | 41.9% | 57.6% | 42.4% |
| 19,714 | FARIBAULT | 8,816 | 4,846 | 3,879 | 91 | 967 R | 55.0% | 44.0% | 55.5% | 44.5% |
| 21,930 | FILLMORE | 9,201 | 5,004 | 4,114 | 83 | 890 R | 54.4% | 44.7% | 54.9% | 45.1% |
| 36,329 | FREEBORN | 16,219 | 7,226 | 8,836 | 157 | 1,610 D | 44.6% | 54.5% | 45.0% | 55.0% |
| 38,749 | GOODHUE | 19,126 | 9,455 | 9,438 | 233 | 17 R | 49.4% | 49.3% | 50.0% | 50.0% |
| 7,171 | GRANT | 3,687 | 1,693 | 1,950 | 44 | 257 D | 45.9% | 52.9% | 46.5% | 53.5% |
| 941,411 | HENNEPIN | 539,788 | 240,209 | 292,909 | 6,670 | 52,700 D | 44.5% | 54.3% | 45.1% | 54.9% |
| 18,382 | HOUSTON | 8,848 | 4,777 | 3,936 | 135 | 841 R | 54.0% | 44.5% | 54.8% | 45.2% |
| 14,098 | HUBBARD | 7,749 | 4,365 | 3,306 | 78 | 1,059 R | 56.3% | 42.7% | 56.9% | 43.1% |
| 23,600 | ISANTI | 11,477 | 5,246 | 6,075 | 156 | 829 D | 45.7% | 52.9% | 46.3% | 53.7% |
| 43,069 | ITASCA | 19,076 | 8,358 | 10,517 | 201 | 2,159 D | 43.8% | 55.1% | 44.3% | 55.7% |
| 13,690 | JACKSON | 5,979 | 2,629 | 3,275 | 75 | 646 D | 44.0% | 54.8% | 44.5% | 55.5% |
| 12,161 | KANABEC | 5,604 | 2,571 | 2,970 | 63 | 399 D | 45.9% | 53.0% | 46.4% | 53.6% |
| 36,763 | KANDIYOHI | 17,878 | 8,634 | 8,962 | 282 | 328 D | 48.3% | 50.1% | 49.1% | 50.9% |
| 6,672 | KITTSON | 3,060 | 1,381 | 1,650 | 29 | 269 D | 45.1% | 53.9% | 45.6% | 54.4% |
| 17,571 | KOOCHICHING | 6,795 | 2,842 | 3,867 | 86 | 1,025 D | 41.8% | 56.9% | 42.4% | 57.6% |
| 10,592 | LAC QUI PARLE | 4,995 | 2,116 | 2,805 | 74 | 689 D | 42.4% | 56.2% | 43.0% | 57.0% |
| 13,043 | LAKE | 5,785 | 1,838 | 3,887 | 60 | 2,049 D | 31.8% | 67.2% | 32.1% | 67.9% |
| 3,764 | LAKE OF THE WOODS | 1,814 | 984 | 798 | 32 | 186 R | 54.2% | 44.0% | 55.2% | 44.8% |
| 23,434 | LE SUEUR | 10,948 | 5,415 | 5,410 | 123 | 5 R | 49.5% | 49.4% | 50.0% | 50.0% |
| 8,207 | LINCOLN | 3,436 | 1,479 | 1,891 | 66 | 412 D | 43.0% | 55.0% | 43.9% | 56.1% |
| 25,207 | LYON | 11,762 | 5,969 | 5,657 | 136 | 312 R | 50.7% | 48.1% | 51.3% | 48.7% |
| 29,657 | MCLEOD | 13,885 | 7,967 | 5,736 | 182 | 2,231 R | 57.4% | 41.3% | 58.1% | 41.9% |
| 5,535 | MAHNOMEN | 2,360 | 1,051 | 1,277 | 32 | 226 D | 44.5% | 54.1% | 45.1% | 54.9% |
| 13,027 | MARSHALL | 5,826 | 2,752 | 3,001 | 73 | 249 D | 47.2% | 51.5% | 47.8% | 52.2% |
| 24,687 | MARTIN | 10,734 | 5,724 | 4,922 | 88 | 802 R | 53.3% | 45.9% | 53.8% | 46.2% |
| 20,594 | MEEKER | 9,728 | 4,999 | 4,544 | 185 | 455 R | 51.4% | 46.7% | 52.4% | 47.6% |
| 18,430 | MILLE LACS | 8,308 | 3,862 | 4,327 | 119 | 465 D | 46.5% | 52.1% | 47.2% | 52.8% |
| 29,311 | MORRISON | 13,246 | 6,598 | 6,469 | 179 | 129 R | 49.8% | 48.8% | 50.5% | 49.5% |
| 40,390 | MOWER | 19,050 | 6,969 | 11,893 | 188 | 4,924 D | 36.6% | 62.4% | 36.9% | 63.1% |
| 11,507 | MURRAY | 5,225 | 2,316 | 2,840 | 69 | 524 D | 44.3% | 54.4% | 44.9% | 55.1% |
| 26,929 | NICOLLET | 13,822 | 6,878 | 6,786 | 158 | 92 R | 49.8% | 49.1% | 50.3% | 49.7% |
| 21,840 | NOBLES | 9,394 | 4,348 | 4,953 | 93 | 605 D | 46.3% | 52.7% | 46.7% | 53.3% |
| 9,379 | NORMAN | 3,964 | 1,789 | 2,149 | 26 | 360 D | 45.1% | 54.2% | 45.4% | 54.6% |
| 92,006 | OLMSTED | 47,609 | 27,683 | 19,423 | 503 | 8,260 R | 58.1% | 40.8% | 58.8% | 41.2% |
| 51,937 | OTTER TAIL | 24,655 | 14,015 | 10,373 | 267 | 3,642 R | 56.8% | 42.1% | 57.5% | 42.5% |
| 15,258 | PENNINGTON | 6,073 | 2,920 | 3,105 | 48 | 185 D | 48.1% | 51.1% | 48.5% | 51.5% |
| 19,871 | PINE | 9,543 | 3,857 | 5,540 | 146 | 1,683 D | 40.4% | 58.1% | 41.0% | 59.0% |
| 11,690 | PIPESTONE | 5,197 | 2,760 | 2,382 | 55 | 378 R | 53.1% | 45.8% | 53.7% | 46.3% |
| 34,844 | POLK | 14,665 | 7,032 | 7,523 | 110 | 491 D | 48.0% | 51.3% | 48.3% | 51.7% |

# MINNESOTA

## PRESIDENT 1988

| 1980 Census Population | County | Total Vote | Republican | Democratic | Other | Rep.-Dem. Plurality | Percentage | | | |
|---|---|---|---|---|---|---|---|---|---|---|
| | | | | | | | Total Vote | | Major Vote | |
| | | | | | | | Rep. | Dem. | Rep. | Dem. |
| 11,657 | POPE | 5,783 | 2,627 | 3,074 | 82 | 447 D | 45.4% | 53.2% | 46.1% | 53.9% |
| 459,784 | RAMSEY | 235,333 | 88,736 | 143,767 | 2,830 | 55,031 D | 37.7% | 61.1% | 38.2% | 61.8% |
| 5,471 | RED LAKE | 2,182 | 918 | 1,229 | 35 | 311 D | 42.1% | 56.3% | 42.8% | 57.2% |
| 19,341 | REDWOOD | 8,379 | 5,076 | 3,178 | 125 | 1,898 R | 60.6% | 37.9% | 61.5% | 38.5% |
| 20,401 | RENVILLE | 8,932 | 4,356 | 4,454 | 122 | 98 D | 48.8% | 49.9% | 49.4% | 50.6% |
| 46,087 | RICE | 21,297 | 9,460 | 11,570 | 267 | 2,110 D | 44.4% | 54.3% | 45.0% | 55.0% |
| 10,703 | ROCK | 5,223 | 2,737 | 2,435 | 51 | 302 R | 52.4% | 46.6% | 52.9% | 47.1% |
| 12,574 | ROSEAU | 6,214 | 3,500 | 2,630 | 84 | 870 R | 56.3% | 42.3% | 57.1% | 42.9% |
| 222,229 | ST. LOUIS | 103,308 | 31,799 | 70,344 | 1,165 | 38,545 D | 30.8% | 68.1% | 31.1% | 68.9% |
| 43,784 | SCOTT | 24,747 | 13,050 | 11,405 | 292 | 1,645 R | 52.7% | 46.1% | 53.4% | 46.6% |
| 29,908 | SHERBURNE | 16,550 | 8,360 | 7,959 | 231 | 401 R | 50.5% | 48.1% | 51.2% | 48.8% |
| 15,448 | SIBLEY | 6,952 | 3,655 | 3,154 | 143 | 501 R | 52.6% | 45.4% | 53.7% | 46.3% |
| 108,161 | STEARNS | 52,166 | 27,529 | 23,798 | 839 | 3,731 R | 52.8% | 45.6% | 53.6% | 46.4% |
| 30,328 | STEELE | 13,620 | 7,981 | 5,496 | 143 | 2,485 R | 58.6% | 40.4% | 59.2% | 40.8% |
| 11,322 | STEVENS | 5,468 | 2,679 | 2,721 | 68 | 42 D | 49.0% | 49.8% | 49.6% | 50.4% |
| 12,920 | SWIFT | 5,806 | 2,156 | 3,579 | 71 | 1,423 D | 37.1% | 61.6% | 37.6% | 62.4% |
| 24,991 | TODD | 10,776 | 5,633 | 5,023 | 120 | 610 R | 52.3% | 46.6% | 52.9% | 47.1% |
| 5,542 | TRAVERSE | 2,478 | 1,061 | 1,399 | 18 | 338 D | 42.8% | 56.5% | 43.1% | 56.9% |
| 19,335 | WABASHA | 9,237 | 4,681 | 4,442 | 114 | 239 R | 50.7% | 48.1% | 51.3% | 48.7% |
| 14,192 | WADENA | 6,309 | 3,733 | 2,484 | 92 | 1,249 R | 59.2% | 39.4% | 60.0% | 40.0% |
| 18,448 | WASECA | 8,294 | 4,471 | 3,721 | 102 | 750 R | 53.9% | 44.9% | 54.6% | 45.4% |
| 113,571 | WASHINGTON | 66,513 | 30,850 | 34,952 | 711 | 4,102 D | 46.4% | 52.5% | 46.9% | 53.1% |
| 12,361 | WATONWAN | 5,430 | 2,821 | 2,544 | 65 | 277 R | 52.0% | 46.9% | 52.6% | 47.4% |
| 8,454 | WILKIN | 3,450 | 1,933 | 1,486 | 31 | 447 R | 56.0% | 43.1% | 56.5% | 43.5% |
| 46,256 | WINONA | 21,652 | 11,012 | 10,310 | 330 | 702 R | 50.9% | 47.6% | 51.6% | 48.4% |
| 58,681 | WRIGHT | 29,601 | 14,987 | 14,177 | 437 | 810 R | 50.6% | 47.9% | 51.4% | 48.6% |
| 13,653 | YELLOW MEDICINE | 6,298 | 2,925 | 3,282 | 91 | 357 D | 46.4% | 52.1% | 47.1% | 52.9% |
| 4,075,970 | TOTAL | 2,096,790 | 962,337 | 1,109,471 | 24,982 | 147,134 D | 45.9% | 52.9% | 46.4% | 53.6% |

# MINNESOTA

## PRESIDENT 1984

| 1980 Census Population | County | Total Vote | Republican | Democratic | Other | Rep.-Dem. Plurality | Percentage Total Vote Rep. | Dem. | Major Vote Rep. | Dem. |
|---|---|---|---|---|---|---|---|---|---|---|
| 13,404 | AITKIN | 7,419 | 3,422 | 3,943 | 54 | 521 D | 46.1% | 53.1% | 46.5% | 53.5% |
| 195,998 | ANOKA | 97,486 | 46,578 | 50,305 | 603 | 3,727 D | 47.8% | 51.6% | 48.1% | 51.9% |
| 29,336 | BECKER | 13,107 | 7,553 | 5,456 | 98 | 2,097 R | 57.6% | 41.6% | 58.1% | 41.9% |
| 30,982 | BELTRAMI | 15,002 | 7,414 | 7,481 | 107 | 67 D | 49.4% | 49.9% | 49.8% | 50.2% |
| 25,187 | BENTON | 11,886 | 6,830 | 4,922 | 134 | 1,908 R | 57.5% | 41.4% | 58.1% | 41.9% |
| 7,716 | BIG STONE | 3,847 | 1,821 | 1,994 | 32 | 173 D | 47.3% | 51.8% | 47.7% | 52.3% |
| 52,314 | BLUE EARTH | 26,353 | 14,298 | 11,877 | 178 | 2,421 R | 54.3% | 45.1% | 54.6% | 45.4% |
| 28,645 | BROWN | 12,977 | 8,399 | 4,469 | 109 | 3,930 R | 64.7% | 34.4% | 65.3% | 34.7% |
| 29,936 | CARLTON | 14,206 | 4,877 | 9,189 | 140 | 4,312 D | 34.3% | 64.7% | 34.7% | 65.3% |
| 37,046 | CARVER | 18,816 | 11,963 | 6,725 | 128 | 5,238 R | 63.6% | 35.7% | 64.0% | 36.0% |
| 21,050 | CASS | 11,482 | 6,619 | 4,773 | 90 | 1,846 R | 57.6% | 41.6% | 58.1% | 41.9% |
| 14,941 | CHIPPEWA | 7,085 | 3,964 | 3,047 | 74 | 917 R | 55.9% | 43.0% | 56.5% | 43.5% |
| 25,717 | CHISAGO | 13,063 | 6,279 | 6,683 | 101 | 404 D | 48.1% | 51.2% | 48.4% | 51.6% |
| 49,327 | CLAY | 21,978 | 11,565 | 10,294 | 119 | 1,271 R | 52.6% | 46.8% | 52.9% | 47.1% |
| 8,761 | CLEARWATER | 4,027 | 2,066 | 1,917 | 44 | 149 R | 51.3% | 47.6% | 51.9% | 48.1% |
| 4,092 | COOK | 2,362 | 1,219 | 1,129 | 14 | 90 R | 51.6% | 47.8% | 51.9% | 48.1% |
| 14,854 | COTTONWOOD | 7,385 | 4,275 | 3,073 | 37 | 1,202 R | 57.9% | 41.6% | 58.2% | 41.8% |
| 41,722 | CROW WING | 20,236 | 11,362 | 8,719 | 155 | 2,643 R | 56.1% | 43.1% | 56.6% | 43.4% |
| 194,279 | DAKOTA | 104,946 | 55,119 | 49,125 | 702 | 5,994 R | 52.5% | 46.8% | 52.9% | 47.1% |
| 14,773 | DODGE | 7,267 | 4,428 | 2,786 | 53 | 1,642 R | 60.9% | 38.3% | 61.4% | 38.6% |
| 27,839 | DOUGLAS | 14,546 | 9,005 | 5,444 | 97 | 3,561 R | 61.9% | 37.4% | 62.3% | 37.7% |
| 19,714 | FARIBAULT | 9,739 | 5,690 | 3,993 | 56 | 1,697 R | 58.4% | 41.0% | 58.8% | 41.2% |
| 21,930 | FILLMORE | 10,762 | 6,342 | 4,351 | 69 | 1,991 R | 58.9% | 40.4% | 59.3% | 40.7% |
| 36,329 | FREEBORN | 17,873 | 8,413 | 9,338 | 122 | 925 D | 47.1% | 52.2% | 47.4% | 52.6% |
| 38,749 | GOODHUE | 19,988 | 11,171 | 8,679 | 138 | 2,492 R | 55.9% | 43.4% | 56.3% | 43.7% |
| 7,171 | GRANT | 3,999 | 2,111 | 1,867 | 21 | 244 R | 52.8% | 46.7% | 53.1% | 46.9% |
| 941,411 | HENNEPIN | 529,485 | 253,921 | 272,401 | 3,163 | 18,480 D | 48.0% | 51.4% | 48.2% | 51.8% |
| 18,382 | HOUSTON | 9,249 | 5,645 | 3,512 | 92 | 2,133 R | 61.0% | 38.0% | 61.6% | 38.4% |
| 14,098 | HUBBARD | 7,483 | 4,621 | 2,806 | 56 | 1,815 R | 61.8% | 37.5% | 62.2% | 37.8% |
| 23,600 | ISANTI | 11,120 | 5,660 | 5,378 | 82 | 282 R | 50.9% | 48.4% | 51.3% | 48.7% |
| 43,069 | ITASCA | 20,958 | 9,306 | 11,455 | 197 | 2,149 D | 44.4% | 54.7% | 44.8% | 55.2% |
| 13,690 | JACKSON | 6,626 | 3,131 | 3,437 | 58 | 306 D | 47.3% | 51.9% | 47.7% | 52.3% |
| 12,161 | KANABEC | 5,725 | 3,027 | 2,660 | 38 | 367 R | 52.9% | 46.5% | 53.2% | 46.8% |
| 36,763 | KANDIYOHI | 18,108 | 9,539 | 8,402 | 167 | 1,137 R | 52.7% | 46.4% | 53.2% | 46.8% |
| 6,672 | KITTSON | 3,351 | 1,716 | 1,610 | 25 | 106 R | 51.2% | 48.0% | 51.6% | 48.4% |
| 17,571 | KOOCHICHING | 7,746 | 3,466 | 4,238 | 42 | 772 D | 44.7% | 54.7% | 45.0% | 55.0% |
| 10,592 | LAC QUI PARLE | 5,497 | 2,731 | 2,685 | 81 | 46 R | 49.7% | 48.8% | 50.4% | 49.6% |
| 13,043 | LAKE | 6,534 | 2,003 | 4,468 | 63 | 2,465 D | 30.7% | 68.4% | 31.0% | 69.0% |
| 3,764 | LAKE OF THE WOODS | 1,940 | 1,094 | 824 | 22 | 270 R | 56.4% | 42.5% | 57.0% | 43.0% |
| 23,434 | LE SUEUR | 11,154 | 6,033 | 5,070 | 51 | 963 R | 54.1% | 45.5% | 54.3% | 45.7% |
| 8,207 | LINCOLN | 3,815 | 1,905 | 1,827 | 83 | 78 R | 49.9% | 47.9% | 51.0% | 49.0% |
| 25,207 | LYON | 12,664 | 7,170 | 5,389 | 105 | 1,781 R | 56.6% | 42.6% | 57.1% | 42.9% |
| 29,657 | MCLEOD | 13,731 | 8,728 | 4,864 | 139 | 3,864 R | 63.6% | 35.4% | 64.2% | 35.8% |
| 5,535 | MAHNOMEN | 2,597 | 1,328 | 1,241 | 28 | 87 R | 51.1% | 47.8% | 51.7% | 48.3% |
| 13,027 | MARSHALL | 6,209 | 3,433 | 2,705 | 71 | 728 R | 55.3% | 43.6% | 55.9% | 44.1% |
| 24,687 | MARTIN | 12,046 | 7,308 | 4,673 | 65 | 2,635 R | 60.7% | 38.8% | 61.0% | 39.0% |
| 20,594 | MEEKER | 9,726 | 5,511 | 4,156 | 59 | 1,355 R | 56.7% | 42.7% | 57.0% | 43.0% |
| 18,430 | MILLE LACS | 8,371 | 4,307 | 4,011 | 53 | 296 R | 51.5% | 47.9% | 51.8% | 48.2% |
| 29,311 | MORRISON | 13,885 | 7,556 | 6,225 | 104 | 1,331 R | 54.4% | 44.8% | 54.8% | 45.2% |
| 40,390 | MOWER | 20,648 | 8,054 | 12,498 | 96 | 4,444 D | 39.0% | 60.5% | 39.2% | 60.8% |
| 11,507 | MURRAY | 5,578 | 2,780 | 2,741 | 57 | 39 R | 49.8% | 49.1% | 50.4% | 49.6% |
| 26,929 | NICOLLET | 13,359 | 7,472 | 5,789 | 98 | 1,683 R | 55.9% | 43.3% | 56.3% | 43.7% |
| 21,840 | NOBLES | 9,605 | 4,876 | 4,619 | 110 | 257 R | 50.8% | 48.1% | 51.4% | 48.6% |
| 9,379 | NORMAN | 4,377 | 2,152 | 2,202 | 23 | 50 D | 49.2% | 50.3% | 49.4% | 50.6% |
| 92,006 | OLMSTED | 44,831 | 28,129 | 16,335 | 367 | 11,794 R | 62.7% | 36.4% | 63.3% | 36.7% |
| 51,937 | OTTER TAIL | 25,554 | 15,664 | 9,714 | 176 | 5,950 R | 61.3% | 38.0% | 61.7% | 38.3% |
| 15,258 | PENNINGTON | 6,489 | 3,536 | 2,913 | 40 | 623 R | 54.5% | 44.9% | 54.8% | 45.2% |
| 19,871 | PINE | 9,780 | 4,493 | 5,223 | 64 | 730 D | 45.9% | 53.4% | 46.2% | 53.8% |
| 11,690 | PIPESTONE | 5,501 | 3,043 | 2,391 | 67 | 652 R | 55.3% | 43.5% | 56.0% | 44.0% |
| 34,844 | POLK | 15,789 | 8,617 | 7,033 | 139 | 1,584 R | 54.6% | 44.5% | 55.1% | 44.9% |

# MINNESOTA

## PRESIDENT 1984

| 1980 Census Population | County | Total Vote | Republican | Democratic | Other | Rep.-Dem. Plurality | | Percentage | | | |
|---|---|---|---|---|---|---|---|---|---|---|---|
| | | | | | | | | Total Vote | | Major Vote | |
| | | | | | | | | Rep. | Dem. | Rep. | Dem. |
| 11,657 | POPE | 5,863 | 3,064 | 2,757 | 42 | 307 | R | 52.3% | 47.0% | 52.6% | 47.4% |
| 459,784 | RAMSEY | 239,511 | 95,667 | 141,623 | 2,221 | 45,956 | D | 39.9% | 59.1% | 40.3% | 59.7% |
| 5,471 | RED LAKE | 2,495 | 1,184 | 1,294 | 17 | 110 | D | 47.5% | 51.9% | 47.8% | 52.2% |
| 19,341 | REDWOOD | 9,061 | 6,020 | 2,957 | 84 | 3,063 | R | 66.4% | 32.6% | 67.1% | 32.9% |
| 20,401 | RENVILLE | 9,632 | 5,571 | 3,972 | 89 | 1,599 | R | 57.8% | 41.2% | 58.4% | 41.6% |
| 46,087 | RICE | 21,537 | 10,456 | 10,880 | 201 | 424 | D | 48.5% | 50.5% | 49.0% | 51.0% |
| 10,703 | ROCK | 5,196 | 2,971 | 2,188 | 37 | 783 | R | 57.2% | 42.1% | 57.6% | 42.4% |
| 12,574 | ROSEAU | 5,811 | 3,445 | 2,319 | 47 | 1,126 | R | 59.3% | 39.9% | 59.8% | 40.2% |
| 222,229 | ST. LOUIS | 112,879 | 34,162 | 77,683 | 1,034 | 43,521 | D | 30.3% | 68.8% | 30.5% | 69.5% |
| 43,784 | SCOTT | 22,133 | 12,573 | 9,452 | 108 | 3,121 | R | 56.8% | 42.7% | 57.1% | 42.9% |
| 29,908 | SHERBURNE | 13,962 | 7,738 | 6,140 | 84 | 1,598 | R | 55.4% | 44.0% | 55.8% | 44.2% |
| 15,448 | SIBLEY | 7,471 | 4,638 | 2,761 | 72 | 1,877 | R | 62.1% | 37.0% | 62.7% | 37.3% |
| 108,161 | STEARNS | 51,663 | 30,216 | 20,944 | 503 | 9,272 | R | 58.5% | 40.5% | 59.1% | 40.9% |
| 30,328 | STEELE | 13,910 | 8,780 | 5,060 | 70 | 3,720 | R | 63.1% | 36.4% | 63.4% | 36.6% |
| 11,322 | STEVENS | 5,752 | 3,251 | 2,451 | 50 | 800 | R | 56.5% | 42.6% | 57.0% | 43.0% |
| 12,920 | SWIFT | 6,488 | 2,893 | 3,531 | 64 | 638 | D | 44.6% | 54.4% | 45.0% | 55.0% |
| 24,991 | TODD | 11,310 | 6,585 | 4,657 | 68 | 1,928 | R | 58.2% | 41.2% | 58.6% | 41.4% |
| 5,542 | TRAVERSE | 2,744 | 1,399 | 1,325 | 20 | 74 | R | 51.0% | 48.3% | 51.4% | 48.6% |
| 19,335 | WABASHA | 9,247 | 5,299 | 3,872 | 76 | 1,427 | R | 57.3% | 41.9% | 57.8% | 42.2% |
| 14,192 | WADENA | 6,794 | 4,306 | 2,454 | 34 | 1,852 | R | 63.4% | 36.1% | 63.7% | 36.3% |
| 18,448 | WASECA | 9,092 | 5,509 | 3,527 | 56 | 1,982 | R | 60.6% | 38.8% | 61.0% | 39.0% |
| 113,571 | WASHINGTON | 57,961 | 29,046 | 28,527 | 388 | 519 | R | 50.1% | 49.2% | 50.5% | 49.5% |
| 12,361 | WATONWAN | 5,978 | 3,526 | 2,425 | 27 | 1,101 | R | 59.0% | 40.6% | 59.3% | 40.7% |
| 8,454 | WILKIN | 3,796 | 2,367 | 1,410 | 19 | 957 | R | 62.4% | 37.1% | 62.7% | 37.3% |
| 46,256 | WINONA | 21,770 | 11,981 | 9,577 | 212 | 2,404 | R | 55.0% | 44.0% | 55.6% | 44.4% |
| 58,681 | WRIGHT | 28,108 | 15,399 | 12,486 | 223 | 2,913 | R | 54.8% | 44.4% | 55.2% | 44.8% |
| 13,653 | YELLOW MEDICINE | 6,917 | 3,819 | 3,018 | 80 | 801 | R | 55.2% | 43.6% | 55.9% | 44.1% |
| 4,075,970 | TOTAL | 2,084,449 | 1,032,603 | 1,036,364 | 15,482 | 3,761 | D | 49.5% | 49.7% | 49.9% | 50.1% |

# MINNESOTA

## PRESIDENT 1980

| 1980 Census Population | County | Total Vote | Republican | Democratic | Other | Rep.-Dem. Plurality | Percentage | | | |
|---|---|---|---|---|---|---|---|---|---|---|
| | | | | | | | Total Vote | | Major Vote | |
| | | | | | | | Rep. | Dem. | Rep. | Dem. |
| 13,404 | AITKIN | 7,670 | 3,396 | 3,677 | 597 | 281 D | 44.3% | 47.9% | 48.0% | 52.0% |
| 195,998 | ANOKA | 87,843 | 33,100 | 45,532 | 9,211 | 12,432 D | 37.7% | 51.8% | 42.1% | 57.9% |
| 29,336 | BECKER | 13,134 | 6,848 | 5,221 | 1,065 | 1,627 R | 52.1% | 39.8% | 56.7% | 43.3% |
| 30,982 | BELTRAMI | 15,537 | 6,481 | 7,432 | 1,624 | 951 D | 41.7% | 47.8% | 46.6% | 53.4% |
| 25,187 | BENTON | 11,782 | 5,513 | 5,272 | 997 | 241 R | 46.8% | 44.7% | 51.1% | 48.9% |
| 7,716 | BIG STONE | 4,091 | 1,950 | 1,814 | 327 | 136 R | 47.7% | 44.3% | 51.8% | 48.2% |
| 52,314 | BLUE EARTH | 26,138 | 11,966 | 10,930 | 3,242 | 1,036 R | 45.8% | 41.8% | 52.3% | 47.7% |
| 28,645 | BROWN | 14,122 | 8,051 | 4,915 | 1,156 | 3,136 R | 57.0% | 34.8% | 62.1% | 37.9% |
| 29,936 | CARLTON | 14,850 | 4,760 | 8,822 | 1,268 | 4,062 D | 32.1% | 59.4% | 35.0% | 65.0% |
| 37,046 | CARVER | 18,481 | 9,909 | 6,621 | 1,951 | 3,288 R | 53.6% | 35.8% | 59.9% | 40.1% |
| 21,050 | CASS | 11,504 | 6,119 | 4,717 | 668 | 1,402 R | 53.2% | 41.0% | 56.5% | 43.5% |
| 14,941 | CHIPPEWA | 8,101 | 4,252 | 3,164 | 685 | 1,088 R | 52.5% | 39.1% | 57.3% | 42.7% |
| 25,717 | CHISAGO | 12,535 | 5,017 | 6,240 | 1,278 | 1,223 D | 40.0% | 49.8% | 44.6% | 55.4% |
| 49,327 | CLAY | 22,508 | 10,447 | 8,940 | 3,121 | 1,507 R | 46.4% | 39.7% | 53.9% | 46.1% |
| 8,761 | CLEARWATER | 4,138 | 1,919 | 1,955 | 264 | 36 D | 46.4% | 47.2% | 49.5% | 50.5% |
| 4,092 | COOK | 2,293 | 1,174 | 871 | 248 | 303 R | 51.2% | 38.0% | 57.4% | 42.6% |
| 14,854 | COTTONWOOD | 7,847 | 4,258 | 2,958 | 631 | 1,300 R | 54.3% | 37.7% | 59.0% | 41.0% |
| 41,722 | CROW WING | 21,677 | 10,844 | 9,323 | 1,510 | 1,521 R | 50.0% | 43.0% | 53.8% | 46.2% |
| 194,279 | DAKOTA | 94,755 | 40,708 | 43,433 | 10,614 | 2,725 D | 43.0% | 45.8% | 48.4% | 51.6% |
| 14,773 | DODGE | 7,100 | 3,900 | 2,698 | 502 | 1,202 R | 54.9% | 38.0% | 59.1% | 40.9% |
| 27,839 | DOUGLAS | 14,445 | 7,778 | 5,530 | 1,137 | 2,248 R | 53.8% | 38.3% | 58.4% | 41.6% |
| 19,714 | FARIBAULT | 10,481 | 6,206 | 3,620 | 655 | 2,586 R | 59.2% | 34.5% | 63.2% | 36.8% |
| 21,930 | FILLMORE | 11,312 | 6,452 | 4,010 | 850 | 2,442 R | 57.0% | 35.4% | 61.7% | 38.3% |
| 36,329 | FREEBORN | 17,785 | 8,475 | 8,212 | 1,098 | 263 R | 47.7% | 46.2% | 50.8% | 49.2% |
| 38,749 | GOODHUE | 20,262 | 9,329 | 8,566 | 2,367 | 763 R | 46.0% | 42.3% | 52.1% | 47.9% |
| 7,171 | GRANT | 4,272 | 2,054 | 1,822 | 396 | 232 R | 48.1% | 42.6% | 53.0% | 47.0% |
| 941,411 | HENNEPIN | 505,372 | 194,898 | 239,592 | 70,882 | 44,694 D | 38.6% | 47.4% | 44.9% | 55.1% |
| 18,382 | HOUSTON | 9,483 | 5,582 | 3,218 | 683 | 2,364 R | 58.9% | 33.9% | 63.4% | 36.6% |
| 14,098 | HUBBARD | 7,524 | 4,172 | 2,840 | 512 | 1,332 R | 55.4% | 37.7% | 59.5% | 40.5% |
| 23,600 | ISANTI | 10,809 | 4,480 | 5,457 | 872 | 977 D | 41.4% | 50.5% | 45.1% | 54.9% |
| 43,069 | ITASCA | 22,256 | 8,368 | 12,134 | 1,754 | 3,766 D | 37.6% | 54.5% | 40.8% | 59.2% |
| 13,690 | JACKSON | 7,064 | 3,391 | 3,062 | 611 | 329 R | 48.0% | 43.3% | 52.5% | 47.5% |
| 12,161 | KANABEC | 5,508 | 2,500 | 2,654 | 354 | 154 D | 45.4% | 48.2% | 48.5% | 51.5% |
| 36,763 | KANDIYOHI | 18,095 | 8,480 | 8,038 | 1,577 | 442 R | 46.9% | 44.4% | 51.3% | 48.7% |
| 6,672 | KITTSON | 3,577 | 1,875 | 1,407 | 295 | 468 R | 52.4% | 39.3% | 57.1% | 42.9% |
| 17,571 | KOOCHICHING | 8,250 | 3,433 | 4,181 | 636 | 748 D | 41.6% | 50.7% | 45.1% | 54.9% |
| 10,592 | LAC QUI PARLE | 5,903 | 2,981 | 2,457 | 465 | 524 R | 50.5% | 41.6% | 54.8% | 45.2% |
| 13,043 | LAKE | 6,931 | 2,414 | 3,864 | 653 | 1,450 D | 34.8% | 55.7% | 38.5% | 61.5% |
| 3,764 | LAKE OF THE WOODS | 2,000 | 1,052 | 763 | 185 | 289 R | 52.6% | 38.2% | 58.0% | 42.0% |
| 23,434 | LE SUEUR | 11,631 | 5,478 | 5,161 | 992 | 317 R | 47.1% | 44.4% | 51.5% | 48.5% |
| 8,207 | LINCOLN | 4,130 | 2,122 | 1,640 | 368 | 482 R | 51.4% | 39.7% | 56.4% | 43.6% |
| 25,207 | LYON | 12,911 | 5,852 | 5,626 | 1,433 | 226 R | 45.3% | 43.6% | 51.0% | 49.0% |
| 29,657 | MCLEOD | 14,040 | 7,819 | 4,987 | 1,234 | 2,832 R | 55.7% | 35.5% | 61.1% | 38.9% |
| 5,535 | MAHNOMEN | 2,637 | 1,275 | 1,175 | 187 | 100 R | 48.4% | 44.6% | 52.0% | 48.0% |
| 13,027 | MARSHALL | 6,775 | 3,638 | 2,636 | 501 | 1,002 R | 53.7% | 38.9% | 58.0% | 42.0% |
| 24,687 | MARTIN | 12,294 | 7,057 | 4,301 | 936 | 2,756 R | 57.4% | 35.0% | 62.1% | 37.9% |
| 20,594 | MEEKER | 10,095 | 5,032 | 4,238 | 825 | 794 R | 49.8% | 42.0% | 54.3% | 45.7% |
| 18,430 | MILLE LACS | 9,013 | 3,860 | 4,443 | 710 | 583 D | 42.8% | 49.3% | 46.5% | 53.5% |
| 29,311 | MORRISON | 14,024 | 6,296 | 6,930 | 798 | 634 D | 44.9% | 49.4% | 47.6% | 52.4% |
| 40,390 | MOWER | 20,335 | 7,908 | 10,538 | 1,889 | 2,630 D | 38.9% | 51.8% | 42.9% | 57.1% |
| 11,507 | MURRAY | 6,186 | 3,004 | 2,714 | 468 | 290 R | 48.6% | 43.9% | 52.5% | 47.5% |
| 26,929 | NICOLLET | 13,643 | 6,436 | 5,400 | 1,807 | 1,036 R | 47.2% | 39.6% | 54.4% | 45.6% |
| 21,840 | NOBLES | 10,365 | 4,706 | 4,703 | 956 | 3 R | 45.4% | 45.4% | 50.0% | 50.0% |
| 9,379 | NORMAN | 4,880 | 2,192 | 2,253 | 435 | 61 D | 44.9% | 46.2% | 49.3% | 50.7% |
| 92,006 | OLMSTED | 40,911 | 22,704 | 13,983 | 4,224 | 8,721 R | 55.5% | 34.2% | 61.9% | 38.1% |
| 51,937 | OTTER TAIL | 26,138 | 15,091 | 9,108 | 1,939 | 5,983 R | 57.7% | 34.8% | 62.4% | 37.6% |
| 15,258 | PENNINGTON | 7,416 | 3,715 | 3,101 | 600 | 614 R | 50.1% | 41.8% | 54.5% | 45.5% |
| 19,871 | PINE | 9,687 | 3,899 | 5,121 | 667 | 1,222 D | 40.2% | 52.9% | 43.2% | 56.8% |
| 11,690 | PIPESTONE | 6,243 | 3,207 | 2,392 | 644 | 815 R | 51.4% | 38.3% | 57.3% | 42.7% |
| 34,844 | POLK | 17,644 | 9,036 | 7,151 | 1,457 | 1,885 R | 51.2% | 40.5% | 55.8% | 44.2% |

# MINNESOTA

## PRESIDENT 1980

| 1980 Census Population | County | Total Vote | Republican | Democratic | Other | Rep.-Dem. Plurality | Percentage | | | |
|---|---|---|---|---|---|---|---|---|---|---|
| | | | | | | | Total Vote | | Major Vote | |
| | | | | | | | Rep. | Dem. | Rep. | Dem. |
| 11,657 | POPE | 6,153 | 3,159 | 2,527 | 467 | 632 R | 51.3% | 41.1% | 55.6% | 44.4% |
| 459,784 | RAMSEY | 232,744 | 78,860 | 124,774 | 29,110 | 45,914 D | 33.9% | 53.6% | 38.7% | 61.3% |
| 5,471 | RED LAKE | 2,707 | 1,223 | 1,318 | 166 | 95 D | 45.2% | 48.7% | 48.1% | 51.9% |
| 19,341 | REDWOOD | 9,699 | 5,993 | 2,952 | 754 | 3,041 R | 61.8% | 30.4% | 67.0% | 33.0% |
| 20,401 | RENVILLE | 10,444 | 5,544 | 4,058 | 842 | 1,486 R | 53.1% | 38.9% | 57.7% | 42.3% |
| 46,087 | RICE | 20,677 | 8,168 | 9,531 | 2,978 | 1,363 D | 39.5% | 46.1% | 46.1% | 53.9% |
| 10,703 | ROCK | 5,713 | 3,164 | 2,089 | 460 | 1,075 R | 55.4% | 36.6% | 60.2% | 39.8% |
| 12,574 | ROSEAU | 6,317 | 3,358 | 2,616 | 343 | 742 R | 53.2% | 41.4% | 56.2% | 43.8% |
| 222,229 | ST. LOUIS | 114,757 | 33,407 | 69,403 | 11,947 | 35,996 D | 29.1% | 60.5% | 32.5% | 67.5% |
| 43,784 | SCOTT | 20,038 | 9,018 | 9,115 | 1,905 | 97 D | 45.0% | 45.5% | 49.7% | 50.3% |
| 29,908 | SHERBURNE | 13,620 | 6,035 | 6,229 | 1,356 | 194 D | 44.3% | 45.7% | 49.2% | 50.8% |
| 15,448 | SIBLEY | 7,642 | 4,460 | 2,521 | 661 | 1,939 R | 58.4% | 33.0% | 63.9% | 36.1% |
| 108,161 | STEARNS | 51,522 | 24,888 | 21,862 | 4,772 | 3,026 R | 48.3% | 42.4% | 53.2% | 46.8% |
| 30,328 | STEELE | 14,279 | 7,805 | 5,095 | 1,379 | 2,710 R | 54.7% | 35.7% | 60.5% | 39.5% |
| 11,322 | STEVENS | 6,487 | 3,283 | 2,559 | 645 | 724 R | 50.6% | 39.4% | 56.2% | 43.8% |
| 12,920 | SWIFT | 6,823 | 2,943 | 3,245 | 635 | 302 D | 43.1% | 47.6% | 47.6% | 52.4% |
| 24,991 | TODD | 12,111 | 6,451 | 4,975 | 685 | 1,476 R | 53.3% | 41.1% | 56.5% | 43.5% |
| 5,542 | TRAVERSE | 3,032 | 1,574 | 1,258 | 200 | 316 R | 51.9% | 41.5% | 55.6% | 44.4% |
| 19,335 | WABASHA | 9,453 | 4,986 | 3,712 | 755 | 1,274 R | 52.7% | 39.3% | 57.3% | 42.7% |
| 14,192 | WADENA | 7,103 | 4,089 | 2,635 | 379 | 1,454 R | 57.6% | 37.1% | 60.8% | 39.2% |
| 18,448 | WASECA | 9,303 | 4,801 | 3,535 | 967 | 1,266 R | 51.6% | 38.0% | 57.6% | 42.4% |
| 113,571 | WASHINGTON | 54,902 | 22,718 | 25,634 | 6,550 | 2,916 D | 41.4% | 46.7% | 47.0% | 53.0% |
| 12,361 | WATONWAN | 6,587 | 3,629 | 2,442 | 516 | 1,187 R | 55.1% | 37.1% | 59.8% | 40.2% |
| 8,454 | WILKIN | 4,113 | 2,224 | 1,496 | 393 | 728 R | 54.1% | 36.4% | 59.8% | 40.2% |
| 46,256 | WINONA | 22,903 | 10,332 | 9,814 | 2,757 | 518 R | 45.1% | 42.9% | 51.3% | 48.7% |
| 58,681 | WRIGHT | 26,991 | 12,293 | 12,383 | 2,315 | 90 D | 45.5% | 45.9% | 49.8% | 50.2% |
| 13,653 | YELLOW MEDICINE | 7,427 | 4,004 | 2,833 | 590 | 1,171 R | 53.9% | 38.1% | 58.6% | 41.4% |
| 4,075,970 | TOTAL | 2,051,980 | 873,268 | 954,174 | 224,538 | 80,906 D | 42.6% | 46.5% | 47.8% | 52.2% |

# MINNESOTA

## PRESIDENT 1976

| 1970 Census Population | County | Total Vote | Republican | Democratic | Other | Rep.-Dem. Plurality | Percentage Total Vote Rep. | Dem. | Major Vote Rep. | Dem. |
|---|---|---|---|---|---|---|---|---|---|---|
| 11,403 | AITKIN | 6,949 | 2,476 | 4,308 | 165 | 1,832 D | 35.6% | 62.0% | 36.5% | 63.5% |
| 154,556 | ANOKA | 78,315 | 27,863 | 48,173 | 2,279 | 20,310 D | 35.6% | 61.5% | 36.6% | 63.4% |
| 24,372 | BECKER | 12,575 | 5,611 | 6,597 | 367 | 986 D | 44.6% | 52.5% | 46.0% | 54.0% |
| 26,373 | BELTRAMI | 13,285 | 5,214 | 7,540 | 531 | 2,326 D | 39.2% | 56.8% | 40.9% | 59.1% |
| 20,841 | BENTON | 10,965 | 4,099 | 6,235 | 631 | 2,136 D | 37.4% | 56.9% | 39.7% | 60.3% |
| 7,941 | BIG STONE | 4,011 | 1,332 | 2,581 | 98 | 1,249 D | 33.2% | 64.3% | 34.0% | 66.0% |
| 52,322 | BLUE EARTH | 25,688 | 11,998 | 12,930 | 760 | 932 D | 46.7% | 50.3% | 48.1% | 51.9% |
| 28,887 | BROWN | 14,039 | 7,479 | 5,792 | 768 | 1,687 R | 53.3% | 41.3% | 56.4% | 43.6% |
| 28,072 | CARLTON | 13,952 | 4,371 | 9,247 | 334 | 4,876 D | 31.3% | 66.3% | 32.1% | 67.9% |
| 28,310 | CARVER | 16,363 | 8,199 | 7,574 | 590 | 625 R | 50.1% | 46.3% | 52.0% | 48.0% |
| 17,323 | CASS | 10,234 | 4,443 | 5,424 | 367 | 981 D | 43.4% | 53.0% | 45.0% | 55.0% |
| 15,109 | CHIPPEWA | 8,051 | 3,254 | 4,648 | 149 | 1,394 D | 40.4% | 57.7% | 41.2% | 58.8% |
| 17,492 | CHISAGO | 10,867 | 3,874 | 6,625 | 368 | 2,751 D | 35.6% | 61.0% | 36.9% | 63.1% |
| 46,585 | CLAY | 21,711 | 10,317 | 10,876 | 518 | 559 D | 47.5% | 50.1% | 48.7% | 51.3% |
| 8,013 | CLEARWATER | 4,016 | 1,374 | 2,437 | 205 | 1,063 D | 34.2% | 60.7% | 36.1% | 63.9% |
| 3,423 | COOK | 2,130 | 1,034 | 1,018 | 78 | 16 R | 48.5% | 47.8% | 50.4% | 49.6% |
| 14,887 | COTTONWOOD | 7,859 | 3,906 | 3,813 | 140 | 93 R | 49.7% | 48.5% | 50.6% | 49.4% |
| 34,826 | CROW WING | 19,608 | 8,072 | 10,653 | 883 | 2,581 D | 41.2% | 54.3% | 43.1% | 56.9% |
| 139,808 | DAKOTA | 84,080 | 37,542 | 44,253 | 2,285 | 6,711 D | 44.7% | 52.6% | 45.9% | 54.1% |
| 13,037 | DODGE | 6,598 | 3,446 | 3,009 | 143 | 437 R | 52.2% | 45.6% | 53.4% | 46.6% |
| 22,892 | DOUGLAS | 13,321 | 5,910 | 7,097 | 314 | 1,187 D | 44.4% | 53.3% | 45.4% | 54.6% |
| 20,896 | FARIBAULT | 10,848 | 5,577 | 5,049 | 222 | 528 R | 51.4% | 46.5% | 52.5% | 47.5% |
| 21,916 | FILLMORE | 10,957 | 5,984 | 4,758 | 215 | 1,226 R | 54.6% | 43.4% | 55.7% | 44.3% |
| 38,064 | FREEBORN | 18,018 | 8,220 | 9,470 | 328 | 1,250 D | 45.6% | 52.6% | 46.5% | 53.5% |
| 34,763 | GOODHUE | 19,352 | 9,967 | 8,926 | 459 | 1,041 R | 51.5% | 46.1% | 52.8% | 47.2% |
| 7,462 | GRANT | 4,338 | 1,635 | 2,624 | 79 | 989 D | 37.7% | 60.5% | 38.4% | 61.6% |
| 960,080 | HENNEPIN | 483,378 | 211,892 | 257,380 | 14,106 | 45,488 D | 43.8% | 53.2% | 45.2% | 54.8% |
| 17,556 | HOUSTON | 8,926 | 4,853 | 3,861 | 212 | 992 R | 54.4% | 43.3% | 55.7% | 44.3% |
| 10,583 | HUBBARD | 6,502 | 2,985 | 3,196 | 321 | 211 D | 45.9% | 49.2% | 48.3% | 51.7% |
| 16,560 | ISANTI | 9,428 | 3,159 | 6,013 | 256 | 2,854 D | 33.5% | 63.8% | 34.4% | 65.6% |
| 35,530 | ITASCA | 20,281 | 6,646 | 12,979 | 656 | 6,333 D | 32.8% | 64.0% | 33.9% | 66.1% |
| 14,352 | JACKSON | 7,298 | 2,870 | 4,311 | 117 | 1,441 D | 39.3% | 59.1% | 40.0% | 60.0% |
| 9,775 | KANABEC | 5,311 | 1,943 | 3,188 | 180 | 1,245 D | 36.6% | 60.0% | 37.9% | 62.1% |
| 30,548 | KANDIYOHI | 17,145 | 6,664 | 9,992 | 489 | 3,328 D | 38.9% | 58.3% | 40.0% | 60.0% |
| 6,853 | KITTSON | 3,629 | 1,555 | 2,008 | 66 | 453 D | 42.8% | 55.3% | 43.6% | 56.4% |
| 17,131 | KOOCHICHING | 8,010 | 2,893 | 4,846 | 271 | 1,953 D | 36.1% | 60.5% | 37.4% | 62.6% |
| 11,164 | LAC QUI PARLE | 6,065 | 2,292 | 3,647 | 126 | 1,355 D | 37.8% | 60.1% | 38.6% | 61.4% |
| 13,351 | LAKE | 6,619 | 2,313 | 3,973 | 333 | 1,660 D | 34.9% | 60.0% | 36.8% | 63.2% |
| 3,987 | LAKE OF THE WOODS | 1,968 | 757 | 1,105 | 106 | 348 D | 38.5% | 56.1% | 40.7% | 59.3% |
| 21,332 | LE SUEUR | 11,396 | 4,565 | 6,556 | 275 | 1,991 D | 40.1% | 57.5% | 41.0% | 59.0% |
| 8,143 | LINCOLN | 4,272 | 1,599 | 2,594 | 79 | 995 D | 37.4% | 60.7% | 38.1% | 61.9% |
| 24,273 | LYON | 12,470 | 5,036 | 7,122 | 312 | 2,086 D | 40.4% | 57.1% | 41.4% | 58.6% |
| 27,662 | MCLEOD | 13,245 | 6,519 | 6,249 | 477 | 270 R | 49.2% | 47.2% | 51.1% | 48.9% |
| 5,638 | MAHNOMEN | 2,621 | 905 | 1,590 | 126 | 685 D | 34.5% | 60.7% | 36.3% | 63.7% |
| 13,060 | MARSHALL | 6,490 | 2,605 | 3,744 | 141 | 1,139 D | 40.1% | 57.7% | 41.0% | 59.0% |
| 24,316 | MARTIN | 12,488 | 6,484 | 5,672 | 332 | 812 R | 51.9% | 45.4% | 53.3% | 46.7% |
| 18,810 | MEEKER | 9,765 | 4,097 | 5,295 | 373 | 1,198 D | 42.0% | 54.2% | 43.6% | 56.4% |
| 15,703 | MILLE LACS | 8,670 | 3,212 | 5,172 | 286 | 1,960 D | 37.0% | 59.7% | 38.3% | 61.7% |
| 26,949 | MORRISON | 13,294 | 4,590 | 8,176 | 528 | 3,586 D | 34.5% | 61.5% | 36.0% | 64.0% |
| 43,783 | MOWER | 21,487 | 8,163 | 12,837 | 487 | 4,674 D | 38.0% | 59.7% | 38.9% | 61.1% |
| 12,508 | MURRAY | 6,399 | 2,605 | 3,685 | 109 | 1,080 D | 40.7% | 57.6% | 41.4% | 58.6% |
| 24,518 | NICOLLET | 12,245 | 6,071 | 5,777 | 397 | 294 R | 49.6% | 47.2% | 51.2% | 48.8% |
| 23,208 | NOBLES | 10,735 | 4,503 | 6,034 | 198 | 1,531 D | 41.9% | 56.2% | 42.7% | 57.3% |
| 10,008 | NORMAN | 5,012 | 1,983 | 2,946 | 83 | 963 D | 39.6% | 58.8% | 40.2% | 59.8% |
| 84,104 | OLMSTED | 39,617 | 24,030 | 14,676 | 911 | 9,354 R | 60.7% | 37.0% | 62.1% | 37.9% |
| 46,097 | OTTER TAIL | 24,510 | 12,113 | 11,881 | 516 | 232 R | 49.4% | 48.5% | 50.5% | 49.5% |
| 13,266 | PENNINGTON | 6,948 | 3,023 | 3,787 | 138 | 764 D | 43.5% | 54.5% | 44.4% | 55.6% |
| 16,821 | PINE | 8,887 | 3,057 | 5,442 | 388 | 2,385 D | 34.4% | 61.2% | 36.0% | 64.0% |
| 12,791 | PIPESTONE | 6,402 | 3,018 | 3,272 | 112 | 254 D | 47.1% | 51.1% | 48.0% | 52.0% |
| 34,435 | POLK | 16,052 | 6,552 | 9,078 | 422 | 2,526 D | 40.8% | 56.6% | 41.9% | 58.1% |

# MINNESOTA

## PRESIDENT 1976

| 1970 Census Population | County | Total Vote | Republican | Democratic | Other | Rep.-Dem. Plurality | | Percentage | | | |
|---|---|---|---|---|---|---|---|---|---|---|---|
| | | | | | | | | Total Vote | | Major Vote | |
| | | | | | | | | Rep. | Dem. | Rep. | Dem. |
| 11,107 | POPE | 6,127 | 2,251 | 3,746 | 130 | 1,495 | D | 36.7% | 61.1% | 37.5% | 62.5% |
| 476,255 | RAMSEY | 228,067 | 86,480 | 133,682 | 7,905 | 47,202 | D | 37.9% | 58.6% | 39.3% | 60.7% |
| 5,388 | RED LAKE | 2,613 | 737 | 1,748 | 128 | 1,011 | D | 28.2% | 66.9% | 29.7% | 70.3% |
| 20,024 | REDWOOD | 9,822 | 4,926 | 4,525 | 371 | 401 | R | 50.2% | 46.1% | 52.1% | 47.9% |
| 21,139 | RENVILLE | 10,545 | 4,482 | 5,762 | 301 | 1,280 | D | 42.5% | 54.6% | 43.8% | 56.2% |
| 41,582 | RICE | 19,607 | 8,311 | 10,590 | 706 | 2,279 | D | 42.4% | 54.0% | 44.0% | 56.0% |
| 11,346 | ROCK | 5,739 | 2,892 | 2,769 | 78 | 123 | R | 50.4% | 48.2% | 51.1% | 48.9% |
| 11,569 | ROSEAU | 5,755 | 2,382 | 3,215 | 158 | 833 | D | 41.4% | 55.9% | 42.6% | 57.4% |
| 220,693 | ST. LOUIS | 114,075 | 35,331 | 75,040 | 3,704 | 39,709 | D | 31.0% | 65.8% | 32.0% | 68.0% |
| 32,423 | SCOTT | 17,622 | 7,154 | 9,912 | 556 | 2,758 | D | 40.6% | 56.2% | 41.9% | 58.1% |
| 18,344 | SHERBURNE | 11,442 | 4,361 | 6,678 | 403 | 2,317 | D | 38.1% | 58.4% | 39.5% | 60.5% |
| 15,845 | SIBLEY | 7,860 | 3,871 | 3,752 | 237 | 119 | R | 49.2% | 47.7% | 50.8% | 49.2% |
| 95,400 | STEARNS | 47,821 | 19,574 | 25,027 | 3,220 | 5,453 | D | 40.9% | 52.3% | 43.9% | 56.1% |
| 26,931 | STEELE | 13,648 | 7,053 | 6,263 | 332 | 790 | R | 51.7% | 45.9% | 53.0% | 47.0% |
| 11,218 | STEVENS | 5,793 | 2,484 | 3,171 | 138 | 687 | D | 42.9% | 54.7% | 43.9% | 56.1% |
| 13,177 | SWIFT | 6,762 | 2,190 | 4,428 | 144 | 2,238 | D | 32.4% | 65.5% | 33.1% | 66.9% |
| 22,114 | TODD | 11,248 | 4,278 | 6,530 | 440 | 2,252 | D | 38.0% | 58.1% | 39.6% | 60.4% |
| 6,254 | TRAVERSE | 3,207 | 1,130 | 2,020 | 57 | 890 | D | 35.2% | 63.0% | 35.9% | 64.1% |
| 17,224 | WABASHA | 9,049 | 4,484 | 4,286 | 279 | 198 | R | 49.6% | 47.4% | 51.1% | 48.9% |
| 12,412 | WADENA | 6,424 | 3,048 | 3,164 | 212 | 116 | D | 47.4% | 49.3% | 49.1% | 50.9% |
| 16,663 | WASECA | 8,805 | 4,582 | 4,002 | 221 | 580 | R | 52.0% | 45.5% | 53.4% | 46.6% |
| 82,948 | WASHINGTON | 48,583 | 20,716 | 26,454 | 1,413 | 5,738 | D | 42.6% | 54.5% | 43.9% | 56.1% |
| 13,298 | WATONWAN | 6,662 | 3,351 | 3,177 | 134 | 174 | R | 50.3% | 47.7% | 51.3% | 48.7% |
| 9,389 | WILKIN | 4,112 | 1,882 | 2,103 | 127 | 221 | D | 45.8% | 51.1% | 47.2% | 52.8% |
| 44,409 | WINONA | 21,914 | 10,436 | 10,939 | 539 | 503 | D | 47.6% | 49.9% | 48.8% | 51.2% |
| 38,933 | WRIGHT | 23,464 | 9,314 | 13,379 | 771 | 4,065 | D | 39.7% | 57.0% | 41.0% | 59.0% |
| 14,516 | YELLOW MEDICINE | 7,470 | 2,946 | 4,337 | 187 | 1,391 | D | 39.4% | 58.1% | 40.5% | 59.5% |
| 3,805,069 | TOTAL | 1,949,931 | 819,395 | 1,070,440 | 60,096 | 251,045 | D | 42.0% | 54.9% | 43.4% | 56.6% |

# MINNESOTA

## PRESIDENT 1972

| 1970 Census Population | County | Total Vote | Republican | Democratic | Other | Rep.-Dem. Plurality | Total Vote Rep. | Total Vote Dem. | Major Vote Rep. | Major Vote Dem. |
|---|---|---|---|---|---|---|---|---|---|---|
| 11,403 | AITKIN | 6,032 | 3,241 | 2,687 | 104 | 554 R | 53.7% | 44.5% | 54.7% | 45.3% |
| 154,556 | ANOKA | 59,360 | 29,546 | 28,031 | 1,783 | 1,515 R | 49.8% | 47.2% | 51.3% | 48.7% |
| 24,372 | BECKER | 10,884 | 6,033 | 4,695 | 156 | 1,338 R | 55.4% | 43.1% | 56.2% | 43.8% |
| 26,373 | BELTRAMI | 11,393 | 5,947 | 5,194 | 252 | 753 R | 52.2% | 45.6% | 53.4% | 46.6% |
| 20,841 | BENTON | 9,426 | 4,652 | 4,282 | 492 | 370 R | 49.4% | 45.4% | 52.1% | 47.9% |
| 7,941 | BIG STONE | 4,017 | 1,748 | 2,185 | 84 | 437 D | 43.5% | 54.4% | 44.4% | 55.6% |
| 52,322 | BLUE EARTH | 23,662 | 12,702 | 10,638 | 322 | 2,064 R | 53.7% | 45.0% | 54.4% | 45.6% |
| 28,887 | BROWN | 12,729 | 7,791 | 4,347 | 591 | 3,444 R | 61.2% | 34.2% | 64.2% | 35.8% |
| 28,072 | CARLTON | 12,730 | 5,445 | 7,116 | 169 | 1,671 D | 42.8% | 55.9% | 43.3% | 56.7% |
| 28,310 | CARVER | 13,905 | 8,546 | 4,852 | 507 | 3,694 R | 61.5% | 34.9% | 63.8% | 36.2% |
| 17,323 | CASS | 8,503 | 4,906 | 3,347 | 250 | 1,559 R | 57.7% | 39.4% | 59.4% | 40.6% |
| 15,109 | CHIPPEWA | 7,547 | 3,787 | 3,630 | 130 | 157 R | 50.2% | 48.1% | 51.1% | 48.9% |
| 17,492 | CHISAGO | 9,241 | 4,718 | 4,174 | 349 | 544 R | 51.1% | 45.2% | 53.1% | 46.9% |
| 46,585 | CLAY | 20,400 | 11,089 | 9,076 | 235 | 2,013 R | 54.4% | 44.5% | 55.0% | 45.0% |
| 8,013 | CLEARWATER | 3,683 | 1,819 | 1,751 | 113 | 68 R | 49.4% | 47.5% | 51.0% | 49.0% |
| 3,423 | COOK | 1,817 | 1,047 | 742 | 28 | 305 R | 57.6% | 40.8% | 58.5% | 41.5% |
| 14,887 | COTTONWOOD | 7,303 | 4,396 | 2,802 | 105 | 1,594 R | 60.2% | 38.4% | 61.1% | 38.9% |
| 34,826 | CROW WING | 16,551 | 8,774 | 7,328 | 449 | 1,446 R | 53.0% | 44.3% | 54.5% | 45.5% |
| 139,808 | DAKOTA | 64,796 | 34,967 | 28,479 | 1,350 | 6,488 R | 54.0% | 44.0% | 55.1% | 44.9% |
| 13,037 | DODGE | 5,936 | 3,863 | 1,921 | 152 | 1,942 R | 65.1% | 32.4% | 66.8% | 33.2% |
| 22,892 | DOUGLAS | 12,606 | 6,678 | 5,501 | 427 | 1,177 R | 53.0% | 43.6% | 54.8% | 45.2% |
| 20,896 | FARIBAULT | 10,153 | 6,503 | 3,519 | 131 | 2,984 R | 64.1% | 34.7% | 64.9% | 35.1% |
| 21,916 | FILLMORE | 10,460 | 7,107 | 3,155 | 198 | 3,952 R | 67.9% | 30.2% | 69.3% | 30.7% |
| 38,064 | FREEBORN | 17,130 | 9,747 | 7,163 | 220 | 2,584 R | 56.9% | 41.8% | 57.6% | 42.4% |
| 34,763 | GOODHUE | 17,631 | 11,107 | 6,147 | 377 | 4,960 R | 63.0% | 34.9% | 64.4% | 35.6% |
| 7,462 | GRANT | 4,054 | 1,899 | 2,085 | 70 | 186 D | 46.8% | 51.4% | 47.7% | 52.3% |
| 960,080 | HENNEPIN | 443,358 | 228,951 | 205,943 | 8,464 | 23,008 R | 51.6% | 46.5% | 52.6% | 47.4% |
| 17,556 | HOUSTON | 7,790 | 5,186 | 2,467 | 137 | 2,719 R | 66.6% | 31.7% | 67.8% | 32.2% |
| 10,583 | HUBBARD | 5,554 | 3,294 | 2,136 | 124 | 1,158 R | 59.3% | 38.5% | 60.7% | 39.3% |
| 16,560 | ISANTI | 7,634 | 3,715 | 3,660 | 259 | 55 R | 48.7% | 47.9% | 50.4% | 49.6% |
| 35,530 | ITASCA | 16,583 | 7,558 | 8,683 | 342 | 1,125 D | 45.6% | 52.4% | 46.5% | 53.5% |
| 14,352 | JACKSON | 6,989 | 3,599 | 3,304 | 86 | 295 R | 51.5% | 47.3% | 52.1% | 47.9% |
| 9,775 | KANABEC | 4,632 | 2,395 | 1,969 | 268 | 426 R | 51.7% | 42.5% | 54.9% | 45.1% |
| 30,548 | KANDIYOHI | 14,481 | 6,624 | 7,241 | 616 | 617 D | 45.7% | 50.0% | 47.8% | 52.2% |
| 6,853 | KITTSON | 3,479 | 1,832 | 1,584 | 63 | 248 R | 52.7% | 45.5% | 53.6% | 46.4% |
| 17,131 | KOOCHICHING | 7,230 | 3,681 | 3,396 | 153 | 285 R | 50.9% | 47.0% | 52.0% | 48.0% |
| 11,164 | LAC QUI PARLE | 5,726 | 2,773 | 2,845 | 108 | 72 D | 48.4% | 49.7% | 49.4% | 50.6% |
| 13,351 | LAKE | 6,327 | 2,575 | 3,640 | 112 | 1,065 D | 40.7% | 57.5% | 41.4% | 58.6% |
| 3,987 | LAKE OF THE WOODS | 1,582 | 877 | 672 | 33 | 205 R | 55.4% | 42.5% | 56.6% | 43.4% |
| 21,332 | LE SUEUR | 10,262 | 5,388 | 4,725 | 149 | 663 R | 52.5% | 46.0% | 53.3% | 46.7% |
| 8,143 | LINCOLN | 4,095 | 1,881 | 2,148 | 66 | 267 D | 45.9% | 52.5% | 46.7% | 53.3% |
| 24,273 | LYON | 11,630 | 5,820 | 5,614 | 196 | 206 R | 50.0% | 48.3% | 50.9% | 49.1% |
| 27,662 | MCLEOD | 12,733 | 7,820 | 4,538 | 375 | 3,282 R | 61.4% | 35.6% | 63.3% | 36.7% |
| 5,638 | MAHNOMEN | 2,691 | 1,246 | 1,397 | 48 | 151 D | 46.3% | 51.9% | 47.1% | 52.9% |
| 13,060 | MARSHALL | 6,190 | 3,264 | 2,790 | 136 | 474 R | 52.7% | 45.1% | 53.9% | 46.1% |
| 24,316 | MARTIN | 11,718 | 7,569 | 3,816 | 333 | 3,753 R | 64.6% | 32.6% | 66.5% | 33.5% |
| 18,810 | MEEKER | 8,933 | 5,097 | 3,601 | 235 | 1,496 R | 57.1% | 40.3% | 58.6% | 41.4% |
| 15,703 | MILLE LACS | 7,686 | 4,291 | 3,221 | 174 | 1,070 R | 55.8% | 41.9% | 57.1% | 42.9% |
| 26,949 | MORRISON | 12,329 | 5,714 | 5,993 | 622 | 279 D | 46.3% | 48.6% | 48.8% | 51.2% |
| 43,783 | MOWER | 20,530 | 9,929 | 10,286 | 315 | 357 D | 48.4% | 50.1% | 49.1% | 50.9% |
| 12,508 | MURRAY | 5,927 | 2,959 | 2,893 | 75 | 66 R | 49.9% | 48.8% | 50.6% | 49.4% |
| 24,518 | NICOLLET | 11,069 | 6,230 | 4,680 | 159 | 1,550 R | 56.3% | 42.3% | 57.1% | 42.9% |
| 23,208 | NOBLES | 10,525 | 4,951 | 5,464 | 110 | 513 D | 47.0% | 51.9% | 47.5% | 52.5% |
| 10,008 | NORMAN | 5,021 | 2,536 | 2,444 | 41 | 92 R | 50.5% | 48.7% | 50.9% | 49.1% |
| 84,104 | OLMSTED | 34,521 | 23,806 | 9,817 | 898 | 13,989 R | 69.0% | 28.4% | 70.8% | 29.2% |
| 46,097 | OTTER TAIL | 21,731 | 13,519 | 7,881 | 331 | 5,638 R | 62.2% | 36.3% | 63.2% | 36.8% |
| 13,266 | PENNINGTON | 6,600 | 3,548 | 2,892 | 160 | 656 R | 53.8% | 43.8% | 55.1% | 44.9% |
| 16,821 | PINE | 8,017 | 3,881 | 3,794 | 342 | 87 R | 48.4% | 47.3% | 50.6% | 49.4% |
| 12,791 | PIPESTONE | 6,376 | 3,543 | 2,758 | 75 | 785 R | 55.6% | 43.3% | 56.2% | 43.8% |
| 34,435 | POLK | 15,885 | 8,139 | 7,366 | 380 | 773 R | 51.2% | 46.4% | 52.5% | 47.5% |

# MINNESOTA

## PRESIDENT 1972

| 1970 Census Population | County | Total Vote | Republican | Democratic | Other | Rep.-Dem. Plurality | Percentage Total Vote Rep. | Dem. | Major Vote Rep. | Dem. |
|---|---|---|---|---|---|---|---|---|---|---|
| 11,107 | POPE | 5,681 | 2,610 | 2,910 | 161 | 300 D | 45.9% | 51.2% | 47.3% | 52.7% |
| 476,255 | RAMSEY | 209,951 | 95,716 | 108,392 | 5,843 | 12,676 D | 45.6% | 51.6% | 46.9% | 53.1% |
| 5,388 | RED LAKE | 2,541 | 1,052 | 1,409 | 80 | 357 D | 41.4% | 55.5% | 42.7% | 57.3% |
| 20,024 | REDWOOD | 9,252 | 5,776 | 3,177 | 299 | 2,599 R | 62.4% | 34.3% | 64.5% | 35.5% |
| 21,139 | RENVILLE | 10,044 | 5,329 | 4,499 | 216 | 830 R | 53.1% | 44.8% | 54.2% | 45.8% |
| 41,582 | RICE | 17,475 | 9,195 | 8,065 | 215 | 1,130 R | 52.6% | 46.2% | 53.3% | 46.7% |
| 11,346 | ROCK | 5,612 | 3,470 | 2,089 | 53 | 1,381 R | 61.8% | 37.2% | 62.4% | 37.6% |
| 11,569 | ROSEAU | 5,344 | 2,844 | 2,396 | 104 | 448 R | 53.2% | 44.8% | 54.3% | 45.7% |
| 220,693 | ST. LOUIS | 104,180 | 41,435 | 61,103 | 1,642 | 19,668 D | 39.8% | 58.7% | 40.4% | 59.6% |
| 32,423 | SCOTT | 14,376 | 7,310 | 6,745 | 321 | 565 R | 50.8% | 46.9% | 52.0% | 48.0% |
| 18,344 | SHERBURNE | 8,658 | 4,332 | 4,070 | 256 | 262 R | 50.0% | 47.0% | 51.6% | 48.4% |
| 15,845 | SIBLEY | 7,080 | 4,543 | 2,433 | 104 | 2,110 R | 64.2% | 34.4% | 65.1% | 34.9% |
| 95,400 | STEARNS | 41,400 | 18,951 | 19,315 | 3,134 | 364 D | 45.8% | 46.7% | 49.5% | 50.5% |
| 26,931 | STEELE | 11,868 | 7,678 | 4,010 | 180 | 3,668 R | 64.7% | 33.8% | 65.7% | 34.3% |
| 11,218 | STEVENS | 5,811 | 2,830 | 2,870 | 111 | 40 D | 48.7% | 49.4% | 49.6% | 50.4% |
| 13,177 | SWIFT | 6,617 | 2,673 | 3,823 | 121 | 1,150 D | 40.4% | 57.8% | 41.1% | 58.9% |
| 22,114 | TODD | 10,137 | 5,387 | 4,270 | 480 | 1,117 R | 53.1% | 42.1% | 55.8% | 44.2% |
| 6,254 | TRAVERSE | 3,055 | 1,276 | 1,744 | 35 | 468 D | 41.8% | 57.1% | 42.3% | 57.7% |
| 17,224 | WABASHA | 8,413 | 5,158 | 3,017 | 238 | 2,141 R | 61.3% | 35.9% | 63.1% | 36.9% |
| 12,412 | WADENA | 5,974 | 3,408 | 2,430 | 136 | 978 R | 57.0% | 40.7% | 58.4% | 41.6% |
| 16,663 | WASECA | 7,926 | 5,064 | 2,767 | 95 | 2,297 R | 63.9% | 34.9% | 64.7% | 35.3% |
| 82,948 | WASHINGTON | 36,098 | 19,142 | 16,102 | 854 | 3,040 R | 53.0% | 44.6% | 54.3% | 45.7% |
| 13,298 | WATONWAN | 6,251 | 3,960 | 2,229 | 62 | 1,731 R | 63.3% | 35.7% | 64.0% | 36.0% |
| 9,389 | WILKIN | 4,093 | 2,292 | 1,739 | 62 | 553 R | 56.0% | 42.5% | 56.9% | 43.1% |
| 44,409 | WINONA | 19,327 | 10,910 | 8,080 | 337 | 2,830 R | 56.4% | 41.8% | 57.5% | 42.5% |
| 38,933 | WRIGHT | 19,386 | 9,996 | 8,695 | 695 | 1,301 R | 51.6% | 44.9% | 53.5% | 46.5% |
| 14,516 | YELLOW MEDICINE | 7,319 | 3,683 | 3,462 | 174 | 221 R | 50.3% | 47.3% | 51.5% | 48.5% |
| 3,805,069 | TOTAL | 1,741,652 | 898,269 | 802,346 | 41,037 | 95,923 R | 51.6% | 46.1% | 52.8% | 47.2% |

# MINNESOTA

## PRESIDENT 1968

| 1960 Census Population | County | Total Vote | Republican | Democratic | AIP | Other | Plurality | Rep. | Dem. | AIP |
|---|---|---|---|---|---|---|---|---|---|---|
| 12,162 | AITKIN | 5,657 | 2,254 | 3,094 | 286 | 23 | 840 D | 39.8% | 54.7% | 5.1% |
| 85,916 | ANOKA | 50,134 | 16,358 | 30,656 | 3,073 | 47 | 14,298 D | 32.6% | 61.1% | 6.1% |
| 23,959 | BECKER | 10,196 | 4,728 | 4,875 | 568 | 25 | 147 D | 46.4% | 47.8% | 5.6% |
| 23,425 | BELTRAMI | 9,565 | 3,912 | 5,034 | 599 | 20 | 1,122 D | 40.9% | 52.6% | 6.3% |
| 17,287 | BENTON | 8,016 | 3,470 | 4,022 | 514 | 10 | 552 D | 43.3% | 50.2% | 6.4% |
| 8,954 | BIG STONE | 3,946 | 1,645 | 2,119 | 176 | 6 | 474 D | 41.7% | 53.7% | 4.5% |
| 44,385 | BLUE EARTH | 19,537 | 9,571 | 9,254 | 686 | 26 | 317 R | 49.0% | 47.4% | 3.5% |
| 27,676 | BROWN | 12,350 | 7,039 | 4,585 | 703 | 23 | 2,454 R | 57.0% | 37.1% | 5.7% |
| 27,932 | CARLTON | 12,018 | 3,016 | 8,538 | 444 | 20 | 5,522 D | 25.1% | 71.0% | 3.7% |
| 21,358 | CARVER | 11,780 | 6,649 | 4,590 | 528 | 13 | 2,059 R | 56.4% | 39.0% | 4.5% |
| 16,720 | CASS | 7,950 | 3,888 | 3,569 | 486 | 7 | 319 R | 48.9% | 44.9% | 6.1% |
| 16,320 | CHIPPEWA | 7,147 | 3,195 | 3,701 | 243 | 8 | 506 D | 44.7% | 51.8% | 3.4% |
| 13,419 | CHISAGO | 7,651 | 3,053 | 4,102 | 492 | 4 | 1,049 D | 39.9% | 53.6% | 6.4% |
| 39,080 | CLAY | 16,560 | 7,910 | 7,987 | 640 | 23 | 77 D | 47.8% | 48.2% | 3.9% |
| 8,864 | CLEARWATER | 3,561 | 1,284 | 2,046 | 217 | 14 | 762 D | 36.1% | 57.5% | 6.1% |
| 3,377 | COOK | 1,729 | 853 | 777 | 96 | 3 | 76 R | 49.3% | 44.9% | 5.6% |
| 16,166 | COTTONWOOD | 7,391 | 4,050 | 3,046 | 293 | 2 | 1,004 R | 54.8% | 41.2% | 4.0% |
| 32,134 | CROW WING | 14,795 | 6,687 | 7,411 | 672 | 25 | 724 D | 45.2% | 50.1% | 4.5% |
| 78,303 | DAKOTA | 49,908 | 19,290 | 28,416 | 2,142 | 60 | 9,126 D | 38.7% | 56.9% | 4.3% |
| 13,259 | DODGE | 5,709 | 3,064 | 2,437 | 201 | 7 | 627 R | 53.7% | 42.7% | 3.5% |
| 21,313 | DOUGLAS | 10,839 | 5,464 | 4,826 | 536 | 13 | 638 R | 50.4% | 44.5% | 4.9% |
| 23,685 | FARIBAULT | 10,384 | 5,662 | 4,335 | 379 | 8 | 1,327 R | 54.5% | 41.7% | 3.6% |
| 23,768 | FILLMORE | 10,607 | 6,257 | 3,918 | 426 | 6 | 2,339 R | 59.0% | 36.9% | 4.0% |
| 37,891 | FREEBORN | 16,563 | 7,315 | 8,671 | 558 | 19 | 1,356 D | 44.2% | 52.4% | 3.4% |
| 33,035 | GOODHUE | 15,964 | 8,283 | 7,220 | 451 | 10 | 1,063 R | 51.9% | 45.2% | 2.8% |
| 8,870 | GRANT | 4,095 | 1,929 | 1,982 | 179 | 5 | 53 D | 47.1% | 48.4% | 4.4% |
| 842,854 | HENNEPIN | 407,024 | 170,002 | 220,078 | 15,659 | 1,285 | 50,076 D | 41.8% | 54.1% | 3.8% |
| 16,588 | HOUSTON | 7,681 | 4,450 | 2,703 | 521 | 7 | 1,747 R | 57.9% | 35.2% | 6.8% |
| 9,962 | HUBBARD | 4,950 | 2,720 | 1,920 | 304 | 6 | 800 R | 54.9% | 38.8% | 6.1% |
| 13,530 | ISANTI | 6,337 | 2,429 | 3,439 | 451 | 18 | 1,010 D | 38.3% | 54.3% | 7.1% |
| 38,006 | ITASCA | 16,206 | 4,898 | 10,512 | 780 | 16 | 5,614 D | 30.2% | 64.9% | 4.8% |
| 15,501 | JACKSON | 6,766 | 2,886 | 3,515 | 359 | 6 | 629 D | 42.7% | 52.0% | 5.3% |
| 9,007 | KANABEC | 4,248 | 1,847 | 2,154 | 240 | 7 | 307 D | 43.5% | 50.7% | 5.6% |
| 29,987 | KANDIYOHI | 13,400 | 5,086 | 7,639 | 658 | 17 | 2,553 D | 38.0% | 57.0% | 4.9% |
| 8,343 | KITTSON | 3,513 | 1,436 | 1,894 | 179 | 4 | 458 D | 40.9% | 53.9% | 5.1% |
| 18,190 | KOOCHICHING | 7,116 | 2,104 | 4,697 | 299 | 16 | 2,593 D | 29.6% | 66.0% | 4.2% |
| 13,330 | LAC QUI PARLE | 5,828 | 2,672 | 2,937 | 212 | 7 | 265 D | 45.8% | 50.4% | 3.6% |
| 13,702 | LAKE | 5,891 | 1,351 | 4,266 | 263 | 11 | 2,915 D | 22.9% | 72.4% | 4.5% |
| 4,304 | LAKE OF THE WOODS | 1,558 | 607 | 875 | 69 | 7 | 268 D | 39.0% | 56.2% | 4.4% |
| 19,906 | LE SUEUR | 9,581 | 4,189 | 5,094 | 292 | 6 | 905 D | 43.7% | 53.2% | 3.0% |
| 9,651 | LINCOLN | 4,030 | 1,732 | 2,109 | 187 | 2 | 377 D | 43.0% | 52.3% | 4.6% |
| 22,655 | LYON | 9,966 | 4,331 | 5,317 | 306 | 12 | 986 D | 43.5% | 53.4% | 3.1% |
| 24,401 | MCLEOD | 12,064 | 6,619 | 4,861 | 576 | 8 | 1,758 R | 54.9% | 40.3% | 4.8% |
| 6,341 | MAHNOMEN | 2,605 | 893 | 1,508 | 201 | 3 | 615 D | 34.3% | 57.9% | 7.7% |
| 14,262 | MARSHALL | 5,956 | 2,367 | 3,161 | 418 | 10 | 794 D | 39.7% | 53.1% | 7.0% |
| 26,986 | MARTIN | 11,973 | 7,115 | 4,271 | 580 | 7 | 2,844 R | 59.4% | 35.7% | 4.8% |
| 18,887 | MEEKER | 8,704 | 4,044 | 4,213 | 438 | 9 | 169 D | 46.5% | 48.4% | 5.0% |
| 14,560 | MILLE LACS | 6,890 | 2,990 | 3,494 | 399 | 7 | 504 D | 43.4% | 50.7% | 5.8% |
| 26,641 | MORRISON | 11,256 | 4,511 | 6,111 | 612 | 22 | 1,600 D | 40.1% | 54.3% | 5.4% |
| 48,498 | MOWER | 19,486 | 7,736 | 11,022 | 692 | 36 | 3,286 D | 39.7% | 56.6% | 3.6% |
| 14,743 | MURRAY | 5,888 | 2,906 | 2,662 | 316 | 4 | 244 R | 49.4% | 45.2% | 5.4% |
| 23,196 | NICOLLET | 9,234 | 4,671 | 4,244 | 312 | 7 | 427 R | 50.6% | 46.0% | 3.4% |
| 23,365 | NOBLES | 10,107 | 4,451 | 5,171 | 477 | 8 | 720 D | 44.0% | 51.2% | 4.7% |
| 11,253 | NORMAN | 5,012 | 1,981 | 2,828 | 200 | 3 | 847 D | 39.5% | 56.4% | 4.0% |
| 65,532 | OLMSTED | 31,840 | 17,292 | 13,417 | 1,103 | 28 | 3,875 R | 54.3% | 42.1% | 3.5% |
| 48,960 | OTTER TAIL | 20,701 | 12,483 | 7,400 | 802 | 16 | 5,083 R | 60.3% | 35.7% | 3.9% |
| 12,468 | PENNINGTON | 5,465 | 2,247 | 2,998 | 212 | 8 | 751 D | 41.1% | 54.9% | 3.9% |
| 17,004 | PINE | 7,117 | 2,591 | 4,044 | 463 | 19 | 1,453 D | 36.4% | 56.8% | 6.5% |
| 13,605 | PIPESTONE | 5,738 | 3,241 | 2,234 | 260 | 3 | 1,007 R | 56.5% | 38.9% | 4.5% |
| 36,182 | POLK | 15,169 | 6,074 | 8,380 | 700 | 15 | 2,306 D | 40.0% | 55.2% | 4.6% |

# MINNESOTA

## PRESIDENT 1968

| 1960 Census Population | County | Total Vote | Republican | Democratic | AIP | Other | Plurality | Percentage Total Vote Rep. | Dem. | AIP |
|---|---|---|---|---|---|---|---|---|---|---|
| 11,914 | POPE | 5,368 | 2,504 | 2,592 | 265 | 7 | 88 D | 46.6% | 48.3% | 4.9% |
| 422,525 | RAMSEY | 195,656 | 64,068 | 122,568 | 8,543 | 477 | 58,500 D | 32.7% | 62.6% | 4.4% |
| 5,830 | RED LAKE | 2,318 | 718 | 1,467 | 130 | 3 | 749 D | 31.0% | 63.3% | 5.6% |
| 21,718 | REDWOOD | 9,285 | 5,134 | 3,680 | 462 | 9 | 1,454 R | 55.3% | 39.6% | 5.0% |
| 23,249 | RENVILLE | 9,906 | 4,821 | 4,535 | 543 | 7 | 286 R | 48.7% | 45.8% | 5.5% |
| 38,988 | RICE | 15,319 | 7,037 | 7,785 | 477 | 20 | 748 D | 45.9% | 50.8% | 3.1% |
| 11,864 | ROCK | 5,374 | 3,056 | 2,084 | 232 | 2 | 972 R | 56.9% | 38.8% | 4.3% |
| 12,154 | ROSEAU | 5,035 | 2,048 | 2,649 | 326 | 12 | 601 D | 40.7% | 52.6% | 6.5% |
| 231,588 | ST. LOUIS | 101,797 | 25,981 | 72,267 | 3,255 | 294 | 46,286 D | 25.5% | 71.0% | 3.2% |
| 21,909 | SCOTT | 11,837 | 4,632 | 6,656 | 540 | 9 | 2,024 D | 39.1% | 56.2% | 4.6% |
| 12,861 | SHERBURNE | 6,593 | 2,737 | 3,481 | 369 | 6 | 744 D | 41.5% | 52.8% | 5.6% |
| 16,228 | SIBLEY | 7,154 | 4,250 | 2,540 | 361 | 3 | 1,710 R | 59.4% | 35.5% | 5.0% |
| 80,345 | STEARNS | 33,580 | 15,422 | 15,990 | 2,081 | 87 | 568 D | 45.9% | 47.6% | 6.2% |
| 25,029 | STEELE | 11,190 | 6,193 | 4,631 | 358 | 8 | 1,562 R | 55.3% | 41.4% | 3.2% |
| 11,262 | STEVENS | 5,062 | 2,560 | 2,247 | 246 | 9 | 313 R | 50.6% | 44.4% | 4.9% |
| 14,936 | SWIFT | 6,451 | 2,476 | 3,716 | 247 | 12 | 1,240 D | 38.4% | 57.6% | 3.8% |
| 23,119 | TODD | 9,460 | 4,883 | 3,992 | 572 | 13 | 891 R | 51.6% | 42.2% | 6.0% |
| 7,503 | TRAVERSE | 3,084 | 1,277 | 1,669 | 137 | 1 | 392 D | 41.4% | 54.1% | 4.4% |
| 17,007 | WABASHA | 7,886 | 4,081 | 3,452 | 346 | 7 | 629 R | 51.7% | 43.8% | 4.4% |
| 12,199 | WADENA | 5,386 | 2,912 | 2,198 | 269 | 7 | 714 R | 54.1% | 40.8% | 5.0% |
| 16,041 | WASECA | 7,605 | 4,292 | 3,057 | 244 | 12 | 1,235 R | 56.4% | 40.2% | 3.2% |
| 52,432 | WASHINGTON | 28,954 | 10,921 | 16,449 | 1,527 | 57 | 5,528 D | 37.7% | 56.8% | 5.3% |
| 14,460 | WATONWAN | 6,433 | 3,446 | 2,701 | 278 | 8 | 745 R | 53.6% | 42.0% | 4.3% |
| 10,650 | WILKIN | 4,165 | 2,037 | 1,946 | 181 | 1 | 91 R | 48.9% | 46.7% | 4.3% |
| 40,937 | WINONA | 17,443 | 7,998 | 8,627 | 781 | 37 | 629 D | 45.9% | 49.5% | 4.5% |
| 29,935 | WRIGHT | 15,753 | 6,321 | 8,793 | 627 | 12 | 2,472 D | 40.1% | 55.8% | 4.0% |
| 15,523 | YELLOW MEDICINE | 7,060 | 3,060 | 3,587 | 406 | 7 | 527 D | 43.3% | 50.8% | 5.8% |
| 3,413,864 | TOTAL | 1,588,506 | 658,643 | 857,738 | 68,931 | 3,194 | 199,095 D | 41.5% | 54.0% | 4.3% |

# MINNESOTA

## PRESIDENT 1964

| 1960 Census Population | County | Total Vote | Republican | Democratic | Other | Rep.-Dem. Plurality | Percentage Total Vote Rep. | Dem. | Major Vote Rep. | Dem. |
|---:|---|---:|---:|---:|---:|---:|---:|---:|---:|---:|
| 12,162 | AITKIN | 5,890 | 2,000 | 3,874 | 16 | 1,874 D | 34.0% | 65.8% | 34.0% | 66.0% |
| 85,916 | ANOKA | 45,005 | 13,201 | 31,714 | 90 | 18,513 D | 29.3% | 70.5% | 29.4% | 70.6% |
| 23,959 | BECKER | 10,220 | 3,751 | 6,453 | 16 | 2,702 D | 36.7% | 63.1% | 36.8% | 63.2% |
| 23,425 | BELTRAMI | 9,166 | 3,184 | 5,967 | 15 | 2,783 D | 34.7% | 65.1% | 34.8% | 65.2% |
| 17,287 | BENTON | 7,520 | 2,818 | 4,679 | 23 | 1,861 D | 37.5% | 62.2% | 37.6% | 62.4% |
| 8,954 | BIG STONE | 4,172 | 1,331 | 2,831 | 10 | 1,500 D | 31.9% | 67.9% | 32.0% | 68.0% |
| 44,385 | BLUE EARTH | 18,797 | 8,009 | 10,687 | 101 | 2,678 D | 42.6% | 56.9% | 42.8% | 57.2% |
| 27,676 | BROWN | 11,937 | 5,851 | 6,069 | 17 | 218 D | 49.0% | 50.8% | 49.1% | 50.9% |
| 27,932 | CARLTON | 12,359 | 2,780 | 9,552 | 27 | 6,772 D | 22.5% | 77.3% | 22.5% | 77.5% |
| 21,358 | CARVER | 10,558 | 5,424 | 5,123 | 11 | 301 R | 51.4% | 48.5% | 51.4% | 48.6% |
| 16,720 | CASS | 7,754 | 3,110 | 4,635 | 9 | 1,525 D | 40.1% | 59.8% | 40.2% | 59.8% |
| 16,320 | CHIPPEWA | 7,365 | 2,806 | 4,550 | 9 | 1,744 D | 38.1% | 61.8% | 38.1% | 61.9% |
| 13,419 | CHISAGO | 6,889 | 2,525 | 4,347 | 17 | 1,822 D | 36.7% | 63.1% | 36.7% | 63.3% |
| 39,080 | CLAY | 16,285 | 6,085 | 10,161 | 39 | 4,076 D | 37.4% | 62.4% | 37.5% | 62.5% |
| 8,864 | CLEARWATER | 3,739 | 1,137 | 2,596 | 6 | 1,459 D | 30.4% | 69.4% | 30.5% | 69.5% |
| 3,377 | COOK | 1,742 | 764 | 976 | 2 | 212 D | 43.9% | 56.0% | 43.9% | 56.1% |
| 16,166 | COTTONWOOD | 7,528 | 3,423 | 4,090 | 15 | 667 D | 45.5% | 54.3% | 45.6% | 54.4% |
| 32,134 | CROW WING | 14,349 | 5,131 | 9,197 | 21 | 4,066 D | 35.8% | 64.1% | 35.8% | 64.2% |
| 78,303 | DAKOTA | 42,328 | 13,856 | 28,391 | 81 | 14,535 D | 32.7% | 67.1% | 32.8% | 67.2% |
| 13,259 | DODGE | 5,620 | 2,474 | 3,138 | 8 | 664 D | 44.0% | 55.8% | 44.1% | 55.9% |
| 21,313 | DOUGLAS | 10,175 | 4,122 | 6,040 | 13 | 1,918 D | 40.5% | 59.4% | 40.6% | 59.4% |
| 23,685 | FARIBAULT | 10,775 | 4,817 | 5,946 | 12 | 1,129 D | 44.7% | 55.2% | 44.8% | 55.2% |
| 23,768 | FILLMORE | 10,651 | 4,824 | 5,813 | 14 | 989 D | 45.3% | 54.6% | 45.4% | 54.6% |
| 37,891 | FREEBORN | 16,709 | 6,136 | 10,554 | 19 | 4,418 D | 36.7% | 63.2% | 36.8% | 63.2% |
| 33,035 | GOODHUE | 15,589 | 6,539 | 9,035 | 15 | 2,496 D | 41.9% | 58.0% | 42.0% | 58.0% |
| 8,870 | GRANT | 4,366 | 1,734 | 2,631 | 1 | 897 D | 39.7% | 60.3% | 39.7% | 60.3% |
| 842,854 | HENNEPIN | 396,727 | 154,736 | 241,020 | 971 | 86,284 D | 39.0% | 60.8% | 39.1% | 60.9% |
| 16,588 | HOUSTON | 7,326 | 3,433 | 3,885 | 8 | 452 D | 46.9% | 53.0% | 46.9% | 53.1% |
| 9,962 | HUBBARD | 4,843 | 2,283 | 2,553 | 7 | 270 D | 47.1% | 52.7% | 47.2% | 52.8% |
| 13,530 | ISANTI | 6,018 | 1,982 | 4,026 | 10 | 2,044 D | 32.9% | 66.9% | 33.0% | 67.0% |
| 38,006 | ITASCA | 16,231 | 4,137 | 12,054 | 40 | 7,917 D | 25.5% | 74.3% | 25.6% | 74.4% |
| 15,501 | JACKSON | 7,021 | 2,441 | 4,576 | 4 | 2,135 D | 34.8% | 65.2% | 34.8% | 65.2% |
| 9,007 | KANABEC | 4,024 | 1,348 | 2,666 | 10 | 1,318 D | 33.5% | 66.3% | 33.6% | 66.4% |
| 29,987 | KANDIYOHI | 13,156 | 4,011 | 9,108 | 37 | 5,097 D | 30.5% | 69.2% | 30.6% | 69.4% |
| 8,343 | KITTSON | 3,945 | 1,153 | 2,790 | 2 | 1,637 D | 29.2% | 70.7% | 29.2% | 70.8% |
| 18,190 | KOOCHICHING | 7,491 | 1,602 | 5,878 | 11 | 4,276 D | 21.4% | 78.5% | 21.4% | 78.6% |
| 13,330 | LAC QUI PARLE | 6,180 | 2,236 | 3,934 | 10 | 1,698 D | 36.2% | 63.7% | 36.2% | 63.8% |
| 13,702 | LAKE | 5,925 | 1,205 | 4,704 | 16 | 3,499 D | 20.3% | 79.4% | 20.4% | 79.6% |
| 4,304 | LAKE OF THE WOODS | 1,765 | 489 | 1,266 | 10 | 777 D | 27.7% | 71.7% | 27.9% | 72.1% |
| 19,906 | LE SUEUR | 9,325 | 3,191 | 6,117 | 17 | 2,926 D | 34.2% | 65.6% | 34.3% | 65.7% |
| 9,651 | LINCOLN | 4,428 | 1,393 | 3,024 | 11 | 1,631 D | 31.5% | 68.3% | 31.5% | 68.5% |
| 22,655 | LYON | 9,822 | 3,165 | 6,649 | 8 | 3,484 D | 32.2% | 67.7% | 32.2% | 67.8% |
| 24,401 | MCLEOD | 11,316 | 5,545 | 5,755 | 16 | 210 D | 49.0% | 50.9% | 49.1% | 50.9% |
| 6,341 | MAHNOMEN | 2,619 | 648 | 1,957 | 4 | 1,319 D | 24.7% | 75.1% | 24.8% | 75.2% |
| 14,262 | MARSHALL | 6,490 | 1,893 | 4,594 | 3 | 2,701 D | 29.2% | 70.8% | 29.2% | 70.8% |
| 26,986 | MARTIN | 12,126 | 6,529 | 5,575 | 22 | 954 R | 53.8% | 46.0% | 53.9% | 46.1% |
| 18,887 | MEEKER | 8,378 | 3,099 | 5,270 | 9 | 2,171 D | 37.0% | 62.9% | 37.0% | 63.0% |
| 14,560 | MILLE LACS | 6,872 | 2,474 | 4,369 | 29 | 1,895 D | 36.0% | 63.6% | 36.2% | 63.8% |
| 26,641 | MORRISON | 11,032 | 3,515 | 7,492 | 25 | 3,977 D | 31.9% | 67.9% | 31.9% | 68.1% |
| 48,498 | MOWER | 20,140 | 6,510 | 13,573 | 57 | 7,063 D | 32.3% | 67.4% | 32.4% | 67.6% |
| 14,743 | MURRAY | 6,152 | 2,325 | 3,822 | 5 | 1,497 D | 37.8% | 62.1% | 37.8% | 62.2% |
| 23,196 | NICOLLET | 8,736 | 3,605 | 5,121 | 10 | 1,516 D | 41.3% | 58.6% | 41.3% | 58.7% |
| 23,365 | NOBLES | 9,960 | 3,517 | 6,431 | 12 | 2,914 D | 35.3% | 64.6% | 35.4% | 64.6% |
| 11,253 | NORMAN | 5,301 | 1,662 | 3,631 | 8 | 1,969 D | 31.4% | 68.5% | 31.4% | 68.6% |
| 65,532 | OLMSTED | 28,950 | 12,699 | 16,195 | 56 | 3,496 D | 43.9% | 55.9% | 44.0% | 56.0% |
| 48,960 | OTTER TAIL | 20,565 | 10,542 | 9,997 | 26 | 545 R | 51.3% | 48.6% | 51.3% | 48.7% |
| 12,468 | PENNINGTON | 5,534 | 1,630 | 3,894 | 10 | 2,264 D | 29.5% | 70.4% | 29.5% | 70.5% |
| 17,004 | PINE | 7,420 | 2,279 | 5,123 | 18 | 2,844 D | 30.7% | 69.0% | 30.8% | 69.2% |
| 13,605 | PIPESTONE | 5,851 | 2,481 | 3,365 | 5 | 884 D | 42.4% | 57.5% | 42.4% | 57.6% |
| 36,182 | POLK | 16,111 | 5,039 | 11,052 | 20 | 6,013 D | 31.3% | 68.6% | 31.3% | 68.7% |

# MINNESOTA

## PRESIDENT 1964

| 1960 Census Population | County | Total Vote | Republican | Democratic | Other | Rep.-Dem. Plurality | Percentage | | | |
|---|---|---|---|---|---|---|---|---|---|---|
| | | | | | | | Total Vote | | Major Vote | |
| | | | | | | | Rep. | Dem. | Rep. | Dem. |
| 11,914 | POPE | 5,764 | 2,213 | 3,549 | 2 | 1,336 D | 38.4% | 61.6% | 38.4% | 61.6% |
| 422,525 | RAMSEY | 191,592 | 56,898 | 133,948 | 746 | 77,050 D | 29.7% | 69.9% | 29.8% | 70.2% |
| 5,830 | RED LAKE | 2,450 | 573 | 1,861 | 16 | 1,288 D | 23.4% | 76.0% | 23.5% | 76.5% |
| 21,718 | REDWOOD | 9,277 | 4,546 | 4,722 | 9 | 176 D | 49.0% | 50.9% | 49.1% | 50.9% |
| 23,249 | RENVILLE | 10,437 | 4,340 | 6,072 | 25 | 1,732 D | 41.6% | 58.2% | 41.7% | 58.3% |
| 38,988 | RICE | 14,843 | 5,518 | 9,299 | 26 | 3,781 D | 37.2% | 62.6% | 37.2% | 62.8% |
| 11,864 | ROCK | 5,287 | 2,389 | 2,896 | 2 | 507 D | 45.2% | 54.8% | 45.2% | 54.8% |
| 12,154 | ROSEAU | 5,293 | 1,651 | 3,636 | 6 | 1,985 D | 31.2% | 68.7% | 31.2% | 68.8% |
| 231,588 | ST. LOUIS | 105,183 | 25,246 | 79,529 | 408 | 54,283 D | 24.0% | 75.6% | 24.1% | 75.9% |
| 21,909 | SCOTT | 10,570 | 3,311 | 7,248 | 11 | 3,937 D | 31.3% | 68.6% | 31.4% | 68.6% |
| 12,861 | SHERBURNE | 5,940 | 2,132 | 3,787 | 21 | 1,655 D | 35.9% | 63.8% | 36.0% | 64.0% |
| 16,228 | SIBLEY | 7,436 | 3,854 | 3,577 | 5 | 277 R | 51.8% | 48.1% | 51.9% | 48.1% |
| 80,345 | STEARNS | 32,166 | 13,009 | 19,063 | 94 | 6,054 D | 40.4% | 59.3% | 40.6% | 59.4% |
| 25,029 | STEELE | 10,939 | 4,882 | 6,022 | 35 | 1,140 D | 44.6% | 55.1% | 44.8% | 55.2% |
| 11,262 | STEVENS | 5,137 | 2,220 | 2,910 | 7 | 690 D | 43.2% | 56.6% | 43.3% | 56.7% |
| 14,936 | SWIFT | 6,524 | 2,132 | 4,380 | 12 | 2,248 D | 32.7% | 67.1% | 32.7% | 67.3% |
| 23,119 | TODD | 9,702 | 4,006 | 5,673 | 23 | 1,667 D | 41.3% | 58.5% | 41.4% | 58.6% |
| 7,503 | TRAVERSE | 3,322 | 1,073 | 2,247 | 2 | 1,174 D | 32.3% | 67.6% | 32.3% | 67.7% |
| 17,007 | WABASHA | 7,504 | 3,133 | 4,367 | 4 | 1,234 D | 41.8% | 58.2% | 41.8% | 58.2% |
| 12,199 | WADENA | 5,334 | 2,418 | 2,908 | 8 | 490 D | 45.3% | 54.5% | 45.4% | 54.6% |
| 16,041 | WASECA | 7,217 | 3,570 | 3,633 | 14 | 63 D | 49.5% | 50.3% | 49.6% | 50.4% |
| 52,432 | WASHINGTON | 27,022 | 8,850 | 18,108 | 64 | 9,258 D | 32.8% | 67.0% | 32.8% | 67.2% |
| 14,460 | WATONWAN | 6,445 | 2,823 | 3,615 | 7 | 792 D | 43.8% | 56.1% | 43.8% | 56.2% |
| 10,650 | WILKIN | 4,391 | 1,636 | 2,751 | 4 | 1,115 D | 37.3% | 62.7% | 37.3% | 62.7% |
| 40,937 | WINONA | 17,770 | 6,345 | 11,397 | 28 | 5,052 D | 35.7% | 64.1% | 35.8% | 64.2% |
| 29,935 | WRIGHT | 14,185 | 5,476 | 8,687 | 22 | 3,211 D | 38.6% | 61.2% | 38.7% | 61.3% |
| 15,523 | YELLOW MEDICINE | 7,464 | 2,751 | 4,707 | 6 | 1,956 D | 36.9% | 63.1% | 36.9% | 63.1% |
| 3,413,864 | TOTAL | 1,554,462 | 559,624 | 991,117 | 3,721 | 431,493 D | 36.0% | 63.8% | 36.1% | 63.9% |

519

# MINNESOTA

## PRESIDENT 1960

| 1960 Census Population | County | Total Vote | Republican | Democratic | Other | Rep.-Dem. Plurality | Total Vote Rep. | Total Vote Dem. | Major Vote Rep. | Major Vote Dem. |
|---|---|---|---|---|---|---|---|---|---|---|
| 12,162 | AITKIN | 6,113 | 3,097 | 2,980 | 36 | 117 R | 50.7% | 48.7% | 51.0% | 49.0% |
| 85,916 | ANOKA | 34,511 | 14,114 | 20,324 | 73 | 6,210 D | 40.9% | 58.9% | 41.0% | 59.0% |
| 23,959 | BECKER | 10,389 | 5,090 | 5,257 | 42 | 167 D | 49.0% | 50.6% | 49.2% | 50.8% |
| 23,425 | BELTRAMI | 9,157 | 4,482 | 4,653 | 22 | 171 D | 48.9% | 50.8% | 49.1% | 50.9% |
| 17,287 | BENTON | 7,515 | 3,324 | 4,175 | 16 | 851 D | 44.2% | 55.6% | 44.3% | 55.7% |
| 8,954 | BIG STONE | 4,282 | 1,834 | 2,437 | 11 | 603 D | 42.8% | 56.9% | 42.9% | 57.1% |
| 44,385 | BLUE EARTH | 19,413 | 11,328 | 8,052 | 33 | 3,276 R | 58.4% | 41.5% | 58.5% | 41.5% |
| 27,676 | BROWN | 12,453 | 7,084 | 5,353 | 16 | 1,731 R | 56.9% | 43.0% | 57.0% | 43.0% |
| 27,932 | CARLTON | 12,224 | 4,613 | 7,576 | 35 | 2,963 D | 37.7% | 62.0% | 37.8% | 62.2% |
| 21,358 | CARVER | 10,227 | 6,231 | 3,982 | 14 | 2,249 R | 60.9% | 38.9% | 61.0% | 39.0% |
| 16,720 | CASS | 7,991 | 4,399 | 3,578 | 14 | 821 R | 55.0% | 44.8% | 55.1% | 44.9% |
| 16,320 | CHIPPEWA | 7,574 | 3,915 | 3,643 | 16 | 272 R | 51.7% | 48.1% | 51.8% | 48.2% |
| 13,419 | CHISAGO | 6,754 | 3,822 | 2,907 | 25 | 915 R | 56.6% | 43.0% | 56.8% | 43.2% |
| 39,080 | CLAY | 15,544 | 8,278 | 7,241 | 25 | 1,037 R | 53.3% | 46.6% | 53.3% | 46.7% |
| 8,864 | CLEARWATER | 4,135 | 1,651 | 2,466 | 18 | 815 D | 39.9% | 59.6% | 40.1% | 59.9% |
| 3,377 | COOK | 1,641 | 987 | 650 | 4 | 337 R | 60.1% | 39.6% | 60.3% | 39.7% |
| 16,166 | COTTONWOOD | 7,872 | 5,087 | 2,768 | 17 | 2,319 R | 64.6% | 35.2% | 64.8% | 35.2% |
| 32,134 | CROW WING | 14,614 | 7,727 | 6,835 | 52 | 892 R | 52.9% | 46.8% | 53.1% | 46.9% |
| 78,303 | DAKOTA | 35,273 | 15,032 | 20,150 | 91 | 5,118 D | 42.6% | 57.1% | 42.7% | 57.3% |
| 13,259 | DODGE | 5,943 | 3,769 | 2,170 | 4 | 1,599 R | 63.4% | 36.5% | 63.5% | 36.5% |
| 21,313 | DOUGLAS | 10,506 | 5,594 | 4,871 | 41 | 723 R | 53.2% | 46.4% | 53.5% | 46.5% |
| 23,685 | FARIBAULT | 11,287 | 6,975 | 4,301 | 11 | 2,674 R | 61.8% | 38.1% | 61.9% | 38.1% |
| 23,768 | FILLMORE | 11,444 | 7,507 | 3,926 | 11 | 3,581 R | 65.6% | 34.3% | 65.7% | 34.3% |
| 37,891 | FREEBORN | 17,010 | 8,970 | 8,018 | 22 | 952 R | 52.7% | 47.1% | 52.8% | 47.2% |
| 33,035 | GOODHUE | 16,073 | 10,473 | 5,562 | 38 | 4,911 R | 65.2% | 34.6% | 65.3% | 34.7% |
| 8,870 | GRANT | 4,576 | 2,239 | 2,333 | 4 | 94 D | 48.9% | 51.0% | 49.0% | 51.0% |
| 842,854 | HENNEPIN | 388,181 | 198,992 | 188,250 | 939 | 10,742 R | 51.3% | 48.5% | 51.4% | 48.6% |
| 16,588 | HOUSTON | 7,890 | 4,807 | 3,080 | 3 | 1,727 R | 60.9% | 39.0% | 60.9% | 39.1% |
| 9,962 | HUBBARD | 4,787 | 2,749 | 2,029 | 9 | 720 R | 57.4% | 42.4% | 57.5% | 42.5% |
| 13,530 | ISANTI | 5,694 | 3,067 | 2,599 | 28 | 468 R | 53.9% | 45.6% | 54.1% | 45.9% |
| 38,006 | ITASCA | 17,408 | 6,615 | 10,761 | 32 | 4,146 D | 38.0% | 61.8% | 38.1% | 61.9% |
| 15,501 | JACKSON | 7,502 | 3,591 | 3,898 | 13 | 307 D | 47.9% | 52.0% | 48.0% | 52.0% |
| 9,007 | KANABEC | 4,193 | 2,278 | 1,890 | 25 | 388 R | 54.3% | 45.1% | 54.7% | 45.3% |
| 29,987 | KANDIYOHI | 13,567 | 6,786 | 6,738 | 43 | 48 R | 50.0% | 49.7% | 50.2% | 49.8% |
| 8,343 | KITTSON | 4,165 | 1,937 | 2,218 | 10 | 281 D | 46.5% | 53.3% | 46.6% | 53.4% |
| 18,190 | KOOCHICHING | 7,656 | 3,055 | 4,578 | 23 | 1,523 D | 39.9% | 59.8% | 40.0% | 60.0% |
| 13,330 | LAC QUI PARLE | 6,449 | 3,185 | 3,253 | 11 | 68 D | 49.4% | 50.4% | 49.5% | 50.5% |
| 13,702 | LAKE | 6,180 | 2,276 | 3,888 | 16 | 1,612 D | 36.8% | 62.9% | 36.9% | 63.1% |
| 4,304 | LAKE OF THE WOODS | 1,904 | 835 | 1,053 | 16 | 218 D | 43.9% | 55.3% | 44.2% | 55.8% |
| 19,906 | LE SUEUR | 9,670 | 4,426 | 5,234 | 10 | 808 D | 45.8% | 54.1% | 45.8% | 54.2% |
| 9,651 | LINCOLN | 4,657 | 2,147 | 2,500 | 10 | 353 D | 46.1% | 53.7% | 46.2% | 53.8% |
| 22,655 | LYON | 10,305 | 4,740 | 5,550 | 15 | 810 D | 46.0% | 53.9% | 46.1% | 53.9% |
| 24,401 | MCLEOD | 11,511 | 7,214 | 4,276 | 21 | 2,938 R | 62.7% | 37.1% | 62.8% | 37.2% |
| 6,341 | MAHNOMEN | 2,749 | 880 | 1,864 | 5 | 984 D | 32.0% | 67.8% | 32.1% | 67.9% |
| 14,262 | MARSHALL | 6,777 | 3,006 | 3,759 | 12 | 753 D | 44.4% | 55.5% | 44.4% | 55.6% |
| 26,986 | MARTIN | 12,692 | 8,479 | 4,194 | 19 | 4,285 R | 66.8% | 33.0% | 66.9% | 33.1% |
| 18,887 | MEEKER | 8,560 | 4,857 | 3,678 | 25 | 1,179 R | 56.7% | 43.0% | 56.9% | 43.1% |
| 14,560 | MILLE LACS | 6,830 | 3,913 | 2,886 | 31 | 1,027 R | 57.3% | 42.3% | 57.6% | 42.4% |
| 26,641 | MORRISON | 11,764 | 4,403 | 7,337 | 24 | 2,934 D | 37.4% | 62.4% | 37.5% | 62.5% |
| 48,498 | MOWER | 21,068 | 11,040 | 9,961 | 67 | 1,079 R | 52.4% | 47.3% | 52.6% | 47.4% |
| 14,743 | MURRAY | 6,377 | 3,357 | 3,009 | 11 | 348 R | 52.6% | 47.2% | 52.7% | 47.3% |
| 23,196 | NICOLLET | 9,255 | 5,283 | 3,961 | 11 | 1,322 R | 57.1% | 42.8% | 57.2% | 42.8% |
| 23,365 | NOBLES | 10,594 | 5,636 | 4,947 | 11 | 689 R | 53.2% | 46.7% | 53.3% | 46.7% |
| 11,253 | NORMAN | 5,586 | 2,642 | 2,932 | 12 | 290 D | 47.3% | 52.5% | 47.4% | 52.6% |
| 65,532 | OLMSTED | 27,065 | 16,080 | 10,918 | 67 | 5,162 R | 59.4% | 40.3% | 59.6% | 40.4% |
| 48,960 | OTTER TAIL | 21,843 | 13,747 | 8,054 | 42 | 5,693 R | 62.9% | 36.9% | 63.1% | 36.9% |
| 12,468 | PENNINGTON | 5,759 | 2,537 | 3,204 | 18 | 667 D | 44.1% | 55.6% | 44.2% | 55.8% |
| 17,004 | PINE | 7,687 | 3,450 | 4,211 | 26 | 761 D | 44.9% | 54.8% | 45.0% | 55.0% |
| 13,605 | PIPESTONE | 6,131 | 3,677 | 2,443 | 11 | 1,234 R | 60.0% | 39.8% | 60.1% | 39.9% |
| 36,182 | POLK | 16,909 | 7,528 | 9,346 | 35 | 1,818 D | 44.5% | 55.3% | 44.6% | 55.4% |

# MINNESOTA

## PRESIDENT 1960

| 1960 Census Population | County | Total Vote | Republican | Democratic | Other | Rep.-Dem. Plurality | Percentage | | | |
|---|---|---|---|---|---|---|---|---|---|---|
| | | | | | | | Total Vote | | Major Vote | |
| | | | | | | | Rep. | Dem. | Rep. | Dem. |
| 11,914 | POPE | 5,958 | 3,062 | 2,883 | 13 | 179 R | 51.4% | 48.4% | 51.5% | 48.5% |
| 422,525 | RAMSEY | 186,527 | 77,408 | 108,464 | 655 | 31,056 D | 41.5% | 58.1% | 41.6% | 58.4% |
| 5,830 | RED LAKE | 2,549 | 679 | 1,865 | 5 | 1,186 D | 26.6% | 73.2% | 26.7% | 73.3% |
| 21,718 | REDWOOD | 9,746 | 5,893 | 3,839 | 14 | 2,054 R | 60.5% | 39.4% | 60.6% | 39.4% |
| 23,249 | RENVILLE | 10,857 | 5,885 | 4,958 | 14 | 927 R | 54.2% | 45.7% | 54.3% | 45.7% |
| 38,988 | RICE | 15,031 | 8,248 | 6,752 | 31 | 1,496 R | 54.9% | 44.9% | 55.0% | 45.0% |
| 11,864 | ROCK | 5,297 | 3,469 | 1,823 | 5 | 1,646 R | 65.5% | 34.4% | 65.6% | 34.4% |
| 12,154 | ROSEAU | 5,482 | 2,274 | 3,198 | 10 | 924 D | 41.5% | 58.3% | 41.6% | 58.4% |
| 231,588 | ST. LOUIS | 109,522 | 39,620 | 69,270 | 632 | 29,650 D | 36.2% | 63.2% | 36.4% | 63.6% |
| 21,909 | SCOTT | 9,743 | 3,671 | 6,061 | 11 | 2,390 D | 37.7% | 62.2% | 37.7% | 62.3% |
| 12,861 | SHERBURNE | 5,417 | 2,837 | 2,568 | 12 | 269 R | 52.4% | 47.4% | 52.5% | 47.5% |
| 16,228 | SIBLEY | 7,542 | 4,987 | 2,541 | 14 | 2,446 R | 66.1% | 33.7% | 66.2% | 33.8% |
| 80,345 | STEARNS | 32,581 | 13,522 | 19,026 | 33 | 5,504 D | 41.5% | 58.4% | 41.5% | 58.5% |
| 25,029 | STEELE | 11,301 | 6,795 | 4,491 | 15 | 2,304 R | 60.1% | 39.7% | 60.2% | 39.8% |
| 11,262 | STEVENS | 5,126 | 2,710 | 2,405 | 11 | 305 R | 52.9% | 46.9% | 53.0% | 47.0% |
| 14,936 | SWIFT | 6,928 | 2,848 | 4,062 | 18 | 1,214 D | 41.1% | 58.6% | 41.2% | 58.8% |
| 23,119 | TODD | 10,334 | 5,255 | 5,051 | 28 | 204 R | 50.9% | 48.9% | 51.0% | 49.0% |
| 7,503 | TRAVERSE | 3,590 | 1,463 | 2,122 | 5 | 659 D | 40.8% | 59.1% | 40.8% | 59.2% |
| 17,007 | WABASHA | 8,197 | 4,566 | 3,628 | 3 | 938 R | 55.7% | 44.3% | 55.7% | 44.3% |
| 12,199 | WADENA | 5,329 | 3,082 | 2,240 | 7 | 842 R | 57.8% | 42.0% | 57.9% | 42.1% |
| 16,041 | WASECA | 7,636 | 4,838 | 2,793 | 5 | 2,045 R | 63.4% | 36.6% | 63.4% | 36.6% |
| 52,432 | WASHINGTON | 23,133 | 11,202 | 11,870 | 61 | 668 D | 48.4% | 51.3% | 48.6% | 51.4% |
| 14,460 | WATONWAN | 6,595 | 4,173 | 2,412 | 10 | 1,761 R | 63.3% | 36.6% | 63.4% | 36.6% |
| 10,650 | WILKIN | 4,667 | 2,340 | 2,319 | 8 | 21 R | 50.1% | 49.7% | 50.2% | 49.8% |
| 40,937 | WINONA | 17,780 | 9,271 | 8,484 | 25 | 787 R | 52.1% | 47.7% | 52.2% | 47.8% |
| 29,935 | WRIGHT | 13,658 | 7,180 | 6,452 | 26 | 728 R | 52.6% | 47.2% | 52.7% | 47.3% |
| 15,523 | YELLOW MEDICINE | 7,475 | 3,800 | 3,649 | 26 | 151 R | 50.8% | 48.8% | 51.0% | 49.0% |
| 3,413,864 | TOTAL | 1,541,887 | 757,915 | 779,933 | 4,039 | 22,018 D | 49.2% | 50.6% | 49.3% | 50.7% |

# MINNESOTA

In Minnesota the Democratic party is known as the Democratic-Farmer-Labor party and the Republican party as the Independent-Republican party. Candidates appear on the ballot with these designations.

## ELECTION NOTES

**2004**      Other vote was 18,683 Better Life (Ralph Nader); 4,639 Libertarian (Michael Badnarik); 4,408 Green (David Cobb); 3,074 Constitution (Michael Peroutka); 2,387 Christian Freedom (Thomas J. Harens); 539 Socialist Equality (Bill Van Auken); 416 Socialist Workers (Roger Calero); 4 write-in (John Joseph Kennedy); 2 write-in (Walter F. Brown); 2 write-in (Debra Joyce Renderos); 2 write-in (Martin Wishnatsky); 1 write-in (Joy Elaina Graham-Pendergast); 2,521 scattered write-in.

**2000**      Other vote was 22,166 Reform Party Minnesota (Buchanan); 5,282 Libertarian (Browne); 3,272 Constitution (Phillips); 2,294 Reform (Hagelin); 1,022 Socialist Workers (Harris); 17 write-in (Marcus); 7 write-in (Mooney); 4 write-in (Strickland).

**1996**      Other vote was 24,908 Green (Nader); 8,271 Libertarian (Browne); 4,898 Grassroots (Peron); 3,416 U.S. Taxpayers (Phillips); 1,808 Natural Law (Hagelin); 787 Independent Grassroots (Birrenbach); 684 Socialist Workers (Harris); 347 Socialist Equality (White); 2,903 scattered write-in.

**1992**      Other vote was 3,374 Marrou (Libertarian); 3,363 Gritz (Constitution); 2,659 Herer (Grassroots); 1,406 Hagelin (Natural Law); 990 Warren (Socialist Workers); 958 Fulani (New Alliance); 733 Phillips (Taxpayers); 622 LaRouche (Independent Economic Recovery); 2,499 scattered write-in.

**1988**      Other vote was 5,403 McCarthy (Minnesota Progressive); 5,109 Paul (Libertarian); 2,155 Warren (Socialist Workers); 1,949 Herer (Grassroots); 1,734 Fulani (New Alliance); 1,702 LaRouche (National Economic Recovery); 1,529 Duke (Populist); 1,298 Dennis (American); 489 Winn (Workers League); 3,614 scattered write-in.

**1984**      Other vote was 3,865 LaRouche (Independent); 3,180 Mason (Socialist Workers); 2,996 Bergland (Libertarian); 2,377 Richards (American Populist); 1,219 Johnson (Citizens); 630 Hall (Communist); 260 Winn (Workers League); 232 Serrette (National Alliance); 723 scattered write-in.

**1980**      Other vote was 174,990 Anderson (Anderson Coalition); 31,592 Clark (Libertarian); 8,407 Commoner (Citizens); 6,139 no Presidential candidate indicated (American); 1,184 Hall (Communist); 711 DeBerry (Socialist Workers); 698 Griswold (Workers World); 536 McReynolds (Socialist); 281 scattered write-in. Early unamended canvass gave the state-wide total votes as 954,173 Democratic; 174,997 Anderson Coalition; 31,593 Libertarian; 8,406 Citizens; 6,136 American; 1,117 Communist.

**1976**      Other vote was 35,490 McCarthy (McCarthy '76 Principle); 13,592 Anderson (American); 4,149 Camejo (Socialist Workers); 3,529 MacBride (Libertarian); 1,092 Hall (Communist); 635 Wright (People's); 543 LaRouche (International Development Bank); 370 Levin (Industrial Government); 354 Zeidler (Socialist); 342 scattered write-in.

**1972**      Other vote was 31,407 Schmitz (American); 4,261 Fisher (Industrial Government); 2,805 Spock (People's); 940 Jenness (Socialist Workers); 662 Hall (Communist); 962 scattered write-in.

**1968**      Wallace on the ballot as American. Other vote was 933 Cleaver (Peace and Freedom); 807 Halstead (Socialist Workers); 415 Mitchell (Communist); 285 Blomen (Industrial Government); 584 McCarthy (write-in); 170 scattered write-in.

**1964**      Other vote was 2,544 Hass (Socialist Labor); 1,177 DeBerry (Socialist Workers).

**1960**      Other vote was 3,077 Dobbs (Socialist Workers); 962 Hass (Socialist Labor).

# MISSISSIPPI

## POPULAR VOTE FOR PRESIDENT 1920 TO 2004

| Year | Total Vote | Republican Vote | Republican Candidate | Democratic Vote | Democratic Candidate | Other Vote | Plurality | Percentage Total Vote Rep. | Percentage Total Vote Dem. | Percentage Major Vote Rep. | Percentage Major Vote Dem. |
|---|---|---|---|---|---|---|---|---|---|---|---|
| 2004 | 1,152,145 | 684,981 | Bush, George W. | 458,094 | Kerry, John | 9,070 | 226,887 R | 59.5% | 39.8% | 59.9% | 40.1% |
| 2000 ** | 994,184 | 572,844 | Bush, George W. | 404,614 | Gore, Al | 16,726 | 168,230 R | 57.6% | 40.7% | 58.6% | 41.4% |
| 1996 ** | 893,857 | 439,838 | Dole, Bob | 394,022 | Clinton, Bill | 59,997 | 45,816 R | 49.2% | 44.1% | 52.7% | 47.3% |
| 1992 ** | 981,793 | 487,793 | Bush, George | 400,258 | Clinton, Bill | 93,742 | 87,535 R | 49.7% | 40.8% | 54.9% | 45.1% |
| 1988 | 931,527 | 557,890 | Bush, George | 363,921 | Dukakis, Michael S. | 9,716 | 193,969 R | 59.9% | 39.1% | 60.5% | 39.5% |
| 1984 | 941,104 | 582,377 | Reagan, Ronald | 352,192 | Mondale, Walter F. | 6,535 | 230,185 R | 61.9% | 37.4% | 62.3% | 37.7% |
| 1980 ** | 892,620 | 441,089 | Reagan, Ronald | 429,281 | Carter, Jimmy | 22,250 | 11,808 R | 49.4% | 48.1% | 50.7% | 49.3% |
| 1976 | 769,361 | 366,846 | Ford, Gerald R. | 381,309 | Carter, Jimmy | 21,206 | 14,463 D | 47.7% | 49.6% | 49.0% | 51.0% |
| 1972 | 645,963 | 505,125 | Nixon, Richard M. | 126,782 | McGovern, George S. | 14,056 | 378,343 R | 78.2% | 19.6% | 79.9% | 20.1% |
| 1968 ** | 654,509 | 88,516 | Nixon, Richard M. | 150,644 | Humphrey, Hubert H. | 415,349 | 264,705 A | 13.5% | 23.0% | 37.0% | 63.0% |
| 1964 | 409,146 | 356,528 | Goldwater, Barry M. | 52,618 | Johnson, Lyndon B. | | 303,910 R | 87.1% | 12.9% | 87.1% | 12.9% |
| 1960 ** | 298,171 | 73,561 | Nixon, Richard M. | 108,362 | Kennedy, John F. | 116,248 | 7,886 U | 24.7% | 36.3% | 40.4% | 59.6% |
| 1956 | 248,104 | 60,685 | Eisenhower, Dwight D. | 144,453 | Stevenson, Adlai E. | 42,966 | 83,768 D | 24.5% | 58.2% | 29.6% | 70.4% |
| 1952 | 285,532 | 112,966 | Eisenhower, Dwight D. | 172,566 | Stevenson, Adlai E. | | 59,600 D | 39.6% | 60.4% | 39.6% | 60.4% |
| 1948 ** | 192,190 | 5,043 | Dewey, Thomas E. | 19,384 | Truman, Harry S. | 167,763 | 148,154 SR | 2.6% | 10.1% | 20.6% | 79.4% |
| 1944 | 180,234 | 11,613 | Dewey, Thomas E. | 168,621 | Roosevelt, Franklin D. | | 157,008 D | 6.4% | 93.6% | 6.4% | 93.6% |
| 1940 | 175,824 | 7,364 | Willkie, Wendell | 168,267 | Roosevelt, Franklin D. | 193 | 160,903 D | 4.2% | 95.7% | 4.2% | 95.8% |
| 1936 | 162,142 | 4,467 | Landon, Alfred M. | 157,333 | Roosevelt, Franklin D. | 342 | 152,866 D | 2.8% | 97.0% | 2.8% | 97.2% |
| 1932 | 146,034 | 5,180 | Hoover, Herbert C. | 140,168 | Roosevelt, Franklin D. | 686 | 134,988 D | 3.5% | 96.0% | 3.6% | 96.4% |
| 1928 | 151,568 | 27,030 | Hoover, Herbert C. | 124,538 | Smith, Alfred E. | | 97,508 D | 17.8% | 82.2% | 17.8% | 82.2% |
| 1924 | 112,442 | 8,494 | Coolidge, Calvin | 100,474 | Davis, John W. | 3,474 | 91,980 D | 7.6% | 89.4% | 7.8% | 92.2% |
| 1920 | 82,351 | 11,576 | Harding, Warren G. | 69,136 | Cox, James M. | 1,639 | 57,560 D | 14.1% | 84.0% | 14.3% | 85.7% |

In 2000 the other vote column includes 8,122 votes cast for Green (Nader). In 1996 the other vote column includes 52,222 votes cast for Perot. In 1992 the other vote column includes 85,626 votes cast for Perot. In 1980 the other column includes 12,036 votes for Independent (Anderson). In 1968 other vote was Independent (Wallace). In 1960 other vote was Unpledged Independent Democratic. In 1948 other vote was 167,538 States Rights and 225 Progressive.

## ELECTORAL COLLEGE VOTE 1920 TO 2004

| Year | Total | Republican | Democratic | Other |
|---|---|---|---|---|
| 2004 | 6 | 6 | | |
| 2000 | 7 | 7 | | |
| 1996 | 7 | 7 | | |
| 1992 | 7 | 7 | | |
| 1988 | 7 | 7 | | |
| 1984 | 7 | 7 | | |
| 1980 | 7 | 7 | | |
| 1976 | 7 | | 7 | |
| 1972 | 7 | 7 | | |
| 1968 | 7 | | | 7 AIP |
| 1964 | 7 | 7 | | |
| 1960 ** | 8 | | | 8 BYRD |
| 1956 | 8 | | 8 | |
| 1952 | 8 | | 8 | |
| 1948 | 9 | | | 9 SR |
| 1944 | 9 | | 9 | |
| 1940 | 9 | | 9 | |
| 1936 | 9 | | 9 | |
| 1932 | 9 | | 9 | |
| 1928 | 10 | | 10 | |
| 1924 | 10 | | 10 | |
| 1920 | 10 | | 10 | |

In 1960 the Unpledged Independent Democratic electors voted in the Electoral College for Harry Flood Byrd and Strom Thurmond.

# MISSISSIPPI

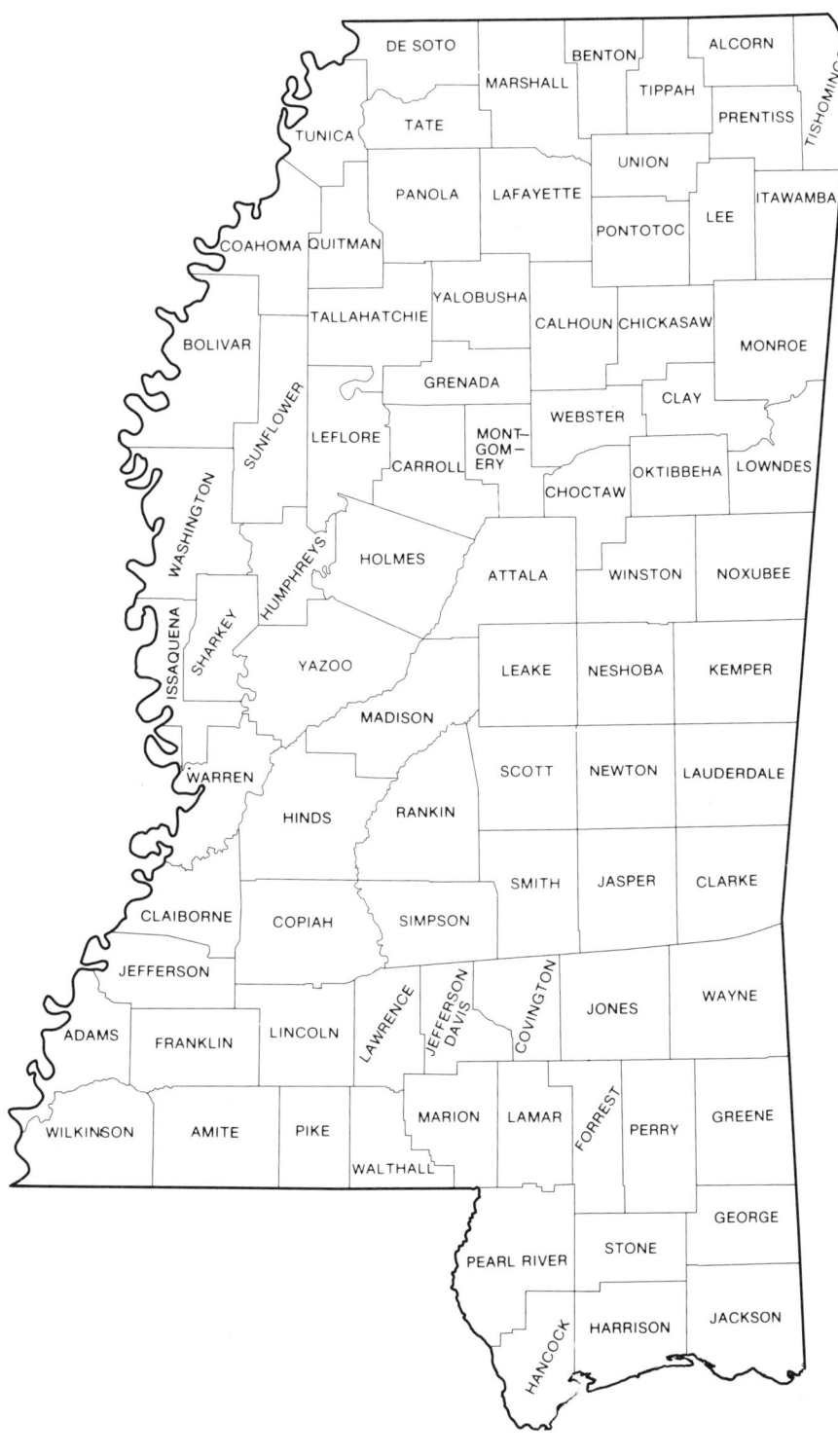

# MISSISSIPPI

## PRESIDENT 2004

| 2000 Census Population | County | Total Vote | Republican | Democratic | Other | Rep.-Dem. Plurality | Percentage | | | |
|---|---|---|---|---|---|---|---|---|---|---|
| | | | | | | | Total Vote | | Major Vote | |
| | | | | | | | Rep. | Dem. | Rep. | Dem. |
| 34,340 | ADAMS | 15,470 | 6,996 | 8,423 | 51 | 1,427 D | 45.2% | 54.4% | 45.4% | 54.6% |
| 34,558 | ALCORN | 14,239 | 8,634 | 5,454 | 151 | 3,180 R | 60.6% | 38.3% | 61.3% | 38.7% |
| 13,599 | AMITE | 7,197 | 4,147 | 3,012 | 38 | 1,135 R | 57.6% | 41.9% | 57.9% | 42.1% |
| 19,661 | ATTALA | 8,207 | 5,014 | 3,145 | 48 | 1,869 R | 61.1% | 38.3% | 61.5% | 38.5% |
| 8,026 | BENTON | 4,247 | 1,969 | 2,245 | 33 | 276 D | 46.4% | 52.9% | 46.7% | 53.3% |
| 40,633 | BOLIVAR | 15,307 | 5,535 | 9,631 | 141 | 4,096 D | 36.2% | 62.9% | 36.5% | 63.5% |
| 15,069 | CALHOUN | 6,389 | 4,131 | 2,234 | 24 | 1,897 R | 64.7% | 35.0% | 64.9% | 35.1% |
| 10,769 | CARROLL | 5,592 | 3,664 | 1,900 | 28 | 1,764 R | 65.5% | 34.0% | 65.9% | 34.1% |
| 19,440 | CHICKASAW | 8,343 | 4,193 | 4,078 | 72 | 115 R | 50.3% | 48.9% | 50.7% | 49.3% |
| 9,758 | CHOCTAW | 4,082 | 2,694 | 1,366 | 22 | 1,328 R | 66.0% | 33.5% | 66.4% | 33.6% |
| 11,831 | CLAIBORNE | 5,355 | 950 | 4,362 | 43 | 3,412 D | 17.7% | 81.5% | 17.9% | 82.1% |
| 17,955 | CLARKE | 7,505 | 5,068 | 2,402 | 35 | 2,666 R | 67.5% | 32.0% | 67.8% | 32.2% |
| 21,979 | CLAY | 9,139 | 4,342 | 4,753 | 44 | 411 D | 47.5% | 52.0% | 47.7% | 52.3% |
| 30,622 | COAHOMA | 10,608 | 3,676 | 6,805 | 127 | 3,129 D | 34.7% | 64.1% | 35.1% | 64.9% |
| 28,757 | COPIAH | 11,388 | 6,374 | 4,961 | 53 | 1,413 R | 56.0% | 43.6% | 56.2% | 43.8% |
| 19,407 | COVINGTON | 8,252 | 5,044 | 3,158 | 50 | 1,886 R | 61.1% | 38.3% | 61.5% | 38.5% |
| 107,199 | DE SOTO | 50,200 | 36,306 | 13,583 | 311 | 22,723 R | 72.3% | 27.1% | 72.8% | 27.2% |
| 72,604 | FORREST | 26,733 | 16,318 | 10,220 | 195 | 6,098 R | 61.0% | 38.2% | 61.5% | 38.5% |
| 8,448 | FRANKLIN | 4,491 | 2,893 | 1,574 | 24 | 1,319 R | 64.4% | 35.0% | 64.8% | 35.2% |
| 19,144 | GEORGE | 8,001 | 6,223 | 1,724 | 54 | 4,499 R | 77.8% | 21.5% | 78.3% | 21.7% |
| 13,299 | GREENE | 5,299 | 3,850 | 1,421 | 28 | 2,429 R | 72.7% | 26.8% | 73.0% | 27.0% |
| 23,263 | GRENADA | 10,105 | 5,872 | 4,180 | 53 | 1,692 R | 58.1% | 41.4% | 58.4% | 41.6% |
| 42,967 | HANCOCK | 17,869 | 12,581 | 5,107 | 181 | 7,474 R | 70.4% | 28.6% | 71.1% | 28.9% |
| 189,601 | HARRISON | 63,267 | 39,703 | 23,076 | 488 | 16,627 R | 62.8% | 36.5% | 63.2% | 36.8% |
| 250,800 | HINDS | 92,500 | 36,975 | 54,845 | 680 | 17,870 D | 40.0% | 59.3% | 40.3% | 59.7% |
| 21,609 | HOLMES | 8,383 | 1,961 | 6,366 | 56 | 4,405 D | 23.4% | 75.9% | 23.5% | 76.5% |
| 11,206 | HUMPHREYS | 4,899 | 1,679 | 3,168 | 52 | 1,489 D | 34.3% | 64.7% | 34.6% | 65.4% |
| 2,274 | ISSAQUENA | 970 | 439 | 516 | 15 | 77 D | 45.3% | 53.2% | 46.0% | 54.0% |
| 22,770 | ITAWAMBA | 9,710 | 6,833 | 2,802 | 75 | 4,031 R | 70.4% | 28.9% | 70.9% | 29.1% |
| 131,420 | JACKSON | 51,049 | 35,134 | 15,572 | 343 | 19,562 R | 68.8% | 30.5% | 69.3% | 30.7% |
| 18,149 | JASPER | 8,009 | 3,855 | 4,117 | 37 | 262 D | 48.1% | 51.4% | 48.4% | 51.6% |
| 9,740 | JEFFERSON | 3,466 | 630 | 2,821 | 15 | 2,191 D | 18.2% | 81.4% | 18.3% | 81.7% |
| 13,962 | JEFFERSON DAVIS | 5,765 | 2,668 | 2,959 | 138 | 291 D | 46.3% | 51.3% | 47.4% | 52.6% |
| 64,958 | JONES | 26,666 | 19,125 | 7,398 | 143 | 11,727 R | 71.7% | 27.7% | 72.1% | 27.9% |
| 10,453 | KEMPER | 4,603 | 2,109 | 2,465 | 29 | 356 D | 45.8% | 53.6% | 46.1% | 53.9% |
| 38,744 | LAFAYETTE | 15,388 | 9,004 | 6,218 | 166 | 2,786 R | 58.5% | 40.4% | 59.2% | 40.8% |
| 39,070 | LAMAR | 20,465 | 16,410 | 3,923 | 132 | 12,487 R | 80.2% | 19.2% | 80.7% | 19.3% |
| 78,161 | LAUDERDALE | 30,166 | 19,736 | 10,292 | 138 | 9,444 R | 65.4% | 34.1% | 65.7% | 34.3% |
| 13,258 | LAWRENCE | 6,306 | 3,956 | 2,308 | 42 | 1,648 R | 62.7% | 36.6% | 63.2% | 36.8% |
| 20,940 | LEAKE | 8,212 | 4,962 | 3,212 | 38 | 1,750 R | 60.4% | 39.1% | 60.7% | 39.3% |
| 75,755 | LEE | 30,621 | 20,254 | 10,127 | 240 | 10,127 R | 66.1% | 33.1% | 66.7% | 33.3% |
| 37,947 | LEFLORE | 12,463 | 4,635 | 7,566 | 262 | 2,931 D | 37.2% | 60.7% | 38.0% | 62.0% |
| 33,166 | LINCOLN | 14,491 | 10,008 | 4,418 | 65 | 5,590 R | 69.1% | 30.5% | 69.4% | 30.6% |
| 61,586 | LOWNDES | 24,268 | 13,690 | 10,408 | 170 | 3,282 R | 56.4% | 42.9% | 56.8% | 43.2% |
| 74,674 | MADISON | 37,724 | 24,257 | 13,268 | 199 | 10,989 R | 64.3% | 35.2% | 64.6% | 35.4% |
| 25,595 | MARION | 11,947 | 7,999 | 3,888 | 60 | 4,111 R | 67.0% | 32.5% | 67.3% | 32.7% |
| 34,993 | MARSHALL | 14,649 | 5,975 | 8,591 | 83 | 2,616 D | 40.8% | 58.6% | 41.0% | 59.0% |
| 38,014 | MONROE | 15,632 | 9,308 | 6,237 | 87 | 3,071 R | 59.5% | 39.9% | 59.9% | 40.1% |
| 12,189 | MONTGOMERY | 5,496 | 3,002 | 2,473 | 21 | 529 R | 54.6% | 45.0% | 54.8% | 45.2% |
| 28,684 | NESHOBA | 10,418 | 7,780 | 2,600 | 38 | 5,180 R | 74.7% | 25.0% | 75.0% | 25.0% |
| 21,838 | NEWTON | 8,487 | 6,165 | 2,280 | 42 | 3,885 R | 72.6% | 26.9% | 73.0% | 27.0% |
| 12,548 | NOXUBEE | 6,097 | 1,723 | 4,346 | 28 | 2,623 D | 28.3% | 71.3% | 28.4% | 71.6% |
| 42,902 | OKTIBBEHA | 16,279 | 9,068 | 7,015 | 196 | 2,053 R | 55.7% | 43.1% | 56.4% | 43.6% |
| 34,274 | PANOLA | 13,440 | 6,769 | 6,615 | 56 | 154 R | 50.4% | 49.2% | 50.6% | 49.4% |
| 48,621 | PEARL RIVER | 19,487 | 14,896 | 4,472 | 119 | 10,424 R | 76.4% | 22.9% | 76.9% | 23.1% |
| 12,138 | PERRY | 5,030 | 3,747 | 1,261 | 22 | 2,486 R | 74.5% | 25.1% | 74.8% | 25.2% |
| 38,940 | PIKE | 16,632 | 8,660 | 7,881 | 91 | 779 R | 52.1% | 47.4% | 52.4% | 47.6% |
| 26,726 | PONTOTOC | 11,240 | 8,480 | 2,660 | 100 | 5,820 R | 75.4% | 23.7% | 76.1% | 23.9% |
| 25,556 | PRENTISS | 9,932 | 6,538 | 3,327 | 67 | 3,211 R | 65.8% | 33.5% | 66.3% | 33.7% |
| 10,117 | QUITMAN | 3,416 | 1,360 | 2,032 | 24 | 672 D | 39.8% | 59.5% | 40.1% | 59.9% |

525

# MISSISSIPPI

## PRESIDENT 2004

| 2000 Census Population | County | Total Vote | Republican | Democratic | Other | Rep.-Dem. Plurality | Percentage Total Vote Rep. | Dem. | Major Vote Rep. | Dem. |
|---|---|---|---|---|---|---|---|---|---|---|
| 115,327 | RANKIN | 54,717 | 43,054 | 11,005 | 658 | 32,049 R | 78.7% | 20.1% | 79.6% | 20.4% |
| 28,423 | SCOTT | 10,228 | 6,395 | 3,802 | 31 | 2,593 R | 62.5% | 37.2% | 62.7% | 37.3% |
| 6,580 | SHARKEY | 3,093 | 1,120 | 1,560 | 413 | 440 D | 36.2% | 50.4% | 41.8% | 58.2% |
| 27,639 | SIMPSON | 10,474 | 7,138 | 3,272 | 64 | 3,866 R | 68.1% | 31.2% | 68.6% | 31.4% |
| 16,182 | SMITH | 7,120 | 5,577 | 1,496 | 47 | 4,081 R | 78.3% | 21.0% | 78.8% | 21.2% |
| 13,622 | STONE | 5,735 | 4,146 | 1,528 | 61 | 2,618 R | 72.3% | 26.6% | 73.1% | 26.9% |
| 34,369 | SUNFLOWER | 10,015 | 3,534 | 6,359 | 122 | 2,825 D | 35.3% | 63.5% | 35.7% | 64.3% |
| 14,903 | TALLAHATCHIE | 6,217 | 2,737 | 3,420 | 60 | 683 D | 44.0% | 55.0% | 44.5% | 55.5% |
| 25,370 | TATE | 11,167 | 6,760 | 4,347 | 60 | 2,413 R | 60.5% | 38.9% | 60.9% | 39.1% |
| 20,826 | TIPPAH | 9,275 | 6,174 | 3,016 | 85 | 3,158 R | 66.6% | 32.5% | 67.2% | 32.8% |
| 19,163 | TISHOMINGO | 8,326 | 5,379 | 2,846 | 101 | 2,533 R | 64.6% | 34.2% | 65.4% | 34.6% |
| 9,227 | TUNICA | 3,129 | 950 | 2,140 | 39 | 1,190 D | 30.4% | 68.4% | 30.7% | 69.3% |
| 25,362 | UNION | 10,819 | 7,906 | 2,839 | 74 | 5,067 R | 73.1% | 26.2% | 73.6% | 26.4% |
| 15,156 | WALTHALL | 6,352 | 3,888 | 2,435 | 29 | 1,453 R | 61.2% | 38.3% | 61.5% | 38.5% |
| 49,644 | WARREN | 19,679 | 11,356 | 8,224 | 99 | 3,132 R | 57.7% | 41.8% | 58.0% | 42.0% |
| 62,977 | WASHINGTON | 19,597 | 7,731 | 11,569 | 297 | 3,838 D | 39.4% | 59.0% | 40.1% | 59.9% |
| 21,216 | WAYNE | 8,794 | 5,562 | 3,193 | 39 | 2,369 R | 63.2% | 36.3% | 63.5% | 36.5% |
| 10,294 | WEBSTER | 5,065 | 3,708 | 1,341 | 16 | 2,367 R | 73.2% | 26.5% | 73.4% | 26.6% |
| 10,312 | WILKINSON | 4,385 | 1,563 | 2,794 | 28 | 1,231 D | 35.6% | 63.7% | 35.9% | 64.1% |
| 20,160 | WINSTON | 9,409 | 5,386 | 3,978 | 45 | 1,408 R | 57.2% | 42.3% | 57.5% | 42.5% |
| 13,051 | YALOBUSHA | 5,971 | 3,278 | 2,656 | 37 | 622 R | 54.9% | 44.5% | 55.2% | 44.8% |
| 28,149 | YAZOO | 10,987 | 5,672 | 5,013 | 302 | 659 R | 51.6% | 45.6% | 53.1% | 46.9% |
| 2,844,658 | TOTAL | 1,152,145 | 684,981 | 458,094 | 9,070 | 226,887 R | 59.5% | 39.8% | 59.9% | 40.1% |

# MISSISSIPPI

## PRESIDENT 2000

| 2000 Census Population | County | Total Vote | Republican | Democratic | Green (Nader) | Other | Rep.-Dem. Plurality | Percentage of Total Vote | | |
|---|---|---|---|---|---|---|---|---|---|---|
| | | | | | | | | Rep. | Dem. | Green |
| 34,340 | ADAMS | 14,879 | 6,691 | 8,065 | 89 | 34 | 1,374 D | 45.0% | 54.2% | 0.6% |
| 34,558 | ALCORN | 12,638 | 7,254 | 5,059 | 101 | 224 | 2,195 R | 57.4% | 40.0% | 0.8% |
| 13,599 | AMITE | 6,408 | 3,677 | 2,673 | 28 | 30 | 1,004 R | 57.4% | 41.7% | 0.4% |
| 19,661 | ATTALA | 7,173 | 4,206 | 2,922 | 22 | 23 | 1,284 R | 58.6% | 40.7% | 0.3% |
| 8,026 | BENTON | 3,481 | 1,561 | 1,886 | 17 | 17 | 325 D | 44.8% | 54.2% | 0.5% |
| 40,633 | BOLIVAR | 13,538 | 4,847 | 8,436 | 64 | 191 | 3,589 D | 35.8% | 62.3% | 0.5% |
| 15,069 | CALHOUN | 5,758 | 3,448 | 2,251 | 31 | 28 | 1,197 R | 59.9% | 39.1% | 0.5% |
| 10,769 | CARROLL | 4,924 | 3,165 | 1,726 | 18 | 15 | 1,439 R | 64.3% | 35.1% | 0.4% |
| 19,440 | CHICKASAW | 7,175 | 3,549 | 3,519 | 36 | 71 | 30 R | 49.5% | 49.0% | 0.5% |
| 9,758 | CHOCTAW | 3,719 | 2,398 | 1,278 | 27 | 16 | 1,120 R | 64.5% | 34.4% | 0.7% |
| 11,831 | CLAIBORNE | 4,615 | 883 | 3,670 | 12 | 50 | 2,787 D | 19.1% | 79.5% | 0.3% |
| 17,955 | CLARKE | 6,919 | 4,503 | 2,368 | 17 | 31 | 2,135 R | 65.1% | 34.2% | 0.2% |
| 21,979 | CLAY | 8,165 | 3,570 | 4,515 | 41 | 39 | 945 D | 43.7% | 55.3% | 0.5% |
| 30,622 | COAHOMA | 9,553 | 3,695 | 5,662 | 48 | 148 | 1,967 D | 38.7% | 59.3% | 0.5% |
| 28,757 | COPIAH | 10,587 | 5,643 | 4,845 | 52 | 47 | 798 R | 53.3% | 45.8% | 0.5% |
| 19,407 | COVINGTON | 6,881 | 4,180 | 2,623 | 30 | 48 | 1,557 R | 60.7% | 38.1% | 0.4% |
| 107,199 | DE SOTO | 34,936 | 24,879 | 9,586 | 302 | 169 | 15,293 R | 71.2% | 27.4% | 0.9% |
| 72,604 | FORREST | 22,251 | 13,281 | 8,500 | 353 | 117 | 4,781 R | 59.7% | 38.2% | 1.6% |
| 8,448 | FRANKLIN | 3,953 | 2,427 | 1,486 | 20 | 20 | 941 R | 61.4% | 37.6% | 0.5% |
| 19,144 | GEORGE | 7,284 | 5,143 | 1,977 | 69 | 95 | 3,166 R | 70.6% | 27.1% | 0.9% |
| 13,299 | GREENE | 4,436 | 3,082 | 1,317 | 14 | 23 | 1,765 R | 69.5% | 29.7% | 0.3% |
| 23,263 | GRENADA | 8,643 | 4,743 | 3,813 | 38 | 49 | 930 R | 54.9% | 44.1% | 0.4% |
| 42,967 | HANCOCK | 14,548 | 9,326 | 4,801 | 285 | 136 | 4,525 R | 64.1% | 33.0% | 2.0% |
| 189,601 | HARRISON | 52,616 | 32,256 | 19,142 | 923 | 295 | 13,114 R | 61.3% | 36.4% | 1.8% |
| 250,800 | HINDS | 87,770 | 37,753 | 46,789 | 711 | 2,517 | 9,036 D | 43.0% | 53.3% | 0.8% |
| 21,609 | HOLMES | 7,422 | 1,937 | 5,447 | 15 | 23 | 3,510 D | 26.1% | 73.4% | 0.2% |
| 11,206 | HUMPHREYS | 3,944 | 1,628 | 2,288 | 17 | 11 | 660 D | 41.3% | 58.0% | 0.4% |
| 2,274 | ISSAQUENA | 941 | 366 | 555 | 4 | 16 | 189 D | 38.9% | 59.0% | 0.4% |
| 22,770 | ITAWAMBA | 8,564 | 5,424 | 2,994 | 70 | 76 | 2,430 R | 63.3% | 35.0% | 0.8% |
| 131,420 | JACKSON | 45,107 | 30,068 | 14,193 | 567 | 279 | 15,875 R | 66.7% | 31.5% | 1.3% |
| 18,149 | JASPER | 6,447 | 3,294 | 3,104 | 23 | 26 | 190 R | 51.1% | 48.1% | 0.4% |
| 9,740 | JEFFERSON | 3,408 | 600 | 2,786 | 6 | 16 | 2,186 D | 17.6% | 81.7% | 0.2% |
| 13,962 | JEFFERSON DAVIS | 5,317 | 2,437 | 2,835 | 11 | 34 | 398 D | 45.8% | 53.3% | 0.2% |
| 64,958 | JONES | 24,340 | 16,341 | 7,713 | 150 | 136 | 8,628 R | 67.1% | 31.7% | 0.6% |
| 10,453 | KEMPER | 4,261 | 1,915 | 2,311 | 18 | 17 | 396 D | 44.9% | 54.2% | 0.4% |
| 38,744 | LAFAYETTE | 12,678 | 7,081 | 5,139 | 385 | 73 | 1,942 R | 55.9% | 40.5% | 3.0% |
| 39,070 | LAMAR | 16,602 | 12,795 | 3,478 | 212 | 117 | 9,317 R | 77.1% | 20.9% | 1.3% |
| 78,161 | LAUDERDALE | 25,970 | 17,315 | 8,412 | 160 | 83 | 8,903 R | 66.7% | 32.4% | 0.6% |
| 13,258 | LAWRENCE | 6,587 | 3,674 | 2,841 | 32 | 40 | 833 R | 55.8% | 43.1% | 0.5% |
| 20,940 | LEAKE | 6,952 | 4,114 | 2,793 | 20 | 25 | 1,321 R | 59.2% | 40.2% | 0.3% |
| 75,755 | LEE | 25,094 | 15,551 | 9,142 | 240 | 161 | 6,409 R | 62.0% | 36.4% | 1.0% |
| 37,947 | LEFLORE | 11,276 | 4,626 | 6,401 | 43 | 206 | 1,775 D | 41.0% | 56.8% | 0.4% |
| 33,166 | LINCOLN | 13,000 | 8,540 | 4,358 | 60 | 42 | 4,182 R | 65.7% | 33.5% | 0.5% |
| 61,586 | LOWNDES | 19,230 | 11,404 | 7,537 | 172 | 117 | 3,867 R | 59.3% | 39.2% | 0.9% |
| 74,674 | MADISON | 29,859 | 19,109 | 10,416 | 219 | 115 | 8,693 R | 64.0% | 34.9% | 0.7% |
| 25,595 | MARION | 10,998 | 6,796 | 4,114 | 58 | 30 | 2,682 R | 61.8% | 37.4% | 0.5% |
| 34,993 | MARSHALL | 12,592 | 4,723 | 7,735 | 73 | 61 | 3,012 D | 37.5% | 61.4% | 0.6% |
| 38,014 | MONROE | 13,360 | 7,397 | 5,783 | 113 | 67 | 1,614 R | 55.4% | 43.3% | 0.8% |
| 12,189 | MONTGOMERY | 4,849 | 2,630 | 2,187 | 15 | 17 | 443 R | 54.2% | 45.1% | 0.3% |
| 28,684 | NESHOBA | 9,066 | 6,409 | 2,563 | 53 | 41 | 3,846 R | 70.7% | 28.3% | 0.6% |
| 21,838 | NEWTON | 7,738 | 5,540 | 2,147 | 28 | 23 | 3,393 R | 71.6% | 27.7% | 0.4% |
| 12,548 | NOXUBEE | 4,954 | 1,530 | 3,383 | 15 | 26 | 1,853 D | 30.9% | 68.3% | 0.3% |
| 42,902 | OKTIBBEHA | 14,804 | 7,959 | 6,443 | 255 | 147 | 1,516 R | 53.8% | 43.5% | 1.7% |
| 34,274 | PANOLA | 11,389 | 5,424 | 5,880 | 41 | 44 | 456 D | 47.6% | 51.6% | 0.4% |
| 48,621 | PEARL RIVER | 16,477 | 11,575 | 4,611 | 173 | 118 | 6,964 R | 70.2% | 28.0% | 1.0% |
| 12,138 | PERRY | 4,359 | 3,026 | 1,285 | 22 | 26 | 1,741 R | 69.4% | 29.5% | 0.5% |
| 38,940 | PIKE | 14,166 | 7,464 | 6,544 | 114 | 44 | 920 R | 52.7% | 46.2% | 0.8% |
| 26,726 | PONTOTOC | 9,510 | 6,601 | 2,771 | 84 | 54 | 3,830 R | 69.4% | 29.1% | 0.9% |
| 25,556 | PRENTISS | 8,482 | 5,101 | 3,287 | 54 | 40 | 1,814 R | 60.1% | 38.8% | 0.6% |
| 10,117 | QUITMAN | 3,413 | 1,280 | 2,103 | 8 | 22 | 823 D | 37.5% | 61.6% | 0.2% |

# MISSISSIPPI

## PRESIDENT 2000

| 2000 Census Population | County | Total Vote | Republican | Democratic | Green (Nader) | Other | Rep.-Dem. Plurality | Percentage of Total Vote | | |
|---|---|---|---|---|---|---|---|---|---|---|
| | | | | | | | | Rep. | Dem. | Green |
| 115,327 | RANKIN | 41,435 | 32,983 | 8,050 | 261 | 141 | 24,933 R | 79.6% | 19.4% | 0.6% |
| 28,423 | SCOTT | 9,206 | 5,601 | 3,548 | 27 | 30 | 2,053 R | 60.8% | 38.5% | 0.3% |
| 6,580 | SHARKEY | 2,903 | 1,074 | 1,706 | 16 | 107 | 632 D | 37.0% | 58.8% | 0.6% |
| 27,639 | SIMPSON | 9,574 | 6,254 | 3,227 | 39 | 54 | 3,027 R | 65.3% | 33.7% | 0.4% |
| 16,182 | SMITH | 6,528 | 4,838 | 1,620 | 26 | 44 | 3,218 R | 74.1% | 24.8% | 0.4% |
| 13,622 | STONE | 5,523 | 3,702 | 1,677 | 65 | 79 | 2,025 R | 67.0% | 30.4% | 1.2% |
| 34,369 | SUNFLOWER | 8,415 | 3,369 | 4,981 | 30 | 35 | 1,612 D | 40.0% | 59.2% | 0.4% |
| 14,903 | TALLAHATCHIE | 5,523 | 2,428 | 3,041 | 20 | 34 | 613 D | 44.0% | 55.1% | 0.4% |
| 25,370 | TATE | 8,693 | 5,148 | 3,441 | 66 | 38 | 1,707 R | 59.2% | 39.6% | 0.8% |
| 20,826 | TIPPAH | 8,403 | 5,381 | 2,908 | 60 | 54 | 2,473 R | 64.0% | 34.6% | 0.7% |
| 19,163 | TISHOMINGO | 6,992 | 4,122 | 2,747 | 64 | 59 | 1,375 R | 59.0% | 39.3% | 0.9% |
| 9,227 | TUNICA | 2,366 | 792 | 1,539 | 9 | 26 | 747 D | 33.5% | 65.0% | 0.4% |
| 25,362 | UNION | 9,311 | 6,087 | 3,094 | 69 | 61 | 2,993 R | 65.4% | 33.2% | 0.7% |
| 15,156 | WALTHALL | 5,895 | 3,476 | 2,356 | 30 | 33 | 1,120 R | 59.0% | 40.0% | 0.5% |
| 49,644 | WARREN | 18,623 | 10,892 | 7,485 | 173 | 73 | 3,407 R | 58.5% | 40.2% | 0.9% |
| 62,977 | WASHINGTON | 18,328 | 7,367 | 10,405 | 70 | 486 | 3,038 D | 40.2% | 56.8% | 0.4% |
| 21,216 | WAYNE | 7,705 | 4,635 | 2,981 | 42 | 47 | 1,654 R | 60.2% | 38.7% | 0.5% |
| 10,294 | WEBSTER | 4,545 | 3,069 | 1,426 | 24 | 26 | 1,643 R | 67.5% | 31.4% | 0.5% |
| 10,312 | WILKINSON | 4,098 | 1,423 | 2,551 | 32 | 92 | 1,128 D | 34.7% | 62.2% | 0.8% |
| 20,160 | WINSTON | 8,368 | 4,645 | 3,672 | 20 | 31 | 973 R | 55.5% | 43.9% | 0.2% |
| 13,051 | YALOBUSHA | 5,228 | 2,470 | 2,674 | 51 | 33 | 204 D | 47.2% | 51.1% | 1.0% |
| 28,149 | YAZOO | 10,516 | 5,254 | 4,997 | 50 | 215 | 257 R | 50.0% | 47.5% | 0.5% |
| 2,844,658 | TOTAL | 994,184 | 572,844 | 404,614 | 8,122 | 8,604 | 168,230 R | 57.6% | 40.7% | 0.8% |

# MISSISSIPPI

## PRESIDENT 1996

| 1995 Census Pop. Est. | County | Total Vote | Republican | Democratic | Reform (Perot) | Other | Rep.-Dem. Plurality | Percentage of Total Vote | | |
|---|---|---|---|---|---|---|---|---|---|---|
| | | | | | | | | Rep. | Dem. | Reform |
| 34,645 | ADAMS | 14,421 | 5,378 | 8,218 | 779 | 46 | 2,840 D | 37.3% | 57.0% | 5.4% |
| 32,781 | ALCORN | 10,962 | 4,960 | 4,964 | 929 | 109 | 4 D | 45.2% | 45.3% | 8.5% |
| 13,581 | AMITE | 5,716 | 2,521 | 2,824 | 351 | 20 | 303 D | 44.1% | 49.4% | 6.1% |
| 18,433 | ATTALA | 6,612 | 3,130 | 3,092 | 383 | 7 | 38 R | 47.3% | 46.8% | 5.8% |
| 7,937 | BENTON | 3,166 | 993 | 1,944 | 209 | 20 | 951 D | 31.4% | 61.4% | 6.6% |
| 41,434 | BOLIVAR | 13,176 | 4,027 | 8,670 | 320 | 159 | 4,643 D | 30.6% | 65.8% | 2.4% |
| 14,862 | CALHOUN | 5,021 | 2,470 | 2,178 | 351 | 22 | 292 R | 49.2% | 43.4% | 7.0% |
| 9,900 | CARROLL | 4,934 | 2,629 | 2,041 | 245 | 19 | 588 R | 53.3% | 41.4% | 5.0% |
| 18,355 | CHICKASAW | 5,930 | 2,535 | 2,971 | 401 | 23 | 436 D | 42.7% | 50.1% | 6.8% |
| 9,123 | CHOCTAW | 3,227 | 1,715 | 1,247 | 247 | 18 | 468 R | 53.1% | 38.6% | 7.7% |
| 11,567 | CLAIBORNE | 4,647 | 784 | 3,739 | 103 | 21 | 2,955 D | 16.9% | 80.5% | 2.2% |
| 17,741 | CLARKE | 6,192 | 3,470 | 2,337 | 366 | 19 | 1,133 R | 56.0% | 37.7% | 5.9% |
| 21,765 | CLAY | 7,564 | 2,948 | 4,267 | 337 | 12 | 1,319 D | 39.0% | 56.4% | 4.5% |
| 31,558 | COAHOMA | 9,611 | 3,441 | 5,776 | 256 | 138 | 2,335 D | 35.8% | 60.1% | 2.7% |
| 28,639 | COPIAH | 8,950 | 4,138 | 4,415 | 375 | 22 | 277 D | 46.2% | 49.3% | 4.2% |
| 17,239 | COVINGTON | 6,305 | 3,219 | 2,628 | 417 | 41 | 591 R | 51.1% | 41.7% | 6.6% |
| 83,567 | DE SOTO | 33,881 | 18,135 | 10,282 | 2,399 | 3,065 | 7,853 R | 53.5% | 30.3% | 7.1% |
| 72,553 | FORREST | 20,442 | 11,278 | 7,965 | 1,094 | 105 | 3,313 R | 55.2% | 39.0% | 5.4% |
| 8,260 | FRANKLIN | 3,339 | 1,586 | 1,381 | 329 | 43 | 205 R | 47.5% | 41.4% | 9.9% |
| 18,230 | GEORGE | 5,943 | 3,311 | 1,888 | 710 | 34 | 1,423 R | 55.7% | 31.8% | 11.9% |
| 11,476 | GREENE | 3,625 | 1,947 | 1,347 | 322 | 9 | 600 R | 53.7% | 37.2% | 8.9% |
| 22,211 | GRENADA | 9,455 | 4,527 | 4,402 | 470 | 56 | 125 R | 47.9% | 46.6% | 5.0% |
| 37,814 | HANCOCK | 11,377 | 5,820 | 4,303 | 1,143 | 111 | 1,517 R | 51.2% | 37.8% | 10.0% |
| 175,240 | HARRISON | 48,235 | 25,486 | 18,775 | 3,726 | 248 | 6,711 R | 52.8% | 38.9% | 7.7% |
| 251,031 | HINDS | 84,509 | 35,653 | 45,410 | 2,929 | 517 | 9,757 D | 42.2% | 53.7% | 3.5% |
| 21,325 | HOLMES | 6,411 | 1,536 | 4,720 | 140 | 15 | 3,184 D | 24.0% | 73.6% | 2.2% |
| 11,533 | HUMPHREYS | 3,813 | 1,382 | 2,305 | 110 | 16 | 923 D | 36.2% | 60.5% | 2.9% |
| 1,676 | ISSAQUENA | 873 | 269 | 546 | 42 | 16 | 277 D | 30.8% | 62.5% | 4.8% |
| 20,902 | ITAWAMBA | 7,237 | 3,490 | 2,987 | 732 | 28 | 503 R | 48.2% | 41.3% | 10.1% |
| 128,494 | JACKSON | 41,625 | 24,918 | 13,598 | 2,947 | 162 | 11,320 R | 59.9% | 32.7% | 7.1% |
| 17,433 | JASPER | 6,153 | 2,615 | 3,170 | 353 | 15 | 555 D | 42.5% | 51.5% | 5.7% |
| 8,549 | JEFFERSON | 3,119 | 489 | 2,531 | 89 | 10 | 2,042 D | 15.7% | 81.1% | 2.9% |
| 14,073 | JEFFERSON DAVIS | 4,866 | 1,890 | 2,663 | 264 | 49 | 773 D | 38.8% | 54.7% | 5.4% |
| 63,001 | JONES | 21,837 | 13,020 | 7,360 | 1,362 | 95 | 5,660 R | 59.6% | 33.7% | 6.2% |
| 10,429 | KEMPER | 3,696 | 1,439 | 2,048 | 188 | 21 | 609 D | 38.9% | 55.4% | 5.1% |
| 33,463 | LAFAYETTE | 10,074 | 4,753 | 4,646 | 580 | 95 | 107 R | 47.2% | 46.1% | 5.8% |
| 33,642 | LAMAR | 12,774 | 8,609 | 3,169 | 925 | 71 | 5,440 R | 67.4% | 24.8% | 7.2% |
| 76,910 | LAUDERDALE | 24,834 | 15,055 | 8,668 | 1,036 | 75 | 6,387 R | 60.6% | 34.9% | 4.2% |
| 12,780 | LAWRENCE | 5,371 | 2,392 | 2,481 | 471 | 27 | 89 D | 44.5% | 46.2% | 8.8% |
| 19,056 | LEAKE | 6,338 | 3,017 | 2,902 | 406 | 13 | 115 R | 47.6% | 45.8% | 6.4% |
| 72,272 | LEE | 21,686 | 11,815 | 8,438 | 1,361 | 72 | 3,377 R | 54.5% | 38.9% | 6.3% |
| 37,410 | LEFLORE | 11,713 | 4,456 | 6,853 | 240 | 164 | 2,397 D | 38.0% | 58.5% | 2.0% |
| 31,417 | LINCOLN | 11,067 | 5,960 | 4,294 | 778 | 35 | 1,666 R | 53.9% | 38.8% | 7.0% |
| 60,823 | LOWNDES | 16,258 | 9,169 | 6,220 | 750 | 119 | 2,949 R | 56.4% | 38.3% | 4.6% |
| 66,282 | MADISON | 24,688 | 14,467 | 9,354 | 759 | 108 | 5,113 R | 58.6% | 37.9% | 3.1% |
| 26,258 | MARION | 9,968 | 5,023 | 4,334 | 585 | 26 | 689 R | 50.4% | 43.5% | 5.9% |
| 32,078 | MARSHALL | 11,340 | 3,272 | 7,521 | 482 | 65 | 4,249 D | 28.9% | 66.3% | 4.3% |
| 37,771 | MONROE | 11,324 | 5,206 | 5,184 | 889 | 45 | 22 R | 46.0% | 45.8% | 7.9% |
| 12,428 | MONTGOMERY | 4,121 | 1,943 | 1,970 | 197 | 11 | 27 D | 47.1% | 47.8% | 4.8% |
| 26,747 | NESHOBA | 7,787 | 4,545 | 2,646 | 560 | 36 | 1,899 R | 58.4% | 34.0% | 7.2% |
| 21,256 | NEWTON | 6,889 | 4,223 | 2,163 | 464 | 39 | 2,060 R | 61.3% | 31.4% | 6.7% |
| 12,407 | NOXUBEE | 4,298 | 1,287 | 2,801 | 119 | 91 | 1,514 D | 29.9% | 65.2% | 2.8% |
| 38,653 | OKTIBBEHA | 12,524 | 6,142 | 5,923 | 395 | 64 | 219 R | 49.0% | 47.3% | 3.2% |
| 32,407 | PANOLA | 9,652 | 3,701 | 5,408 | 513 | 30 | 1,707 D | 38.3% | 56.0% | 5.3% |
| 43,466 | PEARL RIVER | 14,377 | 8,212 | 4,892 | 1,190 | 83 | 3,320 R | 57.1% | 34.0% | 8.3% |
| 11,542 | PERRY | 4,054 | 2,178 | 1,413 | 450 | 13 | 765 R | 53.7% | 34.9% | 11.1% |
| 38,067 | PIKE | 12,435 | 5,403 | 6,302 | 683 | 47 | 899 D | 43.4% | 50.7% | 5.5% |
| 24,236 | PONTOTOC | 7,709 | 4,289 | 2,597 | 774 | 49 | 1,692 R | 55.6% | 33.7% | 10.0% |
| 23,842 | PRENTISS | 7,127 | 3,473 | 3,053 | 574 | 27 | 420 R | 48.7% | 42.8% | 8.1% |
| 10,100 | QUITMAN | 3,445 | 1,121 | 2,186 | 126 | 12 | 1,065 D | 32.5% | 63.5% | 3.7% |

# MISSISSIPPI

## PRESIDENT 1996

| 1995 Census Pop. Est. | County | Total Vote | Republican | Democratic | Reform (Perot) | Other | Rep.-Dem. Plurality | Percentage of Total Vote | | |
|---|---|---|---|---|---|---|---|---|---|---|
| | | | | | | | | Rep. | Dem. | Reform |
| 98,984 | RANKIN | 35,423 | 24,585 | 8,614 | 2,093 | 131 | 15,971 R | 69.4% | 24.3% | 5.9% |
| 25,042 | SCOTT | 7,664 | 4,018 | 3,163 | 466 | 17 | 855 R | 52.4% | 41.3% | 6.1% |
| 6,917 | SHARKEY | 2,619 | 906 | 1,566 | 70 | 77 | 660 D | 34.6% | 59.8% | 2.7% |
| 25,144 | SIMPSON | 7,877 | 4,455 | 2,851 | 525 | 46 | 1,604 R | 56.6% | 36.2% | 6.7% |
| 15,093 | SMITH | 5,765 | 3,371 | 1,858 | 522 | 14 | 1,513 R | 58.5% | 32.2% | 9.1% |
| 12,382 | STONE | 4,281 | 2,288 | 1,551 | 417 | 25 | 737 R | 53.4% | 36.2% | 9.7% |
| 35,752 | SUNFLOWER | 8,225 | 2,926 | 4,960 | 290 | 49 | 2,034 D | 35.6% | 60.3% | 3.5% |
| 15,052 | TALLAHATCHIE | 4,930 | 1,676 | 2,990 | 251 | 13 | 1,314 D | 34.0% | 60.6% | 5.1% |
| 22,737 | TATE | 7,330 | 3,694 | 3,195 | 406 | 35 | 499 R | 50.4% | 43.6% | 5.5% |
| 20,649 | TIPPAH | 6,942 | 3,249 | 2,992 | 661 | 40 | 257 R | 46.8% | 43.1% | 9.5% |
| 18,235 | TISHOMINGO | 6,109 | 2,766 | 2,709 | 609 | 25 | 57 R | 45.3% | 44.3% | 10.0% |
| 8,132 | TUNICA | 1,886 | 557 | 1,263 | 55 | 11 | 706 D | 29.5% | 67.0% | 2.9% |
| 22,875 | UNION | 8,555 | 4,375 | 3,316 | 788 | 76 | 1,059 R | 51.1% | 38.8% | 9.2% |
| 14,304 | WALTHALL | 4,946 | 2,239 | 2,240 | 444 | 23 | 1 D | 45.3% | 45.3% | 9.0% |
| 49,176 | WARREN | 19,385 | 9,261 | 8,774 | 1,259 | 91 | 487 R | 47.8% | 45.3% | 6.5% |
| 66,451 | WASHINGTON | 17,440 | 6,762 | 10,053 | 437 | 188 | 3,291 D | 38.8% | 57.6% | 2.5% |
| 19,864 | WAYNE | 6,490 | 3,219 | 2,652 | 595 | 24 | 567 R | 49.6% | 40.9% | 9.2% |
| 10,500 | WEBSTER | 3,896 | 2,254 | 1,379 | 255 | 8 | 875 R | 57.9% | 35.4% | 6.5% |
| 9,710 | WILKINSON | 4,102 | 1,016 | 2,807 | 226 | 53 | 1,791 D | 24.8% | 68.4% | 5.5% |
| 19,723 | WINSTON | 7,438 | 3,498 | 3,488 | 434 | 18 | 10 R | 47.0% | 46.9% | 5.8% |
| 12,362 | YALOBUSHA | 4,498 | 1,711 | 2,437 | 332 | 18 | 726 D | 38.0% | 54.2% | 7.4% |
| 25,489 | YAZOO | 9,333 | 4,152 | 4,754 | 362 | 65 | 602 D | 44.5% | 50.9% | 3.9% |
| 2,697,243 | TOTAL | 893,857 | 439,838 | 394,022 | 52,222 | 7,775 | 45,816 R | 49.2% | 44.1% | 5.8% |

# MISSISSIPPI

## PRESIDENT 1992

| 1990 Census Population | County | Total Vote | Republican | Democratic | Perot | Other | Plurality | Rep. | Dem. | Perot |
|---|---|---|---|---|---|---|---|---|---|---|
| | | | | | | | | Percentage Total Vote | | |
| 35,356 | ADAMS | 15,877 | 5,831 | 8,255 | 1,753 | 38 | 2,424 D | 36.7% | 52.0% | 11.0% |
| 31,722 | ALCORN | 14,136 | 6,249 | 6,373 | 1,349 | 165 | 124 D | 44.2% | 45.1% | 9.5% |
| 13,328 | AMITE | 5,681 | 2,561 | 2,608 | 498 | 14 | 47 D | 45.1% | 45.9% | 8.8% |
| 18,481 | ATTALA | 7,087 | 3,520 | 3,015 | 529 | 23 | 505 R | 49.7% | 42.5% | 7.5% |
| 8,046 | BENTON | 3,955 | 1,253 | 2,402 | 293 | 7 | 1,149 D | 31.7% | 60.7% | 7.4% |
| 41,875 | BOLIVAR | 14,226 | 4,752 | 8,801 | 593 | 80 | 4,049 D | 33.4% | 61.9% | 4.2% |
| 14,908 | CALHOUN | 6,273 | 3,191 | 2,462 | 607 | 13 | 729 R | 50.9% | 39.2% | 9.7% |
| 9,237 | CARROLL | 3,084 | 1,695 | 1,182 | 200 | 7 | 513 R | 55.0% | 38.3% | 6.5% |
| 18,085 | CHICKASAW | 7,007 | 3,150 | 3,220 | 629 | 8 | 70 D | 45.0% | 46.0% | 9.0% |
| 9,071 | CHOCTAW | 3,768 | 2,026 | 1,435 | 298 | 9 | 591 R | 53.8% | 38.1% | 7.9% |
| 11,370 | CLAIBORNE | 4,412 | 935 | 3,302 | 161 | 14 | 2,367 D | 21.2% | 74.8% | 3.6% |
| 17,313 | CLARKE | 6,934 | 4,207 | 2,259 | 450 | 18 | 1,948 R | 60.7% | 32.6% | 6.5% |
| 21,120 | CLAY | 8,563 | 3,297 | 4,620 | 626 | 20 | 1,323 D | 38.5% | 54.0% | 7.3% |
| 31,665 | COAHOMA | 11,180 | 4,120 | 6,409 | 518 | 133 | 2,289 D | 36.9% | 57.3% | 4.6% |
| 27,592 | COPIAH | 9,449 | 4,600 | 4,397 | 409 | 43 | 203 R | 48.7% | 46.5% | 4.3% |
| 16,527 | COVINGTON | 6,996 | 3,525 | 2,775 | 654 | 42 | 750 R | 50.4% | 39.7% | 9.3% |
| 67,910 | DE SOTO | 27,575 | 16,104 | 8,833 | 2,569 | 69 | 7,271 R | 58.4% | 32.0% | 9.3% |
| 68,314 | FORREST | 22,753 | 12,432 | 8,333 | 1,909 | 79 | 4,099 R | 54.6% | 36.6% | 8.4% |
| 8,377 | FRANKLIN | 3,938 | 1,942 | 1,587 | 393 | 16 | 355 R | 49.3% | 40.3% | 10.0% |
| 16,673 | GEORGE | 9,509 | 4,141 | 2,650 | 1,335 | 1,383 | 1,491 R | 43.5% | 27.9% | 14.0% |
| 10,220 | GREENE | 4,636 | 2,406 | 1,664 | 559 | 7 | 742 R | 51.9% | 35.9% | 12.1% |
| 21,555 | GRENADA | 9,568 | 4,721 | 4,203 | 609 | 35 | 518 R | 49.3% | 43.9% | 6.4% |
| 31,760 | HANCOCK | 13,440 | 6,422 | 4,651 | 2,302 | 65 | 1,771 R | 47.8% | 34.6% | 17.1% |
| 165,365 | HARRISON | 47,407 | 25,049 | 15,268 | 6,855 | 235 | 9,781 R | 52.8% | 32.2% | 14.5% |
| 254,441 | HINDS | 96,024 | 45,031 | 43,434 | 5,341 | 2,218 | 1,597 R | 46.9% | 45.2% | 5.6% |
| 21,604 | HOLMES | 6,014 | 1,694 | 4,092 | 203 | 25 | 2,398 D | 28.2% | 68.0% | 3.4% |
| 12,134 | HUMPHREYS | 4,683 | 1,721 | 2,696 | 258 | 8 | 975 D | 36.7% | 57.6% | 5.5% |
| 1,909 | ISSAQUENA | 990 | 298 | 550 | 79 | 63 | 252 D | 30.1% | 55.6% | 8.0% |
| 20,017 | ITAWAMBA | 8,713 | 4,142 | 3,635 | 918 | 18 | 507 R | 47.5% | 41.7% | 10.5% |
| 115,243 | JACKSON | 44,930 | 25,321 | 13,017 | 6,484 | 108 | 12,304 R | 56.4% | 29.0% | 14.4% |
| 17,114 | JASPER | 6,428 | 2,789 | 3,059 | 568 | 12 | 270 D | 43.4% | 47.6% | 8.8% |
| 8,653 | JEFFERSON | 3,522 | 562 | 2,796 | 156 | 8 | 2,234 D | 16.0% | 79.4% | 4.4% |
| 14,051 | JEFFERSON DAVIS | 5,633 | 2,228 | 2,991 | 382 | 32 | 763 D | 39.6% | 53.1% | 6.8% |
| 62,031 | JONES | 24,430 | 13,824 | 8,035 | 2,523 | 48 | 5,789 R | 56.6% | 32.9% | 10.3% |
| 10,356 | KEMPER | 4,361 | 1,830 | 2,243 | 278 | 10 | 413 D | 42.0% | 51.4% | 6.4% |
| 31,826 | LAFAYETTE | 11,397 | 5,251 | 5,224 | 861 | 61 | 27 R | 46.1% | 45.8% | 7.6% |
| 30,424 | LAMAR | 13,032 | 8,259 | 3,208 | 1,543 | 22 | 5,051 R | 63.4% | 24.6% | 11.8% |
| 75,555 | LAUDERDALE | 27,466 | 17,098 | 8,489 | 1,659 | 220 | 8,609 R | 62.3% | 30.9% | 6.0% |
| 12,458 | LAWRENCE | 6,095 | 2,689 | 2,582 | 765 | 59 | 107 R | 44.1% | 42.4% | 12.6% |
| 18,436 | LEAKE | 7,786 | 3,943 | 3,333 | 497 | 13 | 610 R | 50.6% | 42.8% | 6.4% |
| 65,581 | LEE | 22,501 | 12,231 | 7,710 | 2,041 | 519 | 4,521 R | 54.4% | 34.3% | 9.1% |
| 37,341 | LEFLORE | 12,498 | 5,298 | 6,374 | 611 | 215 | 1,076 D | 42.4% | 51.0% | 4.9% |
| 30,278 | LINCOLN | 13,091 | 7,040 | 4,744 | 1,281 | 26 | 2,296 R | 53.8% | 36.2% | 9.8% |
| 59,308 | LOWNDES | 18,835 | 10,509 | 6,552 | 1,716 | 58 | 3,957 R | 55.8% | 34.8% | 9.1% |
| 53,794 | MADISON | 23,721 | 12,810 | 9,386 | 1,478 | 47 | 3,424 R | 54.0% | 39.6% | 6.2% |
| 25,544 | MARION | 11,613 | 5,776 | 4,654 | 1,162 | 21 | 1,122 R | 49.7% | 40.1% | 10.0% |
| 30,361 | MARSHALL | 12,512 | 3,847 | 7,913 | 689 | 63 | 4,066 D | 30.7% | 63.2% | 5.5% |
| 36,582 | MONROE | 12,224 | 5,994 | 4,933 | 1,255 | 42 | 1,061 R | 49.0% | 40.4% | 10.3% |
| 12,388 | MONTGOMERY | 4,776 | 2,324 | 2,076 | 370 | 6 | 248 R | 48.7% | 43.5% | 7.7% |
| 24,800 | NESHOBA | 10,042 | 6,135 | 3,090 | 794 | 23 | 3,045 R | 61.1% | 30.8% | 7.9% |
| 20,291 | NEWTON | 7,806 | 5,128 | 2,146 | 494 | 38 | 2,982 R | 65.7% | 27.5% | 6.3% |
| 12,604 | NOXUBEE | 5,037 | 1,623 | 3,188 | 203 | 23 | 1,565 D | 32.2% | 63.3% | 4.0% |
| 38,375 | OKTIBBEHA | 13,156 | 6,381 | 5,726 | 984 | 65 | 655 R | 48.5% | 43.5% | 7.5% |
| 29,996 | PANOLA | 11,460 | 4,644 | 6,066 | 729 | 21 | 1,422 D | 40.5% | 52.9% | 6.4% |
| 38,714 | PEARL RIVER | 14,797 | 7,726 | 4,683 | 2,352 | 36 | 3,043 R | 52.2% | 31.6% | 15.9% |
| 10,865 | PERRY | 4,501 | 2,538 | 1,490 | 462 | 11 | 1,048 R | 56.4% | 33.1% | 10.3% |
| 36,882 | PIKE | 13,679 | 6,005 | 6,279 | 1,380 | 15 | 274 D | 43.9% | 45.9% | 10.1% |
| 22,237 | PONTOTOC | 8,366 | 4,595 | 2,965 | 777 | 29 | 1,630 R | 54.9% | 35.4% | 9.3% |
| 23,278 | PRENTISS | 8,526 | 4,317 | 3,385 | 781 | 43 | 932 R | 50.6% | 39.7% | 9.2% |
| 10,490 | QUITMAN | 4,093 | 1,451 | 2,422 | 210 | 10 | 971 D | 35.5% | 59.2% | 5.1% |

# MISSISSIPPI

## PRESIDENT 1992

| 1990 Census Population | County | Total Vote | Republican | Democratic | Perot | Other | Plurality | Percentage Total Vote | | |
|---|---|---|---|---|---|---|---|---|---|---|
| | | | | | | | | Rep. | Dem. | Perot |
| 87,161 | RANKIN | 36,210 | 24,537 | 8,155 | 3,454 | 64 | 16,382 R | 67.8% | 22.5% | 9.5% |
| 24,137 | SCOTT | 9,329 | 5,268 | 3,349 | 691 | 21 | 1,919 R | 56.5% | 35.9% | 7.4% |
| 7,066 | SHARKEY | 2,752 | 1,008 | 1,526 | 145 | 73 | 518 D | 36.6% | 55.5% | 5.3% |
| 23,953 | SIMPSON | 9,326 | 5,358 | 3,213 | 726 | 29 | 2,145 R | 57.5% | 34.5% | 7.8% |
| 14,798 | SMITH | 6,788 | 4,106 | 1,968 | 680 | 34 | 2,138 R | 60.5% | 29.0% | 10.0% |
| 10,750 | STONE | 4,209 | 2,295 | 1,447 | 447 | 20 | 848 R | 54.5% | 34.4% | 10.6% |
| 32,867 | SUNFLOWER | 9,391 | 3,726 | 5,050 | 600 | 15 | 1,324 D | 39.7% | 53.8% | 6.4% |
| 15,210 | TALLAHATCHIE | 5,518 | 2,213 | 2,902 | 380 | 23 | 689 D | 40.1% | 52.6% | 6.9% |
| 21,432 | TATE | 8,371 | 4,196 | 3,519 | 634 | 22 | 677 R | 50.1% | 42.0% | 7.6% |
| 19,523 | TIPPAH | 8,739 | 4,444 | 3,475 | 802 | 18 | 969 R | 50.9% | 39.8% | 9.2% |
| 17,683 | TISHOMINGO | 8,072 | 3,393 | 3,910 | 751 | 18 | 517 D | 42.0% | 48.4% | 9.3% |
| 8,164 | TUNICA | 2,243 | 693 | 1,451 | 96 | 3 | 758 D | 30.9% | 64.7% | 4.3% |
| 22,085 | UNION | 9,742 | 5,173 | 3,714 | 816 | 39 | 1,459 R | 53.1% | 38.1% | 8.4% |
| 14,352 | WALTHALL | 5,967 | 2,728 | 2,476 | 711 | 52 | 252 R | 45.7% | 41.5% | 11.9% |
| 47,880 | WARREN | 20,578 | 10,209 | 8,175 | 2,146 | 48 | 2,034 R | 49.6% | 39.7% | 10.4% |
| 67,935 | WASHINGTON | 19,689 | 7,598 | 10,588 | 795 | 708 | 2,990 D | 38.6% | 53.8% | 4.0% |
| 19,517 | WAYNE | 7,783 | 3,874 | 3,064 | 824 | 21 | 810 R | 49.8% | 39.4% | 10.6% |
| 10,222 | WEBSTER | 4,988 | 2,791 | 1,746 | 444 | 7 | 1,045 R | 56.0% | 35.0% | 8.9% |
| 9,678 | WILKINSON | 4,945 | 1,399 | 3,210 | 307 | 29 | 1,811 D | 28.3% | 64.9% | 6.2% |
| 19,433 | WINSTON | 8,968 | 4,311 | 3,953 | 688 | 16 | 358 R | 48.1% | 44.1% | 7.7% |
| 12,033 | YALOBUSHA | 5,248 | 2,179 | 2,617 | 438 | 14 | 438 D | 41.5% | 49.9% | 8.3% |
| 25,506 | YAZOO | 10,745 | 5,113 | 4,880 | 669 | 83 | 233 R | 47.6% | 45.4% | 6.2% |
| 2,573,216 | TOTAL | 981,793 | 487,793 | 400,258 | 85,626 | 8,116 | 87,535 R | 49.7% | 40.8% | 8.7% |

# MISSISSIPPI

## PRESIDENT 1988

| 1980 Census Population | County | Total Vote | Republican | Democratic | Other | Rep.-Dem. Plurality | | Percentage | | | |
|---|---|---|---|---|---|---|---|---|---|---|---|
| | | | | | | | | Total Vote | | Major Vote | |
| | | | | | | | | Rep. | Dem. | Rep. | Dem. |
| 38,035 | ADAMS | 15,994 | 8,116 | 7,732 | 146 | 384 | R | 50.7% | 48.3% | 51.2% | 48.8% |
| 33,036 | ALCORN | 12,102 | 6,641 | 5,335 | 126 | 1,306 | R | 54.9% | 44.1% | 55.5% | 44.5% |
| 13,369 | AMITE | 6,186 | 3,333 | 2,834 | 19 | 499 | R | 53.9% | 45.8% | 54.0% | 46.0% |
| 19,865 | ATTALA | 7,556 | 4,524 | 2,997 | 35 | 1,527 | R | 59.9% | 39.7% | 60.2% | 39.8% |
| 8,153 | BENTON | 3,309 | 1,565 | 1,718 | 26 | 153 | D | 47.3% | 51.9% | 47.7% | 52.3% |
| 45,965 | BOLIVAR | 14,085 | 6,105 | 7,606 | 374 | 1,501 | D | 43.3% | 54.0% | 44.5% | 55.5% |
| 15,664 | CALHOUN | 5,483 | 3,375 | 2,086 | 22 | 1,289 | R | 61.6% | 38.0% | 61.8% | 38.2% |
| 9,776 | CARROLL | 4,204 | 2,628 | 1,560 | 16 | 1,068 | R | 62.5% | 37.1% | 62.8% | 37.2% |
| 17,853 | CHICKASAW | 6,125 | 3,390 | 2,713 | 22 | 677 | R | 55.3% | 44.3% | 55.5% | 44.5% |
| 8,996 | CHOCTAW | 3,647 | 2,297 | 1,335 | 15 | 962 | R | 63.0% | 36.6% | 63.2% | 36.8% |
| 12,279 | CLAIBORNE | 4,349 | 1,233 | 3,083 | 33 | 1,850 | D | 28.4% | 70.9% | 28.6% | 71.4% |
| 16,945 | CLARKE | 7,098 | 4,522 | 2,576 | | 1,946 | R | 63.7% | 36.3% | 63.7% | 36.3% |
| 21,082 | CLAY | 7,553 | 3,645 | 3,849 | 59 | 204 | D | 48.3% | 51.0% | 48.6% | 51.4% |
| 36,918 | COAHOMA | 11,278 | 4,939 | 6,139 | 200 | 1,200 | D | 43.8% | 54.4% | 44.6% | 55.4% |
| 26,503 | COPIAH | 9,334 | 5,100 | 4,175 | 59 | 925 | R | 54.6% | 44.7% | 55.0% | 45.0% |
| 15,927 | COVINGTON | 6,633 | 4,005 | 2,591 | 37 | 1,414 | R | 60.4% | 39.1% | 60.7% | 39.3% |
| 53,930 | DE SOTO | 20,250 | 14,681 | 5,449 | 120 | 9,232 | R | 72.5% | 26.9% | 72.9% | 27.1% |
| 66,018 | FORREST | 21,318 | 14,249 | 6,953 | 116 | 7,296 | R | 66.8% | 32.6% | 67.2% | 32.8% |
| 8,208 | FRANKLIN | 3,962 | 2,376 | 1,563 | 23 | 813 | R | 60.0% | 39.4% | 60.3% | 39.7% |
| 15,297 | GEORGE | 7,782 | 4,545 | 2,435 | 802 | 2,110 | R | 58.4% | 31.3% | 65.1% | 34.9% |
| 9,827 | GREENE | 4,970 | 2,837 | 1,637 | 496 | 1,200 | R | 57.1% | 32.9% | 63.4% | 36.6% |
| 21,043 | GRENADA | 9,056 | 5,352 | 3,683 | 21 | 1,669 | R | 59.1% | 40.7% | 59.2% | 40.8% |
| 24,537 | HANCOCK | 11,687 | 7,763 | 3,760 | 164 | 4,003 | R | 66.4% | 32.2% | 67.4% | 32.6% |
| 157,665 | HARRISON | 47,754 | 32,892 | 14,439 | 423 | 18,453 | R | 68.9% | 30.2% | 69.5% | 30.5% |
| 250,998 | HINDS | 95,006 | 52,749 | 41,058 | 1,199 | 11,691 | R | 55.5% | 43.2% | 56.2% | 43.8% |
| 22,970 | HOLMES | 8,126 | 2,737 | 5,350 | 39 | 2,613 | D | 33.7% | 65.8% | 33.8% | 66.2% |
| 13,931 | HUMPHREYS | 4,695 | 2,018 | 2,644 | 33 | 626 | D | 43.0% | 56.3% | 43.3% | 56.7% |
| 2,513 | ISSAQUENA | 973 | 424 | 511 | 38 | 87 | D | 43.6% | 52.5% | 45.3% | 54.7% |
| 20,518 | ITAWAMBA | 7,693 | 4,535 | 3,143 | 15 | 1,392 | R | 58.9% | 40.9% | 59.1% | 40.9% |
| 118,015 | JACKSON | 40,364 | 29,830 | 10,328 | 206 | 19,502 | R | 73.9% | 25.6% | 74.3% | 25.7% |
| 17,265 | JASPER | 6,572 | 3,368 | 3,184 | 20 | 184 | R | 51.2% | 48.4% | 51.4% | 48.6% |
| 9,181 | JEFFERSON | 3,401 | 702 | 2,693 | 6 | 1,991 | D | 20.6% | 79.2% | 20.7% | 79.3% |
| 13,846 | JEFFERSON DAVIS | 5,728 | 2,745 | 2,948 | 35 | 203 | D | 47.9% | 51.5% | 48.2% | 51.8% |
| 61,912 | JONES | 24,272 | 16,764 | 7,383 | 125 | 9,381 | R | 69.1% | 30.4% | 69.4% | 30.6% |
| 10,148 | KEMPER | 4,235 | 2,128 | 2,069 | 38 | 59 | R | 50.2% | 48.9% | 50.7% | 49.3% |
| 31,030 | LAFAYETTE | 9,852 | 5,841 | 3,967 | 44 | 1,874 | R | 59.3% | 40.3% | 59.6% | 40.4% |
| 23,821 | LAMAR | 11,746 | 9,145 | 2,535 | 66 | 6,610 | R | 77.9% | 21.6% | 78.3% | 21.7% |
| 77,285 | LAUDERDALE | 26,529 | 18,302 | 7,967 | 260 | 10,335 | R | 69.0% | 30.0% | 69.7% | 30.3% |
| 12,518 | LAWRENCE | 6,223 | 3,682 | 2,517 | 24 | 1,165 | R | 59.2% | 40.4% | 59.4% | 40.6% |
| 18,790 | LEAKE | 6,963 | 4,168 | 2,787 | 8 | 1,381 | R | 59.9% | 40.0% | 59.9% | 40.1% |
| 57,061 | LEE | 20,728 | 13,767 | 6,604 | 357 | 7,163 | R | 66.4% | 31.9% | 67.6% | 32.4% |
| 41,525 | LEFLORE | 12,579 | 6,409 | 5,830 | 340 | 579 | R | 50.9% | 46.3% | 52.4% | 47.6% |
| 30,174 | LINCOLN | 13,297 | 8,710 | 4,534 | 53 | 4,176 | R | 65.5% | 34.1% | 65.8% | 34.2% |
| 57,304 | LOWNDES | 17,331 | 11,258 | 5,993 | 80 | 5,265 | R | 65.0% | 34.6% | 65.3% | 34.7% |
| 41,613 | MADISON | 19,825 | 11,399 | 8,242 | 184 | 3,157 | R | 57.5% | 41.6% | 58.0% | 42.0% |
| 25,708 | MARION | 11,344 | 7,019 | 4,240 | 85 | 2,779 | R | 61.9% | 37.4% | 62.3% | 37.7% |
| 29,296 | MARSHALL | 11,751 | 4,668 | 6,982 | 101 | 2,314 | D | 39.7% | 59.4% | 40.1% | 59.9% |
| 36,404 | MONROE | 11,173 | 6,447 | 4,669 | 57 | 1,778 | R | 57.7% | 41.8% | 58.0% | 42.0% |
| 13,366 | MONTGOMERY | 4,409 | 2,504 | 1,893 | 12 | 611 | R | 56.8% | 42.9% | 56.9% | 43.1% |
| 23,789 | NESHOBA | 9,347 | 6,363 | 2,942 | 42 | 3,421 | R | 68.1% | 31.5% | 68.4% | 31.6% |
| 19,944 | NEWTON | 8,003 | 5,658 | 2,332 | 13 | 3,326 | R | 70.7% | 29.1% | 70.8% | 29.2% |
| 13,212 | NOXUBEE | 4,631 | 1,870 | 2,722 | 39 | 852 | D | 40.4% | 58.8% | 40.7% | 59.3% |
| 36,018 | OKTIBBEHA | 12,289 | 7,126 | 5,100 | 63 | 2,026 | R | 58.0% | 41.5% | 58.3% | 41.7% |
| 28,164 | PANOLA | 10,665 | 5,382 | 5,222 | 61 | 160 | R | 50.5% | 49.0% | 50.8% | 49.2% |
| 33,795 | PEARL RIVER | 14,333 | 10,220 | 3,939 | 174 | 6,281 | R | 71.3% | 27.5% | 72.2% | 27.8% |
| 9,864 | PERRY | 4,347 | 2,983 | 1,326 | 38 | 1,657 | R | 68.6% | 30.5% | 69.2% | 30.8% |
| 36,173 | PIKE | 14,239 | 7,637 | 6,531 | 71 | 1,106 | R | 53.6% | 45.9% | 53.9% | 46.1% |
| 20,918 | PONTOTOC | 7,740 | 4,939 | 2,772 | 29 | 2,167 | R | 63.8% | 35.8% | 64.1% | 35.9% |
| 24,025 | PRENTISS | 7,892 | 4,348 | 3,429 | 115 | 919 | R | 55.1% | 43.4% | 55.9% | 44.1% |
| 12,636 | QUITMAN | 4,351 | 1,832 | 2,497 | 22 | 665 | D | 42.1% | 57.4% | 42.3% | 57.7% |

# MISSISSIPPI

## PRESIDENT 1988

| 1980 Census Population | County | Total Vote | Republican | Democratic | Other | Rep.-Dem. Plurality | Percentage | | | |
|---|---|---|---|---|---|---|---|---|---|---|
| | | | | | | | Total Vote | | Major Vote | |
| | | | | | | | Rep. | Dem. | Rep. | Dem. |
| 69,427 | RANKIN | 29,254 | 22,937 | 6,201 | 116 | 16,736 R | 78.4% | 21.2% | 78.7% | 21.3% |
| 24,556 | SCOTT | 8,488 | 5,522 | 2,939 | 27 | 2,583 R | 65.1% | 34.6% | 65.3% | 34.7% |
| 7,964 | SHARKEY | 2,970 | 1,277 | 1,609 | 84 | 332 D | 43.0% | 54.2% | 44.2% | 55.8% |
| 23,441 | SIMPSON | 9,223 | 6,151 | 3,016 | 56 | 3,135 R | 66.7% | 32.7% | 67.1% | 32.9% |
| 15,077 | SMITH | 6,285 | 4,573 | 1,660 | 52 | 2,913 R | 72.8% | 26.4% | 73.4% | 26.6% |
| 9,716 | STONE | 4,499 | 3,007 | 1,452 | 40 | 1,555 R | 66.8% | 32.3% | 67.4% | 32.6% |
| 34,844 | SUNFLOWER | 9,289 | 4,362 | 4,898 | 29 | 536 D | 47.0% | 52.7% | 47.1% | 52.9% |
| 17,157 | TALLAHATCHIE | 5,547 | 2,633 | 2,881 | 33 | 248 D | 47.5% | 51.9% | 47.8% | 52.2% |
| 20,119 | TATE | 7,449 | 4,553 | 2,872 | 24 | 1,681 R | 61.1% | 38.6% | 61.3% | 38.7% |
| 18,739 | TIPPAH | 7,603 | 4,593 | 2,958 | 52 | 1,635 R | 60.4% | 38.9% | 60.8% | 39.2% |
| 18,434 | TISHOMINGO | 7,052 | 3,646 | 3,378 | 28 | 268 R | 51.7% | 47.9% | 51.9% | 48.1% |
| 9,652 | TUNICA | 2,430 | 896 | 1,510 | 24 | 614 D | 36.9% | 62.1% | 37.2% | 62.8% |
| 21,741 | UNION | 8,591 | 5,511 | 3,044 | 36 | 2,467 R | 64.1% | 35.4% | 64.4% | 35.6% |
| 13,761 | WALTHALL | 5,502 | 3,103 | 2,354 | 45 | 749 R | 56.4% | 42.8% | 56.9% | 43.1% |
| 51,627 | WARREN | 20,170 | 12,507 | 7,437 | 226 | 5,070 R | 62.0% | 36.9% | 62.7% | 37.3% |
| 72,344 | WASHINGTON | 20,687 | 10,229 | 10,222 | 236 | 7 R | 49.4% | 49.4% | 50.0% | 50.0% |
| 19,135 | WAYNE | 7,414 | 4,496 | 2,889 | 29 | 1,607 R | 60.6% | 39.0% | 60.9% | 39.1% |
| 10,300 | WEBSTER | 4,632 | 3,061 | 1,550 | 21 | 1,511 R | 66.1% | 33.5% | 66.4% | 33.6% |
| 10,021 | WILKINSON | 4,223 | 1,528 | 2,678 | 17 | 1,150 D | 36.2% | 63.4% | 36.3% | 63.7% |
| 19,474 | WINSTON | 9,229 | 5,317 | 3,851 | 61 | 1,466 R | 57.6% | 41.7% | 58.0% | 42.0% |
| 13,139 | YALOBUSHA | 5,093 | 2,660 | 2,402 | 31 | 258 R | 52.2% | 47.2% | 52.5% | 47.5% |
| 27,349 | YAZOO | 11,530 | 5,538 | 4,989 | 1,003 | 549 R | 48.0% | 43.3% | 52.6% | 47.4% |
| 2,520,638 | TOTAL | 931,527 | 557,890 | 363,921 | 9,716 | 193,969 R | 59.9% | 39.1% | 60.5% | 39.5% |

# MISSISSIPPI

## PRESIDENT 1984

| 1980 Census Population | County | Total Vote | Republican | Democratic | Other | Rep.-Dem. Plurality | | Percentage | | | |
|---|---|---|---|---|---|---|---|---|---|---|---|
| | | | | | | | | Total Vote | | Major Vote | |
| | | | | | | | | Rep. | Dem. | Rep. | Dem. |
| 38,035 | ADAMS | 17,378 | 9,440 | 7,849 | 89 | 1,591 | R | 54.3% | 45.2% | 54.6% | 45.4% |
| 33,036 | ALCORN | 12,279 | 7,203 | 4,862 | 214 | 2,341 | R | 58.7% | 39.6% | 59.7% | 40.3% |
| 13,369 | AMITE | 6,050 | 3,463 | 2,569 | 18 | 894 | R | 57.2% | 42.5% | 57.4% | 42.6% |
| 19,865 | ATTALA | 8,215 | 4,870 | 3,327 | 18 | 1,543 | R | 59.3% | 40.5% | 59.4% | 40.6% |
| 8,153 | BENTON | 3,466 | 1,737 | 1,715 | 14 | 22 | R | 50.1% | 49.5% | 50.3% | 49.7% |
| 45,965 | BOLIVAR | 15,824 | 6,939 | 8,769 | 116 | 1,830 | D | 43.9% | 55.4% | 44.2% | 55.8% |
| 15,664 | CALHOUN | 5,337 | 3,579 | 1,749 | 9 | 1,830 | R | 67.1% | 32.8% | 67.2% | 32.8% |
| 9,776 | CARROLL | 4,297 | 2,823 | 1,462 | 12 | 1,361 | R | 65.7% | 34.0% | 65.9% | 34.1% |
| 17,853 | CHICKASAW | 5,957 | 3,605 | 2,329 | 23 | 1,276 | R | 60.5% | 39.1% | 60.8% | 39.2% |
| 8,996 | CHOCTAW | 3,663 | 2,491 | 1,166 | 6 | 1,325 | R | 68.0% | 31.8% | 68.1% | 31.9% |
| 12,279 | CLAIBORNE | 4,484 | 1,294 | 3,179 | 11 | 1,885 | D | 28.9% | 70.9% | 28.9% | 71.1% |
| 16,945 | CLARKE | 6,832 | 4,551 | 2,262 | 19 | 2,289 | R | 66.6% | 33.1% | 66.8% | 33.2% |
| 21,082 | CLAY | 8,187 | 4,112 | 4,046 | 29 | 66 | R | 50.2% | 49.4% | 50.4% | 49.6% |
| 36,918 | COAHOMA | 12,810 | 5,759 | 6,839 | 212 | 1,080 | D | 45.0% | 53.4% | 45.7% | 54.3% |
| 26,503 | COPIAH | 10,416 | 5,806 | 4,591 | 19 | 1,215 | R | 55.7% | 44.1% | 55.8% | 44.2% |
| 15,927 | COVINGTON | 6,413 | 4,165 | 2,219 | 29 | 1,946 | R | 64.9% | 34.6% | 65.2% | 34.8% |
| 53,930 | DE SOTO | 17,022 | 12,576 | 4,369 | 77 | 8,207 | R | 73.9% | 25.7% | 74.2% | 25.8% |
| 66,018 | FORREST | 22,576 | 15,719 | 6,786 | 71 | 8,933 | R | 69.6% | 30.1% | 69.8% | 30.2% |
| 8,208 | FRANKLIN | 4,079 | 2,564 | 1,494 | 21 | 1,070 | R | 62.9% | 36.6% | 63.2% | 36.8% |
| 15,297 | GEORGE | 6,028 | 4,346 | 1,655 | 27 | 2,691 | R | 72.1% | 27.5% | 72.4% | 27.6% |
| 9,827 | GREENE | 4,062 | 2,744 | 1,297 | 21 | 1,447 | R | 67.6% | 31.9% | 67.9% | 32.1% |
| 21,043 | GRENADA | 8,521 | 5,181 | 3,325 | 15 | 1,856 | R | 60.8% | 39.0% | 60.9% | 39.1% |
| 24,537 | HANCOCK | 10,344 | 7,662 | 2,630 | 52 | 5,032 | R | 74.1% | 25.4% | 74.4% | 25.6% |
| 157,665 | HARRISON | 46,677 | 33,995 | 12,495 | 187 | 21,500 | R | 72.8% | 26.8% | 73.1% | 26.9% |
| 250,998 | HINDS | 100,468 | 56,953 | 42,373 | 1,142 | 14,580 | R | 56.7% | 42.2% | 57.3% | 42.7% |
| 22,970 | HOLMES | 8,753 | 3,102 | 5,641 | 10 | 2,539 | D | 35.4% | 64.4% | 35.5% | 64.5% |
| 13,931 | HUMPHREYS | 4,914 | 2,309 | 2,596 | 9 | 287 | D | 47.0% | 52.8% | 47.1% | 52.9% |
| 2,513 | ISSAQUENA | 1,034 | 512 | 501 | 21 | 11 | R | 49.5% | 48.5% | 50.5% | 49.5% |
| 20,518 | ITAWAMBA | 7,285 | 4,587 | 2,674 | 24 | 1,913 | R | 63.0% | 36.7% | 63.2% | 36.8% |
| 118,015 | JACKSON | 38,529 | 29,585 | 8,821 | 123 | 20,764 | R | 76.8% | 22.9% | 77.0% | 23.0% |
| 17,265 | JASPER | 6,902 | 3,727 | 3,104 | 71 | 623 | R | 54.0% | 45.0% | 54.6% | 45.4% |
| 9,181 | JEFFERSON | 3,912 | 856 | 3,049 | 7 | 2,193 | D | 21.9% | 77.9% | 21.9% | 78.1% |
| 13,846 | JEFFERSON DAVIS | 5,566 | 2,884 | 2,644 | 38 | 240 | R | 51.8% | 47.5% | 52.2% | 47.8% |
| 61,912 | JONES | 24,954 | 17,586 | 7,298 | 70 | 10,288 | R | 70.5% | 29.2% | 70.7% | 29.3% |
| 10,148 | KEMPER | 4,456 | 2,354 | 2,089 | 13 | 265 | R | 52.8% | 46.9% | 53.0% | 47.0% |
| 31,030 | LAFAYETTE | 9,680 | 6,006 | 3,646 | 28 | 2,360 | R | 62.0% | 37.7% | 62.2% | 37.8% |
| 23,821 | LAMAR | 9,930 | 7,929 | 1,964 | 37 | 5,965 | R | 79.8% | 19.8% | 80.1% | 19.9% |
| 77,285 | LAUDERDALE | 27,267 | 18,807 | 7,534 | 926 | 11,273 | R | 69.0% | 27.6% | 71.4% | 28.6% |
| 12,518 | LAWRENCE | 6,253 | 3,970 | 2,274 | 9 | 1,696 | R | 63.5% | 36.4% | 63.6% | 36.4% |
| 18,790 | LEAKE | 7,516 | 4,663 | 2,845 | 8 | 1,818 | R | 62.0% | 37.9% | 62.1% | 37.9% |
| 57,061 | LEE | 19,730 | 13,312 | 6,208 | 210 | 7,104 | R | 67.5% | 31.5% | 68.2% | 31.8% |
| 41,525 | LEFLORE | 15,212 | 7,550 | 7,443 | 219 | 107 | R | 49.6% | 48.9% | 50.4% | 49.6% |
| 30,174 | LINCOLN | 13,381 | 8,898 | 4,458 | 25 | 4,440 | R | 66.5% | 33.3% | 66.6% | 33.4% |
| 57,304 | LOWNDES | 18,177 | 12,049 | 6,078 | 50 | 5,971 | R | 66.3% | 33.4% | 66.5% | 33.5% |
| 41,613 | MADISON | 17,463 | 9,298 | 8,002 | 163 | 1,296 | R | 53.2% | 45.8% | 53.7% | 46.3% |
| 25,708 | MARION | 11,125 | 7,355 | 3,757 | 13 | 3,598 | R | 66.1% | 33.8% | 66.2% | 33.8% |
| 29,296 | MARSHALL | 10,278 | 4,389 | 5,845 | 44 | 1,456 | D | 42.7% | 56.9% | 42.9% | 57.1% |
| 36,404 | MONROE | 11,860 | 7,387 | 4,437 | 36 | 2,950 | R | 62.3% | 37.4% | 62.5% | 37.5% |
| 13,366 | MONTGOMERY | 4,983 | 3,093 | 1,881 | 9 | 1,212 | R | 62.1% | 37.7% | 62.2% | 37.8% |
| 23,789 | NESHOBA | 9,364 | 6,715 | 2,630 | 19 | 4,085 | R | 71.7% | 28.1% | 71.9% | 28.1% |
| 19,944 | NEWTON | 8,072 | 5,911 | 2,127 | 34 | 3,784 | R | 73.2% | 26.4% | 73.5% | 26.5% |
| 13,212 | NOXUBEE | 5,149 | 2,123 | 2,928 | 98 | 805 | D | 41.2% | 56.9% | 42.0% | 58.0% |
| 36,018 | OKTIBBEHA | 12,697 | 7,574 | 5,097 | 26 | 2,477 | R | 59.7% | 40.1% | 59.8% | 40.2% |
| 28,164 | PANOLA | 11,375 | 5,850 | 5,465 | 60 | 385 | R | 51.4% | 48.0% | 51.7% | 48.3% |
| 33,795 | PEARL RIVER | 13,112 | 9,978 | 3,085 | 49 | 6,893 | R | 76.1% | 23.5% | 76.4% | 23.6% |
| 9,864 | PERRY | 4,744 | 3,098 | 1,415 | 231 | 1,683 | R | 65.3% | 29.8% | 68.6% | 31.4% |
| 36,173 | PIKE | 14,411 | 8,254 | 6,137 | 20 | 2,117 | R | 57.3% | 42.6% | 57.4% | 42.6% |
| 20,918 | PONTOTOC | 7,643 | 5,182 | 2,434 | 27 | 2,748 | R | 67.8% | 31.8% | 68.0% | 32.0% |
| 24,025 | PRENTISS | 7,732 | 4,821 | 2,897 | 14 | 1,924 | R | 62.4% | 37.5% | 62.5% | 37.5% |
| 12,636 | QUITMAN | 4,548 | 2,198 | 2,343 | 7 | 145 | D | 48.3% | 51.5% | 48.4% | 51.6% |

# MISSISSIPPI

## PRESIDENT 1984

| 1980 Census Population | County | Total Vote | Republican | Democratic | Other | Rep.-Dem. Plurality | | Percentage | | | |
|---|---|---|---|---|---|---|---|---|---|---|---|
| | | | | | | | | Total Vote | | Major Vote | |
| | | | | | | | | Rep. | Dem. | Rep. | Dem. |
| 69,427 | RANKIN | 28,308 | 22,393 | 5,874 | 41 | 16,519 R | | 79.1% | 20.8% | 79.2% | 20.8% |
| 24,556 | SCOTT | 9,053 | 5,763 | 3,274 | 16 | 2,489 R | | 63.7% | 36.2% | 63.8% | 36.2% |
| 7,964 | SHARKEY | 3,398 | 1,487 | 1,723 | 188 | 236 D | | 43.8% | 50.7% | 46.3% | 53.7% |
| 23,441 | SIMPSON | 8,924 | 5,983 | 2,894 | 47 | 3,089 R | | 67.0% | 32.4% | 67.4% | 32.6% |
| 15,077 | SMITH | 6,710 | 5,116 | 1,573 | 21 | 3,543 R | | 76.2% | 23.4% | 76.5% | 23.5% |
| 9,716 | STONE | 4,193 | 2,980 | 1,185 | 28 | 1,795 R | | 71.1% | 28.3% | 71.5% | 28.5% |
| 34,844 | SUNFLOWER | 10,111 | 5,178 | 4,913 | 20 | 265 R | | 51.2% | 48.6% | 51.3% | 48.7% |
| 17,157 | TALLAHATCHIE | 5,646 | 2,901 | 2,725 | 20 | 176 R | | 51.4% | 48.3% | 51.6% | 48.4% |
| 20,119 | TATE | 7,557 | 4,677 | 2,846 | 34 | 1,831 R | | 61.9% | 37.7% | 62.2% | 37.8% |
| 18,739 | TIPPAH | 7,301 | 4,706 | 2,566 | 29 | 2,140 R | | 64.5% | 35.1% | 64.7% | 35.3% |
| 18,434 | TISHOMINGO | 6,428 | 3,527 | 2,879 | 22 | 648 R | | 54.9% | 44.8% | 55.1% | 44.9% |
| 9,652 | TUNICA | 2,804 | 1,109 | 1,621 | 74 | 512 D | | 39.6% | 57.8% | 40.6% | 59.4% |
| 21,741 | UNION | 8,617 | 5,837 | 2,766 | 14 | 3,071 R | | 67.7% | 32.1% | 67.8% | 32.2% |
| 13,761 | WALTHALL | 5,541 | 3,305 | 2,219 | 17 | 1,086 R | | 59.6% | 40.0% | 59.8% | 40.2% |
| 51,627 | WARREN | 21,248 | 12,959 | 8,054 | 235 | 4,905 R | | 61.0% | 37.9% | 61.7% | 38.3% |
| 72,344 | WASHINGTON | 23,414 | 12,454 | 10,617 | 343 | 1,837 R | | 53.2% | 45.3% | 54.0% | 46.0% |
| 19,135 | WAYNE | 7,836 | 5,000 | 2,818 | 18 | 2,182 R | | 63.8% | 36.0% | 64.0% | 36.0% |
| 10,300 | WEBSTER | 4,794 | 3,390 | 1,397 | 7 | 1,993 R | | 70.7% | 29.1% | 70.8% | 29.2% |
| 10,021 | WILKINSON | 4,386 | 1,722 | 2,627 | 37 | 905 D | | 39.3% | 59.9% | 39.6% | 60.4% |
| 19,474 | WINSTON | 8,746 | 5,192 | 3,543 | 11 | 1,649 R | | 59.4% | 40.5% | 59.4% | 40.6% |
| 13,139 | YALOBUSHA | 5,285 | 2,934 | 2,337 | 14 | 597 R | | 55.5% | 44.2% | 55.7% | 44.3% |
| 27,349 | YAZOO | 11,412 | 6,275 | 5,037 | 100 | 1,238 R | | 55.0% | 44.1% | 55.5% | 44.5% |
| 2,520,638 | TOTAL | 941,104 | 582,377 | 352,192 | 6,535 | 230,185 R | | 61.9% | 37.4% | 62.3% | 37.7% |

# MISSISSIPPI

## PRESIDENT 1980

| 1980 Census Population | County | Total Vote | Republican | Democratic | Other | Rep.-Dem. Plurality | Percentage Total Vote Rep. | Total Vote Dem. | Major Vote Rep. | Major Vote Dem. |
|---|---|---|---|---|---|---|---|---|---|---|
| 38,035 | ADAMS | 15,363 | 7,523 | 7,228 | 612 | 295 R | 49.0% | 47.0% | 51.0% | 49.0% |
| 33,036 | ALCORN | 12,595 | 5,196 | 6,242 | 1,157 | 1,046 D | 41.3% | 49.6% | 45.4% | 54.6% |
| 13,369 | AMITE | 5,971 | 2,653 | 3,229 | 89 | 576 D | 44.4% | 54.1% | 45.1% | 54.9% |
| 19,865 | ATTALA | 8,214 | 3,975 | 4,117 | 122 | 142 D | 48.4% | 50.1% | 49.1% | 50.9% |
| 8,153 | BENTON | 3,427 | 1,254 | 2,094 | 79 | 840 D | 36.6% | 61.1% | 37.5% | 62.5% |
| 45,965 | BOLIVAR | 14,491 | 5,148 | 8,839 | 504 | 3,691 D | 35.5% | 61.0% | 36.8% | 63.2% |
| 15,664 | CALHOUN | 6,019 | 2,579 | 3,295 | 145 | 716 D | 42.8% | 54.7% | 43.9% | 56.1% |
| 9,776 | CARROLL | 4,228 | 2,153 | 2,037 | 38 | 116 R | 50.9% | 48.2% | 51.4% | 48.6% |
| 17,853 | CHICKASAW | 6,329 | 2,540 | 3,622 | 167 | 1,082 D | 40.1% | 57.2% | 41.2% | 58.8% |
| 8,996 | CHOCTAW | 3,695 | 1,927 | 1,729 | 39 | 198 R | 52.2% | 46.8% | 52.7% | 47.3% |
| 12,279 | CLAIBORNE | 4,228 | 1,129 | 3,032 | 67 | 1,903 D | 26.7% | 71.7% | 27.1% | 72.9% |
| 16,945 | CLARKE | 6,721 | 3,303 | 3,303 | 115 | | 49.1% | 49.1% | 50.0% | 50.0% |
| 21,082 | CLAY | 7,964 | 3,439 | 4,275 | 250 | 836 D | 43.2% | 53.7% | 44.6% | 55.4% |
| 36,918 | COAHOMA | 12,015 | 4,592 | 7,030 | 393 | 2,438 D | 38.2% | 58.5% | 39.5% | 60.5% |
| 26,503 | COPIAH | 10,140 | 4,461 | 5,517 | 162 | 1,056 D | 44.0% | 54.4% | 44.7% | 55.3% |
| 15,927 | COVINGTON | 6,531 | 3,471 | 2,956 | 104 | 515 R | 53.1% | 45.3% | 54.0% | 46.0% |
| 53,930 | DE SOTO | 16,419 | 9,655 | 6,344 | 420 | 3,311 R | 58.8% | 38.6% | 60.3% | 39.7% |
| 66,018 | FORREST | 21,327 | 12,656 | 8,274 | 397 | 4,382 R | 59.3% | 38.8% | 60.5% | 39.5% |
| 8,208 | FRANKLIN | 4,109 | 2,026 | 2,040 | 43 | 14 D | 49.3% | 49.6% | 49.8% | 50.2% |
| 15,297 | GEORGE | 5,932 | 3,052 | 2,757 | 123 | 295 R | 51.4% | 46.5% | 52.5% | 47.5% |
| 9,827 | GREENE | 3,541 | 1,772 | 1,740 | 29 | 32 R | 50.0% | 49.1% | 50.5% | 49.5% |
| 21,043 | GRENADA | 8,300 | 3,993 | 4,182 | 125 | 189 D | 48.1% | 50.4% | 48.8% | 51.2% |
| 24,537 | HANCOCK | 8,915 | 5,088 | 3,544 | 283 | 1,544 R | 57.1% | 39.8% | 58.9% | 41.1% |
| 157,665 | HARRISON | 42,888 | 25,175 | 16,318 | 1,395 | 8,857 R | 58.7% | 38.0% | 60.7% | 39.3% |
| 250,998 | HINDS | 90,074 | 48,135 | 39,369 | 2,570 | 8,766 R | 53.4% | 43.7% | 55.0% | 45.0% |
| 22,970 | HOLMES | 8,336 | 2,693 | 5,463 | 180 | 2,770 D | 32.3% | 65.5% | 33.0% | 67.0% |
| 13,931 | HUMPHREYS | 5,020 | 1,841 | 2,970 | 209 | 1,129 D | 36.7% | 59.2% | 38.3% | 61.7% |
| 2,513 | ISSAQUENA | 968 | 349 | 598 | 21 | 249 D | 36.1% | 61.8% | 36.9% | 63.1% |
| 20,518 | ITAWAMBA | 7,853 | 2,906 | 4,852 | 95 | 1,946 D | 37.0% | 61.8% | 37.5% | 62.5% |
| 118,015 | JACKSON | 35,958 | 22,498 | 12,226 | 1,234 | 10,272 R | 62.6% | 34.0% | 64.8% | 35.2% |
| 17,265 | JASPER | 6,673 | 2,781 | 3,813 | 79 | 1,032 D | 41.7% | 57.1% | 42.2% | 57.8% |
| 9,181 | JEFFERSON | 3,724 | 751 | 2,871 | 102 | 2,120 D | 20.2% | 77.1% | 20.7% | 79.3% |
| 13,846 | JEFFERSON DAVIS | 6,187 | 2,280 | 3,831 | 76 | 1,551 D | 36.9% | 61.9% | 37.3% | 62.7% |
| 61,912 | JONES | 24,289 | 12,900 | 11,117 | 272 | 1,783 R | 53.1% | 45.8% | 53.7% | 46.3% |
| 10,148 | KEMPER | 4,439 | 1,822 | 2,601 | 16 | 779 D | 41.0% | 58.6% | 41.2% | 58.8% |
| 31,030 | LAFAYETTE | 9,571 | 4,366 | 4,887 | 318 | 521 D | 45.6% | 51.1% | 47.2% | 52.8% |
| 23,821 | LAMAR | 8,546 | 5,395 | 3,005 | 146 | 2,390 R | 63.1% | 35.2% | 64.2% | 35.8% |
| 77,285 | LAUDERDALE | 26,119 | 14,727 | 9,918 | 1,474 | 4,809 R | 56.4% | 38.0% | 59.8% | 40.2% |
| 12,518 | LAWRENCE | 5,560 | 2,781 | 2,692 | 87 | 89 R | 50.0% | 48.4% | 50.8% | 49.2% |
| 18,790 | LEAKE | 7,738 | 3,624 | 4,033 | 81 | 409 D | 46.8% | 52.1% | 47.3% | 52.7% |
| 57,061 | LEE | 18,889 | 8,326 | 10,047 | 516 | 1,721 D | 44.1% | 53.2% | 45.3% | 54.7% |
| 41,525 | LEFLORE | 13,675 | 5,798 | 7,498 | 379 | 1,700 D | 42.4% | 54.8% | 43.6% | 56.4% |
| 30,174 | LINCOLN | 12,610 | 7,286 | 5,213 | 111 | 2,073 R | 57.8% | 41.3% | 58.3% | 41.7% |
| 57,304 | LOWNDES | 16,355 | 9,973 | 6,187 | 195 | 3,786 R | 61.0% | 37.8% | 61.7% | 38.3% |
| 41,613 | MADISON | 14,039 | 6,024 | 7,621 | 394 | 1,597 D | 42.9% | 54.3% | 44.1% | 55.9% |
| 25,708 | MARION | 10,707 | 5,218 | 5,366 | 123 | 148 D | 48.7% | 50.1% | 49.3% | 50.7% |
| 29,296 | MARSHALL | 10,848 | 3,455 | 7,153 | 240 | 3,698 D | 31.8% | 65.9% | 32.6% | 67.4% |
| 36,404 | MONROE | 12,239 | 4,793 | 6,998 | 448 | 2,205 D | 39.2% | 57.2% | 40.6% | 59.4% |
| 13,366 | MONTGOMERY | 5,326 | 2,479 | 2,730 | 117 | 251 D | 46.5% | 51.3% | 47.6% | 52.4% |
| 23,789 | NESHOBA | 9,149 | 5,165 | 3,872 | 112 | 1,293 R | 56.5% | 42.3% | 57.2% | 42.8% |
| 19,944 | NEWTON | 7,941 | 4,317 | 3,455 | 169 | 862 R | 54.4% | 43.5% | 55.5% | 44.5% |
| 13,212 | NOXUBEE | 5,555 | 1,970 | 3,434 | 151 | 1,464 D | 35.5% | 61.8% | 36.5% | 63.5% |
| 36,018 | OKTIBBEHA | 12,675 | 6,300 | 6,039 | 336 | 261 R | 49.7% | 47.6% | 51.1% | 48.9% |
| 28,164 | PANOLA | 10,728 | 4,219 | 6,179 | 330 | 1,960 D | 39.3% | 57.6% | 40.6% | 59.4% |
| 33,795 | PEARL RIVER | 12,141 | 6,822 | 5,028 | 291 | 1,794 R | 56.2% | 41.4% | 57.6% | 42.4% |
| 9,864 | PERRY | 4,263 | 2,255 | 1,957 | 51 | 298 R | 52.9% | 45.9% | 53.5% | 46.5% |
| 36,173 | PIKE | 13,716 | 6,661 | 6,694 | 361 | 33 D | 48.6% | 48.8% | 49.9% | 50.1% |
| 20,918 | PONTOTOC | 7,802 | 3,198 | 4,499 | 105 | 1,301 D | 41.0% | 57.7% | 41.5% | 58.5% |
| 24,025 | PRENTISS | 8,178 | 3,264 | 4,832 | 82 | 1,568 D | 39.9% | 59.1% | 40.3% | 59.7% |
| 12,636 | QUITMAN | 4,810 | 1,691 | 2,926 | 193 | 1,235 D | 35.2% | 60.8% | 36.6% | 63.4% |

# MISSISSIPPI

## PRESIDENT 1980

| 1980 Census Population | County | Total Vote | Republican | Democratic | Other | Rep.-Dem. Plurality | Percentage | | | |
|---|---|---|---|---|---|---|---|---|---|---|
| | | | | | | | Total Vote | | Major Vote | |
| | | | | | | | Rep. | Dem. | Rep. | Dem. |
| 69,427 | RANKIN | 25,132 | 16,650 | 8,047 | 435 | 8,603 R | 66.3% | 32.0% | 67.4% | 32.6% |
| 24,556 | SCOTT | 8,832 | 4,645 | 4,043 | 144 | 602 R | 52.6% | 45.8% | 53.5% | 46.5% |
| 7,964 | SHARKEY | 3,021 | 996 | 1,957 | 68 | 961 D | 33.0% | 64.8% | 33.7% | 66.3% |
| 23,441 | SIMPSON | 9,334 | 5,190 | 4,015 | 129 | 1,175 R | 55.6% | 43.0% | 56.4% | 43.6% |
| 15,077 | SMITH | 6,340 | 3,772 | 2,474 | 94 | 1,298 R | 59.5% | 39.0% | 60.4% | 39.6% |
| 9,716 | STONE | 3,837 | 1,888 | 1,821 | 128 | 67 R | 49.2% | 47.5% | 50.9% | 49.1% |
| 34,844 | SUNFLOWER | 8,927 | 3,728 | 5,035 | 164 | 1,307 D | 41.8% | 56.4% | 42.5% | 57.5% |
| 17,157 | TALLAHATCHIE | 5,776 | 2,183 | 3,467 | 126 | 1,284 D | 37.8% | 60.0% | 38.6% | 61.4% |
| 20,119 | TATE | 7,366 | 3,343 | 3,892 | 131 | 549 D | 45.4% | 52.8% | 46.2% | 53.8% |
| 18,739 | TIPPAH | 7,423 | 3,338 | 3,878 | 207 | 540 D | 45.0% | 52.2% | 46.3% | 53.7% |
| 18,434 | TISHOMINGO | 7,221 | 2,489 | 4,595 | 137 | 2,106 D | 34.5% | 63.6% | 35.1% | 64.9% |
| 9,652 | TUNICA | 3,205 | 954 | 2,198 | 53 | 1,244 D | 29.8% | 68.6% | 30.3% | 69.7% |
| 21,741 | UNION | 8,715 | 3,545 | 5,001 | 169 | 1,456 D | 40.7% | 57.4% | 41.5% | 58.5% |
| 13,761 | WALTHALL | 5,762 | 2,703 | 2,960 | 99 | 257 D | 46.9% | 51.4% | 47.7% | 52.3% |
| 51,627 | WARREN | 18,128 | 10,151 | 7,489 | 488 | 2,662 R | 56.0% | 41.3% | 57.5% | 42.5% |
| 72,344 | WASHINGTON | 20,117 | 8,978 | 10,722 | 417 | 1,744 D | 44.6% | 53.3% | 45.6% | 54.4% |
| 19,135 | WAYNE | 7,383 | 3,844 | 3,494 | 45 | 350 R | 52.1% | 47.3% | 52.4% | 47.6% |
| 10,300 | WEBSTER | 4,712 | 2,386 | 2,178 | 148 | 208 R | 50.6% | 46.2% | 52.3% | 47.7% |
| 10,021 | WILKINSON | 4,500 | 1,442 | 2,981 | 77 | 1,539 D | 32.0% | 66.2% | 32.6% | 67.4% |
| 19,474 | WINSTON | 8,545 | 3,998 | 4,416 | 131 | 418 D | 46.8% | 51.7% | 47.5% | 52.5% |
| 13,139 | YALOBUSHA | 5,783 | 2,224 | 3,432 | 127 | 1,208 D | 38.5% | 59.3% | 39.3% | 60.7% |
| 27,349 | YAZOO | 10,498 | 4,819 | 5,468 | 211 | 649 D | 45.9% | 52.1% | 46.8% | 53.2% |
| 2,520,638 | TOTAL | 892,620 | 441,089 | 429,281 | 22,250 | 11,808 R | 49.4% | 48.1% | 50.7% | 49.3% |

# MISSISSIPPI

## PRESIDENT 1976

| 1970 Census Population | County | Total Vote | Republican | Democratic | Other | Rep.-Dem. Plurality | Percentage Total Vote Rep. | Dem. | Major Vote Rep. | Dem. |
|---|---|---|---|---|---|---|---|---|---|---|
| 37,293 | ADAMS | 13,861 | 6,431 | 6,619 | 811 | 188 D | 46.4% | 47.8% | 49.3% | 50.7% |
| 27,179 | ALCORN | 10,770 | 3,430 | 6,995 | 345 | 3,565 D | 31.8% | 64.9% | 32.9% | 67.1% |
| 13,763 | AMITE | 4,999 | 2,256 | 2,574 | 169 | 318 D | 45.1% | 51.5% | 46.7% | 53.3% |
| 19,570 | ATTALA | 7,423 | 3,146 | 4,068 | 209 | 922 D | 42.4% | 54.8% | 43.6% | 56.4% |
| 7,505 | BENTON | 3,209 | 790 | 2,375 | 44 | 1,585 D | 24.6% | 74.0% | 25.0% | 75.0% |
| 49,409 | BOLIVAR | 12,875 | 5,136 | 7,561 | 178 | 2,425 D | 39.9% | 58.7% | 40.5% | 59.5% |
| 14,623 | CALHOUN | 4,788 | 1,892 | 2,724 | 172 | 832 D | 39.5% | 56.9% | 41.0% | 59.0% |
| 9,397 | CARROLL | 3,167 | 1,561 | 1,566 | 40 | 5 D | 49.3% | 49.4% | 49.9% | 50.1% |
| 16,805 | CHICKASAW | 5,723 | 2,581 | 2,891 | 251 | 310 D | 45.1% | 50.5% | 47.2% | 52.8% |
| 8,440 | CHOCTAW | 3,172 | 1,562 | 1,520 | 90 | 42 R | 49.2% | 47.9% | 50.7% | 49.3% |
| 10,086 | CLAIBORNE | 3,852 | 1,078 | 2,657 | 117 | 1,579 D | 28.0% | 69.0% | 28.9% | 71.1% |
| 15,049 | CLARKE | 5,995 | 2,935 | 2,816 | 244 | 119 R | 49.0% | 47.0% | 51.0% | 49.0% |
| 18,840 | CLAY | 6,837 | 3,017 | 3,514 | 306 | 497 D | 44.1% | 51.4% | 46.2% | 53.8% |
| 40,447 | COAHOMA | 11,113 | 4,269 | 6,412 | 432 | 2,143 D | 38.4% | 57.7% | 40.0% | 60.0% |
| 24,749 | COPIAH | 8,646 | 4,108 | 4,267 | 271 | 159 D | 47.5% | 49.4% | 49.1% | 50.9% |
| 14,002 | COVINGTON | 5,568 | 2,591 | 2,862 | 115 | 271 D | 46.5% | 51.4% | 47.5% | 52.5% |
| 35,885 | DE SOTO | 14,312 | 6,240 | 7,756 | 316 | 1,516 D | 43.6% | 54.2% | 44.6% | 55.4% |
| 57,849 | FORREST | 19,120 | 10,770 | 7,914 | 436 | 2,856 R | 56.3% | 41.4% | 57.6% | 42.4% |
| 8,011 | FRANKLIN | 3,395 | 1,719 | 1,578 | 98 | 141 R | 50.6% | 46.5% | 52.1% | 47.9% |
| 12,459 | GEORGE | 5,229 | 1,957 | 3,072 | 200 | 1,115 D | 37.4% | 58.7% | 38.9% | 61.1% |
| 8,545 | GREENE | 3,770 | 1,538 | 2,127 | 105 | 589 D | 40.8% | 56.4% | 42.0% | 58.0% |
| 19,854 | GRENADA | 7,020 | 3,569 | 3,263 | 188 | 306 R | 50.8% | 46.5% | 52.2% | 47.8% |
| 17,387 | HANCOCK | 7,842 | 3,765 | 3,855 | 222 | 90 D | 48.0% | 49.2% | 49.4% | 50.6% |
| 134,582 | HARRISON | 37,139 | 19,207 | 16,569 | 1,363 | 2,638 R | 51.7% | 44.6% | 53.7% | 46.3% |
| 214,973 | HINDS | 75,756 | 45,803 | 28,748 | 1,205 | 17,055 R | 60.5% | 37.9% | 61.4% | 38.6% |
| 23,120 | HOLMES | 7,203 | 2,438 | 4,616 | 149 | 2,178 D | 33.8% | 64.1% | 34.6% | 65.4% |
| 14,601 | HUMPHREYS | 3,774 | 1,445 | 2,172 | 157 | 727 D | 38.3% | 57.6% | 40.0% | 60.0% |
| 2,737 | ISSAQUENA | 954 | 325 | 567 | 62 | 242 D | 34.1% | 59.4% | 36.4% | 63.6% |
| 16,847 | ITAWAMBA | 6,705 | 2,153 | 4,480 | 72 | 2,327 D | 32.1% | 66.8% | 32.5% | 67.5% |
| 87,975 | JACKSON | 31,082 | 17,177 | 12,533 | 1,372 | 4,644 R | 55.3% | 40.3% | 57.8% | 42.2% |
| 15,994 | JASPER | 5,513 | 2,356 | 3,109 | 48 | 753 D | 42.7% | 56.4% | 43.1% | 56.9% |
| 9,295 | JEFFERSON | 3,426 | 782 | 2,562 | 82 | 1,780 D | 22.8% | 74.8% | 23.4% | 76.6% |
| 12,936 | JEFFERSON DAVIS | 4,698 | 1,868 | 2,747 | 83 | 879 D | 39.8% | 58.5% | 40.5% | 59.5% |
| 56,357 | JONES | 21,552 | 11,098 | 10,139 | 315 | 959 R | 51.5% | 47.0% | 52.3% | 47.7% |
| 10,233 | KEMPER | 4,160 | 1,680 | 2,436 | 44 | 756 D | 40.4% | 58.6% | 40.8% | 59.2% |
| 24,181 | LAFAYETTE | 8,351 | 3,735 | 4,375 | 241 | 640 D | 44.7% | 52.4% | 46.1% | 53.9% |
| 15,209 | LAMAR | 7,414 | 4,056 | 3,109 | 249 | 947 R | 54.7% | 41.9% | 56.6% | 43.4% |
| 67,087 | LAUDERDALE | 24,446 | 14,273 | 9,813 | 360 | 4,460 R | 58.4% | 40.1% | 59.3% | 40.7% |
| 11,137 | LAWRENCE | 4,436 | 2,109 | 2,242 | 85 | 133 D | 47.5% | 50.5% | 48.5% | 51.5% |
| 17,085 | LEAKE | 6,508 | 2,952 | 3,415 | 141 | 463 D | 45.4% | 52.5% | 46.4% | 53.6% |
| 46,148 | LEE | 16,333 | 7,366 | 8,504 | 463 | 1,138 D | 45.1% | 52.1% | 46.4% | 53.6% |
| 42,111 | LEFLORE | 12,589 | 5,872 | 6,135 | 582 | 263 D | 46.6% | 48.7% | 48.9% | 51.1% |
| 26,198 | LINCOLN | 10,392 | 6,084 | 4,043 | 265 | 2,041 R | 58.5% | 38.9% | 60.1% | 39.9% |
| 49,700 | LOWNDES | 14,700 | 8,003 | 6,181 | 516 | 1,822 R | 54.4% | 42.0% | 56.4% | 43.6% |
| 29,737 | MADISON | 11,316 | 4,838 | 6,240 | 238 | 1,402 D | 42.8% | 55.1% | 43.7% | 56.3% |
| 22,871 | MARION | 10,737 | 5,300 | 5,283 | 154 | 17 R | 49.4% | 49.2% | 50.1% | 49.9% |
| 24,027 | MARSHALL | 9,226 | 2,242 | 6,769 | 215 | 4,527 D | 24.3% | 73.4% | 24.9% | 75.1% |
| 34,043 | MONROE | 11,234 | 4,737 | 6,097 | 400 | 1,360 D | 42.2% | 54.3% | 43.7% | 56.3% |
| 12,918 | MONTGOMERY | 4,827 | 2,278 | 2,410 | 139 | 132 D | 47.2% | 49.9% | 48.6% | 51.4% |
| 20,802 | NESHOBA | 7,819 | 3,859 | 3,891 | 69 | 32 D | 49.4% | 49.8% | 49.8% | 50.2% |
| 18,983 | NEWTON | 6,690 | 3,813 | 2,741 | 136 | 1,072 R | 57.0% | 41.0% | 58.2% | 41.8% |
| 14,288 | NOXUBEE | 4,136 | 1,860 | 2,121 | 155 | 261 D | 45.0% | 51.3% | 46.7% | 53.3% |
| 28,752 | OKTIBBEHA | 9,725 | 5,194 | 4,339 | 192 | 855 R | 53.4% | 44.6% | 54.5% | 45.5% |
| 26,829 | PANOLA | 9,067 | 3,341 | 5,517 | 209 | 2,176 D | 36.8% | 60.8% | 37.7% | 62.3% |
| 27,802 | PEARL RIVER | 9,665 | 4,332 | 5,024 | 309 | 692 D | 44.8% | 52.0% | 46.3% | 53.7% |
| 9,065 | PERRY | 3,725 | 1,527 | 1,965 | 233 | 438 D | 41.0% | 52.8% | 43.7% | 56.3% |
| 31,756 | PIKE | 11,751 | 5,659 | 5,749 | 343 | 90 D | 48.2% | 48.9% | 49.6% | 50.4% |
| 17,363 | PONTOTOC | 6,491 | 2,245 | 4,066 | 180 | 1,821 D | 34.6% | 62.6% | 35.6% | 64.4% |
| 20,133 | PRENTISS | 6,977 | 2,362 | 4,431 | 184 | 2,069 D | 33.9% | 63.5% | 34.8% | 65.2% |
| 15,888 | QUITMAN | 4,045 | 1,287 | 2,621 | 137 | 1,334 D | 31.8% | 64.8% | 32.9% | 67.1% |

# MISSISSIPPI

## PRESIDENT 1976

| 1970 Census Population | County | Total Vote | Republican | Democratic | Other | Rep.-Dem. Plurality | Percentage | | | |
|---|---|---|---|---|---|---|---|---|---|---|
| | | | | | | | Total Vote | | Major Vote | |
| | | | | | | | Rep. | Dem. | Rep. | Dem. |
| 43,933 | RANKIN | 18,878 | 11,507 | 6,937 | 434 | 4,570 R | 61.0% | 36.7% | 62.4% | 37.6% |
| 21,369 | SCOTT | 7,468 | 3,649 | 3,643 | 176 | 6 R | 48.9% | 48.8% | 50.0% | 50.0% |
| 8,937 | SHARKEY | 2,449 | 1,024 | 1,283 | 142 | 259 D | 41.8% | 52.4% | 44.4% | 55.6% |
| 19,947 | SIMPSON | 7,960 | 4,291 | 3,600 | 69 | 691 R | 53.9% | 45.2% | 54.4% | 45.6% |
| 13,561 | SMITH | 5,748 | 3,147 | 2,434 | 167 | 713 R | 54.7% | 42.3% | 56.4% | 43.6% |
| 8,101 | STONE | 3,278 | 1,575 | 1,648 | 55 | 73 D | 48.0% | 50.3% | 48.9% | 51.1% |
| 37,047 | SUNFLOWER | 8,024 | 3,456 | 4,322 | 246 | 866 D | 43.1% | 53.9% | 44.4% | 55.6% |
| 19,338 | TALLAHATCHIE | 5,252 | 2,146 | 2,991 | 115 | 845 D | 40.9% | 56.9% | 41.8% | 58.2% |
| 18,544 | TATE | 6,436 | 2,497 | 3,747 | 192 | 1,250 D | 38.8% | 58.2% | 40.0% | 60.0% |
| 15,852 | TIPPAH | 6,274 | 1,887 | 4,260 | 127 | 2,373 D | 30.1% | 67.9% | 30.7% | 69.3% |
| 14,940 | TISHOMINGO | 5,839 | 1,969 | 3,734 | 136 | 1,765 D | 33.7% | 63.9% | 34.5% | 65.5% |
| 11,854 | TUNICA | 2,756 | 951 | 1,695 | 110 | 744 D | 34.5% | 61.5% | 35.9% | 64.1% |
| 19,096 | UNION | 7,659 | 2,507 | 5,021 | 131 | 2,514 D | 32.7% | 65.6% | 33.3% | 66.7% |
| 12,500 | WALTHALL | 4,927 | 2,110 | 2,650 | 167 | 540 D | 42.8% | 53.8% | 44.3% | 55.7% |
| 44,981 | WARREN | 15,705 | 8,699 | 6,299 | 707 | 2,400 R | 55.4% | 40.1% | 58.0% | 42.0% |
| 70,581 | WASHINGTON | 18,146 | 7,474 | 9,650 | 1,022 | 2,176 D | 41.2% | 53.2% | 43.6% | 56.4% |
| 16,650 | WAYNE | 6,422 | 3,022 | 3,306 | 94 | 284 D | 47.1% | 51.5% | 47.8% | 52.2% |
| 10,047 | WEBSTER | 4,281 | 1,943 | 2,218 | 120 | 275 D | 45.4% | 51.8% | 46.7% | 53.3% |
| 11,099 | WILKINSON | 3,845 | 1,273 | 2,514 | 58 | 1,241 D | 33.1% | 65.4% | 33.6% | 66.4% |
| 18,406 | WINSTON | 7,792 | 3,659 | 3,956 | 177 | 297 D | 47.0% | 50.8% | 48.0% | 52.0% |
| 11,915 | YALOBUSHA | 4,503 | 1,808 | 2,603 | 92 | 795 D | 40.2% | 57.8% | 41.0% | 59.0% |
| 27,304 | YAZOO | 8,471 | 4,255 | 4,053 | 163 | 202 R | 50.2% | 47.8% | 51.2% | 48.8% |
| 2,216,912 | TOTAL | 769,361 | 366,846 | 381,309 | 21,206 | 14,463 D | 47.7% | 49.6% | 49.0% | 51.0% |

# MISSISSIPPI

## PRESIDENT 1972

| 1970 Census Population | County | Total Vote | Republican | Democratic | Other | Rep.-Dem. Plurality | Percentage | | | |
|---|---|---|---|---|---|---|---|---|---|---|
| | | | | | | | Total Vote | | Major Vote | |
| | | | | | | | Rep. | Dem. | Rep. | Dem. |
| 37,293 | ADAMS | 12,657 | 8,500 | 3,697 | 460 | 4,803 R | 67.2% | 29.2% | 69.7% | 30.3% |
| 27,179 | ALCORN | 6,883 | 5,732 | 982 | 169 | 4,750 R | 83.3% | 14.3% | 85.4% | 14.6% |
| 13,763 | AMITE | 4,128 | 2,846 | 1,185 | 97 | 1,661 R | 68.9% | 28.7% | 70.6% | 29.4% |
| 19,570 | ATTALA | 5,960 | 4,738 | 1,103 | 119 | 3,635 R | 79.5% | 18.5% | 81.1% | 18.9% |
| 7,505 | BENTON | 2,235 | 1,483 | 701 | 51 | 782 R | 66.4% | 31.4% | 67.9% | 32.1% |
| 49,409 | BOLIVAR | 11,187 | 7,397 | 3,616 | 174 | 3,781 R | 66.1% | 32.3% | 67.2% | 32.8% |
| 14,623 | CALHOUN | 3,345 | 3,023 | 245 | 77 | 2,778 R | 90.4% | 7.3% | 92.5% | 7.5% |
| 9,397 | CARROLL | 2,424 | 1,777 | 580 | 67 | 1,197 R | 73.3% | 23.9% | 75.4% | 24.6% |
| 16,805 | CHICKASAW | 4,433 | 3,753 | 579 | 101 | 3,174 R | 84.7% | 13.1% | 86.6% | 13.4% |
| 8,440 | CHOCTAW | 2,658 | 2,301 | 326 | 31 | 1,975 R | 86.6% | 12.3% | 87.6% | 12.4% |
| 10,086 | CLAIBORNE | 3,642 | 1,521 | 2,076 | 45 | 555 D | 41.8% | 57.0% | 42.3% | 57.7% |
| 15,049 | CLARKE | 5,592 | 4,561 | 954 | 77 | 3,607 R | 81.6% | 17.1% | 82.7% | 17.3% |
| 18,840 | CLAY | 5,652 | 4,035 | 1,410 | 207 | 2,625 R | 71.4% | 24.9% | 74.1% | 25.9% |
| 40,447 | COAHOMA | 10,725 | 6,602 | 3,708 | 415 | 2,894 R | 61.6% | 34.6% | 64.0% | 36.0% |
| 24,749 | COPIAH | 7,520 | 5,498 | 1,803 | 219 | 3,695 R | 73.1% | 24.0% | 75.3% | 24.7% |
| 14,002 | COVINGTON | 4,569 | 3,842 | 642 | 85 | 3,200 R | 84.1% | 14.1% | 85.7% | 14.3% |
| 35,885 | DE SOTO | 9,789 | 7,917 | 1,557 | 315 | 6,360 R | 80.9% | 15.9% | 83.6% | 16.4% |
| 57,849 | FORREST | 17,898 | 14,418 | 2,933 | 547 | 11,485 R | 80.6% | 16.4% | 83.1% | 16.9% |
| 8,011 | FRANKLIN | 2,999 | 2,361 | 561 | 77 | 1,800 R | 78.7% | 18.7% | 80.8% | 19.2% |
| 12,459 | GEORGE | 4,283 | 3,979 | 270 | 34 | 3,709 R | 92.9% | 6.3% | 93.6% | 6.4% |
| 8,545 | GREENE | 3,453 | 2,884 | 513 | 56 | 2,371 R | 83.5% | 14.9% | 84.9% | 15.1% |
| 19,854 | GRENADA | 6,392 | 4,800 | 1,471 | 121 | 3,329 R | 75.1% | 23.0% | 76.5% | 23.5% |
| 17,387 | HANCOCK | 5,949 | 5,133 | 745 | 71 | 4,388 R | 86.3% | 12.5% | 87.3% | 12.7% |
| 134,582 | HARRISON | 34,470 | 28,962 | 4,761 | 747 | 24,201 R | 84.0% | 13.8% | 85.9% | 14.1% |
| 214,973 | HINDS | 64,096 | 49,877 | 12,679 | 1,540 | 37,198 R | 77.8% | 19.8% | 79.7% | 20.3% |
| 23,120 | HOLMES | 6,686 | 3,158 | 3,459 | 69 | 301 D | 47.2% | 51.7% | 47.7% | 52.3% |
| 14,601 | HUMPHREYS | 3,382 | 2,334 | 892 | 156 | 1,442 R | 69.0% | 26.4% | 72.3% | 27.7% |
| 2,737 | ISSAQUENA | 1,153 | 701 | 395 | 57 | 306 R | 60.8% | 34.3% | 64.0% | 36.0% |
| 16,847 | ITAWAMBA | 4,954 | 4,419 | 509 | 26 | 3,910 R | 89.2% | 10.3% | 89.7% | 10.3% |
| 87,975 | JACKSON | 25,038 | 22,204 | 2,534 | 300 | 19,670 R | 88.7% | 10.1% | 89.8% | 10.2% |
| 15,994 | JASPER | 4,584 | 3,597 | 935 | 52 | 2,662 R | 78.5% | 20.4% | 79.4% | 20.6% |
| 9,295 | JEFFERSON | 2,608 | 1,131 | 1,457 | 20 | 326 D | 43.4% | 55.9% | 43.7% | 56.3% |
| 12,936 | JEFFERSON DAVIS | 3,886 | 2,830 | 1,005 | 51 | 1,825 R | 72.8% | 25.9% | 73.8% | 26.2% |
| 56,357 | JONES | 19,679 | 16,489 | 2,790 | 400 | 13,699 R | 83.8% | 14.2% | 85.5% | 14.5% |
| 10,233 | KEMPER | 3,652 | 2,748 | 837 | 67 | 1,911 R | 75.2% | 22.9% | 76.7% | 23.3% |
| 24,181 | LAFAYETTE | 7,011 | 5,391 | 1,545 | 75 | 3,846 R | 76.9% | 22.0% | 77.7% | 22.3% |
| 15,209 | LAMAR | 5,682 | 5,022 | 493 | 167 | 4,529 R | 88.4% | 8.7% | 91.1% | 8.9% |
| 67,087 | LAUDERDALE | 22,420 | 18,337 | 3,453 | 630 | 14,884 R | 81.8% | 15.4% | 84.2% | 15.8% |
| 11,137 | LAWRENCE | 4,154 | 3,394 | 709 | 51 | 2,685 R | 81.7% | 17.1% | 82.7% | 17.3% |
| 17,085 | LEAKE | 5,329 | 4,217 | 1,053 | 59 | 3,164 R | 79.1% | 19.8% | 80.0% | 20.0% |
| 46,148 | LEE | 12,991 | 10,730 | 1,632 | 629 | 9,098 R | 82.6% | 12.6% | 86.8% | 13.2% |
| 42,111 | LEFLORE | 8,969 | 6,779 | 2,038 | 152 | 4,741 R | 75.6% | 22.7% | 76.9% | 23.1% |
| 26,198 | LINCOLN | 8,828 | 7,593 | 1,070 | 165 | 6,523 R | 86.0% | 12.1% | 87.6% | 12.4% |
| 49,700 | LOWNDES | 12,831 | 10,098 | 2,398 | 335 | 7,700 R | 78.7% | 18.7% | 80.8% | 19.2% |
| 29,737 | MADISON | 8,824 | 5,047 | 3,464 | 313 | 1,583 R | 57.2% | 39.3% | 59.3% | 40.7% |
| 22,871 | MARION | 8,570 | 6,805 | 1,693 | 72 | 5,112 R | 79.4% | 19.8% | 80.1% | 19.9% |
| 24,027 | MARSHALL | 5,356 | 3,326 | 1,875 | 155 | 1,451 R | 62.1% | 35.0% | 63.9% | 36.1% |
| 34,043 | MONROE | 8,648 | 7,273 | 1,279 | 96 | 5,994 R | 84.1% | 14.8% | 85.0% | 15.0% |
| 12,918 | MONTGOMERY | 4,206 | 3,210 | 925 | 71 | 2,285 R | 76.3% | 22.0% | 77.6% | 22.4% |
| 20,802 | NESHOBA | 7,725 | 6,815 | 812 | 98 | 6,003 R | 88.2% | 10.5% | 89.4% | 10.6% |
| 18,983 | NEWTON | 6,343 | 5,585 | 597 | 161 | 4,988 R | 88.0% | 9.4% | 90.3% | 9.7% |
| 14,288 | NOXUBEE | 3,378 | 2,239 | 1,052 | 87 | 1,187 R | 66.3% | 31.1% | 68.0% | 32.0% |
| 28,752 | OKTIBBEHA | 8,153 | 6,160 | 1,880 | 113 | 4,280 R | 75.6% | 23.1% | 76.6% | 23.4% |
| 26,829 | PANOLA | 7,483 | 5,284 | 2,091 | 108 | 3,193 R | 70.6% | 27.9% | 71.6% | 28.4% |
| 27,802 | PEARL RIVER | 8,504 | 7,487 | 901 | 116 | 6,586 R | 88.0% | 10.6% | 89.3% | 10.7% |
| 9,065 | PERRY | 3,196 | 2,689 | 446 | 61 | 2,243 R | 84.1% | 14.0% | 85.8% | 14.2% |
| 31,756 | PIKE | 9,076 | 6,542 | 2,332 | 202 | 4,210 R | 72.1% | 25.7% | 73.7% | 26.3% |
| 17,363 | PONTOTOC | 5,004 | 4,476 | 488 | 40 | 3,988 R | 89.4% | 9.8% | 90.2% | 9.8% |
| 20,133 | PRENTISS | 5,056 | 4,607 | 398 | 51 | 4,209 R | 91.1% | 7.9% | 92.0% | 8.0% |
| 15,888 | QUITMAN | 3,392 | 2,524 | 790 | 78 | 1,734 R | 74.4% | 23.3% | 76.2% | 23.8% |

# MISSISSIPPI

## PRESIDENT 1972

| 1970 Census Population | County | Total Vote | Republican | Democratic | Other | Rep.-Dem. Plurality | Percentage | | | |
|---|---|---|---|---|---|---|---|---|---|---|
| | | | | | | | Total Vote | | Major Vote | |
| | | | | | | | Rep. | Dem. | Rep. | Dem. |
| 43,933 | RANKIN | 14,305 | 12,187 | 1,913 | 205 | 10,274 R | 85.2% | 13.4% | 86.4% | 13.6% |
| 21,369 | SCOTT | 6,559 | 5,244 | 1,213 | 102 | 4,031 R | 80.0% | 18.5% | 81.2% | 18.8% |
| 8,937 | SHARKEY | 2,099 | 1,426 | 655 | 18 | 771 R | 67.9% | 31.2% | 68.5% | 31.5% |
| 19,947 | SIMPSON | 6,602 | 5,669 | 871 | 62 | 4,798 R | 85.9% | 13.2% | 86.7% | 13.3% |
| 13,561 | SMITH | 4,785 | 4,419 | 329 | 37 | 4,090 R | 92.4% | 6.9% | 93.1% | 6.9% |
| 8,101 | STONE | 2,788 | 2,467 | 293 | 28 | 2,174 R | 88.5% | 10.5% | 89.4% | 10.6% |
| 37,047 | SUNFLOWER | 7,355 | 5,389 | 1,874 | 92 | 3,515 R | 73.3% | 25.5% | 74.2% | 25.8% |
| 19,338 | TALLAHATCHIE | 4,449 | 3,442 | 835 | 172 | 2,607 R | 77.4% | 18.8% | 80.5% | 19.5% |
| 18,544 | TATE | 5,236 | 3,966 | 1,151 | 119 | 2,815 R | 75.7% | 22.0% | 77.5% | 22.5% |
| 15,852 | TIPPAH | 4,585 | 3,937 | 569 | 79 | 3,368 R | 85.9% | 12.4% | 87.4% | 12.6% |
| 14,940 | TISHOMINGO | 4,681 | 4,177 | 443 | 61 | 3,734 R | 89.2% | 9.5% | 90.4% | 9.6% |
| 11,854 | TUNICA | 2,325 | 1,446 | 858 | 21 | 588 R | 62.2% | 36.9% | 62.8% | 37.2% |
| 19,096 | UNION | 6,230 | 5,477 | 658 | 95 | 4,819 R | 87.9% | 10.6% | 89.3% | 10.7% |
| 12,500 | WALTHALL | 3,904 | 3,110 | 747 | 47 | 2,363 R | 79.7% | 19.1% | 80.6% | 19.4% |
| 44,981 | WARREN | 14,478 | 10,420 | 3,480 | 578 | 6,940 R | 72.0% | 24.0% | 75.0% | 25.0% |
| 70,581 | WASHINGTON | 15,104 | 9,634 | 4,623 | 847 | 5,011 R | 63.8% | 30.6% | 67.6% | 32.4% |
| 16,650 | WAYNE | 5,663 | 4,648 | 975 | 40 | 3,673 R | 82.1% | 17.2% | 82.7% | 17.3% |
| 10,047 | WEBSTER | 4,065 | 3,624 | 403 | 38 | 3,221 R | 89.2% | 9.9% | 90.0% | 10.0% |
| 11,099 | WILKINSON | 3,054 | 1,608 | 1,409 | 37 | 199 R | 52.7% | 46.1% | 53.3% | 46.7% |
| 18,406 | WINSTON | 6,555 | 5,155 | 1,354 | 46 | 3,801 R | 78.6% | 20.7% | 79.2% | 20.8% |
| 11,915 | YALOBUSHA | 3,797 | 2,944 | 797 | 56 | 2,147 R | 77.5% | 21.0% | 78.7% | 21.3% |
| 27,304 | YAZOO | 7,654 | 5,555 | 2,008 | 91 | 3,547 R | 72.6% | 26.2% | 73.4% | 26.6% |
| 2,216,912 | TOTAL | 645,963 | 505,125 | 126,782 | 14,056 | 378,343 R | 78.2% | 19.6% | 79.9% | 20.1% |

# MISSISSIPPI

## PRESIDENT 1968

| 1960 Census Population | County | Total Vote | Republican | Democratic | AIP | Other | Plurality | Rep. | Dem. | AIP |
|---|---|---|---|---|---|---|---|---|---|---|
| 37,730 | ADAMS | 13,501 | 1,475 | 5,214 | 6,812 | | 1,598 A | 10.9% | 38.6% | 50.5% |
| 25,282 | ALCORN | 9,186 | 1,760 | 1,122 | 6,304 | | 4,544 A | 19.2% | 12.2% | 68.6% |
| 15,573 | AMITE | 5,132 | 393 | 1,533 | 3,206 | | 1,673 A | 7.7% | 29.9% | 62.5% |
| 21,335 | ATTALA | 6,963 | 599 | 1,588 | 4,776 | | 3,188 A | 8.6% | 22.8% | 68.6% |
| 7,723 | BENTON | 2,665 | 185 | 850 | 1,630 | | 780 A | 6.9% | 31.9% | 61.2% |
| 54,464 | BOLIVAR | 11,504 | 1,790 | 4,696 | 5,018 | | 322 A | 15.6% | 40.8% | 43.6% |
| 15,941 | CALHOUN | 5,493 | 394 | 276 | 4,823 | | 4,429 A | 7.2% | 5.0% | 87.8% |
| 11,177 | CARROLL | 3,194 | 138 | 925 | 2,131 | | 1,206 A | 4.3% | 29.0% | 66.7% |
| 16,891 | CHICKASAW | 5,163 | 381 | 720 | 4,062 | | 3,342 A | 7.4% | 13.9% | 78.7% |
| 8,423 | CHOCTAW | 3,171 | 211 | 417 | 2,543 | | 2,126 A | 6.7% | 13.2% | 80.2% |
| 10,845 | CLAIBORNE | 3,502 | 230 | 2,129 | 1,143 | | 986 D | 6.6% | 60.8% | 32.6% |
| 16,493 | CLARKE | 5,390 | 298 | 878 | 4,214 | | 3,336 A | 5.5% | 16.3% | 78.2% |
| 18,933 | CLAY | 5,509 | 494 | 1,510 | 3,505 | | 1,995 A | 9.0% | 27.4% | 63.6% |
| 46,212 | COAHOMA | 10,898 | 1,875 | 5,352 | 3,671 | | 1,681 D | 17.2% | 49.1% | 33.7% |
| 27,051 | COPIAH | 8,379 | 704 | 2,724 | 4,951 | | 2,227 A | 8.4% | 32.5% | 59.1% |
| 13,637 | COVINGTON | 4,804 | 445 | 691 | 3,668 | | 2,977 A | 9.3% | 14.4% | 76.4% |
| 23,891 | DE SOTO | 8,336 | 1,092 | 1,898 | 5,346 | | 3,448 A | 13.1% | 22.8% | 64.1% |
| 52,722 | FORREST | 16,226 | 3,294 | 2,957 | 9,975 | | 6,681 A | 20.3% | 18.2% | 61.5% |
| 9,286 | FRANKLIN | 3,442 | 231 | 782 | 2,429 | | 1,647 A | 6.7% | 22.7% | 70.6% |
| 11,098 | GEORGE | 4,377 | 171 | 214 | 3,992 | | 3,778 A | 3.9% | 4.9% | 91.2% |
| 8,366 | GREENE | 3,325 | 132 | 449 | 2,744 | | 2,295 A | 4.0% | 13.5% | 82.5% |
| 18,409 | GRENADA | 7,103 | 718 | 2,050 | 4,335 | | 2,285 A | 10.1% | 28.9% | 61.0% |
| 14,039 | HANCOCK | 6,041 | 1,065 | 904 | 4,072 | | 3,007 A | 17.6% | 15.0% | 67.4% |
| 119,489 | HARRISON | 29,248 | 6,542 | 4,549 | 18,157 | | 11,615 A | 22.4% | 15.6% | 62.1% |
| 187,045 | HINDS | 60,734 | 13,488 | 14,880 | 32,366 | | 17,486 A | 22.2% | 24.5% | 53.3% |
| 27,096 | HOLMES | 7,409 | 520 | 3,881 | 3,008 | | 873 D | 7.0% | 52.4% | 40.6% |
| 19,093 | HUMPHREYS | 3,628 | 258 | 1,219 | 2,151 | | 932 A | 7.1% | 33.6% | 59.3% |
| 3,576 | ISSAQUENA | 1,105 | 44 | 527 | 534 | | 7 A | 4.0% | 47.7% | 48.3% |
| 15,080 | ITAWAMBA | 6,190 | 569 | 417 | 5,204 | | 4,635 A | 9.2% | 6.7% | 84.1% |
| 55,522 | JACKSON | 20,439 | 2,942 | 2,236 | 15,261 | | 12,319 A | 14.4% | 10.9% | 74.7% |
| 16,909 | JASPER | 4,460 | 373 | 987 | 3,100 | | 2,113 A | 8.4% | 22.1% | 69.5% |
| 10,142 | JEFFERSON | 3,380 | 147 | 2,121 | 1,112 | | 1,009 D | 4.3% | 62.8% | 32.9% |
| 13,540 | JEFFERSON DAVIS | 4,376 | 297 | 1,465 | 2,614 | | 1,149 A | 6.8% | 33.5% | 59.7% |
| 59,542 | JONES | 17,994 | 3,242 | 2,476 | 12,276 | | 9,034 A | 18.0% | 13.8% | 68.2% |
| 12,277 | KEMPER | 3,352 | 167 | 655 | 2,530 | | 1,875 A | 5.0% | 19.5% | 75.5% |
| 21,355 | LAFAYETTE | 6,142 | 1,235 | 1,578 | 3,329 | | 1,751 A | 20.1% | 25.7% | 54.2% |
| 13,675 | LAMAR | 5,319 | 546 | 351 | 4,422 | | 3,876 A | 10.3% | 6.6% | 83.1% |
| 67,119 | LAUDERDALE | 20,365 | 2,328 | 3,195 | 14,842 | | 11,647 A | 11.4% | 15.7% | 72.9% |
| 10,215 | LAWRENCE | 3,894 | 329 | 740 | 2,825 | | 2,085 A | 8.4% | 19.0% | 72.5% |
| 18,660 | LEAKE | 6,316 | 453 | 1,295 | 4,568 | | 3,273 A | 7.2% | 20.5% | 72.3% |
| 40,589 | LEE | 13,666 | 2,522 | 1,912 | 9,232 | | 6,710 A | 18.5% | 14.0% | 67.6% |
| 47,142 | LEFLORE | 11,632 | 1,514 | 4,386 | 5,732 | | 1,346 A | 13.0% | 37.7% | 49.3% |
| 26,759 | LINCOLN | 9,918 | 1,057 | 1,585 | 7,276 | | 5,691 A | 10.7% | 16.0% | 73.4% |
| 46,639 | LOWNDES | 11,026 | 1,968 | 2,229 | 6,829 | | 4,600 A | 17.8% | 20.2% | 61.9% |
| 32,904 | MADISON | 9,462 | 876 | 4,515 | 4,071 | | 444 D | 9.3% | 47.7% | 43.0% |
| 23,293 | MARION | 8,333 | 763 | 1,722 | 5,848 | | 4,126 A | 9.2% | 20.7% | 70.2% |
| 24,503 | MARSHALL | 6,278 | 577 | 2,907 | 2,794 | | 113 D | 9.2% | 46.3% | 44.5% |
| 33,953 | MONROE | 10,529 | 1,167 | 1,506 | 7,856 | | 6,350 A | 11.1% | 14.3% | 74.6% |
| 13,320 | MONTGOMERY | 4,359 | 475 | 896 | 2,988 | | 2,092 A | 10.9% | 20.6% | 68.5% |
| 20,927 | NESHOBA | 7,815 | 531 | 867 | 6,417 | | 5,550 A | 6.8% | 11.1% | 82.1% |
| 19,517 | NEWTON | 6,902 | 542 | 799 | 5,561 | | 4,762 A | 7.9% | 11.6% | 80.6% |
| 16,826 | NOXUBEE | 3,659 | 232 | 1,387 | 2,040 | | 653 A | 6.3% | 37.9% | 55.8% |
| 26,175 | OKTIBBEHA | 7,229 | 1,276 | 1,826 | 4,127 | | 2,301 A | 17.7% | 25.3% | 57.1% |
| 28,791 | PANOLA | 7,974 | 1,098 | 2,743 | 4,133 | | 1,390 A | 13.8% | 34.4% | 51.8% |
| 22,411 | PEARL RIVER | 8,274 | 1,298 | 926 | 6,050 | | 4,752 A | 15.7% | 11.2% | 73.1% |
| 8,745 | PERRY | 3,207 | 227 | 439 | 2,541 | | 2,102 A | 7.1% | 13.7% | 79.2% |
| 35,063 | PIKE | 10,154 | 1,460 | 2,848 | 5,846 | | 2,998 A | 14.4% | 28.0% | 57.6% |
| 17,232 | PONTOTOC | 6,130 | 733 | 599 | 4,798 | | 4,065 A | 12.0% | 9.8% | 78.3% |
| 17,949 | PRENTISS | 6,218 | 723 | 440 | 5,055 | | 4,332 A | 11.6% | 7.1% | 81.3% |
| 21,019 | QUITMAN | 4,379 | 434 | 1,502 | 2,443 | | 941 A | 9.9% | 34.3% | 55.8% |

# MISSISSIPPI

## PRESIDENT 1968

| 1960 Census Population | County | Total Vote | Republican | Democratic | AIP | Other | Plurality | Percentage Total Vote | | |
|---|---|---|---|---|---|---|---|---|---|---|
| | | | | | | | | Rep. | Dem. | AIP |
| 34,322 | RANKIN | 12,323 | 1,124 | 1,975 | 9,224 | | 7,249 A | 9.1% | 16.0% | 74.9% |
| 21,187 | SCOTT | 6,764 | 604 | 1,067 | 5,093 | | 4,026 A | 8.9% | 15.8% | 75.3% |
| 10,738 | SHARKEY | 2,409 | 249 | 972 | 1,188 | | 216 A | 10.3% | 40.3% | 49.3% |
| 20,454 | SIMPSON | 7,018 | 875 | 1,079 | 5,064 | | 3,985 A | 12.5% | 15.4% | 72.2% |
| 14,303 | SMITH | 5,156 | 437 | 352 | 4,367 | | 3,930 A | 8.5% | 6.8% | 84.7% |
| 7,013 | STONE | 2,712 | 258 | 314 | 2,140 | | 1,826 A | 9.5% | 11.6% | 78.9% |
| 45,750 | SUNFLOWER | 7,570 | 1,036 | 2,602 | 3,932 | | 1,330 A | 13.7% | 34.4% | 51.9% |
| 24,081 | TALLAHATCHIE | 5,130 | 577 | 1,477 | 3,076 | | 1,599 A | 11.2% | 28.8% | 60.0% |
| 18,138 | TATE | 4,577 | 605 | 1,162 | 2,810 | | 1,648 A | 13.2% | 25.4% | 61.4% |
| 15,093 | TIPPAH | 5,879 | 589 | 663 | 4,627 | | 3,964 A | 10.0% | 11.3% | 78.7% |
| 13,889 | TISHOMINGO | 5,544 | 617 | 358 | 4,569 | | 3,952 A | 11.1% | 6.5% | 82.4% |
| 16,826 | TUNICA | 2,329 | 413 | 1,133 | 783 | | 350 D | 17.7% | 48.6% | 33.6% |
| 18,904 | UNION | 6,770 | 948 | 624 | 5,198 | | 4,250 A | 14.0% | 9.2% | 76.8% |
| 13,512 | WALTHALL | 4,806 | 387 | 1,233 | 3,186 | | 1,953 A | 8.1% | 25.7% | 66.3% |
| 42,206 | WARREN | 14,112 | 2,392 | 4,503 | 7,217 | | 2,714 A | 17.0% | 31.9% | 51.1% |
| 78,638 | WASHINGTON | 15,320 | 3,500 | 5,520 | 6,300 | | 780 A | 22.8% | 36.0% | 41.1% |
| 16,258 | WAYNE | 5,075 | 247 | 739 | 4,089 | | 3,350 A | 4.9% | 14.6% | 80.6% |
| 10,580 | WEBSTER | 4,023 | 330 | 295 | 3,398 | | 3,068 A | 8.2% | 7.3% | 84.5% |
| 13,235 | WILKINSON | 3,919 | 272 | 2,144 | 1,503 | | 641 D | 6.9% | 54.7% | 38.4% |
| 19,246 | WINSTON | 6,054 | 508 | 911 | 4,635 | | 3,724 A | 8.4% | 15.0% | 76.6% |
| 12,502 | YALOBUSHA | 4,160 | 562 | 873 | 2,725 | | 1,852 A | 13.5% | 21.0% | 65.5% |
| 31,653 | YAZOO | 8,060 | 958 | 2,163 | 4,939 | | 2,776 A | 11.9% | 26.8% | 61.3% |
| 2,178,141 | TOTAL | 654,509 | 88,516 | 150,644 | 415,349 | | 264,705 A | 13.5% | 23.0% | 63.5% |

# MISSISSIPPI

## PRESIDENT 1964

| 1960 Census Population | County | Total Vote | Republican | Democratic | Other | Rep.-Dem. Plurality | Percentage Total Vote Rep. | Dem. | Major Vote Rep. | Dem. |
|---|---|---|---|---|---|---|---|---|---|---|
| 37,730 | ADAMS | 6,993 | 5,900 | 1,093 | | 4,807 R | 84.4% | 15.6% | 84.4% | 15.6% |
| 25,282 | ALCORN | 5,294 | 3,377 | 1,917 | | 1,460 R | 63.8% | 36.2% | 63.8% | 36.2% |
| 15,573 | AMITE | 2,845 | 2,742 | 103 | | 2,639 R | 96.4% | 3.6% | 96.4% | 3.6% |
| 21,335 | ATTALA | 4,672 | 4,409 | 263 | | 4,146 R | 94.4% | 5.6% | 94.4% | 5.6% |
| 7,723 | BENTON | 1,170 | 934 | 236 | | 698 R | 79.8% | 20.2% | 79.8% | 20.2% |
| 54,464 | BOLIVAR | 5,411 | 4,680 | 731 | | 3,949 R | 86.5% | 13.5% | 86.5% | 13.5% |
| 15,941 | CALHOUN | 3,518 | 3,224 | 294 | | 2,930 R | 91.6% | 8.4% | 91.6% | 8.4% |
| 11,177 | CARROLL | 2,141 | 2,043 | 98 | | 1,945 R | 95.4% | 4.6% | 95.4% | 4.6% |
| 16,891 | CHICKASAW | 3,417 | 3,138 | 279 | | 2,859 R | 91.8% | 8.2% | 91.8% | 8.2% |
| 8,423 | CHOCTAW | 2,246 | 2,096 | 150 | | 1,946 R | 93.3% | 6.7% | 93.3% | 6.7% |
| 10,845 | CLAIBORNE | 1,310 | 1,226 | 84 | | 1,142 R | 93.6% | 6.4% | 93.6% | 6.4% |
| 16,493 | CLARKE | 3,844 | 3,591 | 253 | | 3,338 R | 93.4% | 6.6% | 93.4% | 6.6% |
| 18,933 | CLAY | 3,074 | 2,848 | 226 | | 2,622 R | 92.6% | 7.4% | 92.6% | 7.4% |
| 46,212 | COAHOMA | 5,136 | 4,172 | 964 | | 3,208 R | 81.2% | 18.8% | 81.2% | 18.8% |
| 27,051 | COPIAH | 4,745 | 4,506 | 239 | | 4,267 R | 95.0% | 5.0% | 95.0% | 5.0% |
| 13,637 | COVINGTON | 3,425 | 3,033 | 392 | | 2,641 R | 88.6% | 11.4% | 88.6% | 11.4% |
| 23,891 | DE SOTO | 3,389 | 2,928 | 461 | | 2,467 R | 86.4% | 13.6% | 86.4% | 13.6% |
| 52,722 | FORREST | 10,419 | 9,291 | 1,128 | | 8,163 R | 89.2% | 10.8% | 89.2% | 10.8% |
| 9,286 | FRANKLIN | 2,302 | 2,211 | 91 | | 2,120 R | 96.0% | 4.0% | 96.0% | 4.0% |
| 11,098 | GEORGE | 3,039 | 2,797 | 242 | | 2,555 R | 92.0% | 8.0% | 92.0% | 8.0% |
| 8,366 | GREENE | 2,061 | 1,845 | 216 | | 1,629 R | 89.5% | 10.5% | 89.5% | 10.5% |
| 18,409 | GRENADA | 3,803 | 3,648 | 155 | | 3,493 R | 95.9% | 4.1% | 95.9% | 4.1% |
| 14,039 | HANCOCK | 4,051 | 2,550 | 1,501 | | 1,049 R | 62.9% | 37.1% | 62.9% | 37.1% |
| 119,489 | HARRISON | 21,694 | 16,301 | 5,393 | | 10,908 R | 75.1% | 24.9% | 75.1% | 24.9% |
| 187,045 | HINDS | 41,889 | 36,831 | 5,058 | | 31,773 R | 87.9% | 12.1% | 87.9% | 12.1% |
| 27,096 | HOLMES | 3,225 | 3,115 | 110 | | 3,005 R | 96.6% | 3.4% | 96.6% | 3.4% |
| 19,093 | HUMPHREYS | 1,947 | 1,863 | 84 | | 1,779 R | 95.7% | 4.3% | 95.7% | 4.3% |
| 3,576 | ISSAQUENA | 490 | 456 | 34 | | 422 R | 93.1% | 6.9% | 93.1% | 6.9% |
| 15,080 | ITAWAMBA | 3,267 | 2,140 | 1,127 | | 1,013 R | 65.5% | 34.5% | 65.5% | 34.5% |
| 55,522 | JACKSON | 13,728 | 11,357 | 2,371 | | 8,986 R | 82.7% | 17.3% | 82.7% | 17.3% |
| 16,909 | JASPER | 3,230 | 2,994 | 236 | | 2,758 R | 92.7% | 7.3% | 92.7% | 7.3% |
| 10,142 | JEFFERSON | 1,327 | 1,258 | 69 | | 1,189 R | 94.8% | 5.2% | 94.8% | 5.2% |
| 13,540 | JEFFERSON DAVIS | 2,586 | 2,351 | 235 | | 2,116 R | 90.9% | 9.1% | 90.9% | 9.1% |
| 59,542 | JONES | 14,104 | 12,123 | 1,981 | | 10,142 R | 86.0% | 14.0% | 86.0% | 14.0% |
| 12,277 | KEMPER | 2,376 | 2,185 | 191 | | 1,994 R | 92.0% | 8.0% | 92.0% | 8.0% |
| 21,355 | LAFAYETTE | 3,922 | 3,202 | 720 | | 2,482 R | 81.6% | 18.4% | 81.6% | 18.4% |
| 13,675 | LAMAR | 3,706 | 3,372 | 334 | | 3,038 R | 91.0% | 9.0% | 91.0% | 9.0% |
| 67,119 | LAUDERDALE | 14,874 | 13,291 | 1,583 | | 11,708 R | 89.4% | 10.6% | 89.4% | 10.6% |
| 10,215 | LAWRENCE | 2,609 | 2,373 | 236 | | 2,137 R | 91.0% | 9.0% | 91.0% | 9.0% |
| 18,660 | LEAKE | 4,513 | 4,343 | 170 | | 4,173 R | 96.2% | 3.8% | 96.2% | 3.8% |
| 40,589 | LEE | 7,574 | 5,165 | 2,409 | | 2,756 R | 68.2% | 31.8% | 68.2% | 31.8% |
| 47,142 | LEFLORE | 5,969 | 5,589 | 380 | | 5,209 R | 93.6% | 6.4% | 93.6% | 6.4% |
| 26,759 | LINCOLN | 7,187 | 6,750 | 437 | | 6,313 R | 93.9% | 6.1% | 93.9% | 6.1% |
| 46,639 | LOWNDES | 6,668 | 6,135 | 533 | | 5,602 R | 92.0% | 8.0% | 92.0% | 8.0% |
| 32,904 | MADISON | 3,534 | 3,283 | 251 | | 3,032 R | 92.9% | 7.1% | 92.9% | 7.1% |
| 23,293 | MARION | 5,974 | 5,469 | 505 | | 4,964 R | 91.5% | 8.5% | 91.5% | 8.5% |
| 24,503 | MARSHALL | 2,592 | 2,250 | 342 | | 1,908 R | 86.8% | 13.2% | 86.8% | 13.2% |
| 33,953 | MONROE | 6,612 | 5,627 | 985 | | 4,642 R | 85.1% | 14.9% | 85.1% | 14.9% |
| 13,320 | MONTGOMERY | 3,330 | 3,181 | 149 | | 3,032 R | 95.5% | 4.5% | 95.5% | 4.5% |
| 20,927 | NESHOBA | 5,724 | 5,431 | 293 | | 5,138 R | 94.9% | 5.1% | 94.9% | 5.1% |
| 19,517 | NEWTON | 4,973 | 4,735 | 238 | | 4,497 R | 95.2% | 4.8% | 95.2% | 4.8% |
| 16,826 | NOXUBEE | 2,050 | 1,980 | 70 | | 1,910 R | 96.6% | 3.4% | 96.6% | 3.4% |
| 26,175 | OKTIBBEHA | 4,185 | 3,795 | 390 | | 3,405 R | 90.7% | 9.3% | 90.7% | 9.3% |
| 28,791 | PANOLA | 4,415 | 4,002 | 413 | | 3,589 R | 90.6% | 9.4% | 90.6% | 9.4% |
| 22,411 | PEARL RIVER | 4,744 | 4,009 | 735 | | 3,274 R | 84.5% | 15.5% | 84.5% | 15.5% |
| 8,745 | PERRY | 2,054 | 1,775 | 279 | | 1,496 R | 86.4% | 13.6% | 86.4% | 13.6% |
| 35,063 | PIKE | 6,961 | 6,418 | 543 | | 5,875 R | 92.2% | 7.8% | 92.2% | 7.8% |
| 17,232 | PONTOTOC | 3,401 | 2,699 | 702 | | 1,997 R | 79.4% | 20.6% | 79.4% | 20.6% |
| 17,949 | PRENTISS | 3,302 | 2,289 | 1,013 | | 1,276 R | 69.3% | 30.7% | 69.3% | 30.7% |
| 21,019 | QUITMAN | 2,401 | 2,065 | 336 | | 1,729 R | 86.0% | 14.0% | 86.0% | 14.0% |

# MISSISSIPPI

## PRESIDENT 1964

| 1960 Census Population | County | Total Vote | Republican | Democratic | Other | Rep.-Dem. Plurality | Percentage | | | |
|---|---|---|---|---|---|---|---|---|---|---|
| | | | | | | | Total Vote | | Major Vote | |
| | | | | | | | Rep. | Dem. | Rep. | Dem. |
| 34,322 | RANKIN | 7,873 | 7,541 | 332 | | 7,209 R | 95.8% | 4.2% | 95.8% | 4.2% |
| 21,187 | SCOTT | 4,967 | 4,729 | 238 | | 4,491 R | 95.2% | 4.8% | 95.2% | 4.8% |
| 10,738 | SHARKEY | 1,244 | 1,116 | 128 | | 988 R | 89.7% | 10.3% | 89.7% | 10.3% |
| 20,454 | SIMPSON | 5,220 | 4,949 | 271 | | 4,678 R | 94.8% | 5.2% | 94.8% | 5.2% |
| 14,303 | SMITH | 4,283 | 4,045 | 238 | | 3,807 R | 94.4% | 5.6% | 94.4% | 5.6% |
| 7,013 | STONE | 1,955 | 1,776 | 179 | | 1,597 R | 90.8% | 9.2% | 90.8% | 9.2% |
| 45,750 | SUNFLOWER | 4,378 | 4,127 | 251 | | 3,876 R | 94.3% | 5.7% | 94.3% | 5.7% |
| 24,081 | TALLAHATCHIE | 3,381 | 3,126 | 255 | | 2,871 R | 92.5% | 7.5% | 92.5% | 7.5% |
| 18,138 | TATE | 2,673 | 2,390 | 283 | | 2,107 R | 89.4% | 10.6% | 89.4% | 10.6% |
| 15,093 | TIPPAH | 3,456 | 2,482 | 974 | | 1,508 R | 71.8% | 28.2% | 71.8% | 28.2% |
| 13,889 | TISHOMINGO | 2,911 | 1,934 | 977 | | 957 R | 66.4% | 33.6% | 66.4% | 33.6% |
| 16,826 | TUNICA | 1,044 | 945 | 99 | | 846 R | 90.5% | 9.5% | 90.5% | 9.5% |
| 18,904 | UNION | 4,176 | 2,939 | 1,237 | | 1,702 R | 70.4% | 29.6% | 70.4% | 29.6% |
| 13,512 | WALTHALL | 3,168 | 3,014 | 154 | | 2,860 R | 95.1% | 4.9% | 95.1% | 4.9% |
| 42,206 | WARREN | 9,040 | 7,409 | 1,631 | | 5,778 R | 82.0% | 18.0% | 82.0% | 18.0% |
| 78,638 | WASHINGTON | 7,615 | 5,611 | 2,004 | | 3,607 R | 73.7% | 26.3% | 73.7% | 26.3% |
| 16,258 | WAYNE | 3,815 | 3,539 | 276 | | 3,263 R | 92.8% | 7.2% | 92.8% | 7.2% |
| 10,580 | WEBSTER | 3,121 | 2,884 | 237 | | 2,647 R | 92.4% | 7.6% | 92.4% | 7.6% |
| 13,235 | WILKINSON | 1,576 | 1,473 | 103 | | 1,370 R | 93.5% | 6.5% | 93.5% | 6.5% |
| 19,246 | WINSTON | 4,159 | 3,922 | 237 | | 3,685 R | 94.3% | 5.7% | 94.3% | 5.7% |
| 12,502 | YALOBUSHA | 2,644 | 2,385 | 259 | | 2,126 R | 90.2% | 9.8% | 90.2% | 9.8% |
| 31,653 | YAZOO | 5,005 | 4,801 | 204 | | 4,597 R | 95.9% | 4.1% | 95.9% | 4.1% |
| 2,178,141 | TOTAL | 409,146 | 356,528 | 52,618 | | 303,910 R | 87.1% | 12.9% | 87.1% | 12.9% |

# MISSISSIPPI

## PRESIDENT 1960

| 1960 Census Population | County | Total Vote | Republican | Democratic | Unpledged | Other | Plurality | Percentage Total Vote Rep. | Dem. | Unp. |
|---|---|---|---|---|---|---|---|---|---|---|
| 37,730 | ADAMS | 5,205 | 1,227 | 1,452 | 2,526 | | 1,074 U | 23.6% | 27.9% | 48.5% |
| 25,282 | ALCORN | 4,475 | 820 | 3,054 | 601 | | 2,234 D | 18.3% | 68.2% | 13.4% |
| 15,573 | AMITE | 2,276 | 283 | 338 | 1,655 | | 1,317 U | 12.4% | 14.9% | 72.7% |
| 21,335 | ATTALA | 3,268 | 650 | 1,337 | 1,281 | | 56 D | 19.9% | 40.9% | 39.2% |
| 7,723 | BENTON | 1,091 | 175 | 568 | 348 | | 220 D | 16.0% | 52.1% | 31.9% |
| 54,464 | BOLIVAR | 3,769 | 1,012 | 1,119 | 1,638 | | 519 U | 26.9% | 29.7% | 43.5% |
| 15,941 | CALHOUN | 2,447 | 383 | 765 | 1,299 | | 534 U | 15.7% | 31.3% | 53.1% |
| 11,177 | CARROLL | 1,472 | 207 | 425 | 840 | | 415 U | 14.1% | 28.9% | 57.1% |
| 16,891 | CHICKASAW | 2,538 | 385 | 791 | 1,362 | | 571 U | 15.2% | 31.2% | 53.7% |
| 8,423 | CHOCTAW | 1,646 | 245 | 817 | 584 | | 233 D | 14.9% | 49.6% | 35.5% |
| 10,845 | CLAIBORNE | 1,036 | 180 | 205 | 651 | | 446 U | 17.4% | 19.8% | 62.8% |
| 16,493 | CLARKE | 3,308 | 586 | 1,244 | 1,478 | | 234 U | 17.7% | 37.6% | 44.7% |
| 18,933 | CLAY | 2,372 | 451 | 626 | 1,295 | | 669 U | 19.0% | 26.4% | 54.6% |
| 46,212 | COAHOMA | 3,867 | 1,096 | 1,386 | 1,385 | | 1 D | 28.3% | 35.8% | 35.8% |
| 27,051 | COPIAH | 3,614 | 761 | 896 | 1,957 | | 1,061 U | 21.1% | 24.8% | 54.2% |
| 13,637 | COVINGTON | 2,198 | 371 | 842 | 985 | | 143 U | 16.9% | 38.3% | 44.8% |
| 23,891 | DE SOTO | 2,082 | 553 | 795 | 734 | | 61 D | 26.6% | 38.2% | 35.3% |
| 52,722 | FORREST | 8,632 | 3,412 | 2,068 | 3,152 | | 260 R | 39.5% | 24.0% | 36.5% |
| 9,286 | FRANKLIN | 1,680 | 124 | 441 | 1,115 | | 674 U | 7.4% | 26.3% | 66.4% |
| 11,098 | GEORGE | 2,071 | 310 | 844 | 917 | | 73 U | 15.0% | 40.8% | 44.3% |
| 8,366 | GREENE | 1,578 | 247 | 550 | 781 | | 231 U | 15.7% | 34.9% | 49.5% |
| 18,409 | GRENADA | 2,343 | 682 | 529 | 1,132 | | 450 U | 29.1% | 22.6% | 48.3% |
| 14,039 | HANCOCK | 3,353 | 719 | 2,132 | 502 | | 1,413 D | 21.4% | 63.6% | 15.0% |
| 119,489 | HARRISON | 16,759 | 5,177 | 8,961 | 2,621 | | 3,784 D | 30.9% | 53.5% | 15.6% |
| 187,045 | HINDS | 28,988 | 11,083 | 5,811 | 12,094 | | 1,011 U | 38.2% | 20.0% | 41.7% |
| 27,096 | HOLMES | 2,567 | 455 | 628 | 1,484 | | 856 U | 17.7% | 24.5% | 57.8% |
| 19,093 | HUMPHREYS | 1,422 | 231 | 459 | 732 | | 273 U | 16.2% | 32.3% | 51.5% |
| 3,576 | ISSAQUENA | 423 | 64 | 178 | 181 | | 3 U | 15.1% | 42.1% | 42.8% |
| 15,080 | ITAWAMBA | 2,771 | 366 | 1,752 | 653 | | 1,099 D | 13.2% | 63.2% | 23.6% |
| 55,522 | JACKSON | 9,174 | 2,266 | 5,000 | 1,908 | | 2,734 D | 24.7% | 54.5% | 20.8% |
| 16,909 | JASPER | 2,435 | 362 | 1,147 | 926 | | 221 D | 14.9% | 47.1% | 38.0% |
| 10,142 | JEFFERSON | 1,094 | 137 | 229 | 728 | | 499 U | 12.5% | 20.9% | 66.5% |
| 13,540 | JEFFERSON DAVIS | 1,723 | 225 | 510 | 988 | | 478 U | 13.1% | 29.6% | 57.3% |
| 59,542 | JONES | 10,528 | 2,729 | 4,871 | 2,928 | | 1,943 D | 25.9% | 46.3% | 27.8% |
| 12,277 | KEMPER | 1,711 | 193 | 931 | 587 | | 344 D | 11.3% | 54.4% | 34.3% |
| 21,355 | LAFAYETTE | 2,922 | 705 | 1,308 | 909 | | 399 D | 24.1% | 44.8% | 31.1% |
| 13,675 | LAMAR | 2,333 | 636 | 651 | 1,046 | | 395 U | 27.3% | 27.9% | 44.8% |
| 67,119 | LAUDERDALE | 10,745 | 2,836 | 3,755 | 4,154 | | 399 U | 26.4% | 34.9% | 38.7% |
| 10,215 | LAWRENCE | 1,651 | 259 | 469 | 923 | | 454 U | 15.7% | 28.4% | 55.9% |
| 18,660 | LEAKE | 3,250 | 286 | 953 | 2,011 | | 1,058 U | 8.8% | 29.3% | 61.9% |
| 40,589 | LEE | 6,641 | 1,550 | 3,653 | 1,438 | | 2,103 D | 23.3% | 55.0% | 21.7% |
| 47,142 | LEFLORE | 4,641 | 1,317 | 1,212 | 2,112 | | 795 U | 28.4% | 26.1% | 45.5% |
| 26,759 | LINCOLN | 4,885 | 1,251 | 1,449 | 2,185 | | 736 U | 25.6% | 29.7% | 44.7% |
| 46,639 | LOWNDES | 4,680 | 2,010 | 1,240 | 1,430 | | 580 R | 42.9% | 26.5% | 30.6% |
| 32,904 | MADISON | 2,861 | 525 | 753 | 1,583 | | 830 U | 18.4% | 26.3% | 55.3% |
| 23,293 | MARION | 3,045 | 698 | 1,082 | 1,265 | | 183 U | 22.9% | 35.5% | 41.5% |
| 24,503 | MARSHALL | 1,785 | 404 | 681 | 700 | | 19 U | 22.6% | 38.2% | 39.2% |
| 33,953 | MONROE | 4,860 | 1,400 | 1,901 | 1,559 | | 342 D | 28.8% | 39.1% | 32.1% |
| 13,320 | MONTGOMERY | 1,969 | 585 | 623 | 761 | | 138 U | 29.7% | 31.6% | 38.6% |
| 20,927 | NESHOBA | 4,136 | 580 | 1,840 | 1,716 | | 124 D | 14.0% | 44.5% | 41.5% |
| 19,517 | NEWTON | 3,376 | 508 | 912 | 1,956 | | 1,044 U | 15.0% | 27.0% | 57.9% |
| 16,826 | NOXUBEE | 1,489 | 342 | 277 | 870 | | 528 U | 23.0% | 18.6% | 58.4% |
| 26,175 | OKTIBBEHA | 3,416 | 829 | 915 | 1,672 | | 757 U | 24.3% | 26.8% | 48.9% |
| 28,791 | PANOLA | 2,888 | 643 | 841 | 1,404 | | 563 U | 22.3% | 29.1% | 48.6% |
| 22,411 | PEARL RIVER | 3,483 | 651 | 1,276 | 1,556 | | 280 U | 18.7% | 36.6% | 44.7% |
| 8,745 | PERRY | 1,344 | 274 | 514 | 556 | | 42 U | 20.4% | 38.2% | 41.4% |
| 35,063 | PIKE | 5,357 | 1,467 | 1,258 | 2,632 | | 1,165 U | 27.4% | 23.5% | 49.1% |
| 17,232 | PONTOTOC | 2,704 | 328 | 1,584 | 792 | | 792 D | 12.1% | 58.6% | 29.3% |
| 17,949 | PRENTISS | 2,985 | 740 | 1,777 | 468 | | 1,037 D | 24.8% | 59.5% | 15.7% |
| 21,019 | QUITMAN | 1,556 | 299 | 583 | 674 | | 91 U | 19.2% | 37.5% | 43.3% |

# MISSISSIPPI

## PRESIDENT 1960

| 1960 Census Population | County | Total Vote | Republican | Democratic | Unpledged | Other | Plurality | Percentage Total Vote | | |
|---|---|---|---|---|---|---|---|---|---|---|
| | | | | | | | | Rep. | Dem. | Unp. |
| 34,322 | RANKIN | 4,782 | 818 | 850 | 3,114 | | 2,264 U | 17.1% | 17.8% | 65.1% |
| 21,187 | SCOTT | 3,472 | 607 | 1,024 | 1,841 | | 817 U | 17.5% | 29.5% | 53.0% |
| 10,738 | SHARKEY | 1,007 | 313 | 263 | 431 | | 118 U | 31.1% | 26.1% | 42.8% |
| 20,454 | SIMPSON | 3,208 | 606 | 1,034 | 1,568 | | 534 U | 18.9% | 32.2% | 48.9% |
| 14,303 | SMITH | 2,946 | 353 | 1,568 | 1,025 | | 543 D | 12.0% | 53.2% | 34.8% |
| 7,013 | STONE | 1,436 | 275 | 343 | 818 | | 475 U | 19.2% | 23.9% | 57.0% |
| 45,750 | SUNFLOWER | 3,451 | 1,177 | 1,033 | 1,241 | | 64 U | 34.1% | 29.9% | 36.0% |
| 24,081 | TALLAHATCHIE | 2,597 | 346 | 830 | 1,421 | | 591 U | 13.3% | 32.0% | 54.7% |
| 18,138 | TATE | 1,772 | 241 | 686 | 845 | | 159 U | 13.6% | 38.7% | 47.7% |
| 15,093 | TIPPAH | 2,892 | 486 | 1,939 | 467 | | 1,453 D | 16.8% | 67.0% | 16.1% |
| 13,889 | TISHOMINGO | 2,427 | 536 | 1,222 | 669 | | 553 D | 22.1% | 50.4% | 27.6% |
| 16,826 | TUNICA | 897 | 334 | 323 | 240 | | 11 R | 37.2% | 36.0% | 26.8% |
| 18,904 | UNION | 3,295 | 605 | 2,001 | 689 | | 1,312 D | 18.4% | 60.7% | 20.9% |
| 13,512 | WALTHALL | 2,139 | 310 | 747 | 1,082 | | 335 U | 14.5% | 34.9% | 50.6% |
| 42,206 | WARREN | 6,587 | 2,277 | 2,289 | 2,021 | | 12 D | 34.6% | 34.8% | 30.7% |
| 78,638 | WASHINGTON | 6,655 | 2,292 | 3,105 | 1,258 | | 813 D | 34.4% | 46.7% | 18.9% |
| 16,258 | WAYNE | 2,233 | 490 | 707 | 1,036 | | 329 U | 21.9% | 31.7% | 46.4% |
| 10,580 | WEBSTER | 2,026 | 299 | 553 | 1,174 | | 621 U | 14.8% | 27.3% | 57.9% |
| 13,235 | WILKINSON | 1,222 | 174 | 216 | 832 | | 616 U | 14.2% | 17.7% | 68.1% |
| 19,246 | WINSTON | 2,966 | 405 | 1,056 | 1,505 | | 449 U | 13.7% | 35.6% | 50.7% |
| 12,502 | YALOBUSHA | 1,903 | 549 | 650 | 704 | | 54 U | 28.8% | 34.2% | 37.0% |
| 31,653 | YAZOO | 3,340 | 778 | 715 | 1,847 | | 1,069 U | 23.3% | 21.4% | 55.3% |
| 2,178,141 | TOTAL | 298,171 | 73,561 | 108,362 | 116,248 | | 7,886 U | 24.7% | 36.3% | 39.0% |

# MISSISSIPPI

## ELECTION NOTES

**2004**   Other vote was 3,177 Reform (Ralph Nader); 1,793 Libertarian (Michael Badnarik); 1,759 Constitution (Michael Peroutka); 1,268 Independent (James Harris); 1,073 Green (David Cobb).

**2000**   Other vote was 3,267 Constitution (Phillips); 2,265 Reform (Buchanan); 2,009 Libertarian (Browne); 613 Independent (Harris); 450 Natural Law (Hagelin). Nader was listed on the Mississippi ballot as an independent.

**1996**   Other vote was 2,809 Libertarian (Browne); 2,314 Taxpayers (Phillips); 1,447 Natural Law (Hagelin); 1,205 Independent (Collins).

**1992**   Other vote was 2,625 Fulani (Independent); 2,154 Marrou (Libertarian); 1,652 Phillips (Taxpayers); 1,140 Hagelin (Independent); 545 Gritz (Independent).

**1988**   Other vote was 4,232 Duke (Independent); 3,329 Paul (Libertarian); 2,155 Fulani (Independent).

**1984**   Other vote was 2,336 Bergland (Libertarian); 1,169 Holmes (Independent); 1,032 Mason (Independent); 1,001 LaRouche (Independent); 641 Richards (Independent); 356 Serrette (Independent).

**1980**   Other vote was 12,036 Anderson (Independent); 5,465 Clark (Independent); 2,402 Griswold (Independent); 2,347 Pulley (Independent).

**1976**   Other vote was 6,678 Anderson (American); 4,861 Maddox (Independent); 4,074 McCarthy (Independent); 2,805 Camejo (Independent); 2,788 MacBride (Independent). Early unamended canvass gave the statewide total votes as 381,329 Republican; 2,787 MacBride (Independent); and the Republican vote in Jefferson Davis county as 1,808; the Democratic vote in Noxubee county as 3,121.

**1972**   Other vote was 11,598 Schmitz (Independent); 2,458 Jenness (Independent).

**1968**   Wallace on the ballot as Independent.

**1964**

**1960**   Other vote all cast for an unpledged Independent Democratic slate of electors. This slate carried the state and Mississippi's 8 Electoral College votes were cast for Senator Harry Flood Byrd for President. It should be noted that in using the Republican-Democratic plurality figures, the Independent Democratic electors carried fifty-four of the eighty-two counties and ran second in many others.

# MISSOURI

## POPULAR VOTE FOR PRESIDENT 1920 TO 2004

| Year | Total Vote | Republican Vote | Republican Candidate | Democratic Vote | Democratic Candidate | Other Vote | Plurality | Percentage Total Vote Rep. | Percentage Total Vote Dem. | Percentage Major Vote Rep. | Percentage Major Vote Dem. |
|---|---|---|---|---|---|---|---|---|---|---|---|
| 2004 | 2,731,364 | 1,455,713 | Bush, George W. | 1,259,171 | Kerry, John | 16,480 | 196,542 R | 53.3% | 46.1% | 53.6% | 46.4% |
| 2000 ** | 2,359,892 | 1,189,924 | Bush, George W. | 1,111,138 | Gore, Al | 58,830 | 78,786 R | 50.4% | 47.1% | 51.7% | 48.3% |
| 1996 ** | 2,158,065 | 890,016 | Dole, Bob | 1,025,935 | Clinton, Bill | 242,114 | 135,919 D | 41.2% | 47.5% | 46.5% | 53.5% |
| 1992 ** | 2,391,565 | 811,159 | Bush, George | 1,053,873 | Clinton, Bill | 526,533 | 242,714 D | 33.9% | 44.1% | 43.5% | 56.5% |
| 1988 | 2,093,713 | 1,084,953 | Bush, George | 1,001,619 | Dukakis, Michael S. | 7,141 | 83,334 R | 51.8% | 47.8% | 52.0% | 48.0% |
| 1984 | 2,122,783 | 1,274,188 | Reagan, Ronald | 848,583 | Mondale, Walter F. | 12 | 425,605 R | 60.0% | 40.0% | 60.0% | 40.0% |
| 1980** | 2,099,824 | 1,074,181 | Reagan, Ronald | 931,182 | Carter, Jimmy | 94,461 | 142,999 R | 51.2% | 44.3% | 53.6% | 46.4% |
| 1976 | 1,953,600 | 927,443 | Ford, Gerald R. | 998,387 | Carter, Jimmy | 27,770 | 70,944 D | 47.5% | 51.1% | 48.2% | 51.8% |
| 1972 | 1,855,803 | 1,153,852 | Nixon, Richard M. | 697,147 | McGovern, George S. | 4,804 | 456,705 R | 62.2% | 37.6% | 62.3% | 37.7% |
| 1968 | 1,809,502 | 811,932 | Nixon, Richard M. | 791,444 | Humphrey, Hubert H. | 206,126 | 20,488 R | 44.9% | 43.7% | 50.6% | 49.4% |
| 1964 | 1,817,879 | 653,535 | Goldwater, Barry M. | 1,164,344 | Johnson, Lyndon B. | | 510,809 D | 36.0% | 64.0% | 36.0% | 64.0% |
| 1960 | 1,934,422 | 962,221 | Nixon, Richard M. | 972,201 | Kennedy, John F. | | 9,980 D | 49.7% | 50.3% | 49.7% | 50.3% |
| 1956 | 1,832,562 | 914,289 | Eisenhower, Dwight D. | 918,273 | Stevenson, Adlai E. | | 3,984 D | 49.9% | 50.1% | 49.9% | 50.1% |
| 1952 | 1,892,062 | 959,429 | Eisenhower, Dwight D. | 929,830 | Stevenson, Adlai E. | 2,803 | 29,599 R | 50.7% | 49.1% | 50.8% | 49.2% |
| 1948 | 1,578,628 | 655,039 | Dewey, Thomas E. | 917,315 | Truman, Harry S. | 6,274 | 262,276 D | 41.5% | 58.1% | 41.7% | 58.3% |
| 1944 | 1,571,697 | 761,175 | Dewey, Thomas E. | 807,356 | Roosevelt, Franklin D. | 3,166 | 46,181 D | 48.4% | 51.4% | 48.5% | 51.5% |
| 1940 | 1,833,729 | 871,009 | Willkie, Wendell | 958,476 | Roosevelt, Franklin D. | 4,244 | 87,467 D | 47.5% | 52.3% | 47.6% | 52.4% |
| 1936 | 1,828,635 | 697,891 | Landon, Alfred M. | 1,111,043 | Roosevelt, Franklin D. | 19,701 | 413,152 D | 38.2% | 60.8% | 38.6% | 61.4% |
| 1932 | 1,609,894 | 564,713 | Hoover, Herbert C. | 1,025,406 | Roosevelt, Franklin D. | 19,775 | 460,693 D | 35.1% | 63.7% | 35.5% | 64.5% |
| 1928 | 1,500,845 | 834,080 | Hoover, Herbert C. | 662,684 | Smith, Alfred E. | 4,081 | 171,396 R | 55.6% | 44.2% | 55.7% | 44.3% |
| 1924 | 1,310,095 | 648,488 | Coolidge, Calvin | 574,962 | Davis, John W. | 86,645 | 73,526 R | 49.5% | 43.9% | 53.0% | 47.0% |
| 1920 | 1,332,140 | 727,252 | Harding, Warren G. | 574,699 | Cox, James M. | 30,189 | 152,553 R | 54.6% | 43.1% | 55.9% | 44.1% |

In 2000 the other vote column includes 38,515 votes cast for Green (Nader). In 1996 the other vote column includes 217,188 votes cast for Perot. In 1992 the other vote column includes 518,741 votes cast for Perot. In 1980 the other column includes 77,920 votes for Independent (Anderson).

## ELECTORAL COLLEGE VOTE 1920 TO 2004

| Year | Total | Republican | Democratic | Other |
|---|---|---|---|---|
| 2004 | 11 | 11 | | |
| 2000 | 11 | 11 | | |
| 1996 | 11 | | 11 | |
| 1992 | 11 | | 11 | |
| 1988 | 11 | 11 | | |
| 1984 | 11 | 11 | | |
| 1980 | 12 | 12 | | |
| 1976 | 12 | | 12 | |
| 1972 | 12 | 12 | | |
| 1968 | 12 | 12 | | |
| 1964 | 12 | | 12 | |
| 1960 | 13 | | 13 | |
| 1956 | 13 | | 13 | |
| 1952 | 13 | 13 | | |
| 1948 | 15 | | 15 | |
| 1944 | 15 | | 15 | |
| 1940 | 15 | | 15 | |
| 1936 | 15 | | 15 | |
| 1932 | 15 | | 15 | |
| 1928 | 18 | 18 | | |
| 1924 | 18 | 18 | | |
| 1920 | 18 | 18 | | |

# MISSOURI

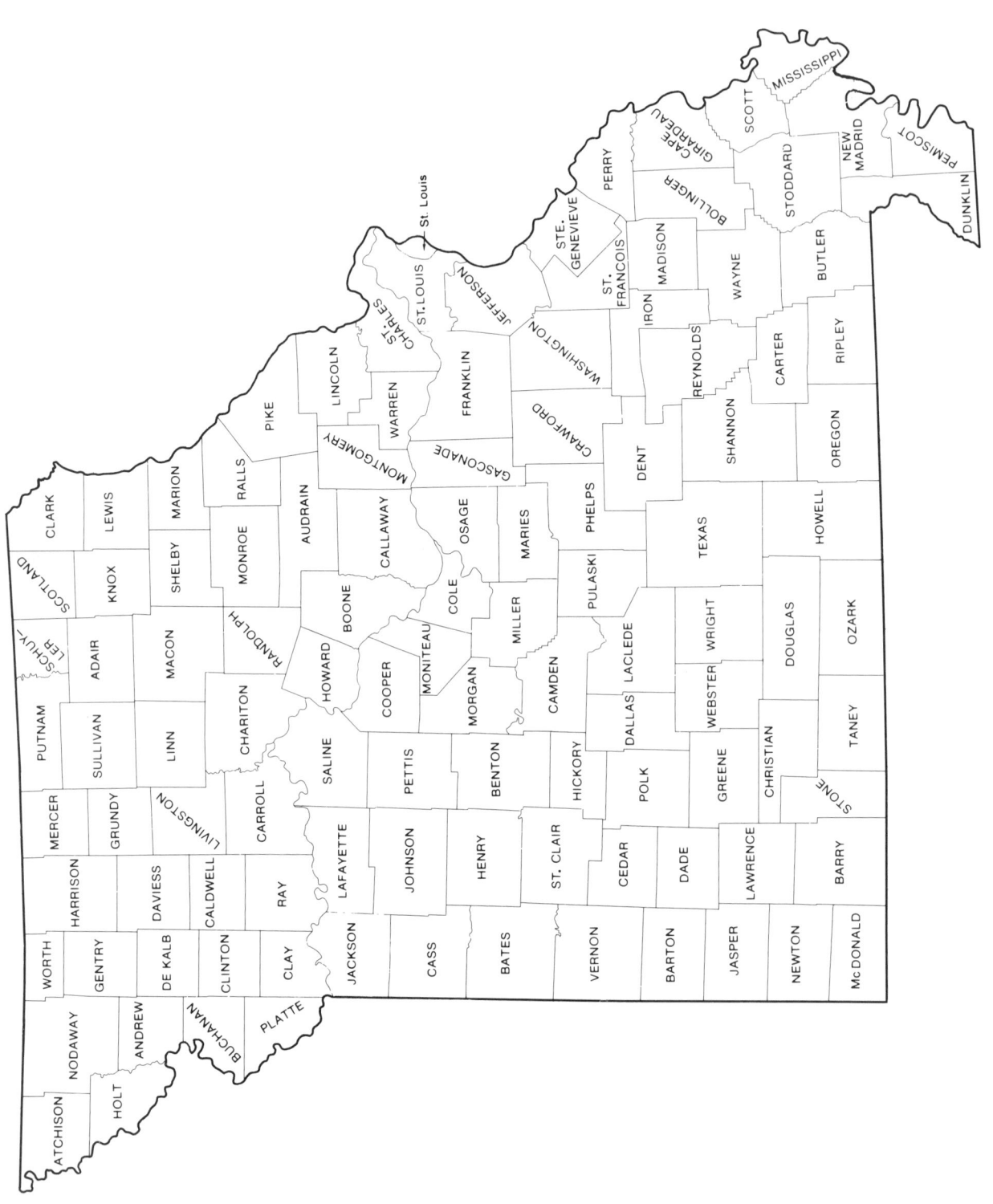

# MISSOURI

## PRESIDENT 2004

| 2000 Census Population | County | Total Vote | Republican | Democratic | Other | Rep.-Dem. Plurality | Percentage | | | |
|---|---|---|---|---|---|---|---|---|---|---|
| | | | | | | | Total Vote | | Major Vote | |
| | | | | | | | Rep. | Dem. | Rep. | Dem. |
| 24,977 | ADAIR | 11,404 | 6,367 | 4,938 | 99 | 1,429 R | 55.8% | 43.3% | 56.3% | 43.7% |
| 16,492 | ANDREW | 8,266 | 5,135 | 3,069 | 62 | 2,066 R | 62.1% | 37.1% | 62.6% | 37.4% |
| 6,430 | ATCHISON | 3,156 | 2,137 | 1,005 | 14 | 1,132 R | 67.7% | 31.8% | 68.0% | 32.0% |
| 25,853 | AUDRAIN | 10,683 | 6,294 | 4,318 | 71 | 1,976 R | 58.9% | 40.4% | 59.3% | 40.7% |
| 34,010 | BARRY | 13,927 | 9,599 | 4,223 | 105 | 5,376 R | 68.9% | 30.3% | 69.4% | 30.6% |
| 12,541 | BARTON | 5,991 | 4,572 | 1,373 | 46 | 3,199 R | 76.3% | 22.9% | 76.9% | 23.1% |
| 16,653 | BATES | 8,466 | 5,004 | 3,398 | 64 | 1,606 R | 59.1% | 40.1% | 59.6% | 40.4% |
| 17,180 | BENTON | 9,009 | 5,575 | 3,381 | 53 | 2,194 R | 61.9% | 37.5% | 62.2% | 37.8% |
| 12,029 | BOLLINGER | 5,895 | 4,102 | 1,754 | 39 | 2,348 R | 69.6% | 29.8% | 70.0% | 30.0% |
| 135,454 | BOONE | 76,046 | 37,801 | 37,643 | 602 | 158 R | 49.7% | 49.5% | 50.1% | 49.9% |
| 85,998 | BUCHANAN | 37,950 | 19,812 | 17,799 | 339 | 2,013 R | 52.2% | 46.9% | 52.7% | 47.3% |
| 40,867 | BUTLER | 16,441 | 11,696 | 4,666 | 79 | 7,030 R | 71.1% | 28.4% | 71.5% | 28.5% |
| 8,969 | CALDWELL | 4,268 | 2,593 | 1,645 | 30 | 948 R | 60.8% | 38.5% | 61.2% | 38.8% |
| 40,766 | CALLAWAY | 17,773 | 11,108 | 6,559 | 106 | 4,549 R | 62.5% | 36.9% | 62.9% | 37.1% |
| 37,051 | CAMDEN | 19,519 | 13,122 | 6,296 | 101 | 6,826 R | 67.2% | 32.3% | 67.6% | 32.4% |
| 68,693 | CAPE GIRARDEAU | 34,565 | 23,814 | 10,568 | 183 | 13,246 R | 68.9% | 30.6% | 69.3% | 30.7% |
| 10,285 | CARROLL | 4,741 | 3,155 | 1,568 | 18 | 1,587 R | 66.5% | 33.1% | 66.8% | 33.2% |
| 5,941 | CARTER | 2,779 | 1,797 | 964 | 18 | 833 R | 64.7% | 34.7% | 65.1% | 34.9% |
| 82,092 | CASS | 44,217 | 27,253 | 16,681 | 283 | 10,572 R | 61.6% | 37.7% | 62.0% | 38.0% |
| 13,733 | CEDAR | 6,203 | 4,238 | 1,910 | 55 | 2,328 R | 68.3% | 30.8% | 68.9% | 31.1% |
| 8,438 | CHARITON | 4,340 | 2,421 | 1,892 | 27 | 529 R | 55.8% | 43.6% | 56.1% | 43.9% |
| 54,285 | CHRISTIAN | 31,348 | 22,102 | 9,059 | 187 | 13,043 R | 70.5% | 28.9% | 70.9% | 29.1% |
| 7,416 | CLARK | 3,736 | 1,899 | 1,794 | 43 | 105 R | 50.8% | 48.0% | 51.4% | 48.6% |
| 184,006 | CLAY | 96,460 | 51,193 | 44,670 | 597 | 6,523 R | 53.1% | 46.3% | 53.4% | 46.6% |
| 18,979 | CLINTON | 9,540 | 5,287 | 4,165 | 88 | 1,122 R | 55.4% | 43.7% | 55.9% | 44.1% |
| 71,397 | COLE | 36,701 | 24,752 | 11,753 | 196 | 12,999 R | 67.4% | 32.0% | 67.8% | 32.2% |
| 16,670 | COOPER | 7,508 | 5,058 | 2,400 | 50 | 2,658 R | 67.4% | 32.0% | 67.8% | 32.2% |
| 22,804 | CRAWFORD | 9,381 | 5,686 | 3,632 | 63 | 2,054 R | 60.6% | 38.7% | 61.0% | 39.0% |
| 7,923 | DADE | 4,089 | 2,963 | 1,104 | 22 | 1,859 R | 72.5% | 27.0% | 72.9% | 27.1% |
| 15,661 | DALLAS | 7,259 | 4,788 | 2,407 | 64 | 2,381 R | 66.0% | 33.2% | 66.5% | 33.5% |
| 8,016 | DAVIESS | 3,794 | 2,351 | 1,402 | 41 | 949 R | 62.0% | 37.0% | 62.6% | 37.4% |
| 11,597 | DE KALB | 4,686 | 2,941 | 1,707 | 38 | 1,234 R | 62.8% | 36.4% | 63.3% | 36.7% |
| 14,927 | DENT | 6,304 | 4,369 | 1,865 | 70 | 2,504 R | 69.3% | 29.6% | 70.1% | 29.9% |
| 13,084 | DOUGLAS | 6,327 | 4,498 | 1,741 | 88 | 2,757 R | 71.1% | 27.5% | 72.1% | 27.9% |
| 33,155 | DUNKLIN | 11,677 | 6,720 | 4,901 | 56 | 1,819 R | 57.5% | 42.0% | 57.8% | 42.2% |
| 93,807 | FRANKLIN | 45,318 | 26,429 | 18,556 | 333 | 7,873 R | 58.3% | 40.9% | 58.8% | 41.2% |
| 15,342 | GASCONADE | 7,171 | 4,753 | 2,355 | 63 | 2,398 R | 66.3% | 32.8% | 66.9% | 33.1% |
| 6,861 | GENTRY | 3,312 | 2,085 | 1,201 | 26 | 884 R | 63.0% | 36.3% | 63.5% | 36.5% |
| 240,391 | GREENE | 125,266 | 77,885 | 46,657 | 724 | 31,228 R | 62.2% | 37.2% | 62.5% | 37.5% |
| 10,432 | GRUNDY | 4,808 | 3,172 | 1,561 | 75 | 1,611 R | 66.0% | 32.5% | 67.0% | 33.0% |
| 8,850 | HARRISON | 4,048 | 2,729 | 1,279 | 40 | 1,450 R | 67.4% | 31.6% | 68.1% | 31.9% |
| 21,997 | HENRY | 10,877 | 6,361 | 4,461 | 55 | 1,900 R | 58.5% | 41.0% | 58.8% | 41.2% |
| 8,940 | HICKORY | 4,866 | 2,791 | 2,043 | 32 | 748 R | 57.4% | 42.0% | 57.7% | 42.3% |
| 5,351 | HOLT | 2,691 | 1,864 | 811 | 16 | 1,053 R | 69.3% | 30.1% | 69.7% | 30.3% |
| 10,212 | HOWARD | 4,921 | 2,915 | 1,972 | 34 | 943 R | 59.2% | 40.1% | 59.6% | 40.4% |
| 37,238 | HOWELL | 16,379 | 11,097 | 5,118 | 164 | 5,979 R | 67.8% | 31.2% | 68.4% | 31.6% |
| 10,697 | IRON | 4,679 | 2,477 | 2,157 | 45 | 320 R | 52.9% | 46.1% | 53.5% | 46.5% |
| 654,880 | JACKSON | 174,570 | 94,439 | 79,029 | 1,102 | 15,410 R | 54.1% | 45.3% | 54.4% | 45.6% |
| 104,686 | JASPER | 45,085 | 31,846 | 13,002 | 237 | 18,844 R | 70.6% | 28.8% | 71.0% | 29.0% |
| 198,099 | JEFFERSON | 93,264 | 46,624 | 46,057 | 583 | 567 R | 50.0% | 49.4% | 50.3% | 49.7% |
| 48,258 | JOHNSON | 20,236 | 12,257 | 7,790 | 189 | 4,467 R | 60.6% | 38.5% | 61.1% | 38.9% |
| *See Note | KANSAS CITY | 141,423 | 36,061 | 104,625 | 737 | 68,564 D | 25.5% | 74.0% | 25.6% | 74.4% |
| 4,361 | KNOX | 1,978 | 1,207 | 761 | 10 | 446 R | 61.0% | 38.5% | 61.3% | 38.7% |
| 32,513 | LACLEDE | 14,869 | 10,578 | 4,213 | 78 | 6,365 R | 71.1% | 28.3% | 71.5% | 28.5% |
| 32,960 | LAFAYETTE | 16,182 | 9,656 | 6,412 | 114 | 3,244 R | 59.7% | 39.6% | 60.1% | 39.9% |
| 35,204 | LAWRENCE | 15,806 | 11,194 | 4,506 | 106 | 6,688 R | 70.8% | 28.5% | 71.3% | 28.7% |
| 10,494 | LEWIS | 4,644 | 2,862 | 1,754 | 28 | 1,108 R | 61.6% | 37.8% | 62.0% | 38.0% |
| 38,944 | LINCOLN | 19,839 | 11,316 | 8,368 | 155 | 2,948 R | 57.0% | 42.2% | 57.5% | 42.5% |
| 13,754 | LINN | 5,898 | 3,422 | 2,440 | 36 | 982 R | 58.0% | 41.4% | 58.4% | 41.6% |
| 14,558 | LIVINGSTON | 6,346 | 4,029 | 2,278 | 39 | 1,751 R | 63.5% | 35.9% | 63.9% | 36.1% |

# MISSOURI

## PRESIDENT 2004

| 2000 Census Population | County | Total Vote | Republican | Democratic | Other | Rep.-Dem. Plurality | Percentage Total Vote Rep. | Dem. | Major Vote Rep. | Dem. |
|---|---|---|---|---|---|---|---|---|---|---|
| 21,681 | MCDONALD | 7,725 | 5,443 | 2,215 | 67 | 3,228 R | 70.5% | 28.7% | 71.1% | 28.9% |
| 15,762 | MACON | 7,570 | 4,673 | 2,856 | 41 | 1,817 R | 61.7% | 37.7% | 62.1% | 37.9% |
| 11,800 | MADISON | 4,918 | 2,905 | 1,972 | 41 | 933 R | 59.1% | 40.1% | 59.6% | 40.4% |
| 8,903 | MARIES | 4,424 | 2,825 | 1,563 | 36 | 1,262 R | 63.9% | 35.3% | 64.4% | 35.6% |
| 28,289 | MARION | 12,453 | 7,815 | 4,568 | 70 | 3,247 R | 62.8% | 36.7% | 63.1% | 36.9% |
| 3,757 | MERCER | 1,817 | 1,207 | 582 | 28 | 625 R | 66.4% | 32.0% | 67.5% | 32.5% |
| 23,564 | MILLER | 10,831 | 7,797 | 2,959 | 75 | 4,838 R | 72.0% | 27.3% | 72.5% | 27.5% |
| 13,427 | MISSISSIPPI | 5,298 | 2,903 | 2,374 | 21 | 529 R | 54.8% | 44.8% | 55.0% | 45.0% |
| 14,827 | MONITEAU | 6,691 | 4,743 | 1,913 | 35 | 2,830 R | 70.9% | 28.6% | 71.3% | 28.7% |
| 9,311 | MONROE | 4,307 | 2,632 | 1,647 | 28 | 985 R | 61.1% | 38.2% | 61.5% | 38.5% |
| 12,136 | MONTGOMERY | 5,760 | 3,563 | 2,147 | 50 | 1,416 R | 61.9% | 37.3% | 62.4% | 37.6% |
| 19,309 | MORGAN | 8,771 | 5,657 | 3,053 | 61 | 2,604 R | 64.5% | 34.8% | 64.9% | 35.1% |
| 19,760 | NEW MADRID | 7,907 | 4,154 | 3,716 | 37 | 438 R | 52.5% | 47.0% | 52.8% | 47.2% |
| 52,636 | NEWTON | 23,889 | 17,187 | 6,564 | 138 | 10,623 R | 71.9% | 27.5% | 72.4% | 27.6% |
| 21,912 | NODAWAY | 10,119 | 6,226 | 3,830 | 63 | 2,396 R | 61.5% | 37.8% | 61.9% | 38.1% |
| 10,344 | OREGON | 4,673 | 2,769 | 1,823 | 81 | 946 R | 59.3% | 39.0% | 60.3% | 39.7% |
| 13,062 | OSAGE | 6,671 | 4,975 | 1,673 | 23 | 3,302 R | 74.6% | 25.1% | 74.8% | 25.2% |
| 9,542 | OZARK | 4,707 | 3,083 | 1,561 | 63 | 1,522 R | 65.5% | 33.2% | 66.4% | 33.6% |
| 20,047 | PEMISCOT | 6,806 | 3,398 | 3,381 | 27 | 17 R | 49.9% | 49.7% | 50.1% | 49.9% |
| 18,132 | PERRY | 8,247 | 5,583 | 2,621 | 43 | 2,962 R | 67.7% | 31.8% | 68.1% | 31.9% |
| 39,403 | PETTIS | 17,496 | 11,603 | 5,801 | 92 | 5,802 R | 66.3% | 33.2% | 66.7% | 33.3% |
| 39,825 | PHELPS | 18,700 | 11,874 | 6,666 | 160 | 5,208 R | 63.5% | 35.6% | 64.0% | 36.0% |
| 18,351 | PIKE | 8,040 | 4,314 | 3,670 | 56 | 644 R | 53.7% | 45.6% | 54.0% | 46.0% |
| 73,781 | PLATTE | 41,970 | 23,302 | 18,412 | 256 | 4,890 R | 55.5% | 43.9% | 55.9% | 44.1% |
| 26,992 | POLK | 12,453 | 8,586 | 3,775 | 92 | 4,811 R | 68.9% | 30.3% | 69.5% | 30.5% |
| 41,165 | PULASKI | 12,221 | 8,618 | 3,551 | 52 | 5,067 R | 70.5% | 29.1% | 70.8% | 29.2% |
| 5,223 | PUTNAM | 2,445 | 1,660 | 772 | 13 | 888 R | 67.9% | 31.6% | 68.3% | 31.7% |
| 9,626 | RALLS | 5,034 | 2,986 | 2,031 | 17 | 955 R | 59.3% | 40.3% | 59.5% | 40.5% |
| 24,663 | RANDOLPH | 10,198 | 6,551 | 3,586 | 61 | 2,965 R | 64.2% | 35.2% | 64.6% | 35.4% |
| 23,354 | RAY | 10,788 | 5,673 | 5,034 | 81 | 639 R | 52.6% | 46.7% | 53.0% | 47.0% |
| 6,689 | REYNOLDS | 3,364 | 1,896 | 1,449 | 19 | 447 R | 56.4% | 43.1% | 56.7% | 43.3% |
| 13,509 | RIPLEY | 5,653 | 3,693 | 1,907 | 53 | 1,786 R | 65.3% | 33.7% | 65.9% | 34.1% |
| 283,883 | ST. CHARLES | 163,488 | 95,826 | 66,855 | 807 | 28,971 R | 58.6% | 40.9% | 58.9% | 41.1% |
| 9,652 | ST. CLAIR | 4,965 | 3,098 | 1,841 | 26 | 1,257 R | 62.4% | 37.1% | 62.7% | 37.3% |
| 55,641 | ST. FRANCOIS | 22,933 | 12,087 | 10,748 | 98 | 1,339 R | 52.7% | 46.9% | 52.9% | 47.1% |
| 1,016,315 | ST. LOUIS COUNTY | 542,983 | 244,969 | 295,284 | 2,730 | 50,315 D | 45.1% | 54.4% | 45.3% | 54.7% |
| 348,189 | ST. LOUIS CITY | 144,638 | 27,793 | 116,133 | 712 | 88,340 D | 19.2% | 80.3% | 19.3% | 80.7% |
| 17,842 | STE. GENEVIEVE | 8,146 | 3,791 | 4,281 | 74 | 490 D | 46.5% | 52.6% | 47.0% | 53.0% |
| 23,756 | SALINE | 9,939 | 5,389 | 4,479 | 71 | 910 R | 54.2% | 45.1% | 54.6% | 45.4% |
| 4,170 | SCHUYLER | 2,031 | 1,124 | 894 | 13 | 230 R | 55.3% | 44.0% | 55.7% | 44.3% |
| 4,983 | SCOTLAND | 2,197 | 1,352 | 828 | 17 | 524 R | 61.5% | 37.7% | 62.0% | 38.0% |
| 40,422 | SCOTT | 17,448 | 11,330 | 6,057 | 61 | 5,273 R | 64.9% | 34.7% | 65.2% | 34.8% |
| 8,324 | SHANNON | 4,167 | 2,511 | 1,618 | 38 | 893 R | 60.3% | 38.8% | 60.8% | 39.2% |
| 6,799 | SHELBY | 3,502 | 2,280 | 1,201 | 21 | 1,079 R | 65.1% | 34.3% | 65.5% | 34.5% |
| 29,705 | STODDARD | 13,252 | 9,242 | 3,946 | 64 | 5,296 R | 69.7% | 29.8% | 70.1% | 29.9% |
| 28,658 | STONE | 15,189 | 10,534 | 4,578 | 77 | 5,956 R | 69.4% | 30.1% | 69.7% | 30.3% |
| 7,219 | SULLIVAN | 3,089 | 1,880 | 1,178 | 31 | 702 R | 60.9% | 38.1% | 61.5% | 38.5% |
| 39,703 | TANEY | 19,280 | 13,578 | 5,601 | 101 | 7,977 R | 70.4% | 29.1% | 70.8% | 29.2% |
| 23,003 | TEXAS | 11,018 | 7,234 | 3,664 | 120 | 3,570 R | 65.7% | 33.3% | 66.4% | 33.6% |
| 20,454 | VERNON | 8,992 | 5,732 | 3,206 | 54 | 2,526 R | 63.7% | 35.7% | 64.1% | 35.9% |
| 24,525 | WARREN | 13,432 | 7,883 | 5,461 | 88 | 2,422 R | 58.7% | 40.7% | 59.1% | 40.9% |
| 23,344 | WASHINGTON | 9,178 | 4,641 | 4,459 | 78 | 182 R | 50.6% | 48.6% | 51.0% | 49.0% |
| 13,259 | WAYNE | 6,204 | 3,919 | 2,250 | 35 | 1,669 R | 63.2% | 36.3% | 63.5% | 36.5% |
| 31,045 | WEBSTER | 14,944 | 10,194 | 4,657 | 93 | 5,537 R | 68.2% | 31.2% | 68.6% | 31.4% |
| 2,382 | WORTH | 1,132 | 691 | 436 | 5 | 255 R | 61.0% | 38.5% | 61.3% | 38.7% |
| 17,955 | WRIGHT | 8,346 | 6,090 | 2,188 | 68 | 3,902 R | 73.0% | 26.2% | 73.6% | 26.4% |
| 5,595,211 | TOTAL | 2,731,364 | 1,455,713 | 1,259,171 | 16,480 | 196,542 R | 53.3% | 46.1% | 53.6% | 46.4% |

Note: Kansas City has established its own election board and reports its results separately from Jackson County.

# MISSOURI

## PRESIDENT 2000

| 2000 Census Population | County | Total Vote | Republican | Democratic | Green (Nader) | Other | Rep.-Dem. Plurality | Percentage of Total Vote | | |
|---|---|---|---|---|---|---|---|---|---|---|
| | | | | | | | | Rep. | Dem. | Green |
| 24,977 | ADAIR | 10,552 | 6,050 | 4,101 | 301 | 100 | 1,949 R | 57.3% | 38.9% | 2.9% |
| 16,492 | ANDREW | 7,274 | 4,257 | 2,795 | 128 | 94 | 1,462 R | 58.5% | 38.4% | 1.8% |
| 6,430 | ATCHISON | 2,871 | 1,798 | 1,013 | 35 | 25 | 785 R | 62.6% | 35.3% | 1.2% |
| 25,853 | AUDRAIN | 9,985 | 5,256 | 4,551 | 113 | 65 | 705 R | 52.6% | 45.6% | 1.1% |
| 34,010 | BARRY | 12,368 | 7,885 | 4,135 | 193 | 155 | 3,750 R | 63.8% | 33.4% | 1.6% |
| 12,541 | BARTON | 5,366 | 3,836 | 1,424 | 75 | 31 | 2,412 R | 71.5% | 26.5% | 1.4% |
| 16,653 | BATES | 7,792 | 4,245 | 3,386 | 84 | 77 | 859 R | 54.5% | 43.5% | 1.1% |
| 17,180 | BENTON | 7,534 | 4,218 | 3,150 | 97 | 69 | 1,068 R | 56.0% | 41.8% | 1.3% |
| 12,029 | BOLLINGER | 5,294 | 3,487 | 1,692 | 41 | 74 | 1,795 R | 65.9% | 32.0% | 0.8% |
| 135,454 | BOONE | 59,609 | 28,426 | 28,811 | 1,894 | 478 | 385 D | 47.7% | 48.3% | 3.2% |
| 85,998 | BUCHANAN | 34,751 | 16,423 | 17,085 | 776 | 467 | 662 D | 47.3% | 49.2% | 2.2% |
| 40,867 | BUTLER | 14,397 | 9,111 | 4,996 | 149 | 141 | 4,115 R | 63.3% | 34.7% | 1.0% |
| 8,969 | CALDWELL | 3,850 | 2,220 | 1,488 | 76 | 66 | 732 R | 57.7% | 38.6% | 2.0% |
| 40,766 | CALLAWAY | 15,308 | 8,238 | 6,708 | 220 | 142 | 1,530 R | 53.8% | 43.8% | 1.4% |
| 37,051 | CAMDEN | 17,099 | 10,358 | 6,323 | 258 | 160 | 4,035 R | 60.6% | 37.0% | 1.5% |
| 68,693 | CAPE GIRARDEAU | 29,859 | 19,832 | 9,334 | 376 | 317 | 10,498 R | 66.4% | 31.3% | 1.3% |
| 10,285 | CARROLL | 4,581 | 2,880 | 1,620 | 54 | 27 | 1,260 R | 62.9% | 35.4% | 1.2% |
| 5,941 | CARTER | 2,808 | 1,730 | 997 | 40 | 41 | 733 R | 61.6% | 35.5% | 1.4% |
| 82,092 | CASS | 35,869 | 20,113 | 14,921 | 511 | 324 | 5,192 R | 56.1% | 41.6% | 1.4% |
| 13,733 | CEDAR | 5,663 | 3,530 | 1,979 | 81 | 73 | 1,551 R | 62.3% | 34.9% | 1.4% |
| 8,438 | CHARITON | 4,154 | 2,300 | 1,792 | 30 | 32 | 508 R | 55.4% | 43.1% | 0.7% |
| 54,285 | CHRISTIAN | 23,228 | 14,824 | 7,896 | 279 | 229 | 6,928 R | 63.8% | 34.0% | 1.2% |
| 7,416 | CLARK | 3,802 | 1,899 | 1,812 | 53 | 38 | 87 R | 49.9% | 47.7% | 1.4% |
| 184,006 | CLAY | 80,173 | 39,083 | 39,084 | 1,427 | 579 | 1 D | 48.7% | 48.7% | 1.8% |
| 18,979 | CLINTON | 8,531 | 4,323 | 3,994 | 124 | 90 | 329 R | 50.7% | 46.8% | 1.5% |
| 71,397 | COLE | 32,775 | 20,167 | 12,056 | 370 | 182 | 8,111 R | 61.5% | 36.8% | 1.1% |
| 16,670 | COOPER | 6,790 | 4,072 | 2,567 | 78 | 73 | 1,505 R | 60.0% | 37.8% | 1.1% |
| 22,804 | CRAWFORD | 8,302 | 4,754 | 3,350 | 100 | 98 | 1,404 R | 57.3% | 40.4% | 1.2% |
| 7,923 | DADE | 3,752 | 2,468 | 1,193 | 42 | 49 | 1,275 R | 65.8% | 31.8% | 1.1% |
| 15,661 | DALLAS | 6,219 | 3,723 | 2,311 | 76 | 109 | 1,412 R | 59.9% | 37.2% | 1.2% |
| 8,016 | DAVIESS | 3,494 | 2,011 | 1,367 | 58 | 58 | 644 R | 57.6% | 39.1% | 1.7% |
| 11,597 | DE KALB | 4,049 | 2,363 | 1,562 | 63 | 61 | 801 R | 58.4% | 38.6% | 1.6% |
| 14,927 | DENT | 5,988 | 3,996 | 1,839 | 66 | 87 | 2,157 R | 66.7% | 30.7% | 1.1% |
| 13,084 | DOUGLAS | 5,281 | 3,599 | 1,546 | 54 | 82 | 2,053 R | 68.1% | 29.3% | 1.0% |
| 33,155 | DUNKLIN | 10,525 | 5,426 | 4,947 | 78 | 74 | 479 R | 51.6% | 47.0% | 0.7% |
| 93,807 | FRANKLIN | 39,194 | 21,863 | 16,172 | 670 | 489 | 5,691 R | 55.8% | 41.3% | 1.7% |
| 15,342 | GASCONADE | 6,629 | 4,190 | 2,257 | 110 | 72 | 1,933 R | 63.2% | 34.0% | 1.7% |
| 6,861 | GENTRY | 3,105 | 1,771 | 1,271 | 39 | 24 | 500 R | 57.0% | 40.9% | 1.3% |
| 240,391 | GREENE | 102,926 | 59,178 | 41,091 | 1,760 | 897 | 18,087 R | 57.5% | 39.9% | 1.7% |
| 10,432 | GRUNDY | 4,708 | 2,976 | 1,563 | 102 | 67 | 1,413 R | 63.2% | 33.2% | 2.2% |
| 8,850 | HARRISON | 3,991 | 2,552 | 1,328 | 62 | 49 | 1,224 R | 63.9% | 33.3% | 1.6% |
| 21,997 | HENRY | 9,778 | 5,120 | 4,459 | 125 | 74 | 661 R | 52.4% | 45.6% | 1.3% |
| 8,940 | HICKORY | 4,238 | 2,172 | 1,961 | 54 | 51 | 211 R | 51.3% | 46.3% | 1.3% |
| 5,351 | HOLT | 2,662 | 1,738 | 871 | 23 | 30 | 867 R | 65.3% | 32.7% | 0.9% |
| 10,212 | HOWARD | 4,512 | 2,414 | 1,944 | 83 | 71 | 470 R | 53.5% | 43.1% | 1.8% |
| 37,238 | HOWELL | 14,075 | 9,018 | 4,641 | 197 | 219 | 4,377 R | 64.1% | 33.0% | 1.4% |
| 10,697 | IRON | 4,414 | 2,237 | 2,044 | 64 | 69 | 193 R | 50.7% | 46.3% | 1.4% |
| 654,880 | JACKSON | 272,062 | 104,418 | 160,419 | 5,041 | 2,184 | 56,001 D | 38.4% | 59.0% | 1.9% |
| 104,686 | JASPER | 37,481 | 24,899 | 11,737 | 574 | 271 | 13,162 R | 66.4% | 31.3% | 1.5% |
| 198,099 | JEFFERSON | 77,204 | 36,766 | 38,616 | 1,182 | 640 | 1,850 D | 47.6% | 50.0% | 1.5% |
| 48,258 | JOHNSON | 16,787 | 9,339 | 6,926 | 321 | 201 | 2,413 R | 55.6% | 41.3% | 1.9% |
| 4,361 | KNOX | 2,055 | 1,226 | 787 | 24 | 18 | 439 R | 59.7% | 38.3% | 1.2% |
| 32,513 | LACLEDE | 13,046 | 8,556 | 4,183 | 142 | 165 | 4,373 R | 65.6% | 32.1% | 1.1% |
| 32,960 | LAFAYETTE | 14,520 | 7,849 | 6,343 | 205 | 123 | 1,506 R | 54.1% | 43.7% | 1.4% |
| 35,204 | LAWRENCE | 12,903 | 8,305 | 4,235 | 177 | 186 | 4,070 R | 64.4% | 32.8% | 1.4% |
| 10,494 | LEWIS | 4,484 | 2,388 | 2,023 | 34 | 39 | 365 R | 53.3% | 45.1% | 0.8% |
| 38,944 | LINCOLN | 15,913 | 8,549 | 6,961 | 224 | 179 | 1,588 R | 53.7% | 43.7% | 1.4% |
| 13,754 | LINN | 6,010 | 3,246 | 2,646 | 66 | 52 | 600 R | 54.0% | 44.0% | 1.1% |
| 14,558 | LIVINGSTON | 6,276 | 3,709 | 2,425 | 98 | 44 | 1,284 R | 59.1% | 38.6% | 1.6% |
| 21,681 | MCDONALD | 6,529 | 4,460 | 1,866 | 107 | 96 | 2,594 R | 68.3% | 28.6% | 1.6% |

# MISSOURI

## PRESIDENT 2000

| 2000 Census Population | County | Total Vote | Republican | Democratic | Green (Nader) | Other | Rep.-Dem. Plurality | Percentage of Total Vote | | |
|---|---|---|---|---|---|---|---|---|---|---|
| | | | | | | | | Rep. | Dem. | Green |
| 15,762 | MACON | 7,175 | 4,232 | 2,817 | 75 | 51 | 1,415 R | 59.0% | 39.3% | 1.0% |
| 11,800 | MADISON | 4,373 | 2,460 | 1,828 | 42 | 43 | 632 R | 56.3% | 41.8% | 1.0% |
| 8,903 | MARIES | 3,854 | 2,216 | 1,554 | 32 | 52 | 662 R | 57.5% | 40.3% | 0.8% |
| 28,289 | MARION | 11,712 | 6,550 | 4,993 | 87 | 82 | 1,557 R | 55.9% | 42.6% | 0.7% |
| 3,757 | MERCER | 1,842 | 1,250 | 555 | 20 | 17 | 695 R | 67.9% | 30.1% | 1.1% |
| 23,564 | MILLER | 9,356 | 5,945 | 3,217 | 133 | 61 | 2,728 R | 63.5% | 34.4% | 1.4% |
| 13,427 | MISSISSIPPI | 5,215 | 2,395 | 2,756 | 29 | 35 | 361 D | 45.9% | 52.8% | 0.6% |
| 14,827 | MONITEAU | 6,065 | 3,764 | 2,176 | 60 | 65 | 1,588 R | 62.1% | 35.9% | 1.0% |
| 9,311 | MONROE | 4,094 | 2,175 | 1,860 | 20 | 39 | 315 R | 53.1% | 45.4% | 0.5% |
| 12,136 | MONTGOMERY | 5,303 | 3,106 | 2,092 | 70 | 35 | 1,014 R | 58.6% | 39.4% | 1.3% |
| 19,309 | MORGAN | 7,881 | 4,460 | 3,235 | 87 | 99 | 1,225 R | 56.6% | 41.0% | 1.1% |
| 19,760 | NEW MADRID | 7,266 | 3,416 | 3,738 | 45 | 67 | 322 D | 47.0% | 51.4% | 0.6% |
| 52,636 | NEWTON | 21,162 | 14,232 | 6,447 | 326 | 157 | 7,785 R | 67.3% | 30.5% | 1.5% |
| 21,912 | NODAWAY | 9,049 | 5,161 | 3,553 | 215 | 120 | 1,608 R | 57.0% | 39.3% | 2.4% |
| 10,344 | OREGON | 4,233 | 2,521 | 1,568 | 60 | 84 | 953 R | 59.6% | 37.0% | 1.4% |
| 13,062 | OSAGE | 6,178 | 4,154 | 1,938 | 50 | 36 | 2,216 R | 67.2% | 31.4% | 0.8% |
| 9,542 | OZARK | 4,292 | 2,663 | 1,432 | 118 | 79 | 1,231 R | 62.0% | 33.4% | 2.7% |
| 20,047 | PEMISCOT | 6,060 | 2,750 | 3,245 | 37 | 28 | 495 D | 45.4% | 53.5% | 0.6% |
| 18,132 | PERRY | 6,903 | 4,667 | 2,085 | 70 | 81 | 2,582 R | 67.6% | 30.2% | 1.0% |
| 39,403 | PETTIS | 15,755 | 9,533 | 5,855 | 223 | 144 | 3,678 R | 60.5% | 37.2% | 1.4% |
| 39,825 | PHELPS | 16,146 | 9,444 | 6,262 | 253 | 187 | 3,182 R | 58.5% | 38.8% | 1.6% |
| 18,351 | PIKE | 7,351 | 3,648 | 3,557 | 79 | 67 | 91 R | 49.6% | 48.4% | 1.1% |
| 73,781 | PLATTE | 34,054 | 17,785 | 15,325 | 648 | 296 | 2,460 R | 52.2% | 45.0% | 1.9% |
| 26,992 | POLK | 10,294 | 6,430 | 3,606 | 119 | 139 | 2,824 R | 62.5% | 35.0% | 1.2% |
| 41,165 | PULASKI | 10,531 | 6,531 | 3,800 | 120 | 80 | 2,731 R | 62.0% | 36.1% | 1.1% |
| 5,223 | PUTNAM | 2,334 | 1,593 | 708 | 19 | 14 | 885 R | 68.3% | 30.3% | 0.8% |
| 9,626 | RALLS | 4,542 | 2,446 | 2,033 | 36 | 27 | 413 R | 53.9% | 44.8% | 0.8% |
| 24,663 | RANDOLPH | 9,186 | 4,844 | 4,116 | 114 | 112 | 728 R | 52.7% | 44.8% | 1.2% |
| 23,354 | RAY | 9,747 | 4,517 | 4,970 | 145 | 115 | 453 D | 46.3% | 51.0% | 1.5% |
| 6,689 | REYNOLDS | 3,131 | 1,762 | 1,298 | 42 | 29 | 464 R | 56.3% | 41.5% | 1.3% |
| 13,509 | RIPLEY | 5,065 | 3,121 | 1,820 | 58 | 66 | 1,301 R | 61.6% | 35.9% | 1.1% |
| 283,883 | ST. CHARLES | 128,686 | 72,114 | 53,806 | 1,900 | 866 | 18,308 R | 56.0% | 41.8% | 1.5% |
| 9,652 | ST. CLAIR | 4,739 | 2,731 | 1,866 | 80 | 62 | 865 R | 57.6% | 39.4% | 1.7% |
| 55,641 | ST. FRANCOIS | 18,841 | 9,327 | 9,075 | 265 | 174 | 252 R | 49.5% | 48.2% | 1.4% |
| 1,016,315 | ST. LOUIS COUNTY | 486,884 | 224,689 | 250,631 | 8,474 | 3,090 | 25,942 D | 46.1% | 51.5% | 1.7% |
| 348,189 | ST. LOUIS CITY | 124,752 | 24,799 | 96,557 | 2,592 | 804 | 71,758 D | 19.9% | 77.4% | 2.1% |
| 17,842 | STE. GENEVIEVE | 7,311 | 3,505 | 3,600 | 127 | 79 | 95 D | 47.9% | 49.2% | 1.7% |
| 23,756 | SALINE | 9,355 | 4,572 | 4,585 | 131 | 67 | 13 D | 48.9% | 49.0% | 1.4% |
| 4,170 | SCHUYLER | 2,006 | 1,159 | 808 | 16 | 23 | 351 R | 57.8% | 40.3% | 0.8% |
| 4,983 | SCOTLAND | 2,179 | 1,335 | 790 | 37 | 17 | 545 R | 61.3% | 36.3% | 1.7% |
| 40,422 | SCOTT | 15,704 | 8,999 | 6,452 | 113 | 140 | 2,547 R | 57.3% | 41.1% | 0.7% |
| 8,324 | SHANNON | 3,781 | 2,245 | 1,430 | 48 | 58 | 815 R | 59.4% | 37.8% | 1.3% |
| 6,799 | SHELBY | 3,257 | 1,936 | 1,262 | 37 | 22 | 674 R | 59.4% | 38.7% | 1.1% |
| 29,705 | STODDARD | 12,454 | 7,727 | 4,476 | 114 | 137 | 3,251 R | 62.0% | 35.9% | 0.9% |
| 28,658 | STONE | 12,151 | 7,793 | 4,055 | 179 | 124 | 3,738 R | 64.1% | 33.4% | 1.5% |
| 7,219 | SULLIVAN | 3,064 | 1,877 | 1,127 | 27 | 33 | 750 R | 61.3% | 36.8% | 0.9% |
| 39,703 | TANEY | 15,112 | 9,647 | 5,092 | 204 | 169 | 4,555 R | 63.8% | 33.7% | 1.3% |
| 23,003 | TEXAS | 9,932 | 6,136 | 3,486 | 137 | 173 | 2,650 R | 61.8% | 35.1% | 1.4% |
| 20,454 | VERNON | 8,408 | 4,985 | 3,156 | 156 | 111 | 1,829 R | 59.3% | 37.5% | 1.9% |
| 24,525 | WARREN | 10,740 | 5,979 | 4,524 | 150 | 87 | 1,455 R | 55.7% | 42.1% | 1.4% |
| 23,344 | WASHINGTON | 8,265 | 4,020 | 4,047 | 95 | 103 | 27 D | 48.6% | 49.0% | 1.1% |
| 13,259 | WAYNE | 5,848 | 3,346 | 2,387 | 55 | 60 | 959 R | 57.2% | 40.8% | 0.9% |
| 31,045 | WEBSTER | 11,880 | 7,350 | 4,174 | 161 | 195 | 3,176 R | 61.9% | 35.1% | 1.4% |
| 2,382 | WORTH | 1,158 | 651 | 469 | 15 | 23 | 182 R | 56.2% | 40.5% | 1.3% |
| 17,955 | WRIGHT | 7,841 | 5,391 | 2,250 | 86 | 114 | 3,141 R | 68.8% | 28.7% | 1.1% |
| 5,595,211 | TOTAL | 2,359,892 | 1,189,924 | 1,111,138 | 38,515 | 20,315 | 78,786 R | 50.4% | 47.1% | 1.6% |

# MISSOURI

## PRESIDENT 1996

| 1995 Census Pop. Est. | County | Total Vote | Republican | Democratic | Reform (Perot) | Other | Rep.-Dem. Plurality | Percentage of Total Vote | | |
|---|---|---|---|---|---|---|---|---|---|---|
| | | | | | | | | Rep. | Dem. | Reform |
| 24,755 | ADAIR | 10,397 | 4,656 | 4,441 | 1,170 | 130 | 215 R | 44.8% | 42.7% | 11.3% |
| 15,202 | ANDREW | 7,101 | 3,281 | 2,807 | 964 | 49 | 474 R | 46.2% | 39.5% | 13.6% |
| 7,137 | ATCHISON | 2,978 | 1,327 | 1,266 | 367 | 18 | 61 R | 44.6% | 42.5% | 12.3% |
| 23,588 | AUDRAIN | 9,778 | 3,955 | 4,690 | 1,046 | 87 | 735 D | 40.4% | 48.0% | 10.7% |
| 31,382 | BARRY | 11,799 | 5,855 | 4,352 | 1,494 | 98 | 1,503 R | 49.6% | 36.9% | 12.7% |
| 11,736 | BARTON | 5,045 | 2,812 | 1,625 | 563 | 45 | 1,187 R | 55.7% | 32.2% | 11.2% |
| 15,425 | BATES | 7,137 | 2,904 | 3,224 | 949 | 60 | 320 D | 40.7% | 45.2% | 13.3% |
| 15,489 | BENTON | 6,715 | 2,895 | 2,996 | 764 | 60 | 101 D | 43.1% | 44.6% | 11.4% |
| 11,253 | BOLLINGER | 5,047 | 2,420 | 2,044 | 506 | 77 | 376 R | 47.9% | 40.5% | 10.0% |
| 123,742 | BOONE | 51,920 | 22,047 | 24,984 | 4,083 | 806 | 2,937 D | 42.5% | 48.1% | 7.9% |
| 82,477 | BUCHANAN | 33,018 | 12,610 | 15,848 | 4,248 | 312 | 3,238 D | 38.2% | 48.0% | 12.9% |
| 40,267 | BUTLER | 14,343 | 6,996 | 5,780 | 1,414 | 153 | 1,216 R | 48.8% | 40.3% | 9.9% |
| 8,569 | CALDWELL | 3,468 | 1,464 | 1,487 | 468 | 49 | 23 D | 42.2% | 42.9% | 13.5% |
| 34,870 | CALLAWAY | 13,137 | 5,567 | 5,880 | 1,530 | 160 | 313 D | 42.4% | 44.8% | 11.6% |
| 31,611 | CAMDEN | 14,694 | 7,190 | 5,566 | 1,809 | 129 | 1,624 R | 48.9% | 37.9% | 12.3% |
| 65,313 | CAPE GIRARDEAU | 27,622 | 15,557 | 9,957 | 1,861 | 247 | 5,600 R | 56.3% | 36.0% | 6.7% |
| 10,378 | CARROLL | 4,515 | 1,839 | 2,080 | 580 | 16 | 241 D | 40.7% | 46.1% | 12.8% |
| 6,024 | CARTER | 2,677 | 1,180 | 1,172 | 301 | 24 | 8 R | 44.1% | 43.8% | 11.2% |
| 73,547 | CASS | 29,010 | 13,495 | 11,743 | 3,474 | 298 | 1,752 R | 46.5% | 40.5% | 12.0% |
| 12,892 | CEDAR | 5,222 | 2,484 | 2,027 | 658 | 53 | 457 R | 47.6% | 38.8% | 12.6% |
| 8,829 | CHARITON | 4,032 | 1,508 | 2,072 | 423 | 29 | 564 D | 37.4% | 51.4% | 10.5% |
| 42,740 | CHRISTIAN | 18,595 | 9,477 | 6,627 | 2,301 | 190 | 2,850 R | 51.0% | 35.6% | 12.4% |
| 7,449 | CLARK | 3,313 | 1,081 | 1,749 | 458 | 25 | 668 D | 32.6% | 52.8% | 13.8% |
| 165,981 | CLAY | 69,147 | 28,935 | 32,603 | 7,048 | 561 | 3,668 D | 41.8% | 47.2% | 10.2% |
| 17,810 | CLINTON | 7,165 | 2,780 | 3,445 | 848 | 92 | 665 D | 38.8% | 48.1% | 11.8% |
| 67,641 | COLE | 29,342 | 16,140 | 10,857 | 2,121 | 224 | 5,283 R | 55.0% | 37.0% | 7.2% |
| 15,989 | COOPER | 6,629 | 2,900 | 2,753 | 891 | 85 | 147 R | 43.7% | 41.5% | 13.4% |
| 21,329 | CRAWFORD | 7,656 | 2,990 | 3,349 | 1,223 | 94 | 359 D | 39.1% | 43.7% | 16.0% |
| 8,010 | DADE | 3,545 | 1,822 | 1,243 | 447 | 33 | 579 R | 51.4% | 35.1% | 12.6% |
| 14,637 | DALLAS | 5,674 | 2,554 | 2,277 | 787 | 56 | 277 R | 45.0% | 40.1% | 13.9% |
| 7,896 | DAVIESS | 3,353 | 1,321 | 1,534 | 466 | 32 | 213 D | 39.4% | 45.8% | 13.9% |
| 10,553 | DE KALB | 3,846 | 1,627 | 1,679 | 492 | 48 | 52 D | 42.3% | 43.7% | 12.8% |
| 14,164 | DENT | 5,538 | 2,542 | 2,234 | 693 | 69 | 308 R | 45.9% | 40.3% | 12.5% |
| 12,120 | DOUGLAS | 5,184 | 2,601 | 1,744 | 775 | 64 | 857 R | 50.2% | 33.6% | 14.9% |
| 32,965 | DUNKLIN | 10,173 | 3,766 | 5,428 | 934 | 45 | 1,662 D | 37.0% | 53.4% | 9.2% |
| 87,769 | FRANKLIN | 33,734 | 13,715 | 13,908 | 5,517 | 594 | 193 D | 40.7% | 41.2% | 16.4% |
| 14,529 | GASCONADE | 5,971 | 2,997 | 2,104 | 820 | 50 | 893 R | 50.2% | 35.2% | 13.7% |
| 6,800 | GENTRY | 3,291 | 1,361 | 1,493 | 416 | 21 | 132 D | 41.4% | 45.4% | 12.6% |
| 224,976 | GREENE | 97,164 | 48,193 | 39,300 | 8,569 | 1,102 | 8,893 R | 49.6% | 40.4% | 8.8% |
| 10,417 | GRUNDY | 4,698 | 1,883 | 2,073 | 631 | 111 | 190 D | 40.1% | 44.1% | 13.4% |
| 8,270 | HARRISON | 3,880 | 1,737 | 1,628 | 484 | 31 | 109 R | 44.8% | 42.0% | 12.5% |
| 20,960 | HENRY | 9,137 | 3,260 | 4,579 | 1,231 | 67 | 1,319 D | 35.7% | 50.1% | 13.5% |
| 8,312 | HICKORY | 3,912 | 1,491 | 1,858 | 531 | 32 | 367 D | 38.1% | 47.5% | 13.6% |
| 5,662 | HOLT | 2,806 | 1,323 | 1,144 | 314 | 25 | 179 R | 47.1% | 40.8% | 11.2% |
| 9,661 | HOWARD | 4,203 | 1,545 | 2,014 | 568 | 76 | 469 D | 36.8% | 47.9% | 13.5% |
| 34,507 | HOWELL | 13,524 | 5,991 | 5,261 | 2,066 | 206 | 730 R | 44.3% | 38.9% | 15.3% |
| 10,886 | IRON | 4,160 | 1,328 | 2,221 | 568 | 43 | 893 D | 31.9% | 53.4% | 13.7% |
| 635,637 | JACKSON | 249,658 | 85,534 | 140,317 | 21,047 | 2,760 | 54,783 D | 34.3% | 56.2% | 8.4% |
| 96,275 | JASPER | 33,761 | 18,361 | 11,462 | 3,545 | 393 | 6,899 R | 54.4% | 34.0% | 10.5% |
| 186,435 | JEFFERSON | 66,102 | 23,877 | 32,073 | 8,893 | 1,259 | 8,196 D | 36.1% | 48.5% | 13.5% |
| 46,603 | JOHNSON | 14,574 | 6,276 | 6,220 | 1,911 | 167 | 56 R | 43.1% | 42.7% | 13.1% |
| 4,347 | KNOX | 2,021 | 862 | 891 | 254 | 14 | 29 D | 42.7% | 44.1% | 12.6% |
| 29,111 | LACLEDE | 11,499 | 5,887 | 4,047 | 1,459 | 106 | 1,840 R | 51.2% | 35.2% | 12.7% |
| 32,191 | LAFAYETTE | 13,203 | 5,489 | 6,118 | 1,516 | 80 | 629 D | 41.6% | 46.3% | 11.5% |
| 31,698 | LAWRENCE | 12,332 | 6,099 | 4,465 | 1,613 | 155 | 1,634 R | 49.5% | 36.2% | 13.1% |
| 10,219 | LEWIS | 4,176 | 1,453 | 2,050 | 644 | 29 | 597 D | 34.8% | 49.1% | 15.4% |
| 32,969 | LINCOLN | 12,611 | 4,897 | 5,644 | 1,881 | 189 | 747 D | 38.8% | 44.8% | 14.9% |
| 14,004 | LINN | 5,891 | 2,097 | 2,967 | 781 | 46 | 870 D | 35.6% | 50.4% | 13.3% |
| 14,349 | LIVINGSTON | 6,130 | 2,384 | 2,913 | 777 | 56 | 529 D | 38.9% | 47.5% | 12.7% |
| 18,553 | MCDONALD | 5,973 | 3,008 | 1,980 | 923 | 62 | 1,028 R | 50.4% | 33.1% | 15.5% |

# MISSOURI

## PRESIDENT 1996

| 1995 Census Pop. Est. | County | Total Vote | Republican | Democratic | Reform (Perot) | Other | Rep.-Dem. Plurality | | Percentage of Total Vote | | |
|---|---|---|---|---|---|---|---|---|---|---|---|
| | | | | | | | | | Rep. | Dem. | Reform |
| 15,213 | MACON | 6,480 | 2,634 | 2,937 | 848 | 61 | 303 | D | 40.6% | 45.3% | 13.1% |
| 11,211 | MADISON | 4,663 | 1,595 | 2,351 | 625 | 92 | 756 | D | 34.2% | 50.4% | 13.4% |
| 8,293 | MARIES | 3,636 | 1,560 | 1,540 | 516 | 20 | 20 | R | 42.9% | 42.4% | 14.2% |
| 27,891 | MARION | 10,721 | 4,653 | 4,924 | 1,082 | 62 | 271 | D | 43.4% | 45.9% | 10.1% |
| 4,087 | MERCER | 1,581 | 660 | 700 | 208 | 13 | 40 | D | 41.7% | 44.3% | 13.2% |
| 21,974 | MILLER | 8,739 | 4,387 | 3,110 | 1,185 | 57 | 1,277 | R | 50.2% | 35.6% | 13.6% |
| 13,817 | MISSISSIPPI | 5,249 | 1,595 | 3,235 | 380 | 39 | 1,640 | D | 30.4% | 61.6% | 7.2% |
| 12,985 | MONITEAU | 5,465 | 2,603 | 2,129 | 693 | 40 | 474 | R | 47.6% | 39.0% | 12.7% |
| 8,821 | MONROE | 3,831 | 1,333 | 1,938 | 532 | 28 | 605 | D | 34.8% | 50.6% | 13.9% |
| 11,609 | MONTGOMERY | 5,225 | 2,124 | 2,277 | 772 | 52 | 153 | D | 40.7% | 43.6% | 14.8% |
| 17,180 | MORGAN | 7,133 | 3,059 | 3,006 | 1,006 | 62 | 53 | R | 42.9% | 42.1% | 14.1% |
| 20,711 | NEW MADRID | 7,570 | 2,417 | 4,451 | 663 | 39 | 2,034 | D | 31.9% | 58.8% | 8.8% |
| 47,529 | NEWTON | 18,085 | 10,067 | 5,840 | 1,995 | 183 | 4,227 | R | 55.7% | 32.3% | 11.0% |
| 21,097 | NODAWAY | 8,461 | 3,362 | 3,966 | 1,043 | 90 | 604 | D | 39.7% | 46.9% | 12.3% |
| 10,029 | OREGON | 3,841 | 1,502 | 1,795 | 475 | 69 | 293 | D | 39.1% | 46.7% | 12.4% |
| 12,374 | OSAGE | 5,568 | 2,890 | 2,045 | 608 | 25 | 845 | R | 51.9% | 36.7% | 10.9% |
| 9,517 | OZARK | 3,989 | 1,882 | 1,445 | 595 | 67 | 437 | R | 47.2% | 36.2% | 14.9% |
| 21,700 | PEMISCOT | 5,677 | 1,820 | 3,371 | 458 | 28 | 1,551 | D | 32.1% | 59.4% | 8.1% |
| 17,318 | PERRY | 6,781 | 3,427 | 2,517 | 777 | 60 | 910 | R | 50.5% | 37.1% | 11.5% |
| 36,641 | PETTIS | 15,263 | 7,336 | 6,057 | 1,716 | 154 | 1,279 | R | 48.1% | 39.7% | 11.2% |
| 37,477 | PHELPS | 15,299 | 6,990 | 6,405 | 1,703 | 201 | 585 | R | 45.7% | 41.9% | 11.1% |
| 16,200 | PIKE | 6,693 | 2,209 | 3,495 | 916 | 73 | 1,286 | D | 33.0% | 52.2% | 13.7% |
| 66,529 | PLATTE | 29,388 | 13,332 | 12,705 | 3,035 | 316 | 627 | R | 45.4% | 43.2% | 10.3% |
| 24,501 | POLK | 9,090 | 4,521 | 3,307 | 1,169 | 93 | 1,214 | R | 49.7% | 36.4% | 12.9% |
| 38,516 | PULASKI | 9,079 | 4,089 | 3,783 | 1,141 | 66 | 306 | R | 45.0% | 41.7% | 12.6% |
| 5,094 | PUTNAM | 2,245 | 1,091 | 857 | 276 | 21 | 234 | R | 48.6% | 38.2% | 12.3% |
| 8,789 | RALLS | 4,052 | 1,513 | 1,998 | 520 | 21 | 485 | D | 37.3% | 49.3% | 12.8% |
| 23,924 | RANDOLPH | 8,985 | 3,274 | 4,502 | 1,130 | 79 | 1,228 | D | 36.4% | 50.1% | 12.6% |
| 22,368 | RAY | 8,787 | 2,884 | 4,714 | 1,113 | 76 | 1,830 | D | 32.8% | 53.6% | 12.7% |
| 6,733 | REYNOLDS | 2,960 | 903 | 1,631 | 386 | 40 | 728 | D | 30.5% | 55.1% | 13.0% |
| 13,450 | RIPLEY | 4,658 | 1,988 | 2,081 | 530 | 59 | 93 | D | 42.7% | 44.7% | 11.4% |
| 248,327 | ST. CHARLES | 102,246 | 47,705 | 41,369 | 11,591 | 1,581 | 6,336 | R | 46.7% | 40.5% | 11.3% |
| 8,880 | ST. CLAIR | 4,473 | 1,815 | 1,974 | 650 | 34 | 159 | D | 40.6% | 44.1% | 14.5% |
| 53,254 | ST. FRANCOIS | 17,726 | 6,200 | 9,034 | 2,266 | 226 | 2,834 | D | 35.0% | 51.0% | 12.8% |
| 1,007,834 | ST. LOUIS COUNTY | 462,278 | 196,096 | 225,524 | 34,850 | 5,808 | 29,428 | D | 42.4% | 48.8% | 7.5% |
| 358,704 | ST. LOUIS CITY | 122,003 | 22,121 | 91,233 | 7,276 | 1,373 | 69,112 | D | 18.1% | 74.8% | 6.0% |
| 16,643 | STE. GENEVIEVE | 6,727 | 2,078 | 3,597 | 942 | 110 | 1,519 | D | 30.9% | 53.5% | 14.0% |
| 23,022 | SALINE | 8,854 | 2,931 | 4,765 | 1,090 | 68 | 1,834 | D | 33.1% | 53.8% | 12.3% |
| 4,333 | SCHUYLER | 1,933 | 777 | 857 | 287 | 12 | 80 | D | 40.2% | 44.3% | 14.8% |
| 4,846 | SCOTLAND | 2,106 | 773 | 990 | 326 | 17 | 217 | D | 36.7% | 47.0% | 15.5% |
| 40,303 | SCOTT | 15,252 | 6,641 | 7,011 | 1,483 | 117 | 370 | D | 43.5% | 46.0% | 9.7% |
| 8,070 | SHANNON | 3,796 | 1,339 | 1,882 | 524 | 51 | 543 | D | 35.3% | 49.6% | 13.8% |
| 6,884 | SHELBY | 3,060 | 1,213 | 1,410 | 413 | 24 | 197 | D | 39.6% | 46.1% | 13.5% |
| 29,573 | STODDARD | 11,176 | 5,020 | 4,883 | 1,185 | 88 | 137 | R | 44.9% | 43.7% | 10.6% |
| 25,079 | STONE | 10,161 | 5,223 | 3,497 | 1,353 | 88 | 1,726 | R | 51.4% | 34.4% | 13.3% |
| 6,553 | SULLIVAN | 3,054 | 1,275 | 1,402 | 340 | 37 | 127 | D | 41.7% | 45.9% | 11.1% |
| 32,260 | TANEY | 13,160 | 6,844 | 4,623 | 1,580 | 113 | 2,221 | R | 52.0% | 35.1% | 12.0% |
| 22,186 | TEXAS | 9,440 | 4,065 | 3,897 | 1,335 | 143 | 168 | R | 43.1% | 41.3% | 14.1% |
| 19,299 | VERNON | 7,674 | 3,123 | 3,363 | 1,135 | 53 | 240 | D | 40.7% | 43.8% | 14.8% |
| 22,574 | WARREN | 8,607 | 3,768 | 3,443 | 1,254 | 142 | 325 | R | 43.8% | 40.0% | 14.6% |
| 21,907 | WASHINGTON | 7,850 | 2,259 | 4,315 | 1,169 | 107 | 2,056 | D | 28.8% | 55.0% | 14.9% |
| 12,646 | WAYNE | 5,649 | 2,172 | 2,754 | 674 | 49 | 582 | D | 38.4% | 48.8% | 11.9% |
| 26,810 | WEBSTER | 10,152 | 4,958 | 3,855 | 1,214 | 125 | 1,103 | R | 48.8% | 38.0% | 12.0% |
| 2,346 | WORTH | 1,273 | 540 | 572 | 150 | 11 | 32 | D | 42.4% | 44.9% | 11.8% |
| 18,702 | WRIGHT | 6,995 | 3,754 | 2,280 | 890 | 71 | 1,474 | R | 53.7% | 32.6% | 12.7% |
| 5,323,523 | TOTAL | 2,158,065 | 890,016 | 1,025,935 | 217,188 | 24,926 | 135,919 | D | 41.2% | 47.5% | 10.1% |

# MISSOURI

## PRESIDENT 1992

| 1990 Census Population | County | Total Vote | Republican | Democratic | Perot | Other | Plurality | Percentage Total Vote | | |
|---|---|---|---|---|---|---|---|---|---|---|
| | | | | | | | | Rep. | Dem. | Perot |
| 24,577 | ADAIR | 10,640 | 4,141 | 4,232 | 2,224 | 43 | 91 D | 38.9% | 39.8% | 20.9% |
| 14,632 | ANDREW | 7,489 | 2,652 | 2,675 | 2,151 | 11 | 23 D | 35.4% | 35.7% | 28.7% |
| 7,457 | ATCHISON | 3,199 | 1,140 | 1,208 | 840 | 11 | 68 D | 35.6% | 37.8% | 26.3% |
| 23,599 | AUDRAIN | 10,654 | 3,798 | 4,731 | 2,099 | 26 | 933 D | 35.6% | 44.4% | 19.7% |
| 27,547 | BARRY | 12,757 | 5,565 | 4,791 | 2,381 | 20 | 774 R | 43.6% | 37.6% | 18.7% |
| 11,312 | BARTON | 5,194 | 2,775 | 1,433 | 971 | 15 | 1,342 R | 53.4% | 27.6% | 18.7% |
| 15,025 | BATES | 7,730 | 2,499 | 2,993 | 2,225 | 13 | 494 D | 32.3% | 38.7% | 28.8% |
| 13,859 | BENTON | 7,276 | 2,511 | 3,195 | 1,551 | 19 | 684 D | 34.5% | 43.9% | 21.3% |
| 10,619 | BOLLINGER | 5,363 | 2,289 | 2,150 | 909 | 15 | 139 R | 42.7% | 40.1% | 16.9% |
| 112,379 | BOONE | 57,890 | 19,405 | 26,176 | 12,040 | 269 | 6,771 D | 33.5% | 45.2% | 20.8% |
| 83,083 | BUCHANAN | 37,365 | 11,275 | 16,570 | 9,404 | 116 | 5,295 D | 30.2% | 44.3% | 25.2% |
| 38,765 | BUTLER | 15,272 | 6,450 | 6,602 | 2,189 | 31 | 152 D | 42.2% | 43.2% | 14.3% |
| 8,380 | CALDWELL | 4,055 | 1,295 | 1,456 | 1,283 | 21 | 161 D | 31.9% | 35.9% | 31.6% |
| 32,809 | CALLAWAY | 13,981 | 4,880 | 5,799 | 3,266 | 36 | 919 D | 34.9% | 41.5% | 23.4% |
| 27,495 | CAMDEN | 14,627 | 5,554 | 5,140 | 3,891 | 42 | 414 R | 38.0% | 35.1% | 26.6% |
| 61,633 | CAPE GIRARDEAU | 28,355 | 13,464 | 9,605 | 5,199 | 87 | 3,859 R | 47.5% | 33.9% | 18.3% |
| 10,748 | CARROLL | 5,378 | 1,774 | 2,100 | 1,495 | 9 | 326 D | 33.0% | 39.0% | 27.8% |
| 5,515 | CARTER | 2,686 | 1,101 | 1,169 | 405 | 11 | 68 D | 41.0% | 43.5% | 15.1% |
| 63,808 | CASS | 29,905 | 10,349 | 10,246 | 9,216 | 94 | 103 R | 34.6% | 34.3% | 30.8% |
| 12,093 | CEDAR | 5,339 | 2,085 | 2,064 | 1,173 | 17 | 21 R | 39.1% | 38.7% | 22.0% |
| 9,202 | CHARITON | 4,601 | 1,378 | 2,141 | 1,067 | 15 | 763 D | 30.0% | 46.5% | 23.2% |
| 32,644 | CHRISTIAN | 17,145 | 7,422 | 6,242 | 3,422 | 59 | 1,180 R | 43.3% | 36.4% | 20.0% |
| 7,547 | CLARK | 3,584 | 1,039 | 1,815 | 725 | 5 | 776 D | 29.0% | 50.6% | 20.2% |
| 153,411 | CLAY | 75,778 | 23,798 | 30,565 | 20,951 | 464 | 6,767 D | 31.4% | 40.3% | 27.6% |
| 16,595 | CLINTON | 8,228 | 2,391 | 3,400 | 2,423 | 14 | 977 D | 29.1% | 41.3% | 29.4% |
| 63,579 | COLE | 31,304 | 15,270 | 10,201 | 5,770 | 63 | 5,069 R | 48.8% | 32.6% | 18.4% |
| 14,835 | COOPER | 7,339 | 2,867 | 2,709 | 1,735 | 28 | 158 R | 39.1% | 36.9% | 23.6% |
| 19,173 | CRAWFORD | 8,385 | 2,831 | 3,515 | 2,002 | 37 | 684 D | 33.8% | 41.9% | 23.9% |
| 7,449 | DADE | 3,751 | 1,577 | 1,332 | 834 | 8 | 245 R | 42.0% | 35.5% | 22.2% |
| 12,646 | DALLAS | 6,051 | 2,116 | 2,533 | 1,392 | 10 | 417 D | 35.0% | 41.9% | 23.0% |
| 7,865 | DAVIESS | 3,732 | 1,107 | 1,477 | 1,143 | 5 | 334 D | 29.7% | 39.6% | 30.6% |
| 9,967 | DE KALB | 4,171 | 1,318 | 1,630 | 1,207 | 16 | 312 D | 31.6% | 39.1% | 28.9% |
| 13,702 | DENT | 5,877 | 2,125 | 2,689 | 1,049 | 14 | 564 D | 36.2% | 45.8% | 17.8% |
| 11,876 | DOUGLAS | 5,792 | 2,569 | 2,126 | 1,081 | 16 | 443 R | 44.4% | 36.7% | 18.7% |
| 33,112 | DUNKLIN | 11,479 | 4,024 | 6,277 | 1,166 | 12 | 2,253 D | 35.1% | 54.7% | 10.2% |
| 80,603 | FRANKLIN | 36,064 | 11,477 | 13,431 | 11,043 | 113 | 1,954 D | 31.8% | 37.2% | 30.6% |
| 14,006 | GASCONADE | 6,334 | 2,690 | 1,952 | 1,672 | 20 | 738 R | 42.5% | 30.8% | 26.4% |
| 6,848 | GENTRY | 3,724 | 1,272 | 1,519 | 921 | 12 | 247 D | 34.2% | 40.8% | 24.7% |
| 207,949 | GREENE | 105,713 | 46,457 | 41,137 | 17,770 | 349 | 5,320 R | 43.9% | 38.9% | 16.8% |
| 10,536 | GRUNDY | 5,105 | 1,749 | 1,968 | 1,372 | 16 | 219 D | 34.3% | 38.6% | 26.9% |
| 8,469 | HARRISON | 4,222 | 1,563 | 1,590 | 1,059 | 10 | 27 D | 37.0% | 37.7% | 25.1% |
| 20,044 | HENRY | 9,740 | 2,681 | 4,232 | 2,807 | 20 | 1,425 D | 27.5% | 43.4% | 28.8% |
| 7,335 | HICKORY | 4,058 | 1,259 | 1,929 | 864 | 6 | 670 D | 31.0% | 47.5% | 21.3% |
| 6,034 | HOLT | 3,044 | 1,202 | 1,050 | 781 | 11 | 152 R | 39.5% | 34.5% | 25.7% |
| 9,631 | HOWARD | 4,443 | 1,253 | 2,085 | 1,090 | 15 | 832 D | 28.2% | 46.9% | 24.5% |
| 31,447 | HOWELL | 13,537 | 5,360 | 5,492 | 2,650 | 35 | 132 D | 39.6% | 40.6% | 19.6% |
| 10,726 | IRON | 4,634 | 1,276 | 2,507 | 841 | 10 | 1,231 D | 27.5% | 54.1% | 18.1% |
| 633,232 | JACKSON | 291,595 | 78,611 | 145,999 | 66,142 | 843 | 67,388 D | 27.0% | 50.1% | 22.7% |
| 90,465 | JASPER | 35,872 | 17,592 | 11,727 | 6,440 | 113 | 5,865 R | 49.0% | 32.7% | 18.0% |
| 171,380 | JEFFERSON | 73,501 | 20,637 | 32,569 | 20,057 | 238 | 11,932 D | 28.1% | 44.3% | 27.3% |
| 42,514 | JOHNSON | 15,203 | 5,032 | 5,546 | 4,578 | 47 | 514 D | 33.1% | 36.5% | 30.1% |
| 4,482 | KNOX | 2,262 | 724 | 1,010 | 523 | 5 | 286 D | 32.0% | 44.7% | 23.1% |
| 27,158 | LACLEDE | 12,222 | 5,176 | 4,179 | 2,852 | 15 | 997 R | 42.3% | 34.2% | 23.3% |
| 31,107 | LAFAYETTE | 13,467 | 4,651 | 5,213 | 3,561 | 42 | 562 D | 34.5% | 38.7% | 26.4% |
| 30,236 | LAWRENCE | 12,891 | 5,608 | 4,666 | 2,570 | 47 | 942 R | 43.5% | 36.2% | 19.9% |
| 10,233 | LEWIS | 4,562 | 1,461 | 2,196 | 892 | 13 | 735 D | 32.0% | 48.1% | 19.6% |
| 28,892 | LINCOLN | 12,765 | 3,718 | 5,453 | 3,572 | 22 | 1,735 D | 29.1% | 42.7% | 28.0% |
| 13,885 | LINN | 6,436 | 1,967 | 2,916 | 1,524 | 29 | 949 D | 30.6% | 45.3% | 23.7% |
| 14,592 | LIVINGSTON | 6,863 | 2,370 | 2,505 | 1,976 | 12 | 135 D | 34.5% | 36.5% | 28.8% |
| 16,938 | MCDONALD | 6,875 | 3,010 | 2,281 | 1,551 | 33 | 729 R | 43.8% | 33.2% | 22.6% |

# MISSOURI

## PRESIDENT 1992

| 1990 Census Population | County | Total Vote | Republican | Democratic | Perot | Other | Plurality | Percentage Total Vote | | |
|---|---|---|---|---|---|---|---|---|---|---|
| | | | | | | | | Rep. | Dem. | Perot |
| 15,345 | MACON | 7,164 | 2,256 | 3,194 | 1,697 | 17 | 938 D | 31.5% | 44.6% | 23.7% |
| 11,127 | MADISON | 5,082 | 1,673 | 2,501 | 899 | 9 | 828 D | 32.9% | 49.2% | 17.7% |
| 7,976 | MARIES | 4,015 | 1,356 | 1,732 | 915 | 12 | 376 D | 33.8% | 43.1% | 22.8% |
| 27,682 | MARION | 11,783 | 4,762 | 5,156 | 1,841 | 24 | 394 D | 40.4% | 43.8% | 15.6% |
| 3,723 | MERCER | 1,849 | 626 | 843 | 378 | 2 | 217 D | 33.9% | 45.6% | 20.4% |
| 20,700 | MILLER | 9,487 | 4,175 | 2,905 | 2,391 | 16 | 1,270 R | 44.0% | 30.6% | 25.2% |
| 14,442 | MISSISSIPPI | 5,687 | 1,675 | 3,226 | 776 | 10 | 1,551 D | 29.5% | 56.7% | 13.6% |
| 12,298 | MONITEAU | 6,088 | 2,566 | 2,018 | 1,499 | 5 | 548 R | 42.1% | 33.1% | 24.6% |
| 9,104 | MONROE | 4,187 | 1,153 | 2,060 | 969 | 5 | 907 D | 27.5% | 49.2% | 23.1% |
| 11,355 | MONTGOMERY | 5,319 | 1,974 | 2,063 | 1,266 | 16 | 89 D | 37.1% | 38.8% | 23.8% |
| 15,574 | MORGAN | 7,770 | 2,819 | 2,906 | 2,028 | 17 | 87 D | 36.3% | 37.4% | 26.1% |
| 20,928 | NEW MADRID | 8,289 | 2,431 | 4,883 | 962 | 13 | 2,452 D | 29.3% | 58.9% | 11.6% |
| 44,445 | NEWTON | 18,479 | 8,804 | 5,987 | 3,567 | 121 | 2,817 R | 47.6% | 32.4% | 19.3% |
| 21,709 | NODAWAY | 9,388 | 3,147 | 3,723 | 2,484 | 34 | 576 D | 33.5% | 39.7% | 26.5% |
| 9,470 | OREGON | 4,236 | 1,402 | 2,258 | 564 | 12 | 856 D | 33.1% | 53.3% | 13.3% |
| 12,018 | OSAGE | 6,073 | 2,784 | 1,860 | 1,423 | 6 | 924 R | 45.8% | 30.6% | 23.4% |
| 8,598 | OZARK | 4,271 | 1,772 | 1,581 | 906 | 12 | 191 R | 41.5% | 37.0% | 21.2% |
| 21,921 | PEMISCOT | 6,768 | 2,161 | 3,924 | 670 | 13 | 1,763 D | 31.9% | 58.0% | 9.9% |
| 16,648 | PERRY | 7,252 | 3,205 | 2,525 | 1,498 | 24 | 680 R | 44.2% | 34.8% | 20.7% |
| 35,437 | PETTIS | 16,470 | 6,823 | 5,314 | 4,278 | 55 | 1,509 R | 41.4% | 32.3% | 26.0% |
| 35,248 | PHELPS | 16,739 | 6,040 | 6,852 | 3,774 | 73 | 812 D | 36.1% | 40.9% | 22.5% |
| 15,969 | PIKE | 7,336 | 2,255 | 3,609 | 1,464 | 8 | 1,354 D | 30.7% | 49.2% | 20.0% |
| 57,867 | PLATTE | 29,478 | 9,380 | 10,920 | 9,062 | 116 | 1,540 D | 31.8% | 37.0% | 30.7% |
| 21,826 | POLK | 8,675 | 3,465 | 3,316 | 1,879 | 15 | 149 R | 39.9% | 38.2% | 21.7% |
| 41,307 | PULASKI | 9,988 | 3,793 | 4,113 | 2,057 | 25 | 320 D | 38.0% | 41.2% | 20.6% |
| 5,079 | PUTNAM | 2,503 | 1,143 | 838 | 522 | | 305 R | 45.7% | 33.5% | 20.9% |
| 8,476 | RALLS | 4,393 | 1,349 | 2,158 | 880 | 6 | 809 D | 30.7% | 49.1% | 20.0% |
| 24,370 | RANDOLPH | 10,210 | 3,025 | 4,951 | 2,212 | 22 | 1,926 D | 29.6% | 48.5% | 21.7% |
| 21,971 | RAY | 9,620 | 2,563 | 4,457 | 2,567 | 33 | 1,890 D | 26.6% | 46.3% | 26.7% |
| 6,661 | REYNOLDS | 3,325 | 776 | 2,014 | 532 | 3 | 1,238 D | 23.3% | 60.6% | 16.0% |
| 12,303 | RIPLEY | 4,860 | 1,814 | 2,300 | 739 | 7 | 486 D | 37.3% | 47.3% | 15.2% |
| 212,907 | ST. CHARLES | 106,563 | 38,673 | 37,263 | 30,351 | 276 | 1,410 R | 36.3% | 35.0% | 28.5% |
| 8,457 | ST. CLAIR | 4,611 | 1,555 | 1,965 | 1,083 | 8 | 410 D | 33.7% | 42.6% | 23.5% |
| 48,904 | ST. FRANCOIS | 18,947 | 5,889 | 9,367 | 3,635 | 56 | 3,478 D | 31.1% | 49.4% | 19.2% |
| 396,685 | ST. LOUIS CITY | 147,404 | 25,441 | 102,356 | 18,864 | 743 | 76,915 D | 17.3% | 69.4% | 12.8% |
| 993,529 | ST. LOUIS COUNTY | 534,763 | 188,285 | 235,760 | 109,099 | 1,619 | 47,475 D | 35.2% | 44.1% | 20.4% |
| 16,037 | STE. GENEVIEVE | 7,137 | 1,780 | 3,795 | 1,547 | 15 | 2,015 D | 24.9% | 53.2% | 21.7% |
| 23,523 | SALINE | 10,166 | 2,688 | 4,643 | 2,815 | 20 | 1,828 D | 26.4% | 45.7% | 27.7% |
| 4,236 | SCHUYLER | 2,170 | 742 | 936 | 487 | 5 | 194 D | 34.2% | 43.1% | 22.4% |
| 4,822 | SCOTLAND | 2,494 | 798 | 1,070 | 617 | 9 | 272 D | 32.0% | 42.9% | 24.7% |
| 39,376 | SCOTT | 16,507 | 6,265 | 7,452 | 2,763 | 27 | 1,187 D | 38.0% | 45.1% | 16.7% |
| 7,613 | SHANNON | 3,952 | 1,224 | 2,135 | 579 | 14 | 911 D | 31.0% | 54.0% | 14.7% |
| 6,942 | SHELBY | 3,394 | 1,169 | 1,435 | 786 | 4 | 266 D | 34.4% | 42.3% | 23.2% |
| 28,895 | STODDARD | 12,308 | 4,608 | 5,720 | 1,977 | 3 | 1,112 D | 37.4% | 46.5% | 16.1% |
| 19,078 | STONE | 9,196 | 4,035 | 3,256 | 1,884 | 21 | 779 R | 43.9% | 35.4% | 20.5% |
| 6,326 | SULLIVAN | 3,436 | 1,326 | 1,510 | 596 | 4 | 184 D | 38.6% | 43.9% | 17.3% |
| 25,561 | TANEY | 13,205 | 6,081 | 4,682 | 2,395 | 47 | 1,399 R | 46.1% | 35.5% | 18.1% |
| 21,476 | TEXAS | 10,001 | 3,470 | 4,597 | 1,900 | 34 | 1,127 D | 34.7% | 46.0% | 19.0% |
| 19,041 | VERNON | 8,303 | 2,851 | 3,546 | 1,890 | 16 | 695 D | 34.3% | 42.7% | 22.8% |
| 19,534 | WARREN | 8,659 | 2,953 | 3,213 | 2,471 | 22 | 260 D | 34.1% | 37.1% | 28.5% |
| 20,380 | WASHINGTON | 8,010 | 2,157 | 4,211 | 1,618 | 24 | 2,054 D | 26.9% | 52.6% | 20.2% |
| 11,543 | WAYNE | 6,019 | 2,101 | 3,073 | 837 | 8 | 972 D | 34.9% | 51.1% | 13.9% |
| 23,753 | WEBSTER | 10,640 | 4,361 | 4,149 | 2,108 | 22 | 212 R | 41.0% | 39.0% | 19.8% |
| 2,440 | WORTH | 1,413 | 483 | 599 | 328 | 3 | 116 D | 34.2% | 42.4% | 23.2% |
| 16,758 | WRIGHT | 7,684 | 3,427 | 2,814 | 1,425 | 18 | 613 R | 44.6% | 36.6% | 18.5% |
| 5,117,073 | TOTAL | 2,391,565 | 811,159 | 1,053,873 | 518,741 | 7,792 | 242,714 D | 33.9% | 44.1% | 21.7% |

# MISSOURI

## PRESIDENT 1988

| 1980 Census Population | County | Total Vote | Republican | Democratic | Other | Rep.-Dem. Plurality | Total Vote Rep. | Total Vote Dem. | Major Vote Rep. | Major Vote Dem. |
|---|---|---|---|---|---|---|---|---|---|---|
| 24,870 | ADAIR | 9,336 | 5,721 | 3,571 | 44 | 2,150 R | 61.3% | 38.2% | 61.6% | 38.4% |
| 13,980 | ANDREW | 6,537 | 3,407 | 3,103 | 27 | 304 R | 52.1% | 47.5% | 52.3% | 47.7% |
| 8,605 | ATCHISON | 3,239 | 1,761 | 1,468 | 10 | 293 R | 54.4% | 45.3% | 54.5% | 45.5% |
| 26,458 | AUDRAIN | 10,327 | 5,072 | 5,226 | 29 | 154 D | 49.1% | 50.6% | 49.3% | 50.7% |
| 24,408 | BARRY | 11,477 | 7,231 | 4,210 | 36 | 3,021 R | 63.0% | 36.7% | 63.2% | 36.8% |
| 11,292 | BARTON | 4,958 | 3,339 | 1,603 | 16 | 1,736 R | 67.3% | 32.3% | 67.6% | 32.4% |
| 15,873 | BATES | 6,930 | 3,574 | 3,332 | 24 | 242 R | 51.6% | 48.1% | 51.8% | 48.2% |
| 12,183 | BENTON | 6,145 | 3,467 | 2,654 | 24 | 813 R | 56.4% | 43.2% | 56.6% | 43.4% |
| 10,301 | BOLLINGER | 4,599 | 2,710 | 1,883 | 6 | 827 R | 58.9% | 40.9% | 59.0% | 41.0% |
| 100,376 | BOONE | 47,458 | 22,948 | 24,370 | 140 | 1,422 D | 48.4% | 51.4% | 48.5% | 51.5% |
| 87,888 | BUCHANAN | 34,089 | 15,336 | 18,601 | 152 | 3,265 D | 45.0% | 54.6% | 45.2% | 54.8% |
| 37,693 | BUTLER | 13,738 | 7,968 | 5,751 | 19 | 2,217 R | 58.0% | 41.9% | 58.1% | 41.9% |
| 8,660 | CALDWELL | 3,815 | 2,074 | 1,726 | 15 | 348 R | 54.4% | 45.2% | 54.6% | 45.4% |
| 32,252 | CALLAWAY | 11,938 | 6,687 | 5,209 | 42 | 1,478 R | 56.0% | 43.6% | 56.2% | 43.8% |
| 20,017 | CAMDEN | 11,759 | 7,773 | 3,930 | 56 | 3,843 R | 66.1% | 33.4% | 66.4% | 33.6% |
| 58,837 | CAPE GIRARDEAU | 24,556 | 16,583 | 7,904 | 69 | 8,679 R | 67.5% | 32.2% | 67.7% | 32.3% |
| 12,131 | CARROLL | 5,150 | 2,811 | 2,330 | 9 | 481 R | 54.6% | 45.2% | 54.7% | 45.3% |
| 5,428 | CARTER | 2,528 | 1,429 | 1,087 | 12 | 342 R | 56.5% | 43.0% | 56.8% | 43.2% |
| 51,029 | CASS | 22,961 | 12,799 | 10,092 | 70 | 2,707 R | 55.7% | 44.0% | 55.9% | 44.1% |
| 11,894 | CEDAR | 4,744 | 2,966 | 1,774 | 4 | 1,192 R | 62.5% | 37.4% | 62.6% | 37.4% |
| 10,489 | CHARITON | 4,555 | 2,193 | 2,347 | 15 | 154 D | 48.1% | 51.5% | 48.3% | 51.7% |
| 22,402 | CHRISTIAN | 12,441 | 7,670 | 4,724 | 47 | 2,946 R | 61.7% | 38.0% | 61.9% | 38.1% |
| 8,493 | CLARK | 3,431 | 1,493 | 1,925 | 13 | 432 D | 43.5% | 56.1% | 43.7% | 56.3% |
| 136,488 | CLAY | 60,287 | 30,293 | 29,620 | 374 | 673 R | 50.2% | 49.1% | 50.6% | 49.4% |
| 15,916 | CLINTON | 6,961 | 3,282 | 3,653 | 26 | 371 D | 47.1% | 52.5% | 47.3% | 52.7% |
| 56,663 | COLE | 26,441 | 18,023 | 8,359 | 59 | 9,664 R | 68.2% | 31.6% | 68.3% | 31.7% |
| 14,643 | COOPER | 6,266 | 3,737 | 2,510 | 19 | 1,227 R | 59.6% | 40.1% | 59.8% | 40.2% |
| 18,300 | CRAWFORD | 6,987 | 3,856 | 3,107 | 24 | 749 R | 55.2% | 44.5% | 55.4% | 44.6% |
| 7,383 | DADE | 3,476 | 2,154 | 1,315 | 7 | 839 R | 62.0% | 37.8% | 62.1% | 37.9% |
| 12,096 | DALLAS | 5,223 | 2,898 | 2,298 | 27 | 600 R | 55.5% | 44.0% | 55.8% | 44.2% |
| 8,905 | DAVIESS | 3,518 | 1,765 | 1,743 | 10 | 22 R | 50.2% | 49.5% | 50.3% | 49.7% |
| 8,222 | DE KALB | 3,843 | 1,863 | 1,970 | 10 | 107 D | 48.5% | 51.3% | 48.6% | 51.4% |
| 14,517 | DENT | 5,417 | 2,975 | 2,421 | 21 | 554 R | 54.9% | 44.7% | 55.1% | 44.9% |
| 11,594 | DOUGLAS | 4,976 | 3,225 | 1,735 | 16 | 1,490 R | 64.8% | 34.9% | 65.0% | 35.0% |
| 36,324 | DUNKLIN | 10,320 | 5,026 | 5,281 | 13 | 255 D | 48.7% | 51.2% | 48.8% | 51.2% |
| 71,233 | FRANKLIN | 28,621 | 16,611 | 11,891 | 119 | 4,720 R | 58.0% | 41.5% | 58.3% | 41.7% |
| 13,181 | GASCONADE | 5,856 | 4,216 | 1,621 | 19 | 2,595 R | 72.0% | 27.7% | 72.2% | 27.8% |
| 7,887 | GENTRY | 3,433 | 1,554 | 1,872 | 7 | 318 D | 45.3% | 54.5% | 45.4% | 54.6% |
| 185,302 | GREENE | 87,959 | 52,211 | 35,475 | 273 | 16,736 R | 59.4% | 40.3% | 59.5% | 40.5% |
| 11,959 | GRUNDY | 4,733 | 2,668 | 2,052 | 13 | 616 R | 56.4% | 43.4% | 56.5% | 43.5% |
| 9,890 | HARRISON | 4,064 | 2,271 | 1,776 | 17 | 495 R | 55.9% | 43.7% | 56.1% | 43.9% |
| 19,672 | HENRY | 8,328 | 4,167 | 4,135 | 26 | 32 R | 50.0% | 49.7% | 50.2% | 49.8% |
| 6,367 | HICKORY | 3,732 | 2,043 | 1,677 | 12 | 366 R | 54.7% | 44.9% | 54.9% | 45.1% |
| 6,882 | HOLT | 2,855 | 1,583 | 1,258 | 14 | 325 R | 55.4% | 44.1% | 55.7% | 44.3% |
| 10,008 | HOWARD | 4,322 | 1,865 | 2,446 | 11 | 581 D | 43.2% | 56.6% | 43.3% | 56.7% |
| 28,807 | HOWELL | 11,645 | 7,277 | 4,324 | 44 | 2,953 R | 62.5% | 37.1% | 62.7% | 37.3% |
| 11,084 | IRON | 4,170 | 1,877 | 2,283 | 10 | 406 D | 45.0% | 54.7% | 45.1% | 54.9% |
| 629,266 | JACKSON | 256,621 | 107,810 | 147,964 | 847 | 40,154 D | 42.0% | 57.7% | 42.2% | 57.8% |
| 86,958 | JASPER | 31,187 | 19,934 | 11,159 | 94 | 8,775 R | 63.9% | 35.8% | 64.1% | 35.9% |
| 146,183 | JEFFERSON | 57,255 | 29,279 | 27,738 | 238 | 1,541 R | 51.1% | 48.4% | 51.4% | 48.6% |
| 39,059 | JOHNSON | 12,921 | 7,512 | 5,373 | 36 | 2,139 R | 58.1% | 41.6% | 58.3% | 41.7% |
| 5,508 | KNOX | 2,472 | 1,212 | 1,255 | 5 | 43 D | 49.0% | 50.8% | 49.1% | 50.9% |
| 24,323 | LACLEDE | 9,536 | 6,070 | 3,442 | 24 | 2,628 R | 63.7% | 36.1% | 63.8% | 36.2% |
| 29,925 | LAFAYETTE | 12,514 | 6,825 | 5,654 | 35 | 1,171 R | 54.5% | 45.2% | 54.7% | 45.3% |
| 28,973 | LAWRENCE | 11,379 | 6,911 | 4,432 | 36 | 2,479 R | 60.7% | 38.9% | 60.9% | 39.1% |
| 10,901 | LEWIS | 4,273 | 1,803 | 2,460 | 10 | 657 D | 42.2% | 57.6% | 42.3% | 57.7% |
| 22,193 | LINCOLN | 9,938 | 5,305 | 4,605 | 28 | 700 R | 53.4% | 46.3% | 53.5% | 46.5% |
| 15,495 | LINN | 6,230 | 3,061 | 3,150 | 19 | 89 D | 49.1% | 50.6% | 49.3% | 50.7% |
| 15,739 | LIVINGSTON | 6,548 | 3,462 | 3,077 | 9 | 385 R | 52.9% | 47.0% | 52.9% | 47.1% |
| 14,917 | MCDONALD | 6,153 | 3,812 | 2,299 | 42 | 1,513 R | 62.0% | 37.4% | 62.4% | 37.6% |

# MISSOURI

## PRESIDENT 1988

| 1980 Census Population | County | Total Vote | Republican | Democratic | Other | Rep.-Dem. Plurality | Percentage Total Vote Rep. | Dem. | Major Vote Rep. | Dem. |
|---|---|---|---|---|---|---|---|---|---|---|
| 16,313 | MACON | 6,639 | 3,406 | 3,215 | 18 | 191 R | 51.3% | 48.4% | 51.4% | 48.6% |
| 10,725 | MADISON | 4,703 | 2,528 | 2,167 | 8 | 361 R | 53.8% | 46.1% | 53.8% | 46.2% |
| 7,551 | MARIES | 3,480 | 1,919 | 1,552 | 9 | 367 R | 55.1% | 44.6% | 55.3% | 44.7% |
| 28,638 | MARION | 10,677 | 5,034 | 5,617 | 26 | 583 D | 47.1% | 52.6% | 47.3% | 52.7% |
| 4,685 | MERCER | 1,756 | 875 | 877 | 4 | 2 D | 49.8% | 49.9% | 49.9% | 50.1% |
| 18,532 | MILLER | 8,228 | 5,662 | 2,555 | 11 | 3,107 R | 68.8% | 31.1% | 68.9% | 31.1% |
| 15,726 | MISSISSIPPI | 5,042 | 2,218 | 2,814 | 10 | 596 D | 44.0% | 55.8% | 44.1% | 55.9% |
| 12,068 | MONITEAU | 5,446 | 3,502 | 1,936 | 8 | 1,566 R | 64.3% | 35.5% | 64.4% | 35.6% |
| 9,716 | MONROE | 4,014 | 1,542 | 2,461 | 11 | 919 D | 38.4% | 61.3% | 38.5% | 61.5% |
| 11,537 | MONTGOMERY | 4,794 | 2,714 | 2,064 | 16 | 650 R | 56.6% | 43.1% | 56.8% | 43.2% |
| 13,807 | MORGAN | 6,586 | 3,958 | 2,604 | 24 | 1,354 R | 60.1% | 39.5% | 60.3% | 39.7% |
| 22,945 | NEW MADRID | 7,208 | 3,387 | 3,812 | 9 | 425 D | 47.0% | 52.9% | 47.0% | 53.0% |
| 40,555 | NEWTON | 16,497 | 10,617 | 5,798 | 82 | 4,819 R | 64.4% | 35.1% | 64.7% | 35.3% |
| 21,996 | NODAWAY | 8,387 | 4,103 | 4,240 | 44 | 137 D | 48.9% | 50.6% | 49.2% | 50.8% |
| 10,238 | OREGON | 3,766 | 1,717 | 2,042 | 7 | 325 D | 45.6% | 54.2% | 45.7% | 54.3% |
| 12,014 | OSAGE | 5,665 | 3,885 | 1,771 | 9 | 2,114 R | 68.6% | 31.3% | 68.7% | 31.3% |
| 7,961 | OZARK | 3,744 | 2,404 | 1,329 | 11 | 1,075 R | 64.2% | 35.5% | 64.4% | 35.6% |
| 24,987 | PEMISCOT | 6,364 | 3,066 | 3,288 | 10 | 222 D | 48.2% | 51.7% | 48.3% | 51.7% |
| 16,784 | PERRY | 5,986 | 3,836 | 2,136 | 14 | 1,700 R | 64.1% | 35.7% | 64.2% | 35.8% |
| 36,378 | PETTIS | 15,200 | 9,648 | 5,486 | 66 | 4,162 R | 63.5% | 36.1% | 63.8% | 36.2% |
| 33,633 | PHELPS | 14,253 | 8,329 | 5,867 | 57 | 2,462 R | 58.4% | 41.2% | 58.7% | 41.3% |
| 17,568 | PIKE | 7,101 | 3,271 | 3,816 | 14 | 545 D | 46.1% | 53.7% | 46.2% | 53.8% |
| 46,341 | PLATTE | 23,134 | 11,838 | 11,225 | 71 | 613 R | 51.2% | 48.5% | 51.3% | 48.7% |
| 18,822 | POLK | 8,471 | 5,030 | 3,419 | 22 | 1,611 R | 59.4% | 40.4% | 59.5% | 40.5% |
| 42,011 | PULASKI | 8,114 | 4,642 | 3,446 | 26 | 1,196 R | 57.2% | 42.5% | 57.4% | 42.6% |
| 6,092 | PUTNAM | 2,176 | 1,365 | 803 | 8 | 562 R | 62.7% | 36.9% | 63.0% | 37.0% |
| 8,911 | RALLS | 3,990 | 1,494 | 2,489 | 7 | 995 D | 37.4% | 62.4% | 37.5% | 62.5% |
| 25,460 | RANDOLPH | 9,695 | 4,384 | 5,291 | 20 | 907 D | 45.2% | 54.6% | 45.3% | 54.7% |
| 21,378 | RAY | 8,662 | 3,763 | 4,879 | 20 | 1,116 D | 43.4% | 56.3% | 43.5% | 56.5% |
| 7,230 | REYNOLDS | 3,035 | 1,162 | 1,864 | 9 | 702 D | 38.3% | 61.4% | 38.4% | 61.6% |
| 12,458 | RIPLEY | 4,620 | 2,647 | 1,961 | 12 | 686 R | 57.3% | 42.4% | 57.4% | 42.6% |
| 144,107 | ST. CHARLES | 79,548 | 50,005 | 29,286 | 257 | 20,719 R | 62.9% | 36.8% | 63.1% | 36.9% |
| 8,622 | ST. CLAIR | 4,183 | 2,312 | 1,864 | 7 | 448 R | 55.3% | 44.6% | 55.4% | 44.6% |
| 42,600 | ST. FRANCOIS | 16,127 | 7,923 | 8,158 | 46 | 235 D | 49.1% | 50.6% | 49.3% | 50.7% |
| 453,085 | ST. LOUIS CITY | 151,758 | 40,906 | 110,076 | 776 | 69,170 D | 27.0% | 72.5% | 27.1% | 72.9% |
| 973,896 | ST. LOUIS COUNTY | 480,897 | 262,784 | 216,534 | 1,579 | 46,250 R | 54.6% | 45.0% | 54.8% | 45.2% |
| 15,180 | STE. GENEVIEVE | 6,164 | 2,532 | 3,612 | 20 | 1,080 D | 41.1% | 58.6% | 41.2% | 58.8% |
| 24,919 | SALINE | 9,696 | 4,625 | 5,039 | 32 | 414 D | 47.7% | 52.0% | 47.9% | 52.1% |
| 4,979 | SCHUYLER | 2,080 | 1,063 | 1,013 | 4 | 50 R | 51.1% | 48.7% | 51.2% | 48.8% |
| 5,415 | SCOTLAND | 2,372 | 1,248 | 1,117 | 7 | 131 R | 52.6% | 47.1% | 52.8% | 47.2% |
| 39,647 | SCOTT | 13,948 | 8,013 | 5,914 | 21 | 2,099 R | 57.4% | 42.4% | 57.5% | 42.5% |
| 7,885 | SHANNON | 3,500 | 1,696 | 1,796 | 8 | 100 D | 48.5% | 51.3% | 48.6% | 51.4% |
| 7,826 | SHELBY | 3,408 | 1,586 | 1,818 | 4 | 232 D | 46.5% | 53.3% | 46.6% | 53.4% |
| 29,009 | STODDARD | 10,538 | 5,822 | 4,701 | 15 | 1,121 R | 55.2% | 44.6% | 55.3% | 44.7% |
| 15,587 | STONE | 8,004 | 5,080 | 2,889 | 35 | 2,191 R | 63.5% | 36.1% | 63.7% | 36.3% |
| 7,434 | SULLIVAN | 3,467 | 1,897 | 1,562 | 8 | 335 R | 54.7% | 45.1% | 54.8% | 45.2% |
| 20,467 | TANEY | 10,978 | 7,043 | 3,888 | 47 | 3,155 R | 64.2% | 35.4% | 64.4% | 35.6% |
| 21,070 | TEXAS | 8,506 | 4,584 | 3,887 | 35 | 697 R | 53.9% | 45.7% | 54.1% | 45.9% |
| 19,806 | VERNON | 7,572 | 4,149 | 3,402 | 21 | 747 R | 54.8% | 44.9% | 54.9% | 45.1% |
| 14,900 | WARREN | 7,411 | 4,452 | 2,935 | 24 | 1,517 R | 60.1% | 39.6% | 60.3% | 39.7% |
| 17,983 | WASHINGTON | 7,000 | 3,240 | 3,744 | 16 | 504 D | 46.3% | 53.5% | 46.4% | 53.6% |
| 11,277 | WAYNE | 5,112 | 2,648 | 2,456 | 8 | 192 R | 51.8% | 48.0% | 51.9% | 48.1% |
| 20,414 | WEBSTER | 9,035 | 5,123 | 3,890 | 22 | 1,233 R | 56.7% | 43.1% | 56.8% | 43.2% |
| 3,008 | WORTH | 1,411 | 677 | 732 | 2 | 55 D | 48.0% | 51.9% | 48.0% | 52.0% |
| 16,188 | WRIGHT | 6,394 | 4,151 | 2,232 | 11 | 1,919 R | 64.9% | 34.9% | 65.0% | 35.0% |
| 4,916,686 | TOTAL | 2,093,713 | 1,084,953 | 1,001,619 | 7,141 | 83,334 R | 51.8% | 47.8% | 52.0% | 48.0% |

# MISSOURI

## PRESIDENT 1984

| 1980 Census Population | County | Total Vote | Republican | Democratic | Other | Rep.-Dem. Plurality | Percentage Total Vote Rep. | Dem. | Major Vote Rep. | Dem. |
|---|---|---|---|---|---|---|---|---|---|---|
| 24,870 | ADAIR | 9,549 | 6,430 | 3,119 | | 3,311 R | 67.3% | 32.7% | 67.3% | 32.7% |
| 13,980 | ANDREW | 6,709 | 4,252 | 2,457 | | 1,795 R | 63.4% | 36.6% | 63.4% | 36.6% |
| 8,605 | ATCHISON | 3,496 | 2,277 | 1,219 | | 1,058 R | 65.1% | 34.9% | 65.1% | 34.9% |
| 26,458 | AUDRAIN | 11,923 | 7,261 | 4,662 | | 2,599 R | 60.9% | 39.1% | 60.9% | 39.1% |
| 24,408 | BARRY | 11,166 | 7,683 | 3,483 | | 4,200 R | 68.8% | 31.2% | 68.8% | 31.2% |
| 11,292 | BARTON | 5,344 | 3,996 | 1,348 | | 2,648 R | 74.8% | 25.2% | 74.8% | 25.2% |
| 15,873 | BATES | 7,112 | 4,223 | 2,889 | | 1,334 R | 59.4% | 40.6% | 59.4% | 40.6% |
| 12,183 | BENTON | 6,056 | 3,805 | 2,251 | | 1,554 R | 62.8% | 37.2% | 62.8% | 37.2% |
| 10,301 | BOLLINGER | 4,701 | 2,778 | 1,923 | | 855 R | 59.1% | 40.9% | 59.1% | 40.9% |
| 100,376 | BOONE | 45,964 | 26,600 | 19,364 | | 7,236 R | 57.9% | 42.1% | 57.9% | 42.1% |
| 87,888 | BUCHANAN | 35,104 | 19,735 | 15,369 | | 4,366 R | 56.2% | 43.8% | 56.2% | 43.8% |
| 37,693 | BUTLER | 13,411 | 8,712 | 4,699 | | 4,013 R | 65.0% | 35.0% | 65.0% | 35.0% |
| 8,660 | CALDWELL | 4,060 | 2,678 | 1,382 | | 1,296 R | 66.0% | 34.0% | 66.0% | 34.0% |
| 32,252 | CALLAWAY | 12,589 | 8,262 | 4,327 | | 3,935 R | 65.6% | 34.4% | 65.6% | 34.4% |
| 20,017 | CAMDEN | 11,145 | 8,057 | 3,088 | | 4,969 R | 72.3% | 27.7% | 72.3% | 27.7% |
| 58,837 | CAPE GIRARDEAU | 24,750 | 17,404 | 7,346 | | 10,058 R | 70.3% | 29.7% | 70.3% | 29.7% |
| 12,131 | CARROLL | 5,475 | 3,495 | 1,980 | | 1,515 R | 63.8% | 36.2% | 63.8% | 36.2% |
| 5,428 | CARTER | 2,318 | 1,402 | 916 | | 486 R | 60.5% | 39.5% | 60.5% | 39.5% |
| 51,029 | CASS | 21,973 | 14,456 | 7,517 | | 6,939 R | 65.8% | 34.2% | 65.8% | 34.2% |
| 11,894 | CEDAR | 4,979 | 3,539 | 1,440 | | 2,099 R | 71.1% | 28.9% | 71.1% | 28.9% |
| 10,489 | CHARITON | 4,988 | 2,744 | 2,244 | | 500 R | 55.0% | 45.0% | 55.0% | 45.0% |
| 22,402 | CHRISTIAN | 10,857 | 7,634 | 3,223 | | 4,411 R | 70.3% | 29.7% | 70.3% | 29.7% |
| 8,493 | CLARK | 3,695 | 2,068 | 1,627 | | 441 R | 56.0% | 44.0% | 56.0% | 44.0% |
| 136,488 | CLAY | 59,116 | 36,529 | 22,586 | 1 | 13,943 R | 61.8% | 38.2% | 61.8% | 38.2% |
| 15,916 | CLINTON | 7,004 | 4,226 | 2,778 | | 1,448 R | 60.3% | 39.7% | 60.3% | 39.7% |
| 56,663 | COLE | 27,068 | 20,366 | 6,702 | | 13,664 R | 75.2% | 24.8% | 75.2% | 24.8% |
| 14,643 | COOPER | 6,822 | 4,603 | 2,219 | | 2,384 R | 67.5% | 32.5% | 67.5% | 32.5% |
| 18,300 | CRAWFORD | 7,326 | 4,716 | 2,610 | | 2,106 R | 64.4% | 35.6% | 64.4% | 35.6% |
| 7,383 | DADE | 3,700 | 2,600 | 1,100 | | 1,500 R | 70.3% | 29.7% | 70.3% | 29.7% |
| 12,096 | DALLAS | 5,479 | 3,577 | 1,902 | | 1,675 R | 65.3% | 34.7% | 65.3% | 34.7% |
| 8,905 | DAVIESS | 3,940 | 2,414 | 1,526 | | 888 R | 61.3% | 38.7% | 61.3% | 38.7% |
| 8,222 | DE KALB | 3,652 | 2,188 | 1,464 | | 724 R | 59.9% | 40.1% | 59.9% | 40.1% |
| 14,517 | DENT | 6,034 | 3,490 | 2,544 | | 946 R | 57.8% | 42.2% | 57.8% | 42.2% |
| 11,594 | DOUGLAS | 5,199 | 3,662 | 1,536 | 1 | 2,126 R | 70.4% | 29.5% | 70.5% | 29.5% |
| 36,324 | DUNKLIN | 11,059 | 6,092 | 4,967 | | 1,125 R | 55.1% | 44.9% | 55.1% | 44.9% |
| 71,233 | FRANKLIN | 26,988 | 18,669 | 8,319 | | 10,350 R | 69.2% | 30.8% | 69.2% | 30.8% |
| 13,181 | GASCONADE | 5,808 | 4,678 | 1,130 | | 3,548 R | 80.5% | 19.5% | 80.5% | 19.5% |
| 7,887 | GENTRY | 3,647 | 2,047 | 1,600 | | 447 R | 56.1% | 43.9% | 56.1% | 43.9% |
| 185,302 | GREENE | 85,215 | 57,250 | 27,965 | | 29,285 R | 67.2% | 32.8% | 67.2% | 32.8% |
| 11,959 | GRUNDY | 5,017 | 3,156 | 1,861 | | 1,295 R | 62.9% | 37.1% | 62.9% | 37.1% |
| 9,890 | HARRISON | 4,493 | 2,844 | 1,649 | | 1,195 R | 63.3% | 36.7% | 63.3% | 36.7% |
| 19,672 | HENRY | 9,160 | 5,419 | 3,741 | | 1,678 R | 59.2% | 40.8% | 59.2% | 40.8% |
| 6,367 | HICKORY | 3,402 | 2,190 | 1,212 | | 978 R | 64.4% | 35.6% | 64.4% | 35.6% |
| 6,882 | HOLT | 3,113 | 2,087 | 1,026 | | 1,061 R | 67.0% | 33.0% | 67.0% | 33.0% |
| 10,008 | HOWARD | 4,374 | 2,360 | 2,014 | | 346 R | 54.0% | 46.0% | 54.0% | 46.0% |
| 28,807 | HOWELL | 11,971 | 8,204 | 3,767 | | 4,437 R | 68.5% | 31.5% | 68.5% | 31.5% |
| 11,084 | IRON | 4,339 | 2,316 | 2,023 | | 293 R | 53.4% | 46.6% | 53.4% | 46.6% |
| 629,266 | JACKSON | 267,347 | 132,271 | 135,067 | 9 | 2,796 D | 49.5% | 50.5% | 49.5% | 50.5% |
| 86,958 | JASPER | 32,325 | 23,066 | 9,259 | | 13,807 R | 71.4% | 28.6% | 71.4% | 28.6% |
| 146,183 | JEFFERSON | 54,551 | 34,525 | 20,026 | | 14,499 R | 63.3% | 36.7% | 63.3% | 36.7% |
| 39,059 | JOHNSON | 12,651 | 8,413 | 4,238 | | 4,175 R | 66.5% | 33.5% | 66.5% | 33.5% |
| 5,508 | KNOX | 2,610 | 1,513 | 1,097 | | 416 R | 58.0% | 42.0% | 58.0% | 42.0% |
| 24,323 | LACLEDE | 9,071 | 6,406 | 2,665 | | 3,741 R | 70.6% | 29.4% | 70.6% | 29.4% |
| 29,925 | LAFAYETTE | 13,429 | 8,581 | 4,848 | | 3,733 R | 63.9% | 36.1% | 63.9% | 36.1% |
| 28,973 | LAWRENCE | 12,090 | 8,370 | 3,720 | | 4,650 R | 69.2% | 30.8% | 69.2% | 30.8% |
| 10,901 | LEWIS | 4,415 | 2,438 | 1,977 | | 461 R | 55.2% | 44.8% | 55.2% | 44.8% |
| 22,193 | LINCOLN | 9,427 | 6,137 | 3,290 | | 2,847 R | 65.1% | 34.9% | 65.1% | 34.9% |
| 15,495 | LINN | 6,934 | 3,822 | 3,112 | | 710 R | 55.1% | 44.9% | 55.1% | 44.9% |
| 15,739 | LIVINGSTON | 6,789 | 4,090 | 2,699 | | 1,391 R | 60.2% | 39.8% | 60.2% | 39.8% |
| 14,917 | MCDONALD | 6,630 | 4,521 | 2,109 | | 2,412 R | 68.2% | 31.8% | 68.2% | 31.8% |

# MISSOURI

## PRESIDENT 1984

| 1980 Census Population | County | Total Vote | Republican | Democratic | Other | Rep.-Dem. Plurality | | Percentage | | | |
|---|---|---|---|---|---|---|---|---|---|---|---|
| | | | | | | | | Total Vote | | Major Vote | |
| | | | | | | | | Rep. | Dem. | Rep. | Dem. |
| 16,313 | MACON | 7,579 | 4,542 | 3,037 | | 1,505 | R | 59.9% | 40.1% | 59.9% | 40.1% |
| 10,725 | MADISON | 4,670 | 2,808 | 1,862 | | 946 | R | 60.1% | 39.9% | 60.1% | 39.9% |
| 7,551 | MARIES | 3,655 | 2,267 | 1,388 | | 879 | R | 62.0% | 38.0% | 62.0% | 38.0% |
| 28,638 | MARION | 11,497 | 6,831 | 4,666 | | 2,165 | R | 59.4% | 40.6% | 59.4% | 40.6% |
| 4,685 | MERCER | 2,104 | 1,229 | 875 | | 354 | R | 58.4% | 41.6% | 58.4% | 41.6% |
| 18,532 | MILLER | 8,760 | 6,706 | 2,054 | | 4,652 | R | 76.6% | 23.4% | 76.6% | 23.4% |
| 15,726 | MISSISSIPPI | 5,026 | 2,502 | 2,524 | | 22 | D | 49.8% | 50.2% | 49.8% | 50.2% |
| 12,068 | MONITEAU | 5,811 | 4,197 | 1,614 | | 2,583 | R | 72.2% | 27.8% | 72.2% | 27.8% |
| 9,716 | MONROE | 4,155 | 2,163 | 1,992 | | 171 | R | 52.1% | 47.9% | 52.1% | 47.9% |
| 11,537 | MONTGOMERY | 4,929 | 3,261 | 1,668 | | 1,593 | R | 66.2% | 33.8% | 66.2% | 33.8% |
| 13,807 | MORGAN | 6,561 | 4,392 | 2,169 | | 2,223 | R | 66.9% | 33.1% | 66.9% | 33.1% |
| 22,945 | NEW MADRID | 8,099 | 4,323 | 3,776 | | 547 | R | 53.4% | 46.6% | 53.4% | 46.6% |
| 40,555 | NEWTON | 16,332 | 11,709 | 4,623 | | 7,086 | R | 71.7% | 28.3% | 71.7% | 28.3% |
| 21,996 | NODAWAY | 9,086 | 5,471 | 3,615 | | 1,856 | R | 60.2% | 39.8% | 60.2% | 39.8% |
| 10,238 | OREGON | 4,005 | 1,979 | 2,026 | | 47 | D | 49.4% | 50.6% | 49.4% | 50.6% |
| 12,014 | OSAGE | 5,724 | 4,381 | 1,343 | | 3,038 | R | 76.5% | 23.5% | 76.5% | 23.5% |
| 7,961 | OZARK | 3,724 | 2,614 | 1,110 | | 1,504 | R | 70.2% | 29.8% | 70.2% | 29.8% |
| 24,987 | PEMISCOT | 7,026 | 3,733 | 3,293 | | 440 | R | 53.1% | 46.9% | 53.1% | 46.9% |
| 16,784 | PERRY | 6,330 | 4,493 | 1,837 | | 2,656 | R | 71.0% | 29.0% | 71.0% | 29.0% |
| 36,378 | PETTIS | 16,404 | 10,991 | 5,413 | | 5,578 | R | 67.0% | 33.0% | 67.0% | 33.0% |
| 33,633 | PHELPS | 14,086 | 9,012 | 5,074 | | 3,938 | R | 64.0% | 36.0% | 64.0% | 36.0% |
| 17,568 | PIKE | 7,246 | 3,933 | 3,313 | | 620 | R | 54.3% | 45.7% | 54.3% | 45.7% |
| 46,341 | PLATTE | 20,527 | 12,859 | 7,668 | | 5,191 | R | 62.6% | 37.4% | 62.6% | 37.4% |
| 18,822 | POLK | 8,286 | 5,467 | 2,819 | | 2,648 | R | 66.0% | 34.0% | 66.0% | 34.0% |
| 42,011 | PULASKI | 8,195 | 5,330 | 2,865 | | 2,465 | R | 65.0% | 35.0% | 65.0% | 35.0% |
| 6,092 | PUTNAM | 2,337 | 1,540 | 797 | | 743 | R | 65.9% | 34.1% | 65.9% | 34.1% |
| 8,911 | RALLS | 4,078 | 2,067 | 2,011 | | 56 | R | 50.7% | 49.3% | 50.7% | 49.3% |
| 25,460 | RANDOLPH | 10,206 | 5,735 | 4,471 | | 1,264 | R | 56.2% | 43.8% | 56.2% | 43.8% |
| 21,378 | RAY | 8,854 | 4,875 | 3,979 | | 896 | R | 55.1% | 44.9% | 55.1% | 44.9% |
| 7,230 | REYNOLDS | 3,356 | 1,330 | 2,026 | | 696 | D | 39.6% | 60.4% | 39.6% | 60.4% |
| 12,458 | RIPLEY | 4,810 | 2,927 | 1,883 | | 1,044 | R | 60.9% | 39.1% | 60.9% | 39.1% |
| 144,107 | ST. CHARLES | 65,401 | 47,784 | 17,617 | | 30,167 | R | 73.1% | 26.9% | 73.1% | 26.9% |
| 8,622 | ST. CLAIR | 4,322 | 2,667 | 1,655 | | 1,012 | R | 61.7% | 38.3% | 61.7% | 38.3% |
| 42,600 | ST. FRANCOIS | 16,929 | 9,792 | 7,137 | | 2,655 | R | 57.8% | 42.2% | 57.8% | 42.2% |
| 453,085 | ST. LOUIS CITY | 173,338 | 61,020 | 112,318 | | 51,298 | D | 35.2% | 64.8% | 35.2% | 64.8% |
| 973,896 | ST. LOUIS COUNTY | 480,828 | 307,684 | 173,144 | | 134,540 | R | 64.0% | 36.0% | 64.0% | 36.0% |
| 15,180 | STE. GENEVIEVE | 5,968 | 3,245 | 2,723 | | 522 | R | 54.4% | 45.6% | 54.4% | 45.6% |
| 24,919 | SALINE | 10,323 | 6,042 | 4,281 | | 1,761 | R | 58.5% | 41.5% | 58.5% | 41.5% |
| 4,979 | SCHUYLER | 2,391 | 1,250 | 1,141 | | 109 | R | 52.3% | 47.7% | 52.3% | 47.7% |
| 5,415 | SCOTLAND | 2,560 | 1,485 | 1,075 | | 410 | R | 58.0% | 42.0% | 58.0% | 42.0% |
| 39,647 | SCOTT | 14,297 | 8,727 | 5,569 | 1 | 3,158 | R | 61.0% | 39.0% | 61.0% | 39.0% |
| 7,885 | SHANNON | 3,359 | 1,779 | 1,580 | | 199 | R | 53.0% | 47.0% | 53.0% | 47.0% |
| 7,826 | SHELBY | 3,816 | 2,243 | 1,573 | | 670 | R | 58.8% | 41.2% | 58.8% | 41.2% |
| 29,009 | STODDARD | 10,995 | 6,701 | 4,294 | | 2,407 | R | 60.9% | 39.1% | 60.9% | 39.1% |
| 15,587 | STONE | 7,825 | 5,706 | 2,119 | | 3,587 | R | 72.9% | 27.1% | 72.9% | 27.1% |
| 7,434 | SULLIVAN | 4,090 | 2,306 | 1,784 | | 522 | R | 56.4% | 43.6% | 56.4% | 43.6% |
| 20,467 | TANEY | 9,994 | 7,082 | 2,912 | | 4,170 | R | 70.9% | 29.1% | 70.9% | 29.1% |
| 21,070 | TEXAS | 9,253 | 5,591 | 3,662 | | 1,929 | R | 60.4% | 39.6% | 60.4% | 39.6% |
| 19,806 | VERNON | 8,165 | 5,181 | 2,984 | | 2,197 | R | 63.5% | 36.5% | 63.5% | 36.5% |
| 14,900 | WARREN | 7,114 | 5,150 | 1,964 | | 3,186 | R | 72.4% | 27.6% | 72.4% | 27.6% |
| 17,983 | WASHINGTON | 6,742 | 3,755 | 2,987 | | 768 | R | 55.7% | 44.3% | 55.7% | 44.3% |
| 11,277 | WAYNE | 5,230 | 2,867 | 2,363 | | 504 | R | 54.8% | 45.2% | 54.8% | 45.2% |
| 20,414 | WEBSTER | 8,511 | 5,529 | 2,982 | | 2,547 | R | 65.0% | 35.0% | 65.0% | 35.0% |
| 3,008 | WORTH | 1,655 | 921 | 734 | | 187 | R | 55.6% | 44.4% | 55.6% | 44.4% |
| 16,188 | WRIGHT | 6,660 | 4,687 | 1,973 | | 2,714 | R | 70.4% | 29.6% | 70.4% | 29.6% |
| 4,916,686 | TOTAL | 2,122,783 | 1,274,188 | 848,583 | 12 | 425,605 | R | 60.0% | 40.0% | 60.0% | 40.0% |

# MISSOURI

## PRESIDENT 1980

| 1980 Census Population | County | Total Vote | Republican | Democratic | Other | Rep.-Dem. Plurality | Percentage | | | |
|---|---|---|---|---|---|---|---|---|---|---|
| | | | | | | | Total Vote | | Major Vote | |
| | | | | | | | Rep. | Dem. | Rep. | Dem. |
| 24,870 | ADAIR | 9,522 | 5,513 | 3,507 | 502 | 2,006 R | 57.9% | 36.8% | 61.1% | 38.9% |
| 13,980 | ANDREW | 6,573 | 3,690 | 2,575 | 308 | 1,115 R | 56.1% | 39.2% | 58.9% | 41.1% |
| 8,605 | ATCHISON | 3,556 | 2,096 | 1,273 | 187 | 823 R | 58.9% | 35.8% | 62.2% | 37.8% |
| 26,458 | AUDRAIN | 11,834 | 6,347 | 5,168 | 319 | 1,179 R | 53.6% | 43.7% | 55.1% | 44.9% |
| 24,408 | BARRY | 11,458 | 7,038 | 4,193 | 227 | 2,845 R | 61.4% | 36.6% | 62.7% | 37.3% |
| 11,292 | BARTON | 5,398 | 3,337 | 1,901 | 160 | 1,436 R | 61.8% | 35.2% | 63.7% | 36.3% |
| 15,873 | BATES | 7,521 | 4,061 | 3,297 | 163 | 764 R | 54.0% | 43.8% | 55.2% | 44.8% |
| 12,183 | BENTON | 5,852 | 3,451 | 2,241 | 160 | 1,210 R | 59.0% | 38.3% | 60.6% | 39.4% |
| 10,301 | BOLLINGER | 5,105 | 2,863 | 2,160 | 82 | 703 R | 56.1% | 42.3% | 57.0% | 43.0% |
| 100,376 | BOONE | 38,837 | 16,313 | 18,527 | 3,997 | 2,214 D | 42.0% | 47.7% | 46.8% | 53.2% |
| 87,888 | BUCHANAN | 35,150 | 16,551 | 16,967 | 1,632 | 416 D | 47.1% | 48.3% | 49.4% | 50.6% |
| 37,693 | BUTLER | 14,181 | 8,342 | 5,605 | 234 | 2,737 R | 58.8% | 39.5% | 59.8% | 40.2% |
| 8,660 | CALDWELL | 4,226 | 2,551 | 1,541 | 134 | 1,010 R | 60.4% | 36.5% | 62.3% | 37.7% |
| 32,252 | CALLAWAY | 12,835 | 6,755 | 5,560 | 520 | 1,195 R | 52.6% | 43.3% | 54.9% | 45.1% |
| 20,017 | CAMDEN | 10,246 | 6,541 | 3,416 | 289 | 3,125 R | 63.8% | 33.3% | 65.7% | 34.3% |
| 58,837 | CAPE GIRARDEAU | 24,549 | 14,861 | 8,625 | 1,063 | 6,236 R | 60.5% | 35.1% | 63.3% | 36.7% |
| 12,131 | CARROLL | 5,583 | 3,291 | 2,130 | 162 | 1,161 R | 58.9% | 38.2% | 60.7% | 39.3% |
| 5,428 | CARTER | 2,368 | 1,218 | 1,087 | 63 | 131 R | 51.4% | 45.9% | 52.8% | 47.2% |
| 51,029 | CASS | 19,134 | 10,105 | 8,198 | 831 | 1,907 R | 52.8% | 42.8% | 55.2% | 44.8% |
| 11,894 | CEDAR | 5,283 | 3,469 | 1,703 | 111 | 1,766 R | 65.7% | 32.2% | 67.1% | 32.9% |
| 10,489 | CHARITON | 4,973 | 2,641 | 2,250 | 82 | 391 R | 53.1% | 45.2% | 54.0% | 46.0% |
| 22,402 | CHRISTIAN | 10,251 | 6,487 | 3,502 | 262 | 2,985 R | 63.3% | 34.2% | 64.9% | 35.1% |
| 8,493 | CLARK | 3,614 | 2,042 | 1,494 | 78 | 548 R | 56.5% | 41.3% | 57.7% | 42.3% |
| 136,488 | CLAY | 56,314 | 28,521 | 24,250 | 3,543 | 4,271 R | 50.6% | 43.1% | 54.0% | 46.0% |
| 15,916 | CLINTON | 6,852 | 3,599 | 3,001 | 252 | 598 R | 52.5% | 43.8% | 54.5% | 45.5% |
| 56,663 | COLE | 26,423 | 16,373 | 9,210 | 840 | 7,163 R | 62.0% | 34.9% | 64.0% | 36.0% |
| 14,643 | COOPER | 6,849 | 3,996 | 2,687 | 166 | 1,309 R | 58.3% | 39.2% | 59.8% | 40.2% |
| 18,300 | CRAWFORD | 7,011 | 4,081 | 2,710 | 220 | 1,371 R | 58.2% | 38.7% | 60.1% | 39.9% |
| 7,383 | DADE | 3,778 | 2,410 | 1,283 | 85 | 1,127 R | 63.8% | 34.0% | 65.3% | 34.7% |
| 12,096 | DALLAS | 5,438 | 3,297 | 2,011 | 130 | 1,286 R | 60.6% | 37.0% | 62.1% | 37.9% |
| 8,905 | DAVIESS | 3,984 | 2,125 | 1,770 | 89 | 355 R | 53.3% | 44.4% | 54.6% | 45.4% |
| 8,222 | DE KALB | 3,885 | 2,062 | 1,677 | 146 | 385 R | 53.1% | 43.2% | 55.1% | 44.9% |
| 14,517 | DENT | 6,131 | 3,477 | 2,528 | 126 | 949 R | 56.7% | 41.2% | 57.9% | 42.1% |
| 11,594 | DOUGLAS | 5,252 | 3,440 | 1,677 | 135 | 1,763 R | 65.5% | 31.9% | 67.2% | 32.8% |
| 36,324 | DUNKLIN | 11,530 | 5,253 | 6,120 | 157 | 867 D | 45.6% | 53.1% | 46.2% | 53.8% |
| 71,233 | FRANKLIN | 26,832 | 15,210 | 10,480 | 1,142 | 4,730 R | 56.7% | 39.1% | 59.2% | 40.8% |
| 13,181 | GASCONADE | 6,203 | 4,481 | 1,550 | 172 | 2,931 R | 72.2% | 25.0% | 74.3% | 25.7% |
| 7,887 | GENTRY | 3,869 | 2,005 | 1,720 | 144 | 285 R | 51.8% | 44.5% | 53.8% | 46.2% |
| 185,302 | GREENE | 77,425 | 43,116 | 30,498 | 3,811 | 12,618 R | 55.7% | 39.4% | 58.6% | 41.4% |
| 11,959 | GRUNDY | 5,106 | 2,890 | 2,064 | 152 | 826 R | 56.6% | 40.4% | 58.3% | 41.7% |
| 9,890 | HARRISON | 4,655 | 2,734 | 1,732 | 189 | 1,002 R | 58.7% | 37.2% | 61.2% | 38.8% |
| 19,672 | HENRY | 9,772 | 4,807 | 4,648 | 317 | 159 R | 49.2% | 47.6% | 50.8% | 49.2% |
| 6,367 | HICKORY | 3,213 | 1,893 | 1,248 | 72 | 645 R | 58.9% | 38.8% | 60.3% | 39.7% |
| 6,882 | HOLT | 3,190 | 1,993 | 1,119 | 78 | 874 R | 62.5% | 35.1% | 64.0% | 36.0% |
| 10,008 | HOWARD | 4,554 | 2,179 | 2,243 | 132 | 64 D | 47.8% | 49.3% | 49.3% | 50.7% |
| 28,807 | HOWELL | 11,903 | 7,149 | 4,472 | 282 | 2,677 R | 60.1% | 37.6% | 61.5% | 38.5% |
| 11,084 | IRON | 4,551 | 2,205 | 2,226 | 120 | 21 D | 48.5% | 48.9% | 49.8% | 50.2% |
| 629,266 | JACKSON | 256,687 | 106,156 | 135,805 | 14,726 | 29,649 D | 41.4% | 52.9% | 43.9% | 56.1% |
| 86,958 | JASPER | 34,666 | 21,664 | 11,953 | 1,049 | 9,711 R | 62.5% | 34.5% | 64.4% | 35.6% |
| 146,183 | JEFFERSON | 54,882 | 28,546 | 24,042 | 2,294 | 4,504 R | 52.0% | 43.8% | 54.3% | 45.7% |
| 39,059 | JOHNSON | 12,585 | 6,449 | 5,441 | 695 | 1,008 R | 51.2% | 43.2% | 54.2% | 45.8% |
| 5,508 | KNOX | 2,710 | 1,475 | 1,187 | 48 | 288 R | 54.4% | 43.8% | 55.4% | 44.6% |
| 24,323 | LACLEDE | 9,282 | 5,642 | 3,443 | 197 | 2,199 R | 60.8% | 37.1% | 62.1% | 37.9% |
| 29,925 | LAFAYETTE | 13,468 | 7,271 | 5,792 | 405 | 1,479 R | 54.0% | 43.0% | 55.7% | 44.3% |
| 28,973 | LAWRENCE | 12,843 | 7,921 | 4,670 | 252 | 3,251 R | 61.7% | 36.4% | 62.9% | 37.1% |
| 10,901 | LEWIS | 4,789 | 2,350 | 2,314 | 125 | 36 R | 49.1% | 48.3% | 50.4% | 49.6% |
| 22,193 | LINCOLN | 9,335 | 4,963 | 4,110 | 262 | 853 R | 53.2% | 44.0% | 54.7% | 45.3% |
| 15,495 | LINN | 7,224 | 3,585 | 3,467 | 172 | 118 R | 49.6% | 48.0% | 50.8% | 49.2% |
| 15,739 | LIVINGSTON | 7,270 | 3,654 | 3,368 | 248 | 286 R | 50.3% | 46.3% | 52.0% | 48.0% |
| 14,917 | MCDONALD | 6,783 | 4,114 | 2,485 | 184 | 1,629 R | 60.7% | 36.6% | 62.3% | 37.7% |

# MISSOURI

## PRESIDENT 1980

| 1980 Census Population | County | Total Vote | Republican | Democratic | Other | Rep.-Dem. Plurality | Percentage Total Vote Rep. | Dem. | Major Vote Rep. | Dem. |
|---:|---|---:|---:|---:|---:|---:|---:|---:|---:|---:|
| 16,313 | MACON | 8,187 | 4,430 | 3,578 | 179 | 852 R | 54.1% | 43.7% | 55.3% | 44.7% |
| 10,725 | MADISON | 4,938 | 2,618 | 2,231 | 89 | 387 R | 53.0% | 45.2% | 54.0% | 46.0% |
| 7,551 | MARIES | 3,789 | 1,985 | 1,732 | 72 | 253 R | 52.4% | 45.7% | 53.4% | 46.6% |
| 28,638 | MARION | 12,186 | 6,036 | 5,890 | 260 | 146 R | 49.5% | 48.3% | 50.6% | 49.4% |
| 4,685 | MERCER | 2,158 | 1,266 | 821 | 71 | 445 R | 58.7% | 38.0% | 60.7% | 39.3% |
| 18,532 | MILLER | 8,185 | 5,560 | 2,469 | 156 | 3,091 R | 67.9% | 30.2% | 69.2% | 30.8% |
| 15,726 | MISSISSIPPI | 5,579 | 2,459 | 3,040 | 80 | 581 D | 44.1% | 54.5% | 44.7% | 55.3% |
| 12,068 | MONITEAU | 5,834 | 3,430 | 2,284 | 120 | 1,146 R | 58.8% | 39.1% | 60.0% | 40.0% |
| 9,716 | MONROE | 4,555 | 2,026 | 2,445 | 84 | 419 D | 44.5% | 53.7% | 45.3% | 54.7% |
| 11,537 | MONTGOMERY | 5,225 | 3,061 | 2,007 | 157 | 1,054 R | 58.6% | 38.4% | 60.4% | 39.6% |
| 13,807 | MORGAN | 6,182 | 3,577 | 2,460 | 145 | 1,117 R | 57.9% | 39.8% | 59.3% | 40.7% |
| 22,945 | NEW MADRID | 8,298 | 4,041 | 4,171 | 86 | 130 D | 48.7% | 50.3% | 49.2% | 50.8% |
| 40,555 | NEWTON | 16,662 | 10,515 | 5,621 | 526 | 4,894 R | 63.1% | 33.7% | 65.2% | 34.8% |
| 21,996 | NODAWAY | 9,290 | 4,544 | 4,257 | 489 | 287 R | 48.9% | 45.8% | 51.6% | 48.4% |
| 10,238 | OREGON | 3,898 | 1,523 | 2,326 | 49 | 803 D | 39.1% | 59.7% | 39.6% | 60.4% |
| 12,014 | OSAGE | 5,822 | 3,679 | 2,045 | 98 | 1,634 R | 63.2% | 35.1% | 64.3% | 35.7% |
| 7,961 | OZARK | 3,770 | 2,434 | 1,242 | 94 | 1,192 R | 64.6% | 32.9% | 66.2% | 33.8% |
| 24,987 | PEMISCOT | 7,732 | 3,519 | 4,140 | 73 | 621 D | 45.5% | 53.5% | 45.9% | 54.1% |
| 16,784 | PERRY | 7,689 | 5,053 | 2,416 | 220 | 2,637 R | 65.7% | 31.4% | 67.7% | 32.3% |
| 36,378 | PETTIS | 15,841 | 8,833 | 6,475 | 533 | 2,358 R | 55.8% | 40.9% | 57.7% | 42.3% |
| 33,633 | PHELPS | 13,566 | 7,366 | 5,470 | 730 | 1,896 R | 54.3% | 40.3% | 57.4% | 42.6% |
| 17,568 | PIKE | 7,591 | 3,932 | 3,454 | 205 | 478 R | 51.8% | 45.5% | 53.2% | 46.8% |
| 46,341 | PLATTE | 18,756 | 10,092 | 7,342 | 1,322 | 2,750 R | 53.8% | 39.1% | 57.9% | 42.1% |
| 18,822 | POLK | 8,368 | 4,842 | 3,336 | 190 | 1,506 R | 57.9% | 39.9% | 59.2% | 40.8% |
| 42,011 | PULASKI | 7,871 | 3,998 | 3,707 | 166 | 291 R | 50.8% | 47.1% | 51.9% | 48.1% |
| 6,092 | PUTNAM | 2,655 | 1,722 | 871 | 62 | 851 R | 64.9% | 32.8% | 66.4% | 33.6% |
| 8,911 | RALLS | 4,142 | 1,968 | 2,069 | 105 | 101 D | 47.5% | 50.0% | 48.7% | 51.3% |
| 25,460 | RANDOLPH | 10,276 | 5,141 | 4,884 | 251 | 257 R | 50.0% | 47.5% | 51.3% | 48.7% |
| 21,378 | RAY | 8,871 | 4,064 | 4,518 | 289 | 454 D | 45.8% | 50.9% | 47.4% | 52.6% |
| 7,230 | REYNOLDS | 3,250 | 1,271 | 1,919 | 60 | 648 D | 39.1% | 59.0% | 39.8% | 60.2% |
| 12,458 | RIPLEY | 4,765 | 2,524 | 2,156 | 85 | 368 R | 53.0% | 45.2% | 53.9% | 46.1% |
| 144,107 | ST. CHARLES | 59,768 | 36,050 | 20,668 | 3,050 | 15,382 R | 60.3% | 34.6% | 63.6% | 36.4% |
| 8,622 | ST. CLAIR | 4,210 | 2,419 | 1,706 | 85 | 713 R | 57.5% | 40.5% | 58.6% | 41.4% |
| 42,600 | ST. FRANCOIS | 16,916 | 8,914 | 7,495 | 507 | 1,419 R | 52.7% | 44.3% | 54.3% | 45.7% |
| 453,085 | ST. LOUIS CITY | 170,751 | 50,333 | 113,697 | 6,721 | 63,364 D | 29.5% | 66.6% | 30.7% | 69.3% |
| 973,896 | ST. LOUIS COUNTY | 484,831 | 263,518 | 192,796 | 28,517 | 70,722 R | 54.4% | 39.8% | 57.7% | 42.3% |
| 15,180 | STE. GENEVIEVE | 6,291 | 2,768 | 3,324 | 199 | 556 D | 44.0% | 52.8% | 45.4% | 54.6% |
| 24,919 | SALINE | 10,576 | 5,218 | 4,943 | 415 | 275 R | 49.3% | 46.7% | 51.4% | 48.6% |
| 4,979 | SCHUYLER | 2,559 | 1,386 | 1,114 | 59 | 272 R | 54.2% | 43.5% | 55.4% | 44.6% |
| 5,415 | SCOTLAND | 2,869 | 1,592 | 1,200 | 77 | 392 R | 55.5% | 41.8% | 57.0% | 43.0% |
| 39,647 | SCOTT | 15,336 | 8,227 | 6,854 | 255 | 1,373 R | 53.6% | 44.7% | 54.6% | 45.4% |
| 7,885 | SHANNON | 3,401 | 1,523 | 1,818 | 60 | 295 D | 44.8% | 53.5% | 45.6% | 54.4% |
| 7,826 | SHELBY | 4,079 | 2,151 | 1,849 | 79 | 302 R | 52.7% | 45.3% | 53.8% | 46.2% |
| 29,009 | STODDARD | 11,512 | 6,199 | 5,128 | 185 | 1,071 R | 53.8% | 44.5% | 54.7% | 45.3% |
| 15,587 | STONE | 7,209 | 4,780 | 2,210 | 219 | 2,570 R | 66.3% | 30.7% | 68.4% | 31.6% |
| 7,434 | SULLIVAN | 4,325 | 2,412 | 1,824 | 89 | 588 R | 55.8% | 42.2% | 56.9% | 43.1% |
| 20,467 | TANEY | 9,854 | 6,230 | 3,389 | 235 | 2,841 R | 63.2% | 34.4% | 64.8% | 35.2% |
| 21,070 | TEXAS | 9,309 | 4,879 | 4,261 | 169 | 618 R | 52.4% | 45.8% | 53.4% | 46.6% |
| 19,806 | VERNON | 8,456 | 4,391 | 3,704 | 361 | 687 R | 51.9% | 43.8% | 54.2% | 45.8% |
| 14,900 | WARREN | 6,743 | 4,366 | 2,132 | 245 | 2,234 R | 64.7% | 31.6% | 67.2% | 32.8% |
| 17,983 | WASHINGTON | 6,465 | 3,439 | 2,873 | 153 | 566 R | 53.2% | 44.4% | 54.5% | 45.5% |
| 11,277 | WAYNE | 5,444 | 2,823 | 2,549 | 72 | 274 R | 51.9% | 46.8% | 52.6% | 47.4% |
| 20,414 | WEBSTER | 8,719 | 5,121 | 3,409 | 189 | 1,712 R | 58.7% | 39.1% | 60.0% | 40.0% |
| 3,008 | WORTH | 1,657 | 833 | 760 | 64 | 73 R | 50.3% | 45.9% | 52.3% | 47.7% |
| 16,188 | WRIGHT | 6,716 | 4,451 | 2,182 | 83 | 2,269 R | 66.3% | 32.5% | 67.1% | 32.9% |
| 4,916,686 | TOTAL | 2,099,824 | 1,074,181 | 931,182 | 94,461 | 142,999 R | 51.2% | 44.3% | 53.6% | 46.4% |

# MISSOURI

## PRESIDENT 1976

| 1970 Census Population | County | Total Vote | Republican | Democratic | Other | Rep.-Dem. Plurality | Percentage | | | |
|---|---|---|---|---|---|---|---|---|---|---|
| | | | | | | | Total Vote | | Major Vote | |
| | | | | | | | Rep. | Dem. | Rep. | Dem. |
| 22,472 | ADAIR | 9,133 | 5,249 | 3,684 | 200 | 1,565 R | 57.5% | 40.3% | 58.8% | 41.2% |
| 11,913 | ANDREW | 6,213 | 3,130 | 3,042 | 41 | 88 R | 50.4% | 49.0% | 50.7% | 49.3% |
| 9,240 | ATCHISON | 3,930 | 1,960 | 1,926 | 44 | 34 R | 49.9% | 49.0% | 50.4% | 49.6% |
| 25,362 | AUDRAIN | 11,032 | 5,378 | 5,600 | 54 | 222 D | 48.7% | 50.8% | 49.0% | 51.0% |
| 19,597 | BARRY | 10,148 | 5,053 | 5,046 | 49 | 7 R | 49.8% | 49.7% | 50.0% | 50.0% |
| 10,431 | BARTON | 5,077 | 2,708 | 2,326 | 43 | 382 R | 53.3% | 45.8% | 53.8% | 46.2% |
| 15,468 | BATES | 7,684 | 3,350 | 4,288 | 46 | 938 D | 43.6% | 55.8% | 43.9% | 56.1% |
| 9,695 | BENTON | 5,587 | 2,875 | 2,684 | 28 | 191 R | 51.5% | 48.0% | 51.7% | 48.3% |
| 8,820 | BOLLINGER | 4,862 | 2,113 | 2,740 | 9 | 627 D | 43.5% | 56.4% | 43.5% | 56.5% |
| 80,911 | BOONE | 34,893 | 16,373 | 17,674 | 846 | 1,301 D | 46.9% | 50.7% | 48.1% | 51.9% |
| 86,915 | BUCHANAN | 34,124 | 16,446 | 17,427 | 251 | 981 D | 48.2% | 51.1% | 48.6% | 51.4% |
| 33,529 | BUTLER | 12,485 | 5,669 | 6,759 | 57 | 1,090 D | 45.4% | 54.1% | 45.6% | 54.4% |
| 8,351 | CALDWELL | 4,233 | 2,094 | 2,113 | 26 | 19 D | 49.5% | 49.9% | 49.8% | 50.2% |
| 25,950 | CALLAWAY | 10,059 | 5,115 | 4,843 | 101 | 272 R | 50.8% | 48.1% | 51.4% | 48.6% |
| 13,315 | CAMDEN | 8,510 | 4,469 | 3,975 | 66 | 494 R | 52.5% | 46.7% | 52.9% | 47.1% |
| 49,350 | CAPE GIRARDEAU | 23,164 | 12,607 | 10,440 | 117 | 2,167 R | 54.4% | 45.1% | 54.7% | 45.3% |
| 12,565 | CARROLL | 6,077 | 2,936 | 3,114 | 27 | 178 D | 48.3% | 51.2% | 48.5% | 51.5% |
| 3,878 | CARTER | 2,007 | 842 | 1,154 | 11 | 312 D | 42.0% | 57.5% | 42.2% | 57.8% |
| 39,448 | CASS | 16,330 | 7,182 | 9,008 | 140 | 1,826 D | 44.0% | 55.2% | 44.4% | 55.6% |
| 9,424 | CEDAR | 4,965 | 2,752 | 2,192 | 21 | 560 R | 55.4% | 44.1% | 55.7% | 44.3% |
| 11,084 | CHARITON | 5,204 | 2,128 | 3,055 | 21 | 927 D | 40.9% | 58.7% | 41.1% | 58.9% |
| 15,124 | CHRISTIAN | 8,442 | 4,553 | 3,830 | 59 | 723 R | 53.9% | 45.4% | 54.3% | 45.7% |
| 8,260 | CLARK | 3,274 | 1,582 | 1,679 | 13 | 97 D | 48.3% | 51.3% | 48.5% | 51.5% |
| 123,644 | CLAY | 52,315 | 24,962 | 26,609 | 744 | 1,647 D | 47.7% | 50.9% | 48.4% | 51.6% |
| 12,462 | CLINTON | 6,272 | 2,807 | 3,424 | 41 | 617 D | 44.8% | 54.6% | 45.0% | 55.0% |
| 46,228 | COLE | 22,503 | 14,370 | 7,949 | 184 | 6,421 R | 63.9% | 35.3% | 64.4% | 35.6% |
| 14,732 | COOPER | 6,809 | 3,694 | 3,087 | 28 | 607 R | 54.3% | 45.3% | 54.5% | 45.5% |
| 14,828 | CRAWFORD | 6,833 | 3,224 | 3,565 | 44 | 341 D | 47.2% | 52.2% | 47.5% | 52.5% |
| 6,850 | DADE | 3,710 | 2,015 | 1,681 | 14 | 334 R | 54.3% | 45.3% | 54.5% | 45.5% |
| 10,054 | DALLAS | 4,910 | 2,430 | 2,453 | 27 | 23 D | 49.5% | 50.0% | 49.8% | 50.2% |
| 8,420 | DAVIESS | 4,191 | 1,919 | 2,250 | 22 | 331 D | 45.8% | 53.7% | 46.0% | 54.0% |
| 7,305 | DE KALB | 3,779 | 1,739 | 2,023 | 17 | 284 D | 46.0% | 53.5% | 46.2% | 53.8% |
| 11,457 | DENT | 5,401 | 2,433 | 2,931 | 37 | 498 D | 45.0% | 54.3% | 45.4% | 54.6% |
| 9,268 | DOUGLAS | 4,667 | 2,652 | 1,981 | 34 | 671 R | 56.8% | 42.4% | 57.2% | 42.8% |
| 33,742 | DUNKLIN | 10,443 | 3,314 | 7,107 | 22 | 3,793 D | 31.7% | 68.1% | 31.8% | 68.2% |
| 55,116 | FRANKLIN | 24,342 | 12,242 | 11,695 | 405 | 547 R | 50.3% | 48.0% | 51.1% | 48.9% |
| 11,878 | GASCONADE | 5,682 | 3,925 | 1,702 | 55 | 2,223 R | 69.1% | 30.0% | 69.8% | 30.2% |
| 8,060 | GENTRY | 4,035 | 1,772 | 2,249 | 14 | 477 D | 43.9% | 55.7% | 44.1% | 55.9% |
| 152,929 | GREENE | 72,205 | 37,691 | 33,824 | 690 | 3,867 R | 52.2% | 46.8% | 52.7% | 47.3% |
| 11,819 | GRUNDY | 5,273 | 2,646 | 2,597 | 30 | 49 R | 50.2% | 49.3% | 50.5% | 49.5% |
| 10,257 | HARRISON | 4,813 | 2,478 | 2,304 | 31 | 174 R | 51.5% | 47.9% | 51.8% | 48.2% |
| 18,451 | HENRY | 9,497 | 4,168 | 5,282 | 47 | 1,114 D | 43.9% | 55.6% | 44.1% | 55.9% |
| 4,481 | HICKORY | 2,822 | 1,403 | 1,398 | 21 | 5 R | 49.7% | 49.5% | 50.1% | 49.9% |
| 6,654 | HOLT | 3,318 | 1,777 | 1,529 | 12 | 248 R | 53.6% | 46.1% | 53.8% | 46.2% |
| 10,561 | HOWARD | 4,494 | 1,690 | 2,769 | 35 | 1,079 D | 37.6% | 61.6% | 37.9% | 62.1% |
| 23,521 | HOWELL | 10,035 | 4,692 | 5,265 | 78 | 573 D | 46.8% | 52.5% | 47.1% | 52.9% |
| 9,529 | IRON | 4,434 | 1,765 | 2,646 | 23 | 881 D | 39.8% | 59.7% | 40.0% | 60.0% |
| 654,558 | JACKSON | 235,441 | 101,401 | 130,120 | 3,920 | 28,719 D | 43.1% | 55.3% | 43.8% | 56.2% |
| 79,852 | JASPER | 32,149 | 17,086 | 14,910 | 153 | 2,176 R | 53.1% | 46.4% | 53.4% | 46.6% |
| 105,248 | JEFFERSON | 43,915 | 18,261 | 25,159 | 495 | 6,898 D | 41.6% | 57.3% | 42.1% | 57.9% |
| 34,172 | JOHNSON | 11,220 | 5,513 | 5,551 | 156 | 38 D | 49.1% | 49.5% | 49.8% | 50.2% |
| 5,692 | KNOX | 2,556 | 1,216 | 1,319 | 21 | 103 D | 47.6% | 51.6% | 48.0% | 52.0% |
| 19,944 | LACLEDE | 8,475 | 4,067 | 4,381 | 27 | 314 D | 48.0% | 51.7% | 48.1% | 51.9% |
| 26,626 | LAFAYETTE | 13,305 | 6,823 | 6,410 | 72 | 413 R | 51.3% | 48.2% | 51.6% | 48.4% |
| 24,585 | LAWRENCE | 11,137 | 5,784 | 5,315 | 38 | 469 R | 51.9% | 47.7% | 52.1% | 47.9% |
| 10,993 | LEWIS | 4,497 | 1,983 | 2,486 | 28 | 503 D | 44.1% | 55.3% | 44.4% | 55.6% |
| 18,041 | LINCOLN | 8,140 | 3,581 | 4,473 | 86 | 892 D | 44.0% | 55.0% | 44.5% | 55.5% |
| 15,125 | LINN | 7,236 | 3,114 | 4,092 | 30 | 978 D | 43.0% | 56.6% | 43.2% | 56.8% |
| 15,368 | LIVINGSTON | 6,857 | 3,010 | 3,819 | 28 | 809 D | 43.9% | 55.7% | 44.1% | 55.9% |
| 12,357 | MCDONALD | 6,108 | 2,949 | 3,111 | 48 | 162 D | 48.3% | 50.9% | 48.7% | 51.3% |

# MISSOURI

## PRESIDENT 1976

| 1970 Census Population | County | Total Vote | Republican | Democratic | Other | Rep.-Dem. Plurality | Percentage Total Vote Rep. | Dem. | Major Vote Rep. | Dem. |
|---|---|---|---|---|---|---|---|---|---|---|
| 15,432 | MACON | 7,688 | 3,360 | 4,296 | 32 | 936 D | 43.7% | 55.9% | 43.9% | 56.1% |
| 8,641 | MADISON | 3,989 | 1,739 | 2,229 | 21 | 490 D | 43.6% | 55.9% | 43.8% | 56.2% |
| 6,851 | MARIES | 3,294 | 1,485 | 1,796 | 13 | 311 D | 45.1% | 54.5% | 45.3% | 54.7% |
| 28,121 | MARION | 11,663 | 5,501 | 6,124 | 38 | 623 D | 47.2% | 52.5% | 47.3% | 52.7% |
| 4,910 | MERCER | 2,207 | 1,025 | 1,177 | 5 | 152 D | 46.4% | 53.3% | 46.5% | 53.5% |
| 15,026 | MILLER | 6,866 | 4,095 | 2,739 | 32 | 1,356 R | 59.6% | 39.9% | 59.9% | 40.1% |
| 16,647 | MISSISSIPPI | 5,116 | 1,733 | 3,366 | 17 | 1,633 D | 33.9% | 65.8% | 34.0% | 66.0% |
| 10,742 | MONITEAU | 5,555 | 3,077 | 2,462 | 16 | 615 R | 55.4% | 44.3% | 55.6% | 44.4% |
| 9,542 | MONROE | 4,650 | 1,585 | 3,039 | 26 | 1,454 D | 34.1% | 65.4% | 34.3% | 65.7% |
| 11,000 | MONTGOMERY | 5,243 | 2,665 | 2,535 | 43 | 130 R | 50.8% | 48.4% | 51.2% | 48.8% |
| 10,068 | MORGAN | 5,595 | 2,831 | 2,738 | 26 | 93 R | 50.6% | 48.9% | 50.8% | 49.2% |
| 23,420 | NEW MADRID | 8,136 | 2,798 | 5,319 | 19 | 2,521 D | 34.4% | 65.4% | 34.5% | 65.5% |
| 32,901 | NEWTON | 14,301 | 7,142 | 7,045 | 114 | 97 R | 49.9% | 49.3% | 50.3% | 49.7% |
| 22,467 | NODAWAY | 9,534 | 4,558 | 4,875 | 101 | 317 D | 47.8% | 51.1% | 48.3% | 51.7% |
| 9,180 | OREGON | 3,712 | 1,122 | 2,564 | 26 | 1,442 D | 30.2% | 69.1% | 30.4% | 69.6% |
| 10,994 | OSAGE | 5,269 | 3,224 | 2,015 | 30 | 1,209 R | 61.2% | 38.2% | 61.5% | 38.5% |
| 6,226 | OZARK | 3,105 | 1,754 | 1,341 | 10 | 413 R | 56.5% | 43.2% | 56.7% | 43.3% |
| 26,373 | PEMISCOT | 7,236 | 2,541 | 4,681 | 14 | 2,140 D | 35.1% | 64.7% | 35.2% | 64.8% |
| 14,393 | PERRY | 6,918 | 4,086 | 2,801 | 31 | 1,285 R | 59.1% | 40.5% | 59.3% | 40.7% |
| 34,137 | PETTIS | 15,296 | 7,344 | 7,887 | 65 | 543 D | 48.0% | 51.6% | 48.2% | 51.8% |
| 29,567 | PHELPS | 12,512 | 6,153 | 6,261 | 98 | 108 D | 49.2% | 50.0% | 49.6% | 50.4% |
| 16,928 | PIKE | 7,162 | 3,355 | 3,770 | 37 | 415 D | 46.8% | 52.6% | 47.1% | 52.9% |
| 32,081 | PLATTE | 17,054 | 8,103 | 8,651 | 300 | 548 D | 47.5% | 50.7% | 48.4% | 51.6% |
| 15,415 | POLK | 7,590 | 3,893 | 3,663 | 34 | 230 R | 51.3% | 48.3% | 51.5% | 48.5% |
| 53,967 | PULASKI | 7,267 | 2,865 | 4,370 | 32 | 1,505 D | 39.4% | 60.1% | 39.6% | 60.4% |
| 5,916 | PUTNAM | 2,550 | 1,444 | 1,097 | 9 | 347 R | 56.6% | 43.0% | 56.8% | 43.2% |
| 7,764 | RALLS | 3,682 | 1,334 | 2,318 | 30 | 984 D | 36.2% | 63.0% | 36.5% | 63.5% |
| 22,434 | RANDOLPH | 9,481 | 3,594 | 5,839 | 48 | 2,245 D | 37.9% | 61.6% | 38.1% | 61.9% |
| 17,599 | RAY | 8,461 | 2,853 | 5,535 | 73 | 2,682 D | 33.7% | 65.4% | 34.0% | 66.0% |
| 6,106 | REYNOLDS | 3,030 | 879 | 2,143 | 8 | 1,264 D | 29.0% | 70.7% | 29.1% | 70.9% |
| 9,803 | RIPLEY | 4,245 | 1,640 | 2,577 | 28 | 937 D | 38.6% | 60.7% | 38.9% | 61.1% |
| 92,954 | ST. CHARLES | 48,704 | 26,105 | 22,063 | 536 | 4,042 R | 53.6% | 45.3% | 54.2% | 45.8% |
| 7,667 | ST. CLAIR | 4,103 | 1,808 | 2,271 | 24 | 463 D | 44.1% | 55.3% | 44.3% | 55.7% |
| 36,818 | ST. FRANCOIS | 15,911 | 7,002 | 8,852 | 57 | 1,850 D | 44.0% | 55.6% | 44.2% | 55.8% |
| 622,236 | ST. LOUIS CITY | 179,784 | 58,367 | 118,703 | 2,714 | 60,336 D | 32.5% | 66.0% | 33.0% | 67.0% |
| 951,353 | ST. LOUIS COUNTY | 452,626 | 246,988 | 196,915 | 8,723 | 50,073 R | 54.6% | 43.5% | 55.6% | 44.4% |
| 12,867 | STE. GENEVIEVE | 5,372 | 2,241 | 3,091 | 40 | 850 D | 41.7% | 57.5% | 42.0% | 58.0% |
| 24,837 | SALINE | 10,845 | 4,883 | 5,890 | 72 | 1,007 D | 45.0% | 54.3% | 45.3% | 54.7% |
| 4,665 | SCHUYLER | 2,620 | 1,193 | 1,417 | 10 | 224 D | 45.5% | 54.1% | 45.7% | 54.3% |
| 5,499 | SCOTLAND | 2,752 | 1,286 | 1,449 | 17 | 163 D | 46.7% | 52.7% | 47.0% | 53.0% |
| 33,250 | SCOTT | 13,576 | 5,473 | 8,075 | 28 | 2,602 D | 40.3% | 59.5% | 40.4% | 59.6% |
| 7,196 | SHANNON | 2,971 | 989 | 1,960 | 22 | 971 D | 33.3% | 66.0% | 33.5% | 66.5% |
| 7,906 | SHELBY | 3,702 | 1,453 | 2,227 | 22 | 774 D | 39.2% | 60.2% | 39.5% | 60.5% |
| 25,771 | STODDARD | 10,111 | 3,989 | 6,097 | 25 | 2,108 D | 39.5% | 60.3% | 39.5% | 60.5% |
| 9,921 | STONE | 5,842 | 3,457 | 2,358 | 27 | 1,099 R | 59.2% | 40.4% | 59.4% | 40.6% |
| 7,572 | SULLIVAN | 4,484 | 2,141 | 2,313 | 30 | 172 D | 47.7% | 51.6% | 48.1% | 51.9% |
| 13,023 | TANEY | 8,344 | 4,696 | 3,626 | 22 | 1,070 R | 56.3% | 43.5% | 56.4% | 43.6% |
| 18,320 | TEXAS | 8,018 | 3,338 | 4,638 | 42 | 1,300 D | 41.6% | 57.8% | 41.9% | 58.1% |
| 19,065 | VERNON | 8,684 | 3,715 | 4,921 | 48 | 1,206 D | 42.8% | 56.7% | 43.0% | 57.0% |
| 9,699 | WARREN | 5,430 | 3,214 | 2,164 | 52 | 1,050 R | 59.2% | 39.9% | 59.8% | 40.2% |
| 15,086 | WASHINGTON | 6,108 | 2,526 | 3,543 | 39 | 1,017 D | 41.4% | 58.0% | 41.6% | 58.4% |
| 8,546 | WAYNE | 4,958 | 1,963 | 2,987 | 8 | 1,024 D | 39.6% | 60.2% | 39.7% | 60.3% |
| 15,562 | WEBSTER | 7,315 | 3,510 | 3,759 | 46 | 249 D | 48.0% | 51.4% | 48.3% | 51.7% |
| 3,359 | WORTH | 1,749 | 771 | 969 | 9 | 198 D | 44.1% | 55.4% | 44.3% | 55.7% |
| 13,667 | WRIGHT | 6,191 | 3,397 | 2,781 | 13 | 616 R | 54.9% | 44.9% | 55.0% | 45.0% |
| 4,677,399 | TOTAL | 1,953,600 | 927,443 | 998,387 | 27,770 | 70,944 D | 47.5% | 51.1% | 48.2% | 51.8% |

# MISSOURI

## PRESIDENT 1972

| 1970 Census Population | County | Total Vote | Republican | Democratic | Other | Rep.-Dem. Plurality | Total Vote Rep. | Total Vote Dem. | Major Vote Rep. | Major Vote Dem. |
|---|---|---|---|---|---|---|---|---|---|---|
| 22,472 | ADAIR | 8,449 | 6,157 | 2,286 | 6 | 3,871 R | 72.9% | 27.1% | 72.9% | 27.1% |
| 11,913 | ANDREW | 5,869 | 4,180 | 1,686 | 3 | 2,494 R | 71.2% | 28.7% | 71.3% | 28.7% |
| 9,240 | ATCHISON | 4,447 | 2,927 | 1,509 | 11 | 1,418 R | 65.8% | 33.9% | 66.0% | 34.0% |
| 25,362 | AUDRAIN | 10,969 | 7,197 | 3,706 | 66 | 3,491 R | 65.6% | 33.8% | 66.0% | 34.0% |
| 19,597 | BARRY | 10,512 | 7,295 | 3,167 | 50 | 4,128 R | 69.4% | 30.1% | 69.7% | 30.3% |
| 10,431 | BARTON | 5,183 | 4,026 | 1,140 | 17 | 2,886 R | 77.7% | 22.0% | 77.9% | 22.1% |
| 15,468 | BATES | 8,346 | 5,314 | 3,020 | 12 | 2,294 R | 63.7% | 36.2% | 63.8% | 36.2% |
| 9,695 | BENTON | 4,990 | 3,537 | 1,423 | 30 | 2,114 R | 70.9% | 28.5% | 71.3% | 28.7% |
| 8,820 | BOLLINGER | 4,890 | 3,069 | 1,818 | 3 | 1,251 R | 62.8% | 37.2% | 62.8% | 37.2% |
| 80,911 | BOONE | 31,154 | 17,488 | 13,666 | | 3,822 R | 56.1% | 43.9% | 56.1% | 43.9% |
| 86,915 | BUCHANAN | 33,582 | 21,850 | 11,395 | 337 | 10,455 R | 65.1% | 33.9% | 65.7% | 34.3% |
| 33,529 | BUTLER | 12,702 | 9,198 | 3,466 | 38 | 5,732 R | 72.4% | 27.3% | 72.6% | 27.4% |
| 8,351 | CALDWELL | 4,408 | 3,167 | 1,231 | 10 | 1,936 R | 71.8% | 27.9% | 72.0% | 28.0% |
| 25,950 | CALLAWAY | 9,380 | 6,313 | 3,036 | 31 | 3,277 R | 67.3% | 32.4% | 67.5% | 32.5% |
| 13,315 | CAMDEN | 6,782 | 4,996 | 1,761 | 25 | 3,235 R | 73.7% | 26.0% | 73.9% | 26.1% |
| 49,350 | CAPE GIRARDEAU | 22,080 | 15,693 | 6,280 | 107 | 9,413 R | 71.1% | 28.4% | 71.4% | 28.6% |
| 12,565 | CARROLL | 6,042 | 4,100 | 1,927 | 15 | 2,173 R | 67.9% | 31.9% | 68.0% | 32.0% |
| 3,878 | CARTER | 1,822 | 1,257 | 565 | | 692 R | 69.0% | 31.0% | 69.0% | 31.0% |
| 39,448 | CASS | 12,973 | 9,242 | 3,731 | | 5,511 R | 71.2% | 28.8% | 71.2% | 28.8% |
| 9,424 | CEDAR | 4,685 | 3,520 | 1,152 | 13 | 2,368 R | 75.1% | 24.6% | 75.3% | 24.7% |
| 11,084 | CHARITON | 4,819 | 2,812 | 1,999 | 8 | 813 R | 58.4% | 41.5% | 58.4% | 41.6% |
| 15,124 | CHRISTIAN | 8,266 | 6,305 | 1,945 | 16 | 4,360 R | 76.3% | 23.5% | 76.4% | 23.6% |
| 8,260 | CLARK | 3,935 | 2,499 | 1,403 | 33 | 1,096 R | 63.5% | 35.7% | 64.0% | 36.0% |
| 123,644 | CLAY | 47,794 | 33,017 | 14,538 | 239 | 18,479 R | 69.1% | 30.4% | 69.4% | 30.6% |
| 12,462 | CLINTON | 5,868 | 3,924 | 1,944 | | 1,980 R | 66.9% | 33.1% | 66.9% | 33.1% |
| 46,228 | COLE | 21,539 | 16,685 | 4,754 | 100 | 11,931 R | 77.5% | 22.1% | 77.8% | 22.2% |
| 14,732 | COOPER | 7,521 | 5,172 | 2,332 | 17 | 2,840 R | 68.8% | 31.0% | 68.9% | 31.1% |
| 14,828 | CRAWFORD | 6,857 | 4,595 | 2,248 | 14 | 2,347 R | 67.0% | 32.8% | 67.1% | 32.9% |
| 6,850 | DADE | 3,375 | 2,624 | 747 | 4 | 1,877 R | 77.7% | 22.1% | 77.8% | 22.2% |
| 10,054 | DALLAS | 4,218 | 3,120 | 1,085 | 13 | 2,035 R | 74.0% | 25.7% | 74.2% | 25.8% |
| 8,420 | DAVIESS | 4,289 | 2,840 | 1,430 | 19 | 1,410 R | 66.2% | 33.3% | 66.5% | 33.5% |
| 7,305 | DE KALB | 4,113 | 2,766 | 1,339 | 8 | 1,427 R | 67.3% | 32.6% | 67.4% | 32.6% |
| 11,457 | DENT | 4,743 | 3,024 | 1,710 | 9 | 1,314 R | 63.8% | 36.1% | 63.9% | 36.1% |
| 9,268 | DOUGLAS | 4,995 | 3,773 | 1,209 | 13 | 2,564 R | 75.5% | 24.2% | 75.7% | 24.3% |
| 33,742 | DUNKLIN | 8,732 | 5,926 | 2,776 | 30 | 3,150 R | 67.9% | 31.8% | 68.1% | 31.9% |
| 55,116 | FRANKLIN | 21,343 | 13,785 | 7,464 | 94 | 6,321 R | 64.6% | 35.0% | 64.9% | 35.1% |
| 11,878 | GASCONADE | 6,175 | 4,944 | 1,226 | 5 | 3,718 R | 80.1% | 19.9% | 80.1% | 19.9% |
| 8,060 | GENTRY | 4,626 | 2,984 | 1,642 | | 1,342 R | 64.5% | 35.5% | 64.5% | 35.5% |
| 152,929 | GREENE | 68,674 | 48,348 | 20,155 | 171 | 28,193 R | 70.4% | 29.3% | 70.6% | 29.4% |
| 11,819 | GRUNDY | 5,439 | 3,969 | 1,428 | 42 | 2,541 R | 73.0% | 26.3% | 73.5% | 26.5% |
| 10,257 | HARRISON | 4,970 | 3,574 | 1,383 | 13 | 2,191 R | 71.9% | 27.8% | 72.1% | 27.9% |
| 18,451 | HENRY | 8,948 | 5,802 | 3,125 | 21 | 2,677 R | 64.8% | 34.9% | 65.0% | 35.0% |
| 4,481 | HICKORY | 2,473 | 1,851 | 622 | | 1,229 R | 74.8% | 25.2% | 74.8% | 25.2% |
| 6,654 | HOLT | 3,620 | 2,578 | 1,011 | 31 | 1,567 R | 71.2% | 27.9% | 71.8% | 28.2% |
| 10,561 | HOWARD | 4,666 | 2,613 | 2,041 | 12 | 572 R | 56.0% | 43.7% | 56.1% | 43.9% |
| 23,521 | HOWELL | 10,078 | 7,253 | 2,795 | 30 | 4,458 R | 72.0% | 27.7% | 72.2% | 27.8% |
| 9,529 | IRON | 3,559 | 2,203 | 1,346 | 10 | 857 R | 61.9% | 37.8% | 62.1% | 37.9% |
| 654,558 | JACKSON | 223,626 | 129,989 | 92,830 | 807 | 37,159 R | 58.1% | 41.5% | 58.3% | 41.7% |
| 79,852 | JASPER | 30,241 | 22,482 | 7,652 | 107 | 14,830 R | 74.3% | 25.3% | 74.6% | 25.4% |
| 105,248 | JEFFERSON | 35,922 | 21,947 | 13,787 | 188 | 8,160 R | 61.1% | 38.4% | 61.4% | 38.6% |
| 34,172 | JOHNSON | 10,288 | 7,228 | 3,044 | 16 | 4,184 R | 70.3% | 29.6% | 70.4% | 29.6% |
| 5,692 | KNOX | 2,929 | 1,896 | 1,031 | 2 | 865 R | 64.7% | 35.2% | 64.8% | 35.2% |
| 19,944 | LACLEDE | 8,370 | 6,152 | 2,186 | 32 | 3,966 R | 73.5% | 26.1% | 73.8% | 26.2% |
| 26,626 | LAFAYETTE | 13,250 | 9,187 | 4,063 | | 5,124 R | 69.3% | 30.7% | 69.3% | 30.7% |
| 24,585 | LAWRENCE | 11,594 | 8,445 | 3,130 | 19 | 5,315 R | 72.8% | 27.0% | 73.0% | 27.0% |
| 10,993 | LEWIS | 4,434 | 2,738 | 1,695 | 1 | 1,043 R | 61.8% | 38.2% | 61.8% | 38.2% |
| 18,041 | LINCOLN | 7,956 | 5,127 | 2,784 | 45 | 2,343 R | 64.4% | 35.0% | 64.8% | 35.2% |
| 15,125 | LINN | 7,702 | 4,595 | 3,073 | 34 | 1,522 R | 59.7% | 39.9% | 59.9% | 40.1% |
| 15,368 | LIVINGSTON | 7,971 | 5,253 | 2,662 | 56 | 2,591 R | 65.9% | 33.4% | 66.4% | 33.6% |
| 12,357 | MCDONALD | 6,137 | 4,339 | 1,787 | 11 | 2,552 R | 70.7% | 29.1% | 70.8% | 29.2% |

# MISSOURI

## PRESIDENT 1972

| 1970 Census Population | County | Total Vote | Republican | Democratic | Other | Rep.-Dem. Plurality | Percentage | | | |
|---|---|---|---|---|---|---|---|---|---|---|
| | | | | | | | Total Vote | | Major Vote | |
| | | | | | | | Rep. | Dem. | Rep. | Dem. |
| 15,432 | MACON | 7,393 | 4,538 | 2,844 | 11 | 1,694 R | 61.4% | 38.5% | 61.5% | 38.5% |
| 8,641 | MADISON | 4,298 | 2,837 | 1,451 | 10 | 1,386 R | 66.0% | 33.8% | 66.2% | 33.8% |
| 6,851 | MARIES | 3,312 | 2,082 | 1,219 | 11 | 863 R | 62.9% | 36.8% | 63.1% | 36.9% |
| 28,121 | MARION | 11,392 | 7,197 | 4,171 | 24 | 3,026 R | 63.2% | 36.6% | 63.3% | 36.7% |
| 4,910 | MERCER | 2,208 | 1,592 | 607 | 9 | 985 R | 72.1% | 27.5% | 72.4% | 27.6% |
| 15,026 | MILLER | 7,280 | 5,682 | 1,598 | | 4,084 R | 78.0% | 22.0% | 78.0% | 22.0% |
| 16,647 | MISSISSIPPI | 4,204 | 2,727 | 1,470 | 7 | 1,257 R | 64.9% | 35.0% | 65.0% | 35.0% |
| 10,742 | MONITEAU | 5,358 | 3,963 | 1,395 | | 2,568 R | 74.0% | 26.0% | 74.0% | 26.0% |
| 9,542 | MONROE | 4,441 | 2,141 | 2,299 | 1 | 158 D | 48.2% | 51.8% | 48.2% | 51.8% |
| 11,000 | MONTGOMERY | 5,419 | 3,707 | 1,691 | 21 | 2,016 R | 68.4% | 31.2% | 68.7% | 31.3% |
| 10,068 | MORGAN | 5,723 | 4,021 | 1,685 | 17 | 2,336 R | 70.3% | 29.4% | 70.5% | 29.5% |
| 23,420 | NEW MADRID | 8,288 | 4,735 | 3,500 | 53 | 1,235 R | 57.1% | 42.2% | 57.5% | 42.5% |
| 32,901 | NEWTON | 15,023 | 10,701 | 4,291 | 31 | 6,410 R | 71.2% | 28.6% | 71.4% | 28.6% |
| 22,467 | NODAWAY | 9,264 | 5,942 | 3,322 | | 2,620 R | 64.1% | 35.9% | 64.1% | 35.9% |
| 9,180 | OREGON | 3,479 | 2,118 | 1,352 | 9 | 766 R | 60.9% | 38.9% | 61.0% | 39.0% |
| 10,994 | OSAGE | 5,751 | 4,266 | 1,485 | | 2,781 R | 74.2% | 25.8% | 74.2% | 25.8% |
| 6,226 | OZARK | 2,748 | 2,119 | 625 | 4 | 1,494 R | 77.1% | 22.7% | 77.2% | 22.8% |
| 26,373 | PEMISCOT | 6,747 | 4,697 | 2,017 | 33 | 2,680 R | 69.6% | 29.9% | 70.0% | 30.0% |
| 14,393 | PERRY | 6,696 | 4,736 | 1,953 | 7 | 2,783 R | 70.7% | 29.2% | 70.8% | 29.2% |
| 34,137 | PETTIS | 15,120 | 10,065 | 5,016 | 39 | 5,049 R | 66.6% | 33.2% | 66.7% | 33.3% |
| 29,567 | PHELPS | 11,192 | 7,598 | 3,567 | 27 | 4,031 R | 67.9% | 31.9% | 68.1% | 31.9% |
| 16,928 | PIKE | 7,146 | 4,452 | 2,659 | 35 | 1,793 R | 62.3% | 37.2% | 62.6% | 37.4% |
| 32,081 | PLATTE | 12,973 | 8,764 | 4,183 | 26 | 4,581 R | 67.6% | 32.2% | 67.7% | 32.3% |
| 15,415 | POLK | 7,676 | 5,409 | 2,245 | 22 | 3,164 R | 70.5% | 29.2% | 70.7% | 29.3% |
| 53,967 | PULASKI | 6,164 | 4,243 | 1,903 | 18 | 2,340 R | 68.8% | 30.9% | 69.0% | 31.0% |
| 5,916 | PUTNAM | 2,684 | 2,112 | 571 | 1 | 1,541 R | 78.7% | 21.3% | 78.7% | 21.3% |
| 7,764 | RALLS | 3,213 | 1,827 | 1,371 | 15 | 456 R | 56.9% | 42.7% | 57.1% | 42.9% |
| 22,434 | RANDOLPH | 9,009 | 5,195 | 3,814 | | 1,381 R | 57.7% | 42.3% | 57.7% | 42.3% |
| 17,599 | RAY | 7,075 | 4,205 | 2,844 | 26 | 1,361 R | 59.4% | 40.2% | 59.7% | 40.3% |
| 6,106 | REYNOLDS | 2,579 | 1,541 | 1,031 | 7 | 510 R | 59.8% | 40.0% | 59.9% | 40.1% |
| 9,803 | RIPLEY | 4,179 | 2,810 | 1,361 | 8 | 1,449 R | 67.2% | 32.6% | 67.4% | 32.6% |
| 92,954 | ST. CHARLES | 36,868 | 25,677 | 11,034 | 157 | 14,643 R | 69.6% | 29.9% | 69.9% | 30.1% |
| 7,667 | ST. CLAIR | 4,257 | 2,847 | 1,410 | | 1,437 R | 66.9% | 33.1% | 66.9% | 33.1% |
| 36,818 | ST. FRANCOIS | 13,518 | 8,812 | 4,658 | 48 | 4,154 R | 65.2% | 34.5% | 65.4% | 34.6% |
| 622,236 | ST. LOUIS CITY | 192,867 | 72,402 | 119,817 | 648 | 47,415 D | 37.5% | 62.1% | 37.7% | 62.3% |
| 951,353 | ST. LOUIS COUNTY | 425,056 | 264,147 | 160,801 | 108 | 103,346 R | 62.1% | 37.8% | 62.2% | 37.8% |
| 12,867 | STE. GENEVIEVE | 5,153 | 2,900 | 2,247 | 6 | 653 R | 56.3% | 43.6% | 56.3% | 43.7% |
| 24,837 | SALINE | 10,148 | 6,641 | 3,460 | 47 | 3,181 R | 65.4% | 34.1% | 65.7% | 34.3% |
| 4,665 | SCHUYLER | 2,491 | 1,495 | 991 | 5 | 504 R | 60.0% | 39.8% | 60.1% | 39.9% |
| 5,499 | SCOTLAND | 3,190 | 1,918 | 1,269 | 3 | 649 R | 60.1% | 39.8% | 60.2% | 39.8% |
| 33,250 | SCOTT | 10,998 | 7,316 | 3,646 | 36 | 3,670 R | 66.5% | 33.2% | 66.7% | 33.3% |
| 7,196 | SHANNON | 2,758 | 1,623 | 1,134 | 1 | 489 R | 58.8% | 41.1% | 58.9% | 41.1% |
| 7,906 | SHELBY | 3,639 | 2,057 | 1,569 | 13 | 488 R | 56.5% | 43.1% | 56.7% | 43.3% |
| 25,771 | STODDARD | 8,933 | 6,282 | 2,636 | 15 | 3,646 R | 70.3% | 29.5% | 70.4% | 29.6% |
| 9,921 | STONE | 5,297 | 4,180 | 1,094 | 23 | 3,086 R | 78.9% | 20.7% | 79.3% | 20.7% |
| 7,572 | SULLIVAN | 4,211 | 2,611 | 1,588 | 12 | 1,023 R | 62.0% | 37.7% | 62.2% | 37.8% |
| 13,023 | TANEY | 6,450 | 4,982 | 1,435 | 33 | 3,547 R | 77.2% | 22.2% | 77.6% | 22.4% |
| 18,320 | TEXAS | 7,870 | 5,104 | 2,737 | 29 | 2,367 R | 64.9% | 34.8% | 65.1% | 34.9% |
| 19,065 | VERNON | 7,974 | 4,892 | 3,057 | 25 | 1,835 R | 61.3% | 38.3% | 61.5% | 38.5% |
| 9,699 | WARREN | 4,775 | 3,530 | 1,225 | 20 | 2,305 R | 73.9% | 25.7% | 74.2% | 25.8% |
| 15,086 | WASHINGTON | 6,085 | 3,818 | 2,229 | 38 | 1,589 R | 62.7% | 36.6% | 63.1% | 36.9% |
| 8,546 | WAYNE | 4,839 | 3,091 | 1,746 | 2 | 1,345 R | 63.9% | 36.1% | 63.9% | 36.1% |
| 15,562 | WEBSTER | 7,447 | 5,095 | 2,343 | 9 | 2,752 R | 68.4% | 31.5% | 68.5% | 31.5% |
| 3,359 | WORTH | 1,900 | 1,170 | 727 | 3 | 443 R | 61.6% | 38.3% | 61.7% | 38.3% |
| 13,667 | WRIGHT | 5,725 | 4,350 | 1,368 | 7 | 2,982 R | 76.0% | 23.9% | 76.1% | 23.9% |
| 4,677,399 | TOTAL | 1,855,803 | 1,153,852 | 697,147 | 4,804 | 456,705 R | 62.2% | 37.6% | 62.3% | 37.7% |

# MISSOURI

## PRESIDENT 1968

| 1960 Census Population | County | Total Vote | Republican | Democratic | AIP | Other | Plurality | Percentage Total Vote Rep. | Dem. | AIP |
|---|---|---|---|---|---|---|---|---|---|---|
| 20,105 | ADAIR | 7,861 | 4,624 | 2,645 | 592 | | 1,979 R | 58.8% | 33.6% | 7.5% |
| 11,062 | ANDREW | 5,762 | 3,398 | 2,005 | 359 | | 1,393 R | 59.0% | 34.8% | 6.2% |
| 9,213 | ATCHISON | 4,295 | 2,206 | 1,752 | 337 | | 454 R | 51.4% | 40.8% | 7.8% |
| 26,079 | AUDRAIN | 10,823 | 5,005 | 4,806 | 1,012 | | 199 R | 46.2% | 44.4% | 9.4% |
| 18,921 | BARRY | 9,693 | 5,537 | 3,398 | 758 | | 2,139 R | 57.1% | 35.1% | 7.8% |
| 11,113 | BARTON | 5,259 | 2,928 | 1,832 | 499 | | 1,096 R | 55.7% | 34.8% | 9.5% |
| 15,905 | BATES | 8,258 | 4,087 | 3,370 | 801 | | 717 R | 49.5% | 40.8% | 9.7% |
| 8,737 | BENTON | 4,742 | 2,899 | 1,345 | 498 | | 1,554 R | 61.1% | 28.4% | 10.5% |
| 9,167 | BOLLINGER | 4,559 | 2,283 | 1,693 | 583 | | 590 R | 50.1% | 37.1% | 12.8% |
| 55,202 | BOONE | 25,703 | 11,917 | 11,771 | 2,015 | | 146 R | 46.4% | 45.8% | 7.8% |
| 90,581 | BUCHANAN | 34,713 | 16,101 | 15,860 | 2,752 | | 241 R | 46.4% | 45.7% | 7.9% |
| 34,656 | BUTLER | 13,464 | 6,326 | 4,379 | 2,759 | | 1,947 R | 47.0% | 32.5% | 20.5% |
| 8,830 | CALDWELL | 4,551 | 2,631 | 1,490 | 430 | | 1,141 R | 57.8% | 32.7% | 9.4% |
| 23,858 | CALLAWAY | 9,291 | 4,277 | 3,738 | 1,276 | | 539 R | 46.0% | 40.2% | 13.7% |
| 9,116 | CAMDEN | 5,738 | 3,500 | 1,605 | 633 | | 1,895 R | 61.0% | 28.0% | 11.0% |
| 42,020 | CAPE GIRARDEAU | 19,305 | 10,298 | 6,656 | 2,351 | | 3,642 R | 53.3% | 34.5% | 12.2% |
| 13,847 | CARROLL | 6,798 | 3,680 | 2,473 | 645 | | 1,207 R | 54.1% | 36.4% | 9.5% |
| 3,973 | CARTER | 1,888 | 861 | 738 | 289 | | 123 R | 45.6% | 39.1% | 15.3% |
| 29,702 | CASS | 11,677 | 5,271 | 4,468 | 1,938 | | 803 R | 45.1% | 38.3% | 16.6% |
| 9,185 | CEDAR | 4,588 | 2,940 | 1,218 | 430 | | 1,722 R | 64.1% | 26.5% | 9.4% |
| 12,720 | CHARITON | 5,284 | 2,404 | 2,371 | 509 | | 33 R | 45.5% | 44.9% | 9.6% |
| 12,359 | CHRISTIAN | 6,238 | 4,019 | 1,586 | 633 | | 2,433 R | 64.4% | 25.4% | 10.1% |
| 8,725 | CLARK | 3,942 | 2,111 | 1,489 | 342 | | 622 R | 53.6% | 37.8% | 8.7% |
| 87,474 | CLAY | 44,162 | 19,643 | 17,547 | 6,972 | | 2,096 R | 44.5% | 39.7% | 15.8% |
| 11,588 | CLINTON | 5,803 | 2,659 | 2,525 | 619 | | 134 R | 45.8% | 43.5% | 10.7% |
| 40,761 | COLE | 19,116 | 11,575 | 5,916 | 1,625 | | 5,659 R | 60.6% | 30.9% | 8.5% |
| 15,448 | COOPER | 7,443 | 4,115 | 2,798 | 530 | | 1,317 R | 55.3% | 37.6% | 7.1% |
| 12,647 | CRAWFORD | 6,319 | 3,525 | 2,123 | 671 | | 1,402 R | 55.8% | 33.6% | 10.6% |
| 7,577 | DADE | 3,497 | 2,250 | 917 | 330 | | 1,333 R | 64.3% | 26.2% | 9.4% |
| 9,314 | DALLAS | 4,537 | 2,835 | 1,237 | 465 | | 1,598 R | 62.5% | 27.3% | 10.2% |
| 9,502 | DAVIESS | 4,298 | 2,288 | 1,676 | 334 | | 612 R | 53.2% | 39.0% | 7.8% |
| 7,226 | DE KALB | 3,849 | 2,112 | 1,452 | 285 | | 660 R | 54.9% | 37.7% | 7.4% |
| 10,445 | DENT | 4,648 | 2,369 | 1,810 | 469 | | 559 R | 51.0% | 38.9% | 10.1% |
| 9,653 | DOUGLAS | 4,226 | 2,836 | 978 | 412 | | 1,858 R | 67.1% | 23.1% | 9.7% |
| 39,139 | DUNKLIN | 12,332 | 4,366 | 5,063 | 2,903 | | 697 D | 35.4% | 41.1% | 23.5% |
| 44,566 | FRANKLIN | 19,349 | 9,823 | 7,566 | 1,960 | | 2,257 R | 50.8% | 39.1% | 10.1% |
| 12,195 | GASCONADE | 5,895 | 4,400 | 1,131 | 364 | | 3,269 R | 74.6% | 19.2% | 6.2% |
| 8,793 | GENTRY | 4,691 | 2,286 | 2,189 | 216 | | 97 R | 48.7% | 46.7% | 4.6% |
| 126,276 | GREENE | 59,048 | 32,638 | 19,659 | 6,751 | | 12,979 R | 55.3% | 33.3% | 11.4% |
| 12,220 | GRUNDY | 5,608 | 3,213 | 1,976 | 419 | | 1,237 R | 57.3% | 35.2% | 7.5% |
| 11,603 | HARRISON | 5,192 | 3,092 | 1,688 | 412 | | 1,404 R | 59.6% | 32.5% | 7.9% |
| 19,226 | HENRY | 8,020 | 3,824 | 3,514 | 682 | | 310 R | 47.7% | 43.8% | 8.5% |
| 4,516 | HICKORY | 2,230 | 1,484 | 537 | 209 | | 947 R | 66.5% | 24.1% | 9.4% |
| 7,885 | HOLT | 3,621 | 2,031 | 1,211 | 379 | | 820 R | 56.1% | 33.4% | 10.5% |
| 10,859 | HOWARD | 4,665 | 1,825 | 2,333 | 507 | | 508 D | 39.1% | 50.0% | 10.9% |
| 22,027 | HOWELL | 9,838 | 5,631 | 2,763 | 1,444 | | 2,868 R | 57.2% | 28.1% | 14.7% |
| 8,041 | IRON | 3,846 | 1,600 | 1,755 | 491 | | 155 D | 41.6% | 45.6% | 12.8% |
| 622,732 | JACKSON | 232,220 | 91,086 | 112,154 | 28,980 | | 21,068 D | 39.2% | 48.3% | 12.5% |
| 78,863 | JASPER | 30,962 | 16,794 | 10,987 | 3,181 | | 5,807 R | 54.2% | 35.5% | 10.3% |
| 66,377 | JEFFERSON | 31,053 | 11,708 | 13,230 | 6,115 | | 1,522 D | 37.7% | 42.6% | 19.7% |
| 28,981 | JOHNSON | 9,336 | 4,834 | 3,484 | 1,018 | | 1,350 R | 51.8% | 37.3% | 10.9% |
| 6,558 | KNOX | 3,169 | 1,562 | 1,257 | 350 | | 305 R | 49.3% | 39.7% | 11.0% |
| 18,991 | LACLEDE | 8,670 | 4,860 | 2,958 | 852 | | 1,902 R | 56.1% | 34.1% | 9.8% |
| 25,274 | LAFAYETTE | 12,804 | 6,840 | 4,859 | 1,105 | | 1,981 R | 53.4% | 37.9% | 8.6% |
| 23,260 | LAWRENCE | 11,442 | 6,834 | 3,710 | 898 | | 3,124 R | 59.7% | 32.4% | 7.8% |
| 10,984 | LEWIS | 4,642 | 2,038 | 2,067 | 537 | | 29 D | 43.9% | 44.5% | 11.6% |
| 14,783 | LINCOLN | 7,624 | 3,185 | 3,142 | 1,297 | | 43 R | 41.8% | 41.2% | 17.0% |
| 16,815 | LINN | 8,241 | 3,795 | 3,933 | 513 | | 138 D | 46.1% | 47.7% | 6.2% |
| 15,771 | LIVINGSTON | 7,812 | 3,827 | 3,467 | 518 | | 360 R | 49.0% | 44.4% | 6.6% |
| 11,798 | MCDONALD | 5,894 | 3,025 | 2,188 | 681 | | 837 R | 51.3% | 37.1% | 11.6% |

# MISSOURI

## PRESIDENT 1968

| 1960 Census Population | County | Total Vote | Republican | Democratic | AIP | Other | Plurality | Percentage Total Vote Rep. | Dem. | AIP |
|---|---|---|---|---|---|---|---|---|---|---|
| 16,473 | MACON | 8,087 | 3,804 | 3,462 | 821 | | 342 R | 47.0% | 42.8% | 10.2% |
| 9,366 | MADISON | 4,300 | 2,164 | 1,521 | 615 | | 643 R | 50.3% | 35.4% | 14.3% |
| 7,282 | MARIES | 3,026 | 1,438 | 1,185 | 403 | | 253 R | 47.5% | 39.2% | 13.3% |
| 29,522 | MARION | 11,369 | 4,732 | 5,416 | 1,221 | | 684 D | 41.6% | 47.6% | 10.7% |
| 5,750 | MERCER | 2,314 | 1,406 | 783 | 125 | | 623 R | 60.8% | 33.8% | 5.4% |
| 13,800 | MILLER | 6,820 | 4,425 | 1,727 | 668 | | 2,698 R | 64.9% | 25.3% | 9.8% |
| 20,695 | MISSISSIPPI | 5,299 | 1,421 | 2,303 | 1,575 | | 728 D | 26.8% | 43.5% | 29.7% |
| 10,500 | MONITEAU | 5,483 | 3,210 | 1,687 | 586 | | 1,523 R | 58.5% | 30.8% | 10.7% |
| 10,688 | MONROE | 4,641 | 1,349 | 2,776 | 516 | | 1,427 D | 29.1% | 59.8% | 11.1% |
| 11,097 | MONTGOMERY | 5,417 | 2,903 | 1,891 | 623 | | 1,012 R | 53.6% | 34.9% | 11.5% |
| 9,476 | MORGAN | 5,059 | 2,906 | 1,649 | 504 | | 1,257 R | 57.4% | 32.6% | 10.0% |
| 31,350 | NEW MADRID | 9,496 | 2,317 | 4,195 | 2,984 | | 1,211 D | 24.4% | 44.2% | 31.4% |
| 30,093 | NEWTON | 13,888 | 7,343 | 5,064 | 1,481 | | 2,279 R | 52.9% | 36.5% | 10.7% |
| 22,215 | NODAWAY | 9,845 | 4,736 | 4,494 | 615 | | 242 R | 48.1% | 45.6% | 6.2% |
| 9,845 | OREGON | 3,564 | 1,213 | 1,726 | 625 | | 513 D | 34.0% | 48.4% | 17.5% |
| 10,867 | OSAGE | 5,041 | 3,107 | 1,540 | 394 | | 1,567 R | 61.6% | 30.5% | 7.8% |
| 6,744 | OZARK | 2,877 | 1,967 | 606 | 304 | | 1,361 R | 68.4% | 21.1% | 10.6% |
| 38,095 | PEMISCOT | 7,822 | 2,191 | 2,681 | 2,950 | | 269 A | 28.0% | 34.3% | 37.7% |
| 14,642 | PERRY | 6,278 | 3,858 | 1,958 | 462 | | 1,900 R | 61.5% | 31.2% | 7.4% |
| 35,120 | PETTIS | 14,621 | 6,738 | 6,334 | 1,549 | | 404 R | 46.1% | 43.3% | 10.6% |
| 25,396 | PHELPS | 11,783 | 5,577 | 4,211 | 1,995 | | 1,366 R | 47.3% | 35.7% | 16.9% |
| 16,706 | PIKE | 7,067 | 3,072 | 3,192 | 803 | | 120 D | 43.5% | 45.2% | 11.4% |
| 23,350 | PLATTE | 11,316 | 4,836 | 4,665 | 1,815 | | 171 R | 42.7% | 41.2% | 16.0% |
| 13,753 | POLK | 6,929 | 4,145 | 2,170 | 614 | | 1,975 R | 59.8% | 31.3% | 8.9% |
| 46,567 | PULASKI | 5,576 | 2,555 | 2,303 | 718 | | 252 R | 45.8% | 41.3% | 12.9% |
| 6,999 | PUTNAM | 3,092 | 1,971 | 952 | 169 | | 1,019 R | 63.7% | 30.8% | 5.5% |
| 8,078 | RALLS | 3,553 | 1,175 | 1,900 | 478 | | 725 D | 33.1% | 53.5% | 13.5% |
| 22,014 | RANDOLPH | 9,285 | 3,582 | 4,810 | 893 | | 1,228 D | 38.6% | 51.8% | 9.6% |
| 16,075 | RAY | 7,206 | 2,587 | 3,541 | 1,078 | | 954 D | 35.9% | 49.1% | 15.0% |
| 5,161 | REYNOLDS | 2,581 | 898 | 1,245 | 438 | | 347 D | 34.8% | 48.2% | 17.0% |
| 9,096 | RIPLEY | 4,090 | 1,973 | 1,440 | 677 | | 533 R | 48.2% | 35.2% | 16.6% |
| 52,970 | ST. CHARLES | 29,659 | 13,533 | 10,374 | 5,752 | | 3,159 R | 45.6% | 35.0% | 19.4% |
| 8,421 | ST. CLAIR | 4,178 | 2,271 | 1,496 | 411 | | 775 R | 54.4% | 35.8% | 9.8% |
| 36,516 | ST. FRANCOIS | 15,738 | 7,492 | 6,379 | 1,867 | | 1,113 R | 47.6% | 40.5% | 11.9% |
| 750,026 | ST. LOUIS CITY | 220,914 | 58,252 | 143,010 | 19,652 | | 84,758 D | 26.4% | 64.7% | 8.9% |
| 703,532 | ST. LOUIS COUNTY | 385,375 | 180,355 | 165,786 | 39,234 | | 14,569 R | 46.8% | 43.0% | 10.2% |
| 12,116 | STE. GENEVIEVE | 4,602 | 1,937 | 2,225 | 440 | | 288 D | 42.1% | 48.3% | 9.6% |
| 25,148 | SALINE | 10,048 | 4,698 | 4,646 | 704 | | 52 R | 46.8% | 46.2% | 7.0% |
| 5,052 | SCHUYLER | 2,428 | 1,291 | 969 | 168 | | 322 R | 53.2% | 39.9% | 6.9% |
| 6,484 | SCOTLAND | 3,104 | 1,554 | 1,340 | 210 | | 214 R | 50.1% | 43.2% | 6.8% |
| 32,748 | SCOTT | 10,643 | 3,856 | 4,313 | 2,474 | | 457 D | 36.2% | 40.5% | 23.2% |
| 7,087 | SHANNON | 2,710 | 1,048 | 1,216 | 446 | | 168 D | 38.7% | 44.9% | 16.5% |
| 9,063 | SHELBY | 4,096 | 1,693 | 2,045 | 358 | | 352 D | 41.3% | 49.9% | 8.7% |
| 29,490 | STODDARD | 8,820 | 3,919 | 3,150 | 1,751 | | 769 R | 44.4% | 35.7% | 19.9% |
| 8,176 | STONE | 4,465 | 3,006 | 1,004 | 455 | | 2,002 R | 67.3% | 22.5% | 10.2% |
| 8,783 | SULLIVAN | 4,464 | 2,332 | 1,907 | 225 | | 425 R | 52.2% | 42.7% | 5.0% |
| 10,238 | TANEY | 4,922 | 3,289 | 1,219 | 414 | | 2,070 R | 66.8% | 24.8% | 8.4% |
| 17,758 | TEXAS | 8,120 | 4,022 | 3,117 | 981 | | 905 R | 49.5% | 38.4% | 12.1% |
| 20,540 | VERNON | 7,930 | 3,590 | 3,557 | 783 | | 33 R | 45.3% | 44.9% | 9.9% |
| 8,750 | WARREN | 4,267 | 2,669 | 1,033 | 565 | | 1,636 R | 62.5% | 24.2% | 13.2% |
| 14,346 | WASHINGTON | 5,709 | 2,641 | 2,292 | 776 | | 349 R | 46.3% | 40.1% | 13.6% |
| 8,638 | WAYNE | 4,511 | 2,156 | 1,714 | 641 | | 442 R | 47.8% | 38.0% | 14.2% |
| 13,753 | WEBSTER | 7,237 | 4,118 | 2,547 | 572 | | 1,571 R | 56.9% | 35.2% | 7.9% |
| 3,936 | WORTH | 1,903 | 924 | 853 | 126 | | 71 R | 48.6% | 44.8% | 6.6% |
| 14,183 | WRIGHT | 5,400 | 3,576 | 1,337 | 487 | | 2,239 R | 66.2% | 24.8% | 9.0% |
| 4,319,813 | TOTAL | 1,809,502 | 811,932 | 791,444 | 206,126 | | 20,488 R | 44.9% | 43.7% | 11.4% |

# MISSOURI

## PRESIDENT 1964

| 1960 Census Population | County | Total Vote | Republican | Democratic | Other | Rep.-Dem. Plurality | Percentage | | | |
|---|---|---|---|---|---|---|---|---|---|---|
| | | | | | | | Total Vote | | Major Vote | |
| | | | | | | | Rep. | Dem. | Rep. | Dem. |
| 20,105 | ADAIR | 7,808 | 3,573 | 4,235 | | 662 D | 45.8% | 54.2% | 45.8% | 54.2% |
| 11,062 | ANDREW | 5,805 | 2,594 | 3,211 | | 617 D | 44.7% | 55.3% | 44.7% | 55.3% |
| 9,213 | ATCHISON | 4,523 | 1,653 | 2,870 | | 1,217 D | 36.5% | 63.5% | 36.5% | 63.5% |
| 26,079 | AUDRAIN | 10,703 | 3,316 | 7,387 | | 4,071 D | 31.0% | 69.0% | 31.0% | 69.0% |
| 18,921 | BARRY | 10,064 | 4,757 | 5,307 | | 550 D | 47.3% | 52.7% | 47.3% | 52.7% |
| 11,113 | BARTON | 5,505 | 2,332 | 3,173 | | 841 D | 42.4% | 57.6% | 42.4% | 57.6% |
| 15,905 | BATES | 8,676 | 3,514 | 5,162 | | 1,648 D | 40.5% | 59.5% | 40.5% | 59.5% |
| 8,737 | BENTON | 4,507 | 2,477 | 2,030 | | 447 R | 55.0% | 45.0% | 55.0% | 45.0% |
| 9,167 | BOLLINGER | 4,917 | 2,125 | 2,792 | | 667 D | 43.2% | 56.8% | 43.2% | 56.8% |
| 55,202 | BOONE | 22,453 | 7,695 | 14,758 | | 7,063 D | 34.3% | 65.7% | 34.3% | 65.7% |
| 90,581 | BUCHANAN | 35,665 | 11,501 | 24,164 | | 12,663 D | 32.2% | 67.8% | 32.2% | 67.8% |
| 34,656 | BUTLER | 13,326 | 5,616 | 7,710 | | 2,094 D | 42.1% | 57.9% | 42.1% | 57.9% |
| 8,830 | CALDWELL | 4,600 | 2,125 | 2,475 | | 350 D | 46.2% | 53.8% | 46.2% | 53.8% |
| 23,858 | CALLAWAY | 8,899 | 2,983 | 5,916 | | 2,933 D | 33.5% | 66.5% | 33.5% | 66.5% |
| 9,116 | CAMDEN | 5,129 | 2,607 | 2,522 | | 85 R | 50.8% | 49.2% | 50.8% | 49.2% |
| 42,020 | CAPE GIRARDEAU | 20,207 | 8,776 | 11,431 | | 2,655 D | 43.4% | 56.6% | 43.4% | 56.6% |
| 13,847 | CARROLL | 7,063 | 2,994 | 4,069 | | 1,075 D | 42.4% | 57.6% | 42.4% | 57.6% |
| 3,973 | CARTER | 1,993 | 761 | 1,232 | | 471 D | 38.2% | 61.8% | 38.2% | 61.8% |
| 29,702 | CASS | 10,323 | 3,665 | 6,658 | | 2,993 D | 35.5% | 64.5% | 35.5% | 64.5% |
| 9,185 | CEDAR | 4,725 | 2,478 | 2,247 | | 231 R | 52.4% | 47.6% | 52.4% | 47.6% |
| 12,720 | CHARITON | 5,794 | 1,932 | 3,862 | | 1,930 D | 33.3% | 66.7% | 33.3% | 66.7% |
| 12,359 | CHRISTIAN | 5,878 | 3,232 | 2,646 | | 586 R | 55.0% | 45.0% | 55.0% | 45.0% |
| 8,725 | CLARK | 3,883 | 1,660 | 2,223 | | 563 D | 42.8% | 57.2% | 42.8% | 57.2% |
| 87,474 | CLAY | 37,990 | 13,997 | 23,993 | | 9,996 D | 36.8% | 63.2% | 36.8% | 63.2% |
| 11,588 | CLINTON | 5,398 | 1,800 | 3,598 | | 1,798 D | 33.3% | 66.7% | 33.3% | 66.7% |
| 40,761 | COLE | 18,195 | 10,068 | 8,127 | | 1,941 R | 55.3% | 44.7% | 55.3% | 44.7% |
| 15,448 | COOPER | 7,731 | 3,530 | 4,201 | | 671 D | 45.7% | 54.3% | 45.7% | 54.3% |
| 12,647 | CRAWFORD | 6,104 | 2,660 | 3,444 | | 784 D | 43.6% | 56.4% | 43.6% | 56.4% |
| 7,577 | DADE | 3,572 | 1,931 | 1,641 | | 290 R | 54.1% | 45.9% | 54.1% | 45.9% |
| 9,314 | DALLAS | 4,251 | 2,268 | 1,983 | | 285 R | 53.4% | 46.6% | 53.4% | 46.6% |
| 9,502 | DAVIESS | 4,613 | 1,874 | 2,739 | | 865 D | 40.6% | 59.4% | 40.6% | 59.4% |
| 7,226 | DE KALB | 4,026 | 1,679 | 2,347 | | 668 D | 41.7% | 58.3% | 41.7% | 58.3% |
| 10,445 | DENT | 4,648 | 1,788 | 2,860 | | 1,072 D | 38.5% | 61.5% | 38.5% | 61.5% |
| 9,653 | DOUGLAS | 3,873 | 2,280 | 1,593 | | 687 R | 58.9% | 41.1% | 58.9% | 41.1% |
| 39,139 | DUNKLIN | 11,932 | 3,465 | 8,467 | | 5,002 D | 29.0% | 71.0% | 29.0% | 71.0% |
| 44,566 | FRANKLIN | 21,777 | 8,313 | 13,464 | | 5,151 D | 38.2% | 61.8% | 38.2% | 61.8% |
| 12,195 | GASCONADE | 5,798 | 3,672 | 2,126 | | 1,546 R | 63.3% | 36.7% | 63.3% | 36.7% |
| 8,793 | GENTRY | 4,875 | 1,677 | 3,198 | | 1,521 D | 34.4% | 65.6% | 34.4% | 65.6% |
| 126,276 | GREENE | 54,119 | 23,989 | 30,130 | | 6,141 D | 44.3% | 55.7% | 44.3% | 55.7% |
| 12,220 | GRUNDY | 5,774 | 2,411 | 3,363 | | 952 D | 41.8% | 58.2% | 41.8% | 58.2% |
| 11,603 | HARRISON | 5,303 | 2,516 | 2,787 | | 271 D | 47.4% | 52.6% | 47.4% | 52.6% |
| 19,226 | HENRY | 8,844 | 3,083 | 5,761 | | 2,678 D | 34.9% | 65.1% | 34.9% | 65.1% |
| 4,516 | HICKORY | 2,011 | 1,157 | 854 | | 303 R | 57.5% | 42.5% | 57.5% | 42.5% |
| 7,885 | HOLT | 3,597 | 1,726 | 1,871 | | 145 D | 48.0% | 52.0% | 48.0% | 52.0% |
| 10,859 | HOWARD | 4,846 | 1,339 | 3,507 | | 2,168 D | 27.6% | 72.4% | 27.6% | 72.4% |
| 22,027 | HOWELL | 9,600 | 4,632 | 4,968 | | 336 D | 48.3% | 51.7% | 48.3% | 51.7% |
| 8,041 | IRON | 3,780 | 1,050 | 2,730 | | 1,680 D | 27.8% | 72.2% | 27.8% | 72.2% |
| 622,732 | JACKSON | 240,056 | 78,766 | 161,290 | | 82,524 D | 32.8% | 67.2% | 32.8% | 67.2% |
| 78,863 | JASPER | 33,526 | 15,481 | 18,045 | | 2,564 D | 46.2% | 53.8% | 46.2% | 53.8% |
| 66,377 | JEFFERSON | 26,803 | 7,887 | 18,916 | | 11,029 D | 29.4% | 70.6% | 29.4% | 70.6% |
| 28,981 | JOHNSON | 10,760 | 4,348 | 6,412 | | 2,064 D | 40.4% | 59.6% | 40.4% | 59.6% |
| 6,558 | KNOX | 3,390 | 1,305 | 2,085 | | 780 D | 38.5% | 61.5% | 38.5% | 61.5% |
| 18,991 | LACLEDE | 8,365 | 3,848 | 4,517 | | 669 D | 46.0% | 54.0% | 46.0% | 54.0% |
| 25,274 | LAFAYETTE | 12,893 | 5,493 | 7,400 | | 1,907 D | 42.6% | 57.4% | 42.6% | 57.4% |
| 23,260 | LAWRENCE | 12,430 | 6,047 | 6,383 | | 336 D | 48.6% | 51.4% | 48.6% | 51.4% |
| 10,984 | LEWIS | 4,520 | 1,239 | 3,281 | | 2,042 D | 27.4% | 72.6% | 27.4% | 72.6% |
| 14,783 | LINCOLN | 7,264 | 2,271 | 4,993 | | 2,722 D | 31.3% | 68.7% | 31.3% | 68.7% |
| 16,815 | LINN | 8,618 | 2,883 | 5,735 | | 2,852 D | 33.5% | 66.5% | 33.5% | 66.5% |
| 15,771 | LIVINGSTON | 8,023 | 2,703 | 5,320 | | 2,617 D | 33.7% | 66.3% | 33.7% | 66.3% |
| 11,798 | MCDONALD | 6,543 | 3,055 | 3,488 | | 433 D | 46.7% | 53.3% | 46.7% | 53.3% |

# MISSOURI

## PRESIDENT 1964

| 1960 Census Population | County | Total Vote | Republican | Democratic | Other | Rep.-Dem. Plurality | Percentage Total Vote Rep. | Dem. | Major Vote Rep. | Dem. |
|---|---|---|---|---|---|---|---|---|---|---|
| 16,473 | MACON | 8,226 | 2,837 | 5,389 | | 2,552 D | 34.5% | 65.5% | 34.5% | 65.5% |
| 9,366 | MADISON | 4,474 | 1,756 | 2,718 | | 962 D | 39.2% | 60.8% | 39.2% | 60.8% |
| 7,282 | MARIES | 3,246 | 1,183 | 2,063 | | 880 D | 36.4% | 63.6% | 36.4% | 63.6% |
| 29,522 | MARION | 11,919 | 3,605 | 8,314 | | 4,709 D | 30.2% | 69.8% | 30.2% | 69.8% |
| 5,750 | MERCER | 2,324 | 1,040 | 1,284 | | 244 D | 44.8% | 55.2% | 44.8% | 55.2% |
| 13,800 | MILLER | 6,642 | 3,784 | 2,858 | | 926 R | 57.0% | 43.0% | 57.0% | 43.0% |
| 20,695 | MISSISSIPPI | 5,680 | 1,665 | 4,015 | | 2,350 D | 29.3% | 70.7% | 29.3% | 70.7% |
| 10,500 | MONITEAU | 5,382 | 2,758 | 2,624 | | 134 R | 51.2% | 48.8% | 51.2% | 48.8% |
| 10,688 | MONROE | 5,031 | 928 | 4,103 | | 3,175 D | 18.4% | 81.6% | 18.4% | 81.6% |
| 11,097 | MONTGOMERY | 5,899 | 2,610 | 3,289 | | 679 D | 44.2% | 55.8% | 44.2% | 55.8% |
| 9,476 | MORGAN | 5,210 | 2,742 | 2,468 | | 274 R | 52.6% | 47.4% | 52.6% | 47.4% |
| 31,350 | NEW MADRID | 9,998 | 2,583 | 7,415 | | 4,832 D | 25.8% | 74.2% | 25.8% | 74.2% |
| 30,093 | NEWTON | 14,799 | 6,660 | 8,139 | | 1,479 D | 45.0% | 55.0% | 45.0% | 55.0% |
| 22,215 | NODAWAY | 10,479 | 3,789 | 6,690 | | 2,901 D | 36.2% | 63.8% | 36.2% | 63.8% |
| 9,845 | OREGON | 3,900 | 992 | 2,908 | | 1,916 D | 25.4% | 74.6% | 25.4% | 74.6% |
| 10,867 | OSAGE | 5,320 | 2,712 | 2,608 | | 104 R | 51.0% | 49.0% | 51.0% | 49.0% |
| 6,744 | OZARK | 2,604 | 1,540 | 1,064 | | 476 R | 59.1% | 40.9% | 59.1% | 40.9% |
| 38,095 | PEMISCOT | 7,741 | 2,658 | 5,083 | | 2,425 D | 34.3% | 65.7% | 34.3% | 65.7% |
| 14,642 | PERRY | 6,293 | 2,837 | 3,456 | | 619 D | 45.1% | 54.9% | 45.1% | 54.9% |
| 35,120 | PETTIS | 14,396 | 5,409 | 8,987 | | 3,578 D | 37.6% | 62.4% | 37.6% | 62.4% |
| 25,396 | PHELPS | 9,531 | 3,755 | 5,776 | | 2,021 D | 39.4% | 60.6% | 39.4% | 60.6% |
| 16,706 | PIKE | 7,217 | 1,944 | 5,273 | | 3,329 D | 26.9% | 73.1% | 26.9% | 73.1% |
| 23,350 | PLATTE | 9,202 | 3,059 | 6,143 | | 3,084 D | 33.2% | 66.8% | 33.2% | 66.8% |
| 13,753 | POLK | 6,641 | 3,288 | 3,353 | | 65 D | 49.5% | 50.5% | 49.5% | 50.5% |
| 46,567 | PULASKI | 5,239 | 1,856 | 3,383 | | 1,527 D | 35.4% | 64.6% | 35.4% | 64.6% |
| 6,999 | PUTNAM | 3,031 | 1,547 | 1,484 | | 63 R | 51.0% | 49.0% | 51.0% | 49.0% |
| 8,078 | RALLS | 3,583 | 736 | 2,847 | | 2,111 D | 20.5% | 79.5% | 20.5% | 79.5% |
| 22,014 | RANDOLPH | 9,473 | 2,485 | 6,988 | | 4,503 D | 26.2% | 73.8% | 26.2% | 73.8% |
| 16,075 | RAY | 6,923 | 1,734 | 5,189 | | 3,455 D | 25.0% | 75.0% | 25.0% | 75.0% |
| 5,161 | REYNOLDS | 2,365 | 530 | 1,835 | | 1,305 D | 22.4% | 77.6% | 22.4% | 77.6% |
| 9,096 | RIPLEY | 4,372 | 1,684 | 2,688 | | 1,004 D | 38.5% | 61.5% | 38.5% | 61.5% |
| 52,970 | ST. CHARLES | 23,550 | 9,020 | 14,530 | | 5,510 D | 38.3% | 61.7% | 38.3% | 61.7% |
| 8,421 | ST. CLAIR | 4,554 | 1,961 | 2,593 | | 632 D | 43.1% | 56.9% | 43.1% | 56.9% |
| 36,516 | ST. FRANCOIS | 16,257 | 5,690 | 10,567 | | 4,877 D | 35.0% | 65.0% | 35.0% | 65.0% |
| 750,026 | ST. LOUIS CITY | 267,562 | 59,604 | 207,958 | | 148,354 D | 22.3% | 77.7% | 22.3% | 77.7% |
| 703,532 | ST. LOUIS COUNTY | 348,620 | 134,962 | 213,658 | | 78,696 D | 38.7% | 61.3% | 38.7% | 61.3% |
| 12,116 | STE. GENEVIEVE | 5,084 | 1,316 | 3,768 | | 2,452 D | 25.9% | 74.1% | 25.9% | 74.1% |
| 25,148 | SALINE | 10,943 | 3,635 | 7,308 | | 3,673 D | 33.2% | 66.8% | 33.2% | 66.8% |
| 5,052 | SCHUYLER | 2,521 | 1,072 | 1,449 | | 377 D | 42.5% | 57.5% | 42.5% | 57.5% |
| 6,484 | SCOTLAND | 3,402 | 1,215 | 2,187 | | 972 D | 35.7% | 64.3% | 35.7% | 64.3% |
| 32,748 | SCOTT | 10,724 | 3,212 | 7,512 | | 4,300 D | 30.0% | 70.0% | 30.0% | 70.0% |
| 7,087 | SHANNON | 3,216 | 904 | 2,312 | | 1,408 D | 28.1% | 71.9% | 28.1% | 71.9% |
| 9,063 | SHELBY | 4,368 | 1,212 | 3,156 | | 1,944 D | 27.7% | 72.3% | 27.7% | 72.3% |
| 29,490 | STODDARD | 8,958 | 3,014 | 5,944 | | 2,930 D | 33.6% | 66.4% | 33.6% | 66.4% |
| 8,176 | STONE | 4,212 | 2,377 | 1,835 | | 542 R | 56.4% | 43.6% | 56.4% | 43.6% |
| 8,783 | SULLIVAN | 4,747 | 2,052 | 2,695 | | 643 D | 43.2% | 56.8% | 43.2% | 56.8% |
| 10,238 | TANEY | 5,285 | 2,741 | 2,544 | | 197 R | 51.9% | 48.1% | 51.9% | 48.1% |
| 17,758 | TEXAS | 7,836 | 2,902 | 4,934 | | 2,032 D | 37.0% | 63.0% | 37.0% | 63.0% |
| 20,540 | VERNON | 9,035 | 3,077 | 5,958 | | 2,881 D | 34.1% | 65.9% | 34.1% | 65.9% |
| 8,750 | WARREN | 4,226 | 2,323 | 1,903 | | 420 R | 55.0% | 45.0% | 55.0% | 45.0% |
| 14,346 | WASHINGTON | 6,194 | 2,286 | 3,908 | | 1,622 D | 36.9% | 63.1% | 36.9% | 63.1% |
| 8,638 | WAYNE | 5,024 | 2,019 | 3,005 | | 986 D | 40.2% | 59.8% | 40.2% | 59.8% |
| 13,753 | WEBSTER | 7,165 | 3,341 | 3,824 | | 483 D | 46.6% | 53.4% | 46.6% | 53.4% |
| 3,936 | WORTH | 2,204 | 831 | 1,373 | | 542 D | 37.7% | 62.3% | 37.7% | 62.3% |
| 14,183 | WRIGHT | 6,758 | 3,466 | 3,292 | | 174 R | 51.3% | 48.7% | 51.3% | 48.7% |
| 4,319,813 | TOTAL | 1,817,879 | 653,535 | 1,164,344 | | 510,809 D | 36.0% | 64.0% | 36.0% | 64.0% |

# MISSOURI

## PRESIDENT 1960

| 1960 Census Population | County | Total Vote | Republican | Democratic | Other | Rep.-Dem. Plurality | Percentage | | | |
|---|---|---|---|---|---|---|---|---|---|---|
| | | | | | | | Total Vote | | Major Vote | |
| | | | | | | | Rep. | Dem. | Rep. | Dem. |
| 20,105 | ADAIR | 8,629 | 5,469 | 3,160 | | 2,309 R | 63.4% | 36.6% | 63.4% | 36.6% |
| 11,062 | ANDREW | 5,886 | 3,716 | 2,170 | | 1,546 R | 63.1% | 36.9% | 63.1% | 36.9% |
| 9,213 | ATCHISON | 4,826 | 2,659 | 2,167 | | 492 R | 55.1% | 44.9% | 55.1% | 44.9% |
| 26,079 | AUDRAIN | 11,365 | 4,955 | 6,410 | | 1,455 D | 43.6% | 56.4% | 43.6% | 56.4% |
| 18,921 | BARRY | 10,625 | 6,706 | 3,919 | | 2,787 R | 63.1% | 36.9% | 63.1% | 36.9% |
| 11,113 | BARTON | 6,120 | 3,703 | 2,417 | | 1,286 R | 60.5% | 39.5% | 60.5% | 39.5% |
| 15,905 | BATES | 9,335 | 5,429 | 3,906 | | 1,523 R | 58.2% | 41.8% | 58.2% | 41.8% |
| 8,737 | BENTON | 4,980 | 3,484 | 1,496 | | 1,988 R | 70.0% | 30.0% | 70.0% | 30.0% |
| 9,167 | BOLLINGER | 4,821 | 2,886 | 1,935 | | 951 R | 59.9% | 40.1% | 59.9% | 40.1% |
| 55,202 | BOONE | 21,967 | 10,453 | 11,514 | | 1,061 D | 47.6% | 52.4% | 47.6% | 52.4% |
| 90,581 | BUCHANAN | 40,796 | 21,448 | 19,348 | | 2,100 R | 52.6% | 47.4% | 52.6% | 47.4% |
| 34,656 | BUTLER | 14,157 | 8,751 | 5,406 | | 3,345 R | 61.8% | 38.2% | 61.8% | 38.2% |
| 8,830 | CALDWELL | 4,851 | 3,115 | 1,736 | | 1,379 R | 64.2% | 35.8% | 64.2% | 35.8% |
| 23,858 | CALLAWAY | 9,398 | 4,054 | 5,344 | | 1,290 D | 43.1% | 56.9% | 43.1% | 56.9% |
| 9,116 | CAMDEN | 5,268 | 3,509 | 1,759 | | 1,750 R | 66.6% | 33.4% | 66.6% | 33.4% |
| 42,020 | CAPE GIRARDEAU | 19,503 | 11,331 | 8,172 | | 3,159 R | 58.1% | 41.9% | 58.1% | 41.9% |
| 13,847 | CARROLL | 7,851 | 4,555 | 3,296 | | 1,259 R | 58.0% | 42.0% | 58.0% | 42.0% |
| 3,973 | CARTER | 1,732 | 1,049 | 683 | | 366 R | 60.6% | 39.4% | 60.6% | 39.4% |
| 29,702 | CASS | 12,241 | 6,523 | 5,718 | | 805 R | 53.3% | 46.7% | 53.3% | 46.7% |
| 9,185 | CEDAR | 5,277 | 3,730 | 1,547 | | 2,183 R | 70.7% | 29.3% | 70.7% | 29.3% |
| 12,720 | CHARITON | 6,652 | 3,102 | 3,550 | | 448 D | 46.6% | 53.4% | 46.6% | 53.4% |
| 12,359 | CHRISTIAN | 6,249 | 4,627 | 1,622 | | 3,005 R | 74.0% | 26.0% | 74.0% | 26.0% |
| 8,725 | CLARK | 4,681 | 2,642 | 2,039 | | 603 R | 56.4% | 43.6% | 56.4% | 43.6% |
| 87,474 | CLAY | 36,273 | 18,955 | 17,318 | | 1,637 R | 52.3% | 47.7% | 52.3% | 47.7% |
| 11,588 | CLINTON | 6,558 | 3,391 | 3,167 | | 224 R | 51.7% | 48.3% | 51.7% | 48.3% |
| 40,761 | COLE | 18,295 | 9,763 | 8,532 | | 1,231 R | 53.4% | 46.6% | 53.4% | 46.6% |
| 15,448 | COOPER | 8,530 | 4,672 | 3,858 | | 814 R | 54.8% | 45.2% | 54.8% | 45.2% |
| 12,647 | CRAWFORD | 6,452 | 4,065 | 2,387 | | 1,678 R | 63.0% | 37.0% | 63.0% | 37.0% |
| 7,577 | DADE | 4,204 | 2,987 | 1,217 | | 1,770 R | 71.1% | 28.9% | 71.1% | 28.9% |
| 9,314 | DALLAS | 5,004 | 3,522 | 1,482 | | 2,040 R | 70.4% | 29.6% | 70.4% | 29.6% |
| 9,502 | DAVIESS | 5,411 | 3,191 | 2,220 | | 971 R | 59.0% | 41.0% | 59.0% | 41.0% |
| 7,226 | DE KALB | 4,181 | 2,484 | 1,697 | | 787 R | 59.4% | 40.6% | 59.4% | 40.6% |
| 10,445 | DENT | 5,805 | 3,212 | 2,593 | | 619 R | 55.3% | 44.7% | 55.3% | 44.7% |
| 9,653 | DOUGLAS | 4,625 | 3,611 | 1,014 | | 2,597 R | 78.1% | 21.9% | 78.1% | 21.9% |
| 39,139 | DUNKLIN | 13,276 | 6,708 | 6,568 | | 140 R | 50.5% | 49.5% | 50.5% | 49.5% |
| 44,566 | FRANKLIN | 21,934 | 11,610 | 10,324 | | 1,286 R | 52.9% | 47.1% | 52.9% | 47.1% |
| 12,195 | GASCONADE | 6,505 | 4,854 | 1,651 | | 3,203 R | 74.6% | 25.4% | 74.6% | 25.4% |
| 8,793 | GENTRY | 5,327 | 2,888 | 2,439 | | 449 R | 54.2% | 45.8% | 54.2% | 45.8% |
| 126,276 | GREENE | 57,400 | 36,943 | 20,457 | | 16,486 R | 64.4% | 35.6% | 64.4% | 35.6% |
| 12,220 | GRUNDY | 6,837 | 4,422 | 2,415 | | 2,007 R | 64.7% | 35.3% | 64.7% | 35.3% |
| 11,603 | HARRISON | 6,366 | 4,166 | 2,200 | | 1,966 R | 65.4% | 34.6% | 65.4% | 34.6% |
| 19,226 | HENRY | 10,613 | 6,012 | 4,601 | | 1,411 R | 56.6% | 43.4% | 56.6% | 43.4% |
| 4,516 | HICKORY | 2,500 | 1,885 | 615 | | 1,270 R | 75.4% | 24.6% | 75.4% | 24.6% |
| 7,885 | HOLT | 4,271 | 2,720 | 1,551 | | 1,169 R | 63.7% | 36.3% | 63.7% | 36.3% |
| 10,859 | HOWARD | 5,377 | 2,075 | 3,302 | | 1,227 D | 38.6% | 61.4% | 38.6% | 61.4% |
| 22,027 | HOWELL | 9,829 | 7,095 | 2,734 | | 4,361 R | 72.2% | 27.8% | 72.2% | 27.8% |
| 8,041 | IRON | 3,973 | 2,122 | 1,851 | | 271 R | 53.4% | 46.6% | 53.4% | 46.6% |
| 622,732 | JACKSON | 266,458 | 123,589 | 142,869 | | 19,280 D | 46.4% | 53.6% | 46.4% | 53.6% |
| 78,863 | JASPER | 36,766 | 21,804 | 14,962 | | 6,842 R | 59.3% | 40.7% | 59.3% | 40.7% |
| 66,377 | JEFFERSON | 29,964 | 12,910 | 17,054 | | 4,144 D | 43.1% | 56.9% | 43.1% | 56.9% |
| 28,981 | JOHNSON | 11,682 | 6,970 | 4,712 | | 2,258 R | 59.7% | 40.3% | 59.7% | 40.3% |
| 6,558 | KNOX | 3,670 | 1,874 | 1,796 | | 78 R | 51.1% | 48.9% | 51.1% | 48.9% |
| 18,991 | LACLEDE | 8,961 | 5,805 | 3,156 | | 2,649 R | 64.8% | 35.2% | 64.8% | 35.2% |
| 25,274 | LAFAYETTE | 13,566 | 8,011 | 5,555 | | 2,456 R | 59.1% | 40.9% | 59.1% | 40.9% |
| 23,260 | LAWRENCE | 12,889 | 8,406 | 4,483 | | 3,923 R | 65.2% | 34.8% | 65.2% | 34.8% |
| 10,984 | LEWIS | 5,286 | 2,560 | 2,726 | | 166 D | 48.4% | 51.6% | 48.4% | 51.6% |
| 14,783 | LINCOLN | 7,264 | 3,471 | 3,793 | | 322 D | 47.8% | 52.2% | 47.8% | 52.2% |
| 16,815 | LINN | 9,620 | 5,086 | 4,534 | | 552 R | 52.9% | 47.1% | 52.9% | 47.1% |
| 15,771 | LIVINGSTON | 8,840 | 5,045 | 3,795 | | 1,250 R | 57.1% | 42.9% | 57.1% | 42.9% |
| 11,798 | MCDONALD | 6,451 | 3,955 | 2,496 | | 1,459 R | 61.3% | 38.7% | 61.3% | 38.7% |

# MISSOURI

## PRESIDENT 1960

| 1960 Census Population | County | Total Vote | Republican | Democratic | Other | Rep.-Dem. Plurality | Percentage Total Vote Rep. | Dem. | Major Vote Rep. | Dem. |
|---|---|---|---|---|---|---|---|---|---|---|
| 16,473 | MACON | 9,133 | 4,925 | 4,208 | | 717 R | 53.9% | 46.1% | 53.9% | 46.1% |
| 9,366 | MADISON | 4,834 | 2,960 | 1,874 | | 1,086 R | 61.2% | 38.8% | 61.2% | 38.8% |
| 7,282 | MARIES | 3,400 | 1,684 | 1,716 | | 32 D | 49.5% | 50.5% | 49.5% | 50.5% |
| 29,522 | MARION | 13,189 | 6,431 | 6,758 | | 327 D | 48.8% | 51.2% | 48.8% | 51.2% |
| 5,750 | MERCER | 3,500 | 2,354 | 1,146 | | 1,208 R | 67.3% | 32.7% | 67.3% | 32.7% |
| 13,800 | MILLER | 7,066 | 4,482 | 2,584 | | 1,898 R | 63.4% | 36.6% | 63.4% | 36.6% |
| 20,695 | MISSISSIPPI | 6,484 | 2,629 | 3,855 | | 1,226 D | 40.5% | 59.5% | 40.5% | 59.5% |
| 10,500 | MONITEAU | 5,724 | 3,453 | 2,271 | | 1,182 R | 60.3% | 39.7% | 60.3% | 39.7% |
| 10,688 | MONROE | 5,530 | 1,519 | 4,011 | | 2,492 D | 27.5% | 72.5% | 27.5% | 72.5% |
| 11,097 | MONTGOMERY | 6,258 | 3,454 | 2,804 | | 650 R | 55.2% | 44.8% | 55.2% | 44.8% |
| 9,476 | MORGAN | 5,218 | 3,239 | 1,979 | | 1,260 R | 62.1% | 37.9% | 62.1% | 37.9% |
| 31,350 | NEW MADRID | 11,578 | 4,205 | 7,373 | | 3,168 D | 36.3% | 63.7% | 36.3% | 63.7% |
| 30,093 | NEWTON | 14,688 | 9,010 | 5,678 | | 3,332 R | 61.3% | 38.7% | 61.3% | 38.7% |
| 22,215 | NODAWAY | 11,311 | 5,993 | 5,318 | | 675 R | 53.0% | 47.0% | 53.0% | 47.0% |
| 9,845 | OREGON | 3,908 | 1,974 | 1,934 | | 40 R | 50.5% | 49.5% | 50.5% | 49.5% |
| 10,867 | OSAGE | 5,578 | 2,678 | 2,900 | | 222 D | 48.0% | 52.0% | 48.0% | 52.0% |
| 6,744 | OZARK | 3,316 | 2,595 | 721 | | 1,874 R | 78.3% | 21.7% | 78.3% | 21.7% |
| 38,095 | PEMISCOT | 11,776 | 4,464 | 7,312 | | 2,848 D | 37.9% | 62.1% | 37.9% | 62.1% |
| 14,642 | PERRY | 6,877 | 3,886 | 2,991 | | 895 R | 56.5% | 43.5% | 56.5% | 43.5% |
| 35,120 | PETTIS | 16,063 | 9,066 | 6,997 | | 2,069 R | 56.4% | 43.6% | 56.4% | 43.6% |
| 25,396 | PHELPS | 10,239 | 5,663 | 4,576 | | 1,087 R | 55.3% | 44.7% | 55.3% | 44.7% |
| 16,706 | PIKE | 7,996 | 3,900 | 4,096 | | 196 D | 48.8% | 51.2% | 48.8% | 51.2% |
| 23,350 | PLATTE | 10,631 | 4,771 | 5,860 | | 1,089 D | 44.9% | 55.1% | 44.9% | 55.1% |
| 13,753 | POLK | 7,289 | 4,849 | 2,440 | | 2,409 R | 66.5% | 33.5% | 66.5% | 33.5% |
| 46,567 | PULASKI | 6,381 | 3,285 | 3,096 | | 189 R | 51.5% | 48.5% | 51.5% | 48.5% |
| 6,999 | PUTNAM | 3,771 | 2,711 | 1,060 | | 1,651 R | 71.9% | 28.1% | 71.9% | 28.1% |
| 8,078 | RALLS | 3,980 | 1,485 | 2,495 | | 1,010 D | 37.3% | 62.7% | 37.3% | 62.7% |
| 22,014 | RANDOLPH | 10,614 | 4,180 | 6,434 | | 2,254 D | 39.4% | 60.6% | 39.4% | 60.6% |
| 16,075 | RAY | 8,107 | 3,542 | 4,565 | | 1,023 D | 43.7% | 56.3% | 43.7% | 56.3% |
| 5,161 | REYNOLDS | 2,183 | 1,139 | 1,044 | | 95 R | 52.2% | 47.8% | 52.2% | 47.8% |
| 9,096 | RIPLEY | 4,528 | 2,811 | 1,717 | | 1,094 R | 62.1% | 37.9% | 62.1% | 37.9% |
| 52,970 | ST. CHARLES | 22,778 | 10,888 | 11,890 | | 1,002 D | 47.8% | 52.2% | 47.8% | 52.2% |
| 8,421 | ST. CLAIR | 5,061 | 3,196 | 1,865 | | 1,331 R | 63.1% | 36.9% | 63.1% | 36.9% |
| 36,516 | ST. FRANCOIS | 17,336 | 10,131 | 7,205 | | 2,926 R | 58.4% | 41.6% | 58.4% | 41.6% |
| 750,026 | ST. LOUIS CITY | 303,650 | 101,331 | 202,319 | | 100,988 D | 33.4% | 66.6% | 33.4% | 66.6% |
| 703,532 | ST. LOUIS COUNTY | 324,500 | 157,992 | 166,508 | | 8,516 D | 48.7% | 51.3% | 48.7% | 51.3% |
| 12,116 | STE. GENEVIEVE | 5,167 | 1,956 | 3,211 | | 1,255 D | 37.9% | 62.1% | 37.9% | 62.1% |
| 25,148 | SALINE | 12,054 | 6,085 | 5,969 | | 116 R | 50.5% | 49.5% | 50.5% | 49.5% |
| 5,052 | SCHUYLER | 3,027 | 1,666 | 1,361 | | 305 R | 55.0% | 45.0% | 55.0% | 45.0% |
| 6,484 | SCOTLAND | 3,783 | 1,899 | 1,884 | | 15 R | 50.2% | 49.8% | 50.2% | 49.8% |
| 32,748 | SCOTT | 12,156 | 5,807 | 6,349 | | 542 D | 47.8% | 52.2% | 47.8% | 52.2% |
| 7,087 | SHANNON | 2,815 | 1,429 | 1,386 | | 43 R | 50.8% | 49.2% | 50.8% | 49.2% |
| 9,063 | SHELBY | 4,932 | 2,062 | 2,870 | | 808 D | 41.8% | 58.2% | 41.8% | 58.2% |
| 29,490 | STODDARD | 11,683 | 6,366 | 5,317 | | 1,049 R | 54.5% | 45.5% | 54.5% | 45.5% |
| 8,176 | STONE | 4,091 | 3,201 | 890 | | 2,311 R | 78.2% | 21.8% | 78.2% | 21.8% |
| 8,783 | SULLIVAN | 5,706 | 3,202 | 2,504 | | 698 R | 56.1% | 43.9% | 56.1% | 43.9% |
| 10,238 | TANEY | 5,131 | 3,692 | 1,439 | | 2,253 R | 72.0% | 28.0% | 72.0% | 28.0% |
| 17,758 | TEXAS | 8,864 | 5,258 | 3,606 | | 1,652 R | 59.3% | 40.7% | 59.3% | 40.7% |
| 20,540 | VERNON | 9,573 | 5,387 | 4,186 | | 1,201 R | 56.3% | 43.7% | 56.3% | 43.7% |
| 8,750 | WARREN | 4,353 | 2,946 | 1,407 | | 1,539 R | 67.7% | 32.3% | 67.7% | 32.3% |
| 14,346 | WASHINGTON | 6,086 | 3,437 | 2,649 | | 788 R | 56.5% | 43.5% | 56.5% | 43.5% |
| 8,638 | WAYNE | 5,221 | 3,069 | 2,152 | | 917 R | 58.8% | 41.2% | 58.8% | 41.2% |
| 13,753 | WEBSTER | 7,310 | 4,603 | 2,707 | | 1,896 R | 63.0% | 37.0% | 63.0% | 37.0% |
| 3,936 | WORTH | 2,678 | 1,355 | 1,323 | | 32 R | 50.6% | 49.4% | 50.6% | 49.4% |
| 14,183 | WRIGHT | 7,144 | 5,191 | 1,953 | | 3,238 R | 72.7% | 27.3% | 72.7% | 27.3% |
| 4,319,813 | TOTAL | 1,934,422 | 962,221 | 972,201 | | 9,980 D | 49.7% | 50.3% | 49.7% | 50.3% |

# MISSOURI

## ELECTION NOTES

**2004**  Other vote was 9,831 Libertarian (Michael Badnarik); 5,355 Constitution (Michael Peroutka); 1,294 write-in (Ralph Nader).

**2000**  Other vote was 9,818 Reform (Buchanan); 7,436 Libertarian (Browne); 1,957 Constitution (Phillips); 1,104 Natural Law (Hagelin).

**1996**  Other vote was 11,521 U.S. Taxpayers (Phillips); 10,522 Libertarian (Browne); 2,287 Natural Law (Hagelin); 596 scattered write-in.

**1992**  Other vote was 7,497 Marrou (Libertarian); 180 Gritz (write-in); 64 Hagelin (write-in); 17 Fulani (write-in); 13 LaRouche (write-in); 12 Daniels (write-in); 6 Warren (write-in); 3 scattered write-in. The total of the other vote column includes these write-ins which were not available by county.

**1988**  Other vote was 6,656 Fulani (New Alliance); 434 Paul (write-in); 44 Duke (write-in); 1 Dennis (write-in); 6 scattered write-in.

**1984**  Other vote was 8 Mason (write-in); 2 Johnson (write-in); 1 Dennis (write-in); 1 scattered write-in.

**1980**  Other vote was 77,920 Anderson (Independent); 14,422 Clark (Libertarian); 1,515 DeBerry (Socialist Workers); 573 Commoner (write-in); 26 Hall (write-in); 5 McCormack (write-in). The state-wide total for the other vote column includes these 604 write-in votes not reported by county.

**1976**  Other vote was 24,029 McCarthy (Independent); 3,741 scattered write-in. Early unamended canvass gave the state-wide totals as 928,808 Republican; 999,163 Democratic; 24,329 McCarthy (Independent). The state-wide total for the other vote column includes the 3,741 write-in votes not reported by county.

**1972**  Other vote was scattered write-in. Unidentified write-in votes cast in the Republican (206) and Democratic (1,384) columns on the ballot are included in the other vote column.

**1968**  Wallace on the ballot as American.

**1964**

**1960**

# MONTANA

## POPULAR VOTE FOR PRESIDENT 1920 TO 2004

| Year | Total Vote | Republican Vote | Candidate | Democratic Vote | Candidate | Other Vote | Plurality | | Percentage | | | |
|------|-----------|-----|-----------|-----|-----------|-----|-----------|---|---|---|---|---|
| | | | | | | | | | Total Vote | | Major Vote | |
| | | | | | | | | | Rep. | Dem. | Rep. | Dem. |
| 2004 | 450,445 | 266,063 | Bush, George W. | 173,710 | Kerry, John | 10,672 | 92,353 | R | 59.1% | 38.6% | 60.5% | 39.5% |
| 2000 ** | 410,997 | 240,178 | Bush, George W. | 137,126 | Gore, Al | 33,693 | 103,052 | R | 58.4% | 33.4% | 63.7% | 36.3% |
| 1996 ** | 407,261 | 179,652 | Dole, Bob | 167,922 | Clinton, Bill | 59,687 | 11,730 | R | 44.1% | 41.2% | 51.7% | 48.3% |
| 1992 ** | 410,611 | 144,207 | Bush, George | 154,507 | Clinton, Bill | 111,897 | 10,300 | D | 35.1% | 37.6% | 48.3% | 51.7% |
| 1988 | 365,674 | 190,412 | Bush, George | 168,936 | Dukakis, Michael S. | 6,326 | 21,476 | R | 52.1% | 46.2% | 53.0% | 47.0% |
| 1984 | 384,377 | 232,450 | Reagan, Ronald | 146,742 | Mondale, Walter F. | 5,185 | 85,708 | R | 60.5% | 38.2% | 61.3% | 38.7% |
| 1980 ** | 363,952 | 206,814 | Reagan, Ronald | 118,032 | Carter, Jimmy | 39,106 | 88,782 | R | 56.8% | 32.4% | 63.7% | 36.3% |
| 1976 | 328,734 | 173,703 | Ford, Gerald R. | 149,259 | Carter, Jimmy | 5,772 | 24,444 | R | 52.8% | 45.4% | 53.8% | 46.2% |
| 1972 | 317,603 | 183,976 | Nixon, Richard M. | 120,197 | McGovern, George S. | 13,430 | 63,779 | R | 57.9% | 37.8% | 60.5% | 39.5% |
| 1968 | 274,404 | 138,835 | Nixon, Richard M. | 114,117 | Humphrey, Hubert H. | 21,452 | 24,718 | R | 50.6% | 41.6% | 54.9% | 45.1% |
| 1964 | 278,628 | 113,032 | Goldwater, Barry M. | 164,246 | Johnson, Lyndon B. | 1,350 | 51,214 | D | 40.6% | 58.9% | 40.8% | 59.2% |
| 1960 | 277,579 | 141,841 | Nixon, Richard M. | 134,891 | Kennedy, John F. | 847 | 6,950 | R | 51.1% | 48.6% | 51.3% | 48.7% |
| 1956 | 271,171 | 154,933 | Eisenhower, Dwight D. | 116,238 | Stevenson, Adlai E. | | 38,695 | R | 57.1% | 42.9% | 57.1% | 42.9% |
| 1952 | 265,037 | 157,394 | Eisenhower, Dwight D. | 106,213 | Stevenson, Adlai E. | 1,430 | 51,181 | R | 59.4% | 40.1% | 59.7% | 40.3% |
| 1948 | 224,278 | 96,770 | Dewey, Thomas E. | 119,071 | Truman, Harry S. | 8,437 | 22,301 | D | 43.1% | 53.1% | 44.8% | 55.2% |
| 1944 | 207,355 | 93,163 | Dewey, Thomas E. | 112,556 | Roosevelt, Franklin D. | 1,636 | 19,393 | D | 44.9% | 54.3% | 45.3% | 54.7% |
| 1940 | 247,873 | 99,579 | Willkie, Wendell | 145,698 | Roosevelt, Franklin D. | 2,596 | 46,119 | D | 40.2% | 58.8% | 40.6% | 59.4% |
| 1936 | 230,502 | 63,598 | Landon, Alfred M. | 159,690 | Roosevelt, Franklin D. | 7,214 | 96,092 | D | 27.6% | 69.3% | 28.5% | 71.5% |
| 1932 | 216,479 | 78,078 | Hoover, Herbert C. | 127,286 | Roosevelt, Franklin D. | 11,115 | 49,208 | D | 36.1% | 58.8% | 38.0% | 62.0% |
| 1928 | 194,108 | 113,300 | Hoover, Herbert C. | 78,578 | Smith, Alfred E. | 2,230 | 34,722 | R | 58.4% | 40.5% | 59.0% | 41.0% |
| 1924 ** | 174,425 | 74,138 | Coolidge, Calvin | 33,805 | Davis, John W. | 66,482 | 8,014 | R | 42.5% | 19.4% | 68.7% | 31.3% |
| 1920 | 179,006 | 109,430 | Harding, Warren G. | 57,372 | Cox, James M. | 12,204 | 52,058 | R | 61.1% | 32.1% | 65.6% | 34.4% |

In 2000 the other vote column includes 24,437 votes cast for Green (Nader). In 1996 the other vote column includes 55,229 votes cast for Perot. In 1992 the other vote column includes 107,225 votes cast for Perot. In 1980 the other column includes 29,281 votes for Independent (Anderson). In 1924 the other vote was 66,124 Progressive and 358 Communist.

## ELECTORAL COLLEGE VOTE 1920 TO 2004

| Year | Total | Republican | Democratic | Other |
|------|-------|-----------|-----------|-------|
| 2004 | 3 | 3 | | |
| 2000 | 3 | 3 | | |
| 1996 | 3 | 3 | | |
| 1992 | 3 | | 3 | |
| 1988 | 4 | 4 | | |
| 1984 | 4 | 4 | | |
| 1980 | 4 | 4 | | |
| 1976 | 4 | 4 | | |
| 1972 | 4 | 4 | | |
| 1968 | 4 | 4 | | |
| 1964 | 4 | | 4 | |
| 1960 | 4 | 4 | | |
| 1956 | 4 | 4 | | |
| 1952 | 4 | 4 | | |
| 1948 | 4 | | 4 | |
| 1944 | 4 | | 4 | |
| 1940 | 4 | | 4 | |
| 1936 | 4 | | 4 | |
| 1932 | 4 | | 4 | |
| 1928 | 4 | 4 | | |
| 1924 | 4 | 4 | | |
| 1920 | 4 | 4 | | |

# MONTANA

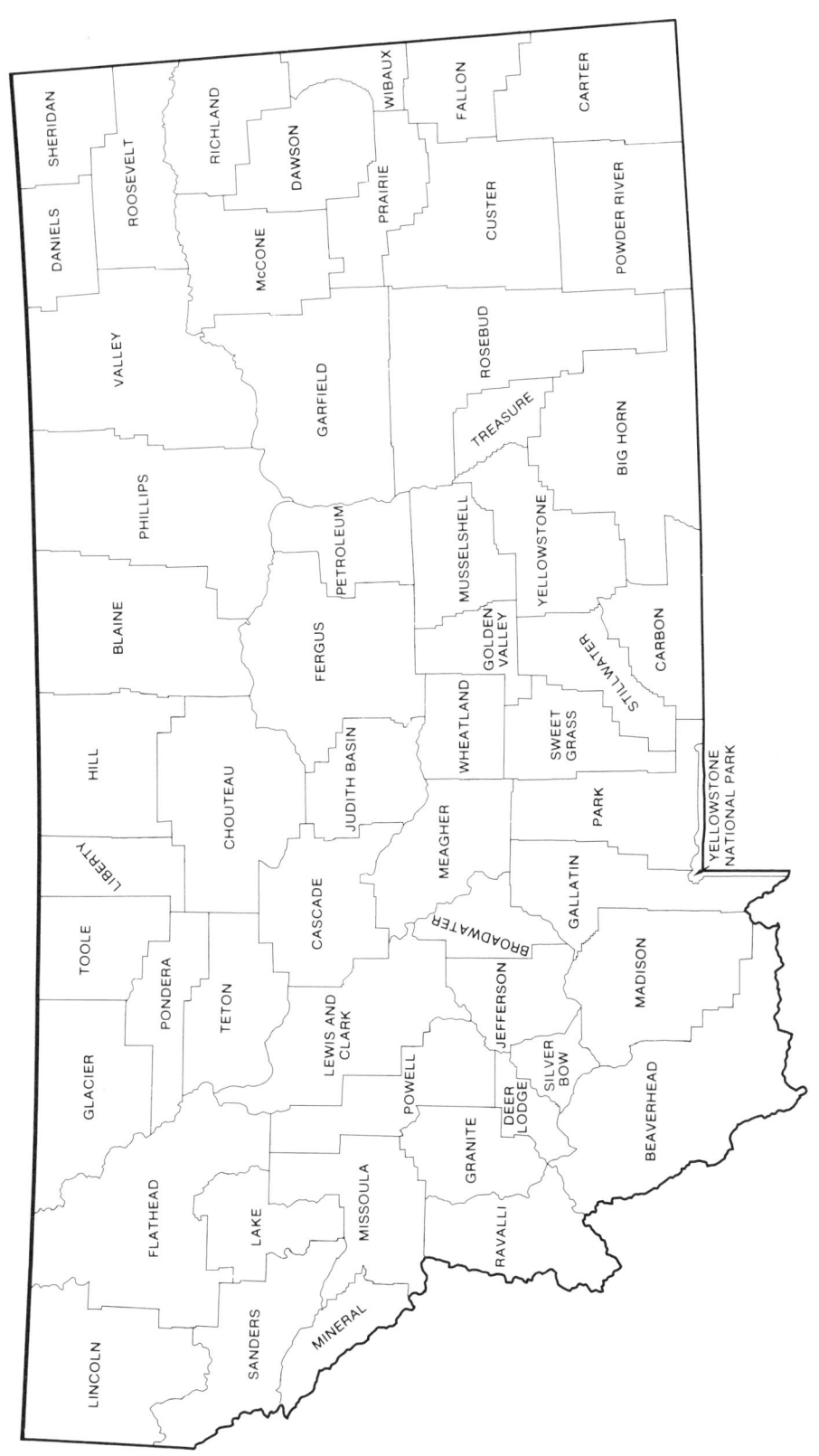

# MONTANA

## PRESIDENT 2004

| 2000 Census Population | County | Total Vote | Republican | Democratic | Other | Rep.-Dem. Plurality | Percentage | | | |
|---|---|---|---|---|---|---|---|---|---|---|
| | | | | | | | Total Vote | | Major Vote | |
| | | | | | | | Rep. | Dem. | Rep. | Dem. |
| 9,202 | BEAVERHEAD | 4,242 | 3,067 | 1,103 | 72 | 1,964 R | 72.3% | 26.0% | 73.5% | 26.5% |
| 12,671 | BIG HORN | 4,311 | 2,028 | 2,215 | 68 | 187 D | 47.0% | 51.4% | 47.8% | 52.2% |
| 7,009 | BLAINE | 2,768 | 1,424 | 1,300 | 44 | 124 R | 51.4% | 47.0% | 52.3% | 47.7% |
| 4,385 | BROADWATER | 2,356 | 1,778 | 533 | 45 | 1,245 R | 75.5% | 22.6% | 76.9% | 23.1% |
| 9,552 | CARBON | 5,321 | 3,342 | 1,847 | 132 | 1,495 R | 62.8% | 34.7% | 64.4% | 35.6% |
| 1,360 | CARTER | 709 | 623 | 76 | 10 | 547 R | 87.9% | 10.7% | 89.1% | 10.9% |
| 80,357 | CASCADE | 33,459 | 19,028 | 13,701 | 730 | 5,327 R | 56.9% | 40.9% | 58.1% | 41.9% |
| 5,970 | CHOUTEAU | 2,921 | 1,913 | 946 | 62 | 967 R | 65.5% | 32.4% | 66.9% | 33.1% |
| 11,696 | CUSTER | 5,048 | 3,297 | 1,630 | 121 | 1,667 R | 65.3% | 32.3% | 66.9% | 33.1% |
| 2,017 | DANIELS | 1,119 | 764 | 326 | 29 | 438 R | 68.3% | 29.1% | 70.1% | 29.9% |
| 9,059 | DAWSON | 4,484 | 2,884 | 1,494 | 106 | 1,390 R | 64.3% | 33.3% | 65.9% | 34.1% |
| 9,417 | DEER LODGE | 4,543 | 1,725 | 2,700 | 118 | 975 D | 38.0% | 59.4% | 39.0% | 61.0% |
| 2,837 | FALLON | 1,491 | 1,178 | 289 | 24 | 889 R | 79.0% | 19.4% | 80.3% | 19.7% |
| 11,893 | FERGUS | 6,127 | 4,425 | 1,582 | 120 | 2,843 R | 72.2% | 25.8% | 73.7% | 26.3% |
| 74,471 | FLATHEAD | 38,678 | 26,019 | 11,587 | 1,072 | 14,432 R | 67.3% | 30.0% | 69.2% | 30.8% |
| 67,831 | GALLATIN | 39,842 | 22,392 | 16,405 | 1,045 | 5,987 R | 56.2% | 41.2% | 57.7% | 42.3% |
| 1,279 | GARFIELD | 655 | 590 | 52 | 13 | 538 R | 90.1% | 7.9% | 91.9% | 8.1% |
| 13,247 | GLACIER | 4,562 | 1,828 | 2,641 | 93 | 813 D | 40.1% | 57.9% | 40.9% | 59.1% |
| 1,042 | GOLDEN VALLEY | 522 | 396 | 119 | 7 | 277 R | 75.9% | 22.8% | 76.9% | 23.1% |
| 2,830 | GRANITE | 1,605 | 1,144 | 404 | 57 | 740 R | 71.3% | 25.2% | 73.9% | 26.1% |
| 16,673 | HILL | 6,657 | 3,505 | 2,997 | 155 | 508 R | 52.7% | 45.0% | 53.9% | 46.1% |
| 10,049 | JEFFERSON | 5,868 | 3,844 | 1,881 | 143 | 1,963 R | 65.5% | 32.1% | 67.1% | 32.9% |
| 2,329 | JUDITH BASIN | 1,286 | 944 | 322 | 20 | 622 R | 73.4% | 25.0% | 74.6% | 25.4% |
| 26,507 | LAKE | 12,576 | 7,245 | 4,960 | 371 | 2,285 R | 57.6% | 39.4% | 59.4% | 40.6% |
| 55,716 | LEWIS AND CLARK | 29,843 | 16,494 | 12,717 | 632 | 3,777 R | 55.3% | 42.6% | 56.5% | 43.5% |
| 2,158 | LIBERTY | 1,033 | 734 | 281 | 18 | 453 R | 71.1% | 27.2% | 72.3% | 27.7% |
| 18,837 | LINCOLN | 8,449 | 5,889 | 2,320 | 240 | 3,569 R | 69.7% | 27.5% | 71.7% | 28.3% |
| 1,977 | MCCONE | 1,137 | 791 | 320 | 26 | 471 R | 69.6% | 28.1% | 71.2% | 28.8% |
| 6,851 | MADISON | 3,933 | 2,868 | 983 | 82 | 1,885 R | 72.9% | 25.0% | 74.5% | 25.5% |
| 1,932 | MEAGHER | 973 | 698 | 247 | 28 | 451 R | 71.7% | 25.4% | 73.9% | 26.1% |
| 3,884 | MINERAL | 1,837 | 1,242 | 542 | 53 | 700 R | 67.6% | 29.5% | 69.6% | 30.4% |
| 95,802 | MISSOULA | 52,454 | 23,989 | 26,983 | 1,482 | 2,994 D | 45.7% | 51.4% | 47.1% | 52.9% |
| 4,497 | MUSSELSHELL | 2,247 | 1,663 | 538 | 46 | 1,125 R | 74.0% | 23.9% | 75.6% | 24.4% |
| 15,694 | PARK | 8,218 | 4,771 | 3,199 | 248 | 1,572 R | 58.1% | 38.9% | 59.9% | 40.1% |
| 493 | PETROLEUM | 292 | 228 | 55 | 9 | 173 R | 78.1% | 18.8% | 80.6% | 19.4% |
| 4,601 | PHILLIPS | 2,170 | 1,677 | 456 | 37 | 1,221 R | 77.3% | 21.0% | 78.6% | 21.4% |
| 6,424 | PONDERA | 2,860 | 1,853 | 956 | 51 | 897 R | 64.8% | 33.4% | 66.0% | 34.0% |
| 1,858 | POWDER RIVER | 1,029 | 856 | 154 | 19 | 702 R | 83.2% | 15.0% | 84.8% | 15.2% |
| 7,180 | POWELL | 2,830 | 1,993 | 761 | 76 | 1,232 R | 70.4% | 26.9% | 72.4% | 27.6% |
| 1,199 | PRAIRIE | 736 | 546 | 181 | 9 | 365 R | 74.2% | 24.6% | 75.1% | 24.9% |
| 36,070 | RAVALLI | 19,867 | 13,279 | 6,144 | 444 | 7,135 R | 66.8% | 30.9% | 68.4% | 31.6% |
| 9,667 | RICHLAND | 4,308 | 3,110 | 1,120 | 78 | 1,990 R | 72.2% | 26.0% | 73.5% | 26.5% |
| 10,620 | ROOSEVELT | 4,028 | 1,762 | 2,195 | 71 | 433 D | 43.7% | 54.5% | 44.5% | 55.5% |
| 9,383 | ROSEBUD | 3,585 | 1,982 | 1,520 | 83 | 462 R | 55.3% | 42.4% | 56.6% | 43.4% |
| 10,227 | SANDERS | 5,153 | 3,461 | 1,502 | 190 | 1,959 R | 67.2% | 29.1% | 69.7% | 30.3% |
| 4,105 | SHERIDAN | 2,038 | 1,159 | 846 | 33 | 313 R | 56.9% | 41.5% | 57.8% | 42.2% |
| 34,606 | SILVER BOW | 16,084 | 6,381 | 9,307 | 396 | 2,926 D | 39.7% | 57.9% | 40.7% | 59.3% |
| 8,195 | STILLWATER | 4,213 | 3,090 | 1,025 | 98 | 2,065 R | 73.3% | 24.3% | 75.1% | 24.9% |
| 3,609 | SWEET GRASS | 1,983 | 1,509 | 445 | 29 | 1,064 R | 76.1% | 22.4% | 77.2% | 22.8% |
| 6,445 | TETON | 3,359 | 2,232 | 1,047 | 80 | 1,185 R | 66.4% | 31.2% | 68.1% | 31.9% |
| 5,267 | TOOLE | 2,311 | 1,583 | 690 | 38 | 893 R | 68.5% | 29.9% | 69.6% | 30.4% |
| 861 | TREASURE | 482 | 348 | 121 | 13 | 227 R | 72.2% | 25.1% | 74.2% | 25.8% |
| 7,675 | VALLEY | 4,018 | 2,476 | 1,431 | 111 | 1,045 R | 61.6% | 35.6% | 63.4% | 36.6% |
| 2,259 | WHEATLAND | 979 | 706 | 250 | 23 | 456 R | 72.1% | 25.5% | 73.8% | 26.2% |
| 1,068 | WIBAUX | 560 | 407 | 144 | 9 | 263 R | 72.7% | 25.7% | 73.9% | 26.1% |
| 129,352 | YELLOWSTONE | 66,286 | 40,903 | 24,120 | 1,263 | 16,783 R | 61.7% | 36.4% | 62.9% | 37.1% |
| 902,195 | TOTAL | 450,445 | 266,063 | 173,710 | 10,672 | 92,353 R | 59.1% | 38.6% | 60.5% | 39.5% |

# MONTANA

## PRESIDENT 2000

| 2000 Census Population | County | Total Vote | Republican | Democratic | Green (Nader) | Other | Rep.-Dem. Plurality | Percentage of Total Vote | | |
|---|---|---|---|---|---|---|---|---|---|---|
| | | | | | | | | Rep. | Dem. | Green |
| 9,202 | BEAVERHEAD | 4,196 | 3,113 | 799 | 218 | 66 | 2,314 R | 74.2% | 19.0% | 5.2% |
| 12,671 | BIG HORN | 4,161 | 1,651 | 2,345 | 101 | 64 | 694 D | 39.7% | 56.4% | 2.4% |
| 7,009 | BLAINE | 2,759 | 1,410 | 1,246 | 58 | 45 | 164 R | 51.1% | 45.2% | 2.1% |
| 4,385 | BROADWATER | 2,074 | 1,488 | 462 | 63 | 61 | 1,026 R | 71.7% | 22.3% | 3.0% |
| 9,552 | CARBON | 4,789 | 3,008 | 1,434 | 237 | 110 | 1,574 R | 62.8% | 29.9% | 4.9% |
| 1,360 | CARTER | 645 | 573 | 53 | 10 | 9 | 520 R | 88.8% | 8.2% | 1.6% |
| 80,357 | CASCADE | 33,328 | 18,164 | 13,137 | 1,202 | 825 | 5,027 R | 54.5% | 39.4% | 3.6% |
| 5,970 | CHOUTEAU | 2,885 | 2,039 | 686 | 86 | 74 | 1,353 R | 70.7% | 23.8% | 3.0% |
| 11,696 | CUSTER | 4,905 | 3,156 | 1,501 | 154 | 94 | 1,655 R | 64.3% | 30.6% | 3.1% |
| 2,017 | DANIELS | 1,110 | 750 | 303 | 39 | 18 | 447 R | 67.6% | 27.3% | 3.5% |
| 9,059 | DAWSON | 4,271 | 2,723 | 1,364 | 115 | 69 | 1,359 R | 63.8% | 31.9% | 2.7% |
| 9,417 | DEER LODGE | 4,534 | 1,493 | 2,672 | 232 | 137 | 1,179 D | 32.9% | 58.9% | 5.1% |
| 2,837 | FALLON | 1,369 | 1,061 | 256 | 31 | 21 | 805 R | 77.5% | 18.7% | 2.3% |
| 11,893 | FERGUS | 5,994 | 4,353 | 1,352 | 165 | 124 | 3,001 R | 72.6% | 22.6% | 2.8% |
| 74,471 | FLATHEAD | 33,839 | 22,519 | 8,329 | 2,037 | 954 | 14,190 R | 66.5% | 24.6% | 6.0% |
| 67,831 | GALLATIN | 32,040 | 18,833 | 10,009 | 2,545 | 653 | 8,824 R | 58.8% | 31.2% | 7.9% |
| 1,279 | GARFIELD | 744 | 651 | 61 | 12 | 20 | 590 R | 87.5% | 8.2% | 1.6% |
| 13,247 | GLACIER | 4,124 | 1,709 | 2,211 | 139 | 65 | 502 D | 41.4% | 53.6% | 3.4% |
| 1,042 | GOLDEN VALLEY | 531 | 405 | 88 | 17 | 21 | 317 R | 76.3% | 16.6% | 3.2% |
| 2,830 | GRANITE | 1,590 | 1,181 | 295 | 75 | 39 | 886 R | 74.3% | 18.6% | 4.7% |
| 16,673 | HILL | 6,558 | 3,392 | 2,760 | 278 | 128 | 632 R | 51.7% | 42.1% | 4.2% |
| 10,049 | JEFFERSON | 5,163 | 3,308 | 1,513 | 189 | 153 | 1,795 R | 64.1% | 29.3% | 3.7% |
| 2,329 | JUDITH BASIN | 1,394 | 1,057 | 278 | 31 | 28 | 779 R | 75.8% | 19.9% | 2.2% |
| 26,507 | LAKE | 11,448 | 6,441 | 3,884 | 762 | 361 | 2,557 R | 56.3% | 33.9% | 6.7% |
| 55,716 | LEWIS AND CLARK | 27,269 | 15,091 | 9,982 | 1,645 | 551 | 5,109 R | 55.3% | 36.6% | 6.0% |
| 2,158 | LIBERTY | 1,044 | 752 | 243 | 24 | 25 | 509 R | 72.0% | 23.3% | 2.3% |
| 18,837 | LINCOLN | 7,846 | 5,578 | 1,629 | 402 | 237 | 3,949 R | 71.1% | 20.8% | 5.1% |
| 1,977 | MCCONE | 1,142 | 827 | 267 | 34 | 14 | 560 R | 72.4% | 23.4% | 3.0% |
| 6,851 | MADISON | 3,656 | 2,656 | 758 | 161 | 81 | 1,898 R | 72.6% | 20.7% | 4.4% |
| 1,932 | MEAGHER | 935 | 698 | 176 | 27 | 34 | 522 R | 74.7% | 18.8% | 2.9% |
| 3,884 | MINERAL | 1,639 | 1,078 | 382 | 127 | 52 | 696 R | 65.8% | 23.3% | 7.7% |
| 95,802 | MISSOULA | 46,576 | 21,474 | 17,241 | 6,999 | 862 | 4,233 R | 46.1% | 37.0% | 15.0% |
| 4,497 | MUSSELSHELL | 2,207 | 1,582 | 512 | 53 | 60 | 1,070 R | 71.7% | 23.2% | 2.4% |
| 15,694 | PARK | 7,406 | 4,523 | 2,154 | 498 | 231 | 2,369 R | 61.1% | 29.1% | 6.7% |
| 493 | PETROLEUM | 306 | 254 | 36 | 6 | 10 | 218 R | 83.0% | 11.8% | 2.0% |
| 4,601 | PHILLIPS | 2,228 | 1,727 | 423 | 44 | 34 | 1,304 R | 77.5% | 19.0% | 2.0% |
| 6,424 | PONDERA | 2,896 | 1,948 | 792 | 96 | 60 | 1,156 R | 67.3% | 27.3% | 3.3% |
| 1,858 | POWDER RIVER | 1,008 | 860 | 115 | 21 | 12 | 745 R | 85.3% | 11.4% | 2.1% |
| 7,180 | POWELL | 2,832 | 1,971 | 638 | 129 | 94 | 1,333 R | 69.6% | 22.5% | 4.6% |
| 1,199 | PRAIRIE | 746 | 541 | 164 | 24 | 17 | 377 R | 72.5% | 22.0% | 3.2% |
| 36,070 | RAVALLI | 17,238 | 11,241 | 4,451 | 1,128 | 418 | 6,790 R | 65.2% | 25.8% | 6.5% |
| 9,667 | RICHLAND | 4,033 | 2,858 | 1,018 | 79 | 78 | 1,840 R | 70.9% | 25.2% | 2.0% |
| 10,620 | ROOSEVELT | 3,813 | 1,605 | 2,059 | 95 | 54 | 454 D | 42.1% | 54.0% | 2.5% |
| 9,383 | ROSEBUD | 3,423 | 1,826 | 1,394 | 130 | 73 | 432 R | 53.3% | 40.7% | 3.8% |
| 10,227 | SANDERS | 4,721 | 3,144 | 1,165 | 305 | 107 | 1,979 R | 66.6% | 24.7% | 6.5% |
| 4,105 | SHERIDAN | 1,965 | 1,176 | 702 | 62 | 25 | 474 R | 59.8% | 35.7% | 3.2% |
| 34,606 | SILVER BOW | 16,703 | 6,299 | 8,967 | 876 | 561 | 2,668 D | 37.7% | 53.7% | 5.2% |
| 8,195 | STILLWATER | 3,918 | 2,765 | 925 | 141 | 87 | 1,840 R | 70.6% | 23.6% | 3.6% |
| 3,609 | SWEET GRASS | 1,846 | 1,450 | 305 | 59 | 32 | 1,145 R | 78.5% | 16.5% | 3.2% |
| 6,445 | TETON | 3,314 | 2,294 | 847 | 102 | 71 | 1,447 R | 69.2% | 25.6% | 3.1% |
| 5,267 | TOOLE | 2,378 | 1,639 | 630 | 77 | 32 | 1,009 R | 68.9% | 26.5% | 3.2% |
| 861 | TREASURE | 479 | 344 | 106 | 12 | 17 | 238 R | 71.8% | 22.1% | 2.5% |
| 7,675 | VALLEY | 3,963 | 2,500 | 1,273 | 103 | 87 | 1,227 R | 63.1% | 32.1% | 2.6% |
| 2,259 | WHEATLAND | 999 | 708 | 243 | 21 | 27 | 465 R | 70.9% | 24.3% | 2.1% |
| 1,068 | WIBAUX | 518 | 369 | 121 | 16 | 12 | 248 R | 71.2% | 23.4% | 3.1% |
| 129,352 | YELLOWSTONE | 57,499 | 33,922 | 20,370 | 2,145 | 1,062 | 13,552 R | 59.0% | 35.4% | 3.7% |
| 902,195 | TOTAL | 410,997 | 240,178 | 137,126 | 24,437 | 9,256 | 103,052 R | 58.4% | 33.4% | 5.9% |

# MONTANA

## PRESIDENT 1996

| 1995 Census Pop. Est. | County | Total Vote | Republican | Democratic | Reform (Perot) | Other | Rep.-Dem. Plurality | Percentage of Total Vote | | |
|---|---|---|---|---|---|---|---|---|---|---|
| | | | | | | | | Rep. | Dem. | Reform |
| 9,008 | BEAVERHEAD | 4,019 | 2,414 | 1,164 | 412 | 29 | 1,250 R | 60.1% | 29.0% | 10.3% |
| 12,215 | BIG HORN | 4,239 | 1,336 | 2,453 | 424 | 26 | 1,117 D | 31.5% | 57.9% | 10.0% |
| 7,032 | BLAINE | 2,893 | 1,127 | 1,316 | 435 | 15 | 189 D | 39.0% | 45.5% | 15.0% |
| 3,885 | BROADWATER | 1,966 | 1,029 | 603 | 318 | 16 | 426 R | 52.3% | 30.7% | 16.2% |
| 9,029 | CARBON | 4,765 | 2,147 | 1,854 | 713 | 51 | 293 R | 45.1% | 38.9% | 15.0% |
| 1,464 | CARTER | 765 | 522 | 150 | 89 | 4 | 372 R | 68.2% | 19.6% | 11.6% |
| 81,091 | CASCADE | 35,042 | 14,291 | 15,707 | 4,749 | 295 | 1,416 D | 40.8% | 44.8% | 13.6% |
| 5,492 | CHOUTEAU | 3,160 | 1,660 | 1,039 | 434 | 27 | 621 R | 52.5% | 32.9% | 13.7% |
| 12,193 | CUSTER | 5,333 | 2,467 | 2,115 | 695 | 56 | 352 R | 46.3% | 39.7% | 13.0% |
| 2,140 | DANIELS | 1,314 | 558 | 510 | 240 | 6 | 48 R | 42.5% | 38.8% | 18.3% |
| 9,095 | DAWSON | 4,677 | 1,890 | 1,903 | 842 | 42 | 13 D | 40.4% | 40.7% | 18.0% |
| 10,149 | DEER LODGE | 5,018 | 883 | 3,331 | 772 | 32 | 2,448 D | 17.6% | 66.4% | 15.4% |
| 3,003 | FALLON | 1,516 | 778 | 452 | 276 | 10 | 326 R | 51.3% | 29.8% | 18.2% |
| 12,689 | FERGUS | 6,198 | 3,671 | 1,866 | 605 | 56 | 1,805 R | 59.2% | 30.1% | 9.8% |
| 69,512 | FLATHEAD | 32,238 | 16,542 | 10,452 | 4,786 | 458 | 6,090 R | 51.3% | 32.4% | 14.8% |
| 59,406 | GALLATIN | 29,083 | 14,559 | 10,972 | 3,146 | 406 | 3,587 R | 50.1% | 37.7% | 10.8% |
| 1,419 | GARFIELD | 746 | 562 | 107 | 69 | 8 | 455 R | 75.3% | 14.3% | 9.2% |
| 12,677 | GLACIER | 4,095 | 1,270 | 2,292 | 491 | 42 | 1,022 D | 31.0% | 56.0% | 12.0% |
| 980 | GOLDEN VALLEY | 490 | 284 | 128 | 73 | 5 | 156 R | 58.0% | 26.1% | 14.9% |
| 2,619 | GRANITE | 1,407 | 733 | 429 | 228 | 17 | 304 R | 52.1% | 30.5% | 16.2% |
| 17,668 | HILL | 7,115 | 2,601 | 3,517 | 950 | 47 | 916 D | 36.6% | 49.4% | 13.4% |
| 9,233 | JEFFERSON | 4,812 | 2,248 | 1,775 | 729 | 60 | 473 R | 46.7% | 36.9% | 15.1% |
| 2,281 | JUDITH BASIN | 1,338 | 753 | 452 | 126 | 7 | 301 R | 56.3% | 33.8% | 9.4% |
| 24,479 | LAKE | 10,857 | 4,723 | 4,195 | 1,804 | 135 | 528 R | 43.5% | 38.6% | 16.6% |
| 52,785 | LEWIS AND CLARK | 26,547 | 11,665 | 11,535 | 3,140 | 207 | 130 R | 43.9% | 43.5% | 11.8% |
| 2,246 | LIBERTY | 1,162 | 634 | 379 | 144 | 5 | 255 R | 54.6% | 32.6% | 12.4% |
| 18,678 | LINCOLN | 7,866 | 3,552 | 2,705 | 1,425 | 184 | 847 R | 45.2% | 34.4% | 18.1% |
| 2,121 | MCCONE | 1,256 | 615 | 390 | 244 | 7 | 225 R | 49.0% | 31.1% | 19.4% |
| 6,662 | MADISON | 3,496 | 1,984 | 955 | 516 | 41 | 1,029 R | 56.8% | 27.3% | 14.8% |
| 1,826 | MEAGHER | 936 | 505 | 281 | 142 | 8 | 224 R | 54.0% | 30.0% | 15.2% |
| 3,626 | MINERAL | 1,615 | 549 | 658 | 383 | 25 | 109 D | 34.0% | 40.7% | 23.7% |
| 87,130 | MISSOULA | 44,397 | 16,034 | 21,874 | 5,586 | 903 | 5,840 D | 36.1% | 49.3% | 12.6% |
| 4,491 | MUSSELSHELL | 2,077 | 1,121 | 652 | 291 | 13 | 469 R | 54.0% | 31.4% | 14.0% |
| 15,856 | PARK | 7,451 | 3,837 | 2,564 | 959 | 91 | 1,273 R | 51.5% | 34.4% | 12.9% |
| 527 | PETROLEUM | 290 | 186 | 62 | 36 | 6 | 124 R | 64.1% | 21.4% | 12.4% |
| 5,151 | PHILLIPS | 2,511 | 1,392 | 705 | 401 | 13 | 687 R | 55.4% | 28.1% | 16.0% |
| 6,274 | PONDERA | 2,963 | 1,438 | 1,123 | 383 | 19 | 315 R | 48.5% | 37.9% | 12.9% |
| 2,011 | POWDER RIVER | 1,048 | 663 | 236 | 137 | 12 | 427 R | 63.3% | 22.5% | 13.1% |
| 6,859 | POWELL | 2,807 | 1,274 | 952 | 531 | 50 | 322 R | 45.4% | 33.9% | 18.9% |
| 1,342 | PRAIRIE | 781 | 417 | 259 | 99 | 6 | 158 R | 53.4% | 33.2% | 12.7% |
| 32,230 | RAVALLI | 16,251 | 8,138 | 5,200 | 2,731 | 182 | 2,938 R | 50.1% | 32.0% | 16.8% |
| 10,351 | RICHLAND | 4,568 | 2,021 | 1,614 | 906 | 27 | 407 R | 44.2% | 35.3% | 19.8% |
| 11,243 | ROOSEVELT | 3,998 | 1,209 | 2,118 | 645 | 26 | 909 D | 30.2% | 53.0% | 16.1% |
| 10,881 | ROSEBUD | 3,686 | 1,413 | 1,681 | 547 | 45 | 268 D | 38.3% | 45.6% | 14.8% |
| 10,089 | SANDERS | 4,661 | 2,043 | 1,573 | 990 | 55 | 470 R | 43.8% | 33.7% | 21.2% |
| 4,431 | SHERIDAN | 2,435 | 832 | 1,187 | 408 | 8 | 355 D | 34.2% | 48.7% | 16.8% |
| 34,795 | SILVER BOW | 17,683 | 3,909 | 11,199 | 2,447 | 128 | 7,290 D | 22.1% | 63.3% | 13.8% |
| 7,466 | STILLWATER | 3,800 | 1,871 | 1,282 | 618 | 29 | 589 R | 49.2% | 33.7% | 16.3% |
| 3,374 | SWEET GRASS | 1,782 | 1,109 | 469 | 186 | 18 | 640 R | 62.2% | 26.3% | 10.4% |
| 6,371 | TETON | 3,327 | 1,701 | 1,188 | 416 | 22 | 513 R | 51.1% | 35.7% | 12.5% |
| 5,103 | TOOLE | 2,482 | 1,203 | 874 | 386 | 19 | 329 R | 48.5% | 35.2% | 15.6% |
| 837 | TREASURE | 498 | 237 | 171 | 87 | 3 | 66 R | 47.6% | 34.3% | 17.5% |
| 8,462 | VALLEY | 4,207 | 1,838 | 1,674 | 645 | 50 | 164 R | 43.7% | 39.8% | 15.3% |
| 2,425 | WHEATLAND | 1,088 | 563 | 391 | 127 | 7 | 172 R | 51.7% | 35.9% | 11.7% |
| 1,170 | WIBAUX | 613 | 284 | 197 | 128 | 4 | 87 R | 46.3% | 32.1% | 20.9% |
| 124,709 | YELLOWSTONE | 55,893 | 26,367 | 22,992 | 6,139 | 395 | 3,375 R | 47.2% | 41.1% | 11.0% |
| 870,281 | TOTAL | 407,261 | 179,652 | 167,922 | 55,229 | 4,458 | 11,730 R | 44.1% | 41.2% | 13.6% |

# MONTANA

## PRESIDENT 1992

| 1990 Census Population | County | Total Vote | Republican | Democratic | Perot | Other | Plurality | Percentage Total Vote | | |
|---:|---|---:|---:|---:|---:|---:|---:|---:|---:|---:|
| | | | | | | | | Rep. | Dem. | Perot |
| 8,424 | BEAVERHEAD | 4,160 | 1,746 | 1,098 | 1,202 | 114 | 544 R | 42.0% | 26.4% | 28.9% |
| 11,337 | BIG HORN | 4,394 | 1,377 | 2,154 | 840 | 23 | 777 D | 31.3% | 49.0% | 19.1% |
| 6,728 | BLAINE | 3,046 | 971 | 1,355 | 699 | 21 | 384 D | 31.9% | 44.5% | 22.9% |
| 3,318 | BROADWATER | 1,842 | 830 | 491 | 505 | 16 | 325 R | 45.1% | 26.7% | 27.4% |
| 8,080 | CARBON | 4,620 | 1,562 | 1,549 | 1,482 | 27 | 13 R | 33.8% | 33.5% | 32.1% |
| 1,503 | CARTER | 874 | 497 | 154 | 220 | 3 | 277 R | 56.9% | 17.6% | 25.2% |
| 77,691 | CASCADE | 36,580 | 12,494 | 14,719 | 9,151 | 216 | 2,225 D | 34.2% | 40.2% | 25.0% |
| 5,452 | CHOUTEAU | 3,236 | 1,380 | 959 | 870 | 27 | 421 R | 42.6% | 29.6% | 26.9% |
| 11,697 | CUSTER | 5,611 | 2,105 | 1,968 | 1,505 | 33 | 137 R | 37.5% | 35.1% | 26.8% |
| 2,266 | DANIELS | 1,363 | 496 | 457 | 402 | 8 | 39 R | 36.4% | 33.5% | 29.5% |
| 9,505 | DAWSON | 4,850 | 1,679 | 1,785 | 1,370 | 16 | 106 D | 34.6% | 36.8% | 28.2% |
| 10,278 | DEER LODGE | 5,269 | 832 | 3,174 | 1,207 | 56 | 1,967 D | 15.8% | 60.2% | 22.9% |
| 3,103 | FALLON | 1,608 | 731 | 446 | 427 | 4 | 285 R | 45.5% | 27.7% | 26.6% |
| 12,083 | FERGUS | 6,491 | 2,736 | 1,615 | 1,934 | 206 | 802 R | 42.2% | 24.9% | 29.8% |
| 59,218 | FLATHEAD | 31,417 | 11,699 | 9,746 | 9,109 | 863 | 1,953 R | 37.2% | 31.0% | 29.0% |
| 50,463 | GALLATIN | 28,787 | 11,109 | 9,535 | 7,711 | 432 | 1,574 R | 38.6% | 33.1% | 26.8% |
| 1,589 | GARFIELD | 819 | 403 | 125 | 281 | 10 | 122 R | 49.2% | 15.3% | 34.3% |
| 12,121 | GLACIER | 4,323 | 1,222 | 2,076 | 997 | 28 | 854 D | 28.3% | 48.0% | 23.1% |
| 912 | GOLDEN VALLEY | 496 | 192 | 142 | 157 | 5 | 35 R | 38.7% | 28.6% | 31.7% |
| 2,548 | GRANITE | 1,323 | 556 | 358 | 386 | 23 | 170 R | 42.0% | 27.1% | 29.2% |
| 17,654 | HILL | 8,082 | 2,408 | 3,618 | 2,017 | 39 | 1,210 D | 29.8% | 44.8% | 25.0% |
| 7,939 | JEFFERSON | 4,225 | 1,541 | 1,415 | 1,172 | 97 | 126 R | 36.5% | 33.5% | 27.7% |
| 2,282 | JUDITH BASIN | 1,447 | 610 | 409 | 415 | 13 | 195 R | 42.2% | 28.3% | 28.7% |
| 21,041 | LAKE | 10,553 | 3,596 | 3,938 | 2,878 | 141 | 342 D | 34.1% | 37.3% | 27.3% |
| 47,495 | LEWIS AND CLARK | 26,181 | 9,351 | 11,117 | 5,560 | 153 | 1,766 D | 35.7% | 42.5% | 21.2% |
| 2,295 | LIBERTY | 1,211 | 512 | 321 | 363 | 15 | 149 R | 42.3% | 26.5% | 30.0% |
| 17,481 | LINCOLN | 8,378 | 2,799 | 2,765 | 2,637 | 177 | 34 R | 33.4% | 33.0% | 31.5% |
| 2,276 | MCCONE | 1,354 | 528 | 424 | 395 | 7 | 104 R | 39.0% | 31.3% | 29.2% |
| 5,989 | MADISON | 3,299 | 1,415 | 779 | 1,043 | 62 | 372 R | 42.9% | 23.6% | 31.6% |
| 1,819 | MEAGHER | 1,002 | 422 | 260 | 310 | 10 | 112 R | 42.1% | 25.9% | 30.9% |
| 3,315 | MINERAL | 1,635 | 403 | 664 | 543 | 25 | 121 D | 24.6% | 40.6% | 33.2% |
| 78,687 | MISSOULA | 43,307 | 12,898 | 20,347 | 9,735 | 327 | 7,449 D | 29.8% | 47.0% | 22.5% |
| 4,106 | MUSSELSHELL | 2,228 | 876 | 648 | 691 | 13 | 185 R | 39.3% | 29.1% | 31.0% |
| 14,562 | PARK | 7,483 | 2,846 | 2,258 | 2,182 | 197 | 588 R | 38.0% | 30.2% | 29.2% |
| 519 | PETROLEUM | 296 | 135 | 61 | 95 | 5 | 40 R | 45.6% | 20.6% | 32.1% |
| 5,163 | PHILLIPS | 2,625 | 1,026 | 634 | 949 | 16 | 77 R | 39.1% | 24.2% | 36.2% |
| 6,433 | PONDERA | 3,165 | 1,252 | 1,046 | 855 | 12 | 206 R | 39.6% | 33.0% | 27.0% |
| 2,090 | POWDER RIVER | 1,156 | 547 | 258 | 340 | 11 | 207 R | 47.3% | 22.3% | 29.4% |
| 6,620 | POWELL | 2,938 | 1,058 | 989 | 872 | 19 | 69 R | 36.0% | 33.7% | 29.7% |
| 1,383 | PRAIRIE | 856 | 412 | 260 | 179 | 5 | 152 R | 48.1% | 30.4% | 20.9% |
| 25,010 | RAVALLI | 15,020 | 5,392 | 4,644 | 4,573 | 411 | 748 R | 35.9% | 30.9% | 30.4% |
| 10,716 | RICHLAND | 4,748 | 1,760 | 1,440 | 1,525 | 23 | 235 R | 37.1% | 30.3% | 32.1% |
| 10,999 | ROOSEVELT | 4,193 | 1,212 | 1,827 | 1,089 | 65 | 615 D | 28.9% | 43.6% | 26.0% |
| 10,505 | ROSEBUD | 3,918 | 1,130 | 1,669 | 1,099 | 20 | 539 D | 28.8% | 42.6% | 28.1% |
| 8,669 | SANDERS | 4,506 | 1,361 | 1,689 | 1,378 | 78 | 311 D | 30.2% | 37.5% | 30.6% |
| 4,732 | SHERIDAN | 2,663 | 795 | 1,077 | 782 | 9 | 282 D | 29.9% | 40.4% | 29.4% |
| 33,941 | SILVER BOW | 18,146 | 3,491 | 9,960 | 4,570 | 125 | 5,390 D | 19.2% | 54.9% | 25.2% |
| 6,536 | STILLWATER | 3,640 | 1,390 | 1,178 | 1,056 | 16 | 212 R | 38.2% | 32.4% | 29.0% |
| 3,154 | SWEET GRASS | 1,802 | 880 | 395 | 507 | 20 | 373 R | 48.8% | 21.9% | 28.1% |
| 6,271 | TETON | 3,405 | 1,364 | 1,043 | 969 | 29 | 321 R | 40.1% | 30.6% | 28.5% |
| 5,046 | TOOLE | 2,717 | 943 | 854 | 903 | 17 | 40 R | 34.7% | 31.4% | 33.2% |
| 874 | TREASURE | 547 | 206 | 157 | 178 | 6 | 28 R | 37.7% | 28.7% | 32.5% |
| 8,239 | VALLEY | 4,568 | 1,497 | 1,715 | 1,320 | 36 | 218 D | 32.8% | 37.5% | 28.9% |
| 2,246 | WHEATLAND | 1,150 | 478 | 384 | 284 | 4 | 94 R | 41.6% | 33.4% | 24.7% |
| 1,191 | WIBAUX | 607 | 234 | 195 | 173 | 5 | 39 R | 38.6% | 32.1% | 28.5% |
| 113,419 | YELLOWSTONE | 56,451 | 22,822 | 20,163 | 13,133 | 333 | 2,659 R | 40.4% | 35.7% | 23.3% |
| 799,065 | TOTAL | 410,611 | 144,207 | 154,507 | 107,225 | 4,672 | 10,300 D | 35.1% | 37.6% | 26.1% |

# MONTANA

## PRESIDENT 1988

| 1980 Census Population | County | Total Vote | Republican | Democratic | Other | Rep.-Dem. Plurality | Percentage | | | |
|---|---|---|---|---|---|---|---|---|---|---|
| | | | | | | | Total Vote | | Major Vote | |
| | | | | | | | Rep. | Dem. | Rep. | Dem. |
| 8,186 | BEAVERHEAD | 3,998 | 2,668 | 1,274 | 56 | 1,394 R | 66.7% | 31.9% | 67.7% | 32.3% |
| 11,096 | BIG HORN | 3,984 | 1,711 | 2,233 | 40 | 522 D | 42.9% | 56.0% | 43.4% | 56.6% |
| 6,999 | BLAINE | 2,912 | 1,402 | 1,460 | 50 | 58 D | 48.1% | 50.1% | 49.0% | 51.0% |
| 3,267 | BROADWATER | 1,683 | 1,054 | 592 | 37 | 462 R | 62.6% | 35.2% | 64.0% | 36.0% |
| 8,099 | CARBON | 4,470 | 2,360 | 2,039 | 71 | 321 R | 52.8% | 45.6% | 53.6% | 46.4% |
| 1,799 | CARTER | 942 | 686 | 242 | 14 | 444 R | 72.8% | 25.7% | 73.9% | 26.1% |
| 80,696 | CASCADE | 32,124 | 15,946 | 15,718 | 460 | 228 R | 49.6% | 48.9% | 50.4% | 49.6% |
| 6,092 | CHOUTEAU | 3,219 | 1,980 | 1,166 | 73 | 814 R | 61.5% | 36.2% | 62.9% | 37.1% |
| 13,109 | CUSTER | 5,462 | 3,007 | 2,343 | 112 | 664 R | 55.1% | 42.9% | 56.2% | 43.8% |
| 2,835 | DANIELS | 1,395 | 802 | 571 | 22 | 231 R | 57.5% | 40.9% | 58.4% | 41.6% |
| 11,805 | DAWSON | 4,886 | 2,658 | 2,120 | 108 | 538 R | 54.4% | 43.4% | 55.6% | 44.4% |
| 12,518 | DEER LODGE | 4,406 | 1,168 | 3,185 | 53 | 2,017 D | 26.5% | 72.3% | 26.8% | 73.2% |
| 3,763 | FALLON | 1,636 | 1,002 | 612 | 22 | 390 R | 61.2% | 37.4% | 62.1% | 37.9% |
| 13,076 | FERGUS | 6,116 | 3,948 | 2,052 | 116 | 1,896 R | 64.6% | 33.6% | 65.8% | 34.2% |
| 51,966 | FLATHEAD | 25,225 | 14,461 | 10,202 | 562 | 4,259 R | 57.3% | 40.4% | 58.6% | 41.4% |
| 42,865 | GALLATIN | 23,205 | 13,214 | 9,527 | 464 | 3,687 R | 56.9% | 41.1% | 58.1% | 41.9% |
| 1,656 | GARFIELD | 851 | 631 | 196 | 24 | 435 R | 74.1% | 23.0% | 76.3% | 23.7% |
| 10,628 | GLACIER | 4,004 | 1,728 | 2,151 | 125 | 423 D | 43.2% | 53.7% | 44.5% | 55.5% |
| 1,026 | GOLDEN VALLEY | 543 | 335 | 203 | 5 | 132 R | 61.7% | 37.4% | 62.3% | 37.7% |
| 2,700 | GRANITE | 1,326 | 789 | 511 | 26 | 278 R | 59.5% | 38.5% | 60.7% | 39.3% |
| 17,985 | HILL | 7,791 | 3,467 | 4,219 | 105 | 752 D | 44.5% | 54.2% | 45.1% | 54.9% |
| 7,029 | JEFFERSON | 3,837 | 2,007 | 1,746 | 84 | 261 R | 52.3% | 45.5% | 53.5% | 46.5% |
| 2,646 | JUDITH BASIN | 1,516 | 902 | 590 | 24 | 312 R | 59.5% | 38.9% | 60.5% | 39.5% |
| 19,056 | LAKE | 9,150 | 4,883 | 4,109 | 158 | 774 R | 53.4% | 44.9% | 54.3% | 45.7% |
| 43,039 | LEWIS AND CLARK | 23,334 | 10,946 | 11,932 | 456 | 986 D | 46.9% | 51.1% | 47.8% | 52.2% |
| 2,329 | LIBERTY | 1,208 | 771 | 418 | 19 | 353 R | 63.8% | 34.6% | 64.8% | 35.2% |
| 17,752 | LINCOLN | 7,294 | 3,500 | 3,601 | 193 | 101 D | 48.0% | 49.4% | 49.3% | 50.7% |
| 2,702 | MCCONE | 1,399 | 814 | 567 | 18 | 247 R | 58.2% | 40.5% | 58.9% | 41.1% |
| 5,448 | MADISON | 2,980 | 2,045 | 878 | 57 | 1,167 R | 68.6% | 29.5% | 70.0% | 30.0% |
| 2,154 | MEAGHER | 1,009 | 656 | 337 | 16 | 319 R | 65.0% | 33.4% | 66.1% | 33.9% |
| 3,675 | MINERAL | 1,428 | 616 | 789 | 23 | 173 D | 43.1% | 55.3% | 43.8% | 56.2% |
| 76,016 | MISSOULA | 35,669 | 15,965 | 19,178 | 526 | 3,213 D | 44.8% | 53.8% | 45.4% | 54.6% |
| 4,428 | MUSSELSHELL | 2,204 | 1,280 | 898 | 26 | 382 R | 58.1% | 40.7% | 58.8% | 41.2% |
| 12,660 | PARK | 6,465 | 3,823 | 2,526 | 116 | 1,297 R | 59.1% | 39.1% | 60.2% | 39.8% |
| 655 | PETROLEUM | 302 | 204 | 91 | 7 | 113 R | 67.5% | 30.1% | 69.2% | 30.8% |
| 5,367 | PHILLIPS | 2,426 | 1,462 | 905 | 59 | 557 R | 60.3% | 37.3% | 61.8% | 38.2% |
| 6,731 | PONDERA | 3,114 | 1,795 | 1,245 | 74 | 550 R | 57.6% | 40.0% | 59.0% | 41.0% |
| 2,520 | POWDER RIVER | 1,232 | 815 | 395 | 22 | 420 R | 66.2% | 32.1% | 67.4% | 32.6% |
| 6,958 | POWELL | 2,795 | 1,574 | 1,174 | 47 | 400 R | 56.3% | 42.0% | 57.3% | 42.7% |
| 1,836 | PRAIRIE | 900 | 541 | 343 | 16 | 198 R | 60.1% | 38.1% | 61.2% | 38.8% |
| 22,493 | RAVALLI | 12,490 | 7,418 | 4,763 | 309 | 2,655 R | 59.4% | 38.1% | 60.9% | 39.1% |
| 12,243 | RICHLAND | 4,546 | 2,628 | 1,824 | 94 | 804 R | 57.8% | 40.1% | 59.0% | 41.0% |
| 10,467 | ROOSEVELT | 4,118 | 1,957 | 2,083 | 78 | 126 D | 47.5% | 50.6% | 48.4% | 51.6% |
| 9,899 | ROSEBUD | 3,792 | 1,822 | 1,869 | 101 | 47 D | 48.0% | 49.3% | 49.4% | 50.6% |
| 8,675 | SANDERS | 4,200 | 2,152 | 1,959 | 89 | 193 R | 51.2% | 46.6% | 52.3% | 47.7% |
| 5,414 | SHERIDAN | 2,763 | 1,381 | 1,354 | 28 | 27 R | 50.0% | 49.0% | 50.5% | 49.5% |
| 38,092 | SILVER BOW | 16,687 | 5,043 | 11,422 | 222 | 6,379 D | 30.2% | 68.4% | 30.6% | 69.4% |
| 5,598 | STILLWATER | 3,379 | 1,920 | 1,407 | 52 | 513 R | 56.8% | 41.6% | 57.7% | 42.3% |
| 3,216 | SWEET GRASS | 1,733 | 1,242 | 462 | 29 | 780 R | 71.7% | 26.7% | 72.9% | 27.1% |
| 6,491 | TETON | 3,244 | 1,876 | 1,303 | 65 | 573 R | 57.8% | 40.2% | 59.0% | 41.0% |
| 5,559 | TOOLE | 2,634 | 1,505 | 1,070 | 59 | 435 R | 57.1% | 40.6% | 58.4% | 41.6% |
| 981 | TREASURE | 536 | 291 | 231 | 14 | 60 R | 54.3% | 43.1% | 55.7% | 44.3% |
| 10,250 | VALLEY | 4,706 | 2,467 | 2,163 | 76 | 304 R | 52.4% | 46.0% | 53.3% | 46.7% |
| 2,359 | WHEATLAND | 1,130 | 667 | 443 | 20 | 224 R | 59.0% | 39.2% | 60.1% | 39.9% |
| 1,476 | WIBAUX | 629 | 358 | 258 | 13 | 100 R | 56.9% | 41.0% | 58.1% | 41.9% |
| 108,035 | YELLOWSTONE | 50,647 | 28,069 | 21,987 | 591 | 6,082 R | 55.4% | 43.4% | 56.1% | 43.9% |
| 786,690 | TOTAL | 365,674 | 190,412 | 168,936 | 6,326 | 21,476 R | 52.1% | 46.2% | 53.0% | 47.0% |

# MONTANA

## PRESIDENT 1984

| 1980 Census Population | County | Total Vote | Republican | Democratic | Other | Rep.-Dem. Plurality | Percentage Total Vote Rep. | Dem. | Major Vote Rep. | Dem. |
|---|---|---|---|---|---|---|---|---|---|---|
| 8,186 | BEAVERHEAD | 4,035 | 3,044 | 942 | 49 | 2,102 R | 75.4% | 23.3% | 76.4% | 23.6% |
| 11,096 | BIG HORN | 5,110 | 2,390 | 2,681 | 39 | 291 D | 46.8% | 52.5% | 47.1% | 52.9% |
| 6,999 | BLAINE | 2,997 | 1,736 | 1,229 | 32 | 507 R | 57.9% | 41.0% | 58.5% | 41.5% |
| 3,267 | BROADWATER | 1,830 | 1,345 | 458 | 27 | 887 R | 73.5% | 25.0% | 74.6% | 25.4% |
| 8,099 | CARBON | 4,587 | 2,877 | 1,657 | 53 | 1,220 R | 62.7% | 36.1% | 63.5% | 36.5% |
| 1,799 | CARTER | 1,028 | 823 | 194 | 11 | 629 R | 80.1% | 18.9% | 80.9% | 19.1% |
| 80,696 | CASCADE | 34,505 | 19,846 | 14,252 | 407 | 5,594 R | 57.5% | 41.3% | 58.2% | 41.8% |
| 6,092 | CHOUTEAU | 3,360 | 2,425 | 896 | 39 | 1,529 R | 72.2% | 26.7% | 73.0% | 27.0% |
| 13,109 | CUSTER | 5,919 | 3,879 | 1,982 | 58 | 1,897 R | 65.5% | 33.5% | 66.2% | 33.8% |
| 2,835 | DANIELS | 1,477 | 984 | 473 | 20 | 511 R | 66.6% | 32.0% | 67.5% | 32.5% |
| 11,805 | DAWSON | 5,314 | 3,468 | 1,776 | 70 | 1,692 R | 65.3% | 33.4% | 66.1% | 33.9% |
| 12,518 | DEER LODGE | 5,505 | 1,901 | 3,539 | 65 | 1,638 D | 34.5% | 64.3% | 34.9% | 65.1% |
| 3,763 | FALLON | 1,829 | 1,237 | 569 | 23 | 668 R | 67.6% | 31.1% | 68.5% | 31.5% |
| 13,076 | FERGUS | 6,459 | 4,585 | 1,804 | 70 | 2,781 R | 71.0% | 27.9% | 71.8% | 28.2% |
| 51,966 | FLATHEAD | 25,803 | 17,012 | 8,310 | 481 | 8,702 R | 65.9% | 32.2% | 67.2% | 32.8% |
| 42,865 | GALLATIN | 24,140 | 15,643 | 8,163 | 334 | 7,480 R | 64.8% | 33.8% | 65.7% | 34.3% |
| 1,656 | GARFIELD | 911 | 770 | 134 | 7 | 636 R | 84.5% | 14.7% | 85.2% | 14.8% |
| 10,628 | GLACIER | 4,435 | 2,228 | 2,167 | 40 | 61 R | 50.2% | 48.9% | 50.7% | 49.3% |
| 1,026 | GOLDEN VALLEY | 600 | 384 | 211 | 5 | 173 R | 64.0% | 35.2% | 64.5% | 35.5% |
| 2,700 | GRANITE | 1,322 | 880 | 417 | 25 | 463 R | 66.6% | 31.5% | 67.8% | 32.2% |
| 17,985 | HILL | 8,390 | 4,635 | 3,657 | 98 | 978 R | 55.2% | 43.6% | 55.9% | 44.1% |
| 7,029 | JEFFERSON | 3,618 | 2,226 | 1,324 | 68 | 902 R | 61.5% | 36.6% | 62.7% | 37.3% |
| 2,646 | JUDITH BASIN | 1,550 | 1,050 | 483 | 17 | 567 R | 67.7% | 31.2% | 68.5% | 31.5% |
| 19,056 | LAKE | 9,348 | 5,754 | 3,473 | 121 | 2,281 R | 61.6% | 37.2% | 62.4% | 37.6% |
| 43,039 | LEWIS AND CLARK | 22,626 | 13,569 | 8,768 | 289 | 4,801 R | 60.0% | 38.8% | 60.7% | 39.3% |
| 2,329 | LIBERTY | 1,229 | 895 | 323 | 11 | 572 R | 72.8% | 26.3% | 73.5% | 26.5% |
| 17,752 | LINCOLN | 7,184 | 4,080 | 2,959 | 145 | 1,121 R | 56.8% | 41.2% | 58.0% | 42.0% |
| 2,702 | MCCONE | 1,497 | 1,015 | 459 | 23 | 556 R | 67.8% | 30.7% | 68.9% | 31.1% |
| 5,448 | MADISON | 3,069 | 2,308 | 708 | 53 | 1,600 R | 75.2% | 23.1% | 76.5% | 23.5% |
| 2,154 | MEAGHER | 1,069 | 771 | 283 | 15 | 488 R | 72.1% | 26.5% | 73.1% | 26.9% |
| 3,675 | MINERAL | 1,704 | 943 | 718 | 43 | 225 R | 55.3% | 42.1% | 56.8% | 43.2% |
| 76,016 | MISSOULA | 36,937 | 19,777 | 16,540 | 620 | 3,237 R | 53.5% | 44.8% | 54.5% | 45.5% |
| 4,428 | MUSSELSHELL | 2,359 | 1,541 | 781 | 37 | 760 R | 65.3% | 33.1% | 66.4% | 33.6% |
| 12,660 | PARK | 6,581 | 4,115 | 2,387 | 79 | 1,728 R | 62.5% | 36.3% | 63.3% | 36.7% |
| 655 | PETROLEUM | 347 | 258 | 86 | 3 | 172 R | 74.4% | 24.8% | 75.0% | 25.0% |
| 5,367 | PHILLIPS | 2,749 | 1,934 | 787 | 28 | 1,147 R | 70.4% | 28.6% | 71.1% | 28.9% |
| 6,731 | PONDERA | 3,316 | 2,239 | 1,039 | 38 | 1,200 R | 67.5% | 31.3% | 68.3% | 31.7% |
| 2,520 | POWDER RIVER | 1,429 | 1,066 | 346 | 17 | 720 R | 74.6% | 24.2% | 75.5% | 24.5% |
| 6,958 | POWELL | 3,012 | 1,877 | 1,066 | 69 | 811 R | 62.3% | 35.4% | 63.8% | 36.2% |
| 1,836 | PRAIRIE | 991 | 693 | 289 | 9 | 404 R | 69.9% | 29.2% | 70.6% | 29.4% |
| 22,493 | RAVALLI | 12,154 | 8,161 | 3,825 | 168 | 4,336 R | 67.1% | 31.5% | 68.1% | 31.9% |
| 12,243 | RICHLAND | 5,281 | 3,847 | 1,382 | 52 | 2,465 R | 72.8% | 26.2% | 73.6% | 26.4% |
| 10,467 | ROOSEVELT | 4,464 | 2,431 | 1,962 | 71 | 469 R | 54.5% | 44.0% | 55.3% | 44.7% |
| 9,899 | ROSEBUD | 4,402 | 2,413 | 1,920 | 69 | 493 R | 54.8% | 43.6% | 55.7% | 44.3% |
| 8,675 | SANDERS | 4,204 | 2,467 | 1,654 | 83 | 813 R | 58.7% | 39.3% | 59.9% | 40.1% |
| 5,414 | SHERIDAN | 2,879 | 1,774 | 1,087 | 18 | 687 R | 61.6% | 37.8% | 62.0% | 38.0% |
| 38,092 | SILVER BOW | 18,010 | 6,637 | 11,095 | 278 | 4,458 D | 36.9% | 61.6% | 37.4% | 62.6% |
| 5,598 | STILLWATER | 3,258 | 2,118 | 1,100 | 40 | 1,018 R | 65.0% | 33.8% | 65.8% | 34.2% |
| 3,216 | SWEET GRASS | 1,803 | 1,417 | 378 | 8 | 1,039 R | 78.6% | 21.0% | 78.9% | 21.1% |
| 6,491 | TETON | 3,384 | 2,257 | 1,102 | 25 | 1,155 R | 66.7% | 32.6% | 67.2% | 32.8% |
| 5,559 | TOOLE | 2,768 | 1,949 | 789 | 30 | 1,160 R | 70.4% | 28.5% | 71.2% | 28.8% |
| 981 | TREASURE | 576 | 353 | 209 | 14 | 144 R | 61.3% | 36.3% | 62.8% | 37.2% |
| 10,250 | VALLEY | 5,046 | 3,123 | 1,849 | 74 | 1,274 R | 61.9% | 36.6% | 62.8% | 37.2% |
| 2,359 | WHEATLAND | 1,173 | 753 | 407 | 13 | 346 R | 64.2% | 34.7% | 64.9% | 35.1% |
| 1,476 | WIBAUX | 651 | 423 | 216 | 12 | 207 R | 65.0% | 33.2% | 66.2% | 33.8% |
| 108,035 | YELLOWSTONE | 54,153 | 34,124 | 19,437 | 592 | 14,687 R | 63.0% | 35.9% | 63.7% | 36.3% |
| 786,690 | TOTAL | 384,377 | 232,450 | 146,742 | 5,185 | 85,708 R | 60.5% | 38.2% | 61.3% | 38.7% |

# MONTANA

## PRESIDENT 1980

| 1980 Census Population | County | Total Vote | Republican | Democratic | Other | Rep.-Dem. Plurality | Percentage | | | |
|---|---|---|---|---|---|---|---|---|---|---|
| | | | | | | | Total Vote | | Major Vote | |
| | | | | | | | Rep. | Dem. | Rep. | Dem. |
| 8,186 | BEAVERHEAD | 4,103 | 2,955 | 842 | 306 | 2,113 R | 72.0% | 20.5% | 77.8% | 22.2% |
| 11,096 | BIG HORN | 3,735 | 1,730 | 1,644 | 361 | 86 R | 46.3% | 44.0% | 51.3% | 48.7% |
| 6,999 | BLAINE | 2,995 | 1,686 | 1,107 | 202 | 579 R | 56.3% | 37.0% | 60.4% | 39.6% |
| 3,267 | BROADWATER | 1,564 | 1,052 | 401 | 111 | 651 R | 67.3% | 25.6% | 72.4% | 27.6% |
| 8,099 | CARBON | 4,363 | 2,471 | 1,468 | 424 | 1,003 R | 56.6% | 33.6% | 62.7% | 37.3% |
| 1,799 | CARTER | 1,058 | 766 | 237 | 55 | 529 R | 72.4% | 22.4% | 76.4% | 23.6% |
| 80,696 | CASCADE | 32,234 | 17,664 | 11,105 | 3,465 | 6,559 R | 54.8% | 34.5% | 61.4% | 38.6% |
| 6,092 | CHOUTEAU | 3,583 | 2,448 | 853 | 282 | 1,595 R | 68.3% | 23.8% | 74.2% | 25.8% |
| 13,109 | CUSTER | 5,816 | 3,533 | 1,822 | 461 | 1,711 R | 60.7% | 31.3% | 66.0% | 34.0% |
| 2,835 | DANIELS | 1,666 | 1,086 | 483 | 97 | 603 R | 65.2% | 29.0% | 69.2% | 30.8% |
| 11,805 | DAWSON | 5,118 | 3,045 | 1,543 | 530 | 1,502 R | 59.5% | 30.1% | 66.4% | 33.6% |
| 12,518 | DEER LODGE | 5,638 | 1,905 | 3,077 | 656 | 1,172 D | 33.8% | 54.6% | 38.2% | 61.8% |
| 3,763 | FALLON | 1,920 | 1,286 | 512 | 122 | 774 R | 67.0% | 26.7% | 71.5% | 28.5% |
| 13,076 | FERGUS | 6,852 | 4,455 | 1,840 | 557 | 2,615 R | 65.0% | 26.9% | 70.8% | 29.2% |
| 51,966 | FLATHEAD | 23,767 | 15,102 | 6,349 | 2,316 | 8,753 R | 63.5% | 26.7% | 70.4% | 29.6% |
| 42,865 | GALLATIN | 21,726 | 12,738 | 5,747 | 3,241 | 6,991 R | 58.6% | 26.5% | 68.9% | 31.1% |
| 1,656 | GARFIELD | 974 | 760 | 169 | 45 | 591 R | 78.0% | 17.4% | 81.8% | 18.2% |
| 10,628 | GLACIER | 4,093 | 2,283 | 1,394 | 416 | 889 R | 55.8% | 34.1% | 62.1% | 37.9% |
| 1,026 | GOLDEN VALLEY | 556 | 362 | 155 | 39 | 207 R | 65.1% | 27.9% | 70.0% | 30.0% |
| 2,700 | GRANITE | 1,371 | 811 | 439 | 121 | 372 R | 59.2% | 32.0% | 64.9% | 35.1% |
| 17,985 | HILL | 8,089 | 4,448 | 2,875 | 766 | 1,573 R | 55.0% | 35.5% | 60.7% | 39.3% |
| 7,029 | JEFFERSON | 3,223 | 1,841 | 1,055 | 327 | 786 R | 57.1% | 32.7% | 63.6% | 36.4% |
| 2,646 | JUDITH BASIN | 1,627 | 1,030 | 480 | 117 | 550 R | 63.3% | 29.5% | 68.2% | 31.8% |
| 19,056 | LAKE | 8,532 | 5,083 | 2,615 | 834 | 2,468 R | 59.6% | 30.6% | 66.0% | 34.0% |
| 43,039 | LEWIS AND CLARK | 21,212 | 12,128 | 6,815 | 2,269 | 5,313 R | 57.2% | 32.1% | 64.0% | 36.0% |
| 2,329 | LIBERTY | 1,256 | 872 | 283 | 101 | 589 R | 69.4% | 22.5% | 75.5% | 24.5% |
| 17,752 | LINCOLN | 7,348 | 4,202 | 2,422 | 724 | 1,780 R | 57.2% | 33.0% | 63.4% | 36.6% |
| 2,702 | MCCONE | 1,471 | 1,000 | 349 | 122 | 651 R | 68.0% | 23.7% | 74.1% | 25.9% |
| 5,448 | MADISON | 3,145 | 2,220 | 676 | 249 | 1,544 R | 70.6% | 21.5% | 76.7% | 23.3% |
| 2,154 | MEAGHER | 990 | 689 | 247 | 54 | 442 R | 69.6% | 24.9% | 73.6% | 26.4% |
| 3,675 | MINERAL | 1,657 | 800 | 660 | 197 | 140 R | 48.3% | 39.8% | 54.8% | 45.2% |
| 76,016 | MISSOULA | 34,594 | 16,161 | 13,115 | 5,318 | 3,046 R | 46.7% | 37.9% | 55.2% | 44.8% |
| 4,428 | MUSSELSHELL | 2,204 | 1,279 | 784 | 141 | 495 R | 58.0% | 35.6% | 62.0% | 38.0% |
| 12,660 | PARK | 6,195 | 3,929 | 1,663 | 603 | 2,266 R | 63.4% | 26.8% | 70.3% | 29.7% |
| 655 | PETROLEUM | 341 | 225 | 90 | 26 | 135 R | 66.0% | 26.4% | 71.4% | 28.6% |
| 5,367 | PHILLIPS | 2,653 | 1,723 | 745 | 185 | 978 R | 64.9% | 28.1% | 69.8% | 30.2% |
| 6,731 | PONDERA | 3,432 | 2,270 | 897 | 265 | 1,373 R | 66.1% | 26.1% | 71.7% | 28.3% |
| 2,520 | POWDER RIVER | 1,443 | 985 | 336 | 122 | 649 R | 68.3% | 23.3% | 74.6% | 25.4% |
| 6,958 | POWELL | 2,993 | 1,770 | 883 | 340 | 887 R | 59.1% | 29.5% | 66.7% | 33.3% |
| 1,836 | PRAIRIE | 927 | 580 | 283 | 64 | 297 R | 62.6% | 30.5% | 67.2% | 32.8% |
| 22,493 | RAVALLI | 11,404 | 7,268 | 3,063 | 1,073 | 4,205 R | 63.7% | 26.9% | 70.4% | 29.6% |
| 12,243 | RICHLAND | 5,038 | 3,348 | 1,252 | 438 | 2,096 R | 66.5% | 24.9% | 72.8% | 27.2% |
| 10,467 | ROOSEVELT | 4,160 | 2,298 | 1,504 | 358 | 794 R | 55.2% | 36.2% | 60.4% | 39.6% |
| 9,899 | ROSEBUD | 3,443 | 1,875 | 1,167 | 401 | 708 R | 54.5% | 33.9% | 61.6% | 38.4% |
| 8,675 | SANDERS | 3,999 | 2,194 | 1,395 | 410 | 799 R | 54.9% | 34.9% | 61.1% | 38.9% |
| 5,414 | SHERIDAN | 2,912 | 1,658 | 955 | 299 | 703 R | 56.9% | 32.8% | 63.5% | 36.5% |
| 38,092 | SILVER BOW | 19,377 | 7,301 | 9,721 | 2,355 | 2,420 D | 37.7% | 50.2% | 42.9% | 57.1% |
| 5,598 | STILLWATER | 2,984 | 1,828 | 919 | 237 | 909 R | 61.3% | 30.8% | 66.5% | 33.5% |
| 3,216 | SWEET GRASS | 1,739 | 1,169 | 440 | 130 | 729 R | 67.2% | 25.3% | 72.7% | 27.3% |
| 6,491 | TETON | 3,564 | 2,415 | 902 | 247 | 1,513 R | 67.8% | 25.3% | 72.8% | 27.2% |
| 5,559 | TOOLE | 2,850 | 2,000 | 634 | 216 | 1,366 R | 70.2% | 22.2% | 75.9% | 24.1% |
| 981 | TREASURE | 554 | 321 | 181 | 52 | 140 R | 57.9% | 32.7% | 63.9% | 36.1% |
| 10,250 | VALLEY | 5,190 | 3,242 | 1,567 | 381 | 1,675 R | 62.5% | 30.2% | 67.4% | 32.6% |
| 2,359 | WHEATLAND | 1,230 | 742 | 381 | 107 | 361 R | 60.3% | 31.0% | 66.1% | 33.9% |
| 1,476 | WIBAUX | 731 | 450 | 219 | 62 | 231 R | 61.6% | 30.0% | 67.3% | 32.7% |
| 108,035 | YELLOWSTONE | 48,313 | 27,332 | 15,272 | 5,709 | 12,060 R | 56.6% | 31.6% | 64.2% | 35.8% |
| 786,690 | TOTAL | 363,952 | 206,814 | 118,032 | 39,106 | 88,782 R | 56.8% | 32.4% | 63.7% | 36.3% |

# MONTANA

## PRESIDENT 1976

| 1970 Census Population | County | Total Vote | Republican | Democratic | Other | Rep.-Dem. Plurality | Percentage Total Vote Rep. | Dem. | Major Vote Rep. | Dem. |
|---|---|---|---|---|---|---|---|---|---|---|
| 8,187 | BEAVERHEAD | 3,543 | 2,461 | 1,013 | 69 | 1,448 R | 69.5% | 28.6% | 70.8% | 29.2% |
| 10,057 | BIG HORN | 3,630 | 1,615 | 1,962 | 53 | 347 D | 44.5% | 54.0% | 45.1% | 54.9% |
| 6,727 | BLAINE | 2,739 | 1,349 | 1,356 | 34 | 7 D | 49.3% | 49.5% | 49.9% | 50.1% |
| 2,526 | BROADWATER | 1,389 | 820 | 557 | 12 | 263 R | 59.0% | 40.1% | 59.5% | 40.5% |
| 7,080 | CARBON | 4,045 | 2,121 | 1,853 | 71 | 268 R | 52.4% | 45.8% | 53.4% | 46.6% |
| 1,956 | CARTER | 972 | 558 | 344 | 70 | 214 R | 57.4% | 35.4% | 61.9% | 38.1% |
| 81,804 | CASCADE | 30,511 | 15,289 | 14,678 | 544 | 611 R | 50.1% | 48.1% | 51.0% | 49.0% |
| 6,473 | CHOUTEAU | 3,465 | 1,814 | 1,568 | 83 | 246 R | 52.4% | 45.3% | 53.6% | 46.4% |
| 12,174 | CUSTER | 5,647 | 3,120 | 2,425 | 102 | 695 R | 55.3% | 42.9% | 56.3% | 43.7% |
| 3,083 | DANIELS | 1,639 | 816 | 797 | 26 | 19 R | 49.8% | 48.6% | 50.6% | 49.4% |
| 11,269 | DAWSON | 4,960 | 2,639 | 2,201 | 120 | 438 R | 53.2% | 44.4% | 54.5% | 45.5% |
| 15,652 | DEER LODGE | 6,176 | 2,197 | 3,859 | 120 | 1,662 D | 35.6% | 62.5% | 36.3% | 63.7% |
| 4,050 | FALLON | 1,797 | 934 | 847 | 16 | 87 R | 52.0% | 47.1% | 52.4% | 47.6% |
| 12,611 | FERGUS | 6,160 | 3,556 | 2,470 | 134 | 1,086 R | 57.7% | 40.1% | 59.0% | 41.0% |
| 39,460 | FLATHEAD | 18,845 | 10,494 | 7,827 | 524 | 2,667 R | 55.7% | 41.5% | 57.3% | 42.7% |
| 32,505 | GALLATIN | 17,460 | 11,062 | 6,215 | 183 | 4,847 R | 63.4% | 35.6% | 64.0% | 36.0% |
| 1,796 | GARFIELD | 922 | 625 | 273 | 24 | 352 R | 67.8% | 29.6% | 69.6% | 30.4% |
| 10,783 | GLACIER | 3,724 | 1,892 | 1,755 | 77 | 137 R | 50.8% | 47.1% | 51.9% | 48.1% |
| 931 | GOLDEN VALLEY | 569 | 302 | 255 | 12 | 47 R | 53.1% | 44.8% | 54.2% | 45.8% |
| 2,737 | GRANITE | 1,272 | 746 | 509 | 17 | 237 R | 58.6% | 40.0% | 59.4% | 40.6% |
| 17,358 | HILL | 7,260 | 3,274 | 3,878 | 108 | 604 D | 45.1% | 53.4% | 45.8% | 54.2% |
| 5,238 | JEFFERSON | 2,654 | 1,387 | 1,210 | 57 | 177 R | 52.3% | 45.6% | 53.4% | 46.6% |
| 2,667 | JUDITH BASIN | 1,614 | 809 | 772 | 33 | 37 R | 50.1% | 47.8% | 51.2% | 48.8% |
| 14,445 | LAKE | 7,210 | 3,809 | 3,253 | 148 | 556 R | 52.8% | 45.1% | 53.9% | 46.1% |
| 33,281 | LEWIS AND CLARK | 18,517 | 10,155 | 8,118 | 244 | 2,037 R | 54.8% | 43.8% | 55.6% | 44.4% |
| 2,359 | LIBERTY | 1,163 | 638 | 506 | 19 | 132 R | 54.9% | 43.5% | 55.8% | 44.2% |
| 18,063 | LINCOLN | 6,283 | 3,017 | 3,146 | 120 | 129 D | 48.0% | 50.1% | 49.0% | 51.0% |
| 2,875 | MCCONE | 1,499 | 730 | 749 | 20 | 19 D | 48.7% | 50.0% | 49.4% | 50.6% |
| 5,014 | MADISON | 2,610 | 1,688 | 870 | 52 | 818 R | 64.7% | 33.3% | 66.0% | 34.0% |
| 2,122 | MEAGHER | 939 | 565 | 364 | 10 | 201 R | 60.2% | 38.8% | 60.8% | 39.2% |
| 2,958 | MINERAL | 1,514 | 679 | 819 | 16 | 140 D | 44.8% | 54.1% | 45.3% | 54.7% |
| 58,263 | MISSOULA | 31,837 | 16,350 | 15,099 | 388 | 1,251 R | 51.4% | 47.4% | 52.0% | 48.0% |
| 3,734 | MUSSELSHELL | 2,065 | 1,117 | 922 | 26 | 195 R | 54.1% | 44.6% | 54.8% | 45.2% |
| 11,197 | PARK | 5,740 | 3,281 | 2,364 | 95 | 917 R | 57.2% | 41.2% | 58.1% | 41.9% |
| 675 | PETROLEUM | 331 | 211 | 110 | 10 | 101 R | 63.7% | 33.2% | 65.7% | 34.3% |
| 5,386 | PHILLIPS | 2,486 | 1,347 | 1,117 | 22 | 230 R | 54.2% | 44.9% | 54.7% | 45.3% |
| 6,611 | PONDERA | 3,150 | 1,666 | 1,413 | 71 | 253 R | 52.9% | 44.9% | 54.1% | 45.9% |
| 2,862 | POWDER RIVER | 1,235 | 683 | 429 | 123 | 254 R | 55.3% | 34.7% | 61.4% | 38.6% |
| 6,660 | POWELL | 2,951 | 1,610 | 1,302 | 39 | 308 R | 54.6% | 44.1% | 55.3% | 44.7% |
| 1,752 | PRAIRIE | 1,019 | 597 | 415 | 7 | 182 R | 58.6% | 40.7% | 59.0% | 41.0% |
| 14,409 | RAVALLI | 8,694 | 4,894 | 3,504 | 296 | 1,390 R | 56.3% | 40.3% | 58.3% | 41.7% |
| 9,837 | RICHLAND | 4,263 | 2,189 | 1,961 | 113 | 228 R | 51.3% | 46.0% | 52.7% | 47.3% |
| 10,365 | ROOSEVELT | 3,928 | 1,822 | 2,061 | 45 | 239 D | 46.4% | 52.5% | 46.9% | 53.1% |
| 6,032 | ROSEBUD | 3,006 | 1,538 | 1,413 | 55 | 125 R | 51.2% | 47.0% | 52.1% | 47.9% |
| 7,093 | SANDERS | 3,576 | 1,738 | 1,725 | 113 | 13 R | 48.6% | 48.2% | 50.2% | 49.8% |
| 5,779 | SHERIDAN | 2,714 | 1,114 | 1,560 | 40 | 446 D | 41.0% | 57.5% | 41.7% | 58.3% |
| 41,981 | SILVER BOW | 19,110 | 7,506 | 11,377 | 227 | 3,871 D | 39.3% | 59.5% | 39.8% | 60.2% |
| 4,632 | STILLWATER | 2,635 | 1,446 | 1,143 | 46 | 303 R | 54.9% | 43.4% | 55.9% | 44.1% |
| 2,980 | SWEET GRASS | 1,659 | 1,135 | 502 | 22 | 633 R | 68.4% | 30.3% | 69.3% | 30.7% |
| 6,116 | TETON | 3,345 | 1,730 | 1,506 | 109 | 224 R | 51.7% | 45.0% | 53.5% | 46.5% |
| 5,839 | TOOLE | 2,603 | 1,469 | 1,080 | 54 | 389 R | 56.4% | 41.5% | 57.6% | 42.4% |
| 1,069 | TREASURE | 564 | 315 | 239 | 10 | 76 R | 55.9% | 42.4% | 56.9% | 43.1% |
| 11,471 | VALLEY | 4,959 | 2,520 | 2,352 | 87 | 168 R | 50.8% | 47.4% | 51.7% | 48.3% |
| 2,529 | WHEATLAND | 1,320 | 755 | 535 | 30 | 220 R | 57.2% | 40.5% | 58.5% | 41.5% |
| 1,465 | WIBAUX | 691 | 308 | 352 | 31 | 44 D | 44.6% | 50.9% | 46.7% | 53.3% |
| 87,367 | YELLOWSTONE | 44,125 | 25,201 | 18,329 | 595 | 6,872 R | 57.1% | 41.5% | 57.9% | 42.1% |
| 694,409 | TOTAL | 328,734 | 173,703 | 149,259 | 5,772 | 24,444 R | 52.8% | 45.4% | 53.8% | 46.2% |

# MONTANA

## PRESIDENT 1972

| 1970 Census Population | County | Total Vote | Republican | Democratic | Other | Rep.-Dem. Plurality | Percentage | | | |
|---|---|---|---|---|---|---|---|---|---|---|
| | | | | | | | Total Vote | | Major Vote | |
| | | | | | | | Rep. | Dem. | Rep. | Dem. |
| 8,187 | BEAVERHEAD | 3,417 | 2,460 | 775 | 182 | 1,685 R | 72.0% | 22.7% | 76.0% | 24.0% |
| 10,057 | BIG HORN | 3,824 | 2,148 | 1,552 | 124 | 596 R | 56.2% | 40.6% | 58.1% | 41.9% |
| 6,727 | BLAINE | 2,779 | 1,513 | 1,151 | 115 | 362 R | 54.4% | 41.4% | 56.8% | 43.2% |
| 2,526 | BROADWATER | 1,376 | 916 | 411 | 49 | 505 R | 66.6% | 29.9% | 69.0% | 31.0% |
| 7,080 | CARBON | 3,841 | 2,378 | 1,292 | 171 | 1,086 R | 61.9% | 33.6% | 64.8% | 35.2% |
| 1,956 | CARTER | 983 | 726 | 218 | 39 | 508 R | 73.9% | 22.2% | 76.9% | 23.1% |
| 81,804 | CASCADE | 30,836 | 16,159 | 12,899 | 1,778 | 3,260 R | 52.4% | 41.8% | 55.6% | 44.4% |
| 6,473 | CHOUTEAU | 3,399 | 2,027 | 1,149 | 223 | 878 R | 59.6% | 33.8% | 63.8% | 36.2% |
| 12,174 | CUSTER | 5,506 | 3,486 | 1,875 | 145 | 1,611 R | 63.3% | 34.1% | 65.0% | 35.0% |
| 3,083 | DANIELS | 1,574 | 973 | 570 | 31 | 403 R | 61.8% | 36.2% | 63.1% | 36.9% |
| 11,269 | DAWSON | 5,014 | 3,207 | 1,685 | 122 | 1,522 R | 64.0% | 33.6% | 65.6% | 34.4% |
| 15,652 | DEER LODGE | 6,604 | 2,373 | 3,979 | 252 | 1,606 D | 35.9% | 60.3% | 37.4% | 62.6% |
| 4,050 | FALLON | 1,604 | 1,034 | 531 | 39 | 503 R | 64.5% | 33.1% | 66.1% | 33.9% |
| 12,611 | FERGUS | 6,049 | 4,082 | 1,652 | 315 | 2,430 R | 67.5% | 27.3% | 71.2% | 28.8% |
| 39,460 | FLATHEAD | 17,156 | 10,417 | 5,412 | 1,327 | 5,005 R | 60.7% | 31.5% | 65.8% | 34.2% |
| 32,505 | GALLATIN | 16,088 | 10,663 | 5,096 | 329 | 5,567 R | 66.3% | 31.7% | 67.7% | 32.3% |
| 1,796 | GARFIELD | 893 | 695 | 173 | 25 | 522 R | 77.8% | 19.4% | 80.1% | 19.9% |
| 10,783 | GLACIER | 3,819 | 2,143 | 1,469 | 207 | 674 R | 56.1% | 38.5% | 59.3% | 40.7% |
| 931 | GOLDEN VALLEY | 553 | 359 | 170 | 24 | 189 R | 64.9% | 30.7% | 67.9% | 32.1% |
| 2,737 | GRANITE | 1,291 | 804 | 422 | 65 | 382 R | 62.3% | 32.7% | 65.6% | 34.4% |
| 17,358 | HILL | 7,085 | 3,759 | 3,061 | 265 | 698 R | 53.1% | 43.2% | 55.1% | 44.9% |
| 5,238 | JEFFERSON | 2,285 | 1,281 | 904 | 100 | 377 R | 56.1% | 39.6% | 58.6% | 41.4% |
| 2,667 | JUDITH BASIN | 1,614 | 961 | 557 | 96 | 404 R | 59.5% | 34.5% | 63.3% | 36.7% |
| 14,445 | LAKE | 6,719 | 4,172 | 2,260 | 287 | 1,912 R | 62.1% | 33.6% | 64.9% | 35.1% |
| 33,281 | LEWIS AND CLARK | 17,316 | 10,719 | 6,081 | 516 | 4,638 R | 61.9% | 35.1% | 63.8% | 36.2% |
| 2,359 | LIBERTY | 1,235 | 808 | 365 | 62 | 443 R | 65.4% | 29.6% | 68.9% | 31.1% |
| 18,063 | LINCOLN | 6,208 | 3,276 | 2,402 | 530 | 874 R | 52.8% | 38.7% | 57.7% | 42.3% |
| 2,875 | MCCONE | 1,465 | 854 | 562 | 49 | 292 R | 58.3% | 38.4% | 60.3% | 39.7% |
| 5,014 | MADISON | 2,588 | 1,780 | 669 | 139 | 1,111 R | 68.8% | 25.9% | 72.7% | 27.3% |
| 2,122 | MEAGHER | 942 | 674 | 230 | 38 | 444 R | 71.5% | 24.4% | 74.6% | 25.4% |
| 2,958 | MINERAL | 1,419 | 706 | 659 | 54 | 47 R | 49.8% | 46.4% | 51.7% | 48.3% |
| 58,263 | MISSOULA | 30,049 | 15,557 | 13,784 | 708 | 1,773 R | 51.8% | 45.9% | 53.0% | 47.0% |
| 3,734 | MUSSELSHELL | 1,967 | 1,202 | 689 | 76 | 513 R | 61.1% | 35.0% | 63.6% | 36.4% |
| 11,197 | PARK | 5,902 | 3,771 | 1,923 | 208 | 1,848 R | 63.9% | 32.6% | 66.2% | 33.8% |
| 675 | PETROLEUM | 325 | 232 | 87 | 6 | 145 R | 71.4% | 26.8% | 72.7% | 27.3% |
| 5,386 | PHILLIPS | 2,557 | 1,659 | 828 | 70 | 831 R | 64.9% | 32.4% | 66.7% | 33.3% |
| 6,611 | PONDERA | 3,292 | 1,890 | 1,215 | 187 | 675 R | 57.4% | 36.9% | 60.9% | 39.1% |
| 2,862 | POWDER RIVER | 1,217 | 844 | 267 | 106 | 577 R | 69.4% | 21.9% | 76.0% | 24.0% |
| 6,660 | POWELL | 2,882 | 1,720 | 1,050 | 112 | 670 R | 59.7% | 36.4% | 62.1% | 37.9% |
| 1,752 | PRAIRIE | 999 | 685 | 303 | 11 | 382 R | 68.6% | 30.3% | 69.3% | 30.7% |
| 14,409 | RAVALLI | 7,458 | 4,611 | 2,480 | 367 | 2,131 R | 61.8% | 33.3% | 65.0% | 35.0% |
| 9,837 | RICHLAND | 4,300 | 2,645 | 1,438 | 217 | 1,207 R | 61.5% | 33.4% | 64.8% | 35.2% |
| 10,365 | ROOSEVELT | 3,907 | 2,304 | 1,464 | 139 | 840 R | 59.0% | 37.5% | 61.1% | 38.9% |
| 6,032 | ROSEBUD | 2,350 | 1,486 | 777 | 87 | 709 R | 63.2% | 33.1% | 65.7% | 34.3% |
| 7,093 | SANDERS | 3,251 | 1,779 | 1,197 | 275 | 582 R | 54.7% | 36.8% | 59.8% | 40.2% |
| 5,779 | SHERIDAN | 2,780 | 1,500 | 1,197 | 83 | 303 R | 54.0% | 43.1% | 55.6% | 44.4% |
| 41,981 | SILVER BOW | 20,404 | 7,967 | 11,704 | 733 | 3,737 D | 39.0% | 57.4% | 40.5% | 59.5% |
| 4,632 | STILLWATER | 2,499 | 1,698 | 716 | 85 | 982 R | 67.9% | 28.7% | 70.3% | 29.7% |
| 2,980 | SWEET GRASS | 1,658 | 1,260 | 350 | 48 | 910 R | 76.0% | 21.1% | 78.3% | 21.7% |
| 6,116 | TETON | 3,321 | 1,991 | 1,121 | 209 | 870 R | 60.0% | 33.8% | 64.0% | 36.0% |
| 5,839 | TOOLE | 2,815 | 1,679 | 897 | 239 | 782 R | 59.6% | 31.9% | 65.2% | 34.8% |
| 1,069 | TREASURE | 574 | 377 | 176 | 21 | 201 R | 65.7% | 30.7% | 68.2% | 31.8% |
| 11,471 | VALLEY | 5,348 | 3,210 | 1,973 | 165 | 1,237 R | 60.0% | 36.9% | 61.9% | 38.1% |
| 2,529 | WHEATLAND | 1,326 | 761 | 445 | 120 | 316 R | 57.4% | 33.6% | 63.1% | 36.9% |
| 1,465 | WIBAUX | 703 | 390 | 283 | 30 | 107 R | 55.5% | 40.3% | 57.9% | 42.1% |
| 87,367 | YELLOWSTONE | 40,237 | 25,205 | 13,602 | 1,430 | 11,603 R | 62.6% | 33.8% | 64.9% | 35.1% |
| 694,409 | TOTAL | 317,603 | 183,976 | 120,197 | 13,430 | 63,779 R | 57.9% | 37.8% | 60.5% | 39.5% |

# MONTANA

## PRESIDENT 1968

| 1960 Census Population | County | Total Vote | Republican | Democratic | AIP | Other | Plurality | Percentage Total Vote | | |
|---|---|---|---|---|---|---|---|---|---|---|
| | | | | | | | | Rep. | Dem. | AIP |
| 7,194 | BEAVERHEAD | 3,106 | 1,896 | 853 | 357 | | 1,043 R | 61.0% | 27.5% | 11.5% |
| 10,007 | BIG HORN | 3,321 | 1,789 | 1,319 | 209 | 4 | 470 R | 53.9% | 39.7% | 6.3% |
| 8,091 | BLAINE | 2,655 | 1,291 | 1,198 | 165 | 1 | 93 R | 48.6% | 45.1% | 6.2% |
| 2,804 | BROADWATER | 1,236 | 671 | 439 | 125 | 1 | 232 R | 54.3% | 35.5% | 10.1% |
| 8,317 | CARBON | 3,587 | 1,972 | 1,353 | 258 | 4 | 619 R | 55.0% | 37.7% | 7.2% |
| 2,493 | CARTER | 1,003 | 624 | 269 | 110 | | 355 R | 62.2% | 26.8% | 11.0% |
| 73,418 | CASCADE | 26,803 | 11,588 | 13,507 | 1,539 | 169 | 1,919 D | 43.2% | 50.4% | 5.7% |
| 7,348 | CHOUTEAU | 3,159 | 1,695 | 1,216 | 247 | 1 | 479 R | 53.7% | 38.5% | 7.8% |
| 13,227 | CUSTER | 4,876 | 2,831 | 1,760 | 275 | 10 | 1,071 R | 58.1% | 36.1% | 5.6% |
| 3,755 | DANIELS | 1,584 | 826 | 688 | 69 | 1 | 138 R | 52.1% | 43.4% | 4.4% |
| 12,314 | DAWSON | 4,568 | 2,650 | 1,695 | 220 | 3 | 955 R | 58.0% | 37.1% | 4.8% |
| 18,640 | DEER LODGE | 6,074 | 1,554 | 4,208 | 308 | 4 | 2,654 D | 25.6% | 69.3% | 5.1% |
| 3,997 | FALLON | 1,565 | 990 | 477 | 97 | 1 | 513 R | 63.3% | 30.5% | 6.2% |
| 14,018 | FERGUS | 6,057 | 3,367 | 2,070 | 616 | 4 | 1,297 R | 55.6% | 34.2% | 10.2% |
| 32,965 | FLATHEAD | 14,000 | 7,215 | 5,253 | 1,524 | 8 | 1,962 R | 51.5% | 37.5% | 10.9% |
| 26,045 | GALLATIN | 11,978 | 7,433 | 3,818 | 706 | 21 | 3,615 R | 62.1% | 31.9% | 5.9% |
| 1,981 | GARFIELD | 844 | 542 | 190 | 112 | | 352 R | 64.2% | 22.5% | 13.3% |
| 11,565 | GLACIER | 3,671 | 1,643 | 1,723 | 295 | 10 | 80 D | 44.8% | 46.9% | 8.0% |
| 1,203 | GOLDEN VALLEY | 553 | 332 | 194 | 26 | 1 | 138 R | 60.0% | 35.1% | 4.7% |
| 3,014 | GRANITE | 1,263 | 626 | 502 | 135 | | 124 R | 49.6% | 39.7% | 10.7% |
| 18,653 | HILL | 6,669 | 2,970 | 3,386 | 305 | 8 | 416 D | 44.5% | 50.8% | 4.6% |
| 4,297 | JEFFERSON | 1,771 | 798 | 820 | 152 | 1 | 22 D | 45.1% | 46.3% | 8.6% |
| 3,085 | JUDITH BASIN | 1,516 | 804 | 606 | 106 | | 198 R | 53.0% | 40.0% | 7.0% |
| 13,104 | LAKE | 5,999 | 3,358 | 1,956 | 679 | 6 | 1,402 R | 56.0% | 32.6% | 11.3% |
| 28,006 | LEWIS AND CLARK | 14,115 | 7,979 | 5,379 | 723 | 34 | 2,600 R | 56.5% | 38.1% | 5.1% |
| 2,624 | LIBERTY | 1,144 | 670 | 390 | 83 | 1 | 280 R | 58.6% | 34.1% | 7.3% |
| 12,537 | LINCOLN | 5,807 | 2,355 | 2,677 | 765 | 10 | 322 D | 40.6% | 46.1% | 13.2% |
| 3,321 | MCCONE | 1,405 | 733 | 589 | 82 | 1 | 144 R | 52.2% | 41.9% | 5.8% |
| 5,211 | MADISON | 2,286 | 1,289 | 734 | 261 | 2 | 555 R | 56.4% | 32.1% | 11.4% |
| 2,616 | MEAGHER | 863 | 543 | 218 | 102 | | 325 R | 62.9% | 25.3% | 11.8% |
| 3,037 | MINERAL | 1,169 | 483 | 576 | 108 | 2 | 93 D | 41.3% | 49.3% | 9.2% |
| 44,663 | MISSOULA | 20,292 | 9,745 | 8,398 | 1,638 | 511 | 1,347 R | 48.0% | 41.4% | 8.1% |
| 4,888 | MUSSELSHELL | 1,863 | 953 | 795 | 111 | 4 | 158 R | 51.2% | 42.7% | 6.0% |
| 13,168 | PARK | 5,340 | 3,063 | 1,815 | 460 | 2 | 1,248 R | 57.4% | 34.0% | 8.6% |
| 894 | PETROLEUM | 335 | 211 | 98 | 26 | 0 | 113 R | 63.0% | 29.3% | 7.8% |
| 6,027 | PHILLIPS | 2,632 | 1,353 | 1,100 | 177 | 2 | 253 R | 51.4% | 41.8% | 6.7% |
| 7,653 | PONDERA | 2,888 | 1,530 | 1,149 | 205 | 4 | 381 R | 53.0% | 39.8% | 7.1% |
| 2,485 | POWDER RIVER | 1,076 | 699 | 258 | 118 | 1 | 441 R | 65.0% | 24.0% | 11.0% |
| 7,002 | POWELL | 2,739 | 1,301 | 1,206 | 231 | 1 | 95 R | 47.5% | 44.0% | 8.4% |
| 2,318 | PRAIRIE | 937 | 635 | 270 | 30 | 2 | 365 R | 67.8% | 28.8% | 3.2% |
| 12,341 | RAVALLI | 5,977 | 3,183 | 2,080 | 709 | 5 | 1,103 R | 53.3% | 34.8% | 11.9% |
| 10,504 | RICHLAND | 4,016 | 2,381 | 1,399 | 228 | 8 | 982 R | 59.3% | 34.8% | 5.7% |
| 11,731 | ROOSEVELT | 3,885 | 1,947 | 1,771 | 162 | 5 | 176 R | 50.1% | 45.6% | 4.2% |
| 6,187 | ROSEBUD | 2,109 | 1,190 | 711 | 204 | 4 | 479 R | 56.4% | 33.7% | 9.7% |
| 6,880 | SANDERS | 2,996 | 1,459 | 1,242 | 292 | 3 | 217 R | 48.7% | 41.5% | 9.7% |
| 6,458 | SHERIDAN | 2,576 | 1,180 | 1,275 | 115 | 6 | 95 D | 45.8% | 49.5% | 4.5% |
| 46,454 | SILVER BOW | 19,617 | 5,488 | 12,626 | 1,120 | 383 | 7,138 D | 28.0% | 64.4% | 5.7% |
| 5,526 | STILLWATER | 2,201 | 1,347 | 676 | 177 | 1 | 671 R | 61.2% | 30.7% | 8.0% |
| 3,290 | SWEET GRASS | 1,490 | 1,043 | 336 | 110 | 1 | 707 R | 70.0% | 22.6% | 7.4% |
| 7,295 | TETON | 3,109 | 1,697 | 1,228 | 179 | 5 | 469 R | 54.6% | 39.5% | 5.8% |
| 7,904 | TOOLE | 2,708 | 1,407 | 1,048 | 249 | 4 | 359 R | 52.0% | 38.7% | 9.2% |
| 1,345 | TREASURE | 527 | 298 | 188 | 41 | | 110 R | 56.5% | 35.7% | 7.8% |
| 17,080 | VALLEY | 4,632 | 2,290 | 1,926 | 393 | 23 | 364 R | 49.4% | 41.6% | 8.5% |
| 3,026 | WHEATLAND | 1,300 | 673 | 525 | 101 | 1 | 148 R | 51.8% | 40.4% | 7.8% |
| 1,698 | WIBAUX | 655 | 347 | 252 | 56 | | 95 R | 53.0% | 38.5% | 8.5% |
| 79,016 | YELLOWSTONE | 33,857 | 19,898 | 11,682 | 2,124 | 153 | 8,216 R | 58.8% | 34.5% | 6.3% |
| 674,767 | TOTAL | 274,404 | 138,835 | 114,117 | 20,015 | 1,437 | 24,718 R | 50.6% | 41.6% | 7.3% |

# MONTANA

## PRESIDENT 1964

| 1960 Census Population | County | Total Vote | Republican | Democratic | Other | Rep.-Dem. Plurality | Percentage |  |  |  |
|---|---|---|---|---|---|---|---|---|---|---|
|  |  |  |  |  |  |  | Total Vote |  | Major Vote |  |
|  |  |  |  |  |  |  | Rep. | Dem. | Rep. | Dem. |
| 7,194 | BEAVERHEAD | 3,231 | 1,754 | 1,469 | 8 | 285 R | 54.3% | 45.5% | 54.4% | 45.6% |
| 10,007 | BIG HORN | 3,993 | 1,481 | 2,509 | 3 | 1,028 D | 37.1% | 62.8% | 37.1% | 62.9% |
| 8,091 | BLAINE | 2,703 | 961 | 1,742 |  | 781 D | 35.6% | 64.4% | 35.6% | 64.4% |
| 2,804 | BROADWATER | 1,204 | 609 | 595 |  | 14 R | 50.6% | 49.4% | 50.6% | 49.4% |
| 8,317 | CARBON | 3,633 | 1,535 | 2,098 |  | 563 D | 42.3% | 57.7% | 42.3% | 57.7% |
| 2,493 | CARTER | 1,029 | 576 | 453 |  | 123 R | 56.0% | 44.0% | 56.0% | 44.0% |
| 73,418 | CASCADE | 26,714 | 8,986 | 17,609 | 119 | 8,623 D | 33.6% | 65.9% | 33.8% | 66.2% |
| 7,348 | CHOUTEAU | 3,276 | 1,444 | 1,827 | 5 | 383 D | 44.1% | 55.8% | 44.1% | 55.9% |
| 13,227 | CUSTER | 5,101 | 2,302 | 2,790 | 9 | 488 D | 45.1% | 54.7% | 45.2% | 54.8% |
| 3,755 | DANIELS | 1,730 | 742 | 987 | 1 | 245 D | 42.9% | 57.1% | 42.9% | 57.1% |
| 12,314 | DAWSON | 4,637 | 1,938 | 2,691 | 8 | 753 D | 41.8% | 58.0% | 41.9% | 58.1% |
| 18,640 | DEER LODGE | 6,259 | 1,415 | 4,835 | 9 | 3,420 D | 22.6% | 77.2% | 22.6% | 77.4% |
| 3,997 | FALLON | 1,595 | 827 | 765 | 3 | 62 R | 51.8% | 48.0% | 51.9% | 48.1% |
| 14,018 | FERGUS | 6,293 | 2,980 | 3,300 | 13 | 320 D | 47.4% | 52.4% | 47.5% | 52.5% |
| 32,965 | FLATHEAD | 14,370 | 6,325 | 8,015 | 30 | 1,690 D | 44.0% | 55.8% | 44.1% | 55.9% |
| 26,045 | GALLATIN | 11,248 | 5,621 | 5,600 | 27 | 21 R | 50.0% | 49.8% | 50.1% | 49.9% |
| 1,981 | GARFIELD | 896 | 509 | 384 | 3 | 125 R | 56.8% | 42.9% | 57.0% | 43.0% |
| 11,565 | GLACIER | 3,697 | 1,458 | 2,218 | 21 | 760 D | 39.4% | 60.0% | 39.7% | 60.3% |
| 1,203 | GOLDEN VALLEY | 604 | 252 | 352 |  | 100 D | 41.7% | 58.3% | 41.7% | 58.3% |
| 3,014 | GRANITE | 1,187 | 527 | 658 | 2 | 131 D | 44.4% | 55.4% | 44.5% | 55.5% |
| 18,653 | HILL | 6,604 | 2,101 | 4,491 | 12 | 2,390 D | 31.8% | 68.0% | 31.9% | 68.1% |
| 4,297 | JEFFERSON | 1,631 | 662 | 967 | 2 | 305 D | 40.6% | 59.3% | 40.6% | 59.4% |
| 3,085 | JUDITH BASIN | 1,502 | 678 | 822 | 2 | 144 D | 45.1% | 54.7% | 45.2% | 54.8% |
| 13,104 | LAKE | 5,986 | 2,828 | 3,148 | 10 | 320 D | 47.2% | 52.6% | 47.3% | 52.7% |
| 28,006 | LEWIS AND CLARK | 13,687 | 6,155 | 7,506 | 26 | 1,351 D | 45.0% | 54.8% | 45.1% | 54.9% |
| 2,624 | LIBERTY | 1,155 | 533 | 619 | 3 | 86 D | 46.1% | 53.6% | 46.3% | 53.7% |
| 12,537 | LINCOLN | 4,709 | 1,554 | 3,140 | 15 | 1,586 D | 33.0% | 66.7% | 33.1% | 66.9% |
| 3,321 | MCCONE | 1,507 | 615 | 891 | 1 | 276 D | 40.8% | 59.1% | 40.8% | 59.2% |
| 5,211 | MADISON | 2,403 | 1,276 | 1,125 | 2 | 151 R | 53.1% | 46.8% | 53.1% | 46.9% |
| 2,616 | MEAGHER | 913 | 506 | 405 | 2 | 101 R | 55.4% | 44.4% | 55.5% | 44.5% |
| 3,037 | MINERAL | 1,274 | 368 | 901 | 5 | 533 D | 28.9% | 70.7% | 29.0% | 71.0% |
| 44,663 | MISSOULA | 21,004 | 8,065 | 12,900 | 39 | 4,835 D | 38.4% | 61.4% | 38.5% | 61.5% |
| 4,888 | MUSSELSHELL | 2,012 | 823 | 1,189 |  | 366 D | 40.9% | 59.1% | 40.9% | 59.1% |
| 13,168 | PARK | 5,453 | 2,619 | 2,824 | 10 | 205 D | 48.0% | 51.8% | 48.1% | 51.9% |
| 894 | PETROLEUM | 401 | 190 | 210 | 1 | 20 D | 47.4% | 52.4% | 47.5% | 52.5% |
| 6,027 | PHILLIPS | 2,857 | 1,242 | 1,612 | 3 | 370 D | 43.5% | 56.4% | 43.5% | 56.5% |
| 7,653 | PONDERA | 2,877 | 1,110 | 1,759 | 8 | 649 D | 38.6% | 61.1% | 38.7% | 61.3% |
| 2,485 | POWDER RIVER | 1,099 | 649 | 449 | 1 | 200 R | 59.1% | 40.9% | 59.1% | 40.9% |
| 7,002 | POWELL | 3,040 | 1,140 | 1,896 | 4 | 756 D | 37.5% | 62.4% | 37.5% | 62.5% |
| 2,318 | PRAIRIE | 1,048 | 555 | 488 | 5 | 67 R | 53.0% | 46.6% | 53.2% | 46.8% |
| 12,341 | RAVALLI | 5,662 | 2,350 | 3,300 | 12 | 950 D | 41.5% | 58.3% | 41.6% | 58.4% |
| 10,504 | RICHLAND | 4,131 | 1,784 | 2,320 | 27 | 536 D | 43.2% | 56.2% | 43.5% | 56.5% |
| 11,731 | ROOSEVELT | 4,078 | 1,612 | 2,463 | 3 | 851 D | 39.5% | 60.4% | 39.6% | 60.4% |
| 6,187 | ROSEBUD | 2,321 | 1,105 | 1,212 | 4 | 107 D | 47.6% | 52.2% | 47.7% | 52.3% |
| 6,880 | SANDERS | 3,013 | 1,163 | 1,836 | 14 | 673 D | 38.6% | 60.9% | 38.8% | 61.2% |
| 6,458 | SHERIDAN | 2,754 | 837 | 1,905 | 12 | 1,068 D | 30.4% | 69.2% | 30.5% | 69.5% |
| 46,454 | SILVER BOW | 21,239 | 4,873 | 15,751 | 615 | 10,878 D | 22.9% | 74.2% | 23.6% | 76.4% |
| 5,526 | STILLWATER | 2,271 | 1,140 | 1,130 | 1 | 10 R | 50.2% | 49.8% | 50.2% | 49.8% |
| 3,290 | SWEET GRASS | 1,514 | 856 | 653 | 5 | 203 R | 56.5% | 43.1% | 56.7% | 43.3% |
| 7,295 | TETON | 3,199 | 1,388 | 1,808 | 3 | 420 D | 43.4% | 56.5% | 43.4% | 56.6% |
| 7,904 | TOOLE | 2,874 | 1,223 | 1,649 | 2 | 426 D | 42.6% | 57.4% | 42.6% | 57.4% |
| 1,345 | TREASURE | 536 | 251 | 285 |  | 34 D | 46.8% | 53.2% | 46.8% | 53.2% |
| 17,080 | VALLEY | 5,125 | 2,077 | 3,032 | 16 | 955 D | 40.5% | 59.2% | 40.7% | 59.3% |
| 3,026 | WHEATLAND | 1,373 | 583 | 790 |  | 207 D | 42.5% | 57.5% | 42.5% | 57.5% |
| 1,698 | WIBAUX | 737 | 308 | 427 | 2 | 119 D | 41.8% | 57.9% | 41.9% | 58.1% |
| 79,016 | YELLOWSTONE | 33,239 | 15,571 | 17,446 | 222 | 1,875 D | 46.8% | 52.5% | 47.2% | 52.8% |
| 674,767 | TOTAL | 278,628 | 113,032 | 164,246 | 1,350 | 51,214 D | 40.6% | 58.9% | 40.8% | 59.2% |

# MONTANA

## PRESIDENT 1960

| 1960 Census Population | County | Total Vote | Republican | Democratic | Other | Rep.-Dem. Plurality | Percentage Total Vote Rep. | Total Vote Dem. | Major Vote Rep. | Major Vote Dem. |
|---|---|---|---|---|---|---|---|---|---|---|
| 7,194 | BEAVERHEAD | 3,043 | 1,731 | 1,307 | 5 | 424 R | 56.9% | 43.0% | 57.0% | 43.0% |
| 10,007 | BIG HORN | 3,224 | 1,724 | 1,497 | 3 | 227 R | 53.5% | 46.4% | 53.5% | 46.5% |
| 8,091 | BLAINE | 2,876 | 1,290 | 1,569 | 17 | 279 D | 44.9% | 54.6% | 45.1% | 54.9% |
| 2,804 | BROADWATER | 1,311 | 680 | 631 | | 49 R | 51.9% | 48.1% | 51.9% | 48.1% |
| 8,317 | CARBON | 3,961 | 2,050 | 1,903 | 8 | 147 R | 51.8% | 48.0% | 51.9% | 48.1% |
| 2,493 | CARTER | 1,075 | 688 | 383 | 4 | 305 R | 64.0% | 35.6% | 64.2% | 35.8% |
| 73,418 | CASCADE | 26,090 | 11,928 | 14,117 | 45 | 2,189 D | 45.7% | 54.1% | 45.8% | 54.2% |
| 7,348 | CHOUTEAU | 3,389 | 1,672 | 1,708 | 9 | 36 D | 49.3% | 50.4% | 49.5% | 50.5% |
| 13,227 | CUSTER | 5,351 | 2,943 | 2,393 | 15 | 550 R | 55.0% | 44.7% | 55.2% | 44.8% |
| 3,755 | DANIELS | 1,724 | 763 | 960 | 1 | 197 D | 44.3% | 55.7% | 44.3% | 55.7% |
| 12,314 | DAWSON | 4,582 | 2,460 | 2,108 | 14 | 352 R | 53.7% | 46.0% | 53.9% | 46.1% |
| 18,640 | DEER LODGE | 7,344 | 2,188 | 5,149 | 7 | 2,961 D | 29.8% | 70.1% | 29.8% | 70.2% |
| 3,997 | FALLON | 1,516 | 918 | 597 | 1 | 321 R | 60.6% | 39.4% | 60.6% | 39.4% |
| 14,018 | FERGUS | 6,306 | 3,294 | 2,999 | 13 | 295 R | 52.2% | 47.6% | 52.3% | 47.7% |
| 32,965 | FLATHEAD | 14,267 | 7,554 | 6,689 | 24 | 865 R | 52.9% | 46.9% | 53.0% | 47.0% |
| 26,045 | GALLATIN | 10,652 | 6,870 | 3,761 | 21 | 3,109 R | 64.5% | 35.3% | 64.6% | 35.4% |
| 1,981 | GARFIELD | 880 | 515 | 363 | 2 | 152 R | 58.5% | 41.3% | 58.7% | 41.3% |
| 11,565 | GLACIER | 4,039 | 1,775 | 2,260 | 4 | 485 D | 43.9% | 56.0% | 44.0% | 56.0% |
| 1,203 | GOLDEN VALLEY | 639 | 362 | 277 | | 85 R | 56.7% | 43.3% | 56.7% | 43.3% |
| 3,014 | GRANITE | 1,323 | 722 | 592 | 9 | 130 R | 54.6% | 44.7% | 54.9% | 45.1% |
| 18,653 | HILL | 6,916 | 3,163 | 3,741 | 12 | 578 D | 45.7% | 54.1% | 45.8% | 54.2% |
| 4,297 | JEFFERSON | 1,590 | 817 | 769 | 4 | 48 R | 51.4% | 48.4% | 51.5% | 48.5% |
| 3,085 | JUDITH BASIN | 1,564 | 721 | 842 | 1 | 121 D | 46.1% | 53.8% | 46.1% | 53.9% |
| 13,104 | LAKE | 5,709 | 3,240 | 2,462 | 7 | 778 R | 56.8% | 43.1% | 56.8% | 43.2% |
| 28,006 | LEWIS AND CLARK | 13,285 | 7,260 | 6,008 | 17 | 1,252 R | 54.6% | 45.2% | 54.7% | 45.3% |
| 2,624 | LIBERTY | 1,100 | 597 | 501 | 2 | 96 R | 54.3% | 45.5% | 54.4% | 45.6% |
| 12,537 | LINCOLN | 4,546 | 1,902 | 2,623 | 21 | 721 D | 41.8% | 57.7% | 42.0% | 58.0% |
| 3,321 | MCCONE | 1,515 | 743 | 764 | 8 | 21 D | 49.0% | 50.4% | 49.3% | 50.7% |
| 5,211 | MADISON | 2,469 | 1,456 | 1,010 | 3 | 446 R | 59.0% | 40.9% | 59.0% | 41.0% |
| 2,616 | MEAGHER | 1,048 | 613 | 431 | 4 | 182 R | 58.5% | 41.1% | 58.7% | 41.3% |
| 3,037 | MINERAL | 1,240 | 549 | 686 | 5 | 137 D | 44.3% | 55.3% | 44.5% | 55.5% |
| 44,663 | MISSOULA | 19,337 | 10,396 | 8,876 | 65 | 1,520 R | 53.8% | 45.9% | 53.9% | 46.1% |
| 4,888 | MUSSELSHELL | 2,210 | 1,107 | 1,100 | 3 | 7 R | 50.1% | 49.8% | 50.2% | 49.8% |
| 13,168 | PARK | 5,601 | 3,329 | 2,249 | 23 | 1,080 R | 59.4% | 40.2% | 59.7% | 40.3% |
| 894 | PETROLEUM | 476 | 255 | 221 | | 34 R | 53.6% | 46.4% | 53.6% | 46.4% |
| 6,027 | PHILLIPS | 2,925 | 1,457 | 1,455 | 13 | 2 R | 49.8% | 49.7% | 50.0% | 50.0% |
| 7,653 | PONDERA | 3,105 | 1,452 | 1,653 | | 201 D | 46.8% | 53.2% | 46.8% | 53.2% |
| 2,485 | POWDER RIVER | 1,105 | 665 | 438 | 2 | 227 R | 60.2% | 39.6% | 60.3% | 39.7% |
| 7,002 | POWELL | 3,025 | 1,497 | 1,522 | 6 | 25 D | 49.5% | 50.3% | 49.6% | 50.4% |
| 2,318 | PRAIRIE | 987 | 649 | 338 | | 311 R | 65.8% | 34.2% | 65.8% | 34.2% |
| 12,341 | RAVALLI | 5,528 | 3,121 | 2,381 | 26 | 740 R | 56.5% | 43.1% | 56.7% | 43.3% |
| 10,504 | RICHLAND | 4,269 | 2,395 | 1,863 | 11 | 532 R | 56.1% | 43.6% | 56.2% | 43.8% |
| 11,731 | ROOSEVELT | 4,132 | 1,876 | 2,227 | 29 | 351 D | 45.4% | 53.9% | 45.7% | 54.3% |
| 6,187 | ROSEBUD | 2,399 | 1,386 | 1,002 | 11 | 384 R | 57.8% | 41.8% | 58.0% | 42.0% |
| 6,880 | SANDERS | 2,984 | 1,497 | 1,469 | 18 | 28 R | 50.2% | 49.2% | 50.5% | 49.5% |
| 6,458 | SHERIDAN | 2,754 | 1,196 | 1,549 | 9 | 353 D | 43.4% | 56.2% | 43.6% | 56.4% |
| 46,454 | SILVER BOW | 21,190 | 7,290 | 13,754 | 146 | 6,464 D | 34.4% | 64.9% | 34.6% | 65.4% |
| 5,526 | STILLWATER | 2,491 | 1,455 | 1,036 | | 419 R | 58.4% | 41.6% | 58.4% | 41.6% |
| 3,390 | SWEET GRASS | 1,617 | 1,096 | 521 | | 575 R | 67.8% | 32.2% | 67.8% | 32.2% |
| 7,295 | TETON | 3,276 | 1,623 | 1,648 | 5 | 25 D | 49.5% | 50.3% | 49.6% | 50.4% |
| 7,904 | TOOLE | 3,348 | 1,577 | 1,767 | 4 | 190 D | 47.1% | 52.8% | 47.2% | 52.8% |
| 1,345 | TREASURE | 570 | 300 | 270 | | 30 R | 52.6% | 47.4% | 52.6% | 47.4% |
| 17,080 | VALLEY | 5,346 | 2,387 | 2,953 | 6 | 566 D | 44.7% | 55.2% | 44.7% | 55.3% |
| 3,026 | WHEATLAND | 1,518 | 793 | 724 | 1 | 69 R | 52.2% | 47.7% | 52.3% | 47.7% |
| 1,698 | WIBAUX | 806 | 387 | 419 | | 32 D | 48.0% | 52.0% | 48.0% | 52.0% |
| 79,016 | YELLOWSTONE | 32,006 | 19,467 | 12,356 | 183 | 7,111 R | 60.8% | 38.6% | 61.2% | 38.8% |
| 674,767 | TOTAL | 277,579 | 141,841 | 134,891 | 847 | 6,950 R | 51.1% | 48.6% | 51.3% | 48.7% |

590

# MONTANA

Population total includes persons living in Yellowstone National Park and not under any county jurisdiction.

## ELECTION NOTES

**2004** Other vote was 6,168 Independent (Ralph Nader); 1,764 Constitution (Michael Peroutka); 1,733 Libertarian (Michael Badnarik); 996 Green (David Cobb); 6 write-in (John Joseph Kennedy); 3 write-in (Robert Leslie Beattie); 2 write-in (Walter F. Brown).

**2000** Other vote was 5,697 Reform (Buchanan); 1,718 Libertarian (Browne); 1,155 Constitution (Phillips); 675 Natural Law (Hagelin); 11 write-in (Laible).

**1996** Other vote was 2,526 Libertarian (Browne); 1,754 Natural Law (Hagelin); 152 write-in (Phillips); 26 other scattered write-in.

**1992** Other vote was 3,658 Gritz (Independent); 986 Marrou (Libertarian); 20 Hagelin (write-in); 8 Fulani (write-in).

**1988** Other vote was 5,047 Paul (Libertarian); 1,279 Fulani (New Alliance). Early unamended returns gave the Democratic (Dukakis) vote as 168,956; Rosebud county was adjusted by 20 votes.

**1984** Other vote was Bergland (Libertarian).

**1980** Other vote was 29,281 Anderson (Independent); 9,825 Clark (Libertarian).

**1976** Other vote was Anderson (Americanist for President).

**1972** Other vote was Schmitz (American).

**1968** Wallace on the ballot as American. Other vote was 510 Munn (Prohibition); 470 no Presidential candidate indicated (New Reformist); 457 Halstead (Socialist Workers).

**1964** Other vote was 519 Kasper (National States Rights); 499 Munn (Prohibition); 332 DeBerry (Socialist Workers).

**1960** Other vote was 456 Decker (Prohibition); 391 Dobbs (Socialist Workers).

# NEBRASKA

## POPULAR VOTE FOR PRESIDENT 1920 TO 2004

| Year | Total Vote | Republican Vote | Republican Candidate | Democratic Vote | Democratic Candidate | Other Vote | Plurality | Percentage Total Vote Rep. | Dem. | Major Vote Rep. | Dem. |
|------|-----------|-----------------|----------------------|-----------------|----------------------|------------|-----------|------------------|------|-----------|------|
| 2004 | 778,186 | 512,814 | Bush, George W. | 254,328 | Kerry, John | 11,044 | 258,486 R | 65.9% | 32.7% | 66.8% | 33.2% |
| 2000 ** | 697,019 | 433,862 | Bush, George W. | 231,780 | Gore, Al | 31,377 | 202,082 R | 62.2% | 33.3% | 65.2% | 34.8% |
| 1996 ** | 677,415 | 363,467 | Dole, Bob | 236,761 | Clinton, Bill | 77,187 | 126,706 R | 53.7% | 35.0% | 60.6% | 39.4% |
| 1992 ** | 737,546 | 343,678 | Bush, George | 216,864 | Clinton, Bill | 177,004 | 126,814 R | 46.6% | 29.4% | 61.3% | 38.7% |
| 1988 | 661,465 | 397,956 | Bush, George | 259,235 | Dukakis, Michael S. | 4,274 | 138,721 R | 60.2% | 39.2% | 60.6% | 39.4% |
| 1984 | 652,090 | 460,054 | Reagan, Ronald | 187,866 | Mondale, Walter F. | 4,170 | 272,188 R | 70.6% | 28.8% | 71.0% | 29.0% |
| 1980 ** | 640,854 | 419,937 | Reagan, Ronald | 166,851 | Carter, Jimmy | 54,066 | 253,086 R | 65.5% | 26.0% | 71.6% | 28.4% |
| 1976 | 607,668 | 359,705 | Ford, Gerald R. | 233,692 | Carter, Jimmy | 14,271 | 126,013 R | 59.2% | 38.5% | 60.6% | 39.4% |
| 1972 | 576,289 | 406,298 | Nixon, Richard M. | 169,991 | McGovern, George S. | | 236,307 R | 70.5% | 29.5% | 70.5% | 29.5% |
| 1968 | 536,851 | 321,163 | Nixon, Richard M. | 170,784 | Humphrey, Hubert H. | 44,904 | 150,379 R | 59.8% | 31.8% | 65.3% | 34.7% |
| 1964 | 584,154 | 276,847 | Goldwater, Barry M. | 307,307 | Johnson, Lyndon B. | | 30,460 D | 47.4% | 52.6% | 47.4% | 52.6% |
| 1960 | 613,095 | 380,553 | Nixon, Richard M. | 232,542 | Kennedy, John F. | | 148,011 R | 62.1% | 37.9% | 62.1% | 37.9% |
| 1956 | 577,137 | 378,108 | Eisenhower, Dwight D. | 199,029 | Stevenson, Adlai E. | | 179,079 R | 65.5% | 34.5% | 65.5% | 34.5% |
| 1952 | 609,660 | 421,603 | Eisenhower, Dwight D. | 188,057 | Stevenson, Adlai E. | | 233,546 R | 69.2% | 30.8% | 69.2% | 30.8% |
| 1948 | 488,940 | 264,774 | Dewey, Thomas E. | 224,165 | Truman, Harry S. | 1 | 40,609 R | 54.2% | 45.8% | 54.2% | 45.8% |
| 1944 | 563,126 | 329,880 | Dewey, Thomas E. | 233,246 | Roosevelt, Franklin D. | | 96,634 R | 58.6% | 41.4% | 58.6% | 41.4% |
| 1940 | 615,878 | 352,201 | Willkie, Wendell | 263,677 | Roosevelt, Franklin D. | | 88,524 R | 57.2% | 42.8% | 57.2% | 42.8% |
| 1936 | 608,023 | 247,731 | Landon, Alfred M. | 347,445 | Roosevelt, Franklin D. | 12,847 | 99,714 D | 40.7% | 57.1% | 41.6% | 58.4% |
| 1932 | 570,135 | 201,177 | Hoover, Herbert C. | 359,082 | Roosevelt, Franklin D. | 9,876 | 157,905 D | 35.3% | 63.0% | 35.9% | 64.1% |
| 1928 | 547,128 | 345,745 | Hoover, Herbert C. | 197,950 | Smith, Alfred E. | 3,433 | 147,795 R | 63.2% | 36.2% | 63.6% | 36.4% |
| 1924 ** | 463,559 | 218,985 | Coolidge, Calvin | 137,299 | Davis, John W. | 107,275 | 81,686 R | 47.2% | 29.6% | 61.5% | 38.5% |
| 1920 | 382,743 | 247,498 | Harding, Warren G. | 119,608 | Cox, James M. | 15,637 | 127,890 R | 64.7% | 31.3% | 67.4% | 32.6% |

In 2000 the other vote column includes 24,540 votes cast for Green (Nader). In 1996 the other vote column includes 71,278 votes cast for Perot. In 1992 the other vote column includes 174,104 votes cast for Perot. In 1980 the other column includes 44,993 votes for Independent (Anderson). In 1924 the other vote was 105,681 Progressive and 1,594 Prohibition.

## ELECTORAL COLLEGE VOTE 1920 TO 2004

| Year | Total | Republican | Democratic | Other |
|------|-------|-----------|-----------|-------|
| 2004 | 5 | 5 | | |
| 2000 | 5 | 5 | | |
| 1996 | 5 | 5 | | |
| 1992 | 5 | 5 | | |
| 1988 | 5 | 5 | | |
| 1984 | 5 | 5 | | |
| 1980 | 5 | 5 | | |
| 1976 | 5 | 5 | | |
| 1972 | 5 | 5 | | |
| 1968 | 5 | 5 | | |
| 1964 | 5 | | 5 | |
| 1960 | 6 | 6 | | |
| 1956 | 6 | 6 | | |
| 1952 | 6 | 6 | | |
| 1948 | 6 | 6 | | |
| 1944 | 6 | 6 | | |
| 1940 | 7 | 7 | | |
| 1936 | 7 | | 7 | |
| 1932 | 7 | | 7 | |
| 1928 | 8 | 8 | | |
| 1924 | 8 | 8 | | |
| 1920 | 8 | 8 | | |

# NEBRASKA

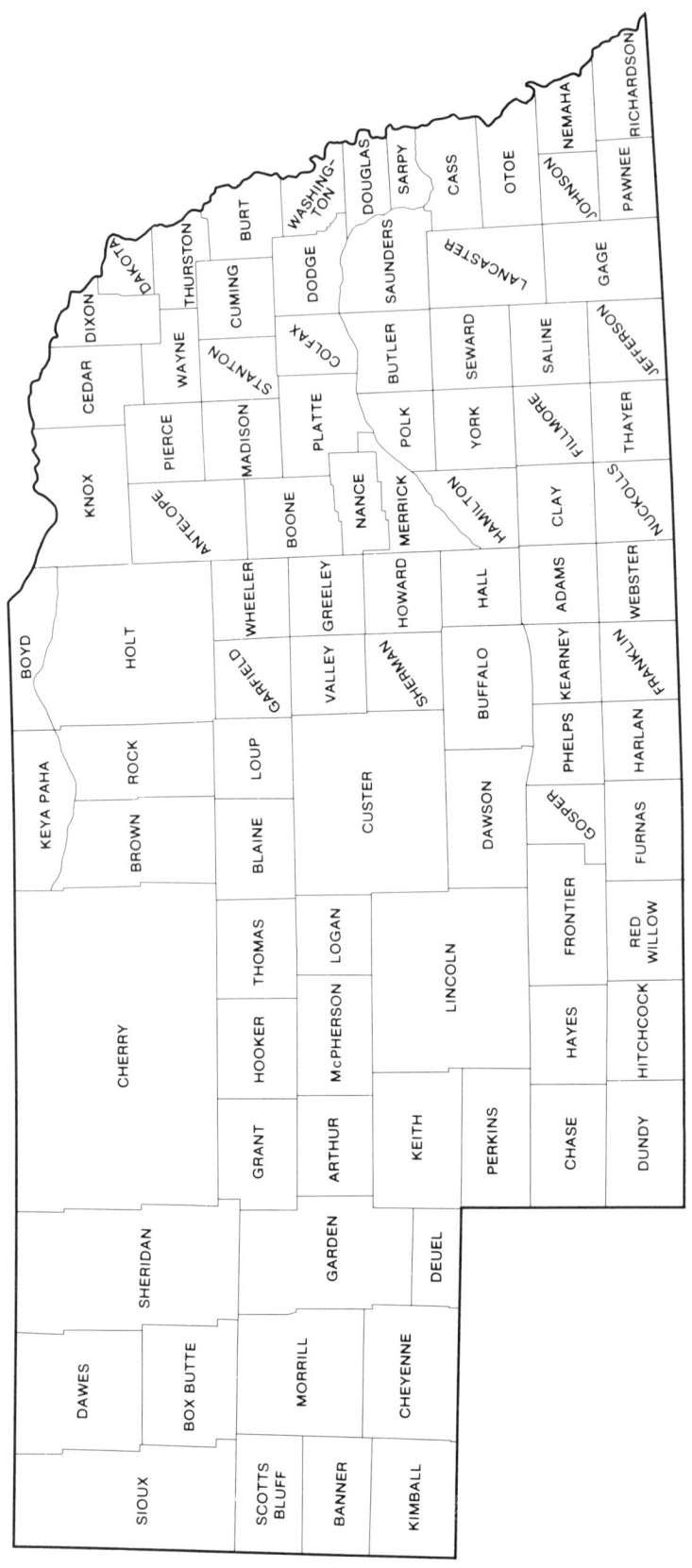

# NEBRASKA

## PRESIDENT 2004

| 2000 Census Population | County | Total Vote | Republican | Democratic | Other | Rep.-Dem. Plurality | Percentage Total Vote Rep. | Dem. | Major Vote Rep. | Dem. |
|---|---|---|---|---|---|---|---|---|---|---|
| 31,151 | ADAMS | 13,286 | 9,233 | 3,791 | 262 | 5,442 R | 69.5% | 28.5% | 70.9% | 29.1% |
| 7,452 | ANTELOPE | 3,424 | 2,761 | 613 | 50 | 2,148 R | 80.6% | 17.9% | 81.8% | 18.2% |
| 444 | ARTHUR | 266 | 240 | 24 | 2 | 216 R | 90.2% | 9.0% | 90.9% | 9.1% |
| 819 | BANNER | 437 | 379 | 56 | 2 | 323 R | 86.7% | 12.8% | 87.1% | 12.9% |
| 583 | BLAINE | 339 | 301 | 38 | | 263 R | 88.8% | 11.2% | 88.8% | 11.2% |
| 6,259 | BOONE | 2,895 | 2,309 | 546 | 40 | 1,763 R | 79.8% | 18.9% | 80.9% | 19.1% |
| 12,158 | BOX BUTTE | 5,152 | 3,396 | 1,657 | 99 | 1,739 R | 65.9% | 32.2% | 67.2% | 32.8% |
| 2,438 | BOYD | 1,148 | 911 | 228 | 9 | 683 R | 79.4% | 19.9% | 80.0% | 20.0% |
| 3,525 | BROWN | 1,733 | 1,426 | 268 | 39 | 1,158 R | 82.3% | 15.5% | 84.2% | 15.8% |
| 42,259 | BUFFALO | 18,608 | 14,222 | 4,100 | 286 | 10,122 R | 76.4% | 22.0% | 77.6% | 22.4% |
| 7,791 | BURT | 3,668 | 2,349 | 1,272 | 47 | 1,077 R | 64.0% | 34.7% | 64.9% | 35.1% |
| 8,767 | BUTLER | 4,168 | 3,016 | 1,068 | 84 | 1,948 R | 72.4% | 25.6% | 73.8% | 26.2% |
| 24,334 | CASS | 11,529 | 7,763 | 3,619 | 147 | 4,144 R | 67.3% | 31.4% | 68.2% | 31.8% |
| 9,615 | CEDAR | 4,536 | 3,387 | 1,083 | 66 | 2,304 R | 74.7% | 23.9% | 75.8% | 24.2% |
| 4,068 | CHASE | 1,973 | 1,652 | 302 | 19 | 1,350 R | 83.7% | 15.3% | 84.5% | 15.5% |
| 6,148 | CHERRY | 3,042 | 2,509 | 483 | 50 | 2,026 R | 82.5% | 15.9% | 83.9% | 16.1% |
| 9,830 | CHEYENNE | 4,746 | 3,791 | 893 | 62 | 2,898 R | 79.9% | 18.8% | 80.9% | 19.1% |
| 7,039 | CLAY | 3,337 | 2,543 | 743 | 51 | 1,800 R | 76.2% | 22.3% | 77.4% | 22.6% |
| 10,441 | COLFAX | 3,633 | 2,589 | 990 | 54 | 1,599 R | 71.3% | 27.3% | 72.3% | 27.7% |
| 10,203 | CUMING | 4,349 | 3,330 | 966 | 53 | 2,364 R | 76.6% | 22.2% | 77.5% | 22.5% |
| 11,793 | CUSTER | 5,612 | 4,518 | 1,040 | 54 | 3,478 R | 80.5% | 18.5% | 81.3% | 18.7% |
| 20,253 | DAKOTA | 6,615 | 3,526 | 3,027 | 62 | 499 R | 53.3% | 45.8% | 53.8% | 46.2% |
| 9,060 | DAWES | 3,994 | 2,809 | 1,119 | 66 | 1,690 R | 70.3% | 28.0% | 71.5% | 28.5% |
| 24,365 | DAWSON | 7,956 | 6,149 | 1,728 | 79 | 4,421 R | 77.3% | 21.7% | 78.1% | 21.9% |
| 2,098 | DEUEL | 1,053 | 820 | 222 | 11 | 598 R | 77.9% | 21.1% | 78.7% | 21.3% |
| 6,339 | DIXON | 3,009 | 2,028 | 938 | 43 | 1,090 R | 67.4% | 31.2% | 68.4% | 31.6% |
| 36,160 | DODGE | 16,172 | 10,716 | 5,250 | 206 | 5,466 R | 66.3% | 32.5% | 67.1% | 32.9% |
| 463,585 | DOUGLAS | 207,071 | 120,813 | 83,330 | 2,928 | 37,483 R | 58.3% | 40.2% | 59.2% | 40.8% |
| 2,292 | DUNDY | 1,053 | 858 | 186 | 9 | 672 R | 81.5% | 17.7% | 82.2% | 17.8% |
| 6,634 | FILLMORE | 3,193 | 2,314 | 828 | 51 | 1,486 R | 72.5% | 25.9% | 73.6% | 26.4% |
| 3,574 | FRANKLIN | 1,714 | 1,277 | 412 | 25 | 865 R | 74.5% | 24.0% | 75.6% | 24.4% |
| 3,099 | FRONTIER | 1,467 | 1,160 | 275 | 32 | 885 R | 79.1% | 18.7% | 80.8% | 19.2% |
| 5,324 | FURNAS | 2,467 | 1,950 | 492 | 25 | 1,458 R | 79.0% | 19.9% | 79.9% | 20.1% |
| 22,993 | GAGE | 10,384 | 6,575 | 3,655 | 154 | 2,920 R | 63.3% | 35.2% | 64.3% | 35.7% |
| 2,292 | GARDEN | 1,183 | 970 | 201 | 12 | 769 R | 82.0% | 17.0% | 82.8% | 17.2% |
| 1,902 | GARFIELD | 1,017 | 806 | 196 | 15 | 610 R | 79.3% | 19.3% | 80.4% | 19.6% |
| 2,143 | GOSPER | 1,119 | 890 | 222 | 7 | 668 R | 79.5% | 19.8% | 80.0% | 20.0% |
| 747 | GRANT | 396 | 352 | 41 | 3 | 311 R | 88.9% | 10.4% | 89.6% | 10.4% |
| 2,714 | GREELEY | 1,248 | 865 | 361 | 22 | 504 R | 69.3% | 28.9% | 70.6% | 29.4% |
| 53,534 | HALL | 21,154 | 14,592 | 6,228 | 334 | 8,364 R | 69.0% | 29.4% | 70.1% | 29.9% |
| 9,403 | HAMILTON | 4,866 | 3,785 | 1,012 | 69 | 2,773 R | 77.8% | 20.8% | 78.9% | 21.1% |
| 3,786 | HARLAN | 1,897 | 1,467 | 398 | 32 | 1,069 R | 77.3% | 21.0% | 78.7% | 21.3% |
| 1,068 | HAYES | 598 | 524 | 66 | 8 | 458 R | 87.6% | 11.0% | 88.8% | 11.2% |
| 3,111 | HITCHCOCK | 1,486 | 1,171 | 296 | 19 | 875 R | 78.8% | 19.9% | 79.8% | 20.2% |
| 11,551 | HOLT | 5,174 | 4,217 | 894 | 63 | 3,323 R | 81.5% | 17.3% | 82.5% | 17.5% |
| 783 | HOOKER | 461 | 392 | 64 | 5 | 328 R | 85.0% | 13.9% | 86.0% | 14.0% |
| 6,567 | HOWARD | 2,979 | 2,020 | 900 | 59 | 1,120 R | 67.8% | 30.2% | 69.2% | 30.8% |
| 8,333 | JEFFERSON | 4,011 | 2,600 | 1,352 | 59 | 1,248 R | 64.8% | 33.7% | 65.8% | 34.2% |
| 4,488 | JOHNSON | 2,394 | 1,470 | 885 | 39 | 585 R | 61.4% | 37.0% | 62.4% | 37.6% |
| 6,882 | KEARNEY | 3,379 | 2,621 | 707 | 51 | 1,914 R | 77.6% | 20.9% | 78.8% | 21.2% |
| 8,875 | KEITH | 4,137 | 3,356 | 743 | 38 | 2,613 R | 81.1% | 18.0% | 81.9% | 18.1% |
| 983 | KEYA PAHA | 549 | 442 | 98 | 9 | 344 R | 80.5% | 17.9% | 81.9% | 18.1% |
| 4,089 | KIMBALL | 1,877 | 1,491 | 366 | 20 | 1,125 R | 79.4% | 19.5% | 80.3% | 19.7% |
| 9,374 | KNOX | 4,213 | 3,062 | 1,086 | 65 | 1,976 R | 72.7% | 25.8% | 73.8% | 26.2% |
| 250,291 | LANCASTER | 124,509 | 69,764 | 52,747 | 1,998 | 17,017 R | 56.0% | 42.4% | 56.9% | 43.1% |
| 34,632 | LINCOLN | 16,199 | 11,056 | 4,905 | 238 | 6,151 R | 68.3% | 30.3% | 69.3% | 30.7% |
| 774 | LOGAN | 429 | 357 | 67 | 5 | 290 R | 83.2% | 15.6% | 84.2% | 15.8% |
| 712 | LOUP | 386 | 314 | 68 | 4 | 246 R | 81.3% | 17.6% | 82.2% | 17.8% |
| 533 | MCPHERSON | 312 | 259 | 49 | 4 | 210 R | 83.0% | 15.7% | 84.1% | 15.9% |
| 35,226 | MADISON | 14,089 | 10,981 | 2,934 | 174 | 8,047 R | 77.9% | 20.8% | 78.9% | 21.1% |

# NEBRASKA

## PRESIDENT 2004

| 2000 Census Population | County | Total Vote | Republican | Democratic | Other | Rep.-Dem. Plurality | Percentage | | | |
|---|---|---|---|---|---|---|---|---|---|---|
| | | | | | | | Total Vote | | Major Vote | |
| | | | | | | | Rep. | Dem. | Rep. | Dem. |
| 8,204 | MERRICK | 3,657 | 2,771 | 833 | 53 | 1,938 R | 75.8% | 22.8% | 76.9% | 23.1% |
| 5,440 | MORRILL | 2,293 | 1,755 | 495 | 43 | 1,260 R | 76.5% | 21.6% | 78.0% | 22.0% |
| 4,038 | NANCE | 1,731 | 1,237 | 459 | 35 | 778 R | 71.5% | 26.5% | 72.9% | 27.1% |
| 7,576 | NEMAHA | 3,715 | 2,595 | 1,066 | 54 | 1,529 R | 69.9% | 28.7% | 70.9% | 29.1% |
| 5,057 | NUCKOLLS | 2,471 | 1,884 | 541 | 46 | 1,343 R | 76.2% | 21.9% | 77.7% | 22.3% |
| 15,396 | OTOE | 7,386 | 5,018 | 2,275 | 93 | 2,743 R | 67.9% | 30.8% | 68.8% | 31.2% |
| 3,087 | PAWNEE | 1,483 | 986 | 481 | 16 | 505 R | 66.5% | 32.4% | 67.2% | 32.8% |
| 3,200 | PERKINS | 1,558 | 1,285 | 262 | 11 | 1,023 R | 82.5% | 16.8% | 83.1% | 16.9% |
| 9,747 | PHELPS | 4,743 | 3,872 | 830 | 41 | 3,042 R | 81.6% | 17.5% | 82.3% | 17.7% |
| 7,857 | PIERCE | 3,398 | 2,824 | 546 | 28 | 2,278 R | 83.1% | 16.1% | 83.8% | 16.2% |
| 31,662 | PLATTE | 13,987 | 11,130 | 2,657 | 200 | 8,473 R | 79.6% | 19.0% | 80.7% | 19.3% |
| 5,639 | POLK | 2,727 | 2,146 | 549 | 32 | 1,597 R | 78.7% | 20.1% | 79.6% | 20.4% |
| 11,448 | RED WILLOW | 5,258 | 4,129 | 1,055 | 74 | 3,074 R | 78.5% | 20.1% | 79.6% | 20.4% |
| 9,531 | RICHARDSON | 4,278 | 2,924 | 1,297 | 57 | 1,627 R | 68.3% | 30.3% | 69.3% | 30.7% |
| 1,756 | ROCK | 883 | 740 | 130 | 13 | 610 R | 83.8% | 14.7% | 85.1% | 14.9% |
| 13,843 | SALINE | 5,566 | 3,071 | 2,420 | 75 | 651 R | 55.2% | 43.5% | 55.9% | 44.1% |
| 122,595 | SARPY | 58,334 | 40,163 | 17,455 | 716 | 22,708 R | 68.9% | 29.9% | 69.7% | 30.3% |
| 19,830 | SAUNDERS | 9,489 | 6,441 | 2,884 | 164 | 3,557 R | 67.9% | 30.4% | 69.1% | 30.9% |
| 36,951 | SCOTTS BLUFF | 14,390 | 10,378 | 3,843 | 169 | 6,535 R | 72.1% | 26.7% | 73.0% | 27.0% |
| 16,496 | SEWARD | 7,565 | 5,353 | 2,114 | 98 | 3,239 R | 70.8% | 27.9% | 71.7% | 28.3% |
| 6,198 | SHERIDAN | 2,599 | 2,136 | 430 | 33 | 1,706 R | 82.2% | 16.5% | 83.2% | 16.8% |
| 3,318 | SHERMAN | 1,643 | 1,072 | 541 | 30 | 531 R | 65.2% | 32.9% | 66.5% | 33.5% |
| 1,475 | SIOUX | 809 | 677 | 123 | 9 | 554 R | 83.7% | 15.2% | 84.6% | 15.4% |
| 6,455 | STANTON | 2,745 | 2,159 | 559 | 27 | 1,600 R | 78.7% | 20.4% | 79.4% | 20.6% |
| 6,055 | THAYER | 2,878 | 2,075 | 764 | 39 | 1,311 R | 72.1% | 26.5% | 73.1% | 26.9% |
| 729 | THOMAS | 444 | 378 | 60 | 6 | 318 R | 85.1% | 13.5% | 86.3% | 13.7% |
| 7,171 | THURSTON | 2,387 | 1,154 | 1,212 | 21 | 58 D | 48.3% | 50.8% | 48.8% | 51.2% |
| 4,647 | VALLEY | 2,391 | 1,801 | 564 | 26 | 1,237 R | 75.3% | 23.6% | 76.2% | 23.8% |
| 18,780 | WASHINGTON | 9,950 | 7,083 | 2,754 | 113 | 4,329 R | 71.2% | 27.7% | 72.0% | 28.0% |
| 9,851 | WAYNE | 4,085 | 2,971 | 1,059 | 55 | 1,912 R | 72.7% | 25.9% | 73.7% | 26.3% |
| 4,061 | WEBSTER | 2,002 | 1,403 | 557 | 42 | 846 R | 70.1% | 27.8% | 71.6% | 28.4% |
| 886 | WHEELER | 453 | 366 | 81 | 6 | 285 R | 80.8% | 17.9% | 81.9% | 18.1% |
| 14,598 | YORK | 6,797 | 5,393 | 1,304 | 100 | 4,089 R | 79.3% | 19.2% | 80.5% | 19.5% |
| 1,711,263 | TOTAL | 778,186 | 512,814 | 254,328 | 11,044 | 258,486 R | 65.9% | 32.7% | 66.8% | 33.2% |

# NEBRASKA

## PRESIDENT 2000

| 2000 Census Population | County | Total Vote | Republican | Democratic | Green (Nader) | Other | Rep.-Dem. Plurality | Percentage of Total Vote | | |
|---|---|---|---|---|---|---|---|---|---|---|
| | | | | | | | | Rep. | Dem. | Green |
| 31,151 | ADAMS | 12,438 | 8,162 | 3,686 | 472 | 118 | 4,476 R | 65.6% | 29.6% | 3.8% |
| 7,452 | ANTELOPE | 3,368 | 2,562 | 678 | 84 | 44 | 1,884 R | 76.1% | 20.1% | 2.5% |
| 444 | ARTHUR | 272 | 235 | 26 | 6 | 5 | 209 R | 86.4% | 9.6% | 2.2% |
| 819 | BANNER | 462 | 390 | 65 | 2 | 5 | 325 R | 84.4% | 14.1% | 0.4% |
| 583 | BLAINE | 349 | 299 | 43 | 5 | 2 | 256 R | 85.7% | 12.3% | 1.4% |
| 6,259 | BOONE | 2,862 | 2,196 | 575 | 65 | 26 | 1,621 R | 76.7% | 20.1% | 2.3% |
| 12,158 | BOX BUTTE | 5,089 | 3,208 | 1,614 | 203 | 64 | 1,594 R | 63.0% | 31.7% | 4.0% |
| 2,438 | BOYD | 1,242 | 931 | 265 | 25 | 21 | 666 R | 75.0% | 21.3% | 2.0% |
| 3,525 | BROWN | 1,684 | 1,375 | 250 | 36 | 23 | 1,125 R | 81.7% | 14.8% | 2.1% |
| 42,259 | BUFFALO | 16,461 | 11,931 | 3,927 | 483 | 120 | 8,004 R | 72.5% | 23.9% | 2.9% |
| 7,791 | BURT | 3,392 | 2,056 | 1,223 | 73 | 40 | 833 R | 60.6% | 36.1% | 2.2% |
| 8,767 | BUTLER | 3,828 | 2,638 | 1,028 | 108 | 54 | 1,610 R | 68.9% | 26.9% | 2.8% |
| 24,334 | CASS | 10,280 | 6,144 | 3,656 | 369 | 111 | 2,488 R | 59.8% | 35.6% | 3.6% |
| 9,615 | CEDAR | 4,269 | 2,989 | 1,062 | 140 | 78 | 1,927 R | 70.0% | 24.9% | 3.3% |
| 4,068 | CHASE | 1,875 | 1,505 | 306 | 38 | 26 | 1,199 R | 80.3% | 16.3% | 2.0% |
| 6,148 | CHERRY | 2,847 | 2,322 | 446 | 50 | 29 | 1,876 R | 81.6% | 15.7% | 1.8% |
| 9,830 | CHEYENNE | 4,186 | 3,207 | 844 | 76 | 59 | 2,363 R | 76.6% | 20.2% | 1.8% |
| 7,039 | CLAY | 3,215 | 2,326 | 774 | 86 | 29 | 1,552 R | 72.3% | 24.1% | 2.7% |
| 10,441 | COLFAX | 3,315 | 2,338 | 863 | 72 | 42 | 1,475 R | 70.5% | 26.0% | 2.2% |
| 10,203 | CUMING | 4,215 | 3,232 | 857 | 91 | 35 | 2,375 R | 76.7% | 20.3% | 2.2% |
| 11,793 | CUSTER | 5,414 | 4,245 | 976 | 140 | 53 | 3,269 R | 78.4% | 18.0% | 2.6% |
| 20,253 | DAKOTA | 6,061 | 3,119 | 2,695 | 141 | 106 | 424 R | 51.5% | 44.5% | 2.3% |
| 9,060 | DAWES | 3,621 | 2,549 | 823 | 212 | 37 | 1,726 R | 70.4% | 22.7% | 5.9% |
| 24,365 | DAWSON | 7,507 | 5,511 | 1,740 | 143 | 113 | 3,771 R | 73.4% | 23.2% | 1.9% |
| 2,098 | DEUEL | 1,033 | 783 | 213 | 27 | 10 | 570 R | 75.8% | 20.6% | 2.6% |
| 6,339 | DIXON | 2,792 | 1,834 | 820 | 60 | 78 | 1,014 R | 65.7% | 29.4% | 2.1% |
| 36,160 | DODGE | 14,472 | 8,871 | 5,021 | 443 | 137 | 3,850 R | 61.3% | 34.7% | 3.1% |
| 463,585 | DOUGLAS | 183,156 | 101,025 | 73,347 | 7,109 | 1,675 | 27,678 R | 55.2% | 40.0% | 3.9% |
| 2,292 | DUNDY | 1,011 | 801 | 179 | 19 | 12 | 622 R | 79.2% | 17.7% | 1.9% |
| 6,634 | FILLMORE | 2,998 | 2,024 | 848 | 103 | 23 | 1,176 R | 67.5% | 28.3% | 3.4% |
| 3,574 | FRANKLIN | 1,668 | 1,196 | 420 | 36 | 16 | 776 R | 71.7% | 25.2% | 2.2% |
| 3,099 | FRONTIER | 1,393 | 1,102 | 244 | 27 | 20 | 858 R | 79.1% | 17.5% | 1.9% |
| 5,324 | FURNAS | 2,431 | 1,849 | 534 | 29 | 19 | 1,315 R | 76.1% | 22.0% | 1.2% |
| 22,993 | GAGE | 9,506 | 5,538 | 3,516 | 355 | 97 | 2,022 R | 58.3% | 37.0% | 3.7% |
| 2,292 | GARDEN | 1,219 | 963 | 203 | 38 | 15 | 760 R | 79.0% | 16.7% | 3.1% |
| 1,902 | GARFIELD | 963 | 718 | 202 | 33 | 10 | 516 R | 74.6% | 21.0% | 3.4% |
| 2,143 | GOSPER | 1,014 | 757 | 228 | 19 | 10 | 529 R | 74.7% | 22.5% | 1.9% |
| 747 | GRANT | 385 | 324 | 49 | 10 | 2 | 275 R | 84.2% | 12.7% | 2.6% |
| 2,714 | GREELEY | 1,310 | 839 | 416 | 37 | 18 | 423 R | 64.0% | 31.8% | 2.8% |
| 53,534 | HALL | 18,546 | 11,803 | 5,952 | 595 | 196 | 5,851 R | 63.6% | 32.1% | 3.2% |
| 9,403 | HAMILTON | 4,491 | 3,251 | 1,066 | 141 | 33 | 2,185 R | 72.4% | 23.7% | 3.1% |
| 3,786 | HARLAN | 1,852 | 1,358 | 438 | 37 | 19 | 920 R | 73.3% | 23.7% | 2.0% |
| 1,068 | HAYES | 571 | 486 | 66 | 8 | 11 | 420 R | 85.1% | 11.6% | 1.4% |
| 3,111 | HITCHCOCK | 1,480 | 1,126 | 312 | 21 | 21 | 814 R | 76.1% | 21.1% | 1.4% |
| 11,551 | HOLT | 4,959 | 3,954 | 846 | 93 | 66 | 3,108 R | 79.7% | 17.1% | 1.9% |
| 783 | HOOKER | 409 | 317 | 74 | 13 | 5 | 243 R | 77.5% | 18.1% | 3.2% |
| 6,567 | HOWARD | 2,827 | 1,760 | 955 | 71 | 41 | 805 R | 62.3% | 33.8% | 2.5% |
| 8,333 | JEFFERSON | 3,847 | 2,351 | 1,361 | 102 | 33 | 990 R | 61.1% | 35.4% | 2.7% |
| 4,488 | JOHNSON | 2,112 | 1,210 | 794 | 74 | 34 | 416 R | 57.3% | 37.6% | 3.5% |
| 6,882 | KEARNEY | 3,122 | 2,333 | 680 | 75 | 34 | 1,653 R | 74.7% | 21.8% | 2.4% |
| 8,875 | KEITH | 3,849 | 2,953 | 778 | 75 | 43 | 2,175 R | 76.7% | 20.2% | 1.9% |
| 983 | KEYA PAHA | 513 | 422 | 78 | 6 | 7 | 344 R | 82.3% | 15.2% | 1.2% |
| 4,089 | KIMBALL | 1,820 | 1,379 | 379 | 41 | 21 | 1,000 R | 75.8% | 20.8% | 2.3% |
| 9,374 | KNOX | 3,978 | 2,784 | 1,037 | 110 | 47 | 1,747 R | 70.0% | 26.1% | 2.8% |
| 250,291 | LANCASTER | 107,132 | 55,514 | 44,650 | 6,182 | 786 | 10,864 R | 51.8% | 41.7% | 5.8% |
| 34,632 | LINCOLN | 15,114 | 9,220 | 5,205 | 502 | 187 | 4,015 R | 61.0% | 34.4% | 3.3% |
| 774 | LOGAN | 412 | 336 | 60 | 11 | 5 | 276 R | 81.6% | 14.6% | 2.7% |
| 712 | LOUP | 378 | 284 | 84 | 7 | 3 | 200 R | 75.1% | 22.2% | 1.9% |
| 533 | MCPHERSON | 301 | 244 | 48 | 1 | 8 | 196 R | 81.1% | 15.9% | 0.3% |
| 35,226 | MADISON | 12,853 | 9,636 | 2,772 | 290 | 155 | 6,864 R | 75.0% | 21.6% | 2.3% |

# NEBRASKA

## PRESIDENT 2000

| 2000 Census Population | County | Total Vote | Republican | Democratic | Green (Nader) | Other | Rep.-Dem. Plurality | Percentage of Total Vote | | |
|---|---|---|---|---|---|---|---|---|---|---|
| | | | | | | | | Rep. | Dem. | Green |
| 8,204 | MERRICK | 3,340 | 2,380 | 848 | 84 | 28 | 1,532 R | 71.3% | 25.4% | 2.5% |
| 5,440 | MORRILL | 2,138 | 1,597 | 460 | 46 | 35 | 1,137 R | 74.7% | 21.5% | 2.2% |
| 4,038 | NANCE | 1,665 | 1,105 | 497 | 46 | 17 | 608 R | 66.4% | 29.8% | 2.8% |
| 7,576 | NEMAHA | 3,369 | 2,177 | 1,063 | 94 | 35 | 1,114 R | 64.6% | 31.6% | 2.8% |
| 5,057 | NUCKOLLS | 2,443 | 1,701 | 644 | 66 | 32 | 1,057 R | 69.6% | 26.4% | 2.7% |
| 15,396 | OTOE | 6,662 | 4,178 | 2,208 | 218 | 58 | 1,970 R | 62.7% | 33.1% | 3.3% |
| 3,087 | PAWNEE | 1,519 | 937 | 522 | 38 | 22 | 415 R | 61.7% | 34.4% | 2.5% |
| 3,200 | PERKINS | 1,452 | 1,170 | 243 | 31 | 8 | 927 R | 80.6% | 16.7% | 2.1% |
| 9,747 | PHELPS | 4,627 | 3,575 | 934 | 86 | 32 | 2,641 R | 77.3% | 20.2% | 1.9% |
| 7,857 | PIERCE | 3,208 | 2,534 | 570 | 52 | 52 | 1,964 R | 79.0% | 17.8% | 1.6% |
| 31,662 | PLATTE | 12,859 | 9,861 | 2,612 | 266 | 120 | 7,249 R | 76.7% | 20.3% | 2.1% |
| 5,639 | POLK | 2,613 | 1,925 | 610 | 52 | 26 | 1,315 R | 73.7% | 23.3% | 2.0% |
| 11,448 | RED WILLOW | 5,025 | 3,680 | 1,188 | 103 | 54 | 2,492 R | 73.2% | 23.6% | 2.0% |
| 9,531 | RICHARDSON | 4,150 | 2,623 | 1,382 | 83 | 62 | 1,241 R | 63.2% | 33.3% | 2.0% |
| 1,756 | ROCK | 894 | 725 | 141 | 17 | 11 | 584 R | 81.1% | 15.8% | 1.9% |
| 13,843 | SALINE | 5,145 | 2,581 | 2,321 | 187 | 56 | 260 R | 50.2% | 45.1% | 3.6% |
| 122,595 | SARPY | 45,278 | 28,979 | 14,637 | 1,308 | 354 | 14,342 R | 64.0% | 32.3% | 2.9% |
| 19,830 | SAUNDERS | 8,919 | 5,688 | 2,852 | 277 | 102 | 2,836 R | 63.8% | 32.0% | 3.1% |
| 36,951 | SCOTTS BLUFF | 13,839 | 9,397 | 3,937 | 400 | 105 | 5,460 R | 67.9% | 28.4% | 2.9% |
| 16,496 | SEWARD | 7,016 | 4,457 | 2,250 | 245 | 64 | 2,207 R | 63.5% | 32.1% | 3.5% |
| 6,198 | SHERIDAN | 2,576 | 2,105 | 392 | 54 | 25 | 1,713 R | 81.7% | 15.2% | 2.1% |
| 3,318 | SHERMAN | 1,705 | 1,072 | 564 | 48 | 21 | 508 R | 62.9% | 33.1% | 2.8% |
| 1,475 | SIOUX | 752 | 629 | 98 | 18 | 7 | 531 R | 83.6% | 13.0% | 2.4% |
| 6,455 | STANTON | 2,486 | 1,895 | 500 | 53 | 38 | 1,395 R | 76.2% | 20.1% | 2.1% |
| 6,055 | THAYER | 3,006 | 2,096 | 821 | 65 | 24 | 1,275 R | 69.7% | 27.3% | 2.2% |
| 729 | THOMAS | 395 | 329 | 55 | 9 | 2 | 274 R | 83.3% | 13.9% | 2.3% |
| 7,171 | THURSTON | 2,082 | 1,040 | 924 | 56 | 62 | 116 R | 50.0% | 44.4% | 2.7% |
| 4,647 | VALLEY | 2,263 | 1,610 | 583 | 45 | 25 | 1,027 R | 71.1% | 25.8% | 2.0% |
| 18,780 | WASHINGTON | 8,626 | 5,758 | 2,550 | 234 | 84 | 3,208 R | 66.8% | 29.6% | 2.7% |
| 9,851 | WAYNE | 3,940 | 2,774 | 1,001 | 119 | 46 | 1,773 R | 70.4% | 25.4% | 3.0% |
| 4,061 | WEBSTER | 1,945 | 1,302 | 584 | 48 | 11 | 718 R | 66.9% | 30.0% | 2.5% |
| 886 | WHEELER | 453 | 351 | 85 | 11 | 6 | 266 R | 77.5% | 18.8% | 2.4% |
| 14,598 | YORK | 6,460 | 4,816 | 1,407 | 161 | 76 | 3,409 R | 74.6% | 21.8% | 2.5% |
| 1,711,263 | TOTAL | 697,019 | 433,862 | 231,780 | 24,540 | 6,837 | 202,082 R | 62.2% | 33.3% | 3.5% |

# NEBRASKA

## PRESIDENT 1996

| 1995 Census Pop. Est. | County | Total Vote | Republican | Democratic | Reform (Perot) | Other | Rep.-Dem. Plurality | Percentage of Total Vote Rep. | Dem. | Reform |
|---:|---|---:|---:|---:|---:|---:|---:|---:|---:|---:|
| 29,728 | ADAMS | 12,496 | 6,924 | 3,935 | 1,513 | 124 | 2,989 R | 55.4% | 31.5% | 12.1% |
| 7,502 | ANTELOPE | 3,370 | 2,005 | 884 | 457 | 24 | 1,121 R | 59.5% | 26.2% | 13.6% |
| 440 | ARTHUR | 258 | 187 | 25 | 46 | | 162 R | 72.5% | 9.7% | 17.8% |
| 848 | BANNER | 406 | 309 | 62 | 30 | 5 | 247 R | 76.1% | 15.3% | 7.4% |
| 667 | BLAINE | 378 | 284 | 53 | 39 | 2 | 231 R | 75.1% | 14.0% | 10.3% |
| 6,517 | BOONE | 2,941 | 1,695 | 806 | 424 | 16 | 889 R | 57.6% | 27.4% | 14.4% |
| 13,006 | BOX BUTTE | 4,975 | 2,458 | 1,782 | 695 | 40 | 676 R | 49.4% | 35.8% | 14.0% |
| 2,763 | BOYD | 1,342 | 778 | 372 | 181 | 11 | 406 R | 58.0% | 27.7% | 13.5% |
| 3,652 | BROWN | 1,766 | 1,105 | 359 | 289 | 13 | 746 R | 62.6% | 20.3% | 16.4% |
| 39,516 | BUFFALO | 15,856 | 10,004 | 4,277 | 1,484 | 91 | 5,727 R | 63.1% | 27.0% | 9.4% |
| 7,970 | BURT | 3,496 | 1,707 | 1,237 | 497 | 55 | 470 R | 48.8% | 35.4% | 14.2% |
| 8,591 | BUTLER | 3,696 | 2,042 | 1,099 | 512 | 43 | 943 R | 55.2% | 29.7% | 13.9% |
| 22,913 | CASS | 9,685 | 4,878 | 3,477 | 1,239 | 91 | 1,401 R | 50.4% | 35.9% | 12.8% |
| 10,071 | CEDAR | 4,159 | 2,171 | 1,218 | 739 | 31 | 953 R | 52.2% | 29.3% | 17.8% |
| 4,287 | CHASE | 1,854 | 1,277 | 365 | 197 | 15 | 912 R | 68.9% | 19.7% | 10.6% |
| 6,374 | CHERRY | 2,800 | 1,905 | 551 | 332 | 12 | 1,354 R | 68.0% | 19.7% | 11.9% |
| 9,573 | CHEYENNE | 3,966 | 2,571 | 1,059 | 287 | 49 | 1,512 R | 64.8% | 26.7% | 7.2% |
| 7,132 | CLAY | 3,311 | 1,982 | 880 | 425 | 24 | 1,102 R | 59.9% | 26.6% | 12.8% |
| 10,140 | COLFAX | 3,538 | 1,954 | 1,065 | 492 | 27 | 889 R | 55.2% | 30.1% | 13.9% |
| 10,147 | CUMING | 4,091 | 2,520 | 1,033 | 503 | 35 | 1,487 R | 61.6% | 25.3% | 12.3% |
| 12,258 | CUSTER | 5,383 | 3,453 | 1,293 | 615 | 22 | 2,160 R | 64.1% | 24.0% | 11.4% |
| 18,206 | DAKOTA | 5,985 | 2,592 | 2,632 | 721 | 40 | 40 D | 43.3% | 44.0% | 12.0% |
| 9,140 | DAWES | 3,575 | 1,991 | 1,108 | 442 | 34 | 883 R | 55.7% | 31.0% | 12.4% |
| 22,688 | DAWSON | 8,065 | 4,794 | 2,180 | 1,044 | 47 | 2,614 R | 59.4% | 27.0% | 12.9% |
| 2,119 | DEUEL | 991 | 629 | 245 | 111 | 6 | 384 R | 63.5% | 24.7% | 11.2% |
| 6,282 | DIXON | 2,845 | 1,478 | 931 | 414 | 22 | 547 R | 52.0% | 32.7% | 14.6% |
| 34,722 | DODGE | 14,688 | 7,484 | 5,181 | 1,894 | 129 | 2,303 R | 51.0% | 35.3% | 12.9% |
| 434,147 | DOUGLAS | 179,721 | 92,334 | 70,708 | 14,863 | 1,816 | 21,626 R | 51.4% | 39.3% | 8.3% |
| 2,441 | DUNDY | 1,101 | 752 | 224 | 112 | 13 | 528 R | 68.3% | 20.3% | 10.2% |
| 6,966 | FILLMORE | 3,095 | 1,696 | 1,058 | 321 | 20 | 638 R | 54.8% | 34.2% | 10.4% |
| 3,715 | FRANKLIN | 1,716 | 1,013 | 483 | 215 | 5 | 530 R | 59.0% | 28.1% | 12.5% |
| 3,168 | FRONTIER | 1,387 | 901 | 310 | 169 | 7 | 591 R | 65.0% | 22.4% | 12.2% |
| 5,658 | FURNAS | 2,411 | 1,475 | 663 | 207 | 66 | 812 R | 61.2% | 27.5% | 8.6% |
| 22,848 | GAGE | 9,843 | 4,413 | 4,008 | 1,346 | 76 | 405 R | 44.8% | 40.7% | 13.7% |
| 2,240 | GARDEN | 1,297 | 851 | 279 | 155 | 12 | 572 R | 65.6% | 21.5% | 12.0% |
| 2,066 | GARFIELD | 988 | 625 | 249 | 111 | 3 | 376 R | 63.3% | 25.2% | 11.2% |
| 2,150 | GOSPER | 1,036 | 609 | 275 | 150 | 2 | 334 R | 58.8% | 26.5% | 14.5% |
| 777 | GRANT | 398 | 258 | 84 | 55 | 1 | 174 R | 64.8% | 21.1% | 13.8% |
| 2,958 | GREELEY | 1,277 | 642 | 472 | 155 | 8 | 170 R | 50.3% | 37.0% | 12.1% |
| 51,178 | HALL | 19,416 | 10,183 | 6,708 | 2,403 | 122 | 3,475 R | 52.4% | 34.5% | 12.4% |
| 9,305 | HAMILTON | 4,274 | 2,623 | 1,172 | 457 | 22 | 1,451 R | 61.4% | 27.4% | 10.7% |
| 3,689 | HARLAN | 1,858 | 1,120 | 520 | 203 | 15 | 600 R | 60.3% | 28.0% | 10.9% |
| 1,140 | HAYES | 570 | 439 | 87 | 39 | 5 | 352 R | 77.0% | 15.3% | 6.8% |
| 3,427 | HITCHCOCK | 1,569 | 977 | 409 | 173 | 10 | 568 R | 62.3% | 26.1% | 11.0% |
| 12,387 | HOLT | 5,264 | 3,436 | 1,107 | 677 | 44 | 2,329 R | 65.3% | 21.0% | 12.9% |
| 733 | HOOKER | 514 | 308 | 115 | 83 | 8 | 193 R | 59.9% | 22.4% | 16.1% |
| 6,339 | HOWARD | 2,583 | 1,294 | 853 | 417 | 19 | 441 R | 50.1% | 33.0% | 16.1% |
| 8,445 | JEFFERSON | 4,025 | 1,979 | 1,520 | 495 | 31 | 459 R | 49.2% | 37.8% | 12.3% |
| 4,583 | JOHNSON | 2,103 | 1,009 | 770 | 309 | 15 | 239 R | 48.0% | 36.6% | 14.7% |
| 6,638 | KEARNEY | 3,048 | 1,953 | 782 | 296 | 17 | 1,171 R | 64.1% | 25.7% | 9.7% |
| 8,622 | KEITH | 3,823 | 2,504 | 830 | 460 | 29 | 1,674 R | 65.5% | 21.7% | 12.0% |
| 1,020 | KEYA PAHA | 534 | 385 | 94 | 47 | 8 | 291 R | 72.1% | 17.6% | 8.8% |
| 4,143 | KIMBALL | 1,784 | 1,011 | 527 | 212 | 34 | 484 R | 56.7% | 29.5% | 11.9% |
| 9,409 | KNOX | 3,938 | 2,123 | 1,266 | 531 | 18 | 857 R | 53.9% | 32.1% | 13.5% |
| 228,638 | LANCASTER | 97,708 | 44,812 | 43,339 | 8,595 | 962 | 1,473 R | 45.9% | 44.4% | 8.8% |
| 33,468 | LINCOLN | 14,804 | 7,482 | 5,165 | 2,043 | 114 | 2,317 R | 50.5% | 34.9% | 13.8% |
| 853 | LOGAN | 448 | 294 | 79 | 72 | 3 | 215 R | 65.6% | 17.6% | 16.1% |
| 695 | LOUP | 333 | 229 | 74 | 28 | 2 | 155 R | 68.8% | 22.2% | 8.4% |
| 544 | MCPHERSON | 322 | 233 | 50 | 33 | 6 | 183 R | 72.4% | 15.5% | 10.2% |
| 34,341 | MADISON | 12,649 | 7,965 | 3,047 | 1,554 | 83 | 4,918 R | 63.0% | 24.1% | 12.3% |

# NEBRASKA

## PRESIDENT 1996

| 1995 Census Pop. Est. | County | Total Vote | Republican | Democratic | Reform (Perot) | Other | Rep.-Dem. Plurality | Percentage of Total Vote | | |
|---|---|---|---|---|---|---|---|---|---|---|
| | | | | | | | | Rep. | Dem. | Reform |
| 8,156 | MERRICK | 3,552 | 2,084 | 997 | 449 | 22 | 1,087 R | 58.7% | 28.1% | 12.6% |
| 5,347 | MORRILL | 2,202 | 1,296 | 620 | 262 | 24 | 676 R | 58.9% | 28.2% | 11.9% |
| 4,241 | NANCE | 1,724 | 892 | 585 | 238 | 9 | 307 R | 51.7% | 33.9% | 13.8% |
| 8,033 | NEMAHA | 3,635 | 1,888 | 1,232 | 485 | 30 | 656 R | 51.9% | 33.9% | 13.3% |
| 5,569 | NUCKOLLS | 2,469 | 1,383 | 757 | 306 | 23 | 626 R | 56.0% | 30.7% | 12.4% |
| 14,346 | OTOE | 6,505 | 3,290 | 2,279 | 877 | 59 | 1,011 R | 50.6% | 35.0% | 13.5% |
| 3,322 | PAWNEE | 1,569 | 766 | 580 | 207 | 16 | 186 R | 48.8% | 37.0% | 13.2% |
| 3,265 | PERKINS | 1,541 | 1,018 | 352 | 163 | 8 | 666 R | 66.1% | 22.8% | 10.6% |
| 9,982 | PHELPS | 4,578 | 3,015 | 1,071 | 465 | 27 | 1,944 R | 65.9% | 23.4% | 10.2% |
| 7,874 | PIERCE | 3,082 | 1,923 | 697 | 446 | 16 | 1,226 R | 62.4% | 22.6% | 14.5% |
| 30,651 | PLATTE | 12,398 | 7,948 | 3,010 | 1,353 | 87 | 4,938 R | 64.1% | 24.3% | 10.9% |
| 5,659 | POLK | 2,556 | 1,504 | 750 | 268 | 34 | 754 R | 58.8% | 29.3% | 10.5% |
| 11,416 | RED WILLOW | 5,011 | 3,112 | 1,365 | 499 | 35 | 1,747 R | 62.1% | 27.2% | 10.0% |
| 9,696 | RICHARDSON | 4,276 | 2,089 | 1,517 | 633 | 37 | 572 R | 48.9% | 35.5% | 14.8% |
| 1,870 | ROCK | 885 | 564 | 180 | 135 | 6 | 384 R | 63.7% | 20.3% | 15.3% |
| 12,938 | SALINE | 5,175 | 1,945 | 2,523 | 689 | 18 | 578 D | 37.6% | 48.8% | 13.3% |
| 111,806 | SARPY | 39,877 | 23,023 | 12,806 | 3,722 | 326 | 10,217 R | 57.7% | 32.1% | 9.3% |
| 19,010 | SAUNDERS | 8,597 | 4,514 | 2,777 | 1,223 | 83 | 1,737 R | 52.5% | 32.3% | 14.2% |
| 37,161 | SCOTTS BLUFF | 13,541 | 7,641 | 4,547 | 1,251 | 102 | 3,094 R | 56.4% | 33.6% | 9.2% |
| 16,267 | SEWARD | 6,709 | 3,479 | 2,432 | 745 | 53 | 1,047 R | 51.9% | 36.2% | 11.1% |
| 6,704 | SHERIDAN | 2,717 | 1,834 | 573 | 289 | 21 | 1,261 R | 67.5% | 21.1% | 10.6% |
| 3,584 | SHERMAN | 1,672 | 822 | 567 | 266 | 17 | 255 R | 49.2% | 33.9% | 15.9% |
| 1,619 | SIOUX | 768 | 551 | 138 | 75 | 4 | 413 R | 71.7% | 18.0% | 9.8% |
| 6,229 | STANTON | 2,443 | 1,457 | 577 | 386 | 23 | 880 R | 59.6% | 23.6% | 15.8% |
| 6,393 | THAYER | 2,989 | 1,698 | 933 | 334 | 24 | 765 R | 56.8% | 31.2% | 11.2% |
| 848 | THOMAS | 429 | 303 | 64 | 62 | | 239 R | 70.6% | 14.9% | 14.5% |
| 7,199 | THURSTON | 2,114 | 835 | 962 | 293 | 24 | 127 D | 39.5% | 45.5% | 13.9% |
| 4,914 | VALLEY | 2,392 | 1,346 | 758 | 274 | 14 | 588 R | 56.3% | 31.7% | 11.5% |
| 17,755 | WASHINGTON | 7,700 | 4,391 | 2,248 | 971 | 90 | 2,143 R | 57.0% | 29.2% | 12.6% |
| 9,561 | WAYNE | 3,676 | 2,150 | 1,048 | 440 | 38 | 1,102 R | 58.5% | 28.5% | 12.0% |
| 4,137 | WEBSTER | 1,955 | 1,094 | 621 | 236 | 4 | 473 R | 56.0% | 31.8% | 12.1% |
| 953 | WHEELER | 418 | 241 | 106 | 69 | 2 | 135 R | 57.7% | 25.4% | 16.5% |
| 14,624 | YORK | 6,507 | 4,266 | 1,653 | 559 | 29 | 2,613 R | 65.6% | 25.4% | 8.6% |
| 1,637,112 | TOTAL | 677,415 | 363,467 | 236,761 | 71,278 | 5,909 | 126,706 R | 53.7% | 35.0% | 10.5% |

# NEBRASKA

## PRESIDENT 1992

| 1990 Census Population | County | Total Vote | Republican | Democratic | Perot | Other | Plurality | Percentage Total Vote | | |
|---|---|---|---|---|---|---|---|---|---|---|
| | | | | | | | | Rep. | Dem. | Perot |
| 29,625 | ADAMS | 13,110 | 6,346 | 3,445 | 3,273 | 46 | 2,901 R | 48.4% | 26.3% | 25.0% |
| 7,965 | ANTELOPE | 3,776 | 1,979 | 650 | 1,134 | 13 | 845 R | 52.4% | 17.2% | 30.0% |
| 462 | ARTHUR | 263 | 148 | 18 | 97 | | 51 R | 56.3% | 6.8% | 36.9% |
| 852 | BANNER | 480 | 284 | 68 | 128 | | 156 R | 59.2% | 14.2% | 26.7% |
| 675 | BLAINE | 453 | 256 | 64 | 130 | 3 | 126 R | 56.5% | 14.1% | 28.7% |
| 6,667 | BOONE | 3,162 | 1,588 | 604 | 956 | 14 | 632 R | 50.2% | 19.1% | 30.2% |
| 13,130 | BOX BUTTE | 5,670 | 2,198 | 1,935 | 1,508 | 29 | 263 R | 38.8% | 34.1% | 26.6% |
| 2,835 | BOYD | 1,571 | 744 | 353 | 468 | 6 | 276 R | 47.4% | 22.5% | 29.8% |
| 3,657 | BROWN | 1,846 | 999 | 311 | 525 | 11 | 474 R | 54.1% | 16.8% | 28.4% |
| 37,447 | BUFFALO | 17,617 | 9,708 | 3,742 | 4,083 | 84 | 5,625 R | 55.1% | 21.2% | 23.2% |
| 7,868 | BURT | 3,912 | 1,667 | 1,224 | 1,009 | 12 | 443 R | 42.6% | 31.3% | 25.8% |
| 8,601 | BUTLER | 4,147 | 1,881 | 1,087 | 1,157 | 22 | 724 R | 45.4% | 26.2% | 27.9% |
| 21,318 | CASS | 9,979 | 4,314 | 2,949 | 2,657 | 59 | 1,365 R | 43.2% | 29.6% | 26.6% |
| 10,131 | CEDAR | 4,518 | 1,981 | 1,007 | 1,507 | 23 | 474 R | 43.8% | 22.3% | 33.4% |
| 4,381 | CHASE | 2,082 | 1,000 | 398 | 674 | 10 | 326 R | 48.0% | 19.1% | 32.4% |
| 6,307 | CHERRY | 3,008 | 1,707 | 563 | 730 | 8 | 977 R | 56.7% | 18.7% | 24.3% |
| 9,494 | CHEYENNE | 4,241 | 2,197 | 967 | 1,061 | 16 | 1,136 R | 51.8% | 22.8% | 25.0% |
| 7,123 | CLAY | 3,581 | 1,818 | 802 | 952 | 9 | 866 R | 50.8% | 22.4% | 26.6% |
| 9,139 | COLFAX | 4,144 | 1,915 | 1,011 | 1,197 | 21 | 718 R | 46.2% | 24.4% | 28.9% |
| 10,117 | CUMING | 4,746 | 2,711 | 835 | 1,192 | 8 | 1,519 R | 57.1% | 17.6% | 25.1% |
| 12,270 | CUSTER | 5,820 | 3,180 | 1,126 | 1,492 | 22 | 1,688 R | 54.6% | 19.3% | 25.6% |
| 16,742 | DAKOTA | 6,414 | 2,771 | 2,322 | 1,307 | 14 | 449 R | 43.2% | 36.2% | 20.4% |
| 9,021 | DAWES | 4,068 | 1,961 | 987 | 1,103 | 17 | 858 R | 48.2% | 24.3% | 27.1% |
| 19,940 | DAWSON | 8,781 | 4,710 | 1,739 | 2,305 | 27 | 2,405 R | 53.6% | 19.8% | 26.2% |
| 2,237 | DEUEL | 1,120 | 558 | 232 | 327 | 3 | 231 R | 49.8% | 20.7% | 29.2% |
| 6,143 | DIXON | 3,054 | 1,484 | 830 | 726 | 14 | 654 R | 48.6% | 27.2% | 23.8% |
| 34,500 | DODGE | 16,408 | 7,269 | 4,665 | 4,432 | 42 | 2,604 R | 44.3% | 28.4% | 27.0% |
| 416,444 | DOUGLAS | 199,880 | 93,421 | 67,003 | 38,641 | 815 | 26,418 R | 46.7% | 33.5% | 19.3% |
| 2,582 | DUNDY | 1,252 | 664 | 244 | 332 | 12 | 332 R | 53.0% | 19.5% | 26.5% |
| 7,103 | FILLMORE | 3,483 | 1,495 | 988 | 993 | 7 | 502 R | 42.9% | 28.4% | 28.5% |
| 3,938 | FRANKLIN | 1,980 | 967 | 477 | 527 | 9 | 440 R | 48.8% | 24.1% | 26.6% |
| 3,101 | FRONTIER | 1,571 | 785 | 302 | 479 | 5 | 306 R | 50.0% | 19.2% | 30.5% |
| 5,553 | FURNAS | 2,801 | 1,365 | 624 | 804 | 8 | 561 R | 48.7% | 22.3% | 28.7% |
| 22,794 | GAGE | 10,073 | 3,995 | 3,309 | 2,726 | 43 | 686 R | 39.7% | 32.9% | 27.1% |
| 2,460 | GARDEN | 1,303 | 697 | 212 | 385 | 9 | 312 R | 53.5% | 16.3% | 29.5% |
| 2,141 | GARFIELD | 1,087 | 595 | 221 | 270 | 1 | 325 R | 54.7% | 20.3% | 24.8% |
| 1,928 | GOSPER | 1,048 | 492 | 254 | 297 | 5 | 195 R | 46.9% | 24.2% | 28.3% |
| 769 | GRANT | 449 | 247 | 75 | 124 | 3 | 123 R | 55.0% | 16.7% | 27.6% |
| 3,006 | GREELEY | 1,418 | 587 | 435 | 395 | 1 | 152 R | 41.4% | 30.7% | 27.9% |
| 48,925 | HALL | 20,692 | 9,264 | 5,519 | 5,822 | 87 | 3,442 R | 44.8% | 26.7% | 28.1% |
| 8,862 | HAMILTON | 4,599 | 2,379 | 992 | 1,213 | 15 | 1,166 R | 51.7% | 21.6% | 26.4% |
| 3,810 | HARLAN | 2,112 | 991 | 488 | 623 | 10 | 368 R | 46.9% | 23.1% | 29.5% |
| 1,222 | HAYES | 654 | 362 | 85 | 207 | | 155 R | 55.4% | 13.0% | 31.7% |
| 3,750 | HITCHCOCK | 1,731 | 824 | 359 | 540 | 8 | 284 R | 47.6% | 20.7% | 31.2% |
| 12,599 | HOLT | 5,703 | 3,131 | 835 | 1,714 | 23 | 1,417 R | 54.9% | 14.6% | 30.1% |
| 793 | HOOKER | 455 | 283 | 70 | 102 | | 181 R | 62.2% | 15.4% | 22.4% |
| 6,055 | HOWARD | 2,868 | 1,138 | 778 | 940 | 12 | 198 R | 39.7% | 27.1% | 32.8% |
| 8,759 | JEFFERSON | 4,491 | 1,783 | 1,506 | 1,177 | 25 | 277 R | 39.7% | 33.5% | 26.2% |
| 4,673 | JOHNSON | 2,360 | 885 | 822 | 642 | 11 | 63 R | 37.5% | 34.8% | 27.2% |
| 6,629 | KEARNEY | 3,254 | 1,751 | 644 | 844 | 15 | 907 R | 53.8% | 19.8% | 25.9% |
| 8,584 | KEITH | 3,897 | 2,019 | 731 | 1,130 | 17 | 889 R | 51.8% | 18.8% | 29.0% |
| 1,029 | KEYA PAHA | 631 | 368 | 105 | 158 | | 210 R | 58.3% | 16.6% | 25.0% |
| 4,108 | KIMBALL | 1,788 | 931 | 408 | 440 | 9 | 491 R | 52.1% | 22.8% | 24.6% |
| 9,534 | KNOX | 4,263 | 2,112 | 968 | 1,166 | 17 | 946 R | 49.5% | 22.7% | 27.4% |
| 213,641 | LANCASTER | 104,843 | 41,400 | 41,207 | 21,783 | 453 | 193 R | 39.5% | 39.3% | 20.8% |
| 32,508 | LINCOLN | 15,593 | 7,025 | 5,142 | 3,384 | 42 | 1,883 R | 45.1% | 33.0% | 21.7% |
| 878 | LOGAN | 451 | 271 | 80 | 98 | 2 | 173 R | 60.1% | 17.7% | 21.7% |
| 683 | LOUP | 389 | 233 | 58 | 96 | 2 | 137 R | 59.9% | 14.9% | 24.7% |
| 546 | MCPHERSON | 329 | 217 | 49 | 62 | 1 | 155 R | 66.0% | 14.9% | 18.8% |
| 32,655 | MADISON | 13,736 | 7,851 | 2,352 | 3,486 | 47 | 4,365 R | 57.2% | 17.1% | 25.4% |

# NEBRASKA

## PRESIDENT 1992

| 1990 Census Population | County | Total Vote | Republican | Democratic | Perot | Other | Plurality | Percentage Total Vote | | |
|---|---|---|---|---|---|---|---|---|---|---|
| | | | | | | | | Rep. | Dem. | Perot |
| 8,042 | MERRICK | 3,811 | 1,854 | 864 | 1,072 | 21 | 782 R | 48.6% | 22.7% | 28.1% |
| 5,423 | MORRILL | 2,525 | 1,184 | 577 | 752 | 12 | 432 R | 46.9% | 22.9% | 29.8% |
| 4,275 | NANCE | 1,987 | 851 | 559 | 569 | 8 | 282 R | 42.8% | 28.1% | 28.6% |
| 7,980 | NEMAHA | 3,854 | 1,696 | 1,110 | 1,020 | 28 | 586 R | 44.0% | 28.8% | 26.5% |
| 5,786 | NUCKOLLS | 2,956 | 1,277 | 834 | 825 | 20 | 443 R | 43.2% | 28.2% | 27.9% |
| 14,252 | OTOE | 6,838 | 2,960 | 2,038 | 1,800 | 40 | 922 R | 43.3% | 29.8% | 26.3% |
| 3,317 | PAWNEE | 1,808 | 670 | 566 | 565 | 7 | 104 R | 37.1% | 31.3% | 31.3% |
| 3,367 | PERKINS | 1,666 | 842 | 300 | 522 | 2 | 320 R | 50.5% | 18.0% | 31.3% |
| 9,715 | PHELPS | 4,894 | 2,748 | 829 | 1,298 | 19 | 1,450 R | 56.2% | 16.9% | 26.5% |
| 7,827 | PIERCE | 3,562 | 1,853 | 611 | 1,084 | 14 | 769 R | 52.0% | 17.2% | 30.4% |
| 29,820 | PLATTE | 13,823 | 7,712 | 2,409 | 3,656 | 46 | 4,056 R | 55.8% | 17.4% | 26.4% |
| 5,675 | POLK | 2,916 | 1,435 | 661 | 812 | 8 | 623 R | 49.2% | 22.7% | 27.8% |
| 11,705 | RED WILLOW | 5,323 | 2,488 | 1,164 | 1,660 | 11 | 828 R | 46.7% | 21.9% | 31.2% |
| 9,937 | RICHARDSON | 4,940 | 2,050 | 1,513 | 1,356 | 21 | 537 R | 41.5% | 30.6% | 27.4% |
| 2,019 | ROCK | 987 | 588 | 162 | 233 | 4 | 355 R | 59.6% | 16.4% | 23.6% |
| 12,715 | SALINE | 5,765 | 1,740 | 2,425 | 1,576 | 24 | 685 D | 30.2% | 42.1% | 27.3% |
| 102,583 | SARPY | 40,604 | 20,482 | 10,720 | 9,270 | 132 | 9,762 R | 50.4% | 26.4% | 22.8% |
| 18,285 | SAUNDERS | 9,152 | 4,037 | 2,509 | 2,567 | 39 | 1,470 R | 44.1% | 27.4% | 28.0% |
| 36,025 | SCOTTS BLUFF | 14,947 | 7,213 | 4,173 | 3,514 | 47 | 3,040 R | 48.3% | 27.9% | 23.5% |
| 15,450 | SEWARD | 6,908 | 3,044 | 2,118 | 1,722 | 24 | 926 R | 44.1% | 30.7% | 24.9% |
| 6,750 | SHERIDAN | 2,996 | 1,698 | 535 | 751 | 12 | 947 R | 56.7% | 17.9% | 25.1% |
| 3,718 | SHERMAN | 1,899 | 736 | 568 | 582 | 13 | 154 R | 38.8% | 29.9% | 30.6% |
| 1,549 | SIOUX | 802 | 445 | 148 | 206 | 3 | 239 R | 55.5% | 18.5% | 25.7% |
| 6,244 | STANTON | 2,563 | 1,274 | 496 | 786 | 7 | 488 R | 49.7% | 19.4% | 30.7% |
| 6,635 | THAYER | 3,403 | 1,387 | 923 | 1,077 | 16 | 310 R | 40.8% | 27.1% | 31.6% |
| 851 | THOMAS | 468 | 283 | 69 | 115 | 1 | 168 R | 60.5% | 14.7% | 24.6% |
| 6,936 | THURSTON | 2,257 | 898 | 865 | 487 | 7 | 33 R | 39.8% | 38.3% | 21.6% |
| 5,169 | VALLEY | 2,590 | 1,173 | 716 | 693 | 8 | 457 R | 45.3% | 27.6% | 26.8% |
| 16,607 | WASHINGTON | 8,307 | 4,035 | 2,108 | 2,148 | 16 | 1,887 R | 48.6% | 25.4% | 25.9% |
| 9,364 | WAYNE | 4,102 | 2,122 | 921 | 1,047 | 12 | 1,075 R | 51.7% | 22.5% | 25.5% |
| 4,279 | WEBSTER | 2,262 | 972 | 624 | 657 | 9 | 315 R | 43.0% | 27.6% | 29.0% |
| 948 | WHEELER | 464 | 246 | 88 | 127 | 3 | 119 R | 53.0% | 19.0% | 27.4% |
| 14,428 | YORK | 7,012 | 3,783 | 1,385 | 1,825 | 19 | 1,958 R | 54.0% | 19.8% | 26.0% |
| 1,578,385 | TOTAL | 737,546 | 343,678 | 216,864 | 174,104 | 2,900 | 126,814 R | 46.6% | 29.4% | 23.6% |

# NEBRASKA

## PRESIDENT 1988

| 1980 Census Population | County | Total Vote | Republican | Democratic | Other | Rep.-Dem. Plurality | Percentage Total Vote Rep. | Dem. | Major Vote Rep. | Dem. |
|---:|---|---:|---:|---:|---:|---:|---:|---:|---:|---:|
| 30,656 | ADAMS | 12,287 | 8,063 | 4,145 | 79 | 3,918 R | 65.6% | 33.7% | 66.0% | 34.0% |
| 8,675 | ANTELOPE | 3,559 | 2,626 | 933 | | 1,693 R | 73.8% | 26.2% | 73.8% | 26.2% |
| 513 | ARTHUR | 269 | 210 | 58 | 1 | 152 R | 78.1% | 21.6% | 78.4% | 21.6% |
| 918 | BANNER | 477 | 361 | 112 | 4 | 249 R | 75.7% | 23.5% | 76.3% | 23.7% |
| 867 | BLAINE | 411 | 338 | 72 | 1 | 266 R | 82.2% | 17.5% | 82.4% | 17.6% |
| 7,391 | BOONE | 3,150 | 2,160 | 976 | 14 | 1,184 R | 68.6% | 31.0% | 68.9% | 31.1% |
| 13,696 | BOX BUTTE | 5,764 | 3,253 | 2,466 | 45 | 787 R | 56.4% | 42.8% | 56.9% | 43.1% |
| 3,331 | BOYD | 1,467 | 967 | 480 | 20 | 487 R | 65.9% | 32.7% | 66.8% | 33.2% |
| 4,377 | BROWN | 1,782 | 1,335 | 435 | 12 | 900 R | 74.9% | 24.4% | 75.4% | 24.6% |
| 34,797 | BUFFALO | 14,825 | 9,980 | 4,700 | 145 | 5,280 R | 67.3% | 31.7% | 68.0% | 32.0% |
| 8,813 | BURT | 3,531 | 2,050 | 1,458 | 23 | 592 R | 58.1% | 41.3% | 58.4% | 41.6% |
| 9,330 | BUTLER | 3,816 | 2,083 | 1,715 | 18 | 368 R | 54.6% | 44.9% | 54.8% | 45.2% |
| 20,297 | CASS | 8,378 | 4,658 | 3,674 | 46 | 984 R | 55.6% | 43.9% | 55.9% | 44.1% |
| 11,375 | CEDAR | 4,238 | 2,462 | 1,759 | 17 | 703 R | 58.1% | 41.5% | 58.3% | 41.7% |
| 4,758 | CHASE | 2,082 | 1,446 | 597 | 39 | 849 R | 69.5% | 28.7% | 70.8% | 29.2% |
| 6,758 | CHERRY | 2,896 | 2,240 | 642 | 14 | 1,598 R | 77.3% | 22.2% | 77.7% | 22.3% |
| 10,057 | CHEYENNE | 4,223 | 2,862 | 1,333 | 28 | 1,529 R | 67.8% | 31.6% | 68.2% | 31.8% |
| 8,106 | CLAY | 3,470 | 2,352 | 1,097 | 21 | 1,255 R | 67.8% | 31.6% | 68.2% | 31.8% |
| 9,890 | COLFAX | 3,898 | 2,329 | 1,542 | 27 | 787 R | 59.7% | 39.6% | 60.2% | 39.8% |
| 11,664 | CUMING | 4,463 | 3,201 | 1,238 | 24 | 1,963 R | 71.7% | 27.7% | 72.1% | 27.9% |
| 13,877 | CUSTER | 5,725 | 4,202 | 1,496 | 27 | 2,706 R | 73.4% | 26.1% | 73.7% | 26.3% |
| 16,573 | DAKOTA | 5,696 | 2,744 | 2,941 | 11 | 197 D | 48.2% | 51.6% | 48.3% | 51.7% |
| 9,609 | DAWES | 3,767 | 2,618 | 1,122 | 27 | 1,496 R | 69.5% | 29.8% | 70.0% | 30.0% |
| 22,304 | DAWSON | 7,755 | 5,529 | 2,184 | 42 | 3,345 R | 71.3% | 28.2% | 71.7% | 28.3% |
| 2,462 | DEUEL | 1,080 | 769 | 302 | 9 | 467 R | 71.2% | 28.0% | 71.8% | 28.2% |
| 7,137 | DIXON | 2,977 | 1,802 | 1,166 | 9 | 636 R | 60.5% | 39.2% | 60.7% | 39.3% |
| 35,847 | DODGE | 14,592 | 8,412 | 6,116 | 64 | 2,296 R | 57.6% | 41.9% | 57.9% | 42.1% |
| 397,038 | DOUGLAS | 177,355 | 99,806 | 76,444 | 1,105 | 23,362 R | 56.3% | 43.1% | 56.6% | 43.4% |
| 2,861 | DUNDY | 1,178 | 828 | 333 | 17 | 495 R | 70.3% | 28.3% | 71.3% | 28.7% |
| 7,920 | FILLMORE | 3,413 | 1,952 | 1,433 | 28 | 519 R | 57.2% | 42.0% | 57.7% | 42.3% |
| 4,377 | FRANKLIN | 2,085 | 1,294 | 768 | 23 | 526 R | 62.1% | 36.8% | 62.8% | 37.2% |
| 3,647 | FRONTIER | 1,459 | 1,057 | 384 | 18 | 673 R | 72.4% | 26.3% | 73.4% | 26.6% |
| 6,486 | FURNAS | 2,645 | 1,830 | 791 | 24 | 1,039 R | 69.2% | 29.9% | 69.8% | 30.2% |
| 24,456 | GAGE | 9,185 | 5,114 | 4,008 | 63 | 1,106 R | 55.7% | 43.6% | 56.1% | 43.9% |
| 2,802 | GARDEN | 1,362 | 986 | 366 | 10 | 620 R | 72.4% | 26.9% | 72.9% | 27.1% |
| 2,363 | GARFIELD | 1,057 | 803 | 234 | 20 | 569 R | 76.0% | 22.1% | 77.4% | 22.6% |
| 2,140 | GOSPER | 1,034 | 694 | 331 | 9 | 363 R | 67.1% | 32.0% | 67.7% | 32.3% |
| 877 | GRANT | 392 | 301 | 89 | 2 | 212 R | 76.8% | 22.7% | 77.2% | 22.8% |
| 3,462 | GREELEY | 1,438 | 763 | 670 | 5 | 93 R | 53.1% | 46.6% | 53.2% | 46.8% |
| 47,690 | HALL | 18,950 | 12,020 | 6,822 | 108 | 5,198 R | 63.4% | 36.0% | 63.8% | 36.2% |
| 9,301 | HAMILTON | 4,331 | 3,019 | 1,289 | 23 | 1,730 R | 69.7% | 29.8% | 70.1% | 29.9% |
| 4,292 | HARLAN | 2,154 | 1,403 | 725 | 26 | 678 R | 65.1% | 33.7% | 65.9% | 34.1% |
| 1,356 | HAYES | 682 | 512 | 160 | 10 | 352 R | 75.1% | 23.5% | 76.2% | 23.8% |
| 4,079 | HITCHCOCK | 1,630 | 1,132 | 480 | 18 | 652 R | 69.4% | 29.4% | 70.2% | 29.8% |
| 13,552 | HOLT | 5,466 | 4,081 | 1,327 | 58 | 2,754 R | 74.7% | 24.3% | 75.5% | 24.5% |
| 990 | HOOKER | 471 | 378 | 91 | 2 | 287 R | 80.3% | 19.3% | 80.6% | 19.4% |
| 6,773 | HOWARD | 2,743 | 1,526 | 1,186 | 31 | 340 R | 55.6% | 43.2% | 56.3% | 43.7% |
| 9,817 | JEFFERSON | 4,322 | 2,470 | 1,819 | 33 | 651 R | 57.1% | 42.1% | 57.6% | 42.4% |
| 5,285 | JOHNSON | 2,354 | 1,182 | 1,162 | 10 | 20 R | 50.2% | 49.4% | 50.4% | 49.6% |
| 7,053 | KEARNEY | 3,213 | 2,120 | 1,056 | 37 | 1,064 R | 66.0% | 32.9% | 66.8% | 33.2% |
| 9,364 | KEITH | 3,976 | 2,879 | 1,067 | 30 | 1,812 R | 72.4% | 26.8% | 73.0% | 27.0% |
| 1,301 | KEYA PAHA | 595 | 446 | 145 | 4 | 301 R | 75.0% | 24.4% | 75.5% | 24.5% |
| 4,882 | KIMBALL | 1,890 | 1,321 | 540 | 29 | 781 R | 69.9% | 28.6% | 71.0% | 29.0% |
| 11,457 | KNOX | 4,147 | 2,644 | 1,477 | 26 | 1,167 R | 63.8% | 35.6% | 64.2% | 35.8% |
| 192,884 | LANCASTER | 89,447 | 44,605 | 44,260 | 582 | 345 R | 49.9% | 49.5% | 50.2% | 49.8% |
| 36,455 | LINCOLN | 14,556 | 8,395 | 6,070 | 91 | 2,325 R | 57.7% | 41.7% | 58.0% | 42.0% |
| 983 | LOGAN | 468 | 373 | 93 | 2 | 280 R | 79.7% | 19.9% | 80.0% | 20.0% |
| 859 | LOUP | 399 | 295 | 97 | 7 | 198 R | 73.9% | 24.3% | 75.3% | 24.7% |
| 593 | MCPHERSON | 292 | 229 | 60 | 3 | 169 R | 78.4% | 20.5% | 79.2% | 20.8% |
| 31,382 | MADISON | 11,973 | 9,135 | 2,779 | 59 | 6,356 R | 76.3% | 23.2% | 76.7% | 23.3% |

# NEBRASKA

## PRESIDENT 1988

| 1980 Census Population | County | Total Vote | Republican | Democratic | Other | Rep.-Dem. Plurality | Percentage Total Vote Rep. | Dem. | Major Vote Rep. | Dem. |
|---|---|---|---|---|---|---|---|---|---|---|
| 8,945 | MERRICK | 3,592 | 2,376 | 1,192 | 24 | 1,184 R | 66.1% | 33.2% | 66.6% | 33.4% |
| 6,085 | MORRILL | 2,328 | 1,554 | 753 | 21 | 801 R | 66.8% | 32.3% | 67.4% | 32.6% |
| 4,740 | NANCE | 1,990 | 1,185 | 794 | 11 | 391 R | 59.5% | 39.9% | 59.9% | 40.1% |
| 8,367 | NEMAHA | 3,785 | 2,293 | 1,457 | 35 | 836 R | 60.6% | 38.5% | 61.1% | 38.9% |
| 6,726 | NUCKOLLS | 2,891 | 1,750 | 1,114 | 27 | 636 R | 60.5% | 38.5% | 61.1% | 38.9% |
| 15,183 | OTOE | 6,366 | 3,724 | 2,616 | 26 | 1,108 R | 58.5% | 41.1% | 58.7% | 41.3% |
| 3,937 | PAWNEE | 1,758 | 975 | 767 | 16 | 208 R | 55.5% | 43.6% | 56.0% | 44.0% |
| 3,637 | PERKINS | 1,602 | 1,117 | 467 | 18 | 650 R | 69.7% | 29.2% | 70.5% | 29.5% |
| 9,769 | PHELPS | 4,387 | 3,316 | 1,047 | 24 | 2,269 R | 75.6% | 23.9% | 76.0% | 24.0% |
| 8,481 | PIERCE | 3,399 | 2,474 | 914 | 11 | 1,560 R | 72.8% | 26.9% | 73.0% | 27.0% |
| 28,852 | PLATTE | 12,385 | 9,029 | 3,285 | 71 | 5,744 R | 72.9% | 26.5% | 73.3% | 26.7% |
| 6,320 | POLK | 2,723 | 1,768 | 944 | 11 | 824 R | 64.9% | 34.7% | 65.2% | 34.8% |
| 12,615 | RED WILLOW | 4,873 | 3,325 | 1,505 | 43 | 1,820 R | 68.2% | 30.9% | 68.8% | 31.2% |
| 11,315 | RICHARDSON | 4,658 | 2,702 | 1,926 | 30 | 776 R | 58.0% | 41.3% | 58.4% | 41.6% |
| 2,383 | ROCK | 956 | 756 | 198 | 2 | 558 R | 79.1% | 20.7% | 79.2% | 20.8% |
| 13,131 | SALINE | 5,500 | 2,352 | 3,119 | 29 | 767 D | 42.8% | 56.7% | 43.0% | 57.0% |
| 86,015 | SARPY | 31,261 | 20,179 | 10,936 | 146 | 9,243 R | 64.6% | 35.0% | 64.9% | 35.1% |
| 18,716 | SAUNDERS | 8,033 | 4,454 | 3,524 | 55 | 930 R | 55.4% | 43.9% | 55.8% | 44.2% |
| 38,344 | SCOTTS BLUFF | 13,142 | 8,594 | 4,454 | 94 | 4,140 R | 65.4% | 33.9% | 65.9% | 34.1% |
| 15,789 | SEWARD | 6,199 | 3,467 | 2,682 | 50 | 785 R | 55.9% | 43.3% | 56.4% | 43.6% |
| 7,544 | SHERIDAN | 2,898 | 2,251 | 612 | 35 | 1,639 R | 77.7% | 21.1% | 78.6% | 21.4% |
| 4,226 | SHERMAN | 1,770 | 914 | 839 | 17 | 75 R | 51.6% | 47.4% | 52.1% | 47.9% |
| 1,845 | SIOUX | 767 | 568 | 194 | 5 | 374 R | 74.1% | 25.3% | 74.5% | 25.5% |
| 6,549 | STANTON | 2,356 | 1,709 | 637 | 10 | 1,072 R | 72.5% | 27.0% | 72.8% | 27.2% |
| 7,582 | THAYER | 3,326 | 1,981 | 1,322 | 23 | 659 R | 59.6% | 39.7% | 60.0% | 40.0% |
| 973 | THOMAS | 466 | 383 | 81 | 2 | 302 R | 82.2% | 17.4% | 82.5% | 17.5% |
| 7,186 | THURSTON | 2,340 | 1,105 | 1,225 | 10 | 120 D | 47.2% | 52.4% | 47.4% | 52.6% |
| 5,633 | VALLEY | 2,502 | 1,603 | 873 | 26 | 730 R | 64.1% | 34.9% | 64.7% | 35.3% |
| 15,508 | WASHINGTON | 7,155 | 4,567 | 2,552 | 36 | 2,015 R | 63.8% | 35.7% | 64.2% | 35.8% |
| 9,858 | WAYNE | 3,614 | 2,473 | 1,111 | 30 | 1,362 R | 68.4% | 30.7% | 69.0% | 31.0% |
| 4,858 | WEBSTER | 2,226 | 1,314 | 891 | 21 | 423 R | 59.0% | 40.0% | 59.6% | 40.4% |
| 1,060 | WHEELER | 455 | 309 | 141 | 5 | 168 R | 67.9% | 31.0% | 68.7% | 31.3% |
| 14,798 | YORK | 6,522 | 4,744 | 1,748 | 30 | 2,996 R | 72.7% | 26.8% | 73.1% | 26.9% |
| 1,569,825 | TOTAL | 661,465 | 397,956 | 259,235 | 4,274 | 138,721 R | 60.2% | 39.2% | 60.6% | 39.4% |

# NEBRASKA

## PRESIDENT 1984

| 1980 Census Population | County | Total Vote | Republican | Democratic | Other | Rep.-Dem. Plurality | Percentage Total Vote Rep. | Dem. | Major Vote Rep. | Dem. |
|---|---|---|---|---|---|---|---|---|---|---|
| 30,656 | ADAMS | 12,155 | 9,127 | 2,945 | 83 | 6,182 R | 75.1% | 24.2% | 75.6% | 24.4% |
| 8,675 | ANTELOPE | 3,939 | 3,222 | 697 | 20 | 2,525 R | 81.8% | 17.7% | 82.2% | 17.8% |
| 513 | ARTHUR | 281 | 248 | 33 | | 215 R | 88.3% | 11.7% | 88.3% | 11.7% |
| 918 | BANNER | 522 | 457 | 58 | 7 | 399 R | 87.5% | 11.1% | 88.7% | 11.3% |
| 867 | BLAINE | 411 | 363 | 48 | | 315 R | 88.3% | 11.7% | 88.3% | 11.7% |
| 7,391 | BOONE | 3,215 | 2,508 | 690 | 17 | 1,818 R | 78.0% | 21.5% | 78.4% | 21.6% |
| 13,696 | BOX BUTTE | 5,525 | 4,011 | 1,471 | 43 | 2,540 R | 72.6% | 26.6% | 73.2% | 26.8% |
| 3,331 | BOYD | 1,496 | 1,175 | 308 | 13 | 867 R | 78.5% | 20.6% | 79.2% | 20.8% |
| 4,377 | BROWN | 1,833 | 1,514 | 312 | 7 | 1,202 R | 82.6% | 17.0% | 82.9% | 17.1% |
| 34,797 | BUFFALO | 14,550 | 11,365 | 3,086 | 99 | 8,279 R | 78.1% | 21.2% | 78.6% | 21.4% |
| 8,813 | BURT | 3,721 | 2,645 | 1,054 | 22 | 1,591 R | 71.1% | 28.3% | 71.5% | 28.5% |
| 9,330 | BUTLER | 3,785 | 2,557 | 1,193 | 35 | 1,364 R | 67.6% | 31.5% | 68.2% | 31.8% |
| 20,297 | CASS | 8,026 | 5,461 | 2,499 | 66 | 2,962 R | 68.0% | 31.1% | 68.6% | 31.4% |
| 11,375 | CEDAR | 4,536 | 3,298 | 1,201 | 37 | 2,097 R | 72.7% | 26.5% | 73.3% | 26.7% |
| 4,758 | CHASE | 2,097 | 1,697 | 368 | 32 | 1,329 R | 80.9% | 17.5% | 82.2% | 17.8% |
| 6,758 | CHERRY | 3,198 | 2,720 | 463 | 15 | 2,257 R | 85.1% | 14.5% | 85.5% | 14.5% |
| 10,057 | CHEYENNE | 4,064 | 3,159 | 857 | 48 | 2,302 R | 77.7% | 21.1% | 78.7% | 21.3% |
| 8,106 | CLAY | 3,756 | 2,920 | 811 | 25 | 2,109 R | 77.7% | 21.6% | 78.3% | 21.7% |
| 9,890 | COLFAX | 4,016 | 2,999 | 981 | 36 | 2,018 R | 74.7% | 24.4% | 75.4% | 24.6% |
| 11,664 | CUMING | 4,740 | 3,931 | 779 | 30 | 3,152 R | 82.9% | 16.4% | 83.5% | 16.5% |
| 13,877 | CUSTER | 5,867 | 4,749 | 1,090 | 28 | 3,659 R | 80.9% | 18.6% | 81.3% | 18.7% |
| 16,573 | DAKOTA | 6,002 | 3,467 | 2,510 | 25 | 957 R | 57.8% | 41.8% | 58.0% | 42.0% |
| 9,609 | DAWES | 4,232 | 3,326 | 865 | 41 | 2,461 R | 78.6% | 20.4% | 79.4% | 20.6% |
| 22,304 | DAWSON | 8,407 | 6,887 | 1,487 | 33 | 5,400 R | 81.9% | 17.7% | 82.2% | 17.8% |
| 2,462 | DEUEL | 1,167 | 962 | 198 | 7 | 764 R | 82.4% | 17.0% | 82.9% | 17.1% |
| 7,137 | DIXON | 3,164 | 2,155 | 986 | 23 | 1,169 R | 68.1% | 31.2% | 68.6% | 31.4% |
| 35,847 | DODGE | 14,541 | 10,201 | 4,266 | 74 | 5,935 R | 70.2% | 29.3% | 70.5% | 29.5% |
| 397,038 | DOUGLAS | 172,658 | 112,676 | 58,979 | 1,003 | 53,697 R | 65.3% | 34.2% | 65.6% | 34.4% |
| 2,861 | DUNDY | 1,225 | 992 | 225 | 8 | 767 R | 81.0% | 18.4% | 81.5% | 18.5% |
| 7,920 | FILLMORE | 3,511 | 2,474 | 1,009 | 28 | 1,465 R | 70.5% | 28.7% | 71.0% | 29.0% |
| 4,377 | FRANKLIN | 2,127 | 1,597 | 522 | 8 | 1,075 R | 75.1% | 24.5% | 75.4% | 24.6% |
| 3,647 | FRONTIER | 1,617 | 1,351 | 258 | 8 | 1,093 R | 83.5% | 16.0% | 84.0% | 16.0% |
| 6,486 | FURNAS | 2,966 | 2,363 | 579 | 24 | 1,784 R | 79.7% | 19.5% | 80.3% | 19.7% |
| 24,456 | GAGE | 8,892 | 6,116 | 2,709 | 67 | 3,407 R | 68.8% | 30.5% | 69.3% | 30.7% |
| 2,802 | GARDEN | 1,351 | 1,158 | 180 | 13 | 978 R | 85.7% | 13.3% | 86.5% | 13.5% |
| 2,363 | GARFIELD | 1,104 | 899 | 196 | 9 | 703 R | 81.4% | 17.8% | 82.1% | 17.9% |
| 2,140 | GOSPER | 1,011 | 802 | 201 | 8 | 601 R | 79.3% | 19.9% | 80.0% | 20.0% |
| 877 | GRANT | 459 | 406 | 51 | 2 | 355 R | 88.5% | 11.1% | 88.8% | 11.2% |
| 3,462 | GREELEY | 1,442 | 948 | 485 | 9 | 463 R | 65.7% | 33.6% | 66.2% | 33.8% |
| 47,690 | HALL | 17,956 | 13,193 | 4,655 | 108 | 8,538 R | 73.5% | 25.9% | 73.9% | 26.1% |
| 9,301 | HAMILTON | 4,285 | 3,418 | 842 | 25 | 2,576 R | 79.8% | 19.6% | 80.2% | 19.8% |
| 4,292 | HARLAN | 2,203 | 1,692 | 493 | 18 | 1,199 R | 76.8% | 22.4% | 77.4% | 22.6% |
| 1,356 | HAYES | 694 | 593 | 101 | | 492 R | 85.4% | 14.6% | 85.4% | 14.6% |
| 4,079 | HITCHCOCK | 1,739 | 1,391 | 341 | 7 | 1,050 R | 80.0% | 19.6% | 80.3% | 19.7% |
| 13,552 | HOLT | 5,545 | 4,613 | 893 | 39 | 3,720 R | 83.2% | 16.1% | 83.8% | 16.2% |
| 990 | HOOKER | 493 | 433 | 55 | 5 | 378 R | 87.8% | 11.2% | 88.7% | 11.3% |
| 6,773 | HOWARD | 2,806 | 1,899 | 887 | 20 | 1,012 R | 67.7% | 31.6% | 68.2% | 31.8% |
| 9,817 | JEFFERSON | 4,523 | 3,116 | 1,367 | 40 | 1,749 R | 68.9% | 30.2% | 69.5% | 30.5% |
| 5,285 | JOHNSON | 2,396 | 1,542 | 821 | 33 | 721 R | 64.4% | 34.3% | 65.3% | 34.7% |
| 7,053 | KEARNEY | 3,262 | 2,508 | 726 | 28 | 1,782 R | 76.9% | 22.3% | 77.6% | 22.4% |
| 9,364 | KEITH | 4,082 | 3,433 | 631 | 18 | 2,802 R | 84.1% | 15.5% | 84.5% | 15.5% |
| 1,301 | KEYA PAHA | 635 | 507 | 128 | | 379 R | 79.8% | 20.2% | 79.8% | 20.2% |
| 4,882 | KIMBALL | 2,087 | 1,734 | 339 | 14 | 1,395 R | 83.1% | 16.2% | 83.6% | 16.4% |
| 11,457 | KNOX | 4,560 | 3,364 | 1,149 | 47 | 2,215 R | 73.8% | 25.2% | 74.5% | 25.5% |
| 192,884 | LANCASTER | 82,245 | 48,778 | 32,898 | 569 | 15,880 R | 59.3% | 40.0% | 59.7% | 40.3% |
| 36,455 | LINCOLN | 15,307 | 10,717 | 4,509 | 81 | 6,208 R | 70.0% | 29.5% | 70.4% | 29.6% |
| 983 | LOGAN | 514 | 446 | 67 | 1 | 379 R | 86.8% | 13.0% | 86.9% | 13.1% |
| 859 | LOUP | 404 | 323 | 79 | 2 | 244 R | 80.0% | 19.6% | 80.3% | 19.7% |
| 593 | MCPHERSON | 356 | 295 | 57 | 4 | 238 R | 82.9% | 16.0% | 83.8% | 16.2% |
| 31,382 | MADISON | 11,589 | 9,790 | 1,757 | 42 | 8,033 R | 84.5% | 15.2% | 84.8% | 15.2% |

# NEBRASKA

## PRESIDENT 1984

| 1980 Census Population | County | Total Vote | Republican | Democratic | Other | Rep.-Dem. Plurality | Percentage | | | |
|---|---|---|---|---|---|---|---|---|---|---|
| | | | | | | | Total Vote | | Major Vote | |
| | | | | | | | Rep. | Dem. | Rep. | Dem. |
| 8,945 | MERRICK | 3,546 | 2,700 | 818 | 28 | 1,882 R | 76.1% | 23.1% | 76.7% | 23.3% |
| 6,085 | MORRILL | 2,366 | 1,888 | 464 | 14 | 1,424 R | 79.8% | 19.6% | 80.3% | 19.7% |
| 4,740 | NANCE | 1,931 | 1,393 | 525 | 13 | 868 R | 72.1% | 27.2% | 72.6% | 27.4% |
| 8,367 | NEMAHA | 3,793 | 2,752 | 1,004 | 37 | 1,748 R | 72.6% | 26.5% | 73.3% | 26.7% |
| 6,726 | NUCKOLLS | 3,098 | 2,132 | 947 | 19 | 1,185 R | 68.8% | 30.6% | 69.2% | 30.8% |
| 15,183 | OTOE | 6,596 | 4,679 | 1,869 | 48 | 2,810 R | 70.9% | 28.3% | 71.5% | 28.5% |
| 3,937 | PAWNEE | 1,884 | 1,306 | 552 | 26 | 754 R | 69.3% | 29.3% | 70.3% | 29.7% |
| 3,637 | PERKINS | 1,736 | 1,420 | 307 | 9 | 1,113 R | 81.8% | 17.7% | 82.2% | 17.8% |
| 9,769 | PHELPS | 4,501 | 3,741 | 740 | 20 | 3,001 R | 83.1% | 16.4% | 83.5% | 16.5% |
| 8,481 | PIERCE | 3,589 | 3,017 | 545 | 27 | 2,472 R | 84.1% | 15.2% | 84.7% | 15.3% |
| 28,852 | PLATTE | 12,222 | 10,069 | 2,061 | 92 | 8,008 R | 82.4% | 16.9% | 83.0% | 17.0% |
| 6,320 | POLK | 2,776 | 2,149 | 610 | 17 | 1,539 R | 77.4% | 22.0% | 77.9% | 22.1% |
| 12,615 | RED WILLOW | 5,184 | 4,131 | 1,026 | 27 | 3,105 R | 79.7% | 19.8% | 80.1% | 19.9% |
| 11,315 | RICHARDSON | 5,098 | 3,634 | 1,422 | 42 | 2,212 R | 71.3% | 27.9% | 71.9% | 28.1% |
| 2,383 | ROCK | 1,023 | 873 | 147 | 3 | 726 R | 85.3% | 14.4% | 85.6% | 14.4% |
| 13,131 | SALINE | 5,394 | 2,942 | 2,385 | 67 | 557 R | 54.5% | 44.2% | 55.2% | 44.8% |
| 86,015 | SARPY | 27,160 | 20,192 | 6,838 | 130 | 13,354 R | 74.3% | 25.2% | 74.7% | 25.3% |
| 18,716 | SAUNDERS | 7,747 | 5,217 | 2,467 | 63 | 2,750 R | 67.3% | 31.8% | 67.9% | 32.1% |
| 38,344 | SCOTTS BLUFF | 13,878 | 10,711 | 3,074 | 93 | 7,637 R | 77.2% | 22.2% | 77.7% | 22.3% |
| 15,789 | SEWARD | 5,937 | 3,983 | 1,911 | 43 | 2,072 R | 67.1% | 32.2% | 67.6% | 32.4% |
| 7,544 | SHERIDAN | 3,061 | 2,661 | 377 | 23 | 2,284 R | 86.9% | 12.3% | 87.6% | 12.4% |
| 4,226 | SHERMAN | 1,862 | 1,144 | 701 | 17 | 443 R | 61.4% | 37.6% | 62.0% | 38.0% |
| 1,845 | SIOUX | 860 | 732 | 121 | 7 | 611 R | 85.1% | 14.1% | 85.8% | 14.2% |
| 6,549 | STANTON | 2,508 | 2,082 | 411 | 15 | 1,671 R | 83.0% | 16.4% | 83.5% | 16.5% |
| 7,582 | THAYER | 3,551 | 2,580 | 946 | 25 | 1,634 R | 72.7% | 26.6% | 73.2% | 26.8% |
| 973 | THOMAS | 374 | 298 | 73 | 3 | 225 R | 79.7% | 19.5% | 80.3% | 19.7% |
| 7,186 | THURSTON | 2,500 | 1,410 | 1,077 | 13 | 333 R | 56.4% | 43.1% | 56.7% | 43.3% |
| 5,633 | VALLEY | 2,807 | 2,055 | 739 | 13 | 1,316 R | 73.2% | 26.3% | 73.6% | 26.4% |
| 15,508 | WASHINGTON | 6,791 | 5,191 | 1,565 | 35 | 3,626 R | 76.4% | 23.0% | 76.8% | 23.2% |
| 9,858 | WAYNE | 3,936 | 3,075 | 833 | 28 | 2,242 R | 78.1% | 21.2% | 78.7% | 21.3% |
| 4,858 | WEBSTER | 2,355 | 1,694 | 645 | 16 | 1,049 R | 71.9% | 27.4% | 72.4% | 27.6% |
| 1,060 | WHEELER | 465 | 365 | 97 | 3 | 268 R | 78.5% | 20.9% | 79.0% | 21.0% |
| 14,798 | YORK | 6,271 | 5,147 | 1,124 | | 4,023 R | 82.1% | 17.9% | 82.1% | 17.9% |
| 1,569,825 | TOTAL | 652,090 | 460,054 | 187,866 | 4,170 | 272,188 R | 70.6% | 28.8% | 71.0% | 29.0% |

# NEBRASKA

## PRESIDENT 1980

| 1980 Census Population | County | Total Vote | Republican | Democratic | Other | Rep.-Dem. Plurality | Total Vote Rep. | Total Vote Dem. | Major Vote Rep. | Major Vote Dem. |
|---|---|---|---|---|---|---|---|---|---|---|
| 30,656 | ADAMS | 12,973 | 8,500 | 3,372 | 1,101 | 5,128 R | 65.5% | 26.0% | 71.6% | 28.4% |
| 8,675 | ANTELOPE | 4,057 | 3,192 | 659 | 206 | 2,533 R | 78.7% | 16.2% | 82.9% | 17.1% |
| 513 | ARTHUR | 319 | 245 | 57 | 17 | 188 R | 76.8% | 17.9% | 81.1% | 18.9% |
| 918 | BANNER | 532 | 481 | 33 | 18 | 448 R | 90.4% | 6.2% | 93.6% | 6.4% |
| 867 | BLAINE | 442 | 361 | 63 | 18 | 298 R | 81.7% | 14.3% | 85.1% | 14.9% |
| 7,391 | BOONE | 3,603 | 2,598 | 769 | 236 | 1,829 R | 72.1% | 21.3% | 77.2% | 22.8% |
| 13,696 | BOX BUTTE | 5,532 | 3,912 | 1,208 | 412 | 2,704 R | 70.7% | 21.8% | 76.4% | 23.6% |
| 3,331 | BOYD | 1,733 | 1,261 | 376 | 96 | 885 R | 72.8% | 21.7% | 77.0% | 23.0% |
| 4,377 | BROWN | 2,087 | 1,615 | 341 | 131 | 1,274 R | 77.4% | 16.3% | 82.6% | 17.4% |
| 34,797 | BUFFALO | 14,243 | 9,769 | 3,167 | 1,307 | 6,602 R | 68.6% | 22.2% | 75.5% | 24.5% |
| 8,813 | BURT | 3,893 | 2,806 | 814 | 273 | 1,992 R | 72.1% | 20.9% | 77.5% | 22.5% |
| 9,330 | BUTLER | 3,929 | 2,596 | 1,112 | 221 | 1,484 R | 66.1% | 28.3% | 70.0% | 30.0% |
| 20,297 | CASS | 7,818 | 5,193 | 2,007 | 618 | 3,186 R | 66.4% | 25.7% | 72.1% | 27.9% |
| 11,375 | CEDAR | 4,858 | 3,259 | 1,265 | 334 | 1,994 R | 67.1% | 26.0% | 72.0% | 28.0% |
| 4,758 | CHASE | 2,103 | 1,593 | 324 | 186 | 1,269 R | 75.7% | 15.4% | 83.1% | 16.9% |
| 6,758 | CHERRY | 3,155 | 2,517 | 489 | 149 | 2,028 R | 79.8% | 15.5% | 83.7% | 16.3% |
| 10,057 | CHEYENNE | 4,108 | 3,073 | 776 | 259 | 2,297 R | 74.8% | 18.9% | 79.8% | 20.2% |
| 8,106 | CLAY | 3,824 | 2,739 | 840 | 245 | 1,899 R | 71.6% | 22.0% | 76.5% | 23.5% |
| 9,890 | COLFAX | 4,454 | 3,259 | 893 | 302 | 2,366 R | 73.2% | 20.0% | 78.5% | 21.5% |
| 11,664 | CUMING | 5,131 | 4,006 | 803 | 322 | 3,203 R | 78.1% | 15.6% | 83.3% | 16.7% |
| 13,877 | CUSTER | 5,934 | 4,563 | 1,011 | 360 | 3,552 R | 76.9% | 17.0% | 81.9% | 18.1% |
| 16,573 | DAKOTA | 5,488 | 3,165 | 1,930 | 393 | 1,235 R | 57.7% | 35.2% | 62.1% | 37.9% |
| 9,609 | DAWES | 4,306 | 3,283 | 705 | 318 | 2,578 R | 76.2% | 16.4% | 82.3% | 17.7% |
| 22,304 | DAWSON | 8,609 | 6,689 | 1,463 | 457 | 5,226 R | 77.7% | 17.0% | 82.1% | 17.9% |
| 2,462 | DEUEL | 1,220 | 946 | 192 | 82 | 754 R | 77.5% | 15.7% | 83.1% | 16.9% |
| 7,137 | DIXON | 3,385 | 2,328 | 822 | 235 | 1,506 R | 68.8% | 24.3% | 73.9% | 26.1% |
| 35,847 | DODGE | 14,250 | 9,522 | 3,564 | 1,164 | 5,958 R | 66.8% | 25.0% | 72.8% | 27.2% |
| 397,038 | DOUGLAS | 163,930 | 96,908 | 51,668 | 15,354 | 45,240 R | 59.1% | 31.5% | 65.2% | 34.8% |
| 2,861 | DUNDY | 1,411 | 1,138 | 192 | 81 | 946 R | 80.7% | 13.6% | 85.6% | 14.4% |
| 7,920 | FILLMORE | 3,746 | 2,435 | 1,025 | 286 | 1,410 R | 65.0% | 27.4% | 70.4% | 29.6% |
| 4,377 | FRANKLIN | 2,265 | 1,675 | 441 | 149 | 1,234 R | 74.0% | 19.5% | 79.2% | 20.8% |
| 3,647 | FRONTIER | 1,698 | 1,346 | 259 | 93 | 1,087 R | 79.3% | 15.3% | 83.9% | 16.1% |
| 6,486 | FURNAS | 3,172 | 2,483 | 536 | 153 | 1,947 R | 78.3% | 16.9% | 82.2% | 17.8% |
| 24,456 | GAGE | 9,201 | 6,089 | 2,259 | 853 | 3,830 R | 66.2% | 24.6% | 72.9% | 27.1% |
| 2,802 | GARDEN | 1,580 | 1,297 | 202 | 81 | 1,095 R | 82.1% | 12.8% | 86.5% | 13.5% |
| 2,363 | GARFIELD | 1,108 | 811 | 238 | 59 | 573 R | 73.2% | 21.5% | 77.3% | 22.7% |
| 2,140 | GOSPER | 1,029 | 783 | 181 | 65 | 602 R | 76.1% | 17.6% | 81.2% | 18.8% |
| 877 | GRANT | 465 | 373 | 76 | 16 | 297 R | 80.2% | 16.3% | 83.1% | 16.9% |
| 3,462 | GREELEY | 1,625 | 1,028 | 495 | 102 | 533 R | 63.3% | 30.5% | 67.5% | 32.5% |
| 47,690 | HALL | 17,857 | 12,166 | 4,422 | 1,269 | 7,744 R | 68.1% | 24.8% | 73.3% | 26.7% |
| 9,301 | HAMILTON | 4,271 | 3,200 | 778 | 293 | 2,422 R | 74.9% | 18.2% | 80.4% | 19.6% |
| 4,292 | HARLAN | 2,317 | 1,690 | 486 | 141 | 1,204 R | 72.9% | 21.0% | 77.7% | 22.3% |
| 1,356 | HAYES | 730 | 617 | 82 | 31 | 535 R | 84.5% | 11.2% | 88.3% | 11.7% |
| 4,079 | HITCHCOCK | 1,963 | 1,474 | 329 | 160 | 1,145 R | 75.1% | 16.8% | 81.8% | 18.2% |
| 13,552 | HOLT | 5,838 | 4,495 | 1,016 | 327 | 3,479 R | 77.0% | 17.4% | 81.6% | 18.4% |
| 990 | HOOKER | 472 | 386 | 63 | 23 | 323 R | 81.8% | 13.3% | 86.0% | 14.0% |
| 6,773 | HOWARD | 2,970 | 1,971 | 789 | 210 | 1,182 R | 66.4% | 26.6% | 71.4% | 28.6% |
| 9,817 | JEFFERSON | 4,572 | 3,090 | 1,125 | 357 | 1,965 R | 67.6% | 24.6% | 73.3% | 26.7% |
| 5,285 | JOHNSON | 2,565 | 1,719 | 626 | 220 | 1,093 R | 67.0% | 24.4% | 73.3% | 26.7% |
| 7,053 | KEARNEY | 3,530 | 2,512 | 726 | 292 | 1,786 R | 71.2% | 20.6% | 77.6% | 22.4% |
| 9,364 | KEITH | 4,354 | 3,381 | 710 | 263 | 2,671 R | 77.7% | 16.3% | 82.6% | 17.4% |
| 1,301 | KEYA PAHA | 688 | 526 | 130 | 32 | 396 R | 76.5% | 18.9% | 80.2% | 19.8% |
| 4,882 | KIMBALL | 2,136 | 1,615 | 385 | 136 | 1,230 R | 75.6% | 18.0% | 80.8% | 19.3% |
| 11,457 | KNOX | 4,789 | 3,404 | 1,057 | 328 | 2,347 R | 71.1% | 22.1% | 76.3% | 23.7% |
| 192,884 | LANCASTER | 76,233 | 38,780 | 27,162 | 10,291 | 11,618 R | 50.9% | 35.6% | 58.8% | 41.2% |
| 36,455 | LINCOLN | 14,479 | 9,643 | 3,768 | 1,068 | 5,875 R | 66.6% | 26.0% | 71.9% | 28.1% |
| 983 | LOGAN | 536 | 442 | 71 | 23 | 371 R | 82.5% | 13.2% | 86.2% | 13.8% |
| 859 | LOUP | 470 | 368 | 74 | 28 | 294 R | 78.3% | 15.7% | 83.3% | 16.7% |
| 593 | MCPHERSON | 343 | 285 | 49 | 9 | 236 R | 83.1% | 14.3% | 85.3% | 14.7% |
| 31,382 | MADISON | 12,329 | 9,718 | 1,926 | 685 | 7,792 R | 78.8% | 15.6% | 83.5% | 16.5% |

# NEBRASKA

## PRESIDENT 1980

| 1980 Census Population | County | Total Vote | Republican | Democratic | Other | Rep.-Dem. Plurality | Percentage | | | |
|---|---|---|---|---|---|---|---|---|---|---|
| | | | | | | | Total Vote | | Major Vote | |
| | | | | | | | Rep. | Dem. | Rep. | Dem. |
| 8,945 | MERRICK | 3,694 | 2,710 | 712 | 272 | 1,998 R | 73.4% | 19.3% | 79.2% | 20.8% |
| 6,085 | MORRILL | 2,540 | 1,893 | 512 | 135 | 1,381 R | 74.5% | 20.2% | 78.7% | 21.3% |
| 4,740 | NANCE | 2,143 | 1,442 | 561 | 140 | 881 R | 67.3% | 26.2% | 72.0% | 28.0% |
| 8,367 | NEMAHA | 3,911 | 2,695 | 930 | 286 | 1,765 R | 68.9% | 23.8% | 74.3% | 25.7% |
| 6,726 | NUCKOLLS | 3,282 | 2,180 | 899 | 203 | 1,281 R | 66.4% | 27.4% | 70.8% | 29.2% |
| 15,183 | OTOE | 6,559 | 4,611 | 1,471 | 477 | 3,140 R | 70.3% | 22.4% | 75.8% | 24.2% |
| 3,937 | PAWNEE | 1,993 | 1,418 | 431 | 144 | 987 R | 71.1% | 21.6% | 76.7% | 23.3% |
| 3,637 | PERKINS | 1,762 | 1,342 | 313 | 107 | 1,029 R | 76.2% | 17.8% | 81.1% | 18.9% |
| 9,769 | PHELPS | 4,445 | 3,465 | 734 | 246 | 2,731 R | 78.0% | 16.5% | 82.5% | 17.5% |
| 8,481 | PIERCE | 3,639 | 2,938 | 517 | 184 | 2,421 R | 80.7% | 14.2% | 85.0% | 15.0% |
| 28,852 | PLATTE | 11,975 | 8,803 | 2,389 | 783 | 6,414 R | 73.5% | 19.9% | 78.7% | 21.3% |
| 6,320 | POLK | 2,936 | 2,206 | 538 | 192 | 1,668 R | 75.1% | 18.3% | 80.4% | 19.6% |
| 12,615 | RED WILLOW | 5,278 | 4,050 | 899 | 329 | 3,151 R | 76.7% | 17.0% | 81.8% | 18.2% |
| 11,315 | RICHARDSON | 5,344 | 3,634 | 1,350 | 360 | 2,284 R | 68.0% | 25.3% | 72.9% | 27.1% |
| 2,383 | ROCK | 1,059 | 855 | 146 | 58 | 709 R | 80.7% | 13.8% | 85.4% | 14.6% |
| 13,131 | SALINE | 5,416 | 2,934 | 1,908 | 574 | 1,026 R | 54.2% | 35.2% | 60.6% | 39.4% |
| 86,015 | SARPY | 23,202 | 15,552 | 5,689 | 1,961 | 9,863 R | 67.0% | 24.5% | 73.2% | 26.8% |
| 18,716 | SAUNDERS | 7,906 | 5,223 | 2,034 | 649 | 3,189 R | 66.1% | 25.7% | 72.0% | 28.0% |
| 38,344 | SCOTTS BLUFF | 13,249 | 9,504 | 2,854 | 891 | 6,650 R | 71.7% | 21.5% | 76.9% | 23.1% |
| 15,789 | SEWARD | 5,965 | 3,527 | 1,803 | 635 | 1,724 R | 59.1% | 30.2% | 66.2% | 33.8% |
| 7,544 | SHERIDAN | 3,271 | 2,749 | 370 | 152 | 2,379 R | 84.0% | 11.3% | 88.1% | 11.9% |
| 4,226 | SHERMAN | 1,970 | 1,254 | 578 | 138 | 676 R | 63.7% | 29.3% | 68.4% | 31.6% |
| 1,845 | SIOUX | 932 | 760 | 120 | 52 | 640 R | 81.5% | 12.9% | 86.4% | 13.6% |
| 6,549 | STANTON | 2,466 | 1,945 | 362 | 159 | 1,583 R | 78.9% | 14.7% | 84.3% | 15.7% |
| 7,582 | THAYER | 3,650 | 2,514 | 926 | 210 | 1,588 R | 68.9% | 25.4% | 73.1% | 26.9% |
| 973 | THOMAS | 402 | 306 | 65 | 31 | 241 R | 76.1% | 16.2% | 82.5% | 17.5% |
| 7,186 | THURSTON | 2,356 | 1,454 | 726 | 176 | 728 R | 61.7% | 30.8% | 66.7% | 33.3% |
| 5,633 | VALLEY | 2,929 | 2,101 | 655 | 173 | 1,446 R | 71.7% | 22.4% | 76.2% | 23.8% |
| 15,508 | WASHINGTON | 6,463 | 4,570 | 1,454 | 439 | 3,116 R | 70.7% | 22.5% | 75.9% | 24.1% |
| 9,858 | WAYNE | 3,921 | 2,844 | 733 | 344 | 2,111 R | 72.5% | 18.7% | 79.5% | 20.5% |
| 4,858 | WEBSTER | 2,403 | 1,676 | 547 | 180 | 1,129 R | 69.7% | 22.8% | 75.4% | 24.6% |
| 1,060 | WHEELER | 501 | 374 | 93 | 34 | 281 R | 74.7% | 18.6% | 80.1% | 19.9% |
| 14,798 | YORK | 6,634 | 5,089 | 1,131 | 414 | 3,958 R | 76.7% | 17.0% | 81.8% | 18.2% |
| 1,569,825 | TOTAL | 640,854 | 419,937 | 166,851 | 54,066 | 253,086 R | 65.5% | 26.0% | 71.6% | 28.4% |

# NEBRASKA

## PRESIDENT 1976

| 1970 Census Population | County | Total Vote | Republican | Democratic | Other | Rep.-Dem. Plurality | Percentage Total Vote Rep. | Dem. | Major Vote Rep. | Dem. |
|---:|---|---:|---:|---:|---:|---:|---:|---:|---:|---:|
| 30,553 | ADAMS | 12,839 | 7,623 | 4,959 | 257 | 2,664 R | 59.4% | 38.6% | 60.6% | 39.4% |
| 9,047 | ANTELOPE | 3,887 | 2,488 | 1,325 | 74 | 1,163 R | 64.0% | 34.1% | 65.3% | 34.7% |
| 606 | ARTHUR | 262 | 193 | 64 | 5 | 129 R | 73.7% | 24.4% | 75.1% | 24.9% |
| 1,034 | BANNER | 513 | 281 | 210 | 22 | 71 R | 54.8% | 40.9% | 57.2% | 42.8% |
| 847 | BLAINE | 422 | 281 | 133 | 8 | 148 R | 66.6% | 31.5% | 67.9% | 32.1% |
| 8,190 | BOONE | 3,437 | 2,035 | 1,329 | 73 | 706 R | 59.2% | 38.7% | 60.5% | 39.5% |
| 10,094 | BOX BUTTE | 4,579 | 2,956 | 1,516 | 107 | 1,440 R | 64.6% | 33.1% | 66.1% | 33.9% |
| 3,752 | BOYD | 1,821 | 1,004 | 792 | 25 | 212 R | 55.1% | 43.5% | 55.9% | 44.1% |
| 4,021 | BROWN | 1,836 | 1,241 | 557 | 38 | 684 R | 67.6% | 30.3% | 69.0% | 31.0% |
| 31,222 | BUFFALO | 12,777 | 8,095 | 4,308 | 374 | 3,787 R | 63.4% | 33.7% | 65.3% | 34.7% |
| 9,247 | BURT | 3,967 | 2,510 | 1,375 | 82 | 1,135 R | 63.3% | 34.7% | 64.6% | 35.4% |
| 9,461 | BUTLER | 4,271 | 1,809 | 2,337 | 125 | 528 D | 42.4% | 54.7% | 43.6% | 56.4% |
| 18,076 | CASS | 7,141 | 3,807 | 3,205 | 129 | 602 R | 53.3% | 44.9% | 54.3% | 45.7% |
| 12,192 | CEDAR | 4,760 | 2,415 | 2,225 | 120 | 190 R | 50.7% | 46.7% | 52.0% | 48.0% |
| 4,129 | CHASE | 1,937 | 1,146 | 725 | 66 | 421 R | 59.2% | 37.4% | 61.3% | 38.7% |
| 6,846 | CHERRY | 3,192 | 2,197 | 906 | 89 | 1,291 R | 68.8% | 28.4% | 70.8% | 29.2% |
| 10,778 | CHEYENNE | 4,052 | 2,285 | 1,665 | 102 | 620 R | 56.4% | 41.1% | 57.8% | 42.2% |
| 8,266 | CLAY | 3,703 | 2,254 | 1,369 | 80 | 885 R | 60.9% | 37.0% | 62.2% | 37.8% |
| 9,498 | COLFAX | 4,123 | 2,364 | 1,666 | 93 | 698 R | 57.3% | 40.4% | 58.7% | 41.3% |
| 12,034 | CUMING | 4,774 | 3,303 | 1,374 | 97 | 1,929 R | 69.2% | 28.8% | 70.6% | 29.4% |
| 14,092 | CUSTER | 6,175 | 3,935 | 1,985 | 255 | 1,950 R | 63.7% | 32.1% | 66.5% | 33.5% |
| 13,137 | DAKOTA | 4,995 | 2,631 | 2,292 | 72 | 339 R | 52.7% | 45.9% | 53.4% | 46.6% |
| 9,761 | DAWES | 3,910 | 2,446 | 1,286 | 178 | 1,160 R | 62.6% | 32.9% | 65.5% | 34.5% |
| 19,467 | DAWSON | 7,985 | 5,413 | 2,395 | 177 | 3,018 R | 67.8% | 30.0% | 69.3% | 30.7% |
| 2,717 | DEUEL | 1,191 | 776 | 398 | 17 | 378 R | 65.2% | 33.4% | 66.1% | 33.9% |
| 7,453 | DIXON | 3,338 | 1,981 | 1,286 | 71 | 695 R | 59.3% | 38.5% | 60.6% | 39.4% |
| 34,782 | DODGE | 14,481 | 8,982 | 5,283 | 216 | 3,699 R | 62.0% | 36.5% | 63.0% | 37.0% |
| 389,455 | DOUGLAS | 158,707 | 93,204 | 61,877 | 3,626 | 31,327 R | 58.7% | 39.0% | 60.1% | 39.9% |
| 2,926 | DUNDY | 1,263 | 774 | 457 | 32 | 317 R | 61.3% | 36.2% | 62.9% | 37.1% |
| 8,137 | FILLMORE | 3,671 | 2,098 | 1,489 | 84 | 609 R | 57.2% | 40.6% | 58.5% | 41.5% |
| 4,566 | FRANKLIN | 2,163 | 1,170 | 941 | 52 | 229 R | 54.1% | 43.5% | 55.4% | 44.6% |
| 3,982 | FRONTIER | 1,635 | 994 | 588 | 53 | 406 R | 60.8% | 36.0% | 62.8% | 37.2% |
| 6,897 | FURNAS | 3,061 | 1,844 | 1,126 | 91 | 718 R | 60.2% | 36.8% | 62.1% | 37.9% |
| 25,719 | GAGE | 9,908 | 5,206 | 4,512 | 190 | 694 R | 52.5% | 45.5% | 53.6% | 46.4% |
| 2,929 | GARDEN | 1,442 | 928 | 445 | 69 | 483 R | 64.4% | 30.9% | 67.6% | 32.4% |
| 2,411 | GARFIELD | 1,121 | 726 | 343 | 52 | 383 R | 64.8% | 30.6% | 67.9% | 32.1% |
| 2,178 | GOSPER | 1,009 | 654 | 332 | 23 | 322 R | 64.8% | 32.9% | 66.3% | 33.7% |
| 1,019 | GRANT | 446 | 314 | 116 | 16 | 198 R | 70.4% | 26.0% | 73.0% | 27.0% |
| 4,000 | GREELEY | 1,709 | 787 | 877 | 45 | 90 D | 46.1% | 51.3% | 47.3% | 52.7% |
| 42,851 | HALL | 17,386 | 10,935 | 6,079 | 372 | 4,856 R | 62.9% | 35.0% | 64.3% | 35.7% |
| 8,867 | HAMILTON | 4,181 | 2,737 | 1,337 | 107 | 1,400 R | 65.5% | 32.0% | 67.2% | 32.8% |
| 4,357 | HARLAN | 2,255 | 1,325 | 879 | 51 | 446 R | 58.8% | 39.0% | 60.1% | 39.9% |
| 1,530 | HAYES | 695 | 411 | 267 | 17 | 144 R | 59.1% | 38.4% | 60.6% | 39.4% |
| 4,051 | HITCHCOCK | 1,732 | 898 | 786 | 48 | 112 R | 51.8% | 45.4% | 53.3% | 46.7% |
| 12,933 | HOLT | 5,278 | 3,389 | 1,751 | 138 | 1,638 R | 64.2% | 33.2% | 65.9% | 34.1% |
| 939 | HOOKER | 427 | 326 | 98 | 3 | 228 R | 76.3% | 23.0% | 76.9% | 23.1% |
| 6,807 | HOWARD | 2,736 | 1,362 | 1,316 | 58 | 46 R | 49.8% | 48.1% | 50.9% | 49.1% |
| 10,436 | JEFFERSON | 4,789 | 2,628 | 2,068 | 93 | 560 R | 54.9% | 43.2% | 56.0% | 44.0% |
| 5,743 | JOHNSON | 2,455 | 1,298 | 1,115 | 42 | 183 R | 52.9% | 45.4% | 53.8% | 46.2% |
| 6,707 | KEARNEY | 3,124 | 1,830 | 1,219 | 75 | 611 R | 58.6% | 39.0% | 60.0% | 40.0% |
| 8,487 | KEITH | 3,760 | 2,485 | 1,139 | 136 | 1,346 R | 66.1% | 30.3% | 68.6% | 31.4% |
| 1,340 | KEYA PAHA | 667 | 405 | 245 | 17 | 160 R | 60.7% | 36.7% | 62.3% | 37.7% |
| 6,009 | KIMBALL | 2,001 | 1,257 | 696 | 48 | 561 R | 62.8% | 34.8% | 64.4% | 35.6% |
| 11,723 | KNOX | 4,654 | 2,610 | 1,922 | 122 | 688 R | 56.1% | 41.3% | 57.6% | 42.4% |
| 167,972 | LANCASTER | 69,131 | 39,041 | 28,301 | 1,789 | 10,740 R | 56.5% | 40.9% | 58.0% | 42.0% |
| 29,538 | LINCOLN | 12,739 | 7,076 | 5,355 | 308 | 1,721 R | 55.5% | 42.0% | 56.9% | 43.1% |
| 991 | LOGAN | 494 | 283 | 196 | 15 | 87 R | 57.3% | 39.7% | 59.1% | 40.9% |
| 854 | LOUP | 456 | 299 | 140 | 17 | 159 R | 65.6% | 30.7% | 68.1% | 31.9% |
| 623 | MCPHERSON | 333 | 221 | 104 | 8 | 117 R | 66.4% | 31.2% | 68.0% | 32.0% |
| 27,402 | MADISON | 11,455 | 7,846 | 3,433 | 176 | 4,413 R | 68.5% | 30.0% | 69.6% | 30.4% |

# NEBRASKA

## PRESIDENT 1976

| 1970 Census Population | County | Total Vote | Republican | Democratic | Other | Rep.-Dem. Plurality | Percentage Total Vote Rep. | Dem. | Major Vote Rep. | Dem. |
|---|---|---|---|---|---|---|---|---|---|---|
| 8,751 | MERRICK | 3,702 | 2,229 | 1,360 | 113 | 869 R | 60.2% | 36.7% | 62.1% | 37.9% |
| 5,813 | MORRILL | 2,379 | 1,351 | 971 | 57 | 380 R | 56.8% | 40.8% | 58.2% | 41.8% |
| 5,142 | NANCE | 2,113 | 1,121 | 936 | 56 | 185 R | 53.1% | 44.3% | 54.5% | 45.5% |
| 8,976 | NEMAHA | 3,544 | 2,093 | 1,406 | 45 | 687 R | 59.1% | 39.7% | 59.8% | 40.2% |
| 7,404 | NUCKOLLS | 3,224 | 1,753 | 1,424 | 47 | 329 R | 54.4% | 44.2% | 55.2% | 44.8% |
| 15,576 | OTOE | 6,237 | 3,715 | 2,436 | 86 | 1,279 R | 59.6% | 39.1% | 60.4% | 39.6% |
| 4,473 | PAWNEE | 1,873 | 990 | 845 | 38 | 145 R | 52.9% | 45.1% | 54.0% | 46.0% |
| 3,423 | PERKINS | 1,649 | 981 | 622 | 46 | 359 R | 59.5% | 37.7% | 61.2% | 38.8% |
| 9,553 | PHELPS | 4,509 | 3,210 | 1,168 | 131 | 2,042 R | 71.2% | 25.9% | 73.3% | 26.7% |
| 8,493 | PIERCE | 3,244 | 2,172 | 1,004 | 68 | 1,168 R | 67.0% | 30.9% | 68.4% | 31.6% |
| 26,508 | PLATTE | 11,179 | 7,217 | 3,693 | 269 | 3,524 R | 64.6% | 33.0% | 66.2% | 33.8% |
| 6,468 | POLK | 3,053 | 1,797 | 1,190 | 66 | 607 R | 58.9% | 39.0% | 60.2% | 39.8% |
| 12,191 | RED WILLOW | 4,810 | 2,978 | 1,722 | 110 | 1,256 R | 61.9% | 35.8% | 63.4% | 36.6% |
| 12,277 | RICHARDSON | 5,627 | 3,119 | 2,416 | 92 | 703 R | 55.4% | 42.9% | 56.4% | 43.6% |
| 2,231 | ROCK | 1,009 | 732 | 255 | 22 | 477 R | 72.5% | 25.3% | 74.2% | 25.8% |
| 12,809 | SALINE | 5,662 | 2,330 | 3,205 | 127 | 875 D | 41.2% | 56.6% | 42.1% | 57.9% |
| 65,007 | SARPY | 19,716 | 11,917 | 7,385 | 414 | 4,532 R | 60.4% | 37.5% | 61.7% | 38.3% |
| 17,018 | SAUNDERS | 7,502 | 3,844 | 3,507 | 151 | 337 R | 51.2% | 46.7% | 52.3% | 47.7% |
| 36,432 | SCOTTS BLUFF | 11,468 | 6,887 | 4,298 | 283 | 2,589 R | 60.1% | 37.5% | 61.6% | 38.4% |
| 14,460 | SEWARD | 5,950 | 3,220 | 2,610 | 120 | 610 R | 54.1% | 43.9% | 55.2% | 44.8% |
| 7,285 | SHERIDAN | 2,953 | 2,003 | 810 | 140 | 1,193 R | 67.8% | 27.4% | 71.2% | 28.8% |
| 4,725 | SHERMAN | 2,093 | 935 | 1,078 | 80 | 143 D | 44.7% | 51.5% | 46.4% | 53.6% |
| 2,034 | SIOUX | 883 | 532 | 329 | 22 | 203 R | 60.2% | 37.3% | 61.8% | 38.2% |
| 5,758 | STANTON | 2,286 | 1,469 | 764 | 53 | 705 R | 64.3% | 33.4% | 65.8% | 34.2% |
| 7,779 | THAYER | 3,360 | 1,994 | 1,315 | 51 | 679 R | 59.3% | 39.1% | 60.3% | 39.7% |
| 954 | THOMAS | 468 | 343 | 103 | 22 | 240 R | 73.3% | 22.0% | 76.9% | 23.1% |
| 6,942 | THURSTON | 2,393 | 1,290 | 1,021 | 82 | 269 R | 53.9% | 42.7% | 55.8% | 44.2% |
| 5,783 | VALLEY | 2,769 | 1,587 | 1,042 | 140 | 545 R | 57.3% | 37.6% | 60.4% | 39.6% |
| 13,310 | WASHINGTON | 6,111 | 3,799 | 2,233 | 79 | 1,566 R | 62.2% | 36.5% | 63.0% | 37.0% |
| 10,400 | WAYNE | 3,708 | 2,521 | 1,089 | 98 | 1,432 R | 68.0% | 29.4% | 69.8% | 30.2% |
| 5,396 | WEBSTER | 2,441 | 1,267 | 1,130 | 44 | 137 R | 51.9% | 46.3% | 52.9% | 47.1% |
| 1,054 | WHEELER | 436 | 274 | 146 | 16 | 128 R | 62.8% | 33.5% | 65.2% | 34.8% |
| 13,685 | YORK | 6,066 | 4,223 | 1,665 | 178 | 2,558 R | 69.6% | 27.4% | 71.7% | 28.3% |
| 1,483,791 | TOTAL | 607,668 | 359,705 | 233,692 | 14,271 | 126,013 R | 59.2% | 38.5% | 60.6% | 39.4% |

# NEBRASKA

## PRESIDENT 1972

| 1970 Census Population | County | Total Vote | Republican | Democratic | Other | Rep.-Dem. Plurality | Percentage | | | |
|---|---|---|---|---|---|---|---|---|---|---|
| | | | | | | | Total Vote | | Major Vote | |
| | | | | | | | Rep. | Dem. | Rep. | Dem. |
| 30,553 | ADAMS | 12,200 | 8,841 | 3,359 | | 5,482 R | 72.5% | 27.5% | 72.5% | 27.5% |
| 9,047 | ANTELOPE | 4,079 | 3,228 | 851 | | 2,377 R | 79.1% | 20.9% | 79.1% | 20.9% |
| 606 | ARTHUR | 281 | 236 | 45 | | 191 R | 84.0% | 16.0% | 84.0% | 16.0% |
| 1,034 | BANNER | 500 | 404 | 96 | | 308 R | 80.8% | 19.2% | 80.8% | 19.2% |
| 847 | BLAINE | 399 | 343 | 56 | | 287 R | 86.0% | 14.0% | 86.0% | 14.0% |
| 8,190 | BOONE | 3,289 | 2,406 | 883 | | 1,523 R | 73.2% | 26.8% | 73.2% | 26.8% |
| 10,094 | BOX BUTTE | 4,391 | 3,431 | 960 | | 2,471 R | 78.1% | 21.9% | 78.1% | 21.9% |
| 3,752 | BOYD | 1,925 | 1,419 | 506 | | 913 R | 73.7% | 26.3% | 73.7% | 26.3% |
| 4,021 | BROWN | 1,792 | 1,462 | 330 | | 1,132 R | 81.6% | 18.4% | 81.6% | 18.4% |
| 31,222 | BUFFALO | 11,575 | 8,587 | 2,988 | | 5,599 R | 74.2% | 25.8% | 74.2% | 25.8% |
| 9,247 | BURT | 3,837 | 2,937 | 900 | | 2,037 R | 76.5% | 23.5% | 76.5% | 23.5% |
| 9,461 | BUTLER | 4,113 | 2,301 | 1,812 | | 489 R | 55.9% | 44.1% | 55.9% | 44.1% |
| 18,076 | CASS | 6,308 | 4,503 | 1,805 | | 2,698 R | 71.4% | 28.6% | 71.4% | 28.6% |
| 12,192 | CEDAR | 4,802 | 2,995 | 1,807 | | 1,188 R | 62.4% | 37.6% | 62.4% | 37.6% |
| 4,129 | CHASE | 1,625 | 1,318 | 307 | | 1,011 R | 81.1% | 18.9% | 81.1% | 18.9% |
| 6,846 | CHERRY | 3,073 | 2,610 | 463 | | 2,147 R | 84.9% | 15.1% | 84.9% | 15.1% |
| 10,778 | CHEYENNE | 4,070 | 3,120 | 950 | | 2,170 R | 76.7% | 23.3% | 76.7% | 23.3% |
| 8,266 | CLAY | 3,403 | 2,542 | 861 | | 1,681 R | 74.7% | 25.3% | 74.7% | 25.3% |
| 9,498 | COLFAX | 3,906 | 2,799 | 1,107 | | 1,692 R | 71.7% | 28.3% | 71.7% | 28.3% |
| 12,034 | CUMING | 4,829 | 3,810 | 1,019 | | 2,791 R | 78.9% | 21.1% | 78.9% | 21.1% |
| 14,092 | CUSTER | 5,983 | 4,836 | 1,147 | | 3,689 R | 80.8% | 19.2% | 80.8% | 19.2% |
| 13,137 | DAKOTA | 4,627 | 2,879 | 1,748 | | 1,131 R | 62.2% | 37.8% | 62.2% | 37.8% |
| 9,761 | DAWES | 3,698 | 2,987 | 711 | | 2,276 R | 80.8% | 19.2% | 80.8% | 19.2% |
| 19,467 | DAWSON | 7,635 | 6,211 | 1,424 | | 4,787 R | 81.3% | 18.7% | 81.3% | 18.7% |
| 2,717 | DEUEL | 1,225 | 1,001 | 224 | | 777 R | 81.7% | 18.3% | 81.7% | 18.3% |
| 7,453 | DIXON | 3,240 | 2,299 | 941 | | 1,358 R | 71.0% | 29.0% | 71.0% | 29.0% |
| 34,782 | DODGE | 13,663 | 9,837 | 3,826 | | 6,011 R | 72.0% | 28.0% | 72.0% | 28.0% |
| 389,455 | DOUGLAS | 149,780 | 101,579 | 48,201 | | 53,378 R | 67.8% | 32.2% | 67.8% | 32.2% |
| 2,926 | DUNDY | 1,224 | 1,003 | 221 | | 782 R | 81.9% | 18.1% | 81.9% | 18.1% |
| 8,137 | FILLMORE | 3,781 | 2,511 | 1,270 | | 1,241 R | 66.4% | 33.6% | 66.4% | 33.6% |
| 4,566 | FRANKLIN | 2,109 | 1,510 | 599 | | 911 R | 71.6% | 28.4% | 71.6% | 28.4% |
| 3,982 | FRONTIER | 1,639 | 1,315 | 324 | | 991 R | 80.2% | 19.8% | 80.2% | 19.8% |
| 6,897 | FURNAS | 2,958 | 2,282 | 676 | | 1,606 R | 77.1% | 22.9% | 77.1% | 22.9% |
| 25,719 | GAGE | 9,886 | 6,298 | 3,588 | | 2,710 R | 63.7% | 36.3% | 63.7% | 36.3% |
| 2,929 | GARDEN | 1,365 | 1,161 | 204 | | 957 R | 85.1% | 14.9% | 85.1% | 14.9% |
| 2,411 | GARFIELD | 1,112 | 903 | 209 | | 694 R | 81.2% | 18.8% | 81.2% | 18.8% |
| 2,178 | GOSPER | 1,071 | 829 | 242 | | 587 R | 77.4% | 22.6% | 77.4% | 22.6% |
| 1,019 | GRANT | 445 | 376 | 69 | | 307 R | 84.5% | 15.5% | 84.5% | 15.5% |
| 4,000 | GREELEY | 1,765 | 1,005 | 760 | | 245 R | 56.9% | 43.1% | 56.9% | 43.1% |
| 42,851 | HALL | 15,205 | 10,987 | 4,218 | | 6,769 R | 72.3% | 27.7% | 72.3% | 27.7% |
| 8,867 | HAMILTON | 3,867 | 2,960 | 907 | | 2,053 R | 76.5% | 23.5% | 76.5% | 23.5% |
| 4,357 | HARLAN | 2,088 | 1,549 | 539 | | 1,010 R | 74.2% | 25.8% | 74.2% | 25.8% |
| 1,530 | HAYES | 609 | 486 | 123 | | 363 R | 79.8% | 20.2% | 79.8% | 20.2% |
| 4,051 | HITCHCOCK | 1,703 | 1,339 | 364 | | 975 R | 78.6% | 21.4% | 78.6% | 21.4% |
| 12,933 | HOLT | 5,200 | 4,147 | 1,053 | | 3,094 R | 79.8% | 20.3% | 79.8% | 20.3% |
| 939 | HOOKER | 446 | 394 | 52 | | 342 R | 88.3% | 11.7% | 88.3% | 11.7% |
| 6,807 | HOWARD | 2,636 | 1,691 | 945 | | 746 R | 64.2% | 35.8% | 64.2% | 35.8% |
| 10,436 | JEFFERSON | 4,484 | 3,008 | 1,476 | | 1,532 R | 67.1% | 32.9% | 67.1% | 32.9% |
| 5,743 | JOHNSON | 2,554 | 1,637 | 917 | | 720 R | 64.1% | 35.9% | 64.1% | 35.9% |
| 6,707 | KEARNEY | 2,962 | 2,203 | 759 | | 1,444 R | 74.4% | 25.6% | 74.4% | 25.6% |
| 8,487 | KEITH | 3,178 | 2,513 | 665 | | 1,848 R | 79.1% | 20.9% | 79.1% | 20.9% |
| 1,340 | KEYA PAHA | 709 | 563 | 146 | | 417 R | 79.4% | 20.6% | 79.4% | 20.6% |
| 6,009 | KIMBALL | 2,087 | 1,650 | 437 | | 1,213 R | 79.1% | 20.9% | 79.1% | 20.9% |
| 11,723 | KNOX | 4,607 | 3,318 | 1,289 | | 2,029 R | 72.0% | 28.0% | 72.0% | 28.0% |
| 167,972 | LANCASTER | 68,497 | 42,573 | 25,924 | | 16,649 R | 62.2% | 37.8% | 62.2% | 37.8% |
| 29,538 | LINCOLN | 10,722 | 7,502 | 3,220 | | 4,282 R | 70.0% | 30.0% | 70.0% | 30.0% |
| 991 | LOGAN | 393 | 320 | 73 | | 247 R | 81.4% | 18.6% | 81.4% | 18.6% |
| 854 | LOUP | 403 | 345 | 58 | | 287 R | 85.6% | 14.4% | 85.6% | 14.4% |
| 623 | MCPHERSON | 289 | 247 | 42 | | 205 R | 85.5% | 14.5% | 85.5% | 14.5% |
| 27,402 | MADISON | 10,804 | 8,580 | 2,224 | | 6,356 R | 79.4% | 20.6% | 79.4% | 20.6% |

# NEBRASKA

## PRESIDENT 1972

| 1970 Census Population | County | Total Vote | Republican | Democratic | Other | Rep.-Dem. Plurality | Percentage Total Vote Rep. | Dem. | Major Vote Rep. | Dem. |
|---|---|---|---|---|---|---|---|---|---|---|
| 8,751 | MERRICK | 3,305 | 2,418 | 887 | | 1,531 R | 73.2% | 26.8% | 73.2% | 26.8% |
| 5,813 | MORRILL | 2,260 | 1,740 | 520 | | 1,220 R | 77.0% | 23.0% | 77.0% | 23.0% |
| 5,142 | NANCE | 2,054 | 1,413 | 641 | | 772 R | 68.8% | 31.2% | 68.8% | 31.2% |
| 8,976 | NEMAHA | 3,509 | 2,600 | 909 | | 1,691 R | 74.1% | 25.9% | 74.1% | 25.9% |
| 7,404 | NUCKOLLS | 3,088 | 2,089 | 999 | | 1,090 R | 67.6% | 32.4% | 67.6% | 32.4% |
| 15,576 | OTOE | 6,533 | 4,815 | 1,718 | | 3,097 R | 73.7% | 26.3% | 73.7% | 26.3% |
| 4,473 | PAWNEE | 1,823 | 1,299 | 524 | | 775 R | 71.3% | 28.7% | 71.3% | 28.7% |
| 3,423 | PERKINS | 1,519 | 1,165 | 354 | | 811 R | 76.7% | 23.3% | 76.7% | 23.3% |
| 9,553 | PHELPS | 4,091 | 3,356 | 735 | | 2,621 R | 82.0% | 18.0% | 82.0% | 18.0% |
| 8,493 | PIERCE | 3,104 | 2,451 | 653 | | 1,798 R | 79.0% | 21.0% | 79.0% | 21.0% |
| 26,508 | PLATTE | 10,726 | 7,871 | 2,855 | | 5,016 R | 73.4% | 26.6% | 73.4% | 26.6% |
| 6,468 | POLK | 2,877 | 2,050 | 827 | | 1,223 R | 71.3% | 28.7% | 71.3% | 28.7% |
| 12,191 | RED WILLOW | 4,632 | 3,701 | 931 | | 2,770 R | 79.9% | 20.1% | 79.9% | 20.1% |
| 12,277 | RICHARDSON | 5,170 | 3,662 | 1,508 | | 2,154 R | 70.8% | 29.2% | 70.8% | 29.2% |
| 2,231 | ROCK | 1,075 | 937 | 138 | | 799 R | 87.2% | 12.8% | 87.2% | 12.8% |
| 12,809 | SALINE | 5,482 | 2,828 | 2,654 | | 174 R | 51.6% | 48.4% | 51.6% | 48.4% |
| 65,007 | SARPY | 15,418 | 11,514 | 3,904 | | 7,610 R | 74.7% | 25.3% | 74.7% | 25.3% |
| 17,018 | SAUNDERS | 6,783 | 4,282 | 2,501 | | 1,781 R | 63.1% | 36.9% | 63.1% | 36.9% |
| 36,432 | SCOTTS BLUFF | 11,413 | 8,649 | 2,764 | | 5,885 R | 75.8% | 24.2% | 75.8% | 24.2% |
| 14,460 | SEWARD | 5,794 | 3,707 | 2,087 | | 1,620 R | 64.0% | 36.0% | 64.0% | 36.0% |
| 7,285 | SHERIDAN | 2,867 | 2,386 | 481 | | 1,905 R | 83.2% | 16.8% | 83.2% | 16.8% |
| 4,725 | SHERMAN | 1,910 | 1,099 | 811 | | 288 R | 57.5% | 42.5% | 57.5% | 42.5% |
| 2,034 | SIOUX | 768 | 639 | 129 | | 510 R | 83.2% | 16.8% | 83.2% | 16.8% |
| 5,758 | STANTON | 2,140 | 1,662 | 478 | | 1,184 R | 77.7% | 22.3% | 77.7% | 22.3% |
| 7,779 | THAYER | 3,252 | 2,274 | 978 | | 1,296 R | 69.9% | 30.1% | 69.9% | 30.1% |
| 954 | THOMAS | 470 | 397 | 73 | | 324 R | 84.5% | 15.5% | 84.5% | 15.5% |
| 6,942 | THURSTON | 2,405 | 1,565 | 840 | | 725 R | 65.1% | 34.9% | 65.1% | 34.9% |
| 5,783 | VALLEY | 2,782 | 2,011 | 771 | | 1,240 R | 72.3% | 27.7% | 72.3% | 27.7% |
| 13,310 | WASHINGTON | 5,691 | 4,290 | 1,401 | | 2,889 R | 75.4% | 24.6% | 75.4% | 24.6% |
| 10,400 | WAYNE | 3,561 | 2,659 | 902 | | 1,757 R | 74.7% | 25.3% | 74.7% | 25.3% |
| 5,396 | WEBSTER | 2,327 | 1,631 | 696 | | 935 R | 70.1% | 29.9% | 70.1% | 29.9% |
| 1,054 | WHEELER | 445 | 361 | 84 | | 277 R | 81.1% | 18.9% | 81.1% | 18.9% |
| 13,685 | YORK | 5,969 | 4,651 | 1,318 | | 3,333 R | 77.9% | 22.1% | 77.9% | 22.1% |
| 1,483,791 | TOTAL | 576,289 | 406,298 | 169,991 | | 236,307 R | 70.5% | 29.5% | 70.5% | 29.5% |

# NEBRASKA

## PRESIDENT 1968

| 1960 Census Population | County | Total Vote | Republican | Democratic | AIP | Other | Plurality | Percentage Total Vote | | |
|---|---|---|---|---|---|---|---|---|---|---|
| | | | | | | | | Rep. | Dem. | AIP |
| 28,944 | ADAMS | 11,362 | 7,191 | 3,524 | 647 | | 3,667 R | 63.3% | 31.0% | 5.7% |
| 10,176 | ANTELOPE | 4,117 | 2,805 | 952 | 360 | | 1,853 R | 68.1% | 23.1% | 8.7% |
| 680 | ARTHUR | 280 | 218 | 47 | 15 | | 171 R | 77.9% | 16.8% | 5.4% |
| 1,269 | BANNER | 491 | 350 | 72 | 69 | | 278 R | 71.3% | 14.7% | 14.1% |
| 1,016 | BLAINE | 433 | 344 | 64 | 25 | | 280 R | 79.4% | 14.8% | 5.8% |
| 9,134 | BOONE | 3,404 | 2,179 | 934 | 291 | | 1,245 R | 64.0% | 27.4% | 8.5% |
| 11,688 | BOX BUTTE | 4,043 | 2,728 | 1,052 | 263 | | 1,676 R | 67.5% | 26.0% | 6.5% |
| 4,513 | BOYD | 1,934 | 1,250 | 437 | 247 | | 813 R | 64.6% | 22.6% | 12.8% |
| 4,436 | BROWN | 1,871 | 1,340 | 369 | 162 | | 971 R | 71.6% | 19.7% | 8.7% |
| 26,236 | BUFFALO | 10,394 | 6,786 | 2,875 | 733 | | 3,911 R | 65.3% | 27.7% | 7.1% |
| 10,192 | BURT | 3,815 | 2,615 | 937 | 263 | | 1,678 R | 68.5% | 24.6% | 6.9% |
| 10,312 | BUTLER | 3,514 | 1,646 | 1,544 | 324 | | 102 R | 46.8% | 43.9% | 9.2% |
| 17,821 | CASS | 5,529 | 3,185 | 1,739 | 605 | | 1,446 R | 57.6% | 31.5% | 10.9% |
| 13,368 | CEDAR | 4,637 | 2,853 | 1,444 | 340 | | 1,409 R | 61.5% | 31.1% | 7.3% |
| 4,317 | CHASE | 1,727 | 1,171 | 363 | 193 | | 808 R | 67.8% | 21.0% | 11.2% |
| 8,218 | CHERRY | 3,003 | 2,199 | 582 | 222 | | 1,617 R | 73.2% | 19.4% | 7.4% |
| 14,828 | CHEYENNE | 4,132 | 2,725 | 993 | 414 | | 1,732 R | 65.9% | 24.0% | 10.0% |
| 8,717 | CLAY | 3,414 | 2,273 | 935 | 206 | | 1,338 R | 66.6% | 27.4% | 6.0% |
| 9,595 | COLFAX | 3,511 | 2,264 | 932 | 315 | | 1,332 R | 64.5% | 26.5% | 9.0% |
| 12,435 | CUMING | 4,485 | 3,254 | 935 | 296 | | 2,319 R | 72.6% | 20.8% | 6.6% |
| 16,517 | CUSTER | 6,133 | 4,325 | 1,407 | 401 | | 2,918 R | 70.5% | 22.9% | 6.5% |
| 12,168 | DAKOTA | 4,210 | 2,383 | 1,541 | 286 | | 842 R | 56.6% | 36.6% | 6.8% |
| 9,536 | DAWES | 3,614 | 2,600 | 741 | 273 | | 1,859 R | 71.9% | 20.5% | 7.6% |
| 19,405 | DAWSON | 7,254 | 5,221 | 1,614 | 419 | | 3,607 R | 72.0% | 22.2% | 5.8% |
| 3,125 | DEUEL | 1,325 | 997 | 250 | 78 | | 747 R | 75.2% | 18.9% | 5.9% |
| 8,106 | DIXON | 3,124 | 2,051 | 890 | 183 | | 1,161 R | 65.7% | 28.5% | 5.9% |
| 32,471 | DODGE | 12,636 | 8,059 | 3,755 | 822 | | 4,304 R | 63.8% | 29.7% | 6.5% |
| 343,490 | DOUGLAS | 137,164 | 69,808 | 51,617 | 15,739 | | 18,191 R | 50.9% | 37.6% | 11.5% |
| 3,570 | DUNDY | 1,390 | 1,001 | 261 | 128 | | 740 R | 72.0% | 18.8% | 9.2% |
| 9,425 | FILLMORE | 3,713 | 2,213 | 1,297 | 203 | | 916 R | 59.6% | 34.9% | 5.5% |
| 5,449 | FRANKLIN | 2,225 | 1,447 | 626 | 152 | | 821 R | 65.0% | 28.1% | 6.8% |
| 4,311 | FRONTIER | 1,685 | 1,183 | 345 | 157 | | 838 R | 70.2% | 20.5% | 9.3% |
| 7,711 | FURNAS | 3,061 | 2,137 | 701 | 223 | | 1,436 R | 69.8% | 22.9% | 7.3% |
| 26,818 | GAGE | 9,806 | 5,465 | 3,704 | 637 | | 1,761 R | 55.7% | 37.8% | 6.5% |
| 3,472 | GARDEN | 1,425 | 1,120 | 206 | 99 | | 914 R | 78.6% | 14.5% | 6.9% |
| 2,699 | GARFIELD | 1,043 | 797 | 183 | 63 | | 614 R | 76.4% | 17.5% | 6.0% |
| 2,489 | GOSPER | 987 | 701 | 229 | 57 | | 472 R | 71.0% | 23.2% | 5.8% |
| 1,009 | GRANT | 415 | 311 | 84 | 20 | | 227 R | 74.9% | 20.2% | 4.8% |
| 4,595 | GREELEY | 1,763 | 882 | 739 | 142 | | 143 R | 50.0% | 41.9% | 8.1% |
| 35,757 | HALL | 13,861 | 8,457 | 4,571 | 833 | | 3,886 R | 61.0% | 33.0% | 6.0% |
| 8,714 | HAMILTON | 3,654 | 2,592 | 918 | 144 | | 1,674 R | 70.9% | 25.1% | 3.9% |
| 5,081 | HARLAN | 2,174 | 1,392 | 579 | 203 | | 813 R | 64.0% | 26.6% | 9.3% |
| 1,919 | HAYES | 696 | 496 | 127 | 73 | | 369 R | 71.3% | 18.2% | 10.5% |
| 4,829 | HITCHCOCK | 1,753 | 1,173 | 387 | 193 | | 786 R | 66.9% | 22.1% | 11.0% |
| 13,722 | HOLT | 5,027 | 3,319 | 1,278 | 430 | | 2,041 R | 66.0% | 25.4% | 8.6% |
| 1,130 | HOOKER | 398 | 350 | 36 | 12 | | 314 R | 87.9% | 9.0% | 3.0% |
| 6,541 | HOWARD | 2,445 | 1,256 | 1,003 | 186 | | 253 R | 51.4% | 41.0% | 7.6% |
| 11,620 | JEFFERSON | 4,637 | 2,793 | 1,572 | 272 | | 1,221 R | 60.2% | 33.9% | 5.9% |
| 6,281 | JOHNSON | 2,482 | 1,508 | 759 | 215 | | 749 R | 60.8% | 30.6% | 8.7% |
| 6,580 | KEARNEY | 2,822 | 1,806 | 825 | 191 | | 981 R | 64.0% | 29.2% | 6.8% |
| 7,958 | KEITH | 2,998 | 2,126 | 694 | 178 | | 1,432 R | 70.9% | 23.1% | 5.9% |
| 1,672 | KEYA PAHA | 690 | 531 | 109 | 50 | | 422 R | 77.0% | 15.8% | 7.2% |
| 7,975 | KIMBALL | 2,074 | 1,423 | 414 | 237 | | 1,009 R | 68.6% | 20.0% | 11.4% |
| 13,300 | KNOX | 4,588 | 3,129 | 1,131 | 328 | | 1,998 R | 68.2% | 24.7% | 7.1% |
| 155,272 | LANCASTER | 59,530 | 33,051 | 23,539 | 2,940 | | 9,512 R | 55.5% | 39.5% | 4.9% |
| 28,491 | LINCOLN | 10,269 | 5,996 | 3,491 | 782 | | 2,505 R | 58.4% | 34.0% | 7.6% |
| 1,108 | LOGAN | 547 | 363 | 130 | 54 | | 233 R | 66.4% | 23.8% | 9.9% |
| 1,097 | LOUP | 433 | 331 | 64 | 38 | | 267 R | 76.4% | 14.8% | 8.8% |
| 735 | MCPHERSON | 310 | 236 | 40 | 34 | | 196 R | 76.1% | 12.9% | 11.0% |
| 25,145 | MADISON | 10,044 | 7,066 | 2,364 | 614 | | 4,702 R | 70.4% | 23.5% | 6.1% |

# NEBRASKA

## PRESIDENT 1968

| 1960 Census Population | County | Total Vote | Republican | Democratic | AIP | Other | Plurality | Percentage Total Vote | | |
|---|---|---|---|---|---|---|---|---|---|---|
| | | | | | | | | Rep. | Dem. | AIP |
| 8,363 | MERRICK | 3,083 | 2,031 | 840 | 212 | | 1,191 R | 65.9% | 27.2% | 6.9% |
| 7,057 | MORRILL | 2,281 | 1,516 | 480 | 285 | | 1,036 R | 66.5% | 21.0% | 12.5% |
| 5,635 | NANCE | 2,165 | 1,316 | 677 | 172 | | 639 R | 60.8% | 31.3% | 7.9% |
| 9,099 | NEMAHA | 3,608 | 2,290 | 1,023 | 295 | | 1,267 R | 63.5% | 28.4% | 8.2% |
| 8,217 | NUCKOLLS | 3,193 | 1,894 | 1,127 | 172 | | 767 R | 59.3% | 35.3% | 5.4% |
| 16,503 | OTOE | 5,822 | 3,840 | 1,508 | 474 | | 2,332 R | 66.0% | 25.9% | 8.1% |
| 5,356 | PAWNEE | 2,005 | 1,209 | 583 | 213 | | 626 R | 60.3% | 29.1% | 10.6% |
| 4,189 | PERKINS | 1,652 | 1,165 | 360 | 127 | | 805 R | 70.5% | 21.8% | 7.7% |
| 9,800 | PHELPS | 4,055 | 2,976 | 825 | 254 | | 2,151 R | 73.4% | 20.3% | 6.3% |
| 8,722 | PIERCE | 3,279 | 2,408 | 674 | 197 | | 1,734 R | 73.4% | 20.6% | 6.0% |
| 23,992 | PLATTE | 9,584 | 5,817 | 2,999 | 768 | | 2,818 R | 60.7% | 31.3% | 8.0% |
| 7,210 | POLK | 2,686 | 1,795 | 690 | 201 | | 1,105 R | 66.8% | 25.7% | 7.5% |
| 12,940 | RED WILLOW | 4,575 | 3,066 | 1,145 | 364 | | 1,921 R | 67.0% | 25.0% | 8.0% |
| 13,903 | RICHARDSON | 5,251 | 3,133 | 1,591 | 527 | | 1,542 R | 59.7% | 30.3% | 10.0% |
| 2,554 | ROCK | 1,031 | 791 | 146 | 94 | | 645 R | 76.7% | 14.2% | 9.1% |
| 12,542 | SALINE | 5,234 | 2,341 | 2,543 | 350 | | 202 D | 44.7% | 48.6% | 6.7% |
| 31,281 | SARPY | 11,470 | 6,019 | 3,506 | 1,945 | | 2,513 R | 52.5% | 30.6% | 17.0% |
| 17,270 | SAUNDERS | 5,975 | 3,429 | 1,990 | 556 | | 1,439 R | 57.4% | 33.3% | 9.3% |
| 33,809 | SCOTTS BLUFF | 10,951 | 7,356 | 2,649 | 946 | | 4,707 R | 67.2% | 24.2% | 8.6% |
| 13,581 | SEWARD | 4,851 | 2,939 | 1,658 | 254 | | 1,281 R | 60.6% | 34.2% | 5.2% |
| 9,049 | SHERIDAN | 2,931 | 2,236 | 454 | 241 | | 1,782 R | 76.3% | 15.5% | 8.2% |
| 5,382 | SHERMAN | 1,986 | 955 | 851 | 180 | | 104 R | 48.1% | 42.8% | 9.1% |
| 2,575 | SIOUX | 791 | 565 | 157 | 69 | | 408 R | 71.4% | 19.8% | 8.7% |
| 5,783 | STANTON | 1,973 | 1,408 | 411 | 154 | | 997 R | 71.4% | 20.8% | 7.8% |
| 9,118 | THAYER | 3,569 | 2,331 | 1,061 | 177 | | 1,270 R | 65.3% | 29.7% | 5.0% |
| 1,078 | THOMAS | 461 | 354 | 76 | 31 | | 278 R | 76.8% | 16.5% | 6.7% |
| 7,237 | THURSTON | 2,353 | 1,341 | 802 | 210 | | 539 R | 57.0% | 34.1% | 8.9% |
| 6,590 | VALLEY | 2,731 | 1,759 | 793 | 179 | | 966 R | 64.4% | 29.0% | 6.6% |
| 12,103 | WASHINGTON | 4,834 | 3,063 | 1,279 | 492 | | 1,784 R | 63.4% | 26.5% | 10.2% |
| 9,959 | WAYNE | 3,560 | 2,582 | 786 | 192 | | 1,796 R | 72.5% | 22.1% | 5.4% |
| 6,224 | WEBSTER | 2,488 | 1,521 | 781 | 186 | | 740 R | 61.1% | 31.4% | 7.5% |
| 1,297 | WHEELER | 503 | 323 | 131 | 49 | | 192 R | 64.2% | 26.0% | 9.7% |
| 13,724 | YORK | 5,419 | 3,923 | 1,237 | 259 | | 2,686 R | 72.4% | 22.8% | 4.8% |
| 1,411,330 | TOTAL | 536,851 | 321,163 | 170,784 | 44,904 | | 150,379 R | 59.8% | 31.8% | 8.4% |

# NEBRASKA

## PRESIDENT 1964

| 1960 Census Population | County | Total Vote | Republican | Democratic | Other | Rep.-Dem. Plurality | Percentage Total Vote Rep. | Dem. | Major Vote Rep. | Dem. |
|---|---|---|---|---|---|---|---|---|---|---|
| 28,944 | ADAMS | 12,027 | 5,586 | 6,441 | | 855 D | 46.4% | 53.6% | 46.4% | 53.6% |
| 10,176 | ANTELOPE | 4,570 | 2,566 | 2,004 | | 562 R | 56.1% | 43.9% | 56.1% | 43.9% |
| 680 | ARTHUR | 369 | 243 | 126 | | 117 R | 65.9% | 34.1% | 65.9% | 34.1% |
| 1,269 | BANNER | 553 | 357 | 196 | | 161 R | 64.6% | 35.4% | 64.6% | 35.4% |
| 1,016 | BLAINE | 521 | 326 | 195 | | 131 R | 62.6% | 37.4% | 62.6% | 37.4% |
| 9,134 | BOONE | 3,798 | 1,893 | 1,905 | | 12 D | 49.8% | 50.2% | 49.8% | 50.2% |
| 11,688 | BOX BUTTE | 4,693 | 2,725 | 1,968 | | 757 R | 58.1% | 41.9% | 58.1% | 41.9% |
| 4,513 | BOYD | 2,008 | 1,100 | 908 | | 192 R | 54.8% | 45.2% | 54.8% | 45.2% |
| 4,436 | BROWN | 2,157 | 1,272 | 885 | | 387 R | 59.0% | 41.0% | 59.0% | 41.0% |
| 26,236 | BUFFALO | 10,861 | 5,425 | 5,436 | | 11 D | 49.9% | 50.1% | 49.9% | 50.1% |
| 10,192 | BURT | 4,533 | 2,459 | 2,074 | | 385 R | 54.2% | 45.8% | 54.2% | 45.8% |
| 10,312 | BUTLER | 4,635 | 1,642 | 2,993 | | 1,351 D | 35.4% | 64.6% | 35.4% | 64.6% |
| 17,821 | CASS | 6,922 | 2,947 | 3,975 | | 1,028 D | 42.6% | 57.4% | 42.6% | 57.4% |
| 13,368 | CEDAR | 5,403 | 2,299 | 3,104 | | 805 D | 42.6% | 57.4% | 42.6% | 57.4% |
| 4,317 | CHASE | 1,988 | 1,081 | 907 | | 174 R | 54.4% | 45.6% | 54.4% | 45.6% |
| 8,218 | CHERRY | 3,672 | 2,244 | 1,428 | | 816 R | 61.1% | 38.9% | 61.1% | 38.9% |
| 14,828 | CHEYENNE | 5,818 | 3,129 | 2,689 | | 440 R | 53.8% | 46.2% | 53.8% | 46.2% |
| 8,717 | CLAY | 3,880 | 1,879 | 2,001 | | 122 D | 48.4% | 51.6% | 48.4% | 51.6% |
| 9,595 | COLFAX | 4,179 | 1,972 | 2,207 | | 235 D | 47.2% | 52.8% | 47.2% | 52.8% |
| 12,435 | CUMING | 5,329 | 3,064 | 2,265 | | 799 R | 57.5% | 42.5% | 57.5% | 42.5% |
| 16,517 | CUSTER | 7,391 | 3,916 | 3,475 | | 441 R | 53.0% | 47.0% | 53.0% | 47.0% |
| 12,168 | DAKOTA | 4,560 | 1,906 | 2,654 | | 748 D | 41.8% | 58.2% | 41.8% | 58.2% |
| 9,536 | DAWES | 4,087 | 2,518 | 1,569 | | 949 R | 61.6% | 38.4% | 61.6% | 38.4% |
| 19,405 | DAWSON | 8,367 | 4,577 | 3,790 | | 787 R | 54.7% | 45.3% | 54.7% | 45.3% |
| 3,125 | DEUEL | 1,505 | 972 | 533 | | 439 R | 64.6% | 35.4% | 64.6% | 35.4% |
| 8,106 | DIXON | 3,757 | 1,845 | 1,912 | | 67 D | 49.1% | 50.9% | 49.1% | 50.9% |
| 32,471 | DODGE | 13,543 | 6,812 | 6,731 | | 81 R | 50.3% | 49.7% | 50.3% | 49.7% |
| 343,490 | DOUGLAS | 139,093 | 61,613 | 77,480 | | 15,867 D | 44.3% | 55.7% | 44.3% | 55.7% |
| 3,570 | DUNDY | 1,623 | 911 | 712 | | 199 R | 56.1% | 43.9% | 56.1% | 43.9% |
| 9,425 | FILLMORE | 4,433 | 1,936 | 2,497 | | 561 D | 43.7% | 56.3% | 43.7% | 56.3% |
| 5,449 | FRANKLIN | 2,650 | 1,241 | 1,409 | | 168 D | 46.8% | 53.2% | 46.8% | 53.2% |
| 4,311 | FRONTIER | 1,931 | 1,090 | 841 | | 249 R | 56.4% | 43.6% | 56.4% | 43.6% |
| 7,711 | FURNAS | 3,680 | 2,011 | 1,669 | | 342 R | 54.6% | 45.4% | 54.6% | 45.4% |
| 26,818 | GAGE | 10,446 | 4,035 | 6,411 | | 2,376 D | 38.6% | 61.4% | 38.6% | 61.4% |
| 3,472 | GARDEN | 1,665 | 1,106 | 559 | | 547 R | 66.4% | 33.6% | 66.4% | 33.6% |
| 2,699 | GARFIELD | 1,244 | 761 | 483 | | 278 R | 61.2% | 38.8% | 61.2% | 38.8% |
| 2,489 | GOSPER | 1,059 | 547 | 512 | | 35 R | 51.7% | 48.3% | 51.7% | 48.3% |
| 1,009 | GRANT | 503 | 304 | 199 | | 105 R | 60.4% | 39.6% | 60.4% | 39.6% |
| 4,595 | GREELEY | 2,080 | 775 | 1,305 | | 530 D | 37.3% | 62.7% | 37.3% | 62.7% |
| 35,757 | HALL | 14,988 | 6,715 | 8,273 | | 1,558 D | 44.8% | 55.2% | 44.8% | 55.2% |
| 8,714 | HAMILTON | 3,991 | 2,105 | 1,886 | | 219 R | 52.7% | 47.3% | 52.7% | 47.3% |
| 5,081 | HARLAN | 2,478 | 1,283 | 1,195 | | 88 R | 51.8% | 48.2% | 51.8% | 48.2% |
| 1,919 | HAYES | 865 | 503 | 362 | | 141 R | 58.2% | 41.8% | 58.2% | 41.8% |
| 4,829 | HITCHCOCK | 2,095 | 1,149 | 946 | | 203 R | 54.8% | 45.2% | 54.8% | 45.2% |
| 13,722 | HOLT | 5,933 | 3,194 | 2,739 | | 455 R | 53.8% | 46.2% | 53.8% | 46.2% |
| 1,130 | HOOKER | 472 | 335 | 137 | | 198 R | 71.0% | 29.0% | 71.0% | 29.0% |
| 6,541 | HOWARD | 3,044 | 1,019 | 2,025 | | 1,006 D | 33.5% | 66.5% | 33.5% | 66.5% |
| 11,620 | JEFFERSON | 5,079 | 2,275 | 2,804 | | 529 D | 44.8% | 55.2% | 44.8% | 55.2% |
| 6,281 | JOHNSON | 2,866 | 1,312 | 1,554 | | 242 D | 45.8% | 54.2% | 45.8% | 54.2% |
| 6,580 | KEARNEY | 3,119 | 1,352 | 1,767 | | 415 D | 43.3% | 56.7% | 43.3% | 56.7% |
| 7,958 | KEITH | 3,711 | 1,927 | 1,784 | | 143 R | 51.9% | 48.1% | 51.9% | 48.1% |
| 1,672 | KEYA PAHA | 826 | 506 | 320 | | 186 R | 61.3% | 38.7% | 61.3% | 38.7% |
| 7,975 | KIMBALL | 2,815 | 1,573 | 1,242 | | 331 R | 55.9% | 44.1% | 55.9% | 44.1% |
| 13,300 | KNOX | 5,369 | 2,752 | 2,617 | | 135 R | 51.3% | 48.7% | 51.3% | 48.7% |
| 155,272 | LANCASTER | 58,390 | 23,887 | 34,503 | | 10,616 D | 40.9% | 59.1% | 40.9% | 59.1% |
| 28,491 | LINCOLN | 11,257 | 4,811 | 6,446 | | 1,635 D | 42.7% | 57.3% | 42.7% | 57.3% |
| 1,108 | LOGAN | 563 | 267 | 296 | | 29 D | 47.4% | 52.6% | 47.4% | 52.6% |
| 1,097 | LOUP | 524 | 348 | 176 | | 172 R | 66.4% | 33.6% | 66.4% | 33.6% |
| 735 | MCPHERSON | 323 | 219 | 104 | | 115 R | 67.8% | 32.2% | 67.8% | 32.2% |
| 25,145 | MADISON | 10,816 | 6,155 | 4,661 | | 1,494 R | 56.9% | 43.1% | 56.9% | 43.1% |

# NEBRASKA

## PRESIDENT 1964

| 1960 Census Population | County | Total Vote | Republican | Democratic | Other | Rep.-Dem. Plurality | Percentage Total Vote Rep. | Dem. | Major Vote Rep. | Dem. |
|---|---|---|---|---|---|---|---|---|---|---|
| 8,363 | MERRICK | 3,539 | 1,798 | 1,741 | | 57 R | 50.8% | 49.2% | 50.8% | 49.2% |
| 7,057 | MORRILL | 2,877 | 1,649 | 1,228 | | 421 R | 57.3% | 42.7% | 57.3% | 42.7% |
| 5,635 | NANCE | 2,478 | 1,155 | 1,323 | | 168 D | 46.6% | 53.4% | 46.6% | 53.4% |
| 9,099 | NEMAHA | 4,020 | 1,936 | 2,084 | | 148 D | 48.2% | 51.8% | 48.2% | 51.8% |
| 8,217 | NUCKOLLS | 3,727 | 1,546 | 2,181 | | 635 D | 41.5% | 58.5% | 41.5% | 58.5% |
| 16,503 | OTOE | 6,795 | 3,626 | 3,169 | | 457 R | 53.4% | 46.6% | 53.4% | 46.6% |
| 5,356 | PAWNEE | 2,277 | 1,166 | 1,111 | | 55 R | 51.2% | 48.8% | 51.2% | 48.8% |
| 4,189 | PERKINS | 1,789 | 912 | 877 | | 35 R | 51.0% | 49.0% | 51.0% | 49.0% |
| 9,800 | PHELPS | 4,593 | 2,440 | 2,153 | | 287 R | 53.1% | 46.9% | 53.1% | 46.9% |
| 8,722 | PIERCE | 3,596 | 1,965 | 1,631 | | 334 R | 54.6% | 45.4% | 54.6% | 45.4% |
| 23,992 | PLATTE | 9,865 | 4,705 | 5,160 | | 455 D | 47.7% | 52.3% | 47.7% | 52.3% |
| 7,210 | POLK | 3,337 | 1,607 | 1,730 | | 123 D | 48.2% | 51.8% | 48.2% | 51.8% |
| 12,940 | RED WILLOW | 5,156 | 2,740 | 2,416 | | 324 R | 53.1% | 46.9% | 53.1% | 46.9% |
| 13,903 | RICHARDSON | 6,095 | 2,850 | 3,245 | | 395 D | 46.8% | 53.2% | 46.8% | 53.2% |
| 2,554 | ROCK | 1,211 | 835 | 376 | | 459 R | 69.0% | 31.0% | 69.0% | 31.0% |
| 12,542 | SALINE | 5,905 | 1,780 | 4,125 | | 2,345 D | 30.1% | 69.9% | 30.1% | 69.9% |
| 31,281 | SARPY | 9,999 | 4,418 | 5,581 | | 1,163 D | 44.2% | 55.8% | 44.2% | 55.8% |
| 17,270 | SAUNDERS | 7,517 | 3,345 | 4,172 | | 827 D | 44.5% | 55.5% | 44.5% | 55.5% |
| 33,809 | SCOTTS BLUFF | 13,333 | 6,965 | 6,368 | | 597 R | 52.2% | 47.8% | 52.2% | 47.8% |
| 13,581 | SEWARD | 5,568 | 2,221 | 3,347 | | 1,126 D | 39.9% | 60.1% | 39.9% | 60.1% |
| 9,049 | SHERIDAN | 3,596 | 2,440 | 1,156 | | 1,284 R | 67.9% | 32.1% | 67.9% | 32.1% |
| 5,382 | SHERMAN | 2,394 | 762 | 1,632 | | 870 D | 31.8% | 68.2% | 31.8% | 68.2% |
| 2,575 | SIOUX | 1,077 | 698 | 379 | | 319 R | 64.8% | 35.2% | 64.8% | 35.2% |
| 5,783 | STANTON | 2,313 | 1,299 | 1,014 | | 285 R | 56.2% | 43.8% | 56.2% | 43.8% |
| 9,118 | THAYER | 4,430 | 2,132 | 2,298 | | 166 D | 48.1% | 51.9% | 48.1% | 51.9% |
| 1,078 | THOMAS | 531 | 319 | 212 | | 107 R | 60.1% | 39.9% | 60.1% | 39.9% |
| 7,237 | THURSTON | 2,894 | 1,194 | 1,700 | | 506 D | 41.3% | 58.7% | 41.3% | 58.7% |
| 6,590 | VALLEY | 3,202 | 1,657 | 1,545 | | 112 R | 51.7% | 48.3% | 51.7% | 48.3% |
| 12,103 | WASHINGTON | 5,339 | 2,638 | 2,701 | | 63 D | 49.4% | 50.6% | 49.4% | 50.6% |
| 9,959 | WAYNE | 3,989 | 2,359 | 1,630 | | 729 R | 59.1% | 40.9% | 59.1% | 40.9% |
| 6,224 | WEBSTER | 2,848 | 1,191 | 1,657 | | 466 D | 41.8% | 58.2% | 41.8% | 58.2% |
| 1,297 | WHEELER | 565 | 317 | 248 | | 69 R | 56.1% | 43.9% | 56.1% | 43.9% |
| 13,724 | YORK | 6,242 | 3,410 | 2,832 | | 578 R | 54.6% | 45.4% | 54.6% | 45.4% |
| 1,411,330 | TOTAL | 584,154 | 276,847 | 307,307 | | 30,460 D | 47.4% | 52.6% | 47.4% | 52.6% |

# NEBRASKA

## PRESIDENT 1960

| 1960 Census Population | County | Total Vote | Republican | Democratic | Other | Rep.-Dem. Plurality | Percentage Total Vote | | Major Vote | |
|---|---|---|---|---|---|---|---|---|---|---|
| | | | | | | | Rep. | Dem. | Rep. | Dem. |
| 28,944 | ADAMS | 12,296 | 7,932 | 4,364 | | 3,568 R | 64.5% | 35.5% | 64.5% | 35.5% |
| 10,176 | ANTELOPE | 5,087 | 3,617 | 1,470 | | 2,147 R | 71.1% | 28.9% | 71.1% | 28.9% |
| 680 | ARTHUR | 351 | 283 | 68 | | 215 R | 80.6% | 19.4% | 80.6% | 19.4% |
| 1,269 | BANNER | 635 | 424 | 211 | | 213 R | 66.8% | 33.2% | 66.8% | 33.2% |
| 1,016 | BLAINE | 533 | 420 | 113 | | 307 R | 78.8% | 21.2% | 78.8% | 21.2% |
| 9,134 | BOONE | 4,356 | 2,809 | 1,547 | | 1,262 R | 64.5% | 35.5% | 64.5% | 35.5% |
| 11,688 | BOX BUTTE | 5,043 | 3,157 | 1,886 | | 1,271 R | 62.6% | 37.4% | 62.6% | 37.4% |
| 4,513 | BOYD | 2,161 | 1,393 | 768 | | 625 R | 64.5% | 35.5% | 64.5% | 35.5% |
| 4,436 | BROWN | 2,249 | 1,735 | 514 | | 1,221 R | 77.1% | 22.9% | 77.1% | 22.9% |
| 26,236 | BUFFALO | 11,486 | 7,595 | 3,891 | | 3,704 R | 66.1% | 33.9% | 66.1% | 33.9% |
| 10,192 | BURT | 4,979 | 3,613 | 1,366 | | 2,247 R | 72.6% | 27.4% | 72.6% | 27.4% |
| 10,312 | BUTLER | 4,995 | 2,253 | 2,742 | | 489 D | 45.1% | 54.9% | 45.1% | 54.9% |
| 17,821 | CASS | 7,305 | 4,506 | 2,799 | | 1,707 R | 61.7% | 38.3% | 61.7% | 38.3% |
| 13,368 | CEDAR | 5,999 | 3,060 | 2,939 | | 121 R | 51.0% | 49.0% | 51.0% | 49.0% |
| 4,317 | CHASE | 2,139 | 1,482 | 657 | | 825 R | 69.3% | 30.7% | 69.3% | 30.7% |
| 8,218 | CHERRY | 3,739 | 2,695 | 1,044 | | 1,651 R | 72.1% | 27.9% | 72.1% | 27.9% |
| 14,828 | CHEYENNE | 6,394 | 3,814 | 2,580 | | 1,234 R | 59.6% | 40.4% | 59.6% | 40.4% |
| 8,717 | CLAY | 4,336 | 3,005 | 1,331 | | 1,674 R | 69.3% | 30.7% | 69.3% | 30.7% |
| 9,595 | COLFAX | 4,479 | 2,504 | 1,975 | | 529 R | 55.9% | 44.1% | 55.9% | 44.1% |
| 12,435 | CUMING | 5,773 | 3,894 | 1,879 | | 2,015 R | 67.5% | 32.5% | 67.5% | 32.5% |
| 16,517 | CUSTER | 8,066 | 5,716 | 2,350 | | 3,366 R | 70.9% | 29.1% | 70.9% | 29.1% |
| 12,168 | DAKOTA | 5,304 | 2,977 | 2,327 | | 650 R | 56.1% | 43.9% | 56.1% | 43.9% |
| 9,536 | DAWES | 4,385 | 3,106 | 1,279 | | 1,827 R | 70.8% | 29.2% | 70.8% | 29.2% |
| 19,405 | DAWSON | 8,868 | 6,480 | 2,388 | | 4,092 R | 73.1% | 26.9% | 73.1% | 26.9% |
| 3,125 | DEUEL | 1,674 | 1,276 | 398 | | 878 R | 76.2% | 23.8% | 76.2% | 23.8% |
| 8,106 | DIXON | 4,097 | 2,713 | 1,384 | | 1,329 R | 66.2% | 33.8% | 66.2% | 33.8% |
| 32,471 | DODGE | 14,340 | 9,638 | 4,702 | | 4,936 R | 67.2% | 32.8% | 67.2% | 32.8% |
| 343,490 | DOUGLAS | 136,065 | 72,005 | 64,060 | | 7,945 R | 52.9% | 47.1% | 52.9% | 47.1% |
| 3,570 | DUNDY | 1,731 | 1,245 | 486 | | 759 R | 71.9% | 28.1% | 71.9% | 28.1% |
| 9,425 | FILLMORE | 4,652 | 2,842 | 1,810 | | 1,032 R | 61.1% | 38.9% | 61.1% | 38.9% |
| 5,449 | FRANKLIN | 2,801 | 1,798 | 1,003 | | 795 R | 64.2% | 35.8% | 64.2% | 35.8% |
| 4,311 | FRONTIER | 2,197 | 1,615 | 582 | | 1,033 R | 73.5% | 26.5% | 73.5% | 26.5% |
| 7,711 | FURNAS | 3,945 | 2,854 | 1,091 | | 1,763 R | 72.3% | 27.7% | 72.3% | 27.7% |
| 26,818 | GAGE | 11,615 | 7,754 | 3,861 | | 3,893 R | 66.8% | 33.2% | 66.8% | 33.2% |
| 3,472 | GARDEN | 1,802 | 1,376 | 426 | | 950 R | 76.4% | 23.6% | 76.4% | 23.6% |
| 2,699 | GARFIELD | 1,352 | 1,047 | 305 | | 742 R | 77.4% | 22.6% | 77.4% | 22.6% |
| 2,489 | GOSPER | 1,193 | 854 | 339 | | 515 R | 71.6% | 28.4% | 71.6% | 28.4% |
| 1,009 | GRANT | 537 | 410 | 127 | | 283 R | 76.4% | 23.6% | 76.4% | 23.6% |
| 4,595 | GREELEY | 2,223 | 960 | 1,263 | | 303 D | 43.2% | 56.8% | 43.2% | 56.8% |
| 35,757 | HALL | 15,259 | 9,763 | 5,496 | | 4,267 R | 64.0% | 36.0% | 64.0% | 36.0% |
| 8,714 | HAMILTON | 4,472 | 3,249 | 1,223 | | 2,026 R | 72.7% | 27.3% | 72.7% | 27.3% |
| 5,081 | HARLAN | 2,659 | 1,766 | 893 | | 873 R | 66.4% | 33.6% | 66.4% | 33.6% |
| 1,919 | HAYES | 980 | 699 | 281 | | 418 R | 71.3% | 28.7% | 71.3% | 28.7% |
| 4,829 | HITCHCOCK | 2,312 | 1,634 | 678 | | 956 R | 70.7% | 29.3% | 70.7% | 29.3% |
| 13,722 | HOLT | 6,588 | 4,150 | 2,438 | | 1,712 R | 63.0% | 37.0% | 63.0% | 37.0% |
| 1,130 | HOOKER | 514 | 443 | 71 | | 372 R | 86.2% | 13.8% | 86.2% | 13.8% |
| 6,541 | HOWARD | 3,194 | 1,676 | 1,518 | | 158 R | 52.5% | 47.5% | 52.5% | 47.5% |
| 11,620 | JEFFERSON | 5,942 | 4,047 | 1,895 | | 2,152 R | 68.1% | 31.9% | 68.1% | 31.9% |
| 6,281 | JOHNSON | 3,249 | 2,098 | 1,151 | | 947 R | 64.6% | 35.4% | 64.6% | 35.4% |
| 6,580 | KEARNEY | 3,328 | 2,065 | 1,263 | | 802 R | 62.0% | 38.0% | 62.0% | 38.0% |
| 7,958 | KEITH | 3,891 | 2,680 | 1,211 | | 1,469 R | 68.9% | 31.1% | 68.9% | 31.1% |
| 1,672 | KEYA PAHA | 887 | 646 | 241 | | 405 R | 72.8% | 27.2% | 72.8% | 27.2% |
| 7,975 | KIMBALL | 3,168 | 2,152 | 1,016 | | 1,136 R | 67.9% | 32.1% | 67.9% | 32.1% |
| 13,300 | KNOX | 5,969 | 3,847 | 2,122 | | 1,725 R | 64.4% | 35.6% | 64.4% | 35.6% |
| 155,272 | LANCASTER | 60,289 | 37,725 | 22,564 | | 15,161 R | 62.6% | 37.4% | 62.6% | 37.4% |
| 28,491 | LINCOLN | 12,497 | 7,685 | 4,812 | | 2,873 R | 61.5% | 38.5% | 61.5% | 38.5% |
| 1,108 | LOGAN | 554 | 391 | 163 | | 228 R | 70.6% | 29.4% | 70.6% | 29.4% |
| 1,097 | LOUP | 574 | 445 | 129 | | 316 R | 77.5% | 22.5% | 77.5% | 22.5% |
| 735 | MCPHERSON | 370 | 303 | 67 | | 236 R | 81.9% | 18.1% | 81.9% | 18.1% |
| 25,145 | MADISON | 11,400 | 8,350 | 3,050 | | 5,300 R | 73.2% | 26.8% | 73.2% | 26.8% |

# NEBRASKA

## PRESIDENT 1960

| 1960 Census Population | County | Total Vote | Republican | Democratic | Other | Rep.-Dem. Plurality | Percentage | | | |
|---|---|---|---|---|---|---|---|---|---|---|
| | | | | | | | Total Vote | | Major Vote | |
| | | | | | | | Rep. | Dem. | Rep. | Dem. |
| 8,363 | MERRICK | 3,978 | 2,744 | 1,234 | | 1,510 R | 69.0% | 31.0% | 69.0% | 31.0% |
| 7,057 | MORRILL | 3,219 | 2,020 | 1,199 | | 821 R | 62.8% | 37.2% | 62.8% | 37.2% |
| 5,635 | NANCE | 2,711 | 1,699 | 1,012 | | 687 R | 62.7% | 37.3% | 62.7% | 37.3% |
| 9,099 | NEMAHA | 4,408 | 3,031 | 1,377 | | 1,654 R | 68.8% | 31.2% | 68.8% | 31.2% |
| 8,217 | NUCKOLLS | 4,011 | 2,441 | 1,570 | | 871 R | 60.9% | 39.1% | 60.9% | 39.1% |
| 16,503 | OTOE | 7,600 | 5,057 | 2,543 | | 2,514 R | 66.5% | 33.5% | 66.5% | 33.5% |
| 5,356 | PAWNEE | 2,737 | 1,728 | 1,009 | | 719 R | 63.1% | 36.9% | 63.1% | 36.9% |
| 4,189 | PERKINS | 1,998 | 1,301 | 697 | | 604 R | 65.1% | 34.9% | 65.1% | 34.9% |
| 9,800 | PHELPS | 5,047 | 3,795 | 1,252 | | 2,543 R | 75.2% | 24.8% | 75.2% | 24.8% |
| 8,722 | PIERCE | 4,070 | 2,963 | 1,107 | | 1,856 R | 72.8% | 27.2% | 72.8% | 27.2% |
| 23,992 | PLATTE | 10,516 | 6,129 | 4,387 | | 1,742 R | 58.3% | 41.7% | 58.3% | 41.7% |
| 7,210 | POLK | 3,581 | 2,397 | 1,184 | | 1,213 R | 66.9% | 33.1% | 66.9% | 33.1% |
| 12,940 | RED WILLOW | 5,812 | 3,890 | 1,922 | | 1,968 R | 66.9% | 33.1% | 66.9% | 33.1% |
| 13,903 | RICHARDSON | 7,151 | 4,481 | 2,670 | | 1,811 R | 62.7% | 37.3% | 62.7% | 37.3% |
| 2,554 | ROCK | 1,337 | 1,084 | 253 | | 831 R | 81.1% | 18.9% | 81.1% | 18.9% |
| 12,542 | SALINE | 6,404 | 2,881 | 3,523 | | 642 D | 45.0% | 55.0% | 45.0% | 55.0% |
| 31,281 | SARPY | 8,449 | 4,672 | 3,777 | | 895 R | 55.3% | 44.7% | 55.3% | 44.7% |
| 17,270 | SAUNDERS | 8,258 | 4,702 | 3,556 | | 1,146 R | 56.9% | 43.1% | 56.9% | 43.1% |
| 33,809 | SCOTTS BLUFF | 14,374 | 8,728 | 5,646 | | 3,082 R | 60.7% | 39.3% | 60.7% | 39.3% |
| 13,581 | SEWARD | 5,683 | 3,588 | 2,095 | | 1,493 R | 63.1% | 36.9% | 63.1% | 36.9% |
| 9,049 | SHERIDAN | 4,014 | 2,870 | 1,144 | | 1,726 R | 71.5% | 28.5% | 71.5% | 28.5% |
| 5,382 | SHERMAN | 2,558 | 1,131 | 1,427 | | 296 D | 44.2% | 55.8% | 44.2% | 55.8% |
| 2,575 | SIOUX | 1,160 | 745 | 415 | | 330 R | 64.2% | 35.8% | 64.2% | 35.8% |
| 5,783 | STANTON | 2,537 | 1,680 | 857 | | 823 R | 66.2% | 33.8% | 66.2% | 33.8% |
| 9,118 | THAYER | 4,752 | 3,202 | 1,550 | | 1,652 R | 67.4% | 32.6% | 67.4% | 32.6% |
| 1,078 | THOMAS | 561 | 420 | 141 | | 279 R | 74.9% | 25.1% | 74.9% | 25.1% |
| 7,237 | THURSTON | 3,072 | 1,757 | 1,315 | | 442 R | 57.2% | 42.8% | 57.2% | 42.8% |
| 6,590 | VALLEY | 3,293 | 2,045 | 1,248 | | 797 R | 62.1% | 37.9% | 62.1% | 37.9% |
| 12,103 | WASHINGTON | 5,466 | 3,772 | 1,694 | | 2,078 R | 69.0% | 31.0% | 69.0% | 31.0% |
| 9,959 | WAYNE | 4,299 | 3,274 | 1,025 | | 2,249 R | 76.2% | 23.8% | 76.2% | 23.8% |
| 6,224 | WEBSTER | 3,129 | 2,026 | 1,103 | | 923 R | 64.7% | 35.3% | 64.7% | 35.3% |
| 1,297 | WHEELER | 663 | 424 | 239 | | 185 R | 64.0% | 36.0% | 64.0% | 36.0% |
| 13,724 | YORK | 6,969 | 5,205 | 1,764 | | 3,441 R | 74.7% | 25.3% | 74.7% | 25.3% |
| 1,411,330 | TOTAL | 613,095 | 380,553 | 232,542 | | 148,011 R | 62.1% | 37.9% | 62.1% | 37.9% |

# NEBRASKA

## ELECTION NOTES

**2004**   Other vote was 5,698 By Petition (Ralph Nader); 2,041 Libertarian (Michael Badnarik); 1,314 Nebraska (Michael Peroutka); 978 Green (David Cobb); 82 By Petition (Roger Calero); 931 scattered write-in.

**2000**   Other vote was 3,646 By Petition (Buchanan); 2,245 Libertarian (Browne); 478 Natural Law (Hagelin); 468 By Petition (Phillips).

**1996**   Other vote was 2,792 Libertarian (Browne); 1,928 Independent (Phillips); 1,189 (Hagelin).

**1992**   Other vote was 1,340 Marrou (Libertarian); 846 Fulani (Independent); 714 Hagelin (Independent).

**1988**   Other vote was 2,534 Paul (Libertarian); 1,740 Fulani (New Alliance).

**1984**   Other vote was 2,079 Bergland (Libertarian); 1,066 Mason (Independent); 1,025 Serrette (Independent). State and county data include new resident votes reported separately.

**1980**   Other vote was 44,993 Anderson (Independent); 9,073 Clark (Libertarian). State and county data include new resident votes reported separately.

**1976**   Other vote was 9,409 McCarthy (Independent); 3,380 Maddox (American); 1,482 MacBride (Libertarian). State and county data include new resident votes reported separately. Due to a printers error in the "Official Report", the Democratic state-wide total vote was given as 233,287.

**1972**

**1968**   Wallace on the ballot as American.

**1964**

**1960**

# NEVADA

## POPULAR VOTE FOR PRESIDENT 1920 TO 2004

| Year | Total Vote | Republican Vote | Republican Candidate | Democratic Vote | Democratic Candidate | Other Vote | Plurality | Percentage Total Vote Rep. | Percentage Total Vote Dem. | Percentage Major Vote Rep. | Percentage Major Vote Dem. |
|---|---|---|---|---|---|---|---|---|---|---|---|
| 2004 | 829,587 | 418,690 | Bush, George W. | 397,190 | Kerry, John | 13,707 | 21,500 R | 50.5% | 47.9% | 51.3% | 48.7% |
| 2000 ** | 608,970 | 301,575 | Bush, George W. | 279,978 | Gore, Al | 27,417 | 21,597 R | 49.5% | 46.0% | 51.9% | 48.1% |
| 1996 ** | 464,279 | 199,244 | Dole, Bob | 203,974 | Clinton, Bill | 61,061 | 4,730 D | 42.9% | 43.9% | 49.4% | 50.6% |
| 1992 ** | 506,318 | 175,828 | Bush, George | 189,148 | Clinton, Bill | 141,342 | 13,320 D | 34.7% | 37.4% | 48.2% | 51.8% |
| 1988 | 350,067 | 206,040 | Bush, George | 132,738 | Dukakis, Michael S. | 11,289 | 73,302 R | 58.9% | 37.9% | 60.8% | 39.2% |
| 1984 | 286,667 | 188,770 | Reagan, Ronald | 91,655 | Mondale, Walter F. | 6,242 | 97,115 R | 65.8% | 32.0% | 67.3% | 32.7% |
| 1980 ** | 247,885 | 155,017 | Reagan, Ronald | 66,666 | Carter, Jimmy | 26,202 | 88,351 R | 62.5% | 26.9% | 69.9% | 30.1% |
| 1976 | 201,876 | 101,273 | Ford, Gerald R. | 92,479 | Carter, Jimmy | 8,124 | 8,794 R | 50.2% | 45.8% | 52.3% | 47.7% |
| 1972 | 181,766 | 115,750 | Nixon, Richard M. | 66,016 | McGovern, George S. | | 49,734 R | 63.7% | 36.3% | 63.7% | 36.3% |
| 1968 | 154,218 | 73,188 | Nixon, Richard M. | 60,598 | Humphrey, Hubert H. | 20,432 | 12,590 R | 47.5% | 39.3% | 54.7% | 45.3% |
| 1964 | 135,433 | 56,094 | Goldwater, Barry M. | 79,339 | Johnson, Lyndon B. | | 23,245 D | 41.4% | 58.6% | 41.4% | 58.6% |
| 1960 | 107,267 | 52,387 | Nixon, Richard M. | 54,880 | Kennedy, John F. | | 2,493 D | 48.8% | 51.2% | 48.8% | 51.2% |
| 1956 | 96,689 | 56,049 | Eisenhower, Dwight D. | 40,640 | Stevenson, Adlai E. | | 15,409 R | 58.0% | 42.0% | 58.0% | 42.0% |
| 1952 | 82,190 | 50,502 | Eisenhower, Dwight D. | 31,688 | Stevenson, Adlai E. | | 18,814 R | 61.4% | 38.6% | 61.4% | 38.6% |
| 1948 | 62,117 | 29,357 | Dewey, Thomas E. | 31,291 | Truman, Harry S. | 1,469 | 1,934 D | 47.3% | 50.4% | 48.4% | 51.6% |
| 1944 | 54,234 | 24,611 | Dewey, Thomas E. | 29,623 | Roosevelt, Franklin D. | | 5,012 D | 45.4% | 54.6% | 45.4% | 54.6% |
| 1940 | 53,174 | 21,229 | Willkie, Wendell | 31,945 | Roosevelt, Franklin D. | | 10,716 D | 39.9% | 60.1% | 39.9% | 60.1% |
| 1936 | 43,848 | 11,923 | Landon, Alfred M. | 31,925 | Roosevelt, Franklin D. | | 20,002 D | 27.2% | 72.8% | 27.2% | 72.8% |
| 1932 | 41,430 | 12,674 | Hoover, Herbert C. | 28,756 | Roosevelt, Franklin D. | | 16,082 D | 30.6% | 69.4% | 30.6% | 69.4% |
| 1928 | 32,417 | 18,327 | Hoover, Herbert C. | 14,090 | Smith, Alfred E. | | 4,237 R | 56.5% | 43.5% | 56.5% | 43.5% |
| 1924 ** | 26,921 | 11,243 | Coolidge, Calvin | 5,909 | Davis, John W. | 9,769 | 1,474 R | 41.8% | 21.9% | 65.5% | 34.5% |
| 1920 | 27,194 | 15,479 | Harding, Warren G. | 9,851 | Cox, James M. | 1,864 | 5,628 R | 56.9% | 36.2% | 61.1% | 38.9% |

In 2000 the other vote column includes 15,008 votes cast for Green (Nader). In 1996 the other vote column includes 43,986 votes cast for Perot. In 1992 the other vote column includes 132,580 votes cast for Perot. In 1980 the other column includes 17,651 votes for Independent (Anderson). In 1924 the other vote was Progressive.

## ELECTORAL COLLEGE VOTE 1920 TO 2004

| Year | Total | Republican | Democratic | Other |
|---|---|---|---|---|
| 2004 | 5 | 5 | | |
| 2000 | 4 | 4 | | |
| 1996 | 4 | | 4 | |
| 1992 | 4 | | 4 | |
| 1988 | 4 | 4 | | |
| 1984 | 4 | 4 | | |
| 1980 | 3 | 3 | | |
| 1976 | 3 | 3 | | |
| 1972 | 3 | 3 | | |
| 1968 | 3 | 3 | | |
| 1964 | 3 | | 3 | |
| 1960 | 3 | | 3 | |
| 1956 | 3 | 3 | | |
| 1952 | 3 | 3 | | |
| 1948 | 3 | | 3 | |
| 1944 | 3 | | 3 | |
| 1940 | 3 | | 3 | |
| 1936 | 3 | | 3 | |
| 1932 | 3 | | 3 | |
| 1928 | 3 | 3 | | |
| 1924 | 3 | 3 | | |
| 1920 | 3 | 3 | | |

# NEVADA

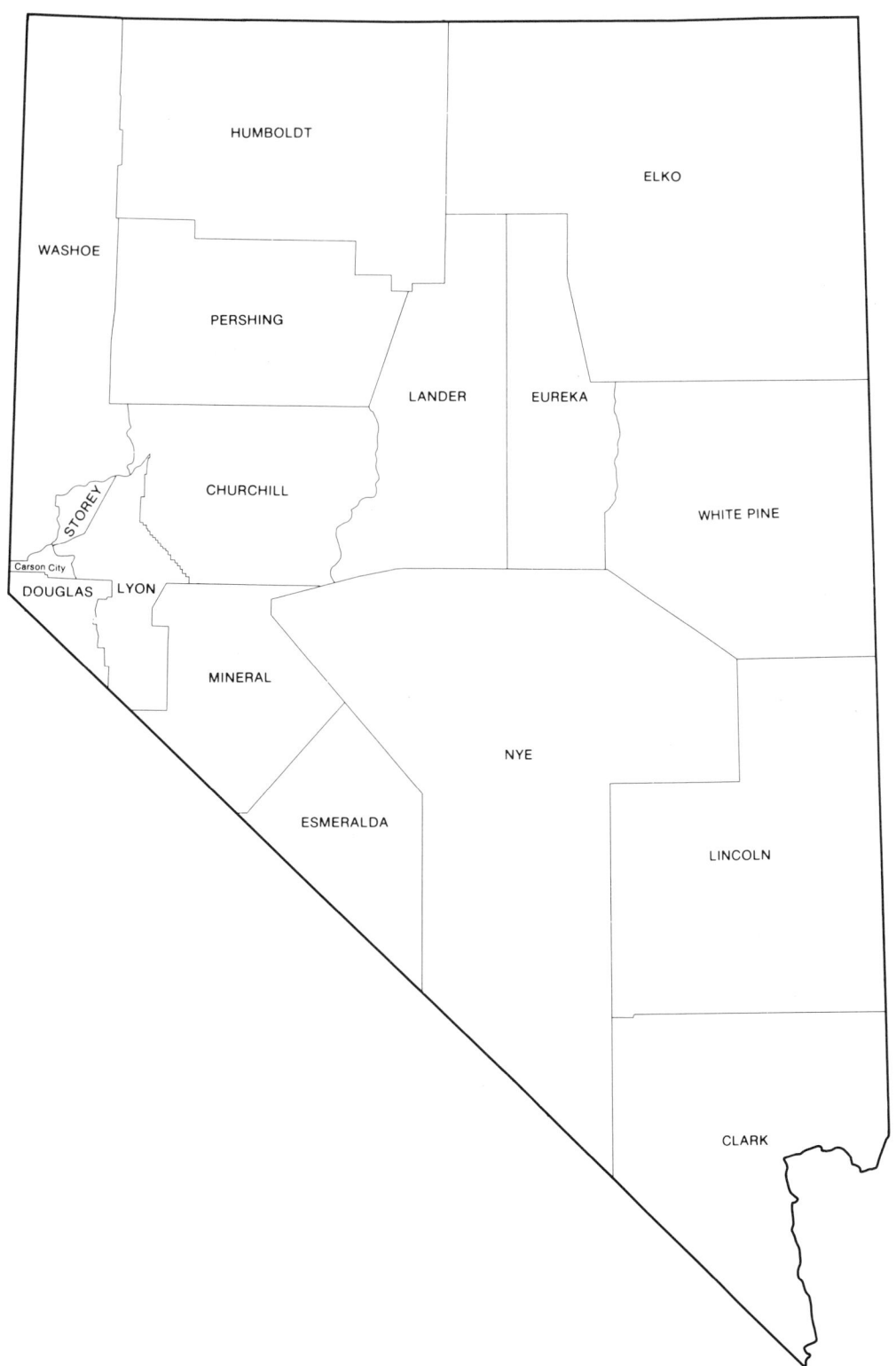

# NEVADA

## PRESIDENT 2004

| 2000 Census Population | County | Total Vote | Republican | Democratic | Other | Rep.-Dem. Plurality | Percentage | | | |
|---|---|---|---|---|---|---|---|---|---|---|
| | | | | | | | Total Vote | | Major Vote | |
| | | | | | | | Rep. | Dem. | Rep. | Dem. |
| 52,457 | CARSON CITY | 23,106 | 13,171 | 9,441 | 494 | 3,730 R | 57.0% | 40.9% | 58.2% | 41.8% |
| 23,982 | CHURCHILL | 10,237 | 7,335 | 2,705 | 197 | 4,630 R | 71.7% | 26.4% | 73.1% | 26.9% |
| 1,375,765 | CLARK | 545,397 | 255,337 | 281,767 | 8,293 | 26,430 D | 46.8% | 51.7% | 47.5% | 52.5% |
| 41,259 | DOUGLAS | 23,898 | 15,192 | 8,275 | 431 | 6,917 R | 63.6% | 34.6% | 64.7% | 35.3% |
| 45,291 | ELKO | 15,309 | 11,938 | 3,050 | 321 | 8,888 R | 78.0% | 19.9% | 79.7% | 20.3% |
| 971 | ESMERALDA | 481 | 367 | 99 | 15 | 268 R | 76.3% | 20.6% | 78.8% | 21.2% |
| 1,651 | EUREKA | 738 | 571 | 144 | 23 | 427 R | 77.4% | 19.5% | 79.9% | 20.1% |
| 16,106 | HUMBOLDT | 5,367 | 3,896 | 1,361 | 110 | 2,535 R | 72.6% | 25.4% | 74.1% | 25.9% |
| 5,794 | LANDER | 2,053 | 1,602 | 414 | 37 | 1,188 R | 78.0% | 20.2% | 79.5% | 20.5% |
| 4,165 | LINCOLN | 2,047 | 1,579 | 418 | 50 | 1,161 R | 77.1% | 20.4% | 79.1% | 20.9% |
| 34,501 | LYON | 17,151 | 11,136 | 5,637 | 378 | 5,499 R | 64.9% | 32.9% | 66.4% | 33.6% |
| 5,071 | MINERAL | 2,327 | 1,336 | 931 | 60 | 405 R | 57.4% | 40.0% | 58.9% | 41.1% |
| 32,485 | NYE | 14,510 | 8,487 | 5,616 | 407 | 2,871 R | 58.5% | 38.7% | 60.2% | 39.8% |
| 6,693 | PERSHING | 1,917 | 1,341 | 538 | 38 | 803 R | 70.0% | 28.1% | 71.4% | 28.6% |
| 3,399 | STOREY | 2,168 | 1,253 | 871 | 44 | 382 R | 57.8% | 40.2% | 59.0% | 41.0% |
| 339,486 | WASHOE | 159,079 | 81,545 | 74,841 | 2,693 | 6,704 R | 51.3% | 47.0% | 52.1% | 47.9% |
| 9,181 | WHITE PINE | 3,802 | 2,604 | 1,082 | 116 | 1,522 R | 68.5% | 28.5% | 70.6% | 29.4% |
| 1,998,257 | TOTAL | 829,587 | 418,690 | 397,190 | 13,707 | 21,500 R | 50.5% | 47.9% | 51.3% | 48.7% |

# NEVADA

## PRESIDENT 2000

| 2000 Census Population | County | Total Vote | Republican | Democratic | Green (Nader) | Other | Rep.-Dem. Plurality | Percentage of Total Vote | | |
|---|---|---|---|---|---|---|---|---|---|---|
| | | | | | | | | Rep. | Dem. | Green |
| 52,457 | CARSON CITY | 19,452 | 11,084 | 7,354 | 605 | 409 | 3,730 R | 57.0% | 37.8% | 3.1% |
| 23,982 | CHURCHILL | 8,823 | 6,237 | 2,191 | 189 | 206 | 4,046 R | 70.7% | 24.8% | 2.1% |
| 1,375,765 | CLARK | 382,198 | 170,932 | 196,100 | 7,942 | 7,224 | 25,168 D | 44.7% | 51.3% | 2.1% |
| 41,259 | DOUGLAS | 17,974 | 11,193 | 5,837 | 593 | 351 | 5,356 R | 62.3% | 32.5% | 3.3% |
| 45,291 | ELKO | 14,180 | 11,025 | 2,542 | 221 | 392 | 8,483 R | 77.8% | 17.9% | 1.6% |
| 971 | ESMERALDA | 491 | 333 | 116 | 14 | 28 | 217 R | 67.8% | 23.6% | 2.9% |
| 1,651 | EUREKA | 837 | 632 | 150 | 15 | 40 | 482 R | 75.5% | 17.9% | 1.8% |
| 16,106 | HUMBOLDT | 5,030 | 3,638 | 1,128 | 137 | 127 | 2,510 R | 72.3% | 22.4% | 2.7% |
| 5,794 | LANDER | 2,119 | 1,619 | 395 | 37 | 68 | 1,224 R | 76.4% | 18.6% | 1.7% |
| 4,165 | LINCOLN | 1,956 | 1,372 | 461 | 40 | 83 | 911 R | 70.1% | 23.6% | 2.0% |
| 34,501 | LYON | 11,992 | 7,270 | 3,955 | 382 | 385 | 3,315 R | 60.6% | 33.0% | 3.2% |
| 5,071 | MINERAL | 2,293 | 1,227 | 916 | 81 | 69 | 311 R | 53.5% | 39.9% | 3.5% |
| 32,485 | NYE | 12,181 | 6,904 | 4,525 | 332 | 420 | 2,379 R | 56.7% | 37.1% | 2.7% |
| 6,693 | PERSHING | 1,802 | 1,221 | 476 | 46 | 59 | 745 R | 67.8% | 26.4% | 2.6% |
| 3,399 | STOREY | 1,798 | 1,014 | 666 | 79 | 39 | 348 R | 56.4% | 37.0% | 4.4% |
| 339,486 | WASHOE | 122,301 | 63,640 | 52,097 | 4,209 | 2,355 | 11,543 R | 52.0% | 42.6% | 3.4% |
| 9,181 | WHITE PINE | 3,543 | 2,234 | 1,069 | 86 | 154 | 1,165 R | 63.1% | 30.2% | 2.4% |
| 1,998,257 | TOTAL | 608,970 | 301,575 | 279,978 | 15,008 | 12,409 | 21,597 R | 49.5% | 46.0% | 2.5% |

# NEVADA

## PRESIDENT 1996

| 1995 Census Pop. Est. | County | Total Vote | Republican | Democratic | Reform (Perot) | Other | Rep.-Dem. Plurality | Percentage of Total Vote | | |
|---|---|---|---|---|---|---|---|---|---|---|
| | | | | | | | | Rep. | Dem. | Reform |
| 46,283 | CARSON CITY | 18,814 | 9,168 | 7,269 | 1,591 | 786 | 1,899 R | 48.7% | 38.6% | 8.5% |
| 21,096 | CHURCHILL | 7,763 | 4,369 | 2,282 | 821 | 291 | 2,087 R | 56.3% | 29.4% | 10.6% |
| 992,593 | CLARK | 262,710 | 103,431 | 127,963 | 23,177 | 8,139 | 24,532 D | 39.4% | 48.7% | 8.8% |
| 34,695 | DOUGLAS | 16,100 | 8,828 | 5,109 | 1,486 | 677 | 3,719 R | 54.8% | 31.7% | 9.2% |
| 41,732 | ELKO | 11,857 | 6,512 | 3,149 | 1,539 | 657 | 3,363 R | 54.9% | 26.6% | 13.0% |
| 1,185 | ESMERALDA | 546 | 277 | 140 | 91 | 38 | 137 R | 50.7% | 25.6% | 16.7% |
| 1,413 | EUREKA | 688 | 412 | 158 | 90 | 28 | 254 R | 59.9% | 23.0% | 13.1% |
| 16,038 | HUMBOLDT | 4,590 | 2,334 | 1,467 | 603 | 186 | 867 R | 50.8% | 32.0% | 13.1% |
| 6,473 | LANDER | 2,215 | 1,107 | 660 | 361 | 87 | 447 R | 50.0% | 29.8% | 16.3% |
| 3,837 | LINCOLN | 1,783 | 936 | 499 | 255 | 93 | 437 R | 52.5% | 28.0% | 14.3% |
| 25,867 | LYON | 9,699 | 4,753 | 3,419 | 1,104 | 423 | 1,334 R | 49.0% | 35.3% | 11.4% |
| 6,182 | MINERAL | 2,318 | 814 | 1,068 | 361 | 75 | 254 D | 35.1% | 46.1% | 15.6% |
| 24,563 | NYE | 9,211 | 3,979 | 3,300 | 1,544 | 388 | 679 R | 43.2% | 35.8% | 16.8% |
| 4,526 | PERSHING | 1,569 | 743 | 565 | 203 | 58 | 178 R | 47.4% | 36.0% | 12.9% |
| 2,835 | STOREY | 1,655 | 705 | 614 | 244 | 92 | 91 R | 42.6% | 37.1% | 14.7% |
| 290,833 | WASHOE | 109,266 | 49,477 | 44,915 | 9,970 | 4,904 | 4,562 R | 45.3% | 41.1% | 9.1% |
| 9,957 | WHITE PINE | 3,495 | 1,399 | 1,397 | 546 | 153 | 2 R | 40.0% | 40.0% | 15.6% |
| 1,530,108 | TOTAL | 464,279 | 199,244 | 203,974 | 43,986 | 17,075 | 4,730 D | 42.9% | 43.9% | 9.5% |

# NEVADA

## PRESIDENT 1992

| 1990 Census Population | County | Total Vote | Republican | Democratic | Perot | Other | Plurality | Percentage Total Vote | | |
|---|---|---|---|---|---|---|---|---|---|---|
| | | | | | | | | Rep. | Dem. | Perot |
| 40,443 | CARSON CITY | 18,803 | 7,302 | 6,035 | 5,195 | 271 | 1,267 R | 38.8% | 32.1% | 27.6% |
| 17,938 | CHURCHILL | 7,663 | 3,789 | 1,770 | 1,964 | 140 | 1,825 R | 49.4% | 23.1% | 25.6% |
| 741,459 | CLARK | 302,782 | 97,403 | 124,586 | 75,364 | 5,429 | 27,183 D | 32.2% | 41.1% | 24.9% |
| 27,637 | DOUGLAS | 15,145 | 6,182 | 3,928 | 4,814 | 221 | 1,368 R | 40.8% | 25.9% | 31.8% |
| 33,530 | ELKO | 11,926 | 5,208 | 2,782 | 3,628 | 308 | 1,580 R | 43.7% | 23.3% | 30.4% |
| 1,344 | ESMERALDA | 584 | 221 | 118 | 220 | 25 | 1 R | 37.8% | 20.2% | 37.7% |
| 1,547 | EUREKA | 690 | 330 | 129 | 214 | 17 | 116 R | 47.8% | 18.7% | 31.0% |
| 12,844 | HUMBOLDT | 3,523 | 1,505 | 810 | 1,149 | 59 | 356 R | 42.7% | 23.0% | 32.6% |
| 6,266 | LANDER | 1,992 | 885 | 423 | 652 | 32 | 233 R | 44.4% | 21.2% | 32.7% |
| 3,775 | LINCOLN | 1,857 | 890 | 511 | 394 | 62 | 379 R | 47.9% | 27.5% | 21.2% |
| 20,001 | LYON | 9,204 | 3,509 | 2,777 | 2,716 | 202 | 732 R | 38.1% | 30.2% | 29.5% |
| 6,475 | MINERAL | 2,641 | 918 | 909 | 746 | 68 | 9 R | 34.8% | 34.4% | 28.2% |
| 17,781 | NYE | 8,022 | 2,743 | 2,561 | 2,501 | 217 | 182 R | 34.2% | 31.9% | 31.2% |
| | ORMSBY | — | — | — | — | — | — | — | — | — |
| 4,336 | PERSHING | 1,566 | 643 | 467 | 429 | 27 | 176 R | 41.1% | 29.8% | 27.4% |
| 2,526 | STOREY | 1,519 | 458 | 488 | 550 | 23 | 62 P | 30.2% | 32.1% | 36.2% |
| 254,667 | WASHOE | 114,671 | 42,636 | 39,500 | 30,974 | 1,561 | 3,136 R | 37.2% | 34.4% | 27.0% |
| 9,264 | WHITE PINE | 3,730 | 1,206 | 1,354 | 1,070 | 100 | 148 D | 32.3% | 36.3% | 28.7% |
| 1,201,833 | TOTAL | 506,318 | 175,828 | 189,148 | 132,580 | 8,762 | 13,320 D | 34.7% | 37.4% | 26.2% |

# NEVADA

## PRESIDENT 1988

| 1980 Census Population | County | Total Vote | Republican | Democratic | Other | Rep.-Dem. Plurality | Percentage | | | |
|---|---|---|---|---|---|---|---|---|---|---|
| | | | | | | | Total Vote | | Major Vote | |
| | | | | | | | Rep. | Dem. | Rep. | Dem. |
| 32,022 | CARSON CITY | 15,291 | 9,701 | 5,088 | 502 | 4,613 R | 63.4% | 33.3% | 65.6% | 34.4% |
| 13,917 | CHURCHILL | 6,283 | 4,578 | 1,481 | 224 | 3,097 R | 72.9% | 23.6% | 75.6% | 24.4% |
| 463,087 | CLARK | 191,779 | 108,110 | 78,359 | 5,310 | 29,751 R | 56.4% | 40.9% | 58.0% | 42.0% |
| 19,421 | DOUGLAS | 10,555 | 7,074 | 3,107 | 374 | 3,967 R | 67.0% | 29.4% | 69.5% | 30.5% |
| 17,269 | ELKO | 8,372 | 5,722 | 2,310 | 340 | 3,412 R | 68.3% | 27.6% | 71.2% | 28.8% |
| 777 | ESMERALDA | 552 | 380 | 143 | 29 | 237 R | 68.8% | 25.9% | 72.7% | 27.3% |
| 1,198 | EUREKA | 582 | 413 | 151 | 18 | 262 R | 71.0% | 25.9% | 73.2% | 26.8% |
| 9,434 | HUMBOLDT | 3,576 | 2,378 | 1,024 | 174 | 1,354 R | 66.5% | 28.6% | 69.9% | 30.1% |
| 4,076 | LANDER | 1,714 | 1,214 | 439 | 61 | 775 R | 70.8% | 25.6% | 73.4% | 26.6% |
| 3,732 | LINCOLN | 1,564 | 1,035 | 466 | 63 | 569 R | 66.2% | 29.8% | 69.0% | 31.0% |
| 13,594 | LYON | 6,987 | 4,390 | 2,301 | 296 | 2,089 R | 62.8% | 32.9% | 65.6% | 34.4% |
| 6,217 | MINERAL | 2,602 | 1,480 | 978 | 144 | 502 R | 56.9% | 37.6% | 60.2% | 39.8% |
| 9,048 | NYE | 5,603 | 3,619 | 1,748 | 236 | 1,871 R | 64.6% | 31.2% | 67.4% | 32.6% |
| | ORMSBY | — | — | — | — | — | — | — | — | — |
| 3,408 | PERSHING | 1,396 | 867 | 458 | 71 | 409 R | 62.1% | 32.8% | 65.4% | 34.6% |
| 1,503 | STOREY | 1,155 | 651 | 432 | 72 | 219 R | 56.4% | 37.4% | 60.1% | 39.9% |
| 193,623 | WASHOE | 88,728 | 52,654 | 32,902 | 3,172 | 19,752 R | 59.3% | 37.1% | 61.5% | 38.5% |
| 8,167 | WHITE PINE | 3,328 | 1,774 | 1,351 | 203 | 423 R | 53.3% | 40.6% | 56.8% | 43.2% |
| 800,493 | TOTAL | 350,067 | 206,040 | 132,738 | 11,289 | 73,302 R | 58.9% | 37.9% | 60.8% | 39.2% |

# NEVADA

## PRESIDENT 1984

| 1980 Census Population | County | Total Vote | Republican | Democratic | Other | Rep.-Dem. Plurality | Percentage | | | |
|---|---|---|---|---|---|---|---|---|---|---|
| | | | | | | | Total Vote | | Major Vote | |
| | | | | | | | Rep. | Dem. | Rep. | Dem. |
| 32,022 | CARSON CITY | 13,536 | 9,477 | 3,790 | 269 | 5,687 R | 70.0% | 28.0% | 71.4% | 28.6% |
| 13,917 | CHURCHILL | 5,930 | 4,479 | 1,304 | 147 | 3,175 R | 75.5% | 22.0% | 77.5% | 22.5% |
| 463,087 | CLARK | 150,363 | 94,133 | 53,386 | 2,844 | 40,747 R | 62.6% | 35.5% | 63.8% | 36.2% |
| 19,421 | DOUGLAS | 8,449 | 6,385 | 1,877 | 187 | 4,508 R | 75.6% | 22.2% | 77.3% | 22.7% |
| 17,269 | ELKO | 6,861 | 5,110 | 1,566 | 185 | 3,544 R | 74.5% | 22.8% | 76.5% | 23.5% |
| 777 | ESMERALDA | 647 | 453 | 158 | 36 | 295 R | 70.0% | 24.4% | 74.1% | 25.9% |
| 1,198 | EUREKA | 578 | 439 | 124 | 15 | 315 R | 76.0% | 21.5% | 78.0% | 22.0% |
| 9,434 | HUMBOLDT | 3,450 | 2,498 | 862 | 90 | 1,636 R | 72.4% | 25.0% | 74.3% | 25.7% |
| 4,076 | LANDER | 1,561 | 1,222 | 301 | 38 | 921 R | 78.3% | 19.3% | 80.2% | 19.8% |
| 3,732 | LINCOLN | 1,616 | 1,175 | 397 | 44 | 778 R | 72.7% | 24.6% | 74.7% | 25.3% |
| 13,594 | LYON | 6,177 | 4,320 | 1,673 | 184 | 2,647 R | 69.9% | 27.1% | 72.1% | 27.9% |
| 6,217 | MINERAL | 2,504 | 1,645 | 766 | 93 | 879 R | 65.7% | 30.6% | 68.2% | 31.8% |
| 9,048 | NYE | 4,989 | 3,573 | 1,269 | 147 | 2,304 R | 71.6% | 25.4% | 73.8% | 26.2% |
| | ORMSBY | — | — | — | — | — | — | — | — | — |
| 3,408 | PERSHING | 1,330 | 956 | 333 | 41 | 623 R | 71.9% | 25.0% | 74.2% | 25.8% |
| 1,503 | STOREY | 854 | 570 | 252 | 32 | 318 R | 66.7% | 29.5% | 69.3% | 30.7% |
| 193,623 | WASHOE | 74,511 | 50,418 | 22,321 | 1,772 | 28,097 R | 67.7% | 30.0% | 69.3% | 30.7% |
| 8,167 | WHITE PINE | 3,311 | 1,917 | 1,276 | 118 | 641 R | 57.9% | 38.5% | 60.0% | 40.0% |
| 800,493 | TOTAL | 286,667 | 188,770 | 91,655 | 6,242 | 97,115 R | 65.8% | 32.0% | 67.3% | 32.7% |

# NEVADA

## PRESIDENT 1980

| 1980 Census Population | County | Total Vote | Republican | Democratic | Other | Rep.-Dem. Plurality | Percentage | | | |
| --- | --- | --- | --- | --- | --- | --- | --- | --- | --- | --- |
| | | | | | | | Total Vote | | Major Vote | |
| | | | | | | | Rep. | Dem. | Rep. | Dem. |
| 32,022 | CARSON CITY | 12,556 | 8,389 | 2,769 | 1,398 | 5,620 R | 66.8% | 22.1% | 75.2% | 24.8% |
| 13,917 | CHURCHILL | 5,273 | 3,841 | 1,055 | 377 | 2,786 R | 72.8% | 20.0% | 78.5% | 21.5% |
| 463,087 | CLARK | 127,424 | 76,194 | 38,313 | 12,917 | 37,881 R | 59.8% | 30.1% | 66.5% | 33.5% |
| 19,421 | DOUGLAS | 7,343 | 5,254 | 1,352 | 737 | 3,902 R | 71.6% | 18.4% | 79.5% | 20.5% |
| 17,269 | ELKO | 6,197 | 4,393 | 1,296 | 508 | 3,097 R | 70.9% | 20.9% | 77.2% | 22.8% |
| 777 | ESMERALDA | 469 | 311 | 110 | 48 | 201 R | 66.3% | 23.5% | 73.9% | 26.1% |
| 1,198 | EUREKA | 564 | 430 | 103 | 31 | 327 R | 76.2% | 18.3% | 80.7% | 19.3% |
| 9,434 | HUMBOLDT | 2,843 | 1,950 | 684 | 209 | 1,266 R | 68.6% | 24.1% | 74.0% | 26.0% |
| 4,076 | LANDER | 1,425 | 935 | 361 | 129 | 574 R | 65.6% | 25.3% | 72.1% | 27.9% |
| 3,732 | LINCOLN | 1,586 | 1,087 | 396 | 103 | 691 R | 68.5% | 25.0% | 73.3% | 26.7% |
| 13,594 | LYON | 5,456 | 3,709 | 1,288 | 459 | 2,421 R | 68.0% | 23.6% | 74.2% | 25.8% |
| 6,217 | MINERAL | 2,546 | 1,628 | 631 | 287 | 997 R | 63.9% | 24.8% | 72.1% | 27.9% |
| 9,048 | NYE | 3,720 | 2,387 | 973 | 360 | 1,414 R | 64.2% | 26.2% | 71.0% | 29.0% |
| | ORMSBY | -- | -- | -- | -- | -- | -- | -- | -- | -- |
| 3,408 | PERSHING | 1,282 | 877 | 311 | 94 | 566 R | 68.4% | 24.3% | 73.8% | 26.2% |
| 1,503 | STOREY | 783 | 460 | 222 | 101 | 238 R | 58.7% | 28.4% | 67.4% | 32.6% |
| 193,623 | WASHOE | 64,956 | 41,276 | 15,621 | 8,059 | 25,655 R | 63.5% | 24.0% | 72.5% | 27.5% |
| 8,167 | WHITE PINE | 3,462 | 1,896 | 1,181 | 385 | 715 R | 54.8% | 34.1% | 61.6% | 38.4% |
| 800,493 | TOTAL | 247,885 | 155,017 | 66,666 | 26,202 | 88,351 R | 62.5% | 26.9% | 69.9% | 30.1% |

# NEVADA

## PRESIDENT 1976

| 1970 Census Population | County | Total Vote | Republican | Democratic | Other | Rep.-Dem. Plurality | Percentage | | | |
| --- | --- | --- | --- | --- | --- | --- | --- | --- | --- | --- |
| | | | | | | | Total Vote | | Major Vote | |
| | | | | | | | Rep. | Dem. | Rep. | Dem. |
| 15,468 | CARSON CITY | 9,761 | 5,282 | 3,874 | 605 | 1,408 R | 54.1% | 39.7% | 57.7% | 42.3% |
| 10,513 | CHURCHILL | 4,446 | 2,358 | 1,800 | 288 | 558 R | 53.0% | 40.5% | 56.7% | 43.3% |
| 273,288 | CLARK | 102,812 | 48,236 | 51,178 | 3,398 | 2,942 D | 46.9% | 49.8% | 48.5% | 51.5% |
| 6,882 | DOUGLAS | 5,282 | 3,095 | 1,934 | 253 | 1,161 R | 58.6% | 36.6% | 61.5% | 38.5% |
| 13,958 | ELKO | 5,459 | 3,293 | 1,955 | 211 | 1,338 R | 60.3% | 35.8% | 62.7% | 37.3% |
| 629 | ESMERALDA | 416 | 181 | 214 | 21 | 33 D | 43.5% | 51.4% | 45.8% | 54.2% |
| 948 | EUREKA | 467 | 272 | 163 | 32 | 109 R | 58.2% | 34.9% | 62.5% | 37.5% |
| 6,375 | HUMBOLDT | 2,585 | 1,380 | 1,074 | 131 | 306 R | 53.4% | 41.5% | 56.2% | 43.8% |
| 2,666 | LANDER | 1,123 | 561 | 518 | 44 | 43 R | 50.0% | 46.1% | 52.0% | 48.0% |
| 2,557 | LINCOLN | 1,399 | 700 | 642 | 57 | 58 R | 50.0% | 45.9% | 52.2% | 47.8% |
| 8,221 | LYON | 4,162 | 2,068 | 1,866 | 228 | 202 R | 49.7% | 44.8% | 52.6% | 47.4% |
| 7,051 | MINERAL | 2,594 | 1,104 | 1,361 | 129 | 257 D | 42.6% | 52.5% | 44.8% | 55.2% |
| 5,599 | NYE | 2,415 | 1,027 | 1,261 | 127 | 234 D | 42.5% | 52.2% | 44.9% | 55.1% |
| | ORMSBY | — | — | — | — | — | — | — | — | — |
| 2,670 | PERSHING | 1,353 | 635 | 633 | 85 | 2 R | 46.9% | 46.8% | 50.1% | 49.9% |
| 695 | STOREY | 636 | 274 | 310 | 52 | 36 D | 43.1% | 48.7% | 46.9% | 53.1% |
| 121,068 | WASHOE | 53,227 | 29,264 | 21,687 | 2,276 | 7,577 R | 55.0% | 40.7% | 57.4% | 42.6% |
| 10,150 | WHITE PINE | 3,739 | 1,543 | 2,009 | 187 | 466 D | 41.3% | 53.7% | 43.4% | 56.6% |
| 488,738 | TOTAL | 201,876 | 101,273 | 92,479 | 8,124 | 8,794 R | 50.2% | 45.8% | 52.3% | 47.7% |

# NEVADA

## PRESIDENT 1972

| 1970 Census Population | County | Total Vote | Republican | Democratic | Other | Rep.-Dem. Plurality | Percentage | | | |
|---|---|---|---|---|---|---|---|---|---|---|
| | | | | | | | Total Vote | | Major Vote | |
| | | | | | | | Rep. | Dem. | Rep. | Dem. |
| 15,468 | CARSON CITY | 7,516 | 5,396 | 2,120 | | 3,276 R | 71.8% | 28.2% | 71.8% | 28.2% |
| 10,513 | CHURCHILL | 4,008 | 2,970 | 1,038 | | 1,932 R | 74.1% | 25.9% | 74.1% | 25.9% |
| 273,288 | CLARK | 89,908 | 53,101 | 36,807 | | 16,294 R | 59.1% | 40.9% | 59.1% | 40.9% |
| 6,882 | DOUGLAS | 3,881 | 2,898 | 983 | | 1,915 R | 74.7% | 25.3% | 74.7% | 25.3% |
| 13,958 | ELKO | 5,353 | 3,886 | 1,467 | | 2,419 R | 72.6% | 27.4% | 72.6% | 27.4% |
| 629 | ESMERALDA | 400 | 273 | 127 | | 146 R | 68.3% | 31.8% | 68.3% | 31.8% |
| 948 | EUREKA | 510 | 371 | 139 | | 232 R | 72.7% | 27.3% | 72.7% | 27.3% |
| 6,375 | HUMBOLDT | 2,372 | 1,659 | 713 | | 946 R | 69.9% | 30.1% | 69.9% | 30.1% |
| 2,666 | LANDER | 1,266 | 798 | 468 | | 330 R | 63.0% | 37.0% | 63.0% | 37.0% |
| 2,557 | LINCOLN | 1,223 | 841 | 382 | | 459 R | 68.8% | 31.2% | 68.8% | 31.2% |
| 8,221 | LYON | 3,772 | 2,813 | 959 | | 1,854 R | 74.6% | 25.4% | 74.6% | 25.4% |
| 7,051 | MINERAL | 2,879 | 2,111 | 768 | | 1,343 R | 73.3% | 26.7% | 73.3% | 26.7% |
| 5,599 | NYE | 2,089 | 1,287 | 802 | | 485 R | 61.6% | 38.4% | 61.6% | 38.4% |
| | ORMSBY | — | — | — | | — | — | — | — | — |
| 2,670 | PERSHING | 1,218 | 853 | 365 | | 488 R | 70.0% | 30.0% | 70.0% | 30.0% |
| 695 | STOREY | 734 | 508 | 226 | | 282 R | 69.2% | 30.8% | 69.2% | 30.8% |
| 121,068 | WASHOE | 50,645 | 33,539 | 17,106 | | 16,433 R | 66.2% | 33.8% | 66.2% | 33.8% |
| 10,150 | WHITE PINE | 3,992 | 2,446 | 1,546 | | 900 R | 61.3% | 38.7% | 61.3% | 38.7% |
| 488,738 | TOTAL | 181,766 | 115,750 | 66,016 | | 49,734 R | 63.7% | 36.3% | 63.7% | 36.3% |

# NEVADA

## PRESIDENT 1968

| 1960 Census Population | County | Total Vote | Republican | Democratic | AIP | Other | Plurality | Percentage Total Vote | | |
|---|---|---|---|---|---|---|---|---|---|---|
| | | | | | | | | Rep. | Dem. | AIP |
| | CARSON CITY | — | — | — | — | | — | — | — | — |
| 8,452 | CHURCHILL | 3,740 | 1,954 | 1,211 | 575 | | 743 R | 52.2% | 32.4% | 15.4% |
| 127,016 | CLARK | 75,065 | 31,522 | 33,225 | 10,318 | | 1,703 D | 42.0% | 44.3% | 13.7% |
| 3,481 | DOUGLAS | 2,798 | 1,801 | 670 | 327 | | 1,131 R | 64.4% | 23.9% | 11.7% |
| 12,011 | ELKO | 4,932 | 2,687 | 1,686 | 559 | | 1,001 R | 54.5% | 34.2% | 11.3% |
| 619 | ESMERALDA | 353 | 138 | 118 | 97 | | 20 R | 39.1% | 33.4% | 27.5% |
| 767 | EUREKA | 490 | 277 | 149 | 64 | | 128 R | 56.5% | 30.4% | 13.1% |
| 5,708 | HUMBOLDT | 2,525 | 1,287 | 885 | 353 | | 402 R | 51.0% | 35.0% | 14.0% |
| 1,566 | LANDER | 909 | 461 | 301 | 147 | | 160 R | 50.7% | 33.1% | 16.2% |
| 2,431 | LINCOLN | 1,113 | 555 | 414 | 144 | | 141 R | 49.9% | 37.2% | 12.9% |
| 6,143 | LYON | 2,999 | 1,616 | 939 | 444 | | 677 R | 53.9% | 31.3% | 14.8% |
| 6,329 | MINERAL | 2,869 | 927 | 1,242 | 700 | | 315 D | 32.3% | 43.3% | 24.4% |
| 4,374 | NYE | 2,071 | 843 | 728 | 500 | | 115 R | 40.7% | 35.2% | 24.1% |
| 8,063 | ORMSBY | 5,601 | 3,169 | 1,770 | 662 | | 1,399 R | 56.6% | 31.6% | 11.8% |
| 3,199 | PERSHING | 1,213 | 567 | 466 | 180 | | 101 R | 46.7% | 38.4% | 14.8% |
| 568 | STOREY | 444 | 222 | 172 | 50 | | 50 R | 50.0% | 38.7% | 11.3% |
| 84,743 | WASHOE | 42,988 | 23,492 | 14,560 | 4,936 | | 8,932 R | 54.6% | 33.9% | 11.5% |
| 9,808 | WHITE PINE | 4,108 | 1,670 | 2,062 | 376 | | 392 D | 40.7% | 50.2% | 9.2% |
| 285,278 | TOTAL | 154,218 | 73,188 | 60,598 | 20,432 | | 12,590 R | 47.5% | 39.3% | 13.2% |

# NEVADA

## PRESIDENT 1964

| 1960 Census Population | County | Total Vote | Republican | Democratic | Other | Rep.-Dem. Plurality | Percentage | | | |
| --- | --- | --- | --- | --- | --- | --- | --- | --- | --- | --- |
| | | | | | | | Total Vote | | Major Vote | |
| | | | | | | | Rep. | Dem. | Rep. | Dem. |
| | CARSON CITY | — | — | — | | — | — | — | — | — |
| 8,452 | CHURCHILL | 3,172 | 1,607 | 1,565 | | 42 R | 50.7% | 49.3% | 50.7% | 49.3% |
| 127,016 | CLARK | 64,681 | 23,921 | 40,760 | | 16,839 D | 37.0% | 63.0% | 37.0% | 63.0% |
| 3,481 | DOUGLAS | 2,137 | 1,127 | 1,010 | | 117 R | 52.7% | 47.3% | 52.7% | 47.3% |
| 12,011 | ELKO | 4,641 | 1,856 | 2,785 | | 929 D | 40.0% | 60.0% | 40.0% | 60.0% |
| 619 | ESMERALDA | 318 | 131 | 187 | | 56 D | 41.2% | 58.8% | 41.2% | 58.8% |
| 767 | EUREKA | 528 | 243 | 285 | | 42 D | 46.0% | 54.0% | 46.0% | 54.0% |
| 5,708 | HUMBOLDT | 2,527 | 1,106 | 1,421 | | 315 D | 43.8% | 56.2% | 43.8% | 56.2% |
| 1,566 | LANDER | 729 | 338 | 391 | | 53 D | 46.4% | 53.6% | 46.4% | 53.6% |
| 2,431 | LINCOLN | 1,225 | 440 | 785 | | 345 D | 35.9% | 64.1% | 35.9% | 64.1% |
| 6,143 | LYON | 2,724 | 1,397 | 1,327 | | 70 R | 51.3% | 48.7% | 51.3% | 48.7% |
| 6,329 | MINERAL | 2,367 | 927 | 1,440 | | 513 D | 39.2% | 60.8% | 39.2% | 60.8% |
| 4,374 | NYE | 2,098 | 822 | 1,276 | | 454 D | 39.2% | 60.8% | 39.2% | 60.8% |
| 8,063 | ORMSBY | 4,126 | 1,997 | 2,129 | | 132 D | 48.4% | 51.6% | 48.4% | 51.6% |
| 3,199 | PERSHING | 1,224 | 486 | 738 | | 252 D | 39.7% | 60.3% | 39.7% | 60.3% |
| 568 | STOREY | 433 | 172 | 261 | | 89 D | 39.7% | 60.3% | 39.7% | 60.3% |
| 84,743 | WASHOE | 38,520 | 18,350 | 20,170 | | 1,820 D | 47.6% | 52.4% | 47.6% | 52.4% |
| 9,808 | WHITE PINE | 3,983 | 1,174 | 2,809 | | 1,635 D | 29.5% | 70.5% | 29.5% | 70.5% |
| 285,278 | TOTAL | 135,433 | 56,094 | 79,339 | | 23,245 D | 41.4% | 58.6% | 41.4% | 58.6% |

# NEVADA

## PRESIDENT 1960

| 1960 Census Population | County | Total Vote | Republican | Democratic | Other | Rep.-Dem. Plurality | Percentage | | | |
| --- | --- | --- | --- | --- | --- | --- | --- | --- | --- | --- |
| | | | | | | | Total Vote | | Major Vote | |
| | | | | | | | Rep. | Dem. | Rep. | Dem. |
| | CARSON CITY | — | — | — | | — | — | — | — | — |
| 8,452 | CHURCHILL | 3,074 | 1,765 | 1,309 | | 456 R | 57.4% | 42.6% | 57.4% | 42.6% |
| 127,016 | CLARK | 42,146 | 18,197 | 23,949 | | 5,752 D | 43.2% | 56.8% | 43.2% | 56.8% |
| 3,481 | DOUGLAS | 1,751 | 1,164 | 587 | | 577 R | 66.5% | 33.5% | 66.5% | 33.5% |
| 12,011 | ELKO | 4,922 | 2,427 | 2,495 | | 68 D | 49.3% | 50.7% | 49.3% | 50.7% |
| 619 | ESMERALDA | 371 | 156 | 215 | | 59 D | 42.0% | 58.0% | 42.0% | 58.0% |
| 767 | EUREKA | 462 | 239 | 223 | | 16 R | 51.7% | 48.3% | 51.7% | 48.3% |
| 5,708 | HUMBOLDT | 2,330 | 1,157 | 1,173 | | 16 D | 49.7% | 50.3% | 49.7% | 50.3% |
| 1,566 | LANDER | 774 | 383 | 391 | | 8 D | 49.5% | 50.5% | 49.5% | 50.5% |
| 2,431 | LINCOLN | 1,301 | 530 | 771 | | 241 D | 40.7% | 59.3% | 40.7% | 59.3% |
| 6,143 | LYON | 2,503 | 1,494 | 1,009 | | 485 R | 59.7% | 40.3% | 59.7% | 40.3% |
| 6,329 | MINERAL | 2,536 | 930 | 1,606 | | 676 D | 36.7% | 63.3% | 36.7% | 63.3% |
| 4,374 | NYE | 1,756 | 763 | 993 | | 230 D | 43.5% | 56.5% | 43.5% | 56.5% |
| 8,063 | ORMSBY | 3,229 | 1,946 | 1,283 | | 663 R | 60.3% | 39.7% | 60.3% | 39.7% |
| 3,199 | PERSHING | 1,364 | 648 | 716 | | 68 D | 47.5% | 52.5% | 47.5% | 52.5% |
| 568 | STOREY | 370 | 203 | 167 | | 36 R | 54.9% | 45.1% | 54.9% | 45.1% |
| 84,743 | WASHOE | 34,113 | 18,833 | 15,280 | | 3,553 R | 55.2% | 44.8% | 55.2% | 44.8% |
| 9,808 | WHITE PINE | 4,265 | 1,552 | 2,713 | | 1,161 D | 36.4% | 63.6% | 36.4% | 63.6% |
| 285,278 | TOTAL | 107,267 | 52,387 | 54,880 | | 2,493 D | 48.8% | 51.2% | 48.8% | 51.2% |

# NEVADA

After a state-wide vote in the General Election of November 1968, Carson City, the state capital, and Ormsby county were combined under the name Carson City.

## ELECTION NOTES

**2004**    Other vote was 4,838 Independent (Ralph Nader); 3,688 "None of these Candidates"; 3,176 Libertarian (Michael Badnarik); 1,152 Independent American (Michael Peroutka); 853 Green (David Cobb).

**2000**    Other vote was 4,747 Citizens First (Buchanan); 3,315 "None of These Candidates"; 3,311 Libertarian (Browne); 621 Independent American (Phillips); 415 Natural Law (Hagelin).

**1996**    Other vote was 5,608 None of These Candidates; 4,730 Green (Nader); 4,460 Libertarian (Browne); 1,732 Independent American (Phillips); 545 Natural Law (Hagelin).

**1992**    Other vote was 2,892 Gritz (Populist); 1,835 Marrou (Libertarian); 677 Phillips (Independent American); 483 Fulani (Independent); 338 Hagelin (Natural Law); 2,537 "None of these Candidates".

**1988**    Other vote was 3,520 Paul (Libertarian); 835 Fulani (New Alliance); 6,934 "None of these Candidates".

**1984**    Other vote was 2,292 Bergland (Libertarian); 3,950 "None of these Candidates".

**1980**    Other vote was 17,651 Anderson (Independent); 4,358 Clark (Libertarian); 4,193 "None of these Candidates".

**1976**    Other vote was 1,519 MacBride (Libertarian); 1,497 Maddox (Independent American); 5,108 "None of these Candidates".

**1972**

**1968**    Wallace on the ballot as Independent American.

**1964**

**1960**

# NEW HAMPSHIRE

## POPULAR VOTE FOR PRESIDENT 1920 TO 2004

| Year | Total Vote | Republican Vote | Republican Candidate | Democratic Vote | Democratic Candidate | Other Vote | Plurality | Percentage Total Vote Rep. | Percentage Total Vote Dem. | Percentage Major Vote Rep. | Percentage Major Vote Dem. |
|------|-----------|-----------------|----------------------|-----------------|----------------------|-----------|-----------|------|------|------|------|
| 2004 | 677,738 | 331,237 | Bush, George W. | 340,511 | Kerry, John | 5,990 | 9,274 D | 48.9% | 50.2% | 49.3% | 50.7% |
| 2000 ** | 569,081 | 273,559 | Bush, George W. | 266,348 | Gore, Al | 29,174 | 7,211 R | 48.1% | 46.8% | 50.7% | 49.3% |
| 1996 ** | 499,175 | 196,532 | Dole, Bob | 246,214 | Clinton, Bill | 56,429 | 49,682 D | 39.4% | 49.3% | 44.4% | 55.6% |
| 1992 ** | 537,943 | 202,484 | Bush, George | 209,040 | Clinton, Bill | 126,419 | 6,556 D | 37.6% | 38.9% | 49.2% | 50.8% |
| 1988 | 451,074 | 281,537 | Bush, George | 163,696 | Dukakis, Michael S. | 5,841 | 117,841 R | 62.4% | 36.3% | 63.2% | 36.8% |
| 1984 | 389,066 | 267,051 | Reagan, Ronald | 120,395 | Mondale, Walter F. | 1,620 | 146,656 R | 68.6% | 30.9% | 68.9% | 31.1% |
| 1980 ** | 383,990 | 221,705 | Reagan, Ronald | 108,864 | Carter, Jimmy | 53,421 | 112,841 R | 57.7% | 28.4% | 67.1% | 32.9% |
| 1976 | 339,618 | 185,935 | Ford, Gerald R. | 147,635 | Carter, Jimmy | 6,048 | 38,300 R | 54.7% | 43.5% | 55.7% | 44.3% |
| 1972 | 334,055 | 213,724 | Nixon, Richard M. | 116,435 | McGovern, George S. | 3,896 | 97,289 R | 64.0% | 34.9% | 64.7% | 35.3% |
| 1968 | 297,298 | 154,903 | Nixon, Richard M. | 130,589 | Humphrey, Hubert H. | 11,806 | 24,314 R | 52.1% | 43.9% | 54.3% | 45.7% |
| 1964 | 288,093 | 104,029 | Goldwater, Barry M. | 184,064 | Johnson, Lyndon B. | | 80,035 D | 36.1% | 63.9% | 36.1% | 63.9% |
| 1960 | 295,761 | 157,989 | Nixon, Richard M. | 137,772 | Kennedy, John F. | | 20,217 R | 53.4% | 46.6% | 53.4% | 46.6% |
| 1956 | 266,994 | 176,519 | Eisenhower, Dwight D. | 90,364 | Stevenson, Adlai E. | 111 | 86,155 R | 66.1% | 33.8% | 66.1% | 33.9% |
| 1952 | 272,950 | 166,287 | Eisenhower, Dwight D. | 106,663 | Stevenson, Adlai E. | | 59,624 R | 60.9% | 39.1% | 60.9% | 39.1% |
| 1948 | 231,440 | 121,299 | Dewey, Thomas E. | 107,995 | Truman, Harry S. | 2,146 | 13,304 R | 52.4% | 46.7% | 52.9% | 47.1% |
| 1944 | 229,625 | 109,916 | Dewey, Thomas E. | 119,663 | Roosevelt, Franklin D. | 46 | 9,747 D | 47.9% | 52.1% | 47.9% | 52.1% |
| 1940 | 235,419 | 110,127 | Willkie, Wendell | 125,292 | Roosevelt, Franklin D. | | 15,165 D | 46.8% | 53.2% | 46.8% | 53.2% |
| 1936 | 218,114 | 104,642 | Landon, Alfred M. | 108,460 | Roosevelt, Franklin D. | 5,012 | 3,818 D | 48.0% | 49.7% | 49.1% | 50.9% |
| 1932 | 205,520 | 103,629 | Hoover, Herbert C. | 100,680 | Roosevelt, Franklin D. | 1,211 | 2,949 R | 50.4% | 49.0% | 50.7% | 49.3% |
| 1928 | 196,757 | 115,404 | Hoover, Herbert C. | 80,715 | Smith, Alfred E. | 638 | 34,689 R | 58.7% | 41.0% | 58.8% | 41.2% |
| 1924 | 164,769 | 98,575 | Coolidge, Calvin | 57,201 | Davis, John W. | 8,993 | 41,374 R | 59.8% | 34.7% | 63.3% | 36.7% |
| 1920 | 159,092 | 95,196 | Harding, Warren G. | 62,662 | Cox, James M. | 1,234 | 32,534 R | 59.8% | 39.4% | 60.3% | 39.7% |

In 2000 the other vote column includes 22,198 votes cast for Green (Nader). In 1996 the other vote column includes 48,390 votes cast for Perot. In 1992 the other vote column includes 121,337 votes cast for Perot. In 1980 the other column includes 49,693 votes for Independent (Anderson).

## ELECTORAL COLLEGE VOTE 1920 TO 2004

| Year | Total | Republican | Democratic | Other |
|------|-------|------------|------------|-------|
| 2004 | 4 | | 4 | |
| 2000 | 4 | 4 | | |
| 1996 | 4 | | 4 | |
| 1992 | 4 | | 4 | |
| 1988 | 4 | 4 | | |
| 1984 | 4 | 4 | | |
| 1980 | 4 | 4 | | |
| 1976 | 4 | 4 | | |
| 1972 | 4 | 4 | | |
| 1968 | 4 | 4 | | |
| 1964 | 4 | | 4 | |
| 1960 | 4 | 4 | | |
| 1956 | 4 | 4 | | |
| 1952 | 4 | 4 | | |
| 1948 | 4 | 4 | | |
| 1944 | 4 | | 4 | |
| 1940 | 4 | | 4 | |
| 1936 | 4 | | 4 | |
| 1932 | 4 | 4 | | |
| 1928 | 4 | 4 | | |
| 1924 | 4 | 4 | | |
| 1920 | 4 | 4 | | |

# NEW HAMPSHIRE

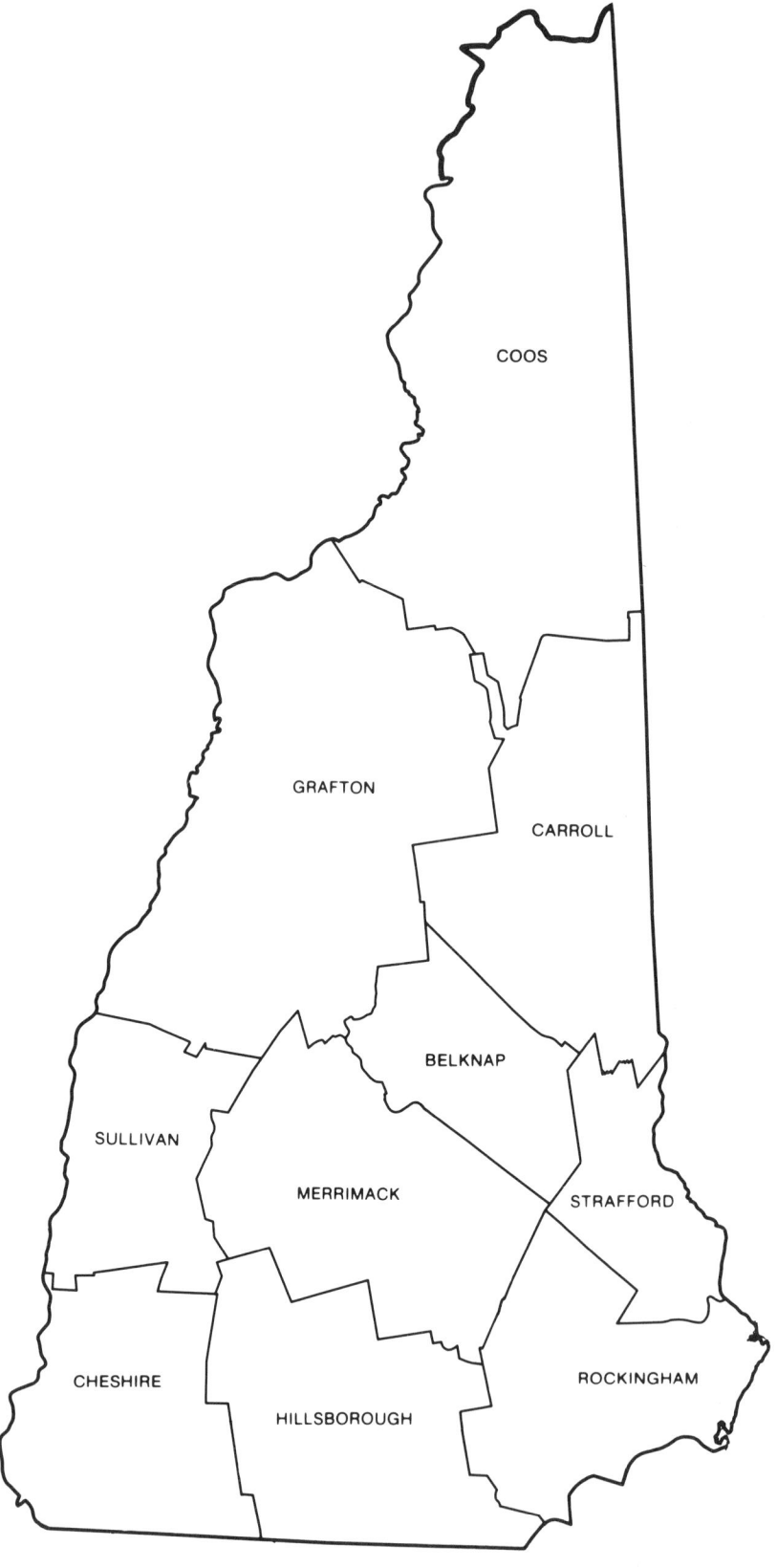

COOS

GRAFTON

CARROLL

BELKNAP

SULLIVAN

MERRIMACK

STRAFFORD

CHESHIRE

HILLSBOROUGH

ROCKINGHAM

# NEW HAMPSHIRE

## PRESIDENT 2004

| 2000 Census Population | County | Total Vote | Republican | Democratic | Other | Rep.-Dem. Plurality | Percentage | | | |
| | | | | | | | Total Vote | | Major Vote | |
| | | | | | | | Rep. | Dem. | Rep. | Dem. |
|---|---|---|---|---|---|---|---|---|---|---|
| 56,325 | BELKNAP | 32,298 | 17,920 | 14,080 | 298 | 3,840 R | 55.5% | 43.6% | 56.0% | 44.0% |
| 43,666 | CARROLL | 28,222 | 14,614 | 13,319 | 289 | 1,295 R | 51.8% | 47.2% | 52.3% | 47.7% |
| 73,825 | CHESHIRE | 41,347 | 16,463 | 24,438 | 446 | 7,975 D | 39.8% | 59.1% | 40.3% | 59.7% |
| 33,111 | COOS | 16,925 | 8,143 | 8,585 | 197 | 442 D | 48.1% | 50.7% | 48.7% | 51.3% |
| 81,743 | GRAFTON | 46,971 | 20,277 | 26,180 | 514 | 5,903 D | 43.2% | 55.7% | 43.6% | 56.4% |
| 380,841 | HILLSBOROUGH | 195,427 | 99,724 | 94,121 | 1,582 | 5,603 R | 51.0% | 48.2% | 51.4% | 48.6% |
| 136,225 | MERRIMACK | 76,647 | 36,060 | 39,975 | 612 | 3,915 D | 47.0% | 52.2% | 47.4% | 52.6% |
| 277,359 | ROCKINGHAM | 158,816 | 82,069 | 75,437 | 1,310 | 6,632 R | 51.7% | 47.5% | 52.1% | 47.9% |
| 112,233 | STRAFFORD | 59,281 | 25,825 | 32,942 | 514 | 7,117 D | 43.6% | 55.6% | 43.9% | 56.1% |
| 40,458 | SULLIVAN | 21,804 | 10,142 | 11,434 | 228 | 1,292 D | 46.5% | 52.4% | 47.0% | 53.0% |
| 1,235,786 | TOTAL | 677,738 | 331,237 | 340,511 | 5,990 | 9,274 D | 48.9% | 50.2% | 49.3% | 50.7% |

# NEW HAMPSHIRE

## PRESIDENT 2000

| 2000 Census Population | County | Total Vote | Republican | Democratic | Green (Nader) | Other | Rep.-Dem. Plurality | Percentage of Total Vote | | |
| | | | | | | | | Rep. | Dem. | Green |
|---|---|---|---|---|---|---|---|---|---|---|
| 56,325 | BELKNAP | 26,795 | 14,799 | 10,719 | 977 | 300 | 4,080 R | 55.2% | 40.0% | 3.6% |
| 43,666 | CARROLL | 23,879 | 12,597 | 9,852 | 1,086 | 344 | 2,745 R | 52.8% | 41.3% | 4.5% |
| 73,825 | CHESHIRE | 33,395 | 13,793 | 17,382 | 1,750 | 470 | 3,589 D | 41.3% | 52.0% | 5.2% |
| 33,111 | COOS | 14,600 | 7,329 | 6,570 | 463 | 238 | 759 R | 50.2% | 45.0% | 3.2% |
| 81,743 | GRAFTON | 38,733 | 18,092 | 18,326 | 1,783 | 532 | 234 D | 46.7% | 47.3% | 4.6% |
| 380,841 | HILLSBOROUGH | 165,761 | 80,649 | 77,625 | 5,465 | 2,022 | 3,024 R | 48.7% | 46.8% | 3.3% |
| 136,225 | MERRIMACK | 63,684 | 30,028 | 30,622 | 2,343 | 691 | 594 D | 47.2% | 48.1% | 3.7% |
| 277,359 | ROCKINGHAM | 134,173 | 65,860 | 61,628 | 5,213 | 1,472 | 4,232 R | 49.1% | 45.9% | 3.9% |
| 112,233 | STRAFFORD | 49,393 | 21,108 | 25,400 | 2,273 | 612 | 4,292 D | 42.7% | 51.4% | 4.6% |
| 40,458 | SULLIVAN | 18,668 | 9,304 | 8,224 | 845 | 295 | 1,080 R | 49.8% | 44.1% | 4.5% |
| 1,235,786 | TOTAL | 569,081 | 273,559 | 266,348 | 22,198 | 6,976 | 7,211 R | 48.1% | 46.8% | 3.9% |

# NEW HAMPSHIRE

## PRESIDENT 1996

| 1995 Census Pop. Est. | County | Total Vote | Republican | Democratic | Reform (Perot) | Other | Rep.-Dem. Plurality | Percentage of Total Vote | | |
| | | | | | | | | Rep. | Dem. | Reform |
|---|---|---|---|---|---|---|---|---|---|---|
| 50,940 | BELKNAP | 23,533 | 10,685 | 10,345 | 2,297 | 206 | 340 R | 45.4% | 44.0% | 9.8% |
| 37,583 | CARROLL | 20,682 | 9,168 | 8,881 | 2,445 | 188 | 287 R | 44.3% | 42.9% | 11.8% |
| 71,158 | CHESHIRE | 29,516 | 10,252 | 16,159 | 2,777 | 328 | 5,907 D | 34.7% | 54.7% | 9.4% |
| 33,580 | COOS | 14,095 | 4,703 | 7,191 | 2,085 | 116 | 2,488 D | 33.4% | 51.0% | 14.8% |
| 77,736 | GRAFTON | 34,562 | 13,543 | 17,476 | 3,237 | 306 | 3,933 D | 39.2% | 50.6% | 9.4% |
| 349,572 | HILLSBOROUGH | 145,925 | 59,441 | 71,282 | 13,411 | 1,791 | 11,841 D | 40.7% | 48.8% | 9.2% |
| 123,348 | MERRIMACK | 55,976 | 21,231 | 29,381 | 4,814 | 550 | 8,150 D | 37.9% | 52.5% | 8.6% |
| 257,579 | ROCKINGHAM | 112,690 | 46,201 | 53,644 | 11,433 | 1,412 | 7,443 D | 41.0% | 47.6% | 10.1% |
| 107,265 | STRAFFORD | 42,561 | 14,484 | 23,475 | 4,088 | 514 | 8,991 D | 34.0% | 55.2% | 9.6% |
| 39,492 | SULLIVAN | 17,179 | 6,824 | 8,380 | 1,803 | 172 | 1,556 D | 39.7% | 48.8% | 10.5% |
| 1,148,253 | TOTAL | 499,175 | 196,532 | 246,214 | 48,390 | 8,039 | 49,682 D | 39.4% | 49.3% | 9.7% |

Note: Total and other vote include 2,456 write-in votes that official election returns did not classify by county or city/town.

# NEW HAMPSHIRE

## PRESIDENT 1992

| 1990 Census Population | County | Total Vote | Republican | Democratic | Perot | Other | Plurality | Percentage Total Vote | | |
|---|---|---|---|---|---|---|---|---|---|---|
| | | | | | | | | Rep. | Dem. | Perot |
| 49,216 | BELKNAP | 25,121 | 10,578 | 8,405 | 5,970 | 168 | 2,173 R | 42.1% | 33.5% | 23.8% |
| 35,410 | CARROLL | 21,715 | 8,715 | 7,258 | 5,546 | 196 | 1,457 R | 40.1% | 33.4% | 25.5% |
| 70,121 | CHESHIRE | 32,505 | 11,037 | 15,037 | 6,195 | 236 | 4,000 D | 34.0% | 46.3% | 19.1% |
| 34,828 | COOS | 15,817 | 5,271 | 6,559 | 3,868 | 119 | 1,288 D | 33.3% | 41.5% | 24.5% |
| 74,929 | GRAFTON | 36,429 | 13,450 | 15,389 | 7,296 | 294 | 1,939 D | 36.9% | 42.2% | 20.0% |
| 336,073 | HILLSBOROUGH | 158,056 | 61,620 | 58,470 | 36,067 | 1,899 | 3,150 R | 39.0% | 37.0% | 22.8% |
| 120,005 | MERRIMACK | 58,904 | 22,114 | 24,437 | 11,860 | 493 | 2,323 D | 37.5% | 41.5% | 20.1% |
| 245,845 | ROCKINGHAM | 123,965 | 47,353 | 44,317 | 31,192 | 1,103 | 3,036 R | 38.2% | 35.7% | 25.2% |
| 104,233 | STRAFFORD | 47,595 | 16,028 | 21,247 | 9,920 | 400 | 5,219 D | 33.7% | 44.6% | 20.8% |
| 38,592 | SULLIVAN | 17,836 | 6,318 | 7,921 | 3,423 | 174 | 1,603 D | 35.4% | 44.4% | 19.2% |
| 1,109,252 | TOTAL | 537,943 | 202,484 | 209,040 | 121,337 | 5,082 | 6,556 D | 37.6% | 38.9% | 22.6% |

# NEW HAMPSHIRE

## PRESIDENT 1988

| 1980 Census Population | County | Total Vote | Republican | Democratic | Other | Rep.-Dem. Plurality | Percentage | | | |
|---|---|---|---|---|---|---|---|---|---|---|
| | | | | | | | Total Vote | | Major Vote | |
| | | | | | | | Rep. | Dem. | Rep. | Dem. |
| 42,884 | BELKNAP | 21,280 | 14,454 | 6,603 | 223 | 7,851 R | 67.9% | 31.0% | 68.6% | 31.4% |
| 27,931 | CARROLL | 18,344 | 12,983 | 5,153 | 208 | 7,830 R | 70.8% | 28.1% | 71.6% | 28.4% |
| 62,116 | CHESHIRE | 27,512 | 15,002 | 12,339 | 171 | 2,663 R | 54.5% | 44.8% | 54.9% | 45.1% |
| 35,147 | COOS | 13,900 | 8,763 | 4,981 | 156 | 3,782 R | 63.0% | 35.8% | 63.8% | 36.2% |
| 65,806 | GRAFTON | 30,699 | 19,033 | 11,484 | 182 | 7,549 R | 62.0% | 37.4% | 62.4% | 37.6% |
| 276,608 | HILLSBOROUGH | 135,778 | 88,261 | 45,799 | 1,718 | 42,462 R | 65.0% | 33.7% | 65.8% | 34.2% |
| 98,302 | MERRIMACK | 48,686 | 29,535 | 18,637 | 514 | 10,898 R | 60.7% | 38.3% | 61.3% | 38.7% |
| 190,345 | ROCKINGHAM | 101,747 | 64,034 | 35,775 | 1,938 | 28,259 R | 62.9% | 35.2% | 64.2% | 35.8% |
| 85,408 | STRAFFORD | 37,845 | 20,636 | 16,547 | 662 | 4,089 R | 54.5% | 43.7% | 55.5% | 44.5% |
| 36,063 | SULLIVAN | 15,283 | 8,836 | 6,378 | 69 | 2,458 R | 57.8% | 41.7% | 58.1% | 41.9% |
| 920,610 | TOTAL | 451,074 | 281,537 | 163,696 | 5,841 | 117,841 R | 62.4% | 36.3% | 63.2% | 36.8% |

# NEW HAMPSHIRE

## PRESIDENT 1984

| 1980 Census Population | County | Total Vote | Republican | Democratic | Other | Rep.-Dem. Plurality | Percentage | | | |
|---|---|---|---|---|---|---|---|---|---|---|
| | | | | | | | Total Vote | | Major Vote | |
| | | | | | | | Rep. | Dem. | Rep. | Dem. |
| 42,884 | BELKNAP | 19,065 | 14,200 | 4,743 | 122 | 9,457 R | 74.5% | 24.9% | 75.0% | 25.0% |
| 27,931 | CARROLL | 15,764 | 11,891 | 3,806 | 67 | 8,085 R | 75.4% | 24.1% | 75.8% | 24.2% |
| 62,116 | CHESHIRE | 24,943 | 15,851 | 8,990 | 102 | 6,861 R | 63.5% | 36.0% | 63.8% | 36.2% |
| 35,147 | COOS | 14,059 | 10,013 | 4,004 | 42 | 6,009 R | 71.2% | 28.5% | 71.4% | 28.6% |
| 65,806 | GRAFTON | 27,300 | 18,451 | 8,757 | 92 | 9,694 R | 67.6% | 32.1% | 67.8% | 32.2% |
| 276,608 | HILLSBOROUGH | 115,278 | 81,462 | 33,314 | 502 | 48,148 R | 70.7% | 28.9% | 71.0% | 29.0% |
| 98,302 | MERRIMACK | 41,591 | 27,925 | 13,510 | 156 | 14,415 R | 67.1% | 32.5% | 67.4% | 32.6% |
| 190,345 | ROCKINGHAM | 83,439 | 57,586 | 25,557 | 296 | 32,029 R | 69.0% | 30.6% | 69.3% | 30.7% |
| 85,408 | STRAFFORD | 33,388 | 20,452 | 12,752 | 184 | 7,700 R | 61.3% | 38.2% | 61.6% | 38.4% |
| 36,063 | SULLIVAN | 14,239 | 9,220 | 4,962 | 57 | 4,258 R | 64.8% | 34.8% | 65.0% | 35.0% |
| 920,610 | TOTAL | 389,066 | 267,051 | 120,395 | 1,620 | 146,656 R | 68.6% | 30.9% | 68.9% | 31.1% |

# NEW HAMPSHIRE

## PRESIDENT 1980

| 1980 Census Population | County | Total Vote | Republican | Democratic | Other | Rep.-Dem. Plurality | Percentage Total Vote Rep. | Dem. | Major Vote Rep. | Dem. |
|---|---|---|---|---|---|---|---|---|---|---|
| 42,884 | BELKNAP | 18,558 | 12,077 | 4,365 | 2,116 | 7,712 R | 65.1% | 23.5% | 73.5% | 26.5% |
| 27,931 | CARROLL | 14,853 | 9,980 | 3,119 | 1,754 | 6,861 R | 67.2% | 21.0% | 76.2% | 23.8% |
| 62,116 | CHESHIRE | 25,467 | 13,242 | 7,835 | 4,390 | 5,407 R | 52.0% | 30.8% | 62.8% | 37.2% |
| 35,147 | COOS | 14,520 | 8,724 | 4,749 | 1,047 | 3,975 R | 60.1% | 32.7% | 64.8% | 35.2% |
| 65,806 | GRAFTON | 27,142 | 15,273 | 7,282 | 4,587 | 7,991 R | 56.3% | 26.8% | 67.7% | 32.3% |
| 276,608 | HILLSBOROUGH | 115,343 | 68,994 | 31,789 | 14,560 | 37,205 R | 59.8% | 27.6% | 68.5% | 31.5% |
| 98,302 | MERRIMACK | 41,963 | 23,584 | 12,083 | 6,296 | 11,501 R | 56.2% | 28.8% | 66.1% | 33.9% |
| 190,345 | ROCKINGHAM | 79,474 | 45,960 | 21,712 | 11,802 | 24,248 R | 57.8% | 27.3% | 67.9% | 32.1% |
| 85,408 | STRAFFORD | 32,533 | 16,399 | 11,041 | 5,093 | 5,358 R | 50.4% | 33.9% | 59.8% | 40.2% |
| 36,063 | SULLIVAN | 14,137 | 7,472 | 4,889 | 1,776 | 2,583 R | 52.9% | 34.6% | 60.4% | 39.6% |
| 920,610 | TOTAL | 383,990 | 221,705 | 108,864 | 53,421 | 112,841 R | 57.7% | 28.4% | 67.1% | 32.9% |

# NEW HAMPSHIRE

## PRESIDENT 1976

| 1970 Census Population | County | Total Vote | Republican | Democratic | Other | Rep.-Dem. Plurality | Percentage Total Vote Rep. | Dem. | Major Vote Rep. | Dem. |
|---|---|---|---|---|---|---|---|---|---|---|
| 32,367 | BELKNAP | 16,249 | 9,876 | 6,143 | 230 | 3,733 R | 60.8% | 37.8% | 61.7% | 38.3% |
| 18,548 | CARROLL | 12,198 | 8,561 | 3,374 | 263 | 5,187 R | 70.2% | 27.7% | 71.7% | 28.3% |
| 52,364 | CHESHIRE | 23,305 | 12,554 | 10,388 | 363 | 2,166 R | 53.9% | 44.6% | 54.7% | 45.3% |
| 34,291 | COOS | 14,638 | 7,094 | 7,385 | 159 | 291 D | 48.5% | 50.5% | 49.0% | 51.0% |
| 54,914 | GRAFTON | 23,914 | 14,430 | 8,996 | 488 | 5,434 R | 60.3% | 37.6% | 61.6% | 38.4% |
| 223,941 | HILLSBOROUGH | 100,880 | 53,581 | 45,544 | 1,755 | 8,037 R | 53.1% | 45.1% | 54.1% | 45.9% |
| 80,925 | MERRIMACK | 37,282 | 21,853 | 14,865 | 564 | 6,988 R | 58.6% | 39.9% | 59.5% | 40.5% |
| 138,951 | ROCKINGHAM | 68,130 | 36,738 | 30,051 | 1,341 | 6,687 R | 53.9% | 44.1% | 55.0% | 45.0% |
| 70,431 | STRAFFORD | 29,815 | 14,569 | 14,566 | 680 | 3 R | 48.9% | 48.9% | 50.0% | 50.0% |
| 30,949 | SULLIVAN | 13,207 | 6,679 | 6,323 | 205 | 356 R | 50.6% | 47.9% | 51.4% | 48.6% |
| 737,681 | TOTAL | 339,618 | 185,935 | 147,635 | 6,048 | 38,300 R | 54.7% | 43.5% | 55.7% | 44.3% |

# NEW HAMPSHIRE

## PRESIDENT 1972

| 1970 Census Population | County | Total Vote | Republican | Democratic | Other | Rep.-Dem. Plurality | Percentage Total Vote Rep. | Dem. | Major Vote Rep. | Dem. |
|---|---|---|---|---|---|---|---|---|---|---|
| 32,367 | BELKNAP | 16,312 | 11,536 | 4,610 | 166 | 6,926 R | 70.7% | 28.3% | 71.4% | 28.6% |
| 18,548 | CARROLL | 11,070 | 8,525 | 2,395 | 150 | 6,130 R | 77.0% | 21.6% | 78.1% | 21.9% |
| 52,364 | CHESHIRE | 22,703 | 13,390 | 9,157 | 156 | 4,233 R | 59.0% | 40.3% | 59.4% | 40.6% |
| 34,291 | COOS | 15,563 | 9,468 | 5,829 | 266 | 3,639 R | 60.8% | 37.5% | 61.9% | 38.1% |
| 54,914 | GRAFTON | 25,319 | 16,605 | 8,388 | 326 | 8,217 R | 65.6% | 33.1% | 66.4% | 33.6% |
| 223,941 | HILLSBOROUGH | 101,377 | 65,274 | 34,739 | 1,364 | 30,535 R | 64.4% | 34.3% | 65.3% | 34.7% |
| 80,925 | MERRIMACK | 37,449 | 25,354 | 11,737 | 358 | 13,617 R | 67.7% | 31.3% | 68.4% | 31.6% |
| 138,951 | ROCKINGHAM | 61,541 | 38,825 | 21,998 | 718 | 16,827 R | 63.1% | 35.7% | 63.8% | 36.2% |
| 70,431 | STRAFFORD | 29,129 | 16,846 | 12,028 | 255 | 4,818 R | 57.8% | 41.3% | 58.3% | 41.7% |
| 30,949 | SULLIVAN | 13,592 | 7,901 | 5,554 | 137 | 2,347 R | 58.1% | 40.9% | 58.7% | 41.3% |
| 737,681 | TOTAL | 334,055 | 213,724 | 116,435 | 3,896 | 97,289 R | 64.0% | 34.9% | 64.7% | 35.3% |

# NEW HAMPSHIRE

## PRESIDENT 1968

| 1960 Census Population | County | Total Vote | Republican | Democratic | AIP | Other | Plurality | Percentage Total Vote | | |
|---|---|---|---|---|---|---|---|---|---|---|
| | | | | | | | | Rep. | Dem. | AIP |
| 28,912 | BELKNAP | 14,071 | 8,642 | 4,942 | 454 | 33 | 3,700 R | 61.4% | 35.1% | 3.2% |
| 15,829 | CARROLL | 9,317 | 6,795 | 2,163 | 348 | 11 | 4,632 R | 72.9% | 23.2% | 3.7% |
| 43,342 | CHESHIRE | 20,332 | 10,702 | 9,135 | 441 | 54 | 1,567 R | 52.6% | 44.9% | 2.2% |
| 37,140 | COOS | 15,497 | 6,822 | 8,261 | 399 | 15 | 1,439 D | 44.0% | 53.3% | 2.6% |
| 48,857 | GRAFTON | 21,554 | 12,881 | 7,813 | 727 | 133 | 5,068 R | 59.8% | 36.2% | 3.4% |
| 178,161 | HILLSBOROUGH | 92,169 | 42,409 | 45,423 | 4,231 | 106 | 3,014 D | 46.0% | 49.3% | 4.6% |
| 67,785 | MERRIMACK | 33,291 | 19,289 | 12,711 | 1,201 | 90 | 6,578 R | 57.9% | 38.2% | 3.6% |
| 99,029 | ROCKINGHAM | 52,456 | 28,842 | 21,195 | 2,333 | 86 | 7,647 R | 55.0% | 40.4% | 4.4% |
| 59,799 | STRAFFORD | 26,283 | 12,427 | 13,129 | 650 | 77 | 702 D | 47.3% | 50.0% | 2.5% |
| 28,067 | SULLIVAN | 12,328 | 6,094 | 5,817 | 389 | 28 | 277 R | 49.4% | 47.2% | 3.2% |
| 606,921 | TOTAL | 297,298 | 154,903 | 130,589 | 11,173 | 633 | 24,314 R | 52.1% | 43.9% | 3.8% |

# NEW HAMPSHIRE

## PRESIDENT 1964

| 1960 Census Population | County | Total Vote | Republican | Democratic | Other | Rep.-Dem. Plurality | Percentage | | | |
|---|---|---|---|---|---|---|---|---|---|---|
| | | | | | | | Total Vote | | Major Vote | |
| | | | | | | | Rep. | Dem. | Rep. | Dem. |
| 28,912 | BELKNAP | 13,932 | 5,908 | 8,024 | | 2,116 D | 42.4% | 57.6% | 42.4% | 57.6% |
| 15,829 | CARROLL | 9,015 | 4,957 | 4,058 | | 899 R | 55.0% | 45.0% | 55.0% | 45.0% |
| 43,342 | CHESHIRE | 19,584 | 5,958 | 13,626 | | 7,668 D | 30.4% | 69.6% | 30.4% | 69.6% |
| 37,140 | COOS | 16,819 | 4,863 | 11,956 | | 7,093 D | 28.9% | 71.1% | 28.9% | 71.1% |
| 48,857 | GRAFTON | 21,027 | 8,461 | 12,566 | | 4,105 D | 40.2% | 59.8% | 40.2% | 59.8% |
| 178,161 | HILLSBOROUGH | 89,739 | 29,503 | 60,236 | | 30,733 D | 32.9% | 67.1% | 32.9% | 67.1% |
| 67,785 | MERRIMACK | 32,382 | 12,564 | 19,818 | | 7,254 D | 38.8% | 61.2% | 38.8% | 61.2% |
| 99,029 | ROCKINGHAM | 46,754 | 19,498 | 27,256 | | 7,758 D | 41.7% | 58.3% | 41.7% | 58.3% |
| 59,799 | STRAFFORD | 26,079 | 8,342 | 17,737 | | 9,395 D | 32.0% | 68.0% | 32.0% | 68.0% |
| 28,067 | SULLIVAN | 12,762 | 3,975 | 8,787 | | 4,812 D | 31.1% | 68.9% | 31.1% | 68.9% |
| 606,921 | TOTAL | 288,093 | 104,029 | 184,064 | | 80,035 D | 36.1% | 63.9% | 36.1% | 63.9% |

# NEW HAMPSHIRE

## PRESIDENT 1960

| 1960 Census Population | County | Total Vote | Republican | Democratic | Other | Rep.-Dem. Plurality | Percentage | | | |
|---|---|---|---|---|---|---|---|---|---|---|
| | | | | | | | Total Vote | | Major Vote | |
| | | | | | | | Rep. | Dem. | Rep. | Dem. |
| 28,912 | BELKNAP | 14,786 | 9,156 | 5,630 | | 3,526 R | 61.9% | 38.1% | 61.9% | 38.1% |
| 15,829 | CARROLL | 9,405 | 7,487 | 1,918 | | 5,569 R | 79.6% | 20.4% | 79.6% | 20.4% |
| 43,342 | CHESHIRE | 20,262 | 11,594 | 8,668 | | 2,926 R | 57.2% | 42.8% | 57.2% | 42.8% |
| 37,140 | COOS | 18,252 | 7,797 | 10,455 | | 2,658 D | 42.7% | 57.3% | 42.7% | 57.3% |
| 48,857 | GRAFTON | 22,275 | 14,454 | 7,821 | | 6,633 R | 64.9% | 35.1% | 64.9% | 35.1% |
| 178,161 | HILLSBOROUGH | 90,565 | 38,430 | 52,135 | | 13,705 D | 42.4% | 57.6% | 42.4% | 57.6% |
| 67,785 | MERRIMACK | 33,673 | 20,395 | 13,278 | | 7,117 R | 60.6% | 39.4% | 60.6% | 39.4% |
| 99,029 | ROCKINGHAM | 45,095 | 28,032 | 17,063 | | 10,969 R | 62.2% | 37.8% | 62.2% | 37.8% |
| 59,799 | STRAFFORD | 27,874 | 13,539 | 14,335 | | 796 D | 48.6% | 51.4% | 48.6% | 51.4% |
| 28,067 | SULLIVAN | 13,574 | 7,105 | 6,469 | | 636 R | 52.3% | 47.7% | 52.3% | 47.7% |
| 606,921 | TOTAL | 295,761 | 157,989 | 137,772 | | 20,217 R | 53.4% | 46.6% | 53.4% | 46.6% |

# NEW HAMPSHIRE

## ELECTION NOTES

**2004**     Other vote was 4,479 Independent (Ralph Nader); 372 write-in (Michael Badnarik); 357 write-in (John McCain); 161 write-in (Michael Peroutka); 42 write-in (Howard Dean); 14 write-in (Wesley Clark); 14 write-in (Wesley Powell); 8 write-in (Dennis Kucinich); 5 write-in (John Edwards); 538 scattered write-in.

**2000**     Other vote was 2,757 Libertarian (Browne); 2,615 Independence Party (Buchanan); 328 Constitution (Phillips); 55 write-in (Hagelin); 1,221 scattered write-in.

**1996**     Other vote was 4,237 Libertarian (Browne); 1,346 Taxpayers (Phillips); 2,456 scattered write-in.

**1992**     Other vote was 3,548 Marrou (Libertarian); 512 Fulani (New Alliance); 292 Hagelin (Natural Law); 730 scattered write-in.

**1988**     Other vote was 4,502 Paul (Libertarian); 790 Fulani (New Alliance); 549 scattered write-in.

**1984**     Other vote was 735 Bergland (Libertarian); 467 LaRouche (Independent); 305 Serrette (Alliance); 113 scattered write-in. Early unamended canvass gave the Republican state-wide total vote as 267,050 and the Democratic state-wide total vote as 120,347; vote totals in Hillsborough and Grafton counties were amended.

**1980**     Other vote was 49,693 Anderson (Independent); 2,064 Clark (Libertarian); 1,320 Commoner (Citizens); 129 Hall (Communist); 76 Griswold (Workers World); 71 DeBerry (Socialist Workers); 68 scattered write-in. Data published in the "Manual for the General Court" amended the minor party vote slightly to read 2,067 Libertarian; 1,325 Citizens; the original canvass is used here in the data table.

**1976**     Other vote was 4,095 McCarthy (McCarthy '76); 936 MacBride (Libertarian); 186 LaRouche (U.S. Labor); 161 Camejo (Socialist Workers); 66 Levin (Socialist Labor); 604 scattered write-in. Early unamended canvass gave the Democratic state-wide total vote as 147,645 and the state-wide total vote for other as 6,047; the vote in Hillsborough county was amended from 45,554 Democratic and 1,754 other.

**1972**     Other vote was 3,386 Schmitz (American); 368 Jenness (Socialist Workers); 142 scattered write-in.

**1968**     Wallace on the ballot as George Wallace party. Other vote was 421 no Presidential candidate indicated (New Party); 104 Halstead (Socialist Workers); 108 scattered write-in.

**1964**     Early uncorrected canvass reports under-counted the Democratic (Johnson) vote in Hillsborough county by 1,999.

**1960**

# NEW JERSEY

## POPULAR VOTE FOR PRESIDENT 1920 TO 2004

| Year | Total Vote | Republican Vote | Candidate | Democratic Vote | Candidate | Other Vote | Plurality | Percentage Total Vote Rep. | Dem. | Major Vote Rep. | Dem. |
|------|-----------|------|-----------|------|-----------|------|-----------|------|------|------|------|
| 2004 | 3,611,691 | 1,670,003 | Bush, George W. | 1,911,430 | Kerry, John | 30,258 | 241,427 D | 46.2% | 52.9% | 46.6% | 53.4% |
| 2000** | 3,187,226 | 1,284,173 | Bush, George W. | 1,788,850 | Gore, Al | 114,203 | 504,677 D | 40.3% | 56.1% | 41.8% | 58.2% |
| 1996 ** | 3,075,807 | 1,103,078 | Dole, Bob | 1,652,329 | Clinton, Bill | 320,400 | 549,251 D | 35.9% | 53.7% | 40.0% | 60.0% |
| 1992 ** | 3,343,594 | 1,356,865 | Bush, George | 1,436,206 | Clinton, Bill | 550,523 | 79,341 D | 40.6% | 43.0% | 48.6% | 51.4% |
| 1988 | 3,099,553 | 1,743,192 | Bush, George | 1,320,352 | Dukakis, Michael S. | 36,009 | 422,840 R | 56.2% | 42.6% | 56.9% | 43.1% |
| 1984 | 3,217,862 | 1,933,630 | Reagan, Ronald | 1,261,323 | Mondale, Walter F. | 22,909 | 672,307 R | 60.1% | 39.2% | 60.5% | 39.5% |
| 1980 ** | 2,975,684 | 1,546,557 | Reagan, Ronald | 1,147,364 | Carter, Jimmy | 281,763 | 399,193 R | 52.0% | 38.6% | 57.4% | 42.6% |
| 1976 | 3,014,472 | 1,509,688 | Ford, Gerald R. | 1,444,653 | Carter, Jimmy | 60,131 | 65,035 R | 50.1% | 47.9% | 51.1% | 48.9% |
| 1972 | 2,997,229 | 1,845,502 | Nixon, Richard M. | 1,102,211 | McGovern, George S. | 49,516 | 743,291 R | 61.6% | 36.8% | 62.6% | 37.4% |
| 1968 | 2,875,395 | 1,325,467 | Nixon, Richard M. | 1,264,206 | Humphrey, Hubert H. | 285,722 | 61,261 R | 46.1% | 44.0% | 51.2% | 48.8% |
| 1964 | 2,847,663 | 964,174 | Goldwater, Barry M. | 1,868,231 | Johnson, Lyndon B. | 15,258 | 904,057 D | 33.9% | 65.6% | 34.0% | 66.0% |
| 1960 | 2,773,111 | 1,363,324 | Nixon, Richard M. | 1,385,415 | Kennedy, John F. | 24,372 | 22,091 D | 49.2% | 50.0% | 49.6% | 50.4% |
| 1956 | 2,484,312 | 1,606,942 | Eisenhower, Dwight D. | 850,337 | Stevenson, Adlai E. | 27,033 | 756,605 R | 64.7% | 34.2% | 65.4% | 34.6% |
| 1952 | 2,418,554 | 1,373,613 | Eisenhower, Dwight D. | 1,015,902 | Stevenson, Adlai E. | 29,039 | 357,711 R | 56.8% | 42.0% | 57.5% | 42.5% |
| 1948 | 1,949,555 | 981,124 | Dewey, Thomas E. | 895,455 | Truman, Harry S. | 72,976 | 85,669 R | 50.3% | 45.9% | 52.3% | 47.7% |
| 1944 | 1,963,761 | 961,335 | Dewey, Thomas E. | 987,874 | Roosevelt, Franklin D. | 14,552 | 26,539 D | 49.0% | 50.3% | 49.3% | 50.7% |
| 1940 | 1,972,552 | 945,475 | Willkie, Wendell | 1,016,808 | Roosevelt, Franklin D. | 10,269 | 71,333 D | 47.9% | 51.5% | 48.2% | 51.8% |
| 1936 | 1,820,437 | 720,322 | Landon, Alfred M. | 1,083,850 | Roosevelt, Franklin D. | 16,265 | 363,528 D | 39.6% | 59.5% | 39.9% | 60.1% |
| 1932 | 1,630,063 | 775,684 | Hoover, Herbert C. | 806,630 | Roosevelt, Franklin D. | 47,749 | 30,946 D | 47.6% | 49.5% | 49.0% | 51.0% |
| 1928 | 1,549,381 | 926,050 | Hoover, Herbert C. | 616,517 | Smith, Alfred E. | 6,814 | 309,533 R | 59.8% | 39.8% | 60.0% | 40.0% |
| 1924 ** | 1,088,054 | 676,277 | Coolidge, Calvin | 298,043 | Davis, John W. | 113,734 | 378,234 R | 62.2% | 27.4% | 69.4% | 30.6% |
| 1920 | 910,251 | 615,333 | Harding, Warren G. | 258,761 | Cox, James M. | 36,157 | 356,572 R | 67.6% | 28.4% | 70.4% | 29.6% |

In 2000 the other vote column includes 94,554 votes cast for Green (Nader). In 1996 the other vote column includes 262,134 votes cast for Perot. In 1992 the other vote column includes 521,829 votes cast for Perot. In 1980 the other column includes 234,632 votes for Independent (Anderson). In 1924 the other vote was 109,028 Progressive; 1,660 Prohibition; 1,560 Communist; 853 Socialist Labor; 368 American; and 265 Commonwealth Land.

## ELECTORAL COLLEGE VOTE 1920 TO 2004

| Year | Total | Republican | Democratic | Other |
|------|-------|-----------|-----------|-------|
| 2004 | 15 | | 15 | |
| 2000 | 15 | | 15 | |
| 1996 | 15 | | 15 | |
| 1992 | 15 | | 15 | |
| 1988 | 16 | 16 | | |
| 1984 | 16 | 16 | | |
| 1980 | 17 | 17 | | |
| 1976 | 17 | 17 | | |
| 1972 | 17 | 17 | | |
| 1968 | 17 | 17 | | |
| 1964 | 17 | | 17 | |
| 1960 | 16 | | 16 | |
| 1956 | 16 | 16 | | |
| 1952 | 16 | 16 | | |
| 1948 | 16 | 16 | | |
| 1944 | 16 | | 16 | |
| 1940 | 16 | | 16 | |
| 1936 | 16 | | 16 | |
| 1932 | 16 | | 16 | |
| 1928 | 14 | 14 | | |
| 1924 | 14 | 14 | | |
| 1920 | 14 | 14 | | |

# NEW JERSEY

# NEW JERSEY

## PRESIDENT 2004

| 2000 Census Population | County | Total Vote | Republican | Democratic | Other | Rep.-Dem. Plurality | Percentage | | | |
|---|---|---|---|---|---|---|---|---|---|---|
| | | | | | | | Total Vote | | Major Vote | |
| | | | | | | | Rep. | Dem. | Rep. | Dem. |
| 252,552 | ATLANTIC | 106,097 | 49,487 | 55,746 | 864 | 6,259 D | 46.6% | 52.5% | 47.0% | 53.0% |
| 884,118 | BERGEN | 400,244 | 189,833 | 207,666 | 2,745 | 17,833 D | 47.4% | 51.9% | 47.8% | 52.2% |
| 423,394 | BURLINGTON | 207,956 | 95,936 | 110,411 | 1,609 | 14,475 D | 46.1% | 53.1% | 46.5% | 53.5% |
| 508,932 | CAMDEN | 220,933 | 81,427 | 137,765 | 1,741 | 56,338 D | 36.9% | 62.4% | 37.1% | 62.9% |
| 102,326 | CAPE MAY | 50,762 | 28,832 | 21,475 | 455 | 7,357 R | 56.8% | 42.3% | 57.3% | 42.7% |
| 146,438 | CUMBERLAND | 53,185 | 24,362 | 27,875 | 948 | 3,513 D | 45.8% | 52.4% | 46.6% | 53.4% |
| 793,633 | ESSEX | 289,348 | 83,374 | 203,681 | 2,293 | 120,307 D | 28.8% | 70.4% | 29.0% | 71.0% |
| 254,673 | GLOUCESTER | 127,964 | 60,033 | 66,835 | 1,096 | 6,802 D | 46.9% | 52.2% | 47.3% | 52.7% |
| 608,975 | HUDSON | 189,446 | 60,646 | 127,447 | 1,353 | 66,801 D | 32.0% | 67.3% | 32.2% | 67.8% |
| 121,989 | HUNTERDON | 66,680 | 39,888 | 26,050 | 742 | 13,838 R | 59.8% | 39.1% | 60.5% | 39.5% |
| 350,761 | MERCER | 149,510 | 56,604 | 91,580 | 1,326 | 34,976 D | 37.9% | 61.3% | 38.2% | 61.8% |
| 750,162 | MIDDLESEX | 295,805 | 126,492 | 166,628 | 2,685 | 40,136 D | 42.8% | 56.3% | 43.2% | 56.8% |
| 615,301 | MONMOUTH | 299,939 | 163,650 | 133,773 | 2,516 | 29,877 R | 54.6% | 44.6% | 55.0% | 45.0% |
| 470,212 | MORRIS | 235,154 | 135,241 | 98,066 | 1,847 | 37,175 R | 57.5% | 41.7% | 58.0% | 42.0% |
| 510,916 | OCEAN | 256,306 | 154,204 | 99,839 | 2,263 | 54,365 R | 60.2% | 39.0% | 60.7% | 39.3% |
| 489,049 | PASSAIC | 171,311 | 75,200 | 94,962 | 1,149 | 19,762 D | 43.9% | 55.4% | 44.2% | 55.8% |
| 64,285 | SALEM | 29,781 | 15,721 | 13,749 | 311 | 1,972 R | 52.8% | 46.2% | 53.3% | 46.7% |
| 297,490 | SOMERSET | 140,279 | 72,508 | 66,476 | 1,295 | 6,032 R | 51.7% | 47.4% | 52.2% | 47.8% |
| 144,166 | SUSSEX | 69,396 | 44,506 | 23,990 | 900 | 20,516 R | 64.1% | 34.6% | 65.0% | 35.0% |
| 522,541 | UNION | 203,387 | 82,517 | 119,372 | 1,498 | 36,855 D | 40.6% | 58.7% | 40.9% | 59.1% |
| 102,437 | WARREN | 48,208 | 29,542 | 18,044 | 622 | 11,498 R | 61.3% | 37.4% | 62.1% | 37.9% |
| 8,414,350 | TOTAL | 3,611,691 | 1,670,003 | 1,911,430 | 30,258 | 241,427 D | 46.2% | 52.9% | 46.6% | 53.4% |

# NEW JERSEY

## PRESIDENT 2000

| 2000 Census Population | County | Total Vote | Republican | Democratic | Green (Nader) | Other | Rep.-Dem. Plurality | Percentage of Total Vote | | |
|---|---|---|---|---|---|---|---|---|---|---|
| | | | | | | | | Rep. | Dem. | Green |
| 252,552 | ATLANTIC | 91,102 | 35,593 | 52,880 | 2,188 | 441 | 17,287 D | 39.1% | 58.0% | 2.4% |
| 884,118 | BERGEN | 366,721 | 152,731 | 202,682 | 9,688 | 1,620 | 49,951 D | 41.6% | 55.3% | 2.6% |
| 423,394 | BURLINGTON | 177,541 | 72,254 | 99,506 | 4,894 | 887 | 27,252 D | 40.7% | 56.0% | 2.8% |
| 508,932 | CAMDEN | 196,861 | 62,464 | 127,166 | 6,124 | 1,107 | 64,702 D | 31.7% | 64.6% | 3.1% |
| 102,326 | CAPE MAY | 47,594 | 23,794 | 22,189 | 1,291 | 320 | 1,605 R | 50.0% | 46.6% | 2.7% |
| 146,438 | CUMBERLAND | 48,684 | 18,882 | 28,188 | 1,004 | 610 | 9,306 D | 38.8% | 57.9% | 2.1% |
| 793,633 | ESSEX | 259,573 | 66,842 | 185,505 | 5,641 | 1,585 | 118,663 D | 25.8% | 71.5% | 2.2% |
| 254,673 | GLOUCESTER | 107,298 | 42,315 | 61,095 | 3,196 | 692 | 18,780 D | 39.4% | 56.9% | 3.0% |
| 608,975 | HUDSON | 167,361 | 43,804 | 118,206 | 4,436 | 915 | 74,402 D | 26.2% | 70.6% | 2.7% |
| 121,989 | HUNTERDON | 56,455 | 32,210 | 21,387 | 2,459 | 399 | 10,823 R | 57.1% | 37.9% | 4.4% |
| 350,761 | MERCER | 135,559 | 46,670 | 83,256 | 4,561 | 1,072 | 36,586 D | 34.4% | 61.4% | 3.4% |
| 750,162 | MIDDLESEX | 258,849 | 93,545 | 154,998 | 8,934 | 1,372 | 61,453 D | 36.1% | 59.9% | 3.5% |
| 615,301 | MONMOUTH | 262,141 | 119,291 | 131,476 | 9,059 | 2,315 | 12,185 D | 45.5% | 50.2% | 3.5% |
| 470,212 | MORRIS | 206,508 | 111,066 | 88,039 | 6,333 | 1,070 | 23,027 R | 53.8% | 42.6% | 3.1% |
| 510,916 | OCEAN | 216,393 | 105,684 | 102,104 | 7,354 | 1,251 | 3,580 R | 48.8% | 47.2% | 3.4% |
| 489,049 | PASSAIC | 156,573 | 61,043 | 90,324 | 3,752 | 1,454 | 29,281 D | 39.0% | 57.7% | 2.4% |
| 64,285 | SALEM | 26,972 | 12,257 | 13,718 | 714 | 283 | 1,461 D | 45.4% | 50.9% | 2.6% |
| 297,490 | SOMERSET | 120,377 | 59,725 | 56,232 | 3,776 | 644 | 3,493 R | 49.6% | 46.7% | 3.1% |
| 144,166 | SUSSEX | 57,490 | 33,277 | 21,353 | 2,399 | 461 | 11,924 R | 57.9% | 37.1% | 4.2% |
| 522,541 | UNION | 186,373 | 68,554 | 112,003 | 4,945 | 871 | 43,449 D | 36.8% | 60.1% | 2.7% |
| 102,437 | WARREN | 40,801 | 22,172 | 16,543 | 1,806 | 280 | 5,629 R | 54.3% | 40.5% | 4.4% |
| 8,414,350 | TOTAL | 3,187,226 | 1,284,173 | 1,788,850 | 94,554 | 19,649 | 504,677 D | 40.3% | 56.1% | 3.0% |

# NEW JERSEY

## PRESIDENT 1996

| 1995 Census Pop. Est. | County | Total Vote | Republican | Democratic | Reform (Perot) | Other | Rep.-Dem. Plurality | Percentage of Total Vote | | |
|---|---|---|---|---|---|---|---|---|---|---|
| | | | | | | | | Rep. | Dem. | Reform |
| 233,996 | ATLANTIC | 83,601 | 29,538 | 44,434 | 8,261 | 1,368 | 14,896 D | 35.3% | 53.2% | 9.9% |
| 845,189 | BERGEN | 362,887 | 141,164 | 191,085 | 25,512 | 5,126 | 49,921 D | 38.9% | 52.7% | 7.0% |
| 403,337 | BURLINGTON | 163,809 | 57,337 | 85,086 | 18,407 | 2,979 | 27,749 D | 35.0% | 51.9% | 11.2% |
| 507,157 | CAMDEN | 189,723 | 52,791 | 114,962 | 17,433 | 4,537 | 62,171 D | 27.8% | 60.6% | 9.2% |
| 98,340 | CAPE MAY | 45,036 | 19,357 | 19,849 | 4,978 | 852 | 492 D | 43.0% | 44.1% | 11.1% |
| 138,058 | CUMBERLAND | 46,533 | 14,744 | 25,444 | 5,348 | 997 | 10,700 D | 31.7% | 54.7% | 11.5% |
| 758,626 | ESSEX | 254,196 | 65,162 | 175,368 | 9,513 | 4,153 | 110,206 D | 25.6% | 69.0% | 3.7% |
| 243,748 | GLOUCESTER | 100,495 | 32,116 | 51,915 | 14,361 | 2,103 | 19,799 D | 32.0% | 51.7% | 14.3% |
| 550,183 | HUDSON | 166,009 | 38,288 | 116,121 | 8,965 | 2,635 | 77,833 D | 23.1% | 69.9% | 5.4% |
| 116,516 | HUNTERDON | 51,727 | 26,379 | 18,446 | 5,686 | 1,216 | 7,933 R | 51.0% | 35.7% | 11.0% |
| 330,305 | MERCER | 131,726 | 40,559 | 77,641 | 10,536 | 2,990 | 37,082 D | 30.8% | 58.9% | 8.0% |
| 698,494 | MIDDLESEX | 258,386 | 82,433 | 145,201 | 24,643 | 6,109 | 62,768 D | 31.9% | 56.2% | 9.5% |
| 585,230 | MONMOUTH | 248,961 | 99,975 | 120,414 | 22,754 | 5,818 | 20,439 D | 40.2% | 48.4% | 9.1% |
| 444,354 | MORRIS | 195,745 | 95,830 | 81,092 | 15,299 | 3,524 | 14,738 R | 49.0% | 41.4% | 7.8% |
| 464,822 | OCEAN | 202,976 | 82,830 | 94,243 | 22,864 | 3,039 | 11,413 D | 40.8% | 46.4% | 11.3% |
| 463,466 | PASSAIC | 152,951 | 53,594 | 85,879 | 10,944 | 2,534 | 32,285 D | 35.0% | 56.1% | 7.2% |
| 64,921 | SALEM | 25,992 | 9,294 | 12,044 | 4,124 | 530 | 2,750 D | 35.8% | 46.3% | 15.9% |
| 265,440 | SOMERSET | 112,929 | 51,869 | 50,673 | 8,377 | 2,010 | 1,196 R | 45.9% | 44.9% | 7.4% |
| 140,198 | SUSSEX | 54,183 | 26,746 | 19,525 | 6,705 | 1,207 | 7,221 R | 49.4% | 36.0% | 12.4% |
| 496,310 | UNION | 190,241 | 65,912 | 108,102 | 12,432 | 3,795 | 42,190 D | 34.6% | 56.8% | 6.5% |
| 96,608 | WARREN | 37,701 | 17,160 | 14,805 | 4,992 | 744 | 2,355 R | 45.5% | 39.3% | 13.2% |
| 7,945,298 | TOTAL | 3,075,807 | 1,103,078 | 1,652,329 | 262,134 | 58,266 | 549,251 D | 35.9% | 53.7% | 8.5% |

# NEW JERSEY

## PRESIDENT 1992

| 1990 Census Population | County | Total Vote | Republican | Democratic | Perot | Other | Plurality | Percentage Total Vote | | |
|---|---|---|---|---|---|---|---|---|---|---|
| | | | | | | | | Rep. | Dem. | Perot |
| 224,327 | ATLANTIC | 90,298 | 34,279 | 39,633 | 15,890 | 496 | 5,354 D | 38.0% | 43.9% | 17.6% |
| 825,380 | BERGEN | 403,137 | 178,223 | 171,104 | 52,082 | 1,728 | 7,119 R | 44.2% | 42.4% | 12.9% |
| 395,066 | BURLINGTON | 173,357 | 63,709 | 72,845 | 35,322 | 1,481 | 9,136 D | 36.8% | 42.0% | 20.4% |
| 502,824 | CAMDEN | 210,886 | 67,205 | 104,915 | 37,144 | 1,622 | 37,710 D | 31.9% | 49.7% | 17.6% |
| 95,089 | CAPE MAY | 48,856 | 21,502 | 17,324 | 9,798 | 232 | 4,178 R | 44.0% | 35.5% | 20.1% |
| 138,053 | CUMBERLAND | 52,116 | 19,253 | 22,220 | 9,901 | 742 | 2,967 D | 36.9% | 42.6% | 19.0% |
| 778,206 | ESSEX | 276,858 | 89,146 | 158,130 | 26,961 | 2,621 | 68,984 D | 32.2% | 57.1% | 9.7% |
| 230,082 | GLOUCESTER | 104,619 | 37,335 | 42,425 | 24,132 | 727 | 5,090 D | 35.7% | 40.6% | 23.1% |
| 553,099 | HUDSON | 185,057 | 66,505 | 99,799 | 14,569 | 4,184 | 33,294 D | 35.9% | 53.9% | 7.9% |
| 107,776 | HUNTERDON | 53,974 | 25,130 | 15,423 | 12,736 | 685 | 9,707 R | 46.6% | 28.6% | 23.6% |
| 325,824 | MERCER | 145,260 | 50,473 | 71,383 | 22,503 | 901 | 20,910 D | 34.7% | 49.1% | 15.5% |
| 671,780 | MIDDLESEX | 285,271 | 108,701 | 128,824 | 45,055 | 2,691 | 20,123 D | 38.1% | 45.2% | 15.8% |
| 553,124 | MONMOUTH | 266,116 | 117,715 | 101,750 | 45,445 | 1,206 | 15,965 R | 44.2% | 38.2% | 17.1% |
| 421,353 | MORRIS | 209,232 | 108,431 | 67,593 | 32,447 | 761 | 40,838 R | 51.8% | 32.3% | 15.5% |
| 433,203 | OCEAN | 216,243 | 95,984 | 75,431 | 41,668 | 3,160 | 20,553 R | 44.4% | 34.9% | 19.3% |
| 453,060 | PASSAIC | 164,888 | 71,147 | 70,030 | 21,494 | 2,217 | 1,117 R | 43.1% | 42.5% | 13.0% |
| 65,294 | SALEM | 27,935 | 10,363 | 10,062 | 7,274 | 236 | 301 R | 37.1% | 36.0% | 26.0% |
| 240,279 | SOMERSET | 120,813 | 56,044 | 42,867 | 21,014 | 888 | 13,177 R | 46.4% | 35.5% | 17.4% |
| 130,943 | SUSSEX | 57,064 | 29,510 | 14,775 | 12,537 | 242 | 14,735 R | 51.7% | 25.9% | 22.0% |
| 493,819 | UNION | 210,112 | 87,742 | 96,671 | 23,991 | 1,708 | 8,929 D | 41.8% | 46.0% | 11.4% |
| 91,607 | WARREN | 41,502 | 18,468 | 13,002 | 9,866 | 166 | 5,466 R | 44.5% | 31.3% | 23.8% |
| 7,730,188 | TOTAL | 3,343,594 | 1,356,865 | 1,436,206 | 521,829 | 28,694 | 79,341 D | 40.6% | 43.0% | 15.6% |

# NEW JERSEY

## PRESIDENT 1988

| 1980 Census Population | County | Total Vote | Republican | Democratic | Other | Rep.-Dem. Plurality | Percentage | | | |
| --- | --- | --- | --- | --- | --- | --- | --- | --- | --- | --- |
| | | | | | | | Total Vote | | Major Vote | |
| | | | | | | | Rep. | Dem. | Rep. | Dem. |
| 194,119 | ATLANTIC | 79,442 | 44,748 | 34,047 | 647 | 10,701 R | 56.3% | 42.9% | 56.8% | 43.2% |
| 845,385 | BERGEN | 389,933 | 226,885 | 160,655 | 2,393 | 66,230 R | 58.2% | 41.2% | 58.5% | 41.5% |
| 362,542 | BURLINGTON | 149,949 | 87,416 | 61,140 | 1,393 | 26,276 R | 58.3% | 40.8% | 58.8% | 41.2% |
| 471,650 | CAMDEN | 192,515 | 100,072 | 90,704 | 1,739 | 9,368 R | 52.0% | 47.1% | 52.5% | 47.5% |
| 82,266 | CAPE MAY | 44,117 | 28,738 | 15,105 | 274 | 13,633 R | 65.1% | 34.2% | 65.5% | 34.5% |
| 132,866 | CUMBERLAND | 48,349 | 26,024 | 21,869 | 456 | 4,155 R | 53.8% | 45.2% | 54.3% | 45.7% |
| 851,116 | ESSEX | 276,967 | 111,491 | 156,098 | 9,378 | 44,607 D | 40.3% | 56.4% | 41.7% | 58.3% |
| 199,917 | GLOUCESTER | 88,117 | 51,708 | 35,479 | 930 | 16,229 R | 58.7% | 40.3% | 59.3% | 40.7% |
| 556,972 | HUDSON | 184,463 | 84,334 | 98,507 | 1,622 | 14,173 D | 45.7% | 53.4% | 46.1% | 53.9% |
| 87,361 | HUNTERDON | 46,182 | 31,907 | 13,758 | 517 | 18,149 R | 69.1% | 29.8% | 69.9% | 30.1% |
| 307,863 | MERCER | 135,345 | 65,384 | 68,712 | 1,249 | 3,328 D | 48.3% | 50.8% | 48.8% | 51.2% |
| 595,893 | MIDDLESEX | 264,119 | 143,422 | 117,149 | 3,548 | 26,273 R | 54.3% | 44.4% | 55.0% | 45.0% |
| 503,173 | MONMOUTH | 240,957 | 147,320 | 91,844 | 1,793 | 55,476 R | 61.1% | 38.1% | 61.6% | 38.4% |
| 407,630 | MORRIS | 187,249 | 127,420 | 58,721 | 1,108 | 68,699 R | 68.0% | 31.4% | 68.5% | 31.5% |
| 346,038 | OCEAN | 190,558 | 124,587 | 64,474 | 1,497 | 60,113 R | 65.4% | 33.8% | 65.9% | 34.1% |
| 447,585 | PASSAIC | 157,513 | 88,070 | 66,254 | 3,189 | 21,816 R | 55.9% | 42.1% | 57.1% | 42.9% |
| 64,676 | SALEM | 25,606 | 15,240 | 9,956 | 410 | 5,284 R | 59.5% | 38.9% | 60.5% | 39.5% |
| 203,129 | SOMERSET | 106,193 | 67,658 | 37,406 | 1,129 | 30,252 R | 63.7% | 35.2% | 64.4% | 35.6% |
| 116,119 | SUSSEX | 50,160 | 36,086 | 13,676 | 398 | 22,410 R | 71.9% | 27.3% | 72.5% | 27.5% |
| 504,094 | UNION | 208,153 | 112,967 | 93,158 | 2,028 | 19,809 R | 54.3% | 44.8% | 54.8% | 45.2% |
| 84,429 | WARREN | 33,666 | 21,715 | 11,640 | 311 | 10,075 R | 64.5% | 34.6% | 65.1% | 34.9% |
| 7,364,823 | TOTAL | 3,099,553 | 1,743,192 | 1,320,352 | 36,009 | 422,840 R | 56.2% | 42.6% | 56.9% | 43.1% |

# NEW JERSEY

## PRESIDENT 1984

| 1980 Census Population | County | Total Vote | Republican | Democratic | Other | Rep.-Dem. Plurality | Percentage | | | |
| --- | --- | --- | --- | --- | --- | --- | --- | --- | --- | --- |
| | | | | | | | Total Vote | | Major Vote | |
| | | | | | | | Rep. | Dem. | Rep. | Dem. |
| 194,119 | ATLANTIC | 82,851 | 49,158 | 33,240 | 453 | 15,918 R | 59.3% | 40.1% | 59.7% | 40.3% |
| 845,385 | BERGEN | 424,718 | 268,507 | 155,039 | 1,172 | 113,468 R | 63.2% | 36.5% | 63.4% | 36.6% |
| 362,542 | BURLINGTON | 147,659 | 89,815 | 57,467 | 377 | 32,348 R | 60.8% | 38.9% | 61.0% | 39.0% |
| 471,650 | CAMDEN | 200,886 | 109,749 | 90,233 | 904 | 19,516 R | 54.6% | 44.9% | 54.9% | 45.1% |
| 82,266 | CAPE MAY | 42,297 | 28,786 | 13,378 | 133 | 15,408 R | 68.1% | 31.6% | 68.3% | 31.7% |
| 132,866 | CUMBERLAND | 51,155 | 29,398 | 21,141 | 616 | 8,257 R | 57.5% | 41.3% | 58.2% | 41.8% |
| 851,116 | ESSEX | 314,543 | 136,798 | 173,295 | 4,450 | 36,497 D | 43.5% | 55.1% | 44.1% | 55.9% |
| 199,917 | GLOUCESTER | 87,050 | 54,041 | 32,702 | 307 | 21,339 R | 62.1% | 37.6% | 62.3% | 37.7% |
| 556,972 | HUDSON | 208,244 | 112,834 | 94,304 | 1,106 | 18,530 R | 54.2% | 45.3% | 54.5% | 45.5% |
| 87,361 | HUNTERDON | 41,079 | 29,737 | 10,972 | 370 | 18,765 R | 72.4% | 26.7% | 73.0% | 27.0% |
| 307,863 | MERCER | 138,121 | 71,195 | 66,398 | 528 | 4,797 R | 51.5% | 48.1% | 51.7% | 48.3% |
| 595,893 | MIDDLESEX | 267,853 | 160,221 | 104,905 | 2,727 | 55,316 R | 59.8% | 39.2% | 60.4% | 39.6% |
| 503,173 | MONMOUTH | 232,909 | 152,595 | 79,382 | 932 | 73,213 R | 65.5% | 34.1% | 65.8% | 34.2% |
| 407,630 | MORRIS | 191,504 | 137,719 | 53,201 | 584 | 84,518 R | 71.9% | 27.8% | 72.1% | 27.9% |
| 346,038 | OCEAN | 177,113 | 124,391 | 51,012 | 1,710 | 73,379 R | 70.2% | 28.8% | 70.9% | 29.1% |
| 447,585 | PASSAIC | 174,940 | 101,951 | 69,590 | 3,399 | 32,361 R | 58.3% | 39.8% | 59.4% | 40.6% |
| 64,676 | SALEM | 26,452 | 17,368 | 8,935 | 149 | 8,433 R | 65.7% | 33.8% | 66.0% | 34.0% |
| 203,129 | SOMERSET | 99,296 | 66,303 | 31,924 | 1,069 | 34,379 R | 66.8% | 32.2% | 67.5% | 32.5% |
| 116,119 | SUSSEX | 47,345 | 35,680 | 11,502 | 163 | 24,178 R | 75.4% | 24.3% | 75.6% | 24.4% |
| 504,094 | UNION | 229,140 | 135,446 | 92,056 | 1,638 | 43,390 R | 59.1% | 40.2% | 59.5% | 40.5% |
| 84,429 | WARREN | 32,707 | 21,938 | 10,647 | 122 | 11,291 R | 67.1% | 32.6% | 67.3% | 32.7% |
| 7,364,823 | TOTAL | 3,217,862 | 1,933,630 | 1,261,323 | 22,909 | 672,307 R | 60.1% | 39.2% | 60.5% | 39.5% |

# NEW JERSEY

## PRESIDENT 1980

| 1980 Census Population | County | Total Vote | Republican | Democratic | Other | Rep.-Dem. Plurality | Percentage — Total Vote Rep. | Dem. | Major Vote Rep. | Dem. |
|---|---|---|---|---|---|---|---|---|---|---|
| 194,119 | ATLANTIC | 76,202 | 37,973 | 31,286 | 6,943 | 6,687 R | 49.8% | 41.1% | 54.8% | 45.2% |
| 845,385 | BERGEN | 415,157 | 232,043 | 139,474 | 43,640 | 92,569 R | 55.9% | 33.6% | 62.5% | 37.5% |
| 362,542 | BURLINGTON | 131,709 | 68,415 | 50,083 | 13,211 | 18,332 R | 51.9% | 38.0% | 57.7% | 42.3% |
| 471,650 | CAMDEN | 186,808 | 87,939 | 80,033 | 18,836 | 7,906 R | 47.1% | 42.8% | 52.4% | 47.6% |
| 82,266 | CAPE MAY | 38,471 | 22,729 | 12,708 | 3,034 | 10,021 R | 59.1% | 33.0% | 64.1% | 35.9% |
| 132,866 | CUMBERLAND | 46,403 | 23,242 | 19,356 | 3,805 | 3,886 R | 50.1% | 41.7% | 54.6% | 45.4% |
| 851,116 | ESSEX | 287,166 | 117,222 | 145,281 | 24,663 | 28,059 D | 40.8% | 50.6% | 44.7% | 55.3% |
| 199,917 | GLOUCESTER | 78,903 | 40,306 | 29,804 | 8,793 | 10,502 R | 51.1% | 37.8% | 57.5% | 42.5% |
| 556,972 | HUDSON | 198,688 | 91,207 | 95,622 | 11,859 | 4,415 D | 45.9% | 48.1% | 48.8% | 51.2% |
| 87,361 | HUNTERDON | 36,430 | 21,403 | 10,029 | 4,998 | 11,374 R | 58.8% | 27.5% | 68.1% | 31.9% |
| 307,863 | MERCER | 128,582 | 53,450 | 60,888 | 14,244 | 7,438 D | 41.6% | 47.4% | 46.7% | 53.3% |
| 595,893 | MIDDLESEX | 241,206 | 122,354 | 97,304 | 21,548 | 25,050 R | 50.7% | 40.3% | 55.7% | 44.3% |
| 503,173 | MONMOUTH | 211,971 | 120,173 | 71,328 | 20,470 | 48,845 R | 56.7% | 33.6% | 62.8% | 37.2% |
| 407,630 | MORRIS | 173,604 | 105,260 | 48,965 | 19,379 | 56,295 R | 60.6% | 28.2% | 68.3% | 31.7% |
| 346,038 | OCEAN | 157,568 | 98,433 | 46,923 | 12,212 | 51,510 R | 62.5% | 29.8% | 67.7% | 32.3% |
| 447,585 | PASSAIC | 158,951 | 82,531 | 61,486 | 14,934 | 21,045 R | 51.9% | 38.7% | 57.3% | 42.7% |
| 64,676 | SALEM | 25,474 | 13,000 | 10,209 | 2,265 | 2,791 R | 51.0% | 40.1% | 56.0% | 44.0% |
| 203,129 | SOMERSET | 91,928 | 52,591 | 29,470 | 9,867 | 23,121 R | 57.2% | 32.1% | 64.1% | 35.9% |
| 116,119 | SUSSEX | 42,327 | 27,063 | 10,531 | 4,733 | 16,532 R | 63.9% | 24.9% | 72.0% | 28.0% |
| 504,094 | UNION | 217,339 | 112,288 | 86,074 | 18,977 | 26,214 R | 51.7% | 39.6% | 56.6% | 43.4% |
| 84,429 | WARREN | 30,797 | 16,935 | 10,510 | 3,352 | 6,425 R | 55.0% | 34.1% | 61.7% | 38.3% |
| 7,364,823 | TOTAL | 2,975,684 | 1,546,557 | 1,147,364 | 281,763 | 399,193 R | 52.0% | 38.6% | 57.4% | 42.6% |

# NEW JERSEY

## PRESIDENT 1976

| 1970 Census Population | County | Total Vote | Republican | Democratic | Other | Rep.-Dem. Plurality | Percentage — Total Vote Rep. | Dem. | Major Vote Rep. | Dem. |
|---|---|---|---|---|---|---|---|---|---|---|
| 175,043 | ATLANTIC | 80,630 | 36,733 | 41,965 | 1,932 | 5,232 D | 45.6% | 52.0% | 46.7% | 53.3% |
| 898,012 | BERGEN | 424,853 | 237,331 | 180,738 | 6,784 | 56,593 R | 55.9% | 42.5% | 56.8% | 43.2% |
| 323,132 | BURLINGTON | 126,820 | 60,960 | 63,309 | 2,551 | 2,349 D | 48.1% | 49.9% | 49.1% | 50.9% |
| 456,291 | CAMDEN | 195,611 | 82,801 | 108,854 | 3,956 | 26,053 D | 42.3% | 55.6% | 43.2% | 56.8% |
| 59,554 | CAPE MAY | 36,667 | 19,498 | 16,489 | 680 | 3,009 R | 53.2% | 45.0% | 54.2% | 45.8% |
| 121,374 | CUMBERLAND | 50,287 | 20,535 | 29,165 | 587 | 8,630 D | 40.8% | 58.0% | 41.3% | 58.7% |
| 929,986 | ESSEX | 315,812 | 133,911 | 174,434 | 7,467 | 40,523 D | 42.4% | 55.2% | 43.4% | 56.6% |
| 172,681 | GLOUCESTER | 75,302 | 34,888 | 38,726 | 1,688 | 3,838 D | 46.3% | 51.4% | 47.4% | 52.6% |
| 609,266 | HUDSON | 212,730 | 92,636 | 116,241 | 3,853 | 23,605 D | 43.5% | 54.6% | 44.3% | 55.7% |
| 69,718 | HUNTERDON | 32,966 | 19,616 | 12,592 | 758 | 7,024 R | 59.5% | 38.2% | 60.9% | 39.1% |
| 303,968 | MERCER | 130,856 | 58,453 | 69,621 | 2,782 | 11,168 D | 44.7% | 53.2% | 45.6% | 54.4% |
| 583,813 | MIDDLESEX | 240,864 | 113,539 | 122,859 | 4,466 | 9,320 D | 47.1% | 51.0% | 48.0% | 52.0% |
| 459,379 | MONMOUTH | 202,790 | 110,104 | 88,956 | 3,730 | 21,148 R | 54.3% | 43.9% | 55.3% | 44.7% |
| 383,454 | MORRIS | 172,373 | 105,921 | 63,749 | 2,703 | 42,172 R | 61.4% | 37.0% | 62.4% | 37.6% |
| 208,470 | OCEAN | 136,781 | 77,875 | 56,413 | 2,493 | 21,462 R | 56.9% | 41.2% | 58.0% | 42.0% |
| 460,782 | PASSAIC | 166,226 | 85,102 | 76,194 | 4,930 | 8,908 R | 51.2% | 45.8% | 52.8% | 47.2% |
| 60,346 | SALEM | 24,977 | 11,639 | 12,826 | 512 | 1,187 D | 46.6% | 51.4% | 47.6% | 52.4% |
| 198,372 | SOMERSET | 89,691 | 51,260 | 36,258 | 2,173 | 15,002 R | 57.2% | 40.4% | 58.6% | 41.4% |
| 77,528 | SUSSEX | 39,229 | 23,613 | 14,759 | 857 | 8,854 R | 60.2% | 37.6% | 61.5% | 38.5% |
| 543,116 | UNION | 228,902 | 118,019 | 106,267 | 4,616 | 11,752 R | 51.6% | 46.4% | 52.6% | 47.4% |
| 73,879 | WARREN | 30,105 | 15,254 | 14,238 | 613 | 1,016 R | 50.7% | 47.3% | 51.7% | 48.3% |
| 7,168,164 | TOTAL | 3,014,472 | 1,509,688 | 1,444,653 | 60,131 | 65,035 R | 50.1% | 47.9% | 51.1% | 48.9% |

# NEW JERSEY

## PRESIDENT 1972

| 1970 Census Population | County | Total Vote | Republican | Democratic | Other | Rep.-Dem. Plurality | Percentage | | | |
| --- | --- | --- | --- | --- | --- | --- | --- | --- | --- | --- |
| | | | | | | | Total Vote | | Major Vote | |
| | | | | | | | Rep. | Dem. | Rep. | Dem. |
| 175,043 | ATLANTIC | 76,700 | 45,667 | 28,203 | 2,830 | 17,464 R | 59.5% | 36.8% | 61.8% | 38.2% |
| 898,012 | BERGEN | 436,894 | 285,458 | 147,155 | 4,281 | 138,303 R | 65.3% | 33.7% | 66.0% | 34.0% |
| 323,132 | BURLINGTON | 114,260 | 70,805 | 41,520 | 1,935 | 29,285 R | 62.0% | 36.3% | 63.0% | 37.0% |
| 456,291 | CAMDEN | 190,207 | 111,935 | 75,202 | 3,070 | 36,733 R | 58.8% | 39.5% | 59.8% | 40.2% |
| 59,554 | CAPE MAY | 32,069 | 22,621 | 8,729 | 719 | 13,892 R | 70.5% | 27.2% | 72.2% | 27.8% |
| 121,374 | CUMBERLAND | 45,392 | 26,409 | 18,692 | 291 | 7,717 R | 58.2% | 41.2% | 58.6% | 41.4% |
| 929,986 | ESSEX | 338,888 | 170,036 | 161,270 | 7,582 | 8,766 R | 50.2% | 47.6% | 51.3% | 48.7% |
| 172,681 | GLOUCESTER | 71,209 | 44,806 | 25,509 | 894 | 19,297 R | 62.9% | 35.8% | 63.7% | 36.3% |
| 609,266 | HUDSON | 227,600 | 136,895 | 87,977 | 2,728 | 48,918 R | 60.1% | 38.7% | 60.9% | 39.1% |
| 69,718 | HUNTERDON | 30,856 | 21,282 | 9,031 | 543 | 12,251 R | 69.0% | 29.3% | 70.2% | 29.8% |
| 303,968 | MERCER | 133,191 | 69,303 | 62,180 | 1,708 | 7,123 R | 52.0% | 46.7% | 52.7% | 47.3% |
| 583,813 | MIDDLESEX | 242,694 | 149,033 | 88,397 | 5,264 | 60,636 R | 61.4% | 36.4% | 62.8% | 37.2% |
| 459,379 | MONMOUTH | 189,977 | 124,830 | 63,176 | 1,971 | 61,654 R | 65.7% | 33.3% | 66.4% | 33.6% |
| 383,454 | MORRIS | 166,434 | 113,469 | 50,937 | 2,028 | 62,532 R | 68.2% | 30.6% | 69.0% | 31.0% |
| 208,470 | OCEAN | 107,667 | 77,979 | 27,710 | 1,978 | 50,269 R | 72.4% | 25.7% | 73.8% | 26.2% |
| 460,782 | PASSAIC | 174,923 | 108,511 | 62,302 | 4,110 | 46,209 R | 62.0% | 35.6% | 63.5% | 36.5% |
| 60,346 | SALEM | 25,249 | 16,371 | 8,609 | 269 | 7,762 R | 64.8% | 34.1% | 65.5% | 34.5% |
| 198,372 | SOMERSET | 85,605 | 56,524 | 26,537 | 2,544 | 29,987 R | 66.0% | 31.0% | 68.1% | 31.9% |
| 77,528 | SUSSEX | 34,898 | 25,977 | 8,585 | 336 | 17,392 R | 74.4% | 24.6% | 75.2% | 24.8% |
| 543,116 | UNION | 242,973 | 148,290 | 90,482 | 4,201 | 57,808 R | 61.0% | 37.2% | 62.1% | 37.9% |
| 73,879 | WARREN | 29,543 | 19,301 | 10,008 | 234 | 9,293 R | 65.3% | 33.9% | 65.9% | 34.1% |
| 7,168,164 | TOTAL | 2,997,229 | 1,845,502 | 1,102,211 | 49,516 | 743,291 R | 61.6% | 36.8% | 62.6% | 37.4% |

# NEW JERSEY

## PRESIDENT 1968

| 1960 Census Population | County | Total Vote | Republican | Democratic | AIP | Other | Plurality | Percentage Total Vote | | |
| --- | --- | --- | --- | --- | --- | --- | --- | --- | --- | --- |
| | | | | | | | | Rep. | Dem. | AIP |
| 160,880 | ATLANTIC | 77,834 | 32,807 | 35,581 | 7,528 | 1,918 | 2,774 D | 42.1% | 45.7% | 9.7% |
| 780,255 | BERGEN | 413,037 | 224,911 | 162,182 | 23,663 | 2,281 | 62,729 R | 54.5% | 39.3% | 5.7% |
| 224,499 | BURLINGTON | 99,747 | 46,177 | 41,651 | 11,635 | 284 | 4,526 R | 46.3% | 41.8% | 11.7% |
| 392,035 | CAMDEN | 188,887 | 77,642 | 87,347 | 23,111 | 787 | 9,705 D | 41.1% | 46.2% | 12.2% |
| 48,555 | CAPE MAY | 28,172 | 14,970 | 9,664 | 3,498 | 40 | 5,306 R | 53.1% | 34.3% | 12.4% |
| 106,850 | CUMBERLAND | 45,488 | 18,388 | 21,661 | 5,356 | 83 | 3,273 D | 40.4% | 47.6% | 11.8% |
| 923,545 | ESSEX | 357,095 | 140,084 | 185,440 | 26,823 | 4,748 | 45,356 D | 39.2% | 51.9% | 7.5% |
| 134,840 | GLOUCESTER | 68,731 | 30,596 | 27,438 | 10,626 | 71 | 3,158 D | 44.5% | 39.9% | 15.5% |
| 610,734 | HUDSON | 244,560 | 91,324 | 124,939 | 23,138 | 5,159 | 33,615 D | 37.3% | 51.1% | 9.5% |
| 54,107 | HUNTERDON | 27,439 | 15,851 | 8,755 | 2,749 | 84 | 7,096 R | 57.8% | 31.9% | 10.0% |
| 266,392 | MERCER | 125,529 | 45,354 | 63,218 | 16,104 | 853 | 17,864 D | 36.1% | 50.4% | 12.8% |
| 433,856 | MIDDLESEX | 225,530 | 96,515 | 103,339 | 24,138 | 1,538 | 6,824 D | 42.8% | 45.8% | 10.7% |
| 334,401 | MONMOUTH | 170,456 | 87,311 | 69,669 | 13,047 | 429 | 17,642 R | 51.2% | 40.9% | 7.7% |
| 261,620 | MORRIS | 148,062 | 85,512 | 52,398 | 9,659 | 493 | 33,114 R | 57.8% | 35.4% | 6.5% |
| 108,241 | OCEAN | 77,963 | 41,995 | 26,909 | 8,520 | 539 | 15,086 R | 53.9% | 34.5% | 10.9% |
| 406,618 | PASSAIC | 172,657 | 79,862 | 74,442 | 16,617 | 1,736 | 5,420 R | 46.3% | 43.1% | 9.6% |
| 58,711 | SALEM | 26,251 | 11,407 | 11,172 | 3,647 | 25 | 235 R | 43.5% | 42.6% | 13.9% |
| 143,913 | SOMERSET | 78,475 | 42,459 | 27,580 | 7,331 | 1,105 | 14,879 R | 54.1% | 35.1% | 9.3% |
| 49,255 | SUSSEX | 29,240 | 18,043 | 8,325 | 2,843 | 29 | 9,718 R | 61.7% | 28.5% | 9.7% |
| 504,255 | UNION | 241,256 | 110,309 | 109,674 | 19,963 | 1,310 | 635 R | 45.7% | 45.5% | 8.3% |
| 63,220 | WARREN | 28,986 | 13,950 | 12,822 | 2,191 | 23 | 1,128 R | 48.1% | 44.2% | 7.6% |
| 6,066,782 | TOTAL | 2,875,395 | 1,325,467 | 1,264,206 | 262,187 | 23,535 | 61,261 R | 46.1% | 44.0% | 9.1% |

# NEW JERSEY

## PRESIDENT 1964

| 1960 Census Population | County | Total Vote | Republican | Democratic | Other | Rep.-Dem. Plurality | Percentage | | | |
|---|---|---|---|---|---|---|---|---|---|---|
| | | | | | | | Total Vote | | Major Vote | |
| | | | | | | | Rep. | Dem. | Rep. | Dem. |
| 160,880 | ATLANTIC | 78,019 | 25,626 | 50,945 | 1,448 | 25,319 D | 32.8% | 65.3% | 33.5% | 66.5% |
| 780,255 | BERGEN | 394,358 | 158,230 | 235,409 | 719 | 77,179 D | 40.1% | 59.7% | 40.2% | 59.8% |
| 224,499 | BURLINGTON | 88,945 | 31,215 | 57,638 | 92 | 26,423 D | 35.1% | 64.8% | 35.1% | 64.9% |
| 392,035 | CAMDEN | 185,761 | 60,844 | 124,620 | 297 | 63,776 D | 32.8% | 67.1% | 32.8% | 67.2% |
| 48,555 | CAPE MAY | 26,380 | 11,390 | 14,943 | 47 | 3,553 D | 43.2% | 56.6% | 43.3% | 56.7% |
| 106,850 | CUMBERLAND | 46,215 | 12,611 | 33,593 | 11 | 20,982 D | 27.3% | 72.7% | 27.3% | 72.7% |
| 923,545 | ESSEX | 396,477 | 116,172 | 277,042 | 3,263 | 160,870 D | 29.3% | 69.9% | 29.5% | 70.5% |
| 134,840 | GLOUCESTER | 64,052 | 23,702 | 40,305 | 45 | 16,603 D | 37.0% | 62.9% | 37.0% | 63.0% |
| 610,734 | HUDSON | 272,009 | 69,515 | 200,051 | 2,443 | 130,536 D | 25.6% | 73.5% | 25.8% | 74.2% |
| 54,107 | HUNTERDON | 25,283 | 10,173 | 15,091 | 19 | 4,918 D | 40.2% | 59.7% | 40.3% | 59.7% |
| 266,392 | MERCER | 122,214 | 35,081 | 86,985 | 148 | 51,904 D | 28.7% | 71.2% | 28.7% | 71.3% |
| 433,856 | MIDDLESEX | 215,618 | 63,370 | 151,196 | 1,052 | 87,826 D | 29.4% | 70.1% | 29.5% | 70.5% |
| 334,401 | MONMOUTH | 157,055 | 61,367 | 95,320 | 368 | 33,953 D | 39.1% | 60.7% | 39.2% | 60.8% |
| 261,620 | MORRIS | 128,913 | 55,024 | 73,684 | 205 | 18,660 D | 42.7% | 57.2% | 42.8% | 57.2% |
| 108,241 | OCEAN | 63,714 | 25,985 | 36,892 | 837 | 10,907 D | 40.8% | 57.9% | 41.3% | 58.7% |
| 406,618 | PASSAIC | 179,699 | 63,114 | 113,919 | 2,666 | 50,805 D | 35.1% | 63.4% | 35.7% | 64.3% |
| 58,711 | SALEM | 26,545 | 8,682 | 17,846 | 17 | 9,164 D | 32.7% | 67.2% | 32.7% | 67.3% |
| 143,913 | SOMERSET | 72,270 | 28,416 | 43,659 | 195 | 15,243 D | 39.3% | 60.4% | 39.4% | 60.6% |
| 49,255 | SUSSEX | 26,197 | 11,836 | 14,349 | 12 | 2,513 D | 45.2% | 54.8% | 45.2% | 54.8% |
| 504,255 | UNION | 249,347 | 82,999 | 164,989 | 1,359 | 81,990 D | 33.3% | 66.2% | 33.5% | 66.5% |
| 63,220 | WARREN | 28,592 | 8,822 | 19,755 | 15 | 10,933 D | 30.9% | 69.1% | 30.9% | 69.1% |
| 6,066,782 | TOTAL | 2,847,663 | 964,174 | 1,868,231 | 15,258 | 904,057 D | 33.9% | 65.6% | 34.0% | 66.0% |

# NEW JERSEY

## PRESIDENT 1960

| 1960 Census Population | County | Total Vote | Republican | Democratic | Other | Rep.-Dem. Plurality | Percentage | | | |
|---|---|---|---|---|---|---|---|---|---|---|
| | | | | | | | Total Vote | | Major Vote | |
| | | | | | | | Rep. | Dem. | Rep. | Dem. |
| 160,880 | ATLANTIC | 76,969 | 39,158 | 36,129 | 1,682 | 3,029 R | 50.9% | 46.9% | 52.0% | 48.0% |
| 780,255 | BERGEN | 381,808 | 224,969 | 156,165 | 674 | 68,804 R | 58.9% | 40.9% | 59.0% | 41.0% |
| 224,499 | BURLINGTON | 81,539 | 42,112 | 39,321 | 106 | 2,791 R | 51.6% | 48.2% | 51.7% | 48.3% |
| 392,035 | CAMDEN | 186,515 | 84,066 | 102,083 | 366 | 18,017 D | 45.1% | 54.7% | 45.2% | 54.8% |
| 48,555 | CAPE MAY | 26,222 | 16,076 | 10,137 | 9 | 5,939 R | 61.3% | 38.7% | 61.3% | 38.7% |
| 106,850 | CUMBERLAND | 44,512 | 21,283 | 23,199 | 30 | 1,916 D | 47.8% | 52.1% | 47.8% | 52.2% |
| 923,545 | ESSEX | 393,623 | 167,848 | 217,878 | 7,897 | 50,030 D | 42.6% | 55.4% | 43.5% | 56.5% |
| 134,840 | GLOUCESTER | 62,259 | 32,474 | 29,752 | 33 | 2,722 R | 52.2% | 47.8% | 52.2% | 47.8% |
| 610,734 | HUDSON | 291,292 | 113,972 | 174,754 | 2,566 | 60,782 D | 39.1% | 60.0% | 39.5% | 60.5% |
| 54,107 | HUNTERDON | 24,731 | 15,842 | 8,863 | 26 | 6,979 R | 64.1% | 35.8% | 64.1% | 35.9% |
| 266,392 | MERCER | 121,269 | 46,924 | 74,166 | 179 | 27,242 D | 38.7% | 61.2% | 38.8% | 61.2% |
| 433,856 | MIDDLESEX | 199,556 | 83,025 | 116,095 | 436 | 33,070 D | 41.6% | 58.2% | 41.7% | 58.3% |
| 334,401 | MONMOUTH | 144,060 | 81,382 | 62,434 | 244 | 18,948 R | 56.5% | 43.3% | 56.6% | 43.4% |
| 261,620 | MORRIS | 117,883 | 75,039 | 42,698 | 146 | 32,341 R | 63.7% | 36.2% | 63.7% | 36.3% |
| 108,241 | OCEAN | 51,898 | 31,430 | 20,113 | 355 | 11,317 R | 60.6% | 38.8% | 61.0% | 39.0% |
| 406,618 | PASSAIC | 179,402 | 80,853 | 90,950 | 7,599 | 10,097 D | 45.1% | 50.7% | 47.1% | 52.9% |
| 58,711 | SALEM | 26,607 | 14,192 | 12,394 | 21 | 1,798 R | 53.3% | 46.6% | 53.4% | 46.6% |
| 143,913 | SOMERSET | 64,863 | 36,200 | 28,489 | 174 | 7,711 R | 55.8% | 43.9% | 56.0% | 44.0% |
| 49,255 | SUSSEX | 23,642 | 16,362 | 7,269 | 11 | 9,093 R | 69.2% | 30.7% | 69.2% | 30.8% |
| 504,255 | UNION | 245,008 | 123,224 | 119,986 | 1,798 | 3,238 R | 50.3% | 49.0% | 50.7% | 49.3% |
| 63,220 | WARREN | 29,453 | 16,893 | 12,540 | 20 | 4,353 R | 57.4% | 42.6% | 57.4% | 42.6% |
| 6,066,782 | TOTAL | 2,773,111 | 1,363,324 | 1,385,415 | 24,372 | 22,091 D | 49.2% | 50.0% | 49.6% | 50.4% |

642

# NEW JERSEY

## ELECTION NOTES

**2004**  Other vote was 19,418 Independent (Ralph Nader); 4,514 Libertarian (Michael Badnarik); 2,750 Constitution (Michael Peroutka); 1,807 Green (David Cobb); 664 Socialist (Walter F. Brown); 575 Socialist Equality (Bill Van Auken); 530 Socialist Workers (Roger Calero).

**2000**  Other vote was 6,989 Reform (Buchanan); 6,312 Libertarian (Browne); 2,215 Independent (Hagelin); 1,880 Socialist (McReynolds); 1,409 Constitution (Phillips); 844 Socialist Workers (Harris). All of these candidates, including Nader, were listed on the ballot as Independent, with their partisan designation indicated as a "Slogan."

**1996**  Other vote was 32,465 Green (Nader); 14,763 Libertarian (Browne); 3,887 Natural Law (Hagelin); 3,440 U.S. Taxpayers (Phillips); 1,837 Socialist Workers (Harris); 1,337 Workers World (Moorehead); 537 Socialist Equality (White).

**1992**  Other vote was 6,822 Marrou (Libertarian); 4,749 Bradford (Independent); 3,513 Fulani (New Alliance); 2,670 Phillips (Taxpayers); 2,095 LaRouche (Six Million Jobs); 2,011 Warren (Socialist Workers); 1,996 Daniels (Independent); 1,867 Gritz (Populist); 1,618 Halyard (Workers League); 1,353 Hagelin (Natural Law).

**1988**  Other vote was 9,953 Lewin (Peace and Freedom); 8,421 Paul (Libertarian); 5,139 Fulani (New Alliance); 3,454 McCarthy (Consumer); 2,587 Kenoyer (Socialist); 2,446 Duke (Pupulist); 2,298 Warren (Socialist Workers); 1,020 Holmes (Workers World); 691 Winn (Workers League). Statistics presented are the final, official amended returns with adjustments in Hudson and Middlesex counties.

**1984**  Other vote was 8,404 Holmes (Workers World); 6,416 Bergland (Libertarian); 2,293 Serrette (New Alliance); 1,721 Winn (Workers League); 1,564 Hall (Communist); 1,264 Mason (Socialist Workers); 1,247 Johnson (Citizens).

**1980**  Other vote was 234,632 Anderson (The Anderson Alternative); 20,652 Clark (Libertarian); 8,203 Commoner (Citizens); 3,927 McCormack (Right to Life); 3,694 Lynen (Middle Class Candidate); 2,555 Hall (Communist); 2,198 Pulley (Socialist Workers); 1,973 McReynolds (Socialist); 1,718 Gahres (Down with Lawyers); 1,288 Griswold (Workers World); 923 Wendelken (Independent).

**1976**  Other vote was 32,717 McCarthy (Independent); 9,449 MacBride (Libertarian); 7,716 Maddox (American); 3,686 Levin (Socialist Labor); 1,662 Hall (Communist); 1,650 LaRouche (Labor); 1,184 Camejo (Socialist Workers); 1,044 Wright (People's); 554 Bubar (Prohibition); 469 Zeidler (Socialist).

**1972**  Other vote was 34,378 Schmitz (American); 5,355 Spock (People's); 4,544 Fisher (Socialist Labor); 2,233 Jenness (Socialist Workers); 1,743 Mahalchik (America First); 1,263 Hall (Communist).

**1968**  Wallace on the ballot as George Wallace party. Other vote was 8,667 Halstead (Socialist Workers); 8,084 Gregory (Peace and Freedom Alternative); 6,784 Blomen (Socialist Labor).

**1964**  Other vote was 8,183 DeBerry (Socialist Workers); 7,075 Hass (Socialist Labor). The original state canvass did not include votes cast in one precinct of Paramus borough (Bergen county). These votes have been included in the Bergen county data and the state totals adjusted to reflect this addition.

**1960**  Other vote was 11,402 Dobbs (Socialist Workers); 8,708 Lee (Conservative); 4,262 Hass (Socialist Labor).

# NEW MEXICO

## POPULAR VOTE FOR PRESIDENT 1920 TO 2004

| Year | Total Vote | Republican | | Democratic | | Other Vote | Plurality | Percentage | | | |
|------|-----------|------|-----------|------|-----------|-----------|-----------|------|------|------|------|
| | | | | | | | | Total Vote | | Major Vote | |
| | | Vote | Candidate | Vote | Candidate | | | Rep. | Dem. | Rep. | Dem. |
| 2004 | 756,304 | 376,930 | Bush, George W. | 370,942 | Kerry, John | 8,432 | 5,988 R | 49.8% | 49.0% | 50.4% | 49.6% |
| 2000 ** | 598,605 | 286,417 | Bush, George W. | 286,783 | Gore, Al | 25,405 | 366 D | 47.8% | 47.9% | 50.0% | 50.0% |
| 1996 ** | 556,074 | 232,751 | Dole, Bob | 273,495 | Clinton, Bill | 49,828 | 40,744 D | 41.9% | 49.2% | 46.0% | 54.0% |
| 1992 ** | 569,986 | 212,824 | Bush, George | 261,617 | Clinton, Bill | 95,545 | 48,793 D | 37.3% | 45.9% | 44.9% | 55.1% |
| 1988 | 521,287 | 270,341 | Bush, George | 244,497 | Dukakis, Michael S. | 6,449 | 25,844 R | 51.9% | 46.9% | 52.5% | 47.5% |
| 1984 | 514,370 | 307,101 | Reagan, Ronald | 201,769 | Mondale, Walter F. | 5,500 | 105,332 R | 59.7% | 39.2% | 60.3% | 39.7% |
| 1980 ** | 456,971 | 250,779 | Reagan, Ronald | 167,826 | Carter, Jimmy | 38,366 | 82,953 R | 54.9% | 36.7% | 59.9% | 40.1% |
| 1976 | 418,409 | 211,419 | Ford, Gerald R. | 201,148 | Carter, Jimmy | 5,842 | 10,271 R | 50.5% | 48.1% | 51.2% | 48.8% |
| 1972 | 386,241 | 235,606 | Nixon, Richard M. | 141,084 | McGovern, George S. | 9,551 | 94,522 R | 61.0% | 36.5% | 62.5% | 37.5% |
| 1968 | 327,350 | 169,692 | Nixon, Richard M. | 130,081 | Humphrey, Hubert H. | 27,577 | 39,611 R | 51.8% | 39.7% | 56.6% | 43.4% |
| 1964 | 328,645 | 132,838 | Goldwater, Barry M. | 194,015 | Johnson, Lyndon B. | 1,792 | 61,177 D | 40.4% | 59.0% | 40.6% | 59.4% |
| 1960 | 311,107 | 153,733 | Nixon, Richard M. | 156,027 | Kennedy, John F. | 1,347 | 2,294 D | 49.4% | 50.2% | 49.6% | 50.4% |
| 1956 | 253,926 | 146,788 | Eisenhower, Dwight D. | 106,098 | Stevenson, Adlai E. | 1,040 | 40,690 R | 57.8% | 41.8% | 58.0% | 42.0% |
| 1952 | 238,608 | 132,170 | Eisenhower, Dwight D. | 105,661 | Stevenson, Adlai E. | 777 | 26,509 R | 55.4% | 44.3% | 55.6% | 44.4% |
| 1948 | 187,063 | 80,303 | Dewey, Thomas E. | 105,464 | Truman, Harry S. | 1,296 | 25,161 D | 42.9% | 56.4% | 43.2% | 56.8% |
| 1944 | 152,225 | 70,688 | Dewey, Thomas E. | 81,389 | Roosevelt, Franklin D. | 148 | 10,701 D | 46.4% | 53.5% | 46.5% | 53.5% |
| 1940 | 183,258 | 79,315 | Willkie, Wendell | 103,699 | Roosevelt, Franklin D. | 244 | 24,384 D | 43.3% | 56.6% | 43.3% | 56.7% |
| 1036 | 169,135 | 61,727 | Landon, Alfred M. | 106,037 | Roosevelt, Franklin D. | 1,371 | 44,310 D | 36.5% | 62.7% | 36.8% | 63.2% |
| 1932 | 151,606 | 54,217 | Hoover, Herbert C. | 95,089 | Roosevelt, Franklin D. | 2,300 | 40,872 D | 35.8% | 62.7% | 36.3% | 63.7% |
| 1928 | 118,077 | 69,708 | Hoover, Herbert C. | 48,211 | Smith, Alfred E. | 158 | 21,497 R | 59.0% | 40.8% | 59.1% | 40.9% |
| 1924 | 112,830 | 54,745 | Coolidge, Calvin | 48,542 | Davis, John W. | 9,543 | 6,203 R | 48.5% | 43.0% | 53.0% | 47.0% |
| 1920 | 105,412 | 57,634 | Harding, Warren G. | 46,668 | Cox, James M. | 1,110 | 10,966 R | 54.7% | 44.3% | 55.3% | 44.7% |

In 2000 the other vote column includes 21,251 votes cast for Green (Nader). In 1996 the other vote column includes 32,257 votes cast for Perot. In 1992 the other vote column includes 91,895 votes cast for Perot. In 1980 the other column includes 29,459 votes for Independent (Anderson).

## ELECTORAL COLLEGE VOTE 1920 TO 2004

| Year | Total | Republican | Democratic | Other |
|------|-------|-----------|-----------|-------|
| 2004 | 5 | 5 | | |
| 2000 | 5 | | 5 | |
| 1996 | 5 | | 5 | |
| 1992 | 5 | | 5 | |
| 1988 | 5 | 5 | | |
| 1984 | 5 | 5 | | |
| 1980 | 4 | 4 | | |
| 1976 | 4 | 4 | | |
| 1972 | 4 | 4 | | |
| 1968 | 4 | 4 | | |
| 1964 | 4 | | 4 | |
| 1960 | 4 | | 4 | |
| 1956 | 4 | 4 | | |
| 1952 | 4 | 4 | | |
| 1948 | 4 | | 4 | |
| 1944 | 4 | | 4 | |
| 1940 | 3 | | 3 | |
| 1936 | 3 | | 3 | |
| 1932 | 3 | | 3 | |
| 1928 | 3 | 3 | | |
| 1924 | 3 | 3 | | |
| 1920 | 3 | 3 | | |

644

# NEW MEXICO

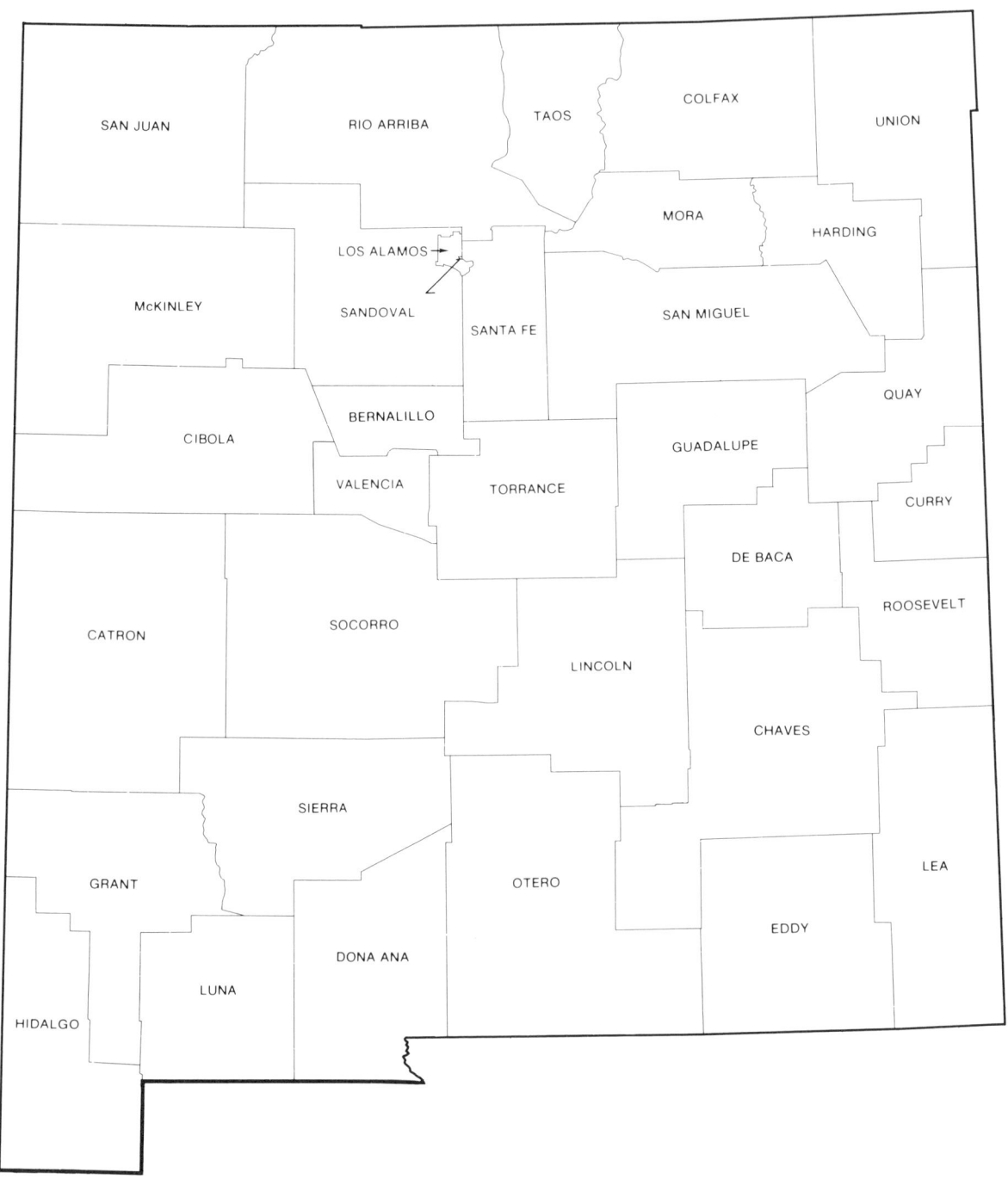

# NEW MEXICO

## PRESIDENT 2004

| 2000 Census Population | County | Total Vote | Republican | Democratic | Other | Rep.-Dem. Plurality | Percentage Total Vote Rep. | Dem. | Major Vote Rep. | Dem. |
|---|---|---|---|---|---|---|---|---|---|---|
| 556,678 | BERNALILLO | 256,811 | 121,454 | 132,252 | 3,105 | 10,798 D | 47.3% | 51.5% | 47.9% | 52.1% |
| 3,543 | CATRON | 1,993 | 1,427 | 551 | 15 | 876 R | 71.6% | 27.6% | 72.1% | 27.9% |
| 61,382 | CHAVES | 21,705 | 14,773 | 6,726 | 206 | 8,047 R | 68.1% | 31.0% | 68.7% | 31.3% |
| 25,595 | CIBOLA | 7,487 | 3,477 | 3,913 | 97 | 436 D | 46.4% | 52.3% | 47.1% | 52.9% |
| 14,189 | COLFAX | 5,968 | 3,082 | 2,824 | 62 | 258 R | 51.6% | 47.3% | 52.2% | 47.8% |
| 45,044 | CURRY | 14,286 | 10,649 | 3,541 | 96 | 7,108 R | 74.5% | 24.8% | 75.0% | 25.0% |
| 2,240 | DE BACA | 993 | 706 | 281 | 6 | 425 R | 71.1% | 28.3% | 71.5% | 28.5% |
| 174,682 | DONA ANA | 61,960 | 29,548 | 31,762 | 650 | 2,214 D | 47.7% | 51.3% | 48.2% | 51.8% |
| 51,658 | EDDY | 20,270 | 13,268 | 6,880 | 122 | 6,388 R | 65.5% | 33.9% | 65.9% | 34.1% |
| 31,002 | GRANT | 13,392 | 6,135 | 7,095 | 162 | 960 D | 45.8% | 53.0% | 46.4% | 53.6% |
| 4,680 | GUADALUPE | 2,267 | 914 | 1,340 | 13 | 426 D | 40.3% | 59.1% | 40.6% | 59.4% |
| 810 | HARDING | 644 | 380 | 259 | 5 | 121 R | 59.0% | 40.2% | 59.5% | 40.5% |
| 5,932 | HIDALGO | 1,964 | 1,081 | 861 | 22 | 220 R | 55.0% | 43.8% | 55.7% | 44.3% |
| 55,511 | LEA | 18,181 | 14,430 | 3,646 | 105 | 10,784 R | 79.4% | 20.1% | 79.8% | 20.2% |
| 19,411 | LINCOLN | 9,014 | 6,070 | 2,822 | 122 | 3,248 R | 67.3% | 31.3% | 68.3% | 31.7% |
| 18,343 | LOS ALAMOS | 11,197 | 5,810 | 5,206 | 181 | 604 R | 51.9% | 46.5% | 52.7% | 47.3% |
| 25,016 | LUNA | 7,593 | 4,164 | 3,340 | 89 | 824 R | 54.8% | 44.0% | 55.5% | 44.5% |
| 74,798 | MCKINLEY | 20,623 | 7,351 | 13,051 | 221 | 5,700 D | 35.6% | 63.3% | 36.0% | 64.0% |
| 5,180 | MORA | 2,826 | 928 | 1,876 | 22 | 948 D | 32.8% | 66.4% | 33.1% | 66.9% |
| 62,298 | OTERO | 20,764 | 14,066 | 6,433 | 265 | 7,633 R | 67.7% | 31.0% | 68.6% | 31.4% |
| 10,155 | QUAY | 4,117 | 2,661 | 1,422 | 34 | 1,239 R | 64.6% | 34.5% | 65.2% | 34.8% |
| 41,190 | RIO ARRIBA | 14,999 | 5,149 | 9,753 | 97 | 4,604 D | 34.3% | 65.0% | 34.6% | 65.4% |
| 18,018 | ROOSEVELT | 7,144 | 4,997 | 2,082 | 65 | 2,915 R | 69.9% | 29.1% | 70.6% | 29.4% |
| 89,908 | SANDOVAL | 44,541 | 22,628 | 21,421 | 492 | 1,207 R | 50.8% | 48.1% | 51.4% | 48.6% |
| 113,801 | SAN JUAN | 45,006 | 29,525 | 14,843 | 638 | 14,682 R | 65.6% | 33.0% | 66.5% | 33.5% |
| 30,126 | SAN MIGUEL | 12,116 | 3,313 | 8,683 | 120 | 5,370 D | 27.3% | 71.7% | 27.6% | 72.4% |
| 129,292 | SANTA FE | 66,200 | 18,466 | 47,074 | 660 | 28,608 D | 27.9% | 71.1% | 28.2% | 71.8% |
| 13,270 | SIERRA | 5,157 | 3,162 | 1,926 | 69 | 1,236 R | 61.3% | 37.3% | 62.1% | 37.9% |
| 18,078 | SOCORRO | 7,851 | 3,696 | 4,025 | 130 | 329 D | 47.1% | 51.3% | 47.9% | 52.1% |
| 29,979 | TAOS | 14,835 | 3,666 | 10,987 | 182 | 7,321 D | 24.7% | 74.1% | 25.0% | 75.0% |
| 16,911 | TORRANCE | 6,507 | 4,026 | 2,386 | 95 | 1,640 R | 61.9% | 36.7% | 62.8% | 37.2% |
| 4,174 | UNION | 1,881 | 1,454 | 411 | 16 | 1,043 R | 77.3% | 21.9% | 78.0% | 22.0% |
| 66,152 | VALENCIA | 26,012 | 14,474 | 11,270 | 268 | 3,204 R | 55.6% | 43.3% | 56.2% | 43.8% |
| 1,819,046 | TOTAL | 756,304 | 376,930 | 370,942 | 8,432 | 5,988 R | 49.8% | 49.0% | 50.4% | 49.6% |

# NEW MEXICO

## PRESIDENT 2000

| 2000 Census Population | County | Total Vote | Republican | Democratic | Green (Nader) | Other | Rep.-Dem. Plurality | Percentage of Total Vote | | |
|---|---|---|---|---|---|---|---|---|---|---|
| | | | | | | | | Rep. | Dem. | Green |
| 556,678 | BERNALILLO | 204,319 | 95,249 | 99,461 | 8,274 | 1,335 | 4,212 D | 46.6% | 48.7% | 4.0% |
| 3,543 | CATRON | 1,711 | 1,273 | 353 | 57 | 28 | 920 R | 74.4% | 20.6% | 3.3% |
| 61,382 | CHAVES | 18,149 | 11,378 | 6,340 | 307 | 124 | 5,038 R | 62.7% | 34.9% | 1.7% |
| 25,595 | CIBOLA | 7,088 | 2,752 | 4,127 | 164 | 45 | 1,375 D | 38.8% | 58.2% | 2.3% |
| 14,189 | COLFAX | 5,461 | 2,600 | 2,653 | 163 | 45 | 53 D | 47.6% | 48.6% | 3.0% |
| 45,044 | CURRY | 11,969 | 8,301 | 3,471 | 147 | 50 | 4,830 R | 69.4% | 29.0% | 1.2% |
| 2,240 | DE BACA | 982 | 612 | 349 | 12 | 9 | 263 R | 62.3% | 35.5% | 1.2% |
| 174,682 | DONA ANA | 46,653 | 21,263 | 23,912 | 1,158 | 320 | 2,649 D | 45.6% | 51.3% | 2.5% |
| 51,658 | EDDY | 17,787 | 10,335 | 7,108 | 256 | 88 | 3,227 R | 58.1% | 40.0% | 1.4% |
| 31,002 | GRANT | 11,241 | 4,961 | 5,673 | 530 | 77 | 712 D | 44.1% | 50.5% | 4.7% |
| 4,680 | GUADALUPE | 1,651 | 548 | 1,076 | 24 | 3 | 528 D | 33.2% | 65.2% | 1.5% |
| 810 | HARDING | 593 | 366 | 214 | 9 | 4 | 152 R | 61.7% | 36.1% | 1.5% |
| 5,932 | HIDALGO | 1,834 | 954 | 839 | 28 | 13 | 115 R | 52.0% | 45.7% | 1.5% |
| 55,511 | LEA | 14,256 | 10,157 | 3,855 | 169 | 75 | 6,302 R | 71.2% | 27.0% | 1.2% |
| 19,411 | LINCOLN | 6,772 | 4,458 | 2,027 | 168 | 119 | 2,431 R | 65.8% | 29.9% | 2.5% |
| 18,343 | LOS ALAMOS | 10,218 | 5,623 | 4,149 | 329 | 117 | 1,474 R | 55.0% | 40.6% | 3.2% |
| 25,016 | LUNA | 6,612 | 3,395 | 2,975 | 186 | 56 | 420 R | 51.3% | 45.0% | 2.8% |
| 74,798 | MCKINLEY | 15,879 | 5,070 | 10,281 | 392 | 136 | 5,211 D | 31.9% | 64.7% | 2.5% |
| 5,180 | MORA | 2,191 | 668 | 1,456 | 49 | 18 | 788 D | 30.5% | 66.5% | 2.2% |
| 62,298 | OTERO | 16,204 | 10,258 | 5,465 | 338 | 143 | 4,793 R | 63.3% | 33.7% | 2.1% |
| 10,155 | QUAY | 3,844 | 2,292 | 1,471 | 51 | 30 | 821 R | 59.6% | 38.3% | 1.3% |
| 41,190 | RIO ARRIBA | 12,097 | 3,495 | 8,169 | 377 | 56 | 4,674 D | 28.9% | 67.5% | 3.1% |
| 18,018 | ROOSEVELT | 5,651 | 3,762 | 1,762 | 98 | 29 | 2,000 R | 66.6% | 31.2% | 1.7% |
| 89,908 | SANDOVAL | 31,755 | 15,423 | 14,899 | 1,211 | 222 | 524 R | 48.6% | 46.9% | 3.8% |
| 113,801 | SAN JUAN | 34,657 | 21,434 | 11,980 | 923 | 320 | 9,454 R | 61.8% | 34.6% | 2.7% |
| 30,126 | SAN MIGUEL | 9,161 | 2,215 | 6,540 | 344 | 62 | 4,325 D | 24.2% | 71.4% | 3.8% |
| 129,292 | SANTA FE | 49,471 | 13,974 | 32,017 | 3,215 | 265 | 18,043 D | 28.2% | 64.7% | 6.5% |
| 13,270 | SIERRA | 4,586 | 2,721 | 1,689 | 132 | 44 | 1,032 R | 59.3% | 36.8% | 2.9% |
| 18,078 | SOCORRO | 6,826 | 3,173 | 3,294 | 279 | 80 | 121 D | 46.5% | 48.3% | 4.1% |
| 29,979 | TAOS | 10,895 | 2,744 | 7,039 | 1,064 | 48 | 4,295 D | 25.2% | 64.6% | 9.8% |
| 16,911 | TORRANCE | 4,960 | 2,891 | 1,868 | 163 | 38 | 1,023 R | 58.3% | 37.7% | 3.3% |
| 4,174 | UNION | 1,755 | 1,269 | 452 | 19 | 15 | 817 R | 72.3% | 25.8% | 1.1% |
| 66,152 | VALENCIA | 21,377 | 10,803 | 9,819 | 615 | 140 | 984 R | 50.5% | 45.9% | 2.9% |
| 1,819,046 | TOTAL | 598,605 | 286,417 | 286,783 | 21,251 | 4,154 | 366 D | 47.8% | 47.9% | 3.6% |

# NEW MEXICO

## PRESIDENT 1996

| 1995 Census Pop. Est. | County | Total Vote | Republican | Democratic | Reform (Perot) | Other | Rep.-Dem. Plurality | Percentage of Total Vote Rep. | Dem. | Reform |
|---|---|---|---|---|---|---|---|---|---|---|
| 522,328 | BERNALILLO | 182,543 | 78,832 | 88,140 | 8,708 | 6,863 | 9,308 D | 43.2% | 48.3% | 4.8% |
| 2,719 | CATRON | 1,524 | 923 | 423 | 114 | 64 | 500 R | 60.6% | 27.8% | 7.5% |
| 61,770 | CHAVES | 18,519 | 9,991 | 7,014 | 1,271 | 243 | 2,977 R | 53.9% | 37.9% | 6.9% |
| 25,166 | CIBOLA | 6,880 | 2,245 | 4,030 | 488 | 117 | 1,785 D | 32.6% | 58.6% | 7.1% |
| 13,860 | COLFAX | 5,166 | 1,975 | 2,659 | 411 | 121 | 684 D | 38.2% | 51.5% | 8.0% |
| 47,464 | CURRY | 12,447 | 7,378 | 4,116 | 842 | 111 | 3,262 R | 59.3% | 33.1% | 6.8% |
| 2,373 | DE BACA | 1,093 | 489 | 509 | 86 | 9 | 20 D | 44.7% | 46.6% | 7.9% |
| 158,849 | DONA ANA | 43,564 | 17,541 | 22,766 | 2,269 | 988 | 5,225 D | 40.3% | 52.3% | 5.2% |
| 52,758 | EDDY | 18,998 | 8,534 | 8,959 | 1,297 | 208 | 425 D | 44.9% | 47.2% | 6.8% |
| 30,076 | GRANT | 10,928 | 3,993 | 5,860 | 778 | 297 | 1,867 D | 36.5% | 53.6% | 7.1% |
| 4,075 | GUADALUPE | 1,736 | 436 | 1,208 | 79 | 13 | 772 D | 25.1% | 69.6% | 4.6% |
| 913 | HARDING | 616 | 321 | 264 | 28 | 3 | 57 R | 52.1% | 42.9% | 4.5% |
| 6,259 | HIDALGO | 1,952 | 789 | 943 | 209 | 11 | 154 D | 40.4% | 48.3% | 10.7% |
| 56,793 | LEA | 14,666 | 7,661 | 5,393 | 1,465 | 147 | 2,268 R | 52.2% | 36.8% | 10.0% |
| 14,853 | LINCOLN | 6,411 | 3,396 | 2,209 | 666 | 140 | 1,187 R | 53.0% | 34.5% | 10.4% |
| 18,604 | LOS ALAMOS | 9,932 | 4,999 | 3,983 | 560 | 390 | 1,016 R | 50.3% | 40.1% | 5.6% |
| 22,121 | LUNA | 6,326 | 2,616 | 3,001 | 598 | 111 | 385 D | 41.4% | 47.4% | 9.5% |
| 66,991 | MCKINLEY | 15,526 | 4,470 | 10,124 | 650 | 282 | 5,654 D | 28.8% | 65.2% | 4.2% |
| 4,581 | MORA | 2,394 | 561 | 1,646 | 131 | 56 | 1,085 D | 23.4% | 68.8% | 5.5% |
| 55,027 | OTERO | 16,337 | 9,065 | 5,938 | 1,096 | 238 | 3,127 R | 55.5% | 36.3% | 6.7% |
| 10,488 | QUAY | 4,176 | 1,943 | 1,830 | 377 | 26 | 113 R | 46.5% | 43.8% | 9.0% |
| 36,959 | RIO ARRIBA | 11,305 | 2,551 | 7,965 | 469 | 320 | 5,414 D | 22.6% | 70.5% | 4.1% |
| 18,465 | ROOSEVELT | 5,869 | 3,245 | 2,097 | 467 | 60 | 1,148 R | 55.3% | 35.7% | 8.0% |
| 79,781 | SANDOVAL | 26,448 | 11,015 | 13,081 | 1,482 | 870 | 2,066 D | 41.6% | 49.5% | 5.6% |
| 100,470 | SAN JUAN | 32,553 | 17,478 | 12,070 | 2,355 | 650 | 5,408 R | 53.7% | 37.1% | 7.2% |
| 28,490 | SAN MIGUEL | 9,647 | 1,938 | 6,995 | 405 | 309 | 5,057 D | 20.1% | 72.5% | 4.2% |
| 116,414 | SANTA FE | 42,446 | 10,857 | 26,349 | 1,846 | 3,394 | 15,492 D | 25.6% | 62.1% | 4.3% |
| 10,600 | SIERRA | 4,805 | 2,140 | 2,154 | 431 | 80 | 14 D | 44.5% | 44.8% | 9.0% |
| 15,853 | SOCORRO | 6,364 | 2,315 | 3,374 | 455 | 220 | 1,059 D | 36.4% | 53.0% | 7.1% |
| 25,581 | TAOS | 10,053 | 2,126 | 6,635 | 545 | 747 | 4,509 D | 21.1% | 66.0% | 5.4% |
| 12,835 | TORRANCE | 4,655 | 2,154 | 2,072 | 332 | 97 | 82 R | 46.3% | 44.5% | 7.1% |
| 4,139 | UNION | 1,650 | 995 | 519 | 125 | 11 | 476 R | 60.3% | 31.5% | 7.6% |
| 57,746 | VALENCIA | 18,545 | 7,779 | 9,169 | 1,222 | 375 | 1,390 D | 41.9% | 49.4% | 6.6% |
| 1,685,401 | TOTAL | 556,074 | 232,751 | 273,495 | 32,257 | 17,571 | 40,744 D | 41.9% | 49.2% | 5.8% |

# NEW MEXICO

## PRESIDENT 1992

| 1990 Census Population | County | Total Vote | Republican | Democratic | Perot | Other | Plurality | Percentage Total Vote | | |
|---|---|---|---|---|---|---|---|---|---|---|
| | | | | | | | | Rep. | Dem. | Perot |
| 480,577 | BERNALILLO | 200,698 | 77,304 | 90,863 | 31,241 | 1,290 | 13,559 D | 38.5% | 45.3% | 15.6% |
| 2,563 | CATRON | 1,553 | 771 | 465 | 289 | 28 | 306 R | 49.6% | 29.9% | 18.6% |
| 57,849 | CHAVES | 18,898 | 8,872 | 6,360 | 3,590 | 76 | 2,512 R | 46.9% | 33.7% | 19.0% |
| 23,794 | CIBOLA | 6,284 | 2,051 | 3,334 | 847 | 52 | 1,283 D | 32.6% | 53.1% | 13.5% |
| 12,925 | COLFAX | 5,228 | 1,730 | 2,607 | 871 | 20 | 877 D | 33.1% | 49.9% | 16.7% |
| 42,207 | CURRY | 12,633 | 6,831 | 3,699 | 2,056 | 47 | 3,132 R | 54.1% | 29.3% | 16.3% |
| 2,252 | DE BACA | 1,185 | 526 | 451 | 204 | 4 | 75 R | 44.4% | 38.1% | 17.2% |
| 135,510 | DONA ANA | 44,217 | 16,308 | 19,894 | 7,682 | 333 | 3,586 D | 36.9% | 45.0% | 17.4% |
| 48,605 | EDDY | 18,202 | 7,313 | 7,409 | 3,430 | 50 | 96 D | 40.2% | 40.7% | 18.8% |
| 27,676 | GRANT | 10,277 | 2,917 | 5,603 | 1,685 | 72 | 2,686 D | 28.4% | 54.5% | 16.4% |
| 4,156 | GUADALUPE | 2,102 | 691 | 1,225 | 173 | 13 | 534 D | 32.9% | 58.3% | 8.2% |
| 987 | HARDING | 678 | 312 | 268 | 98 | | 44 R | 46.0% | 39.5% | 14.5% |
| 5,958 | HIDALGO | 2,315 | 871 | 995 | 442 | 7 | 124 D | 37.6% | 43.0% | 19.1% |
| 55,765 | LEA | 16,311 | 7,921 | 5,047 | 3,233 | 110 | 2,874 R | 48.6% | 30.9% | 19.8% |
| 12,219 | LINCOLN | 5,857 | 2,669 | 1,730 | 1,431 | 27 | 939 R | 45.6% | 29.5% | 24.4% |
| 18,115 | LOS ALAMOS | 10,642 | 4,320 | 3,897 | 2,339 | 86 | 423 R | 40.6% | 36.6% | 22.0% |
| 18,110 | LUNA | 6,272 | 2,166 | 2,637 | 1,445 | 24 | 471 D | 34.5% | 42.0% | 23.0% |
| 60,686 | MCKINLEY | 15,531 | 4,720 | 9,405 | 1,304 | 102 | 4,685 D | 30.4% | 60.6% | 8.4% |
| 4,264 | MORA | 2,421 | 668 | 1,555 | 188 | 10 | 887 D | 27.6% | 64.2% | 7.8% |
| 51,928 | OTERO | 16,203 | 7,481 | 5,377 | 3,257 | 88 | 2,104 R | 46.2% | 33.2% | 20.1% |
| 10,823 | QUAY | 4,289 | 1,759 | 1,758 | 755 | 17 | 1 R | 41.0% | 41.0% | 17.6% |
| 34,365 | RIO ARRIBA | 11,542 | 2,680 | 7,832 | 984 | 46 | 5,152 D | 23.2% | 67.9% | 8.5% |
| 16,702 | ROOSEVELT | 6,513 | 3,215 | 2,172 | 1,085 | 41 | 1,043 R | 49.4% | 33.3% | 16.7% |
| 63,319 | SANDOVAL | 23,574 | 8,491 | 10,951 | 3,954 | 178 | 2,460 D | 36.0% | 46.5% | 16.8% |
| 91,605 | SAN JUAN | 30,281 | 13,415 | 11,302 | 5,351 | 213 | 2,113 R | 44.3% | 37.3% | 17.7% |
| 25,743 | SAN MIGUEL | 9,387 | 2,183 | 6,186 | 965 | 53 | 4,003 D | 23.3% | 65.9% | 10.3% |
| 98,928 | SANTA FE | 42,917 | 9,684 | 27,189 | 5,656 | 388 | 17,505 D | 22.6% | 63.4% | 13.2% |
| 9,912 | SIERRA | 4,418 | 1,562 | 1,771 | 1,055 | 30 | 209 D | 35.4% | 40.1% | 23.9% |
| 14,764 | SOCORRO | 6,088 | 2,186 | 2,908 | 918 | 76 | 722 D | 35.9% | 47.8% | 15.1% |
| 23,118 | TAOS | 10,681 | 2,260 | 7,051 | 1,300 | 70 | 4,791 D | 21.2% | 66.0% | 12.2% |
| 10,285 | TORRANCE | 4,167 | 1,667 | 1,662 | 810 | 28 | 5 R | 40.0% | 39.9% | 19.4% |
| 4,124 | UNION | 1,854 | 975 | 519 | 355 | 5 | 456 R | 52.6% | 28.0% | 19.1% |
| 45,235 | VALENCIA | 16,768 | 6,305 | 7,495 | 2,902 | 66 | 1,190 D | 37.6% | 44.7% | 17.3% |
| 1,515,069 | TOTAL | 569,986 | 212,824 | 261,617 | 91,895 | 3,650 | 48,793 D | 37.3% | 45.9% | 16.1% |

# NEW MEXICO

## PRESIDENT 1988

| 1980 Census Population | County | Total Vote | Republican | Democratic | Other | Rep.-Dem. Plurality | Percentage | | | |
|---|---|---|---|---|---|---|---|---|---|---|
| | | | | | | | Total Vote | | Major Vote | |
| | | | | | | | Rep. | Dem. | Rep. | Dem. |
| 419,700 | BERNALILLO | 173,135 | 92,830 | 78,346 | 1,959 | 14,484 R | 53.6% | 45.3% | 54.2% | 45.8% |
| 2,720 | CATRON | 1,486 | 925 | 490 | 71 | 435 R | 62.2% | 33.0% | 65.4% | 34.6% |
| 51,103 | CHAVES | 20,303 | 13,367 | 6,730 | 206 | 6,637 R | 65.8% | 33.1% | 66.5% | 33.5% |
| 30,364 | CIBOLA | 6,137 | 2,640 | 3,458 | 39 | 818 D | 43.0% | 56.3% | 43.3% | 56.7% |
| 13,667 | COLFAX | 5,085 | 2,256 | 2,785 | 44 | 529 D | 44.4% | 54.8% | 44.8% | 55.2% |
| 42,019 | CURRY | 12,138 | 8,032 | 3,995 | 111 | 4,037 R | 66.2% | 32.9% | 66.8% | 33.2% |
| 2,454 | DE BACA | 1,136 | 643 | 480 | 13 | 163 R | 56.6% | 42.3% | 57.3% | 42.7% |
| 96,340 | DONA ANA | 41,747 | 21,582 | 19,608 | 557 | 1,974 R | 51.7% | 47.0% | 52.4% | 47.6% |
| 47,855 | EDDY | 18,535 | 9,805 | 8,544 | 186 | 1,261 R | 52.9% | 46.1% | 53.4% | 46.6% |
| 26,204 | GRANT | 9,735 | 4,196 | 5,443 | 96 | 1,247 D | 43.1% | 55.9% | 43.5% | 56.5% |
| 4,496 | GUADALUPE | 2,119 | 861 | 1,243 | 15 | 382 D | 40.6% | 58.7% | 40.9% | 59.1% |
| 1,090 | HARDING | 672 | 377 | 291 | 4 | 86 R | 56.1% | 43.3% | 56.4% | 43.6% |
| 6,049 | HIDALGO | 2,020 | 1,100 | 901 | 19 | 199 R | 54.5% | 44.6% | 55.0% | 45.0% |
| 55,993 | LEA | 17,303 | 11,309 | 5,879 | 115 | 5,430 R | 65.4% | 34.0% | 65.8% | 34.2% |
| 10,997 | LINCOLN | 5,288 | 3,511 | 1,690 | 87 | 1,821 R | 66.4% | 32.0% | 67.5% | 32.5% |
| 17,599 | LOS ALAMOS | 10,153 | 6,622 | 3,275 | 256 | 3,347 R | 65.2% | 32.3% | 66.9% | 33.1% |
| 15,585 | LUNA | 6,636 | 3,415 | 3,066 | 155 | 349 R | 51.5% | 46.2% | 52.7% | 47.3% |
| 56,449 | MCKINLEY | 15,467 | 5,694 | 9,595 | 178 | 3,901 D | 36.8% | 62.0% | 37.2% | 62.8% |
| 4,205 | MORA | 2,545 | 923 | 1,601 | 21 | 678 D | 36.3% | 62.9% | 36.6% | 63.4% |
| 44,665 | OTERO | 15,478 | 9,984 | 5,284 | 210 | 4,700 R | 64.5% | 34.1% | 65.4% | 34.6% |
| 10,577 | QUAY | 4,412 | 2,454 | 1,901 | 57 | 553 R | 55.6% | 43.1% | 56.3% | 43.7% |
| 29,282 | RIO ARRIBA | 10,626 | 3,024 | 7,503 | 99 | 4,479 D | 28.5% | 70.6% | 28.7% | 71.3% |
| 15,695 | ROOSEVELT | 5,681 | 3,589 | 2,033 | 59 | 1,556 R | 63.2% | 35.8% | 63.8% | 36.2% |
| 34,799 | SANDOVAL | 19,011 | 9,411 | 9,332 | 268 | 79 R | 49.5% | 49.1% | 50.2% | 49.8% |
| 81,433 | SAN JUAN | 27,750 | 16,202 | 11,094 | 454 | 5,108 R | 58.4% | 40.0% | 59.4% | 40.6% |
| 22,751 | SAN MIGUEL | 9,023 | 2,763 | 6,131 | 129 | 3,368 D | 30.6% | 67.9% | 31.1% | 68.9% |
| 75,360 | SANTA FE | 36,927 | 12,891 | 23,581 | 455 | 10,690 D | 34.9% | 63.9% | 35.3% | 64.7% |
| 8,454 | SIERRA | 4,165 | 2,507 | 1,595 | 63 | 912 R | 60.2% | 38.3% | 61.1% | 38.9% |
| 12,566 | SOCORRO | 6,217 | 3,114 | 2,960 | 143 | 154 R | 50.1% | 47.6% | 51.3% | 48.7% |
| 19,456 | TAOS | 9,259 | 2,897 | 6,271 | 91 | 3,374 D | 31.3% | 67.7% | 31.6% | 68.4% |
| 7,491 | TORRANCE | 3,938 | 2,252 | 1,618 | 68 | 634 R | 57.2% | 41.1% | 58.2% | 41.8% |
| 4,725 | UNION | 1,960 | 1,291 | 638 | 31 | 653 R | 65.9% | 32.6% | 66.9% | 33.1% |
| 30,751 | VALENCIA | 15,200 | 7,874 | 7,136 | 190 | 738 R | 51.8% | 46.9% | 52.5% | 47.5% |
| 1,302,894 | TOTAL | 521,287 | 270,341 | 244,497 | 6,449 | 25,844 R | 51.9% | 46.9% | 52.5% | 47.5% |

650

# NEW MEXICO

## PRESIDENT 1984

| 1980 Census Population | County | Total Vote | Republican | Democratic | Other | Rep.-Dem. Plurality | | Percentage Total Vote Rep. | Dem. | Major Vote Rep. | Dem. |
|---|---|---|---|---|---|---|---|---|---|---|---|
| 419,700 | BERNALILLO | 174,262 | 104,694 | 67,789 | 1,779 | 36,905 | R | 60.1% | 38.9% | 60.7% | 39.3% |
| 2,720 | CATRON | 1,415 | 970 | 418 | 27 | 552 | R | 68.6% | 29.5% | 69.9% | 30.1% |
| 51,103 | CHAVES | 20,782 | 15,248 | 5,332 | 202 | 9,916 | R | 73.4% | 25.7% | 74.1% | 25.9% |
| 30,364 | CIBOLA | 6,740 | 3,578 | 3,140 | 22 | 438 | R | 53.1% | 46.6% | 53.3% | 46.7% |
| 13,667 | COLFAX | 5,485 | 2,994 | 2,435 | 56 | 559 | R | 54.6% | 44.4% | 55.1% | 44.9% |
| 42,019 | CURRY | 12,415 | 9,188 | 3,108 | 119 | 6,080 | R | 74.0% | 25.0% | 74.7% | 25.3% |
| 2,454 | DE BACA | 1,159 | 756 | 386 | 17 | 370 | R | 65.2% | 33.3% | 66.2% | 33.8% |
| 96,340 | DONA ANA | 36,393 | 22,153 | 13,878 | 362 | 8,275 | R | 60.9% | 38.1% | 61.5% | 38.5% |
| 47,855 | EDDY | 19,365 | 11,810 | 7,364 | 191 | 4,446 | R | 61.0% | 38.0% | 61.6% | 38.4% |
| 26,204 | GRANT | 10,840 | 4,979 | 5,755 | 106 | 776 | D | 45.9% | 53.1% | 46.4% | 53.6% |
| 4,496 | GUADALUPE | 1,966 | 990 | 946 | 30 | 44 | R | 50.4% | 48.1% | 51.1% | 48.9% |
| 1,090 | HARDING | 631 | 401 | 224 | 6 | 177 | R | 63.5% | 35.5% | 64.2% | 35.8% |
| 6,049 | HIDALGO | 2,161 | 1,282 | 860 | 19 | 422 | R | 59.3% | 39.8% | 59.9% | 40.1% |
| 55,993 | LEA | 19,357 | 14,569 | 4,558 | 230 | 10,011 | R | 75.3% | 23.5% | 76.2% | 23.8% |
| 10,997 | LINCOLN | 5,182 | 3,992 | 1,134 | 56 | 2,858 | R | 77.0% | 21.9% | 77.9% | 22.1% |
| 17,599 | LOS ALAMOS | 9,888 | 6,882 | 2,859 | 147 | 4,023 | R | 69.6% | 28.9% | 70.6% | 29.4% |
| 15,585 | LUNA | 6,776 | 4,145 | 2,557 | 74 | 1,588 | R | 61.2% | 37.7% | 61.8% | 38.2% |
| 56,449 | MCKINLEY | 14,643 | 6,557 | 7,915 | 171 | 1,358 | D | 44.8% | 54.1% | 45.3% | 54.7% |
| 4,205 | MORA | 2,287 | 1,017 | 1,235 | 35 | 218 | D | 44.5% | 54.0% | 45.2% | 54.8% |
| 44,665 | OTERO | 14,087 | 9,751 | 4,167 | 169 | 5,584 | R | 69.2% | 29.6% | 70.1% | 29.9% |
| 10,577 | QUAY | 4,253 | 2,842 | 1,368 | 43 | 1,474 | R | 66.8% | 32.2% | 67.5% | 32.5% |
| 29,282 | RIO ARRIBA | 11,146 | 4,116 | 6,938 | 92 | 2,822 | D | 36.9% | 62.2% | 37.2% | 62.8% |
| 15,695 | ROOSEVELT | 6,363 | 4,598 | 1,696 | 69 | 2,902 | R | 72.3% | 26.7% | 73.1% | 26.9% |
| 34,799 | SANDOVAL | 16,246 | 9,005 | 7,080 | 161 | 1,925 | R | 55.4% | 43.6% | 56.0% | 44.0% |
| 81,433 | SAN JUAN | 27,910 | 18,690 | 8,963 | 257 | 9,727 | R | 67.0% | 32.1% | 67.6% | 32.4% |
| 22,751 | SAN MIGUEL | 8,850 | 3,485 | 5,227 | 138 | 1,742 | D | 39.4% | 59.1% | 40.0% | 60.0% |
| 75,360 | SANTA FE | 34,552 | 15,886 | 18,262 | 404 | 2,376 | D | 46.0% | 52.9% | 46.5% | 53.5% |
| 8,454 | SIERRA | 4,035 | 2,663 | 1,335 | 37 | 1,328 | R | 66.0% | 33.1% | 66.6% | 33.4% |
| 12,566 | SOCORRO | 6,048 | 3,403 | 2,541 | 104 | 862 | R | 56.3% | 42.0% | 57.3% | 42.7% |
| 19,456 | TAOS | 9,432 | 4,154 | 5,144 | 134 | 990 | D | 44.0% | 54.5% | 44.7% | 55.3% |
| 7,491 | TORRANCE | 3,633 | 2,326 | 1,274 | 33 | 1,052 | R | 64.0% | 35.1% | 64.6% | 35.4% |
| 4,725 | UNION | 2,019 | 1,503 | 488 | 28 | 1,015 | R | 74.4% | 24.2% | 75.5% | 24.5% |
| 30,751 | VALENCIA | 14,049 | 8,474 | 5,393 | 182 | 3,081 | R | 60.3% | 38.4% | 61.1% | 38.9% |
| 1,302,894 | TOTAL | 514,370 | 307,101 | 201,769 | 5,500 | 105,332 | R | 59.7% | 39.2% | 60.3% | 39.7% |

# NEW MEXICO

## PRESIDENT 1980

| 1980 Census Population | County | Total Vote | Republican | Democratic | Other | Rep.-Dem. Plurality | Total Vote Rep. | Dem. | Major Vote Rep. | Dem. |
|---|---|---|---|---|---|---|---|---|---|---|
| 419,700 | BERNALILLO | 157,284 | 83,956 | 54,841 | 18,487 | 29,115 R | 53.4% | 34.9% | 60.5% | 39.5% |
| 2,720 | CATRON | 1,448 | 906 | 466 | 76 | 440 R | 62.6% | 32.2% | 66.0% | 34.0% |
| 51,103 | CHAVES | 18,657 | 12,502 | 5,350 | 805 | 7,152 R | 67.0% | 28.7% | 70.0% | 30.0% |
|  | CIBOLA | -- | -- | -- | -- | -- | -- | -- | -- | -- |
| 13,667 | COLFAX | 5,094 | 2,537 | 2,266 | 291 | 271 R | 49.8% | 44.5% | 52.8% | 47.2% |
| 42,019 | CURRY | 12,070 | 8,132 | 3,622 | 316 | 4,510 R | 67.4% | 30.0% | 69.2% | 30.8% |
| 2,454 | DE BACA | 1,167 | 655 | 484 | 28 | 171 R | 56.1% | 41.5% | 57.5% | 42.5% |
| 96,340 | DONA ANA | 28,852 | 15,539 | 10,839 | 2,474 | 4,700 R | 53.9% | 37.6% | 58.9% | 41.1% |
| 47,855 | EDDY | 17,417 | 9,817 | 7,028 | 572 | 2,789 R | 56.4% | 40.4% | 58.3% | 41.7% |
| 26,204 | GRANT | 9,778 | 4,628 | 4,600 | 550 | 28 R | 47.3% | 47.0% | 50.2% | 49.8% |
| 4,496 | GUADALUPE | 2,145 | 1,065 | 980 | 100 | 85 R | 49.7% | 45.7% | 52.1% | 47.9% |
| 1,090 | HARDING | 601 | 356 | 225 | 20 | 131 R | 59.2% | 37.4% | 61.3% | 38.7% |
| 6,049 | HIDALGO | 1,993 | 1,059 | 840 | 94 | 219 R | 53.1% | 42.1% | 55.8% | 44.2% |
| 55,993 | LEA | 16,261 | 10,727 | 5,006 | 528 | 5,721 R | 66.0% | 30.8% | 68.2% | 31.8% |
| 10,997 | LINCOLN | 4,393 | 3,009 | 1,127 | 257 | 1,882 R | 68.5% | 25.7% | 72.8% | 27.2% |
| 17,599 | LOS ALAMOS | 9,383 | 5,460 | 2,368 | 1,555 | 3,092 R | 58.2% | 25.2% | 69.7% | 30.3% |
| 15,585 | LUNA | 6,373 | 3,636 | 2,443 | 294 | 1,193 R | 57.1% | 38.3% | 59.8% | 40.2% |
| 56,449 | MCKINLEY | 12,934 | 7,329 | 4,869 | 736 | 2,460 R | 56.7% | 37.6% | 60.1% | 39.9% |
| 4,205 | MORA | 2,385 | 1,037 | 1,274 | 74 | 237 D | 43.5% | 53.4% | 44.9% | 55.1% |
| 44,665 | OTERO | 11,995 | 7,210 | 4,111 | 674 | 3,099 R | 60.1% | 34.3% | 63.7% | 36.3% |
| 10,577 | QUAY | 4,026 | 2,499 | 1,422 | 105 | 1,077 R | 62.1% | 35.3% | 63.7% | 36.3% |
| 29,282 | RIO ARRIBA | 10,594 | 3,794 | 6,245 | 555 | 2,451 D | 35.8% | 58.9% | 37.8% | 62.2% |
| 15,695 | ROOSEVELT | 6,497 | 3,950 | 2,240 | 307 | 1,710 R | 60.8% | 34.5% | 63.8% | 36.2% |
| 34,799 | SANDOVAL | 12,597 | 6,762 | 4,740 | 1,095 | 2,022 R | 53.7% | 37.6% | 58.8% | 41.2% |
| 81,433 | SAN JUAN | 23,556 | 15,579 | 6,705 | 1,272 | 8,874 R | 66.1% | 28.5% | 69.9% | 30.1% |
| 22,751 | SAN MIGUEL | 8,369 | 3,292 | 4,514 | 563 | 1,222 D | 39.3% | 53.9% | 42.2% | 57.8% |
| 75,360 | SANTA FE | 28,871 | 12,361 | 12,658 | 3,852 | 297 D | 42.8% | 43.8% | 49.4% | 50.6% |
| 8,454 | SIERRA | 3,567 | 2,222 | 1,169 | 176 | 1,053 R | 62.3% | 32.8% | 65.5% | 34.5% |
| 12,566 | SOCORRO | 5,427 | 2,685 | 2,226 | 516 | 459 R | 49.5% | 41.0% | 54.7% | 45.3% |
| 19,456 | TAOS | 8,603 | 3,584 | 4,346 | 673 | 762 D | 41.7% | 50.5% | 45.2% | 54.8% |
| 7,491 | TORRANCE | 3,322 | 1,907 | 1,261 | 154 | 646 R | 57.4% | 38.0% | 60.2% | 39.8% |
| 4,725 | UNION | 2,140 | 1,407 | 675 | 58 | 732 R | 65.7% | 31.5% | 67.6% | 32.4% |
| 61,115 | VALENCIA | 19,172 | 11,177 | 6,886 | 1,109 | 4,291 R | 58.3% | 35.9% | 61.9% | 38.1% |
| 1,302,894 | TOTAL | 456,971 | 250,779 | 167,826 | 38,366 | 82,953 R | 54.9% | 36.7% | 59.9% | 40.1% |

# NEW MEXICO

## PRESIDENT 1976

| 1970 Census Population | County | Total Vote | Republican | Democratic | Other | Rep.-Dem. Plurality | | Percentage | | | |
|---|---|---|---|---|---|---|---|---|---|---|---|
| | | | | | | | | Total Vote | | Major Vote | |
| | | | | | | | | Rep. | Dem. | Rep. | Dem. |
| 315,774 | BERNALILLO | 142,921 | 76,614 | 63,949 | 2,358 | 12,665 | R | 53.6% | 44.7% | 54.5% | 45.5% |
| 2,198 | CATRON | 1,135 | 602 | 517 | 16 | 85 | R | 53.0% | 45.6% | 53.8% | 46.2% |
| 43,335 | CHAVES | 17,985 | 10,631 | 7,139 | 215 | 3,492 | R | 59.1% | 39.7% | 59.8% | 40.2% |
| | CIBOLA | — | — | — | — | — | | — | — | — | — |
| 12,170 | COLFAX | 5,018 | 2,259 | 2,718 | 41 | 459 | D | 45.0% | 54.2% | 45.4% | 54.6% |
| 39,517 | CURRY | 11,374 | 6,232 | 5,004 | 138 | 1,228 | R | 54.8% | 44.0% | 55.5% | 44.5% |
| 2,547 | DE BACA | 1,160 | 556 | 597 | 7 | 41 | D | 47.9% | 51.5% | 48.2% | 51.8% |
| 69,773 | DONA ANA | 26,261 | 13,888 | 12,036 | 337 | 1,852 | R | 52.9% | 45.8% | 53.6% | 46.4% |
| 41,119 | EDDY | 16,905 | 7,698 | 9,073 | 134 | 1,375 | D | 45.5% | 53.7% | 45.9% | 54.1% |
| 22,030 | GRANT | 9,349 | 4,095 | 5,176 | 78 | 1,081 | D | 43.8% | 55.4% | 44.2% | 55.8% |
| 4,969 | GUADALUPE | 2,456 | 1,047 | 1,379 | 30 | 332 | D | 42.6% | 56.1% | 43.2% | 56.8% |
| 1,348 | HARDING | 678 | 387 | 285 | 6 | 102 | R | 57.1% | 42.0% | 57.6% | 42.4% |
| 4,734 | HIDALGO | 1,837 | 891 | 938 | 8 | 47 | D | 48.5% | 51.1% | 48.7% | 51.3% |
| 49,554 | LEA | 15,457 | 8,773 | 6,533 | 151 | 2,240 | R | 56.8% | 42.3% | 57.3% | 42.7% |
| 7,560 | LINCOLN | 3,772 | 2,320 | 1,415 | 37 | 905 | R | 61.5% | 37.5% | 62.1% | 37.9% |
| 15,198 | LOS ALAMOS | 8,429 | 5,383 | 2,890 | 156 | 2,493 | R | 63.9% | 34.3% | 65.1% | 34.9% |
| 11,706 | LUNA | 5,914 | 2,966 | 2,872 | 76 | 94 | R | 50.2% | 48.6% | 50.8% | 49.2% |
| 43,208 | MCKINLEY | 11,624 | 4,617 | 6,856 | 151 | 2,239 | D | 39.7% | 59.0% | 40.2% | 59.8% |
| 4,673 | MORA | 2,361 | 904 | 1,438 | 19 | 534 | D | 38.3% | 60.9% | 38.6% | 61.4% |
| 41,097 | OTERO | 11,380 | 5,914 | 5,333 | 133 | 581 | R | 52.0% | 46.9% | 52.6% | 47.4% |
| 10,903 | QUAY | 4,197 | 2,059 | 2,095 | 43 | 36 | D | 49.1% | 49.9% | 49.6% | 50.4% |
| 25,170 | RIO ARRIBA | 10,455 | 3,213 | 7,125 | 117 | 3,912 | D | 30.7% | 68.1% | 31.1% | 68.9% |
| 16,479 | ROOSEVELT | 6,445 | 3,269 | 3,111 | 65 | 158 | R | 50.7% | 48.3% | 51.2% | 48.8% |
| 17,492 | SANDOVAL | 9,319 | 4,110 | 5,072 | 137 | 962 | D | 44.1% | 54.4% | 44.8% | 55.2% |
| 52,517 | SAN JUAN | 19,742 | 10,852 | 8,615 | 275 | 2,237 | R | 55.0% | 43.6% | 55.7% | 44.3% |
| 21,951 | SAN MIGUEL | 8,523 | 3,162 | 5,204 | 157 | 2,042 | D | 37.1% | 61.1% | 37.8% | 62.2% |
| 53,756 | SANTA FE | 26,165 | 11,576 | 14,127 | 462 | 2,551 | D | 44.2% | 54.0% | 45.0% | 55.0% |
| 7,189 | SIERRA | 3,264 | 1,665 | 1,564 | 35 | 101 | R | 51.0% | 47.9% | 51.6% | 48.4% |
| 9,763 | SOCORRO | 4,980 | 2,265 | 2,606 | 109 | 341 | D | 45.5% | 52.3% | 46.5% | 53.5% |
| 17,516 | TAOS | 7,532 | 3,012 | 4,414 | 106 | 1,402 | D | 40.0% | 58.6% | 40.6% | 59.4% |
| 5,290 | TORRANCE | 3,015 | 1,462 | 1,526 | 27 | 64 | D | 48.5% | 50.6% | 48.9% | 51.1% |
| 4,925 | UNION | 2,152 | 1,146 | 975 | 31 | 171 | R | 53.3% | 45.3% | 54.0% | 46.0% |
| 40,539 | VALENCIA | 16,604 | 7,851 | 8,566 | 187 | 715 | D | 47.3% | 51.6% | 47.8% | 52.2% |
| 1,016,000 | TOTAL | 418,409 | 211,419 | 201,148 | 5,842 | 10,271 | R | 50.5% | 48.1% | 51.2% | 48.8% |

# NEW MEXICO

## PRESIDENT 1972

| 1970 Census Population | County | Total Vote | Republican | Democratic | Other | Rep.-Dem. Plurality | Percentage | | | |
|---|---|---|---|---|---|---|---|---|---|---|
| | | | | | | | Total Vote | | Major Vote | |
| | | | | | | | Rep. | Dem. | Rep. | Dem. |
| 315,774 | BERNALILLO | 131,703 | 79,993 | 48,753 | 2,957 | 31,240 R | 60.7% | 37.0% | 62.1% | 37.9% |
| 2,198 | CATRON | 1,132 | 829 | 271 | 32 | 558 R | 73.2% | 23.9% | 75.4% | 24.6% |
| 43,335 | CHAVES | 16,227 | 11,493 | 4,296 | 438 | 7,197 R | 70.8% | 26.5% | 72.8% | 27.2% |
| | CIBOLA | — | — | — | — | — | — | — | — | — |
| 12,170 | COLFAX | 4,603 | 2,663 | 1,855 | 85 | 808 R | 57.9% | 40.3% | 58.9% | 41.1% |
| 39,517 | CURRY | 11,068 | 8,392 | 2,416 | 260 | 5,976 R | 75.8% | 21.8% | 77.6% | 22.4% |
| 2,547 | DE BACA | 1,047 | 752 | 270 | 25 | 482 R | 71.8% | 25.8% | 73.6% | 26.4% |
| 69,773 | DONA ANA | 24,397 | 14,562 | 9,416 | 419 | 5,146 R | 59.7% | 38.6% | 60.7% | 39.3% |
| 41,119 | EDDY | 15,357 | 9,921 | 5,040 | 396 | 4,881 R | 64.6% | 32.8% | 66.3% | 33.7% |
| 22,030 | GRANT | 8,784 | 4,431 | 4,081 | 272 | 350 R | 50.4% | 46.5% | 52.1% | 47.9% |
| 4,969 | GUADALUPE | 2,525 | 1,297 | 1,202 | 26 | 95 R | 51.4% | 47.6% | 51.9% | 48.1% |
| 1,348 | HARDING | 760 | 522 | 220 | 18 | 302 R | 68.7% | 28.9% | 70.4% | 29.6% |
| 4,734 | HIDALGO | 1,657 | 1,051 | 562 | 44 | 489 R | 63.4% | 33.9% | 65.2% | 34.8% |
| 49,554 | LEA | 16,343 | 12,478 | 3,429 | 436 | 9,049 R | 76.4% | 21.0% | 78.4% | 21.6% |
| 7,560 | LINCOLN | 3,285 | 2,528 | 696 | 61 | 1,832 R | 77.0% | 21.2% | 78.4% | 21.6% |
| 15,198 | LOS ALAMOS | 7,647 | 5,039 | 2,435 | 173 | 2,604 R | 65.9% | 31.8% | 67.4% | 32.6% |
| 11,706 | LUNA | 4,680 | 2,958 | 1,560 | 162 | 1,398 R | 63.2% | 33.3% | 65.5% | 34.5% |
| 43,208 | MCKINLEY | 10,798 | 5,366 | 5,124 | 308 | 242 R | 49.7% | 47.5% | 51.2% | 48.8% |
| 4,673 | MORA | 2,318 | 1,165 | 1,135 | 18 | 30 R | 50.3% | 49.0% | 50.7% | 49.3% |
| 41,097 | OTERO | 10,677 | 7,033 | 2,981 | 663 | 4,052 R | 65.9% | 27.9% | 70.2% | 29.8% |
| 10,903 | QUAY | 4,522 | 3,224 | 1,161 | 137 | 2,063 R | 71.3% | 25.7% | 73.5% | 26.5% |
| 25,170 | RIO ARRIBA | 10,195 | 4,351 | 5,642 | 202 | 1,291 D | 42.7% | 55.3% | 43.5% | 56.5% |
| 16,479 | ROOSEVELT | 6,478 | 4,727 | 1,612 | 139 | 3,115 R | 73.0% | 24.9% | 74.6% | 25.4% |
| 17,492 | SANDOVAL | 6,979 | 3,507 | 3,293 | 179 | 214 R | 50.3% | 47.2% | 51.6% | 48.4% |
| 52,517 | SAN JUAN | 15,983 | 10,788 | 4,296 | 899 | 6,492 R | 67.5% | 26.9% | 71.5% | 28.5% |
| 21,951 | SAN MIGUEL | 9,302 | 4,434 | 4,663 | 205 | 229 D | 47.7% | 50.1% | 48.7% | 51.3% |
| 53,756 | SANTA FE | 23,258 | 12,211 | 10,761 | 286 | 1,450 R | 52.5% | 46.3% | 53.2% | 46.8% |
| 7,189 | SIERRA | 3,075 | 2,074 | 934 | 67 | 1,140 R | 67.4% | 30.4% | 68.9% | 31.1% |
| 9,763 | SOCORRO | 4,732 | 2,658 | 1,994 | 80 | 664 R | 56.2% | 42.1% | 57.1% | 42.9% |
| 17,516 | TAOS | 7,164 | 3,617 | 3,472 | 75 | 145 R | 50.5% | 48.5% | 51.0% | 49.0% |
| 5,290 | TORRANCE | 2,726 | 1,758 | 908 | 60 | 850 R | 64.5% | 33.3% | 65.9% | 34.1% |
| 4,925 | UNION | 2,131 | 1,545 | 496 | 90 | 1,049 R | 72.5% | 23.3% | 75.7% | 24.3% |
| 40,539 | VALENCIA | 14,688 | 8,239 | 6,110 | 339 | 2,129 R | 56.1% | 41.6% | 57.4% | 42.6% |
| 1,016,000 | TOTAL | 386,241 | 235,606 | 141,084 | 9,551 | 94,522 R | 61.0% | 36.5% | 62.5% | 37.5% |

# NEW MEXICO

## PRESIDENT 1968

| 1960 Census Population | County | Total Vote | Republican | Democratic | AIP | Other | Plurality | Percentage Total Vote Rep. | Dem. | AIP |
|---|---|---|---|---|---|---|---|---|---|---|
| 262,199 | BERNALILLO | 102,321 | 56,234 | 40,835 | 4,920 | 332 | 15,399 R | 55.0% | 39.9% | 4.8% |
| 2,773 | CATRON | 1,082 | 674 | 278 | 128 | 2 | 396 R | 62.3% | 25.7% | 11.8% |
| 57,649 | CHAVES | 13,938 | 8,866 | 3,612 | 1,425 | 35 | 5,254 R | 63.6% | 25.9% | 10.2% |
| | CIBOLA | — | — | — | — | — | — | — | — | — |
| 13,806 | COLFAX | 4,983 | 2,212 | 2,477 | 263 | 31 | 265 D | 44.4% | 49.7% | 5.3% |
| 32,691 | CURRY | 10,304 | 5,562 | 2,915 | 1,754 | 73 | 2,647 R | 54.0% | 28.3% | 17.0% |
| 2,991 | DE BACA | 1,141 | 658 | 345 | 130 | 8 | 313 R | 57.7% | 30.2% | 11.4% |
| 59,948 | DONA ANA | 19,990 | 10,824 | 7,658 | 1,453 | 55 | 3,166 R | 54.1% | 38.3% | 7.3% |
| 50,783 | EDDY | 15,071 | 7,193 | 6,093 | 1,671 | 114 | 1,100 R | 47.7% | 40.4% | 11.1% |
| 18,700 | GRANT | 7,549 | 2,908 | 3,817 | 793 | 31 | 909 D | 38.5% | 50.6% | 10.5% |
| 5,610 | GUADALUPE | 2,288 | 1,176 | 1,027 | 77 | 8 | 149 R | 51.4% | 44.9% | 3.4% |
| 1,874 | HARDING | 780 | 450 | 284 | 44 | 2 | 166 R | 57.7% | 36.4% | 5.6% |
| 4,961 | HIDALGO | 1,544 | 606 | 678 | 257 | 3 | 72 D | 39.2% | 43.9% | 16.6% |
| 53,429 | LEA | 15,382 | 7,415 | 4,751 | 3,025 | 191 | 2,664 R | 48.2% | 30.9% | 19.7% |
| 7,744 | LINCOLN | 3,107 | 2,004 | 802 | 287 | 14 | 1,202 R | 64.5% | 25.8% | 9.2% |
| 13,037 | LOS ALAMOS | 6,288 | 3,447 | 2,552 | 268 | 21 | 895 R | 54.8% | 40.6% | 4.3% |
| 9,839 | LUNA | 3,896 | 1,952 | 1,438 | 490 | 16 | 514 R | 50.1% | 36.9% | 12.6% |
| 37,209 | MCKINLEY | 9,573 | 4,376 | 4,491 | 547 | 159 | 115 D | 45.7% | 46.9% | 5.7% |
| 6,028 | MORA | 2,266 | 1,155 | 1,069 | 35 | 7 | 86 R | 51.0% | 47.2% | 1.5% |
| 36,976 | OTERO | 10,229 | 4,475 | 3,978 | 1,688 | 88 | 497 R | 43.7% | 38.9% | 16.5% |
| 12,279 | QUAY | 4,132 | 2,123 | 1,399 | 567 | 43 | 724 R | 51.4% | 33.9% | 13.7% |
| 24,193 | RIO ARRIBA | 9,102 | 3,935 | 4,799 | 269 | 99 | 864 D | 43.2% | 52.7% | 3.0% |
| 16,198 | ROOSEVELT | 5,607 | 3,256 | 1,547 | 773 | 31 | 1,709 R | 58.1% | 27.6% | 13.8% |
| 14,201 | SANDOVAL | 4,731 | 1,959 | 2,609 | 129 | 34 | 650 D | 41.4% | 55.1% | 2.7% |
| 53,306 | SAN JUAN | 14,192 | 7,664 | 4,036 | 2,304 | 188 | 3,628 R | 54.0% | 28.4% | 16.2% |
| 23,468 | SAN MIGUEL | 8,368 | 4,027 | 4,088 | 195 | 58 | 61 D | 48.1% | 48.9% | 2.3% |
| 44,970 | SANTA FE | 19,475 | 9,359 | 9,544 | 492 | 80 | 185 D | 48.1% | 49.0% | 2.5% |
| 6,409 | SIERRA | 2,846 | 1,624 | 930 | 282 | 10 | 694 R | 57.1% | 32.7% | 9.9% |
| 10,168 | SOCORRO | 4,283 | 2,230 | 1,871 | 173 | 9 | 359 R | 52.1% | 43.7% | 4.0% |
| 15,934 | TAOS | 6,252 | 3,119 | 2,993 | 124 | 16 | 126 R | 49.9% | 47.9% | 2.0% |
| 6,497 | TORRANCE | 2,486 | 1,316 | 974 | 188 | 8 | 342 R | 52.9% | 39.2% | 7.6% |
| 6,068 | UNION | 2,197 | 1,217 | 678 | 279 | 23 | 539 R | 55.4% | 30.9% | 12.7% |
| 39,085 | VALENCIA | 11,947 | 5,676 | 5,513 | 707 | 51 | 163 R | 47.5% | 46.1% | 5.9% |
| 951,023 | TOTAL | 327,350 | 169,692 | 130,081 | 25,737 | 1,840 | 39,611 R | 51.8% | 39.7% | 7.9% |

# NEW MEXICO

## PRESIDENT 1964

| 1960 Census Population | County | Total Vote | Republican | Democratic | Other | Rep.-Dem. Plurality | Percentage | | | |
|---|---|---|---|---|---|---|---|---|---|---|
| | | | | | | | Total Vote | | Major Vote | |
| | | | | | | | Rep. | Dem. | Rep. | Dem. |
| 262,199 | BERNALILLO | 98,317 | 42,583 | 55,036 | 698 | 12,453 D | 43.3% | 56.0% | 43.6% | 56.4% |
| 2,773 | CATRON | 1,209 | 584 | 624 | 1 | 40 D | 48.3% | 51.6% | 48.3% | 51.7% |
| 57,649 | CHAVES | 17,113 | 8,419 | 8,650 | 44 | 231 D | 49.2% | 50.5% | 49.3% | 50.7% |
| | CIBOLA | — | — | — | — | — | — | — | — | — |
| 13,806 | COLFAX | 5,029 | 1,636 | 3,367 | 26 | 1,731 D | 32.5% | 67.0% | 32.7% | 67.3% |
| 32,691 | CURRY | 10,378 | 5,120 | 5,228 | 30 | 108 D | 49.3% | 50.4% | 49.5% | 50.5% |
| 2,991 | DE BACA | 1,240 | 559 | 674 | 7 | 115 D | 45.1% | 54.4% | 45.3% | 54.7% |
| 59,948 | DONA ANA | 18,085 | 7,280 | 10,748 | 57 | 3,468 D | 40.3% | 59.4% | 40.4% | 59.6% |
| 50,783 | EDDY | 18,032 | 6,747 | 11,216 | 69 | 4,469 D | 37.4% | 62.2% | 37.6% | 62.4% |
| 18,700 | GRANT | 7,314 | 2,042 | 5,253 | 19 | 3,211 D | 27.9% | 71.8% | 28.0% | 72.0% |
| 5,610 | GUADALUPE | 2,713 | 1,058 | 1,649 | 6 | 591 D | 39.0% | 60.8% | 39.1% | 60.9% |
| 1,874 | HARDING | 905 | 473 | 431 | 1 | 42 R | 52.3% | 47.6% | 52.3% | 47.7% |
| 4,961 | HIDALGO | 1,635 | 628 | 995 | 12 | 367 D | 38.4% | 60.9% | 38.7% | 61.3% |
| 53,429 | LEA | 15,948 | 7,033 | 8,862 | 53 | 1,829 D | 44.1% | 55.6% | 44.2% | 55.8% |
| 7,744 | LINCOLN | 3,351 | 1,761 | 1,565 | 25 | 196 R | 52.6% | 46.7% | 52.9% | 47.1% |
| 13,037 | LOS ALAMOS | 5,711 | 1,895 | 3,767 | 49 | 1,872 D | 33.2% | 66.0% | 33.5% | 66.5% |
| 9,839 | LUNA | 3,969 | 1,665 | 2,286 | 18 | 621 D | 42.0% | 57.6% | 42.1% | 57.9% |
| 37,209 | MCKINLEY | 10,000 | 2,965 | 6,913 | 122 | 3,948 D | 29.7% | 69.1% | 30.0% | 70.0% |
| 6,028 | MORA | 2,527 | 1,014 | 1,509 | 4 | 495 D | 40.1% | 59.7% | 40.2% | 59.8% |
| 36,976 | OTERO | 9,560 | 3,498 | 6,035 | 27 | 2,537 D | 36.6% | 63.1% | 36.7% | 63.3% |
| 12,279 | QUAY | 4,515 | 2,161 | 2,333 | 21 | 172 D | 47.9% | 51.7% | 48.1% | 51.9% |
| 24,193 | RIO ARRIBA | 9,757 | 2,906 | 6,787 | 64 | 3,881 D | 29.8% | 69.6% | 30.0% | 70.0% |
| 16,198 | ROOSEVELT | 5,635 | 2,732 | 2,875 | 28 | 143 D | 48.5% | 51.0% | 48.7% | 51.3% |
| 14,201 | SANDOVAL | 4,420 | 1,077 | 3,332 | 11 | 2,255 D | 24.4% | 75.4% | 24.4% | 75.6% |
| 53,306 | SAN JUAN | 13,892 | 6,808 | 6,901 | 183 | 93 D | 49.0% | 49.7% | 49.7% | 50.3% |
| 23,468 | SAN MIGUEL | 8,505 | 2,714 | 5,767 | 24 | 3,053 D | 31.9% | 67.8% | 32.0% | 68.0% |
| 44,970 | SANTA FE | 18,524 | 5,834 | 12,616 | 74 | 6,782 D | 31.5% | 68.1% | 31.6% | 68.4% |
| 6,409 | SIERRA | 3,149 | 1,501 | 1,633 | 15 | 132 D | 47.7% | 51.9% | 47.9% | 52.1% |
| 10,168 | SOCORRO | 4,181 | 1,774 | 2,397 | 10 | 623 D | 42.4% | 57.3% | 42.5% | 57.5% |
| 15,934 | TAOS | 6,238 | 2,006 | 4,204 | 28 | 2,198 D | 32.2% | 67.4% | 32.3% | 67.7% |
| 6,497 | TORRANCE | 2,635 | 1,183 | 1,446 | 6 | 263 D | 44.9% | 54.9% | 45.0% | 55.0% |
| 6,068 | UNION | 2,401 | 1,232 | 1,159 | 10 | 73 R | 51.3% | 48.3% | 51.5% | 48.5% |
| 39,085 | VALENCIA | 11,757 | 3,950 | 7,757 | 50 | 3,807 D | 33.6% | 66.0% | 33.7% | 66.3% |
| 951,023 | TOTAL | 328,645 | 132,838 | 194,015 | 1,792 | 61,177 D | 40.4% | 59.0% | 40.6% | 59.4% |

# NEW MEXICO

## PRESIDENT 1960

| 1960 Census Population | County | Total Vote | Republican | Democratic | Other | Rep.-Dem. Plurality | Percentage Total Vote Rep. | Dem. | Major Vote Rep. | Dem. |
|---|---|---|---|---|---|---|---|---|---|---|
| 262,199 | BERNALILLO | 86,061 | 44,805 | 40,908 | 348 | 3,897 R | 52.1% | 47.5% | 52.3% | 47.7% |
| 2,773 | CATRON | 1,245 | 671 | 573 | 1 | 98 R | 53.9% | 46.0% | 53.9% | 46.1% |
| 57,649 | CHAVES | 15,392 | 9,089 | 6,212 | 91 | 2,877 R | 59.1% | 40.4% | 59.4% | 40.6% |
| | CIBOLA | — | — | — | — | — | — | — | — | — |
| 13,806 | COLFAX | 5,528 | 2,316 | 3,187 | 25 | 871 D | 41.9% | 57.7% | 42.1% | 57.9% |
| 32,691 | CURRY | 9,639 | 6,153 | 3,421 | 65 | 2,732 R | 63.8% | 35.5% | 64.3% | 35.7% |
| 2,991 | DE BACA | 1,355 | 734 | 619 | 2 | 115 R | 54.2% | 45.7% | 54.2% | 45.8% |
| 59,948 | DONA ANA | 16,755 | 7,789 | 8,905 | 61 | 1,116 D | 46.5% | 53.1% | 46.7% | 53.3% |
| 50,783 | EDDY | 16,780 | 7,986 | 8,707 | 87 | 721 D | 47.6% | 51.9% | 47.8% | 52.2% |
| 18,700 | GRANT | 6,868 | 2,468 | 4,378 | 22 | 1,910 D | 35.9% | 63.7% | 36.1% | 63.9% |
| 5,610 | GUADALUPE | 2,834 | 1,242 | 1,589 | 3 | 347 D | 43.8% | 56.1% | 43.9% | 56.1% |
| 1,874 | HARDING | 1,012 | 616 | 396 | | 220 R | 60.9% | 39.1% | 60.9% | 39.1% |
| 4,961 | HIDALGO | 1,643 | 750 | 889 | 4 | 139 D | 45.6% | 54.1% | 45.8% | 54.2% |
| 53,429 | LEA | 15,474 | 7,548 | 7,806 | 120 | 258 D | 48.8% | 50.4% | 49.2% | 50.8% |
| 7,744 | LINCOLN | 3,503 | 2,042 | 1,459 | 2 | 583 R | 58.3% | 41.7% | 58.3% | 41.7% |
| 13,037 | LOS ALAMOS | 5,283 | 2,574 | 2,692 | 17 | 118 D | 48.7% | 51.0% | 48.9% | 51.1% |
| 9,839 | LUNA | 3,306 | 1,583 | 1,708 | 15 | 125 D | 47.9% | 51.7% | 48.1% | 51.9% |
| 37,209 | MCKINLEY | 9,893 | 4,262 | 5,599 | 32 | 1,337 D | 43.1% | 56.6% | 43.2% | 56.8% |
| 6,028 | MORA | 2,807 | 1,349 | 1,458 | | 109 D | 48.1% | 51.9% | 48.1% | 51.9% |
| 36,976 | OTERO | 9,426 | 4,507 | 4,916 | 3 | 409 D | 47.8% | 52.2% | 47.8% | 52.2% |
| 12,279 | QUAY | 4,704 | 2,652 | 2,050 | 2 | 602 R | 56.4% | 43.6% | 56.4% | 43.6% |
| 24,193 | RIO ARRIBA | 9,969 | 3,716 | 6,250 | 3 | 2,534 D | 37.3% | 62.7% | 37.3% | 62.7% |
| 16,198 | ROOSEVELT | 5,804 | 4,039 | 1,761 | 4 | 2,278 R | 69.6% | 30.3% | 69.6% | 30.4% |
| 14,201 | SANDOVAL | 4,119 | 1,447 | 2,672 | | 1,225 D | 35.1% | 64.9% | 35.1% | 64.9% |
| 53,306 | SAN JUAN | 13,185 | 7,521 | 5,370 | 294 | 2,151 R | 57.0% | 40.7% | 58.3% | 41.7% |
| 23,468 | SAN MIGUEL | 9,514 | 3,988 | 5,520 | 6 | 1,532 D | 41.9% | 58.0% | 41.9% | 58.1% |
| 44,970 | SANTA FE | 17,890 | 7,411 | 10,385 | 94 | 2,974 D | 41.4% | 58.0% | 41.6% | 58.4% |
| 6,409 | SIERRA | 3,117 | 1,890 | 1,220 | 7 | 670 R | 60.6% | 39.1% | 60.8% | 39.2% |
| 10,168 | SOCORRO | 4,128 | 1,796 | 2,327 | 5 | 531 D | 43.5% | 56.4% | 43.6% | 56.4% |
| 15,934 | TAOS | 6,257 | 2,620 | 3,631 | 6 | 1,011 D | 41.9% | 58.0% | 41.9% | 58.1% |
| 6,497 | TORRANCE | 2,884 | 1,554 | 1,308 | 22 | 246 R | 53.9% | 45.4% | 54.3% | 45.7% |
| 6,068 | UNION | 2,756 | 1,686 | 1,068 | 2 | 618 R | 61.2% | 38.8% | 61.2% | 38.8% |
| 39,085 | VALENCIA | 11,976 | 4,929 | 7,043 | 4 | 2,114 D | 41.2% | 58.8% | 41.2% | 58.8% |
| 951,023 | TOTAL | 311,107 | 153,733 | 156,027 | 1,347 | 2,294 D | 49.4% | 50.2% | 49.6% | 50.4% |

# NEW MEXICO

Cibola county was created by the state legislature in 1981 from the western part of Valencia county.

## ELECTION NOTES

**2004**   Other vote was 4,053 Independent (Ralph Nader); 2,382 Libertarian (Michael Badnarik); 1,226 Green (David Cobb); 771 Constitution (Michael Peroutka).

**2000**   Other vote was 2,058 Libertarian (Browne); 1,392 Reform (Buchanan); 361 Natural Law (Hagelin); 343 Constitution (Phillips).

**1996**   Other vote was 13,218 Green (Nader); 2,996 Libertarian (Browne); 713 Taxpayers (Phillips); 644 Natural Law (Hagelin).

**1992**   Other vote was 1,615 Marrou (Libertarian); 620 Phillips (Taxpayers); 562 Hagelin (Natural Law); 369 Fulani (New Alliance); 183 Warren (Socialist Workers); 181 LaRiva (Workers World); 120 Dodge (Prohibition).

**1988**   Other vote was 3,268 Paul (Libertarian); 2,237 Fulani (New Alliance); 344 Warren (Socialist Workers); 258 Holmes (Workers World); 249 Dodge (Prohibition); 93 scattered write-in.

**1984**   Other vote was 4,459 Bergland (Libertarian); 455 Johnson (Citizens); 224 Mason (Socialist Workers); 206 Dodge (Prohibition); 155 Serrette (Alliance); 1 scattered write-in.

**1980**   Other vote was 29,459 Anderson (Independent); 4,365 Clark (Libertarian); 2,202 Commoner (Citizens); 1,281 Bubar (Statesman); 325 Pulley (Socialist Workers); 734 scattered write-in.

**1976**   Other vote was 2,462 Camejo (Socialist Workers); 1,161 McCarthy (write-in); 1,110 MacBride (Libertarian); 240 Zeidler (Socialist); 211 Bubar (Prohibition); 106 Anderson (write-in); 31 Maddox (write-in); 19 Hall (write-in); 1 LaRouche (write-in); 501 scattered write-in.

**1972**   Other vote was 8,767 Schmitz (American Independent); 474 Jenness (Socialist Workers); 310 scattered write-in.

**1968**   Wallace on the ballot as American Independent.  Other vote was 1,519 Chavez (People's Constitutional party); 252 Halstead (Socialist Workers); 69 scattered write-in.

**1964**   Other vote was 1,217 Hass (Socialist Labor); 543 Munn (Prohibition); 32 scattered write-in. The data presented are from amended returns and reflect minor corrections from the early canvass.

**1960**   Other vote was 777 Decker (Prohibition; 570 Hass (Socialist Labor).

# NEW YORK

## POPULAR VOTE FOR PRESIDENT 1920 TO 2004

| Year | Total Vote | Republican | | Democratic | | Other Vote | Plurality | Percentage | | | |
|------|-----------|------|-----------|------|-----------|------|-----------|------|------|------|------|
| | | | | | | | | Total Vote | | Major Vote | |
| | | Vote | Candidate | Vote | Candidate | | | Rep. | Dem. | Rep. | Dem. |
| 2004 | 7,391,036 | 2,962,567 | Bush, George W. | 4,314,280 | Kerry, John | 114,189 | 1,351,713 D | 40.1% | 58.4% | 40.7% | 59.3% |
| 2000 ** | 6,821,999 | 2,403,374 | Bush, George W. | 4,107,697 | Gore, Al | 310,928 | 1,704,323 D | 35.2% | 60.2% | 36.9% | 63.1% |
| 1996 ** | 6,316,129 | 1,933,492 | Dole, Bob | 3,756,177 | Clinton, Bill | 626,460 | 1,822,685 D | 30.6% | 59.5% | 34.0% | 66.0% |
| 1992 ** | 6,926,925 | 2,346,649 | Bush, George | 3,444,450 | Clinton, Bill | 1,135,826 | 1,097,801 D | 33.9% | 49.7% | 40.5% | 59.5% |
| 1988 | 6,485,683 | 3,081,871 | Bush, George | 3,347,882 | Dukakis, Michael S. | 55,930 | 266,011 D | 47.5% | 51.6% | 47.9% | 52.1% |
| 1984 | 6,806,810 | 3,664,763 | Reagan, Ronald | 3,119,609 | Mondale, Walter F. | 22,438 | 545,154 R | 53.8% | 45.8% | 54.0% | 46.0% |
| 1980** | 6,201,959 | 2,893,831 | Reagan, Ronald | 2,728,372 | Carter, Jimmy | 579,756 | 165,459 R | 46.7% | 44.0% | 51.5% | 48.5% |
| 1976 | 6,534,170 | 3,100,791 | Ford, Gerald R. | 3,389,558 | Carter, Jimmy | 43,821 | 288,767 D | 47.5% | 51.9% | 47.8% | 52.2% |
| 1972 | 7,165,919 | 4,192,778 | Nixon, Richard M. | 2,951,084 | McGovern, George S. | 22,057 | 1,241,694 R | 58.5% | 41.2% | 58.7% | 41.3% |
| 1968 | 6,791,688 | 3,007,932 | Nixon, Richard M. | 3,378,470 | Humphrey, Hubert H. | 405,286 | 370,538 D | 44.3% | 49.7% | 47.1% | 52.9% |
| 1964 | 7,166,275 | 2,243,559 | Goldwater, Barry M. | 4,913,102 | Johnson, Lyndon B. | 9,614 | 2,669,543 D | 31.3% | 68.6% | 31.3% | 68.7% |
| 1960 | 7,291,079 | 3,446,419 | Nixon, Richard M. | 3,830,085 | Kennedy, John F. | 14,575 | 383,666 D | 47.3% | 52.5% | 47.4% | 52.6% |
| 1956 | 7,095,971 | 4,345,506 | Eisenhower, Dwight D. | 2,747,944 | Stevenson, Adlai E. | 2,521 | 1,597,562 R | 61.2% | 38.7% | 61.3% | 38.7% |
| 1952 | 7,128,239 | 3,952,813 | Eisenhower, Dwight D. | 3,104,601 | Stevenson, Adlai E. | 70,825 | 848,212 R | 55.5% | 43.6% | 56.0% | 44.0% |
| 1948 | 6,177,337 | 2,841,163 | Dewey, Thomas E. | 2,780,204 | Truman, Harry S. | 555,970 | 60,959 R | 46.0% | 45.0% | 50.5% | 49.5% |
| 1944 | 6,316,790 | 2,987,647 | Dewey, Thomas E. | 3,304,238 | Roosevelt, Franklin D. | 24,905 | 316,591 D | 47.3% | 52.3% | 47.5% | 52.5% |
| 1940 | 6,301,596 | 3,027,478 | Willkie, Wendell | 3,251,918 | Roosevelt, Franklin D. | 22,200 | 224,440 D | 48.0% | 51.6% | 48.2% | 51.8% |
| 1936 | 5,596,398 | 2,180,670 | Landon, Alfred M. | 3,293,222 | Roosevelt, Franklin D. | 122,506 | 1,112,552 D | 39.0% | 58.8% | 39.8% | 60.2% |
| 1932 | 4,688,614 | 1,937,963 | Hoover, Herbert C. | 2,534,959 | Roosevelt, Franklin D. | 215,692 | 596,996 D | 41.3% | 54.1% | 43.3% | 56.7% |
| 1928 | 4,405,626 | 2,193,344 | Hoover, Herbert C. | 2,089,863 | Smith, Alfred E. | 122,419 | 103,481 R | 49.8% | 47.4% | 51.2% | 48.8% |
| 1924 ** | 3,263,939 | 1,820,058 | Coolidge, Calvin | 950,796 | Davis, John W. | 493,085 | 869,262 R | 55.8% | 29.1% | 65.7% | 34.3% |
| 1920 | 2,898,513 | 1,871,167 | Harding, Warren G. | 781,238 | Cox, James M. | 246,108 | 1,089,929 R | 64.6% | 27.0% | 70.5% | 29.5% |

In 2000 the other vote column includes 244,030 votes cast for Green (Nader). In 1996 the other vote column includes 503,458 votes cast for Perot. In 1992 the other vote column includes 1,090,721 votes cast for Perot. In 1980 the other column includes 467,801 votes for Independent (Anderson). In 1924 the other vote was 474,913 Progressive; 9,928 Socialist Labor; and 8,244 Communist.

## ELECTORAL COLLEGE VOTE 1920 TO 2004

| Year | Total | Republican | Democratic | Other |
|------|-------|-----------|-----------|-------|
| 2004 | 31 | | 31 | |
| 2000 | 33 | | 33 | |
| 1996 | 33 | | 33 | |
| 1992 | 33 | | 33 | |
| 1988 | 36 | | 36 | |
| 1984 | 36 | 36 | | |
| 1980 | 41 | 41 | | |
| 1976 | 41 | | 41 | |
| 1972 | 41 | 41 | | |
| 1968 | 43 | | 43 | |
| 1964 | 43 | | 43 | |
| 1960 | 45 | | 45 | |
| 1956 | 45 | 45 | | |
| 1952 | 45 | 45 | | |
| 1948 | 47 | 47 | | |
| 1944 | 47 | | 47 | |
| 1940 | 47 | | 47 | |
| 1936 | 47 | | 47 | |
| 1932 | 47 | | 47 | |
| 1928 | 45 | 45 | | |
| 1924 | 45 | 45 | | |
| 1920 | 45 | 45 | | |

# NEW YORK

# NEW YORK

## PRESIDENT 2004

| 2000 Census Population | County | Total Vote | Republican | Democratic | Other | Rep.-Dem. Plurality | Percentage Total Vote Rep. | Dem. | Major Vote Rep. | Dem. |
|---|---|---|---|---|---|---|---|---|---|---|
| 294,565 | ALBANY | 147,199 | 54,872 | 89,323 | 3,004 | 34,451 D | 37.3% | 60.7% | 38.1% | 61.9% |
| 49,927 | ALLEGANY | 19,270 | 12,310 | 6,566 | 394 | 5,744 R | 63.9% | 34.1% | 65.2% | 34.8% |
| 1,332,650 | BRONX | 342,929 | 56,701 | 283,994 | 2,234 | 227,293 D | 16.5% | 82.8% | 16.6% | 83.4% |
| 200,536 | BROOME | 91,890 | 43,568 | 46,281 | 2,041 | 2,713 D | 47.4% | 50.4% | 48.5% | 51.5% |
| 83,955 | CATTARAUGUS | 34,262 | 20,051 | 13,514 | 697 | 6,537 R | 58.5% | 39.4% | 59.7% | 40.3% |
| 81,963 | CAYUGA | 36,052 | 17,743 | 17,534 | 775 | 209 R | 49.2% | 48.6% | 50.3% | 49.7% |
| 139,750 | CHAUTAUQUA | 60,942 | 32,434 | 27,257 | 1,251 | 5,177 R | 53.2% | 44.7% | 54.3% | 45.7% |
| 91,070 | CHEMUNG | 39,075 | 21,321 | 17,080 | 674 | 4,241 R | 54.6% | 43.7% | 55.5% | 44.5% |
| 51,401 | CHENANGO | 21,341 | 11,582 | 9,277 | 482 | 2,305 R | 54.3% | 43.5% | 55.5% | 44.5% |
| 79,894 | CLINTON | 33,736 | 15,330 | 17,624 | 782 | 2,294 D | 45.4% | 52.2% | 46.5% | 53.5% |
| 63,094 | COLUMBIA | 31,103 | 14,457 | 15,929 | 717 | 1,472 D | 46.5% | 51.2% | 47.6% | 52.4% |
| 48,599 | CORTLAND | 22,760 | 11,613 | 10,670 | 477 | 943 R | 51.0% | 46.9% | 52.1% | 47.9% |
| 48,055 | DELAWARE | 21,166 | 11,958 | 8,724 | 484 | 3,234 R | 56.5% | 41.2% | 57.8% | 42.2% |
| 280,150 | DUTCHESS | 123,881 | 63,372 | 58,232 | 2,277 | 5,140 R | 51.2% | 47.0% | 52.1% | 47.9% |
| 950,265 | ERIE | 445,138 | 184,423 | 251,090 | 9,625 | 66,667 D | 41.4% | 56.4% | 42.3% | 57.7% |
| 38,851 | ESSEX | 19,082 | 9,869 | 8,768 | 445 | 1,101 R | 51.7% | 45.9% | 53.0% | 47.0% |
| 51,134 | FRANKLIN | 18,316 | 8,383 | 9,543 | 390 | 1,160 D | 45.8% | 52.1% | 46.8% | 53.2% |
| 55,073 | FULTON | 22,215 | 12,570 | 9,202 | 443 | 3,368 R | 56.6% | 41.4% | 57.7% | 42.3% |
| 60,370 | GENESEE | 27,580 | 16,725 | 10,331 | 524 | 6,394 R | 60.6% | 37.5% | 61.8% | 38.2% |
| 48,195 | GREENE | 22,398 | 12,996 | 8,933 | 469 | 4,063 R | 58.0% | 39.9% | 59.3% | 40.7% |
| 5,379 | HAMILTON | 3,692 | 2,475 | 1,145 | 72 | 1,330 R | 67.0% | 31.0% | 68.4% | 31.6% |
| 64,427 | HERKIMER | 28,310 | 16,024 | 11,675 | 611 | 4,349 R | 56.6% | 41.2% | 57.9% | 42.1% |
| 111,738 | JEFFERSON | 38,800 | 21,231 | 16,860 | 709 | 4,371 R | 54.7% | 43.5% | 55.7% | 44.3% |
| 2,465,326 | KINGS | 687,780 | 167,149 | 514,973 | 5,658 | 347,824 D | 24.3% | 74.9% | 24.5% | 75.5% |
| 26,944 | LEWIS | 11,397 | 6,624 | 4,546 | 227 | 2,078 R | 58.1% | 39.9% | 59.3% | 40.7% |
| 64,328 | LIVINGSTON | 29,948 | 17,729 | 11,504 | 715 | 6,225 R | 59.2% | 38.4% | 60.6% | 39.4% |
| 69,441 | MADISON | 30,287 | 16,537 | 13,121 | 629 | 3,416 R | 54.6% | 43.3% | 55.8% | 44.2% |
| 735,343 | MONROE | 342,981 | 163,545 | 173,497 | 5,939 | 9,952 D | 47.7% | 50.6% | 48.5% | 51.5% |
| 49,708 | MONTGOMERY | 21,221 | 11,338 | 9,449 | 434 | 1,889 R | 53.4% | 44.5% | 54.5% | 45.5% |
| 1,334,544 | NASSAU | 618,343 | 288,355 | 323,070 | 6,918 | 34,715 D | 46.6% | 52.2% | 47.2% | 52.8% |
| 1,537,195 | NEW YORK | 641,747 | 107,405 | 526,765 | 7,577 | 419,360 D | 16.7% | 82.1% | 16.9% | 83.1% |
| 219,846 | NIAGARA | 96,580 | 47,111 | 47,602 | 1,867 | 491 D | 48.8% | 49.3% | 49.7% | 50.3% |
| 235,469 | ONEIDA | 95,369 | 52,392 | 40,792 | 2,185 | 11,600 R | 54.9% | 42.8% | 56.2% | 43.8% |
| 458,336 | ONONDAGA | 214,589 | 94,006 | 116,381 | 4,202 | 22,375 D | 43.8% | 54.2% | 44.7% | 55.3% |
| 100,224 | ONTARIO | 50,102 | 27,999 | 21,166 | 937 | 6,833 R | 55.9% | 42.2% | 56.9% | 43.1% |
| 341,367 | ORANGE | 144,673 | 79,089 | 63,394 | 2,190 | 15,695 R | 54.7% | 43.8% | 55.5% | 44.5% |
| 44,171 | ORLEANS | 16,573 | 10,317 | 5,959 | 297 | 4,358 R | 62.3% | 36.0% | 63.4% | 36.6% |
| 122,377 | OSWEGO | 51,607 | 26,325 | 24,133 | 1,149 | 2,192 R | 51.0% | 46.8% | 52.2% | 47.8% |
| 61,676 | OTSEGO | 26,652 | 13,342 | 12,723 | 587 | 619 R | 50.1% | 47.7% | 51.2% | 48.8% |
| 95,745 | PUTNAM | 46,563 | 26,356 | 19,575 | 632 | 6,781 R | 56.6% | 42.0% | 57.4% | 42.6% |
| 2,229,379 | QUEENS | 605,062 | 165,954 | 433,835 | 5,273 | 267,881 D | 27.4% | 71.7% | 27.7% | 72.3% |
| 152,538 | RENSSELAER | 72,514 | 34,734 | 36,075 | 1,705 | 1,341 D | 47.9% | 49.7% | 49.1% | 50.9% |
| 443,728 | RICHMOND | 160,126 | 90,325 | 68,448 | 1,353 | 21,877 R | 56.4% | 42.7% | 56.9% | 43.1% |
| 286,753 | ROCKLAND | 131,231 | 65,130 | 64,191 | 1,910 | 939 R | 49.6% | 48.9% | 50.4% | 49.6% |
| 111,931 | ST. LAWRENCE | 41,755 | 18,029 | 22,857 | 869 | 4,828 D | 43.2% | 54.7% | 44.1% | 55.9% |
| 200,635 | SARATOGA | 106,873 | 56,158 | 48,730 | 1,985 | 7,428 R | 52.5% | 45.6% | 53.5% | 46.5% |
| 146,555 | SCHENECTADY | 69,469 | 32,066 | 35,971 | 1,432 | 3,905 D | 46.2% | 51.8% | 47.1% | 52.9% |
| 31,582 | SCHOHARIE | 14,557 | 8,591 | 5,630 | 336 | 2,961 R | 59.0% | 38.7% | 60.4% | 39.6% |
| 19,224 | SCHUYLER | 8,590 | 4,960 | 3,445 | 185 | 1,515 R | 57.7% | 40.1% | 59.0% | 41.0% |
| 33,342 | SENECA | 15,325 | 7,981 | 6,979 | 365 | 1,002 R | 52.1% | 45.5% | 53.3% | 46.7% |
| 98,726 | STEUBEN | 42,284 | 26,980 | 14,523 | 781 | 12,457 R | 63.8% | 34.3% | 65.0% | 35.0% |
| 1,419,369 | SUFFOLK | 638,712 | 309,949 | 315,909 | 12,854 | 5,960 D | 48.5% | 49.5% | 49.5% | 50.5% |
| 73,966 | SULLIVAN | 30,966 | 15,319 | 15,034 | 613 | 285 R | 49.5% | 48.6% | 50.5% | 49.5% |
| 51,784 | TIOGA | 23,902 | 13,762 | 9,694 | 446 | 4,068 R | 57.6% | 40.6% | 58.7% | 41.3% |
| 96,501 | TOMPKINS | 42,402 | 13,994 | 27,229 | 1,179 | 13,235 D | 33.0% | 64.2% | 33.9% | 66.1% |
| 177,749 | ULSTER | 87,712 | 37,821 | 47,602 | 2,289 | 9,781 D | 43.1% | 54.3% | 44.3% | 55.7% |
| 63,303 | WARREN | 31,059 | 16,969 | 13,405 | 685 | 3,564 R | 54.6% | 43.2% | 55.9% | 44.1% |
| 61,042 | WASHINGTON | 25,103 | 13,827 | 10,624 | 652 | 3,203 R | 55.1% | 42.3% | 56.5% | 43.5% |
| 93,765 | WAYNE | 41,200 | 24,709 | 15,709 | 782 | 9,000 R | 60.0% | 38.1% | 61.1% | 38.9% |
| 923,459 | WESTCHESTER | 395,770 | 159,628 | 229,849 | 6,293 | 70,221 D | 40.3% | 58.1% | 41.0% | 59.0% |
| 43,424 | WYOMING | 18,164 | 11,745 | 6,134 | 285 | 5,611 R | 64.7% | 33.8% | 65.7% | 34.3% |
| 24,621 | YATES | 10,711 | 6,309 | 4,205 | 197 | 2,104 R | 58.9% | 39.3% | 60.0% | 40.0% |
| 18,976,457 | TOTAL | 7,391,036 | 2,962,567 | 4,314,280 | 114,189 | 1,351,713 D | 40.1% | 58.4% | 40.7% | 59.3% |

# NEW YORK

## PRESIDENT 2000

| 2000 Census Population | County | Total Vote | Republican | Democratic | Green (Nader) | Other | Rep.-Dem. Plurality | Percentage of Total Vote | | |
|---|---|---|---|---|---|---|---|---|---|---|
| | | | | | | | | Rep. | Dem. | Green |
| 294,565 | ALBANY | 141,969 | 47,624 | 85,617 | 7,182 | 1,546 | 37,993 D | 33.5% | 60.3% | 5.1% |
| 49,927 | ALLEGANY | 18,689 | 11,436 | 6,336 | 657 | 260 | 5,100 R | 61.2% | 33.9% | 3.5% |
| 1,332,650 | BRONX | 308,048 | 36,245 | 265,801 | 4,265 | 1,737 | 229,556 D | 11.8% | 86.3% | 1.4% |
| 200,536 | BROOME | 87,063 | 36,946 | 45,381 | 3,826 | 910 | 8,435 D | 42.4% | 52.1% | 4.4% |
| 83,955 | CATTARAUGUS | 33,733 | 18,382 | 13,697 | 1,094 | 560 | 4,685 R | 54.5% | 40.6% | 3.2% |
| 81,963 | CAYUGA | 33,978 | 14,988 | 17,031 | 1,448 | 511 | 2,043 D | 44.1% | 50.1% | 4.3% |
| 139,750 | CHAUTAUQUA | 58,720 | 29,064 | 27,016 | 1,888 | 752 | 2,048 R | 49.5% | 46.0% | 3.2% |
| 91,070 | CHEMUNG | 37,710 | 18,779 | 17,424 | 1,195 | 312 | 1,355 R | 49.8% | 46.2% | 3.2% |
| 51,401 | CHENANGO | 20,250 | 10,033 | 9,112 | 869 | 236 | 921 R | 49.5% | 45.0% | 4.3% |
| 79,894 | CLINTON | 30,555 | 13,274 | 15,542 | 1,205 | 534 | 2,268 D | 43.4% | 50.9% | 3.9% |
| 63,094 | COLUMBIA | 28,691 | 13,153 | 13,489 | 1,707 | 342 | 336 D | 45.8% | 47.0% | 5.9% |
| 48,599 | CORTLAND | 20,723 | 9,857 | 9,691 | 943 | 232 | 166 R | 47.6% | 46.8% | 4.6% |
| 48,055 | DELAWARE | 20,175 | 10,662 | 8,450 | 833 | 230 | 2,212 R | 52.8% | 41.9% | 4.1% |
| 280,150 | DUTCHESS | 111,762 | 52,669 | 52,390 | 5,553 | 1,150 | 279 R | 47.1% | 46.9% | 5.0% |
| 950,265 | ERIE | 424,654 | 160,176 | 240,176 | 18,166 | 6,136 | 80,000 D | 37.7% | 56.6% | 4.3% |
| 38,851 | ESSEX | 17,932 | 8,822 | 7,927 | 848 | 335 | 895 R | 49.2% | 44.2% | 4.7% |
| 51,134 | FRANKLIN | 17,447 | 7,643 | 8,870 | 658 | 276 | 1,227 D | 43.8% | 50.8% | 3.8% |
| 55,073 | FULTON | 21,671 | 11,434 | 9,314 | 668 | 255 | 2,120 R | 52.8% | 43.0% | 3.1% |
| 60,370 | GENESEE | 26,069 | 14,459 | 10,191 | 924 | 495 | 4,268 R | 55.5% | 39.1% | 3.5% |
| 48,195 | GREENE | 21,094 | 11,332 | 8,480 | 924 | 358 | 2,852 R | 53.7% | 40.2% | 4.4% |
| 5,379 | HAMILTON | 3,682 | 2,388 | 1,114 | 133 | 47 | 1,274 R | 64.9% | 30.3% | 3.6% |
| 64,427 | HERKIMER | 27,705 | 14,147 | 12,224 | 969 | 365 | 1,923 R | 51.1% | 44.1% | 3.5% |
| 111,738 | JEFFERSON | 36,418 | 18,192 | 16,799 | 1,029 | 398 | 1,393 R | 50.0% | 46.1% | 2.8% |
| 2,465,326 | KINGS | 617,105 | 96,605 | 497,468 | 19,977 | 3,055 | 400,863 D | 15.7% | 80.6% | 3.2% |
| 26,944 | LEWIS | 10,923 | 6,103 | 4,333 | 324 | 163 | 1,770 R | 55.9% | 39.7% | 3.0% |
| 64,328 | LIVINGSTON | 27,223 | 15,244 | 10,476 | 1,053 | 450 | 4,768 R | 56.0% | 38.5% | 3.9% |
| 69,441 | MADISON | 28,366 | 14,879 | 12,017 | 1,092 | 378 | 2,862 R | 52.5% | 42.4% | 3.8% |
| 735,343 | MONROE | 317,762 | 141,266 | 161,743 | 11,520 | 3,233 | 20,477 D | 44.5% | 50.9% | 3.6% |
| 49,708 | MONTGOMERY | 20,809 | 9,765 | 10,249 | 487 | 308 | 484 D | 46.9% | 49.3% | 2.3% |
| 1,334,544 | NASSAU | 589,707 | 226,954 | 341,610 | 14,780 | 6,363 | 114,656 D | 38.5% | 57.9% | 2.5% |
| 1,537,195 | NEW YORK | 563,232 | 79,921 | 449,300 | 30,923 | 3,088 | 369,379 D | 14.2% | 79.8% | 5.5% |
| 219,846 | NIAGARA | 93,257 | 40,952 | 47,781 | 3,257 | 1,267 | 6,829 D | 43.9% | 51.2% | 3.5% |
| 235,469 | ONEIDA | 95,996 | 47,603 | 43,933 | 3,160 | 1,300 | 3,670 R | 49.6% | 45.8% | 3.3% |
| 458,336 | ONONDAGA | 203,629 | 83,678 | 109,896 | 7,670 | 2,385 | 26,218 D | 41.1% | 54.0% | 3.8% |
| 100,224 | ONTARIO | 45,948 | 23,885 | 19,761 | 1,793 | 509 | 4,124 R | 52.0% | 43.0% | 3.9% |
| 341,367 | ORANGE | 126,549 | 62,852 | 58,170 | 4,192 | 1,335 | 4,682 R | 49.7% | 46.0% | 3.3% |
| 44,171 | ORLEANS | 15,843 | 9,202 | 5,991 | 474 | 176 | 3,211 R | 58.1% | 37.8% | 3.0% |
| 122,377 | OSWEGO | 48,473 | 23,249 | 22,857 | 1,699 | 668 | 392 R | 48.0% | 47.2% | 3.5% |
| 61,676 | OTSEGO | 25,358 | 12,219 | 11,460 | 1,419 | 260 | 759 R | 48.2% | 45.2% | 5.6% |
| 95,745 | PUTNAM | 42,547 | 21,853 | 18,525 | 1,730 | 439 | 3,328 R | 51.4% | 43.5% | 4.1% |
| 2,229,379 | QUEENS | 555,930 | 122,052 | 416,967 | 13,720 | 3,191 | 294,915 D | 22.0% | 75.0% | 2.5% |
| 152,538 | RENSSELAER | 68,436 | 29,562 | 34,808 | 3,291 | 775 | 5,246 D | 43.2% | 50.9% | 4.8% |
| 443,728 | RICHMOND | 142,121 | 63,903 | 73,828 | 3,550 | 840 | 9,925 D | 45.0% | 51.9% | 2.5% |
| 286,753 | ROCKLAND | 122,580 | 48,441 | 69,530 | 3,502 | 1,107 | 21,089 D | 39.5% | 56.7% | 2.9% |
| 111,931 | ST. LAWRENCE | 39,779 | 16,449 | 21,386 | 1,488 | 456 | 4,937 D | 41.4% | 53.8% | 3.7% |
| 200,635 | SARATOGA | 95,057 | 46,623 | 43,359 | 4,149 | 926 | 3,264 R | 49.0% | 45.6% | 4.4% |
| 146,555 | SCHENECTADY | 66,946 | 27,961 | 35,534 | 2,750 | 701 | 7,573 D | 41.8% | 53.1% | 4.1% |
| 31,582 | SCHOHARIE | 13,548 | 7,459 | 5,390 | 551 | 148 | 2,069 R | 55.1% | 39.8% | 4.1% |
| 19,224 | SCHUYLER | 8,153 | 4,381 | 3,301 | 369 | 102 | 1,080 R | 53.7% | 40.5% | 4.5% |
| 33,342 | SENECA | 14,333 | 6,734 | 6,841 | 560 | 198 | 107 D | 47.0% | 47.7% | 3.9% |
| 98,726 | STEUBEN | 40,563 | 24,200 | 14,600 | 1,248 | 515 | 9,600 R | 59.7% | 36.0% | 3.1% |
| 1,419,369 | SUFFOLK | 573,866 | 240,992 | 306,306 | 18,130 | 8,438 | 65,314 D | 42.0% | 53.4% | 3.2% |
| 73,966 | SULLIVAN | 28,524 | 12,703 | 14,348 | 1,156 | 317 | 1,645 D | 44.5% | 50.3% | 4.1% |
| 51,784 | TIOGA | 22,454 | 12,239 | 9,170 | 846 | 199 | 3,069 R | 54.5% | 40.8% | 3.8% |
| 96,501 | TOMPKINS | 40,060 | 13,351 | 21,807 | 4,548 | 354 | 8,456 D | 33.3% | 54.4% | 11.4% |
| 177,749 | ULSTER | 78,225 | 33,447 | 38,162 | 5,732 | 884 | 4,715 D | 42.8% | 48.8% | 7.3% |
| 63,303 | WARREN | 28,621 | 14,993 | 12,193 | 1,177 | 258 | 2,800 R | 52.4% | 42.6% | 4.1% |
| 61,042 | WASHINGTON | 23,555 | 12,596 | 9,641 | 997 | 321 | 2,955 R | 53.5% | 40.9% | 4.2% |
| 93,765 | WAYNE | 38,329 | 21,701 | 14,977 | 1,202 | 449 | 6,724 R | 56.6% | 39.1% | 3.1% |
| 923,459 | WESTCHESTER | 371,775 | 139,278 | 218,010 | 11,596 | 2,891 | 78,732 D | 37.5% | 58.6% | 3.1% |
| 43,424 | WYOMING | 17,627 | 10,809 | 5,935 | 548 | 335 | 4,874 R | 61.3% | 33.7% | 3.1% |
| 24,621 | YATES | 10,052 | 5,565 | 3,962 | 386 | 139 | 1,603 R | 55.4% | 39.4% | 3.8% |
| 18,976,457 | TOTAL | 6,821,999 | 2,403,374 | 4,107,697 | 244,030 | 66,898 | 1,704,323 D | 35.2% | 60.2% | 3.6% |

# NEW YORK

## PRESIDENT 1996

| 1995 Census Pop. Est. | County | Total Vote | Republican | Democratic | Reform (Perot) | Other | Rep.-Dem. Plurality | Percentage of Total Vote | | |
|---|---|---|---|---|---|---|---|---|---|---|
| | | | | | | | | Rep. | Dem. | Reform |
| 289,549 | ALBANY | 140,991 | 39,785 | 85,993 | 11,957 | 3,256 | 46,208 D | 28.2% | 61.0% | 8.5% |
| 51,390 | ALLEGANY | 17,703 | 8,107 | 6,621 | 2,730 | 245 | 1,486 R | 45.8% | 37.4% | 15.4% |
| 1,187,798 | BRONX | 289,350 | 30,435 | 248,276 | 7,186 | 3,453 | 217,841 D | 10.5% | 85.8% | 2.5% |
| 204,436 | BROOME | 86,814 | 31,327 | 44,407 | 9,114 | 1,966 | 13,080 D | 36.1% | 51.2% | 10.5% |
| 85,596 | CATTARAUGUS | 31,643 | 12,971 | 13,029 | 5,151 | 492 | 58 D | 41.0% | 41.2% | 16.3% |
| 82,988 | CAYUGA | 31,894 | 11,093 | 15,879 | 4,420 | 502 | 4,786 D | 34.8% | 49.8% | 13.9% |
| 141,677 | CHAUTAUQUA | 56,290 | 21,261 | 26,831 | 7,484 | 714 | 5,570 D | 37.8% | 47.7% | 13.3% |
| 94,082 | CHEMUNG | 35,813 | 14,287 | 16,977 | 3,967 | 582 | 2,690 D | 39.9% | 47.4% | 11.1% |
| 51,977 | CHENANGO | 19,279 | 7,319 | 8,797 | 2,822 | 341 | 1,478 D | 38.0% | 45.6% | 14.6% |
| 83,370 | CLINTON | 29,060 | 9,759 | 15,386 | 3,488 | 427 | 5,627 D | 33.6% | 52.9% | 12.0% |
| 63,703 | COLUMBIA | 27,403 | 10,324 | 12,910 | 3,466 | 703 | 2,586 D | 37.7% | 47.1% | 12.6% |
| 49,052 | CORTLAND | 19,449 | 7,606 | 9,130 | 2,398 | 315 | 1,524 D | 39.1% | 46.9% | 12.3% |
| 47,584 | DELAWARE | 19,394 | 7,684 | 8,724 | 2,601 | 385 | 1,040 D | 39.6% | 45.0% | 13.4% |
| 262,062 | DUTCHESS | 103,821 | 41,929 | 47,339 | 12,294 | 2,259 | 5,410 D | 40.4% | 45.6% | 11.8% |
| 962,046 | ERIE | 410,234 | 132,343 | 224,554 | 45,679 | 7,658 | 92,211 D | 32.3% | 54.7% | 11.1% |
| 37,887 | ESSEX | 16,986 | 6,379 | 7,893 | 2,363 | 351 | 1,514 D | 37.6% | 46.5% | 13.9% |
| 49,400 | FRANKLIN | 16,394 | 5,072 | 8,494 | 2,499 | 329 | 3,422 D | 30.9% | 51.8% | 15.2% |
| 54,106 | FULTON | 21,130 | 7,881 | 9,779 | 3,214 | 256 | 1,898 D | 37.3% | 46.3% | 15.2% |
| 61,316 | GENESEE | 24,238 | 10,821 | 10,074 | 2,996 | 347 | 747 R | 44.6% | 41.6% | 12.4% |
| 47,660 | GREENE | 20,124 | 8,712 | 8,251 | 2,790 | 371 | 461 R | 43.3% | 41.0% | 13.9% |
| 5,208 | HAMILTON | 3,612 | 1,841 | 1,228 | 492 | 51 | 613 R | 51.0% | 34.0% | 13.6% |
| 66,354 | HERKIMER | 26,626 | 10,085 | 11,910 | 4,235 | 396 | 1,825 D | 37.9% | 44.7% | 15.9% |
| 114,712 | JEFFERSON | 34,127 | 12,362 | 16,783 | 4,561 | 421 | 4,421 D | 36.2% | 49.2% | 13.4% |
| 2,244,021 | KINGS | 539,833 | 81,406 | 432,232 | 15,031 | 11,164 | 350,826 D | 15.1% | 80.1% | 2.8% |
| 27,711 | LEWIS | 10,185 | 3,965 | 4,402 | 1,669 | 149 | 437 D | 38.9% | 43.2% | 16.4% |
| 65,770 | LIVINGSTON | 25,138 | 10,981 | 10,868 | 2,889 | 400 | 113 R | 43.7% | 43.2% | 11.5% |
| 71,490 | MADISON | 26,988 | 11,324 | 11,832 | 3,379 | 453 | 508 D | 42.0% | 43.8% | 12.5% |
| 723,177 | MONROE | 309,994 | 115,694 | 164,858 | 23,936 | 5,506 | 49,164 D | 37.3% | 53.2% | 7.7% |
| 52,068 | MONTGOMERY | 21,166 | 7,172 | 10,485 | 3,253 | 256 | 3,313 D | 33.9% | 49.5% | 15.4% |
| 1,305,772 | NASSAU | 544,664 | 196,820 | 303,587 | 36,122 | 8,135 | 106,767 D | 36.1% | 55.7% | 6.6% |
| 1,518,910 | NEW YORK | 492,989 | 67,839 | 394,131 | 11,144 | 19,875 | 326,292 D | 13.8% | 79.9% | 2.3% |
| 222,006 | NIAGARA | 89,444 | 31,438 | 44,203 | 12,564 | 1,239 | 12,765 D | 35.1% | 49.4% | 14.0% |
| 242,208 | ONEIDA | 94,929 | 37,996 | 44,399 | 11,296 | 1,238 | 6,403 D | 40.0% | 46.8% | 11.9% |
| 469,818 | ONONDAGA | 194,939 | 73,771 | 100,190 | 17,602 | 3,376 | 26,419 D | 37.8% | 51.4% | 9.0% |
| 99,138 | ONTARIO | 41,439 | 17,237 | 19,156 | 4,391 | 655 | 1,919 D | 41.6% | 46.2% | 10.6% |
| 322,892 | ORANGE | 114,538 | 45,956 | 54,995 | 11,778 | 1,809 | 9,039 D | 40.1% | 48.0% | 10.3% |
| 45,144 | ORLEANS | 15,268 | 6,865 | 6,233 | 1,986 | 184 | 632 R | 45.0% | 40.8% | 13.0% |
| 125,794 | OSWEGO | 45,673 | 17,159 | 20,440 | 7,499 | 575 | 3,281 D | 37.6% | 44.8% | 16.4% |
| 61,575 | OTSEGO | 24,126 | 8,774 | 11,470 | 3,217 | 665 | 2,696 D | 36.4% | 47.5% | 13.3% |
| 90,320 | PUTNAM | 38,432 | 17,452 | 16,173 | 4,032 | 775 | 1,279 R | 45.4% | 42.1% | 10.5% |
| 1,963,628 | QUEENS | 511,206 | 107,650 | 372,925 | 22,288 | 8,343 | 265,275 D | 21.1% | 73.0% | 4.4% |
| 155,684 | RENSSELAER | 67,625 | 23,482 | 34,273 | 8,405 | 1,465 | 10,791 D | 34.7% | 50.7% | 12.4% |
| 397,719 | RICHMOND | 128,007 | 52,207 | 64,684 | 8,968 | 2,148 | 12,477 D | 40.8% | 50.5% | 7.0% |
| 276,898 | ROCKLAND | 112,241 | 40,395 | 63,127 | 6,798 | 1,921 | 22,732 D | 36.0% | 56.2% | 6.1% |
| 115,482 | ST. LAWRENCE | 38,477 | 10,827 | 21,798 | 5,309 | 543 | 10,971 D | 28.1% | 56.7% | 13.8% |
| 194,332 | SARATOGA | 85,665 | 34,337 | 39,832 | 10,141 | 1,355 | 5,495 D | 40.1% | 46.5% | 11.8% |
| 148,888 | SCHENECTADY | 66,709 | 22,106 | 35,404 | 7,865 | 1,334 | 13,298 D | 33.1% | 53.1% | 11.8% |
| 32,840 | SCHOHARIE | 13,261 | 5,353 | 5,902 | 1,796 | 210 | 549 D | 40.4% | 44.5% | 13.5% |
| 19,247 | SCHUYLER | 7,635 | 3,134 | 3,303 | 1,037 | 161 | 169 D | 41.0% | 43.3% | 13.6% |
| 32,593 | SENECA | 13,955 | 5,004 | 6,825 | 1,889 | 237 | 1,821 D | 35.9% | 48.9% | 13.5% |
| 99,949 | STEUBEN | 38,171 | 17,710 | 14,481 | 5,496 | 484 | 3,229 R | 46.4% | 37.9% | 14.4% |
| 1,353,704 | SUFFOLK | 505,213 | 182,510 | 261,828 | 52,209 | 8,666 | 79,318 D | 36.1% | 51.8% | 10.3% |
| 70,452 | SULLIVAN | 28,244 | 9,321 | 15,052 | 3,453 | 418 | 5,731 D | 33.0% | 53.3% | 12.2% |
| 52,967 | TIOGA | 21,282 | 9,416 | 8,769 | 2,721 | 376 | 647 R | 44.2% | 41.2% | 12.8% |
| 96,384 | TOMPKINS | 37,124 | 11,532 | 20,772 | 2,623 | 2,197 | 9,240 D | 31.1% | 56.0% | 7.1% |
| 167,862 | ULSTER | 73,851 | 26,212 | 35,852 | 9,246 | 2,541 | 9,640 D | 35.5% | 48.5% | 12.5% |
| 61,544 | WARREN | 26,791 | 11,152 | 11,603 | 3,623 | 413 | 451 D | 41.6% | 43.3% | 13.5% |
| 61,015 | WASHINGTON | 22,544 | 8,954 | 9,572 | 3,648 | 370 | 618 D | 39.7% | 42.5% | 16.2% |
| 93,971 | WAYNE | 35,997 | 15,837 | 15,145 | 4,619 | 396 | 692 R | 44.0% | 42.1% | 12.8% |
| 890,918 | WESTCHESTER | 344,863 | 123,719 | 196,310 | 18,028 | 6,806 | 72,591 D | 35.9% | 56.9% | 5.2% |
| 44,083 | WYOMING | 15,821 | 7,477 | 5,735 | 2,411 | 198 | 1,742 R | 47.3% | 36.2% | 15.2% |
| 24,154 | YATES | 9,327 | 3,925 | 4,066 | 1,190 | 146 | 141 D | 42.1% | 43.6% | 12.8% |
| 18,136,081 | TOTAL | 6,316,129 | 1,933,492 | 3,756,177 | 503,458 | 123,002 | 1,822,685 D | 30.6% | 59.5% | 8.0% |

# NEW YORK

## PRESIDENT 1992

| 1990 Census Population | County | Total Vote | Republican | Democratic | Perot | Other | Plurality | Percentage Total Vote | | |
|---|---|---|---|---|---|---|---|---|---|---|
| | | | | | | | | Rep. | Dem. | Perot |
| 292,594 | ALBANY | 155,357 | 49,452 | 80,641 | 24,064 | 1,200 | 31,189 D | 31.8% | 51.9% | 15.5% |
| 50,470 | ALLEGANY | 18,719 | 8,976 | 4,848 | 4,703 | 192 | 4,128 R | 48.0% | 25.9% | 25.1% |
| 1,203,789 | BRONX | 305,460 | 63,310 | 225,038 | 15,115 | 1,997 | 161,728 D | 20.7% | 73.7% | 4.9% |
| 212,160 | BROOME | 99,846 | 34,653 | 43,444 | 21,280 | 469 | 8,791 D | 34.7% | 43.5% | 21.3% |
| 84,234 | CATTARAUGUS | 35,092 | 13,944 | 10,150 | 10,662 | 336 | 3,282 R | 39.7% | 28.9% | 30.4% |
| 82,313 | CAYUGA | 35,671 | 12,065 | 13,088 | 10,279 | 239 | 1,023 D | 33.8% | 36.7% | 28.8% |
| 141,895 | CHAUTAUQUA | 62,785 | 21,222 | 22,645 | 18,455 | 463 | 1,423 D | 33.8% | 36.1% | 29.4% |
| 95,195 | CHEMUNG | 39,135 | 16,088 | 15,099 | 7,493 | 455 | 989 R | 41.1% | 38.6% | 19.1% |
| 51,768 | CHENANGO | 21,787 | 8,114 | 8,017 | 5,356 | 300 | 97 R | 37.2% | 36.8% | 24.6% |
| 85,969 | CLINTON | 31,987 | 13,455 | 12,881 | 5,389 | 262 | 574 R | 42.1% | 40.3% | 16.8% |
| 62,982 | COLUMBIA | 29,056 | 11,568 | 11,368 | 5,829 | 291 | 200 R | 39.8% | 39.1% | 20.1% |
| 48,963 | CORTLAND | 20,851 | 7,782 | 7,815 | 5,098 | 156 | 33 D | 37.3% | 37.5% | 24.4% |
| 47,225 | DELAWARE | 20,530 | 8,829 | 7,152 | 4,404 | 145 | 1,677 R | 43.0% | 34.8% | 21.5% |
| 259,462 | DUTCHESS | 115,328 | 46,709 | 41,655 | 26,320 | 644 | 5,054 R | 40.5% | 36.1% | 22.8% |
| 968,532 | ERIE | 451,496 | 129,444 | 196,233 | 123,358 | 2,461 | 66,789 D | 28.7% | 43.5% | 27.3% |
| 37,152 | ESSEX | 18,973 | 8,278 | 6,717 | 3,784 | 194 | 1,561 R | 43.6% | 35.4% | 19.9% |
| 46,540 | FRANKLIN | 18,365 | 6,635 | 7,654 | 3,857 | 219 | 1,019 D | 36.1% | 41.7% | 21.0% |
| 54,191 | FULTON | 22,845 | 9,137 | 8,400 | 5,120 | 188 | 737 R | 40.0% | 36.8% | 22.4% |
| 60,060 | GENESEE | 26,222 | 11,663 | 8,071 | 6,192 | 296 | 3,592 R | 44.5% | 30.8% | 23.6% |
| 44,739 | GREENE | 21,190 | 9,390 | 6,924 | 4,689 | 187 | 2,466 R | 44.3% | 32.7% | 22.1% |
| 5,279 | HAMILTON | 3,817 | 2,038 | 963 | 793 | 23 | 1,075 R | 53.4% | 25.2% | 20.8% |
| 65,797 | HERKIMER | 29,939 | 12,052 | 10,880 | 6,866 | 141 | 1,172 R | 40.3% | 36.3% | 22.9% |
| 110,943 | JEFFERSON | 37,426 | 14,227 | 13,380 | 9,461 | 358 | 847 R | 38.0% | 35.8% | 25.3% |
| 2,300,664 | KINGS | 581,594 | 133,344 | 411,183 | 33,014 | 4,053 | 277,839 D | 22.9% | 70.7% | 5.7% |
| 26,796 | LEWIS | 11,032 | 4,101 | 3,676 | 3,164 | 91 | 425 R | 37.2% | 33.3% | 28.7% |
| 62,372 | LIVINGSTON | 26,813 | 12,122 | 8,648 | 5,775 | 268 | 3,474 R | 45.2% | 32.3% | 21.5% |
| 69,120 | MADISON | 29,033 | 11,293 | 10,099 | 7,391 | 250 | 1,194 R | 38.9% | 34.8% | 25.5% |
| 713,968 | MONROE | 340,369 | 134,021 | 141,502 | 63,229 | 1,617 | 7,481 D | 39.4% | 41.6% | 18.6% |
| 51,981 | MONTGOMERY | 23,443 | 8,802 | 9,509 | 5,020 | 112 | 707 D | 37.5% | 40.6% | 21.4% |
| 1,287,348 | NASSAU | 609,326 | 246,881 | 282,593 | 77,097 | 2,755 | 35,712 D | 40.5% | 46.4% | 12.7% |
| 1,487,536 | NEW YORK | 531,753 | 84,501 | 416,142 | 27,689 | 3,421 | 331,641 D | 15.9% | 78.3% | 5.2% |
| 220,756 | NIAGRA | 96,584 | 30,401 | 35,649 | 30,126 | 408 | 5,248 D | 31.5% | 36.9% | 31.2% |
| 250,836 | ONEIDA | 108,342 | 43,806 | 40,966 | 22,717 | 853 | 2,840 R | 40.4% | 37.8% | 21.0% |
| 468,973 | ONONDAGA | 214,886 | 77,642 | 90,645 | 45,175 | 1,424 | 13,003 D | 36.1% | 42.2% | 21.0% |
| 95,101 | ONTARIO | 44,889 | 18,995 | 16,064 | 9,571 | 259 | 2,931 R | 42.3% | 35.8% | 21.3% |
| 307,647 | ORANGE | 122,520 | 53,493 | 45,946 | 22,499 | 582 | 7,547 R | 43.7% | 37.5% | 18.4% |
| 41,846 | ORLEANS | 16,749 | 7,468 | 4,927 | 4,275 | 79 | 2,541 R | 44.6% | 29.4% | 25.5% |
| 121,771 | OSWEGO | 50,931 | 18,530 | 16,990 | 14,853 | 558 | 1,540 R | 36.4% | 33.4% | 29.2% |
| 60,517 | OTSEGO | 26,606 | 10,141 | 10,471 | 5,841 | 153 | 330 D | 38.1% | 39.4% | 22.0% |
| 83,941 | PUTNAM | 41,263 | 18,934 | 14,048 | 8,011 | 270 | 4,886 R | 45.9% | 34.0% | 19.4% |
| 1,951,598 | QUEENS | 555,956 | 157,561 | 349,520 | 46,014 | 2,861 | 191,959 D | 28.3% | 62.9% | 8.3% |
| 154,429 | RENSSELAER | 74,579 | 28,937 | 29,793 | 15,198 | 651 | 856 D | 38.8% | 39.9% | 20.4% |
| 378,977 | RICHMOND | 147,760 | 70,707 | 56,901 | 19,678 | 474 | 13,806 R | 47.9% | 38.5% | 13.3% |
| 265,475 | ROCKLAND | 121,831 | 49,608 | 56,759 | 15,026 | 438 | 7,151 D | 40.7% | 46.6% | 12.3% |
| 111,974 | ST. LAWRENCE | 42,317 | 13,901 | 18,197 | 9,758 | 461 | 4,296 D | 32.8% | 43.0% | 23.1% |
| 181,276 | SARATOGA | 89,810 | 36,917 | 33,011 | 19,091 | 791 | 3,906 R | 41.1% | 36.8% | 21.3% |
| 149,285 | SCHENECTADY | 73,869 | 26,258 | 32,335 | 14,838 | 438 | 6,077 D | 35.5% | 43.8% | 20.1% |
| 31,859 | SCHOHARIE | 14,147 | 5,678 | 4,997 | 3,327 | 145 | 681 R | 40.1% | 35.3% | 23.5% |
| 18,662 | SCHUYLER | 8,199 | 3,226 | 2,859 | 2,051 | 63 | 367 R | 39.3% | 34.9% | 25.0% |
| 33,683 | SENECA | 14,974 | 5,432 | 5,810 | 3,660 | 72 | 378 D | 36.3% | 38.8% | 24.4% |
| 99,088 | STEUBEN | 41,408 | 19,761 | 12,043 | 9,378 | 226 | 7,718 R | 47.7% | 29.1% | 22.6% |
| 1,321,864 | SUFFOLK | 567,953 | 229,467 | 220,811 | 112,973 | 4,702 | 8,656 R | 40.4% | 38.9% | 19.9% |
| 69,277 | SULLIVAN | 31,635 | 11,396 | 13,717 | 6,336 | 186 | 2,321 D | 36.0% | 43.4% | 20.0% |
| 52,337 | TIOGA | 23,065 | 9,287 | 7,791 | 5,867 | 120 | 1,496 R | 40.3% | 33.8% | 25.4% |
| 94,097 | TOMPKINS | 41,658 | 11,520 | 23,197 | 6,704 | 237 | 11,677 D | 27.7% | 55.7% | 16.1% |
| 165,304 | ULSTER | 80,821 | 29,223 | 32,886 | 17,952 | 760 | 3,663 D | 36.2% | 40.7% | 22.2% |
| 59,209 | WARREN | 28,767 | 12,260 | 9,820 | 6,401 | 286 | 2,440 R | 42.6% | 34.1% | 22.3% |
| 59,330 | WASHINGTON | 25,135 | 10,305 | 8,429 | 6,143 | 258 | 1,876 R | 41.0% | 33.5% | 24.4% |
| 89,123 | WAYNE | 39,306 | 18,019 | 11,866 | 9,188 | 233 | 6,153 R | 45.8% | 30.2% | 23.4% |
| 874,866 | WESTCHESTER | 378,815 | 151,990 | 184,300 | 39,933 | 2,592 | 32,310 D | 40.1% | 48.7% | 10.5% |
| 42,507 | WYOMING | 16,374 | 7,324 | 4,045 | 4,837 | 168 | 2,487 R | 44.7% | 24.7% | 29.5% |
| 22,810 | YATES | 10,092 | 4,366 | 3,242 | 2,354 | 130 | 1,124 R | 43.3% | 32.1% | 23.3% |
| 17,990,455 | TOTAL | 6,926,925 | 2,346,649 | 3,444,450 | 1,090,721 | 45,105 | 1,097,801 D | 33.9% | 49.7% | 15.7% |

# NEW YORK

## PRESIDENT 1988

| 1980 Census Population | County | Total Vote | Republican | Democratic | Other | Rep.-Dem. Plurality | Percentage Total Vote Rep. | Dem. | Major Vote Rep. | Dem. |
|---|---|---|---|---|---|---|---|---|---|---|
| 285,909 | ALBANY | 147,461 | 59,534 | 86,564 | 1,363 | 27,030 D | 40.4% | 58.7% | 40.7% | 59.3% |
| 51,742 | ALLEGANY | 17,626 | 11,880 | 5,614 | 132 | 6,266 R | 67.4% | 31.9% | 67.9% | 32.1% |
| 1,168,972 | BRONX | 298,081 | 76,043 | 218,245 | 3,793 | 142,202 D | 25.5% | 73.2% | 25.8% | 74.2% |
| 213,648 | BROOME | 96,365 | 47,610 | 48,130 | 625 | 520 D | 49.4% | 49.9% | 49.7% | 50.3% |
| 85,697 | CATTARAUGUS | 32,428 | 19,691 | 12,447 | 290 | 7,244 R | 60.7% | 38.4% | 61.3% | 38.7% |
| 79,894 | CAYUGA | 32,285 | 16,934 | 15,044 | 307 | 1,890 R | 52.5% | 46.6% | 53.0% | 47.0% |
| 146,925 | CHAUTAUQUA | 57,867 | 31,642 | 25,814 | 411 | 5,828 R | 54.7% | 44.6% | 55.1% | 44.9% |
| 97,656 | CHEMUNG | 37,139 | 20,951 | 15,966 | 222 | 4,985 R | 56.4% | 43.0% | 56.8% | 43.2% |
| 49,344 | CHENANGO | 19,902 | 11,727 | 8,021 | 154 | 3,706 R | 58.9% | 40.3% | 59.4% | 40.6% |
| 80,750 | CLINTON | 28,563 | 15,702 | 12,670 | 191 | 3,032 R | 55.0% | 44.4% | 55.3% | 44.7% |
| 59,487 | COLUMBIA | 26,924 | 15,111 | 11,585 | 228 | 3,526 R | 56.1% | 43.0% | 56.6% | 43.4% |
| 48,820 | CORTLAND | 18,769 | 10,934 | 7,673 | 162 | 3,261 R | 58.3% | 40.9% | 58.8% | 41.2% |
| 46,824 | DELAWARE | 19,010 | 11,391 | 7,463 | 156 | 3,928 R | 59.9% | 39.3% | 60.4% | 39.6% |
| 245,055 | DUTCHESS | 101,959 | 62,165 | 38,968 | 826 | 23,197 R | 61.0% | 38.2% | 61.5% | 38.5% |
| 1,015,472 | ERIE | 430,792 | 188,796 | 238,779 | 3,217 | 49,983 D | 43.8% | 55.4% | 44.2% | 55.8% |
| 36,176 | ESSEX | 17,113 | 10,350 | 6,623 | 140 | 3,727 R | 60.5% | 38.7% | 61.0% | 39.0% |
| 44,929 | FRANKLIN | 17,192 | 9,135 | 7,928 | 129 | 1,207 R | 53.1% | 46.1% | 53.5% | 46.5% |
| 55,153 | FULTON | 20,931 | 11,757 | 9,012 | 162 | 2,745 R | 56.2% | 43.1% | 56.6% | 43.4% |
| 59,400 | GENESEE | 24,332 | 14,182 | 9,945 | 205 | 4,237 R | 58.3% | 40.9% | 58.8% | 41.2% |
| 40,861 | GREENE | 19,319 | 11,874 | 7,265 | 180 | 4,609 R | 61.5% | 37.6% | 62.0% | 38.0% |
| 5,034 | HAMILTON | 3,317 | 2,320 | 976 | 21 | 1,344 R | 69.9% | 29.4% | 70.4% | 29.6% |
| 66,714 | HERKIMER | 28,022 | 15,104 | 12,694 | 224 | 2,410 R | 53.9% | 45.3% | 54.3% | 45.7% |
| 88,151 | JEFFERSON | 33,622 | 19,304 | 14,137 | 181 | 5,167 R | 57.4% | 42.0% | 57.7% | 42.3% |
| 2,230,936 | KINGS | 549,019 | 178,961 | 363,916 | 6,142 | 184,955 D | 32.6% | 66.3% | 33.0% | 67.0% |
| 25,035 | LEWIS | 10,138 | 5,787 | 4,252 | 99 | 1,535 R | 57.1% | 41.9% | 57.6% | 42.4% |
| 57,006 | LIVINGSTON | 23,697 | 14,004 | 9,506 | 187 | 4,498 R | 59.1% | 40.1% | 59.6% | 40.4% |
| 65,150 | MADISON | 25,754 | 14,902 | 10,665 | 187 | 4,237 R | 57.9% | 41.4% | 58.3% | 41.7% |
| 702,238 | MONROE | 311,466 | 155,271 | 153,650 | 2,545 | 1,621 R | 49.9% | 49.3% | 50.3% | 49.7% |
| 53,439 | MONTGOMERY | 22,685 | 11,128 | 11,371 | 186 | 243 D | 49.1% | 50.1% | 49.5% | 50.5% |
| 1,321,582 | NASSAU | 592,418 | 337,430 | 250,130 | 4,858 | 87,300 R | 57.0% | 42.2% | 57.4% | 42.6% |
| 1,428,285 | NEW YORK | 506,551 | 115,927 | 385,675 | 4,949 | 269,748 D | 22.9% | 76.1% | 23.1% | 76.9% |
| 227,354 | NIAGARA | 86,868 | 42,537 | 43,801 | 530 | 1,264 D | 49.0% | 50.4% | 49.3% | 50.7% |
| 253,466 | ONEIDA | 103,461 | 55,039 | 47,665 | 757 | 7,374 R | 53.2% | 46.1% | 53.6% | 46.4% |
| 463,920 | ONONDAGA | 200,485 | 104,080 | 94,751 | 1,654 | 9,329 R | 51.9% | 47.3% | 52.3% | 47.7% |
| 88,909 | ONTARIO | 39,435 | 21,780 | 17,341 | 314 | 4,439 R | 55.2% | 44.0% | 55.7% | 44.3% |
| 259,603 | ORANGE | 104,810 | 65,446 | 38,465 | 899 | 26,981 R | 62.4% | 36.7% | 63.0% | 37.0% |
| 38,496 | ORLEANS | 15,055 | 9,028 | 5,913 | 114 | 3,115 R | 60.0% | 39.3% | 60.4% | 39.6% |
| 113,901 | OSWEGO | 44,211 | 25,362 | 18,430 | 419 | 6,932 R | 57.4% | 41.7% | 57.9% | 42.1% |
| 59,075 | OTSEGO | 24,335 | 13,021 | 11,069 | 245 | 1,952 R | 53.5% | 45.5% | 54.1% | 45.9% |
| 77,193 | PUTNAM | 36,500 | 24,086 | 12,158 | 256 | 11,928 R | 66.0% | 33.3% | 66.5% | 33.5% |
| 1,891,325 | QUEENS | 546,729 | 217,049 | 325,147 | 4,533 | 108,098 D | 39.7% | 59.5% | 40.0% | 60.0% |
| 151,966 | RENSSELAER | 69,197 | 35,412 | 33,066 | 719 | 2,346 R | 51.2% | 47.8% | 51.7% | 48.3% |
| 352,121 | RICHMOND | 125,975 | 77,427 | 47,812 | 736 | 29,615 R | 61.5% | 38.0% | 61.8% | 38.2% |
| 259,530 | ROCKLAND | 112,301 | 63,825 | 47,634 | 842 | 16,191 R | 56.8% | 42.4% | 57.3% | 42.7% |
| 114,254 | ST. LAWRENCE | 39,481 | 20,290 | 18,921 | 270 | 1,369 R | 51.4% | 47.9% | 51.7% | 48.3% |
| 153,759 | SARATOGA | 75,788 | 43,498 | 31,684 | 606 | 11,814 R | 57.4% | 41.8% | 57.9% | 42.1% |
| 149,946 | SCHENECTADY | 70,386 | 33,364 | 36,483 | 539 | 3,119 D | 47.4% | 51.8% | 47.8% | 52.2% |
| 29,710 | SCHOHARIE | 12,536 | 7,008 | 5,389 | 139 | 1,619 R | 55.9% | 43.0% | 56.5% | 43.5% |
| 17,686 | SCHUYLER | 7,242 | 4,291 | 2,900 | 51 | 1,391 R | 59.3% | 40.0% | 59.7% | 40.3% |
| 33,733 | SENECA | 13,571 | 7,221 | 6,215 | 135 | 1,006 R | 53.2% | 45.8% | 53.7% | 46.3% |
| 99,217 | STEUBEN | 38,466 | 25,359 | 12,824 | 283 | 12,535 R | 65.9% | 33.3% | 66.4% | 33.6% |
| 1,284,231 | SUFFOLK | 514,350 | 311,242 | 199,215 | 3,893 | 112,027 R | 60.5% | 38.7% | 61.0% | 39.0% |
| 65,155 | SULLIVAN | 27,568 | 15,713 | 11,635 | 220 | 4,078 R | 57.0% | 42.2% | 57.5% | 42.5% |
| 49,812 | TIOGA | 20,946 | 12,670 | 8,102 | 174 | 4,568 R | 60.5% | 38.7% | 61.0% | 39.0% |
| 87,085 | TOMPKINS | 36,699 | 14,932 | 21,455 | 312 | 6,523 D | 40.7% | 58.5% | 41.0% | 59.0% |
| 158,158 | ULSTER | 72,557 | 41,173 | 30,744 | 640 | 10,429 R | 56.7% | 42.4% | 57.3% | 42.7% |
| 54,854 | WARREN | 24,622 | 15,860 | 8,580 | 182 | 7,280 R | 64.4% | 34.8% | 64.9% | 35.1% |
| 54,795 | WASHINGTON | 22,515 | 14,103 | 8,201 | 211 | 5,902 R | 62.6% | 36.4% | 63.2% | 36.8% |
| 84,581 | WAYNE | 33,902 | 20,613 | 12,959 | 330 | 7,654 R | 60.8% | 38.2% | 61.4% | 38.6% |
| 866,599 | WESTCHESTER | 371,008 | 197,956 | 169,860 | 3,192 | 28,096 R | 53.4% | 45.8% | 53.8% | 46.2% |
| 39,895 | WYOMING | 14,863 | 9,451 | 5,228 | 184 | 4,223 R | 63.6% | 35.2% | 64.4% | 35.6% |
| 21,459 | YATES | 9,074 | 5,488 | 3,507 | 79 | 1,981 R | 60.5% | 38.6% | 61.0% | 39.0% |
| 17,558,072 | TOTAL | 6,485,683 | 3,081,871 | 3,347,882 | 55,930 | 266,011 D | 47.5% | 51.6% | 47.9% | 52.1% |

# NEW YORK

## PRESIDENT 1984

| 1980 Census Population | County | Total Vote | Republican | Democratic | Other | Rep.-Dem. Plurality | | Percentage | | | |
|---|---|---|---|---|---|---|---|---|---|---|---|
| | | | | | | | | Total Vote | | Major Vote | |
| | | | | | | | | Rep. | Dem. | Rep. | Dem. |
| 285,909 | ALBANY | 150,592 | 74,542 | 75,447 | 603 | 905 | D | 49.5% | 50.1% | 49.7% | 50.3% |
| 51,742 | ALLEGANY | 19,304 | 14,527 | 4,720 | 57 | 9,807 | R | 75.3% | 24.5% | 75.5% | 24.5% |
| 1,168,972 | BRONX | 333,683 | 109,308 | 223,112 | 1,263 | 113,804 | D | 32.8% | 66.9% | 32.9% | 67.1% |
| 213,648 | BROOME | 96,089 | 58,109 | 37,658 | 322 | 20,451 | R | 60.5% | 39.2% | 60.7% | 39.3% |
| 85,697 | CATTARAUGUS | 34,468 | 24,162 | 10,194 | 112 | 13,968 | R | 70.1% | 29.6% | 70.3% | 29.7% |
| 79,894 | CAYUGA | 33,779 | 21,451 | 12,207 | 121 | 9,244 | R | 63.5% | 36.1% | 63.7% | 36.3% |
| 146,925 | CHAUTAUQUA | 62,724 | 39,597 | 22,986 | 141 | 16,611 | R | 63.1% | 36.6% | 63.3% | 36.7% |
| 97,656 | CHEMUNG | 39,647 | 24,909 | 14,638 | 100 | 10,271 | R | 62.8% | 36.9% | 63.0% | 37.0% |
| 49,344 | CHENANGO | 20,648 | 14,254 | 6,343 | 51 | 7,911 | R | 69.0% | 30.7% | 69.2% | 30.8% |
| 80,750 | CLINTON | 30,443 | 19,549 | 10,804 | 90 | 8,745 | R | 64.2% | 35.5% | 64.4% | 35.6% |
| 59,487 | COLUMBIA | 27,891 | 18,814 | 8,960 | 117 | 9,854 | R | 67.5% | 32.1% | 67.7% | 32.3% |
| 48,820 | CORTLAND | 20,224 | 13,691 | 6,438 | 95 | 7,253 | R | 67.7% | 31.8% | 68.0% | 32.0% |
| 46,824 | DELAWARE | 19,830 | 14,002 | 5,745 | 83 | 8,257 | R | 70.6% | 29.0% | 70.9% | 29.1% |
| 245,055 | DUTCHESS | 103,580 | 70,324 | 32,867 | 389 | 37,457 | R | 67.9% | 31.7% | 68.1% | 31.9% |
| 1,015,472 | ERIE | 461,671 | 222,882 | 237,631 | 1,158 | 14,749 | D | 48.3% | 51.5% | 48.4% | 51.6% |
| 36,176 | ESSEX | 17,320 | 12,114 | 5,119 | 87 | 6,995 | R | 69.9% | 29.6% | 70.3% | 29.7% |
| 44,929 | FRANKLIN | 17,064 | 10,617 | 6,400 | 47 | 4,217 | R | 62.2% | 37.5% | 62.4% | 37.6% |
| 55,153 | FULTON | 22,618 | 14,887 | 7,644 | 87 | 7,243 | R | 65.8% | 33.8% | 66.1% | 33.9% |
| 59,400 | GENESEE | 25,210 | 16,582 | 8,549 | 79 | 8,033 | R | 65.8% | 33.9% | 66.0% | 34.0% |
| 40,861 | GREENE | 20,070 | 14,150 | 5,858 | 62 | 8,292 | R | 70.5% | 29.2% | 70.7% | 29.3% |
| 5,034 | HAMILTON | 3,382 | 2,637 | 737 | 8 | 1,900 | R | 78.0% | 21.8% | 78.2% | 21.8% |
| 66,714 | HERKIMER | 29,258 | 18,827 | 10,346 | 85 | 8,481 | R | 64.3% | 35.4% | 64.5% | 35.5% |
| 88,151 | JEFFERSON | 34,496 | 23,445 | 10,960 | 91 | 12,485 | R | 68.0% | 31.8% | 68.1% | 31.9% |
| 2,230,936 | KINGS | 600,771 | 230,064 | 368,518 | 2,189 | 138,454 | D | 38.3% | 61.3% | 38.4% | 61.6% |
| 25,035 | LEWIS | 9,860 | 7,069 | 2,757 | 34 | 4,312 | R | 71.7% | 28.0% | 71.9% | 28.1% |
| 57,006 | LIVINGSTON | 23,892 | 16,389 | 7,399 | 104 | 8,990 | R | 68.6% | 31.0% | 68.9% | 31.1% |
| 65,150 | MADISON | 25,963 | 17,568 | 8,291 | 104 | 9,277 | R | 67.7% | 31.9% | 67.9% | 32.1% |
| 702,238 | MONROE | 316,277 | 182,696 | 132,109 | 1,472 | 50,587 | R | 57.8% | 41.8% | 58.0% | 42.0% |
| 53,439 | MONTGOMERY | 23,520 | 14,398 | 9,044 | 78 | 5,354 | R | 61.2% | 38.5% | 61.4% | 38.6% |
| 1,321,582 | NASSAU | 634,063 | 392,017 | 240,697 | 1,349 | 151,320 | R | 61.8% | 38.0% | 62.0% | 38.0% |
| 1,428,285 | NEW YORK | 526,671 | 144,281 | 379,521 | 2,869 | 235,240 | D | 27.4% | 72.1% | 27.5% | 72.5% |
| 227,354 | NIAGARA | 92,858 | 51,289 | 41,368 | 201 | 9,921 | R | 55.2% | 44.5% | 55.4% | 44.6% |
| 253,466 | ONEIDA | 108,269 | 65,377 | 42,603 | 289 | 22,774 | R | 60.4% | 39.3% | 60.5% | 39.5% |
| 463,920 | ONONDAGA | 204,314 | 121,857 | 81,777 | 680 | 40,080 | R | 59.6% | 40.0% | 59.8% | 40.2% |
| 88,909 | ONTARIO | 37,494 | 24,507 | 12,844 | 143 | 11,663 | R | 65.4% | 34.3% | 65.6% | 34.4% |
| 259,603 | ORANGE | 102,413 | 69,413 | 32,663 | 337 | 36,750 | R | 67.8% | 31.9% | 68.0% | 32.0% |
| 38,496 | ORLEANS | 15,024 | 10,543 | 4,429 | 52 | 6,114 | R | 70.2% | 29.5% | 70.4% | 29.6% |
| 113,901 | OSWEGO | 46,034 | 31,481 | 14,347 | 206 | 17,134 | R | 68.4% | 31.2% | 68.7% | 31.3% |
| 59,075 | OTSEGO | 26,511 | 16,777 | 9,582 | 152 | 7,195 | R | 63.3% | 36.1% | 63.6% | 36.4% |
| 77,193 | PUTNAM | 35,277 | 25,707 | 9,473 | 97 | 16,234 | R | 72.9% | 26.9% | 73.1% | 26.9% |
| 1,891,325 | QUEENS | 615,578 | 285,477 | 328,379 | 1,722 | 42,902 | D | 46.4% | 53.3% | 46.5% | 53.5% |
| 151,966 | RENSSELAER | 70,864 | 43,892 | 26,755 | 217 | 17,137 | R | 61.9% | 37.8% | 62.1% | 37.9% |
| 352,121 | RICHMOND | 127,826 | 83,187 | 44,345 | 294 | 38,842 | R | 65.1% | 34.7% | 65.2% | 34.8% |
| 259,530 | ROCKLAND | 115,018 | 70,020 | 44,687 | 311 | 25,333 | R | 60.9% | 38.9% | 61.0% | 39.0% |
| 114,254 | ST. LAWRENCE | 42,149 | 26,062 | 15,963 | 124 | 10,099 | R | 61.8% | 37.9% | 62.0% | 38.0% |
| 153,759 | SARATOGA | 69,788 | 47,394 | 22,166 | 228 | 25,228 | R | 67.9% | 31.8% | 68.1% | 31.9% |
| 149,946 | SCHENECTADY | 73,697 | 42,808 | 30,612 | 277 | 12,196 | R | 58.1% | 41.5% | 58.3% | 41.7% |
| 29,710 | SCHOHARIE | 12,788 | 8,692 | 3,996 | 100 | 4,696 | R | 68.0% | 31.2% | 68.5% | 31.5% |
| 17,686 | SCHUYLER | 7,660 | 5,207 | 2,422 | 31 | 2,785 | R | 68.0% | 31.6% | 68.3% | 31.7% |
| 33,733 | SENECA | 14,307 | 9,420 | 4,825 | 62 | 4,595 | R | 65.8% | 33.7% | 66.1% | 33.9% |
| 99,217 | STEUBEN | 39,417 | 28,848 | 10,471 | 98 | 18,377 | R | 73.2% | 26.6% | 73.4% | 26.6% |
| 1,284,231 | SUFFOLK | 508,056 | 335,485 | 171,295 | 1,276 | 164,190 | R | 66.0% | 33.7% | 66.2% | 33.8% |
| 65,155 | SULLIVAN | 28,590 | 18,037 | 10,475 | 78 | 7,562 | R | 63.1% | 36.6% | 63.3% | 36.7% |
| 49,812 | TIOGA | 20,817 | 14,856 | 5,860 | 101 | 8,996 | R | 71.4% | 28.2% | 71.7% | 28.3% |
| 87,085 | TOMPKINS | 37,777 | 18,255 | 19,357 | 165 | 1,102 | D | 48.3% | 51.2% | 48.5% | 51.5% |
| 158,158 | ULSTER | 74,102 | 47,372 | 26,445 | 285 | 20,927 | R | 63.9% | 35.7% | 64.2% | 35.8% |
| 54,854 | WARREN | 23,568 | 17,616 | 5,886 | 66 | 11,730 | R | 74.7% | 25.0% | 75.0% | 25.0% |
| 54,795 | WASHINGTON | 22,563 | 16,580 | 5,909 | 74 | 10,671 | R | 73.5% | 26.2% | 73.7% | 26.3% |
| 84,581 | WAYNE | 34,051 | 24,171 | 9,700 | 180 | 14,471 | R | 71.0% | 28.5% | 71.4% | 28.6% |
| 866,599 | WESTCHESTER | 390,308 | 229,005 | 160,225 | 1,078 | 68,780 | R | 58.7% | 41.1% | 58.8% | 41.2% |
| 39,895 | WYOMING | 15,622 | 11,199 | 4,381 | 42 | 6,818 | R | 71.7% | 28.0% | 71.9% | 28.1% |
| 21,459 | YATES | 9,062 | 6,367 | 2,670 | 25 | 3,697 | R | 70.3% | 29.5% | 70.5% | 29.5% |
| 17,558,072 | TOTAL | 6,806,810 | 3,664,763 | 3,119,609 | 22,438 | 545,154 | R | 53.8% | 45.8% | 54.0% | 46.0% |

# NEW YORK

## PRESIDENT 1980

| 1980 Census Population | County | Total Vote | Republican | Democratic | Other | Rep.-Dem. Plurality | Percentage Total Vote Rep. | Dem. | Major Vote Rep. | Dem. |
|---|---|---|---|---|---|---|---|---|---|---|
| 285,909 | ALBANY | 144,364 | 52,354 | 74,429 | 17,581 | 22,075 D | 36.3% | 51.6% | 41.3% | 58.7% |
| 51,742 | ALLEGANY | 17,640 | 10,423 | 5,879 | 1,338 | 4,544 R | 59.1% | 33.3% | 63.9% | 36.1% |
| 1,168,972 | BRONX | 282,847 | 86,843 | 181,090 | 14,914 | 94,247 D | 30.7% | 64.0% | 32.4% | 67.6% |
| 213,648 | BROOME | 89,280 | 39,275 | 37,013 | 12,992 | 2,262 R | 44.0% | 41.5% | 51.5% | 48.5% |
| 85,697 | CATTARAUGUS | 32,709 | 17,222 | 12,917 | 2,570 | 4,305 R | 52.7% | 39.5% | 57.1% | 42.9% |
| 79,894 | CAYUGA | 32,756 | 17,945 | 11,708 | 3,103 | 6,237 R | 54.8% | 35.7% | 60.5% | 39.5% |
| 146,925 | CHAUTAUQUA | 58,756 | 30,081 | 22,871 | 5,804 | 7,210 R | 51.2% | 38.9% | 56.8% | 43.2% |
| 97,656 | CHEMUNG | 37,209 | 19,674 | 14,565 | 2,970 | 5,109 R | 52.9% | 39.1% | 57.5% | 42.5% |
| 49,344 | CHENANGO | 19,592 | 10,400 | 6,917 | 2,275 | 3,483 R | 53.1% | 35.3% | 60.1% | 39.9% |
| 80,750 | CLINTON | 26,890 | 13,120 | 11,498 | 2,272 | 1,622 R | 48.8% | 42.8% | 53.3% | 46.7% |
| 59,487 | COLUMBIA | 26,274 | 13,946 | 9,500 | 2,828 | 4,446 R | 53.1% | 36.2% | 59.5% | 40.5% |
| 48,820 | CORTLAND | 18,048 | 9,885 | 6,176 | 1,987 | 3,709 R | 54.8% | 34.2% | 61.5% | 38.5% |
| 46,824 | DELAWARE | 19,164 | 10,609 | 6,333 | 2,222 | 4,276 R | 55.4% | 33.0% | 62.6% | 37.4% |
| 245,055 | DUTCHESS | 93,007 | 53,616 | 28,616 | 10,775 | 25,000 R | 57.6% | 30.8% | 65.2% | 34.8% |
| 1,015,472 | ERIE | 420,473 | 169,209 | 215,283 | 35,981 | 46,074 D | 40.2% | 51.2% | 44.0% | 56.0% |
| 36,176 | ESSEX | 16,978 | 9,025 | 6,443 | 1,510 | 2,582 R | 53.2% | 37.9% | 58.3% | 41.7% |
| 44,929 | FRANKLIN | 16,292 | 7,620 | 7,281 | 1,391 | 339 R | 46.8% | 44.7% | 51.1% | 48.9% |
| 55,153 | FULTON | 21,522 | 11,448 | 8,105 | 1,969 | 3,343 R | 53.2% | 37.7% | 58.5% | 41.5% |
| 59,400 | GENESEE | 24,489 | 11,650 | 10,677 | 2,162 | 973 R | 47.6% | 43.6% | 52.2% | 47.8% |
| 40,861 | GREENE | 19,498 | 11,286 | 6,488 | 1,724 | 4,798 R | 57.9% | 33.3% | 63.5% | 36.5% |
| 5,034 | HAMILTON | 3,230 | 2,038 | 925 | 267 | 1,113 R | 63.1% | 28.6% | 68.8% | 31.2% |
| 66,714 | HERKIMER | 27,888 | 14,105 | 11,497 | 2,286 | 2,608 R | 50.6% | 41.2% | 55.1% | 44.9% |
| 88,151 | JEFFERSON | 33,128 | 16,455 | 13,271 | 3,402 | 3,184 R | 49.7% | 40.1% | 55.4% | 44.6% |
| 2,230,936 | KINGS | 521,109 | 200,306 | 288,893 | 31,910 | 88,587 D | 38.4% | 55.4% | 40.9% | 59.1% |
| 25,035 | LEWIS | 9,822 | 4,937 | 3,973 | 912 | 964 R | 50.3% | 40.5% | 55.4% | 44.6% |
| 57,006 | LIVINGSTON | 22,454 | 11,193 | 9,030 | 2,231 | 2,163 R | 49.8% | 40.2% | 55.3% | 44.7% |
| 65,150 | MADISON | 23,937 | 13,369 | 7,843 | 2,725 | 5,526 R | 55.9% | 32.8% | 63.0% | 37.0% |
| 702,238 | MONROE | 306,733 | 128,615 | 142,423 | 35,695 | 13,808 D | 41.9% | 46.4% | 47.5% | 52.5% |
| 53,439 | MONTGOMERY | 24,088 | 11,917 | 9,645 | 2,526 | 2,272 R | 49.5% | 40.0% | 55.3% | 44.7% |
| 1,321,582 | NASSAU | 596,154 | 333,567 | 207,602 | 54,985 | 125,965 R | 56.0% | 34.8% | 61.6% | 38.4% |
| 1,428,285 | NEW YORK | 441,901 | 115,911 | 275,742 | 50,248 | 159,831 D | 26.2% | 62.4% | 29.6% | 70.4% |
| 227,354 | NIAGARA | 86,409 | 38,760 | 40,405 | 7,244 | 1,645 D | 44.9% | 46.8% | 49.0% | 51.0% |
| 253,466 | ONEIDA | 104,799 | 51,968 | 44,292 | 8,539 | 7,676 R | 49.6% | 42.3% | 54.0% | 46.0% |
| 463,920 | ONONDAGA | 193,372 | 97,887 | 73,453 | 22,032 | 24,434 R | 50.6% | 38.0% | 57.1% | 42.9% |
| 88,909 | ONTARIO | 35,506 | 17,036 | 14,477 | 3,993 | 2,559 R | 48.0% | 40.8% | 54.1% | 45.9% |
| 259,603 | ORANGE | 90,470 | 51,268 | 30,022 | 9,180 | 21,246 R | 56.7% | 33.2% | 63.1% | 36.9% |
| 38,496 | ORLEANS | 14,611 | 7,536 | 5,767 | 1,308 | 1,769 R | 51.6% | 39.5% | 56.6% | 43.4% |
| 113,901 | OSWEGO | 42,541 | 22,816 | 15,343 | 4,382 | 7,473 R | 53.6% | 36.1% | 59.8% | 40.2% |
| 59,075 | OTSEGO | 23,907 | 11,814 | 8,795 | 3,298 | 3,019 R | 49.4% | 36.8% | 57.3% | 42.7% |
| 77,193 | PUTNAM | 31,819 | 20,193 | 8,691 | 2,935 | 11,502 R | 63.5% | 27.3% | 69.9% | 30.1% |
| 1,891,325 | QUEENS | 560,923 | 251,333 | 269,147 | 40,443 | 17,814 D | 44.8% | 48.0% | 48.3% | 51.7% |
| 151,966 | RENSSELAER | 69,747 | 32,005 | 29,880 | 7,862 | 2,125 R | 45.9% | 42.8% | 51.7% | 48.3% |
| 352,121 | RICHMOND | 110,651 | 64,885 | 37,306 | 8,460 | 27,579 R | 58.6% | 33.7% | 63.5% | 36.5% |
| 259,530 | ROCKLAND | 104,995 | 59,068 | 35,277 | 10,650 | 23,791 R | 56.3% | 33.6% | 62.6% | 37.4% |
| 114,254 | ST. LAWRENCE | 39,624 | 18,437 | 17,006 | 4,181 | 1,431 R | 46.5% | 42.9% | 52.0% | 48.0% |
| 153,759 | SARATOGA | 65,362 | 34,184 | 23,641 | 7,537 | 10,543 R | 52.3% | 36.2% | 59.1% | 40.9% |
| 149,946 | SCHENECTADY | 70,534 | 32,003 | 29,932 | 8,599 | 2,071 R | 45.4% | 42.4% | 51.7% | 48.3% |
| 29,710 | SCHOHARIE | 12,262 | 6,382 | 4,715 | 1,165 | 1,667 R | 52.0% | 38.5% | 57.5% | 42.5% |
| 17,686 | SCHUYLER | 6,957 | 3,838 | 2,514 | 605 | 1,324 R | 55.2% | 36.1% | 60.4% | 39.6% |
| 33,733 | SENECA | 13,690 | 7,174 | 5,010 | 1,506 | 2,164 R | 52.4% | 36.6% | 58.9% | 41.1% |
| 99,217 | STEUBEN | 38,170 | 22,418 | 12,826 | 2,926 | 9,592 R | 58.7% | 33.6% | 63.6% | 36.4% |
| 1,284,231 | SUFFOLK | 449,655 | 256,294 | 149,945 | 43,416 | 106,349 R | 57.0% | 33.3% | 63.1% | 36.9% |
| 65,155 | SULLIVAN | 27,218 | 15,089 | 9,553 | 2,576 | 5,536 R | 55.4% | 35.1% | 61.2% | 38.8% |
| 49,812 | TIOGA | 19,214 | 10,291 | 6,690 | 2,233 | 3,601 R | 53.6% | 34.8% | 60.6% | 39.4% |
| 87,085 | TOMPKINS | 29,668 | 12,448 | 11,970 | 5,250 | 478 R | 42.0% | 40.3% | 51.0% | 49.0% |
| 158,158 | ULSTER | 66,726 | 36,709 | 22,179 | 7,838 | 14,530 R | 55.0% | 33.2% | 62.3% | 37.7% |
| 54,854 | WARREN | 22,377 | 13,264 | 6,971 | 2,142 | 6,293 R | 59.3% | 31.2% | 65.5% | 34.5% |
| 54,795 | WASHINGTON | 21,906 | 12,835 | 7,144 | 1,927 | 5,691 R | 58.6% | 32.6% | 64.2% | 35.8% |
| 84,581 | WAYNE | 32,512 | 16,498 | 12,590 | 3,424 | 3,908 R | 50.7% | 38.7% | 56.7% | 43.3% |
| 866,599 | WESTCHESTER | 365,166 | 198,552 | 130,136 | 36,478 | 68,416 R | 54.4% | 35.6% | 60.4% | 39.6% |
| 39,895 | WYOMING | 14,552 | 8,108 | 5,234 | 1,210 | 2,874 R | 55.7% | 36.0% | 60.8% | 39.2% |
| 21,459 | YATES | 8,384 | 4,694 | 2,828 | 862 | 1,866 R | 56.0% | 33.7% | 62.4% | 37.6% |
| 17,558,072 | TOTAL | 6,201,959 | 2,893,831 | 2,728,372 | 579,756 | 165,459 R | 46.7% | 44.0% | 51.5% | 48.5% |

# NEW YORK

## PRESIDENT 1976

| 1970 Census Population | County | Total Vote | Republican | Democratic | Other | Rep.-Dem. Plurality | Percentage Total Vote Rep. | Percentage Total Vote Dem. | Percentage Major Vote Rep. | Percentage Major Vote Dem. |
|---|---|---|---|---|---|---|---|---|---|---|
| 285,618 | ALBANY | 142,409 | 69,592 | 71,616 | 1,201 | 2,024 D | 48.9% | 50.3% | 49.3% | 50.7% |
| 46,458 | ALLEGANY | 18,010 | 11,769 | 6,134 | 107 | 5,635 R | 65.3% | 34.1% | 65.7% | 34.3% |
| 1,472,216 | BRONX | 337,391 | 96,842 | 238,786 | 1,763 | 141,944 D | 28.7% | 70.8% | 28.9% | 71.1% |
| 221,815 | BROOME | 90,658 | 50,340 | 39,827 | 491 | 10,513 R | 55.5% | 43.9% | 55.8% | 44.2% |
| 81,666 | CATTARAUGUS | 33,422 | 19,469 | 13,768 | 185 | 5,701 R | 58.3% | 41.2% | 58.6% | 41.4% |
| 77,439 | CAYUGA | 33,343 | 19,775 | 13,348 | 220 | 6,427 R | 59.3% | 40.0% | 59.7% | 40.3% |
| 147,305 | CHAUTAUQUA | 61,436 | 33,730 | 27,447 | 259 | 6,283 R | 54.9% | 44.7% | 55.1% | 44.9% |
| 101,537 | CHEMUNG | 38,026 | 20,640 | 17,207 | 179 | 3,433 R | 54.3% | 45.3% | 54.5% | 45.5% |
| 46,368 | CHENANGO | 19,837 | 12,384 | 7,356 | 97 | 5,028 R | 62.4% | 37.1% | 62.7% | 37.3% |
| 72,934 | CLINTON | 27,103 | 15,433 | 11,555 | 115 | 3,878 R | 56.9% | 42.6% | 57.2% | 42.8% |
| 51,519 | COLUMBIA | 26,574 | 15,871 | 10,514 | 189 | 5,357 R | 59.7% | 39.6% | 60.2% | 39.8% |
| 45,894 | CORTLAND | 18,300 | 11,222 | 6,947 | 131 | 4,275 R | 61.3% | 38.0% | 61.8% | 38.2% |
| 44,718 | DELAWARE | 19,827 | 12,443 | 7,254 | 130 | 5,189 R | 62.8% | 36.6% | 63.2% | 36.8% |
| 222,295 | DUTCHESS | 89,505 | 51,312 | 37,531 | 662 | 13,781 R | 57.3% | 41.9% | 57.8% | 42.2% |
| 1,113,491 | ERIE | 452,843 | 220,310 | 229,397 | 3,136 | 9,087 D | 48.7% | 50.7% | 49.0% | 51.0% |
| 34,631 | ESSEX | 16,824 | 10,194 | 6,556 | 74 | 3,638 R | 60.6% | 39.0% | 60.9% | 39.1% |
| 43,931 | FRANKLIN | 16,152 | 8,846 | 7,248 | 58 | 1,598 R | 54.8% | 44.9% | 55.0% | 45.0% |
| 52,637 | FULTON | 21,629 | 12,161 | 9,323 | 145 | 2,838 R | 56.2% | 43.1% | 56.6% | 43.4% |
| 58,722 | GENESEE | 25,536 | 14,567 | 10,803 | 166 | 3,764 R | 57.0% | 42.3% | 57.4% | 42.6% |
| 33,136 | GREENE | 19,264 | 11,370 | 7,740 | 154 | 3,630 R | 59.0% | 40.2% | 59.5% | 40.5% |
| 4,714 | HAMILTON | 3,370 | 2,306 | 1,052 | 12 | 1,254 R | 68.4% | 31.2% | 68.7% | 31.3% |
| 67,440 | HERKIMER | 28,377 | 15,362 | 12,875 | 140 | 2,487 R | 54.1% | 45.4% | 54.4% | 45.6% |
| 88,508 | JEFFERSON | 34,028 | 20,401 | 13,503 | 124 | 6,898 R | 60.0% | 39.7% | 60.2% | 39.8% |
| 2,601,852 | KINGS | 613,643 | 190,728 | 419,382 | 3,533 | 228,654 D | 31.1% | 68.3% | 31.3% | 68.7% |
| 23,644 | LEWIS | 9,633 | 5,840 | 3,764 | 29 | 2,076 R | 60.6% | 39.1% | 60.8% | 39.2% |
| 54,041 | LIVINGSTON | 23,819 | 14,044 | 9,629 | 146 | 4,415 R | 59.0% | 40.4% | 59.3% | 40.7% |
| 62,864 | MADISON | 24,591 | 15,674 | 8,822 | 95 | 6,852 R | 63.7% | 35.9% | 64.0% | 36.0% |
| 711,917 | MONROE | 303,434 | 167,303 | 134,739 | 1,392 | 32,564 R | 55.1% | 44.4% | 55.4% | 44.6% |
| 55,883 | MONTGOMERY | 24,730 | 13,281 | 11,271 | 178 | 2,010 R | 53.7% | 45.6% | 54.1% | 45.9% |
| 1,422,905 | NASSAU | 637,438 | 329,176 | 302,869 | 5,393 | 26,307 R | 51.6% | 47.5% | 52.1% | 47.9% |
| 1,524,541 | NEW YORK | 460,838 | 117,702 | 337,438 | 5,698 | 219,736 D | 25.5% | 73.2% | 25.9% | 74.1% |
| 235,720 | NIAGARA | 90,239 | 46,101 | 43,667 | 471 | 2,434 R | 51.1% | 48.4% | 51.4% | 48.6% |
| 273,037 | ONEIDA | 105,988 | 57,655 | 47,779 | 554 | 9,876 R | 54.4% | 45.1% | 54.7% | 45.3% |
| 472,185 | ONONDAGA | 192,578 | 115,474 | 76,097 | 1,007 | 39,377 R | 60.0% | 39.5% | 60.3% | 39.7% |
| 78,849 | ONTARIO | 35,441 | 21,118 | 14,044 | 279 | 7,074 R | 59.6% | 39.6% | 60.1% | 39.9% |
| 220,558 | ORANGE | 90,677 | 49,685 | 40,362 | 630 | 9,323 R | 54.8% | 44.5% | 55.2% | 44.8% |
| 37,305 | ORLEANS | 15,023 | 8,994 | 5,927 | 102 | 3,067 R | 59.9% | 39.5% | 60.3% | 39.7% |
| 100,897 | OSWEGO | 40,463 | 23,949 | 16,332 | 182 | 7,617 R | 59.2% | 40.4% | 59.5% | 40.5% |
| 56,181 | OTSEGO | 24,754 | 14,796 | 9,787 | 171 | 5,009 R | 59.8% | 39.5% | 60.2% | 39.8% |
| 56,696 | PUTNAM | 30,711 | 18,523 | 11,963 | 225 | 6,560 R | 60.3% | 39.0% | 60.8% | 39.2% |
| 1,973,708 | QUEENS | 627,352 | 244,396 | 379,907 | 3,049 | 135,511 D | 39.0% | 60.6% | 39.1% | 60.9% |
| 152,510 | RENSSELAER | 69,653 | 40,229 | 28,979 | 445 | 11,250 R | 57.8% | 41.6% | 58.1% | 41.9% |
| 295,443 | RICHMOND | 105,477 | 56,995 | 47,867 | 615 | 9,128 R | 54.0% | 45.4% | 54.4% | 45.6% |
| 229,903 | ROCKLAND | 101,489 | 52,087 | 48,673 | 729 | 3,414 R | 51.3% | 48.0% | 51.7% | 48.3% |
| 111,991 | ST. LAWRENCE | 39,934 | 22,249 | 17,503 | 182 | 4,746 R | 55.7% | 43.8% | 56.0% | 44.0% |
| 121,679 | SARATOGA | 62,486 | 38,296 | 23,768 | 422 | 14,528 R | 61.3% | 38.0% | 61.7% | 38.3% |
| 160,979 | SCHENECTADY | 73,450 | 40,789 | 31,838 | 823 | 8,951 R | 55.5% | 43.3% | 56.2% | 43.8% |
| 24,750 | SCHOHARIE | 12,515 | 7,154 | 5,250 | 111 | 1,904 R | 57.2% | 41.9% | 57.7% | 42.3% |
| 16,737 | SCHUYLER | 7,189 | 4,267 | 2,885 | 37 | 1,382 R | 59.4% | 40.1% | 59.7% | 40.3% |
| 35,083 | SENECA | 13,508 | 7,659 | 5,745 | 104 | 1,914 R | 56.7% | 42.5% | 57.1% | 42.9% |
| 99,546 | STEUBEN | 38,015 | 23,164 | 14,685 | 166 | 8,479 R | 60.9% | 38.6% | 61.2% | 38.8% |
| 1,116,672 | SUFFOLK | 460,048 | 248,908 | 208,263 | 2,877 | 40,645 R | 54.1% | 45.3% | 54.4% | 45.6% |
| 52,580 | SULLIVAN | 28,096 | 13,709 | 14,189 | 198 | 480 D | 48.8% | 50.5% | 49.1% | 50.9% |
| 46,513 | TIOGA | 18,893 | 11,824 | 6,969 | 100 | 4,855 R | 62.6% | 36.9% | 62.9% | 37.1% |
| 76,879 | TOMPKINS | 28,671 | 15,463 | 12,808 | 400 | 2,655 R | 53.9% | 44.7% | 54.7% | 45.3% |
| 141,241 | ULSTER | 66,155 | 35,353 | 30,190 | 612 | 5,163 R | 53.4% | 45.6% | 53.9% | 46.1% |
| 49,402 | WARREN | 21,912 | 14,548 | 7,264 | 100 | 7,284 R | 66.4% | 33.2% | 66.7% | 33.3% |
| 52,725 | WASHINGTON | 21,324 | 13,946 | 7,262 | 116 | 6,684 R | 65.4% | 34.1% | 65.8% | 34.2% |
| 79,404 | WAYNE | 31,562 | 19,324 | 12,061 | 177 | 7,263 R | 61.2% | 38.2% | 61.6% | 38.4% |
| 891,409 | WESTCHESTER | 384,296 | 208,527 | 173,153 | 2,616 | 35,374 R | 54.3% | 45.1% | 54.6% | 45.4% |
| 37,688 | WYOMING | 15,539 | 9,726 | 5,737 | 76 | 3,989 R | 62.6% | 36.9% | 62.9% | 37.1% |
| 19,831 | YATES | 8,742 | 5,796 | 2,903 | 43 | 2,893 R | 66.3% | 33.2% | 66.6% | 33.4% |
| 18,190,740 | TOTAL | 6,534,170 | 3,100,791 | 3,389,558 | 43,821 | 288,767 D | 47.5% | 51.9% | 47.8% | 52.2% |

# NEW YORK

## PRESIDENT 1972

| 1970 Census Population | County | Total Vote | Republican | Democratic | Other | Rep.-Dem. Plurality | Percentage Total Vote Rep. | Dem. | Major Vote Rep. | Dem. |
|---|---|---|---|---|---|---|---|---|---|---|
| 285,618 | ALBANY | 149,562 | 81,848 | 67,297 | 417 | 14,551 R | 54.7% | 45.0% | 54.9% | 45.1% |
| 46,458 | ALLEGANY | 18,320 | 13,426 | 4,812 | 82 | 8,614 R | 73.3% | 26.3% | 73.6% | 26.4% |
| 1,472,216 | BRONX | 441,199 | 196,754 | 243,345 | 1,100 | 46,591 D | 44.6% | 55.2% | 44.7% | 55.3% |
| 221,815 | BROOME | 93,135 | 55,736 | 37,154 | 245 | 18,582 R | 59.8% | 39.9% | 60.0% | 40.0% |
| 81,666 | CATTARAUGUS | 32,950 | 21,906 | 10,909 | 135 | 10,997 R | 66.5% | 33.1% | 66.8% | 33.2% |
| 77,439 | CAYUGA | 34,030 | 22,774 | 11,097 | 159 | 11,677 R | 66.9% | 32.6% | 67.2% | 32.8% |
| 147,305 | CHAUTAUQUA | 63,583 | 37,158 | 26,253 | 172 | 10,905 R | 58.4% | 41.3% | 58.6% | 41.4% |
| 101,537 | CHEMUNG | 38,944 | 26,200 | 12,650 | 94 | 13,550 R | 67.3% | 32.5% | 67.4% | 32.6% |
| 46,368 | CHENANGO | 19,509 | 13,770 | 5,695 | 44 | 8,075 R | 70.6% | 29.2% | 70.7% | 29.3% |
| 72,934 | CLINTON | 26,844 | 17,048 | 9,703 | 93 | 7,345 R | 63.5% | 36.1% | 63.7% | 36.3% |
| 51,519 | COLUMBIA | 25,643 | 17,995 | 7,558 | 90 | 10,437 R | 70.2% | 29.5% | 70.4% | 29.6% |
| 45,894 | CORTLAND | 18,180 | 12,885 | 5,234 | 61 | 7,651 R | 70.9% | 28.8% | 71.1% | 28.9% |
| 44,718 | DELAWARE | 20,449 | 15,136 | 5,243 | 70 | 9,893 R | 74.0% | 25.6% | 74.3% | 25.7% |
| 222,295 | DUTCHESS | 92,987 | 64,864 | 27,872 | 251 | 36,992 R | 69.8% | 30.0% | 69.9% | 30.1% |
| 1,113,491 | ERIE | 476,424 | 256,462 | 218,105 | 1,857 | 38,357 R | 53.8% | 45.8% | 54.0% | 46.0% |
| 34,631 | ESSEX | 16,759 | 11,763 | 4,955 | 41 | 6,808 R | 70.2% | 29.6% | 70.4% | 29.6% |
| 43,931 | FRANKLIN | 16,282 | 10,959 | 5,266 | 57 | 5,693 R | 67.3% | 32.3% | 67.5% | 32.5% |
| 52,637 | FULTON | 22,599 | 15,200 | 7,303 | 96 | 7,897 R | 67.3% | 32.3% | 67.5% | 32.5% |
| 58,722 | GENESEE | 25,843 | 17,107 | 8,631 | 105 | 8,476 R | 66.2% | 33.4% | 66.5% | 33.5% |
| 33,136 | GREENE | 19,675 | 14,313 | 5,260 | 102 | 9,053 R | 72.7% | 26.7% | 73.1% | 26.9% |
| 4,714 | HAMILTON | 3,334 | 2,597 | 731 | 6 | 1,866 R | 77.9% | 21.9% | 78.0% | 22.0% |
| 67,440 | HERKIMER | 29,775 | 20,194 | 9,487 | 94 | 10,707 R | 67.8% | 31.9% | 68.0% | 32.0% |
| 88,508 | JEFFERSON | 34,827 | 23,123 | 11,629 | 75 | 11,494 R | 66.4% | 33.4% | 66.5% | 33.5% |
| 2,601,852 | KINGS | 763,742 | 373,903 | 387,768 | 2,071 | 13,865 D | 49.0% | 50.8% | 49.1% | 50.9% |
| 23,644 | LEWIS | 9,608 | 6,591 | 2,987 | 30 | 3,604 R | 68.6% | 31.1% | 68.8% | 31.2% |
| 54,041 | LIVINGSTON | 22,999 | 15,886 | 7,031 | 82 | 8,855 R | 69.1% | 30.6% | 69.3% | 30.7% |
| 62,864 | MADISON | 24,697 | 18,392 | 6,241 | 64 | 12,151 R | 74.5% | 25.3% | 74.7% | 25.3% |
| 711,917 | MONROE | 317,905 | 196,579 | 120,031 | 1,295 | 76,548 R | 61.8% | 37.8% | 62.1% | 37.9% |
| 55,883 | MONTGOMERY | 26,210 | 16,640 | 9,460 | 110 | 7,180 R | 63.5% | 36.1% | 63.8% | 36.2% |
| 1,422,905 | NASSAU | 693,429 | 438,723 | 252,831 | 1,875 | 185,892 R | 63.3% | 36.5% | 63.4% | 36.6% |
| 1,524,541 | NEW YORK | 534,972 | 178,515 | 354,326 | 2,131 | 175,811 D | 33.4% | 66.2% | 33.5% | 66.5% |
| 235,720 | NIAGARA | 94,096 | 54,777 | 38,991 | 328 | 15,786 R | 58.2% | 41.4% | 58.4% | 41.6% |
| 273,037 | ONEIDA | 112,444 | 78,549 | 33,642 | 253 | 44,907 R | 69.9% | 29.9% | 70.0% | 30.0% |
| 472,185 | ONONDAGA | 202,421 | 140,039 | 61,895 | 487 | 78,144 R | 69.2% | 30.6% | 69.3% | 30.7% |
| 78,849 | ONTARIO | 34,968 | 23,828 | 11,012 | 128 | 12,816 R | 68.1% | 31.5% | 68.4% | 31.6% |
| 220,558 | ORANGE | 89,533 | 63,556 | 25,778 | 199 | 37,778 R | 71.0% | 28.8% | 71.1% | 28.9% |
| 37,305 | ORLEANS | 15,347 | 10,938 | 4,371 | 38 | 6,567 R | 71.3% | 28.5% | 71.4% | 28.6% |
| 100,897 | OSWEGO | 40,528 | 29,109 | 11,317 | 102 | 17,792 R | 71.8% | 27.9% | 72.0% | 28.0% |
| 56,181 | OTSEGO | 25,337 | 17,364 | 7,898 | 75 | 9,466 R | 68.5% | 31.2% | 68.7% | 31.3% |
| 56,696 | PUTNAM | 29,557 | 21,673 | 7,747 | 137 | 13,926 R | 73.3% | 26.2% | 73.7% | 26.3% |
| 1,973,708 | QUEENS | 756,369 | 426,015 | 328,316 | 2,038 | 97,699 R | 56.3% | 43.4% | 56.5% | 43.5% |
| 152,510 | RENSSELAER | 73,166 | 48,864 | 24,019 | 283 | 24,845 R | 66.8% | 32.8% | 67.0% | 33.0% |
| 295,443 | RICHMOND | 114,181 | 84,686 | 29,241 | 254 | 55,445 R | 74.2% | 25.6% | 74.3% | 25.7% |
| 229,903 | ROCKLAND | 100,806 | 64,753 | 35,771 | 282 | 28,982 R | 64.2% | 35.5% | 64.4% | 35.6% |
| 111,991 | ST. LAWRENCE | 41,503 | 26,145 | 15,286 | 72 | 10,859 R | 63.0% | 36.8% | 63.1% | 36.9% |
| 121,679 | SARATOGA | 58,685 | 40,582 | 17,899 | 204 | 22,683 R | 69.2% | 30.5% | 69.4% | 30.6% |
| 160,979 | SCHENECTADY | 77,503 | 47,529 | 29,619 | 355 | 17,910 R | 61.3% | 38.2% | 61.6% | 38.4% |
| 24,750 | SCHOHARIE | 12,408 | 8,644 | 3,730 | 34 | 4,914 R | 69.7% | 30.1% | 69.9% | 30.1% |
| 16,737 | SCHUYLER | 6,927 | 4,945 | 1,937 | 45 | 3,008 R | 71.4% | 28.0% | 71.9% | 28.1% |
| 35,083 | SENECA | 13,842 | 9,368 | 4,441 | 33 | 4,927 R | 67.7% | 32.1% | 67.8% | 32.2% |
| 99,546 | STEUBEN | 38,253 | 28,708 | 9,462 | 83 | 19,246 R | 75.0% | 24.7% | 75.2% | 24.8% |
| 1,116,672 | SUFFOLK | 450,186 | 316,452 | 132,441 | 1,293 | 184,011 R | 70.3% | 29.4% | 70.5% | 29.5% |
| 52,580 | SULLIVAN | 26,938 | 17,035 | 9,847 | 56 | 7,188 R | 63.2% | 36.6% | 63.4% | 36.6% |
| 46,513 | TIOGA | 18,927 | 13,396 | 5,470 | 61 | 7,926 R | 70.8% | 28.9% | 71.0% | 29.0% |
| 76,879 | TOMPKINS | 30,038 | 17,605 | 12,344 | 89 | 5,261 R | 58.6% | 41.1% | 58.8% | 41.2% |
| 141,241 | ULSTER | 68,467 | 46,883 | 21,371 | 213 | 25,512 R | 68.5% | 31.2% | 68.7% | 31.3% |
| 49,402 | WARREN | 22,480 | 16,649 | 5,760 | 71 | 10,889 R | 74.1% | 25.6% | 74.3% | 25.7% |
| 52,725 | WASHINGTON | 21,895 | 16,136 | 5,677 | 82 | 10,459 R | 73.7% | 25.9% | 74.0% | 26.0% |
| 79,404 | WAYNE | 31,679 | 23,379 | 8,203 | 97 | 15,176 R | 73.8% | 25.9% | 74.0% | 26.0% |
| 891,409 | WESTCHESTER | 418,814 | 262,901 | 154,412 | 1,501 | 108,489 R | 62.8% | 36.9% | 63.0% | 37.0% |
| 37,688 | WYOMING | 15,588 | 11,184 | 4,365 | 39 | 6,819 R | 71.7% | 28.0% | 71.9% | 28.1% |
| 19,831 | YATES | 8,618 | 6,639 | 1,958 | 21 | 4,681 R | 77.0% | 22.7% | 77.2% | 22.8% |
| 18,190,740 | TOTAL | 7,165,919 | 4,192,778 | 2,951,084 | 22,057 | 1,241,694 R | 58.5% | 41.2% | 58.7% | 41.3% |

# NEW YORK

## PRESIDENT 1968

| 1960 Census Population | County | Total Vote | Republican | Democratic | AIP | Other | Plurality | Percentage Total Vote | | |
|---|---|---|---|---|---|---|---|---|---|---|
| | | | | | | | | Rep. | Dem. | AIP |
| 272,926 | ALBANY | 139,394 | 52,948 | 80,724 | 5,025 | 697 | 27,776 D | 38.0% | 57.9% | 3.6% |
| 43,978 | ALLEGANY | 17,156 | 11,222 | 4,986 | 851 | 97 | 6,236 R | 65.4% | 29.1% | 5.0% |
| 1,424,815 | BRONX | 444,532 | 142,314 | 277,385 | 21,950 | 2,883 | 135,071 D | 32.0% | 62.4% | 4.9% |
| 212,661 | BROOME | 89,372 | 46,872 | 37,451 | 4,618 | 431 | 9,421 R | 52.4% | 41.9% | 5.2% |
| 80,187 | CATTARAUGUS | 31,157 | 16,594 | 12,733 | 1,674 | 156 | 3,861 R | 53.3% | 40.9% | 5.4% |
| 73,942 | CAYUGA | 32,670 | 16,167 | 14,604 | 1,826 | 73 | 1,563 R | 49.5% | 44.7% | 5.6% |
| 145,377 | CHAUTAUQUA | 58,507 | 28,561 | 26,431 | 3,273 | 242 | 2,130 R | 48.8% | 45.2% | 5.6% |
| 98,706 | CHEMUNG | 39,553 | 20,693 | 15,820 | 2,807 | 233 | 4,873 R | 52.3% | 40.0% | 7.1% |
| 43,243 | CHENANGO | 18,455 | 11,785 | 5,706 | 887 | 77 | 6,079 R | 63.9% | 30.9% | 4.8% |
| 72,722 | CLINTON | 23,176 | 11,951 | 10,153 | 931 | 141 | 1,798 R | 51.6% | 43.8% | 4.0% |
| 47,322 | COLUMBIA | 23,086 | 13,857 | 7,762 | 1,372 | 95 | 6,095 R | 60.0% | 33.6% | 5.9% |
| 41,113 | CORTLAND | 16,818 | 10,209 | 5,791 | 720 | 98 | 4,418 R | 60.7% | 34.4% | 4.3% |
| 43,540 | DELAWARE | 18,898 | 12,366 | 5,360 | 1,121 | 51 | 7,006 R | 65.4% | 28.4% | 5.9% |
| 176,008 | DUTCHESS | 82,122 | 45,032 | 31,025 | 5,662 | 403 | 14,007 R | 54.8% | 37.8% | 6.9% |
| 1,064,688 | ERIE | 453,271 | 167,853 | 250,054 | 33,402 | 1,962 | 82,201 D | 37.0% | 55.2% | 7.4% |
| 35,300 | ESSEX | 15,361 | 9,377 | 5,218 | 701 | 65 | 4,159 R | 61.0% | 34.0% | 4.6% |
| 44,742 | FRANKLIN | 15,604 | 8,314 | 6,678 | 544 | 68 | 1,636 R | 53.3% | 42.8% | 3.5% |
| 51,304 | FULTON | 21,818 | 11,895 | 8,871 | 989 | 63 | 3,024 R | 54.5% | 40.7% | 4.5% |
| 53,994 | GENESEE | 23,150 | 12,418 | 9,533 | 1,141 | 58 | 2,885 R | 53.6% | 41.2% | 4.9% |
| 31,372 | GREENE | 18,021 | 10,954 | 5,499 | 1,421 | 147 | 5,455 R | 60.8% | 30.5% | 7.9% |
| 4,267 | HAMILTON | 3,053 | 2,123 | 762 | 163 | 5 | 1,361 R | 69.5% | 25.0% | 5.3% |
| 66,370 | HERKIMER | 27,677 | 15,192 | 10,940 | 1,455 | 90 | 4,252 R | 54.9% | 39.5% | 5.3% |
| 87,835 | JEFFERSON | 33,123 | 18,552 | 13,438 | 1,016 | 117 | 5,114 R | 56.0% | 40.6% | 3.1% |
| 2,627,319 | KINGS | 775,067 | 247,936 | 489,174 | 33,563 | 4,394 | 241,238 D | 32.0% | 63.1% | 4.3% |
| 23,249 | LEWIS | 9,180 | 5,524 | 3,205 | 430 | 21 | 2,319 R | 60.2% | 34.9% | 4.7% |
| 44,053 | LIVINGSTON | 19,516 | 11,659 | 6,989 | 775 | 93 | 4,670 R | 59.7% | 35.8% | 4.0% |
| 54,635 | MADISON | 22,010 | 13,819 | 7,056 | 1,053 | 82 | 6,763 R | 62.8% | 32.1% | 4.8% |
| 586,387 | MONROE | 296,755 | 143,233 | 141,437 | 10,875 | 1,210 | 1,796 R | 48.3% | 47.7% | 3.7% |
| 57,240 | MONTGOMERY | 25,257 | 12,566 | 11,449 | 1,147 | 95 | 1,117 R | 49.8% | 45.3% | 4.5% |
| 1,300,171 | NASSAU | 643,582 | 329,792 | 278,599 | 30,860 | 4,331 | 51,193 R | 51.2% | 43.3% | 4.8% |
| 1,698,281 | NEW YORK | 529,464 | 135,458 | 370,806 | 12,958 | 10,242 | 235,348 D | 25.6% | 70.0% | 2.4% |
| 242,269 | NIAGARA | 87,925 | 38,796 | 41,999 | 6,617 | 513 | 3,203 D | 44.1% | 47.8% | 7.5% |
| 264,401 | ONEIDA | 103,761 | 52,875 | 44,685 | 5,666 | 535 | 8,190 R | 51.0% | 43.1% | 5.5% |
| 423,028 | ONONDAGA | 189,880 | 95,806 | 83,576 | 9,459 | 1,039 | 12,230 R | 50.5% | 44.0% | 5.0% |
| 68,070 | ONTARIO | 30,098 | 17,114 | 11,719 | 1,180 | 85 | 5,395 R | 56.9% | 38.9% | 3.9% |
| 183,734 | ORANGE | 80,181 | 44,955 | 28,122 | 6,473 | 631 | 16,833 R | 56.1% | 35.1% | 8.1% |
| 34,159 | ORLEANS | 14,032 | 8,509 | 4,786 | 696 | 41 | 3,723 R | 60.6% | 34.1% | 5.0% |
| 86,118 | OSWEGO | 36,845 | 20,041 | 14,636 | 1,962 | 206 | 5,405 R | 54.4% | 39.7% | 5.3% |
| 51,942 | OTSEGO | 22,708 | 13,543 | 7,981 | 1,091 | 93 | 5,562 R | 59.6% | 35.1% | 4.8% |
| 31,722 | PUTNAM | 24,327 | 13,293 | 8,472 | 2,388 | 174 | 4,821 R | 54.6% | 34.8% | 9.8% |
| 1,809,578 | QUEENS | 766,012 | 306,620 | 410,546 | 44,198 | 4,648 | 103,926 D | 40.0% | 53.6% | 5.8% |
| 142,585 | RENSSELAER | 68,681 | 34,674 | 30,232 | 3,461 | 314 | 4,442 R | 50.5% | 44.0% | 5.0% |
| 221,991 | RICHMOND | 98,838 | 54,631 | 34,770 | 9,112 | 325 | 19,861 R | 55.3% | 35.2% | 9.2% |
| 136,803 | ROCKLAND | 83,337 | 40,880 | 36,948 | 5,028 | 481 | 3,932 R | 49.1% | 44.3% | 6.0% |
| 111,239 | ST. LAWRENCE | 37,937 | 20,982 | 15,662 | 1,178 | 115 | 5,320 R | 55.3% | 41.3% | 3.1% |
| 89,096 | SARATOGA | 45,935 | 25,658 | 17,766 | 2,220 | 291 | 7,892 R | 55.9% | 38.7% | 4.8% |
| 152,896 | SCHENECTADY | 72,052 | 33,687 | 34,786 | 3,246 | 333 | 1,099 D | 46.8% | 48.3% | 4.5% |
| 22,616 | SCHOHARIE | 10,777 | 6,166 | 3,883 | 689 | 39 | 2,283 R | 57.2% | 36.0% | 6.4% |
| 15,044 | SCHUYLER | 6,696 | 4,105 | 2,034 | 522 | 35 | 2,071 R | 61.3% | 30.4% | 7.8% |
| 31,984 | SENECA | 13,008 | 7,083 | 5,222 | 635 | 68 | 1,861 R | 54.5% | 40.1% | 4.9% |
| 97,691 | STEUBEN | 38,690 | 24,189 | 12,229 | 2,194 | 78 | 11,960 R | 62.5% | 31.6% | 5.7% |
| 666,784 | SUFFOLK | 374,875 | 218,027 | 122,590 | 31,304 | 2,954 | 95,437 R | 58.2% | 32.7% | 8.4% |
| 45,272 | SULLIVAN | 24,198 | 11,657 | 10,860 | 1,487 | 194 | 797 R | 48.2% | 44.9% | 6.1% |
| 37,802 | TIOGA | 16,956 | 10,441 | 5,336 | 1,127 | 52 | 5,105 R | 61.6% | 31.5% | 6.6% |
| 66,164 | TOMPKINS | 25,310 | 13,446 | 10,343 | 1,236 | 285 | 3,103 R | 53.1% | 40.9% | 4.9% |
| 118,804 | ULSTER | 60,452 | 34,798 | 20,886 | 4,183 | 585 | 13,912 R | 57.6% | 34.5% | 6.9% |
| 44,002 | WARREN | 20,280 | 12,963 | 6,460 | 807 | 50 | 6,503 R | 63.9% | 31.9% | 4.0% |
| 48,476 | WASHINGTON | 20,570 | 12,694 | 6,806 | 930 | 140 | 5,888 R | 61.7% | 33.1% | 4.5% |
| 67,989 | WAYNE | 27,695 | 17,470 | 8,907 | 1,211 | 107 | 8,563 R | 63.1% | 32.2% | 4.4% |
| 808,891 | WESTCHESTER | 400,945 | 201,652 | 173,954 | 22,115 | 3,224 | 27,698 R | 50.3% | 43.4% | 5.5% |
| 34,793 | WYOMING | 13,765 | 8,459 | 4,477 | 799 | 30 | 3,982 R | 61.5% | 32.5% | 5.8% |
| 18,614 | YATES | 8,117 | 5,482 | 2,158 | 440 | 37 | 3,324 R | 67.5% | 26.6% | 5.4% |
| 16,782,304 | TOTAL | 6,791,688 | 3,007,932 | 3,378,470 | 358,864 | 46,422 | 370,538 D | 44.3% | 49.7% | 5.3% |

# NEW YORK

## PRESIDENT 1964

| 1960 Census Population | County | Total Vote | Republican | Democratic | Other | Rep.-Dem. Plurality | Percentage Total Vote Rep. | Dem. | Major Vote Rep. | Dem. |
|---|---|---|---|---|---|---|---|---|---|---|
| 272,926 | ALBANY | 147,152 | 32,224 | 114,827 | 101 | 82,603 D | 21.9% | 78.0% | 21.9% | 78.1% |
| 43,978 | ALLEGANY | 18,039 | 7,688 | 10,329 | 22 | 2,641 D | 42.6% | 57.3% | 42.7% | 57.3% |
| 1,424,815 | BRONX | 539,559 | 135,780 | 402,960 | 819 | 267,180 D | 25.2% | 74.7% | 25.2% | 74.8% |
| 212,661 | BROOME | 91,139 | 32,048 | 59,021 | 70 | 26,973 D | 35.2% | 64.8% | 35.2% | 64.8% |
| 80,187 | CATTARAUGUS | 32,933 | 10,907 | 21,994 | 32 | 11,087 D | 33.1% | 66.8% | 33.2% | 66.8% |
| 73,942 | CAYUGA | 35,566 | 11,453 | 24,090 | 23 | 12,637 D | 32.2% | 67.7% | 32.2% | 67.8% |
| 145,377 | CHAUTAUQUA | 62,064 | 19,069 | 42,924 | 71 | 23,855 D | 30.7% | 69.2% | 30.8% | 69.2% |
| 98,706 | CHEMUNG | 41,082 | 14,716 | 26,332 | 34 | 11,616 D | 35.8% | 64.1% | 35.9% | 64.1% |
| 43,243 | CHENANGO | 18,952 | 7,293 | 11,653 | 6 | 4,360 D | 38.5% | 61.5% | 38.5% | 61.5% |
| 72,722 | CLINTON | 24,492 | 6,078 | 18,398 | 16 | 12,320 D | 24.8% | 75.1% | 24.8% | 75.2% |
| 47,322 | COLUMBIA | 23,558 | 9,023 | 14,516 | 19 | 5,493 D | 38.3% | 61.6% | 38.3% | 61.7% |
| 41,113 | CORTLAND | 17,272 | 6,149 | 11,110 | 13 | 4,961 D | 35.6% | 64.3% | 35.6% | 64.4% |
| 43,540 | DELAWARE | 20,064 | 8,359 | 11,686 | 19 | 3,327 D | 41.7% | 58.2% | 41.7% | 58.3% |
| 176,008 | DUTCHESS | 79,735 | 29,503 | 50,179 | 53 | 20,676 D | 37.0% | 62.9% | 37.0% | 63.0% |
| 1,064,688 | ERIE | 471,576 | 125,962 | 344,910 | 704 | 218,948 D | 26.7% | 73.1% | 26.8% | 73.2% |
| 35,300 | ESSEX | 16,585 | 5,837 | 10,739 | 9 | 4,902 D | 35.2% | 64.8% | 35.2% | 64.8% |
| 44,742 | FRANKLIN | 17,329 | 4,846 | 12,467 | 16 | 7,621 D | 28.0% | 71.9% | 28.0% | 72.0% |
| 51,304 | FULTON | 23,149 | 7,278 | 15,846 | 25 | 8,568 D | 31.4% | 68.5% | 31.5% | 68.5% |
| 53,994 | GENESEE | 23,841 | 8,114 | 15,713 | 14 | 7,599 D | 34.0% | 65.9% | 34.1% | 65.9% |
| 31,372 | GREENE | 17,895 | 7,842 | 10,034 | 19 | 2,192 D | 43.8% | 56.1% | 43.9% | 56.1% |
| 4,267 | HAMILTON | 2,873 | 1,269 | 1,603 | 1 | 334 D | 44.2% | 55.8% | 44.2% | 55.8% |
| 66,370 | HERKIMER | 30,317 | 10,159 | 20,136 | 22 | 9,977 D | 33.5% | 66.4% | 33.5% | 66.5% |
| 87,835 | JEFFERSON | 35,922 | 10,718 | 25,175 | 29 | 14,457 D | 29.8% | 70.1% | 29.9% | 70.1% |
| 2,627,319 | KINGS | 915,510 | 229,291 | 684,839 | 1,380 | 455,548 D | 25.0% | 74.8% | 25.1% | 74.9% |
| 23,249 | LEWIS | 9,779 | 3,185 | 6,584 | 10 | 3,399 D | 32.6% | 67.3% | 32.6% | 67.4% |
| 44,053 | LIVINGSTON | 20,619 | 7,120 | 13,481 | 18 | 6,361 D | 34.5% | 65.4% | 34.6% | 65.4% |
| 54,635 | MADISON | 23,180 | 8,858 | 14,313 | 9 | 5,455 D | 38.2% | 61.7% | 38.2% | 61.8% |
| 586,387 | MONROE | 285,582 | 80,099 | 205,226 | 257 | 125,127 D | 28.0% | 71.9% | 28.1% | 71.9% |
| 57,240 | MONTGOMERY | 27,861 | 8,471 | 19,370 | 20 | 10,899 D | 30.4% | 69.5% | 30.4% | 69.6% |
| 1,300,171 | NASSAU | 632,115 | 248,886 | 382,590 | 639 | 133,704 D | 39.4% | 60.5% | 39.4% | 60.6% |
| 1,698,281 | NEW YORK | 625,772 | 120,125 | 503,848 | 1,799 | 383,723 D | 19.2% | 80.5% | 19.3% | 80.7% |
| 242,269 | NIAGARA | 95,985 | 28,663 | 67,260 | 62 | 38,597 D | 29.9% | 70.1% | 29.9% | 70.1% |
| 264,401 | ONEIDA | 113,210 | 39,737 | 73,359 | 114 | 33,622 D | 35.1% | 64.8% | 35.1% | 64.9% |
| 423,028 | ONONDAGA | 192,014 | 63,205 | 128,630 | 179 | 65,425 D | 32.9% | 67.0% | 32.9% | 67.1% |
| 68,070 | ONTARIO | 30,788 | 10,847 | 19,922 | 19 | 9,075 D | 35.2% | 64.7% | 35.3% | 64.7% |
| 183,734 | ORANGE | 78,932 | 30,610 | 48,244 | 78 | 17,634 D | 38.8% | 61.1% | 38.8% | 61.2% |
| 34,159 | ORLEANS | 14,896 | 5,567 | 9,304 | 25 | 3,737 D | 37.4% | 62.5% | 37.4% | 62.6% |
| 86,118 | OSWEGO | 37,226 | 12,415 | 24,788 | 23 | 12,373 D | 33.4% | 66.6% | 33.4% | 66.6% |
| 51,942 | OTSEGO | 23,859 | 8,643 | 15,190 | 26 | 6,547 D | 36.2% | 63.7% | 36.3% | 63.7% |
| 31,722 | PUTNAM | 21,879 | 9,219 | 12,636 | 24 | 3,417 D | 42.1% | 57.8% | 42.2% | 57.8% |
| 1,809,578 | QUEENS | 816,875 | 274,351 | 541,418 | 1,106 | 267,067 D | 33.6% | 66.3% | 33.6% | 66.4% |
| 142,585 | RENSSELAER | 72,060 | 20,814 | 51,170 | 76 | 30,356 D | 28.9% | 71.0% | 28.9% | 71.1% |
| 221,991 | RICHMOND | 92,946 | 42,330 | 50,524 | 92 | 8,194 D | 45.5% | 54.4% | 45.6% | 54.4% |
| 136,803 | ROCKLAND | 72,460 | 26,187 | 46,173 | 100 | 19,986 D | 36.1% | 63.7% | 36.2% | 63.8% |
| 111,239 | ST. LAWRENCE | 41,307 | 12,102 | 29,173 | 32 | 17,071 D | 29.3% | 70.6% | 29.3% | 70.7% |
| 89,096 | SARATOGA | 42,688 | 13,364 | 29,264 | 60 | 15,900 D | 31.3% | 68.6% | 31.4% | 68.6% |
| 152,896 | SCHENECTADY | 73,868 | 21,848 | 51,892 | 128 | 30,044 D | 29.6% | 70.2% | 29.6% | 70.4% |
| 22,616 | SCHOHARIE | 11,391 | 4,193 | 7,187 | 11 | 2,994 D | 36.8% | 63.1% | 36.8% | 63.2% |
| 15,044 | SCHUYLER | 7,256 | 2,925 | 4,326 | 5 | 1,401 D | 40.3% | 59.6% | 40.3% | 59.7% |
| 31,984 | SENECA | 13,376 | 4,473 | 8,890 | 13 | 4,417 D | 33.4% | 66.5% | 33.5% | 66.5% |
| 97,691 | STEUBEN | 40,645 | 15,988 | 24,634 | 23 | 8,646 D | 39.3% | 60.6% | 39.4% | 60.6% |
| 666,784 | SUFFOLK | 325,333 | 144,350 | 180,598 | 385 | 36,248 D | 44.4% | 55.5% | 44.4% | 55.6% |
| 45,272 | SULLIVAN | 24,775 | 8,006 | 16,728 | 41 | 8,722 D | 32.3% | 67.5% | 32.4% | 67.6% |
| 37,802 | TIOGA | 17,569 | 7,147 | 10,411 | 11 | 3,264 D | 40.7% | 59.3% | 40.7% | 59.3% |
| 66,164 | TOMPKINS | 25,203 | 9,070 | 16,103 | 30 | 7,033 D | 36.0% | 63.9% | 36.0% | 64.0% |
| 118,804 | ULSTER | 59,326 | 23,749 | 35,486 | 91 | 11,737 D | 40.0% | 59.8% | 40.1% | 59.9% |
| 44,002 | WARREN | 20,620 | 7,834 | 12,772 | 14 | 4,938 D | 38.0% | 61.9% | 38.0% | 62.0% |
| 48,476 | WASHINGTON | 21,994 | 8,160 | 13,826 | 8 | 5,666 D | 37.1% | 62.9% | 37.1% | 62.9% |
| 67,989 | WAYNE | 29,342 | 10,586 | 18,729 | 27 | 8,143 D | 36.1% | 63.8% | 36.1% | 63.9% |
| 808,891 | WESTCHESTER | 393,297 | 149,052 | 243,723 | 522 | 94,671 D | 37.9% | 62.0% | 37.9% | 62.1% |
| 34,793 | WYOMING | 14,980 | 6,099 | 8,866 | 15 | 2,767 D | 40.7% | 59.2% | 40.8% | 59.2% |
| 18,614 | YATES | 8,663 | 3,675 | 4,983 | 5 | 1,308 D | 42.4% | 57.5% | 42.4% | 57.6% |
| 16,782,304 | TOTAL | 7,166,275 | 2,243,559 | 4,913,102 | 9,614 | 2,669,543 D | 31.3% | 68.6% | 31.3% | 68.7% |

# NEW YORK

## PRESIDENT 1960

| 1960 Census Population | County | Total Vote | Republican | Democratic | Other | Rep.-Dem. Plurality | Percentage | | | |
|---|---|---|---|---|---|---|---|---|---|---|
| | | | | | | | Total Vote | | Major Vote | |
| | | | | | | | Rep. | Dem. | Rep. | Dem. |
| 272,926 | ALBANY | 153,692 | 61,600 | 91,973 | 119 | 30,373 D | 40.1% | 59.8% | 40.1% | 59.9% |
| 43,978 | ALLEGANY | 19,695 | 14,408 | 5,280 | 7 | 9,128 R | 73.2% | 26.8% | 73.2% | 26.8% |
| 1,424,815 | BRONX | 574,282 | 182,393 | 389,818 | 2,071 | 207,425 D | 31.8% | 67.9% | 31.9% | 68.1% |
| 212,661 | BROOME | 94,991 | 56,467 | 38,462 | 62 | 18,005 R | 59.4% | 40.5% | 59.5% | 40.5% |
| 80,187 | CATTARAUGUS | 36,573 | 21,749 | 14,797 | 27 | 6,952 R | 59.5% | 40.5% | 59.5% | 40.5% |
| 73,942 | CAYUGA | 37,722 | 20,437 | 17,257 | 28 | 3,180 R | 54.2% | 45.7% | 54.2% | 45.8% |
| 145,377 | CHAUTAUQUA | 66,031 | 37,836 | 28,143 | 52 | 9,693 R | 57.3% | 42.6% | 57.3% | 42.7% |
| 98,706 | CHEMUNG | 44,396 | 26,469 | 17,899 | 28 | 8,570 R | 59.6% | 40.3% | 59.7% | 40.3% |
| 43,243 | CHENANGO | 20,204 | 14,533 | 5,659 | 12 | 8,874 R | 71.9% | 28.0% | 72.0% | 28.0% |
| 72,722 | CLINTON | 24,951 | 11,154 | 13,782 | 15 | 2,628 D | 44.7% | 55.2% | 44.7% | 55.3% |
| 47,322 | COLUMBIA | 24,664 | 15,893 | 8,747 | 24 | 7,146 R | 64.4% | 35.5% | 64.5% | 35.5% |
| 41,113 | CORTLAND | 18,235 | 12,305 | 5,921 | 9 | 6,384 R | 67.5% | 32.5% | 67.5% | 32.5% |
| 43,540 | DELAWARE | 22,013 | 16,336 | 5,662 | 15 | 10,674 R | 74.2% | 25.7% | 74.3% | 25.7% |
| 176,008 | DUTCHESS | 76,004 | 46,109 | 29,842 | 53 | 16,267 R | 60.7% | 39.3% | 60.7% | 39.3% |
| 1,064,688 | ERIE | 489,564 | 211,957 | 277,203 | 404 | 65,246 D | 43.3% | 56.6% | 43.3% | 56.7% |
| 35,300 | ESSEX | 17,901 | 11,557 | 6,334 | 10 | 5,223 R | 64.6% | 35.4% | 64.6% | 35.4% |
| 44,742 | FRANKLIN | 19,358 | 9,385 | 9,946 | 27 | 561 D | 48.5% | 51.4% | 48.5% | 51.5% |
| 51,304 | FULTON | 24,883 | 14,455 | 10,409 | 19 | 4,046 R | 58.1% | 41.8% | 58.1% | 41.9% |
| 53,994 | GENESEE | 25,085 | 14,724 | 10,343 | 18 | 4,381 R | 58.7% | 41.2% | 58.7% | 41.3% |
| 31,372 | GREENE | 18,320 | 11,878 | 6,441 | 1 | 5,437 R | 64.8% | 35.2% | 64.8% | 35.2% |
| 4,267 | HAMILTON | 2,964 | 2,168 | 795 | 1 | 1,373 R | 73.1% | 26.8% | 73.2% | 26.8% |
| 66,370 | HERKIMER | 32,768 | 17,758 | 14,977 | 33 | 2,781 R | 54.2% | 45.7% | 54.2% | 45.8% |
| 87,835 | JEFFERSON | 40,115 | 24,290 | 15,800 | 25 | 8,490 R | 60.6% | 39.4% | 60.6% | 39.4% |
| 2,627,319 | KINGS | 977,306 | 327,497 | 646,582 | 3,227 | 319,085 D | 33.5% | 66.2% | 33.6% | 66.4% |
| 23,249 | LEWIS | 10,697 | 6,632 | 4,056 | 9 | 2,576 R | 62.0% | 37.9% | 62.1% | 37.9% |
| 44,053 | LIVINGSTON | 21,454 | 13,681 | 7,765 | 8 | 5,916 R | 63.8% | 36.2% | 63.8% | 36.2% |
| 54,635 | MADISON | 24,697 | 16,245 | 8,433 | 19 | 7,812 R | 65.8% | 34.1% | 65.8% | 34.2% |
| 586,387 | MONROE | 289,948 | 148,423 | 141,378 | 147 | 7,045 R | 51.2% | 48.8% | 51.2% | 48.8% |
| 57,240 | MONTGOMERY | 30,827 | 14,837 | 15,976 | 14 | 1,139 D | 48.1% | 51.8% | 48.2% | 51.8% |
| 1,300,171 | NASSAU | 588,319 | 324,255 | 263,303 | 761 | 60,952 R | 55.1% | 44.8% | 55.2% | 44.8% |
| 1,698,281 | NEW YORK | 635,567 | 217,271 | 414,902 | 3,394 | 197,631 D | 34.2% | 65.3% | 34.4% | 65.6% |
| 242,269 | NIAGARA | 101,765 | 50,001 | 51,680 | 84 | 1,679 D | 49.1% | 50.8% | 49.2% | 50.8% |
| 264,401 | ONEIDA | 122,981 | 59,513 | 63,368 | 100 | 3,855 D | 48.4% | 51.5% | 48.4% | 51.6% |
| 423,028 | ONONDAGA | 198,156 | 107,170 | 90,836 | 150 | 16,334 R | 54.1% | 45.8% | 54.1% | 45.9% |
| 68,070 | ONTARIO | 31,931 | 19,654 | 12,251 | 26 | 7,403 R | 61.6% | 38.4% | 61.6% | 38.4% |
| 183,734 | ORANGE | 80,182 | 48,646 | 31,471 | 65 | 17,175 R | 60.7% | 39.2% | 60.7% | 39.3% |
| 34,159 | ORLEANS | 15,864 | 10,344 | 5,515 | 5 | 4,829 R | 65.2% | 34.8% | 65.2% | 34.8% |
| 86,118 | OSWEGO | 39,568 | 24,013 | 15,544 | 11 | 8,469 R | 60.7% | 39.3% | 60.7% | 39.3% |
| 51,942 | OTSEGO | 25,347 | 17,422 | 7,899 | 26 | 9,523 R | 68.7% | 31.2% | 68.8% | 31.2% |
| 31,722 | PUTNAM | 19,987 | 11,946 | 8,013 | 28 | 3,933 R | 59.8% | 40.1% | 59.9% | 40.1% |
| 1,809,578 | QUEENS | 815,899 | 367,688 | 446,348 | 1,863 | 78,660 D | 45.1% | 54.7% | 45.2% | 54.8% |
| 142,585 | RENSSELAER | 76,294 | 40,124 | 36,109 | 61 | 4,015 R | 52.6% | 47.3% | 52.6% | 47.4% |
| 221,991 | RICHMOND | 89,123 | 50,356 | 38,673 | 94 | 11,683 R | 56.5% | 43.4% | 56.6% | 43.4% |
| 136,803 | ROCKLAND | 60,398 | 33,107 | 27,178 | 113 | 5,929 R | 54.8% | 45.0% | 54.9% | 45.1% |
| 111,239 | ST. LAWRENCE | 45,302 | 25,848 | 19,430 | 24 | 6,418 R | 57.1% | 42.9% | 57.1% | 42.9% |
| 89,096 | SARATOGA | 43,250 | 25,035 | 18,179 | 36 | 6,856 R | 57.9% | 42.0% | 57.9% | 42.1% |
| 152,896 | SCHENECTADY | 77,253 | 40,180 | 37,003 | 70 | 3,177 R | 52.0% | 47.9% | 52.1% | 47.9% |
| 22,616 | SCHOHARIE | 12,002 | 7,644 | 4,342 | 16 | 3,302 R | 63.7% | 36.2% | 63.8% | 36.2% |
| 15,044 | SCHUYLER | 7,527 | 5,201 | 2,315 | 11 | 2,886 R | 69.1% | 30.8% | 69.2% | 30.8% |
| 31,984 | SENECA | 14,435 | 8,741 | 5,693 | 1 | 3,048 R | 60.6% | 39.4% | 60.6% | 39.4% |
| 97,691 | STEUBEN | 43,549 | 29,638 | 13,898 | 13 | 15,740 R | 68.1% | 31.9% | 68.1% | 31.9% |
| 666,784 | SUFFOLK | 280,945 | 166,644 | 114,033 | 268 | 52,611 R | 59.3% | 40.6% | 59.4% | 40.6% |
| 45,272 | SULLIVAN | 25,279 | 13,744 | 11,486 | 49 | 2,258 R | 54.4% | 45.4% | 54.5% | 45.5% |
| 37,802 | TIOGA | 17,431 | 12,572 | 4,855 | 4 | 7,717 R | 72.1% | 27.9% | 72.1% | 27.9% |
| 66,164 | TOMPKINS | 25,733 | 17,061 | 8,659 | 13 | 8,402 R | 66.3% | 33.6% | 66.3% | 33.7% |
| 118,804 | ULSTER | 59,502 | 36,418 | 23,017 | 67 | 13,401 R | 61.2% | 38.7% | 61.3% | 38.7% |
| 44,002 | WARREN | 21,778 | 14,433 | 7,328 | 17 | 7,105 R | 66.3% | 33.6% | 66.3% | 33.7% |
| 48,476 | WASHINGTON | 23,317 | 15,037 | 8,274 | 6 | 6,763 R | 64.5% | 35.5% | 64.5% | 35.5% |
| 67,989 | WAYNE | 30,777 | 21,290 | 9,476 | 11 | 11,814 R | 69.2% | 30.8% | 69.2% | 30.8% |
| 808,891 | WESTCHESTER | 396,663 | 224,562 | 171,410 | 691 | 53,152 R | 56.6% | 43.2% | 56.7% | 43.3% |
| 34,793 | WYOMING | 16,307 | 10,793 | 5,508 | 6 | 5,285 R | 66.2% | 33.8% | 66.2% | 33.8% |
| 18,614 | YATES | 9,308 | 6,892 | 2,409 | 7 | 4,483 R | 74.0% | 25.9% | 74.1% | 25.9% |
| 16,782,304 | TOTAL | 7,291,079 | 3,446,419 | 3,830,085 | 14,575 | 383,666 D | 47.3% | 52.5% | 47.4% | 52.6% |

# NEW YORK

## ELECTION NOTES

**2004**     Other vote was 99,873 Ralph Nader (84,247 on the Independence Party line; 15,626 on the Peace and Justice line); 11,607 Libertarian (Michael Badnarik); 2,405 Socialist Workers (Roger Calero); 207 write-in (Michael Peroutka); 87 write-in (David Cobb); 4 write-in (Michael Halpin); 4 write-in (John Joseph Kennedy); 2 write-in (Bill Van Auken).

**2000**     Other vote was 31,599 Right to Life (Buchanan)/Reform (Buchanan); 24,361 Independence Party (Hagelin); 7,649 Libertarian (Browne); 1,789 Socialist Workers (Harris); 1,498 Constitution (Phillips); 2 write-in (McReynolds).

**1996**     Other vote was 75,956 Green (Nader); 23,580 Right to Life (Phillips); 12,220 Libertarian (Browne); 5,011 Natural Law (Hagelin); 3,473 Workers World (Moorehead); 2,762 Socialist Workers (Harris).

**1992**     Other vote was 15,472 Warren (Socialist Workers); 13,451 Marrou (Libertarian); 11,318 Fulani (New Alliance); 4,420 Hagelin (Natural Law); 385 Daniels (write-in); 23 Gritz (write-in); 20 LaRouche (write-in); 16 Brisben (write-in). The total of the other vote column includes the 444 write-in votes not available by county. The Republican candidate was also the Conservative and Right to Life nominee; 177,000 of his votes were received as the Conservative candidate and 127,959 as the Right to Life candidate. The Democratic candidate was also the Liberal nominee and 97,556 of his votes were received as the Liberal candidate.

**1988**     Other vote was 20,497 Marra (Right to Life); 15,845 Fulani (New Alliance); 12,109 Paul (Libertarian); 4,179 Holmes (Workers World); 3,287 Warren (Socialist Workers); 10 Winn (write-in); 3 Kenoyer (write-in). The Republican candidate was also the Conservative nominee and 243,457 of his votes were received as the Conservative candidate. The Democratic candidate was also the Liberal nominee and 92,395 of his votes were received as the Liberal candidate.

**1984**     Other vote was 11,949 Bergland (Free Libertarian); 4,226 Hall (Communist); 3,200 Serrette (New Alliance); 2,226 Holmes (Workers World); 837 scattered write-in.  The Republican candidate was also the Conservative nominee and 288,244 of his votes were received as the Conservative candidate. The Democratic candidate was also the Liberal nominee and 118,324 of his votes were received as the Liberal candidate.

**1980**     Other vote was 467,801 Anderson (Liberal); 52,648 Clark (Free Libertarian); 24,159 McCormack (Right to Life); 23,186 Commoner (Citizens); 7,414 Hall (Communist); 2,068 DeBerry (Socialist Workers); 1,416 Griswold (Workers World); 1,064 scattered write-in. The Republican candidate was also the Conservative nominee and 256,131 of his votes were received as the Conservative candidate. Early unamended canvass gave the Republican vote in Oswego county as 31,151.

**1976**     Other vote was 12,197 MacBride (Free Libertarian); 10,270 Hall (Communist); 6,996 Camejo (Socialist Workers); 5,413 LaRouche (Labor); 4,303 McCarthy (write-in); 451 Anderson (write-in); 97 Maddox (write-in); 28 Levin (write-in); 14 Zeidler (write-in); 4,052 scattered write-in. The Republican candidate was also the Conservative nominee and 274,878 of his votes were received as the Conservative candidate. The Democratic candidate was also the Liberal nominee and 145,393 of his votes were received as the Liberal candidate. Early unamended canvass gave the total write-in votes as 8,975.

**1972**     Other vote was 7,797 Reed (Socialist Workers); 4,530 Fisher (Socialist Labor); 5,641 Hall (Communist); 4,089 scattered write-in. The Republican candidate was also the Conservative nominee and 368,136 of his votes were received as the Conservative candidate. The Democratic candidate was also the Liberal nominee and 183,128 of his votes were received as the Liberal candidate.

**1968**     Wallace on the ballot as Courage. Other vote was 24,517 Gregory (Freedom and Peace); 11,851 Halstead (Socialist Workers); 8,432 Blomen (Socialist Labor); 1,622 scattered write-in. The Democratic candidate was also the Liberal nominee and 311,622 of his votes were received as the Liberal candidate.

# NEW YORK

## ELECTION NOTES

**1964**    Other vote was 6,118 Hass (Socialist Labor); 3,228 DeBerry (Socialist Workers); 268 scattered write-in. The Democratic candidate was also the Liberal nominee and 342,432 of his votes were received as the Liberal candidate.

**1960**    Other vote was 14,319 Dobbs (Socialist Workers); 256 scattered write-in. The Democratic candidate was also the Liberal nominee and 406,176 of his votes were received as the Liberal candidate.

# NORTH CAROLINA

## POPULAR VOTE FOR PRESIDENT 1920 TO 2004

| Year | Total Vote | Republican | | Democratic | | Other Vote | Plurality | Percentage | | | |
|------|------------|------|-----------|------|-----------|------|-----------|------|------|------|------|
| | | | | | | | | Total Vote | | Major Vote | |
| | | Vote | Candidate | Vote | Candidate | | | Rep. | Dem. | Rep. | Dem. |
| 2004 | 3,501,007 | 1,961,166 | Bush, George W. | 1,525,849 | Kerry, John | 13,992 | 435,317 R | 56.0% | 43.6% | 56.2% | 43.8% |
| 2000 | 2,911,262 | 1,631,163 | Bush, George W. | 1,257,692 | Gore, Al | 22,407 | 373,471 R | 56.0% | 43.2% | 56.5% | 43.5% |
| 1996 ** | 2,515,807 | 1,225,938 | Dole, Bob | 1,107,849 | Clinton, Bill | 182,020 | 118,089 R | 48.7% | 44.0% | 52.5% | 47.5% |
| 1992 ** | 2,611,850 | 1,134,661 | Bush, George | 1,114,042 | Clinton, Bill | 363,147 | 20,619 R | 43.4% | 42.7% | 50.5% | 49.5% |
| 1988 | 2,134,370 | 1,237,258 | Bush, George | 890,167 | Dukakis, Michael S. | 6,945 | 347,091 R | 58.0% | 41.7% | 58.2% | 41.8% |
| 1984 | 2,175,361 | 1,346,481 | Reagan, Ronald | 824,287 | Mondale, Walter F. | 4,593 | 522,194 R | 61.9% | 37.9% | 62.0% | 38.0% |
| 1980** | 1,855,833 | 915,018 | Reagan, Ronald | 875,635 | Carter, Jimmy | 65,180 | 39,383 R | 49.3% | 47.2% | 51.1% | 48.9% |
| 1976 | 1,678,914 | 741,960 | Ford, Gerald R. | 927,365 | Carter, Jimmy | 9,589 | 185,405 D | 44.2% | 55.2% | 44.4% | 55.6% |
| 1972 | 1,518,612 | 1,054,889 | Nixon, Richard M. | 438,705 | McGovern, George S. | 25,018 | 616,184 R | 69.5% | 28.9% | 70.6% | 29.4% |
| 1968 ** | 1,587,493 | 627,192 | Nixon, Richard M. | 464,113 | Humphrey, Hubert H. | 496,188 | 131,004 R | 39.5% | 29.2% | 57.5% | 42.5% |
| 1964 | 1,424,983 | 624,844 | Goldwater, Barry M. | 800,139 | Johnson, Lyndon B. | | 175,295 D | 43.8% | 56.2% | 43.8% | 56.2% |
| 1960 | 1,368,556 | 655,420 | Nixon, Richard M. | 713,136 | Kennedy, John F. | | 57,716 D | 47.9% | 52.1% | 47.9% | 52.1% |
| 1956 | 1,165,592 | 575,062 | Eisenhower, Dwight D. | 590,530 | Stevenson, Adlai E. | 15,468 | | 49.3% | 50.7% | 49.3% | 50.7% |
| 1952 | 1,210,910 | 558,107 | Eisenhower, Dwight D. | 652,803 | Stevenson, Adlai E. | | 94,696 D | 46.1% | 53.9% | 46.1% | 53.9% |
| 1948 | 791,209 | 258,572 | Dewey, Thomas E. | 459,070 | Truman, Harry S. | 73,567 | 200,498 D | 32.7% | 58.0% | 36.0% | 64.0% |
| 1944 | 790,554 | 263,155 | Dewey, Thomas E. | 527,399 | Roosevelt, Franklin D. | | 264,244 D | 33.3% | 66.7% | 33.3% | 66.7% |
| 1940 | 822,648 | 213,633 | Willkie, Wendell | 609,015 | Roosevelt, Franklin D. | | 395,382 D | 26.0% | 74.0% | 26.0% | 74.0% |
| 1936 | 839,475 | 223,294 | Landon, Alfred M. | 616,141 | Roosevelt, Franklin D. | 40 | 392,847 D | 26.6% | 73.4% | 26.6% | 73.4% |
| 1932 | 711,498 | 208,344 | Hoover, Herbert C. | 497,566 | Roosevelt, Franklin D. | 5,588 | 289,222 D | 29.3% | 69.9% | 29.5% | 70.5% |
| 1928 | 635,150 | 348,923 | Hoover, Herbert C. | 286,227 | Smith, Alfred E. | | 62,696 R | 54.9% | 45.1% | 54.9% | 45.1% |
| 1924 | 481,608 | 190,754 | Coolidge, Calvin | 284,190 | Davis, John W. | 6,664 | 93,436 D | 39.6% | 59.0% | 40.2% | 59.8% |
| 1920 | 538,649 | 232,819 | Harding, Warren G. | 305,367 | Cox, James M. | 463 | 72,548 D | 43.2% | 56.7% | 43.3% | 56.7% |

In 1996 the other vote column includes 168,059 votes cast for Perot. In 1992 the other vote column includes 357,864 votes cast for Perot. In 1980 the other column includes 52,800 votes for Independent (Anderson). In 1968 other vote was American (Wallace).

## ELECTORAL COLLEGE VOTE 1920 TO 2004

| Year | Total | Republican | Democratic | Other |
|------|-------|------------|------------|-------|
| 2004 | 15 | 15 | | |
| 2000 | 14 | 14 | | |
| 1996 | 14 | 14 | | |
| 1992 | 14 | 14 | | |
| 1988 | 13 | 13 | | |
| 1984 | 13 | 13 | | |
| 1980 | 13 | 13 | | |
| 1976 | 13 | | 13 | |
| 1972 | 13 | 13 | | |
| 1968 ** | 13 | 12 | | 1 AIP |
| 1964 | 13 | | 13 | |
| 1960 | 14 | | 14 | |
| 1956 | 14 | | 14 | |
| 1952 | 14 | | 14 | |
| 1948 | 14 | | 14 | |
| 1944 | 14 | | 14 | |
| 1940 | 13 | | 13 | |
| 1936 | 13 | | 13 | |
| 1932 | 13 | | 13 | |
| 1928 | 12 | 12 | | |
| 1924 | 12 | | 12 | |
| 1920 | 12 | | 12 | |

In 1968 one of the thirteen Republican electors voted in the Electoral College for the American Independent party candidates rather than for the national Republican candidates.

# NORTH CAROLINA

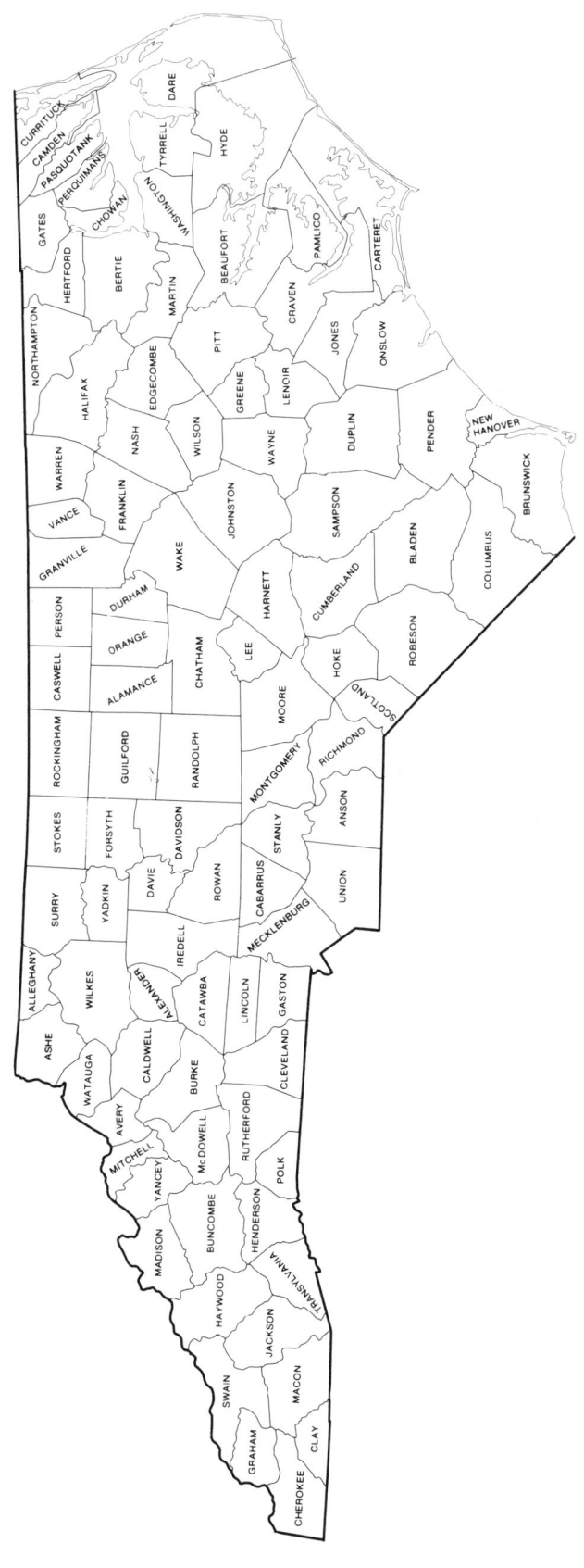

# NORTH CAROLINA

## PRESIDENT 2004

| 2000 Census Population | County | Total Vote | Republican | Democratic | Other | Rep.-Dem. Plurality | Percentage | | | |
|---|---|---|---|---|---|---|---|---|---|---|
| | | | | | | | Total Vote | | Major Vote | |
| | | | | | | | Rep. | Dem. | Rep. | Dem. |
| 130,800 | ALAMANCE | 54,175 | 33,302 | 20,686 | 187 | 12,616 R | 61.5% | 38.2% | 61.7% | 38.3% |
| 33,603 | ALEXANDER | 15,600 | 10,928 | 4,618 | 54 | 6,310 R | 70.1% | 29.6% | 70.3% | 29.7% |
| 10,677 | ALLEGHANY | 4,827 | 2,883 | 1,922 | 22 | 961 R | 59.7% | 39.8% | 60.0% | 40.0% |
| 25,275 | ANSON | 9,225 | 3,796 | 5,413 | 16 | 1,617 D | 41.1% | 58.7% | 41.2% | 58.8% |
| 24,384 | ASHE | 11,823 | 7,292 | 4,477 | 54 | 2,815 R | 61.7% | 37.9% | 62.0% | 38.0% |
| 17,167 | AVERY | 7,524 | 5,678 | 1,805 | 41 | 3,873 R | 75.5% | 24.0% | 75.9% | 24.1% |
| 44,958 | BEAUFORT | 19,522 | 12,432 | 7,025 | 65 | 5,407 R | 63.7% | 36.0% | 63.9% | 36.1% |
| 19,773 | BERTIE | 8,032 | 3,057 | 4,938 | 37 | 1,881 D | 38.1% | 61.5% | 38.2% | 61.8% |
| 32,278 | BLADEN | 12,313 | 6,174 | 6,109 | 30 | 65 R | 50.1% | 49.6% | 50.3% | 49.7% |
| 73,143 | BRUNSWICK | 37,977 | 22,925 | 14,903 | 149 | 8,022 R | 60.4% | 39.2% | 60.6% | 39.4% |
| 206,330 | BUNCOMBE | 105,013 | 52,491 | 51,868 | 654 | 623 R | 50.0% | 49.4% | 50.3% | 49.7% |
| 89,148 | BURKE | 30,762 | 18,922 | 11,728 | 112 | 7,194 R | 61.5% | 38.1% | 61.7% | 38.3% |
| 131,063 | CABARRUS | 60,824 | 40,780 | 19,803 | 241 | 20,977 R | 67.0% | 32.6% | 67.3% | 32.7% |
| 77,415 | CALDWELL | 31,348 | 21,186 | 9,999 | 163 | 11,187 R | 67.6% | 31.9% | 67.9% | 32.1% |
| 6,885 | CAMDEN | 3,830 | 2,480 | 1,339 | 11 | 1,141 R | 64.8% | 35.0% | 64.9% | 35.1% |
| 59,383 | CARTERET | 25,575 | 17,716 | 7,732 | 127 | 9,984 R | 69.3% | 30.2% | 69.6% | 30.4% |
| 23,501 | CASWELL | 9,437 | 4,868 | 4,539 | 30 | 329 R | 51.6% | 48.1% | 51.7% | 48.3% |
| 141,685 | CATAWBA | 58,688 | 39,602 | 18,858 | 228 | 20,744 R | 67.5% | 32.1% | 67.7% | 32.3% |
| 49,329 | CHATHAM | 25,922 | 12,892 | 12,897 | 133 | 5 D | 49.7% | 49.8% | 50.0% | 50.0% |
| 24,298 | CHEROKEE | 11,199 | 7,517 | 3,635 | 47 | 3,882 R | 67.1% | 32.5% | 67.4% | 32.6% |
| 14,526 | CHOWAN | 5,386 | 2,967 | 2,406 | 13 | 561 R | 55.1% | 44.7% | 55.2% | 44.8% |
| 8,775 | CLAY | 4,866 | 3,209 | 1,628 | 29 | 1,581 R | 65.9% | 33.5% | 66.3% | 33.7% |
| 96,287 | CLEVELAND | 37,079 | 22,750 | 14,215 | 114 | 8,535 R | 61.4% | 38.3% | 61.5% | 38.5% |
| 54,749 | COLUMBUS | 21,191 | 10,773 | 10,343 | 75 | 430 R | 50.8% | 48.8% | 51.0% | 49.0% |
| 91,436 | CRAVEN | 37,756 | 23,575 | 14,019 | 162 | 9,556 R | 62.4% | 37.1% | 62.7% | 37.3% |
| 302,963 | CUMBERLAND | 95,226 | 49,139 | 45,788 | 299 | 3,351 R | 51.6% | 48.1% | 51.8% | 48.2% |
| 18,190 | CURRITUCK | 8,976 | 6,013 | 2,909 | 54 | 3,104 R | 67.0% | 32.4% | 67.4% | 32.6% |
| 29,967 | DARE | 15,548 | 9,345 | 6,136 | 67 | 3,209 R | 60.1% | 39.5% | 60.4% | 39.6% |
| 147,246 | DAVIDSON | 59,496 | 42,075 | 17,191 | 230 | 24,884 R | 70.7% | 28.9% | 71.0% | 29.0% |
| 34,835 | DAVIE | 16,680 | 12,372 | 4,233 | 75 | 8,139 R | 74.2% | 25.4% | 74.5% | 25.5% |
| 49,063 | DUPLIN | 16,583 | 9,611 | 6,923 | 49 | 2,688 R | 58.0% | 41.7% | 58.1% | 41.9% |
| 223,314 | DURHAM | 109,651 | 34,614 | 74,524 | 513 | 39,910 D | 31.6% | 68.0% | 31.7% | 68.3% |
| 55,606 | EDGECOMBE | 21,079 | 8,163 | 12,877 | 39 | 4,714 D | 38.7% | 61.1% | 38.8% | 61.2% |
| 306,067 | FORSYTH | 139,125 | 75,294 | 63,340 | 491 | 11,954 R | 54.1% | 45.5% | 54.3% | 45.7% |
| 47,260 | FRANKLIN | 20,918 | 11,540 | 9,286 | 92 | 2,254 R | 55.2% | 44.4% | 55.4% | 44.6% |
| 190,365 | GASTON | 63,755 | 43,252 | 20,254 | 249 | 22,998 R | 67.8% | 31.8% | 68.1% | 31.9% |
| 10,516 | GATES | 4,053 | 1,924 | 2,121 | 8 | 197 D | 47.5% | 52.3% | 47.6% | 52.4% |
| 7,993 | GRAHAM | 3,987 | 2,693 | 1,272 | 22 | 1,421 R | 67.5% | 31.9% | 67.9% | 32.1% |
| 48,498 | GRANVILLE | 18,601 | 9,491 | 9,057 | 53 | 434 R | 51.0% | 48.7% | 51.2% | 48.8% |
| 18,974 | GREENE | 6,472 | 3,800 | 2,665 | 7 | 1,135 R | 58.7% | 41.2% | 58.8% | 41.2% |
| 421,048 | GUILFORD | 199,314 | 98,254 | 100,042 | 1,018 | 1,788 D | 49.3% | 50.2% | 49.5% | 50.5% |
| 57,370 | HALIFAX | 19,647 | 8,088 | 11,528 | 31 | 3,440 D | 41.2% | 58.7% | 41.2% | 58.8% |
| 91,025 | HARNETT | 32,571 | 20,922 | 11,563 | 86 | 9,359 R | 64.2% | 35.5% | 64.4% | 35.6% |
| 54,033 | HAYWOOD | 25,932 | 14,545 | 11,237 | 150 | 3,308 R | 56.1% | 43.3% | 56.4% | 43.6% |
| 89,173 | HENDERSON | 43,234 | 28,025 | 15,003 | 206 | 13,022 R | 64.8% | 34.7% | 65.1% | 34.9% |
| 22,601 | HERTFORD | 8,132 | 2,942 | 5,141 | 49 | 2,199 D | 36.2% | 63.2% | 36.4% | 63.6% |
| 33,646 | HOKE | 11,088 | 5,257 | 5,794 | 37 | 537 D | 47.4% | 52.3% | 47.6% | 52.4% |
| 5,826 | HYDE | 2,293 | 1,235 | 1,048 | 10 | 187 R | 53.9% | 45.7% | 54.1% | 45.9% |
| 122,660 | IREDELL | 56,973 | 38,675 | 18,065 | 233 | 20,610 R | 67.9% | 31.7% | 68.2% | 31.8% |
| 33,121 | JACKSON | 14,174 | 7,351 | 6,737 | 86 | 614 R | 51.9% | 47.5% | 52.2% | 47.8% |
| 121,965 | JOHNSTON | 54,357 | 36,903 | 17,266 | 188 | 19,637 R | 67.9% | 31.8% | 68.1% | 31.9% |
| 10,381 | JONES | 4,513 | 2,607 | 1,893 | 13 | 714 R | 57.8% | 41.9% | 57.9% | 42.1% |
| 49,040 | LEE | 19,543 | 11,834 | 7,657 | 52 | 4,177 R | 60.6% | 39.2% | 60.7% | 39.3% |
| 59,648 | LENOIR | 23,179 | 12,939 | 10,207 | 33 | 2,732 R | 55.8% | 44.0% | 55.9% | 44.1% |
| 63,780 | LINCOLN | 29,579 | 20,052 | 9,434 | 93 | 10,618 R | 67.8% | 31.9% | 68.0% | 32.0% |
| 42,151 | MCDOWELL | 16,002 | 10,590 | 5,330 | 82 | 5,260 R | 66.2% | 33.3% | 66.5% | 33.5% |
| 29,811 | MACON | 15,024 | 9,448 | 5,489 | 87 | 3,959 R | 62.9% | 36.5% | 63.3% | 36.7% |
| 19,635 | MADISON | 9,463 | 5,175 | 4,234 | 54 | 941 R | 54.7% | 44.7% | 55.0% | 45.0% |
| 25,593 | MARTIN | 10,452 | 5,334 | 5,102 | 16 | 232 R | 51.0% | 48.8% | 51.1% | 48.9% |
| 695,454 | MECKLENBURG | 323,102 | 155,084 | 166,828 | 1,190 | 11,744 D | 48.0% | 51.6% | 48.2% | 51.8% |

# NORTH CAROLINA

## PRESIDENT 2004

| 2000 Census Population | County | Total Vote | Republican | Democratic | Other | Rep.-Dem. Plurality | Percentage | | | |
|---|---|---|---|---|---|---|---|---|---|---|
| | | | | | | | Total Vote | | Major Vote | |
| | | | | | | | Rep. | Dem. | Rep. | Dem. |
| 15,687 | MITCHELL | 7,798 | 5,686 | 2,080 | 32 | 3,606 R | 72.9% | 26.7% | 73.2% | 26.8% |
| 26,822 | MONTGOMERY | 10,080 | 5,745 | 4,313 | 22 | 1,432 R | 57.0% | 42.8% | 57.1% | 42.9% |
| 74,769 | MOORE | 38,382 | 24,714 | 13,555 | 113 | 11,159 R | 64.4% | 35.3% | 64.6% | 35.4% |
| 87,420 | NASH | 37,673 | 21,902 | 15,693 | 78 | 6,209 R | 58.1% | 41.7% | 58.3% | 41.7% |
| 160,307 | NEW HANOVER | 81,247 | 45,351 | 35,572 | 324 | 9,779 R | 55.8% | 43.8% | 56.0% | 44.0% |
| 22,086 | NORTHAMPTON | 8,770 | 3,176 | 5,584 | 10 | 2,408 D | 36.2% | 63.7% | 36.3% | 63.7% |
| 150,355 | ONSLOW | 37,277 | 25,890 | 11,250 | 137 | 14,640 R | 69.5% | 30.2% | 69.7% | 30.3% |
| 118,227 | ORANGE | 64,153 | 20,771 | 42,910 | 472 | 22,139 D | 32.4% | 66.9% | 32.6% | 67.4% |
| 12,934 | PAMLICO | 6,038 | 3,679 | 2,335 | 24 | 1,344 R | 60.9% | 38.7% | 61.2% | 38.8% |
| 34,897 | PASQUOTANK | 13,648 | 6,609 | 6,984 | 55 | 375 D | 48.4% | 51.2% | 48.6% | 51.4% |
| 41,082 | PENDER | 17,085 | 10,037 | 6,999 | 49 | 3,038 R | 58.7% | 41.0% | 58.9% | 41.1% |
| 11,368 | PERQUIMANS | 4,958 | 2,965 | 1,971 | 22 | 994 R | 59.8% | 39.8% | 60.1% | 39.9% |
| 35,623 | PERSON | 15,214 | 8,973 | 6,198 | 43 | 2,775 R | 59.0% | 40.7% | 59.1% | 40.9% |
| 133,798 | PITT | 53,643 | 28,590 | 24,924 | 129 | 3,666 R | 53.3% | 46.5% | 53.4% | 46.6% |
| 18,324 | POLK | 9,021 | 5,140 | 3,787 | 94 | 1,353 R | 57.0% | 42.0% | 57.6% | 42.4% |
| 130,454 | RANDOLPH | 50,910 | 37,771 | 12,966 | 173 | 24,805 R | 74.2% | 25.5% | 74.4% | 25.6% |
| 46,564 | RICHMOND | 16,145 | 7,709 | 8,383 | 53 | 674 D | 47.7% | 51.9% | 47.9% | 52.1% |
| 123,339 | ROBESON | 33,871 | 15,909 | 17,868 | 94 | 1,959 D | 47.0% | 52.8% | 47.1% | 52.9% |
| 91,928 | ROCKINGHAM | 37,388 | 22,840 | 14,430 | 118 | 8,410 R | 61.1% | 38.6% | 61.3% | 38.7% |
| 130,340 | ROWAN | 51,867 | 34,915 | 16,735 | 217 | 18,180 R | 67.3% | 32.3% | 67.6% | 32.4% |
| 62,899 | RUTHERFORD | 24,658 | 16,343 | 8,184 | 131 | 8,159 R | 66.3% | 33.2% | 66.6% | 33.4% |
| 60,161 | SAMPSON | 22,288 | 12,600 | 9,649 | 39 | 2,951 R | 56.5% | 43.3% | 56.6% | 43.4% |
| 35,998 | SCOTLAND | 11,547 | 5,141 | 6,386 | 20 | 1,245 D | 44.5% | 55.3% | 44.6% | 55.4% |
| 58,100 | STANLY | 25,553 | 17,814 | 7,650 | 89 | 10,164 R | 69.7% | 29.9% | 70.0% | 30.0% |
| 44,711 | STOKES | 19,414 | 13,583 | 5,767 | 64 | 7,816 R | 70.0% | 29.7% | 70.2% | 29.8% |
| 71,219 | SURRY | 25,992 | 17,587 | 8,304 | 101 | 9,283 R | 67.7% | 31.9% | 67.9% | 32.1% |
| 12,968 | SWAIN | 5,044 | 2,593 | 2,419 | 32 | 174 R | 51.4% | 48.0% | 51.7% | 48.3% |
| 29,334 | TRANSYLVANIA | 15,588 | 9,386 | 6,097 | 105 | 3,289 R | 60.2% | 39.1% | 60.6% | 39.4% |
| 4,149 | TYRRELL | 1,590 | 855 | 731 | 4 | 124 R | 53.8% | 46.0% | 53.9% | 46.1% |
| 123,677 | UNION | 61,001 | 42,820 | 17,974 | 207 | 24,846 R | 70.2% | 29.5% | 70.4% | 29.6% |
| 42,954 | VANCE | 15,677 | 6,884 | 8,762 | 31 | 1,878 D | 43.9% | 55.9% | 44.0% | 56.0% |
| 627,846 | WAKE | 348,844 | 177,324 | 169,909 | 1,611 | 7,415 R | 50.8% | 48.7% | 51.1% | 48.9% |
| 19,972 | WARREN | 8,027 | 2,840 | 5,171 | 16 | 2,331 D | 35.4% | 64.4% | 35.5% | 64.5% |
| 13,723 | WASHINGTON | 5,471 | 2,484 | 2,969 | 18 | 485 D | 45.4% | 54.3% | 45.6% | 54.4% |
| 42,695 | WATAUGA | 24,050 | 12,659 | 11,232 | 159 | 1,427 R | 52.6% | 46.7% | 53.0% | 47.0% |
| 113,329 | WAYNE | 40,046 | 24,883 | 15,076 | 87 | 9,807 R | 62.1% | 37.6% | 62.3% | 37.7% |
| 65,632 | WILKES | 27,154 | 19,197 | 7,862 | 95 | 11,335 R | 70.7% | 29.0% | 70.9% | 29.1% |
| 73,814 | WILSON | 30,535 | 16,264 | 14,206 | 65 | 2,058 R | 53.3% | 46.5% | 53.4% | 46.6% |
| 36,348 | YADKIN | 15,313 | 11,816 | 3,451 | 46 | 8,365 R | 77.2% | 22.5% | 77.4% | 22.6% |
| 17,774 | YANCEY | 9,431 | 4,940 | 4,434 | 57 | 506 R | 52.4% | 47.0% | 52.7% | 47.3% |
| 8,049,313 | TOTAL | 3,501,007 | 1,961,166 | 1,525,849 | 13,992 | 435,317 R | 56.0% | 43.6% | 56.2% | 43.8% |

# NORTH CAROLINA

## PRESIDENT 2000

| 2000 Census Population | County | Total Vote | Republican | Democratic | Green (Nader) | Other | Rep.-Dem. Plurality | Percentage of Total Vote | | |
|---|---|---|---|---|---|---|---|---|---|---|
| | | | | | | | | Rep. | Dem. | Green |
| 130,800 | ALAMANCE | 47,091 | 29,305 | 17,459 | | 327 | 11,846 R | 62.2% | 37.1% | |
| 33,603 | ALEXANDER | 13,492 | 9,242 | 4,166 | | 84 | 5,076 R | 68.5% | 30.9% | |
| 10,677 | ALLEGHANY | 4,313 | 2,531 | 1,715 | | 67 | 816 R | 58.7% | 39.8% | |
| 25,275 | ANSON | 7,985 | 3,161 | 4,792 | | 32 | 1,631 D | 39.6% | 60.0% | |
| 24,384 | ASHE | 10,316 | 6,226 | 4,011 | | 79 | 2,215 R | 60.4% | 38.9% | |
| 17,167 | AVERY | 6,694 | 4,956 | 1,686 | | 52 | 3,270 R | 74.0% | 25.2% | |
| 44,958 | BEAUFORT | 17,313 | 10,531 | 6,634 | | 148 | 3,897 R | 60.8% | 38.3% | |
| 19,773 | BERTIE | 7,176 | 2,488 | 4,660 | | 28 | 2,172 D | 34.7% | 64.9% | |
| 32,278 | BLADEN | 10,908 | 4,977 | 5,889 | | 42 | 912 D | 45.6% | 54.0% | |
| 73,143 | BRUNSWICK | 28,839 | 15,427 | 13,118 | | 294 | 2,309 R | 53.5% | 45.5% | |
| 206,330 | BUNCOMBE | 85,476 | 46,101 | 38,545 | | 830 | 7,556 R | 53.9% | 45.1% | |
| 89,148 | BURKE | 30,658 | 18,466 | 11,924 | | 268 | 6,542 R | 60.2% | 38.9% | |
| 131,063 | CABARRUS | 49,381 | 32,704 | 16,284 | | 343 | 16,420 R | 66.2% | 33.0% | |
| 77,415 | CALDWELL | 26,115 | 17,337 | 8,588 | | 190 | 8,749 R | 66.4% | 32.9% | |
| 6,885 | CAMDEN | 2,831 | 1,628 | 1,187 | | 16 | 441 R | 57.5% | 41.9% | |
| 59,383 | CARTERET | 26,461 | 17,381 | 8,839 | | 241 | 8,542 R | 65.7% | 33.4% | |
| 23,501 | CASWELL | 8,422 | 4,270 | 4,091 | | 61 | 179 R | 50.7% | 48.6% | |
| 141,685 | CATAWBA | 50,841 | 34,244 | 16,246 | | 351 | 17,998 R | 67.4% | 32.0% | |
| 49,329 | CHATHAM | 20,931 | 10,248 | 10,461 | | 222 | 213 D | 49.0% | 50.0% | |
| 24,298 | CHEROKEE | 9,674 | 6,305 | 3,239 | | 130 | 3,066 R | 65.2% | 33.5% | |
| 14,526 | CHOWAN | 4,890 | 2,415 | 2,430 | | 45 | 15 D | 49.4% | 49.7% | |
| 8,775 | CLAY | 3,852 | 2,416 | 1,361 | | 75 | 1,055 R | 62.7% | 35.3% | |
| 96,287 | CLEVELAND | 32,746 | 19,064 | 13,455 | | 227 | 5,609 R | 58.2% | 41.1% | |
| 54,749 | COLUMBUS | 18,425 | 8,342 | 9,986 | | 97 | 1,644 D | 45.3% | 54.2% | |
| 91,436 | CRAVEN | 31,985 | 19,494 | 12,213 | | 278 | 7,281 R | 60.9% | 38.2% | |
| 302,963 | CUMBERLAND | 77,151 | 38,129 | 38,626 | | 396 | 497 D | 49.4% | 50.1% | |
| 18,190 | CURRITUCK | 6,739 | 4,095 | 2,595 | | 49 | 1,500 R | 60.8% | 38.5% | |
| 29,967 | DARE | 13,002 | 7,301 | 5,589 | | 112 | 1,712 R | 56.2% | 43.0% | |
| 147,246 | DAVIDSON | 52,047 | 35,387 | 16,199 | | 461 | 19,188 R | 68.0% | 31.1% | |
| 34,835 | DAVIE | 13,998 | 10,184 | 3,651 | | 163 | 6,533 R | 72.8% | 26.1% | |
| 49,063 | DUPLIN | 14,390 | 7,840 | 6,475 | | 75 | 1,365 R | 54.5% | 45.0% | |
| 223,314 | DURHAM | 84,604 | 30,150 | 53,907 | | 547 | 23,757 D | 35.6% | 63.7% | |
| 55,606 | EDGECOMBE | 18,202 | 6,836 | 11,315 | | 51 | 4,479 D | 37.6% | 62.2% | |
| 306,067 | FORSYTH | 120,942 | 67,700 | 52,457 | | 785 | 15,243 R | 56.0% | 43.4% | |
| 47,260 | FRANKLIN | 16,051 | 8,501 | 7,454 | | 96 | 1,047 R | 53.0% | 46.4% | |
| 190,365 | GASTON | 59,179 | 39,453 | 19,281 | | 445 | 20,172 R | 66.7% | 32.6% | |
| 10,516 | GATES | 3,446 | 1,480 | 1,944 | | 22 | 464 D | 42.9% | 56.4% | |
| 7,993 | GRAHAM | 3,361 | 2,304 | 1,006 | | 51 | 1,298 R | 68.6% | 29.9% | |
| 48,498 | GRANVILLE | 15,194 | 7,364 | 7,733 | | 97 | 369 D | 48.5% | 50.9% | |
| 18,974 | GREENE | 5,870 | 3,353 | 2,478 | | 39 | 875 R | 57.1% | 42.2% | |
| 421,048 | GUILFORD | 166,264 | 84,394 | 80,787 | | 1,083 | 3,607 R | 50.8% | 48.6% | |
| 57,370 | HALIFAX | 16,970 | 6,698 | 10,222 | | 50 | 3,524 D | 39.5% | 60.2% | |
| 91,025 | HARNETT | 24,167 | 14,762 | 9,155 | | 250 | 5,607 R | 61.1% | 37.9% | |
| 54,033 | HAYWOOD | 22,273 | 12,118 | 9,793 | | 362 | 2,325 R | 54.4% | 44.0% | |
| 89,173 | HENDERSON | 38,607 | 25,688 | 12,562 | | 357 | 13,126 R | 66.5% | 32.5% | |
| 22,601 | HERTFORD | 7,897 | 2,382 | 5,484 | | 31 | 3,102 D | 30.2% | 69.4% | |
| 33,646 | HOKE | 8,582 | 3,439 | 5,017 | | 126 | 1,578 D | 40.1% | 58.5% | |
| 5,826 | HYDE | 2,237 | 1,132 | 1,088 | | 17 | 44 R | 50.6% | 48.6% | |
| 122,660 | IREDELL | 45,586 | 29,853 | 15,434 | | 299 | 14,419 R | 65.5% | 33.9% | |
| 33,121 | JACKSON | 12,121 | 6,237 | 5,722 | | 162 | 515 R | 51.5% | 47.2% | |
| 121,965 | JOHNSTON | 41,155 | 27,212 | 13,704 | | 239 | 13,508 R | 66.1% | 33.3% | |
| 10,381 | JONES | 3,964 | 2,114 | 1,822 | | 28 | 292 R | 53.3% | 46.0% | |
| 49,040 | LEE | 16,283 | 9,406 | 6,785 | | 92 | 2,621 R | 57.8% | 41.7% | |
| 59,648 | LENOIR | 21,163 | 11,512 | 9,527 | | 124 | 1,985 R | 54.4% | 45.0% | |
| 63,780 | LINCOLN | 24,529 | 15,951 | 8,412 | | 166 | 7,539 R | 65.0% | 34.3% | |
| 42,151 | MCDOWELL | 14,011 | 9,109 | 4,747 | | 155 | 4,362 R | 65.0% | 33.9% | |
| 29,811 | MACON | 13,234 | 8,406 | 4,683 | | 145 | 3,723 R | 63.5% | 35.4% | |
| 19,635 | MADISON | 8,325 | 4,676 | 3,505 | | 144 | 1,171 R | 56.2% | 42.1% | |
| 25,593 | MARTIN | 9,366 | 4,420 | 4,929 | | 17 | 509 D | 47.2% | 52.6% | |
| 695,454 | MECKLENBURG | 263,036 | 134,068 | 126,911 | | 2,057 | 7,157 R | 51.0% | 48.2% | |

# NORTH CAROLINA

## PRESIDENT 2000

| 2000 Census Population | County | Total Vote | Republican | Democratic | Green (Nader) | Other | Rep.-Dem. Plurality | Percentage of Total Vote Rep. | Dem. | Green |
|---|---|---|---|---|---|---|---|---|---|---|
| 15,687 | MITCHELL | 6,600 | 4,984 | 1,535 | | 81 | 3,449 R | 75.5% | 23.3% | |
| 26,822 | MONTGOMERY | 8,974 | 4,946 | 3,979 | | 49 | 967 R | 55.1% | 44.3% | |
| 74,769 | MOORE | 31,301 | 19,882 | 11,232 | | 187 | 8,650 R | 63.5% | 35.9% | |
| 87,420 | NASH | 30,513 | 17,995 | 12,376 | | 142 | 5,619 R | 59.0% | 40.6% | |
| 160,307 | NEW HANOVER | 66,319 | 36,503 | 29,292 | | 524 | 7,211 R | 55.0% | 44.2% | |
| 22,086 | NORTHAMPTON | 8,200 | 2,667 | 5,513 | | 20 | 2,846 D | 32.5% | 67.2% | |
| 150,355 | ONSLOW | 30,215 | 19,657 | 10,269 | | 289 | 9,388 R | 65.1% | 34.0% | |
| 118,227 | ORANGE | 49,344 | 17,930 | 30,921 | | 493 | 12,991 D | 36.3% | 62.7% | |
| 12,934 | PAMLICO | 5,242 | 2,999 | 2,188 | | 55 | 811 R | 57.2% | 41.7% | |
| 34,897 | PASQUOTANK | 10,903 | 4,943 | 5,874 | | 86 | 931 D | 45.3% | 53.9% | |
| 41,082 | PENDER | 14,154 | 7,661 | 6,415 | | 78 | 1,246 R | 54.1% | 45.3% | |
| 11,368 | PERQUIMANS | 4,306 | 2,230 | 2,033 | | 43 | 197 R | 51.8% | 47.2% | |
| 35,623 | PERSON | 11,833 | 6,722 | 5,042 | | 69 | 1,680 R | 56.8% | 42.6% | |
| 133,798 | PITT | 43,075 | 23,192 | 19,685 | | 198 | 3,507 R | 53.8% | 45.7% | |
| 18,324 | POLK | 8,303 | 5,074 | 3,114 | | 115 | 1,960 R | 61.1% | 37.5% | |
| 130,454 | RANDOLPH | 42,696 | 30,959 | 11,366 | | 371 | 19,593 R | 72.5% | 26.6% | |
| 46,564 | RICHMOND | 14,269 | 6,263 | 7,935 | | 71 | 1,672 D | 43.9% | 55.6% | |
| 123,339 | ROBESON | 29,747 | 11,721 | 17,834 | | 192 | 6,113 D | 39.4% | 60.0% | |
| 91,928 | ROCKINGHAM | 32,528 | 18,979 | 13,260 | | 289 | 5,719 R | 58.3% | 40.8% | |
| 130,340 | ROWAN | 44,133 | 28,922 | 14,891 | | 320 | 14,031 R | 65.5% | 33.7% | |
| 62,899 | RUTHERFORD | 21,716 | 13,755 | 7,697 | | 264 | 6,058 R | 63.3% | 35.4% | |
| 60,161 | SAMPSON | 19,239 | 10,410 | 8,768 | | 61 | 1,642 R | 54.1% | 45.6% | |
| 35,998 | SCOTLAND | 9,403 | 3,740 | 5,627 | | 36 | 1,887 D | 39.8% | 59.8% | |
| 58,100 | STANLY | 22,818 | 15,548 | 7,066 | | 204 | 8,482 R | 68.1% | 31.0% | |
| 44,711 | STOKES | 17,182 | 12,028 | 5,030 | | 124 | 6,998 R | 70.0% | 29.3% | |
| 71,219 | SURRY | 23,358 | 15,401 | 7,757 | | 200 | 7,644 R | 65.9% | 33.2% | |
| 12,968 | SWAIN | 4,370 | 2,224 | 2,097 | | 49 | 127 R | 50.9% | 48.0% | |
| 29,334 | TRANSYLVANIA | 14,225 | 9,011 | 5,044 | | 170 | 3,967 R | 63.3% | 35.5% | |
| 4,149 | TYRRELL | 1,566 | 706 | 849 | | 11 | 143 D | 45.1% | 54.2% | |
| 123,677 | UNION | 47,161 | 31,876 | 14,890 | | 395 | 16,986 R | 67.6% | 31.6% | |
| 42,954 | VANCE | 12,701 | 5,564 | 7,092 | | 45 | 1,528 D | 43.8% | 55.8% | |
| 627,846 | WAKE | 268,220 | 142,494 | 123,466 | | 2,260 | 19,028 R | 53.1% | 46.0% | |
| 19,972 | WARREN | 6,795 | 2,202 | 4,576 | | 17 | 2,374 D | 32.4% | 67.3% | |
| 13,723 | WASHINGTON | 4,890 | 2,169 | 2,704 | | 17 | 535 D | 44.4% | 55.3% | |
| 42,695 | WATAUGA | 18,723 | 10,438 | 7,959 | | 326 | 2,479 R | 55.7% | 42.5% | |
| 113,329 | WAYNE | 33,884 | 20,758 | 13,005 | | 121 | 7,753 R | 61.3% | 38.4% | |
| 65,632 | WILKES | 24,323 | 16,826 | 7,226 | | 271 | 9,600 R | 69.2% | 29.7% | |
| 73,814 | WILSON | 24,826 | 13,466 | 11,266 | | 94 | 2,200 R | 54.2% | 45.4% | |
| 36,348 | YADKIN | 13,682 | 10,435 | 3,127 | | 120 | 7,308 R | 76.3% | 22.9% | |
| 17,774 | YANCEY | 8,764 | 4,970 | 3,714 | | 80 | 1,256 R | 56.7% | 42.4% | |
| 8,049,313 | TOTAL | 2,911,262 | 1,631,163 | 1,257,692 | | 22,407 | 373,471 R | 56.0% | 43.2% | |

Note: No votes were tallied for Nader in North Carolina. He qualified neither for the ballot nor as a write-in candidate.

# NORTH CAROLINA

## PRESIDENT 1996

| 1995 Census Pop. Est. | County | Total Vote | Republican | Democratic | Reform (Perot) | Other | Rep.-Dem. Plurality | Percentage of Total Vote | | |
|---|---|---|---|---|---|---|---|---|---|---|
| | | | | | | | | Rep. | Dem. | Reform |
| 115,062 | ALAMANCE | 41,861 | 22,461 | 15,814 | 3,395 | 191 | 6,647 R | 53.7% | 37.8% | 8.1% |
| 29,892 | ALEXANDER | 11,730 | 6,748 | 3,955 | 1,004 | 23 | 2,793 R | 57.5% | 33.7% | 8.6% |
| 9,893 | ALLEGHANY | 4,235 | 1,936 | 1,801 | 458 | 40 | 135 R | 45.7% | 42.5% | 10.8% |
| 24,177 | ANSON | 7,613 | 2,193 | 4,890 | 512 | 18 | 2,697 D | 28.8% | 64.2% | 6.7% |
| 23,371 | ASHE | 9,942 | 5,203 | 3,825 | 865 | 49 | 1,378 R | 52.3% | 38.5% | 8.7% |
| 15,323 | AVERY | 6,159 | 3,870 | 1,586 | 655 | 48 | 2,284 R | 62.8% | 25.8% | 10.6% |
| 44,123 | BEAUFORT | 15,215 | 8,154 | 6,172 | 834 | 55 | 1,982 R | 53.6% | 40.6% | 5.5% |
| 20,847 | BERTIE | 6,271 | 1,745 | 4,202 | 316 | 8 | 2,457 D | 27.8% | 67.0% | 5.0% |
| 29,963 | BLADEN | 8,960 | 3,335 | 4,952 | 655 | 18 | 1,617 D | 37.2% | 55.3% | 7.3% |
| 60,795 | BRUNSWICK | 22,023 | 10,065 | 10,041 | 1,815 | 102 | 24 R | 45.7% | 45.6% | 8.2% |
| 189,506 | BUNCOMBE | 69,067 | 30,518 | 31,658 | 6,254 | 637 | 1,140 D | 44.2% | 45.8% | 9.1% |
| 79,859 | BURKE | 28,291 | 13,853 | 11,678 | 2,654 | 106 | 2,175 R | 49.0% | 41.3% | 9.4% |
| 110,030 | CABARRUS | 41,310 | 23,035 | 14,447 | 3,626 | 202 | 8,588 R | 55.8% | 35.0% | 8.8% |
| 74,060 | CALDWELL | 22,931 | 12,653 | 8,050 | 2,099 | 129 | 4,603 R | 55.2% | 35.1% | 9.2% |
| 6,453 | CAMDEN | 2,566 | 1,074 | 1,186 | 293 | 13 | 112 D | 41.9% | 46.2% | 11.4% |
| 57,880 | CARTERET | 20,876 | 11,721 | 7,566 | 1,467 | 122 | 4,155 R | 56.1% | 36.2% | 7.0% |
| 21,324 | CASWELL | 8,158 | 3,310 | 4,312 | 510 | 26 | 1,002 D | 40.6% | 52.9% | 6.3% |
| 126,425 | CATAWBA | 46,354 | 26,898 | 15,601 | 3,629 | 226 | 11,297 R | 58.0% | 33.7% | 7.8% |
| 42,536 | CHATHAM | 18,396 | 7,731 | 9,353 | 1,113 | 199 | 1,622 D | 42.0% | 50.8% | 6.1% |
| 21,602 | CHEROKEE | 7,883 | 3,883 | 3,129 | 785 | 86 | 754 R | 49.3% | 39.7% | 10.0% |
| 14,013 | CHOWAN | 4,276 | 1,659 | 2,239 | 359 | 19 | 580 D | 38.8% | 52.4% | 8.4% |
| 7,858 | CLAY | 3,655 | 1,769 | 1,462 | 387 | 37 | 307 R | 48.4% | 40.0% | 10.6% |
| 89,772 | CLEVELAND | 28,241 | 13,474 | 12,728 | 1,931 | 108 | 746 R | 47.7% | 45.1% | 6.8% |
| 51,400 | COLUMBUS | 16,280 | 6,017 | 9,019 | 1,170 | 74 | 3,002 D | 37.0% | 55.4% | 7.2% |
| 85,518 | CRAVEN | 25,191 | 13,264 | 10,317 | 1,528 | 82 | 2,947 R | 52.7% | 41.0% | 6.1% |
| 285,869 | CUMBERLAND | 66,479 | 29,804 | 32,739 | 3,776 | 160 | 2,935 D | 44.8% | 49.2% | 5.7% |
| 16,274 | CURRITUCK | 5,645 | 2,569 | 2,277 | 770 | 29 | 292 R | 45.5% | 40.3% | 13.6% |
| 26,047 | DARE | 10,820 | 4,977 | 4,522 | 1,258 | 63 | 455 R | 46.0% | 41.8% | 11.6% |
| 135,373 | DAVIDSON | 42,207 | 24,797 | 13,593 | 3,698 | 119 | 11,204 R | 58.8% | 32.2% | 8.8% |
| 29,610 | DAVIE | 12,620 | 8,141 | 3,525 | 915 | 39 | 4,616 R | 64.5% | 27.9% | 7.3% |
| 41,987 | DUPLIN | 12,392 | 5,432 | 6,179 | 766 | 15 | 747 D | 43.8% | 49.9% | 6.2% |
| 195,261 | DURHAM | 80,910 | 27,825 | 49,186 | 3,122 | 777 | 21,361 D | 34.4% | 60.8% | 3.9% |
| 56,371 | EDGECOMBE | 17,278 | 6,010 | 10,568 | 660 | 40 | 4,558 D | 34.8% | 61.2% | 3.8% |
| 281,052 | FORSYTH | 112,033 | 59,160 | 46,543 | 5,747 | 583 | 12,617 R | 52.8% | 41.5% | 5.1% |
| 41,395 | FRANKLIN | 13,026 | 5,648 | 6,448 | 891 | 39 | 800 D | 43.4% | 49.5% | 6.8% |
| 181,466 | GASTON | 56,739 | 33,149 | 19,458 | 3,921 | 211 | 13,691 R | 58.4% | 34.3% | 6.9% |
| 9,854 | GATES | 3,542 | 1,072 | 2,155 | 307 | 8 | 1,083 D | 30.3% | 60.8% | 8.7% |
| 7,622 | GRAHAM | 3,289 | 1,801 | 1,210 | 270 | 8 | 591 R | 54.8% | 36.8% | 8.2% |
| 40,911 | GRANVILLE | 12,800 | 5,498 | 6,747 | 432 | 123 | 1,249 D | 43.0% | 52.7% | 3.4% |
| 16,942 | GREENE | 5,198 | 2,689 | 2,224 | 280 | 5 | 465 R | 51.7% | 42.8% | 5.4% |
| 374,438 | GUILFORD | 147,587 | 67,727 | 69,208 | 9,739 | 913 | 1,481 D | 45.9% | 46.9% | 6.6% |
| 57,497 | HALIFAX | 16,103 | 5,700 | 9,551 | 816 | 36 | 3,851 D | 35.4% | 59.3% | 5.1% |
| 76,310 | HARNETT | 21,739 | 11,596 | 8,767 | 1,287 | 89 | 2,829 R | 53.3% | 40.3% | 5.9% |
| 49,737 | HAYWOOD | 20,069 | 7,995 | 9,350 | 2,594 | 130 | 1,355 D | 39.8% | 46.6% | 12.9% |
| 76,704 | HENDERSON | 32,676 | 19,182 | 10,626 | 2,679 | 189 | 8,556 R | 58.7% | 32.5% | 8.2% |
| 22,587 | HERTFORD | 7,049 | 1,823 | 4,856 | 356 | 14 | 3,033 D | 25.9% | 68.9% | 5.1% |
| 27,627 | HOKE | 5,929 | 1,914 | 3,510 | 481 | 24 | 1,596 D | 32.3% | 59.2% | 8.1% |
| 5,366 | HYDE | 2,042 | 782 | 1,109 | 143 | 8 | 327 D | 38.3% | 54.3% | 7.0% |
| 103,412 | IREDELL | 37,409 | 21,163 | 13,102 | 2,970 | 174 | 8,061 R | 56.6% | 35.0% | 7.9% |
| 29,029 | JACKSON | 10,506 | 4,244 | 5,211 | 970 | 81 | 967 D | 40.4% | 49.6% | 9.2% |
| 94,777 | JOHNSTON | 32,119 | 18,704 | 11,175 | 2,163 | 77 | 7,529 R | 58.2% | 34.8% | 6.7% |
| 9,797 | JONES | 3,715 | 1,682 | 1,829 | 197 | 7 | 147 D | 45.3% | 49.2% | 5.3% |
| 45,945 | LEE | 14,630 | 7,321 | 6,290 | 980 | 39 | 1,031 R | 50.0% | 43.0% | 6.7% |
| 59,257 | LENOIR | 18,925 | 9,433 | 8,635 | 822 | 35 | 798 R | 49.8% | 45.6% | 4.3% |
| 56,017 | LINCOLN | 20,850 | 11,439 | 7,721 | 1,619 | 71 | 3,718 R | 54.9% | 37.0% | 7.8% |
| 37,471 | MCDOWELL | 12,278 | 6,407 | 4,553 | 1,275 | 43 | 1,854 R | 52.2% | 37.1% | 10.4% |
| 26,180 | MACON | 10,675 | 5,267 | 4,209 | 1,121 | 78 | 1,058 R | 49.3% | 39.4% | 10.5% |
| 17,942 | MADISON | 7,030 | 3,110 | 3,333 | 538 | 49 | 223 D | 44.2% | 47.4% | 7.7% |
| 26,396 | MARTIN | 8,552 | 3,590 | 4,500 | 445 | 17 | 910 D | 42.0% | 52.6% | 5.2% |
| 579,473 | MECKLENBURG | 212,845 | 97,719 | 103,429 | 10,473 | 1,224 | 5,710 D | 45.9% | 48.6% | 4.9% |

# NORTH CAROLINA

## PRESIDENT 1996

| 1995 Census Pop. Est. | County | Total Vote | Republican | Democratic | Reform (Perot) | Other | Rep.-Dem. Plurality | Percentage of Total Vote | | |
|---|---|---|---|---|---|---|---|---|---|---|
| | | | | | | | | Rep. | Dem. | Reform |
| 14,699 | MITCHELL | 5,946 | 3,874 | 1,496 | 549 | 27 | 2,378 R | 65.2% | 25.2% | 9.2% |
| 23,487 | MONTGOMERY | 7,838 | 3,379 | 3,856 | 587 | 16 | 477 D | 43.1% | 49.2% | 7.5% |
| 67,174 | MOORE | 26,479 | 14,760 | 9,847 | 1,761 | 111 | 4,913 R | 55.7% | 37.2% | 6.7% |
| 85,561 | NASH | 28,262 | 15,309 | 11,142 | 1,751 | 60 | 4,167 R | 54.2% | 39.4% | 6.2% |
| 139,815 | NEW HANOVER | 54,769 | 27,889 | 22,839 | 3,615 | 426 | 5,050 R | 50.9% | 41.7% | 6.6% |
| 20,905 | NORTHAMPTON | 7,499 | 1,881 | 5,207 | 402 | 9 | 3,326 D | 25.1% | 69.4% | 5.4% |
| 143,324 | ONSLOW | 24,049 | 13,396 | 8,685 | 1,857 | 111 | 4,711 R | 55.7% | 36.1% | 7.7% |
| 107,648 | ORANGE | 46,765 | 15,053 | 28,674 | 1,534 | 1,504 | 13,621 D | 32.2% | 61.3% | 3.3% |
| 12,066 | PAMLICO | 4,790 | 2,270 | 2,204 | 297 | 19 | 66 R | 47.4% | 46.0% | 6.2% |
| 33,866 | PASQUOTANK | 7,822 | 2,999 | 4,233 | 565 | 25 | 1,234 D | 38.3% | 54.1% | 7.2% |
| 35,080 | PENDER | 11,940 | 5,538 | 5,409 | 945 | 48 | 129 R | 46.4% | 45.3% | 7.9% |
| 10,798 | PERQUIMANS | 4,015 | 1,561 | 2,069 | 369 | 16 | 508 D | 38.9% | 51.5% | 9.2% |
| 32,376 | PERSON | 10,030 | 4,883 | 4,540 | 591 | 16 | 343 R | 48.7% | 45.3% | 5.9% |
| 117,740 | PITT | 38,011 | 18,227 | 17,555 | 2,037 | 192 | 672 R | 48.0% | 46.2% | 5.4% |
| 15,800 | POLK | 6,756 | 3,516 | 2,704 | 493 | 43 | 812 R | 52.0% | 40.0% | 7.3% |
| 114,624 | RANDOLPH | 37,535 | 23,030 | 10,783 | 3,593 | 129 | 12,247 R | 61.4% | 28.7% | 9.6% |
| 45,660 | RICHMOND | 12,801 | 3,973 | 7,564 | 1,230 | 34 | 3,591 D | 31.0% | 59.1% | 9.6% |
| 112,038 | ROBESON | 27,671 | 8,146 | 17,361 | 2,105 | 59 | 9,215 D | 29.4% | 62.7% | 7.6% |
| 88,414 | ROCKINGHAM | 28,959 | 14,255 | 12,096 | 2,528 | 80 | 2,159 R | 49.2% | 41.8% | 8.7% |
| 119,211 | ROWAN | 39,273 | 22,754 | 13,461 | 2,902 | 156 | 9,293 R | 57.9% | 34.3% | 7.4% |
| 59,210 | RUTHERFORD | 18,571 | 9,792 | 7,162 | 1,585 | 32 | 2,630 R | 52.7% | 38.6% | 8.5% |
| 50,485 | SAMPSON | 17,232 | 8,241 | 8,150 | 825 | 16 | 91 R | 47.8% | 47.3% | 4.8% |
| 35,304 | SCOTLAND | 8,299 | 2,858 | 4,870 | 548 | 23 | 2,012 D | 34.4% | 58.7% | 6.6% |
| 54,172 | STANLY | 20,333 | 11,446 | 7,131 | 1,690 | 66 | 4,315 R | 56.3% | 35.1% | 8.3% |
| 40,723 | STOKES | 15,320 | 9,471 | 4,769 | 1,025 | 55 | 4,702 R | 61.8% | 31.1% | 6.7% |
| 65,159 | SURRY | 20,021 | 11,117 | 7,303 | 1,538 | 63 | 3,814 R | 55.5% | 36.5% | 7.7% |
| 11,815 | SWAIN | 3,722 | 1,444 | 1,869 | 401 | 8 | 425 D | 38.8% | 50.2% | 10.8% |
| 27,339 | TRANSYLVANIA | 12,877 | 6,734 | 4,842 | 1,183 | 118 | 1,892 R | 52.3% | 37.6% | 9.2% |
| 3,894 | TYRRELL | 1,513 | 488 | 908 | 112 | 5 | 420 D | 32.3% | 60.0% | 7.4% |
| 99,155 | UNION | 32,970 | 18,802 | 11,525 | 2,477 | 166 | 7,277 R | 57.0% | 35.0% | 7.5% |
| 40,720 | VANCE | 11,635 | 4,651 | 6,385 | 575 | 24 | 1,734 D | 40.0% | 54.9% | 4.9% |
| 513,639 | WAKE | 225,755 | 108,780 | 103,574 | 11,811 | 1,590 | 5,206 R | 48.2% | 45.9% | 5.2% |
| 17,984 | WARREN | 6,339 | 1,861 | 4,141 | 319 | 18 | 2,280 D | 29.4% | 65.3% | 5.0% |
| 14,119 | WASHINGTON | 4,532 | 1,562 | 2,790 | 171 | 9 | 1,228 D | 34.5% | 61.6% | 3.8% |
| 39,799 | WATAUGA | 17,222 | 8,146 | 7,349 | 1,415 | 312 | 797 R | 47.3% | 42.7% | 8.2% |
| 110,174 | WAYNE | 29,390 | 16,588 | 11,580 | 1,178 | 44 | 5,008 R | 56.4% | 39.4% | 4.0% |
| 60,922 | WILKES | 21,228 | 12,395 | 6,793 | 1,967 | 73 | 5,602 R | 58.4% | 32.0% | 9.3% |
| 67,362 | WILSON | 21,451 | 10,518 | 9,779 | 1,100 | 54 | 739 R | 49.0% | 45.6% | 5.1% |
| 32,958 | YADKIN | 12,313 | 8,439 | 2,927 | 913 | 34 | 5,512 R | 68.5% | 23.8% | 7.4% |
| 16,241 | YANCEY | 8,684 | 3,973 | 3,956 | 720 | 35 | 17 R | 45.8% | 45.6% | 8.3% |
| 7,195,138 | TOTAL | 2,515,807 | 1,225,938 | 1,107,849 | 168,059 | 13,961 | 118,089 R | 48.7% | 44.0% | 6.7% |

# NORTH CAROLINA

## PRESIDENT 1992

| 1990 Census Population | County | Total Vote | Republican | Democratic | Perot | Other | Plurality | Percentage Total Vote Rep. | Dem. | Perot |
|---|---|---|---|---|---|---|---|---|---|---|
| 108,213 | ALAMANCE | 42,701 | 20,637 | 15,521 | 6,444 | 99 | 5,116 R | 48.3% | 36.3% | 15.1% |
| 27,544 | ALEXANDER | 13,626 | 6,764 | 4,849 | 2,002 | 11 | 1,915 R | 49.6% | 35.6% | 14.7% |
| 9,590 | ALLEGHANY | 4,730 | 1,853 | 2,271 | 600 | 6 | 418 D | 39.2% | 48.0% | 12.7% |
| 23,474 | ANSON | 8,539 | 2,334 | 5,269 | 921 | 15 | 2,935 D | 27.3% | 61.7% | 10.8% |
| 22,209 | ASHE | 11,070 | 5,200 | 4,624 | 1,220 | 26 | 576 R | 47.0% | 41.8% | 11.0% |
| 14,867 | AVERY | 6,787 | 3,895 | 1,755 | 1,123 | 14 | 2,140 R | 57.4% | 25.9% | 16.5% |
| 42,283 | BEAUFORT | 15,980 | 7,337 | 6,445 | 2,174 | 24 | 892 R | 45.9% | 40.3% | 13.6% |
| 20,388 | BERTIE | 6,743 | 1,756 | 4,382 | 600 | 5 | 2,626 D | 26.0% | 65.0% | 8.9% |
| 28,663 | BLADEN | 10,177 | 3,214 | 5,700 | 1,248 | 15 | 2,486 D | 31.6% | 56.0% | 12.3% |
| 50,985 | BRUNSWICK | 22,400 | 8,833 | 10,177 | 3,349 | 41 | 1,344 D | 39.4% | 45.4% | 15.0% |
| 174,821 | BUNCOMBE | 75,492 | 30,892 | 32,955 | 11,481 | 164 | 2,063 D | 40.9% | 43.7% | 15.2% |
| 75,744 | BURKE | 30,122 | 13,397 | 12,565 | 4,124 | 36 | 832 R | 44.5% | 41.7% | 13.7% |
| 98,935 | CABARRUS | 41,123 | 21,281 | 13,513 | 6,251 | 78 | 7,768 R | 51.7% | 32.9% | 15.2% |
| 70,709 | CALDWELL | 25,576 | 12,543 | 9,033 | 3,965 | 35 | 3,510 R | 49.0% | 35.3% | 15.5% |
| 5,904 | CAMDEN | 2,675 | 1,039 | 1,153 | 479 | 4 | 114 D | 38.8% | 43.1% | 17.9% |
| 52,556 | CARTERET | 21,819 | 10,334 | 8,028 | 3,401 | 56 | 2,306 R | 47.4% | 36.8% | 15.6% |
| 20,693 | CASWELL | 8,363 | 2,793 | 4,725 | 827 | 18 | 1,932 D | 33.4% | 56.5% | 9.9% |
| 118,412 | CATAWBA | 49,409 | 25,466 | 16,334 | 7,523 | 86 | 9,132 R | 51.5% | 33.1% | 15.2% |
| 38,759 | CHATHAM | 18,577 | 6,568 | 9,520 | 2,425 | 64 | 2,952 D | 35.4% | 51.2% | 13.1% |
| 20,170 | CHEROKEE | 8,758 | 4,021 | 3,686 | 1,040 | 11 | 335 R | 45.9% | 42.1% | 11.9% |
| 13,506 | CHOWAN | 4,506 | 1,661 | 2,136 | 700 | 9 | 475 D | 36.9% | 47.4% | 15.5% |
| 7,155 | CLAY | 3,960 | 1,890 | 1,600 | 465 | 5 | 290 R | 47.7% | 40.4% | 11.7% |
| 84,714 | CLEVELAND | 30,522 | 13,650 | 13,037 | 3,784 | 51 | 613 R | 44.7% | 42.7% | 12.4% |
| 49,587 | COLUMBUS | 18,916 | 5,462 | 11,469 | 1,963 | 22 | 6,007 D | 28.9% | 60.6% | 10.4% |
| 81,613 | CRAVEN | 25,287 | 11,575 | 9,998 | 3,679 | 35 | 1,577 R | 45.8% | 39.5% | 14.5% |
| 274,566 | CUMBERLAND | 64,470 | 27,139 | 30,291 | 6,792 | 248 | 3,152 D | 42.1% | 47.0% | 10.5% |
| 13,736 | CURRITUCK | 5,297 | 2,188 | 1,935 | 1,163 | 11 | 253 R | 41.3% | 36.5% | 22.0% |
| 22,746 | DARE | 10,696 | 4,357 | 3,925 | 2,388 | 26 | 432 R | 40.7% | 36.7% | 22.3% |
| 126,677 | DAVIDSON | 49,725 | 24,869 | 16,462 | 8,324 | 70 | 8,407 R | 50.0% | 33.1% | 16.7% |
| 27,859 | DAVIE | 12,387 | 6,796 | 3,675 | 1,903 | 13 | 3,121 R | 54.9% | 29.7% | 15.4% |
| 39,995 | DUPLIN | 13,747 | 5,286 | 6,816 | 1,636 | 9 | 1,530 D | 38.5% | 49.6% | 11.9% |
| 181,835 | DURHAM | 82,682 | 27,581 | 47,331 | 7,504 | 266 | 19,750 D | 33.4% | 57.2% | 9.1% |
| 56,558 | EDGECOMBE | 19,657 | 6,275 | 11,174 | 2,175 | 33 | 4,899 D | 31.9% | 56.8% | 11.1% |
| 265,878 | FORSYTH | 116,274 | 52,787 | 49,006 | 14,262 | 219 | 3,781 R | 45.4% | 42.1% | 12.3% |
| 36,414 | FRANKLIN | 13,266 | 4,669 | 6,517 | 2,062 | 18 | 1,848 D | 35.2% | 49.1% | 15.5% |
| 175,093 | GASTON | 61,435 | 34,714 | 19,121 | 7,490 | 110 | 15,593 R | 56.5% | 31.1% | 12.2% |
| 9,305 | GATES | 3,834 | 1,158 | 2,206 | 466 | 4 | 1,048 D | 30.2% | 57.5% | 12.2% |
| 7,196 | GRAHAM | 3,876 | 1,919 | 1,551 | 403 | 3 | 368 R | 49.5% | 40.0% | 10.4% |
| 38,345 | GRANVILLE | 12,128 | 4,538 | 6,178 | 1,321 | 91 | 1,640 D | 37.4% | 50.9% | 10.9% |
| 15,384 | GREENE | 5,732 | 2,180 | 2,768 | 780 | 4 | 588 D | 38.0% | 48.3% | 13.6% |
| 347,420 | GUILFORD | 146,399 | 60,140 | 66,319 | 19,601 | 339 | 6,179 D | 41.1% | 45.3% | 13.4% |
| 55,516 | HALIFAX | 17,804 | 5,769 | 9,960 | 2,047 | 28 | 4,191 D | 32.4% | 55.9% | 11.5% |
| 67,822 | HARNETT | 20,932 | 9,751 | 8,473 | 2,684 | 24 | 1,278 R | 46.6% | 40.5% | 12.8% |
| 46,942 | HAYWOOD | 21,009 | 7,292 | 10,385 | 3,303 | 29 | 3,093 D | 34.7% | 49.4% | 15.7% |
| 69,285 | HENDERSON | 33,072 | 17,010 | 10,747 | 5,260 | 55 | 6,263 R | 51.4% | 32.5% | 15.9% |
| 22,523 | HERTFORD | 7,672 | 2,208 | 4,609 | 846 | 9 | 2,401 D | 28.8% | 60.1% | 11.0% |
| 22,856 | HOKE | 6,337 | 1,711 | 3,730 | 887 | 9 | 2,019 D | 27.0% | 58.9% | 14.0% |
| 5,411 | HYDE | 2,288 | 740 | 1,206 | 340 | 2 | 466 D | 32.3% | 52.7% | 14.9% |
| 92,931 | IREDELL | 38,980 | 19,411 | 13,263 | 6,204 | 102 | 6,148 R | 49.8% | 34.0% | 15.9% |
| 26,846 | JACKSON | 11,558 | 4,275 | 5,753 | 1,516 | 14 | 1,478 D | 37.0% | 49.8% | 13.1% |
| 81,306 | JOHNSTON | 31,679 | 15,418 | 11,284 | 4,939 | 38 | 4,134 R | 48.7% | 35.6% | 15.6% |
| 9,414 | JONES | 3,846 | 1,438 | 1,962 | 444 | 2 | 524 D | 37.4% | 51.0% | 11.5% |
| 41,374 | LEE | 14,659 | 6,658 | 5,852 | 2,125 | 24 | 806 R | 45.4% | 39.9% | 14.5% |
| 57,274 | LENOIR | 19,842 | 8,932 | 8,793 | 2,107 | 10 | 139 R | 45.0% | 44.3% | 10.6% |
| 50,319 | LINCOLN | 22,355 | 11,018 | 8,150 | 3,142 | 45 | 2,868 R | 49.3% | 36.5% | 14.1% |
| 35,681 | MCDOWELL | 13,295 | 6,090 | 5,309 | 1,881 | 15 | 781 R | 45.8% | 39.9% | 14.1% |
| 23,499 | MACON | 11,279 | 4,797 | 4,624 | 1,829 | 29 | 173 R | 42.5% | 41.0% | 16.2% |
| 16,953 | MADISON | 7,989 | 3,121 | 3,980 | 857 | 31 | 859 D | 39.1% | 49.8% | 10.7% |
| 25,078 | MARTIN | 8,016 | 2,958 | 4,069 | 981 | 8 | 1,111 D | 36.9% | 50.8% | 12.2% |
| 511,433 | MECKLENBURG | 228,375 | 99,496 | 97,065 | 31,283 | 531 | 2,431 R | 43.6% | 42.5% | 13.7% |

# NORTH CAROLINA

## PRESIDENT 1992

| 1990 Census Population | County | Total Vote | Republican | Democratic | Perot | Other | Plurality | Percentage Total Vote Rep. | Dem. | Perot |
|---|---|---|---|---|---|---|---|---|---|---|
| 14,433 | MITCHELL | 7,015 | 4,405 | 1,727 | 877 | 6 | 2,678 R | 62.8% | 24.6% | 12.5% |
| 23,346 | MONTGOMERY | 9,161 | 3,543 | 4,422 | 1,185 | 11 | 879 D | 38.7% | 48.3% | 12.9% |
| 59,013 | MOORE | 26,591 | 12,448 | 9,649 | 4,448 | 46 | 2,799 R | 46.8% | 36.3% | 16.7% |
| 76,677 | NASH | 29,886 | 14,446 | 10,809 | 4,544 | 87 | 3,637 R | 48.3% | 36.2% | 15.2% |
| 120,284 | NEW HANOVER | 52,154 | 24,338 | 20,291 | 7,401 | 124 | 4,047 R | 46.7% | 38.9% | 14.2% |
| 20,798 | NORTHAMPTON | 7,967 | 1,845 | 5,195 | 916 | 11 | 3,350 D | 23.2% | 65.2% | 11.5% |
| 149,838 | ONSLOW | 24,318 | 11,842 | 8,045 | 4,387 | 44 | 3,797 R | 48.7% | 33.1% | 18.0% |
| 93,851 | ORANGE | 47,300 | 13,009 | 28,595 | 5,535 | 161 | 15,586 D | 27.5% | 60.5% | 11.7% |
| 11,372 | PAMLICO | 4,975 | 1,929 | 2,229 | 809 | 8 | 300 D | 38.8% | 44.8% | 16.3% |
| 31,298 | PASQUOTANK | 9,581 | 3,419 | 4,709 | 1,434 | 19 | 1,290 D | 35.7% | 49.1% | 15.0% |
| 28,855 | PENDER | 12,430 | 4,857 | 5,825 | 1,725 | 23 | 968 D | 39.1% | 46.9% | 13.9% |
| 10,447 | PERQUIMANS | 3,878 | 1,429 | 1,818 | 624 | 7 | 389 D | 36.8% | 46.9% | 16.1% |
| 30,180 | PERSON | 10,230 | 4,460 | 4,323 | 1,431 | 16 | 137 R | 43.6% | 42.3% | 14.0% |
| 107,924 | PITT | 39,895 | 16,609 | 17,959 | 5,262 | 65 | 1,350 D | 41.6% | 45.0% | 13.2% |
| 14,416 | POLK | 7,533 | 3,448 | 2,939 | 1,134 | 12 | 509 R | 45.8% | 39.0% | 15.1% |
| 106,546 | RANDOLPH | 38,902 | 20,697 | 11,274 | 6,870 | 61 | 9,423 R | 53.2% | 29.0% | 17.7% |
| 44,518 | RICHMOND | 15,553 | 4,356 | 9,163 | 2,015 | 19 | 4,807 D | 28.0% | 58.9% | 13.0% |
| 105,179 | ROBESON | 30,474 | 7,777 | 19,378 | 3,277 | 42 | 11,601 D | 25.5% | 63.6% | 10.8% |
| 86,064 | ROCKINGHAM | 31,269 | 12,678 | 13,880 | 4,671 | 40 | 1,202 D | 40.5% | 44.4% | 14.9% |
| 110,605 | ROWAN | 42,732 | 21,297 | 14,308 | 7,053 | 74 | 6,989 R | 49.8% | 33.5% | 16.5% |
| 56,918 | RUTHERFORD | 20,329 | 9,748 | 7,855 | 2,695 | 31 | 1,893 R | 48.0% | 38.6% | 13.3% |
| 47,297 | SAMPSON | 18,568 | 8,007 | 8,698 | 1,852 | 11 | 691 D | 43.1% | 46.8% | 10.0% |
| 33,754 | SCOTLAND | 9,360 | 2,980 | 5,175 | 1,196 | 9 | 2,195 D | 31.8% | 55.3% | 12.8% |
| 51,765 | STANLY | 21,664 | 11,030 | 7,735 | 2,855 | 44 | 3,295 R | 50.9% | 35.7% | 13.2% |
| 37,223 | STOKES | 16,657 | 7,979 | 6,463 | 2,183 | 32 | 1,516 R | 47.9% | 38.8% | 13.1% |
| 61,704 | SURRY | 23,453 | 10,866 | 9,392 | 3,164 | 31 | 1,474 R | 46.3% | 40.0% | 13.5% |
| 11,268 | SWAIN | 4,330 | 1,640 | 2,117 | 568 | 5 | 477 D | 37.9% | 48.9% | 13.1% |
| 25,520 | TRANSYLVANIA | 13,137 | 5,984 | 5,120 | 2,006 | 27 | 864 R | 45.6% | 39.0% | 15.3% |
| 3,856 | TYRRELL | 1,674 | 553 | 928 | 189 | 4 | 375 D | 33.0% | 55.4% | 11.3% |
| 84,211 | UNION | 31,992 | 16,542 | 10,789 | 4,601 | 60 | 5,753 R | 51.7% | 33.7% | 14.4% |
| 38,892 | VANCE | 12,800 | 4,747 | 6,598 | 1,444 | 11 | 1,851 D | 37.1% | 51.5% | 11.3% |
| 423,380 | WAKE | 207,467 | 86,798 | 88,979 | 31,140 | 550 | 2,181 D | 41.8% | 42.9% | 15.0% |
| 17,265 | WARREN | 7,125 | 1,767 | 4,656 | 693 | 9 | 2,889 D | 24.8% | 65.3% | 9.7% |
| 13,997 | WASHINGTON | 5,253 | 1,780 | 2,902 | 563 | 8 | 1,122 D | 33.9% | 55.2% | 10.7% |
| 36,952 | WATAUGA | 19,225 | 7,899 | 8,262 | 3,007 | 57 | 363 D | 41.1% | 43.0% | 15.6% |
| 104,666 | WAYNE | 27,532 | 14,397 | 10,307 | 2,798 | 30 | 4,090 R | 52.3% | 37.4% | 10.2% |
| 59,393 | WILKES | 23,868 | 12,547 | 7,991 | 3,307 | 23 | 4,556 R | 52.6% | 33.5% | 13.9% |
| 66,061 | WILSON | 22,937 | 10,176 | 10,105 | 2,630 | 26 | 71 R | 44.4% | 44.1% | 11.5% |
| 30,488 | YADKIN | 12,977 | 7,311 | 3,913 | 1,725 | 28 | 3,398 R | 56.3% | 30.2% | 13.3% |
| 15,419 | YANCEY | 9,208 | 3,994 | 4,285 | 917 | 12 | 291 D | 43.4% | 46.5% | 10.0% |
| 6,628,637 | TOTAL | 2,611,850 | 1,134,661 | 1,114,042 | 357,864 | 5,283 | 20,619 R | 43.4% | 42.7% | 13.7% |

# NORTH CAROLINA

## PRESIDENT 1988

| 1980 Census Population | County | Total Vote | Republican | Democratic | Other | Rep.-Dem. Plurality | Percentage Total Vote Rep. | Dem. | Major Vote Rep. | Dem. |
|---|---|---|---|---|---|---|---|---|---|---|
| 99,319 | ALAMANCE | 36,851 | 24,131 | 12,642 | 78 | 11,489 R | 65.5% | 34.3% | 65.6% | 34.4% |
| 24,999 | ALEXANDER | 12,154 | 7,968 | 4,148 | 38 | 3,820 R | 65.6% | 34.1% | 65.8% | 34.2% |
| 9,587 | ALLEGHANY | 4,264 | 2,174 | 2,087 | 3 | 87 R | 51.0% | 48.9% | 51.0% | 49.0% |
| 25,649 | ANSON | 7,633 | 2,782 | 4,831 | 20 | 2,049 D | 36.4% | 63.3% | 36.5% | 63.5% |
| 22,325 | ASHE | 10,083 | 6,019 | 4,034 | 30 | 1,985 R | 59.7% | 40.0% | 59.9% | 40.1% |
| 14,409 | AVERY | 5,678 | 4,277 | 1,367 | 34 | 2,910 R | 75.3% | 24.1% | 75.8% | 24.2% |
| 40,355 | BEAUFORT | 13,570 | 8,190 | 5,352 | 28 | 2,838 R | 60.4% | 39.4% | 60.5% | 39.5% |
| 21,024 | BERTIE | 5,919 | 2,145 | 3,762 | 12 | 1,617 D | 36.2% | 63.6% | 36.3% | 63.7% |
| 30,491 | BLADEN | 8,814 | 3,770 | 5,031 | 13 | 1,261 D | 42.8% | 57.1% | 42.8% | 57.2% |
| 35,777 | BRUNSWICK | 17,939 | 10,007 | 7,881 | 51 | 2,126 R | 55.8% | 43.9% | 55.9% | 44.1% |
| 160,934 | BUNCOMBE | 63,992 | 36,828 | 26,964 | 200 | 9,864 R | 57.6% | 42.1% | 57.7% | 42.3% |
| 72,504 | BURKE | 26,819 | 15,933 | 10,848 | 38 | 5,085 R | 59.4% | 40.4% | 59.5% | 40.5% |
| 85,895 | CABARRUS | 33,284 | 22,524 | 10,686 | 74 | 11,838 R | 67.7% | 32.1% | 67.8% | 32.2% |
| 67,746 | CALDWELL | 23,071 | 15,176 | 7,862 | 33 | 7,314 R | 65.8% | 34.1% | 65.9% | 34.1% |
| 5,829 | CAMDEN | 2,249 | 1,144 | 1,081 | 24 | 63 R | 50.9% | 48.1% | 51.4% | 48.6% |
| 41,092 | CARTERET | 17,994 | 11,076 | 6,859 | 59 | 4,217 R | 61.6% | 38.1% | 61.8% | 38.2% |
| 20,705 | CASWELL | 7,509 | 3,299 | 4,189 | 21 | 890 D | 43.9% | 55.8% | 44.1% | 55.9% |
| 105,208 | CATAWBA | 41,838 | 28,872 | 12,922 | 44 | 15,950 R | 69.0% | 30.9% | 69.1% | 30.9% |
| 33,415 | CHATHAM | 14,639 | 6,999 | 7,600 | 40 | 601 D | 47.8% | 51.9% | 47.9% | 52.1% |
| 18,933 | CHEROKEE | 7,145 | 4,557 | 2,567 | 21 | 1,990 R | 63.8% | 35.9% | 64.0% | 36.0% |
| 12,558 | CHOWAN | 3,654 | 1,884 | 1,756 | 14 | 128 R | 51.6% | 48.1% | 51.8% | 48.2% |
| 6,619 | CLAY | 3,480 | 2,174 | 1,289 | 17 | 885 R | 62.5% | 37.0% | 62.8% | 37.2% |
| 83,435 | CLEVELAND | 24,397 | 14,039 | 10,321 | 37 | 3,718 R | 57.5% | 42.3% | 57.6% | 42.4% |
| 51,037 | COLUMBUS | 15,882 | 6,659 | 9,172 | 51 | 2,513 D | 41.9% | 57.8% | 42.1% | 57.9% |
| 71,043 | CRAVEN | 19,417 | 12,057 | 7,313 | 47 | 4,744 R | 62.1% | 37.7% | 62.2% | 37.8% |
| 247,160 | CUMBERLAND | 50,979 | 27,057 | 23,789 | 133 | 3,268 R | 53.1% | 46.7% | 53.2% | 46.8% |
| 11,089 | CURRITUCK | 4,006 | 2,443 | 1,555 | 8 | 888 R | 61.0% | 38.8% | 61.1% | 38.9% |
| 13,377 | DARE | 8,071 | 5,234 | 2,806 | 31 | 2,428 R | 64.8% | 34.8% | 65.1% | 34.9% |
| 113,162 | DAVIDSON | 41,662 | 28,374 | 13,215 | 73 | 15,159 R | 68.1% | 31.7% | 68.2% | 31.8% |
| 24,599 | DAVIE | 11,192 | 7,988 | 3,166 | 38 | 4,822 R | 71.4% | 28.3% | 71.6% | 28.4% |
| 40,952 | DUPLIN | 11,726 | 5,774 | 5,945 | 7 | 171 D | 49.2% | 50.7% | 49.3% | 50.7% |
| 152,785 | DURHAM | 65,883 | 29,928 | 35,441 | 514 | 5,513 D | 45.4% | 53.8% | 45.8% | 54.2% |
| 55,988 | EDGECOMBE | 15,916 | 6,831 | 9,044 | 41 | 2,213 D | 42.9% | 56.8% | 43.0% | 57.0% |
| 243,683 | FORSYTH | 97,735 | 57,688 | 39,726 | 321 | 17,962 R | 59.0% | 40.6% | 59.2% | 40.8% |
| 30,055 | FRANKLIN | 10,960 | 5,499 | 5,438 | 23 | 61 R | 50.2% | 49.6% | 50.3% | 49.7% |
| 162,568 | GASTON | 49,451 | 34,775 | 14,582 | 94 | 20,193 R | 70.3% | 29.5% | 70.5% | 29.5% |
| 8,875 | GATES | 3,485 | 1,451 | 2,024 | 10 | 573 D | 41.6% | 58.1% | 41.8% | 58.2% |
| 7,217 | GRAHAM | 3,419 | 2,091 | 1,313 | 15 | 778 R | 61.2% | 38.4% | 61.4% | 38.6% |
| 34,043 | GRANVILLE | 10,439 | 4,880 | 5,280 | 279 | 400 D | 46.7% | 50.6% | 48.0% | 52.0% |
| 16,117 | GREENE | 5,238 | 2,498 | 2,729 | 11 | 231 D | 47.7% | 52.1% | 47.8% | 52.2% |
| 317,154 | GUILFORD | 117,232 | 66,060 | 50,351 | 821 | 15,709 R | 56.3% | 42.9% | 56.7% | 43.3% |
| 55,286 | HALIFAX | 16,211 | 7,462 | 8,726 | 23 | 1,264 D | 46.0% | 53.8% | 46.1% | 53.9% |
| 59,570 | HARNETT | 17,029 | 9,749 | 7,259 | 21 | 2,490 R | 57.2% | 42.6% | 57.3% | 42.7% |
| 46,495 | HAYWOOD | 18,028 | 8,957 | 9,010 | 61 | 53 D | 49.7% | 50.0% | 49.9% | 50.1% |
| 58,580 | HENDERSON | 29,125 | 19,711 | 9,338 | 76 | 10,373 R | 67.7% | 32.1% | 67.9% | 32.1% |
| 23,368 | HERTFORD | 7,930 | 2,977 | 4,943 | 10 | 1,966 D | 37.5% | 62.3% | 37.6% | 62.4% |
| 20,383 | HOKE | 5,333 | 2,020 | 3,281 | 32 | 1,261 D | 37.9% | 61.5% | 38.1% | 61.9% |
| 5,873 | HYDE | 2,264 | 940 | 1,316 | 8 | 376 D | 41.5% | 58.1% | 41.7% | 58.3% |
| 82,538 | IREDELL | 32,135 | 21,536 | 10,530 | 69 | 11,006 R | 67.0% | 32.8% | 67.2% | 32.8% |
| 25,811 | JACKSON | 10,123 | 5,166 | 4,933 | 24 | 233 R | 51.0% | 48.7% | 51.2% | 48.8% |
| 70,599 | JOHNSTON | 24,329 | 15,563 | 8,717 | 49 | 6,846 R | 64.0% | 35.8% | 64.1% | 35.9% |
| 9,705 | JONES | 3,602 | 1,649 | 1,946 | 7 | 297 D | 45.8% | 54.0% | 45.9% | 54.1% |
| 36,718 | LEE | 11,371 | 7,104 | 4,231 | 36 | 2,873 R | 62.5% | 37.2% | 62.7% | 37.3% |
| 59,819 | LENOIR | 18,353 | 10,669 | 7,649 | 35 | 3,020 R | 58.1% | 41.7% | 58.2% | 41.8% |
| 42,372 | LINCOLN | 18,130 | 11,651 | 6,444 | 35 | 5,207 R | 64.3% | 35.5% | 64.4% | 35.6% |
| 35,135 | MCDOWELL | 10,997 | 6,526 | 4,449 | 22 | 2,077 R | 59.3% | 40.5% | 59.5% | 40.5% |
| 20,178 | MACON | 9,816 | 6,026 | 3,773 | 17 | 2,253 R | 61.4% | 38.4% | 61.5% | 38.5% |
| 16,827 | MADISON | 6,506 | 3,453 | 3,033 | 20 | 420 R | 53.1% | 46.6% | 53.2% | 46.8% |
| 25,948 | MARTIN | 6,756 | 3,149 | 3,598 | 9 | 449 D | 46.6% | 53.3% | 46.7% | 53.3% |
| 404,270 | MECKLENBURG | 178,796 | 106,236 | 71,907 | 653 | 34,329 R | 59.4% | 40.2% | 59.6% | 40.4% |

# NORTH CAROLINA

## PRESIDENT 1988

| 1980 Census Population | County | Total Vote | Republican | Democratic | Other | Rep.-Dem. Plurality | Percentage | | | |
|---|---|---|---|---|---|---|---|---|---|---|
| | | | | | | | Total Vote | | Major Vote | |
| | | | | | | | Rep. | Dem. | Rep. | Dem. |
| 14,428 | MITCHELL | 6,014 | 4,620 | 1,377 | 17 | 3,243 R | 76.8% | 22.9% | 77.0% | 23.0% |
| 22,469 | MONTGOMERY | 8,530 | 4,504 | 3,995 | 31 | 509 R | 52.8% | 46.8% | 53.0% | 47.0% |
| 50,505 | MOORE | 22,248 | 14,543 | 7,642 | 63 | 6,901 R | 65.4% | 34.3% | 65.6% | 34.4% |
| 67,153 | NASH | 24,722 | 15,906 | 8,740 | 76 | 7,166 R | 64.3% | 35.4% | 64.5% | 35.5% |
| 103,471 | NEW HANOVER | 39,313 | 23,807 | 15,401 | 105 | 8,406 R | 60.6% | 39.2% | 60.7% | 39.3% |
| 22,584 | NORTHAMPTON | 7,033 | 2,415 | 4,599 | 19 | 2,184 D | 34.3% | 65.4% | 34.4% | 65.6% |
| 112,784 | ONSLOW | 19,488 | 12,253 | 7,162 | 73 | 5,091 R | 62.9% | 36.8% | 63.1% | 36.9% |
| 77,055 | ORANGE | 37,067 | 14,503 | 22,326 | 238 | 7,823 D | 39.1% | 60.2% | 39.4% | 60.6% |
| 10,398 | PAMLICO | 4,506 | 2,297 | 2,188 | 21 | 109 R | 51.0% | 48.6% | 51.2% | 48.8% |
| 28,462 | PASQUOTANK | 7,892 | 4,006 | 3,860 | 26 | 146 R | 50.8% | 48.9% | 50.9% | 49.1% |
| 22,215 | PENDER | 9,323 | 4,926 | 4,377 | 20 | 549 R | 52.8% | 46.9% | 53.0% | 47.0% |
| 9,486 | PERQUIMANS | 3,340 | 1,781 | 1,543 | 16 | 238 R | 53.3% | 46.2% | 53.6% | 46.4% |
| 29,164 | PERSON | 8,628 | 4,832 | 3,777 | 19 | 1,055 R | 56.0% | 43.8% | 56.1% | 43.9% |
| 90,146 | PITT | 33,127 | 18,245 | 14,777 | 105 | 3,468 R | 55.1% | 44.6% | 55.3% | 44.7% |
| 12,984 | POLK | 6,423 | 3,874 | 2,534 | 15 | 1,340 R | 60.3% | 39.5% | 60.5% | 39.5% |
| 91,728 | RANDOLPH | 32,571 | 23,881 | 8,641 | 49 | 15,240 R | 73.3% | 26.5% | 73.4% | 26.6% |
| 45,481 | RICHMOND | 12,257 | 5,073 | 7,151 | 33 | 2,078 D | 41.4% | 58.3% | 41.5% | 58.5% |
| 101,610 | ROBESON | 27,000 | 9,908 | 16,988 | 104 | 7,080 D | 36.7% | 62.9% | 36.8% | 63.2% |
| 83,426 | ROCKINGHAM | 26,164 | 14,591 | 11,551 | 22 | 3,040 R | 55.8% | 44.1% | 55.8% | 44.2% |
| 99,186 | ROWAN | 35,416 | 23,192 | 12,127 | 97 | 11,065 R | 65.5% | 34.2% | 65.7% | 34.3% |
| 53,787 | RUTHERFORD | 17,306 | 10,337 | 6,926 | 43 | 3,411 R | 59.7% | 40.0% | 59.9% | 40.1% |
| 49,687 | SAMPSON | 16,555 | 8,524 | 8,009 | 22 | 515 R | 51.5% | 48.4% | 51.6% | 48.4% |
| 32,273 | SCOTLAND | 7,084 | 3,199 | 3,865 | 20 | 666 D | 45.2% | 54.6% | 45.3% | 54.7% |
| 48,517 | STANLY | 18,532 | 11,885 | 6,627 | 20 | 5,258 R | 64.1% | 35.8% | 64.2% | 35.8% |
| 33,086 | STOKES | 14,012 | 8,661 | 5,319 | 32 | 3,342 R | 61.8% | 38.0% | 62.0% | 38.0% |
| 59,449 | SURRY | 18,660 | 11,393 | 7,245 | 22 | 4,148 R | 61.1% | 38.8% | 61.1% | 38.9% |
| 10,283 | SWAIN | 3,625 | 1,795 | 1,821 | 9 | 26 D | 49.5% | 50.2% | 49.6% | 50.4% |
| 23,417 | TRANSYLVANIA | 11,330 | 7,009 | 4,280 | 41 | 2,729 R | 61.9% | 37.8% | 62.1% | 37.9% |
| 3,975 | TYRRELL | 1,425 | 637 | 785 | 3 | 148 D | 44.7% | 55.1% | 44.8% | 55.2% |
| 70,380 | UNION | 25,896 | 17,015 | 8,820 | 61 | 8,195 R | 65.7% | 34.1% | 65.9% | 34.1% |
| 36,748 | VANCE | 11,276 | 5,625 | 5,631 | 20 | 6 D | 49.9% | 49.9% | 50.0% | 50.0% |
| 301,327 | WAKE | 143,504 | 81,613 | 61,352 | 539 | 20,261 R | 56.9% | 42.8% | 57.1% | 42.9% |
| 16,232 | WARREN | 6,429 | 2,163 | 4,249 | 17 | 2,086 D | 33.6% | 66.1% | 33.7% | 66.3% |
| 14,801 | WASHINGTON | 5,004 | 2,186 | 2,806 | 12 | 620 D | 43.7% | 56.1% | 43.8% | 56.2% |
| 31,666 | WATAUGA | 14,785 | 8,662 | 6,048 | 75 | 2,614 R | 58.6% | 40.9% | 58.9% | 41.1% |
| 97,054 | WAYNE | 24,474 | 15,292 | 9,135 | 47 | 6,157 R | 62.5% | 37.3% | 62.6% | 37.4% |
| 58,657 | WILKES | 22,514 | 15,231 | 7,230 | 53 | 8,001 R | 67.7% | 32.1% | 67.8% | 32.2% |
| 63,132 | WILSON | 19,257 | 10,997 | 8,214 | 46 | 2,783 R | 57.1% | 42.7% | 57.2% | 42.8% |
| 28,439 | YADKIN | 11,137 | 7,918 | 3,195 | 24 | 4,723 R | 71.1% | 28.7% | 71.2% | 28.8% |
| 14,934 | YANCEY | 8,000 | 4,160 | 3,803 | 37 | 357 R | 52.0% | 47.5% | 52.2% | 47.8% |
| 5,881,766 | TOTAL | 2,134,370 | 1,237,258 | 890,167 | 6,945 | 347,091 R | 58.0% | 41.7% | 58.2% | 41.8% |

# NORTH CAROLINA

## PRESIDENT 1984

| 1980 Census Population | County | Total Vote | Republican | Democratic | Other | Rep.-Dem. Plurality | | Percentage | | | |
|---|---|---|---|---|---|---|---|---|---|---|---|
| | | | | | | | | Total Vote | | Major Vote | |
| | | | | | | | | Rep. | Dem. | Rep. | Dem. |
| 99,319 | ALAMANCE | 37,370 | 26,063 | 11,230 | 77 | 14,833 | R | 69.7% | 30.1% | 69.9% | 30.1% |
| 24,999 | ALEXANDER | 12,107 | 8,502 | 3,581 | 24 | 4,921 | R | 70.2% | 29.6% | 70.4% | 29.6% |
| 9,587 | ALLEGHANY | 4,617 | 2,589 | 2,013 | 15 | 576 | R | 56.1% | 43.6% | 56.3% | 43.7% |
| 25,649 | ANSON | 8,760 | 3,719 | 5,015 | 26 | 1,296 | D | 42.5% | 57.2% | 42.6% | 57.4% |
| 22,325 | ASHE | 10,645 | 6,611 | 4,009 | 25 | 2,602 | R | 62.1% | 37.7% | 62.3% | 37.7% |
| 14,409 | AVERY | 5,886 | 4,702 | 1,159 | 25 | 3,543 | R | 79.9% | 19.7% | 80.2% | 19.8% |
| 40,355 | BEAUFORT | 15,304 | 9,284 | 5,987 | 33 | 3,297 | R | 60.7% | 39.1% | 60.8% | 39.2% |
| 21,024 | BERTIE | 6,870 | 2,879 | 3,953 | 38 | 1,074 | D | 41.9% | 57.5% | 42.1% | 57.9% |
| 30,491 | BLADEN | 9,779 | 4,701 | 5,064 | 14 | 363 | D | 48.1% | 51.8% | 48.1% | 51.9% |
| 35,777 | BRUNSWICK | 16,488 | 9,673 | 6,774 | 41 | 2,899 | R | 58.7% | 41.1% | 58.8% | 41.2% |
| 160,934 | BUNCOMBE | 61,183 | 37,698 | 23,337 | 148 | 14,361 | R | 61.6% | 38.1% | 61.8% | 38.2% |
| 72,504 | BURKE | 29,178 | 18,766 | 10,353 | 59 | 8,413 | R | 64.3% | 35.5% | 64.4% | 35.6% |
| 85,895 | CABARRUS | 31,058 | 22,528 | 8,477 | 53 | 14,051 | R | 72.5% | 27.3% | 72.7% | 27.3% |
| 67,746 | CALDWELL | 24,394 | 17,024 | 7,311 | 59 | 9,713 | R | 69.8% | 30.0% | 70.0% | 30.0% |
| 5,829 | CAMDEN | 2,363 | 1,282 | 1,075 | 6 | 207 | R | 54.3% | 45.5% | 54.4% | 45.6% |
| 41,092 | CARTERET | 17,557 | 11,637 | 5,882 | 38 | 5,755 | R | 66.3% | 33.5% | 66.4% | 33.6% |
| 20,705 | CASWELL | 8,174 | 3,992 | 4,157 | 25 | 165 | D | 48.8% | 50.9% | 49.0% | 51.0% |
| 105,208 | CATAWBA | 43,250 | 31,476 | 11,700 | 74 | 19,776 | R | 72.8% | 27.1% | 72.9% | 27.1% |
| 33,415 | CHATHAM | 16,099 | 8,595 | 7,458 | 46 | 1,137 | R | 53.4% | 46.3% | 53.5% | 46.5% |
| 18,933 | CHEROKEE | 7,679 | 4,894 | 2,776 | 9 | 2,118 | R | 63.7% | 36.2% | 63.8% | 36.2% |
| 12,558 | CHOWAN | 3,918 | 2,171 | 1,736 | 11 | 435 | R | 55.4% | 44.3% | 55.6% | 44.4% |
| 6,619 | CLAY | 3,619 | 2,259 | 1,340 | 20 | 919 | R | 62.4% | 37.0% | 62.8% | 37.2% |
| 83,435 | CLEVELAND | 27,472 | 17,095 | 10,288 | 89 | 6,807 | R | 62.2% | 37.4% | 62.4% | 37.6% |
| 51,037 | COLUMBUS | 17,904 | 9,150 | 8,728 | 26 | 422 | R | 51.1% | 48.7% | 51.2% | 48.8% |
| 71,043 | CRAVEN | 20,134 | 12,893 | 7,186 | 55 | 5,707 | R | 64.0% | 35.7% | 64.2% | 35.8% |
| 247,160 | CUMBERLAND | 54,319 | 31,602 | 22,614 | 103 | 8,988 | R | 58.2% | 41.6% | 58.3% | 41.7% |
| 11,089 | CURRITUCK | 4,562 | 2,885 | 1,668 | 9 | 1,217 | R | 63.2% | 36.6% | 63.4% | 36.6% |
| 13,377 | DARE | 6,596 | 4,738 | 1,839 | 19 | 2,899 | R | 71.8% | 27.9% | 72.0% | 28.0% |
| 113,162 | DAVIDSON | 42,001 | 30,471 | 11,469 | 61 | 19,002 | R | 72.5% | 27.3% | 72.7% | 27.3% |
| 24,599 | DAVIE | 11,125 | 8,201 | 2,911 | 13 | 5,290 | R | 73.7% | 26.2% | 73.8% | 26.2% |
| 40,952 | DUPLIN | 14,555 | 7,708 | 6,830 | 17 | 878 | R | 53.0% | 46.9% | 53.0% | 47.0% |
| 152,785 | DURHAM | 61,584 | 29,185 | 32,244 | 155 | 3,059 | D | 47.4% | 52.4% | 47.5% | 52.5% |
| 55,988 | EDGECOMBE | 20,216 | 9,635 | 10,545 | 36 | 910 | D | 47.7% | 52.2% | 47.7% | 52.3% |
| 243,683 | FORSYTH | 96,211 | 59,208 | 36,814 | 189 | 22,394 | R | 61.5% | 38.3% | 61.7% | 38.3% |
| 30,055 | FRANKLIN | 10,768 | 5,984 | 4,766 | 18 | 1,218 | R | 55.6% | 44.3% | 55.7% | 44.3% |
| 162,568 | GASTON | 53,392 | 39,167 | 14,142 | 83 | 25,025 | R | 73.4% | 26.5% | 73.5% | 26.5% |
| 8,875 | GATES | 3,930 | 1,694 | 2,225 | 11 | 531 | D | 43.1% | 56.6% | 43.2% | 56.8% |
| 7,217 | GRAHAM | 4,014 | 2,514 | 1,494 | 6 | 1,020 | R | 62.6% | 37.2% | 62.7% | 37.3% |
| 34,043 | GRANVILLE | 11,580 | 6,302 | 5,217 | 61 | 1,085 | R | 54.4% | 45.1% | 54.7% | 45.3% |
| 16,117 | GREENE | 5,975 | 3,195 | 2,772 | 8 | 423 | R | 53.5% | 46.4% | 53.5% | 46.5% |
| 317,154 | GUILFORD | 119,336 | 73,096 | 46,027 | 213 | 27,069 | R | 61.3% | 38.6% | 61.4% | 38.6% |
| 55,286 | HALIFAX | 18,153 | 8,832 | 9,278 | 43 | 446 | D | 48.7% | 51.1% | 48.8% | 51.2% |
| 59,570 | HARNETT | 18,323 | 11,198 | 7,106 | 19 | 4,092 | R | 61.1% | 38.8% | 61.2% | 38.8% |
| 46,495 | HAYWOOD | 18,131 | 10,146 | 7,958 | 27 | 2,188 | R | 56.0% | 43.9% | 56.0% | 44.0% |
| 58,580 | HENDERSON | 26,697 | 19,369 | 7,222 | 106 | 12,147 | R | 72.6% | 27.1% | 72.8% | 27.2% |
| 23,368 | HERTFORD | 7,695 | 3,176 | 4,498 | 21 | 1,322 | D | 41.3% | 58.5% | 41.4% | 58.6% |
| 20,383 | HOKE | 5,677 | 2,449 | 3,214 | 14 | 765 | D | 43.1% | 56.6% | 43.2% | 56.8% |
| 5,873 | HYDE | 2,202 | 1,195 | 1,004 | 3 | 191 | R | 54.3% | 45.6% | 54.3% | 45.7% |
| 82,538 | IREDELL | 33,704 | 23,641 | 9,999 | 64 | 13,642 | R | 70.1% | 29.7% | 70.3% | 29.7% |
| 25,811 | JACKSON | 9,974 | 5,582 | 4,367 | 25 | 1,215 | R | 56.0% | 43.8% | 56.1% | 43.9% |
| 70,599 | JOHNSTON | 24,080 | 16,210 | 7,833 | 37 | 8,377 | R | 67.3% | 32.5% | 67.4% | 32.6% |
| 9,705 | JONES | 4,099 | 2,062 | 2,025 | 12 | 37 | R | 50.3% | 49.4% | 50.5% | 49.5% |
| 36,718 | LEE | 12,151 | 8,198 | 3,925 | 28 | 4,273 | R | 67.5% | 32.3% | 67.6% | 32.4% |
| 59,819 | LENOIR | 21,914 | 13,321 | 8,556 | 37 | 4,765 | R | 60.8% | 39.0% | 60.9% | 39.1% |
| 42,372 | LINCOLN | 18,659 | 12,621 | 5,996 | 42 | 6,625 | R | 67.6% | 32.1% | 67.8% | 32.2% |
| 35,135 | MCDOWELL | 11,736 | 7,639 | 4,076 | 21 | 3,563 | R | 65.1% | 34.7% | 65.2% | 34.8% |
| 20,178 | MACON | 10,256 | 6,661 | 3,570 | 25 | 3,091 | R | 64.9% | 34.8% | 65.1% | 34.9% |
| 16,827 | MADISON | 6,689 | 3,666 | 2,988 | 35 | 678 | R | 54.8% | 44.7% | 55.1% | 44.9% |
| 25,948 | MARTIN | 8,153 | 4,266 | 3,870 | 17 | 396 | R | 52.3% | 47.5% | 52.4% | 47.6% |
| 404,270 | MECKLENBURG | 170,337 | 106,754 | 63,190 | 393 | 43,564 | R | 62.7% | 37.1% | 62.8% | 37.2% |

# NORTH CAROLINA

## PRESIDENT 1984

| 1980 Census Population | County | Total Vote | Republican | Democratic | Other | Rep.-Dem. Plurality | Percentage | | | |
|---|---|---|---|---|---|---|---|---|---|---|
| | | | | | | | Total Vote | | Major Vote | |
| | | | | | | | Rep. | Dem. | Rep. | Dem. |
| 14,428 | MITCHELL | 6,034 | 4,737 | 1,286 | 11 | 3,451 R | 78.5% | 21.3% | 78.6% | 21.4% |
| 22,469 | MONTGOMERY | 8,952 | 5,109 | 3,831 | 12 | 1,278 R | 57.1% | 42.8% | 57.1% | 42.9% |
| 50,505 | MOORE | 21,782 | 14,681 | 7,063 | 38 | 7,618 R | 67.4% | 32.4% | 67.5% | 32.5% |
| 67,153 | NASH | 25,917 | 17,295 | 8,588 | 34 | 8,707 R | 66.7% | 33.1% | 66.8% | 33.2% |
| 103,471 | NEW HANOVER | 36,452 | 23,771 | 12,591 | 90 | 11,180 R | 65.2% | 34.5% | 65.4% | 34.6% |
| 22,584 | NORTHAMPTON | 8,330 | 3,198 | 5,094 | 38 | 1,896 D | 38.4% | 61.2% | 38.6% | 61.4% |
| 112,784 | ONSLOW | 19,687 | 13,928 | 5,713 | 46 | 8,215 R | 70.7% | 29.0% | 70.9% | 29.1% |
| 77,055 | ORANGE | 36,277 | 15,585 | 20,564 | 128 | 4,979 D | 43.0% | 56.7% | 43.1% | 56.9% |
| 10,398 | PAMLICO | 4,717 | 2,554 | 2,152 | 11 | 402 R | 54.1% | 45.6% | 54.3% | 45.7% |
| 28,462 | PASQUOTANK | 8,513 | 4,646 | 3,854 | 13 | 792 R | 54.6% | 45.3% | 54.7% | 45.3% |
| 22,215 | PENDER | 9,453 | 5,079 | 4,354 | 20 | 725 R | 53.7% | 46.1% | 53.8% | 46.2% |
| 9,486 | PERQUIMANS | 3,385 | 1,939 | 1,441 | 5 | 498 R | 57.3% | 42.6% | 57.4% | 42.6% |
| 29,164 | PERSON | 9,397 | 5,854 | 3,528 | 15 | 2,326 R | 62.3% | 37.5% | 62.4% | 37.6% |
| 90,146 | PITT | 32,526 | 18,983 | 13,481 | 62 | 5,502 R | 58.4% | 41.4% | 58.5% | 41.5% |
| 12,984 | POLK | 6,251 | 4,046 | 2,169 | 36 | 1,877 R | 64.7% | 34.7% | 65.1% | 34.9% |
| 91,728 | RANDOLPH | 33,299 | 25,759 | 7,511 | 29 | 18,248 R | 77.4% | 22.6% | 77.4% | 22.6% |
| 45,481 | RICHMOND | 14,330 | 6,807 | 7,494 | 29 | 687 D | 47.5% | 52.3% | 47.6% | 52.4% |
| 101,610 | ROBESON | 28,291 | 12,947 | 15,257 | 87 | 2,310 D | 45.8% | 53.9% | 45.9% | 54.1% |
| 83,426 | ROCKINGHAM | 28,539 | 17,895 | 10,605 | 39 | 7,290 R | 62.7% | 37.2% | 62.8% | 37.2% |
| 99,186 | ROWAN | 35,907 | 25,207 | 10,643 | 57 | 14,564 R | 70.2% | 29.6% | 70.3% | 29.7% |
| 53,787 | RUTHERFORD | 18,268 | 11,369 | 6,862 | 37 | 4,507 R | 62.2% | 37.6% | 62.4% | 37.6% |
| 49,687 | SAMPSON | 19,796 | 10,665 | 9,115 | 16 | 1,550 R | 53.9% | 46.0% | 53.9% | 46.1% |
| 32,273 | SCOTLAND | 8,117 | 4,077 | 4,028 | 12 | 49 R | 50.2% | 49.6% | 50.3% | 49.7% |
| 48,517 | STANLY | 19,289 | 13,116 | 6,138 | 35 | 6,978 R | 68.0% | 31.8% | 68.1% | 31.9% |
| 33,086 | STOKES | 14,498 | 9,515 | 4,950 | 33 | 4,565 R | 65.6% | 34.1% | 65.8% | 34.2% |
| 59,449 | SURRY | 20,562 | 13,340 | 7,188 | 34 | 6,152 R | 64.9% | 35.0% | 65.0% | 35.0% |
| 10,283 | SWAIN | 4,022 | 2,012 | 2,000 | 10 | 12 R | 50.0% | 49.7% | 50.1% | 49.9% |
| 23,417 | TRANSYLVANIA | 10,717 | 6,956 | 3,733 | 28 | 3,223 R | 64.9% | 34.8% | 65.1% | 34.9% |
| 3,975 | TYRRELL | 1,583 | 774 | 807 | 2 | 33 D | 48.9% | 51.0% | 49.0% | 51.0% |
| 70,380 | UNION | 23,968 | 16,885 | 7,048 | 35 | 9,837 R | 70.4% | 29.4% | 70.6% | 29.4% |
| 36,748 | VANCE | 12,734 | 6,836 | 5,880 | 18 | 956 R | 53.7% | 46.2% | 53.8% | 46.2% |
| 301,327 | WAKE | 131,871 | 81,251 | 50,323 | 297 | 30,928 R | 61.6% | 38.2% | 61.8% | 38.2% |
| 16,232 | WARREN | 6,618 | 2,664 | 3,946 | 8 | 1,282 D | 40.3% | 59.6% | 40.3% | 59.7% |
| 14,801 | WASHINGTON | 5,852 | 2,731 | 3,114 | 7 | 383 D | 46.7% | 53.2% | 46.7% | 53.3% |
| 31,666 | WATAUGA | 14,579 | 9,370 | 5,163 | 46 | 4,207 R | 64.3% | 35.4% | 64.5% | 35.5% |
| 97,054 | WAYNE | 28,008 | 17,961 | 10,011 | 36 | 7,950 R | 64.1% | 35.7% | 64.2% | 35.8% |
| 58,657 | WILKES | 25,564 | 18,670 | 6,852 | 42 | 11,818 R | 73.0% | 26.8% | 73.2% | 26.8% |
| 63,132 | WILSON | 20,643 | 12,243 | 8,343 | 57 | 3,900 R | 59.3% | 40.4% | 59.5% | 40.5% |
| 28,439 | YADKIN | 12,070 | 8,976 | 3,075 | 19 | 5,901 R | 74.4% | 25.5% | 74.5% | 25.5% |
| 14,934 | YANCEY | 7,961 | 4,296 | 3,651 | 14 | 645 R | 54.0% | 45.9% | 54.1% | 45.9% |
| 5,881,766 | TOTAL | 2,175,361 | 1,346,481 | 824,287 | 4,593 | 522,194 R | 61.9% | 37.9% | 62.0% | 38.0% |

# NORTH CAROLINA

## PRESIDENT 1980

| 1980 Census Population | County | Total Vote | Republican | Democratic | Other | Rep.-Dem. Plurality | Percentage Total Vote Rep. | Dem. | Major Vote Rep. | Dem. |
|---|---|---|---|---|---|---|---|---|---|---|
| 99,319 | ALAMANCE | 34,066 | 18,077 | 15,042 | 947 | 3,035 R | 53.1% | 44.2% | 54.6% | 45.4% |
| 24,999 | ALEXANDER | 11,109 | 6,376 | 4,546 | 187 | 1,830 R | 57.4% | 40.9% | 58.4% | 41.6% |
| 9,587 | ALLEGHANY | 4,310 | 1,995 | 2,198 | 117 | 203 D | 46.3% | 51.0% | 47.6% | 52.4% |
| 25,649 | ANSON | 7,087 | 1,968 | 4,973 | 146 | 3,005 D | 27.8% | 70.2% | 28.4% | 71.6% |
| 22,325 | ASHE | 10,312 | 5,643 | 4,461 | 208 | 1,182 R | 54.7% | 43.3% | 55.8% | 44.2% |
| 14,409 | AVERY | 5,182 | 3,480 | 1,527 | 175 | 1,953 R | 67.2% | 29.5% | 69.5% | 30.5% |
| 40,355 | BEAUFORT | 13,037 | 6,773 | 6,024 | 240 | 749 R | 52.0% | 46.2% | 52.9% | 47.1% |
| 21,024 | BERTIE | 5,632 | 1,695 | 3,863 | 74 | 2,168 D | 30.1% | 68.6% | 30.5% | 69.5% |
| 30,491 | BLADEN | 8,941 | 2,745 | 6,104 | 92 | 3,359 D | 30.7% | 68.3% | 31.0% | 69.0% |
| 35,777 | BRUNSWICK | 13,003 | 5,897 | 6,761 | 345 | 864 D | 45.4% | 52.0% | 46.6% | 53.4% |
| 160,934 | BUNCOMBE | 53,530 | 26,124 | 24,837 | 2,569 | 1,287 R | 48.8% | 46.4% | 51.3% | 48.7% |
| 72,504 | BURKE | 25,417 | 12,956 | 11,680 | 781 | 1,276 R | 51.0% | 46.0% | 52.6% | 47.4% |
| 85,895 | CABARRUS | 25,585 | 15,143 | 9,768 | 674 | 5,375 R | 59.2% | 38.2% | 60.8% | 39.2% |
| 67,746 | CALDWELL | 22,310 | 12,965 | 8,738 | 607 | 4,227 R | 58.1% | 39.2% | 59.7% | 40.3% |
| 5,829 | CAMDEN | 2,088 | 813 | 1,212 | 63 | 399 D | 38.9% | 58.0% | 40.1% | 59.9% |
| 41,092 | CARTERET | 14,767 | 7,733 | 6,485 | 549 | 1,248 R | 52.4% | 43.9% | 54.4% | 45.6% |
| 20,705 | CASWELL | 5,777 | 2,156 | 3,529 | 92 | 1,373 D | 37.3% | 61.1% | 37.9% | 62.1% |
| 105,208 | CATAWBA | 37,878 | 22,873 | 13,873 | 1,132 | 9,000 R | 60.4% | 36.6% | 62.2% | 37.8% |
| 33,415 | CHATHAM | 13,205 | 5,414 | 7,144 | 647 | 1,730 D | 41.0% | 54.1% | 43.1% | 56.9% |
| 18,933 | CHEROKEE | 7,079 | 3,849 | 3,114 | 116 | 735 R | 54.4% | 44.0% | 55.3% | 44.7% |
| 12,558 | CHOWAN | 3,660 | 1,424 | 2,146 | 90 | 722 D | 38.9% | 58.6% | 39.9% | 60.1% |
| 6,619 | CLAY | 3,547 | 2,136 | 1,324 | 87 | 812 R | 60.2% | 37.3% | 61.7% | 38.3% |
| 83,435 | CLEVELAND | 23,498 | 10,828 | 12,219 | 451 | 1,391 D | 46.1% | 52.0% | 47.0% | 53.0% |
| 51,037 | COLUMBUS | 15,940 | 5,522 | 10,212 | 206 | 4,690 D | 34.6% | 64.1% | 35.1% | 64.9% |
| 71,043 | CRAVEN | 16,783 | 8,554 | 7,781 | 448 | 773 R | 51.0% | 46.4% | 52.4% | 47.6% |
| 247,160 | CUMBERLAND | 45,228 | 21,540 | 22,073 | 1,615 | 533 D | 47.6% | 48.8% | 49.4% | 50.6% |
| 11,089 | CURRITUCK | 3,786 | 1,668 | 1,980 | 138 | 312 D | 44.1% | 52.3% | 45.7% | 54.3% |
| 13,377 | DARE | 5,615 | 2,794 | 2,497 | 324 | 297 R | 49.8% | 44.5% | 52.8% | 47.2% |
| 113,162 | DAVIDSON | 38,269 | 22,794 | 14,579 | 896 | 8,215 R | 59.6% | 38.1% | 61.0% | 39.0% |
| 24,599 | DAVIE | 9,880 | 6,302 | 3,289 | 289 | 3,013 R | 63.8% | 33.3% | 65.7% | 34.3% |
| 40,952 | DUPLIN | 13,069 | 5,403 | 7,524 | 142 | 2,121 D | 41.3% | 57.6% | 41.8% | 58.2% |
| 152,785 | DURHAM | 47,901 | 19,276 | 24,969 | 3,656 | 5,693 D | 40.2% | 52.1% | 43.6% | 56.4% |
| 55,988 | EDGECOMBE | 14,056 | 5,916 | 7,945 | 195 | 2,029 D | 42.1% | 56.5% | 42.7% | 57.3% |
| 243,683 | FORSYTH | 84,798 | 42,389 | 38,870 | 3,539 | 3,519 R | 50.0% | 45.8% | 52.2% | 47.8% |
| 30,055 | FRANKLIN | 9,081 | 3,508 | 5,427 | 146 | 1,919 D | 38.6% | 59.8% | 39.3% | 60.7% |
| 162,568 | GASTON | 45,204 | 25,139 | 19,016 | 1,049 | 6,123 R | 55.6% | 42.1% | 56.9% | 43.1% |
| 8,875 | GATES | 3,467 | 957 | 2,435 | 75 | 1,478 D | 27.6% | 70.2% | 28.2% | 71.8% |
| 7,217 | GRAHAM | 3,615 | 1,961 | 1,608 | 46 | 353 R | 54.2% | 44.5% | 54.9% | 45.1% |
| 34,043 | GRANVILLE | 9,246 | 3,513 | 5,556 | 177 | 2,043 D | 38.0% | 60.1% | 38.7% | 61.3% |
| 16,117 | GREENE | 5,113 | 2,221 | 2,835 | 57 | 614 D | 43.4% | 55.4% | 43.9% | 56.1% |
| 317,154 | GUILFORD | 102,622 | 53,291 | 44,516 | 4,815 | 8,775 R | 51.9% | 43.4% | 54.5% | 45.5% |
| 55,286 | HALIFAX | 14,648 | 6,033 | 8,364 | 251 | 2,331 D | 41.2% | 57.1% | 41.9% | 58.1% |
| 59,570 | HARNETT | 16,295 | 7,284 | 8,791 | 220 | 1,507 D | 44.7% | 53.9% | 45.3% | 54.7% |
| 46,495 | HAYWOOD | 17,462 | 7,217 | 9,814 | 431 | 2,597 D | 41.3% | 56.2% | 42.4% | 57.6% |
| 58,580 | HENDERSON | 22,181 | 13,573 | 7,578 | 1,030 | 5,995 R | 61.2% | 34.2% | 64.2% | 35.8% |
| 23,368 | HERTFORD | 6,060 | 1,854 | 4,102 | 104 | 2,248 D | 30.6% | 67.7% | 31.1% | 68.9% |
| 20,383 | HOKE | 4,628 | 1,168 | 3,376 | 84 | 2,208 D | 25.2% | 72.9% | 25.7% | 74.3% |
| 5,873 | HYDE | 2,072 | 807 | 1,221 | 44 | 414 D | 38.9% | 58.9% | 39.8% | 60.2% |
| 82,538 | IREDELL | 27,794 | 14,926 | 12,067 | 801 | 2,859 R | 53.7% | 43.4% | 55.3% | 44.7% |
| 25,811 | JACKSON | 9,310 | 4,140 | 4,857 | 313 | 717 D | 44.5% | 52.2% | 46.0% | 54.0% |
| 70,599 | JOHNSTON | 20,376 | 10,444 | 9,601 | 331 | 843 R | 51.3% | 47.1% | 52.1% | 47.9% |
| 9,705 | JONES | 3,630 | 1,401 | 2,198 | 31 | 797 D | 38.6% | 60.6% | 38.9% | 61.1% |
| 36,718 | LEE | 10,574 | 4,847 | 5,426 | 301 | 579 D | 45.8% | 51.3% | 47.2% | 52.8% |
| 59,819 | LENOIR | 17,714 | 9,832 | 7,546 | 336 | 2,286 R | 55.5% | 42.6% | 56.6% | 43.4% |
| 42,372 | LINCOLN | 17,196 | 9,009 | 7,796 | 391 | 1,213 R | 52.4% | 45.3% | 53.6% | 46.4% |
| 35,135 | MCDOWELL | 10,606 | 5,680 | 4,703 | 223 | 977 R | 53.6% | 44.3% | 54.7% | 45.3% |
| 20,178 | MACON | 9,031 | 4,727 | 4,105 | 199 | 622 R | 52.3% | 45.5% | 53.5% | 46.5% |
| 16,827 | MADISON | 5,972 | 2,629 | 3,202 | 141 | 573 D | 44.0% | 53.6% | 45.1% | 54.9% |
| 25,948 | MARTIN | 7,412 | 2,564 | 4,750 | 98 | 2,186 D | 34.6% | 64.1% | 35.1% | 64.9% |
| 404,270 | MECKLENBURG | 143,058 | 68,384 | 66,995 | 7,679 | 1,389 R | 47.8% | 46.8% | 50.5% | 49.5% |

# NORTH CAROLINA

## PRESIDENT 1980

| 1980 Census Population | County | Total Vote | Republican | Democratic | Other | Rep.-Dem. Plurality | Percentage | | | |
|---|---|---|---|---|---|---|---|---|---|---|
| | | | | | | | Total Vote | | Major Vote | |
| | | | | | | | Rep. | Dem. | Rep. | Dem. |
| 14,428 | MITCHELL | 6,270 | 4,322 | 1,765 | 183 | 2,557 R | 68.9% | 28.1% | 71.0% | 29.0% |
| 22,469 | MONTGOMERY | 7,842 | 3,587 | 4,129 | 126 | 542 D | 45.7% | 52.7% | 46.5% | 53.5% |
| 50,505 | MOORE | 18,911 | 10,158 | 8,084 | 669 | 2,074 R | 53.7% | 42.7% | 55.7% | 44.3% |
| 67,153 | NASH | 19,601 | 11,043 | 8,184 | 374 | 2,859 R | 56.3% | 41.8% | 57.4% | 42.6% |
| 103,471 | NEW HANOVER | 32,244 | 17,243 | 13,670 | 1,331 | 3,573 R | 53.5% | 42.4% | 55.8% | 44.2% |
| 22,584 | NORTHAMPTON | 6,861 | 1,847 | 4,933 | 81 | 3,086 D | 26.9% | 71.9% | 27.2% | 72.8% |
| 112,784 | ONSLOW | 16,736 | 8,861 | 7,371 | 504 | 1,490 R | 52.9% | 44.0% | 54.6% | 45.4% |
| 77,055 | ORANGE | 28,589 | 9,261 | 15,226 | 4,102 | 5,965 D | 32.4% | 53.3% | 37.8% | 62.2% |
| 10,398 | PAMLICO | 3,803 | 1,504 | 2,224 | 75 | 720 D | 39.5% | 58.5% | 40.3% | 59.7% |
| 28,462 | PASQUOTANK | 7,698 | 3,340 | 4,128 | 230 | 788 D | 43.4% | 53.6% | 44.7% | 55.3% |
| 22,215 | PENDER | 7,536 | 3,018 | 4,382 | 136 | 1,364 D | 40.0% | 58.1% | 40.8% | 59.2% |
| 9,486 | PERQUIMANS | 2,854 | 1,210 | 1,560 | 84 | 350 D | 42.4% | 54.7% | 43.7% | 56.3% |
| 29,164 | PERSON | 7,534 | 3,281 | 4,111 | 142 | 830 D | 43.5% | 54.6% | 44.4% | 55.6% |
| 90,146 | PITT | 26,371 | 12,816 | 12,590 | 965 | 226 R | 48.6% | 47.7% | 50.4% | 49.6% |
| 12,984 | POLK | 5,609 | 3,021 | 2,375 | 213 | 646 R | 53.9% | 42.3% | 56.0% | 44.0% |
| 91,728 | RANDOLPH | 30,717 | 19,881 | 10,107 | 729 | 9,774 R | 64.7% | 32.9% | 66.3% | 33.7% |
| 45,481 | RICHMOND | 11,609 | 3,911 | 7,416 | 282 | 3,505 D | 33.7% | 63.9% | 34.5% | 65.5% |
| 101,610 | ROBESON | 25,030 | 6,982 | 17,618 | 430 | 10,636 D | 27.9% | 70.4% | 28.4% | 71.6% |
| 83,426 | ROCKINGHAM | 23,522 | 11,205 | 11,708 | 609 | 503 D | 47.6% | 49.8% | 48.9% | 51.1% |
| 99,186 | ROWAN | 31,109 | 18,566 | 11,671 | 872 | 6,895 R | 59.7% | 37.5% | 61.4% | 38.6% |
| 53,787 | RUTHERFORD | 16,966 | 8,363 | 8,315 | 288 | 48 R | 49.3% | 49.0% | 50.1% | 49.9% |
| 49,687 | SAMPSON | 17,578 | 8,097 | 9,090 | 391 | 993 D | 46.1% | 51.7% | 47.1% | 52.9% |
| 32,273 | SCOTLAND | 6,782 | 2,133 | 4,446 | 203 | 2,313 D | 31.5% | 65.6% | 32.4% | 67.6% |
| 48,517 | STANLY | 17,846 | 9,734 | 7,784 | 328 | 1,950 R | 54.5% | 43.6% | 55.6% | 44.4% |
| 33,086 | STOKES | 13,245 | 7,275 | 5,764 | 206 | 1,511 R | 54.9% | 43.5% | 55.8% | 44.2% |
| 59,449 | SURRY | 19,408 | 10,065 | 8,987 | 356 | 1,078 R | 51.9% | 46.3% | 52.8% | 47.2% |
| 10,283 | SWAIN | 3,520 | 1,457 | 1,987 | 76 | 530 D | 41.4% | 56.4% | 42.3% | 57.7% |
| 23,417 | TRANSYLVANIA | 9,175 | 4,826 | 4,008 | 341 | 818 R | 52.6% | 43.7% | 54.6% | 45.4% |
| 3,975 | TYRRELL | 1,370 | 466 | 887 | 17 | 421 D | 34.0% | 64.7% | 34.4% | 65.6% |
| 70,380 | UNION | 19,688 | 9,012 | 10,073 | 603 | 1,061 D | 45.8% | 51.2% | 47.2% | 52.8% |
| 36,748 | VANCE | 9,774 | 4,217 | 5,415 | 142 | 1,198 D | 43.1% | 55.4% | 43.8% | 56.2% |
| 301,327 | WAKE | 105,193 | 49,768 | 49,003 | 6,422 | 765 R | 47.3% | 46.6% | 50.4% | 49.6% |
| 16,232 | WARREN | 5,430 | 1,582 | 3,750 | 98 | 2,168 D | 29.1% | 69.1% | 29.7% | 70.3% |
| 14,801 | WASHINGTON | 5,037 | 1,943 | 3,008 | 86 | 1,065 D | 38.6% | 59.7% | 39.2% | 60.8% |
| 31,666 | WATAUGA | 11,958 | 6,149 | 5,022 | 787 | 1,127 R | 51.4% | 42.0% | 55.0% | 45.0% |
| 97,054 | WAYNE | 22,836 | 12,860 | 9,586 | 390 | 3,274 R | 56.3% | 42.0% | 57.3% | 42.7% |
| 58,657 | WILKES | 23,049 | 14,462 | 8,184 | 403 | 6,278 R | 62.7% | 35.5% | 63.9% | 36.1% |
| 63,132 | WILSON | 16,704 | 8,329 | 8,042 | 333 | 287 R | 49.9% | 48.1% | 50.9% | 49.1% |
| 28,439 | YADKIN | 11,570 | 7,530 | 3,850 | 190 | 3,680 R | 65.1% | 33.3% | 66.2% | 33.8% |
| 14,934 | YANCEY | 7,546 | 3,363 | 4,010 | 173 | 647 D | 44.6% | 53.1% | 45.6% | 54.4% |
| 5,881,766 | TOTAL | 1,855,833 | 915,018 | 875,635 | 65,180 | 39,383 R | 49.3% | 47.2% | 51.1% | 48.9% |

# NORTH CAROLINA

## PRESIDENT 1976

| 1970 Census Population | County | Total Vote | Republican | Democratic | Other | Rep.-Dem. Plurality | Percentage | | | |
|---|---|---|---|---|---|---|---|---|---|---|
| | | | | | | | Total Vote | | Major Vote | |
| | | | | | | | Rep. | Dem. | Rep. | Dem. |
| 96,362 | ALAMANCE | 30,247 | 12,680 | 17,371 | 196 | 4,691 D | 41.9% | 57.4% | 42.2% | 57.8% |
| 19,466 | ALEXANDER | 9,975 | 4,661 | 5,287 | 27 | 626 D | 46.7% | 53.0% | 46.9% | 53.1% |
| 8,134 | ALLEGHANY | 4,099 | 1,532 | 2,550 | 17 | 1,018 D | 37.4% | 62.2% | 37.5% | 62.5% |
| 23,488 | ANSON | 6,425 | 1,608 | 4,796 | 21 | 3,188 D | 25.0% | 74.6% | 25.1% | 74.9% |
| 19,571 | ASHE | 10,155 | 4,937 | 5,193 | 25 | 256 D | 48.6% | 51.1% | 48.7% | 51.3% |
| 12,655 | AVERY | 4,995 | 3,085 | 1,869 | 41 | 1,216 R | 61.8% | 37.4% | 62.3% | 37.7% |
| 35,980 | BEAUFORT | 10,467 | 4,677 | 5,728 | 62 | 1,051 D | 44.7% | 54.7% | 44.9% | 55.1% |
| 20,528 | BERTIE | 5,470 | 1,332 | 4,117 | 21 | 2,785 D | 24.4% | 75.3% | 24.4% | 75.6% |
| 26,477 | BLADEN | 7,589 | 1,546 | 6,009 | 34 | 4,463 D | 20.4% | 79.2% | 20.5% | 79.5% |
| 24,223 | BRUNSWICK | 11,066 | 3,636 | 7,377 | 53 | 3,741 D | 32.9% | 66.7% | 33.0% | 67.0% |
| 145,056 | BUNCOMBE | 49,426 | 22,461 | 26,633 | 332 | 4,172 D | 45.4% | 53.9% | 45.8% | 54.2% |
| 60,364 | BURKE | 24,440 | 10,070 | 14,254 | 116 | 4,184 D | 41.2% | 58.3% | 41.4% | 58.6% |
| 74,629 | CABARRUS | 24,644 | 12,455 | 12,049 | 140 | 406 R | 50.5% | 48.9% | 50.8% | 49.2% |
| 56,699 | CALDWELL | 21,875 | 9,872 | 11,894 | 109 | 2,022 D | 45.1% | 54.4% | 45.4% | 54.6% |
| 5,453 | CAMDEN | 1,809 | 562 | 1,231 | 16 | 669 D | 31.1% | 68.0% | 31.3% | 68.7% |
| 31,603 | CARTERET | 12,939 | 5,786 | 7,080 | 73 | 1,294 D | 44.7% | 54.7% | 45.0% | 55.0% |
| 19,055 | CASWELL | 5,489 | 1,761 | 3,707 | 21 | 1,946 D | 32.1% | 67.5% | 32.2% | 67.8% |
| 90,873 | CATAWBA | 35,718 | 18,696 | 16,862 | 160 | 1,834 R | 52.3% | 47.2% | 52.6% | 47.4% |
| 29,554 | CHATHAM | 10,730 | 4,279 | 6,397 | 54 | 2,118 D | 39.9% | 59.6% | 40.1% | 59.9% |
| 16,330 | CHEROKEE | 6,849 | 3,210 | 3,571 | 68 | 361 D | 46.9% | 52.1% | 47.3% | 52.7% |
| 10,764 | CHOWAN | 2,890 | 1,019 | 1,862 | 9 | 843 D | 35.3% | 64.4% | 35.4% | 64.6% |
| 5,180 | CLAY | 3,012 | 1,428 | 1,569 | 15 | 141 D | 47.4% | 52.1% | 47.6% | 52.4% |
| 72,556 | CLEVELAND | 22,605 | 8,106 | 14,406 | 93 | 6,300 D | 35.9% | 63.7% | 36.0% | 64.0% |
| 46,937 | COLUMBUS | 14,401 | 3,184 | 11,148 | 69 | 7,964 D | 22.1% | 77.4% | 22.2% | 77.8% |
| 62,554 | CRAVEN | 13,549 | 5,881 | 7,553 | 115 | 1,672 D | 43.4% | 55.7% | 43.8% | 56.2% |
| 212,042 | CUMBERLAND | 38,694 | 14,226 | 24,297 | 171 | 10,071 D | 36.8% | 62.8% | 36.9% | 63.1% |
| 6,976 | CURRITUCK | 2,972 | 954 | 1,999 | 19 | 1,045 D | 32.1% | 67.3% | 32.3% | 67.7% |
| 6,995 | DARE | 3,891 | 1,680 | 2,191 | 20 | 511 D | 43.2% | 56.3% | 43.4% | 56.6% |
| 95,627 | DAVIDSON | 36,863 | 18,813 | 17,859 | 191 | 954 R | 51.0% | 48.4% | 51.3% | 48.7% |
| 18,855 | DAVIE | 8,463 | 4,772 | 3,635 | 56 | 1,137 R | 56.4% | 43.0% | 56.8% | 43.2% |
| 38,015 | DUPLIN | 11,694 | 3,912 | 7,696 | 86 | 3,784 D | 33.5% | 65.8% | 33.7% | 66.3% |
| 132,681 | DURHAM | 41,575 | 18,945 | 22,425 | 205 | 3,480 D | 45.6% | 53.9% | 45.8% | 54.2% |
| 52,341 | EDGECOMBE | 12,970 | 4,850 | 8,001 | 119 | 3,151 D | 37.4% | 61.7% | 37.7% | 62.3% |
| 214,348 | FORSYTH | 78,934 | 38,886 | 39,561 | 487 | 675 D | 49.3% | 50.1% | 49.6% | 50.4% |
| 26,820 | FRANKLIN | 8,097 | 2,630 | 5,405 | 62 | 2,775 D | 32.5% | 66.8% | 32.7% | 67.3% |
| 148,415 | GASTON | 42,776 | 19,727 | 22,878 | 171 | 3,151 D | 46.1% | 53.5% | 46.3% | 53.7% |
| 8,524 | GATES | 3,028 | 722 | 2,291 | 15 | 1,569 D | 23.8% | 75.7% | 24.0% | 76.0% |
| 6,562 | GRAHAM | 3,424 | 1,621 | 1,791 | 12 | 170 D | 47.3% | 52.3% | 47.5% | 52.5% |
| 32,762 | GRANVILLE | 8,251 | 2,955 | 5,244 | 52 | 2,289 D | 35.8% | 63.6% | 36.0% | 64.0% |
| 14,967 | GREENE | 4,126 | 1,356 | 2,740 | 30 | 1,384 D | 32.9% | 66.4% | 33.1% | 66.9% |
| 288,590 | GUILFORD | 92,740 | 45,441 | 46,826 | 473 | 1,385 D | 49.0% | 50.5% | 49.2% | 50.8% |
| 53,884 | HALIFAX | 13,254 | 5,257 | 7,892 | 105 | 2,635 D | 39.7% | 59.5% | 40.0% | 60.0% |
| 49,667 | HARNETT | 14,988 | 5,935 | 8,992 | 61 | 3,057 D | 39.6% | 60.0% | 39.8% | 60.2% |
| 41,710 | HAYWOOD | 16,655 | 5,885 | 10,692 | 78 | 4,807 D | 35.3% | 64.2% | 35.5% | 64.5% |
| 42,804 | HENDERSON | 19,156 | 10,830 | 8,155 | 171 | 2,675 R | 56.5% | 42.6% | 57.0% | 43.0% |
| 23,529 | HERTFORD | 5,511 | 1,517 | 3,986 | 8 | 2,469 D | 27.5% | 72.3% | 27.6% | 72.4% |
| 16,436 | HOKE | 4,123 | 920 | 3,186 | 17 | 2,266 D | 22.3% | 77.3% | 22.4% | 77.6% |
| 5,571 | HYDE | 1,718 | 623 | 1,084 | 11 | 461 D | 36.3% | 63.1% | 36.5% | 63.5% |
| 72,197 | IREDELL | 25,142 | 11,573 | 13,295 | 274 | 1,722 D | 46.0% | 52.9% | 46.5% | 53.5% |
| 21,593 | JACKSON | 8,798 | 3,536 | 5,223 | 39 | 1,687 D | 40.2% | 59.4% | 40.4% | 59.6% |
| 61,737 | JOHNSTON | 18,881 | 8,511 | 10,301 | 69 | 1,790 D | 45.1% | 54.6% | 45.2% | 54.8% |
| 9,779 | JONES | 3,011 | 948 | 2,016 | 47 | 1,068 D | 31.5% | 67.0% | 32.0% | 68.0% |
| 30,467 | LEE | 8,834 | 3,691 | 5,104 | 39 | 1,413 D | 41.8% | 57.8% | 42.0% | 58.0% |
| 55,204 | LENOIR | 15,484 | 7,715 | 7,650 | 119 | 65 R | 49.8% | 49.4% | 50.2% | 49.8% |
| 32,682 | LINCOLN | 16,214 | 6,682 | 9,462 | 70 | 2,780 D | 41.2% | 58.4% | 41.4% | 58.6% |
| 30,648 | MCDOWELL | 10,750 | 4,450 | 6,246 | 54 | 1,796 D | 41.4% | 58.1% | 41.6% | 58.4% |
| 15,788 | MACON | 8,123 | 3,673 | 4,406 | 44 | 733 D | 45.2% | 54.2% | 45.5% | 54.5% |
| 16,003 | MADISON | 5,896 | 2,446 | 3,433 | 17 | 987 D | 41.5% | 58.2% | 41.6% | 58.4% |
| 24,730 | MARTIN | 6,478 | 1,931 | 4,518 | 29 | 2,587 D | 29.8% | 69.7% | 29.9% | 70.1% |
| 354,656 | MECKLENBURG | 125,549 | 61,715 | 63,198 | 636 | 1,483 D | 49.2% | 50.3% | 49.4% | 50.6% |

# NORTH CAROLINA

## PRESIDENT 1976

| 1970 Census Population | County | Total Vote | Republican | Democratic | Other | Rep.-Dem. Plurality | Percentage Total Vote Rep. | Dem. | Major Vote Rep. | Dem. |
|---|---|---|---|---|---|---|---|---|---|---|
| 13,447 | MITCHELL | 5,781 | 3,728 | 2,031 | 22 | 1,697 R | 64.5% | 35.1% | 64.7% | 35.3% |
| 19,267 | MONTGOMERY | 7,214 | 2,872 | 4,308 | 34 | 1,436 D | 39.8% | 59.7% | 40.0% | 60.0% |
| 39,048 | MOORE | 15,030 | 7,577 | 7,373 | 80 | 204 R | 50.4% | 49.1% | 50.7% | 49.3% |
| 59,122 | NASH | 17,617 | 8,477 | 8,937 | 203 | 460 D | 48.1% | 50.7% | 48.7% | 51.3% |
| 82,996 | NEW HANOVER | 28,502 | 13,687 | 14,504 | 311 | 817 D | 48.0% | 50.9% | 48.6% | 51.4% |
| 24,009 | NORTHAMPTON | 6,380 | 1,238 | 5,118 | 24 | 3,880 D | 19.4% | 80.2% | 19.5% | 80.5% |
| 103,126 | ONSLOW | 13,978 | 5,953 | 7,954 | 71 | 2,001 D | 42.6% | 56.9% | 42.8% | 57.2% |
| 57,707 | ORANGE | 25,297 | 9,302 | 15,755 | 240 | 6,453 D | 36.8% | 62.3% | 37.1% | 62.9% |
| 9,467 | PAMLICO | 3,209 | 1,068 | 2,113 | 28 | 1,045 D | 33.3% | 65.8% | 33.6% | 66.4% |
| 26,824 | PASQUOTANK | 6,996 | 2,651 | 4,302 | 43 | 1,651 D | 37.9% | 61.5% | 38.1% | 61.9% |
| 18,149 | PENDER | 6,538 | 2,063 | 4,422 | 53 | 2,359 D | 31.6% | 67.6% | 31.8% | 68.2% |
| 8,351 | PERQUIMANS | 2,581 | 909 | 1,666 | 6 | 757 D | 35.2% | 64.5% | 35.3% | 64.7% |
| 25,914 | PERSON | 7,038 | 3,038 | 3,977 | 23 | 939 D | 43.2% | 56.5% | 43.3% | 56.7% |
| 73,900 | PITT | 21,309 | 9,532 | 11,636 | 141 | 2,104 D | 44.7% | 54.6% | 45.0% | 55.0% |
| 11,735 | POLK | 5,812 | 2,605 | 3,155 | 52 | 550 D | 44.8% | 54.3% | 45.2% | 54.8% |
| 76,358 | RANDOLPH | 27,212 | 14,337 | 12,714 | 161 | 1,623 R | 52.7% | 46.7% | 53.0% | 47.0% |
| 39,889 | RICHMOND | 11,665 | 2,848 | 8,793 | 24 | 5,945 D | 24.4% | 75.4% | 24.5% | 75.5% |
| 84,842 | ROBESON | 25,699 | 4,907 | 20,695 | 97 | 15,788 D | 19.1% | 80.5% | 19.2% | 80.8% |
| 72,402 | ROCKINGHAM | 22,872 | 9,362 | 13,413 | 97 | 4,051 D | 40.9% | 58.6% | 41.1% | 58.9% |
| 90,035 | ROWAN | 30,248 | 14,644 | 15,363 | 241 | 719 D | 48.4% | 50.8% | 48.8% | 51.2% |
| 47,337 | RUTHERFORD | 17,124 | 6,718 | 10,361 | 45 | 3,643 D | 39.2% | 60.5% | 39.3% | 60.7% |
| 44,954 | SAMPSON | 15,902 | 6,968 | 8,869 | 65 | 1,901 D | 43.8% | 55.8% | 44.0% | 56.0% |
| 26,929 | SCOTLAND | 6,391 | 1,932 | 4,430 | 29 | 2,498 D | 30.2% | 69.3% | 30.4% | 69.6% |
| 42,822 | STANLY | 18,190 | 8,845 | 9,262 | 83 | 417 D | 48.6% | 50.9% | 48.8% | 51.2% |
| 23,782 | STOKES | 12,711 | 6,029 | 6,647 | 35 | 618 D | 47.4% | 52.3% | 47.6% | 52.4% |
| 51,415 | SURRY | 17,490 | 7,403 | 10,024 | 63 | 2,621 D | 42.3% | 57.3% | 42.5% | 57.5% |
| 7,861 | SWAIN | 3,771 | 1,608 | 2,151 | 12 | 543 D | 42.6% | 57.0% | 42.8% | 57.2% |
| 19,713 | TRANSYLVANIA | 8,795 | 4,089 | 4,636 | 70 | 547 D | 46.5% | 52.7% | 46.9% | 53.1% |
| 3,806 | TYRRELL | 1,305 | 403 | 900 | 2 | 497 D | 30.9% | 69.0% | 30.9% | 69.1% |
| 54,714 | UNION | 16,847 | 6,184 | 10,578 | 85 | 4,394 D | 36.7% | 62.8% | 36.9% | 63.1% |
| 32,691 | VANCE | 9,461 | 3,813 | 5,620 | 28 | 1,807 D | 40.3% | 59.4% | 40.4% | 59.6% |
| 228,453 | WAKE | 88,947 | 44,291 | 44,005 | 651 | 286 R | 49.8% | 49.5% | 50.2% | 49.8% |
| 15,810 | WARREN | 4,635 | 1,427 | 3,185 | 23 | 1,758 D | 30.8% | 68.7% | 30.9% | 69.1% |
| 14,038 | WASHINGTON | 4,364 | 1,486 | 2,840 | 38 | 1,354 D | 34.1% | 65.1% | 34.4% | 65.6% |
| 23,404 | WATAUGA | 10,834 | 5,400 | 5,358 | 76 | 42 R | 49.8% | 49.5% | 50.2% | 49.8% |
| 85,408 | WAYNE | 19,002 | 9,607 | 9,265 | 130 | 342 R | 50.6% | 48.8% | 50.9% | 49.1% |
| 49,524 | WILKES | 22,032 | 11,768 | 10,176 | 88 | 1,592 R | 53.4% | 46.2% | 53.6% | 46.4% |
| 57,486 | WILSON | 15,087 | 6,795 | 8,209 | 83 | 1,414 D | 45.0% | 54.4% | 45.3% | 54.7% |
| 24,599 | YADKIN | 10,471 | 5,916 | 4,497 | 58 | 1,419 R | 56.5% | 42.9% | 56.8% | 43.2% |
| 12,629 | YANCEY | 6,650 | 2,688 | 3,932 | 30 | 1,244 D | 40.4% | 59.1% | 40.6% | 59.4% |
| 5,082,059 | TOTAL | 1,678,914 | 741,960 | 927,365 | 9,589 | 185,405 D | 44.2% | 55.2% | 44.4% | 55.6% |

# NORTH CAROLINA

## PRESIDENT 1972

| 1970 Census Population | County | Total Vote | Republican | Democratic | Other | Rep.-Dem. Plurality | Percentage | | | |
|---|---|---|---|---|---|---|---|---|---|---|
| | | | | | | | Total Vote | | Major Vote | |
| | | | | | | | Rep. | Dem. | Rep. | Dem. |
| 96,362 | ALAMANCE | 29,549 | 22,046 | 6,833 | 670 | 15,213 R | 74.6% | 23.1% | 76.3% | 23.7% |
| 19,466 | ALEXANDER | 8,506 | 5,865 | 2,468 | 173 | 3,397 R | 69.0% | 29.0% | 70.4% | 29.6% |
| 8,134 | ALLEGHANY | 3,521 | 2,158 | 1,304 | 59 | 854 R | 61.3% | 37.0% | 62.3% | 37.7% |
| 23,488 | ANSON | 5,833 | 3,551 | 2,188 | 94 | 1,363 R | 60.9% | 37.5% | 61.9% | 38.1% |
| 19,571 | ASHE | 9,188 | 5,784 | 3,313 | 91 | 2,471 R | 63.0% | 36.1% | 63.6% | 36.4% |
| 12,655 | AVERY | 4,179 | 3,510 | 627 | 42 | 2,883 R | 84.0% | 15.0% | 84.8% | 15.2% |
| 35,980 | BEAUFORT | 9,928 | 6,915 | 2,901 | 112 | 4,014 R | 69.7% | 29.2% | 70.4% | 29.6% |
| 20,528 | BERTIE | 4,747 | 2,874 | 1,819 | 54 | 1,055 R | 60.5% | 38.3% | 61.2% | 38.8% |
| 26,477 | BLADEN | 6,497 | 4,205 | 2,201 | 91 | 2,004 R | 64.7% | 33.9% | 65.6% | 34.4% |
| 24,223 | BRUNSWICK | 8,909 | 6,153 | 2,500 | 256 | 3,653 R | 69.1% | 28.1% | 71.1% | 28.9% |
| 145,056 | BUNCOMBE | 45,594 | 32,091 | 12,626 | 877 | 19,465 R | 70.4% | 27.7% | 71.8% | 28.2% |
| 60,364 | BURKE | 20,950 | 14,447 | 6,197 | 306 | 8,250 R | 69.0% | 29.6% | 70.0% | 30.0% |
| 74,629 | CABARRUS | 24,048 | 18,384 | 5,336 | 328 | 13,048 R | 76.4% | 22.2% | 77.5% | 22.5% |
| 56,699 | CALDWELL | 18,171 | 12,976 | 4,886 | 309 | 8,090 R | 71.4% | 26.9% | 72.6% | 27.4% |
| 5,453 | CAMDEN | 1,510 | 909 | 556 | 45 | 353 R | 60.2% | 36.8% | 62.0% | 38.0% |
| 31,603 | CARTERET | 11,415 | 8,463 | 2,805 | 147 | 5,658 R | 74.1% | 24.6% | 75.1% | 24.9% |
| 19,055 | CASWELL | 5,001 | 2,983 | 1,922 | 96 | 1,061 R | 59.6% | 38.4% | 60.8% | 39.2% |
| 90,873 | CATAWBA | 32,375 | 24,106 | 7,744 | 525 | 16,362 R | 74.5% | 23.9% | 75.7% | 24.3% |
| 29,554 | CHATHAM | 9,941 | 6,175 | 3,624 | 142 | 2,551 R | 62.1% | 36.5% | 63.0% | 37.0% |
| 16,330 | CHEROKEE | 6,604 | 4,113 | 2,411 | 80 | 1,702 R | 62.3% | 36.5% | 63.0% | 37.0% |
| 10,764 | CHOWAN | 2,871 | 1,906 | 936 | 29 | 970 R | 66.4% | 32.6% | 67.1% | 32.9% |
| 5,180 | CLAY | 2,370 | 1,545 | 797 | 28 | 748 R | 65.2% | 33.6% | 66.0% | 34.0% |
| 72,556 | CLEVELAND | 19,048 | 13,726 | 4,994 | 328 | 8,732 R | 72.1% | 26.2% | 73.3% | 26.7% |
| 46,937 | COLUMBUS | 11,987 | 8,468 | 3,305 | 214 | 5,163 R | 70.6% | 27.6% | 71.9% | 28.1% |
| 62,554 | CRAVEN | 11,903 | 9,372 | 2,384 | 147 | 6,988 R | 78.7% | 20.0% | 79.7% | 20.3% |
| 212,042 | CUMBERLAND | 34,595 | 24,376 | 9,853 | 366 | 14,523 R | 70.5% | 28.5% | 71.2% | 28.8% |
| 6,976 | CURRITUCK | 2,367 | 1,578 | 718 | 71 | 860 R | 66.7% | 30.3% | 68.7% | 31.3% |
| 6,995 | DARE | 2,641 | 1,986 | 634 | 21 | 1,352 R | 75.2% | 24.0% | 75.8% | 24.2% |
| 95,627 | DAVIDSON | 33,262 | 24,875 | 7,691 | 696 | 17,184 R | 74.8% | 23.1% | 76.4% | 23.6% |
| 18,855 | DAVIE | 7,416 | 5,613 | 1,578 | 225 | 4,035 R | 75.7% | 21.3% | 78.1% | 21.9% |
| 38,015 | DUPLIN | 10,130 | 7,153 | 2,857 | 120 | 4,296 R | 70.6% | 28.2% | 71.5% | 28.5% |
| 132,681 | DURHAM | 41,667 | 25,576 | 15,566 | 525 | 10,010 R | 61.4% | 37.4% | 62.2% | 37.8% |
| 52,341 | EDGECOMBE | 13,184 | 8,244 | 4,635 | 305 | 3,609 R | 62.5% | 35.2% | 64.0% | 36.0% |
| 214,348 | FORSYTH | 68,569 | 46,415 | 20,928 | 1,226 | 25,487 R | 67.7% | 30.5% | 68.9% | 31.1% |
| 26,820 | FRANKLIN | 7,944 | 5,431 | 2,341 | 172 | 3,090 R | 68.4% | 29.5% | 69.9% | 30.1% |
| 148,415 | GASTON | 36,901 | 27,956 | 8,462 | 483 | 19,494 R | 75.8% | 22.9% | 76.8% | 23.2% |
| 8,524 | GATES | 2,478 | 1,264 | 1,177 | 37 | 87 R | 51.0% | 47.5% | 51.8% | 48.2% |
| 6,562 | GRAHAM | 2,783 | 1,699 | 1,057 | 27 | 642 R | 61.0% | 38.0% | 61.6% | 38.4% |
| 32,762 | GRANVILLE | 9,035 | 6,037 | 2,918 | 80 | 3,119 R | 66.8% | 32.3% | 67.4% | 32.6% |
| 14,967 | GREENE | 3,684 | 2,788 | 847 | 49 | 1,941 R | 75.7% | 23.0% | 76.7% | 23.3% |
| 288,590 | GUILFORD | 88,366 | 61,381 | 25,800 | 1,185 | 35,581 R | 69.5% | 29.2% | 70.4% | 29.6% |
| 53,884 | HALIFAX | 13,375 | 8,908 | 4,241 | 226 | 4,667 R | 66.6% | 31.7% | 67.7% | 32.3% |
| 49,667 | HARNETT | 13,744 | 10,259 | 3,347 | 138 | 6,912 R | 74.6% | 24.4% | 75.4% | 24.6% |
| 41,710 | HAYWOOD | 13,731 | 8,903 | 4,515 | 313 | 4,388 R | 64.8% | 32.9% | 66.4% | 33.6% |
| 42,804 | HENDERSON | 15,135 | 12,134 | 2,701 | 300 | 9,433 R | 80.2% | 17.8% | 81.8% | 18.2% |
| 23,529 | HERTFORD | 4,789 | 2,794 | 1,928 | 67 | 866 R | 58.3% | 40.3% | 59.2% | 40.8% |
| 16,436 | HOKE | 3,426 | 1,927 | 1,466 | 33 | 461 R | 56.2% | 42.8% | 56.8% | 43.2% |
| 5,571 | HYDE | 1,545 | 1,112 | 403 | 30 | 709 R | 72.0% | 26.1% | 73.4% | 26.6% |
| 72,197 | IREDELL | 22,682 | 16,736 | 5,088 | 858 | 11,648 R | 73.8% | 22.4% | 76.7% | 23.3% |
| 21,593 | JACKSON | 7,967 | 4,709 | 3,169 | 89 | 1,540 R | 59.1% | 39.8% | 59.8% | 40.2% |
| 61,737 | JOHNSTON | 18,011 | 14,272 | 3,488 | 251 | 10,784 R | 79.2% | 19.4% | 80.4% | 19.6% |
| 9,779 | JONES | 2,800 | 1,650 | 1,093 | 57 | 557 R | 58.9% | 39.0% | 60.2% | 39.8% |
| 30,467 | LEE | 8,026 | 5,836 | 2,024 | 166 | 3,812 R | 72.7% | 25.2% | 74.2% | 25.8% |
| 55,204 | LENOIR | 14,975 | 11,065 | 3,672 | 238 | 7,393 R | 73.9% | 24.5% | 75.1% | 24.9% |
| 32,682 | LINCOLN | 13,892 | 8,597 | 5,100 | 195 | 3,497 R | 61.9% | 36.7% | 62.8% | 37.2% |
| 30,648 | MCDOWELL | 9,114 | 6,570 | 2,348 | 196 | 4,222 R | 72.1% | 25.8% | 73.7% | 26.3% |
| 15,788 | MACON | 5,974 | 4,134 | 1,749 | 91 | 2,385 R | 69.2% | 29.3% | 70.3% | 29.7% |
| 16,003 | MADISON | 5,350 | 3,273 | 2,039 | 38 | 1,234 R | 61.2% | 38.1% | 61.6% | 38.4% |
| 24,730 | MARTIN | 6,091 | 4,188 | 1,840 | 63 | 2,348 R | 68.8% | 30.2% | 69.5% | 30.5% |
| 354,656 | MECKLENBURG | 113,176 | 77,546 | 33,730 | 1,900 | 43,816 R | 68.5% | 29.8% | 69.7% | 30.3% |

# NORTH CAROLINA

## PRESIDENT 1972

| 1970 Census Population | County | Total Vote | Republican | Democratic | Other | Rep.-Dem. Plurality | Percentage | | | |
|---|---|---|---|---|---|---|---|---|---|---|
| | | | | | | | Total Vote | | Major Vote | |
| | | | | | | | Rep. | Dem. | Rep. | Dem. |
| 13,447 | MITCHELL | 5,081 | 4,240 | 800 | 41 | 3,440 R | 83.4% | 15.7% | 84.1% | 15.9% |
| 19,267 | MONTGOMERY | 6,726 | 4,417 | 2,175 | 134 | 2,242 R | 65.7% | 32.3% | 67.0% | 33.0% |
| 39,048 | MOORE | 13,308 | 9,406 | 3,627 | 275 | 5,779 R | 70.7% | 27.3% | 72.2% | 27.8% |
| 59,122 | NASH | 17,761 | 12,679 | 4,503 | 579 | 8,176 R | 71.4% | 25.4% | 73.8% | 26.2% |
| 82,996 | NEW HANOVER | 25,615 | 19,060 | 5,894 | 661 | 13,166 R | 74.4% | 23.0% | 76.4% | 23.6% |
| 24,009 | NORTHAMPTON | 6,282 | 2,997 | 3,233 | 52 | 236 D | 47.7% | 51.5% | 48.1% | 51.9% |
| 103,126 | ONSLOW | 12,921 | 10,343 | 2,424 | 154 | 7,919 R | 80.0% | 18.8% | 81.0% | 19.0% |
| 57,707 | ORANGE | 24,408 | 11,632 | 12,634 | 142 | 1,002 D | 47.7% | 51.8% | 47.9% | 52.1% |
| 9,467 | PAMLICO | 2,794 | 1,847 | 919 | 28 | 928 R | 66.1% | 32.9% | 66.8% | 33.2% |
| 26,824 | PASQUOTANK | 6,193 | 3,906 | 2,115 | 172 | 1,791 R | 63.1% | 34.2% | 64.9% | 35.1% |
| 18,149 | PENDER | 4,829 | 3,327 | 1,415 | 87 | 1,912 R | 68.9% | 29.3% | 70.2% | 29.8% |
| 8,351 | PERQUIMANS | 2,076 | 1,299 | 723 | 54 | 576 R | 62.6% | 34.8% | 64.2% | 35.8% |
| 25,914 | PERSON | 8,264 | 5,941 | 2,246 | 77 | 3,695 R | 71.9% | 27.2% | 72.6% | 27.4% |
| 73,900 | PITT | 20,459 | 14,406 | 5,858 | 195 | 8,548 R | 70.4% | 28.6% | 71.1% | 28.9% |
| 11,735 | POLK | 4,637 | 3,121 | 1,416 | 100 | 1,705 R | 67.3% | 30.5% | 68.8% | 31.2% |
| 76,358 | RANDOLPH | 24,629 | 18,724 | 5,346 | 559 | 13,378 R | 76.0% | 21.7% | 77.8% | 22.2% |
| 39,889 | RICHMOND | 9,356 | 5,692 | 3,508 | 156 | 2,184 R | 60.8% | 37.5% | 61.9% | 38.1% |
| 84,842 | ROBESON | 18,941 | 11,362 | 7,391 | 188 | 3,971 R | 60.0% | 39.0% | 60.6% | 39.4% |
| 72,402 | ROCKINGHAM | 20,407 | 14,519 | 5,530 | 358 | 8,989 R | 71.1% | 27.1% | 72.4% | 27.6% |
| 90,035 | ROWAN | 28,274 | 20,735 | 6,834 | 705 | 13,901 R | 73.3% | 24.2% | 75.2% | 24.8% |
| 47,337 | RUTHERFORD | 13,816 | 9,506 | 4,140 | 170 | 5,366 R | 68.8% | 30.0% | 69.7% | 30.3% |
| 44,954 | SAMPSON | 14,726 | 9,684 | 4,888 | 154 | 4,796 R | 65.8% | 33.2% | 66.5% | 33.5% |
| 26,929 | SCOTLAND | 5,472 | 3,485 | 1,938 | 49 | 1,547 R | 63.7% | 35.4% | 64.3% | 35.7% |
| 42,822 | STANLY | 17,972 | 12,459 | 5,218 | 295 | 7,241 R | 69.3% | 29.0% | 70.5% | 29.5% |
| 23,782 | STOKES | 10,646 | 7,118 | 3,254 | 274 | 3,864 R | 66.9% | 30.6% | 68.6% | 31.4% |
| 51,415 | SURRY | 15,487 | 10,497 | 4,706 | 284 | 5,791 R | 67.8% | 30.4% | 69.0% | 31.0% |
| 7,861 | SWAIN | 3,184 | 2,052 | 1,101 | 31 | 951 R | 64.4% | 34.6% | 65.1% | 34.9% |
| 19,713 | TRANSYLVANIA | 8,404 | 5,860 | 2,321 | 223 | 3,539 R | 69.7% | 27.6% | 71.6% | 28.4% |
| 3,806 | TYRRELL | 1,140 | 676 | 459 | 5 | 217 R | 59.3% | 40.3% | 59.6% | 40.4% |
| 54,714 | UNION | 14,336 | 10,264 | 3,886 | 186 | 6,378 R | 71.6% | 27.1% | 72.5% | 27.5% |
| 32,691 | VANCE | 9,710 | 6,491 | 3,117 | 102 | 3,374 R | 66.8% | 32.1% | 67.6% | 32.4% |
| 228,453 | WAKE | 80,789 | 56,808 | 22,807 | 1,174 | 34,001 R | 70.3% | 28.2% | 71.4% | 28.6% |
| 15,810 | WARREN | 4,366 | 2,603 | 1,698 | 65 | 905 R | 59.6% | 38.9% | 60.5% | 39.5% |
| 14,038 | WASHINGTON | 4,151 | 2,559 | 1,546 | 46 | 1,013 R | 61.6% | 37.2% | 62.3% | 37.7% |
| 23,404 | WATAUGA | 9,573 | 6,017 | 3,451 | 105 | 2,566 R | 62.9% | 36.0% | 63.6% | 36.4% |
| 85,408 | WAYNE | 19,842 | 14,352 | 5,234 | 256 | 9,118 R | 72.3% | 26.4% | 73.3% | 26.7% |
| 49,524 | WILKES | 17,994 | 13,105 | 4,634 | 255 | 8,471 R | 72.8% | 25.8% | 73.9% | 26.1% |
| 57,486 | WILSON | 16,512 | 12,060 | 4,166 | 286 | 7,894 R | 73.0% | 25.2% | 74.3% | 25.7% |
| 24,599 | YADKIN | 8,621 | 6,824 | 1,592 | 205 | 5,232 R | 79.2% | 18.5% | 81.1% | 18.9% |
| 12,629 | YANCEY | 5,440 | 3,106 | 2,278 | 56 | 828 R | 57.1% | 41.9% | 57.7% | 42.3% |
| 5,082,059 | TOTAL | 1,518,612 | 1,054,889 | 438,705 | 25,018 | 616,184 R | 69.5% | 28.9% | 70.6% | 29.4% |

# NORTH CAROLINA

## PRESIDENT 1968

| 1960 Census Population | County | Total Vote | Republican | Democratic | AIP | Other | Plurality | Percentage Total Vote Rep. | Dem. | AIP |
|---|---|---|---|---|---|---|---|---|---|---|
| 85,674 | ALAMANCE | 33,690 | 12,310 | 8,241 | 13,139 | | 829 A | 36.5% | 24.5% | 39.0% |
| 15,625 | ALEXANDER | 8,416 | 4,379 | 1,834 | 2,203 | | 2,176 R | 52.0% | 21.8% | 26.2% |
| 7,734 | ALLEGHANY | 3,701 | 1,695 | 1,102 | 904 | | 593 R | 45.8% | 29.8% | 24.4% |
| 24,962 | ANSON | 8,014 | 1,474 | 2,969 | 3,571 | | 602 A | 18.4% | 37.0% | 44.6% |
| 19,768 | ASHE | 9,208 | 4,894 | 3,426 | 888 | | 1,468 R | 53.1% | 37.2% | 9.6% |
| 12,009 | AVERY | 4,518 | 3,197 | 631 | 690 | | 2,507 R | 70.8% | 14.0% | 15.3% |
| 36,014 | BEAUFORT | 11,587 | 2,669 | 3,232 | 5,686 | | 2,454 A | 23.0% | 27.9% | 49.1% |
| 24,350 | BERTIE | 7,126 | 811 | 3,207 | 3,108 | | 99 D | 11.4% | 45.0% | 43.6% |
| 28,881 | BLADEN | 8,397 | 1,746 | 2,754 | 3,897 | | 1,143 A | 20.8% | 32.8% | 46.4% |
| 20,278 | BRUNSWICK | 8,734 | 2,404 | 2,972 | 3,358 | | 386 A | 27.5% | 34.0% | 38.4% |
| 130,074 | BUNCOMBE | 47,544 | 21,031 | 14,624 | 11,889 | | 6,407 R | 44.2% | 30.8% | 25.0% |
| 52,701 | BURKE | 22,664 | 11,068 | 5,704 | 5,892 | | 5,176 R | 48.8% | 25.2% | 26.0% |
| 68,137 | CABARRUS | 25,265 | 13,226 | 5,501 | 6,538 | | 6,688 R | 52.3% | 21.8% | 25.9% |
| 49,552 | CALDWELL | 20,274 | 10,433 | 4,746 | 5,095 | | 5,338 R | 51.5% | 23.4% | 25.1% |
| 5,598 | CAMDEN | 1,987 | 180 | 707 | 1,100 | | 393 A | 9.1% | 35.6% | 55.4% |
| 30,940 | CARTERET | 11,416 | 4,593 | 3,762 | 3,061 | | 831 R | 40.2% | 33.0% | 26.8% |
| 19,912 | CASWELL | 6,024 | 1,036 | 2,137 | 2,851 | | 714 A | 17.2% | 35.5% | 47.3% |
| 73,191 | CATAWBA | 32,652 | 18,393 | 6,974 | 7,285 | | 11,108 R | 56.3% | 21.4% | 22.3% |
| 26,785 | CHATHAM | 10,616 | 3,845 | 3,532 | 3,239 | | 313 R | 36.2% | 33.3% | 30.5% |
| 16,335 | CHEROKEE | 7,085 | 3,768 | 2,402 | 915 | | 1,366 R | 53.2% | 33.9% | 12.9% |
| 11,729 | CHOWAN | 3,695 | 798 | 1,201 | 1,696 | | 495 A | 21.6% | 32.5% | 45.9% |
| 5,526 | CLAY | 2,530 | 1,390 | 847 | 293 | | 543 R | 54.9% | 33.5% | 11.6% |
| 66,048 | CLEVELAND | 22,608 | 7,298 | 5,661 | 9,649 | | 2,351 A | 32.3% | 25.0% | 42.7% |
| 48,973 | COLUMBUS | 14,817 | 3,881 | 4,243 | 6,693 | | 2,450 A | 26.2% | 28.6% | 45.2% |
| 58,773 | CRAVEN | 13,740 | 2,991 | 4,240 | 6,509 | | 2,269 A | 21.8% | 30.9% | 47.4% |
| 148,418 | CUMBERLAND | 28,620 | 9,143 | 9,938 | 9,539 | | 399 D | 31.9% | 34.7% | 33.3% |
| 6,601 | CURRITUCK | 2,572 | 363 | 738 | 1,471 | | 733 A | 14.1% | 28.7% | 57.2% |
| 5,935 | DARE | 2,579 | 1,035 | 700 | 844 | | 191 R | 40.1% | 27.1% | 32.7% |
| 79,493 | DAVIDSON | 35,816 | 16,678 | 7,594 | 11,544 | | 5,134 R | 46.6% | 21.2% | 32.2% |
| 16,728 | DAVIE | 7,883 | 3,866 | 1,502 | 2,515 | | 1,351 R | 49.0% | 19.1% | 31.9% |
| 40,270 | DUPLIN | 12,257 | 2,724 | 3,451 | 6,082 | | 2,631 A | 22.2% | 28.2% | 49.6% |
| 111,995 | DURHAM | 42,810 | 12,705 | 16,563 | 13,542 | | 3,021 D | 29.7% | 38.7% | 31.6% |
| 54,228 | EDGECOMBE | 14,302 | 3,198 | 5,243 | 5,861 | | 618 A | 22.4% | 36.7% | 41.0% |
| 189,426 | FORSYTH | 67,585 | 31,623 | 20,281 | 15,681 | | 11,342 R | 46.8% | 30.0% | 23.2% |
| 28,755 | FRANKLIN | 9,755 | 1,375 | 2,855 | 5,525 | | 2,670 A | 14.1% | 29.3% | 56.6% |
| 127,074 | GASTON | 42,814 | 18,741 | 10,100 | 13,973 | | 4,768 R | 43.8% | 23.6% | 32.6% |
| 9,254 | GATES | 2,784 | 406 | 1,151 | 1,227 | | 76 A | 14.6% | 41.3% | 44.1% |
| 6,432 | GRAHAM | 2,994 | 1,570 | 1,061 | 363 | | 509 R | 52.4% | 35.4% | 12.1% |
| 33,110 | GRANVILLE | 8,546 | 1,837 | 2,638 | 4,071 | | 1,433 A | 21.5% | 30.9% | 47.6% |
| 16,741 | GREENE | 5,116 | 650 | 1,560 | 2,906 | | 1,346 A | 12.7% | 30.5% | 56.8% |
| 246,520 | GUILFORD | 84,351 | 38,996 | 25,604 | 19,751 | | 13,392 R | 46.2% | 30.4% | 23.4% |
| 58,956 | HALIFAX | 15,191 | 3,148 | 4,927 | 7,116 | | 2,189 A | 20.7% | 32.4% | 46.8% |
| 48,236 | HARNETT | 15,722 | 5,184 | 4,007 | 6,531 | | 1,347 A | 33.0% | 25.5% | 41.5% |
| 39,711 | HAYWOOD | 15,806 | 6,205 | 5,703 | 3,898 | | 502 R | 39.3% | 36.1% | 24.7% |
| 36,163 | HENDERSON | 16,248 | 9,334 | 3,053 | 3,861 | | 5,473 R | 57.4% | 18.8% | 23.8% |
| 22,718 | HERTFORD | 6,603 | 1,125 | 3,275 | 2,203 | | 1,072 D | 17.0% | 49.6% | 33.4% |
| 16,356 | HOKE | 4,542 | 812 | 2,185 | 1,545 | | 640 D | 17.9% | 48.1% | 34.0% |
| 5,765 | HYDE | 2,003 | 401 | 769 | 833 | | 64 A | 20.0% | 38.4% | 41.6% |
| 62,526 | IREDELL | 24,456 | 10,557 | 4,878 | 9,021 | | 1,536 R | 43.2% | 19.9% | 36.9% |
| 17,780 | JACKSON | 7,783 | 3,747 | 2,956 | 1,080 | | 791 R | 48.1% | 38.0% | 13.9% |
| 62,936 | JOHNSTON | 20,468 | 6,764 | 4,492 | 9,212 | | 2,448 A | 33.0% | 21.9% | 45.0% |
| 11,005 | JONES | 3,366 | 361 | 1,225 | 1,780 | | 555 A | 10.7% | 36.4% | 52.9% |
| 26,561 | LEE | 8,821 | 2,586 | 2,524 | 3,711 | | 1,125 A | 29.3% | 28.6% | 42.1% |
| 55,276 | LENOIR | 15,733 | 3,844 | 3,853 | 8,036 | | 4,183 A | 24.4% | 24.5% | 51.1% |
| 28,814 | LINCOLN | 13,393 | 6,188 | 4,044 | 3,161 | | 2,144 R | 46.2% | 30.2% | 23.6% |
| 26,742 | MCDOWELL | 10,301 | 4,740 | 2,543 | 3,018 | | 1,722 R | 46.0% | 24.7% | 29.3% |
| 14,935 | MACON | 6,527 | 3,295 | 2,070 | 1,162 | | 1,225 R | 50.5% | 31.7% | 17.8% |
| 17,217 | MADISON | 6,365 | 3,130 | 2,201 | 1,034 | | 929 R | 49.2% | 34.6% | 16.2% |
| 27,139 | MARTIN | 8,157 | 1,221 | 3,118 | 3,818 | | 700 A | 15.0% | 38.2% | 46.8% |
| 272,111 | MECKLENBURG | 107,497 | 56,325 | 31,102 | 20,070 | | 25,223 R | 52.4% | 28.9% | 18.7% |

# NORTH CAROLINA

## PRESIDENT 1968

| 1960 Census Population | County | Total Vote | Republican | Democratic | AIP | Other | Plurality | Percentage Total Vote | | |
|---|---|---|---|---|---|---|---|---|---|---|
| | | | | | | | | Rep. | Dem. | AIP |
| 13,906 | MITCHELL | 5,200 | 3,778 | 819 | 603 | | 2,959 R | 72.7% | 15.8% | 11.6% |
| 18,408 | MONTGOMERY | 7,739 | 3,070 | 2,410 | 2,259 | | 660 R | 39.7% | 31.1% | 29.2% |
| 36,733 | MOORE | 12,168 | 5,322 | 3,583 | 3,263 | | 1,739 R | 43.7% | 29.4% | 26.8% |
| 61,002 | NASH | 19,115 | 4,602 | 5,283 | 9,230 | | 3,947 A | 24.1% | 27.6% | 48.3% |
| 71,742 | NEW HANOVER | 27,061 | 10,020 | 7,750 | 9,291 | | 729 R | 37.0% | 28.6% | 34.3% |
| 26,811 | NORTHAMPTON | 7,918 | 860 | 4,072 | 2,986 | | 1,086 D | 10.9% | 51.4% | 37.7% |
| 82,706 | ONSLOW | 12,267 | 3,444 | 3,281 | 5,542 | | 2,098 A | 28.1% | 26.7% | 45.2% |
| 42,970 | ORANGE | 18,308 | 6,097 | 8,366 | 3,845 | | 2,269 D | 33.3% | 45.7% | 21.0% |
| 9,850 | PAMLICO | 3,472 | 745 | 1,280 | 1,447 | | 167 A | 21.5% | 36.9% | 41.7% |
| 25,630 | PASQUOTANK | 7,591 | 1,430 | 2,564 | 3,597 | | 1,033 A | 18.8% | 33.8% | 47.4% |
| 18,508 | PENDER | 5,669 | 1,007 | 1,942 | 2,720 | | 778 A | 17.8% | 34.3% | 48.0% |
| 9,178 | PERQUIMANS | 3,045 | 468 | 1,023 | 1,554 | | 531 A | 15.4% | 33.6% | 51.0% |
| 26,394 | PERSON | 8,847 | 2,138 | 2,644 | 4,065 | | 1,421 A | 24.2% | 29.9% | 45.9% |
| 69,942 | PITT | 22,608 | 5,745 | 7,696 | 9,167 | | 1,471 A | 25.4% | 34.0% | 40.5% |
| 11,395 | POLK | 5,557 | 2,550 | 1,523 | 1,484 | | 1,027 R | 45.9% | 27.4% | 26.7% |
| 61,497 | RANDOLPH | 25,693 | 13,450 | 5,351 | 6,892 | | 6,558 R | 52.3% | 20.8% | 26.8% |
| 39,202 | RICHMOND | 12,579 | 2,865 | 4,257 | 5,457 | | 1,200 A | 22.8% | 33.8% | 43.4% |
| 89,102 | ROBESON | 19,215 | 4,526 | 8,248 | 6,441 | | 1,807 D | 23.6% | 42.9% | 33.5% |
| 69,629 | ROCKINGHAM | 24,193 | 8,095 | 6,774 | 9,324 | | 1,229 A | 33.5% | 28.0% | 38.5% |
| 82,817 | ROWAN | 32,501 | 15,207 | 8,074 | 9,220 | | 5,987 R | 46.8% | 24.8% | 28.4% |
| 45,091 | RUTHERFORD | 16,883 | 7,785 | 4,622 | 4,476 | | 3,163 R | 46.1% | 27.4% | 26.5% |
| 48,013 | SAMPSON | 15,921 | 6,597 | 4,797 | 4,527 | | 1,800 R | 41.4% | 30.1% | 28.4% |
| 25,183 | SCOTLAND | 5,985 | 1,717 | 2,252 | 2,016 | | 236 D | 28.7% | 37.6% | 33.7% |
| 40,873 | STANLY | 18,333 | 9,428 | 4,199 | 4,706 | | 4,722 R | 51.4% | 22.9% | 25.7% |
| 22,314 | STOKES | 10,565 | 4,781 | 2,374 | 3,410 | | 1,371 R | 45.3% | 22.5% | 32.3% |
| 48,205 | SURRY | 18,829 | 9,638 | 5,088 | 4,103 | | 4,550 R | 51.2% | 27.0% | 21.8% |
| 8,387 | SWAIN | 3,258 | 1,494 | 1,227 | 537 | | 267 R | 45.9% | 37.7% | 16.5% |
| 16,372 | TRANSYLVANIA | 8,608 | 4,033 | 2,210 | 2,365 | | 1,668 R | 46.9% | 25.7% | 27.5% |
| 4,520 | TYRRELL | 1,287 | 291 | 581 | 415 | | 166 D | 22.6% | 45.1% | 32.2% |
| 44,670 | UNION | 13,681 | 5,290 | 3,630 | 4,761 | | 529 R | 38.7% | 26.5% | 34.8% |
| 32,002 | VANCE | 11,348 | 2,252 | 3,852 | 5,244 | | 1,392 A | 19.8% | 33.9% | 46.2% |
| 169,082 | WAKE | 67,157 | 28,928 | 20,979 | 17,250 | | 7,949 R | 43.1% | 31.2% | 25.7% |
| 19,652 | WARREN | 5,383 | 796 | 2,293 | 2,294 | | 1 A | 14.8% | 42.6% | 42.6% |
| 13,488 | WASHINGTON | 4,780 | 1,016 | 1,898 | 1,866 | | 32 D | 21.3% | 39.7% | 39.0% |
| 17,529 | WATAUGA | 9,093 | 5,081 | 2,952 | 1,060 | | 2,129 R | 55.9% | 32.5% | 11.7% |
| 82,059 | WAYNE | 19,725 | 5,678 | 5,338 | 8,709 | | 3,031 A | 28.8% | 27.1% | 44.2% |
| 45,269 | WILKES | 18,568 | 11,195 | 4,497 | 2,876 | | 6,698 R | 60.3% | 24.2% | 15.5% |
| 57,716 | WILSON | 16,129 | 4,053 | 4,173 | 7,903 | | 3,730 A | 25.1% | 25.9% | 49.0% |
| 22,804 | YADKIN | 9,725 | 5,885 | 1,443 | 2,397 | | 3,488 R | 60.5% | 14.8% | 24.6% |
| 14,008 | YANCEY | 5,415 | 2,448 | 2,215 | 752 | | 233 R | 45.2% | 40.9% | 13.9% |
| 4,556,155 | TOTAL | 1,587,493 | 627,192 | 464,113 | 496,188 | | 131,004 R | 39.5% | 29.2% | 31.3% |

# NORTH CAROLINA

## PRESIDENT 1964

| 1960 Census Population | County | Total Vote | Republican | Democratic | Other | Rep.-Dem. Plurality | Total Vote Rep. | Total Vote Dem. | Major Vote Rep. | Major Vote Dem. |
|---|---|---|---|---|---|---|---|---|---|---|
| 85,674 | ALAMANCE | 30,574 | 15,177 | 15,397 | | 220 D | 49.6% | 50.4% | 49.6% | 50.4% |
| 15,625 | ALEXANDER | 7,482 | 3,760 | 3,722 | | 38 R | 50.3% | 49.7% | 50.3% | 49.7% |
| 7,734 | ALLEGHANY | 3,941 | 1,573 | 2,368 | | 795 D | 39.9% | 60.1% | 39.9% | 60.1% |
| 24,962 | ANSON | 5,865 | 1,721 | 4,144 | | 2,423 D | 29.3% | 70.7% | 29.3% | 70.7% |
| 19,768 | ASHE | 9,156 | 4,191 | 4,965 | | 774 D | 45.8% | 54.2% | 45.8% | 54.2% |
| 12,009 | AVERY | 4,179 | 2,656 | 1,523 | | 1,133 R | 63.6% | 36.4% | 63.6% | 36.4% |
| 36,014 | BEAUFORT | 9,685 | 3,595 | 6,090 | | 2,495 D | 37.1% | 62.9% | 37.1% | 62.9% |
| 24,350 | BERTIE | 4,263 | 931 | 3,332 | | 2,401 D | 21.8% | 78.2% | 21.8% | 78.2% |
| 28,881 | BLADEN | 6,685 | 2,169 | 4,516 | | 2,347 D | 32.4% | 67.6% | 32.4% | 67.6% |
| 20,278 | BRUNSWICK | 7,961 | 3,721 | 4,240 | | 519 D | 46.7% | 53.3% | 46.7% | 53.3% |
| 130,074 | BUNCOMBE | 50,995 | 19,372 | 31,623 | | 12,251 D | 38.0% | 62.0% | 38.0% | 62.0% |
| 52,701 | BURKE | 22,896 | 10,081 | 12,815 | | 2,734 D | 44.0% | 56.0% | 44.0% | 56.0% |
| 68,137 | CABARRUS | 25,099 | 13,178 | 11,921 | | 1,257 R | 52.5% | 47.5% | 52.5% | 47.5% |
| 49,552 | CALDWELL | 19,579 | 8,733 | 10,846 | | 2,113 D | 44.6% | 55.4% | 44.6% | 55.4% |
| 5,598 | CAMDEN | 1,404 | 534 | 870 | | 336 D | 38.0% | 62.0% | 38.0% | 62.0% |
| 30,940 | CARTERET | 10,520 | 4,289 | 6,231 | | 1,942 D | 40.8% | 59.2% | 40.8% | 59.2% |
| 19,912 | CASWELL | 4,306 | 1,793 | 2,513 | | 720 D | 41.6% | 58.4% | 41.6% | 58.4% |
| 73,191 | CATAWBA | 32,930 | 17,116 | 15,814 | | 1,302 R | 52.0% | 48.0% | 52.0% | 48.0% |
| 26,785 | CHATHAM | 9,406 | 4,111 | 5,295 | | 1,184 D | 43.7% | 56.3% | 43.7% | 56.3% |
| 16,335 | CHEROKEE | 6,929 | 3,106 | 3,823 | | 717 D | 44.8% | 55.2% | 44.8% | 55.2% |
| 11,729 | CHOWAN | 2,483 | 787 | 1,696 | | 909 D | 31.7% | 68.3% | 31.7% | 68.3% |
| 5,526 | CLAY | 2,743 | 1,286 | 1,457 | | 171 D | 46.9% | 53.1% | 46.9% | 53.1% |
| 66,048 | CLEVELAND | 18,710 | 7,874 | 10,836 | | 2,962 D | 42.1% | 57.9% | 42.1% | 57.9% |
| 48,973 | COLUMBUS | 13,475 | 4,471 | 9,004 | | 4,533 D | 33.2% | 66.8% | 33.2% | 66.8% |
| 58,773 | CRAVEN | 12,113 | 4,691 | 7,422 | | 2,731 D | 38.7% | 61.3% | 38.7% | 61.3% |
| 148,418 | CUMBERLAND | 22,957 | 9,093 | 13,864 | | 4,771 D | 39.6% | 60.4% | 39.6% | 60.4% |
| 6,601 | CURRITUCK | 2,196 | 741 | 1,455 | | 714 D | 33.7% | 66.3% | 33.7% | 66.3% |
| 5,935 | DARE | 2,343 | 867 | 1,476 | | 609 D | 37.0% | 63.0% | 37.0% | 63.0% |
| 79,493 | DAVIDSON | 31,027 | 17,292 | 13,735 | | 3,557 R | 55.7% | 44.3% | 55.7% | 44.3% |
| 16,728 | DAVIE | 7,546 | 4,460 | 3,086 | | 1,374 R | 59.1% | 40.9% | 59.1% | 40.9% |
| 40,270 | DUPLIN | 10,990 | 3,821 | 7,169 | | 3,348 D | 34.8% | 65.2% | 34.8% | 65.2% |
| 111,995 | DURHAM | 38,138 | 15,264 | 22,874 | | 7,610 D | 40.0% | 60.0% | 40.0% | 60.0% |
| 54,228 | EDGECOMBE | 11,766 | 3,932 | 7,834 | | 3,902 D | 33.4% | 66.6% | 33.4% | 66.6% |
| 189,426 | FORSYTH | 61,891 | 30,276 | 31,615 | | 1,339 D | 48.9% | 51.1% | 48.9% | 51.1% |
| 28,755 | FRANKLIN | 6,651 | 2,097 | 4,554 | | 2,457 D | 31.5% | 68.5% | 31.5% | 68.5% |
| 127,074 | GASTON | 37,326 | 17,129 | 20,197 | | 3,068 D | 45.9% | 54.1% | 45.9% | 54.1% |
| 9,254 | GATES | 2,258 | 556 | 1,702 | | 1,146 D | 24.6% | 75.4% | 24.6% | 75.4% |
| 6,432 | GRAHAM | 3,135 | 1,398 | 1,737 | | 339 D | 44.6% | 55.4% | 44.6% | 55.4% |
| 33,110 | GRANVILLE | 7,220 | 2,624 | 4,596 | | 1,972 D | 36.3% | 63.7% | 36.3% | 63.7% |
| 16,741 | GREENE | 3,613 | 901 | 2,712 | | 1,811 D | 24.9% | 75.1% | 24.9% | 75.1% |
| 246,520 | GUILFORD | 75,604 | 35,635 | 39,969 | | 4,334 D | 47.1% | 52.9% | 47.1% | 52.9% |
| 58,956 | HALIFAX | 13,709 | 4,757 | 8,952 | | 4,195 D | 34.7% | 65.3% | 34.7% | 65.3% |
| 48,236 | HARNETT | 13,360 | 5,883 | 7,477 | | 1,594 D | 44.0% | 56.0% | 44.0% | 56.0% |
| 39,711 | HAYWOOD | 16,239 | 5,575 | 10,664 | | 5,089 D | 34.3% | 65.7% | 34.3% | 65.7% |
| 36,163 | HENDERSON | 14,846 | 8,780 | 6,066 | | 2,714 R | 59.1% | 40.9% | 59.1% | 40.9% |
| 22,718 | HERTFORD | 4,947 | 994 | 3,953 | | 2,959 D | 20.1% | 79.9% | 20.1% | 79.9% |
| 16,356 | HOKE | 3,033 | 779 | 2,254 | | 1,475 D | 25.7% | 74.3% | 25.7% | 74.3% |
| 5,765 | HYDE | 1,641 | 514 | 1,127 | | 613 D | 31.3% | 68.7% | 31.3% | 68.7% |
| 62,526 | IREDELL | 24,123 | 12,892 | 11,231 | | 1,661 R | 53.4% | 46.6% | 53.4% | 46.6% |
| 17,780 | JACKSON | 8,088 | 3,183 | 4,905 | | 1,722 D | 39.4% | 60.6% | 39.4% | 60.6% |
| 62,936 | JOHNSTON | 17,849 | 7,523 | 10,326 | | 2,803 D | 42.1% | 57.9% | 42.1% | 57.9% |
| 11,005 | JONES | 2,905 | 776 | 2,129 | | 1,353 D | 26.7% | 73.3% | 26.7% | 73.3% |
| 26,561 | LEE | 7,483 | 2,753 | 4,730 | | 1,977 D | 36.8% | 63.2% | 36.8% | 63.2% |
| 55,276 | LENOIR | 13,234 | 5,617 | 7,617 | | 2,000 D | 42.4% | 57.6% | 42.4% | 57.6% |
| 28,814 | LINCOLN | 13,173 | 5,869 | 7,304 | | 1,435 D | 44.6% | 55.4% | 44.6% | 55.4% |
| 26,742 | MCDOWELL | 10,488 | 4,174 | 6,314 | | 2,140 D | 39.8% | 60.2% | 39.8% | 60.2% |
| 14,935 | MACON | 6,674 | 2,900 | 3,774 | | 874 D | 43.5% | 56.5% | 43.5% | 56.5% |
| 17,217 | MADISON | 7,165 | 3,336 | 3,829 | | 493 D | 46.6% | 53.4% | 46.6% | 53.4% |
| 27,139 | MARTIN | 6,332 | 1,511 | 4,821 | | 3,310 D | 23.9% | 76.1% | 23.9% | 76.1% |
| 272,111 | MECKLENBURG | 96,171 | 46,589 | 49,582 | | 2,993 D | 48.4% | 51.6% | 48.4% | 51.6% |

# NORTH CAROLINA

## PRESIDENT 1964

| 1960 Census Population | County | Total Vote | Republican | Democratic | Other | Rep.-Dem. Plurality | Percentage Total Vote Rep. | Dem. | Major Vote Rep. | Dem. |
|---|---|---|---|---|---|---|---|---|---|---|
| 13,906 | MITCHELL | 4,999 | 3,263 | 1,736 | | 1,527 R | 65.3% | 34.7% | 65.3% | 34.7% |
| 18,408 | MONTGOMERY | 7,318 | 3,385 | 3,933 | | 548 D | 46.3% | 53.7% | 46.3% | 53.7% |
| 36,733 | MOORE | 11,546 | 5,162 | 6,384 | | 1,222 D | 44.7% | 55.3% | 44.7% | 55.3% |
| 61,002 | NASH | 15,559 | 6,396 | 9,163 | | 2,767 D | 41.1% | 58.9% | 41.1% | 58.9% |
| 71,742 | NEW HANOVER | 24,724 | 12,140 | 12,584 | | 444 D | 49.1% | 50.9% | 49.1% | 50.9% |
| 26,811 | NORTHAMPTON | 6,233 | 1,187 | 5,046 | | 3,859 D | 19.0% | 81.0% | 19.0% | 81.0% |
| 82,706 | ONSLOW | 9,726 | 3,771 | 5,955 | | 2,184 D | 38.8% | 61.2% | 38.8% | 61.2% |
| 42,970 | ORANGE | 14,991 | 5,785 | 9,206 | | 3,421 D | 38.6% | 61.4% | 38.6% | 61.4% |
| 9,850 | PAMLICO | 2,900 | 1,036 | 1,864 | | 828 D | 35.7% | 64.3% | 35.7% | 64.3% |
| 25,630 | PASQUOTANK | 6,649 | 2,380 | 4,269 | | 1,889 D | 35.8% | 64.2% | 35.8% | 64.2% |
| 18,508 | PENDER | 5,166 | 1,961 | 3,205 | | 1,244 D | 38.0% | 62.0% | 38.0% | 62.0% |
| 9,178 | PERQUIMANS | 2,399 | 941 | 1,458 | | 517 D | 39.2% | 60.8% | 39.2% | 60.8% |
| 26,394 | PERSON | 6,902 | 2,162 | 4,740 | | 2,578 D | 31.3% | 68.7% | 31.3% | 68.7% |
| 69,942 | PITT | 16,466 | 5,149 | 11,317 | | 6,168 D | 31.3% | 68.7% | 31.3% | 68.7% |
| 11,395 | POLK | 5,782 | 2,765 | 3,017 | | 252 D | 47.8% | 52.2% | 47.8% | 52.2% |
| 61,497 | RANDOLPH | 24,377 | 13,739 | 10,638 | | 3,101 R | 56.4% | 43.6% | 56.4% | 43.6% |
| 39,202 | RICHMOND | 11,639 | 3,123 | 8,516 | | 5,393 D | 26.8% | 73.2% | 26.8% | 73.2% |
| 89,102 | ROBESON | 17,387 | 3,591 | 13,796 | | 10,205 D | 20.7% | 79.3% | 20.7% | 79.3% |
| 69,629 | ROCKINGHAM | 20,495 | 9,063 | 11,432 | | 2,369 D | 44.2% | 55.8% | 44.2% | 55.8% |
| 82,817 | ROWAN | 29,738 | 14,804 | 14,934 | | 130 D | 49.8% | 50.2% | 49.8% | 50.2% |
| 45,091 | RUTHERFORD | 16,656 | 7,115 | 9,541 | | 2,426 D | 42.7% | 57.3% | 42.7% | 57.3% |
| 48,013 | SAMPSON | 15,701 | 7,634 | 8,067 | | 433 D | 48.6% | 51.4% | 48.6% | 51.4% |
| 25,183 | SCOTLAND | 5,073 | 1,229 | 3,844 | | 2,615 D | 24.2% | 75.8% | 24.2% | 75.8% |
| 40,873 | STANLY | 16,855 | 8,924 | 7,931 | | 993 R | 52.9% | 47.1% | 52.9% | 47.1% |
| 22,314 | STOKES | 9,562 | 4,664 | 4,898 | | 234 D | 48.8% | 51.2% | 48.8% | 51.2% |
| 48,205 | SURRY | 17,780 | 7,970 | 9,810 | | 1,840 D | 44.8% | 55.2% | 44.8% | 55.2% |
| 8,387 | SWAIN | 3,828 | 1,534 | 2,294 | | 760 D | 40.1% | 59.9% | 40.1% | 59.9% |
| 16,372 | TRANSYLVANIA | 8,030 | 3,547 | 4,483 | | 936 D | 44.2% | 55.8% | 44.2% | 55.8% |
| 4,520 | TYRRELL | 1,370 | 374 | 996 | | 622 D | 27.3% | 72.7% | 27.3% | 72.7% |
| 44,670 | UNION | 11,437 | 4,229 | 7,208 | | 2,979 D | 37.0% | 63.0% | 37.0% | 63.0% |
| 32,002 | VANCE | 8,638 | 3,452 | 5,186 | | 1,734 D | 40.0% | 60.0% | 40.0% | 60.0% |
| 169,082 | WAKE | 54,195 | 22,542 | 31,653 | | 9,111 D | 41.6% | 58.4% | 41.6% | 58.4% |
| 19,652 | WARREN | 4,758 | 1,909 | 2,849 | | 940 D | 40.1% | 59.9% | 40.1% | 59.9% |
| 13,488 | WASHINGTON | 3,649 | 1,144 | 2,505 | | 1,361 D | 31.4% | 68.6% | 31.4% | 68.6% |
| 17,529 | WATAUGA | 7,963 | 3,932 | 4,031 | | 99 D | 49.4% | 50.6% | 49.4% | 50.6% |
| 82,059 | WAYNE | 17,346 | 7,555 | 9,791 | | 2,236 D | 43.6% | 56.4% | 43.6% | 56.4% |
| 45,269 | WILKES | 20,190 | 11,014 | 9,176 | | 1,838 R | 54.6% | 45.4% | 54.6% | 45.4% |
| 57,716 | WILSON | 12,240 | 5,002 | 7,238 | | 2,236 D | 40.9% | 59.1% | 40.9% | 59.1% |
| 22,804 | YADKIN | 9,498 | 5,860 | 3,638 | | 2,222 R | 61.7% | 38.3% | 61.7% | 38.3% |
| 14,008 | YANCEY | 5,718 | 2,004 | 3,714 | | 1,710 D | 35.0% | 65.0% | 35.0% | 65.0% |
| 4,556,155 | TOTAL | 1,424,983 | 624,844 | 800,139 | | 175,295 D | 43.8% | 56.2% | 43.8% | 56.2% |

# NORTH CAROLINA

## PRESIDENT 1960

| 1960 Census Population | County | Total Vote | Republican | Democratic | Other | Rep.-Dem. Plurality | Percentage | | | |
|---|---|---|---|---|---|---|---|---|---|---|
| | | | | | | | Total Vote | | Major Vote | |
| | | | | | | | Rep. | Dem. | Rep. | Dem. |
| 85,674 | ALAMANCE | 28,417 | 14,818 | 13,599 | | 1,219 R | 52.1% | 47.9% | 52.1% | 47.9% |
| 15,625 | ALEXANDER | 8,131 | 4,175 | 3,956 | | 219 R | 51.3% | 48.7% | 51.3% | 48.7% |
| 7,734 | ALLEGHANY | 4,099 | 1,978 | 2,121 | | 143 D | 48.3% | 51.7% | 48.3% | 51.7% |
| 24,962 | ANSON | 5,717 | 1,597 | 4,120 | | 2,523 D | 27.9% | 72.1% | 27.9% | 72.1% |
| 19,768 | ASHE | 9,300 | 4,823 | 4,477 | | 346 R | 51.9% | 48.1% | 51.9% | 48.1% |
| 12,009 | AVERY | 5,223 | 4,176 | 1,047 | | 3,129 R | 80.0% | 20.0% | 80.0% | 20.0% |
| 36,014 | BEAUFORT | 8,733 | 2,694 | 6,039 | | 3,345 D | 30.8% | 69.2% | 30.8% | 69.2% |
| 24,350 | BERTIE | 4,259 | 577 | 3,682 | | 3,105 D | 13.5% | 86.5% | 13.5% | 86.5% |
| 28,881 | BLADEN | 6,207 | 1,854 | 4,353 | | 2,499 D | 29.9% | 70.1% | 29.9% | 70.1% |
| 20,278 | BRUNSWICK | 7,220 | 2,915 | 4,305 | | 1,390 D | 40.4% | 59.6% | 40.4% | 59.6% |
| 130,074 | BUNCOMBE | 51,343 | 28,040 | 23,303 | | 4,737 R | 54.6% | 45.4% | 54.6% | 45.4% |
| 52,701 | BURKE | 22,940 | 12,925 | 10,015 | | 2,910 R | 56.3% | 43.7% | 56.3% | 43.7% |
| 68,137 | CABARRUS | 24,358 | 15,678 | 8,680 | | 6,998 R | 64.4% | 35.6% | 64.4% | 35.6% |
| 49,552 | CALDWELL | 20,275 | 11,553 | 8,722 | | 2,831 R | 57.0% | 43.0% | 57.0% | 43.0% |
| 5,598 | CAMDEN | 1,352 | 338 | 1,014 | | 676 D | 25.0% | 75.0% | 25.0% | 75.0% |
| 30,940 | CARTERET | 9,757 | 4,493 | 5,264 | | 771 D | 46.0% | 54.0% | 46.0% | 54.0% |
| 19,912 | CASWELL | 4,104 | 1,272 | 2,832 | | 1,560 D | 31.0% | 69.0% | 31.0% | 69.0% |
| 73,191 | CATAWBA | 32,626 | 19,135 | 13,491 | | 5,644 R | 58.6% | 41.4% | 58.6% | 41.4% |
| 26,785 | CHATHAM | 8,991 | 4,308 | 4,683 | | 375 D | 47.9% | 52.1% | 47.9% | 52.1% |
| 16,335 | CHEROKEE | 7,491 | 4,294 | 3,197 | | 1,097 R | 57.3% | 42.7% | 57.3% | 42.7% |
| 11,729 | CHOWAN | 2,453 | 533 | 1,920 | | 1,387 D | 21.7% | 78.3% | 21.7% | 78.3% |
| 5,526 | CLAY | 2,921 | 1,657 | 1,264 | | 393 R | 56.7% | 43.3% | 56.7% | 43.3% |
| 66,048 | CLEVELAND | 18,802 | 8,257 | 10,545 | | 2,288 D | 43.9% | 56.1% | 43.9% | 56.1% |
| 48,973 | COLUMBUS | 14,110 | 3,655 | 10,455 | | 6,800 D | 25.9% | 74.1% | 25.9% | 74.1% |
| 58,773 | CRAVEN | 10,838 | 3,680 | 7,158 | | 3,478 D | 34.0% | 66.0% | 34.0% | 66.0% |
| 148,418 | CUMBERLAND | 19,673 | 8,072 | 11,601 | | 3,529 D | 41.0% | 59.0% | 41.0% | 59.0% |
| 6,601 | CURRITUCK | 2,115 | 464 | 1,651 | | 1,187 D | 21.9% | 78.1% | 21.9% | 78.1% |
| 5,935 | DARE | 2,305 | 1,058 | 1,247 | | 189 D | 45.9% | 54.1% | 45.9% | 54.1% |
| 79,493 | DAVIDSON | 31,915 | 18,797 | 13,118 | | 5,679 R | 58.9% | 41.1% | 58.9% | 41.1% |
| 16,728 | DAVIE | 7,259 | 4,788 | 2,471 | | 2,317 R | 66.0% | 34.0% | 66.0% | 34.0% |
| 40,270 | DUPLIN | 10,222 | 2,953 | 7,269 | | 4,316 D | 28.9% | 71.1% | 28.9% | 71.1% |
| 111,995 | DURHAM | 33,620 | 14,322 | 19,298 | | 4,976 D | 42.6% | 57.4% | 42.6% | 57.4% |
| 54,228 | EDGECOMBE | 10,325 | 2,279 | 8,046 | | 5,767 D | 22.1% | 77.9% | 22.1% | 77.9% |
| 189,426 | FORSYTH | 57,409 | 33,374 | 24,035 | | 9,339 R | 58.1% | 41.9% | 58.1% | 41.9% |
| 28,755 | FRANKLIN | 6,189 | 1,108 | 5,081 | | 3,973 D | 17.9% | 82.1% | 17.9% | 82.1% |
| 127,074 | GASTON | 41,354 | 21,250 | 20,104 | | 1,146 R | 51.4% | 48.6% | 51.4% | 48.6% |
| 9,254 | GATES | 1,934 | 385 | 1,549 | | 1,164 D | 19.9% | 80.1% | 19.9% | 80.1% |
| 6,432 | GRAHAM | 3,056 | 1,721 | 1,335 | | 386 R | 56.3% | 43.7% | 56.3% | 43.7% |
| 33,110 | GRANVILLE | 6,743 | 1,798 | 4,945 | | 3,147 D | 26.7% | 73.3% | 26.7% | 73.3% |
| 16,741 | GREENE | 3,543 | 451 | 3,092 | | 2,641 D | 12.7% | 87.3% | 12.7% | 87.3% |
| 246,520 | GUILFORD | 71,843 | 41,357 | 30,486 | | 10,871 R | 57.6% | 42.4% | 57.6% | 42.4% |
| 58,956 | HALIFAX | 11,215 | 2,343 | 8,872 | | 6,529 D | 20.9% | 79.1% | 20.9% | 79.1% |
| 48,236 | HARNETT | 13,193 | 5,301 | 7,892 | | 2,591 D | 40.2% | 59.8% | 40.2% | 59.8% |
| 39,711 | HAYWOOD | 16,627 | 8,583 | 8,044 | | 539 R | 51.6% | 48.4% | 51.6% | 48.4% |
| 36,163 | HENDERSON | 15,446 | 10,835 | 4,611 | | 6,224 R | 70.1% | 29.9% | 70.1% | 29.9% |
| 22,718 | HERTFORD | 3,886 | 781 | 3,105 | | 2,324 D | 20.1% | 79.9% | 20.1% | 79.9% |
| 16,356 | HOKE | 2,702 | 596 | 2,106 | | 1,510 D | 22.1% | 77.9% | 22.1% | 77.9% |
| 5,765 | HYDE | 1,628 | 481 | 1,147 | | 666 D | 29.5% | 70.5% | 29.5% | 70.5% |
| 62,526 | IREDELL | 21,058 | 12,085 | 8,973 | | 3,112 R | 57.4% | 42.6% | 57.4% | 42.6% |
| 17,780 | JACKSON | 7,917 | 4,017 | 3,900 | | 117 R | 50.7% | 49.3% | 50.7% | 49.3% |
| 62,936 | JOHNSTON | 16,574 | 6,660 | 9,914 | | 3,254 D | 40.2% | 59.8% | 40.2% | 59.8% |
| 11,005 | JONES | 2,505 | 585 | 1,920 | | 1,335 D | 23.4% | 76.6% | 23.4% | 76.6% |
| 26,561 | LEE | 7,236 | 2,563 | 4,673 | | 2,110 D | 35.4% | 64.6% | 35.4% | 64.6% |
| 55,276 | LENOIR | 11,784 | 3,658 | 8,126 | | 4,468 D | 31.0% | 69.0% | 31.0% | 69.0% |
| 28,814 | LINCOLN | 13,544 | 6,816 | 6,728 | | 88 R | 50.3% | 49.7% | 50.3% | 49.7% |
| 26,742 | MCDOWELL | 11,037 | 6,148 | 4,889 | | 1,259 R | 55.7% | 44.3% | 55.7% | 44.3% |
| 14,935 | MACON | 6,833 | 3,735 | 3,098 | | 637 R | 54.7% | 45.3% | 54.7% | 45.3% |
| 17,217 | MADISON | 8,968 | 4,422 | 4,546 | | 124 D | 49.3% | 50.7% | 49.3% | 50.7% |
| 27,139 | MARTIN | 6,563 | 737 | 5,826 | | 5,089 D | 11.2% | 88.8% | 11.2% | 88.8% |
| 272,111 | MECKLENBURG | 87,612 | 48,250 | 39,362 | | 8,888 R | 55.1% | 44.9% | 55.1% | 44.9% |

# NORTH CAROLINA

## PRESIDENT 1960

| 1960 Census Population | County | Total Vote | Republican | Democratic | Other | Rep.-Dem. Plurality | Percentage Total Vote Rep. | Dem. | Major Vote Rep. | Dem. |
|---|---|---|---|---|---|---|---|---|---|---|
| 13,906 | MITCHELL | 6,005 | 4,831 | 1,174 | | 3,657 R | 80.4% | 19.6% | 80.4% | 19.6% |
| 18,408 | MONTGOMERY | 6,946 | 3,649 | 3,297 | | 352 R | 52.5% | 47.5% | 52.5% | 47.5% |
| 36,733 | MOORE | 11,363 | 5,815 | 5,548 | | 267 R | 51.2% | 48.8% | 51.2% | 48.8% |
| 61,002 | NASH | 13,982 | 3,896 | 10,086 | | 6,190 D | 27.9% | 72.1% | 27.9% | 72.1% |
| 71,742 | NEW HANOVER | 22,957 | 9,775 | 13,182 | | 3,407 D | 42.6% | 57.4% | 42.6% | 57.4% |
| 26,811 | NORTHAMPTON | 5,434 | 678 | 4,756 | | 4,078 D | 12.5% | 87.5% | 12.5% | 87.5% |
| 82,706 | ONSLOW | 8,376 | 2,812 | 5,564 | | 2,752 D | 33.6% | 66.4% | 33.6% | 66.4% |
| 42,970 | ORANGE | 12,411 | 5,231 | 7,180 | | 1,949 D | 42.1% | 57.9% | 42.1% | 57.9% |
| 9,850 | PAMLICO | 2,758 | 1,061 | 1,697 | | 636 D | 38.5% | 61.5% | 38.5% | 61.5% |
| 25,630 | PASQUOTANK | 6,357 | 1,827 | 4,530 | | 2,703 D | 28.7% | 71.3% | 28.7% | 71.3% |
| 18,508 | PENDER | 4,018 | 1,274 | 2,744 | | 1,470 D | 31.7% | 68.3% | 31.7% | 68.3% |
| 9,178 | PERQUIMANS | 2,097 | 637 | 1,460 | | 823 D | 30.4% | 69.6% | 30.4% | 69.6% |
| 26,394 | PERSON | 6,231 | 1,926 | 4,305 | | 2,379 D | 30.9% | 69.1% | 30.9% | 69.1% |
| 69,942 | PITT | 15,984 | 3,458 | 12,526 | | 9,068 D | 21.6% | 78.4% | 21.6% | 78.4% |
| 11,395 | POLK | 5,618 | 2,856 | 2,762 | | 94 R | 50.8% | 49.2% | 50.8% | 49.2% |
| 61,497 | RANDOLPH | 25,561 | 15,772 | 9,789 | | 5,983 R | 61.7% | 38.3% | 61.7% | 38.3% |
| 39,202 | RICHMOND | 11,578 | 3,285 | 8,293 | | 5,008 D | 28.4% | 71.6% | 28.4% | 71.6% |
| 89,102 | ROBESON | 15,203 | 3,580 | 11,623 | | 8,043 D | 23.5% | 76.5% | 23.5% | 76.5% |
| 69,629 | ROCKINGHAM | 20,663 | 9,456 | 11,207 | | 1,751 D | 45.8% | 54.2% | 45.8% | 54.2% |
| 82,817 | ROWAN | 30,645 | 17,726 | 12,919 | | 4,807 R | 57.8% | 42.2% | 57.8% | 42.2% |
| 45,091 | RUTHERFORD | 17,547 | 8,993 | 8,554 | | 439 R | 51.3% | 48.7% | 51.3% | 48.7% |
| 48,013 | SAMPSON | 14,970 | 7,338 | 7,632 | | 294 D | 49.0% | 51.0% | 49.0% | 51.0% |
| 25,183 | SCOTLAND | 4,922 | 1,279 | 3,643 | | 2,364 D | 26.0% | 74.0% | 26.0% | 74.0% |
| 40,873 | STANLY | 19,339 | 11,080 | 8,259 | | 2,821 R | 57.3% | 42.7% | 57.3% | 42.7% |
| 22,314 | STOKES | 9,359 | 4,872 | 4,487 | | 385 R | 52.1% | 47.9% | 52.1% | 47.9% |
| 48,205 | SURRY | 18,220 | 10,035 | 8,185 | | 1,850 R | 55.1% | 44.9% | 55.1% | 44.9% |
| 8,387 | SWAIN | 4,283 | 2,112 | 2,171 | | 59 D | 49.3% | 50.7% | 49.3% | 50.7% |
| 16,372 | TRANSYLVANIA | 7,609 | 4,221 | 3,388 | | 833 R | 55.5% | 44.5% | 55.5% | 44.5% |
| 4,520 | TYRRELL | 1,275 | 349 | 926 | | 577 D | 27.4% | 72.6% | 27.4% | 72.6% |
| 44,670 | UNION | 11,423 | 4,030 | 7,393 | | 3,363 D | 35.3% | 64.7% | 35.3% | 64.7% |
| 32,002 | VANCE | 7,706 | 2,012 | 5,694 | | 3,682 D | 26.1% | 73.9% | 26.1% | 73.9% |
| 169,082 | WAKE | 44,486 | 18,436 | 26,050 | | 7,614 D | 41.4% | 58.6% | 41.4% | 58.6% |
| 19,652 | WARREN | 3,714 | 717 | 2,997 | | 2,280 D | 19.3% | 80.7% | 19.3% | 80.7% |
| 13,488 | WASHINGTON | 3,442 | 1,027 | 2,415 | | 1,388 D | 29.8% | 70.2% | 29.8% | 70.2% |
| 17,529 | WATAUGA | 8,460 | 5,020 | 3,440 | | 1,580 R | 59.3% | 40.7% | 59.3% | 40.7% |
| 82,059 | WAYNE | 13,330 | 5,474 | 7,856 | | 2,382 D | 41.1% | 58.9% | 41.1% | 58.9% |
| 45,269 | WILKES | 21,002 | 13,016 | 7,986 | | 5,030 R | 62.0% | 38.0% | 62.0% | 38.0% |
| 57,716 | WILSON | 11,135 | 3,114 | 8,021 | | 4,907 D | 28.0% | 72.0% | 28.0% | 72.0% |
| 22,804 | YADKIN | 10,053 | 7,268 | 2,785 | | 4,483 R | 72.3% | 27.7% | 72.3% | 27.7% |
| 14,008 | YANCEY | 6,594 | 3,284 | 3,310 | | 26 D | 49.8% | 50.2% | 49.8% | 50.2% |
| 4,556,155 | TOTAL | 1,368,556 | 655,420 | 713,136 | | 57,716 D | 47.9% | 52.1% | 47.9% | 52.1% |

# NORTH CAROLINA

## ELECTION NOTES

**2004**    Other vote was 11,731 Libertarian (Michael Badnarik); 1,805 write-in (Ralph Nader); 348 write-in (Walter F. Brown); 108 write-in (David Cobb).

**2000**    Other vote was 12,307 Libertarian (Browne); 8,874 Reform (Buchanan); 1,226 write-in (McReynolds).

**1996**    Other vote was 8,740 Libertarian (Browne); 2,771 Natural Law (Hagelin); 2,108 write-in (Nader); 258 write-in (Phillips); 84 write-in (Harris).

**1992**    Other vote was 5,171 Marrou (Libertarian); 59 Fulani (write-in); 41 Hagelin (write-in); 12 Warren (write-in).

**1988**    Other vote was 5,682 Fulani (New Alliance); 1,263 Paul (write-in).

**1984**    Other vote was 3,794 Bergland (Libertarian); 799 Mason (Socialist Workers).

**1980**    Other vote was 52,800 Anderson (Independent); 9,677 Clark (Libertarian); 2,287 Commoner (Citizens); 416 DeBerry (Socialist Workers).

**1976**    Other vote was 5,607 Anderson (American); 2,219 MacBride (Libertarian); 755 LaRouche (Labor); 780 McCarthy (write-in); 228 scattered write-in.

**1972**    Other vote was Schmitz (American).

**1968**    Wallace on the ballot as American.

**1964**

**1960**

# NORTH DAKOTA

## POPULAR VOTE FOR PRESIDENT 1920 TO 2004

| Year | Total Vote | Republican Vote | Republican Candidate | Democratic Vote | Democratic Candidate | Other Vote | Plurality | Total Vote Rep. | Total Vote Dem. | Major Vote Rep. | Major Vote Dem. |
|---|---|---|---|---|---|---|---|---|---|---|---|
| 2004 | 312,833 | 196,651 | Bush, George W. | 111,052 | Kerry, John | 5,130 | 85,599 R | 62.9% | 35.5% | 63.9% | 36.1% |
| 2000 ** | 288,256 | 174,852 | Bush, George W. | 95,284 | Gore, Al | 18,120 | 79,568 R | 60.7% | 33.1% | 64.7% | 35.3% |
| 1996 ** | 266,411 | 125,050 | Dole, Bob | 106,905 | Clinton, Bill | 34,456 | 18,145 R | 46.9% | 40.1% | 53.9% | 46.1% |
| 1992 ** | 308,133 | 136,244 | Bush, George | 99,168 | Clinton, Bill | 72,721 | 37,076 R | 44.2% | 32.2% | 57.9% | 42.1% |
| 1988 | 297,261 | 166,559 | Bush, George | 127,739 | Dukakis, Michael S. | 2,963 | 38,820 R | 56.0% | 43.0% | 56.6% | 43.4% |
| 1984 | 308,971 | 200,336 | Reagan, Ronald | 104,429 | Mondale, Walter F. | 4,206 | 95,907 R | 64.8% | 33.8% | 65.7% | 34.3% |
| 1980 ** | 301,545 | 193,695 | Reagan, Ronald | 79,189 | Carter, Jimmy | 28,661 | 114,506 R | 64.2% | 26.3% | 71.0% | 29.0% |
| 1976 | 297,188 | 153,470 | Ford, Gerald R. | 136,078 | Carter, Jimmy | 7,640 | 17,392 R | 51.6% | 45.8% | 53.0% | 47.0% |
| 1972 | 280,514 | 174,109 | Nixon, Richard M. | 100,384 | McGovern, George S. | 6,021 | 73,725 R | 62.1% | 35.8% | 63.4% | 36.6% |
| 1968 | 247,882 | 138,669 | Nixon, Richard M. | 94,769 | Humphrey, Hubert H. | 14,444 | 43,900 R | 55.9% | 38.2% | 59.4% | 40.6% |
| 1964 | 258,389 | 108,207 | Goldwater, Barry M. | 149,784 | Johnson, Lyndon B. | 398 | 41,577 D | 41.9% | 58.0% | 41.9% | 58.1% |
| 1960 | 278,431 | 154,310 | Nixon, Richard M. | 123,963 | Kennedy, John F. | 158 | 30,347 R | 55.4% | 44.5% | 55.5% | 44.5% |
| 1956 | 253,991 | 156,766 | Eisenhower, Dwight D. | 96,742 | Stevenson, Adlai E. | 483 | 60,024 R | 61.7% | 38.1% | 61.8% | 38.2% |
| 1952 | 270,127 | 191,712 | Eisenhower, Dwight D. | 76,694 | Stevenson, Adlai E. | 1,721 | 115,018 R | 71.0% | 28.4% | 71.4% | 28.6% |
| 1948 | 220,716 | 115,139 | Dewey, Thomas E. | 95,812 | Truman, Harry S. | 9,765 | 19,327 R | 52.2% | 43.4% | 54.6% | 45.4% |
| 1944 | 220,182 | 118,535 | Dewey, Thomas E. | 100,144 | Roosevelt, Franklin D. | 1,503 | 18,391 R | 53.8% | 45.5% | 54.2% | 45.8% |
| 1940 | 280,775 | 154,590 | Willkie, Wendell | 124,036 | Roosevelt, Franklin D. | 2,149 | 30,554 R | 55.1% | 44.2% | 55.5% | 44.5% |
| 1936 | 273,716 | 72,751 | Landon, Alfred M. | 163,148 | Roosevelt, Franklin D. | 37,817 | 90,397 D | 26.6% | 59.6% | 30.8% | 69.2% |
| 1932 | 256,290 | 71,772 | Hoover, Herbert C. | 178,350 | Roosevelt, Franklin D. | 6,168 | 106,578 D | 28.0% | 69.6% | 28.7% | 71.3% |
| 1928 | 239,845 | 131,419 | Hoover, Herbert C. | 106,648 | Smith, Alfred E. | 1,778 | 24,771 R | 54.8% | 44.5% | 55.2% | 44.8% |
| 1924 ** | 199,081 | 94,931 | Coolidge, Calvin | 13,858 | Davis, John W. | 90,292 | 5,009 R | 47.7% | 7.0% | 87.3% | 12.7% |
| 1920 | 205,786 | 160,082 | Harding, Warren G. | 37,422 | Cox, James M. | 8,282 | 122,660 R | 77.8% | 18.2% | 81.1% | 18.9% |

In 2000 the other vote column includes 9,486 votes cast for Green (Nader). In 1996 the other vote column includes 32,515 votes cast for Perot. In 1992 the other vote column includes 71,084 votes cast for Perot. In 1980 the other column includes 23,640 votes for Independent (Anderson). In 1924 the other vote was 89,922 Progressive and 370 Communist.

## ELECTORAL COLLEGE VOTE 1920 TO 2004

| Year | Total | Republican | Democratic | Other |
|---|---|---|---|---|
| 2004 | 3 | 3 | | |
| 2000 | 3 | 3 | | |
| 1996 | 3 | 3 | | |
| 1992 | 3 | 3 | | |
| 1988 | 3 | 3 | | |
| 1984 | 3 | 3 | | |
| 1980 | 3 | 3 | | |
| 1976 | 3 | 3 | | |
| 1972 | 3 | 3 | | |
| 1968 | 4 | 4 | | |
| 1964 | 4 | | 4 | |
| 1960 | 4 | 4 | | |
| 1956 | 4 | 4 | | |
| 1952 | 4 | 4 | | |
| 1948 | 4 | 4 | | |
| 1944 | 4 | 4 | | |
| 1940 | 4 | 4 | | |
| 1936 | 4 | | 4 | |
| 1932 | 4 | | 4 | |
| 1928 | 5 | 5 | | |
| 1924 | 5 | 5 | | |
| 1920 | 5 | 5 | | |

# NORTH DAKOTA

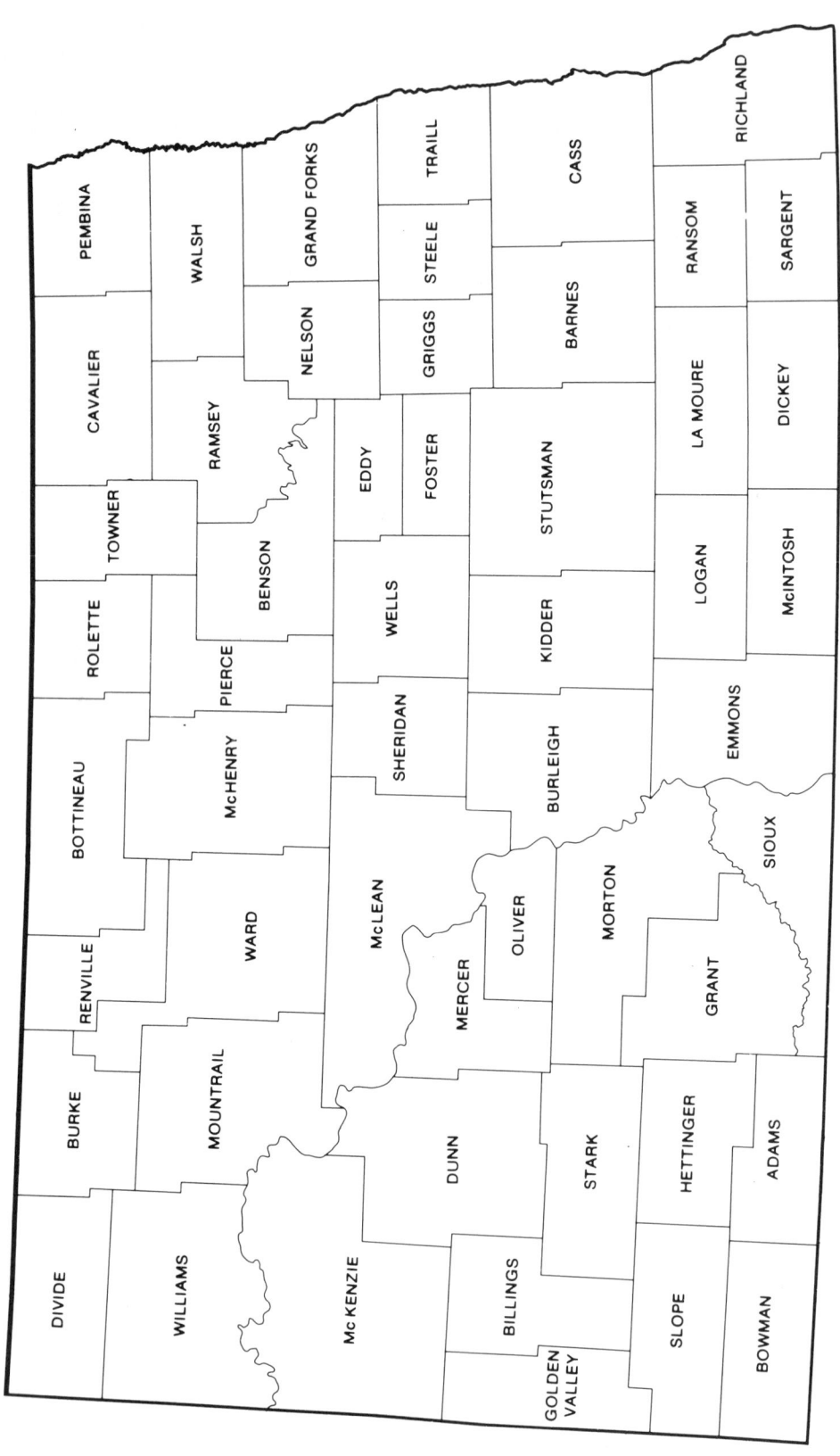

# NORTH DAKOTA

## PRESIDENT 2004

| 2000 Census Population | County | Total Vote | Republican | Democratic | Other | Rep.-Dem. Plurality | Percentage | | | |
|---|---|---|---|---|---|---|---|---|---|---|
| | | | | | | | Total Vote | | Major Vote | |
| | | | | | | | Rep. | Dem. | Rep. | Dem. |
| 2,593 | ADAMS | 1,291 | 915 | 353 | 23 | 562 R | 70.9% | 27.3% | 72.2% | 27.8% |
| 11,775 | BARNES | 5,813 | 3,541 | 2,186 | 86 | 1,355 R | 60.9% | 37.6% | 61.8% | 38.2% |
| 6,964 | BENSON | 2,246 | 1,002 | 1,196 | 48 | 194 D | 44.6% | 53.3% | 45.6% | 54.4% |
| 888 | BILLINGS | 564 | 449 | 99 | 16 | 350 R | 79.6% | 17.6% | 81.9% | 18.1% |
| 7,149 | BOTTINEAU | 3,674 | 2,468 | 1,168 | 38 | 1,300 R | 67.2% | 31.8% | 67.9% | 32.1% |
| 3,242 | BOWMAN | 1,716 | 1,280 | 397 | 39 | 883 R | 74.6% | 23.1% | 76.3% | 23.7% |
| 2,242 | BURKE | 1,165 | 808 | 336 | 21 | 472 R | 69.4% | 28.8% | 70.6% | 29.4% |
| 69,416 | BURLEIGH | 38,814 | 26,577 | 11,621 | 616 | 14,956 R | 68.5% | 29.9% | 69.6% | 30.4% |
| 123,138 | CASS | 66,711 | 39,619 | 26,010 | 1,082 | 13,609 R | 59.4% | 39.0% | 60.4% | 39.6% |
| 4,831 | CAVALIER | 2,444 | 1,522 | 887 | 35 | 635 R | 62.3% | 36.3% | 63.2% | 36.8% |
| 5,757 | DICKEY | 2,821 | 1,890 | 883 | 48 | 1,007 R | 67.0% | 31.3% | 68.2% | 31.8% |
| 2,283 | DIVIDE | 1,268 | 751 | 487 | 30 | 264 R | 59.2% | 38.4% | 60.7% | 39.3% |
| 3,600 | DUNN | 1,774 | 1,178 | 571 | 25 | 607 R | 66.4% | 32.2% | 67.4% | 32.6% |
| 2,757 | EDDY | 1,213 | 655 | 534 | 24 | 121 R | 54.0% | 44.0% | 55.1% | 44.9% |
| 4,331 | EMMONS | 2,113 | 1,449 | 611 | 53 | 838 R | 68.6% | 28.9% | 70.3% | 29.7% |
| 3,759 | FOSTER | 1,766 | 1,219 | 518 | 29 | 701 R | 69.0% | 29.3% | 70.2% | 29.8% |
| 1,924 | GOLDEN VALLEY | 927 | 719 | 195 | 13 | 524 R | 77.6% | 21.0% | 78.7% | 21.3% |
| 66,109 | GRAND FORKS | 30,470 | 17,298 | 12,646 | 526 | 4,652 R | 56.8% | 41.5% | 57.8% | 42.2% |
| 2,841 | GRANT | 1,242 | 952 | 264 | 26 | 688 R | 76.7% | 21.3% | 78.3% | 21.7% |
| 2,754 | GRIGGS | 1,439 | 907 | 505 | 27 | 402 R | 63.0% | 35.1% | 64.2% | 35.8% |
| 2,715 | HETTINGER | 1,494 | 1,044 | 405 | 45 | 639 R | 69.9% | 27.1% | 72.0% | 28.0% |
| 2,753 | KIDDER | 1,369 | 902 | 433 | 34 | 469 R | 65.9% | 31.6% | 67.6% | 32.4% |
| 4,701 | LA MOURE | 2,335 | 1,592 | 712 | 31 | 880 R | 68.2% | 30.5% | 69.1% | 30.9% |
| 2,308 | LOGAN | 1,130 | 844 | 265 | 21 | 579 R | 74.7% | 23.5% | 76.1% | 23.9% |
| 5,987 | MCHENRY | 2,820 | 1,744 | 1,030 | 46 | 714 R | 61.8% | 36.5% | 62.9% | 37.1% |
| 3,390 | MCINTOSH | 1,722 | 1,254 | 436 | 32 | 818 R | 72.8% | 25.3% | 74.2% | 25.8% |
| 5,737 | MCKENZIE | 2,762 | 1,897 | 847 | 18 | 1,050 R | 68.7% | 30.7% | 69.1% | 30.9% |
| 9,311 | MCLEAN | 4,750 | 3,014 | 1,664 | 72 | 1,350 R | 63.5% | 35.0% | 64.4% | 35.6% |
| 8,644 | MERCER | 4,617 | 3,285 | 1,245 | 87 | 2,040 R | 71.2% | 27.0% | 72.5% | 27.5% |
| 25,303 | MORTON | 12,633 | 8,325 | 4,073 | 235 | 4,252 R | 65.9% | 32.2% | 67.1% | 32.9% |
| 6,631 | MOUNTRAIL | 3,030 | 1,527 | 1,465 | 38 | 62 R | 50.4% | 48.3% | 51.0% | 49.0% |
| 3,715 | NELSON | 1,922 | 1,107 | 778 | 37 | 329 R | 57.6% | 40.5% | 58.7% | 41.3% |
| 2,065 | OLIVER | 1,119 | 790 | 310 | 19 | 480 R | 70.6% | 27.7% | 71.8% | 28.2% |
| 8,585 | PEMBINA | 3,856 | 2,466 | 1,321 | 69 | 1,145 R | 64.0% | 34.3% | 65.1% | 34.9% |
| 4,675 | PIERCE | 2,195 | 1,475 | 686 | 34 | 789 R | 67.2% | 31.3% | 68.3% | 31.7% |
| 12,066 | RAMSEY | 4,900 | 2,943 | 1,885 | 72 | 1,058 R | 60.1% | 38.5% | 61.0% | 39.0% |
| 5,890 | RANSOM | 2,602 | 1,352 | 1,199 | 51 | 153 R | 52.0% | 46.1% | 53.0% | 47.0% |
| 2,610 | RENVILLE | 1,469 | 953 | 497 | 19 | 456 R | 64.9% | 33.8% | 65.7% | 34.3% |
| 17,998 | RICHLAND | 8,215 | 5,264 | 2,821 | 130 | 2,443 R | 64.1% | 34.3% | 65.1% | 34.9% |
| 13,674 | ROLETTE | 4,044 | 1,392 | 2,564 | 88 | 1,172 D | 34.4% | 63.4% | 35.2% | 64.8% |
| 4,366 | SARGENT | 2,200 | 1,147 | 1,021 | 32 | 126 R | 52.1% | 46.4% | 52.9% | 47.1% |
| 1,710 | SHERIDAN | 944 | 727 | 200 | 17 | 527 R | 77.0% | 21.2% | 78.4% | 21.6% |
| 4,044 | SIOUX | 1,140 | 319 | 804 | 17 | 485 D | 28.0% | 70.5% | 28.4% | 71.6% |
| 767 | SLOPE | 432 | 335 | 89 | 8 | 246 R | 77.5% | 20.6% | 79.0% | 21.0% |
| 22,636 | STARK | 10,400 | 7,220 | 3,013 | 167 | 4,207 R | 69.4% | 29.0% | 70.6% | 29.4% |
| 2,258 | STEELE | 1,213 | 586 | 616 | 11 | 30 D | 48.3% | 50.8% | 48.8% | 51.2% |
| 21,908 | STUTSMAN | 10,122 | 6,517 | 3,438 | 167 | 3,079 R | 64.4% | 34.0% | 65.5% | 34.5% |
| 2,876 | TOWNER | 1,391 | 754 | 606 | 31 | 148 R | 54.2% | 43.6% | 55.4% | 44.6% |
| 8,477 | TRAILL | 4,248 | 2,543 | 1,651 | 54 | 892 R | 59.9% | 38.9% | 60.6% | 39.4% |
| 12,389 | WALSH | 5,186 | 3,194 | 1,905 | 87 | 1,289 R | 61.6% | 36.7% | 62.6% | 37.4% |
| 58,795 | WARD | 25,612 | 17,008 | 8,236 | 368 | 8,772 R | 66.4% | 32.2% | 67.4% | 32.6% |
| 5,102 | WELLS | 2,561 | 1,654 | 858 | 49 | 796 R | 64.6% | 33.5% | 65.8% | 34.2% |
| 19,761 | WILLIAMS | 8,929 | 6,278 | 2,512 | 139 | 3,766 R | 70.3% | 28.1% | 71.4% | 28.6% |
| 642,200 | TOTAL | 312,833 | 196,651 | 111,052 | 5,130 | 85,599 R | 62.9% | 35.5% | 63.9% | 36.1% |

704

# NORTH DAKOTA

## PRESIDENT 2000

| 2000 Census Population | County | Total Vote | Republican | Democratic | Green (Nader) | Other | Rep.-Dem. Plurality | Percentage of Total Vote | | |
|---|---|---|---|---|---|---|---|---|---|---|
| | | | | | | | | Rep. | Dem. | Green |
| 2,593 | ADAMS | 1,160 | 826 | 286 | 23 | 25 | 540 R | 71.2% | 24.7% | 2.0% |
| 11,775 | BARNES | 5,748 | 3,452 | 1,933 | 160 | 203 | 1,519 R | 60.1% | 33.6% | 2.8% |
| 6,964 | BENSON | 2,154 | 1,055 | 952 | 50 | 97 | 103 R | 49.0% | 44.2% | 2.3% |
| 888 | BILLINGS | 525 | 394 | 82 | 15 | 34 | 312 R | 75.0% | 15.6% | 2.9% |
| 7,149 | BOTTINEAU | 3,690 | 2,349 | 1,173 | 95 | 73 | 1,176 R | 63.7% | 31.8% | 2.6% |
| 3,242 | BOWMAN | 1,471 | 1,080 | 330 | 40 | 21 | 750 R | 73.4% | 22.4% | 2.7% |
| 2,242 | BURKE | 1,039 | 698 | 296 | 20 | 25 | 402 R | 67.2% | 28.5% | 1.9% |
| 69,416 | BURLEIGH | 34,482 | 22,467 | 9,842 | 1,142 | 1,031 | 12,625 R | 65.2% | 28.5% | 3.3% |
| 123,138 | CASS | 58,995 | 33,536 | 21,451 | 2,560 | 1,448 | 12,085 R | 56.8% | 36.4% | 4.3% |
| 4,831 | CAVALIER | 2,371 | 1,513 | 618 | 73 | 167 | 895 R | 63.8% | 26.1% | 3.1% |
| 5,757 | DICKEY | 2,786 | 1,853 | 806 | 52 | 75 | 1,047 R | 66.5% | 28.9% | 1.9% |
| 2,283 | DIVIDE | 794 | 443 | 306 | 24 | 21 | 137 R | 55.8% | 38.5% | 3.0% |
| 3,600 | DUNN | 1,728 | 1,124 | 474 | 54 | 76 | 650 R | 65.0% | 27.4% | 3.1% |
| 2,757 | EDDY | 1,268 | 703 | 458 | 36 | 71 | 245 R | 55.4% | 36.1% | 2.8% |
| 4,331 | EMMONS | 1,992 | 1,430 | 405 | 42 | 115 | 1,025 R | 71.8% | 20.3% | 2.1% |
| 3,759 | FOSTER | 1,743 | 1,172 | 474 | 46 | 51 | 698 R | 67.2% | 27.2% | 2.6% |
| 1,924 | GOLDEN VALLEY | 812 | 611 | 156 | 26 | 19 | 455 R | 75.2% | 19.2% | 3.2% |
| 66,109 | GRAND FORKS | 28,385 | 15,875 | 10,593 | 1,367 | 550 | 5,282 R | 55.9% | 37.3% | 4.8% |
| 2,841 | GRANT | 1,427 | 1,077 | 235 | 27 | 88 | 842 R | 75.5% | 16.5% | 1.9% |
| 2,754 | GRIGGS | 1,469 | 920 | 484 | 19 | 46 | 436 R | 62.6% | 32.9% | 1.3% |
| 2,715 | HETTINGER | 1,519 | 1,057 | 353 | 44 | 65 | 704 R | 69.6% | 23.2% | 2.9% |
| 2,753 | KIDDER | 1,276 | 837 | 283 | 29 | 127 | 554 R | 65.6% | 22.2% | 2.3% |
| 4,701 | LA MOURE | 2,468 | 1,590 | 689 | 50 | 139 | 901 R | 64.4% | 27.9% | 2.0% |
| 2,308 | LOGAN | 1,145 | 812 | 223 | 14 | 96 | 589 R | 70.9% | 19.5% | 1.2% |
| 5,987 | MCHENRY | 2,737 | 1,682 | 888 | 79 | 88 | 794 R | 61.5% | 32.4% | 2.9% |
| 3,390 | MCINTOSH | 1,626 | 1,178 | 350 | 25 | 73 | 828 R | 72.4% | 21.5% | 1.5% |
| 5,737 | MCKENZIE | 2,364 | 1,634 | 653 | 45 | 32 | 981 R | 69.1% | 27.6% | 1.9% |
| 9,311 | MCLEAN | 4,646 | 2,891 | 1,465 | 117 | 173 | 1,426 R | 62.2% | 31.5% | 2.5% |
| 8,644 | MERCER | 4,353 | 2,984 | 1,011 | 157 | 201 | 1,973 R | 68.6% | 23.2% | 3.6% |
| 25,303 | MORTON | 11,223 | 6,993 | 3,439 | 341 | 450 | 3,554 R | 62.3% | 30.6% | 3.0% |
| 6,631 | MOUNTRAIL | 2,896 | 1,466 | 1,256 | 105 | 69 | 210 R | 50.6% | 43.4% | 3.6% |
| 3,715 | NELSON | 1,840 | 1,031 | 687, | 49 | 73 | 344 R | 56.0% | 37.3% | 2.7% |
| 2,065 | OLIVER | 1,051 | 709 | 244 | 36 | 62 | 465 R | 67.5% | 23.2% | 3.4% |
| 8,585 | PEMBINA | 3,779 | 2,430 | 1,093 | 110 | 146 | 1,337 R | 64.3% | 28.9% | 2.9% |
| 4,675 | PIERCE | 1,971 | 1,348 | 500 | 54 | 69 | 848 R | 68.4% | 25.4% | 2.7% |
| 12,066 | RAMSEY | 4,977 | 3,005 | 1,658 | 161 | 153 | 1,347 R | 60.4% | 33.3% | 3.2% |
| 5,890 | RANSOM | 2,719 | 1,488 | 1,080 | 67 | 84 | 408 R | 54.7% | 39.7% | 2.5% |
| 2,610 | RENVILLE | 1,332 | 820 | 443 | 37 | 32 | 377 R | 61.6% | 33.3% | 2.8% |
| 17,998 | RICHLAND | 8,015 | 4,999 | 2,490 | 240 | 286 | 2,509 R | 62.4% | 31.1% | 3.0% |
| 13,674 | ROLETTE | 4,398 | 1,416 | 2,681 | 137 | 164 | 1,265 D | 32.2% | 61.0% | 3.1% |
| 4,366 | SARGENT | 2,184 | 1,103 | 959 | 48 | 74 | 144 R | 50.5% | 43.9% | 2.2% |
| 1,710 | SHERIDAN | 928 | 707 | 161 | 13 | 47 | 546 R | 76.2% | 17.3% | 1.4% |
| 4,044 | SIOUX | 1,041 | 269 | 724 | 16 | 32 | 455 D | 25.8% | 69.5% | 1.5% |
| 767 | SLOPE | 442 | 316 | 85 | 17 | 24 | 231 R | 71.5% | 19.2% | 3.8% |
| 22,636 | STARK | 9,777 | 6,387 | 2,784 | 301 | 305 | 3,603 R | 65.3% | 28.5% | 3.1% |
| 2,258 | STEELE | 1,210 | 655 | 475 | 28 | 52 | 180 R | 54.1% | 39.3% | 2.3% |
| 21,908 | STUTSMAN | 9,118 | 5,488 | 3,067 | 256 | 307 | 2,421 R | 60.2% | 33.6% | 2.8% |
| 2,876 | TOWNER | 1,189 | 694 | 410 | 31 | 54 | 284 R | 58.4% | 34.5% | 2.6% |
| 8,477 | TRAILL | 4,112 | 2,392 | 1,512 | 95 | 113 | 880 R | 58.2% | 36.8% | 2.3% |
| 12,389 | WALSH | 5,182 | 3,099 | 1,743 | 107 | 233 | 1,356 R | 59.8% | 33.6% | 2.1% |
| 58,795 | WARD | 22,482 | 13,997 | 7,533 | 598 | 354 | 6,464 R | 62.3% | 33.5% | 2.7% |
| 5,102 | WELLS | 2,410 | 1,610 | 661 | 51 | 88 | 949 R | 66.8% | 27.4% | 2.1% |
| 19,761 | WILLIAMS | 7,807 | 5,187 | 2,330 | 157 | 133 | 2,857 R | 66.4% | 29.8% | 2.0% |
| 642,200 | TOTAL | 288,256 | 174,852 | 95,284 | 9,486 | 8,634 | 79,568 R | 60.7% | 33.1% | 3.3% |

# NORTH DAKOTA

## PRESIDENT 1996

| 1995 Census Pop. Est. | County | Total Vote | Republican | Democratic | Reform (Perot) | Other | Rep.-Dem. Plurality | Percentage of Total Vote Rep. | Dem. | Reform |
|---|---|---|---|---|---|---|---|---|---|---|
| 2,593 | ADAMS | 1,152 | 575 | 366 | 200 | 11 | 209 R | 49.9% | 31.8% | 17.4% |
| 12,042 | BARNES | 5,468 | 2,449 | 2,317 | 666 | 36 | 132 R | 44.8% | 42.4% | 12.2% |
| 6,990 | BENSON | 2,172 | 850 | 1,059 | 252 | 11 | 209 D | 39.1% | 48.8% | 11.6% |
| 1,157 | BILLINGS | 507 | 281 | 116 | 107 | 3 | 165 R | 55.4% | 22.9% | 21.1% |
| 7,706 | BOTTINEAU | 3,519 | 1,682 | 1,280 | 536 | 21 | 402 R | 47.8% | 36.4% | 15.2% |
| 3,229 | BOWMAN | 1,473 | 710 | 489 | 261 | 13 | 221 R | 48.2% | 33.2% | 17.7% |
| 2,501 | BURKE | 1,089 | 483 | 416 | 176 | 14 | 67 R | 44.4% | 38.2% | 16.2% |
| 64,807 | BURLEIGH | 29,890 | 15,464 | 10,679 | 3,535 | 212 | 4,785 R | 51.7% | 35.7% | 11.8% |
| 111,440 | CASS | 50,471 | 24,238 | 21,693 | 4,116 | 424 | 2,545 R | 48.0% | 43.0% | 8.2% |
| 5,474 | CAVALIER | 2,483 | 1,188 | 941 | 326 | 28 | 247 R | 47.8% | 37.9% | 13.1% |
| 5,775 | DICKEY | 2,665 | 1,418 | 953 | 276 | 18 | 465 R | 53.2% | 35.8% | 10.4% |
| 2,558 | DIVIDE | 1,340 | 488 | 637 | 209 | 6 | 149 D | 36.4% | 47.5% | 15.6% |
| 3,790 | DUNN | 1,743 | 830 | 587 | 304 | 22 | 243 R | 47.6% | 33.7% | 17.4% |
| 2,851 | EDDY | 1,281 | 517 | 553 | 201 | 10 | 36 D | 40.4% | 43.2% | 15.7% |
| 4,564 | EMMONS | 2,144 | 1,148 | 544 | 441 | 11 | 604 R | 53.5% | 25.4% | 20.6% |
| 3,892 | FOSTER | 1,744 | 801 | 664 | 265 | 14 | 137 R | 45.9% | 38.1% | 15.2% |
| 1,962 | GOLDEN VALLEY | 924 | 520 | 235 | 163 | 6 | 285 R | 56.3% | 25.4% | 17.6% |
| 71,879 | GRAND FORKS | 25,836 | 11,606 | 11,376 | 2,663 | 191 | 230 R | 44.9% | 44.0% | 10.3% |
| 3,235 | GRANT | 1,369 | 760 | 300 | 295 | 14 | 460 R | 55.5% | 21.9% | 21.5% |
| 3,036 | GRIGGS | 1,571 | 731 | 670 | 162 | 8 | 61 R | 46.5% | 42.6% | 10.3% |
| 3,020 | HETTINGER | 1,426 | 765 | 418 | 238 | 5 | 347 R | 53.6% | 29.3% | 16.7% |
| 3,036 | KIDDER | 1,382 | 691 | 434 | 242 | 15 | 257 R | 50.0% | 31.4% | 17.5% |
| 5,026 | LA MOURE | 2,385 | 1,220 | 880 | 276 | 9 | 340 R | 51.2% | 36.9% | 11.6% |
| 2,477 | LOGAN | 1,328 | 705 | 360 | 254 | 9 | 345 R | 53.1% | 27.1% | 19.1% |
| 6,322 | MCHENRY | 2,756 | 1,187 | 1,096 | 453 | 20 | 91 R | 43.1% | 39.8% | 16.4% |
| 3,649 | MCINTOSH | 1,781 | 1,005 | 470 | 295 | 11 | 535 R | 56.4% | 26.4% | 16.6% |
| 5,779 | MCKENZIE | 2,703 | 1,338 | 928 | 428 | 9 | 410 R | 49.5% | 34.3% | 15.8% |
| 9,847 | MCLEAN | 4,380 | 1,988 | 1,759 | 618 | 15 | 229 R | 45.4% | 40.2% | 14.1% |
| 9,466 | MERCER | 4,042 | 1,953 | 1,300 | 764 | 25 | 653 R | 48.3% | 32.2% | 18.9% |
| 24,633 | MORTON | 10,070 | 4,699 | 3,745 | 1,566 | 60 | 954 R | 46.7% | 37.2% | 15.6% |
| 6,797 | MOUNTRAIL | 2,615 | 965 | 1,277 | 360 | 13 | 312 D | 36.9% | 48.8% | 13.8% |
| 4,065 | NELSON | 1,799 | 745 | 827 | 206 | 21 | 82 D | 41.4% | 46.0% | 11.5% |
| 2,186 | OLIVER | 1,022 | 499 | 333 | 183 | 7 | 166 R | 48.8% | 32.6% | 17.9% |
| 8,791 | PEMBINA | 3,294 | 1,678 | 1,191 | 400 | 25 | 487 R | 50.9% | 36.2% | 12.1% |
| 4,675 | PIERCE | 1,974 | 1,017 | 671 | 270 | 16 | 346 R | 51.5% | 34.0% | 13.7% |
| 12,680 | RAMSEY | 4,774 | 2,077 | 2,123 | 549 | 25 | 46 D | 43.5% | 44.5% | 11.5% |
| 5,887 | RANSOM | 2,435 | 920 | 1,199 | 303 | 13 | 279 D | 37.8% | 49.2% | 12.4% |
| 2,843 | RENVILLE | 1,354 | 576 | 562 | 210 | 6 | 14 R | 42.5% | 41.5% | 15.5% |
| 18,177 | RICHLAND | 7,069 | 3,345 | 2,890 | 782 | 52 | 455 R | 47.3% | 40.9% | 11.1% |
| 13,779 | ROLETTE | 3,601 | 823 | 2,299 | 448 | 31 | 1,476 D | 22.9% | 63.8% | 12.4% |
| 4,564 | SARGENT | 2,067 | 814 | 1,003 | 241 | 9 | 189 D | 39.4% | 48.5% | 11.7% |
| 1,895 | SHERIDAN | 941 | 566 | 252 | 121 | 2 | 314 R | 60.1% | 26.8% | 12.9% |
| 3,994 | SIOUX | 690 | 207 | 393 | 82 | 8 | 186 D | 30.0% | 57.0% | 11.9% |
| 821 | SLOPE | 445 | 260 | 123 | 60 | 2 | 137 R | 58.4% | 27.6% | 13.5% |
| 22,434 | STARK | 8,705 | 4,086 | 3,095 | 1,456 | 68 | 991 R | 46.9% | 35.6% | 16.7% |
| 2,312 | STEELE | 1,225 | 486 | 620 | 115 | 4 | 134 D | 39.7% | 50.6% | 9.4% |
| 21,457 | STUTSMAN | 8,593 | 3,784 | 3,589 | 1,141 | 79 | 195 R | 44.0% | 41.8% | 13.3% |
| 3,212 | TOWNER | 1,387 | 542 | 649 | 187 | 9 | 107 D | 39.1% | 46.8% | 13.5% |
| 8,695 | TRAILL | 4,042 | 1,820 | 1,822 | 380 | 20 | 2 D | 45.0% | 45.1% | 9.4% |
| 12,789 | WALSH | 4,939 | 2,222 | 2,082 | 599 | 36 | 140 R | 45.0% | 42.2% | 12.1% |
| 58,778 | WARD | 21,964 | 10,546 | 8,660 | 2,587 | 171 | 1,886 R | 48.0% | 39.4% | 11.8% |
| 5,254 | WELLS | 2,542 | 1,192 | 962 | 373 | 15 | 230 R | 46.9% | 37.8% | 14.7% |
| 20,546 | WILLIAMS | 7,840 | 3,590 | 3,018 | 1,174 | 58 | 572 R | 45.8% | 38.5% | 15.0% |
| 641,367 | TOTAL | 266,411 | 125,050 | 106,905 | 32,515 | 1,941 | 18,145 R | 46.9% | 40.1% | 12.2% |

# NORTH DAKOTA

## PRESIDENT 1992

| 1990 Census Population | County | Total Vote | Republican | Democratic | Perot | Other | Plurality | Percentage Total Vote Rep. | Dem. | Perot |
|---|---|---|---|---|---|---|---|---|---|---|
| 3,174 | ADAMS | 1,626 | 647 | 469 | 499 | 11 | 148 R | 39.8% | 28.8% | 30.7% |
| 12,545 | BARNES | 6,449 | 2,728 | 2,124 | 1,568 | 29 | 604 R | 42.3% | 32.9% | 24.3% |
| 7,198 | BENSON | 2,625 | 874 | 1,126 | 610 | 15 | 252 D | 33.3% | 42.9% | 23.2% |
| 1,108 | BILLINGS | 678 | 279 | 123 | 270 | 6 | 9 R | 41.2% | 18.1% | 39.8% |
| 8,011 | BOTTINEAU | 4,104 | 1,787 | 1,266 | 1,036 | 15 | 521 R | 43.5% | 30.8% | 25.2% |
| 3,596 | BOWMAN | 1,907 | 712 | 506 | 678 | 11 | 34 R | 37.3% | 26.5% | 35.6% |
| 3,002 | BURKE | 1,524 | 551 | 458 | 506 | 9 | 45 R | 36.2% | 30.1% | 33.2% |
| 60,131 | BURLEIGH | 32,384 | 16,484 | 8,940 | 6,780 | 180 | 7,544 R | 50.9% | 27.6% | 20.9% |
| 102,874 | CASS | 53,116 | 25,312 | 18,077 | 9,513 | 214 | 7,235 R | 47.7% | 34.0% | 17.9% |
| 6,064 | CAVALIER | 3,126 | 1,527 | 866 | 723 | 10 | 661 R | 48.8% | 27.7% | 23.1% |
| 6,107 | DICKEY | 3,060 | 1,514 | 918 | 616 | 12 | 596 R | 49.5% | 30.0% | 20.1% |
| 2,899 | DIVIDE | 1,620 | 515 | 634 | 456 | 15 | 119 D | 31.8% | 39.1% | 28.1% |
| 4,005 | DUNN | 2,105 | 784 | 667 | 637 | 17 | 117 R | 37.2% | 31.7% | 30.3% |
| 2,951 | EDDY | 1,615 | 591 | 575 | 432 | 17 | 16 R | 36.6% | 35.6% | 26.7% |
| 4,830 | EMMONS | 2,430 | 1,047 | 595 | 774 | 14 | 273 R | 43.1% | 24.5% | 31.9% |
| 3,983 | FOSTER | 1,940 | 803 | 565 | 556 | 16 | 238 R | 41.4% | 29.1% | 28.7% |
| 2,108 | GOLDEN VALLEY | 1,114 | 503 | 255 | 352 | 4 | 151 R | 45.2% | 22.9% | 31.6% |
| 70,683 | GRAND FORKS | 31,104 | 13,705 | 10,930 | 6,349 | 120 | 2,775 R | 44.1% | 35.1% | 20.4% |
| 3,549 | GRANT | 1,959 | 900 | 415 | 629 | 15 | 271 R | 45.9% | 21.2% | 32.1% |
| 3,303 | GRIGGS | 1,756 | 773 | 647 | 330 | 6 | 126 R | 44.0% | 36.8% | 18.8% |
| 3,445 | HETTINGER | 1,838 | 854 | 465 | 500 | 19 | 354 R | 46.5% | 25.3% | 27.2% |
| 3,332 | KIDDER | 1,711 | 739 | 468 | 489 | 15 | 250 R | 43.2% | 27.4% | 28.6% |
| 5,383 | LA MOURE | 2,763 | 1,270 | 797 | 679 | 17 | 473 R | 46.0% | 28.8% | 24.6% |
| 2,847 | LOGAN | 1,486 | 703 | 383 | 390 | 10 | 313 R | 47.3% | 25.8% | 26.2% |
| 6,528 | MCHENRY | 3,396 | 1,321 | 1,173 | 886 | 16 | 148 R | 38.9% | 34.5% | 26.1% |
| 4,021 | MCINTOSH | 2,054 | 1,134 | 450 | 454 | 16 | 680 R | 55.2% | 21.9% | 22.1% |
| 6,383 | MCKENZIE | 3,090 | 1,324 | 787 | 969 | 10 | 355 R | 42.8% | 25.5% | 31.4% |
| 10,457 | MCLEAN | 5,303 | 2,124 | 1,808 | 1,330 | 41 | 316 R | 40.1% | 34.1% | 25.1% |
| 9,808 | MERCER | 5,017 | 2,274 | 1,323 | 1,378 | 42 | 896 R | 45.3% | 26.4% | 27.5% |
| 23,700 | MORTON | 11,522 | 5,042 | 3,594 | 2,787 | 99 | 1,448 R | 43.8% | 31.2% | 24.2% |
| 7,021 | MOUNTRAIL | 3,289 | 1,017 | 1,393 | 861 | 18 | 376 D | 30.9% | 42.4% | 26.2% |
| 4,410 | NELSON | 2,206 | 864 | 841 | 486 | 15 | 23 R | 39.2% | 38.1% | 22.0% |
| 2,381 | OLIVER | 1,228 | 503 | 306 | 407 | 12 | 96 R | 41.0% | 24.9% | 33.1% |
| 9,238 | PEMBINA | 4,127 | 1,917 | 1,186 | 991 | 33 | 731 R | 46.5% | 28.7% | 24.0% |
| 5,052 | PIERCE | 2,431 | 1,099 | 761 | 554 | 17 | 338 R | 45.2% | 31.3% | 22.8% |
| 12,681 | RAMSEY | 6,054 | 2,516 | 2,008 | 1,507 | 23 | 508 R | 41.6% | 33.2% | 24.9% |
| 5,921 | RANSOM | 2,903 | 1,102 | 1,166 | 625 | 10 | 64 D | 38.0% | 40.2% | 21.5% |
| 3,160 | RENVILLE | 1,670 | 655 | 580 | 429 | 6 | 75 R | 39.2% | 34.7% | 25.7% |
| 18,148 | RICHLAND | 8,301 | 3,873 | 2,688 | 1,698 | 42 | 1,185 R | 46.7% | 32.4% | 20.5% |
| 12,772 | ROLETTE | 3,606 | 895 | 2,002 | 660 | 49 | 1,107 D | 24.8% | 55.5% | 18.3% |
| 4,549 | SARGENT | 2,254 | 816 | 961 | 463 | 14 | 145 D | 36.2% | 42.6% | 20.5% |
| 2,148 | SHERIDAN | 1,175 | 589 | 276 | 304 | 6 | 285 R | 50.1% | 23.5% | 25.9% |
| 3,761 | SIOUX | 984 | 264 | 463 | 244 | 13 | 199 D | 26.8% | 47.1% | 24.8% |
| 907 | SLOPE | 535 | 226 | 145 | 162 | 2 | 64 R | 42.2% | 27.1% | 30.3% |
| 22,832 | STARK | 10,678 | 4,491 | 3,003 | 3,123 | 61 | 1,368 R | 42.1% | 28.1% | 29.2% |
| 2,420 | STEELE | 1,370 | 503 | 598 | 267 | 2 | 95 D | 36.7% | 43.6% | 19.5% |
| 22,241 | STUTSMAN | 10,001 | 4,039 | 3,313 | 2,580 | 69 | 726 R | 40.4% | 33.1% | 25.8% |
| 3,627 | TOWNER | 1,757 | 600 | 748 | 402 | 7 | 148 D | 34.1% | 42.6% | 22.9% |
| 8,752 | TRAILL | 4,553 | 2,019 | 1,638 | 875 | 21 | 381 R | 44.3% | 36.0% | 19.2% |
| 13,840 | WALSH | 5,904 | 2,544 | 1,936 | 1,384 | 40 | 608 R | 43.1% | 32.8% | 23.4% |
| 57,921 | WARD | 25,852 | 12,056 | 7,856 | 5,856 | 84 | 4,200 R | 46.6% | 30.4% | 22.7% |
| 5,864 | WELLS | 2,916 | 1,171 | 888 | 850 | 7 | 283 R | 40.2% | 30.5% | 29.1% |
| 21,129 | WILLIAMS | 9,917 | 3,664 | 3,008 | 3,180 | 65 | 484 R | 36.9% | 30.3% | 32.1% |
| 638,800 | TOTAL | 308,133 | 136,244 | 99,168 | 71,084 | 1,637 | 37,076 R | 44.2% | 32.2% | 23.1% |

# NORTH DAKOTA

## PRESIDENT 1988

| 1980 Census Population | County | Total Vote | Republican | Democratic | Other | Rep.-Dem. Plurality | Percentage | | | |
|---|---|---|---|---|---|---|---|---|---|---|
| | | | | | | | Total Vote | | Major Vote | |
| | | | | | | | Rep. | Dem. | Rep. | Dem. |
| 3,584 | ADAMS | 1,737 | 1,018 | 708 | 11 | 310 R | 58.6% | 40.8% | 59.0% | 41.0% |
| 13,960 | BARNES | 6,546 | 3,631 | 2,858 | 57 | 773 R | 55.5% | 43.7% | 56.0% | 44.0% |
| 7,944 | BENSON | 3,031 | 1,316 | 1,691 | 24 | 375 D | 43.4% | 55.8% | 43.8% | 56.2% |
| 1,138 | BILLINGS | 659 | 437 | 211 | 11 | 226 R | 66.3% | 32.0% | 67.4% | 32.6% |
| 9,239 | BOTTINEAU | 4,251 | 2,530 | 1,684 | 37 | 846 R | 59.5% | 39.6% | 60.0% | 40.0% |
| 4,229 | BOWMAN | 1,867 | 1,111 | 737 | 19 | 374 R | 59.5% | 39.5% | 60.1% | 39.9% |
| 3,822 | BURKE | 1,690 | 971 | 693 | 26 | 278 R | 57.5% | 41.0% | 58.4% | 41.6% |
| 54,811 | BURLEIGH | 29,084 | 18,000 | 10,760 | 324 | 7,240 R | 61.9% | 37.0% | 62.6% | 37.4% |
| 88,247 | CASS | 49,137 | 26,699 | 22,107 | 331 | 4,592 R | 54.3% | 45.0% | 54.7% | 45.3% |
| 7,636 | CAVALIER | 3,457 | 2,096 | 1,333 | 28 | 763 R | 60.6% | 38.6% | 61.1% | 38.9% |
| 7,207 | DICKEY | 3,336 | 2,064 | 1,249 | 23 | 815 R | 61.9% | 37.4% | 62.3% | 37.7% |
| 3,494 | DIVIDE | 1,768 | 869 | 875 | 24 | 6 D | 49.2% | 49.5% | 49.8% | 50.2% |
| 4,627 | DUNN | 2,178 | 1,263 | 892 | 23 | 371 R | 58.0% | 41.0% | 58.6% | 41.4% |
| 3,554 | EDDY | 1,658 | 891 | 748 | 19 | 143 R | 53.7% | 45.1% | 54.4% | 45.6% |
| 5,877 | EMMONS | 2,596 | 1,634 | 925 | 37 | 709 R | 62.9% | 35.6% | 63.9% | 36.1% |
| 4,611 | FOSTER | 2,070 | 1,218 | 837 | 15 | 381 R | 58.8% | 40.4% | 59.3% | 40.7% |
| 2,391 | GOLDEN VALLEY | 1,183 | 781 | 388 | 14 | 393 R | 66.0% | 32.8% | 66.8% | 33.2% |
| 66,100 | GRAND FORKS | 27,531 | 14,801 | 12,494 | 236 | 2,307 R | 53.8% | 45.4% | 54.2% | 45.8% |
| 4,274 | GRANT | 2,043 | 1,351 | 654 | 38 | 697 R | 66.1% | 32.0% | 67.4% | 32.6% |
| 3,714 | GRIGGS | 1,885 | 1,020 | 846 | 19 | 174 R | 54.1% | 44.9% | 54.7% | 45.3% |
| 4,275 | HETTINGER | 2,111 | 1,395 | 698 | 18 | 697 R | 66.1% | 33.1% | 66.7% | 33.3% |
| 3,833 | KIDDER | 1,761 | 1,039 | 678 | 44 | 361 R | 59.0% | 38.5% | 60.5% | 39.5% |
| 6,473 | LA MOURE | 2,901 | 1,642 | 1,223 | 36 | 419 R | 56.6% | 42.2% | 57.3% | 42.7% |
| 3,493 | LOGAN | 1,671 | 1,111 | 540 | 20 | 571 R | 66.5% | 32.3% | 67.3% | 32.7% |
| 7,858 | MCHENRY | 3,583 | 1,888 | 1,665 | 30 | 223 R | 52.7% | 46.5% | 53.1% | 46.9% |
| 4,800 | MCINTOSH | 2,347 | 1,726 | 598 | 23 | 1,128 R | 73.5% | 25.5% | 74.3% | 25.7% |
| 7,132 | MCKENZIE | 3,253 | 1,949 | 1,273 | 31 | 676 R | 59.9% | 39.1% | 60.5% | 39.5% |
| 12,383 | MCLEAN | 5,396 | 2,906 | 2,428 | 62 | 478 R | 53.9% | 45.0% | 54.5% | 45.5% |
| 9,404 | MERCER | 4,902 | 3,013 | 1,843 | 46 | 1,170 R | 61.5% | 37.6% | 62.0% | 38.0% |
| 25,177 | MORTON | 10,447 | 5,588 | 4,708 | 151 | 880 R | 53.5% | 45.1% | 54.3% | 45.7% |
| 7,679 | MOUNTRAIL | 3,458 | 1,443 | 1,977 | 38 | 534 D | 41.7% | 57.2% | 42.2% | 57.8% |
| 5,233 | NELSON | 2,243 | 1,078 | 1,151 | 14 | 73 D | 48.1% | 51.3% | 48.4% | 51.6% |
| 2,495 | OLIVER | 1,237 | 696 | 526 | 15 | 170 R | 56.3% | 42.5% | 57.0% | 43.0% |
| 10,399 | PEMBINA | 4,149 | 2,471 | 1,616 | 62 | 855 R | 59.6% | 38.9% | 60.5% | 39.5% |
| 6,166 | PIERCE | 2,477 | 1,422 | 1,008 | 47 | 414 R | 57.4% | 40.7% | 58.5% | 41.5% |
| 13,048 | RAMSEY | 5,841 | 3,103 | 2,665 | 73 | 438 R | 53.1% | 45.6% | 53.8% | 46.2% |
| 6,698 | RANSOM | 2,858 | 1,362 | 1,459 | 37 | 97 D | 47.7% | 51.0% | 48.3% | 51.7% |
| 3,608 | RENVILLE | 1,750 | 893 | 837 | 20 | 56 R | 51.0% | 47.8% | 51.6% | 48.4% |
| 19,207 | RICHLAND | 8,274 | 4,670 | 3,523 | 81 | 1,147 R | 56.4% | 42.6% | 57.0% | 43.0% |
| 12,177 | ROLETTE | 3,606 | 1,126 | 2,426 | 54 | 1,300 D | 31.2% | 67.3% | 31.7% | 68.3% |
| 5,512 | SARGENT | 2,436 | 1,119 | 1,306 | 11 | 187 D | 45.9% | 53.6% | 46.1% | 53.9% |
| 2,819 | SHERIDAN | 1,318 | 885 | 428 | 5 | 457 R | 67.1% | 32.5% | 67.4% | 32.6% |
| 3,620 | SIOUX | 1,042 | 325 | 701 | 16 | 376 D | 31.2% | 67.3% | 31.7% | 68.3% |
| 1,157 | SLOPE | 530 | 315 | 202 | 13 | 113 R | 59.4% | 38.1% | 60.9% | 39.1% |
| 23,697 | STARK | 10,003 | 6,137 | 3,678 | 188 | 2,459 R | 61.4% | 36.8% | 62.5% | 37.5% |
| 3,106 | STEELE | 1,595 | 690 | 895 | 10 | 205 D | 43.3% | 56.1% | 43.5% | 56.5% |
| 24,154 | STUTSMAN | 9,669 | 5,375 | 4,214 | 80 | 1,161 R | 55.6% | 43.6% | 56.1% | 43.9% |
| 4,052 | TOWNER | 1,934 | 946 | 970 | 18 | 24 D | 48.9% | 50.2% | 49.4% | 50.6% |
| 9,624 | TRAILL | 4,559 | 2,562 | 1,940 | 57 | 622 R | 56.2% | 42.6% | 56.9% | 43.1% |
| 15,371 | WALSH | 5,966 | 3,250 | 2,646 | 70 | 604 R | 54.5% | 44.4% | 55.1% | 44.9% |
| 58,392 | WARD | 23,228 | 13,179 | 9,906 | 143 | 3,273 R | 56.7% | 42.6% | 57.1% | 42.9% |
| 6,979 | WELLS | 3,241 | 1,901 | 1,317 | 23 | 584 R | 58.7% | 40.6% | 59.1% | 40.9% |
| 22,237 | WILLIAMS | 9,768 | 5,653 | 4,004 | 111 | 1,649 R | 57.9% | 41.0% | 58.5% | 41.5% |
| 652,717 | TOTAL | 297,261 | 166,559 | 127,739 | 2,963 | 38,820 R | 56.0% | 43.0% | 56.6% | 43.4% |

# NORTH DAKOTA

## PRESIDENT 1984

| 1980 Census Population | County | Total Vote | Republican | Democratic | Other | Rep.-Dem. Plurality | | Percentage | | | |
|---|---|---|---|---|---|---|---|---|---|---|---|
| | | | | | | | | Total Vote | | Major Vote | |
| | | | | | | | | Rep. | Dem. | Rep. | Dem. |
| 3,584 | ADAMS | 1,900 | 1,343 | 530 | 27 | 813 | R | 70.7% | 27.9% | 71.7% | 28.3% |
| 13,960 | BARNES | 6,925 | 4,348 | 2,507 | 70 | 1,841 | R | 62.8% | 36.2% | 63.4% | 36.6% |
| 7,944 | BENSON | 3,363 | 1,729 | 1,599 | 35 | 130 | R | 51.4% | 47.5% | 52.0% | 48.0% |
| 1,138 | BILLINGS | 653 | 505 | 133 | 15 | 372 | R | 77.3% | 20.4% | 79.2% | 20.8% |
| 9,239 | BOTTINEAU | 4,688 | 3,356 | 1,279 | 53 | 2,077 | R | 71.6% | 27.3% | 72.4% | 27.6% |
| 4,229 | BOWMAN | 2,149 | 1,559 | 562 | 28 | 997 | R | 72.5% | 26.2% | 73.5% | 26.5% |
| 3,822 | BURKE | 1,869 | 1,298 | 543 | 28 | 755 | R | 69.4% | 29.1% | 70.5% | 29.5% |
| 54,811 | BURLEIGH | 29,176 | 19,913 | 8,781 | 482 | 11,132 | R | 68.3% | 30.1% | 69.4% | 30.6% |
| 88,247 | CASS | 47,629 | 29,221 | 18,054 | 354 | 11,167 | R | 61.4% | 37.9% | 61.8% | 38.2% |
| 7,636 | CAVALIER | 3,804 | 2,661 | 1,110 | 33 | 1,551 | R | 70.0% | 29.2% | 70.6% | 29.4% |
| 7,207 | DICKEY | 3,546 | 2,460 | 1,051 | 35 | 1,409 | R | 69.4% | 29.6% | 70.1% | 29.9% |
| 3,494 | DIVIDE | 1,840 | 1,165 | 626 | 49 | 539 | R | 63.3% | 34.0% | 65.0% | 35.0% |
| 4,627 | DUNN | 2,324 | 1,583 | 716 | 25 | 867 | R | 68.1% | 30.8% | 68.9% | 31.1% |
| 3,554 | EDDY | 1,860 | 1,049 | 796 | 15 | 253 | R | 56.4% | 42.8% | 56.9% | 43.1% |
| 5,877 | EMMONS | 2,566 | 1,885 | 620 | 61 | 1,265 | R | 73.5% | 24.2% | 75.2% | 24.8% |
| 4,611 | FOSTER | 2,214 | 1,422 | 765 | 27 | 657 | R | 64.2% | 34.6% | 65.0% | 35.0% |
| 2,391 | GOLDEN VALLEY | 1,319 | 964 | 325 | 30 | 639 | R | 73.1% | 24.6% | 74.8% | 25.2% |
| 66,100 | GRAND FORKS | 26,191 | 15,898 | 10,050 | 243 | 5,848 | R | 60.7% | 38.4% | 61.3% | 38.7% |
| 4,274 | GRANT | 2,145 | 1,607 | 507 | 31 | 1,100 | R | 74.9% | 23.6% | 76.0% | 24.0% |
| 3,714 | GRIGGS | 2,094 | 1,254 | 828 | 12 | 426 | R | 59.9% | 39.5% | 60.2% | 39.8% |
| 4,275 | HETTINGER | 2,202 | 1,646 | 524 | 32 | 1,122 | R | 74.8% | 23.8% | 75.9% | 24.1% |
| 3,833 | KIDDER | 1,807 | 1,240 | 506 | 61 | 734 | R | 68.6% | 28.0% | 71.0% | 29.0% |
| 6,473 | LA MOURE | 3,108 | 1,978 | 1,086 | 44 | 892 | R | 63.6% | 34.9% | 64.6% | 35.4% |
| 3,493 | LOGAN | 1,676 | 1,222 | 401 | 53 | 821 | R | 72.9% | 23.9% | 75.3% | 24.7% |
| 7,858 | MCHENRY | 3,801 | 2,485 | 1,283 | 33 | 1,202 | R | 65.4% | 33.8% | 66.0% | 34.0% |
| 4,800 | MCINTOSH | 2,513 | 2,047 | 427 | 39 | 1,620 | R | 81.5% | 17.0% | 82.7% | 17.3% |
| 7,132 | MCKENZIE | 3,627 | 2,610 | 974 | 43 | 1,636 | R | 72.0% | 26.9% | 72.8% | 27.2% |
| 12,383 | MCLEAN | 5,847 | 3,673 | 2,062 | 112 | 1,611 | R | 62.8% | 35.3% | 64.0% | 36.0% |
| 9,404 | MERCER | 5,510 | 3,705 | 1,729 | 76 | 1,976 | R | 67.2% | 31.4% | 68.2% | 31.8% |
| 25,177 | MORTON | 11,356 | 7,146 | 3,996 | 214 | 3,150 | R | 62.9% | 35.2% | 64.1% | 35.9% |
| 7,679 | MOUNTRAIL | 3,555 | 1,959 | 1,565 | 31 | 394 | R | 55.1% | 44.0% | 55.6% | 44.4% |
| 5,233 | NELSON | 2,513 | 1,445 | 1,026 | 42 | 419 | R | 57.5% | 40.8% | 58.5% | 41.5% |
| 2,495 | OLIVER | 1,357 | 915 | 419 | 23 | 496 | R | 67.4% | 30.9% | 68.6% | 31.4% |
| 10,399 | PEMBINA | 4,387 | 2,895 | 1,367 | 125 | 1,528 | R | 66.0% | 31.2% | 67.9% | 32.1% |
| 6,166 | PIERCE | 2,626 | 1,883 | 691 | 52 | 1,192 | R | 71.7% | 26.3% | 73.2% | 26.8% |
| 13,048 | RAMSEY | 6,553 | 4,150 | 2,304 | 99 | 1,846 | R | 63.3% | 35.2% | 64.3% | 35.7% |
| 6,698 | RANSOM | 2,973 | 1,706 | 1,222 | 45 | 484 | R | 57.4% | 41.1% | 58.3% | 41.7% |
| 3,608 | RENVILLE | 1,774 | 1,163 | 592 | 19 | 571 | R | 65.6% | 33.4% | 66.3% | 33.7% |
| 19,207 | RICHLAND | 9,133 | 5,980 | 3,047 | 106 | 2,933 | R | 65.5% | 33.4% | 66.2% | 33.8% |
| 12,177 | ROLETTE | 3,751 | 1,479 | 2,179 | 93 | 700 | D | 39.4% | 58.1% | 40.4% | 59.6% |
| 5,512 | SARGENT | 2,725 | 1,385 | 1,295 | 45 | 90 | R | 50.8% | 47.5% | 51.7% | 48.3% |
| 2,819 | SHERIDAN | 1,396 | 1,075 | 306 | 15 | 769 | R | 77.0% | 21.9% | 77.8% | 22.2% |
| 3,620 | SIOUX | 1,118 | 442 | 655 | 21 | 213 | D | 39.5% | 58.6% | 40.3% | 59.7% |
| 1,157 | SLOPE | 605 | 419 | 174 | 12 | 245 | R | 69.3% | 28.8% | 70.7% | 29.3% |
| 23,697 | STARK | 10,740 | 7,641 | 2,759 | 340 | 4,882 | R | 71.1% | 25.7% | 73.5% | 26.5% |
| 3,106 | STEELE | 1,740 | 941 | 781 | 18 | 160 | R | 54.1% | 44.9% | 54.6% | 45.4% |
| 24,154 | STUTSMAN | 10,208 | 6,591 | 3,495 | 122 | 3,096 | R | 64.6% | 34.2% | 65.3% | 34.7% |
| 4,052 | TOWNER | 2,065 | 1,242 | 789 | 34 | 453 | R | 60.1% | 38.2% | 61.2% | 38.8% |
| 9,624 | TRAILL | 4,694 | 3,037 | 1,580 | 77 | 1,457 | R | 64.7% | 33.7% | 65.8% | 34.2% |
| 15,371 | WALSH | 6,704 | 4,347 | 2,264 | 93 | 2,083 | R | 64.8% | 33.8% | 65.8% | 34.2% |
| 58,392 | WARD | 23,623 | 16,077 | 7,336 | 210 | 8,741 | R | 68.1% | 31.1% | 68.7% | 31.3% |
| 6,979 | WELLS | 3,506 | 2,426 | 1,036 | 44 | 1,390 | R | 69.2% | 29.5% | 70.1% | 29.9% |
| 22,237 | WILLIAMS | 11,523 | 8,166 | 3,177 | 180 | 4,989 | R | 70.9% | 27.6% | 72.0% | 28.0% |
| 652,717 | TOTAL | 308,971 | 200,336 | 104,429 | 4,206 | 95,907 | R | 64.8% | 33.8% | 65.7% | 34.3% |

# NORTH DAKOTA

## PRESIDENT 1980

| 1980 Census Population | County | Total Vote | Republican | Democratic | Other | Rep.-Dem. Plurality | Percentage Total Vote Rep. | Dem. | Major Vote Rep. | Dem. |
|---|---|---|---|---|---|---|---|---|---|---|
| 3,584 | ADAMS | 1,941 | 1,334 | 470 | 137 | 864 R | 68.7% | 24.2% | 73.9% | 26.1% |
| 13,960 | BARNES | 7,346 | 4,392 | 2,128 | 826 | 2,264 R | 59.8% | 29.0% | 67.4% | 32.6% |
| 7,944 | BENSON | 3,587 | 2,149 | 1,119 | 319 | 1,030 R | 59.9% | 31.2% | 65.8% | 34.2% |
| 1,138 | BILLINGS | 689 | 524 | 122 | 43 | 402 R | 76.1% | 17.7% | 81.1% | 18.9% |
| 9,239 | BOTTINEAU | 4,828 | 3,394 | 1,090 | 344 | 2,304 R | 70.3% | 22.6% | 75.7% | 24.3% |
| 4,229 | BOWMAN | 2,138 | 1,507 | 454 | 177 | 1,053 R | 70.5% | 21.2% | 76.8% | 23.2% |
| 3,822 | BURKE | 1,968 | 1,442 | 418 | 108 | 1,024 R | 73.3% | 21.2% | 77.5% | 22.5% |
| 54,811 | BURLEIGH | 27,137 | 18,437 | 6,129 | 2,571 | 12,308 R | 67.9% | 22.6% | 75.1% | 24.9% |
| 88,247 | CASS | 43,620 | 23,886 | 13,562 | 6,172 | 10,324 R | 54.8% | 31.1% | 63.8% | 36.2% |
| 7,636 | CAVALIER | 3,977 | 2,582 | 1,105 | 290 | 1,477 R | 64.9% | 27.8% | 70.0% | 30.0% |
| 7,207 | DICKEY | 3,574 | 2,455 | 917 | 202 | 1,538 R | 68.7% | 25.7% | 72.8% | 27.2% |
| 3,494 | DIVIDE | 1,918 | 1,267 | 509 | 142 | 758 R | 66.1% | 26.5% | 71.3% | 28.7% |
| 4,627 | DUNN | 2,386 | 1,706 | 532 | 148 | 1,174 R | 71.5% | 22.3% | 76.2% | 23.8% |
| 3,554 | EDDY | 1,883 | 1,153 | 539 | 191 | 614 R | 61.2% | 28.6% | 68.1% | 31.9% |
| 5,877 | EMMONS | 3,054 | 2,369 | 502 | 183 | 1,867 R | 77.6% | 16.4% | 82.5% | 17.5% |
| 4,611 | FOSTER | 2,303 | 1,534 | 586 | 183 | 948 R | 66.6% | 25.4% | 72.4% | 27.6% |
| 2,391 | GOLDEN VALLEY | 1,349 | 1,006 | 259 | 84 | 747 R | 74.6% | 19.2% | 79.5% | 20.5% |
| 66,100 | GRAND FORKS | 24,731 | 14,257 | 6,997 | 3,477 | 7,260 R | 57.6% | 28.3% | 67.1% | 32.9% |
| 4,274 | GRANT | 2,339 | 1,891 | 317 | 131 | 1,574 R | 80.8% | 13.6% | 85.6% | 14.4% |
| 3,714 | GRIGGS | 2,170 | 1,342 | 636 | 192 | 706 R | 61.8% | 29.3% | 67.8% | 32.2% |
| 4,275 | HETTINGER | 2,257 | 1,699 | 434 | 124 | 1,265 R | 75.3% | 19.2% | 79.7% | 20.3% |
| 3,833 | KIDDER | 1,913 | 1,474 | 326 | 113 | 1,148 R | 77.1% | 17.0% | 81.9% | 18.1% |
| 6,473 | LA MOURE | 3,292 | 2,136 | 850 | 306 | 1,286 R | 64.9% | 25.8% | 71.5% | 28.5% |
| 3,493 | LOGAN | 1,865 | 1,474 | 283 | 108 | 1,191 R | 79.0% | 15.2% | 83.9% | 16.1% |
| 7,858 | MCHENRY | 4,104 | 2,922 | 939 | 243 | 1,983 R | 71.2% | 22.9% | 75.7% | 24.3% |
| 4,800 | MCINTOSH | 2,873 | 2,471 | 308 | 94 | 2,163 R | 86.0% | 10.7% | 88.9% | 11.1% |
| 7,132 | MCKENZIE | 3,368 | 2,265 | 867 | 236 | 1,398 R | 67.3% | 25.7% | 72.3% | 27.7% |
| 12,383 | MCLEAN | 6,246 | 4,234 | 1,613 | 399 | 2,621 R | 67.8% | 25.8% | 72.4% | 27.6% |
| 9,404 | MERCER | 4,741 | 3,224 | 1,209 | 308 | 2,015 R | 68.0% | 25.5% | 72.7% | 27.3% |
| 25,177 | MORTON | 11,458 | 7,659 | 2,861 | 938 | 4,798 R | 66.8% | 25.0% | 72.8% | 27.2% |
| 7,679 | MOUNTRAIL | 3,587 | 2,165 | 1,183 | 239 | 982 R | 60.4% | 33.0% | 64.7% | 35.3% |
| 5,233 | NELSON | 2,595 | 1,611 | 726 | 258 | 885 R | 62.1% | 28.0% | 68.9% | 31.1% |
| 2,495 | OLIVER | 1,316 | 966 | 270 | 80 | 696 R | 73.4% | 20.5% | 78.2% | 21.8% |
| 10,399 | PEMBINA | 4,718 | 3,101 | 1,239 | 378 | 1,862 R | 65.7% | 26.3% | 71.5% | 28.5% |
| 6,166 | PIERCE | 2,988 | 2,273 | 517 | 198 | 1,756 R | 76.1% | 17.3% | 81.5% | 18.5% |
| 13,048 | RAMSEY | 6,285 | 4,078 | 1,607 | 600 | 2,471 R | 64.9% | 25.6% | 71.7% | 28.3% |
| 6,698 | RANSOM | 3,142 | 1,883 | 974 | 285 | 909 R | 59.9% | 31.0% | 65.9% | 34.1% |
| 3,608 | RENVILLE | 1,842 | 1,154 | 570 | 118 | 584 R | 62.6% | 30.9% | 66.9% | 33.1% |
| 19,207 | RICHLAND | 9,337 | 5,711 | 2,698 | 928 | 3,013 R | 61.2% | 28.9% | 67.9% | 32.1% |
| 12,177 | ROLETTE | 3,566 | 1,599 | 1,660 | 307 | 61 D | 44.8% | 46.6% | 49.1% | 50.9% |
| 5,512 | SARGENT | 2,823 | 1,565 | 1,048 | 210 | 517 R | 55.4% | 37.1% | 59.9% | 40.1% |
| 2,819 | SHERIDAN | 1,607 | 1,326 | 208 | 73 | 1,118 R | 82.5% | 12.9% | 86.4% | 13.6% |
| 3,620 | SIOUX | 1,090 | 620 | 383 | 87 | 237 R | 56.9% | 35.1% | 61.8% | 38.2% |
| 1,157 | SLOPE | 647 | 462 | 128 | 57 | 334 R | 71.4% | 19.8% | 78.3% | 21.7% |
| 23,697 | STARK | 9,003 | 6,312 | 2,016 | 675 | 4,296 R | 70.1% | 22.4% | 75.8% | 24.2% |
| 3,106 | STEELE | 1,870 | 997 | 617 | 256 | 380 R | 53.3% | 33.0% | 61.8% | 38.2% |
| 24,154 | STUTSMAN | 10,249 | 6,545 | 2,573 | 1,131 | 3,972 R | 63.9% | 25.1% | 71.8% | 28.2% |
| 4,052 | TOWNER | 2,119 | 1,375 | 568 | 176 | 807 R | 64.9% | 26.8% | 70.8% | 29.2% |
| 9,624 | TRAILL | 5,076 | 3,092 | 1,428 | 556 | 1,664 R | 60.9% | 28.1% | 68.4% | 31.6% |
| 15,371 | WALSH | 6,938 | 4,488 | 1,850 | 600 | 2,638 R | 64.7% | 26.7% | 70.8% | 29.2% |
| 58,392 | WARD | 22,189 | 14,997 | 5,554 | 1,638 | 9,443 R | 67.6% | 25.0% | 73.0% | 27.0% |
| 6,979 | WELLS | 3,599 | 2,660 | 746 | 193 | 1,914 R | 73.9% | 20.7% | 78.1% | 21.9% |
| 22,237 | WILLIAMS | 9,904 | 6,530 | 2,545 | 829 | 3,985 R | 65.9% | 25.7% | 72.0% | 28.0% |
| 652,717 | TOTAL | 301,545 | 193,695 | 79,189 | 28,661 | 114,506 R | 64.2% | 26.3% | 71.0% | 29.0% |

# NORTH DAKOTA

## PRESIDENT 1976

| 1970 Census Population | County | Total Vote | Republican | Democratic | Other | Rep.-Dem. Plurality | Percentage Total Vote Rep. | Dem. | Major Vote Rep. | Dem. |
|---|---|---|---|---|---|---|---|---|---|---|
| 3,832 | ADAMS | 1,937 | 940 | 959 | 38 | 19 D | 48.5% | 49.5% | 49.5% | 50.5% |
| 14,669 | BARNES | 7,462 | 4,011 | 3,321 | 130 | 690 R | 53.8% | 44.5% | 54.7% | 45.3% |
| 8,245 | BENSON | 3,725 | 1,689 | 1,973 | 63 | 284 D | 45.3% | 53.0% | 46.1% | 53.9% |
| 1,198 | BILLINGS | 684 | 351 | 285 | 48 | 66 R | 51.3% | 41.7% | 55.2% | 44.8% |
| 9,496 | BOTTINEAU | 4,700 | 2,638 | 1,987 | 75 | 651 R | 56.1% | 42.3% | 57.0% | 43.0% |
| 3,901 | BOWMAN | 1,998 | 1,033 | 911 | 54 | 122 R | 51.7% | 45.6% | 53.1% | 46.9% |
| 4,739 | BURKE | 2,089 | 1,087 | 899 | 103 | 188 R | 52.0% | 43.0% | 54.7% | 45.3% |
| 40,714 | BURLEIGH | 23,549 | 13,680 | 9,188 | 681 | 4,492 R | 58.1% | 39.0% | 59.8% | 40.2% |
| 73,653 | CASS | 41,411 | 22,583 | 17,879 | 949 | 4,704 R | 54.5% | 43.2% | 55.8% | 44.2% |
| 8,213 | CAVALIER | 4,300 | 2,046 | 2,178 | 76 | 132 D | 47.6% | 50.7% | 48.4% | 51.6% |
| 6,976 | DICKEY | 3,709 | 2,027 | 1,612 | 70 | 415 R | 54.7% | 43.5% | 55.7% | 44.3% |
| 4,564 | DIVIDE | 1,978 | 881 | 1,057 | 40 | 176 D | 44.5% | 53.4% | 45.5% | 54.5% |
| 4,895 | DUNN | 2,157 | 1,041 | 1,051 | 65 | 10 D | 48.3% | 48.7% | 49.8% | 50.2% |
| 4,103 | EDDY | 2,054 | 890 | 1,123 | 41 | 233 D | 43.3% | 54.7% | 44.2% | 55.8% |
| 7,200 | EMMONS | 2,984 | 1,370 | 1,459 | 155 | 89 D | 45.9% | 48.9% | 48.4% | 51.6% |
| 4,832 | FOSTER | 2,305 | 1,120 | 1,147 | 38 | 27 D | 48.6% | 49.8% | 49.4% | 50.6% |
| 2,611 | GOLDEN VALLEY | 1,208 | 633 | 479 | 96 | 154 R | 52.4% | 39.7% | 56.9% | 43.1% |
| 61,102 | GRAND FORKS | 26,218 | 13,820 | 11,545 | 853 | 2,275 R | 52.7% | 44.0% | 54.5% | 45.5% |
| 5,009 | GRANT | 2,258 | 1,205 | 952 | 101 | 253 R | 53.4% | 42.2% | 55.9% | 44.1% |
| 4,184 | GRIGGS | 2,262 | 1,086 | 1,122 | 54 | 36 D | 48.0% | 49.6% | 49.2% | 50.8% |
| 5,075 | HETTINGER | 2,302 | 1,135 | 1,095 | 72 | 40 R | 49.3% | 47.6% | 50.9% | 49.1% |
| 4,362 | KIDDER | 2,023 | 954 | 936 | 133 | 18 R | 47.2% | 46.3% | 50.5% | 49.5% |
| 7,117 | LA MOURE | 3,538 | 1,735 | 1,718 | 85 | 17 R | 49.0% | 48.6% | 50.2% | 49.8% |
| 4,245 | LOGAN | 1,876 | 944 | 809 | 123 | 135 R | 50.3% | 43.1% | 53.9% | 46.1% |
| 8,977 | MCHENRY | 4,111 | 2,043 | 1,994 | 74 | 49 R | 49.7% | 48.5% | 50.6% | 49.4% |
| 5,545 | MCINTOSH | 2,776 | 1,785 | 912 | 79 | 873 R | 64.3% | 32.9% | 66.2% | 33.8% |
| 6,127 | MCKENZIE | 2,978 | 1,595 | 1,335 | 48 | 260 R | 53.6% | 44.8% | 54.4% | 45.6% |
| 11,251 | MCLEAN | 5,665 | 2,729 | 2,815 | 121 | 86 D | 48.2% | 49.7% | 49.2% | 50.8% |
| 6,175 | MERCER | 3,414 | 1,982 | 1,298 | 134 | 684 R | 58.1% | 38.0% | 60.4% | 39.6% |
| 20,310 | MORTON | 10,462 | 4,921 | 5,241 | 300 | 320 D | 47.0% | 50.1% | 48.4% | 51.6% |
| 8,437 | MOUNTRAIL | 3,708 | 1,430 | 2,189 | 89 | 759 D | 38.6% | 59.0% | 39.5% | 60.5% |
| 5,776 | NELSON | 3,015 | 1,336 | 1,610 | 69 | 274 D | 44.3% | 53.4% | 45.3% | 54.7% |
| 2,322 | OLIVER | 1,140 | 575 | 529 | 36 | 46 R | 50.4% | 46.4% | 52.1% | 47.9% |
| 10,728 | PEMBINA | 5,209 | 2,810 | 2,274 | 125 | 536 R | 53.9% | 43.7% | 55.3% | 44.7% |
| 6,323 | PIERCE | 2,887 | 1,396 | 1,434 | 57 | 38 D | 48.4% | 49.7% | 49.3% | 50.7% |
| 12,915 | RAMSEY | 6,502 | 3,293 | 3,096 | 113 | 197 R | 50.6% | 47.6% | 51.5% | 48.5% |
| 7,102 | RANSOM | 3,456 | 1,696 | 1,715 | 45 | 19 D | 49.1% | 49.6% | 49.7% | 50.3% |
| 3,828 | RENVILLE | 1,846 | 812 | 1,008 | 26 | 196 D | 44.0% | 54.6% | 44.6% | 55.4% |
| 18,089 | RICHLAND | 9,785 | 4,991 | 4,592 | 202 | 399 R | 51.0% | 46.9% | 52.1% | 47.9% |
| 11,549 | ROLETTE | 3,693 | 1,094 | 2,531 | 68 | 1,437 D | 29.6% | 68.5% | 30.2% | 69.8% |
| 5,937 | SARGENT | 3,031 | 1,344 | 1,644 | 43 | 300 D | 44.3% | 54.2% | 45.0% | 55.0% |
| 3,232 | SHERIDAN | 1,536 | 935 | 569 | 32 | 366 R | 60.9% | 37.0% | 62.2% | 37.8% |
| 3,632 | SIOUX | 1,081 | 354 | 697 | 30 | 343 D | 32.7% | 64.5% | 33.7% | 66.3% |
| 1,484 | SLOPE | 726 | 355 | 347 | 24 | 8 R | 48.9% | 47.8% | 50.6% | 49.4% |
| 19,613 | STARK | 8,760 | 4,374 | 4,076 | 310 | 298 R | 49.9% | 46.5% | 51.8% | 48.2% |
| 3,749 | STEELE | 1,926 | 835 | 1,066 | 25 | 231 D | 43.4% | 55.3% | 43.9% | 56.1% |
| 23,550 | STUTSMAN | 10,780 | 5,653 | 4,883 | 244 | 770 R | 52.4% | 45.3% | 53.7% | 46.3% |
| 4,645 | TOWNER | 2,234 | 993 | 1,216 | 25 | 223 D | 44.4% | 54.4% | 45.0% | 55.0% |
| 9,571 | TRAILL | 5,251 | 2,800 | 2,352 | 99 | 448 R | 53.3% | 44.8% | 54.3% | 45.7% |
| 16,251 | WALSH | 7,309 | 3,518 | 3,555 | 236 | 37 D | 48.1% | 48.6% | 49.7% | 50.3% |
| 58,560 | WARD | 22,721 | 12,751 | 9,484 | 486 | 3,267 R | 56.1% | 41.7% | 57.3% | 42.7% |
| 7,847 | WELLS | 3,767 | 1,941 | 1,742 | 84 | 199 R | 51.5% | 46.2% | 52.7% | 47.3% |
| 19,301 | WILLIAMS | 8,692 | 4,230 | 4,189 | 273 | 41 R | 48.7% | 48.2% | 50.2% | 49.8% |
| 617,761 | TOTAL | 297,188 | 153,470 | 136,078 | 7,640 | 17,392 R | 51.6% | 45.8% | 53.0% | 47.0% |

# NORTH DAKOTA

## PRESIDENT 1972

| 1970 Census Population | County | Total Vote | Republican | Democratic | Other | Rep.-Dem. Plurality | Percentage Total Vote Rep. | Dem. | Major Vote Rep. | Dem. |
|---|---|---|---|---|---|---|---|---|---|---|
| 3,832 | ADAMS | 1,875 | 1,177 | 665 | 33 | 512 R | 62.8% | 35.5% | 63.9% | 36.1% |
| 14,669 | BARNES | 7,389 | 4,518 | 2,804 | 67 | 1,714 R | 61.1% | 37.9% | 61.7% | 38.3% |
| 8,245 | BENSON | 3,721 | 2,050 | 1,635 | 36 | 415 R | 55.1% | 43.9% | 55.6% | 44.4% |
| 1,198 | BILLINGS | 729 | 509 | 192 | 28 | 317 R | 69.8% | 26.3% | 72.6% | 27.4% |
| 9,496 | BOTTINEAU | 4,688 | 3,263 | 1,369 | 56 | 1,894 R | 69.6% | 29.2% | 70.4% | 29.6% |
| 3,901 | BOWMAN | 1,801 | 1,111 | 643 | 47 | 468 R | 61.7% | 35.7% | 63.3% | 36.7% |
| 4,739 | BURKE | 2,179 | 1,446 | 651 | 82 | 795 R | 66.4% | 29.9% | 69.0% | 31.0% |
| 40,714 | BURLEIGH | 20,644 | 13,909 | 5,841 | 894 | 8,068 R | 67.4% | 28.3% | 70.4% | 29.6% |
| 73,653 | CASS | 36,306 | 21,770 | 14,073 | 463 | 7,697 R | 60.0% | 38.8% | 60.7% | 39.3% |
| 8,213 | CAVALIER | 4,824 | 2,898 | 1,867 | 59 | 1,031 R | 60.1% | 38.7% | 60.8% | 39.2% |
| 6,976 | DICKEY | 3,581 | 2,277 | 1,266 | 38 | 1,011 R | 63.6% | 35.4% | 64.3% | 35.7% |
| 4,564 | DIVIDE | 2,040 | 1,230 | 774 | 36 | 456 R | 60.3% | 37.9% | 61.4% | 38.6% |
| 4,895 | DUNN | 2,197 | 1,438 | 644 | 115 | 794 R | 65.5% | 29.3% | 69.1% | 30.9% |
| 4,103 | EDDY | 1,964 | 1,022 | 911 | 31 | 111 R | 52.0% | 46.4% | 52.9% | 47.1% |
| 7,200 | EMMONS | 3,400 | 2,194 | 1,115 | 91 | 1,079 R | 64.5% | 32.8% | 66.3% | 33.7% |
| 4,832 | FOSTER | 2,243 | 1,352 | 861 | 30 | 491 R | 60.3% | 38.4% | 61.1% | 38.9% |
| 2,611 | GOLDEN VALLEY | 1,229 | 774 | 362 | 93 | 412 R | 63.0% | 29.5% | 68.1% | 31.9% |
| 61,102 | GRAND FORKS | 23,475 | 13,361 | 9,416 | 698 | 3,945 R | 56.9% | 40.1% | 58.7% | 41.3% |
| 5,009 | GRANT | 2,236 | 1,569 | 596 | 71 | 973 R | 70.2% | 26.7% | 72.5% | 27.5% |
| 4,184 | GRIGGS | 2,258 | 1,312 | 901 | 45 | 411 R | 58.1% | 39.9% | 59.3% | 40.7% |
| 5,075 | HETTINGER | 2,327 | 1,511 | 726 | 90 | 785 R | 64.9% | 31.2% | 67.5% | 32.5% |
| 4,362 | KIDDER | 1,961 | 1,315 | 557 | 89 | 758 R | 67.1% | 28.4% | 70.2% | 29.8% |
| 7,117 | LA MOURE | 3,539 | 2,110 | 1,399 | 30 | 711 R | 59.6% | 39.5% | 60.1% | 39.9% |
| 4,245 | LOGAN | 2,031 | 1,408 | 554 | 69 | 854 R | 69.3% | 27.3% | 71.8% | 28.2% |
| 8,977 | MCHENRY | 4,346 | 2,765 | 1,554 | 27 | 1,211 R | 63.6% | 35.8% | 64.0% | 36.0% |
| 5,545 | MCINTOSH | 2,990 | 2,440 | 521 | 29 | 1,919 R | 81.6% | 17.4% | 82.4% | 17.6% |
| 6,127 | MCKENZIE | 2,904 | 1,913 | 937 | 54 | 976 R | 65.9% | 32.3% | 67.1% | 32.9% |
| 11,251 | MCLEAN | 5,398 | 3,575 | 1,703 | 120 | 1,872 R | 66.2% | 31.5% | 67.7% | 32.3% |
| 6,175 | MERCER | 3,456 | 2,567 | 784 | 105 | 1,783 R | 74.3% | 22.7% | 76.6% | 23.4% |
| 20,310 | MORTON | 9,177 | 5,494 | 3,312 | 371 | 2,182 R | 59.9% | 36.1% | 62.4% | 37.6% |
| 8,437 | MOUNTRAIL | 3,496 | 2,038 | 1,391 | 67 | 647 R | 58.3% | 39.8% | 59.4% | 40.6% |
| 5,776 | NELSON | 3,028 | 1,625 | 1,358 | 45 | 267 R | 53.7% | 44.8% | 54.5% | 45.5% |
| 2,322 | OLIVER | 1,027 | 669 | 293 | 65 | 376 R | 65.1% | 28.5% | 69.5% | 30.5% |
| 10,728 | PEMBINA | 5,203 | 3,317 | 1,801 | 85 | 1,516 R | 63.8% | 34.6% | 64.8% | 35.2% |
| 6,323 | PIERCE | 2,978 | 1,970 | 973 | 35 | 997 R | 66.2% | 32.7% | 66.9% | 33.1% |
| 12,915 | RAMSEY | 6,400 | 3,954 | 2,384 | 62 | 1,570 R | 61.8% | 37.3% | 62.4% | 37.6% |
| 7,102 | RANSOM | 3,435 | 2,056 | 1,355 | 24 | 701 R | 59.9% | 39.4% | 60.3% | 39.7% |
| 3,828 | RENVILLE | 1,835 | 1,121 | 702 | 12 | 419 R | 61.1% | 38.3% | 61.5% | 38.5% |
| 18,089 | RICHLAND | 8,624 | 5,194 | 3,367 | 63 | 1,827 R | 60.2% | 39.0% | 60.7% | 39.3% |
| 11,549 | ROLETTE | 3,559 | 1,713 | 1,803 | 43 | 90 D | 48.1% | 50.7% | 48.7% | 51.3% |
| 5,937 | SARGENT | 2,966 | 1,616 | 1,331 | 19 | 285 R | 54.5% | 44.9% | 54.8% | 45.2% |
| 3,232 | SHERIDAN | 1,809 | 1,460 | 334 | 15 | 1,126 R | 80.7% | 18.5% | 81.4% | 18.6% |
| 3,632 | SIOUX | 1,142 | 561 | 557 | 24 | 4 R | 49.1% | 48.8% | 50.2% | 49.8% |
| 1,484 | SLOPE | 690 | 413 | 249 | 28 | 164 R | 59.9% | 36.1% | 62.4% | 37.6% |
| 19,613 | STARK | 8,131 | 5,115 | 2,636 | 380 | 2,479 R | 62.9% | 32.4% | 66.0% | 34.0% |
| 3,749 | STEELE | 1,970 | 1,063 | 892 | 15 | 171 R | 54.0% | 45.3% | 54.4% | 45.6% |
| 23,550 | STUTSMAN | 10,028 | 6,269 | 3,589 | 170 | 2,680 R | 62.5% | 35.8% | 63.6% | 36.4% |
| 4,645 | TOWNER | 2,325 | 1,349 | 944 | 32 | 405 R | 58.0% | 40.6% | 58.8% | 41.2% |
| 9,571 | TRAILL | 5,078 | 3,118 | 1,892 | 68 | 1,226 R | 61.4% | 37.3% | 62.2% | 37.8% |
| 16,251 | WALSH | 7,090 | 3,991 | 2,908 | 191 | 1,083 R | 56.3% | 41.0% | 57.8% | 42.2% |
| 58,560 | WARD | 20,868 | 13,900 | 6,706 | 262 | 7,194 R | 66.6% | 32.1% | 67.5% | 32.5% |
| 7,847 | WELLS | 3,910 | 2,519 | 1,297 | 94 | 1,222 R | 64.4% | 33.2% | 66.0% | 34.0% |
| 19,301 | WILLIAMS | 8,014 | 4,800 | 2,989 | 225 | 1,811 R | 59.9% | 37.3% | 61.6% | 38.4% |
| 617,761 | TOTAL | 280,514 | 174,109 | 100,384 | 6,021 | 73,725 R | 62.1% | 35.8% | 63.4% | 36.6% |

# NORTH DAKOTA

## PRESIDENT 1968

| 1960 Census Population | County | Total Vote | Republican | Democratic | AIP | Other | Plurality | Percentage Total Vote Rep. | Dem. | AIP |
|---|---|---|---|---|---|---|---|---|---|---|
| 4,449 | ADAMS | 1,781 | 1,020 | 641 | 116 | 4 | 379 R | 57.3% | 36.0% | 6.5% |
| 16,719 | BARNES | 6,805 | 3,831 | 2,623 | 348 | 3 | 1,208 R | 56.3% | 38.5% | 5.1% |
| 9,435 | BENSON | 3,643 | 1,707 | 1,772 | 164 | | 65 D | 46.9% | 48.6% | 4.5% |
| 1,513 | BILLINGS | 638 | 395 | 174 | 69 | | 221 R | 61.9% | 27.3% | 10.8% |
| 11,315 | BOTTINEAU | 4,384 | 2,633 | 1,520 | 230 | 1 | 1,113 R | 60.1% | 34.7% | 5.2% |
| 4,154 | BOWMAN | 1,642 | 927 | 559 | 156 | | 368 R | 56.5% | 34.0% | 9.5% |
| 5,886 | BURKE | 2,180 | 1,239 | 808 | 132 | 1 | 431 R | 56.8% | 37.1% | 6.1% |
| 34,016 | BURLEIGH | 16,649 | 10,661 | 5,139 | 818 | 31 | 5,522 R | 64.0% | 30.9% | 4.9% |
| 66,947 | CASS | 27,271 | 15,240 | 10,819 | 1,167 | 45 | 4,421 R | 55.9% | 39.7% | 4.3% |
| 10,064 | CAVALIER | 3,841 | 1,953 | 1,631 | 257 | | 322 R | 50.8% | 42.5% | 6.7% |
| 8,147 | DICKEY | 3,348 | 2,087 | 1,098 | 161 | 2 | 989 R | 62.3% | 32.8% | 4.8% |
| 5,566 | DIVIDE | 2,048 | 1,032 | 914 | 102 | | 118 R | 50.4% | 44.6% | 5.0% |
| 6,350 | DUNN | 2,149 | 1,207 | 772 | 169 | 1 | 435 R | 56.2% | 35.9% | 7.9% |
| 4,936 | EDDY | 1,992 | 1,018 | 893 | 76 | 5 | 125 R | 51.1% | 44.8% | 3.8% |
| 8,462 | EMMONS | 3,061 | 1,991 | 756 | 311 | 3 | 1,235 R | 65.0% | 24.7% | 10.2% |
| 5,361 | FOSTER | 2,139 | 1,119 | 897 | 123 | | 222 R | 52.3% | 41.9% | 5.8% |
| 3,100 | GOLDEN VALLEY | 1,199 | 735 | 348 | 115 | 1 | 387 R | 61.3% | 29.0% | 9.6% |
| 48,677 | GRAND FORKS | 18,849 | 9,802 | 7,695 | 1,332 | 20 | 2,107 R | 52.0% | 40.8% | 7.1% |
| 6,248 | GRANT | 2,296 | 1,648 | 488 | 157 | 3 | 1,160 R | 71.8% | 21.3% | 6.8% |
| 5,023 | GRIGGS | 2,227 | 1,110 | 1,008 | 109 | | 102 R | 49.8% | 45.3% | 4.9% |
| 6,317 | HETTINGER | 2,226 | 1,424 | 638 | 163 | 1 | 786 R | 64.0% | 28.7% | 7.3% |
| 5,386 | KIDDER | 1,947 | 1,204 | 548 | 192 | 3 | 656 R | 61.8% | 28.1% | 9.9% |
| 8,705 | LA MOURE | 3,468 | 2,008 | 1,269 | 189 | 2 | 739 R | 57.9% | 36.6% | 5.4% |
| 5,369 | LOGAN | 2,010 | 1,416 | 459 | 135 | | 957 R | 70.4% | 22.8% | 6.7% |
| 11,099 | MCHENRY | 4,106 | 2,226 | 1,595 | 281 | 4 | 631 R | 54.2% | 38.8% | 6.8% |
| 6,702 | MCINTOSH | 2,732 | 2,258 | 342 | 129 | 3 | 1,916 R | 82.7% | 12.5% | 4.7% |
| 7,296 | MCKENZIE | 2,725 | 1,625 | 935 | 164 | 1 | 690 R | 59.6% | 34.3% | 6.0% |
| 14,030 | MCLEAN | 5,030 | 2,764 | 2,050 | 216 | | 714 R | 55.0% | 40.8% | 4.3% |
| 6,805 | MERCER | 2,939 | 2,039 | 730 | 169 | 1 | 1,309 R | 69.4% | 24.8% | 5.8% |
| 20,992 | MORTON | 8,115 | 4,465 | 3,156 | 489 | 5 | 1,309 R | 55.0% | 38.9% | 6.0% |
| 10,077 | MOUNTRAIL | 3,370 | 1,494 | 1,662 | 212 | 2 | 168 D | 44.3% | 49.3% | 6.3% |
| 7,034 | NELSON | 3,162 | 1,526 | 1,477 | 157 | 2 | 49 R | 48.3% | 46.7% | 5.0% |
| 2,610 | OLIVER | 971 | 616 | 269 | 85 | 1 | 347 R | 63.4% | 27.7% | 8.8% |
| 12,946 | PEMBINA | 4,596 | 2,574 | 1,686 | 335 | 1 | 888 R | 56.0% | 36.7% | 7.3% |
| 7,394 | PIERCE | 2,979 | 1,700 | 1,048 | 229 | 2 | 652 R | 57.1% | 35.2% | 7.7% |
| 13,443 | RAMSEY | 5,845 | 3,189 | 2,384 | 269 | 3 | 805 R | 54.6% | 40.8% | 4.6% |
| 8,078 | RANSOM | 3,383 | 1,943 | 1,286 | 153 | 1 | 657 R | 57.4% | 38.0% | 4.5% |
| 4,698 | RENVILLE | 1,816 | 851 | 880 | 84 | 1 | 29 D | 46.9% | 48.5% | 4.6% |
| 18,824 | RICHLAND | 7,767 | 4,224 | 3,098 | 443 | 2 | 1,126 R | 54.4% | 39.9% | 5.7% |
| 10,641 | ROLETTE | 3,253 | 1,211 | 1,870 | 172 | | 659 D | 37.2% | 57.5% | 5.3% |
| 6,856 | SARGENT | 2,849 | 1,386 | 1,308 | 154 | 1 | 78 R | 48.6% | 45.9% | 5.4% |
| 4,350 | SHERIDAN | 1,727 | 1,295 | 350 | 79 | 3 | 945 R | 75.0% | 20.3% | 4.6% |
| 3,662 | SIOUX | 1,065 | 482 | 525 | 58 | | 43 D | 45.3% | 49.3% | 5.4% |
| 1,893 | SLOPE | 682 | 379 | 238 | 64 | 1 | 141 R | 55.6% | 34.9% | 9.4% |
| 18,451 | STARK | 7,444 | 4,365 | 2,577 | 500 | 2 | 1,788 R | 58.6% | 34.6% | 6.7% |
| 4,719 | STEELE | 2,031 | 952 | 991 | 88 | | 39 D | 46.9% | 48.8% | 4.3% |
| 25,137 | STUTSMAN | 9,184 | 5,162 | 3,532 | 477 | 13 | 1,630 R | 56.2% | 38.5% | 5.2% |
| 5,624 | TOWNER | 2,225 | 1,109 | 990 | 124 | 2 | 119 R | 49.8% | 44.5% | 5.6% |
| 10,583 | TRAILL | 4,678 | 2,692 | 1,740 | 243 | 3 | 952 R | 57.5% | 37.2% | 5.2% |
| 17,997 | WALSH | 6,812 | 3,410 | 2,948 | 453 | 1 | 462 R | 50.1% | 43.3% | 6.7% |
| 47,072 | WARD | 17,095 | 9,079 | 7,105 | 896 | 15 | 1,974 R | 53.1% | 41.6% | 5.2% |
| 9,237 | WELLS | 3,782 | 2,266 | 1,265 | 247 | 4 | 1,001 R | 59.9% | 33.4% | 6.5% |
| 22,051 | WILLIAMS | 7,726 | 3,980 | 3,263 | 483 | | 717 R | 51.5% | 42.2% | 6.3% |
| 632,446 | TOTAL | 247,882 | 138,669 | 94,769 | 14,244 | 200 | 43,900 R | 55.9% | 38.2% | 5.7% |

# NORTH DAKOTA

## PRESIDENT 1964

| 1960 Census Population | County | Total Vote | Republican | Democratic | Other | Rep.-Dem. Plurality | Percentage | | | |
|---|---|---|---|---|---|---|---|---|---|---|
| | | | | | | | Total Vote | | Major Vote | |
| | | | | | | | Rep. | Dem. | Rep. | Dem. |
| 4,449 | ADAMS | 1,888 | 877 | 1,010 | 1 | 133 D | 46.5% | 53.5% | 46.5% | 53.5% |
| 16,719 | BARNES | 7,008 | 2,987 | 4,007 | 14 | 1,020 D | 42.6% | 57.2% | 42.7% | 57.3% |
| 9,435 | BENSON | 4,060 | 1,489 | 2,566 | 5 | 1,077 D | 36.7% | 63.2% | 36.7% | 63.3% |
| 1,513 | BILLINGS | 688 | 340 | 348 | | 8 D | 49.4% | 50.6% | 49.4% | 50.6% |
| 11,315 | BOTTINEAU | 4,607 | 2,060 | 2,546 | 1 | 486 D | 44.7% | 55.3% | 44.7% | 55.3% |
| 4,154 | BOWMAN | 1,827 | 756 | 1,070 | 1 | 314 D | 41.4% | 58.6% | 41.4% | 58.6% |
| 5,886 | BURKE | 2,434 | 974 | 1,454 | 6 | 480 D | 40.0% | 59.7% | 40.1% | 59.9% |
| 34,016 | BURLEIGH | 15,419 | 7,239 | 8,120 | 60 | 881 D | 46.9% | 52.7% | 47.1% | 52.9% |
| 66,947 | CASS | 28,669 | 12,972 | 15,674 | 23 | 2,702 D | 45.2% | 54.7% | 45.3% | 54.7% |
| 10,064 | CAVALIER | 4,231 | 1,417 | 2,810 | 4 | 1,393 D | 33.5% | 66.4% | 33.5% | 66.5% |
| 8,147 | DICKEY | 3,630 | 1,808 | 1,818 | 4 | 10 D | 49.8% | 50.1% | 49.9% | 50.1% |
| 5,566 | DIVIDE | 2,281 | 779 | 1,498 | 4 | 719 D | 34.2% | 65.7% | 34.2% | 65.8% |
| 6,350 | DUNN | 2,432 | 1,079 | 1,351 | 2 | 272 D | 44.4% | 55.6% | 44.4% | 55.6% |
| 4,936 | EDDY | 2,088 | 747 | 1,337 | 4 | 590 D | 35.8% | 64.0% | 35.8% | 64.2% |
| 8,462 | EMMONS | 3,315 | 1,759 | 1,556 | | 203 R | 53.1% | 46.9% | 53.1% | 46.9% |
| 5,361 | FOSTER | 2,244 | 927 | 1,315 | 2 | 388 D | 41.3% | 58.6% | 41.3% | 58.7% |
| 3,100 | GOLDEN VALLEY | 1,324 | 722 | 602 | | 120 R | 54.5% | 45.5% | 54.5% | 45.5% |
| 48,677 | GRAND FORKS | 18,175 | 7,367 | 10,740 | 68 | 3,373 D | 40.5% | 59.1% | 40.7% | 59.3% |
| 6,248 | GRANT | 2,488 | 1,421 | 1,063 | 4 | 358 R | 57.1% | 42.7% | 57.2% | 42.8% |
| 5,023 | GRIGGS | 2,390 | 885 | 1,505 | | 620 D | 37.0% | 63.0% | 37.0% | 63.0% |
| 6,317 | HETTINGER | 2,465 | 1,188 | 1,275 | 2 | 87 D | 48.2% | 51.7% | 48.2% | 51.8% |
| 5,386 | KIDDER | 2,151 | 1,104 | 1,047 | | 57 R | 51.3% | 48.7% | 51.3% | 48.7% |
| 8,705 | LA MOURE | 3,755 | 1,604 | 2,145 | 6 | 541 D | 42.7% | 57.1% | 42.8% | 57.2% |
| 5,369 | LOGAN | 2,141 | 1,187 | 951 | 3 | 236 R | 55.4% | 44.4% | 55.5% | 44.5% |
| 11,099 | MCHENRY | 4,379 | 1,728 | 2,643 | 8 | 915 D | 39.5% | 60.4% | 39.5% | 60.5% |
| 6,702 | MCINTOSH | 2,841 | 1,891 | 950 | | 941 R | 66.6% | 33.4% | 66.6% | 33.4% |
| 7,296 | MCKENZIE | 2,938 | 1,352 | 1,584 | 2 | 232 D | 46.0% | 53.9% | 46.0% | 54.0% |
| 14,030 | MCLEAN | 5,547 | 2,204 | 3,339 | 4 | 1,135 D | 39.7% | 60.2% | 39.8% | 60.2% |
| 6,805 | MERCER | 2,850 | 1,540 | 1,310 | | 230 R | 54.0% | 46.0% | 54.0% | 46.0% |
| 20,992 | MORTON | 8,138 | 2,955 | 5,173 | 10 | 2,218 D | 36.3% | 63.6% | 36.4% | 63.6% |
| 10,077 | MOUNTRAIL | 3,683 | 1,131 | 2,548 | 4 | 1,417 D | 30.7% | 69.2% | 30.7% | 69.3% |
| 7,034 | NELSON | 3,287 | 1,101 | 2,186 | | 1,085 D | 33.5% | 66.5% | 33.5% | 66.5% |
| 2,610 | OLIVER | 1,017 | 469 | 548 | | 79 D | 46.1% | 53.9% | 46.1% | 53.9% |
| 12,946 | PEMBINA | 5,167 | 1,961 | 3,198 | 8 | 1,237 D | 38.0% | 61.9% | 38.0% | 62.0% |
| 7,394 | PIERCE | 3,073 | 1,178 | 1,893 | 2 | 715 D | 38.3% | 61.6% | 38.4% | 61.6% |
| 13,443 | RAMSEY | 5,987 | 2,409 | 3,572 | 6 | 1,163 D | 40.2% | 59.7% | 40.3% | 59.7% |
| 8,078 | RANSOM | 3,717 | 1,647 | 2,063 | 7 | 416 D | 44.3% | 55.5% | 44.4% | 55.6% |
| 4,698 | RENVILLE | 1,997 | 640 | 1,356 | 1 | 716 D | 32.0% | 67.9% | 32.1% | 67.9% |
| 18,824 | RICHLAND | 7,955 | 3,425 | 4,525 | 5 | 1,100 D | 43.1% | 56.9% | 43.1% | 56.9% |
| 10,641 | ROLETTE | 3,458 | 892 | 2,566 | | 1,674 D | 25.8% | 74.2% | 25.8% | 74.2% |
| 6,856 | SARGENT | 3,033 | 1,189 | 1,840 | 4 | 651 D | 39.2% | 60.7% | 39.3% | 60.7% |
| 4,350 | SHERIDAN | 1,911 | 1,187 | 724 | | 463 R | 62.1% | 37.9% | 62.1% | 37.9% |
| 3,662 | SIOUX | 1,013 | 314 | 695 | 4 | 381 D | 31.0% | 68.6% | 31.1% | 68.9% |
| 1,893 | SLOPE | 765 | 329 | 436 | | 107 D | 43.0% | 57.0% | 43.0% | 57.0% |
| 18,451 | STARK | 7,161 | 2,888 | 4,270 | 3 | 1,382 D | 40.3% | 59.6% | 40.3% | 59.7% |
| 4,719 | STEELE | 2,203 | 796 | 1,404 | 3 | 608 D | 36.1% | 63.7% | 36.2% | 63.8% |
| 25,137 | STUTSMAN | 9,474 | 3,990 | 5,463 | 21 | 1,473 D | 42.1% | 57.7% | 42.2% | 57.8% |
| 5,624 | TOWNER | 2,417 | 788 | 1,628 | 1 | 840 D | 32.6% | 67.4% | 32.6% | 67.4% |
| 10,583 | TRAILL | 4,929 | 2,312 | 2,614 | 3 | 302 D | 46.9% | 53.0% | 46.9% | 53.1% |
| 17,997 | WALSH | 7,376 | 2,454 | 4,911 | 11 | 2,457 D | 33.3% | 66.6% | 33.3% | 66.7% |
| 47,072 | WARD | 17,735 | 6,798 | 10,871 | 66 | 4,073 D | 38.3% | 61.3% | 38.5% | 61.5% |
| 9,237 | WELLS | 4,189 | 1,875 | 2,314 | | 439 D | 44.8% | 55.2% | 44.8% | 55.2% |
| 22,051 | WILLIAMS | 8,439 | 3,076 | 5,352 | 11 | 2,276 D | 36.4% | 63.4% | 36.5% | 63.5% |
| 632,446 | TOTAL | 258,389 | 108,207 | 149,784 | 398 | 41,577 D | 41.9% | 58.0% | 41.9% | 58.1% |

# NORTH DAKOTA

## PRESIDENT 1960

| 1960 Census Population | County | Total Vote | Republican | Democratic | Other | Rep.-Dem. Plurality | Percentage Total Vote Rep. | Total Vote Dem. | Major Vote Rep. | Major Vote Dem. |
|---|---|---|---|---|---|---|---|---|---|---|
| 4,449 | ADAMS | 2,064 | 1,232 | 832 | | 400 R | 59.7% | 40.3% | 59.7% | 40.3% |
| 16,719 | BARNES | 7,629 | 4,403 | 3,223 | 3 | 1,180 R | 57.7% | 42.2% | 57.7% | 42.3% |
| 9,435 | BENSON | 4,443 | 2,259 | 2,181 | 3 | 78 R | 50.8% | 49.1% | 50.9% | 49.1% |
| 1,513 | BILLINGS | 768 | 368 | 400 | | 32 D | 47.9% | 52.1% | 47.9% | 52.1% |
| 11,315 | BOTTINEAU | 5,069 | 3,092 | 1,974 | 3 | 1,118 R | 61.0% | 38.9% | 61.0% | 39.0% |
| 4,154 | BOWMAN | 1,888 | 1,038 | 847 | 3 | 191 R | 55.0% | 44.9% | 55.1% | 44.9% |
| 5,886 | BURKE | 2,687 | 1,609 | 1,076 | 2 | 533 R | 59.9% | 40.0% | 59.9% | 40.1% |
| 34,016 | BURLEIGH | 15,278 | 9,492 | 5,761 | 25 | 3,731 R | 62.1% | 37.7% | 62.2% | 37.8% |
| 66,947 | CASS | 29,711 | 17,498 | 12,213 | | 5,285 R | 58.9% | 41.1% | 58.9% | 41.1% |
| 10,064 | CAVALIER | 4,743 | 2,430 | 2,312 | 1 | 118 R | 51.2% | 48.7% | 51.2% | 48.8% |
| 8,147 | DICKEY | 3,856 | 2,420 | 1,433 | 3 | 987 R | 62.8% | 37.2% | 62.8% | 37.2% |
| 5,566 | DIVIDE | 2,595 | 1,348 | 1,243 | 4 | 105 R | 51.9% | 47.9% | 52.0% | 48.0% |
| 6,350 | DUNN | 2,783 | 1,462 | 1,321 | | 141 R | 52.5% | 47.5% | 52.5% | 47.5% |
| 4,936 | EDDY | 2,342 | 1,188 | 1,152 | 2 | 36 R | 50.7% | 49.2% | 50.8% | 49.2% |
| 8,462 | EMMONS | 3,845 | 1,785 | 2,058 | 2 | 273 D | 46.4% | 53.5% | 46.4% | 53.6% |
| 5,361 | FOSTER | 2,533 | 1,351 | 1,182 | | 169 R | 53.3% | 46.7% | 53.3% | 46.7% |
| 3,100 | GOLDEN VALLEY | 1,499 | 825 | 672 | 2 | 153 R | 55.0% | 44.8% | 55.1% | 44.9% |
| 48,677 | GRAND FORKS | 19,343 | 10,997 | 8,341 | 5 | 2,656 R | 56.9% | 43.1% | 56.9% | 43.1% |
| 6,248 | GRANT | 2,751 | 1,794 | 955 | 2 | 839 R | 65.2% | 34.7% | 65.3% | 34.7% |
| 5,023 | GRIGGS | 2,561 | 1,278 | 1,279 | 4 | 1 D | 49.9% | 49.9% | 50.0% | 50.0% |
| 6,317 | HETTINGER | 2,762 | 1,541 | 1,219 | 2 | 322 R | 55.8% | 44.1% | 55.8% | 44.2% |
| 5,386 | KIDDER | 2,443 | 1,574 | 868 | 1 | 706 R | 64.4% | 35.5% | 64.5% | 35.5% |
| 8,705 | LA MOURE | 4,090 | 2,511 | 1,575 | 4 | 936 R | 61.4% | 38.5% | 61.5% | 38.5% |
| 5,369 | LOGAN | 2,499 | 1,601 | 898 | | 703 R | 64.1% | 35.9% | 64.1% | 35.9% |
| 11,099 | MCHENRY | 4,948 | 2,715 | 2,231 | 2 | 484 R | 54.9% | 45.1% | 54.9% | 45.1% |
| 6,702 | MCINTOSH | 3,322 | 2,694 | 628 | | 2,066 R | 81.1% | 18.9% | 81.1% | 18.9% |
| 7,296 | MCKENZIE | 3,231 | 1,715 | 1,514 | 2 | 201 R | 53.1% | 46.9% | 53.1% | 46.9% |
| 14,030 | MCLEAN | 6,173 | 3,398 | 2,771 | 4 | 627 R | 55.0% | 44.9% | 55.1% | 44.9% |
| 6,805 | MERCER | 3,239 | 2,395 | 844 | | 1,551 R | 73.9% | 26.1% | 73.9% | 26.1% |
| 20,992 | MORTON | 8,895 | 4,028 | 4,866 | 1 | 838 D | 45.3% | 54.7% | 45.3% | 54.7% |
| 10,077 | MOUNTRAIL | 4,163 | 1,894 | 2,264 | 5 | 370 D | 45.5% | 54.4% | 45.6% | 54.4% |
| 7,034 | NELSON | 3,719 | 1,934 | 1,783 | 2 | 151 R | 52.0% | 47.9% | 52.0% | 48.0% |
| 2,610 | OLIVER | 1,198 | 703 | 494 | 1 | 209 R | 58.7% | 41.2% | 58.7% | 41.3% |
| 12,946 | PEMBINA | 5,810 | 3,348 | 2,460 | 2 | 888 R | 57.6% | 42.3% | 57.6% | 42.4% |
| 7,394 | PIERCE | 3,313 | 1,464 | 1,848 | 1 | 384 D | 44.2% | 55.8% | 44.2% | 55.8% |
| 13,443 | RAMSEY | 6,413 | 3,599 | 2,813 | 1 | 786 R | 56.1% | 43.9% | 56.1% | 43.9% |
| 8,078 | RANSOM | 4,131 | 2,324 | 1,806 | 1 | 518 R | 56.3% | 43.7% | 56.3% | 43.7% |
| 4,698 | RENVILLE | 2,230 | 1,012 | 1,217 | 1 | 205 D | 45.4% | 54.6% | 45.4% | 54.6% |
| 18,824 | RICHLAND | 8,718 | 4,711 | 4,003 | 4 | 708 R | 54.0% | 45.9% | 54.1% | 45.9% |
| 10,641 | ROLETTE | 3,615 | 1,277 | 2,335 | 3 | 1,058 D | 35.3% | 64.6% | 35.4% | 64.6% |
| 6,856 | SARGENT | 3,248 | 1,591 | 1,655 | 2 | 64 D | 49.0% | 51.0% | 49.0% | 51.0% |
| 4,350 | SHERIDAN | 2,098 | 1,552 | 539 | 7 | 1,013 R | 74.0% | 25.7% | 74.2% | 25.8% |
| 3,662 | SIOUX | 1,259 | 571 | 688 | | 117 D | 45.4% | 54.6% | 45.4% | 54.6% |
| 1,893 | SLOPE | 906 | 475 | 431 | | 44 R | 52.4% | 47.6% | 52.4% | 47.6% |
| 18,451 | STARK | 7,421 | 3,223 | 4,197 | 1 | 974 D | 43.4% | 56.6% | 43.4% | 56.6% |
| 4,719 | STEELE | 2,382 | 1,209 | 1,173 | | 36 R | 50.8% | 49.2% | 50.8% | 49.2% |
| 25,137 | STUTSMAN | 10,399 | 5,905 | 4,481 | 13 | 1,424 R | 56.8% | 43.1% | 56.9% | 43.1% |
| 5,624 | TOWNER | 2,703 | 1,410 | 1,292 | 1 | 118 R | 52.2% | 47.8% | 52.2% | 47.8% |
| 10,583 | TRAILL | 5,303 | 3,218 | 2,084 | 1 | 1,134 R | 60.7% | 39.3% | 60.7% | 39.3% |
| 17,997 | WALSH | 8,047 | 4,036 | 4,009 | 2 | 27 R | 50.2% | 49.8% | 50.2% | 49.8% |
| 47,072 | WARD | 17,653 | 9,680 | 7,954 | 19 | 1,726 R | 54.8% | 45.1% | 54.9% | 45.1% |
| 9,237 | WELLS | 4,535 | 2,641 | 1,885 | 9 | 756 R | 58.2% | 41.6% | 58.4% | 41.6% |
| 22,051 | WILLIAMS | 9,177 | 4,492 | 4,683 | 2 | 191 D | 48.9% | 51.0% | 49.0% | 51.0% |
| 632,446 | TOTAL | 278,431 | 154,310 | 123,963 | 158 | 30,347 R | 55.4% | 44.5% | 55.5% | 44.5% |

# NORTH DAKOTA

## ELECTION NOTES

**2004**    Other vote was 3,756 Independent (Ralph Nader); 851 Libertarian (Michael Badnarik); 514 Constitution (Michael Peroutka); 9 write-in (Martin Wishnatsky).

**2000**    Other vote was 7,288 Reform (Buchanan); 660 Independent Nomination (Browne); 373 Constitution (Phillips); 313 Independent Nomination (Hagelin). Nader was listed on the ballot as an Independent Nomination.

**1996**    Other vote was 847 Libertarian (Browne); 745 Independent (Phillips); 349 Natural Law (Hagelin).

**1992**    Other vote was 642 LaRouche (Independent); 416 Marrou (Independent); 240 Hagelin (Independent); 193 Warren (Independent); 143 Fulani (Independent); 3 Dodge (write-in).

**1988**    Other vote was 1,315 Paul (Libertarian); 905 LaRouche (National Economic Recovery; 396 Fulani (New Alliance); 347 Warren (Socialist Workers).

**1984**    Other vote was 1,278 LaRouche (Independent); 1,077 Richards (Populist); 703 Bergland (Libertarian); 368 Johnson (Citizens); 239 Mason (Socialist Workers); 220 Dodge (Prohibition); 169 Hall (Communist); 152 Serrette (New Alliance).

**1980**    Other vote was 23,640 Anderson (Independent); 3,743 Clark (Libertarian); 429 Commoner (Citizens); 296 McLain (Natural Peoples League); 235 Greaves (American); 93 Hall (Communist); 89 DeBerry (Socialist Workers); 82 McReynolds (Socialist); 54 Bubar (Statesman).

**1976**    Other vote was 3,796 Anderson (American); 2,952 McCarthy (Independent); 269 Maddox (American Independent); 253 MacBride (Libertarian); 142 LaRouche (U.S. Labor); 84 Hall (Communist); 63 Bubar (Prohibition); 43 Camejo (Socialist Workers); 38 Zeidler (Socialist). Early unamended canvass gave the Communist vote as 85; the Libertarian vote as 256 and the American vote as 3,698 (98 votes cast for Anderson had been omitted in Mercer county).

**1972**    Other vote was 5,646 Schmitz (American); 288 Jenness (Socialist Workers); 87 Hall (Communist).

**1968**    Wallace on the ballot as American. Other vote was 128 Halstead (Socialist Workers); 38 Munn (Prohibition); 34 Troxell (Constitution).

**1964**    Other vote was 224 DeBerry (Socialist Workers); 174 Munn (Prohibition).

**1960**    Other vote was Dobbs (Socialist Workers).

# OHIO

## POPULAR VOTE FOR PRESIDENT 1920 TO 2004

| Year | Total Vote | Republican Vote | Republican Candidate | Democratic Vote | Democratic Candidate | Other Vote | Plurality | Total Vote Rep. | Total Vote Dem. | Major Vote Rep. | Major Vote Dem. |
|------|-----------|-----------------|----------------------|-----------------|----------------------|------------|-----------|------|------|------|------|
| 2004 | 5,627,908 | 2,859,768 | Bush, George W. | 2,741,167 | Kerry, John | 26,973 | 118,601 R | 50.8% | 48.7% | 51.1% | 48.9% |
| 2000 ** | 4,701,998 | 2,350,363 | Bush, George W. | 2,183,628 | Gore, Al | 168,007 | 166,735 R | 50.0% | 46.4% | 51.8% | 48.2% |
| 1996 ** | 4,534,434 | 1,859,883 | Dole, Bob | 2,148,222 | Clinton, Bill | 526,329 | 288,339 D | 41.0% | 47.4% | 46.4% | 53.6% |
| 1992 ** | 4,939,967 | 1,894,310 | Bush, George | 1,984,942 | Clinton, Bill | 1,060,715 | 90,632 D | 38.3% | 40.2% | 48.8% | 51.2% |
| 1988 | 4,393,699 | 2,416,549 | Bush, George | 1,939,629 | Dukakis, Michael S. | 37,521 | 476,920 R | 55.0% | 44.1% | 55.5% | 44.5% |
| 1984 | 4,547,619 | 2,678,560 | Reagan, Ronald | 1,825,440 | Mondale, Walter F. | 43,619 | 853,120 R | 58.9% | 40.1% | 59.5% | 40.5% |
| 1980 ** | 4,283,603 | 2,206,545 | Reagan, Ronald | 1,752,414 | Carter, Jimmy | 324,644 | 454,131 R | 51.5% | 40.9% | 55.7% | 44.3% |
| 1976 | 4,111,873 | 2,000,505 | Ford, Gerald R. | 2,011,621 | Carter, Jimmy | 99,747 | 11,116 D | 48.7% | 48.9% | 49.9% | 50.1% |
| 1972 | 4,094,787 | 2,441,827 | Nixon, Richard M. | 1,558,889 | McGovern, George S. | 94,071 | 882,938 R | 59.6% | 38.1% | 61.0% | 39.0% |
| 1968 | 3,959,698 | 1,791,014 | Nixon, Richard M. | 1,700,586 | Humphrey, Hubert H. | 468,098 | 90,428 R | 45.2% | 42.9% | 51.3% | 48.7% |
| 1964 | 3,969,196 | 1,470,865 | Goldwater, Barry M. | 2,498,331 | Johnson, Lyndon B. | | 1,027,466 D | 37.1% | 62.9% | 37.1% | 62.9% |
| 1960 | 4,161,859 | 2,217,611 | Nixon, Richard M. | 1,944,248 | Kennedy, John F. | | 273,363 R | 53.3% | 46.7% | 53.3% | 46.7% |
| 1956 | 3,702,265 | 2,262,610 | Eisenhower, Dwight D. | 1,439,655 | Stevenson, Adlai E. | | 822,955 R | 61.1% | 38.9% | 61.1% | 38.9% |
| 1952 | 3,700,758 | 2,100,391 | Eisenhower, Dwight D. | 1,600,367 | Stevenson, Adlai E. | | 500,024 R | 56.8% | 43.2% | 56.8% | 43.2% |
| 1948 | 2,936,071 | 1,445,684 | Dewey, Thomas E. | 1,452,791 | Truman, Harry S. | 37,596 | 7,107 D | 49.2% | 49.5% | 49.9% | 50.1% |
| 1944 | 3,153,056 | 1,582,293 | Dewey, Thomas E. | 1,570,763 | Roosevelt, Franklin D. | | 11,530 R | 50.2% | 49.8% | 50.2% | 49.8% |
| 1940 | 3,319,912 | 1,586,773 | Willkie, Wendell | 1,733,139 | Roosevelt, Franklin D. | | 146,366 D | 47.8% | 52.2% | 47.8% | 52.2% |
| 1936 | 3,012,660 | 1,127,855 | Landon, Alfred M. | 1,747,140 | Roosevelt, Franklin D. | 137,665 | 619,285 D | 37.4% | 58.0% | 39.2% | 60.8% |
| 1932 | 2,609,728 | 1,227,319 | Hoover, Herbert C. | 1,301,695 | Roosevelt, Franklin D. | 80,714 | 74,376 D | 47.0% | 49.9% | 48.5% | 51.5% |
| 1928 | 2,508,346 | 1,627,546 | Hoover, Herbert C. | 864,210 | Smith, Alfred E. | 16,590 | 763,336 R | 64.9% | 34.5% | 65.3% | 34.7% |
| 1924 ** | 2,016,296 | 1,176,130 | Coolidge, Calvin | 477,887 | Davis, John W. | 362,279 | 698,243 R | 58.3% | 23.7% | 71.1% | 28.9% |
| 1920 | 2,021,653 | 1,182,022 | Harding, Warren G. | 780,037 | Cox, James M. | 59,594 | 401,985 R | 58.5% | 38.6% | 60.2% | 39.8% |

In 2000 the other vote column includes 117,799 votes cast for Green (Nader). In 1996 the other vote column includes 483,207 votes cast for Perot. In 1992 the other vote column includes 1,036,426 votes cast for Perot. In 1980 the other column includes 254,472 votes for Independent (Anderson). In 1924 the other vote was 358,008 Progressive; 3,025 Socialist Labor; and 1,246 Commonwealth Land.

## ELECTORAL COLLEGE VOTE 1920 TO 2004

| Year | Total | Republican | Democratic | Other |
|------|-------|------------|------------|-------|
| 2004 | 20 | 20 | | |
| 2000 | 21 | 21 | | |
| 1996 | 21 | | 21 | |
| 1992 | 21 | | 21 | |
| 1988 | 23 | 23 | | |
| 1984 | 23 | 23 | | |
| 1980 | 25 | 25 | | |
| 1976 | 25 | | 25 | |
| 1972 | 25 | 25 | | |
| 1968 | 26 | 26 | | |
| 1964 | 26 | | 26 | |
| 1960 | 25 | 25 | | |
| 1956 | 25 | 25 | | |
| 1952 | 25 | 25 | | |
| 1948 | 25 | | 25 | |
| 1944 | 25 | 25 | | |
| 1940 | 26 | | 26 | |
| 1936 | 26 | | 26 | |
| 1932 | 26 | | 26 | |
| 1928 | 24 | 24 | | |
| 1924 | 24 | 24 | | |
| 1920 | 24 | 24 | | |

# OHIO

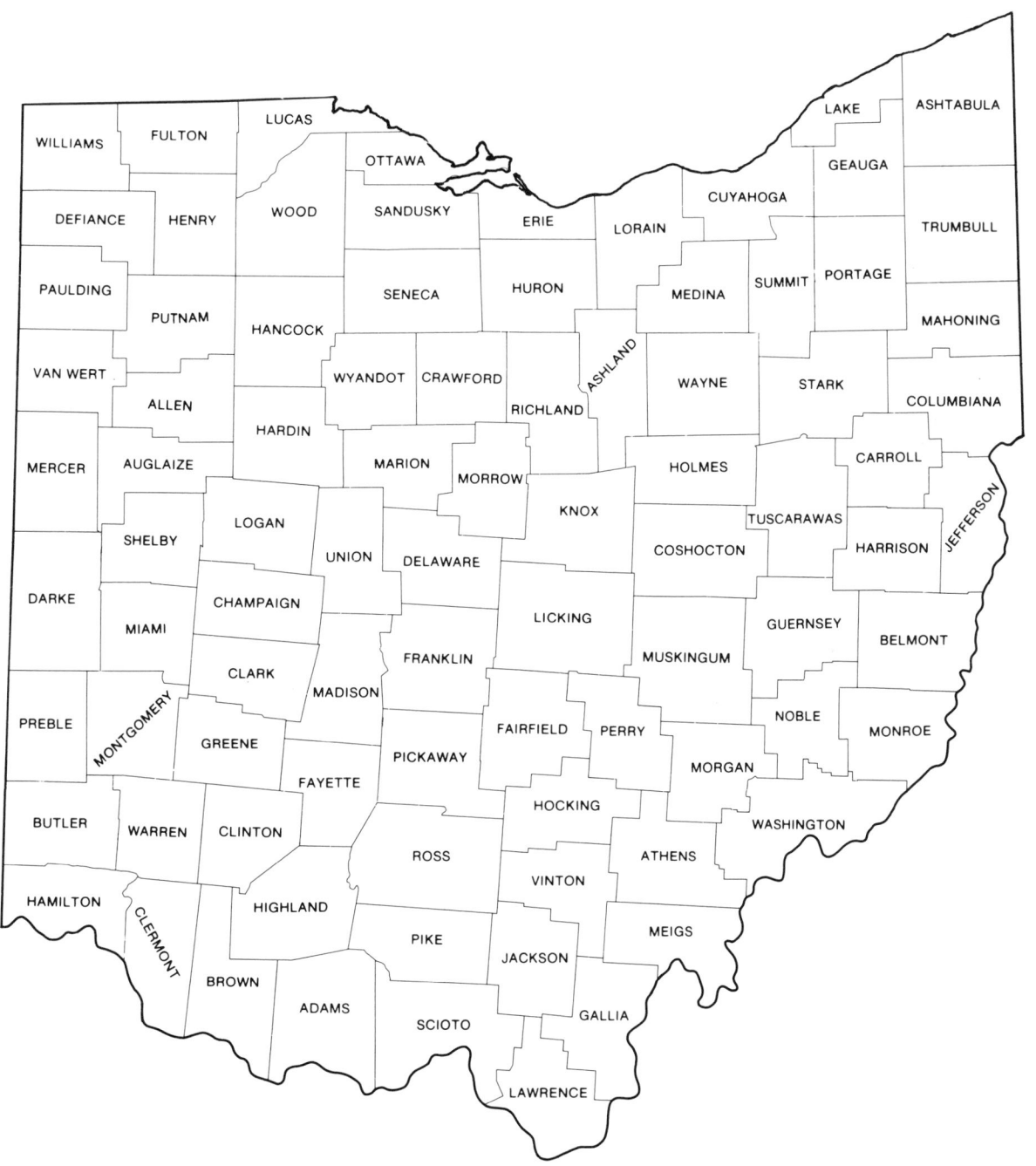

# OHIO

## PRESIDENT 2004

| 2000 Census Population | County | Total Vote | Republican | Democratic | Other | Rep.-Dem. Plurality | Percentage Total Vote Rep. | Dem. | Major Vote Rep. | Dem. |
|---|---|---|---|---|---|---|---|---|---|---|
| 27,330 | ADAMS | 12,000 | 7,653 | 4,281 | 66 | 3,372 R | 63.8% | 35.7% | 64.1% | 35.9% |
| 108,473 | ALLEN | 49,256 | 32,580 | 16,470 | 206 | 16,110 R | 66.1% | 33.4% | 66.4% | 33.6% |
| 52,523 | ASHLAND | 24,979 | 16,209 | 8,576 | 194 | 7,633 R | 64.9% | 34.3% | 65.4% | 34.6% |
| 102,728 | ASHTABULA | 45,407 | 21,038 | 24,060 | 309 | 3,022 D | 46.3% | 53.0% | 46.6% | 53.4% |
| 62,223 | ATHENS | 30,045 | 10,847 | 18,998 | 200 | 8,151 D | 36.1% | 63.2% | 36.3% | 63.7% |
| 46,611 | AUGLAIZE | 23,034 | 17,016 | 5,903 | 115 | 11,113 R | 73.9% | 25.6% | 74.2% | 25.8% |
| 70,226 | BELMONT | 33,322 | 15,589 | 17,576 | 157 | 1,987 D | 46.8% | 52.7% | 47.0% | 53.0% |
| 42,285 | BROWN | 19,892 | 12,647 | 7,140 | 105 | 5,507 R | 63.6% | 35.9% | 63.9% | 36.1% |
| 332,807 | BUTLER | 166,819 | 109,872 | 56,243 | 704 | 53,629 R | 65.9% | 33.7% | 66.1% | 33.9% |
| 28,836 | CARROLL | 14,112 | 7,695 | 6,300 | 117 | 1,395 R | 54.5% | 44.6% | 55.0% | 45.0% |
| 38,890 | CHAMPAIGN | 18,776 | 11,718 | 6,968 | 90 | 4,750 R | 62.4% | 37.1% | 62.7% | 37.3% |
| 144,742 | CLARK | 68,807 | 34,941 | 33,535 | 331 | 1,406 R | 50.8% | 48.7% | 51.0% | 49.0% |
| 177,977 | CLERMONT | 89,079 | 62,949 | 25,887 | 243 | 37,062 R | 70.7% | 29.1% | 70.9% | 29.1% |
| 40,543 | CLINTON | 18,414 | 12,938 | 5,417 | 59 | 7,521 R | 70.3% | 29.4% | 70.5% | 29.5% |
| 112,075 | COLUMBIANA | 49,465 | 25,753 | 23,429 | 283 | 2,324 R | 52.1% | 47.4% | 52.4% | 47.6% |
| 36,655 | COSHOCTON | 17,303 | 9,839 | 7,378 | 86 | 2,461 R | 56.9% | 42.6% | 57.1% | 42.9% |
| 46,966 | CRAWFORD | 21,801 | 13,885 | 7,773 | 143 | 6,112 R | 63.7% | 35.7% | 64.1% | 35.9% |
| 1,393,978 | CUYAHOGA | 673,777 | 221,600 | 448,503 | 3,674 | 226,903 D | 32.9% | 66.6% | 33.1% | 66.9% |
| 53,309 | DARKE | 26,313 | 18,306 | 7,846 | 161 | 10,460 R | 69.6% | 29.8% | 70.0% | 30.0% |
| 39,500 | DEFIANCE | 18,516 | 11,397 | 6,975 | 144 | 4,422 R | 61.6% | 37.7% | 62.0% | 38.0% |
| 109,989 | DELAWARE | 80,456 | 53,143 | 27,048 | 265 | 26,095 R | 66.1% | 33.6% | 66.3% | 33.7% |
| 79,551 | ERIE | 40,085 | 18,597 | 21,421 | 67 | 2,824 D | 46.4% | 53.4% | 46.5% | 53.5% |
| 122,759 | FAIRFIELD | 67,882 | 42,715 | 24,783 | 384 | 17,932 R | 62.9% | 36.5% | 63.3% | 36.7% |
| 28,433 | FAYETTE | 11,757 | 7,376 | 4,334 | 47 | 3,042 R | 62.7% | 36.9% | 63.0% | 37.0% |
| 1,068,978 | FRANKLIN | 525,827 | 237,253 | 285,801 | 2,773 | 48,548 D | 45.1% | 54.4% | 45.4% | 54.6% |
| 42,084 | FULTON | 21,954 | 13,640 | 8,224 | 90 | 5,416 R | 62.1% | 37.5% | 62.4% | 37.6% |
| 31,069 | GALLIA | 13,993 | 8,576 | 5,366 | 51 | 3,210 R | 61.3% | 38.3% | 61.5% | 38.5% |
| 90,895 | GEAUGA | 50,442 | 30,370 | 19,850 | 222 | 10,520 R | 60.2% | 39.4% | 60.5% | 39.5% |
| 147,886 | GREENE | 79,282 | 48,388 | 30,531 | 363 | 17,857 R | 61.0% | 38.5% | 61.3% | 38.7% |
| 40,792 | GUERNSEY | 17,840 | 9,962 | 7,768 | 110 | 2,194 R | 55.8% | 43.5% | 56.2% | 43.8% |
| 845,303 | HAMILTON | 424,025 | 222,616 | 199,679 | 1,730 | 22,937 R | 52.5% | 47.1% | 52.7% | 47.3% |
| 71,295 | HANCOCK | 35,619 | 25,105 | 10,352 | 162 | 14,753 R | 70.5% | 29.1% | 70.8% | 29.2% |
| 31,945 | HARDIN | 13,392 | 8,441 | 4,891 | 60 | 3,550 R | 63.0% | 36.5% | 63.3% | 36.7% |
| 15,856 | HARRISON | 8,109 | 4,274 | 3,780 | 55 | 494 R | 52.7% | 46.6% | 53.1% | 46.9% |
| 29,210 | HENRY | 15,105 | 9,902 | 5,111 | 92 | 4,791 R | 65.6% | 33.8% | 66.0% | 34.0% |
| 40,875 | HIGHLAND | 18,481 | 12,211 | 6,194 | 76 | 6,017 R | 66.1% | 33.5% | 66.3% | 33.7% |
| 28,241 | HOCKING | 13,199 | 6,936 | 6,175 | 88 | 761 R | 52.5% | 46.8% | 52.9% | 47.1% |
| 38,943 | HOLMES | 11,220 | 8,468 | 2,697 | 55 | 5,771 R | 75.5% | 24.0% | 75.8% | 24.2% |
| 59,487 | HURON | 25,558 | 14,817 | 10,568 | 173 | 4,249 R | 58.0% | 41.3% | 58.4% | 41.6% |
| 32,641 | JACKSON | 14,334 | 8,585 | 5,700 | 49 | 2,885 R | 59.9% | 39.8% | 60.1% | 39.9% |
| 73,894 | JEFFERSON | 36,372 | 17,185 | 19,024 | 163 | 1,839 D | 47.2% | 52.3% | 47.5% | 52.5% |
| 54,500 | KNOX | 27,045 | 17,068 | 9,820 | 157 | 7,248 R | 63.1% | 36.3% | 63.5% | 36.5% |
| 227,511 | LAKE | 121,823 | 62,193 | 59,049 | 581 | 3,144 R | 51.1% | 48.5% | 51.3% | 48.7% |
| 62,319 | LAWRENCE | 27,710 | 15,455 | 12,120 | 135 | 3,335 R | 55.8% | 43.7% | 56.0% | 44.0% |
| 145,491 | LICKING | 79,420 | 49,016 | 30,053 | 351 | 18,963 R | 61.7% | 37.8% | 62.0% | 38.0% |
| 46,005 | LOGAN | 21,398 | 14,471 | 6,825 | 102 | 7,646 R | 67.6% | 31.9% | 68.0% | 32.0% |
| 284,664 | LORAIN | 140,742 | 61,203 | 78,970 | 569 | 17,767 D | 43.5% | 56.1% | 43.7% | 56.3% |
| 455,054 | LUCAS | 220,430 | 87,160 | 132,715 | 555 | 45,555 D | 39.5% | 60.2% | 39.6% | 60.4% |
| 40,213 | MADISON | 17,398 | 11,117 | 6,203 | 78 | 4,914 R | 63.9% | 35.7% | 64.2% | 35.8% |
| 257,555 | MAHONING | 132,904 | 48,761 | 83,194 | 949 | 34,433 D | 36.7% | 62.6% | 37.0% | 63.0% |
| 66,217 | MARION | 29,258 | 17,171 | 11,930 | 157 | 5,241 R | 58.7% | 40.8% | 59.0% | 41.0% |
| 151,095 | MEDINA | 84,878 | 48,196 | 36,272 | 410 | 11,924 R | 56.8% | 42.7% | 57.1% | 42.9% |
| 23,072 | MEIGS | 10,771 | 6,272 | 4,438 | 61 | 1,834 R | 58.2% | 41.2% | 58.6% | 41.4% |
| 40,924 | MERCER | 20,890 | 15,650 | 5,118 | 122 | 10,532 R | 74.9% | 24.5% | 75.4% | 24.6% |
| 98,868 | MIAMI | 51,760 | 33,992 | 17,606 | 162 | 16,386 R | 65.7% | 34.0% | 65.9% | 34.1% |
| 15,180 | MONROE | 7,729 | 3,424 | 4,243 | 62 | 819 D | 44.3% | 54.9% | 44.7% | 55.3% |
| 559,062 | MONTGOMERY | 282,584 | 138,371 | 142,997 | 1,216 | 4,626 D | 49.0% | 50.6% | 49.2% | 50.8% |
| 14,897 | MORGAN | 6,703 | 3,758 | 2,875 | 70 | 883 R | 56.1% | 42.9% | 56.7% | 43.3% |
| 31,628 | MORROW | 16,328 | 10,474 | 5,775 | 79 | 4,699 R | 64.1% | 35.4% | 64.5% | 35.5% |
| 84,585 | MUSKINGUM | 38,866 | 22,254 | 16,421 | 191 | 5,833 R | 57.3% | 42.3% | 57.5% | 42.5% |

# OHIO

## PRESIDENT 2004

| 2000 Census Population | County | Total Vote | Republican | Democratic | Other | Rep.-Dem. Plurality | Percentage | | | |
|---|---|---|---|---|---|---|---|---|---|---|
| | | | | | | | Total Vote | | Major Vote | |
| | | | | | | | Rep. | Dem. | Rep. | Dem. |
| 14,058 | NOBLE | 6,540 | 3,841 | 2,654 | 45 | 1,187 R | 58.7% | 40.6% | 59.1% | 40.9% |
| 40,985 | OTTAWA | 23,259 | 12,073 | 11,118 | 68 | 955 R | 51.9% | 47.8% | 52.1% | 47.9% |
| 20,293 | PAULDING | 9,879 | 6,206 | 3,610 | 63 | 2,596 R | 62.8% | 36.5% | 63.2% | 36.8% |
| 34,078 | PERRY | 15,189 | 7,856 | 7,257 | 76 | 599 R | 51.7% | 47.8% | 52.0% | 48.0% |
| 52,727 | PICKAWAY | 22,852 | 14,161 | 8,579 | 112 | 5,582 R | 62.0% | 37.5% | 62.3% | 37.7% |
| 27,695 | PIKE | 12,576 | 6,520 | 5,989 | 67 | 531 R | 51.8% | 47.6% | 52.1% | 47.9% |
| 152,061 | PORTAGE | 76,647 | 35,583 | 40,675 | 389 | 5,092 D | 46.4% | 53.1% | 46.7% | 53.3% |
| 42,337 | PREBLE | 21,127 | 13,734 | 7,274 | 119 | 6,460 R | 65.0% | 34.4% | 65.4% | 34.6% |
| 34,726 | PUTNAM | 18,849 | 14,370 | 4,392 | 87 | 9,978 R | 76.2% | 23.3% | 76.6% | 23.4% |
| 128,852 | RICHLAND | 61,840 | 36,872 | 24,638 | 330 | 12,234 R | 59.6% | 39.8% | 59.9% | 40.1% |
| 73,345 | ROSS | 31,671 | 17,231 | 13,978 | 462 | 3,253 R | 54.4% | 44.1% | 55.2% | 44.8% |
| 61,792 | SANDUSKY | 29,014 | 16,224 | 12,686 | 104 | 3,538 R | 55.9% | 43.7% | 56.1% | 43.9% |
| 79,195 | SCIOTO | 35,203 | 18,259 | 16,827 | 117 | 1,432 R | 51.9% | 47.8% | 52.0% | 48.0% |
| 58,683 | SENECA | 26,991 | 15,886 | 10,957 | 148 | 4,929 R | 58.9% | 40.6% | 59.2% | 40.8% |
| 47,910 | SHELBY | 22,855 | 16,204 | 6,535 | 116 | 9,669 R | 70.9% | 28.6% | 71.3% | 28.7% |
| 378,098 | STARK | 188,459 | 92,215 | 95,337 | 907 | 3,122 D | 48.9% | 50.6% | 49.2% | 50.8% |
| 542,899 | SUMMIT | 276,320 | 118,558 | 156,587 | 1,175 | 38,029 D | 42.9% | 56.7% | 43.1% | 56.9% |
| 225,116 | TRUMBULL | 108,145 | 40,977 | 66,673 | 495 | 25,696 D | 37.9% | 61.7% | 38.1% | 61.9% |
| 90,914 | TUSCARAWAS | 42,906 | 23,829 | 18,853 | 224 | 4,976 R | 55.5% | 43.9% | 55.8% | 44.2% |
| 40,909 | UNION | 22,631 | 15,870 | 6,665 | 96 | 9,205 R | 70.1% | 29.5% | 70.4% | 29.6% |
| 29,659 | VAN WERT | 14,827 | 10,678 | 4,095 | 54 | 6,583 R | 72.0% | 27.6% | 72.3% | 27.7% |
| 12,806 | VINTON | 5,928 | 3,249 | 2,651 | 28 | 598 R | 54.8% | 44.7% | 55.1% | 44.9% |
| 158,383 | WARREN | 94,422 | 68,037 | 26,044 | 341 | 41,993 R | 72.1% | 27.6% | 72.3% | 27.7% |
| 63,251 | WASHINGTON | 30,216 | 17,532 | 12,538 | 146 | 4,994 R | 58.0% | 41.5% | 58.3% | 41.7% |
| 111,564 | WAYNE | 51,848 | 31,879 | 19,786 | 183 | 12,093 R | 61.5% | 38.2% | 61.7% | 38.3% |
| 39,188 | WILLIAMS | 18,639 | 12,040 | 6,481 | 118 | 5,559 R | 64.6% | 34.8% | 65.0% | 35.0% |
| 121,065 | WOOD | 63,346 | 33,592 | 29,401 | 353 | 4,191 R | 53.0% | 46.4% | 53.3% | 46.7% |
| 22,908 | WYANDOT | 11,043 | 7,254 | 3,708 | 81 | 3,546 R | 65.7% | 33.6% | 66.2% | 33.8% |
| 11,353,140 | TOTAL | 5,627,908 | 2,859,768 | 2,741,167 | 26,973 | 118,601 R | 50.8% | 48.7% | 51.1% | 48.9% |

# OHIO

## PRESIDENT 2000

| 2000 Census Population | County | Total Vote | Republican | Democratic | Green (Nader) | Other | Rep.-Dem. Plurality | Percentage of Total Vote | | |
|---|---|---|---|---|---|---|---|---|---|---|
| | | | | | | | | Rep. | Dem. | Green |
| 27,330 | ADAMS | 10,235 | 6,380 | 3,581 | 162 | 112 | 2,799 R | 62.3% | 35.0% | 1.6% |
| 108,473 | ALLEN | 43,795 | 28,647 | 13,996 | 760 | 392 | 14,651 R | 65.4% | 32.0% | 1.7% |
| 52,523 | ASHLAND | 21,258 | 13,533 | 6,685 | 563 | 477 | 6,848 R | 63.7% | 31.4% | 2.6% |
| 102,728 | ASHTABULA | 39,472 | 17,940 | 19,831 | 1,109 | 592 | 1,891 D | 45.4% | 50.2% | 2.8% |
| 62,223 | ATHENS | 25,447 | 9,703 | 13,158 | 1,663 | 923 | 3,455 D | 38.1% | 51.7% | 6.5% |
| 46,611 | AUGLAIZE | 19,892 | 13,770 | 5,564 | 372 | 186 | 8,206 R | 69.2% | 28.0% | 1.9% |
| 70,226 | BELMONT | 30,141 | 12,625 | 15,980 | 723 | 813 | 3,355 D | 41.9% | 53.0% | 2.4% |
| 42,285 | BROWN | 16,429 | 10,027 | 5,972 | 269 | 161 | 4,055 R | 61.0% | 36.4% | 1.6% |
| 332,807 | BUTLER | 136,737 | 86,587 | 46,390 | 2,708 | 1,052 | 40,197 R | 63.3% | 33.9% | 2.0% |
| 28,836 | CARROLL | 12,261 | 6,732 | 4,960 | 271 | 298 | 1,772 R | 54.9% | 40.5% | 2.2% |
| 38,890 | CHAMPAIGN | 15,680 | 9,220 | 5,955 | 346 | 159 | 3,265 R | 58.8% | 38.0% | 2.2% |
| 144,742 | CLARK | 57,559 | 27,660 | 27,984 | 1,347 | 568 | 324 D | 48.1% | 48.6% | 2.3% |
| 177,977 | CLERMONT | 69,877 | 47,129 | 20,927 | 1,303 | 518 | 26,202 R | 67.4% | 29.9% | 1.9% |
| 40,543 | CLINTON | 15,070 | 9,824 | 4,791 | 325 | 130 | 5,033 R | 65.2% | 31.8% | 2.2% |
| 112,075 | COLUMBIANA | 44,427 | 21,804 | 20,657 | 1,217 | 749 | 1,147 R | 49.1% | 46.5% | 2.7% |
| 36,655 | COSHOCTON | 14,268 | 8,243 | 5,594 | 295 | 136 | 2,649 R | 57.8% | 39.2% | 2.1% |
| 46,966 | CRAWFORD | 19,176 | 11,666 | 6,721 | 536 | 253 | 4,945 R | 60.8% | 35.0% | 2.8% |
| 1,393,978 | CUYAHOGA | 571,323 | 191,253 | 357,351 | 16,898 | 5,821 | 166,098 D | 33.5% | 62.5% | 3.0% |
| 53,309 | DARKE | 23,267 | 14,817 | 7,741 | 452 | 257 | 7,076 R | 63.7% | 33.3% | 1.9% |
| 39,500 | DEFIANCE | 16,242 | 9,540 | 6,175 | 365 | 162 | 3,365 R | 58.7% | 38.0% | 2.2% |
| 109,989 | DELAWARE | 55,403 | 36,639 | 17,134 | 1,212 | 418 | 19,505 R | 66.1% | 30.9% | 2.2% |
| 79,551 | ERIE | 35,015 | 16,105 | 17,732 | 872 | 306 | 1,627 D | 46.0% | 50.6% | 2.5% |
| 122,759 | FAIRFIELD | 54,094 | 33,523 | 19,065 | 1,115 | 391 | 14,458 R | 62.0% | 35.2% | 2.1% |
| 28,433 | FAYETTE | 9,278 | 5,685 | 3,363 | 165 | 65 | 2,322 R | 61.3% | 36.2% | 1.8% |
| 1,068,978 | FRANKLIN | 414,074 | 197,862 | 202,018 | 10,702 | 3,492 | 4,156 D | 47.8% | 48.8% | 2.6% |
| 42,084 | FULTON | 18,896 | 11,546 | 6,805 | 376 | 169 | 4,741 R | 61.1% | 36.0% | 2.0% |
| 31,069 | GALLIA | 12,776 | 7,511 | 4,872 | 215 | 178 | 2,639 R | 58.8% | 38.1% | 1.7% |
| 90,895 | GEAUGA | 42,600 | 25,417 | 15,327 | 1,405 | 451 | 10,090 R | 59.7% | 36.0% | 3.3% |
| 147,886 | GREENE | 65,204 | 37,946 | 25,059 | 1,592 | 607 | 12,887 R | 58.2% | 38.4% | 2.4% |
| 40,792 | GUERNSEY | 15,430 | 8,181 | 6,643 | 405 | 201 | 1,538 R | 53.0% | 43.1% | 2.6% |
| 845,303 | HAMILTON | 377,899 | 204,175 | 161,578 | 9,222 | 2,924 | 42,597 R | 54.0% | 42.8% | 2.4% |
| 71,295 | HANCOCK | 30,617 | 20,985 | 8,798 | 592 | 242 | 12,187 R | 68.5% | 28.7% | 1.9% |
| 31,945 | HARDIN | 12,068 | 7,124 | 4,557 | 243 | 144 | 2,567 R | 59.0% | 37.8% | 2.0% |
| 15,856 | HARRISON | 7,161 | 3,417 | 3,351 | 192 | 201 | 66 R | 47.7% | 46.8% | 2.7% |
| 29,210 | HENRY | 13,252 | 8,530 | 4,367 | 258 | 97 | 4,163 R | 64.4% | 33.0% | 1.9% |
| 40,875 | HIGHLAND | 15,447 | 9,728 | 5,328 | 245 | 146 | 4,400 R | 63.0% | 34.5% | 1.6% |
| 28,241 | HOCKING | 10,756 | 5,702 | 4,474 | 291 | 289 | 1,228 R | 53.0% | 41.6% | 2.7% |
| 38,943 | HOLMES | 9,145 | 6,754 | 2,066 | 172 | 153 | 4,688 R | 73.9% | 22.6% | 1.9% |
| 59,487 | HURON | 21,360 | 12,286 | 8,183 | 560 | 331 | 4,103 R | 57.5% | 38.3% | 2.6% |
| 32,641 | JACKSON | 12,490 | 6,958 | 5,131 | 222 | 179 | 1,827 R | 55.7% | 41.1% | 1.8% |
| 73,894 | JEFFERSON | 34,636 | 15,038 | 17,488 | 897 | 1,213 | 2,450 D | 43.4% | 50.5% | 2.6% |
| 54,500 | KNOX | 21,260 | 13,393 | 7,133 | 452 | 282 | 6,260 R | 63.0% | 33.6% | 2.1% |
| 227,511 | LAKE | 102,564 | 51,747 | 46,497 | 3,166 | 1,154 | 5,250 R | 50.5% | 45.3% | 3.1% |
| 62,319 | LAWRENCE | 24,452 | 12,531 | 11,307 | 402 | 212 | 1,224 R | 51.2% | 46.2% | 1.6% |
| 145,491 | LICKING | 62,466 | 37,180 | 23,196 | 1,498 | 592 | 13,984 R | 59.5% | 37.1% | 2.4% |
| 46,005 | LOGAN | 18,455 | 11,849 | 5,945 | 449 | 212 | 5,904 R | 64.2% | 32.2% | 2.4% |
| 284,664 | LORAIN | 112,180 | 47,957 | 59,809 | 3,183 | 1,231 | 11,852 D | 42.8% | 53.3% | 2.8% |
| 455,054 | LUCAS | 187,350 | 73,342 | 108,344 | 4,227 | 1,437 | 35,002 D | 39.1% | 57.8% | 2.3% |
| 40,213 | MADISON | 14,667 | 8,892 | 5,287 | 299 | 189 | 3,605 R | 60.6% | 36.0% | 2.0% |
| 257,555 | MAHONING | 114,119 | 40,460 | 69,212 | 3,322 | 1,125 | 28,752 D | 35.5% | 60.6% | 2.9% |
| 66,217 | MARION | 24,815 | 13,617 | 10,370 | 588 | 240 | 3,247 R | 54.9% | 41.8% | 2.4% |
| 151,095 | MEDINA | 66,883 | 37,349 | 26,635 | 1,960 | 939 | 10,714 R | 55.8% | 39.8% | 2.9% |
| 23,072 | MEIGS | 9,795 | 5,750 | 3,674 | 226 | 145 | 2,076 R | 58.7% | 37.5% | 2.3% |
| 40,924 | MERCER | 18,294 | 12,485 | 5,212 | 392 | 205 | 7,273 R | 68.2% | 28.5% | 2.1% |
| 98,868 | MIAMI | 42,841 | 26,037 | 15,584 | 879 | 341 | 10,453 R | 60.8% | 36.4% | 2.1% |
| 15,180 | MONROE | 7,115 | 3,145 | 3,605 | 149 | 216 | 460 D | 44.2% | 50.7% | 2.1% |
| 559,062 | MONTGOMERY | 230,987 | 109,792 | 114,597 | 4,690 | 1,908 | 4,805 D | 47.5% | 49.6% | 2.0% |
| 14,897 | MORGAN | 5,993 | 3,451 | 2,261 | 177 | 104 | 1,190 R | 57.6% | 37.7% | 3.0% |
| 31,628 | MORROW | 12,839 | 7,842 | 4,529 | 305 | 163 | 3,313 R | 61.1% | 35.3% | 2.4% |
| 84,585 | MUSKINGUM | 32,624 | 17,995 | 13,415 | 882 | 332 | 4,580 R | 55.2% | 41.1% | 2.7% |

# OHIO

## PRESIDENT 2000

| 2000 Census Population | County | Total Vote | Republican | Democratic | Green (Nader) | Other | Rep.-Dem. Plurality | Percentage of Total Vote | | |
|---|---|---|---|---|---|---|---|---|---|---|
| | | | | | | | | Rep. | Dem. | Green |
| 14,058 | NOBLE | 5,988 | 3,435 | 2,296 | 154 | 103 | 1,139 R | 57.4% | 38.3% | 2.6% |
| 40,985 | OTTAWA | 19,968 | 9,917 | 9,485 | 432 | 134 | 432 R | 49.7% | 47.5% | 2.2% |
| 20,293 | PAULDING | 8,946 | 5,210 | 3,384 | 242 | 110 | 1,826 R | 58.2% | 37.8% | 2.7% |
| 34,078 | PERRY | 12,828 | 6,440 | 5,895 | 334 | 159 | 545 R | 50.2% | 46.0% | 2.6% |
| 52,727 | PICKAWAY | 17,740 | 10,717 | 6,598 | 276 | 149 | 4,119 R | 60.4% | 37.2% | 1.6% |
| 27,695 | PIKE | 10,560 | 5,333 | 4,923 | 176 | 128 | 410 R | 50.5% | 46.6% | 1.7% |
| 152,061 | PORTAGE | 62,899 | 28,271 | 31,446 | 2,340 | 842 | 3,175 D | 44.9% | 50.0% | 3.7% |
| 42,337 | PREBLE | 18,166 | 11,176 | 6,375 | 404 | 211 | 4,801 R | 61.5% | 35.1% | 2.2% |
| 34,726 | PUTNAM | 17,344 | 12,837 | 4,063 | 254 | 190 | 8,774 R | 74.0% | 23.4% | 1.5% |
| 128,852 | RICHLAND | 52,779 | 30,138 | 20,572 | 1,306 | 763 | 9,566 R | 57.1% | 39.0% | 2.5% |
| 73,345 | ROSS | 26,016 | 13,706 | 11,662 | 421 | 227 | 2,044 R | 52.7% | 44.8% | 1.6% |
| 61,792 | SANDUSKY | 25,744 | 13,699 | 11,146 | 587 | 312 | 2,553 R | 53.2% | 43.3% | 2.3% |
| 79,195 | SCIOTO | 29,945 | 15,022 | 13,997 | 590 | 336 | 1,025 R | 50.2% | 46.7% | 2.0% |
| 58,683 | SENECA | 24,351 | 13,863 | 9,512 | 666 | 310 | 4,351 R | 56.9% | 39.1% | 2.7% |
| 47,910 | SHELBY | 19,670 | 12,476 | 6,593 | 392 | 209 | 5,883 R | 63.4% | 33.5% | 2.0% |
| 378,098 | STARK | 159,844 | 78,153 | 75,308 | 4,032 | 2,351 | 2,845 R | 48.9% | 47.1% | 2.5% |
| 542,899 | SUMMIT | 224,839 | 96,721 | 119,759 | 5,955 | 2,404 | 23,038 D | 43.0% | 53.3% | 2.6% |
| 225,116 | TRUMBULL | 96,239 | 34,654 | 57,643 | 2,749 | 1,193 | 22,989 D | 36.0% | 59.9% | 2.9% |
| 90,914 | TUSCARAWAS | 37,118 | 19,549 | 15,879 | 1,061 | 629 | 3,670 R | 52.7% | 42.8% | 2.9% |
| 40,909 | UNION | 17,024 | 11,502 | 5,040 | 336 | 146 | 6,462 R | 67.6% | 29.6% | 2.0% |
| 29,659 | VAN WERT | 13,219 | 8,679 | 4,209 | 216 | 115 | 4,470 R | 65.7% | 31.8% | 1.6% |
| 12,806 | VINTON | 4,946 | 2,720 | 2,037 | 110 | 79 | 683 R | 55.0% | 41.2% | 2.2% |
| 158,383 | WARREN | 69,078 | 48,318 | 19,142 | 1,067 | 551 | 29,176 R | 69.9% | 27.7% | 1.5% |
| 63,251 | WASHINGTON | 26,515 | 15,342 | 10,383 | 571 | 219 | 4,959 R | 57.9% | 39.2% | 2.2% |
| 111,564 | WAYNE | 42,436 | 25,901 | 14,779 | 1,171 | 585 | 11,122 R | 61.0% | 34.8% | 2.8% |
| 39,188 | WILLIAMS | 15,919 | 9,941 | 5,454 | 347 | 177 | 4,487 R | 62.4% | 34.3% | 2.2% |
| 121,065 | WOOD | 52,194 | 27,504 | 22,687 | 1,536 | 467 | 4,817 R | 52.7% | 43.5% | 2.9% |
| 22,908 | WYANDOT | 9,827 | 6,113 | 3,397 | 191 | 126 | 2,716 R | 62.2% | 34.6% | 1.9% |
| 11,353,140 | TOTAL | 4,701,998 | 2,350,363 | 2,183,628 | 117,799 | 50,208 | 166,735 R | 50.0% | 46.4% | 2.5% |

# OHIO

## PRESIDENT 1996

| 1995 Census Pop. Est. | County | Total Vote | Republican | Democratic | Reform (Perot) | Other | Rep.-Dem. Plurality | Percentage of Total Vote | | |
|---|---|---|---|---|---|---|---|---|---|---|
| | | | | | | | | Rep. | Dem. | Reform |
| 27,670 | ADAMS | 10,381 | 4,763 | 4,317 | 1,223 | 78 | 446 R | 45.9% | 41.6% | 11.8% |
| 109,399 | ALLEN | 43,948 | 24,325 | 15,529 | 3,799 | 295 | 8,796 R | 55.3% | 35.3% | 8.6% |
| 51,240 | ASHLAND | 19,773 | 10,402 | 6,573 | 2,630 | 168 | 3,829 R | 52.6% | 33.2% | 13.3% |
| 102,360 | ASHTABULA | 38,722 | 13,287 | 19,341 | 5,700 | 394 | 6,054 D | 34.3% | 49.9% | 14.7% |
| 60,687 | ATHENS | 23,954 | 7,154 | 13,418 | 2,777 | 605 | 6,264 D | 29.9% | 56.0% | 11.6% |
| 46,877 | AUGLAIZE | 19,632 | 10,169 | 6,652 | 2,641 | 170 | 3,517 R | 51.8% | 33.9% | 13.5% |
| 70,379 | BELMONT | 30,639 | 8,213 | 17,705 | 4,452 | 269 | 9,492 D | 26.8% | 57.8% | 14.5% |
| 38,850 | BROWN | 15,366 | 6,970 | 6,318 | 1,941 | 137 | 652 R | 45.4% | 41.1% | 12.6% |
| 315,601 | BUTLER | 122,398 | 67,023 | 43,690 | 10,540 | 1,145 | 23,333 R | 54.8% | 35.7% | 8.6% |
| 28,142 | CARROLL | 11,790 | 4,449 | 4,792 | 2,445 | 104 | 343 D | 37.7% | 40.6% | 20.7% |
| 37,686 | CHAMPAIGN | 14,893 | 6,568 | 5,990 | 2,219 | 116 | 578 R | 44.1% | 40.2% | 14.9% |
| 147,731 | CLARK | 57,802 | 22,297 | 27,890 | 7,083 | 532 | 5,593 D | 38.6% | 48.3% | 12.3% |
| 166,941 | CLERMONT | 64,174 | 36,457 | 21,329 | 5,795 | 593 | 15,128 R | 56.8% | 33.2% | 9.0% |
| 38,019 | CLINTON | 14,521 | 7,504 | 5,303 | 1,588 | 126 | 2,201 R | 51.7% | 36.5% | 10.9% |
| 111,853 | COLUMBIANA | 43,629 | 15,386 | 20,716 | 7,127 | 400 | 5,330 D | 35.3% | 47.5% | 16.3% |
| 36,244 | COSHOCTON | 14,330 | 6,018 | 6,005 | 2,183 | 124 | 13 R | 42.0% | 41.9% | 15.2% |
| 47,733 | CRAWFORD | 19,451 | 8,730 | 7,449 | 3,072 | 200 | 1,281 R | 44.9% | 38.3% | 15.8% |
| 1,398,169 | CUYAHOGA | 561,892 | 163,770 | 341,357 | 50,691 | 6,074 | 177,587 D | 29.1% | 60.8% | 9.0% |
| 54,318 | DARKE | 23,032 | 10,798 | 8,871 | 3,168 | 195 | 1,927 R | 46.9% | 38.5% | 13.8% |
| 40,115 | DEFIANCE | 15,893 | 7,469 | 6,343 | 1,929 | 152 | 1,126 R | 47.0% | 39.9% | 12.1% |
| 78,956 | DELAWARE | 41,415 | 24,123 | 13,463 | 3,471 | 358 | 10,660 R | 58.2% | 32.5% | 8.4% |
| 78,805 | ERIE | 33,449 | 12,204 | 16,730 | 4,225 | 290 | 4,526 D | 36.5% | 50.0% | 12.6% |
| 117,556 | FAIRFIELD | 50,684 | 26,850 | 18,821 | 4,660 | 353 | 8,029 R | 53.0% | 37.1% | 9.2% |
| 28,431 | FAYETTE | 9,607 | 4,831 | 3,665 | 1,047 | 64 | 1,166 R | 50.3% | 38.1% | 10.9% |
| 1,011,019 | FRANKLIN | 400,515 | 178,412 | 192,795 | 25,400 | 3,908 | 14,383 D | 44.5% | 48.1% | 6.3% |
| 40,846 | FULTON | 17,907 | 8,703 | 6,662 | 2,412 | 130 | 2,041 R | 48.6% | 37.2% | 13.5% |
| 32,582 | GALLIA | 12,466 | 5,135 | 5,386 | 1,839 | 106 | 251 D | 41.2% | 43.2% | 14.8% |
| 84,260 | GEAUGA | 39,089 | 19,662 | 14,143 | 4,848 | 436 | 5,519 R | 50.3% | 36.2% | 12.4% |
| 141,181 | GREENE | 61,782 | 30,677 | 25,082 | 5,246 | 777 | 5,595 R | 49.7% | 40.6% | 8.5% |
| 40,246 | GUERNSEY | 15,108 | 5,970 | 6,731 | 2,251 | 156 | 761 D | 39.5% | 44.6% | 14.9% |
| 863,908 | HAMILTON | 372,068 | 186,493 | 160,458 | 21,335 | 3,782 | 26,035 R | 50.1% | 43.1% | 5.7% |
| 68,239 | HANCOCK | 29,908 | 17,252 | 9,334 | 2,904 | 418 | 7,918 R | 57.7% | 31.2% | 9.7% |
| 31,558 | HARDIN | 11,876 | 5,506 | 4,930 | 1,365 | 75 | 576 R | 46.4% | 41.5% | 11.5% |
| 16,100 | HARRISON | 7,402 | 2,310 | 3,721 | 1,302 | 69 | 1,411 D | 31.2% | 50.3% | 17.6% |
| 29,814 | HENRY | 12,785 | 6,385 | 4,762 | 1,550 | 88 | 1,623 R | 49.9% | 37.2% | 12.1% |
| 39,245 | HIGHLAND | 14,674 | 7,102 | 5,837 | 1,629 | 106 | 1,265 R | 48.4% | 39.8% | 11.1% |
| 27,997 | HOCKING | 10,356 | 4,017 | 4,646 | 1,564 | 129 | 629 D | 38.8% | 44.9% | 15.1% |
| 36,160 | HOLMES | 9,084 | 5,213 | 2,531 | 1,276 | 64 | 2,682 R | 57.4% | 27.9% | 14.0% |
| 58,613 | HURON | 21,161 | 8,750 | 8,858 | 3,338 | 215 | 108 D | 41.3% | 41.9% | 15.8% |
| 31,927 | JACKSON | 12,095 | 4,922 | 5,538 | 1,529 | 106 | 616 D | 40.7% | 45.8% | 12.6% |
| 78,262 | JEFFERSON | 34,623 | 10,212 | 19,402 | 4,748 | 261 | 9,190 D | 29.5% | 56.0% | 13.7% |
| 51,009 | KNOX | 20,068 | 10,159 | 7,562 | 2,138 | 209 | 2,597 R | 50.6% | 37.7% | 10.7% |
| 223,003 | LAKE | 97,736 | 40,974 | 43,186 | 12,507 | 1,069 | 2,212 D | 41.9% | 44.2% | 12.8% |
| 64,206 | LAWRENCE | 23,926 | 8,832 | 11,595 | 3,232 | 267 | 2,763 D | 36.9% | 48.5% | 13.5% |
| 136,593 | LICKING | 57,967 | 28,276 | 22,624 | 6,516 | 551 | 5,652 R | 48.8% | 39.0% | 11.2% |
| 45,204 | LOGAN | 17,145 | 8,325 | 6,397 | 2,264 | 159 | 1,928 R | 48.6% | 37.3% | 13.2% |
| 281,447 | LORAIN | 106,445 | 34,937 | 55,744 | 14,889 | 875 | 20,807 D | 32.8% | 52.4% | 14.0% |
| 455,018 | LUCAS | 181,747 | 58,120 | 104,911 | 17,282 | 1,434 | 46,791 D | 32.0% | 57.7% | 9.5% |
| 40,878 | MADISON | 13,421 | 6,871 | 5,072 | 1,386 | 92 | 1,799 R | 51.2% | 37.8% | 10.3% |
| 262,338 | MAHONING | 118,178 | 31,397 | 72,716 | 13,213 | 852 | 41,319 D | 26.6% | 61.5% | 11.2% |
| 65,781 | MARION | 24,674 | 11,112 | 10,482 | 2,897 | 183 | 630 R | 45.0% | 42.5% | 11.7% |
| 135,735 | MEDINA | 59,086 | 26,120 | 23,727 | 8,700 | 539 | 2,393 R | 44.2% | 40.2% | 14.7% |
| 24,066 | MEIGS | 9,465 | 3,622 | 4,275 | 1,453 | 115 | 653 D | 38.3% | 45.2% | 15.4% |
| 40,906 | MERCER | 17,653 | 8,832 | 6,300 | 2,361 | 160 | 2,532 R | 50.0% | 35.7% | 13.4% |
| 97,010 | MIAMI | 40,005 | 19,509 | 15,540 | 4,599 | 357 | 3,969 R | 48.8% | 38.8% | 11.5% |
| 15,388 | MONROE | 6,967 | 1,856 | 3,914 | 1,128 | 69 | 2,058 D | 26.6% | 56.2% | 16.2% |
| 570,490 | MONTGOMERY | 230,957 | 95,391 | 115,469 | 18,298 | 1,799 | 20,078 D | 41.3% | 50.0% | 7.9% |
| 14,602 | MORGAN | 5,971 | 2,566 | 2,385 | 922 | 98 | 181 R | 43.0% | 39.9% | 15.4% |
| 30,136 | MORROW | 12,275 | 5,655 | 4,627 | 1,745 | 248 | 1,028 R | 46.1% | 37.7% | 14.2% |
| 84,169 | MUSKINGUM | 32,972 | 13,861 | 13,813 | 4,880 | 418 | 48 R | 42.0% | 41.9% | 14.8% |

# OHIO

## PRESIDENT 1996

| 1995 Census Pop. Est. | County | Total Vote | Republican | Democratic | Reform (Perot) | Other | Rep.-Dem. Plurality | Percentage of Total Vote | | |
|---|---|---|---|---|---|---|---|---|---|---|
| | | | | | | | | Rep. | Dem. | Reform |
| 12,096 | NOBLE | 5,514 | 2,183 | 2,366 | 899 | 66 | 183 D | 39.6% | 42.9% | 16.3% |
| 40,591 | OTTAWA | 18,888 | 6,991 | 9,321 | 2,438 | 138 | 2,330 D | 37.0% | 49.3% | 12.9% |
| 20,443 | PAULDING | 8,596 | 3,760 | 3,449 | 1,292 | 95 | 311 R | 43.7% | 40.1% | 15.0% |
| 33,550 | PERRY | 12,447 | 4,606 | 5,819 | 1,854 | 168 | 1,213 D | 37.0% | 46.8% | 14.9% |
| 52,510 | PICKAWAY | 17,501 | 8,666 | 7,042 | 1,702 | 91 | 1,624 R | 49.5% | 40.2% | 9.7% |
| 26,775 | PIKE | 10,787 | 3,759 | 5,542 | 1,402 | 84 | 1,783 D | 34.8% | 51.4% | 13.0% |
| 148,699 | PORTAGE | 58,238 | 18,939 | 29,441 | 9,178 | 680 | 10,502 D | 32.5% | 50.6% | 15.8% |
| 42,174 | PREBLE | 17,133 | 8,139 | 6,611 | 2,235 | 148 | 1,528 R | 47.5% | 38.6% | 13.0% |
| 35,089 | PUTNAM | 16,158 | 9,294 | 4,972 | 1,767 | 125 | 4,322 R | 57.5% | 30.8% | 10.9% |
| 128,421 | RICHLAND | 51,451 | 23,697 | 20,832 | 6,613 | 309 | 2,865 R | 46.1% | 40.5% | 12.9% |
| 73,941 | ROSS | 25,797 | 10,286 | 12,649 | 2,648 | 214 | 2,363 D | 39.9% | 49.0% | 10.3% |
| 62,997 | SANDUSKY | 25,413 | 10,033 | 11,547 | 3,617 | 216 | 1,514 D | 39.5% | 45.4% | 14.2% |
| 81,414 | SCIOTO | 31,328 | 11,679 | 15,041 | 4,418 | 190 | 3,362 D | 37.3% | 48.0% | 14.1% |
| 60,369 | SENECA | 23,511 | 9,713 | 10,044 | 3,498 | 256 | 331 D | 41.3% | 42.7% | 14.9% |
| 47,079 | SHELBY | 18,362 | 8,773 | 6,729 | 2,686 | 174 | 2,044 R | 47.8% | 36.6% | 14.6% |
| 375,553 | STARK | 158,346 | 60,212 | 73,437 | 23,004 | 1,693 | 13,225 D | 38.0% | 46.4% | 14.5% |
| 530,135 | SUMMIT | 215,195 | 73,555 | 112,050 | 27,723 | 1,867 | 38,495 D | 34.2% | 52.1% | 12.9% |
| 228,417 | TRUMBULL | 94,745 | 24,811 | 55,604 | 13,563 | 767 | 30,793 D | 26.2% | 58.7% | 14.3% |
| 87,323 | TUSCARAWAS | 34,755 | 13,388 | 15,244 | 5,682 | 441 | 1,856 D | 38.5% | 43.9% | 16.3% |
| 36,528 | UNION | 15,003 | 8,290 | 4,989 | 1,596 | 128 | 3,301 R | 55.3% | 33.3% | 10.6% |
| 30,463 | VAN WERT | 13,041 | 6,999 | 4,453 | 1,487 | 102 | 2,546 R | 53.7% | 34.1% | 11.4% |
| 12,072 | VINTON | 4,811 | 1,673 | 2,350 | 728 | 60 | 677 D | 34.8% | 48.8% | 15.1% |
| 131,295 | WARREN | 55,409 | 33,210 | 17,089 | 4,689 | 421 | 16,121 R | 59.9% | 30.8% | 8.5% |
| 63,836 | WASHINGTON | 25,977 | 11,965 | 10,945 | 2,832 | 235 | 1,020 R | 46.1% | 42.1% | 10.9% |
| 107,526 | WAYNE | 40,548 | 19,628 | 14,850 | 5,771 | 299 | 4,778 R | 48.4% | 36.6% | 14.2% |
| 37,846 | WILLIAMS | 15,598 | 7,747 | 5,524 | 2,121 | 206 | 2,223 R | 49.7% | 35.4% | 13.6% |
| 116,934 | WOOD | 49,343 | 20,518 | 23,183 | 5,065 | 577 | 2,665 D | 41.6% | 47.0% | 10.3% |
| 22,732 | WYANDOT | 9,607 | 4,473 | 3,677 | 1,347 | 110 | 796 R | 46.6% | 38.3% | 14.0% |
| 11,150,506 | TOTAL | 4,534,434 | 1,859,883 | 2,148,222 | 483,207 | 43,122 | 288,339 D | 41.0% | 47.4% | 10.7% |

# OHIO

## PRESIDENT 1992

| 1990 Census Population | County | Total Vote | Republican | Democratic | Perot | Other | Plurality | Percentage Total Vote | | |
|---|---|---|---|---|---|---|---|---|---|---|
| | | | | | | | | Rep. | Dem. | Perot |
| 25,371 | ADAMS | 10,758 | 4,722 | 3,998 | 1,993 | 45 | 724 R | 43.9% | 37.2% | 18.5% |
| 109,755 | ALLEN | 47,350 | 25,322 | 13,777 | 8,131 | 120 | 11,545 R | 53.5% | 29.1% | 17.2% |
| 47,507 | ASHLAND | 20,855 | 9,864 | 5,985 | 4,950 | 56 | 3,879 R | 47.3% | 28.7% | 23.7% |
| 99,821 | ASHTABULA | 43,028 | 13,254 | 18,843 | 10,765 | 166 | 5,589 D | 30.8% | 43.8% | 25.0% |
| 59,549 | ATHENS | 25,793 | 7,184 | 13,423 | 5,074 | 112 | 6,239 D | 27.9% | 52.0% | 19.7% |
| 44,585 | AUGLAIZE | 20,306 | 10,455 | 4,960 | 4,840 | 51 | 5,495 R | 51.5% | 24.4% | 23.8% |
| 71,074 | BELMONT | 33,421 | 8,614 | 18,527 | 6,142 | 138 | 9,913 D | 25.8% | 55.4% | 18.4% |
| 34,966 | BROWN | 15,186 | 5,912 | 5,540 | 3,676 | 58 | 372 R | 38.9% | 36.5% | 24.2% |
| 291,479 | BUTLER | 131,112 | 63,375 | 39,682 | 27,527 | 528 | 23,693 R | 48.3% | 30.3% | 21.0% |
| 26,521 | CARROLL | 12,463 | 4,224 | 4,731 | 3,434 | 74 | 507 D | 33.9% | 38.0% | 27.6% |
| 36,019 | CHAMPAIGN | 16,252 | 7,004 | 5,201 | 3,992 | 55 | 1,803 R | 43.1% | 32.0% | 24.6% |
| 147,548 | CLARK | 63,538 | 24,011 | 26,692 | 12,571 | 264 | 2,681 D | 37.8% | 42.0% | 19.8% |
| 150,187 | CLERMONT | 64,142 | 32,065 | 17,558 | 14,279 | 240 | 14,507 R | 50.0% | 27.4% | 22.3% |
| 35,415 | CLINTON | 15,391 | 7,290 | 4,638 | 3,402 | 61 | 2,652 R | 47.4% | 30.1% | 22.1% |
| 108,276 | COLUMBIANA | 47,554 | 15,016 | 19,765 | 12,611 | 162 | 4,749 D | 31.6% | 41.6% | 26.5% |
| 35,427 | COSHOCTON | 16,173 | 5,705 | 6,212 | 4,081 | 175 | 507 D | 35.3% | 38.4% | 25.2% |
| 47,870 | CRAWFORD | 20,835 | 8,618 | 6,351 | 5,764 | 102 | 2,267 R | 41.4% | 30.5% | 27.7% |
| 1,412,140 | CUYAHOGA | 640,241 | 187,186 | 337,548 | 112,352 | 3,155 | 150,362 D | 29.2% | 52.7% | 17.5% |
| 53,619 | DARKE | 24,426 | 11,098 | 7,016 | 6,217 | 95 | 4,082 R | 45.4% | 28.7% | 25.5% |
| 39,350 | DEFIANCE | 17,211 | 7,195 | 5,735 | 4,187 | 94 | 1,460 R | 41.8% | 33.3% | 24.3% |
| 66,929 | DELAWARE | 36,873 | 18,225 | 9,263 | 9,244 | 141 | 8,962 R | 49.4% | 25.1% | 25.1% |
| 76,779 | ERIE | 35,828 | 12,459 | 14,531 | 8,720 | 118 | 2,072 D | 34.8% | 40.6% | 24.3% |
| 103,461 | FAIRFIELD | 50,789 | 24,125 | 14,249 | 12,246 | 169 | 9,876 R | 47.5% | 28.1% | 24.1% |
| 27,466 | FAYETTE | 10,086 | 4,916 | 2,976 | 2,162 | 32 | 1,940 R | 48.7% | 29.5% | 21.4% |
| 961,437 | FRANKLIN | 444,801 | 186,324 | 176,656 | 79,049 | 2,772 | 9,668 R | 41.9% | 39.7% | 17.8% |
| 38,498 | FULTON | 18,804 | 8,358 | 5,576 | 4,798 | 72 | 2,782 R | 44.4% | 29.7% | 25.5% |
| 30,954 | GALLIA | 13,738 | 5,776 | 5,350 | 2,549 | 63 | 426 R | 42.0% | 38.9% | 18.6% |
| 81,129 | GEAUGA | 40,518 | 18,200 | 11,466 | 10,577 | 275 | 6,734 R | 44.9% | 28.3% | 26.1% |
| 136,731 | GREENE | 59,502 | 27,651 | 20,139 | 11,459 | 253 | 7,512 R | 46.5% | 33.8% | 19.3% |
| 39,024 | GUERNSEY | 16,348 | 5,749 | 6,428 | 4,103 | 68 | 679 D | 35.2% | 39.3% | 25.1% |
| 866,228 | HAMILTON | 403,420 | 192,447 | 148,409 | 60,145 | 2,419 | 44,038 R | 47.7% | 36.8% | 14.9% |
| 65,536 | HANCOCK | 31,963 | 16,821 | 7,944 | 7,002 | 196 | 8,877 R | 52.6% | 24.9% | 21.9% |
| 31,111 | HARDIN | 13,215 | 5,851 | 4,364 | 2,867 | 133 | 1,487 R | 44.3% | 33.0% | 21.7% |
| 16,085 | HARRISON | 7,827 | 2,289 | 3,830 | 1,679 | 29 | 1,541 D | 29.2% | 48.9% | 21.5% |
| 29,108 | HENRY | 13,359 | 6,196 | 3,933 | 3,178 | 52 | 2,263 R | 46.4% | 29.4% | 23.8% |
| 35,728 | HIGHLAND | 15,242 | 7,020 | 4,866 | 3,315 | 41 | 2,154 R | 46.1% | 31.9% | 21.7% |
| 25,533 | HOCKING | 10,574 | 3,761 | 3,935 | 2,831 | 47 | 174 D | 35.6% | 37.2% | 26.8% |
| 32,849 | HOLMES | 9,056 | 5,079 | 1,969 | 1,945 | 63 | 3,110 R | 56.1% | 21.7% | 21.5% |
| 56,240 | HURON | 24,471 | 9,480 | 7,930 | 6,751 | 310 | 1,550 R | 38.7% | 32.4% | 27.6% |
| 30,230 | JACKSON | 12,883 | 5,422 | 5,016 | 2,389 | 56 | 406 R | 42.1% | 38.9% | 18.5% |
| 80,298 | JEFFERSON | 38,798 | 10,764 | 20,978 | 6,910 | 146 | 10,214 D | 27.7% | 54.1% | 17.8% |
| 47,473 | KNOX | 21,745 | 9,044 | 7,259 | 5,282 | 160 | 1,785 R | 41.6% | 33.4% | 24.3% |
| 215,499 | LAKE | 105,990 | 40,766 | 37,682 | 26,878 | 664 | 3,084 R | 38.5% | 35.6% | 25.4% |
| 61,834 | LAWRENCE | 27,021 | 10,044 | 12,325 | 4,536 | 116 | 2,281 .D | 37.2% | 45.6% | 16.8% |
| 128,300 | LICKING | 60,434 | 26,918 | 18,898 | 13,806 | 812 | 8,020 R | 44.5% | 31.3% | 22.8% |
| 42,310 | LOGAN | 18,787 | 9,364 | 4,889 | 4,472 | 62 | 4,475 R | 49.8% | 26.0% | 23.8% |
| 271,126 | LORAIN | 118,605 | 36,803 | 50,962 | 30,425 | 415 | 14,159 D | 31.0% | 43.0% | 25.7% |
| 462,361 | LUCAS | 203,019 | 63,297 | 99,989 | 38,108 | 1,625 | 36,692 D | 31.2% | 49.3% | 18.8% |
| 37,068 | MADISON | 14,071 | 6,865 | 3,998 | 3,170 | 38 | 2,867 R | 48.8% | 28.4% | 22.5% |
| 264,806 | MAHONING | 125,650 | 31,191 | 64,731 | 29,417 | 311 | 33,540 D | 24.8% | 51.5% | 23.4% |
| 64,274 | MARION | 27,715 | 11,675 | 9,444 | 6,471 | 125 | 2,231 R | 42.1% | 34.1% | 23.3% |
| 122,354 | MEDINA | 60,601 | 24,090 | 18,995 | 17,290 | 226 | 5,095 R | 39.8% | 31.3% | 28.5% |
| 22,987 | MEIGS | 10,286 | 3,916 | 4,226 | 2,098 | 46 | 310 D | 38.1% | 41.1% | 20.4% |
| 39,443 | MERCER | 18,548 | 8,683 | 4,883 | 4,913 | 69 | 3,770 R | 46.8% | 26.3% | 26.5% |
| 93,182 | MIAMI | 43,006 | 19,741 | 12,547 | 10,544 | 174 | 7,194 R | 45.9% | 29.2% | 24.5% |
| 15,497 | MONROE | 7,591 | 1,823 | 4,235 | 1,505 | 28 | 2,412 D | 24.0% | 55.8% | 19.8% |
| 573,809 | MONTGOMERY | 261,720 | 104,751 | 108,017 | 47,854 | 1,098 | 3,266 D | 40.0% | 41.3% | 18.3% |
| 14,194 | MORGAN | 6,707 | 2,719 | 2,402 | 1,551 | 35 | 317 R | 40.5% | 35.8% | 23.1% |
| 27,749 | MORROW | 12,791 | 5,208 | 3,907 | 3,623 | 53 | 1,301 R | 40.7% | 30.5% | 28.3% |
| 82,068 | MUSKINGUM | 34,720 | 14,168 | 11,670 | 8,731 | 151 | 2,498 R | 40.8% | 33.6% | 25.1% |

# OHIO

## PRESIDENT 1992

| 1990 Census Population | County | Total Vote | Republican | Democratic | Perot | Other | Plurality | Percentage Total Vote | | |
|---|---|---|---|---|---|---|---|---|---|---|
| | | | | | | | | Rep. | Dem. | Perot |
| 11,336 | NOBLE | 5,883 | 2,223 | 2,201 | 1,429 | 30 | 22 R | 37.8% | 37.4% | 24.3% |
| 40,029 | OTTAWA | 19,795 | 6,782 | 8,128 | 4,832 | 53 | 1,346 D | 34.3% | 41.1% | 24.4% |
| 20,488 | PAULDING | 9,510 | 3,652 | 3,293 | 2,510 | 55 | 359 R | 38.4% | 34.6% | 26.4% |
| 31,557 | PERRY | 13,547 | 4,712 | 4,972 | 3,810 | 53 | 260 D | 34.8% | 36.7% | 28.1% |
| 48,255 | PICKAWAY | 18,930 | 8,690 | 5,765 | 4,319 | 156 | 2,925 R | 45.9% | 30.5% | 22.8% |
| 24,249 | PIKE | 11,393 | 4,094 | 5,057 | 2,192 | 50 | 963 D | 35.9% | 44.4% | 19.2% |
| 142,585 | PORTAGE | 62,135 | 18,447 | 26,325 | 17,065 | 298 | 7,878 D | 29.7% | 42.4% | 27.5% |
| 40,113 | PREBLE | 18,098 | 8,023 | 5,557 | 4,460 | 58 | 2,466 R | 44.3% | 30.7% | 24.6% |
| 33,819 | PUTNAM | 17,004 | 9,338 | 3,962 | 3,648 | 56 | 5,376 R | 54.9% | 23.3% | 21.5% |
| 126,137 | RICHLAND | 56,697 | 23,532 | 19,606 | 13,370 | 189 | 3,926 R | 41.5% | 34.6% | 23.6% |
| 69,330 | ROSS | 27,173 | 10,825 | 10,452 | 5,616 | 280 | 373 R | 39.8% | 38.5% | 20.7% |
| 61,963 | SANDUSKY | 27,472 | 10,772 | 9,878 | 6,682 | 140 | 894 R | 39.2% | 36.0% | 24.3% |
| 80,327 | SCIOTO | 33,624 | 11,931 | 14,715 | 6,860 | 118 | 2,784 D | 35.5% | 43.8% | 20.4% |
| 59,733 | SENECA | 26,150 | 9,763 | 9,280 | 6,967 | 140 | 483 R | 37.3% | 35.5% | 26.6% |
| 44,915 | SHELBY | 20,011 | 8,854 | 5,262 | 5,835 | 60 | 3,019 R | 44.2% | 26.3% | 29.2% |
| 367,585 | STARK | 175,092 | 61,863 | 70,064 | 42,413 | 752 | 8,201 D | 35.3% | 40.0% | 24.2% |
| 514,990 | SUMMIT | 241,492 | 77,530 | 107,881 | 55,151 | 930 | 30,351 D | 32.1% | 44.7% | 22.8% |
| 227,813 | TRUMBULL | 107,606 | 25,831 | 54,591 | 26,791 | 393 | 27,800 D | 24.0% | 50.7% | 24.9% |
| 84,090 | TUSCARAWAS | 36,894 | 13,179 | 14,787 | 8,785 | 143 | 1,608 D | 35.7% | 40.1% | 23.8% |
| 31,969 | UNION | 14,777 | 7,818 | 3,465 | 3,433 | 61 | 4,353 R | 52.9% | 23.4% | 23.2% |
| 30,464 | VAN WERT | 14,217 | 7,227 | 3,822 | 3,102 | 66 | 3,405 R | 50.8% | 26.9% | 21.8% |
| 11,098 | VINTON | 5,363 | 1,975 | 2,308 | 1,050 | 30 | 333 D | 36.8% | 43.0% | 19.6% |
| 113,909 | WARREN | 52,802 | 27,998 | 13,542 | 11,115 | 147 | 14,456 R | 53.0% | 25.6% | 21.1% |
| 62,254 | WASHINGTON | 28,073 | 12,204 | 10,380 | 5,415 | 74 | 1,824 R | 43.5% | 37.0% | 19.3% |
| 101,461 | WAYNE | 41,982 | 18,350 | 13,953 | 9,482 | 197 | 4,397 R | 43.7% | 33.2% | 22.6% |
| 36,956 | WILLIAMS | 17,464 | 7,614 | 4,862 | 4,902 | 86 | 2,712 R | 43.6% | 27.8% | 28.1% |
| 113,269 | WOOD | 53,203 | 20,579 | 20,754 | 11,682 | 188 | 175 D | 38.7% | 39.0% | 22.0% |
| 22,254 | WYANDOT | 10,443 | 4,411 | 3,031 | 2,929 | 72 | 1,380 R | 42.2% | 29.0% | 28.0% |
| 10,847,115 | TOTAL | 4,939,967 | 1,894,310 | 1,984,942 | 1,036,426 | 24,289 | 90,632 D | 38.3% | 40.2% | 21.0% |

# OHIO

## PRESIDENT 1988

| 1980 Census Population | County | Total Vote | Republican | Democratic | Other | Rep.-Dem. Plurality | Percentage Total Vote Rep. | Dem. | Major Vote Rep. | Dem. |
|---|---|---|---|---|---|---|---|---|---|---|
| 24,328 | ADAMS | 9,744 | 5,916 | 3,740 | 88 | 2,176 R | 60.7% | 38.4% | 61.3% | 38.7% |
| 112,241 | ALLEN | 44,975 | 31,021 | 13,727 | 227 | 17,294 R | 69.0% | 30.5% | 69.3% | 30.7% |
| 46,178 | ASHLAND | 18,939 | 12,726 | 6,072 | 141 | 6,654 R | 67.2% | 32.1% | 67.7% | 32.3% |
| 104,215 | ASHTABULA | 38,556 | 17,654 | 20,536 | 366 | 2,882 D | 45.8% | 53.3% | 46.2% | 53.8% |
| 56,399 | ATHENS | 20,281 | 9,314 | 10,795 | 172 | 1,481 D | 45.9% | 53.2% | 46.3% | 53.7% |
| 42,554 | AUGLAIZE | 18,479 | 13,562 | 4,756 | 161 | 8,806 R | 73.4% | 25.7% | 74.0% | 26.0% |
| 82,569 | BELMONT | 31,973 | 12,214 | 19,515 | 244 | 7,301 D | 38.2% | 61.0% | 38.5% | 61.5% |
| 31,920 | BROWN | 12,698 | 7,539 | 5,047 | 112 | 2,492 R | 59.4% | 39.7% | 59.9% | 40.1% |
| 258,787 | BUTLER | 110,208 | 75,725 | 33,770 | 713 | 41,955 R | 68.7% | 30.6% | 69.2% | 30.8% |
| 25,598 | CARROLL | 10,994 | 6,179 | 4,667 | 148 | 1,512 R | 56.2% | 42.5% | 57.0% | 43.0% |
| 33,649 | CHAMPAIGN | 13,368 | 8,995 | 4,272 | 101 | 4,723 R | 67.3% | 32.0% | 67.8% | 32.2% |
| 150,236 | CLARK | 56,503 | 32,729 | 23,247 | 527 | 9,482 R | 57.9% | 41.1% | 58.5% | 41.5% |
| 128,483 | CLERMONT | 53,085 | 37,417 | 15,352 | 316 | 22,065 R | 70.5% | 28.9% | 70.9% | 29.1% |
| 34,603 | CLINTON | 12,699 | 8,856 | 3,746 | 97 | 5,110 R | 69.7% | 29.5% | 70.3% | 29.7% |
| 113,572 | COLUMBIANA | 43,140 | 21,175 | 21,581 | 384 | 406 D | 49.1% | 50.0% | 49.5% | 50.5% |
| 36,024 | COSHOCTON | 14,506 | 8,282 | 6,020 | 204 | 2,262 R | 57.1% | 41.5% | 57.9% | 42.1% |
| 50,075 | CRAWFORD | 18,700 | 12,472 | 6,018 | 210 | 6,454 R | 66.7% | 32.2% | 67.5% | 32.5% |
| 1,498,400 | CUYAHOGA | 601,117 | 242,439 | 353,401 | 5,277 | 110,962 D | 40.3% | 58.8% | 40.7% | 59.3% |
| 55,096 | DARKE | 21,954 | 14,914 | 6,851 | 189 | 8,063 R | 67.9% | 31.2% | 68.5% | 31.5% |
| 39,987 | DEFIANCE | 15,153 | 9,566 | 5,448 | 139 | 4,118 R | 63.1% | 36.0% | 63.7% | 36.3% |
| 53,840 | DELAWARE | 28,498 | 20,693 | 7,590 | 215 | 13,103 R | 72.6% | 26.6% | 73.2% | 26.8% |
| 79,655 | ERIE | 32,198 | 16,670 | 15,097 | 431 | 1,573 R | 51.8% | 46.9% | 52.5% | 47.5% |
| 93,678 | FAIRFIELD | 42,051 | 29,208 | 12,504 | 339 | 16,704 R | 69.5% | 29.7% | 70.0% | 30.0% |
| 27,467 | FAYETTE | 8,873 | 6,186 | 2,623 | 64 | 3,563 R | 69.7% | 29.6% | 70.2% | 29.8% |
| 869,132 | FRANKLIN | 377,357 | 226,265 | 147,585 | 3,507 | 78,680 R | 60.0% | 39.1% | 60.5% | 39.5% |
| 37,751 | FULTON | 15,428 | 10,230 | 5,076 | 122 | 5,154 R | 66.3% | 32.9% | 66.8% | 33.2% |
| 30,098 | GALLIA | 12,349 | 7,399 | 4,834 | 116 | 2,565 R | 59.9% | 39.1% | 60.5% | 39.5% |
| 74,474 | GEAUGA | 34,608 | 22,339 | 11,874 | 395 | 10,465 R | 64.5% | 34.3% | 65.3% | 34.7% |
| 129,769 | GREENE | 52,856 | 34,432 | 18,025 | 399 | 16,407 R | 65.1% | 34.1% | 65.6% | 34.4% |
| 42,024 | GUERNSEY | 14,563 | 8,507 | 5,926 | 130 | 2,581 R | 58.4% | 40.7% | 58.9% | 41.1% |
| 873,224 | HAMILTON | 370,384 | 227,004 | 140,354 | 3,026 | 86,650 R | 61.3% | 37.9% | 61.8% | 38.2% |
| 64,581 | HANCOCK | 27,643 | 19,896 | 7,435 | 312 | 12,461 R | 72.0% | 26.9% | 72.8% | 27.2% |
| 32,719 | HARDIN | 11,606 | 7,291 | 4,145 | 170 | 3,146 R | 62.8% | 35.7% | 63.8% | 36.2% |
| 18,152 | HARRISON | 7,252 | 3,298 | 3,881 | 73 | 583 D | 45.5% | 53.5% | 45.9% | 54.1% |
| 28,383 | HENRY | 12,468 | 8,618 | 3,764 | 86 | 4,854 R | 69.1% | 30.2% | 69.6% | 30.4% |
| 33,477 | HIGHLAND | 13,178 | 8,776 | 4,278 | 124 | 4,498 R | 66.6% | 32.5% | 67.2% | 32.8% |
| 24,304 | HOCKING | 9,243 | 5,426 | 3,706 | 111 | 1,720 R | 58.7% | 40.1% | 59.4% | 40.6% |
| 29,416 | HOLMES | 7,316 | 5,064 | 2,179 | 73 | 2,885 R | 69.2% | 29.8% | 69.9% | 30.1% |
| 54,608 | HURON | 20,642 | 12,633 | 7,794 | 215 | 4,839 R | 61.2% | 37.8% | 61.8% | 38.2% |
| 30,592 | JACKSON | 11,267 | 6,671 | 4,505 | 91 | 2,166 R | 59.2% | 40.0% | 59.7% | 40.3% |
| 91,564 | JEFFERSON | 36,509 | 14,141 | 22,095 | 273 | 7,954 D | 38.7% | 60.5% | 39.0% | 61.0% |
| 46,304 | KNOX | 19,200 | 12,180 | 6,882 | 138 | 5,298 R | 63.4% | 35.8% | 63.9% | 36.1% |
| 212,801 | LAKE | 93,524 | 52,963 | 39,667 | 894 | 13,296 R | 56.6% | 42.4% | 57.2% | 42.8% |
| 63,849 | LAWRENCE | 24,768 | 12,937 | 11,628 | 203 | 1,309 R | 52.2% | 46.9% | 52.7% | 47.3% |
| 120,981 | LICKING | 51,767 | 34,540 | 16,793 | 434 | 17,747 R | 66.7% | 32.4% | 67.3% | 32.7% |
| 39,155 | LOGAN | 15,697 | 11,099 | 4,484 | 114 | 6,615 R | 70.7% | 28.6% | 71.2% | 28.8% |
| 274,909 | LORAIN | 106,926 | 50,410 | 55,600 | 916 | 5,190 D | 47.1% | 52.0% | 47.6% | 52.4% |
| 471,741 | LUCAS | 185,095 | 83,788 | 99,755 | 1,552 | 15,967 D | 45.3% | 53.9% | 45.7% | 54.3% |
| 33,004 | MADISON | 11,817 | 8,303 | 3,421 | 93 | 4,882 R | 70.3% | 28.9% | 70.8% | 29.2% |
| 289,487 | MAHONING | 120,126 | 43,722 | 75,524 | 880 | 31,802 D | 36.4% | 62.9% | 36.7% | 63.3% |
| 67,974 | MARION | 24,718 | 14,864 | 9,596 | 258 | 5,268 R | 60.1% | 38.8% | 60.8% | 39.2% |
| 113,150 | MEDINA | 49,874 | 29,962 | 19,505 | 407 | 10,457 R | 60.1% | 39.1% | 60.6% | 39.4% |
| 23,641 | MEIGS | 9,276 | 5,486 | 3,699 | 91 | 1,787 R | 59.1% | 39.9% | 59.7% | 40.3% |
| 38,334 | MERCER | 16,286 | 11,162 | 4,978 | 146 | 6,184 R | 68.5% | 30.6% | 69.2% | 30.8% |
| 90,381 | MIAMI | 36,434 | 24,915 | 11,138 | 381 | 13,777 R | 68.4% | 30.6% | 69.1% | 30.9% |
| 17,382 | MONROE | 6,874 | 2,557 | 4,269 | 48 | 1,712 D | 37.2% | 62.1% | 37.5% | 62.5% |
| 571,697 | MONTGOMERY | 228,943 | 131,596 | 95,737 | 1,610 | 35,859 R | 57.5% | 41.8% | 57.9% | 42.1% |
| 14,241 | MORGAN | 5,859 | 3,713 | 2,085 | 61 | 1,628 R | 63.4% | 35.6% | 64.0% | 36.0% |
| 26,480 | MORROW | 10,760 | 7,130 | 3,515 | 115 | 3,615 R | 66.3% | 32.7% | 67.0% | 33.0% |
| 83,340 | MUSKINGUM | 31,674 | 19,736 | 11,691 | 247 | 8,045 R | 62.3% | 36.9% | 62.8% | 37.2% |

# OHIO

## PRESIDENT 1988

| 1980 Census Population | County | Total Vote | Republican | Democratic | Other | Rep.-Dem. Plurality | Percentage Total Vote Rep. | Dem. | Major Vote Rep. | Dem. |
|---|---|---|---|---|---|---|---|---|---|---|
| 11,310 | NOBLE | 5,308 | 3,155 | 2,079 | 74 | 1,076 R | 59.4% | 39.2% | 60.3% | 39.7% |
| 40,076 | OTTAWA | 17,517 | 9,352 | 8,038 | 127 | 1,314 R | 53.4% | 45.9% | 53.8% | 46.2% |
| 21,302 | PAULDING | 8,571 | 5,381 | 3,114 | 76 | 2,267 R | 62.8% | 36.3% | 63.3% | 36.7% |
| 31,032 | PERRY | 11,731 | 6,602 | 5,011 | 118 | 1,591 R | 56.3% | 42.7% | 56.9% | 43.1% |
| 43,662 | PICKAWAY | 15,794 | 10,796 | 4,905 | 93 | 5,891 R | 68.4% | 31.1% | 68.8% | 31.2% |
| 22,802 | PIKE | 10,919 | 5,611 | 5,191 | 117 | 420 R | 51.4% | 47.5% | 51.9% | 48.1% |
| 135,856 | PORTAGE | 52,480 | 26,334 | 25,607 | 539 | 727 R | 50.2% | 48.8% | 50.7% | 49.3% |
| 38,223 | PREBLE | 15,381 | 10,297 | 4,937 | 147 | 5,360 R | 66.9% | 32.1% | 67.6% | 32.4% |
| 32,991 | PUTNAM | 15,301 | 11,183 | 4,004 | 114 | 7,179 R | 73.1% | 26.2% | 73.6% | 26.4% |
| 131,205 | RICHLAND | 50,047 | 30,047 | 19,617 | 383 | 10,430 R | 60.0% | 39.2% | 60.5% | 39.5% |
| 65,004 | ROSS | 24,113 | 14,563 | 9,271 | 279 | 5,292 R | 60.4% | 38.4% | 61.1% | 38.9% |
| 63,267 | SANDUSKY | 24,232 | 14,203 | 9,709 | 320 | 4,494 R | 58.6% | 40.1% | 59.4% | 40.6% |
| 84,545 | SCIOTO | 30,760 | 16,029 | 14,442 | 289 | 1,587 R | 52.1% | 47.0% | 52.6% | 47.4% |
| 61,901 | SENECA | 23,430 | 13,704 | 9,504 | 222 | 4,200 R | 58.5% | 40.6% | 59.0% | 41.0% |
| 43,089 | SHELBY | 17,425 | 12,198 | 5,065 | 162 | 7,133 R | 70.0% | 29.1% | 70.7% | 29.3% |
| 378,823 | STARK | 158,096 | 87,087 | 69,639 | 1,370 | 17,448 R | 55.1% | 44.0% | 55.6% | 44.4% |
| 524,472 | SUMMIT | 215,589 | 101,155 | 112,612 | 1,822 | 11,457 D | 46.9% | 52.2% | 47.3% | 52.7% |
| 241,863 | TRUMBULL | 98,250 | 38,815 | 58,674 | 761 | 19,859 D | 39.5% | 59.7% | 39.8% | 60.2% |
| 84,614 | TUSCARAWAS | 31,589 | 17,145 | 14,185 | 259 | 2,960 R | 54.3% | 44.9% | 54.7% | 45.3% |
| 29,536 | UNION | 12,071 | 8,846 | 3,130 | 95 | 5,716 R | 73.3% | 25.9% | 73.9% | 26.1% |
| 30,458 | VAN WERT | 13,336 | 9,410 | 3,848 | 78 | 5,562 R | 70.6% | 28.9% | 71.0% | 29.0% |
| 11,584 | VINTON | 5,081 | 2,652 | 2,385 | 44 | 267 R | 52.2% | 46.9% | 52.7% | 47.3% |
| 99,276 | WARREN | 42,818 | 31,419 | 11,145 | 254 | 20,274 R | 73.4% | 26.0% | 73.8% | 26.2% |
| 64,266 | WASHINGTON | 24,916 | 14,767 | 9,967 | 182 | 4,800 R | 59.3% | 40.0% | 59.7% | 40.3% |
| 97,408 | WAYNE | 36,208 | 22,320 | 13,571 | 317 | 8,749 R | 61.6% | 37.5% | 62.2% | 37.8% |
| 36,369 | WILLIAMS | 15,585 | 10,782 | 4,666 | 137 | 6,116 R | 69.2% | 29.9% | 69.8% | 30.2% |
| 107,372 | WOOD | 44,933 | 26,013 | 18,579 | 341 | 7,434 R | 57.9% | 41.3% | 58.3% | 41.7% |
| 22,651 | WYANDOT | 9,239 | 6,178 | 2,936 | 125 | 3,242 R | 66.9% | 31.8% | 67.8% | 32.2% |
| 10,797,630 | TOTAL | 4,393,699 | 2,416,549 | 1,939,629 | 37,521 | 476,920 R | 55.0% | 44.1% | 55.5% | 44.5% |

# OHIO

## PRESIDENT 1984

| 1980 Census Population | County | Total Vote | Republican | Democratic | Other | Rep.-Dem. Plurality | Percentage |||| 
| | | | | | | | Total Vote || Major Vote ||
| | | | | | | | Rep. | Dem. | Rep. | Dem. |
|---|---|---|---|---|---|---|---|---|---|---|
| 24,328 | ADAMS | 9,729 | 6,113 | 3,534 | 82 | 2,579 R | 62.8% | 36.3% | 63.4% | 36.6% |
| 112,241 | ALLEN | 45,911 | 33,506 | 12,176 | 229 | 21,330 R | 73.0% | 26.5% | 73.3% | 26.7% |
| 46,178 | ASHLAND | 19,272 | 14,339 | 4,786 | 147 | 9,553 R | 74.4% | 24.8% | 75.0% | 25.0% |
| 104,215 | ASHTABULA | 41,397 | 21,669 | 19,344 | 384 | 2,325 R | 52.3% | 46.7% | 52.8% | 47.2% |
| 56,399 | ATHENS | 21,958 | 11,548 | 10,201 | 209 | 1,347 R | 52.6% | 46.5% | 53.1% | 46.9% |
| 42,554 | AUGLAIZE | 19,000 | 14,766 | 4,102 | 132 | 10,664 R | 77.7% | 21.6% | 78.3% | 21.7% |
| 82,569 | BELMONT | 34,856 | 15,170 | 19,458 | 228 | 4,288 D | 43.5% | 55.8% | 43.8% | 56.2% |
| 31,920 | BROWN | 12,404 | 8,221 | 4,067 | 116 | 4,154 R | 66.3% | 32.8% | 66.9% | 33.1% |
| 258,787 | BUTLER | 104,514 | 76,216 | 27,700 | 598 | 48,516 R | 72.9% | 26.5% | 73.3% | 26.7% |
| 25,598 | CARROLL | 10,584 | 6,703 | 3,771 | 110 | 2,932 R | 63.3% | 35.6% | 64.0% | 36.0% |
| 33,649 | CHAMPAIGN | 13,600 | 9,935 | 3,544 | 121 | 6,391 R | 73.1% | 26.1% | 73.7% | 26.3% |
| 150,236 | CLARK | 57,744 | 35,831 | 21,154 | 759 | 14,677 R | 62.1% | 36.6% | 62.9% | 37.1% |
| 128,483 | CLERMONT | 47,319 | 35,316 | 11,713 | 290 | 23,603 R | 74.6% | 24.8% | 75.1% | 24.9% |
| 34,603 | CLINTON | 13,018 | 9,603 | 3,332 | 83 | 6,271 R | 73.8% | 25.6% | 74.2% | 25.8% |
| 113,572 | COLUMBIANA | 45,110 | 24,552 | 20,155 | 403 | 4,397 R | 54.4% | 44.7% | 54.9% | 45.1% |
| 36,024 | COSHOCTON | 14,323 | 9,842 | 4,392 | 89 | 5,450 R | 68.7% | 30.7% | 69.1% | 30.9% |
| 50,075 | CRAWFORD | 19,820 | 14,682 | 4,932 | 206 | 9,750 R | 74.1% | 24.9% | 74.9% | 25.1% |
| 1,498,400 | CUYAHOGA | 651,633 | 284,094 | 362,626 | 4,913 | 78,532 D | 43.6% | 55.6% | 43.9% | 56.1% |
| 55,096 | DARKE | 22,494 | 16,379 | 5,904 | 211 | 10,475 R | 72.8% | 26.2% | 73.5% | 26.5% |
| 39,987 | DEFIANCE | 16,130 | 10,951 | 5,004 | 175 | 5,947 R | 67.9% | 31.0% | 68.6% | 31.4% |
| 53,840 | DELAWARE | 24,989 | 19,050 | 5,773 | 166 | 13,277 R | 76.2% | 23.1% | 76.7% | 23.3% |
| 79,655 | ERIE | 33,154 | 19,174 | 13,508 | 472 | 5,666 R | 57.8% | 40.7% | 58.7% | 41.3% |
| 93,678 | FAIRFIELD | 41,033 | 30,843 | 9,817 | 373 | 21,026 R | 75.2% | 23.9% | 75.9% | 24.1% |
| 27,467 | FAYETTE | 9,021 | 6,838 | 2,126 | 57 | 4,712 R | 75.8% | 23.6% | 76.3% | 23.7% |
| 869,132 | FRANKLIN | 390,474 | 250,360 | 131,530 | 8,584 | 118,830 R | 64.1% | 33.7% | 65.6% | 34.4% |
| 37,751 | FULTON | 15,730 | 11,412 | 4,217 | 101 | 7,195 R | 72.5% | 26.8% | 73.0% | 27.0% |
| 30,098 | GALLIA | 12,554 | 8,194 | 4,251 | 109 | 3,943 R | 65.3% | 33.9% | 65.8% | 34.2% |
| 74,474 | GEAUGA | 32,754 | 22,369 | 9,954 | 431 | 12,415 R | 68.3% | 30.4% | 69.2% | 30.8% |
| 129,769 | GREENE | 51,711 | 34,267 | 17,129 | 315 | 17,138 R | 66.3% | 33.1% | 66.7% | 33.3% |
| 42,024 | GUERNSEY | 15,344 | 10,252 | 4,967 | 125 | 5,285 R | 66.8% | 32.4% | 67.4% | 32.6% |
| 873,224 | HAMILTON | 388,817 | 246,288 | 140,350 | 2,179 | 105,938 R | 63.3% | 36.1% | 63.7% | 36.3% |
| 64,581 | HANCOCK | 28,295 | 22,169 | 5,758 | 368 | 16,411 R | 78.3% | 20.3% | 79.4% | 20.6% |
| 32,719 | HARDIN | 12,620 | 8,722 | 3,813 | 85 | 4,909 R | 69.1% | 30.2% | 69.6% | 30.4% |
| 18,152 | HARRISON | 7,712 | 4,276 | 3,370 | 66 | 906 R | 55.4% | 43.7% | 55.9% | 44.1% |
| 28,383 | HENRY | 12,173 | 9,317 | 2,779 | 77 | 6,538 R | 76.5% | 22.8% | 77.0% | 23.0% |
| 33,477 | HIGHLAND | 12,875 | 9,000 | 3,784 | 91 | 5,216 R | 69.9% | 29.4% | 70.4% | 29.6% |
| 24,304 | HOCKING | 9,463 | 6,071 | 3,280 | 112 | 2,791 R | 64.2% | 34.7% | 64.9% | 35.1% |
| 29,416 | HOLMES | 6,944 | 5,146 | 1,737 | 61 | 3,409 R | 74.1% | 25.0% | 74.8% | 25.2% |
| 54,608 | HURON | 21,171 | 14,388 | 6,609 | 174 | 7,779 R | 68.0% | 31.2% | 68.5% | 31.5% |
| 30,592 | JACKSON | 11,908 | 7,411 | 4,369 | 128 | 3,042 R | 62.2% | 36.7% | 62.9% | 37.1% |
| 91,564 | JEFFERSON | 40,277 | 17,105 | 22,832 | 340 | 5,727 D | 42.5% | 56.7% | 42.8% | 57.2% |
| 46,304 | KNOX | 19,901 | 14,062 | 5,730 | 109 | 8,332 R | 70.7% | 28.8% | 71.0% | 29.0% |
| 212,801 | LAKE | 92,325 | 54,587 | 36,711 | 1,027 | 17,876 R | 59.1% | 39.8% | 59.8% | 40.2% |
| 63,849 | LAWRENCE | 26,437 | 14,793 | 11,431 | 213 | 3,362 R | 56.0% | 43.2% | 56.4% | 43.6% |
| 120,981 | LICKING | 51,976 | 37,560 | 13,995 | 421 | 23,565 R | 72.3% | 26.9% | 72.9% | 27.1% |
| 39,155 | LOGAN | 15,979 | 12,230 | 3,645 | 104 | 8,585 R | 76.5% | 22.8% | 77.0% | 23.0% |
| 274,909 | LORAIN | 113,021 | 57,379 | 52,970 | 2,672 | 4,409 R | 50.8% | 46.9% | 52.0% | 48.0% |
| 471,741 | LUCAS | 199,554 | 100,285 | 97,293 | 1,976 | 2,992 R | 50.3% | 48.8% | 50.8% | 49.2% |
| 33,004 | MADISON | 11,987 | 8,979 | 2,928 | 80 | 6,051 R | 74.9% | 24.4% | 75.4% | 24.6% |
| 289,487 | MAHONING | 131,438 | 53,424 | 76,514 | 1,500 | 23,090 D | 40.6% | 58.2% | 41.1% | 58.9% |
| 67,974 | MARION | 26,443 | 17,392 | 8,827 | 224 | 8,565 R | 65.8% | 33.4% | 66.3% | 33.7% |
| 113,150 | MEDINA | 46,944 | 30,690 | 15,897 | 357 | 14,793 R | 65.4% | 33.9% | 65.9% | 34.1% |
| 23,641 | MEIGS | 9,929 | 6,307 | 3,549 | 73 | 2,758 R | 63.5% | 35.7% | 64.0% | 36.0% |
| 38,334 | MERCER | 16,144 | 11,542 | 4,422 | 180 | 7,120 R | 71.5% | 27.4% | 72.3% | 27.7% |
| 90,381 | MIAMI | 36,315 | 26,300 | 9,695 | 320 | 16,605 R | 72.4% | 26.7% | 73.1% | 26.9% |
| 17,382 | MONROE | 6,978 | 3,302 | 3,611 | 65 | 309 D | 47.3% | 51.7% | 47.8% | 52.2% |
| 571,697 | MONTGOMERY | 232,402 | 137,053 | 94,016 | 1,333 | 43,037 R | 59.0% | 40.5% | 59.3% | 40.7% |
| 14,241 | MORGAN | 5,903 | 3,994 | 1,868 | 41 | 2,126 R | 67.7% | 31.6% | 68.1% | 31.9% |
| 26,480 | MORROW | 11,042 | 8,116 | 2,839 | 87 | 5,277 R | 73.5% | 25.7% | 74.1% | 25.9% |
| 83,340 | MUSKINGUM | 32,101 | 21,821 | 10,037 | 243 | 11,784 R | 68.0% | 31.3% | 68.5% | 31.5% |

# OHIO

## PRESIDENT 1984

| 1980 Census Population | County | Total Vote | Republican | Democratic | Other | Rep.-Dem. Plurality | Percentage Total Vote Rep. | Dem. | Major Vote Rep. | Dem. |
|---|---|---|---|---|---|---|---|---|---|---|
| 11,310 | NOBLE | 5,691 | 3,853 | 1,777 | 61 | 2,076 R | 67.7% | 31.2% | 68.4% | 31.6% |
| 40,076 | OTTAWA | 18,075 | 10,920 | 7,053 | 102 | 3,867 R | 60.4% | 39.0% | 60.8% | 39.2% |
| 21,302 | PAULDING | 8,439 | 5,545 | 2,811 | 83 | 2,734 R | 65.7% | 33.3% | 66.4% | 33.6% |
| 31,032 | PERRY | 11,597 | 7,548 | 3,961 | 88 | 3,587 R | 65.1% | 34.2% | 65.6% | 34.4% |
| 43,662 | PICKAWAY | 16,160 | 11,942 | 4,110 | 108 | 7,832 R | 73.9% | 25.4% | 74.4% | 25.6% |
| 22,802 | PIKE | 11,302 | 6,318 | 4,895 | 89 | 1,423 R | 55.9% | 43.3% | 56.3% | 43.7% |
| 135,856 | PORTAGE | 51,687 | 29,536 | 21,719 | 432 | 7,817 R | 57.1% | 42.0% | 57.6% | 42.4% |
| 38,223 | PREBLE | 15,403 | 11,065 | 4,198 | 140 | 6,867 R | 71.8% | 27.3% | 72.5% | 27.5% |
| 32,991 | PUTNAM | 15,252 | 11,937 | 3,194 | 121 | 8,743 R | 78.3% | 20.9% | 78.9% | 21.1% |
| 131,205 | RICHLAND | 51,836 | 35,299 | 16,141 | 396 | 19,158 R | 68.1% | 31.1% | 68.6% | 31.4% |
| 65,004 | ROSS | 25,548 | 17,015 | 8,020 | 513 | 8,995 R | 66.6% | 31.4% | 68.0% | 32.0% |
| 63,267 | SANDUSKY | 26,020 | 17,214 | 8,564 | 242 | 8,650 R | 66.2% | 32.9% | 66.8% | 33.2% |
| 84,545 | SCIOTO | 33,219 | 18,818 | 14,120 | 281 | 4,698 R | 56.6% | 42.5% | 57.1% | 42.9% |
| 61,901 | SENECA | 24,642 | 16,520 | 7,905 | 217 | 8,615 R | 67.0% | 32.1% | 67.6% | 32.4% |
| 43,089 | SHELBY | 17,983 | 13,509 | 4,315 | 159 | 9,194 R | 75.1% | 24.0% | 75.8% | 24.2% |
| 378,823 | STARK | 164,916 | 98,434 | 65,157 | 1,325 | 33,277 R | 59.7% | 39.5% | 60.2% | 39.8% |
| 524,472 | SUMMIT | 226,780 | 115,637 | 109,569 | 1,574 | 6,068 R | 51.0% | 48.3% | 51.3% | 48.7% |
| 241,863 | TRUMBULL | 103,259 | 45,623 | 56,902 | 734 | 11,279 D | 44.2% | 55.1% | 44.5% | 55.5% |
| 84,614 | TUSCARAWAS | 32,754 | 19,366 | 13,149 | 239 | 6,217 R | 59.1% | 40.1% | 59.6% | 40.4% |
| 29,536 | UNION | 12,001 | 9,336 | 2,579 | 86 | 6,757 R | 77.8% | 21.5% | 78.4% | 21.6% |
| 30,458 | VAN WERT | 12,988 | 9,570 | 3,338 | 80 | 6,232 R | 73.7% | 25.7% | 74.1% | 25.9% |
| 11,584 | VINTON | 5,085 | 3,041 | 1,990 | 54 | 1,051 R | 59.8% | 39.1% | 60.4% | 39.6% |
| 99,276 | WARREN | 39,070 | 29,848 | 9,031 | 191 | 20,817 R | 76.4% | 23.1% | 76.8% | 23.2% |
| 64,266 | WASHINGTON | 24,993 | 16,529 | 7,920 | 544 | 8,609 R | 66.1% | 31.7% | 67.6% | 32.4% |
| 97,408 | WAYNE | 36,104 | 24,475 | 11,323 | 306 | 13,152 R | 67.8% | 31.4% | 68.4% | 31.6% |
| 36,369 | WILLIAMS | 14,577 | 10,804 | 3,624 | 149 | 7,180 R | 74.1% | 24.9% | 74.9% | 25.1% |
| 107,372 | WOOD | 45,954 | 29,750 | 15,907 | 297 | 13,843 R | 64.7% | 34.6% | 65.2% | 34.8% |
| 22,651 | WYANDOT | 9,630 | 7,204 | 2,342 | 84 | 4,862 R | 74.8% | 24.3% | 75.5% | 24.5% |
| 10,797,630 | TOTAL | 4,547,619 | 2,678,560 | 1,825,440 | 43,619 | 853,120 R | 58.9% | 40.1% | 59.5% | 40.5% |

# OHIO

## PRESIDENT 1980

| 1980 Census Population | County | Total Vote | Republican | Democratic | Other | Rep.-Dem. Plurality | Percentage | | | |
|---|---|---|---|---|---|---|---|---|---|---|
| | | | | | | | Total Vote | | Major Vote | |
| | | | | | | | Rep. | Dem. | Rep. | Dem. |
| 24,328 | ADAMS | 9,928 | 5,336 | 4,161 | 431 | 1,175 R | 53.7% | 41.9% | 56.2% | 43.8% |
| 112,241 | ALLEN | 44,154 | 29,070 | 13,140 | 1,944 | 15,930 R | 65.8% | 29.8% | 68.9% | 31.1% |
| 46,178 | ASHLAND | 18,689 | 11,691 | 5,142 | 1,856 | 6,549 R | 62.6% | 27.5% | 69.5% | 30.5% |
| 104,215 | ASHTABULA | 40,467 | 19,847 | 17,363 | 3,257 | 2,484 R | 49.0% | 42.9% | 53.3% | 46.7% |
| 56,399 | ATHENS | 19,801 | 8,170 | 9,514 | 2,117 | 1,344 D | 41.3% | 48.0% | 46.2% | 53.8% |
| 42,554 | AUGLAIZE | 17,657 | 11,537 | 5,022 | 1,098 | 6,515 R | 65.3% | 28.4% | 69.7% | 30.3% |
| 82,569 | BELMONT | 32,024 | 13,601 | 16,653 | 1,770 | 3,052 D | 42.5% | 52.0% | 45.0% | 55.0% |
| 31,920 | BROWN | 11,337 | 6,065 | 4,706 | 566 | 1,359 R | 53.5% | 41.5% | 56.3% | 43.7% |
| 258,787 | BUTLER | 98,901 | 61,231 | 31,796 | 5,874 | 29,435 R | 61.9% | 32.1% | 65.8% | 34.2% |
| 25,598 | CARROLL | 9,851 | 5,806 | 3,476 | 569 | 2,330 R | 58.9% | 35.3% | 62.6% | 37.4% |
| 33,649 | CHAMPAIGN | 12,225 | 7,356 | 4,109 | 760 | 3,247 R | 60.2% | 33.6% | 64.2% | 35.8% |
| 150,236 | CLARK | 54,015 | 27,237 | 22,630 | 4,148 | 4,607 R | 50.4% | 41.9% | 54.6% | 45.4% |
| 128,483 | CLERMONT | 42,091 | 26,674 | 13,199 | 2,218 | 13,475 R | 63.4% | 31.4% | 66.9% | 33.1% |
| 34,603 | CLINTON | 12,400 | 7,675 | 3,967 | 758 | 3,708 R | 61.9% | 32.0% | 65.9% | 34.1% |
| 113,572 | COLUMBIANA | 41,143 | 20,798 | 17,459 | 2,886 | 3,339 R | 50.6% | 42.4% | 54.4% | 45.6% |
| 36,024 | COSHOCTON | 13,856 | 8,359 | 4,725 | 772 | 3,634 R | 60.3% | 34.1% | 63.9% | 36.1% |
| 50,075 | CRAWFORD | 19,755 | 12,424 | 6,058 | 1,273 | 6,366 R | 62.9% | 30.7% | 67.2% | 32.8% |
| 1,498,400 | CUYAHOGA | 614,682 | 254,883 | 307,448 | 52,351 | 52,565 D | 41.5% | 50.0% | 45.3% | 54.7% |
| 55,096 | DARKE | 21,958 | 12,773 | 7,635 | 1,550 | 5,138 R | 58.2% | 34.8% | 62.6% | 37.4% |
| 39,987 | DEFIANCE | 15,639 | 9,358 | 5,096 | 1,185 | 4,262 R | 59.8% | 32.6% | 64.7% | 35.3% |
| 53,840 | DELAWARE | 22,861 | 14,740 | 6,417 | 1,704 | 8,323 R | 64.5% | 28.1% | 69.7% | 30.3% |
| 79,655 | ERIE | 30,470 | 15,628 | 12,343 | 2,499 | 3,285 R | 51.3% | 40.5% | 55.9% | 44.1% |
| 93,678 | FAIRFIELD | 39,515 | 24,096 | 13,144 | 2,275 | 10,952 R | 61.0% | 33.3% | 64.7% | 35.3% |
| 27,467 | FAYETTE | 9,068 | 5,827 | 2,810 | 431 | 3,017 R | 64.3% | 31.0% | 67.5% | 32.5% |
| 869,132 | FRANKLIN | 373,045 | 200,948 | 143,932 | 28,165 | 57,016 R | 53.9% | 38.6% | 58.3% | 41.7% |
| 37,751 | FULTON | 14,707 | 9,519 | 3,972 | 1,216 | 5,547 R | 64.7% | 27.0% | 70.6% | 29.4% |
| 30,098 | GALLIA | 11,404 | 6,469 | 4,406 | 529 | 2,063 R | 56.7% | 38.6% | 59.5% | 40.5% |
| 74,474 | GEAUGA | 30,204 | 17,762 | 9,542 | 2,900 | 8,220 R | 58.8% | 31.6% | 65.1% | 34.9% |
| 129,769 | GREENE | 48,842 | 24,922 | 20,068 | 3,852 | 4,854 R | 51.0% | 41.1% | 55.4% | 44.6% |
| 42,024 | GUERNSEY | 14,084 | 8,180 | 5,121 | 783 | 3,059 R | 58.1% | 36.4% | 61.5% | 38.5% |
| 873,224 | HAMILTON | 358,541 | 206,979 | 129,114 | 22,448 | 77,865 R | 57.7% | 36.0% | 61.6% | 38.4% |
| 64,581 | HANCOCK | 27,010 | 18,264 | 6,843 | 1,903 | 11,421 R | 67.6% | 25.3% | 72.7% | 27.3% |
| 32,719 | HARDIN | 12,123 | 7,457 | 3,863 | 803 | 3,594 R | 61.5% | 31.9% | 65.9% | 34.1% |
| 18,152 | HARRISON | 6,916 | 3,639 | 2,848 | 429 | 791 R | 52.6% | 41.2% | 56.1% | 43.9% |
| 28,383 | HENRY | 11,489 | 7,584 | 3,059 | 846 | 4,525 R | 66.0% | 26.6% | 71.3% | 28.7% |
| 33,477 | HIGHLAND | 12,400 | 7,359 | 4,363 | 678 | 2,996 R | 59.3% | 35.2% | 62.8% | 37.2% |
| 24,304 | HOCKING | 8,819 | 4,588 | 3,765 | 466 | 823 R | 52.0% | 42.7% | 54.9% | 45.1% |
| 29,416 | HOLMES | 6,394 | 3,860 | 2,094 | 440 | 1,766 R | 60.4% | 32.7% | 64.8% | 35.2% |
| 54,608 | HURON | 19,159 | 11,173 | 6,537 | 1,449 | 4,636 R | 58.3% | 34.1% | 63.1% | 36.9% |
| 30,592 | JACKSON | 10,719 | 5,902 | 4,409 | 408 | 1,493 R | 55.1% | 41.1% | 57.2% | 42.8% |
| 91,564 | JEFFERSON | 38,491 | 15,777 | 20,382 | 2,332 | 4,605 D | 41.0% | 53.0% | 43.6% | 56.4% |
| 46,304 | KNOX | 18,195 | 10,384 | 6,586 | 1,225 | 3,798 R | 57.1% | 36.2% | 61.2% | 38.8% |
| 212,801 | LAKE | 86,428 | 43,485 | 35,246 | 7,697 | 8,239 R | 50.3% | 40.8% | 55.2% | 44.8% |
| 63,849 | LAWRENCE | 26,194 | 13,799 | 11,366 | 1,029 | 2,433 R | 52.7% | 43.4% | 54.8% | 45.2% |
| 120,981 | LICKING | 48,769 | 28,425 | 17,208 | 3,136 | 11,217 R | 58.3% | 35.3% | 62.3% | 37.7% |
| 39,155 | LOGAN | 14,994 | 9,727 | 4,319 | 948 | 5,408 R | 64.9% | 28.8% | 69.3% | 30.7% |
| 274,909 | LORAIN | 103,084 | 51,034 | 40,919 | 11,131 | 10,115 R | 49.5% | 39.7% | 55.5% | 44.5% |
| 471,741 | LUCAS | 191,298 | 86,653 | 85,341 | 19,304 | 1,312 R | 45.3% | 44.6% | 50.4% | 49.6% |
| 33,004 | MADISON | 11,350 | 7,166 | 3,565 | 619 | 3,601 R | 63.1% | 31.4% | 66.8% | 33.2% |
| 289,487 | MAHONING | 125,161 | 50,153 | 63,677 | 11,331 | 13,524 D | 40.1% | 50.9% | 44.1% | 55.9% |
| 67,974 | MARION | 25,631 | 14,605 | 9,419 | 1,607 | 5,186 R | 57.0% | 36.7% | 60.8% | 39.2% |
| 113,150 | MEDINA | 42,050 | 24,723 | 13,573 | 3,754 | 11,150 R | 58.8% | 32.3% | 64.6% | 35.4% |
| 23,641 | MEIGS | 9,170 | 4,911 | 3,827 | 432 | 1,084 R | 53.6% | 41.7% | 56.2% | 43.8% |
| 38,334 | MERCER | 15,339 | 8,673 | 5,506 | 1,160 | 3,167 R | 56.5% | 35.9% | 61.2% | 38.8% |
| 90,381 | MIAMI | 35,808 | 19,928 | 12,893 | 2,987 | 7,035 R | 55.7% | 36.0% | 60.7% | 39.3% |
| 17,382 | MONROE | 6,373 | 2,870 | 3,166 | 337 | 296 D | 45.0% | 49.7% | 47.5% | 52.5% |
| 571,697 | MONTGOMERY | 223,009 | 101,443 | 105,110 | 16,456 | 3,667 D | 45.5% | 47.1% | 49.1% | 50.9% |
| 14,241 | MORGAN | 5,366 | 3,236 | 1,875 | 255 | 1,361 R | 60.3% | 34.9% | 63.3% | 36.7% |
| 26,480 | MORROW | 9,972 | 6,179 | 3,239 | 554 | 2,940 R | 62.0% | 32.5% | 65.6% | 34.4% |
| 83,340 | MUSKINGUM | 32,688 | 17,921 | 12,584 | 2,183 | 5,337 R | 54.8% | 38.5% | 58.7% | 41.3% |

# OHIO

## PRESIDENT 1980

| 1980 Census Population | County | Total Vote | Republican | Democratic | Other | Rep.-Dem. Plurality | Percentage | | | |
|---|---|---|---|---|---|---|---|---|---|---|
| | | | | | | | Total Vote | | Major Vote | |
| | | | | | | | Rep. | Dem. | Rep. | Dem. |
| 11,310 | NOBLE | 5,272 | 3,025 | 1,944 | 303 | 1,081 R | 57.4% | 36.9% | 60.9% | 39.1% |
| 40,076 | OTTAWA | 16,883 | 8,641 | 6,753 | 1,489 | 1,888 R | 51.2% | 40.0% | 56.1% | 43.9% |
| 21,302 | PAULDING | 8,494 | 4,971 | 2,778 | 745 | 2,193 R | 58.5% | 32.7% | 64.2% | 35.8% |
| 31,032 | PERRY | 10,648 | 5,725 | 4,383 | 540 | 1,342 R | 53.8% | 41.2% | 56.6% | 43.4% |
| 43,662 | PICKAWAY | 15,170 | 9,289 | 5,052 | 829 | 4,237 R | 61.2% | 33.3% | 64.8% | 35.2% |
| 22,802 | PIKE | 9,818 | 4,426 | 4,938 | 454 | 512 D | 45.1% | 50.3% | 47.3% | 52.7% |
| 135,856 | PORTAGE | 48,190 | 22,829 | 20,570 | 4,791 | 2,259 R | 47.4% | 42.7% | 52.6% | 47.4% |
| 38,223 | PREBLE | 14,723 | 8,376 | 5,416 | 931 | 2,960 R | 56.9% | 36.8% | 60.7% | 39.3% |
| 32,991 | PUTNAM | 14,193 | 9,752 | 3,742 | 699 | 6,010 R | 68.7% | 26.4% | 72.3% | 27.7% |
| 131,205 | RICHLAND | 50,824 | 29,213 | 18,253 | 3,358 | 10,960 R | 57.5% | 35.9% | 61.5% | 38.5% |
| 65,004 | ROSS | 23,859 | 13,251 | 9,355 | 1,253 | 3,896 R | 55.5% | 39.2% | 58.6% | 41.4% |
| 63,267 | SANDUSKY | 24,166 | 13,420 | 8,482 | 2,264 | 4,938 R | 55.5% | 35.1% | 61.3% | 38.7% |
| 84,545 | SCIOTO | 32,568 | 15,881 | 15,552 | 1,135 | 329 R | 48.8% | 47.8% | 50.5% | 49.5% |
| 61,901 | SENECA | 23,259 | 14,172 | 7,303 | 1,784 | 6,869 R | 60.9% | 31.4% | 66.0% | 34.0% |
| 43,089 | SHELBY | 16,544 | 8,988 | 6,425 | 1,131 | 2,563 R | 54.3% | 38.8% | 58.3% | 41.7% |
| 378,823 | STARK | 157,106 | 87,769 | 59,005 | 10,332 | 28,764 R | 55.9% | 37.6% | 59.8% | 40.2% |
| 524,472 | SUMMIT | 212,919 | 92,299 | 102,459 | 18,161 | 10,160 D | 43.3% | 48.1% | 47.4% | 52.6% |
| 241,863 | TRUMBULL | 93,002 | 41,056 | 44,366 | 7,580 | 3,310 D | 44.1% | 47.7% | 48.1% | 51.9% |
| 84,614 | TUSCARAWAS | 30,086 | 15,708 | 12,117 | 2,261 | 3,591 R | 52.2% | 40.3% | 56.5% | 43.5% |
| 29,536 | UNION | 11,186 | 7,576 | 3,038 | 572 | 4,538 R | 67.7% | 27.2% | 71.4% | 28.6% |
| 30,458 | VAN WERT | 12,872 | 7,866 | 4,070 | 936 | 3,796 R | 61.1% | 31.6% | 65.9% | 34.1% |
| 11,584 | VINTON | 5,064 | 2,484 | 2,381 | 199 | 103 R | 49.1% | 47.0% | 51.1% | 48.9% |
| 99,276 | WARREN | 35,522 | 22,430 | 11,306 | 1,786 | 11,124 R | 63.1% | 31.8% | 66.5% | 33.5% |
| 64,266 | WASHINGTON | 23,971 | 14,310 | 7,936 | 1,725 | 6,374 R | 59.7% | 33.1% | 64.3% | 35.7% |
| 97,408 | WAYNE | 33,942 | 18,962 | 12,129 | 2,851 | 6,833 R | 55.9% | 35.7% | 61.0% | 39.0% |
| 36,369 | WILLIAMS | 14,221 | 9,146 | 4,015 | 1,060 | 5,131 R | 64.3% | 28.2% | 69.5% | 30.5% |
| 107,372 | WOOD | 42,213 | 23,315 | 14,139 | 4,759 | 9,176 R | 55.2% | 33.5% | 62.2% | 37.8% |
| 22,651 | WYANDOT | 9,175 | 5,786 | 2,757 | 632 | 3,029 R | 63.1% | 30.0% | 67.7% | 32.3% |
| 10,797,630 | TOTAL | 4,283,603 | 2,206,545 | 1,752,414 | 324,644 | 454,131 R | 51.5% | 40.9% | 55.7% | 44.3% |

# OHIO

## PRESIDENT 1976

| 1970 Census Population | County | Total Vote | Republican | Democratic | Other | Rep.-Dem. Plurality | Percentage | | | |
|---|---|---|---|---|---|---|---|---|---|---|
| | | | | | | | Total Vote | | Major Vote | |
| | | | | | | | Rep. | Dem. | Rep. | Dem. |
| 18,957 | ADAMS | 8,780 | 4,197 | 4,450 | 133 | 253 D | 47.8% | 50.7% | 48.5% | 51.5% |
| 111,144 | ALLEN | 39,167 | 23,721 | 14,627 | 819 | 9,094 R | 60.6% | 37.3% | 61.9% | 38.1% |
| 43,303 | ASHLAND | 17,354 | 9,761 | 7,205 | 388 | 2,556 R | 56.2% | 41.5% | 57.5% | 42.5% |
| 98,237 | ASHTABULA | 38,625 | 16,885 | 20,883 | 857 | 3,998 D | 43.7% | 54.1% | 44.7% | 55.3% |
| 54,889 | ATHENS | 19,016 | 8,387 | 9,896 | 733 | 1,509 D | 44.1% | 52.0% | 45.9% | 54.1% |
| 38,602 | AUGLAIZE | 15,965 | 9,772 | 5,840 | 353 | 3,932 R | 61.2% | 36.6% | 62.6% | 37.4% |
| 80,917 | BELMONT | 35,219 | 13,550 | 21,162 | 507 | 7,612 D | 38.5% | 60.1% | 39.0% | 61.0% |
| 26,635 | BROWN | 10,126 | 4,549 | 5,432 | 145 | 883 D | 44.9% | 53.6% | 45.6% | 54.4% |
| 226,207 | BUTLER | 86,217 | 49,625 | 35,123 | 1,469 | 14,502 R | 57.6% | 40.7% | 58.6% | 41.4% |
| 21,579 | CARROLL | 10,325 | 5,091 | 5,006 | 228 | 85 R | 49.3% | 48.5% | 50.4% | 49.6% |
| 30,491 | CHAMPAIGN | 11,502 | 6,526 | 4,748 | 228 | 1,778 R | 56.7% | 41.3% | 57.9% | 42.1% |
| 157,115 | CLARK | 54,660 | 26,745 | 26,135 | 1,780 | 610 R | 48.9% | 47.8% | 50.6% | 49.4% |
| 95,725 | CLERMONT | 35,037 | 19,616 | 14,850 | 571 | 4,766 R | 56.0% | 42.4% | 56.9% | 43.1% |
| 31,464 | CLINTON | 11,737 | 6,597 | 4,959 | 181 | 1,638 R | 56.2% | 42.3% | 57.1% | 42.9% |
| 108,310 | COLUMBIANA | 46,367 | 22,318 | 23,096 | 953 | 778 D | 48.1% | 49.8% | 49.1% | 50.9% |
| 33,486 | COSHOCTON | 12,496 | 6,361 | 5,827 | 308 | 534 R | 50.9% | 46.6% | 52.2% | 47.8% |
| 50,364 | CRAWFORD | 18,870 | 10,801 | 7,553 | 516 | 3,248 R | 57.2% | 40.0% | 58.8% | 41.2% |
| 1,721,300 | CUYAHOGA | 623,222 | 255,594 | 349,186 | 18,442 | 93,592 D | 41.0% | 56.0% | 42.3% | 57.7% |
| 49,141 | DARKE | 21,953 | 11,580 | 9,901 | 472 | 1,679 R | 52.7% | 45.1% | 53.9% | 46.1% |
| 36,949 | DEFIANCE | 13,679 | 7,526 | 5,850 | 303 | 1,676 R | 55.0% | 42.8% | 56.3% | 43.7% |
| 42,908 | DELAWARE | 19,853 | 12,285 | 7,058 | 510 | 5,227 R | 61.9% | 35.6% | 63.5% | 36.5% |
| 75,909 | ERIE | 29,478 | 14,742 | 13,843 | 893 | 899 R | 50.0% | 47.0% | 51.6% | 48.4% |
| 73,301 | FAIRFIELD | 33,079 | 19,098 | 13,361 | 620 | 5,737 R | 57.7% | 40.4% | 58.8% | 41.2% |
| 25,461 | FAYETTE | 10,364 | 5,719 | 4,477 | 168 | 1,242 R | 55.2% | 43.2% | 56.1% | 43.9% |
| 833,249 | FRANKLIN | 340,712 | 189,645 | 141,624 | 9,443 | 48,021 R | 55.7% | 41.6% | 57.2% | 42.8% |
| 33,071 | FULTON | 12,949 | 7,891 | 4,850 | 208 | 3,041 R | 60.9% | 37.5% | 61.9% | 38.1% |
| 25,239 | GALLIA | 10,317 | 5,198 | 4,971 | 148 | 227 R | 50.4% | 48.2% | 51.1% | 48.9% |
| 62,977 | GEAUGA | 26,269 | 15,004 | 10,449 | 816 | 4,555 R | 57.1% | 39.8% | 58.9% | 41.1% |
| 125,057 | GREENE | 44,077 | 22,598 | 20,245 | 1,234 | 2,353 R | 51.3% | 45.9% | 52.7% | 47.3% |
| 37,665 | GUERNSEY | 15,524 | 7,746 | 7,573 | 205 | 173 R | 49.9% | 48.8% | 50.6% | 49.4% |
| 924,018 | HAMILTON | 353,079 | 211,267 | 135,605 | 6,207 | 75,662 R | 59.8% | 38.4% | 60.9% | 39.1% |
| 61,217 | HANCOCK | 25,333 | 15,983 | 8,548 | 802 | 7,435 R | 63.1% | 33.7% | 65.2% | 34.8% |
| 30,813 | HARDIN | 11,075 | 6,076 | 4,650 | 349 | 1,426 R | 54.9% | 42.0% | 56.6% | 43.4% |
| 17,013 | HARRISON | 7,681 | 3,509 | 4,070 | 102 | 561 D | 45.7% | 53.0% | 46.3% | 53.7% |
| 27,058 | HENRY | 12,470 | 7,656 | 4,592 | 222 | 3,064 R | 61.4% | 36.8% | 62.5% | 37.5% |
| 28,996 | HIGHLAND | 13,331 | 6,853 | 6,327 | 151 | 526 R | 51.4% | 47.5% | 52.0% | 48.0% |
| 20,322 | HOCKING | 9,396 | 4,114 | 5,126 | 156 | 1,012 D | 43.8% | 54.6% | 44.5% | 55.5% |
| 23,024 | HOLMES | 5,299 | 2,870 | 2,242 | 187 | 628 R | 54.2% | 42.3% | 56.1% | 43.9% |
| 49,587 | HURON | 18,066 | 9,386 | 7,742 | 938 | 1,644 R | 52.0% | 42.9% | 54.8% | 45.2% |
| 27,174 | JACKSON | 12,822 | 5,987 | 6,699 | 136 | 712 D | 46.7% | 52.2% | 47.2% | 52.8% |
| 96,193 | JEFFERSON | 37,825 | 14,839 | 22,318 | 668 | 7,479 D | 39.2% | 59.0% | 39.9% | 60.1% |
| 41,795 | KNOX | 17,081 | 9,290 | 7,361 | 430 | 1,929 R | 54.4% | 43.1% | 55.8% | 44.2% |
| 197,200 | LAKE | 79,408 | 36,390 | 40,734 | 2,284 | 4,344 D | 45.8% | 51.3% | 47.2% | 52.8% |
| 56,868 | LAWRENCE | 22,995 | 10,668 | 12,072 | 255 | 1,404 D | 46.4% | 52.5% | 46.9% | 53.1% |
| 107,799 | LICKING | 43,733 | 23,518 | 19,247 | 968 | 4,271 R | 53.8% | 44.0% | 55.0% | 45.0% |
| 35,072 | LOGAN | 15,402 | 9,092 | 5,949 | 361 | 3,143 R | 59.0% | 38.6% | 60.4% | 39.6% |
| 256,843 | LORAIN | 94,711 | 39,459 | 52,387 | 2,865 | 12,928 D | 41.7% | 55.3% | 43.0% | 57.0% |
| 484,370 | LUCAS | 183,907 | 76,069 | 103,658 | 4,180 | 27,589 D | 41.4% | 56.4% | 42.3% | 57.7% |
| 28,318 | MADISON | 12,161 | 7,074 | 4,885 | 202 | 2,189 R | 58.2% | 40.2% | 59.2% | 40.8% |
| 303,424 | MAHONING | 125,294 | 46,314 | 75,837 | 3,143 | 29,523 D | 37.0% | 60.5% | 37.9% | 62.1% |
| 64,724 | MARION | 24,620 | 13,141 | 10,962 | 517 | 2,179 R | 53.4% | 44.5% | 54.5% | 45.5% |
| 82,717 | MEDINA | 36,249 | 19,066 | 16,251 | 932 | 2,815 R | 52.6% | 44.8% | 54.0% | 46.0% |
| 19,799 | MEIGS | 10,348 | 4,942 | 5,262 | 144 | 320 D | 47.8% | 50.9% | 48.4% | 51.6% |
| 35,265 | MERCER | 14,849 | 7,678 | 6,724 | 447 | 954 R | 51.7% | 45.3% | 53.3% | 46.7% |
| 84,342 | MIAMI | 32,413 | 18,686 | 13,074 | 653 | 5,612 R | 57.6% | 40.3% | 58.8% | 41.2% |
| 15,739 | MONROE | 7,132 | 2,728 | 4,296 | 108 | 1,568 D | 38.3% | 60.2% | 38.8% | 61.2% |
| 606,148 | MONTGOMERY | 211,436 | 100,223 | 106,468 | 4,745 | 6,245 D | 47.4% | 50.4% | 48.5% | 51.5% |
| 12,375 | MORGAN | 5,809 | 2,971 | 2,727 | 111 | 244 R | 51.1% | 46.9% | 52.1% | 47.9% |
| 21,348 | MORROW | 10,912 | 5,814 | 4,870 | 228 | 944 R | 53.3% | 44.6% | 54.4% | 45.6% |
| 77,826 | MUSKINGUM | 30,070 | 15,358 | 14,178 | 534 | 1,180 R | 51.1% | 47.1% | 52.0% | 48.0% |

# OHIO

## PRESIDENT 1976

| 1970 Census Population | County | Total Vote | Republican | Democratic | Other | Rep.-Dem. Plurality | Percentage | | | |
|---|---|---|---|---|---|---|---|---|---|---|
| | | | | | | | Total Vote | | Major Vote | |
| | | | | | | | Rep. | Dem. | Rep. | Dem. |
| 10,428 | NOBLE | 5,730 | 3,007 | 2,612 | 111 | 395 R | 52.5% | 45.6% | 53.5% | 46.5% |
| 37,099 | OTTAWA | 18,299 | 8,241 | 9,646 | 412 | 1,405 D | 45.0% | 52.7% | 46.1% | 53.9% |
| 19,329 | PAULDING | 6,987 | 3,593 | 3,229 | 165 | 364 R | 51.4% | 46.2% | 52.7% | 47.3% |
| 27,434 | PERRY | 12,138 | 5,637 | 6,268 | 233 | 631 D | 46.4% | 51.6% | 47.3% | 52.7% |
| 40,071 | PICKAWAY | 14,045 | 7,695 | 5,907 | 443 | 1,788 R | 54.8% | 42.1% | 56.6% | 43.4% |
| 19,114 | PIKE | 9,574 | 3,729 | 5,734 | 111 | 2,005 D | 38.9% | 59.9% | 39.4% | 60.6% |
| 125,868 | PORTAGE | 43,824 | 17,927 | 24,417 | 1,480 | 6,490 D | 40.9% | 55.7% | 42.3% | 57.7% |
| 34,719 | PREBLE | 12,747 | 6,654 | 5,850 | 243 | 804 R | 52.2% | 45.9% | 53.2% | 46.8% |
| 31,134 | PUTNAM | 12,710 | 7,332 | 5,035 | 343 | 2,297 R | 57.7% | 39.6% | 59.3% | 40.7% |
| 129,997 | RICHLAND | 49,251 | 24,310 | 23,065 | 1,876 | 1,245 R | 49.4% | 46.8% | 51.3% | 48.7% |
| 61,211 | ROSS | 22,751 | 11,477 | 10,743 | 531 | 734 R | 50.4% | 47.2% | 51.7% | 48.3% |
| 60,983 | SANDUSKY | 24,867 | 13,074 | 11,202 | 591 | 1,872 R | 52.6% | 45.0% | 53.9% | 46.1% |
| 76,951 | SCIOTO | 31,488 | 13,021 | 18,019 | 448 | 4,998 D | 41.4% | 57.2% | 41.9% | 58.1% |
| 60,696 | SENECA | 22,516 | 11,730 | 10,074 | 712 | 1,656 R | 52.1% | 44.7% | 53.8% | 46.2% |
| 37,748 | SHELBY | 14,859 | 8,011 | 6,414 | 434 | 1,597 R | 53.9% | 43.2% | 55.5% | 44.5% |
| 372,210 | STARK | 145,709 | 72,607 | 70,012 | 3,090 | 2,595 R | 49.8% | 48.0% | 50.9% | 49.1% |
| 553,371 | SUMMIT | 209,350 | 80,415 | 123,711 | 5,224 | 43,296 D | 38.4% | 59.1% | 39.4% | 60.6% |
| 232,579 | TRUMBULL | 92,544 | 36,469 | 53,828 | 2,247 | 17,359 D | 39.4% | 58.2% | 40.4% | 59.6% |
| 77,211 | TUSCARAWAS | 31,841 | 14,279 | 16,880 | 682 | 2,601 D | 44.8% | 53.0% | 45.8% | 54.2% |
| 23,786 | UNION | 12,043 | 7,464 | 4,377 | 202 | 3,087 R | 62.0% | 36.3% | 63.0% | 37.0% |
| 29,194 | VAN WERT | 14,284 | 8,344 | 5,689 | 251 | 2,655 R | 58.4% | 39.8% | 59.5% | 40.5% |
| 9,420 | VINTON | 4,846 | 2,148 | 2,629 | 69 | 481 D | 44.3% | 54.3% | 45.0% | 55.0% |
| 84,925 | WARREN | 29,935 | 16,115 | 13,349 | 471 | 2,766 R | 53.8% | 44.6% | 54.7% | 45.3% |
| 57,160 | WASHINGTON | 21,096 | 11,513 | 8,914 | 669 | 2,599 R | 54.6% | 42.3% | 56.4% | 43.6% |
| 87,123 | WAYNE | 30,754 | 16,976 | 13,087 | 691 | 3,889 R | 55.2% | 42.6% | 56.5% | 43.5% |
| 33,669 | WILLIAMS | 12,762 | 7,596 | 4,920 | 246 | 2,676 R | 59.5% | 38.6% | 60.7% | 39.3% |
| 89,722 | WOOD | 37,131 | 19,331 | 16,926 | 874 | 2,405 R | 52.1% | 45.6% | 53.3% | 46.7% |
| 21,826 | WYANDOT | 9,946 | 5,661 | 4,043 | 242 | 1,618 R | 56.9% | 40.6% | 58.3% | 41.7% |
| 10,652,017 | TOTAL | 4,111,873 | 2,000,505 | 2,011,621 | 99,747 | 11,116 D | 48.7% | 48.9% | 49.9% | 50.1% |

# OHIO

## PRESIDENT 1972

| 1970 Census Population | County | Total Vote | Republican | Democratic | Other | Rep.-Dem. Plurality | Percentage | | | |
|---|---|---|---|---|---|---|---|---|---|---|
| | | | | | | | Total Vote | | Major Vote | |
| | | | | | | | Rep. | Dem. | Rep. | Dem. |
| 18,957 | ADAMS | 7,882 | 4,980 | 2,709 | 193 | 2,271 R | 63.2% | 34.4% | 64.8% | 35.2% |
| 111,144 | ALLEN | 38,543 | 26,966 | 10,184 | 1,393 | 16,782 R | 70.0% | 26.4% | 72.6% | 27.4% |
| 43,303 | ASHLAND | 17,074 | 12,470 | 4,302 | 302 | 8,168 R | 73.0% | 25.2% | 74.4% | 25.6% |
| 98,237 | ASHTABULA | 38,608 | 22,762 | 15,052 | 794 | 7,710 R | 59.0% | 39.0% | 60.2% | 39.8% |
| 54,889 | ATHENS | 19,915 | 9,735 | 9,977 | 203 | 242 D | 48.9% | 50.1% | 49.4% | 50.6% |
| 38,602 | AUGLAIZE | 17,047 | 11,900 | 4,617 | 530 | 7,283 R | 69.8% | 27.1% | 72.0% | 28.0% |
| 80,917 | BELMONT | 32,878 | 17,628 | 14,800 | 450 | 2,828 R | 53.6% | 45.0% | 54.4% | 45.6% |
| 26,635 | BROWN | 10,804 | 6,772 | 3,770 | 262 | 3,002 R | 62.7% | 34.9% | 64.2% | 35.8% |
| 226,207 | BUTLER | 73,635 | 50,380 | 21,194 | 2,061 | 29,186 R | 68.4% | 28.8% | 70.4% | 29.6% |
| 21,579 | CARROLL | 9,014 | 5,984 | 2,755 | 275 | 3,229 R | 66.4% | 30.6% | 68.5% | 31.5% |
| 30,491 | CHAMPAIGN | 12,603 | 8,756 | 3,626 | 221 | 5,130 R | 69.5% | 28.8% | 70.7% | 29.3% |
| 157,115 | CLARK | 55,750 | 34,447 | 19,725 | 1,578 | 14,722 R | 61.8% | 35.4% | 63.6% | 36.4% |
| 95,725 | CLERMONT | 31,989 | 22,936 | 8,276 | 777 | 14,660 R | 71.7% | 25.9% | 73.5% | 26.5% |
| 31,464 | CLINTON | 10,988 | 8,140 | 2,709 | 139 | 5,431 R | 74.1% | 24.7% | 75.0% | 25.0% |
| 108,310 | COLUMBIANA | 43,602 | 27,308 | 15,683 | 611 | 11,625 R | 62.6% | 36.0% | 63.5% | 36.5% |
| 33,486 | COSHOCTON | 12,206 | 8,082 | 3,790 | 334 | 4,292 R | 66.2% | 31.1% | 68.1% | 31.9% |
| 50,364 | CRAWFORD | 21,053 | 14,632 | 5,518 | 903 | 9,114 R | 69.5% | 26.2% | 72.6% | 27.4% |
| 1,721,300 | CUYAHOGA | 659,751 | 329,493 | 317,670 | 12,588 | 11,823 R | 49.9% | 48.1% | 50.9% | 49.1% |
| 49,141 | DARKE | 21,096 | 13,862 | 6,534 | 700 | 7,328 R | 65.7% | 31.0% | 68.0% | 32.0% |
| 36,949 | DEFIANCE | 13,630 | 8,914 | 4,377 | 339 | 4,537 R | 65.4% | 32.1% | 67.1% | 32.9% |
| 42,908 | DELAWARE | 17,886 | 12,950 | 4,452 | 484 | 8,498 R | 72.4% | 24.9% | 74.4% | 25.6% |
| 75,909 | ERIE | 28,591 | 16,714 | 10,889 | 988 | 5,825 R | 58.5% | 38.1% | 60.6% | 39.4% |
| 73,301 | FAIRFIELD | 30,568 | 21,909 | 7,746 | 913 | 14,163 R | 71.7% | 25.3% | 73.9% | 26.1% |
| 25,461 | FAYETTE | 9,515 | 6,970 | 2,344 | 201 | 4,626 R | 73.3% | 24.6% | 74.8% | 25.2% |
| 833,249 | FRANKLIN | 344,808 | 219,771 | 117,562 | 7,475 | 102,209 R | 63.7% | 34.1% | 65.1% | 34.9% |
| 33,071 | FULTON | 12,234 | 8,387 | 3,615 | 232 | 4,772 R | 68.6% | 29.5% | 69.9% | 30.1% |
| 25,239 | GALLIA | 8,986 | 6,506 | 2,341 | 139 | 4,165 R | 72.4% | 26.1% | 73.5% | 26.5% |
| 62,977 | GEAUGA | 23,577 | 15,624 | 7,329 | 624 | 8,295 R | 66.3% | 31.1% | 68.1% | 31.9% |
| 125,057 | GREENE | 38,909 | 25,349 | 12,736 | 824 | 12,613 R | 65.1% | 32.7% | 66.6% | 33.4% |
| 37,665 | GUERNSEY | 14,619 | 9,648 | 4,757 | 214 | 4,891 R | 66.0% | 32.5% | 67.0% | 33.0% |
| 924,018 | HAMILTON | 364,385 | 239,212 | 119,054 | 6,119 | 120,158 R | 65.6% | 32.7% | 66.8% | 33.2% |
| 61,217 | HANCOCK | 25,624 | 18,111 | 6,084 | 1,429 | 12,027 R | 70.7% | 23.7% | 74.9% | 25.1% |
| 30,813 | HARDIN | 12,602 | 8,713 | 3,535 | 354 | 5,178 R | 69.1% | 28.1% | 71.1% | 28.9% |
| 17,013 | HARRISON | 7,010 | 4,554 | 2,388 | 68 | 2,166 R | 65.0% | 34.1% | 65.6% | 34.4% |
| 27,058 | HENRY | 11,475 | 8,099 | 3,145 | 231 | 4,954 R | 70.6% | 27.4% | 72.0% | 28.0% |
| 28,996 | HIGHLAND | 12,226 | 8,524 | 3,464 | 238 | 5,060 R | 69.7% | 28.3% | 71.1% | 28.9% |
| 20,322 | HOCKING | 8,492 | 5,407 | 2,874 | 211 | 2,533 R | 63.7% | 33.8% | 65.3% | 34.7% |
| 23,024 | HOLMES | 5,362 | 3,752 | 1,507 | 103 | 2,245 R | 70.0% | 28.1% | 71.3% | 28.7% |
| 49,587 | HURON | 17,340 | 10,942 | 5,491 | 907 | 5,451 R | 63.1% | 31.7% | 66.6% | 33.4% |
| 27,174 | JACKSON | 10,923 | 7,351 | 3,410 | 162 | 3,941 R | 67.3% | 31.2% | 68.3% | 31.7% |
| 96,193 | JEFFERSON | 38,274 | 21,531 | 16,198 | 545 | 5,333 R | 56.3% | 42.3% | 57.1% | 42.9% |
| 41,795 | KNOX | 16,739 | 10,705 | 5,370 | 664 | 5,335 R | 64.0% | 32.1% | 66.6% | 33.4% |
| 197,200 | LAKE | 72,141 | 42,488 | 27,523 | 2,130 | 14,965 R | 58.9% | 38.2% | 60.7% | 39.3% |
| 56,868 | LAWRENCE | 22,567 | 15,125 | 7,112 | 330 | 8,013 R | 67.0% | 31.5% | 68.0% | 32.0% |
| 107,799 | LICKING | 42,232 | 28,070 | 12,460 | 1,702 | 15,610 R | 66.5% | 29.5% | 69.3% | 30.7% |
| 35,072 | LOGAN | 15,380 | 10,938 | 3,786 | 656 | 7,152 R | 71.1% | 24.6% | 74.3% | 25.7% |
| 256,843 | LORAIN | 91,016 | 51,102 | 36,634 | 3,280 | 14,468 R | 56.1% | 40.3% | 58.2% | 41.8% |
| 484,370 | LUCAS | 182,709 | 88,401 | 90,142 | 4,166 | 1,741 D | 48.4% | 49.3% | 49.5% | 50.5% |
| 28,318 | MADISON | 11,064 | 8,372 | 2,484 | 208 | 5,888 R | 75.7% | 22.5% | 77.1% | 22.9% |
| 303,424 | MAHONING | 129,088 | 64,144 | 62,428 | 2,516 | 1,716 R | 49.7% | 48.4% | 50.7% | 49.3% |
| 64,724 | MARION | 25,659 | 17,197 | 7,970 | 492 | 9,227 R | 67.0% | 31.1% | 68.3% | 31.7% |
| 82,717 | MEDINA | 32,411 | 21,010 | 10,643 | 758 | 10,367 R | 64.8% | 32.8% | 66.4% | 33.6% |
| 19,799 | MEIGS | 8,433 | 5,961 | 2,335 | 137 | 3,626 R | 70.7% | 27.7% | 71.9% | 28.1% |
| 35,265 | MERCER | 14,907 | 8,587 | 5,798 | 522 | 2,789 R | 57.6% | 38.9% | 59.7% | 40.3% |
| 84,342 | MIAMI | 31,012 | 21,226 | 9,121 | 665 | 12,105 R | 68.4% | 29.4% | 69.9% | 30.1% |
| 15,739 | MONROE | 6,292 | 3,721 | 2,483 | 88 | 1,238 R | 59.1% | 39.5% | 60.0% | 40.0% |
| 606,148 | MONTGOMERY | 208,552 | 120,998 | 82,231 | 5,323 | 38,767 R | 58.0% | 39.4% | 59.5% | 40.5% |
| 12,375 | MORGAN | 5,371 | 3,679 | 1,554 | 138 | 2,125 R | 68.5% | 28.9% | 70.3% | 29.7% |
| 21,348 | MORROW | 9,759 | 6,886 | 2,527 | 346 | 4,359 R | 70.6% | 25.9% | 73.2% | 26.8% |
| 77,826 | MUSKINGUM | 31,094 | 19,897 | 10,313 | 884 | 9,584 R | 64.0% | 33.2% | 65.9% | 34.1% |

# OHIO

## PRESIDENT 1972

| 1970 Census Population | County | Total Vote | Republican | Democratic | Other | Rep.-Dem. Plurality | Percentage | | | |
|---|---|---|---|---|---|---|---|---|---|---|
| | | | | | | | Total Vote | | Major Vote | |
| | | | | | | | Rep. | Dem. | Rep. | Dem. |
| 10,428 | NOBLE | 4,799 | 3,274 | 1,449 | 76 | 1,825 R | 68.2% | 30.2% | 69.3% | 30.7% |
| 37,099 | OTTAWA | 16,889 | 9,772 | 6,465 | 652 | 3,307 R | 57.9% | 38.3% | 60.2% | 39.8% |
| 19,329 | PAULDING | 7,025 | 4,553 | 2,283 | 189 | 2,270 R | 64.8% | 32.5% | 66.6% | 33.4% |
| 27,434 | PERRY | 10,809 | 6,716 | 3,728 | 365 | 2,988 R | 62.1% | 34.5% | 64.3% | 35.7% |
| 40,071 | PICKAWAY | 13,002 | 9,661 | 2,978 | 363 | 6,683 R | 74.3% | 22.9% | 76.4% | 23.6% |
| 19,114 | PIKE | 8,761 | 5,037 | 3,531 | 193 | 1,506 R | 57.5% | 40.3% | 58.8% | 41.2% |
| 125,868 | PORTAGE | 45,002 | 23,294 | 20,769 | 939 | 2,525 R | 51.8% | 46.2% | 52.9% | 47.1% |
| 34,719 | PREBLE | 12,795 | 8,993 | 3,472 | 330 | 5,521 R | 70.3% | 27.1% | 72.1% | 27.9% |
| 31,134 | PUTNAM | 12,342 | 8,185 | 3,729 | 428 | 4,456 R | 66.3% | 30.2% | 68.7% | 31.3% |
| 129,997 | RICHLAND | 45,641 | 31,117 | 13,468 | 1,056 | 17,649 R | 68.2% | 29.5% | 69.8% | 30.2% |
| 61,211 | ROSS | 21,888 | 15,573 | 5,879 | 436 | 9,694 R | 71.1% | 26.9% | 72.6% | 27.4% |
| 60,983 | SANDUSKY | 24,343 | 15,489 | 8,308 | 546 | 7,181 R | 63.6% | 34.1% | 65.1% | 34.9% |
| 76,951 | SCIOTO | 31,679 | 19,998 | 11,008 | 673 | 8,990 R | 63.1% | 34.7% | 64.5% | 35.5% |
| 60,696 | SENECA | 22,918 | 13,939 | 8,180 | 799 | 5,759 R | 60.8% | 35.7% | 63.0% | 37.0% |
| 37,748 | SHELBY | 14,703 | 9,089 | 4,721 | 893 | 4,368 R | 61.8% | 32.1% | 65.8% | 34.2% |
| 372,210 | STARK | 146,810 | 92,110 | 51,565 | 3,135 | 40,545 R | 62.7% | 35.1% | 64.1% | 35.9% |
| 553,371 | SUMMIT | 225,216 | 112,419 | 108,534 | 4,263 | 3,885 R | 49.9% | 48.2% | 50.9% | 49.1% |
| 232,579 | TRUMBULL | 85,266 | 47,680 | 35,278 | 2,308 | 12,402 R | 55.9% | 41.4% | 57.5% | 42.5% |
| 77,211 | TUSCARAWAS | 31,169 | 18,413 | 12,255 | 501 | 6,158 R | 59.1% | 39.3% | 60.0% | 40.0% |
| 23,786 | UNION | 11,054 | 8,389 | 2,447 | 218 | 5,942 R | 75.9% | 22.1% | 77.4% | 22.6% |
| 29,194 | VAN WERT | 13,391 | 9,545 | 3,644 | 202 | 5,901 R | 71.3% | 27.2% | 72.4% | 27.6% |
| 9,420 | VINTON | 4,336 | 2,725 | 1,537 | 74 | 1,188 R | 62.8% | 35.4% | 63.9% | 36.1% |
| 84,925 | WARREN | 27,897 | 20,210 | 6,941 | 746 | 13,269 R | 72.4% | 24.9% | 74.4% | 25.6% |
| 57,160 | WASHINGTON | 20,434 | 14,023 | 5,814 | 597 | 8,209 R | 68.6% | 28.5% | 70.7% | 29.3% |
| 87,123 | WAYNE | 30,076 | 20,368 | 9,260 | 448 | 11,108 R | 67.7% | 30.8% | 68.7% | 31.3% |
| 33,669 | WILLIAMS | 13,605 | 9,083 | 4,278 | 244 | 4,805 R | 66.8% | 31.4% | 68.0% | 32.0% |
| 89,722 | WOOD | 35,625 | 21,080 | 13,494 | 1,051 | 7,586 R | 59.2% | 37.9% | 61.0% | 39.0% |
| 21,826 | WYANDOT | 9,412 | 6,414 | 2,771 | 227 | 3,643 R | 68.1% | 29.4% | 69.8% | 30.2% |
| 10,652,017 | TOTAL | 4,094,787 | 2,441,827 | 1,558,889 | 94,071 | 882,938 R | 59.6% | 38.1% | 61.0% | 39.0% |

# OHIO

## PRESIDENT 1968

| 1960 Census Population | County | Total Vote | Republican | Democratic | AIP | Other | Plurality | Rep. | Dem. | AIP |
|---|---|---|---|---|---|---|---|---|---|---|
| 19,982 | ADAMS | 7,708 | 3,973 | 2,685 | 1,049 | 1 | 1,288 R | 51.5% | 34.8% | 13.6% |
| 103,691 | ALLEN | 38,349 | 23,124 | 10,994 | 4,231 | | 12,130 R | 60.3% | 28.7% | 11.0% |
| 38,771 | ASHLAND | 15,594 | 9,745 | 4,526 | 1,323 | | 5,219 R | 62.5% | 29.0% | 8.5% |
| 93,067 | ASHTABULA | 36,555 | 17,058 | 16,738 | 2,753 | 6 | 320 R | 46.7% | 45.8% | 7.5% |
| 46,998 | ATHENS | 16,400 | 7,837 | 7,351 | 1,207 | 5 | 486 R | 47.8% | 44.8% | 7.4% |
| 36,147 | AUGLAIZE | 16,447 | 9,368 | 5,550 | 1,528 | 1 | 3,818 R | 57.0% | 33.7% | 9.3% |
| 83,864 | BELMONT | 36,046 | 11,512 | 22,056 | 2,478 | | 10,544 D | 31.9% | 61.2% | 6.9% |
| 25,178 | BROWN | 10,617 | 4,700 | 3,610 | 2,307 | | 1,090 R | 44.3% | 34.0% | 21.7% |
| 199,076 | BUTLER | 73,802 | 35,962 | 23,649 | 14,188 | 3 | 12,313 R | 48.7% | 32.0% | 19.2% |
| 20,857 | CARROLL | 8,846 | 4,634 | 3,119 | 1,092 | 1 | 1,515 R | 52.4% | 35.3% | 12.3% |
| 29,714 | CHAMPAIGN | 12,750 | 6,863 | 4,264 | 1,621 | 2 | 2,599 R | 53.8% | 33.4% | 12.7% |
| 131,440 | CLARK | 54,491 | 23,748 | 24,029 | 6,710 | 4 | 281 D | 43.6% | 44.1% | 12.3% |
| 80,530 | CLERMONT | 31,849 | 15,299 | 8,859 | 7,690 | 1 | 6,440 R | 48.0% | 27.8% | 24.1% |
| 30,004 | CLINTON | 11,077 | 6,265 | 2,982 | 1,830 | | 3,283 R | 56.6% | 26.9% | 16.5% |
| 107,004 | COLUMBIANA | 43,170 | 19,947 | 19,382 | 3,832 | 9 | 565 R | 46.2% | 44.9% | 8.9% |
| 32,224 | COSHOCTON | 13,539 | 7,256 | 5,013 | 1,270 | | 2,243 R | 53.6% | 37.0% | 9.4% |
| 46,775 | CRAWFORD | 21,008 | 11,898 | 6,737 | 2,373 | | 5,161 R | 56.6% | 32.1% | 11.3% |
| 1,647,895 | CUYAHOGA | 673,839 | 238,791 | 363,540 | 71,360 | 148 | 124,749 D | 35.4% | 54.0% | 10.6% |
| 45,612 | DARKE | 20,315 | 10,926 | 7,371 | 2,015 | 3 | 3,555 R | 53.8% | 36.3% | 9.9% |
| 31,508 | DEFIANCE | 13,959 | 7,348 | 5,686 | 925 | | 1,662 R | 52.6% | 40.7% | 6.6% |
| 36,107 | DELAWARE | 15,644 | 9,029 | 4,056 | 2,557 | 2 | 4,973 R | 57.7% | 25.9% | 16.3% |
| 68,000 | ERIE | 26,849 | 13,023 | 11,388 | 2,437 | 1 | 1,635 R | 48.5% | 42.4% | 9.1% |
| 63,912 | FAIRFIELD | 28,467 | 14,810 | 9,533 | 4,124 | | 5,277 R | 52.0% | 33.5% | 14.5% |
| 24,775 | FAYETTE | 10,269 | 5,339 | 2,966 | 1,962 | 2 | 2,373 R | 52.0% | 28.9% | 19.1% |
| 682,962 | FRANKLIN | 287,624 | 148,933 | 101,240 | 37,390 | 61 | 47,693 R | 51.8% | 35.2% | 13.0% |
| 29,301 | FULTON | 12,188 | 7,817 | 3,338 | 1,033 | | 4,479 R | 64.1% | 27.4% | 8.5% |
| 26,120 | GALLIA | 8,836 | 5,134 | 2,660 | 1,039 | 3 | 2,474 R | 58.1% | 30.1% | 11.8% |
| 47,573 | GEAUGA | 22,908 | 11,857 | 7,825 | 3,226 | | 4,032 R | 51.8% | 34.2% | 14.1% |
| 94,642 | GREENE | 38,775 | 17,589 | 15,178 | 5,999 | 9 | 2,411 R | 45.4% | 39.1% | 15.5% |
| 38,579 | GUERNSEY | 14,837 | 7,336 | 5,815 | 1,685 | 1 | 1,521 R | 49.4% | 39.2% | 11.4% |
| 864,121 | HAMILTON | 365,483 | 183,611 | 135,057 | 46,742 | 73 | 48,554 R | 50.2% | 37.0% | 12.8% |
| 53,686 | HANCOCK | 24,609 | 15,032 | 6,918 | 2,659 | | 8,114 R | 61.1% | 28.1% | 10.8% |
| 29,633 | HARDIN | 12,937 | 6,963 | 4,180 | 1,794 | | 2,783 R | 53.8% | 32.3% | 13.9% |
| 17,995 | HARRISON | 7,700 | 3,532 | 3,594 | 574 | | 62 D | 45.9% | 46.7% | 7.5% |
| 25,392 | HENRY | 11,026 | 6,970 | 3,256 | 799 | 1 | 3,714 R | 63.2% | 29.5% | 7.2% |
| 29,716 | HIGHLAND | 12,525 | 6,489 | 3,828 | 2,208 | | 2,661 R | 51.8% | 30.6% | 17.6% |
| 20,168 | HOCKING | 8,702 | 3,998 | 3,701 | 1,003 | | 297 R | 45.9% | 42.5% | 11.5% |
| 21,591 | HOLMES | 5,729 | 3,350 | 1,898 | 479 | 2 | 1,452 R | 58.5% | 33.1% | 8.4% |
| 47,326 | HURON | 17,714 | 9,456 | 6,515 | 1,741 | 2 | 2,941 R | 53.4% | 36.8% | 9.8% |
| 29,372 | JACKSON | 10,968 | 5,870 | 4,021 | 1,077 | | 1,849 R | 53.5% | 36.7% | 9.8% |
| 99,201 | JEFFERSON | 38,615 | 12,949 | 21,917 | 3,740 | 9 | 8,968 D | 33.5% | 56.8% | 9.7% |
| 38,808 | KNOX | 16,492 | 9,072 | 5,725 | 1,695 | | 3,347 R | 55.0% | 34.7% | 10.3% |
| 148,700 | LAKE | 65,559 | 28,450 | 27,932 | 9,160 | 17 | 518 R | 43.4% | 42.6% | 14.0% |
| 55,438 | LAWRENCE | 20,923 | 9,782 | 8,671 | 2,470 | | 1,111 R | 46.8% | 41.4% | 11.8% |
| 90,242 | LICKING | 39,970 | 19,542 | 15,021 | 5,405 | 2 | 4,521 R | 48.9% | 37.6% | 13.5% |
| 34,803 | LOGAN | 14,899 | 8,362 | 4,889 | 1,647 | 1 | 3,473 R | 56.1% | 32.8% | 11.1% |
| 217,500 | LORAIN | 85,727 | 34,252 | 42,642 | 8,825 | 8 | 8,390 D | 40.0% | 49.7% | 10.3% |
| 456,931 | LUCAS | 178,037 | 69,403 | 91,346 | 17,260 | 28 | 21,943 D | 39.0% | 51.3% | 9.7% |
| 26,454 | MADISON | 10,293 | 5,882 | 2,780 | 1,631 | | 3,102 R | 57.1% | 27.0% | 15.8% |
| 300,480 | MAHONING | 123,578 | 42,948 | 68,433 | 12,189 | 8 | 25,485 D | 34.8% | 55.4% | 9.9% |
| 60,221 | MARION | 24,271 | 12,887 | 8,611 | 2,772 | 1 | 4,276 R | 53.1% | 35.5% | 11.4% |
| 65,315 | MEDINA | 26,933 | 14,089 | 9,194 | 3,632 | 18 | 4,895 R | 52.3% | 34.1% | 13.5% |
| 22,159 | MEIGS | 8,455 | 4,759 | 2,921 | 774 | 1 | 1,838 R | 56.3% | 34.5% | 9.2% |
| 32,559 | MERCER | 14,209 | 6,313 | 6,801 | 1,095 | | 488 D | 44.4% | 47.9% | 7.7% |
| 72,901 | MIAMI | 33,577 | 16,997 | 13,228 | 3,348 | 4 | 3,769 R | 50.6% | 39.4% | 10.0% |
| 15,268 | MONROE | 6,354 | 2,686 | 3,105 | 562 | 1 | 419 D | 42.3% | 48.9% | 8.8% |
| 527,080 | MONTGOMERY | 207,120 | 84,766 | 96,082 | 26,232 | 40 | 11,316 D | 40.9% | 46.4% | 12.7% |
| 12,747 | MORGAN | 5,269 | 3,030 | 1,789 | 450 | | 1,241 R | 57.5% | 34.0% | 8.5% |
| 19,405 | MORROW | 8,812 | 4,898 | 2,405 | 1,509 | | 2,493 R | 55.6% | 27.3% | 17.1% |
| 79,159 | MUSKINGUM | 31,705 | 15,260 | 13,089 | 3,356 | | 2,171 R | 48.1% | 41.3% | 10.6% |

# OHIO

## PRESIDENT 1968

| 1960 Census Population | County | Total Vote | Republican | Democratic | AIP | Other | Plurality | Percentage Total Vote Rep. | Dem. | AIP |
|---|---|---|---|---|---|---|---|---|---|---|
| 10,982 | NOBLE | 4,928 | 2,615 | 1,726 | 587 | | 889 R | 53.1% | 35.0% | 11.9% |
| 35,323 | OTTAWA | 15,115 | 7,149 | 6,319 | 1,647 | | 830 R | 47.3% | 41.8% | 10.9% |
| 16,792 | PAULDING | 7,685 | 4,074 | 2,703 | 908 | | 1,371 R | 53.0% | 35.2% | 11.8% |
| 27,864 | PERRY | 10,710 | 4,815 | 4,811 | 1,084 | | 4 R | 45.0% | 44.9% | 10.1% |
| 35,855 | PICKAWAY | 12,564 | 6,690 | 3,536 | 2,335 | 3 | 3,154 R | 53.2% | 28.1% | 18.6% |
| 19,380 | PIKE | 8,115 | 3,247 | 3,445 | 1,423 | | 198 D | 40.0% | 42.5% | 17.5% |
| 91,798 | PORTAGE | 36,505 | 15,064 | 16,348 | 5,093 | | 1,284 D | 41.3% | 44.8% | 14.0% |
| 32,498 | PREBLE | 12,434 | 6,544 | 3,817 | 2,073 | | 2,727 R | 52.6% | 30.7% | 16.7% |
| 28,331 | PUTNAM | 12,105 | 7,188 | 3,530 | 1,387 | | 3,658 R | 59.4% | 29.2% | 11.5% |
| 117,761 | RICHLAND | 43,787 | 23,484 | 14,988 | 5,311 | 4 | 8,496 R | 53.6% | 34.2% | 12.1% |
| 61,215 | ROSS | 22,246 | 11,284 | 6,873 | 4,087 | 2 | 4,411 R | 50.7% | 30.9% | 18.4% |
| 56,486 | SANDUSKY | 22,025 | 11,696 | 8,581 | 1,745 | 3 | 3,115 R | 53.1% | 39.0% | 7.9% |
| 84,216 | SCIOTO | 32,317 | 15,310 | 13,836 | 3,171 | | 1,474 R | 47.4% | 42.8% | 9.8% |
| 59,326 | SENECA | 23,020 | 12,040 | 8,970 | 2,010 | | 3,070 R | 52.3% | 39.0% | 8.7% |
| 33,586 | SHELBY | 15,226 | 7,248 | 6,479 | 1,499 | | 769 R | 47.6% | 42.6% | 9.8% |
| 340,345 | STARK | 142,888 | 68,414 | 57,675 | 16,775 | 24 | 10,739 R | 47.9% | 40.4% | 11.7% |
| 513,569 | SUMMIT | 208,941 | 82,649 | 100,068 | 26,157 | 67 | 17,419 D | 39.6% | 47.9% | 12.5% |
| 208,526 | TRUMBULL | 82,760 | 33,076 | 40,365 | 9,314 | 5 | 7,289 D | 40.0% | 48.8% | 11.3% |
| 76,789 | TUSCARAWAS | 32,461 | 14,102 | 15,617 | 2,741 | 1 | 1,515 D | 43.4% | 48.1% | 8.4% |
| 22,853 | UNION | 10,238 | 6,415 | 2,431 | 1,392 | | 3,984 R | 62.7% | 23.7% | 13.6% |
| 28,840 | VAN WERT | 13,527 | 7,835 | 4,360 | 1,332 | | 3,475 R | 57.9% | 32.2% | 9.8% |
| 10,274 | VINTON | 4,242 | 2,219 | 1,608 | 414 | 1 | 611 R | 52.3% | 37.9% | 9.8% |
| 65,711 | WARREN | 26,014 | 12,663 | 6,756 | 6,595 | | 5,907 R | 48.7% | 26.0% | 25.4% |
| 51,689 | WASHINGTON | 20,408 | 11,888 | 6,922 | 1,597 | 1 | 4,966 R | 58.3% | 33.9% | 7.8% |
| 75,497 | WAYNE | 25,970 | 15,151 | 8,891 | 1,924 | 4 | 6,260 R | 58.3% | 34.2% | 7.4% |
| 29,968 | WILLIAMS | 13,485 | 8,059 | 4,456 | 970 | | 3,603 R | 59.8% | 33.0% | 7.2% |
| 72,596 | WOOD | 29,939 | 16,111 | 10,867 | 2,952 | 9 | 5,244 R | 53.8% | 36.3% | 9.9% |
| 21,648 | WYANDOT | 9,094 | 5,265 | 2,919 | 910 | | 2,346 R | 57.9% | 32.1% | 10.0% |
| 9,706,397 | TOTAL | 3,959,698 | 1,791,014 | 1,700,586 | 467,495 | 603 | 90,428 R | 45.2% | 42.9% | 11.8% |

# OHIO

## PRESIDENT 1964

| 1960 Census Population | County | Total Vote | Republican | Democratic | Other | Rep.-Dem. Plurality | Percentage | | | |
|---|---|---|---|---|---|---|---|---|---|---|
| | | | | | | | Total Vote | | Major Vote | |
| | | | | | | | Rep. | Dem. | Rep. | Dem. |
| 19,982 | ADAMS | 8,707 | 3,702 | 5,005 | | 1,303 D | 42.5% | 57.5% | 42.5% | 57.5% |
| 103,691 | ALLEN | 38,887 | 19,897 | 18,990 | | 907 R | 51.2% | 48.8% | 51.2% | 48.8% |
| 38,771 | ASHLAND | 15,801 | 7,308 | 8,493 | | 1,185 D | 46.3% | 53.7% | 46.3% | 53.7% |
| 93,067 | ASHTABULA | 37,287 | 13,183 | 24,104 | | 10,921 D | 35.4% | 64.6% | 35.4% | 64.6% |
| 46,998 | ATHENS | 16,844 | 6,211 | 10,633 | | 4,422 D | 36.9% | 63.1% | 36.9% | 63.1% |
| 36,147 | AUGLAIZE | 16,586 | 7,954 | 8,632 | | 678 D | 48.0% | 52.0% | 48.0% | 52.0% |
| 83,864 | BELMONT | 37,873 | 9,693 | 28,180 | | 18,487 D | 25.6% | 74.4% | 25.6% | 74.4% |
| 25,178 | BROWN | 10,887 | 3,904 | 6,983 | | 3,079 D | 35.9% | 64.1% | 35.9% | 64.1% |
| 199,076 | BUTLER | 73,691 | 31,413 | 42,278 | | 10,865 D | 42.6% | 57.4% | 42.6% | 57.4% |
| 20,857 | CARROLL | 8,705 | 3,655 | 5,050 | | 1,395 D | 42.0% | 58.0% | 42.0% | 58.0% |
| 29,714 | CHAMPAIGN | 12,726 | 5,588 | 7,138 | | 1,550 D | 43.9% | 56.1% | 43.9% | 56.1% |
| 131,440 | CLARK | 53,387 | 19,112 | 34,275 | | 15,163 D | 35.8% | 64.2% | 35.8% | 64.2% |
| 80,530 | CLERMONT | 29,890 | 13,367 | 16,523 | | 3,156 D | 44.7% | 55.3% | 44.7% | 55.3% |
| 30,004 | CLINTON | 12,596 | 6,082 | 6,514 | | 432 D | 48.3% | 51.7% | 48.3% | 51.7% |
| 107,004 | COLUMBIANA | 44,533 | 15,827 | 28,706 | | 12,879 D | 35.5% | 64.5% | 35.5% | 64.5% |
| 32,224 | COSHOCTON | 14,347 | 5,965 | 8,382 | | 2,417 D | 41.6% | 58.4% | 41.6% | 58.4% |
| 46,775 | CRAWFORD | 20,938 | 8,970 | 11,968 | | 2,998 D | 42.8% | 57.2% | 42.8% | 57.2% |
| 1,647,895 | CUYAHOGA | 689,347 | 196,436 | 492,911 | | 296,475 D | 28.5% | 71.5% | 28.5% | 71.5% |
| 45,612 | DARKE | 21,014 | 8,581 | 12,433 | | 3,852 D | 40.8% | 59.2% | 40.8% | 59.2% |
| 31,508 | DEFIANCE | 13,755 | 5,048 | 8,707 | | 3,659 D | 36.7% | 63.3% | 36.7% | 63.3% |
| 36,107 | DELAWARE | 16,475 | 8,395 | 8,080 | | 315 R | 51.0% | 49.0% | 51.0% | 49.0% |
| 68,000 | ERIE | 25,949 | 9,981 | 15,968 | | 5,987 D | 38.5% | 61.5% | 38.5% | 61.5% |
| 63,912 | FAIRFIELD | 27,091 | 11,480 | 15,611 | | 4,131 D | 42.4% | 57.6% | 42.4% | 57.6% |
| 24,775 | FAYETTE | 10,695 | 4,567 | 6,128 | | 1,561 D | 42.7% | 57.3% | 42.7% | 57.3% |
| 682,962 | FRANKLIN | 285,872 | 131,345 | 154,527 | | 23,182 D | 45.9% | 54.1% | 45.9% | 54.1% |
| 29,301 | FULTON | 11,577 | 5,973 | 5,604 | | 369 R | 51.6% | 48.4% | 51.6% | 48.4% |
| 26,120 | GALLIA | 9,148 | 4,408 | 4,740 | | 332 D | 48.2% | 51.8% | 48.2% | 51.8% |
| 47,573 | GEAUGA | 21,635 | 9,423 | 12,212 | | 2,789 D | 43.6% | 56.4% | 43.6% | 56.4% |
| 94,642 | GREENE | 35,847 | 14,571 | 21,276 | | 6,705 D | 40.6% | 59.4% | 40.6% | 59.4% |
| 38,579 | GUERNSEY | 15,932 | 6,429 | 9,503 | | 3,074 D | 40.4% | 59.6% | 40.4% | 59.6% |
| 864,121 | HAMILTON | 360,306 | 161,179 | 199,127 | | 37,948 D | 44.7% | 55.3% | 44.7% | 55.3% |
| 53,686 | HANCOCK | 23,157 | 11,610 | 11,547 | | 63 R | 50.1% | 49.9% | 50.1% | 49.9% |
| 29,633 | HARDIN | 13,003 | 5,679 | 7,324 | | 1,645 D | 43.7% | 56.3% | 43.7% | 56.3% |
| 17,995 | HARRISON | 8,087 | 2,928 | 5,159 | | 2,231 D | 36.2% | 63.8% | 36.2% | 63.8% |
| 25,392 | HENRY | 10,939 | 5,094 | 5,845 | | 751 D | 46.6% | 53.4% | 46.6% | 53.4% |
| 29,716 | HIGHLAND | 13,266 | 5,985 | 7,281 | | 1,296 D | 45.1% | 54.9% | 45.1% | 54.9% |
| 20,168 | HOCKING | 8,809 | 2,858 | 5,951 | | 3,093 D | 32.4% | 67.6% | 32.4% | 67.6% |
| 21,591 | HOLMES | 5,665 | 2,106 | 3,559 | | 1,453 D | 37.2% | 62.8% | 37.2% | 62.8% |
| 47,326 | HURON | 18,435 | 7,655 | 10,780 | | 3,125 D | 41.5% | 58.5% | 41.5% | 58.5% |
| 29,372 | JACKSON | 12,005 | 4,949 | 7,056 | | 2,107 D | 41.2% | 58.8% | 41.2% | 58.8% |
| 99,201 | JEFFERSON | 44,823 | 11,784 | 33,039 | | 21,255 D | 26.3% | 73.7% | 26.3% | 73.7% |
| 38,808 | KNOX | 18,480 | 7,258 | 11,222 | | 3,964 D | 39.3% | 60.7% | 39.3% | 60.7% |
| 148,700 | LAKE | 61,834 | 23,282 | 38,552 | | 15,270 D | 37.7% | 62.3% | 37.7% | 62.3% |
| 55,438 | LAWRENCE | 20,392 | 7,757 | 12,635 | | 4,878 D | 38.0% | 62.0% | 38.0% | 62.0% |
| 90,242 | LICKING | 38,460 | 15,096 | 23,364 | | 8,268 D | 39.3% | 60.7% | 39.3% | 60.7% |
| 34,803 | LOGAN | 15,167 | 6,683 | 8,484 | | 1,801 D | 44.1% | 55.9% | 44.1% | 55.9% |
| 217,500 | LORAIN | 82,438 | 26,683 | 55,755 | | 29,072 D | 32.4% | 67.6% | 32.4% | 67.6% |
| 456,931 | LUCAS | 185,892 | 57,782 | 128,110 | | 70,328 D | 31.1% | 68.9% | 31.1% | 68.9% |
| 26,454 | MADISON | 10,209 | 4,945 | 5,264 | | 319 D | 48.4% | 51.6% | 48.4% | 51.6% |
| 300,480 | MAHONING | 124,709 | 33,775 | 90,934 | | 57,159 D | 27.1% | 72.9% | 27.1% | 72.9% |
| 60,221 | MARION | 24,450 | 10,050 | 14,400 | | 4,350 D | 41.1% | 58.9% | 41.1% | 58.9% |
| 65,315 | MEDINA | 24,950 | 10,221 | 14,729 | | 4,508 D | 41.0% | 59.0% | 41.0% | 59.0% |
| 22,159 | MEIGS | 9,106 | 3,973 | 5,133 | | 1,160 D | 43.6% | 56.4% | 43.6% | 56.4% |
| 32,559 | MERCER | 14,454 | 4,373 | 10,081 | | 5,708 D | 30.3% | 69.7% | 30.3% | 69.7% |
| 72,901 | MIAMI | 32,364 | 12,985 | 19,379 | | 6,394 D | 40.1% | 59.9% | 40.1% | 59.9% |
| 15,268 | MONROE | 6,720 | 1,944 | 4,776 | | 2,832 D | 28.9% | 71.1% | 28.9% | 71.1% |
| 527,080 | MONTGOMERY | 198,612 | 71,979 | 126,633 | | 54,654 D | 36.2% | 63.8% | 36.2% | 63.8% |
| 12,747 | MORGAN | 5,334 | 2,281 | 3,053 | | 772 D | 42.8% | 57.2% | 42.8% | 57.2% |
| 19,405 | MORROW | 8,766 | 4,194 | 4,572 | | 378 D | 47.8% | 52.2% | 47.8% | 52.2% |
| 79,159 | MUSKINGUM | 32,427 | 11,635 | 20,792 | | 9,157 D | 35.9% | 64.1% | 35.9% | 64.1% |

# OHIO

## PRESIDENT 1964

| 1960 Census Population | County | Total Vote | Republican | Democratic | Other | Rep.-Dem. Plurality | Percentage Total Vote Rep. | Total Vote Dem. | Major Vote Rep. | Major Vote Dem. |
|---|---|---|---|---|---|---|---|---|---|---|
| 10,982 | NOBLE | 5,175 | 2,250 | 2,925 | | 675 D | 43.5% | 56.5% | 43.5% | 56.5% |
| 35,323 | OTTAWA | 15,257 | 5,639 | 9,618 | | 3,979 D | 37.0% | 63.0% | 37.0% | 63.0% |
| 16,792 | PAULDING | 7,719 | 3,254 | 4,465 | | 1,211 D | 42.2% | 57.8% | 42.2% | 57.8% |
| 27,864 | PERRY | 11,711 | 3,895 | 7,816 | | 3,921 D | 33.3% | 66.7% | 33.3% | 66.7% |
| 35,855 | PICKAWAY | 12,627 | 5,317 | 7,310 | | 1,993 D | 42.1% | 57.9% | 42.1% | 57.9% |
| 19,380 | PIKE | 7,898 | 2,567 | 5,331 | | 2,764 D | 32.5% | 67.5% | 32.5% | 67.5% |
| 91,798 | PORTAGE | 34,150 | 10,842 | 23,308 | | 12,466 D | 31.7% | 68.3% | 31.7% | 68.3% |
| 32,498 | PREBLE | 13,413 | 5,839 | 7,574 | | 1,735 D | 43.5% | 56.5% | 43.5% | 56.5% |
| 28,331 | PUTNAM | 12,235 | 5,221 | 7,014 | | 1,793 D | 42.7% | 57.3% | 42.7% | 57.3% |
| 117,761 | RICHLAND | 43,632 | 18,833 | 24,799 | | 5,966 D | 43.2% | 56.8% | 43.2% | 56.8% |
| 61,215 | ROSS | 22,327 | 9,623 | 12,704 | | 3,081 D | 43.1% | 56.9% | 43.1% | 56.9% |
| 56,486 | SANDUSKY | 21,735 | 8,254 | 13,481 | | 5,227 D | 38.0% | 62.0% | 38.0% | 62.0% |
| 84,216 | SCIOTO | 35,024 | 13,465 | 21,559 | | 8,094 D | 38.4% | 61.6% | 38.4% | 61.6% |
| 59,326 | SENECA | 24,054 | 9,536 | 14,518 | | 4,982 D | 39.6% | 60.4% | 39.6% | 60.4% |
| 33,586 | SHELBY | 15,194 | 5,190 | 10,004 | | 4,814 D | 34.2% | 65.8% | 34.2% | 65.8% |
| 340,345 | STARK | 142,336 | 53,632 | 88,704 | | 35,072 D | 37.7% | 62.3% | 37.7% | 62.3% |
| 513,569 | SUMMIT | 210,319 | 68,000 | 142,319 | | 74,319 D | 32.3% | 67.7% | 32.3% | 67.7% |
| 208,526 | TRUMBULL | 81,401 | 27,059 | 54,342 | | 27,283 D | 33.2% | 66.8% | 33.2% | 66.8% |
| 76,789 | TUSCARAWAS | 33,585 | 9,962 | 23,623 | | 13,661 D | 29.7% | 70.3% | 29.7% | 70.3% |
| 22,853 | UNION | 10,489 | 5,504 | 4,985 | | 519 R | 52.5% | 47.5% | 52.5% | 47.5% |
| 28,840 | VAN WERT | 13,889 | 6,194 | 7,695 | | 1,501 D | 44.6% | 55.4% | 44.6% | 55.4% |
| 10,274 | VINTON | 4,537 | 1,919 | 2,618 | | 699 D | 42.3% | 57.7% | 42.3% | 57.7% |
| 65,711 | WARREN | 23,388 | 10,982 | 12,406 | | 1,424 D | 47.0% | 53.0% | 47.0% | 53.0% |
| 51,689 | WASHINGTON | 20,066 | 8,873 | 11,193 | | 2,320 D | 44.2% | 55.8% | 44.2% | 55.8% |
| 75,497 | WAYNE | 24,696 | 9,890 | 14,806 | | 4,916 D | 40.0% | 60.0% | 40.0% | 60.0% |
| 29,968 | WILLIAMS | 13,200 | 5,653 | 7,547 | | 1,894 D | 42.8% | 57.2% | 42.8% | 57.2% |
| 72,596 | WOOD | 28,446 | 12,142 | 16,304 | | 4,162 D | 42.7% | 57.3% | 42.7% | 57.3% |
| 21,648 | WYANDOT | 9,412 | 4,139 | 5,273 | | 1,134 D | 44.0% | 56.0% | 44.0% | 56.0% |
| 9,706,397 | TOTAL | 3,969,196 | 1,470,865 | 2,498,331 | | 1,027,466 D | 37.1% | 62.9% | 37.1% | 62.9% |

# OHIO

## PRESIDENT 1960

| 1960 Census Population | County | Total Vote | Republican | Democratic | Other | Rep.-Dem. Plurality | Percentage Total Vote Rep. | Dem. | Major Vote Rep. | Dem. |
|---|---|---|---|---|---|---|---|---|---|---|
| 19,982 | ADAMS | 9,896 | 5,996 | 3,900 | | 2,096 R | 60.6% | 39.4% | 60.6% | 39.4% |
| 103,691 | ALLEN | 42,732 | 28,007 | 14,725 | | 13,282 R | 65.5% | 34.5% | 65.5% | 34.5% |
| 38,771 | ASHLAND | 18,812 | 13,112 | 5,700 | | 7,412 R | 69.7% | 30.3% | 69.7% | 30.3% |
| 93,067 | ASHTABULA | 41,561 | 22,406 | 19,155 | | 3,251 R | 53.9% | 46.1% | 53.9% | 46.1% |
| 46,998 | ATHENS | 18,289 | 10,747 | 7,542 | | 3,205 R | 58.8% | 41.2% | 58.8% | 41.2% |
| 36,147 | AUGLAIZE | 17,465 | 11,183 | 6,282 | | 4,901 R | 64.0% | 36.0% | 64.0% | 36.0% |
| 83,864 | BELMONT | 41,951 | 18,146 | 23,805 | | 5,659 D | 43.3% | 56.7% | 43.3% | 56.7% |
| 25,178 | BROWN | 11,594 | 6,461 | 5,133 | | 1,328 R | 55.7% | 44.3% | 55.7% | 44.3% |
| 199,076 | BUTLER | 79,296 | 46,518 | 32,778 | | 13,740 R | 58.7% | 41.3% | 58.7% | 41.3% |
| 20,857 | CARROLL | 9,583 | 6,095 | 3,488 | | 2,607 R | 63.6% | 36.4% | 63.6% | 36.4% |
| 29,714 | CHAMPAIGN | 13,701 | 9,141 | 4,560 | | 4,581 R | 66.7% | 33.3% | 66.7% | 33.3% |
| 131,440 | CLARK | 53,044 | 30,588 | 22,456 | | 8,132 R | 57.7% | 42.3% | 57.7% | 42.3% |
| 80,530 | CLERMONT | 30,525 | 18,802 | 11,723 | | 7,079 R | 61.6% | 38.4% | 61.6% | 38.4% |
| 30,004 | CLINTON | 12,962 | 8,464 | 4,498 | | 3,966 R | 65.3% | 34.7% | 65.3% | 34.7% |
| 107,004 | COLUMBIANA | 48,451 | 28,414 | 20,037 | | 8,377 R | 58.6% | 41.4% | 58.6% | 41.4% |
| 32,224 | COSHOCTON | 15,309 | 9,913 | 5,396 | | 4,517 R | 64.8% | 35.2% | 64.8% | 35.2% |
| 46,775 | CRAWFORD | 21,539 | 14,558 | 6,981 | | 7,577 R | 67.6% | 32.4% | 67.6% | 32.4% |
| 1,647,895 | CUYAHOGA | 717,086 | 288,056 | 429,030 | | 140,974 D | 40.2% | 59.8% | 40.2% | 59.8% |
| 45,612 | DARKE | 21,763 | 14,048 | 7,715 | | 6,333 R | 64.5% | 35.5% | 64.5% | 35.5% |
| 31,508 | DEFIANCE | 14,119 | 8,912 | 5,207 | | 3,705 R | 63.1% | 36.9% | 63.1% | 36.9% |
| 36,107 | DELAWARE | 16,725 | 11,391 | 5,334 | | 6,057 R | 68.1% | 31.9% | 68.1% | 31.9% |
| 68,000 | ERIE | 26,046 | 15,092 | 10,954 | | 4,138 R | 57.9% | 42.1% | 57.9% | 42.1% |
| 63,912 | FAIRFIELD | 26,871 | 17,743 | 9,128 | | 8,615 R | 66.0% | 34.0% | 66.0% | 34.0% |
| 24,775 | FAYETTE | 11,051 | 7,085 | 3,966 | | 3,119 R | 64.1% | 35.9% | 64.1% | 35.9% |
| 682,962 | FRANKLIN | 271,461 | 161,178 | 110,283 | | 50,895 R | 59.4% | 40.6% | 59.4% | 40.6% |
| 29,301 | FULTON | 12,969 | 9,695 | 3,274 | | 6,421 R | 74.8% | 25.2% | 74.8% | 25.2% |
| 26,120 | GALLIA | 11,100 | 7,602 | 3,498 | | 4,104 R | 68.5% | 31.5% | 68.5% | 31.5% |
| 47,573 | GEAUGA | 21,013 | 12,491 | 8,522 | | 3,969 R | 59.4% | 40.6% | 59.4% | 40.6% |
| 94,642 | GREENE | 33,797 | 19,642 | 14,155 | | 5,487 R | 58.1% | 41.9% | 58.1% | 41.9% |
| 38,579 | GUERNSEY | 16,928 | 10,396 | 6,532 | | 3,864 R | 61.4% | 38.6% | 61.4% | 38.6% |
| 864,121 | HAMILTON | 387,283 | 211,068 | 176,215 | | 34,853 R | 54.5% | 45.5% | 54.5% | 45.5% |
| 53,686 | HANCOCK | 23,771 | 17,059 | 6,712 | | 10,347 R | 71.8% | 28.2% | 71.8% | 28.2% |
| 29,633 | HARDIN | 14,038 | 9,042 | 4,996 | | 4,046 R | 64.4% | 35.6% | 64.4% | 35.6% |
| 17,995 | HARRISON | 8,832 | 5,191 | 3,641 | | 1,550 R | 58.8% | 41.2% | 58.8% | 41.2% |
| 25,392 | HENRY | 11,666 | 8,251 | 3,415 | | 4,836 R | 70.7% | 29.3% | 70.7% | 29.3% |
| 29,716 | HIGHLAND | 14,371 | 8,948 | 5,423 | | 3,525 R | 62.3% | 37.7% | 62.3% | 37.7% |
| 20,168 | HOCKING | 9,319 | 5,262 | 4,057 | | 1,205 R | 56.5% | 43.5% | 56.5% | 43.5% |
| 21,591 | HOLMES | 6,385 | 4,432 | 1,953 | | 2,479 R | 69.4% | 30.6% | 69.4% | 30.6% |
| 47,326 | HURON | 19,795 | 12,261 | 7,534 | | 4,727 R | 61.9% | 38.1% | 61.9% | 38.1% |
| 29,372 | JACKSON | 13,522 | 7,973 | 5,549 | | 2,424 R | 59.0% | 41.0% | 59.0% | 41.0% |
| 99,201 | JEFFERSON | 48,141 | 21,186 | 26,955 | | 5,769 D | 44.0% | 56.0% | 44.0% | 56.0% |
| 38,808 | KNOX | 19,276 | 12,711 | 6,565 | | 6,146 R | 65.9% | 34.1% | 65.9% | 34.1% |
| 148,700 | LAKE | 65,463 | 32,038 | 33,425 | | 1,387 D | 48.9% | 51.1% | 48.9% | 51.1% |
| 55,438 | LAWRENCE | 21,815 | 13,159 | 8,656 | | 4,503 R | 60.3% | 39.7% | 60.3% | 39.7% |
| 90,242 | LICKING | 36,988 | 23,653 | 13,335 | | 10,318 R | 63.9% | 36.1% | 63.9% | 36.1% |
| 34,803 | LOGAN | 16,590 | 11,311 | 5,279 | | 6,032 R | 68.2% | 31.8% | 68.2% | 31.8% |
| 217,500 | LORAIN | 82,848 | 39,361 | 43,487 | | 4,126 D | 47.5% | 52.5% | 47.5% | 52.5% |
| 456,931 | LUCAS | 197,504 | 94,679 | 102,825 | | 8,146 D | 47.9% | 52.1% | 47.9% | 52.1% |
| 26,454 | MADISON | 10,933 | 7,256 | 3,677 | | 3,579 R | 66.4% | 33.6% | 66.4% | 33.6% |
| 300,480 | MAHONING | 134,070 | 51,927 | 82,143 | | 30,216 D | 38.7% | 61.3% | 38.7% | 61.3% |
| 60,221 | MARION | 24,808 | 15,210 | 9,598 | | 5,612 R | 61.3% | 38.7% | 61.3% | 38.7% |
| 65,315 | MEDINA | 25,919 | 16,123 | 9,796 | | 6,327 R | 62.2% | 37.8% | 62.2% | 37.8% |
| 22,159 | MEIGS | 10,448 | 6,976 | 3,472 | | 3,504 R | 66.8% | 33.2% | 66.8% | 33.2% |
| 32,559 | MERCER | 15,465 | 7,735 | 7,730 | | 5 R | 50.0% | 50.0% | 50.0% | 50.0% |
| 72,901 | MIAMI | 33,921 | 22,151 | 11,770 | | 10,381 R | 65.3% | 34.7% | 65.3% | 34.7% |
| 15,268 | MONROE | 7,250 | 4,106 | 3,144 | | 962 R | 56.6% | 43.4% | 56.6% | 43.4% |
| 527,080 | MONTGOMERY | 207,927 | 109,602 | 98,325 | | 11,277 R | 52.7% | 47.3% | 52.7% | 47.3% |
| 12,747 | MORGAN | 6,247 | 4,424 | 1,823 | | 2,601 R | 70.8% | 29.2% | 70.8% | 29.2% |
| 19,405 | MORROW | 9,093 | 6,357 | 2,736 | | 3,621 R | 69.9% | 30.1% | 69.9% | 30.1% |
| 79,159 | MUSKINGUM | 34,772 | 21,518 | 13,254 | | 8,264 R | 61.9% | 38.1% | 61.9% | 38.1% |

# OHIO

## PRESIDENT 1960

| 1960 Census Population | County | Total Vote | Republican | Democratic | Other | Rep.-Dem. Plurality | Percentage | | | |
|---|---|---|---|---|---|---|---|---|---|---|
| | | | | | | | Total Vote | | Major Vote | |
| | | | | | | | Rep. | Dem. | Rep. | Dem. |
| 10,982 | NOBLE | 5,987 | 3,951 | 2,036 | | 1,915 R | 66.0% | 34.0% | 66.0% | 34.0% |
| 35,323 | OTTAWA | 15,872 | 9,260 | 6,612 | | 2,648 R | 58.3% | 41.7% | 58.3% | 41.7% |
| 16,792 | PAULDING | 7,786 | 4,961 | 2,825 | | 2,136 R | 63.7% | 36.3% | 63.7% | 36.3% |
| 27,864 | PERRY | 12,849 | 7,658 | 5,191 | | 2,467 R | 59.6% | 40.4% | 59.6% | 40.4% |
| 35,855 | PICKAWAY | 12,691 | 7,821 | 4,870 | | 2,951 R | 61.6% | 38.4% | 61.6% | 38.4% |
| 19,380 | PIKE | 8,023 | 3,684 | 4,339 | | 655 D | 45.9% | 54.1% | 45.9% | 54.1% |
| 91,798 | PORTAGE | 38,162 | 19,634 | 18,528 | | 1,106 R | 51.4% | 48.6% | 51.4% | 48.6% |
| 32,498 | PREBLE | 14,269 | 8,802 | 5,467 | | 3,335 R | 61.7% | 38.3% | 61.7% | 38.3% |
| 28,331 | PUTNAM | 12,873 | 6,834 | 6,039 | | 795 R | 53.1% | 46.9% | 53.1% | 46.9% |
| 117,761 | RICHLAND | 46,962 | 27,317 | 19,645 | | 7,672 R | 58.2% | 41.8% | 58.2% | 41.8% |
| 61,215 | ROSS | 23,111 | 14,075 | 9,036 | | 5,039 R | 60.9% | 39.1% | 60.9% | 39.1% |
| 56,486 | SANDUSKY | 22,737 | 14,566 | 8,171 | | 6,395 R | 64.1% | 35.9% | 64.1% | 35.9% |
| 84,216 | SCIOTO | 38,418 | 21,771 | 16,647 | | 5,124 R | 56.7% | 43.3% | 56.7% | 43.3% |
| 59,326 | SENECA | 25,773 | 15,772 | 10,001 | | 5,771 R | 61.2% | 38.8% | 61.2% | 38.8% |
| 33,586 | SHELBY | 15,632 | 8,766 | 6,866 | | 1,900 R | 56.1% | 43.9% | 56.1% | 43.9% |
| 340,345 | STARK | 150,086 | 82,881 | 67,205 | | 15,676 R | 55.2% | 44.8% | 55.2% | 44.8% |
| 513,569 | SUMMIT | 219,918 | 109,066 | 110,852 | | 1,786 D | 49.6% | 50.4% | 49.6% | 50.4% |
| 208,526 | TRUMBULL | 87,652 | 40,724 | 46,928 | | 6,204 D | 46.5% | 53.5% | 46.5% | 53.5% |
| 76,789 | TUSCARAWAS | 36,720 | 20,637 | 16,083 | | 4,554 R | 56.2% | 43.8% | 56.2% | 43.8% |
| 22,853 | UNION | 10,954 | 7,838 | 3,116 | | 4,722 R | 71.6% | 28.4% | 71.6% | 28.4% |
| 28,840 | VAN WERT | 14,716 | 9,666 | 5,050 | | 4,616 R | 65.7% | 34.3% | 65.7% | 34.3% |
| 10,274 | VINTON | 5,074 | 3,043 | 2,031 | | 1,012 R | 60.0% | 40.0% | 60.0% | 40.0% |
| 65,711 | WARREN | 22,450 | 14,505 | 7,945 | | 6,560 R | 64.6% | 35.4% | 64.6% | 35.4% |
| 51,689 | WASHINGTON | 22,053 | 14,197 | 7,856 | | 6,341 R | 64.4% | 35.6% | 64.4% | 35.6% |
| 75,497 | WAYNE | 30,784 | 21,273 | 9,511 | | 11,762 R | 69.1% | 30.9% | 69.1% | 30.9% |
| 29,968 | WILLIAMS | 14,363 | 10,319 | 4,044 | | 6,275 R | 71.8% | 28.2% | 71.8% | 28.2% |
| 72,596 | WOOD | 29,533 | 18,952 | 10,581 | | 8,371 R | 64.2% | 35.8% | 64.2% | 35.8% |
| 21,648 | WYANDOT | 10,312 | 6,786 | 3,526 | | 3,260 R | 65.8% | 34.2% | 65.8% | 34.2% |
| 9,706,397 | TOTAL | 4,161,859 | 2,217,611 | 1,944,248 | | 273,363 R | 53.3% | 46.7% | 53.3% | 46.7% |

# OHIO

## ELECTION NOTES

**2004**  Other vote was 14,676 Other Party Candidate (Michael Badnarik); 11,939 Other Party Candidate (Michael Peroutka); 192 write-in (David Cobb); 114 write-in (Joe Schriner); 22 write-in (James Harris); 17 write-in (Richard A. Duncan); 11 write-in (Thomas F. Zych); 2 write-in (John Parker).

**2000**  Other vote was 26,721 no designation (Buchanan); 13,473 Libertarian (Browne); 6,181 Natural Law (Hagelin); 3,823 no designation (Phillips); 10 write-in (Harris). Nader was listed on the ballot with no designation.

**1996**  Other vote was 12,851 Independent (Hagelin); 10,813 Independent (Moorehead); 9,120 Natural Law (Hagelin); 7,361 Independent (Phillips); 2,962 write-in (Nader); 15 scattered write-in.

**1992**  Other vote was 7,252 Marrou (Independent); 6,413 Fulani (Independent); 4,699 Gritz (Independent); 3,437 Hagelin (Independent); 2,446 LaRouche (Independent); 32 Warren (write-in); 10 scattered write-in. The final, official returns as amended by the Ohio Secretary of State are presented in the table. The vote from Clermont county was corrected for the three major candidates and the state totals reflect this minor adjustment.

**1988**  Minor party candidates appeared on the ballot without party designation. Other vote was 12,017 Fulani; 11,989 Paul; 7,733 LaRouche; 5,432 Winn; 134 Holmes (write-in); 216 scattered write-in. In the final canvass used in the table, the Sandusky county votes for LaRouche, Paul and Winn reflect minor adjustments made by the Secretary of State.

**1984**  Other vote was 12,090 Serrette (Independent); 10,693 LaRouche (Independent); 5,886 Bergland (Independent); 4,438 Hall (Independent); 4,344 Mason (Independent); 3,565 Winn (Independent); 2,565 Holmes (Independent); 4 Dodge (write-in); 34 scattered write-in. Early unamended canvass gave the Serrette (Independent) vote as 24,180 and the Winn (Independent) vote as 7,130.

**1980**  Other vote was 254,472 Anderson (Independent); 49,033 Clark (Independent); 8,564 Commoner (Independent); 4,729 Hall (Independent); 4,029 Congress (Independent); 3,790 Griswold (Independent); 27 Bubar (write-in). The vote for Congress (Independent) was with Zimmermann for Vice President who was the Socialist Workers candidate in other states.

**1976**  Other vote was 58,258 McCarthy (Independent); 15,529 Maddox (American); 8,961 MacBride (Independent); 7,817 Hall (Independent); 4,717 Camejo (Independent); 4,335 LaRouche (Independent); 68 Levin (write-in); 62 Bubar (write-in). Vote detailed in the table is for the recount.

**1972**  Other vote was 80,067 Schmitz (American Independent); 7,107 Fisher (Socialist Labor); 6,437 Hall (no party label on the ballot); 460 Edward Wallace (write-in).

**1968**  Wallace on the ballot as American Independent. Other vote was 372 Gregory (write-in); 120 Blomen (write-in); 69 Halstead (write-in); 23 Mitchell (write-in); 19 Munn (write-in).

**1964**

**1960**

# OKLAHOMA

## POPULAR VOTE FOR PRESIDENT 1920 TO 2004

| Year | Total Vote | Republican Vote | Republican Candidate | Democratic Vote | Democratic Candidate | Other Vote | Plurality | Percentage Total Vote Rep. | Percentage Total Vote Dem. | Percentage Major Vote Rep. | Percentage Major Vote Dem. |
|---|---|---|---|---|---|---|---|---|---|---|---|
| 2004 | 1,463,758 | 959,792 | Bush, George W. | 503,966 | Kerry, John | | 455,826 R | 65.6% | 34.4% | 65.6% | 34.4% |
| 2000 | 1,234,229 | 744,337 | Bush, George W. | 474,276 | Gore, Al | 15,616 | 270,061 R | 60.3% | 38.4% | 61.1% | 38.9% |
| 1996 ** | 1,206,713 | 582,315 | Dole, Bob | 488,105 | Clinton, Bill | 136,293 | 94,210 R | 48.3% | 40.4% | 54.4% | 45.6% |
| 1992 ** | 1,390,359 | 592,929 | Bush, George | 473,066 | Clinton, Bill | 324,364 | 119,863 R | 42.6% | 34.0% | 55.6% | 44.4% |
| 1988 | 1,171,036 | 678,367 | Bush, George | 483,423 | Dukakis, Michael S. | 9,246 | 194,944 R | 57.9% | 41.3% | 58.4% | 41.6% |
| 1984 | 1,255,676 | 861,530 | Reagan, Ronald | 385,080 | Mondale, Walter F. | 9,066 | 476,450 R | 68.6% | 30.7% | 69.1% | 30.9% |
| 1980 ** | 1,149,708 | 695,570 | Reagan, Ronald | 402,026 | Carter, Jimmy | 52,112 | 293,544 R | 60.5% | 35.0% | 63.4% | 36.6% |
| 1976 | 1,092,251 | 545,708 | Ford, Gerald R. | 532,442 | Carter, Jimmy | 14,101 | 13,266 R | 50.0% | 48.7% | 50.6% | 49.4% |
| 1972 | 1,029,900 | 759,025 | Nixon, Richard M. | 247,147 | McGovern, George S. | 23,728 | 511,878 R | 73.7% | 24.0% | 75.4% | 24.6% |
| 1968 | 943,086 | 449,697 | Nixon, Richard M. | 301,658 | Humphrey, Hubert H. | 191,731 | 148,039 R | 47.7% | 32.0% | 59.9% | 40.1% |
| 1964 | 932,499 | 412,665 | Goldwater, Barry M. | 519,834 | Johnson, Lyndon B. | | 107,169 D | 44.3% | 55.7% | 44.3% | 55.7% |
| 1960 | 903,150 | 533,039 | Nixon, Richard M. | 370,111 | Kennedy, John F. | | 162,928 R | 59.0% | 41.0% | 59.0% | 41.0% |
| 1956 | 859,350 | 473,769 | Eisenhower, Dwight D. | 385,581 | Stevenson, Adlai E. | | 88,188 R | 55.1% | 44.9% | 55.1% | 44.9% |
| 1952 | 948,984 | 518,045 | Eisenhower, Dwight D. | 430,939 | Stevenson, Adlai E. | | 87,106 R | 54.6% | 45.4% | 54.6% | 45.4% |
| 1948 | 721,599 | 268,817 | Dewey, Thomas E. | 452,782 | Truman, Harry S. | | 183,965 D | 37.3% | 62.7% | 37.3% | 62.7% |
| 1944 | 722,636 | 319,424 | Dewey, Thomas E. | 401,549 | Roosevelt, Franklin D. | 1,663 | 82,125 D | 44.2% | 55.6% | 44.3% | 55.7% |
| 1940 | 826,212 | 348,872 | Willkie, Wendell | 474,313 | Roosevelt, Franklin D. | 3,027 | 125,441 D | 42.2% | 57.4% | 42.4% | 57.6% |
| 1936 | 749,740 | 245,122 | Landon, Alfred M. | 501,069 | Roosevelt, Franklin D. | 3,549 | 255,947 D | 32.7% | 66.8% | 32.8% | 67.2% |
| 1932 | 704,633 | 188,165 | Hoover, Herbert C. | 516,468 | Roosevelt, Franklin D. | | 328,303 D | 26.7% | 73.3% | 26.7% | 73.3% |
| 1928 | 618,427 | 394,046 | Hoover, Herbert C. | 219,174 | Smith, Alfred E. | 5,207 | 174,872 R | 63.7% | 35.4% | 64.3% | 35.7% |
| 1924 | 527,828 | 225,756 | Coolidge, Calvin | 255,798 | Davis, John W. | 46,274 | 30,042 D | 42.8% | 48.5% | 46.9% | 53.1% |
| 1920 | 485,678 | 243,840 | Harding, Warren G. | 216,122 | Cox, James M. | 25,716 | 27,718 R | 50.2% | 44.5% | 53.0% | 47.0% |

In 1996 the other vote column includes 130,788 votes cast for Perot. In 1992 the other vote column includes 319,878 votes cast for Perot. In 1980 the other column includes 38,284 votes for Independent (Anderson).

## ELECTORAL COLLEGE VOTE 1920 TO 2004

| Year | Total | Republican | Democratic | Other |
|---|---|---|---|---|
| 2004 | 7 | 7 | | |
| 2000 | 8 | 8 | | |
| 1996 | 8 | 8 | | |
| 1992 | 8 | 8 | | |
| 1988 | 8 | 8 | | |
| 1984 | 8 | 8 | | |
| 1980 | 8 | 8 | | |
| 1976 | 8 | 8 | | |
| 1972 | 8 | 8 | | |
| 1968 | 8 | 8 | | |
| 1964 | 8 | | 8 | |
| 1960 ** | 8 | 7 | | 1 BYRD |
| 1956 | 8 | 8 | | |
| 1952 | 8 | 8 | | |
| 1948 | 10 | | 10 | |
| 1944 | 10 | | 10 | |
| 1940 | 11 | | 11 | |
| 1936 | 11 | | 11 | |
| 1932 | 11 | | 11 | |
| 1928 | 10 | 10 | | |
| 1924 | 10 | | 10 | |
| 1920 | 10 | 10 | | |

In 1960 one of the eight Republican electors voted in the Electoral College for Senator Harry Flood Byrd and Senator Barry M. Goldwater rather than for the national Republican candidates.

# OKLAHOMA

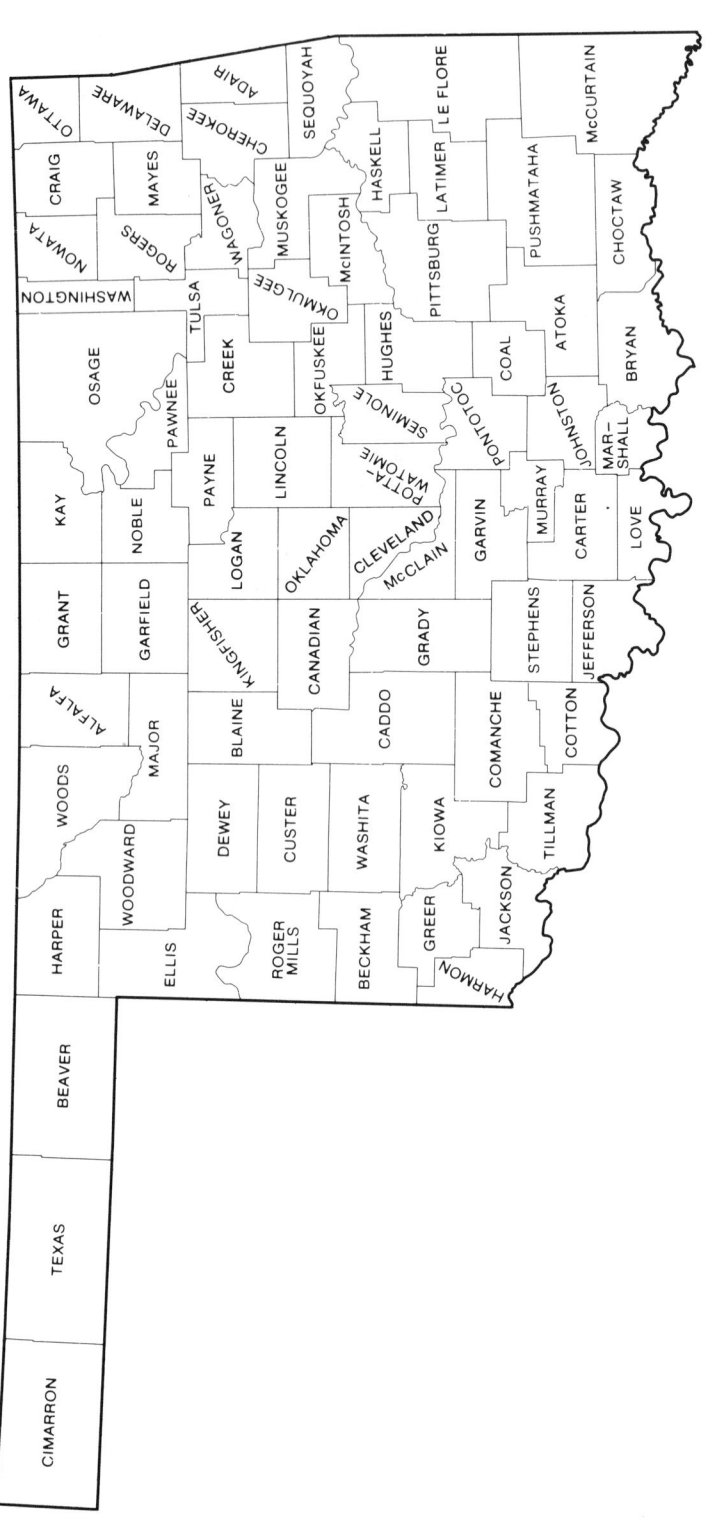

# OKLAHOMA

## PRESIDENT 2004

| 2000 Census Population | County | Total Vote | Republican | Democratic | Other | Rep.-Dem. Plurality | Percentage Total Vote Rep. | Dem. | Major Vote Rep. | Dem. |
|---|---|---|---|---|---|---|---|---|---|---|
| 21,038 | ADAIR | 7,533 | 4,971 | 2,562 | | 2,409 R | 66.0% | 34.0% | 66.0% | 34.0% |
| 6,105 | ALFALFA | 2,671 | 2,201 | 470 | | 1,731 R | 82.4% | 17.6% | 82.4% | 17.6% |
| 13,879 | ATOKA | 5,088 | 3,142 | 1,946 | | 1,196 R | 61.8% | 38.2% | 61.8% | 38.2% |
| 5,857 | BEAVER | 2,569 | 2,272 | 297 | | 1,975 R | 88.4% | 11.6% | 88.4% | 11.6% |
| 19,799 | BECKHAM | 7,385 | 5,454 | 1,931 | | 3,523 R | 73.9% | 26.1% | 73.9% | 26.1% |
| 11,976 | BLAINE | 4,421 | 3,199 | 1,222 | | 1,977 R | 72.4% | 27.6% | 72.4% | 27.6% |
| 36,534 | BRYAN | 14,360 | 8,615 | 5,745 | | 2,870 R | 60.0% | 40.0% | 60.0% | 40.0% |
| 30,150 | CADDO | 10,407 | 6,491 | 3,916 | | 2,575 R | 62.4% | 37.6% | 62.4% | 37.6% |
| 87,697 | CANADIAN | 43,009 | 33,297 | 9,712 | | 23,585 R | 77.4% | 22.6% | 77.4% | 22.6% |
| 45,621 | CARTER | 18,644 | 12,178 | 6,466 | | 5,712 R | 65.3% | 34.7% | 65.3% | 34.7% |
| 42,521 | CHEROKEE | 18,192 | 9,569 | 8,623 | | 946 R | 52.6% | 47.4% | 52.6% | 47.4% |
| 15,342 | CHOCTAW | 5,807 | 3,168 | 2,639 | | 529 R | 54.6% | 45.4% | 54.6% | 45.4% |
| 3,148 | CIMARRON | 1,426 | 1,242 | 184 | | 1,058 R | 87.1% | 12.9% | 87.1% | 12.9% |
| 208,016 | CLEVELAND | 99,727 | 65,720 | 34,007 | | 31,713 R | 65.9% | 34.1% | 65.9% | 34.1% |
| 6,031 | COAL | 2,599 | 1,396 | 1,203 | | 193 R | 53.7% | 46.3% | 53.7% | 46.3% |
| 114,996 | COMANCHE | 33,192 | 21,170 | 12,022 | | 9,148 R | 63.8% | 36.2% | 63.8% | 36.2% |
| 6,614 | COTTON | 2,640 | 1,742 | 898 | | 844 R | 66.0% | 34.0% | 66.0% | 34.0% |
| 14,950 | CRAIG | 6,398 | 3,894 | 2,504 | | 1,390 R | 60.9% | 39.1% | 60.9% | 39.1% |
| 67,367 | CREEK | 28,777 | 18,848 | 9,929 | | 8,919 R | 65.5% | 34.5% | 65.5% | 34.5% |
| 26,142 | CUSTER | 10,640 | 7,839 | 2,801 | | 5,038 R | 73.7% | 26.3% | 73.7% | 26.3% |
| 37,077 | DELAWARE | 15,608 | 10,017 | 5,591 | | 4,426 R | 64.2% | 35.8% | 64.2% | 35.8% |
| 4,743 | DEWEY | 2,251 | 1,843 | 408 | | 1,435 R | 81.9% | 18.1% | 81.9% | 18.1% |
| 4,075 | ELLIS | 2,080 | 1,685 | 395 | | 1,290 R | 81.0% | 19.0% | 81.0% | 19.0% |
| 57,813 | GARFIELD | 23,271 | 17,685 | 5,586 | | 12,099 R | 76.0% | 24.0% | 76.0% | 24.0% |
| 27,210 | GARVIN | 11,317 | 7,610 | 3,707 | | 3,903 R | 67.2% | 32.8% | 67.2% | 32.8% |
| 45,516 | GRADY | 20,106 | 14,136 | 5,970 | | 8,166 R | 70.3% | 29.7% | 70.3% | 29.7% |
| 5,144 | GRANT | 2,521 | 1,950 | 571 | | 1,379 R | 77.4% | 22.6% | 77.4% | 22.6% |
| 6,061 | GREER | 2,248 | 1,529 | 719 | | 810 R | 68.0% | 32.0% | 68.0% | 32.0% |
| 3,283 | HARMON | 1,192 | 838 | 354 | | 484 R | 70.3% | 29.7% | 70.3% | 29.7% |
| 3,562 | HARPER | 1,665 | 1,397 | 268 | | 1,129 R | 83.9% | 16.1% | 83.9% | 16.1% |
| 11,792 | HASKELL | 5,324 | 2,946 | 2,378 | | 568 R | 55.3% | 44.7% | 55.3% | 44.7% |
| 14,154 | HUGHES | 5,349 | 3,066 | 2,283 | | 783 R | 57.3% | 42.7% | 57.3% | 42.7% |
| 28,439 | JACKSON | 9,256 | 7,024 | 2,232 | | 4,792 R | 75.9% | 24.1% | 75.9% | 24.1% |
| 6,818 | JEFFERSON | 2,603 | 1,546 | 1,057 | | 489 R | 59.4% | 40.6% | 59.4% | 40.6% |
| 10,513 | JOHNSTON | 4,348 | 2,635 | 1,713 | | 922 R | 60.6% | 39.4% | 60.6% | 39.4% |
| 48,080 | KAY | 20,078 | 14,121 | 5,957 | | 8,164 R | 70.3% | 29.7% | 70.3% | 29.7% |
| 13,926 | KINGFISHER | 6,652 | 5,630 | 1,022 | | 4,608 R | 84.6% | 15.4% | 84.6% | 15.4% |
| 10,227 | KIOWA | 4,023 | 2,610 | 1,413 | | 1,197 R | 64.9% | 35.1% | 64.9% | 35.1% |
| 10,692 | LATIMER | 4,480 | 2,535 | 1,945 | | 590 R | 56.6% | 43.4% | 56.6% | 43.4% |
| 48,109 | LE FLORE | 17,424 | 10,683 | 6,741 | | 3,942 R | 61.3% | 38.7% | 61.3% | 38.7% |
| 32,080 | LINCOLN | 14,190 | 10,149 | 4,041 | | 6,108 R | 71.5% | 28.5% | 71.5% | 28.5% |
| 33,924 | LOGAN | 16,343 | 11,474 | 4,869 | | 6,605 R | 70.2% | 29.8% | 70.2% | 29.8% |
| 8,831 | LOVE | 3,833 | 2,295 | 1,538 | | 757 R | 59.9% | 40.1% | 59.9% | 40.1% |
| 27,740 | MCCLAIN | 13,783 | 10,041 | 3,742 | | 6,299 R | 72.9% | 27.1% | 72.9% | 27.1% |
| 34,402 | MCCURTAIN | 11,156 | 7,472 | 3,684 | | 3,788 R | 67.0% | 33.0% | 67.0% | 33.0% |
| 19,456 | MCINTOSH | 9,180 | 4,692 | 4,488 | | 204 R | 51.1% | 48.9% | 51.1% | 48.9% |
| 7,545 | MAJOR | 3,659 | 3,122 | 537 | | 2,585 R | 85.3% | 14.7% | 85.3% | 14.7% |
| 13,184 | MARSHALL | 5,451 | 3,363 | 2,088 | | 1,275 R | 61.7% | 38.3% | 61.7% | 38.3% |
| 38,369 | MAYES | 16,879 | 9,946 | 6,933 | | 3,013 R | 58.9% | 41.1% | 58.9% | 41.1% |
| 12,623 | MURRAY | 5,795 | 3,665 | 2,130 | | 1,535 R | 63.2% | 36.8% | 63.2% | 36.8% |
| 69,451 | MUSKOGEE | 27,709 | 15,124 | 12,585 | | 2,539 R | 54.6% | 45.4% | 54.6% | 45.4% |
| 11,411 | NOBLE | 5,328 | 3,993 | 1,335 | | 2,658 R | 74.9% | 25.1% | 74.9% | 25.1% |
| 10,569 | NOWATA | 4,465 | 2,805 | 1,660 | | 1,145 R | 62.8% | 37.2% | 62.8% | 37.2% |
| 11,814 | OKFUSKEE | 4,285 | 2,542 | 1,743 | | 799 R | 59.3% | 40.7% | 59.3% | 40.7% |
| 660,448 | OKLAHOMA | 272,039 | 174,741 | 97,298 | | 77,443 R | 64.2% | 35.8% | 64.2% | 35.8% |
| 39,685 | OKMULGEE | 15,730 | 8,363 | 7,367 | | 996 R | 53.2% | 46.8% | 53.2% | 46.8% |
| 44,437 | OSAGE | 19,535 | 11,467 | 8,068 | | 3,399 R | 58.7% | 41.3% | 58.7% | 41.3% |
| 33,194 | OTTAWA | 12,529 | 7,443 | 5,086 | | 2,357 R | 59.4% | 40.6% | 59.4% | 40.6% |
| 16,612 | PAWNEE | 6,976 | 4,412 | 2,564 | | 1,848 R | 63.2% | 36.8% | 63.2% | 36.8% |
| 68,190 | PAYNE | 29,661 | 19,560 | 10,101 | | 9,459 R | 65.9% | 34.1% | 65.9% | 34.1% |

# OKLAHOMA

## PRESIDENT 2004

| 2000 Census Population | County | Total Vote | Republican | Democratic | Other | Rep.-Dem. Plurality | Percentage | | | |
|---|---|---|---|---|---|---|---|---|---|---|
| | | | | | | | Total Vote | | Major Vote | |
| | | | | | | | Rep. | Dem. | Rep. | Dem. |
| 43,953 | PITTSBURG | 18,586 | 11,134 | 7,452 | | 3,682 R | 59.9% | 40.1% | 59.9% | 40.1% |
| 35,143 | PONTOTOC | 14,812 | 9,647 | 5,165 | | 4,482 R | 65.1% | 34.9% | 65.1% | 34.9% |
| 65,521 | POTTAWATOMIE | 25,853 | 17,215 | 8,638 | | 8,577 R | 66.6% | 33.4% | 66.6% | 33.4% |
| 11,667 | PUSHMATAHA | 4,797 | 2,863 | 1,934 | | 929 R | 59.7% | 40.3% | 59.7% | 40.3% |
| 3,436 | ROGER MILLS | 1,770 | 1,388 | 382 | | 1,006 R | 78.4% | 21.6% | 78.4% | 21.6% |
| 70,641 | ROGERS | 36,894 | 24,976 | 11,918 | | 13,058 R | 67.7% | 32.3% | 67.7% | 32.3% |
| 24,894 | SEMINOLE | 9,272 | 5,624 | 3,648 | | 1,976 R | 60.7% | 39.3% | 60.7% | 39.3% |
| 38,972 | SEQUOYAH | 14,775 | 8,865 | 5,910 | | 2,955 R | 60.0% | 40.0% | 60.0% | 40.0% |
| 43,182 | STEPHENS | 19,161 | 13,646 | 5,515 | | 8,131 R | 71.2% | 28.8% | 71.2% | 28.8% |
| 20,107 | TEXAS | 6,466 | 5,450 | 1,016 | | 4,434 R | 84.3% | 15.7% | 84.3% | 15.7% |
| 9,287 | TILLMAN | 3,448 | 2,273 | 1,175 | | 1,098 R | 65.9% | 34.1% | 65.9% | 34.1% |
| 563,299 | TULSA | 253,672 | 163,452 | 90,220 | | 73,232 R | 64.4% | 35.6% | 64.4% | 35.6% |
| 57,491 | WAGONER | 28,238 | 19,081 | 9,157 | | 9,924 R | 67.6% | 32.4% | 67.6% | 32.4% |
| 48,996 | WASHINGTON | 23,413 | 16,551 | 6,862 | | 9,689 R | 70.7% | 29.3% | 70.7% | 29.3% |
| 11,508 | WASHITA | 5,045 | 3,705 | 1,340 | | 2,365 R | 73.4% | 26.6% | 73.4% | 26.6% |
| 9,089 | WOODS | 4,098 | 3,166 | 932 | | 2,234 R | 77.3% | 22.7% | 77.3% | 22.7% |
| 18,486 | WOODWARD | 7,651 | 6,193 | 1,458 | | 4,735 R | 80.9% | 19.1% | 80.9% | 19.1% |
| 3,450,654 | TOTAL | 1,463,758 | 959,792 | 503,966 | | 455,826 R | 65.6% | 34.4% | 65.6% | 34.4% |

# OKLAHOMA

## PRESIDENT 2000

| 2000 Census Population | County | Total Vote | Republican | Democratic | Green (Nader) | Other | Rep.-Dem. Plurality | Percentage of Total Vote | | |
|---|---|---|---|---|---|---|---|---|---|---|
| | | | | | | | | Rep. | Dem. | Green |
| 21,038 | ADAIR | 5,977 | 3,503 | 2,361 | | 113 | 1,142 R | 58.6% | 39.5% | |
| 6,105 | ALFALFA | 2,507 | 1,886 | 583 | | 38 | 1,303 R | 75.2% | 23.3% | |
| 13,879 | ATOKA | 4,324 | 2,375 | 1,906 | | 43 | 469 R | 54.9% | 44.1% | |
| 5,857 | BEAVER | 2,456 | 2,092 | 339 | | 25 | 1,753 R | 85.2% | 13.8% | |
| 19,799 | BECKHAM | 6,532 | 4,067 | 2,408 | | 57 | 1,659 R | 62.3% | 36.9% | |
| 11,976 | BLAINE | 4,094 | 2,633 | 1,402 | | 59 | 1,231 R | 64.3% | 34.2% | |
| 36,534 | BRYAN | 11,746 | 6,084 | 5,554 | | 108 | 530 R | 51.8% | 47.3% | |
| 30,150 | CADDO | 9,210 | 4,835 | 4,272 | | 103 | 563 R | 52.5% | 46.4% | |
| 87,697 | CANADIAN | 31,360 | 22,679 | 8,367 | | 314 | 14,312 R | 72.3% | 26.7% | |
| 45,621 | CARTER | 16,458 | 9,667 | 6,659 | | 132 | 3,008 R | 58.7% | 40.5% | |
| 42,521 | CHEROKEE | 14,468 | 6,918 | 7,256 | | 294 | 338 D | 47.8% | 50.2% | |
| 15,342 | CHOCTAW | 5,315 | 2,461 | 2,799 | | 55 | 338 D | 46.3% | 52.7% | |
| 3,148 | CIMARRON | 1,484 | 1,230 | 227 | | 27 | 1,003 R | 82.9% | 15.3% | |
| 208,016 | CLEVELAND | 76,171 | 47,393 | 27,792 | | 986 | 19,601 R | 62.2% | 36.5% | |
| 6,031 | COAL | 2,362 | 1,196 | 1,148 | | 18 | 48 R | 50.6% | 48.6% | |
| 114,996 | COMANCHE | 29,333 | 17,103 | 11,971 | | 259 | 5,132 R | 58.3% | 40.8% | |
| 6,614 | COTTON | 2,482 | 1,388 | 1,068 | | 26 | 320 R | 55.9% | 43.0% | |
| 14,950 | CRAIG | 5,484 | 2,815 | 2,568 | | 101 | 247 R | 51.3% | 46.8% | |
| 67,367 | CREEK | 23,741 | 13,580 | 9,753 | | 408 | 3,827 R | 57.2% | 41.1% | |
| 26,142 | CUSTER | 9,743 | 6,527 | 3,115 | | 101 | 3,412 R | 67.0% | 32.0% | |
| 37,077 | DELAWARE | 13,353 | 7,618 | 5,514 | | 221 | 2,104 R | 57.1% | 41.3% | |
| 4,743 | DEWEY | 2,220 | 1,607 | 599 | | 14 | 1,008 R | 72.4% | 27.0% | |
| 4,075 | ELLIS | 2,013 | 1,513 | 468 | | 32 | 1,045 R | 75.2% | 23.2% | |
| 57,813 | GARFIELD | 21,683 | 14,902 | 6,543 | | 238 | 8,359 R | 68.7% | 30.2% | |
| 27,210 | GARVIN | 9,843 | 5,536 | 4,189 | | 118 | 1,347 R | 56.2% | 42.6% | |
| 45,516 | GRADY | 16,276 | 10,040 | 6,037 | | 199 | 4,003 R | 61.7% | 37.1% | |
| 5,144 | GRANT | 2,503 | 1,762 | 709 | | 32 | 1,053 R | 70.4% | 28.3% | |
| 6,061 | GREER | 2,152 | 1,287 | 839 | | 26 | 448 R | 59.8% | 39.0% | |
| 3,283 | HARMON | 1,205 | 692 | 507 | | 6 | 185 R | 57.4% | 42.1% | |
| 3,562 | HARPER | 1,683 | 1,296 | 374 | | 13 | 922 R | 77.0% | 22.2% | |
| 11,792 | HASKELL | 4,628 | 2,039 | 2,510 | | 79 | 471 D | 44.1% | 54.2% | |
| 14,154 | HUGHES | 4,585 | 2,196 | 2,334 | | 55 | 138 D | 47.9% | 50.9% | |
| 28,439 | JACKSON | 8,159 | 5,591 | 2,515 | | 53 | 3,076 R | 68.5% | 30.8% | |
| 6,818 | JEFFERSON | 2,593 | 1,320 | 1,245 | | 28 | 75 R | 50.9% | 48.0% | |
| 10,513 | JOHNSTON | 3,930 | 2,072 | 1,809 | | 49 | 263 R | 52.7% | 46.0% | |
| 48,080 | KAY | 18,162 | 11,768 | 6,122 | | 272 | 5,646 R | 64.8% | 33.7% | |
| 13,926 | KINGFISHER | 6,056 | 4,693 | 1,304 | | 59 | 3,389 R | 77.5% | 21.5% | |
| 10,227 | KIOWA | 3,750 | 2,173 | 1,544 | | 33 | 629 R | 57.9% | 41.2% | |
| 10,692 | LATIMER | 3,669 | 1,739 | 1,865 | | 65 | 126 D | 47.4% | 50.8% | |
| 48,109 | LE FLORE | 14,985 | 8,215 | 6,536 | | 234 | 1,679 R | 54.8% | 43.6% | |
| 32,080 | LINCOLN | 11,701 | 7,387 | 4,140 | | 174 | 3,247 R | 63.1% | 35.4% | |
| 33,924 | LOGAN | 12,870 | 8,187 | 4,510 | | 173 | 3,677 R | 63.6% | 35.0% | |
| 8,831 | LOVE | 3,372 | 1,807 | 1,530 | | 35 | 277 R | 53.6% | 45.4% | |
| 27,740 | MCCLAIN | 10,539 | 6,750 | 3,679 | | 110 | 3,071 R | 64.0% | 34.9% | |
| 34,402 | MCCURTAIN | 10,482 | 6,601 | 3,752 | | 129 | 2,849 R | 63.0% | 35.8% | |
| 19,456 | MCINTOSH | 7,781 | 3,444 | 4,206 | | 131 | 762 D | 44.3% | 54.1% | |
| 7,545 | MAJOR | 3,352 | 2,672 | 635 | | 45 | 2,037 R | 79.7% | 18.9% | |
| 13,184 | MARSHALL | 4,900 | 2,641 | 2,210 | | 49 | 431 R | 53.9% | 45.1% | |
| 38,369 | MAYES | 14,001 | 7,132 | 6,618 | | 251 | 514 R | 50.9% | 47.3% | |
| 12,623 | MURRAY | 4,922 | 2,609 | 2,263 | | 50 | 346 R | 53.0% | 46.0% | |
| 69,451 | MUSKOGEE | 24,693 | 11,820 | 12,520 | | 353 | 700 D | 47.9% | 50.7% | |
| 11,411 | NOBLE | 4,697 | 3,230 | 1,416 | | 51 | 1,814 R | 68.8% | 30.1% | |
| 10,569 | NOWATA | 3,849 | 2,069 | 1,703 | | 77 | 366 R | 53.8% | 44.2% | |
| 11,814 | OKFUSKEE | 3,788 | 1,910 | 1,814 | | 64 | 96 R | 50.4% | 47.9% | |
| 660,448 | OKLAHOMA | 223,111 | 139,078 | 81,590 | | 2,443 | 57,488 R | 62.3% | 36.6% | |
| 39,685 | OKMULGEE | 13,178 | 5,797 | 7,186 | | 195 | 1,389 D | 44.0% | 54.5% | |
| 44,437 | OSAGE | 15,909 | 8,138 | 7,540 | | 231 | 598 R | 51.2% | 47.4% | |
| 33,194 | OTTAWA | 11,411 | 5,625 | 5,647 | | 139 | 22 D | 49.3% | 49.5% | |
| 16,612 | PAWNEE | 5,925 | 3,386 | 2,435 | | 104 | 951 R | 57.1% | 41.1% | |
| 68,190 | PAYNE | 24,947 | 15,256 | 9,319 | | 372 | 5,937 R | 61.2% | 37.4% | |

# OKLAHOMA

## PRESIDENT 2000

| 2000 Census Population | County | Total Vote | Republican | Democratic | Green (Nader) | Other | Rep.-Dem. Plurality | Percentage of Total Vote | | |
|---|---|---|---|---|---|---|---|---|---|---|
| | | | | | | | | Rep. | Dem. | Green |
| 43,953 | PITTSBURG | 16,357 | 8,514 | 7,627 | | 216 | 887 R | 52.1% | 46.6% | |
| 35,143 | PONTOTOC | 12,836 | 7,299 | 5,387 | | 150 | 1,912 R | 56.9% | 42.0% | |
| 65,521 | POTTAWATOMIE | 22,316 | 13,235 | 8,763 | | 318 | 4,472 R | 59.3% | 39.3% | |
| 11,667 | PUSHMATAHA | 4,348 | 2,331 | 1,969 | | 48 | 362 R | 53.6% | 45.3% | |
| 3,436 | ROGER MILLS | 1,687 | 1,234 | 441 | | 12 | 793 R | 73.1% | 26.1% | |
| 70,641 | ROGERS | 28,951 | 17,713 | 10,813 | | 425 | 6,900 R | 61.2% | 37.3% | |
| 24,894 | SEMINOLE | 7,866 | 4,011 | 3,783 | | 72 | 228 R | 51.0% | 48.1% | |
| 38,972 | SEQUOYAH | 12,254 | 6,614 | 5,425 | | 215 | 1,189 R | 54.0% | 44.3% | |
| 43,182 | STEPHENS | 17,488 | 10,860 | 6,467 | | 161 | 4,393 R | 62.1% | 37.0% | |
| 20,107 | TEXAS | 6,088 | 4,964 | 1,084 | | 40 | 3,880 R | 81.5% | 17.8% | |
| 9,287 | TILLMAN | 3,349 | 1,920 | 1,400 | | 29 | 520 R | 57.3% | 41.8% | |
| 563,299 | TULSA | 218,691 | 134,152 | 81,656 | | 2,883 | 52,496 R | 61.3% | 37.3% | |
| 57,491 | WAGONER | 21,517 | 12,981 | 8,244 | | 292 | 4,737 R | 60.3% | 38.3% | |
| 48,996 | WASHINGTON | 20,744 | 13,788 | 6,644 | | 312 | 7,144 R | 66.5% | 32.0% | |
| 11,508 | WASHITA | 4,468 | 2,850 | 1,564 | | 54 | 1,286 R | 63.8% | 35.0% | |
| 9,089 | WOODS | 4,046 | 2,774 | 1,235 | | 37 | 1,539 R | 68.6% | 30.5% | |
| 18,486 | WOODWARD | 7,100 | 5,067 | 1,950 | | 83 | 3,117 R | 71.4% | 27.5% | |
| 3,450,654 | TOTAL | 1,234,229 | 744,337 | 474,276 | | 15,616 | 270,061 R | 60.3% | 38.4% | |

Note: No votes for Nader were tallied in Oklahoma. He did not qualify for the ballot and write-in votes were not allowed.

# OKLAHOMA

## PRESIDENT 1996

| 1995 Census Pop. Est. | County | Total Vote | Republican | Democratic | Reform (Perot) | Other | Rep.-Dem. Plurality | Percentage of Total Vote | | |
|---|---|---|---|---|---|---|---|---|---|---|
| | | | | | | | | Rep. | Dem. | Reform |
| 19,904 | ADAIR | 6,521 | 2,956 | 2,792 | 751 | 22 | 164 R | 45.3% | 42.8% | 11.5% |
| 6,110 | ALFALFA | 2,663 | 1,504 | 796 | 348 | 15 | 708 R | 56.5% | 29.9% | 13.1% |
| 13,263 | ATOKA | 4,373 | 1,542 | 2,281 | 532 | 18 | 739 D | 35.3% | 52.2% | 12.2% |
| 5,883 | BEAVER | 2,611 | 1,893 | 515 | 199 | 4 | 1,378 R | 72.5% | 19.7% | 7.6% |
| 18,568 | BECKHAM | 6,551 | 2,912 | 2,797 | 817 | 25 | 115 R | 44.5% | 42.7% | 12.5% |
| 10,896 | BLAINE | 4,537 | 2,127 | 1,832 | 563 | 15 | 295 R | 46.9% | 40.4% | 12.4% |
| 33,720 | BRYAN | 11,335 | 3,943 | 5,962 | 1,396 | 34 | 2,019 D | 34.8% | 52.6% | 12.3% |
| 30,625 | CADDO | 9,670 | 3,422 | 4,844 | 1,358 | 46 | 1,422 D | 35.4% | 50.1% | 14.0% |
| 81,593 | CANADIAN | 30,536 | 18,139 | 8,977 | 3,297 | 123 | 9,162 R | 59.4% | 29.4% | 10.8% |
| 44,137 | CARTER | 15,804 | 6,769 | 6,979 | 1,997 | 59 | 210 D | 42.8% | 44.2% | 12.6% |
| 37,098 | CHEROKEE | 13,696 | 5,046 | 6,817 | 1,777 | 56 | 1,771 D | 36.8% | 49.8% | 13.0% |
| 15,263 | CHOCTAW | 5,379 | 1,580 | 3,198 | 589 | 12 | 1,618 D | 29.4% | 59.5% | 10.9% |
| 3,018 | CIMARRON | 1,455 | 986 | 361 | 102 | 6 | 625 R | 67.8% | 24.8% | 7.0% |
| 191,059 | CLEVELAND | 69,783 | 36,457 | 26,038 | 6,785 | 503 | 10,419 R | 52.2% | 37.3% | 9.7% |
| 6,014 | COAL | 2,276 | 734 | 1,205 | 323 | 14 | 471 D | 32.2% | 52.9% | 14.2% |
| 115,672 | COMANCHE | 30,278 | 14,461 | 12,841 | 2,819 | 157 | 1,620 R | 47.8% | 42.4% | 9.3% |
| 6,891 | COTTON | 2,698 | 1,042 | 1,258 | 381 | 17 | 216 D | 38.6% | 46.6% | 14.1% |
| 14,211 | CRAIG | 5,486 | 2,058 | 2,649 | 758 | 21 | 591 D | 37.5% | 48.3% | 13.8% |
| 64,299 | CREEK | 22,457 | 9,861 | 9,674 | 2,837 | 85 | 187 R | 43.9% | 43.1% | 12.6% |
| 26,320 | CUSTER | 9,879 | 4,723 | 4,027 | 1,101 | 28 | 696 R | 47.8% | 40.8% | 11.1% |
| 32,401 | DELAWARE | 11,939 | 5,230 | 5,094 | 1,573 | 42 | 136 R | 43.8% | 42.7% | 13.2% |
| 5,126 | DEWEY | 2,301 | 1,179 | 816 | 292 | 14 | 363 R | 51.2% | 35.5% | 12.7% |
| 4,251 | ELLIS | 1,996 | 1,090 | 619 | 279 | 8 | 471 R | 54.6% | 31.0% | 14.0% |
| 57,330 | GARFIELD | 21,841 | 11,712 | 7,504 | 2,523 | 102 | 4,208 R | 53.6% | 34.4% | 11.6% |
| 26,849 | GARVIN | 9,767 | 3,745 | 4,639 | 1,345 | 38 | 894 D | 38.3% | 47.5% | 13.8% |
| 43,817 | GRADY | 15,598 | 7,228 | 6,256 | 2,048 | 66 | 972 R | 46.3% | 40.1% | 13.1% |
| 5,503 | GRANT | 2,653 | 1,382 | 867 | 384 | 20 | 515 R | 52.1% | 32.7% | 14.5% |
| 6,556 | GREER | 2,517 | 905 | 1,240 | 361 | 11 | 335 D | 36.0% | 49.3% | 14.3% |
| 3,669 | HARMON | 1,327 | 448 | 729 | 143 | 7 | 281 D | 33.8% | 54.9% | 10.8% |
| 3,814 | HARPER | 1,778 | 1,036 | 511 | 219 | 12 | 525 R | 58.3% | 28.7% | 12.3% |
| 11,125 | HASKELL | 4,805 | 1,442 | 2,762 | 590 | 11 | 1,320 D | 30.0% | 57.5% | 12.3% |
| 12,932 | HUGHES | 5,012 | 1,510 | 2,748 | 730 | 24 | 1,238 D | 30.1% | 54.8% | 14.6% |
| 29,754 | JACKSON | 8,582 | 4,422 | 3,245 | 892 | 23 | 1,177 R | 51.5% | 37.8% | 10.4% |
| 6,877 | JEFFERSON | 2,646 | 865 | 1,430 | 337 | 14 | 565 D | 32.7% | 54.0% | 12.7% |
| 10,283 | JOHNSTON | 3,767 | 1,229 | 1,998 | 532 | 8 | 769 D | 32.6% | 53.0% | 14.1% |
| 47,676 | KAY | 19,514 | 9,741 | 6,882 | 2,785 | 106 | 2,859 R | 49.9% | 35.3% | 14.3% |
| 13,377 | KINGFISHER | 5,679 | 3,423 | 1,626 | 621 | 9 | 1,797 R | 60.3% | 28.6% | 10.9% |
| 11,105 | KIOWA | 4,128 | 1,638 | 1,973 | 510 | 7 | 335 D | 39.7% | 47.8% | 12.4% |
| 10,416 | LATIMER | 4,003 | 1,189 | 2,222 | 578 | 14 | 1,033 D | 29.7% | 55.5% | 14.4% |
| 45,641 | LE FLORE | 14,316 | 5,689 | 6,831 | 1,721 | 75 | 1,142 D | 39.7% | 47.7% | 12.0% |
| 30,528 | LINCOLN | 11,122 | 5,243 | 4,332 | 1,500 | 47 | 911 R | 47.1% | 38.9% | 13.5% |
| 31,189 | LOGAN | 12,277 | 5,949 | 4,854 | 1,410 | 64 | 1,095 R | 48.5% | 39.5% | 11.5% |
| 8,735 | LOVE | 3,304 | 1,224 | 1,675 | 385 | 20 | 451 D | 37.0% | 50.7% | 11.7% |
| 25,162 | MCCLAIN | 9,439 | 4,363 | 3,753 | 1,289 | 34 | 610 R | 46.2% | 39.8% | 13.7% |
| 34,477 | MCCURTAIN | 9,774 | 3,892 | 4,350 | 1,483 | 49 | 458 D | 39.8% | 44.5% | 15.2% |
| 18,407 | MCINTOSH | 7,691 | 2,400 | 4,219 | 1,044 | 28 | 1,819 D | 31.2% | 54.9% | 13.6% |
| 7,703 | MAJOR | 3,512 | 2,188 | 900 | 410 | 14 | 1,288 R | 62.3% | 25.6% | 11.7% |
| 11,718 | MARSHALL | 4,913 | 1,605 | 2,624 | 663 | 21 | 1,019 D | 32.7% | 53.4% | 13.5% |
| 36,047 | MAYES | 13,308 | 5,268 | 6,377 | 1,617 | 46 | 1,109 D | 39.6% | 47.9% | 12.2% |
| 12,213 | MURRAY | 5,068 | 1,712 | 2,620 | 723 | 13 | 908 D | 33.8% | 51.7% | 14.3% |
| 69,297 | MUSKOGEE | 25,180 | 8,974 | 12,963 | 3,163 | 80 | 3,989 D | 35.6% | 51.5% | 12.6% |
| 11,333 | NOBLE | 4,791 | 2,318 | 1,756 | 694 | 23 | 562 R | 48.4% | 36.7% | 14.5% |
| 9,966 | NOWATA | 3,854 | 1,457 | 1,788 | 586 | 23 | 331 D | 37.8% | 46.4% | 15.2% |
| 11,339 | OKFUSKEE | 4,010 | 1,380 | 2,074 | 536 | 20 | 694 D | 34.4% | 51.7% | 13.4% |
| 625,337 | OKLAHOMA | 220,253 | 120,429 | 80,438 | 18,411 | 975 | 39,991 R | 54.7% | 36.5% | 8.4% |
| 37,760 | OKMULGEE | 13,337 | 4,246 | 7,555 | 1,487 | 49 | 3,309 D | 31.8% | 56.6% | 11.1% |
| 42,577 | OSAGE | 15,183 | 5,827 | 7,342 | 1,938 | 76 | 1,515 D | 38.4% | 48.4% | 12.8% |
| 30,649 | OTTAWA | 11,504 | 4,127 | 5,844 | 1,496 | 37 | 1,717 D | 35.9% | 50.8% | 13.0% |
| 15,918 | PAWNEE | 6,006 | 2,560 | 2,663 | 756 | 27 | 103 D | 42.6% | 44.3% | 12.6% |
| 63,577 | PAYNE | 24,308 | 11,686 | 9,985 | 2,472 | 165 | 1,701 R | 48.1% | 41.1% | 10.2% |

# OKLAHOMA

## PRESIDENT 1996

| 1995 Census Pop. Est. | County | Total Vote | Republican | Democratic | Reform (Perot) | Other | Rep.-Dem. Plurality | Percentage of Total Vote | | |
|---|---|---|---|---|---|---|---|---|---|---|
| | | | | | | | | Rep. | Dem. | Reform |
| 42,819 | PITTSBURG | 16,766 | 5,966 | 8,475 | 2,217 | 108 | 2,509 D | 35.6% | 50.5% | 13.2% |
| 34,689 | PONTOTOC | 13,613 | 5,366 | 6,470 | 1,712 | 65 | 1,104 D | 39.4% | 47.5% | 12.6% |
| 60,834 | POTTAWATOMIE | 21,753 | 9,802 | 9,141 | 2,724 | 86 | 661 R | 45.1% | 42.0% | 12.5% |
| 11,481 | PUSHMATAHA | 4,341 | 1,458 | 2,270 | 588 | 25 | 812 D | 33.6% | 52.3% | 13.5% |
| 3,880 | ROGER MILLS | 1,933 | 959 | 733 | 233 | 8 | 226 R | 49.6% | 37.9% | 12.1% |
| 62,095 | ROGERS | 25,554 | 12,883 | 9,544 | 3,022 | 105 | 3,339 R | 50.4% | 37.3% | 11.8% |
| 25,000 | SEMINOLE | 8,229 | 2,935 | 4,225 | 1,041 | 28 | 1,290 D | 35.7% | 51.3% | 12.7% |
| 36,070 | SEQUOYAH | 12,124 | 4,733 | 5,665 | 1,673 | 53 | 932 D | 39.0% | 46.7% | 13.8% |
| 42,929 | STEPHENS | 17,776 | 8,144 | 7,248 | 2,312 | 72 | 896 R | 45.8% | 40.8% | 13.0% |
| 16,759 | TEXAS | 6,091 | 4,139 | 1,408 | 518 | 26 | 2,731 R | 68.0% | 23.1% | 8.5% |
| 9,775 | TILLMAN | 3,659 | 1,346 | 1,827 | 471 | 15 | 481 D | 36.8% | 49.9% | 12.9% |
| 525,115 | TULSA | 207,356 | 111,243 | 76,924 | 18,201 | 988 | 34,319 R | 53.6% | 37.1% | 8.8% |
| 52,414 | WAGONER | 19,558 | 9,392 | 7,749 | 2,357 | 60 | 1,643 R | 48.0% | 39.6% | 12.1% |
| 47,594 | WASHINGTON | 20,694 | 11,605 | 6,732 | 2,255 | 102 | 4,873 R | 56.1% | 32.5% | 10.9% |
| 11,779 | WASHITA | 4,675 | 1,994 | 1,913 | 748 | 20 | 81 R | 42.7% | 40.9% | 16.0% |
| 8,611 | WOODS | 4,102 | 2,151 | 1,431 | 497 | 23 | 720 R | 52.4% | 34.9% | 12.1% |
| 18,865 | WOODWARD | 7,498 | 4,093 | 2,403 | 963 | 39 | 1,690 R | 54.6% | 32.0% | 12.8% |
| 3,277,687 | TOTAL | 1,206,713 | 582,315 | 488,105 | 130,788 | 5,505 | 94,210 R | 48.3% | 40.4% | 10.8% |

# OKLAHOMA

## PRESIDENT 1992

| 1990 Census Population | County | Total Vote | Republican | Democratic | Perot | Other | Plurality | Percentage Total Vote | | |
|---|---|---|---|---|---|---|---|---|---|---|
| | | | | | | | | Rep. | Dem. | Perot |
| 18,421 | ADAIR | 6,583 | 2,994 | 2,645 | 914 | 30 | 349 R | 45.5% | 40.2% | 13.9% |
| 6,416 | ALFALFA | 3,045 | 1,567 | 741 | 722 | 15 | 826 R | 51.5% | 24.3% | 23.7% |
| 12,778 | ATOKA | 5,167 | 1,561 | 2,336 | 1,255 | 15 | 775 D | 30.2% | 45.2% | 24.3% |
| 6,023 | BEAVER | 2,850 | 1,699 | 580 | 565 | 6 | 1,119 R | 59.6% | 20.4% | 19.8% |
| 18,812 | BECKHAM | 7,820 | 2,913 | 2,947 | 1,929 | 31 | 34 D | 37.3% | 37.7% | 24.7% |
| 11,470 | BLAINE | 5,052 | 2,209 | 1,564 | 1,258 | 21 | 645 R | 43.7% | 31.0% | 24.9% |
| 32,089 | BRYAN | 13,468 | 3,452 | 6,259 | 3,713 | 44 | 2,546 D | 25.6% | 46.5% | 27.6% |
| 29,550 | CADDO | 11,488 | 3,664 | 4,861 | 2,911 | 52 | 1,197 D | 31.9% | 42.3% | 25.3% |
| 74,409 | CANADIAN | 33,050 | 16,756 | 7,215 | 8,985 | 94 | 7,771 R | 50.7% | 21.8% | 27.2% |
| 42,919 | CARTER | 18,368 | 5,947 | 7,171 | 5,188 | 62 | 1,224 D | 32.4% | 39.0% | 28.2% |
| 34,049 | CHEROKEE | 15,111 | 4,977 | 6,794 | 3,297 | 43 | 1,817 D | 32.9% | 45.0% | 21.8% |
| 15,302 | CHOCTAW | 6,377 | 1,641 | 3,413 | 1,298 | 25 | 1,772 D | 25.7% | 53.5% | 20.4% |
| 3,301 | CIMARRON | 1,624 | 965 | 395 | 254 | 10 | 570 R | 59.4% | 24.3% | 15.6% |
| 174,253 | CLEVELAND | 80,629 | 35,561 | 24,404 | 20,352 | 312 | 11,157 R | 44.1% | 30.3% | 25.2% |
| 5,780 | COAL | 2,800 | 714 | 1,448 | 618 | 20 | 734 D | 25.5% | 51.7% | 22.1% |
| 111,486 | COMANCHE | 35,520 | 15,704 | 12,237 | 7,463 | 116 | 3,467 R | 44.2% | 34.5% | 21.0% |
| 6,651 | COTTON | 3,091 | 910 | 1,314 | 853 | 14 | 404 D | 29.4% | 42.5% | 27.6% |
| 14,104 | CRAIG | 6,219 | 2,106 | 2,780 | 1,316 | 17 | 674 D | 33.9% | 44.7% | 21.2% |
| 60,915 | CREEK | 25,238 | 10,055 | 9,118 | 5,984 | 81 | 937 R | 39.8% | 36.1% | 23.7% |
| 26,897 | CUSTER | 11,694 | 5,362 | 3,540 | 2,741 | 51 | 1,822 R | 45.9% | 30.3% | 23.4% |
| 28,070 | DELAWARE | 12,426 | 4,840 | 4,842 | 2,689 | 55 | 2 D | 39.0% | 39.0% | 21.6% |
| 5,551 | DEWEY | 2,782 | 1,244 | 845 | 684 | 9 | 399 R | 44.7% | 30.4% | 24.6% |
| 4,497 | ELLIS | 2,307 | 1,072 | 594 | 632 | 9 | 440 R | 46.5% | 25.7% | 27.4% |
| 56,735 | GARFIELD | 25,485 | 13,095 | 6,720 | 5,559 | 111 | 6,375 R | 51.4% | 26.4% | 21.8% |
| 26,605 | GARVIN | 11,863 | 3,983 | 4,811 | 3,014 | 55 | 828 D | 33.6% | 40.6% | 25.4% |
| 41,747 | GRADY | 17,757 | 6,997 | 6,177 | 4,528 | 55 | 820 R | 39.4% | 34.8% | 25.5% |
| 5,689 | GRANT | 3,056 | 1,311 | 864 | 871 | 10 | 440 R | 42.9% | 28.3% | 28.5% |
| 6,559 | GREER | 2,779 | 964 | 1,162 | 640 | 13 | 198 D | 34.7% | 41.8% | 23.0% |
| 3,793 | HARMON | 1,611 | 496 | 783 | 326 | 6 | 287 D | 30.8% | 48.6% | 20.2% |
| 4,063 | HARPER | 2,035 | 1,038 | 486 | 501 | 10 | 537 R | 51.0% | 23.9% | 24.6% |
| 10,940 | HASKELL | 5,546 | 1,461 | 3,069 | 995 | 21 | 1,608 D | 26.3% | 55.3% | 17.9% |
| 13,023 | HUGHES | 5,554 | 1,522 | 2,850 | 1,158 | 24 | 1,328 D | 27.4% | 51.3% | 20.8% |
| 28,764 | JACKSON | 9,420 | 3,893 | 3,273 | 2,227 | 27 | 620 R | 41.3% | 34.7% | 23.6% |
| 7,010 | JEFFERSON | 3,019 | 671 | 1,580 | 758 | 10 | 822 D | 22.2% | 52.3% | 25.1% |
| 10,032 | JOHNSTON | 4,339 | 1,191 | 2,096 | 1,040 | 12 | 905 D | 27.4% | 48.3% | 24.0% |
| 48,056 | KAY | 22,828 | 9,115 | 6,643 | 6,984 | 86 | 2,131 R | 39.9% | 29.1% | 30.6% |
| 13,212 | KINGFISHER | 6,411 | 3,479 | 1,379 | 1,534 | 19 | 1,945 R | 54.3% | 21.5% | 23.9% |
| 11,347 | KIOWA | 4,910 | 1,635 | 2,143 | 1,114 | 18 | 508 D | 33.3% | 43.6% | 22.7% |
| 10,333 | LATIMER | 4,885 | 1,212 | 2,606 | 1,049 | 18 | 1,394 D | 24.8% | 53.3% | 21.5% |
| 43,270 | LE FLORE | 16,763 | 5,850 | 7,843 | 3,021 | 49 | 1,993 D | 34.9% | 46.8% | 18.0% |
| 29,216 | LINCOLN | 12,423 | 5,315 | 3,904 | 3,160 | 44 | 1,411 R | 42.8% | 31.4% | 25.4% |
| 29,011 | LOGAN | 13,806 | 6,071 | 4,453 | 3,239 | 43 | 1,618 R | 44.0% | 32.3% | 23.5% |
| 8,157 | LOVE | 3,679 | 922 | 1,708 | 1,033 | 16 | 675 D | 25.1% | 46.4% | 28.1% |
| 22,795 | MCCLAIN | 10,776 | 4,377 | 3,378 | 2,996 | 25 | 999 R | 40.6% | 31.3% | 27.8% |
| 33,433 | MCCURTAIN | 11,494 | 3,519 | 5,082 | 2,852 | 41 | 1,563 D | 30.6% | 44.2% | 24.8% |
| 16,779 | MCINTOSH | 7,893 | 2,225 | 4,184 | 1,469 | 15 | 1,959 D | 28.2% | 53.0% | 18.6% |
| 8,055 | MAJOR | 3,755 | 2,154 | 731 | 857 | 13 | 1,297 R | 57.4% | 19.5% | 22.8% |
| 10,829 | MARSHALL | 5,498 | 1,478 | 2,519 | 1,486 | 15 | 1,033 D | 26.9% | 45.8% | 27.0% |
| 33,366 | MAYES | 15,171 | 5,445 | 6,432 | 3,235 | 59 | 987 D | 35.9% | 42.4% | 21.3% |
| 12,042 | MURRAY | 5,588 | 1,536 | 2,594 | 1,447 | 11 | 1,058 D | 27.5% | 46.4% | 25.9% |
| 68,078 | MUSKOGEE | 27,932 | 8,782 | 13,619 | 5,454 | 77 | 4,837 D | 31.4% | 48.8% | 19.5% |
| 11,045 | NOBLE | 5,283 | 2,474 | 1,333 | 1,449 | 27 | 1,025 R | 46.8% | 25.2% | 27.4% |
| 9,992 | NOWATA | 4,524 | 1,531 | 1,912 | 1,063 | 18 | 381 D | 33.8% | 42.3% | 23.5% |
| 11,551 | OKFUSKEE | 4,630 | 1,580 | 2,141 | 889 | 20 | 561 D | 34.1% | 46.2% | 19.2% |
| 599,611 | OKLAHOMA | 259,923 | 126,788 | 76,271 | 56,139 | 725 | 50,517 R | 48.8% | 29.3% | 21.6% |
| 36,490 | OKMULGEE | 15,421 | 4,586 | 7,767 | 3,013 | 55 | 3,181 D | 29.7% | 50.4% | 19.5% |
| 41,645 | OSAGE | 17,322 | 5,891 | 6,894 | 4,477 | 60 | 1,003 D | 34.0% | 39.8% | 25.8% |
| 30,561 | OTTAWA | 13,209 | 4,141 | 6,304 | 2,721 | 43 | 2,163 D | 31.3% | 47.7% | 20.6% |
| 15,575 | PAWNEE | 6,973 | 2,675 | 2,612 | 1,656 | 30 | 63 R | 38.4% | 37.5% | 23.7% |
| 61,507 | PAYNE | 30,880 | 13,032 | 9,886 | 7,852 | 110 | 3,146 R | 42.2% | 32.0% | 25.4% |

# OKLAHOMA

## PRESIDENT 1992

| 1990 Census Population | County | Total Vote | Republican | Democratic | Perot | Other | Plurality | Percentage Total Vote | | |
|---:|---|---:|---:|---:|---:|---:|---:|---:|---:|---:|
| | | | | | | | | Rep. | Dem. | Perot |
| 40,581 | PITTSBURG | 18,827 | 5,659 | 8,523 | 4,594 | 51 | 2,864 D | 30.1% | 45.3% | 24.4% |
| 34,119 | PONTOTOC | 15,521 | 5,206 | 6,350 | 3,916 | 49 | 1,144 D | 33.5% | 40.9% | 25.2% |
| 58,760 | POTTAWATOMIE | 25,572 | 10,350 | 8,616 | 6,520 | 86 | 1,734 R | 40.5% | 33.7% | 25.5% |
| 10,997 | PUSHMATAHA | 4,897 | 1,319 | 2,553 | 1,000 | 25 | 1,234 D | 26.9% | 52.1% | 20.4% |
| 4,147 | ROGER MILLS | 2,173 | 890 | 767 | 505 | 11 | 123 R | 41.0% | 35.3% | 23.2% |
| 55,170 | ROGERS | 27,892 | 12,455 | 8,257 | 7,101 | 79 | 4,198 R | 44.7% | 29.6% | 25.5% |
| 25,412 | SEMINOLE | 10,240 | 3,253 | 4,624 | 2,330 | 33 | 1,371 D | 31.8% | 45.2% | 22.8% |
| 33,828 | SEQUOYAH | 13,556 | 4,925 | 6,092 | 2,486 | 53 | 1,167 D | 36.3% | 44.9% | 18.3% |
| 42,299 | STEPHENS | 20,471 | 7,085 | 7,644 | 5,692 | 50 | 559 D | 34.6% | 37.3% | 27.8% |
| 16,419 | TEXAS | 6,980 | 4,059 | 1,487 | 1,417 | 17 | 2,572 R | 58.2% | 21.3% | 20.3% |
| 10,384 | TILLMAN | 4,178 | 1,377 | 1,749 | 1,039 | 13 | 372 D | 33.0% | 41.9% | 24.9% |
| 503,341 | TULSA | 239,068 | 117,465 | 71,165 | 49,760 | 678 | 46,300 R | 49.1% | 29.8% | 20.8% |
| 47,883 | WAGONER | 21,529 | 9,053 | 7,041 | 5,381 | 54 | 2,012 R | 42.1% | 32.7% | 25.0% |
| 48,066 | WASHINGTON | 23,663 | 11,342 | 6,593 | 5,664 | 64 | 4,749 R | 47.9% | 27.9% | 23.9% |
| 11,441 | WASHITA | 5,339 | 1,912 | 1,929 | 1,468 | 30 | 17 D | 35.8% | 36.1% | 27.5% |
| 9,103 | WOODS | 4,777 | 2,225 | 1,361 | 1,167 | 24 | 864 R | 46.6% | 28.5% | 24.4% |
| 18,976 | WOODWARD | 8,526 | 4,006 | 2,063 | 2,411 | 46 | 1,595 R | 47.0% | 24.2% | 28.3% |
| 3,145,585 | TOTAL | 1,390,359 | 592,929 | 473,066 | 319,878 | 4,486 | 119,863 R | 42.6% | 34.0% | 23.0% |

# OKLAHOMA

## PRESIDENT 1988

| 1980 Census Population | County | Total Vote | Republican | Democratic | Other | Rep.-Dem. Plurality | Percentage | | | |
|---|---|---|---|---|---|---|---|---|---|---|
| | | | | | | | Total Vote | | Major Vote | |
| | | | | | | | Rep. | Dem. | Rep. | Dem. |
| 18,575 | ADAIR | 6,240 | 3,558 | 2,624 | 58 | 934 R | 57.0% | 42.1% | 57.6% | 42.4% |
| 7,077 | ALFALFA | 3,132 | 1,960 | 1,117 | 55 | 843 R | 62.6% | 35.7% | 63.7% | 36.3% |
| 12,748 | ATOKA | 4,570 | 1,971 | 2,565 | 34 | 594 D | 43.1% | 56.1% | 43.5% | 56.5% |
| 6,806 | BEAVER | 2,834 | 2,013 | 777 | 44 | 1,236 R | 71.0% | 27.4% | 72.2% | 27.8% |
| 19,243 | BECKHAM | 6,915 | 3,463 | 3,388 | 64 | 75 R | 50.1% | 49.0% | 50.5% | 49.5% |
| 13,443 | BLAINE | 4,734 | 2,889 | 1,775 | 70 | 1,114 R | 61.0% | 37.5% | 61.9% | 38.1% |
| 30,535 | BRYAN | 11,501 | 4,615 | 6,849 | 37 | 2,234 D | 40.1% | 59.6% | 40.3% | 59.7% |
| 30,905 | CADDO | 10,177 | 4,689 | 5,387 | 101 | 698 D | 46.1% | 52.9% | 46.5% | 53.5% |
| 56,452 | CANADIAN | 25,530 | 17,872 | 7,453 | 205 | 10,419 R | 70.0% | 29.2% | 70.6% | 29.4% |
| 43,610 | CARTER | 16,535 | 8,430 | 7,988 | 117 | 442 R | 51.0% | 48.3% | 51.3% | 48.7% |
| 30,684 | CHEROKEE | 12,424 | 5,838 | 6,483 | 103 | 645 D | 47.0% | 52.2% | 47.4% | 52.6% |
| 17,203 | CHOCTAW | 5,599 | 2,217 | 3,362 | 20 | 1,145 D | 39.6% | 60.0% | 39.7% | 60.3% |
| 3,648 | CIMARRON | 1,647 | 1,153 | 470 | 24 | 683 R | 70.0% | 28.5% | 71.0% | 29.0% |
| 133,173 | CLEVELAND | 58,933 | 36,313 | 22,067 | 553 | 14,246 R | 61.6% | 37.4% | 62.2% | 37.8% |
| 6,041 | COAL | 2,270 | 891 | 1,365 | 14 | 474 D | 39.3% | 60.1% | 39.5% | 60.5% |
| 112,456 | COMANCHE | 29,099 | 17,464 | 11,441 | 194 | 6,023 R | 60.0% | 39.3% | 60.4% | 39.6% |
| 7,338 | COTTON | 2,775 | 1,266 | 1,482 | 27 | 216 D | 45.6% | 53.4% | 46.1% | 53.9% |
| 15,014 | CRAIG | 5,446 | 2,463 | 2,940 | 43 | 477 D | 45.2% | 54.0% | 45.6% | 54.4% |
| 59,016 | CREEK | 20,982 | 11,308 | 9,512 | 162 | 1,796 R | 53.9% | 45.3% | 54.3% | 45.7% |
| 25,995 | CUSTER | 10,527 | 6,735 | 3,697 | 95 | 3,038 R | 64.0% | 35.1% | 64.6% | 35.4% |
| 23,946 | DELAWARE | 10,212 | 5,248 | 4,889 | 75 | 359 R | 51.4% | 47.9% | 51.8% | 48.2% |
| 5,922 | DEWEY | 2,551 | 1,543 | 963 | 45 | 580 R | 60.5% | 37.7% | 61.6% | 38.4% |
| 5,596 | ELLIS | 2,244 | 1,422 | 786 | 36 | 636 R | 63.4% | 35.0% | 64.4% | 35.6% |
| 62,820 | GARFIELD | 23,538 | 15,248 | 8,067 | 223 | 7,181 R | 64.8% | 34.3% | 65.4% | 34.6% |
| 27,856 | GARVIN | 10,656 | 5,109 | 5,438 | 109 | 329 D | 47.9% | 51.0% | 48.4% | 51.6% |
| 39,490 | GRADY | 14,848 | 7,994 | 6,689 | 165 | 1,305 R | 53.8% | 45.0% | 54.4% | 45.6% |
| 6,518 | GRANT | 2,980 | 1,690 | 1,249 | 41 | 441 R | 56.7% | 41.9% | 57.5% | 42.5% |
| 7,028 | GREER | 2,503 | 1,225 | 1,256 | 22 | 31 D | 48.9% | 50.2% | 49.4% | 50.6% |
| 4,519 | HARMON | 1,504 | 611 | 890 | 3 | 279 D | 40.6% | 59.2% | 40.7% | 59.3% |
| 4,715 | HARPER | 1,900 | 1,281 | 593 | 26 | 688 R | 67.4% | 31.2% | 68.4% | 31.6% |
| 11,010 | HASKELL | 4,829 | 1,822 | 2,963 | 44 | 1,141 D | 37.7% | 61.4% | 38.1% | 61.9% |
| 14,338 | HUGHES | 5,327 | 2,037 | 3,259 | 31 | 1,222 D | 38.2% | 61.2% | 38.5% | 61.5% |
| 30,356 | JACKSON | 8,001 | 4,423 | 3,542 | 36 | 881 R | 55.3% | 44.3% | 55.5% | 44.5% |
| 8,183 | JEFFERSON | 2,846 | 1,063 | 1,767 | 16 | 704 D | 37.4% | 62.1% | 37.6% | 62.4% |
| 10,356 | JOHNSTON | 3,581 | 1,518 | 2,042 | 21 | 524 D | 42.4% | 57.0% | 42.6% | 57.4% |
| 49,852 | KAY | 20,564 | 12,646 | 7,751 | 167 | 4,895 R | 61.5% | 37.7% | 62.0% | 38.0% |
| 14,187 | KINGFISHER | 5,852 | 4,011 | 1,777 | 64 | 2,234 R | 68.5% | 30.4% | 69.3% | 30.7% |
| 12,711 | KIOWA | 4,358 | 2,030 | 2,296 | 32 | 266 D | 46.6% | 52.7% | 46.9% | 53.1% |
| 9,840 | LATIMER | 4,233 | 1,830 | 2,365 | 38 | 535 D | 43.2% | 55.9% | 43.6% | 56.4% |
| 40,698 | LE FLORE | 13,641 | 6,964 | 6,594 | 83 | 370 R | 51.1% | 48.3% | 51.4% | 48.6% |
| 26,601 | LINCOLN | 10,740 | 6,409 | 4,225 | 106 | 2,184 R | 59.7% | 39.3% | 60.3% | 39.7% |
| 26,881 | LOGAN | 11,704 | 6,947 | 4,603 | 154 | 2,344 R | 59.4% | 39.3% | 60.1% | 39.9% |
| 7,469 | LOVE | 3,267 | 1,361 | 1,889 | 17 | 528 D | 41.7% | 57.8% | 41.9% | 58.1% |
| 20,291 | MCCLAIN | 8,453 | 4,771 | 3,594 | 88 | 1,177 R | 56.4% | 42.5% | 57.0% | 43.0% |
| 36,151 | MCCURTAIN | 9,911 | 4,920 | 4,928 | 63 | 8 D | 49.6% | 49.7% | 50.0% | 50.0% |
| 15,562 | MCINTOSH | 6,742 | 2,665 | 4,041 | 36 | 1,376 D | 39.5% | 59.9% | 39.7% | 60.3% |
| 8,772 | MAJOR | 3,671 | 2,638 | 982 | 51 | 1,656 R | 71.9% | 26.8% | 72.9% | 27.1% |
| 10,550 | MARSHALL | 4,669 | 1,911 | 2,730 | 28 | 819 D | 40.9% | 58.5% | 41.2% | 58.8% |
| 32,261 | MAYES | 12,901 | 6,115 | 6,691 | 95 | 576 D | 47.4% | 51.9% | 47.8% | 52.2% |
| 12,147 | MURRAY | 4,794 | 2,056 | 2,697 | 41 | 641 D | 42.9% | 56.3% | 43.3% | 56.7% |
| 66,939 | MUSKOGEE | 25,068 | 11,147 | 13,760 | 161 | 2,613 D | 44.5% | 54.9% | 44.8% | 55.2% |
| 11,573 | NOBLE | 4,726 | 3,015 | 1,661 | 50 | 1,354 R | 63.8% | 35.1% | 64.5% | 35.5% |
| 11,486 | NOWATA | 4,234 | 2,000 | 2,203 | 31 | 203 D | 47.2% | 52.0% | 47.6% | 52.4% |
| 11,125 | OKFUSKEE | 4,098 | 1,851 | 2,209 | 38 | 358 D | 45.2% | 53.9% | 45.6% | 54.4% |
| 568,933 | OKLAHOMA | 212,891 | 135,376 | 75,812 | 1,703 | 59,564 R | 63.6% | 35.6% | 64.1% | 35.9% |
| 39,169 | OKMULGEE | 14,004 | 5,674 | 8,262 | 68 | 2,588 D | 40.5% | 59.0% | 40.7% | 59.3% |
| 39,327 | OSAGE | 15,055 | 7,162 | 7,778 | 115 | 616 D | 47.6% | 51.7% | 47.9% | 52.1% |
| 32,870 | OTTAWA | 11,729 | 5,026 | 6,658 | 45 | 1,632 D | 42.9% | 56.8% | 43.0% | 57.0% |
| 15,310 | PAWNEE | 6,162 | 3,324 | 2,781 | 57 | 543 R | 53.9% | 45.1% | 54.4% | 45.6% |
| 62,435 | PAYNE | 26,905 | 16,027 | 10,568 | 310 | 5,459 R | 59.6% | 39.3% | 60.3% | 39.7% |

# OKLAHOMA

## PRESIDENT 1988

| 1980 Census Population | County | Total Vote | Republican | Democratic | Other | Rep.-Dem. Plurality | Percentage | | | |
|---|---|---|---|---|---|---|---|---|---|---|
| | | | | | | | Total Vote | | Major Vote | |
| | | | | | | | Rep. | Dem. | Rep. | Dem. |
| 40,524 | PITTSBURG | 16,342 | 7,594 | 8,623 | 125 | 1,029 D | 46.5% | 52.8% | 46.8% | 53.2% |
| 32,598 | PONTOTOC | 13,239 | 6,609 | 6,484 | 146 | 125 R | 49.9% | 49.0% | 50.5% | 49.5% |
| 55,239 | POTTAWATOMIE | 21,169 | 12,099 | 8,873 | 197 | 3,226 R | 57.2% | 41.9% | 57.7% | 42.3% |
| 11,773 | PUSHMATAHA | 4,301 | 1,841 | 2,430 | 30 | 589 D | 42.8% | 56.5% | 43.1% | 56.9% |
| 4,799 | ROGER MILLS | 2,012 | 1,132 | 866 | 14 | 266 R | 56.3% | 43.0% | 56.7% | 43.3% |
| 46,436 | ROGERS | 21,851 | 12,940 | 8,771 | 140 | 4,169 R | 59.2% | 40.1% | 59.6% | 40.4% |
| 27,473 | SEMINOLE | 9,073 | 4,078 | 4,911 | 84 | 833 D | 44.9% | 54.1% | 45.4% | 54.6% |
| 30,749 | SEQUOYAH | 10,729 | 5,710 | 4,951 | 68 | 759 R | 53.2% | 46.1% | 53.6% | 46.4% |
| 43,419 | STEPHENS | 17,795 | 9,844 | 7,833 | 118 | 2,011 R | 55.3% | 44.0% | 55.7% | 44.3% |
| 17,727 | TEXAS | 6,752 | 4,971 | 1,717 | 64 | 3,254 R | 73.6% | 25.4% | 74.3% | 25.7% |
| 12,398 | TILLMAN | 3,928 | 1,754 | 2,148 | 26 | 394 D | 44.7% | 54.7% | 45.0% | 55.0% |
| 470,593 | TULSA | 197,763 | 127,512 | 69,044 | 1,207 | 58,468 R | 64.5% | 34.9% | 64.9% | 35.1% |
| 41,801 | WAGONER | 17,718 | 10,219 | 7,378 | 121 | 2,841 R | 57.7% | 41.6% | 58.1% | 41.9% |
| 48,113 | WASHINGTON | 21,713 | 14,613 | 6,971 | 129 | 7,642 R | 67.3% | 32.1% | 67.7% | 32.3% |
| 13,798 | WASHITA | 4,745 | 2,402 | 2,290 | 53 | 112 R | 50.6% | 48.3% | 51.2% | 48.8% |
| 10,923 | WOODS | 4,651 | 2,835 | 1,735 | 81 | 1,100 R | 61.0% | 37.3% | 62.0% | 38.0% |
| 21,172 | WOODWARD | 7,493 | 4,996 | 2,408 | 89 | 2,588 R | 66.7% | 32.1% | 67.5% | 32.5% |
| 3,025,290 | TOTAL | 1,171,036 | 678,367 | 483,423 | 9,246 | 194,944 R | 57.9% | 41.3% | 58.4% | 41.6% |

# OKLAHOMA

## PRESIDENT 1984

| 1980 Census Population | County | Total Vote | Republican | Democratic | Other | Rep.-Dem. Plurality | Percentage | | | |
|---|---|---|---|---|---|---|---|---|---|---|
| | | | | | | | Total Vote | | Major Vote | |
| | | | | | | | Rep. | Dem. | Rep. | Dem. |
| 18,575 | ADAIR | 6,745 | 4,423 | 2,266 | 56 | 2,157 R | 65.6% | 33.6% | 66.1% | 33.9% |
| 7,077 | ALFALFA | 3,608 | 2,715 | 866 | 27 | 1,849 R | 75.2% | 24.0% | 75.8% | 24.2% |
| 12,748 | ATOKA | 4,444 | 2,361 | 2,047 | 36 | 314 R | 53.1% | 46.1% | 53.6% | 46.4% |
| 6,806 | BEAVER | 3,252 | 2,689 | 536 | 27 | 2,153 R | 82.7% | 16.5% | 83.4% | 16.6% |
| 19,243 | BECKHAM | 7,654 | 5,005 | 2,601 | 48 | 2,404 R | 65.4% | 34.0% | 65.8% | 34.2% |
| 13,443 | BLAINE | 5,554 | 4,037 | 1,484 | 33 | 2,553 R | 72.7% | 26.7% | 73.1% | 26.9% |
| 30,535 | BRYAN | 11,769 | 6,246 | 5,475 | 48 | 771 R | 53.1% | 46.5% | 53.3% | 46.7% |
| 30,905 | CADDO | 11,341 | 6,811 | 4,463 | 67 | 2,348 R | 60.1% | 39.4% | 60.4% | 39.6% |
| 56,452 | CANADIAN | 26,320 | 20,929 | 5,245 | 146 | 15,684 R | 79.5% | 19.9% | 80.0% | 20.0% |
| 43,610 | CARTER | 17,822 | 11,578 | 6,161 | 83 | 5,417 R | 65.0% | 34.6% | 65.3% | 34.7% |
| 30,684 | CHEROKEE | 13,015 | 7,614 | 5,307 | 94 | 2,307 R | 58.5% | 40.8% | 58.9% | 41.1% |
| 17,203 | CHOCTAW | 5,987 | 3,155 | 2,801 | 31 | 354 R | 52.7% | 46.8% | 53.0% | 47.0% |
| 3,648 | CIMARRON | 1,794 | 1,420 | 359 | 15 | 1,061 R | 79.2% | 20.0% | 79.8% | 20.2% |
| 133,173 | CLEVELAND | 59,705 | 42,806 | 16,512 | 387 | 26,294 R | 71.7% | 27.7% | 72.2% | 27.8% |
| 6,041 | COAL | 2,564 | 1,259 | 1,284 | 21 | 25 D | 49.1% | 50.1% | 49.5% | 50.5% |
| 112,456 | COMANCHE | 30,394 | 21,382 | 8,890 | 122 | 12,492 R | 70.3% | 29.2% | 70.6% | 29.4% |
| 7,338 | COTTON | 3,080 | 1,796 | 1,264 | 20 | 532 R | 58.3% | 41.0% | 58.7% | 41.3% |
| 15,014 | CRAIG | 6,190 | 3,629 | 2,515 | 46 | 1,114 R | 58.6% | 40.6% | 59.1% | 40.9% |
| 59,016 | CREEK | 22,628 | 15,011 | 7,465 | 152 | 7,546 R | 66.3% | 33.0% | 66.8% | 33.2% |
| 25,995 | CUSTER | 10,940 | 8,191 | 2,700 | 49 | 5,491 R | 74.9% | 24.7% | 75.2% | 24.8% |
| 23,946 | DELAWARE | 10,542 | 6,690 | 3,789 | 63 | 2,901 R | 63.5% | 35.9% | 63.8% | 36.2% |
| 5,922 | DEWEY | 2,777 | 2,098 | 664 | 15 | 1,434 R | 75.5% | 23.9% | 76.0% | 24.0% |
| 5,596 | ELLIS | 2,460 | 1,881 | 562 | 17 | 1,319 R | 76.5% | 22.8% | 77.0% | 23.0% |
| 62,820 | GARFIELD | 25,534 | 19,642 | 5,730 | 162 | 13,912 R | 76.9% | 22.4% | 77.4% | 22.6% |
| 27,856 | GARVIN | 11,811 | 7,505 | 4,215 | 91 | 3,290 R | 63.5% | 35.7% | 64.0% | 36.0% |
| 39,490 | GRADY | 15,960 | 11,042 | 4,846 | 72 | 6,196 R | 69.2% | 30.4% | 69.5% | 30.5% |
| 6,518 | GRANT | 3,324 | 2,470 | 825 | 29 | 1,645 R | 74.3% | 24.8% | 75.0% | 25.0% |
| 7,028 | GREEN | 2,901 | 1,664 | 1,220 | 17 | 444 R | 57.4% | 42.1% | 57.7% | 42.3% |
| 4,519 | HARMON | 1,805 | 1,009 | 785 | 11 | 224 R | 55.9% | 43.5% | 56.2% | 43.8% |
| 4,715 | HARPER | 2,146 | 1,748 | 373 | 25 | 1,375 R | 81.5% | 17.4% | 82.4% | 17.6% |
| 11,010 | HASKELL | 4,981 | 2,417 | 2,535 | 29 | 118 D | 48.5% | 50.9% | 48.8% | 51.2% |
| 14,338 | HUGHES | 5,598 | 2,663 | 2,901 | 34 | 238 D | 47.6% | 51.8% | 47.9% | 52.1% |
| 30,356 | JACKSON | 8,795 | 5,773 | 2,996 | 26 | 2,777 R | 65.6% | 34.1% | 65.8% | 34.2% |
| 8,183 | JEFFERSON | 3,179 | 1,656 | 1,496 | 27 | 160 R | 52.1% | 47.1% | 52.5% | 47.5% |
| 10,356 | JOHNSTON | 4,038 | 2,195 | 1,820 | 23 | 375 R | 54.4% | 45.1% | 54.7% | 45.3% |
| 49,852 | KAY | 22,911 | 16,731 | 6,044 | 136 | 10,687 R | 73.0% | 26.4% | 73.5% | 26.5% |
| 14,187 | KINGFISHER | 6,686 | 5,528 | 1,125 | 33 | 4,403 R | 82.7% | 16.8% | 83.1% | 16.9% |
| 12,711 | KIOWA | 4,995 | 2,951 | 2,016 | 28 | 935 R | 59.1% | 40.4% | 59.4% | 40.6% |
| 9,840 | LATIMER | 4,100 | 2,210 | 1,858 | 32 | 352 R | 53.9% | 45.3% | 54.3% | 45.7% |
| 40,698 | LE FLORE | 14,698 | 8,604 | 5,990 | 104 | 2,614 R | 58.5% | 40.8% | 59.0% | 41.0% |
| 26,601 | LINCOLN | 11,189 | 8,088 | 3,020 | 81 | 5,068 R | 72.3% | 27.0% | 72.8% | 27.2% |
| 26,881 | LOGAN | 11,978 | 8,356 | 3,551 | 71 | 4,805 R | 69.8% | 29.6% | 70.2% | 29.8% |
| 7,469 | LOVE | 3,209 | 1,833 | 1,359 | 17 | 474 R | 57.1% | 42.3% | 57.4% | 42.6% |
| 20,291 | MCCLAIN | 8,672 | 6,056 | 2,549 | 67 | 3,507 R | 69.8% | 29.4% | 70.4% | 29.6% |
| 36,151 | MCCURTAIN | 10,416 | 6,381 | 3,994 | 41 | 2,387 R | 61.3% | 38.3% | 61.5% | 38.5% |
| 15,562 | MCINTOSH | 7,165 | 3,646 | 3,479 | 40 | 167 R | 50.9% | 48.6% | 51.2% | 48.8% |
| 8,772 | MAJOR | 4,035 | 3,385 | 619 | 31 | 2,766 R | 83.9% | 15.3% | 84.5% | 15.5% |
| 10,550 | MARSHALL | 4,560 | 2,488 | 2,039 | 33 | 449 R | 54.6% | 44.7% | 55.0% | 45.0% |
| 32,261 | MAYES | 13,838 | 8,585 | 5,154 | 99 | 3,431 R | 62.0% | 37.2% | 62.5% | 37.5% |
| 12,147 | MURRAY | 5,347 | 3,073 | 2,229 | 45 | 844 R | 57.5% | 41.7% | 58.0% | 42.0% |
| 66,939 | MUSKOGEE | 27,183 | 14,652 | 12,343 | 188 | 2,309 R | 53.9% | 45.4% | 54.3% | 45.7% |
| 11,573 | NOBLE | 5,279 | 4,018 | 1,238 | 23 | 2,780 R | 76.1% | 23.5% | 76.4% | 23.6% |
| 11,486 | NOWATA | 4,761 | 3,030 | 1,687 | 44 | 1,343 R | 63.6% | 35.4% | 64.2% | 35.8% |
| 11,125 | OKFUSKEE | 4,145 | 2,443 | 1,684 | 18 | 759 R | 58.9% | 40.6% | 59.2% | 40.8% |
| 568,933 | OKLAHOMA | 223,261 | 159,974 | 60,235 | 3,052 | 99,739 R | 71.7% | 27.0% | 72.6% | 27.4% |
| 39,169 | OKMULGEE | 16,189 | 8,704 | 7,380 | 105 | 1,324 R | 53.8% | 45.6% | 54.1% | 45.9% |
| 39,327 | OSAGE | 16,257 | 10,083 | 6,095 | 79 | 3,988 R | 62.0% | 37.5% | 62.3% | 37.7% |
| 32,870 | OTTAWA | 13,505 | 7,666 | 5,781 | 58 | 1,885 R | 56.8% | 42.8% | 57.0% | 43.0% |
| 15,310 | PAWNEE | 6,928 | 4,699 | 2,165 | 64 | 2,534 R | 67.8% | 31.3% | 68.5% | 31.5% |
| 62,435 | PAYNE | 28,648 | 20,811 | 7,653 | 184 | 13,158 R | 72.6% | 26.7% | 73.1% | 26.9% |

# OKLAHOMA

## PRESIDENT 1984

| 1980 Census Population | County | Total Vote | Republican | Democratic | Other | Rep.-Dem. Plurality | | Percentage | | | |
|---|---|---|---|---|---|---|---|---|---|---|---|
| | | | | | | | | Total Vote | | Major Vote | |
| | | | | | | | | Rep. | Dem. | Rep. | Dem. |
| 40,524 | PITTSBURG | 16,760 | 9,778 | 6,860 | 122 | 2,918 | R | 58.3% | 40.9% | 58.8% | 41.2% |
| 32,598 | PONTOTOC | 13,907 | 8,301 | 5,526 | 80 | 2,775 | R | 59.7% | 39.7% | 60.0% | 40.0% |
| 55,239 | POTTAWATOMIE | 23,261 | 16,143 | 6,966 | 152 | 9,177 | R | 69.4% | 29.9% | 69.9% | 30.1% |
| 11,773 | PUSHMATAHA | 4,614 | 2,499 | 2,079 | 36 | 420 | R | 54.2% | 45.1% | 54.6% | 45.4% |
| 4,799 | ROGER MILLS | 2,243 | 1,550 | 680 | 13 | 870 | R | 69.1% | 30.3% | 69.5% | 30.5% |
| 46,436 | ROGERS | 22,288 | 16,137 | 6,013 | 138 | 10,124 | R | 72.4% | 27.0% | 72.9% | 27.1% |
| 27,473 | SEMINOLE | 10,030 | 6,009 | 3,957 | 64 | 2,052 | R | 59.9% | 39.5% | 60.3% | 39.7% |
| 30,749 | SEQUOYAH | 11,300 | 7,042 | 4,202 | 56 | 2,840 | R | 62.3% | 37.2% | 62.6% | 37.4% |
| 43,419 | STEPHENS | 19,333 | 12,871 | 6,359 | 103 | 6,512 | R | 66.6% | 32.9% | 66.9% | 33.1% |
| 17,727 | TEXAS | 7,039 | 5,968 | 1,033 | 38 | 4,935 | R | 84.8% | 14.7% | 85.2% | 14.8% |
| 12,398 | TILLMAN | 4,326 | 2,637 | 1,674 | 15 | 963 | R | 61.0% | 38.7% | 61.2% | 38.8% |
| 470,593 | TULSA | 218,872 | 159,549 | 58,274 | 1,049 | 101,275 | R | 72.9% | 26.6% | 73.2% | 26.8% |
| 41,801 | WAGONER | 17,913 | 12,534 | 5,271 | 108 | 7,263 | R | 70.0% | 29.4% | 70.4% | 29.6% |
| 48,113 | WASHINGTON | 24,667 | 19,043 | 5,476 | 148 | 13,567 | R | 77.2% | 22.2% | 77.7% | 22.3% |
| 13,798 | WASHITA | 5,430 | 3,847 | 1,547 | 36 | 2,300 | R | 70.8% | 28.5% | 71.3% | 28.7% |
| 10,923 | WOODS | 5,018 | 3,741 | 1,231 | 46 | 2,510 | R | 74.6% | 24.5% | 75.2% | 24.8% |
| 21,172 | WOODWARD | 8,063 | 6,376 | 1,647 | 40 | 4,729 | R | 79.1% | 20.4% | 79.5% | 20.5% |
| 3,025,290 | TOTAL | 1,255,676 | 861,530 | 385,080 | 9,066 | 476,450 | R | 68.6% | 30.7% | 69.1% | 30.9% |

# OKLAHOMA

## PRESIDENT 1980

| 1980 Census Population | County | Total Vote | Republican | Democratic | Other | Rep.-Dem. Plurality | Percentage | | | |
|---|---|---|---|---|---|---|---|---|---|---|
| | | | | | | | Total Vote | | Major Vote | |
| | | | | | | | Rep. | Dem. | Rep. | Dem. |
| 18,575 | ADAIR | 6,341 | 3,429 | 2,761 | 151 | 668 R | 54.1% | 43.5% | 55.4% | 44.6% |
| 7,077 | ALFALFA | 3,642 | 2,628 | 899 | 115 | 1,729 R | 72.2% | 24.7% | 74.5% | 25.5% |
| 12,748 | ATOKA | 4,216 | 1,613 | 2,505 | 98 | 892 D | 38.3% | 59.4% | 39.2% | 60.8% |
| 6,806 | BEAVER | 3,218 | 2,430 | 696 | 92 | 1,734 R | 75.5% | 21.6% | 77.7% | 22.3% |
| 19,243 | BECKHAM | 7,113 | 3,637 | 3,298 | 178 | 339 R | 51.1% | 46.4% | 52.4% | 47.6% |
| 13,443 | BLAINE | 5,264 | 3,708 | 1,399 | 157 | 2,309 R | 70.4% | 26.6% | 72.6% | 27.4% |
| 30,535 | BRYAN | 10,582 | 3,980 | 6,410 | 192 | 2,430 D | 37.6% | 60.6% | 38.3% | 61.7% |
| 30,905 | CADDO | 10,995 | 5,945 | 4,695 | 355 | 1,250 R | 54.1% | 42.7% | 55.9% | 44.1% |
| 56,452 | CANADIAN | 21,041 | 15,272 | 4,889 | 880 | 10,383 R | 72.6% | 23.2% | 75.8% | 24.2% |
| 43,610 | CARTER | 16,154 | 9,262 | 6,509 | 383 | 2,753 R | 57.3% | 40.3% | 58.7% | 41.3% |
| 30,684 | CHEROKEE | 11,308 | 5,594 | 5,215 | 499 | 379 R | 49.5% | 46.1% | 51.8% | 48.2% |
| 17,203 | CHOCTAW | 6,009 | 2,394 | 3,507 | 108 | 1,113 D | 39.8% | 58.4% | 40.6% | 59.4% |
| 3,648 | CIMARRON | 1,821 | 1,404 | 373 | 44 | 1,031 R | 77.1% | 20.5% | 79.0% | 21.0% |
| 133,173 | CLEVELAND | 50,401 | 31,178 | 14,536 | 4,687 | 16,642 R | 61.9% | 28.8% | 68.2% | 31.8% |
| 6,041 | COAL | 2,431 | 926 | 1,442 | 63 | 516 D | 38.1% | 59.3% | 39.1% | 60.9% |
| 112,456 | COMANCHE | 27,910 | 16,609 | 9,972 | 1,329 | 6,637 R | 59.5% | 35.7% | 62.5% | 37.5% |
| 7,338 | COTTON | 3,206 | 1,702 | 1,410 | 94 | 292 R | 53.1% | 44.0% | 54.7% | 45.3% |
| 15,014 | CRAIG | 5,952 | 2,956 | 2,801 | 195 | 155 R | 49.7% | 47.1% | 51.3% | 48.7% |
| 59,016 | CREEK | 19,729 | 11,749 | 7,339 | 641 | 4,410 R | 59.6% | 37.2% | 61.6% | 38.4% |
| 25,995 | CUSTER | 9,854 | 6,469 | 3,008 | 377 | 3,461 R | 65.6% | 30.5% | 68.3% | 31.7% |
| 23,946 | DELAWARE | 9,819 | 5,302 | 4,244 | 273 | 1,058 R | 54.0% | 43.2% | 55.5% | 44.5% |
| 5,922 | DEWEY | 2,876 | 1,943 | 826 | 107 | 1,117 R | 67.6% | 28.7% | 70.2% | 29.8% |
| 5,596 | ELLIS | 2,550 | 1,908 | 561 | 81 | 1,347 R | 74.8% | 22.0% | 77.3% | 22.7% |
| 62,820 | GARFIELD | 24,828 | 17,989 | 5,718 | 1,121 | 12,271 R | 72.5% | 23.0% | 75.9% | 24.1% |
| 27,856 | GARVIN | 10,860 | 5,520 | 5,033 | 307 | 487 R | 50.8% | 46.3% | 52.3% | 47.7% |
| 39,490 | GRADY | 13,971 | 8,131 | 5,330 | 510 | 2,801 R | 58.2% | 38.2% | 60.4% | 39.6% |
| 6,518 | GRANT | 3,472 | 2,411 | 927 | 134 | 1,484 R | 69.4% | 26.7% | 72.2% | 27.8% |
| 7,028 | GREEN | 3,099 | 1,535 | 1,492 | 72 | 43 R | 49.5% | 48.1% | 50.7% | 49.3% |
| 4,519 | HARMON | 1,670 | 676 | 961 | 33 | 285 D | 40.5% | 57.5% | 41.3% | 58.7% |
| 4,715 | HARPER | 2,230 | 1,652 | 517 | 61 | 1,135 R | 74.1% | 23.2% | 76.2% | 23.8% |
| 11,010 | HASKELL | 5,011 | 2,024 | 2,874 | 113 | 850 D | 40.4% | 57.4% | 41.3% | 58.7% |
| 14,338 | HUGHES | 5,515 | 2,170 | 3,211 | 134 | 1,041 D | 39.3% | 58.2% | 40.3% | 59.7% |
| 30,356 | JACKSON | 8,554 | 4,327 | 4,031 | 196 | 296 R | 50.6% | 47.1% | 51.8% | 48.2% |
| 8,183 | JEFFERSON | 3,332 | 1,440 | 1,812 | 80 | 372 D | 43.2% | 54.4% | 44.3% | 55.7% |
| 10,356 | JOHNSTON | 3,857 | 1,701 | 2,066 | 90 | 365 D | 44.1% | 53.6% | 45.2% | 54.8% |
| 49,852 | KAY | 22,337 | 15,004 | 6,449 | 884 | 8,555 R | 67.2% | 28.9% | 69.9% | 30.1% |
| 14,187 | KINGFISHER | 6,418 | 4,962 | 1,282 | 174 | 3,680 R | 77.3% | 20.0% | 79.5% | 20.5% |
| 12,711 | KIOWA | 5,124 | 2,636 | 2,372 | 116 | 264 R | 51.4% | 46.3% | 52.6% | 47.4% |
| 9,840 | LATIMER | 3,966 | 1,737 | 2,105 | 124 | 368 D | 43.8% | 53.1% | 45.2% | 54.8% |
| 40,698 | LE FLORE | 13,759 | 6,807 | 6,668 | 284 | 139 R | 49.5% | 48.5% | 50.5% | 49.5% |
| 26,601 | LINCOLN | 9,585 | 6,064 | 3,231 | 290 | 2,833 R | 63.3% | 33.7% | 65.2% | 34.8% |
| 26,881 | LOGAN | 9,992 | 6,311 | 3,246 | 435 | 3,065 R | 63.2% | 32.5% | 66.0% | 34.0% |
| 7,469 | LOVE | 3,075 | 1,449 | 1,578 | 48 | 129 D | 47.1% | 51.3% | 47.9% | 52.1% |
| 20,291 | MCCLAIN | 7,533 | 4,284 | 2,990 | 259 | 1,294 R | 56.9% | 39.7% | 58.9% | 41.1% |
| 36,151 | MCCURTAIN | 11,372 | 5,189 | 5,953 | 230 | 764 D | 45.6% | 52.3% | 46.6% | 53.4% |
| 15,562 | MCINTOSH | 6,763 | 2,925 | 3,654 | 184 | 729 D | 43.3% | 54.0% | 44.5% | 55.5% |
| 8,772 | MAJOR | 3,739 | 3,059 | 584 | 96 | 2,475 R | 81.8% | 15.6% | 84.0% | 16.0% |
| 10,550 | MARSHALL | 4,195 | 1,961 | 2,157 | 77 | 196 D | 46.7% | 51.4% | 47.6% | 52.4% |
| 32,261 | MAYES | 12,358 | 6,633 | 5,344 | 381 | 1,289 R | 53.7% | 43.2% | 55.4% | 44.6% |
| 12,147 | MURRAY | 5,067 | 2,494 | 2,384 | 189 | 110 R | 49.2% | 47.0% | 51.1% | 48.9% |
| 66,939 | MUSKOGEE | 25,715 | 11,511 | 13,341 | 863 | 1,830 D | 44.8% | 51.9% | 46.3% | 53.7% |
| 11,573 | NOBLE | 5,240 | 3,663 | 1,398 | 179 | 2,265 R | 69.9% | 26.7% | 72.4% | 27.6% |
| 11,486 | NOWATA | 4,470 | 2,640 | 1,694 | 136 | 946 R | 59.1% | 37.9% | 60.9% | 39.1% |
| 11,125 | OKFUSKEE | 4,401 | 2,126 | 2,177 | 98 | 51 D | 48.3% | 49.5% | 49.4% | 50.6% |
| 568,933 | OKLAHOMA | 211,273 | 139,538 | 58,765 | 12,970 | 80,773 R | 66.0% | 27.8% | 70.4% | 29.6% |
| 39,169 | OKMULGEE | 14,285 | 6,652 | 7,236 | 397 | 584 D | 46.6% | 50.7% | 47.9% | 52.1% |
| 39,327 | OSAGE | 14,246 | 8,044 | 5,687 | 515 | 2,357 R | 56.5% | 39.9% | 58.6% | 41.4% |
| 32,870 | OTTAWA | 12,919 | 6,362 | 6,143 | 414 | 219 R | 49.2% | 47.6% | 50.9% | 49.1% |
| 15,310 | PAWNEE | 6,151 | 3,902 | 2,020 | 229 | 1,882 R | 63.4% | 32.8% | 65.9% | 34.1% |
| 62,435 | PAYNE | 25,691 | 15,955 | 7,466 | 2,270 | 8,489 R | 62.1% | 29.1% | 68.1% | 31.9% |

# OKLAHOMA

## PRESIDENT 1980

| 1980 Census Population | County | Total Vote | Republican | Democratic | Other | Rep.-Dem. Plurality | Percentage | | | |
|---|---|---|---|---|---|---|---|---|---|---|
| | | | | | | | Total Vote | | Major Vote | |
| | | | | | | | Rep. | Dem. | Rep. | Dem. |
| 40,524 | PITTSBURG | 15,857 | 7,062 | 8,292 | 503 | 1,230 D | 44.5% | 52.3% | 46.0% | 54.0% |
| 32,598 | PONTOTOC | 12,631 | 6,232 | 5,942 | 457 | 290 R | 49.3% | 47.0% | 51.2% | 48.8% |
| 55,239 | POTTAWATOMIE | 21,850 | 12,466 | 8,526 | 858 | 3,940 R | 57.1% | 39.0% | 59.4% | 40.6% |
| 11,773 | PUSHMATAHA | 4,775 | 1,989 | 2,666 | 120 | 677 D | 41.7% | 55.8% | 42.7% | 57.3% |
| 4,799 | ROGER MILLS | 2,171 | 1,221 | 877 | 73 | 344 R | 56.2% | 40.4% | 58.2% | 41.8% |
| 46,436 | ROGERS | 18,642 | 11,581 | 6,399 | 662 | 5,182 R | 62.1% | 34.3% | 64.4% | 35.6% |
| 27,473 | SEMINOLE | 10,145 | 5,067 | 4,726 | 352 | 341 R | 49.9% | 46.6% | 51.7% | 48.3% |
| 30,749 | SEQUOYAH | 11,246 | 5,987 | 4,983 | 276 | 1,004 R | 53.2% | 44.3% | 54.6% | 45.4% |
| 43,419 | STEPHENS | 17,852 | 10,199 | 7,191 | 462 | 3,008 R | 57.1% | 40.3% | 58.6% | 41.4% |
| 17,727 | TEXAS | 7,099 | 5,503 | 1,451 | 145 | 4,052 R | 77.5% | 20.4% | 79.1% | 20.9% |
| 12,398 | TILLMAN | 4,687 | 2,450 | 2,144 | 93 | 306 R | 52.3% | 45.7% | 53.3% | 46.7% |
| 470,593 | TULSA | 188,148 | 124,643 | 53,438 | 10,067 | 71,205 R | 66.2% | 28.4% | 70.0% | 30.0% |
| 41,801 | WAGONER | 14,727 | 8,969 | 5,235 | 523 | 3,734 R | 60.9% | 35.5% | 63.1% | 36.9% |
| 48,113 | WASHINGTON | 23,503 | 16,563 | 5,854 | 1,086 | 10,709 R | 70.5% | 24.9% | 73.9% | 26.1% |
| 13,798 | WASHITA | 5,373 | 3,206 | 2,044 | 123 | 1,162 R | 59.7% | 38.0% | 61.1% | 38.9% |
| 10,923 | WOODS | 5,208 | 3,592 | 1,364 | 252 | 2,228 R | 69.0% | 26.2% | 72.5% | 27.5% |
| 21,172 | WOODWARD | 7,289 | 5,318 | 1,703 | 268 | 3,615 R | 73.0% | 23.4% | 75.7% | 24.3% |
| 3,025,290 | TOTAL | 1,149,708 | 695,570 | 402,026 | 52,112 | 293,544 R | 60.5% | 35.0% | 63.4% | 36.6% |

# OKLAHOMA

## PRESIDENT 1976

| 1970 Census Population | County | Total Vote | Republican | Democratic | Other | Rep.-Dem. Plurality | Percentage Total Vote Rep. | Total Vote Dem. | Major Vote Rep. | Major Vote Dem. |
|---|---|---|---|---|---|---|---|---|---|---|
| 15,141 | ADAIR | 6,259 | 3,013 | 3,183 | 63 | 170 D | 48.1% | 50.9% | 48.6% | 51.4% |
| 7,224 | ALFALFA | 3,897 | 2,113 | 1,725 | 59 | 388 R | 54.2% | 44.3% | 55.1% | 44.9% |
| 10,972 | ATOKA | 4,402 | 1,098 | 3,276 | 28 | 2,178 D | 24.9% | 74.4% | 25.1% | 74.9% |
| 6,282 | BEAVER | 3,061 | 1,801 | 1,213 | 47 | 588 R | 58.8% | 39.6% | 59.8% | 40.2% |
| 15,754 | BECKHAM | 6,935 | 2,351 | 4,530 | 54 | 2,179 D | 33.9% | 65.3% | 34.2% | 65.8% |
| 11,794 | BLAINE | 5,056 | 2,682 | 2,297 | 77 | 385 R | 53.0% | 45.4% | 53.9% | 46.1% |
| 25,552 | BRYAN | 10,293 | 2,848 | 7,410 | 35 | 4,562 D | 27.7% | 72.0% | 27.8% | 72.2% |
| 28,931 | CADDO | 11,327 | 3,854 | 7,382 | 91 | 3,528 D | 34.0% | 65.2% | 34.3% | 65.7% |
| 32,245 | CANADIAN | 17,339 | 9,766 | 7,288 | 285 | 2,478 R | 56.3% | 42.0% | 57.3% | 42.7% |
| 37,349 | CARTER | 15,070 | 6,668 | 8,319 | 83 | 1,651 D | 44.2% | 55.2% | 44.5% | 55.5% |
| 23,174 | CHEROKEE | 10,564 | 4,443 | 6,006 | 115 | 1,563 D | 42.1% | 56.9% | 42.5% | 57.5% |
| 15,141 | CHOCTAW | 6,140 | 1,821 | 4,269 | 50 | 2,448 D | 29.7% | 69.5% | 29.9% | 70.1% |
| 4,145 | CIMARRON | 1,879 | 872 | 962 | 45 | 90 D | 46.4% | 51.2% | 47.5% | 52.5% |
| 81,839 | CLEVELAND | 43,281 | 22,098 | 20,054 | 1,129 | 2,044 R | 51.1% | 46.3% | 52.4% | 47.6% |
| 5,525 | COAL | 2,566 | 769 | 1,774 | 23 | 1,005 D | 30.0% | 69.1% | 30.2% | 69.8% |
| 108,144 | COMANCHE | 26,303 | 13,163 | 12,910 | 230 | 253 R | 50.0% | 49.1% | 50.5% | 49.5% |
| 6,832 | COTTON | 3,064 | 1,127 | 1,911 | 26 | 784 D | 36.8% | 62.4% | 37.1% | 62.9% |
| 14,722 | CRAIG | 6,178 | 2,540 | 3,577 | 61 | 1,037 D | 41.1% | 57.9% | 41.5% | 58.5% |
| 45,532 | CREEK | 17,591 | 8,458 | 8,964 | 169 | 506 D | 48.1% | 51.0% | 48.5% | 51.5% |
| 22,665 | CUSTER | 9,546 | 4,847 | 4,597 | 102 | 250 R | 50.8% | 48.2% | 51.3% | 48.7% |
| 17,767 | DELAWARE | 8,657 | 3,642 | 4,924 | 91 | 1,282 D | 42.1% | 56.9% | 42.5% | 57.5% |
| 5,656 | DEWEY | 2,825 | 1,230 | 1,540 | 55 | 310 D | 43.5% | 54.5% | 44.4% | 55.6% |
| 5,129 | ELLIS | 2,746 | 1,429 | 1,256 | 61 | 173 R | 52.0% | 45.7% | 53.2% | 46.8% |
| 56,343 | GARFIELD | 23,474 | 14,202 | 8,969 | 303 | 5,233 R | 60.5% | 38.2% | 61.3% | 38.7% |
| 24,874 | GARVIN | 10,785 | 3,905 | 6,797 | 83 | 2,892 D | 36.2% | 63.0% | 36.5% | 63.5% |
| 29,354 | GRADY | 11,955 | 4,686 | 7,155 | 114 | 2,469 D | 39.2% | 59.8% | 39.6% | 60.4% |
| 7,117 | GRANT | 3,588 | 1,685 | 1,853 | 50 | 168 D | 47.0% | 51.6% | 47.6% | 52.4% |
| 7,979 | GREEN | 3,308 | 1,164 | 2,113 | 31 | 949 D | 35.2% | 63.9% | 35.5% | 64.5% |
| 5,136 | HARMON | 2,045 | 666 | 1,371 | 8 | 705 D | 32.6% | 67.0% | 32.7% | 67.3% |
| 5,151 | HARPER | 2,320 | 1,303 | 978 | 39 | 325 R | 56.2% | 42.2% | 57.1% | 42.9% |
| 9,578 | HASKELL | 4,818 | 1,401 | 3,388 | 29 | 1,987 D | 29.1% | 70.3% | 29.3% | 70.7% |
| 13,228 | HUGHES | 5,956 | 1,715 | 4,185 | 56 | 2,470 D | 28.8% | 70.3% | 29.1% | 70.9% |
| 30,902 | JACKSON | 8,163 | 3,189 | 4,914 | 60 | 1,725 D | 39.1% | 60.2% | 39.4% | 60.6% |
| 7,125 | JEFFERSON | 3,285 | 956 | 2,303 | 26 | 1,347 D | 29.1% | 70.1% | 29.3% | 70.7% |
| 7,870 | JOHNSTON | 3,934 | 1,127 | 2,765 | 42 | 1,638 D | 28.6% | 70.3% | 29.0% | 71.0% |
| 48,791 | KAY | 22,086 | 12,441 | 9,371 | 274 | 3,070 R | 56.3% | 42.4% | 57.0% | 43.0% |
| 12,857 | KINGFISHER | 5,897 | 3,443 | 2,372 | 82 | 1,071 R | 58.4% | 40.2% | 59.2% | 40.8% |
| 12,532 | KIOWA | 5,420 | 1,971 | 3,403 | 46 | 1,432 D | 36.4% | 62.8% | 36.7% | 63.3% |
| 8,601 | LATIMER | 4,028 | 1,312 | 2,661 | 55 | 1,349 D | 32.6% | 66.1% | 33.0% | 67.0% |
| 32,137 | LE FLORE | 13,085 | 4,907 | 8,033 | 145 | 3,126 D | 37.5% | 61.4% | 37.9% | 62.1% |
| 19,482 | LINCOLN | 9,550 | 4,429 | 4,988 | 133 | 559 D | 46.4% | 52.2% | 47.0% | 53.0% |
| 19,645 | LOGAN | 9,136 | 4,382 | 4,594 | 160 | 212 D | 48.0% | 50.3% | 48.8% | 51.2% |
| 5,637 | LOVE | 2,778 | 846 | 1,923 | 9 | 1,077 D | 30.5% | 69.2% | 30.6% | 69.4% |
| 14,157 | MCCLAIN | 6,572 | 2,444 | 4,048 | 80 | 1,604 D | 37.2% | 61.6% | 37.6% | 62.4% |
| 28,642 | MCCURTAIN | 11,080 | 3,423 | 7,560 | 97 | 4,137 D | 30.9% | 68.2% | 31.2% | 68.8% |
| 12,472 | MCINTOSH | 6,015 | 1,822 | 4,145 | 48 | 2,323 D | 30.3% | 68.9% | 30.5% | 69.5% |
| 7,529 | MAJOR | 3,697 | 2,282 | 1,357 | 58 | 925 R | 61.7% | 36.7% | 62.7% | 37.3% |
| 7,682 | MARSHALL | 4,324 | 1,358 | 2,939 | 27 | 1,581 D | 31.4% | 68.0% | 31.6% | 68.4% |
| 23,302 | MAYES | 11,419 | 5,040 | 6,298 | 81 | 1,258 D | 44.1% | 55.2% | 44.5% | 55.5% |
| 10,669 | MURRAY | 4,536 | 1,563 | 2,932 | 41 | 1,369 D | 34.5% | 64.6% | 34.8% | 65.2% |
| 59,542 | MUSKOGEE | 25,155 | 10,287 | 14,678 | 190 | 4,391 D | 40.9% | 58.4% | 41.2% | 58.8% |
| 10,043 | NOBLE | 4,965 | 2,634 | 2,278 | 53 | 356 R | 53.1% | 45.9% | 53.6% | 46.4% |
| 9,773 | NOWATA | 4,311 | 2,077 | 2,195 | 39 | 118 D | 48.2% | 50.9% | 48.6% | 51.4% |
| 10,683 | OKFUSKEE | 4,325 | 1,630 | 2,663 | 32 | 1,033 D | 37.7% | 61.6% | 38.0% | 62.0% |
| 526,805 | OKLAHOMA | 210,113 | 119,120 | 87,185 | 3,808 | 31,935 R | 56.7% | 41.5% | 57.7% | 42.3% |
| 35,358 | OKMULGEE | 13,963 | 5,333 | 8,499 | 131 | 3,166 D | 38.2% | 60.9% | 38.6% | 61.4% |
| 29,750 | OSAGE | 13,348 | 6,398 | 6,832 | 118 | 434 D | 47.9% | 51.2% | 48.4% | 51.6% |
| 29,800 | OTTAWA | 12,515 | 4,985 | 7,446 | 84 | 2,461 D | 39.8% | 59.5% | 40.1% | 59.9% |
| 11,338 | PAWNEE | 6,201 | 3,111 | 3,031 | 59 | 80 R | 50.2% | 48.9% | 50.7% | 49.3% |
| 50,654 | PAYNE | 23,888 | 13,481 | 9,987 | 420 | 3,494 R | 56.4% | 41.8% | 57.4% | 42.6% |

# OKLAHOMA

## PRESIDENT 1976

| 1970 Census Population | County | Total Vote | Republican | Democratic | Other | Rep.-Dem. Plurality | Percentage | | | |
|---:|---|---:|---:|---:|---:|---:|---|---|---|---|
| | | | | | | | Total Vote | | Major Vote | |
| | | | | | | | Rep. | Dem. | Rep. | Dem. |
| 37,521 | PITTSBURG | 15,692 | 4,807 | 10,743 | 142 | 5,936 D | 30.6% | 68.5% | 30.9% | 69.1% |
| 27,867 | PONTOTOC | 12,486 | 4,895 | 7,466 | 125 | 2,571 D | 39.2% | 59.8% | 39.6% | 60.4% |
| 43,134 | POTTAWATOMIE | 20,571 | 9,090 | 11,255 | 226 | 2,165 D | 44.2% | 54.7% | 44.7% | 55.3% |
| 9,385 | PUSHMATAHA | 4,376 | 1,360 | 2,987 | 29 | 1,627 D | 31.1% | 68.3% | 31.3% | 68.7% |
| 4,452 | ROGER MILLS | 2,243 | 873 | 1,346 | 24 | 473 D | 38.9% | 60.0% | 39.3% | 60.7% |
| 28,425 | ROGERS | 14,815 | 7,318 | 7,368 | 129 | 50 D | 49.4% | 49.7% | 49.8% | 50.2% |
| 25,144 | SEMINOLE | 10,202 | 4,237 | 5,874 | 91 | 1,637 D | 41.5% | 57.6% | 41.9% | 58.1% |
| 23,370 | SEQUOYAH | 9,884 | 3,938 | 5,873 | 73 | 1,935 D | 39.8% | 59.4% | 40.1% | 59.9% |
| 35,902 | STEPHENS | 17,020 | 7,099 | 9,795 | 126 | 2,696 D | 41.7% | 57.5% | 42.0% | 58.0% |
| 16,352 | TEXAS | 6,580 | 3,919 | 2,591 | 70 | 1,328 R | 59.6% | 39.4% | 60.2% | 39.8% |
| 12,901 | TILLMAN | 4,695 | 1,802 | 2,852 | 41 | 1,050 D | 38.4% | 60.7% | 38.7% | 61.3% |
| 400,709 | TULSA | 176,300 | 108,653 | 65,298 | 2,349 | 43,355 R | 61.6% | 37.0% | 62.5% | 37.5% |
| 22,163 | WAGONER | 11,057 | 5,071 | 5,879 | 107 | 808 D | 45.9% | 53.2% | 46.3% | 53.7% |
| 42,277 | WASHINGTON | 21,670 | 14,560 | 6,898 | 212 | 7,662 R | 67.2% | 31.8% | 67.9% | 32.1% |
| 12,141 | WASHITA | 5,531 | 2,165 | 3,304 | 62 | 1,139 D | 39.1% | 59.7% | 39.6% | 60.4% |
| 11,920 | WOODS | 5,421 | 2,788 | 2,530 | 103 | 258 R | 51.4% | 46.7% | 52.4% | 47.6% |
| 15,537 | WOODWARD | 6,691 | 3,782 | 2,807 | 102 | 975 R | 56.5% | 42.0% | 57.4% | 42.6% |
| 2,559,253 | TOTAL | 1,092,251 | 545,708 | 532,442 | 14,101 | 13,266 R | 50.0% | 48.7% | 50.6% | 49.4% |

# OKLAHOMA

## PRESIDENT 1972

| 1970 Census Population | County | Total Vote | Republican | Democratic | Other | Rep.-Dem. Plurality | Percentage Total Vote Rep. | Dem. | Major Vote Rep. | Dem. |
|---|---|---|---|---|---|---|---|---|---|---|
| 15,141 | ADAIR | 6,455 | 4,720 | 1,601 | 134 | 3,119 R | 73.1% | 24.8% | 74.7% | 25.3% |
| 7,224 | ALFALFA | 3,937 | 3,208 | 641 | 88 | 2,567 R | 81.5% | 16.3% | 83.3% | 16.7% |
| 10,972 | ATOKA | 3,987 | 2,905 | 993 | 89 | 1,912 R | 72.9% | 24.9% | 74.5% | 25.5% |
| 6,282 | BEAVER | 3,186 | 2,562 | 522 | 102 | 2,040 R | 80.4% | 16.4% | 83.1% | 16.9% |
| 15,754 | BECKHAM | 6,235 | 4,472 | 1,608 | 155 | 2,864 R | 71.7% | 25.8% | 73.6% | 26.4% |
| 11,794 | BLAINE | 5,092 | 3,958 | 963 | 171 | 2,995 R | 77.7% | 18.9% | 80.4% | 19.6% |
| 25,552 | BRYAN | 8,718 | 5,397 | 3,144 | 177 | 2,253 R | 61.9% | 36.1% | 63.2% | 36.8% |
| 28,931 | CADDO | 10,912 | 7,683 | 2,921 | 308 | 4,762 R | 70.4% | 26.8% | 72.5% | 27.5% |
| 32,245 | CANADIAN | 14,564 | 11,400 | 2,751 | 413 | 8,649 R | 78.3% | 18.9% | 80.6% | 19.4% |
| 37,349 | CARTER | 14,106 | 9,368 | 4,577 | 161 | 4,791 R | 66.4% | 32.4% | 67.2% | 32.8% |
| 23,174 | CHEROKEE | 10,206 | 7,080 | 2,899 | 227 | 4,181 R | 69.4% | 28.4% | 70.9% | 29.1% |
| 15,141 | CHOCTAW | 5,278 | 3,399 | 1,798 | 81 | 1,601 R | 64.4% | 34.1% | 65.4% | 34.6% |
| 4,145 | CIMARRON | 1,885 | 1,350 | 323 | 212 | 1,027 R | 71.6% | 17.1% | 80.7% | 19.3% |
| 81,839 | CLEVELAND | 37,518 | 25,777 | 11,126 | 615 | 14,651 R | 68.7% | 29.7% | 69.9% | 30.1% |
| 5,525 | COAL | 2,179 | 1,461 | 680 | 38 | 781 R | 67.0% | 31.2% | 68.2% | 31.8% |
| 108,144 | COMANCHE | 24,745 | 19,759 | 4,559 | 427 | 15,200 R | 79.9% | 18.4% | 81.3% | 18.7% |
| 6,832 | COTTON | 2,919 | 2,050 | 798 | 71 | 1,252 R | 70.2% | 27.3% | 72.0% | 28.0% |
| 14,722 | CRAIG | 5,917 | 4,163 | 1,642 | 112 | 2,521 R | 70.4% | 27.8% | 71.7% | 28.3% |
| 45,532 | CREEK | 16,503 | 12,396 | 3,705 | 402 | 8,691 R | 75.1% | 22.5% | 77.0% | 23.0% |
| 22,665 | CUSTER | 9,780 | 7,267 | 2,298 | 215 | 4,969 R | 74.3% | 23.5% | 76.0% | 24.0% |
| 17,767 | DELAWARE | 7,789 | 5,476 | 2,135 | 178 | 3,341 R | 70.3% | 27.4% | 71.9% | 28.1% |
| 5,656 | DEWEY | 2,816 | 2,106 | 626 | 84 | 1,480 R | 74.8% | 22.2% | 77.1% | 22.9% |
| 5,129 | ELLIS | 2,648 | 2,059 | 473 | 116 | 1,586 R | 77.8% | 17.9% | 81.3% | 18.7% |
| 56,343 | GARFIELD | 24,469 | 19,348 | 4,557 | 564 | 14,791 R | 79.1% | 18.6% | 80.9% | 19.1% |
| 24,874 | GARVIN | 10,245 | 7,245 | 2,685 | 315 | 4,560 R | 70.7% | 26.2% | 73.0% | 27.0% |
| 29,354 | GRADY | 11,499 | 7,762 | 3,440 | 297 | 4,322 R | 67.5% | 29.9% | 69.3% | 30.7% |
| 7,117 | GRANT | 3,755 | 2,829 | 805 | 121 | 2,024 R | 75.3% | 21.4% | 77.8% | 22.2% |
| 7,979 | GREEN | 3,244 | 2,154 | 1,004 | 86 | 1,150 R | 66.4% | 30.9% | 68.2% | 31.8% |
| 5,136 | HARMON | 1,929 | 1,319 | 568 | 42 | 751 R | 68.4% | 29.4% | 69.9% | 30.1% |
| 5,151 | HARPER | 2,475 | 1,976 | 385 | 114 | 1,591 R | 79.8% | 15.6% | 83.7% | 16.3% |
| 9,578 | HASKELL | 4,460 | 2,815 | 1,408 | 237 | 1,407 R | 63.1% | 31.6% | 66.7% | 33.3% |
| 13,228 | HUGHES | 5,392 | 3,497 | 1,787 | 108 | 1,710 R | 64.9% | 33.1% | 66.2% | 33.8% |
| 30,902 | JACKSON | 7,707 | 5,519 | 2,054 | 134 | 3,465 R | 71.6% | 26.7% | 72.9% | 27.1% |
| 7,125 | JEFFERSON | 2,751 | 1,709 | 969 | 73 | 740 R | 62.1% | 35.2% | 63.8% | 36.2% |
| 7,870 | JOHNSTON | 3,256 | 2,205 | 983 | 68 | 1,222 R | 67.7% | 30.2% | 69.2% | 30.8% |
| 48,791 | KAY | 21,984 | 17,244 | 4,246 | 494 | 12,998 R | 78.4% | 19.3% | 80.2% | 19.8% |
| 12,857 | KINGFISHER | 5,935 | 4,861 | 912 | 162 | 3,949 R | 81.9% | 15.4% | 84.2% | 15.8% |
| 12,532 | KIOWA | 5,316 | 3,711 | 1,495 | 110 | 2,216 R | 69.8% | 28.1% | 71.3% | 28.7% |
| 8,601 | LATIMER | 3,889 | 2,520 | 1,239 | 130 | 1,281 R | 64.8% | 31.9% | 67.0% | 33.0% |
| 32,137 | LE FLORE | 11,759 | 7,932 | 3,433 | 394 | 4,499 R | 67.5% | 29.2% | 69.8% | 30.2% |
| 19,482 | LINCOLN | 8,685 | 6,512 | 1,919 | 254 | 4,593 R | 75.0% | 22.1% | 77.2% | 22.8% |
| 19,645 | LOGAN | 9,503 | 6,543 | 2,760 | 200 | 3,783 R | 68.9% | 29.0% | 70.3% | 29.7% |
| 5,637 | LOVE | 2,108 | 1,407 | 671 | 30 | 736 R | 66.7% | 31.8% | 67.7% | 32.3% |
| 14,157 | MCCLAIN | 5,797 | 4,241 | 1,350 | 206 | 2,891 R | 73.2% | 23.3% | 75.9% | 24.1% |
| 28,642 | MCCURTAIN | 9,175 | 6,441 | 2,568 | 166 | 3,873 R | 70.2% | 28.0% | 71.5% | 28.5% |
| 12,472 | MCINTOSH | 5,034 | 3,216 | 1,686 | 132 | 1,530 R | 63.9% | 33.5% | 65.6% | 34.4% |
| 7,529 | MAJOR | 3,818 | 3,203 | 512 | 103 | 2,691 R | 83.9% | 13.4% | 86.2% | 13.8% |
| 7,682 | MARSHALL | 3,477 | 2,273 | 1,113 | 91 | 1,160 R | 65.4% | 32.0% | 67.1% | 32.9% |
| 23,302 | MAYES | 10,454 | 7,535 | 2,656 | 263 | 4,879 R | 72.1% | 25.4% | 73.9% | 26.1% |
| 10,669 | MURRAY | 4,372 | 2,983 | 1,294 | 95 | 1,689 R | 68.2% | 29.6% | 69.7% | 30.3% |
| 59,542 | MUSKOGEE | 23,092 | 15,161 | 7,380 | 551 | 7,781 R | 65.7% | 32.0% | 67.3% | 32.7% |
| 10,043 | NOBLE | 5,212 | 4,085 | 999 | 128 | 3,086 R | 78.4% | 19.2% | 80.4% | 19.6% |
| 9,773 | NOWATA | 4,535 | 3,293 | 1,096 | 146 | 2,197 R | 72.6% | 24.2% | 75.0% | 25.0% |
| 10,683 | OKFUSKEE | 4,289 | 2,862 | 1,328 | 99 | 1,534 R | 66.7% | 31.0% | 68.3% | 31.7% |
| 526,805 | OKLAHOMA | 207,925 | 156,437 | 46,986 | 4,502 | 109,451 R | 75.2% | 22.6% | 76.9% | 23.1% |
| 35,358 | OKMULGEE | 13,642 | 8,706 | 4,494 | 442 | 4,212 R | 63.8% | 32.9% | 66.0% | 34.0% |
| 29,750 | OSAGE | 12,591 | 9,288 | 2,968 | 335 | 6,320 R | 73.8% | 23.6% | 75.8% | 24.2% |
| 29,800 | OTTAWA | 12,163 | 8,348 | 3,657 | 158 | 4,691 R | 68.6% | 30.1% | 69.5% | 30.5% |
| 11,338 | PAWNEE | 5,537 | 4,280 | 1,135 | 122 | 3,145 R | 77.3% | 20.5% | 79.0% | 21.0% |
| 50,654 | PAYNE | 23,070 | 17,019 | 5,644 | 407 | 11,375 R | 73.8% | 24.5% | 75.1% | 24.9% |

# OKLAHOMA

## PRESIDENT 1972

| 1970 Census Population | County | Total Vote | Republican | Democratic | Other | Rep.-Dem. Plurality | Percentage Total Vote Rep. | Dem. | Major Vote Rep. | Dem. |
|---|---|---|---|---|---|---|---|---|---|---|
| 37,521 | PITTSBURG | 15,040 | 9,989 | 4,748 | 303 | 5,241 R | 66.4% | 31.6% | 67.8% | 32.2% |
| 27,867 | PONTOTOC | 12,162 | 8,762 | 3,160 | 240 | 5,602 R | 72.0% | 26.0% | 73.5% | 26.5% |
| 43,134 | POTTAWATOMIE | 18,664 | 13,308 | 4,822 | 534 | 8,486 R | 71.3% | 25.8% | 73.4% | 26.6% |
| 9,385 | PUSHMATAHA | 3,599 | 2,456 | 1,016 | 127 | 1,440 R | 68.2% | 28.2% | 70.7% | 29.3% |
| 4,452 | ROGER MILLS | 2,170 | 1,696 | 420 | 54 | 1,276 R | 78.2% | 19.4% | 80.2% | 19.8% |
| 28,425 | ROGERS | 12,728 | 9,697 | 2,607 | 424 | 7,090 R | 76.2% | 20.5% | 78.8% | 21.2% |
| 25,144 | SEMINOLE | 9,824 | 6,879 | 2,746 | 199 | 4,133 R | 70.0% | 28.0% | 71.5% | 28.5% |
| 23,370 | SEQUOYAH | 9,551 | 6,842 | 2,519 | 190 | 4,323 R | 71.6% | 26.4% | 73.1% | 26.9% |
| 35,902 | STEPHENS | 14,396 | 10,309 | 3,623 | 464 | 6,686 R | 71.6% | 25.2% | 74.0% | 26.0% |
| 16,352 | TEXAS | 6,937 | 5,726 | 924 | 287 | 4,802 R | 82.5% | 13.3% | 86.1% | 13.9% |
| 12,901 | TILLMAN | 4,697 | 3,331 | 1,256 | 110 | 2,075 R | 70.9% | 26.7% | 72.6% | 27.4% |
| 400,709 | TULSA | 161,126 | 125,278 | 32,779 | 3,069 | 92,499 R | 77.8% | 20.3% | 79.3% | 20.7% |
| 22,163 | WAGONER | 9,107 | 6,569 | 2,257 | 281 | 4,312 R | 72.1% | 24.8% | 74.4% | 25.6% |
| 42,277 | WASHINGTON | 20,500 | 16,347 | 3,658 | 495 | 12,689 R | 79.7% | 17.8% | 81.7% | 18.3% |
| 12,141 | WASHITA | 5,008 | 3,578 | 1,305 | 125 | 2,273 R | 71.4% | 26.1% | 73.3% | 26.7% |
| 11,920 | WOODS | 5,789 | 4,413 | 1,234 | 142 | 3,179 R | 76.2% | 21.3% | 78.1% | 21.9% |
| 15,537 | WOODWARD | 6,683 | 5,350 | 1,104 | 229 | 4,246 R | 80.1% | 16.5% | 82.9% | 17.1% |
| 2,559,253 | TOTAL | 1,029,900 | 759,025 | 247,147 | 23,728 | 511,878 R | 73.7% | 24.0% | 75.4% | 24.6% |

# OKLAHOMA

## PRESIDENT 1968

| 1960 Census Population | County | Total Vote | Republican | Democratic | AIP | Other | Plurality | Percentage Total Vote Rep. | Dem. | AIP |
|---|---|---|---|---|---|---|---|---|---|---|
| 13,112 | ADAIR | 5,426 | 2,877 | 1,549 | 1,000 | | 1,328 R | 53.0% | 28.5% | 18.4% |
| 8,445 | ALFALFA | 3,847 | 2,672 | 865 | 310 | | 1,807 R | 69.5% | 22.5% | 8.1% |
| 10,352 | ATOKA | 4,144 | 1,131 | 1,400 | 1,613 | | 213 A | 27.3% | 33.8% | 38.9% |
| 6,965 | BEAVER | 3,077 | 2,114 | 624 | 339 | | 1,490 R | 68.7% | 20.3% | 11.0% |
| 17,782 | BECKHAM | 6,839 | 2,935 | 2,354 | 1,550 | | 581 R | 42.9% | 34.4% | 22.7% |
| 12,077 | BLAINE | 5,053 | 3,036 | 1,285 | 732 | | 1,751 R | 60.1% | 25.4% | 14.5% |
| 24,252 | BRYAN | 8,205 | 2,727 | 3,214 | 2,264 | | 487 D | 33.2% | 39.2% | 27.6% |
| 28,621 | CADDO | 10,782 | 4,712 | 4,212 | 1,858 | | 500 R | 43.7% | 39.1% | 17.2% |
| 24,727 | CANADIAN | 11,993 | 5,891 | 3,577 | 2,525 | | 2,314 R | 49.1% | 29.8% | 21.1% |
| 39,044 | CARTER | 14,348 | 5,127 | 5,807 | 3,414 | | 680 D | 35.7% | 40.5% | 23.8% |
| 17,762 | CHEROKEE | 8,391 | 3,971 | 2,554 | 1,866 | | 1,417 R | 47.3% | 30.4% | 22.2% |
| 15,637 | CHOCTAW | 5,433 | 1,414 | 2,268 | 1,751 | | 517 D | 26.0% | 41.7% | 32.2% |
| 4,496 | CIMARRON | 2,085 | 1,122 | 436 | 527 | | 595 R | 53.8% | 20.9% | 25.3% |
| 47,600 | CLEVELAND | 25,774 | 12,446 | 8,617 | 4,711 | | 3,829 R | 48.3% | 33.4% | 18.3% |
| 5,546 | COAL | 2,257 | 669 | 963 | 625 | | 294 D | 29.6% | 42.7% | 27.7% |
| 90,803 | COMANCHE | 23,165 | 9,225 | 8,061 | 5,879 | | 1,164 R | 39.8% | 34.8% | 25.4% |
| 8,031 | COTTON | 3,113 | 1,016 | 1,192 | 905 | | 176 D | 32.6% | 38.3% | 29.1% |
| 16,303 | CRAIG | 6,013 | 2,686 | 2,098 | 1,229 | | 588 R | 44.7% | 34.9% | 20.4% |
| 40,495 | CREEK | 15,998 | 6,934 | 5,151 | 3,913 | | 1,783 R | 43.3% | 32.2% | 24.5% |
| 21,040 | CUSTER | 8,362 | 4,709 | 2,717 | 936 | | 1,992 R | 56.3% | 32.5% | 11.2% |
| 13,198 | DELAWARE | 6,699 | 3,168 | 2,129 | 1,402 | | 1,039 R | 47.3% | 31.8% | 20.9% |
| 6,051 | DEWEY | 2,821 | 1,508 | 773 | 540 | | 735 R | 53.5% | 27.4% | 19.1% |
| 5,457 | ELLIS | 2,560 | 1,601 | 533 | 426 | | 1,068 R | 62.5% | 20.8% | 16.6% |
| 52,975 | GARFIELD | 23,183 | 14,370 | 5,802 | 3,011 | | 8,568 R | 62.0% | 25.0% | 13.0% |
| 28,290 | GARVIN | 10,301 | 3,786 | 3,845 | 2,670 | | 59 D | 36.8% | 37.3% | 25.9% |
| 29,590 | GRADY | 11,119 | 4,242 | 4,760 | 2,117 | | 518 D | 38.2% | 42.8% | 19.0% |
| 8,140 | GRANT | 3,887 | 2,403 | 1,047 | 437 | | 1,356 R | 61.8% | 26.9% | 11.2% |
| 8,877 | GREEN | 3,474 | 1,225 | 1,419 | 830 | | 194 D | 35.3% | 40.8% | 23.9% |
| 5,852 | HARMON | 2,144 | 644 | 1,097 | 403 | | 453 D | 30.0% | 51.2% | 18.8% |
| 5,956 | HARPER | 2,354 | 1,483 | 518 | 353 | | 965 R | 63.0% | 22.0% | 15.0% |
| 9,121 | HASKELL | 4,092 | 1,516 | 1,563 | 1,013 | | 47 D | 37.0% | 38.2% | 24.8% |
| 15,144 | HUGHES | 5,645 | 1,897 | 2,578 | 1,170 | | 681 D | 33.6% | 45.7% | 20.7% |
| 29,736 | JACKSON | 7,405 | 2,248 | 3,371 | 1,786 | | 1,123 D | 30.4% | 45.5% | 24.1% |
| 8,192 | JEFFERSON | 3,109 | 780 | 1,628 | 701 | | 848 D | 25.1% | 52.4% | 22.5% |
| 8,517 | JOHNSTON | 3,238 | 1,048 | 1,216 | 974 | | 168 D | 32.4% | 37.6% | 30.1% |
| 51,042 | KAY | 21,591 | 12,751 | 6,031 | 2,809 | | 6,720 R | 59.1% | 27.9% | 13.0% |
| 10,635 | KINGFISHER | 5,504 | 3,558 | 1,226 | 720 | | 2,332 R | 64.6% | 22.3% | 13.1% |
| 14,825 | KIOWA | 5,594 | 2,418 | 2,219 | 957 | | 199 R | 43.2% | 39.7% | 17.1% |
| 7,738 | LATIMER | 3,333 | 1,091 | 1,350 | 892 | | 259 D | 32.7% | 40.5% | 26.8% |
| 29,106 | LE FLORE | 10,965 | 3,600 | 4,020 | 3,345 | | 420 D | 32.8% | 36.7% | 30.5% |
| 18,783 | LINCOLN | 8,128 | 3,855 | 2,304 | 1,969 | | 1,551 R | 47.4% | 28.3% | 24.2% |
| 18,662 | LOGAN | 8,157 | 3,960 | 2,508 | 1,689 | | 1,452 R | 48.5% | 30.7% | 20.7% |
| 5,862 | LOVE | 2,374 | 677 | 931 | 766 | | 165 D | 28.5% | 39.2% | 32.3% |
| 12,740 | MCCLAIN | 5,536 | 2,047 | 1,842 | 1,647 | | 205 D | 37.0% | 33.3% | 29.8% |
| 25,851 | MCCURTAIN | 8,619 | 2,795 | 2,944 | 2,880 | | 64 D | 32.4% | 34.2% | 33.4% |
| 12,371 | MCINTOSH | 4,545 | 1,532 | 1,759 | 1,254 | | 227 D | 33.7% | 38.7% | 27.6% |
| 7,808 | MAJOR | 3,501 | 2,550 | 594 | 357 | | 1,956 R | 72.8% | 17.0% | 10.2% |
| 7,263 | MARSHALL | 3,386 | 1,209 | 1,191 | 986 | | 18 R | 35.7% | 35.2% | 29.1% |
| 20,073 | MAYES | 9,546 | 4,260 | 2,855 | 2,431 | | 1,405 R | 44.6% | 29.9% | 25.5% |
| 10,622 | MURRAY | 4,254 | 1,454 | 1,773 | 1,027 | | 319 D | 34.2% | 41.7% | 24.1% |
| 61,866 | MUSKOGEE | 22,680 | 8,707 | 9,377 | 4,596 | | 670 D | 38.4% | 41.3% | 20.3% |
| 10,376 | NOBLE | 4,941 | 2,911 | 1,412 | 618 | | 1,499 R | 58.9% | 28.6% | 12.5% |
| 10,848 | NOWATA | 4,510 | 2,116 | 1,314 | 1,080 | | 802 R | 46.9% | 29.1% | 23.9% |
| 11,706 | OKFUSKEE | 4,444 | 1,686 | 1,777 | 981 | | 91 D | 37.9% | 40.0% | 22.1% |
| 439,506 | OKLAHOMA | 187,441 | 93,212 | 60,395 | 33,834 | | 32,817 R | 49.7% | 32.2% | 18.1% |
| 36,945 | OKMULGEE | 13,526 | 4,709 | 6,089 | 2,728 | | 1,380 D | 34.8% | 45.0% | 20.2% |
| 32,441 | OSAGE | 11,825 | 5,499 | 3,919 | 2,407 | | 1,580 R | 46.5% | 33.1% | 20.4% |
| 28,301 | OTTAWA | 11,241 | 5,000 | 4,820 | 1,421 | | 180 R | 44.5% | 42.9% | 12.6% |
| 10,884 | PAWNEE | 4,770 | 2,437 | 1,343 | 990 | | 1,094 R | 51.1% | 28.2% | 20.8% |
| 44,231 | PAYNE | 17,824 | 9,577 | 5,772 | 2,475 | | 3,805 R | 53.7% | 32.4% | 13.9% |

# OKLAHOMA

## PRESIDENT 1968

| 1960 Census Population | County | Total Vote | Republican | Democratic | AIP | Other | Plurality | Percentage Total Vote | | |
|---:|---|---:|---:|---:|---:|---|---:|---:|---:|---:|
| | | | | | | | | Rep. | Dem. | AIP |
| 34,360 | PITTSBURG | 13,816 | 3,978 | 6,112 | 3,726 | | 2,134 D | 28.8% | 44.2% | 27.0% |
| 28,089 | PONTOTOC | 10,877 | 4,161 | 4,291 | 2,425 | | 130 D | 38.3% | 39.5% | 22.3% |
| 41,486 | POTTAWATOMIE | 17,493 | 6,899 | 6,721 | 3,873 | | 178 R | 39.4% | 38.4% | 22.1% |
| 9,088 | PUSHMATAHA | 3,744 | 1,225 | 1,232 | 1,287 | | 55 A | 32.7% | 32.9% | 34.4% |
| 5,090 | ROGER MILLS | 2,432 | 1,102 | 720 | 610 | | 382 R | 45.3% | 29.6% | 25.1% |
| 20,614 | ROGERS | 10,437 | 4,631 | 2,665 | 3,141 | | 1,490 R | 44.4% | 25.5% | 30.1% |
| 28,066 | SEMINOLE | 9,742 | 3,711 | 3,889 | 2,142 | | 178 D | 38.1% | 39.9% | 22.0% |
| 18,001 | SEQUOYAH | 7,573 | 2,797 | 2,618 | 2,158 | | 179 R | 36.9% | 34.6% | 28.5% |
| 37,990 | STEPHENS | 14,323 | 5,508 | 5,249 | 3,566 | | 259 R | 38.5% | 36.6% | 24.9% |
| 14,162 | TEXAS | 5,859 | 3,729 | 1,176 | 954 | | 2,553 R | 63.6% | 20.1% | 16.3% |
| 14,654 | TILLMAN | 4,895 | 1,748 | 1,771 | 1,376 | | 23 D | 35.7% | 36.2% | 28.1% |
| 346,038 | TULSA | 142,667 | 81,476 | 32,748 | 28,443 | | 48,728 R | 57.1% | 23.0% | 19.9% |
| 15,673 | WAGONER | 7,632 | 3,187 | 2,183 | 2,262 | | 925 R | 41.8% | 28.6% | 29.6% |
| 42,347 | WASHINGTON | 20,544 | 12,812 | 4,641 | 3,091 | | 8,171 R | 62.4% | 22.6% | 15.0% |
| 18,121 | WASHITA | 5,221 | 2,592 | 1,771 | 858 | | 821 R | 49.6% | 33.9% | 16.4% |
| 11,932 | WOODS | 5,405 | 3,449 | 1,439 | 517 | | 2,010 R | 63.8% | 26.6% | 9.6% |
| 13,902 | WOODWARD | 5,855 | 3,748 | 1,444 | 663 | | 2,304 R | 64.0% | 24.7% | 11.3% |
| 2,328,284 | TOTAL | 943,086 | 449,697 | 301,658 | 191,731 | | 148,039 R | 47.7% | 32.0% | 20.3% |

# OKLAHOMA

## PRESIDENT 1964

| 1960 Census Population | County | Total Vote | Republican | Democratic | Other | Rep.-Dem. Plurality | Percentage Total Vote Rep. | Dem. | Major Vote Rep. | Dem. |
|---|---|---|---|---|---|---|---|---|---|---|
| 13,112 | ADAIR | 5,862 | 2,859 | 3,003 | | 144 D | 48.8% | 51.2% | 48.8% | 51.2% |
| 8,445 | ALFALFA | 4,180 | 2,450 | 1,730 | | 720 R | 58.6% | 41.4% | 58.6% | 41.4% |
| 10,352 | ATOKA | 3,883 | 1,424 | 2,459 | | 1,035 D | 36.7% | 63.3% | 36.7% | 63.3% |
| 6,965 | BEAVER | 3,490 | 1,982 | 1,508 | | 474 R | 56.8% | 43.2% | 56.8% | 43.2% |
| 17,782 | BECKHAM | 6,672 | 2,557 | 4,115 | | 1,558 D | 38.3% | 61.7% | 38.3% | 61.7% |
| 12,077 | BLAINE | 5,125 | 2,741 | 2,384 | | 357 R | 53.5% | 46.5% | 53.5% | 46.5% |
| 24,252 | BRYAN | 8,586 | 2,652 | 5,934 | | 3,282 D | 30.9% | 69.1% | 30.9% | 69.1% |
| 28,621 | CADDO | 11,171 | 3,724 | 7,447 | | 3,723 D | 33.3% | 66.7% | 33.3% | 66.7% |
| 24,727 | CANADIAN | 10,940 | 5,193 | 5,747 | | 554 D | 47.5% | 52.5% | 47.5% | 52.5% |
| 39,044 | CARTER | 15,631 | 4,986 | 10,645 | | 5,659 D | 31.9% | 68.1% | 31.9% | 68.1% |
| 17,762 | CHEROKEE | 7,916 | 3,467 | 4,449 | | 982 D | 43.8% | 56.2% | 43.8% | 56.2% |
| 15,637 | CHOCTAW | 5,687 | 1,718 | 3,969 | | 2,251 D | 30.2% | 69.8% | 30.2% | 69.8% |
| 4,496 | CIMARRON | 2,103 | 1,225 | 878 | | 347 R | 58.3% | 41.7% | 58.3% | 41.7% |
| 47,600 | CLEVELAND | 21,255 | 9,656 | 11,599 | | 1,943 D | 45.4% | 54.6% | 45.4% | 54.6% |
| 5,546 | COAL | 2,334 | 721 | 1,613 | | 892 D | 30.9% | 69.1% | 30.9% | 69.1% |
| 90,803 | COMANCHE | 21,521 | 7,936 | 13,585 | | 5,649 D | 36.9% | 63.1% | 36.9% | 63.1% |
| 8,031 | COTTON | 3,339 | 1,123 | 2,216 | | 1,093 D | 33.6% | 66.4% | 33.6% | 66.4% |
| 16,303 | CRAIG | 6,379 | 2,541 | 3,838 | | 1,297 D | 39.8% | 60.2% | 39.8% | 60.2% |
| 40,495 | CREEK | 16,191 | 6,355 | 9,836 | | 3,481 D | 39.3% | 60.7% | 39.3% | 60.7% |
| 21,040 | CUSTER | 7,826 | 3,362 | 4,464 | | 1,102 D | 43.0% | 57.0% | 43.0% | 57.0% |
| 13,198 | DELAWARE | 6,445 | 2,743 | 3,702 | | 959 D | 42.6% | 57.4% | 42.6% | 57.4% |
| 6,051 | DEWEY | 3,055 | 1,438 | 1,617 | | 179 D | 47.1% | 52.9% | 47.1% | 52.9% |
| 5,457 | ELLIS | 2,572 | 1,452 | 1,120 | | 332 R | 56.5% | 43.5% | 56.5% | 43.5% |
| 52,975 | GARFIELD | 22,472 | 12,297 | 10,175 | | 2,122 R | 54.7% | 45.3% | 54.7% | 45.3% |
| 28,290 | GARVIN | 10,483 | 3,470 | 7,013 | | 3,543 D | 33.1% | 66.9% | 33.1% | 66.9% |
| 29,590 | GRADY | 11,162 | 3,569 | 7,593 | | 4,024 D | 32.0% | 68.0% | 32.0% | 68.0% |
| 8,140 | GRANT | 4,112 | 1,992 | 2,120 | | 128 D | 48.4% | 51.6% | 48.4% | 51.6% |
| 8,877 | GREER | 3,918 | 1,247 | 2,671 | | 1,424 D | 31.8% | 68.2% | 31.8% | 68.2% |
| 5,852 | HARMON | 2,267 | 602 | 1,665 | | 1,063 D | 26.6% | 73.4% | 26.6% | 73.4% |
| 5,956 | HARPER | 2,619 | 1,379 | 1,240 | | 139 R | 52.7% | 47.3% | 52.7% | 47.3% |
| 9,121 | HASKELL | 3,897 | 1,355 | 2,542 | | 1,187 D | 34.8% | 65.2% | 34.8% | 65.2% |
| 15,144 | HUGHES | 6,169 | 1,692 | 4,477 | | 2,785 D | 27.4% | 72.6% | 27.4% | 72.6% |
| 29,736 | JACKSON | 8,260 | 2,366 | 5,894 | | 3,528 D | 28.6% | 71.4% | 28.6% | 71.4% |
| 8,192 | JEFFERSON | 3,366 | 811 | 2,555 | | 1,744 D | 24.1% | 75.9% | 24.1% | 75.9% |
| 8,517 | JOHNSTON | 3,435 | 1,065 | 2,370 | | 1,305 D | 31.0% | 69.0% | 31.0% | 69.0% |
| 51,042 | KAY | 23,329 | 12,033 | 11,296 | | 737 R | 51.6% | 48.4% | 51.6% | 48.4% |
| 10,635 | KINGFISHER | 5,629 | 3,117 | 2,512 | | 605 R | 55.4% | 44.6% | 55.4% | 44.6% |
| 14,825 | KIOWA | 5,892 | 2,206 | 3,686 | | 1,480 D | 37.4% | 62.6% | 37.4% | 62.6% |
| 7,738 | LATIMER | 3,146 | 849 | 2,297 | | 1,448 D | 27.0% | 73.0% | 27.0% | 73.0% |
| 29,106 | LE FLORE | 11,009 | 3,904 | 7,105 | | 3,201 D | 35.5% | 64.5% | 35.5% | 64.5% |
| 18,783 | LINCOLN | 8,900 | 3,854 | 5,046 | | 1,192 D | 43.3% | 56.7% | 43.3% | 56.7% |
| 18,662 | LOGAN | 8,066 | 3,787 | 4,279 | | 492 D | 47.0% | 53.0% | 47.0% | 53.0% |
| 5,862 | LOVE | 2,526 | 663 | 1,863 | | 1,200 D | 26.2% | 73.8% | 26.2% | 73.8% |
| 12,740 | MCCLAIN | 5,276 | 1,638 | 3,638 | | 2,000 D | 31.0% | 69.0% | 31.0% | 69.0% |
| 25,851 | MCCURTAIN | 8,963 | 2,981 | 5,982 | | 3,001 D | 33.3% | 66.7% | 33.3% | 66.7% |
| 12,371 | MCINTOSH | 4,925 | 1,428 | 3,497 | | 2,069 D | 29.0% | 71.0% | 29.0% | 71.0% |
| 7,808 | MAJOR | 3,727 | 2,436 | 1,291 | | 1,145 R | 65.4% | 34.6% | 65.4% | 34.6% |
| 7,263 | MARSHALL | 3,419 | 1,101 | 2,318 | | 1,217 D | 32.2% | 67.8% | 32.2% | 67.8% |
| 20,073 | MAYES | 9,578 | 4,157 | 5,421 | | 1,264 D | 43.4% | 56.6% | 43.4% | 56.6% |
| 10,622 | MURRAY | 4,319 | 1,236 | 3,083 | | 1,847 D | 28.6% | 71.4% | 28.6% | 71.4% |
| 61,866 | MUSKOGEE | 24,838 | 8,508 | 16,330 | | 7,822 D | 34.3% | 65.7% | 34.3% | 65.7% |
| 10,376 | NOBLE | 4,870 | 2,157 | 2,713 | | 556 D | 44.3% | 55.7% | 44.3% | 55.7% |
| 10,848 | NOWATA | 4,786 | 2,142 | 2,644 | | 502 D | 44.8% | 55.2% | 44.8% | 55.2% |
| 11,706 | OKFUSKEE | 4,534 | 1,629 | 2,905 | | 1,276 D | 35.9% | 64.1% | 35.9% | 64.1% |
| 439,506 | OKLAHOMA | 174,301 | 83,660 | 90,641 | | 6,981 D | 48.0% | 52.0% | 48.0% | 52.0% |
| 36,945 | OKMULGEE | 14,899 | 4,704 | 10,195 | | 5,491 D | 31.6% | 68.4% | 31.6% | 68.4% |
| 32,441 | OSAGE | 13,090 | 5,695 | 7,395 | | 1,700 D | 43.5% | 56.5% | 43.5% | 56.5% |
| 28,301 | OTTAWA | 11,679 | 4,090 | 7,589 | | 3,499 D | 35.0% | 65.0% | 35.0% | 65.0% |
| 10,884 | PAWNEE | 4,667 | 2,278 | 2,389 | | 111 D | 48.8% | 51.2% | 48.8% | 51.2% |
| 44,231 | PAYNE | 16,842 | 7,936 | 8,906 | | 970 D | 47.1% | 52.9% | 47.1% | 52.9% |

# OKLAHOMA

## PRESIDENT 1964

| 1960 Census Population | County | Total Vote | Republican | Democratic | Other | Rep.-Dem. Plurality | Percentage | | | |
|---|---|---|---|---|---|---|---|---|---|---|
| | | | | | | | Total Vote | | Major Vote | |
| | | | | | | | Rep. | Dem. | Rep. | Dem. |
| 34,360 | PITTSBURG | 13,458 | 3,555 | 9,903 | | 6,348 D | 26.4% | 73.6% | 26.4% | 73.6% |
| 28,089 | PONTOTOC | 11,615 | 4,166 | 7,449 | | 3,283 D | 35.9% | 64.1% | 35.9% | 64.1% |
| 41,486 | POTTAWATOMIE | 17,725 | 6,841 | 10,884 | | 4,043 D | 38.6% | 61.4% | 38.6% | 61.4% |
| 9,088 | PUSHMATAHA | 3,895 | 1,332 | 2,563 | | 1,231 D | 34.2% | 65.8% | 34.2% | 65.8% |
| 5,090 | ROGER MILLS | 2,271 | 926 | 1,345 | | 419 D | 40.8% | 59.2% | 40.8% | 59.2% |
| 20,614 | ROGERS | 9,651 | 4,202 | 5,449 | | 1,247 D | 43.5% | 56.5% | 43.5% | 56.5% |
| 28,066 | SEMINOLE | 10,258 | 3,676 | 6,582 | | 2,906 D | 35.8% | 64.2% | 35.8% | 64.2% |
| 18,001 | SEQUOYAH | 7,150 | 2,846 | 4,304 | | 1,458 D | 39.8% | 60.2% | 39.8% | 60.2% |
| 37,990 | STEPHENS | 14,595 | 5,323 | 9,272 | | 3,949 D | 36.5% | 63.5% | 36.5% | 63.5% |
| 14,162 | TEXAS | 5,839 | 3,339 | 2,500 | | 839 R | 57.2% | 42.8% | 57.2% | 42.8% |
| 14,654 | TILLMAN | 5,355 | 2,001 | 3,354 | | 1,353 D | 37.4% | 62.6% | 37.4% | 62.6% |
| 346,038 | TULSA | 138,254 | 76,770 | 61,484 | | 15,286 R | 55.5% | 44.5% | 55.5% | 44.5% |
| 15,673 | WAGONER | 6,797 | 2,840 | 3,957 | | 1,117 D | 41.8% | 58.2% | 41.8% | 58.2% |
| 42,347 | WASHINGTON | 20,953 | 12,382 | 8,571 | | 3,811 R | 59.1% | 40.9% | 59.1% | 40.9% |
| 18,121 | WASHITA | 5,486 | 2,147 | 3,339 | | 1,192 D | 39.1% | 60.9% | 39.1% | 60.9% |
| 11,932 | WOODS | 5,636 | 2,886 | 2,750 | | 136 R | 51.2% | 48.8% | 51.2% | 48.8% |
| 13,902 | WOODWARD | 6,028 | 3,094 | 2,934 | | 160 R | 51.3% | 48.7% | 51.3% | 48.7% |
| 2,328,284 | TOTAL | 932,499 | 412,665 | 519,834 | | 107,169 D | 44.3% | 55.7% | 44.3% | 55.7% |

# OKLAHOMA

## PRESIDENT 1960

| 1960 Census Population | County | Total Vote | Republican | Democratic | Other | Rep.-Dem. Plurality | Percentage Total Vote Rep. | Dem. | Major Vote Rep. | Dem. |
|---|---|---|---|---|---|---|---|---|---|---|
| 13,112 | ADAIR | 5,558 | 3,655 | 1,903 | | 1,752 R | 65.8% | 34.2% | 65.8% | 34.2% |
| 8,445 | ALFALFA | 4,399 | 3,332 | 1,067 | | 2,265 R | 75.7% | 24.3% | 75.7% | 24.3% |
| 10,352 | ATOKA | 3,651 | 1,892 | 1,759 | | 133 R | 51.8% | 48.2% | 51.8% | 48.2% |
| 6,965 | BEAVER | 3,329 | 2,442 | 887 | | 1,555 R | 73.4% | 26.6% | 73.4% | 26.6% |
| 17,782 | BECKHAM | 6,979 | 4,258 | 2,721 | | 1,537 R | 61.0% | 39.0% | 61.0% | 39.0% |
| 12,077 | BLAINE | 5,371 | 3,646 | 1,725 | | 1,921 R | 67.9% | 32.1% | 67.9% | 32.1% |
| 24,252 | BRYAN | 8,273 | 3,845 | 4,428 | | 583 D | 46.5% | 53.5% | 46.5% | 53.5% |
| 28,621 | CADDO | 11,035 | 5,920 | 5,115 | | 805 R | 53.6% | 46.4% | 53.6% | 46.4% |
| 24,727 | CANADIAN | 9,931 | 5,697 | 4,234 | | 1,463 R | 57.4% | 42.6% | 57.4% | 42.6% |
| 39,044 | CARTER | 14,729 | 6,288 | 8,441 | | 2,153 D | 42.7% | 57.3% | 42.7% | 57.3% |
| 17,762 | CHEROKEE | 6,258 | 3,571 | 2,687 | | 884 R | 57.1% | 42.9% | 57.1% | 42.9% |
| 15,637 | CHOCTAW | 5,472 | 2,531 | 2,941 | | 410 D | 46.3% | 53.7% | 46.3% | 53.7% |
| 4,496 | CIMARRON | 2,012 | 1,316 | 696 | | 620 R | 65.4% | 34.6% | 65.4% | 34.6% |
| 47,600 | CLEVELAND | 15,689 | 9,292 | 6,397 | | 2,895 R | 59.2% | 40.8% | 59.2% | 40.8% |
| 5,546 | COAL | 2,288 | 1,019 | 1,269 | | 250 D | 44.5% | 55.5% | 44.5% | 55.5% |
| 90,803 | COMANCHE | 20,253 | 10,691 | 9,562 | | 1,129 R | 52.8% | 47.2% | 52.8% | 47.2% |
| 8,031 | COTTON | 3,253 | 1,619 | 1,634 | | 15 D | 49.8% | 50.2% | 49.8% | 50.2% |
| 16,303 | CRAIG | 6,562 | 3,770 | 2,792 | | 978 R | 57.5% | 42.5% | 57.5% | 42.5% |
| 40,495 | CREEK | 14,990 | 8,785 | 6,205 | | 2,580 R | 58.6% | 41.4% | 58.6% | 41.4% |
| 21,040 | CUSTER | 7,793 | 5,050 | 2,743 | | 2,307 R | 64.8% | 35.2% | 64.8% | 35.2% |
| 13,198 | DELAWARE | 5,921 | 3,639 | 2,282 | | 1,357 R | 61.5% | 38.5% | 61.5% | 38.5% |
| 6,051 | DEWEY | 3,197 | 2,115 | 1,082 | | 1,033 R | 66.2% | 33.8% | 66.2% | 33.8% |
| 5,457 | ELLIS | 2,794 | 2,085 | 709 | | 1,376 R | 74.6% | 25.4% | 74.6% | 25.4% |
| 52,975 | GARFIELD | 21,442 | 14,860 | 6,582 | | 8,278 R | 69.3% | 30.7% | 69.3% | 30.7% |
| 28,290 | GARVIN | 9,920 | 5,125 | 4,795 | | 330 R | 51.7% | 48.3% | 51.7% | 48.3% |
| 29,590 | GRADY | 11,359 | 5,913 | 5,446 | | 467 R | 52.1% | 47.9% | 52.1% | 47.9% |
| 8,140 | GRANT | 4,533 | 2,810 | 1,723 | | 1,087 R | 62.0% | 38.0% | 62.0% | 38.0% |
| 8,877 | GREER | 3,856 | 2,158 | 1,698 | | 460 R | 56.0% | 44.0% | 56.0% | 44.0% |
| 5,852 | HARMON | 2,407 | 1,142 | 1,265 | | 123 D | 47.4% | 52.6% | 47.4% | 52.6% |
| 5,956 | HARPER | 2,801 | 2,057 | 744 | | 1,313 R | 73.4% | 26.6% | 73.4% | 26.6% |
| 9,121 | HASKELL | 3,570 | 1,858 | 1,712 | | 146 R | 52.0% | 48.0% | 52.0% | 48.0% |
| 15,144 | HUGHES | 6,174 | 3,117 | 3,057 | | 60 R | 50.5% | 49.5% | 50.5% | 49.5% |
| 29,736 | JACKSON | 7,136 | 3,375 | 3,761 | | 386 D | 47.3% | 52.7% | 47.3% | 52.7% |
| 8,192 | JEFFERSON | 3,288 | 1,343 | 1,945 | | 602 D | 40.8% | 59.2% | 40.8% | 59.2% |
| 8,517 | JOHNSTON | 3,263 | 1,441 | 1,822 | | 381 D | 44.2% | 55.8% | 44.2% | 55.8% |
| 51,042 | KAY | 23,405 | 15,156 | 8,249 | | 6,907 R | 64.8% | 35.2% | 64.8% | 35.2% |
| 10,635 | KINGFISHER | 5,322 | 3,501 | 1,821 | | 1,680 R | 65.8% | 34.2% | 65.8% | 34.2% |
| 14,825 | KIOWA | 6,153 | 3,515 | 2,638 | | 877 R | 57.1% | 42.9% | 57.1% | 42.9% |
| 7,738 | LATIMER | 2,988 | 1,454 | 1,534 | | 80 D | 48.7% | 51.3% | 48.7% | 51.3% |
| 29,106 | LE FLORE | 10,146 | 5,302 | 4,844 | | 458 R | 52.3% | 47.7% | 52.3% | 47.7% |
| 18,783 | LINCOLN | 8,783 | 5,528 | 3,255 | | 2,273 R | 62.9% | 37.1% | 62.9% | 37.1% |
| 18,662 | LOGAN | 7,941 | 5,121 | 2,820 | | 2,301 R | 64.5% | 35.5% | 64.5% | 35.5% |
| 5,862 | LOVE | 2,375 | 932 | 1,443 | | 511 D | 39.2% | 60.8% | 39.2% | 60.8% |
| 12,740 | MCCLAIN | 4,912 | 2,547 | 2,365 | | 182 R | 51.9% | 48.1% | 51.9% | 48.1% |
| 25,851 | MCCURTAIN | 7,764 | 3,562 | 4,202 | | 640 D | 45.9% | 54.1% | 45.9% | 54.1% |
| 12,371 | MCINTOSH | 4,406 | 2,221 | 2,185 | | 36 R | 50.4% | 49.6% | 50.4% | 49.6% |
| 7,808 | MAJOR | 3,608 | 2,892 | 716 | | 2,176 R | 80.2% | 19.8% | 80.2% | 19.8% |
| 7,263 | MARSHALL | 3,118 | 1,325 | 1,793 | | 468 D | 42.5% | 57.5% | 42.5% | 57.5% |
| 20,073 | MAYES | 8,915 | 5,194 | 3,721 | | 1,473 R | 58.3% | 41.7% | 58.3% | 41.7% |
| 10,622 | MURRAY | 4,122 | 1,993 | 2,129 | | 136 D | 48.4% | 51.6% | 48.4% | 51.6% |
| 61,866 | MUSKOGEE | 23,485 | 12,403 | 11,082 | | 1,321 R | 52.8% | 47.2% | 52.8% | 47.2% |
| 10,376 | NOBLE | 5,108 | 3,198 | 1,910 | | 1,288 R | 62.6% | 37.4% | 62.6% | 37.4% |
| 10,848 | NOWATA | 5,139 | 3,014 | 2,125 | | 889 R | 58.6% | 41.4% | 58.6% | 41.4% |
| 11,706 | OKFUSKEE | 4,478 | 2,510 | 1,968 | | 542 R | 56.1% | 43.9% | 56.1% | 43.9% |
| 439,506 | OKLAHOMA | 167,640 | 102,992 | 64,648 | | 38,344 R | 61.4% | 38.6% | 61.4% | 38.6% |
| 36,945 | OKMULGEE | 14,369 | 7,107 | 7,262 | | 155 D | 49.5% | 50.5% | 49.5% | 50.5% |
| 32,441 | OSAGE | 13,309 | 7,508 | 5,801 | | 1,707 R | 56.4% | 43.6% | 56.4% | 43.6% |
| 28,301 | OTTAWA | 12,225 | 6,520 | 5,705 | | 815 R | 53.3% | 46.7% | 53.3% | 46.7% |
| 10,884 | PAWNEE | 4,792 | 3,153 | 1,639 | | 1,514 R | 65.8% | 34.2% | 65.8% | 34.2% |
| 44,231 | PAYNE | 15,637 | 9,943 | 5,694 | | 4,249 R | 63.6% | 36.4% | 63.6% | 36.4% |

# OKLAHOMA

## PRESIDENT 1960

| 1960 Census Population | County | Total Vote | Republican | Democratic | Other | Rep.-Dem. Plurality | Percentage | | | |
|---|---|---|---|---|---|---|---|---|---|---|
| | | | | | | | Total Vote | | Major Vote | |
| | | | | | | | Rep. | Dem. | Rep. | Dem. |
| 34,360 | PITTSBURG | 13,144 | 5,834 | 7,310 | | 1,476 D | 44.4% | 55.6% | 44.4% | 55.6% |
| 28,089 | PONTOTOC | 10,517 | 5,863 | 4,654 | | 1,209 R | 55.7% | 44.3% | 55.7% | 44.3% |
| 41,486 | POTTAWATOMIE | 17,488 | 9,421 | 8,067 | | 1,354 R | 53.9% | 46.1% | 53.9% | 46.1% |
| 9,088 | PUSHMATAHA | 3,358 | 1,728 | 1,630 | | 98 R | 51.5% | 48.5% | 51.5% | 48.5% |
| 5,090 | ROGER MILLS | 2,272 | 1,463 | 809 | | 654 R | 64.4% | 35.6% | 64.4% | 35.6% |
| 20,614 | ROGERS | 8,579 | 5,412 | 3,167 | | 2,245 R | 63.1% | 36.9% | 63.1% | 36.9% |
| 28,066 | SEMINOLE | 9,761 | 5,505 | 4,256 | | 1,249 R | 56.4% | 43.6% | 56.4% | 43.6% |
| 18,001 | SEQUOYAH | 6,804 | 3,862 | 2,942 | | 920 R | 56.8% | 43.2% | 56.8% | 43.2% |
| 37,990 | STEPHENS | 14,983 | 8,084 | 6,899 | | 1,185 R | 54.0% | 46.0% | 54.0% | 46.0% |
| 14,162 | TEXAS | 5,863 | 4,314 | 1,549 | | 2,765 R | 73.6% | 26.4% | 73.6% | 26.4% |
| 14,654 | TILLMAN | 5,414 | 2,678 | 2,736 | | 58 D | 49.5% | 50.5% | 49.5% | 50.5% |
| 346,038 | TULSA | 142,624 | 89,899 | 52,725 | | 37,174 R | 63.0% | 37.0% | 63.0% | 37.0% |
| 15,673 | WAGONER | 6,277 | 3,570 | 2,707 | | 863 R | 56.9% | 43.1% | 56.9% | 43.1% |
| 42,347 | WASHINGTON | 19,179 | 13,700 | 5,479 | | 8,221 R | 71.4% | 28.6% | 71.4% | 28.6% |
| 18,121 | WASHITA | 5,623 | 3,209 | 2,414 | | 795 R | 57.1% | 42.9% | 57.1% | 42.9% |
| 11,932 | WOODS | 5,966 | 4,064 | 1,902 | | 2,162 R | 68.1% | 31.9% | 68.1% | 31.9% |
| 13,902 | WOODWARD | 5,672 | 4,185 | 1,487 | | 2,698 R | 73.8% | 26.2% | 73.8% | 26.2% |
| 2,328,284 | TOTAL | 903,150 | 533,039 | 370,111 | | 162,928 R | 59.0% | 41.0% | 59.0% | 41.0% |

# OKLAHOMA

## ELECTION NOTES

**2004**

**2000**      Other vote was 9,014 Reform (Buchanan); 6,602 Libertarian (Browne).

**1996**      Other vote was 5,505 Libertarian (Browne).

**1992**      Other vote was Marrou (Libertarian).

**1988**      Other vote was 6,261 Paul (Libertarian); 2,985 Fulani (New Alliance).

**1984**      Other vote was Bergland (Libertarian).

**1980**      Other vote was 38,284 Anderson (Independent); 13,828 Clark (Libertarian).

**1976**      Other vote was McCarthy (Independent).

**1972**      Other vote was Schmitz (American).

**1968**      Wallace on the ballot as American.

**1964**

**1960**

# OREGON

## POPULAR VOTE FOR PRESIDENT 1920 TO 2004

| Year | Total Vote | Republican | | Democratic | | Other Vote | Plurality | Percentage | | | |
|------|-----------|------|-----------|------|-----------|------------|-----------|------------|------|------------|------|
| | | | | | | | | Total Vote | | Major Vote | |
| | | Vote | Candidate | Vote | Candidate | | | Rep. | Dem. | Rep. | Dem. |
| 2004 | 1,836,782 | 866,831 | Bush, George W. | 943,163 | Kerry, John | 26,788 | 76,332 D | 47.2% | 51.3% | 47.9% | 52.1% |
| 2000 ** | 1,533,968 | 713,577 | Bush, George W. | 720,342 | Gore, Al | 100,049 | 6,765 D | 46.5% | 47.0% | 49.8% | 50.2% |
| 1996 ** | 1,377,760 | 538,152 | Dole, Bob | 649,641 | Clinton, Bill | 189,967 | 111,489 D | 39.1% | 47.2% | 45.3% | 54.7% |
| 1992 ** | 1,462,643 | 475,757 | Bush, George | 621,314 | Clinton, Bill | 365,572 | 145,557 D | 32.5% | 42.5% | 43.4% | 56.6% |
| 1988 | 1,201,694 | 560,126 | Bush, George | 616,206 | Dukakis, Michael S. | 25,362 | 56,080 D | 46.6% | 51.3% | 47.6% | 52.4% |
| 1984 | 1,226,527 | 685,700 | Reagan, Ronald | 536,479 | Mondale, Walter F. | 4,348 | 149,221 R | 55.9% | 43.7% | 56.1% | 43.9% |
| 1980 ** | 1,181,516 | 571,044 | Reagan, Ronald | 456,890 | Carter, Jimmy | 153,582 | 114,154 R | 48.3% | 38.7% | 55.6% | 44.4% |
| 1976 | 1,029,876 | 492,120 | Ford, Gerald R. | 490,407 | Carter, Jimmy | 47,349 | 1,713 R | 47.8% | 47.6% | 50.1% | 49.9% |
| 1972 | 927,946 | 486,686 | Nixon, Richard M. | 392,760 | McGovern, George S. | 48,500 | 93,926 R | 52.4% | 42.3% | 55.3% | 44.7% |
| 1968 | 819,622 | 408,433 | Nixon, Richard M. | 358,866 | Humphrey, Hubert H. | 52,323 | 49,567 R | 49.8% | 43.8% | 53.2% | 46.8% |
| 1964 | 786,305 | 282,779 | Goldwater, Barry M. | 501,017 | Johnson, Lyndon B. | 2,509 | 218,238 D | 36.0% | 63.7% | 36.1% | 63.9% |
| 1960 | 776,421 | 408,060 | Nixon, Richard M. | 367,402 | Kennedy, John F. | 959 | 40,658 R | 52.6% | 47.3% | 52.6% | 47.4% |
| 1956 | 736,132 | 406,393 | Eisenhower, Dwight D. | 329,204 | Stevenson, Adlai E. | 535 | 77,189 R | 55.2% | 44.7% | 55.2% | 44.8% |
| 1952 | 695,059 | 420,815 | Eisenhower, Dwight D. | 270,579 | Stevenson, Adlai E. | 3,665 | 150,236 R | 60.5% | 38.9% | 60.9% | 39.1% |
| 1948 | 524,080 | 260,904 | Dewey, Thomas E. | 243,147 | Truman, Harry S. | 20,029 | 17,757 R | 49.8% | 46.4% | 51.8% | 48.2% |
| 1944 | 480,147 | 225,365 | Dewey, Thomas E. | 248,635 | Roosevelt, Franklin D. | 6,147 | 23,270 D | 46.9% | 51.8% | 47.5% | 52.5% |
| 1940 | 481,240 | 219,555 | Willkie, Wendell | 258,415 | Roosevelt, Franklin D. | 3,270 | 38,860 D | 45.6% | 53.7% | 45.9% | 54.1% |
| 1936 | 414,021 | 122,706 | Landon, Alfred M. | 266,733 | Roosevelt, Franklin D. | 24,582 | 144,027 D | 29.6% | 64.4% | 31.5% | 68.5% |
| 1932 | 368,751 | 136,019 | Hoover, Herbert C. | 213,871 | Roosevelt, Franklin D. | 18,861 | 77,852 D | 36.9% | 58.0% | 38.9% | 61.1% |
| 1928 | 319,942 | 205,341 | Hoover, Herbert C. | 109,223 | Smith, Alfred E. | 5,378 | 96,118 R | 64.2% | 34.1% | 65.3% | 34.7% |
| 1924 ** | 279,488 | 142,579 | Coolidge, Calvin | 67,589 | Davis, John W. | 69,320 | 74,176 R | 51.0% | 24.2% | 67.8% | 32.2% |
| 1920 | 238,522 | 143,592 | Harding, Warren G. | 80,019 | Cox, James M. | 14,911 | 63,573 R | 60.2% | 33.5% | 64.2% | 35.8% |

In 2000 the other vote column includes 77,357 votes cast for Green (Nader). In 1996 the other vote column includes 121,221 votes cast for Perot. In 1992 the other vote column includes 354,091 votes cast for Perot. In 1980 the other column includes 112,389 votes for Independent (Anderson). In 1924 the other vote was 68,403 Progressive and 917 Socialist Labor.

## ELECTORAL COLLEGE VOTE 1920 TO 2004

| Year | Total | Republican | Democratic | Other |
|------|-------|-----------|------------|-------|
| 2004 | 7 | | 7 | |
| 2000 | 7 | | 7 | |
| 1996 | 7 | | 7 | |
| 1992 | 7 | | 7 | |
| 1988 | 7 | | 7 | |
| 1984 | 7 | 7 | | |
| 1980 | 6 | 6 | | |
| 1976 | 6 | 6 | | |
| 1972 | 6 | 6 | | |
| 1968 | 6 | 6 | | |
| 1964 | 6 | | 6 | |
| 1960 | 6 | 6 | | |
| 1956 | 6 | 6 | | |
| 1952 | 6 | 6 | | |
| 1948 | 6 | 6 | | |
| 1944 | 6 | | 6 | |
| 1940 | 5 | | 5 | |
| 1936 | 5 | | 5 | |
| 1932 | 5 | | 5 | |
| 1928 | 5 | 5 | | |
| 1924 | 5 | 5 | | |
| 1920 | 5 | 5 | | |

# OREGON

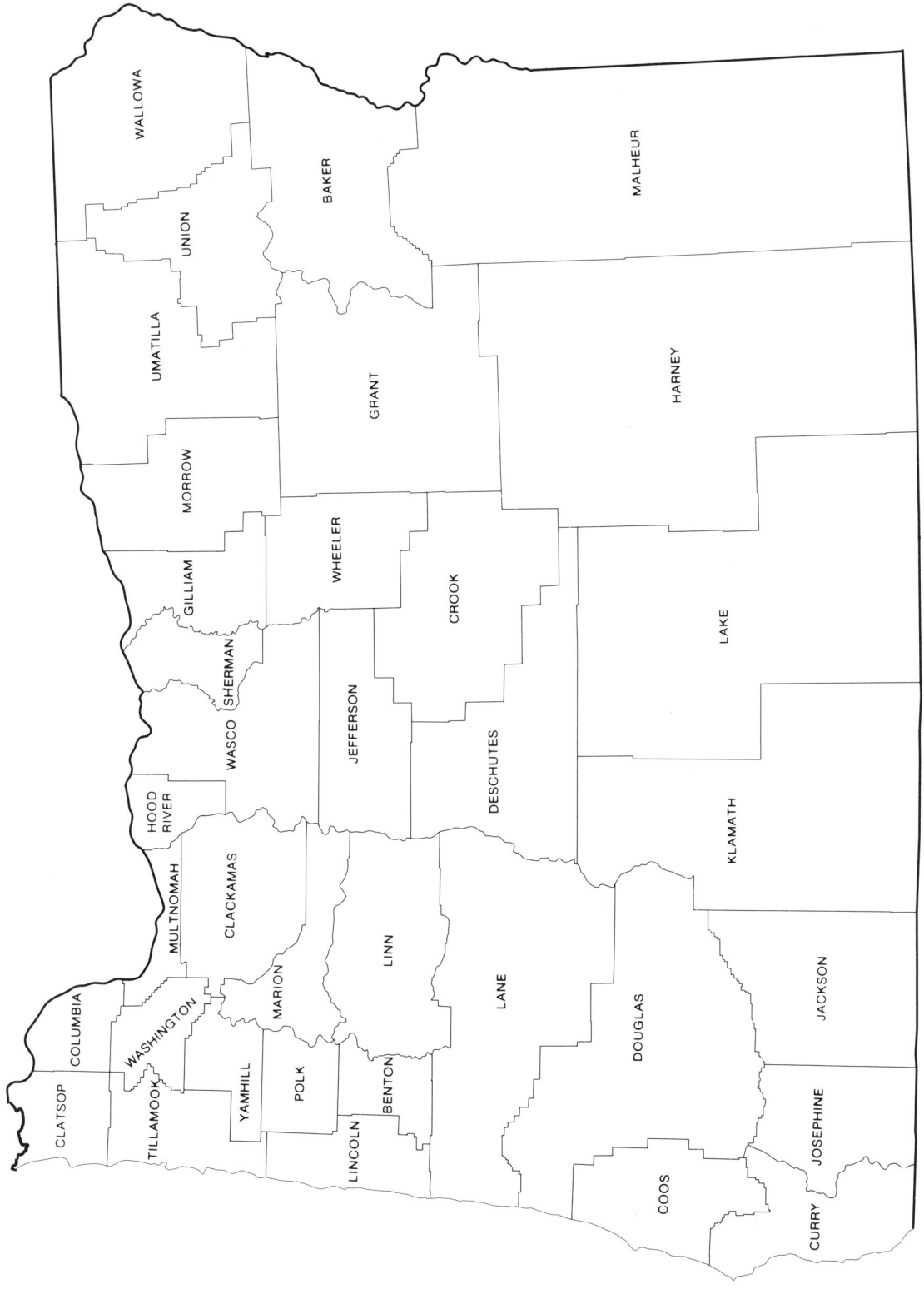

# OREGON

## PRESIDENT 2004

| 2000 Census Population | County | Total Vote | Republican | Democratic | Other | Rep.-Dem. Plurality | Percentage | | | |
|---|---|---|---|---|---|---|---|---|---|---|
| | | | | | | | Total Vote | | Major Vote | |
| | | | | | | | Rep. | Dem. | Rep. | Dem. |
| 16,741 | BAKER | 9,034 | 6,253 | 2,616 | 165 | 3,637 R | 69.2% | 29.0% | 70.5% | 29.5% |
| 78,153 | BENTON | 45,735 | 18,460 | 26,515 | 760 | 8,055 D | 40.4% | 58.0% | 41.0% | 59.0% |
| 338,391 | CLACKAMAS | 195,000 | 97,691 | 95,129 | 2,180 | 2,562 R | 50.1% | 48.8% | 50.7% | 49.3% |
| 35,630 | CLATSOP | 19,309 | 8,503 | 10,461 | 345 | 1,958 D | 44.0% | 54.2% | 44.8% | 55.2% |
| 43,560 | COLUMBIA | 24,917 | 11,868 | 12,563 | 486 | 695 D | 47.6% | 50.4% | 48.6% | 51.4% |
| 62,779 | COOS | 33,362 | 18,291 | 14,393 | 678 | 3,898 R | 54.8% | 43.1% | 56.0% | 44.0% |
| 19,182 | CROOK | 10,051 | 6,830 | 3,024 | 197 | 3,806 R | 68.0% | 30.1% | 69.3% | 30.7% |
| 21,137 | CURRY | 12,799 | 7,332 | 5,220 | 247 | 2,112 R | 57.3% | 40.8% | 58.4% | 41.6% |
| 115,367 | DESCHUTES | 74,048 | 41,757 | 31,179 | 1,112 | 10,578 R | 56.4% | 42.1% | 57.3% | 42.7% |
| 100,399 | DOUGLAS | 54,984 | 35,956 | 18,089 | 939 | 17,867 R | 65.4% | 32.9% | 66.5% | 33.5% |
| 1,915 | GILLIAM | 1,138 | 755 | 370 | 13 | 385 R | 66.3% | 32.5% | 67.1% | 32.9% |
| 7,935 | GRANT | 4,061 | 3,204 | 780 | 77 | 2,424 R | 78.9% | 19.2% | 80.4% | 19.6% |
| 7,609 | HARNEY | 3,702 | 2,815 | 839 | 48 | 1,976 R | 76.0% | 22.7% | 77.0% | 23.0% |
| 20,411 | HOOD RIVER | 9,859 | 4,124 | 5,587 | 148 | 1,463 D | 41.8% | 56.7% | 42.5% | 57.5% |
| 181,269 | JACKSON | 102,189 | 56,519 | 44,366 | 1,304 | 12,153 R | 55.3% | 43.4% | 56.0% | 44.0% |
| 19,009 | JEFFERSON | 8,115 | 4,762 | 3,243 | 110 | 1,519 R | 58.7% | 40.0% | 59.5% | 40.5% |
| 75,726 | JOSEPHINE | 42,275 | 26,241 | 15,214 | 820 | 11,027 R | 62.1% | 36.0% | 63.3% | 36.7% |
| 63,775 | KLAMATH | 31,515 | 22,733 | 8,264 | 518 | 14,469 R | 72.1% | 26.2% | 73.3% | 26.7% |
| 7,422 | LAKE | 3,905 | 3,039 | 802 | 64 | 2,237 R | 77.8% | 20.5% | 79.1% | 20.9% |
| 322,959 | LANE | 185,872 | 75,007 | 107,769 | 3,096 | 32,762 D | 40.4% | 58.0% | 41.0% | 59.0% |
| 44,479 | LINCOLN | 24,325 | 10,160 | 13,753 | 412 | 3,593 D | 41.8% | 56.5% | 42.5% | 57.5% |
| 103,069 | LINN | 52,041 | 31,260 | 19,940 | 841 | 11,320 R | 60.1% | 38.3% | 61.1% | 38.9% |
| 31,615 | MALHEUR | 10,846 | 8,123 | 2,577 | 146 | 5,546 R | 74.9% | 23.8% | 75.9% | 24.1% |
| 284,834 | MARION | 129,619 | 69,900 | 57,671 | 2,048 | 12,229 R | 53.9% | 44.5% | 54.8% | 45.2% |
| 10,995 | MORROW | 4,149 | 2,732 | 1,361 | 56 | 1,371 R | 65.8% | 32.8% | 66.7% | 33.3% |
| 660,486 | MULTNOMAH | 362,694 | 98,439 | 259,585 | 4,670 | 161,146 D | 27.1% | 71.6% | 27.5% | 72.5% |
| 62,380 | POLK | 35,489 | 19,508 | 15,484 | 497 | 4,024 R | 55.0% | 43.6% | 55.7% | 44.3% |
| 1,934 | SHERMAN | 1,104 | 694 | 390 | 20 | 304 R | 62.9% | 35.3% | 64.0% | 36.0% |
| 24,262 | TILLAMOOK | 13,951 | 7,003 | 6,750 | 198 | 253 R | 50.2% | 48.4% | 50.9% | 49.1% |
| 70,548 | UMATILLA | 26,322 | 17,068 | 8,884 | 370 | 8,184 R | 64.8% | 33.8% | 65.8% | 34.2% |
| 24,530 | UNION | 13,519 | 8,879 | 4,428 | 212 | 4,451 R | 65.7% | 32.8% | 66.7% | 33.3% |
| 7,226 | WALLOWA | 4,521 | 3,132 | 1,269 | 120 | 1,863 R | 69.3% | 28.1% | 71.2% | 28.8% |
| 23,791 | WASCO | 12,002 | 6,119 | 5,691 | 192 | 428 R | 51.0% | 47.4% | 51.8% | 48.2% |
| 445,342 | WASHINGTON | 231,308 | 107,223 | 121,140 | 2,945 | 13,917 D | 46.4% | 52.4% | 47.0% | 53.0% |
| 1,547 | WHEELER | 880 | 612 | 245 | 23 | 367 R | 69.5% | 27.8% | 71.4% | 28.6% |
| 84,992 | YAMHILL | 42,142 | 23,839 | 17,572 | 731 | 6,267 R | 56.6% | 41.7% | 57.6% | 42.4% |
| 3,421,399 | TOTAL | 1,836,782 | 866,831 | 943,163 | 26,788 | 76,332 D | 47.2% | 51.3% | 47.9% | 52.1% |

# OREGON

## PRESIDENT 2000

| 2000 Census Population | County | Total Vote | Republican | Democratic | Green (Nader) | Other | Rep.-Dem. Plurality | Percentage of Total Vote | | |
|---|---|---|---|---|---|---|---|---|---|---|
| | | | | | | | | Rep. | Dem. | Green |
| 16,741 | BAKER | 8,258 | 5,618 | 2,195 | 289 | 156 | 3,423 R | 68.0% | 26.6% | 3.5% |
| 78,153 | BENTON | 38,226 | 15,825 | 19,444 | 2,463 | 494 | 3,619 D | 41.4% | 50.9% | 6.4% |
| 338,391 | CLACKAMAS | 162,262 | 77,539 | 76,421 | 6,357 | 1,945 | 1,118 R | 47.8% | 47.1% | 3.9% |
| 35,630 | CLATSOP | 16,474 | 6,950 | 8,296 | 939 | 289 | 1,346 D | 42.2% | 50.4% | 5.7% |
| 43,560 | COLUMBIA | 21,195 | 9,369 | 10,331 | 970 | 525 | 962 D | 44.2% | 48.7% | 4.6% |
| 62,779 | COOS | 29,379 | 15,626 | 11,610 | 1,410 | 733 | 4,016 R | 53.2% | 39.5% | 4.8% |
| 19,182 | CROOK | 8,277 | 5,363 | 2,474 | 258 | 182 | 2,889 R | 64.8% | 29.9% | 3.1% |
| 21,137 | CURRY | 11,513 | 6,551 | 4,090 | 603 | 269 | 2,461 R | 56.9% | 35.5% | 5.2% |
| 115,367 | DESCHUTES | 57,885 | 32,132 | 22,061 | 2,799 | 893 | 10,071 R | 55.5% | 38.1% | 4.8% |
| 100,399 | DOUGLAS | 47,220 | 30,294 | 14,193 | 1,768 | 965 | 16,101 R | 64.2% | 30.1% | 3.7% |
| 1,915 | GILLIAM | 1,090 | 679 | 359 | 37 | 15 | 320 R | 62.3% | 32.9% | 3.4% |
| 7,935 | GRANT | 3,846 | 3,078 | 589 | 98 | 81 | 2,489 R | 80.0% | 15.3% | 2.5% |
| 7,609 | HARNEY | 3,734 | 2,799 | 766 | 84 | 85 | 2,033 R | 75.0% | 20.5% | 2.2% |
| 20,411 | HOOD RIVER | 8,549 | 3,721 | 4,072 | 645 | 111 | 351 D | 43.5% | 47.6% | 7.5% |
| 181,269 | JACKSON | 84,796 | 46,052 | 33,153 | 4,207 | 1,384 | 12,899 R | 54.3% | 39.1% | 5.0% |
| 19,009 | JEFFERSON | 6,897 | 3,838 | 2,681 | 247 | 131 | 1,157 R | 55.6% | 38.9% | 3.6% |
| 75,726 | JOSEPHINE | 36,733 | 22,186 | 11,864 | 1,783 | 900 | 10,322 R | 60.4% | 32.3% | 4.9% |
| 63,775 | KLAMATH | 27,844 | 18,855 | 7,541 | 867 | 581 | 11,314 R | 67.7% | 27.1% | 3.1% |
| 7,422 | LAKE | 3,729 | 2,830 | 707 | 108 | 84 | 2,123 R | 75.9% | 19.0% | 2.9% |
| 322,959 | LANE | 152,188 | 61,578 | 78,583 | 10,245 | 1,782 | 17,005 D | 40.5% | 51.6% | 6.7% |
| 44,479 | LINCOLN | 21,118 | 8,446 | 10,861 | 1,435 | 376 | 2,415 D | 40.0% | 51.4% | 6.8% |
| 103,069 | LINN | 44,388 | 25,359 | 16,682 | 1,617 | 730 | 8,677 R | 57.1% | 37.6% | 3.6% |
| 31,615 | MALHEUR | 10,404 | 7,624 | 2,336 | 248 | 196 | 5,288 R | 73.3% | 22.5% | 2.4% |
| 284,834 | MARION | 113,334 | 57,443 | 49,430 | 4,679 | 1,782 | 8,013 R | 50.7% | 43.6% | 4.1% |
| 10,995 | MORROW | 3,609 | 2,224 | 1,197 | 87 | 101 | 1,027 R | 61.6% | 33.2% | 2.4% |
| 660,486 | MULTNOMAH | 296,685 | 83,677 | 188,441 | 21,048 | 3,519 | 104,764 D | 28.2% | 63.5% | 7.1% |
| 62,380 | POLK | 28,449 | 14,988 | 11,921 | 1,201 | 339 | 3,067 R | 52.7% | 41.9% | 4.2% |
| 1,934 | SHERMAN | 1,062 | 679 | 326 | 36 | 21 | 353 R | 63.9% | 30.7% | 3.4% |
| 24,262 | TILLAMOOK | 12,376 | 5,775 | 5,762 | 613 | 226 | 13 R | 46.7% | 46.6% | 5.0% |
| 70,548 | UMATILLA | 23,060 | 14,140 | 7,809 | 655 | 456 | 6,331 R | 61.3% | 33.9% | 2.8% |
| 24,530 | UNION | 12,076 | 7,836 | 3,577 | 436 | 227 | 4,259 R | 64.9% | 29.6% | 3.6% |
| 7,226 | WALLOWA | 4,294 | 3,279 | 836 | 114 | 65 | 2,443 R | 76.4% | 19.5% | 2.7% |
| 23,791 | WASCO | 10,664 | 5,356 | 4,616 | 513 | 179 | 740 R | 50.2% | 43.3% | 4.8% |
| 445,342 | WASHINGTON | 185,974 | 86,091 | 90,662 | 6,985 | 2,236 | 4,571 D | 46.3% | 48.7% | 3.8% |
| 1,547 | WHEELER | 841 | 584 | 202 | 27 | 28 | 382 R | 69.4% | 24.0% | 3.2% |
| 84,992 | YAMHILL | 35,539 | 19,193 | 14,254 | 1,486 | 606 | 4,939 R | 54.0% | 40.1% | 4.2% |
| 3,421,399 | TOTAL | 1,533,968 | 713,577 | 720,342 | 77,357 | 22,692 | 6,765 D | 46.5% | 47.0% | 5.0% |

# OREGON

## PRESIDENT 1996

| 1995 Census Pop. Est. | County | Total Vote | Republican | Democratic | Reform (Perot) | Other | Rep.-Dem. Plurality | Percentage of Total Vote | | |
|---|---|---|---|---|---|---|---|---|---|---|
| | | | | | | | | Rep. | Dem. | Reform |
| 16,471 | BAKER | 7,703 | 3,975 | 2,547 | 900 | 281 | 1,428 R | 51.6% | 33.1% | 11.7% |
| 75,235 | BENTON | 34,500 | 12,450 | 17,211 | 2,445 | 2,394 | 4,761 D | 36.1% | 49.9% | 7.1% |
| 316,428 | CLACKAMAS | 145,146 | 59,443 | 67,709 | 12,304 | 5,690 | 8,266 D | 41.0% | 46.6% | 8.5% |
| 35,372 | CLATSOP | 15,405 | 5,334 | 7,732 | 1,582 | 757 | 2,398 D | 34.6% | 50.2% | 10.3% |
| 41,816 | COLUMBIA | 18,476 | 6,205 | 9,275 | 2,330 | 666 | 3,070 D | 33.6% | 50.2% | 12.6% |
| 62,822 | COOS | 27,638 | 10,886 | 12,171 | 3,460 | 1,121 | 1,285 D | 39.4% | 44.0% | 12.5% |
| 16,386 | CROOK | 6,989 | 3,250 | 2,607 | 948 | 184 | 643 R | 46.5% | 37.3% | 13.6% |
| 21,243 | CURRY | 10,972 | 4,790 | 4,202 | 1,560 | 420 | 588 R | 43.7% | 38.3% | 14.2% |
| 94,974 | DESCHUTES | 45,282 | 21,135 | 17,151 | 5,306 | 1,690 | 3,984 R | 46.7% | 37.9% | 11.7% |
| 99,906 | DOUGLAS | 42,769 | 21,855 | 15,250 | 4,465 | 1,199 | 6,605 R | 51.1% | 35.7% | 10.4% |
| 1,861 | GILLIAM | 1,040 | 398 | 485 | 143 | 14 | 87 D | 38.3% | 46.6% | 13.8% |
| 7,976 | GRANT | 3,837 | 2,110 | 1,180 | 432 | 115 | 930 R | 55.0% | 30.8% | 11.3% |
| 7,075 | HARNEY | 3,515 | 1,948 | 980 | 506 | 81 | 968 R | 55.4% | 27.9% | 14.4% |
| 18,589 | HOOD RIVER | 7,574 | 2,794 | 3,654 | 721 | 405 | 860 D | 36.9% | 48.2% | 9.5% |
| 166,060 | JACKSON | 73,647 | 33,771 | 29,230 | 7,470 | 3,176 | 4,541 R | 45.9% | 39.7% | 10.1% |
| 15,969 | JEFFERSON | 6,195 | 2,634 | 2,555 | 813 | 193 | 79 R | 42.5% | 41.2% | 13.1% |
| 71,335 | JOSEPHINE | 32,111 | 16,048 | 11,113 | 3,546 | 1,404 | 4,935 R | 50.0% | 34.6% | 11.0% |
| 61,043 | KLAMATH | 22,360 | 12,116 | 7,207 | 2,538 | 499 | 4,909 R | 54.2% | 32.2% | 11.4% |
| 7,421 | LAKE | 3,652 | 2,239 | 962 | 385 | 66 | 1,277 R | 61.3% | 26.3% | 10.5% |
| 303,426 | LANE | 139,787 | 48,253 | 69,461 | 11,498 | 10,575 | 21,208 D | 34.5% | 49.7% | 8.2% |
| 44,347 | LINCOLN | 20,607 | 6,717 | 10,552 | 2,269 | 1,069 | 3,835 D | 32.6% | 51.2% | 11.0% |
| 100,130 | LINN | 41,325 | 18,331 | 17,041 | 4,773 | 1,180 | 1,290 R | 44.4% | 41.2% | 11.5% |
| 27,860 | MALHEUR | 9,892 | 6,045 | 2,827 | 844 | 176 | 3,218 R | 61.1% | 28.6% | 8.5% |
| 255,044 | MARION | 107,463 | 46,415 | 48,637 | 8,802 | 3,609 | 2,222 D | 43.2% | 45.3% | 8.2% |
| 8,922 | MORROW | 3,331 | 1,381 | 1,426 | 455 | 69 | 45 D | 41.5% | 42.8% | 13.7% |
| 614,104 | MULTNOMAH | 269,961 | 71,094 | 159,878 | 17,536 | 21,453 | 88,784 D | 26.3% | 59.2% | 6.5% |
| 56,678 | POLK | 25,331 | 11,478 | 10,942 | 2,093 | 818 | 536 R | 45.3% | 43.2% | 8.3% |
| 1,886 | SHERMAN | 1,067 | 476 | 444 | 126 | 21 | 32 R | 44.6% | 41.6% | 11.8% |
| 23,767 | TILLAMOOK | 11,332 | 3,884 | 5,775 | 1,263 | 410 | 1,891 D | 34.3% | 51.0% | 11.1% |
| 64,040 | UMATILLA | 21,495 | 9,703 | 8,774 | 2,500 | 518 | 929 R | 45.1% | 40.8% | 11.6% |
| 24,948 | UNION | 11,345 | 5,414 | 4,379 | 1,241 | 311 | 1,035 R | 47.7% | 38.6% | 10.9% |
| 7,535 | WALLOWA | 4,297 | 2,379 | 1,321 | 483 | 114 | 1,058 R | 55.4% | 30.7% | 11.2% |
| 22,737 | WASCO | 9,952 | 3,662 | 4,967 | 1,004 | 319 | 1,305 D | 36.8% | 49.9% | 10.1% |
| 370,197 | WASHINGTON | 159,755 | 65,221 | 76,619 | 11,446 | 6,469 | 11,398 D | 40.8% | 48.0% | 7.2% |
| 1,539 | WHEELER | 874 | 418 | 299 | 121 | 36 | 119 R | 47.8% | 34.2% | 13.8% |
| 75,443 | YAMHILL | 31,135 | 13,900 | 13,078 | 2,913 | 1,244 | 822 R | 44.6% | 42.0% | 9.4% |
| 3,140,585 | TOTAL | 1,377,760 | 538,152 | 649,641 | 121,221 | 68,746 | 111,489 D | 39.1% | 47.2% | 8.8% |

# OREGON

## PRESIDENT 1992

| 1990 Census Population | County | Total Vote | Republican | Democratic | Perot | Other | Plurality | Percentage Total Vote | | |
|---:|---|---:|---:|---:|---:|---:|---:|---:|---:|---:|
| | | | | | | | | Rep. | Dem. | Perot |
| 15,317 | BAKER | 7,530 | 2,862 | 2,395 | 2,191 | 82 | 467 R | 38.0% | 31.8% | 29.1% |
| 70,811 | BENTON | 37,923 | 11,550 | 17,966 | 8,103 | 304 | 6,416 D | 30.5% | 47.4% | 21.4% |
| 278,850 | CLACKAMAS | 154,538 | 53,724 | 60,310 | 39,776 | 728 | 6,586 D | 34.8% | 39.0% | 25.7% |
| 33,301 | CLATSOP | 16,812 | 4,683 | 7,700 | 4,316 | 113 | 3,017 D | 27.9% | 45.8% | 25.7% |
| 37,557 | COLUMBIA | 19,402 | 5,227 | 8,298 | 5,670 | 207 | 2,628 D | 26.9% | 42.8% | 29.2% |
| 60,273 | COOS | 29,659 | 9,284 | 12,072 | 7,989 | 314 | 2,788 D | 31.3% | 40.7% | 26.9% |
| 14,111 | CROOK | 7,271 | 2,703 | 2,508 | 2,024 | 36 | 195 R | 37.2% | 34.5% | 27.8% |
| 19,327 | CURRY | 11,050 | 3,809 | 3,841 | 3,310 | 90 | 32 D | 34.5% | 34.8% | 30.0% |
| 74,958 | DESCHUTES | 43,918 | 15,655 | 15,693 | 12,293 | 277 | 38 D | 35.6% | 35.7% | 28.0% |
| 94,649 | DOUGLAS | 45,860 | 19,011 | 14,137 | 12,377 | 335 | 4,874 R | 41.5% | 30.8% | 27.0% |
| 1,717 | GILLIAM | 1,038 | 377 | 374 | 283 | 4 | 3 R | 36.3% | 36.0% | 27.3% |
| 7,853 | GRANT | 3,986 | 1,496 | 1,135 | 1,302 | 53 | 194 R | 37.5% | 28.5% | 32.7% |
| 7,060 | HARNEY | 3,372 | 1,350 | 973 | 1,024 | 25 | 326 R | 40.0% | 28.9% | 30.4% |
| 16,903 | HOOD RIVER | 7,841 | 2,453 | 3,106 | 2,235 | 47 | 653 D | 31.3% | 39.6% | 28.5% |
| 146,389 | JACKSON | 77,096 | 28,704 | 29,146 | 18,633 | 613 | 442 D | 37.2% | 37.8% | 24.2% |
| 13,676 | JEFFERSON | 5,906 | 1,962 | 2,161 | 1,741 | 42 | 199 D | 33.2% | 36.6% | 29.5% |
| 62,649 | JOSEPHINE | 33,559 | 13,003 | 11,007 | 8,426 | 1,123 | 1,996 R | 38.7% | 32.8% | 25.1% |
| 57,702 | KLAMATH | 26,593 | 11,864 | 7,918 | 6,636 | 175 | 3,946 R | 44.6% | 29.8% | 25.0% |
| 7,186 | LAKE | 3,802 | 1,791 | 1,019 | 980 | 12 | 772 R | 47.1% | 26.8% | 25.8% |
| 282,912 | LANE | 151,862 | 41,789 | 74,083 | 34,906 | 1,084 | 32,294 D | 27.5% | 48.8% | 23.0% |
| 38,889 | LINCOLN | 21,623 | 5,716 | 9,603 | 6,127 | 177 | 3,476 D | 26.4% | 44.4% | 28.3% |
| 91,227 | LINN | 45,287 | 16,461 | 15,399 | 13,256 | 171 | 1,062 R | 36.3% | 34.0% | 29.3% |
| 26,038 | MALHEUR | 10,663 | 5,374 | 2,539 | 2,654 | 96 | 2,720 R | 50.4% | 23.8% | 24.9% |
| 228,483 | MARION | 110,334 | 42,145 | 41,137 | 26,156 | 896 | 1,008 R | 38.2% | 37.3% | 23.7% |
| 7,625 | MORROW | 3,474 | 1,187 | 1,174 | 1,089 | 24 | 13 R | 34.2% | 33.8% | 31.3% |
| 583,887 | MULTNOMAH | 298,291 | 72,326 | 165,081 | 58,236 | 2,648 | 92,755 D | 24.2% | 55.3% | 19.5% |
| 49,541 | POLK | 25,614 | 10,082 | 9,551 | 5,818 | 163 | 531 R | 39.4% | 37.3% | 22.7% |
| 1,918 | SHERMAN | 1,116 | 424 | 362 | 326 | 4 | 62 R | 38.0% | 32.4% | 29.2% |
| 21,570 | TILLAMOOK | 11,484 | 3,359 | 5,040 | 2,997 | 88 | 1,681 D | 29.2% | 43.9% | 26.1% |
| 59,249 | UMATILLA | 19,643 | 7,095 | 6,787 | 5,581 | 180 | 308 R | 36.1% | 34.6% | 28.4% |
| 23,598 | UNION | 11,588 | 4,223 | 3,990 | 3,305 | 70 | 233 R | 36.4% | 34.4% | 28.5% |
| 6,911 | WALLOWA | 4,074 | 1,630 | 1,203 | 1,209 | 32 | 421 R | 40.0% | 29.5% | 29.7% |
| 21,683 | WASCO | 10,973 | 3,242 | 4,663 | 3,008 | 60 | 1,421 D | 29.5% | 42.5% | 27.4% |
| 311,554 | WASHINGTON | 167,195 | 57,146 | 67,528 | 41,575 | 946 | 10,382 D | 34.2% | 40.4% | 24.9% |
| 1,396 | WHEELER | 860 | 357 | 267 | 227 | 9 | 90 R | 41.5% | 31.0% | 26.4% |
| 65,551 | YAMHILL | 31,406 | 11,693 | 11,148 | 8,312 | 253 | 545 R | 37.2% | 35.5% | 26.5% |
| 2,842,321 | TOTAL | 1,462,643 | 475,757 | 621,314 | 354,091 | 11,481 | 145,557 D | 32.5% | 42.5% | 24.2% |

# OREGON

## PRESIDENT 1988

| 1980 Census Population | County | Total Vote | Republican | Democratic | Other | Rep.-Dem. Plurality | Percentage | | | |
|---|---|---|---|---|---|---|---|---|---|---|
| | | | | | | | Total Vote | | Major Vote | |
| | | | | | | | Rep. | Dem. | Rep. | Dem. |
| 16,134 | BAKER | 6,826 | 3,696 | 2,896 | 234 | 800 R | 54.1% | 42.4% | 56.1% | 43.9% |
| 68,211 | BENTON | 31,610 | 14,004 | 16,930 | 676 | 2,926 D | 44.3% | 53.6% | 45.3% | 54.7% |
| 241,919 | CLACKAMAS | 123,351 | 61,381 | 59,799 | 2,171 | 1,582 R | 49.8% | 48.5% | 50.7% | 49.3% |
| 32,489 | CLATSOP | 14,316 | 5,956 | 8,074 | 286 | 2,118 D | 41.6% | 56.4% | 42.5% | 57.5% |
| 35,646 | COLUMBIA | 15,806 | 6,424 | 8,983 | 399 | 2,559 D | 40.6% | 56.8% | 41.7% | 58.3% |
| 64,047 | COOS | 24,836 | 10,153 | 13,996 | 687 | 3,843 D | 40.9% | 56.4% | 42.0% | 58.0% |
| 13,091 | CROOK | 5,882 | 3,049 | 2,719 | 114 | 330 R | 51.8% | 46.2% | 52.9% | 47.1% |
| 16,992 | CURRY | 9,012 | 4,761 | 4,015 | 236 | 746 R | 52.8% | 44.6% | 54.3% | 45.7% |
| 62,142 | DESCHUTES | 31,366 | 16,425 | 14,264 | 677 | 2,161 R | 52.4% | 45.5% | 53.5% | 46.5% |
| 93,748 | DOUGLAS | 38,415 | 20,120 | 17,255 | 1,040 | 2,865 R | 52.4% | 44.9% | 53.8% | 46.2% |
| 2,057 | GILLIAM | 897 | 470 | 417 | 10 | 53 R | 52.4% | 46.5% | 53.0% | 47.0% |
| 8,210 | GRANT | 3,844 | 2,264 | 1,437 | 143 | 827 R | 58.9% | 37.4% | 61.2% | 38.8% |
| 8,314 | HARNEY | 3,330 | 1,833 | 1,379 | 118 | 454 R | 55.0% | 41.4% | 57.1% | 42.9% |
| 15,835 | HOOD RIVER | 6,689 | 3,257 | 3,275 | 157 | 18 D | 48.7% | 49.0% | 49.9% | 50.1% |
| 132,456 | JACKSON | 61,912 | 32,516 | 28,028 | 1,368 | 4,488 R | 52.5% | 45.3% | 53.7% | 46.3% |
| 11,599 | JEFFERSON | 4,995 | 2,509 | 2,346 | 140 | 163 R | 50.2% | 47.0% | 51.7% | 48.3% |
| 58,855 | JOSEPHINE | 27,272 | 15,876 | 10,646 | 750 | 5,230 R | 58.2% | 39.0% | 59.9% | 40.1% |
| 59,117 | KLAMATH | 22,470 | 13,484 | 8,429 | 557 | 5,055 R | 60.0% | 37.5% | 61.5% | 38.5% |
| 7,532 | LAKE | 3,463 | 2,161 | 1,237 | 65 | 924 R | 62.4% | 35.7% | 63.6% | 36.4% |
| 275,226 | LANE | 119,702 | 47,563 | 69,883 | 2,256 | 22,320 D | 39.7% | 58.4% | 40.5% | 59.5% |
| 35,264 | LINCOLN | 17,443 | 7,364 | 9,598 | 481 | 2,234 D | 42.2% | 55.0% | 43.4% | 56.6% |
| 89,495 | LINN | 36,122 | 18,312 | 17,007 | 803 | 1,305 R | 50.7% | 47.1% | 51.8% | 48.2% |
| 26,896 | MALHEUR | 9,443 | 6,285 | 2,965 | 193 | 3,320 R | 66.6% | 31.4% | 67.9% | 32.1% |
| 204,692 | MARION | 88,492 | 45,292 | 41,193 | 2,007 | 4,099 R | 51.2% | 46.5% | 52.4% | 47.6% |
| 7,519 | MORROW | 2,970 | 1,529 | 1,375 | 66 | 154 R | 51.5% | 46.3% | 52.7% | 47.3% |
| 562,640 | MULTNOMAH | 261,843 | 95,561 | 161,361 | 4,921 | 65,800 D | 36.5% | 61.6% | 37.2% | 62.8% |
| 45,203 | POLK | 20,621 | 10,553 | 9,626 | 442 | 927 R | 51.2% | 46.7% | 52.3% | 47.7% |
| 2,172 | SHERMAN | 1,016 | 555 | 435 | 26 | 120 R | 54.6% | 42.8% | 56.1% | 43.9% |
| 21,164 | TILLAMOOK | 10,070 | 4,297 | 5,529 | 244 | 1,232 D | 42.7% | 54.9% | 43.7% | 56.3% |
| 58,861 | UMATILLA | 18,981 | 10,254 | 8,327 | 400 | 1,927 R | 54.0% | 43.9% | 55.2% | 44.8% |
| 23,921 | UNION | 10,090 | 5,061 | 4,682 | 347 | 379 R | 50.2% | 46.4% | 51.9% | 48.1% |
| 7,273 | WALLOWA | 3,503 | 1,993 | 1,425 | 85 | 568 R | 56.9% | 40.7% | 58.3% | 41.7% |
| 21,732 | WASCO | 9,834 | 4,462 | 5,141 | 231 | 679 D | 45.4% | 52.3% | 46.5% | 53.5% |
| 245,808 | WASHINGTON | 129,211 | 67,018 | 59,837 | 2,356 | 7,181 R | 51.9% | 46.3% | 52.8% | 47.2% |
| 1,513 | WHEELER | 673 | 367 | 274 | 32 | 93 R | 54.5% | 40.7% | 57.3% | 42.7% |
| 55,332 | YAMHILL | 25,388 | 13,321 | 11,423 | 644 | 1,898 R | 52.5% | 45.0% | 53.8% | 46.2% |
| 2,633,105 | TOTAL | 1,201,694 | 560,126 | 616,206 | 25,362 | 56,080 D | 46.6% | 51.3% | 47.6% | 52.4% |

# OREGON

## PRESIDENT 1984

| 1980 Census Population | County | Total Vote | Republican | Democratic | Other | Rep.-Dem. Plurality | Percentage | | | |
|---|---|---|---|---|---|---|---|---|---|---|
| | | | | | | | Total Vote | | Major Vote | |
| | | | | | | | Rep. | Dem. | Rep. | Dem. |
| 16,134 | BAKER | 7,812 | 5,204 | 2,591 | 17 | 2,613 R | 66.6% | 33.2% | 66.8% | 33.2% |
| 68,211 | BENTON | 34,062 | 17,836 | 16,073 | 153 | 1,763 R | 52.4% | 47.2% | 52.6% | 47.4% |
| 241,919 | CLACKAMAS | 116,173 | 68,630 | 47,254 | 289 | 21,376 R | 59.1% | 40.7% | 59.2% | 40.8% |
| 32,489 | CLATSOP | 15,085 | 7,522 | 7,525 | 38 | 3 D | 49.9% | 49.9% | 50.0% | 50.0% |
| 35,646 | COLUMBIA | 16,105 | 7,811 | 8,219 | 75 | 408 D | 48.5% | 51.0% | 48.7% | 51.3% |
| 64,047 | COOS | 27,339 | 13,637 | 13,582 | 120 | 55 R | 49.9% | 49.7% | 50.1% | 49.9% |
| 13,091 | CROOK | 6,064 | 3,773 | 2,268 | 23 | 1,505 R | 62.2% | 37.4% | 62.5% | 37.5% |
| 16,992 | CURRY | 8,815 | 5,363 | 3,423 | 29 | 1,940 R | 60.8% | 38.8% | 61.0% | 39.0% |
| 62,142 | DESCHUTES | 31,066 | 19,323 | 11,671 | 72 | 7,652 R | 62.2% | 37.6% | 62.3% | 37.7% |
| 93,748 | DOUGLAS | 39,996 | 25,243 | 14,609 | 144 | 10,634 R | 63.1% | 36.5% | 63.3% | 36.7% |
| 2,057 | GILLIAM | 1,073 | 700 | 369 | 4 | 331 R | 65.2% | 34.4% | 65.5% | 34.5% |
| 8,210 | GRANT | 4,041 | 2,695 | 1,344 | 2 | 1,351 R | 66.7% | 33.3% | 66.7% | 33.3% |
| 8,314 | HARNEY | 3,512 | 2,197 | 1,290 | 25 | 907 R | 62.6% | 36.7% | 63.0% | 37.0% |
| 15,835 | HOOD RIVER | 7,571 | 4,531 | 3,022 | 18 | 1,509 R | 59.8% | 39.9% | 60.0% | 40.0% |
| 132,456 | JACKSON | 61,359 | 37,895 | 23,230 | 234 | 14,665 R | 61.8% | 37.9% | 62.0% | 38.0% |
| 11,599 | JEFFERSON | 5,216 | 3,283 | 1,920 | 13 | 1,363 R | 62.9% | 36.8% | 63.1% | 36.9% |
| 58,855 | JOSEPHINE | 28,062 | 19,470 | 8,539 | 53 | 10,931 R | 69.4% | 30.4% | 69.5% | 30.5% |
| 59,117 | KLAMATH | 25,335 | 17,686 | 7,575 | 74 | 10,111 R | 69.8% | 29.9% | 70.0% | 30.0% |
| 7,532 | LAKE | 3,653 | 2,466 | 1,184 | 3 | 1,282 R | 67.5% | 32.4% | 67.6% | 32.4% |
| 275,226 | LANE | 125,852 | 61,493 | 63,999 | 360 | 2,506 D | 48.9% | 50.9% | 49.0% | 51.0% |
| 35,264 | LINCOLN | 17,804 | 9,110 | 8,637 | 57 | 473 R | 51.2% | 48.5% | 51.3% | 48.7% |
| 89,495 | LINN | 39,699 | 23,463 | 16,161 | 75 | 7,302 R | 59.1% | 40.7% | 59.2% | 40.8% |
| 26,896 | MALHEUR | 11,071 | 8,441 | 2,611 | 19 | 5,830 R | 76.2% | 23.6% | 76.4% | 23.6% |
| 204,692 | MARION | 91,209 | 54,535 | 36,440 | 234 | 18,095 R | 59.8% | 40.0% | 59.9% | 40.1% |
| 7,519 | MORROW | 3,397 | 2,130 | 1,254 | 13 | 876 R | 62.7% | 36.9% | 62.9% | 37.1% |
| 562,640 | MULTNOMAH | 265,539 | 119,932 | 144,179 | 1,428 | 24,247 D | 45.2% | 54.3% | 45.4% | 54.6% |
| 45,203 | POLK | 21,432 | 12,678 | 8,709 | 45 | 3,969 R | 59.2% | 40.6% | 59.3% | 40.7% |
| 2,172 | SHERMAN | 1,227 | 828 | 398 | 1 | 430 R | 67.5% | 32.4% | 67.5% | 32.5% |
| 21,164 | TILLAMOOK | 10,308 | 5,267 | 4,988 | 53 | 279 R | 51.1% | 48.4% | 51.4% | 48.6% |
| 58,861 | UMATILLA | 22,514 | 14,211 | 8,246 | 57 | 5,965 R | 63.1% | 36.6% | 63.3% | 36.7% |
| 23,921 | UNION | 10,829 | 6,645 | 4,134 | 50 | 2,511 R | 61.4% | 38.2% | 61.6% | 38.4% |
| 7,273 | WALLOWA | 3,831 | 2,619 | 1,204 | 8 | 1,415 R | 68.4% | 31.4% | 68.5% | 31.5% |
| 21,732 | WASCO | 12,472 | 6,905 | 5,526 | 41 | 1,379 R | 55.4% | 44.3% | 55.5% | 44.5% |
| 245,808 | WASHINGTON | 120,896 | 75,877 | 44,602 | 417 | 31,275 R | 62.8% | 36.9% | 63.0% | 37.0% |
| 1,513 | WHEELER | 757 | 504 | 253 | | 251 R | 66.6% | 33.4% | 66.6% | 33.4% |
| 55,332 | YAMHILL | 25,351 | 15,797 | 9,450 | 104 | 6,347 R | 62.3% | 37.3% | 62.6% | 37.4% |
| 2,633,105 | TOTAL | 1,226,527 | 685,700 | 536,479 | 4,348 | 149,221 R | 55.9% | 43.7% | 56.1% | 43.9% |

# OREGON

## PRESIDENT 1980

| 1980 Census Population | County | Total Vote | Republican | Democratic | Other | Rep.-Dem. Plurality | Percentage Total Vote Rep. | Dem. | Major Vote Rep. | Dɛm. |
|---|---|---|---|---|---|---|---|---|---|---|
| 16,134 | BAKER | 8,013 | 4,747 | 2,515 | 751 | 2,232 R | 59.2% | 31.4% | 65.4% | 34.6% |
| 68,211 | BENTON | 34,507 | 14,982 | 13,150 | 6,375 | 1,832 R | 43.4% | 38.1% | 53.3% | 46.7% |
| 241,919 | CLACKAMAS | 109,483 | 54,111 | 40,462 | 14,910 | 13,649 R | 49.4% | 37.0% | 57.2% | 42.8% |
| 32,489 | CLATSOP | 14,959 | 6,124 | 6,482 | 2,353 | 358 D | 40.9% | 43.3% | 48.6% | 51.4% |
| 35,646 | COLUMBIA | 15,505 | 6,623 | 7,124 | 1,758 | 501 D | 42.7% | 45.9% | 48.2% | 51.8% |
| 64,047 | COOS | 28,176 | 13,041 | 11,817 | 3,318 | 1,224 R | 46.3% | 41.9% | 52.5% | 47.5% |
| 13,091 | CROOK | 5,862 | 3,113 | 2,162 | 587 | 951 R | 53.1% | 36.9% | 59.0% | 41.0% |
| 16,992 | CURRY | 8,488 | 4,910 | 2,656 | 922 | 2,254 R | 57.8% | 31.3% | 64.9% | 35.1% |
| 62,142 | DESCHUTES | 28,715 | 15,186 | 9,641 | 3,888 | 5,545 R | 52.9% | 33.6% | 61.2% | 38.8% |
| 93,748 | DOUGLAS | 39,516 | 23,101 | 12,564 | 3,851 | 10,537 R | 58.5% | 31.8% | 64.8% | 35.2% |
| 2,057 | GILLIAM | 1,140 | 622 | 394 | 124 | 228 R | 54.6% | 34.6% | 61.2% | 38.8% |
| 8,210 | GRANT | 4,187 | 2,519 | 1,274 | 394 | 1,245 R | 60.2% | 30.4% | 66.4% | 33.6% |
| 8,314 | HARNEY | 3,785 | 2,313 | 1,110 | 362 | 1,203 R | 61.1% | 29.3% | 67.6% | 32.4% |
| 15,835 | HOOD RIVER | 7,092 | 3,450 | 2,924 | 718 | 526 R | 48.6% | 41.2% | 54.1% | 45.9% |
| 132,456 | JACKSON | 58,740 | 32,879 | 19,903 | 5,958 | 12,976 R | 56.0% | 33.9% | 62.3% | 37.7% |
| 11,599 | JEFFERSON | 4,737 | 2,523 | 1,654 | 560 | 869 R | 53.3% | 34.9% | 60.4% | 39.6% |
| 58,855 | JOSEPHINE | 26,336 | 16,827 | 7,116 | 2,393 | 9,711 R | 63.9% | 27.0% | 70.3% | 29.7% |
| 59,117 | KLAMATH | 25,592 | 16,060 | 7,371 | 2,161 | 8,689 R | 62.8% | 28.8% | 68.5% | 31.5% |
| 7,532 | LAKE | 3,689 | 2,234 | 1,147 | 308 | 1,087 R | 60.6% | 31.1% | 66.1% | 33.9% |
| 275,226 | LANE | 125,604 | 54,750 | 52,240 | 18,614 | 2,510 R | 43.6% | 41.6% | 51.2% | 48.8% |
| 35,264 | LINCOLN | 17,127 | 7,637 | 7,009 | 2,481 | 628 R | 44.6% | 40.9% | 52.1% | 47.9% |
| 89,495 | LINN | 36,293 | 18,943 | 13,516 | 3,834 | 5,427 R | 52.2% | 37.2% | 58.4% | 41.6% |
| 26,896 | MALHEUR | 11,364 | 7,705 | 2,937 | 722 | 4,768 R | 67.8% | 25.8% | 72.4% | 27.6% |
| 204,692 | MARION | 85,449 | 42,191 | 32,134 | 11,124 | 10,057 R | 49.4% | 37.6% | 56.8% | 43.2% |
| 7,519 | MORROW | 3,141 | 1,728 | 1,077 | 336 | 651 R | 55.0% | 34.3% | 61.6% | 38.4% |
| 562,640 | MULTNOMAH | 258,968 | 101,606 | 120,487 | 36,875 | 18,881 D | 39.2% | 46.5% | 45.7% | 54.3% |
| 45,203 | POLK | 20,531 | 10,006 | 7,833 | 2,692 | 2,173 R | 48.7% | 38.2% | 56.1% | 43.9% |
| 2,172 | SHERMAN | 1,170 | 677 | 389 | 104 | 288 R | 57.9% | 33.2% | 63.5% | 36.5% |
| 21,164 | TILLAMOOK | 9,903 | 4,123 | 4,521 | 1,259 | 398 D | 41.6% | 45.7% | 47.7% | 52.3% |
| 58,861 | UMATILLA | 22,414 | 12,950 | 7,382 | 2,082 | 5,568 R | 57.8% | 32.9% | 63.7% | 36.3% |
| 23,921 | UNION | 11,272 | 6,514 | 3,677 | 1,081 | 2,837 R | 57.8% | 32.6% | 63.9% | 36.1% |
| 7,273 | WALLOWA | 3,792 | 2,485 | 995 | 312 | 1,490 R | 65.5% | 26.2% | 71.4% | 28.6% |
| 21,732 | WASCO | 10,235 | 4,703 | 4,336 | 1,196 | 367 R | 46.0% | 42.4% | 52.0% | 48.0% |
| 245,808 | WASHINGTON | 111,355 | 57,165 | 37,915 | 16,275 | 19,250 R | 51.3% | 34.0% | 60.1% | 39.9% |
| 1,513 | WHEELER | 808 | 442 | 282 | 84 | 160 R | 54.7% | 34.9% | 61.0% | 39.0% |
| 55,332 | YAMHILL | 23,568 | 12,054 | 8,694 | 2,820 | 3,360 R | 51.1% | 36.9% | 58.1% | 41.9% |
| 2,633,105 | TOTAL | 1,181,516 | 571,044 | 456,890 | 153,582 | 114,154 R | 48.3% | 38.7% | 55.6% | 44.4% |

# OREGON

## PRESIDENT 1976

| 1970 Census Population | County | Total Vote | Republican | Democratic | Other | Rep.-Dem. Plurality | Percentage | | | |
|---|---|---|---|---|---|---|---|---|---|---|
| | | | | | | | Total Vote | | Major Vote | |
| | | | | | | | Rep. | Dem. | Rep. | Dem. |
| 14,919 | BAKER | 6,919 | 3,340 | 3,306 | 273 | 34 R | 48.3% | 47.8% | 50.3% | 49.7% |
| 53,776 | BENTON | 29,307 | 15,555 | 11,887 | 1,865 | 3,668 R | 53.1% | 40.6% | 56.7% | 43.3% |
| 166,088 | CLACKAMAS | 93,959 | 47,671 | 42,504 | 3,784 | 5,167 R | 50.7% | 45.2% | 52.9% | 47.1% |
| 28,473 | CLATSOP | 13,616 | 6,178 | 6,690 | 748 | 512 D | 45.4% | 49.1% | 48.0% | 52.0% |
| 28,790 | COLUMBIA | 13,859 | 5,226 | 8,005 | 628 | 2,779 D | 37.7% | 57.8% | 39.5% | 60.5% |
| 56,515 | COOS | 24,725 | 9,481 | 14,168 | 1,076 | 4,687 D | 38.3% | 57.3% | 40.1% | 59.9% |
| 9,985 | CROOK | 4,777 | 2,093 | 2,536 | 148 | 443 D | 43.8% | 53.1% | 45.2% | 54.8% |
| 13,006 | CURRY | 6,507 | 2,962 | 3,227 | 318 | 265 D | 45.5% | 49.6% | 47.9% | 52.1% |
| 30,442 | DESCHUTES | 19,382 | 9,054 | 9,480 | 848 | 426 D | 46.7% | 48.9% | 48.9% | 51.1% |
| 71,743 | DOUGLAS | 32,973 | 16,500 | 14,965 | 1,508 | 1,535 R | 50.0% | 45.4% | 52.4% | 47.6% |
| 2,342 | GILLIAM | 1,166 | 612 | 508 | 46 | 104 R | 52.5% | 43.6% | 54.6% | 45.4% |
| 6,996 | GRANT | 3,206 | 1,640 | 1,393 | 173 | 247 R | 51.2% | 43.4% | 54.1% | 45.9% |
| 7,215 | HARNEY | 3,407 | 1,652 | 1,567 | 188 | 85 R | 48.5% | 46.0% | 51.3% | 48.7% |
| 13,187 | HOOD RIVER | 6,636 | 3,210 | 3,114 | 312 | 96 R | 48.4% | 46.9% | 50.8% | 49.2% |
| 94,533 | JACKSON | 50,236 | 24,237 | 23,384 | 2,615 | 853 R | 48.2% | 46.5% | 50.9% | 49.1% |
| 8,548 | JEFFERSON | 3,777 | 1,810 | 1,769 | 198 | 41 R | 47.9% | 46.8% | 50.6% | 49.4% |
| 35,746 | JOSEPHINE | 21,110 | 10,726 | 9,061 | 1,323 | 1,665 R | 50.8% | 42.9% | 54.2% | 45.8% |
| 50,021 | KLAMATH | 22,187 | 11,649 | 9,659 | 879 | 1,990 R | 52.5% | 43.5% | 54.7% | 45.3% |
| 6,343 | LAKE | 3,088 | 1,575 | 1,381 | 132 | 194 R | 51.0% | 44.7% | 53.3% | 46.7% |
| 213,358 | LANE | 108,367 | 46,245 | 56,479 | 5,643 | 10,234 D | 42.7% | 52.1% | 45.0% | 55.0% |
| 25,755 | LINCOLN | 13,199 | 5,755 | 6,685 | 759 | 930 D | 43.6% | 50.6% | 46.3% | 53.7% |
| 71,914 | LINN | 31,241 | 14,128 | 15,776 | 1,337 | 1,648 D | 45.2% | 50.5% | 47.2% | 52.8% |
| 23,169 | MALHEUR | 9,610 | 5,682 | 3,507 | 421 | 2,175 R | 59.1% | 36.5% | 61.8% | 38.2% |
| 151,309 | MARION | 72,331 | 35,497 | 33,781 | 3,053 | 1,716 R | 49.1% | 46.7% | 51.2% | 48.8% |
| 4,465 | MORROW | 2,367 | 1,091 | 1,162 | 114 | 71 D | 46.1% | 49.1% | 48.4% | 51.6% |
| 556,667 | MULTNOMAH | 253,159 | 112,400 | 129,060 | 11,699 | 16,660 D | 44.4% | 51.0% | 46.6% | 53.4% |
| 35,349 | POLK | 17,530 | 8,528 | 8,141 | 861 | 387 R | 48.6% | 46.4% | 51.2% | 48.8% |
| 2,139 | SHERMAN | 1,109 | 567 | 491 | 51 | 76 R | 51.1% | 44.3% | 53.6% | 46.4% |
| 17,930 | TILLAMOOK | 8,867 | 4,033 | 4,456 | 378 | 423 D | 45.5% | 50.3% | 47.5% | 52.5% |
| 44,923 | UMATILLA | 18,031 | 9,345 | 7,985 | 701 | 1,360 R | 51.8% | 44.3% | 53.9% | 46.1% |
| 19,377 | UNION | 9,829 | 5,111 | 4,280 | 438 | 831 R | 52.0% | 43.5% | 54.4% | 45.6% |
| 6,247 | WALLOWA | 3,149 | 1,693 | 1,310 | 146 | 383 R | 53.8% | 41.6% | 56.4% | 43.6% |
| 20,133 | WASCO | 9,240 | 4,258 | 4,560 | 422 | 302 D | 46.1% | 49.4% | 48.3% | 51.7% |
| 157,920 | WASHINGTON | 90,611 | 52,376 | 34,847 | 3,388 | 17,529 R | 57.8% | 38.5% | 60.0% | 40.0% |
| 1,849 | WHEELER | 779 | 355 | 402 | 22 | 47 D | 45.6% | 51.6% | 46.9% | 53.1% |
| 40,213 | YAMHILL | 19,620 | 9,885 | 8,881 | 854 | 1,004 R | 50.4% | 45.3% | 52.7% | 47.3% |
| 2,091,385 | TOTAL | 1,029,876 | 492,120 | 490,407 | 47,349 | 1,713 R | 47.8% | 47.6% | 50.1% | 49.9% |

# OREGON

## PRESIDENT 1972

| 1970 Census Population | County | Total Vote | Republican | Democratic | Other | Rep.-Dem. Plurality | Percentage Total Vote Rep. | Dem. | Major Vote Rep. | Dem. |
|---:|---|---:|---:|---:|---:|---:|---:|---:|---:|---:|
| 14,919 | BAKER | 6,220 | 3,441 | 2,047 | 732 | 1,394 R | 55.3% | 32.9% | 62.7% | 37.3% |
| 53,776 | BENTON | 26,456 | 14,906 | 10,842 | 708 | 4,064 R | 56.3% | 41.0% | 57.9% | 42.1% |
| 166,088 | CLACKAMAS | 78,089 | 41,767 | 32,540 | 3,782 | 9,227 R | 53.5% | 41.7% | 56.2% | 43.8% |
| 28,473 | CLATSOP | 12,647 | 5,998 | 6,017 | 632 | 19 D | 47.4% | 47.6% | 49.9% | 50.1% |
| 28,790 | COLUMBIA | 12,284 | 5,348 | 5,997 | 939 | 649 D | 43.5% | 48.8% | 47.1% | 52.9% |
| 56,515 | COOS | 23,213 | 10,370 | 11,778 | 1,065 | 1,408 D | 44.7% | 50.7% | 46.8% | 53.2% |
| 9,985 | CROOK | 4,123 | 2,167 | 1,743 | 213 | 424 R | 52.6% | 42.3% | 55.4% | 44.6% |
| 13,006 | CURRY | 5,470 | 2,832 | 2,108 | 530 | 724 R | 51.8% | 38.5% | 57.3% | 42.7% |
| 30,442 | DESCHUTES | 14,819 | 7,747 | 6,319 | 753 | 1,428 R | 52.3% | 42.6% | 55.1% | 44.9% |
| 71,743 | DOUGLAS | 27,508 | 15,881 | 9,009 | 2,618 | 6,872 R | 57.7% | 32.8% | 63.8% | 36.2% |
| 2,342 | GILLIAM | 1,069 | 665 | 355 | 49 | 310 R | 62.2% | 33.2% | 65.2% | 34.8% |
| 6,996 | GRANT | 2,951 | 1,781 | 932 | 238 | 849 R | 60.4% | 31.6% | 65.6% | 34.4% |
| 7,215 | HARNEY | 2,863 | 1,693 | 1,004 | 166 | 689 R | 59.1% | 35.1% | 62.8% | 37.2% |
| 13,187 | HOOD RIVER | 5,841 | 3,152 | 2,330 | 359 | 822 R | 54.0% | 39.9% | 57.5% | 42.5% |
| 94,533 | JACKSON | 41,561 | 24,003 | 14,529 | 3,029 | 9,474 R | 57.8% | 35.0% | 62.3% | 37.7% |
| 8,548 | JEFFERSON | 3,221 | 1,816 | 1,229 | 176 | 587 R | 56.4% | 38.2% | 59.6% | 40.4% |
| 35,746 | JOSEPHINE | 16,927 | 9,911 | 5,090 | 1,926 | 4,821 R | 58.6% | 30.1% | 66.1% | 33.9% |
| 50,021 | KLAMATH | 18,954 | 11,169 | 5,719 | 2,066 | 5,450 R | 58.9% | 30.2% | 66.1% | 33.9% |
| 6,343 | LAKE | 2,653 | 1,619 | 777 | 257 | 842 R | 61.0% | 29.3% | 67.6% | 32.4% |
| 213,358 | LANE | 98,187 | 47,739 | 46,177 | 4,271 | 1,562 R | 48.6% | 47.0% | 50.8% | 49.2% |
| 25,755 | LINCOLN | 11,854 | 6,112 | 5,117 | 625 | 995 R | 51.6% | 43.2% | 54.4% | 45.6% |
| 71,914 | LINN | 27,814 | 15,079 | 11,178 | 1,557 | 3,901 R | 54.2% | 40.2% | 57.4% | 42.6% |
| 23,169 | MALHEUR | 8,771 | 5,908 | 1,870 | 993 | 4,038 R | 67.4% | 21.3% | 76.0% | 24.0% |
| 151,309 | MARION | 63,361 | 36,441 | 23,908 | 3,012 | 12,533 R | 57.5% | 37.7% | 60.4% | 39.6% |
| 4,465 | MORROW | 2,007 | 1,059 | 718 | 230 | 341 R | 52.8% | 35.8% | 59.6% | 40.4% |
| 556,667 | MULTNOMAH | 252,958 | 118,219 | 125,470 | 9,269 | 7,251 D | 46.7% | 49.6% | 48.5% | 51.5% |
| 35,349 | POLK | 15,609 | 8,985 | 5,908 | 716 | 3,077 R | 57.6% | 37.8% | 60.3% | 39.7% |
| 2,139 | SHERMAN | 1,043 | 677 | 330 | 36 | 347 R | 64.9% | 31.6% | 67.2% | 32.8% |
| 17,930 | TILLAMOOK | 8,044 | 4,120 | 3,544 | 380 | 576 R | 51.2% | 44.1% | 53.8% | 46.2% |
| 44,923 | UMATILLA | 18,071 | 10,470 | 6,090 | 1,511 | 4,380 R | 57.9% | 33.7% | 63.2% | 36.8% |
| 19,377 | UNION | 8,985 | 5,073 | 3,272 | 640 | 1,801 R | 56.5% | 36.4% | 60.8% | 39.2% |
| 6,247 | WALLOWA | 3,065 | 1,909 | 899 | 257 | 1,010 R | 62.3% | 29.3% | 68.0% | 32.0% |
| 20,133 | WASCO | 8,775 | 4,537 | 3,749 | 489 | 788 R | 51.7% | 42.7% | 54.8% | 45.2% |
| 157,920 | WASHINGTON | 75,238 | 43,958 | 27,890 | 3,390 | 16,068 R | 58.4% | 37.1% | 61.2% | 38.8% |
| 1,849 | WHEELER | 786 | 474 | 267 | 45 | 207 R | 60.3% | 34.0% | 64.0% | 36.0% |
| 40,213 | YAMHILL | 16,509 | 9,660 | 6,008 | 841 | 3,652 R | 58.5% | 36.4% | 61.7% | 38.3% |
| 2,091,385 | TOTAL | 927,946 | 486,686 | 392,760 | 48,500 | 93,926 R | 52.4% | 42.3% | 55.3% | 44.7% |

# OREGON

## PRESIDENT 1968

| 1960 Census Population | County | Total Vote | Republican | Democratic | AIP | Other | Plurality | Percentage Total Vote Rep. | Dem. | AIP |
|---|---|---|---|---|---|---|---|---|---|---|
| 17,295 | BAKER | 6,255 | 3,311 | 2,464 | 480 | | 847 R | 52.9% | 39.4% | 7.7% |
| 39,165 | BENTON | 19,016 | 11,654 | 6,538 | 749 | 75 | 5,116 R | 61.3% | 34.4% | 3.9% |
| 113,038 | CLACKAMAS | 63,961 | 32,363 | 27,939 | 3,659 | | 4,424 R | 50.6% | 43.7% | 5.7% |
| 27,380 | CLATSOP | 12,738 | 5,810 | 6,243 | 651 | 34 | 433 D | 45.6% | 49.0% | 5.1% |
| 22,379 | COLUMBIA | 11,047 | 4,208 | 6,064 | 728 | 47 | 1,856 D | 38.1% | 54.9% | 6.6% |
| 54,955 | COOS | 20,890 | 8,230 | 10,884 | 1,767 | 9 | 2,654 D | 39.4% | 52.1% | 8.5% |
| 9,430 | CROOK | 3,607 | 1,727 | 1,611 | 256 | 13 | 116 R | 47.9% | 44.7% | 7.1% |
| 13,983 | CURRY | 4,729 | 2,323 | 1,934 | 436 | 36 | 389 R | 49.1% | 40.9% | 9.2% |
| 23,100 | DESCHUTES | 11,230 | 5,599 | 4,859 | 738 | 34 | 740 R | 49.9% | 43.3% | 6.6% |
| 68,458 | DOUGLAS | 26,092 | 13,410 | 9,186 | 3,433 | 63 | 4,224 R | 51.4% | 35.2% | 13.2% |
| 3,069 | GILLIAM | 1,120 | 619 | 436 | 65 | | 183 R | 55.3% | 38.9% | 5.8% |
| 7,726 | GRANT | 2,814 | 1,632 | 934 | 239 | 9 | 698 R | 58.0% | 33.2% | 8.5% |
| 6,744 | HARNEY | 2,858 | 1,617 | 1,036 | 197 | 8 | 581 R | 56.6% | 36.2% | 6.9% |
| 13,395 | HOOD RIVER | 5,317 | 2,597 | 2,385 | 323 | 12 | 212 R | 48.8% | 44.9% | 6.1% |
| 73,962 | JACKSON | 34,842 | 19,577 | 12,714 | 2,446 | 105 | 6,863 R | 56.2% | 36.5% | 7.0% |
| 7,130 | JEFFERSON | 3,020 | 1,669 | 1,160 | 180 | 11 | 509 R | 55.3% | 38.4% | 6.0% |
| 29,917 | JOSEPHINE | 14,671 | 8,456 | 4,351 | 1,800 | 64 | 4,105 R | 57.6% | 29.7% | 12.3% |
| 47,475 | KLAMATH | 17,017 | 9,604 | 5,629 | 1,735 | 49 | 3,975 R | 56.4% | 33.1% | 10.2% |
| 7,158 | LAKE | 2,505 | 1,538 | 730 | 229 | 8 | 808 R | 61.4% | 29.1% | 9.1% |
| 162,890 | LANE | 80,549 | 39,563 | 34,521 | 5,830 | 635 | 5,042 R | 49.1% | 42.9% | 7.2% |
| 24,635 | LINCOLN | 10,699 | 5,031 | 5,009 | 659 | | 22 R | 47.0% | 46.8% | 6.2% |
| 58,867 | LINN | 24,284 | 12,604 | 10,032 | 1,648 | | 2,572 R | 51.9% | 41.3% | 6.8% |
| 22,764 | MALHEUR | 8,360 | 5,447 | 2,021 | 892 | | 3,426 R | 65.2% | 24.2% | 10.7% |
| 120,888 | MARION | 55,502 | 30,417 | 22,327 | 2,756 | 2 | 8,090 R | 54.8% | 40.2% | 5.0% |
| 4,871 | MORROW | 1,967 | 1,068 | 797 | 102 | | 271 R | 54.3% | 40.5% | 5.2% |
| 522,813 | MULTNOMAH | 243,518 | 106,831 | 124,651 | 11,054 | 982 | 17,820 D | 43.9% | 51.2% | 4.5% |
| 26,523 | POLK | 12,571 | 6,997 | 4,961 | 581 | 32 | 2,036 R | 55.7% | 39.5% | 4.6% |
| 2,446 | SHERMAN | 1,089 | 646 | 384 | 59 | | 262 R | 59.3% | 35.3% | 5.4% |
| 18,955 | TILLAMOOK | 7,291 | 3,261 | 3,609 | 394 | 27 | 348 D | 44.7% | 49.5% | 5.4% |
| 44,352 | UMATILLA | 16,379 | 8,975 | 6,402 | 956 | 46 | 2,573 R | 54.8% | 39.1% | 5.8% |
| 18,180 | UNION | 7,747 | 3,796 | 3,409 | 521 | 21 | 387 R | 49.0% | 44.0% | 6.7% |
| 7,102 | WALLOWA | 2,742 | 1,527 | 1,006 | 194 | 15 | 521 R | 55.7% | 36.7% | 7.1% |
| 20,205 | WASCO | 8,306 | 3,842 | 3,918 | 514 | 32 | 76 D | 46.3% | 47.2% | 6.2% |
| 92,237 | WASHINGTON | 59,842 | 34,105 | 22,943 | 2,566 | 228 | 11,162 R | 57.0% | 38.3% | 4.3% |
| 2,722 | WHEELER | 762 | 443 | 292 | 27 | | 151 R | 58.1% | 38.3% | 3.5% |
| 32,478 | YAMHILL | 14,285 | 7,936 | 5,487 | 819 | 43 | 2,449 R | 55.6% | 38.4% | 5.7% |
| 1,768,687 | TOTAL | 819,622 | 408,433 | 358,866 | 49,683 | 2,640 | 49,567 R | 49.8% | 43.8% | 6.1% |

# OREGON

## PRESIDENT 1964

| 1960 Census Population | County | Total Vote | Republican | Democratic | Other | Rep.-Dem. Plurality | Percentage | | | |
|---|---|---|---|---|---|---|---|---|---|---|
| | | | | | | | Total Vote | | Major Vote | |
| | | | | | | | Rep. | Dem. | Rep. | Dem. |
| 17,295 | BAKER | 6,585 | 2,670 | 3,903 | 12 | 1,233 D | 40.5% | 59.3% | 40.6% | 59.4% |
| 39,165 | BENTON | 16,486 | 7,250 | 8,971 | 265 | 1,721 D | 44.0% | 54.4% | 44.7% | 55.3% |
| 113,038 | CLACKAMAS | 57,043 | 21,299 | 35,711 | 33 | 14,412 D | 37.3% | 62.6% | 37.4% | 62.6% |
| 27,380 | CLATSOP | 12,413 | 4,023 | 8,371 | 19 | 4,348 D | 32.4% | 67.4% | 32.5% | 67.5% |
| 22,379 | COLUMBIA | 10,268 | 2,489 | 7,728 | 51 | 5,239 D | 24.2% | 75.3% | 24.4% | 75.6% |
| 54,955 | COOS | 21,149 | 5,032 | 16,109 | 8 | 11,077 D | 23.8% | 76.2% | 23.8% | 76.2% |
| 9,430 | CROOK | 3,586 | 1,161 | 2,419 | 6 | 1,258 D | 32.4% | 67.5% | 32.4% | 67.6% |
| 13,983 | CURRY | 4,686 | 1,467 | 3,195 | 24 | 1,728 D | 31.3% | 68.2% | 31.5% | 68.5% |
| 23,100 | DESCHUTES | 10,095 | 3,148 | 6,947 | | 3,799 D | 31.2% | 68.8% | 31.2% | 68.8% |
| 68,458 | DOUGLAS | 25,717 | 9,806 | 15,909 | 2 | 6,103 D | 38.1% | 61.9% | 38.1% | 61.9% |
| 3,069 | GILLIAM | 1,220 | 442 | 775 | 3 | 333 D | 36.2% | 63.5% | 36.3% | 63.7% |
| 7,726 | GRANT | 3,032 | 1,149 | 1,877 | 6 | 728 D | 37.9% | 61.9% | 38.0% | 62.0% |
| 6,744 | HARNEY | 2,759 | 1,172 | 1,577 | 10 | 405 D | 42.5% | 57.2% | 42.6% | 57.4% |
| 13,395 | HOOD RIVER | 5,472 | 1,786 | 3,564 | 122 | 1,778 D | 32.6% | 65.1% | 33.4% | 66.6% |
| 73,962 | JACKSON | 34,084 | 14,598 | 19,486 | | 4,888 D | 42.8% | 57.2% | 42.8% | 57.2% |
| 7,130 | JEFFERSON | 2,938 | 1,197 | 1,739 | 2 | 542 D | 40.7% | 59.2% | 40.8% | 59.2% |
| 29,917 | JOSEPHINE | 13,801 | 6,918 | 6,857 | 26 | 61 R | 50.1% | 49.7% | 50.2% | 49.8% |
| 47,475 | KLAMATH | 17,599 | 8,530 | 9,066 | 3 | 536 D | 48.5% | 51.5% | 48.5% | 51.5% |
| 7,158 | LAKE | 2,723 | 1,304 | 1,419 | | 115 D | 47.9% | 52.1% | 47.9% | 52.1% |
| 162,890 | LANE | 74,200 | 24,139 | 49,785 | 276 | 25,646 D | 32.5% | 67.1% | 32.7% | 67.3% |
| 24,635 | LINCOLN | 10,323 | 3,200 | 7,101 | 22 | 3,901 D | 31.0% | 68.8% | 31.1% | 68.9% |
| 58,867 | LINN | 23,308 | 8,382 | 14,926 | | 6,544 D | 36.0% | 64.0% | 36.0% | 64.0% |
| 22,764 | MALHEUR | 7,983 | 4,177 | 3,798 | 8 | 379 R | 52.3% | 47.6% | 52.4% | 47.6% |
| 120,888 | MARION | 51,209 | 18,897 | 32,091 | 221 | 13,194 D | 36.9% | 62.7% | 37.1% | 62.9% |
| 4,871 | MORROW | 2,097 | 627 | 1,470 | | 843 D | 29.9% | 70.1% | 29.9% | 70.1% |
| 522,813 | MULTNOMAH | 243,739 | 81,683 | 161,040 | 1,016 | 79,357 D | 33.5% | 66.1% | 33.7% | 66.3% |
| 26,523 | POLK | 11,629 | 4,319 | 7,292 | 18 | 2,973 D | 37.1% | 62.7% | 37.2% | 62.8% |
| 2,446 | SHERMAN | 1,353 | 494 | 859 | | 365 D | 36.5% | 63.5% | 36.5% | 63.5% |
| 18,955 | TILLAMOOK | 7,573 | 2,318 | 5,246 | 9 | 2,928 D | 30.6% | 69.3% | 30.6% | 69.4% |
| 44,352 | UMATILLA | 16,859 | 6,138 | 10,689 | 32 | 4,551 D | 36.4% | 63.4% | 36.5% | 63.5% |
| 18,180 | UNION | 7,489 | 2,553 | 4,929 | 7 | 2,376 D | 34.1% | 65.8% | 34.1% | 65.9% |
| 7,102 | WALLOWA | 2,848 | 1,055 | 1,790 | 3 | 735 D | 37.0% | 62.9% | 37.1% | 62.9% |
| 20,205 | WASCO | 8,597 | 2,695 | 5,890 | 12 | 3,195 D | 31.3% | 68.5% | 31.4% | 68.6% |
| 92,237 | WASHINGTON | 50,181 | 20,813 | 29,081 | 287 | 8,268 D | 41.5% | 58.0% | 41.7% | 58.3% |
| 2,722 | WHEELER | 798 | 340 | 458 | | 118 D | 42.6% | 57.4% | 42.6% | 57.4% |
| 32,478 | YAMHILL | 14,463 | 5,508 | 8,949 | 6 | 3,441 D | 38.1% | 61.9% | 38.1% | 61.9% |
| 1,768,687 | TOTAL | 786,305 | 282,779 | 501,017 | 2,509 | 218,238 D | 36.0% | 63.7% | 36.1% | 63.9% |

# OREGON

## PRESIDENT 1960

| 1960 Census Population | County | Total Vote | Republican | Democratic | Other | Rep.-Dem. Plurality | Percentage | | | |
|---|---|---|---|---|---|---|---|---|---|---|
| | | | | | | | Total Vote | | Major Vote | |
| | | | | | | | Rep. | Dem. | Rep. | Dem. |
| 17,295 | BAKER | 7,251 | 3,514 | 3,734 | 3 | 220 D | 48.5% | 51.5% | 48.5% | 51.5% |
| 39,165 | BENTON | 15,125 | 9,734 | 5,391 | | 4,343 R | 64.4% | 35.6% | 64.4% | 35.6% |
| 113,038 | CLACKAMAS | 52,319 | 28,531 | 23,679 | 109 | 4,852 R | 54.5% | 45.3% | 54.6% | 45.4% |
| 27,380 | CLATSOP | 12,866 | 6,286 | 6,530 | 50 | 244 D | 48.9% | 50.8% | 49.0% | 51.0% |
| 22,379 | COLUMBIA | 9,908 | 4,356 | 5,546 | 6 | 1,190 D | 44.0% | 56.0% | 44.0% | 56.0% |
| 54,955 | COOS | 21,705 | 8,751 | 12,893 | 61 | 4,142 D | 40.3% | 59.4% | 40.4% | 59.6% |
| 9,430 | CROOK | 3,737 | 1,732 | 2,005 | | 273 D | 46.3% | 53.7% | 46.3% | 53.7% |
| 13,983 | CURRY | 5,153 | 2,382 | 2,767 | 4 | 385 D | 46.2% | 53.7% | 46.3% | 53.7% |
| 23,100 | DESCHUTES | 9,944 | 5,145 | 4,776 | 23 | 369 R | 51.7% | 48.0% | 51.9% | 48.1% |
| 68,458 | DOUGLAS | 25,815 | 12,493 | 13,322 | | 829 D | 48.4% | 51.6% | 48.4% | 51.6% |
| 3,069 | GILLIAM | 1,318 | 712 | 606 | | 106 R | 54.0% | 46.0% | 54.0% | 46.0% |
| 7,726 | GRANT | 3,135 | 1,697 | 1,438 | | 259 R | 54.1% | 45.9% | 54.1% | 45.9% |
| 6,744 | HARNEY | 2,691 | 1,464 | 1,220 | 7 | 244 R | 54.4% | 45.3% | 54.5% | 45.5% |
| 13,395 | HOOD RIVER | 5,555 | 3,103 | 2,450 | 2 | 653 R | 55.9% | 44.1% | 55.9% | 44.1% |
| 73,962 | JACKSON | 32,157 | 17,554 | 14,531 | 72 | 3,023 R | 54.6% | 45.2% | 54.7% | 45.3% |
| 7,130 | JEFFERSON | 2,629 | 1,413 | 1,214 | 2 | 199 R | 53.7% | 46.2% | 53.8% | 46.2% |
| 29,917 | JOSEPHINE | 12,831 | 7,387 | 5,419 | 25 | 1,968 R | 57.6% | 42.2% | 57.7% | 42.3% |
| 47,475 | KLAMATH | 18,023 | 9,095 | 8,928 | | 167 R | 50.5% | 49.5% | 50.5% | 49.5% |
| 7,158 | LAKE | 2,996 | 1,555 | 1,441 | | 114 R | 51.9% | 48.1% | 51.9% | 48.1% |
| 162,890 | LANE | 68,862 | 36,148 | 32,596 | 118 | 3,552 R | 52.5% | 47.3% | 52.6% | 47.4% |
| 24,635 | LINCOLN | 10,483 | 5,231 | 5,243 | 9 | 12 D | 49.9% | 50.0% | 49.9% | 50.1% |
| 58,867 | LINN | 23,934 | 12,899 | 11,035 | | 1,864 R | 53.9% | 46.1% | 53.9% | 46.1% |
| 22,764 | MALHEUR | 8,424 | 5,043 | 3,381 | | 1,662 R | 59.9% | 40.1% | 59.9% | 40.1% |
| 120,888 | MARION | 49,970 | 29,124 | 20,791 | 55 | 8,333 R | 58.3% | 41.6% | 58.3% | 41.7% |
| 4,871 | MORROW | 2,042 | 1,003 | 1,039 | | 36 D | 49.1% | 50.9% | 49.1% | 50.9% |
| 522,813 | MULTNOMAH | 251,882 | 127,271 | 124,273 | 338 | 2,998 R | 50.5% | 49.3% | 50.6% | 49.4% |
| 26,523 | POLK | 11,298 | 6,709 | 4,578 | 11 | 2,131 R | 59.4% | 40.5% | 59.4% | 40.6% |
| 2,446 | SHERMAN | 1,165 | 659 | 506 | | 153 R | 56.6% | 43.4% | 56.6% | 43.4% |
| 18,955 | TILLAMOOK | 8,044 | 3,935 | 4,098 | 11 | 163 D | 48.9% | 50.9% | 49.0% | 51.0% |
| 44,352 | UMATILLA | 17,433 | 9,374 | 8,053 | 6 | 1,321 R | 53.8% | 46.2% | 53.8% | 46.2% |
| 18,180 | UNION | 7,770 | 3,689 | 4,081 | | 392 D | 47.5% | 52.5% | 47.5% | 52.5% |
| 7,102 | WALLOWA | 3,125 | 1,440 | 1,682 | 3 | 242 D | 46.1% | 53.8% | 46.1% | 53.9% |
| 20,205 | WASCO | 8,784 | 4,355 | 4,426 | 3 | 71 D | 49.6% | 50.4% | 49.6% | 50.4% |
| 92,237 | WASHINGTON | 43,186 | 25,415 | 17,736 | 35 | 7,679 R | 58.9% | 41.1% | 58.9% | 41.1% |
| 2,722 | WHEELER | 1,032 | 566 | 466 | | 100 R | 54.8% | 45.2% | 54.8% | 45.2% |
| 32,478 | YAMHILL | 13,829 | 8,295 | 5,528 | 6 | 2,767 R | 60.0% | 40.0% | 60.0% | 40.0% |
| 1,768,687 | TOTAL | 776,421 | 408,060 | 367,402 | 959 | 40,658 R | 52.6% | 47.3% | 52.6% | 47.4% |

# OREGON

## ELECTION NOTES

**2004**    Other vote was 7,260 Libertarian (Michael Badnarik); 5,315 Pacific Green (David Cobb); 5,257 Constitution (Michael Peroutka); 8,956 write-in.

**2000**    Other vote was 7,447 Libertarian (Browne); 7,063 Independent (Buchanan); 2,574 Reform (Hagelin); 2,189 Constitution (Phillips); 3,419 scattered write-in. Nader was listed on the ballot as Pacific Green.

**1996**    Other vote was 49,415 Pacific (Nader); 8,903 Libertarian (Browne); 3,379 U.S. Taxpayers (Phillips); 2,798 Natural Law (Hagelin); 1,922 Socialist (Hollis); 2,329 scattered write-in.

**1992**    Other vote was 4,277 Marrou (Libertarian); 3,030 Fulani (New Alliance); 1,470 Gritz (write-in); 91 Hagelin (write-in); 4 Brisben (write-in); 2,609 scattered write-in.

**1988**    Other vote was 14,811 Paul (Libertarian); 6,487 Fulani (Independent); 90 Duke (write-in); 3,974 scattered write-in.

**1984**    Other vote was scattered write-in.

**1980**    Other vote was 112,389 Anderson (Independent); 25,838 Clark (Libertarian); 13,642 Commoner (Independent); 1,713 scattered write-in.

**1976**    Other vote was 40,207 McCarthy (Independent); 1,035 Anderson (write-in); 6,107 scattered write-in. Early unamended canvass gave the McCarthy (Independent) vote as 40,192. Vote detailed in the table is for the recount.

**1972**    Other vote was 46,211 Schmitz (Independent); 2,289 scattered write-in.

**1968**    Wallace on the ballot as Independent. Other vote was 1,496 McCarthy (write-in); 1,144 scattered write-in.

**1964**    Other vote was scattered write-in.

**1960**    Other vote was scattered write-in.

# PENNSYLVANIA

## POPULAR VOTE FOR PRESIDENT 1920 TO 2004

| Year | Total Vote | Republican Vote | Republican Candidate | Democratic Vote | Democratic Candidate | Other Vote | Plurality | Percentage Total Vote Rep. | Percentage Total Vote Dem. | Percentage Major Vote Rep. | Percentage Major Vote Dem. |
|------|-----------|-----------------|---------------------|-----------------|---------------------|-----------|-----------|------|------|------|------|
| 2004 | 5,769,590 | 2,793,847 | Bush, George W. | 2,938,095 | Kerry, John | 37,648 | 144,248 D | 48.4% | 50.9% | 48.7% | 51.3% |
| 2000** | 4,913,119 | 2,281,127 | Bush, George W. | 2,485,967 | Gore, Al | 146,025 | 204,840 D | 46.4% | 50.6% | 47.9% | 52.1% |
| 1996 ** | 4,506,118 | 1,801,169 | Dole, Bob | 2,215,819 | Clinton, Bill | 489,130 | 414,650 D | 40.0% | 49.2% | 44.8% | 55.2% |
| 1992 ** | 4,959,810 | 1,791,841 | Bush, George | 2,239,164 | Clinton, Bill | 928,805 | 447,323 D | 36.1% | 45.1% | 44.5% | 55.5% |
| 1988 | 4,536,251 | 2,300,087 | Bush, George | 2,194,944 | Dukakis, Michael S. | 41,220 | 105,143 R | 50.7% | 48.4% | 51.2% | 48.8% |
| 1984 | 4,844,903 | 2,584,323 | Reagan, Ronald | 2,228,131 | Mondale, Walter F. | 32,449 | 356,192 R | 53.3% | 46.0% | 53.7% | 46.3% |
| 1980 ** | 4,561,501 | 2,261,872 | Reagan, Ronald | 1,937,540 | Carter, Jimmy | 362,089 | 324,332 R | 49.6% | 42.5% | 53.9% | 46.1% |
| 1976 | 4,620,787 | 2,205,604 | Ford, Gerald R. | 2,328,677 | Carter, Jimmy | 86,506 | 123,073 D | 47.7% | 50.4% | 48.6% | 51.4% |
| 1972 | 4,592,106 | 2,714,521 | Nixon, Richard M. | 1,796,951 | McGovern, George S. | 80,634 | 917,570 R | 59.1% | 39.1% | 60.2% | 39.8% |
| 1968 | 4,747,928 | 2,090,017 | Nixon, Richard M. | 2,259,405 | Humphrey, Hubert H. | 398,506 | 169,388 D | 44.0% | 47.6% | 48.1% | 51.9% |
| 1964 | 4,822,690 | 1,673,657 | Goldwater, Barry M. | 3,130,954 | Johnson, Lyndon B. | 18,079 | 1,457,297 D | 34.7% | 64.9% | 34.8% | 65.2% |
| 1960 | 5,006,541 | 2,439,956 | Nixon, Richard M. | 2,556,282 | Kennedy, John F. | 10,303 | 116,326 D | 48.7% | 51.1% | 48.8% | 51.2% |
| 1956 | 4,576,503 | 2,585,252 | Eisenhower, Dwight D. | 1,981,769 | Stevenson, Adlai E. | 9,482 | 603,483 R | 56.5% | 43.3% | 56.6% | 43.4% |
| 1952 | 4,580,969 | 2,415,789 | Eisenhower, Dwight D. | 2,146,269 | Stevenson, Adlai E. | 18,911 | 269,520 R | 52.7% | 46.9% | 53.0% | 47.0% |
| 1948 | 3,735,348 | 1,902,197 | Dewey, Thomas E. | 1,752,426 | Truman, Harry S. | 80,725 | 149,771 R | 50.9% | 46.9% | 52.0% | 48.0% |
| 1944 | 3,794,793 | 1,835,054 | Dewey, Thomas E. | 1,940,479 | Roosevelt, Franklin D. | 19,260 | 105,425 D | 48.4% | 51.1% | 48.6% | 51.4% |
| 1940 | 4,078,714 | 1,889,848 | Willkie, Wendell | 2,171,035 | Roosevelt, Franklin D. | 17,831 | 281,187 D | 46.3% | 53.2% | 46.5% | 53.5% |
| 1936 | 4,138,105 | 1,690,300 | Landon, Alfred M. | 2,353,788 | Roosevelt, Franklin D. | 94,017 | 663,488 D | 40.8% | 56.9% | 41.8% | 58.2% |
| 1932 | 2,859,021 | 1,453,540 | Hoover, Herbert C. | 1,295,948 | Roosevelt, Franklin D. | 109,533 | 157,592 R | 50.8% | 45.3% | 52.9% | 47.1% |
| 1928 | 3,150,612 | 2,055,382 | Hoover, Herbert C. | 1,067,586 | Smith, Alfred E. | 27,644 | 987,796 R | 65.2% | 33.9% | 65.8% | 34.2% |
| 1924 ** | 2,144,850 | 1,401,481 | Coolidge, Calvin | 409,192 | Davis, John W. | 334,177 | 992,289 R | 65.3% | 19.1% | 77.4% | 22.6% |
| 1920 | 1,851,248 | 1,218,215 | Harding, Warren G. | 503,202 | Cox, James M. | 129,831 | 715,013 R | 65.8% | 27.2% | 70.8% | 29.2% |

In 2000 the other vote column includes 103,392 votes cast for Green (Nader). In 1996 the other vote column includes 430,984 votes cast for Perot. In 1992 the other vote column includes 902,667 votes cast for Perot. In 1980 the other column includes 292,921 votes for Independent (Anderson). In 1924 the other vote was 307,567 Progressive; 13,035 American; 9,779 Prohibition; 2,735 Communist; 634 Socialist Labor; 296 Commonwealth Land; and 131 scattered.

## ELECTORAL COLLEGE VOTE 1920 TO 2004

| Year | Total | Republican | Democratic | Other |
|------|-------|-----------|-----------|-------|
| 2004 | 21 | | 21 | |
| 2000 | 23 | | 23 | |
| 1996 | 23 | | 23 | |
| 1992 | 23 | | 23 | |
| 1988 | 25 | 25 | | |
| 1984 | 25 | 25 | | |
| 1980 | 27 | 27 | | |
| 1976 | 27 | | 27 | |
| 1972 | 27 | 27 | | |
| 1968 | 29 | | 29 | |
| 1964 | 29 | | 29 | |
| 1960 | 32 | | 32 | |
| 1956 | 32 | 32 | | |
| 1952 | 32 | 32 | | |
| 1948 | 35 | 35 | | |
| 1944 | 35 | | 35 | |
| 1940 | 36 | | 36 | |
| 1936 | 36 | | 36 | |
| 1932 | 36 | 36 | | |
| 1928 | 38 | 38 | | |
| 1924 | 38 | 38 | | |
| 1920 | 38 | 38 | | |

# PENNSYLVANIA

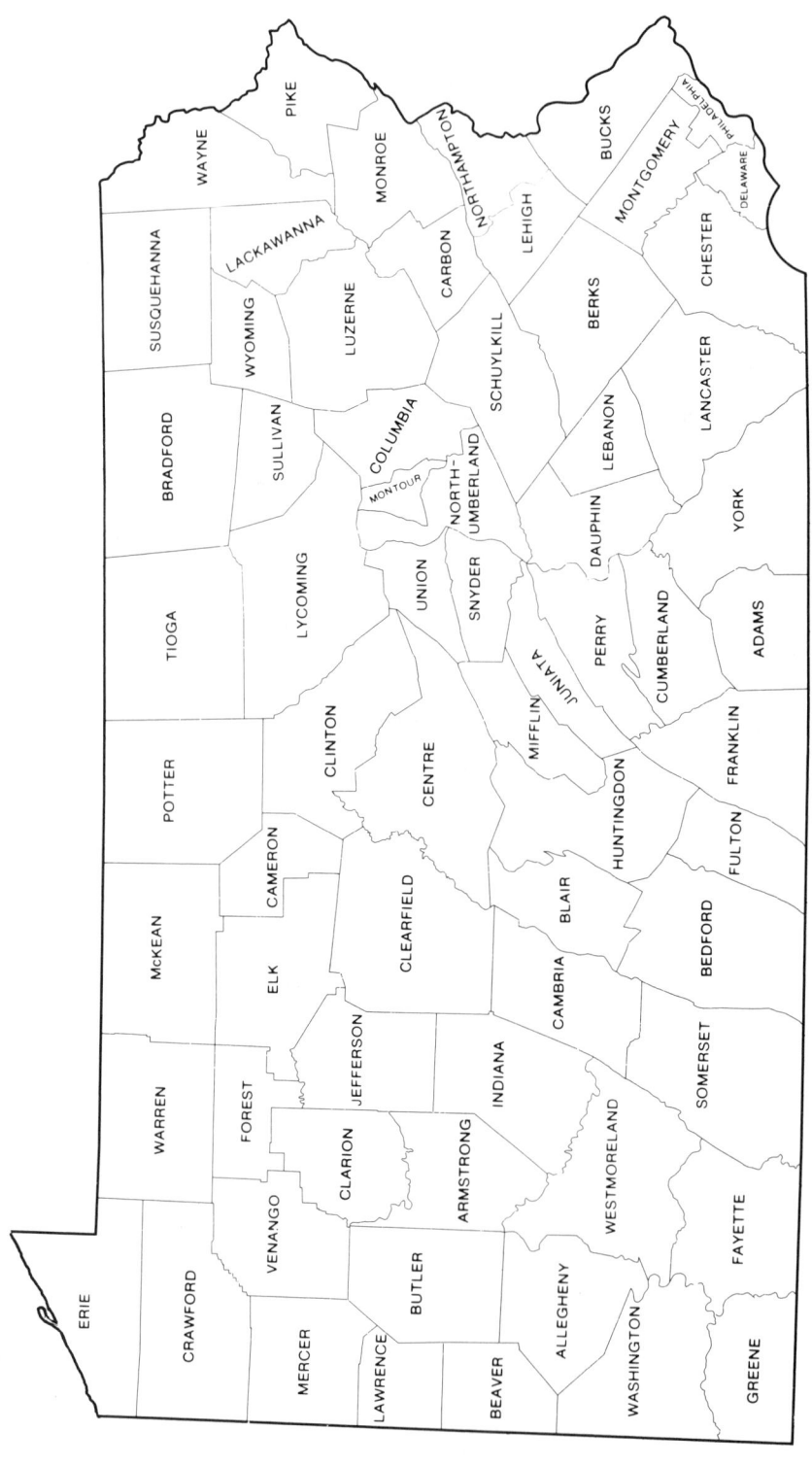

# PENNSYLVANIA

## PRESIDENT 2004

| 2000 Census Population | County | Total Vote | Republican | Democratic | Other | Rep.-Dem. Plurality | Percentage | | | |
|---|---|---|---|---|---|---|---|---|---|---|
| | | | | | | | Total Vote | | Major Vote | |
| | | | | | | | Rep. | Dem. | Rep. | Dem. |
| 91,292 | ADAMS | 42,228 | 28,247 | 13,764 | 217 | 14,483 R | 66.9% | 32.6% | 67.2% | 32.8% |
| 1,281,666 | ALLEGHENY | 645,469 | 271,925 | 368,912 | 4,632 | 96,987 D | 42.1% | 57.2% | 42.4% | 57.6% |
| 72,392 | ARMSTRONG | 31,097 | 18,925 | 12,025 | 147 | 6,900 R | 60.9% | 38.7% | 61.1% | 38.9% |
| 181,412 | BEAVER | 82,543 | 39,916 | 42,146 | 481 | 2,230 D | 48.4% | 51.1% | 48.6% | 51.4% |
| 49,984 | BEDFORD | 22,679 | 16,606 | 6,016 | 57 | 10,590 R | 73.2% | 26.5% | 73.4% | 26.6% |
| 373,638 | BERKS | 164,487 | 87,122 | 76,309 | 1,056 | 10,813 R | 53.0% | 46.4% | 53.3% | 46.7% |
| 129,144 | BLAIR | 54,178 | 35,751 | 18,105 | 322 | 17,646 R | 66.0% | 33.4% | 66.4% | 33.6% |
| 62,761 | BRADFORD | 25,652 | 16,942 | 8,590 | 120 | 8,352 R | 66.0% | 33.5% | 66.4% | 33.6% |
| 597,635 | BUCKS | 319,816 | 154,469 | 163,438 | 1,909 | 8,969 D | 48.3% | 51.1% | 48.6% | 51.4% |
| 174,083 | BUTLER | 85,425 | 54,959 | 30,090 | 376 | 24,869 R | 64.3% | 35.2% | 64.6% | 35.4% |
| 152,598 | CAMBRIA | 66,983 | 34,048 | 32,591 | 344 | 1,457 R | 50.8% | 48.7% | 51.1% | 48.9% |
| 5,974 | CAMERON | 2,406 | 1,599 | 794 | 13 | 805 R | 66.5% | 33.0% | 66.8% | 33.2% |
| 58,802 | CARBON | 25,043 | 12,519 | 12,223 | 301 | 296 R | 50.0% | 48.8% | 50.6% | 49.4% |
| 135,758 | CENTRE | 64,253 | 33,133 | 30,733 | 387 | 2,400 R | 51.6% | 47.8% | 51.9% | 48.1% |
| 433,501 | CHESTER | 230,823 | 120,036 | 109,708 | 1,079 | 10,328 R | 52.0% | 47.5% | 52.2% | 47.8% |
| 41,765 | CLARION | 17,184 | 11,063 | 6,049 | 72 | 5,014 R | 64.4% | 35.2% | 64.7% | 35.3% |
| 83,382 | CLEARFIELD | 34,233 | 20,533 | 13,518 | 182 | 7,015 R | 60.0% | 39.5% | 60.3% | 39.7% |
| 37,914 | CLINTON | 13,967 | 8,035 | 5,823 | 109 | 2,212 R | 57.5% | 41.7% | 58.0% | 42.0% |
| 64,151 | COLUMBIA | 26,869 | 16,052 | 10,679 | 138 | 5,373 R | 59.7% | 39.7% | 60.1% | 39.9% |
| 90,366 | CRAWFORD | 38,322 | 21,965 | 16,013 | 344 | 5,952 R | 57.3% | 41.8% | 57.8% | 42.2% |
| 213,674 | CUMBERLAND | 106,082 | 67,648 | 37,928 | 506 | 29,720 R | 63.8% | 35.8% | 64.1% | 35.9% |
| 251,798 | DAUPHIN | 121,208 | 65,296 | 55,299 | 613 | 9,997 R | 53.9% | 45.6% | 54.1% | 45.9% |
| 550,864 | DELAWARE | 284,538 | 120,425 | 162,601 | 1,512 | 42,176 D | 42.3% | 57.1% | 42.5% | 57.5% |
| 35,112 | ELK | 14,550 | 7,872 | 6,602 | 76 | 1,270 R | 54.1% | 45.4% | 54.4% | 45.6% |
| 280,843 | ERIE | 125,898 | 57,372 | 67,921 | 605 | 10,549 D | 45.6% | 53.9% | 45.8% | 54.2% |
| 148,644 | FAYETTE | 54,707 | 25,045 | 29,120 | 542 | 4,075 D | 45.8% | 53.2% | 46.2% | 53.8% |
| 4,946 | FOREST | 2,573 | 1,571 | 989 | 13 | 582 R | 61.1% | 38.4% | 61.4% | 38.6% |
| 129,313 | FRANKLIN | 58,569 | 41,817 | 16,562 | 190 | 25,255 R | 71.4% | 28.3% | 71.6% | 28.4% |
| 14,261 | FULTON | 6,271 | 4,772 | 1,475 | 24 | 3,297 R | 76.1% | 23.5% | 76.4% | 23.6% |
| 40,672 | GREENE | 15,565 | 7,786 | 7,674 | 105 | 112 R | 50.0% | 49.3% | 50.4% | 49.6% |
| 45,586 | HUNTINGDON | 18,058 | 12,126 | 5,879 | 53 | 6,247 R | 67.2% | 32.6% | 67.3% | 32.7% |
| 89,605 | INDIANA | 36,248 | 20,254 | 15,831 | 163 | 4,423 R | 55.9% | 43.7% | 56.1% | 43.9% |
| 45,932 | JEFFERSON | 19,560 | 13,371 | 6,073 | 116 | 7,298 R | 68.4% | 31.0% | 68.8% | 31.2% |
| 22,821 | JUNIATA | 10,006 | 7,144 | 2,797 | 65 | 4,347 R | 71.4% | 28.0% | 71.9% | 28.1% |
| 213,295 | LACKAWANNA | 105,819 | 44,766 | 59,573 | 1,480 | 14,807 D | 42.3% | 56.3% | 42.9% | 57.1% |
| 470,658 | LANCASTER | 221,278 | 145,591 | 74,328 | 1,359 | 71,263 R | 65.8% | 33.6% | 66.2% | 33.8% |
| 94,643 | LAWRENCE | 43,442 | 21,938 | 21,387 | 117 | 551 R | 50.5% | 49.2% | 50.6% | 49.4% |
| 120,327 | LEBANON | 55,665 | 37,089 | 18,109 | 467 | 18,980 R | 66.6% | 32.5% | 67.2% | 32.8% |
| 312,090 | LEHIGH | 145,091 | 70,160 | 73,940 | 991 | 3,780 D | 48.4% | 51.0% | 48.7% | 51.3% |
| 319,250 | LUZERNE | 136,028 | 64,953 | 69,573 | 1,502 | 4,620 D | 47.7% | 51.1% | 48.3% | 51.7% |
| 120,044 | LYCOMING | 50,049 | 33,961 | 15,681 | 407 | 18,280 R | 67.9% | 31.3% | 68.4% | 31.6% |
| 45,936 | MCKEAN | 17,426 | 10,941 | 6,294 | 191 | 4,647 R | 62.8% | 36.1% | 63.5% | 36.5% |
| 120,293 | MERCER | 51,564 | 26,311 | 24,831 | 422 | 1,480 R | 51.0% | 48.2% | 51.4% | 48.6% |
| 46,486 | MIFFLIN | 16,802 | 11,726 | 4,889 | 187 | 6,837 R | 69.8% | 29.1% | 70.6% | 29.4% |
| 138,687 | MONROE | 56,342 | 27,971 | 27,967 | 404 | 4 R | 49.6% | 49.6% | 50.0% | 50.0% |
| 750,097 | MONTGOMERY | 399,591 | 175,741 | 222,048 | 1,802 | 46,307 D | 44.0% | 55.6% | 44.2% | 55.8% |
| 18,236 | MONTOUR | 7,624 | 4,903 | 2,666 | 55 | 2,237 R | 64.3% | 35.0% | 64.8% | 35.2% |
| 267,066 | NORTHAMPTON | 126,740 | 62,102 | 63,446 | 1,192 | 1,344 D | 49.0% | 50.1% | 49.5% | 50.5% |
| 94,556 | NORTHUMBERLAND | 37,134 | 22,262 | 14,602 | 270 | 7,660 R | 60.0% | 39.3% | 60.4% | 39.6% |
| 43,602 | PERRY | 19,427 | 13,919 | 5,423 | 85 | 8,496 R | 71.6% | 27.9% | 72.0% | 28.0% |
| 1,517,550 | PHILADELPHIA | 674,069 | 130,099 | 542,205 | 1,765 | 412,106 D | 19.3% | 80.4% | 19.4% | 80.6% |
| 46,302 | PIKE | 21,299 | 12,444 | 8,656 | 199 | 3,788 R | 58.4% | 40.6% | 59.0% | 41.0% |
| 18,080 | POTTER | 7,962 | 5,640 | 2,268 | 54 | 3,372 R | 70.8% | 28.5% | 71.3% | 28.7% |
| 150,336 | SCHUYLKILL | 65,269 | 35,640 | 29,231 | 398 | 6,409 R | 54.6% | 44.8% | 54.9% | 45.1% |
| 37,546 | SNYDER | 14,983 | 10,566 | 4,348 | 69 | 6,218 R | 70.5% | 29.0% | 70.8% | 29.2% |
| 80,023 | SOMERSET | 36,778 | 23,802 | 12,842 | 134 | 10,960 R | 64.7% | 34.9% | 65.0% | 35.0% |
| 6,556 | SULLIVAN | 3,285 | 2,056 | 1,213 | 16 | 843 R | 62.6% | 36.9% | 62.9% | 37.1% |
| 42,238 | SUSQUEHANNA | 19,040 | 11,573 | 7,351 | 116 | 4,222 R | 60.8% | 38.6% | 61.2% | 38.8% |
| 41,373 | TIOGA | 17,571 | 12,019 | 5,437 | 115 | 6,582 R | 68.4% | 30.9% | 68.9% | 31.1% |
| 41,624 | UNION | 16,123 | 10,334 | 5,700 | 89 | 4,634 R | 64.1% | 35.4% | 64.5% | 35.5% |

# PENNSYLVANIA

## PRESIDENT 2004

| 2000 Census Population | County | Total Vote | Republican | Democratic | Other | Rep.-Dem. Plurality | Percentage | | | |
|---|---|---|---|---|---|---|---|---|---|---|
| | | | | | | | Total Vote | | Major Vote | |
| | | | | | | | Rep. | Dem. | Rep. | Dem. |
| 57,565 | VENANGO | 23,659 | 14,472 | 9,024 | 163 | 5,448 R | 61.2% | 38.1% | 61.6% | 38.4% |
| 43,863 | WARREN | 19,273 | 10,999 | 8,044 | 230 | 2,955 R | 57.1% | 41.7% | 57.8% | 42.2% |
| 202,897 | WASHINGTON | 96,177 | 47,673 | 48,225 | 279 | 552 D | 49.6% | 50.1% | 49.7% | 50.3% |
| 47,722 | WAYNE | 21,967 | 13,713 | 8,060 | 194 | 5,653 R | 62.4% | 36.7% | 63.0% | 37.0% |
| 369,993 | WESTMORELAND | 178,696 | 100,087 | 77,774 | 835 | 22,313 R | 56.0% | 43.5% | 56.3% | 43.7% |
| 28,080 | WYOMING | 12,832 | 7,782 | 4,982 | 68 | 2,800 R | 60.6% | 38.8% | 61.0% | 39.0% |
| 381,751 | YORK | 179,269 | 114,270 | 63,701 | 1,298 | 50,569 R | 63.7% | 35.5% | 64.2% | 35.8% |
| 12,281,054 | TOTAL | 5,769,590 | 2,793,847 | 2,938,095 | 37,648 | 144,248 D | 48.4% | 50.9% | 48.7% | 51.3% |

Note: The statewide totals for "Total Vote" and "Other" include 2,656 write-in votes for Ralph Nader and 1,170 scattered write-ins that were not included in the county-by-county returns.

# PENNSYLVANIA

## PRESIDENT 2000

| 2000 Census Population | County | Total Vote | Republican | Democratic | Green (Nader) | Other | Rep.-Dem. Plurality | Percentage of Total Vote | | |
|---|---|---|---|---|---|---|---|---|---|---|
| | | | | | | | | Rep. | Dem. | Green |
| 91,292 | ADAMS | 33,433 | 20,848 | 11,682 | 696 | 207 | 9,166 R | 62.4% | 34.9% | 2.1% |
| 1,281,666 | ALLEGHENY | 582,478 | 235,361 | 329,963 | 10,575 | 6,579 | 94,602 D | 40.4% | 56.6% | 1.8% |
| 72,392 | ARMSTRONG | 27,423 | 15,508 | 11,127 | 485 | 303 | 4,381 R | 56.6% | 40.6% | 1.8% |
| 181,412 | BEAVER | 73,593 | 32,491 | 38,925 | 1,450 | 727 | 6,434 D | 44.1% | 52.9% | 2.0% |
| 49,984 | BEDFORD | 19,435 | 13,598 | 5,474 | 265 | 98 | 8,124 R | 70.0% | 28.2% | 1.4% |
| 373,638 | BERKS | 135,163 | 71,273 | 59,150 | 3,494 | 1,246 | 12,123 R | 52.7% | 43.8% | 2.6% |
| 129,144 | BLAIR | 45,140 | 28,376 | 15,774 | 693 | 297 | 12,602 R | 62.9% | 34.9% | 1.5% |
| 62,761 | BRADFORD | 23,330 | 14,660 | 7,911 | 600 | 159 | 6,749 R | 62.8% | 33.9% | 2.6% |
| 597,635 | BUCKS | 263,422 | 121,927 | 132,914 | 6,294 | 2,287 | 10,987 D | 46.3% | 50.5% | 2.4% |
| 174,083 | BUTLER | 70,824 | 44,009 | 25,037 | 1,287 | 491 | 18,972 R | 62.1% | 35.4% | 1.8% |
| 152,598 | CAMBRIA | 60,286 | 28,001 | 30,308 | 1,369 | 608 | 2,307 D | 46.4% | 50.3% | 2.3% |
| 5,974 | CAMERON | 2,246 | 1,383 | 779 | 50 | 34 | 604 R | 61.6% | 34.7% | 2.2% |
| 58,802 | CARBON | 21,277 | 9,717 | 10,668 | 574 | 318 | 951 D | 45.7% | 50.1% | 2.7% |
| 135,758 | CENTRE | 49,538 | 26,172 | 21,409 | 1,623 | 334 | 4,763 R | 52.8% | 43.2% | 3.3% |
| 433,501 | CHESTER | 187,562 | 100,080 | 82,047 | 4,302 | 1,133 | 18,033 R | 53.4% | 43.7% | 2.3% |
| 41,765 | CLARION | 15,843 | 9,796 | 5,605 | 293 | 149 | 4,191 R | 61.8% | 35.4% | 1.8% |
| 83,382 | CLEARFIELD | 30,609 | 18,019 | 11,718 | 570 | 302 | 6,301 R | 58.9% | 38.3% | 1.9% |
| 37,914 | CLINTON | 11,994 | 6,064 | 5,521 | 307 | 102 | 543 R | 50.6% | 46.0% | 2.6% |
| 64,151 | COLUMBIA | 21,894 | 12,095 | 8,975 | 663 | 161 | 3,120 R | 55.2% | 41.0% | 3.0% |
| 90,366 | CRAWFORD | 33,321 | 18,858 | 13,250 | 854 | 359 | 5,608 R | 56.6% | 39.8% | 2.6% |
| 213,674 | CUMBERLAND | 88,062 | 54,802 | 31,053 | 1,749 | 458 | 23,749 R | 62.2% | 35.3% | 2.0% |
| 251,798 | DAUPHIN | 100,658 | 53,631 | 44,390 | 2,059 | 578 | 9,241 R | 53.3% | 44.1% | 2.0% |
| 550,864 | DELAWARE | 248,077 | 105,836 | 134,861 | 5,348 | 2,032 | 29,025 D | 42.7% | 54.4% | 2.2% |
| 35,112 | ELK | 13,578 | 7,347 | 5,754 | 352 | 125 | 1,593 R | 54.1% | 42.4% | 2.6% |
| 280,843 | ERIE | 112,335 | 49,027 | 59,399 | 2,980 | 929 | 10,372 D | 43.6% | 52.9% | 2.7% |
| 148,644 | FAYETTE | 49,532 | 20,013 | 28,152 | 798 | 569 | 8,139 D | 40.4% | 56.8% | 1.6% |
| 4,946 | FOREST | 2,283 | 1,371 | 843 | 57 | 12 | 528 R | 60.1% | 36.9% | 2.5% |
| 129,313 | FRANKLIN | 48,969 | 33,042 | 14,922 | 761 | 244 | 18,120 R | 67.5% | 30.5% | 1.6% |
| 14,261 | FULTON | 5,285 | 3,753 | 1,425 | 77 | 30 | 2,328 R | 71.0% | 27.0% | 1.5% |
| 40,672 | GREENE | 13,634 | 5,890 | 7,230 | 337 | 177 | 1,340 D | 43.2% | 53.0% | 2.5% |
| 45,586 | HUNTINGDON | 15,957 | 10,408 | 5,073 | 340 | 136 | 5,335 R | 65.2% | 31.8% | 2.1% |
| 89,605 | INDIANA | 31,401 | 16,799 | 13,667 | 711 | 224 | 3,132 R | 53.5% | 43.5% | 2.3% |
| 45,932 | JEFFERSON | 17,574 | 11,473 | 5,566 | 339 | 196 | 5,907 R | 65.3% | 31.7% | 1.9% |
| 22,821 | JUNIATA | 8,667 | 5,795 | 2,656 | 158 | 58 | 3,139 R | 66.9% | 30.6% | 1.8% |
| 213,295 | LACKAWANNA | 96,381 | 35,096 | 57,471 | 2,134 | 1,680 | 22,375 D | 36.4% | 59.6% | 2.2% |
| 470,658 | LANCASTER | 175,317 | 115,900 | 54,968 | 3,341 | 1,108 | 60,932 R | 66.1% | 31.4% | 1.9% |
| 94,643 | LAWRENCE | 39,640 | 18,060 | 20,593 | 653 | 334 | 2,533 D | 45.6% | 52.0% | 1.6% |
| 120,327 | LEBANON | 45,880 | 28,534 | 16,093 | 873 | 380 | 12,441 R | 62.2% | 35.1% | 1.9% |
| 312,090 | LEHIGH | 116,280 | 55,492 | 56,667 | 3,278 | 843 | 1,175 D | 47.7% | 48.7% | 2.8% |
| 319,250 | LUZERNE | 119,586 | 52,328 | 62,199 | 3,456 | 1,603 | 9,871 D | 43.8% | 52.0% | 2.9% |
| 120,044 | LYCOMING | 43,183 | 27,137 | 14,663 | 965 | 418 | 12,474 R | 62.8% | 34.0% | 2.2% |
| 45,936 | MCKEAN | 15,804 | 9,661 | 5,510 | 403 | 230 | 4,151 R | 61.1% | 34.9% | 2.5% |
| 120,293 | MERCER | 48,725 | 23,132 | 23,817 | 1,073 | 703 | 685 D | 47.5% | 48.9% | 2.2% |
| 46,486 | MIFFLIN | 14,614 | 9,400 | 4,835 | 264 | 115 | 4,565 R | 64.3% | 33.1% | 1.8% |
| 138,687 | MONROE | 46,878 | 23,265 | 21,939 | 1,319 | 355 | 1,326 R | 49.6% | 46.8% | 2.8% |
| 750,097 | MONTGOMERY | 332,422 | 145,623 | 177,990 | 6,816 | 1,993 | 32,367 D | 43.8% | 53.5% | 2.1% |
| 18,236 | MONTOUR | 6,492 | 3,960 | 2,356 | 132 | 44 | 1,604 R | 61.0% | 36.3% | 2.0% |
| 267,066 | NORTHAMPTON | 104,690 | 47,396 | 53,097 | 3,012 | 1,185 | 5,701 D | 45.3% | 50.7% | 2.9% |
| 94,556 | NORTHUMBERLAND | 33,251 | 18,142 | 13,670 | 956 | 483 | 4,472 R | 54.6% | 41.1% | 2.9% |
| 43,602 | PERRY | 16,071 | 11,184 | 4,459 | 309 | 119 | 6,725 R | 69.6% | 27.7% | 1.9% |
| 1,517,550 | PHILADELPHIA | 561,180 | 100,959 | 449,182 | 8,206 | 2,833 | 348,223 D | 18.0% | 80.0% | 1.5% |
| 46,302 | PIKE | 17,364 | 9,339 | 7,330 | 498 | 197 | 2,009 R | 53.8% | 42.2% | 2.9% |
| 18,080 | POTTER | 7,090 | 4,858 | 2,037 | 146 | 49 | 2,821 R | 68.5% | 28.7% | 2.1% |
| 150,336 | SCHUYLKILL | 58,300 | 29,841 | 26,215 | 1,713 | 531 | 3,626 R | 51.2% | 45.0% | 2.9% |
| 37,546 | SNYDER | 12,841 | 8,963 | 3,536 | 271 | 71 | 5,427 R | 69.8% | 27.5% | 2.1% |
| 80,023 | SOMERSET | 32,985 | 20,218 | 12,028 | 487 | 252 | 8,190 R | 61.3% | 36.5% | 1.5% |
| 6,556 | SULLIVAN | 3,105 | 1,928 | 1,066 | 91 | 20 | 862 R | 62.1% | 34.3% | 2.9% |
| 42,238 | SUSQUEHANNA | 17,271 | 10,226 | 6,481 | 459 | 105 | 3,745 R | 59.2% | 37.5% | 2.7% |
| 41,373 | TIOGA | 14,772 | 9,635 | 4,617 | 404 | 116 | 5,018 R | 65.2% | 31.3% | 2.7% |
| 41,624 | UNION | 13,175 | 8,523 | 4,209 | 373 | 70 | 4,314 R | 64.7% | 31.9% | 2.8% |

# PENNSYLVANIA

## PRESIDENT 2000

| 2000 Census Population | County | Total Vote | Republican | Democratic | Green (Nader) | Other | Rep.-Dem. Plurality | Percentage of Total Vote | | |
|---|---|---|---|---|---|---|---|---|---|---|
| | | | | | | | | Rep. | Dem. | Green |
| 57,565 | VENANGO | 20,523 | 11,642 | 8,196 | 467 | 218 | 3,446 R | 56.7% | 39.9% | 2.3% |
| 43,863 | WARREN | 17,541 | 9,290 | 7,537 | 466 | 248 | 1,753 R | 53.0% | 43.0% | 2.7% |
| 202,897 | WASHINGTON | 84,441 | 37,339 | 44,961 | 1,442 | 699 | 7,622 D | 44.2% | 53.2% | 1.7% |
| 47,722 | WAYNE | 18,914 | 11,201 | 6,904 | 625 | 184 | 4,297 R | 59.2% | 36.5% | 3.3% |
| 369,993 | WESTMORELAND | 156,709 | 80,858 | 71,792 | 2,601 | 1,458 | 9,066 R | 51.6% | 45.8% | 1.7% |
| 28,080 | WYOMING | 11,693 | 6,922 | 4,363 | 344 | 64 | 2,559 R | 59.2% | 37.3% | 2.9% |
| 381,751 | YORK | 144,244 | 87,652 | 51,958 | 3,305 | 1,329 | 35,694 R | 60.8% | 36.0% | 2.3% |
| 12,281,054 | TOTAL | 4,913,119 | 2,281,127 | 2,485,967 | 103,392 | 42,633 | 204,840 D | 46.4% | 50.6% | 2.1% |

Note: The statewide totals for "Total Vote" and "Other" include 934 scattered write-in votes that are not included in the county-by-county results.

# PENNSYLVANIA

## PRESIDENT 1996

| 1995 Census Pop. Est. | County | Total Vote | Republican | Democratic | Reform (Perot) | Other | Rep.-Dem. Plurality | Percentage of Total Vote | | |
|---|---|---|---|---|---|---|---|---|---|---|
| | | | | | | | | Rep. | Dem. | Reform |
| 83,998 | ADAMS | 29,508 | 15,338 | 10,774 | 3,186 | 210 | 4,564 R | 52.0% | 36.5% | 10.8% |
| 1,309,821 | ALLEGHENY | 538,615 | 204,067 | 284,480 | 42,309 | 7,759 | 80,413 D | 37.9% | 52.8% | 7.9% |
| 74,569 | ARMSTRONG | 25,779 | 11,052 | 11,130 | 3,452 | 145 | 78 D | 42.9% | 43.2% | 13.4% |
| 187,979 | BEAVER | 74,279 | 26,048 | 39,578 | 8,276 | 377 | 13,530 D | 35.1% | 53.3% | 11.1% |
| 49,192 | BEDFORD | 18,127 | 10,064 | 5,954 | 2,041 | 68 | 4,110 R | 55.5% | 32.8% | 11.3% |
| 349,583 | BERKS | 121,718 | 56,289 | 49,887 | 13,788 | 1,754 | 6,402 R | 46.2% | 41.0% | 11.3% |
| 131,647 | BLAIR | 40,691 | 21,282 | 15,036 | 4,014 | 359 | 6,246 R | 52.3% | 37.0% | 9.9% |
| 62,260 | BRADFORD | 21,008 | 10,393 | 7,736 | 2,712 | 167 | 2,657 R | 49.5% | 36.8% | 12.9% |
| 573,901 | BUCKS | 227,363 | 94,899 | 103,313 | 24,544 | 4,607 | 8,414 D | 41.7% | 45.4% | 10.8% |
| 165,557 | BUTLER | 60,591 | 32,038 | 21,990 | 6,145 | 418 | 10,048 R | 52.9% | 36.3% | 10.1% |
| 160,531 | CAMBRIA | 59,275 | 20,341 | 30,391 | 7,837 | 706 | 10,050 D | 34.3% | 51.3% | 13.2% |
| 5,707 | CAMERON | 2,231 | 1,113 | 822 | 283 | 13 | 291 R | 49.9% | 36.8% | 12.7% |
| 58,832 | CARBON | 19,829 | 7,193 | 9,457 | 2,992 | 187 | 2,264 D | 36.3% | 47.7% | 15.1% |
| 131,968 | CENTRE | 46,826 | 20,935 | 21,145 | 4,173 | 573 | 210 D | 44.7% | 45.2% | 8.9% |
| 404,945 | CHESTER | 158,366 | 77,029 | 64,783 | 14,067 | 2,487 | 12,246 R | 48.6% | 40.9% | 8.9% |
| 42,338 | CLARION | 15,071 | 6,916 | 5,954 | 2,064 | 137 | 962 R | 45.9% | 39.5% | 13.7% |
| 79,724 | CLEARFIELD | 28,955 | 12,987 | 11,991 | 3,758 | 219 | 996 R | 44.9% | 41.4% | 13.0% |
| 37,215 | CLINTON | 11,483 | 4,293 | 5,658 | 1,424 | 108 | 1,365 D | 37.4% | 49.3% | 12.4% |
| 64,492 | COLUMBIA | 20,372 | 8,234 | 8,379 | 3,654 | 105 | 145 D | 40.4% | 41.1% | 17.9% |
| 89,173 | CRAWFORD | 31,446 | 14,659 | 12,943 | 3,519 | 325 | 1,716 R | 46.6% | 41.2% | 11.2% |
| 205,959 | CUMBERLAND | 78,985 | 43,943 | 28,749 | 5,669 | 624 | 15,194 R | 55.6% | 36.4% | 7.2% |
| 246,338 | DAUPHIN | 92,971 | 44,417 | 40,936 | 6,967 | 651 | 3,481 R | 47.8% | 44.0% | 7.5% |
| 548,708 | DELAWARE | 234,748 | 92,628 | 115,946 | 21,883 | 4,291 | 23,318 D | 39.5% | 49.4% | 9.3% |
| 35,125 | ELK | 13,013 | 4,889 | 5,749 | 2,293 | 82 | 860 D | 37.6% | 44.2% | 17.6% |
| 280,460 | ERIE | 108,791 | 39,884 | 57,508 | 10,386 | 1,013 | 17,624 D | 36.7% | 52.9% | 9.5% |
| 146,827 | FAYETTE | 46,532 | 14,019 | 26,359 | 5,722 | 432 | 12,340 D | 30.1% | 56.6% | 12.3% |
| 5,001 | FOREST | 2,201 | 902 | 964 | 325 | 10 | 62 D | 41.0% | 43.8% | 14.8% |
| 126,444 | FRANKLIN | 44,730 | 25,392 | 14,980 | 4,127 | 231 | 10,412 R | 56.8% | 33.5% | 9.2% |
| 14,362 | FULTON | 4,868 | 2,665 | 1,620 | 554 | 29 | 1,045 R | 54.7% | 33.3% | 11.4% |
| 41,114 | GREENE | 13,736 | 4,002 | 7,620 | 2,052 | 62 | 3,618 D | 29.1% | 55.5% | 14.9% |
| 44,933 | HUNTINGDON | 14,495 | 7,324 | 5,285 | 1,813 | 73 | 2,039 R | 50.5% | 36.5% | 12.5% |
| 90,604 | INDIANA | 30,583 | 12,874 | 13,868 | 3,674 | 167 | 994 D | 42.1% | 45.3% | 12.0% |
| 46,620 | JEFFERSON | 16,457 | 8,156 | 5,846 | 2,322 | 133 | 2,310 R | 49.6% | 35.5% | 14.1% |
| 21,701 | JUNIATA | 7,984 | 4,128 | 2,896 | 911 | 49 | 1,232 R | 51.7% | 36.3% | 11.4% |
| 215,688 | LACKAWANNA | 82,681 | 26,930 | 46,377 | 8,189 | 1,185 | 19,447 D | 32.6% | 56.1% | 9.9% |
| 447,521 | LANCASTER | 155,286 | 92,875 | 49,120 | 11,601 | 1,690 | 43,755 R | 59.8% | 31.6% | 7.5% |
| 96,604 | LAWRENCE | 36,259 | 13,088 | 18,993 | 4,002 | 176 | 5,905 D | 36.1% | 52.4% | 11.0% |
| 116,789 | LEBANON | 40,735 | 21,885 | 14,187 | 4,235 | 428 | 7,698 R | 53.7% | 34.8% | 10.4% |
| 297,838 | LEHIGH | 106,110 | 45,103 | 48,568 | 10,947 | 1,492 | 3,465 D | 42.5% | 45.8% | 10.3% |
| 326,063 | LUZERNE | 116,817 | 43,577 | 60,174 | 12,424 | 642 | 16,597 D | 37.3% | 51.5% | 10.6% |
| 120,194 | LYCOMING | 39,241 | 21,535 | 13,516 | 3,855 | 335 | 8,019 R | 54.9% | 34.4% | 9.8% |
| 48,503 | MCKEAN | 14,869 | 6,838 | 5,509 | 2,350 | 172 | 1,329 R | 46.0% | 37.1% | 15.8% |
| 122,254 | MERCER | 45,779 | 17,213 | 23,003 | 5,108 | 455 | 5,790 D | 37.6% | 50.2% | 11.2% |
| 47,066 | MIFFLIN | 13,718 | 6,888 | 5,327 | 1,392 | 111 | 1,561 R | 50.2% | 38.8% | 10.1% |
| 116,091 | MONROE | 39,065 | 17,326 | 16,547 | 4,650 | 542 | 779 R | 44.4% | 42.4% | 11.9% |
| 705,178 | MONTGOMERY | 293,961 | 121,047 | 143,664 | 24,392 | 4,858 | 22,617 D | 41.2% | 48.9% | 8.3% |
| 18,223 | MONTOUR | 5,811 | 2,785 | 2,183 | 784 | 59 | 602 R | 47.9% | 37.6% | 13.5% |
| 256,796 | NORTHAMPTON | 91,002 | 35,726 | 43,959 | 9,848 | 1,469 | 8,233 D | 39.3% | 48.3% | 10.8% |
| 96,260 | NORTHUMBERLAND | 32,400 | 13,551 | 13,418 | 5,173 | 258 | 133 R | 41.8% | 41.4% | 16.0% |
| 43,531 | PERRY | 14,515 | 8,156 | 4,611 | 1,609 | 139 | 3,545 R | 56.2% | 31.8% | 11.1% |
| 1,498,971 | PHILADELPHIA | 533,277 | 85,345 | 412,988 | 29,329 | 5,615 | 327,643 D | 16.0% | 77.4% | 5.5% |
| 36,852 | PIKE | 14,244 | 6,697 | 5,509 | 1,873 | 165 | 1,188 R | 47.0% | 38.7% | 13.1% |
| 17,090 | POTTER | 6,817 | 3,714 | 2,146 | 925 | 32 | 1,568 R | 54.5% | 31.5% | 13.6% |
| 153,616 | SCHUYLKILL | 56,629 | 22,920 | 24,860 | 8,471 | 378 | 1,940 D | 40.5% | 43.9% | 15.0% |
| 37,845 | SNYDER | 11,642 | 6,742 | 3,405 | 1,451 | 44 | 3,337 R | 57.9% | 29.2% | 12.5% |
| 80,113 | SOMERSET | 31,591 | 14,735 | 12,719 | 3,968 | 169 | 2,016 R | 46.6% | 40.3% | 12.6% |
| 6,184 | SULLIVAN | 2,858 | 1,352 | 1,071 | 418 | 17 | 281 R | 47.3% | 37.5% | 14.6% |
| 41,800 | SUSQUEHANNA | 15,636 | 7,354 | 5,912 | 2,266 | 104 | 1,442 R | 47.0% | 37.8% | 14.5% |
| 41,534 | TIOGA | 14,425 | 7,382 | 4,961 | 1,993 | 89 | 2,421 R | 51.2% | 34.4% | 13.8% |
| 40,928 | UNION | 11,724 | 6,570 | 3,658 | 1,431 | 65 | 2,912 R | 56.0% | 31.2% | 12.2% |

# PENNSYLVANIA

## PRESIDENT 1996

| 1995 Census Pop. Est. | County | Total Vote | Republican | Democratic | Reform (Perot) | Other | Rep.-Dem. Plurality | Percentage of Total Vote | | |
|---|---|---|---|---|---|---|---|---|---|---|
| | | | | | | | | Rep. | Dem. | Reform |
| 59,057 | VENANGO | 19,549 | 8,398 | 8,205 | 2,777 | 169 | 193 R | 43.0% | 42.0% | 14.2% |
| 44,928 | WARREN | 17,067 | 7,056 | 7,291 | 2,504 | 216 | 235 D | 41.3% | 42.7% | 14.7% |
| 208,017 | WASHINGTON | 77,745 | 27,777 | 40,952 | 8,661 | 355 | 13,175 D | 35.7% | 52.7% | 11.1% |
| 44,070 | WAYNE | 16,334 | 8,077 | 5,928 | 2,126 | 203 | 2,149 R | 49.4% | 36.3% | 13.0% |
| 376,501 | WESTMORELAND | 143,329 | 62,058 | 63,686 | 16,230 | 1,355 | 1,628 D | 43.3% | 44.4% | 11.3% |
| 29,316 | WYOMING | 10,408 | 4,888 | 4,049 | 1,414 | 57 | 839 R | 47.0% | 38.9% | 13.6% |
| 362,793 | YORK | 128,156 | 65,188 | 49,596 | 11,652 | 1,720 | 15,592 R | 50.9% | 38.7% | 9.1% |
| 12,071,842 | TOTAL | 4,506,118 | 1,801,169 | 2,215,819 | 430,984 | 58,146 | 414,650 D | 40.0% | 49.2% | 9.6% |

Note: The statewide totals for "Other" and "Total Vote" include 3,086 write-in votes for Ralph Nader and 1,725 scattered write-in votes that are not included in the county-by-county results.

# PENNSYLVANIA

## PRESIDENT 1992

| 1990 Census Population | County | Total Vote | Republican | Democratic | Perot | Other | Plurality | Percentage Total Vote Rep. | Dem. | Perot |
|---|---|---|---|---|---|---|---|---|---|---|
| 78,274 | ADAMS | 29,501 | 13,552 | 9,576 | 6,313 | 60 | 3,976 R | 45.9% | 32.5% | 21.4% |
| 1,336,449 | ALLEGHENY | 614,187 | 183,035 | 324,004 | 103,470 | 3,678 | 140,969 D | 29.8% | 52.8% | 16.8% |
| 73,478 | ARMSTRONG | 28,333 | 9,122 | 12,995 | 6,166 | 50 | 3,873 D | 32.2% | 45.9% | 21.8% |
| 186,093 | BEAVER | 82,340 | 21,361 | 44,877 | 15,954 | 148 | 23,516 D | 25.9% | 54.5% | 19.4% |
| 47,919 | BEDFORD | 18,817 | 9,216 | 5,840 | 3,731 | 30 | 3,376 R | 49.0% | 31.0% | 19.8% |
| 336,523 | BERKS | 131,407 | 52,939 | 46,031 | 31,663 | 774 | 6,908 R | 40.3% | 35.0% | 24.1% |
| 130,542 | BLAIR | 44,758 | 21,447 | 14,857 | 8,284 | 170 | 6,590 R | 47.9% | 33.2% | 18.5% |
| 60,967 | BRADFORD | 22,628 | 10,221 | 6,903 | 5,452 | 52 | 3,318 R | 45.2% | 30.5% | 24.1% |
| 541,174 | BUCKS | 248,507 | 94,584 | 97,902 | 53,931 | 2,090 | 3,318 D | 38.1% | 39.4% | 21.7% |
| 152,013 | BUTLER | 61,130 | 23,656 | 22,303 | 15,013 | 158 | 1,353 R | 38.7% | 36.5% | 24.6% |
| 163,029 | CAMBRIA | 66,349 | 20,770 | 34,334 | 11,070 | 175 | 13,564 D | 31.3% | 51.7% | 16.7% |
| 5,913 | CAMERON | 2,678 | 1,173 | 824 | 676 | 5 | 349 R | 43.8% | 30.8% | 25.2% |
| 56,846 | CARBON | 21,659 | 7,243 | 9,072 | 5,222 | 122 | 1,829 D | 33.4% | 41.9% | 24.1% |
| 123,786 | CENTRE | 51,225 | 20,478 | 21,177 | 9,356 | 214 | 699 D | 40.0% | 41.3% | 18.3% |
| 376,396 | CHESTER | 169,208 | 74,002 | 59,643 | 34,536 | 1,027 | 14,359 R | 43.7% | 35.2% | 20.4% |
| 41,699 | CLARION | 15,718 | 6,477 | 5,584 | 3,619 | 38 | 893 R | 41.2% | 35.5% | 23.0% |
| 78,097 | CLEARFIELD | 30,847 | 11,553 | 12,247 | 6,989 | 58 | 694 D | 37.5% | 39.7% | 22.7% |
| 37,182 | CLINTON | 12,569 | 4,471 | 5,397 | 2,654 | 47 | 926 D | 35.6% | 42.9% | 21.1% |
| 63,202 | COLUMBIA | 23,739 | 9,742 | 8,261 | 5,683 | 53 | 1,481 R | 41.0% | 34.8% | 23.9% |
| 86,169 | CRAWFORD | 34,628 | 14,112 | 12,813 | 7,392 | 311 | 1,299 R | 40.8% | 37.0% | 21.3% |
| 195,257 | CUMBERLAND | 84,573 | 43,447 | 26,635 | 14,344 | 147 | 16,812 R | 51.4% | 31.5% | 17.0% |
| 237,813 | DAUPHIN | 98,910 | 45,479 | 36,990 | 16,063 | 378 | 8,489 R | 46.0% | 37.4% | 16.2% |
| 547,651 | DELAWARE | 266,074 | 108,587 | 111,210 | 43,728 | 2,549 | 2,623 D | 40.8% | 41.8% | 16.4% |
| 34,878 | ELK | 13,832 | 4,908 | 5,016 | 3,885 | 23 | 108 D | 35.5% | 36.3% | 28.1% |
| 275,572 | ERIE | 117,804 | 39,283 | 56,381 | 21,510 | 630 | 17,098 D | 33.3% | 47.9% | 18.3% |
| 145,351 | FAYETTE | 53,861 | 12,820 | 30,577 | 10,162 | 302 | 17,757 D | 23.8% | 56.8% | 18.9% |
| 4,802 | FOREST | 2,144 | 801 | 890 | 448 | 5 | 89 D | 37.4% | 41.5% | 20.9% |
| 121,082 | FRANKLIN | 43,834 | 23,387 | 13,440 | 6,941 | 66 | 9,947 R | 53.4% | 30.7% | 15.8% |
| 13,837 | FULTON | 5,023 | 2,558 | 1,588 | 869 | 8 | 970 R | 50.9% | 31.6% | 17.3% |
| 39,550 | GREENE | 15,135 | 3,482 | 8,438 | 3,186 | 29 | 4,956 D | 23.0% | 55.8% | 21.1% |
| 44,164 | HUNTINGDON | 15,700 | 7,249 | 5,153 | 3,273 | 25 | 2,096 R | 46.2% | 32.8% | 20.8% |
| 89,994 | INDIANA | 33,314 | 10,966 | 15,194 | 7,089 | 65 | 4,228 D | 32.9% | 45.6% | 21.3% |
| 46,083 | JEFFERSON | 17,711 | 7,271 | 5,998 | 4,403 | 39 | 1,273 R | 41.1% | 33.9% | 24.9% |
| 20,625 | JUNIATA | 8,420 | 3,980 | 2,601 | 1,819 | 20 | 1,379 R | 47.3% | 30.9% | 21.6% |
| 219,039 | LACKAWANNA | 94,968 | 33,443 | 45,054 | 15,667 | 804 | 11,611 D | 35.2% | 47.4% | 16.5% |
| 422,822 | LANCASTER | 160,180 | 88,447 | 44,255 | 26,807 | 671 | 44,192 R | 55.2% | 27.6% | 16.7% |
| 96,246 | LAWRENCE | 41,203 | 12,359 | 20,830 | 7,950 | 64 | 8,471 D | 30.0% | 50.6% | 19.3% |
| 113,744 | LEBANON | 43,021 | 21,512 | 12,350 | 9,005 | 154 | 9,162 R | 50.0% | 28.7% | 20.9% |
| 291,130 | LEHIGH | 114,836 | 42,631 | 46,711 | 24,853 | 641 | 4,080 D | 37.1% | 40.7% | 21.6% |
| 328,149 | LUZERNE | 127,146 | 49,285 | 56,623 | 21,007 | 231 | 7,338 D | 38.8% | 44.5% | 16.5% |
| 118,710 | LYCOMING | 43,172 | 20,536 | 13,315 | 9,170 | 151 | 7,221 R | 47.6% | 30.8% | 21.2% |
| 47,131 | MCKEAN | 16,400 | 6,965 | 5,331 | 4,019 | 85 | 1,634 R | 42.5% | 32.5% | 24.5% |
| 121,003 | MERCER | 49,836 | 16,081 | 23,264 | 10,277 | 214 | 7,183 D | 32.3% | 46.7% | 20.6% |
| 46,197 | MIFFLIN | 14,688 | 6,300 | 4,946 | 3,382 | 60 | 1,354 R | 42.9% | 33.7% | 23.0% |
| 95,709 | MONROE | 37,500 | 14,557 | 13,468 | 9,257 | 218 | 1,089 R | 38.8% | 35.9% | 24.7% |
| 678,111 | MONTGOMERY | 318,576 | 125,704 | 136,572 | 53,738 | 2,562 | 10,868 D | 39.5% | 42.9% | 16.9% |
| 17,735 | MONTOUR | 6,646 | 3,096 | 2,150 | 1,373 | 27 | 946 R | 46.6% | 32.4% | 20.7% |
| 247,105 | NORTHAMPTON | 97,525 | 34,429 | 42,203 | 20,234 | 659 | 7,774 D | 35.3% | 43.3% | 20.7% |
| 96,771 | NORTHUMBERLAND | 35,792 | 15,057 | 12,814 | 7,782 | 139 | 2,243 R | 42.1% | 35.8% | 21.7% |
| 41,172 | PERRY | 15,327 | 7,871 | 4,086 | 3,334 | 36 | 3,785 R | 51.4% | 26.7% | 21.8% |
| 1,585,577 | PHILADELPHIA | 638,058 | 133,328 | 434,904 | 65,455 | 4,371 | 301,576 D | 20.9% | 68.2% | 10.3% |
| 27,966 | PIKE | 13,603 | 6,084 | 4,382 | 3,019 | 118 | 1,702 R | 44.7% | 32.2% | 22.2% |
| 16,717 | POTTER | 7,044 | 3,452 | 1,892 | 1,687 | 13 | 1,560 R | 49.0% | 26.9% | 23.9% |
| 152,585 | SCHUYLKILL | 63,029 | 25,780 | 23,679 | 13,398 | 172 | 2,101 R | 40.9% | 37.6% | 21.3% |
| 36,680 | SNYDER | 12,596 | 6,934 | 2,952 | 2,686 | 24 | 3,982 R | 55.0% | 23.4% | 21.3% |
| 78,218 | SOMERSET | 32,759 | 13,858 | 12,493 | 6,333 | 75 | 1,365 R | 42.3% | 38.1% | 19.3% |
| 6,104 | SULLIVAN | 3,113 | 1,340 | 1,030 | 731 | 12 | 310 R | 43.0% | 33.1% | 23.5% |
| 40,380 | SUSQUEHANNA | 16,709 | 7,356 | 5,368 | 3,946 | 39 | 1,988 R | 44.0% | 32.1% | 23.6% |
| 41,126 | TIOGA | 16,543 | 7,823 | 4,868 | 3,804 | 48 | 2,955 R | 47.3% | 29.4% | 23.0% |
| 36,176 | UNION | 12,265 | 6,362 | 3,623 | 2,255 | 25 | 2,739 R | 51.9% | 29.5% | 18.4% |

# PENNSYLVANIA

## PRESIDENT 1992

| 1990 Census Population | County | Total Vote | Republican | Democratic | Perot | Other | Plurality | Percentage Total Vote | | |
|---|---|---|---|---|---|---|---|---|---|---|
| | | | | | | | | Rep. | Dem. | Perot |
| 59,381 | VENANGO | 21,554 | 8,545 | 8,230 | 4,695 | 84 | 315 R | 39.6% | 38.2% | 21.8% |
| 45,050 | WARREN | 18,426 | 6,585 | 6,972 | 4,795 | 74 | 387 D | 35.7% | 37.8% | 26.0% |
| 204,584 | WASHINGTON | 84,364 | 21,977 | 46,143 | 16,083 | 161 | 24,166 D | 26.1% | 54.7% | 19.1% |
| 39,944 | WAYNE | 16,822 | 8,184 | 4,817 | 3,727 | 94 | 3,367 R | 48.7% | 28.6% | 22.2% |
| 370,321 | WESTMORELAND | 154,451 | 47,315 | 69,817 | 37,036 | 283 | 22,502 D | 30.6% | 45.2% | 24.0% |
| 28,076 | WYOMING | 10,850 | 5,143 | 3,158 | 2,525 | 24 | 1,985 R | 47.4% | 29.1% | 23.3% |
| 339,574 | YORK | 134,245 | 60,130 | 46,113 | 27,743 | 259 | 14,017 R | 44.8% | 34.3% | 20.7% |
| 11,881,643 | TOTAL | 4,959,810 | 1,791,841 | 2,239,164 | 902,667 | 26,138 | 447,323 D | 36.1% | 45.1% | 18.2% |

# PENNSYLVANIA

## PRESIDENT 1988

| 1980 Census Population | County | Total Vote | Republican | Democratic | Other | Rep.-Dem. Plurality | Percentage | | | |
|---|---|---|---|---|---|---|---|---|---|---|
| | | | | | | | Total Vote | | Major Vote | |
| | | | | | | | Rep. | Dem. | Rep. | Dem. |
| 68,292 | ADAMS | 24,105 | 15,650 | 8,299 | 156 | 7,351 R | 64.9% | 34.4% | 65.3% | 34.7% |
| 1,450,085 | ALLEGHENY | 586,151 | 231,137 | 348,814 | 6,200 | 117,677 D | 39.4% | 59.5% | 39.9% | 60.1% |
| 77,768 | ARMSTRONG | 25,683 | 11,509 | 13,892 | 282 | 2,383 D | 44.8% | 54.1% | 45.3% | 54.7% |
| 204,441 | BEAVER | 76,469 | 25,764 | 50,327 | 378 | 24,563 D | 33.7% | 65.8% | 33.9% | 66.1% |
| 46,784 | BEDFORD | 16,969 | 11,123 | 5,754 | 92 | 5,369 R | 65.5% | 33.9% | 65.9% | 34.1% |
| 312,509 | BERKS | 112,444 | 70,153 | 41,040 | 1,251 | 29,113 R | 62.4% | 36.5% | 63.1% | 36.9% |
| 136,621 | BLAIR | 41,662 | 25,623 | 15,588 | 451 | 10,035 R | 61.5% | 37.4% | 62.2% | 37.8% |
| 62,919 | BRADFORD | 20,337 | 13,568 | 6,635 | 134 | 6,933 R | 66.7% | 32.6% | 67.2% | 32.8% |
| 479,211 | BUCKS | 212,640 | 127,563 | 82,472 | 2,605 | 45,091 R | 60.0% | 38.8% | 60.7% | 39.3% |
| 147,912 | BUTLER | 50,667 | 27,777 | 22,341 | 549 | 5,436 R | 54.8% | 44.1% | 55.4% | 44.6% |
| 183,263 | CAMBRIA | 64,552 | 25,626 | 38,517 | 409 | 12,891 D | 39.7% | 59.7% | 40.0% | 60.0% |
| 6,674 | CAMERON | 2,655 | 1,731 | 901 | 23 | 830 R | 65.2% | 33.9% | 65.8% | 34.2% |
| 53,285 | CARBON | 19,547 | 10,232 | 9,104 | 211 | 1,128 R | 52.3% | 46.6% | 52.9% | 47.1% |
| 112,760 | CENTRE | 42,527 | 23,875 | 18,357 | 295 | 5,518 R | 56.1% | 43.2% | 56.5% | 43.5% |
| 316,660 | CHESTER | 139,585 | 93,522 | 44,853 | 1,210 | 48,669 R | 67.0% | 32.1% | 67.6% | 32.4% |
| 43,362 | CLARION | 13,751 | 8,026 | 5,616 | 109 | 2,410 R | 58.4% | 40.8% | 58.8% | 41.2% |
| 83,578 | CLEARFIELD | 26,713 | 14,296 | 12,235 | 182 | 2,061 R | 53.5% | 45.8% | 53.9% | 46.1% |
| 38,971 | CLINTON | 11,613 | 5,735 | 5,759 | 119 | 24 D | 49.4% | 49.6% | 49.9% | 50.1% |
| 61,967 | COLUMBIA | 20,021 | 12,114 | 7,767 | 140 | 4,347 R | 60.5% | 38.8% | 60.9% | 39.1% |
| 88,869 | CRAWFORD | 30,628 | 17,249 | 13,021 | 358 | 4,228 R | 56.3% | 42.5% | 57.0% | 43.0% |
| 178,541 | CUMBERLAND | 72,433 | 47,292 | 24,613 | 528 | 22,679 R | 65.3% | 34.0% | 65.8% | 34.2% |
| 232,317 | DAUPHIN | 84,677 | 48,917 | 35,079 | 681 | 13,838 R | 57.8% | 41.4% | 58.2% | 41.8% |
| 555,007 | DELAWARE | 246,305 | 147,656 | 96,144 | 2,505 | 51,512 R | 59.9% | 39.0% | 60.6% | 39.4% |
| 38,338 | ELK | 12,744 | 6,737 | 5,879 | 128 | 858 R | 52.9% | 46.1% | 53.4% | 46.6% |
| 279,780 | ERIE | 103,300 | 48,306 | 53,913 | 1,081 | 5,607 D | 46.8% | 52.2% | 47.3% | 52.7% |
| 159,417 | FAYETTE | 50,349 | 16,915 | 33,098 | 336 | 16,183 D | 33.6% | 65.7% | 33.8% | 66.2% |
| 5,072 | FOREST | 2,065 | 1,159 | 895 | 11 | 264 R | 56.1% | 43.3% | 56.4% | 43.6% |
| 113,629 | FRANKLIN | 39,644 | 27,086 | 12,368 | 190 | 14,718 R | 68.3% | 31.2% | 68.7% | 31.3% |
| 12,842 | FULTON | 4,646 | 3,086 | 1,532 | 28 | 1,554 R | 66.4% | 33.0% | 66.8% | 33.2% |
| 40,476 | GREENE | 14,095 | 4,879 | 9,126 | 90 | 4,247 D | 34.6% | 64.7% | 34.8% | 65.2% |
| 42,253 | HUNTINGDON | 13,631 | 8,800 | 4,752 | 79 | 4,048 R | 64.6% | 34.9% | 64.9% | 35.1% |
| 92,281 | INDIANA | 31,739 | 14,983 | 16,514 | 242 | 1,531 D | 47.2% | 52.0% | 47.6% | 52.4% |
| 48,303 | JEFFERSON | 16,109 | 9,743 | 6,235 | 131 | 3,508 R | 60.5% | 38.7% | 61.0% | 39.0% |
| 19,188 | JUNIATA | 7,764 | 4,881 | 2,834 | 49 | 2,047 R | 62.9% | 36.5% | 63.3% | 36.7% |
| 227,908 | LACKAWANNA | 88,741 | 42,083 | 45,591 | 1,067 | 3,508 D | 47.4% | 51.4% | 48.0% | 52.0% |
| 362,346 | LANCASTER | 137,029 | 96,979 | 38,982 | 1,068 | 57,997 R | 70.8% | 28.4% | 71.3% | 28.7% |
| 107,150 | LAWRENCE | 37,904 | 15,829 | 21,884 | 191 | 6,055 D | 41.8% | 57.7% | 42.0% | 58.0% |
| 108,582 | LEBANON | 36,608 | 24,415 | 11,912 | 281 | 12,503 R | 66.7% | 32.5% | 67.2% | 32.8% |
| 272,349 | LEHIGH | 100,107 | 56,363 | 42,801 | 943 | 13,562 R | 56.3% | 42.8% | 56.8% | 43.2% |
| 343,079 | LUZERNE | 118,092 | 59,059 | 58,553 | 480 | 506 R | 50.0% | 49.6% | 50.2% | 49.8% |
| 118,416 | LYCOMING | 38,735 | 24,792 | 13,528 | 415 | 11,264 R | 64.0% | 34.9% | 64.7% | 35.3% |
| 50,635 | MCKEAN | 14,747 | 9,323 | 5,300 | 124 | 4,023 R | 63.2% | 35.9% | 63.8% | 36.2% |
| 128,299 | MERCER | 45,880 | 21,301 | 24,278 | 301 | 2,977 D | 46.4% | 52.9% | 46.7% | 53.3% |
| 46,908 | MIFFLIN | 13,075 | 8,170 | 4,790 | 115 | 3,380 R | 62.5% | 36.6% | 63.0% | 37.0% |
| 69,409 | MONROE | 27,371 | 17,185 | 9,859 | 327 | 7,326 R | 62.8% | 36.0% | 63.5% | 36.5% |
| 643,621 | MONTGOMERY | 282,870 | 170,294 | 109,834 | 2,742 | 60,460 R | 60.2% | 38.8% | 60.8% | 39.2% |
| 16,675 | MONTOUR | 5,696 | 3,617 | 2,031 | 48 | 1,586 R | 63.5% | 35.7% | 64.0% | 36.0% |
| 225,418 | NORTHAMPTON | 82,978 | 42,748 | 39,264 | 966 | 3,484 R | 51.5% | 47.3% | 52.1% | 47.9% |
| 100,381 | NORTHUMBERLAND | 34,800 | 20,207 | 14,255 | 338 | 5,952 R | 58.1% | 41.0% | 58.6% | 41.4% |
| 35,718 | PERRY | 12,533 | 8,545 | 3,910 | 78 | 4,635 R | 68.2% | 31.2% | 68.6% | 31.4% |
| 1,688,210 | PHILADELPHIA | 674,977 | 219,053 | 449,566 | 6,358 | 230,513 D | 32.5% | 66.6% | 32.8% | 67.2% |
| 18,271 | PIKE | 9,917 | 6,659 | 3,097 | 161 | 3,562 R | 67.1% | 31.2% | 68.3% | 31.7% |
| 17,726 | POTTER | 6,592 | 4,432 | 2,119 | 41 | 2,313 R | 67.2% | 32.1% | 67.7% | 32.3% |
| 160,630 | SCHUYLKILL | 57,842 | 32,666 | 24,797 | 379 | 7,869 R | 56.5% | 42.9% | 56.8% | 43.2% |
| 33,584 | SNYDER | 11,779 | 9,054 | 2,658 | 67 | 6,396 R | 76.9% | 22.6% | 77.3% | 22.7% |
| 81,243 | SOMERSET | 30,768 | 16,809 | 13,815 | 144 | 2,994 R | 54.6% | 44.9% | 54.9% | 45.1% |
| 6,349 | SULLIVAN | 2,922 | 1,808 | 1,091 | 23 | 717 R | 61.9% | 37.3% | 62.4% | 37.6% |
| 37,876 | SUSQUEHANNA | 14,056 | 9,077 | 4,871 | 108 | 4,206 R | 64.6% | 34.7% | 65.1% | 34.9% |
| 40,973 | TIOGA | 14,350 | 9,471 | 4,807 | 72 | 4,664 R | 66.0% | 33.5% | 66.3% | 33.7% |
| 32,870 | UNION | 11,136 | 7,912 | 3,163 | 61 | 4,749 R | 71.0% | 28.4% | 71.4% | 28.6% |

# PENNSYLVANIA

## PRESIDENT 1988

| 1980 Census Population | County | Total Vote | Republican | Democratic | Other | Rep.-Dem. Plurality | Percentage | | | |
| --- | --- | --- | --- | --- | --- | --- | --- | --- | --- | --- |
| | | | | | | | Total Vote | | Major Vote | |
| | | | | | | | Rep. | Dem. | Rep. | Dem. |
| 64,444 | VENANGO | 20,263 | 11,468 | 8,624 | 171 | 2,844 R | 56.6% | 42.6% | 57.1% | 42.9% |
| 47,449 | WARREN | 15,995 | 8,991 | 6,790 | 214 | 2,201 R | 56.2% | 42.5% | 57.0% | 43.0% |
| 217,074 | WASHINGTON | 76,553 | 28,651 | 47,527 | 375 | 18,876 D | 37.4% | 62.1% | 37.6% | 62.4% |
| 35,237 | WAYNE | 13,862 | 9,926 | 3,775 | 161 | 6,151 R | 71.6% | 27.2% | 72.4% | 27.6% |
| 392,294 | WESTMORELAND | 139,290 | 61,472 | 76,710 | 1,108 | 15,238 D | 44.1% | 55.1% | 44.5% | 55.5% |
| 26,433 | WYOMING | 9,447 | 6,607 | 2,797 | 43 | 3,810 R | 69.9% | 29.6% | 70.3% | 29.7% |
| 312,963 | YORK | 111,116 | 72,408 | 37,691 | 1,017 | 34,717 R | 65.2% | 33.9% | 65.8% | 34.2% |
| 11,863,895 | TOTAL | 4,536,251 | 2,300,087 | 2,194,944 | 41,220 | 105,143 R | 50.7% | 48.4% | 51.2% | 48.8% |

# PENNSYLVANIA

## PRESIDENT 1984

| 1980 Census Population | County | Total Vote | Republican | Democratic | Other | Rep.-Dem. Plurality | | Total Vote Rep. | Total Vote Dem. | Major Vote Rep. | Major Vote Dem. |
|---|---|---|---|---|---|---|---|---|---|---|---|
| 68,292 | ADAMS | 24,174 | 16,786 | 7,289 | 99 | 9,497 | R | 69.4% | 30.2% | 69.7% | 30.3% |
| 1,450,085 | ALLEGHENY | 665,748 | 284,692 | 372,576 | 8,480 | 87,884 | D | 42.8% | 56.0% | 43.3% | 56.7% |
| 77,768 | ARMSTRONG | 28,344 | 13,709 | 14,525 | 110 | 816 | D | 48.4% | 51.2% | 48.6% | 51.4% |
| 204,441 | BEAVER | 87,117 | 32,052 | 54,765 | 300 | 22,713 | D | 36.8% | 62.9% | 36.9% | 63.1% |
| 46,784 | BEDFORD | 18,543 | 13,085 | 5,424 | 34 | 7,661 | R | 70.6% | 29.3% | 70.7% | 29.3% |
| 312,509 | BERKS | 113,145 | 74,605 | 37,849 | 691 | 36,756 | R | 65.9% | 33.5% | 66.3% | 33.7% |
| 136,621 | BLAIR | 45,945 | 30,104 | 15,651 | 190 | 14,453 | R | 65.5% | 34.1% | 65.8% | 34.2% |
| 62,919 | BRADFORD | 20,367 | 14,808 | 5,474 | 85 | 9,334 | R | 72.7% | 26.9% | 73.0% | 27.0% |
| 479,211 | BUCKS | 205,719 | 130,119 | 74,568 | 1,032 | 55,551 | R | 63.3% | 36.2% | 63.6% | 36.4% |
| 147,912 | BUTLER | 56,626 | 31,676 | 24,735 | 215 | 6,941 | R | 55.9% | 43.7% | 56.2% | 43.8% |
| 183,263 | CAMBRIA | 72,296 | 32,173 | 39,865 | 258 | 7,692 | D | 44.5% | 55.1% | 44.7% | 55.3% |
| 6,674 | CAMERON | 3,029 | 2,031 | 990 | 8 | 1,041 | R | 67.1% | 32.7% | 67.2% | 32.8% |
| 53,285 | CARBON | 19,668 | 10,701 | 8,836 | 131 | 1,865 | R | 54.4% | 44.9% | 54.8% | 45.2% |
| 112,760 | CENTRE | 44,236 | 27,802 | 16,194 | 240 | 11,608 | R | 62.8% | 36.6% | 63.2% | 36.8% |
| 316,660 | CHESTER | 131,531 | 92,221 | 38,870 | 440 | 53,351 | R | 70.1% | 29.6% | 70.3% | 29.7% |
| 43,362 | CLARION | 15,304 | 9,836 | 5,407 | 61 | 4,429 | R | 64.3% | 35.3% | 64.5% | 35.5% |
| 83,578 | CLEARFIELD | 30,769 | 18,653 | 11,963 | 153 | 6,690 | R | 60.6% | 38.9% | 60.9% | 39.1% |
| 38,971 | CLINTON | 11,273 | 6,678 | 4,525 | 70 | 2,153 | R | 59.2% | 40.1% | 59.6% | 40.4% |
| 61,967 | COLUMBIA | 22,718 | 14,402 | 8,254 | 62 | 6,148 | R | 63.4% | 36.3% | 63.6% | 36.4% |
| 88,869 | CRAWFORD | 33,195 | 20,181 | 12,792 | 222 | 7,389 | R | 60.8% | 38.5% | 61.2% | 38.8% |
| 178,541 | CUMBERLAND | 71,123 | 49,282 | 21,374 | 467 | 27,908 | R | 69.3% | 30.1% | 69.7% | 30.3% |
| 232,317 | DAUPHIN | 88,658 | 54,330 | 33,576 | 752 | 20,754 | R | 61.3% | 37.9% | 61.8% | 38.2% |
| 555,007 | DELAWARE | 261,782 | 161,754 | 98,207 | 1,821 | 63,547 | R | 61.8% | 37.5% | 62.2% | 37.8% |
| 38,338 | ELK | 14,007 | 8,470 | 5,486 | 51 | 2,984 | R | 60.5% | 39.2% | 60.7% | 39.3% |
| 279,780 | ERIE | 109,266 | 55,860 | 52,471 | 935 | 3,389 | R | 51.1% | 48.0% | 51.6% | 48.4% |
| 159,417 | FAYETTE | 56,547 | 21,314 | 35,098 | 135 | 13,784 | D | 37.7% | 62.1% | 37.8% | 62.2% |
| 5,072 | FOREST | 2,317 | 1,468 | 839 | 10 | 629 | R | 63.4% | 36.2% | 63.6% | 36.4% |
| 113,629 | FRANKLIN | 38,845 | 27,243 | 11,480 | 122 | 15,763 | R | 70.1% | 29.6% | 70.4% | 29.6% |
| 12,842 | FULTON | 4,574 | 3,254 | 1,309 | 11 | 1,945 | R | 71.1% | 28.6% | 71.3% | 28.7% |
| 40,476 | GREENE | 15,784 | 6,376 | 9,365 | 43 | 2,989 | D | 40.4% | 59.3% | 40.5% | 59.5% |
| 42,253 | HUNTINGDON | 14,691 | 10,220 | 4,430 | 41 | 5,790 | R | 69.6% | 30.2% | 69.8% | 30.2% |
| 92,281 | INDIANA | 34,759 | 18,845 | 15,791 | 123 | 3,054 | R | 54.2% | 45.4% | 54.4% | 45.6% |
| 48,303 | JEFFERSON | 17,355 | 11,334 | 5,950 | 71 | 5,384 | R | 65.3% | 34.3% | 65.6% | 34.4% |
| 19,188 | JUNIATA | 7,705 | 5,059 | 2,624 | 22 | 2,435 | R | 65.7% | 34.1% | 65.8% | 34.2% |
| 227,908 | LACKAWANNA | 95,185 | 48,132 | 45,851 | 1,202 | 2,281 | R | 50.6% | 48.2% | 51.2% | 48.8% |
| 362,346 | LANCASTER | 131,016 | 99,090 | 31,308 | 618 | 67,782 | R | 75.6% | 23.9% | 76.0% | 24.0% |
| 107,150 | LAWRENCE | 43,386 | 19,277 | 23,981 | 128 | 4,704 | D | 44.4% | 55.3% | 44.6% | 55.4% |
| 108,582 | LEBANON | 37,716 | 27,008 | 10,520 | 188 | 16,488 | R | 71.6% | 27.9% | 72.0% | 28.0% |
| 272,349 | LEHIGH | 103,537 | 61,799 | 41,089 | 649 | 20,710 | R | 59.7% | 39.7% | 60.1% | 39.9% |
| 343,079 | LUZERNE | 129,291 | 69,169 | 58,482 | 1,640 | 10,687 | R | 53.5% | 45.2% | 54.2% | 45.8% |
| 118,416 | LYCOMING | 41,895 | 28,498 | 13,147 | 250 | 15,351 | R | 68.0% | 31.4% | 68.4% | 31.6% |
| 50,635 | MCKEAN | 15,839 | 10,963 | 4,818 | 58 | 6,145 | R | 69.2% | 30.4% | 69.5% | 30.5% |
| 128,299 | MERCER | 49,303 | 24,211 | 24,658 | 434 | 447 | D | 49.1% | 50.0% | 49.5% | 50.5% |
| 46,908 | MIFFLIN | 14,373 | 9,106 | 5,178 | 89 | 3,928 | R | 63.4% | 36.0% | 63.7% | 36.3% |
| 69,409 | MONROE | 24,474 | 16,109 | 8,193 | 172 | 7,916 | R | 65.8% | 33.5% | 66.3% | 33.7% |
| 643,621 | MONTGOMERY | 282,666 | 181,426 | 99,741 | 1,499 | 81,685 | R | 64.2% | 35.3% | 64.5% | 35.5% |
| 16,675 | MONTOUR | 6,248 | 4,174 | 2,055 | 19 | 2,119 | R | 66.8% | 32.9% | 67.0% | 33.0% |
| 225,418 | NORTHAMPTON | 83,467 | 44,648 | 37,979 | 840 | 6,669 | R | 53.5% | 45.5% | 54.0% | 46.0% |
| 100,381 | NORTHUMBERLAND | 36,165 | 22,109 | 13,748 | 308 | 8,361 | R | 61.1% | 38.0% | 61.7% | 38.3% |
| 35,718 | PERRY | 13,113 | 9,365 | 3,692 | 56 | 5,673 | R | 71.4% | 28.2% | 71.7% | 28.3% |
| 1,688,210 | PHILADELPHIA | 772,102 | 267,178 | 501,369 | 3,555 | 234,191 | D | 34.6% | 64.9% | 34.8% | 65.2% |
| 18,271 | PIKE | 8,913 | 6,343 | 2,503 | 67 | 3,840 | R | 71.2% | 28.1% | 71.7% | 28.3% |
| 17,726 | POTTER | 6,984 | 5,164 | 1,789 | 31 | 3,375 | R | 73.9% | 25.6% | 74.3% | 25.7% |
| 160,630 | SCHUYLKILL | 63,312 | 37,330 | 25,758 | 224 | 11,572 | R | 59.0% | 40.7% | 59.2% | 40.8% |
| 33,584 | SNYDER | 11,391 | 8,968 | 2,383 | 40 | 6,585 | R | 78.7% | 20.9% | 79.0% | 21.0% |
| 81,243 | SOMERSET | 33,491 | 19,502 | 13,900 | 89 | 5,602 | R | 58.2% | 41.5% | 58.4% | 41.6% |
| 6,349 | SULLIVAN | 2,889 | 1,926 | 952 | 11 | 974 | R | 66.7% | 33.0% | 66.9% | 33.1% |
| 37,876 | SUSQUEHANNA | 15,104 | 10,566 | 4,471 | 67 | 6,095 | R | 70.0% | 29.6% | 70.3% | 29.7% |
| 40,973 | TIOGA | 14,644 | 10,532 | 4,060 | 52 | 6,472 | R | 71.9% | 27.7% | 72.2% | 27.8% |
| 32,870 | UNION | 10,579 | 7,792 | 2,747 | 40 | 5,045 | R | 73.7% | 26.0% | 73.9% | 26.1% |

# PENNSYLVANIA

## PRESIDENT 1984

| 1980 Census Population | County | Total Vote | Republican | Democratic | Other | Rep.-Dem. Plurality | Percentage | | | |
| --- | --- | --- | --- | --- | --- | --- | --- | --- | --- | --- |
| | | | | | | | Total Vote | | Major Vote | |
| | | | | | | | Rep. | Dem. | Rep. | Dem. |
| 64,444 | VENANGO | 22,725 | 13,507 | 9,114 | 104 | 4,393 R | 59.4% | 40.1% | 59.7% | 40.3% |
| 47,449 | WARREN | 17,221 | 10,838 | 6,244 | 139 | 4,594 R | 62.9% | 36.3% | 63.4% | 36.6% |
| 217,074 | WASHINGTON | 85,937 | 34,782 | 50,911 | 244 | 16,129 D | 40.5% | 59.2% | 40.6% | 59.4% |
| 35,237 | WAYNE | 13,297 | 10,061 | 3,155 | 81 | 6,906 R | 75.7% | 23.7% | 76.1% | 23.9% |
| 392,294 | WESTMORELAND | 152,464 | 71,377 | 79,906 | 1,181 | 8,529 D | 46.8% | 52.4% | 47.2% | 52.8% |
| 26,433 | WYOMING | 9,769 | 7,230 | 2,518 | 21 | 4,712 R | 74.0% | 25.8% | 74.2% | 25.8% |
| 312,963 | YORK | 109,247 | 75,020 | 33,359 | 868 | 41,661 R | 68.7% | 30.5% | 69.2% | 30.8% |
| 11,863,895 | TOTAL | 4,844,903 | 2,584,323 | 2,228,131 | 32,449 | 356,192 R | 53.3% | 46.0% | 53.7% | 46.3% |

# PENNSYLVANIA

## PRESIDENT 1980

| 1980 Census Population | County | Total Vote | Republican | Democratic | Other | Rep.-Dem. Plurality | Percentage | | | |
|---|---|---|---|---|---|---|---|---|---|---|
| | | | | | | | Total Vote | | Major Vote | |
| | | | | | | | Rep. | Dem. | Rep. | Dem. |
| 68,292 | ADAMS | 22,404 | 13,760 | 7,266 | 1,378 | 6,494 R | 61.4% | 32.4% | 65.4% | 34.6% |
| 1,450,085 | ALLEGHENY | 621,418 | 271,850 | 297,464 | 52,104 | 25,614 D | 43.7% | 47.9% | 47.8% | 52.2% |
| 77,768 | ARMSTRONG | 27,104 | 12,955 | 12,718 | 1,431 | 237 R | 47.8% | 46.9% | 50.5% | 49.5% |
| 204,441 | BEAVER | 79,765 | 30,496 | 43,955 | 5,314 | 13,459 D | 38.2% | 55.1% | 41.0% | 59.0% |
| 46,784 | BEDFORD | 16,419 | 10,930 | 4,950 | 539 | 5,980 R | 66.6% | 30.1% | 68.8% | 31.2% |
| 312,509 | BERKS | 107,385 | 60,576 | 36,449 | 10,360 | 24,127 R | 56.4% | 33.9% | 62.4% | 37.6% |
| 136,621 | BLAIR | 46,359 | 28,931 | 15,014 | 2,414 | 13,917 R | 62.4% | 32.4% | 65.8% | 34.2% |
| 62,919 | BRADFORD | 20,865 | 13,139 | 6,439 | 1,287 | 6,700 R | 63.0% | 30.9% | 67.1% | 32.9% |
| 479,211 | BUCKS | 181,164 | 100,536 | 59,120 | 21,508 | 41,416 R | 55.5% | 32.6% | 63.0% | 37.0% |
| 147,912 | BUTLER | 52,689 | 28,821 | 19,711 | 4,157 | 9,110 R | 54.7% | 37.4% | 59.4% | 40.6% |
| 183,263 | CAMBRIA | 72,131 | 33,072 | 36,121 | 2,938 | 3,049 D | 45.8% | 50.1% | 47.8% | 52.2% |
| 6,674 | CAMERON | 3,030 | 1,795 | 1,112 | 123 | 683 R | 59.2% | 36.7% | 61.7% | 38.3% |
| 53,285 | CARBON | 19,329 | 10,042 | 8,009 | 1,278 | 2,033 R | 52.0% | 41.4% | 55.6% | 44.4% |
| 112,760 | CENTRE | 42,631 | 20,605 | 15,987 | 6,039 | 4,618 R | 48.3% | 37.5% | 56.3% | 43.7% |
| 316,660 | CHESTER | 119,896 | 73,046 | 34,307 | 12,543 | 38,739 R | 60.9% | 28.6% | 68.0% | 32.0% |
| 43,362 | CLARION | 15,101 | 8,812 | 5,472 | 817 | 3,340 R | 58.4% | 36.2% | 61.7% | 38.3% |
| 83,578 | CLEARFIELD | 28,192 | 15,299 | 11,647 | 1,246 | 3,652 R | 54.3% | 41.3% | 56.8% | 43.2% |
| 38,971 | CLINTON | 12,010 | 6,288 | 4,842 | 880 | 1,446 R | 52.4% | 40.3% | 56.5% | 43.5% |
| 61,967 | COLUMBIA | 23,313 | 12,426 | 9,449 | 1,438 | 2,977 R | 53.3% | 40.5% | 56.8% | 43.2% |
| 88,869 | CRAWFORD | 30,909 | 16,552 | 11,778 | 2,579 | 4,774 R | 53.6% | 38.1% | 58.4% | 41.6% |
| 178,541 | CUMBERLAND | 67,260 | 41,152 | 19,789 | 6,319 | 21,363 R | 61.2% | 29.4% | 67.5% | 32.5% |
| 232,317 | DAUPHIN | 78,387 | 44,039 | 27,252 | 7,096 | 16,787 R | 56.2% | 34.8% | 61.8% | 38.2% |
| 555,007 | DELAWARE | 256,859 | 143,282 | 88,314 | 25,263 | 54,968 R | 55.8% | 34.4% | 61.9% | 38.1% |
| 38,338 | ELK | 13,669 | 7,175 | 5,898 | 596 | 1,277 R | 52.5% | 43.1% | 54.9% | 45.1% |
| 279,780 | ERIE | 103,162 | 48,918 | 45,946 | 8,298 | 2,972 R | 47.4% | 44.5% | 51.6% | 48.4% |
| 159,417 | FAYETTE | 49,383 | 19,252 | 27,963 | 2,168 | 8,711 D | 39.0% | 56.6% | 40.8% | 59.2% |
| 5,072 | FOREST | 2,149 | 1,206 | 819 | 124 | 387 R | 56.1% | 38.1% | 59.6% | 40.4% |
| 113,629 | FRANKLIN | 36,741 | 22,716 | 12,061 | 1,964 | 10,655 R | 61.8% | 32.8% | 65.3% | 34.7% |
| 12,842 | FULTON | 4,222 | 2,740 | 1,342 | 140 | 1,398 R | 64.9% | 31.8% | 67.1% | 32.9% |
| 40,476 | GREENE | 14,121 | 5,336 | 8,193 | 592 | 2,857 D | 37.8% | 58.0% | 39.4% | 60.6% |
| 42,253 | HUNTINGDON | 13,928 | 8,140 | 5,094 | 694 | 3,046 R | 58.4% | 36.6% | 61.5% | 38.5% |
| 92,281 | INDIANA | 31,451 | 15,607 | 13,828 | 2,016 | 1,779 R | 49.6% | 44.0% | 53.0% | 47.0% |
| 48,303 | JEFFERSON | 16,778 | 9,628 | 6,296 | 854 | 3,332 R | 57.4% | 37.5% | 60.5% | 39.5% |
| 19,188 | JUNIATA | 7,161 | 4,139 | 2,696 | 326 | 1,443 R | 57.8% | 37.6% | 60.6% | 39.4% |
| 227,908 | LACKAWANNA | 95,447 | 44,242 | 45,257 | 5,948 | 1,015 D | 46.4% | 47.4% | 49.4% | 50.6% |
| 362,346 | LANCASTER | 118,897 | 79,963 | 30,026 | 8,908 | 49,937 R | 67.3% | 25.3% | 72.7% | 27.3% |
| 107,150 | LAWRENCE | 40,213 | 18,404 | 19,506 | 2,303 | 1,102 D | 45.8% | 48.5% | 48.5% | 51.5% |
| 108,582 | LEBANON | 35,507 | 24,495 | 8,281 | 2,731 | 16,214 R | 69.0% | 23.3% | 74.7% | 25.3% |
| 272,349 | LEHIGH | 95,985 | 50,782 | 34,827 | 10,376 | 15,955 R | 52.9% | 36.3% | 59.3% | 40.7% |
| 343,079 | LUZERNE | 135,080 | 67,822 | 59,976 | 7,282 | 7,846 R | 50.2% | 44.4% | 53.1% | 46.9% |
| 118,416 | LYCOMING | 40,553 | 23,415 | 14,609 | 2,529 | 8,806 R | 57.7% | 36.0% | 61.6% | 38.4% |
| 50,635 | MCKEAN | 15,166 | 9,229 | 5,064 | 873 | 4,165 R | 60.9% | 33.4% | 64.6% | 35.4% |
| 128,299 | MERCER | 46,090 | 22,372 | 19,716 | 4,002 | 2,656 R | 48.5% | 42.8% | 53.2% | 46.8% |
| 46,908 | MIFFLIN | 13,520 | 7,541 | 5,226 | 753 | 2,315 R | 55.8% | 38.7% | 59.1% | 40.9% |
| 69,409 | MONROE | 22,289 | 12,357 | 7,551 | 2,381 | 4,806 R | 55.4% | 33.9% | 62.1% | 37.9% |
| 643,621 | MONTGOMERY | 271,553 | 156,996 | 84,289 | 30,268 | 72,707 R | 57.8% | 31.0% | 65.1% | 34.9% |
| 16,675 | MONTOUR | 6,096 | 3,399 | 2,272 | 425 | 1,127 R | 55.8% | 37.3% | 59.9% | 40.1% |
| 225,418 | NORTHAMPTON | 76,037 | 35,787 | 31,920 | 8,330 | 3,867 R | 47.1% | 42.0% | 52.9% | 47.1% |
| 100,381 | NORTHUMBERLAND | 36,290 | 20,608 | 13,750 | 1,932 | 6,858 R | 56.8% | 37.9% | 60.0% | 40.0% |
| 35,718 | PERRY | 12,599 | 8,026 | 3,681 | 892 | 4,345 R | 63.7% | 29.2% | 68.6% | 31.4% |
| 1,688,210 | PHILADELPHIA | 718,100 | 244,108 | 421,253 | 52,739 | 177,145 D | 34.0% | 58.7% | 36.7% | 63.3% |
| 18,271 | PIKE | 7,973 | 5,249 | 2,132 | 592 | 3,117 R | 65.8% | 26.7% | 71.1% | 28.9% |
| 17,726 | POTTER | 6,669 | 4,073 | 2,299 | 297 | 1,774 R | 61.1% | 34.5% | 63.9% | 36.1% |
| 160,630 | SCHUYLKILL | 64,969 | 36,273 | 24,968 | 3,728 | 11,305 R | 55.8% | 38.4% | 59.2% | 40.8% |
| 33,584 | SNYDER | 10,591 | 7,634 | 2,418 | 539 | 5,216 R | 72.1% | 22.8% | 75.9% | 24.1% |
| 81,243 | SOMERSET | 30,455 | 17,729 | 11,695 | 1,031 | 6,034 R | 58.2% | 38.4% | 60.3% | 39.7% |
| 6,349 | SULLIVAN | 2,902 | 1,676 | 1,074 | 152 | 602 R | 57.8% | 37.0% | 60.9% | 39.1% |
| 37,876 | SUSQUEHANNA | 14,689 | 8,994 | 4,660 | 1,035 | 4,334 R | 61.2% | 31.7% | 65.9% | 34.1% |
| 40,973 | TIOGA | 13,849 | 8,770 | 4,273 | 806 | 4,497 R | 63.3% | 30.9% | 67.2% | 32.8% |
| 32,870 | UNION | 10,256 | 6,798 | 2,687 | 771 | 4,111 R | 66.3% | 26.2% | 71.7% | 28.3% |

# PENNSYLVANIA

## PRESIDENT 1980

| 1980 Census Population | County | Total Vote | Republican | Democratic | Other | Rep.-Dem. Plurality | Percentage | | | |
|---|---|---|---|---|---|---|---|---|---|---|
| | | | | | | | Total Vote | | Major Vote | |
| | | | | | | | Rep. | Dem. | Rep. | Dem. |
| 64,444 | VENANGO | 20,604 | 11,547 | 7,800 | 1,257 | 3,747 R | 56.0% | 37.9% | 59.7% | 40.3% |
| 47,449 | WARREN | 15,974 | 9,165 | 5,560 | 1,249 | 3,605 R | 57.4% | 34.8% | 62.2% | 37.8% |
| 217,074 | WASHINGTON | 82,018 | 32,532 | 45,295 | 4,191 | 12,763 D | 39.7% | 55.2% | 41.8% | 58.2% |
| 35,237 | WAYNE | 12,548 | 8,468 | 3,375 | 705 | 5,093 R | 67.5% | 26.9% | 71.5% | 28.5% |
| 392,294 | WESTMORELAND | 140,139 | 63,140 | 68,627 | 8,372 | 5,487 D | 45.1% | 49.0% | 47.9% | 52.1% |
| 26,433 | WYOMING | 9,167 | 5,919 | 2,766 | 482 | 3,153 R | 64.6% | 30.2% | 68.2% | 31.8% |
| 312,963 | YORK | 101,891 | 61,098 | 33,406 | 7,387 | 27,692 R | 60.0% | 32.8% | 64.7% | 35.3% |
| 11,863,895 | TOTAL | 4,561,501 | 2,261,872 | 1,937,540 | 362,089 | 324,332 R | 49.6% | 42.5% | 53.9% | 46.1% |

# PENNSYLVANIA

## PRESIDENT 1976

| 1970 Census Population | County | Total Vote | Republican | Democratic | Other | Rep.-Dem. Plurality | Percentage Total Vote | | Major Vote | |
|---|---|---|---|---|---|---|---|---|---|---|
| | | | | | | | Rep. | Dem. | Rep. | Dem. |
| 56,937 | ADAMS | 21,322 | 12,133 | 8,771 | 418 | 3,362 R | 56.9% | 41.1% | 58.0% | 42.0% |
| 1,605,016 | ALLEGHENY | 647,857 | 303,127 | 328,343 | 16,387 | 25,216 D | 46.8% | 50.7% | 48.0% | 52.0% |
| 75,590 | ARMSTRONG | 29,050 | 13,378 | 15,179 | 493 | 1,801 D | 46.1% | 52.3% | 46.8% | 53.2% |
| 208,418 | BEAVER | 81,150 | 33,593 | 46,117 | 1,440 | 12,524 D | 41.4% | 56.8% | 42.1% | 57.9% |
| 42,353 | BEDFORD | 16,138 | 9,355 | 6,652 | 131 | 2,703 R | 58.0% | 41.2% | 58.4% | 41.6% |
| 296,382 | BERKS | 107,553 | 54,452 | 50,994 | 2,107 | 3,458 R | 50.6% | 47.4% | 51.6% | 48.4% |
| 135,356 | BLAIR | 47,366 | 28,290 | 18,397 | 679 | 9,893 R | 59.7% | 38.8% | 60.6% | 39.4% |
| 57,962 | BRADFORD | 21,034 | 12,851 | 7,913 | 270 | 4,938 R | 61.1% | 37.6% | 61.9% | 38.1% |
| 415,056 | BUCKS | 168,923 | 85,628 | 79,838 | 3,457 | 5,790 R | 50.7% | 47.3% | 51.7% | 48.3% |
| 127,941 | BUTLER | 50,198 | 26,366 | 22,611 | 1,221 | 3,755 R | 52.5% | 45.0% | 53.8% | 46.2% |
| 186,785 | CAMBRIA | 72,128 | 32,469 | 38,797 | 862 | 6,328 D | 45.0% | 53.8% | 45.6% | 54.4% |
| 7,096 | CAMERON | 2,977 | 1,616 | 1,319 | 42 | 297 R | 54.3% | 44.3% | 55.1% | 44.9% |
| 50,573 | CARBON | 19,973 | 8,883 | 10,791 | 299 | 1,908 D | 44.5% | 54.0% | 45.2% | 54.8% |
| 99,267 | CENTRE | 40,437 | 21,177 | 17,867 | 1,393 | 3,310 R | 52.4% | 44.2% | 54.2% | 45.8% |
| 278,311 | CHESTER | 112,026 | 67,686 | 42,712 | 1,628 | 24,974 R | 60.4% | 38.1% | 61.3% | 38.7% |
| 38,414 | CLARION | 15,210 | 8,360 | 6,585 | 265 | 1,775 R | 55.0% | 43.3% | 55.9% | 44.1% |
| 74,619 | CLEARFIELD | 27,685 | 13,626 | 13,714 | 345 | 88 D | 49.2% | 49.5% | 49.8% | 50.2% |
| 37,721 | CLINTON | 12,564 | 5,858 | 6,532 | 174 | 674 D | 46.6% | 52.0% | 47.3% | 52.7% |
| 55,114 | COLUMBIA | 23,925 | 11,508 | 12,051 | 366 | 543 D | 48.1% | 50.4% | 48.8% | 51.2% |
| 81,342 | CRAWFORD | 30,610 | 15,301 | 14,712 | 597 | 589 R | 50.0% | 48.1% | 51.0% | 49.0% |
| 158,177 | CUMBERLAND | 64,270 | 39,950 | 23,008 | 1,312 | 16,942 R | 62.2% | 35.8% | 63.5% | 36.5% |
| 223,834 | DAUPHIN | 83,122 | 46,819 | 34,342 | 1,961 | 12,477 R | 56.3% | 41.3% | 57.7% | 42.3% |
| 600,035 | DELAWARE | 270,894 | 148,679 | 117,252 | 4,963 | 31,427 R | 54.9% | 43.3% | 55.9% | 44.1% |
| 37,770 | ELK | 13,109 | 6,159 | 6,713 | 237 | 554 D | 47.0% | 51.2% | 47.8% | 52.2% |
| 263,654 | ERIE | 107,439 | 49,641 | 55,385 | 2,413 | 5,744 D | 46.2% | 51.6% | 47.3% | 52.7% |
| 154,667 | FAYETTE | 53,244 | 20,021 | 32,232 | 991 | 12,211 D | 37.6% | 60.5% | 38.3% | 61.7% |
| 4,926 | FOREST | 2,187 | 1,135 | 1,017 | 35 | 118 R | 51.9% | 46.5% | 52.7% | 47.3% |
| 100,833 | FRANKLIN | 35,389 | 20,009 | 14,643 | 737 | 5,366 R | 56.5% | 41.4% | 57.7% | 42.3% |
| 10,776 | FULTON | 4,052 | 2,219 | 1,737 | 96 | 482 R | 54.8% | 42.9% | 56.1% | 43.9% |
| 36,090 | GREENE | 14,219 | 5,293 | 8,769 | 157 | 3,476 D | 37.2% | 61.7% | 37.6% | 62.4% |
| 39,108 | HUNTINGDON | 13,462 | 7,843 | 5,410 | 209 | 2,433 R | 58.3% | 40.2% | 59.2% | 40.8% |
| 79,451 | INDIANA | 30,949 | 15,786 | 14,650 | 513 | 1,136 R | 51.0% | 47.3% | 51.9% | 48.1% |
| 43,695 | JEFFERSON | 17,130 | 9,437 | 7,456 | 237 | 1,981 R | 55.1% | 43.5% | 55.9% | 44.1% |
| 16,712 | JUNIATA | 7,206 | 3,991 | 3,105 | 110 | 886 R | 55.4% | 43.1% | 56.2% | 43.8% |
| 234,107 | LACKAWANNA | 102,797 | 43,354 | 57,685 | 1,758 | 14,331 D | 42.2% | 56.1% | 42.9% | 57.1% |
| 319,693 | LANCASTER | 109,676 | 72,106 | 35,533 | 2,037 | 36,573 R | 65.7% | 32.4% | 67.0% | 33.0% |
| 107,374 | LAWRENCE | 42,640 | 18,546 | 23,337 | 757 | 4,791 D | 43.5% | 54.7% | 44.3% | 55.7% |
| 99,665 | LEBANON | 33,330 | 20,880 | 11,785 | 665 | 9,095 R | 62.6% | 35.4% | 63.9% | 36.1% |
| 255,304 | LEHIGH | 95,308 | 46,895 | 46,620 | 1,793 | 275 R | 49.2% | 48.9% | 50.1% | 49.9% |
| 342,301 | LUZERNE | 136,009 | 60,058 | 74,655 | 1,296 | 14,597 D | 44.2% | 54.9% | 44.6% | 55.4% |
| 113,296 | LYCOMING | 42,082 | 22,648 | 18,635 | 799 | 4,013 R | 53.8% | 44.3% | 54.9% | 45.1% |
| 51,915 | MCKEAN | 16,926 | 10,305 | 6,424 | 197 | 3,881 R | 60.9% | 38.0% | 61.6% | 38.4% |
| 127,175 | MERCER | 48,235 | 22,469 | 25,041 | 725 | 2,572 D | 46.6% | 51.9% | 47.3% | 52.7% |
| 45,268 | MIFFLIN | 14,109 | 7,698 | 6,210 | 201 | 1,488 R | 54.6% | 44.0% | 55.3% | 44.7% |
| 45,422 | MONROE | 20,165 | 10,228 | 9,544 | 393 | 684 R | 50.7% | 47.3% | 51.7% | 48.3% |
| 623,799 | MONTGOMERY | 273,169 | 155,480 | 112,644 | 5,045 | 42,836 R | 56.9% | 41.2% | 58.0% | 42.0% |
| 16,508 | MONTOUR | 6,075 | 3,259 | 2,727 | 89 | 532 R | 53.6% | 44.9% | 54.4% | 45.6% |
| 214,368 | NORTHAMPTON | 76,961 | 32,926 | 42,514 | 1,521 | 9,588 D | 42.8% | 55.2% | 43.6% | 56.4% |
| 99,190 | NORTHUMBERLAND | 38,876 | 19,283 | 18,939 | 654 | 344 R | 49.6% | 48.7% | 50.5% | 49.5% |
| 28,615 | PERRY | 12,320 | 7,454 | 4,605 | 261 | 2,849 R | 60.5% | 37.4% | 61.8% | 38.2% |
| 1,948,609 | PHILADELPHIA | 746,197 | 239,000 | 494,579 | 12,618 | 255,579 D | 32.0% | 66.3% | 32.6% | 67.4% |
| 11,818 | PIKE | 7,146 | 4,241 | 2,775 | 130 | 1,466 R | 59.3% | 38.8% | 60.4% | 39.6% |
| 16,395 | POTTER | 6,891 | 3,828 | 2,983 | 80 | 845 R | 55.6% | 43.3% | 56.2% | 43.8% |
| 160,089 | SCHUYLKILL | 66,948 | 31,944 | 33,905 | 1,099 | 1,961 D | 47.7% | 50.6% | 48.5% | 51.5% |
| 29,269 | SNYDER | 9,929 | 6,557 | 3,097 | 275 | 3,460 R | 66.0% | 31.2% | 67.9% | 32.1% |
| 76,037 | SOMERSET | 29,685 | 15,960 | 13,452 | 273 | 2,508 R | 53.8% | 45.3% | 54.3% | 45.7% |
| 5,961 | SULLIVAN | 2,951 | 1,584 | 1,347 | 20 | 237 R | 53.7% | 45.6% | 54.0% | 46.0% |
| 34,344 | SUSQUEHANNA | 14,682 | 8,331 | 6,075 | 276 | 2,256 R | 56.7% | 41.4% | 57.8% | 42.2% |
| 39,691 | TIOGA | 14,405 | 8,417 | 5,795 | 193 | 2,622 R | 58.4% | 40.2% | 59.2% | 40.8% |
| 28,603 | UNION | 9,902 | 6,309 | 3,405 | 188 | 2,904 R | 63.7% | 34.4% | 64.9% | 35.1% |

# PENNSYLVANIA

## PRESIDENT 1976

| 1970 Census Population | County | Total Vote | Republican | Democratic | Other | Rep.-Dem. Plurality | Percentage | | | |
|---|---|---|---|---|---|---|---|---|---|---|
| | | | | | | | Total Vote | | Major Vote | |
| | | | | | | | Rep. | Dem. | Rep. | Dem. |
| 62,353 | VENANGO | 21,311 | 12,270 | 8,653 | 388 | 3,617 R | 57.6% | 40.6% | 58.6% | 41.4% |
| 47,682 | WARREN | 16,170 | 8,508 | 7,412 | 250 | 1,096 R | 52.6% | 45.8% | 53.4% | 46.6% |
| 210,876 | WASHINGTON | 83,251 | 32,827 | 49,317 | 1,107 | 16,490 D | 39.4% | 59.2% | 40.0% | 60.0% |
| 29,581 | WAYNE | 12,310 | 7,811 | 4,244 | 255 | 3,567 R | 63.5% | 34.5% | 64.8% | 35.2% |
| 376,935 | WESTMORELAND | 136,134 | 59,172 | 74,217 | 2,745 | 15,045 D | 43.5% | 54.5% | 44.4% | 55.6% |
| 19,082 | WYOMING | 9,455 | 5,705 | 3,628 | 122 | 2,077 R | 60.3% | 38.4% | 61.1% | 38.9% |
| 272,603 | YORK | 99,944 | 56,912 | 41,281 | 1,751 | 15,631 R | 56.9% | 41.3% | 58.0% | 42.0% |
| 11,793,909 | TOTAL | 4,620,787 | 2,205,604 | 2,328,677 | 86,506 | 123,073 D | 47.7% | 50.4% | 48.6% | 51.4% |

# PENNSYLVANIA

## PRESIDENT 1972

| 1970 Census Population | County | Total Vote | Republican | Democratic | Other | Rep.-Dem. Plurality | Percentage | | | |
|---|---|---|---|---|---|---|---|---|---|---|
| | | | | | | | Total Vote | | Major Vote | |
| | | | | | | | Rep. | Dem. | Rep. | Dem. |
| 56,937 | ADAMS | 19,365 | 13,593 | 5,529 | 243 | 8,064 R | 70.2% | 28.6% | 71.1% | 28.9% |
| 1,605,016 | ALLEGHENY | 668,535 | 371,737 | 282,496 | 14,302 | 89,241 R | 55.6% | 42.3% | 56.8% | 43.2% |
| 75,590 | ARMSTRONG | 28,498 | 17,557 | 10,490 | 451 | 7,067 R | 61.6% | 36.8% | 62.6% | 37.4% |
| 208,418 | BEAVER | 77,337 | 43,637 | 31,570 | 2,130 | 12,067 R | 56.4% | 40.8% | 58.0% | 42.0% |
| 42,353 | BEDFORD | 15,338 | 11,243 | 3,836 | 259 | 7,407 R | 73.3% | 25.0% | 74.6% | 25.4% |
| 296,382 | BERKS | 106,127 | 66,172 | 36,563 | 3,392 | 29,609 R | 62.4% | 34.5% | 64.4% | 35.6% |
| 135,356 | BLAIR | 44,110 | 33,126 | 10,023 | 961 | 23,103 R | 75.1% | 22.7% | 76.8% | 23.2% |
| 57,962 | BRADFORD | 20,458 | 15,050 | 5,204 | 204 | 9,846 R | 73.6% | 25.4% | 74.3% | 25.7% |
| 415,056 | BUCKS | 160,059 | 99,684 | 56,784 | 3,591 | 42,900 R | 62.3% | 35.5% | 63.7% | 36.3% |
| 127,941 | BUTLER | 45,574 | 29,665 | 14,695 | 1,214 | 14,970 R | 65.1% | 32.2% | 66.9% | 33.1% |
| 186,785 | CAMBRIA | 72,975 | 43,825 | 27,950 | 1,200 | 15,875 R | 60.1% | 38.3% | 61.1% | 38.9% |
| 7,096 | CAMERON | 2,827 | 1,935 | 828 | 64 | 1,107 R | 68.4% | 29.3% | 70.0% | 30.0% |
| 50,573 | CARBON | 19,712 | 11,639 | 7,774 | 299 | 3,865 R | 59.0% | 39.4% | 60.0% | 40.0% |
| 99,267 | CENTRE | 34,197 | 20,683 | 13,194 | 320 | 7,489 R | 60.5% | 38.6% | 61.1% | 38.9% |
| 278,311 | CHESTER | 106,259 | 72,726 | 31,118 | 2,415 | 41,608 R | 68.4% | 29.3% | 70.0% | 30.0% |
| 38,414 | CLARION | 14,821 | 10,073 | 4,509 | 239 | 5,564 R | 68.0% | 30.4% | 69.1% | 30.9% |
| 74,619 | CLEARFIELD | 26,409 | 16,780 | 9,246 | 383 | 7,534 R | 63.5% | 35.0% | 64.5% | 35.5% |
| 37,721 | CLINTON | 13,119 | 8,205 | 4,772 | 142 | 3,433 R | 62.5% | 36.4% | 63.2% | 36.8% |
| 55,114 | COLUMBIA | 22,309 | 14,187 | 7,222 | 900 | 6,965 R | 63.6% | 32.4% | 66.3% | 33.7% |
| 81,342 | CRAWFORD | 28,569 | 18,393 | 9,371 | 805 | 9,022 R | 64.4% | 32.8% | 66.2% | 33.8% |
| 158,177 | CUMBERLAND | 57,775 | 42,099 | 14,562 | 1,114 | 27,537 R | 72.9% | 25.2% | 74.3% | 25.7% |
| 223,834 | DAUPHIN | 78,270 | 54,307 | 22,587 | 1,376 | 31,720 R | 69.4% | 28.9% | 70.6% | 29.4% |
| 600,035 | DELAWARE | 274,451 | 175,414 | 94,144 | 4,893 | 81,270 R | 63.9% | 34.3% | 65.1% | 34.9% |
| 37,770 | ELK | 12,908 | 7,900 | 4,710 | 298 | 3,190 R | 61.2% | 36.5% | 62.6% | 37.4% |
| 263,654 | ERIE | 105,713 | 61,542 | 42,022 | 2,149 | 19,520 R | 58.2% | 39.8% | 59.4% | 40.6% |
| 154,667 | FAYETTE | 50,479 | 27,288 | 22,475 | 716 | 4,813 R | 54.1% | 44.5% | 54.8% | 45.2% |
| 4,926 | FOREST | 1,915 | 1,374 | 509 | 32 | 865 R | 71.7% | 26.6% | 73.0% | 27.0% |
| 100,833 | FRANKLIN | 34,415 | 24,093 | 9,456 | 866 | 14,637 R | 70.0% | 27.5% | 71.8% | 28.2% |
| 10,776 | FULTON | 3,797 | 2,515 | 1,192 | 90 | 1,323 R | 66.2% | 31.4% | 67.8% | 32.2% |
| 36,090 | GREENE | 13,543 | 7,790 | 5,562 | 191 | 2,228 R | 57.5% | 41.1% | 58.3% | 41.7% |
| 39,108 | HUNTINGDON | 13,216 | 9,606 | 3,394 | 216 | 6,212 R | 72.7% | 25.7% | 73.9% | 26.1% |
| 79,451 | INDIANA | 29,274 | 18,122 | 10,833 | 319 | 7,289 R | 61.9% | 37.0% | 62.6% | 37.4% |
| 43,695 | JEFFERSON | 16,876 | 11,631 | 5,024 | 221 | 6,607 R | 68.9% | 29.8% | 69.8% | 30.2% |
| 16,712 | JUNIATA | 6,653 | 4,412 | 2,156 | 85 | 2,256 R | 66.3% | 32.4% | 67.2% | 32.8% |
| 234,107 | LACKAWANNA | 104,869 | 58,838 | 45,465 | 566 | 13,373 R | 56.1% | 43.4% | 56.4% | 43.6% |
| 319,693 | LANCASTER | 107,138 | 81,036 | 24,223 | 1,879 | 56,813 R | 75.6% | 22.6% | 77.0% | 23.0% |
| 107,374 | LAWRENCE | 42,297 | 23,712 | 17,595 | 990 | 6,117 R | 56.1% | 41.6% | 57.4% | 42.6% |
| 99,665 | LEBANON | 32,320 | 25,008 | 6,683 | 629 | 18,325 R | 77.4% | 20.7% | 78.9% | 21.1% |
| 255,304 | LEHIGH | 93,002 | 58,023 | 33,325 | 1,654 | 24,698 R | 62.4% | 35.8% | 63.5% | 36.5% |
| 342,301 | LUZERNE | 133,606 | 81,358 | 51,128 | 1,120 | 30,230 R | 60.9% | 38.3% | 61.4% | 38.6% |
| 113,296 | LYCOMING | 42,087 | 28,913 | 11,999 | 1,175 | 16,914 R | 68.7% | 28.5% | 70.7% | 29.3% |
| 51,915 | MCKEAN | 16,673 | 11,958 | 4,513 | 202 | 7,445 R | 71.7% | 27.1% | 72.6% | 27.4% |
| 127,175 | MERCER | 47,100 | 27,961 | 18,087 | 1,052 | 9,874 R | 59.4% | 38.4% | 60.7% | 39.3% |
| 45,268 | MIFFLIN | 13,855 | 9,989 | 3,667 | 199 | 6,322 R | 72.1% | 26.5% | 73.1% | 26.9% |
| 45,422 | MONROE | 18,814 | 12,701 | 5,619 | 494 | 7,082 R | 67.5% | 29.9% | 69.3% | 30.7% |
| 623,799 | MONTGOMERY | 270,018 | 173,662 | 91,959 | 4,397 | 81,703 R | 64.3% | 34.1% | 65.4% | 34.6% |
| 16,508 | MONTOUR | 6,298 | 4,386 | 1,755 | 157 | 2,631 R | 69.6% | 27.9% | 71.4% | 28.6% |
| 214,368 | NORTHAMPTON | 74,281 | 41,822 | 32,335 | 124 | 9,487 R | 56.3% | 43.5% | 56.4% | 43.6% |
| 99,190 | NORTHUMBERLAND | 40,385 | 25,912 | 13,885 | 588 | 12,027 R | 64.2% | 34.4% | 65.1% | 34.9% |
| 28,615 | PERRY | 11,025 | 8,082 | 2,731 | 212 | 5,351 R | 73.3% | 24.8% | 74.7% | 25.3% |
| 1,948,609 | PHILADELPHIA | 783,970 | 344,096 | 431,736 | 8,138 | 87,640 D | 43.9% | 55.1% | 44.4% | 55.6% |
| 11,818 | PIKE | 6,108 | 4,568 | 1,385 | 155 | 3,183 R | 74.8% | 22.7% | 76.7% | 23.3% |
| 16,395 | POTTER | 6,236 | 4,422 | 1,710 | 104 | 2,712 R | 70.9% | 27.4% | 72.1% | 27.9% |
| 160,089 | SCHUYLKILL | 71,595 | 44,071 | 26,077 | 1,447 | 17,994 R | 61.6% | 36.4% | 62.8% | 37.2% |
| 29,269 | SNYDER | 9,345 | 7,308 | 1,834 | 203 | 5,474 R | 78.2% | 19.6% | 79.9% | 20.1% |
| 76,037 | SOMERSET | 28,841 | 19,739 | 8,743 | 359 | 10,996 R | 68.4% | 30.3% | 69.3% | 30.7% |
| 5,961 | SULLIVAN | 2,808 | 1,886 | 885 | 37 | 1,001 R | 67.2% | 31.5% | 68.1% | 31.9% |
| 34,344 | SUSQUEHANNA | 13,979 | 9,476 | 4,154 | 349 | 5,322 R | 67.8% | 29.7% | 69.5% | 30.5% |
| 39,691 | TIOGA | 13,918 | 10,028 | 3,733 | 157 | 6,295 R | 72.1% | 26.8% | 72.9% | 27.1% |
| 28,603 | UNION | 9,385 | 6,905 | 2,278 | 202 | 4,627 R | 73.6% | 24.3% | 75.2% | 24.8% |

# PENNSYLVANIA

## PRESIDENT 1972

| 1970 Census Population | County | Total Vote | Republican | Democratic | Other | Rep.-Dem. Plurality | Percentage | | | |
|---|---|---|---|---|---|---|---|---|---|---|
| | | | | | | | Total Vote | | Major Vote | |
| | | | | | | | Rep. | Dem. | Rep. | Dem. |
| 62,353 | VENANGO | 20,794 | 13,991 | 6,302 | 501 | 7,689 R | 67.3% | 30.3% | 68.9% | 31.1% |
| 47,682 | WARREN | 15,167 | 10,018 | 4,877 | 272 | 5,141 R | 66.1% | 32.2% | 67.3% | 32.7% |
| 210,876 | WASHINGTON | 78,862 | 42,587 | 34,781 | 1,494 | 7,806 R | 54.0% | 44.1% | 55.0% | 45.0% |
| 29,581 | WAYNE | 12,009 | 8,948 | 2,733 | 328 | 6,215 R | 74.5% | 22.8% | 76.6% | 23.4% |
| 376,935 | WESTMORELAND | 137,527 | 75,085 | 59,322 | 3,120 | 15,763 R | 54.6% | 43.1% | 55.9% | 44.1% |
| 19,082 | WYOMING | 8,631 | 6,423 | 2,112 | 96 | 4,311 R | 74.4% | 24.5% | 75.3% | 24.7% |
| 272,603 | YORK | 93,280 | 63,606 | 27,520 | 2,154 | 36,086 R | 68.2% | 29.5% | 69.8% | 30.2% |
| 11,793,909 | TOTAL | 4,592,106 | 2,714,521 | 1,796,951 | 80,634 | 917,570 R | 59.1% | 39.1% | 60.2% | 39.8% |

# PENNSYLVANIA

## PRESIDENT 1968

| 1960 Census Population | County | Total Vote | Republican | Democratic | AIP | Other | Plurality | Percentage Total Vote Rep. | Dem. | AIP |
|---|---|---|---|---|---|---|---|---|---|---|
| 51,906 | ADAMS | 18,907 | 11,303 | 5,993 | 1,579 | 32 | 5,310 R | 59.8% | 31.7% | 8.4% |
| 1,628,587 | ALLEGHENY | 713,817 | 264,790 | 364,906 | 79,776 | 4,345 | 100,116 D | 37.1% | 51.1% | 11.2% |
| 79,524 | ARMSTRONG | 30,353 | 14,132 | 13,921 | 2,256 | 44 | 211 R | 46.6% | 45.9% | 7.4% |
| 206,948 | BEAVER | 82,028 | 28,264 | 45,396 | 7,974 | 394 | 17,132 D | 34.5% | 55.3% | 9.7% |
| 42,451 | BEDFORD | 16,518 | 10,482 | 4,725 | 1,301 | 10 | 5,757 R | 63.5% | 28.6% | 7.9% |
| 275,414 | BERKS | 108,924 | 50,623 | 49,877 | 8,093 | 331 | 746 R | 46.5% | 45.8% | 7.4% |
| 137,270 | BLAIR | 48,296 | 28,780 | 15,803 | 3,644 | 69 | 12,977 R | 59.6% | 32.7% | 7.5% |
| 54,925 | BRADFORD | 21,058 | 13,308 | 6,373 | 1,347 | 30 | 6,935 R | 63.2% | 30.3% | 6.4% |
| 308,567 | BUCKS | 143,211 | 69,646 | 57,634 | 15,211 | 720 | 12,012 R | 48.6% | 40.2% | 10.6% |
| 114,639 | BUTLER | 45,291 | 21,618 | 19,415 | 4,139 | 119 | 2,203 R | 47.7% | 42.9% | 9.1% |
| 203,283 | CAMBRIA | 79,150 | 33,280 | 41,225 | 4,485 | 160 | 7,945 D | 42.0% | 52.1% | 5.7% |
| 7,586 | CAMERON | 3,090 | 1,822 | 1,104 | 159 | 5 | 718 R | 59.0% | 35.7% | 5.1% |
| 52,889 | CARBON | 21,579 | 9,954 | 10,634 | 952 | 39 | 680 D | 46.1% | 49.3% | 4.4% |
| 78,580 | CENTRE | 28,527 | 15,865 | 11,163 | 1,389 | 110 | 4,702 R | 55.6% | 39.1% | 4.9% |
| 210,608 | CHESTER | 98,051 | 56,073 | 32,606 | 9,142 | 230 | 23,467 R | 57.2% | 33.3% | 9.3% |
| 37,408 | CLARION | 14,423 | 8,077 | 5,341 | 981 | 24 | 2,736 R | 56.0% | 37.0% | 6.8% |
| 81,534 | CLEARFIELD | 29,163 | 14,471 | 12,369 | 2,252 | 71 | 2,102 R | 49.6% | 42.4% | 7.7% |
| 37,619 | CLINTON | 13,508 | 6,563 | 6,301 | 625 | 19 | 262 R | 48.6% | 46.6% | 4.6% |
| 53,489 | COLUMBIA | 22,229 | 12,202 | 8,187 | 1,797 | 43 | 4,015 R | 54.9% | 36.8% | 8.1% |
| 77,956 | CRAWFORD | 28,226 | 14,991 | 11,345 | 1,832 | 58 | 3,646 R | 53.1% | 40.2% | 6.5% |
| 124,816 | CUMBERLAND | 53,472 | 32,908 | 15,467 | 4,893 | 204 | 17,441 R | 61.5% | 28.9% | 9.2% |
| 220,255 | DAUPHIN | 81,788 | 48,394 | 25,480 | 7,534 | 380 | 22,914 R | 59.2% | 31.2% | 9.2% |
| 553,154 | DELAWARE | 266,436 | 133,777 | 106,695 | 25,051 | 913 | 27,082 R | 50.2% | 40.0% | 9.4% |
| 37,328 | ELK | 14,046 | 6,193 | 6,886 | 945 | 22 | 693 D | 44.1% | 49.0% | 6.7% |
| 250,682 | ERIE | 99,847 | 43,134 | 51,604 | 4,868 | 241 | 8,470 D | 43.2% | 51.7% | 4.9% |
| 169,340 | FAYETTE | 59,450 | 18,921 | 34,340 | 5,984 | 205 | 15,419 D | 31.8% | 57.8% | 10.1% |
| 4,485 | FOREST | 1,973 | 1,172 | 669 | 129 | 3 | 503 R | 59.4% | 33.9% | 6.5% |
| 88,172 | FRANKLIN | 35,195 | 19,146 | 11,451 | 4,557 | 41 | 7,695 R | 54.4% | 32.5% | 12.9% |
| 10,597 | FULTON | 3,973 | 2,200 | 1,174 | 592 | 7 | 1,026 R | 55.4% | 29.5% | 14.9% |
| 39,424 | GREENE | 14,401 | 5,099 | 8,198 | 1,094 | 10 | 3,099 D | 35.4% | 56.9% | 7.6% |
| 39,457 | HUNTINGDON | 13,388 | 8,276 | 4,128 | 962 | 22 | 4,148 R | 61.8% | 30.8% | 7.2% |
| 75,366 | INDIANA | 29,196 | 14,899 | 12,175 | 2,078 | 44 | 2,724 R | 51.0% | 41.7% | 7.1% |
| 46,792 | JEFFERSON | 18,347 | 10,214 | 6,839 | 1,278 | 16 | 3,375 R | 55.7% | 37.3% | 7.0% |
| 15,874 | JUNIATA | 6,874 | 4,039 | 2,321 | 507 | 7 | 1,718 R | 58.8% | 33.8% | 7.4% |
| 234,531 | LACKAWANNA | 114,391 | 44,388 | 66,297 | 3,538 | 168 | 21,909 D | 38.8% | 58.0% | 3.1% |
| 278,359 | LANCASTER | 108,307 | 69,953 | 29,870 | 8,194 | 290 | 40,083 R | 64.6% | 27.6% | 7.6% |
| 112,965 | LAWRENCE | 43,103 | 18,360 | 21,027 | 3,635 | 81 | 2,667 D | 42.6% | 48.8% | 8.4% |
| 90,853 | LEBANON | 34,025 | 21,832 | 9,529 | 2,584 | 80 | 12,303 R | 64.2% | 28.0% | 7.6% |
| 227,536 | LEHIGH | 95,408 | 47,255 | 44,033 | 3,900 | 220 | 3,222 R | 49.5% | 46.2% | 4.1% |
| 346,972 | LUZERNE | 143,380 | 57,044 | 79,040 | 6,857 | 439 | 21,996 D | 39.8% | 55.1% | 4.8% |
| 109,367 | LYCOMING | 43,566 | 23,830 | 16,888 | 2,761 | 87 | 6,942 R | 54.7% | 38.8% | 6.3% |
| 54,517 | MCKEAN | 17,607 | 10,506 | 6,326 | 745 | 30 | 4,180 R | 59.7% | 35.9% | 4.2% |
| 127,519 | MERCER | 49,105 | 23,131 | 22,814 | 3,033 | 127 | 317 R | 47.1% | 46.5% | 6.2% |
| 44,348 | MIFFLIN | 14,698 | 8,133 | 5,681 | 859 | 25 | 2,452 R | 55.3% | 38.7% | 5.8% |
| 39,567 | MONROE | 17,747 | 9,465 | 6,946 | 1,267 | 69 | 2,519 R | 53.3% | 39.1% | 7.1% |
| 516,682 | MONTGOMERY | 260,732 | 141,621 | 102,464 | 15,599 | 1,048 | 39,157 R | 54.3% | 39.3% | 6.0% |
| 16,730 | MONTOUR | 5,976 | 3,289 | 2,239 | 438 | 10 | 1,050 R | 55.0% | 37.5% | 7.3% |
| 201,412 | NORTHAMPTON | 78,130 | 32,033 | 42,554 | 3,276 | 267 | 10,521 D | 41.0% | 54.5% | 4.2% |
| 104,138 | NORTHUMBERLAND | 41,899 | 22,366 | 17,013 | 2,456 | 64 | 5,353 R | 53.4% | 40.6% | 5.9% |
| 26,582 | PERRY | 10,849 | 6,655 | 2,944 | 1,222 | 28 | 3,711 R | 61.3% | 27.1% | 11.3% |
| 2,002,512 | PHILADELPHIA | 850,117 | 254,153 | 525,768 | 63,506 | 6,690 | 271,615 D | 29.9% | 61.8% | 7.5% |
| 9,158 | PIKE | 5,790 | 3,719 | 1,617 | 441 | 13 | 2,102 R | 64.2% | 27.9% | 7.6% |
| 16,483 | POTTER | 6,339 | 4,019 | 1,860 | 451 | 9 | 2,159 R | 63.4% | 29.3% | 7.1% |
| 173,027 | SCHUYLKILL | 76,645 | 37,194 | 34,982 | 4,381 | 88 | 2,212 R | 48.5% | 45.6% | 5.7% |
| 25,922 | SNYDER | 9,469 | 6,784 | 1,993 | 676 | 16 | 4,791 R | 71.6% | 21.0% | 7.1% |
| 77,450 | SOMERSET | 30,921 | 17,511 | 11,515 | 1,845 | 50 | 5,996 R | 56.6% | 37.2% | 6.0% |
| 6,251 | SULLIVAN | 2,870 | 1,629 | 1,035 | 200 | 6 | 594 R | 56.8% | 36.1% | 7.0% |
| 33,137 | SUSQUEHANNA | 14,032 | 8,705 | 4,364 | 929 | 34 | 4,341 R | 62.0% | 31.1% | 6.6% |
| 36,614 | TIOGA | 13,863 | 9,298 | 3,488 | 1,065 | 12 | 5,810 R | 67.1% | 25.2% | 7.7% |
| 25,646 | UNION | 9,215 | 6,422 | 2,178 | 581 | 34 | 4,244 R | 69.7% | 23.6% | 6.3% |

# PENNSYLVANIA

## PRESIDENT 1968

| 1960 Census Population | County | Total Vote | Republican | Democratic | AIP | Other | Plurality | Percentage Total Vote | | |
|---|---|---|---|---|---|---|---|---|---|---|
| | | | | | | | | Rep. | Dem. | AIP |
| 65,295 | VENANGO | 21,949 | 12,323 | 8,319 | 1,262 | 45 | 4,004 R | 56.1% | 37.9% | 5.7% |
| 45,582 | WARREN | 15,968 | 8,889 | 6,368 | 676 | 35 | 2,521 R | 55.7% | 39.9% | 4.2% |
| 217,271 | WASHINGTON | 84,968 | 28,023 | 47,805 | 9,016 | 124 | 19,782 D | 33.0% | 56.3% | 10.6% |
| 28,237 | WAYNE | 11,790 | 7,827 | 3,176 | 754 | 33 | 4,651 R | 66.4% | 26.9% | 6.4% |
| 352,629 | WESTMORELAND | 148,839 | 52,206 | 81,833 | 14,436 | 364 | 29,627 D | 35.1% | 55.0% | 9.7% |
| 16,813 | WYOMING | 8,124 | 5,207 | 2,366 | 539 | 12 | 2,841 R | 64.1% | 29.1% | 6.6% |
| 238,336 | YORK | 93,371 | 51,631 | 33,328 | 8,054 | 358 | 18,303 R | 55.3% | 35.7% | 8.6% |
| 11,319,366 | TOTAL | 4,747,928 | 2,090,017 | 2,259,405 | 378,582 | 19,924 | 169,388 D | 44.0% | 47.6% | 8.0% |

# PENNSYLVANIA

## PRESIDENT 1964

| 1960 Census Population | County | Total Vote | Republican | Democratic | Other | Rep.-Dem. Plurality | Percentage Total Vote Rep. | Dem. | Major Vote Rep. | Dem. |
|---|---|---|---|---|---|---|---|---|---|---|
| 51,906 | ADAMS | 19,860 | 8,617 | 11,148 | 95 | 2,531 D | 43.4% | 56.1% | 43.6% | 56.4% |
| 1,628,587 | ALLEGHENY | 719,725 | 241,707 | 475,207 | 2,811 | 233,500 D | 33.6% | 66.0% | 33.7% | 66.3% |
| 79,524 | ARMSTRONG | 31,790 | 10,618 | 21,098 | 74 | 10,480 D | 33.4% | 66.4% | 33.5% | 66.5% |
| 206,948 | BEAVER | 83,993 | 23,174 | 60,492 | 327 | 37,318 D | 27.6% | 72.0% | 27.7% | 72.3% |
| 42,451 | BEDFORD | 17,147 | 7,968 | 9,165 | 14 | 1,197 D | 46.5% | 53.4% | 46.5% | 53.5% |
| 275,414 | BERKS | 110,646 | 36,726 | 73,444 | 476 | 36,718 D | 33.2% | 66.4% | 33.3% | 66.7% |
| 137,270 | BLAIR | 50,531 | 24,301 | 26,157 | 73 | 1,856 D | 48.1% | 51.8% | 48.2% | 51.8% |
| 54,925 | BRADFORD | 21,162 | 10,434 | 10,714 | 14 | 280 D | 49.3% | 50.6% | 49.3% | 50.7% |
| 308,567 | BUCKS | 129,176 | 50,243 | 78,287 | 646 | 28,044 D | 38.9% | 60.6% | 39.1% | 60.9% |
| 114,639 | BUTLER | 44,722 | 17,360 | 27,267 | 95 | 9,907 D | 38.8% | 61.0% | 38.9% | 61.1% |
| 203,283 | CAMBRIA | 81,598 | 26,281 | 55,183 | 134 | 28,902 D | 32.2% | 67.6% | 32.3% | 67.7% |
| 7,586 | CAMERON | 3,285 | 1,376 | 1,904 | 5 | 528 D | 41.9% | 58.0% | 42.0% | 58.0% |
| 52,889 | CARBON | 22,841 | 7,309 | 15,416 | 116 | 8,107 D | 32.0% | 67.5% | 32.2% | 67.8% |
| 78,580 | CENTRE | 26,195 | 9,481 | 16,556 | 158 | 7,075 D | 36.2% | 63.2% | 36.4% | 63.6% |
| 210,608 | CHESTER | 88,610 | 40,280 | 47,940 | 390 | 7,660 D | 45.5% | 54.1% | 45.7% | 54.3% |
| 37,408 | CLARION | 15,389 | 6,143 | 9,235 | 11 | 3,092 D | 39.9% | 60.0% | 39.9% | 60.1% |
| 81,534 | CLEARFIELD | 30,652 | 11,338 | 19,211 | 103 | 7,873 D | 37.0% | 62.7% | 37.1% | 62.9% |
| 37,619 | CLINTON | 14,372 | 4,298 | 10,038 | 36 | 5,740 D | 29.9% | 69.8% | 30.0% | 70.0% |
| 53,489 | COLUMBIA | 22,903 | 8,982 | 13,885 | 36 | 4,903 D | 39.2% | 60.6% | 39.3% | 60.7% |
| 77,956 | CRAWFORD | 28,991 | 10,664 | 18,212 | 115 | 7,548 D | 36.8% | 62.8% | 36.9% | 63.1% |
| 124,816 | CUMBERLAND | 50,525 | 23,685 | 26,633 | 207 | 2,948 D | 46.9% | 52.7% | 47.1% | 52.9% |
| 220,255 | DAUPHIN | 89,431 | 42,718 | 46,119 | 594 | 3,401 D | 47.8% | 51.6% | 48.1% | 51.9% |
| 553,154 | DELAWARE | 259,095 | 111,189 | 147,189 | 717 | 36,000 D | 42.9% | 56.8% | 43.0% | 57.0% |
| 37,328 | ELK | 14,828 | 4,354 | 10,455 | 19 | 6,101 D | 29.4% | 70.5% | 29.4% | 70.6% |
| 250,682 | ERIE | 104,886 | 31,393 | 72,944 | 549 | 41,551 D | 29.9% | 69.5% | 30.1% | 69.9% |
| 169,340 | FAYETTE | 61,558 | 16,127 | 45,155 | 276 | 29,028 D | 26.2% | 73.4% | 26.3% | 73.7% |
| 4,485 | FOREST | 2,154 | 900 | 1,249 | 5 | 349 D | 41.8% | 58.0% | 41.9% | 58.1% |
| 88,172 | FRANKLIN | 32,942 | 13,525 | 19,332 | 85 | 5,807 D | 41.1% | 58.7% | 41.2% | 58.8% |
| 10,597 | FULTON | 3,937 | 1,747 | 2,180 | 10 | 433 D | 44.4% | 55.4% | 44.5% | 55.5% |
| 39,424 | GREENE | 15,327 | 3,896 | 11,412 | 19 | 7,516 D | 25.4% | 74.5% | 25.5% | 74.5% |
| 39,457 | HUNTINGDON | 14,039 | 6,571 | 7,435 | 33 | 864 D | 46.8% | 53.0% | 46.9% | 53.1% |
| 75,366 | INDIANA | 29,320 | 11,706 | 17,568 | 46 | 5,862 D | 39.9% | 59.9% | 40.0% | 60.0% |
| 46,792 | JEFFERSON | 19,261 | 8,373 | 10,851 | 37 | 2,478 D | 43.5% | 56.3% | 43.6% | 56.4% |
| 15,874 | JUNIATA | 7,235 | 3,087 | 4,138 | 10 | 1,051 D | 42.7% | 57.2% | 42.7% | 57.3% |
| 234,531 | LACKAWANNA | 119,540 | 31,272 | 88,131 | 137 | 56,859 D | 26.2% | 73.7% | 26.2% | 73.8% |
| 278,359 | LANCASTER | 105,508 | 52,243 | 53,041 | 224 | 798 D | 49.5% | 50.3% | 49.6% | 50.4% |
| 112,965 | LAWRENCE | 45,207 | 15,998 | 29,092 | 117 | 13,094 D | 35.4% | 64.4% | 35.5% | 64.5% |
| 90,853 | LEBANON | 33,845 | 17,891 | 15,882 | 72 | 2,009 R | 52.9% | 46.9% | 53.0% | 47.0% |
| 227,536 | LEHIGH | 93,093 | 32,245 | 60,377 | 471 | 28,132 D | 34.6% | 64.9% | 34.8% | 65.2% |
| 346,972 | LUZERNE | 152,071 | 43,895 | 106,397 | 1,779 | 62,502 D | 28.9% | 70.0% | 29.2% | 70.8% |
| 109,367 | LYCOMING | 44,945 | 19,011 | 25,879 | 55 | 6,868 D | 42.3% | 57.6% | 42.4% | 57.6% |
| 54,517 | MCKEAN | 19,007 | 7,948 | 10,950 | 109 | 3,002 D | 41.8% | 57.6% | 42.1% | 57.9% |
| 127,519 | MERCER | 50,563 | 18,153 | 32,199 | 211 | 14,046 D | 35.9% | 63.7% | 36.1% | 63.9% |
| 44,348 | MIFFLIN | 14,856 | 6,006 | 8,811 | 39 | 2,805 D | 40.4% | 59.3% | 40.5% | 59.5% |
| 39,567 | MONROE | 17,019 | 6,281 | 10,622 | 116 | 4,341 D | 36.9% | 62.4% | 37.2% | 62.8% |
| 516,682 | MONTGOMERY | 239,075 | 102,714 | 135,657 | 704 | 32,943 D | 43.0% | 56.7% | 43.1% | 56.9% |
| 16,730 | MONTOUR | 6,214 | 2,527 | 3,683 | 4 | 1,156 D | 40.7% | 59.3% | 40.7% | 59.3% |
| 201,412 | NORTHAMPTON | 80,485 | 21,048 | 58,818 | 619 | 37,770 D | 26.2% | 73.1% | 26.4% | 73.6% |
| 104,138 | NORTHUMBERLAND | 45,244 | 17,046 | 28,082 | 116 | 11,036 D | 37.7% | 62.1% | 37.8% | 62.2% |
| 26,582 | PERRY | 11,452 | 5,364 | 6,054 | 34 | 690 D | 46.8% | 52.9% | 47.0% | 53.0% |
| 2,002,512 | PHILADELPHIA | 913,472 | 239,733 | 670,645 | 3,094 | 430,912 D | 26.2% | 73.4% | 26.3% | 73.7% |
| 9,158 | PIKE | 5,426 | 2,651 | 2,753 | 22 | 102 D | 48.9% | 50.7% | 49.1% | 50.9% |
| 16,483 | POTTER | 6,909 | 3,232 | 3,652 | 25 | 420 D | 46.8% | 52.9% | 46.9% | 53.1% |
| 173,027 | SCHUYLKILL | 77,042 | 26,386 | 50,560 | 96 | 24,174 D | 34.2% | 65.6% | 34.3% | 65.7% |
| 25,922 | SNYDER | 9,416 | 5,195 | 4,199 | 22 | 996 R | 55.2% | 44.6% | 55.3% | 44.7% |
| 77,450 | SOMERSET | 32,814 | 14,817 | 17,934 | 63 | 3,117 D | 45.2% | 54.7% | 45.2% | 54.8% |
| 6,251 | SULLIVAN | 3,038 | 1,344 | 1,690 | 4 | 346 D | 44.2% | 55.6% | 44.3% | 55.7% |
| 33,137 | SUSQUEHANNA | 14,417 | 6,567 | 7,838 | 12 | 1,271 D | 45.6% | 54.4% | 45.6% | 54.4% |
| 36,614 | TIOGA | 14,495 | 7,064 | 7,415 | 16 | 351 D | 48.7% | 51.2% | 48.8% | 51.2% |
| 25,646 | UNION | 9,216 | 4,944 | 4,262 | 10 | 682 R | 53.6% | 46.2% | 53.7% | 46.3% |

# PENNSYLVANIA

## PRESIDENT 1964

| 1960 Census Population | County | Total Vote | Republican | Democratic | Other | Rep.-Dem. Plurality | Percentage | | | |
|---|---|---|---|---|---|---|---|---|---|---|
| | | | | | | | Total Vote | | Major Vote | |
| | | | | | | | Rep. | Dem. | Rep. | Dem. |
| 65,295 | VENANGO | 23,022 | 9,873 | 13,065 | 84 | 3,192 D | 42.9% | 56.8% | 43.0% | 57.0% |
| 45,582 | WARREN | 16,657 | 5,965 | 10,598 | 94 | 4,633 D | 35.8% | 63.6% | 36.0% | 64.0% |
| 217,271 | WASHINGTON | 87,756 | 24,127 | 63,482 | 147 | 39,355 D | 27.5% | 72.3% | 27.5% | 72.5% |
| 28,237 | WAYNE | 12,328 | 6,512 | 5,781 | 35 | 731 R | 52.8% | 46.9% | 53.0% | 47.0% |
| 352,629 | WESTMORELAND | 149,416 | 41,493 | 107,131 | 792 | 65,638 D | 27.8% | 71.7% | 27.9% | 72.1% |
| 16,813 | WYOMING | 8,144 | 3,864 | 4,268 | 12 | 404 D | 47.4% | 52.4% | 47.5% | 52.5% |
| 238,336 | YORK | 92,872 | 33,677 | 58,787 | 408 | 25,110 D | 36.3% | 63.3% | 36.4% | 63.6% |
| 11,319,366 | TOTAL | 4,822,690 | 1,673,657 | 3,130,954 | 18,079 | 1,457,297 D | 34.7% | 64.9% | 34.8% | 65.2% |

# PENNSYLVANIA

## PRESIDENT 1960

| 1960 Census Population | County | Total Vote | Republican | Democratic | Other | Rep.-Dem. Plurality | Percentage | | | |
|---|---|---|---|---|---|---|---|---|---|---|
| | | | | | | | Total Vote | | Major Vote | |
| | | | | | | | Rep. | Dem. | Rep. | Dem. |
| 51,906 | ADAMS | 20,854 | 12,933 | 7,895 | 26 | 5,038 R | 62.0% | 37.9% | 62.1% | 37.9% |
| 1,628,587 | ALLEGHENY | 750,718 | 320,970 | 428,455 | 1,293 | 107,485 D | 42.8% | 57.1% | 42.8% | 57.2% |
| 79,524 | ARMSTRONG | 34,745 | 19,883 | 14,799 | 63 | 5,084 R | 57.2% | 42.6% | 57.3% | 42.7% |
| 206,948 | BEAVER | 84,190 | 36,796 | 47,182 | 212 | 10,386 D | 43.7% | 56.0% | 43.8% | 56.2% |
| 42,451 | BEDFORD | 18,604 | 12,542 | 6,030 | 32 | 6,512 R | 67.4% | 32.4% | 67.5% | 32.5% |
| 275,414 | BERKS | 112,706 | 61,743 | 50,572 | 391 | 11,171 R | 54.8% | 44.9% | 55.0% | 45.0% |
| 137,270 | BLAIR | 54,809 | 35,297 | 19,445 | 67 | 15,852 R | 64.4% | 35.5% | 64.5% | 35.5% |
| 54,925 | BRADFORD | 23,205 | 16,252 | 6,920 | 33 | 9,332 R | 70.0% | 29.8% | 70.1% | 29.9% |
| 308,567 | BUCKS | 125,116 | 67,501 | 57,177 | 438 | 10,324 R | 54.0% | 45.7% | 54.1% | 45.9% |
| 114,639 | BUTLER | 46,305 | 28,348 | 17,805 | 152 | 10,543 R | 61.2% | 38.5% | 61.4% | 38.6% |
| 203,283 | CAMBRIA | 89,622 | 37,062 | 52,409 | 151 | 15,347 D | 41.4% | 58.5% | 41.4% | 58.6% |
| 7,586 | CAMERON | 3,487 | 2,129 | 1,353 | 5 | 776 R | 61.1% | 38.8% | 61.1% | 38.9% |
| 52,889 | CARBON | 25,032 | 12,586 | 12,391 | 55 | 195 R | 50.3% | 49.5% | 50.4% | 49.6% |
| 78,580 | CENTRE | 27,004 | 18,357 | 8,601 | 46 | 9,756 R | 68.0% | 31.9% | 68.1% | 31.9% |
| 210,608 | CHESTER | 83,373 | 53,059 | 30,167 | 147 | 22,892 R | 63.6% | 36.2% | 63.8% | 36.2% |
| 37,408 | CLARION | 15,847 | 10,307 | 5,506 | 34 | 4,801 R | 65.0% | 34.7% | 65.2% | 34.8% |
| 81,534 | CLEARFIELD | 33,195 | 18,911 | 14,212 | 72 | 4,699 R | 57.0% | 42.8% | 57.1% | 42.9% |
| 37,619 | CLINTON | 15,161 | 9,184 | 5,965 | 12 | 3,219 R | 60.6% | 39.3% | 60.6% | 39.4% |
| 53,489 | COLUMBIA | 24,651 | 15,310 | 9,322 | 19 | 5,988 R | 62.1% | 37.8% | 62.2% | 37.8% |
| 77,956 | CRAWFORD | 30,906 | 18,754 | 12,050 | 102 | 6,704 R | 60.7% | 39.0% | 60.9% | 39.1% |
| 124,816 | CUMBERLAND | 51,801 | 35,636 | 15,968 | 197 | 19,668 R | 68.8% | 30.8% | 69.1% | 30.9% |
| 220,255 | DAUPHIN | 96,115 | 61,726 | 33,962 | 427 | 27,764 R | 64.2% | 35.3% | 64.5% | 35.5% |
| 553,154 | DELAWARE | 260,783 | 135,672 | 124,629 | 482 | 11,043 R | 52.0% | 47.8% | 52.1% | 47.9% |
| 37,328 | ELK | 15,567 | 7,155 | 8,398 | 14 | 1,243 D | 46.0% | 53.9% | 46.0% | 54.0% |
| 250,682 | ERIE | 105,543 | 51,525 | 53,723 | 295 | 2,198 D | 48.8% | 50.9% | 49.0% | 51.0% |
| 169,340 | FAYETTE | 68,861 | 27,120 | 41,560 | 181 | 14,440 D | 39.4% | 60.4% | 39.5% | 60.5% |
| 4,485 | FOREST | 2,332 | 1,497 | 828 | 7 | 669 R | 64.2% | 35.5% | 64.4% | 35.6% |
| 88,172 | FRANKLIN | 34,134 | 22,010 | 12,088 | 36 | 9,922 R | 64.5% | 35.4% | 64.5% | 35.5% |
| 10,597 | FULTON | 4,379 | 2,698 | 1,672 | 9 | 1,026 R | 61.6% | 38.2% | 61.7% | 38.3% |
| 39,424 | GREENE | 17,159 | 7,498 | 9,645 | 16 | 2,147 D | 43.7% | 56.2% | 43.7% | 56.3% |
| 39,457 | HUNTINGDON | 15,864 | 11,116 | 4,710 | 38 | 6,406 R | 70.1% | 29.7% | 70.2% | 29.8% |
| 75,366 | INDIANA | 32,013 | 18,756 | 13,174 | 83 | 5,582 R | 58.6% | 41.2% | 58.7% | 41.3% |
| 46,792 | JEFFERSON | 21,694 | 13,845 | 7,811 | 38 | 6,034 R | 63.8% | 36.0% | 63.9% | 36.1% |
| 15,874 | JUNIATA | 7,431 | 4,805 | 2,615 | 11 | 2,190 R | 64.7% | 35.2% | 64.8% | 35.2% |
| 234,531 | LACKAWANNA | 129,783 | 49,636 | 80,098 | 49 | 30,462 D | 38.2% | 61.7% | 38.3% | 61.7% |
| 278,359 | LANCASTER | 111,889 | 78,390 | 33,233 | 266 | 45,157 R | 70.1% | 29.7% | 70.2% | 29.8% |
| 112,965 | LAWRENCE | 48,064 | 23,646 | 24,309 | 109 | 663 D | 49.2% | 50.6% | 49.3% | 50.7% |
| 90,853 | LEBANON | 37,353 | 25,525 | 11,761 | 67 | 13,764 R | 68.3% | 31.5% | 68.5% | 31.5% |
| 227,536 | LEHIGH | 94,167 | 54,278 | 39,640 | 249 | 14,638 R | 57.6% | 42.1% | 57.8% | 42.2% |
| 346,972 | LUZERNE | 174,271 | 70,711 | 102,998 | 562 | 32,287 D | 40.6% | 59.1% | 40.7% | 59.3% |
| 109,367 | LYCOMING | 48,482 | 30,083 | 18,351 | 48 | 11,732 R | 62.0% | 37.9% | 62.1% | 37.9% |
| 54,517 | MCKEAN | 21,532 | 13,699 | 7,767 | 66 | 5,932 R | 63.6% | 36.1% | 63.8% | 36.2% |
| 127,519 | MERCER | 53,480 | 29,109 | 24,243 | 128 | 4,866 R | 54.4% | 45.3% | 54.6% | 45.4% |
| 44,348 | MIFFLIN | 15,203 | 10,315 | 4,816 | 72 | 5,499 R | 67.8% | 31.7% | 68.2% | 31.8% |
| 39,567 | MONROE | 17,726 | 11,299 | 6,312 | 115 | 4,987 R | 63.7% | 35.6% | 64.2% | 35.8% |
| 516,682 | MONTGOMERY | 235,326 | 142,796 | 92,212 | 318 | 50,584 R | 60.7% | 39.2% | 60.8% | 39.2% |
| 16,730 | MONTOUR | 6,791 | 4,154 | 2,629 | 8 | 1,525 R | 61.2% | 38.7% | 61.2% | 38.8% |
| 201,412 | NORTHAMPTON | 82,306 | 40,683 | 41,552 | 71 | 869 D | 49.4% | 50.5% | 49.5% | 50.5% |
| 104,138 | NORTHUMBERLAND | 49,841 | 27,568 | 22,233 | 40 | 5,335 R | 55.3% | 44.6% | 55.4% | 44.6% |
| 26,582 | PERRY | 11,570 | 8,134 | 3,413 | 23 | 4,721 R | 70.3% | 29.5% | 70.4% | 29.6% |
| 2,002,512 | PHILADELPHIA | 915,277 | 291,000 | 622,544 | 1,733 | 331,544 D | 31.8% | 68.0% | 31.9% | 68.1% |
| 9,158 | PIKE | 5,683 | 4,000 | 1,676 | 7 | 2,324 R | 70.4% | 29.5% | 70.5% | 29.5% |
| 16,483 | POTTER | 7,830 | 5,099 | 2,715 | 16 | 2,384 R | 65.1% | 34.7% | 65.3% | 34.7% |
| 173,027 | SCHUYLKILL | 88,687 | 44,187 | 44,430 | 70 | 243 D | 49.8% | 50.1% | 49.9% | 50.1% |
| 25,922 | SNYDER | 10,117 | 8,103 | 1,998 | 16 | 6,105 R | 80.1% | 19.7% | 80.2% | 19.8% |
| 77,450 | SOMERSET | 35,335 | 20,554 | 14,739 | 42 | 5,815 R | 58.2% | 41.7% | 58.2% | 41.8% |
| 6,251 | SULLIVAN | 3,284 | 1,808 | 1,471 | 5 | 337 R | 55.1% | 44.8% | 55.1% | 44.9% |
| 33,137 | SUSQUEHANNA | 15,970 | 10,201 | 5,760 | 9 | 4,441 R | 63.9% | 36.1% | 63.9% | 36.1% |
| 36,614 | TIOGA | 15,173 | 11,082 | 4,076 | 15 | 7,006 R | 73.0% | 26.9% | 73.1% | 26.9% |
| 25,646 | UNION | 9,472 | 7,466 | 1,993 | 13 | 5,473 R | 78.8% | 21.0% | 78.9% | 21.1% |

# PENNSYLVANIA

## PRESIDENT 1960

| 1960 Census Population | County | Total Vote | Republican | Democratic | Other | Rep.-Dem. Plurality | Percentage | | | |
|---|---|---|---|---|---|---|---|---|---|---|
| | | | | | | | Total Vote | | Major Vote | |
| | | | | | | | Rep. | Dem. | Rep. | Dem. |
| 65,295 | VENANGO | 25,280 | 17,193 | 8,064 | 23 | 9,129 R | 68.0% | 31.9% | 68.1% | 31.9% |
| 45,582 | WARREN | 18,195 | 11,611 | 6,525 | 59 | 5,086 R | 63.8% | 35.9% | 64.0% | 36.0% |
| 217,271 | WASHINGTON | 92,197 | 38,348 | 53,729 | 120 | 15,381 D | 41.6% | 58.3% | 41.6% | 58.4% |
| 28,237 | WAYNE | 13,811 | 9,360 | 4,425 | 26 | 4,935 R | 67.8% | 32.0% | 67.9% | 32.1% |
| 352,629 | WESTMORELAND | 154,840 | 68,825 | 85,641 | 374 | 16,816 D | 44.4% | 55.3% | 44.6% | 55.4% |
| 16,813 | WYOMING | 8,921 | 6,188 | 2,726 | 7 | 3,462 R | 69.4% | 30.6% | 69.4% | 30.6% |
| 238,336 | YORK | 95,479 | 55,922 | 39,164 | 393 | 16,758 R | 58.6% | 41.0% | 58.8% | 41.2% |
| 11,319,366 | TOTAL | 5,006,541 | 2,439,956 | 2,556,282 | 10,303 | 116,326 D | 48.7% | 51.1% | 48.8% | 51.2% |

# PENNSYLVANIA

## ELECTION NOTES

**2004**    Other vote was 21,185 Libertarian (Michael Badnarik); 6,319 Green (David Cobb); 6,318 Constitution (Michael Peroutka); 2,656 write-in (Ralph Nader); 1,170 scattered write-in.

**2000**    Other vote was 16,023 Reform (Buchanan); 14,428 Constitution (Phillips); 11,248 Libertarian (Browne); 934 scattered write-in.

**1996**    Other vote was 28,000 Libertarian (Browne); 19,552 Constitutional (Phillips); 5,783 Natural Law (Hagelin); 3,086 write-in (Nader); 1,725 scattered write-in.

**1992**    Other vote was 21,477 Marrou (Libertarian); 4,661 Fulani (New Alliance). The Perot vote in Huntingdon county was amended from 7,273 to 3,273 thereby changing his statewide vote from 906,667 to 902,667.

**1988**    Other vote was 19,158 McCarthy (Consumer); 12,051 Paul (Libertarian); 4,379 Fulani (New Alliance); 3,444 Duke (Populist); 2,188 Winn (Workers World).

**1984**    Other vote was 21,628 Johnson (Consumer); 6,982 Bergland (Libertarian); 2,059 Winn (Workers League); 1,780 Hall (Communist).

**1980**    Other vote was 292,921 Anderson (Anderson Coalition); 33,263 Clark (Libertarian); 20,291 DeBerry (Socialist Workers); 10,430 Commoner (Consumer); 5,184 Hall (Communist).

**1976**    Other vote was 50,584 McCarthy (McCarthy '76); 25,344 Maddox (Constitutional); 3,009 Camejo (Socialist Workers); 2,744 LaRouche (Labor); 1,891 Hall (Communist); 2,934 scattered write-in.

**1972**    Other vote was 70,593 Schmitz (Constitutional); 4,639 Jenness (Socialist Workers); 2,686 Hall (Communist); 2,716 scattered write-in. Early unamended canvass gave the scattered write-in vote as 2,715.

**1968**    Wallace on the ballot as American Independent. Other vote was 7,821 Gregory (Peace and Freedom); 4,977 Blomen (Socialist Labor); 4,862 Halstead (Militant Workers); 2,264 scattered write-in.

**1964**    Other vote was 10,456 DeBerry (Militant Workers); 5,092 Hass (Socialist Labor); 2,531 scattered write-in.

**1960**    Other vote was 7,185 Hass (Socialist Labor); 2,678 Dobbs (Militant Workers); 440 scattered write-in.

# RHODE ISLAND

## POPULAR VOTE FOR PRESIDENT 1920 TO 2004

| Year | Total Vote | Republican Vote | Republican Candidate | Democratic Vote | Democratic Candidate | Other Vote | Plurality | Total Vote Rep. | Total Vote Dem. | Major Vote Rep. | Major Vote Dem. |
|------|-----------|-----------------|---------------------|-----------------|----------------------|-----------|-----------|-----------------|-----------------|-----------------|-----------------|
| 2004 | 437,134 | 169,046 | Bush, George W. | 259,760 | Kerry, John | 8,328 | 90,714 D | 38.7% | 59.4% | 39.4% | 60.6% |
| 2000 ** | 409,047 | 130,555 | Bush, George W. | 249,508 | Gore, Al | 28,984 | 118,953 D | 31.9% | 61.0% | 34.4% | 65.6% |
| 1996 ** | 390,284 | 104,683 | Dole, Bob | 233,050 | Clinton, Bill | 52,551 | 128,367 D | 26.8% | 59.7% | 31.0% | 69.0% |
| 1992 ** | 453,477 | 131,601 | Bush, George | 213,299 | Clinton, Bill | 108,577 | 81,698 D | 29.0% | 47.0% | 38.2% | 61.8% |
| 1988 | 404,620 | 177,761 | Bush, George | 225,123 | Dukakis, Michael S. | 1,736 | 47,362 D | 43.9% | 55.6% | 44.1% | 55.9% |
| 1984 | 410,492 | 212,080 | Reagan, Ronald | 197,106 | Mondale, Walter F. | 1,306 | 14,974 R | 51.7% | 48.0% | 51.8% | 48.2% |
| 1980 ** | 416,072 | 154,793 | Reagan, Ronald | 198,342 | Carter, Jimmy | 62,937 | 43,549 D | 37.2% | 47.7% | 43.8% | 56.2% |
| 1976 | 411,170 | 181,249 | Ford, Gerald R. | 227,636 | Carter, Jimmy | 2,285 | 46,387 D | 44.1% | 55.4% | 44.3% | 55.7% |
| 1972 | 415,808 | 220,383 | Nixon, Richard M. | 194,645 | McGovern, George S. | 780 | 25,738 R | 53.0% | 46.8% | 53.1% | 46.9% |
| 1968 | 385,000 | 122,359 | Nixon, Richard M. | 246,518 | Humphrey, Hubert H. | 16,123 | 124,159 D | 31.8% | 64.0% | 33.2% | 66.8% |
| 1964 | 390,091 | 74,615 | Goldwater, Barry M. | 315,463 | Johnson, Lyndon B. | 13 | 240,848 D | 19.1% | 80.9% | 19.1% | 80.9% |
| 1960 | 405,535 | 147,502 | Nixon, Richard M. | 258,032 | Kennedy, John F. | 1 | 110,530 D | 36.4% | 63.6% | 36.4% | 63.6% |
| 1956 | 387,609 | 225,819 | Eisenhower, Dwight D. | 161,790 | Stevenson, Adlai E. | | 64,029 R | 58.3% | 41.7% | 58.3% | 41.7% |
| 1952 | 414,498 | 210,935 | Eisenhower, Dwight D. | 203,293 | Stevenson, Adlai E. | 270 | 7,642 R | 50.9% | 49.0% | 50.9% | 49.1% |
| 1948 | 327,702 | 135,787 | Dewey, Thomas E. | 188,736 | Truman, Harry S. | 3,179 | 52,949 D | 41.4% | 57.6% | 41.8% | 58.2% |
| 1944 | 299,276 | 123,487 | Dewey, Thomas E. | 175,356 | Roosevelt, Franklin D. | 433 | 51,869 D | 41.3% | 58.6% | 41.3% | 58.7% |
| 1940 | 321,152 | 138,654 | Willkie, Wendell | 182,181 | Roosevelt, Franklin D. | 317 | 43,527 D | 43.2% | 56.7% | 43.2% | 56.8% |
| 1936 | 310,278 | 125,031 | Landon, Alfred M. | 164,338 | Roosevelt, Franklin D. | 20,909 | 39,307 D | 40.3% | 53.0% | 43.2% | 56.8% |
| 1932 | 266,170 | 115,266 | Hoover, Herbert C. | 146,604 | Roosevelt, Franklin D. | 4,300 | 31,338 D | 43.3% | 55.1% | 44.0% | 56.0% |
| 1928 | 237,194 | 117,522 | Hoover, Herbert C. | 118,973 | Smith, Alfred E. | 699 | 1,451 D | 49.5% | 50.2% | 49.7% | 50.3% |
| 1924 | 210,115 | 125,286 | Coolidge, Calvin | 76,606 | Davis, John W. | 8,223 | 48,680 R | 59.6% | 36.5% | 62.1% | 37.9% |
| 1920 | 167,981 | 107,463 | Harding, Warren G. | 55,062 | Cox, James M. | 5,456 | 52,401 R | 64.0% | 32.8% | 66.1% | 33.9% |

In 2000 the other vote column includes 25,052 votes cast for Green (Nader). In 1996 the other vote column includes 43,723 votes cast for Perot. In 1992 the other vote column includes 105,045 votes cast for Perot. In 1980 the other column includes 59,819 votes for Independent (Anderson).

## ELECTORAL COLLEGE VOTE 1920 TO 2004

| Year | Total | Republican | Democratic | Other |
|------|-------|-----------|-----------|-------|
| 2004 | 4 | | 4 | |
| 2000 | 4 | | 4 | |
| 1996 | 4 | | 4 | |
| 1992 | 4 | | 4 | |
| 1988 | 4 | | 4 | |
| 1984 | 4 | 4 | | |
| 1980 | 4 | | 4 | |
| 1976 | 4 | | 4 | |
| 1972 | 4 | 4 | | |
| 1968 | 4 | | 4 | |
| 1964 | 4 | | 4 | |
| 1960 | 4 | | 4 | |
| 1956 | 4 | 4 | | |
| 1952 | 4 | 4 | | |
| 1948 | 4 | | 4 | |
| 1944 | 4 | | 4 | |
| 1940 | 4 | | 4 | |
| 1936 | 4 | | 4 | |
| 1932 | 4 | | 4 | |
| 1928 | 5 | | 5 | |
| 1924 | 5 | 5 | | |
| 1920 | 5 | 5 | | |

# RHODE ISLAND

PROVIDENCE

KENT

BRISTOL

NEWPORT

WASHINGTON
(PART)

WASHINGTON
(PART)

# RHODE ISLAND

## PRESIDENT 2004

| 2000 Census Population | County | Total Vote | Republican | Democratic | Other | Rep.-Dem. Plurality | Percentage | | | |
|---|---|---|---|---|---|---|---|---|---|---|
| | | | | | | | Total Vote | | Major Vote | |
| | | | | | | | Rep. | Dem. | Rep. | Dem. |
| 50,648 | BRISTOL | 24,677 | 9,855 | 14,448 | 374 | 4,593 D | 39.9% | 58.5% | 40.6% | 59.4% |
| 167,090 | KENT | 77,842 | 33,699 | 42,830 | 1,313 | 9,131 D | 43.3% | 55.0% | 44.0% | 56.0% |
| 85,433 | NEWPORT | 40,337 | 16,622 | 22,992 | 723 | 6,370 D | 41.2% | 57.0% | 42.0% | 58.0% |
| 621,602 | PROVIDENCE | 230,947 | 82,337 | 144,811 | 3,799 | 62,474 D | 35.7% | 62.7% | 36.2% | 63.8% |
| 123,546 | WASHINGTON | 62,486 | 26,533 | 34,679 | 1,274 | 8,146 D | 42.5% | 55.5% | 43.3% | 56.7% |
| 1,048,319 | TOTAL | 437,134 | 169,046 | 259,760 | 8,328 | 90,714 D | 38.7% | 59.4% | 39.4% | 60.6% |

Note: The statewide totals for "Total Vote" and "Other" include 845 scattered write-in votes that were not included in the county-by-county returns.

# RHODE ISLAND

## PRESIDENT 2000

| 2000 Census Population | County | Total Vote | Republican | Democratic | Green (Nader) | Other | Rep.-Dem. Plurality | Percentage of Total Vote | | |
|---|---|---|---|---|---|---|---|---|---|---|
| | | | | | | | | Rep. | Dem. | Green |
| 50,648 | BRISTOL | 23,252 | 8,375 | 13,424 | 1,283 | 170 | 5,049 D | 36.0% | 57.7% | 5.5% |
| 167,090 | KENT | 73,414 | 25,291 | 43,265 | 4,140 | 718 | 17,974 D | 34.4% | 58.9% | 5.6% |
| 85,433 | NEWPORT | 37,796 | 14,258 | 20,790 | 2,427 | 321 | 6,532 D | 37.7% | 55.0% | 6.4% |
| 621,602 | PROVIDENCE | 218,160 | 61,378 | 142,469 | 12,352 | 1,961 | 81,091 D | 28.1% | 65.3% | 5.7% |
| 123,546 | WASHINGTON | 56,161 | 21,253 | 29,560 | 4,850 | 498 | 8,307 D | 37.8% | 52.6% | 8.6% |
| 1,048,319 | TOTAL | 409,047 | 130,555 | 249,508 | 25,052 | 3,932 | 118,953 D | 31.9% | 61.0% | 6.1% |

Note: The statewide totals for "Total Vote" and "Other" include 264 scattered write-in votes that are not included in the county-by-county results.

# RHODE ISLAND

## PRESIDENT 1996

| 1995 Census Pop. Est. | County | Total Vote | Republican | Democratic | Reform (Perot) | Other | Rep.-Dem. Plurality | Percentage of Total Vote | | |
|---|---|---|---|---|---|---|---|---|---|---|
| | | | | | | | | Rep. | Dem. | Reform |
| 48,781 | BRISTOL | 21,671 | 6,988 | 12,257 | 1,990 | 436 | 5,269 D | 32.2% | 56.6% | 9.2% |
| 162,143 | KENT | 71,526 | 19,992 | 41,018 | 9,240 | 1,276 | 21,026 D | 28.0% | 57.3% | 12.9% |
| 81,993 | NEWPORT | 35,096 | 11,500 | 18,951 | 3,785 | 860 | 7,451 D | 32.8% | 54.0% | 10.8% |
| 580,015 | PROVIDENCE | 212,122 | 49,901 | 134,866 | 22,724 | 4,631 | 84,965 D | 23.5% | 63.6% | 10.7% |
| 116,862 | WASHINGTON | 49,832 | 16,302 | 25,958 | 5,984 | 1,588 | 9,656 D | 32.7% | 52.1% | 12.0% |
| 989,794 | TOTAL | 390,284 | 104,683 | 233,050 | 43,723 | 8,828 | 128,367 D | 26.8% | 59.7% | 11.2% |

# RHODE ISLAND

## PRESIDENT 1992

| 1990 Census Population | County | Total Vote | Republican | Democratic | Perot | Other | Plurality | Percentage Total Vote | | |
|---|---|---|---|---|---|---|---|---|---|---|
| | | | | | | | | Rep. | Dem. | Perot |
| 48,859 | BRISTOL | 24,911 | 8,208 | 11,414 | 5,132 | 157 | 3,206 D | 32.9% | 45.8% | 20.6% |
| 161,135 | KENT | 82,425 | 25,217 | 35,934 | 20,690 | 584 | 10,717 D | 30.6% | 43.6% | 25.1% |
| 87,194 | NEWPORT | 39,644 | 12,386 | 17,584 | 9,366 | 308 | 5,198 D | 31.2% | 44.4% | 23.6% |
| 596,270 | PROVIDENCE | 253,441 | 69,579 | 125,358 | 56,575 | 1,929 | 55,779 D | 27.5% | 49.5% | 22.3% |
| 110,006 | WASHINGTON | 52,944 | 16,211 | 23,009 | 13,282 | 442 | 6,798 D | 30.6% | 43.5% | 25.1% |
| 1,003,464 | TOTAL | 453,477 | 131,601 | 213,299 | 105,045 | 3,532 | 81,698 D | 29.0% | 47.0% | 23.2% |

# RHODE ISLAND

## PRESIDENT 1988

| 1980 Census Population | County | Total Vote | Republican | Democratic | Other | Rep.-Dem. Plurality | Percentage | | | |
|---|---|---|---|---|---|---|---|---|---|---|
| | | | | | | | Total Vote | | Major Vote | |
| | | | | | | | Rep. | Dem. | Rep. | Dem. |
| 46,942 | BRISTOL | 21,883 | 10,626 | 11,168 | 89 | 542 D | 48.6% | 51.0% | 48.8% | 51.2% |
| 154,163 | KENT | 71,801 | 34,314 | 37,221 | 266 | 2,907 D | 47.8% | 51.8% | 48.0% | 52.0% |
| 81,383 | NEWPORT | 34,664 | 16,923 | 17,597 | 144 | 674 D | 48.8% | 50.8% | 49.0% | 51.0% |
| 571,349 | PROVIDENCE | 231,159 | 94,248 | 135,927 | 984 | 41,679 D | 40.8% | 58.8% | 40.9% | 59.1% |
| 93,317 | WASHINGTON | 45,062 | 21,650 | 23,210 | 202 | 1,560 D | 48.0% | 51.5% | 48.3% | 51.7% |
| 947,154 | TOTAL | 404,620 | 177,761 | 225,123 | 1,736 | 47,362 D | 43.9% | 55.6% | 44.1% | 55.9% |

# RHODE ISLAND

## PRESIDENT 1984

| 1980 Census Population | County | Total Vote | Republican | Democratic | Other | Rep.-Dem. Plurality | Percentage | | | |
|---|---|---|---|---|---|---|---|---|---|---|
| | | | | | | | Total Vote | | Major Vote | |
| | | | | | | | Rep. | Dem. | Rep. | Dem. |
| 46,942 | BRISTOL | 21,084 | 11,635 | 9,386 | 63 | 2,249 R | 55.2% | 44.5% | 55.3% | 44.7% |
| 154,163 | KENT | 71,993 | 40,427 | 31,352 | 214 | 9,075 R | 56.2% | 43.5% | 56.3% | 43.7% |
| 81,383 | NEWPORT | 34,209 | 19,629 | 14,466 | 114 | 5,163 R | 57.4% | 42.3% | 57.6% | 42.4% |
| 571,349 | PROVIDENCE | 240,898 | 116,024 | 124,109 | 765 | 8,085 D | 48.2% | 51.5% | 48.3% | 51.7% |
| 93,317 | WASHINGTON | 42,305 | 24,365 | 17,793 | 147 | 6,572 R | 57.6% | 42.1% | 57.8% | 42.2% |
| 947,154 | TOTAL | 410,492 | 212,080 | 197,106 | 1,306 | 14,974 R | 51.7% | 48.0% | 51.8% | 48.2% |

# RHODE ISLAND

## PRESIDENT 1980

| 1980 Census Population | County | Total Vote | Republican | Democratic | Other | Rep.-Dem. Plurality | Percentage | | | |
|---|---|---|---|---|---|---|---|---|---|---|
| | | | | | | | Total Vote | | Major Vote | |
| | | | | | | | Rep. | Dem. | Rep. | Dem. |
| 46,942 | BRISTOL | 21,852 | 8,508 | 9,851 | 3,493 | 1,343 D | 38.9% | 45.1% | 46.3% | 53.7% |
| 154,163 | KENT | 71,005 | 28,331 | 31,350 | 11,324 | 3,019 D | 39.9% | 44.2% | 47.5% | 52.5% |
| 81,383 | NEWPORT | 34,356 | 14,555 | 13,904 | 5,897 | 651 R | 42.4% | 40.5% | 51.1% | 48.9% |
| 571,349 | PROVIDENCE | 247,927 | 86,467 | 126,808 | 34,652 | 40,341 D | 34.9% | 51.1% | 40.5% | 59.5% |
| 93,317 | WASHINGTON | 40,827 | 16,932 | 16,429 | 7,466 | 503 R | 41.5% | 40.2% | 50.8% | 49.2% |
| 947,154 | TOTAL | 416,072 | 154,793 | 198,342 | 62,937 | 43,549 D | 37.2% | 47.7% | 43.8% | 56.2% |

# RHODE ISLAND

## PRESIDENT 1976

| 1970 Census Population | County | Total Vote | Republican | Democratic | Other | Rep.-Dem. Plurality | Percentage | | | |
|---|---|---|---|---|---|---|---|---|---|---|
| | | | | | | | Total Vote | | Major Vote | |
| | | | | | | | Rep. | Dem. | Rep. | Dem. |
| 45,937 | BRISTOL | 21,425 | 10,131 | 11,228 | 66 | 1,097 D | 47.3% | 52.4% | 47.4% | 52.6% |
| 142,382 | KENT | 70,213 | 34,131 | 35,855 | 227 | 1,724 D | 48.6% | 51.1% | 48.8% | 51.2% |
| 94,228 | NEWPORT | 33,107 | 15,155 | 17,768 | 184 | 2,613 D | 45.8% | 53.7% | 46.0% | 54.0% |
| 581,470 | PROVIDENCE | 249,817 | 103,976 | 144,805 | 1,036 | 40,829 D | 41.6% | 58.0% | 41.8% | 58.2% |
| 85,706 | WASHINGTON | 36,022 | 17,856 | 17,980 | 186 | 124 D | 49.6% | 49.9% | 49.8% | 50.2% |
| 949,723 | TOTAL | 411,170 | 181,249 | 227,636 | 2,285 | 46,387 D | 44.1% | 55.4% | 44.3% | 55.7% |

# RHODE ISLAND

## PRESIDENT 1972

| 1970 Census Population | County | Total Vote | Republican | Democratic | Other | Rep.-Dem. Plurality | Percentage | | | |
|---|---|---|---|---|---|---|---|---|---|---|
| | | | | | | | Total Vote | | Major Vote | |
| | | | | | | | Rep. | Dem. | Rep. | Dem. |
| 45,937 | BRISTOL | 21,985 | 12,009 | 9,928 | 48 | 2,081 R | 54.6% | 45.2% | 54.7% | 45.3% |
| 142,382 | KENT | 69,653 | 40,534 | 29,004 | 115 | 11,530 R | 58.2% | 41.6% | 58.3% | 41.7% |
| 94,228 | NEWPORT | 32,035 | 19,142 | 12,844 | 49 | 6,298 R | 59.8% | 40.1% | 59.8% | 40.2% |
| 581,470 | PROVIDENCE | 259,156 | 129,418 | 129,232 | 506 | 186 R | 49.9% | 49.9% | 50.0% | 50.0% |
| 85,706 | WASHINGTON | 32,979 | 19,280 | 13,637 | 62 | 5,643 R | 58.5% | 41.4% | 58.6% | 41.4% |
| 949,723 | TOTAL | 415,808 | 220,383 | 194,645 | 780 | 25,738 R | 53.0% | 46.8% | 53.1% | 46.9% |

# RHODE ISLAND

## PRESIDENT 1968

| 1960 Census Population | County | Total Vote | Republican | Democratic | AIP | Other | Plurality | Percentage Total Vote | | |
|---|---|---|---|---|---|---|---|---|---|---|
| | | | | | | | | Rep. | Dem. | AIP |
| 37,146 | BRISTOL | 19,475 | 7,403 | 11,561 | 483 | 28 | 4,158 D | 38.0% | 59.4% | 2.5% |
| 112,619 | KENT | 60,678 | 22,493 | 35,609 | 2,519 | 57 | 13,116 D | 37.1% | 58.7% | 4.2% |
| 81,891 | NEWPORT | 27,830 | 10,504 | 16,251 | 1,043 | 32 | 5,747 D | 37.7% | 58.4% | 3.7% |
| 568,778 | PROVIDENCE | 250,199 | 70,320 | 169,246 | 10,347 | 286 | 98,926 D | 28.1% | 67.6% | 4.1% |
| 59,054 | WASHINGTON | 26,818 | 11,639 | 13,851 | 1,286 | 42 | 2,212 D | 43.4% | 51.6% | 4.8% |
| 859,488 | TOTAL | 385,000 | 122,359 | 246,518 | 15,678 | 445 | 124,159 D | 31.8% | 64.0% | 4.1% |

# RHODE ISLAND

## PRESIDENT 1964

| 1960 Census Population | County | Total Vote | Republican | Democratic | Other | Rep.-Dem. Plurality | Percentage | | | |
|---|---|---|---|---|---|---|---|---|---|---|
| | | | | | | | Total Vote | | Major Vote | |
| | | | | | | | Rep. | Dem. | Rep. | Dem. |
| 37,146 | BRISTOL | 18,772 | 4,466 | 14,306 | | 9,840 D | 23.8% | 76.2% | 23.8% | 76.2% |
| 112,619 | KENT | 56,773 | 12,297 | 44,476 | | 32,179 D | 21.7% | 78.3% | 21.7% | 78.3% |
| 81,891 | NEWPORT | 27,371 | 7,286 | 20,085 | | 12,799 D | 26.6% | 73.4% | 26.6% | 73.4% |
| 568,778 | PROVIDENCE | 262,910 | 43,432 | 219,465 | 13 | 176,033 D | 16.5% | 83.5% | 16.5% | 83.5% |
| 59,054 | WASHINGTON | 24,265 | 7,134 | 17,131 | | 9,997 D | 29.4% | 70.6% | 29.4% | 70.6% |
| 859,488 | TOTAL | 390,091 | 74,615 | 315,463 | 13 | 240,848 D | 19.1% | 80.9% | 19.1% | 80.9% |

# RHODE ISLAND

## PRESIDENT 1960

| 1960 Census Population | County | Total Vote | Republican | Democratic | Other | Rep.-Dem. Plurality | Percentage | | | |
|---|---|---|---|---|---|---|---|---|---|---|
| | | | | | | | Total Vote | | Major Vote | |
| | | | | | | | Rep. | Dem. | Rep. | Dem. |
| 37,146 | BRISTOL | 18,636 | 7,537 | 11,099 | | 3,562 D | 40.4% | 59.6% | 40.4% | 59.6% |
| 112,619 | KENT | 55,006 | 24,344 | 30,662 | | 6,318 D | 44.3% | 55.7% | 44.3% | 55.7% |
| 81,891 | NEWPORT | 27,619 | 11,942 | 15,677 | | 3,735 D | 43.2% | 56.8% | 43.2% | 56.8% |
| 568,778 | PROVIDENCE | 280,043 | 91,028 | 189,014 | 1 | 97,986 D | 32.5% | 67.5% | 32.5% | 67.5% |
| 59,054 | WASHINGTON | 24,231 | 12,651 | 11,580 | | 1,071 R | 52.2% | 47.8% | 52.2% | 47.8% |
| 859,488 | TOTAL | 405,535 | 147,502 | 258,032 | 1 | 110,530 D | 36.4% | 63.6% | 36.4% | 63.6% |

# RHODE ISLAND

## ELECTION NOTES

**2004**   Other vote was 4,651 Reform (Ralph Nader); 1,333 Green (David Cobb); 907 Libertarian (Michael Badnarik); 339 Constitution (Michael Peroutka); 253 Workers World (John Parker); 845 write-in.

**2000**   Other vote was 2,273 Reform (Buchanan); 742 Libertarian (Browne); 271 Natural Law (Hagelin); 199 Workers World (Moorehead); 97 Constitution (Phillips); 52 Socialist (McReynolds); 34 Socialist Workers (Harris); 264 scattered write-in.

**1996**   Other vote was 6,040 Green (Nader); 1,109 Libertarian (Browne); 1,021 U.S. Taxpayers (Phillips); 435 Natural Law (Hagelin); 186 Workers World (Moorehead); 37 scattered write-in.

**1992**   Other vote was 1,878 Fulani (New Alliance); 571 Marrou (Libertarian); 494 LaRouche (Independent); 262 Hagelin (Natural Law); 215 Phillips (Taxpayers); 3 Gritz (write-in); 2 Brisben (write-in); 1 Daniels (write-in); 106 scattered write-in.

**1988**   Other vote was 825 Paul (Libertarian); 280 Fulani (New Alliance); 195 Lewin (Peace and Freedom); 159 Duke (Populist); 130 Warren (Socialist Workers); 96 Kenoyer (Socialist); 51 scattered write-in.

**1984**   Other vote was 510 Richards (American Independent); 277 Bergland (Libertarian); 240 Johnson (Citizens); 91 Holmes (Workers World); 75 Hall (Communist); 61 Mason (Socialist Workers); 49 Serrette (Alliance); 3 scattered write-in. The state-wide total for the other vote column includes the 3 scattered write-in votes not reported by county.

**1980**   Other vote was 59,819 Anderson (Independent); 2,458 Clark (Libertarian); 218 Hall (Communist); 170 McReynolds (Socialist); 90 DeBerry (Socialist Workers); 77 Griswold (Workers World); 67 Commoner (write-in); 1 McCormack (write-in); 37 scattered write-in. The state-wide total for the other vote column includes the 105 write-in votes not reported by county.

**1976**   Other vote was 715 MacBride (Libertarian); 479 McCarthy (write-in); 462 Camejo (Socialist Workers); 334 Hall (Communist); 188 Levin (Socialist Labor); 24 Anderson (write-in); 1 Maddox (write-in); 82 scattered write-in. The state-wide total for the other vote column includes the 586 write-in votes not available by county.

**1972**   Other vote was 729 Jenness (Socialist Workers); 25 Schmitz (write-in); 5 Spock (write-in); 2 Hospers (write-in); 19 scattered write-in.

**1968**   Wallace on the ballot as George Wallace Independent. Other vote was 383 Halstead (Socialist Workers); 62 scattered write-in.

**1964**   Other vote was scattered write-in.

**1960**   Other vote was scattered write-in.

# SOUTH CAROLINA

## POPULAR VOTE FOR PRESIDENT 1920 TO 2004

| Year | Total Vote | Republican Vote | Candidate | Democratic Vote | Candidate | Other Vote | Plurality | Total Vote Rep. | Total Vote Dem. | Major Vote Rep. | Major Vote Dem. |
|---|---|---|---|---|---|---|---|---|---|---|---|
| 2004 | 1,617,730 | 937,974 | Bush, George W. | 661,699 | Kerry, John | 18,057 | 276,275 R | 58.0% | 40.9% | 58.6% | 41.4% |
| 2000 ** | 1,382,717 | 785,937 | Bush, George W. | 565,561 | Gore, Al | 31,219 | 220,376 R | 56.8% | 40.9% | 58.2% | 41.8% |
| 1996 ** | 1,151,689 | 573,458 | Dole, Bob | 506,283 | Clinton, Bill | 71,948 | 67,175 R | 49.8% | 44.0% | 53.1% | 46.9% |
| 1992 ** | 1,202,527 | 577,507 | Bush, George | 479,514 | Clinton, Bill | 145,506 | 97,993 R | 48.0% | 39.9% | 54.6% | 45.4% |
| 1988 | 986,009 | 606,443 | Bush, George | 370,554 | Dukakis, Michael S. | 9,012 | 235,889 R | 61.5% | 37.6% | 62.1% | 37.9% |
| 1984 | 968,529 | 615,539 | Reagan, Ronald | 344,459 | Mondale, Walter F. | 8,531 | 271,080 R | 63.6% | 35.6% | 64.1% | 35.9% |
| 1980** | 894,071 | 441,841 | Reagan, Ronald | 430,385 | Carter, Jimmy | 21,845 | 11,456 R | 49.4% | 48.1% | 50.7% | 49.3% |
| 1976 | 802,583 | 346,149 | Ford, Gerald R. | 450,807 | Carter, Jimmy | 5,627 | 104,658 D | 43.1% | 56.2% | 43.4% | 56.6% |
| 1972 | 673,960 | 477,044 | Nixon, Richard M. | 186,824 | McGovern, George S. | 10,092 | 290,220 R | 70.8% | 27.7% | 71.9% | 28.1% |
| 1968 ** | 666,978 | 254,062 | Nixon, Richard M. | 197,486 | Humphrey, Hubert H. | 215,430 | 38,632 R | 38.1% | 29.6% | 56.3% | 43.7% |
| 1964 | 524,779 | 309,048 | Goldwater, Barry M. | 215,723 | Johnson, Lyndon B. | 8 | 93,325 R | 58.9% | 41.1% | 58.9% | 41.1% |
| 1960 | 386,688 | 188,558 | Nixon, Richard M. | 198,129 | Kennedy, John F. | 1 | 9,571 D | 48.8% | 51.2% | 48.8% | 51.2% |
| 1956 ** | 300,583 | 75,700 | Eisenhower, Dwight D. | 136,372 | Stevenson, Adlai E. | 88,511 | 47,863 D | 25.2% | 45.4% | 35.7% | 64.3% |
| 1952 | 341,087 | 168,082 | Eisenhower, Dwight D. | 173,004 | Stevenson, Adlai E. | 1 | 4,922 D | 49.3% | 50.7% | 49.3% | 50.7% |
| 1948 ** | 142,571 | 5,386 | Dewey, Thomas E. | 34,423 | Truman, Harry S. | 102,762 | 68,184 SR | 3.8% | 24.1% | 13.5% | 86.5% |
| 1944 ** | 103,382 | 4,617 | Dewey, Thomas E. | 90,601 | Roosevelt, Franklin D. | 8,164 | 82,802 D | 4.5% | 87.6% | 4.8% | 95.2% |
| 1940 | 99,830 | 4,360 | Willkie, Wendell | 95,470 | Roosevelt, Franklin D. | | 91,110 D | 4.4% | 95.6% | 4.4% | 95.6% |
| 1936 | 115,437 | 1,646 | Landon, Alfred M. | 113,791 | Roosevelt, Franklin D. | | 112,145 D | 1.4% | 98.6% | 1.4% | 98.6% |
| 1932 | 104,407 | 1,978 | Hoover, Herbert C. | 102,347 | Roosevelt, Franklin D. | 82 | 100,369 D | 1.9% | 98.0% | 1.9% | 98.1% |
| 1928 | 68,605 | 5,858 | Hoover, Herbert C. | 62,700 | Smith, Alfred E. | 47 | 56,842 D | 8.5% | 91.4% | 8.5% | 91.5% |
| 1924 | 50,755 | 1,123 | Coolidge, Calvin | 49,008 | Davis, John W. | 624 | 47,885 D | 2.2% | 96.6% | 2.2% | 97.8% |
| 1920 | 66,808 | 2,610 | Harding, Warren G. | 64,170 | Cox, James M. | 28 | 61,560 D | 3.9% | 96.1% | 3.9% | 96.1% |

In 2000 the other vote column includes 20,200 votes cast for Green (Nader). In 1996 the other vote column includes 64,386 votes cast for Perot. In 1992 the other vote column includes 138,872 votes cast for Perot. In 1980 the other column includes 14,153 votes for Independent (Anderson). In 1968 other vote was Independent (Wallace). In 1956 other vote was 88,509 Independent (Uncommitted States Rights) and 2 scattered. In 1948 other vote was 102,607 States Rights; 154 Progressive and 1 Socialist. In 1944 the other vote was 7,799 Southern Democratic and 365 Prohibition.

## ELECTORAL COLLEGE VOTE 1920 TO 2004

| Year | Total | Republican | Democratic | Other |
|---|---|---|---|---|
| 2004 | 8 | 8 | | |
| 2000 | 8 | 8 | | |
| 1996 | 8 | 8 | | |
| 1992 | 8 | 8 | | |
| 1988 | 8 | 8 | | |
| 1984 | 8 | 8 | | |
| 1980 | 8 | 8 | | |
| 1976 | 8 | | 8 | |
| 1972 | 8 | 8 | | |
| 1968 | 8 | 8 | | |
| 1964 | 8 | 8 | | |
| 1960 | 8 | | 8 | |
| 1956 | 8 | | 8 | |
| 1952 | 8 | | 8 | |
| 1948 | 8 | | | 8 SR |
| 1944 | 8 | | 8 | |
| 1940 | 8 | | 8 | |
| 1936 | 8 | | 8 | |
| 1932 | 8 | | 8 | |
| 1928 | 9 | | 9 | |
| 1924 | 9 | | 9 | |
| 1920 | 9 | | 9 | |

# SOUTH CAROLINA

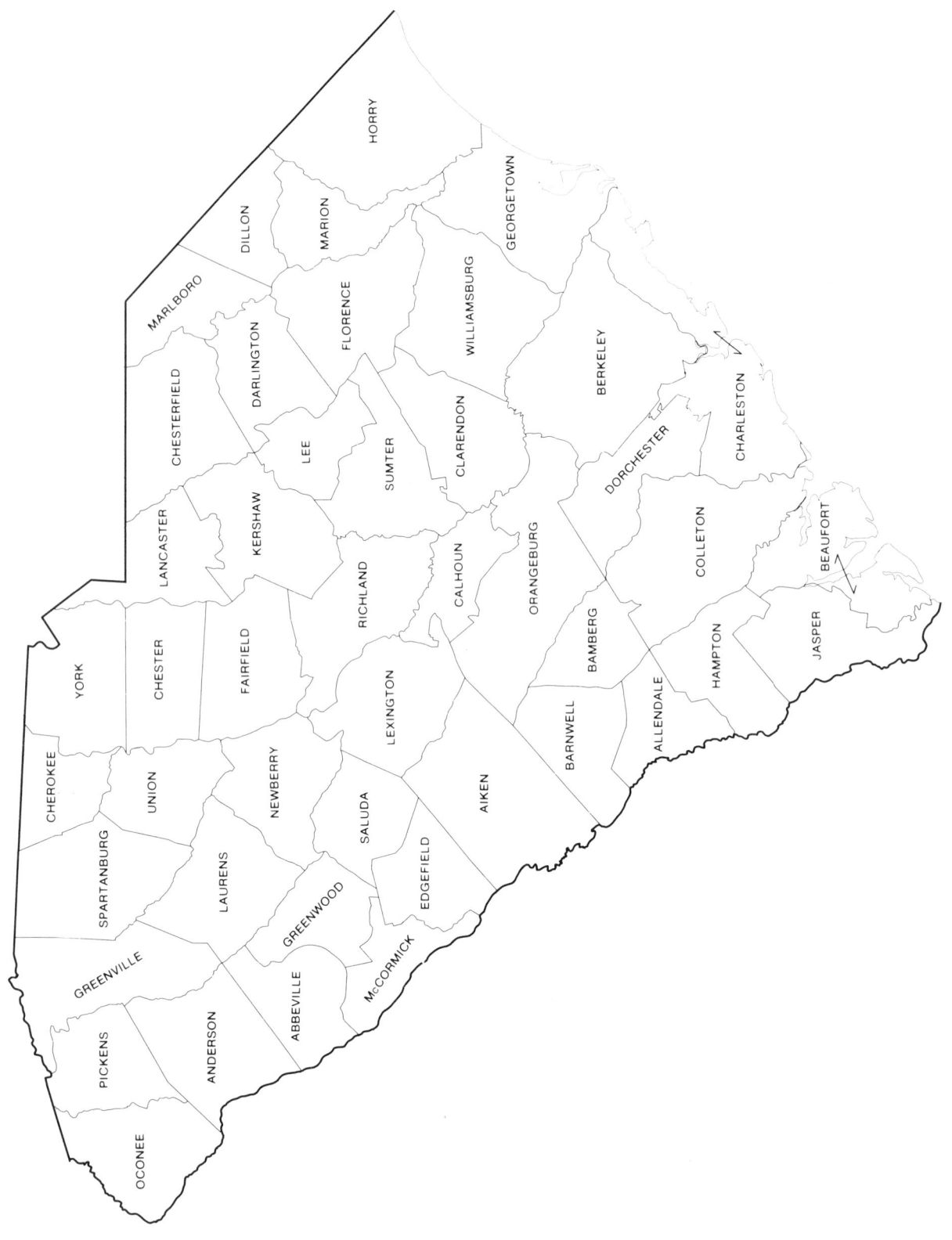

# SOUTH CAROLINA

## PRESIDENT 2004

| 2000 Census Population | County | Total Vote | Republican | Democratic | Other | Rep.-Dem. Plurality | Percentage | | | |
|---|---|---|---|---|---|---|---|---|---|---|
| | | | | | | | Total Vote | | Major Vote | |
| | | | | | | | Rep. | Dem. | Rep. | Dem. |
| 26,167 | ABBEVILLE | 9,925 | 5,436 | 4,389 | 100 | 1,047 R | 54.8% | 44.2% | 55.3% | 44.7% |
| 142,552 | AIKEN | 59,492 | 39,077 | 19,799 | 616 | 19,278 R | 65.7% | 33.3% | 66.4% | 33.6% |
| 11,211 | ALLENDALE | 3,591 | 985 | 2,565 | 41 | 1,580 D | 27.4% | 71.4% | 27.7% | 72.3% |
| 165,740 | ANDERSON | 64,722 | 43,355 | 20,697 | 670 | 22,658 R | 67.0% | 32.0% | 67.7% | 32.3% |
| 16,658 | BAMBERG | 6,036 | 2,138 | 3,841 | 57 | 1,703 D | 35.4% | 63.6% | 35.8% | 64.2% |
| 23,478 | BARNWELL | 8,685 | 4,606 | 3,982 | 97 | 624 R | 53.0% | 45.8% | 53.6% | 46.4% |
| 120,937 | BEAUFORT | 55,235 | 33,331 | 21,505 | 399 | 11,826 R | 60.3% | 38.9% | 60.8% | 39.2% |
| 142,651 | BERKELEY | 52,937 | 32,104 | 20,142 | 691 | 11,962 R | 60.6% | 38.0% | 61.4% | 38.6% |
| 15,185 | CALHOUN | 6,919 | 3,448 | 3,393 | 78 | 55 R | 49.8% | 49.0% | 50.4% | 49.6% |
| 309,969 | CHARLESTON | 136,316 | 70,297 | 63,758 | 2,261 | 6,539 R | 51.6% | 46.8% | 52.4% | 47.6% |
| 52,537 | CHEROKEE | 18,714 | 12,090 | 6,466 | 158 | 5,624 R | 64.6% | 34.6% | 65.2% | 34.8% |
| 34,068 | CHESTER | 11,729 | 5,798 | 5,790 | 141 | 8 R | 49.4% | 49.4% | 50.0% | 50.0% |
| 42,768 | CHESTERFIELD | 14,049 | 7,252 | 6,729 | 68 | 523 R | 51.6% | 47.9% | 51.9% | 48.1% |
| 32,502 | CLARENDON | 13,200 | 6,061 | 7,087 | 52 | 1,026 D | 45.9% | 53.7% | 46.1% | 53.9% |
| 38,264 | COLLETON | 14,106 | 7,264 | 6,699 | 143 | 565 R | 51.5% | 47.5% | 52.0% | 48.0% |
| 67,394 | DARLINGTON | 25,454 | 13,416 | 11,829 | 209 | 1,587 R | 52.7% | 46.5% | 53.1% | 46.9% |
| 30,722 | DILLON | 9,235 | 4,301 | 4,832 | 102 | 531 D | 46.6% | 52.3% | 47.1% | 52.9% |
| 96,413 | DORCHESTER | 41,317 | 26,006 | 14,733 | 578 | 11,273 R | 62.9% | 35.7% | 63.8% | 36.2% |
| 24,595 | EDGEFIELD | 9,746 | 5,611 | 4,051 | 84 | 1,560 R | 57.6% | 41.6% | 58.1% | 41.9% |
| 23,454 | FAIRFIELD | 9,435 | 3,531 | 5,764 | 140 | 2,233 D | 37.4% | 61.1% | 38.0% | 62.0% |
| 125,761 | FLORENCE | 49,545 | 27,689 | 21,442 | 414 | 6,247 R | 55.9% | 43.3% | 56.4% | 43.6% |
| 55,797 | GEORGETOWN | 23,593 | 12,606 | 10,602 | 385 | 2,004 R | 53.4% | 44.9% | 54.3% | 45.7% |
| 379,616 | GREENVILLE | 168,833 | 111,481 | 55,347 | 2,005 | 56,134 R | 66.0% | 32.8% | 66.8% | 33.2% |
| 66,271 | GREENWOOD | 23,442 | 14,264 | 8,954 | 224 | 5,310 R | 60.8% | 38.2% | 61.4% | 38.6% |
| 21,386 | HAMPTON | 8,016 | 3,097 | 4,832 | 87 | 1,735 D | 38.6% | 60.3% | 39.1% | 60.9% |
| 196,629 | HORRY | 81,347 | 50,447 | 29,547 | 1,353 | 20,900 R | 62.0% | 36.3% | 63.1% | 36.9% |
| 20,678 | JASPER | 6,846 | 2,933 | 3,840 | 73 | 907 D | 42.8% | 56.1% | 43.3% | 56.7% |
| 52,647 | KERSHAW | 22,915 | 14,160 | 8,515 | 240 | 5,645 R | 61.8% | 37.2% | 62.4% | 37.6% |
| 61,351 | LANCASTER | 20,814 | 12,916 | 7,631 | 267 | 5,285 R | 62.1% | 36.7% | 62.9% | 37.1% |
| 69,567 | LAURENS | 23,829 | 14,466 | 9,205 | 158 | 5,261 R | 60.7% | 38.6% | 61.1% | 38.9% |
| 20,119 | LEE | 7,898 | 2,901 | 4,960 | 37 | 2,059 D | 36.7% | 62.8% | 36.9% | 63.1% |
| 216,014 | LEXINGTON | 93,432 | 67,132 | 25,393 | 907 | 41,739 R | 71.9% | 27.2% | 72.6% | 27.4% |
| 9,958 | MCCORMICK | 5,122 | 2,396 | 2,648 | 78 | 252 D | 46.8% | 51.7% | 47.5% | 52.5% |
| 35,466 | MARION | 13,507 | 5,589 | 7,767 | 151 | 2,178 D | 41.4% | 57.5% | 41.8% | 58.2% |
| 28,818 | MARLBORO | 8,560 | 3,423 | 4,984 | 153 | 1,561 D | 40.0% | 58.2% | 40.7% | 59.3% |
| 36,108 | NEWBERRY | 12,409 | 7,654 | 4,483 | 272 | 3,171 R | 61.7% | 36.1% | 63.1% | 36.9% |
| 66,215 | OCONEE | 27,532 | 18,811 | 8,395 | 326 | 10,416 R | 68.3% | 30.5% | 69.1% | 30.9% |
| 91,582 | ORANGEBURG | 37,564 | 12,695 | 24,698 | 171 | 12,003 D | 33.8% | 65.7% | 34.0% | 66.0% |
| 110,757 | PICKENS | 40,510 | 29,759 | 10,287 | 464 | 19,472 R | 73.5% | 25.4% | 74.3% | 25.7% |
| 320,677 | RICHLAND | 133,801 | 56,212 | 76,283 | 1,306 | 20,071 D | 42.0% | 57.0% | 42.4% | 57.6% |
| 19,181 | SALUDA | 7,578 | 4,537 | 3,001 | 40 | 1,536 R | 59.9% | 39.6% | 60.2% | 39.8% |
| 253,791 | SPARTANBURG | 96,758 | 62,004 | 33,633 | 1,121 | 28,371 R | 64.1% | 34.8% | 64.8% | 35.2% |
| 104,646 | SUMTER | 37,003 | 18,074 | 18,695 | 234 | 621 D | 48.8% | 50.5% | 49.2% | 50.8% |
| 29,881 | UNION | 11,934 | 6,592 | 5,236 | 106 | 1,356 R | 55.2% | 43.9% | 55.7% | 44.3% |
| 37,217 | WILLIAMSBURG | 13,918 | 4,795 | 9,044 | 79 | 4,249 D | 34.5% | 65.0% | 34.6% | 65.4% |
| 164,614 | YORK | 70,181 | 45,234 | 24,226 | 721 | 21,008 R | 64.5% | 34.5% | 65.1% | 34.9% |
| 4,012,012 | TOTAL | 1,617,730 | 937,974 | 661,699 | 18,057 | 276,275 R | 58.0% | 40.9% | 58.6% | 41.4% |

# SOUTH CAROLINA

## PRESIDENT 2000

| 2000 Census Population | County | Total Vote | Republican | Democratic | Green (Nader) | Other | Rep.-Dem. Plurality | Percentage of Total Vote | | |
|---|---|---|---|---|---|---|---|---|---|---|
| | | | | | | | | Rep. | Dem. | Green |
| 26,167 | ABBEVILLE | 8,374 | 4,450 | 3,766 | 66 | 92 | 684 R | 53.1% | 45.0% | 0.8% |
| 142,552 | AIKEN | 50,782 | 33,203 | 16,409 | 676 | 494 | 16,794 R | 65.4% | 32.3% | 1.3% |
| 11,211 | ALLENDALE | 3,340 | 967 | 2,338 | 17 | 18 | 1,371 D | 29.0% | 70.0% | 0.5% |
| 165,740 | ANDERSON | 56,681 | 35,827 | 19,606 | 777 | 471 | 16,221 R | 63.2% | 34.6% | 1.4% |
| 16,658 | BAMBERG | 5,551 | 2,047 | 3,451 | 19 | 34 | 1,404 D | 36.9% | 62.2% | 0.3% |
| 23,478 | BARNWELL | 8,276 | 4,521 | 3,661 | 43 | 51 | 860 R | 54.6% | 44.2% | 0.5% |
| 120,937 | BEAUFORT | 44,148 | 25,561 | 17,487 | 846 | 254 | 8,074 R | 57.9% | 39.6% | 1.9% |
| 142,651 | BERKELEY | 43,316 | 24,796 | 17,707 | 464 | 349 | 7,089 R | 57.2% | 40.9% | 1.1% |
| 15,185 | CALHOUN | 6,373 | 3,216 | 3,063 | 60 | 34 | 153 R | 50.5% | 48.1% | 0.9% |
| 309,969 | CHARLESTON | 111,476 | 58,229 | 49,520 | 2,631 | 1,096 | 8,709 R | 52.2% | 44.4% | 2.4% |
| 52,537 | CHEROKEE | 16,323 | 9,900 | 6,138 | 144 | 141 | 3,762 R | 60.7% | 37.6% | 0.9% |
| 34,068 | CHESTER | 10,432 | 4,986 | 5,242 | 98 | 106 | 256 D | 47.8% | 50.2% | 0.9% |
| 42,768 | CHESTERFIELD | 12,526 | 6,266 | 6,111 | 105 | 44 | 155 R | 50.0% | 48.8% | 0.8% |
| 32,502 | CLARENDON | 11,290 | 5,186 | 5,999 | 64 | 41 | 813 D | 45.9% | 53.1% | 0.6% |
| 38,264 | COLLETON | 13,390 | 6,767 | 6,449 | 104 | 70 | 318 R | 50.5% | 48.2% | 0.8% |
| 67,394 | DARLINGTON | 21,863 | 11,290 | 10,253 | 166 | 154 | 1,037 R | 51.6% | 46.9% | 0.8% |
| 30,722 | DILLON | 8,990 | 3,975 | 4,930 | 46 | 39 | 955 D | 44.2% | 54.8% | 0.5% |
| 96,413 | DORCHESTER | 33,641 | 20,734 | 12,168 | 476 | 263 | 8,566 R | 61.6% | 36.2% | 1.4% |
| 24,595 | EDGEFIELD | 8,834 | 4,760 | 3,950 | 65 | 59 | 810 R | 53.9% | 44.7% | 0.7% |
| 23,454 | FAIRFIELD | 8,398 | 3,011 | 5,263 | 70 | 54 | 2,252 D | 35.9% | 62.7% | 0.8% |
| 125,761 | FLORENCE | 41,437 | 23,678 | 17,157 | 394 | 208 | 6,521 R | 57.1% | 41.4% | 1.0% |
| 55,797 | GEORGETOWN | 20,351 | 10,535 | 9,445 | 270 | 101 | 1,090 R | 51.8% | 46.4% | 1.3% |
| 379,616 | GREENVILLE | 140,293 | 92,714 | 43,810 | 2,388 | 1,381 | 48,904 R | 66.1% | 31.2% | 1.7% |
| 66,271 | GREENWOOD | 20,860 | 12,193 | 8,139 | 263 | 265 | 4,054 R | 58.5% | 39.0% | 1.3% |
| 21,386 | HAMPTON | 7,759 | 2,798 | 4,896 | 39 | 26 | 2,098 D | 36.1% | 63.1% | 0.5% |
| 196,629 | HORRY | 71,265 | 40,300 | 29,113 | 1,405 | 447 | 11,187 R | 56.5% | 40.9% | 2.0% |
| 20,678 | JASPER | 6,469 | 2,414 | 3,646 | 134 | 275 | 1,232 D | 37.3% | 56.4% | 2.1% |
| 52,647 | KERSHAW | 19,677 | 11,911 | 7,428 | 211 | 127 | 4,483 R | 60.5% | 37.7% | 1.1% |
| 61,351 | LANCASTER | 20,705 | 11,676 | 8,782 | 161 | 86 | 2,894 R | 56.4% | 42.4% | 0.8% |
| 69,567 | LAURENS | 20,410 | 12,102 | 7,920 | 213 | 175 | 4,182 R | 59.3% | 38.8% | 1.0% |
| 20,119 | LEE | 6,642 | 2,675 | 3,899 | 32 | 36 | 1,224 D | 40.3% | 58.7% | 0.5% |
| 216,014 | LEXINGTON | 83,081 | 58,095 | 22,830 | 1,444 | 712 | 35,265 R | 69.9% | 27.5% | 1.7% |
| 9,958 | MCCORMICK | 3,661 | 1,704 | 1,896 | 38 | 23 | 192 D | 46.5% | 51.8% | 1.0% |
| 35,466 | MARION | 12,149 | 4,687 | 7,358 | 53 | 51 | 2,671 D | 38.6% | 60.6% | 0.4% |
| 28,818 | MARLBORO | 7,883 | 2,699 | 5,060 | 52 | 72 | 2,361 D | 34.2% | 64.2% | 0.7% |
| 36,108 | NEWBERRY | 12,372 | 7,492 | 4,428 | 210 | 242 | 3,064 R | 60.6% | 35.8% | 1.7% |
| 66,215 | OCONEE | 23,575 | 15,364 | 7,571 | 451 | 189 | 7,793 R | 65.2% | 32.1% | 1.9% |
| 91,582 | ORANGEBURG | 32,734 | 12,657 | 19,802 | 170 | 105 | 7,145 D | 38.7% | 60.5% | 0.5% |
| 110,757 | PICKENS | 34,582 | 24,681 | 8,927 | 606 | 368 | 15,754 R | 71.4% | 25.8% | 1.8% |
| 320,677 | RICHLAND | 115,421 | 49,675 | 62,701 | 2,277 | 768 | 13,026 D | 43.0% | 54.3% | 2.0% |
| 19,181 | SALUDA | 6,891 | 4,098 | 2,682 | 56 | 55 | 1,416 R | 59.5% | 38.9% | 0.8% |
| 253,791 | SPARTANBURG | 83,553 | 52,114 | 29,559 | 1,150 | 730 | 22,555 R | 62.4% | 35.4% | 1.4% |
| 104,646 | SUMTER | 30,672 | 15,915 | 14,365 | 270 | 122 | 1,550 R | 51.9% | 46.8% | 0.9% |
| 29,881 | UNION | 10,589 | 5,768 | 4,662 | 90 | 69 | 1,106 R | 54.5% | 44.0% | 0.8% |
| 37,217 | WILLIAMSBURG | 11,331 | 4,524 | 6,723 | 46 | 38 | 2,199 D | 39.9% | 59.3% | 0.4% |
| 164,614 | YORK | 54,351 | 33,776 | 19,251 | 840 | 484 | 14,525 R | 62.1% | 35.4% | 1.5% |
| 4,012,012 | TOTAL | 1,382,717 | 785,937 | 565,561 | 20,200 | 11,019 | 220,376 R | 56.8% | 40.9% | 1.5% |

# SOUTH CAROLINA

## PRESIDENT 1996

| 1995 Census Pop. Est. | County | Total Vote | Republican | Democratic | Reform (Perot) | Other | Rep.-Dem. Plurality | Percentage of Total Vote | | |
|---|---|---|---|---|---|---|---|---|---|---|
| | | | | | | | | Rep. | Dem. | Reform |
| 24,258 | ABBEVILLE | 7,100 | 3,054 | 3,493 | 537 | 16 | 439 D | 43.0% | 49.2% | 7.6% |
| 133,059 | AIKEN | 43,074 | 26,539 | 14,314 | 1,984 | 237 | 12,225 R | 61.6% | 33.2% | 4.6% |
| 11,580 | ALLENDALE | 3,273 | 941 | 2,222 | 87 | 23 | 1,281 D | 28.8% | 67.9% | 2.7% |
| 154,478 | ANDERSON | 45,769 | 24,137 | 17,460 | 3,896 | 276 | 6,677 R | 52.7% | 38.1% | 8.5% |
| 16,698 | BAMBERG | 5,312 | 1,715 | 3,380 | 192 | 25 | 1,665 D | 32.3% | 63.6% | 3.6% |
| 21,478 | BARNWELL | 7,774 | 3,808 | 3,620 | 310 | 36 | 188 R | 49.0% | 46.6% | 4.0% |
| 99,841 | BEAUFORT | 35,394 | 17,575 | 15,764 | 1,838 | 217 | 1,811 R | 49.7% | 44.5% | 5.2% |
| 135,337 | BERKELEY | 33,242 | 17,691 | 13,358 | 1,922 | 271 | 4,333 R | 53.2% | 40.2% | 5.8% |
| 13,369 | CALHOUN | 5,598 | 2,520 | 2,716 | 316 | 46 | 196 D | 45.0% | 48.5% | 5.6% |
| 281,983 | CHARLESTON | 96,688 | 48,675 | 43,571 | 3,514 | 928 | 5,104 R | 50.3% | 45.1% | 3.6% |
| 47,184 | CHEROKEE | 13,639 | 6,689 | 5,821 | 1,064 | 65 | 868 R | 49.0% | 42.7% | 7.8% |
| 33,050 | CHESTER | 9,072 | 3,157 | 5,108 | 758 | 49 | 1,951 D | 34.8% | 56.3% | 8.4% |
| 39,365 | CHESTERFIELD | 10,569 | 4,028 | 5,734 | 768 | 39 | 1,706 D | 38.1% | 54.3% | 7.3% |
| 29,415 | CLARENDON | 10,198 | 3,841 | 5,930 | 395 | 32 | 2,089 D | 37.7% | 58.1% | 3.9% |
| 36,738 | COLLETON | 10,401 | 4,462 | 5,329 | 550 | 60 | 867 D | 42.9% | 51.2% | 5.3% |
| 64,997 | DARLINGTON | 18,194 | 8,220 | 8,943 | 898 | 133 | 723 D | 45.2% | 49.2% | 4.9% |
| 29,759 | DILLON | 7,061 | 2,774 | 3,992 | 275 | 20 | 1,218 D | 39.3% | 56.5% | 3.9% |
| 89,100 | DORCHESTER | 26,987 | 15,283 | 9,931 | 1,591 | 182 | 5,352 R | 56.6% | 36.8% | 5.9% |
| 19,341 | EDGEFIELD | 7,486 | 3,640 | 3,576 | 244 | 26 | 64 R | 48.6% | 47.8% | 3.3% |
| 22,504 | FAIRFIELD | 7,476 | 2,414 | 4,719 | 284 | 59 | 2,305 D | 32.3% | 63.1% | 3.8% |
| 122,769 | FLORENCE | 36,070 | 18,490 | 15,804 | 1,563 | 213 | 2,686 R | 51.3% | 43.8% | 4.3% |
| 50,890 | GEORGETOWN | 16,352 | 7,023 | 8,298 | 950 | 81 | 1,275 D | 42.9% | 50.7% | 5.8% |
| 339,908 | GREENVILLE | 120,420 | 71,210 | 41,605 | 6,761 | 844 | 29,605 R | 59.1% | 34.5% | 5.6% |
| 61,954 | GREENWOOD | 18,163 | 8,865 | 8,193 | 985 | 120 | 672 R | 48.8% | 45.1% | 5.4% |
| 19,120 | HAMPTON | 7,317 | 2,111 | 4,828 | 344 | 34 | 2,717 D | 28.9% | 66.0% | 4.7% |
| 157,902 | HORRY | 54,653 | 26,159 | 23,722 | 4,446 | 326 | 2,437 R | 47.9% | 43.4% | 8.1% |
| 16,404 | JASPER | 6,468 | 2,024 | 4,053 | 348 | 43 | 2,029 D | 31.3% | 62.7% | 5.4% |
| 46,768 | KERSHAW | 16,354 | 8,513 | 6,764 | 996 | 81 | 1,749 R | 52.1% | 41.4% | 6.1% |
| 56,325 | LANCASTER | 17,957 | 7,544 | 8,752 | 1,598 | 63 | 1,208 D | 42.0% | 48.7% | 8.9% |
| 60,804 | LAURENS | 16,547 | 8,057 | 7,055 | 1,341 | 94 | 1,002 R | 48.7% | 42.6% | 8.1% |
| 18,672 | LEE | 5,908 | 1,973 | 3,588 | 320 | 27 | 1,615 D | 33.4% | 60.7% | 5.4% |
| 191,879 | LEXINGTON | 62,720 | 39,658 | 18,907 | 3,703 | 452 | 20,751 R | 63.2% | 30.1% | 5.9% |
| 9,224 | MCCORMICK | 3,123 | 1,104 | 1,858 | 148 | 13 | 754 D | 35.4% | 59.5% | 4.7% |
| 35,203 | MARION | 10,451 | 3,595 | 6,359 | 356 | 141 | 2,764 D | 34.4% | 60.8% | 3.4% |
| 29,963 | MARLBORO | 8,027 | 2,148 | 5,348 | 494 | 37 | 3,200 D | 26.8% | 66.6% | 6.2% |
| 34,215 | NEWBERRY | 11,232 | 5,670 | 4,804 | 682 | 76 | 866 R | 50.5% | 42.8% | 6.1% |
| 61,605 | OCONEE | 19,952 | 10,503 | 7,398 | 1,961 | 90 | 3,105 R | 52.6% | 37.1% | 9.8% |
| 87,719 | ORANGEBURG | 30,315 | 10,494 | 18,610 | 1,112 | 99 | 8,116 D | 34.6% | 61.4% | 3.7% |
| 102,407 | PICKENS | 27,900 | 17,151 | 8,369 | 2,211 | 169 | 8,782 R | 61.5% | 30.0% | 7.9% |
| 289,839 | RICHLAND | 95,230 | 39,092 | 52,222 | 3,158 | 758 | 13,130 D | 41.1% | 54.8% | 3.3% |
| 16,903 | SALUDA | 5,700 | 2,825 | 2,486 | 371 | 18 | 339 R | 49.6% | 43.6% | 6.5% |
| 240,329 | SPARTANBURG | 67,196 | 35,972 | 26,814 | 3,885 | 525 | 9,158 R | 53.5% | 39.9% | 5.8% |
| 106,823 | SUMTER | 25,392 | 12,080 | 12,198 | 933 | 181 | 118 D | 47.6% | 48.0% | 3.7% |
| 30,836 | UNION | 10,055 | 3,855 | 5,407 | 749 | 44 | 1,552 D | 38.3% | 53.8% | 7.4% |
| 37,467 | WILLIAMSBURG | 11,357 | 3,957 | 6,987 | 375 | 38 | 3,030 D | 34.8% | 61.5% | 3.3% |
| 143,825 | YORK | 42,523 | 22,222 | 16,873 | 3,173 | 255 | 5,349 R | 52.3% | 39.7% | 7.5% |
| 3,673,287 | TOTAL | 1,151,689 | 573,458 | 506,283 | 64,386 | 7,562 | 67,175 R | 49.8% | 44.0% | 5.6% |

# SOUTH CAROLINA

## PRESIDENT 1992

| 1990 Census Population | County | Total Vote | Republican | Democratic | Perot | Other | Plurality | Percentage Total Vote | | |
|---|---|---|---|---|---|---|---|---|---|---|
| | | | | | | | | Rep. | Dem. | Perot |
| 23,862 | ABBEVILLE | 8,343 | 3,317 | 3,968 | 1,036 | 22 | 651 D | 39.8% | 47.6% | 12.4% |
| 120,940 | AIKEN | 46,778 | 25,731 | 14,802 | 6,056 | 189 | 10,929 R | 55.0% | 31.6% | 12.9% |
| 11,722 | ALLENDALE | 3,455 | 1,049 | 2,159 | 212 | 35 | 1,110 D | 30.4% | 62.5% | 6.1% |
| 145,196 | ANDERSON | 47,971 | 24,793 | 16,072 | 6,966 | 140 | 8,721 R | 51.7% | 33.5% | 14.5% |
| 16,902 | BAMBERG | 5,727 | 1,906 | 3,426 | 360 | 35 | 1,520 D | 33.3% | 59.8% | 6.3% |
| 20,293 | BARNWELL | 8,177 | 4,026 | 3,344 | 752 | 55 | 682 R | 49.2% | 40.9% | 9.2% |
| 86,425 | BEAUFORT | 31,287 | 14,735 | 11,466 | 4,966 | 120 | 3,269 R | 47.1% | 36.6% | 15.9% |
| 128,776 | BERKELEY | 35,479 | 18,048 | 12,533 | 4,632 | 266 | 5,515 R | 50.9% | 35.3% | 13.1% |
| 12,753 | CALHOUN | 5,778 | 2,418 | 2,770 | 564 | 26 | 352 D | 41.8% | 47.9% | 9.8% |
| 295,039 | CHARLESTON | 98,749 | 47,403 | 40,095 | 10,354 | 897 | 7,308 R | 48.0% | 40.6% | 10.5% |
| 44,506 | CHEROKEE | 14,557 | 6,887 | 5,453 | 2,186 | 31 | 1,434 R | 47.3% | 37.5% | 15.0% |
| 32,170 | CHESTER | 10,288 | 3,451 | 5,458 | 1,350 | 29 | 2,007 D | 33.5% | 53.1% | 13.1% |
| 38,577 | CHESTERFIELD | 11,212 | 4,183 | 5,691 | 1,315 | 23 | 1,508 D | 37.3% | 50.8% | 11.7% |
| 28,450 | CLARENDON | 10,945 | 4,147 | 6,033 | 744 | 21 | 1,886 D | 37.9% | 55.1% | 6.8% |
| 34,377 | COLLETON | 11,314 | 4,545 | 5,455 | 1,245 | 69 | 910 D | 40.2% | 48.2% | 11.0% |
| 61,851 | DARLINGTON | 20,253 | 8,912 | 9,090 | 1,863 | 388 | 178 D | 44.0% | 44.9% | 9.2% |
| 29,114 | DILLON | 9,390 | 3,575 | 4,953 | 831 | 31 | 1,378 D | 38.1% | 52.7% | 8.8% |
| 83,060 | DORCHESTER | 28,029 | 15,004 | 9,160 | 3,648 | 217 | 5,844 R | 53.5% | 32.7% | 13.0% |
| 18,375 | EDGEFIELD | 7,396 | 3,339 | 3,433 | 596 | 28 | 94 D | 45.1% | 46.4% | 8.1% |
| 22,295 | FAIRFIELD | 8,091 | 2,518 | 4,867 | 652 | 54 | 2,349 D | 31.1% | 60.2% | 8.1% |
| 114,344 | FLORENCE | 39,003 | 19,802 | 15,569 | 3,499 | 133 | 4,233 R | 50.8% | 39.9% | 9.0% |
| 46,302 | GEORGETOWN | 16,272 | 6,870 | 7,494 | 1,840 | 68 | 624 D | 42.2% | 46.1% | 11.3% |
| 320,167 | GREENVILLE | 113,907 | 65,066 | 34,651 | 13,699 | 491 | 30,415 R | 57.1% | 30.4% | 12.0% |
| 59,567 | GREENWOOD | 18,923 | 9,079 | 7,621 | 2,101 | 122 | 1,458 R | 48.0% | 40.3% | 11.1% |
| 18,191 | HAMPTON | 7,361 | 2,402 | 4,332 | 564 | 63 | 1,930 D | 32.6% | 58.9% | 7.7% |
| 144,053 | HORRY | 51,204 | 23,489 | 18,896 | 8,472 | 347 | 4,593 R | 45.9% | 36.9% | 16.5% |
| 15,487 | JASPER | 5,763 | 1,725 | 3,453 | 549 | 36 | 1,728 D | 29.9% | 59.9% | 9.5% |
| 43,599 | KERSHAW | 17,301 | 8,499 | 6,585 | 2,150 | 67 | 1,914 R | 49.1% | 38.1% | 12.4% |
| 54,516 | LANCASTER | 18,655 | 7,757 | 8,307 | 2,563 | 28 | 550 D | 41.6% | 44.5% | 13.7% |
| 58,092 | LAURENS | 17,200 | 8,347 | 6,638 | 2,157 | 58 | 1,709 R | 48.5% | 38.6% | 12.5% |
| 18,437 | LEE | 7,822 | 2,730 | 4,454 | 611 | 27 | 1,724 D | 34.9% | 56.9% | 7.8% |
| 167,611 | LEXINGTON | 69,022 | 41,759 | 18,312 | 8,652 | 299 | 23,447 R | 60.5% | 26.5% | 12.5% |
| 8,868 | MCCORMICK | 3,052 | 899 | 1,846 | 295 | 12 | 947 D | 29.5% | 60.5% | 9.7% |
| 33,899 | MARION | 10,376 | 3,647 | 5,843 | 822 | 64 | 2,196 D | 35.1% | 56.3% | 7.9% |
| 29,361 | MARLBORO | 8,570 | 2,526 | 5,111 | 895 | 38 | 2,585 D | 29.5% | 59.6% | 10.4% |
| 33,172 | NEWBERRY | 12,329 | 5,980 | 4,896 | 1,393 | 60 | 1,084 R | 48.5% | 39.7% | 11.3% |
| 57,494 | OCONEE | 20,479 | 10,379 | 6,617 | 3,405 | 78 | 3,762 R | 50.7% | 32.3% | 16.6% |
| 84,803 | ORANGEBURG | 32,234 | 11,328 | 18,440 | 2,383 | 83 | 7,112 D | 35.1% | 57.2% | 7.4% |
| 93,894 | PICKENS | 29,494 | 17,008 | 8,275 | 4,128 | 83 | 8,733 R | 57.7% | 28.1% | 14.0% |
| 285,720 | RICHLAND | 106,250 | 43,744 | 53,648 | 7,918 | 940 | 9,904 D | 41.2% | 50.5% | 7.5% |
| 16,357 | SALUDA | 6,209 | 2,968 | 2,393 | 833 | 15 | 575 R | 47.8% | 38.5% | 13.4% |
| 226,800 | SPARTANBURG | 72,635 | 37,707 | 25,488 | 8,900 | 540 | 12,219 R | 51.9% | 35.1% | 12.3% |
| 102,637 | SUMTER | 26,596 | 12,576 | 11,852 | 2,062 | 106 | 724 R | 47.3% | 44.6% | 7.8% |
| 30,337 | UNION | 10,680 | 4,647 | 4,644 | 1,371 | 18 | 3 R | 43.5% | 43.5% | 12.8% |
| 36,815 | WILLIAMSBURG | 14,277 | 5,289 | 8,077 | 864 | 47 | 2,788 D | 37.0% | 56.6% | 6.1% |
| 131,497 | YORK | 43,694 | 21,297 | 15,844 | 6,418 | 135 | 5,453 R | 48.7% | 36.3% | 14.7% |
| 3,486,703 | TOTAL | 1,202,527 | 577,507 | 479,514 | 138,872 | 6,634 | 97,993 R | 48.0% | 39.9% | 11.5% |

# SOUTH CAROLINA

## PRESIDENT 1988

| 1980 Census Population | County | Total Vote | Republican | Democratic | Other | Rep.-Dem. Plurality | Total Vote Rep. | Total Vote Dem. | Major Vote Rep. | Major Vote Dem. |
|---|---|---|---|---|---|---|---|---|---|---|
| 22,627 | ABBEVILLE | 7,401 | 3,738 | 3,629 | 34 | 109 R | 50.5% | 49.0% | 50.7% | 49.3% |
| 105,625 | AIKEN | 38,507 | 27,665 | 10,598 | 244 | 17,067 R | 71.8% | 27.5% | 72.3% | 27.7% |
| 10,700 | ALLENDALE | 3,114 | 1,295 | 1,796 | 23 | 501 D | 41.6% | 57.7% | 41.9% | 58.1% |
| 133,235 | ANDERSON | 38,383 | 25,939 | 12,281 | 163 | 13,658 R | 67.6% | 32.0% | 67.9% | 32.1% |
| 18,118 | BAMBERG | 5,255 | 2,403 | 2,830 | 22 | 427 D | 45.7% | 53.9% | 45.9% | 54.1% |
| 19,868 | BARNWELL | 7,075 | 4,467 | 2,564 | 44 | 1,903 R | 63.1% | 36.2% | 63.5% | 36.5% |
| 65,364 | BEAUFORT | 25,021 | 16,184 | 8,691 | 146 | 7,493 R | 64.7% | 34.7% | 65.1% | 34.9% |
| 94,727 | BERKELEY | 26,297 | 16,779 | 9,312 | 206 | 7,467 R | 63.8% | 35.4% | 64.3% | 35.7% |
| 12,206 | CALHOUN | 4,787 | 2,585 | 2,175 | 27 | 410 R | 54.0% | 45.4% | 54.3% | 45.7% |
| 276,974 | CHARLESTON | 82,916 | 49,149 | 32,977 | 790 | 16,172 R | 59.3% | 39.8% | 59.8% | 40.2% |
| 40,983 | CHEROKEE | 12,151 | 7,763 | 4,322 | 66 | 3,441 R | 63.9% | 35.6% | 64.2% | 35.8% |
| 30,148 | CHESTER | 7,748 | 3,968 | 3,737 | 43 | 231 R | 51.2% | 48.2% | 51.5% | 48.5% |
| 38,161 | CHESTERFIELD | 9,735 | 4,999 | 4,699 | 37 | 300 R | 51.4% | 48.3% | 51.5% | 48.5% |
| 27,464 | CLARENDON | 9,397 | 4,337 | 5,030 | 30 | 693 D | 46.2% | 53.5% | 46.3% | 53.7% |
| 31,776 | COLLETON | 9,547 | 4,962 | 4,508 | 77 | 454 R | 52.0% | 47.2% | 52.4% | 47.6% |
| 62,717 | DARLINGTON | 17,843 | 9,854 | 7,625 | 364 | 2,229 R | 55.2% | 42.7% | 56.4% | 43.6% |
| 31,083 | DILLON | 7,069 | 3,793 | 3,251 | 25 | 542 R | 53.7% | 46.0% | 53.8% | 46.2% |
| 58,761 | DORCHESTER | 22,232 | 14,756 | 7,371 | 105 | 7,385 R | 66.4% | 33.2% | 66.7% | 33.3% |
| 17,528 | EDGEFIELD | 6,863 | 3,814 | 3,020 | 29 | 794 R | 55.6% | 44.0% | 55.8% | 44.2% |
| 20,700 | FAIRFIELD | 6,583 | 2,714 | 3,827 | 42 | 1,113 D | 41.2% | 58.1% | 41.5% | 58.5% |
| 110,163 | FLORENCE | 32,214 | 19,490 | 12,531 | 193 | 6,959 R | 60.5% | 38.9% | 60.9% | 39.1% |
| 42,461 | GEORGETOWN | 12,506 | 7,032 | 5,402 | 72 | 1,630 R | 56.2% | 43.2% | 56.6% | 43.4% |
| 287,913 | GREENVILLE | 95,126 | 67,371 | 27,188 | 567 | 40,183 R | 70.8% | 28.6% | 71.2% | 28.8% |
| 57,847 | GREENWOOD | 15,704 | 9,096 | 6,511 | 97 | 2,585 R | 57.9% | 41.5% | 58.3% | 41.7% |
| 18,159 | HAMPTON | 6,306 | 2,826 | 3,435 | 45 | 609 D | 44.8% | 54.5% | 45.1% | 54.9% |
| 101,419 | HORRY | 38,409 | 24,843 | 13,316 | 250 | 11,527 R | 64.7% | 34.7% | 65.1% | 34.9% |
| 14,504 | JASPER | 4,929 | 2,004 | 2,894 | 31 | 890 D | 40.7% | 58.7% | 40.9% | 59.1% |
| 39,015 | KERSHAW | 13,473 | 8,877 | 4,494 | 102 | 4,383 R | 65.9% | 33.4% | 66.4% | 33.6% |
| 53,361 | LANCASTER | 15,393 | 9,152 | 6,181 | 60 | 2,971 R | 59.5% | 40.2% | 59.7% | 40.3% |
| 52,214 | LAURENS | 15,702 | 9,731 | 5,930 | 41 | 3,801 R | 62.0% | 37.8% | 62.1% | 37.9% |
| 18,929 | LEE | 6,359 | 2,936 | 3,423 | | 487 D | 46.2% | 53.8% | 46.2% | 53.8% |
| 140,353 | LEXINGTON | 53,238 | 41,467 | 11,366 | 405 | 30,101 R | 77.9% | 21.3% | 78.5% | 21.5% |
| 7,797 | MCCORMICK | 2,914 | 1,172 | 1,722 | 20 | 550 D | 40.2% | 59.1% | 40.5% | 59.5% |
| 34,179 | MARION | 9,486 | 4,403 | 5,008 | 75 | 605 D | 46.4% | 52.8% | 46.8% | 53.2% |
| 31,634 | MARLBORO | 6,870 | 2,921 | 3,937 | 12 | 1,016 D | 42.5% | 57.3% | 42.6% | 57.4% |
| 31,242 | NEWBERRY | 10,305 | 6,427 | 3,825 | 53 | 2,602 R | 62.4% | 37.1% | 62.7% | 37.3% |
| 48,611 | OCONEE | 14,585 | 10,184 | 4,299 | 102 | 5,885 R | 69.8% | 29.5% | 70.3% | 29.7% |
| 82,276 | ORANGEBURG | 28,049 | 13,281 | 14,655 | 113 | 1,374 D | 47.3% | 52.2% | 47.5% | 52.5% |
| 79,292 | PICKENS | 23,696 | 17,448 | 6,103 | 145 | 11,345 R | 73.6% | 25.8% | 74.1% | 25.9% |
| 269,735 | RICHLAND | 83,123 | 43,841 | 36,420 | 2,862 | 7,421 R | 52.7% | 43.8% | 54.6% | 45.4% |
| 16,150 | SALUDA | 5,232 | 3,225 | 1,984 | 23 | 1,241 R | 61.6% | 37.9% | 61.9% | 38.1% |
| 201,861 | SPARTANBURG | 64,568 | 40,801 | 22,964 | 803 | 17,837 R | 63.2% | 35.6% | 64.0% | 36.0% |
| 88,243 | SUMTER | 22,801 | 13,161 | 9,502 | 138 | 3,659 R | 57.7% | 41.7% | 58.1% | 41.9% |
| 30,751 | UNION | 10,465 | 6,019 | 4,420 | 26 | 1,599 R | 57.5% | 42.2% | 57.7% | 42.3% |
| 38,226 | WILLIAMSBURG | 13,324 | 5,914 | 7,343 | 67 | 1,429 D | 44.4% | 55.1% | 44.6% | 55.4% |
| 106,720 | YORK | 33,308 | 21,657 | 11,458 | 193 | 10,199 R | 65.0% | 34.4% | 65.4% | 34.6% |
| 3,121,820 | TOTAL | 986,009 | 606,443 | 370,554 | 9,012 | 235,889 R | 61.5% | 37.6% | 62.1% | 37.9% |

826

# SOUTH CAROLINA

## PRESIDENT 1984

| 1980 Census Population | County | Total Vote | Republican | Democratic | Other | Rep.-Dem. Plurality | | Percentage Total Vote Rep. | Dem. | Major Vote Rep. | Dem. |
|---|---|---|---|---|---|---|---|---|---|---|---|
| 22,627 | ABBEVILLE | 6,875 | 3,798 | 3,051 | 26 | 747 | R | 55.2% | 44.4% | 55.5% | 44.5% |
| 105,625 | AIKEN | 36,133 | 25,872 | 9,892 | 369 | 15,980 | R | 71.6% | 27.4% | 72.3% | 27.7% |
| 10,700 | ALLENDALE | 3,769 | 1,570 | 2,170 | 29 | 600 | D | 41.7% | 57.6% | 42.0% | 58.0% |
| 133,235 | ANDERSON | 34,691 | 24,123 | 10,324 | 244 | 13,799 | R | 69.5% | 29.8% | 70.0% | 30.0% |
| 18,118 | BAMBERG | 5,831 | 2,908 | 2,892 | 31 | 16 | R | 49.9% | 49.6% | 50.1% | 49.9% |
| 19,868 | BARNWELL | 7,189 | 4,346 | 2,811 | 32 | 1,535 | R | 60.5% | 39.1% | 60.7% | 39.3% |
| 65,364 | BEAUFORT | 21,118 | 13,668 | 7,347 | 103 | 6,321 | R | 64.7% | 34.8% | 65.0% | 35.0% |
| 94,727 | BERKELEY | 24,511 | 16,972 | 7,380 | 159 | 9,592 | R | 69.2% | 30.1% | 69.7% | 30.3% |
| 12,206 | CALHOUN | 5,094 | 2,742 | 2,315 | 37 | 427 | R | 53.8% | 45.4% | 54.2% | 45.8% |
| 276,974 | CHARLESTON | 84,249 | 53,779 | 29,470 | 1,000 | 24,309 | R | 63.8% | 35.0% | 64.6% | 35.4% |
| 40,983 | CHEROKEE | 12,809 | 8,655 | 4,101 | 53 | 4,554 | R | 67.6% | 32.0% | 67.9% | 32.1% |
| 30,148 | CHESTER | 8,045 | 4,441 | 3,559 | 45 | 882 | R | 55.2% | 44.2% | 55.5% | 44.5% |
| 38,161 | CHESTERFIELD | 10,067 | 5,451 | 4,593 | 23 | 858 | R | 54.1% | 45.6% | 54.3% | 45.7% |
| 27,464 | CLARENDON | 10,746 | 5,102 | 5,591 | 53 | 489 | D | 47.5% | 52.0% | 47.7% | 52.3% |
| 31,776 | COLLETON | 11,145 | 6,200 | 4,910 | 35 | 1,290 | R | 55.6% | 44.1% | 55.8% | 44.2% |
| 62,717 | DARLINGTON | 18,910 | 11,100 | 7,456 | 354 | 3,644 | R | 58.7% | 39.4% | 59.8% | 40.2% |
| 31,083 | DILLON | 8,050 | 4,646 | 3,360 | 44 | 1,286 | R | 57.7% | 41.7% | 58.0% | 42.0% |
| 58,761 | DORCHESTER | 22,399 | 15,289 | 7,037 | 73 | 8,252 | R | 68.3% | 31.4% | 68.5% | 31.5% |
| 17,528 | EDGEFIELD | 6,478 | 3,224 | 3,227 | 27 | 3 | D | 49.8% | 49.8% | 50.0% | 50.0% |
| 20,700 | FAIRFIELD | 7,287 | 3,147 | 4,117 | 23 | 970 | D | 43.2% | 56.5% | 43.3% | 56.7% |
| 110,163 | FLORENCE | 37,600 | 22,753 | 14,639 | 208 | 8,114 | R | 60.5% | 38.9% | 60.8% | 39.2% |
| 42,461 | GEORGETOWN | 13,830 | 7,370 | 6,392 | 68 | 978 | R | 53.3% | 46.2% | 53.6% | 46.4% |
| 287,913 | GREENVILLE | 91,369 | 66,766 | 24,137 | 466 | 42,629 | R | 73.1% | 26.4% | 73.4% | 26.6% |
| 57,847 | GREENWOOD | 17,307 | 10,887 | 6,339 | 81 | 4,548 | R | 62.9% | 36.6% | 63.2% | 36.8% |
| 18,159 | HAMPTON | 7,228 | 3,464 | 3,736 | 28 | 272 | D | 47.9% | 51.7% | 48.1% | 51.9% |
| 101,419 | HORRY | 29,463 | 20,396 | 8,940 | 127 | 11,456 | R | 69.2% | 30.3% | 69.5% | 30.5% |
| 14,504 | JASPER | 6,879 | 3,102 | 3,753 | 24 | 651 | D | 45.1% | 54.6% | 45.3% | 54.7% |
| 39,015 | KERSHAW | 13,226 | 8,822 | 4,323 | 81 | 4,499 | R | 66.7% | 32.7% | 67.1% | 32.9% |
| 53,361 | LANCASTER | 16,244 | 10,383 | 5,804 | 57 | 4,579 | R | 63.9% | 35.7% | 64.1% | 35.9% |
| 52,214 | LAURENS | 15,086 | 9,729 | 5,312 | 45 | 4,417 | R | 64.5% | 35.2% | 64.7% | 35.3% |
| 18,929 | LEE | 7,500 | 3,548 | 3,912 | 40 | 364 | D | 47.3% | 52.2% | 47.6% | 52.4% |
| 140,353 | LEXINGTON | 47,721 | 38,628 | 8,828 | 265 | 29,800 | R | 80.9% | 18.5% | 81.4% | 18.6% |
| 7,797 | MCCORMICK | 2,726 | 1,186 | 1,526 | 14 | 340 | D | 43.5% | 56.0% | 43.7% | 56.3% |
| 34,179 | MARION | 9,773 | 4,698 | 5,043 | 32 | 345 | D | 48.1% | 51.6% | 48.2% | 51.8% |
| 31,634 | MARLBORO | 8,283 | 3,951 | 4,294 | 38 | 343 | D | 47.7% | 51.8% | 47.9% | 52.1% |
| 31,242 | NEWBERRY | 11,008 | 7,176 | 3,790 | 42 | 3,386 | R | 65.2% | 34.4% | 65.4% | 34.6% |
| 48,611 | OCONEE | 12,044 | 8,625 | 3,333 | 86 | 5,292 | R | 71.6% | 27.7% | 72.1% | 27.9% |
| 82,276 | ORANGEBURG | 29,635 | 14,286 | 15,121 | 228 | 835 | D | 48.2% | 51.0% | 48.6% | 51.4% |
| 79,292 | PICKENS | 19,764 | 15,155 | 4,481 | 128 | 10,674 | R | 76.7% | 22.7% | 77.2% | 22.8% |
| 269,735 | RICHLAND | 81,429 | 46,773 | 32,212 | 2,444 | 14,561 | R | 57.4% | 39.6% | 59.2% | 40.8% |
| 16,150 | SALUDA | 5,501 | 3,515 | 1,962 | 24 | 1,553 | R | 63.9% | 35.7% | 64.2% | 35.8% |
| 201,861 | SPARTANBURG | 62,575 | 41,553 | 20,130 | 892 | 21,423 | R | 66.4% | 32.2% | 67.4% | 32.6% |
| 88,243 | SUMTER | 22,591 | 12,909 | 9,566 | 116 | 3,343 | R | 57.1% | 42.3% | 57.4% | 42.6% |
| 30,751 | UNION | 10,796 | 6,331 | 4,424 | 41 | 1,907 | R | 58.6% | 41.0% | 58.9% | 41.1% |
| 38,226 | WILLIAMSBURG | 14,128 | 6,492 | 7,586 | 50 | 1,094 | D | 46.0% | 53.7% | 46.1% | 53.9% |
| 106,720 | YORK | 29,427 | 20,008 | 9,273 | 146 | 10,735 | R | 68.0% | 31.5% | 68.3% | 31.7% |
| 3,121,820 | TOTAL | 968,529 | 615,539 | 344,459 | 8,531 | 271,080 | R | 63.6% | 35.6% | 64.1% | 35.9% |

# SOUTH CAROLINA

## PRESIDENT 1980

| 1980 Census Population | County | Total Vote | Republican | Democratic | Other | Rep.-Dem. Plurality | Percentage | | | |
|---|---|---|---|---|---|---|---|---|---|---|
| | | | | | | | Total Vote | | Major Vote | |
| | | | | | | | Rep. | Dem. | Rep. | Dem. |
| 22,627 | ABBEVILLE | 6,530 | 2,261 | 4,049 | 220 | 1,788 D | 34.6% | 62.0% | 35.8% | 64.2% |
| 105,625 | AIKEN | 32,369 | 18,570 | 13,014 | 785 | 5,556 R | 57.4% | 40.2% | 58.8% | 41.2% |
| 10,700 | ALLENDALE | 3,991 | 1,184 | 2,775 | 32 | 1,591 D | 29.7% | 69.5% | 29.9% | 70.1% |
| 133,235 | ANDERSON | 35,300 | 15,667 | 18,801 | 832 | 3,134 D | 44.4% | 53.3% | 45.5% | 54.5% |
| 18,118 | BAMBERG | 5,422 | 2,099 | 3,294 | 29 | 1,195 D | 38.7% | 60.8% | 38.9% | 61.1% |
| 19,868 | BARNWELL | 6,705 | 3,228 | 3,399 | 78 | 171 D | 48.1% | 50.7% | 48.7% | 51.3% |
| 65,364 | BEAUFORT | 16,684 | 8,620 | 7,415 | 649 | 1,205 R | 51.7% | 44.4% | 53.8% | 46.2% |
| 94,727 | BERKELEY | 23,024 | 12,790 | 9,850 | 384 | 2,940 R | 55.6% | 42.8% | 56.5% | 43.5% |
| 12,206 | CALHOUN | 3,850 | 1,767 | 2,044 | 39 | 277 D | 45.9% | 53.1% | 46.4% | 53.6% |
| 276,974 | CHARLESTON | 81,260 | 44,833 | 33,057 | 3,370 | 11,776 R | 55.2% | 40.7% | 57.6% | 42.4% |
| 40,983 | CHEROKEE | 12,437 | 5,392 | 6,894 | 151 | 1,502 D | 43.4% | 55.4% | 43.9% | 56.1% |
| 30,148 | CHESTER | 8,363 | 3,104 | 5,145 | 114 | 2,041 D | 37.1% | 61.5% | 37.6% | 62.4% |
| 38,161 | CHESTERFIELD | 9,973 | 3,479 | 6,393 | 101 | 2,914 D | 34.9% | 64.1% | 35.2% | 64.8% |
| 27,464 | CLARENDON | 10,203 | 4,162 | 5,983 | 58 | 1,821 D | 40.8% | 58.6% | 41.0% | 59.0% |
| 31,776 | COLLETON | 10,543 | 4,719 | 5,745 | 79 | 1,026 D | 44.8% | 54.5% | 45.1% | 54.9% |
| 62,717 | DARLINGTON | 17,650 | 8,290 | 9,011 | 349 | 721 D | 47.0% | 51.1% | 47.9% | 52.1% |
| 31,083 | DILLON | 7,998 | 3,385 | 4,520 | 93 | 1,135 D | 42.3% | 56.5% | 42.8% | 57.2% |
| 58,761 | DORCHESTER | 18,298 | 10,893 | 7,237 | 168 | 3,656 R | 59.5% | 39.6% | 60.1% | 39.9% |
| 17,528 | EDGEFIELD | 5,945 | 2,422 | 3,464 | 59 | 1,042 D | 40.7% | 58.3% | 41.1% | 58.9% |
| 20,700 | FAIRFIELD | 6,323 | 2,098 | 4,153 | 72 | 2,055 D | 33.2% | 65.7% | 33.6% | 66.4% |
| 110,163 | FLORENCE | 33,992 | 17,069 | 16,391 | 532 | 678 R | 50.2% | 48.2% | 51.0% | 49.0% |
| 42,461 | GEORGETOWN | 12,041 | 5,151 | 6,701 | 189 | 1,550 D | 42.8% | 55.7% | 43.5% | 56.5% |
| 287,913 | GREENVILLE | 80,415 | 46,168 | 32,135 | 2,112 | 14,033 R | 57.4% | 40.0% | 59.0% | 41.0% |
| 57,847 | GREENWOOD | 16,886 | 7,291 | 9,285 | 310 | 1,994 D | 43.2% | 55.0% | 44.0% | 56.0% |
| 18,159 | HAMPTON | 6,612 | 2,220 | 4,332 | 60 | 2,112 D | 33.6% | 65.5% | 33.9% | 66.1% |
| 101,419 | HORRY | 28,871 | 14,331 | 13,897 | 643 | 434 R | 49.6% | 48.1% | 50.8% | 49.2% |
| 14,504 | JASPER | 4,977 | 1,618 | 3,316 | 43 | 1,698 D | 32.5% | 66.6% | 32.8% | 67.2% |
| 39,015 | KERSHAW | 11,970 | 6,652 | 5,103 | 215 | 1,549 R | 55.6% | 42.6% | 56.6% | 43.4% |
| 53,361 | LANCASTER | 15,166 | 6,410 | 8,283 | 473 | 1,873 D | 42.3% | 54.6% | 43.6% | 56.4% |
| 52,214 | LAURENS | 14,100 | 6,041 | 7,862 | 197 | 1,821 D | 42.8% | 55.8% | 43.5% | 56.5% |
| 18,929 | LEE | 7,795 | 2,952 | 4,816 | 27 | 1,864 D | 37.9% | 61.8% | 38.0% | 62.0% |
| 140,353 | LEXINGTON | 41,711 | 28,313 | 12,334 | 1,064 | 15,979 R | 67.9% | 29.6% | 69.7% | 30.3% |
| 7,797 | MCCORMICK | 2,610 | 800 | 1,775 | 35 | 975 D | 30.7% | 68.0% | 31.1% | 68.9% |
| 34,179 | MARION | 8,816 | 3,323 | 5,389 | 104 | 2,066 D | 37.7% | 61.1% | 38.1% | 61.9% |
| 31,634 | MARLBORO | 8,040 | 2,585 | 5,378 | 77 | 2,793 D | 32.2% | 66.9% | 32.5% | 67.5% |
| 31,242 | NEWBERRY | 10,508 | 5,568 | 4,825 | 115 | 743 R | 53.0% | 45.9% | 53.6% | 46.4% |
| 48,611 | OCONEE | 13,588 | 5,652 | 7,678 | 258 | 2,026 D | 41.6% | 56.5% | 42.4% | 57.6% |
| 82,276 | ORANGEBURG | 27,733 | 11,313 | 16,178 | 242 | 4,865 D | 40.8% | 58.3% | 41.2% | 58.8% |
| 79,292 | PICKENS | 17,919 | 9,575 | 7,789 | 555 | 1,786 R | 53.4% | 43.5% | 55.1% | 44.9% |
| 269,735 | RICHLAND | 73,911 | 36,450 | 33,916 | 3,545 | 2,534 R | 49.3% | 45.9% | 51.8% | 48.2% |
| 16,150 | SALUDA | 5,173 | 2,450 | 2,653 | 70 | 203 D | 47.4% | 51.3% | 48.0% | 52.0% |
| 201,861 | SPARTANBURG | 60,027 | 29,979 | 28,414 | 1,634 | 1,565 R | 49.9% | 47.3% | 51.3% | 48.7% |
| 88,243 | SUMTER | 20,126 | 10,557 | 9,205 | 364 | 1,352 R | 52.5% | 45.7% | 53.4% | 46.6% |
| 30,751 | UNION | 10,450 | 4,035 | 6,274 | 141 | 2,239 D | 38.6% | 60.0% | 39.1% | 60.9% |
| 38,226 | WILLIAMSBURG | 13,347 | 5,110 | 8,138 | 99 | 3,028 D | 38.3% | 61.0% | 38.6% | 61.4% |
| 106,720 | YORK | 24,043 | 11,265 | 12,075 | 703 | 810 D | 46.9% | 50.2% | 48.3% | 51.7% |
| 3,121,820 | TOTAL | 894,071 | 441,841 | 430,385 | 21,845 | 11,456 R | 49.4% | 48.1% | 50.7% | 49.3% |

# SOUTH CAROLINA

## PRESIDENT 1976

| 1970 Census Population | County | Total Vote | Republican | Democratic | Other | Rep.-Dem. Plurality | Percentage Total Vote Rep. | Dem. | Major Vote Rep. | Dem. |
|---|---|---|---|---|---|---|---|---|---|---|
| 21,112 | ABBEVILLE | 6,527 | 1,791 | 4,700 | 36 | 2,909 D | 27.4% | 72.0% | 27.6% | 72.4% |
| 91,023 | AIKEN | 31,173 | 16,011 | 14,927 | 235 | 1,084 R | 51.4% | 47.9% | 51.8% | 48.2% |
| 9,692 | ALLENDALE | 3,709 | 1,064 | 2,634 | 11 | 1,570 D | 28.7% | 71.0% | 28.8% | 71.2% |
| 105,474 | ANDERSON | 28,654 | 9,496 | 19,002 | 156 | 9,506 D | 33.1% | 66.3% | 33.3% | 66.7% |
| 15,950 | BAMBERG | 5,218 | 1,849 | 3,330 | 39 | 1,481 D | 35.4% | 63.8% | 35.7% | 64.3% |
| 17,176 | BARNWELL | 6,652 | 2,569 | 4,083 |  | 1,514 D | 38.6% | 61.4% | 38.6% | 61.4% |
| 51,136 | BEAUFORT | 12,052 | 5,935 | 6,049 | 68 | 114 D | 49.2% | 50.2% | 49.5% | 50.5% |
| 56,199 | BERKELEY | 16,795 | 6,981 | 9,741 | 73 | 2,760 D | 41.6% | 58.0% | 41.7% | 58.3% |
| 10,780 | CALHOUN | 3,468 | 1,382 | 2,055 | 31 | 673 D | 39.9% | 59.3% | 40.2% | 59.8% |
| 247,650 | CHARLESTON | 69,265 | 34,010 | 34,328 | 927 | 318 D | 49.1% | 49.6% | 49.8% | 50.2% |
| 36,791 | CHEROKEE | 11,732 | 3,931 | 7,765 | 36 | 3,834 D | 33.5% | 66.2% | 33.6% | 66.4% |
| 29,811 | CHESTER | 8,212 | 2,982 | 5,200 | 30 | 2,218 D | 36.3% | 63.3% | 36.4% | 63.6% |
| 33,667 | CHESTERFIELD | 10,250 | 2,537 | 7,687 | 26 | 5,150 D | 24.8% | 75.0% | 24.8% | 75.2% |
| 25,604 | CLARENDON | 8,561 | 3,040 | 5,489 | 32 | 2,449 D | 35.5% | 64.1% | 35.6% | 64.4% |
| 27,622 | COLLETON | 8,522 | 3,324 | 5,134 | 64 | 1,810 D | 39.0% | 60.2% | 39.3% | 60.7% |
| 53,442 | DARLINGTON | 16,899 | 6,678 | 10,165 | 56 | 3,487 D | 39.5% | 60.2% | 39.6% | 60.4% |
| 28,838 | DILLON | 7,639 | 2,527 | 5,089 | 23 | 2,562 D | 33.1% | 66.6% | 33.2% | 66.8% |
| 32,421 | DORCHESTER | 14,779 | 6,695 | 8,046 | 38 | 1,351 D | 45.3% | 54.4% | 45.4% | 54.6% |
| 15,692 | EDGEFIELD | 5,144 | 1,878 | 3,216 | 50 | 1,338 D | 36.5% | 62.5% | 36.9% | 63.1% |
| 19,999 | FAIRFIELD | 5,990 | 1,817 | 4,155 | 18 | 2,338 D | 30.3% | 69.4% | 30.4% | 69.6% |
| 89,636 | FLORENCE | 29,938 | 13,539 | 16,294 | 105 | 2,755 D | 45.2% | 54.4% | 45.4% | 54.6% |
| 33,500 | GEORGETOWN | 11,293 | 4,068 | 7,169 | 56 | 3,101 D | 36.0% | 63.5% | 36.2% | 63.8% |
| 240,546 | GREENVILLE | 75,961 | 39,099 | 35,923 | 939 | 3,176 R | 51.5% | 47.3% | 52.1% | 47.9% |
| 49,686 | GREENWOOD | 15,991 | 5,974 | 9,976 | 41 | 4,002 D | 37.4% | 62.4% | 37.5% | 62.5% |
| 15,878 | HAMPTON | 5,725 | 1,773 | 3,923 | 29 | 2,150 D | 31.0% | 68.5% | 31.1% | 68.9% |
| 69,992 | HORRY | 25,117 | 9,339 | 15,720 | 58 | 6,381 D | 37.2% | 62.6% | 37.3% | 62.7% |
| 11,885 | JASPER | 4,140 | 1,221 | 2,903 | 16 | 1,682 D | 29.5% | 70.1% | 29.6% | 70.4% |
| 34,727 | KERSHAW | 12,402 | 6,126 | 6,211 | 65 | 85 D | 49.4% | 50.1% | 49.7% | 50.3% |
| 43,328 | LANCASTER | 13,394 | 4,997 | 8,324 | 73 | 3,327 D | 37.3% | 62.1% | 37.5% | 62.5% |
| 49,713 | LAURENS | 12,831 | 5,300 | 7,440 | 91 | 2,140 D | 41.3% | 58.0% | 41.6% | 58.4% |
| 18,323 | LEE | 6,257 | 2,357 | 3,869 | 31 | 1,512 D | 37.7% | 61.8% | 37.9% | 62.1% |
| 89,012 | LEXINGTON | 36,143 | 21,442 | 14,339 | 362 | 7,103 R | 59.3% | 39.7% | 59.9% | 40.1% |
| 7,955 | MCCORMICK | 2,431 | 640 | 1,774 | 17 | 1,134 D | 26.3% | 73.0% | 26.5% | 73.5% |
| 30,270 | MARION | 9,024 | 3,076 | 5,927 | 21 | 2,851 D | 34.1% | 65.7% | 34.2% | 65.8% |
| 27,151 | MARLBORO | 7,377 | 1,961 | 5,409 | 7 | 3,448 D | 26.6% | 73.3% | 26.6% | 73.4% |
| 29,273 | NEWBERRY | 10,024 | 4,931 | 5,034 | 59 | 103 D | 49.2% | 50.2% | 49.5% | 50.5% |
| 40,728 | OCONEE | 12,333 | 3,805 | 8,447 | 81 | 4,642 D | 30.9% | 68.5% | 31.1% | 68.9% |
| 69,789 | ORANGEBURG | 22,604 | 8,794 | 13,652 | 158 | 4,858 D | 38.9% | 60.4% | 39.2% | 60.8% |
| 58,956 | PICKENS | 16,655 | 8,029 | 8,505 | 121 | 476 D | 48.2% | 51.1% | 48.6% | 51.4% |
| 233,868 | RICHLAND | 70,153 | 32,727 | 36,855 | 571 | 4,128 D | 46.7% | 52.5% | 47.0% | 53.0% |
| 14,528 | SALUDA | 4,853 | 2,085 | 2,715 | 53 | 630 D | 43.0% | 55.9% | 43.4% | 56.6% |
| 173,631 | SPARTANBURG | 48,820 | 20,456 | 27,925 | 439 | 7,469 D | 41.9% | 57.2% | 42.3% | 57.7% |
| 78,885 | SUMTER | 19,949 | 9,332 | 10,471 | 146 | 1,139 D | 46.8% | 52.5% | 47.1% | 52.9% |
| 29,133 | UNION | 9,867 | 3,463 | 6,363 | 41 | 2,900 D | 35.1% | 64.5% | 35.2% | 64.8% |
| 34,203 | WILLIAMSBURG | 14,055 | 5,275 | 8,745 | 35 | 3,470 D | 37.5% | 62.2% | 37.6% | 62.4% |
| 85,216 | YORK | 24,005 | 9,843 | 14,099 | 63 | 4,256 D | 41.0% | 58.7% | 41.1% | 58.9% |
| 2,589,891 | TOTAL | 802,583 | 346,149 | 450,807 | 5,627 | 104,658 D | 43.1% | 56.2% | 43.4% | 56.6% |

# SOUTH CAROLINA

## PRESIDENT 1972

| 1970 Census Population | County | Total Vote | Republican | Democratic | Other | Rep.-Dem. Plurality | Percentage | | | |
|---|---|---|---|---|---|---|---|---|---|---|
| | | | | | | | Total Vote | | Major Vote | |
| | | | | | | | Rep. | Dem. | Rep. | Dem. |
| 21,112 | ABBEVILLE | 4,733 | 3,265 | 1,347 | 121 | 1,918 R | 69.0% | 28.5% | 70.8% | 29.2% |
| 91,023 | AIKEN | 27,407 | 21,117 | 5,745 | 545 | 15,372 R | 77.0% | 21.0% | 78.6% | 21.4% |
| 9,692 | ALLENDALE | 3,141 | 1,740 | 1,383 | 18 | 357 R | 55.4% | 44.0% | 55.7% | 44.3% |
| 105,474 | ANDERSON | 23,292 | 17,514 | 5,241 | 537 | 12,273 R | 75.2% | 22.5% | 77.0% | 23.0% |
| 15,950 | BAMBERG | 4,253 | 2,537 | 1,680 | 36 | 857 R | 59.7% | 39.5% | 60.2% | 39.8% |
| 17,176 | BARNWELL | 5,515 | 3,955 | 1,560 | | 2,395 R | 71.7% | 28.3% | 71.7% | 28.3% |
| 51,136 | BEAUFORT | 9,247 | 5,929 | 3,237 | 81 | 2,692 R | 64.1% | 35.0% | 64.7% | 35.3% |
| 56,199 | BERKELEY | 14,019 | 9,345 | 4,497 | 177 | 4,848 R | 66.7% | 32.1% | 67.5% | 32.5% |
| 10,780 | CALHOUN | 3,069 | 1,867 | 1,148 | 54 | 719 R | 60.8% | 37.4% | 61.9% | 38.1% |
| 247,650 | CHARLESTON | 57,912 | 39,832 | 16,856 | 1,224 | 22,976 R | 68.8% | 29.1% | 70.3% | 29.7% |
| 36,791 | CHEROKEE | 9,800 | 7,570 | 2,107 | 123 | 5,463 R | 77.2% | 21.5% | 78.2% | 21.8% |
| 29,811 | CHESTER | 7,136 | 4,724 | 2,352 | 60 | 2,372 R | 66.2% | 33.0% | 66.8% | 33.2% |
| 33,667 | CHESTERFIELD | 8,229 | 5,230 | 2,938 | 61 | 2,292 R | 63.6% | 35.7% | 64.0% | 36.0% |
| 25,604 | CLARENDON | 7,284 | 3,958 | 3,276 | 50 | 682 R | 54.3% | 45.0% | 54.7% | 45.3% |
| 27,622 | COLLETON | 8,248 | 5,738 | 2,376 | 134 | 3,362 R | 69.6% | 28.8% | 70.7% | 29.3% |
| 53,442 | DARLINGTON | 16,319 | 11,756 | 4,414 | 149 | 7,342 R | 72.0% | 27.0% | 72.7% | 27.3% |
| 28,838 | DILLON | 6,034 | 4,364 | 1,604 | 66 | 2,760 R | 72.3% | 26.6% | 73.1% | 26.9% |
| 32,421 | DORCHESTER | 11,886 | 8,095 | 3,606 | 185 | 4,489 R | 68.1% | 30.3% | 69.2% | 30.8% |
| 15,692 | EDGEFIELD | 4,218 | 2,812 | 1,326 | 80 | 1,486 R | 66.7% | 31.4% | 68.0% | 32.0% |
| 19,999 | FAIRFIELD | 5,146 | 2,608 | 2,491 | 47 | 117 R | 50.7% | 48.4% | 51.1% | 48.9% |
| 89,636 | FLORENCE | 25,723 | 18,107 | 7,451 | 165 | 10,656 R | 70.4% | 29.0% | 70.8% | 29.2% |
| 33,500 | GEORGETOWN | 10,676 | 6,114 | 4,446 | 116 | 1,668 R | 57.3% | 41.6% | 57.9% | 42.1% |
| 240,546 | GREENVILLE | 58,249 | 46,360 | 10,163 | 1,726 | 36,197 R | 79.6% | 17.4% | 82.0% | 18.0% |
| 49,686 | GREENWOOD | 12,975 | 9,370 | 3,400 | 205 | 5,970 R | 72.2% | 26.2% | 73.4% | 26.6% |
| 15,878 | HAMPTON | 5,036 | 2,891 | 2,086 | 59 | 805 R | 57.4% | 41.4% | 58.1% | 41.9% |
| 69,992 | HORRY | 19,944 | 15,324 | 4,437 | 183 | 10,887 R | 76.8% | 22.2% | 77.5% | 22.5% |
| 11,885 | JASPER | 2,884 | 1,650 | 1,203 | 31 | 447 R | 57.2% | 41.7% | 57.8% | 42.2% |
| 34,727 | KERSHAW | 10,744 | 8,035 | 2,531 | 178 | 5,504 R | 74.8% | 23.6% | 76.0% | 24.0% |
| 43,328 | LANCASTER | 11,580 | 9,016 | 2,461 | 103 | 6,555 R | 77.9% | 21.3% | 78.6% | 21.4% |
| 49,713 | LAURENS | 10,933 | 8,141 | 2,650 | 142 | 5,491 R | 74.5% | 24.2% | 75.4% | 24.6% |
| 18,323 | LEE | 5,100 | 3,076 | 1,996 | 28 | 1,080 R | 60.3% | 39.1% | 60.6% | 39.4% |
| 89,012 | LEXINGTON | 29,886 | 25,327 | 4,069 | 490 | 21,258 R | 84.7% | 13.6% | 86.2% | 13.8% |
| 7,955 | MCCORMICK | 2,162 | 1,302 | 844 | 16 | 458 R | 60.2% | 39.0% | 60.7% | 39.3% |
| 30,270 | MARION | 7,310 | 4,719 | 2,545 | 46 | 2,174 R | 64.6% | 34.8% | 65.0% | 35.0% |
| 27,151 | MARLBORO | 5,852 | 3,838 | 1,999 | 15 | 1,839 R | 65.6% | 34.2% | 65.8% | 34.2% |
| 29,273 | NEWBERRY | 9,521 | 7,325 | 2,035 | 161 | 5,290 R | 76.9% | 21.4% | 78.3% | 21.7% |
| 40,728 | OCONEE | 8,728 | 6,825 | 1,739 | 164 | 5,086 R | 78.2% | 19.9% | 79.7% | 20.3% |
| 69,789 | ORANGEBURG | 19,745 | 11,711 | 7,652 | 382 | 4,059 R | 59.3% | 38.8% | 60.5% | 39.5% |
| 58,956 | PICKENS | 14,296 | 11,776 | 2,255 | 265 | 9,521 R | 82.4% | 15.8% | 83.9% | 16.1% |
| 233,868 | RICHLAND | 60,065 | 38,500 | 20,875 | 690 | 17,625 R | 64.1% | 34.8% | 64.8% | 35.2% |
| 14,528 | SALUDA | 4,191 | 3,095 | 1,022 | 74 | 2,073 R | 73.8% | 24.4% | 75.2% | 24.8% |
| 173,631 | SPARTANBURG | 41,572 | 31,187 | 9,723 | 662 | 21,464 R | 75.0% | 23.4% | 76.2% | 23.8% |
| 78,885 | SUMTER | 16,794 | 10,892 | 5,795 | 107 | 5,097 R | 64.9% | 34.5% | 65.3% | 34.7% |
| 29,133 | UNION | 11,065 | 8,337 | 2,676 | 52 | 5,661 R | 75.3% | 24.2% | 75.7% | 24.3% |
| 34,203 | WILLIAMSBURG | 11,015 | 5,729 | 5,213 | 73 | 516 R | 52.0% | 47.3% | 52.4% | 47.6% |
| 85,216 | YORK | 21,026 | 14,441 | 6,374 | 211 | 8,067 R | 68.7% | 30.3% | 69.4% | 30.6% |
| 2,589,891 | TOTAL | 673,960 | 477,044 | 186,824 | 10,092 | 290,220 R | 70.8% | 27.7% | 71.9% | 28.1% |

# SOUTH CAROLINA

## PRESIDENT 1968

| 1960 Census Population | County | Total Vote | Republican | Democratic | AIP | Other | Plurality | Percentage Total Vote | | |
|---|---|---|---|---|---|---|---|---|---|---|
| | | | | | | | | Rep. | Dem. | AIP |
| 21,417 | ABBEVILLE | 5,839 | 1,213 | 1,425 | 3,201 | | 1,776 A | 20.8% | 24.4% | 54.8% |
| 81,038 | AIKEN | 27,398 | 12,264 | 6,319 | 8,815 | | 3,449 R | 44.8% | 23.1% | 32.2% |
| 11,362 | ALLENDALE | 3,355 | 997 | 1,538 | 820 | | 541 D | 29.7% | 45.8% | 24.4% |
| 98,478 | ANDERSON | 23,263 | 5,661 | 5,218 | 12,384 | | 6,723 A | 24.3% | 22.4% | 53.2% |
| 16,274 | BAMBERG | 4,790 | 1,327 | 1,845 | 1,618 | | 227 D | 27.7% | 38.5% | 33.8% |
| 17,659 | BARNWELL | 5,916 | 1,849 | 1,716 | 2,351 | | 502 A | 31.3% | 29.0% | 39.7% |
| 44,187 | BEAUFORT | 8,221 | 2,983 | 3,740 | 1,498 | | 757 D | 36.3% | 45.5% | 18.2% |
| 38,196 | BERKELEY | 13,918 | 4,021 | 5,089 | 4,808 | | 281 D | 28.9% | 36.6% | 34.5% |
| 12,256 | CALHOUN | 3,079 | 885 | 1,216 | 978 | | 238 D | 28.7% | 39.5% | 31.8% |
| 216,382 | CHARLESTON | 55,880 | 24,282 | 18,343 | 13,255 | | 5,939 R | 43.5% | 32.8% | 23.7% |
| 35,205 | CHEROKEE | 10,493 | 2,853 | 1,998 | 5,642 | | 2,789 A | 27.2% | 19.0% | 53.8% |
| 30,888 | CHESTER | 8,489 | 2,862 | 2,865 | 2,762 | | 3 D | 33.7% | 33.7% | 32.5% |
| 33,717 | CHESTERFIELD | 10,068 | 2,564 | 3,180 | 4,324 | | 1,144 A | 25.5% | 31.6% | 42.9% |
| 29,490 | CLARENDON | 7,904 | 2,201 | 3,606 | 2,097 | | 1,405 D | 27.8% | 45.6% | 26.5% |
| 27,816 | COLLETON | 8,145 | 2,824 | 2,651 | 2,670 | | 154 R | 34.7% | 32.5% | 32.8% |
| 52,928 | DARLINGTON | 13,981 | 4,947 | 3,803 | 5,231 | | 284 A | 35.4% | 27.2% | 37.4% |
| 30,584 | DILLON | 6,706 | 2,396 | 2,178 | 2,132 | | 218 R | 35.7% | 32.5% | 31.8% |
| 24,383 | DORCHESTER | 10,748 | 3,354 | 3,855 | 3,539 | | 316 D | 31.2% | 35.9% | 32.9% |
| 15,735 | EDGEFIELD | 3,919 | 1,688 | 1,225 | 1,006 | | 463 R | 43.1% | 31.3% | 25.7% |
| 20,713 | FAIRFIELD | 5,966 | 1,619 | 3,011 | 1,336 | | 1,392 D | 27.1% | 50.5% | 22.4% |
| 84,438 | FLORENCE | 24,638 | 8,917 | 8,079 | 7,642 | | 838 R | 36.2% | 32.8% | 31.0% |
| 34,798 | GEORGETOWN | 10,021 | 3,269 | 4,110 | 2,642 | | 841 D | 32.6% | 41.0% | 26.4% |
| 209,776 | GREENVILLE | 59,821 | 31,652 | 12,928 | 15,241 | | 16,411 R | 52.9% | 21.6% | 25.5% |
| 44,346 | GREENWOOD | 14,656 | 4,891 | 3,741 | 6,024 | | 1,133 A | 33.4% | 25.5% | 41.1% |
| 17,425 | HAMPTON | 5,230 | 1,671 | 2,107 | 1,452 | | 436 D | 32.0% | 40.3% | 27.8% |
| 68,247 | HORRY | 14,549 | 3,924 | 3,924 | 6,701 | | 2,777 A | 27.0% | 27.0% | 46.1% |
| 12,237 | JASPER | 3,116 | 633 | 1,402 | 1,081 | | 321 D | 20.3% | 45.0% | 34.7% |
| 33,585 | KERSHAW | 10,578 | 4,079 | 2,539 | 3,960 | | 119 R | 38.6% | 24.0% | 37.4% |
| 39,352 | LANCASTER | 12,911 | 4,874 | 3,151 | 4,886 | | 12 A | 37.8% | 24.4% | 37.8% |
| 47,609 | LAURENS | 12,108 | 4,813 | 3,016 | 4,279 | | 534 R | 39.8% | 24.9% | 35.3% |
| 21,832 | LEE | 5,483 | 1,219 | 2,151 | 2,113 | | 38 D | 22.2% | 39.2% | 38.5% |
| 60,726 | LEXINGTON | 25,169 | 12,204 | 4,058 | 8,907 | | 3,297 R | 48.5% | 16.1% | 35.4% |
| 8,629 | MCCORMICK | 2,211 | 466 | 988 | 757 | | 231 D | 21.1% | 44.7% | 34.2% |
| 32,014 | MARION | 6,817 | 2,512 | 2,821 | 1,484 | | 309 D | 36.8% | 41.4% | 21.8% |
| 28,529 | MARLBORO | 6,458 | 2,024 | 2,294 | 2,140 | | 154 D | 31.3% | 35.5% | 33.1% |
| 29,416 | NEWBERRY | 10,716 | 4,538 | 2,444 | 3,734 | | 804 R | 42.3% | 22.8% | 34.8% |
| 40,204 | OCONEE | 9,369 | 2,618 | 2,009 | 4,742 | | 2,124 A | 27.9% | 21.4% | 50.6% |
| 68,559 | ORANGEBURG | 21,259 | 5,144 | 8,971 | 7,144 | | 1,827 D | 24.2% | 42.2% | 33.6% |
| 46,030 | PICKENS | 13,313 | 6,873 | 2,016 | 4,424 | | 2,449 R | 51.6% | 15.1% | 33.2% |
| 200,102 | RICHLAND | 51,443 | 26,215 | 18,198 | 7,030 | | 8,017 R | 51.0% | 35.4% | 13.7% |
| 14,554 | SALUDA | 4,802 | 1,466 | 1,200 | 2,136 | | 670 A | 30.5% | 25.0% | 44.5% |
| 156,830 | SPARTANBURG | 46,996 | 18,183 | 11,467 | 17,346 | | 837 R | 38.7% | 24.4% | 36.9% |
| 74,941 | SUMTER | 16,308 | 5,451 | 6,103 | 4,754 | | 652 D | 33.4% | 37.4% | 29.2% |
| 30,015 | UNION | 9,872 | 3,011 | 2,271 | 4,590 | | 1,579 A | 30.5% | 23.0% | 46.5% |
| 40,932 | WILLIAMSBURG | 10,787 | 3,029 | 5,106 | 2,652 | | 2,077 D | 28.1% | 47.3% | 24.6% |
| 78,760 | YORK | 20,269 | 7,596 | 5,571 | 7,102 | | 494 R | 37.5% | 27.5% | 35.0% |
| 2,382,594 | TOTAL | 666,978 | 254,062 | 197,486 | 215,430 | | 38,632 R | 38.1% | 29.6% | 32.3% |

# SOUTH CAROLINA

## PRESIDENT 1964

| 1960 Census Population | County | Total Vote | Republican | Democratic | Other | Rep.-Dem. Plurality | Percentage Total Vote Rep. | Dem. | Major Vote Rep. | Dem. |
|---|---|---|---|---|---|---|---|---|---|---|
| 21,417 | ABBEVILLE | 4,137 | 1,448 | 2,689 | | 1,241 D | 35.0% | 65.0% | 35.0% | 65.0% |
| 81,038 | AIKEN | 25,089 | 17,467 | 7,622 | | 9,845 R | 69.6% | 30.4% | 69.6% | 30.4% |
| 11,362 | ALLENDALE | 2,512 | 1,740 | 772 | | 968 R | 69.3% | 30.7% | 69.3% | 30.7% |
| 98,478 | ANDERSON | 20,068 | 8,398 | 11,670 | | 3,272 D | 41.8% | 58.2% | 41.8% | 58.2% |
| 16,274 | BAMBERG | 3,785 | 2,366 | 1,419 | | 947 R | 62.5% | 37.5% | 62.5% | 37.5% |
| 17,659 | BARNWELL | 5,052 | 3,670 | 1,382 | | 2,288 R | 72.6% | 27.4% | 72.6% | 27.4% |
| 44,187 | BEAUFORT | 6,179 | 3,432 | 2,747 | | 685 R | 55.5% | 44.5% | 55.5% | 44.5% |
| 38,196 | BERKELEY | 9,637 | 6,100 | 3,537 | | 2,563 R | 63.3% | 36.7% | 63.3% | 36.7% |
| 12,256 | CALHOUN | 2,203 | 1,591 | 612 | | 979 R | 72.2% | 27.8% | 72.2% | 27.8% |
| 216,382 | CHARLESTON | 47,073 | 32,509 | 14,564 | | 17,945 R | 69.1% | 30.9% | 69.1% | 30.9% |
| 35,205 | CHEROKEE | 7,885 | 3,627 | 4,258 | | 631 D | 46.0% | 54.0% | 46.0% | 54.0% |
| 30,888 | CHESTER | 6,797 | 2,915 | 3,882 | | 967 D | 42.9% | 57.1% | 42.9% | 57.1% |
| 33,717 | CHESTERFIELD | 7,083 | 2,449 | 4,634 | | 2,185 D | 34.6% | 65.4% | 34.6% | 65.4% |
| 29,490 | CLARENDON | 3,793 | 2,960 | 833 | | 2,127 R | 78.0% | 22.0% | 78.0% | 22.0% |
| 27,816 | COLLETON | 6,688 | 4,637 | 2,051 | | 2,586 R | 69.3% | 30.7% | 69.3% | 30.7% |
| 52,928 | DARLINGTON | 11,727 | 6,717 | 5,010 | | 1,707 R | 57.3% | 42.7% | 57.3% | 42.7% |
| 30,584 | DILLON | 5,515 | 2,742 | 2,773 | | 31 D | 49.7% | 50.3% | 49.7% | 50.3% |
| 24,383 | DORCHESTER | 6,713 | 5,109 | 1,604 | | 3,505 R | 76.1% | 23.9% | 76.1% | 23.9% |
| 15,735 | EDGEFIELD | 3,313 | 2,489 | 824 | | 1,665 R | 75.1% | 24.9% | 75.1% | 24.9% |
| 20,713 | FAIRFIELD | 4,625 | 1,997 | 2,628 | | 631 D | 43.2% | 56.8% | 43.2% | 56.8% |
| 84,438 | FLORENCE | 17,503 | 10,346 | 7,157 | | 3,189 R | 59.1% | 40.9% | 59.1% | 40.9% |
| 34,798 | GEORGETOWN | 8,128 | 4,705 | 3,423 | | 1,282 R | 57.9% | 42.1% | 57.9% | 42.1% |
| 209,776 | GREENVILLE | 46,656 | 29,358 | 17,298 | | 12,060 R | 62.9% | 37.1% | 62.9% | 37.1% |
| 44,346 | GREENWOOD | 11,132 | 5,653 | 5,479 | | 174 R | 50.8% | 49.2% | 50.8% | 49.2% |
| 17,425 | HAMPTON | 3,698 | 2,259 | 1,439 | | 820 R | 61.1% | 38.9% | 61.1% | 38.9% |
| 68,247 | HORRY | 13,737 | 8,293 | 5,444 | | 2,849 R | 60.4% | 39.6% | 60.4% | 39.6% |
| 12,237 | JASPER | 2,595 | 1,593 | 1,002 | | 591 R | 61.4% | 38.6% | 61.4% | 38.6% |
| 33,585 | KERSHAW | 8,785 | 5,617 | 3,168 | | 2,449 R | 63.9% | 36.1% | 63.9% | 36.1% |
| 39,352 | LANCASTER | 9,712 | 4,742 | 4,970 | | 228 D | 48.8% | 51.2% | 48.8% | 51.2% |
| 47,609 | LAURENS | 9,446 | 5,081 | 4,365 | | 716 R | 53.8% | 46.2% | 53.8% | 46.2% |
| 21,832 | LEE | 3,645 | 2,489 | 1,156 | | 1,333 R | 68.3% | 31.7% | 68.3% | 31.7% |
| 60,726 | LEXINGTON | 16,848 | 12,041 | 4,807 | | 7,234 R | 71.5% | 28.5% | 71.5% | 28.5% |
| 8,629 | MCCORMICK | 1,437 | 939 | 498 | | 441 R | 65.3% | 34.7% | 65.3% | 34.7% |
| 32,014 | MARION | 5,243 | 3,197 | 2,046 | | 1,151 R | 61.0% | 39.0% | 61.0% | 39.0% |
| 28,529 | MARLBORO | 4,286 | 1,864 | 2,422 | | 558 D | 43.5% | 56.5% | 43.5% | 56.5% |
| 29,416 | NEWBERRY | 8,794 | 5,571 | 3,222 | 1 | 2,349 R | 63.4% | 36.6% | 63.4% | 36.6% |
| 40,204 | OCONEE | 8,272 | 2,712 | 5,560 | | 2,848 D | 32.8% | 67.2% | 32.8% | 67.2% |
| 68,559 | ORANGEBURG | 16,063 | 10,456 | 5,607 | | 4,849 R | 65.1% | 34.9% | 65.1% | 34.9% |
| 46,030 | PICKENS | 9,391 | 5,882 | 3,506 | 3 | 2,376 R | 62.6% | 37.3% | 62.7% | 37.3% |
| 200,102 | RICHLAND | 45,245 | 27,306 | 17,939 | | 9,367 R | 60.4% | 39.6% | 60.4% | 39.6% |
| 14,554 | SALUDA | 3,933 | 2,524 | 1,409 | | 1,115 R | 64.2% | 35.8% | 64.2% | 35.8% |
| 156,830 | SPARTANBURG | 38,445 | 18,411 | 20,034 | | 1,623 D | 47.9% | 52.1% | 47.9% | 52.1% |
| 74,941 | SUMTER | 11,504 | 7,729 | 3,775 | | 3,954 R | 67.2% | 32.8% | 67.2% | 32.8% |
| 30,015 | UNION | 7,707 | 3,815 | 3,892 | | 77 D | 49.5% | 50.5% | 49.5% | 50.5% |
| 40,932 | WILLIAMSBURG | 7,058 | 4,810 | 2,248 | | 2,562 R | 68.1% | 31.9% | 68.1% | 31.9% |
| 78,760 | YORK | 15,642 | 7,292 | 8,346 | 4 | 1,054 D | 46.6% | 53.4% | 46.6% | 53.4% |
| 2,382,594 | TOTAL | 524,779 | 309,048 | 215,723 | 8 | 93,325 R | 58.9% | 41.1% | 58.9% | 41.1% |

# SOUTH CAROLINA

## PRESIDENT 1960

| 1960 Census Population | County | Total Vote | Republican | Democratic | Other | Rep.-Dem. Plurality | Percentage | | | |
|---|---|---|---|---|---|---|---|---|---|---|
| | | | | | | | Total Vote | | Major Vote | |
| | | | | | | | Rep. | Dem. | Rep. | Dem. |
| 21,417 | ABBEVILLE | 3,909 | 845 | 3,064 | | 2,219 D | 21.6% | 78.4% | 21.6% | 78.4% |
| 81,038 | AIKEN | 17,389 | 10,715 | 6,674 | | 4,041 R | 61.6% | 38.4% | 61.6% | 38.4% |
| 11,362 | ALLENDALE | 1,471 | 888 | 583 | | 305 R | 60.4% | 39.6% | 60.4% | 39.6% |
| 98,478 | ANDERSON | 17,746 | 3,845 | 13,901 | | 10,056 D | 21.7% | 78.3% | 21.7% | 78.3% |
| 16,274 | BAMBERG | 2,560 | 1,652 | 908 | | 744 R | 64.5% | 35.5% | 64.5% | 35.5% |
| 17,659 | BARNWELL | 3,173 | 1,842 | 1,331 | | 511 R | 58.1% | 41.9% | 58.1% | 41.9% |
| 44,187 | BEAUFORT | 3,821 | 2,021 | 1,800 | | 221 R | 52.9% | 47.1% | 52.9% | 47.1% |
| 38,196 | BERKELEY | 4,964 | 2,422 | 2,542 | | 120 D | 48.8% | 51.2% | 48.8% | 51.2% |
| 12,256 | CALHOUN | 1,388 | 852 | 536 | | 316 R | 61.4% | 38.6% | 61.4% | 38.6% |
| 216,382 | CHARLESTON | 33,233 | 21,223 | 12,010 | | 9,213 R | 63.9% | 36.1% | 63.9% | 36.1% |
| 35,205 | CHEROKEE | 6,956 | 1,565 | 5,391 | | 3,826 D | 22.5% | 77.5% | 22.5% | 77.5% |
| 30,888 | CHESTER | 5,922 | 1,660 | 4,262 | | 2,602 D | 28.0% | 72.0% | 28.0% | 72.0% |
| 33,717 | CHESTERFIELD | 5,822 | 1,372 | 4,450 | | 3,078 D | 23.6% | 76.4% | 23.6% | 76.4% |
| 29,490 | CLARENDON | 2,579 | 1,445 | 1,134 | | 311 R | 56.0% | 44.0% | 56.0% | 44.0% |
| 27,816 | COLLETON | 4,483 | 2,521 | 1,962 | | 559 R | 56.2% | 43.8% | 56.2% | 43.8% |
| 52,928 | DARLINGTON | 8,162 | 3,494 | 4,668 | | 1,174 D | 42.8% | 57.2% | 42.8% | 57.2% |
| 30,584 | DILLON | 4,091 | 1,439 | 2,652 | | 1,213 D | 35.2% | 64.8% | 35.2% | 64.8% |
| 24,383 | DORCHESTER | 5,882 | 3,525 | 2,357 | | 1,168 R | 59.9% | 40.1% | 59.9% | 40.1% |
| 15,735 | EDGEFIELD | 2,294 | 1,448 | 846 | | 602 R | 63.1% | 36.9% | 63.1% | 36.9% |
| 20,713 | FAIRFIELD | 3,182 | 1,549 | 1,633 | | 84 D | 48.7% | 51.3% | 48.7% | 51.3% |
| 84,438 | FLORENCE | 11,906 | 5,815 | 6,090 | 1 | 275 D | 48.8% | 51.2% | 48.8% | 51.2% |
| 34,798 | GEORGETOWN | 5,418 | 2,607 | 2,811 | | 204 D | 48.1% | 51.9% | 48.1% | 51.9% |
| 209,776 | GREENVILLE | 36,633 | 22,657 | 13,976 | | 8,681 R | 61.8% | 38.2% | 61.8% | 38.2% |
| 44,346 | GREENWOOD | 8,251 | 2,968 | 5,283 | | 2,315 D | 36.0% | 64.0% | 36.0% | 64.0% |
| 17,425 | HAMPTON | 2,112 | 1,322 | 790 | | 532 R | 62.6% | 37.4% | 62.6% | 37.4% |
| 68,247 | HORRY | 9,774 | 3,768 | 6,006 | | 2,238 D | 38.6% | 61.4% | 38.6% | 61.4% |
| 12,237 | JASPER | 1,500 | 779 | 721 | | 58 R | 51.9% | 48.1% | 51.9% | 48.1% |
| 33,585 | KERSHAW | 6,643 | 3,465 | 3,178 | | 287 R | 52.2% | 47.8% | 52.2% | 47.8% |
| 39,352 | LANCASTER | 8,470 | 2,909 | 5,561 | | 2,652 D | 34.3% | 65.7% | 34.3% | 65.7% |
| 47,609 | LAURENS | 7,846 | 3,299 | 4,547 | | 1,248 D | 42.0% | 58.0% | 42.0% | 58.0% |
| 21,832 | LEE | 2,784 | 1,297 | 1,487 | | 190 D | 46.6% | 53.4% | 46.6% | 53.4% |
| 60,726 | LEXINGTON | 10,670 | 6,511 | 4,159 | | 2,352 R | 61.0% | 39.0% | 61.0% | 39.0% |
| 8,629 | MCCORMICK | 1,027 | 347 | 680 | | 333 D | 33.8% | 66.2% | 33.8% | 66.2% |
| 32,014 | MARION | 4,043 | 1,646 | 2,397 | | 751 D | 40.7% | 59.3% | 40.7% | 59.3% |
| 28,529 | MARLBORO | 3,877 | 1,291 | 2,586 | | 1,295 D | 33.3% | 66.7% | 33.3% | 66.7% |
| 29,416 | NEWBERRY | 5,984 | 2,841 | 3,143 | | 302 D | 47.5% | 52.5% | 47.5% | 52.5% |
| 40,204 | OCONEE | 6,214 | 1,886 | 4,328 | | 2,442 D | 30.4% | 69.6% | 30.4% | 69.6% |
| 68,559 | ORANGEBURG | 9,123 | 5,233 | 3,890 | | 1,343 R | 57.4% | 42.6% | 57.4% | 42.6% |
| 46,030 | PICKENS | 6,747 | 4,201 | 2,546 | | 1,655 R | 62.3% | 37.7% | 62.3% | 37.7% |
| 200,102 | RICHLAND | 32,430 | 20,736 | 11,694 | | 9,042 R | 63.9% | 36.1% | 63.9% | 36.1% |
| 14,554 | SALUDA | 2,621 | 1,268 | 1,353 | | 85 D | 48.4% | 51.6% | 48.4% | 51.6% |
| 156,830 | SPARTANBURG | 31,074 | 10,940 | 20,134 | | 9,194 D | 35.2% | 64.8% | 35.2% | 64.8% |
| 74,941 | SUMTER | 7,249 | 4,633 | 2,616 | | 2,017 R | 63.9% | 36.1% | 63.9% | 36.1% |
| 30,015 | UNION | 7,209 | 1,980 | 5,229 | | 3,249 D | 27.5% | 72.5% | 27.5% | 72.5% |
| 40,932 | WILLIAMSBURG | 3,837 | 2,324 | 1,513 | | 811 R | 60.6% | 39.4% | 60.6% | 39.4% |
| 78,760 | YORK | 14,219 | 5,512 | 8,707 | | 3,195 D | 38.8% | 61.2% | 38.8% | 61.2% |
| 2,382,594 | TOTAL | 386,688 | 188,558 | 198,129 | 1 | 9,571 D | 48.8% | 51.2% | 48.8% | 51.2% |

# SOUTH CAROLINA

## ELECTION NOTES

**2004** Other vote was 5,520 Independence (Ralph Nader); 5,317 Constitution (Michael Peroutka); 3,608 Libertarian (Michael Badnarik); 2,124 United Citizens (Walter F. Brown); 1,488 Green (David Cobb).

**2000** Other vote was 4,876 Libertarian (Browne); 3,519 Reform (Buchanan); 1,682 Constitution (Phillips); 942 Natural Law (Hagelin). Nader was listed on the ballot under the designation United Citizens.

**1996** Other vote was 4,271 Libertarian (Browne); 2,043 U.S. Taxpayers (Phillips); 1,248 Natural Law (Hagelin).

**1992** Other vote was 2,719 Marrou (Libertarian); 2,680 Phillips (American); 1,235 Fulani (United Citizens).

**1988** Other vote was 4,935 Paul (Libertarian); 4,077 Fulani (United Citizens).

**1984** Other vote was 4,359 Bergland (Libertarian); 3,490 Dennis (American); 682 Serrette (United Citizens). Small adjustments were made to the original canvass when the returns were printed in the "Annual Report of the South Carolina Election Commission". The Democratic vote in Charleston county was amended to read 29,481; the Libertarian vote in Orangeburg county was increased by one to 55; the United Citizens vote in Sumter county was decreased by one to 16. The data used in the table are from the original canvass.

**1980** Other vote was 14,153 Anderson (Independent); 5,139 Clark (Libertarian); 2,177 Rarick (Independent); 376 scattered write-in. The state-wide total for the other vote column includes these 376 scattered write-in votes not reported by county.

**1976** Other vote was 2,996 Anderson (American); 1,950 Maddox (Independent); 289 McCarthy (write-in); 53 MacBride (write-in); 8 Camejo (write-in); 2 LaRouche (write-in); 1 Hall (write-in); 328 scattered write-in.

**1972** Other vote was 10,075 Schmitz (Independent); 17 scattered write-in. The Democratic candidate was also the United Citizens nominee and 2,265 of his votes were received as the United Citizens candidate. Early unamended canvass gave the Democratic vote in Marlboro county as 2,990.

**1968** Wallace on the ballot as Independent.

**1964** Other vote was scattered write-in.

**1960** Other vote was scattered write-in.

# SOUTH DAKOTA

## POPULAR VOTE FOR PRESIDENT 1920 TO 2004

| Year | Total Vote | Republican Vote | Republican Candidate | Democratic Vote | Democratic Candidate | Other Vote | Plurality | Percentage Total Vote Rep. | Total Vote Dem. | Major Vote Rep. | Major Vote Dem. |
|------|-----------|-----------------|----------------------|-----------------|----------------------|------------|-----------|-------|------|------|------|
| 2004 | 388,215 | 232,584 | Bush, George W. | 149,244 | Kerry, John | 6,387 | 83,340 R | 59.9% | 38.4% | 60.9% | 39.1% |
| 2000 | 316,269 | 190,700 | Bush, George W. | 118,804 | Gore, Al | 6,765 | 71,896 R | 60.3% | 37.6% | 61.6% | 38.4% |
| 1996 ** | 323,826 | 150,543 | Dole, Bob | 139,333 | Clinton, Bill | 33,950 | 11,210 R | 46.5% | 43.0% | 51.9% | 48.1% |
| 1992 ** | 336,254 | 136,718 | Bush, George | 124,888 | Clinton, Bill | 74,648 | 11,830 R | 40.7% | 37.1% | 52.3% | 47.7% |
| 1988 | 312,991 | 165,415 | Bush, George | 145,560 | Dukakis, Michael S. | 2,016 | 19,855 R | 52.8% | 46.5% | 53.2% | 46.8% |
| 1984 | 317,867 | 200,267 | Reagan, Ronald | 116,113 | Mondale, Walter F. | 1,487 | 84,154 R | 63.0% | 36.5% | 63.3% | 36.7% |
| 1980 ** | 327,703 | 198,343 | Reagan, Ronald | 103,855 | Carter, Jimmy | 25,505 | 94,488 R | 60.5% | 31.7% | 65.6% | 34.4% |
| 1976 | 300,678 | 151,505 | Ford, Gerald R. | 147,068 | Carter, Jimmy | 2,105 | 4,437 R | 50.4% | 48.9% | 50.7% | 49.3% |
| 1972 | 307,415 | 166,476 | Nixon, Richard M. | 139,945 | McGovern, George S. | 994 | 26,531 R | 54.2% | 45.5% | 54.3% | 45.7% |
| 1968 | 281,264 | 149,841 | Nixon, Richard M. | 118,023 | Humphrey, Hubert H. | 13,400 | 31,818 R | 53.3% | 42.0% | 55.9% | 44.1% |
| 1964 | 293,118 | 130,108 | Goldwater, Barry M. | 163,010 | Johnson, Lyndon B. | | 32,902 D | 44.4% | 55.6% | 44.4% | 55.6% |
| 1960 | 306,487 | 178,417 | Nixon, Richard M. | 128,070 | Kennedy, John F. | | 50,347 R | 58.2% | 41.8% | 58.2% | 41.8% |
| 1956 | 293,857 | 171,569 | Eisenhower, Dwight D. | 122,288 | Stevenson, Adlai E. | | 49,281 R | 58.4% | 41.6% | 58.4% | 41.6% |
| 1952 | 294,283 | 203,857 | Eisenhower, Dwight D. | 90,426 | Stevenson, Adlai E. | | 113,431 R | 69.3% | 30.7% | 69.3% | 30.7% |
| 1948 | 250,105 | 129,651 | Dewey, Thomas E. | 117,653 | Truman, Harry S. | 2,801 | 11,998 R | 51.8% | 47.0% | 52.4% | 47.6% |
| 1944 | 232,076 | 135,365 | Dewey, Thomas E. | 96,711 | Roosevelt, Franklin D. | | 38,654 R | 58.3% | 41.7% | 58.3% | 41.7% |
| 1940 | 308,427 | 177,065 | Willkie, Wendell | 131,362 | Roosevelt, Franklin D. | | 45,703 R | 57.4% | 42.6% | 57.4% | 42.6% |
| 1936 | 296,452 | 125,977 | Landon, Alfred M. | 160,137 | Roosevelt, Franklin D. | 10,338 | 34,160 D | 42.5% | 54.0% | 44.0% | 56.0% |
| 1932 | 288,438 | 99,212 | Hoover, Herbert C. | 183,515 | Roosevelt, Franklin D. | 5,711 | 84,303 D | 34.4% | 63.6% | 35.1% | 64.9% |
| 1928 | 261,857 | 157,603 | Hoover, Herbert C. | 102,660 | Smith, Alfred E. | 1,594 | 54,943 R | 60.2% | 39.2% | 60.6% | 39.4% |
| 1924 ** | 203,868 | 101,299 | Coolidge, Calvin | 27,214 | Davis, John W. | 75,355 | 25,944 R | 49.7% | 13.3% | 78.8% | 21.2% |
| 1920 ** | 182,237 | 110,692 | Harding, Warren G. | 35,938 | Cox, James M. | 35,607 | 74,754 R | 60.7% | 19.7% | 75.5% | 24.5% |

In 1996 the other vote column includes 31,250 votes cast for Perot. In 1992 the other vote column includes 73,295 votes cast for Perot. In 1980 the other column includes 21,431 votes for Independent (Anderson). In 1924 the other vote was Progressive. In 1920 the other vote was 34,707 Farmer-Labor and 900 Prohibition.

## ELECTORAL COLLEGE VOTE 1920 TO 2004

| Year | Total | Republican | Democratic | Other |
|------|-------|------------|------------|-------|
| 2004 | 3 | 3 | | |
| 2000 | 3 | 3 | | |
| 1996 | 3 | 3 | | |
| 1992 | 3 | 3 | | |
| 1988 | 3 | 3 | | |
| 1984 | 3 | 3 | | |
| 1980 | 4 | 4 | | |
| 1976 | 4 | 4 | | |
| 1972 | 4 | 4 | | |
| 1968 | 4 | 4 | | |
| 1964 | 4 | | 4 | |
| 1960 | 4 | 4 | | |
| 1956 | 4 | 4 | | |
| 1952 | 4 | 4 | | |
| 1948 | 4 | 4 | | |
| 1944 | 4 | 4 | | |
| 1940 | 4 | 4 | | |
| 1936 | 4 | | 4 | |
| 1932 | 4 | | 4 | |
| 1928 | 5 | 5 | | |
| 1924 | 5 | 5 | | |
| 1920 | 5 | 5 | | |

# SOUTH DAKOTA

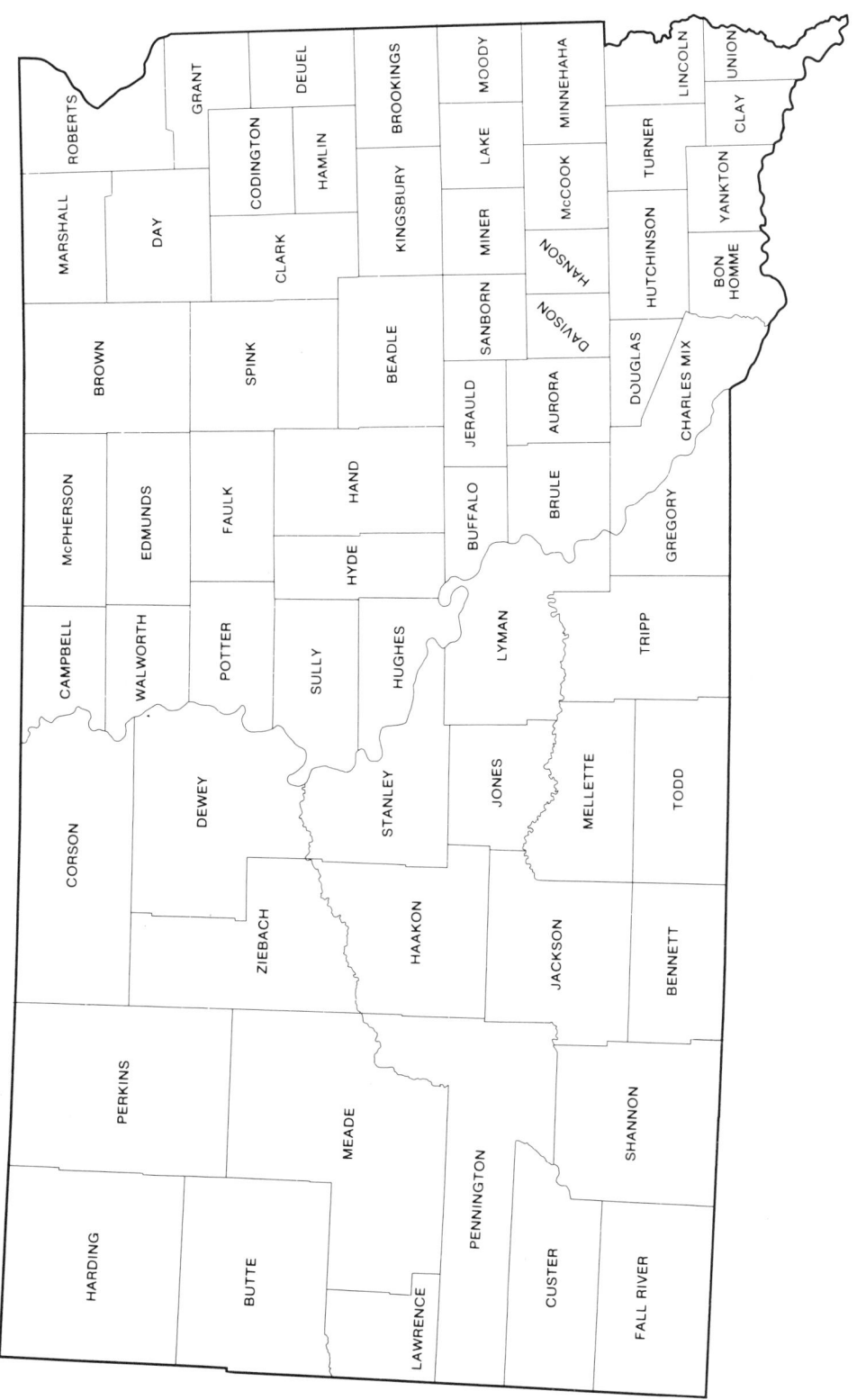

# SOUTH DAKOTA

## PRESIDENT 2004

| 2000 Census Population | County | Total Vote | Republican | Democratic | Other | Rep.-Dem. Plurality | Percentage Total Vote Rep. | Dem. | Major Vote Rep. | Dem. |
|---|---|---|---|---|---|---|---|---|---|---|
| 3,058 | AURORA | 1,649 | 1,009 | 620 | 20 | 389 R | 61.2% | 37.6% | 61.9% | 38.1% |
| 17,023 | BEADLE | 8,480 | 4,917 | 3,443 | 120 | 1,474 R | 58.0% | 40.6% | 58.8% | 41.2% |
| 3,574 | BENNETT | 1,630 | 833 | 759 | 38 | 74 R | 51.1% | 46.6% | 52.3% | 47.7% |
| 7,260 | BON HOMME | 3,408 | 2,063 | 1,293 | 52 | 770 R | 60.5% | 37.9% | 61.5% | 38.5% |
| 28,220 | BROOKINGS | 13,375 | 7,662 | 5,443 | 270 | 2,219 R | 57.3% | 40.7% | 58.5% | 41.5% |
| 35,460 | BROWN | 18,599 | 10,386 | 7,943 | 270 | 2,443 R | 55.8% | 42.7% | 56.7% | 43.3% |
| 5,364 | BRULE | 2,629 | 1,544 | 1,040 | 45 | 504 R | 58.7% | 39.6% | 59.8% | 40.2% |
| 2,032 | BUFFALO | 841 | 223 | 603 | 15 | 380 D | 26.5% | 71.7% | 27.0% | 73.0% |
| 9,094 | BUTTE | 4,271 | 3,166 | 1,009 | 96 | 2,157 R | 74.1% | 23.6% | 75.8% | 24.2% |
| 1,782 | CAMPBELL | 959 | 708 | 239 | 12 | 469 R | 73.8% | 24.9% | 74.8% | 25.2% |
| 9,350 | CHARLES MIX | 4,798 | 2,556 | 2,155 | 87 | 401 R | 53.3% | 44.9% | 54.3% | 45.7% |
| 4,143 | CLARK | 2,327 | 1,435 | 875 | 17 | 560 R | 61.7% | 37.6% | 62.1% | 37.9% |
| 13,537 | CLAY | 6,136 | 2,692 | 3,315 | 129 | 623 D | 43.9% | 54.0% | 44.8% | 55.2% |
| 25,897 | CODINGTON | 12,751 | 7,778 | 4,803 | 170 | 2,975 R | 61.0% | 37.7% | 61.8% | 38.2% |
| 4,181 | CORSON | 1,724 | 720 | 972 | 32 | 252 D | 41.8% | 56.4% | 42.6% | 57.4% |
| 7,275 | CUSTER | 4,304 | 2,922 | 1,272 | 110 | 1,650 R | 67.9% | 29.6% | 69.7% | 30.3% |
| 18,741 | DAVISON | 8,952 | 5,561 | 3,263 | 128 | 2,298 R | 62.1% | 36.4% | 63.0% | 37.0% |
| 6,267 | DAY | 3,540 | 1,671 | 1,817 | 52 | 146 D | 47.2% | 51.3% | 47.9% | 52.1% |
| 4,498 | DEUEL | 2,412 | 1,406 | 961 | 45 | 445 R | 58.3% | 39.8% | 59.4% | 40.6% |
| 5,972 | DEWEY | 2,564 | 921 | 1,606 | 37 | 685 D | 35.9% | 62.6% | 36.4% | 63.6% |
| 3,458 | DOUGLAS | 2,012 | 1,596 | 393 | 23 | 1,203 R | 79.3% | 19.5% | 80.2% | 19.8% |
| 4,367 | EDMUNDS | 2,234 | 1,434 | 765 | 35 | 669 R | 64.2% | 34.2% | 65.2% | 34.8% |
| 7,453 | FALL RIVER | 3,845 | 2,413 | 1,326 | 106 | 1,087 R | 62.8% | 34.5% | 64.5% | 35.5% |
| 2,640 | FAULK | 1,369 | 945 | 418 | 6 | 527 R | 69.0% | 30.5% | 69.3% | 30.7% |
| 7,847 | GRANT | 4,090 | 2,392 | 1,633 | 65 | 759 R | 58.5% | 39.9% | 59.4% | 40.6% |
| 4,792 | GREGORY | 2,546 | 1,685 | 813 | 48 | 872 R | 66.2% | 31.9% | 67.5% | 32.5% |
| 2,196 | HAAKON | 1,240 | 1,007 | 219 | 14 | 788 R | 81.2% | 17.7% | 82.1% | 17.9% |
| 5,540 | HAMLIN | 3,011 | 1,946 | 1,015 | 50 | 931 R | 64.6% | 33.7% | 65.7% | 34.3% |
| 3,741 | HAND | 2,187 | 1,482 | 668 | 37 | 814 R | 67.8% | 30.5% | 68.9% | 31.1% |
| 3,139 | HANSON | 2,150 | 1,379 | 745 | 26 | 634 R | 64.1% | 34.7% | 64.9% | 35.1% |
| 1,353 | HARDING | 815 | 704 | 94 | 17 | 610 R | 86.4% | 11.5% | 88.2% | 11.8% |
| 16,481 | HUGHES | 8,835 | 6,017 | 2,697 | 121 | 3,320 R | 68.1% | 30.5% | 69.0% | 31.0% |
| 8,075 | HUTCHINSON | 4,147 | 2,899 | 1,177 | 71 | 1,722 R | 69.9% | 28.4% | 71.1% | 28.9% |
| 1,671 | HYDE | 900 | 631 | 259 | 10 | 372 R | 70.1% | 28.8% | 70.9% | 29.1% |
| 2,930 | JACKSON | 1,271 | 726 | 508 | 37 | 218 R | 57.1% | 40.0% | 58.8% | 41.2% |
| 2,295 | JERAULD | 1,236 | 736 | 482 | 18 | 254 R | 59.5% | 39.0% | 60.4% | 39.6% |
| 1,193 | JONES | 717 | 565 | 134 | 18 | 431 R | 78.8% | 18.7% | 80.8% | 19.2% |
| 5,815 | KINGSBURY | 3,014 | 1,804 | 1,163 | 47 | 641 R | 59.9% | 38.6% | 60.8% | 39.2% |
| 11,276 | LAKE | 6,007 | 3,359 | 2,509 | 139 | 850 R | 55.9% | 41.8% | 57.2% | 42.8% |
| 21,802 | LAWRENCE | 11,619 | 7,489 | 3,857 | 273 | 3,632 R | 64.5% | 33.2% | 66.0% | 34.0% |
| 24,131 | LINCOLN | 17,066 | 11,161 | 5,703 | 202 | 5,458 R | 65.4% | 33.4% | 66.2% | 33.8% |
| 3,895 | LYMAN | 1,940 | 1,029 | 872 | 39 | 157 R | 53.0% | 44.9% | 54.1% | 45.9% |
| 5,832 | MCCOOK | 3,271 | 2,017 | 1,201 | 53 | 816 R | 61.7% | 36.7% | 62.7% | 37.3% |
| 2,904 | MCPHERSON | 1,579 | 1,180 | 369 | 30 | 811 R | 74.7% | 23.4% | 76.2% | 23.8% |
| 4,576 | MARSHALL | 2,364 | 1,242 | 1,099 | 23 | 143 R | 52.5% | 46.5% | 53.1% | 46.9% |
| 24,253 | MEADE | 11,504 | 8,347 | 2,941 | 216 | 5,406 R | 72.6% | 25.6% | 73.9% | 26.1% |
| 2,083 | MELLETTE | 931 | 553 | 361 | 17 | 192 R | 59.4% | 38.8% | 60.5% | 39.5% |
| 2,884 | MINER | 1,470 | 810 | 641 | 19 | 169 R | 55.1% | 43.6% | 55.8% | 44.2% |
| 148,281 | MINNEHAHA | 77,632 | 44,189 | 32,314 | 1,129 | 11,875 R | 56.9% | 41.6% | 57.8% | 42.2% |
| 6,595 | MOODY | 3,451 | 1,790 | 1,609 | 52 | 181 R | 51.9% | 46.6% | 52.7% | 47.3% |
| 88,565 | PENNINGTON | 44,968 | 29,976 | 14,213 | 779 | 15,763 R | 66.7% | 31.6% | 67.8% | 32.2% |
| 3,363 | PERKINS | 1,813 | 1,329 | 418 | 66 | 911 R | 73.3% | 23.1% | 76.1% | 23.9% |
| 2,693 | POTTER | 1,618 | 1,143 | 463 | 12 | 680 R | 70.6% | 28.6% | 71.2% | 28.8% |
| 10,016 | ROBERTS | 4,982 | 2,396 | 2,527 | 59 | 131 D | 48.1% | 50.7% | 48.7% | 51.3% |
| 2,675 | SANBORN | 1,426 | 817 | 581 | 28 | 236 R | 57.3% | 40.7% | 58.4% | 41.6% |
| 12,466 | SHANNON | 4,214 | 526 | 3,566 | 122 | 3,040 D | 12.5% | 84.6% | 12.9% | 87.1% |
| 7,454 | SPINK | 3,774 | 2,259 | 1,478 | 37 | 781 R | 59.9% | 39.2% | 60.4% | 39.6% |
| 2,772 | STANLEY | 1,623 | 1,129 | 464 | 30 | 665 R | 69.6% | 28.6% | 70.9% | 29.1% |
| 1,556 | SULLY | 917 | 702 | 201 | 14 | 501 R | 76.6% | 21.9% | 77.7% | 22.3% |
| 9,050 | TODD | 3,524 | 889 | 2,543 | 92 | 1,654 D | 25.2% | 72.2% | 25.9% | 74.1% |

# SOUTH DAKOTA

## PRESIDENT 2004

| 2000 Census Population | County | Total Vote | Republican | Democratic | Other | Rep.-Dem. Plurality | Percentage | | | |
| | | | | | | | Total Vote | | Major Vote | |
| | | | | | | | Rep. | Dem. | Rep. | Dem. |
|---|---|---|---|---|---|---|---|---|---|---|
| 6,430 | TRIPP | 3,245 | 2,230 | 972 | 43 | 1,258 R | 68.7% | 30.0% | 69.6% | 30.4% |
| 8,849 | TURNER | 4,834 | 3,084 | 1,646 | 104 | 1,438 R | 63.8% | 34.1% | 65.2% | 34.8% |
| 12,584 | UNION | 7,048 | 3,987 | 3,000 | 61 | 987 R | 56.6% | 42.6% | 57.1% | 42.9% |
| 5,974 | WALWORTH | 2,880 | 1,967 | 878 | 35 | 1,089 R | 68.3% | 30.5% | 69.1% | 30.9% |
| 21,652 | YANKTON | 10,431 | 6,003 | 4,237 | 191 | 1,766 R | 57.5% | 40.6% | 58.6% | 41.4% |
| 2,519 | ZIEBACH | 1,116 | 447 | 641 | 28 | 194 D | 40.1% | 57.4% | 41.1% | 58.9% |
| 754,844 | TOTAL | 388,215 | 232,584 | 149,244 | 6,387 | 83,340 R | 59.9% | 38.4% | 60.9% | 39.1% |

# SOUTH DAKOTA

## PRESIDENT 2000

| 2000 Census Population | County | Total Vote | Republican | Democratic | Green (Nader) | Other | Rep.-Dem. Plurality | Percentage of Total Vote | | |
|---|---|---|---|---|---|---|---|---|---|---|
| | | | | | | | | Rep. | Dem. | Green |
| 3,058 | AURORA | 1,413 | 847 | 513 | | 53 | 334 R | 59.9% | 36.3% | |
| 17,023 | BEADLE | 7,739 | 4,347 | 3,216 | | 176 | 1,131 R | 56.2% | 41.6% | |
| 3,574 | BENNETT | 1,116 | 712 | 377 | | 27 | 335 R | 63.8% | 33.8% | |
| 7,260 | BON HOMME | 3,139 | 1,901 | 1,162 | | 76 | 739 R | 60.6% | 37.0% | |
| 28,220 | BROOKINGS | 10,984 | 6,212 | 4,546 | | 226 | 1,666 R | 56.6% | 41.4% | |
| 35,460 | BROWN | 16,556 | 9,060 | 7,173 | | 323 | 1,887 R | 54.7% | 43.3% | |
| 5,364 | BRULE | 2,167 | 1,268 | 818 | | 81 | 450 R | 58.5% | 37.7% | |
| 2,032 | BUFFALO | 408 | 140 | 256 | | 12 | 116 D | 34.3% | 62.7% | |
| 9,094 | BUTTE | 3,689 | 2,760 | 840 | | 89 | 1,920 R | 74.8% | 22.8% | |
| 1,782 | CAMPBELL | 917 | 739 | 147 | | 31 | 592 R | 80.6% | 16.0% | |
| 9,350 | CHARLES MIX | 3,579 | 2,205 | 1,300 | | 74 | 905 R | 61.6% | 36.3% | |
| 4,143 | CLARK | 2,108 | 1,272 | 791 | | 45 | 481 R | 60.3% | 37.5% | |
| 13,537 | CLAY | 5,105 | 2,363 | 2,638 | | 104 | 275 D | 46.3% | 51.7% | |
| 25,897 | CODINGTON | 11,138 | 6,718 | 4,192 | | 228 | 2,526 R | 60.3% | 37.6% | |
| 4,181 | CORSON | 1,243 | 629 | 549 | | 65 | 80 R | 50.6% | 44.2% | |
| 7,275 | CUSTER | 3,573 | 2,495 | 955 | | 123 | 1,540 R | 69.8% | 26.7% | |
| 18,741 | DAVISON | 7,528 | 4,445 | 2,936 | | 147 | 1,509 R | 59.0% | 39.0% | |
| 6,267 | DAY | 3,197 | 1,623 | 1,492 | | 82 | 131 R | 50.8% | 46.7% | |
| 4,498 | DEUEL | 2,224 | 1,245 | 926 | | 53 | 319 R | 56.0% | 41.6% | |
| 5,972 | DEWEY | 1,681 | 761 | 880 | | 40 | 119 D | 45.3% | 52.3% | |
| 3,458 | DOUGLAS | 1,709 | 1,311 | 363 | | 35 | 948 R | 76.7% | 21.2% | |
| 4,367 | EDMUNDS | 1,986 | 1,257 | 676 | | 53 | 581 R | 63.3% | 34.0% | |
| 7,453 | FALL RIVER | 3,429 | 2,185 | 1,133 | | 111 | 1,052 R | 63.7% | 33.0% | |
| 2,640 | FAULK | 1,329 | 904 | 388 | | 37 | 516 R | 68.0% | 29.2% | |
| 7,847 | GRANT | 3,830 | 2,235 | 1,475 | | 120 | 760 R | 58.4% | 38.5% | |
| 4,792 | GREGORY | 2,257 | 1,487 | 718 | | 52 | 769 R | 65.9% | 31.8% | |
| 2,196 | HAAKON | 1,129 | 938 | 164 | | 27 | 774 R | 83.1% | 14.5% | |
| 5,540 | HAMLIN | 2,723 | 1,731 | 923 | | 69 | 808 R | 63.6% | 33.9% | |
| 3,741 | HAND | 2,031 | 1,419 | 565 | | 47 | 854 R | 69.9% | 27.8% | |
| 3,139 | HANSON | 1,421 | 944 | 457 | | 20 | 487 R | 66.4% | 32.2% | |
| 1,353 | HARDING | 731 | 650 | 64 | | 17 | 586 R | 88.9% | 8.8% | |
| 16,481 | HUGHES | 7,534 | 5,188 | 2,212 | | 134 | 2,976 R | 68.9% | 29.4% | |
| 8,075 | HUTCHINSON | 3,625 | 2,497 | 1,052 | | 76 | 1,445 R | 68.9% | 29.0% | |
| 1,671 | HYDE | 835 | 592 | 218 | | 25 | 374 R | 70.9% | 26.1% | |
| 2,930 | JACKSON | 1,040 | 687 | 319 | | 34 | 368 R | 66.1% | 30.7% | |
| 2,295 | JERAULD | 1,122 | 624 | 468 | | 30 | 156 R | 55.6% | 41.7% | |
| 1,193 | JONES | 664 | 509 | 137 | | 18 | 372 R | 76.7% | 20.6% | |
| 5,815 | KINGSBURY | 2,727 | 1,612 | 1,049 | | 66 | 563 R | 59.1% | 38.5% | |
| 11,276 | LAKE | 5,154 | 2,724 | 2,331 | | 99 | 393 R | 52.9% | 45.2% | |
| 21,802 | LAWRENCE | 9,406 | 6,327 | 2,797 | | 282 | 3,530 R | 67.3% | 29.7% | |
| 24,131 | LINCOLN | 10,556 | 6,546 | 3,844 | | 166 | 2,702 R | 62.0% | 36.4% | |
| 3,895 | LYMAN | 1,386 | 875 | 482 | | 29 | 393 R | 63.1% | 34.8% | |
| 5,832 | MCCOOK | 2,631 | 1,610 | 965 | | 56 | 645 R | 61.2% | 36.7% | |
| 2,904 | MCPHERSON | 1,417 | 1,073 | 295 | | 49 | 778 R | 75.7% | 20.8% | |
| 4,576 | MARSHALL | 2,079 | 1,097 | 939 | | 43 | 158 R | 52.8% | 45.2% | |
| 24,253 | MEADE | 9,366 | 6,870 | 2,267 | | 229 | 4,603 R | 73.4% | 24.2% | |
| 2,083 | MELLETTE | 733 | 495 | 222 | | 16 | 273 R | 67.5% | 30.3% | |
| 2,884 | MINER | 1,266 | 724 | 523 | | 19 | 201 R | 57.2% | 41.3% | |
| 148,281 | MINNEHAHA | 61,369 | 33,428 | 27,042 | | 899 | 6,386 R | 54.5% | 44.1% | |
| 6,595 | MOODY | 2,735 | 1,361 | 1,318 | | 56 | 43 R | 49.8% | 48.2% | |
| 88,565 | PENNINGTON | 36,557 | 24,696 | 11,123 | | 738 | 13,573 R | 67.6% | 30.4% | |
| 3,363 | PERKINS | 1,614 | 1,237 | 297 | | 80 | 940 R | 76.6% | 18.4% | |
| 2,693 | POTTER | 1,494 | 1,112 | 356 | | 26 | 756 R | 74.4% | 23.8% | |
| 10,016 | ROBERTS | 4,074 | 2,237 | 1,700 | | 137 | 537 R | 54.9% | 41.7% | |
| 2,675 | SANBORN | 1,268 | 767 | 468 | | 33 | 299 R | 60.5% | 36.9% | |
| 12,466 | SHANNON | 1,953 | 252 | 1,667 | | 34 | 1,415 D | 12.9% | 85.4% | |
| 7,454 | SPINK | 3,284 | 1,957 | 1,274 | | 53 | 683 R | 59.6% | 38.8% | |
| 2,772 | STANLEY | 1,381 | 955 | 402 | | 24 | 553 R | 69.2% | 29.1% | |
| 1,556 | SULLY | 871 | 633 | 209 | | 29 | 424 R | 72.7% | 24.0% | |
| 9,050 | TODD | 1,494 | 478 | 993 | | 23 | 515 D | 32.0% | 66.5% | |

# SOUTH DAKOTA

## PRESIDENT 2000

| 2000 Census Population | County | Total Vote | Republican | Democratic | Green (Nader) | Other | Rep.-Dem. Plurality | Percentage of Total Vote | | |
|---|---|---|---|---|---|---|---|---|---|---|
| | | | | | | | | Rep. | Dem. | Green |
| 6,430 | TRIPP | 2,765 | 1,909 | 799 | | 57 | 1,110 R | 69.0% | 28.9% | |
| 8,849 | TURNER | 4,004 | 2,514 | 1,414 | | 76 | 1,100 R | 62.8% | 35.3% | |
| 12,584 | UNION | 5,772 | 3,265 | 2,358 | | 149 | 907 R | 56.6% | 40.9% | |
| 5,974 | WALWORTH | 2,553 | 1,758 | 721 | | 74 | 1,037 R | 68.9% | 28.2% | |
| 21,652 | YANKTON | 8,740 | 4,904 | 3,596 | | 240 | 1,308 R | 56.1% | 41.1% | |
| 2,519 | ZIEBACH | 721 | 384 | 314 | | 23 | 70 R | 53.3% | 43.6% | |
| 754,844 | TOTAL | 316,269 | 190,700 | 118,804 | | 6,765 | 71,896 R | 60.3% | 37.6% | |

Note: No votes were tallied for Nader in South Dakota. He did not qualify for the ballot and write-in votes were not allowed.

# SOUTH DAKOTA

## PRESIDENT 1996

| 1995 Census Pop. Est. | County | Total Vote | Republican | Democratic | Reform (Perot) | Other | Rep.-Dem. Plurality | Percentage of Total Vote | | |
|---|---|---|---|---|---|---|---|---|---|---|
| | | | | | | | | Rep. | Dem. | Reform |
| 3,091 | AURORA | 1,587 | 709 | 664 | 199 | 15 | 45 R | 44.7% | 41.8% | 12.5% |
| 18,143 | BEADLE | 8,581 | 3,670 | 3,984 | 842 | 85 | 314 D | 42.8% | 46.4% | 9.8% |
| 3,313 | BENNETT | 1,145 | 539 | 507 | 93 | 6 | 32 R | 47.1% | 44.3% | 8.1% |
| 7,008 | BON HOMME | 3,436 | 1,428 | 1,569 | 391 | 48 | 141 D | 41.6% | 45.7% | 11.4% |
| 26,450 | BROOKINGS | 11,272 | 5,112 | 5,105 | 979 | 76 | 7 R | 45.4% | 45.3% | 8.7% |
| 35,734 | BROWN | 16,447 | 6,801 | 7,913 | 1,622 | 111 | 1,112 D | 41.4% | 48.1% | 9.9% |
| 5,633 | BRULE | 2,404 | 981 | 1,091 | 281 | 51 | 110 D | 40.8% | 45.4% | 11.7% |
| 1,832 | BUFFALO | 640 | 134 | 465 | 35 | 6 | 331 D | 20.9% | 72.7% | 5.5% |
| 8,896 | BUTTE | 3,657 | 1,947 | 1,132 | 541 | 37 | 815 R | 53.2% | 31.0% | 14.8% |
| 1,881 | CAMPBELL | 970 | 623 | 202 | 140 | 5 | 421 R | 64.2% | 20.8% | 14.4% |
| 9,479 | CHARLES MIX | 4,035 | 1,711 | 1,913 | 390 | 21 | 202 D | 42.4% | 47.4% | 9.7% |
| 4,382 | CLARK | 2,242 | 998 | 956 | 272 | 16 | 42 R | 44.5% | 42.6% | 12.1% |
| 13,606 | CLAY | 5,572 | 2,008 | 2,980 | 505 | 79 | 972 D | 36.0% | 53.5% | 9.1% |
| 24,829 | CODINGTON | 11,055 | 4,995 | 4,722 | 1,239 | 99 | 273 R | 45.2% | 42.7% | 11.2% |
| 4,258 | CORSON | 1,300 | 533 | 539 | 216 | 12 | 6 D | 41.0% | 41.5% | 16.6% |
| 6,675 | CUSTER | 3,357 | 1,740 | 1,122 | 418 | 77 | 618 R | 51.8% | 33.4% | 12.5% |
| 17,823 | DAVISON | 7,528 | 3,371 | 3,364 | 737 | 56 | 7 R | 44.8% | 44.7% | 9.8% |
| 6,713 | DAY | 3,533 | 1,282 | 1,840 | 395 | 16 | 558 D | 36.3% | 52.1% | 11.2% |
| 4,449 | DEUEL | 2,349 | 955 | 1,090 | 275 | 29 | 135 D | 40.7% | 46.4% | 11.7% |
| 5,783 | DEWEY | 1,979 | 657 | 1,114 | 195 | 13 | 457 D | 33.2% | 56.3% | 9.9% |
| 3,615 | DOUGLAS | 1,909 | 1,210 | 524 | 161 | 14 | 686 R | 63.4% | 27.4% | 8.4% |
| 4,344 | EDMUNDS | 2,310 | 1,055 | 973 | 263 | 19 | 82 R | 45.7% | 42.1% | 11.4% |
| 7,089 | FALL RIVER | 3,458 | 1,636 | 1,357 | 417 | 48 | 279 R | 47.3% | 39.2% | 12.1% |
| 2,592 | FAULK | 1,389 | 726 | 493 | 165 | 5 | 233 R | 52.3% | 35.5% | 11.9% |
| 8,237 | GRANT | 4,083 | 1,782 | 1,805 | 471 | 25 | 23 D | 43.6% | 44.2% | 11.5% |
| 5,112 | GREGORY | 2,433 | 1,208 | 923 | 286 | 16 | 285 R | 49.7% | 37.9% | 11.8% |
| 2,548 | HAAKON | 1,289 | 887 | 284 | 110 | 8 | 603 R | 68.8% | 22.0% | 8.5% |
| 5,372 | HAMLIN | 2,758 | 1,352 | 1,101 | 285 | 20 | 251 R | 49.0% | 39.9% | 10.3% |
| 4,202 | HAND | 2,268 | 1,187 | 803 | 250 | 28 | 384 R | 52.3% | 35.4% | 11.0% |
| 2,935 | HANSON | 1,534 | 801 | 541 | 170 | 22 | 260 R | 52.2% | 35.3% | 11.1% |
| 1,542 | HARDING | 785 | 537 | 151 | 90 | 7 | 386 R | 68.4% | 19.2% | 11.5% |
| 15,537 | HUGHES | 7,868 | 4,469 | 2,788 | 531 | 80 | 1,681 R | 56.8% | 35.4% | 6.7% |
| 8,016 | HUTCHINSON | 3,911 | 2,177 | 1,285 | 409 | 40 | 892 R | 55.7% | 32.9% | 10.5% |
| 1,675 | HYDE | 904 | 493 | 309 | 95 | 7 | 184 R | 54.5% | 34.2% | 10.5% |
| 2,867 | JACKSON | 1,169 | 646 | 423 | 88 | 12 | 223 R | 55.3% | 36.2% | 7.5% |
| 2,338 | JERAULD | 1,364 | 530 | 656 | 151 | 27 | 126 D | 38.9% | 48.1% | 11.1% |
| 1,318 | JONES | 729 | 463 | 184 | 75 | 7 | 279 R | 63.5% | 25.2% | 10.3% |
| 5,745 | KINGSBURY | 3,001 | 1,297 | 1,357 | 320 | 27 | 60 D | 43.2% | 45.2% | 10.7% |
| 10,797 | LAKE | 5,118 | 1,966 | 2,526 | 593 | 33 | 560 D | 38.4% | 49.4% | 11.6% |
| 22,452 | LAWRENCE | 9,442 | 4,430 | 3,568 | 1,308 | 136 | 862 R | 46.9% | 37.8% | 13.9% |
| 17,666 | LINCOLN | 8,587 | 4,201 | 3,643 | 682 | 61 | 558 R | 48.9% | 42.4% | 7.9% |
| 3,779 | LYMAN | 1,523 | 726 | 646 | 130 | 21 | 80 R | 47.7% | 42.4% | 8.5% |
| 5,824 | MCCOOK | 2,723 | 1,292 | 1,166 | 245 | 20 | 126 R | 47.4% | 42.8% | 9.0% |
| 3,036 | MCPHERSON | 1,735 | 1,080 | 463 | 182 | 10 | 617 R | 62.2% | 26.7% | 10.5% |
| 4,714 | MARSHALL | 2,246 | 861 | 1,185 | 189 | 11 | 324 D | 38.3% | 52.8% | 8.4% |
| 23,084 | MEADE | 9,176 | 4,984 | 2,960 | 1,133 | 99 | 2,024 R | 54.3% | 32.3% | 12.3% |
| 2,002 | MELLETTE | 798 | 417 | 302 | 67 | 12 | 115 R | 52.3% | 37.8% | 8.4% |
| 3,064 | MINER | 1,489 | 571 | 739 | 170 | 9 | 168 D | 38.3% | 49.6% | 11.4% |
| 135,641 | MINNEHAHA | 62,004 | 27,432 | 29,790 | 4,425 | 357 | 2,358 D | 44.2% | 48.0% | 7.1% |
| 6,616 | MOODY | 2,767 | 1,024 | 1,443 | 284 | 16 | 419 D | 37.0% | 52.2% | 10.3% |
| 87,304 | PENNINGTON | 35,516 | 19,293 | 12,784 | 3,149 | 290 | 6,509 R | 54.3% | 36.0% | 8.9% |
| 3,703 | PERKINS | 1,692 | 983 | 460 | 225 | 24 | 523 R | 58.1% | 27.2% | 13.3% |
| 2,990 | POTTER | 1,702 | 979 | 534 | 181 | 8 | 445 R | 57.5% | 31.4% | 10.6% |
| 9,949 | ROBERTS | 4,333 | 1,646 | 2,186 | 474 | 27 | 540 D | 38.0% | 50.5% | 10.9% |
| 2,798 | SANBORN | 1,438 | 630 | 647 | 151 | 10 | 17 D | 43.8% | 45.0% | 10.5% |
| 11,675 | SHANNON | 2,284 | 253 | 1,926 | 87 | 18 | 1,673 D | 11.1% | 84.3% | 3.8% |
| 7,844 | SPINK | 3,669 | 1,651 | 1,636 | 360 | 22 | 15 R | 45.0% | 44.6% | 9.8% |
| 2,823 | STANLEY | 1,382 | 795 | 454 | 121 | 12 | 341 R | 57.5% | 32.9% | 8.8% |
| 1,573 | SULLY | 1,025 | 592 | 321 | 106 | 6 | 271 R | 57.8% | 31.3% | 10.3% |
| 9,105 | TODD | 1,991 | 482 | 1,380 | 108 | 21 | 898 D | 24.2% | 69.3% | 5.4% |

# SOUTH DAKOTA

## PRESIDENT 1996

| 1995 Census Pop. Est. | County | Total Vote | Republican | Democratic | Reform (Perot) | Other | Rep.-Dem. Plurality | Percentage of Total Vote | | |
|---|---|---|---|---|---|---|---|---|---|---|
| | | | | | | | | Rep. | Dem. | Reform |
| 6,902 | TRIPP | 3,132 | 1,680 | 1,088 | 337 | 27 | 592 R | 53.6% | 34.7% | 10.8% |
| 8,603 | TURNER | 4,051 | 1,970 | 1,682 | 385 | 14 | 288 R | 48.6% | 41.5% | 9.5% |
| 11,225 | UNION | 5,207 | 2,234 | 2,378 | 555 | 40 | 144 D | 42.9% | 45.7% | 10.7% |
| 5,834 | WALWORTH | 2,789 | 1,461 | 939 | 366 | 23 | 522 R | 52.4% | 33.7% | 13.1% |
| 20,754 | YANKTON | 8,826 | 3,885 | 3,775 | 1,073 | 93 | 110 R | 44.0% | 42.8% | 12.2% |
| 2,215 | ZIEBACH | 930 | 375 | 483 | 62 | 10 | 108 D | 40.3% | 51.9% | 6.7% |
| 729,034 | TOTAL | 323,826 | 150,543 | 139,333 | 31,250 | 2,700 | 11,210 R | 46.5% | 43.0% | 9.7% |

# SOUTH DAKOTA

## PRESIDENT 1992

| 1990 Census Population | County | Total Vote | Republican | Democratic | Perot | Other | Plurality | Percentage Total Vote | | |
|---|---|---|---|---|---|---|---|---|---|---|
| | | | | | | | | Rep. | Dem. | Perot |
| 3,135 | AURORA | 1,712 | 594 | 680 | 435 | 3 | 86 D | 34.7% | 39.7% | 25.4% |
| 18,253 | BEADLE | 9,136 | 3,363 | 3,925 | 1,819 | 29 | 562 D | 36.8% | 43.0% | 19.9% |
| 3,206 | BENNETT | 1,197 | 556 | 413 | 221 | 7 | 143 R | 46.4% | 34.5% | 18.5% |
| 7,089 | BONHOMME | 3,367 | 1,212 | 1,294 | 836 | 25 | 82 D | 36.0% | 38.4% | 24.8% |
| 25,207 | BROOKINGS | 12,002 | 4,698 | 4,645 | 2,614 | 45 | 53 R | 39.1% | 38.7% | 21.8% |
| 35,580 | BROWN | 18,047 | 6,665 | 7,521 | 3,812 | 49 | 856 D | 36.9% | 41.7% | 21.1% |
| 5,485 | BRULE | 2,676 | 908 | 1,060 | 687 | 21 | 152 D | 33.9% | 39.6% | 25.7% |
| 1,759 | BUFFALO | 496 | 137 | 282 | 72 | 5 | 145 D | 27.6% | 56.9% | 14.5% |
| 7,914 | BUTTE | 3,700 | 1,674 | 973 | 1,039 | 14 | 635 R | 45.2% | 26.3% | 28.1% |
| 1,965 | CAMPBELL | 1,053 | 574 | 222 | 252 | 5 | 322 R | 54.5% | 21.1% | 23.9% |
| 9,131 | CHARLES MIX | 4,099 | 1,570 | 1,639 | 886 | 4 | 69 D | 38.3% | 40.0% | 21.6% |
| 4,403 | CLARK | 2,375 | 803 | 799 | 761 | 12 | 4 R | 33.8% | 33.6% | 32.0% |
| 13,186 | CLAY | 6,036 | 1,869 | 2,826 | 1,303 | 38 | 957 D | 31.0% | 46.8% | 21.6% |
| 22,698 | CODINGTON | 10,943 | 3,943 | 3,701 | 3,262 | 37 | 242 R | 36.0% | 33.8% | 29.8% |
| 4,195 | CORSON | 1,251 | 483 | 444 | 321 | 3 | 39 R | 38.6% | 35.5% | 25.7% |
| 6,179 | CUSTER | 3,363 | 1,422 | 1,078 | 845 | 18 | 344 R | 42.3% | 32.1% | 25.1% |
| 17,503 | DAVISON | 8,146 | 3,111 | 3,285 | 1,706 | 44 | 174 D | 38.2% | 40.3% | 20.9% |
| 6,978 | DAY | 3,725 | 1,161 | 1,578 | 973 | 13 | 417 D | 31.2% | 42.4% | 26.1% |
| 4,522 | DEUEL | 2,423 | 778 | 880 | 761 | 4 | 102 D | 32.1% | 36.3% | 31.4% |
| 5,523 | DEWEY | 1,752 | 642 | 766 | 340 | 4 | 124 D | 36.6% | 43.7% | 19.4% |
| 3,746 | DOUGLAS | 2,067 | 1,175 | 481 | 403 | 8 | 694 R | 56.8% | 23.3% | 19.5% |
| 4,356 | EDMUNDS | 2,260 | 944 | 894 | 415 | 7 | 50 R | 41.8% | 39.6% | 18.4% |
| 7,353 | FALL RIVER | 3,754 | 1,533 | 1,416 | 792 | 13 | 117 R | 40.8% | 37.7% | 21.1% |
| 2,744 | FAULK | 1,434 | 658 | 488 | 281 | 7 | 170 R | 45.9% | 34.0% | 19.6% |
| 8,372 | GRANT | 4,110 | 1,595 | 1,484 | 1,018 | 13 | 111 R | 38.8% | 36.1% | 24.8% |
| 5,359 | GREGORY | 2,615 | 1,027 | 879 | 688 | 21 | 148 R | 39.3% | 33.6% | 26.3% |
| 2,624 | HAAKON | 1,318 | 860 | 209 | 245 | 4 | 615 R | 65.3% | 15.9% | 18.6% |
| 4,974 | HAMLIN | 2,740 | 1,133 | 826 | 774 | 7 | 307 R | 41.4% | 30.1% | 28.2% |
| 4,272 | HAND | 2,546 | 1,130 | 785 | 624 | 7 | 345 R | 44.4% | 30.8% | 24.5% |
| 2,994 | HANSON | 1,435 | 522 | 566 | 341 | 6 | 44 D | 36.4% | 39.4% | 23.8% |
| 1,669 | HARDING | 881 | 515 | 139 | 225 | 2 | 290 R | 58.5% | 15.8% | 25.5% |
| 14,817 | HUGHES | 8,121 | 4,325 | 2,578 | 1,160 | 58 | 1,747 R | 53.3% | 31.7% | 14.3% |
| 8,262 | HUTCHINSON | 4,156 | 2,002 | 1,211 | 920 | 23 | 791 R | 48.2% | 29.1% | 22.1% |
| 1,696 | HYDE | 955 | 440 | 301 | 211 | 3 | 139 R | 46.1% | 31.5% | 22.1% |
| 2,811 | JACKSON | 1,168 | 627 | 351 | 184 | 6 | 276 R | 53.7% | 30.1% | 15.8% |
| 2,425 | JERAULD | 1,467 | 518 | 600 | 346 | 3 | 82 D | 35.3% | 40.9% | 23.6% |
| 1,324 | JONES | 779 | 454 | 166 | 154 | 5 | 288 R | 58.3% | 21.3% | 19.8% |
| 5,925 | KINGSBURY | 3,143 | 1,113 | 1,267 | 744 | 19 | 154 D | 35.4% | 40.3% | 23.7% |
| 10,550 | LAKE | 5,590 | 1,890 | 2,388 | 1,299 | 13 | 498 D | 33.8% | 42.7% | 23.2% |
| 20,655 | LAWRENCE | 9,659 | 3,770 | 3,157 | 2,673 | 59 | 613 R | 39.0% | 32.7% | 27.7% |
| 15,427 | LINCOLN | 7,923 | 3,365 | 2,943 | 1,593 | 22 | 422 R | 42.5% | 37.1% | 20.1% |
| 3,638 | LYMAN | 1,480 | 669 | 486 | 311 | 14 | 183 R | 45.2% | 32.8% | 21.0% |
| 5,688 | MCCOOK | 2,984 | 1,177 | 1,167 | 617 | 23 | 10 R | 39.4% | 39.1% | 20.7% |
| 3,228 | MCPHERSON | 1,752 | 945 | 478 | 322 | 7 | 467 R | 53.9% | 27.3% | 18.4% |
| 4,844 | MARSHALL | 2,297 | 810 | 1,056 | 427 | 4 | 246 D | 35.3% | 46.0% | 18.6% |
| 21,878 | MEADE | 10,075 | 4,724 | 2,694 | 2,611 | 46 | 2,030 R | 46.9% | 26.7% | 25.9% |
| 2,137 | MELLETTE | 841 | 417 | 277 | 140 | 7 | 140 R | 49.6% | 32.9% | 16.6% |
| 3,272 | MINER | 1,584 | 543 | 698 | 332 | 11 | 155 D | 34.3% | 44.1% | 21.0% |
| 123,809 | MINNEHAHA | 63,786 | 25,081 | 27,016 | 11,496 | 193 | 1,935 D | 39.3% | 42.4% | 18.0% |
| 6,507 | MOODY | 3,104 | 898 | 1,473 | 715 | 18 | 575 D | 28.9% | 47.5% | 23.0% |
| 81,343 | PENNINGTON | 37,669 | 18,052 | 11,106 | 8,358 | 153 | 6,946 R | 47.9% | 29.5% | 22.2% |
| 3,932 | PERKINS | 1,991 | 872 | 566 | 541 | 12 | 306 R | 43.8% | 28.4% | 27.2% |
| 3,190 | POTTER | 1,778 | 901 | 493 | 375 | 9 | 408 R | 50.7% | 27.7% | 21.1% |
| 9,914 | ROBERTS | 4,121 | 1,437 | 1,716 | 954 | 14 | 279 D | 34.9% | 41.6% | 23.1% |
| 2,833 | SANBORN | 1,610 | 595 | 632 | 376 | 7 | 37 D | 37.0% | 39.3% | 23.4% |
| 9,902 | SHANNON | 1,651 | 225 | 1,267 | 137 | 22 | 1,042 D | 13.6% | 76.7% | 8.3% |
| 7,981 | SPINK | 4,112 | 1,527 | 1,732 | 839 | 14 | 205 D | 37.1% | 42.1% | 20.4% |
| 2,453 | STANLEY | 1,399 | 719 | 427 | 240 | 13 | 292 R | 51.4% | 30.5% | 17.2% |
| 1,589 | SULLY | 1,010 | 565 | 273 | 167 | 5 | 292 R | 55.9% | 27.0% | 16.5% |
| 8,352 | TODD | 1,630 | 456 | 915 | 246 | 13 | 459 D | 28.0% | 56.1% | 15.1% |

# SOUTH DAKOTA

## PRESIDENT 1992

| 1990 Census Population | County | Total Vote | Republican | Democratic | Perot | Other | Plurality | Percentage Total Vote | | |
|---|---|---|---|---|---|---|---|---|---|---|
| | | | | | | | | Rep. | Dem. | Perot |
| 6,924 | TRIPP | 3,363 | 1,459 | 1,046 | 848 | 10 | 413 R | 43.4% | 31.1% | 25.2% |
| 8,576 | TURNER | 4,290 | 1,906 | 1,507 | 867 | 10 | 399 R | 44.4% | 35.1% | 20.2% |
| 10,189 | UNION | 5,097 | 1,784 | 2,210 | 1,085 | 18 | 426 D | 35.0% | 43.4% | 21.3% |
| 6,087 | WALWORTH | 2,908 | 1,439 | 829 | 628 | 12 | 610 R | 49.5% | 28.5% | 21.6% |
| | WASHABAUGH | — | — | — | — | — | — | — | — | — |
| 19,252 | YANKTON | 9,372 | 3,430 | 3,404 | 2,511 | 27 | 26 R | 36.6% | 36.3% | 26.8% |
| 2,220 | ZIEBACH | 730 | 328 | 280 | 117 | 5 | 48 R | 44.9% | 38.4% | 16.0% |
| 696,004 | TOTAL | 336,254 | 136,718 | 124,888 | 73,295 | 1,353 | 11,830 R | 40.7% | 37.1% | 21.8% |

# SOUTH DAKOTA

## PRESIDENT 1988

| 1980 Census Population | County | Total Vote | Republican | Democratic | Other | Rep.-Dem. Plurality | Percentage Total Vote Rep. | Dem. | Major Vote Rep. | Dem. |
|---|---|---|---|---|---|---|---|---|---|---|
| 3,628 | AURORA | 1,854 | 856 | 987 | 11 | 131 D | 46.2% | 53.2% | 46.4% | 53.6% |
| 19,195 | BEADLE | 9,180 | 4,611 | 4,523 | 46 | 88 R | 50.2% | 49.3% | 50.5% | 49.5% |
| 3,044 | BENNETT | 1,262 | 663 | 579 | 20 | 84 R | 52.5% | 45.9% | 53.4% | 46.6% |
| 8,059 | BONHOMME | 3,417 | 1,826 | 1,574 | 17 | 252 R | 53.4% | 46.1% | 53.7% | 46.3% |
| 24,332 | BROOKINGS | 10,305 | 5,394 | 4,860 | 51 | 534 R | 52.3% | 47.2% | 52.6% | 47.4% |
| 36,962 | BROWN | 17,302 | 8,537 | 8,673 | 92 | 136 D | 49.3% | 50.1% | 49.6% | 50.4% |
| 5,245 | BRULE | 1,974 | 971 | 991 | 12 | 20 D | 49.2% | 50.2% | 49.5% | 50.5% |
| 1,795 | BUFFALO | 490 | 151 | 334 | 5 | 183 D | 30.8% | 68.2% | 31.1% | 68.9% |
| 8,372 | BUTTE | 3,582 | 2,291 | 1,256 | 35 | 1,035 R | 64.0% | 35.1% | 64.6% | 35.4% |
| 2,243 | CAMPBELL | 1,252 | 909 | 334 | 9 | 575 R | 72.6% | 26.7% | 73.1% | 26.9% |
| 9,680 | CHARLES MIX | 4,184 | 1,966 | 2,205 | 13 | 239 D | 47.0% | 52.7% | 47.1% | 52.9% |
| 4,894 | CLARK | 2,424 | 1,247 | 1,164 | 13 | 83 R | 51.4% | 48.0% | 51.7% | 48.3% |
| 13,689 | CLAY | 5,200 | 2,307 | 2,859 | 34 | 552 D | 44.4% | 55.0% | 44.7% | 55.3% |
| 20,885 | CODINGTON | 9,714 | 5,050 | 4,570 | 94 | 480 R | 52.0% | 47.0% | 52.5% | 47.5% |
| 5,196 | CORSON | 1,448 | 710 | 722 | 16 | 12 D | 49.0% | 49.9% | 49.6% | 50.4% |
| 6,000 | CUSTER | 3,036 | 1,806 | 1,180 | 50 | 626 R | 59.5% | 38.9% | 60.5% | 39.5% |
| 17,820 | DAVISON | 7,786 | 4,024 | 3,705 | 57 | 319 R | 51.7% | 47.6% | 52.1% | 47.9% |
| 8,133 | DAY | 3,774 | 1,616 | 2,137 | 21 | 521 D | 42.8% | 56.6% | 43.1% | 56.9% |
| 5,289 | DEUEL | 2,528 | 1,251 | 1,246 | 31 | 5 R | 49.5% | 49.3% | 50.1% | 49.9% |
| 5,366 | DEWEY | 1,789 | 765 | 1,007 | 17 | 242 D | 42.8% | 56.3% | 43.2% | 56.8% |
| 4,181 | DOUGLAS | 2,139 | 1,438 | 695 | 6 | 743 R | 67.2% | 32.5% | 67.4% | 32.6% |
| 5,159 | EDMUNDS | 2,599 | 1,327 | 1,259 | 13 | 68 R | 51.1% | 48.4% | 51.3% | 48.7% |
| 8,439 | FALL RIVER | 3,417 | 2,002 | 1,380 | 35 | 622 R | 58.6% | 40.4% | 59.2% | 40.8% |
| 3,327 | FAULK | 1,561 | 842 | 714 | 5 | 128 R | 53.9% | 45.7% | 54.1% | 45.9% |
| 9,013 | GRANT | 4,172 | 2,148 | 1,988 | 36 | 160 R | 51.5% | 47.7% | 51.9% | 48.1% |
| 6,015 | GREGORY | 2,722 | 1,566 | 1,138 | 18 | 428 R | 57.5% | 41.8% | 57.9% | 42.1% |
| 2,794 | HAAKON | 1,351 | 958 | 379 | 14 | 579 R | 70.9% | 28.1% | 71.7% | 28.3% |
| 5,261 | HAMLIN | 2,651 | 1,380 | 1,258 | 13 | 122 R | 52.1% | 47.5% | 52.3% | 47.7% |
| 4,948 | HAND | 2,578 | 1,461 | 1,101 | 16 | 360 R | 56.7% | 42.7% | 57.0% | 43.0% |
| 3,415 | HANSON | 1,572 | 786 | 776 | 10 | 10 R | 50.0% | 49.4% | 50.3% | 49.7% |
| 1,700 | HARDING | 900 | 633 | 259 | 8 | 374 R | 70.3% | 28.8% | 71.0% | 29.0% |
| 14,220 | HUGHES | 7,442 | 4,545 | 2,853 | 44 | 1,692 R | 61.1% | 38.3% | 61.4% | 38.6% |
| 9,350 | HUTCHINSON | 4,316 | 2,700 | 1,594 | 22 | 1,106 R | 62.6% | 36.9% | 62.9% | 37.1% |
| 2,069 | HYDE | 1,019 | 546 | 436 | 37 | 110 R | 53.6% | 42.8% | 55.6% | 44.4% |
| 3,437 | JACKSON | 1,141 | 671 | 450 | 20 | 221 R | 58.8% | 39.4% | 59.9% | 40.1% |
| 2,929 | JERAULD | 1,534 | 777 | 751 | 6 | 26 R | 50.7% | 49.0% | 50.9% | 49.1% |
| 1,463 | JONES | 786 | 521 | 261 | 4 | 260 R | 66.3% | 33.2% | 66.6% | 33.4% |
| 6,679 | KINGSBURY | 3,087 | 1,592 | 1,472 | 23 | 120 R | 51.6% | 47.7% | 52.0% | 48.0% |
| 10,724 | LAKE | 5,122 | 2,439 | 2,663 | 20 | 224 D | 47.6% | 52.0% | 47.8% | 52.2% |
| 18,339 | LAWRENCE | 9,379 | 5,570 | 3,705 | 104 | 1,865 R | 59.4% | 39.5% | 60.1% | 39.9% |
| 13,942 | LINCOLN | 6,757 | 3,537 | 3,190 | 30 | 347 R | 52.3% | 47.2% | 52.6% | 47.4% |
| 3,864 | LYMAN | 1,480 | 843 | 631 | 6 | 212 R | 57.0% | 42.6% | 57.2% | 42.8% |
| 6,444 | MCCOOK | 3,002 | 1,501 | 1,492 | 9 | 9 R | 50.0% | 49.7% | 50.2% | 49.8% |
| 4,027 | MCPHERSON | 1,936 | 1,358 | 571 | 7 | 787 R | 70.1% | 29.5% | 70.4% | 29.6% |
| 5,404 | MARSHALL | 2,525 | 1,142 | 1,372 | 11 | 230 D | 45.2% | 54.3% | 45.4% | 54.6% |
| 20,717 | MEADE | 8,473 | 5,189 | 3,212 | 72 | 1,977 R | 61.2% | 37.9% | 61.8% | 38.2% |
| 2,249 | MELLETTE | 852 | 460 | 385 | 7 | 75 R | 54.0% | 45.2% | 54.4% | 45.6% |
| 3,739 | MINER | 1,755 | 795 | 955 | 5 | 160 D | 45.3% | 54.4% | 45.4% | 54.6% |
| 109,435 | MINNEHAHA | 56,095 | 26,765 | 29,135 | 195 | 2,370 D | 47.7% | 51.9% | 47.9% | 52.1% |
| 6,692 | MOODY | 2,889 | 1,161 | 1,715 | 13 | 554 D | 40.2% | 59.4% | 40.4% | 59.6% |
| 70,361 | PENNINGTON | 31,757 | 19,510 | 12,068 | 179 | 7,442 R | 61.4% | 38.0% | 61.8% | 38.2% |
| 4,700 | PERKINS | 2,197 | 1,326 | 851 | 20 | 475 R | 60.4% | 38.7% | 60.9% | 39.1% |
| 3,674 | POTTER | 1,893 | 1,175 | 701 | 17 | 474 R | 62.1% | 37.0% | 62.6% | 37.4% |
| 10,911 | ROBERTS | 4,311 | 2,012 | 2,267 | 32 | 255 D | 46.7% | 52.6% | 47.0% | 53.0% |
| 3,213 | SANBORN | 1,595 | 815 | 770 | 10 | 45 R | 51.1% | 48.3% | 51.4% | 48.6% |
| 11,323 | SHANNON | 1,479 | 256 | 1,206 | 17 | 950 D | 17.3% | 81.5% | 17.5% | 82.5% |
| 9,201 | SPINK | 4,062 | 1,969 | 2,071 | 22 | 102 D | 48.5% | 51.0% | 48.7% | 51.3% |
| 2,533 | STANLEY | 1,219 | 698 | 511 | 10 | 187 R | 57.3% | 41.9% | 57.7% | 42.3% |
| 1,990 | SULLY | 1,006 | 571 | 393 | 42 | 178 R | 56.8% | 39.1% | 59.2% | 40.8% |
| 7,328 | TODD | 1,676 | 535 | 1,117 | 24 | 582 D | 31.9% | 66.6% | 32.4% | 67.6% |

# SOUTH DAKOTA

## PRESIDENT 1988

| 1980 Census Population | County | Total Vote | Republican | Democratic | Other | Rep.-Dem. Plurality | Percentage | | | |
|---|---|---|---|---|---|---|---|---|---|---|
| | | | | | | | Total Vote | | Major Vote | |
| | | | | | | | Rep. | Dem. | Rep. | Dem. |
| 7,268 | TRIPP | 3,356 | 2,113 | 1,219 | 24 | 894 R | 63.0% | 36.3% | 63.4% | 36.6% |
| 9,255 | TURNER | 4,239 | 2,436 | 1,780 | 23 | 656 R | 57.5% | 42.0% | 57.8% | 42.2% |
| 10,938 | UNION | 4,550 | 1,907 | 2,612 | 31 | 705 D | 41.9% | 57.4% | 42.2% | 57.8% |
| 7,011 | WALWORTH | 3,060 | 1,940 | 1,094 | 26 | 846 R | 63.4% | 35.8% | 63.9% | 36.1% |
| | WASHABAUGH | — | — | — | — | — | — | — | — | — |
| 18,952 | YANKTON | 8,043 | 4,186 | 3,777 | 80 | 409 R | 52.0% | 47.0% | 52.6% | 47.4% |
| 2,308 | ZIEBACH | 795 | 362 | 427 | 6 | 65 D | 45.5% | 53.7% | 45.9% | 54.1% |
| 690,768 | TOTAL | 312,991 | 165,415 | 145,560 | 2,016 | 19,855 R | 52.8% | 46.5% | 53.2% | 46.8% |

846

# SOUTH DAKOTA

## PRESIDENT 1984

| 1980 Census Population | County | Total Vote | Republican | Democratic | Other | Rep.-Dem. Plurality | Total Vote Rep. | Total Vote Dem. | Major Vote Rep. | Major Vote Dem. |
|---|---|---|---|---|---|---|---|---|---|---|
| 3,628 | AURORA | 1,883 | 1,029 | 840 | 14 | 189 R | 54.6% | 44.6% | 55.1% | 44.9% |
| 19,195 | BEADLE | 9,422 | 5,876 | 3,523 | 23 | 2,353 R | 62.4% | 37.4% | 62.5% | 37.5% |
| 3,044 | BENNETT | 1,316 | 856 | 453 | 7 | 403 R | 65.0% | 34.4% | 65.4% | 34.6% |
| 8,059 | BONHOMME | 3,906 | 2,478 | 1,408 | 20 | 1,070 R | 63.4% | 36.0% | 63.8% | 36.2% |
| 24,332 | BROOKINGS | 10,814 | 6,679 | 4,089 | 46 | 2,590 R | 61.8% | 37.8% | 62.0% | 38.0% |
| 36,962 | BROWN | 17,465 | 10,541 | 6,852 | 72 | 3,689 R | 60.4% | 39.2% | 60.6% | 39.4% |
| 5,245 | BRULE | 2,556 | 1,578 | 961 | 17 | 617 R | 61.7% | 37.6% | 62.2% | 37.8% |
| 1,795 | BUFFALO | 494 | 253 | 236 | 5 | 17 R | 51.2% | 47.8% | 51.7% | 48.3% |
| 8,372 | BUTTE | 3,667 | 2,865 | 784 | 18 | 2,081 R | 78.1% | 21.4% | 78.5% | 21.5% |
| 2,243 | CAMPBELL | 1,255 | 1,035 | 214 | 6 | 821 R | 82.5% | 17.1% | 82.9% | 17.1% |
| 9,680 | CHARLES MIX | 4,563 | 2,660 | 1,879 | 24 | 781 R | 58.3% | 41.2% | 58.6% | 41.4% |
| 4,894 | CLARK | 2,718 | 1,748 | 960 | 10 | 788 R | 64.3% | 35.3% | 64.5% | 35.5% |
| 13,689 | CLAY | 5,808 | 3,057 | 2,711 | 40 | 346 R | 52.6% | 46.7% | 53.0% | 47.0% |
| 20,885 | CODINGTON | 9,678 | 6,108 | 3,528 | 42 | 2,580 R | 63.1% | 36.5% | 63.4% | 36.6% |
| 5,196 | CORSON | 1,753 | 955 | 792 | 6 | 163 R | 54.5% | 45.2% | 54.7% | 45.3% |
| 6,000 | CUSTER | 3,063 | 2,183 | 858 | 22 | 1,325 R | 71.3% | 28.0% | 71.8% | 28.2% |
| 17,820 | DAVISON | 8,048 | 4,783 | 3,248 | 17 | 1,535 R | 59.4% | 40.4% | 59.6% | 40.4% |
| 8,133 | DAY | 4,101 | 2,150 | 1,932 | 19 | 218 R | 52.4% | 47.1% | 52.7% | 47.3% |
| 5,289 | DEUEL | 2,490 | 1,537 | 941 | 12 | 596 R | 61.7% | 37.8% | 62.0% | 38.0% |
| 5,366 | DEWEY | 1,727 | 941 | 772 | 14 | 169 R | 54.5% | 44.7% | 54.9% | 45.1% |
| 4,181 | DOUGLAS | 2,254 | 1,713 | 536 | 5 | 1,177 R | 76.0% | 23.8% | 76.2% | 23.8% |
| 5,159 | EDMUNDS | 2,570 | 1,553 | 1,007 | 10 | 546 R | 60.4% | 39.2% | 60.7% | 39.3% |
| 8,439 | FALL RIVER | 3,905 | 2,748 | 1,135 | 22 | 1,613 R | 70.4% | 29.1% | 70.8% | 29.2% |
| 3,327 | FAULK | 1,706 | 1,124 | 579 | 3 | 545 R | 65.9% | 33.9% | 66.0% | 34.0% |
| 9,013 | GRANT | 4,360 | 2,738 | 1,606 | 16 | 1,132 R | 62.8% | 36.8% | 63.0% | 37.0% |
| 6,015 | GREGORY | 2,569 | 1,777 | 780 | 12 | 997 R | 69.2% | 30.4% | 69.5% | 30.5% |
| 2,794 | HAAKON | 1,410 | 1,168 | 237 | 5 | 931 R | 82.8% | 16.8% | 83.1% | 16.9% |
| 5,261 | HAMLIN | 2,761 | 1,782 | 963 | 16 | 819 R | 64.5% | 34.9% | 64.9% | 35.1% |
| 4,948 | HAND | 2,886 | 2,030 | 846 | 10 | 1,184 R | 70.3% | 29.3% | 70.6% | 29.4% |
| 3,415 | HANSON | 1,530 | 898 | 625 | 7 | 273 R | 58.7% | 40.8% | 59.0% | 41.0% |
| 1,700 | HARDING | 912 | 723 | 186 | 3 | 537 R | 79.3% | 20.4% | 79.5% | 20.5% |
| 14,220 | HUGHES | 7,089 | 4,985 | 2,072 | 32 | 2,913 R | 70.3% | 29.2% | 70.6% | 29.4% |
| 9,350 | HUTCHINSON | 4,624 | 3,372 | 1,237 | 15 | 2,135 R | 72.9% | 26.8% | 73.2% | 26.8% |
| 2,069 | HYDE | 1,148 | 797 | 350 | 1 | 447 R | 69.4% | 30.5% | 69.5% | 30.5% |
| 3,437 | JACKSON | 1,275 | 903 | 365 | 7 | 538 R | 70.8% | 28.6% | 71.2% | 28.8% |
| 2,929 | JERAULD | 1,562 | 1,012 | 542 | 8 | 470 R | 64.8% | 34.7% | 65.1% | 34.9% |
| 1,463 | JONES | 899 | 689 | 206 | 4 | 483 R | 76.6% | 22.9% | 77.0% | 23.0% |
| 6,679 | KINGSBURY | 3,383 | 2,121 | 1,249 | 13 | 872 R | 62.7% | 36.9% | 62.9% | 37.1% |
| 10,724 | LAKE | 5,413 | 3,027 | 2,367 | 19 | 660 R | 55.9% | 43.7% | 56.1% | 43.9% |
| 18,339 | LAWRENCE | 8,569 | 5,949 | 2,565 | 55 | 3,384 R | 69.4% | 29.9% | 69.9% | 30.1% |
| 13,942 | LINCOLN | 6,636 | 3,988 | 2,626 | 22 | 1,362 R | 60.1% | 39.6% | 60.3% | 39.7% |
| 3,864 | LYMAN | 1,605 | 1,120 | 478 | 7 | 642 R | 69.8% | 29.8% | 70.1% | 29.9% |
| 6,444 | MCCOOK | 3,362 | 1,902 | 1,448 | 12 | 454 R | 56.6% | 43.1% | 56.8% | 43.2% |
| 4,027 | MCPHERSON | 2,236 | 1,813 | 418 | 5 | 1,395 R | 81.1% | 18.7% | 81.3% | 18.7% |
| 5,404 | MARSHALL | 2,649 | 1,529 | 1,111 | 9 | 418 R | 57.7% | 41.9% | 57.9% | 42.1% |
| 20,717 | MEADE | 8,041 | 5,908 | 2,093 | 40 | 3,815 R | 73.5% | 26.0% | 73.8% | 26.2% |
| 2,249 | MELLETTE | 927 | 616 | 303 | 8 | 313 R | 66.5% | 32.7% | 67.0% | 33.0% |
| 3,739 | MINER | 1,977 | 1,004 | 960 | 13 | 44 R | 50.8% | 48.6% | 51.1% | 48.9% |
| 109,435 | MINNEHAHA | 53,171 | 29,908 | 23,042 | 221 | 6,866 R | 56.2% | 43.3% | 56.5% | 43.5% |
| 6,692 | MOODY | 3,228 | 1,633 | 1,586 | 9 | 47 R | 50.6% | 49.1% | 50.7% | 49.3% |
| 70,361 | PENNINGTON | 30,389 | 21,947 | 8,224 | 218 | 13,723 R | 72.2% | 27.1% | 72.7% | 27.3% |
| 4,700 | PERKINS | 2,411 | 1,686 | 714 | 11 | 972 R | 69.9% | 29.6% | 70.3% | 29.8% |
| 3,674 | POTTER | 2,035 | 1,551 | 482 | 2 | 1,069 R | 76.2% | 23.7% | 76.3% | 23.7% |
| 10,911 | ROBERTS | 4,840 | 2,767 | 2,063 | 10 | 704 R | 57.2% | 42.6% | 57.3% | 42.7% |
| 3,213 | SANBORN | 1,695 | 1,080 | 611 | 4 | 469 R | 63.7% | 36.0% | 63.9% | 36.1% |
| 11,323 | SHANNON | 1,829 | 324 | 1,489 | 16 | 1,165 D | 17.7% | 81.4% | 17.9% | 82.1% |
| 9,201 | SPINK | 4,324 | 2,627 | 1,680 | 17 | 947 R | 60.8% | 38.9% | 61.0% | 39.0% |
| 2,533 | STANLEY | 1,299 | 942 | 351 | 6 | 591 R | 72.5% | 27.0% | 72.9% | 27.1% |
| 1,990 | SULLY | 1,107 | 836 | 266 | 5 | 570 R | 75.5% | 24.0% | 75.9% | 24.1% |
| 7,328 | TODD | 1,714 | 679 | 1,022 | 13 | 343 D | 39.6% | 59.6% | 39.9% | 60.1% |

# SOUTH DAKOTA

## PRESIDENT 1984

| 1980 Census Population | County | Total Vote | Republican | Democratic | Other | Rep.-Dem. Plurality | Percentage | | | |
|---|---|---|---|---|---|---|---|---|---|---|
| | | | | | | | Total Vote | | Major Vote | |
| | | | | | | | Rep. | Dem. | Rep. | Dem. |
| 7,268 | TRIPP | 3,440 | 2,483 | 935 | 22 | 1,548 R | 72.2% | 27.2% | 72.6% | 27.4% |
| 9,255 | TURNER | 4,592 | 3,086 | 1,486 | 20 | 1,600 R | 67.2% | 32.4% | 67.5% | 32.5% |
| 10,938 | UNION | 4,677 | 2,431 | 2,221 | 25 | 210 R | 52.0% | 47.5% | 52.3% | 47.7% |
| 7,011 | WALWORTH | 3,194 | 2,396 | 779 | 19 | 1,617 R | 75.0% | 24.4% | 75.5% | 24.5% |
| | WASHABAUGH | — | — | — | — | — | — | — | — | — |
| 18,952 | YANKTON | 8,145 | 5,161 | 2,932 | 52 | 2,229 R | 63.4% | 36.0% | 63.8% | 36.2% |
| 2,308 | ZIEBACH | 792 | 429 | 359 | 4 | 70 R | 54.2% | 45.3% | 54.4% | 45.6% |
| 690,768 | TOTAL | 317,867 | 200,267 | 116,113 | 1,487 | 84,154 R | 63.0% | 36.5% | 63.3% | 36.7% |

# SOUTH DAKOTA

## PRESIDENT 1980

| 1980 Census Population | County | Total Vote | Republican | Democratic | Other | Rep.-Dem. Plurality | Percentage — Total Vote | | Percentage — Major Vote | |
|---|---|---|---|---|---|---|---|---|---|---|
| | | | | | | | Rep. | Dem. | Rep. | Dem. |
| 3,628 | AURORA | 2,123 | 1,251 | 709 | 163 | 542 R | 58.9% | 33.4% | 63.8% | 36.2% |
| 19,195 | BEADLE | 10,104 | 5,921 | 3,521 | 662 | 2,400 R | 58.6% | 34.8% | 62.7% | 37.3% |
| 3,044 | BENNETT | 1,324 | 919 | 350 | 55 | 569 R | 69.4% | 26.4% | 72.4% | 27.6% |
| 8,059 | BONHOMME | 4,239 | 2,794 | 1,191 | 254 | 1,603 R | 65.9% | 28.1% | 70.1% | 29.9% |
| 24,332 | BROOKINGS | 10,981 | 5,727 | 3,934 | 1,320 | 1,793 R | 52.2% | 35.8% | 59.3% | 40.7% |
| 36,962 | BROWN | 17,999 | 10,550 | 6,050 | 1,399 | 4,500 R | 58.6% | 33.6% | 63.6% | 36.4% |
| 5,245 | BRULE | 2,800 | 1,674 | 925 | 201 | 749 R | 59.8% | 33.0% | 64.4% | 35.6% |
| 1,795 | BUFFALO | 456 | 272 | 147 | 37 | 125 R | 59.6% | 32.2% | 64.9% | 35.1% |
| 8,372 | BUTTE | 3,898 | 2,850 | 843 | 205 | 2,007 R | 73.1% | 21.6% | 77.2% | 22.8% |
| 2,243 | CAMPBELL | 1,498 | 1,271 | 182 | 45 | 1,089 R | 84.8% | 12.1% | 87.5% | 12.5% |
| 9,680 | CHARLES MIX | 4,599 | 2,608 | 1,741 | 250 | 867 R | 56.7% | 37.9% | 60.0% | 40.0% |
| 4,894 | CLARK | 2,911 | 1,963 | 774 | 174 | 1,189 R | 67.4% | 26.6% | 71.7% | 28.3% |
| 13,689 | CLAY | 6,316 | 3,004 | 2,271 | 1,041 | 733 R | 47.6% | 36.0% | 56.9% | 43.1% |
| 20,885 | CODINGTON | 9,990 | 5,903 | 3,353 | 734 | 2,550 R | 59.1% | 33.6% | 63.8% | 36.2% |
| 5,196 | CORSON | 1,855 | 1,233 | 522 | 100 | 711 R | 66.5% | 28.1% | 70.3% | 29.7% |
| 6,000 | CUSTER | 2,955 | 2,057 | 708 | 190 | 1,349 R | 69.6% | 24.0% | 74.4% | 25.6% |
| 17,820 | DAVISON | 8,512 | 4,743 | 3,107 | 662 | 1,636 R | 55.7% | 36.5% | 60.4% | 39.6% |
| 8,133 | DAY | 4,543 | 2,507 | 1,720 | 316 | 787 R | 55.2% | 37.9% | 59.3% | 40.7% |
| 5,289 | DEUEL | 2,744 | 1,657 | 891 | 196 | 766 R | 60.4% | 32.5% | 65.0% | 35.0% |
| 5,366 | DEWEY | 1,767 | 1,045 | 600 | 122 | 445 R | 59.1% | 34.0% | 63.5% | 36.5% |
| 4,181 | DOUGLAS | 2,463 | 1,855 | 508 | 100 | 1,347 R | 75.3% | 20.6% | 78.5% | 21.5% |
| 5,159 | EDMUNDS | 2,914 | 1,881 | 883 | 150 | 998 R | 64.6% | 30.3% | 68.1% | 31.9% |
| 8,439 | FALL RIVER | 4,067 | 2,831 | 982 | 254 | 1,849 R | 69.6% | 24.1% | 74.2% | 25.8% |
| 3,327 | FAULK | 1,945 | 1,300 | 520 | 125 | 780 R | 66.8% | 26.7% | 71.4% | 28.6% |
| 9,013 | GRANT | 4,594 | 2,691 | 1,602 | 301 | 1,089 R · | 58.6% | 34.9% | 62.7% | 37.3% |
| 6,015 | GREGORY | 3,340 | 2,283 | 883 | 174 | 1,400 R | 68.4% | 26.4% | 72.1% | 27.9% |
| 2,794 | HAAKON | 1,465 | 1,162 | 255 | 48 | 907 R | 79.3% | 17.4% | 82.0% | 18.0% |
| 5,261 | HAMLIN | 3,007 | 1,885 | 903 | 219 | 982 R | 62.7% | 30.0% | 67.6% | 32.4% |
| 4,948 | HAND | 3,066 | 2,066 | 803 | 197 | 1,263 R | 67.4% | 26.2% | 72.0% | 28.0% |
| 3,415 | HANSON | 1,725 | 1,015 | 598 | 112 | 417 R | 58.8% | 34.7% | 62.9% | 37.1% |
| 1,700 | HARDING | 974 | 727 | 205 | 42 | 522 R | 74.6% | 21.0% | 78.0% | 22.0% |
| 14,220 | HUGHES | 7,048 | 4,652 | 1,751 | 645 | 2,901 R | 66.0% | 24.8% | 72.7% | 27.3% |
| 9,350 | HUTCHINSON | 5,180 | 3,789 | 1,145 | 246 | 2,644 R | 73.1% | 22.1% | 76.8% | 23.2% |
| 2,069 | HYDE | 1,221 | 864 | 273 | 84 | 591 R | 70.8% | 22.4% | 76.0% | 24.0% |
| 3,437 | JACKSON | 1,352 | 929 | 354 | 69 | 575 R | 68.7% | 26.2% | 72.4% | 27.6% |
| 2,929 | JERAULD | 1,729 | 1,018 | 595 | 116 | 423 R | 58.9% | 34.4% | 63.1% | 36.9% |
| 1,463 | JONES | 919 | 689 | 189 | 41 | 500 R | 75.0% | 20.6% | 78.5% | 21.5% |
| 6,679 | KINGSBURY | 3,807 | 2,376 | 1,132 | 299 | 1,244 R | 62.4% | 29.7% | 67.7% | 32.3% |
| 10,724 | LAKE | 5,852 | 3,093 | 2,207 | 552 | 886 R | 52.9% | 37.7% | 58.4% | 41.6% |
| 18,339 | LAWRENCE | 8,403 | 5,306 | 2,259 | 838 | 3,047 R | 63.1% | 26.9% | 70.1% | 29.9% |
| 13,942 | LINCOLN | 6,698 | 3,848 | 2,261 | 589 | 1,587 R | 57.4% | 33.8% | 63.0% | 37.0% |
| 3,864 | LYMAN | 1,878 | 1,256 | 486 | 136 | 770 R | 66.9% | 25.9% | 72.1% | 27.9% |
| 6,444 | MCCOOK | 3,544 | 2,014 | 1,223 | 307 | 791 R | 56.8% | 34.5% | 62.2% | 37.8% |
| 4,027 | MCPHERSON | 2,402 | 2,056 | 287 | 59 | 1,769 R | 85.6% | 11.9% | 87.8% | 12.2% |
| 5,404 | MARSHALL | 3,001 | 1,710 | 1,120 | 171 | 590 R | 57.0% | 37.3% | 60.4% | 39.6% |
| 20,717 | MEADE | 7,541 | 5,349 | 1,721 | 471 | 3,628 R | 70.9% | 22.8% | 75.7% | 24.3% |
| 2,249 | MELLETTE | 963 | 624 | 279 | 60 | 345 R | 64.8% | 29.0% | 69.1% | 30.9% |
| 3,739 | MINER | 2,171 | 1,172 | 833 | 166 | 339 R | 54.0% | 38.4% | 58.5% | 41.5% |
| 109,435 | MINNEHAHA | 51,478 | 26,256 | 20,008 | 5,214 | 6,248 R | 51.0% | 38.9% | 56.8% | 43.2% |
| 6,692 | MOODY | 3,480 | 1,807 | 1,364 | 309 | 443 R | 51.9% | 39.2% | 57.0% | 43.0% |
| 70,361 | PENNINGTON | 28,204 | 18,991 | 7,121 | 2,092 | 11,870 R | 67.3% | 25.2% | 72.7% | 27.3% |
| 4,700 | PERKINS | 2,655 | 1,931 | 595 | 129 | 1,336 R | 72.7% | 22.4% | 76.4% | 23.6% |
| 3,674 | POTTER | 2,169 | 1,633 | 436 | 100 | 1,197 R | 75.3% | 20.1% | 78.9% | 21.1% |
| 10,911 | ROBERTS | 5,009 | 2,904 | 1,829 | 276 | 1,075 R | 58.0% | 36.5% | 61.4% | 38.6% |
| 3,213 | SANBORN | 1,932 | 1,178 | 628 | 126 | 550 R | 61.0% | 32.5% | 65.2% | 34.8% |
| 11,323 | SHANNON | 1,687 | 438 | 1,132 | 117 | 694 D | 26.0% | 67.1% | 27.9% | 72.1% |
| 9,201 | SPINK | 4,834 | 2,915 | 1,572 | 347 | 1,343 R | 60.3% | 32.5% | 65.0% | 35.0% |
| 2,533 | STANLEY | 1,299 | 892 | 339 | 68 | 553 R | 68.7% | 26.1% | 72.5% | 27.5% |
| 1,990 | SULLY | 1,149 | 852 | 220 | 77 | 632 R | 74.2% | 19.1% | 79.5% | 20.5% |
| 7,328 | TODD | 1,923 | 803 | 972 | 148 | 169 D | 41.8% | 50.5% | 45.2% | 54.8% |

# SOUTH DAKOTA

## PRESIDENT 1980

| 1980 Census Population | County | Total Vote | Republican | Democratic | Other | Rep.-Dem. Plurality | Percentage | | | |
|---|---|---|---|---|---|---|---|---|---|---|
| | | | | | | | Total Vote | | Major Vote | |
| | | | | | | | Rep. | Dem. | Rep. | Dem. |
| 7,268 | TRIPP | 3,776 | 2,669 | 947 | 160 | 1,722 R | 70.7% | 25.1% | 73.8% | 26.2% |
| 9,255 | TURNER | 5,032 | 3,343 | 1,369 | 320 | 1,974 R | 66.4% | 27.2% | 70.9% | 29.1% |
| 10,938 | UNION | 5,054 | 2,788 | 1,830 | 436 | 958 R | 55.2% | 36.2% | 60.4% | 39.6% |
| 7,011 | WALWORTH | 3,588 | 2,675 | 753 | 160 | 1,922 R | 74.6% | 21.0% | 78.0% | 22.0% |
| | WASHABAUGH | -- | -- | -- | -- | -- | -- | -- | -- | -- |
| 18,952 | YANKTON | 8,747 | 5,355 | 2,698 | 694 | 2,657 R | 61.2% | 30.8% | 66.5% | 33.5% |
| 2,308 | ZIEBACH | 804 | 523 | 246 | 35 | 277 R | 65.0% | 30.6% | 68.0% | 32.0% |
| 690,768 | TOTAL | 327,703 | 198,343 | 103,855 | 25,505 | 94,488 R | 60.5% | 31.7% | 65.6% | 34.4% |

# SOUTH DAKOTA

## PRESIDENT 1976

| 1970 Census Population | County | Total Vote | Republican | Democratic | Other | Rep.-Dem. Plurality | Percentage | | | |
|---|---|---|---|---|---|---|---|---|---|---|
| | | | | | | | Total Vote | | Major Vote | |
| | | | | | | | Rep. | Dem. | Rep. | Dem. |
| 4,183 | AURORA | 2,109 | 831 | 1,269 | 9 | 438 D | 39.4% | 60.2% | 39.6% | 60.4% |
| 20,877 | BEADLE | 9,666 | 4,758 | 4,846 | 62 | 88 D | 49.2% | 50.1% | 49.5% | 50.5% |
| 3,088 | BENNETT | 1,111 | 610 | 481 | 20 | 129 R | 54.9% | 43.3% | 55.9% | 44.1% |
| 8,577 | BONHOMME | 4,073 | 1,897 | 2,154 | 22 | 257 D | 46.6% | 52.9% | 46.8% | 53.2% |
| 22,158 | BROOKINGS | 10,026 | 5,278 | 4,685 | 63 | 593 R | 52.6% | 46.7% | 53.0% | 47.0% |
| 36,920 | BROWN | 16,633 | 7,609 | 8,888 | 136 | 1,279 D | 45.7% | 53.4% | 46.1% | 53.9% |
| 5,870 | BRULE | 2,723 | 1,175 | 1,534 | 14 | 359 D | 43.2% | 56.3% | 43.4% | 56.6% |
| 1,739 | BUFFALO | 434 | 194 | 240 | | 46 D | 44.7% | 55.3% | 44.7% | 55.3% |
| 7,825 | BUTTE | 3,472 | 2,055 | 1,366 | 51 | 689 R | 59.2% | 39.3% | 60.1% | 39.9% |
| 2,866 | CAMPBELL | 1,391 | 897 | 489 | 5 | 408 R | 64.5% | 35.2% | 64.7% | 35.3% |
| 9,994 | CHARLES MIX | 4,394 | 1,779 | 2,593 | 22 | 814 D | 40.5% | 59.0% | 40.7% | 59.3% |
| 5,515 | CLARK | 2,838 | 1,449 | 1,376 | 13 | 73 R | 51.1% | 48.5% | 51.3% | 48.7% |
| 12,923 | CLAY | 5,301 | 2,647 | 2,593 | 61 | 54 R | 49.9% | 48.9% | 50.5% | 49.5% |
| 19,140 | CODINGTON | 9,213 | 4,504 | 4,680 | 29 | 176 D | 48.9% | 50.8% | 49.0% | 51.0% |
| 4,994 | CORSON | 1,823 | 846 | 967 | 10 | 121 D | 46.4% | 53.0% | 46.7% | 53.3% |
| 4,698 | CUSTER | 2,405 | 1,373 | 995 | 37 | 378 R | 57.1% | 41.4% | 58.0% | 42.0% |
| 17,319 | DAVISON | 8,248 | 3,688 | 4,510 | 50 | 822 D | 44.7% | 54.7% | 45.0% | 55.0% |
| 8,713 | DAY | 4,257 | 1,617 | 2,610 | 30 | 993 D | 38.0% | 61.3% | 38.3% | 61.7% |
| 5,686 | DEUEL | 2,652 | 1,177 | 1,465 | 10 | 288 D | 44.4% | 55.2% | 44.5% | 55.5% |
| 5,170 | DEWEY | 1,534 | 820 | 706 | 8 | 114 R | 53.5% | 46.0% | 53.7% | 46.3% |
| 4,569 | DOUGLAS | 2,295 | 1,315 | 975 | 5 | 340 R | 57.3% | 42.5% | 57.4% | 42.6% |
| 5,548 | EDMUNDS | 2,932 | 1,294 | 1,629 | 9 | 335 D | 44.1% | 55.6% | 44.3% | 55.7% |
| 7,505 | FALL RIVER | 3,615 | 2,046 | 1,537 | 32 | 509 R | 56.6% | 42.5% | 57.1% | 42.9% |
| 3,893 | FAULK | 1,937 | 868 | 1,063 | 6 | 195 D | 44.8% | 54.9% | 45.0% | 55.0% |
| 9,005 | GRANT | 4,464 | 2,051 | 2,398 | 15 | 347 D | 45.9% | 53.7% | 46.1% | 53.9% |
| 6,710 | GREGORY | 3,145 | 1,475 | 1,658 | 12 | 183 D | 46.9% | 52.7% | 47.1% | 52.9% |
| 2,802 | HAAKON | 1,312 | 812 | 477 | 23 | 335 R | 61.9% | 36.4% | 63.0% | 37.0% |
| 5,520 | HAMLIN | 2,866 | 1,452 | 1,402 | 12 | 50 R | 50.7% | 48.9% | 50.9% | 49.1% |
| 5,883 | HAND | 2,994 | 1,510 | 1,477 | 7 | 33 R | 50.4% | 49.3% | 50.6% | 49.4% |
| 3,781 | HANSON | 1,707 | 693 | 1,005 | 9 | 312 D | 40.6% | 58.9% | 40.8% | 59.2% |
| 1,855 | HARDING | 945 | 470 | 459 | 16 | 11 R | 49.7% | 48.6% | 50.6% | 49.4% |
| 11,632 | HUGHES | 6,536 | 3,997 | 2,506 | 33 | 1,491 R | 61.2% | 38.3% | 61.5% | 38.5% |
| 10,379 | HUTCHINSON | 4,906 | 2,822 | 2,062 | 22 | 760 R | 57.5% | 42.0% | 57.8% | 42.2% |
| 2,515 | HYDE | 1,263 | 687 | 572 | 4 | 115 R | 54.4% | 45.3% | 54.6% | 45.4% |
| 1,531 | JACKSON | 865 | 532 | 313 | 20 | 219 R | 61.5% | 36.2% | 63.0% | 37.0% |
| 3,310 | JERAULD | 1,669 | 821 | 845 | 3 | 24 D | 49.2% | 50.6% | 49.3% | 50.7% |
| 1,882 | JONES | 890 | 515 | 374 | 1 | 141 R | 57.9% | 42.0% | 57.9% | 42.1% |
| 7,657 | KINGSBURY | 3,617 | 1,844 | 1,762 | 11 | 82 R | 51.0% | 48.7% | 51.1% | 48.9% |
| 11,456 | LAKE | 5,476 | 2,530 | 2,930 | 16 | 400 D | 46.2% | 53.5% | 46.3% | 53.7% |
| 17,453 | LAWRENCE | 7,449 | 4,206 | 3,102 | 141 | 1,104 R | 56.5% | 41.6% | 57.6% | 42.4% |
| 11,761 | LINCOLN | 6,084 | 3,105 | 2,957 | 22 | 148 R | 51.0% | 48.6% | 51.2% | 48.8% |
| 4,060 | LYMAN | 1,739 | 892 | 831 | 16 | 61 R | 51.3% | 47.8% | 51.8% | 48.2% |
| 7,246 | MCCOOK | 3,578 | 1,744 | 1,822 | 12 | 78 D | 48.7% | 50.9% | 48.9% | 51.1% |
| 5,022 | MCPHERSON | 2,367 | 1,662 | 693 | 12 | 969 R | 70.2% | 29.3% | 70.6% | 29.4% |
| 5,965 | MARSHALL | 2,967 | 1,233 | 1,721 | 13 | 488 D | 41.6% | 58.0% | 41.7% | 58.3% |
| 17,020 | MEADE | 5,690 | 3,096 | 2,478 | 116 | 618 R | 54.4% | 43.6% | 55.5% | 44.5% |
| 2,420 | MELLETTE | 949 | 508 | 429 | 12 | 79 R | 53.5% | 45.2% | 54.2% | 45.8% |
| 4,454 | MINER | 2,140 | 839 | 1,289 | 12 | 450 D | 39.2% | 60.2% | 39.4% | 60.6% |
| 95,209 | MINNEHAHA | 45,556 | 23,286 | 22,068 | 202 | 1,218 R | 51.1% | 48.4% | 51.3% | 48.7% |
| 7,622 | MOODY | 3,428 | 1,475 | 1,942 | 11 | 467 D | 43.0% | 56.7% | 43.2% | 56.8% |
| 59,349 | PENNINGTON | 23,699 | 13,352 | 10,058 | 289 | 3,294 R | 56.3% | 42.4% | 57.0% | 43.0% |
| 4,769 | PERKINS | 2,592 | 1,298 | 1,262 | 32 | 36 R | 50.1% | 48.7% | 50.7% | 49.3% |
| 4,449 | POTTER | 2,052 | 1,136 | 908 | 8 | 228 R | 55.4% | 44.2% | 55.6% | 44.4% |
| 11,678 | ROBERTS | 4,820 | 1,915 | 2,890 | 15 | 975 D | 39.7% | 60.0% | 39.9% | 60.1% |
| 3,697 | SANBORN | 1,912 | 881 | 1,025 | 6 | 144 D | 46.1% | 53.6% | 46.2% | 53.8% |
| 8,198 | SHANNON | 1,081 | 301 | 756 | 24 | 455 D | 27.8% | 69.9% | 28.5% | 71.5% |
| 10,595 | SPINK | 4,679 | 2,003 | 2,650 | 26 | 647 D | 42.8% | 56.6% | 43.0% | 57.0% |
| 2,457 | STANLEY | 1,189 | 637 | 548 | 4 | 89 R | 53.6% | 46.1% | 53.8% | 46.2% |
| 2,362 | SULLY | 1,139 | 630 | 505 | 4 | 125 R | 55.3% | 44.3% | 55.5% | 44.5% |
| 6,606 | TODD | 1,434 | 583 | 826 | 25 | 243 D | 40.7% | 57.6% | 41.4% | 58.6% |

# SOUTH DAKOTA

## PRESIDENT 1976

| 1970 Census Population | County | Total Vote | Republican | Democratic | Other | Rep.-Dem. Plurality | Percentage | | | |
|---|---|---|---|---|---|---|---|---|---|---|
| | | | | | | | Total Vote | | Major Vote | |
| | | | | | | | Rep. | Dem. | Rep. | Dem. |
| 8,171 | TRIPP | 3,817 | 1,980 | 1,822 | 15 | 158 R | 51.9% | 47.7% | 52.1% | 47.9% |
| 9,872 | TURNER | 4,618 | 2,694 | 1,906 | 18 | 788 R | 58.3% | 41.3% | 58.6% | 41.4% |
| 9,643 | UNION | 4,860 | 2,297 | 2,540 | 23 | 243 D | 47.3% | 52.3% | 47.5% | 52.5% |
| 7,842 | WALWORTH | 3,728 | 2,187 | 1,516 | 25 | 671 R | 58.7% | 40.7% | 59.1% | 40.9% |
| 1,389 | WASHABAUGH | 526 | 229 | 276 | 21 | 47 D | 43.5% | 52.5% | 45.3% | 54.7% |
| 19,039 | YANKTON | 8,087 | 4,029 | 3,987 | 71 | 42 R | 49.8% | 49.3% | 50.3% | 49.7% |
| 2,221 | ZIEBACH | 761 | 369 | 370 | 22 | 1 D | 48.5% | 48.6% | 49.9% | 50.1% |
| 666,257 | TOTAL | 300,678 | 151,505 | 147,068 | 2,105 | 4,437 R | 50.4% | 48.9% | 50.7% | 49.3% |

# SOUTH DAKOTA

## PRESIDENT 1972

| 1970 Census Population | County | Total Vote | Republican | Democratic | Other | Rep.-Dem. Plurality | Percentage Total Vote Rep. | Dem. | Major Vote Rep. | Dem. |
|---|---|---|---|---|---|---|---|---|---|---|
| 4,183 | AURORA | 2,339 | 1,075 | 1,257 | 7 | 182 D | 46.0% | 53.7% | 46.1% | 53.9% |
| 20,877 | BEADLE | 10,244 | 5,922 | 4,297 | 25 | 1,625 R | 57.8% | 41.9% | 58.0% | 42.0% |
| 3,088 | BENNETT | 1,286 | 808 | 476 | 2 | 332 R | 62.8% | 37.0% | 62.9% | 37.1% |
| 8,577 | BONHOMME | 4,493 | 2,116 | 2,368 | 9 | 252 D | 47.1% | 52.7% | 47.2% | 52.8% |
| 22,158 | BROOKINGS | 9,916 | 5,182 | 4,701 | 33 | 481 R | 52.3% | 47.4% | 52.4% | 47.6% |
| 36,920 | BROWN | 16,451 | 8,134 | 8,216 | 101 | 82 D | 49.4% | 49.9% | 49.7% | 50.3% |
| 5,870 | BRULE | 3,097 | 1,421 | 1,665 | 11 | 244 D | 45.9% | 53.8% | 46.0% | 54.0% |
| 1,739 | BUFFALO | 497 | 221 | 275 | 1 | 54 D | 44.5% | 55.3% | 44.6% | 55.4% |
| 7,825 | BUTTE | 3,563 | 2,452 | 1,085 | 26 | 1,367 R | 68.8% | 30.5% | 69.3% | 30.7% |
| 2,866 | CAMPBELL | 1,537 | 1,169 | 361 | 7 | 808 R | 76.1% | 23.5% | 76.4% | 23.6% |
| 9,994 | CHARLES MIX | 4,721 | 2,020 | 2,691 | 10 | 671 D | 42.8% | 57.0% | 42.9% | 57.1% |
| 5,515 | CLARK | 2,962 | 1,617 | 1,336 | 9 | 281 R | 54.6% | 45.1% | 54.8% | 45.2% |
| 12,923 | CLAY | 5,352 | 2,518 | 2,821 | 13 | 303 D | 47.0% | 52.7% | 47.2% | 52.8% |
| 19,140 | CODINGTON | 9,564 | 4,936 | 4,601 | 27 | 335 R | 51.6% | 48.1% | 51.8% | 48.2% |
| 4,994 | CORSON | 1,673 | 975 | 689 | 9 | 286 R | 58.3% | 41.2% | 58.6% | 41.4% |
| 4,698 | CUSTER | 2,289 | 1,476 | 798 | 15 | 678 R | 64.5% | 34.9% | 64.9% | 35.1% |
| 17,319 | DAVISON | 8,531 | 3,796 | 4,710 | 25 | 914 D | 44.5% | 55.2% | 44.6% | 55.4% |
| 8,713 | DAY | 4,699 | 1,971 | 2,719 | 9 | 748 D | 41.9% | 57.9% | 42.0% | 58.0% |
| 5,686 | DEUEL | 2,736 | 1,357 | 1,370 | 9 | 13 D | 49.6% | 50.1% | 49.8% | 50.2% |
| 5,170 | DEWEY | 1,712 | 1,008 | 699 | 5 | 309 R | 58.9% | 40.8% | 59.1% | 40.9% |
| 4,569 | DOUGLAS | 2,325 | 1,434 | 887 | 4 | 547 R | 61.7% | 38.2% | 61.8% | 38.2% |
| 5,548 | EDMUNDS | 3,216 | 1,567 | 1,646 | 3 | 79 D | 48.7% | 51.2% | 48.8% | 51.2% |
| 7,505 | FALL RIVER | 3,497 | 2,374 | 1,107 | 16 | 1,267 R | 67.9% | 31.7% | 68.2% | 31.8% |
| 3,893 | FAULK | 2,005 | 1,004 | 986 | 15 | 18 R | 50.1% | 49.2% | 50.5% | 49.5% |
| 9,005 | GRANT | 4,490 | 2,247 | 2,231 | 12 | 16 R | 50.0% | 49.7% | 50.2% | 49.8% |
| 6,710 | GREGORY | 3,237 | 1,670 | 1,555 | 12 | 115 R | 51.6% | 48.0% | 51.8% | 48.2% |
| 2,802 | HAAKON | 1,396 | 1,021 | 366 | 9 | 655 R | 73.1% | 26.2% | 73.6% | 26.4% |
| 5,520 | HAMLIN | 2,978 | 1,693 | 1,276 | 9 | 417 R | 56.9% | 42.8% | 57.0% | 43.0% |
| 5,883 | HAND | 3,119 | 1,806 | 1,307 | 6 | 499 R | 57.9% | 41.9% | 58.0% | 42.0% |
| 3,781 | HANSON | 1,906 | 876 | 1,022 | 8 | 146 D | 46.0% | 53.6% | 46.2% | 53.8% |
| 1,855 | HARDING | 890 | 637 | 253 | | 384 R | 71.6% | 28.4% | 71.6% | 28.4% |
| 11,632 | HUGHES | 6,282 | 4,231 | 2,037 | 14 | 2,194 R | 67.4% | 32.4% | 67.5% | 32.5% |
| 10,379 | HUTCHINSON | 5,348 | 3,092 | 2,248 | 8 | 844 R | 57.8% | 42.0% | 57.9% | 42.1% |
| 2,515 | HYDE | 1,326 | 789 | 533 | 4 | 256 R | 59.5% | 40.2% | 59.7% | 40.3% |
| 1,531 | JACKSON | 846 | 581 | 261 | 4 | 320 R | 68.7% | 30.9% | 69.0% | 31.0% |
| 3,310 | JERAULD | 1,820 | 988 | 829 | 3 | 159 R | 54.3% | 45.5% | 54.4% | 45.6% |
| 1,882 | JONES | 997 | 642 | 346 | 9 | 296 R | 64.4% | 34.7% | 65.0% | 35.0% |
| 7,657 | KINGSBURY | 3,958 | 2,320 | 1,632 | 6 | 688 R | 58.6% | 41.2% | 58.7% | 41.3% |
| 11,456 | LAKE | 5,822 | 2,919 | 2,886 | 17 | 33 R | 50.1% | 49.6% | 50.3% | 49.7% |
| 17,453 | LAWRENCE | 7,352 | 4,795 | 2,533 | 24 | 2,262 R | 65.2% | 34.5% | 65.4% | 34.6% |
| 11,761 | LINCOLN | 5,828 | 3,201 | 2,617 | 10 | 584 R | 54.9% | 44.9% | 55.0% | 45.0% |
| 4,060 | LYMAN | 1,944 | 1,166 | 774 | 4 | 392 R | 60.0% | 39.8% | 60.1% | 39.9% |
| 7,246 | MCCOOK | 3,963 | 1,963 | 1,993 | 7 | 30 D | 49.5% | 50.3% | 49.6% | 50.4% |
| 5,022 | MCPHERSON | 2,535 | 1,950 | 579 | 6 | 1,371 R | 76.9% | 22.8% | 77.1% | 22.9% |
| 5,965 | MARSHALL | 3,147 | 1,500 | 1,646 | 1 | 146 D | 47.7% | 52.3% | 47.7% | 52.3% |
| 17,020 | MEADE | 5,080 | 3,416 | 1,633 | 31 | 1,783 R | 67.2% | 32.1% | 67.7% | 32.3% |
| 2,420 | MELLETTE | 1,076 | 637 | 433 | 6 | 204 R | 59.2% | 40.2% | 59.5% | 40.5% |
| 4,454 | MINER | 2,405 | 1,059 | 1,337 | 9 | 278 D | 44.0% | 55.6% | 44.2% | 55.8% |
| 95,209 | MINNEHAHA | 44,988 | 22,447 | 22,386 | 155 | 61 R | 49.9% | 49.8% | 50.1% | 49.9% |
| 7,622 | MOODY | 3,554 | 1,648 | 1,895 | 11 | 247 D | 46.4% | 53.3% | 46.5% | 53.5% |
| 59,349 | PENNINGTON | 22,326 | 13,654 | 8,592 | 80 | 5,062 R | 61.2% | 38.5% | 61.4% | 38.6% |
| 4,769 | PERKINS | 2,598 | 1,691 | 900 | 7 | 791 R | 65.1% | 34.6% | 65.3% | 34.7% |
| 4,449 | POTTER | 2,253 | 1,389 | 858 | 6 | 531 R | 61.7% | 38.1% | 61.8% | 38.2% |
| 11,678 | ROBERTS | 5,172 | 2,187 | 2,976 | 9 | 789 D | 42.3% | 57.5% | 42.4% | 57.6% |
| 3,697 | SANBORN | 2,145 | 1,064 | 1,074 | 7 | 10 D | 49.6% | 50.1% | 49.8% | 50.2% |
| 8,198 | SHANNON | 1,611 | 356 | 1,246 | 9 | 890 D | 22.1% | 77.3% | 22.2% | 77.8% |
| 10,595 | SPINK | 4,880 | 2,547 | 2,321 | 12 | 226 R | 52.2% | 47.6% | 52.3% | 47.7% |
| 2,457 | STANLEY | 1,278 | 779 | 492 | 7 | 287 R | 61.0% | 38.5% | 61.3% | 38.7% |
| 2,362 | SULLY | 1,191 | 773 | 414 | 4 | 359 R | 64.9% | 34.8% | 65.1% | 34.9% |
| 6,606 | TODD | 1,723 | 806 | 907 | 10 | 101 D | 46.8% | 52.6% | 47.1% | 52.9% |

# SOUTH DAKOTA

## PRESIDENT 1972

| 1970 Census Population | County | Total Vote | Republican | Democratic | Other | Rep.-Dem. Plurality | Percentage | | | |
|---|---|---|---|---|---|---|---|---|---|---|
| | | | | | | | Total Vote | | Major Vote | |
| | | | | | | | Rep. | Dem. | Rep. | Dem. |
| 8,171 | TRIPP | 4,132 | 2,592 | 1,538 | 2 | 1,054 R | 62.7% | 37.2% | 62.8% | 37.2% |
| 9,872 | TURNER | 5,010 | 3,007 | 1,993 | 10 | 1,014 R | 60.0% | 39.8% | 60.1% | 39.9% |
| 9,643 | UNION | 4,842 | 2,271 | 2,554 | 17 | 283 D | 46.9% | 52.7% | 47.1% | 52.9% |
| 7,842 | WALWORTH | 3,711 | 2,416 | 1,287 | 8 | 1,129 R | 65.1% | 34.7% | 65.2% | 34.8% |
| 1,389 | WASHABAUGH | 456 | 245 | 211 | | 34 R | 53.7% | 46.3% | 53.7% | 46.3% |
| 19,039 | YANKTON | 8,225 | 4,366 | 3,835 | 24 | 531 R | 53.1% | 46.6% | 53.2% | 46.8% |
| 2,221 | ZIEBACH | 870 | 486 | 378 | 6 | 108 R | 55.9% | 43.4% | 56.3% | 43.8% |
| 666,257 | TOTAL | 307,415 | 166,476 | 139,945 | 994 | 26,531 R | 54.2% | 45.5% | 54.3% | 45.7% |

# SOUTH DAKOTA

## PRESIDENT 1968

| 1960 Census Population | County | Total Vote | Republican | Democratic | AIP | Other | Plurality | Percentage Total Vote | | |
|---|---|---|---|---|---|---|---|---|---|---|
| | | | | | | | | Rep. | Dem. | AIP |
| 4,749 | AURORA | 2,233 | 1,043 | 1,060 | 130 | | 17 D | 46.7% | 47.5% | 5.8% |
| 21,682 | BEADLE | 9,878 | 4,214 | 5,357 | 307 | | 1,143 D | 42.7% | 54.2% | 3.1% |
| 3,053 | BENNETT | 1,233 | 665 | 457 | 111 | | 208 R | 53.9% | 37.1% | 9.0% |
| 9,229 | BONHOMME | 4,383 | 2,411 | 1,773 | 199 | | 638 R | 55.0% | 40.5% | 4.5% |
| 20,046 | BROOKINGS | 8,081 | 4,674 | 3,202 | 205 | | 1,472 R | 57.8% | 39.6% | 2.5% |
| 34,106 | BROWN | 14,547 | 6,685 | 7,302 | 560 | | 617 D | 46.0% | 50.2% | 3.8% |
| 6,319 | BRULE | 2,815 | 1,237 | 1,425 | 153 | | 188 D | 43.9% | 50.6% | 5.4% |
| 1,547 | BUFFALO | 554 | 261 | 265 | 28 | | 4 D | 47.1% | 47.8% | 5.1% |
| 8,592 | BUTTE | 3,303 | 2,090 | 1,017 | 196 | | 1,073 R | 63.3% | 30.8% | 5.9% |
| 3,531 | CAMPBELL | 1,534 | 1,216 | 245 | 73 | | 971 R | 79.3% | 16.0% | 4.8% |
| 11,785 | CHARLES MIX | 4,675 | 2,093 | 2,369 | 213 | | 276 D | 44.8% | 50.7% | 4.6% |
| 7,134 | CLARK | 3,040 | 1,596 | 1,325 | 119 | | 271 R | 52.5% | 43.6% | 3.9% |
| 10,810 | CLAY | 4,386 | 2,249 | 2,006 | 131 | | 243 R | 51.3% | 45.7% | 3.0% |
| 20,220 | CODINGTON | 8,452 | 3,929 | 4,235 | 288 | | 306 D | 46.5% | 50.1% | 3.4% |
| 5,798 | CORSON | 2,009 | 1,108 | 821 | 80 | | 287 R | 55.2% | 40.9% | 4.0% |
| 4,906 | CUSTER | 2,064 | 1,143 | 727 | 194 | | 416 R | 55.4% | 35.2% | 9.4% |
| 16,681 | DAVISON | 7,719 | 3,869 | 3,585 | 265 | | 284 R | 50.1% | 46.4% | 3.4% |
| 10,516 | DAY | 4,707 | 2,062 | 2,463 | 182 | | 401 D | 43.8% | 52.3% | 3.9% |
| 6,782 | DEUEL | 2,625 | 1,398 | 1,076 | 151 | | 322 R | 53.3% | 41.0% | 5.8% |
| 5,257 | DEWEY | 1,785 | 941 | 721 | 123 | | 220 R | 52.7% | 40.4% | 6.9% |
| 5,113 | DOUGLAS | 2,282 | 1,613 | 592 | 77 | | 1,021 R | 70.7% | 25.9% | 3.4% |
| 6,079 | EDMUNDS | 2,940 | 1,534 | 1,225 | 181 | | 309 R | 52.2% | 41.7% | 6.2% |
| 10,688 | FALL RIVER | 3,094 | 1,843 | 965 | 286 | | 878 R | 59.6% | 31.2% | 9.2% |
| 4,397 | FAULK | 2,015 | 997 | 819 | 199 | | 178 R | 49.5% | 40.6% | 9.9% |
| 9,913 | GRANT | 4,360 | 2,259 | 1,890 | 211 | | 369 R | 51.8% | 43.3% | 4.8% |
| 7,399 | GREGORY | 3,327 | 1,810 | 1,266 | 251 | | 544 R | 54.4% | 38.1% | 7.5% |
| 3,303 | HAAKON | 1,245 | 759 | 377 | 109 | | 382 R | 61.0% | 30.3% | 8.8% |
| 6,303 | HAMLIN | 2,926 | 1,649 | 1,149 | 128 | | 500 R | 56.4% | 39.3% | 4.4% |
| 6,712 | HAND | 3,012 | 1,650 | 1,136 | 226 | | 514 R | 54.8% | 37.7% | 7.5% |
| 4,584 | HANSON | 1,799 | 901 | 826 | 72 | | 75 R | 50.1% | 45.9% | 4.0% |
| 2,371 | HARDING | 895 | 564 | 266 | 65 | | 298 R | 63.0% | 29.7% | 7.3% |
| 12,725 | HUGHES | 5,213 | 3,204 | 1,666 | 343 | | 1,538 R | 61.5% | 32.0% | 6.6% |
| 11,085 | HUTCHINSON | 5,131 | 3,544 | 1,412 | 175 | | 2,132 R | 69.1% | 27.5% | 3.4% |
| 2,602 | HYDE | 1,325 | 713 | 499 | 113 | | 214 R | 53.8% | 37.7% | 8.5% |
| 1,985 | JACKSON | 845 | 480 | 267 | 98 | | 213 R | 56.8% | 31.6% | 11.6% |
| 4,048 | JERAULD | 1,803 | 1,002 | 745 | 56 | | 257 R | 55.6% | 41.3% | 3.1% |
| 2,066 | JONES | 1,008 | 562 | 358 | 88 | | 204 R | 55.8% | 35.5% | 8.7% |
| 9,227 | KINGSBURY | 3,937 | 2,300 | 1,491 | 146 | | 809 R | 58.4% | 37.9% | 3.7% |
| 11,764 | LAKE | 5,358 | 2,876 | 2,294 | 188 | | 582 R | 53.7% | 42.8% | 3.5% |
| 17,075 | LAWRENCE | 6,948 | 4,185 | 2,425 | 338 | | 1,760 R | 60.2% | 34.9% | 4.9% |
| 12,371 | LINCOLN | 5,442 | 3,259 | 1,961 | 222 | | 1,298 R | 59.9% | 36.0% | 4.1% |
| 4,428 | LYMAN | 1,837 | 1,063 | 643 | 131 | | 420 R | 57.9% | 35.0% | 7.1% |
| 8,268 | MCCOOK | 3,800 | 1,959 | 1,653 | 188 | | 306 R | 51.6% | 43.5% | 4.9% |
| 5,821 | MCPHERSON | 2,620 | 2,105 | 389 | 126 | | 1,716 R | 80.3% | 14.8% | 4.8% |
| 6,663 | MARSHALL | 3,129 | 1,471 | 1,518 | 140 | | 47 D | 47.0% | 48.5% | 4.5% |
| 12,044 | MEADE | 4,257 | 2,392 | 1,522 | 343 | | 870 R | 56.2% | 35.8% | 8.1% |
| 2,664 | MELLETTE | 1,097 | 611 | 407 | 79 | | 204 R | 55.7% | 37.1% | 7.2% |
| 5,398 | MINER | 2,392 | 1,045 | 1,255 | 92 | | 210 D | 43.7% | 52.5% | 3.8% |
| 86,575 | MINNEHAHA | 37,780 | 20,141 | 16,462 | 1,177 | | 3,679 R | 53.3% | 43.6% | 3.1% |
| 8,810 | MOODY | 3,456 | 1,689 | 1,614 | 153 | | 75 R | 48.9% | 46.7% | 4.4% |
| 58,195 | PENNINGTON | 18,148 | 9,671 | 7,303 | 1,174 | | 2,368 R | 53.3% | 40.2% | 6.5% |
| 5,977 | PERKINS | 2,481 | 1,498 | 869 | 114 | | 629 R | 60.4% | 35.0% | 4.6% |
| 4,926 | POTTER | 2,202 | 1,273 | 780 | 149 | | 493 R | 57.8% | 35.4% | 6.8% |
| 13,190 | ROBERTS | 5,213 | 2,225 | 2,651 | 337 | | 426 D | 42.7% | 50.9% | 6.5% |
| 4,641 | SANBORN | 2,060 | 1,024 | 956 | 80 | | 68 R | 49.7% | 46.4% | 3.9% |
| 6,000 | SHANNON | 1,796 | 533 | 1,202 | 61 | | 669 D | 29.7% | 66.9% | 3.4% |
| 11,706 | SPINK | 4,915 | 2,068 | 2,669 | 178 | | 601 D | 42.1% | 54.3% | 3.6% |
| 4,085 | STANLEY | 1,109 | 572 | 439 | 98 | | 133 R | 51.6% | 39.6% | 8.8% |
| 2,607 | SULLY | 1,125 | 676 | 356 | 93 | | 320 R | 60.1% | 31.6% | 8.3% |
| 4,661 | TODD | 1,761 | 683 | 987 | 91 | | 304 D | 38.8% | 56.0% | 5.2% |

# SOUTH DAKOTA

## PRESIDENT 1968

| 1960 Census Population | County | Total Vote | Republican | Democratic | AIP | Other | Plurality | Percentage Total Vote | | |
|---|---|---|---|---|---|---|---|---|---|---|
| | | | | | | | | Rep. | Dem. | AIP |
| 8,761 | TRIPP | 3,849 | 2,242 | 1,362 | 245 | | 880 R | 58.2% | 35.4% | 6.4% |
| 11,159 | TURNER | 4,801 | 3,246 | 1,350 | 205 | | 1,896 R | 67.6% | 28.1% | 4.3% |
| 10,197 | UNION | 4,451 | 2,212 | 2,014 | 225 | | 198 R | 49.7% | 45.2% | 5.1% |
| 8,097 | WALWORTH | 3,662 | 2,204 | 1,276 | 182 | | 928 R | 60.2% | 34.8% | 5.0% |
| 1,042 | WASHABAUGH | 449 | 224 | 203 | 22 | | 21 R | 49.9% | 45.2% | 4.9% |
| 17,551 | YANKTON | 7,092 | 3,977 | 2,733 | 382 | | 1,244 R | 56.1% | 38.5% | 5.4% |
| 2,495 | ZIEBACH | 854 | 449 | 350 | 55 | | 99 R | 52.6% | 41.0% | 6.4% |
| 680,514 | TOTAL | 281,264 | 149,841 | 118,023 | 13,400 | | 31,818 R | 53.3% | 42.0% | 4.8% |

# SOUTH DAKOTA

## PRESIDENT 1964

| 1960 Census Population | County | Total Vote | Republican | Democratic | Other | Rep.-Dem. Plurality | Percentage | | | |
|---|---|---|---|---|---|---|---|---|---|---|
| | | | | | | | Total Vote | | Major Vote | |
| | | | | | | | Rep. | Dem. | Rep. | Dem. |
| 4,749 | AURORA | 2,426 | 871 | 1,555 | | 684 D | 35.9% | 64.1% | 35.9% | 64.1% |
| 21,682 | BEADLE | 10,019 | 4,051 | 5,968 | | 1,917 D | 40.4% | 59.6% | 40.4% | 59.6% |
| 3,053 | BENNETT | 1,399 | 624 | 775 | | 151 D | 44.6% | 55.4% | 44.6% | 55.4% |
| 9,229 | BONHOMME | 4,278 | 1,784 | 2,494 | | 710 D | 41.7% | 58.3% | 41.7% | 58.3% |
| 20,046 | BROOKINGS | 7,883 | 3,692 | 4,191 | | 499 D | 46.8% | 53.2% | 46.8% | 53.2% |
| 34,106 | BROWN | 14,631 | 5,524 | 9,107 | | 3,583 D | 37.8% | 62.2% | 37.8% | 62.2% |
| 6,319 | BRULE | 3,173 | 968 | 2,205 | | 1,237 D | 30.5% | 69.5% | 30.5% | 69.5% |
| 1,547 | BUFFALO | 779 | 278 | 501 | | 223 D | 35.7% | 64.3% | 35.7% | 64.3% |
| 8,592 | BUTTE | 3,740 | 1,877 | 1,863 | | 14 R | 50.2% | 49.8% | 50.2% | 49.8% |
| 3,531 | CAMPBELL | 1,573 | 1,162 | 411 | | 751 R | 73.9% | 26.1% | 73.9% | 26.1% |
| 11,785 | CHARLES MIX | 5,113 | 1,625 | 3,488 | | 1,863 D | 31.8% | 68.2% | 31.8% | 68.2% |
| 7,134 | CLARK | 3,282 | 1,511 | 1,771 | | 260 D | 46.0% | 54.0% | 46.0% | 54.0% |
| 10,810 | CLAY | 4,401 | 1,802 | 2,599 | | 797 D | 40.9% | 59.1% | 40.9% | 59.1% |
| 20,220 | CODINGTON | 8,946 | 3,593 | 5,353 | | 1,760 D | 40.2% | 59.8% | 40.2% | 59.8% |
| 5,798 | CORSON | 2,362 | 1,034 | 1,328 | | 294 D | 43.8% | 56.2% | 43.8% | 56.2% |
| 4,906 | CUSTER | 2,318 | 1,142 | 1,176 | | 34 D | 49.3% | 50.7% | 49.3% | 50.7% |
| 16,681 | DAVISON | 7,650 | 2,789 | 4,861 | | 2,072 D | 36.5% | 63.5% | 36.5% | 63.5% |
| 10,516 | DAY | 5,149 | 1,914 | 3,235 | | 1,321 D | 37.2% | 62.8% | 37.2% | 62.8% |
| 6,782 | DEUEL | 2,841 | 1,317 | 1,524 | | 207 D | 46.4% | 53.6% | 46.4% | 53.6% |
| 5,257 | DEWEY | 2,240 | 981 | 1,259 | | 278 D | 43.8% | 56.2% | 43.8% | 56.2% |
| 5,113 | DOUGLAS | 2,338 | 1,189 | 1,149 | | 40 R | 50.9% | 49.1% | 50.9% | 49.1% |
| 6,079 | EDMUNDS | 3,150 | 1,442 | 1,708 | | 266 D | 45.8% | 54.2% | 45.8% | 54.2% |
| 10,688 | FALL RIVER | 3,732 | 2,026 | 1,706 | | 320 R | 54.3% | 45.7% | 54.3% | 45.7% |
| 4,397 | FAULK | 2,199 | 974 | 1,225 | | 251 D | 44.3% | 55.7% | 44.3% | 55.7% |
| 9,913 | GRANT | 4,437 | 1,854 | 2,583 | | 729 D | 41.8% | 58.2% | 41.8% | 58.2% |
| 7,399 | GREGORY | 3,639 | 1,644 | 1,995 | | 351 D | 45.2% | 54.8% | 45.2% | 54.8% |
| 3,303 | HAAKON | 1,457 | 795 | 662 | | 133 R | 54.6% | 45.4% | 54.6% | 45.4% |
| 6,303 | HAMLIN | 3,086 | 1,525 | 1,561 | | 36 D | 49.4% | 50.6% | 49.4% | 50.6% |
| 6,712 | HAND | 3,029 | 1,466 | 1,563 | | 97 D | 48.4% | 51.6% | 48.4% | 51.6% |
| 4,584 | HANSON | 2,034 | 802 | 1,232 | | 430 D | 39.4% | 60.6% | 39.4% | 60.6% |
| 2,371 | HARDING | 976 | 489 | 487 | | 2 R | 50.1% | 49.9% | 50.1% | 49.9% |
| 12,725 | HUGHES | 5,338 | 2,732 | 2,606 | | 126 R | 51.2% | 48.8% | 51.2% | 48.8% |
| 11,085 | HUTCHINSON | 5,073 | 2,884 | 2,189 | | 695 R | 56.8% | 43.2% | 56.8% | 43.2% |
| 2,602 | HYDE | 1,402 | 666 | 736 | | 70 D | 47.5% | 52.5% | 47.5% | 52.5% |
| 1,985 | JACKSON | 928 | 448 | 480 | | 32 D | 48.3% | 51.7% | 48.3% | 51.7% |
| 4,048 | JERAULD | 1,856 | 857 | 999 | | 142 D | 46.2% | 53.8% | 46.2% | 53.8% |
| 2,066 | JONES | 963 | 415 | 548 | | 133 D | 43.1% | 56.9% | 43.1% | 56.9% |
| 9,227 | KINGSBURY | 4,131 | 2,126 | 2,005 | | 121 R | 51.5% | 48.5% | 51.5% | 48.5% |
| 11,764 | LAKE | 5,405 | 2,417 | 2,988 | | 571 D | 44.7% | 55.3% | 44.7% | 55.3% |
| 17,075 | LAWRENCE | 7,211 | 3,743 | 3,468 | | 275 R | 51.9% | 48.1% | 51.9% | 48.1% |
| 12,371 | LINCOLN | 5,576 | 2,740 | 2,836 | | 96 D | 49.1% | 50.9% | 49.1% | 50.9% |
| 4,428 | LYMAN | 1,919 | 862 | 1,057 | | 195 D | 44.9% | 55.1% | 44.9% | 55.1% |
| 8,268 | MCCOOK | 3,937 | 1,756 | 2,181 | | 425 D | 44.6% | 55.4% | 44.6% | 55.4% |
| 5,821 | MCPHERSON | 2,614 | 1,891 | 723 | | 1,168 R | 72.3% | 27.7% | 72.3% | 27.7% |
| 6,663 | MARSHALL | 3,246 | 1,183 | 2,063 | | 880 D | 36.4% | 63.6% | 36.4% | 63.6% |
| 12,044 | MEADE | 4,463 | 2,140 | 2,323 | | 183 D | 47.9% | 52.1% | 47.9% | 52.1% |
| 2,664 | MELLETTE | 1,183 | 525 | 658 | | 133 D | 44.4% | 55.6% | 44.4% | 55.6% |
| 5,398 | MINER | 2,624 | 945 | 1,679 | | 734 D | 36.0% | 64.0% | 36.0% | 64.0% |
| 86,575 | MINNEHAHA | 37,695 | 16,766 | 20,929 | | 4,163 D | 44.5% | 55.5% | 44.5% | 55.5% |
| 8,810 | MOODY | 3,762 | 1,461 | 2,301 | | 840 D | 38.8% | 61.2% | 38.8% | 61.2% |
| 58,195 | PENNINGTON | 18,807 | 8,926 | 9,881 | | 955 D | 47.5% | 52.5% | 47.5% | 52.5% |
| 5,977 | PERKINS | 2,664 | 1,409 | 1,255 | | 154 R | 52.9% | 47.1% | 52.9% | 47.1% |
| 4,926 | POTTER | 2,214 | 954 | 1,260 | | 306 D | 43.1% | 56.9% | 43.1% | 56.9% |
| 13,190 | ROBERTS | 5,498 | 1,931 | 3,567 | | 1,636 D | 35.1% | 64.9% | 35.1% | 64.9% |
| 4,641 | SANBORN | 2,313 | 912 | 1,401 | | 489 D | 39.4% | 60.6% | 39.4% | 60.6% |
| 6,000 | SHANNON | 2,305 | 557 | 1,748 | | 1,191 D | 24.2% | 75.8% | 24.2% | 75.8% |
| 11,706 | SPINK | 5,073 | 1,953 | 3,120 | | 1,167 D | 38.5% | 61.5% | 38.5% | 61.5% |
| 4,085 | STANLEY | 1,299 | 549 | 750 | | 201 D | 42.3% | 57.7% | 42.3% | 57.7% |
| 2,607 | SULLY | 1,263 | 667 | 596 | | 71 R | 52.8% | 47.2% | 52.8% | 47.2% |
| 4,661 | TODD | 1,997 | 723 | 1,274 | | 551 D | 36.2% | 63.8% | 36.2% | 63.8% |

# SOUTH DAKOTA

## PRESIDENT 1964

| 1960 Census Population | County | Total Vote | Republican | Democratic | Other | Rep.-Dem. Plurality | Percentage | | | |
|---|---|---|---|---|---|---|---|---|---|---|
| | | | | | | | Total Vote | | Major Vote | |
| | | | | | | | Rep. | Dem. | Rep. | Dem. |
| 8,761 | TRIPP | 4,178 | 1,937 | 2,241 | | 304 D | 46.4% | 53.6% | 46.4% | 53.6% |
| 11,159 | TURNER | 5,030 | 2,846 | 2,184 | | 662 R | 56.6% | 43.4% | 56.6% | 43.4% |
| 10,197 | UNION | 4,555 | 1,727 | 2,828 | | 1,101 D | 37.9% | 62.1% | 37.9% | 62.1% |
| 8,097 | WALWORTH | 3,801 | 1,849 | 1,952 | | 103 D | 48.6% | 51.4% | 48.6% | 51.4% |
| 1,042 | WASHABAUGH | 559 | 211 | 348 | | 137 D | 37.7% | 62.3% | 37.7% | 62.3% |
| 17,551 | YANKTON | 6,955 | 3,208 | 3,747 | | 539 D | 46.1% | 53.9% | 46.1% | 53.9% |
| 2,495 | ZIEBACH | 1,001 | 447 | 554 | | 107 D | 44.7% | 55.3% | 44.7% | 55.3% |
| 680,514 | TOTAL | 293,118 | 130,108 | 163,010 | | 32,902 D | 44.4% | 55.6% | 44.4% | 55.6% |

# SOUTH DAKOTA

## PRESIDENT 1960

| 1960 Census Population | County | Total Vote | Republican | Democratic | Other | Rep.-Dem. Plurality | Percentage Total Vote Rep. | Dem. | Major Vote Rep. | Dem. |
|---|---|---|---|---|---|---|---|---|---|---|
| 4,749 | AURORA | 2,537 | 1,267 | 1,270 | | 3 D | 49.9% | 50.1% | 49.9% | 50.1% |
| 21,682 | BEADLE | 9,990 | 5,911 | 4,079 | | 1,832 R | 59.2% | 40.8% | 59.2% | 40.8% |
| 3,053 | BENNETT | 1,386 | 779 | 607 | | 172 R | 56.2% | 43.8% | 56.2% | 43.8% |
| 9,229 | BONHOMME | 4,782 | 2,730 | 2,052 | | 678 R | 57.1% | 42.9% | 57.1% | 42.9% |
| 20,046 | BROOKINGS | 8,684 | 5,710 | 2,974 | | 2,736 R | 65.8% | 34.2% | 65.8% | 34.2% |
| 34,106 | BROWN | 15,930 | 8,037 | 7,893 | | 144 R | 50.5% | 49.5% | 50.5% | 49.5% |
| 6,319 | BRULE | 3,003 | 1,403 | 1,600 | | 197 D | 46.7% | 53.3% | 46.7% | 53.3% |
| 1,547 | BUFFALO | 628 | 294 | 334 | | 40 D | 46.8% | 53.2% | 46.8% | 53.2% |
| 8,592 | BUTTE | 3,814 | 2,496 | 1,318 | | 1,178 R | 65.4% | 34.6% | 65.4% | 34.6% |
| 3,531 | CAMPBELL | 1,692 | 1,330 | 362 | | 968 R | 78.6% | 21.4% | 78.6% | 21.4% |
| 11,785 | CHARLES MIX | 5,200 | 2,446 | 2,754 | | 308 D | 47.0% | 53.0% | 47.0% | 53.0% |
| 7,134 | CLARK | 3,610 | 2,204 | 1,406 | | 798 R | 61.1% | 38.9% | 61.1% | 38.9% |
| 10,810 | CLAY | 4,650 | 2,772 | 1,878 | | 894 R | 59.6% | 40.4% | 59.6% | 40.4% |
| 20,220 | CODINGTON | 9,613 | 5,309 | 4,304 | | 1,005 R | 55.2% | 44.8% | 55.2% | 44.8% |
| 5,798 | CORSON | 2,383 | 1,290 | 1,093 | | 197 R | 54.1% | 45.9% | 54.1% | 45.9% |
| 4,906 | CUSTER | 2,411 | 1,533 | 878 | | 655 R | 63.6% | 36.4% | 63.6% | 36.4% |
| 16,681 | DAVISON | 8,213 | 4,105 | 4,108 | | 3 D | 50.0% | 50.0% | 50.0% | 50.0% |
| 10,516 | DAY | 5,461 | 2,626 | 2,835 | | 209 D | 48.1% | 51.9% | 48.1% | 51.9% |
| 6,782 | DEUEL | 3,080 | 1,907 | 1,173 | | 734 R | 61.9% | 38.1% | 61.9% | 38.1% |
| 5,257 | DEWEY | 2,212 | 1,168 | 1,044 | | 124 R | 52.8% | 47.2% | 52.8% | 47.2% |
| 5,113 | DOUGLAS | 2,543 | 2,002 | 541 | | 1,461 R | 78.7% | 21.3% | 78.7% | 21.3% |
| 6,079 | EDMUNDS | 3,337 | 1,728 | 1,609 | | 119 R | 51.8% | 48.2% | 51.8% | 48.2% |
| 10,688 | FALL RIVER | 3,918 | 2,492 | 1,426 | | 1,066 R | 63.6% | 36.4% | 63.6% | 36.4% |
| 4,397 | FAULK | 2,283 | 1,240 | 1,043 | | 197 R | 54.3% | 45.7% | 54.3% | 45.7% |
| 9,913 | GRANT | 4,725 | 2,611 | 2,114 | | 497 R | 55.3% | 44.7% | 55.3% | 44.7% |
| 7,399 | GREGORY | 3,841 | 2,063 | 1,778 | | 285 R | 53.7% | 46.3% | 53.7% | 46.3% |
| 3,303 | HAAKON | 1,575 | 980 | 595 | | 385 R | 62.2% | 37.8% | 62.2% | 37.8% |
| 6,303 | HAMLIN | 3,369 | 2,139 | 1,230 | | 909 R | 63.5% | 36.5% | 63.5% | 36.5% |
| 6,712 | HAND | 3,269 | 1,872 | 1,397 | | 475 R | 57.3% | 42.7% | 57.3% | 42.7% |
| 4,584 | HANSON | 2,240 | 1,087 | 1,153 | | 66 D | 48.5% | 51.5% | 48.5% | 51.5% |
| 2,371 | HARDING | 1,058 | 676 | 382 | | 294 R | 63.9% | 36.1% | 63.9% | 36.1% |
| 12,725 | HUGHES | 5,356 | 3,320 | 2,036 | | 1,284 R | 62.0% | 38.0% | 62.0% | 38.0% |
| 11,085 | HUTCHINSON | 5,505 | 3,948 | 1,557 | | 2,391 R | 71.7% | 28.3% | 71.7% | 28.3% |
| 2,602 | HYDE | 1,433 | 773 | 660 | | 113 R | 53.9% | 46.1% | 53.9% | 46.1% |
| 1,985 | JACKSON | 947 | 581 | 366 | | 215 R | 61.4% | 38.6% | 61.4% | 38.6% |
| 4,048 | JERAULD | 2,028 | 1,165 | 863 | | 302 R | 57.4% | 42.6% | 57.4% | 42.6% |
| 2,066 | JONES | 1,067 | 644 | 423 | | 221 R | 60.4% | 39.6% | 60.4% | 39.6% |
| 9,227 | KINGSBURY | 4,564 | 2,887 | 1,677 | | 1,210 R | 63.3% | 36.7% | 63.3% | 36.7% |
| 11,764 | LAKE | 5,744 | 3,520 | 2,224 | | 1,296 R | 61.3% | 38.7% | 61.3% | 38.7% |
| 17,075 | LAWRENCE | 7,695 | 5,083 | 2,612 | | 2,471 R | 66.1% | 33.9% | 66.1% | 33.9% |
| 12,371 | LINCOLN | 5,538 | 3,553 | 1,985 | | 1,568 R | 64.2% | 35.8% | 64.2% | 35.8% |
| 4,428 | LYMAN | 2,018 | 1,166 | 852 | | 314 R | 57.8% | 42.2% | 57.8% | 42.2% |
| 8,268 | MCCOOK | 4,172 | 2,375 | 1,797 | | 578 R | 56.9% | 43.1% | 56.9% | 43.1% |
| 5,821 | MCPHERSON | 2,970 | 2,354 | 616 | | 1,738 R | 79.3% | 20.7% | 79.3% | 20.7% |
| 6,663 | MARSHALL | 3,378 | 1,704 | 1,674 | | 30 R | 50.4% | 49.6% | 50.4% | 49.6% |
| 12,044 | MEADE | 4,567 | 2,644 | 1,923 | | 721 R | 57.9% | 42.1% | 57.9% | 42.1% |
| 2,664 | MELLETTE | 1,284 | 774 | 510 | | 264 R | 60.3% | 39.7% | 60.3% | 39.7% |
| 5,398 | MINER | 2,693 | 1,377 | 1,316 | | 61 R | 51.1% | 48.9% | 51.1% | 48.9% |
| 86,575 | MINNEHAHA | 38,390 | 23,238 | 15,152 | | 8,086 R | 60.5% | 39.5% | 60.5% | 39.5% |
| 8,810 | MOODY | 4,037 | 2,119 | 1,918 | | 201 R | 52.5% | 47.5% | 52.5% | 47.5% |
| 58,195 | PENNINGTON | 18,842 | 11,364 | 7,478 | | 3,886 R | 60.3% | 39.7% | 60.3% | 39.7% |
| 5,977 | PERKINS | 2,931 | 1,767 | 1,164 | | 603 R | 60.3% | 39.7% | 60.3% | 39.7% |
| 4,926 | POTTER | 2,330 | 1,326 | 1,004 | | 322 R | 56.9% | 43.1% | 56.9% | 43.1% |
| 13,190 | ROBERTS | 5,946 | 2,857 | 3,089 | | 232 D | 48.0% | 52.0% | 48.0% | 52.0% |
| 4,641 | SANBORN | 2,503 | 1,254 | 1,249 | | 5 R | 50.1% | 49.9% | 50.1% | 49.9% |
| 6,000 | SHANNON | 1,790 | 655 | 1,135 | | 480 D | 36.6% | 63.4% | 36.6% | 63.4% |
| 11,706 | SPINK | 5,301 | 2,738 | 2,563 | | 175 R | 51.7% | 48.3% | 51.7% | 48.3% |
| 4,085 | STANLEY | 1,408 | 678 | 730 | | 52 D | 48.2% | 51.8% | 48.2% | 51.8% |
| 2,607 | SULLY | 1,347 | 864 | 483 | | 381 R | 64.1% | 35.9% | 64.1% | 35.9% |
| 4,661 | TODD | 1,813 | 909 | 904 | | 5 R | 50.1% | 49.9% | 50.1% | 49.9% |

# SOUTH DAKOTA

## PRESIDENT 1960

| 1960 Census Population | County | Total Vote | Republican | Democratic | Other | Rep.-Dem. Plurality | Percentage | | | |
|---|---|---|---|---|---|---|---|---|---|---|
| | | | | | | | Total Vote | | Major Vote | |
| | | | | | | | Rep. | Dem. | Rep. | Dem. |
| 8,761 | TRIPP | 4,214 | 2,466 | 1,748 | | 718 R | 58.5% | 41.5% | 58.5% | 41.5% |
| 11,159 | TURNER | 5,667 | 4,120 | 1,547 | | 2,573 R | 72.7% | 27.3% | 72.7% | 27.3% |
| 10,197 | UNION | 5,019 | 2,688 | 2,331 | | 357 R | 53.6% | 46.4% | 53.6% | 46.4% |
| 8,097 | WALWORTH | 3,874 | 2,406 | 1,468 | | 938 R | 62.1% | 37.9% | 62.1% | 37.9% |
| 1,042 | WASHABAUGH | 473 | 260 | 213 | | 47 R | 55.0% | 45.0% | 55.0% | 45.0% |
| 17,551 | YANKTON | 7,126 | 4,065 | 3,061 | | 1,004 R | 57.0% | 43.0% | 57.0% | 43.0% |
| 2,495 | ZIEBACH | 1,080 | 568 | 512 | | 56 R | 52.6% | 47.4% | 52.6% | 47.4% |
| 680,514 | TOTAL | 306,487 | 178,417 | 128,070 | | 50,347 R | 58.2% | 41.8% | 58.2% | 41.8% |

# SOUTH DAKOTA

Jackson and Washabaugh counties were consolidated in 1978 under the name Jackson county.

## ELECTION NOTES

**2004**    Other vote was 4,320 Independent (Ralph Nader); 1,103 Constitution (Michael Peroutka); 964 Libertarian (Michael Badnarik).

**2000**    Other vote was 3,322 Reform (Buchanan); 1,781 Independent (Phillips); 1,662 Libertarian (Browne).

**1996**    Other vote was 1,472 Libertarian (Browne); 912 Independent (Phillips); 316 Independent (Hagelin).

**1992**    Other vote was 814 Marrou (Libertarian); 429 Hagelin (Natural law); 110 Fulani (New Alliance).

**1988**    Other vote was 1,060 Paul (Libertarian); 730 Fulani (New Alliance); 226 Warren (Socialist Workers).

**1984**    Other vote was 1,150 Serrette (Independent); 337 Mason (Independent).

**1980**    Other vote was 21,431 Anderson (Independent); 3,824 Clark (Independent); 250 Pulley (Independent).

**1976**    Other vote was 1,619 MacBride (Independent); 318 Hall (Independent); 168 Camejo (Independent). Early unamended canvass gave the Democratic vote in Clay county as 2,589.

**1972**    Other vote was Jenness (Independent).

**1968**    Wallace on the ballot as Independent.

**1964**

**1960**

# TENNESSEE

## POPULAR VOTE FOR PRESIDENT 1920 TO 2004

| Year | Total Vote | Republican | | Democratic | | Other Vote | Plurality | Percentage | | | |
| | | Vote | Candidate | Vote | Candidate | | | Total Vote | | Major Vote | |
| | | | | | | | | Rep. | Dem. | Rep. | Dem. |
|------|-----------|-----------|-----------|----------|----------|-----------|-----------|------|------|------|------|
| 2004 | 2,437,319 | 1,384,375 | Bush, George W. | 1,036,477 | Kerry, John | 16,467 | 347,898 R | 56.8% | 42.5% | 57.2% | 42.8% |
| 2000 ** | 2,076,181 | 1,061,949 | Bush, George W. | 981,720 | Gore, Al | 32,512 | 80,229 R | 51.1% | 47.3% | 52.0% | 48.0% |
| 1996 ** | 1,894,105 | 863,530 | Dole, Bob | 909,146 | Clinton, Bill | 121,429 | 45,616 D | 45.6% | 48.0% | 48.7% | 51.3% |
| 1992 ** | 1,982,638 | 841,300 | Bush, George | 933,521 | Clinton, Bill | 207,817 | 92,221 D | 42.4% | 47.1% | 47.4% | 52.6% |
| 1988 | 1,636,250 | 947,233 | Bush, George | 679,794 | Dukakis, Michael S. | 9,223 | 267,439 R | 57.9% | 41.5% | 58.2% | 41.8% |
| 1984 | 1,711,994 | 990,212 | Reagan, Ronald | 711,714 | Mondale, Walter F. | 10,068 | 278,498 R | 57.8% | 41.6% | 58.2% | 41.8% |
| 1980 ** | 1,617,616 | 787,761 | Reagan, Ronald | 783,051 | Carter, Jimmy | 46,804 | 4,710 R | 48.7% | 48.4% | 50.1% | 49.9% |
| 1976 | 1,476,345 | 633,969 | Ford, Gerald R. | 825,879 | Carter, Jimmy | 16,497 | 191,910 D | 42.9% | 55.9% | 43.4% | 56.6% |
| 1972 | 1,201,182 | 813,147 | Nixon, Richard M. | 357,293 | McGovern, George S. | 30,742 | 455,854 R | 67.7% | 29.7% | 69.5% | 30.5% |
| 1968 ** | 1,248,617 | 472,592 | Nixon, Richard M. | 351,233 | Humphrey, Hubert H. | 424,792 | 47,800 R | 37.8% | 28.1% | 57.4% | 42.6% |
| 1964 | 1,143,946 | 508,965 | Goldwater, Barry M. | 634,947 | Johnson, Lyndon B. | 34 | 125,982 D | 44.5% | 55.5% | 44.5% | 55.5% |
| 1960 | 1,051,792 | 556,577 | Nixon, Richard M. | 481,453 | Kennedy, John F. | 13,762 | 75,124 R | 52.9% | 45.8% | 53.6% | 46.4% |
| 1956 | 939,404 | 462,288 | Eisenhower, Dwight D. | 456,507 | Stevenson, Adlai E. | 20,609 | 5,781 R | 49.2% | 48.6% | 50.3% | 49.7% |
| 1952 | 892,553 | 446,147 | Eisenhower, Dwight D. | 443,710 | Stevenson, Adlai E. | 2,696 | 2,437 R | 50.0% | 49.7% | 50.1% | 49.9% |
| 1948 | 550,283 | 202,914 | Dewey, Thomas E. | 270,402 | Truman, Harry S. | 76,967 | 67,488 D | 36.9% | 49.1% | 42.9% | 57.1% |
| 1944 | 510,692 | 200,311 | Dewey, Thomas E. | 308,707 | Roosevelt, Franklin D. | 1,674 | 108,396 D | 39.2% | 60.4% | 39.4% | 60.6% |
| 1940 | 522,823 | 169,153 | Willkie, Wendell | 351,601 | Roosevelt, Franklin D. | 2,069 | 182,448 D | 32.4% | 67.3% | 32.5% | 67.5% |
| 1936 | 477,086 | 147,055 | Landon, Alfred M. | 328,083 | Roosevelt, Franklin D. | 1,948 | 181,028 D | 30.8% | 68.8% | 30.9% | 69.1% |
| 1932 | 390,273 | 126,752 | Hoover, Herbert C. | 259,473 | Roosevelt, Franklin D. | 4,048 | 132,721 D | 32.5% | 66.5% | 32.8% | 67.2% |
| 1928 | 353,192 | 195,388 | Hoover, Herbert C. | 157,143 | Smith, Alfred E. | 661 | 38,245 R | 55.3% | 44.5% | 55.4% | 44.6% |
| 1924 | 301,030 | 130,831 | Coolidge, Calvin | 159,339 | Davis, John W. | 10,860 | 28,508 D | 43.5% | 52.9% | 45.1% | 54.9% |
| 1920 | 428,036 | 219,229 | Harding, Warren G. | 206,558 | Cox, James M. | 2,249 | 12,671 R | 51.2% | 48.3% | 51.5% | 48.5% |

In 2000 the other vote column includes 19,781 votes cast for Green (Nader). In 1996 the other vote column includes 105,918 votes cast for Perot. In 1992 the other vote column includes 199,968 votes cast for Perot. In 1980 the other column includes 35,991 votes for Independent (Anderson). In 1968 other vote was American (Wallace).

## ELECTORAL COLLEGE VOTE 1920 TO 2004

| Year | Total | Republican | Democratic | Other |
|------|-------|-----------|-----------|-------|
| 2004 | 11 | 11 | | |
| 2000 | 11 | 11 | | |
| 1996 | 11 | | 11 | |
| 1992 | 11 | | 11 | |
| 1988 | 11 | 11 | | |
| 1984 | 11 | 11 | | |
| 1980 | 10 | 10 | | |
| 1976 | 10 | | 10 | |
| 1972 | 10 | 10 | | |
| 1968 | 11 | 11 | | |
| 1964 | 11 | | 11 | |
| 1960 | 11 | 11 | | |
| 1956 | 11 | 11 | | |
| 1952 | 11 | 11 | | |
| 1948 ** | 12 | | 11 | 1  SR |
| 1944 | 12 | | 12 | |
| 1940 | 11 | | 11 | |
| 1936 | 11 | | 11 | |
| 1932 | 11 | | 11 | |
| 1928 | 12 | 12 | | |
| 1924 | 12 | | 12 | |
| 1920 | 12 | 12 | | |

In 1948 one of the twelve Democratic electors voted in the Electoral College for the States Rights candidates rather than for the national Democratic candidates.

# TENNESSEE

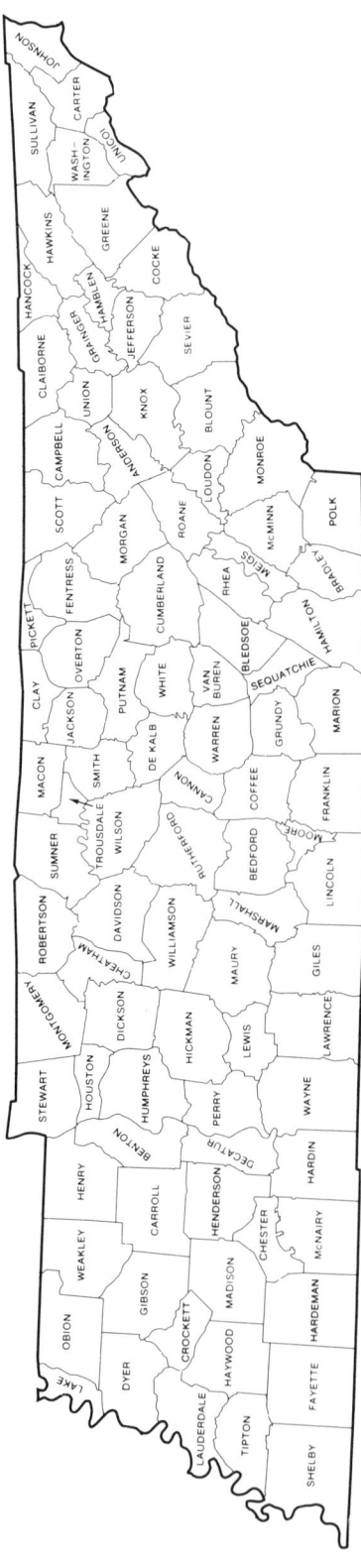

# TENNESSEE

## PRESIDENT 2004

| 2000 Census Population | County | Total Vote | Republican | Democratic | Other | Rep.-Dem. Plurality | Total Vote Rep. | Total Vote Dem. | Major Vote Rep. | Major Vote Dem. |
|---|---|---|---|---|---|---|---|---|---|---|
| 71,330 | ANDERSON | 31,682 | 18,510 | 12,896 | 276 | 5,614 R | 58.4% | 40.7% | 58.9% | 41.1% |
| 37,586 | BEDFORD | 13,706 | 8,351 | 5,268 | 87 | 3,083 R | 60.9% | 38.4% | 61.3% | 38.7% |
| 16,537 | BENTON | 7,090 | 3,161 | 3,869 | 60 | 708 D | 44.6% | 54.6% | 45.0% | 55.0% |
| 12,367 | BLEDSOE | 4,809 | 2,849 | 1,927 | 33 | 922 R | 59.2% | 40.1% | 59.7% | 40.3% |
| 105,823 | BLOUNT | 48,712 | 33,241 | 15,047 | 424 | 18,194 R | 68.2% | 30.9% | 68.8% | 31.2% |
| 87,965 | BRADLEY | 35,637 | 25,951 | 9,431 | 255 | 16,520 R | 72.8% | 26.5% | 73.3% | 26.7% |
| 39,854 | CAMPBELL | 14,118 | 7,859 | 6,163 | 96 | 1,696 R | 55.7% | 43.7% | 56.0% | 44.0% |
| 12,826 | CANNON | 5,481 | 2,931 | 2,515 | 35 | 416 R | 53.5% | 45.9% | 53.8% | 46.2% |
| 29,475 | CARROLL | 11,757 | 6,605 | 5,070 | 82 | 1,535 R | 56.2% | 43.1% | 56.6% | 43.4% |
| 56,742 | CARTER | 22,313 | 15,768 | 6,395 | 150 | 9,373 R | 70.7% | 28.7% | 71.1% | 28.9% |
| 35,912 | CHEATHAM | 15,697 | 9,676 | 5,918 | 103 | 3,758 R | 61.6% | 37.7% | 62.0% | 38.0% |
| 15,540 | CHESTER | 6,357 | 4,086 | 2,242 | 29 | 1,844 R | 64.3% | 35.3% | 64.6% | 35.4% |
| 29,862 | CLAIBORNE | 10,540 | 6,448 | 4,034 | 58 | 2,414 R | 61.2% | 38.3% | 61.5% | 38.5% |
| 7,976 | CLAY | 3,357 | 1,650 | 1,675 | 32 | 25 D | 49.2% | 49.9% | 49.6% | 50.4% |
| 33,565 | COCKE | 12,311 | 8,297 | 3,935 | 79 | 4,362 R | 67.4% | 32.0% | 67.8% | 32.2% |
| 48,014 | COFFEE | 20,167 | 11,793 | 8,243 | 131 | 3,550 R | 58.5% | 40.9% | 58.9% | 41.1% |
| 14,532 | CROCKETT | 5,722 | 3,242 | 2,459 | 21 | 783 R | 56.7% | 43.0% | 56.9% | 43.1% |
| 46,802 | CUMBERLAND | 23,637 | 15,144 | 8,327 | 166 | 6,817 R | 64.1% | 35.2% | 64.5% | 35.5% |
| 569,891 | DAVIDSON | 242,302 | 107,839 | 132,737 | 1,726 | 24,898 D | 44.5% | 54.8% | 44.8% | 55.2% |
| 11,731 | DECATUR | 4,879 | 2,566 | 2,268 | 45 | 298 R | 52.6% | 46.5% | 53.1% | 46.9% |
| 17,423 | DE KALB | 7,173 | 3,685 | 3,445 | 43 | 240 R | 51.4% | 48.0% | 51.7% | 48.3% |
| 43,156 | DICKSON | 19,298 | 10,567 | 8,597 | 134 | 1,970 R | 54.8% | 44.5% | 55.1% | 44.9% |
| 37,279 | DYER | 13,809 | 8,447 | 5,287 | 75 | 3,160 R | 61.2% | 38.3% | 61.5% | 38.5% |
| 28,806 | FAYETTE | 14,737 | 8,962 | 5,696 | 79 | 3,266 R | 60.8% | 38.7% | 61.1% | 38.9% |
| 16,625 | FENTRESS | 6,700 | 4,293 | 2,371 | 36 | 1,922 R | 64.1% | 35.4% | 64.4% | 35.6% |
| 39,270 | FRANKLIN | 17,077 | 9,129 | 7,800 | 148 | 1,329 R | 53.5% | 45.7% | 53.9% | 46.1% |
| 48,152 | GIBSON | 19,221 | 10,596 | 8,511 | 114 | 2,085 R | 55.1% | 44.3% | 55.5% | 44.5% |
| 29,447 | GILES | 11,537 | 6,163 | 5,273 | 101 | 890 R | 53.4% | 45.7% | 53.9% | 46.1% |
| 20,659 | GRAINGER | 7,527 | 4,907 | 2,569 | 51 | 2,338 R | 65.2% | 34.1% | 65.6% | 34.4% |
| 62,909 | GREENE | 24,194 | 16,382 | 7,635 | 177 | 8,747 R | 67.7% | 31.6% | 68.2% | 31.8% |
| 14,332 | GRUNDY | 4,929 | 2,107 | 2,789 | 33 | 682 D | 42.7% | 56.6% | 43.0% | 57.0% |
| 58,128 | HAMBLEN | 22,318 | 14,742 | 7,433 | 143 | 7,309 R | 66.1% | 33.3% | 66.5% | 33.5% |
| 307,896 | HAMILTON | 136,936 | 78,547 | 57,302 | 1,087 | 21,245 R | 57.4% | 41.8% | 57.8% | 42.2% |
| 6,786 | HANCOCK | 2,551 | 1,756 | 777 | 18 | 979 R | 68.8% | 30.5% | 69.3% | 30.7% |
| 28,105 | HARDEMAN | 10,466 | 4,704 | 5,685 | 77 | 981 D | 44.9% | 54.3% | 45.3% | 54.7% |
| 25,578 | HARDIN | 9,954 | 6,087 | 3,834 | 33 | 2,253 R | 61.2% | 38.5% | 61.4% | 38.6% |
| 53,563 | HAWKINS | 20,233 | 13,447 | 6,684 | 102 | 6,763 R | 66.5% | 33.0% | 66.8% | 33.2% |
| 19,797 | HAYWOOD | 7,548 | 3,140 | 4,359 | 49 | 1,219 D | 41.6% | 57.8% | 41.9% | 58.1% |
| 25,522 | HENDERSON | 10,096 | 6,585 | 3,448 | 63 | 3,137 R | 65.2% | 34.2% | 65.6% | 34.4% |
| 31,115 | HENRY | 13,177 | 7,340 | 5,732 | 105 | 1,608 R | 55.7% | 43.5% | 56.2% | 43.8% |
| 22,295 | HICKMAN | 8,673 | 4,359 | 4,263 | 51 | 96 R | 50.3% | 49.2% | 50.6% | 49.4% |
| 8,088 | HOUSTON | 3,598 | 1,440 | 2,126 | 32 | 686 D | 40.0% | 59.1% | 40.4% | 59.6% |
| 17,929 | HUMPHREYS | 7,793 | 3,261 | 4,485 | 47 | 1,224 D | 41.8% | 57.6% | 42.1% | 57.9% |
| 10,984 | JACKSON | 5,056 | 2,026 | 2,998 | 32 | 972 D | 40.1% | 59.3% | 40.3% | 59.7% |
| 44,294 | JEFFERSON | 17,215 | 11,625 | 5,469 | 121 | 6,156 R | 67.5% | 31.8% | 68.0% | 32.0% |
| 17,499 | JOHNSON | 6,480 | 4,634 | 1,812 | 34 | 2,822 R | 71.5% | 28.0% | 71.9% | 28.1% |
| 382,032 | KNOX | 178,419 | 110,803 | 66,013 | 1,603 | 44,790 R | 62.1% | 37.0% | 62.7% | 37.3% |
| 7,954 | LAKE | 4,740 | 2,078 | 2,634 | 28 | 556 D | 43.8% | 55.6% | 44.1% | 55.9% |
| 27,101 | LAUDERDALE | 8,682 | 4,164 | 4,474 | 44 | 310 D | 48.0% | 51.5% | 48.2% | 51.8% |
| 39,926 | LAWRENCE | 16,658 | 9,959 | 6,592 | 107 | 3,367 R | 59.8% | 39.6% | 60.2% | 39.8% |
| 11,367 | LEWIS | 5,054 | 2,819 | 2,192 | 43 | 627 R | 55.8% | 43.4% | 56.3% | 43.7% |
| 31,340 | LINCOLN | 12,457 | 7,829 | 4,546 | 82 | 3,283 R | 62.8% | 36.5% | 63.3% | 36.7% |
| 39,086 | LOUDON | 19,864 | 14,041 | 5,708 | 115 | 8,333 R | 70.7% | 28.7% | 71.1% | 28.9% |
| 49,015 | MCMINN | 18,003 | 11,980 | 5,891 | 132 | 6,089 R | 66.5% | 32.7% | 67.0% | 33.0% |
| 24,653 | MCNAIRY | 9,924 | 5,787 | 4,101 | 36 | 1,686 R | 58.3% | 41.3% | 58.5% | 41.5% |
| 20,386 | MACON | 7,433 | 4,670 | 2,738 | 25 | 1,932 R | 62.8% | 36.8% | 63.0% | 37.0% |
| 91,837 | MADISON | 38,675 | 21,679 | 16,840 | 156 | 4,839 R | 56.1% | 43.5% | 56.3% | 43.7% |
| 27,776 | MARION | 11,492 | 5,862 | 5,548 | 82 | 314 R | 51.0% | 48.3% | 51.4% | 48.6% |
| 26,767 | MARSHALL | 10,615 | 5,825 | 4,722 | 68 | 1,103 R | 54.9% | 44.5% | 55.2% | 44.8% |
| 69,498 | MAURY | 30,043 | 17,505 | 12,379 | 159 | 5,126 R | 58.3% | 41.2% | 58.6% | 41.4% |

# TENNESSEE

## PRESIDENT 2004

| 2000 Census Population | County | Total Vote | Republican | Democratic | Other | Rep.-Dem. Plurality | Percentage | | | |
|---|---|---|---|---|---|---|---|---|---|---|
| | | | | | | | Total Vote | | Major Vote | |
| | | | | | | | Rep. | Dem. | Rep. | Dem. |
| 11,086 | MEIGS | 4,132 | 2,500 | 1,595 | 37 | 905 R | 60.5% | 38.6% | 61.1% | 38.9% |
| 38,961 | MONROE | 15,568 | 10,123 | 5,354 | 91 | 4,769 R | 65.0% | 34.4% | 65.4% | 34.6% |
| 134,768 | MONTGOMERY | 48,998 | 28,627 | 20,070 | 301 | 8,557 R | 58.4% | 41.0% | 58.8% | 41.2% |
| 5,740 | MOORE | 2,774 | 1,668 | 1,084 | 22 | 584 R | 60.1% | 39.1% | 60.6% | 39.4% |
| 19,757 | MORGAN | 7,360 | 4,401 | 2,924 | 35 | 1,477 R | 59.8% | 39.7% | 60.1% | 39.9% |
| 32,450 | OBION | 13,535 | 7,859 | 5,549 | 127 | 2,310 R | 58.1% | 41.0% | 58.6% | 41.4% |
| 20,118 | OVERTON | 8,510 | 3,941 | 4,518 | 51 | 577 D | 46.3% | 53.1% | 46.6% | 53.4% |
| 7,631 | PERRY | 3,150 | 1,522 | 1,579 | 49 | 57 D | 48.3% | 50.1% | 49.1% | 50.9% |
| 4,945 | PICKETT | 2,645 | 1,600 | 1,033 | 12 | 567 R | 60.5% | 39.1% | 60.8% | 39.2% |
| 16,050 | POLK | 6,700 | 3,924 | 2,724 | 52 | 1,200 R | 58.6% | 40.7% | 59.0% | 41.0% |
| 62,315 | PUTNAM | 26,442 | 15,637 | 10,566 | 239 | 5,071 R | 59.1% | 40.0% | 59.7% | 40.3% |
| 28,400 | RHEA | 11,054 | 7,301 | 3,665 | 88 | 3,636 R | 66.0% | 33.2% | 66.6% | 33.4% |
| 51,910 | ROANE | 23,338 | 14,467 | 8,706 | 165 | 5,761 R | 62.0% | 37.3% | 62.4% | 37.6% |
| 54,433 | ROBERTSON | 25,323 | 15,331 | 9,865 | 127 | 5,466 R | 60.5% | 39.0% | 60.8% | 39.2% |
| 182,023 | RUTHERFORD | 84,409 | 52,200 | 31,647 | 562 | 20,553 R | 61.8% | 37.5% | 62.3% | 37.7% |
| 21,127 | SCOTT | 7,628 | 4,509 | 3,086 | 33 | 1,423 R | 59.1% | 40.5% | 59.4% | 40.6% |
| 11,370 | SEQUATCHIE | 4,983 | 2,951 | 1,986 | 46 | 965 R | 59.2% | 39.9% | 59.8% | 40.2% |
| 71,170 | SEVIER | 30,970 | 22,143 | 8,621 | 206 | 13,522 R | 71.5% | 27.8% | 72.0% | 28.0% |
| 897,472 | SHELBY | 377,282 | 158,137 | 216,945 | 2,200 | 58,808 D | 41.9% | 57.5% | 42.2% | 57.8% |
| 17,712 | SMITH | 7,828 | 3,739 | 4,044 | 45 | 305 D | 47.8% | 51.7% | 48.0% | 52.0% |
| 12,370 | STEWART | 5,583 | 2,675 | 2,860 | 48 | 185 D | 47.9% | 51.2% | 48.3% | 51.7% |
| 153,048 | SULLIVAN | 62,639 | 42,555 | 19,637 | 447 | 22,918 R | 67.9% | 31.3% | 68.4% | 31.6% |
| 130,449 | SUMNER | 61,968 | 40,181 | 21,458 | 329 | 18,723 R | 64.8% | 34.6% | 65.2% | 34.8% |
| 51,271 | TIPTON | 21,677 | 14,178 | 7,379 | 120 | 6,799 R | 65.4% | 34.0% | 65.8% | 34.2% |
| 7,259 | TROUSDALE | 3,191 | 1,314 | 1,851 | 26 | 537 D | 41.2% | 58.0% | 41.5% | 58.5% |
| 17,667 | UNICOI | 7,463 | 5,030 | 2,374 | 59 | 2,656 R | 67.4% | 31.8% | 67.9% | 32.1% |
| 17,808 | UNION | 6,710 | 4,145 | 2,524 | 41 | 1,621 R | 61.8% | 37.6% | 62.2% | 37.8% |
| 5,508 | VAN BUREN | 2,347 | 1,120 | 1,209 | 18 | 89 D | 47.7% | 51.5% | 48.1% | 51.9% |
| 38,276 | WARREN | 14,400 | 7,503 | 6,808 | 89 | 695 R | 52.1% | 47.3% | 52.4% | 47.6% |
| 107,198 | WASHINGTON | 45,006 | 29,735 | 14,944 | 327 | 14,791 R | 66.1% | 33.2% | 66.6% | 33.4% |
| 16,842 | WAYNE | 5,984 | 3,999 | 1,951 | 34 | 2,048 R | 66.8% | 32.6% | 67.2% | 32.8% |
| 34,895 | WEAKLEY | 13,496 | 7,817 | 5,588 | 91 | 2,229 R | 57.9% | 41.4% | 58.3% | 41.7% |
| 23,102 | WHITE | 9,495 | 5,269 | 4,147 | 79 | 1,122 R | 55.5% | 43.7% | 56.0% | 44.0% |
| 126,638 | WILLIAMSON | 79,650 | 57,451 | 21,732 | 467 | 35,719 R | 72.1% | 27.3% | 72.6% | 27.4% |
| 88,809 | WILSON | 44,452 | 28,924 | 15,277 | 251 | 13,647 R | 65.1% | 34.4% | 65.4% | 34.6% |
| 5,689,283 | TOTAL | 2,437,319 | 1,384,375 | 1,036,477 | 16,467 | 347,898 R | 56.8% | 42.5% | 57.2% | 42.8% |

# TENNESSEE

## PRESIDENT 2000

| 2000 Census Population | County | Total Vote | Republican | Democratic | Green (Nader) | Other | Rep.-Dem. Plurality | Percentage of Total Vote | | |
|---|---|---|---|---|---|---|---|---|---|---|
| | | | | | | | | Rep. | Dem. | Green |
| 71,330 | ANDERSON | 28,779 | 14,688 | 13,556 | 316 | 219 | 1,132 R | 51.0% | 47.1% | 1.1% |
| 37,586 | BEDFORD | 12,207 | 5,911 | 6,136 | 80 | 80 | 225 D | 48.4% | 50.3% | 0.7% |
| 16,537 | BENTON | 6,311 | 2,484 | 3,700 | 62 | 65 | 1,216 D | 39.4% | 58.6% | 1.0% |
| 12,367 | BLEDSOE | 4,196 | 2,380 | 1,756 | 35 | 25 | 624 R | 56.7% | 41.8% | 0.8% |
| 105,823 | BLOUNT | 40,662 | 25,273 | 14,688 | 379 | 322 | 10,585 R | 62.2% | 36.1% | 0.9% |
| 87,965 | BRADLEY | 29,443 | 20,167 | 8,768 | 271 | 237 | 11,399 R | 68.5% | 29.8% | 0.9% |
| 39,854 | CAMPBELL | 12,421 | 5,784 | 6,492 | 74 | 71 | 708 D | 46.6% | 52.3% | 0.6% |
| 12,826 | CANNON | 4,697 | 1,924 | 2,697 | 45 | 31 | 773 D | 41.0% | 57.4% | 1.0% |
| 29,475 | CARROLL | 10,827 | 5,465 | 5,239 | 65 | 58 | 226 R | 50.5% | 48.4% | 0.6% |
| 56,742 | CARTER | 19,102 | 12,111 | 6,724 | 157 | 110 | 5,387 R | 63.4% | 35.2% | 0.8% |
| 35,912 | CHEATHAM | 12,616 | 6,356 | 6,062 | 139 | 59 | 294 R | 50.4% | 48.1% | 1.1% |
| 15,540 | CHESTER | 5,728 | 3,487 | 2,192 | 25 | 24 | 1,295 R | 60.9% | 38.3% | 0.4% |
| 29,862 | CLAIBORNE | 9,000 | 5,023 | 3,841 | 60 | 76 | 1,182 R | 55.8% | 42.7% | 0.7% |
| 7,976 | CLAY | 3,442 | 1,468 | 1,931 | 19 | 24 | 463 D | 42.6% | 56.1% | 0.6% |
| 33,565 | COCKE | 10,239 | 6,185 | 3,872 | 93 | 89 | 2,313 R | 60.4% | 37.8% | 0.9% |
| 48,014 | COFFEE | 17,788 | 8,788 | 8,741 | 151 | 108 | 47 R | 49.4% | 49.1% | 0.8% |
| 14,532 | CROCKETT | 5,440 | 2,676 | 2,705 | 42 | 17 | 29 D | 49.2% | 49.7% | 0.8% |
| 46,802 | CUMBERLAND | 19,017 | 10,994 | 7,644 | 223 | 156 | 3,350 R | 57.8% | 40.2% | 1.2% |
| 569,891 | DAVIDSON | 208,588 | 84,117 | 120,508 | 2,920 | 1,043 | 36,391 D | 40.3% | 57.8% | 1.4% |
| 11,731 | DECATUR | 4,370 | 2,046 | 2,278 | 22 | 24 | 232 D | 46.8% | 52.1% | 0.5% |
| 17,423 | DE KALB | 6,265 | 2,411 | 3,765 | 63 | 26 | 1,354 D | 38.5% | 60.1% | 1.0% |
| 43,156 | DICKSON | 15,556 | 7,016 | 8,332 | 120 | 88 | 1,316 D | 45.1% | 53.6% | 0.8% |
| 37,279 | DYER | 11,841 | 6,282 | 5,425 | 88 | 46 | 857 R | 53.1% | 45.8% | 0.7% |
| 28,806 | FAYETTE | 11,529 | 6,402 | 5,037 | 44 | 46 | 1,365 R | 55.5% | 43.7% | 0.4% |
| 16,625 | FENTRESS | 6,029 | 3,417 | 2,529 | 28 | 55 | 888 R | 56.7% | 41.9% | 0.5% |
| 39,270 | FRANKLIN | 14,691 | 6,560 | 7,828 | 190 | 113 | 1,268 D | 44.7% | 53.3% | 1.3% |
| 48,152 | GIBSON | 17,137 | 8,286 | 8,663 | 101 | 87 | 377 D | 48.4% | 50.6% | 0.6% |
| 29,447 | GILES | 10,066 | 4,377 | 5,527 | 79 | 83 | 1,150 D | 43.5% | 54.9% | 0.8% |
| 20,659 | GRAINGER | 6,194 | 3,746 | 2,361 | 46 | 41 | 1,385 R | 60.5% | 38.1% | 0.7% |
| 62,909 | GREENE | 20,816 | 12,540 | 7,909 | 185 | 182 | 4,631 R | 60.2% | 38.0% | 0.9% |
| 14,332 | GRUNDY | 4,596 | 1,553 | 2,970 | 37 | 36 | 1,417 D | 33.8% | 64.6% | 0.8% |
| 58,128 | HAMBLEN | 19,699 | 11,824 | 7,564 | 181 | 130 | 4,260 R | 60.0% | 38.4% | 0.9% |
| 307,896 | HAMILTON | 120,379 | 66,605 | 51,708 | 1,290 | 776 | 14,897 R | 55.3% | 43.0% | 1.1% |
| 6,786 | HANCOCK | 2,075 | 1,343 | 690 | 17 | 25 | 653 R | 64.7% | 33.3% | 0.8% |
| 28,105 | HARDEMAN | 8,803 | 3,729 | 4,953 | 38 | 83 | 1,224 D | 42.4% | 56.3% | 0.4% |
| 25,578 | HARDIN | 8,782 | 4,951 | 3,735 | 49 | 47 | 1,216 R | 56.4% | 42.5% | 0.6% |
| 53,563 | HAWKINS | 17,098 | 10,071 | 6,753 | 147 | 127 | 3,318 R | 58.9% | 39.5% | 0.9% |
| 19,797 | HAYWOOD | 6,478 | 2,554 | 3,887 | 20 | 17 | 1,333 D | 39.4% | 60.0% | 0.3% |
| 25,522 | HENDERSON | 8,399 | 5,153 | 3,166 | 46 | 34 | 1,987 R | 61.4% | 37.7% | 0.5% |
| 31,115 | HENRY | 12,309 | 5,944 | 6,093 | 125 | 147 | 149 D | 48.3% | 49.5% | 1.0% |
| 22,295 | HICKMAN | 7,264 | 2,914 | 4,239 | 58 | 53 | 1,325 D | 40.1% | 58.4% | 0.8% |
| 8,088 | HOUSTON | 3,127 | 993 | 2,081 | 16 | 37 | 1,088 D | 31.8% | 66.5% | 0.5% |
| 17,929 | HUMPHREYS | 6,681 | 2,387 | 4,205 | 65 | 24 | 1,818 D | 35.7% | 62.9% | 1.0% |
| 10,984 | JACKSON | 4,754 | 1,384 | 3,304 | 36 | 30 | 1,920 D | 29.1% | 69.5% | 0.8% |
| 44,294 | JEFFERSON | 14,087 | 8,657 | 5,226 | 121 | 83 | 3,431 R | 61.5% | 37.1% | 0.9% |
| 17,499 | JOHNSON | 5,657 | 3,740 | 1,813 | 54 | 50 | 1,927 R | 66.1% | 32.0% | 1.0% |
| 382,032 | KNOX | 150,586 | 86,851 | 60,969 | 1,772 | 994 | 25,882 R | 57.7% | 40.5% | 1.2% |
| 7,954 | LAKE | 2,224 | 781 | 1,419 | 11 | 13 | 638 D | 35.1% | 63.8% | 0.5% |
| 27,101 | LAUDERDALE | 7,618 | 3,329 | 4,224 | 27 | 38 | 895 D | 43.7% | 55.4% | 0.4% |
| 39,926 | LAWRENCE | 14,470 | 7,613 | 6,643 | 98 | 116 | 970 R | 52.6% | 45.9% | 0.7% |
| 11,367 | LEWIS | 4,420 | 2,037 | 2,281 | 63 | 39 | 244 D | 46.1% | 51.6% | 1.4% |
| 31,340 | LINCOLN | 10,659 | 5,435 | 5,060 | 72 | 92 | 375 R | 51.0% | 47.5% | 0.7% |
| 39,086 | LOUDON | 16,406 | 10,266 | 5,905 | 132 | 103 | 4,361 R | 62.6% | 36.0% | 0.8% |
| 49,015 | MCMINN | 16,600 | 10,155 | 6,142 | 142 | 161 | 4,013 R | 61.2% | 37.0% | 0.9% |
| 24,653 | MCNAIRY | 8,989 | 4,897 | 4,003 | 47 | 42 | 894 R | 54.5% | 44.5% | 0.5% |
| 20,386 | MACON | 6,491 | 3,366 | 3,059 | 30 | 36 | 307 R | 51.9% | 47.1% | 0.5% |
| 91,837 | MADISON | 33,930 | 17,862 | 15,781 | 173 | 114 | 2,081 R | 52.6% | 46.5% | 0.5% |
| 27,776 | MARION | 10,250 | 4,651 | 5,441 | 74 | 84 | 790 D | 45.4% | 53.1% | 0.7% |
| 26,767 | MARSHALL | 9,359 | 4,105 | 5,107 | 94 | 53 | 1,002 D | 43.9% | 54.6% | 1.0% |
| 69,498 | MAURY | 23,400 | 11,930 | 11,127 | 207 | 136 | 803 R | 51.0% | 47.6% | 0.9% |

# TENNESSEE

## PRESIDENT 2000

| 2000 Census Population | County | Total Vote | Republican | Democratic | Green (Nader) | Other | Rep.-Dem. Plurality | Percentage of Total Vote | | |
|---|---|---|---|---|---|---|---|---|---|---|
| | | | | | | | | Rep. | Dem. | Green |
| 11,086 | MEIGS | 3,390 | 1,797 | 1,555 | 12 | 26 | 242 R | 53.0% | 45.9% | 0.4% |
| 38,961 | MONROE | 13,003 | 7,514 | 5,327 | 78 | 84 | 2,187 R | 57.8% | 41.0% | 0.6% |
| 134,768 | MONTGOMERY | 39,044 | 19,644 | 18,818 | 359 | 223 | 826 R | 50.3% | 48.2% | 0.9% |
| 5,740 | MOORE | 2,301 | 1,145 | 1,107 | 27 | 22 | 38 R | 49.8% | 48.1% | 1.2% |
| 19,757 | MORGAN | 6,162 | 3,144 | 2,921 | 39 | 58 | 223 R | 51.0% | 47.4% | 0.6% |
| 32,450 | OBION | 12,440 | 6,168 | 6,056 | 99 | 117 | 112 R | 49.6% | 48.7% | 0.8% |
| 20,118 | OVERTON | 7,496 | 2,875 | 4,507 | 46 | 68 | 1,632 D | 38.4% | 60.1% | 0.6% |
| 7,631 | PERRY | 2,866 | 1,165 | 1,650 | 28 | 23 | 485 D | 40.6% | 57.6% | 1.0% |
| 4,945 | PICKETT | 2,239 | 1,281 | 939 | 12 | 7 | 342 R | 57.2% | 41.9% | 0.5% |
| 16,050 | POLK | 5,594 | 2,907 | 2,574 | 46 | 67 | 333 R | 52.0% | 46.0% | 0.8% |
| 62,315 | PUTNAM | 22,438 | 11,248 | 10,785 | 228 | 177 | 463 R | 50.1% | 48.1% | 1.0% |
| 28,400 | RHEA | 9,772 | 5,900 | 3,722 | 74 | 76 | 2,178 R | 60.4% | 38.1% | 0.8% |
| 51,910 | ROANE | 21,326 | 11,345 | 9,575 | 211 | 195 | 1,770 R | 53.2% | 44.9% | 1.0% |
| 54,433 | ROBERTSON | 20,164 | 9,675 | 10,249 | 148 | 92 | 574 D | 48.0% | 50.8% | 0.7% |
| 182,023 | RUTHERFORD | 62,182 | 33,445 | 27,360 | 1,024 | 353 | 6,085 R | 53.8% | 44.0% | 1.6% |
| 21,127 | SCOTT | 6,615 | 3,579 | 2,967 | 31 | 38 | 612 R | 54.1% | 44.9% | 0.5% |
| 11,370 | SEQUATCHIE | 3,887 | 2,169 | 1,648 | 37 | 33 | 521 R | 55.8% | 42.4% | 1.0% |
| 71,170 | SEVIER | 25,365 | 16,734 | 8,208 | 259 | 164 | 8,526 R | 66.0% | 32.4% | 1.0% |
| 897,472 | SHELBY | 336,755 | 141,756 | 190,404 | 2,860 | 1,735 | 48,648 D | 42.1% | 56.5% | 0.8% |
| 17,712 | SMITH | 7,348 | 2,384 | 4,884 | 42 | 38 | 2,500 D | 32.4% | 66.5% | 0.6% |
| 12,370 | STEWART | 4,782 | 1,826 | 2,870 | 50 | 36 | 1,044 D | 38.2% | 60.0% | 1.0% |
| 153,048 | SULLIVAN | 55,727 | 33,482 | 21,354 | 520 | 371 | 12,128 R | 60.1% | 38.3% | 0.9% |
| 130,449 | SUMNER | 50,477 | 27,601 | 22,118 | 482 | 276 | 5,483 R | 54.7% | 43.8% | 1.0% |
| 51,271 | TIPTON | 16,552 | 10,070 | 6,300 | 96 | 86 | 3,770 R | 60.8% | 38.1% | 0.6% |
| 7,259 | TROUSDALE | 2,945 | 950 | 1,966 | 15 | 14 | 1,016 D | 32.3% | 66.8% | 0.5% |
| 17,667 | UNICOI | 6,429 | 3,780 | 2,566 | 40 | 43 | 1,214 R | 58.8% | 39.9% | 0.6% |
| 17,808 | UNION | 5,821 | 3,199 | 2,564 | 30 | 28 | 635 R | 55.0% | 44.0% | 0.5% |
| 5,508 | VAN BUREN | 2,131 | 845 | 1,255 | 8 | 23 | 410 D | 39.7% | 58.9% | 0.4% |
| 38,276 | WARREN | 13,131 | 5,552 | 7,378 | 105 | 96 | 1,826 D | 42.3% | 56.2% | 0.8% |
| 107,198 | WASHINGTON | 37,942 | 22,579 | 14,769 | 375 | 219 | 7,810 R | 59.5% | 38.9% | 1.0% |
| 16,842 | WAYNE | 5,306 | 3,370 | 1,859 | 43 | 34 | 1,511 R | 63.5% | 35.0% | 0.8% |
| 34,895 | WEAKLEY | 11,844 | 6,106 | 5,570 | 91 | 77 | 536 R | 51.6% | 47.0% | 0.8% |
| 23,102 | WHITE | 7,775 | 3,525 | 4,135 | 58 | 57 | 610 D | 45.3% | 53.2% | 0.7% |
| 126,638 | WILLIAMSON | 58,429 | 38,901 | 18,745 | 536 | 247 | 20,156 R | 66.6% | 32.1% | 0.9% |
| 88,809 | WILSON | 35,916 | 18,844 | 16,561 | 308 | 203 | 2,283 R | 52.5% | 46.1% | 0.9% |
| 5,689,283 | TOTAL | 2,076,181 | 1,061,949 | 981,720 | 19,781 | 12,731 | 80,229 R | 51.1% | 47.3% | 1.0% |

# TENNESSEE

## PRESIDENT 1996

| 1995 Census Pop. Est. | County | Total Vote | Republican | Democratic | Reform (Perot) | Other | Rep.-Dem. Plurality | Percentage of Total Vote | | |
|---|---|---|---|---|---|---|---|---|---|---|
| | | | | | | | | Rep. | Dem. | Reform |
| 71,663 | ANDERSON | 27,516 | 11,943 | 13,457 | 1,817 | 299 | 1,514 D | 43.4% | 48.9% | 6.6% |
| 33,126 | BEDFORD | 11,284 | 4,634 | 5,735 | 823 | 92 | 1,101 D | 41.1% | 50.8% | 7.3% |
| 15,770 | BENTON | 7,450 | 2,395 | 4,341 | 663 | 51 | 1,946 D | 32.1% | 58.3% | 8.9% |
| 10,173 | BLEDSOE | 3,532 | 1,626 | 1,621 | 251 | 34 | 5 R | 46.0% | 45.9% | 7.1% |
| 97,014 | BLOUNT | 36,930 | 19,310 | 14,687 | 2,556 | 377 | 4,623 R | 52.3% | 39.8% | 6.9% |
| 78,830 | BRADLEY | 26,628 | 15,478 | 9,095 | 1,856 | 199 | 6,383 R | 58.1% | 34.2% | 7.0% |
| 37,033 | CAMPBELL | 11,385 | 4,393 | 6,122 | 785 | 85 | 1,729 D | 38.6% | 53.8% | 6.9% |
| 11,399 | CANNON | 4,185 | 1,468 | 2,318 | 361 | 38 | 850 D | 35.1% | 55.4% | 8.6% |
| 28,617 | CARROLL | 9,849 | 4,206 | 4,912 | 697 | 34 | 706 D | 42.7% | 49.9% | 7.1% |
| 52,791 | CARTER | 18,282 | 10,540 | 6,218 | 1,383 | 141 | 4,322 R | 57.7% | 34.0% | 7.6% |
| 32,248 | CHEATHAM | 9,964 | 4,283 | 4,883 | 705 | 93 | 600 D | 43.0% | 49.0% | 7.1% |
| 13,703 | CHESTER | 4,901 | 2,746 | 1,922 | 203 | 30 | 824 R | 56.0% | 39.2% | 4.1% |
| 28,542 | CLAIBORNE | 8,679 | 4,023 | 3,861 | 727 | 68 | 162 R | 46.4% | 44.5% | 8.4% |
| 7,230 | CLAY | 3,006 | 1,108 | 1,559 | 316 | 23 | 451 D | 36.9% | 51.9% | 10.5% |
| 31,110 | COCKE | 8,691 | 4,481 | 3,326 | 798 | 86 | 1,155 R | 51.6% | 38.3% | 9.2% |
| 43,696 | COFFEE | 16,301 | 7,038 | 7,951 | 1,205 | 107 | 913 D | 43.2% | 48.8% | 7.4% |
| 13,589 | CROCKETT | 4,342 | 1,872 | 2,256 | 201 | 13 | 384 D | 43.1% | 52.0% | 4.6% |
| 40,445 | CUMBERLAND | 16,347 | 8,096 | 6,676 | 1,399 | 176 | 1,420 R | 49.5% | 40.8% | 8.6% |
| 530,796 | DAVIDSON | 200,382 | 78,453 | 110,805 | 9,018 | 2,106 | 32,352 D | 39.2% | 55.3% | 4.5% |
| 10,788 | DECATUR | 4,224 | 1,712 | 2,262 | 229 | 21 | 550 D | 40.5% | 53.6% | 5.4% |
| 15,290 | DE KALB | 5,302 | 1,696 | 3,213 | 342 | 51 | 1,517 D | 32.0% | 60.6% | 6.5% |
| 38,740 | DICKSON | 13,829 | 5,283 | 7,458 | 996 | 92 | 2,175 D | 38.2% | 53.9% | 7.2% |
| 35,900 | DYER | 11,374 | 5,059 | 5,602 | 676 | 37 | 543 D | 44.5% | 49.3% | 5.9% |
| 26,954 | FAYETTE | 9,519 | 4,406 | 4,655 | 416 | 42 | 249 D | 46.3% | 48.9% | 4.4% |
| 15,565 | FENTRESS | 5,056 | 2,307 | 2,332 | 386 | 31 | 25 D | 45.6% | 46.1% | 7.6% |
| 36,442 | FRANKLIN | 13,379 | 5,296 | 6,929 | 1,057 | 97 | 1,633 D | 39.6% | 51.8% | 7.9% |
| 47,728 | GIBSON | 16,428 | 6,614 | 8,851 | 891 | 72 | 2,237 D | 40.3% | 53.9% | 5.4% |
| 28,168 | GILES | 9,030 | 3,269 | 4,948 | 733 | 80 | 1,679 D | 36.2% | 54.8% | 8.1% |
| 18,667 | GRAINGER | 5,453 | 2,875 | 2,162 | 382 | 34 | 713 R | 52.7% | 39.6% | 7.0% |
| 58,095 | GREENE | 18,416 | 9,779 | 6,885 | 1,604 | 148 | 2,894 R | 53.1% | 37.4% | 8.7% |
| 13,695 | GRUNDY | 4,047 | 1,094 | 2,596 | 326 | 31 | 1,502 D | 27.0% | 64.1% | 8.1% |
| 52,763 | HAMBLEN | 18,099 | 9,797 | 7,006 | 1,106 | 190 | 2,791 R | 54.1% | 38.7% | 6.1% |
| 293,771 | HAMILTON | 110,831 | 55,205 | 48,008 | 6,699 | 919 | 7,197 R | 49.8% | 43.3% | 6.0% |
| 6,844 | HANCOCK | 2,154 | 1,259 | 760 | 116 | 19 | 499 R | 58.4% | 35.3% | 5.4% |
| 24,184 | HARDEMAN | 8,231 | 2,961 | 4,859 | 346 | 65 | 1,898 D | 36.0% | 59.0% | 4.2% |
| 24,399 | HARDIN | 8,117 | 3,980 | 3,508 | 594 | 35 | 472 R | 49.0% | 43.2% | 7.3% |
| 47,724 | HAWKINS | 15,941 | 8,164 | 6,367 | 1,282 | 128 | 1,797 R | 51.2% | 39.9% | 8.0% |
| 19,608 | HAYWOOD | 6,030 | 2,293 | 3,565 | 154 | 18 | 1,272 D | 38.0% | 59.1% | 2.6% |
| 23,245 | HENDERSON | 7,282 | 4,002 | 2,841 | 408 | 31 | 1,161 R | 55.0% | 39.0% | 5.6% |
| 29,429 | HENRY | 11,501 | 4,272 | 6,153 | 992 | 84 | 1,881 D | 37.1% | 53.5% | 8.6% |
| 19,068 | HICKMAN | 6,418 | 2,002 | 3,917 | 460 | 39 | 1,915 D | 31.2% | 61.0% | 7.2% |
| 7,579 | HOUSTON | 2,817 | 742 | 1,868 | 182 | 25 | 1,126 D | 26.3% | 66.3% | 6.5% |
| 16,532 | HUMPHREYS | 6,020 | 1,892 | 3,675 | 423 | 30 | 1,783 D | 31.4% | 61.0% | 7.0% |
| 9,326 | JACKSON | 4,161 | 944 | 2,889 | 289 | 39 | 1,945 D | 22.7% | 69.4% | 6.9% |
| 38,838 | JEFFERSON | 12,155 | 6,446 | 4,688 | 882 | 139 | 1,758 R | 53.0% | 38.6% | 7.3% |
| 16,341 | JOHNSON | 5,359 | 3,137 | 1,698 | 489 | 35 | 1,439 R | 58.5% | 31.7% | 9.1% |
| 361,407 | KNOX | 140,045 | 70,761 | 61,158 | 6,402 | 1,724 | 9,603 R | 50.5% | 43.7% | 4.6% |
| 8,539 | LAKE | 1,982 | 589 | 1,273 | 110 | 10 | 684 D | 29.7% | 64.2% | 5.5% |
| 24,103 | LAUDERDALE | 7,164 | 2,481 | 4,349 | 308 | 26 | 1,868 D | 34.6% | 60.7% | 4.3% |
| 38,292 | LAWRENCE | 13,359 | 6,115 | 6,188 | 973 | 83 | 73 D | 45.8% | 46.3% | 7.3% |
| 10,292 | LEWIS | 3,598 | 1,298 | 1,971 | 316 | 13 | 673 D | 36.1% | 54.8% | 8.8% |
| 28,785 | LINCOLN | 9,747 | 4,551 | 4,361 | 761 | 74 | 190 R | 46.7% | 44.7% | 7.8% |
| 35,927 | LOUDON | 13,730 | 7,097 | 5,552 | 889 | 192 | 1,545 R | 51.7% | 40.4% | 6.5% |
| 45,001 | MCMINN | 14,784 | 7,655 | 5,987 | 1,033 | 109 | 1,668 R | 51.8% | 40.5% | 7.0% |
| 23,410 | MCNAIRY | 8,576 | 3,960 | 4,050 | 519 | 47 | 90 D | 46.2% | 47.2% | 6.1% |
| 16,927 | MACON | 5,166 | 2,481 | 2,240 | 421 | 24 | 241 R | 48.0% | 43.4% | 8.1% |
| 83,715 | MADISON | 29,565 | 14,908 | 13,577 | 968 | 112 | 1,331 R | 50.4% | 45.9% | 3.3% |
| 26,469 | MARION | 9,191 | 3,166 | 5,194 | 768 | 63 | 2,028 D | 34.4% | 56.5% | 8.4% |
| 24,900 | MARSHALL | 7,913 | 2,781 | 4,447 | 603 | 82 | 1,666 D | 35.1% | 56.2% | 7.6% |
| 65,207 | MAURY | 20,574 | 8,737 | 10,367 | 1,366 | 104 | 1,630 D | 42.5% | 50.4% | 6.6% |

# TENNESSEE

## PRESIDENT 1996

| 1995 Census Pop. Est. | County | Total Vote | Republican | Democratic | Reform (Perot) | Other | Rep.-Dem. Plurality | Percentage of Total Vote | | |
|---|---|---|---|---|---|---|---|---|---|---|
| | | | | | | | | Rep. | Dem. | Reform |
| 9,198 | MEIGS | 2,968 | 1,228 | 1,476 | 245 | 19 | 248 D | 41.4% | 49.7% | 8.3% |
| 32,867 | MONROE | 10,928 | 5,257 | 4,872 | 713 | 86 | 385 R | 48.1% | 44.6% | 6.5% |
| 123,811 | MONTGOMERY | 33,625 | 15,133 | 16,498 | 1,781 | 213 | 1,365 D | 45.0% | 49.1% | 5.3% |
| 5,189 | MOORE | 1,980 | 846 | 935 | 177 | 22 | 89 D | 42.7% | 47.2% | 8.9% |
| 18,280 | MORGAN | 5,324 | 2,070 | 2,767 | 446 | 41 | 697 D | 38.9% | 52.0% | 8.4% |
| 32,413 | OBION | 11,536 | 4,310 | 6,226 | 932 | 68 | 1,916 D | 37.4% | 54.0% | 8.1% |
| 18,309 | OVERTON | 6,032 | 1,756 | 3,800 | 431 | 45 | 2,044 D | 29.1% | 63.0% | 7.1% |
| 7,055 | PERRY | 2,386 | 747 | 1,444 | 178 | 17 | 697 D | 31.3% | 60.5% | 7.5% |
| 4,583 | PICKETT | 2,071 | 1,046 | 901 | 116 | 8 | 145 R | 50.5% | 43.5% | 5.6% |
| 14,263 | POLK | 4,770 | 1,910 | 2,450 | 377 | 33 | 540 D | 40.0% | 51.4% | 7.9% |
| 57,319 | PUTNAM | 20,888 | 9,093 | 10,047 | 1,487 | 261 | 954 D | 43.5% | 48.1% | 7.1% |
| 26,833 | RHEA | 9,188 | 4,476 | 3,969 | 694 | 49 | 507 R | 48.7% | 43.2% | 7.6% |
| 48,607 | ROANE | 20,485 | 9,044 | 9,744 | 1,438 | 259 | 700 D | 44.1% | 47.6% | 7.0% |
| 47,955 | ROBERTSON | 16,229 | 6,685 | 8,465 | 993 | 86 | 1,780 D | 41.2% | 52.2% | 6.1% |
| 148,041 | RUTHERFORD | 51,594 | 24,565 | 22,815 | 3,787 | 427 | 1,750 R | 47.6% | 44.2% | 7.3% |
| 19,550 | SCOTT | 5,637 | 2,646 | 2,506 | 431 | 54 | 140 R | 46.9% | 44.5% | 7.6% |
| 9,648 | SEQUATCHIE | 3,298 | 1,391 | 1,598 | 288 | 21 | 207 D | 42.2% | 48.5% | 8.7% |
| 59,542 | SEVIER | 20,846 | 11,847 | 7,136 | 1,650 | 213 | 4,711 R | 56.8% | 34.2% | 7.9% |
| 865,058 | SHELBY | 326,380 | 136,315 | 179,663 | 8,307 | 2,095 | 43,348 D | 41.8% | 55.0% | 2.5% |
| 15,356 | SMITH | 6,057 | 1,857 | 3,812 | 346 | 42 | 1,955 D | 30.7% | 62.9% | 5.7% |
| 10,586 | STEWART | 4,700 | 1,306 | 2,962 | 386 | 46 | 1,656 D | 27.8% | 63.0% | 8.2% |
| 148,783 | SULLIVAN | 53,837 | 29,296 | 20,571 | 3,555 | 415 | 8,725 R | 54.4% | 38.2% | 6.6% |
| 116,845 | SUMNER | 43,154 | 20,863 | 19,205 | 2,783 | 303 | 1,658 R | 48.3% | 44.5% | 6.4% |
| 43,423 | TIPTON | 15,051 | 7,585 | 6,596 | 799 | 71 | 989 R | 50.4% | 43.8% | 5.3% |
| 6,449 | TROUSDALE | 2,499 | 683 | 1,615 | 190 | 11 | 932 D | 27.3% | 64.6% | 7.6% |
| 16,819 | UNICOI | 5,755 | 3,122 | 2,131 | 447 | 55 | 991 R | 54.2% | 37.0% | 7.8% |
| 15,147 | UNION | 5,111 | 2,253 | 2,421 | 385 | 52 | 168 D | 44.1% | 47.4% | 7.5% |
| 5,095 | VAN BUREN | 1,663 | 504 | 1,010 | 128 | 21 | 506 D | 30.3% | 60.7% | 7.7% |
| 35,225 | WARREN | 11,633 | 4,226 | 6,389 | 917 | 101 | 2,163 D | 36.3% | 54.9% | 7.9% |
| 98,477 | WASHINGTON | 34,840 | 18,960 | 13,259 | 2,237 | 384 | 5,701 R | 54.4% | 38.1% | 6.4% |
| 16,032 | WAYNE | 4,650 | 2,715 | 1,574 | 323 | 38 | 1,141 R | 58.4% | 33.8% | 6.9% |
| 32,346 | WEAKLEY | 11,215 | 4,622 | 5,657 | 873 | 63 | 1,035 D | 41.2% | 50.4% | 7.8% |
| 21,304 | WHITE | 6,635 | 2,498 | 3,592 | 505 | 40 | 1,094 D | 37.6% | 54.1% | 7.6% |
| 102,061 | WILLIAMSON | 45,376 | 27,699 | 15,231 | 2,071 | 375 | 12,468 R | 61.0% | 33.6% | 4.6% |
| 77,150 | WILSON | 29,543 | 13,817 | 13,655 | 1,841 | 230 | 162 R | 46.8% | 46.2% | 6.2% |
| 5,256,051 | TOTAL | 1,894,105 | 863,530 | 909,146 | 105,918 | 15,511 | 45,616 D | 45.6% | 48.0% | 5.6% |

# TENNESSEE

## PRESIDENT 1992

| 1990 Census Population | County | Total Vote | Republican | Democratic | Perot | Other | Plurality | Percentage Total Vote | | |
|---|---|---|---|---|---|---|---|---|---|---|
| | | | | | | | | Rep. | Dem. | Perot |
| 68,250 | ANDERSON | 28,611 | 11,838 | 13,482 | 3,149 | 142 | 1,644 D | 41.4% | 47.1% | 11.0% |
| 30,411 | BEDFORD | 11,421 | 3,836 | 5,978 | 1,541 | 66 | 2,142 D | 33.6% | 52.3% | 13.5% |
| 14,524 | BENTON | 6,114 | 1,625 | 3,896 | 559 | 34 | 2,271 D | 26.6% | 63.7% | 9.1% |
| 9,669 | BLEDSOE | 4,018 | 1,776 | 1,884 | 352 | 6 | 108 D | 44.2% | 46.9% | 8.8% |
| 85,969 | BLOUNT | 37,651 | 18,415 | 14,655 | 4,468 | 113 | 3,760 R | 48.9% | 38.9% | 11.9% |
| 73,712 | BRADLEY | 29,696 | 16,528 | 9,889 | 3,212 | 67 | 6,639 R | 55.7% | 33.3% | 10.8% |
| 35,079 | CAMPBELL | 12,931 | 4,897 | 6,756 | 1,240 | 38 | 1,859 D | 37.9% | 52.2% | 9.6% |
| 10,467 | CANNON | 4,331 | 1,229 | 2,593 | 495 | 14 | 1,364 D | 28.4% | 59.9% | 11.4% |
| 27,514 | CARROLL | 11,799 | 4,842 | 5,741 | 1,139 | 77 | 899 D | 41.0% | 48.7% | 9.7% |
| 51,505 | CARTER | 19,190 | 10,712 | 6,502 | 1,898 | 78 | 4,210 R | 55.8% | 33.9% | 9.9% |
| 27,140 | CHEATHAM | 9,788 | 3,496 | 4,817 | 1,433 | 42 | 1,321 D | 35.7% | 49.2% | 14.6% |
| 12,819 | CHESTER | 5,596 | 2,834 | 2,317 | 439 | 6 | 517 R | 50.6% | 41.4% | 7.8% |
| 26,137 | CLAIBORNE | 9,485 | 4,065 | 4,509 | 860 | 51 | 444 D | 42.9% | 47.5% | 9.1% |
| 7,238 | CLAY | 3,226 | 1,072 | 1,922 | 223 | 9 | 850 D | 33.2% | 59.6% | 6.9% |
| 29,141 | COCKE | 10,000 | 5,298 | 3,495 | 1,124 | 83 | 1,803 R | 53.0% | 35.0% | 11.2% |
| 40,339 | COFFEE | 17,044 | 6,047 | 8,534 | 2,420 | 43 | 2,487 D | 35.5% | 50.1% | 14.2% |
| 13,378 | CROCKETT | 5,357 | 2,180 | 2,657 | 507 | 13 | 477 D | 40.7% | 49.6% | 9.5% |
| 34,736 | CUMBERLAND | 15,792 | 7,116 | 6,393 | 2,200 | 83 | 723 R | 45.1% | 40.5% | 13.9% |
| 510,784 | DAVIDSON | 203,807 | 76,567 | 106,355 | 20,184 | 701 | 29,788 D | 37.6% | 52.2% | 9.9% |
| 10,472 | DECATUR | 4,661 | 1,667 | 2,633 | 351 | 10 | 966 D | 35.8% | 56.5% | 7.5% |
| 14,360 | DE KALB | 6,722 | 1,714 | 4,382 | 608 | 18 | 2,668 D | 25.5% | 65.2% | 9.0% |
| 35,061 | DICKSON | 14,093 | 4,450 | 7,863 | 1,730 | 50 | 3,413 D | 31.6% | 55.8% | 12.3% |
| 34,854 | DYER | 12,787 | 5,668 | 5,845 | 1,241 | 33 | 177 D | 44.3% | 45.7% | 9.7% |
| 25,559 | FAYETTE | 8,609 | 3,713 | 4,211 | 657 | 28 | 498 D | 43.1% | 48.9% | 7.6% |
| 14,669 | FENTRESS | 5,759 | 2,391 | 2,730 | 606 | 32 | 339 D | 41.5% | 47.4% | 10.5% |
| 34,725 | FRANKLIN | 14,176 | 4,507 | 7,773 | 1,837 | 59 | 3,266 D | 31.8% | 54.8% | 13.0% |
| 46,315 | GIBSON | 18,332 | 7,161 | 9,555 | 1,536 | 80 | 2,394 D | 39.1% | 52.1% | 8.4% |
| 25,741 | GILES | 9,781 | 2,827 | 5,601 | 1,309 | 44 | 2,774 D | 28.9% | 57.3% | 13.4% |
| 17,095 | GRAINGER | 5,553 | 2,772 | 2,242 | 513 | 26 | 530 R | 49.9% | 40.4% | 9.2% |
| 55,853 | GREENE | 20,875 | 9,912 | 7,857 | 2,930 | 176 | 2,055 R | 47.5% | 37.6% | 14.0% |
| 13,362 | GRUNDY | 4,386 | 1,004 | 2,997 | 366 | 19 | 1,993 D | 22.9% | 68.3% | 8.3% |
| 50,480 | HAMBLEN | 17,854 | 8,898 | 7,114 | 1,760 | 82 | 1,784 R | 49.8% | 39.8% | 9.9% |
| 285,536 | HAMILTON | 115,085 | 53,476 | 46,770 | 14,400 | 439 | 6,706 R | 46.5% | 40.6% | 12.5% |
| 6,739 | HANCOCK | 2,449 | 1,274 | 1,000 | 151 | 24 | 274 R | 52.0% | 40.8% | 6.2% |
| 23,377 | HARDEMAN | 8,627 | 3,122 | 4,832 | 594 | 79 | 1,710 D | 36.2% | 56.0% | 6.9% |
| 22,633 | HARDIN | 8,592 | 3,875 | 3,922 | 734 | 61 | 47 D | 45.1% | 45.6% | 8.5% |
| 44,565 | HAWKINS | 16,285 | 7,758 | 6,623 | 1,847 | 57 | 1,135 R | 47.6% | 40.7% | 11.3% |
| 19,437 | HAYWOOD | 6,376 | 2,518 | 3,511 | 331 | 16 | 993 D | 39.5% | 55.1% | 5.2% |
| 21,844 | HENDERSON | 9,024 | 4,719 | 3,502 | 785 | 18 | 1,217 R | 52.3% | 38.8% | 8.7% |
| 27,888 | HENRY | 12,095 | 3,661 | 6,797 | 1,588 | 49 | 3,136 D | 30.3% | 56.2% | 13.1% |
| 16,754 | HICKMAN | 6,727 | 1,820 | 4,093 | 795 | 19 | 2,273 D | 27.1% | 60.8% | 11.8% |
| 7,018 | HOUSTON | 2,951 | 648 | 2,012 | 280 | 11 | 1,364 D | 22.0% | 68.2% | 9.5% |
| 15,795 | HUMPHREYS | 6,135 | 1,641 | 3,875 | 609 | 10 | 2,234 D | 26.7% | 63.2% | 9.9% |
| 9,297 | JACKSON | 4,258 | 708 | 3,208 | 332 | 10 | 2,500 D | 16.6% | 75.3% | 7.8% |
| 33,016 | JEFFERSON | 12,362 | 6,184 | 4,740 | 1,385 | 53 | 1,444 R | 50.0% | 38.3% | 11.2% |
| 13,766 | JOHNSON | 5,563 | 3,170 | 1,781 | 574 | 38 | 1,389 R | 57.0% | 32.0% | 10.3% |
| 335,749 | KNOX | 142,476 | 66,607 | 59,702 | 15,669 | 498 | 6,905 R | 46.7% | 41.9% | 11.0% |
| 7,129 | LAKE | 2,306 | 680 | 1,449 | 151 | 26 | 769 D | 29.5% | 62.8% | 6.5% |
| 23,491 | LAUDERDALE | 7,958 | 2,928 | 4,452 | 561 | 17 | 1,524 D | 36.8% | 55.9% | 7.0% |
| 35,303 | LAWRENCE | 13,864 | 5,608 | 6,816 | 1,403 | 37 | 1,208 D | 40.5% | 49.2% | 10.1% |
| 9,247 | LEWIS | 4,152 | 1,218 | 2,491 | 434 | 9 | 1,273 D | 29.3% | 60.0% | 10.5% |
| 28,157 | LINCOLN | 10,302 | 3,814 | 5,063 | 1,371 | 54 | 1,249 D | 37.0% | 49.1% | 13.3% |
| 31,255 | LOUDON | 13,510 | 6,444 | 5,414 | 1,602 | 50 | 1,030 R | 47.7% | 40.1% | 11.9% |
| 42,383 | MCMINN | 15,990 | 7,453 | 6,682 | 1,812 | 43 | 771 R | 46.6% | 41.8% | 11.3% |
| 22,422 | MCNAIRY | 9,595 | 4,093 | 4,691 | 774 | 37 | 598 D | 42.7% | 48.9% | 8.1% |
| 15,906 | MACON | 5,726 | 2,299 | 2,961 | 443 | 23 | 662 D | 40.2% | 51.7% | 7.7% |
| 77,982 | MADISON | 31,196 | 14,869 | 13,629 | 2,634 | 64 | 1,240 R | 47.7% | 43.7% | 8.4% |
| 24,860 | MARION | 10,068 | 3,262 | 5,589 | 1,186 | 31 | 2,327 D | 32.4% | 55.5% | 11.8% |
| 21,539 | MARSHALL | 8,098 | 2,516 | 4,491 | 1,050 | 41 | 1,975 D | 31.1% | 55.5% | 13.0% |
| 54,812 | MAURY | 20,459 | 7,440 | 9,997 | 2,821 | 201 | 2,557 D | 36.4% | 48.9% | 13.8% |

# TENNESSEE

## PRESIDENT 1992

| 1990 Census Population | County | Total Vote | Republican | Democratic | Perot | Other | Plurality | Percentage Total Vote | | |
|---|---|---|---|---|---|---|---|---|---|---|
| | | | | | | | | Rep. | Dem. | Perot |
| 8,033 | MEIGS | 3,484 | 1,355 | 1,673 | 453 | 3 | 318 D | 38.9% | 48.0% | 13.0% |
| 30,541 | MONROE | 12,411 | 6,025 | 5,384 | 936 | 66 | 641 R | 48.5% | 43.4% | 7.5% |
| 100,498 | MONTGOMERY | 31,341 | 13,011 | 14,507 | 3,753 | 70 | 1,496 D | 41.5% | 46.3% | 12.0% |
| 4,721 | MOORE | 2,145 | 661 | 1,151 | 327 | 6 | 490 D | 30.8% | 53.7% | 15.2% |
| 17,300 | MORGAN | 6,184 | 2,306 | 3,190 | 658 | 30 | 884 D | 37.3% | 51.6% | 10.6% |
| 31,717 | OBION | 12,864 | 4,812 | 6,497 | 1,494 | 61 | 1,685 D | 37.4% | 50.5% | 11.6% |
| 17,636 | OVERTON | 6,651 | 1,657 | 4,489 | 468 | 37 | 2,832 D | 24.9% | 67.5% | 7.0% |
| 6,612 | PERRY | 2,919 | 708 | 1,889 | 317 | 5 | 1,181 D | 24.3% | 64.7% | 10.9% |
| 4,548 | PICKETT | 2,368 | 1,094 | 1,144 | 121 | 9 | 50 D | 46.2% | 48.3% | 5.1% |
| 13,643 | POLK | 4,610 | 1,584 | 2,583 | 419 | 24 | 999 D | 34.4% | 56.0% | 9.1% |
| 51,373 | PUTNAM | 21,482 | 7,998 | 10,858 | 2,473 | 153 | 2,860 D | 37.2% | 50.5% | 11.5% |
| 24,344 | RHEA | 10,348 | 4,860 | 4,289 | 1,163 | 36 | 571 R | 47.0% | 41.4% | 11.2% |
| 47,227 | ROANE | 20,999 | 8,719 | 9,812 | 2,396 | 72 | 1,093 D | 41.5% | 46.7% | 11.4% |
| 41,494 | ROBERTSON | 15,779 | 5,271 | 8,498 | 1,978 | 32 | 3,227 D | 33.4% | 53.9% | 12.5% |
| 118,570 | RUTHERFORD | 47,140 | 18,877 | 21,084 | 7,005 | 174 | 2,207 D | 40.0% | 44.7% | 14.9% |
| 18,358 | SCOTT | 6,418 | 3,011 | 2,730 | 643 | 34 | 281 R | 46.9% | 42.5% | 10.0% |
| 8,863 | SEQUATCHIE | 3,559 | 1,381 | 1,754 | 405 | 19 | 373 D | 38.8% | 49.3% | 11.4% |
| 51,043 | SEVIER | 21,266 | 11,714 | 6,719 | 2,760 | 73 | 4,995 R | 55.1% | 31.6% | 13.0% |
| 826,330 | SHELBY | 366,110 | 153,310 | 191,322 | 20,223 | 1,255 | 38,012 D | 41.9% | 52.3% | 5.5% |
| 14,143 | SMITH | 7,044 | 1,482 | 5,061 | 486 | 15 | 3,579 D | 21.0% | 71.8% | 6.9% |
| 9,479 | STEWART | 4,323 | 1,046 | 2,779 | 487 | 11 | 1,733 D | 24.2% | 64.3% | 11.3% |
| 143,596 | SULLIVAN | 56,980 | 28,801 | 20,935 | 6,730 | 514 | 7,866 R | 50.5% | 36.7% | 11.8% |
| 103,281 | SUMNER | 42,132 | 17,401 | 19,387 | 5,177 | 167 | 1,986 D | 41.3% | 46.0% | 12.3% |
| 37,568 | TIPTON | 13,717 | 6,757 | 5,652 | 1,279 | 29 | 1,105 R | 49.3% | 41.2% | 9.3% |
| 5,920 | TROUSDALE | 2,664 | 565 | 1,846 | 243 | 10 | 1,281 D | 21.2% | 69.3% | 9.1% |
| 16,549 | UNICOI | 6,447 | 3,344 | 2,375 | 709 | 19 | 969 R | 51.9% | 36.8% | 11.0% |
| 13,694 | UNION | 5,354 | 2,274 | 2,478 | 580 | 22 | 204 D | 42.5% | 46.3% | 10.8% |
| 4,846 | VAN BUREN | 2,080 | 555 | 1,329 | 191 | 5 | 774 D | 26.7% | 63.9% | 9.2% |
| 32,992 | WARREN | 12,355 | 3,704 | 7,189 | 1,415 | 47 | 3,485 D | 30.0% | 58.2% | 11.5% |
| 92,315 | WASHINGTON | 35,483 | 18,206 | 13,071 | 4,002 | 204 | 5,135 R | 51.3% | 36.8% | 11.3% |
| 13,935 | WAYNE | 5,266 | 2,955 | 1,868 | 424 | 19 | 1,087 R | 56.1% | 35.5% | 8.1% |
| 31,972 | WEAKLEY | 11,869 | 4,800 | 5,691 | 1,355 | 23 | 891 D | 40.4% | 47.9% | 11.4% |
| 20,090 | WHITE | 7,074 | 2,118 | 4,102 | 821 | 33 | 1,984 D | 29.9% | 58.0% | 11.6% |
| 81,021 | WILLIAMSON | 40,195 | 22,015 | 13,053 | 5,026 | 101 | 8,962 R | 54.8% | 32.5% | 12.5% |
| 67,675 | WILSON | 29,903 | 12,061 | 13,861 | 3,848 | 133 | 1,800 D | 40.3% | 46.4% | 12.9% |
| 4,877,185 | TOTAL | 1,982,638 | 841,300 | 933,521 | 199,968 | 7,849 | 92,221 D | 42.4% | 47.1% | 10.1% |

# TENNESSEE

## PRESIDENT 1988

| 1980 Census Population | County | Total Vote | Republican | Democratic | Other | Rep.-Dem. Plurality | Percentage | | | |
|---|---|---|---|---|---|---|---|---|---|---|
| | | | | | | | Total Vote | | Major Vote | |
| | | | | | | | Rep. | Dem. | Rep. | Dem. |
| 67,346 | ANDERSON | 24,788 | 15,056 | 9,589 | 143 | 5,467 R | 60.7% | 38.7% | 61.1% | 38.9% |
| 27,916 | BEDFORD | 8,939 | 4,856 | 4,046 | 37 | 810 R | 54.3% | 45.3% | 54.5% | 45.5% |
| 14,901 | BENTON | 5,009 | 2,167 | 2,826 | 16 | 659 D | 43.3% | 56.4% | 43.4% | 56.6% |
| 9,478 | BLEDSOE | 3,147 | 1,858 | 1,274 | 15 | 584 R | 59.0% | 40.5% | 59.3% | 40.7% |
| 77,770 | BLOUNT | 29,776 | 20,027 | 9,602 | 147 | 10,425 R | 67.3% | 32.2% | 67.6% | 32.4% |
| 67,547 | BRADLEY | 22,031 | 15,829 | 6,122 | 80 | 9,707 R | 71.8% | 27.8% | 72.1% | 27.9% |
| 34,923 | CAMPBELL | 9,416 | 5,197 | 4,188 | 31 | 1,009 R | 55.2% | 44.5% | 55.4% | 44.6% |
| 10,234 | CANNON | 3,348 | 1,604 | 1,726 | 18 | 122 D | 47.9% | 51.6% | 48.2% | 51.8% |
| 28,285 | CARROLL | 9,830 | 5,635 | 4,151 | 44 | 1,484 R | 57.3% | 42.2% | 57.6% | 42.4% |
| 50,205 | CARTER | 16,778 | 12,036 | 4,634 | 108 | 7,402 R | 71.7% | 27.6% | 72.2% | 27.8% |
| 21,616 | CHEATHAM | 7,250 | 4,132 | 3,067 | 51 | 1,065 R | 57.0% | 42.3% | 57.4% | 42.6% |
| 12,727 | CHESTER | 4,555 | 2,781 | 1,757 | 17 | 1,024 R | 61.1% | 38.6% | 61.3% | 38.7% |
| 24,595 | CLAIBORNE | 7,082 | 4,071 | 2,977 | 34 | 1,094 R | 57.5% | 42.0% | 57.8% | 42.2% |
| 7,676 | CLAY | 2,493 | 1,291 | 1,183 | 19 | 108 R | 51.8% | 47.5% | 52.2% | 47.8% |
| 28,792 | COCKE | 7,579 | 5,430 | 2,115 | 34 | 3,315 R | 71.6% | 27.9% | 72.0% | 28.0% |
| 38,311 | COFFEE | 13,615 | 7,837 | 5,686 | 92 | 2,151 R | 57.6% | 41.8% | 58.0% | 42.0% |
| 14,941 | CROCKETT | 3,970 | 2,214 | 1,742 | 14 | 472 R | 55.8% | 43.9% | 56.0% | 44.0% |
| 28,676 | CUMBERLAND | 11,594 | 7,557 | 3,964 | 73 | 3,593 R | 65.2% | 34.2% | 65.6% | 34.4% |
| 477,811 | DAVIDSON | 188,946 | 98,599 | 89,270 | 1,077 | 9,329 R | 52.2% | 47.2% | 52.5% | 47.5% |
| 10,857 | DECATUR | 4,191 | 2,286 | 1,880 | 25 | 406 R | 54.5% | 44.9% | 54.9% | 45.1% |
| 13,589 | DE KALB | 4,581 | 2,098 | 2,452 | 31 | 354 D | 45.8% | 53.5% | 46.1% | 53.9% |
| 30,037 | DICKSON | 10,536 | 5,343 | 5,129 | 64 | 214 R | 50.7% | 48.7% | 51.0% | 49.0% |
| 34,663 | DYER | 10,243 | 6,508 | 3,690 | 45 | 2,818 R | 63.5% | 36.0% | 63.8% | 36.2% |
| 25,305 | FAYETTE | 6,921 | 3,573 | 3,292 | 56 | 281 R | 51.6% | 47.6% | 52.0% | 48.0% |
| 14,826 | FENTRESS | 4,992 | 3,103 | 1,856 | 33 | 1,247 R | 62.2% | 37.2% | 62.6% | 37.4% |
| 31,983 | FRANKLIN | 10,886 | 5,381 | 5,442 | 63 | 61 D | 49.4% | 50.0% | 49.7% | 50.3% |
| 49,467 | GIBSON | 16,038 | 8,415 | 7,542 | 81 | 873 R | 52.5% | 47.0% | 52.7% | 47.3% |
| 24,625 | GILES | 7,478 | 3,518 | 3,918 | 42 | 400 D | 47.0% | 52.4% | 47.3% | 52.7% |
| 16,751 | GRAINGER | 4,174 | 2,734 | 1,423 | 17 | 1,311 R | 65.5% | 34.1% | 65.8% | 34.2% |
| 54,422 | GREENE | 17,132 | 11,947 | 5,077 | 108 | 6,870 R | 69.7% | 29.6% | 70.2% | 29.8% |
| 13,787 | GRUNDY | 3,857 | 1,429 | 2,415 | 13 | 986 D | 37.0% | 62.6% | 37.2% | 62.8% |
| 49,300 | HAMBLEN | 15,565 | 10,418 | 5,061 | 86 | 5,357 R | 66.9% | 32.5% | 67.3% | 32.7% |
| 287,740 | HAMILTON | 109,709 | 68,111 | 40,990 | 608 | 27,121 R | 62.1% | 37.4% | 62.4% | 37.6% |
| 6,887 | HANCOCK | 2,082 | 1,303 | 737 | 42 | 566 R | 62.6% | 35.4% | 63.9% | 36.1% |
| 23,873 | HARDEMAN | 7,138 | 3,547 | 3,526 | 65 | 21 R | 49.7% | 49.4% | 50.1% | 49.9% |
| 22,280 | HARDIN | 7,089 | 4,252 | 2,808 | 29 | 1,444 R | 60.0% | 39.6% | 60.2% | 39.8% |
| 43,751 | HAWKINS | 14,646 | 9,356 | 5,212 | 78 | 4,144 R | 63.9% | 35.6% | 64.2% | 35.8% |
| 20,318 | HAYWOOD | 5,640 | 2,687 | 2,923 | 30 | 236 D | 47.6% | 51.8% | 47.9% | 52.1% |
| 21,390 | HENDERSON | 7,819 | 5,418 | 2,296 | 105 | 3,122 R | 69.3% | 29.4% | 70.2% | 29.8% |
| 28,656 | HENRY | 9,975 | 4,784 | 5,138 | 53 | 354 D | 48.0% | 51.5% | 48.2% | 51.8% |
| 15,151 | HICKMAN | 4,918 | 2,246 | 2,643 | 29 | 397 D | 45.7% | 53.7% | 45.9% | 54.1% |
| 6,871 | HOUSTON | 2,367 | 882 | 1,467 | 18 | 585 D | 37.3% | 62.0% | 37.5% | 62.5% |
| 15,957 | HUMPHREYS | 5,188 | 2,132 | 3,037 | 19 | 905 D | 41.1% | 58.5% | 41.2% | 58.8% |
| 9,398 | JACKSON | 3,144 | 1,168 | 1,962 | 14 | 794 D | 37.2% | 62.4% | 37.3% | 62.7% |
| 31,284 | JEFFERSON | 10,069 | 6,832 | 3,168 | 69 | 3,664 R | 67.9% | 31.5% | 68.3% | 31.7% |
| 13,745 | JOHNSON | 5,079 | 3,715 | 1,329 | 35 | 2,386 R | 73.1% | 26.2% | 73.7% | 26.3% |
| 319,694 | KNOX | 115,521 | 73,092 | 41,829 | 600 | 31,263 R | 63.3% | 36.2% | 63.6% | 36.4% |
| 7,455 | LAKE | 1,750 | 806 | 935 | 9 | 129 D | 46.1% | 53.4% | 46.3% | 53.7% |
| 24,555 | LAUDERDALE | 6,639 | 3,308 | 3,296 | 35 | 12 R | 49.8% | 49.6% | 50.1% | 49.9% |
| 34,110 | LAWRENCE | 11,183 | 6,273 | 4,903 | 7 | 1,370 R | 56.1% | 43.8% | 56.1% | 43.9% |
| 9,700 | LEWIS | 2,761 | 1,324 | 1,419 | 18 | 95 D | 48.0% | 51.4% | 48.3% | 51.7% |
| 26,483 | LINCOLN | 8,017 | 4,288 | 3,672 | 57 | 616 R | 53.5% | 45.8% | 53.9% | 46.1% |
| 28,553 | LOUDON | 10,679 | 7,122 | 3,480 | 77 | 3,642 R | 66.7% | 32.6% | 67.2% | 32.8% |
| 41,878 | MCMINN | 13,078 | 8,462 | 4,568 | 48 | 3,894 R | 64.7% | 34.9% | 64.9% | 35.1% |
| 22,525 | MCNAIRY | 8,191 | 4,625 | 3,510 | 56 | 1,115 R | 56.5% | 42.9% | 56.9% | 43.1% |
| 15,700 | MACON | 4,531 | 2,962 | 1,538 | 31 | 1,424 R | 65.4% | 33.9% | 65.8% | 34.2% |
| 74,546 | MADISON | 28,039 | 16,952 | 11,001 | 86 | 5,951 R | 60.5% | 39.2% | 60.6% | 39.4% |
| 24,416 | MARION | 8,618 | 4,407 | 4,175 | 36 | 232 R | 51.1% | 48.4% | 51.4% | 48.6% |
| 19,698 | MARSHALL | 5,791 | 2,975 | 2,795 | 21 | 180 R | 51.4% | 48.3% | 51.6% | 48.4% |
| 51,095 | MAURY | 14,788 | 8,397 | 6,280 | 111 | 2,117 R | 56.8% | 42.5% | 57.2% | 42.8% |

# TENNESSEE

## PRESIDENT 1988

| 1980 Census Population | County | Total Vote | Republican | Democratic | Other | Rep.-Dem. Plurality | Percentage | | | |
|---|---|---|---|---|---|---|---|---|---|---|
| | | | | | | | Total Vote | | Major Vote | |
| | | | | | | | Rep. | Dem. | Rep. | Dem. |
| 7,431 | MEIGS | 2,568 | 1,507 | 1,048 | 13 | 459 R | 58.7% | 40.8% | 59.0% | 41.0% |
| 28,700 | MONROE | 10,393 | 6,355 | 4,000 | 38 | 2,355 R | 61.1% | 38.5% | 61.4% | 38.6% |
| 83,342 | MONTGOMERY | 21,855 | 12,599 | 9,145 | 111 | 3,454 R | 57.6% | 41.8% | 57.9% | 42.1% |
| 4,510 | MOORE | 1,530 | 786 | 731 | 13 | 55 R | 51.4% | 47.8% | 51.8% | 48.2% |
| 16,604 | MORGAN | 4,546 | 2,576 | 1,941 | 29 | 635 R | 56.7% | 42.7% | 57.0% | 43.0% |
| 32,781 | OBION | 10,858 | 6,037 | 4,785 | 36 | 1,252 R | 55.6% | 44.1% | 55.8% | 44.2% |
| 17,575 | OVERTON | 4,397 | 1,873 | 2,511 | 13 | 638 D | 42.6% | 57.1% | 42.7% | 57.3% |
| 6,111 | PERRY | 2,076 | 854 | 1,208 | 14 | 354 D | 41.1% | 58.2% | 41.4% | 58.6% |
| 4,358 | PICKETT | 1,756 | 1,118 | 634 | 4 | 484 R | 63.7% | 36.1% | 63.8% | 36.2% |
| 13,602 | POLK | 4,391 | 2,297 | 2,073 | 21 | 224 R | 52.3% | 47.2% | 52.6% | 47.4% |
| 47,690 | PUTNAM | 16,285 | 9,547 | 6,606 | 132 | 2,941 R | 58.6% | 40.6% | 59.1% | 40.9% |
| 24,235 | RHEA | 7,776 | 5,144 | 2,595 | 37 | 2,549 R | 66.2% | 33.4% | 66.5% | 33.5% |
| 48,425 | ROANE | 17,497 | 10,881 | 6,535 | 81 | 4,346 R | 62.2% | 37.3% | 62.5% | 37.5% |
| 37,021 | ROBERTSON | 11,672 | 5,714 | 5,884 | 74 | 170 D | 49.0% | 50.4% | 49.3% | 50.7% |
| 84,058 | RUTHERFORD | 32,801 | 20,397 | 12,245 | 159 | 8,152 R | 62.2% | 37.3% | 62.5% | 37.5% |
| 19,259 | SCOTT | 4,193 | 2,562 | 1,611 | 20 | 951 R | 61.1% | 38.4% | 61.4% | 38.6% |
| 8,605 | SEQUATCHIE | 2,869 | 1,659 | 1,196 | 14 | 463 R | 57.8% | 41.7% | 58.1% | 41.9% |
| 41,418 | SEVIER | 15,631 | 11,920 | 3,643 | 68 | 8,277 R | 76.3% | 23.3% | 76.6% | 23.4% |
| 777,113 | SHELBY | 308,988 | 157,457 | 149,759 | 1,772 | 7,698 R | 51.0% | 48.5% | 51.3% | 48.7% |
| 14,935 | SMITH | 4,686 | 2,138 | 2,522 | 26 | 384 D | 45.6% | 53.8% | 45.9% | 54.1% |
| 8,665 | STEWART | 3,296 | 1,302 | 1,979 | 15 | 677 D | 39.5% | 60.0% | 39.7% | 60.3% |
| 143,968 | SULLIVAN | 50,977 | 32,996 | 17,396 | 585 | 15,600 R | 64.7% | 34.1% | 65.5% | 34.5% |
| 85,790 | SUMNER | 31,389 | 19,523 | 11,702 | 164 | 7,821 R | 62.2% | 37.3% | 62.5% | 37.5% |
| 32,930 | TIPTON | 9,918 | 6,052 | 3,824 | 42 | 2,228 R | 61.0% | 38.6% | 61.3% | 38.7% |
| 6,137 | TROUSDALE | 2,173 | 969 | 1,193 | 11 | 224 D | 44.6% | 54.9% | 44.8% | 55.2% |
| 16,362 | UNICOI | 5,486 | 3,664 | 1,794 | 28 | 1,870 R | 66.8% | 32.7% | 67.1% | 32.9% |
| 11,707 | UNION | 3,564 | 2,110 | 1,431 | 23 | 679 R | 59.2% | 40.2% | 59.6% | 40.4% |
| 4,728 | VAN BUREN | 1,580 | 780 | 796 | 4 | 16 D | 49.4% | 50.4% | 49.5% | 50.5% |
| 32,653 | WARREN | 9,218 | 4,529 | 4,646 | 43 | 117 D | 49.1% | 50.4% | 49.4% | 50.6% |
| 88,755 | WASHINGTON | 29,887 | 19,615 | 10,087 | 185 | 9,528 R | 65.6% | 33.8% | 66.0% | 34.0% |
| 13,946 | WAYNE | 4,951 | 3,405 | 1,516 | 30 | 1,889 R | 68.8% | 30.6% | 69.2% | 30.8% |
| 32,896 | WEAKLEY | 9,989 | 5,701 | 4,239 | 49 | 1,462 R | 57.1% | 42.4% | 57.4% | 42.6% |
| 19,567 | WHITE | 5,249 | 2,646 | 2,562 | 41 | 84 R | 50.4% | 48.8% | 50.8% | 49.2% |
| 58,108 | WILLIAMSON | 28,823 | 20,847 | 7,864 | 112 | 12,983 R | 72.3% | 27.3% | 72.6% | 27.4% |
| 56,064 | WILSON | 21,793 | 13,317 | 8,360 | 116 | 4,957 R | 61.1% | 38.4% | 61.4% | 38.6% |
| 4,591,120 | TOTAL | 1,636,250 | 947,233 | 679,794 | 9,223 | 267,439 R | 57.9% | 41.5% | 58.2% | 41.8% |

# TENNESSEE

## PRESIDENT 1984

| 1980 Census Population | County | Total Vote | Republican | Democratic | Other | Rep.-Dem. Plurality | Percentage Total Vote Rep. | Dem. | Major Vote Rep. | Dem. |
|---|---|---|---|---|---|---|---|---|---|---|
| 67,346 | ANDERSON | 27,374 | 16,783 | 10,415 | 176 | 6,368 R | 61.3% | 38.0% | 61.7% | 38.3% |
| 27,916 | BEDFORD | 9,296 | 4,699 | 4,499 | 98 | 200 R | 50.5% | 48.4% | 51.1% | 48.9% |
| 14,901 | BENTON | 5,897 | 2,481 | 3,398 | 18 | 917 D | 42.1% | 57.6% | 42.2% | 57.8% |
| 9,478 | BLEDSOE | 3,286 | 1,950 | 1,316 | 20 | 634 R | 59.3% | 40.0% | 59.7% | 40.3% |
| 77,770 | BLOUNT | 29,859 | 20,525 | 9,188 | 146 | 11,337 R | 68.7% | 30.8% | 69.1% | 30.9% |
| 67,547 | BRADLEY | 22,502 | 16,322 | 6,085 | 95 | 10,237 R | 72.5% | 27.0% | 72.8% | 27.2% |
| 34,923 | CAMPBELL | 10,444 | 5,685 | 4,692 | 67 | 993 R | 54.4% | 44.9% | 54.8% | 45.2% |
| 10,234 | CANNON | 3,560 | 1,669 | 1,846 | 45 | 177 D | 46.9% | 51.9% | 47.5% | 52.5% |
| 28,285 | CARROLL | 10,662 | 6,017 | 4,568 | 77 | 1,449 R | 56.4% | 42.8% | 56.8% | 43.2% |
| 50,205 | CARTER | 17,933 | 13,153 | 4,642 | 138 | 8,511 R | 73.3% | 25.9% | 73.9% | 26.1% |
| 21,616 | CHEATHAM | 7,169 | 4,109 | 3,007 | 53 | 1,102 R | 57.3% | 41.9% | 57.7% | 42.3% |
| 12,727 | CHESTER | 4,680 | 2,793 | 1,854 | 33 | 939 R | 59.7% | 39.6% | 60.1% | 39.9% |
| 24,595 | CLAIBORNE | 7,371 | 4,474 | 2,870 | 27 | 1,604 R | 60.7% | 38.9% | 60.9% | 39.1% |
| 7,676 | CLAY | 2,634 | 1,338 | 1,281 | 15 | 57 R | 50.8% | 48.6% | 51.1% | 48.9% |
| 28,792 | COCKE | 8,828 | 6,665 | 2,068 | 95 | 4,597 R | 75.5% | 23.4% | 76.3% | 23.7% |
| 38,311 | COFFEE | 13,468 | 7,695 | 5,691 | 82 | 2,004 R | 57.1% | 42.3% | 57.5% | 42.5% |
| 14,941 | CROCKETT | 4,429 | 2,479 | 1,937 | 13 | 542 R | 56.0% | 43.7% | 56.1% | 43.9% |
| 28,676 | CUMBERLAND | 10,756 | 7,083 | 3,605 | 68 | 3,478 R | 65.9% | 33.5% | 66.3% | 33.7% |
| 477,811 | DAVIDSON | 188,814 | 98,155 | 89,498 | 1,161 | 8,657 R | 52.0% | 47.4% | 52.3% | 47.7% |
| 10,857 | DECATUR | 4,441 | 2,390 | 2,031 | 20 | 359 R | 53.8% | 45.7% | 54.1% | 45.9% |
| 13,589 | DE KALB | 5,010 | 2,337 | 2,645 | 28 | 308 D | 46.6% | 52.8% | 46.9% | 53.1% |
| 30,037 | DICKSON | 11,805 | 5,846 | 5,809 | 150 | 37 R | 49.5% | 49.2% | 50.2% | 49.8% |
| 34,663 | DYER | 10,642 | 6,610 | 3,991 | 41 | 2,619 R | 62.1% | 37.5% | 62.4% | 37.6% |
| 25,305 | FAYETTE | 7,401 | 3,733 | 3,634 | 34 | 99 R | 50.4% | 49.1% | 50.7% | 49.3% |
| 14,826 | FENTRESS | 4,699 | 2,922 | 1,755 | 22 | 1,167 R | 62.2% | 37.3% | 62.5% | 37.5% |
| 31,983 | FRANKLIN | 11,621 | 5,705 | 5,846 | 70 | 141 D | 49.1% | 50.3% | 49.4% | 50.6% |
| 49,467 | GIBSON | 17,992 | 9,484 | 8,334 | 174 | 1,150 R | 52.7% | 46.3% | 53.2% | 46.8% |
| 24,625 | GILES | 7,739 | 3,875 | 3,812 | 52 | 63 R | 50.1% | 49.3% | 50.4% | 49.6% |
| 16,751 | GRAINGER | 4,814 | 3,212 | 1,565 | 37 | 1,647 R | 66.7% | 32.5% | 67.2% | 32.8% |
| 54,422 | GREENE | 18,065 | 13,215 | 4,763 | 87 | 8,452 R | 73.2% | 26.4% | 73.5% | 26.5% |
| 13,787 | GRUNDY | 4,015 | 1,396 | 2,596 | 23 | 1,200 D | 34.8% | 64.7% | 35.0% | 65.0% |
| 49,300 | HAMBLEN | 16,158 | 11,144 | 4,922 | 92 | 6,222 R | 69.0% | 30.5% | 69.4% | 30.6% |
| 287,740 | HAMILTON | 111,622 | 69,626 | 41,449 | 547 | 28,177 R | 62.4% | 37.1% | 62.7% | 37.3% |
| 6,887 | HANCOCK | 2,134 | 1,491 | 619 | 24 | 872 R | 69.9% | 29.0% | 70.7% | 29.3% |
| 23,873 | HARDEMAN | 7,626 | 3,712 | 3,797 | 117 | 85 D | 48.7% | 49.8% | 49.4% | 50.6% |
| 22,280 | HARDIN | 7,773 | 4,632 | 3,051 | 90 | 1,581 R | 59.6% | 39.3% | 60.3% | 39.7% |
| 43,751 | HAWKINS | 14,793 | 9,863 | 4,802 | 128 | 5,061 R | 66.7% | 32.5% | 67.3% | 32.7% |
| 20,318 | HAYWOOD | 6,166 | 2,839 | 3,308 | 19 | 469 D | 46.0% | 53.6% | 46.2% | 53.8% |
| 21,390 | HENDERSON | 7,821 | 5,362 | 2,426 | 33 | 2,936 R | 68.6% | 31.0% | 68.8% | 31.2% |
| 28,656 | HENRY | 10,837 | 5,376 | 5,407 | 54 | 31 D | 49.6% | 49.9% | 49.9% | 50.1% |
| 15,151 | HICKMAN | 5,334 | 2,370 | 2,941 | 23 | 571 D | 44.4% | 55.1% | 44.6% | 55.4% |
| 6,871 | HOUSTON | 2,619 | 882 | 1,716 | 21 | 834 D | 33.7% | 65.5% | 33.9% | 66.1% |
| 15,957 | HUMPHREYS | 5,933 | 2,249 | 3,668 | 16 | 1,419 D | 37.9% | 61.8% | 38.0% | 62.0% |
| 9,398 | JACKSON | 4,486 | 1,544 | 2,894 | 48 | 1,350 D | 34.4% | 64.5% | 34.8% | 65.2% |
| 31,284 | JEFFERSON | 10,975 | 7,721 | 3,185 | 69 | 4,536 R | 70.4% | 29.0% | 70.8% | 29.2% |
| 13,745 | JOHNSON | 4,871 | 3,853 | 999 | 19 | 2,854 R | 79.1% | 20.5% | 79.4% | 20.6% |
| 319,694 | KNOX | 120,987 | 76,965 | 43,448 | 574 | 33,517 R | 63.6% | 35.9% | 63.9% | 36.1% |
| 7,455 | LAKE | 2,092 | 878 | 1,191 | 23 | 313 D | 42.0% | 56.9% | 42.4% | 57.6% |
| 24,555 | LAUDERDALE | 7,099 | 3,566 | 3,506 | 27 | 60 R | 50.2% | 49.4% | 50.4% | 49.6% |
| 34,110 | LAWRENCE | 11,563 | 6,034 | 5,458 | 71 | 576 R | 52.2% | 47.2% | 52.5% | 47.5% |
| 9,700 | LEWIS | 3,306 | 1,733 | 1,556 | 17 | 177 R | 52.4% | 47.1% | 52.7% | 47.3% |
| 26,483 | LINCOLN | 8,114 | 3,982 | 4,103 | 29 | 121 D | 49.1% | 50.6% | 49.3% | 50.7% |
| 28,553 | LOUDON | 10,405 | 7,113 | 3,227 | 65 | 3,886 R | 68.4% | 31.0% | 68.8% | 31.2% |
| 41,878 | MCMINN | 14,813 | 9,604 | 5,141 | 68 | 4,463 R | 64.8% | 34.7% | 65.1% | 34.9% |
| 22,525 | MCNAIRY | 8,631 | 4,776 | 3,825 | 30 | 951 R | 55.3% | 44.3% | 55.5% | 44.5% |
| 15,700 | MACON | 5,105 | 3,330 | 1,747 | 28 | 1,583 R | 65.2% | 34.2% | 65.6% | 34.4% |
| 74,546 | MADISON | 29,880 | 17,819 | 12,006 | 55 | 5,813 R | 59.6% | 40.2% | 59.7% | 40.3% |
| 24,416 | MARION | 8,331 | 4,337 | 3,942 | 52 | 395 R | 52.1% | 47.3% | 52.4% | 47.6% |
| 19,698 | MARSHALL | 6,393 | 3,416 | 2,935 | 42 | 481 R | 53.4% | 45.9% | 53.8% | 46.2% |
| 51,095 | MAURY | 16,033 | 9,008 | 6,950 | 75 | 2,058 R | 56.2% | 43.3% | 56.4% | 43.6% |

# TENNESSEE

## PRESIDENT 1984

| 1980 Census Population | County | Total Vote | Republican | Democratic | Other | Rep.-Dem. Plurality | | Percentage | | | |
|---|---|---|---|---|---|---|---|---|---|---|---|
| | | | | | | | | Total Vote | | Major Vote | |
| | | | | | | | | Rep. | Dem. | Rep. | Dem. |
| 7,431 | MEIGS | 2,602 | 1,575 | 1,012 | 15 | 563 | R | 60.5% | 38.9% | 60.9% | 39.1% |
| 28,700 | MONROE | 10,947 | 6,665 | 4,223 | 59 | 2,442 | R | 60.9% | 38.6% | 61.2% | 38.8% |
| 83,342 | MONTGOMERY | 23,365 | 13,228 | 9,939 | 198 | 3,289 | R | 56.6% | 42.5% | 57.1% | 42.9% |
| 4,510 | MOORE | 1,680 | 863 | 808 | 9 | 55 | R | 51.4% | 48.1% | 51.6% | 48.4% |
| 16,604 | MORGAN | 5,076 | 2,903 | 2,121 | 52 | 782 | R | 57.2% | 41.8% | 57.8% | 42.2% |
| 32,781 | OBION | 11,252 | 6,384 | 4,769 | 99 | 1,615 | R | 56.7% | 42.4% | 57.2% | 42.8% |
| 17,575 | OVERTON | 4,830 | 2,054 | 2,749 | 27 | 695 | D | 42.5% | 56.9% | 42.8% | 57.2% |
| 6,111 | PERRY | 2,267 | 948 | 1,316 | 3 | 368 | D | 41.8% | 58.1% | 41.9% | 58.1% |
| 4,358 | PICKETT | 1,957 | 1,246 | 706 | 5 | 540 | R | 63.7% | 36.1% | 63.8% | 36.2% |
| 13,602 | POLK | 4,960 | 2,785 | 2,112 | 63 | 673 | R | 56.1% | 42.6% | 56.9% | 43.1% |
| 47,690 | PUTNAM | 16,541 | 8,999 | 7,443 | 99 | 1,556 | R | 54.4% | 45.0% | 54.7% | 45.3% |
| 24,235 | RHEA | 8,587 | 5,692 | 2,804 | 91 | 2,888 | R | 66.3% | 32.7% | 67.0% | 33.0% |
| 48,425 | ROANE | 18,614 | 11,882 | 6,623 | 109 | 5,259 | R | 63.8% | 35.6% | 64.2% | 35.8% |
| 37,021 | ROBERTSON | 11,263 | 5,445 | 5,756 | 62 | 311 | D | 48.3% | 51.1% | 48.6% | 51.4% |
| 84,058 | RUTHERFORD | 31,469 | 19,503 | 11,618 | 348 | 7,885 | R | 62.0% | 36.9% | 62.7% | 37.3% |
| 19,259 | SCOTT | 4,961 | 3,107 | 1,810 | 44 | 1,297 | R | 62.6% | 36.5% | 63.2% | 36.8% |
| 8,605 | SEQUATCHIE | 3,042 | 1,785 | 1,238 | 19 | 547 | R | 58.7% | 40.7% | 59.0% | 41.0% |
| 41,418 | SEVIER | 16,041 | 12,517 | 3,384 | 140 | 9,133 | R | 78.0% | 21.1% | 78.7% | 21.3% |
| 777,113 | SHELBY | 337,302 | 169,717 | 165,947 | 1,638 | 3,770 | R | 50.3% | 49.2% | 50.6% | 49.4% |
| 14,935 | SMITH | 5,691 | 2,393 | 3,258 | 40 | 865 | D | 42.0% | 57.2% | 42.3% | 57.7% |
| 8,665 | STEWART | 3,490 | 1,285 | 2,174 | 31 | 889 | D | 36.8% | 62.3% | 37.1% | 62.9% |
| 143,968 | SULLIVAN | 53,835 | 36,516 | 16,925 | 394 | 19,591 | R | 67.8% | 31.4% | 68.3% | 31.7% |
| 85,790 | SUMNER | 30,186 | 18,442 | 11,535 | 209 | 6,907 | R | 61.1% | 38.2% | 61.5% | 38.5% |
| 32,930 | TIPTON | 9,874 | 5,945 | 3,895 | 34 | 2,050 | R | 60.2% | 39.4% | 60.4% | 39.6% |
| 6,137 | TROUSDALE | 1,935 | 781 | 1,142 | 12 | 361 | D | 40.4% | 59.0% | 40.6% | 59.4% |
| 16,362 | UNICOI | 5,979 | 4,249 | 1,696 | 34 | 2,553 | R | 71.1% | 28.4% | 71.5% | 28.5% |
| 11,707 | UNION | 3,978 | 2,447 | 1,495 | 36 | 952 | R | 61.5% | 37.6% | 62.1% | 37.9% |
| 4,728 | VAN BUREN | 1,535 | 718 | 810 | 7 | 92 | D | 46.8% | 52.8% | 47.0% | 53.0% |
| 32,653 | WARREN | 9,691 | 4,811 | 4,813 | 67 | 2 | D | 49.6% | 49.7% | 50.0% | 50.0% |
| 88,755 | WASHINGTON | 31,368 | 21,762 | 9,452 | 154 | 12,310 | R | 69.4% | 30.1% | 69.7% | 30.3% |
| 13,946 | WAYNE | 4,879 | 3,332 | 1,534 | 13 | 1,798 | R | 68.3% | 31.4% | 68.5% | 31.5% |
| 32,896 | WEAKLEY | 11,287 | 6,480 | 4,752 | 55 | 1,728 | R | 57.4% | 42.1% | 57.7% | 42.3% |
| 19,567 | WHITE | 5,958 | 2,895 | 3,033 | 30 | 138 | D | 48.6% | 50.9% | 48.8% | 51.2% |
| 58,108 | WILLIAMSON | 24,997 | 17,975 | 6,929 | 93 | 11,046 | R | 71.9% | 27.7% | 72.2% | 27.8% |
| 56,064 | WILSON | 21,449 | 12,858 | 8,433 | 158 | 4,425 | R | 59.9% | 39.3% | 60.4% | 39.6% |
| 4,591,120 | TOTAL | 1,711,994 | 990,212 | 711,714 | 10,068 | 278,498 | R | 57.8% | 41.6% | 58.2% | 41.8% |

# TENNESSEE

## PRESIDENT 1980

| 1980 Census Population | County | Total Vote | Republican | Democratic | Other | Rep.-Dem. Plurality | Percentage | | | |
|---|---|---|---|---|---|---|---|---|---|---|
| | | | | | | | Total Vote | | Major Vote | |
| | | | | | | | Rep. | Dem. | Rep. | Dem. |
| 67,346 | ANDERSON | 25,736 | 14,235 | 10,194 | 1,307 | 4,041 R | 55.3% | 39.6% | 58.3% | 41.7% |
| 27,916 | BEDFORD | 9,583 | 3,377 | 5,987 | 219 | 2,610 D | 35.2% | 62.5% | 36.1% | 63.9% |
| 14,901 | BENTON | 6,193 | 2,281 | 3,811 | 101 | 1,530 D | 36.8% | 61.5% | 37.4% | 62.6% |
| 9,478 | BLEDSOE | 3,586 | 1,970 | 1,585 | 31 | 385 R | 54.9% | 44.2% | 55.4% | 44.6% |
| 77,770 | BLOUNT | 28,144 | 17,959 | 9,412 | 773 | 8,547 R | 63.8% | 33.4% | 65.6% | 34.4% |
| 67,547 | BRADLEY | 19,905 | 11,869 | 7,638 | 398 | 4,231 R | 59.6% | 38.4% | 60.8% | 39.2% |
| 34,923 | CAMPBELL | 10,450 | 5,537 | 4,752 | 161 | 785 R | 53.0% | 45.5% | 53.8% | 46.2% |
| 10,234 | CANNON | 3,817 | 1,403 | 2,351 | 63 | 948 D | 36.8% | 61.6% | 37.4% | 62.6% |
| 28,285 | CARROLL | 11,143 | 5,681 | 5,277 | 185 | 404 R | 51.0% | 47.4% | 51.8% | 48.2% |
| 50,205 | CARTER | 18,077 | 11,648 | 6,006 | 423 | 5,642 R | 64.4% | 33.2% | 66.0% | 34.0% |
| 21,616 | CHEATHAM | 6,201 | 2,296 | 3,771 | 134 | 1,475 D | 37.0% | 60.8% | 37.8% | 62.2% |
| 12,727 | CHESTER | 4,940 | 2,751 | 2,123 | 66 | 628 R | 55.7% | 43.0% | 56.4% | 43.6% |
| 24,595 | CLAIBORNE | 7,263 | 4,289 | 2,844 | 130 | 1,445 R | 59.1% | 39.2% | 60.1% | 39.9% |
| 7,676 | CLAY | 2,765 | 1,344 | 1,376 | 45 | 32 D | 48.6% | 49.8% | 49.4% | 50.6% |
| 28,792 | COCKE | 9,144 | 6,802 | 2,139 | 203 | 4,663 R | 74.4% | 23.4% | 76.1% | 23.9% |
| 38,311 | COFFEE | 13,393 | 5,454 | 7,612 | 327 | 2,158 D | 40.7% | 56.8% | 41.7% | 58.3% |
| 14,941 | CROCKETT | 4,588 | 2,117 | 2,422 | 49 | 305 D | 46.1% | 52.8% | 46.6% | 53.4% |
| 28,676 | CUMBERLAND | 10,436 | 6,354 | 3,775 | 307 | 2,579 R | 60.9% | 36.2% | 62.7% | 37.3% |
| 477,811 | DAVIDSON | 175,606 | 65,772 | 103,741 | 6,093 | 37,969 D | 37.5% | 59.1% | 38.8% | 61.2% |
| 10,857 | DECATUR | 4,280 | 2,095 | 2,139 | 46 | 44 D | 48.9% | 50.0% | 49.5% | 50.5% |
| 13,589 | DE KALB | 4,868 | 1,841 | 2,948 | 79 | 1,107 D | 37.8% | 60.6% | 38.4% | 61.6% |
| 30,037 | DICKSON | 10,467 | 3,636 | 6,622 | 209 | 2,986 D | 34.7% | 63.3% | 35.4% | 64.6% |
| 34,663 | DYER | 11,407 | 5,475 | 5,713 | 219 | 238 D | 48.0% | 50.1% | 48.9% | 51.1% |
| 25,305 | FAYETTE | 7,195 | 2,944 | 4,141 | 110 | 1,197 D | 40.9% | 57.6% | 41.6% | 58.4% |
| 14,826 | FENTRESS | 4,103 | 2,493 | 1,543 | 67 | 950 R | 60.8% | 37.6% | 61.8% | 38.2% |
| 31,983 | FRANKLIN | 11,090 | 3,995 | 6,760 | 335 | 2,765 D | 36.0% | 61.0% | 37.1% | 62.9% |
| 49,467 | GIBSON | 16,923 | 6,792 | 9,829 | 302 | 3,037 D | 40.1% | 58.1% | 40.9% | 59.1% |
| 24,625 | GILES | 7,537 | 2,757 | 4,653 | 127 | 1,896 D | 36.6% | 61.7% | 37.2% | 62.8% |
| 16,751 | GRAINGER | 4,848 | 3,254 | 1,495 | 99 | 1,759 R | 67.1% | 30.8% | 68.5% | 31.5% |
| 54,422 | GREENE | 16,956 | 10,704 | 5,822 | 430 | 4,882 R | 63.1% | 34.3% | 64.8% | 35.2% |
| 13,787 | GRUNDY | 4,019 | 1,139 | 2,837 | 43 | 1,698 D | 28.3% | 70.6% | 28.6% | 71.4% |
| 49,300 | HAMBLEN | 16,073 | 9,741 | 5,890 | 442 | 3,851 R | 60.6% | 36.6% | 62.3% | 37.7% |
| 287,740 | HAMILTON | 102,092 | 57,575 | 41,913 | 2,604 | 15,662 R | 56.4% | 41.1% | 57.9% | 42.1% |
| 6,887 | HANCOCK | 2,487 | 1,734 | 704 | 49 | 1,030 R | 69.7% | 28.3% | 71.1% | 28.9% |
| 23,873 | HARDEMAN | 7,205 | 2,931 | 4,153 | 121 | 1,222 D | 40.7% | 57.6% | 41.4% | 58.6% |
| 22,280 | HARDIN | 7,435 | 4,152 | 3,164 | 119 | 988 R | 55.8% | 42.6% | 56.8% | 43.2% |
| 43,751 | HAWKINS | 13,529 | 7,836 | 5,283 | 410 | 2,553 R | 57.9% | 39.0% | 59.7% | 40.3% |
| 20,318 | HAYWOOD | 5,943 | 2,435 | 3,445 | 63 | 1,010 D | 41.0% | 58.0% | 41.4% | 58.6% |
| 21,390 | HENDERSON | 7,926 | 5,108 | 2,702 | 116 | 2,406 R | 64.4% | 34.1% | 65.4% | 34.6% |
| 28,656 | HENRY | 11,168 | 4,299 | 6,601 | 268 | 2,302 D | 38.5% | 59.1% | 39.4% | 60.6% |
| 15,151 | HICKMAN | 5,230 | 1,903 | 3,225 | 102 | 1,322 D | 36.4% | 61.7% | 37.1% | 62.9% |
| 6,871 | HOUSTON | 2,541 | 738 | 1,757 | 46 | 1,019 D | 29.0% | 69.1% | 29.6% | 70.4% |
| 15,957 | HUMPHREYS | 5,966 | 1,897 | 3,974 | 95 | 2,077 D | 31.8% | 66.6% | 32.3% | 67.7% |
| 9,398 | JACKSON | 3,535 | 995 | 2,480 | 60 | 1,485 D | 28.1% | 70.2% | 28.6% | 71.4% |
| 31,284 | JEFFERSON | 10,392 | 6,944 | 3,180 | 268 | 3,764 R | 66.8% | 30.6% | 68.6% | 31.4% |
| 13,745 | JOHNSON | 4,955 | 3,716 | 1,141 | 98 | 2,575 R | 75.0% | 23.0% | 76.5% | 23.5% |
| 319,694 | KNOX | 117,585 | 66,153 | 45,634 | 5,798 | 20,519 R | 56.3% | 38.8% | 59.2% | 40.8% |
| 7,455 | LAKE | 2,563 | 823 | 1,718 | 22 | 895 D | 32.1% | 67.0% | 32.4% | 67.6% |
| 24,555 | LAUDERDALE | 7,235 | 2,818 | 4,318 | 99 | 1,500 D | 38.9% | 59.7% | 39.5% | 60.5% |
| 34,110 | LAWRENCE | 13,477 | 6,532 | 6,082 | 863 | 450 R | 48.5% | 45.1% | 51.8% | 48.2% |
| 9,700 | LEWIS | 3,309 | 1,076 | 2,190 | 43 | 1,114 D | 32.5% | 66.2% | 32.9% | 67.1% |
| 26,483 | LINCOLN | 8,409 | 2,856 | 5,387 | 166 | 2,531 D | 34.0% | 64.1% | 34.6% | 65.4% |
| 28,553 | LOUDON | 10,376 | 6,382 | 3,699 | 295 | 2,683 R | 61.5% | 35.6% | 63.3% | 36.7% |
| 41,878 | MCMINN | 13,547 | 7,825 | 5,460 | 262 | 2,365 R | 57.8% | 40.3% | 58.9% | 41.1% |
| 22,525 | MCNAIRY | 8,514 | 4,603 | 3,801 | 110 | 802 R | 54.1% | 44.6% | 54.8% | 45.2% |
| 15,700 | MACON | 4,961 | 2,925 | 1,947 | 89 | 978 R | 59.0% | 39.2% | 60.0% | 40.0% |
| 74,546 | MADISON | 27,187 | 13,667 | 12,986 | 534 | 681 R | 50.3% | 47.8% | 51.3% | 48.7% |
| 24,416 | MARION | 8,651 | 3,902 | 4,623 | 126 | 721 D | 45.1% | 53.4% | 45.8% | 54.2% |
| 19,698 | MARSHALL | 6,666 | 2,282 | 4,277 | 107 | 1,995 D | 34.2% | 64.2% | 34.8% | 65.2% |
| 51,095 | MAURY | 15,030 | 6,637 | 7,957 | 436 | 1,320 D | 44.2% | 52.9% | 45.5% | 54.5% |

# TENNESSEE

## PRESIDENT 1980

| 1980 Census Population | County | Total Vote | Republican | Democratic | Other | Rep.-Dem. Plurality | Percentage | | | |
|---|---|---|---|---|---|---|---|---|---|---|
| | | | | | | | Total Vote | | Major Vote | |
| | | | | | | | Rep. | Dem. | Rep. | Dem. |
| 7,431 | MEIGS | 2,316 | 1,278 | 999 | 39 | 279 R | 55.2% | 43.1% | 56.1% | 43.9% |
| 28,700 | MONROE | 11,065 | 6,246 | 4,612 | 207 | 1,634 R | 56.4% | 41.7% | 57.5% | 42.5% |
| 83,342 | MONTGOMERY | 20,698 | 8,503 | 11,573 | 622 | 3,070 D | 41.1% | 55.9% | 42.4% | 57.6% |
| 4,510 | MOORE | 1,595 | 551 | 993 | 51 | 442 D | 34.5% | 62.3% | 35.7% | 64.3% |
| 16,604 | MORGAN | 5,015 | 2,823 | 2,094 | 98 | 729 R | 56.3% | 41.8% | 57.4% | 42.6% |
| 32,781 | OBION | 11,365 | 5,397 | 5,766 | 202 | 369 D | 47.5% | 50.7% | 48.3% | 51.7% |
| 17,575 | OVERTON | 5,267 | 1,869 | 3,343 | 55 | 1,474 D | 35.5% | 63.5% | 35.9% | 64.1% |
| 6,111 | PERRY | 2,232 | 783 | 1,401 | 48 | 618 D | 35.1% | 62.8% | 35.9% | 64.1% |
| 4,358 | PICKETT | 2,102 | 1,319 | 758 | 25 | 561 R | 62.7% | 36.1% | 63.5% | 36.5% |
| 13,602 | POLK | 4,960 | 2,414 | 2,470 | 76 | 56 D | 48.7% | 49.8% | 49.4% | 50.6% |
| 47,690 | PUTNAM | 14,753 | 6,235 | 8,084 | 434 | 1,849 D | 42.3% | 54.8% | 43.5% | 56.5% |
| 24,235 | RHEA | 7,889 | 4,689 | 3,070 | 130 | 1,619 R | 59.4% | 38.9% | 60.4% | 39.6% |
| 48,425 | ROANE | 18,182 | 11,096 | 6,473 | 613 | 4,623 R | 61.0% | 35.6% | 63.2% | 36.8% |
| 37,021 | ROBERTSON | 11,126 | 3,560 | 7,381 | 185 | 3,821 D | 32.0% | 66.3% | 32.5% | 67.5% |
| 84,058 | RUTHERFORD | 27,350 | 11,208 | 15,213 | 929 | 4,005 D | 41.0% | 55.6% | 42.4% | 57.6% |
| 19,259 | SCOTT | 4,832 | 3,014 | 1,724 | 94 | 1,290 R | 62.4% | 35.7% | 63.6% | 36.4% |
| 8,605 | SEQUATCHIE | 3,052 | 1,512 | 1,509 | 31 | 3 R | 49.5% | 49.4% | 50.0% | 50.0% |
| 41,418 | SEVIER | 14,439 | 10,576 | 3,450 | 413 | 7,126 R | 73.2% | 23.9% | 75.4% | 24.6% |
| 777,113 | SHELBY | 308,517 | 140,157 | 159,240 | 9,120 | 19,083 D | 45.4% | 51.6% | 46.8% | 53.2% |
| 14,935 | SMITH | 5,531 | 1,755 | 3,674 | 102 | 1,919 D | 31.7% | 66.4% | 32.3% | 67.7% |
| 8,665 | STEWART | 3,318 | 985 | 2,274 | 59 | 1,289 D | 29.7% | 68.5% | 30.2% | 69.8% |
| 143,968 | SULLIVAN | 50,470 | 25,963 | 22,341 | 2,166 | 3,622 R | 51.4% | 44.3% | 53.7% | 46.3% |
| 85,790 | SUMNER | 26,735 | 11,876 | 14,150 | 709 | 2,274 D | 44.4% | 52.9% | 45.6% | 54.4% |
| 32,930 | TIPTON | 9,401 | 4,339 | 4,934 | 128 | 595 D | 46.2% | 52.5% | 46.8% | 53.2% |
| 6,137 | TROUSDALE | 2,354 | 629 | 1,674 | 51 | 1,045 D | 26.7% | 71.1% | 27.3% | 72.7% |
| 16,362 | UNICOI | 5,844 | 3,828 | 1,880 | 136 | 1,948 R | 65.5% | 32.2% | 67.1% | 32.9% |
| 11,707 | UNION | 3,951 | 2,453 | 1,435 | 63 | 1,018 R | 62.1% | 36.3% | 63.1% | 36.9% |
| 4,728 | VAN BUREN | 1,404 | 499 | 886 | 19 | 387 D | 35.5% | 63.1% | 36.0% | 64.0% |
| 32,653 | WARREN | 9,904 | 3,680 | 6,021 | 203 | 2,341 D | 37.2% | 60.8% | 37.9% | 62.1% |
| 88,755 | WASHINGTON | 30,249 | 17,457 | 11,599 | 1,193 | 5,858 R | 57.7% | 38.3% | 60.1% | 39.9% |
| 13,946 | WAYNE | 5,297 | 3,418 | 1,633 | 246 | 1,785 R | 64.5% | 30.8% | 67.7% | 32.3% |
| 32,896 | WEAKLEY | 11,771 | 5,668 | 5,910 | 193 | 242 D | 48.2% | 50.2% | 49.0% | 51.0% |
| 19,567 | WHITE | 5,613 | 2,100 | 3,415 | 98 | 1,315 D | 37.4% | 60.8% | 38.1% | 61.9% |
| 58,108 | WILLIAMSON | 21,095 | 11,597 | 8,815 | 683 | 2,782 R | 55.0% | 41.8% | 56.8% | 43.2% |
| 56,064 | WILSON | 19,274 | 7,535 | 11,248 | 491 | 3,713 D | 39.1% | 58.4% | 40.1% | 59.9% |
| 4,591,120 | TOTAL | 1,617,616 | 787,761 | 783,051 | 46,804 | 4,710 R | 48.7% | 48.4% | 50.1% | 49.9% |

# TENNESSEE

## PRESIDENT 1976

| 1970 Census Population | County | Total Vote | Republican | Democratic | Other | Rep.-Dem. Plurality | Percentage | | | |
|---|---|---|---|---|---|---|---|---|---|---|
| | | | | | | | Total Vote | | Major Vote | |
| | | | | | | | Rep. | Dem. | Rep. | Dem. |
| 60,300 | ANDERSON | 24,242 | 10,494 | 13,455 | 293 | 2,961 D | 43.3% | 55.5% | 43.8% | 56.2% |
| 25,039 | BEDFORD | 10,357 | 3,023 | 7,228 | 106 | 4,205 D | 29.2% | 69.8% | 29.5% | 70.5% |
| 12,126 | BENTON | 5,806 | 1,678 | 4,088 | 40 | 2,410 D | 28.9% | 70.4% | 29.1% | 70.9% |
| 7,643 | BLEDSOE | 3,401 | 1,620 | 1,757 | 24 | 137 D | 47.6% | 51.7% | 48.0% | 52.0% |
| 63,744 | BLOUNT | 26,240 | 13,851 | 12,096 | 293 | 1,755 R | 52.8% | 46.1% | 53.4% | 46.6% |
| 50,686 | BRADLEY | 18,051 | 9,136 | 8,776 | 139 | 360 R | 50.6% | 48.6% | 51.0% | 49.0% |
| 26,045 | CAMPBELL | 9,557 | 4,277 | 5,206 | 74 | 929 D | 44.8% | 54.5% | 45.1% | 54.9% |
| 8,467 | CANNON | 3,399 | 908 | 2,463 | 28 | 1,555 D | 26.7% | 72.5% | 26.9% | 73.1% |
| 25,741 | CARROLL | 9,721 | 4,031 | 5,581 | 109 | 1,550 D | 41.5% | 57.4% | 41.9% | 58.1% |
| 43,259 | CARTER | 16,510 | 8,934 | 7,443 | 133 | 1,491 R | 54.1% | 45.1% | 54.6% | 45.4% |
| 13,199 | CHEATHAM | 5,664 | 1,376 | 4,225 | 63 | 2,849 D | 24.3% | 74.6% | 24.6% | 75.4% |
| 9,927 | CHESTER | 4,517 | 1,949 | 2,532 | 36 | 583 D | 43.1% | 56.1% | 43.5% | 56.5% |
| 19,420 | CLAIBORNE | 6,743 | 3,227 | 3,461 | 55 | 234 D | 47.9% | 51.3% | 48.3% | 51.7% |
| 6,624 | CLAY | 2,678 | 982 | 1,671 | 25 | 689 D | 36.7% | 62.4% | 37.0% | 63.0% |
| 25,283 | COCKE | 8,219 | 5,004 | 3,141 | 74 | 1,863 R | 60.9% | 38.2% | 61.4% | 38.6% |
| 32,572 | COFFEE | 12,005 | 3,848 | 8,017 | 140 | 4,169 D | 32.1% | 66.8% | 32.4% | 67.6% |
| 14,402 | CROCKETT | 4,697 | 1,694 | 2,963 | 40 | 1,269 D | 36.1% | 63.1% | 36.4% | 63.6% |
| 20,733 | CUMBERLAND | 8,763 | 4,119 | 4,543 | 101 | 424 D | 47.0% | 51.8% | 47.6% | 52.4% |
| 447,877 | DAVIDSON | 161,598 | 60,662 | 99,007 | 1,929 | 38,345 D | 37.5% | 61.3% | 38.0% | 62.0% |
| 9,457 | DECATUR | 4,116 | 1,637 | 2,432 | 47 | 795 D | 39.8% | 59.1% | 40.2% | 59.8% |
| 11,151 | DE KALB | 4,702 | 1,443 | 3,222 | 37 | 1,779 D | 30.7% | 68.5% | 30.9% | 69.1% |
| 21,977 | DICKSON | 8,922 | 2,285 | 6,551 | 86 | 4,266 D | 25.6% | 73.4% | 25.9% | 74.1% |
| 30,427 | DYER | 10,478 | 4,391 | 5,937 | 150 | 1,546 D | 41.9% | 56.7% | 42.5% | 57.5% |
| 22,692 | FAYETTE | 6,040 | 2,133 | 3,853 | 54 | 1,720 D | 35.3% | 63.8% | 35.6% | 64.4% |
| 12,593 | FENTRESS | 3,758 | 1,767 | 1,953 | 38 | 186 D | 47.0% | 52.0% | 47.5% | 52.5% |
| 27,244 | FRANKLIN | 9,524 | 2,619 | 6,788 | 117 | 4,169 D | 27.5% | 71.3% | 27.8% | 72.2% |
| 47,871 | GIBSON | 16,031 | 5,563 | 10,356 | 112 | 4,793 D | 34.7% | 64.6% | 34.9% | 65.1% |
| 22,138 | GILES | 7,248 | 1,952 | 5,225 | 71 | 3,273 D | 26.9% | 72.1% | 27.2% | 72.8% |
| 13,948 | GRAINGER | 4,863 | 2,805 | 2,018 | 40 | 787 R | 57.7% | 41.5% | 58.2% | 41.8% |
| 47,630 | GREENE | 15,880 | 8,664 | 7,070 | 146 | 1,594 R | 54.6% | 44.5% | 55.1% | 44.9% |
| 10,631 | GRUNDY | 3,721 | 850 | 2,850 | 21 | 2,000 D | 22.8% | 76.6% | 23.0% | 77.0% |
| 38,696 | HAMBLEN | 14,628 | 6,989 | 7,504 | 135 | 515 D | 47.8% | 51.3% | 48.2% | 51.8% |
| 254,236 | HAMILTON | 94,421 | 47,969 | 45,348 | 1,104 | 2,621 R | 50.8% | 48.0% | 51.4% | 48.6% |
| 6,719 | HANCOCK | 2,090 | 1,309 | 764 | 17 | 545 R | 62.6% | 36.6% | 63.1% | 36.9% |
| 22,435 | HARDEMAN | 6,270 | 2,254 | 3,934 | 82 | 1,680 D | 35.9% | 62.7% | 36.4% | 63.6% |
| 18,212 | HARDIN | 6,852 | 3,362 | 3,438 | 52 | 76 D | 49.1% | 50.2% | 49.4% | 50.6% |
| 33,726 | HAWKINS | 12,412 | 6,407 | 5,931 | 74 | 476 R | 51.6% | 47.8% | 51.9% | 48.1% |
| 19,596 | HAYWOOD | 5,661 | 1,952 | 3,681 | 28 | 1,729 D | 34.5% | 65.0% | 34.7% | 65.3% |
| 17,291 | HENDERSON | 7,586 | 4,152 | 3,366 | 68 | 786 R | 54.7% | 44.4% | 55.2% | 44.8% |
| 23,749 | HENRY | 9,881 | 2,585 | 7,162 | 134 | 4,577 D | 26.2% | 72.5% | 26.5% | 73.5% |
| 12,096 | HICKMAN | 4,787 | 1,154 | 3,590 | 43 | 2,436 D | 24.1% | 75.0% | 24.3% | 75.7% |
| 5,845 | HOUSTON | 2,427 | 407 | 1,990 | 30 | 1,583 D | 16.8% | 82.0% | 17.0% | 83.0% |
| 13,560 | HUMPHREYS | 5,413 | 1,338 | 4,021 | 54 | 2,683 D | 24.7% | 74.3% | 25.0% | 75.0% |
| 8,141 | JACKSON | 3,569 | 591 | 2,959 | 19 | 2,368 D | 16.6% | 82.9% | 16.6% | 83.4% |
| 24,940 | JEFFERSON | 9,538 | 5,459 | 3,995 | 84 | 1,464 R | 57.2% | 41.9% | 57.7% | 42.3% |
| 11,569 | JOHNSON | 4,478 | 2,986 | 1,464 | 28 | 1,522 R | 66.7% | 32.7% | 67.1% | 32.9% |
| 276,293 | KNOX | 110,409 | 56,013 | 53,034 | 1,362 | 2,979 R | 50.7% | 48.0% | 51.4% | 48.6% |
| 7,896 | LAKE | 2,549 | 591 | 1,933 | 25 | 1,342 D | 23.2% | 75.8% | 23.4% | 76.6% |
| 20,271 | LAUDERDALE | 6,877 | 2,105 | 4,747 | 25 | 2,642 D | 30.6% | 69.0% | 30.7% | 69.3% |
| 29,097 | LAWRENCE | 12,190 | 4,967 | 7,140 | 83 | 2,173 D | 40.7% | 58.6% | 41.0% | 59.0% |
| 6,761 | LEWIS | 3,036 | 617 | 2,391 | 28 | 1,774 D | 20.3% | 78.8% | 20.5% | 79.5% |
| 24,318 | LINCOLN | 7,518 | 1,724 | 5,732 | 62 | 4,008 D | 22.9% | 76.2% | 23.1% | 76.9% |
| 24,266 | LOUDON | 9,233 | 4,458 | 4,683 | 92 | 225 D | 48.3% | 50.7% | 48.8% | 51.2% |
| 35,462 | MCMINN | 13,732 | 6,638 | 7,020 | 74 | 382 D | 48.3% | 51.1% | 48.6% | 51.4% |
| 18,369 | MCNAIRY | 7,736 | 3,388 | 4,293 | 55 | 905 D | 43.8% | 55.5% | 44.1% | 55.9% |
| 12,315 | MACON | 4,051 | 2,063 | 1,951 | 37 | 112 R | 50.9% | 48.2% | 51.4% | 48.6% |
| 65,727 | MADISON | 24,659 | 11,364 | 12,989 | 306 | 1,625 D | 46.1% | 52.7% | 46.7% | 53.3% |
| 20,577 | MARION | 7,642 | 2,965 | 4,615 | 62 | 1,650 D | 38.8% | 60.4% | 39.1% | 60.9% |
| 17,319 | MARSHALL | 6,209 | 1,674 | 4,457 | 78 | 2,783 D | 27.0% | 71.8% | 27.3% | 72.7% |
| 44,028 | MAURY | 14,265 | 5,327 | 8,747 | 191 | 3,420 D | 37.3% | 61.3% | 37.8% | 62.2% |

# TENNESSEE

## PRESIDENT 1976

| 1970 Census Population | County | Total Vote | Republican | Democratic | Other | Rep.-Dem. Plurality | Percentage | | | |
|---|---|---|---|---|---|---|---|---|---|---|
| | | | | | | | Total Vote | | Major Vote | |
| | | | | | | | Rep. | Dem. | Rep. | Dem. |
| 5,219 | MEIGS | 2,242 | 975 | 1,254 | 13 | 279 D | 43.5% | 55.9% | 43.7% | 56.3% |
| 23,475 | MONROE | 10,756 | 5,335 | 5,368 | 53 | 33 D | 49.6% | 49.9% | 49.8% | 50.2% |
| 62,721 | MONTGOMERY | 18,448 | 5,923 | 12,310 | 215 | 6,387 D | 32.1% | 66.7% | 32.5% | 67.5% |
| 3,568 | MOORE | 1,448 | 331 | 1,101 | 16 | 770 D | 22.9% | 76.0% | 23.1% | 76.9% |
| 13,619 | MORGAN | 4,939 | 1,949 | 2,953 | 37 | 1,004 D | 39.5% | 59.8% | 39.8% | 60.2% |
| 29,936 | OBION | 10,320 | 2,986 | 7,204 | 130 | 4,218 D | 28.9% | 69.8% | 29.3% | 70.7% |
| 14,866 | OVERTON | 5,047 | 1,115 | 3,897 | 35 | 2,782 D | 22.1% | 77.2% | 22.2% | 77.8% |
| 5,238 | PERRY | 2,201 | 520 | 1,660 | 21 | 1,140 D | 23.6% | 75.4% | 23.9% | 76.1% |
| 3,774 | PICKETT | 1,944 | 986 | 948 | 10 | 38 R | 50.7% | 48.8% | 51.0% | 49.0% |
| 11,669 | POLK | 5,155 | 1,835 | 3,284 | 36 | 1,449 D | 35.6% | 63.7% | 35.8% | 64.2% |
| 35,487 | PUTNAM | 12,708 | 4,079 | 8,485 | 144 | 4,406 D | 32.1% | 66.8% | 32.5% | 67.5% |
| 17,202 | RHEA | 7,241 | 3,449 | 3,735 | 57 | 286 D | 47.6% | 51.6% | 48.0% | 52.0% |
| 38,881 | ROANE | 16,491 | 7,121 | 9,216 | 154 | 2,095 D | 43.2% | 55.9% | 43.6% | 56.4% |
| 29,102 | ROBERTSON | 10,114 | 2,505 | 7,547 | 62 | 5,042 D | 24.8% | 74.6% | 24.9% | 75.1% |
| 59,428 | RUTHERFORD | 23,082 | 7,921 | 14,854 | 307 | 6,933 D | 34.3% | 64.4% | 34.8% | 65.2% |
| 14,762 | SCOTT | 4,730 | 2,432 | 2,260 | 38 | 172 R | 51.4% | 47.8% | 51.8% | 48.2% |
| 6,331 | SEQUATCHIE | 2,842 | 1,065 | 1,733 | 44 | 668 D | 37.5% | 61.0% | 38.1% | 61.9% |
| 28,241 | SEVIER | 11,814 | 7,608 | 3,993 | 213 | 3,615 R | 64.4% | 33.8% | 65.6% | 34.4% |
| 722,014 | SHELBY | 279,601 | 128,646 | 147,893 | 3,062 | 19,247 D | 46.0% | 52.9% | 46.5% | 53.5% |
| 12,509 | SMITH | 5,136 | 1,332 | 3,753 | 51 | 2,421 D | 25.9% | 73.1% | 26.2% | 73.8% |
| 7,319 | STEWART | 2,972 | 510 | 2,442 | 20 | 1,932 D | 17.2% | 82.2% | 17.3% | 82.7% |
| 127,329 | SULLIVAN | 46,762 | 22,087 | 23,353 | 1,322 | 1,266 D | 47.2% | 49.9% | 48.6% | 51.4% |
| 56,106 | SUMNER | 22,007 | 7,946 | 13,848 | 213 | 5,902 D | 36.1% | 62.9% | 36.5% | 63.5% |
| 28,001 | TIPTON | 9,072 | 3,329 | 5,667 | 76 | 2,338 D | 36.7% | 62.5% | 37.0% | 63.0% |
| 5,155 | TROUSDALE | 1,726 | 332 | 1,385 | 9 | 1,053 D | 19.2% | 80.2% | 19.3% | 80.7% |
| 15,254 | UNICOI | 5,782 | 3,211 | 2,526 | 45 | 685 R | 55.5% | 43.7% | 56.0% | 44.0% |
| 9,072 | UNION | 3,457 | 1,801 | 1,631 | 25 | 170 R | 52.1% | 47.2% | 52.5% | 47.5% |
| 3,758 | VAN BUREN | 1,442 | 346 | 1,085 | 11 | 739 D | 24.0% | 75.2% | 24.2% | 75.8% |
| 26,972 | WARREN | 9,115 | 2,364 | 6,666 | 85 | 4,302 D | 25.9% | 73.1% | 26.2% | 73.8% |
| 73,924 | WASHINGTON | 29,032 | 14,770 | 13,951 | 311 | 819 R | 50.9% | 48.1% | 51.4% | 48.6% |
| 12,365 | WAYNE | 4,511 | 2,597 | 1,891 | 23 | 706 R | 57.6% | 41.9% | 57.9% | 42.1% |
| 28,827 | WEAKLEY | 9,696 | 2,875 | 6,605 | 216 | 3,730 D | 29.7% | 68.1% | 30.3% | 69.7% |
| 16,355 | WHITE | 5,314 | 1,382 | 3,874 | 58 | 2,492 D | 26.0% | 72.9% | 26.3% | 73.7% |
| 34,330 | WILLIAMSON | 16,266 | 7,880 | 8,183 | 203 | 303 D | 48.4% | 50.3% | 49.1% | 50.9% |
| 36,999 | WILSON | 15,362 | 4,696 | 10,537 | 129 | 5,841 D | 30.6% | 68.6% | 30.8% | 69.2% |
| 3,924,164 | TOTAL | 1,476,345 | 633,969 | 825,879 | 16,497 | 191,910 D | 42.9% | 55.9% | 43.4% | 56.6% |

# TENNESSEE

## PRESIDENT 1972

| 1970 Census Population | County | Total Vote | Republican | Democratic | Other | Rep.-Dem. Plurality | Percentage Total Vote | | Major Vote | |
|---|---|---|---|---|---|---|---|---|---|---|
| | | | | | | | Rep. | Dem. | Rep. | Dem. |
| 60,300 | ANDERSON | 20,999 | 13,865 | 6,713 | 421 | 7,152 R | 66.0% | 32.0% | 67.4% | 32.6% |
| 25,039 | BEDFORD | 7,135 | 4,262 | 2,565 | 308 | 1,697 R | 59.7% | 35.9% | 62.4% | 37.6% |
| 12,126 | BENTON | 4,228 | 2,614 | 1,479 | 135 | 1,135 R | 61.8% | 35.0% | 63.9% | 36.1% |
| 7,643 | BLEDSOE | 2,962 | 1,952 | 899 | 111 | 1,053 R | 65.9% | 30.4% | 68.5% | 31.5% |
| 63,744 | BLOUNT | 21,771 | 16,078 | 5,303 | 390 | 10,775 R | 73.9% | 24.4% | 75.2% | 24.8% |
| 50,686 | BRADLEY | 13,513 | 10,440 | 2,804 | 269 | 7,636 R | 77.3% | 20.8% | 78.8% | 21.2% |
| 26,045 | CAMPBELL | 6,687 | 4,909 | 1,629 | 149 | 3,280 R | 73.4% | 24.4% | 75.1% | 24.9% |
| 8,467 | CANNON | 2,589 | 1,615 | 911 | 63 | 704 R | 62.4% | 35.2% | 63.9% | 36.1% |
| 25,741 | CARROLL | 8,349 | 5,784 | 2,290 | 275 | 3,494 R | 69.3% | 27.4% | 71.6% | 28.4% |
| 43,259 | CARTER | 13,514 | 11,102 | 2,191 | 221 | 8,911 R | 82.2% | 16.2% | 83.5% | 16.5% |
| 13,199 | CHEATHAM | 3,719 | 2,235 | 1,321 | 163 | 914 R | 60.1% | 35.5% | 62.9% | 37.1% |
| 9,927 | CHESTER | 3,887 | 2,787 | 961 | 139 | 1,826 R | 71.7% | 24.7% | 74.4% | 25.6% |
| 19,420 | CLAIBORNE | 4,912 | 3,632 | 1,230 | 50 | 2,402 R | 73.9% | 25.0% | 74.7% | 25.3% |
| 6,624 | CLAY | 1,664 | 982 | 648 | 34 | 334 R | 59.0% | 38.9% | 60.2% | 39.8% |
| 25,283 | COCKE | 6,153 | 5,268 | 805 | 80 | 4,463 R | 85.6% | 13.1% | 86.7% | 13.3% |
| 32,572 | COFFEE | 9,695 | 6,416 | 2,973 | 306 | 3,443 R | 66.2% | 30.7% | 68.3% | 31.7% |
| 14,402 | CROCKETT | 3,504 | 2,642 | 735 | 127 | 1,907 R | 75.4% | 21.0% | 78.2% | 21.8% |
| 20,733 | CUMBERLAND | 6,225 | 4,593 | 1,482 | 150 | 3,111 R | 73.8% | 23.8% | 75.6% | 24.4% |
| 447,877 | DAVIDSON | 134,797 | 82,636 | 48,869 | 3,292 | 33,767 R | 61.3% | 36.3% | 62.8% | 37.2% |
| 9,457 | DECATUR | 3,655 | 2,368 | 1,187 | 100 | 1,181 R | 64.8% | 32.5% | 66.6% | 33.4% |
| 11,151 | DE KALB | 3,320 | 2,014 | 1,243 | 63 | 771 R | 60.7% | 37.4% | 61.8% | 38.2% |
| 21,977 | DICKSON | 6,446 | 3,645 | 2,619 | 182 | 1,026 R | 56.5% | 40.6% | 58.2% | 41.8% |
| 30,427 | DYER | 7,988 | 6,066 | 1,600 | 322 | 4,466 R | 75.9% | 20.0% | 79.1% | 20.9% |
| 22,692 | FAYETTE | 5,463 | 3,264 | 2,067 | 132 | 1,197 R | 59.7% | 37.8% | 61.2% | 38.8% |
| 12,593 | FENTRESS | 2,853 | 2,154 | 665 | 34 | 1,489 R | 75.5% | 23.3% | 76.4% | 23.6% |
| 27,244 | FRANKLIN | 7,192 | 4,136 | 2,896 | 160 | 1,240 R | 57.5% | 40.3% | 58.8% | 41.2% |
| 47,871 | GIBSON | 13,934 | 9,900 | 3,625 | 409 | 6,275 R | 71.0% | 26.0% | 73.2% | 26.8% |
| 22,138 | GILES | 5,051 | 2,914 | 1,875 | 262 | 1,039 R | 57.7% | 37.1% | 60.8% | 39.2% |
| 13,948 | GRAINGER | 3,713 | 2,842 | 828 | 43 | 2,014 R | 76.5% | 22.3% | 77.4% | 22.6% |
| 47,630 | GREENE | 12,709 | 9,772 | 2,764 | 173 | 7,008 R | 76.9% | 21.7% | 78.0% | 22.0% |
| 10,631 | GRUNDY | 2,503 | 1,364 | 1,005 | 134 | 359 R | 54.5% | 40.2% | 57.6% | 42.4% |
| 38,696 | HAMBLEN | 11,624 | 8,879 | 2,563 | 182 | 6,316 R | 76.4% | 22.0% | 77.6% | 22.4% |
| 254,236 | HAMILTON | 82,794 | 58,469 | 20,657 | 3,668 | 37,812 R | 70.6% | 24.9% | 73.9% | 26.1% |
| 6,719 | HANCOCK | 2,222 | 1,813 | 393 | 16 | 1,420 R | 81.6% | 17.7% | 82.2% | 17.8% |
| 22,435 | HARDEMAN | 5,294 | 3,494 | 1,550 | 250 | 1,944 R | 66.0% | 29.3% | 69.3% | 30.7% |
| 18,212 | HARDIN | 5,769 | 4,401 | 1,202 | 166 | 3,199 R | 76.3% | 20.8% | 78.5% | 21.5% |
| 33,726 | HAWKINS | 10,775 | 7,791 | 2,608 | 376 | 5,183 R | 72.3% | 24.2% | 74.9% | 25.1% |
| 19,596 | HAYWOOD | 5,253 | 3,123 | 1,966 | 164 | 1,157 R | 59.5% | 37.4% | 61.4% | 38.6% |
| 17,291 | HENDERSON | 6,597 | 5,122 | 1,313 | 162 | 3,809 R | 77.6% | 19.9% | 79.6% | 20.4% |
| 23,749 | HENRY | 7,611 | 4,613 | 2,694 | 304 | 1,919 R | 60.6% | 35.4% | 63.1% | 36.9% |
| 12,096 | HICKMAN | 3,466 | 1,943 | 1,393 | 130 | 550 R | 56.1% | 40.2% | 58.2% | 41.8% |
| 5,845 | HOUSTON | 1,725 | 800 | 870 | 55 | 70 D | 46.4% | 50.4% | 47.9% | 52.1% |
| 13,560 | HUMPHREYS | 4,338 | 2,263 | 1,973 | 102 | 290 R | 52.2% | 45.5% | 53.4% | 46.6% |
| 8,141 | JACKSON | 2,079 | 956 | 1,085 | 38 | 129 D | 46.0% | 52.2% | 46.8% | 53.2% |
| 24,940 | JEFFERSON | 7,382 | 5,925 | 1,357 | 100 | 4,568 R | 80.3% | 18.4% | 81.4% | 18.6% |
| 11,569 | JOHNSON | 3,861 | 3,362 | 450 | 49 | 2,912 R | 87.1% | 11.7% | 88.2% | 11.8% |
| 276,293 | KNOX | 90,484 | 64,747 | 24,076 | 1,661 | 40,671 R | 71.6% | 26.6% | 72.9% | 27.1% |
| 7,896 | LAKE | 1,746 | 1,147 | 536 | 63 | 611 R | 65.7% | 30.7% | 68.2% | 31.8% |
| 20,271 | LAUDERDALE | 5,585 | 3,597 | 1,771 | 217 | 1,826 R | 64.4% | 31.7% | 67.0% | 33.0% |
| 29,097 | LAWRENCE | 9,482 | 6,438 | 2,824 | 220 | 3,614 R | 67.9% | 29.8% | 69.5% | 30.5% |
| 6,761 | LEWIS | 2,248 | 1,056 | 1,138 | 54 | 82 D | 47.0% | 50.6% | 48.1% | 51.9% |
| 24,318 | LINCOLN | 5,281 | 3,266 | 1,867 | 148 | 1,399 R | 61.8% | 35.4% | 63.6% | 36.4% |
| 24,266 | LOUDON | 7,131 | 5,357 | 1,604 | 170 | 3,753 R | 75.1% | 22.5% | 77.0% | 23.0% |
| 35,462 | MCMINN | 10,520 | 7,423 | 2,838 | 259 | 4,585 R | 70.6% | 27.0% | 72.3% | 27.7% |
| 18,369 | MCNAIRY | 6,519 | 4,774 | 1,610 | 135 | 3,164 R | 73.2% | 24.7% | 74.8% | 25.2% |
| 12,315 | MACON | 3,033 | 2,295 | 653 | 85 | 1,642 R | 75.7% | 21.5% | 77.8% | 22.2% |
| 65,727 | MADISON | 21,409 | 15,481 | 5,203 | 725 | 10,278 R | 72.3% | 24.3% | 74.8% | 25.2% |
| 20,577 | MARION | 5,839 | 3,711 | 1,929 | 199 | 1,782 R | 63.6% | 33.0% | 65.8% | 34.2% |
| 17,319 | MARSHALL | 4,378 | 2,593 | 1,526 | 259 | 1,067 R | 59.2% | 34.9% | 63.0% | 37.0% |
| 44,028 | MAURY | 11,121 | 7,371 | 3,262 | 488 | 4,109 R | 66.3% | 29.3% | 69.3% | 30.7% |

# TENNESSEE

## PRESIDENT 1972

| 1970 Census Population | County | Total Vote | Republican | Democratic | Other | Rep.-Dem. Plurality | Percentage | | | |
|---|---|---|---|---|---|---|---|---|---|---|
| | | | | | | | Total Vote | | Major Vote | |
| | | | | | | | Rep. | Dem. | Rep. | Dem. |
| 5,219 | MEIGS | 1,635 | 1,052 | 539 | 44 | 513 R | 64.3% | 33.0% | 66.1% | 33.9% |
| 23,475 | MONROE | 8,634 | 5,657 | 2,870 | 107 | 2,787 R | 65.5% | 33.2% | 66.3% | 33.7% |
| 62,721 | MONTGOMERY | 13,899 | 7,839 | 5,691 | 369 | 2,148 R | 56.4% | 40.9% | 57.9% | 42.1% |
| 3,568 | MOORE | 996 | 608 | 356 | 32 | 252 R | 61.0% | 35.7% | 63.1% | 36.9% |
| 13,619 | MORGAN | 3,703 | 2,531 | 1,084 | 88 | 1,447 R | 68.3% | 29.3% | 70.0% | 30.0% |
| 29,936 | OBION | 8,243 | 5,800 | 2,243 | 200 | 3,557 R | 70.4% | 27.2% | 72.1% | 27.9% |
| 14,866 | OVERTON | 3,594 | 1,947 | 1,573 | 74 | 374 R | 54.2% | 43.8% | 55.3% | 44.7% |
| 5,238 | PERRY | 1,871 | 900 | 937 | 34 | 37 D | 48.1% | 50.1% | 49.0% | 51.0% |
| 3,774 | PICKETT | 1,325 | 957 | 357 | 11 | 600 R | 72.2% | 26.9% | 72.8% | 27.2% |
| 11,669 | POLK | 3,772 | 2,285 | 1,431 | 56 | 854 R | 60.6% | 37.9% | 61.5% | 38.5% |
| 35,487 | PUTNAM | 9,999 | 6,038 | 3,738 | 223 | 2,300 R | 60.4% | 37.4% | 61.8% | 38.2% |
| 17,202 | RHEA | 5,299 | 3,842 | 1,312 | 145 | 2,530 R | 72.5% | 24.8% | 74.5% | 25.5% |
| 38,881 | ROANE | 12,470 | 8,742 | 3,433 | 295 | 5,309 R | 70.1% | 27.5% | 71.8% | 28.2% |
| 29,102 | ROBERTSON | 7,399 | 4,175 | 2,985 | 239 | 1,190 R | 56.4% | 40.3% | 58.3% | 41.7% |
| 59,428 | RUTHERFORD | 17,554 | 11,256 | 5,811 | 487 | 5,445 R | 64.1% | 33.1% | 66.0% | 34.0% |
| 14,762 | SCOTT | 3,502 | 2,775 | 679 | 48 | 2,096 R | 79.2% | 19.4% | 80.3% | 19.7% |
| 6,331 | SEQUATCHIE | 2,010 | 1,298 | 629 | 83 | 669 R | 64.6% | 31.3% | 67.4% | 32.6% |
| 28,241 | SEVIER | 9,578 | 8,273 | 1,128 | 177 | 7,145 R | 86.4% | 11.8% | 88.0% | 12.0% |
| 722,014 | SHELBY | 247,882 | 161,922 | 81,089 | 4,871 | 80,833 R | 65.3% | 32.7% | 66.6% | 33.4% |
| 12,509 | SMITH | 3,188 | 1,812 | 1,260 | 116 | 552 R | 56.8% | 39.5% | 59.0% | 41.0% |
| 7,319 | STEWART | 1,935 | 790 | 1,098 | 47 | 308 D | 40.8% | 56.7% | 41.8% | 58.2% |
| 127,329 | SULLIVAN | 38,517 | 27,593 | 10,007 | 917 | 17,586 R | 71.6% | 26.0% | 73.4% | 26.6% |
| 56,106 | SUMNER | 15,157 | 10,020 | 4,596 | 541 | 5,424 R | 66.1% | 30.3% | 68.6% | 31.4% |
| 28,001 | TIPTON | 7,749 | 5,542 | 1,853 | 354 | 3,689 R | 71.5% | 23.9% | 74.9% | 25.1% |
| 5,155 | TROUSDALE | 1,230 | 663 | 539 | 28 | 124 R | 53.9% | 43.8% | 55.2% | 44.8% |
| 15,254 | UNICOI | 4,766 | 3,877 | 822 | 67 | 3,055 R | 81.3% | 17.2% | 82.5% | 17.5% |
| 9,072 | UNION | 2,527 | 1,927 | 570 | 30 | 1,357 R | 76.3% | 22.6% | 77.2% | 22.8% |
| 3,758 | VAN BUREN | 1,021 | 629 | 364 | 28 | 265 R | 61.6% | 35.7% | 63.3% | 36.7% |
| 26,972 | WARREN | 5,894 | 3,565 | 2,118 | 211 | 1,447 R | 60.5% | 35.9% | 62.7% | 37.3% |
| 73,924 | WASHINGTON | 23,188 | 17,343 | 5,284 | 561 | 12,059 R | 74.8% | 22.8% | 76.6% | 23.4% |
| 12,365 | WAYNE | 3,632 | 2,898 | 673 | 61 | 2,225 R | 79.8% | 18.5% | 81.2% | 18.8% |
| 28,827 | WEAKLEY | 8,165 | 5,836 | 2,027 | 302 | 3,809 R | 71.5% | 24.8% | 74.2% | 25.8% |
| 16,355 | WHITE | 3,727 | 2,252 | 1,392 | 83 | 860 R | 60.4% | 37.3% | 61.8% | 38.2% |
| 34,330 | WILLIAMSON | 10,564 | 7,556 | 2,616 | 392 | 4,940 R | 71.5% | 24.8% | 74.3% | 25.7% |
| 36,999 | WILSON | 9,861 | 6,486 | 3,096 | 279 | 3,390 R | 65.8% | 31.4% | 67.7% | 32.3% |
| 3,924,164 | TOTAL | 1,201,182 | 813,147 | 357,293 | 30,742 | 455,854 R | 67.7% | 29.7% | 69.5% | 30.5% |

# TENNESSEE

## PRESIDENT 1968

| 1960 Census Population | County | Total Vote | Republican | Democratic | AIP | Other | Plurality | Percentage Total Vote | | |
|---|---|---|---|---|---|---|---|---|---|---|
| | | | | | | | | Rep. | Dem. | AIP |
| 60,032 | ANDERSON | 21,754 | 10,233 | 7,198 | 4,323 | | 3,035 R | 47.0% | 33.1% | 19.9% |
| 23,150 | BEDFORD | 8,385 | 1,870 | 2,416 | 4,099 | | 1,683 A | 22.3% | 28.8% | 48.9% |
| 10,662 | BENTON | 4,782 | 1,468 | 1,059 | 2,255 | | 787 A | 30.7% | 22.1% | 47.2% |
| 7,811 | BLEDSOE | 3,166 | 1,477 | 957 | 732 | | 520 R | 46.7% | 30.2% | 23.1% |
| 57,525 | BLOUNT | 22,336 | 12,753 | 5,176 | 4,407 | | 7,577 R | 57.1% | 23.2% | 19.7% |
| 38,324 | BRADLEY | 13,845 | 6,924 | 2,762 | 4,159 | | 2,765 R | 50.0% | 19.9% | 30.0% |
| 27,936 | CAMPBELL | 7,659 | 4,024 | 2,268 | 1,367 | | 1,756 R | 52.5% | 29.6% | 17.8% |
| 8,537 | CANNON | 3,053 | 780 | 809 | 1,464 | | 655 A | 25.5% | 26.5% | 48.0% |
| 23,476 | CARROLL | 8,987 | 3,757 | 1,932 | 3,298 | | 459 R | 41.8% | 21.5% | 36.7% |
| 41,578 | CARTER | 14,636 | 9,467 | 2,160 | 3,009 | | 6,458 R | 64.7% | 14.8% | 20.6% |
| 9,428 | CHEATHAM | 3,944 | 669 | 778 | 2,497 | | 1,719 A | 17.0% | 19.7% | 63.3% |
| 9,569 | CHESTER | 4,294 | 1,408 | 849 | 2,037 | | 629 A | 32.8% | 19.8% | 47.4% |
| 19,067 | CLAIBORNE | 5,190 | 3,101 | 1,314 | 775 | | 1,787 R | 59.7% | 25.3% | 14.9% |
| 7,289 | CLAY | 1,932 | 814 | 667 | 451 | | 147 R | 42.1% | 34.5% | 23.3% |
| 23,390 | COCKE | 7,754 | 5,645 | 950 | 1,159 | | 4,486 R | 72.8% | 12.3% | 14.9% |
| 28,603 | COFFEE | 11,171 | 3,337 | 3,040 | 4,794 | | 1,457 A | 29.9% | 27.2% | 42.9% |
| 14,594 | CROCKETT | 4,500 | 932 | 703 | 2,865 | | 1,933 A | 20.7% | 15.6% | 63.7% |
| 19,135 | CUMBERLAND | 6,012 | 3,115 | 1,428 | 1,469 | | 1,646 R | 51.8% | 23.8% | 24.4% |
| 399,743 | DAVIDSON | 136,607 | 44,175 | 44,543 | 47,889 | | 3,346 A | 32.3% | 32.6% | 35.1% |
| 8,324 | DECATUR | 3,830 | 1,409 | 877 | 1,544 | | 135 A | 36.8% | 22.9% | 40.3% |
| 10,774 | DE KALB | 3,895 | 1,532 | 847 | 1,516 | | 16 R | 39.3% | 21.7% | 38.9% |
| 18,839 | DICKSON | 6,800 | 1,291 | 2,034 | 3,475 | | 1,441 A | 19.0% | 29.9% | 51.1% |
| 29,537 | DYER | 10,701 | 2,826 | 2,033 | 5,842 | | 3,016 A | 26.4% | 19.0% | 54.6% |
| 24,577 | FAYETTE | 5,546 | 740 | 2,236 | 2,570 | | 334 A | 13.3% | 40.3% | 46.3% |
| 13,288 | FENTRESS | 3,505 | 2,026 | 671 | 808 | | 1,218 R | 57.8% | 19.1% | 23.1% |
| 25,528 | FRANKLIN | 9,128 | 1,700 | 2,489 | 4,939 | | 2,450 A | 18.6% | 27.3% | 54.1% |
| 44,699 | GIBSON | 15,288 | 4,093 | 3,962 | 7,233 | | 3,140 A | 26.8% | 25.9% | 47.3% |
| 22,410 | GILES | 7,433 | 1,264 | 2,203 | 3,966 | | 1,763 A | 17.0% | 29.6% | 53.4% |
| 12,506 | GRAINGER | 4,145 | 2,788 | 761 | 596 | | 2,027 R | 67.3% | 18.4% | 14.4% |
| 42,163 | GREENE | 13,657 | 7,957 | 2,947 | 2,753 | | 5,010 R | 58.3% | 21.6% | 20.2% |
| 11,512 | GRUNDY | 3,567 | 618 | 1,307 | 1,642 | | 335 A | 17.3% | 36.6% | 46.0% |
| 33,092 | HAMBLEN | 11,031 | 6,382 | 2,390 | 2,259 | | 3,992 R | 57.9% | 21.7% | 20.5% |
| 237,905 | HAMILTON | 84,823 | 29,302 | 23,441 | 32,080 | | 2,778 A | 34.5% | 27.6% | 37.8% |
| 7,757 | HANCOCK | 2,043 | 1,489 | 318 | 236 | | 1,171 R | 72.9% | 15.6% | 11.6% |
| 21,517 | HARDEMAN | 5,804 | 1,171 | 1,709 | 2,924 | | 1,215 A | 20.2% | 29.4% | 50.4% |
| 17,397 | HARDIN | 6,388 | 2,910 | 1,153 | 2,325 | | 585 R | 45.6% | 18.0% | 36.4% |
| 30,468 | HAWKINS | 10,228 | 6,217 | 2,213 | 1,798 | | 4,004 R | 60.8% | 21.6% | 17.6% |
| 23,393 | HAYWOOD | 5,618 | 1,152 | 1,709 | 2,757 | | 1,048 A | 20.5% | 30.4% | 49.1% |
| 16,115 | HENDERSON | 6,907 | 3,591 | 1,230 | 2,086 | | 1,505 R | 52.0% | 17.8% | 30.2% |
| 22,275 | HENRY | 8,656 | 2,068 | 3,149 | 3,439 | | 290 A | 23.9% | 36.4% | 39.7% |
| 11,862 | HICKMAN | 4,385 | 760 | 1,152 | 2,473 | | 1,321 A | 17.3% | 26.3% | 56.4% |
| 4,794 | HOUSTON | 1,809 | 232 | 636 | 941 | | 305 A | 12.8% | 35.2% | 52.0% |
| 11,511 | HUMPHREYS | 4,352 | 866 | 1,391 | 2,095 | | 704 A | 19.9% | 32.0% | 48.1% |
| 9,233 | JACKSON | 2,703 | 673 | 1,122 | 908 | | 214 D | 24.9% | 41.5% | 33.6% |
| 21,493 | JEFFERSON | 8,187 | 5,494 | 1,494 | 1,199 | | 4,000 R | 67.1% | 18.2% | 14.6% |
| 10,765 | JOHNSON | 3,932 | 3,107 | 450 | 375 | | 2,657 R | 79.0% | 11.4% | 9.5% |
| 250,523 | KNOX | 90,007 | 47,202 | 24,528 | 18,277 | | 22,674 R | 52.4% | 27.3% | 20.3% |
| 9,572 | LAKE | 2,408 | 409 | 737 | 1,262 | | 525 A | 17.0% | 30.6% | 52.4% |
| 21,844 | LAUDERDALE | 6,754 | 1,080 | 2,108 | 3,566 | | 1,458 A | 16.0% | 31.2% | 52.8% |
| 28,049 | LAWRENCE | 10,527 | 4,343 | 2,191 | 3,993 | | 350 R | 41.3% | 20.8% | 37.9% |
| 6,269 | LEWIS | 2,540 | 455 | 1,088 | 997 | | 91 D | 17.9% | 42.8% | 39.3% |
| 23,829 | LINCOLN | 7,229 | 1,167 | 1,848 | 4,214 | | 2,366 A | 16.1% | 25.6% | 58.3% |
| 23,757 | LOUDON | 7,876 | 4,299 | 1,581 | 1,996 | | 2,303 R | 54.6% | 20.1% | 25.3% |
| 33,662 | MCMINN | 11,522 | 6,098 | 2,889 | 2,535 | | 3,209 R | 52.9% | 25.1% | 22.0% |
| 18,085 | MCNAIRY | 7,228 | 2,979 | 1,377 | 2,872 | | 107 R | 41.2% | 19.1% | 39.7% |
| 12,197 | MACON | 3,744 | 2,173 | 530 | 1,041 | | 1,132 R | 58.0% | 14.2% | 27.8% |
| 60,655 | MADISON | 21,080 | 6,143 | 5,517 | 9,420 | | 3,277 A | 29.1% | 26.2% | 44.7% |
| 21,036 | MARION | 6,404 | 1,959 | 1,661 | 2,784 | | 825 A | 30.6% | 25.9% | 43.5% |
| 16,859 | MARSHALL | 6,108 | 1,202 | 1,527 | 3,379 | | 1,852 A | 19.7% | 25.0% | 55.3% |
| 41,699 | MAURY | 14,597 | 3,048 | 3,401 | 8,148 | | 4,747 A | 20.9% | 23.3% | 55.8% |

# TENNESSEE

## PRESIDENT 1968

| 1960 Census Population | County | Total Vote | Republican | Democratic | AIP | Other | Plurality | Percentage Total Vote Rep. | Dem. | AIP |
|---|---|---|---|---|---|---|---|---|---|---|
| 5,160 | MEIGS | 1,664 | 729 | 493 | 442 | | 236 R | 43.8% | 29.6% | 26.6% |
| 23,316 | MONROE | 8,897 | 4,749 | 2,926 | 1,222 | | 1,823 R | 53.4% | 32.9% | 13.7% |
| 55,645 | MONTGOMERY | 14,424 | 3,248 | 5,538 | 5,638 | | 100 A | 22.5% | 38.4% | 39.1% |
| 3,454 | MOORE | 1,426 | 224 | 346 | 856 | | 510 A | 15.7% | 24.3% | 60.0% |
| 14,304 | MORGAN | 3,799 | 1,803 | 968 | 1,028 | | 775 R | 47.5% | 25.5% | 27.1% |
| 26,957 | OBION | 9,335 | 2,420 | 2,235 | 4,680 | | 2,260 A | 25.9% | 23.9% | 50.1% |
| 14,661 | OVERTON | 4,026 | 1,258 | 1,592 | 1,176 | | 334 D | 31.2% | 39.5% | 29.2% |
| 5,273 | PERRY | 2,029 | 519 | 726 | 784 | | 58 A | 25.6% | 35.8% | 38.6% |
| 4,431 | PICKETT | 1,488 | 884 | 405 | 199 | | 479 R | 59.4% | 27.2% | 13.4% |
| 12,160 | POLK | 4,016 | 1,808 | 1,454 | 754 | | 354 R | 45.0% | 36.2% | 18.8% |
| 29,236 | PUTNAM | 10,307 | 3,693 | 3,541 | 3,073 | | 152 R | 35.8% | 34.4% | 29.8% |
| 15,863 | RHEA | 5,966 | 2,428 | 1,301 | 2,237 | | 191 R | 40.7% | 21.8% | 37.5% |
| 39,133 | ROANE | 13,189 | 6,033 | 3,258 | 3,898 | | 2,135 R | 45.7% | 24.7% | 29.6% |
| 27,335 | ROBERTSON | 8,021 | 1,802 | 2,315 | 3,904 | | 1,589 A | 22.5% | 28.9% | 48.7% |
| 52,368 | RUTHERFORD | 16,862 | 4,168 | 4,921 | 7,773 | | 2,852 A | 24.7% | 29.2% | 46.1% |
| 15,413 | SCOTT | 4,131 | 2,406 | 991 | 734 | | 1,415 R | 58.2% | 24.0% | 17.8% |
| 5,915 | SEQUATCHIE | 2,223 | 663 | 549 | 1,011 | | 348 A | 29.8% | 24.7% | 45.5% |
| 24,251 | SEVIER | 10,217 | 7,629 | 1,112 | 1,476 | | 6,153 R | 74.7% | 10.9% | 14.4% |
| 627,019 | SHELBY | 231,898 | 73,416 | 81,486 | 76,996 | | 4,490 D | 31.7% | 35.1% | 33.2% |
| 12,059 | SMITH | 4,363 | 1,089 | 1,443 | 1,831 | | 388 A | 25.0% | 33.1% | 42.0% |
| 7,851 | STEWART | 2,541 | 443 | 1,041 | 1,057 | | 16 A | 17.4% | 41.0% | 41.6% |
| 114,139 | SULLIVAN | 40,025 | 20,251 | 9,783 | 9,991 | | 10,260 R | 50.6% | 24.4% | 25.0% |
| 36,217 | SUMNER | 16,487 | 4,519 | 4,376 | 7,592 | | 3,073 A | 27.4% | 26.5% | 46.0% |
| 28,564 | TIPTON | 8,436 | 1,422 | 2,071 | 4,943 | | 2,872 A | 16.9% | 24.5% | 58.6% |
| 4,914 | TROUSDALE | 1,595 | 252 | 694 | 649 | | 45 D | 15.8% | 43.5% | 40.7% |
| 15,082 | UNICOI | 5,080 | 3,327 | 910 | 843 | | 2,417 R | 65.5% | 17.9% | 16.6% |
| 8,498 | UNION | 2,932 | 1,956 | 527 | 449 | | 1,429 R | 66.7% | 18.0% | 15.3% |
| 3,671 | VAN BUREN | 1,116 | 327 | 282 | 507 | | 180 A | 29.3% | 25.3% | 45.4% |
| 23,102 | WARREN | 7,718 | 1,858 | 2,046 | 3,814 | | 1,768 A | 24.1% | 26.5% | 49.4% |
| 64,832 | WASHINGTON | 22,737 | 12,882 | 4,930 | 4,925 | | 7,952 R | 56.7% | 21.7% | 21.7% |
| 11,908 | WAYNE | 4,131 | 2,417 | 506 | 1,208 | | 1,209 R | 58.5% | 12.2% | 29.2% |
| 24,227 | WEAKLEY | 9,371 | 2,858 | 1,988 | 4,525 | | 1,667 A | 30.5% | 21.2% | 48.3% |
| 15,577 | WHITE | 4,757 | 1,423 | 1,584 | 1,750 | | 166 A | 29.9% | 33.3% | 36.8% |
| 25,267 | WILLIAMSON | 9,718 | 2,788 | 2,063 | 4,867 | | 2,079 A | 28.7% | 21.2% | 50.1% |
| 27,668 | WILSON | 11,300 | 2,736 | 2,916 | 5,648 | | 2,732 A | 24.2% | 25.8% | 50.0% |
| 3,567,089 | TOTAL | 1,248,617 | 472,592 | 351,233 | 424,792 | | 47,800 R | 37.8% | 28.1% | 34.0% |

# TENNESSEE

## PRESIDENT 1964

| 1960 Census Population | County | Total Vote | Republican | Democratic | Other | Rep.-Dem. Plurality | Percentage Total Vote Rep. | Dem. | Major Vote Rep. | Dem. |
|---|---|---|---|---|---|---|---|---|---|---|
| 60,032 | ANDERSON | 21,008 | 8,860 | 12,146 | 2 | 3,286 D | 42.2% | 57.8% | 42.2% | 57.8% |
| 23,150 | BEDFORD | 7,882 | 2,272 | 5,610 | | 3,338 D | 28.8% | 71.2% | 28.8% | 71.2% |
| 10,662 | BENTON | 3,974 | 1,363 | 2,611 | | 1,248 D | 34.3% | 65.7% | 34.3% | 65.7% |
| 7,811 | BLEDSOE | 2,843 | 1,431 | 1,412 | | 19 R | 50.3% | 49.7% | 50.3% | 49.7% |
| 57,525 | BLOUNT | 20,343 | 11,876 | 8,459 | 8 | 3,417 R | 58.4% | 41.6% | 58.4% | 41.6% |
| 38,324 | BRADLEY | 12,410 | 6,717 | 5,693 | | 1,024 R | 54.1% | 45.9% | 54.1% | 45.9% |
| 27,936 | CAMPBELL | 8,644 | 4,232 | 4,412 | | 180 D | 49.0% | 51.0% | 49.0% | 51.0% |
| 8,537 | CANNON | 2,936 | 746 | 2,190 | | 1,444 D | 25.4% | 74.6% | 25.4% | 74.6% |
| 23,476 | CARROLL | 7,790 | 3,734 | 4,056 | | 322 D | 47.9% | 52.1% | 47.9% | 52.1% |
| 41,578 | CARTER | 13,798 | 8,472 | 5,326 | | 3,146 R | 61.4% | 38.6% | 61.4% | 38.6% |
| 9,428 | CHEATHAM | 3,554 | 803 | 2,750 | 1 | 1,947 D | 22.6% | 77.4% | 22.6% | 77.4% |
| 9,569 | CHESTER | 3,530 | 1,767 | 1,763 | | 4 R | 50.1% | 49.9% | 50.1% | 49.9% |
| 19,067 | CLAIBORNE | 5,433 | 2,852 | 2,581 | | 271 R | 52.5% | 47.5% | 52.5% | 47.5% |
| 7,289 | CLAY | 1,818 | 622 | 1,196 | | 574 D | 34.2% | 65.8% | 34.2% | 65.8% |
| 23,390 | COCKE | 7,193 | 5,084 | 2,109 | | 2,975 R | 70.7% | 29.3% | 70.7% | 29.3% |
| 28,603 | COFFEE | 9,849 | 3,012 | 6,837 | | 3,825 D | 30.6% | 69.4% | 30.6% | 69.4% |
| 14,594 | CROCKETT | 3,690 | 1,873 | 1,817 | | 56 R | 50.8% | 49.2% | 50.8% | 49.2% |
| 19,135 | CUMBERLAND | 6,048 | 2,975 | 3,073 | | 98 D | 49.2% | 50.8% | 49.2% | 50.8% |
| 399,743 | DAVIDSON | 124,722 | 45,335 | 79,387 | | 34,052 D | 36.3% | 63.7% | 36.3% | 63.7% |
| 8,324 | DECATUR | 3,242 | 1,429 | 1,813 | | 384 D | 44.1% | 55.9% | 44.1% | 55.9% |
| 10,774 | DE KALB | 3,693 | 1,402 | 2,291 | | 889 D | 38.0% | 62.0% | 38.0% | 62.0% |
| 18,839 | DICKSON | 6,005 | 1,281 | 4,724 | | 3,443 D | 21.3% | 78.7% | 21.3% | 78.7% |
| 29,537 | DYER | 9,236 | 4,517 | 4,717 | 2 | 200 D | 48.9% | 51.1% | 48.9% | 51.1% |
| 24,577 | FAYETTE | 5,558 | 2,922 | 2,636 | | 286 R | 52.6% | 47.4% | 52.6% | 47.4% |
| 13,288 | FENTRESS | 3,519 | 1,969 | 1,550 | | 419 R | 56.0% | 44.0% | 56.0% | 44.0% |
| 25,528 | FRANKLIN | 8,291 | 2,262 | 6,029 | | 3,767 D | 27.3% | 72.7% | 27.3% | 72.7% |
| 44,699 | GIBSON | 12,733 | 4,614 | 8,119 | | 3,505 D | 36.2% | 63.8% | 36.2% | 63.8% |
| 22,410 | GILES | 6,318 | 1,378 | 4,940 | | 3,562 D | 21.8% | 78.2% | 21.8% | 78.2% |
| 12,506 | GRAINGER | 3,943 | 2,634 | 1,309 | | 1,325 R | 66.8% | 33.2% | 66.8% | 33.2% |
| 42,163 | GREENE | 12,829 | 6,913 | 5,916 | | 997 R | 53.9% | 46.1% | 53.9% | 46.1% |
| 11,512 | GRUNDY | 3,461 | 686 | 2,775 | | 2,089 D | 19.8% | 80.2% | 19.8% | 80.2% |
| 33,092 | HAMBLEN | 9,803 | 5,196 | 4,607 | | 589 R | 53.0% | 47.0% | 53.0% | 47.0% |
| 237,905 | HAMILTON | 78,746 | 40,200 | 38,546 | | 1,654 R | 51.1% | 48.9% | 51.1% | 48.9% |
| 7,757 | HANCOCK | 2,204 | 1,517 | 687 | | 830 R | 68.8% | 31.2% | 68.8% | 31.2% |
| 21,517 | HARDEMAN | 5,125 | 2,450 | 2,675 | | 225 D | 47.8% | 52.2% | 47.8% | 52.2% |
| 17,397 | HARDIN | 5,645 | 3,025 | 2,620 | | 405 R | 53.6% | 46.4% | 53.6% | 46.4% |
| 30,468 | HAWKINS | 9,903 | 5,712 | 4,191 | | 1,521 R | 57.7% | 42.3% | 57.7% | 42.3% |
| 23,393 | HAYWOOD | 4,697 | 2,407 | 2,290 | | 117 R | 51.2% | 48.8% | 51.2% | 48.8% |
| 16,115 | HENDERSON | 5,088 | 3,133 | 1,955 | | 1,178 R | 61.6% | 38.4% | 61.6% | 38.4% |
| 22,275 | HENRY | 8,135 | 2,261 | 5,874 | | 3,613 D | 27.8% | 72.2% | 27.8% | 72.2% |
| 11,862 | HICKMAN | 3,896 | 1,019 | 2,877 | | 1,858 D | 26.2% | 73.8% | 26.2% | 73.8% |
| 4,794 | HOUSTON | 1,859 | 287 | 1,572 | | 1,285 D | 15.4% | 84.6% | 15.4% | 84.6% |
| 11,511 | HUMPHREYS | 4,146 | 916 | 3,230 | | 2,314 D | 22.1% | 77.9% | 22.1% | 77.9% |
| 9,233 | JACKSON | 2,842 | 551 | 2,291 | | 1,740 D | 19.4% | 80.6% | 19.4% | 80.6% |
| 21,493 | JEFFERSON | 7,523 | 4,923 | 2,600 | | 2,323 R | 65.4% | 34.6% | 65.4% | 34.6% |
| 10,765 | JOHNSON | 3,816 | 2,889 | 927 | | 1,962 R | 75.7% | 24.3% | 75.7% | 24.3% |
| 250,523 | KNOX | 85,260 | 42,797 | 42,463 | | 334 R | 50.2% | 49.8% | 50.2% | 49.8% |
| 9,572 | LAKE | 2,404 | 736 | 1,667 | 1 | 931 D | 30.6% | 69.3% | 30.6% | 69.4% |
| 21,844 | LAUDERDALE | 5,727 | 1,880 | 3,847 | | 1,967 D | 32.8% | 67.2% | 32.8% | 67.2% |
| 28,049 | LAWRENCE | 10,039 | 4,590 | 5,449 | | 859 D | 45.7% | 54.3% | 45.7% | 54.3% |
| 6,269 | LEWIS | 2,449 | 388 | 2,061 | | 1,673 D | 15.8% | 84.2% | 15.8% | 84.2% |
| 23,829 | LINCOLN | 6,590 | 1,728 | 4,861 | 1 | 3,133 D | 26.2% | 73.8% | 26.2% | 73.8% |
| 23,757 | LOUDON | 7,524 | 4,148 | 3,365 | 11 | 783 R | 55.1% | 44.7% | 55.2% | 44.8% |
| 33,662 | MCMINN | 10,831 | 5,624 | 5,207 | | 417 R | 51.9% | 48.1% | 51.9% | 48.1% |
| 18,085 | MCNAIRY | 6,103 | 3,109 | 2,994 | | 115 R | 50.9% | 49.1% | 50.9% | 49.1% |
| 12,197 | MACON | 3,292 | 1,846 | 1,446 | | 400 R | 56.1% | 43.9% | 56.1% | 43.9% |
| 60,655 | MADISON | 21,505 | 10,932 | 10,573 | | 359 R | 50.8% | 49.2% | 50.8% | 49.2% |
| 21,036 | MARION | 6,503 | 2,728 | 3,775 | | 1,047 D | 41.9% | 58.1% | 41.9% | 58.1% |
| 16,859 | MARSHALL | 5,329 | 1,340 | 3,989 | | 2,649 D | 25.1% | 74.9% | 25.1% | 74.9% |
| 41,699 | MAURY | 12,322 | 4,605 | 7,716 | 1 | 3,111 D | 37.4% | 62.6% | 37.4% | 62.6% |

# TENNESSEE

## PRESIDENT 1964

| 1960 Census Population | County | Total Vote | Republican | Democratic | Other | Rep.-Dem. Plurality | Percentage | | | |
|---|---|---|---|---|---|---|---|---|---|---|
| | | | | | | | Total Vote | | Major Vote | |
| | | | | | | | Rep. | Dem. | Rep. | Dem. |
| 5,160 | MEIGS | 1,640 | 824 | 816 | | 8 R | 50.2% | 49.8% | 50.2% | 49.8% |
| 23,316 | MONROE | 8,449 | 4,349 | 4,100 | | 249 R | 51.5% | 48.5% | 51.5% | 48.5% |
| 55,645 | MONTGOMERY | 12,992 | 2,814 | 10,178 | | 7,364 D | 21.7% | 78.3% | 21.7% | 78.3% |
| 3,454 | MOORE | 1,298 | 264 | 1,034 | | 770 D | 20.3% | 79.7% | 20.3% | 79.7% |
| 14,304 | MORGAN | 3,799 | 1,842 | 1,957 | | 115 D | 48.5% | 51.5% | 48.5% | 51.5% |
| 26,957 | OBION | 8,474 | 2,802 | 5,672 | | 2,870 D | 33.1% | 66.9% | 33.1% | 66.9% |
| 14,661 | OVERTON | 4,413 | 1,155 | 3,258 | | 2,103 D | 26.2% | 73.8% | 26.2% | 73.8% |
| 5,273 | PERRY | 1,954 | 514 | 1,440 | | 926 D | 26.3% | 73.7% | 26.3% | 73.7% |
| 4,431 | PICKETT | 1,663 | 935 | 728 | | 207 R | 56.2% | 43.8% | 56.2% | 43.8% |
| 12,160 | POLK | 3,798 | 1,685 | 2,113 | | 428 D | 44.4% | 55.6% | 44.4% | 55.6% |
| 29,236 | PUTNAM | 9,304 | 2,993 | 6,309 | 2 | 3,316 D | 32.2% | 67.8% | 32.2% | 67.8% |
| 15,863 | RHEA | 5,367 | 2,730 | 2,637 | | 93 R | 50.9% | 49.1% | 50.9% | 49.1% |
| 39,133 | ROANE | 11,843 | 5,735 | 6,108 | | 373 D | 48.4% | 51.6% | 48.4% | 51.6% |
| 27,335 | ROBERTSON | 7,581 | 1,797 | 5,784 | | 3,987 D | 23.7% | 76.3% | 23.7% | 76.3% |
| 52,368 | RUTHERFORD | 13,668 | 4,088 | 9,580 | | 5,492 D | 29.9% | 70.1% | 29.9% | 70.1% |
| 15,413 | SCOTT | 4,413 | 2,406 | 2,007 | | 399 R | 54.5% | 45.5% | 54.5% | 45.5% |
| 5,915 | SEQUATCHIE | 1,966 | 804 | 1,162 | | 358 D | 40.9% | 59.1% | 40.9% | 59.1% |
| 24,251 | SEVIER | 9,816 | 6,821 | 2,995 | | 3,826 R | 69.5% | 30.5% | 69.5% | 30.5% |
| 627,019 | SHELBY | 212,026 | 100,527 | 111,496 | 3 | 10,969 D | 47.4% | 52.6% | 47.4% | 52.6% |
| 12,059 | SMITH | 4,018 | 1,084 | 2,934 | | 1,850 D | 27.0% | 73.0% | 27.0% | 73.0% |
| 7,851 | STEWART | 2,885 | 441 | 2,444 | | 2,003 D | 15.3% | 84.7% | 15.3% | 84.7% |
| 114,139 | SULLIVAN | 37,199 | 17,703 | 19,496 | | 1,793 D | 47.6% | 52.4% | 47.6% | 52.4% |
| 36,217 | SUMNER | 12,539 | 3,437 | 9,102 | | 5,665 D | 27.4% | 72.6% | 27.4% | 72.6% |
| 28,564 | TIPTON | 6,894 | 3,073 | 3,821 | | 748 D | 44.6% | 55.4% | 44.6% | 55.4% |
| 4,914 | TROUSDALE | 1,475 | 205 | 1,270 | | 1,065 D | 13.9% | 86.1% | 13.9% | 86.1% |
| 15,082 | UNICOI | 4,731 | 2,731 | 2,000 | | 731 R | 57.7% | 42.3% | 57.7% | 42.3% |
| 8,498 | UNION | 2,861 | 1,770 | 1,091 | | 679 R | 61.9% | 38.1% | 61.9% | 38.1% |
| 3,671 | VAN BUREN | 1,158 | 293 | 865 | | 572 D | 25.3% | 74.7% | 25.3% | 74.7% |
| 23,102 | WARREN | 6,782 | 1,754 | 5,027 | 1 | 3,273 D | 25.9% | 74.1% | 25.9% | 74.1% |
| 64,832 | WASHINGTON | 20,865 | 10,612 | 10,253 | | 359 R | 50.9% | 49.1% | 50.9% | 49.1% |
| 11,908 | WAYNE | 3,688 | 2,510 | 1,178 | | 1,332 R | 68.1% | 31.9% | 68.1% | 31.9% |
| 24,227 | WEAKLEY | 7,845 | 2,684 | 5,161 | | 2,477 D | 34.2% | 65.8% | 34.2% | 65.8% |
| 15,577 | WHITE | 4,186 | 1,199 | 2,987 | | 1,788 D | 28.6% | 71.4% | 28.6% | 71.4% |
| 25,267 | WILLIAMSON | 7,783 | 2,707 | 5,075 | 1 | 2,368 D | 34.8% | 65.2% | 34.8% | 65.2% |
| 27,668 | WILSON | 8,974 | 2,707 | 6,267 | | 3,560 D | 30.2% | 69.8% | 30.2% | 69.8% |
| 3,567,089 | TOTAL | 1,143,946 | 508,965 | 634,947 | 34 | 125,982 D | 44.5% | 55.5% | 44.5% | 55.5% |

# TENNESSEE

## PRESIDENT 1960

| 1960 Census Population | County | Total Vote | Republican | Democratic | Other | Rep.-Dem. Plurality | Percentage | | | |
|---|---|---|---|---|---|---|---|---|---|---|
| | | | | | | | Total Vote | | Major Vote | |
| | | | | | | | Rep. | Dem. | Rep. | Dem. |
| 60,032 | ANDERSON | 21,221 | 11,153 | 9,878 | 190 | 1,275 R | 52.6% | 46.5% | 53.0% | 47.0% |
| 23,150 | BEDFORD | 7,152 | 2,633 | 4,457 | 62 | 1,824 D | 36.8% | 62.3% | 37.1% | 62.9% |
| 10,662 | BENTON | 3,923 | 1,773 | 2,030 | 120 | 257 D | 45.2% | 51.7% | 46.6% | 53.4% |
| 7,811 | BLEDSOE | 2,452 | 1,439 | 981 | 32 | 458 R | 58.7% | 40.0% | 59.5% | 40.5% |
| 57,525 | BLOUNT | 19,872 | 13,552 | 6,213 | 107 | 7,339 R | 68.2% | 31.3% | 68.6% | 31.4% |
| 38,324 | BRADLEY | 11,285 | 7,865 | 3,307 | 113 | 4,558 R | 69.7% | 29.3% | 70.4% | 29.6% |
| 27,936 | CAMPBELL | 8,297 | 5,079 | 3,134 | 84 | 1,945 R | 61.2% | 37.8% | 61.8% | 38.2% |
| 8,537 | CANNON | 2,487 | 1,195 | 1,275 | 17 | 80 D | 48.0% | 51.3% | 48.4% | 51.6% |
| 23,476 | CARROLL | 7,609 | 4,517 | 2,961 | 131 | 1,556 R | 59.4% | 38.9% | 60.4% | 39.6% |
| 41,578 | CARTER | 15,798 | 12,214 | 3,412 | 172 | 8,802 R | 77.3% | 21.6% | 78.2% | 21.8% |
| 9,428 | CHEATHAM | 2,607 | 683 | 1,883 | 41 | 1,200 D | 26.2% | 72.2% | 26.6% | 73.4% |
| 9,569 | CHESTER | 3,060 | 1,807 | 1,192 | 61 | 615 R | 59.1% | 39.0% | 60.3% | 39.7% |
| 19,067 | CLAIBORNE | 6,056 | 3,888 | 2,142 | 26 | 1,746 R | 64.2% | 35.4% | 64.5% | 35.5% |
| 7,289 | CLAY | 2,106 | 1,098 | 976 | 32 | 122 R | 52.1% | 46.3% | 52.9% | 47.1% |
| 23,390 | COCKE | 8,095 | 6,581 | 1,442 | 72 | 5,139 R | 81.3% | 17.8% | 82.0% | 18.0% |
| 28,603 | COFFEE | 7,686 | 3,058 | 4,555 | 73 | 1,497 D | 39.8% | 59.3% | 40.2% | 59.8% |
| 14,594 | CROCKETT | 3,013 | 1,467 | 1,438 | 108 | 29 R | 48.7% | 47.7% | 50.5% | 49.5% |
| 19,135 | CUMBERLAND | 5,804 | 3,523 | 2,189 | 92 | 1,334 R | 60.7% | 37.7% | 61.7% | 38.3% |
| 399,743 | DAVIDSON | 112,597 | 52,077 | 59,649 | 871 | 7,572 D | 46.3% | 53.0% | 46.6% | 53.4% |
| 8,324 | DECATUR | 3,075 | 1,684 | 1,321 | 70 | 363 R | 54.8% | 43.0% | 56.0% | 44.0% |
| 10,774 | DE KALB | 3,026 | 1,440 | 1,547 | 39 | 107 D | 47.6% | 51.1% | 48.2% | 51.8% |
| 18,839 | DICKSON | 5,894 | 1,928 | 3,930 | 36 | 2,002 D | 32.7% | 66.7% | 32.9% | 67.1% |
| 29,537 | DYER | 8,203 | 4,097 | 3,868 | 238 | 229 R | 49.9% | 47.2% | 51.4% | 48.6% |
| 24,577 | FAYETTE | 2,799 | 1,370 | 892 | 537 | 478 R | 48.9% | 31.9% | 60.6% | 39.4% |
| 13,288 | FENTRESS | 3,792 | 2,726 | 1,014 | 52 | 1,712 R | 71.9% | 26.7% | 72.9% | 27.1% |
| 25,528 | FRANKLIN | 7,139 | 2,041 | 5,041 | 57 | 3,000 D | 28.6% | 70.6% | 28.8% | 71.2% |
| 44,699 | GIBSON | 11,329 | 5,173 | 5,796 | 360 | 623 D | 45.7% | 51.2% | 47.2% | 52.8% |
| 22,410 | GILES | 6,513 | 1,598 | 4,879 | 36 | 3,281 D | 24.5% | 74.9% | 24.7% | 75.3% |
| 12,506 | GRAINGER | 3,977 | 3,017 | 939 | 21 | 2,078 R | 75.9% | 23.6% | 76.3% | 23.7% |
| 42,163 | GREENE | 13,276 | 8,835 | 4,406 | 35 | 4,429 R | 66.5% | 33.2% | 66.7% | 33.3% |
| 11,512 | GRUNDY | 2,960 | 786 | 2,143 | 31 | 1,357 D | 26.6% | 72.4% | 26.8% | 73.2% |
| 33,092 | HAMBLEN | 10,245 | 7,093 | 3,122 | 30 | 3,971 R | 69.2% | 30.5% | 69.4% | 30.6% |
| 237,905 | HAMILTON | 71,277 | 39,703 | 30,482 | 1,092 | 9,221 R | 55.7% | 42.8% | 56.6% | 43.4% |
| 7,757 | HANCOCK | 2,552 | 2,107 | 438 | 7 | 1,669 R | 82.6% | 17.2% | 82.8% | 17.2% |
| 21,517 | HARDEMAN | 3,604 | 1,601 | 1,711 | 292 | 110 D | 44.4% | 47.5% | 48.3% | 51.7% |
| 17,397 | HARDIN | 5,098 | 3,323 | 1,690 | 85 | 1,633 R | 65.2% | 33.2% | 66.3% | 33.7% |
| 30,468 | HAWKINS | 9,672 | 7,010 | 2,586 | 76 | 4,424 R | 72.5% | 26.7% | 73.1% | 26.9% |
| 23,393 | HAYWOOD | 3,334 | 1,188 | 1,867 | 279 | 679 D | 35.6% | 56.0% | 38.9% | 61.1% |
| 16,115 | HENDERSON | 5,128 | 3,597 | 1,490 | 41 | 2,107 R | 70.1% | 29.1% | 70.7% | 29.3% |
| 22,275 | HENRY | 8,213 | 3,033 | 5,049 | 131 | 2,016 D | 36.9% | 61.5% | 37.5% | 62.5% |
| 11,862 | HICKMAN | 3,687 | 1,224 | 2,401 | 62 | 1,177 D | 33.2% | 65.1% | 33.8% | 66.2% |
| 4,794 | HOUSTON | 1,533 | 366 | 1,150 | 17 | 784 D | 23.9% | 75.0% | 24.1% | 75.9% |
| 11,511 | HUMPHREYS | 3,766 | 1,126 | 2,592 | 48 | 1,466 D | 29.9% | 68.8% | 30.3% | 69.7% |
| 9,233 | JACKSON | 2,636 | 1,049 | 1,539 | 48 | 490 D | 39.8% | 58.4% | 40.5% | 59.5% |
| 21,493 | JEFFERSON | 7,794 | 6,141 | 1,620 | 33 | 4,521 R | 78.8% | 20.8% | 79.1% | 20.9% |
| 10,765 | JOHNSON | 4,443 | 3,854 | 571 | 18 | 3,283 R | 86.7% | 12.9% | 87.1% | 12.9% |
| 250,523 | KNOX | 83,300 | 50,811 | 31,990 | 499 | 18,821 R | 61.0% | 38.4% | 61.4% | 38.6% |
| 9,572 | LAKE | 2,151 | 732 | 1,346 | 73 | 614 D | 34.0% | 62.6% | 35.2% | 64.8% |
| 21,844 | LAUDERDALE | 4,832 | 1,322 | 3,462 | 48 | 2,140 D | 27.4% | 71.6% | 27.6% | 72.4% |
| 28,049 | LAWRENCE | 10,639 | 5,709 | 4,862 | 68 | 847 R | 53.7% | 45.7% | 54.0% | 46.0% |
| 6,269 | LEWIS | 2,312 | 580 | 1,723 | 9 | 1,143 D | 25.1% | 74.5% | 25.2% | 74.8% |
| 23,829 | LINCOLN | 6,346 | 1,428 | 4,862 | 56 | 3,434 D | 22.5% | 76.6% | 22.7% | 77.3% |
| 23,757 | LOUDON | 8,181 | 5,356 | 2,722 | 103 | 2,634 R | 65.5% | 33.3% | 66.3% | 33.7% |
| 33,662 | MCMINN | 10,766 | 6,585 | 4,111 | 70 | 2,474 R | 61.2% | 38.2% | 61.6% | 38.4% |
| 18,085 | MCNAIRY | 5,604 | 3,310 | 2,173 | 121 | 1,137 R | 59.1% | 38.8% | 60.4% | 39.6% |
| 12,197 | MACON | 3,782 | 2,829 | 915 | 38 | 1,914 R | 74.8% | 24.2% | 75.6% | 24.4% |
| 60,655 | MADISON | 17,693 | 8,863 | 8,083 | 747 | 780 R | 50.1% | 45.7% | 52.3% | 47.7% |
| 21,036 | MARION | 5,865 | 2,657 | 3,124 | 84 | 467 D | 45.3% | 53.3% | 46.0% | 54.0% |
| 16,859 | MARSHALL | 5,387 | 1,717 | 3,625 | 45 | 1,908 D | 31.9% | 67.3% | 32.1% | 67.9% |
| 41,699 | MAURY | 10,879 | 4,133 | 6,615 | 131 | 2,482 D | 38.0% | 60.8% | 38.5% | 61.5% |

# TENNESSEE

## PRESIDENT 1960

| 1960 Census Population | County | Total Vote | Republican | Democratic | Other | Rep.-Dem. Plurality | Percentage | | | |
|---|---|---|---|---|---|---|---|---|---|---|
| | | | | | | | Total Vote | | Major Vote | |
| | | | | | | | Rep. | Dem. | Rep. | Dem. |
| 5,160 | MEIGS | 1,605 | 901 | 691 | 13 | 210 R | 56.1% | 43.1% | 56.6% | 43.4% |
| 23,316 | MONROE | 8,452 | 4,991 | 3,375 | 86 | 1,616 R | 59.1% | 39.9% | 59.7% | 40.3% |
| 55,645 | MONTGOMERY | 10,270 | 2,550 | 7,635 | 85 | 5,085 D | 24.8% | 74.3% | 25.0% | 75.0% |
| 3,454 | MOORE | 1,187 | 313 | 863 | 11 | 550 D | 26.4% | 72.7% | 26.6% | 73.4% |
| 14,304 | MORGAN | 3,855 | 2,241 | 1,576 | 38 | 665 R | 58.1% | 40.9% | 58.7% | 41.3% |
| 26,957 | OBION | 8,196 | 3,800 | 4,244 | 152 | 444 D | 46.4% | 51.8% | 47.2% | 52.8% |
| 14,661 | OVERTON | 4,252 | 1,831 | 2,389 | 32 | 558 D | 43.1% | 56.2% | 43.4% | 56.6% |
| 5,273 | PERRY | 1,737 | 645 | 1,076 | 16 | 431 D | 37.1% | 61.9% | 37.5% | 62.5% |
| 4,431 | PICKETT | 1,721 | 1,154 | 567 | | 587 R | 67.1% | 32.9% | 67.1% | 32.9% |
| 12,160 | POLK | 3,751 | 2,187 | 1,532 | 32 | 655 R | 58.3% | 40.8% | 58.8% | 41.2% |
| 29,236 | PUTNAM | 8,715 | 4,240 | 4,443 | 32 | 203 D | 48.7% | 51.0% | 48.8% | 51.2% |
| 15,863 | RHEA | 4,552 | 2,721 | 1,761 | 70 | 960 R | 59.8% | 38.7% | 60.7% | 39.3% |
| 39,133 | ROANE | 11,626 | 6,540 | 4,953 | 133 | 1,587 R | 56.3% | 42.6% | 56.9% | 43.1% |
| 27,335 | ROBERTSON | 5,891 | 1,776 | 4,053 | 62 | 2,277 D | 30.1% | 68.8% | 30.5% | 69.5% |
| 52,368 | RUTHERFORD | 11,052 | 4,526 | 6,410 | 116 | 1,884 D | 41.0% | 58.0% | 41.4% | 58.6% |
| 15,413 | SCOTT | 4,411 | 3,301 | 1,098 | 12 | 2,203 R | 74.8% | 24.9% | 75.0% | 25.0% |
| 5,915 | SEQUATCHIE | 1,655 | 703 | 930 | 22 | 227 D | 42.5% | 56.2% | 43.0% | 57.0% |
| 24,251 | SEVIER | 9,192 | 7,818 | 1,341 | 33 | 6,477 R | 85.1% | 14.6% | 85.4% | 14.6% |
| 627,019 | SHELBY | 176,607 | 87,191 | 86,270 | 3,146 | 921 R | 49.4% | 48.8% | 50.3% | 49.7% |
| 12,059 | SMITH | 4,060 | 1,601 | 2,411 | 48 | 810 D | 39.4% | 59.4% | 39.9% | 60.1% |
| 7,851 | STEWART | 2,386 | 539 | 1,810 | 37 | 1,271 D | 22.6% | 75.9% | 22.9% | 77.1% |
| 114,139 | SULLIVAN | 37,598 | 22,354 | 14,731 | 513 | 7,623 R | 59.5% | 39.2% | 60.3% | 39.7% |
| 36,217 | SUMNER | 10,261 | 3,491 | 6,687 | 83 | 3,196 D | 34.0% | 65.2% | 34.3% | 65.7% |
| 28,564 | TIPTON | 5,917 | 1,829 | 3,853 | 235 | 2,024 D | 30.9% | 65.1% | 32.2% | 67.8% |
| 4,914 | TROUSDALE | 1,356 | 308 | 1,036 | 12 | 728 D | 22.7% | 76.4% | 22.9% | 77.1% |
| 15,082 | UNICOI | 5,336 | 4,004 | 1,322 | 10 | 2,682 R | 75.0% | 24.8% | 75.2% | 24.8% |
| 8,498 | UNION | 2,753 | 2,082 | 652 | 19 | 1,430 R | 75.6% | 23.7% | 76.2% | 23.8% |
| 3,671 | VAN BUREN | 995 | 401 | 577 | 17 | 176 D | 40.3% | 58.0% | 41.0% | 59.0% |
| 23,102 | WARREN | 5,841 | 2,682 | 3,119 | 40 | 437 D | 45.9% | 53.4% | 46.2% | 53.8% |
| 64,832 | WASHINGTON | 21,236 | 14,851 | 6,283 | 102 | 8,568 R | 69.9% | 29.6% | 70.3% | 29.7% |
| 11,908 | WAYNE | 3,872 | 2,912 | 931 | 29 | 1,981 R | 75.2% | 24.0% | 75.8% | 24.2% |
| 24,227 | WEAKLEY | 8,109 | 3,543 | 4,488 | 78 | 945 D | 43.7% | 55.3% | 44.1% | 55.9% |
| 15,577 | WHITE | 3,998 | 1,725 | 2,207 | 66 | 482 D | 43.1% | 55.2% | 43.9% | 56.1% |
| 25,267 | WILLIAMSON | 7,228 | 2,699 | 4,471 | 58 | 1,772 D | 37.3% | 61.9% | 37.6% | 62.4% |
| 27,668 | WILSON | 8,297 | 3,383 | 4,857 | 57 | 1,474 D | 40.8% | 58.5% | 41.1% | 58.9% |
| 3,567,089 | TOTAL | 1,051,792 | 556,577 | 481,453 | 13,762 | 75,124 R | 52.9% | 45.8% | 53.6% | 46.4% |

# TENNESSEE

## ELECTION NOTES

**2004**    Other vote was 8,992 Independent (Ralph Nader); 4,866 Independent (Michael Badnarik); 2,570 Independent (Michael Peroutka); 33 write-in (David Cobb); 6 write-in (Walter F. Brown).

**2000**    Other vote was 4,284 Libertarian (Browne); 4,250 Reform (Buchanan); 1,606 Independent (Brown); 1,015 Independent (Phillips); 613 Reform (Hagelin); 535 Independent (Venson); 428 scattered write-in. All of these candidates, including Nader, were listed as Independent, with partisan designations, where applicable, indicated in parentheses.

**1996**    Other vote was 6,427 Independent (Nader); 5,020 Independent (Browne); 1,818 Independent (Phillips); 688 Independent (Collins); 636 Independent (Hagelin); 408 Independent (Michael); 324 Independent (Dodge); 190 scattered write-in.

**1992**    Other vote was 1,847 Marrou (Independent); 1,356 Brisben (Independent); 756 Gritz (Independent); 727 Fulani (Independent); 599 Hagelin (Independent); 579 Phillips (Independent); 511 Daniels (Independent); 460 LaRouche (Independent); 343 Dodge (Independent); 277 Warren (Independent); 233 Yiamouyiannis (Independent); 161 scattered write-in.

**1988**    Other vote was 2,041 Paul (Independent); 1,807 Dodge (Independent); 1,807 Duke (Independent); 1,334 Fulani (Independent); 873 LaRouche (Independent); 718 Warren (Independent); 358 Kenoyer (Independent); 285 scattered write-in.

**1984**    Other vote was 3,072 Bergland (Independent); 1,852 LaRouche (Independent); 1,763 Richards (Independent); 1,036 Hall (Independent); 978 Johnson (Independent); 715 Mason (Independent); 524 Serrette (Independent); 4 Anderson (write-in); 7 Dennis (write-in); 117 scattered write-in.

**1980**    Other vote was 35,991 Anderson (Independent); 7,116 Clark (Independent); 1,112 Commoner (Independent); 521 Bubar (Independent); 519 McReynolds (Independent); 503 Hall (Independent); 490 DeBerry (Independent); 400 Griswold (Independent); 152 scattered write-in.

**1976**    Other vote was 5,769 Anderson (Independent); 5,004 McCarthy (Independent); 2,303 Maddox (Independent); 1,375 MacBride (Independent); 547 Hall (Independent); 512 LaRouche (Independent); 442 Bubar (Independent); 316 Miller (Independent); 229 scattered write-in. Early unamended canvass gave the scattered write-in vote total as 230.

**1972**    Other vote was 30,373 Schmitz (American); 369 scattered write-in.

**1968**    Wallace on the ballot as American.

**1964**    Other vote was scattered write-in.

**1960**    Other vote was 11,304 Faubus (National States Rights); 2,458 Decker (Prohibition).

# TEXAS

## POPULAR VOTE FOR PRESIDENT 1920 TO 2004

| Year | Total Vote | Republican | | Democratic | | Other Vote | Plurality | Percentage | | | |
|---|---|---|---|---|---|---|---|---|---|---|---|
| | | | | | | | | Total Vote | | Major Vote | |
| | | Vote | Candidate | Vote | Candidate | | | Rep. | Dem. | Rep. | Dem. |
| 2004 | 7,410,765 | 4,526,917 | Bush, George W. | 2,832,704 | Kerry, John | 51,144 | 1,694,213 R | 61.1% | 38.2% | 61.5% | 38.5% |
| 2000 ** | 6,407,637 | 3,799,639 | Bush, George W. | 2,433,746 | Gore, Al | 174,252 | 1,365,893 R | 59.3% | 38.0% | 61.0% | 39.0% |
| 1996 ** | 5,611,644 | 2,736,167 | Dole, Bob | 2,459,683 | Clinton, Bill | 415,794 | 276,484 R | 48.8% | 43.8% | 52.7% | 47.3% |
| 1992 ** | 6,154,018 | 2,496,071 | Bush, George | 2,281,815 | Clinton, Bill | 1,376,132 | 214,256 R | 40.6% | 37.1% | 52.2% | 47.8% |
| 1988 | 5,427,410 | 3,036,829 | Bush, George | 2,352,748 | Dukakis, Michael S. | 37,833 | 684,081 R | 56.0% | 43.3% | 56.3% | 43.7% |
| 1984 | 5,397,571 | 3,433,428 | Reagan, Ronald | 1,949,276 | Mondale, Walter F. | 14,867 | 1,484,152 R | 63.6% | 36.1% | 63.8% | 36.2% |
| 1980 ** | 4,541,636 | 2,510,705 | Reagan, Ronald | 1,881,147 | Carter, Jimmy | 149,784 | 629,558 R | 55.3% | 41.4% | 57.2% | 42.8% |
| 1976 | 4,071,884 | 1,953,300 | Ford, Gerald R. | 2,082,319 | Carter, Jimmy | 36,265 | 129,019 D | 48.0% | 51.1% | 48.4% | 51.6% |
| 1972 | 3,471,281 | 2,298,896 | Nixon, Richard M. | 1,154,289 | McGovern, George S. | 18,096 | 1,144,607 R | 66.2% | 33.3% | 66.6% | 33.4% |
| 1968 ** | 3,079,216 | 1,227,844 | Nixon, Richard M. | 1,266,804 | Humphrey, Hubert H. | 584,568 | 38,960 D | 39.9% | 41.1% | 49.2% | 50.8% |
| 1964 | 2,626,811 | 958,566 | Goldwater, Barry M. | 1,663,185 | Johnson, Lyndon B. | 5,060 | 704,619 D | 36.5% | 63.3% | 36.6% | 63.4% |
| 1960 | 2,311,084 | 1,121,310 | Nixon, Richard M. | 1,167,567 | Kennedy, John F. | 22,207 | 46,257 D | 48.5% | 50.5% | 49.0% | 51.0% |
| 1956 | 1,955,168 | 1,080,619 | Eisenhower, Dwight D. | 859,958 | Stevenson, Adlai E. | 14,591 | 220,661 R | 55.3% | 44.0% | 55.7% | 44.3% |
| 1952 | 2,075,946 | 1,102,878 | Eisenhower, Dwight D. | 969,228 | Stevenson, Adlai E. | 3,840 | 133,650 R | 53.1% | 46.7% | 53.2% | 46.8% |
| 1948 | 1,249,577 | 303,467 | Dewey, Thomas E. | 824,235 | Truman, Harry S. | 121,875 | 520,768 D | 24.3% | 66.0% | 26.9% | 73.1% |
| 1944 | 1,150,334 | 191,423 | Dewey, Thomas E. | 821,605 | Roosevelt, Franklin D. | 137,306 | 630,182 D | 16.6% | 71.4% | 18.9% | 81.1% |
| 1940 | 1,124,437 | 212,692 | Willkie, Wendell | 909,974 | Roosevelt, Franklin D. | 1,771 | 697,282 D | 18.9% | 80.9% | 18.9% | 81.1% |
| 1936 | 849,701 | 104,661 | Landon, Alfred M. | 739,952 | Roosevelt, Franklin D. | 5,088 | 635,291 D | 12.3% | 87.1% | 12.4% | 87.6% |
| 1932 | 874,382 | 98,218 | Hoover, Herbert C. | 771,109 | Roosevelt, Franklin D. | 5,055 | 672,891 D | 11.2% | 88.2% | 11.3% | 88.7% |
| 1928 | 717,733 | 372,324 | Hoover, Herbert C. | 344,542 | Smith, Alfred E. | 867 | 27,782 R | 51.9% | 48.0% | 51.9% | 48.1% |
| 1924 | 657,054 | 130,794 | Coolidge, Calvin | 483,381 | Davis, John W. | 42,879 | 352,587 D | 19.9% | 73.6% | 21.3% | 78.7% |
| 1920 | 486,109 | 114,658 | Harding, Warren G. | 287,920 | Cox, James M. | 83,531 | 173,262 D | 23.6% | 59.2% | 28.5% | 71.5% |

In 2000 the other vote column includes 137,994 votes cast for Green (Nader). In 1996 the other vote column includes 378,537 votes cast for Perot. In 1992 the other vote column includes 1,354,781 votes cast for Perot. In 1980 the other column includes 111,613 votes for Independent (Anderson). In 1968 other vote was 584,269 American (Wallace) and 299 scattered.

## ELECTORAL COLLEGE VOTE 1920 TO 2004

| Year | Total | Republican | Democratic | Other |
|---|---|---|---|---|
| 2004 | 34 | 34 | | |
| 2000 | 32 | 32 | | |
| 1996 | 32 | 32 | | |
| 1992 | 32 | 32 | | |
| 1988 | 29 | 29 | | |
| 1984 | 29 | 29 | | |
| 1980 | 26 | 26 | | |
| 1976 | 26 | | 26 | |
| 1972 | 26 | 26 | | |
| 1968 | 25 | | 25 | |
| 1964 | 25 | | 25 | |
| 1960 | 24 | | 24 | |
| 1956 | 24 | 24 | | |
| 1952 | 24 | 24 | | |
| 1948 | 23 | | 23 | |
| 1944 | 23 | | 23 | |
| 1940 | 23 | | 23 | |
| 1936 | 23 | | 23 | |
| 1932 | 23 | | 23 | |
| 1928 | 20 | 20 | | |
| 1924 | 20 | | 20 | |
| 1920 | 20 | | 20 | |

# TEXAS

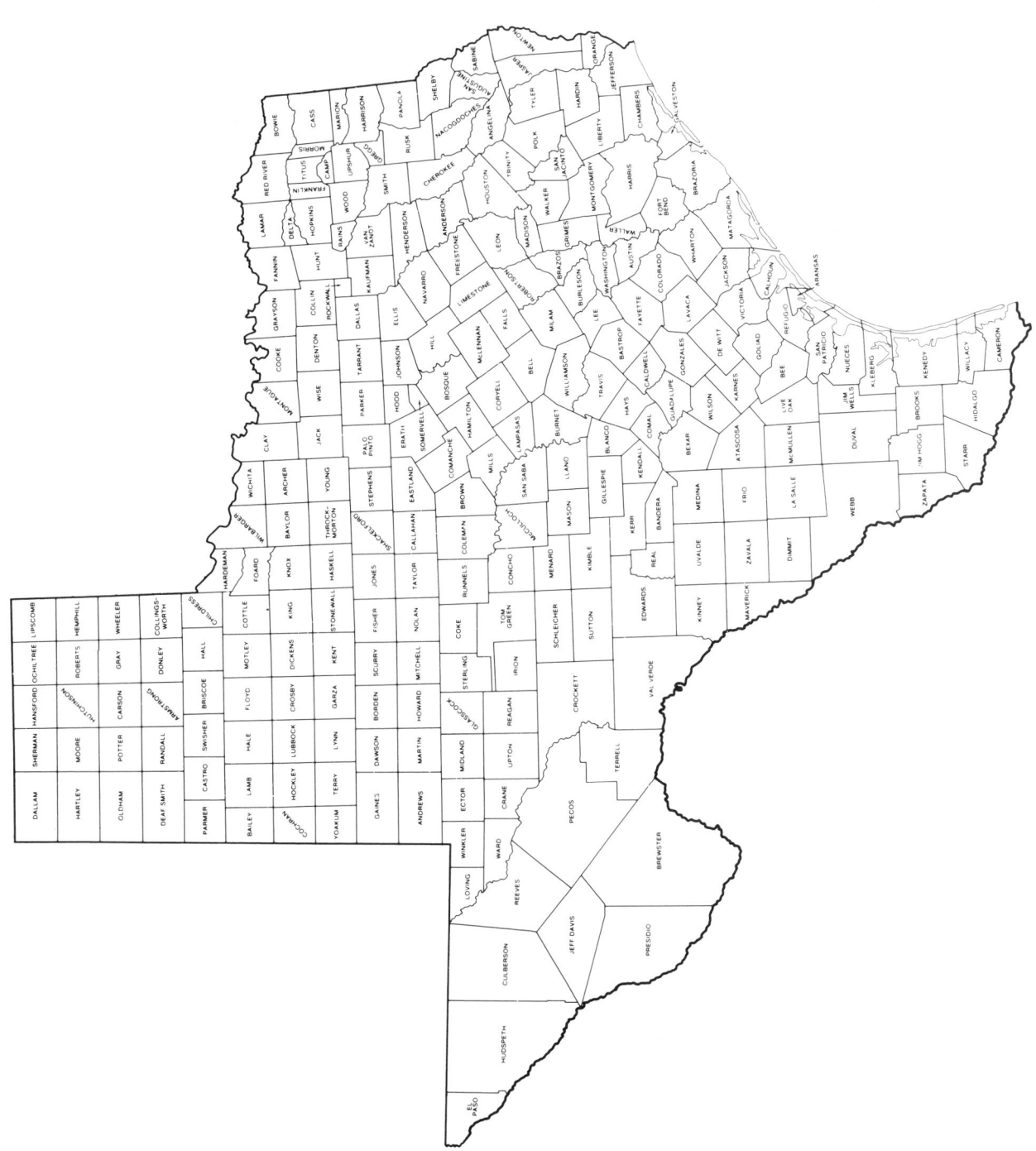

# TEXAS

## PRESIDENT 2004

| 2000 Census Population | County | Total Vote | Republican | Democratic | Other | Rep.-Dem. Plurality | Percentage | | | |
|---|---|---|---|---|---|---|---|---|---|---|
| | | | | | | | Total Vote | | Major Vote | |
| | | | | | | | Rep. | Dem. | Rep. | Dem. |
| 55,109 | ANDERSON | 16,301 | 11,525 | 4,678 | 98 | 6,847 R | 70.7% | 28.7% | 71.1% | 28.9% |
| 13,004 | ANDREWS | 4,536 | 3,837 | 677 | 22 | 3,160 R | 84.6% | 14.9% | 85.0% | 15.0% |
| 80,130 | ANGELINA | 28,364 | 18,932 | 9,302 | 130 | 9,630 R | 66.7% | 32.8% | 67.1% | 32.9% |
| 22,497 | ARANSAS | 9,268 | 6,569 | 2,640 | 59 | 3,929 R | 70.9% | 28.5% | 71.3% | 28.7% |
| 8,854 | ARCHER | 4,451 | 3,556 | 878 | 17 | 2,678 R | 79.9% | 19.7% | 80.2% | 19.8% |
| 2,148 | ARMSTRONG | 1,004 | 830 | 170 | 4 | 660 R | 82.7% | 16.9% | 83.0% | 17.0% |
| 38,628 | ATASCOSA | 12,116 | 7,635 | 4,421 | 60 | 3,214 R | 63.0% | 36.5% | 63.3% | 36.7% |
| 23,590 | AUSTIN | 10,702 | 8,072 | 2,582 | 48 | 5,490 R | 75.4% | 24.1% | 75.8% | 24.2% |
| 6,594 | BAILEY | 2,412 | 1,882 | 525 | 5 | 1,357 R | 78.0% | 21.8% | 78.2% | 21.8% |
| 17,645 | BANDERA | 8,741 | 6,933 | 1,738 | 70 | 5,195 R | 79.3% | 19.9% | 80.0% | 20.0% |
| 57,733 | BASTROP | 23,441 | 13,290 | 9,794 | 357 | 3,496 R | 56.7% | 41.8% | 57.6% | 42.4% |
| 4,093 | BAYLOR | 1,640 | 1,169 | 467 | 4 | 702 R | 71.3% | 28.5% | 71.5% | 28.5% |
| 32,359 | BEE | 9,518 | 5,428 | 4,045 | 45 | 1,383 R | 57.0% | 42.5% | 57.3% | 42.7% |
| 237,974 | BELL | 79,724 | 52,135 | 27,165 | 424 | 24,970 R | 65.4% | 34.1% | 65.7% | 34.3% |
| 1,392,931 | BEXAR | 475,314 | 260,698 | 210,976 | 3,640 | 49,722 R | 54.8% | 44.4% | 55.3% | 44.7% |
| 8,418 | BLANCO | 4,584 | 3,277 | 1,267 | 40 | 2,010 R | 71.5% | 27.6% | 72.1% | 27.9% |
| 729 | BORDEN | 359 | 303 | 55 | 1 | 248 R | 84.4% | 15.3% | 84.6% | 15.4% |
| 17,204 | BOSQUE | 7,586 | 5,737 | 1,815 | 34 | 3,922 R | 75.6% | 23.9% | 76.0% | 24.0% |
| 89,306 | BOWIE | 33,760 | 21,791 | 11,880 | 89 | 9,911 R | 64.5% | 35.2% | 64.7% | 35.3% |
| 241,767 | BRAZORIA | 93,248 | 63,662 | 28,904 | 682 | 34,758 R | 68.3% | 31.0% | 68.8% | 31.2% |
| 152,415 | BRAZOS | 54,309 | 37,594 | 16,128 | 587 | 21,466 R | 69.2% | 29.7% | 70.0% | 30.0% |
| 8,866 | BREWSTER | 3,760 | 1,980 | 1,729 | 51 | 251 R | 52.7% | 46.0% | 53.4% | 46.6% |
| 1,790 | BRISCOE | 811 | 620 | 191 | | 429 R | 76.4% | 23.6% | 76.4% | 23.6% |
| 7,976 | BROOKS | 2,674 | 845 | 1,823 | 6 | 978 D | 31.6% | 68.2% | 31.7% | 68.3% |
| 37,674 | BROWN | 14,253 | 11,640 | 2,523 | 90 | 9,117 R | 81.7% | 17.7% | 82.2% | 17.8% |
| 16,470 | BURLESON | 6,721 | 4,405 | 2,276 | 40 | 2,129 R | 65.5% | 33.9% | 65.9% | 34.1% |
| 34,147 | BURNET | 15,742 | 11,456 | 4,147 | 139 | 7,309 R | 72.8% | 26.3% | 73.4% | 26.6% |
| 32,194 | CALDWELL | 11,587 | 6,436 | 5,052 | 99 | 1,384 R | 55.5% | 43.6% | 56.0% | 44.0% |
| 20,647 | CALHOUN | 6,929 | 4,348 | 2,561 | 20 | 1,787 R | 62.8% | 37.0% | 62.9% | 37.1% |
| 12,905 | CALLAHAN | 5,654 | 4,542 | 1,073 | 39 | 3,469 R | 80.3% | 19.0% | 80.9% | 19.1% |
| 335,227 | CAMERON | 69,156 | 34,801 | 33,998 | 357 | 803 R | 50.3% | 49.2% | 50.6% | 49.4% |
| 11,549 | CAMP | 4,439 | 2,638 | 1,778 | 23 | 860 R | 59.4% | 40.1% | 59.7% | 40.3% |
| 6,516 | CARSON | 2,944 | 2,450 | 485 | 9 | 1,965 R | 83.2% | 16.5% | 83.5% | 16.5% |
| 30,438 | CASS | 12,049 | 7,383 | 4,630 | 36 | 2,753 R | 61.3% | 38.4% | 61.5% | 38.5% |
| 8,285 | CASTRO | 2,430 | 1,794 | 631 | 5 | 1,163 R | 73.8% | 26.0% | 74.0% | 26.0% |
| 26,031 | CHAMBERS | 11,649 | 8,618 | 2,953 | 78 | 5,665 R | 74.0% | 25.3% | 74.5% | 25.5% |
| 46,659 | CHEROKEE | 15,839 | 11,329 | 4,439 | 71 | 6,890 R | 71.5% | 28.0% | 71.8% | 28.2% |
| 7,688 | CHILDRESS | 2,144 | 1,629 | 511 | 4 | 1,118 R | 76.0% | 23.8% | 76.1% | 23.9% |
| 11,006 | CLAY | 5,288 | 3,971 | 1,299 | 18 | 2,672 R | 75.1% | 24.6% | 75.4% | 24.6% |
| 3,730 | COCHRAN | 1,110 | 856 | 249 | 5 | 607 R | 77.1% | 22.4% | 77.5% | 22.5% |
| 3,864 | COKE | 1,610 | 1,338 | 266 | 6 | 1,072 R | 83.1% | 16.5% | 83.4% | 16.6% |
| 9,235 | COLEMAN | 3,826 | 3,035 | 778 | 13 | 2,257 R | 79.3% | 20.3% | 79.6% | 20.4% |
| 491,675 | COLLIN | 245,154 | 174,435 | 68,935 | 1,784 | 105,500 R | 71.2% | 28.1% | 71.7% | 28.3% |
| 3,206 | COLLINGSWORTH | 1,398 | 1,051 | 346 | 1 | 705 R | 75.2% | 24.7% | 75.2% | 24.8% |
| 20,390 | COLORADO | 7,690 | 5,488 | 2,161 | 41 | 3,327 R | 71.4% | 28.1% | 71.7% | 28.3% |
| 78,021 | COMAL | 41,043 | 31,574 | 9,153 | 316 | 22,421 R | 76.9% | 22.3% | 77.5% | 22.5% |
| 14,026 | COMANCHE | 5,268 | 3,813 | 1,431 | 24 | 2,382 R | 72.4% | 27.2% | 72.7% | 27.3% |
| 3,966 | CONCHO | 1,193 | 911 | 270 | 12 | 641 R | 76.4% | 22.6% | 77.1% | 22.9% |
| 36,363 | COOKE | 15,107 | 11,908 | 3,142 | 57 | 8,766 R | 78.8% | 20.8% | 79.1% | 20.9% |
| 74,978 | CORYELL | 17,625 | 12,421 | 5,122 | 82 | 7,299 R | 70.5% | 29.1% | 70.8% | 29.2% |
| 1,904 | COTTLE | 768 | 549 | 214 | 5 | 335 R | 71.5% | 27.9% | 72.0% | 28.0% |
| 3,996 | CRANE | 1,574 | 1,314 | 254 | 6 | 1,060 R | 83.5% | 16.1% | 83.8% | 16.2% |
| 4,099 | CROCKETT | 1,728 | 1,248 | 473 | 7 | 775 R | 72.2% | 27.4% | 72.5% | 27.5% |
| 7,072 | CROSBY | 2,275 | 1,647 | 622 | 6 | 1,025 R | 72.4% | 27.3% | 72.6% | 27.4% |
| 2,975 | CULBERSON | 788 | 407 | 375 | 6 | 32 R | 51.6% | 47.6% | 52.0% | 48.0% |
| 6,222 | DALLAM | 1,782 | 1,473 | 305 | 4 | 1,168 R | 82.7% | 17.1% | 82.8% | 17.2% |
| 2,218,899 | DALLAS | 687,709 | 346,246 | 336,641 | 4,822 | 9,605 R | 50.3% | 49.0% | 50.7% | 49.3% |
| 14,985 | DAWSON | 4,545 | 3,419 | 1,114 | 12 | 2,305 R | 75.2% | 24.5% | 75.4% | 24.6% |
| 18,561 | DEAF SMITH | 5,291 | 4,139 | 1,133 | 19 | 3,006 R | 78.2% | 21.4% | 78.5% | 21.5% |
| 5,327 | DELTA | 2,082 | 1,447 | 627 | 8 | 820 R | 69.5% | 30.1% | 69.8% | 30.2% |

# TEXAS

## PRESIDENT 2004

| 2000 Census Population | County | Total Vote | Republican | Democratic | Other | Rep.-Dem. Plurality | Percentage | | | |
|---|---|---|---|---|---|---|---|---|---|---|
| | | | | | | | Total Vote | | Major Vote | |
| | | | | | | | Rep. | Dem. | Rep. | Dem. |
| 432,976 | DENTON | 201,410 | 140,891 | 59,346 | 1,173 | 81,545 R | 70.0% | 29.5% | 70.4% | 29.6% |
| 20,013 | DE WITT | 6,732 | 5,100 | 1,610 | 22 | 3,490 R | 75.8% | 23.9% | 76.0% | 24.0% |
| 2,762 | DICKENS | 1,063 | 815 | 245 | 3 | 570 R | 76.7% | 23.0% | 76.9% | 23.1% |
| 10,248 | DIMMIT | 3,566 | 1,188 | 2,365 | 13 | 1,177 D | 33.3% | 66.3% | 33.4% | 66.6% |
| 3,828 | DONLEY | 1,784 | 1,429 | 349 | 6 | 1,080 R | 80.1% | 19.6% | 80.4% | 19.6% |
| 13,120 | DUVAL | 4,091 | 1,160 | 2,916 | 15 | 1,756 D | 28.4% | 71.3% | 28.5% | 71.5% |
| 18,297 | EASTLAND | 6,857 | 5,249 | 1,582 | 26 | 3,667 R | 76.5% | 23.1% | 76.8% | 23.2% |
| 121,123 | ECTOR | 36,310 | 27,502 | 8,579 | 229 | 18,923 R | 75.7% | 23.6% | 76.2% | 23.8% |
| 2,162 | EDWARDS | 963 | 745 | 217 | 1 | 528 R | 77.4% | 22.5% | 77.4% | 22.6% |
| 111,360 | ELLIS | 46,444 | 34,602 | 11,640 | 202 | 22,962 R | 74.5% | 25.1% | 74.8% | 25.2% |
| 679,622 | EL PASO | 169,573 | 73,261 | 95,142 | 1,170 | 21,881 D | 43.2% | 56.1% | 43.5% | 56.5% |
| 33,001 | ERATH | 12,281 | 9,506 | 2,710 | 65 | 6,796 R | 77.4% | 22.1% | 77.8% | 22.2% |
| 18,576 | FALLS | 5,902 | 3,454 | 2,427 | 21 | 1,027 R | 58.5% | 41.1% | 58.7% | 41.3% |
| 31,242 | FANNIN | 11,960 | 7,893 | 4,001 | 66 | 3,892 R | 66.0% | 33.5% | 66.4% | 33.6% |
| 21,804 | FAYETTE | 10,397 | 7,527 | 2,803 | 67 | 4,724 R | 72.4% | 27.0% | 72.9% | 27.1% |
| 4,344 | FISHER | 1,923 | 1,161 | 758 | 4 | 403 R | 60.4% | 39.4% | 60.5% | 39.5% |
| 7,771 | FLOYD | 2,584 | 2,032 | 545 | 7 | 1,487 R | 78.6% | 21.1% | 78.9% | 21.1% |
| 1,622 | FOARD | 587 | 347 | 235 | 5 | 112 R | 59.1% | 40.0% | 59.6% | 40.4% |
| 354,452 | FORT BEND | 163,169 | 93,625 | 68,722 | 822 | 24,903 R | 57.4% | 42.1% | 57.7% | 42.3% |
| 9,458 | FRANKLIN | 4,217 | 3,185 | 1,011 | 21 | 2,174 R | 75.5% | 24.0% | 75.9% | 24.1% |
| 17,867 | FREESTONE | 7,161 | 5,057 | 2,070 | 34 | 2,987 R | 70.6% | 28.9% | 71.0% | 29.0% |
| 16,252 | FRIO | 3,930 | 1,991 | 1,931 | 8 | 60 R | 50.7% | 49.1% | 50.8% | 49.2% |
| 14,467 | GAINES | 4,164 | 3,540 | 608 | 16 | 2,932 R | 85.0% | 14.6% | 85.3% | 14.7% |
| 250,158 | GALVESTON | 105,981 | 61,290 | 43,919 | 772 | 17,371 R | 57.8% | 41.4% | 58.3% | 41.7% |
| 4,872 | GARZA | 1,812 | 1,480 | 326 | 6 | 1,154 R | 81.7% | 18.0% | 81.9% | 18.1% |
| 20,814 | GILLESPIE | 11,553 | 9,297 | 2,104 | 152 | 7,193 R | 80.5% | 18.2% | 81.5% | 18.5% |
| 1,406 | GLASSCOCK | 533 | 488 | 44 | 1 | 444 R | 91.6% | 8.3% | 91.7% | 8.3% |
| 6,928 | GOLIAD | 3,501 | 2,267 | 1,219 | 15 | 1,048 R | 64.8% | 34.8% | 65.0% | 35.0% |
| 18,628 | GONZALES | 6,022 | 4,291 | 1,709 | 22 | 2,582 R | 71.3% | 28.4% | 71.5% | 28.5% |
| 22,744 | GRAY | 8,572 | 7,260 | 1,289 | 23 | 5,971 R | 84.7% | 15.0% | 84.9% | 15.1% |
| 110,595 | GRAYSON | 44,423 | 30,777 | 13,452 | 194 | 17,325 R | 69.3% | 30.3% | 69.6% | 30.4% |
| 111,379 | GREGG | 42,398 | 29,939 | 12,306 | 153 | 17,633 R | 70.6% | 29.0% | 70.9% | 29.1% |
| 23,552 | GRIMES | 8,030 | 5,263 | 2,713 | 54 | 2,550 R | 65.5% | 33.8% | 66.0% | 34.0% |
| 89,023 | GUADALUPE | 38,752 | 28,208 | 10,290 | 254 | 17,918 R | 72.8% | 26.6% | 73.3% | 26.7% |
| 36,602 | HALE | 10,154 | 8,025 | 2,078 | 51 | 5,947 R | 79.0% | 20.5% | 79.4% | 20.6% |
| 3,782 | HALL | 1,277 | 860 | 413 | 4 | 447 R | 67.3% | 32.3% | 67.6% | 32.4% |
| 8,229 | HAMILTON | 3,730 | 2,856 | 845 | 29 | 2,011 R | 76.6% | 22.7% | 77.2% | 22.8% |
| 5,369 | HANSFORD | 2,147 | 1,903 | 240 | 4 | 1,663 R | 88.6% | 11.2% | 88.8% | 11.2% |
| 4,724 | HARDEMAN | 1,702 | 1,214 | 480 | 8 | 734 R | 71.3% | 28.2% | 71.7% | 28.3% |
| 48,073 | HARDIN | 20,710 | 15,030 | 5,608 | 72 | 9,422 R | 72.6% | 27.1% | 72.8% | 27.2% |
| 3,400,578 | HARRIS | 1,067,968 | 584,723 | 475,865 | 7,380 | 108,858 R | 54.8% | 44.6% | 55.1% | 44.9% |
| 62,110 | HARRISON | 26,223 | 16,473 | 9,642 | 108 | 6,831 R | 62.8% | 36.8% | 63.1% | 36.9% |
| 5,537 | HARTLEY | 2,059 | 1,736 | 315 | 8 | 1,421 R | 84.3% | 15.3% | 84.6% | 15.4% |
| 6,093 | HASKELL | 2,416 | 1,539 | 867 | 10 | 672 R | 63.7% | 35.9% | 64.0% | 36.0% |
| 97,589 | HAYS | 47,823 | 27,021 | 20,110 | 692 | 6,911 R | 56.5% | 42.1% | 57.3% | 42.7% |
| 3,351 | HEMPHILL | 1,643 | 1,380 | 257 | 6 | 1,123 R | 84.0% | 15.6% | 84.3% | 15.7% |
| 73,277 | HENDERSON | 28,849 | 20,210 | 8,505 | 134 | 11,705 R | 70.1% | 29.5% | 70.4% | 29.6% |
| 569,463 | HIDALGO | 113,683 | 50,931 | 62,369 | 383 | 11,438 D | 44.8% | 54.9% | 45.0% | 55.0% |
| 32,321 | HILL | 13,053 | 9,225 | 3,751 | 77 | 5,474 R | 70.7% | 28.7% | 71.1% | 28.9% |
| 22,716 | HOCKLEY | 7,577 | 6,160 | 1,385 | 32 | 4,775 R | 81.3% | 18.3% | 81.6% | 18.4% |
| 41,100 | HOOD | 21,293 | 16,280 | 4,865 | 148 | 11,415 R | 76.5% | 22.8% | 77.0% | 23.0% |
| 31,960 | HOPKINS | 12,062 | 8,582 | 3,443 | 37 | 5,139 R | 71.1% | 28.5% | 71.4% | 28.6% |
| 23,185 | HOUSTON | 8,806 | 5,848 | 2,921 | 37 | 2,927 R | 66.4% | 33.2% | 66.7% | 33.3% |
| 33,627 | HOWARD | 10,201 | 7,480 | 2,663 | 58 | 4,817 R | 73.3% | 26.1% | 73.7% | 26.3% |
| 3,344 | HUDSPETH | 886 | 577 | 302 | 7 | 275 R | 65.1% | 34.1% | 65.6% | 34.4% |
| 76,596 | HUNT | 28,194 | 20,065 | 7,971 | 158 | 12,094 R | 71.2% | 28.3% | 71.6% | 28.4% |
| 23,857 | HUTCHINSON | 9,369 | 7,839 | 1,503 | 27 | 6,336 R | 83.7% | 16.0% | 83.9% | 16.1% |
| 1,771 | IRION | 828 | 684 | 141 | 3 | 543 R | 82.6% | 17.0% | 82.9% | 17.1% |
| 8,763 | JACK | 3,126 | 2,470 | 643 | 13 | 1,827 R | 79.0% | 20.6% | 79.3% | 20.7% |
| 14,391 | JACKSON | 5,077 | 3,766 | 1,296 | 15 | 2,470 R | 74.2% | 25.5% | 74.4% | 25.6% |

# TEXAS

## PRESIDENT 2004

| 2000 Census Population | County | Total Vote | Republican | Democratic | Other | Rep.-Dem. Plurality | Percentage | | | |
|---|---|---|---|---|---|---|---|---|---|---|
| | | | | | | | Total Vote | | Major Vote | |
| | | | | | | | Rep. | Dem. | Rep. | Dem. |
| 35,604 | JASPER | 12,873 | 8,347 | 4,471 | 55 | 3,876 R | 64.8% | 34.7% | 65.1% | 34.9% |
| 2,207 | JEFF DAVIS | 1,167 | 764 | 378 | 25 | 386 R | 65.5% | 32.4% | 66.9% | 33.1% |
| 252,051 | JEFFERSON | 91,866 | 44,423 | 47,066 | 377 | 2,643 D | 48.4% | 51.2% | 48.6% | 51.4% |
| 5,281 | JIM HOGG | 2,065 | 712 | 1,344 | 9 | 632 D | 34.5% | 65.1% | 34.6% | 65.4% |
| 39,326 | JIM WELLS | 12,691 | 5,817 | 6,824 | 50 | 1,007 D | 45.8% | 53.8% | 46.0% | 54.0% |
| 126,811 | JOHNSON | 47,422 | 34,818 | 12,325 | 279 | 22,493 R | 73.4% | 26.0% | 73.9% | 26.1% |
| 20,785 | JONES | 5,931 | 4,254 | 1,658 | 19 | 2,596 R | 71.7% | 28.0% | 72.0% | 28.0% |
| 15,446 | KARNES | 4,673 | 3,114 | 1,543 | 16 | 1,571 R | 66.6% | 33.0% | 66.9% | 33.1% |
| 71,313 | KAUFMAN | 30,366 | 21,304 | 8,947 | 115 | 12,357 R | 70.2% | 29.5% | 70.4% | 29.6% |
| 23,743 | KENDALL | 14,072 | 11,434 | 2,532 | 106 | 8,902 R | 81.3% | 18.0% | 81.9% | 18.1% |
| 414 | KENEDY | 169 | 82 | 85 | 2 | 3 D | 48.5% | 50.3% | 49.1% | 50.9% |
| 859 | KENT | 522 | 382 | 138 | 2 | 244 R | 73.2% | 26.4% | 73.5% | 26.5% |
| 43,653 | KERR | 21,246 | 16,538 | 4,557 | 151 | 11,981 R | 77.8% | 21.4% | 78.4% | 21.6% |
| 4,468 | KIMBLE | 1,816 | 1,482 | 324 | 10 | 1,158 R | 81.6% | 17.8% | 82.1% | 17.9% |
| 356 | KING | 156 | 137 | 18 | 1 | 119 R | 87.8% | 11.5% | 88.4% | 11.6% |
| 3,379 | KINNEY | 1,600 | 1,051 | 542 | 7 | 509 R | 65.7% | 33.9% | 66.0% | 34.0% |
| 31,549 | KLEBERG | 9,973 | 5,366 | 4,550 | 57 | 816 R | 53.8% | 45.6% | 54.1% | 45.9% |
| 4,253 | KNOX | 1,552 | 1,081 | 464 | 7 | 617 R | 69.7% | 29.9% | 70.0% | 30.0% |
| 48,499 | LAMAR | 17,470 | 12,054 | 5,338 | 78 | 6,716 R | 69.0% | 30.6% | 69.3% | 30.7% |
| 14,709 | LAMB | 4,271 | 3,410 | 857 | 4 | 2,553 R | 79.8% | 20.1% | 79.9% | 20.1% |
| 17,762 | LAMPASAS | 7,025 | 5,422 | 1,593 | 10 | 3,829 R | 77.2% | 22.7% | 77.3% | 22.7% |
| 5,866 | LA SALLE | 2,230 | 989 | 1,229 | 12 | 240 D | 44.3% | 55.1% | 44.6% | 55.4% |
| 19,210 | LAVACA | 8,177 | 5,974 | 2,152 | 51 | 3,822 R | 73.1% | 26.3% | 73.5% | 26.5% |
| 15,657 | LEE | 6,088 | 4,160 | 1,899 | 29 | 2,261 R | 68.3% | 31.2% | 68.7% | 31.3% |
| 15,335 | LEON | 6,799 | 5,023 | 1,754 | 22 | 3,269 R | 73.9% | 25.8% | 74.1% | 25.9% |
| 70,154 | LIBERTY | 21,691 | 14,821 | 6,780 | 90 | 8,041 R | 68.3% | 31.3% | 68.6% | 31.4% |
| 22,051 | LIMESTONE | 7,818 | 5,028 | 2,752 | 38 | 2,276 R | 64.3% | 35.2% | 64.6% | 35.4% |
| 3,057 | LIPSCOMB | 1,337 | 1,147 | 184 | 6 | 963 R | 85.8% | 13.8% | 86.2% | 13.8% |
| 12,309 | LIVE OAK | 4,201 | 3,147 | 1,036 | 18 | 2,111 R | 74.9% | 24.7% | 75.2% | 24.8% |
| 17,044 | LLANO | 9,563 | 7,241 | 2,257 | 65 | 4,984 R | 75.7% | 23.6% | 76.2% | 23.8% |
| 67 | LOVING | 80 | 65 | 12 | 3 | 53 R | 81.3% | 15.0% | 84.4% | 15.6% |
| 242,628 | LUBBOCK | 93,151 | 70,135 | 22,472 | 544 | 47,663 R | 75.3% | 24.1% | 75.7% | 24.3% |
| 6,550 | LYNN | 2,271 | 1,776 | 490 | 5 | 1,286 R | 78.2% | 21.6% | 78.4% | 21.6% |
| 8,205 | MCCULLOCH | 3,220 | 2,465 | 745 | 10 | 1,720 R | 76.6% | 23.1% | 76.8% | 23.2% |
| 213,517 | MCLENNAN | 79,254 | 52,090 | 26,760 | 404 | 25,330 R | 65.7% | 33.8% | 66.1% | 33.9% |
| 851 | MCMULLEN | 564 | 467 | 95 | 2 | 372 R | 82.8% | 16.8% | 83.1% | 16.9% |
| 12,940 | MADISON | 4,101 | 2,837 | 1,235 | 29 | 1,602 R | 69.2% | 30.1% | 69.7% | 30.3% |
| 10,941 | MARION | 4,348 | 2,441 | 1,884 | 23 | 557 R | 56.1% | 43.3% | 56.4% | 43.6% |
| 4,746 | MARTIN | 1,807 | 1,514 | 288 | 5 | 1,226 R | 83.8% | 15.9% | 84.0% | 16.0% |
| 3,738 | MASON | 2,077 | 1,600 | 459 | 18 | 1,141 R | 77.0% | 22.1% | 77.7% | 22.3% |
| 37,957 | MATAGORDA | 12,521 | 8,119 | 4,355 | 47 | 3,764 R | 64.8% | 34.8% | 65.1% | 34.9% |
| 47,297 | MAVERICK | 10,034 | 4,025 | 5,948 | 61 | 1,923 D | 40.1% | 59.3% | 40.4% | 59.6% |
| 39,304 | MEDINA | 14,826 | 10,389 | 4,322 | 115 | 6,067 R | 70.1% | 29.2% | 70.6% | 29.4% |
| 2,360 | MENARD | 1,103 | 761 | 331 | 11 | 430 R | 69.0% | 30.0% | 69.7% | 30.3% |
| 116,009 | MIDLAND | 44,834 | 36,585 | 8,005 | 244 | 28,580 R | 81.6% | 17.9% | 82.0% | 18.0% |
| 24,238 | MILAM | 8,783 | 5,291 | 3,445 | 47 | 1,846 R | 60.2% | 39.2% | 60.6% | 39.4% |
| 5,151 | MILLS | 2,231 | 1,794 | 416 | 21 | 1,378 R | 80.4% | 18.6% | 81.2% | 18.8% |
| 9,698 | MITCHELL | 2,558 | 1,912 | 639 | 7 | 1,273 R | 74.7% | 25.0% | 75.0% | 25.0% |
| 19,117 | MONTAGUE | 7,897 | 5,910 | 1,946 | 41 | 3,964 R | 74.8% | 24.6% | 75.2% | 24.8% |
| 293,768 | MONTGOMERY | 133,988 | 104,654 | 28,628 | 706 | 76,026 R | 78.1% | 21.4% | 78.5% | 21.5% |
| 20,121 | MOORE | 5,628 | 4,601 | 1,009 | 18 | 3,592 R | 81.8% | 17.9% | 82.0% | 18.0% |
| 13,048 | MORRIS | 5,278 | 2,818 | 2,437 | 23 | 381 R | 53.4% | 46.2% | 53.6% | 46.4% |
| 1,426 | MOTLEY | 684 | 564 | 113 | 7 | 451 R | 82.5% | 16.5% | 83.3% | 16.7% |
| 59,203 | NACOGDOCHES | 21,466 | 14,160 | 7,152 | 154 | 7,008 R | 66.0% | 33.3% | 66.4% | 33.6% |
| 45,124 | NAVARRO | 16,034 | 10,715 | 5,259 | 60 | 5,456 R | 66.8% | 32.8% | 67.1% | 32.9% |
| 15,072 | NEWTON | 5,700 | 3,159 | 2,513 | 28 | 646 R | 55.4% | 44.1% | 55.7% | 44.3% |
| 15,802 | NOLAN | 5,289 | 3,722 | 1,541 | 26 | 2,181 R | 70.4% | 29.1% | 70.7% | 29.3% |
| 313,645 | NUECES | 104,560 | 59,359 | 44,439 | 762 | 14,920 R | 56.8% | 42.5% | 57.2% | 42.8% |
| 9,006 | OCHILTREE | 3,177 | 2,922 | 251 | 4 | 2,671 R | 92.0% | 7.9% | 92.1% | 7.9% |
| 2,185 | OLDHAM | 843 | 733 | 108 | 2 | 625 R | 87.0% | 12.8% | 87.2% | 12.8% |

# TEXAS

## PRESIDENT 2004

| 2000 Census Population | County | Total Vote | Republican | Democratic | Other | Rep.-Dem. Plurality | Percentage | | | |
|---|---|---|---|---|---|---|---|---|---|---|
| | | | | | | | Total Vote | | Major Vote | |
| | | | | | | | Rep. | Dem. | Rep. | Dem. |
| 84,966 | ORANGE | 31,908 | 20,292 | 11,476 | 140 | 8,816 R | 63.6% | 36.0% | 63.9% | 36.1% |
| 27,026 | PALO PINTO | 10,014 | 7,137 | 2,816 | 61 | 4,321 R | 71.3% | 28.1% | 71.7% | 28.3% |
| 22,756 | PANOLA | 10,007 | 7,021 | 2,958 | 28 | 4,063 R | 70.2% | 29.6% | 70.4% | 29.6% |
| 88,495 | PARKER | 40,957 | 31,795 | 8,966 | 196 | 22,829 R | 77.6% | 21.9% | 78.0% | 22.0% |
| 10,016 | PARMER | 2,773 | 2,375 | 389 | 9 | 1,986 R | 85.6% | 14.0% | 85.9% | 14.1% |
| 16,809 | PECOS | 4,428 | 3,167 | 1,242 | 19 | 1,925 R | 71.5% | 28.0% | 71.8% | 28.2% |
| 41,133 | POLK | 20,846 | 13,778 | 6,964 | 104 | 6,814 R | 66.1% | 33.4% | 66.4% | 33.6% |
| 113,546 | POTTER | 29,056 | 21,401 | 7,489 | 166 | 13,912 R | 73.7% | 25.8% | 74.1% | 25.9% |
| 7,304 | PRESIDIO | 1,890 | 715 | 1,159 | 16 | 444 D | 37.8% | 61.3% | 38.2% | 61.8% |
| 9,139 | RAINS | 4,229 | 2,998 | 1,213 | 18 | 1,785 R | 70.9% | 28.7% | 71.2% | 28.8% |
| 104,312 | RANDALL | 48,587 | 40,520 | 7,849 | 218 | 32,671 R | 83.4% | 16.2% | 83.8% | 16.2% |
| 3,326 | REAGAN | 1,143 | 956 | 184 | 3 | 772 R | 83.6% | 16.1% | 83.9% | 16.1% |
| 3,047 | REAL | 1,645 | 1,314 | 325 | 6 | 989 R | 79.9% | 19.8% | 80.2% | 19.8% |
| 14,314 | RED RIVER | 5,490 | 3,379 | 2,097 | 14 | 1,282 R | 61.5% | 38.2% | 61.7% | 38.3% |
| 13,137 | REEVES | 3,395 | 1,777 | 1,600 | 18 | 177 R | 52.3% | 47.1% | 52.6% | 47.4% |
| 7,828 | REFUGIO | 3,455 | 2,212 | 1,232 | 11 | 980 R | 64.0% | 35.7% | 64.2% | 35.8% |
| 887 | ROBERTS | 507 | 461 | 46 | | 415 R | 90.9% | 9.1% | 90.9% | 9.1% |
| 16,000 | ROBERTSON | 6,795 | 3,792 | 2,979 | 24 | 813 R | 55.8% | 43.8% | 56.0% | 44.0% |
| 43,080 | ROCKWALL | 25,581 | 20,120 | 5,320 | 141 | 14,800 R | 78.7% | 20.8% | 79.1% | 20.9% |
| 11,495 | RUNNELS | 4,049 | 3,239 | 792 | 18 | 2,447 R | 80.0% | 19.6% | 80.4% | 19.6% |
| 47,372 | RUSK | 18,344 | 13,390 | 4,899 | 55 | 8,491 R | 73.0% | 26.7% | 73.2% | 26.8% |
| 10,469 | SABINE | 4,639 | 3,138 | 1,476 | 25 | 1,662 R | 67.6% | 31.8% | 68.0% | 32.0% |
| 8,946 | SAN AUGUSTINE | 3,757 | 2,235 | 1,506 | 16 | 729 R | 59.5% | 40.1% | 59.7% | 40.3% |
| 22,246 | SAN JACINTO | 8,125 | 5,394 | 2,688 | 43 | 2,706 R | 66.4% | 33.1% | 66.7% | 33.3% |
| 67,138 | SAN PATRICIO | 21,320 | 13,474 | 7,764 | 82 | 5,710 R | 63.2% | 36.4% | 63.4% | 36.6% |
| 6,186 | SAN SABA | 2,431 | 1,894 | 529 | 8 | 1,365 R | 77.9% | 21.8% | 78.2% | 21.8% |
| 2,935 | SCHLEICHER | 1,329 | 1,012 | 312 | 5 | 700 R | 76.1% | 23.5% | 76.4% | 23.6% |
| 16,361 | SCURRY | 5,572 | 4,576 | 981 | 15 | 3,595 R | 82.1% | 17.6% | 82.3% | 17.7% |
| 3,302 | SHACKELFORD | 1,527 | 1,292 | 229 | 6 | 1,063 R | 84.6% | 15.0% | 84.9% | 15.1% |
| 25,224 | SHELBY | 9,279 | 6,295 | 2,951 | 33 | 3,344 R | 67.8% | 31.8% | 68.1% | 31.9% |
| 3,186 | SHERMAN | 1,066 | 942 | 124 | | 818 R | 88.4% | 11.6% | 88.4% | 11.6% |
| 174,706 | SMITH | 73,664 | 53,392 | 19,970 | 302 | 33,422 R | 72.5% | 27.1% | 72.8% | 27.2% |
| 6,809 | SOMERVELL | 3,551 | 2,701 | 831 | 19 | 1,870 R | 76.1% | 23.4% | 76.5% | 23.5% |
| 53,597 | STARR | 9,781 | 2,552 | 7,199 | 30 | 4,647 D | 26.1% | 73.6% | 26.2% | 73.8% |
| 9,674 | STEPHENS | 3,519 | 2,803 | 703 | 13 | 2,100 R | 79.7% | 20.0% | 79.9% | 20.1% |
| 1,393 | STERLING | 615 | 544 | 71 | | 473 R | 88.5% | 11.5% | 88.5% | 11.5% |
| 1,693 | STONEWALL | 752 | 499 | 250 | 3 | 249 R | 66.4% | 33.2% | 66.6% | 33.4% |
| 4,077 | SUTTON | 1,453 | 1,173 | 280 | | 893 R | 80.7% | 19.3% | 80.7% | 19.3% |
| 8,378 | SWISHER | 2,120 | 1,487 | 626 | 7 | 861 R | 70.1% | 29.5% | 70.4% | 29.6% |
| 1,446,219 | TARRANT | 560,141 | 349,462 | 207,286 | 3,393 | 142,176 R | 62.4% | 37.0% | 62.8% | 37.2% |
| 126,555 | TAYLOR | 48,099 | 37,197 | 10,648 | 254 | 26,549 R | 77.3% | 22.1% | 77.7% | 22.3% |
| 1,081 | TERRELL | 469 | 306 | 159 | 4 | 147 R | 65.2% | 33.9% | 65.8% | 34.2% |
| 12,761 | TERRY | 3,970 | 3,166 | 794 | 10 | 2,372 R | 79.7% | 20.0% | 79.9% | 20.1% |
| 1,850 | THROCKMORTON | 863 | 656 | 202 | 5 | 454 R | 76.0% | 23.4% | 76.5% | 23.5% |
| 28,118 | TITUS | 8,907 | 5,709 | 3,173 | 25 | 2,536 R | 64.1% | 35.6% | 64.3% | 35.7% |
| 104,010 | TOM GREEN | 37,417 | 28,185 | 9,007 | 225 | 19,178 R | 75.3% | 24.1% | 75.8% | 24.2% |
| 812,280 | TRAVIS | 352,113 | 147,885 | 197,235 | 6,993 | 49,350 D | 42.0% | 56.0% | 42.9% | 57.1% |
| 13,779 | TRINITY | 6,213 | 3,985 | 2,204 | 24 | 1,781 R | 64.1% | 35.5% | 64.4% | 35.6% |
| 20,871 | TYLER | 7,745 | 5,043 | 2,659 | 43 | 2,384 R | 65.1% | 34.3% | 65.5% | 34.5% |
| 35,291 | UPSHUR | 14,526 | 10,232 | 4,225 | 69 | 6,007 R | 70.4% | 29.1% | 70.8% | 29.2% |
| 3,404 | UPTON | 1,197 | 1,009 | 185 | 3 | 824 R | 84.3% | 15.5% | 84.5% | 15.5% |
| 25,926 | UVALDE | 8,483 | 5,148 | 3,298 | 37 | 1,850 R | 60.7% | 38.9% | 61.0% | 39.0% |
| 44,856 | VAL VERDE | 11,795 | 6,968 | 4,757 | 70 | 2,211 R | 59.1% | 40.3% | 59.4% | 40.6% |
| 48,140 | VAN ZANDT | 19,856 | 14,976 | 4,822 | 58 | 10,154 R | 75.4% | 24.3% | 75.6% | 24.4% |
| 84,088 | VICTORIA | 29,602 | 20,875 | 8,553 | 174 | 12,322 R | 70.5% | 28.9% | 70.9% | 29.1% |
| 61,758 | WALKER | 17,822 | 11,710 | 5,977 | 135 | 5,733 R | 65.7% | 33.5% | 66.2% | 33.8% |
| 32,663 | WALLER | 13,881 | 7,679 | 6,145 | 57 | 1,534 R | 55.3% | 44.3% | 55.5% | 44.5% |
| 10,909 | WARD | 3,768 | 2,856 | 901 | 11 | 1,955 R | 75.8% | 23.9% | 76.0% | 24.0% |
| 30,373 | WASHINGTON | 13,063 | 9,597 | 3,389 | 77 | 6,208 R | 73.5% | 25.9% | 73.9% | 26.1% |
| 193,117 | WEBB | 41,556 | 17,753 | 23,654 | 149 | 5,901 D | 42.7% | 56.9% | 42.9% | 57.1% |

# TEXAS

## PRESIDENT 2004

| 2000 Census Population | County | Total Vote | Republican | Democratic | Other | Rep.-Dem. Plurality | Percentage | | | |
|---|---|---|---|---|---|---|---|---|---|---|
| | | | | | | | Total Vote | | Major Vote | |
| | | | | | | | Rep. | Dem. | Rep. | Dem. |
| 41,188 | WHARTON | 14,039 | 9,288 | 4,702 | 49 | 4,586 R | 66.2% | 33.5% | 66.4% | 33.6% |
| 5,284 | WHEELER | 2,394 | 1,960 | 420 | 14 | 1,540 R | 81.9% | 17.5% | 82.4% | 17.6% |
| 131,664 | WICHITA | 45,545 | 32,472 | 12,819 | 254 | 19,653 R | 71.3% | 28.1% | 71.7% | 28.3% |
| 14,676 | WILBARGER | 4,990 | 3,685 | 1,284 | 21 | 2,401 R | 73.8% | 25.7% | 74.2% | 25.8% |
| 20,082 | WILLACY | 4,962 | 2,209 | 2,734 | 19 | 525 D | 44.5% | 55.1% | 44.7% | 55.3% |
| 249,967 | WILLIAMSON | 128,198 | 83,284 | 43,117 | 1,797 | 40,167 R | 65.0% | 33.6% | 65.9% | 34.1% |
| 32,408 | WILSON | 14,885 | 10,400 | 4,409 | 76 | 5,991 R | 69.9% | 29.6% | 70.2% | 29.8% |
| 7,173 | WINKLER | 2,002 | 1,604 | 391 | 7 | 1,213 R | 80.1% | 19.5% | 80.4% | 19.6% |
| 48,793 | WISE | 20,047 | 15,177 | 4,783 | 87 | 10,394 R | 75.7% | 23.9% | 76.0% | 24.0% |
| 36,752 | WOOD | 16,929 | 12,831 | 4,034 | 64 | 8,797 R | 75.8% | 23.8% | 76.1% | 23.9% |
| 7,322 | YOAKUM | 2,613 | 2,228 | 376 | 9 | 1,852 R | 85.3% | 14.4% | 85.6% | 14.4% |
| 17,943 | YOUNG | 7,409 | 5,874 | 1,511 | 24 | 4,363 R | 79.3% | 20.4% | 79.5% | 20.5% |
| 12,182 | ZAPATA | 2,898 | 1,228 | 1,662 | 8 | 434 D | 42.4% | 57.3% | 42.5% | 57.5% |
| 11,600 | ZAVALA | 3,118 | 777 | 2,332 | 9 | 1,555 D | 24.9% | 74.8% | 25.0% | 75.0% |
| 20,851,820 | TOTAL | 7,410,765 | 4,526,917 | 2,832,704 | 51,144 | 1,694,213 R | 61.1% | 38.2% | 61.5% | 38.5% |

# TEXAS

## PRESIDENT 2000

| 2000 Census Population | County | Total Vote | Republican | Democratic | Green (Nader) | Other | Rep.-Dem. Plurality | Percentage of Total Vote | | |
|---|---|---|---|---|---|---|---|---|---|---|
| | | | | | | | | Rep. | Dem. | Green |
| 55,109 | ANDERSON | 15,080 | 9,835 | 5,041 | 131 | 73 | 4,794 R | 65.2% | 33.4% | 0.9% |
| 13,004 | ANDREWS | 4,024 | 3,091 | 876 | 28 | 29 | 2,215 R | 76.8% | 21.8% | 0.7% |
| 80,130 | ANGELINA | 26,974 | 16,648 | 9,957 | 245 | 124 | 6,691 R | 61.7% | 36.9% | 0.9% |
| 22,497 | ARANSAS | 8,247 | 5,390 | 2,637 | 182 | 38 | 2,753 R | 65.4% | 32.0% | 2.2% |
| 8,854 | ARCHER | 3,997 | 2,951 | 993 | 36 | 17 | 1,958 R | 73.8% | 24.8% | 0.9% |
| 2,148 | ARMSTRONG | 938 | 772 | 150 | 11 | 5 | 622 R | 82.3% | 16.0% | 1.2% |
| 38,628 | ATASCOSA | 10,746 | 6,231 | 4,322 | 130 | 63 | 1,909 R | 58.0% | 40.2% | 1.2% |
| 23,590 | AUSTIN | 9,227 | 6,661 | 2,407 | 112 | 47 | 4,254 R | 72.2% | 26.1% | 1.2% |
| 6,594 | BAILEY | 2,090 | 1,589 | 488 | 6 | 7 | 1,101 R | 76.0% | 23.3% | 0.3% |
| 17,645 | BANDERA | 7,273 | 5,613 | 1,426 | 157 | 77 | 4,187 R | 77.2% | 19.6% | 2.2% |
| 57,733 | BASTROP | 18,308 | 10,310 | 6,973 | 871 | 154 | 3,337 R | 56.3% | 38.1% | 4.8% |
| 4,093 | BAYLOR | 1,984 | 1,285 | 663 | 26 | 10 | 622 R | 64.8% | 33.4% | 1.3% |
| 32,359 | BEE | 8,330 | 4,429 | 3,795 | 66 | 40 | 634 R | 53.2% | 45.6% | 0.8% |
| 237,974 | BELL | 63,291 | 41,208 | 21,011 | 728 | 344 | 20,197 R | 65.1% | 33.2% | 1.2% |
| 1,392,931 | BEXAR | 412,726 | 215,613 | 185,158 | 9,790 | 2,165 | 30,455 R | 52.2% | 44.9% | 2.4% |
| 8,418 | BLANCO | 3,767 | 2,777 | 811 | 140 | 39 | 1,966 R | 73.7% | 21.5% | 3.7% |
| 729 | BORDEN | 353 | 283 | 62 | 5 | 3 | 221 R | 80.2% | 17.6% | 1.4% |
| 17,204 | BOSQUE | 6,770 | 4,745 | 1,930 | 65 | 30 | 2,815 R | 70.1% | 28.5% | 1.0% |
| 89,306 | BOWIE | 30,320 | 18,325 | 11,662 | 238 | 95 | 6,663 R | 60.4% | 38.5% | 0.8% |
| 241,767 | BRAZORIA | 80,019 | 53,445 | 24,883 | 1,212 | 479 | 28,562 R | 66.8% | 31.1% | 1.5% |
| 152,415 | BRAZOS | 46,941 | 32,864 | 12,359 | 1,351 | 367 | 20,505 R | 70.0% | 26.3% | 2.9% |
| 8,866 | BREWSTER | 3,580 | 1,867 | 1,349 | 306 | 58 | 518 R | 52.2% | 37.7% | 8.5% |
| 1,790 | BRISCOE | 772 | 544 | 224 | 1 | 3 | 320 R | 70.5% | 29.0% | 0.1% |
| 7,976 | BROOKS | 2,431 | 556 | 1,854 | 14 | 7 | 1,298 D | 22.9% | 76.3% | 0.6% |
| 37,674 | BROWN | 12,920 | 9,609 | 3,138 | 125 | 48 | 6,471 R | 74.4% | 24.3% | 1.0% |
| 16,470 | BURLESON | 5,866 | 3,542 | 2,235 | 60 | 29 | 1,307 R | 60.4% | 38.1% | 1.0% |
| 34,147 | BURNET | 13,232 | 9,286 | 3,557 | 292 | 97 | 5,729 R | 70.2% | 26.9% | 2.2% |
| 32,194 | CALDWELL | 9,425 | 5,216 | 3,872 | 266 | 71 | 1,344 R | 55.3% | 41.1% | 2.8% |
| 20,647 | CALHOUN | 6,563 | 3,724 | 2,766 | 43 | 30 | 958 R | 56.7% | 42.1% | 0.7% |
| 12,905 | CALLAHAN | 4,896 | 3,656 | 1,174 | 34 | 32 | 2,482 R | 74.7% | 24.0% | 0.7% |
| 335,227 | CAMERON | 62,057 | 27,800 | 33,214 | 699 | 344 | 5,414 D | 44.8% | 53.5% | 1.1% |
| 11,549 | CAMP | 3,784 | 2,121 | 1,625 | 31 | 7 | 496 R | 56.1% | 42.9% | 0.8% |
| 6,516 | CARSON | 2,742 | 2,216 | 480 | 29 | 17 | 1,736 R | 80.8% | 17.5% | 1.1% |
| 30,438 | CASS | 11,019 | 6,295 | 4,618 | 68 | 38 | 1,677 R | 57.1% | 41.9% | 0.6% |
| 8,285 | CASTRO | 2,354 | 1,607 | 727 | 7 | 13 | 880 R | 68.3% | 30.9% | 0.3% |
| 26,031 | CHAMBERS | 9,806 | 6,769 | 2,888 | 111 | 38 | 3,881 R | 69.0% | 29.5% | 1.1% |
| 46,659 | CHEROKEE | 14,537 | 9,599 | 4,755 | 122 | 61 | 4,844 R | 66.0% | 32.7% | 0.8% |
| 7,688 | CHILDRESS | 2,126 | 1,506 | 602 | 11 | 7 | 904 R | 70.8% | 28.3% | 0.5% |
| 11,006 | CLAY | 4,637 | 3,112 | 1,460 | 39 | 26 | 1,652 R | 67.1% | 31.5% | 0.8% |
| 3,730 | COCHRAN | 1,171 | 807 | 344 | 11 | 9 | 463 R | 68.9% | 29.4% | 0.9% |
| 3,864 | COKE | 1,515 | 1,137 | 355 | 14 | 9 | 782 R | 75.0% | 23.4% | 0.9% |
| 9,235 | COLEMAN | 3,578 | 2,687 | 853 | 27 | 11 | 1,834 R | 75.1% | 23.8% | 0.8% |
| 491,675 | COLLIN | 175,420 | 128,179 | 42,884 | 3,195 | 1,162 | 85,295 R | 73.1% | 24.4% | 1.8% |
| 3,206 | COLLINGSWORTH | 1,415 | 974 | 429 | 6 | 6 | 545 R | 68.8% | 30.3% | 0.4% |
| 20,390 | COLORADO | 7,249 | 4,913 | 2,229 | 84 | 23 | 2,684 R | 67.8% | 30.7% | 1.2% |
| 78,021 | COMAL | 32,748 | 24,599 | 7,131 | 787 | 231 | 17,468 R | 75.1% | 21.8% | 2.4% |
| 14,026 | COMANCHE | 5,022 | 3,334 | 1,636 | 33 | 19 | 1,698 R | 66.4% | 32.6% | 0.7% |
| 3,966 | CONCHO | 1,103 | 818 | 268 | 10 | 7 | 550 R | 74.2% | 24.3% | 0.9% |
| 36,363 | COOKE | 13,469 | 10,128 | 3,153 | 124 | 64 | 6,975 R | 75.2% | 23.4% | 0.9% |
| 74,978 | CORYELL | 15,087 | 10,321 | 4,493 | 202 | 71 | 5,828 R | 68.4% | 29.8% | 1.3% |
| 1,904 | COTTLE | 757 | 502 | 241 | 3 | 11 | 261 R | 66.3% | 31.8% | 0.4% |
| 3,996 | CRANE | 1,654 | 1,246 | 387 | 16 | 5 | 859 R | 75.3% | 23.4% | 1.0% |
| 4,099 | CROCKETT | 1,398 | 924 | 467 | 2 | 5 | 457 R | 66.1% | 33.4% | 0.1% |
| 7,072 | CROSBY | 2,002 | 1,270 | 705 | 23 | 4 | 565 R | 63.4% | 35.2% | 1.1% |
| 2,975 | CULBERSON | 1,012 | 413 | 577 | 12 | 10 | 164 D | 40.8% | 57.0% | 1.2% |
| 6,222 | DALLAM | 1,744 | 1,385 | 341 | 11 | 7 | 1,044 R | 79.4% | 19.6% | 0.6% |
| 2,218,899 | DALLAS | 613,039 | 322,345 | 275,308 | 11,671 | 3,715 | 47,037 R | 52.6% | 44.9% | 1.9% |
| 14,985 | DAWSON | 4,839 | 3,337 | 1,463 | 17 | 22 | 1,874 R | 69.0% | 30.2% | 0.4% |
| 18,561 | DEAF SMITH | 4,984 | 3,687 | 1,240 | 27 | 30 | 2,447 R | 74.0% | 24.9% | 0.5% |
| 5,327 | DELTA | 1,900 | 1,143 | 726 | 16 | 15 | 417 R | 60.2% | 38.2% | 0.8% |

# TEXAS

## PRESIDENT 2000

| 2000 Census Population | County | Total Vote | Republican | Democratic | Green (Nader) | Other | Rep.-Dem. Plurality | Percentage of Total Vote | | |
|---|---|---|---|---|---|---|---|---|---|---|
| | | | | | | | | Rep. | Dem. | Green |
| 432,976 | DENTON | 146,790 | 102,171 | 40,144 | 3,430 | 1,045 | 62,027 R | 69.6% | 27.3% | 2.3% |
| 20,013 | DE WITT | 6,183 | 4,541 | 1,570 | 53 | 19 | 2,971 R | 73.4% | 25.4% | 0.9% |
| 2,762 | DICKENS | 881 | 589 | 284 | 3 | 5 | 305 R | 66.9% | 32.2% | 0.3% |
| 10,248 | DIMMIT | 3,753 | 1,032 | 2,678 | 20 | 23 | 1,646 D | 27.5% | 71.4% | 0.5% |
| 3,828 | DONLEY | 1,719 | 1,333 | 360 | 18 | 8 | 973 R | 77.5% | 20.9% | 1.0% |
| 13,120 | DUVAL | 5,030 | 1,010 | 3,990 | 22 | 8 | 2,980 D | 20.1% | 79.3% | 0.4% |
| 18,297 | EASTLAND | 6,414 | 4,531 | 1,774 | 56 | 53 | 2,757 R | 70.6% | 27.7% | 0.9% |
| 121,123 | ECTOR | 32,901 | 22,893 | 9,425 | 378 | 205 | 13,468 R | 69.6% | 28.6% | 1.1% |
| 2,162 | EDWARDS | 937 | 663 | 261 | 6 | 7 | 402 R | 70.8% | 27.9% | 0.6% |
| 111,360 | ELLIS | 37,307 | 26,091 | 10,629 | 377 | 210 | 15,462 R | 69.9% | 28.5% | 1.0% |
| 679,622 | EL PASO | 145,042 | 57,574 | 83,848 | 2,840 | 780 | 26,274 D | 39.7% | 57.8% | 2.0% |
| 33,001 | ERATH | 11,115 | 8,126 | 2,804 | 129 | 56 | 5,322 R | 73.1% | 25.2% | 1.2% |
| 18,576 | FALLS | 5,715 | 3,239 | 2,417 | 33 | 26 | 822 R | 56.7% | 42.3% | 0.6% |
| 31,242 | FANNIN | 10,340 | 6,074 | 4,102 | 110 | 54 | 1,972 R | 58.7% | 39.7% | 1.1% |
| 21,804 | FAYETTE | 9,387 | 6,658 | 2,542 | 132 | 55 | 4,116 R | 70.9% | 27.1% | 1.4% |
| 4,344 | FISHER | 1,872 | 968 | 884 | 11 | 9 | 84 R | 51.7% | 47.2% | 0.6% |
| 7,771 | FLOYD | 2,420 | 1,830 | 580 | 8 | 2 | 1,250 R | 75.6% | 24.0% | 0.3% |
| 1,622 | FOARD | 556 | 286 | 263 | 5 | 2 | 23 R | 51.4% | 47.3% | 0.9% |
| 354,452 | FORT BEND | 123,509 | 73,567 | 47,569 | 1,953 | 420 | 25,998 R | 59.6% | 38.5% | 1.6% |
| 9,458 | FRANKLIN | 3,472 | 2,420 | 1,018 | 22 | 12 | 1,402 R | 69.7% | 29.3% | 0.6% |
| 17,867 | FREESTONE | 6,641 | 4,247 | 2,316 | 46 | 32 | 1,931 R | 64.0% | 34.9% | 0.7% |
| 16,252 | FRIO | 4,128 | 1,774 | 2,317 | 23 | 14 | 543 D | 43.0% | 56.1% | 0.6% |
| 14,467 | GAINES | 3,459 | 2,691 | 723 | 23 | 22 | 1,968 R | 77.8% | 20.9% | 0.7% |
| 250,158 | GALVESTON | 92,983 | 50,397 | 40,020 | 2,150 | 416 | 10,377 R | 54.2% | 43.0% | 2.3% |
| 4,872 | GARZA | 1,770 | 1,302 | 454 | 8 | 6 | 848 R | 73.6% | 25.6% | 0.5% |
| 20,814 | GILLESPIE | 9,920 | 8,096 | 1,511 | 220 | 93 | 6,585 R | 81.6% | 15.2% | 2.2% |
| 1,406 | GLASSCOCK | 571 | 528 | 39 | 3 | 1 | 489 R | 92.5% | 6.8% | 0.5% |
| 6,928 | GOLIAD | 3,392 | 2,108 | 1,233 | 27 | 24 | 875 R | 62.1% | 36.4% | 0.8% |
| 18,628 | GONZALES | 6,069 | 4,092 | 1,877 | 72 | 28 | 2,215 R | 67.4% | 30.9% | 1.2% |
| 22,744 | GRAY | 8,185 | 6,732 | 1,376 | 40 | 37 | 5,356 R | 82.2% | 16.8% | 0.5% |
| 110,595 | GRAYSON | 39,940 | 25,596 | 13,647 | 484 | 213 | 11,949 R | 64.1% | 34.2% | 1.2% |
| 111,379 | GREGG | 38,433 | 26,739 | 11,244 | 324 | 126 | 15,495 R | 69.6% | 29.3% | 0.8% |
| 23,552 | GRIMES | 6,802 | 4,197 | 2,450 | 98 | 57 | 1,747 R | 61.7% | 36.0% | 1.4% |
| 89,023 | GUADALUPE | 30,567 | 21,499 | 8,311 | 545 | 212 | 13,188 R | 70.3% | 27.2% | 1.8% |
| 36,602 | HALE | 9,110 | 6,868 | 2,158 | 45 | 39 | 4,710 R | 75.4% | 23.7% | 0.5% |
| 3,782 | HALL | 1,446 | 966 | 472 | 6 | 2 | 494 R | 66.8% | 32.6% | 0.4% |
| 8,229 | HAMILTON | 3,376 | 2,447 | 878 | 27 | 24 | 1,569 R | 72.5% | 26.0% | 0.8% |
| 5,369 | HANSFORD | 2,088 | 1,874 | 198 | 12 | 4 | 1,676 R | 89.8% | 9.5% | 0.6% |
| 4,724 | HARDEMAN | 1,557 | 976 | 566 | 10 | 5 | 410 R | 62.7% | 36.4% | 0.6% |
| 48,073 | HARDIN | 17,836 | 11,962 | 5,595 | 185 | 94 | 6,367 R | 67.1% | 31.4% | 1.0% |
| 3,400,578 | HARRIS | 974,822 | 529,159 | 418,267 | 22,994 | 4,402 | 110,892 R | 54.3% | 42.9% | 2.4% |
| 62,110 | HARRISON | 22,970 | 13,834 | 8,878 | 164 | 94 | 4,956 R | 60.2% | 38.7% | 0.7% |
| 5,537 | HARTLEY | 2,031 | 1,645 | 359 | 16 | 11 | 1,286 R | 81.0% | 17.7% | 0.8% |
| 6,093 | HASKELL | 2,927 | 1,488 | 1,401 | 23 | 15 | 87 R | 50.8% | 47.9% | 0.8% |
| 97,589 | HAYS | 34,317 | 20,170 | 11,387 | 2,451 | 309 | 8,783 R | 58.8% | 33.2% | 7.1% |
| 3,351 | HEMPHILL | 1,474 | 1,203 | 251 | 13 | 7 | 952 R | 81.6% | 17.0% | 0.9% |
| 73,277 | HENDERSON | 25,627 | 16,607 | 8,704 | 201 | 115 | 7,903 R | 64.8% | 34.0% | 0.8% |
| 569,463 | HIDALGO | 101,050 | 38,301 | 61,390 | 968 | 391 | 23,089 D | 37.9% | 60.8% | 1.0% |
| 32,321 | HILL | 10,735 | 7,054 | 3,524 | 100 | 57 | 3,530 R | 65.7% | 32.8% | 0.9% |
| 22,716 | HOCKLEY | 6,745 | 5,250 | 1,419 | 41 | 35 | 3,831 R | 77.8% | 21.0% | 0.6% |
| 41,100 | HOOD | 17,505 | 12,429 | 4,704 | 239 | 133 | 7,725 R | 71.0% | 26.9% | 1.4% |
| 31,960 | HOPKINS | 10,910 | 7,076 | 3,692 | 82 | 60 | 3,384 R | 64.9% | 33.8% | 0.8% |
| 23,185 | HOUSTON | 8,236 | 5,308 | 2,833 | 51 | 44 | 2,475 R | 64.4% | 34.4% | 0.6% |
| 33,627 | HOWARD | 9,548 | 6,668 | 2,744 | 75 | 61 | 3,924 R | 69.8% | 28.7% | 0.8% |
| 3,344 | HUDSPETH | 922 | 514 | 380 | 15 | 13 | 134 R | 55.7% | 41.2% | 1.6% |
| 76,596 | HUNT | 24,466 | 16,177 | 7,857 | 283 | 149 | 8,320 R | 66.1% | 32.1% | 1.2% |
| 23,857 | HUTCHINSON | 9,351 | 7,443 | 1,796 | 59 | 53 | 5,647 R | 79.6% | 19.2% | 0.6% |
| 1,771 | IRION | 793 | 624 | 162 | 2 | 5 | 462 R | 78.7% | 20.4% | 0.3% |
| 8,763 | JACK | 2,974 | 2,107 | 822 | 26 | 19 | 1,285 R | 70.8% | 27.6% | 0.9% |
| 14,391 | JACKSON | 4,856 | 3,365 | 1,446 | 33 | 12 | 1,919 R | 69.3% | 29.8% | 0.7% |

# TEXAS

## PRESIDENT 2000

| 2000 Census Population | County | Total Vote | Republican | Democratic | Green (Nader) | Other | Rep.-Dem. Plurality | Percentage of Total Vote | | |
|---|---|---|---|---|---|---|---|---|---|---|
| | | | | | | | | Rep. | Dem. | Green |
| 35,604 | JASPER | 11,742 | 7,071 | 4,533 | 87 | 51 | 2,538 R | 60.2% | 38.6% | 0.7% |
| 2,207 | JEFF DAVIS | 1,060 | 708 | 283 | 46 | 23 | 425 R | 66.8% | 26.7% | 4.3% |
| 252,051 | JEFFERSON | 86,909 | 40,320 | 45,409 | 796 | 384 | 5,089 D | 46.4% | 52.2% | 0.9% |
| 5,281 | JIM HOGG | 2,157 | 623 | 1,512 | 9 | 13 | 889 D | 28.9% | 70.1% | 0.4% |
| 39,326 | JIM WELLS | 12,023 | 4,498 | 7,418 | 73 | 34 | 2,920 D | 37.4% | 61.7% | 0.6% |
| 126,811 | JOHNSON | 38,726 | 26,202 | 11,778 | 513 | 233 | 14,424 R | 67.7% | 30.4% | 1.3% |
| 20,785 | JONES | 6,048 | 4,080 | 1,899 | 50 | 19 | 2,181 R | 67.5% | 31.4% | 0.8% |
| 15,446 | KARNES | 4,308 | 2,638 | 1,617 | 25 | 28 | 1,021 R | 61.2% | 37.5% | 0.6% |
| 71,313 | KAUFMAN | 23,063 | 15,290 | 7,455 | 207 | 111 | 7,835 R | 66.3% | 32.3% | 0.9% |
| 23,743 | KENDALL | 11,073 | 8,788 | 1,901 | 286 | 98 | 6,887 R | 79.4% | 17.2% | 2.6% |
| 414 | KENEDY | 228 | 106 | 119 | 2 | 1 | 13 D | 46.5% | 52.2% | 0.9% |
| 859 | KENT | 536 | 346 | 185 | | 5 | 161 R | 64.6% | 34.5% | |
| 43,653 | KERR | 19,228 | 14,637 | 4,002 | 463 | 126 | 10,635 R | 76.1% | 20.8% | 2.4% |
| 4,468 | KIMBLE | 1,666 | 1,313 | 328 | 15 | 10 | 985 R | 78.8% | 19.7% | 0.9% |
| 356 | KING | 137 | 120 | 14 | | 3 | 106 R | 87.6% | 10.2% | |
| 3,379 | KINNEY | 1,444 | 932 | 486 | 16 | 10 | 446 R | 64.5% | 33.7% | 1.1% |
| 31,549 | KLEBERG | 9,194 | 4,526 | 4,481 | 131 | 56 | 45 R | 49.2% | 48.7% | 1.4% |
| 4,253 | KNOX | 1,576 | 947 | 617 | 8 | 4 | 330 R | 60.1% | 39.1% | 0.5% |
| 48,499 | LAMAR | 15,430 | 9,775 | 5,553 | 99 | 3 | 4,222 R | 63.4% | 36.0% | 0.6% |
| 14,709 | LAMB | 4,598 | 3,451 | 1,114 | 15 | 18 | 2,337 R | 75.1% | 24.2% | 0.3% |
| 17,762 | LAMPASAS | 6,214 | 4,526 | 1,569 | 78 | 41 | 2,957 R | 72.8% | 25.2% | 1.3% |
| 5,866 | LA SALLE | 2,014 | 731 | 1,266 | 5 | 12 | 535 D | 36.3% | 62.9% | 0.2% |
| 19,210 | LAVACA | 7,546 | 5,288 | 2,171 | 53 | 34 | 3,117 R | 70.1% | 28.8% | 0.7% |
| 15,657 | LEE | 5,536 | 3,699 | 1,733 | 76 | 28 | 1,966 R | 66.8% | 31.3% | 1.4% |
| 15,335 | LEON | 6,326 | 4,362 | 1,893 | 46 | 25 | 2,469 R | 69.0% | 29.9% | 0.7% |
| 70,154 | LIBERTY | 20,077 | 12,458 | 7,311 | 199 | 109 | 5,147 R | 62.1% | 36.4% | 1.0% |
| 22,051 | LIMESTONE | 7,075 | 4,212 | 2,768 | 57 | 38 | 1,444 R | 59.5% | 39.1% | 0.8% |
| 3,057 | LIPSCOMB | 1,294 | 1,072 | 206 | 9 | 7 | 866 R | 82.8% | 15.9% | 0.7% |
| 12,309 | LIVE OAK | 4,004 | 2,828 | 1,114 | 35 | 27 | 1,714 R | 70.6% | 27.8% | 0.9% |
| 17,044 | LLANO | 8,627 | 6,295 | 2,143 | 142 | 47 | 4,152 R | 73.0% | 24.8% | 1.6% |
| 67 | LOVING | 156 | 124 | 29 | 1 | 2 | 95 R | 79.5% | 18.6% | 0.6% |
| 242,628 | LUBBOCK | 76,008 | 56,054 | 18,469 | 1,042 | 443 | 37,585 R | 73.7% | 24.3% | 1.4% |
| 6,550 | LYNN | 2,084 | 1,507 | 562 | 7 | 8 | 945 R | 72.3% | 27.0% | 0.3% |
| 8,205 | MCCULLOCH | 2,920 | 2,084 | 794 | 29 | 13 | 1,290 R | 71.4% | 27.2% | 1.0% |
| 213,517 | MCLENNAN | 68,789 | 43,955 | 23,462 | 1,032 | 340 | 20,493 R | 63.9% | 34.1% | 1.5% |
| 851 | MCMULLEN | 439 | 358 | 77 | 4 | | 281 R | 81.5% | 17.5% | 0.9% |
| 12,940 | MADISON | 3,623 | 2,333 | 1,241 | 27 | 22 | 1,092 R | 64.4% | 34.3% | 0.7% |
| 10,941 | MARION | 3,930 | 2,039 | 1,852 | 31 | 8 | 187 R | 51.9% | 47.1% | 0.8% |
| 4,746 | MARTIN | 1,949 | 1,520 | 415 | 6 | 8 | 1,105 R | 78.0% | 21.3% | 0.3% |
| 3,738 | MASON | 1,801 | 1,352 | 417 | 18 | 14 | 935 R | 75.1% | 23.2% | 1.0% |
| 37,957 | MATAGORDA | 12,459 | 7,584 | 4,696 | 141 | 38 | 2,888 R | 60.9% | 37.7% | 1.1% |
| 47,297 | MAVERICK | 9,229 | 3,143 | 5,995 | 53 | 38 | 2,852 D | 34.1% | 65.0% | 0.6% |
| 39,304 | MEDINA | 12,873 | 8,590 | 4,025 | 171 | 87 | 4,565 R | 66.7% | 31.3% | 1.3% |
| 2,360 | MENARD | 990 | 642 | 334 | 9 | 5 | 308 R | 64.8% | 33.7% | 0.9% |
| 116,009 | MIDLAND | 39,740 | 31,514 | 7,534 | 475 | 217 | 23,980 R | 79.3% | 19.0% | 1.2% |
| 24,238 | MILAM | 8,269 | 4,706 | 3,429 | 84 | 50 | 1,277 R | 56.9% | 41.5% | 1.0% |
| 5,151 | MILLS | 2,314 | 1,738 | 548 | 14 | 14 | 1,190 R | 75.1% | 23.7% | 0.6% |
| 9,698 | MITCHELL | 2,574 | 1,708 | 837 | 20 | 9 | 871 R | 66.4% | 32.5% | 0.8% |
| 19,117 | MONTAGUE | 7,330 | 4,951 | 2,256 | 66 | 57 | 2,695 R | 67.5% | 30.8% | 0.9% |
| 293,768 | MONTGOMERY | 106,213 | 80,600 | 23,286 | 1,825 | 502 | 57,314 R | 75.9% | 21.9% | 1.7% |
| 20,121 | MOORE | 5,290 | 4,201 | 1,040 | 24 | 25 | 3,161 R | 79.4% | 19.7% | 0.5% |
| 13,048 | MORRIS | 4,889 | 2,381 | 2,455 | 31 | 22 | 74 D | 48.7% | 50.2% | 0.6% |
| 1,426 | MOTLEY | 642 | 514 | 118 | 5 | 5 | 396 R | 80.1% | 18.4% | 0.8% |
| 59,203 | NACOGDOCHES | 19,799 | 13,145 | 6,204 | 387 | 63 | 6,941 R | 66.4% | 31.3% | 2.0% |
| 45,124 | NAVARRO | 13,890 | 8,358 | 5,366 | 105 | 61 | 2,992 R | 60.2% | 38.6% | 0.8% |
| 15,072 | NEWTON | 4,990 | 2,423 | 2,503 | 38 | 26 | 80 D | 48.6% | 50.2% | 0.8% |
| 15,802 | NOLAN | 5,312 | 3,337 | 1,874 | 60 | 41 | 1,463 R | 62.8% | 35.3% | 1.1% |
| 313,645 | NUECES | 97,326 | 49,906 | 45,349 | 1,574 | 497 | 4,557 R | 51.3% | 46.6% | 1.6% |
| 9,006 | OCHILTREE | 2,962 | 2,687 | 251 | 19 | 5 | 2,436 R | 90.7% | 8.5% | 0.6% |
| 2,185 | OLDHAM | 774 | 659 | 108 | 6 | 1 | 551 R | 85.1% | 14.0% | 0.8% |

# TEXAS

## PRESIDENT 2000

| 2000 Census Population | County | Total Vote | Republican | Democratic | Green (Nader) | Other | Rep.-Dem. Plurality | Percentage of Total Vote | | |
|---|---|---|---|---|---|---|---|---|---|---|
| | | | | | | | | Rep. | Dem. | Green |
| 84,966 | ORANGE | 29,654 | 17,325 | 11,887 | 290 | 152 | 5,438 R | 58.4% | 40.1% | 1.0% |
| 27,026 | PALO PINTO | 9,118 | 5,690 | 3,263 | 86 | 79 | 2,427 R | 62.4% | 35.8% | 0.9% |
| 22,756 | PANOLA | 9,074 | 5,975 | 3,011 | 50 | 38 | 2,964 R | 65.8% | 33.2% | 0.6% |
| 88,495 | PARKER | 33,225 | 23,651 | 8,878 | 485 | 211 | 14,773 R | 71.2% | 26.7% | 1.5% |
| 10,016 | PARMER | 2,744 | 2,274 | 447 | 15 | 8 | 1,827 R | 82.9% | 16.3% | 0.5% |
| 16,809 | PECOS | 4,303 | 2,700 | 1,539 | 44 | 20 | 1,161 R | 62.7% | 35.8% | 1.0% |
| 41,133 | POLK | 18,994 | 11,746 | 6,877 | 259 | 112 | 4,869 R | 61.8% | 36.2% | 1.4% |
| 113,546 | POTTER | 25,376 | 17,629 | 7,242 | 362 | 143 | 10,387 R | 69.5% | 28.5% | 1.4% |
| 7,304 | PRESIDIO | 1,757 | 618 | 1,064 | 65 | 10 | 446 D | 35.2% | 60.6% | 3.7% |
| 9,139 | RAINS | 3,333 | 2,049 | 1,225 | 34 | 25 | 824 R | 61.5% | 36.8% | 1.0% |
| 104,312 | RANDALL | 41,790 | 33,921 | 7,209 | 448 | 212 | 26,712 R | 81.2% | 17.3% | 1.1% |
| 3,326 | REAGAN | 1,255 | 959 | 282 | 6 | 8 | 677 R | 76.4% | 22.5% | 0.5% |
| 3,047 | REAL | 1,490 | 1,146 | 316 | 16 | 12 | 830 R | 76.9% | 21.2% | 1.1% |
| 14,314 | RED RIVER | 5,202 | 2,941 | 2,219 | 19 | 23 | 722 R | 56.5% | 42.7% | 0.4% |
| 13,137 | REEVES | 3,176 | 1,273 | 1,872 | 22 | 9 | 599 D | 40.1% | 58.9% | 0.7% |
| 7,828 | REFUGIO | 2,921 | 1,721 | 1,172 | 22 | 6 | 549 R | 58.9% | 40.1% | 0.8% |
| 887 | ROBERTS | 549 | 472 | 72 | 3 | 2 | 400 R | 86.0% | 13.1% | 0.5% |
| 16,000 | ROBERTSON | 6,369 | 3,007 | 3,283 | 41 | 38 | 276 D | 47.2% | 51.5% | 0.6% |
| 43,080 | ROCKWALL | 17,652 | 13,666 | 3,642 | 231 | 113 | 10,024 R | 77.4% | 20.6% | 1.3% |
| 11,495 | RUNNELS | 4,046 | 3,020 | 969 | 31 | 26 | 2,051 R | 74.6% | 23.9% | 0.8% |
| 47,372 | RUSK | 16,633 | 11,611 | 4,841 | 112 | 69 | 6,770 R | 69.8% | 29.1% | 0.7% |
| 10,469 | SABINE | 4,591 | 2,764 | 1,753 | 40 | 34 | 1,011 R | 60.2% | 38.2% | 0.9% |
| 8,946 | SAN AUGUSTINE | 3,805 | 2,116 | 1,636 | 34 | 19 | 480 R | 55.6% | 43.0% | 0.9% |
| 22,246 | SAN JACINTO | 7,714 | 4,623 | 2,946 | 103 | 42 | 1,677 R | 59.9% | 38.2% | 1.3% |
| 67,138 | SAN PATRICIO | 18,699 | 10,599 | 7,840 | 179 | 81 | 2,759 R | 56.7% | 41.9% | 1.0% |
| 6,186 | SAN SABA | 2,333 | 1,691 | 618 | 12 | 12 | 1,073 R | 72.5% | 26.5% | 0.5% |
| 2,935 | SCHLEICHER | 1,173 | 826 | 338 | 4 | 5 | 488 R | 70.4% | 28.8% | 0.3% |
| 16,361 | SCURRY | 5,326 | 4,060 | 1,193 | 45 | 28 | 2,867 R | 76.2% | 22.4% | 0.8% |
| 3,302 | SHACKELFORD | 1,347 | 1,066 | 264 | 9 | 8 | 802 R | 79.1% | 19.6% | 0.7% |
| 25,224 | SHELBY | 9,005 | 5,692 | 3,227 | 55 | 31 | 2,465 R | 63.2% | 35.8% | 0.6% |
| 3,186 | SHERMAN | 1,163 | 998 | 144 | 11 | 10 | 854 R | 85.8% | 12.4% | 0.9% |
| 174,706 | SMITH | 60,624 | 43,320 | 16,470 | 548 | 286 | 26,850 R | 71.5% | 27.2% | 0.9% |
| 6,809 | SOMERVELL | 2,918 | 2,120 | 752 | 37 | 9 | 1,368 R | 72.7% | 25.8% | 1.3% |
| 53,597 | STARR | 8,464 | 1,911 | 6,505 | 19 | 29 | 4,594 D | 22.6% | 76.9% | 0.2% |
| 9,674 | STEPHENS | 3,291 | 2,425 | 811 | 32 | 23 | 1,614 R | 73.7% | 24.6% | 1.0% |
| 1,393 | STERLING | 659 | 520 | 132 | 3 | 4 | 388 R | 78.9% | 20.0% | 0.5% |
| 1,693 | STONEWALL | 799 | 496 | 294 | 7 | 2 | 202 R | 62.1% | 36.8% | 0.9% |
| 4,077 | SUTTON | 1,540 | 1,063 | 468 | 6 | 3 | 595 R | 69.0% | 30.4% | 0.4% |
| 8,378 | SWISHER | 2,501 | 1,612 | 856 | 20 | 13 | 756 R | 64.5% | 34.2% | 0.8% |
| 1,446,219 | TARRANT | 472,389 | 286,921 | 173,758 | 8,808 | 2,902 | 113,163 R | 60.7% | 36.8% | 1.9% |
| 126,555 | TAYLOR | 43,020 | 31,701 | 10,504 | 589 | 226 | 21,197 R | 73.7% | 24.4% | 1.4% |
| 1,081 | TERRELL | 477 | 243 | 219 | 7 | 8 | 24 R | 50.9% | 45.9% | 1.5% |
| 12,761 | TERRY | 4,054 | 2,910 | 1,108 | 18 | 18 | 1,802 R | 71.8% | 27.3% | 0.4% |
| 1,850 | THROCKMORTON | 842 | 608 | 228 | 4 | 2 | 380 R | 72.2% | 27.1% | 0.5% |
| 28,118 | TITUS | 8,103 | 4,995 | 3,008 | 65 | 35 | 1,987 R | 61.6% | 37.1% | 0.8% |
| 104,010 | TOM GREEN | 34,626 | 24,733 | 9,288 | 454 | 151 | 15,445 R | 71.4% | 26.8% | 1.3% |
| 812,280 | TRAVIS | 301,263 | 141,235 | 125,526 | 31,243 | 3,259 | 15,709 R | 46.9% | 41.7% | 10.4% |
| 13,779 | TRINITY | 5,297 | 3,093 | 2,142 | 40 | 22 | 951 R | 58.4% | 40.4% | 0.8% |
| 20,871 | TYLER | 7,116 | 4,236 | 2,775 | 65 | 40 | 1,461 R | 59.5% | 39.0% | 0.9% |
| 35,291 | UPSHUR | 12,808 | 8,448 | 4,180 | 116 | 64 | 4,268 R | 66.0% | 32.6% | 0.9% |
| 3,404 | UPTON | 1,273 | 982 | 266 | 11 | 14 | 716 R | 77.1% | 20.9% | 0.9% |
| 25,926 | UVALDE | 8,420 | 4,855 | 3,436 | 36 | 93 | 1,419 R | 57.7% | 40.8% | 0.4% |
| 44,856 | VAL VERDE | 11,474 | 6,223 | 5,056 | 129 | 66 | 1,167 R | 54.2% | 44.1% | 1.1% |
| 48,140 | VAN ZANDT | 17,891 | 12,383 | 5,245 | 141 | 122 | 7,138 R | 69.2% | 29.3% | 0.8% |
| 84,088 | VICTORIA | 27,408 | 18,787 | 8,176 | 215 | 230 | 10,611 R | 68.5% | 29.8% | 0.8% |
| 61,758 | WALKER | 14,374 | 9,076 | 4,943 | 274 | 81 | 4,133 R | 63.1% | 34.4% | 1.9% |
| 32,663 | WALLER | 10,858 | 5,686 | 5,046 | 95 | 31 | 640 R | 52.4% | 46.5% | 0.9% |
| 10,909 | WARD | 3,874 | 2,534 | 1,256 | 58 | 26 | 1,278 R | 65.4% | 32.4% | 1.5% |
| 30,373 | WASHINGTON | 11,809 | 8,645 | 2,996 | 133 | 35 | 5,649 R | 73.2% | 25.4% | 1.1% |
| 193,117 | WEBB | 31,571 | 13,076 | 18,120 | 256 | 119 | 5,044 D | 41.4% | 57.4% | 0.8% |

# TEXAS

## PRESIDENT 2000

| 2000 Census Population | County | Total Vote | Republican | Democratic | Green (Nader) | Other | Rep.-Dem. Plurality | Percentage of Total Vote | | |
|---|---|---|---|---|---|---|---|---|---|---|
| | | | | | | | | Rep. | Dem. | Green |
| 41,188 | WHARTON | 13,426 | 8,455 | 4,838 | 103 | 30 | 3,617 R | 63.0% | 36.0% | 0.8% |
| 5,284 | WHEELER | 2,389 | 1,787 | 579 | 15 | 8 | 1,208 R | 74.8% | 24.2% | 0.6% |
| 131,664 | WICHITA | 42,713 | 27,802 | 14,108 | 518 | 285 | 13,694 R | 65.1% | 33.0% | 1.2% |
| 14,676 | WILBARGER | 4,577 | 3,138 | 1,356 | 43 | 40 | 1,782 R | 68.6% | 29.6% | 0.9% |
| 20,082 | WILLACY | 5,062 | 1,789 | 3,218 | 24 | 31 | 1,429 D | 35.3% | 63.6% | 0.5% |
| 249,967 | WILLIAMSON | 95,935 | 65,041 | 26,591 | 3,486 | 817 | 38,450 R | 67.8% | 27.7% | 3.6% |
| 32,408 | WILSON | 11,698 | 7,509 | 3,997 | 130 | 62 | 3,512 R | 64.2% | 34.2% | 1.1% |
| 7,173 | WINKLER | 2,043 | 1,468 | 556 | 5 | 14 | 912 R | 71.9% | 27.2% | 0.2% |
| 48,793 | WISE | 16,368 | 11,234 | 4,830 | 185 | 119 | 6,404 R | 68.6% | 29.5% | 1.1% |
| 36,752 | WOOD | 13,884 | 9,810 | 3,893 | 128 | 53 | 5,917 R | 70.7% | 28.0% | 0.9% |
| 7,322 | YOAKUM | 2,465 | 1,911 | 531 | 10 | 13 | 1,380 R | 77.5% | 21.5% | 0.4% |
| 17,943 | YOUNG | 6,954 | 5,022 | 1,843 | 46 | 43 | 3,179 R | 72.2% | 26.5% | 0.7% |
| 12,182 | ZAPATA | 2,616 | 953 | 1,638 | 11 | 14 | 685 D | 36.4% | 62.6% | 0.4% |
| 11,600 | ZAVALA | 3,391 | 751 | 2,616 | 14 | 10 | 1,865 D | 22.1% | 77.1% | 0.4% |
| 20,851,820 | TOTAL | 6,407,637 | 3,799,639 | 2,433,746 | 137,994 | 36,258 | 1,365,893 R | 59.3% | 38.0% | 2.2% |

Note: A blank in a candidate's column in a particular county indicates that no votes were cast for that candidate.

# TEXAS

## PRESIDENT 1996

| 1995 Census Pop. Est. | County | Total Vote | Republican | Democratic | Reform (Perot) | Other | Rep.-Dem. Plurality | Percentage of Total Vote Rep. | Dem. | Reform |
|---|---|---|---|---|---|---|---|---|---|---|
| 50,708 | ANDERSON | 13,400 | 6,458 | 5,693 | 1,170 | 79 | 765 R | 48.2% | 42.5% | 8.7% |
| 14,228 | ANDREWS | 4,001 | 2,360 | 1,181 | 431 | 29 | 1,179 R | 59.0% | 29.5% | 10.8% |
| 75,488 | ANGELINA | 25,421 | 11,789 | 11,346 | 2,160 | 126 | 443 R | 46.4% | 44.6% | 8.5% |
| 21,179 | ARANSAS | 7,440 | 3,769 | 2,964 | 655 | 52 | 805 R | 50.7% | 39.8% | 8.8% |
| 8,147 | ARCHER | 3,655 | 1,974 | 1,235 | 437 | 9 | 739 R | 54.0% | 33.8% | 12.0% |
| 2,111 | ARMSTRONG | 936 | 582 | 272 | 75 | 7 | 310 R | 62.2% | 29.1% | 8.0% |
| 33,808 | ATASCOSA | 9,254 | 4,102 | 4,259 | 813 | 80 | 157 D | 44.3% | 46.0% | 8.8% |
| 22,373 | AUSTIN | 8,001 | 4,669 | 2,719 | 577 | 36 | 1,950 R | 58.4% | 34.0% | 7.2% |
| 6,891 | BAILEY | 2,066 | 1,246 | 706 | 109 | 5 | 540 R | 60.3% | 34.2% | 5.3% |
| 13,482 | BANDERA | 5,673 | 3,700 | 1,383 | 520 | 70 | 2,317 R | 65.2% | 24.4% | 9.2% |
| 44,487 | BASTROP | 14,585 | 6,323 | 6,773 | 1,342 | 147 | 450 D | 43.4% | 46.4% | 9.2% |
| 4,250 | BAYLOR | 2,086 | 860 | 955 | 262 | 9 | 95 D | 41.2% | 45.8% | 12.6% |
| 26,874 | BEE | 8,766 | 3,611 | 4,561 | 539 | 55 | 950 D | 41.2% | 52.0% | 6.1% |
| 217,891 | BELL | 57,049 | 30,348 | 22,638 | 3,666 | 397 | 7,710 R | 53.2% | 39.7% | 6.4% |
| 1,296,731 | BEXAR | 362,489 | 161,619 | 180,308 | 17,822 | 2,740 | 18,689 D | 44.6% | 49.7% | 4.9% |
| 7,651 | BLANCO | 3,316 | 1,919 | 1,028 | 330 | 39 | 891 R | 57.9% | 31.0% | 10.0% |
| 799 | BORDEN | 334 | 194 | 93 | 45 | 2 | 101 R | 58.1% | 27.8% | 13.5% |
| 16,502 | BOSQUE | 6,026 | 2,840 | 2,427 | 739 | 20 | 413 R | 47.1% | 40.3% | 12.3% |
| 83,909 | BOWIE | 29,270 | 12,750 | 13,657 | 2,760 | 103 | 907 D | 43.6% | 46.7% | 9.4% |
| 216,016 | BRAZORIA | 65,638 | 36,392 | 22,959 | 5,869 | 418 | 13,433 R | 55.4% | 35.0% | 8.9% |
| 130,486 | BRAZOS | 38,644 | 22,082 | 13,968 | 2,215 | 379 | 8,114 R | 57.1% | 36.1% | 5.7% |
| 9,120 | BREWSTER | 3,452 | 1,438 | 1,643 | 299 | 72 | 205 D | 41.7% | 47.6% | 8.7% |
| 1,849 | BRISCOE | 892 | 416 | 408 | 65 | 3 | 8 R | 46.6% | 45.7% | 7.3% |
| 8,412 | BROOKS | 3,488 | 413 | 2,945 | 108 | 22 | 2,532 D | 11.8% | 84.4% | 3.1% |
| 35,960 | BROWN | 11,787 | 6,524 | 4,138 | 1,081 | 44 | 2,386 R | 55.3% | 35.1% | 9.2% |
| 15,011 | BURLESON | 4,953 | 2,174 | 2,419 | 347 | 13 | 245 D | 43.9% | 48.8% | 7.0% |
| 27,257 | BURNET | 11,049 | 5,744 | 4,123 | 1,108 | 74 | 1,621 R | 52.0% | 37.3% | 10.0% |
| 29,091 | CALDWELL | 7,821 | 3,239 | 3,961 | 545 | 76 | 722 D | 41.4% | 50.6% | 7.0% |
| 20,469 | CALHOUN | 6,113 | 2,832 | 2,753 | 507 | 21 | 79 R | 46.3% | 45.0% | 8.3% |
| 12,308 | CALLAHAN | 4,695 | 2,480 | 1,666 | 534 | 15 | 814 R | 52.8% | 35.5% | 11.4% |
| 309,578 | CAMERON | 56,493 | 18,434 | 34,891 | 2,760 | 408 | 16,457 D | 32.6% | 61.8% | 4.9% |
| 10,518 | CAMP | 3,662 | 1,488 | 1,912 | 252 | 10 | 424 D | 40.6% | 52.2% | 6.9% |
| 6,639 | CARSON | 2,730 | 1,742 | 742 | 227 | 19 | 1,000 R | 63.8% | 27.2% | 8.3% |
| 30,654 | CASS | 10,839 | 4,066 | 5,691 | 1,038 | 44 | 1,625 D | 37.5% | 52.5% | 9.6% |
| 8,616 | CASTRO | 2,501 | 1,231 | 1,107 | 144 | 19 | 124 R | 49.2% | 44.3% | 5.8% |
| 22,042 | CHAMBERS | 7,831 | 4,101 | 2,876 | 818 | 36 | 1,225 R | 52.4% | 36.7% | 10.4% |
| 41,155 | CHEROKEE | 12,694 | 6,483 | 5,185 | 971 | 55 | 1,298 R | 51.1% | 40.8% | 7.6% |
| 6,529 | CHILDRESS | 1,962 | 1,072 | 719 | 165 | 6 | 353 R | 54.6% | 36.6% | 8.4% |
| 10,157 | CLAY | 4,160 | 1,997 | 1,690 | 465 | 8 | 307 R | 48.0% | 40.6% | 11.2% |
| 4,188 | COCHRAN | 1,336 | 667 | 541 | 127 | 1 | 126 R | 49.9% | 40.5% | 9.5% |
| 3,473 | COKE | 1,546 | 790 | 595 | 157 | 4 | 195 R | 51.1% | 38.5% | 10.2% |
| 9,623 | COLEMAN | 3,645 | 1,793 | 1,488 | 349 | 15 | 305 R | 49.2% | 40.8% | 9.6% |
| 346,232 | COLLIN | 132,925 | 83,750 | 37,854 | 10,443 | 878 | 45,896 R | 63.0% | 28.5% | 7.9% |
| 3,371 | COLLINGSWORTH | 1,431 | 729 | 581 | 118 | 3 | 148 R | 50.9% | 40.6% | 8.2% |
| 18,799 | COLORADO | 6,775 | 3,381 | 2,795 | 574 | 25 | 586 R | 49.9% | 41.3% | 8.5% |
| 64,155 | COMAL | 26,057 | 16,763 | 7,132 | 1,903 | 259 | 9,631 R | 64.3% | 27.4% | 7.3% |
| 13,532 | COMANCHE | 4,779 | 2,123 | 2,138 | 511 | 7 | 15 D | 44.4% | 44.7% | 10.7% |
| 2,993 | CONCHO | 1,032 | 488 | 434 | 107 | 3 | 54 R | 47.3% | 42.1% | 10.4% |
| 31,733 | COOKE | 12,297 | 7,320 | 3,782 | 1,150 | 45 | 3,538 R | 59.5% | 30.8% | 9.4% |
| 72,012 | CORYELL | 13,944 | 7,143 | 5,300 | 1,443 | 58 | 1,843 R | 51.2% | 38.0% | 10.3% |
| 2,048 | COTTLE | 818 | 331 | 404 | 77 | 6 | 73 D | 40.5% | 49.4% | 9.4% |
| 4,515 | CRANE | 1,815 | 984 | 616 | 201 | 14 | 368 R | 54.2% | 33.9% | 11.1% |
| 4,403 | CROCKETT | 1,553 | 714 | 684 | 147 | 8 | 30 R | 46.0% | 44.0% | 9.5% |
| 7,269 | CROSBY | 2,287 | 968 | 1,122 | 189 | 8 | 154 D | 42.3% | 49.1% | 8.3% |
| 3,245 | CULBERSON | 1,241 | 329 | 804 | 99 | 9 | 475 D | 26.5% | 64.8% | 8.0% |
| 6,379 | DALLAM | 1,634 | 970 | 483 | 170 | 11 | 487 R | 59.4% | 29.6% | 10.4% |
| 1,959,281 | DALLAS | 555,953 | 260,058 | 255,766 | 36,759 | 3,370 | 4,292 R | 46.8% | 46.0% | 6.6% |
| 15,051 | DAWSON | 4,176 | 2,319 | 1,612 | 232 | 13 | 707 R | 55.5% | 38.6% | 5.6% |
| 19,422 | DEAF SMITH | 5,048 | 3,051 | 1,655 | 310 | 32 | 1,396 R | 60.4% | 32.8% | 6.1% |
| 4,877 | DELTA | 1,743 | 744 | 849 | 146 | 4 | 105 D | 42.7% | 48.7% | 8.4% |

# TEXAS

## PRESIDENT 1996

| 1995 Census Pop. Est. | County | Total Vote | Republican | Democratic | Reform (Perot) | Other | Rep.-Dem. Plurality | Percentage of Total Vote | | |
|---|---|---|---|---|---|---|---|---|---|---|
| | | | | | | | | Rep. | Dem. | Reform |
| 334,070 | DENTON | 111,596 | 65,313 | 36,138 | 9,294 | 851 | 29,175 R | 58.5% | 32.4% | 8.3% |
| 18,481 | DE WITT | 6,164 | 3,577 | 2,074 | 483 | 30 | 1,503 R | 58.0% | 33.6% | 7.8% |
| 2,419 | DICKENS | 1,053 | 421 | 509 | 117 | 6 | 88 D | 40.0% | 48.3% | 11.1% |
| 10,508 | DIMMIT | 2,991 | 604 | 2,242 | 128 | 17 | 1,638 D | 20.2% | 75.0% | 4.3% |
| 3,743 | DONLEY | 1,585 | 988 | 495 | 97 | 5 | 493 R | 62.3% | 31.2% | 6.1% |
| 12,994 | DUVAL | 4,660 | 543 | 3,958 | 136 | 23 | 3,415 D | 11.7% | 84.9% | 2.9% |
| 17,873 | EASTLAND | 6,596 | 3,272 | 2,594 | 705 | 25 | 678 R | 49.6% | 39.3% | 10.7% |
| 123,450 | ECTOR | 32,686 | 17,746 | 12,017 | 2,511 | 412 | 5,729 R | 54.3% | 36.8% | 7.7% |
| 3,110 | EDWARDS | 1,013 | 511 | 437 | 60 | 5 | 74 R | 50.4% | 43.1% | 5.9% |
| 94,223 | ELLIS | 29,766 | 16,046 | 10,832 | 2,750 | 138 | 5,214 R | 53.9% | 36.4% | 9.2% |
| 678,313 | EL PASO | 134,710 | 43,255 | 83,964 | 6,300 | 1,191 | 40,709 D | 32.1% | 62.3% | 4.7% |
| 30,352 | ERATH | 9,598 | 4,750 | 3,664 | 1,134 | 50 | 1,086 R | 49.5% | 38.2% | 11.8% |
| 17,950 | FALLS | 6,012 | 2,260 | 3,256 | 479 | 17 | 996 D | 37.6% | 54.2% | 8.0% |
| 25,638 | FANNIN | 8,796 | 3,495 | 4,276 | 980 | 45 | 781 D | 39.7% | 48.6% | 11.1% |
| 21,113 | FAYETTE | 8,068 | 4,195 | 3,119 | 708 | 46 | 1,076 R | 52.0% | 38.7% | 8.8% |
| 4,539 | FISHER | 1,849 | 537 | 1,142 | 170 | | 605 D | 29.0% | 61.8% | 9.2% |
| 8,392 | FLOYD | 2,648 | 1,530 | 986 | 126 | 6 | 544 R | 57.8% | 37.2% | 4.8% |
| 1,662 | FOARD | 573 | 166 | 355 | 52 | | 189 D | 29.0% | 62.0% | 9.1% |
| 292,765 | FORT BEND | 92,856 | 49,945 | 38,163 | 4,363 | 385 | 11,782 R | 53.8% | 41.1% | 4.7% |
| 8,934 | FRANKLIN | 3,452 | 1,575 | 1,484 | 386 | 7 | 91 R | 45.6% | 43.0% | 11.2% |
| 17,035 | FREESTONE | 6,097 | 2,888 | 2,630 | 568 | 11 | 258 R | 47.4% | 43.1% | 9.3% |
| 15,250 | FRIO | 4,092 | 1,225 | 2,593 | 253 | 21 | 1,368 D | 29.9% | 63.4% | 6.2% |
| 14,479 | GAINES | 3,194 | 1,812 | 1,012 | 353 | 17 | 800 R | 56.7% | 31.7% | 11.1% |
| 237,533 | GALVESTON | 80,089 | 35,251 | 38,458 | 5,897 | 483 | 3,207 D | 44.0% | 48.0% | 7.4% |
| 4,742 | GARZA | 1,754 | 946 | 703 | 103 | 2 | 243 R | 53.9% | 40.1% | 5.9% |
| 19,408 | GILLESPIE | 8,151 | 5,867 | 1,655 | 542 | 87 | 4,212 R | 72.0% | 20.3% | 6.6% |
| 1,390 | GLASSCOCK | 484 | 382 | 70 | 30 | 2 | 312 R | 78.9% | 14.5% | 6.2% |
| 6,363 | GOLIAD | 2,635 | 1,335 | 1,135 | 148 | 17 | 200 R | 50.7% | 43.1% | 5.6% |
| 17,378 | GONZALES | 5,182 | 2,687 | 2,110 | 354 | 31 | 577 R | 51.9% | 40.7% | 6.8% |
| 23,155 | GRAY | 8,824 | 6,102 | 2,114 | 568 | 40 | 3,988 R | 69.2% | 24.0% | 6.4% |
| 98,336 | GRAYSON | 35,411 | 17,169 | 14,338 | 3,745 | 159 | 2,831 R | 48.5% | 40.5% | 10.6% |
| 110,725 | GREGG | 37,478 | 21,611 | 13,659 | 2,079 | 129 | 7,952 R | 57.7% | 36.4% | 5.5% |
| 21,624 | GRIMES | 5,701 | 2,564 | 2,584 | 538 | 15 | 20 D | 45.0% | 45.3% | 9.4% |
| 72,632 | GUADALUPE | 24,403 | 14,254 | 8,079 | 1,811 | 259 | 6,175 R | 58.4% | 33.1% | 7.4% |
| 36,223 | HALE | 9,746 | 5,905 | 3,204 | 605 | 32 | 2,701 R | 60.6% | 32.9% | 6.2% |
| 3,632 | HALL | 1,472 | 626 | 750 | 94 | 2 | 124 D | 42.5% | 51.0% | 6.4% |
| 7,662 | HAMILTON | 3,031 | 1,493 | 1,200 | 323 | 15 | 293 R | 49.3% | 39.6% | 10.7% |
| 5,264 | HANSFORD | 1,944 | 1,493 | 343 | 105 | 3 | 1,150 R | 76.8% | 17.6% | 5.4% |
| 4,872 | HARDEMAN | 1,531 | 610 | 750 | 168 | 3 | 140 D | 39.8% | 49.0% | 11.0% |
| 46,607 | HARDIN | 17,900 | 8,529 | 7,179 | 2,112 | 80 | 1,350 R | 47.6% | 40.1% | 11.8% |
| 3,076,867 | HARRIS | 855,893 | 421,462 | 386,726 | 42,364 | 5,341 | 34,736 R | 49.2% | 45.2% | 4.9% |
| 58,703 | HARRISON | 21,655 | 9,835 | 10,307 | 1,427 | 86 | 472 D | 45.4% | 47.6% | 6.6% |
| 3,815 | HARTLEY | 1,809 | 1,242 | 463 | 101 | 3 | 779 R | 68.7% | 25.6% | 5.6% |
| 6,358 | HASKELL | 2,572 | 966 | 1,374 | 225 | 7 | 408 D | 37.6% | 53.4% | 8.7% |
| 77,522 | HAYS | 26,840 | 12,865 | 11,580 | 1,990 | 405 | 1,285 R | 47.9% | 43.1% | 7.4% |
| 3,594 | HEMPHILL | 1,438 | 986 | 344 | 104 | 4 | 642 R | 68.6% | 23.9% | 7.2% |
| 64,293 | HENDERSON | 22,772 | 10,345 | 10,085 | 2,274 | 68 | 260 R | 45.4% | 44.3% | 10.0% |
| 479,783 | HIDALGO | 84,727 | 24,437 | 56,335 | 3,536 | 419 | 31,898 D | 28.8% | 66.5% | 4.2% |
| 28,759 | HILL | 9,473 | 4,401 | 3,988 | 1,052 | 32 | 413 R | 46.5% | 42.1% | 11.1% |
| 24,245 | HOCKLEY | 6,950 | 4,230 | 2,170 | 519 | 31 | 2,060 R | 60.9% | 31.2% | 7.5% |
| 33,384 | HOOD | 14,550 | 7,575 | 5,459 | 1,445 | 71 | 2,116 R | 52.1% | 37.5% | 9.9% |
| 29,738 | HOPKINS | 9,929 | 4,341 | 4,522 | 1,034 | 32 | 181 D | 43.7% | 45.5% | 10.4% |
| 21,917 | HOUSTON | 7,439 | 3,443 | 3,383 | 585 | 28 | 60 R | 46.3% | 45.5% | 7.9% |
| 32,450 | HOWARD | 9,857 | 5,007 | 3,732 | 1,037 | 81 | 1,275 R | 50.8% | 37.9% | 10.5% |
| 3,194 | HUDSPETH | 898 | 367 | 427 | 92 | 12 | 60 D | 40.9% | 47.6% | 10.2% |
| 66,972 | HUNT | 21,876 | 10,746 | 8,801 | 2,225 | 104 | 1,945 R | 49.1% | 40.2% | 10.2% |
| 24,522 | HUTCHINSON | 9,803 | 6,350 | 2,553 | 864 | 36 | 3,797 R | 64.8% | 26.0% | 8.8% |
| 1,631 | IRION | 690 | 386 | 213 | 86 | 5 | 173 R | 55.9% | 30.9% | 12.5% |
| 6,953 | JACK | 2,488 | 1,162 | 1,019 | 301 | 6 | 143 R | 46.7% | 41.0% | 12.1% |
| 13,649 | JACKSON | 4,639 | 2,533 | 1,785 | 309 | 12 | 748 R | 54.6% | 38.5% | 6.7% |

# TEXAS

## PRESIDENT 1996

| 1995 Census Pop. Est. | County | Total Vote | Republican | Democratic | Reform (Perot) | Other | Rep.-Dem. Plurality | Percentage of Total Vote | | |
|---|---|---|---|---|---|---|---|---|---|---|
| | | | | | | | | Rep. | Dem. | Reform |
| 32,825 | JASPER | 10,640 | 4,523 | 5,039 | 1,041 | 37 | 516 D | 42.5% | 47.4% | 9.8% |
| 2,122 | JEFF DAVIS | 963 | 482 | 370 | 99 | 12 | 112 R | 50.1% | 38.4% | 10.3% |
| 243,339 | JEFFERSON | 84,426 | 32,821 | 45,854 | 5,314 | 437 | 13,033 D | 38.9% | 54.3% | 6.3% |
| 5,096 | JIM HOGG | 1,812 | 307 | 1,437 | 64 | 4 | 1,130 D | 16.9% | 79.3% | 3.5% |
| 39,923 | JIM WELLS | 10,572 | 2,989 | 7,116 | 430 | 37 | 4,127 D | 28.3% | 67.3% | 4.1% |
| 106,181 | JOHNSON | 32,473 | 16,246 | 12,817 | 3,250 | 160 | 3,429 R | 50.0% | 39.5% | 10.0% |
| 18,058 | JONES | 5,410 | 2,351 | 2,422 | 614 | 23 | 71 D | 43.5% | 44.8% | 11.3% |
| 12,477 | KARNES | 4,334 | 1,869 | 2,154 | 291 | 20 | 285 D | 43.1% | 49.7% | 6.7% |
| 60,114 | KAUFMAN | 17,993 | 8,697 | 7,383 | 1,831 | 82 | 1,314 R | 48.3% | 41.0% | 10.2% |
| 19,413 | KENDALL | 8,781 | 5,940 | 2,092 | 620 | 129 | 3,848 R | 67.6% | 23.8% | 7.1% |
| 442 | KENEDY | 208 | 71 | 133 | 4 | | 62 D | 34.1% | 63.9% | 1.9% |
| 912 | KENT | 515 | 187 | 260 | 67 | 1 | 73 D | 36.3% | 50.5% | 13.0% |
| 40,264 | KERR | 16,775 | 11,173 | 4,192 | 1,236 | 174 | 6,981 R | 66.6% | 25.0% | 7.4% |
| 4,104 | KIMBLE | 1,563 | 898 | 521 | 131 | 13 | 377 R | 57.5% | 33.3% | 8.4% |
| 316 | KING | 182 | 97 | 46 | 29 | 10 | 51 R | 53.3% | 25.3% | 15.9% |
| 3,289 | KINNEY | 1,256 | 650 | 503 | 97 | 6 | 147 R | 51.8% | 40.0% | 7.7% |
| 30,629 | KLEBERG | 8,999 | 3,391 | 5,136 | 431 | 41 | 1,745 D | 37.7% | 57.1% | 4.8% |
| 4,620 | KNOX | 1,537 | 599 | 785 | 149 | 4 | 186 D | 39.0% | 51.1% | 9.7% |
| 45,214 | LAMAR | 13,722 | 6,393 | 6,075 | 1,198 | 56 | 318 R | 46.6% | 44.3% | 8.7% |
| 14,796 | LAMB | 4,574 | 2,593 | 1,683 | 283 | 15 | 910 R | 56.7% | 36.8% | 6.2% |
| 16,606 | LAMPASAS | 5,362 | 3,008 | 1,819 | 509 | 26 | 1,189 R | 56.1% | 33.9% | 9.5% |
| 6,055 | LA SALLE | 2,184 | 570 | 1,522 | 85 | 7 | 952 D | 26.1% | 69.7% | 3.9% |
| 18,614 | LAVACA | 6,855 | 3,697 | 2,575 | 551 | 32 | 1,122 R | 53.9% | 37.6% | 8.0% |
| 13,934 | LEE | 4,804 | 2,354 | 2,008 | 421 | 21 | 346 R | 49.0% | 41.8% | 8.8% |
| 13,738 | LEON | 5,566 | 2,839 | 2,217 | 499 | 11 | 622 R | 51.0% | 39.8% | 9.0% |
| 59,054 | LIBERTY | 16,773 | 7,784 | 6,877 | 2,011 | 101 | 907 R | 46.4% | 41.0% | 12.0% |
| 20,896 | LIMESTONE | 6,646 | 2,691 | 3,236 | 693 | 26 | 545 D | 40.5% | 48.7% | 10.4% |
| 3,054 | LIPSCOMB | 1,344 | 869 | 357 | 115 | 3 | 512 R | 64.7% | 26.6% | 8.6% |
| 10,254 | LIVE OAK | 3,612 | 1,929 | 1,372 | 292 | 19 | 557 R | 53.4% | 38.0% | 8.1% |
| 12,698 | LLANO | 7,737 | 4,290 | 2,633 | 762 | 52 | 1,657 R | 55.4% | 34.0% | 9.8% |
| 140 | LOVING | 77 | 48 | 14 | 15 | | 34 R | 62.3% | 18.2% | 19.5% |
| 232,276 | LUBBOCK | 74,489 | 47,304 | 22,786 | 3,996 | 403 | 24,518 R | 63.5% | 30.6% | 5.4% |
| 6,448 | LYNN | 2,197 | 1,151 | 903 | 136 | 7 | 248 R | 52.4% | 41.1% | 6.2% |
| 8,589 | MCCULLOCH | 3,008 | 1,465 | 1,231 | 296 | 16 | 234 R | 48.7% | 40.9% | 9.8% |
| 200,111 | MCLENNAN | 63,083 | 30,666 | 27,050 | 5,131 | 236 | 3,616 R | 48.6% | 42.9% | 8.1% |
| 794 | MCMULLEN | 430 | 274 | 117 | 35 | 4 | 157 R | 63.7% | 27.2% | 8.1% |
| 11,911 | MADISON | 3,351 | 1,576 | 1,470 | 293 | 12 | 106 R | 47.0% | 43.9% | 8.7% |
| 10,370 | MARION | 3,657 | 1,260 | 2,028 | 353 | 16 | 768 D | 34.5% | 55.5% | 9.7% |
| 4,956 | MARTIN | 1,773 | 973 | 643 | 140 | 17 | 330 R | 54.9% | 36.3% | 7.9% |
| 3,590 | MASON | 1,735 | 949 | 618 | 151 | 17 | 331 R | 54.7% | 35.6% | 8.7% |
| 38,297 | MATAGORDA | 12,494 | 5,876 | 5,374 | 1,190 | 54 | 502 R | 47.0% | 43.0% | 9.5% |
| 45,766 | MAVERICK | 6,586 | 1,050 | 5,307 | 202 | 27 | 4,257 D | 15.9% | 80.6% | 3.1% |
| 32,918 | MEDINA | 10,377 | 5,710 | 3,880 | 715 | 72 | 1,830 R | 55.0% | 37.4% | 6.9% |
| 2,382 | MENARD | 1,043 | 443 | 490 | 102 | 8 | 47 D | 42.5% | 47.0% | 9.8% |
| 115,795 | MIDLAND | 37,320 | 25,382 | 9,513 | 2,079 | 346 | 15,869 R | 68.0% | 25.5% | 5.6% |
| 23,644 | MILAM | 7,567 | 3,019 | 3,869 | 657 | 22 | 850 D | 39.9% | 51.1% | 8.7% |
| 4,730 | MILLS | 2,033 | 1,044 | 748 | 230 | 11 | 296 R | 51.4% | 36.8% | 11.3% |
| 8,713 | MITCHELL | 2,405 | 949 | 1,213 | 232 | 11 | 264 D | 39.5% | 50.4% | 9.6% |
| 17,844 | MONTAGUE | 6,626 | 3,029 | 2,718 | 842 | 37 | 311 R | 45.7% | 41.0% | 12.7% |
| 233,684 | MONTGOMERY | 78,202 | 51,011 | 20,722 | 6,065 | 404 | 30,289 R | 65.2% | 26.5% | 7.8% |
| 19,157 | MOORE | 5,083 | 3,353 | 1,358 | 359 | 13 | 1,995 R | 66.0% | 26.7% | 7.1% |
| 13,169 | MORRIS | 4,828 | 1,449 | 2,973 | 402 | 4 | 1,524 D | 30.0% | 61.6% | 8.3% |
| 1,308 | MOTLEY | 605 | 380 | 164 | 56 | 5 | 216 R | 62.8% | 27.1% | 9.3% |
| 56,380 | NACOGDOCHES | 19,458 | 10,361 | 7,641 | 1,352 | 104 | 2,720 R | 53.2% | 39.3% | 6.9% |
| 40,849 | NAVARRO | 12,502 | 5,236 | 6,078 | 1,140 | 48 | 842 D | 41.9% | 48.6% | 9.1% |
| 14,358 | NEWTON | 4,456 | 1,409 | 2,554 | 474 | 19 | 1,145 D | 31.6% | 57.3% | 10.6% |
| 16,251 | NOLAN | 5,391 | 2,166 | 2,582 | 613 | 30 | 416 D | 40.2% | 47.9% | 11.4% |
| 312,708 | NUECES | 93,168 | 37,470 | 50,009 | 5,103 | 586 | 12,539 D | 40.2% | 53.7% | 5.5% |
| 8,652 | OCHILTREE | 3,091 | 2,448 | 467 | 167 | 9 | 1,981 R | 79.2% | 15.1% | 5.4% |
| 2,218 | OLDHAM | 881 | 583 | 213 | 77 | 8 | 370 R | 66.2% | 24.2% | 8.7% |

# TEXAS

## PRESIDENT 1996

| 1995 Census Pop. Est. | County | Total Vote | Republican | Democratic | Reform (Perot) | Other | Rep.-Dem. Plurality | Percentage of Total Vote | | |
|---|---|---|---|---|---|---|---|---|---|---|
| | | | | | | | | Rep. | Dem. | Reform |
| 84,691 | ORANGE | 29,311 | 12,560 | 13,741 | 2,836 | 174 | 1,181 D | 42.9% | 46.9% | 9.7% |
| 25,051 | PALO PINTO | 8,655 | 3,666 | 3,938 | 1,011 | 40 | 272 D | 42.4% | 45.5% | 11.7% |
| 22,969 | PANOLA | 8,988 | 4,008 | 4,168 | 777 | 35 | 160 D | 44.6% | 46.4% | 8.6% |
| 73,794 | PARKER | 26,855 | 14,580 | 9,447 | 2,703 | 125 | 5,133 R | 54.3% | 35.2% | 10.1% |
| 10,242 | PARMER | 2,888 | 2,042 | 676 | 160 | 10 | 1,366 R | 70.7% | 23.4% | 5.5% |
| 15,427 | PECOS | 3,942 | 1,730 | 1,816 | 369 | 27 | 86 D | 43.9% | 46.1% | 9.4% |
| 39,756 | POLK | 14,244 | 6,473 | 6,360 | 1,347 | 64 | 113 R | 45.4% | 44.7% | 9.5% |
| 104,574 | POTTER | 26,245 | 14,995 | 9,273 | 1,799 | 178 | 5,722 R | 57.1% | 35.3% | 6.9% |
| 7,656 | PRESIDIO | 1,716 | 383 | 1,205 | 111 | 17 | 822 D | 22.3% | 70.2% | 6.5% |
| 7,634 | RAINS | 2,733 | 1,123 | 1,265 | 335 | 10 | 142 D | 41.1% | 46.3% | 12.3% |
| 96,438 | RANDALL | 39,627 | 28,266 | 9,177 | 1,985 | 199 | 19,089 R | 71.3% | 23.2% | 5.0% |
| 4,364 | REAGAN | 1,168 | 645 | 407 | 101 | 15 | 238 R | 55.2% | 34.8% | 8.6% |
| 2,590 | REAL | 1,447 | 845 | 414 | 178 | 10 | 431 R | 58.4% | 28.6% | 12.3% |
| 14,036 | RED RIVER | 4,565 | 1,783 | 2,339 | 433 | 10 | 556 D | 39.1% | 51.2% | 9.5% |
| 15,373 | REEVES | 3,546 | 1,007 | 2,279 | 245 | 15 | 1,272 D | 28.4% | 64.3% | 6.9% |
| 7,834 | REFUGIO | 3,249 | 1,376 | 1,635 | 222 | 16 | 259 D | 42.4% | 50.3% | 6.8% |
| 977 | ROBERTS | 584 | 421 | 122 | 40 | 1 | 299 R | 72.1% | 20.9% | 6.8% |
| 15,535 | ROBERTSON | 5,175 | 1,944 | 2,912 | 315 | 4 | 968 D | 37.6% | 56.3% | 6.1% |
| 32,725 | ROCKWALL | 12,796 | 8,319 | 3,289 | 1,121 | 67 | 5,030 R | 65.0% | 25.7% | 8.8% |
| 11,271 | RUNNELS | 3,763 | 1,941 | 1,417 | 396 | 9 | 524 R | 51.6% | 37.7% | 10.5% |
| 44,670 | RUSK | 15,534 | 8,423 | 5,988 | 1,072 | 51 | 2,435 R | 54.2% | 38.5% | 6.9% |
| 10,487 | SABINE | 3,925 | 1,660 | 1,913 | 334 | 18 | 253 D | 42.3% | 48.7% | 8.5% |
| 8,016 | SAN AUGUSTINE | 3,561 | 1,296 | 1,924 | 324 | 17 | 628 D | 36.4% | 54.0% | 9.1% |
| 19,236 | SAN JACINTO | 6,485 | 2,878 | 2,771 | 810 | 26 | 107 R | 44.4% | 42.7% | 12.5% |
| 66,228 | SAN PATRICIO | 16,983 | 7,678 | 8,132 | 1,085 | 88 | 454 D | 45.2% | 47.9% | 6.4% |
| 6,031 | SAN SABA | 1,916 | 991 | 726 | 194 | 5 | 265 R | 51.7% | 37.9% | 10.1% |
| 3,057 | SCHLEICHER | 1,206 | 587 | 505 | 111 | 3 | 82 R | 48.7% | 41.9% | 9.2% |
| 18,105 | SCURRY | 5,864 | 2,929 | 2,099 | 813 | 23 | 830 R | 49.9% | 35.8% | 13.9% |
| 3,221 | SHACKELFORD | 1,471 | 792 | 502 | 169 | 8 | 290 R | 53.8% | 34.1% | 11.5% |
| 22,436 | SHELBY | 8,048 | 3,482 | 3,720 | 815 | 31 | 238 D | 43.3% | 46.2% | 10.1% |
| 2,857 | SHERMAN | 1,143 | 809 | 243 | 89 | 2 | 566 R | 70.8% | 21.3% | 7.8% |
| 161,986 | SMITH | 53,643 | 32,171 | 18,265 | 2,933 | 274 | 13,906 R | 60.0% | 34.0% | 5.5% |
| 5,952 | SOMERVELL | 2,377 | 1,099 | 993 | 273 | 12 | 106 R | 46.2% | 41.8% | 11.5% |
| 51,482 | STARR | 7,260 | 756 | 6,312 | 157 | 35 | 5,556 D | 10.4% | 86.9% | 2.2% |
| 9,166 | STEPHENS | 3,279 | 1,714 | 1,218 | 336 | 11 | 496 R | 52.3% | 37.1% | 10.2% |
| 1,460 | STERLING | 669 | 394 | 186 | 86 | 3 | 208 R | 58.9% | 27.8% | 12.9% |
| 1,892 | STONEWALL | 917 | 323 | 487 | 105 | 2 | 164 D | 35.2% | 53.1% | 11.5% |
| 4,414 | SUTTON | 1,302 | 688 | 508 | 102 | 4 | 180 R | 52.8% | 39.0% | 7.8% |
| 8,597 | SWISHER | 2,592 | 1,159 | 1,224 | 195 | 14 | 65 D | 44.7% | 47.2% | 7.5% |
| 1,278,606 | TARRANT | 409,644 | 208,312 | 170,431 | 28,715 | 2,186 | 37,881 R | 50.9% | 41.6% | 7.0% |
| 122,791 | TAYLOR | 40,021 | 23,682 | 13,213 | 2,912 | 214 | 10,469 R | 59.2% | 33.0% | 7.3% |
| 1,299 | TERRELL | 519 | 185 | 278 | 47 | 9 | 93 D | 35.6% | 53.6% | 9.1% |
| 12,796 | TERRY | 3,567 | 2,013 | 1,272 | 269 | 13 | 741 R | 56.4% | 35.7% | 7.5% |
| 1,836 | THROCKMORTON | 737 | 360 | 285 | 90 | 2 | 75 R | 48.8% | 38.7% | 12.2% |
| 24,782 | TITUS | 7,928 | 3,438 | 3,725 | 744 | 21 | 287 D | 43.4% | 47.0% | 9.4% |
| 101,555 | TOM GREEN | 32,808 | 18,112 | 11,782 | 2,757 | 157 | 6,330 R | 55.2% | 35.9% | 8.4% |
| 664,802 | TRAVIS | 246,301 | 98,454 | 128,970 | 14,008 | 4,869 | 30,516 D | 40.0% | 52.4% | 5.7% |
| 12,294 | TRINITY | 5,310 | 2,058 | 2,774 | 460 | 18 | 716 D | 38.8% | 52.2% | 8.7% |
| 18,933 | TYLER | 6,821 | 2,804 | 3,340 | 645 | 32 | 536 D | 41.1% | 49.0% | 9.5% |
| 34,521 | UPSHUR | 11,320 | 5,174 | 5,032 | 1,086 | 28 | 142 R | 45.7% | 44.5% | 9.6% |
| 4,054 | UPTON | 1,204 | 685 | 424 | 88 | 7 | 261 R | 56.9% | 35.2% | 7.3% |
| 25,331 | UVALDE | 7,333 | 3,494 | 3,397 | 403 | 39 | 97 R | 47.6% | 46.3% | 5.5% |
| 43,690 | VAL VERDE | 10,600 | 4,357 | 5,623 | 548 | 72 | 1,266 D | 41.1% | 53.0% | 5.2% |
| 41,494 | VAN ZANDT | 15,026 | 7,453 | 5,752 | 1,756 | 65 | 1,701 R | 49.6% | 38.3% | 11.7% |
| 79,992 | VICTORIA | 24,119 | 14,457 | 8,238 | 1,197 | 227 | 6,219 R | 59.9% | 34.2% | 5.0% |
| 54,666 | WALKER | 14,567 | 7,177 | 6,088 | 1,186 | 116 | 1,089 R | 49.3% | 41.8% | 8.1% |
| 26,432 | WALLER | 8,622 | 3,559 | 4,535 | 499 | 29 | 976 D | 41.3% | 52.6% | 5.8% |
| 12,152 | WARD | 3,732 | 1,620 | 1,644 | 446 | 22 | 24 D | 43.4% | 44.1% | 12.0% |
| 28,020 | WASHINGTON | 10,419 | 6,319 | 3,460 | 601 | 39 | 2,859 R | 60.6% | 33.2% | 5.8% |
| 170,863 | WEBB | 24,777 | 4,712 | 18,997 | 936 | 132 | 14,285 D | 19.0% | 76.7% | 3.8% |

# TEXAS

## PRESIDENT 1996

| 1995 Census Pop. Est. | County | Total Vote | Republican | Democratic | Reform (Perot) | Other | Rep.-Dem. Plurality | Percentage of Total Vote | | |
|---|---|---|---|---|---|---|---|---|---|---|
| | | | | | | | | Rep. | Dem. | Reform |
| 40,376 | WHARTON | 12,234 | 6,163 | 5,176 | 871 | 24 | 987 R | 50.4% | 42.3% | 7.1% |
| 5,462 | WHEELER | 2,289 | 1,355 | 750 | 174 | 10 | 605 R | 59.2% | 32.8% | 7.6% |
| 125,239 | WICHITA | 39,950 | 20,495 | 15,775 | 3,371 | 309 | 4,720 R | 51.3% | 39.5% | 8.4% |
| 14,356 | WILBARGER | 4,268 | 2,037 | 1,730 | 465 | 36 | 307 R | 47.7% | 40.5% | 10.9% |
| 19,500 | WILLACY | 5,411 | 1,332 | 3,789 | 241 | 49 | 2,457 D | 24.6% | 70.0% | 4.5% |
| 184,034 | WILLIAMSON | 66,522 | 36,836 | 24,175 | 4,931 | 580 | 12,661 R | 55.4% | 36.3% | 7.4% |
| 27,291 | WILSON | 9,067 | 4,530 | 3,713 | 760 | 64 | 817 R | 50.0% | 41.0% | 8.4% |
| 7,981 | WINKLER | 2,103 | 1,009 | 872 | 218 | 4 | 137 R | 48.0% | 41.5% | 10.4% |
| 38,594 | WISE | 12,968 | 6,330 | 5,056 | 1,516 | 66 | 1,274 R | 48.8% | 39.0% | 11.7% |
| 32,305 | WOOD | 12,161 | 6,228 | 4,711 | 1,184 | 38 | 1,517 R | 51.2% | 38.7% | 9.7% |
| 8,235 | YOAKUM | 2,454 | 1,485 | 738 | 218 | 13 | 747 R | 60.5% | 30.1% | 8.9% |
| 17,781 | YOUNG | 6,697 | 3,647 | 2,394 | 639 | 17 | 1,253 R | 54.5% | 35.7% | 9.5% |
| 11,075 | ZAPATA | 2,450 | 521 | 1,786 | 131 | 12 | 1,265 D | 21.3% | 72.9% | 5.3% |
| 12,413 | ZAVALA | 3,193 | 463 | 2,629 | 91 | 10 | 2,166 D | 14.5% | 82.3% | 2.8% |
| 18,723,991 | TOTAL | 5,611,644 | 2,736,167 | 2,459,683 | 378,537 | 37,257 | 276,484 R | 48.8% | 43.8% | 6.7% |

# TEXAS

## PRESIDENT 1992

| 1990 Census Population | County | Total Vote | Republican | Democratic | Perot | Other | Plurality | Percentage Total Vote | | |
|---|---|---|---|---|---|---|---|---|---|---|
| | | | | | | | | Rep. | Dem. | Perot |
| 48,024 | ANDERSON | 14,466 | 5,598 | 5,322 | 3,519 | 27 | 276 R | 38.7% | 36.8% | 24.3% |
| 14,338 | ANDREWS | 4,228 | 2,266 | 1,081 | 875 | 6 | 1,185 R | 53.6% | 25.6% | 20.7% |
| 69,884 | ANGELINA | 26,281 | 9,722 | 10,318 | 6,204 | 37 | 596 D | 37.0% | 39.3% | 23.6% |
| 17,892 | ARANSAS | 6,770 | 2,826 | 2,246 | 1,676 | 22 | 580 R | 41.7% | 33.2% | 24.8% |
| 7,973 | ARCHER | 3,967 | 1,560 | 1,284 | 1,106 | 17 | 276 R | 39.3% | 32.4% | 27.9% |
| 2,021 | ARMSTRONG | 1,028 | 561 | 278 | 187 | 2 | 283 R | 54.6% | 27.0% | 18.2% |
| 30,533 | ATASCOSA | 9,658 | 3,806 | 3,766 | 2,035 | 51 | 40 R | 39.4% | 39.0% | 21.1% |
| 19,832 | AUSTIN | 7,890 | 4,015 | 2,278 | 1,585 | 12 | 1,737 R | 50.9% | 28.9% | 20.1% |
| 7,064 | BAILEY | 2,365 | 1,308 | 677 | 376 | 4 | 631 R | 55.3% | 28.6% | 15.9% |
| 10,562 | BANDERA | 5,322 | 2,674 | 1,059 | 1,537 | 52 | 1,137 R | 50.2% | 19.9% | 28.9% |
| 38,263 | BASTROP | 14,474 | 4,980 | 6,252 | 3,240 | 2 | 1,272 D | 34.4% | 43.2% | 22.4% |
| 4,385 | BAYLOR | 2,132 | 611 | 990 | 529 | 2 | 379 D | 28.7% | 46.4% | 24.8% |
| 25,135 | BEE | 9,108 | 3,633 | 4,083 | 1,367 | 25 | 450 D | 39.9% | 44.8% | 15.0% |
| 191,088 | BELL | 55,077 | 24,936 | 18,684 | 11,026 | 431 | 6,252 R | 45.3% | 33.9% | 20.0% |
| 1,185,394 | BEXAR | 415,276 | 168,816 | 172,513 | 72,110 | 1,837 | 3,697 D | 40.7% | 41.5% | 17.4% |
| 5,972 | BLANCO | 3,109 | 1,370 | 891 | 830 | 18 | 479 R | 44.1% | 28.7% | 26.7% |
| 799 | BORDEN | 378 | 184 | 106 | 87 | 1 | 78 R | 48.7% | 28.0% | 23.0% |
| 15,125 | BOSQUE | 6,489 | 2,300 | 2,173 | 1,999 | 17 | 127 R | 35.4% | 33.5% | 30.8% |
| 81,665 | BOWIE | 30,365 | 11,776 | 11,825 | 6,659 | 105 | 49 D | 38.8% | 38.9% | 21.9% |
| 191,707 | BRAZORIA | 71,467 | 30,384 | 21,861 | 18,954 | 268 | 8,523 R | 42.5% | 30.6% | 26.5% |
| 121,862 | BRAZOS | 49,340 | 23,943 | 14,819 | 10,372 | 206 | 9,124 R | 48.5% | 30.0% | 21.0% |
| 8,681 | BREWSTER | 3,247 | 1,127 | 1,383 | 712 | 25 | 256 D | 34.7% | 42.6% | 21.9% |
| 1,971 | BRISCOE | 957 | 360 | 430 | 164 | 3 | 70 D | 37.6% | 44.9% | 17.1% |
| 8,204 | BROOKS | 3,765 | 585 | 2,856 | 318 | 6 | 2,271 D | 15.5% | 75.9% | 8.4% |
| 34,371 | BROWN | 12,630 | 5,313 | 4,264 | 3,034 | 19 | 1,049 R | 42.1% | 33.8% | 24.0% |
| 13,625 | BURLESON | 5,711 | 2,013 | 2,511 | 1,179 | 8 | 498 D | 35.2% | 44.0% | 20.6% |
| 22,677 | BURNET | 10,807 | 4,272 | 3,638 | 2,865 | 32 | 634 R | 39.5% | 33.7% | 26.5% |
| 26,392 | CALDWELL | 8,344 | 2,749 | 3,794 | 1,776 | 25 | 1,045 D | 32.9% | 45.5% | 21.3% |
| 19,053 | CALHOUN | 6,779 | 2,640 | 2,550 | 1,579 | 10 | 90 R | 38.9% | 37.6% | 23.3% |
| 11,859 | CALLAHAN | 5,285 | 2,134 | 1,694 | 1,452 | 5 | 440 R | 40.4% | 32.1% | 27.5% |
| 260,120 | CAMERON | 59,057 | 20,123 | 29,435 | 9,286 | 213 | 9,312 D | 34.1% | 49.8% | 15.7% |
| 9,904 | CAMP | 3,980 | 1,219 | 1,938 | 821 | 2 | 719 D | 30.6% | 48.7% | 20.6% |
| 6,576 | CARSON | 3,057 | 1,647 | 825 | 578 | 7 | 822 R | 53.9% | 27.0% | 18.9% |
| 29,982 | CASS | 11,660 | 3,999 | 5,476 | 2,168 | 17 | 1,477 D | 34.3% | 47.0% | 18.6% |
| 9,070 | CASTRO | 2,910 | 1,307 | 1,113 | 485 | 5 | 194 R | 44.9% | 38.2% | 16.7% |
| 20,088 | CHAMBERS | 8,366 | 3,398 | 2,832 | 2,122 | 14 | 566 R | 40.6% | 33.9% | 25.4% |
| 41,049 | CHEROKEE | 14,138 | 5,847 | 5,003 | 3,273 | 15 | 844 R | 41.4% | 35.4% | 23.2% |
| 5,953 | CHILDRESS | 2,338 | 1,033 | 881 | 421 | 3 | 152 R | 44.2% | 37.7% | 18.0% |
| 10,024 | CLAY | 4,910 | 1,586 | 1,919 | 1,397 | 8 | 333 D | 32.3% | 39.1% | 28.5% |
| 4,377 | COCHRAN | 1,461 | 750 | 454 | 255 | 2 | 296 R | 51.3% | 31.1% | 17.5% |
| 3,424 | COKE | 1,614 | 640 | 580 | 393 | 1 | 60 R | 39.7% | 35.9% | 24.3% |
| 9,710 | COLEMAN | 4,138 | 1,462 | 1,579 | 1,095 | 2 | 117 D | 35.3% | 38.2% | 26.5% |
| 264,036 | COLLIN | 128,833 | 60,514 | 24,508 | 43,287 | 524 | 17,227 R | 47.0% | 19.0% | 33.6% |
| 3,573 | COLLINGSWORTH | 1,600 | 697 | 635 | 265 | 3 | 62 R | 43.6% | 39.7% | 16.6% |
| 18,383 | COLORADO | 7,162 | 3,286 | 2,442 | 1,421 | 13 | 844 R | 45.9% | 34.1% | 19.8% |
| 51,832 | COMAL | 24,941 | 12,651 | 6,312 | 5,841 | 137 | 6,339 R | 50.7% | 25.3% | 23.4% |
| 13,381 | COMANCHE | 5,248 | 1,666 | 2,296 | 1,281 | 5 | 630 D | 31.7% | 43.8% | 24.4% |
| 3,044 | CONCHO | 1,236 | 414 | 489 | 329 | 4 | 75 D | 33.5% | 39.6% | 26.6% |
| 30,777 | COOKE | 13,084 | 5,299 | 3,105 | 4,658 | 22 | 641 R | 40.5% | 23.7% | 35.6% |
| 64,213 | CORYELL | 14,312 | 6,144 | 4,157 | 3,974 | 37 | 1,987 R | 42.9% | 29.0% | 27.8% |
| 2,247 | COTTLE | 1,025 | 245 | 542 | 235 | 3 | 297 D | 23.9% | 52.9% | 22.9% |
| 4,652 | CRANE | 1,845 | 918 | 514 | 412 | 1 | 404 R | 49.8% | 27.9% | 22.3% |
| 4,078 | CROCKETT | 1,645 | 623 | 653 | 368 | 1 | 30 D | 37.9% | 39.7% | 22.4% |
| 7,304 | CROSBY | 2,335 | 1,006 | 1,010 | 313 | 6 | 4 D | 43.1% | 43.3% | 13.4% |
| 3,407 | CULBERSON | 847 | 251 | 424 | 171 | 1 | 173 D | 29.6% | 50.1% | 20.2% |
| 5,461 | DALLAM | 1,683 | 922 | 434 | 325 | 2 | 488 R | 54.8% | 25.8% | 19.3% |
| 1,852,810 | DALLAS | 661,252 | 256,007 | 231,412 | 170,571 | 3,262 | 24,595 R | 38.7% | 35.0% | 25.8% |
| 14,349 | DAWSON | 4,855 | 2,691 | 1,639 | 518 | 7 | 1,052 R | 55.4% | 33.8% | 10.7% |
| 19,153 | DEAF SMITH | 5,559 | 3,137 | 1,642 | 772 | 8 | 1,495 R | 56.4% | 29.5% | 13.9% |
| 4,857 | DELTA | 2,015 | 599 | 864 | 551 | 1 | 265 D | 29.7% | 42.9% | 27.3% |

# TEXAS

## PRESIDENT 1992

| 1990 Census Population | County | Total Vote | Republican | Democratic | Perot | Other | Plurality | Percentage Total Vote Rep. | Dem. | Perot |
|---|---|---|---|---|---|---|---|---|---|---|
| 273,525 | DENTON | 116,576 | 48,492 | 27,891 | 39,653 | 540 | 8,839 R | 41.6% | 23.9% | 34.0% |
| 18,840 | DE WITT | 6,730 | 3,238 | 2,127 | 1,346 | 19 | 1,111 R | 48.1% | 31.6% | 20.0% |
| 2,571 | DICKENS | 1,160 | 373 | 536 | 250 | 1 | 163 D | 32.2% | 46.2% | 21.6% |
| 10,433 | DIMMIT | 4,380 | 844 | 3,172 | 361 | 3 | 2,328 D | 19.3% | 72.4% | 8.2% |
| 3,696 | DONLEY | 1,735 | 893 | 578 | 260 | 4 | 315 R | 51.5% | 33.3% | 15.0% |
| 12,918 | DUVAL | 5,035 | 698 | 4,006 | 326 | 5 | 3,308 D | 13.9% | 79.6% | 6.5% |
| 18,488 | EASTLAND | 7,281 | 2,830 | 2,738 | 1,698 | 15 | 92 R | 38.9% | 37.6% | 23.3% |
| 118,934 | ECTOR | 36,073 | 18,161 | 11,130 | 6,668 | 114 | 7,031 R | 50.3% | 30.9% | 18.5% |
| 2,266 | EDWARDS | 887 | 460 | 254 | 171 | 2 | 206 R | 51.9% | 28.6% | 19.3% |
| 85,167 | ELLIS | 33,495 | 13,564 | 9,537 | 10,303 | 91 | 3,261 R | 40.5% | 28.5% | 30.8% |
| 591,610 | EL PASO | 135,163 | 47,224 | 67,715 | 19,738 | 486 | 20,491 D | 34.9% | 50.1% | 14.6% |
| 27,991 | ERATH | 10,431 | 3,835 | 3,531 | 3,046 | 19 | 304 R | 36.8% | 33.9% | 29.2% |
| 17,712 | FALLS | 5,773 | 1,826 | 2,761 | 1,185 | 1 | 935 D | 31.6% | 47.8% | 20.5% |
| 24,804 | FANNIN | 9,615 | 2,510 | 4,164 | 2,919 | 22 | 1,245 D | 26.1% | 43.3% | 30.4% |
| 20,095 | FAYETTE | 8,823 | 3,789 | 2,923 | 2,088 | 23 | 866 R | 42.9% | 33.1% | 23.7% |
| 4,842 | FISHER | 2,225 | 539 | 1,242 | 442 | 2 | 703 D | 24.2% | 55.8% | 19.9% |
| 8,497 | FLOYD | 3,009 | 1,676 | 947 | 385 | 1 | 729 R | 55.7% | 31.5% | 12.8% |
| 1,794 | FOARD | 796 | 207 | 435 | 152 | 2 | 228 D | 26.0% | 54.6% | 19.1% |
| 225,421 | FORT BEND | 88,031 | 41,039 | 29,992 | 16,853 | 147 | 11,047 R | 46.6% | 34.1% | 19.1% |
| 7,802 | FRANKLIN | 3,342 | 1,058 | 1,338 | 942 | 4 | 280 D | 31.7% | 40.0% | 28.2% |
| 15,818 | FREESTONE | 6,365 | 2,316 | 2,445 | 1,596 | 8 | 129 D | 36.4% | 38.4% | 25.1% |
| 13,472 | FRIO | 4,319 | 1,275 | 2,377 | 654 | 13 | 1,102 D | 29.5% | 55.0% | 15.1% |
| 14,123 | GAINES | 3,933 | 2,138 | 1,095 | 696 | 4 | 1,043 R | 54.4% | 27.8% | 17.7% |
| 217,399 | GALVESTON | 90,242 | 31,303 | 38,623 | 20,103 | 213 | 7,320 D | 34.7% | 42.8% | 22.3% |
| 5,143 | GARZA | 1,888 | 982 | 558 | 345 | 3 | 424 R | 52.0% | 29.6% | 18.3% |
| 17,204 | GILLESPIE | 8,372 | 4,712 | 1,600 | 2,018 | 42 | 2,694 R | 56.3% | 19.1% | 24.1% |
| 1,447 | GLASSCOCK | 574 | 379 | 100 | 93 | 2 | 279 R | 66.0% | 17.4% | 16.2% |
| 5,980 | GOLIAD | 2,831 | 1,236 | 1,069 | 521 | 5 | 167 R | 43.7% | 37.8% | 18.4% |
| 17,205 | GONZALES | 5,557 | 2,502 | 2,006 | 1,018 | 31 | 496 R | 45.0% | 36.1% | 18.3% |
| 23,967 | GRAY | 10,372 | 6,105 | 2,426 | 1,810 | 31 | 3,679 R | 58.9% | 23.4% | 17.5% |
| 95,021 | GRAYSON | 38,332 | 12,322 | 12,547 | 13,327 | 136 | 780 P | 32.1% | 32.7% | 34.8% |
| 104,948 | GREGG | 41,829 | 20,542 | 12,797 | 8,437 | 53 | 7,745 R | 49.1% | 30.6% | 20.2% |
| 18,828 | GRIMES | 6,217 | 2,402 | 2,594 | 1,213 | 8 | 192 D | 38.6% | 41.7% | 19.5% |
| 64,873 | GUADALUPE | 23,120 | 10,818 | 6,567 | 5,618 | 117 | 4,251 R | 46.8% | 28.4% | 24.3% |
| 34,671 | HALE | 10,234 | 6,098 | 2,761 | 1,357 | 18 | 3,337 R | 59.6% | 27.0% | 13.3% |
| 3,905 | HALL | 1,714 | 631 | 819 | 263 | 1 | 188 D | 36.8% | 47.8% | 15.3% |
| 7,733 | HAMILTON | 3,259 | 1,232 | 1,100 | 921 | 6 | 132 R | 37.8% | 33.8% | 28.3% |
| 5,848 | HANSFORD | 2,403 | 1,660 | 345 | 398 | | 1,262 R | 69.1% | 14.4% | 16.6% |
| 5,283 | HARDEMAN | 1,936 | 614 | 954 | 362 | 6 | 340 D | 31.7% | 49.3% | 18.7% |
| 41,320 | HARDIN | 16,793 | 5,885 | 6,753 | 4,129 | 26 | 868 D | 35.0% | 40.2% | 24.6% |
| 2,818,199 | HARRIS | 942,947 | 406,778 | 360,171 | 172,922 | 3,076 | 46,607 R | 43.1% | 38.2% | 18.3% |
| 57,483 | HARRISON | 22,683 | 8,733 | 9,538 | 4,371 | 41 | 805 D | 38.5% | 42.0% | 19.3% |
| 3,634 | HARTLEY | 1,797 | 1,081 | 406 | 308 | 2 | 675 R | 60.2% | 22.6% | 17.1% |
| 6,820 | HASKELL | 2,853 | 852 | 1,438 | 562 | 1 | 586 D | 29.9% | 50.4% | 19.7% |
| 65,614 | HAYS | 27,267 | 10,008 | 10,842 | 6,252 | 165 | 834 D | 36.7% | 39.8% | 22.9% |
| 3,720 | HEMPHILL | 1,700 | 989 | 479 | 232 | | 510 R | 58.2% | 28.2% | 13.6% |
| 58,543 | HENDERSON | 24,261 | 8,368 | 9,105 | 6,746 | 42 | 737 D | 34.5% | 37.5% | 27.8% |
| 383,545 | HIDALGO | 88,160 | 26,976 | 51,205 | 9,757 | 222 | 24,229 D | 30.6% | 58.1% | 11.1% |
| 27,146 | HILL | 10,376 | 3,669 | 3,929 | 2,752 | 26 | 260 D | 35.4% | 37.9% | 26.5% |
| 24,199 | HOCKLEY | 7,868 | 4,261 | 2,301 | 1,291 | 15 | 1,960 R | 54.2% | 29.2% | 16.4% |
| 28,981 | HOOD | 14,162 | 5,313 | 4,359 | 4,457 | 33 | 856 R | 37.5% | 30.8% | 31.5% |
| 28,833 | HOPKINS | 10,643 | 3,398 | 4,085 | 3,147 | 13 | 687 D | 31.9% | 38.4% | 29.6% |
| 21,375 | HOUSTON | 8,020 | 3,067 | 3,250 | 1,690 | 13 | 183 D | 38.2% | 40.5% | 21.1% |
| 32,343 | HOWARD | 10,873 | 5,129 | 3,735 | 1,984 | 25 | 1,394 R | 47.2% | 34.4% | 18.2% |
| 2,915 | HUDSPETH | 869 | 325 | 364 | 178 | 2 | 39 D | 37.4% | 41.9% | 20.5% |
| 64,343 | HUNT | 24,650 | 9,739 | 7,452 | 7,387 | 72 | 2,287 R | 39.5% | 30.2% | 30.0% |
| 25,689 | HUTCHINSON | 10,888 | 6,034 | 2,833 | 1,993 | 28 | 3,201 R | 55.4% | 26.0% | 18.3% |
| 1,629 | IRION | 831 | 283 | 256 | 290 | 2 | 7 P | 34.1% | 30.8% | 34.9% |
| 6,981 | JACK | 3,347 | 1,041 | 1,254 | 1,045 | 7 | 209 D | 31.1% | 37.5% | 31.2% |
| 13,039 | JACKSON | 5,152 | 2,451 | 1,722 | 976 | 3 | 729 R | 47.6% | 33.4% | 18.9% |

# TEXAS

## PRESIDENT 1992

| 1990 Census Population | County | Total Vote | Republican | Democratic | Perot | Other | Plurality | Percentage Total Vote Rep. | Dem. | Perot |
|---|---|---|---|---|---|---|---|---|---|---|
| 31,102 | JASPER | 12,087 | 3,870 | 5,658 | 2,539 | 20 | 1,788 D | 32.0% | 46.8% | 21.0% |
| 1,946 | JEFF DAVIS | 876 | 360 | 321 | 187 | 8 | 39 R | 41.1% | 36.6% | 21.3% |
| 239,397 | JEFFERSON | 95,543 | 29,622 | 48,405 | 17,242 | 274 | 18,783 D | 31.0% | 50.7% | 18.0% |
| 5,109 | JIM HOGG | 2,110 | 478 | 1,520 | 107 | 5 | 1,042 D | 22.7% | 72.0% | 5.1% |
| 37,679 | JIM WELLS | 12,561 | 3,311 | 7,812 | 1,413 | 25 | 4,501 D | 26.4% | 62.2% | 11.2% |
| 97,165 | JOHNSON | 37,202 | 13,473 | 12,030 | 11,573 | 126 | 1,443 R | 36.2% | 32.3% | 31.1% |
| 16,490 | JONES | 5,932 | 2,088 | 2,400 | 1,436 | 8 | 312 D | 35.2% | 40.5% | 24.2% |
| 12,455 | KARNES | 4,700 | 1,990 | 1,897 | 802 | 11 | 93 R | 42.3% | 40.4% | 17.1% |
| 52,220 | KAUFMAN | 19,060 | 6,578 | 6,498 | 5,913 | 71 | 80 R | 34.5% | 34.1% | 31.0% |
| 14,589 | KENDALL | 7,354 | 4,162 | 1,374 | 1,773 | 45 | 2,389 R | 56.6% | 18.7% | 24.1% |
| 460 | KENEDY | 174 | 69 | 87 | 18 | | 18 D | 39.7% | 50.0% | 10.3% |
| 1,010 | KENT | 610 | 175 | 271 | 163 | 1 | 96 D | 28.7% | 44.4% | 26.7% |
| 36,304 | KERR | 16,358 | 8,787 | 3,707 | 3,790 | 74 | 4,997 R | 53.7% | 22.7% | 23.2% |
| 4,122 | KIMBLE | 1,613 | 790 | 467 | 354 | 2 | 323 R | 49.0% | 29.0% | 21.9% |
| 354 | KING | 189 | 79 | 54 | 56 | | 23 R | 41.8% | 28.6% | 29.6% |
| 3,119 | KINNEY | 1,539 | 634 | 598 | 299 | 8 | 36 R | 41.2% | 38.9% | 19.4% |
| 30,274 | KLEBERG | 10,564 | 3,897 | 5,109 | 1,470 | 88 | 1,212 D | 36.9% | 48.4% | 13.9% |
| 4,837 | KNOX | 1,815 | 521 | 854 | 438 | 2 | 333 D | 28.7% | 47.1% | 24.1% |
| 43,949 | LAMAR | 16,243 | 5,778 | 6,328 | 4,093 | 44 | 550 D | 35.6% | 39.0% | 25.2% |
| 15,072 | LAMB | 5,450 | 2,998 | 1,737 | 709 | 6 | 1,261 R | 55.0% | 31.9% | 13.0% |
| 13,521 | LAMPASAS | 5,185 | 2,233 | 1,508 | 1,432 | 12 | 725 R | 43.1% | 29.1% | 27.6% |
| 5,254 | LA SALLE | 2,319 | 586 | 1,522 | 211 | | 936 D | 25.3% | 65.6% | 9.1% |
| 18,690 | LAVACA | 7,776 | 3,362 | 2,700 | 1,696 | 18 | 662 R | 43.2% | 34.7% | 21.8% |
| 12,854 | LEE | 5,058 | 2,108 | 1,847 | 1,088 | 15 | 261 R | 41.7% | 36.5% | 21.5% |
| 12,665 | LEON | 5,508 | 2,212 | 2,042 | 1,251 | 3 | 170 R | 40.2% | 37.1% | 22.7% |
| 52,726 | LIBERTY | 18,339 | 6,959 | 7,036 | 4,311 | 33 | 77 D | 37.9% | 38.4% | 23.5% |
| 20,946 | LIMESTONE | 7,060 | 2,358 | 3,188 | 1,505 | 9 | 830 D | 33.4% | 45.2% | 21.3% |
| 3,143 | LIPSCOMB | 1,453 | 839 | 338 | 270 | 6 | 501 R | 57.7% | 23.3% | 18.6% |
| 9,556 | LIVE OAK | 3,965 | 1,805 | 1,345 | 806 | 9 | 460 R | 45.5% | 33.9% | 20.3% |
| 11,631 | LLANO | 7,283 | 3,056 | 2,409 | 1,799 | 19 | 647 R | 42.0% | 33.1% | 24.7% |
| 107 | LOVING | 96 | 31 | 20 | 45 | | 14 P | 32.3% | 20.8% | 46.9% |
| 222,636 | LUBBOCK | 82,858 | 48,847 | 22,240 | 11,618 | 153 | 26,607 R | 59.0% | 26.8% | 14.0% |
| 6,758 | LYNN | 2,428 | 1,233 | 902 | 291 | 2 | 331 R | 50.8% | 37.1% | 12.0% |
| 8,778 | MCCULLOCH | 3,491 | 1,108 | 1,393 | 986 | 4 | 285 D | 31.7% | 39.9% | 28.2% |
| 189,123 | MCLENNAN | 70,016 | 28,473 | 25,903 | 15,505 | 135 | 2,570 R | 40.7% | 37.0% | 22.1% |
| 817 | MCMULLEN | 443 | 274 | 78 | 89 | 2 | 185 R | 61.9% | 17.6% | 20.1% |
| 10,931 | MADISON | 3,883 | 1,544 | 1,553 | 778 | 8 | 9 D | 39.8% | 40.0% | 20.0% |
| 9,984 | MARION | 4,288 | 1,245 | 2,156 | 882 | 5 | 911 D | 29.0% | 50.3% | 20.6% |
| 4,956 | MARTIN | 1,988 | 986 | 641 | 356 | 5 | 345 R | 49.6% | 32.2% | 17.9% |
| 3,423 | MASON | 1,722 | 776 | 570 | 364 | 12 | 206 R | 45.1% | 33.1% | 21.1% |
| 36,928 | MATAGORDA | 13,165 | 5,328 | 4,759 | 3,045 | 33 | 569 R | 40.5% | 36.1% | 23.1% |
| 36,378 | MAVERICK | 7,339 | 2,002 | 4,540 | 771 | 26 | 2,538 D | 27.3% | 61.9% | 10.5% |
| 27,312 | MEDINA | 10,785 | 4,912 | 3,650 | 2,167 | 56 | 1,262 R | 45.5% | 33.8% | 20.1% |
| 2,252 | MENARD | 1,277 | 354 | 553 | 367 | 3 | 186 D | 27.7% | 43.3% | 28.7% |
| 106,611 | MIDLAND | 41,347 | 24,143 | 9,160 | 7,880 | 164 | 14,983 R | 58.4% | 22.2% | 19.1% |
| 22,946 | MILAM | 7,468 | 2,414 | 3,542 | 1,495 | 17 | 1,128 D | 32.3% | 47.4% | 20.0% |
| 4,531 | MILLS | 1,990 | 702 | 753 | 530 | 5 | 51 D | 35.3% | 37.8% | 26.6% |
| 8,016 | MITCHELL | 3,093 | 1,128 | 1,353 | 604 | 8 | 225 D | 36.5% | 43.7% | 19.5% |
| 17,274 | MONTAGUE | 7,526 | 2,304 | 2,885 | 2,330 | 7 | 555 D | 30.6% | 38.3% | 31.0% |
| 182,201 | MONTGOMERY | 77,958 | 39,976 | 18,551 | 19,203 | 228 | 20,773 R | 51.3% | 23.8% | 24.6% |
| 17,865 | MOORE | 5,498 | 3,147 | 1,361 | 976 | 14 | 1,786 R | 57.2% | 24.8% | 17.8% |
| 13,200 | MORRIS | 5,569 | 1,400 | 3,028 | 1,138 | 3 | 1,628 D | 25.1% | 54.4% | 20.4% |
| 1,532 | MOTLEY | 819 | 446 | 256 | 117 | | 190 R | 54.5% | 31.3% | 14.3% |
| 54,753 | NACOGDOCHES | 21,643 | 9,864 | 6,937 | 4,803 | 39 | 2,927 R | 45.6% | 32.1% | 22.2% |
| 39,926 | NAVARRO | 14,721 | 4,897 | 6,006 | 3,800 | 18 | 1,109 D | 33.3% | 40.8% | 25.8% |
| 13,569 | NEWTON | 5,508 | 1,212 | 3,249 | 1,032 | 15 | 2,037 D | 22.0% | 59.0% | 18.7% |
| 16,594 | NOLAN | 5,952 | 1,993 | 2,490 | 1,455 | 14 | 497 D | 33.5% | 41.8% | 24.4% |
| 291,145 | NUECES | 100,791 | 36,781 | 46,317 | 17,374 | 319 | 9,536 D | 36.5% | 46.0% | 17.2% |
| 9,128 | OCHILTREE | 3,554 | 2,419 | 557 | 576 | 2 | 1,843 R | 68.1% | 15.7% | 16.2% |
| 2,278 | OLDHAM | 987 | 583 | 225 | 177 | 2 | 358 R | 59.1% | 22.8% | 17.9% |

# TEXAS

## PRESIDENT 1992

| 1990 Census Population | County | Total Vote | Republican | Democratic | Perot | Other | Plurality | Percentage Total Vote Rep. | Dem. | Perot |
|---|---|---|---|---|---|---|---|---|---|---|
| 80,509 | ORANGE | 32,490 | 9,793 | 15,305 | 7,321 | 71 | 5,512 D | 30.1% | 47.1% | 22.5% |
| 25,055 | PALO PINTO | 9,275 | 2,852 | 3,392 | 3,010 | 21 | 382 D | 30.7% | 36.6% | 32.5% |
| 22,035 | PANOLA | 9,332 | 3,473 | 3,950 | 1,906 | 3 | 477 D | 37.2% | 42.3% | 20.4% |
| 64,785 | PARKER | 27,494 | 10,321 | 7,934 | 9,148 | 91 | 1,173 R | 37.5% | 28.9% | 33.3% |
| 9,863 | PARMER | 3,033 | 1,829 | 637 | 564 | 3 | 1,192 R | 60.3% | 21.0% | 18.6% |
| 14,675 | PECOS | 4,523 | 1,836 | 1,778 | 895 | 14 | 58 R | 40.6% | 39.3% | 19.8% |
| 30,687 | POLK | 14,254 | 5,390 | 5,942 | 2,884 | 38 | 552 D | 37.8% | 41.7% | 20.2% |
| 97,874 | POTTER | 27,775 | 13,510 | 9,527 | 4,655 | 83 | 3,983 R | 48.6% | 34.3% | 16.8% |
| 6,637 | PRESIDIO | 1,891 | 400 | 1,189 | 290 | 12 | 789 D | 21.2% | 62.9% | 15.3% |
| 6,715 | RAINS | 2,983 | 975 | 1,108 | 890 | 10 | 133 D | 32.7% | 37.1% | 29.8% |
| 89,673 | RANDALL | 40,537 | 24,971 | 9,119 | 6,340 | 107 | 15,852 R | 61.6% | 22.5% | 15.6% |
| 4,514 | REAGAN | 1,250 | 651 | 337 | 259 | 3 | 314 R | 52.1% | 27.0% | 20.7% |
| 2,412 | REAL | 1,640 | 787 | 463 | 386 | 4 | 324 R | 48.0% | 28.2% | 23.5% |
| 14,317 | RED RIVER | 5,655 | 1,735 | 2,686 | 1,228 | 6 | 951 D | 30.7% | 47.5% | 21.7% |
| 15,852 | REEVES | 4,557 | 1,244 | 2,569 | 734 | 10 | 1,325 D | 27.3% | 56.4% | 16.1% |
| 7,976 | REFUGIO | 3,732 | 1,469 | 1,531 | 716 | 16 | 62 D | 39.4% | 41.0% | 19.2% |
| 1,025 | ROBERTS | 617 | 391 | 126 | 99 | 1 | 265 R | 63.4% | 20.4% | 16.0% |
| 15,511 | ROBERTSON | 5,604 | 1,707 | 2,927 | 963 | 7 | 1,220 D | 30.5% | 52.2% | 17.2% |
| 25,604 | ROCKWALL | 13,269 | 6,427 | 2,397 | 4,393 | 52 | 2,034 R | 48.4% | 18.1% | 33.1% |
| 11,294 | RUNNELS | 4,340 | 1,653 | 1,401 | 1,279 | 7 | 252 R | 38.1% | 32.3% | 29.5% |
| 43,735 | RUSK | 16,574 | 7,560 | 5,391 | 3,575 | 48 | 2,169 R | 45.6% | 32.5% | 21.6% |
| 9,586 | SABINE | 4,678 | 1,490 | 2,288 | 894 | 6 | 798 D | 31.9% | 48.9% | 19.1% |
| 7,999 | SAN AUGUSTINE | 3,649 | 1,243 | 1,737 | 667 | 2 | 494 D | 34.1% | 47.6% | 18.3% |
| 16,372 | SAN JACINTO | 7,011 | 2,494 | 2,846 | 1,653 | 18 | 352 D | 35.6% | 40.6% | 23.6% |
| 58,749 | SAN PATRICIO | 18,887 | 7,456 | 8,202 | 3,178 | 51 | 746 D | 39.5% | 43.4% | 16.8% |
| 5,401 | SAN SABA | 2,103 | 723 | 716 | 660 | 4 | 7 R | 34.4% | 34.0% | 31.4% |
| 2,990 | SCHLEICHER | 1,231 | 452 | 420 | 355 | 4 | 32 R | 36.7% | 34.1% | 28.8% |
| 18,634 | SCURRY | 6,121 | 2,670 | 1,609 | 1,826 | 16 | 844 R | 43.6% | 26.3% | 29.8% |
| 3,316 | SHACKELFORD | 1,533 | 623 | 484 | 422 | 4 | 139 R | 40.6% | 31.6% | 27.5% |
| 22,034 | SHELBY | 8,705 | 3,217 | 3,986 | 1,487 | 15 | 769 D | 37.0% | 45.8% | 17.1% |
| 2,858 | SHERMAN | 1,369 | 851 | 261 | 256 | 1 | 590 R | 62.2% | 19.1% | 18.7% |
| 151,309 | SMITH | 59,006 | 27,753 | 17,514 | 13,569 | 170 | 10,239 R | 47.0% | 29.7% | 23.0% |
| 5,360 | SOMERVELL | 2,568 | 872 | 782 | 903 | 11 | 31 P | 34.0% | 30.5% | 35.2% |
| 40,518 | STARR | 9,261 | 1,209 | 7,668 | 345 | 39 | 6,459 D | 13.1% | 82.8% | 3.7% |
| 9,010 | STEPHENS | 3,756 | 1,573 | 1,115 | 1,062 | 6 | 458 R | 41.9% | 29.7% | 28.3% |
| 1,438 | STERLING | 634 | 322 | 127 | 182 | 3 | 140 R | 50.8% | 20.0% | 28.7% |
| 2,013 | STONEWALL | 1,125 | 242 | 561 | 322 | | 239 D | 21.5% | 49.9% | 28.6% |
| 4,135 | SUTTON | 1,598 | 687 | 524 | 387 | | 163 R | 43.0% | 32.8% | 24.2% |
| 8,133 | SWISHER | 2,949 | 989 | 1,413 | 541 | 6 | 424 D | 33.5% | 47.9% | 18.3% |
| 1,170,103 | TARRANT | 471,396 | 183,387 | 156,230 | 129,998 | 1,781 | 27,157 R | 38.9% | 33.1% | 27.6% |
| 119,655 | TAYLOR | 45,454 | 22,614 | 12,382 | 10,331 | 127 | 10,232 R | 49.8% | 27.2% | 22.7% |
| 1,410 | TERRELL | 631 | 176 | 325 | 128 | 2 | 149 D | 27.9% | 51.5% | 20.3% |
| 13,218 | TERRY | 4,395 | 2,309 | 1,461 | 619 | 6 | 848 R | 52.5% | 33.2% | 14.1% |
| 1,880 | THROCKMORTON | 1,018 | 389 | 401 | 228 | | 12 D | 38.2% | 39.4% | 22.4% |
| 24,009 | TITUS | 8,810 | 3,024 | 3,625 | 2,146 | 15 | 601 D | 34.3% | 41.1% | 24.4% |
| 98,458 | TOM GREEN | 36,739 | 14,989 | 11,437 | 10,244 | 69 | 3,552 R | 40.8% | 31.1% | 27.9% |
| 576,407 | TRAVIS | 276,235 | 88,105 | 130,546 | 56,158 | 1,426 | 42,441 D | 31.9% | 47.3% | 20.3% |
| 11,445 | TRINITY | 5,909 | 1,988 | 2,784 | 1,133 | 4 | 796 D | 33.6% | 47.1% | 19.2% |
| 16,646 | TYLER | 7,360 | 2,357 | 3,465 | 1,529 | 9 | 1,108 D | 32.0% | 47.1% | 20.8% |
| 31,370 | UPSHUR | 12,208 | 4,511 | 4,776 | 2,896 | 25 | 265 D | 37.0% | 39.1% | 23.7% |
| 4,447 | UPTON | 1,756 | 908 | 489 | 313 | 46 | 419 R | 51.7% | 27.8% | 17.8% |
| 23,340 | UVALDE | 8,543 | 3,635 | 3,482 | 1,387 | 39 | 153 R | 42.5% | 40.8% | 16.2% |
| 38,721 | VAL VERDE | 10,996 | 4,102 | 4,748 | 2,093 | 53 | 646 D | 37.3% | 43.2% | 19.0% |
| 37,944 | VAN ZANDT | 16,396 | 5,810 | 5,310 | 5,239 | 37 | 500 R | 35.4% | 32.4% | 32.0% |
| 74,361 | VICTORIA | 26,037 | 13,086 | 7,604 | 5,136 | 211 | 5,482 R | 50.3% | 29.2% | 19.7% |
| 50,917 | WALKER | 15,924 | 6,662 | 5,619 | 3,619 | 24 | 1,043 R | 41.8% | 35.3% | 22.7% |
| 23,390 | WALLER | 9,058 | 3,065 | 4,270 | 1,692 | 31 | 1,205 D | 33.8% | 47.1% | 18.7% |
| 13,115 | WARD | 4,422 | 1,769 | 1,695 | 948 | 10 | 74 R | 40.0% | 38.3% | 21.4% |
| 26,154 | WASHINGTON | 10,853 | 5,817 | 3,283 | 1,738 | 15 | 2,534 R | 53.6% | 30.2% | 16.0% |
| 133,239 | WEBB | 24,866 | 7,789 | 14,509 | 2,517 | 51 | 6,720 D | 31.3% | 58.3% | 10.1% |

# TEXAS

## PRESIDENT 1992

| 1990 Census Population | County | Total Vote | Republican | Democratic | Perot | Other | Plurality | Percentage Total Vote | | |
|---|---|---|---|---|---|---|---|---|---|---|
| | | | | | | | | Rep. | Dem. | Perot |
| 39,955 | WHARTON | 12,797 | 5,503 | 4,643 | 2,624 | 27 | 860 R | 43.0% | 36.3% | 20.5% |
| 5,879 | WHEELER | 2,767 | 1,458 | 938 | 367 | 4 | 520 R | 52.7% | 33.9% | 13.3% |
| 122,378 | WICHITA | 46,608 | 17,956 | 17,021 | 11,478 | 153 | 935 R | 38.5% | 36.5% | 24.6% |
| 15,121 | WILBARGER | 5,340 | 1,959 | 1,924 | 1,453 | 4 | 35 R | 36.7% | 36.0% | 27.2% |
| 17,705 | WILLACY | 5,510 | 1,490 | 3,359 | 652 | 9 | 1,869 D | 27.0% | 61.0% | 11.8% |
| 139,551 | WILLIAMSON | 61,254 | 26,208 | 19,437 | 15,415 | 194 | 6,771 R | 42.8% | 31.7% | 25.2% |
| 22,650 | WILSON | 9,625 | 3,766 | 3,711 | 2,105 | 43 | 55 R | 39.1% | 38.6% | 21.9% |
| 8,626 | WINKLER | 2,702 | 1,173 | 942 | 582 | 5 | 231 R | 43.4% | 34.9% | 21.5% |
| 34,679 | WISE | 13,568 | 4,555 | 4,478 | 4,485 | 50 | 70 R | 33.6% | 33.0% | 33.1% |
| 29,380 | WOOD | 12,318 | 4,708 | 4,084 | 3,494 | 32 | 624 R | 38.2% | 33.2% | 28.4% |
| 8,786 | YOAKUM | 2,575 | 1,486 | 595 | 484 | 10 | 891 R | 57.7% | 23.1% | 18.8% |
| 18,126 | YOUNG | 7,675 | 2,894 | 2,464 | 2,302 | 15 | 430 R | 37.7% | 32.1% | 30.0% |
| 9,279 | ZAPATA | 3,249 | 866 | 2,052 | 326 | 5 | 1,186 D | 26.7% | 63.2% | 10.0% |
| 12,162 | ZAVALA | 3,868 | 571 | 3,058 | 237 | 2 | 2,487 D | 14.8% | 79.1% | 6.1% |
| 16,986,510 | TOTAL | 6,154,018 | 2,496,071 | 2,281,815 | 1,354,781 | 21,351 | 214,256 R | 40.6% | 37.1% | 22.0% |

# TEXAS

## PRESIDENT 1988

| 1980 Census Population | County | Total Vote | Republican | Democratic | Other | Rep.-Dem. Plurality | Percentage Total Vote Rep. | Dem. | Major Vote Rep. | Dem. |
|---|---|---|---|---|---|---|---|---|---|---|
| 38,381 | ANDERSON | 14,045 | 7,858 | 6,128 | 59 | 1,730 R | 55.9% | 43.6% | 56.2% | 43.8% |
| 13,323 | ANDREWS | 4,191 | 3,052 | 1,122 | 17 | 1,930 R | 72.8% | 26.8% | 73.1% | 26.9% |
| 64,172 | ANGELINA | 23,852 | 12,738 | 10,849 | 265 | 1,889 R | 53.4% | 45.5% | 54.0% | 46.0% |
| 14,260 | ARANSAS | 6,196 | 3,858 | 2,305 | 33 | 1,553 R | 62.3% | 37.2% | 62.6% | 37.4% |
| 7,266 | ARCHER | 3,646 | 2,010 | 1,627 | 9 | 383 R | 55.1% | 44.6% | 55.3% | 44.7% |
| 1,994 | ARMSTRONG | 1,040 | 720 | 314 | 6 | 406 R | 69.2% | 30.2% | 69.6% | 30.4% |
| 25,055 | ATASCOSA | 9,504 | 4,777 | 4,657 | 70 | 120 R | 50.3% | 49.0% | 50.6% | 49.4% |
| 17,726 | AUSTIN | 7,160 | 4,524 | 2,593 | 43 | 1,931 R | 63.2% | 36.2% | 63.6% | 36.4% |
| 8,168 | BAILEY | 2,343 | 1,459 | 876 | 8 | 583 R | 62.3% | 37.4% | 62.5% | 37.5% |
| 7,084 | BANDERA | 4,761 | 3,435 | 1,251 | 75 | 2,184 R | 72.1% | 26.3% | 73.3% | 26.7% |
| 24,726 | BASTROP | 14,092 | 5,991 | 8,004 | 97 | 2,013 D | 42.5% | 56.8% | 42.8% | 57.2% |
| 4,919 | BAYLOR | 2,070 | 914 | 1,153 | 3 | 239 D | 44.2% | 55.7% | 44.2% | 55.8% |
| 26,030 | BEE | 9,281 | 4,620 | 4,616 | 45 | 4 R | 49.8% | 49.7% | 50.0% | 50.0% |
| 157,889 | BELL | 47,551 | 29,382 | 17,751 | 418 | 11,631 R | 61.8% | 37.3% | 62.3% | 37.7% |
| 988,800 | BEXAR | 369,749 | 193,192 | 174,036 | 2,521 | 19,156 R | 52.2% | 47.1% | 52.6% | 47.4% |
| 4,681 | BLANCO | 2,719 | 1,680 | 1,012 | 27 | 668 R | 61.8% | 37.2% | 62.4% | 37.6% |
| 859 | BORDEN | 454 | 283 | 169 | 2 | 114 R | 62.3% | 37.2% | 62.6% | 37.4% |
| 13,401 | BOSQUE | 6,147 | 3,458 | 2,670 | 19 | 788 R | 56.3% | 43.4% | 56.4% | 43.6% |
| 75,301 | BOWIE | 27,941 | 15,454 | 12,331 | 156 | 3,123 R | 55.3% | 44.1% | 55.6% | 44.4% |
| 169,587 | BRAZORIA | 59,081 | 34,028 | 23,436 | 1,617 | 10,592 R | 57.6% | 39.7% | 59.2% | 40.8% |
| 93,588 | BRAZOS | 44,690 | 29,369 | 14,885 | 436 | 14,484 R | 65.7% | 33.3% | 66.4% | 33.6% |
| 7,573 | BREWSTER | 3,313 | 1,708 | 1,569 | 36 | 139 R | 51.6% | 47.4% | 52.1% | 47.9% |
| 2,579 | BRISCOE | 1,048 | 464 | 574 | 10 | 110 D | 44.3% | 54.8% | 44.7% | 55.3% |
| 8,428 | BROOKS | 3,489 | 608 | 2,859 | 22 | 2,251 D | 17.4% | 81.9% | 17.5% | 82.5% |
| 33,057 | BROWN | 11,606 | 6,810 | 4,763 | 33 | 2,047 R | 58.7% | 41.0% | 58.8% | 41.2% |
| 12,313 | BURLESON | 5,339 | 2,242 | 3,085 | 12 | 843 D | 42.0% | 57.8% | 42.1% | 57.9% |
| 17,803 | BURNET | 9,508 | 5,120 | 4,343 | 45 | 777 R | 53.8% | 45.7% | 54.1% | 45.9% |
| 23,637 | CALDWELL | 8,262 | 3,553 | 4,649 | 60 | 1,096 D | 43.0% | 56.3% | 43.3% | 56.7% |
| 19,574 | CALHOUN | 6,524 | 3,183 | 3,314 | 27 | 131 D | 48.8% | 50.8% | 49.0% | 51.0% |
| 10,992 | CALLAHAN | 4,921 | 2,887 | 2,017 | 17 | 870 R | 58.7% | 41.0% | 58.9% | 41.1% |
| 209,727 | CAMERON | 55,552 | 24,263 | 30,972 | 317 | 6,709 D | 43.7% | 55.8% | 43.9% | 56.1% |
| 9,275 | CAMP | 4,042 | 1,908 | 2,121 | 13 | 213 D | 47.2% | 52.5% | 47.4% | 52.6% |
| 6,672 | CARSON | 3,148 | 2,100 | 1,034 | 14 | 1,066 R | 66.7% | 32.8% | 67.0% | 33.0% |
| 29,430 | CASS | 11,262 | 5,305 | 5,941 | 16 | 636 D | 47.1% | 52.8% | 47.2% | 52.8% |
| 10,556 | CASTRO | 3,049 | 1,604 | 1,436 | 9 | 168 R | 52.6% | 47.1% | 52.8% | 47.2% |
| 18,538 | CHAMBERS | 6,781 | 3,694 | 3,035 | 52 | 659 R | 54.5% | 44.8% | 54.9% | 45.1% |
| 38,127 | CHEROKEE | 13,165 | 7,520 | 5,604 | 41 | 1,916 R | 57.1% | 42.6% | 57.3% | 42.7% |
| 6,950 | CHILDRESS | 2,267 | 1,201 | 1,060 | 6 | 141 R | 53.0% | 46.8% | 53.1% | 46.9% |
| 9,582 | CLAY | 4,340 | 2,043 | 2,288 | 9 | 245 D | 47.1% | 52.7% | 47.2% | 52.8% |
| 4,825 | COCHRAN | 1,462 | 771 | 681 | 10 | 90 R | 52.7% | 46.6% | 53.1% | 46.9% |
| 3,196 | COKE | 1,542 | 863 | 674 | 5 | 189 R | 56.0% | 43.7% | 56.1% | 43.9% |
| 10,439 | COLEMAN | 4,321 | 2,340 | 1,978 | 3 | 362 R | 54.2% | 45.8% | 54.2% | 45.8% |
| 144,576 | COLLIN | 91,230 | 67,776 | 22,934 | 520 | 44,842 R | 74.3% | 25.1% | 74.7% | 25.3% |
| 4,648 | COLLINGSWORTH | 1,683 | 872 | 809 | 2 | 63 R | 51.8% | 48.1% | 51.9% | 48.1% |
| 18,823 | COLORADO | 6,600 | 3,723 | 2,847 | 30 | 876 R | 56.4% | 43.1% | 56.7% | 43.3% |
| 36,446 | COMAL | 19,980 | 13,994 | 5,716 | 270 | 8,278 R | 70.0% | 28.6% | 71.0% | 29.0% |
| 12,617 | COMANCHE | 4,761 | 2,120 | 2,622 | 19 | 502 D | 44.5% | 55.1% | 44.7% | 55.3% |
| 2,915 | CONCHO | 1,263 | 617 | 643 | 3 | 26 D | 48.9% | 50.9% | 49.0% | 51.0% |
| 27,656 | COOKE | 11,452 | 7,196 | 4,217 | 39 | 2,979 R | 62.8% | 36.8% | 63.1% | 36.9% |
| 56,767 | CORYELL | 11,627 | 7,461 | 4,026 | 140 | 3,435 R | 64.2% | 34.6% | 65.0% | 35.0% |
| 2,947 | COTTLE | 1,083 | 379 | 690 | 14 | 311 D | 35.0% | 63.7% | 35.5% | 64.5% |
| 4,600 | CRANE | 1,818 | 1,219 | 596 | 3 | 623 R | 67.1% | 32.8% | 67.2% | 32.8% |
| 4,608 | CROCKETT | 1,819 | 932 | 881 | 6 | 51 R | 51.2% | 48.4% | 51.4% | 48.6% |
| 8,859 | CROSBY | 2,562 | 1,121 | 1,435 | 6 | 314 D | 43.8% | 56.0% | 43.9% | 56.1% |
| 3,315 | CULBERSON | 982 | 417 | 557 | 8 | 140 D | 42.5% | 56.7% | 42.8% | 57.2% |
| 6,531 | DALLAM | 1,862 | 1,205 | 645 | 12 | 560 R | 64.7% | 34.6% | 65.1% | 34.9% |
| 1,556,390 | DALLAS | 594,538 | 347,094 | 243,198 | 4,246 | 103,896 R | 58.4% | 40.9% | 58.8% | 41.2% |
| 16,184 | DAWSON | 5,317 | 3,154 | 2,155 | 8 | 999 R | 59.3% | 40.5% | 59.4% | 40.6% |
| 21,165 | DEAF SMITH | 5,726 | 3,744 | 1,930 | 52 | 1,814 R | 65.4% | 33.7% | 66.0% | 34.0% |
| 4,839 | DELTA | 2,101 | 849 | 1,244 | 8 | 395 D | 40.4% | 59.2% | 40.6% | 59.4% |

# TEXAS

## PRESIDENT 1988

| 1980 Census Population | County | Total Vote | Republican | Democratic | Other | Rep.-Dem. Plurality | Total Vote Rep. | Total Vote Dem. | Major Vote Rep. | Major Vote Dem. |
|---|---|---|---|---|---|---|---|---|---|---|
| 143,126 | DENTON | 84,210 | 57,444 | 26,204 | 562 | 31,240 R | 68.2% | 31.1% | 68.7% | 31.3% |
| 18,903 | DE WITT | 6,255 | 3,628 | 2,579 | 48 | 1,049 R | 58.0% | 41.2% | 58.5% | 41.5% |
| 3,539 | DICKENS | 1,141 | 435 | 696 | 10 | 261 D | 38.1% | 61.0% | 38.5% | 61.5% |
| 11,367 | DIMMIT | 3,651 | 900 | 2,735 | 16 | 1,835 D | 24.7% | 74.9% | 24.8% | 75.2% |
| 4,075 | DONLEY | 1,713 | 1,043 | 661 | 9 | 382 R | 60.9% | 38.6% | 61.2% | 38.8% |
| 12,517 | DUVAL | 5,097 | 907 | 4,177 | 13 | 3,270 D | 17.8% | 82.0% | 17.8% | 82.2% |
| 19,480 | EASTLAND | 7,166 | 3,929 | 3,215 | 22 | 714 R | 54.8% | 44.9% | 55.0% | 45.0% |
| 115,374 | ECTOR | 34,152 | 23,155 | 10,825 | 172 | 12,330 R | 67.8% | 31.7% | 68.1% | 31.9% |
| 2,033 | EDWARDS | 930 | 556 | 368 | 6 | 188 R | 59.8% | 39.6% | 60.2% | 39.8% |
| 59,743 | ELLIS | 27,749 | 16,422 | 11,169 | 158 | 5,253 R | 59.2% | 40.3% | 59.5% | 40.5% |
| 479,899 | EL PASO | 118,781 | 55,573 | 62,622 | 586 | 7,049 D | 46.8% | 52.7% | 47.0% | 53.0% |
| 22,560 | ERATH | 9,570 | 5,427 | 4,113 | 30 | 1,314 R | 56.7% | 43.0% | 56.9% | 43.1% |
| 17,946 | FALLS | 5,237 | 2,344 | 2,877 | 16 | 533 D | 44.8% | 54.9% | 44.9% | 55.1% |
| 24,285 | FANNIN | 9,214 | 4,024 | 5,163 | 27 | 1,139 D | 43.7% | 56.0% | 43.8% | 56.2% |
| 18,832 | FAYETTE | 7,971 | 4,551 | 3,390 | 30 | 1,161 R | 57.1% | 42.5% | 57.3% | 42.7% |
| 5,891 | FISHER | 2,240 | 721 | 1,516 | 3 | 795 D | 32.2% | 67.7% | 32.2% | 67.8% |
| 9,834 | FLOYD | 3,138 | 1,741 | 1,391 | 6 | 350 R | 55.5% | 44.3% | 55.6% | 44.4% |
| 2,158 | FOARD | 820 | 306 | 513 | 1 | 207 D | 37.3% | 62.6% | 37.4% | 62.6% |
| 130,846 | FORT BEND | 63,784 | 39,818 | 23,351 | 615 | 16,467 R | 62.4% | 36.6% | 63.0% | 37.0% |
| 6,893 | FRANKLIN | 2,896 | 1,439 | 1,453 | 4 | 14 D | 49.7% | 50.2% | 49.8% | 50.2% |
| 14,830 | FREESTONE | 6,092 | 3,159 | 2,916 | 17 | 243 R | 51.9% | 47.9% | 52.0% | 48.0% |
| 13,785 | FRIO | 4,538 | 1,505 | 3,016 | 17 | 1,511 D | 33.2% | 66.5% | 33.3% | 66.7% |
| 13,150 | GAINES | 3,606 | 2,265 | 1,310 | 31 | 955 R | 62.8% | 36.3% | 63.4% | 36.6% |
| 195,940 | GALVESTON | 74,042 | 34,913 | 38,633 | 496 | 3,720 D | 47.2% | 52.2% | 47.5% | 52.5% |
| 5,336 | GARZA | 2,190 | 1,183 | 989 | 18 | 194 R | 54.0% | 45.2% | 54.5% | 45.5% |
| 13,532 | GILLESPIE | 7,313 | 5,662 | 1,588 | 63 | 4,074 R | 77.4% | 21.7% | 78.1% | 21.9% |
| 1,304 | GLASSCOCK | 528 | 384 | 143 | 1 | 241 R | 72.7% | 27.1% | 72.9% | 27.1% |
| 5,193 | GOLIAD | 2,792 | 1,427 | 1,358 | 7 | 69 R | 51.1% | 48.6% | 51.2% | 48.8% |
| 16,883 | GONZALES | 5,916 | 2,983 | 2,897 | 36 | 86 R | 50.4% | 49.0% | 50.7% | 49.3% |
| 26,386 | GRAY | 9,781 | 7,259 | 2,460 | 62 | 4,799 R | 74.2% | 25.2% | 74.7% | 25.3% |
| 89,796 | GRAYSON | 33,287 | 18,825 | 14,347 | 115 | 4,478 R | 56.6% | 43.1% | 56.7% | 43.3% |
| 99,487 | GREGG | 39,387 | 26,465 | 12,486 | 436 | 13,979 R | 67.2% | 31.7% | 67.9% | 32.1% |
| 13,580 | GRIMES | 5,582 | 2,820 | 2,735 | 27 | 85 R | 50.5% | 49.0% | 50.8% | 49.2% |
| 46,708 | GUADALUPE | 20,609 | 13,265 | 7,111 | 233 | 6,154 R | 64.4% | 34.5% | 65.1% | 34.9% |
| 37,592 | HALE | 9,811 | 6,284 | 3,502 | 25 | 2,782 R | 64.1% | 35.7% | 64.2% | 35.8% |
| 5,594 | HALL | 1,743 | 714 | 1,029 | | 315 D | 41.0% | 59.0% | 41.0% | 59.0% |
| 8,297 | HAMILTON | 3,086 | 1,718 | 1,355 | 13 | 363 R | 55.7% | 43.9% | 55.9% | 44.1% |
| 6,209 | HANSFORD | 2,421 | 1,967 | 443 | 11 | 1,524 R | 81.2% | 18.3% | 81.6% | 18.4% |
| 6,368 | HARDEMAN | 2,001 | 855 | 1,143 | 3 | 288 D | 42.7% | 57.1% | 42.8% | 57.2% |
| 40,721 | HARDIN | 15,173 | 6,897 | 8,245 | 31 | 1,348 D | 45.5% | 54.3% | 45.5% | 54.5% |
| 2,409,547 | HARRIS | 814,160 | 464,217 | 342,919 | 7,024 | 121,298 R | 57.0% | 42.1% | 57.5% | 42.5% |
| 52,265 | HARRISON | 21,285 | 11,957 | 8,974 | 354 | 2,983 R | 56.2% | 42.2% | 57.1% | 42.9% |
| 3,987 | HARTLEY | 1,747 | 1,229 | 505 | 13 | 724 R | 70.3% | 28.9% | 70.9% | 29.1% |
| 7,725 | HASKELL | 2,915 | 1,193 | 1,715 | 7 | 522 D | 40.9% | 58.8% | 41.0% | 59.0% |
| 40,594 | HAYS | 23,264 | 11,716 | 11,187 | 361 | 529 R | 50.4% | 48.1% | 51.2% | 48.8% |
| 5,304 | HEMPHILL | 1,705 | 1,170 | 527 | 8 | 643 R | 68.6% | 30.9% | 68.9% | 31.1% |
| 42,606 | HENDERSON | 20,918 | 11,005 | 9,819 | 94 | 1,186 R | 52.6% | 46.9% | 52.8% | 47.2% |
| 283,229 | HIDALGO | 83,870 | 29,246 | 54,330 | 294 | 25,084 D | 34.9% | 64.8% | 35.0% | 65.0% |
| 25,024 | HILL | 9,198 | 4,796 | 4,381 | 21 | 415 R | 52.1% | 47.6% | 52.3% | 47.7% |
| 23,230 | HOCKLEY | 7,250 | 4,368 | 2,850 | 32 | 1,518 R | 60.2% | 39.3% | 60.5% | 39.5% |
| 17,714 | HOOD | 11,716 | 7,400 | 4,255 | 61 | 3,145 R | 63.2% | 36.3% | 63.5% | 36.5% |
| 25,247 | HOPKINS | 10,142 | 5,133 | 4,984 | 25 | 149 R | 50.6% | 49.1% | 50.7% | 49.3% |
| 22,299 | HOUSTON | 7,764 | 3,882 | 3,846 | 36 | 36 R | 50.0% | 49.5% | 50.2% | 49.8% |
| 33,142 | HOWARD | 10,517 | 6,024 | 4,445 | 48 | 1,579 R | 57.3% | 42.3% | 57.5% | 42.5% |
| 2,728 | HUDSPETH | 816 | 405 | 406 | 5 | 1 D | 49.6% | 49.8% | 49.9% | 50.1% |
| 55,248 | HUNT | 21,238 | 12,331 | 8,820 | 87 | 3,511 R | 58.1% | 41.5% | 58.3% | 41.7% |
| 26,304 | HUTCHINSON | 10,526 | 7,526 | 2,950 | 50 | 4,576 R | 71.5% | 28.0% | 71.8% | 28.2% |
| 1,386 | IRION | 867 | 539 | 326 | 2 | 213 R | 62.2% | 37.6% | 62.3% | 37.7% |
| 7,408 | JACK | 3,074 | 1,542 | 1,521 | 11 | 21 R | 50.2% | 49.5% | 50.3% | 49.7% |
| 13,352 | JACKSON | 5,115 | 2,954 | 2,141 | 20 | 813 R | 57.8% | 41.9% | 58.0% | 42.0% |

# TEXAS

## PRESIDENT 1988

| 1980 Census Population | County | Total Vote | Republican | Democratic | Other | Rep.-Dem. Plurality | Percentage Total Vote Rep. | Dem. | Major Vote Rep. | Dem. |
|---|---|---|---|---|---|---|---|---|---|---|
| 30,781 | JASPER | 11,629 | 4,985 | 6,613 | 31 | 1,628 D | 42.9% | 56.9% | 43.0% | 57.0% |
| 1,647 | JEFF DAVIS | 870 | 524 | 325 | 21 | 199 R | 60.2% | 37.4% | 61.7% | 38.3% |
| 250,938 | JEFFERSON | 91,693 | 35,754 | 55,649 | 290 | 19,895 D | 39.0% | 60.7% | 39.1% | 60.9% |
| 5,168 | JIM HOGG | 2,143 | 510 | 1,630 | 3 | 1,120 D | 23.8% | 76.1% | 23.8% | 76.2% |
| 36,498 | JIM WELLS | 12,886 | 4,335 | 8,495 | 56 | 4,160 D | 33.6% | 65.9% | 33.8% | 66.2% |
| 67,649 | JOHNSON | 30,171 | 17,509 | 12,507 | 155 | 5,002 R | 58.0% | 41.5% | 58.3% | 41.7% |
| 17,268 | JONES | 5,916 | 3,000 | 2,898 | 18 | 102 R | 50.7% | 49.0% | 50.9% | 49.1% |
| 13,593 | KARNES | 4,933 | 2,383 | 2,529 | 21 | 146 D | 48.3% | 51.3% | 48.5% | 51.5% |
| 39,015 | KAUFMAN | 15,916 | 8,466 | 7,358 | 92 | 1,108 R | 53.2% | 46.2% | 53.5% | 46.5% |
| 10,635 | KENDALL | 6,398 | 4,875 | 1,446 | 77 | 3,429 R | 76.2% | 22.6% | 77.1% | 22.9% |
| 543 | KENEDY | 196 | 76 | 119 | 1 | 43 D | 38.8% | 60.7% | 39.0% | 61.0% |
| 1,145 | KENT | 674 | 274 | 398 | 2 | 124 D | 40.7% | 59.1% | 40.8% | 59.2% |
| 28,780 | KERR | 14,937 | 11,207 | 3,587 | 143 | 7,620 R | 75.0% | 24.0% | 75.8% | 24.2% |
| 4,063 | KIMBLE | 1,617 | 1,061 | 551 | 5 | 510 R | 65.6% | 34.1% | 65.8% | 34.2% |
| 425 | KING | 175 | 111 | 64 | | 47 R | 63.4% | 36.6% | 63.4% | 36.6% |
| 2,279 | KINNEY | 1,450 | 771 | 669 | 10 | 102 R | 53.2% | 46.1% | 53.5% | 46.5% |
| 33,358 | KLEBERG | 9,946 | 4,443 | 5,367 | 136 | 924 D | 44.7% | 54.0% | 45.3% | 54.7% |
| 5,329 | KNOX | 1,782 | 765 | 1,013 | 4 | 248 D | 42.9% | 56.8% | 43.0% | 57.0% |
| 42,156 | LAMAR | 15,598 | 8,021 | 7,553 | 24 | 468 R | 51.4% | 48.4% | 51.5% | 48.5% |
| 18,669 | LAMB | 5,316 | 3,064 | 2,230 | 22 | 834 R | 57.6% | 41.9% | 57.9% | 42.1% |
| 12,005 | LAMPASAS | 4,966 | 3,000 | 1,954 | 12 | 1,046 R | 60.4% | 39.3% | 60.6% | 39.4% |
| 5,514 | LA SALLE | 2,352 | 693 | 1,651 | 8 | 958 D | 29.5% | 70.2% | 29.6% | 70.4% |
| 19,004 | LAVACA | 7,962 | 4,377 | 3,531 | 54 | 846 R | 55.0% | 44.3% | 55.3% | 44.7% |
| 10,952 | LEE | 5,067 | 2,513 | 2,527 | 27 | 14 D | 49.6% | 49.9% | 49.9% | 50.1% |
| 9,594 | LEON | 5,115 | 2,778 | 2,316 | 21 | 462 R | 54.3% | 45.3% | 54.5% | 45.5% |
| 47,088 | LIBERTY | 16,973 | 8,524 | 8,343 | 106 | 181 R | 50.2% | 49.2% | 50.5% | 49.5% |
| 20,224 | LIMESTONE | 6,763 | 3,257 | 3,476 | 30 | 219 D | 48.2% | 51.4% | 48.4% | 51.6% |
| 3,766 | LIPSCOMB | 1,499 | 1,111 | 377 | 11 | 734 R | 74.1% | 25.2% | 74.7% | 25.3% |
| 9,606 | LIVE OAK | 3,880 | 2,277 | 1,573 | 30 | 704 R | 58.7% | 40.5% | 59.1% | 40.9% |
| 10,144 | LLANO | 6,202 | 3,550 | 2,629 | 23 | 921 R | 57.2% | 42.4% | 57.5% | 42.5% |
| 91 | LOVING | 77 | 54 | 23 | | 31 R | 70.1% | 29.9% | 70.1% | 29.9% |
| 211,651 | LUBBOCK | 73,292 | 50,760 | 22,202 | 330 | 28,558 R | 69.3% | 30.3% | 69.6% | 30.4% |
| 8,605 | LYNN | 2,367 | 1,279 | 1,086 | 2 | 193 R | 54.0% | 45.9% | 54.1% | 45.9% |
| 8,735 | MCCULLOCH | 3,293 | 1,618 | 1,665 | 10 | 47 D | 49.1% | 50.6% | 49.3% | 50.7% |
| 170,755 | MCLENNAN | 66,423 | 38,606 | 27,545 | 272 | 11,061 R | 58.1% | 41.5% | 58.4% | 41.6% |
| 789 | MCMULLEN | 398 | 302 | 94 | 2 | 208 R | 75.9% | 23.6% | 76.3% | 23.7% |
| 10,649 | MADISON | 3,747 | 1,896 | 1,835 | 16 | 61 R | 50.6% | 49.0% | 50.8% | 49.2% |
| 10,360 | MARION | 4,129 | 1,857 | 2,255 | 17 | 398 D | 45.0% | 54.6% | 45.2% | 54.8% |
| 4,684 | MARTIN | 1,651 | 1,017 | 632 | 2 | 385 R | 61.6% | 38.3% | 61.7% | 38.3% |
| 3,683 | MASON | 1,655 | 975 | 671 | 9 | 304 R | 58.9% | 40.5% | 59.2% | 40.8% |
| 37,828 | MATAGORDA | 12,566 | 6,787 | 5,675 | 104 | 1,112 R | 54.0% | 45.2% | 54.5% | 45.5% |
| 31,398 | MAVERICK | 6,003 | 1,592 | 4,395 | 16 | 2,803 D | 26.5% | 73.2% | 26.6% | 73.4% |
| 23,164 | MEDINA | 10,029 | 5,722 | 4,227 | 80 | 1,495 R | 57.1% | 42.1% | 57.5% | 42.5% |
| 2,346 | MENARD | 1,171 | 552 | 614 | 5 | 62 D | 47.1% | 52.4% | 47.3% | 52.7% |
| 82,636 | MIDLAND | 39,326 | 30,618 | 8,487 | 221 | 22,131 R | 77.9% | 21.6% | 78.3% | 21.7% |
| 22,732 | MILAM | 8,396 | 3,512 | 4,865 | 19 | 1,353 D | 41.8% | 57.9% | 41.9% | 58.1% |
| 4,477 | MILLS | 1,888 | 1,043 | 842 | 3 | 201 R | 55.2% | 44.6% | 55.3% | 44.7% |
| 9,088 | MITCHELL | 3,376 | 1,596 | 1,773 | 7 | 177 D | 47.3% | 52.5% | 47.4% | 52.6% |
| 17,410 | MONTAGUE | 7,186 | 3,475 | 3,689 | 22 | 214 D | 48.4% | 51.3% | 48.5% | 51.5% |
| 128,487 | MONTGOMERY | 59,146 | 40,360 | 18,394 | 392 | 21,966 R | 68.2% | 31.1% | 68.7% | 31.3% |
| 16,575 | MOORE | 5,281 | 3,710 | 1,537 | 34 | 2,173 R | 70.3% | 29.1% | 70.7% | 29.3% |
| 14,629 | MORRIS | 5,630 | 2,104 | 3,522 | 4 | 1,418 D | 37.4% | 62.6% | 37.4% | 62.6% |
| 1,950 | MOTLEY | 692 | 429 | 262 | 1 | 167 R | 62.0% | 37.9% | 62.1% | 37.9% |
| 46,786 | NACOGDOCHES | 18,883 | 11,767 | 6,886 | 230 | 4,881 R | 62.3% | 36.5% | 63.1% | 36.9% |
| 35,323 | NAVARRO | 13,232 | 6,445 | 6,749 | 38 | 304 D | 48.7% | 51.0% | 48.8% | 51.2% |
| 13,254 | NEWTON | 5,309 | 1,659 | 3,640 | 10 | 1,981 D | 31.2% | 68.6% | 31.3% | 68.7% |
| 17,359 | NOLAN | 5,609 | 2,734 | 2,853 | 22 | 119 D | 48.7% | 50.9% | 48.9% | 51.1% |
| 268,215 | NUECES | 95,932 | 46,337 | 49,209 | 386 | 2,872 D | 48.3% | 51.3% | 48.5% | 51.5% |
| 9,588 | OCHILTREE | 3,517 | 2,928 | 579 | 10 | 2,349 R | 83.3% | 16.5% | 83.5% | 16.5% |
| 2,283 | OLDHAM | 1,004 | 691 | 303 | 10 | 388 R | 68.8% | 30.2% | 69.5% | 30.5% |

# TEXAS

## PRESIDENT 1988

| 1980 Census Population | County | Total Vote | Republican | Democratic | Other | Rep.-Dem. Plurality | Percentage | | | |
|---|---|---|---|---|---|---|---|---|---|---|
| | | | | | | | Total Vote | | Major Vote | |
| | | | | | | | Rep. | Dem. | Rep. | Dem. |
| 83,838 | ORANGE | 29,908 | 11,959 | 17,834 | 115 | 5,875 D | 40.0% | 59.6% | 40.1% | 59.9% |
| 24,062 | PALO PINTO | 8,634 | 4,649 | 3,930 | 55 | 719 R | 53.8% | 45.5% | 54.2% | 45.8% |
| 20,724 | PANOLA | 8,780 | 4,642 | 4,123 | 15 | 519 R | 52.9% | 47.0% | 53.0% | 47.0% |
| 44,609 | PARKER | 22,723 | 14,090 | 8,517 | 116 | 5,573 R | 62.0% | 37.5% | 62.3% | 37.7% |
| 11,038 | PARMER | 2,839 | 2,061 | 764 | 14 | 1,297 R | 72.6% | 26.9% | 73.0% | 27.0% |
| 14,618 | PECOS | 4,460 | 2,483 | 1,960 | 17 | 523 R | 55.7% | 43.9% | 55.9% | 44.1% |
| 24,407 | POLK | 11,929 | 5,831 | 5,943 | 155 | 112 D | 48.9% | 49.8% | 49.5% | 50.5% |
| 98,637 | POTTER | 26,131 | 16,400 | 9,563 | 168 | 6,837 R | 62.8% | 36.6% | 63.2% | 36.8% |
| 5,188 | PRESIDIO | 1,771 | 586 | 1,176 | 9 | 590 D | 33.1% | 66.4% | 33.3% | 66.7% |
| 4,839 | RAINS | 2,736 | 1,281 | 1,448 | 7 | 167 D | 46.8% | 52.9% | 46.9% | 53.1% |
| 75,062 | RANDALL | 36,666 | 27,986 | 8,492 | 188 | 19,494 R | 76.3% | 23.2% | 76.7% | 23.3% |
| 4,135 | REAGAN | 1,355 | 935 | 418 | 2 | 517 R | 69.0% | 30.8% | 69.1% | 30.9% |
| 2,469 | REAL | 1,291 | 795 | 483 | 13 | 312 R | 61.6% | 37.4% | 62.2% | 37.8% |
| 16,101 | RED RIVER | 5,652 | 2,475 | 3,165 | 12 | 690 D | 43.8% | 56.0% | 43.9% | 56.1% |
| 15,801 | REEVES | 4,554 | 1,724 | 2,812 | 18 | 1,088 D | 37.9% | 61.7% | 38.0% | 62.0% |
| 9,289 | REFUGIO | 3,724 | 1,883 | 1,831 | 10 | 52 R | 50.6% | 49.2% | 50.7% | 49.3% |
| 1,187 | ROBERTS | 581 | 441 | 135 | 5 | 306 R | 75.9% | 23.2% | 76.6% | 23.4% |
| 14,653 | ROBERTSON | 5,832 | 2,184 | 3,630 | 18 | 1,446 D | 37.4% | 62.2% | 37.6% | 62.4% |
| 14,528 | ROCKWALL | 9,939 | 7,214 | 2,659 | 66 | 4,555 R | 72.6% | 26.8% | 73.1% | 26.9% |
| 11,872 | RUNNELS | 4,147 | 2,417 | 1,720 | 10 | 697 R | 58.3% | 41.5% | 58.4% | 41.6% |
| 41,382 | RUSK | 14,313 | 9,117 | 5,140 | 56 | 3,977 R | 63.7% | 35.9% | 63.9% | 36.1% |
| 8,702 | SABINE | 3,987 | 1,925 | 2,053 | 9 | 128 D | 48.3% | 51.5% | 48.4% | 51.6% |
| 8,785 | SAN AUGUSTINE | 4,084 | 1,946 | 2,118 | 20 | 172 D | 47.6% | 51.9% | 47.9% | 52.1% |
| 11,434 | SAN JACINTO | 5,688 | 2,691 | 2,972 | 25 | 281 D | 47.3% | 52.3% | 47.5% | 52.5% |
| 58,013 | SAN PATRICIO | 19,458 | 9,159 | 9,920 | 379 | 761 D | 47.1% | 51.0% | 48.0% | 52.0% |
| 6,204 | SAN SABA | 2,277 | 1,099 | 1,165 | 13 | 66 D | 48.3% | 51.2% | 48.5% | 51.5% |
| 2,820 | SCHLEICHER | 1,157 | 653 | 494 | 10 | 159 R | 56.4% | 42.7% | 56.9% | 43.1% |
| 18,192 | SCURRY | 5,894 | 3,749 | 2,119 | 26 | 1,630 R | 63.6% | 36.0% | 63.9% | 36.1% |
| 3,915 | SHACKELFORD | 1,554 | 865 | 681 | 8 | 184 R | 55.7% | 43.8% | 56.0% | 44.0% |
| 23,084 | SHELBY | 8,273 | 3,999 | 4,261 | 13 | 262 D | 48.3% | 51.5% | 48.4% | 51.6% |
| 3,174 | SHERMAN | 1,499 | 1,145 | 340 | 14 | 805 R | 76.4% | 22.7% | 77.1% | 22.9% |
| 128,366 | SMITH | 53,592 | 34,658 | 18,719 | 215 | 15,939 R | 64.7% | 34.9% | 64.9% | 35.1% |
| 4,154 | SOMERVELL | 2,296 | 1,304 | 983 | 9 | 321 R | 56.8% | 42.8% | 57.0% | 43.0% |
| 27,266 | STARR | 8,211 | 1,218 | 6,958 | 35 | 5,740 D | 14.8% | 84.7% | 14.9% | 85.1% |
| 9,926 | STEPHENS | 3,874 | 2,342 | 1,519 | 13 | 823 R | 60.5% | 39.2% | 60.7% | 39.3% |
| 1,206 | STERLING | 656 | 464 | 188 | 4 | 276 R | 70.7% | 28.7% | 71.2% | 28.8% |
| 2,406 | STONEWALL | 1,147 | 421 | 724 | 2 | 303 D | 36.7% | 63.1% | 36.8% | 63.2% |
| 5,130 | SUTTON | 1,570 | 996 | 571 | 3 | 425 R | 63.4% | 36.4% | 63.6% | 36.4% |
| 9,723 | SWISHER | 3,179 | 1,271 | 1,893 | 15 | 622 D | 40.0% | 59.5% | 40.2% | 59.8% |
| 860,880 | TARRANT | 396,237 | 242,660 | 151,310 | 2,267 | 91,350 R | 61.2% | 38.2% | 61.6% | 38.4% |
| 110,932 | TAYLOR | 42,024 | 28,563 | 13,073 | 388 | 15,490 R | 68.0% | 31.1% | 68.6% | 31.4% |
| 1,595 | TERRELL | 689 | 296 | 390 | 3 | 94 D | 43.0% | 56.6% | 43.1% | 56.9% |
| 14,581 | TERRY | 4,600 | 2,645 | 1,941 | 14 | 704 R | 57.5% | 42.2% | 57.7% | 42.3% |
| 2,053 | THROCKMORTON | 998 | 455 | 534 | 9 | 79 D | 45.6% | 53.5% | 46.0% | 54.0% |
| 21,442 | TITUS | 8,620 | 4,247 | 4,357 | 16 | 110 D | 49.3% | 50.5% | 49.4% | 50.6% |
| 84,784 | TOM GREEN | 34,012 | 21,463 | 12,283 | 266 | 9,180 R | 63.1% | 36.1% | 63.6% | 36.4% |
| 419,573 | TRAVIS | 236,084 | 105,915 | 127,783 | 2,386 | 21,868 D | 44.9% | 54.1% | 45.3% | 54.7% |
| 9,450 | TRINITY | 5,137 | 2,448 | 2,657 | 32 | 209 D | 47.7% | 51.7% | 48.0% | 52.0% |
| 16,223 | TYLER | 7,292 | 3,070 | 4,198 | 24 | 1,128 D | 42.1% | 57.6% | 42.2% | 57.8% |
| 28,595 | UPSHUR | 11,265 | 5,991 | 5,242 | 32 | 749 R | 53.2% | 46.5% | 53.3% | 46.7% |
| 4,619 | UPTON | 1,740 | 1,189 | 544 | 7 | 645 R | 68.3% | 31.3% | 68.6% | 31.4% |
| 22,441 | UVALDE | 8,001 | 4,266 | 3,684 | 51 | 582 R | 53.3% | 46.0% | 53.7% | 46.3% |
| 35,910 | VAL VERDE | 10,211 | 5,109 | 5,044 | 58 | 65 R | 50.0% | 49.4% | 50.3% | 49.7% |
| 31,426 | VAN ZANDT | 13,559 | 7,371 | 6,153 | 35 | 1,218 R | 54.4% | 45.4% | 54.5% | 45.5% |
| 68,807 | VICTORIA | 24,253 | 15,056 | 8,923 | 274 | 6,133 R | 62.1% | 36.8% | 62.8% | 37.2% |
| 41,789 | WALKER | 14,391 | 8,473 | 5,826 | 92 | 2,647 R | 58.9% | 40.5% | 59.3% | 40.7% |
| 19,798 | WALLER | 7,624 | 3,607 | 3,957 | 60 | 350 D | 47.3% | 51.9% | 47.7% | 52.3% |
| 13,976 | WARD | 4,590 | 2,709 | 1,858 | 23 | 851 R | 59.0% | 40.5% | 59.3% | 40.7% |
| 21,998 | WASHINGTON | 9,037 | 6,041 | 2,960 | 36 | 3,081 R | 66.8% | 32.8% | 67.1% | 32.9% |
| 99,258 | WEBB | 23,832 | 7,528 | 16,227 | 77 | 8,699 D | 31.6% | 68.1% | 31.7% | 68.3% |

# TEXAS

## PRESIDENT 1988

| 1980 Census Population | County | Total Vote | Republican | Democratic | Other | Rep.-Dem. Plurality | Percentage | | | |
|---|---|---|---|---|---|---|---|---|---|---|
| | | | | | | | Total Vote | | Major Vote | |
| | | | | | | | Rep. | Dem. | Rep. | Dem. |
| 40,242 | WHARTON | 12,991 | 6,978 | 5,935 | 78 | 1,043 R | 53.7% | 45.7% | 54.0% | 46.0% |
| 7,137 | WHEELER | 2,777 | 1,703 | 1,067 | 7 | 636 R | 61.3% | 38.4% | 61.5% | 38.5% |
| 121,082 | WICHITA | 41,590 | 23,324 | 17,956 | 310 | 5,368 R | 56.1% | 43.2% | 56.5% | 43.5% |
| 15,931 | WILBARGER | 4,929 | 2,669 | 2,248 | 12 | 421 R | 54.1% | 45.6% | 54.3% | 45.7% |
| 17,495 | WILLACY | 4,940 | 1,750 | 3,165 | 25 | 1,415 D | 35.4% | 64.1% | 35.6% | 64.4% |
| 76,521 | WILLIAMSON | 47,230 | 27,322 | 19,589 | 319 | 7,733 R | 57.8% | 41.5% | 58.2% | 41.8% |
| 16,756 | WILSON | 8,425 | 4,436 | 3,953 | 36 | 483 R | 52.7% | 46.9% | 52.9% | 47.1% |
| 9,944 | WINKLER | 2,611 | 1,656 | 947 | 8 | 709 R | 63.4% | 36.3% | 63.6% | 36.4% |
| 26,575 | WISE | 11,395 | 6,064 | 5,288 | 43 | 776 R | 53.2% | 46.4% | 53.4% | 46.6% |
| 24,697 | WOOD | 11,366 | 6,216 | 4,553 | 597 | 1,663 R | 54.7% | 40.1% | 57.7% | 42.3% |
| 8,299 | YOAKUM | 2,507 | 1,762 | 727 | 18 | 1,035 R | 70.3% | 29.0% | 70.8% | 29.2% |
| 19,083 | YOUNG | 7,193 | 4,156 | 3,007 | 30 | 1,149 R | 57.8% | 41.8% | 58.0% | 42.0% |
| 6,628 | ZAPATA | 3,135 | 958 | 2,171 | 6 | 1,213 D | 30.6% | 69.3% | 30.6% | 69.4% |
| 11,666 | ZAVALA | 3,973 | 628 | 3,338 | 7 | 2,710 D | 15.8% | 84.0% | 15.8% | 84.2% |
| 14,229,191 | TOTAL | 5,427,410 | 3,036,829 | 2,352,748 | 37,833 | 684,081 R | 56.0% | 43.3% | 56.3% | 43.7% |

# TEXAS

## PRESIDENT 1984

| 1980 Census Population | County | Total Vote | Republican | Democratic | Other | Rep.-Dem. Plurality | Total Vote Rep. | Total Vote Dem. | Major Vote Rep. | Major Vote Dem. |
|---|---|---|---|---|---|---|---|---|---|---|
| 38,381 | ANDERSON | 13,423 | 8,634 | 4,747 | 42 | 3,887 R | 64.3% | 35.4% | 64.5% | 35.5% |
| 13,323 | ANDREWS | 4,750 | 3,918 | 820 | 12 | 3,098 R | 82.5% | 17.3% | 82.7% | 17.3% |
| 64,172 | ANGELINA | 23,831 | 14,685 | 9,054 | 92 | 5,631 R | 61.6% | 38.0% | 61.9% | 38.1% |
| 14,260 | ARANSAS | 6,067 | 4,352 | 1,696 | 19 | 2,656 R | 71.7% | 28.0% | 72.0% | 28.0% |
| 7,266 | ARCHER | 3,587 | 2,487 | 1,089 | 11 | 1,398 R | 69.3% | 30.4% | 69.5% | 30.5% |
| 1,994 | ARMSTRONG | 1,034 | 791 | 238 | 5 | 553 R | 76.5% | 23.0% | 76.9% | 23.1% |
| 25,055 | ATASCOSA | 8,845 | 5,279 | 3,547 | 19 | 1,732 R | 59.7% | 40.1% | 59.8% | 40.2% |
| 17,726 | AUSTIN | 6,834 | 4,872 | 1,941 | 21 | 2,931 R | 71.3% | 28.4% | 71.5% | 28.5% |
| 8,168 | BAILEY | 2,586 | 1,888 | 684 | 14 | 1,204 R | 73.0% | 26.5% | 73.4% | 26.6% |
| 7,084 | BANDERA | 3,938 | 3,152 | 771 | 15 | 2,381 R | 80.0% | 19.6% | 80.3% | 19.7% |
| 24,726 | BASTROP | 11,221 | 6,439 | 4,744 | 38 | 1,695 R | 57.4% | 42.3% | 57.6% | 42.4% |
| 4,919 | BAYLOR | 2,346 | 1,314 | 1,019 | 13 | 295 R | 56.0% | 43.4% | 56.3% | 43.7% |
| 26,030 | BEE | 9,064 | 5,377 | 3,659 | 28 | 1,718 R | 59.3% | 40.4% | 59.5% | 40.5% |
| 157,889 | BELL | 44,762 | 31,117 | 13,322 | 323 | 17,795 R | 69.5% | 29.8% | 70.0% | 30.0% |
| 988,800 | BEXAR | 340,826 | 203,319 | 136,947 | 560 | 66,372 R | 59.7% | 40.2% | 59.8% | 40.2% |
| 4,681 | BLANCO | 2,665 | 1,957 | 700 | 8 | 1,257 R | 73.4% | 26.3% | 73.7% | 26.3% |
| 859 | BORDEN | 468 | 325 | 140 | 3 | 185 R | 69.4% | 29.9% | 69.9% | 30.1% |
| 13,401 | BOSQUE | 5,983 | 3,923 | 2,046 | 14 | 1,877 R | 65.6% | 34.2% | 65.7% | 34.3% |
| 75,301 | BOWIE | 28,409 | 18,244 | 10,077 | 88 | 8,167 R | 64.2% | 35.5% | 64.4% | 35.6% |
| 169,587 | BRAZORIA | 58,009 | 39,166 | 18,609 | 234 | 20,557 R | 67.5% | 32.1% | 67.8% | 32.2% |
| 93,588 | BRAZOS | 47,221 | 34,733 | 12,348 | 140 | 22,385 R | 73.6% | 26.1% | 73.8% | 26.2% |
| 7,573 | BREWSTER | 3,545 | 2,066 | 1,462 | 17 | 604 R | 58.3% | 41.2% | 58.6% | 41.4% |
| 2,579 | BRISCOE | 1,017 | 538 | 471 | 8 | 67 R | 52.9% | 46.3% | 53.3% | 46.7% |
| 8,428 | BROOKS | 3,614 | 896 | 2,702 | 16 | 1,806 D | 24.8% | 74.8% | 24.9% | 75.1% |
| 33,057 | BROWN | 12,585 | 8,468 | 4,070 | 47 | 4,398 R | 67.3% | 32.3% | 67.5% | 32.5% |
| 12,313 | BURLESON | 5,666 | 3,076 | 2,578 | 12 | 498 R | 54.3% | 45.5% | 54.4% | 45.6% |
| 17,803 | BURNET | 8,907 | 5,895 | 2,983 | 29 | 2,912 R | 66.2% | 33.5% | 66.4% | 33.6% |
| 23,637 | CALDWELL | 7,732 | 4,315 | 3,401 | 16 | 914 R | 55.8% | 44.0% | 55.9% | 44.1% |
| 19,574 | CALHOUN | 7,039 | 4,434 | 2,586 | 19 | 1,848 R | 63.0% | 36.7% | 63.2% | 36.8% |
| 10,992 | CALLAHAN | 4,867 | 3,538 | 1,305 | 24 | 2,233 R | 72.7% | 26.8% | 73.1% | 26.9% |
| 209,727 | CAMERON | 56,126 | 29,545 | 26,394 | 187 | 3,151 R | 52.6% | 47.0% | 52.8% | 47.2% |
| 9,275 | CAMP | 4,168 | 2,238 | 1,917 | 13 | 321 R | 53.7% | 46.0% | 53.9% | 46.1% |
| 6,672 | CARSON | 3,254 | 2,412 | 826 | 16 | 1,586 R | 74.1% | 25.4% | 74.5% | 25.5% |
| 29,430 | CASS | 11,760 | 6,677 | 5,053 | 30 | 1,624 R | 56.8% | 43.0% | 56.9% | 43.1% |
| 10,556 | CASTRO | 3,056 | 2,026 | 1,009 | 21 | 1,017 R | 66.3% | 33.0% | 66.8% | 33.2% |
| 18,538 | CHAMBERS | 6,989 | 4,322 | 2,632 | 35 | 1,690 R | 61.8% | 37.7% | 62.2% | 37.8% |
| 38,127 | CHEROKEE | 12,711 | 8,187 | 4,494 | 30 | 3,693 R | 64.4% | 35.4% | 64.6% | 35.4% |
| 6,950 | CHILDRESS | 2,481 | 1,574 | 900 | 7 | 674 R | 63.4% | 36.3% | 63.6% | 36.4% |
| 9,582 | CLAY | 4,426 | 2,569 | 1,844 | 13 | 725 R | 58.0% | 41.7% | 58.2% | 41.8% |
| 4,825 | COCHRAN | 1,689 | 1,117 | 557 | 15 | 560 R | 66.1% | 33.0% | 66.7% | 33.3% |
| 3,196 | COKE | 1,600 | 1,060 | 532 | 8 | 528 R | 66.3% | 33.3% | 66.6% | 33.4% |
| 10,439 | COLEMAN | 4,217 | 2,790 | 1,420 | 7 | 1,370 R | 66.2% | 33.7% | 66.3% | 33.7% |
| 144,576 | COLLIN | 74,838 | 61,095 | 13,604 | 139 | 47,491 R | 81.6% | 18.2% | 81.8% | 18.2% |
| 4,648 | COLLINGSWORTH | 2,149 | 1,396 | 742 | 11 | 654 R | 65.0% | 34.5% | 65.3% | 34.7% |
| 18,823 | COLORADO | 6,971 | 4,528 | 2,428 | 15 | 2,100 R | 65.0% | 34.8% | 65.1% | 34.9% |
| 36,446 | COMAL | 17,683 | 13,452 | 4,179 | 52 | 9,273 R | 76.1% | 23.6% | 76.3% | 23.7% |
| 12,617 | COMANCHE | 4,948 | 2,678 | 2,248 | 22 | 430 R | 54.1% | 45.4% | 54.4% | 45.6% |
| 2,915 | CONCHO | 1,408 | 821 | 580 | 7 | 241 R | 58.3% | 41.2% | 58.6% | 41.4% |
| 27,656 | COOKE | 11,564 | 8,260 | 3,278 | 26 | 4,982 R | 71.4% | 28.3% | 71.6% | 28.4% |
| 56,767 | CORYELL | 12,199 | 9,056 | 3,113 | 30 | 5,943 R | 74.2% | 25.5% | 74.4% | 25.6% |
| 2,947 | COTTLE | 1,150 | 507 | 623 | 20 | 116 D | 44.1% | 54.2% | 44.9% | 55.1% |
| 4,600 | CRANE | 1,874 | 1,473 | 392 | 9 | 1,081 R | 78.6% | 20.9% | 79.0% | 21.0% |
| 4,608 | CROCKETT | 1,684 | 1,094 | 589 | 1 | 505 R | 65.0% | 35.0% | 65.0% | 35.0% |
| 8,859 | CROSBY | 2,599 | 1,376 | 1,212 | 11 | 164 R | 52.9% | 46.6% | 53.2% | 46.8% |
| 3,315 | CULBERSON | 917 | 509 | 407 | 1 | 102 R | 55.5% | 44.4% | 55.6% | 44.4% |
| 6,531 | DALLAM | 2,103 | 1,594 | 496 | 13 | 1,098 R | 75.8% | 23.6% | 76.3% | 23.7% |
| 1,556,390 | DALLAS | 610,496 | 405,444 | 203,592 | 1,460 | 201,852 R | 66.4% | 33.3% | 66.6% | 33.4% |
| 16,184 | DAWSON | 5,483 | 3,685 | 1,781 | 17 | 1,904 R | 67.2% | 32.5% | 67.4% | 32.6% |
| 21,165 | DEAF SMITH | 6,283 | 4,762 | 1,485 | 36 | 3,277 R | 75.8% | 23.6% | 76.2% | 23.8% |
| 4,839 | DELTA | 2,001 | 1,024 | 973 | 4 | 51 R | 51.2% | 48.6% | 51.3% | 48.7% |

# TEXAS

## PRESIDENT 1984

| 1980 Census Population | County | Total Vote | Republican | Democratic | Other | Rep.-Dem. Plurality | | Percentage | | | |
|---|---|---|---|---|---|---|---|---|---|---|---|
| | | | | | | | | Total Vote | | Major Vote | |
| | | | | | | | | Rep. | Dem. | Rep. | Dem. |
| 143,126 | DENTON | 69,796 | 52,865 | 16,772 | 159 | 36,093 | R | 75.7% | 24.0% | 75.9% | 24.1% |
| 18,903 | DE WITT | 6,292 | 4,401 | 1,882 | 9 | 2,519 | R | 69.9% | 29.9% | 70.0% | 30.0% |
| 3,539 | DICKENS | 1,294 | 594 | 692 | 8 | 98 | D | 45.9% | 53.5% | 46.2% | 53.8% |
| 11,367 | DIMMIT | 3,892 | 1,338 | 2,546 | 8 | 1,208 | D | 34.4% | 65.4% | 34.4% | 65.6% |
| 4,075 | DONLEY | 1,831 | 1,297 | 529 | 5 | 768 | R | 70.8% | 28.9% | 71.0% | 29.0% |
| 12,517 | DUVAL | 4,959 | 1,201 | 3,748 | 10 | 2,547 | D | 24.2% | 75.6% | 24.3% | 75.7% |
| 19,480 | EASTLAND | 7,389 | 4,841 | 2,522 | 26 | 2,319 | R | 65.5% | 34.1% | 65.7% | 34.3% |
| 115,374 | ECTOR | 40,342 | 31,228 | 8,913 | 201 | 22,315 | R | 77.4% | 22.1% | 77.8% | 22.2% |
| 2,033 | EDWARDS | 786 | 626 | 159 | 1 | 467 | R | 79.6% | 20.2% | 79.7% | 20.3% |
| 59,743 | ELLIS | 24,945 | 16,873 | 8,029 | 43 | 8,844 | R | 67.6% | 32.2% | 67.8% | 32.2% |
| 479,899 | EL PASO | 118,459 | 66,114 | 51,917 | 428 | 14,197 | R | 55.8% | 43.8% | 56.0% | 44.0% |
| 22,560 | ERATH | 9,395 | 6,122 | 3,234 | 39 | 2,888 | R | 65.2% | 34.4% | 65.4% | 34.6% |
| 17,946 | FALLS | 5,986 | 3,133 | 2,834 | 19 | 299 | R | 52.3% | 47.3% | 52.5% | 47.5% |
| 24,285 | FANNIN | 9,106 | 4,692 | 4,399 | 15 | 293 | R | 51.5% | 48.3% | 51.6% | 48.4% |
| 18,832 | FAYETTE | 8,112 | 5,711 | 2,379 | 22 | 3,332 | R | 70.4% | 29.3% | 70.6% | 29.4% |
| 5,891 | FISHER | 2,357 | 965 | 1,384 | 8 | 419 | D | 40.9% | 58.7% | 41.1% | 58.9% |
| 9,834 | FLOYD | 3,134 | 2,092 | 1,023 | 19 | 1,069 | R | 66.8% | 32.6% | 67.2% | 32.8% |
| 2,158 | FOARD | 925 | 472 | 448 | 5 | 24 | R | 51.0% | 48.4% | 51.3% | 48.7% |
| 130,846 | FORT BEND | 60,209 | 41,370 | 18,729 | 110 | 22,641 | R | 68.7% | 31.1% | 68.8% | 31.2% |
| 6,893 | FRANKLIN | 2,948 | 1,836 | 1,104 | 8 | 732 | R | 62.3% | 37.4% | 62.4% | 37.6% |
| 14,830 | FREESTONE | 6,122 | 3,624 | 2,489 | 9 | 1,135 | R | 59.2% | 40.7% | 59.3% | 40.7% |
| 13,785 | FRIO | 4,669 | 2,003 | 2,656 | 10 | 653 | D | 42.9% | 56.9% | 43.0% | 57.0% |
| 13,150 | GAINES | 3,533 | 2,714 | 797 | 22 | 1,917 | R | 76.8% | 22.6% | 77.3% | 22.7% |
| 195,940 | GALVESTON | 76,836 | 40,262 | 36,092 | 482 | 4,170 | R | 52.4% | 47.0% | 52.7% | 47.3% |
| 5,336 | GARZA | 1,750 | 1,219 | 521 | 10 | 698 | R | 69.7% | 29.8% | 70.1% | 29.9% |
| 13,532 | GILLESPIE | 6,651 | 5,496 | 1,137 | 18 | 4,359 | R | 82.6% | 17.1% | 82.9% | 17.1% |
| 1,304 | GLASSCOCK | 536 | 403 | 128 | 5 | 275 | R | 75.2% | 23.9% | 75.9% | 24.1% |
| 5,193 | GOLIAD | 2,377 | 1,540 | 836 | 1 | 704 | R | 64.8% | 35.2% | 64.8% | 35.2% |
| 16,883 | GONZALES | 6,172 | 3,962 | 2,196 | 14 | 1,766 | R | 64.2% | 35.6% | 64.3% | 35.7% |
| 26,386 | GRAY | 10,988 | 8,955 | 2,003 | 30 | 6,952 | R | 81.5% | 18.2% | 81.7% | 18.3% |
| 89,796 | GRAYSON | 34,450 | 22,554 | 11,803 | 93 | 10,751 | R | 65.5% | 34.3% | 65.6% | 34.4% |
| 99,487 | GREGG | 40,643 | 29,697 | 10,700 | 246 | 18,997 | R | 73.1% | 26.3% | 73.5% | 26.5% |
| 13,580 | GRIMES | 5,752 | 3,365 | 2,370 | 17 | 995 | R | 58.5% | 41.2% | 58.7% | 41.3% |
| 46,708 | GUADALUPE | 19,488 | 14,382 | 5,060 | 46 | 9,322 | R | 73.8% | 26.0% | 74.0% | 26.0% |
| 37,592 | HALE | 10,891 | 7,670 | 3,202 | 19 | 4,468 | R | 70.4% | 29.4% | 70.5% | 29.5% |
| 5,594 | HALL | 2,045 | 1,058 | 984 | 3 | 74 | R | 51.7% | 48.1% | 51.8% | 48.2% |
| 8,297 | HAMILTON | 3,258 | 2,118 | 1,130 | 10 | 988 | R | 65.0% | 34.7% | 65.2% | 34.8% |
| 6,209 | HANSFORD | 2,476 | 2,213 | 259 | 4 | 1,954 | R | 89.4% | 10.5% | 89.5% | 10.5% |
| 6,368 | HARDEMAN | 2,173 | 1,238 | 927 | 8 | 311 | R | 57.0% | 42.7% | 57.2% | 42.8% |
| 40,721 | HARDIN | 15,206 | 8,380 | 6,782 | 44 | 1,598 | R | 55.1% | 44.6% | 55.3% | 44.7% |
| 2,409,547 | HARRIS | 872,167 | 536,029 | 334,135 | 2,003 | 201,894 | R | 61.5% | 38.3% | 61.6% | 38.4% |
| 52,265 | HARRISON | 20,509 | 12,618 | 7,773 | 118 | 4,845 | R | 61.5% | 37.9% | 61.9% | 38.1% |
| 3,987 | HARTLEY | 1,786 | 1,419 | 356 | 11 | 1,063 | R | 79.5% | 19.9% | 79.9% | 20.1% |
| 7,725 | HASKELL | 3,151 | 1,701 | 1,434 | 16 | 267 | R | 54.0% | 45.5% | 54.3% | 45.7% |
| 40,594 | HAYS | 19,187 | 12,467 | 6,663 | 57 | 5,804 | R | 65.0% | 34.7% | 65.2% | 34.8% |
| 5,304 | HEMPHILL | 2,067 | 1,650 | 413 | 4 | 1,237 | R | 79.8% | 20.0% | 80.0% | 20.0% |
| 42,606 | HENDERSON | 20,076 | 12,725 | 7,302 | 49 | 5,423 | R | 63.4% | 36.4% | 63.5% | 36.5% |
| 283,229 | HIDALGO | 79,432 | 35,059 | 44,147 | 226 | 9,088 | D | 44.1% | 55.6% | 44.3% | 55.7% |
| 25,024 | HILL | 8,790 | 5,344 | 3,420 | 26 | 1,924 | R | 60.8% | 38.9% | 61.0% | 39.0% |
| 23,230 | HOCKLEY | 7,545 | 5,462 | 2,044 | 39 | 3,418 | R | 72.4% | 27.1% | 72.8% | 27.2% |
| 17,714 | HOOD | 9,921 | 6,817 | 3,063 | 41 | 3,754 | R | 68.7% | 30.9% | 69.0% | 31.0% |
| 25,247 | HOPKINS | 9,493 | 5,772 | 3,707 | 14 | 2,065 | R | 60.8% | 39.0% | 60.9% | 39.1% |
| 22,299 | HOUSTON | 7,834 | 4,542 | 3,275 | 17 | 1,267 | R | 58.0% | 41.8% | 58.1% | 41.9% |
| 33,142 | HOWARD | 11,691 | 7,519 | 4,115 | 57 | 3,404 | R | 64.3% | 35.2% | 64.6% | 35.4% |
| 2,728 | HUDSPETH | 923 | 557 | 362 | 4 | 195 | R | 60.3% | 39.2% | 60.6% | 39.4% |
| 55,248 | HUNT | 21,322 | 14,303 | 6,971 | 48 | 7,332 | R | 67.1% | 32.7% | 67.2% | 32.8% |
| 26,304 | HUTCHINSON | 11,171 | 9,078 | 2,052 | 41 | 7,026 | R | 81.3% | 18.4% | 81.6% | 18.4% |
| 1,386 | IRION | 822 | 619 | 199 | 4 | 420 | R | 75.3% | 24.2% | 75.7% | 24.3% |
| 7,408 | JACK | 2,779 | 1,825 | 945 | 9 | 880 | R | 65.7% | 34.0% | 65.9% | 34.1% |
| 13,352 | JACKSON | 5,478 | 3,661 | 1,804 | 13 | 1,857 | R | 66.8% | 32.9% | 67.0% | 33.0% |

# TEXAS

## PRESIDENT 1984

| 1980 Census Population | County | Total Vote | Republican | Democratic | Other | Rep.-Dem. Plurality | Percentage Total Vote Rep. | Dem. | Major Vote Rep. | Dem. |
|---|---|---|---|---|---|---|---|---|---|---|
| 30,781 | JASPER | 11,779 | 5,965 | 5,787 | 27 | 178 R | 50.6% | 49.1% | 50.8% | 49.2% |
| 1,647 | JEFF DAVIS | 815 | 511 | 299 | 5 | 212 R | 62.7% | 36.7% | 63.1% | 36.9% |
| 250,938 | JEFFERSON | 100,215 | 45,124 | 54,846 | 245 | 9,722 D | 45.0% | 54.7% | 45.1% | 54.9% |
| 5,168 | JIM HOGG | 2,313 | 608 | 1,703 | 2 | 1,095 D | 26.3% | 73.6% | 26.3% | 73.7% |
| 36,498 | JIM WELLS | 13,715 | 5,896 | 7,795 | 24 | 1,899 D | 43.0% | 56.8% | 43.1% | 56.9% |
| 67,649 | JOHNSON | 27,474 | 18,254 | 9,148 | 72 | 9,106 R | 66.4% | 33.3% | 66.6% | 33.4% |
| 17,268 | JONES | 6,383 | 4,017 | 2,343 | 23 | 1,674 R | 62.9% | 36.7% | 63.2% | 36.8% |
| 13,593 | KARNES | 4,882 | 3,068 | 1,802 | 12 | 1,266 R | 62.8% | 36.9% | 63.0% | 37.0% |
| 39,015 | KAUFMAN | 14,938 | 9,343 | 5,554 | 41 | 3,789 R | 62.5% | 37.2% | 62.7% | 37.3% |
| 10,635 | KENDALL | 5,522 | 4,568 | 938 | 16 | 3,630 R | 82.7% | 17.0% | 83.0% | 17.0% |
| 543 | KENEDY | 207 | 96 | 110 | 1 | 14 D | 46.4% | 53.1% | 46.6% | 53.4% |
| 1,145 | KENT | 588 | 332 | 253 | 3 | 79 R | 56.5% | 43.0% | 56.8% | 43.2% |
| 28,780 | KERR | 14,974 | 11,829 | 3,102 | 43 | 8,727 R | 79.0% | 20.7% | 79.2% | 20.8% |
| 4,063 | KIMBLE | 1,784 | 1,333 | 442 | 9 | 891 R | 74.7% | 24.8% | 75.1% | 24.9% |
| 425 | KING | 194 | 141 | 53 | | 88 R | 72.7% | 27.3% | 72.7% | 27.3% |
| 2,279 | KINNEY | 1,263 | 774 | 486 | 3 | 288 R | 61.3% | 38.5% | 61.4% | 38.6% |
| 33,358 | KLEBERG | 10,681 | 5,712 | 4,924 | 45 | 788 R | 53.5% | 46.1% | 53.7% | 46.3% |
| 5,329 | KNOX | 1,952 | 1,027 | 921 | 4 | 106 R | 52.6% | 47.2% | 52.7% | 47.3% |
| 42,156 | LAMAR | 14,820 | 9,273 | 5,504 | 43 | 3,769 R | 62.6% | 37.1% | 62.8% | 37.2% |
| 18,669 | LAMB | 5,828 | 3,892 | 1,919 | 17 | 1,973 R | 66.8% | 32.9% | 67.0% | 33.0% |
| 12,005 | LAMPASAS | 4,653 | 3,285 | 1,356 | 12 | 1,929 R | 70.6% | 29.1% | 70.8% | 29.2% |
| 5,514 | LA SALLE | 2,514 | 1,007 | 1,504 | 3 | 497 D | 40.1% | 59.8% | 40.1% | 59.9% |
| 19,004 | LAVACA | 7,532 | 5,058 | 2,464 | 10 | 2,594 R | 67.2% | 32.7% | 67.2% | 32.8% |
| 10,952 | LEE | 4,632 | 2,967 | 1,659 | 6 | 1,308 R | 64.1% | 35.8% | 64.1% | 35.9% |
| 9,594 | LEON | 5,038 | 3,207 | 1,821 | 10 | 1,386 R | 63.7% | 36.1% | 63.8% | 36.2% |
| 47,088 | LIBERTY | 16,866 | 10,504 | 6,292 | 70 | 4,212 R | 62.3% | 37.3% | 62.5% | 37.5% |
| 20,224 | LIMESTONE | 7,305 | 4,063 | 3,228 | 14 | 835 R | 55.6% | 44.2% | 55.7% | 44.3% |
| 3,766 | LIPSCOMB | 1,708 | 1,461 | 241 | 6 | 1,220 R | 85.5% | 14.1% | 85.8% | 14.2% |
| 9,606 | LIVE OAK | 3,759 | 2,481 | 1,260 | 18 | 1,221 R | 66.0% | 33.5% | 66.3% | 33.7% |
| 10,144 | LLANO | 5,954 | 4,042 | 1,894 | 18 | 2,148 R | 67.9% | 31.8% | 68.1% | 31.9% |
| 91 | LOVING | 73 | 57 | 16 | | 41 R | 78.1% | 21.9% | 78.1% | 21.9% |
| 211,651 | LUBBOCK | 76,219 | 57,151 | 18,793 | 275 | 38,358 R | 75.0% | 24.7% | 75.3% | 24.7% |
| 8,605 | LYNN | 2,630 | 1,617 | 1,009 | 4 | 608 R | 61.5% | 38.4% | 61.6% | 38.4% |
| 8,735 | MCCULLOCH | 3,502 | 2,060 | 1,433 | 9 | 627 R | 58.8% | 40.9% | 59.0% | 41.0% |
| 170,755 | MCLENNAN | 65,578 | 42,232 | 23,206 | 140 | 19,026 R | 64.4% | 35.4% | 64.5% | 35.5% |
| 789 | MCMULLEN | 398 | 337 | 61 | | 276 R | 84.7% | 15.3% | 84.7% | 15.3% |
| 10,649 | MADISON | 3,553 | 2,158 | 1,384 | 11 | 774 R | 60.7% | 39.0% | 60.9% | 39.1% |
| 10,360 | MARION | 4,463 | 2,336 | 2,111 | 16 | 225 R | 52.3% | 47.3% | 52.5% | 47.5% |
| 4,684 | MARTIN | 1,740 | 1,218 | 512 | 10 | 706 R | 70.0% | 29.4% | 70.4% | 29.6% |
| 3,683 | MASON | 1,743 | 1,168 | 570 | 5 | 598 R | 67.0% | 32.7% | 67.2% | 32.8% |
| 37,828 | MATAGORDA | 13,694 | 8,452 | 5,201 | 41 | 3,251 R | 61.7% | 38.0% | 61.9% | 38.1% |
| 31,398 | MAVERICK | 4,861 | 1,783 | 3,063 | 15 | 1,280 D | 36.7% | 63.0% | 36.8% | 63.2% |
| 23,164 | MEDINA | 8,803 | 5,737 | 3,053 | 13 | 2,684 R | 65.2% | 34.7% | 65.3% | 34.7% |
| 2,346 | MENARD | 1,125 | 725 | 394 | 6 | 331 R | 64.4% | 35.0% | 64.8% | 35.2% |
| 82,636 | MIDLAND | 41,039 | 33,706 | 7,214 | 119 | 26,492 R | 82.1% | 17.6% | 82.4% | 17.6% |
| 22,732 | MILAM | 8,140 | 4,384 | 3,734 | 22 | 650 R | 53.9% | 45.9% | 54.0% | 46.0% |
| 4,477 | MILLS | 1,960 | 1,262 | 688 | 10 | 574 R | 64.4% | 35.1% | 64.7% | 35.3% |
| 9,088 | MITCHELL | 3,357 | 2,007 | 1,332 | 18 | 675 R | 59.8% | 39.7% | 60.1% | 39.9% |
| 17,410 | MONTAGUE | 7,030 | 4,406 | 2,602 | 22 | 1,804 R | 62.7% | 37.0% | 62.9% | 37.1% |
| 128,487 | MONTGOMERY | 54,690 | 41,230 | 13,293 | 167 | 27,937 R | 75.4% | 24.3% | 75.6% | 24.4% |
| 16,575 | MOORE | 5,796 | 4,649 | 1,129 | 18 | 3,520 R | 80.2% | 19.5% | 80.5% | 19.5% |
| 14,629 | MORRIS | 5,727 | 2,778 | 2,925 | 24 | 147 D | 48.5% | 51.1% | 48.7% | 51.3% |
| 1,950 | MOTLEY | 819 | 533 | 282 | 4 | 251 R | 65.1% | 34.4% | 65.4% | 34.6% |
| 46,786 | NACOGDOCHES | 18,812 | 13,063 | 5,694 | 55 | 7,369 R | 69.4% | 30.3% | 69.6% | 30.4% |
| 35,323 | NAVARRO | 13,509 | 7,816 | 5,672 | 21 | 2,144 R | 57.9% | 42.0% | 57.9% | 42.1% |
| 13,254 | NEWTON | 5,439 | 2,123 | 3,296 | 20 | 1,173 D | 39.0% | 60.6% | 39.2% | 60.8% |
| 17,359 | NOLAN | 6,136 | 3,608 | 2,524 | 4 | 1,084 R | 58.8% | 41.1% | 58.8% | 41.2% |
| 268,215 | NUECES | 101,213 | 54,333 | 46,721 | 159 | 7,612 R | 53.7% | 46.2% | 53.8% | 46.2% |
| 9,588 | OCHILTREE | 3,917 | 3,492 | 419 | 6 | 3,073 R | 89.1% | 10.7% | 89.3% | 10.7% |
| 2,283 | OLDHAM | 990 | 762 | 226 | 2 | 536 R | 77.0% | 22.8% | 77.1% | 22.9% |

# TEXAS

## PRESIDENT 1984

| 1980 Census Population | County | Total Vote | Republican | Democratic | Other | Rep.-Dem. Plurality | | Percentage | | | |
|---|---|---|---|---|---|---|---|---|---|---|---|
| | | | | | | | | Total Vote | | Major Vote | |
| | | | | | | | | Rep. | Dem. | Rep. | Dem. |
| 83,838 | ORANGE | 32,303 | 15,386 | 16,816 | 101 | 1,430 | D | 47.6% | 52.1% | 47.8% | 52.2% |
| 24,062 | PALO PINTO | 9,077 | 5,701 | 3,349 | 27 | 2,352 | R | 62.8% | 36.9% | 63.0% | 37.0% |
| 20,724 | PANOLA | 8,885 | 5,676 | 3,179 | 30 | 2,497 | R | 63.9% | 35.8% | 64.1% | 35.9% |
| 44,609 | PARKER | 19,759 | 13,647 | 6,050 | 62 | 7,597 | R | 69.1% | 30.6% | 69.3% | 30.7% |
| 11,038 | PARMER | 3,102 | 2,524 | 567 | 11 | 1,957 | R | 81.4% | 18.3% | 81.7% | 18.3% |
| 14,618 | PECOS | 5,080 | 3,451 | 1,596 | 33 | 1,855 | R | 67.9% | 31.4% | 68.4% | 31.6% |
| 24,407 | POLK | 9,918 | 5,987 | 3,898 | 33 | 2,089 | R | 60.4% | 39.3% | 60.6% | 39.4% |
| 98,637 | POTTER | 28,902 | 20,396 | 8,365 | 141 | 12,031 | R | 70.6% | 28.9% | 70.9% | 29.1% |
| 5,188 | PRESIDIO | 1,902 | 837 | 992 | 73 | 155 | D | 44.0% | 52.2% | 45.8% | 54.2% |
| 4,839 | RAINS | 2,591 | 1,560 | 1,027 | 4 | 533 | R | 60.2% | 39.6% | 60.3% | 39.7% |
| 75,062 | RANDALL | 36,409 | 30,249 | 6,044 | 116 | 24,205 | R | 83.1% | 16.6% | 83.3% | 16.7% |
| 4,135 | REAGAN | 1,324 | 1,079 | 243 | 2 | 836 | R | 81.5% | 18.4% | 81.6% | 18.4% |
| 2,469 | REAL | 1,369 | 1,004 | 360 | 5 | 644 | R | 73.3% | 26.3% | 73.6% | 26.4% |
| 16,101 | RED RIVER | 5,512 | 2,979 | 2,518 | 15 | 461 | R | 54.0% | 45.7% | 54.2% | 45.8% |
| 15,801 | REEVES | 4,872 | 2,461 | 2,396 | 15 | 65 | R | 50.5% | 49.2% | 50.7% | 49.3% |
| 9,289 | REFUGIO | 3,988 | 2,421 | 1,559 | 8 | 862 | R | 60.7% | 39.1% | 60.8% | 39.2% |
| 1,187 | ROBERTS | 645 | 539 | 106 | | 433 | R | 83.6% | 16.4% | 83.6% | 16.4% |
| 14,653 | ROBERTSON | 6,016 | 2,663 | 3,339 | 14 | 676 | D | 44.3% | 55.5% | 44.4% | 55.6% |
| 14,528 | ROCKWALL | 8,349 | 6,688 | 1,639 | 22 | 5,049 | R | 80.1% | 19.6% | 80.3% | 19.7% |
| 11,872 | RUNNELS | 4,177 | 2,968 | 1,179 | 30 | 1,789 | R | 71.1% | 28.2% | 71.6% | 28.4% |
| 41,382 | RUSK | 15,741 | 11,081 | 4,599 | 61 | 6,482 | R | 70.4% | 29.2% | 70.7% | 29.3% |
| 8,702 | SABINE | 3,993 | 2,045 | 1,940 | 8 | 105 | R | 51.2% | 48.6% | 51.3% | 48.7% |
| 8,785 | SAN AUGUSTINE | 3,529 | 1,937 | 1,583 | 9 | 354 | R | 54.9% | 44.9% | 55.0% | 45.0% |
| 11,434 | SAN JACINTO | 5,659 | 3,174 | 2,466 | 19 | 708 | R | 56.1% | 43.6% | 56.3% | 43.7% |
| 58,013 | SAN PATRICIO | 19,962 | 11,074 | 8,838 | 50 | 2,236 | R | 55.5% | 44.3% | 55.6% | 44.4% |
| 6,204 | SAN SABA | 2,647 | 1,566 | 1,070 | 11 | 496 | R | 59.2% | 40.4% | 59.4% | 40.6% |
| 2,820 | SCHLEICHER | 1,187 | 854 | 326 | 7 | 528 | R | 71.9% | 27.5% | 72.4% | 27.6% |
| 18,192 | SCURRY | 6,629 | 5,028 | 1,564 | 37 | 3,464 | R | 75.8% | 23.6% | 76.3% | 23.7% |
| 3,915 | SHACKELFORD | 1,604 | 1,181 | 415 | 8 | 766 | R | 73.6% | 25.9% | 74.0% | 26.0% |
| 23,084 | SHELBY | 8,501 | 4,863 | 3,610 | 28 | 1,253 | R | 57.2% | 42.5% | 57.4% | 42.6% |
| 3,174 | SHERMAN | 1,524 | 1,269 | 246 | 9 | 1,023 | R | 83.3% | 16.1% | 83.8% | 16.2% |
| 128,366 | SMITH | 56,119 | 40,740 | 15,227 | 152 | 25,513 | R | 72.6% | 27.1% | 72.8% | 27.2% |
| 4,154 | SOMERVELL | 2,061 | 1,422 | 635 | 4 | 787 | R | 69.0% | 30.8% | 69.1% | 30.9% |
| 27,266 | STARR | 6,713 | 1,658 | 5,047 | 8 | 3,389 | D | 24.7% | 75.2% | 24.7% | 75.3% |
| 9,926 | STEPHENS | 3,955 | 2,898 | 1,046 | 11 | 1,852 | R | 73.3% | 26.4% | 73.5% | 26.5% |
| 1,206 | STERLING | 710 | 577 | 129 | 4 | 448 | R | 81.3% | 18.2% | 81.7% | 18.3% |
| 2,406 | STONEWALL | 1,244 | 599 | 643 | 2 | 44 | D | 48.2% | 51.7% | 48.2% | 51.8% |
| 5,130 | SUTTON | 1,721 | 1,251 | 465 | 5 | 786 | R | 72.7% | 27.0% | 72.9% | 27.1% |
| 9,723 | SWISHER | 3,261 | 1,611 | 1,642 | 8 | 31 | D | 49.4% | 50.4% | 49.5% | 50.5% |
| 860,880 | TARRANT | 368,862 | 248,050 | 120,147 | 665 | 127,903 | R | 67.2% | 32.6% | 67.4% | 32.6% |
| 110,932 | TAYLOR | 44,202 | 34,444 | 9,628 | 130 | 24,816 | R | 77.9% | 21.8% | 78.2% | 21.8% |
| 1,595 | TERRELL | 698 | 407 | 289 | 2 | 118 | R | 58.3% | 41.4% | 58.5% | 41.5% |
| 14,581 | TERRY | 4,724 | 3,181 | 1,535 | 8 | 1,646 | R | 67.3% | 32.5% | 67.5% | 32.5% |
| 2,053 | THROCKMORTON | 979 | 586 | 388 | 5 | 198 | R | 59.9% | 39.6% | 60.2% | 39.8% |
| 21,442 | TITUS | 8,727 | 5,069 | 3,631 | 27 | 1,438 | R | 58.1% | 41.6% | 58.3% | 41.7% |
| 84,784 | TOM GREEN | 32,910 | 23,847 | 8,981 | 82 | 14,866 | R | 72.5% | 27.3% | 72.6% | 27.4% |
| 419,573 | TRAVIS | 219,813 | 124,944 | 94,124 | 745 | 30,820 | R | 56.8% | 42.8% | 57.0% | 43.0% |
| 9,450 | TRINITY | 4,735 | 2,599 | 2,115 | 21 | 484 | R | 54.9% | 44.7% | 55.1% | 44.9% |
| 16,223 | TYLER | 6,785 | 3,638 | 3,119 | 28 | 519 | R | 53.6% | 46.0% | 53.8% | 46.2% |
| 28,595 | UPSHUR | 11,976 | 7,325 | 4,614 | 37 | 2,711 | R | 61.2% | 38.5% | 61.4% | 38.6% |
| 4,619 | UPTON | 1,994 | 1,603 | 380 | 11 | 1,223 | R | 80.4% | 19.1% | 80.8% | 19.2% |
| 22,441 | UVALDE | 7,287 | 4,790 | 2,482 | 15 | 2,308 | R | 65.7% | 34.1% | 65.9% | 34.1% |
| 35,910 | VAL VERDE | 9,787 | 5,909 | 3,857 | 21 | 2,052 | R | 60.4% | 39.4% | 60.5% | 39.5% |
| 31,426 | VAN ZANDT | 13,003 | 8,474 | 4,506 | 23 | 3,968 | R | 65.2% | 34.7% | 65.3% | 34.7% |
| 68,807 | VICTORIA | 25,945 | 18,787 | 7,037 | 121 | 11,750 | R | 72.4% | 27.1% | 72.8% | 27.2% |
| 41,789 | WALKER | 13,100 | 8,809 | 4,263 | 28 | 4,546 | R | 67.2% | 32.5% | 67.4% | 32.6% |
| 19,798 | WALLER | 7,963 | 4,116 | 3,828 | 19 | 288 | R | 51.7% | 48.1% | 51.8% | 48.2% |
| 13,976 | WARD | 4,693 | 3,474 | 1,188 | 31 | 2,286 | R | 74.0% | 25.3% | 74.5% | 25.5% |
| 21,998 | WASHINGTON | 8,996 | 6,506 | 2,483 | 7 | 4,023 | R | 72.3% | 27.6% | 72.4% | 27.6% |
| 99,258 | WEBB | 20,936 | 8,582 | 12,308 | 46 | 3,726 | D | 41.0% | 58.8% | 41.1% | 58.9% |

# TEXAS

## PRESIDENT 1984

| 1980 Census Population | County | Total Vote | Republican | Democratic | Other | Rep.-Dem. Plurality | | Percentage | | | |
|---|---|---|---|---|---|---|---|---|---|---|---|
| | | | | | | | | Total Vote | | Major Vote | |
| | | | | | | | | Rep. | Dem. | Rep. | Dem. |
| 40,242 | WHARTON | 13,584 | 8,495 | 5,072 | 17 | 3,423 | R | 62.5% | 37.3% | 62.6% | 37.4% |
| 7,137 | WHEELER | 3,062 | 2,251 | 805 | 6 | 1,446 | R | 73.5% | 26.3% | 73.7% | 26.3% |
| 121,082 | WICHITA | 45,080 | 28,932 | 16,009 | 139 | 12,923 | R | 64.2% | 35.5% | 64.4% | 35.6% |
| 15,931 | WILBARGER | 5,673 | 3,644 | 2,011 | 18 | 1,633 | R | 64.2% | 35.4% | 64.4% | 35.6% |
| 17,495 | WILLACY | 5,391 | 2,340 | 3,037 | 14 | 697 | D | 43.4% | 56.3% | 43.5% | 56.5% |
| 76,521 | WILLIAMSON | 35,784 | 25,774 | 9,911 | 99 | 15,863 | R | 72.0% | 27.7% | 72.2% | 27.8% |
| 16,756 | WILSON | 7,434 | 4,588 | 2,829 | 17 | 1,759 | R | 61.7% | 38.1% | 61.9% | 38.1% |
| 9,944 | WINKLER | 2,974 | 2,213 | 752 | 9 | 1,461 | R | 74.4% | 25.3% | 74.6% | 25.4% |
| 26,575 | WISE | 10,853 | 6,958 | 3,856 | 39 | 3,102 | R | 64.1% | 35.5% | 64.3% | 35.7% |
| 24,697 | WOOD | 10,612 | 7,144 | 3,449 | 19 | 3,695 | R | 67.3% | 32.5% | 67.4% | 32.6% |
| 8,299 | YOAKUM | 2,668 | 2,204 | 456 | 8 | 1,748 | R | 82.6% | 17.1% | 82.9% | 17.1% |
| 19,083 | YOUNG | 7,503 | 5,282 | 2,203 | 18 | 3,079 | R | 70.4% | 29.4% | 70.6% | 29.4% |
| 6,628 | ZAPATA | 2,801 | 1,214 | 1,577 | 10 | 363 | D | 43.3% | 56.3% | 43.5% | 56.5% |
| 11,666 | ZAVALA | 3,868 | 924 | 2,937 | 7 | 2,013 | D | 23.9% | 75.9% | 23.9% | 76.1% |
| 14,229,191 | TOTAL | 5,397,571 | 3,433,428 | 1,949,276 | 14,867 | 1,484,152 | R | 63.6% | 36.1% | 63.8% | 36.2% |

# TEXAS

## PRESIDENT 1980

| 1980 Census Population | County | Total Vote | Republican | Democratic | Other | Rep.-Dem. Plurality | Percentage Total Vote Rep. | Dem. | Major Vote Rep. | Dem. |
|---|---|---|---|---|---|---|---|---|---|---|
| 38,381 | ANDERSON | 11,330 | 5,970 | 5,163 | 197 | 807 R | 52.7% | 45.6% | 53.6% | 46.4% |
| 13,323 | ANDREWS | 4,013 | 2,800 | 1,155 | 58 | 1,645 R | 69.8% | 28.8% | 70.8% | 29.2% |
| 64,172 | ANGELINA | 20,394 | 9,900 | 10,140 | 354 | 240 D | 48.5% | 49.7% | 49.4% | 50.6% |
| 14,260 | ARANSAS | 5,068 | 3,081 | 1,800 | 187 | 1,281 R | 60.8% | 35.5% | 63.1% | 36.9% |
| 7,266 | ARCHER | 3,289 | 1,804 | 1,444 | 41 | 360 R | 54.8% | 43.9% | 55.5% | 44.5% |
| 1,994 | ARMSTRONG | 1,065 | 709 | 333 | 23 | 376 R | 66.6% | 31.3% | 68.0% | 32.0% |
| 25,055 | ATASCOSA | 8,469 | 4,364 | 3,980 | 125 | 384 R | 51.5% | 47.0% | 52.3% | 47.7% |
| 17,726 | AUSTIN | 5,753 | 3,734 | 1,893 | 126 | 1,841 R | 64.9% | 32.9% | 66.4% | 33.6% |
| 8,168 | BAILEY | 2,655 | 1,809 | 800 | 46 | 1,009 R | 68.1% | 30.1% | 69.3% | 30.7% |
| 7,084 | BANDERA | 3,360 | 2,373 | 894 | 93 | 1,479 R | 70.6% | 26.6% | 72.6% | 27.4% |
| 24,726 | BASTROP | 8,748 | 3,768 | 4,716 | 264 | 948 D | 43.1% | 53.9% | 44.4% | 55.6% |
| 4,919 | BAYLOR | 2,306 | 1,098 | 1,183 | 25 | 85 D | 47.6% | 51.3% | 48.1% | 51.9% |
| 26,030 | BEE | 7,931 | 4,171 | 3,606 | 154 | 565 R | 52.6% | 45.5% | 53.6% | 46.4% |
| 157,889 | BELL | 37,885 | 20,729 | 15,823 | 1,333 | 4,906 R | 54.7% | 41.8% | 56.7% | 43.3% |
| 988,800 | BEXAR | 308,474 | 159,578 | 137,729 | 11,167 | 21,849 R | 51.7% | 44.6% | 53.7% | 46.3% |
| 4,681 | BLANCO | 2,301 | 1,434 | 794 | 73 | 640 R | 62.3% | 34.5% | 64.4% | 35.6% |
| 859 | BORDEN | 415 | 279 | 131 | 5 | 148 R | 67.2% | 31.6% | 68.0% | 32.0% |
| 13,401 | BOSQUE | 5,437 | 2,908 | 2,431 | 98 | 477 R | 53.5% | 44.7% | 54.5% | 45.5% |
| 75,301 | BOWIE | 25,650 | 13,942 | 11,339 | 369 | 2,603 R | 54.4% | 44.2% | 55.1% | 44.9% |
| 169,587 | BRAZORIA | 47,544 | 27,614 | 18,253 | 1,677 | 9,361 R | 58.1% | 38.4% | 60.2% | 39.8% |
| 93,588 | BRAZOS | 29,539 | 17,798 | 9,856 | 1,885 | 7,942 R | 60.3% | 33.4% | 64.4% | 35.6% |
| 7,573 | BREWSTER | 2,892 | 1,496 | 1,271 | 125 | 225 R | 51.7% | 43.9% | 54.1% | 45.9% |
| 2,579 | BRISCOE | 1,150 | 562 | 561 | 27 | 1 R | 48.9% | 48.8% | 50.0% | 50.0% |
| 8,428 | BROOKS | 3,333 | 780 | 2,488 | 65 | 1,708 D | 23.4% | 74.6% | 23.9% | 76.1% |
| 33,057 | BROWN | 11,549 | 6,515 | 4,867 | 167 | 1,648 R | 56.4% | 42.1% | 57.2% | 42.8% |
| 12,313 | BURLESON | 4,609 | 1,943 | 2,615 | 51 | 672 D | 42.2% | 56.7% | 42.6% | 57.4% |
| 17,803 | BURNET | 7,933 | 4,033 | 3,711 | 189 | 322 R | 50.8% | 46.8% | 52.1% | 47.9% |
| 23,637 | CALDWELL | 6,184 | 2,879 | 3,155 | 150 | 276 D | 46.6% | 51.0% | 47.7% | 52.3% |
| 19,574 | CALHOUN | 6,549 | 3,312 | 3,034 | 203 | 278 R | 50.6% | 46.3% | 52.2% | 47.8% |
| 10,992 | CALLAHAN | 4,331 | 2,284 | 2,002 | 45 | 282 R | 52.7% | 46.2% | 53.3% | 46.7% |
| 209,727 | CAMERON | 46,285 | 22,041 | 23,200 | 1,044 | 1,159 D | 47.6% | 50.1% | 48.7% | 51.3% |
| 9,275 | CAMP | 3,618 | 1,531 | 2,052 | 35 | 521 D | 42.3% | 56.7% | 42.7% | 57.3% |
| 6,672 | CARSON | 2,942 | 1,888 | 1,006 | 48 | 882 R | 64.2% | 34.2% | 65.2% | 34.8% |
| 29,430 | CASS | 10,672 | 4,993 | 5,578 | 101 | 585 D | 46.8% | 52.3% | 47.2% | 52.8% |
| 10,556 | CASTRO | 3,218 | 1,955 | 1,199 | 64 | 756 R | 60.8% | 37.3% | 62.0% | 38.0% |
| 18,538 | CHAMBERS | 5,806 | 3,140 | 2,517 | 149 | 623 R | 54.1% | 43.4% | 55.5% | 44.5% |
| 38,127 | CHEROKEE | 11,486 | 5,629 | 5,726 | 131 | 97 D | 49.0% | 49.9% | 49.6% | 50.4% |
| 6,950 | CHILDRESS | 2,713 | 1,443 | 1,222 | 48 | 221 R | 53.2% | 45.0% | 54.1% | 45.9% |
| 9,582 | CLAY | 4,109 | 1,824 | 2,233 | 52 | 409 D | 44.4% | 54.3% | 45.0% | 55.0% |
| 4,825 | COCHRAN | 1,607 | 1,064 | 513 | 30 | 551 R | 66.2% | 31.9% | 67.5% | 32.5% |
| 3,196 | COKE | 1,558 | 708 | 838 | 12 | 130 D | 45.4% | 53.8% | 45.8% | 54.2% |
| 10,439 | COLEMAN | 3,994 | 2,228 | 1,719 | 47 | 509 R | 55.8% | 43.0% | 56.4% | 43.6% |
| 144,576 | COLLIN | 53,861 | 36,559 | 15,187 | 2,115 | 21,372 R | 67.9% | 28.2% | 70.7% | 29.3% |
| 4,648 | COLLINGSWORTH | 1,851 | 1,020 | 798 | 33 | 222 R | 55.1% | 43.1% | 56.1% | 43.9% |
| 18,823 | COLORADO | 5,991 | 3,520 | 2,377 | 94 | 1,143 R | 58.8% | 39.7% | 59.7% | 40.3% |
| 36,446 | COMAL | 13,714 | 9,758 | 3,554 | 402 | 6,204 R | 71.2% | 25.9% | 73.3% | 26.7% |
| 12,617 | COMANCHE | 4,588 | 1,977 | 2,550 | 61 | 573 D | 43.1% | 55.6% | 43.7% | 56.3% |
| 2,915 | CONCHO | 1,417 | 700 | 702 | 15 | 2 D | 49.4% | 49.5% | 49.9% | 50.1% |
| 27,656 | COOKE | 10,802 | 6,760 | 3,842 | 200 | 2,918 R | 62.6% | 35.6% | 63.8% | 36.2% |
| 56,767 | CORYELL | 9,920 | 5,494 | 4,097 | 329 | 1,397 R | 55.4% | 41.3% | 57.3% | 42.7% |
| 2,947 | COTTLE | 1,266 | 511 | 732 | 23 | 221 D | 40.4% | 57.8% | 41.1% | 58.9% |
| 4,600 | CRANE | 1,951 | 1,310 | 607 | 34 | 703 R | 67.1% | 31.1% | 68.3% | 31.7% |
| 4,608 | CROCKETT | 1,494 | 885 | 595 | 14 | 290 R | 59.2% | 39.8% | 59.8% | 40.2% |
| 8,859 | CROSBY | 2,806 | 1,361 | 1,408 | 37 | 47 D | 48.5% | 50.2% | 49.2% | 50.8% |
| 3,315 | CULBERSON | 976 | 541 | 423 | 12 | 118 R | 55.4% | 43.3% | 56.1% | 43.9% |
| 6,531 | DALLAM | 1,639 | 965 | 632 | 42 | 333 R | 58.9% | 38.6% | 60.4% | 39.6% |
| 1,556,390 | DALLAS | 518,213 | 306,682 | 190,459 | 21,072 | 116,223 R | 59.2% | 36.8% | 61.7% | 38.3% |
| 16,184 | DAWSON | 5,205 | 3,267 | 1,867 | 71 | 1,400 R | 62.8% | 35.9% | 63.6% | 36.4% |
| 21,165 | DEAF SMITH | 5,864 | 4,073 | 1,666 | 125 | 2,407 R | 69.5% | 28.4% | 71.0% | 29.0% |
| 4,839 | DELTA | 2,142 | 767 | 1,347 | 28 | 580 D | 35.8% | 62.9% | 36.3% | 63.7% |

# TEXAS

## PRESIDENT 1980

| 1980 Census Population | County | Total Vote | Republican | Democratic | Other | Rep.-Dem. Plurality | Percentage | | | |
|---|---|---|---|---|---|---|---|---|---|---|
| | | | | | | | Total Vote | | Major Vote | |
| | | | | | | | Rep. | Dem. | Rep. | Dem. |
| 143,126 | DENTON | 49,908 | 29,908 | 17,381 | 2,619 | 12,527 R | 59.9% | 34.8% | 63.2% | 36.8% |
| 18,903 | DE WITT | 5,580 | 3,450 | 2,044 | 86 | 1,406 R | 61.8% | 36.6% | 62.8% | 37.2% |
| 3,539 | DICKENS | 1,481 | 554 | 912 | 15 | 358 D | 37.4% | 61.6% | 37.8% | 62.2% |
| 11,367 | DIMMIT | 3,323 | 1,173 | 2,102 | 48 | 929 D | 35.3% | 63.3% | 35.8% | 64.2% |
| 4,075 | DONLEY | 1,888 | 1,106 | 751 | 31 | 355 R | 58.6% | 39.8% | 59.6% | 40.4% |
| 12,517 | DUVAL | 4,757 | 1,012 | 3,706 | 39 | 2,694 D | 21.3% | 77.9% | 21.4% | 78.6% |
| 19,480 | EASTLAND | 6,877 | 3,442 | 3,346 | 89 | 96 R | 50.1% | 48.7% | 50.7% | 49.3% |
| 115,374 | ECTOR | 36,179 | 26,188 | 9,069 | 922 | 17,119 R | 72.4% | 25.1% | 74.3% | 25.7% |
| 2,033 | EDWARDS | 824 | 575 | 237 | 12 | 338 R | 69.8% | 28.8% | 70.8% | 29.2% |
| 59,743 | ELLIS | 19,580 | 10,046 | 9,219 | 315 | 827 R | 51.3% | 47.1% | 52.1% | 47.9% |
| 479,899 | EL PASO | 99,526 | 53,276 | 40,082 | 6,168 | 13,194 R | 53.5% | 40.3% | 57.1% | 42.9% |
| 22,560 | ERATH | 8,306 | 3,981 | 4,156 | 169 | 175 D | 47.9% | 50.0% | 48.9% | 51.1% |
| 17,946 | FALLS | 6,007 | 2,606 | 3,328 | 73 | 722 D | 43.4% | 55.4% | 43.9% | 56.1% |
| 24,285 | FANNIN | 8,611 | 3,196 | 5,284 | 131 | 2,088 D | 37.1% | 61.4% | 37.7% | 62.3% |
| 18,832 | FAYETTE | 6,804 | 4,104 | 2,590 | 110 | 1,514 R | 60.3% | 38.1% | 61.3% | 38.7% |
| 5,891 | FISHER | 2,437 | 838 | 1,564 | 35 | 726 D | 34.4% | 64.2% | 34.9% | 65.1% |
| 9,834 | FLOYD | 3,556 | 2,043 | 1,477 | 36 | 566 R | 57.5% | 41.5% | 58.0% | 42.0% |
| 2,158 | FOARD | 978 | 349 | 617 | 12 | 268 D | 35.7% | 63.1% | 36.1% | 63.9% |
| 130,846 | FORT BEND | 38,286 | 25,366 | 11,583 | 1,337 | 13,783 R | 66.3% | 30.3% | 68.7% | 31.3% |
| 6,893 | FRANKLIN | 2,633 | 1,105 | 1,487 | 41 | 382 D | 42.0% | 56.5% | 42.6% | 57.4% |
| 14,830 | FREESTONE | 5,265 | 2,468 | 2,739 | 58 | 271 D | 46.9% | 52.0% | 47.4% | 52.6% |
| 13,785 | FRIO | 4,668 | 1,753 | 2,849 | 66 | 1,096 D | 37.6% | 61.0% | 38.1% | 61.9% |
| 13,150 | GAINES | 3,656 | 2,390 | 1,182 | 84 | 1,208 R | 65.4% | 32.3% | 66.9% | 33.1% |
| 195,940 | GALVESTON | 63,297 | 29,527 | 30,778 | 2,992 | 1,251 D | 46.6% | 48.6% | 49.0% | 51.0% |
| 5,336 | GARZA | 1,897 | 1,188 | 677 | 32 | 511 R | 62.6% | 35.7% | 63.7% | 36.3% |
| 13,532 | GILLESPIE | 6,018 | 4,736 | 1,170 | 112 | 3,566 R | 78.7% | 19.4% | 80.2% | 19.8% |
| 1,304 | GLASSCOCK | 535 | 416 | 116 | 3 | 300 R | 77.8% | 21.7% | 78.2% | 21.8% |
| 5,193 | GOLIAD | 2,287 | 1,170 | 1,081 | 36 | 89 R | 51.2% | 47.3% | 52.0% | 48.0% |
| 16,883 | GONZALES | 5,922 | 2,931 | 2,896 | 95 | 35 R | 49.5% | 48.9% | 50.3% | 49.7% |
| 26,386 | GRAY | 10,149 | 7,187 | 2,786 | 176 | 4,401 R | 70.8% | 27.5% | 72.1% | 27.9% |
| 89,796 | GRAYSON | 31,326 | 16,811 | 13,807 | 708 | 3,004 R | 53.7% | 44.1% | 54.9% | 45.1% |
| 99,487 | GREGG | 34,190 | 23,399 | 10,219 | 572 | 13,180 R | 68.4% | 29.9% | 69.6% | 30.4% |
| 13,580 | GRIMES | 4,602 | 2,087 | 2,440 | 75 | 353 D | 45.3% | 53.0% | 46.1% | 53.9% |
| 46,708 | GUADALUPE | 15,428 | 9,901 | 5,049 | 478 | 4,852 R | 64.2% | 32.7% | 66.2% | 33.8% |
| 37,592 | HALE | 11,050 | 7,277 | 3,610 | 163 | 3,667 R | 65.9% | 32.7% | 66.8% | 33.2% |
| 5,594 | HALL | 2,220 | 1,141 | 1,057 | 22 | 84 R | 51.4% | 47.6% | 51.9% | 48.1% |
| 8,297 | HAMILTON | 3,267 | 1,683 | 1,526 | 58 | 157 R | 51.5% | 46.7% | 52.4% | 47.6% |
| 6,209 | HANSFORD | 2,596 | 2,046 | 518 | 32 | 1,528 R | 78.8% | 20.0% | 79.8% | 20.2% |
| 6,368 | HARDEMAN | 2,273 | 1,056 | 1,174 | 43 | 118 D | 46.5% | 51.6% | 47.4% | 52.6% |
| 40,721 | HARDIN | 13,732 | 6,087 | 7,358 | 287 | 1,271 D | 44.3% | 53.6% | 45.3% | 54.7% |
| 2,409,547 | HARRIS | 720,014 | 416,655 | 274,061 | 29,298 | 142,594 R | 57.9% | 38.1% | 60.3% | 39.7% |
| 52,265 | HARRISON | 17,493 | 9,328 | 7,746 | 419 | 1,582 R | 53.3% | 44.3% | 54.6% | 45.4% |
| 3,987 | HARTLEY | 1,757 | 1,248 | 470 | 39 | 778 R | 71.0% | 26.8% | 72.6% | 27.4% |
| 7,725 | HASKELL | 3,436 | 1,447 | 1,951 | 38 | 504 D | 42.1% | 56.8% | 42.6% | 57.4% |
| 40,594 | HAYS | 13,289 | 6,517 | 6,013 | 759 | 504 R | 49.0% | 45.2% | 52.0% | 48.0% |
| 5,304 | HEMPHILL | 1,780 | 1,152 | 592 | 36 | 560 R | 64.7% | 33.3% | 66.1% | 33.9% |
| 42,606 | HENDERSON | 16,305 | 7,903 | 8,199 | 203 | 296 D | 48.5% | 50.3% | 49.1% | 50.9% |
| 283,229 | HIDALGO | 61,717 | 25,808 | 34,542 | 1,367 | 8,734 D | 41.8% | 56.0% | 42.8% | 57.2% |
| 25,024 | HILL | 8,936 | 4,113 | 4,688 | 135 | 575 D | 46.0% | 52.5% | 46.7% | 53.3% |
| 23,230 | HOCKLEY | 7,183 | 4,599 | 2,447 | 137 | 2,152 R | 64.0% | 34.1% | 65.3% | 34.7% |
| 17,714 | HOOD | 6,940 | 3,755 | 3,001 | 184 | 754 R | 54.1% | 43.2% | 55.6% | 44.4% |
| 25,247 | HOPKINS | 8,318 | 3,834 | 4,344 | 140 | 510 D | 46.1% | 52.2% | 46.9% | 53.1% |
| 22,299 | HOUSTON | 7,144 | 2,889 | 4,181 | 74 | 1,292 D | 40.4% | 58.5% | 40.9% | 59.1% |
| 33,142 | HOWARD | 11,312 | 6,658 | 4,451 | 203 | 2,207 R | 58.9% | 39.3% | 59.9% | 40.1% |
| 2,728 | HUDSPETH | 884 | 471 | 394 | 19 | 77 R | 53.3% | 44.6% | 54.5% | 45.5% |
| 55,248 | HUNT | 18,501 | 9,283 | 8,773 | 445 | 510 R | 50.2% | 47.4% | 51.4% | 48.6% |
| 26,304 | HUTCHINSON | 10,632 | 7,439 | 2,935 | 258 | 4,504 R | 70.0% | 27.6% | 71.7% | 28.3% |
| 1,386 | IRION | 670 | 427 | 239 | 4 | 188 R | 63.7% | 35.7% | 64.1% | 35.9% |
| 7,408 | JACK | 2,877 | 1,482 | 1,349 | 46 | 133 R | 51.5% | 46.9% | 52.3% | 47.7% |
| 13,352 | JACKSON | 4,463 | 2,540 | 1,826 | 97 | 714 R | 56.9% | 40.9% | 58.2% | 41.8% |

# TEXAS

## PRESIDENT 1980

| 1980 Census Population | County | Total Vote | Republican | Democratic | Other | Rep.-Dem. Plurality | Percentage | | | |
|---|---|---|---|---|---|---|---|---|---|---|
| | | | | | | | Total Vote | | Major Vote | |
| | | | | | | | Rep. | Dem. | Rep. | Dem. |
| 30,781 | JASPER | 10,257 | 4,396 | 5,707 | 154 | 1,311 D | 42.9% | 55.6% | 43.5% | 56.5% |
| 1,647 | JEFF DAVIS | 729 | 409 | 300 | 20 | 109 R | 56.1% | 41.2% | 57.7% | 42.3% |
| 250,938 | JEFFERSON | 84,602 | 36,763 | 45,642 | 2,197 | 8,879 D | 43.5% | 53.9% | 44.6% | 55.4% |
| 5,168 | JIM HOGG | 1,997 | 535 | 1,437 | 25 | 902 D | 26.8% | 72.0% | 27.1% | 72.9% |
| 36,498 | JIM WELLS | 12,013 | 4,606 | 7,267 | 140 | 2,661 D | 38.3% | 60.5% | 38.8% | 61.2% |
| 67,649 | JOHNSON | 22,454 | 11,411 | 10,542 | 501 | 869 R | 50.8% | 46.9% | 52.0% | 48.0% |
| 17,268 | JONES | 5,874 | 2,765 | 3,043 | 66 | 278 D | 47.1% | 51.8% | 47.6% | 52.4% |
| 13,593 | KARNES | 5,074 | 2,719 | 2,284 | 71 | 435 R | 53.6% | 45.0% | 54.3% | 45.7% |
| 39,015 | KAUFMAN | 12,287 | 5,852 | 6,266 | 169 | 414 D | 47.6% | 51.0% | 48.3% | 51.7% |
| 10,635 | KENDALL | 5,086 | 3,890 | 1,075 | 121 | 2,815 R | 76.5% | 21.1% | 78.3% | 21.7% |
| 543 | KENEDY | 187 | 76 | 106 | 5 | 30 D | 40.6% | 56.7% | 41.8% | 58.2% |
| 1,145 | KENT | 694 | 339 | 351 | 4 | 12 D | 48.8% | 50.6% | 49.1% | 50.9% |
| 28,780 | KERR | 12,855 | 9,090 | 3,387 | 378 | 5,703 R | 70.7% | 26.3% | 72.9% | 27.1% |
| 4,063 | KIMBLE | 1,651 | 1,011 | 608 | 32 | 403 R | 61.2% | 36.8% | 62.4% | 37.6% |
| 425 | KING | 205 | 144 | 55 | 6 | 89 R | 70.2% | 26.8% | 72.4% | 27.6% |
| 2,279 | KINNEY | 1,046 | 543 | 472 | 31 | 71 R | 51.9% | 45.1% | 53.5% | 46.5% |
| 33,358 | KLEBERG | 10,053 | 4,608 | 5,125 | 320 | 517 D | 45.8% | 51.0% | 47.3% | 52.7% |
| 5,329 | KNOX | 1,968 | 783 | 1,163 | 22 | 380 D | 39.8% | 59.1% | 40.2% | 59.8% |
| 42,156 | LAMAR | 13,490 | 6,094 | 7,178 | 218 | 1,084 D | 45.2% | 53.2% | 45.9% | 54.1% |
| 18,669 | LAMB | 5,933 | 3,723 | 2,132 | 78 | 1,591 R | 62.8% | 35.9% | 63.6% | 36.4% |
| 12,005 | LAMPASAS | 4,381 | 2,323 | 1,979 | 79 | 344 R | 53.0% | 45.2% | 54.0% | 46.0% |
| 5,514 | LA SALLE | 2,248 | 773 | 1,442 | 33 | 669 D | 34.4% | 64.1% | 34.9% | 65.1% |
| 19,004 | LAVACA | 5,999 | 3,254 | 2,678 | 67 | 576 R | 54.2% | 44.6% | 54.9% | 45.1% |
| 10,952 | LEE | 3,462 | 1,803 | 1,581 | 78 | 222 R | 52.1% | 45.7% | 53.3% | 46.7% |
| 9,594 | LEON | 4,053 | 1,821 | 2,190 | 42 | 369 D | 44.9% | 54.0% | 45.4% | 54.6% |
| 47,088 | LIBERTY | 13,561 | 6,470 | 6,810 | 281 | 340 D | 47.7% | 50.2% | 48.7% | 51.3% |
| 20,224 | LIMESTONE | 6,319 | 2,835 | 3,403 | 81 | 568 D | 44.9% | 53.9% | 45.4% | 54.6% |
| 3,766 | LIPSCOMB | 1,733 | 1,343 | 338 | 52 | 1,005 R | 77.5% | 19.5% | 79.9% | 20.1% |
| 9,606 | LIVE OAK | 3,618 | 2,193 | 1,380 | 45 | 813 R | 60.6% | 38.1% | 61.4% | 38.6% |
| 10,144 | LLANO | 5,097 | 2,866 | 2,130 | 101 | 736 R | 56.2% | 41.8% | 57.4% | 42.6% |
| 91 | LOVING | 72 | 50 | 22 | | 28 R | 69.4% | 30.6% | 69.4% | 30.6% |
| 211,651 | LUBBOCK | 67,867 | 46,711 | 18,732 | 2,424 | 27,979 R | 68.8% | 27.6% | 71.4% | 28.6% |
| 8,605 | LYNN | 2,874 | 1,603 | 1,236 | 35 | 367 R | 55.8% | 43.0% | 56.5% | 43.5% |
| 8,735 | MCCULLOCH | 3,366 | 1,572 | 1,750 | 44 | 178 D | 46.7% | 52.0% | 47.3% | 52.7% |
| 170,755 | MCLENNAN | 59,515 | 31,968 | 26,305 | 1,242 | 5,663 R | 53.7% | 44.2% | 54.9% | 45.1% |
| 789 | MCMULLEN | 398 | 271 | 122 | 5 | 149 R | 68.1% | 30.7% | 69.0% | 31.0% |
| 10,649 | MADISON | 3,018 | 1,389 | 1,583 | 46 | 194 D | 46.0% | 52.5% | 46.7% | 53.3% |
| 10,360 | MARION | 3,730 | 1,666 | 2,015 | 49 | 349 D | 44.7% | 54.0% | 45.3% | 54.7% |
| 4,684 | MARTIN | 1,716 | 1,093 | 605 | 18 | 488 R | 63.7% | 35.3% | 64.4% | 35.6% |
| 3,683 | MASON | 1,621 | 966 | 630 | 25 | 336 R | 59.6% | 38.9% | 60.5% | 39.5% |
| 37,828 | MATAGORDA | 10,382 | 5,545 | 4,585 | 252 | 960 R | 53.4% | 44.2% | 54.7% | 45.3% |
| 31,398 | MAVERICK | 4,367 | 1,370 | 2,932 | 65 | 1,562 D | 31.4% | 67.1% | 31.8% | 68.2% |
| 23,164 | MEDINA | 7,888 | 4,742 | 3,034 | 112 | 1,708 R | 60.1% | 38.5% | 61.0% | 39.0% |
| 2,346 | MENARD | 1,050 | 548 | 489 | 13 | 59 R | 52.2% | 46.6% | 52.8% | 47.2% |
| 82,636 | MIDLAND | 32,692 | 25,027 | 6,839 | 826 | 18,188 R | 76.6% | 20.9% | 78.5% | 21.5% |
| 22,732 | MILAM | 7,627 | 3,251 | 4,230 | 146 | 979 D | 42.6% | 55.5% | 43.5% | 56.5% |
| 4,477 | MILLS | 2,059 | 985 | 1,028 | 46 | 43 D | 47.8% | 49.9% | 48.9% | 51.1% |
| 9,088 | MITCHELL | 2,926 | 1,455 | 1,446 | 25 | 9 R | 49.7% | 49.4% | 50.2% | 49.8% |
| 17,410 | MONTAGUE | 6,472 | 3,143 | 3,233 | 96 | 90 D | 48.6% | 50.0% | 49.3% | 50.7% |
| 128,487 | MONTGOMERY | 39,971 | 26,237 | 12,593 | 1,141 | 13,644 R | 65.6% | 31.5% | 67.6% | 32.4% |
| 16,575 | MOORE | 5,583 | 3,736 | 1,743 | 104 | 1,993 R | 66.9% | 31.2% | 68.2% | 31.8% |
| 14,629 | MORRIS | 5,280 | 2,133 | 3,105 | 42 | 972 D | 40.4% | 58.8% | 40.7% | 59.3% |
| 1,950 | MOTLEY | 929 | 573 | 341 | 15 | 232 R | 61.7% | 36.7% | 62.7% | 37.3% |
| 46,786 | NACOGDOCHES | 15,150 | 8,626 | 5,981 | 543 | 2,645 R | 56.9% | 39.5% | 59.1% | 40.9% |
| 35,323 | NAVARRO | 12,591 | 5,400 | 6,988 | 203 | 1,588 D | 42.9% | 55.5% | 43.6% | 56.4% |
| 13,254 | NEWTON | 4,714 | 1,379 | 3,284 | 51 | 1,905 D | 29.3% | 69.7% | 29.6% | 70.4% |
| 17,359 | NOLAN | 5,695 | 2,781 | 2,796 | 118 | 15 D | 48.8% | 49.1% | 49.9% | 50.1% |
| 268,215 | NUECES | 86,644 | 40,586 | 43,424 | 2,634 | 2,838 D | 46.8% | 50.1% | 48.3% | 51.7% |
| 9,588 | OCHILTREE | 3,702 | 3,032 | 594 | 76 | 2,438 R | 81.9% | 16.0% | 83.6% | 16.4% |
| 2,283 | OLDHAM | 874 | 557 | 290 | 27 | 267 R | 63.7% | 33.2% | 65.8% | 34.2% |

# TEXAS

## PRESIDENT 1980

| 1980 Census Population | County | Total Vote | Republican | Democratic | Other | Rep.-Dem. Plurality | Percentage Total Vote Rep. | Dem. | Major Vote Rep. | Dem. |
|---:|---|---:|---:|---:|---:|---:|---:|---:|---:|---:|
| 83,838 | ORANGE | 27,887 | 12,389 | 14,928 | 570 | 2,539 D | 44.4% | 53.5% | 45.4% | 54.6% |
| 24,062 | PALO PINTO | 8,484 | 4,068 | 4,244 | 172 | 176 D | 47.9% | 50.0% | 48.9% | 51.1% |
| 20,724 | PANOLA | 7,747 | 4,022 | 3,637 | 88 | 385 R | 51.9% | 46.9% | 52.5% | 47.5% |
| 44,609 | PARKER | 16,155 | 8,505 | 7,336 | 314 | 1,169 R | 52.6% | 45.4% | 53.7% | 46.3% |
| 11,038 | PARMER | 3,398 | 2,640 | 707 | 51 | 1,933 R | 77.7% | 20.8% | 78.9% | 21.1% |
| 14,618 | PECOS | 4,395 | 2,723 | 1,602 | 70 | 1,121 R | 62.0% | 36.5% | 63.0% | 37.0% |
| 24,407 | POLK | 8,108 | 3,771 | 4,213 | 124 | 442 D | 46.5% | 52.0% | 47.2% | 52.8% |
| 98,637 | POTTER | 26,831 | 16,327 | 9,633 | 871 | 6,694 R | 60.9% | 35.9% | 62.9% | 37.1% |
| 5,188 | PRESIDIO | 1,799 | 723 | 1,039 | 37 | 316 D | 40.2% | 57.8% | 41.0% | 59.0% |
| 4,839 | RAINS | 2,022 | 813 | 1,174 | 35 | 361 D | 40.2% | 58.1% | 40.9% | 59.1% |
| 75,062 | RANDALL | 31,382 | 23,136 | 7,323 | 923 | 15,813 R | 73.7% | 23.3% | 76.0% | 24.0% |
| 4,135 | REAGAN | 1,351 | 917 | 414 | 20 | 503 R | 67.9% | 30.6% | 68.9% | 31.1% |
| 2,469 | REAL | 1,453 | 832 | 603 | 18 | 229 R | 57.3% | 41.5% | 58.0% | 42.0% |
| 16,101 | RED RIVER | 5,773 | 2,225 | 3,501 | 47 | 1,276 D | 38.5% | 60.6% | 38.9% | 61.1% |
| 15,801 | REEVES | 4,544 | 2,315 | 2,138 | 91 | 177 R | 50.9% | 47.1% | 52.0% | 48.0% |
| 9,289 | REFUGIO | 4,251 | 1,944 | 2,224 | 83 | 280 D | 45.7% | 52.3% | 46.6% | 53.4% |
| 1,187 | ROBERTS | 642 | 482 | 150 | 10 | 332 R | 75.1% | 23.4% | 76.3% | 23.7% |
| 14,653 | ROBERTSON | 5,310 | 1,661 | 3,572 | 77 | 1,911 D | 31.3% | 67.3% | 31.7% | 68.3% |
| 14,528 | ROCKWALL | 6,184 | 4,036 | 1,985 | 163 | 2,051 R | 65.3% | 32.1% | 67.0% | 33.0% |
| 11,872 | RUNNELS | 4,233 | 2,532 | 1,648 | 53 | 884 R | 59.8% | 38.9% | 60.6% | 39.4% |
| 41,382 | RUSK | 14,467 | 8,705 | 5,582 | 180 | 3,123 R | 60.2% | 38.6% | 60.9% | 39.1% |
| 8,702 | SABINE | 3,398 | 1,387 | 1,983 | 28 | 596 D | 40.8% | 58.4% | 41.2% | 58.8% |
| 8,785 | SAN AUGUSTINE | 3,091 | 1,397 | 1,674 | 20 | 277 D | 45.2% | 54.2% | 45.5% | 54.5% |
| 11,434 | SAN JACINTO | 4,193 | 1,726 | 2,376 | 91 | 650 D | 41.2% | 56.7% | 42.1% | 57.9% |
| 58,013 | SAN PATRICIO | 17,494 | 8,326 | 8,627 | 541 | 301 D | 47.6% | 49.3% | 49.1% | 50.9% |
| 6,204 | SAN SABA | 2,385 | 948 | 1,405 | 32 | 457 D | 39.7% | 58.9% | 40.3% | 59.7% |
| 2,820 | SCHLEICHER | 1,131 | 672 | 444 | 15 | 228 R | 59.4% | 39.3% | 60.2% | 39.8% |
| 18,192 | SCURRY | 5,846 | 3,745 | 2,003 | 98 | 1,742 R | 64.1% | 34.3% | 65.2% | 34.8% |
| 3,915 | SHACKELFORD | 1,581 | 959 | 606 | 16 | 353 R | 60.7% | 38.3% | 61.3% | 38.7% |
| 23,084 | SHELBY | 7,804 | 3,500 | 4,215 | 89 | 715 D | 44.8% | 54.0% | 45.4% | 54.6% |
| 3,174 | SHERMAN | 1,456 | 1,128 | 286 | 42 | 842 R | 77.5% | 19.6% | 79.8% | 20.2% |
| 128,366 | SMITH | 43,700 | 28,236 | 14,838 | 626 | 13,398 R | 64.6% | 34.0% | 65.6% | 34.4% |
| 4,154 | SOMERVELL | 1,852 | 792 | 1,015 | 45 | 223 D | 42.8% | 54.8% | 43.8% | 56.2% |
| 27,266 | STARR | 6,253 | 1,389 | 4,782 | 82 | 3,393 D | 22.2% | 76.5% | 22.5% | 77.5% |
| 9,926 | STEPHENS | 3,608 | 2,161 | 1,372 | 75 | 789 R | 59.9% | 38.0% | 61.2% | 38.8% |
| 1,206 | STERLING | 586 | 364 | 218 | 4 | 146 R | 62.1% | 37.2% | 62.5% | 37.5% |
| 2,406 | STONEWALL | 1,219 | 488 | 719 | 12 | 231 D | 40.0% | 59.0% | 40.4% | 59.6% |
| 5,130 | SUTTON | 1,511 | 1,000 | 485 | 26 | 515 R | 66.2% | 32.1% | 67.3% | 32.7% |
| 9,723 | SWISHER | 3,366 | 1,450 | 1,854 | 62 | 404 D | 43.1% | 55.1% | 43.9% | 56.1% |
| 860,880 | TARRANT | 305,066 | 173,466 | 121,068 | 10,532 | 52,398 R | 56.9% | 39.7% | 58.9% | 41.1% |
| 110,932 | TAYLOR | 37,032 | 22,961 | 13,245 | 826 | 9,716 R | 62.0% | 35.8% | 63.4% | 36.6% |
| 1,595 | TERRELL | 686 | 411 | 260 | 15 | 151 R | 59.9% | 37.9% | 61.3% | 38.7% |
| 14,581 | TERRY | 5,195 | 3,178 | 1,945 | 72 | 1,233 R | 61.2% | 37.4% | 62.0% | 38.0% |
| 2,053 | THROCKMORTON | 908 | 444 | 455 | 9 | 11 D | 48.9% | 50.1% | 49.4% | 50.6% |
| 21,442 | TITUS | 7,700 | 3,747 | 3,872 | 81 | 125 D | 48.7% | 50.3% | 49.2% | 50.8% |
| 84,784 | TOM GREEN | 27,271 | 16,555 | 9,892 | 824 | 6,663 R | 60.7% | 36.3% | 62.6% | 37.4% |
| 419,573 | TRAVIS | 160,093 | 73,151 | 75,028 | 11,914 | 1,877 D | 45.7% | 46.9% | 49.4% | 50.6% |
| 9,450 | TRINITY | 4,068 | 1,503 | 2,510 | 55 | 1,007 D | 36.9% | 61.7% | 37.5% | 62.5% |
| 16,223 | TYLER | 6,195 | 2,545 | 3,540 | 110 | 995 D | 41.1% | 57.1% | 41.8% | 58.2% |
| 28,595 | UPSHUR | 9,852 | 4,836 | 4,894 | 122 | 58 D | 49.1% | 49.7% | 49.7% | 50.3% |
| 4,619 | UPTON | 1,684 | 1,169 | 485 | 30 | 684 R | 69.4% | 28.8% | 70.7% | 29.3% |
| 22,441 | UVALDE | 6,366 | 3,887 | 2,402 | 77 | 1,485 R | 61.1% | 37.7% | 61.8% | 38.2% |
| 35,910 | VAL VERDE | 9,353 | 5,055 | 4,116 | 182 | 939 R | 54.0% | 44.0% | 55.1% | 44.9% |
| 31,426 | VAN ZANDT | 11,340 | 5,495 | 5,707 | 138 | 212 D | 48.5% | 50.3% | 49.1% | 50.9% |
| 68,807 | VICTORIA | 21,269 | 13,392 | 7,382 | 495 | 6,010 R | 63.0% | 34.7% | 64.5% | 35.5% |
| 41,789 | WALKER | 10,906 | 5,657 | 4,869 | 380 | 788 R | 51.9% | 44.6% | 53.7% | 46.3% |
| 19,798 | WALLER | 6,463 | 3,019 | 3,329 | 115 | 310 D | 46.7% | 51.5% | 47.6% | 52.4% |
| 13,976 | WARD | 4,396 | 2,912 | 1,405 | 79 | 1,507 R | 66.2% | 32.0% | 67.5% | 32.5% |
| 21,998 | WASHINGTON | 7,495 | 4,821 | 2,518 | 156 | 2,303 R | 64.3% | 33.6% | 65.7% | 34.3% |
| 99,258 | WEBB | 17,593 | 5,421 | 11,856 | 316 | 6,435 D | 30.8% | 67.4% | 31.4% | 68.6% |

# TEXAS

## PRESIDENT 1980

| 1980 Census Population | County | Total Vote | Republican | Democratic | Other | Rep.-Dem. Plurality | Percentage | | | |
|---|---|---|---|---|---|---|---|---|---|---|
| | | | | | | | Total Vote | | Major Vote | |
| | | | | | | | Rep. | Dem. | Rep. | Dem. |
| 40,242 | WHARTON | 11,958 | 6,598 | 5,138 | 222 | 1,460 R | 55.2% | 43.0% | 56.2% | 43.8% |
| 7,137 | WHEELER | 2,743 | 1,626 | 1,090 | 27 | 536 R | 59.3% | 39.7% | 59.9% | 40.1% |
| 121,082 | WICHITA | 41,625 | 22,884 | 17,657 | 1,084 | 5,227 R | 55.0% | 42.4% | 56.4% | 43.6% |
| 15,931 | WILBARGER | 5,463 | 3,031 | 2,347 | 85 | 684 R | 55.5% | 43.0% | 56.4% | 43.6% |
| 17,495 | WILLACY | 5,108 | 1,995 | 3,047 | 66 | 1,052 D | 39.1% | 59.7% | 39.6% | 60.4% |
| 76,521 | WILLIAMSON | 26,661 | 15,035 | 10,408 | 1,218 | 4,627 R | 56.4% | 39.0% | 59.1% | 40.9% |
| 16,756 | WILSON | 6,632 | 3,443 | 3,097 | 92 | 346 R | 51.9% | 46.7% | 52.6% | 47.4% |
| 9,944 | WINKLER | 3,232 | 2,160 | 1,021 | 51 | 1,139 R | 66.8% | 31.6% | 67.9% | 32.1% |
| 26,575 | WISE | 9,205 | 4,350 | 4,674 | 181 | 324 D | 47.3% | 50.8% | 48.2% | 51.8% |
| 24,697 | WOOD | 8,671 | 4,515 | 4,033 | 123 | 482 R | 52.1% | 46.5% | 52.8% | 47.2% |
| 8,299 | YOAKUM | 2,694 | 1,937 | 715 | 42 | 1,222 R | 71.9% | 26.5% | 73.0% | 27.0% |
| 19,083 | YOUNG | 7,022 | 4,153 | 2,740 | 129 | 1,413 R | 59.1% | 39.0% | 60.2% | 39.8% |
| 6,628 | ZAPATA | 2,131 | 874 | 1,218 | 39 | 344 D | 41.0% | 57.2% | 41.8% | 58.2% |
| 11,666 | ZAVALA | 3,538 | 831 | 2,621 | 86 | 1,790 D | 23.5% | 74.1% | 24.1% | 75.9% |
| 14,229,191 | TOTAL | 4,541,636 | 2,510,705 | 1,881,147 | 149,784 | 629,558 R | 55.3% | 41.4% | 57.2% | 42.8% |

# TEXAS

## PRESIDENT 1976

| 1970 Census Population | County | Total Vote | Republican | Democratic | Other | Rep.-Dem. Plurality | Percentage Total Vote Rep. | Total Vote Dem. | Major Vote Rep. | Major Vote Dem. |
|---|---|---|---|---|---|---|---|---|---|---|
| 27,789 | ANDERSON | 9,715 | 4,172 | 5,499 | 44 | 1,327 D | 42.9% | 56.6% | 43.1% | 56.9% |
| 10,372 | ANDREWS | 3,937 | 2,127 | 1,777 | 33 | 350 R | 54.0% | 45.1% | 54.5% | 45.5% |
| 49,349 | ANGELINA | 17,112 | 7,223 | 9,750 | 139 | 2,527 D | 42.2% | 57.0% | 42.6% | 57.4% |
| 8,902 | ARANSAS | 4,181 | 1,985 | 2,136 | 60 | 151 D | 47.5% | 51.1% | 48.2% | 51.8% |
| 5,759 | ARCHER | 2,561 | 966 | 1,577 | 18 | 611 D | 37.7% | 61.6% | 38.0% | 62.0% |
| 1,895 | ARMSTRONG | 1,027 | 506 | 513 | 8 | 7 D | 49.3% | 50.0% | 49.7% | 50.3% |
| 18,696 | ATASCOSA | 7,072 | 2,415 | 4,565 | 92 | 2,150 D | 34.1% | 64.6% | 34.6% | 65.4% |
| 13,831 | AUSTIN | 5,033 | 2,686 | 2,313 | 34 | 373 R | 53.4% | 46.0% | 53.7% | 46.3% |
| 8,487 | BAILEY | 2,627 | 1,255 | 1,356 | 16 | 101 D | 47.8% | 51.6% | 48.1% | 51.9% |
| 4,747 | BANDERA | 2,766 | 1,554 | 1,183 | 29 | 371 R | 56.2% | 42.8% | 56.8% | 43.2% |
| 17,297 | BASTROP | 7,204 | 2,383 | 4,788 | 33 | 2,405 D | 33.1% | 66.5% | 33.2% | 66.8% |
| 5,221 | BAYLOR | 2,130 | 783 | 1,335 | 12 | 552 D | 36.8% | 62.7% | 37.0% | 63.0% |
| 22,737 | BEE | 6,722 | 2,953 | 3,690 | 79 | 737 D | 43.9% | 54.9% | 44.5% | 55.5% |
| 124,483 | BELL | 32,912 | 15,126 | 17,499 | 287 | 2,373 D | 46.0% | 53.2% | 46.4% | 53.6% |
| 830,460 | BEXAR | 271,430 | 121,176 | 146,581 | 3,673 | 25,405 D | 44.6% | 54.0% | 45.3% | 54.7% |
| 3,567 | BLANCO | 1,956 | 1,015 | 923 | 18 | 92 R | 51.9% | 47.2% | 52.4% | 47.6% |
| 888 | BORDEN | 390 | 150 | 234 | 6 | 84 D | 38.5% | 60.0% | 39.1% | 60.9% |
| 10,966 | BOSQUE | 4,883 | 1,912 | 2,954 | 17 | 1,042 D | 39.2% | 60.5% | 39.3% | 60.7% |
| 67,813 | BOWIE | 22,214 | 9,590 | 12,445 | 179 | 2,855 D | 43.2% | 56.0% | 43.5% | 56.5% |
| 108,312 | BRAZORIA | 41,744 | 19,475 | 21,711 | 558 | 2,236 D | 46.7% | 52.0% | 47.3% | 52.7% |
| 57,978 | BRAZOS | 26,700 | 15,685 | 10,628 | 387 | 5,057 R | 58.7% | 39.8% | 59.6% | 40.4% |
| 7,780 | BREWSTER | 2,624 | 1,368 | 1,227 | 29 | 141 R | 52.1% | 46.8% | 52.7% | 47.3% |
| 2,794 | BRISCOE | 1,119 | 285 | 823 | 11 | 538 D | 25.5% | 73.5% | 25.7% | 74.3% |
| 8,005 | BROOKS | 3,429 | 641 | 2,782 | 6 | 2,141 D | 18.7% | 81.1% | 18.7% | 81.3% |
| 25,877 | BROWN | 10,095 | 4,483 | 5,577 | 35 | 1,094 D | 44.4% | 55.2% | 44.6% | 55.4% |
| 9,999 | BURLESON | 4,081 | 1,142 | 2,924 | 15 | 1,782 D | 28.0% | 71.6% | 28.1% | 71.9% |
| 11,420 | BURNET | 6,636 | 2,777 | 3,818 | 41 | 1,041 D | 41.8% | 57.5% | 42.1% | 57.9% |
| 21,178 | CALDWELL | 5,921 | 2,235 | 3,647 | 39 | 1,412 D | 37.7% | 61.6% | 38.0% | 62.0% |
| 17,831 | CALHOUN | 6,061 | 2,377 | 3,642 | 42 | 1,265 D | 39.2% | 60.1% | 39.5% | 60.5% |
| 8,205 | CALLAHAN | 3,864 | 1,581 | 2,241 | 42 | 660 D | 40.9% | 58.0% | 41.4% | 58.6% |
| 140,368 | CAMERON | 42,111 | 16,448 | 25,310 | 353 | 8,862 D | 39.1% | 60.1% | 39.4% | 60.6% |
| 8,005 | CAMP | 3,285 | 1,133 | 2,146 | 6 | 1,013 D | 34.5% | 65.3% | 34.6% | 65.4% |
| 6,358 | CARSON | 2,824 | 1,269 | 1,542 | 13 | 273 D | 44.9% | 54.6% | 45.1% | 54.9% |
| 24,133 | CASS | 8,875 | 3,712 | 5,134 | 29 | 1,422 D | 41.8% | 57.8% | 42.0% | 58.0% |
| 10,394 | CASTRO | 3,076 | 1,007 | 2,033 | 36 | 1,026 D | 32.7% | 66.1% | 33.1% | 66.9% |
| 12,187 | CHAMBERS | 4,852 | 1,835 | 2,927 | 90 | 1,092 D | 37.8% | 60.3% | 38.5% | 61.5% |
| 32,008 | CHEROKEE | 10,465 | 3,921 | 6,509 | 35 | 2,588 D | 37.5% | 62.2% | 37.6% | 62.4% |
| 6,605 | CHILDRESS | 2,626 | 1,043 | 1,578 | 5 | 535 D | 39.7% | 60.1% | 39.8% | 60.2% |
| 8,079 | CLAY | 3,783 | 1,200 | 2,568 | 15 | 1,368 D | 31.7% | 67.9% | 31.8% | 68.2% |
| 5,326 | COCHRAN | 1,739 | 701 | 1,031 | 7 | 330 D | 40.3% | 59.3% | 40.5% | 59.5% |
| 3,087 | COKE | 1,377 | 517 | 844 | 16 | 327 D | 37.5% | 61.3% | 38.0% | 62.0% |
| 10,288 | COLEMAN | 3,955 | 1,669 | 2,264 | 22 | 595 D | 42.2% | 57.2% | 42.4% | 57.6% |
| 66,920 | COLLIN | 36,000 | 21,608 | 14,039 | 353 | 7,569 R | 60.0% | 39.0% | 60.6% | 39.4% |
| 4,755 | COLLINGSWORTH | 1,804 | 629 | 1,169 | 6 | 540 D | 34.9% | 64.8% | 35.0% | 65.0% |
| 17,638 | COLORADO | 6,075 | 2,991 | 3,028 | 56 | 37 D | 49.2% | 49.8% | 49.7% | 50.3% |
| 24,165 | COMAL | 10,554 | 6,377 | 4,068 | 109 | 2,309 R | 60.4% | 38.5% | 61.1% | 38.9% |
| 11,898 | COMANCHE | 4,731 | 1,297 | 3,414 | 20 | 2,117 D | 27.4% | 72.2% | 27.5% | 72.5% |
| 2,937 | CONCHO | 1,195 | 474 | 715 | 6 | 241 D | 39.7% | 59.8% | 39.9% | 60.1% |
| 23,471 | COOKE | 9,329 | 4,804 | 4,483 | 42 | 321 R | 51.5% | 48.1% | 51.7% | 48.3% |
| 35,311 | CORYELL | 8,929 | 4,140 | 4,710 | 79 | 570 D | 46.4% | 52.7% | 46.8% | 53.2% |
| 3,204 | COTTLE | 1,361 | 311 | 1,047 | 3 | 736 D | 22.9% | 76.9% | 22.9% | 77.1% |
| 4,172 | CRANE | 1,680 | 963 | 664 | 53 | 299 R | 57.3% | 39.5% | 59.2% | 40.8% |
| 3,885 | CROCKETT | 1,608 | 802 | 804 | 2 | 2 D | 49.9% | 50.0% | 49.9% | 50.1% |
| 9,085 | CROSBY | 3,092 | 897 | 2,176 | 19 | 1,279 D | 29.0% | 70.4% | 29.2% | 70.8% |
| 3,429 | CULBERSON | 787 | 373 | 407 | 7 | 34 D | 47.4% | 51.7% | 47.8% | 52.2% |
| 6,012 | DALLAM | 2,007 | 936 | 1,029 | 42 | 93 D | 46.6% | 51.3% | 47.6% | 52.4% |
| 1,327,321 | DALLAS | 464,385 | 263,081 | 196,303 | 5,001 | 66,778 R | 56.7% | 42.3% | 57.3% | 42.7% |
| 16,604 | DAWSON | 4,653 | 2,474 | 2,162 | 17 | 312 R | 53.2% | 46.5% | 53.4% | 46.6% |
| 18,999 | DEAF SMITH | 5,435 | 2,776 | 2,613 | 46 | 163 R | 51.1% | 48.1% | 51.5% | 48.5% |
| 4,927 | DELTA | 1,991 | 421 | 1,563 | 7 | 1,142 D | 21.1% | 78.5% | 21.2% | 78.8% |

# TEXAS

## PRESIDENT 1976

| 1970 Census Population | County | Total Vote | Republican | Democratic | Other | Rep.-Dem. Plurality | Percentage Total Vote Rep. | Total Vote Dem. | Major Vote Rep. | Major Vote Dem. |
|---|---|---|---|---|---|---|---|---|---|---|
| 75,633 | DENTON | 39,692 | 20,440 | 18,887 | 365 | 1,553 R | 51.5% | 47.6% | 52.0% | 48.0% |
| 18,660 | DE WITT | 5,327 | 2,754 | 2,540 | 33 | 214 R | 51.7% | 47.7% | 52.0% | 48.0% |
| 3,737 | DICKENS | 1,571 | 343 | 1,222 | 6 | 879 D | 21.8% | 77.8% | 21.9% | 78.1% |
| 9,039 | DIMMIT | 2,624 | 890 | 1,721 | 13 | 831 D | 33.9% | 65.6% | 34.1% | 65.9% |
| 3,641 | DONLEY | 1,804 | 704 | 1,095 | 5 | 391 D | 39.0% | 60.7% | 39.1% | 60.9% |
| 11,722 | DUVAL | 4,941 | 661 | 4,267 | 13 | 3,606 D | 13.4% | 86.4% | 13.4% | 86.6% |
| 18,092 | EASTLAND | 6,695 | 2,340 | 4,320 | 35 | 1,980 D | 35.0% | 64.5% | 35.1% | 64.9% |
| 91,805 | ECTOR | 30,328 | 18,973 | 10,802 | 553 | 8,171 R | 62.6% | 35.6% | 63.7% | 36.3% |
| 2,107 | EDWARDS | 672 | 412 | 258 | 2 | 154 R | 61.3% | 38.4% | 61.5% | 38.5% |
| 46,638 | ELLIS | 17,055 | 6,996 | 9,991 | 68 | 2,995 D | 41.0% | 58.6% | 41.2% | 58.8% |
| 359,291 | EL PASO | 89,465 | 42,697 | 45,477 | 1,291 | 2,780 D | 47.7% | 50.8% | 48.4% | 51.6% |
| 18,141 | ERATH | 7,790 | 2,925 | 4,821 | 44 | 1,896 D | 37.5% | 61.9% | 37.8% | 62.2% |
| 17,300 | FALLS | 6,567 | 2,261 | 4,277 | 29 | 2,016 D | 34.4% | 65.1% | 34.6% | 65.4% |
| 22,705 | FANNIN | 7,985 | 2,102 | 5,845 | 38 | 3,743 D | 26.3% | 73.2% | 26.5% | 73.5% |
| 17,650 | FAYETTE | 6,493 | 3,030 | 3,428 | 35 | 398 D | 46.7% | 52.8% | 46.9% | 53.1% |
| 6,344 | FISHER | 2,576 | 573 | 1,993 | 10 | 1,420 D | 22.2% | 77.4% | 22.3% | 77.7% |
| 11,044 | FLOYD | 3,414 | 1,402 | 1,991 | 21 | 589 D | 41.1% | 58.3% | 41.3% | 58.7% |
| 2,211 | FOARD | 950 | 240 | 706 | 4 | 466 D | 25.3% | 74.3% | 25.4% | 74.6% |
| 52,314 | FORT BEND | 28,787 | 17,354 | 11,264 | 169 | 6,090 R | 60.3% | 39.1% | 60.6% | 39.4% |
| 5,291 | FRANKLIN | 2,404 | 758 | 1,636 | 10 | 878 D | 31.5% | 68.1% | 31.7% | 68.3% |
| 11,116 | FREESTONE | 4,361 | 1,674 | 2,679 | 8 | 1,005 D | 38.4% | 61.4% | 38.5% | 61.5% |
| 11,159 | FRIO | 3,908 | 1,280 | 2,598 | 30 | 1,318 D | 32.8% | 66.5% | 33.0% | 67.0% |
| 11,593 | GAINES | 3,544 | 1,643 | 1,880 | 21 | 237 D | 46.4% | 53.0% | 46.6% | 53.4% |
| 169,812 | GALVESTON | 63,735 | 25,251 | 37,873 | 611 | 12,622 D | 39.6% | 59.4% | 40.0% | 60.0% |
| 5,289 | GARZA | 1,725 | 755 | 957 | 13 | 202 D | 43.8% | 55.5% | 44.1% | 55.9% |
| 10,553 | GILLESPIE | 4,885 | 3,541 | 1,260 | 84 | 2,281 R | 72.5% | 25.8% | 73.8% | 26.2% |
| 1,155 | GLASSCOCK | 413 | 218 | 190 | 5 | 28 R | 52.8% | 46.0% | 53.4% | 46.6% |
| 4,869 | GOLIAD | 1,731 | 846 | 875 | 10 | 29 D | 48.9% | 50.5% | 49.2% | 50.8% |
| 16,375 | GONZALES | 5,026 | 1,789 | 3,219 | 18 | 1,430 D | 35.6% | 64.0% | 35.7% | 64.3% |
| 26,949 | GRAY | 9,962 | 6,010 | 3,872 | 80 | 2,138 R | 60.3% | 38.9% | 60.8% | 39.2% |
| 83,225 | GRAYSON | 29,095 | 11,981 | 17,015 | 99 | 5,034 D | 41.2% | 58.5% | 41.3% | 58.7% |
| 75,929 | GREGG | 27,612 | 17,582 | 9,827 | 203 | 7,755 R | 63.7% | 35.6% | 64.1% | 35.9% |
| 11,855 | GRIMES | 4,148 | 1,473 | 2,656 | 19 | 1,183 D | 35.5% | 64.0% | 35.7% | 64.3% |
| 33,554 | GUADALUPE | 12,935 | 6,766 | 6,054 | 115 | 712 R | 52.3% | 46.8% | 52.8% | 47.2% |
| 34,137 | HALE | 11,007 | 5,390 | 5,580 | 37 | 190 D | 49.0% | 50.7% | 49.1% | 50.9% |
| 6,015 | HALL | 2,314 | 671 | 1,633 | 10 | 962 D | 29.0% | 70.6% | 29.1% | 70.9% |
| 7,198 | HAMILTON | 3,189 | 1,176 | 1,981 | 32 | 805 D | 36.9% | 62.1% | 37.3% | 62.7% |
| 6,351 | HANSFORD | 2,406 | 1,401 | 983 | 22 | 418 R | 58.2% | 40.9% | 58.8% | 41.2% |
| 6,795 | HARDEMAN | 2,225 | 805 | 1,403 | 17 | 598 D | 36.2% | 63.1% | 36.5% | 63.5% |
| 29,996 | HARDIN | 10,688 | 4,046 | 6,558 | 84 | 2,512 D | 37.9% | 61.4% | 38.2% | 61.8% |
| 1,741,912 | HARRIS | 685,264 | 357,536 | 321,897 | 5,831 | 35,639 R | 52.2% | 47.0% | 52.6% | 47.4% |
| 44,841 | HARRISON | 15,639 | 7,787 | 7,796 | 56 | 9 D | 49.8% | 49.8% | 50.0% | 50.0% |
| 2,782 | HARTLEY | 1,597 | 811 | 774 | 12 | 37 R | 50.8% | 48.5% | 51.2% | 48.8% |
| 8,512 | HASKELL | 3,359 | 838 | 2,512 | 9 | 1,674 D | 24.9% | 74.8% | 25.0% | 75.0% |
| 27,642 | HAYS | 12,875 | 5,714 | 7,005 | 156 | 1,291 D | 44.4% | 54.4% | 44.9% | 55.1% |
| 3,084 | HEMPHILL | 1,578 | 858 | 707 | 13 | 151 R | 54.4% | 44.8% | 54.8% | 45.2% |
| 26,466 | HENDERSON | 12,937 | 4,658 | 8,245 | 34 | 3,587 D | 36.0% | 63.7% | 36.1% | 63.9% |
| 181,535 | HIDALGO | 54,593 | 19,199 | 35,021 | 373 | 15,822 D | 35.2% | 64.1% | 35.4% | 64.6% |
| 22,596 | HILL | 8,032 | 2,680 | 5,327 | 25 | 2,647 D | 33.4% | 66.3% | 33.5% | 66.5% |
| 20,396 | HOCKLEY | 7,130 | 3,137 | 3,949 | 44 | 812 D | 44.0% | 55.4% | 44.3% | 55.7% |
| 6,368 | HOOD | 5,061 | 1,857 | 3,181 | 23 | 1,324 D | 36.7% | 62.9% | 36.9% | 63.1% |
| 20,710 | HOPKINS | 7,592 | 2,556 | 4,992 | 44 | 2,436 D | 33.7% | 65.8% | 33.9% | 66.1% |
| 17,855 | HOUSTON | 5,421 | 2,229 | 3,179 | 13 | 950 D | 41.1% | 58.6% | 41.2% | 58.8% |
| 37,796 | HOWARD | 11,972 | 4,899 | 6,984 | 89 | 2,085 D | 40.9% | 58.3% | 41.2% | 58.8% |
| 2,392 | HUDSPETH | 881 | 395 | 479 | 7 | 84 D | 44.8% | 54.4% | 45.2% | 54.8% |
| 47,948 | HUNT | 15,314 | 6,676 | 8,543 | 95 | 1,867 D | 43.6% | 55.8% | 43.9% | 56.1% |
| 24,443 | HUTCHINSON | 9,933 | 6,137 | 3,691 | 105 | 2,446 R | 61.8% | 37.2% | 62.4% | 37.6% |
| 1,070 | IRION | 604 | 302 | 297 | 5 | 5 R | 50.0% | 49.2% | 50.4% | 49.6% |
| 6,711 | JACK | 2,871 | 1,049 | 1,814 | 8 | 765 D | 36.5% | 63.2% | 36.6% | 63.4% |
| 12,975 | JACKSON | 4,433 | 1,884 | 2,524 | 25 | 640 D | 42.5% | 56.9% | 42.7% | 57.3% |

# TEXAS

## PRESIDENT 1976

| 1970 Census Population | County | Total Vote | Republican | Democratic | Other | Rep.-Dem. Plurality | Percentage | | | |
|---|---|---|---|---|---|---|---|---|---|---|
| | | | | | | | Total Vote | | Major Vote | |
| | | | | | | | Rep. | Dem. | Rep. | Dem. |
| 24,692 | JASPER | 8,607 | 3,167 | 5,422 | 18 | 2,255 D | 36.8% | 63.0% | 36.9% | 63.1% |
| 1,527 | JEFF DAVIS | 607 | 288 | 309 | 10 | 21 D | 47.4% | 50.9% | 48.2% | 51.8% |
| 244,773 | JEFFERSON | 80,546 | 32,451 | 47,581 | 514 | 15,130 D | 40.3% | 59.1% | 40.5% | 59.5% |
| 4,654 | JIM HOGG | 2,074 | 429 | 1,645 | | 1,216 D | 20.7% | 79.3% | 20.7% | 79.3% |
| 33,032 | JIM WELLS | 11,550 | 3,547 | 7,961 | 42 | 4,414 D | 30.7% | 68.9% | 30.8% | 69.2% |
| 45,769 | JOHNSON | 18,127 | 7,194 | 10,864 | 69 | 3,670 D | 39.7% | 59.9% | 39.8% | 60.2% |
| 16,106 | JONES | 5,416 | 2,072 | 3,318 | 26 | 1,246 D | 38.3% | 61.3% | 38.4% | 61.6% |
| 13,462 | KARNES | 4,718 | 1,675 | 2,996 | 47 | 1,321 D | 35.5% | 63.5% | 35.9% | 64.1% |
| 32,392 | KAUFMAN | 10,204 | 3,867 | 6,302 | 35 | 2,435 D | 37.9% | 61.8% | 38.0% | 62.0% |
| 6,964 | KENDALL | 3,793 | 2,543 | 1,190 | 60 | 1,353 R | 67.0% | 31.4% | 68.1% | 31.9% |
| 678 | KENEDY | 205 | 65 | 139 | 1 | 74 D | 31.7% | 67.8% | 31.9% | 68.1% |
| 1,434 | KENT | 647 | 171 | 474 | 2 | 303 D | 26.4% | 73.3% | 26.5% | 73.5% |
| 19,454 | KERR | 9,978 | 6,021 | 3,767 | 190 | 2,254 R | 60.3% | 37.8% | 61.5% | 38.5% |
| 3,904 | KIMBLE | 1,632 | 846 | 759 | 27 | 87 R | 51.8% | 46.5% | 52.7% | 47.3% |
| 464 | KING | 197 | 96 | 100 | 1 | 4 D | 48.7% | 50.8% | 49.0% | 51.0% |
| 2,006 | KINNEY | 843 | 318 | 516 | 9 | 198 D | 37.7% | 61.2% | 38.1% | 61.9% |
| 33,166 | KLEBERG | 9,647 | 3,771 | 5,803 | 73 | 2,032 D | 39.1% | 60.2% | 39.4% | 60.6% |
| 5,972 | KNOX | 2,060 | 551 | 1,498 | 11 | 947 D | 26.7% | 72.7% | 26.9% | 73.1% |
| 36,062 | LAMAR | 13,076 | 4,443 | 8,601 | 32 | 4,158 D | 34.0% | 65.8% | 34.1% | 65.9% |
| 17,770 | LAMB | 5,815 | 2,413 | 3,374 | 28 | 961 D | 41.5% | 58.0% | 41.7% | 58.3% |
| 9,323 | LAMPASAS | 3,982 | 1,563 | 2,376 | 43 | 813 D | 39.3% | 59.7% | 39.7% | 60.3% |
| 5,014 | LA SALLE | 1,983 | 677 | 1,294 | 12 | 617 D | 34.1% | 65.3% | 34.3% | 65.7% |
| 17,903 | LAVACA | 5,964 | 2,466 | 3,458 | 40 | 992 D | 41.3% | 58.0% | 41.6% | 58.4% |
| 8,048 | LEE | 3,303 | 1,348 | 1,937 | 18 | 589 D | 40.8% | 58.6% | 41.0% | 59.0% |
| 8,738 | LEON | 3,261 | 1,161 | 2,085 | 15 | 924 D | 35.6% | 63.9% | 35.8% | 64.2% |
| 33,014 | LIBERTY | 11,704 | 4,552 | 7,086 | 66 | 2,534 D | 38.9% | 60.5% | 39.1% | 60.9% |
| 18,100 | LIMESTONE | 5,900 | 2,045 | 3,825 | 30 | 1,780 D | 34.7% | 64.8% | 34.8% | 65.2% |
| 3,486 | LIPSCOMB | 1,569 | 911 | 644 | 14 | 267 R | 58.1% | 41.0% | 58.6% | 41.4% |
| 6,697 | LIVE OAK | 2,961 | 1,287 | 1,656 | 18 | 369 D | 43.5% | 55.9% | 43.7% | 56.3% |
| 6,979 | LLANO | 4,324 | 1,947 | 2,361 | 16 | 414 D | 45.0% | 54.6% | 45.2% | 54.8% |
| 164 | LOVING | 86 | 47 | 35 | 4 | 12 R | 54.7% | 40.7% | 57.3% | 42.7% |
| 179,295 | LUBBOCK | 63,707 | 38,478 | 24,797 | 432 | 13,681 R | 60.4% | 38.9% | 60.8% | 39.2% |
| 9,107 | LYNN | 2,757 | 1,166 | 1,575 | 16 | 409 D | 42.3% | 57.1% | 42.5% | 57.5% |
| 8,571 | MCCULLOCH | 3,207 | 1,300 | 1,888 | 19 | 588 D | 40.5% | 58.9% | 40.8% | 59.2% |
| 147,553 | MCLENNAN | 55,970 | 25,370 | 30,091 | 509 | 4,721 D | 45.3% | 53.8% | 45.7% | 54.3% |
| 1,095 | MCMULLEN | 411 | 217 | 194 | | 23 R | 52.8% | 47.2% | 52.8% | 47.2% |
| 7,693 | MADISON | 2,961 | 1,062 | 1,885 | 14 | 823 D | 35.9% | 63.7% | 36.0% | 64.0% |
| 8,517 | MARION | 3,167 | 1,291 | 1,860 | 16 | 569 D | 40.8% | 58.7% | 41.0% | 59.0% |
| 4,774 | MARTIN | 1,618 | 698 | 907 | 13 | 209 D | 43.1% | 56.1% | 43.5% | 56.5% |
| 3,356 | MASON | 1,640 | 805 | 814 | 21 | 9 D | 49.1% | 49.6% | 49.7% | 50.3% |
| 27,913 | MATAGORDA | 8,731 | 3,679 | 4,971 | 81 | 1,292 D | 42.1% | 56.9% | 42.5% | 57.5% |
| 18,093 | MAVERICK | 3,802 | 924 | 2,840 | 38 | 1,916 D | 24.3% | 74.7% | 24.5% | 75.5% |
| 20,249 | MEDINA | 6,988 | 3,252 | 3,681 | 55 | 429 D | 46.5% | 52.7% | 46.9% | 53.1% |
| 2,646 | MENARD | 1,000 | 441 | 543 | 16 | 102 D | 44.1% | 54.3% | 44.8% | 55.2% |
| 65,433 | MIDLAND | 27,195 | 19,178 | 7,725 | 292 | 11,453 R | 70.5% | 28.4% | 71.3% | 28.7% |
| 20,028 | MILAM | 7,315 | 2,404 | 4,871 | 40 | 2,467 D | 32.9% | 66.6% | 33.0% | 67.0% |
| 4,212 | MILLS | 1,710 | 684 | 1,012 | 14 | 328 D | 40.0% | 59.2% | 40.3% | 59.7% |
| 9,073 | MITCHELL | 2,804 | 1,058 | 1,730 | 16 | 672 D | 37.7% | 61.7% | 37.9% | 62.1% |
| 15,326 | MONTAGUE | 6,294 | 2,182 | 4,087 | 25 | 1,905 D | 34.7% | 64.9% | 34.8% | 65.2% |
| 49,479 | MONTGOMERY | 29,659 | 15,739 | 13,718 | 202 | 2,021 R | 53.1% | 46.3% | 53.4% | 46.6% |
| 14,060 | MOORE | 5,575 | 2,759 | 2,767 | 49 | 8 D | 49.5% | 49.6% | 49.9% | 50.1% |
| 12,310 | MORRIS | 4,931 | 1,843 | 3,071 | 17 | 1,228 D | 37.4% | 62.3% | 37.5% | 62.5% |
| 2,178 | MOTLEY | 961 | 428 | 522 | 11 | 94 D | 44.5% | 54.3% | 45.1% | 54.9% |
| 36,362 | NACOGDOCHES | 14,141 | 7,315 | 6,697 | 129 | 618 R | 51.7% | 47.4% | 52.2% | 47.8% |
| 31,150 | NAVARRO | 11,068 | 4,012 | 6,995 | 61 | 2,983 D | 36.2% | 63.2% | 36.4% | 63.6% |
| 11,657 | NEWTON | 4,502 | 1,011 | 3,468 | 23 | 2,457 D | 22.5% | 77.0% | 22.6% | 77.4% |
| 16,220 | NOLAN | 5,545 | 2,431 | 3,094 | 20 | 663 D | 43.8% | 55.8% | 44.0% | 56.0% |
| 237,544 | NUECES | 86,325 | 32,797 | 52,755 | 773 | 19,958 D | 38.0% | 61.1% | 38.3% | 61.7% |
| 9,704 | OCHILTREE | 3,587 | 2,471 | 1,084 | 32 | 1,387 R | 68.9% | 30.2% | 69.5% | 30.5% |
| 2,258 | OLDHAM | 911 | 354 | 554 | 3 | 200 D | 38.9% | 60.8% | 39.0% | 61.0% |

# TEXAS

## PRESIDENT 1976

| 1970 Census Population | County | Total Vote | Republican | Democratic | Other | Rep.-Dem. Plurality | Percentage | | | |
|---|---|---|---|---|---|---|---|---|---|---|
| | | | | | | | Total Vote | | Major Vote | |
| | | | | | | | Rep. | Dem. | Rep. | Dem. |
| 71,170 | ORANGE | 24,484 | 9,147 | 15,177 | 160 | 6,030 D | 37.4% | 62.0% | 37.6% | 62.4% |
| 28,962 | PALO PINTO | 7,905 | 2,684 | 5,170 | 51 | 2,486 D | 34.0% | 65.4% | 34.2% | 65.8% |
| 15,894 | PANOLA | 6,977 | 3,218 | 3,731 | 28 | 513 D | 46.1% | 53.5% | 46.3% | 53.7% |
| 33,888 | PARKER | 12,969 | 4,692 | 8,186 | 91 | 3,494 D | 36.2% | 63.1% | 36.4% | 63.6% |
| 10,509 | PARMER | 3,417 | 1,487 | 1,914 | 16 | 427 D | 43.5% | 56.0% | 43.7% | 56.3% |
| 13,748 | PECOS | 4,233 | 2,234 | 1,971 | 28 | 263 R | 52.8% | 46.6% | 53.1% | 46.9% |
| 14,457 | POLK | 6,967 | 2,529 | 4,384 | 54 | 1,855 D | 36.3% | 62.9% | 36.6% | 63.4% |
| 90,511 | POTTER | 26,036 | 13,819 | 11,917 | 300 | 1,902 R | 53.1% | 45.8% | 53.7% | 46.3% |
| 4,842 | PRESIDIO | 1,936 | 687 | 1,232 | 17 | 545 D | 35.5% | 63.6% | 35.8% | 64.2% |
| 3,752 | RAINS | 1,855 | 510 | 1,339 | 6 | 829 D | 27.5% | 72.2% | 27.6% | 72.4% |
| 53,885 | RANDALL | 26,524 | 17,115 | 9,074 | 335 | 8,041 R | 64.5% | 34.2% | 65.4% | 34.6% |
| 3,239 | REAGAN | 1,234 | 666 | 563 | 5 | 103 R | 54.0% | 45.6% | 54.2% | 45.8% |
| 2,013 | REAL | 969 | 448 | 510 | 11 | 62 D | 46.2% | 52.6% | 46.8% | 53.2% |
| 14,298 | RED RIVER | 5,533 | 1,852 | 3,670 | 11 | 1,818 D | 33.5% | 66.3% | 33.5% | 66.5% |
| 16,526 | REEVES | 4,342 | 1,711 | 2,613 | 18 | 902 D | 39.4% | 60.2% | 39.6% | 60.4% |
| 9,494 | REFUGIO | 3,765 | 1,537 | 2,218 | 10 | 681 D | 40.8% | 58.9% | 40.9% | 59.1% |
| 967 | ROBERTS | 562 | 350 | 202 | 10 | 148 R | 62.3% | 35.9% | 63.4% | 36.6% |
| 14,389 | ROBERTSON | 4,996 | 1,244 | 3,741 | 11 | 2,497 D | 24.9% | 74.9% | 25.0% | 75.0% |
| 7,046 | ROCKWALL | 3,936 | 2,087 | 1,828 | 21 | 259 R | 53.0% | 46.4% | 53.3% | 46.7% |
| 12,108 | RUNNELS | 4,282 | 2,203 | 2,068 | 11 | 135 R | 51.4% | 48.3% | 51.6% | 48.4% |
| 34,102 | RUSK | 12,915 | 6,800 | 6,063 | 52 | 737 R | 52.7% | 46.9% | 52.9% | 47.1% |
| 7,187 | SABINE | 3,296 | 904 | 2,391 | 1 | 1,487 D | 27.4% | 72.5% | 27.4% | 72.6% |
| 7,858 | SAN AUGUSTINE | 2,870 | 1,047 | 1,817 | 6 | 770 D | 36.5% | 63.3% | 36.6% | 63.4% |
| 6,702 | SAN JACINTO | 3,529 | 1,094 | 2,406 | 29 | 1,312 D | 31.0% | 68.2% | 31.3% | 68.7% |
| 47,288 | SAN PATRICIO | 15,395 | 5,853 | 9,469 | 73 | 3,616 D | 38.0% | 61.5% | 38.2% | 61.8% |
| 5,540 | SAN SABA | 2,005 | 582 | 1,408 | 15 | 826 D | 29.0% | 70.2% | 29.2% | 70.8% |
| 2,277 | SCHLEICHER | 993 | 516 | 468 | 9 | 48 R | 52.0% | 47.1% | 52.4% | 47.6% |
| 15,760 | SCURRY | 5,459 | 2,797 | 2,639 | 23 | 158 R | 51.2% | 48.3% | 51.5% | 48.5% |
| 3,323 | SHACKELFORD | 1,518 | 748 | 764 | 6 | 16 D | 49.3% | 50.3% | 49.5% | 50.5% |
| 19,672 | SHELBY | 7,387 | 2,695 | 4,680 | 12 | 1,985 D | 36.5% | 63.4% | 36.5% | 63.5% |
| 3,657 | SHERMAN | 1,416 | 679 | 718 | 19 | 39 D | 48.0% | 50.7% | 48.6% | 51.4% |
| 97,096 | SMITH | 39,275 | 22,238 | 16,856 | 181 | 5,382 R | 56.6% | 42.9% | 56.9% | 43.1% |
| 2,793 | SOMERVELL | 1,391 | 332 | 1,054 | 5 | 722 D | 23.9% | 75.8% | 24.0% | 76.0% |
| 17,707 | STARR | 5,325 | 664 | 4,646 | 15 | 3,982 D | 12.5% | 87.2% | 12.5% | 87.5% |
| 8,414 | STEPHENS | 3,429 | 1,621 | 1,796 | 12 | 175 D | 47.3% | 52.4% | 47.4% | 52.6% |
| 1,056 | STERLING | 381 | 202 | 174 | 5 | 28 R | 53.0% | 45.7% | 53.7% | 46.3% |
| 2,397 | STONEWALL | 1,070 | 252 | 812 | 6 | 560 D | 23.6% | 75.9% | 23.7% | 76.3% |
| 3,175 | SUTTON | 1,609 | 831 | 768 | 10 | 63 R | 51.6% | 47.7% | 52.0% | 48.0% |
| 10,373 | SWISHER | 3,577 | 753 | 2,811 | 13 | 2,058 D | 21.1% | 78.6% | 21.1% | 78.9% |
| 716,317 | TARRANT | 248,631 | 124,433 | 122,287 | 1,911 | 2,146 R | 50.0% | 49.2% | 50.4% | 49.6% |
| 97,853 | TAYLOR | 34,543 | 19,822 | 14,453 | 268 | 5,369 R | 57.4% | 41.8% | 57.8% | 42.2% |
| 1,940 | TERRELL | 642 | 317 | 321 | 4 | 4 D | 49.4% | 50.0% | 49.7% | 50.3% |
| 14,118 | TERRY | 5,001 | 2,113 | 2,859 | 29 | 746 D | 42.3% | 57.2% | 42.5% | 57.5% |
| 2,205 | THROCKMORTON | 1,016 | 356 | 658 | 2 | 302 D | 35.0% | 64.8% | 35.1% | 64.9% |
| 16,702 | TITUS | 6,822 | 2,603 | 4,205 | 14 | 1,602 D | 38.2% | 61.6% | 38.2% | 61.8% |
| 71,047 | TOM GREEN | 23,554 | 12,316 | 11,064 | 174 | 1,252 R | 52.3% | 47.0% | 52.7% | 47.3% |
| 295,516 | TRAVIS | 152,213 | 71,031 | 78,585 | 2,597 | 7,554 D | 46.7% | 51.6% | 47.5% | 52.5% |
| 7,628 | TRINITY | 3,154 | 1,042 | 2,100 | 12 | 1,058 D | 33.0% | 66.6% | 33.2% | 66.8% |
| 12,417 | TYLER | 5,318 | 1,965 | 3,322 | 31 | 1,357 D | 36.9% | 62.5% | 37.2% | 62.8% |
| 20,976 | UPSHUR | 8,211 | 3,272 | 4,902 | 37 | 1,630 D | 39.8% | 59.7% | 40.0% | 60.0% |
| 4,697 | UPTON | 1,561 | 869 | 686 | 6 | 183 R | 55.7% | 43.9% | 55.9% | 44.1% |
| 17,348 | UVALDE | 5,449 | 3,103 | 2,299 | 47 | 804 R | 56.9% | 42.2% | 57.4% | 42.6% |
| 27,471 | VAL VERDE | 8,152 | 3,476 | 4,603 | 73 | 1,127 D | 42.6% | 56.5% | 43.0% | 57.0% |
| 22,155 | VAN ZANDT | 9,898 | 3,385 | 6,449 | 64 | 3,064 D | 34.2% | 65.2% | 34.4% | 65.6% |
| 53,766 | VICTORIA | 17,028 | 9,594 | 7,326 | 108 | 2,268 R | 56.3% | 43.0% | 56.7% | 43.3% |
| 27,680 | WALKER | 10,171 | 4,974 | 5,105 | 92 | 131 D | 48.9% | 50.2% | 49.4% | 50.6% |
| 14,285 | WALLER | 4,862 | 1,992 | 2,828 | 42 | 836 D | 41.0% | 58.2% | 41.3% | 58.7% |
| 13,019 | WARD | 4,218 | 2,123 | 2,046 | 49 | 77 R | 50.3% | 48.5% | 50.9% | 49.1% |
| 18,842 | WASHINGTON | 6,500 | 3,820 | 2,635 | 45 | 1,185 R | 58.8% | 40.5% | 59.2% | 40.8% |
| 72,859 | WEBB | 14,698 | 4,222 | 10,362 | 114 | 6,140 D | 28.7% | 70.5% | 28.9% | 71.1% |

# TEXAS

## PRESIDENT 1976

| 1970 Census Population | County | Total Vote | Republican | Democratic | Other | Rep.-Dem. Plurality | Total Vote | | Major Vote | |
|---|---|---|---|---|---|---|---|---|---|---|
| | | | | | | | Rep. | Dem. | Rep. | Dem. |
| 36,729 | WHARTON | 10,644 | 4,682 | 5,914 | 48 | 1,232 D | 44.0% | 55.6% | 44.2% | 55.8% |
| 6,434 | WHEELER | 2,888 | 1,273 | 1,598 | 17 | 325 D | 44.1% | 55.3% | 44.3% | 55.7% |
| 121,862 | WICHITA | 41,266 | 19,024 | 22,017 | 225 | 2,993 D | 46.1% | 53.4% | 46.4% | 53.6% |
| 15,355 | WILBARGER | 5,476 | 2,145 | 3,280 | 51 | 1,135 D | 39.2% | 59.9% | 39.5% | 60.5% |
| 15,570 | WILLACY | 4,557 | 1,542 | 2,984 | 31 | 1,442 D | 33.8% | 65.5% | 34.1% | 65.9% |
| 37,305 | WILLIAMSON | 17,010 | 7,481 | 9,355 | 174 | 1,874 D | 44.0% | 55.0% | 44.4% | 55.6% |
| 13,041 | WILSON | 5,902 | 1,926 | 3,973 | 3 | 2,047 D | 32.6% | 67.3% | 32.6% | 67.4% |
| 9,640 | WINKLER | 3,266 | 1,842 | 1,382 | 42 | 460 R | 56.4% | 42.3% | 57.1% | 42.9% |
| 19,687 | WISE | 8,013 | 2,856 | 5,133 | 24 | 2,277 D | 35.6% | 64.1% | 35.7% | 64.3% |
| 18,589 | WOOD | 7,226 | 3,076 | 4,107 | 43 | 1,031 D | 42.6% | 56.8% | 42.8% | 57.2% |
| 7,344 | YOAKUM | 2,680 | 1,477 | 1,181 | 22 | 296 R | 55.1% | 44.1% | 55.6% | 44.4% |
| 15,400 | YOUNG | 6,166 | 2,652 | 3,473 | 41 | 821 D | 43.0% | 56.3% | 43.3% | 56.7% |
| 4,352 | ZAPATA | 1,682 | 462 | 1,216 | 4 | 754 D | 27.5% | 72.3% | 27.5% | 72.5% |
| 11,370 | ZAVALA | 2,578 | 735 | 1,822 | 21 | 1,087 D | 28.5% | 70.7% | 28.7% | 71.3% |
| 11,196,730 | TOTAL | 4,071,884 | 1,953,300 | 2,082,319 | 36,265 | 129,019 D | 48.0% | 51.1% | 48.4% | 51.6% |

# TEXAS

## PRESIDENT 1972

| 1970 Census Population | County | Total Vote | Republican | Democratic | Other | Rep.-Dem. Plurality | Percentage Total Vote Rep. | Dem. | Major Vote Rep. | Dem. |
|---|---|---|---|---|---|---|---|---|---|---|
| 27,789 | ANDERSON | 8,065 | 5,826 | 2,233 | 6 | 3,593 R | 72.2% | 27.7% | 72.3% | 27.7% |
| 10,372 | ANDREWS | 3,310 | 2,615 | 677 | 18 | 1,938 R | 79.0% | 20.5% | 79.4% | 20.6% |
| 49,349 | ANGELINA | 16,589 | 11,453 | 4,970 | 166 | 6,483 R | 69.0% | 30.0% | 69.7% | 30.3% |
| 8,902 | ARANSAS | 2,890 | 2,037 | 844 | 9 | 1,193 R | 70.5% | 29.2% | 70.7% | 29.3% |
| 5,759 | ARCHER | 2,152 | 1,494 | 632 | 26 | 862 R | 69.4% | 29.4% | 70.3% | 29.7% |
| 1,895 | ARMSTRONG | 951 | 768 | 177 | 6 | 591 R | 80.8% | 18.6% | 81.3% | 18.7% |
| 18,696 | ATASCOSA | 5,208 | 3,400 | 1,804 | 4 | 1,596 R | 65.3% | 34.6% | 65.3% | 34.7% |
| 13,831 | AUSTIN | 4,154 | 3,084 | 1,043 | 27 | 2,041 R | 74.2% | 25.1% | 74.7% | 25.3% |
| 8,487 | BAILEY | 2,305 | 1,837 | 465 | 3 | 1,372 R | 79.7% | 20.2% | 79.8% | 20.2% |
| 4,747 | BANDERA | 2,259 | 1,796 | 434 | 29 | 1,362 R | 79.5% | 19.2% | 80.5% | 19.5% |
| 17,297 | BASTROP | 5,010 | 3,097 | 1,906 | 7 | 1,191 R | 61.8% | 38.0% | 61.9% | 38.1% |
| 5,221 | BAYLOR | 1,789 | 1,190 | 598 | 1 | 592 R | 66.5% | 33.4% | 66.6% | 33.4% |
| 22,737 | BEE | 5,866 | 3,779 | 2,067 | 20 | 1,712 R | 64.4% | 35.2% | 64.6% | 35.4% |
| 124,483 | BELL | 24,411 | 17,525 | 6,848 | 38 | 10,677 R | 71.8% | 28.1% | 71.9% | 28.1% |
| 830,460 | BEXAR | 230,193 | 137,572 | 91,662 | 959 | 45,910 R | 59.8% | 39.8% | 60.0% | 40.0% |
| 3,567 | BLANCO | 1,695 | 1,215 | 460 | 20 | 755 R | 71.7% | 27.1% | 72.5% | 27.5% |
| 888 | BORDEN | 433 | 330 | 96 | 7 | 234 R | 76.2% | 22.2% | 77.5% | 22.5% |
| 10,966 | BOSQUE | 3,976 | 2,947 | 1,014 | 15 | 1,933 R | 74.1% | 25.5% | 74.4% | 25.6% |
| 67,813 | BOWIE | 20,015 | 14,722 | 5,227 | 66 | 9,495 R | 73.6% | 26.1% | 73.8% | 26.2% |
| 108,312 | BRAZORIA | 32,432 | 21,045 | 11,350 | 37 | 9,695 R | 64.9% | 35.0% | 65.0% | 35.0% |
| 57,978 | BRAZOS | 20,051 | 14,243 | 5,692 | 116 | 8,551 R | 71.0% | 28.4% | 71.4% | 28.6% |
| 7,780 | BREWSTER | 2,446 | 1,524 | 904 | 18 | 620 R | 62.3% | 37.0% | 62.8% | 37.2% |
| 2,794 | BRISCOE | 1,000 | 642 | 349 | 9 | 293 R | 64.2% | 34.9% | 64.8% | 35.2% |
| 8,005 | BROOKS | 2,781 | 1,117 | 1,657 | 7 | 540 D | 40.2% | 59.6% | 40.3% | 59.7% |
| 25,877 | BROWN | 8,233 | 5,990 | 2,171 | 72 | 3,819 R | 72.8% | 26.4% | 73.4% | 26.6% |
| 9,999 | BURLESON | 3,125 | 1,762 | 1,361 | 2 | 401 R | 56.4% | 43.6% | 56.4% | 43.6% |
| 11,420 | BURNET | 4,688 | 3,438 | 1,227 | 23 | 2,211 R | 73.3% | 26.2% | 73.7% | 26.3% |
| 21,178 | CALDWELL | 5,160 | 3,171 | 1,974 | 15 | 1,197 R | 61.5% | 38.3% | 61.6% | 38.4% |
| 17,831 | CALHOUN | 5,566 | 3,614 | 1,936 | 16 | 1,678 R | 64.9% | 34.8% | 65.1% | 34.9% |
| 8,205 | CALLAHAN | 2,939 | 2,223 | 665 | 51 | 1,558 R | 75.6% | 22.6% | 77.0% | 23.0% |
| 140,368 | CAMERON | 34,300 | 20,816 | 13,340 | 144 | 7,476 R | 60.7% | 38.9% | 60.9% | 39.1% |
| 8,005 | CAMP | 2,641 | 1,599 | 1,041 | 1 | 558 R | 60.5% | 39.4% | 60.6% | 39.4% |
| 6,358 | CARSON | 2,466 | 1,868 | 561 | 37 | 1,307 R | 75.8% | 22.7% | 76.9% | 23.1% |
| 24,133 | CASS | 7,288 | 5,303 | 1,981 | 4 | 3,322 R | 72.8% | 27.2% | 72.8% | 27.2% |
| 10,394 | CASTRO | 2,451 | 1,685 | 751 | 15 | 934 R | 68.7% | 30.6% | 69.2% | 30.8% |
| 12,187 | CHAMBERS | 3,602 | 2,390 | 1,206 | 6 | 1,184 R | 66.4% | 33.5% | 66.5% | 33.5% |
| 32,008 | CHEROKEE | 8,288 | 5,743 | 2,467 | 78 | 3,276 R | 69.3% | 29.8% | 70.0% | 30.0% |
| 6,605 | CHILDRESS | 2,458 | 1,716 | 729 | 13 | 987 R | 69.8% | 29.7% | 70.2% | 29.8% |
| 8,079 | CLAY | 2,945 | 1,893 | 1,023 | 29 | 870 R | 64.3% | 34.7% | 64.9% | 35.1% |
| 5,326 | COCHRAN | 1,536 | 1,106 | 415 | 15 | 691 R | 72.0% | 27.0% | 72.7% | 27.3% |
| 3,087 | COKE | 1,134 | 761 | 358 | 15 | 403 R | 67.1% | 31.6% | 68.0% | 32.0% |
| 10,288 | COLEMAN | 3,112 | 2,386 | 721 | 5 | 1,665 R | 76.7% | 23.2% | 76.8% | 23.2% |
| 66,920 | COLLIN | 22,637 | 17,667 | 4,783 | 187 | 12,884 R | 78.0% | 21.1% | 78.7% | 21.3% |
| 4,755 | COLLINGSWORTH | 1,751 | 1,250 | 501 | | 749 R | 71.4% | 28.6% | 71.4% | 28.6% |
| 17,638 | COLORADO | 5,017 | 3,495 | 1,502 | 20 | 1,993 R | 69.7% | 29.9% | 69.9% | 30.1% |
| 24,165 | COMAL | 8,628 | 6,761 | 1,823 | 44 | 4,938 R | 78.4% | 21.1% | 78.8% | 21.2% |
| 11,898 | COMANCHE | 3,818 | 2,608 | 1,176 | 34 | 1,432 R | 68.3% | 30.8% | 68.9% | 31.1% |
| 2,937 | CONCHO | 1,059 | 709 | 350 | | 359 R | 66.9% | 33.1% | 66.9% | 33.1% |
| 23,471 | COOKE | 8,070 | 6,317 | 1,702 | 51 | 4,615 R | 78.3% | 21.1% | 78.8% | 21.2% |
| 35,311 | CORYELL | 6,366 | 5,077 | 1,235 | 54 | 3,842 R | 79.8% | 19.4% | 80.4% | 19.6% |
| 3,204 | COTTLE | 1,135 | 564 | 571 | | 7 D | 49.7% | 50.3% | 49.7% | 50.3% |
| 4,172 | CRANE | 1,522 | 1,123 | 349 | 50 | 774 R | 73.8% | 22.9% | 76.3% | 23.7% |
| 3,885 | CROCKETT | 1,180 | 851 | 329 | | 522 R | 72.1% | 27.9% | 72.1% | 27.9% |
| 9,085 | CROSBY | 2,541 | 1,503 | 1,021 | 17 | 482 R | 59.1% | 40.2% | 59.5% | 40.5% |
| 3,429 | CULBERSON | 803 | 555 | 238 | 10 | 317 R | 69.1% | 29.6% | 70.0% | 30.0% |
| 6,012 | DALLAM | 1,629 | 1,271 | 327 | 31 | 944 R | 78.0% | 20.1% | 79.5% | 20.5% |
| 1,327,321 | DALLAS | 438,795 | 305,112 | 129,662 | 4,021 | 175,450 R | 69.5% | 29.5% | 70.2% | 29.8% |
| 16,604 | DAWSON | 4,095 | 3,247 | 846 | 2 | 2,401 R | 79.3% | 20.7% | 79.3% | 20.7% |
| 18,999 | DEAF SMITH | 5,009 | 3,690 | 1,240 | 79 | 2,450 R | 73.7% | 24.8% | 74.8% | 25.2% |
| 4,927 | DELTA | 1,546 | 957 | 581 | 8 | 376 R | 61.9% | 37.6% | 62.2% | 37.8% |

# TEXAS

## PRESIDENT 1972

| 1970 Census Population | County | Total Vote | Republican | Democratic | Other | Rep.-Dem. Plurality | Total Vote Rep. | Dem. | Major Vote Rep. | Dem. |
|---|---|---|---|---|---|---|---|---|---|---|
| 75,633 | DENTON | 28,920 | 19,138 | 9,720 | 62 | 9,418 R | 66.2% | 33.6% | 66.3% | 33.7% |
| 18,660 | DE WITT | 5,147 | 3,755 | 1,357 | 35 | 2,398 R | 73.0% | 26.4% | 73.5% | 26.5% |
| 3,737 | DICKENS | 1,245 | 708 | 534 | 3 | 174 R | 56.9% | 42.9% | 57.0% | 43.0% |
| 9,039 | DIMMIT | 2,262 | 1,172 | 1,078 | 12 | 94 R | 51.8% | 47.7% | 52.1% | 47.9% |
| 3,641 | DONLEY | 1,581 | 1,229 | 350 | 2 | 879 R | 77.7% | 22.1% | 77.8% | 22.2% |
| 11,722 | DUVAL | 4,352 | 623 | 3,729 | | 3,106 D | 14.3% | 85.7% | 14.3% | 85.7% |
| 18,092 | EASTLAND | 5,743 | 4,106 | 1,630 | 7 | 2,476 R | 71.5% | 28.4% | 71.6% | 28.4% |
| 91,805 | ECTOR | 26,960 | 21,386 | 5,449 | 125 | 15,937 R | 79.3% | 20.2% | 79.7% | 20.3% |
| 2,107 | EDWARDS | 634 | 520 | 109 | 5 | 411 R | 82.0% | 17.2% | 82.7% | 17.3% |
| 46,638 | ELLIS | 12,626 | 8,779 | 3,839 | 8 | 4,940 R | 69.5% | 30.4% | 69.6% | 30.4% |
| 359,291 | EL PASO | 83,090 | 49,981 | 32,435 | 674 | 17,546 R | 60.2% | 39.0% | 60.6% | 39.4% |
| 18,141 | ERATH | 6,433 | 4,777 | 1,648 | 8 | 3,129 R | 74.3% | 25.6% | 74.4% | 25.6% |
| 17,300 | FALLS | 4,857 | 3,017 | 1,825 | 15 | 1,192 R | 62.1% | 37.6% | 62.3% | 37.7% |
| 22,705 | FANNIN | 6,181 | 3,826 | 2,295 | 60 | 1,531 R | 61.9% | 37.1% | 62.5% | 37.5% |
| 17,650 | FAYETTE | 5,291 | 3,882 | 1,400 | 9 | 2,482 R | 73.4% | 26.5% | 73.5% | 26.5% |
| 6,344 | FISHER | 2,147 | 1,207 | 933 | 7 | 274 R | 56.2% | 43.5% | 56.4% | 43.6% |
| 11,044 | FLOYD | 3,022 | 2,181 | 841 | | 1,340 R | 72.2% | 27.8% | 72.2% | 27.8% |
| 2,211 | FOARD | 685 | 369 | 312 | 4 | 57 R | 53.9% | 45.5% | 54.2% | 45.8% |
| 52,314 | FORT BEND | 15,089 | 10,475 | 4,541 | 73 | 5,934 R | 69.4% | 30.1% | 69.8% | 30.2% |
| 5,291 | FRANKLIN | 1,607 | 1,059 | 546 | 2 | 513 R | 65.9% | 34.0% | 66.0% | 34.0% |
| 11,116 | FREESTONE | 3,748 | 2,459 | 1,283 | 6 | 1,176 R | 65.6% | 34.2% | 65.7% | 34.3% |
| 11,159 | FRIO | 3,511 | 1,904 | 1,588 | 19 | 316 R | 54.2% | 45.2% | 54.5% | 45.5% |
| 11,593 | GAINES | 2,625 | 1,923 | 669 | 33 | 1,254 R | 73.3% | 25.5% | 74.2% | 25.8% |
| 169,812 | GALVESTON | 53,811 | 30,936 | 22,565 | 310 | 8,371 R | 57.5% | 41.9% | 57.8% | 42.2% |
| 5,289 | GARZA | 1,599 | 1,153 | 446 | | 707 R | 72.1% | 27.9% | 72.1% | 27.9% |
| 10,553 | GILLESPIE | 4,074 | 3,490 | 526 | 58 | 2,964 R | 85.7% | 12.9% | 86.9% | 13.1% |
| 1,155 | GLASSCOCK | 369 | 288 | 75 | 6 | 213 R | 78.0% | 20.3% | 79.3% | 20.7% |
| 4,869 | GOLIAD | 1,484 | 1,018 | 464 | 2 | 554 R | 68.6% | 31.3% | 68.7% | 31.3% |
| 16,375 | GONZALES | 3,876 | 2,707 | 1,164 | 5 | 1,543 R | 69.8% | 30.0% | 69.9% | 30.1% |
| 26,949 | GRAY | 9,444 | 7,968 | 1,367 | 109 | 6,601 R | 84.4% | 14.5% | 85.4% | 14.6% |
| 83,225 | GRAYSON | 23,734 | 16,769 | 6,952 | 13 | 9,817 R | 70.7% | 29.3% | 70.7% | 29.3% |
| 75,929 | GREGG | 25,716 | 19,927 | 5,325 | 464 | 14,602 R | 77.5% | 20.7% | 78.9% | 21.1% |
| 11,855 | GRIMES | 3,376 | 2,243 | 1,116 | 17 | 1,127 R | 66.4% | 33.1% | 66.8% | 33.2% |
| 33,554 | GUADALUPE | 11,698 | 8,287 | 3,404 | 7 | 4,883 R | 70.8% | 29.1% | 70.9% | 29.1% |
| 34,137 | HALE | 9,273 | 7,051 | 2,135 | 87 | 4,916 R | 76.0% | 23.0% | 76.8% | 23.2% |
| 6,015 | HALL | 1,934 | 1,303 | 607 | 24 | 696 R | 67.4% | 31.4% | 68.2% | 31.8% |
| 7,198 | HAMILTON | 2,617 | 1,931 | 685 | 1 | 1,246 R | 73.8% | 26.2% | 73.8% | 26.2% |
| 6,351 | HANSFORD | 2,190 | 1,947 | 202 | 41 | 1,745 R | 88.9% | 9.2% | 90.6% | 9.4% |
| 6,795 | HARDEMAN | 1,987 | 1,357 | 614 | 16 | 743 R | 68.3% | 30.9% | 68.8% | 31.2% |
| 29,996 | HARDIN | 8,157 | 5,190 | 2,952 | 15 | 2,238 R | 63.6% | 36.2% | 63.7% | 36.3% |
| 1,741,912 | HARRIS | 584,531 | 365,672 | 215,916 | 2,943 | 149,756 R | 62.6% | 36.9% | 62.9% | 37.1% |
| 44,841 | HARRISON | 14,060 | 9,600 | 4,333 | 127 | 5,267 R | 68.3% | 30.8% | 68.9% | 31.1% |
| 2,782 | HARTLEY | 1,180 | 946 | 206 | 28 | 740 R | 80.2% | 17.5% | 82.1% | 17.9% |
| 8,512 | HASKELL | 2,694 | 1,744 | 950 | | 794 R | 64.7% | 35.3% | 64.7% | 35.3% |
| 27,642 | HAYS | 9,519 | 5,406 | 4,068 | 45 | 1,338 R | 56.8% | 42.7% | 57.1% | 42.9% |
| 3,084 | HEMPHILL | 1,157 | 942 | 214 | 1 | 728 R | 81.4% | 18.5% | 81.5% | 18.5% |
| 26,466 | HENDERSON | 9,013 | 6,263 | 2,741 | 9 | 3,522 R | 69.5% | 30.4% | 69.6% | 30.4% |
| 181,535 | HIDALGO | 41,499 | 22,920 | 18,366 | 213 | 4,554 R | 55.2% | 44.3% | 55.5% | 44.5% |
| 22,596 | HILL | 6,379 | 4,481 | 1,882 | 16 | 2,599 R | 70.2% | 29.5% | 70.4% | 29.6% |
| 20,396 | HOCKLEY | 5,765 | 4,084 | 1,625 | 56 | 2,459 R | 70.8% | 28.2% | 71.5% | 28.5% |
| 6,368 | HOOD | 2,710 | 1,743 | 949 | 18 | 794 R | 64.3% | 35.0% | 64.7% | 35.3% |
| 20,710 | HOPKINS | 5,640 | 3,903 | 1,710 | 27 | 2,193 R | 69.2% | 30.3% | 69.5% | 30.5% |
| 17,855 | HOUSTON | 5,187 | 3,317 | 1,844 | 26 | 1,473 R | 63.9% | 35.6% | 64.3% | 35.7% |
| 37,796 | HOWARD | 10,080 | 7,343 | 2,714 | 23 | 4,629 R | 72.8% | 26.9% | 73.0% | 27.0% |
| 2,392 | HUDSPETH | 727 | 467 | 250 | 10 | 217 R | 64.2% | 34.4% | 65.1% | 34.9% |
| 47,948 | HUNT | 13,239 | 9,535 | 3,655 | 49 | 5,880 R | 72.0% | 27.6% | 72.3% | 27.7% |
| 24,443 | HUTCHINSON | 9,121 | 7,411 | 1,405 | 305 | 6,006 R | 81.3% | 15.4% | 84.1% | 15.9% |
| 1,070 | IRION | 477 | 363 | 111 | 3 | 252 R | 76.1% | 23.3% | 76.6% | 23.4% |
| 6,711 | JACK | 2,507 | 1,719 | 775 | 13 | 944 R | 68.6% | 30.9% | 68.9% | 31.1% |
| 12,975 | JACKSON | 3,929 | 2,743 | 1,163 | 23 | 1,580 R | 69.8% | 29.6% | 70.2% | 29.8% |

# TEXAS

## PRESIDENT 1972

| 1970 Census Population | County | Total Vote | Republican | Democratic | Other | Rep.-Dem. Plurality | Percentage Total Vote Rep. | Dem. | Major Vote Rep. | Dem. |
|---|---|---|---|---|---|---|---|---|---|---|
| 24,692 | JASPER | 7,325 | 4,575 | 2,746 | 4 | 1,829 R | 62.5% | 37.5% | 62.5% | 37.5% |
| 1,527 | JEFF DAVIS | 595 | 382 | 202 | 11 | 180 R | 64.2% | 33.9% | 65.4% | 34.6% |
| 244,773 | JEFFERSON | 75,837 | 45,819 | 29,909 | 109 | 15,910 R | 60.4% | 39.4% | 60.5% | 39.5% |
| 4,654 | JIM HOGG | 1,618 | 765 | 848 | 5 | 83 D | 47.3% | 52.4% | 47.4% | 52.6% |
| 33,032 | JIM WELLS | 9,698 | 5,283 | 4,404 | 11 | 879 R | 54.5% | 45.4% | 54.5% | 45.5% |
| 45,769 | JOHNSON | 14,136 | 10,042 | 3,968 | 126 | 6,074 R | 71.0% | 28.1% | 71.7% | 28.3% |
| 16,106 | JONES | 4,263 | 3,202 | 1,050 | 11 | 2,152 R | 75.1% | 24.6% | 75.3% | 24.7% |
| 13,462 | KARNES | 4,428 | 2,639 | 1,780 | 9 | 859 R | 59.6% | 40.2% | 59.7% | 40.3% |
| 32,392 | KAUFMAN | 7,906 | 5,100 | 2,795 | 11 | 2,305 R | 64.5% | 35.4% | 64.6% | 35.4% |
| 6,964 | KENDALL | 3,183 | 2,681 | 484 | 18 | 2,197 R | 84.2% | 15.2% | 84.7% | 15.3% |
| 678 | KENEDY | 213 | 124 | 88 | 1 | 36 R | 58.2% | 41.3% | 58.5% | 41.5% |
| 1,434 | KENT | 688 | 465 | 223 | | 242 R | 67.6% | 32.4% | 67.6% | 32.4% |
| 19,454 | KERR | 7,760 | 6,039 | 1,511 | 210 | 4,528 R | 77.8% | 19.5% | 80.0% | 20.0% |
| 3,904 | KIMBLE | 1,243 | 971 | 266 | 6 | 705 R | 78.1% | 21.4% | 78.5% | 21.5% |
| 464 | KING | 219 | 143 | 75 | 1 | 68 R | 65.3% | 34.2% | 65.6% | 34.4% |
| 2,006 | KINNEY | 660 | 425 | 234 | 1 | 191 R | 64.4% | 35.5% | 64.5% | 35.5% |
| 33,166 | KLEBERG | 9,803 | 5,312 | 4,481 | 10 | 831 R | 54.2% | 45.7% | 54.2% | 45.8% |
| 5,972 | KNOX | 1,800 | 1,148 | 638 | 14 | 510 R | 63.8% | 35.4% | 64.3% | 35.7% |
| 36,062 | LAMAR | 10,652 | 7,736 | 2,865 | 51 | 4,871 R | 72.6% | 26.9% | 73.0% | 27.0% |
| 17,770 | LAMB | 5,366 | 3,981 | 1,350 | 35 | 2,631 R | 74.2% | 25.2% | 74.7% | 25.3% |
| 9,323 | LAMPASAS | 2,949 | 2,251 | 688 | 10 | 1,563 R | 76.3% | 23.3% | 76.6% | 23.4% |
| 5,014 | LA SALLE | 1,648 | 1,073 | 567 | 8 | 506 R | 65.1% | 34.4% | 65.4% | 34.6% |
| 17,903 | LAVACA | 4,721 | 3,288 | 1,429 | 4 | 1,859 R | 69.6% | 30.3% | 69.7% | 30.3% |
| 8,048 | LEE | 2,814 | 1,877 | 920 | 17 | 957 R | 66.7% | 32.7% | 67.1% | 32.9% |
| 8,738 | LEON | 2,568 | 1,699 | 863 | 6 | 836 R | 66.2% | 33.6% | 66.3% | 33.7% |
| 33,014 | LIBERTY | 9,432 | 6,111 | 3,311 | 10 | 2,800 R | 64.8% | 35.1% | 64.9% | 35.1% |
| 18,100 | LIMESTONE | 4,423 | 2,949 | 1,452 | 22 | 1,497 R | 66.7% | 32.8% | 67.0% | 33.0% |
| 3,486 | LIPSCOMB | 1,400 | 1,226 | 156 | 18 | 1,070 R | 87.6% | 11.1% | 88.7% | 11.3% |
| 6,697 | LIVE OAK | 2,359 | 1,745 | 610 | 4 | 1,135 R | 74.0% | 25.9% | 74.1% | 25.9% |
| 6,979 | LLANO | 2,943 | 2,164 | 766 | 13 | 1,398 R | 73.5% | 26.0% | 73.9% | 26.1% |
| 164 | LOVING | 62 | 55 | 7 | | 48 R | 88.7% | 11.3% | 88.7% | 11.3% |
| 179,295 | LUBBOCK | 59,296 | 43,564 | 15,353 | 379 | 28,211 R | 73.5% | 25.9% | 73.9% | 26.1% |
| 9,107 | LYNN | 2,471 | 1,766 | 697 | 8 | 1,069 R | 71.5% | 28.2% | 71.7% | 28.3% |
| 8,571 | MCCULLOCH | 2,525 | 1,769 | 753 | 3 | 1,016 R | 70.1% | 29.8% | 70.1% | 29.9% |
| 147,553 | MCLENNAN | 49,485 | 33,377 | 15,947 | 161 | 17,430 R | 67.4% | 32.2% | 67.7% | 32.3% |
| 1,095 | MCMULLEN | 396 | 304 | 88 | 4 | 216 R | 76.8% | 22.2% | 77.6% | 22.4% |
| 7,693 | MADISON | 2,101 | 1,540 | 561 | | 979 R | 73.3% | 26.7% | 73.3% | 26.7% |
| 8,517 | MARION | 2,790 | 1,680 | 1,106 | 4 | 574 R | 60.2% | 39.6% | 60.3% | 39.7% |
| 4,774 | MARTIN | 1,243 | 935 | 287 | 21 | 648 R | 75.2% | 23.1% | 76.5% | 23.5% |
| 3,356 | MASON | 1,487 | 1,096 | 369 | 22 | 727 R | 73.7% | 24.8% | 74.8% | 25.2% |
| 27,913 | MATAGORDA | 7,495 | 5,003 | 2,473 | 19 | 2,530 R | 66.8% | 33.0% | 66.9% | 33.1% |
| 18,093 | MAVERICK | 3,197 | 1,477 | 1,710 | 10 | 233 D | 46.2% | 53.5% | 46.3% | 53.7% |
| 20,249 | MEDINA | 5,649 | 4,059 | 1,507 | 83 | 2,552 R | 71.9% | 26.7% | 72.9% | 27.1% |
| 2,646 | MENARD | 921 | 644 | 273 | 4 | 371 R | 69.9% | 29.6% | 70.2% | 29.8% |
| 65,433 | MIDLAND | 23,750 | 18,905 | 4,388 | 457 | 14,517 R | 79.6% | 18.5% | 81.2% | 18.8% |
| 20,028 | MILAM | 5,719 | 3,554 | 2,159 | 6 | 1,395 R | 62.1% | 37.8% | 62.2% | 37.8% |
| 4,212 | MILLS | 1,483 | 1,089 | 388 | 6 | 701 R | 73.4% | 26.2% | 73.7% | 26.3% |
| 9,073 | MITCHELL | 2,492 | 1,790 | 699 | 3 | 1,091 R | 71.8% | 28.0% | 71.9% | 28.1% |
| 15,326 | MONTAGUE | 4,768 | 3,463 | 1,286 | 19 | 2,177 R | 72.6% | 27.0% | 72.9% | 27.1% |
| 49,479 | MONTGOMERY | 19,447 | 15,067 | 4,358 | 22 | 10,709 R | 77.5% | 22.4% | 77.6% | 22.4% |
| 14,060 | MOORE | 4,538 | 3,620 | 863 | 55 | 2,757 R | 79.8% | 19.0% | 80.7% | 19.3% |
| 12,310 | MORRIS | 3,885 | 2,699 | 1,162 | 24 | 1,537 R | 69.5% | 29.9% | 69.9% | 30.1% |
| 2,178 | MOTLEY | 906 | 657 | 230 | 19 | 427 R | 72.5% | 25.4% | 74.1% | 25.9% |
| 36,362 | NACOGDOCHES | 12,437 | 8,757 | 3,656 | 24 | 5,101 R | 70.4% | 29.4% | 70.5% | 29.5% |
| 31,150 | NAVARRO | 9,303 | 6,039 | 3,246 | 18 | 2,793 R | 64.9% | 34.9% | 65.0% | 35.0% |
| 11,657 | NEWTON | 3,605 | 1,946 | 1,636 | 23 | 310 R | 54.0% | 45.4% | 54.3% | 45.7% |
| 16,220 | NOLAN | 4,976 | 3,634 | 1,338 | 4 | 2,296 R | 73.0% | 26.9% | 73.1% | 26.9% |
| 237,544 | NUECES | 75,250 | 41,682 | 33,277 | 291 | 8,405 R | 55.4% | 44.2% | 55.6% | 44.4% |
| 9,704 | OCHILTREE | 3,202 | 2,861 | 298 | 43 | 2,563 R | 89.4% | 9.3% | 90.6% | 9.4% |
| 2,258 | OLDHAM | 863 | 666 | 173 | 24 | 493 R | 77.2% | 20.0% | 79.4% | 20.6% |

# TEXAS

## PRESIDENT 1972

| 1970 Census Population | County | Total Vote | Republican | Democratic | Other | Rep.-Dem. Plurality | Total Vote Rep. | Dem. | Major Vote Rep. | Dem. |
|---|---|---|---|---|---|---|---|---|---|---|
| 71,170 | ORANGE | 20,478 | 13,234 | 7,172 | 72 | 6,062 R | 64.6% | 35.0% | 64.9% | 35.1% |
| 28,962 | PALO PINTO | 7,247 | 5,058 | 2,181 | 8 | 2,877 R | 69.8% | 30.1% | 69.9% | 30.1% |
| 15,894 | PANOLA | 5,864 | 4,324 | 1,511 | 29 | 2,813 R | 73.7% | 25.8% | 74.1% | 25.9% |
| 33,888 | PARKER | 10,349 | 7,152 | 3,184 | 13 | 3,968 R | 69.1% | 30.8% | 69.2% | 30.8% |
| 10,509 | PARMER | 2,823 | 2,304 | 495 | 24 | 1,809 R | 81.6% | 17.5% | 82.3% | 17.7% |
| 13,748 | PECOS | 3,309 | 2,419 | 847 | 43 | 1,572 R | 73.1% | 25.6% | 74.1% | 25.9% |
| 14,457 | POLK | 4,828 | 3,048 | 1,760 | 20 | 1,288 R | 63.1% | 36.5% | 63.4% | 36.6% |
| 90,511 | POTTER | 25,335 | 18,891 | 6,264 | 180 | 12,627 R | 74.6% | 24.7% | 75.1% | 24.9% |
| 4,842 | PRESIDIO | 1,462 | 785 | 674 | 3 | 111 R | 53.7% | 46.1% | 53.8% | 46.2% |
| 3,752 | RAINS | 1,404 | 865 | 532 | 7 | 333 R | 61.6% | 37.9% | 61.9% | 38.1% |
| 53,885 | RANDALL | 22,323 | 18,557 | 3,470 | 296 | 15,087 R | 83.1% | 15.5% | 84.2% | 15.8% |
| 3,239 | REAGAN | 955 | 703 | 244 | 8 | 459 R | 73.6% | 25.5% | 74.2% | 25.8% |
| 2,013 | REAL | 642 | 483 | 150 | 9 | 333 R | 75.2% | 23.4% | 76.3% | 23.7% |
| 14,298 | RED RIVER | 4,475 | 3,112 | 1,361 | 2 | 1,751 R | 69.5% | 30.4% | 69.6% | 30.4% |
| 16,526 | REEVES | 3,942 | 2,427 | 1,510 | 5 | 917 R | 61.6% | 38.3% | 61.6% | 38.4% |
| 9,494 | REFUGIO | 3,000 | 1,937 | 1,060 | 3 | 877 R | 64.6% | 35.3% | 64.6% | 35.4% |
| 967 | ROBERTS | 550 | 467 | 71 | 12 | 396 R | 84.9% | 12.9% | 86.8% | 13.2% |
| 14,389 | ROBERTSON | 3,953 | 1,977 | 1,976 | | 1 R | 50.0% | 50.0% | 50.0% | 50.0% |
| 7,046 | ROCKWALL | 2,518 | 1,890 | 610 | 18 | 1,280 R | 75.1% | 24.2% | 75.6% | 24.4% |
| 12,108 | RUNNELS | 3,491 | 2,752 | 739 | | 2,013 R | 78.8% | 21.2% | 78.8% | 21.2% |
| 34,102 | RUSK | 11,072 | 8,179 | 2,867 | 26 | 5,312 R | 73.9% | 25.9% | 74.0% | 26.0% |
| 7,187 | SABINE | 2,273 | 1,333 | 936 | 4 | 397 R | 58.6% | 41.2% | 58.7% | 41.3% |
| 7,858 | SAN AUGUSTINE | 2,268 | 1,508 | 753 | 7 | 755 R | 66.5% | 33.2% | 66.7% | 33.3% |
| 6,702 | SAN JACINTO | 2,322 | 1,296 | 1,020 | 6 | 276 R | 55.8% | 43.9% | 56.0% | 44.0% |
| 47,288 | SAN PATRICIO | 12,502 | 7,179 | 5,097 | 226 | 2,082 R | 57.4% | 40.8% | 58.5% | 41.5% |
| 5,540 | SAN SABA | 1,681 | 1,106 | 567 | 8 | 539 R | 65.8% | 33.7% | 66.1% | 33.9% |
| 2,277 | SCHLEICHER | 881 | 630 | 250 | 1 | 380 R | 71.5% | 28.4% | 71.6% | 28.4% |
| 15,760 | SCURRY | 5,050 | 3,777 | 1,223 | 50 | 2,554 R | 74.8% | 24.2% | 75.5% | 24.5% |
| 3,323 | SHACKELFORD | 1,244 | 909 | 331 | 4 | 578 R | 73.1% | 26.6% | 73.3% | 26.7% |
| 19,672 | SHELBY | 6,092 | 4,292 | 1,792 | 8 | 2,500 R | 70.5% | 29.4% | 70.5% | 29.5% |
| 3,657 | SHERMAN | 1,181 | 996 | 169 | 16 | 827 R | 84.3% | 14.3% | 85.5% | 14.5% |
| 97,096 | SMITH | 31,827 | 23,671 | 8,041 | 115 | 15,630 R | 74.4% | 25.3% | 74.6% | 25.4% |
| 2,793 | SOMERVELL | 987 | 703 | 284 | | 419 R | 71.2% | 28.8% | 71.2% | 28.8% |
| 17,707 | STARR | 5,713 | 2,389 | 3,320 | 4 | 931 D | 41.8% | 58.1% | 41.8% | 58.2% |
| 8,414 | STEPHENS | 2,944 | 2,259 | 678 | 7 | 1,581 R | 76.7% | 23.0% | 76.9% | 23.1% |
| 1,056 | STERLING | 383 | 286 | 94 | 3 | 192 R | 74.7% | 24.5% | 75.3% | 24.7% |
| 2,397 | STONEWALL | 1,075 | 662 | 394 | 19 | 268 R | 61.6% | 36.7% | 62.7% | 37.3% |
| 3,175 | SUTTON | 957 | 705 | 245 | 7 | 460 R | 73.7% | 25.6% | 74.2% | 25.8% |
| 10,373 | SWISHER | 3,122 | 1,790 | 1,300 | 32 | 490 R | 57.3% | 41.6% | 57.9% | 42.1% |
| 716,317 | TARRANT | 221,138 | 151,596 | 69,187 | 355 | 82,409 R | 68.6% | 31.3% | 68.7% | 31.3% |
| 97,853 | TAYLOR | 28,731 | 22,417 | 6,024 | 290 | 16,393 R | 78.0% | 21.0% | 78.8% | 21.2% |
| 1,940 | TERRELL | 591 | 467 | 124 | | 343 R | 79.0% | 21.0% | 79.0% | 21.0% |
| 14,118 | TERRY | 4,190 | 3,057 | 1,099 | 34 | 1,958 R | 73.0% | 26.2% | 73.6% | 26.4% |
| 2,205 | THROCKMORTON | 919 | 568 | 348 | 3 | 220 R | 61.8% | 37.9% | 62.0% | 38.0% |
| 16,702 | TITUS | 5,393 | 3,671 | 1,703 | 19 | 1,968 R | 68.1% | 31.6% | 68.3% | 31.7% |
| 71,047 | TOM GREEN | 21,961 | 15,784 | 6,082 | 95 | 9,702 R | 71.9% | 27.7% | 72.2% | 27.8% |
| 295,516 | TRAVIS | 125,329 | 70,561 | 54,157 | 611 | 16,404 R | 56.3% | 43.2% | 56.6% | 43.4% |
| 7,628 | TRINITY | 2,295 | 1,467 | 826 | 2 | 641 R | 63.9% | 36.0% | 64.0% | 36.0% |
| 12,417 | TYLER | 4,290 | 2,955 | 1,321 | 14 | 1,634 R | 68.9% | 30.8% | 69.1% | 30.9% |
| 20,976 | UPSHUR | 6,624 | 4,736 | 1,879 | 9 | 2,857 R | 71.5% | 28.4% | 71.6% | 28.4% |
| 4,697 | UPTON | 1,463 | 1,186 | 256 | 21 | 930 R | 81.1% | 17.5% | 82.2% | 17.8% |
| 17,348 | UVALDE | 5,327 | 3,883 | 1,438 | 6 | 2,445 R | 72.9% | 27.0% | 73.0% | 27.0% |
| 27,471 | VAL VERDE | 6,124 | 4,052 | 2,049 | 23 | 2,003 R | 66.2% | 33.5% | 66.4% | 33.6% |
| 22,155 | VAN ZANDT | 6,784 | 4,839 | 1,939 | 6 | 2,900 R | 71.3% | 28.6% | 71.4% | 28.6% |
| 53,766 | VICTORIA | 15,498 | 11,246 | 4,226 | 26 | 7,020 R | 72.6% | 27.3% | 72.7% | 27.3% |
| 27,680 | WALKER | 8,041 | 5,082 | 2,940 | 19 | 2,142 R | 63.2% | 36.6% | 63.4% | 36.6% |
| 14,285 | WALLER | 3,839 | 2,263 | 1,538 | 38 | 725 R | 58.9% | 40.1% | 59.5% | 40.5% |
| 13,019 | WARD | 3,792 | 2,687 | 1,049 | 56 | 1,638 R | 70.9% | 27.7% | 71.9% | 28.1% |
| 18,842 | WASHINGTON | 5,198 | 3,862 | 1,323 | 13 | 2,539 R | 74.3% | 25.5% | 74.5% | 25.5% |
| 72,859 | WEBB | 14,458 | 6,011 | 8,435 | 12 | 2,424 D | 41.6% | 58.3% | 41.6% | 58.4% |

# TEXAS

## PRESIDENT 1972

| 1970 Census Population | County | Total Vote | Republican | Democratic | Other | Rep.-Dem. Plurality | Percentage | | | |
|---|---|---|---|---|---|---|---|---|---|---|
| | | | | | | | Total Vote | | Major Vote | |
| | | | | | | | Rep. | Dem. | Rep. | Dem. |
| 36,729 | WHARTON | 9,757 | 6,271 | 3,481 | 5 | 2,790 R | 64.3% | 35.7% | 64.3% | 35.7% |
| 6,434 | WHEELER | 2,268 | 1,766 | 502 | | 1,264 R | 77.9% | 22.1% | 77.9% | 22.1% |
| 121,862 | WICHITA | 36,682 | 25,197 | 10,948 | 537 | 14,249 R | 68.7% | 29.8% | 69.7% | 30.3% |
| 15,355 | WILBARGER | 4,519 | 3,183 | 1,139 | 197 | 2,044 R | 70.4% | 25.2% | 73.6% | 26.4% |
| 15,570 | WILLACY | 3,730 | 2,317 | 1,384 | 29 | 933 R | 62.1% | 37.1% | 62.6% | 37.4% |
| 37,305 | WILLIAMSON | 10,867 | 6,998 | 3,806 | 63 | 3,192 R | 64.4% | 35.0% | 64.8% | 35.2% |
| 13,041 | WILSON | 5,032 | 2,953 | 2,072 | 7 | 881 R | 58.7% | 41.2% | 58.8% | 41.2% |
| 9,640 | WINKLER | 3,095 | 2,467 | 602 | 26 | 1,865 R | 79.7% | 19.5% | 80.4% | 19.6% |
| 19,687 | WISE | 6,006 | 4,230 | 1,741 | 35 | 2,489 R | 70.4% | 29.0% | 70.8% | 29.2% |
| 18,589 | WOOD | 6,658 | 4,746 | 1,842 | 70 | 2,904 R | 71.3% | 27.7% | 72.0% | 28.0% |
| 7,344 | YOAKUM | 2,443 | 1,952 | 457 | 34 | 1,495 R | 79.9% | 18.7% | 81.0% | 19.0% |
| 15,400 | YOUNG | 4,840 | 3,353 | 1,486 | 1 | 1,867 R | 69.3% | 30.7% | 69.3% | 30.7% |
| 4,352 | ZAPATA | 1,463 | 695 | 768 | | 73 D | 47.5% | 52.5% | 47.5% | 52.5% |
| 11,370 | ZAVALA | 2,432 | 1,288 | 1,122 | 22 | 166 R | 53.0% | 46.1% | 53.4% | 46.6% |
| 11,196,730 | TOTAL | 3,471,281 | 2,298,896 | 1,154,289 | 18,096 | 1,144,607 R | 66.2% | 33.3% | 66.6% | 33.4% |

# TEXAS

## PRESIDENT 1968

| 1960 Census Population | County | Total Vote | Republican | Democratic | AIP | Other | Plurality | Rep. | Dem. | AIP |
|---|---|---|---|---|---|---|---|---|---|---|
| 28,162 | ANDERSON | 9,471 | 2,828 | 3,447 | 3,196 | | 251 D | 29.9% | 36.4% | 33.7% |
| 13,450 | ANDREWS | 3,634 | 1,400 | 922 | 1,312 | | 88 R | 38.5% | 25.4% | 36.1% |
| 39,814 | ANGELINA | 15,930 | 4,645 | 5,174 | 6,111 | | 937 A | 29.2% | 32.5% | 38.4% |
| 7,006 | ARANSAS | 2,715 | 1,076 | 1,222 | 417 | | 146 D | 39.6% | 45.0% | 15.4% |
| 6,110 | ARCHER | 2,357 | 636 | 1,308 | 413 | | 672 D | 27.0% | 55.5% | 17.5% |
| 1,966 | ARMSTRONG | 941 | 434 | 301 | 206 | | 133 R | 46.1% | 32.0% | 21.9% |
| 18,828 | ATASCOSA | 5,098 | 1,805 | 2,522 | 771 | | 717 D | 35.4% | 49.5% | 15.1% |
| 13,777 | AUSTIN | 4,354 | 1,971 | 1,299 | 1,084 | | 672 R | 45.3% | 29.8% | 24.9% |
| 9,090 | BAILEY | 2,558 | 1,174 | 820 | 563 | 1 | 354 R | 45.9% | 32.1% | 22.0% |
| 3,892 | BANDERA | 1,800 | 842 | 535 | 423 | | 307 R | 46.8% | 29.7% | 23.5% |
| 16,925 | BASTROP | 5,117 | 1,455 | 2,687 | 975 | | 1,232 D | 28.4% | 52.5% | 19.1% |
| 5,893 | BAYLOR | 2,164 | 657 | 1,064 | 443 | | 407 D | 30.4% | 49.2% | 20.5% |
| 23,755 | BEE | 5,544 | 1,995 | 2,957 | 589 | 3 | 962 D | 36.0% | 53.3% | 10.6% |
| 94,097 | BELL | 21,145 | 5,705 | 11,893 | 3,547 | | 6,188 D | 27.0% | 56.2% | 16.8% |
| 687,151 | BEXAR | 184,874 | 72,951 | 95,325 | 16,598 | | 22,374 D | 39.5% | 51.6% | 9.0% |
| 3,657 | BLANCO | 1,457 | 614 | 620 | 223 | | 6 D | 42.1% | 42.6% | 15.3% |
| 1,076 | BORDEN | 386 | 117 | 157 | 112 | | 40 D | 30.3% | 40.7% | 29.0% |
| 10,809 | BOSQUE | 3,921 | 1,377 | 1,817 | 727 | | 440 D | 35.1% | 46.3% | 18.5% |
| 59,971 | BOWIE | 19,599 | 5,966 | 6,468 | 7,165 | | 697 A | 30.4% | 33.0% | 36.6% |
| 76,204 | BRAZORIA | 30,103 | 10,631 | 11,439 | 8,026 | 7 | 808 D | 35.3% | 38.0% | 26.7% |
| 44,895 | BRAZOS | 15,579 | 6,839 | 6,299 | 2,437 | 4 | 540 R | 43.9% | 40.4% | 15.6% |
| 6,434 | BREWSTER | 2,091 | 790 | 958 | 342 | 1 | 168 D | 37.8% | 45.8% | 16.4% |
| 3,577 | BRISCOE | 1,158 | 411 | 528 | 219 | | 117 D | 35.5% | 45.6% | 18.9% |
| 8,609 | BROOKS | 2,604 | 534 | 1,904 | 166 | | 1,370 D | 20.5% | 73.1% | 6.4% |
| 24,728 | BROWN | 8,602 | 2,997 | 3,999 | 1,606 | | 1,002 D | 34.8% | 46.5% | 18.7% |
| 11,177 | BURLESON | 3,263 | 891 | 1,678 | 694 | | 787 D | 27.3% | 51.4% | 21.3% |
| 9,265 | BURNET | 3,978 | 1,459 | 1,876 | 643 | | 417 D | 36.7% | 47.2% | 16.2% |
| 17,222 | CALDWELL | 5,130 | 1,402 | 2,889 | 837 | 2 | 1,487 D | 27.3% | 56.3% | 16.3% |
| 16,592 | CALHOUN | 5,350 | 1,672 | 2,612 | 1,065 | 1 | 940 D | 31.3% | 48.8% | 19.9% |
| 7,929 | CALLAHAN | 3,096 | 921 | 1,437 | 737 | 1 | 516 D | 29.7% | 46.4% | 23.8% |
| 151,098 | CAMERON | 29,527 | 11,759 | 15,726 | 2,042 | | 3,967 D | 39.8% | 53.3% | 6.9% |
| 7,849 | CAMP | 2,901 | 555 | 1,272 | 1,074 | | 198 D | 19.1% | 43.8% | 37.0% |
| 7,781 | CARSON | 2,685 | 1,211 | 904 | 570 | | 307 R | 45.1% | 33.7% | 21.2% |
| 23,496 | CASS | 7,350 | 1,930 | 2,536 | 2,883 | 1 | 347 A | 26.3% | 34.5% | 39.2% |
| 8,923 | CASTRO | 2,838 | 1,033 | 1,181 | 623 | 1 | 148 D | 36.4% | 41.6% | 22.0% |
| 10,379 | CHAMBERS | 3,607 | 1,061 | 1,217 | 1,329 | | 112 A | 29.4% | 33.7% | 36.8% |
| 33,120 | CHEROKEE | 9,608 | 2,575 | 3,242 | 3,791 | | 549 A | 26.8% | 33.7% | 39.5% |
| 8,421 | CHILDRESS | 2,759 | 1,045 | 1,093 | 621 | | 48 D | 37.9% | 39.6% | 22.5% |
| 8,351 | CLAY | 3,174 | 936 | 1,573 | 665 | | 637 D | 29.5% | 49.6% | 21.0% |
| 6,417 | COCHRAN | 1,630 | 548 | 633 | 449 | | 85 D | 33.6% | 38.8% | 27.5% |
| 3,589 | COKE | 1,159 | 387 | 563 | 208 | 1 | 176 D | 33.4% | 48.6% | 17.9% |
| 12,458 | COLEMAN | 4,109 | 1,507 | 1,449 | 1,153 | | 58 R | 36.7% | 35.3% | 28.1% |
| 41,247 | COLLIN | 16,262 | 6,494 | 5,918 | 3,850 | | 576 R | 39.9% | 36.4% | 23.7% |
| 6,276 | COLLINGSWORTH | 1,933 | 712 | 746 | 475 | | 34 D | 36.8% | 38.6% | 24.6% |
| 18,463 | COLORADO | 5,438 | 2,296 | 1,976 | 1,163 | 3 | 320 R | 42.2% | 36.3% | 21.4% |
| 19,844 | COMAL | 6,710 | 3,646 | 2,338 | 724 | 2 | 1,308 R | 54.3% | 34.8% | 10.8% |
| 11,865 | COMANCHE | 4,125 | 1,436 | 1,980 | 708 | 1 | 544 D | 34.8% | 48.0% | 17.2% |
| 3,672 | CONCHO | 1,110 | 411 | 502 | 197 | | 91 D | 37.0% | 45.2% | 17.7% |
| 22,560 | COOKE | 7,922 | 3,799 | 2,711 | 1,412 | | 1,088 R | 48.0% | 34.2% | 17.8% |
| 23,961 | CORYELL | 5,857 | 1,698 | 2,987 | 1,172 | | 1,289 D | 29.0% | 51.0% | 20.0% |
| 4,207 | COTTLE | 1,276 | 268 | 742 | 266 | | 474 D | 21.0% | 58.2% | 20.8% |
| 4,699 | CRANE | 1,703 | 493 | 498 | 712 | | 214 A | 28.9% | 29.2% | 41.8% |
| 4,209 | CROCKETT | 1,359 | 509 | 571 | 279 | | 62 D | 37.5% | 42.0% | 20.5% |
| 10,347 | CROSBY | 2,840 | 865 | 1,574 | 401 | | 709 D | 30.5% | 55.4% | 14.1% |
| 2,794 | CULBERSON | 773 | 298 | 330 | 145 | | 32 D | 38.6% | 42.7% | 18.8% |
| 6,302 | DALLAM | 2,008 | 990 | 588 | 430 | | 402 R | 49.3% | 29.3% | 21.4% |
| 951,527 | DALLAS | 363,554 | 184,193 | 123,809 | 55,552 | | 60,384 R | 50.7% | 34.1% | 15.3% |
| 19,185 | DAWSON | 4,513 | 2,091 | 1,522 | 900 | | 569 R | 46.3% | 33.7% | 19.9% |
| 13,187 | DEAF SMITH | 4,713 | 2,474 | 1,545 | 691 | 3 | 929 R | 52.5% | 32.8% | 14.7% |
| 5,860 | DELTA | 1,882 | 370 | 1,037 | 475 | | 562 D | 19.7% | 55.1% | 25.2% |

# TEXAS

## PRESIDENT 1968

| 1960 Census Population | County | Total Vote | Republican | Democratic | AIP | Other | Plurality | Percentage Total Vote Rep. | Dem. | AIP |
|---|---|---|---|---|---|---|---|---|---|---|
| 47,432 | DENTON | 18,863 | 8,222 | 7,463 | 3,178 | | 759 R | 43.6% | 39.6% | 16.8% |
| 20,683 | DE WITT | 5,244 | 2,589 | 1,871 | 784 | | 718 R | 49.4% | 35.7% | 15.0% |
| 4,963 | DICKENS | 1,534 | 428 | 811 | 295 | | 383 D | 27.9% | 52.9% | 19.2% |
| 10,095 | DIMMIT | 1,660 | 584 | 896 | 177 | 3 | 312 D | 35.2% | 54.0% | 10.7% |
| 4,449 | DONLEY | 1,627 | 816 | 543 | 268 | | 273 R | 50.2% | 33.4% | 16.5% |
| 13,398 | DUVAL | 4,483 | 384 | 3,978 | 121 | | 3,594 D | 8.6% | 88.7% | 2.7% |
| 19,526 | EASTLAND | 6,350 | 2,453 | 2,884 | 1,013 | | 431 D | 38.6% | 45.4% | 16.0% |
| 90,995 | ECTOR | 24,540 | 10,557 | 5,312 | 8,671 | | 1,886 R | 43.0% | 21.6% | 35.3% |
| 2,317 | EDWARDS | 639 | 409 | 148 | 82 | | 261 R | 64.0% | 23.2% | 12.8% |
| 43,395 | ELLIS | 12,067 | 3,794 | 5,431 | 2,838 | 4 | 1,637 D | 31.4% | 45.0% | 23.5% |
| 314,070 | EL PASO | 68,116 | 30,347 | 32,658 | 5,111 | | 2,311 D | 44.6% | 47.9% | 7.5% |
| 16,236 | ERATH | 6,059 | 2,209 | 2,915 | 935 | | 706 D | 36.5% | 48.1% | 15.4% |
| 21,263 | FALLS | 5,699 | 1,345 | 2,990 | 1,364 | | 1,626 D | 23.6% | 52.5% | 23.9% |
| 23,880 | FANNIN | 7,177 | 1,585 | 3,931 | 1,661 | | 2,270 D | 22.1% | 54.8% | 23.1% |
| 20,384 | FAYETTE | 5,775 | 2,380 | 1,833 | 1,562 | | 547 R | 41.2% | 31.7% | 27.0% |
| 7,865 | FISHER | 2,385 | 555 | 1,560 | 268 | 2 | 1,005 D | 23.3% | 65.4% | 11.2% |
| 12,369 | FLOYD | 3,617 | 1,465 | 1,305 | 847 | | 160 R | 40.5% | 36.1% | 23.4% |
| 3,125 | FOARD | 978 | 216 | 594 | 168 | | 378 D | 22.1% | 60.7% | 17.2% |
| 40,527 | FORT BEND | 11,514 | 4,573 | 4,493 | 2,447 | 1 | 80 R | 39.7% | 39.0% | 21.3% |
| 5,101 | FRANKLIN | 1,989 | 481 | 1,001 | 507 | | 494 D | 24.2% | 50.3% | 25.5% |
| 12,525 | FREESTONE | 4,093 | 958 | 2,066 | 1,069 | | 997 D | 23.4% | 50.5% | 26.1% |
| 10,112 | FRIO | 2,432 | 795 | 1,330 | 307 | | 535 D | 32.7% | 54.7% | 12.6% |
| 12,267 | GAINES | 3,525 | 1,401 | 1,087 | 1,037 | | 314 R | 39.7% | 30.8% | 29.4% |
| 140,364 | GALVESTON | 52,598 | 16,229 | 26,041 | 10,322 | 6 | 9,812 D | 30.9% | 49.5% | 19.6% |
| 6,611 | GARZA | 1,660 | 615 | 662 | 383 | | 47 D | 37.0% | 39.9% | 23.1% |
| 10,048 | GILLESPIE | 4,105 | 2,945 | 725 | 432 | 3 | 2,220 R | 71.7% | 17.7% | 10.5% |
| 1,118 | GLASSCOCK | 447 | 169 | 106 | 172 | | 3 A | 37.8% | 23.7% | 38.5% |
| 5,429 | GOLIAD | 1,553 | 707 | 690 | 156 | | 17 R | 45.5% | 44.4% | 10.0% |
| 17,845 | GONZALES | 4,389 | 1,476 | 1,930 | 983 | | 454 D | 33.6% | 44.0% | 22.4% |
| 31,535 | GRAY | 10,795 | 5,994 | 2,374 | 2,427 | | 3,567 R | 55.5% | 22.0% | 22.5% |
| 73,043 | GRAYSON | 23,001 | 8,007 | 10,379 | 4,615 | | 2,372 D | 34.8% | 45.1% | 20.1% |
| 69,436 | GREGG | 23,120 | 9,278 | 5,733 | 8,109 | | 1,169 R | 40.1% | 24.8% | 35.1% |
| 12,709 | GRIMES | 3,525 | 1,076 | 1,473 | 976 | | 397 D | 30.5% | 41.8% | 27.7% |
| 29,017 | GUADALUPE | 9,102 | 4,332 | 3,529 | 1,241 | | 803 R | 47.6% | 38.8% | 13.6% |
| 36,798 | HALE | 10,298 | 4,696 | 3,293 | 2,309 | | 1,403 R | 45.6% | 32.0% | 22.4% |
| 7,322 | HALL | 2,225 | 753 | 1,038 | 434 | | 285 D | 33.8% | 46.7% | 19.5% |
| 8,488 | HAMILTON | 2,834 | 1,266 | 1,116 | 452 | | 150 R | 44.7% | 39.4% | 15.9% |
| 6,208 | HANSFORD | 2,188 | 1,359 | 392 | 437 | | 922 R | 62.1% | 17.9% | 20.0% |
| 8,275 | HARDEMAN | 2,549 | 873 | 1,145 | 531 | | 272 D | 34.2% | 44.9% | 20.8% |
| 24,629 | HARDIN | 8,862 | 1,986 | 2,894 | 3,979 | 3 | 1,085 A | 22.4% | 32.7% | 44.9% |
| 1,243,158 | HARRIS | 471,037 | 202,079 | 182,546 | 86,412 | | 19,533 R | 42.9% | 38.8% | 18.3% |
| 45,594 | HARRISON | 13,951 | 3,668 | 4,959 | 5,324 | | 365 A | 26.3% | 35.5% | 38.2% |
| 2,171 | HARTLEY | 1,160 | 597 | 299 | 264 | | 298 R | 51.5% | 25.8% | 22.8% |
| 11,174 | HASKELL | 3,211 | 713 | 1,888 | 610 | | 1,175 D | 22.2% | 58.8% | 19.0% |
| 19,934 | HAYS | 6,183 | 1,993 | 3,546 | 643 | 1 | 1,553 D | 32.2% | 57.4% | 10.4% |
| 3,185 | HEMPHILL | 1,300 | 699 | 400 | 201 | | 299 R | 53.8% | 30.8% | 15.5% |
| 21,786 | HENDERSON | 7,932 | 2,315 | 3,119 | 2,497 | 1 | 622 D | 29.2% | 39.3% | 31.5% |
| 180,904 | HIDALGO | 37,111 | 14,455 | 20,087 | 2,569 | | 5,632 D | 39.0% | 54.1% | 6.9% |
| 23,650 | HILL | 6,977 | 1,809 | 3,415 | 1,751 | 2 | 1,606 D | 25.9% | 48.9% | 25.1% |
| 22,340 | HOCKLEY | 6,147 | 2,265 | 2,426 | 1,456 | | 161 D | 36.8% | 39.5% | 23.7% |
| 5,443 | HOOD | 2,161 | 593 | 1,155 | 411 | 2 | 562 D | 27.4% | 53.4% | 19.0% |
| 18,594 | HOPKINS | 6,492 | 1,860 | 2,700 | 1,932 | | 768 D | 28.7% | 41.6% | 29.8% |
| 19,376 | HOUSTON | 6,237 | 1,391 | 2,782 | 2,062 | 2 | 720 D | 22.3% | 44.6% | 33.1% |
| 40,139 | HOWARD | 10,501 | 3,812 | 3,897 | 2,789 | 3 | 85 D | 36.3% | 37.1% | 26.6% |
| 3,343 | HUDSPETH | 707 | 285 | 289 | 132 | 1 | 4 D | 40.3% | 40.9% | 18.7% |
| 39,399 | HUNT | 12,905 | 4,651 | 4,785 | 3,469 | | 134 D | 36.0% | 37.1% | 26.9% |
| 34,419 | HUTCHINSON | 10,148 | 4,813 | 2,416 | 2,919 | | 1,894 R | 47.4% | 23.8% | 28.8% |
| 1,183 | IRION | 490 | 211 | 187 | 92 | | 24 R | 43.1% | 38.2% | 18.8% |
| 7,418 | JACK | 2,611 | 966 | 1,133 | 512 | | 167 D | 37.0% | 43.4% | 19.6% |
| 14,040 | JACKSON | 4,286 | 1,438 | 1,698 | 1,145 | 5 | 260 D | 33.6% | 39.6% | 26.7% |

# TEXAS

## PRESIDENT 1968

| 1960 Census Population | County | Total Vote | Republican | Democratic | AIP | Other | Plurality | | Percentage Total Vote | | |
|---|---|---|---|---|---|---|---|---|---|---|---|
| | | | | | | | | | Rep. | Dem. | AIP |
| 22,100 | JASPER | 7,183 | 1,839 | 2,438 | 2,906 | | 468 | A | 25.6% | 33.9% | 40.5% |
| 1,582 | JEFF DAVIS | 496 | 191 | 239 | 66 | | 48 | D | 38.5% | 48.2% | 13.3% |
| 245,659 | JEFFERSON | 77,868 | 26,007 | 30,032 | 21,824 | 5 | 4,025 | D | 33.4% | 38.6% | 28.0% |
| 5,022 | JIM HOGG | 1,552 | 223 | 1,276 | 53 | | 1,053 | D | 14.4% | 82.2% | 3.4% |
| 34,548 | JIM WELLS | 10,047 | 2,827 | 6,304 | 913 | 3 | 3,477 | D | 28.1% | 62.7% | 9.1% |
| 34,720 | JOHNSON | 12,417 | 4,372 | 5,330 | 2,709 | 6 | 958 | D | 35.2% | 42.9% | 21.8% |
| 19,299 | JONES | 4,979 | 1,676 | 2,372 | 931 | | 696 | D | 33.7% | 47.6% | 18.7% |
| 14,995 | KARNES | 4,299 | 1,342 | 2,271 | 686 | | 929 | D | 31.2% | 52.8% | 16.0% |
| 29,931 | KAUFMAN | 8,092 | 2,431 | 3,311 | 2,350 | | 880 | D | 30.0% | 40.9% | 29.0% |
| 5,889 | KENDALL | 2,471 | 1,569 | 538 | 364 | | 1,031 | R | 63.5% | 21.8% | 14.7% |
| 884 | KENEDY | 183 | 76 | 100 | 7 | | 24 | D | 41.5% | 54.6% | 3.8% |
| 1,727 | KENT | 634 | 143 | 303 | 188 | | 115 | D | 22.6% | 47.8% | 29.7% |
| 16,800 | KERR | 6,643 | 3,692 | 1,878 | 1,073 | | 1,814 | R | 55.6% | 28.3% | 16.2% |
| 3,943 | KIMBLE | 1,368 | 640 | 463 | 264 | 1 | 177 | R | 46.8% | 33.8% | 19.3% |
| 640 | KING | 224 | 44 | 109 | 71 | | 38 | D | 19.6% | 48.7% | 31.7% |
| 2,452 | KINNEY | 599 | 198 | 333 | 68 | | 135 | D | 33.1% | 55.6% | 11.4% |
| 30,052 | KLEBERG | 8,016 | 2,713 | 4,633 | 670 | | 1,920 | D | 33.8% | 57.8% | 8.4% |
| 7,857 | KNOX | 2,127 | 580 | 1,222 | 325 | | 642 | D | 27.3% | 57.5% | 15.3% |
| 34,234 | LAMAR | 10,933 | 3,395 | 4,635 | 2,903 | | 1,240 | D | 31.1% | 42.4% | 26.6% |
| 21,896 | LAMB | 6,322 | 2,595 | 2,267 | 1,460 | | 328 | R | 41.0% | 35.9% | 23.1% |
| 9,418 | LAMPASAS | 2,818 | 935 | 1,423 | 460 | | 488 | D | 33.2% | 50.5% | 16.3% |
| 5,972 | LA SALLE | 1,081 | 324 | 645 | 112 | | 321 | D | 30.0% | 59.7% | 10.4% |
| 20,174 | LAVACA | 5,314 | 1,698 | 2,165 | 1,451 | | 467 | D | 32.0% | 40.7% | 27.3% |
| 8,949 | LEE | 2,989 | 1,075 | 1,283 | 631 | | 208 | D | 36.0% | 42.9% | 21.1% |
| 9,951 | LEON | 3,075 | 659 | 1,536 | 880 | | 656 | D | 21.4% | 50.0% | 28.6% |
| 31,595 | LIBERTY | 9,608 | 2,746 | 3,469 | 3,393 | | 76 | D | 28.6% | 36.1% | 35.3% |
| 20,413 | LIMESTONE | 5,683 | 1,485 | 2,796 | 1,402 | | 1,311 | D | 26.1% | 49.2% | 24.7% |
| 3,406 | LIPSCOMB | 1,545 | 1,079 | 279 | 187 | | 800 | R | 69.8% | 18.1% | 12.1% |
| 7,846 | LIVE OAK | 2,344 | 938 | 922 | 484 | | 16 | R | 40.0% | 39.3% | 20.6% |
| 5,240 | LLANO | 2,825 | 1,079 | 1,282 | 464 | | 203 | D | 38.2% | 45.4% | 16.4% |
| 226 | LOVING | 81 | 23 | 18 | 40 | | 17 | A | 28.4% | 22.2% | 49.4% |
| 156,271 | LUBBOCK | 50,154 | 25,646 | 15,430 | 9,078 | | 10,216 | R | 51.1% | 30.8% | 18.1% |
| 10,914 | LYNN | 2,882 | 1,005 | 1,333 | 544 | | 328 | D | 34.9% | 46.3% | 18.9% |
| 8,815 | MCCULLOCH | 2,659 | 947 | 1,353 | 359 | | 406 | D | 35.6% | 50.9% | 13.5% |
| 150,091 | MCLENNAN | 46,639 | 15,958 | 22,388 | 8,268 | 25 | 6,430 | D | 34.2% | 48.0% | 17.7% |
| 1,116 | MCMULLEN | 428 | 169 | 160 | 99 | | 9 | R | 39.5% | 37.4% | 23.1% |
| 6,749 | MADISON | 2,367 | 608 | 994 | 765 | | 229 | D | 25.7% | 42.0% | 32.3% |
| 8,049 | MARION | 2,854 | 637 | 1,260 | 957 | | 303 | D | 22.3% | 44.1% | 33.5% |
| 5,068 | MARTIN | 1,255 | 343 | 373 | 539 | | 166 | A | 27.3% | 29.7% | 42.9% |
| 3,780 | MASON | 1,518 | 789 | 560 | 169 | | 229 | R | 52.0% | 36.9% | 11.1% |
| 25,744 | MATAGORDA | 8,466 | 3,094 | 3,595 | 1,777 | | 501 | D | 36.5% | 42.5% | 21.0% |
| 14,508 | MAVERICK | 2,506 | 771 | 1,570 | 165 | | 799 | D | 30.8% | 62.6% | 6.6% |
| 18,904 | MEDINA | 5,251 | 2,058 | 2,471 | 722 | | 413 | D | 39.2% | 47.1% | 13.7% |
| 2,964 | MENARD | 971 | 491 | 362 | 118 | | 129 | R | 50.6% | 37.3% | 12.2% |
| 67,717 | MIDLAND | 23,222 | 12,789 | 4,756 | 5,675 | 2 | 7,114 | R | 55.1% | 20.5% | 24.4% |
| 22,263 | MILAM | 6,409 | 1,614 | 3,269 | 1,525 | 1 | 1,655 | D | 25.2% | 51.0% | 23.8% |
| 4,467 | MILLS | 1,663 | 645 | 722 | 296 | | 77 | D | 38.8% | 43.4% | 17.8% |
| 11,255 | MITCHELL | 2,981 | 893 | 1,589 | 499 | | 696 | D | 30.0% | 53.3% | 16.7% |
| 14,893 | MONTAGUE | 5,205 | 1,736 | 2,555 | 914 | | 819 | D | 33.4% | 49.1% | 17.6% |
| 26,839 | MONTGOMERY | 13,255 | 4,353 | 4,021 | 4,879 | 2 | 526 | A | 32.8% | 30.3% | 36.8% |
| 14,773 | MOORE | 4,996 | 2,378 | 1,359 | 1,258 | 1 | 1,019 | R | 47.6% | 27.2% | 25.2% |
| 12,576 | MORRIS | 4,088 | 1,064 | 1,701 | 1,323 | | 378 | D | 26.0% | 41.6% | 32.4% |
| 2,870 | MOTLEY | 1,107 | 415 | 397 | 295 | | 18 | R | 37.5% | 35.9% | 26.6% |
| 28,046 | NACOGDOCHES | 9,880 | 3,235 | 3,449 | 3,196 | | 214 | D | 32.7% | 34.9% | 32.3% |
| 34,423 | NAVARRO | 10,388 | 2,845 | 5,296 | 2,245 | 2 | 2,451 | D | 27.4% | 51.0% | 21.6% |
| 10,372 | NEWTON | 3,541 | 555 | 1,476 | 1,509 | 1 | 33 | A | 15.7% | 41.7% | 42.6% |
| 18,963 | NOLAN | 5,938 | 1,969 | 2,784 | 1,185 | | 815 | D | 33.2% | 46.9% | 20.0% |
| 221,573 | NUECES | 67,491 | 21,307 | 39,025 | 7,159 | | 17,718 | D | 31.6% | 57.8% | 10.6% |
| 9,380 | OCHILTREE | 3,132 | 2,208 | 432 | 492 | | 1,716 | R | 70.5% | 13.8% | 15.7% |
| 1,928 | OLDHAM | 788 | 320 | 237 | 230 | 1 | 83 | R | 40.6% | 30.1% | 29.2% |

# TEXAS

## PRESIDENT 1968

| 1960 Census Population | County | Total Vote | Republican | Democratic | AIP | Other | Plurality | Percentage Total Vote | | |
|---|---|---|---|---|---|---|---|---|---|---|
| | | | | | | | | Rep. | Dem. | AIP |
| 60,357 | ORANGE | 21,216 | 5,886 | 6,485 | 8,845 | | 2,360 A | 27.7% | 30.6% | 41.7% |
| 20,516 | PALO PINTO | 7,436 | 2,627 | 3,552 | 1,257 | | 925 D | 35.3% | 47.8% | 16.9% |
| 16,870 | PANOLA | 5,947 | 1,586 | 1,711 | 2,650 | | 939 A | 26.7% | 28.8% | 44.6% |
| 22,880 | PARKER | 9,303 | 3,068 | 4,301 | 1,934 | | 1,233 D | 33.0% | 46.2% | 20.8% |
| 9,583 | PARMER | 3,102 | 1,539 | 833 | 730 | | 706 R | 49.6% | 26.9% | 23.5% |
| 11,957 | PECOS | 4,019 | 1,524 | 1,592 | 900 | 3 | 68 D | 37.9% | 39.6% | 22.4% |
| 13,861 | POLK | 4,567 | 1,013 | 1,841 | 1,712 | 1 | 129 D | 22.2% | 40.3% | 37.5% |
| 115,580 | POTTER | 27,072 | 13,338 | 8,238 | 5,486 | 10 | 5,100 R | 49.3% | 30.4% | 20.3% |
| 5,460 | PRESIDIO | 1,582 | 481 | 969 | 132 | | 488 D | 30.4% | 61.3% | 8.3% |
| 2,993 | RAINS | 1,204 | 340 | 558 | 306 | | 218 D | 28.2% | 46.3% | 25.4% |
| 33,913 | RANDALL | 18,592 | 11,400 | 4,060 | 3,128 | 4 | 7,340 R | 61.3% | 21.8% | 16.8% |
| 3,782 | REAGAN | 1,112 | 454 | 370 | 288 | | 84 R | 40.8% | 33.3% | 25.9% |
| 2,079 | REAL | 703 | 290 | 277 | 136 | | 13 R | 41.3% | 39.4% | 19.3% |
| 15,682 | RED RIVER | 5,104 | 1,305 | 2,245 | 1,554 | | 691 D | 25.6% | 44.0% | 30.4% |
| 17,644 | REEVES | 3,509 | 1,310 | 1,456 | 743 | | 146 D | 37.3% | 41.5% | 21.2% |
| 10,975 | REFUGIO | 3,299 | 1,114 | 1,699 | 486 | | 585 D | 33.8% | 51.5% | 14.7% |
| 1,075 | ROBERTS | 514 | 311 | 90 | 113 | | 198 R | 60.5% | 17.5% | 22.0% |
| 16,157 | ROBERTSON | 4,742 | 965 | 2,833 | 944 | | 1,868 D | 20.4% | 59.7% | 19.9% |
| 5,878 | ROCKWALL | 1,975 | 614 | 778 | 582 | 1 | 164 D | 31.1% | 39.4% | 29.5% |
| 15,016 | RUNNELS | 3,823 | 1,707 | 1,448 | 668 | | 259 R | 44.7% | 37.9% | 17.5% |
| 36,421 | RUSK | 12,546 | 3,739 | 4,078 | 4,729 | | 651 A | 29.8% | 32.5% | 37.7% |
| 7,302 | SABINE | 2,468 | 455 | 1,078 | 935 | | 143 D | 18.4% | 43.7% | 37.9% |
| 7,722 | SAN AUGUSTINE | 2,460 | 506 | 817 | 1,137 | | 320 A | 20.6% | 33.2% | 46.2% |
| 6,153 | SAN JACINTO | 2,309 | 381 | 1,235 | 693 | | 542 D | 16.5% | 53.5% | 30.0% |
| 45,021 | SAN PATRICIO | 12,411 | 3,717 | 6,818 | 1,876 | | 3,101 D | 29.9% | 54.9% | 15.1% |
| 6,381 | SAN SABA | 2,140 | 535 | 1,140 | 465 | | 605 D | 25.0% | 53.3% | 21.7% |
| 2,791 | SCHLEICHER | 952 | 396 | 378 | 178 | | 18 R | 41.6% | 39.7% | 18.7% |
| 20,369 | SCURRY | 4,861 | 1,745 | 2,031 | 1,084 | 1 | 286 D | 35.9% | 41.8% | 22.3% |
| 3,990 | SHACKELFORD | 1,507 | 557 | 673 | 277 | | 116 D | 37.0% | 44.7% | 18.4% |
| 20,479 | SHELBY | 6,923 | 1,127 | 2,511 | 3,285 | | 774 A | 16.3% | 36.3% | 47.5% |
| 2,605 | SHERMAN | 1,396 | 723 | 297 | 376 | | 347 R | 51.8% | 21.3% | 26.9% |
| 86,350 | SMITH | 30,571 | 12,079 | 8,897 | 9,595 | | 2,484 R | 39.5% | 29.1% | 31.4% |
| 2,577 | SOMERVELL | 901 | 313 | 384 | 204 | | 71 D | 34.7% | 42.6% | 22.6% |
| 17,137 | STARR | 5,367 | 1,374 | 3,922 | 71 | | 2,548 D | 25.6% | 73.1% | 1.3% |
| 8,885 | STEPHENS | 3,051 | 1,287 | 1,239 | 525 | | 48 R | 42.2% | 40.6% | 17.2% |
| 1,177 | STERLING | 375 | 170 | 151 | 54 | | 19 R | 45.3% | 40.3% | 14.4% |
| 3,017 | STONEWALL | 1,110 | 213 | 635 | 262 | | 373 D | 19.2% | 57.2% | 23.6% |
| 3,738 | SUTTON | 910 | 412 | 351 | 147 | | 61 R | 45.3% | 38.6% | 16.2% |
| 10,607 | SWISHER | 3,560 | 1,177 | 1,760 | 623 | | 583 D | 33.1% | 49.4% | 17.5% |
| 538,495 | TARRANT | 190,747 | 81,786 | 79,705 | 29,256 | | 2,081 R | 42.9% | 41.8% | 15.3% |
| 101,078 | TAYLOR | 25,626 | 12,218 | 9,107 | 4,289 | 12 | 3,111 R | 47.7% | 35.5% | 16.7% |
| 2,600 | TERRELL | 601 | 250 | 201 | 149 | 1 | 49 R | 41.6% | 33.4% | 24.8% |
| 16,286 | TERRY | 4,427 | 1,948 | 1,625 | 854 | | 323 R | 44.0% | 36.7% | 19.3% |
| 2,767 | THROCKMORTON | 1,061 | 317 | 618 | 126 | | 301 D | 29.9% | 58.2% | 11.9% |
| 16,785 | TITUS | 5,775 | 1,572 | 2,317 | 1,886 | | 431 D | 27.2% | 40.1% | 32.7% |
| 64,630 | TOM GREEN | 19,536 | 9,682 | 6,774 | 3,074 | 6 | 2,908 R | 49.6% | 34.7% | 15.7% |
| 212,136 | TRAVIS | 82,520 | 34,309 | 39,667 | 8,424 | 120 | 5,358 D | 41.6% | 48.1% | 10.2% |
| 7,539 | TRINITY | 2,779 | 636 | 1,146 | 997 | | 149 D | 22.9% | 41.2% | 35.9% |
| 10,666 | TYLER | 3,786 | 1,120 | 1,204 | 1,462 | | 258 A | 29.6% | 31.8% | 38.6% |
| 19,793 | UPSHUR | 6,885 | 1,519 | 2,480 | 2,886 | | 406 A | 22.1% | 36.0% | 41.9% |
| 6,239 | UPTON | 1,586 | 664 | 463 | 459 | | 201 R | 41.9% | 29.2% | 28.9% |
| 16,814 | UVALDE | 4,759 | 2,252 | 1,736 | 768 | 3 | 516 R | 47.3% | 36.5% | 16.1% |
| 24,461 | VAL VERDE | 5,698 | 1,914 | 3,205 | 573 | 6 | 1,291 D | 33.6% | 56.2% | 10.1% |
| 19,091 | VAN ZANDT | 6,751 | 1,954 | 2,706 | 2,091 | | 615 D | 28.9% | 40.1% | 31.0% |
| 46,475 | VICTORIA | 14,730 | 6,352 | 6,042 | 2,336 | | 310 R | 43.1% | 41.0% | 15.9% |
| 21,475 | WALKER | 5,789 | 1,946 | 2,391 | 1,452 | | 445 D | 33.6% | 41.3% | 25.1% |
| 12,071 | WALLER | 3,439 | 958 | 1,684 | 797 | | 726 D | 27.9% | 49.0% | 23.2% |
| 14,917 | WARD | 4,265 | 1,552 | 1,331 | 1,382 | | 170 D | 36.4% | 31.2% | 32.4% |
| 19,145 | WASHINGTON | 5,607 | 3,244 | 1,686 | 677 | | 1,558 R | 57.9% | 30.1% | 12.1% |
| 64,791 | WEBB | 11,826 | 2,103 | 9,419 | 304 | | 7,316 D | 17.8% | 79.6% | 2.6% |

# TEXAS

## PRESIDENT 1968

| 1960 Census Population | County | Total Vote | Republican | Democratic | AIP | Other | Plurality | Percentage Total Vote | | |
|---|---|---|---|---|---|---|---|---|---|---|
| | | | | | | | | Rep. | Dem. | AIP |
| 38,152 | WHARTON | 9,959 | 3,773 | 4,304 | 1,882 | | 531 D | 37.9% | 43.2% | 18.9% |
| 7,947 | WHEELER | 2,558 | 1,176 | 812 | 570 | | 364 R | 46.0% | 31.7% | 22.3% |
| 123,528 | WICHITA | 33,414 | 11,937 | 15,387 | 6,087 | 3 | 3,450 D | 35.7% | 46.0% | 18.2% |
| 17,748 | WILBARGER | 5,198 | 1,909 | 1,996 | 1,292 | 1 | 87 D | 36.7% | 38.4% | 24.9% |
| 20,084 | WILLACY | 3,638 | 1,243 | 1,930 | 465 | | 687 D | 34.2% | 53.1% | 12.8% |
| 35,044 | WILLIAMSON | 10,123 | 2,923 | 5,528 | 1,669 | 3 | 2,605 D | 28.9% | 54.6% | 16.5% |
| 13,267 | WILSON | 4,199 | 1,321 | 2,336 | 542 | | 1,015 D | 31.5% | 55.6% | 12.9% |
| 13,652 | WINKLER | 3,579 | 1,391 | 938 | 1,249 | 1 | 142 R | 38.9% | 26.2% | 34.9% |
| 17,012 | WISE | 5,864 | 1,983 | 2,774 | 1,107 | | 791 D | 33.8% | 47.3% | 18.9% |
| 17,653 | WOOD | 6,259 | 2,046 | 2,192 | 2,020 | 1 | 146 D | 32.7% | 35.0% | 32.3% |
| 8,032 | YOAKUM | 2,462 | 1,123 | 615 | 724 | | 399 R | 45.6% | 25.0% | 29.4% |
| 17,254 | YOUNG | 5,346 | 1,860 | 2,482 | 1,004 | | 622 D | 34.8% | 46.4% | 18.8% |
| 4,393 | ZAPATA | 1,212 | 251 | 909 | 52 | | 658 D | 20.7% | 75.0% | 4.3% |
| 12,696 | ZAVALA | 2,215 | 693 | 1,307 | 214 | 1 | 614 D | 31.3% | 59.0% | 9.7% |
| 9,579,677 | TOTAL | 3,079,216 | 1,227,844 | 1,266,804 | 584,269 | 299 | 38,960 D | 39.9% | 41.1% | 19.0% |

# TEXAS

## PRESIDENT 1964

| 1960 Census Population | County | Total Vote | Republican | Democratic | Other | Rep.-Dem. Plurality | Percentage Total Vote Rep. | Dem. | Major Vote Rep. | Dem. |
|---|---|---|---|---|---|---|---|---|---|---|
| 28,162 | ANDERSON | 8,181 | 3,362 | 4,809 | 10 | 1,447 D | 41.1% | 58.8% | 41.1% | 58.9% |
| 13,450 | ANDREWS | 3,585 | 1,442 | 2,133 | 10 | 691 D | 40.2% | 59.5% | 40.3% | 59.7% |
| 39,814 | ANGELINA | 13,484 | 5,262 | 8,194 | 28 | 2,932 D | 39.0% | 60.8% | 39.1% | 60.9% |
| 7,006 | ARANSAS | 2,101 | 602 | 1,492 | 7 | 890 D | 28.7% | 71.0% | 28.7% | 71.3% |
| 6,110 | ARCHER | 2,207 | 441 | 1,766 | | 1,325 D | 20.0% | 80.0% | 20.0% | 80.0% |
| 1,966 | ARMSTRONG | 909 | 365 | 544 | | 179 D | 40.2% | 59.8% | 40.2% | 59.8% |
| 18,828 | ATASCOSA | 4,516 | 1,283 | 3,224 | 9 | 1,941 D | 28.4% | 71.4% | 28.5% | 71.5% |
| 13,777 | AUSTIN | 3,915 | 1,545 | 2,365 | 5 | 820 D | 39.5% | 60.4% | 39.5% | 60.5% |
| 9,090 | BAILEY | 2,562 | 1,056 | 1,503 | 3 | 447 D | 41.2% | 58.7% | 41.3% | 58.7% |
| 3,892 | BANDERA | 1,639 | 762 | 876 | 1 | 114 D | 46.5% | 53.4% | 46.5% | 53.5% |
| 16,925 | BASTROP | 5,049 | 1,130 | 3,912 | 7 | 2,782 D | 22.4% | 77.5% | 22.4% | 77.6% |
| 5,893 | BAYLOR | 1,794 | 389 | 1,403 | 2 | 1,014 D | 21.7% | 78.2% | 21.7% | 78.3% |
| 23,755 | BEE | 4,832 | 1,509 | 3,314 | 9 | 1,805 D | 31.2% | 68.6% | 31.3% | 68.7% |
| 94,097 | BELL | 17,512 | 2,938 | 14,557 | 17 | 11,619 D | 16.8% | 83.1% | 16.8% | 83.2% |
| 687,151 | BEXAR | 162,520 | 53,469 | 108,658 | 393 | 55,189 D | 32.9% | 66.9% | 33.0% | 67.0% |
| 3,657 | BLANCO | 1,488 | 290 | 1,197 | 1 | 907 D | 19.5% | 80.4% | 19.5% | 80.5% |
| 1,076 | BORDEN | 419 | 152 | 266 | 1 | 114 D | 36.3% | 63.5% | 36.4% | 63.6% |
| 10,809 | BOSQUE | 3,721 | 1,024 | 2,690 | 7 | 1,666 D | 27.5% | 72.3% | 27.6% | 72.4% |
| 59,971 | BOWIE | 17,410 | 7,018 | 10,368 | 24 | 3,350 D | 40.3% | 59.6% | 40.4% | 59.6% |
| 76,204 | BRAZORIA | 24,497 | 8,477 | 15,917 | 103 | 7,440 D | 34.6% | 65.0% | 34.8% | 65.2% |
| 44,895 | BRAZOS | 12,019 | 4,003 | 7,998 | 18 | 3,995 D | 33.3% | 66.5% | 33.4% | 66.6% |
| 6,434 | BREWSTER | 1,887 | 635 | 1,251 | 1 | 616 D | 33.7% | 66.3% | 33.7% | 66.3% |
| 3,577 | BRISCOE | 1,317 | 348 | 966 | 3 | 618 D | 26.4% | 73.3% | 26.5% | 73.5% |
| 8,609 | BROOKS | 2,703 | 402 | 2,299 | 2 | 1,897 D | 14.9% | 85.1% | 14.9% | 85.1% |
| 24,728 | BROWN | 7,293 | 2,070 | 5,214 | 9 | 3,144 D | 28.4% | 71.5% | 28.4% | 71.6% |
| 11,177 | BURLESON | 3,147 | 617 | 2,527 | 3 | 1,910 D | 19.6% | 80.3% | 19.6% | 80.4% |
| 9,265 | BURNET | 3,410 | 821 | 2,585 | 4 | 1,764 D | 24.1% | 75.8% | 24.1% | 75.9% |
| 17,222 | CALDWELL | 4,629 | 1,046 | 3,580 | 3 | 2,534 D | 22.6% | 77.3% | 22.6% | 77.4% |
| 16,592 | CALHOUN | 4,434 | 1,031 | 3,398 | 5 | 2,367 D | 23.3% | 76.6% | 23.3% | 76.7% |
| 7,929 | CALLAHAN | 3,037 | 849 | 2,178 | 10 | 1,329 D | 28.0% | 71.7% | 28.0% | 72.0% |
| 151,098 | CAMERON | 25,659 | 9,531 | 16,056 | 72 | 6,525 D | 37.1% | 62.6% | 37.2% | 62.8% |
| 7,849 | CAMP | 2,577 | 729 | 1,841 | 7 | 1,112 D | 28.3% | 71.4% | 28.4% | 71.6% |
| 7,781 | CARSON | 2,621 | 1,044 | 1,574 | 3 | 530 D | 39.8% | 60.1% | 39.9% | 60.1% |
| 23,496 | CASS | 6,292 | 2,681 | 3,603 | 8 | 922 D | 42.6% | 57.3% | 42.7% | 57.3% |
| 8,923 | CASTRO | 2,494 | 626 | 1,865 | 3 | 1,239 D | 25.1% | 74.8% | 25.1% | 74.9% |
| 10,379 | CHAMBERS | 2,956 | 1,023 | 1,921 | 12 | 898 D | 34.6% | 65.0% | 34.7% | 65.3% |
| 33,120 | CHEROKEE | 8,537 | 3,043 | 5,485 | 9 | 2,442 D | 35.6% | 64.2% | 35.7% | 64.3% |
| 8,421 | CHILDRESS | 2,931 | 952 | 1,977 | 2 | 1,025 D | 32.5% | 67.5% | 32.5% | 67.5% |
| 8,351 | CLAY | 3,020 | 659 | 2,357 | 4 | 1,698 D | 21.8% | 78.0% | 21.9% | 78.1% |
| 6,417 | COCHRAN | 1,761 | 497 | 1,260 | 4 | 763 D | 28.2% | 71.6% | 28.3% | 71.7% |
| 3,589 | COKE | 1,269 | 366 | 900 | 3 | 534 D | 28.8% | 70.9% | 23.9% | 71.1% |
| 12,458 | COLEMAN | 4,105 | 1,434 | 2,670 | 1 | 1,236 D | 34.9% | 65.0% | 34.9% | 65.1% |
| 41,247 | COLLIN | 11,193 | 3,341 | 7,833 | 19 | 4,492 D | 29.8% | 70.0% | 29.9% | 70.1% |
| 6,276 | COLLINGSWORTH | 1,872 | 724 | 1,145 | 3 | 421 D | 38.7% | 61.2% | 38.7% | 61.3% |
| 18,463 | COLORADO | 5,574 | 1,918 | 3,650 | 6 | 1,732 D | 34.4% | 65.5% | 34.4% | 65.6% |
| 19,844 | COMAL | 5,875 | 2,223 | 3,644 | 8 | 1,421 D | 37.8% | 62.0% | 37.9% | 62.1% |
| 11,865 | COMANCHE | 3,819 | 962 | 2,851 | 6 | 1,889 D | 25.2% | 74.7% | 25.2% | 74.8% |
| 3,672 | CONCHO | 1,256 | 307 | 948 | 1 | 641 D | 24.4% | 75.5% | 24.5% | 75.5% |
| 22,560 | COOKE | 7,211 | 3,117 | 4,083 | 11 | 966 D | 43.2% | 56.6% | 43.3% | 56.7% |
| 23,961 | CORYELL | 4,564 | 877 | 3,679 | 8 | 2,802 D | 19.2% | 80.6% | 19.2% | 80.8% |
| 4,207 | COTTLE | 1,353 | 230 | 1,122 | 1 | 892 D | 17.0% | 82.9% | 17.0% | 83.0% |
| 4,699 | CRANE | 1,559 | 637 | 919 | 3 | 282 D | 40.9% | 58.9% | 40.9% | 59.1% |
| 4,209 | CROCKETT | 1,211 | 409 | 799 | 3 | 390 D | 33.8% | 66.0% | 33.9% | 66.1% |
| 10,347 | CROSBY | 2,892 | 611 | 2,278 | 3 | 1,667 D | 21.1% | 78.8% | 21.1% | 78.9% |
| 2,794 | CULBERSON | 787 | 314 | 473 | | 159 D | 39.9% | 60.1% | 39.9% | 60.1% |
| 6,302 | DALLAM | 1,759 | 700 | 1,058 | 1 | 358 D | 39.8% | 60.1% | 39.8% | 60.2% |
| 951,527 | DALLAS | 304,158 | 137,065 | 166,472 | 621 | 29,407 D | 45.1% | 54.7% | 45.2% | 54.8% |
| 19,185 | DAWSON | 4,868 | 1,691 | 3,171 | 6 | 1,480 D | 34.7% | 65.1% | 34.8% | 65.2% |
| 13,187 | DEAF SMITH | 3,897 | 1,793 | 2,094 | 10 | 301 D | 46.0% | 53.7% | 46.1% | 53.9% |
| 5,860 | DELTA | 1,960 | 339 | 1,619 | 2 | 1,280 D | 17.3% | 82.6% | 17.3% | 82.7% |

# TEXAS

## PRESIDENT 1964

| 1960 Census Population | County | Total Vote | Republican | Democratic | Other | Rep.-Dem. Plurality | Percentage | | | |
|---|---|---|---|---|---|---|---|---|---|---|
| | | | | | | | Total Vote | | Major Vote | |
| | | | | | | | Rep. | Dem. | Rep. | Dem. |
| 47,432 | DENTON | 13,494 | 4,335 | 9,137 | 22 | 4,802 D | 32.1% | 67.7% | 32.2% | 67.8% |
| 20,683 | DE WITT | 5,573 | 2,283 | 3,286 | 4 | 1,003 D | 41.0% | 59.0% | 41.0% | 59.0% |
| 4,963 | DICKENS | 1,667 | 339 | 1,324 | 4 | 985 D | 20.3% | 79.4% | 20.4% | 79.6% |
| 10,095 | DIMMIT | 1,688 | 501 | 1,184 | 3 | 683 D | 29.7% | 70.1% | 29.7% | 70.3% |
| 4,449 | DONLEY | 1,776 | 708 | 1,068 | | 360 D | 39.9% | 60.1% | 39.9% | 60.1% |
| 13,398 | DUVAL | 4,789 | 353 | 4,432 | 4 | 4,079 D | 7.4% | 92.5% | 7.4% | 92.6% |
| 19,526 | EASTLAND | 6,752 | 2,049 | 4,692 | 11 | 2,643 D | 30.3% | 69.5% | 30.4% | 69.6% |
| 90,995 | ECTOR | 22,386 | 11,497 | 10,826 | 63 | 671 R | 51.4% | 48.4% | 51.5% | 48.5% |
| 2,317 | EDWARDS | 712 | 371 | 337 | 4 | 34 R | 52.1% | 47.3% | 52.4% | 47.6% |
| 43,395 | ELLIS | 10,062 | 2,779 | 7,278 | 5 | 4,499 D | 27.6% | 72.3% | 27.6% | 72.4% |
| 314,070 | EL PASO | 55,927 | 20,687 | 35,050 | 190 | 14,363 D | 37.0% | 62.7% | 37.1% | 62.9% |
| 16,236 | ERATH | 5,498 | 1,642 | 3,851 | 5 | 2,209 D | 29.9% | 70.0% | 29.9% | 70.1% |
| 21,263 | FALLS | 5,151 | 1,216 | 3,933 | 2 | 2,717 D | 23.6% | 76.4% | 23.6% | 76.4% |
| 23,880 | FANNIN | 7,200 | 1,219 | 5,976 | 5 | 4,757 D | 16.9% | 83.0% | 16.9% | 83.1% |
| 20,384 | FAYETTE | 5,677 | 2,036 | 3,630 | 11 | 1,594 D | 35.9% | 63.9% | 35.9% | 64.1% |
| 7,865 | FISHER | 2,567 | 454 | 2,108 | 5 | 1,654 D | 17.7% | 82.1% | 17.7% | 82.3% |
| 12,369 | FLOYD | 3,621 | 1,229 | 2,383 | 9 | 1,154 D | 33.9% | 65.8% | 34.0% | 66.0% |
| 3,125 | FOARD | 980 | 146 | 833 | 1 | 687 D | 14.9% | 85.0% | 14.9% | 85.1% |
| 40,527 | FORT BEND | 9,699 | 3,493 | 6,186 | 20 | 2,693 D | 36.0% | 63.8% | 36.1% | 63.9% |
| 5,101 | FRANKLIN | 1,944 | 424 | 1,520 | | 1,096 D | 21.8% | 78.2% | 21.8% | 78.2% |
| 12,525 | FREESTONE | 3,892 | 1,074 | 2,816 | 2 | 1,742 D | 27.6% | 72.4% | 27.6% | 72.4% |
| 10,112 | FRIO | 2,117 | 607 | 1,507 | 3 | 900 D | 28.7% | 71.2% | 28.7% | 71.3% |
| 12,267 | GAINES | 3,201 | 1,153 | 2,045 | 3 | 892 D | 36.0% | 63.9% | 36.1% | 63.9% |
| 140,364 | GALVESTON | 43,173 | 12,365 | 30,672 | 136 | 18,307 D | 28.6% | 71.0% | 28.7% | 71.3% |
| 6,611 | GARZA | 1,827 | 567 | 1,254 | 6 | 687 D | 31.0% | 68.6% | 31.1% | 68.9% |
| 10,048 | GILLESPIE | 3,960 | 1,695 | 2,264 | 1 | 569 D | 42.8% | 57.2% | 42.8% | 57.2% |
| 1,118 | GLASSCOCK | 363 | 183 | 179 | 1 | 4 R | 50.4% | 49.3% | 50.6% | 49.4% |
| 5,429 | GOLIAD | 1,541 | 549 | 990 | 2 | 441 D | 35.6% | 64.2% | 35.7% | 64.3% |
| 17,845 | GONZALES | 4,545 | 1,190 | 3,348 | 7 | 2,158 D | 26.2% | 73.7% | 26.2% | 73.8% |
| 31,535 | GRAY | 8,650 | 5,011 | 3,633 | 6 | 1,378 R | 57.9% | 42.0% | 58.0% | 42.0% |
| 73,043 | GRAYSON | 19,728 | 5,500 | 14,207 | 21 | 8,707 D | 27.9% | 72.0% | 27.9% | 72.1% |
| 69,436 | GREGG | 20,584 | 11,761 | 8,741 | 82 | 3,020 R | 57.1% | 42.5% | 57.4% | 42.6% |
| 12,709 | GRIMES | 3,247 | 1,014 | 2,229 | 4 | 1,215 D | 31.2% | 68.6% | 31.3% | 68.7% |
| 29,017 | GUADALUPE | 7,308 | 2,731 | 4,568 | 9 | 1,837 D | 37.4% | 62.5% | 37.4% | 62.6% |
| 36,798 | HALE | 9,594 | 3,666 | 5,910 | 18 | 2,244 D | 38.2% | 61.6% | 38.3% | 61.7% |
| 7,322 | HALL | 2,453 | 667 | 1,785 | 1 | 1,118 D | 27.2% | 72.8% | 27.2% | 72.8% |
| 8,488 | HAMILTON | 3,056 | 1,006 | 2,048 | 2 | 1,042 D | 32.9% | 67.0% | 32.9% | 67.1% |
| 6,208 | HANSFORD | 2,056 | 1,193 | 860 | 3 | 333 R | 58.0% | 41.8% | 58.1% | 41.9% |
| 8,275 | HARDEMAN | 2,532 | 697 | 1,835 | | 1,138 D | 27.5% | 72.5% | 27.5% | 72.5% |
| 24,629 | HARDIN | 7,146 | 1,987 | 5,143 | 16 | 3,156 D | 27.8% | 72.0% | 27.9% | 72.1% |
| 1,243,158 | HARRIS | 382,985 | 154,401 | 227,819 | 765 | 73,418 D | 40.3% | 59.5% | 40.4% | 59.6% |
| 45,594 | HARRISON | 11,930 | 5,568 | 6,351 | 11 | 783 D | 46.7% | 53.2% | 46.7% | 53.3% |
| 2,171 | HARTLEY | 1,003 | 437 | 565 | 1 | 128 D | 43.6% | 56.3% | 43.6% | 56.4% |
| 11,174 | HASKELL | 3,421 | 512 | 2,903 | 6 | 2,391 D | 15.0% | 84.9% | 15.0% | 85.0% |
| 19,934 | HAYS | 5,064 | 1,279 | 3,780 | 5 | 2,501 D | 25.3% | 74.6% | 25.3% | 74.7% |
| 3,185 | HEMPHILL | 1,213 | 563 | 649 | 1 | 86 D | 46.4% | 53.5% | 46.5% | 53.5% |
| 21,786 | HENDERSON | 6,714 | 1,988 | 4,697 | 29 | 2,709 D | 29.6% | 70.0% | 29.7% | 70.3% |
| 180,904 | HIDALGO | 33,756 | 11,563 | 22,110 | 83 | 10,547 D | 34.3% | 65.5% | 34.3% | 65.7% |
| 23,650 | HILL | 6,696 | 1,557 | 5,130 | 9 | 3,573 D | 23.3% | 76.6% | 23.3% | 76.7% |
| 22,340 | HOCKLEY | 5,733 | 1,674 | 4,049 | 10 | 2,375 D | 29.2% | 70.6% | 29.3% | 70.7% |
| 5,443 | HOOD | 2,087 | 423 | 1,661 | 3 | 1,238 D | 20.3% | 79.6% | 20.3% | 79.7% |
| 18,594 | HOPKINS | 5,651 | 1,518 | 4,133 | | 2,615 D | 26.9% | 73.1% | 26.9% | 73.1% |
| 19,376 | HOUSTON | 5,366 | 1,675 | 3,681 | 10 | 2,006 D | 31.2% | 68.6% | 31.3% | 68.7% |
| 40,139 | HOWARD | 9,367 | 3,272 | 6,083 | 12 | 2,811 D | 34.9% | 64.9% | 35.0% | 65.0% |
| 3,343 | HUDSPETH | 665 | 224 | 438 | 3 | 214 D | 33.7% | 65.9% | 33.8% | 66.2% |
| 39,399 | HUNT | 9,879 | 3,302 | 6,567 | 10 | 3,265 D | 33.4% | 66.5% | 33.5% | 66.5% |
| 34,419 | HUTCHINSON | 10,000 | 5,358 | 4,625 | 17 | 733 R | 53.6% | 46.3% | 53.7% | 46.3% |
| 1,183 | IRION | 550 | 199 | 351 | | 152 D | 36.2% | 63.8% | 36.2% | 63.8% |
| 7,418 | JACK | 2,444 | 847 | 1,594 | 3 | 747 D | 34.7% | 65.2% | 34.7% | 65.3% |
| 14,040 | JACKSON | 3,952 | 1,168 | 2,775 | 9 | 1,607 D | 29.6% | 70.2% | 29.6% | 70.4% |

# TEXAS

## PRESIDENT 1964

| 1960 Census Population | County | Total Vote | Republican | Democratic | Other | Rep.-Dem. Plurality | Percentage Total Vote Rep. | Dem. | Major Vote Rep. | Dem. |
|---|---|---|---|---|---|---|---|---|---|---|
| 22,100 | JASPER | 5,537 | 1,919 | 3,600 | 18 | 1,681 D | 34.7% | 65.0% | 34.8% | 65.2% |
| 1,582 | JEFF DAVIS | 479 | 174 | 304 | 1 | 130 D | 36.3% | 63.5% | 36.4% | 63.6% |
| 245,659 | JEFFERSON | 73,594 | 28,771 | 44,584 | 239 | 15,813 D | 39.1% | 60.6% | 39.2% | 60.8% |
| 5,022 | JIM HOGG | 1,530 | 152 | 1,375 | 3 | 1,223 D | 9.9% | 89.9% | 10.0% | 90.0% |
| 34,548 | JIM WELLS | 8,837 | 1,988 | 6,849 | | 4,861 D | 22.5% | 77.5% | 22.5% | 77.5% |
| 34,720 | JOHNSON | 9,642 | 3,251 | 6,381 | 10 | 3,130 D | 33.7% | 66.2% | 33.8% | 66.2% |
| 19,299 | JONES | 4,920 | 1,295 | 3,622 | 3 | 2,327 D | 26.3% | 73.6% | 26.3% | 73.7% |
| 14,995 | KARNES | 4,177 | 993 | 3,178 | 6 | 2,185 D | 23.8% | 76.1% | 23.8% | 76.2% |
| 29,931 | KAUFMAN | 6,694 | 1,922 | 4,766 | 6 | 2,844 D | 28.7% | 71.2% | 28.7% | 71.3% |
| 5,889 | KENDALL | 2,173 | 1,200 | 970 | 3 | 230 R | 55.2% | 44.6% | 55.3% | 44.7% |
| 884 | KENEDY | 146 | 30 | 115 | 1 | 85 D | 20.5% | 78.8% | 20.7% | 79.3% |
| 1,727 | KENT | 678 | 115 | 563 | | 448 D | 17.0% | 83.0% | 17.0% | 83.0% |
| 16,800 | KERR | 5,608 | 2,706 | 2,894 | 8 | 188 D | 48.3% | 51.6% | 48.3% | 51.7% |
| 3,943 | KIMBLE | 1,383 | 520 | 862 | 1 | 342 D | 37.6% | 62.3% | 37.6% | 62.4% |
| 640 | KING | 214 | 34 | 180 | | 146 D | 15.9% | 84.1% | 15.9% | 84.1% |
| 2,452 | KINNEY | 594 | 155 | 439 | | 284 D | 26.1% | 73.9% | 26.1% | 73.9% |
| 30,052 | KLEBERG | 6,230 | 1,652 | 4,568 | 10 | 2,916 D | 26.5% | 73.3% | 26.6% | 73.4% |
| 7,857 | KNOX | 2,216 | 439 | 1,773 | 4 | 1,334 D | 19.8% | 80.0% | 19.8% | 80.2% |
| 34,234 | LAMAR | 8,905 | 2,594 | 6,303 | 8 | 3,709 D | 29.1% | 70.8% | 29.2% | 70.8% |
| 21,896 | LAMB | 6,349 | 2,022 | 4,318 | 9 | 2,296 D | 31.8% | 68.0% | 31.9% | 68.1% |
| 9,418 | LAMPASAS | 2,970 | 744 | 2,224 | 2 | 1,480 D | 25.1% | 74.9% | 25.1% | 74.9% |
| 5,972 | LA SALLE | 1,212 | 223 | 988 | 1 | 765 D | 18.4% | 81.5% | 18.4% | 81.6% |
| 20,174 | LAVACA | 5,517 | 1,480 | 4,031 | 6 | 2,551 D | 26.8% | 73.1% | 26.9% | 73.1% |
| 8,949 | LEE | 2,809 | 923 | 1,884 | 2 | 961 D | 32.9% | 67.1% | 32.9% | 67.1% |
| 9,951 | LEON | 3,022 | 642 | 2,373 | 7 | 1,731 D | 21.2% | 78.5% | 21.3% | 78.7% |
| 31,595 | LIBERTY | 8,257 | 2,884 | 5,357 | 16 | 2,473 D | 34.9% | 64.9% | 35.0% | 65.0% |
| 20,413 | LIMESTONE | 5,263 | 1,478 | 3,777 | 8 | 2,299 D | 28.1% | 71.8% | 28.1% | 71.9% |
| 3,406 | LIPSCOMB | 1,352 | 763 | 589 | | 174 R | 56.4% | 43.6% | 56.4% | 43.6% |
| 7,846 | LIVE OAK | 2,226 | 795 | 1,423 | 8 | 628 D | 35.7% | 63.9% | 35.8% | 64.2% |
| 5,240 | LLANO | 2,384 | 655 | 1,727 | 2 | 1,072 D | 27.5% | 72.4% | 27.5% | 72.5% |
| 226 | LOVING | 79 | 32 | 46 | 1 | 14 D | 40.5% | 58.2% | 41.0% | 59.0% |
| 156,271 | LUBBOCK | 39,463 | 17,372 | 22,057 | 34 | 4,685 D | 44.0% | 55.9% | 44.1% | 55.9% |
| 10,914 | LYNN | 3,030 | 745 | 2,281 | 4 | 1,536 D | 24.6% | 75.3% | 24.6% | 75.4% |
| 8,815 | MCCULLOCH | 2,761 | 655 | 2,100 | 6 | 1,445 D | 23.7% | 76.1% | 23.8% | 76.2% |
| 150,091 | MCLENNAN | 39,346 | 10,892 | 28,429 | 25 | 17,537 D | 27.7% | 72.3% | 27.7% | 72.3% |
| 1,116 | MCMULLEN | 443 | 175 | 267 | 1 | 92 D | 39.5% | 60.3% | 39.6% | 60.4% |
| 6,749 | MADISON | 1,945 | 644 | 1,298 | 3 | 654 D | 33.1% | 66.7% | 33.2% | 66.8% |
| 8,049 | MARION | 2,303 | 927 | 1,372 | 4 | 445 D | 40.3% | 59.6% | 40.3% | 59.7% |
| 5,068 | MARTIN | 1,297 | 402 | 892 | 3 | 490 D | 31.0% | 68.8% | 31.1% | 68.9% |
| 3,780 | MASON | 1,535 | 590 | 941 | 4 | 351 D | 38.4% | 61.3% | 38.5% | 61.5% |
| 25,744 | MATAGORDA | 6,555 | 2,407 | 4,143 | 5 | 1,736 D | 36.7% | 63.2% | 36.7% | 63.3% |
| 14,508 | MAVERICK | 2,661 | 545 | 2,113 | 3 | 1,568 D | 20.5% | 79.4% | 20.5% | 79.5% |
| 18,904 | MEDINA | 4,992 | 1,583 | 3,408 | 1 | 1,825 D | 31.7% | 68.3% | 31.7% | 68.3% |
| 2,964 | MENARD | 985 | 397 | 588 | | 191 D | 40.3% | 59.7% | 40.3% | 59.7% |
| 67,717 | MIDLAND | 20,605 | 11,906 | 8,646 | 53 | 3,260 R | 57.8% | 42.0% | 57.9% | 42.1% |
| 22,263 | MILAM | 5,709 | 1,334 | 4,368 | 7 | 3,034 D | 23.4% | 76.5% | 23.4% | 76.6% |
| 4,467 | MILLS | 1,723 | 495 | 1,228 | | 733 D | 28.7% | 71.3% | 28.7% | 71.3% |
| 11,255 | MITCHELL | 3,159 | 737 | 2,420 | 2 | 1,683 D | 23.3% | 76.6% | 23.3% | 76.7% |
| 14,893 | MONTAGUE | 4,856 | 1,106 | 3,746 | 4 | 2,640 D | 22.8% | 77.1% | 22.8% | 77.2% |
| 26,839 | MONTGOMERY | 8,196 | 3,167 | 4,989 | 40 | 1,822 D | 38.6% | 60.9% | 38.8% | 61.2% |
| 14,773 | MOORE | 4,159 | 1,762 | 2,393 | 4 | 631 D | 42.4% | 57.5% | 42.4% | 57.6% |
| 12,576 | MORRIS | 3,594 | 1,218 | 2,366 | 10 | 1,148 D | 33.9% | 65.8% | 34.0% | 66.0% |
| 2,870 | MOTLEY | 1,004 | 324 | 678 | 2 | 354 D | 32.3% | 67.5% | 32.3% | 67.7% |
| 28,046 | NACOGDOCHES | 7,519 | 2,976 | 4,524 | 19 | 1,548 D | 39.6% | 60.2% | 39.7% | 60.3% |
| 34,423 | NAVARRO | 8,953 | 2,139 | 6,811 | 3 | 4,672 D | 23.9% | 76.1% | 23.9% | 76.1% |
| 10,372 | NEWTON | 2,955 | 738 | 2,211 | 6 | 1,473 D | 25.0% | 74.8% | 25.0% | 75.0% |
| 18,963 | NOLAN | 5,162 | 1,610 | 3,540 | 12 | 1,930 D | 31.2% | 68.6% | 31.3% | 68.7% |
| 221,573 | NUECES | 54,558 | 14,048 | 40,426 | 84 | 26,378 D | 25.7% | 74.1% | 25.8% | 74.2% |
| 9,380 | OCHILTREE | 2,737 | 1,814 | 920 | 3 | 894 R | 66.3% | 33.6% | 66.3% | 33.7% |
| 1,928 | OLDHAM | 670 | 269 | 397 | 4 | 128 D | 40.1% | 59.3% | 40.4% | 59.6% |

# TEXAS

## PRESIDENT 1964

| 1960 Census Population | County | Total Vote | Republican | Democratic | Other | Rep.-Dem. Plurality | Percentage Total Vote Rep. | Dem. | Major Vote Rep. | Dem. |
|---|---|---|---|---|---|---|---|---|---|---|
| 60,357 | ORANGE | 15,645 | 6,216 | 9,390 | 39 | 3,174 D | 39.7% | 60.0% | 39.8% | 60.2% |
| 20,516 | PALO PINTO | 5,541 | 1,748 | 3,791 | 2 | 2,043 D | 31.5% | 68.4% | 31.6% | 68.4% |
| 16,870 | PANOLA | 5,437 | 2,818 | 2,608 | 11 | 210 R | 51.8% | 48.0% | 51.9% | 48.1% |
| 22,880 | PARKER | 7,458 | 2,175 | 5,270 | 13 | 3,095 D | 29.2% | 70.7% | 29.2% | 70.8% |
| 9,583 | PARMER | 2,779 | 1,216 | 1,556 | 7 | 340 D | 43.8% | 56.0% | 43.9% | 56.1% |
| 11,957 | PECOS | 3,473 | 1,393 | 2,068 | 12 | 675 D | 40.1% | 59.5% | 40.2% | 59.8% |
| 13,861 | POLK | 3,700 | 1,199 | 2,492 | 9 | 1,293 D | 32.4% | 67.4% | 32.5% | 67.5% |
| 115,580 | POTTER | 24,419 | 11,505 | 12,850 | 64 | 1,345 D | 47.1% | 52.6% | 47.2% | 52.8% |
| 5,460 | PRESIDIO | 1,588 | 431 | 1,156 | 1 | 725 D | 27.1% | 72.8% | 27.2% | 72.8% |
| 2,993 | RAINS | 1,168 | 272 | 893 | 3 | 621 D | 23.3% | 76.5% | 23.3% | 76.7% |
| 33,913 | RANDALL | 13,881 | 7,843 | 6,016 | 22 | 1,827 R | 56.5% | 43.3% | 56.6% | 43.4% |
| 3,782 | REAGAN | 1,022 | 406 | 614 | 2 | 208 D | 39.7% | 60.1% | 39.8% | 60.2% |
| 2,079 | REAL | 743 | 255 | 487 | 1 | 232 D | 34.3% | 65.5% | 34.4% | 65.6% |
| 15,682 | RED RIVER | 4,654 | 1,257 | 3,391 | 6 | 2,134 D | 27.0% | 72.9% | 27.0% | 73.0% |
| 17,644 | REEVES | 3,595 | 1,251 | 2,340 | 4 | 1,089 D | 34.8% | 65.1% | 34.8% | 65.2% |
| 10,975 | REFUGIO | 3,091 | 772 | 2,319 | | 1,547 D | 25.0% | 75.0% | 25.0% | 75.0% |
| 1,075 | ROBERTS | 495 | 297 | 198 | | 99 R | 60.0% | 40.0% | 60.0% | 40.0% |
| 16,157 | ROBERTSON | 4,247 | 895 | 3,350 | 2 | 2,455 D | 21.1% | 78.9% | 21.1% | 78.9% |
| 5,878 | ROCKWALL | 1,755 | 445 | 1,305 | 5 | 860 D | 25.4% | 74.4% | 25.4% | 74.6% |
| 15,016 | RUNNELS | 4,132 | 1,480 | 2,645 | 7 | 1,165 D | 35.8% | 64.0% | 35.9% | 64.1% |
| 36,421 | RUSK | 12,033 | 5,488 | 6,528 | 17 | 1,040 D | 45.6% | 54.3% | 45.7% | 54.3% |
| 7,302 | SABINE | 2,230 | 428 | 1,801 | 1 | 1,373 D | 19.2% | 80.8% | 19.2% | 80.8% |
| 7,722 | SAN AUGUSTINE | 1,940 | 760 | 1,173 | 7 | 413 D | 39.2% | 60.5% | 39.3% | 60.7% |
| 6,153 | SAN JACINTO | 2,026 | 343 | 1,680 | 3 | 1,337 D | 16.9% | 82.9% | 17.0% | 83.0% |
| 45,021 | SAN PATRICIO | 9,384 | 2,188 | 7,176 | 20 | 4,988 D | 23.3% | 76.5% | 23.4% | 76.6% |
| 6,381 | SAN SABA | 2,277 | 418 | 1,859 | | 1,441 D | 18.4% | 81.6% | 18.4% | 81.6% |
| 2,791 | SCHLEICHER | 903 | 388 | 514 | 1 | 126 D | 43.0% | 56.9% | 43.0% | 57.0% |
| 20,369 | SCURRY | 5,137 | 1,741 | 3,381 | 15 | 1,640 D | 33.9% | 65.8% | 34.0% | 66.0% |
| 3,990 | SHACKELFORD | 1,424 | 487 | 934 | 3 | 447 D | 34.2% | 65.6% | 34.3% | 65.7% |
| 20,479 | SHELBY | 5,711 | 2,220 | 3,487 | 4 | 1,267 D | 38.9% | 61.1% | 38.9% | 61.1% |
| 2,605 | SHERMAN | 1,092 | 629 | 462 | 1 | 167 R | 57.6% | 42.3% | 57.7% | 42.3% |
| 86,350 | SMITH | 25,472 | 12,960 | 12,474 | 38 | 486 R | 50.9% | 49.0% | 51.0% | 49.0% |
| 2,577 | SOMERVELL | 854 | 210 | 641 | 3 | 431 D | 24.6% | 75.1% | 24.7% | 75.3% |
| 17,137 | STARR | 4,742 | 678 | 4,056 | 8 | 3,378 D | 14.3% | 85.5% | 14.3% | 85.7% |
| 8,885 | STEPHENS | 2,874 | 1,119 | 1,753 | 2 | 634 D | 38.9% | 61.0% | 39.0% | 61.0% |
| 1,177 | STERLING | 384 | 140 | 243 | 1 | 103 D | 36.5% | 63.3% | 36.6% | 63.4% |
| 3,017 | STONEWALL | 1,199 | 219 | 978 | 2 | 759 D | 18.3% | 81.6% | 18.3% | 81.7% |
| 3,738 | SUTTON | 1,051 | 357 | 694 | | 337 D | 34.0% | 66.0% | 34.0% | 66.0% |
| 10,607 | SWISHER | 3,230 | 815 | 2,410 | 5 | 1,595 D | 25.2% | 74.6% | 25.3% | 74.7% |
| 538,495 | TARRANT | 154,158 | 56,593 | 97,092 | 473 | 40,499 D | 36.7% | 63.0% | 36.8% | 63.2% |
| 101,078 | TAYLOR | 22,620 | 9,220 | 13,366 | 34 | 4,146 D | 40.8% | 59.1% | 40.8% | 59.2% |
| 2,600 | TERRELL | 658 | 294 | 364 | | 70 D | 44.7% | 55.3% | 44.7% | 55.3% |
| 16,286 | TERRY | 4,632 | 1,592 | 3,034 | 6 | 1,442 D | 34.4% | 65.5% | 34.4% | 65.6% |
| 2,767 | THROCKMORTON | 1,130 | 247 | 883 | | 636 D | 21.9% | 78.1% | 21.9% | 78.1% |
| 16,785 | TITUS | 5,219 | 1,687 | 3,528 | 4 | 1,841 D | 32.3% | 67.6% | 32.3% | 67.7% |
| 64,630 | TOM GREEN | 16,443 | 6,664 | 9,767 | 12 | 3,103 D | 40.5% | 59.4% | 40.6% | 59.4% |
| 212,136 | TRAVIS | 63,958 | 19,838 | 44,058 | 62 | 24,220 D | 31.0% | 68.9% | 31.0% | 69.0% |
| 7,539 | TRINITY | 2,428 | 763 | 1,654 | 11 | 891 D | 31.4% | 68.1% | 31.6% | 68.4% |
| 10,666 | TYLER | 3,037 | 1,216 | 1,818 | 3 | 602 D | 40.0% | 59.9% | 40.1% | 59.9% |
| 19,793 | UPSHUR | 6,262 | 2,222 | 4,027 | 13 | 1,805 D | 35.5% | 64.3% | 35.6% | 64.4% |
| 6,239 | UPTON | 1,604 | 636 | 958 | 10 | 322 D | 39.7% | 59.7% | 39.9% | 60.1% |
| 16,814 | UVALDE | 4,326 | 1,963 | 2,358 | 5 | 395 D | 45.4% | 54.5% | 45.4% | 54.6% |
| 24,461 | VAL VERDE | 4,902 | 1,346 | 3,555 | 1 | 2,209 D | 27.5% | 72.5% | 27.5% | 72.5% |
| 19,091 | VAN ZANDT | 5,676 | 1,614 | 4,047 | 15 | 2,433 D | 28.4% | 71.3% | 28.5% | 71.5% |
| 46,475 | VICTORIA | 12,367 | 4,201 | 8,141 | 25 | 3,940 D | 34.0% | 65.8% | 34.0% | 66.0% |
| 21,475 | WALKER | 4,436 | 1,557 | 2,877 | 2 | 1,320 D | 35.1% | 64.9% | 35.1% | 64.9% |
| 12,071 | WALLER | 3,149 | 980 | 2,167 | 2 | 1,187 D | 31.1% | 68.8% | 31.1% | 68.9% |
| 14,917 | WARD | 3,954 | 1,730 | 2,221 | 3 | 491 D | 43.8% | 56.2% | 43.8% | 56.2% |
| 19,145 | WASHINGTON | 4,962 | 2,019 | 2,938 | 5 | 919 D | 40.7% | 59.2% | 40.7% | 59.3% |
| 64,791 | WEBB | 11,182 | 1,094 | 10,073 | 15 | 8,979 D | 9.8% | 90.1% | 9.8% | 90.2% |

# TEXAS

## PRESIDENT 1964

| 1960 Census Population | County | Total Vote | Republican | Democratic | Other | Rep.-Dem. Plurality | Percentage | | | |
|---|---|---|---|---|---|---|---|---|---|---|
| | | | | | | | Total Vote | | Major Vote | |
| | | | | | | | Rep. | Dem. | Rep. | Dem. |
| 38,152 | WHARTON | 9,020 | 2,775 | 6,234 | 11 | 3,459 D | 30.8% | 69.1% | 30.8% | 69.2% |
| 7,947 | WHEELER | 2,580 | 1,138 | 1,440 | 2 | 302 D | 44.1% | 55.8% | 44.1% | 55.9% |
| 123,528 | WICHITA | 27,730 | 8,585 | 19,131 | 14 | 10,546 D | 31.0% | 69.0% | 31.0% | 69.0% |
| 17,748 | WILBARGER | 4,742 | 1,539 | 3,200 | 3 | 1,661 D | 32.5% | 67.5% | 32.5% | 67.5% |
| 20,084 | WILLACY | 3,388 | 1,230 | 2,152 | 6 | 922 D | 36.3% | 63.5% | 36.4% | 63.6% |
| 35,044 | WILLIAMSON | 9,202 | 1,766 | 7,430 | 6 | 5,664 D | 19.2% | 80.7% | 19.2% | 80.8% |
| 13,267 | WILSON | 4,195 | 718 | 3,472 | 5 | 2,754 D | 17.1% | 82.8% | 17.1% | 82.9% |
| 13,652 | WINKLER | 3,679 | 1,617 | 2,059 | 3 | 442 D | 44.0% | 56.0% | 44.0% | 56.0% |
| 17,012 | WISE | 5,241 | 1,386 | 3,852 | 3 | 2,466 D | 26.4% | 73.5% | 26.5% | 73.5% |
| 17,653 | WOOD | 5,606 | 2,068 | 3,528 | 10 | 1,460 D | 36.9% | 62.9% | 37.0% | 63.0% |
| 8,032 | YOAKUM | 2,280 | 859 | 1,415 | 6 | 556 D | 37.7% | 62.1% | 37.8% | 62.2% |
| 17,254 | YOUNG | 4,996 | 1,600 | 3,395 | 1 | 1,795 D | 32.0% | 68.0% | 32.0% | 68.0% |
| 4,393 | ZAPATA | 1,147 | 135 | 1,009 | 3 | 874 D | 11.8% | 88.0% | 11.8% | 88.2% |
| 12,696 | ZAVALA | 2,385 | 598 | 1,784 | 3 | 1,186 D | 25.1% | 74.8% | 25.1% | 74.9% |
| 9,579,677 | TOTAL | 2,626,811 | 958,566 | 1,663,185 | 5,060 | 704,619 D | 36.5% | 63.3% | 36.6% | 63.4% |

# TEXAS

## PRESIDENT 1960

| 1960 Census Population | County | Total Vote | Republican | Democratic | Other | Rep.-Dem. Plurality | Percentage | | | |
|---|---|---|---|---|---|---|---|---|---|---|
| | | | | | | | Total Vote | | Major Vote | |
| | | | | | | | Rep. | Dem. | Rep. | Dem. |
| 28,162 | ANDERSON | 6,982 | 3,642 | 3,296 | 44 | 346 R | 52.2% | 47.2% | 52.5% | 47.5% |
| 13,450 | ANDREWS | 3,409 | 1,550 | 1,821 | 38 | 271 D | 45.5% | 53.4% | 46.0% | 54.0% |
| 39,814 | ANGELINA | 12,510 | 5,169 | 7,046 | 295 | 1,877 D | 41.3% | 56.3% | 42.3% | 57.7% |
| 7,006 | ARANSAS | 1,748 | 792 | 948 | 8 | 156 D | 45.3% | 54.2% | 45.5% | 54.5% |
| 6,110 | ARCHER | 2,023 | 680 | 1,341 | 2 | 661 D | 33.6% | 66.3% | 33.6% | 66.4% |
| 1,966 | ARMSTRONG | 860 | 488 | 365 | 7 | 123 R | 56.7% | 42.4% | 57.2% | 42.8% |
| 18,828 | ATASCOSA | 4,361 | 1,812 | 2,544 | 5 | 732 D | 41.6% | 58.3% | 41.6% | 58.4% |
| 13,777 | AUSTIN | 3,738 | 1,978 | 1,725 | 35 | 253 R | 52.9% | 46.1% | 53.4% | 46.6% |
| 9,090 | BAILEY | 2,271 | 1,180 | 1,064 | 27 | 116 R | 52.0% | 46.9% | 52.6% | 47.4% |
| 3,892 | BANDERA | 1,484 | 942 | 539 | 3 | 403 R | 63.5% | 36.3% | 63.6% | 36.4% |
| 16,925 | BASTROP | 4,080 | 1,208 | 2,866 | 6 | 1,658 D | 29.6% | 70.2% | 29.7% | 70.3% |
| 5,893 | BAYLOR | 1,913 | 713 | 1,199 | 1 | 486 D | 37.3% | 62.7% | 37.3% | 62.7% |
| 23,755 | BEE | 4,787 | 2,220 | 2,557 | 10 | 337 D | 46.4% | 53.4% | 46.5% | 53.5% |
| 94,097 | BELL | 15,288 | 4,606 | 10,651 | 31 | 6,045 D | 30.1% | 69.7% | 30.2% | 69.8% |
| 687,151 | BEXAR | 140,245 | 63,934 | 75,373 | 938 | 11,439 D | 45.6% | 53.7% | 45.9% | 54.1% |
| 3,657 | BLANCO | 1,394 | 557 | 830 | 7 | 273 D | 40.0% | 59.5% | 40.2% | 59.8% |
| 1,076 | BORDEN | 411 | 166 | 230 | 15 | 64 D | 40.4% | 56.0% | 41.9% | 58.1% |
| 10,809 | BOSQUE | 3,525 | 1,653 | 1,852 | 20 | 199 D | 46.9% | 52.5% | 47.2% | 52.8% |
| 59,971 | BOWIE | 15,193 | 5,927 | 9,198 | 68 | 3,271 D | 39.0% | 60.5% | 39.2% | 60.8% |
| 76,204 | BRAZORIA | 21,705 | 10,880 | 10,561 | 264 | 319 R | 50.1% | 48.7% | 50.7% | 49.3% |
| 44,895 | BRAZOS | 10,477 | 4,553 | 5,907 | 17 | 1,354 D | 43.5% | 56.4% | 43.5% | 56.5% |
| 6,434 | BREWSTER | 1,457 | 736 | 716 | 5 | 20 R | 50.5% | 49.1% | 50.7% | 49.3% |
| 3,577 | BRISCOE | 1,112 | 533 | 570 | 9 | 37 D | 47.9% | 51.3% | 48.3% | 51.7% |
| 8,609 | BROOKS | 2,511 | 567 | 1,934 | 10 | 1,367 D | 22.6% | 77.0% | 22.7% | 77.3% |
| 24,728 | BROWN | 7,278 | 3,512 | 3,720 | 46 | 208 D | 48.3% | 51.1% | 48.6% | 51.4% |
| 11,177 | BURLESON | 3,143 | 672 | 2,466 | 5 | 1,794 D | 21.4% | 78.5% | 21.4% | 78.6% |
| 9,265 | BURNET | 2,976 | 1,189 | 1,770 | 17 | 581 D | 40.0% | 59.5% | 40.2% | 59.8% |
| 17,222 | CALDWELL | 4,222 | 1,482 | 2,729 | 11 | 1,247 D | 35.1% | 64.6% | 35.2% | 64.8% |
| 16,592 | CALHOUN | 3,594 | 1,599 | 1,961 | 34 | 362 D | 44.5% | 54.6% | 44.9% | 55.1% |
| 7,929 | CALLAHAN | 2,838 | 1,261 | 1,559 | 18 | 298 D | 44.4% | 54.9% | 44.7% | 55.3% |
| 151,098 | CAMERON | 22,640 | 10,190 | 12,416 | 34 | 2,226 D | 45.0% | 54.8% | 45.1% | 54.9% |
| 7,849 | CAMP | 2,200 | 873 | 1,307 | 20 | 434 D | 39.7% | 59.4% | 40.0% | 60.0% |
| 7,781 | CARSON | 2,407 | 1,387 | 1,009 | 11 | 378 R | 57.6% | 41.9% | 57.9% | 42.1% |
| 23,496 | CASS | 5,290 | 2,322 | 2,934 | 34 | 612 D | 43.9% | 55.5% | 44.2% | 55.8% |
| 8,923 | CASTRO | 2,382 | 810 | 1,544 | 28 | 734 D | 34.0% | 64.8% | 34.4% | 65.6% |
| 10,379 | CHAMBERS | 2,816 | 1,260 | 1,524 | 32 | 264 D | 44.7% | 54.1% | 45.3% | 54.7% |
| 33,120 | CHEROKEE | 7,882 | 3,233 | 4,544 | 105 | 1,311 D | 41.0% | 57.7% | 41.6% | 58.4% |
| 8,421 | CHILDRESS | 2,767 | 1,571 | 1,189 | 7 | 382 R | 56.8% | 43.0% | 56.9% | 43.1% |
| 8,351 | CLAY | 2,718 | 1,019 | 1,692 | 7 | 673 D | 37.5% | 62.3% | 37.6% | 62.4% |
| 6,417 | COCHRAN | 1,674 | 646 | 1,028 | | 382 D | 38.6% | 61.4% | 38.6% | 61.4% |
| 3,589 | COKE | 1,388 | 575 | 799 | 14 | 224 D | 41.4% | 57.6% | 41.8% | 58.2% |
| 12,458 | COLEMAN | 3,977 | 2,127 | 1,835 | 15 | 292 R | 53.5% | 46.1% | 53.7% | 46.3% |
| 41,247 | COLLIN | 9,158 | 3,865 | 5,229 | 64 | 1,364 D | 42.2% | 57.1% | 42.5% | 57.5% |
| 6,276 | COLLINGSWORTH | 1,782 | 1,084 | 691 | 7 | 393 R | 60.8% | 38.8% | 61.1% | 38.9% |
| 18,463 | COLORADO | 4,247 | 1,909 | 2,299 | 39 | 390 D | 44.9% | 54.1% | 45.4% | 54.6% |
| 19,844 | COMAL | 4,941 | 3,082 | 1,845 | 14 | 1,237 R | 62.4% | 37.3% | 62.6% | 37.4% |
| 11,865 | COMANCHE | 3,830 | 1,828 | 1,979 | 23 | 151 D | 47.7% | 51.7% | 48.0% | 52.0% |
| 3,672 | CONCHO | 1,242 | 522 | 718 | 2 | 196 D | 42.0% | 57.8% | 42.1% | 57.9% |
| 22,560 | COOKE | 7,176 | 3,983 | 3,168 | 25 | 815 R | 55.5% | 44.1% | 55.7% | 44.3% |
| 23,961 | CORYELL | 4,192 | 1,477 | 2,700 | 15 | 1,223 D | 35.2% | 64.4% | 35.4% | 64.6% |
| 4,207 | COTTLE | 1,361 | 370 | 986 | 5 | 616 D | 27.2% | 72.4% | 27.3% | 72.7% |
| 4,699 | CRANE | 1,568 | 678 | 848 | 42 | 170 D | 43.2% | 54.1% | 44.4% | 55.6% |
| 4,209 | CROCKETT | 1,156 | 635 | 517 | 4 | 118 R | 54.9% | 44.7% | 55.1% | 44.9% |
| 10,347 | CROSBY | 2,683 | 889 | 1,783 | 11 | 894 D | 33.1% | 66.5% | 33.3% | 66.7% |
| 2,794 | CULBERSON | 650 | 300 | 343 | 7 | 43 D | 46.2% | 52.8% | 46.7% | 53.3% |
| 6,302 | DALLAM | 1,808 | 961 | 835 | 12 | 126 R | 53.2% | 46.2% | 53.5% | 46.5% |
| 951,527 | DALLAS | 240,299 | 149,369 | 88,876 | 2,054 | 60,493 R | 62.2% | 37.0% | 62.7% | 37.3% |
| 19,185 | DAWSON | 4,246 | 2,161 | 2,063 | 22 | 98 R | 50.9% | 48.6% | 51.2% | 48.8% |
| 13,187 | DEAF SMITH | 3,349 | 2,024 | 1,299 | 26 | 725 R | 60.4% | 38.8% | 60.9% | 39.1% |
| 5,860 | DELTA | 1,832 | 460 | 1,360 | 12 | 900 D | 25.1% | 74.2% | 25.3% | 74.7% |

# TEXAS

## PRESIDENT 1960

| 1960 Census Population | County | Total Vote | Republican | Democratic | Other | Rep.-Dem. Plurality | Percentage Total Vote Rep. | Dem. | Major Vote Rep. | Dem. |
|---|---|---|---|---|---|---|---|---|---|---|
| 47,432 | DENTON | 11,119 | 5,724 | 5,366 | 29 | 358 R | 51.5% | 48.3% | 51.6% | 48.4% |
| 20,683 | DE WITT | 5,029 | 2,763 | 2,253 | 13 | 510 R | 54.9% | 44.8% | 55.1% | 44.9% |
| 4,963 | DICKENS | 1,607 | 521 | 1,075 | 11 | 554 D | 32.4% | 66.9% | 32.6% | 67.4% |
| 10,095 | DIMMIT | 1,537 | 648 | 886 | 3 | 238 D | 42.2% | 57.6% | 42.2% | 57.8% |
| 4,449 | DONLEY | 1,720 | 951 | 764 | 5 | 187 R | 55.3% | 44.4% | 55.5% | 44.5% |
| 13,398 | DUVAL | 4,614 | 809 | 3,803 | 2 | 2,994 D | 17.5% | 82.4% | 17.5% | 82.5% |
| 19,526 | EASTLAND | 6,449 | 3,359 | 3,058 | 32 | 301 R | 52.1% | 47.4% | 52.3% | 47.7% |
| 90,995 | ECTOR | 20,672 | 11,145 | 8,996 | 531 | 2,149 R | 53.9% | 43.5% | 55.3% | 44.7% |
| 2,317 | EDWARDS | 639 | 463 | 168 | 8 | 295 R | 72.5% | 26.3% | 73.4% | 26.6% |
| 43,395 | ELLIS | 9,543 | 3,666 | 5,841 | 36 | 2,175 D | 38.4% | 61.2% | 38.6% | 61.4% |
| 314,070 | EL PASO | 47,677 | 21,551 | 26,027 | 99 | 4,476 D | 45.2% | 54.6% | 45.3% | 54.7% |
| 16,236 | ERATH | 5,216 | 2,696 | 2,490 | 30 | 206 R | 51.7% | 47.7% | 52.0% | 48.0% |
| 21,263 | FALLS | 4,965 | 1,559 | 3,399 | 7 | 1,840 D | 31.4% | 68.5% | 31.4% | 68.6% |
| 23,880 | FANNIN | 6,138 | 1,844 | 4,282 | 12 | 2,438 D | 30.0% | 69.8% | 30.1% | 69.9% |
| 20,384 | FAYETTE | 5,699 | 2,213 | 3,462 | 24 | 1,249 D | 38.8% | 60.7% | 39.0% | 61.0% |
| 7,865 | FISHER | 2,655 | 679 | 1,966 | 10 | 1,287 D | 25.6% | 74.0% | 25.7% | 74.3% |
| 12,369 | FLOYD | 3,042 | 1,580 | 1,437 | 25 | 143 R | 51.9% | 47.2% | 52.4% | 47.6% |
| 3,125 | FOARD | 995 | 270 | 723 | 2 | 453 D | 27.1% | 72.7% | 27.2% | 72.8% |
| 40,527 | FORT BEND | 7,711 | 3,301 | 4,339 | 71 | 1,038 D | 42.8% | 56.3% | 43.2% | 56.8% |
| 5,101 | FRANKLIN | 1,774 | 620 | 1,148 | 6 | 528 D | 34.9% | 64.7% | 35.1% | 64.9% |
| 12,525 | FREESTONE | 3,650 | 1,629 | 1,997 | 24 | 368 D | 44.6% | 54.7% | 44.9% | 55.1% |
| 10,112 | FRIO | 1,790 | 713 | 1,068 | 9 | 355 D | 39.8% | 59.7% | 40.0% | 60.0% |
| 12,267 | GAINES | 3,041 | 1,520 | 1,498 | 23 | 22 R | 50.0% | 49.3% | 50.4% | 49.6% |
| 140,364 | GALVESTON | 40,828 | 16,373 | 23,940 | 515 | 7,567 D | 40.1% | 58.6% | 40.6% | 59.4% |
| 6,611 | GARZA | 1,576 | 737 | 829 | 10 | 92 D | 46.8% | 52.6% | 47.1% | 52.9% |
| 10,048 | GILLESPIE | 3,507 | 2,687 | 816 | 4 | 1,871 R | 76.6% | 23.3% | 76.7% | 23.3% |
| 1,118 | GLASSCOCK | 366 | 152 | 207 | 7 | 55 D | 41.5% | 56.6% | 42.3% | 57.7% |
| 5,429 | GOLIAD | 1,455 | 741 | 711 | 3 | 30 R | 50.9% | 48.9% | 51.0% | 49.0% |
| 17,845 | GONZALES | 4,291 | 1,554 | 2,730 | 7 | 1,176 D | 36.2% | 63.6% | 36.3% | 63.7% |
| 31,535 | GRAY | 9,013 | 6,197 | 2,802 | 14 | 3,395 R | 68.8% | 31.1% | 68.9% | 31.1% |
| 73,043 | GRAYSON | 17,231 | 7,312 | 9,866 | 53 | 2,554 D | 42.4% | 57.3% | 42.6% | 57.4% |
| 69,436 | GREGG | 18,737 | 10,679 | 7,765 | 293 | 2,914 R | 57.0% | 41.4% | 57.9% | 42.1% |
| 12,709 | GRIMES | 2,778 | 1,053 | 1,713 | 12 | 660 D | 37.9% | 61.7% | 38.1% | 61.9% |
| 29,017 | GUADALUPE | 6,787 | 3,657 | 3,116 | 14 | 541 R | 53.9% | 45.9% | 54.0% | 46.0% |
| 36,798 | HALE | 8,532 | 4,784 | 3,695 | 53 | 1,089 R | 56.1% | 43.3% | 56.4% | 43.6% |
| 7,322 | HALL | 2,133 | 939 | 1,192 | 2 | 253 D | 44.0% | 55.9% | 44.1% | 55.9% |
| 8,488 | HAMILTON | 2,737 | 1,592 | 1,136 | 9 | 456 R | 58.2% | 41.5% | 58.4% | 41.6% |
| 6,208 | HANSFORD | 1,839 | 1,322 | 512 | 5 | 810 R | 71.9% | 27.8% | 72.1% | 27.9% |
| 8,275 | HARDEMAN | 2,655 | 1,472 | 1,182 | 1 | 290 R | 55.4% | 44.5% | 55.5% | 44.5% |
| 24,629 | HARDIN | 6,451 | 2,115 | 4,315 | 21 | 2,200 D | 32.8% | 66.9% | 32.9% | 67.1% |
| 1,243,158 | HARRIS | 325,399 | 168,170 | 148,275 | 8,954 | 19,895 R | 51.7% | 45.6% | 53.1% | 46.9% |
| 45,594 | HARRISON | 9,945 | 4,613 | 5,108 | 224 | 495 D | 46.4% | 51.4% | 47.5% | 52.5% |
| 2,171 | HARTLEY | 815 | 413 | 397 | 5 | 16 R | 50.7% | 48.7% | 51.0% | 49.0% |
| 11,174 | HASKELL | 3,650 | 866 | 2,776 | 8 | 1,910 D | 23.7% | 76.1% | 23.8% | 76.2% |
| 19,934 | HAYS | 4,529 | 1,606 | 2,916 | 7 | 1,310 D | 35.5% | 64.4% | 35.5% | 64.5% |
| 3,185 | HEMPHILL | 1,181 | 847 | 333 | 1 | 514 R | 71.7% | 28.2% | 71.8% | 28.2% |
| 21,786 | HENDERSON | 5,970 | 2,521 | 3,411 | 38 | 890 D | 42.2% | 57.1% | 42.5% | 57.5% |
| 180,904 | HIDALGO | 32,406 | 13,628 | 18,663 | 115 | 5,035 D | 42.1% | 57.6% | 42.2% | 57.8% |
| 23,650 | HILL | 6,593 | 2,226 | 4,340 | 27 | 2,114 D | 33.8% | 65.8% | 33.9% | 66.1% |
| 22,340 | HOCKLEY | 5,358 | 2,159 | 3,169 | 30 | 1,010 D | 40.3% | 59.1% | 40.5% | 59.5% |
| 5,443 | HOOD | 2,187 | 943 | 1,238 | 6 | 295 D | 43.1% | 56.6% | 43.2% | 56.8% |
| 18,594 | HOPKINS | 5,357 | 2,117 | 3,228 | 12 | 1,111 D | 39.5% | 60.3% | 39.6% | 60.4% |
| 19,376 | HOUSTON | 4,383 | 1,591 | 2,703 | 89 | 1,112 D | 36.3% | 61.7% | 37.1% | 62.9% |
| 40,139 | HOWARD | 8,335 | 3,403 | 4,844 | 88 | 1,441 D | 40.8% | 58.1% | 41.3% | 58.7% |
| 3,343 | HUDSPETH | 685 | 267 | 409 | 9 | 142 D | 39.0% | 59.7% | 39.5% | 60.5% |
| 39,399 | HUNT | 8,242 | 4,084 | 4,116 | 42 | 32 D | 49.6% | 49.9% | 49.8% | 50.2% |
| 34,419 | HUTCHINSON | 9,747 | 6,432 | 3,295 | 20 | 3,137 R | 66.0% | 33.8% | 66.1% | 33.9% |
| 1,183 | IRION | 487 | 238 | 246 | 3 | 8 D | 48.9% | 50.5% | 49.2% | 50.8% |
| 7,418 | JACK | 2,432 | 1,342 | 1,079 | 11 | 263 R | 55.2% | 44.4% | 55.4% | 44.6% |
| 14,040 | JACKSON | 3,972 | 1,670 | 2,268 | 34 | 598 D | 42.0% | 57.1% | 42.4% | 57.6% |

# TEXAS

## PRESIDENT 1960

| 1960 Census Population | County | Total Vote | Republican | Democratic | Other | Rep.-Dem. Plurality | Percentage | | | |
|---|---|---|---|---|---|---|---|---|---|---|
| | | | | | | | Total Vote | | Major Vote | |
| | | | | | | | Rep. | Dem. | Rep. | Dem. |
| 22,100 | JASPER | 5,123 | 2,102 | 3,004 | 17 | 902 D | 41.0% | 58.6% | 41.2% | 58.8% |
| 1,582 | JEFF DAVIS | 381 | 182 | 195 | 4 | 13 D | 47.8% | 51.2% | 48.3% | 51.7% |
| 245,659 | JEFFERSON | 70,331 | 29,395 | 40,533 | 403 | 11,138 D | 41.8% | 57.6% | 42.0% | 58.0% |
| 5,022 | JIM HOGG | 1,479 | 224 | 1,255 | | 1,031 D | 15.1% | 84.9% | 15.1% | 84.9% |
| 34,548 | JIM WELLS | 8,112 | 2,773 | 5,330 | 9 | 2,557 D | 34.2% | 65.7% | 34.2% | 65.8% |
| 34,720 | JOHNSON | 8,431 | 4,510 | 3,844 | 77 | 666 R | 53.5% | 45.6% | 54.0% | 46.0% |
| 19,299 | JONES | 4,986 | 2,196 | 2,772 | 18 | 576 D | 44.0% | 55.6% | 44.2% | 55.8% |
| 14,995 | KARNES | 4,085 | 1,526 | 2,556 | 3 | 1,030 D | 37.4% | 62.6% | 37.4% | 62.6% |
| 29,931 | KAUFMAN | 5,768 | 2,717 | 3,008 | 43 | 291 D | 47.1% | 52.1% | 47.5% | 52.5% |
| 5,889 | KENDALL | 2,100 | 1,544 | 549 | 7 | 995 R | 73.5% | 26.1% | 73.8% | 26.2% |
| 884 | KENEDY | 152 | 74 | 78 | | 4 D | 48.7% | 51.3% | 48.7% | 51.3% |
| 1,727 | KENT | 698 | 205 | 491 | 2 | 286 D | 29.4% | 70.3% | 29.5% | 70.5% |
| 16,800 | KERR | 4,596 | 3,252 | 1,323 | 21 | 1,929 R | 70.8% | 28.8% | 71.1% | 28.9% |
| 3,943 | KIMBLE | 1,253 | 699 | 550 | 4 | 149 R | 55.8% | 43.9% | 56.0% | 44.0% |
| 640 | KING | 173 | 39 | 133 | 1 | 94 D | 22.5% | 76.9% | 22.7% | 77.3% |
| 2,452 | KINNEY | 569 | 211 | 358 | | 147 D | 37.1% | 62.9% | 37.1% | 62.9% |
| 30,052 | KLEBERG | 5,866 | 2,092 | 3,773 | 1 | 1,681 D | 35.7% | 64.3% | 35.7% | 64.3% |
| 7,857 | KNOX | 2,098 | 729 | 1,365 | 4 | 636 D | 34.7% | 65.1% | 34.8% | 65.2% |
| 34,234 | LAMAR | 9,076 | 3,964 | 5,084 | 28 | 1,120 D | 43.7% | 56.0% | 43.8% | 56.2% |
| 21,896 | LAMB | 6,007 | 2,764 | 3,089 | 154 | 325 D | 46.0% | 51.4% | 47.2% | 52.8% |
| 9,418 | LAMPASAS | 2,609 | 1,222 | 1,372 | 15 | 150 D | 46.8% | 52.6% | 47.1% | 52.9% |
| 5,972 | LA SALLE | 1,046 | 326 | 718 | 2 | 392 D | 31.2% | 68.6% | 31.2% | 68.8% |
| 20,174 | LAVACA | 5,522 | 1,507 | 4,002 | 13 | 2,495 D | 27.3% | 72.5% | 27.4% | 72.6% |
| 8,949 | LEE | 2,451 | 1,048 | 1,369 | 34 | 321 D | 42.8% | 55.9% | 43.4% | 56.6% |
| 9,951 | LEON | 2,684 | 868 | 1,803 | 13 | 935 D | 32.3% | 67.2% | 32.5% | 67.5% |
| 31,595 | LIBERTY | 7,345 | 3,361 | 3,902 | 82 | 541 D | 45.8% | 53.1% | 46.3% | 53.7% |
| 20,413 | LIMESTONE | 5,511 | 2,023 | 3,472 | 16 | 1,449 D | 36.7% | 63.0% | 36.8% | 63.2% |
| 3,406 | LIPSCOMB | 1,209 | 939 | 267 | 3 | 672 R | 77.7% | 22.1% | 77.9% | 22.1% |
| 7,846 | LIVE OAK | 1,822 | 1,048 | 770 | 4 | 278 R | 57.5% | 42.3% | 57.6% | 42.4% |
| 5,240 | LLANO | 1,840 | 704 | 1,131 | 5 | 427 D | 38.3% | 61.5% | 38.4% | 61.6% |
| 226 | LOVING | 95 | 42 | 46 | 7 | 4 D | 44.2% | 48.4% | 47.7% | 52.3% |
| 156,271 | LUBBOCK | 35,607 | 20,065 | 15,340 | 202 | 4,725 R | 56.4% | 43.1% | 56.7% | 43.3% |
| 10,914 | LYNN | 2,843 | 953 | 1,872 | 18 | 919 D | 33.5% | 65.8% | 33.7% | 66.3% |
| 8,815 | MCCULLOCH | 2,748 | 1,165 | 1,579 | 4 | 414 D | 42.4% | 57.5% | 42.5% | 57.5% |
| 150,091 | MCLENNAN | 35,156 | 14,926 | 20,100 | 130 | 5,174 D | 42.5% | 57.2% | 42.6% | 57.4% |
| 1,116 | MCMULLEN | 481 | 241 | 240 | | 1 R | 50.1% | 49.9% | 50.1% | 49.9% |
| 6,749 | MADISON | 1,552 | 607 | 909 | 36 | 302 D | 39.1% | 58.6% | 40.0% | 60.0% |
| 8,049 | MARION | 1,691 | 742 | 904 | 45 | 162 D | 43.9% | 53.5% | 45.1% | 54.9% |
| 5,068 | MARTIN | 1,203 | 350 | 831 | 22 | 481 D | 29.1% | 69.1% | 29.6% | 70.4% |
| 3,780 | MASON | 1,417 | 833 | 575 | 9 | 258 R | 58.8% | 40.6% | 59.2% | 40.8% |
| 25,744 | MATAGORDA | 5,998 | 2,975 | 2,971 | 52 | 4 R | 49.6% | 49.5% | 50.0% | 50.0% |
| 14,508 | MAVERICK | 2,139 | 639 | 1,498 | 2 | 859 D | 29.9% | 70.0% | 29.9% | 70.1% |
| 18,904 | MEDINA | 4,368 | 2,028 | 2,325 | 15 | 297 D | 46.4% | 53.2% | 46.6% | 53.4% |
| 2,964 | MENARD | 1,099 | 608 | 491 | | 117 R | 55.3% | 44.7% | 55.3% | 44.7% |
| 67,717 | MIDLAND | 17,645 | 11,343 | 5,842 | 460 | 5,501 R | 64.3% | 33.1% | 66.0% | 34.0% |
| 22,263 | MILAM | 5,556 | 1,898 | 3,640 | 18 | 1,742 D | 34.2% | 65.5% | 34.3% | 65.7% |
| 4,467 | MILLS | 1,887 | 1,012 | 869 | 6 | 143 R | 53.6% | 46.1% | 53.8% | 46.2% |
| 11,255 | MITCHELL | 3,350 | 1,208 | 2,131 | 11 | 923 D | 36.1% | 63.6% | 36.2% | 63.8% |
| 14,893 | MONTAGUE | 4,465 | 2,101 | 2,346 | 18 | 245 D | 47.1% | 52.5% | 47.2% | 52.8% |
| 26,839 | MONTGOMERY | 6,937 | 3,309 | 3,510 | 118 | 201 D | 47.7% | 50.6% | 48.5% | 51.5% |
| 14,773 | MOORE | 4,025 | 2,463 | 1,547 | 15 | 916 R | 61.2% | 38.4% | 61.4% | 38.6% |
| 12,576 | MORRIS | 3,544 | 1,569 | 1,952 | 23 | 383 D | 44.3% | 55.1% | 44.6% | 55.4% |
| 2,870 | MOTLEY | 932 | 480 | 439 | 13 | 41 R | 51.5% | 47.1% | 52.2% | 47.8% |
| 28,046 | NACOGDOCHES | 6,732 | 3,042 | 3,522 | 168 | 480 D | 45.2% | 52.3% | 46.3% | 53.7% |
| 34,423 | NAVARRO | 8,901 | 3,361 | 5,540 | | 2,179 D | 37.8% | 62.2% | 37.8% | 62.2% |
| 10,372 | NEWTON | 2,590 | 756 | 1,815 | 19 | 1,059 D | 29.2% | 70.1% | 29.4% | 70.6% |
| 18,963 | NOLAN | 5,675 | 2,421 | 3,247 | 7 | 826 D | 42.7% | 57.2% | 42.7% | 57.3% |
| 221,573 | NUECES | 48,368 | 18,907 | 29,361 | 100 | 10,454 D | 39.1% | 60.7% | 39.2% | 60.8% |
| 9,380 | OCHILTREE | 2,394 | 1,870 | 521 | 3 | 1,349 R | 78.1% | 21.8% | 78.2% | 21.8% |
| 1,928 | OLDHAM | 643 | 313 | 326 | 4 | 13 D | 48.7% | 50.7% | 49.0% | 51.0% |

# TEXAS

## PRESIDENT 1960

| 1960 Census Population | County | Total Vote | Republican | Democratic | Other | Rep.-Dem. Plurality | Percentage Total Vote Rep. | Dem. | Major Vote Rep. | Dem. |
|---|---|---|---|---|---|---|---|---|---|---|
| 60,357 | ORANGE | 14,637 | 5,483 | 9,078 | 76 | 3,595 D | 37.5% | 62.0% | 37.7% | 62.3% |
| 20,516 | PALO PINTO | 5,742 | 2,695 | 3,022 | 25 | 327 D | 46.9% | 52.6% | 47.1% | 52.9% |
| 16,870 | PANOLA | 4,518 | 2,264 | 2,187 | 67 | 77 R | 50.1% | 48.4% | 50.9% | 49.1% |
| 22,880 | PARKER | 7,148 | 3,467 | 3,629 | 52 | 162 D | 48.5% | 50.8% | 48.9% | 51.1% |
| 9,583 | PARMER | 2,786 | 1,674 | 1,090 | 22 | 584 R | 60.1% | 39.1% | 60.6% | 39.4% |
| 11,957 | PECOS | 3,167 | 1,412 | 1,724 | 31 | 312 D | 44.6% | 54.4% | 45.0% | 55.0% |
| 13,861 | POLK | 3,360 | 1,268 | 2,037 | 55 | 769 D | 37.7% | 60.6% | 38.4% | 61.6% |
| 115,580 | POTTER | 23,229 | 14,202 | 8,989 | 38 | 5,213 R | 61.1% | 38.7% | 61.2% | 38.8% |
| 5,460 | PRESIDIO | 1,248 | 376 | 866 | 6 | 490 D | 30.1% | 69.4% | 30.3% | 69.7% |
| 2,993 | RAINS | 1,081 | 401 | 680 | | 279 D | 37.1% | 62.9% | 37.1% | 62.9% |
| 33,913 | RANDALL | 10,269 | 6,958 | 3,282 | 29 | 3,676 R | 67.8% | 32.0% | 67.9% | 32.1% |
| 3,782 | REAGAN | 1,131 | 489 | 621 | 21 | 132 D | 43.2% | 54.9% | 44.1% | 55.9% |
| 2,079 | REAL | 653 | 377 | 273 | 3 | 104 R | 57.7% | 41.8% | 58.0% | 42.0% |
| 15,682 | RED RIVER | 4,389 | 1,527 | 2,850 | 12 | 1,323 D | 34.8% | 64.9% | 34.9% | 65.1% |
| 17,644 | REEVES | 3,822 | 1,549 | 2,235 | 38 | 686 D | 40.5% | 58.5% | 40.9% | 59.1% |
| 10,975 | REFUGIO | 2,842 | 1,062 | 1,777 | 3 | 715 D | 37.4% | 62.5% | 37.4% | 62.6% |
| 1,075 | ROBERTS | 445 | 339 | 104 | 2 | 235 R | 76.2% | 23.4% | 76.5% | 23.5% |
| 16,157 | ROBERTSON | 3,616 | 935 | 2,669 | 12 | 1,734 D | 25.9% | 73.8% | 25.9% | 74.1% |
| 5,878 | ROCKWALL | 1,583 | 652 | 917 | 14 | 265 D | 41.2% | 57.9% | 41.6% | 58.4% |
| 15,016 | RUNNELS | 4,075 | 2,128 | 1,938 | 9 | 190 R | 52.2% | 47.6% | 52.3% | 47.7% |
| 36,421 | RUSK | 10,840 | 6,001 | 4,390 | 449 | 1,611 R | 55.4% | 40.5% | 57.8% | 42.2% |
| 7,302 | SABINE | 1,843 | 619 | 1,208 | 16 | 589 D | 33.6% | 65.5% | 33.9% | 66.1% |
| 7,722 | SAN AUGUSTINE | 1,961 | 638 | 1,269 | 54 | 631 D | 32.5% | 64.7% | 33.5% | 66.5% |
| 6,153 | SAN JACINTO | 1,570 | 448 | 1,115 | 7 | 667 D | 28.5% | 71.0% | 28.7% | 71.3% |
| 45,021 | SAN PATRICIO | 8,391 | 3,129 | 5,246 | 16 | 2,117 D | 37.3% | 62.5% | 37.4% | 62.6% |
| 6,381 | SAN SABA | 2,108 | 849 | 1,251 | 8 | 402 D | 40.3% | 59.3% | 40.4% | 59.6% |
| 2,791 | SCHLEICHER | 809 | 455 | 351 | 3 | 104 R | 56.2% | 43.4% | 56.5% | 43.5% |
| 20,369 | SCURRY | 5,290 | 2,235 | 3,020 | 35 | 785 D | 42.2% | 57.1% | 42.5% | 57.5% |
| 3,990 | SHACKELFORD | 1,397 | 684 | 713 | | 29 D | 49.0% | 51.0% | 49.0% | 51.0% |
| 20,479 | SHELBY | 4,993 | 1,679 | 3,266 | 48 | 1,587 D | 33.6% | 65.4% | 34.0% | 66.0% |
| 2,605 | SHERMAN | 993 | 686 | 305 | 2 | 381 R | 69.1% | 30.7% | 69.2% | 30.8% |
| 86,350 | SMITH | 20,821 | 12,042 | 8,494 | 285 | 3,548 R | 57.8% | 40.8% | 58.6% | 41.4% |
| 2,577 | SOMERVELL | 800 | 441 | 345 | 14 | 96 R | 55.1% | 43.1% | 56.1% | 43.9% |
| 17,137 | STARR | 4,333 | 280 | 4,051 | 2 | 3,771 D | 6.5% | 93.5% | 6.5% | 93.5% |
| 8,885 | STEPHENS | 3,029 | 1,664 | 1,357 | 8 | 307 R | 54.9% | 44.8% | 55.1% | 44.9% |
| 1,177 | STERLING | 375 | 182 | 193 | | 11 D | 48.5% | 51.5% | 48.5% | 51.5% |
| 3,017 | STONEWALL | 1,173 | 306 | 864 | 3 | 558 D | 26.1% | 73.7% | 26.2% | 73.8% |
| 3,738 | SUTTON | 911 | 437 | 474 | | 37 D | 48.0% | 52.0% | 48.0% | 52.0% |
| 10,607 | SWISHER | 3,103 | 1,310 | 1,777 | 16 | 467 D | 42.2% | 57.3% | 42.4% | 57.6% |
| 538,495 | TARRANT | 132,986 | 72,813 | 59,385 | 788 | 13,428 R | 54.8% | 44.7% | 55.1% | 44.9% |
| 101,078 | TAYLOR | 21,650 | 12,258 | 9,347 | 45 | 2,911 R | 56.6% | 43.2% | 56.7% | 43.3% |
| 2,600 | TERRELL | 646 | 291 | 352 | 3 | 61 D | 45.0% | 54.5% | 45.3% | 54.7% |
| 16,286 | TERRY | 4,162 | 1,908 | 2,237 | 17 | 329 D | 45.8% | 53.7% | 46.0% | 54.0% |
| 2,767 | THROCKMORTON | 1,134 | 442 | 689 | 3 | 247 D | 39.0% | 60.8% | 39.1% | 60.9% |
| 16,785 | TITUS | 4,946 | 2,216 | 2,701 | 29 | 485 D | 44.8% | 54.6% | 45.1% | 54.9% |
| 64,630 | TOM GREEN | 15,246 | 8,176 | 7,031 | 39 | 1,145 R | 53.6% | 46.1% | 53.8% | 46.2% |
| 212,136 | TRAVIS | 49,264 | 22,107 | 27,022 | 135 | 4,915 D | 44.9% | 54.9% | 45.0% | 55.0% |
| 7,539 | TRINITY | 2,264 | 707 | 1,521 | 36 | 814 D | 31.2% | 67.2% | 31.7% | 68.3% |
| 10,666 | TYLER | 2,656 | 1,401 | 1,242 | 13 | 159 R | 52.7% | 46.8% | 53.0% | 47.0% |
| 19,793 | UPSHUR | 5,554 | 2,262 | 3,248 | 44 | 986 D | 40.7% | 58.5% | 41.1% | 58.9% |
| 6,239 | UPTON | 1,760 | 798 | 930 | 32 | 132 D | 45.3% | 52.8% | 46.2% | 53.8% |
| 16,814 | UVALDE | 3,552 | 2,214 | 1,324 | 14 | 890 R | 62.3% | 37.3% | 62.6% | 37.4% |
| 24,461 | VAL VERDE | 3,603 | 1,551 | 2,049 | 3 | 498 D | 43.0% | 56.9% | 43.1% | 56.9% |
| 19,091 | VAN ZANDT | 4,967 | 2,120 | 2,825 | 22 | 705 D | 42.7% | 56.9% | 42.9% | 57.1% |
| 46,475 | VICTORIA | 10,397 | 4,591 | 5,779 | 27 | 1,188 D | 44.2% | 55.6% | 44.3% | 55.7% |
| 21,475 | WALKER | 3,604 | 1,750 | 1,832 | 22 | 82 D | 48.6% | 50.8% | 48.9% | 51.1% |
| 12,071 | WALLER | 2,267 | 1,115 | 1,101 | 51 | 14 R | 49.2% | 48.6% | 50.3% | 49.7% |
| 14,917 | WARD | 3,852 | 1,763 | 2,018 | 71 | 255 D | 45.8% | 52.4% | 46.6% | 53.4% |
| 19,145 | WASHINGTON | 4,489 | 2,613 | 1,864 | 12 | 749 R | 58.2% | 41.5% | 58.4% | 41.6% |
| 64,791 | WEBB | 11,865 | 1,802 | 10,059 | 4 | 8,257 D | 15.2% | 84.8% | 15.2% | 84.8% |

# TEXAS

## PRESIDENT 1960

| 1960 Census Population | County | Total Vote | Republican | Democratic | Other | Rep.-Dem. Plurality | Percentage | | | |
|---|---|---|---|---|---|---|---|---|---|---|
| | | | | | | | Total Vote | | Major Vote | |
| | | | | | | | Rep. | Dem. | Rep. | Dem. |
| 38,152 | WHARTON | 8,458 | 3,387 | 5,004 | 67 | 1,617 D | 40.0% | 59.2% | 40.4% | 59.6% |
| 7,947 | WHEELER | 2,444 | 1,428 | 1,011 | 5 | 417 R | 58.4% | 41.4% | 58.5% | 41.5% |
| 123,528 | WICHITA | 27,213 | 12,587 | 14,587 | 39 | 2,000 D | 46.3% | 53.6% | 46.3% | 53.7% |
| 17,748 | WILBARGER | 5,129 | 2,796 | 2,319 | 14 | 477 R | 54.5% | 45.2% | 54.7% | 45.3% |
| 20,084 | WILLACY | 3,487 | 1,367 | 2,109 | 11 | 742 D | 39.2% | 60.5% | 39.3% | 60.7% |
| 35,044 | WILLIAMSON | 7,870 | 2,429 | 5,410 | 31 | 2,981 D | 30.9% | 68.7% | 31.0% | 69.0% |
| 13,267 | WILSON | 4,157 | 1,248 | 2,905 | 4 | 1,657 D | 30.0% | 69.9% | 30.1% | 69.9% |
| 13,652 | WINKLER | 3,253 | 1,562 | 1,642 | 49 | 80 D | 48.0% | 50.5% | 48.8% | 51.2% |
| 17,012 | WISE | 5,051 | 2,562 | 2,470 | 19 | 92 R | 50.7% | 48.9% | 50.9% | 49.1% |
| 17,653 | WOOD | 5,112 | 2,400 | 2,633 | 79 | 233 D | 46.9% | 51.5% | 47.7% | 52.3% |
| 8,032 | YOAKUM | 2,215 | 1,207 | 994 | 14 | 213 R | 54.5% | 44.9% | 54.8% | 45.2% |
| 17,254 | YOUNG | 4,509 | 2,067 | 2,419 | 23 | 352 D | 45.8% | 53.6% | 46.1% | 53.9% |
| 4,393 | ZAPATA | 935 | 260 | 675 | | 415 D | 27.8% | 72.2% | 27.8% | 72.2% |
| 12,696 | ZAVALA | 1,475 | 761 | 706 | 8 | 55 R | 51.6% | 47.9% | 51.9% | 48.1% |
| 9,579,677 | TOTAL | 2,311,084 | 1,121,310 | 1,167,567 | 22,207 | 46,257 D | 48.5% | 50.5% | 49.0% | 51.0% |

950

# TEXAS

## ELECTION NOTES

**2004**     Other vote was 38,787 Libertarian (Michael Badnarik); 9,159 write-in (Ralph Nader); 1,636 write-in (Michael Peroutka); 1,014 write-in (David Cobb); 219 write-in (Andrew J. Falk); 126 write-in (John Joseph Kennedy); 111 write-in (Walter F. Brown); 92 write-in (Deborah Elaine Allen).

**2000**     Other vote was 23,160 Libertarian (Browne); 12,394 Independent (Buchanan); 567 write-in (Phillips); 74 write-in (Wright); 63 write-in (McReynolds).

**1996**     Other vote was 20,256 Libertarian (Browne); 7,472 Taxpayers (Phillips); 4,810 write-in (Nader); 4,422 Natural Law (Hagelin); 297 write-in (Hollis).

**1992**     Other vote was 19,699 Marrou (Libertarian); 505 Gritz (write-in); 359 Phillips (write-in); 301 Fulani (write-in); 217 Hagelin (write-in); 169 LaRouche (write-in); 78 Brisben (write-in); 23 scattered write-in.

**1988**     Other vote was 30,355 Paul (Libertarian); 7,208 Fulani (New Alliance); 110 Warren (write-in); 62 Kanoyer (write-in); 98 scattered write-in.

**1984**     Other vote was 14,613 LaRouche (Independent); 126 Hall (write-in); 87 Johnson (write-in); 41 Serrette (write-in).

**1980**     Other vote was 111,613 Anderson (Independent); 37,643 Clark (Libertarian); 453 Commoner (write-in); 49 Hall (write-in); 15 Perkins (write-in); 11 Griswold (write-in).  There is a discrepancy of one vote in the total of the other vote column.

**1976**     Other vote was 20,118 McCarthy (Independent); 11,442 Anderson (American); 1,723 Camejo (Socialist Workers); 189 MacBride (write-in); 41 Maddox (write-in); 2,752 scattered write-in. Early unamended canvass gave the Republican vote in Lamar county as 4,437 and the Republican state-wide total vote as 1,953,294.

**1972**     Other vote was 8,664 Jenness (Socialist Workers); 6,039 Schmitz (write-in); 3,393 scattered write-in. Although the addition of the various county totals for the Democratic and other vote columns shows a small discrepancy, the official state certified totals are used here.

**1968**     Wallace on the ballot as American. Other vote was scattered write-in. Early unamended canvass gave the scattered write-in vote as 489.

**1964**     Other vote was Lightburn (Constitution).

**1960**     Other vote was 18,162 Sullivan (Constitutional); 3,870 Decker (Prohibition); 175 scattered write-in.

# UTAH

## POPULAR VOTE FOR PRESIDENT 1920 TO 2004

| Year | Total Vote | Republican Vote | Candidate | Democratic Vote | Candidate | Other Vote | Plurality | Percentage Total Vote Rep. | Dem. | Major Vote Rep. | Dem. |
|---|---|---|---|---|---|---|---|---|---|---|---|
| 2004 | 927,844 | 663,742 | Bush, George W. | 241,199 | Kerry, John | 22,903 | 422,543 R | 71.5% | 26.0% | 73.3% | 26.7% |
| 2000 ** | 770,754 | 515,096 | Bush, George W. | 203,053 | Gore, Al | 52,605 | 312,043 R | 66.8% | 26.3% | 71.7% | 28.3% |
| 1996 ** | 665,629 | 361,911 | Dole, Bob | 221,633 | Clinton, Bill | 82,085 | 140,278 R | 54.4% | 33.3% | 62.0% | 38.0% |
| 1992 ** | 743,999 | 322,632 | Bush, George | 183,429 | Clinton, Bill | 237,938 | 119,232 R | 43.4% | 24.7% | 63.8% | 36.2% |
| 1988 | 647,008 | 428,442 | Bush, George | 207,343 | Dukakis, Michael S. | 11,223 | 221,099 R | 66.2% | 32.0% | 67.4% | 32.6% |
| 1984 | 629,656 | 469,105 | Reagan, Ronald | 155,369 | Mondale, Walter F. | 5,182 | 313,736 R | 74.5% | 24.7% | 75.1% | 24.9% |
| 1980 ** | 604,222 | 439,687 | Reagan, Ronald | 124,266 | Carter, Jimmy | 40,269 | 315,421 R | 72.8% | 20.6% | 78.0% | 22.0% |
| 1976 | 541,198 | 337,908 | Ford, Gerald R. | 182,110 | Carter, Jimmy | 21,180 | 155,798 R | 62.4% | 33.6% | 65.0% | 35.0% |
| 1972 | 478,476 | 323,643 | Nixon, Richard M. | 126,284 | McGovern, George S. | 28,549 | 197,359 R | 67.6% | 26.4% | 71.9% | 28.1% |
| 1968 | 422,568 | 238,728 | Nixon, Richard M. | 156,665 | Humphrey, Hubert H. | 27,175 | 82,063 R | 56.5% | 37.1% | 60.4% | 39.6% |
| 1964 | 401,413 | 181,785 | Goldwater, Barry M. | 219,628 | Johnson, Lyndon B. | | 37,843 D | 45.3% | 54.7% | 45.3% | 54.7% |
| 1960 | 374,709 | 205,361 | Nixon, Richard M. | 169,248 | Kennedy, John F. | 100 | 36,113 R | 54.8% | 45.2% | 54.8% | 45.2% |
| 1956 | 333,995 | 215,631 | Eisenhower, Dwight D. | 118,364 | Stevenson, Adlai E. | | 97,267 R | 64.6% | 35.4% | 64.6% | 35.4% |
| 1952 | 329,554 | 194,190 | Eisenhower, Dwight D. | 135,364 | Stevenson, Adlai E. | | 58,826 R | 58.9% | 41.1% | 58.9% | 41.1% |
| 1948 | 276,306 | 124,402 | Dewey, Thomas E. | 149,151 | Truman, Harry S. | 2,753 | 24,749 D | 45.0% | 54.0% | 45.5% | 54.5% |
| 1944 | 248,319 | 97,891 | Dewey, Thomas E. | 150,088 | Roosevelt, Franklin D. | 340 | 52,197 D | 39.4% | 60.4% | 39.5% | 60.5% |
| 1940 | 247,819 | 93,151 | Willkie, Wendell | 154,277 | Roosevelt, Franklin D. | 391 | 61,126 D | 37.6% | 62.3% | 37.6% | 62.4% |
| 1936 | 216,679 | 64,555 | Landon, Alfred M. | 150,248 | Roosevelt, Franklin D. | 1,876 | 85,693 D | 29.8% | 69.3% | 30.1% | 69.9% |
| 1932 | 206,578 | 84,795 | Hoover, Herbert C. | 116,750 | Roosevelt, Franklin D. | 5,033 | 31,955 D | 41.0% | 56.5% | 42.1% | 57.9% |
| 1928 | 176,603 | 94,618 | Hoover, Herbert C. | 80,985 | Smith, Alfred E. | 1,000 | 13,633 R | 53.6% | 45.9% | 53.9% | 46.1% |
| 1924 ** | 156,990 | 77,327 | Coolidge, Calvin | 47,001 | Davis, John W. | 32,662 | 30,326 R | 49.3% | 29.9% | 62.2% | 37.8% |
| 1920 | 145,828 | 81,555 | Harding, Warren G. | 56,639 | Cox, James M. | 7,634 | 24,916 R | 55.9% | 38.8% | 59.0% | 41.0% |

In 2000 the other vote column includes 35,850 votes cast for Green (Nader). In 1996 the other vote column includes 66,461 votes cast for Perot. In 1992 the other vote column includes 203,400 votes cast for Perot who came in second. In 1980 the other column includes 30,284 votes for Independent (Anderson). In 1924 the other vote was Progressive.

## ELECTORAL COLLEGE VOTE 1920 TO 2004

| Year | Total | Republican | Democratic | Other |
|---|---|---|---|---|
| 2004 | 5 | 5 | | |
| 2000 | 5 | 5 | | |
| 1996 | 5 | 5 | | |
| 1992 | 5 | 5 | | |
| 1988 | 5 | 5 | | |
| 1984 | 5 | 5 | | |
| 1980 | 4 | 4 | | |
| 1976 | 4 | 4 | | |
| 1972 | 4 | 4 | | |
| 1968 | 4 | 4 | | |
| 1964 | 4 | | 4 | |
| 1960 | 4 | 4 | | |
| 1956 | 4 | 4 | | |
| 1952 | 4 | 4 | | |
| 1948 | 4 | | 4 | |
| 1944 | 4 | | 4 | |
| 1940 | 4 | | 4 | |
| 1936 | 4 | | 4 | |
| 1932 | 4 | | 4 | |
| 1928 | 4 | 4 | | |
| 1924 | 4 | 4 | | |
| 1920 | 4 | 4 | | |

# UTAH

BOX ELDER

CACHE

RICH

WEBER

MORGAN

DAVIS

SUMMIT

DAGGETT

SALT LAKE

TOOELE

WASATCH

DUCHESNE

UINTAH

UTAH

JUAB

CARBON

SANPETE

MILLARD

EMERY

GRAND

SEVIER

BEAVER

PIUTE

WAYNE

IRON

GARFIELD

SAN JUAN

WASHINGTON

KANE

# UTAH

## PRESIDENT 2004

| 2000 Census Population | County | Total Vote | Republican | Democratic | Other | Rep.-Dem. Plurality | Percentage | | | |
|---|---|---|---|---|---|---|---|---|---|---|
| | | | | | | | Total Vote | | Major Vote | |
| | | | | | | | Rep. | Dem. | Rep. | Dem. |
| 6,005 | BEAVER | 2,544 | 2,023 | 493 | 28 | 1,530 R | 79.5% | 19.4% | 80.4% | 19.6% |
| 42,745 | BOX ELDER | 18,368 | 15,751 | 2,244 | 373 | 13,507 R | 85.8% | 12.2% | 87.5% | 12.5% |
| 91,391 | CACHE | 39,731 | 32,486 | 6,375 | 870 | 26,111 R | 81.8% | 16.0% | 83.6% | 16.4% |
| 20,422 | CARBON | 8,508 | 4,950 | 3,415 | 143 | 1,535 R | 58.2% | 40.1% | 59.2% | 40.8% |
| 921 | DAGGETT | 499 | 380 | 108 | 11 | 272 R | 76.2% | 21.6% | 77.9% | 22.1% |
| 238,994 | DAVIS | 109,268 | 86,187 | 20,893 | 2,188 | 65,294 R | 78.9% | 19.1% | 80.5% | 19.5% |
| 14,371 | DUCHESNE | 5,556 | 4,742 | 738 | 76 | 4,004 R | 85.3% | 13.3% | 86.5% | 13.5% |
| 10,860 | EMERY | 4,678 | 3,781 | 831 | 66 | 2,950 R | 80.8% | 17.8% | 82.0% | 18.0% |
| 4,735 | GARFIELD | 2,162 | 1,848 | 264 | 50 | 1,584 R | 85.5% | 12.2% | 87.5% | 12.5% |
| 8,485 | GRAND | 4,165 | 2,130 | 1,858 | 177 | 272 R | 51.1% | 44.6% | 53.4% | 46.6% |
| 33,779 | IRON | 15,446 | 12,815 | 2,267 | 364 | 10,548 R | 83.0% | 14.7% | 85.0% | 15.0% |
| 8,238 | JUAB | 3,417 | 2,681 | 605 | 131 | 2,076 R | 78.5% | 17.7% | 81.6% | 18.4% |
| 6,046 | KANE | 3,051 | 2,414 | 576 | 61 | 1,838 R | 79.1% | 18.9% | 80.7% | 19.3% |
| 12,405 | MILLARD | 4,877 | 4,084 | 626 | 167 | 3,458 R | 83.7% | 12.8% | 86.7% | 13.3% |
| 7,129 | MORGAN | 3,841 | 3,301 | 472 | 68 | 2,829 R | 85.9% | 12.3% | 87.5% | 12.5% |
| 1,435 | PIUTE | 773 | 646 | 123 | 4 | 523 R | 83.6% | 15.9% | 84.0% | 16.0% |
| 1,961 | RICH | 1,037 | 922 | 109 | 6 | 813 R | 88.9% | 10.5% | 89.4% | 10.6% |
| 898,387 | SALT LAKE | 362,138 | 215,728 | 135,949 | 10,461 | 79,779 R | 59.6% | 37.5% | 61.3% | 38.7% |
| 14,413 | SAN JUAN | 4,950 | 2,971 | 1,906 | 73 | 1,065 R | 60.0% | 38.5% | 60.9% | 39.1% |
| 22,763 | SANPETE | 8,507 | 7,004 | 1,189 | 314 | 5,815 R | 82.3% | 14.0% | 85.5% | 14.5% |
| 18,842 | SEVIER | 7,641 | 6,597 | 920 | 124 | 5,677 R | 86.3% | 12.0% | 87.8% | 12.2% |
| 29,736 | SUMMIT | 15,312 | 7,936 | 6,977 | 399 | 959 R | 51.8% | 45.6% | 53.2% | 46.8% |
| 40,735 | TOOELE | 16,664 | 12,181 | 4,130 | 353 | 8,051 R | 73.1% | 24.8% | 74.7% | 25.3% |
| 25,224 | UINTAH | 9,957 | 8,518 | 1,266 | 173 | 7,252 R | 85.5% | 12.7% | 87.1% | 12.9% |
| 368,536 | UTAH | 149,173 | 128,269 | 17,357 | 3,547 | 110,912 R | 86.0% | 11.6% | 88.1% | 11.9% |
| 15,215 | WASATCH | 7,512 | 5,503 | 1,854 | 155 | 3,649 R | 73.3% | 24.7% | 74.8% | 25.2% |
| 90,354 | WASHINGTON | 44,018 | 35,633 | 7,513 | 872 | 28,120 R | 81.0% | 17.1% | 82.6% | 17.4% |
| 2,509 | WAYNE | 1,360 | 1,062 | 279 | 19 | 783 R | 78.1% | 20.5% | 79.2% | 20.8% |
| 196,533 | WEBER | 72,691 | 51,199 | 19,862 | 1,630 | 31,337 R | 70.4% | 27.3% | 72.0% | 28.0% |
| 2,233,169 | TOTAL | 927,844 | 663,742 | 241,199 | 22,903 | 422,543 R | 71.5% | 26.0% | 73.3% | 26.7% |

# UTAH

## PRESIDENT 2000

| 2000 Census Population | County | Total Vote | Republican | Democratic | Green (Nader) | Other | Rep.-Dem. Plurality | Percentage of Total Vote | | |
|---|---|---|---|---|---|---|---|---|---|---|
| | | | | | | | | Rep. | Dem. | Green |
| 6,005 | BEAVER | 2,252 | 1,653 | 541 | 38 | 20 | 1,112 R | 73.4% | 24.0% | 1.7% |
| 42,745 | BOX ELDER | 15,483 | 12,288 | 2,555 | 326 | 314 | 9,733 R | 79.4% | 16.5% | 2.1% |
| 91,391 | CACHE | 33,142 | 25,920 | 5,170 | 1,511 | 541 | 20,750 R | 78.2% | 15.6% | 4.6% |
| 20,422 | CARBON | 7,384 | 3,758 | 3,298 | 213 | 115 | 460 R | 50.9% | 44.7% | 2.9% |
| 921 | DAGGETT | 435 | 317 | 104 | 9 | 5 | 213 R | 72.9% | 23.9% | 2.1% |
| 238,994 | DAVIS | 87,855 | 64,375 | 18,845 | 2,891 | 1,744 | 45,530 R | 73.3% | 21.5% | 3.3% |
| 14,371 | DUCHESNE | 4,546 | 3,622 | 779 | 76 | 69 | 2,843 R | 79.7% | 17.1% | 1.7% |
| 10,860 | EMERY | 4,398 | 3,243 | 958 | 81 | 116 | 2,285 R | 73.7% | 21.8% | 1.8% |
| 4,735 | GARFIELD | 1,968 | 1,719 | 178 | 43 | 28 | 1,541 R | 87.3% | 9.0% | 2.2% |
| 8,485 | GRAND | 3,614 | 1,822 | 1,158 | 540 | 94 | 664 R | 50.4% | 32.0% | 14.9% |
| 33,779 | IRON | 12,594 | 10,106 | 1,789 | 341 | 358 | 8,317 R | 80.2% | 14.2% | 2.7% |
| 8,238 | JUAB | 2,785 | 2,023 | 619 | 60 | 83 | 1,404 R | 72.6% | 22.2% | 2.2% |
| 6,046 | KANE | 2,802 | 2,254 | 387 | 102 | 59 | 1,867 R | 80.4% | 13.8% | 3.6% |
| 12,405 | MILLARD | 4,775 | 3,850 | 696 | 73 | 156 | 3,154 R | 80.6% | 14.6% | 1.5% |
| 7,129 | MORGAN | 3,171 | 2,464 | 553 | 80 | 74 | 1,911 R | 77.7% | 17.4% | 2.5% |
| 1,435 | PIUTE | 781 | 626 | 133 | 10 | 12 | 493 R | 80.2% | 17.0% | 1.3% |
| 1,961 | RICH | 903 | 736 | 152 | 10 | 5 | 584 R | 81.5% | 16.8% | 1.1% |
| 898,387 | SALT LAKE | 307,258 | 171,585 | 107,576 | 21,252 | 6,845 | 64,009 R | 55.8% | 35.0% | 6.9% |
| 14,413 | SAN JUAN | 4,744 | 2,721 | 1,838 | 107 | 78 | 883 R | 57.4% | 38.7% | 2.3% |
| 22,763 | SANPETE | 7,430 | 5,781 | 1,211 | 153 | 285 | 4,570 R | 77.8% | 16.3% | 2.1% |
| 18,842 | SEVIER | 7,077 | 5,763 | 1,046 | 125 | 143 | 4,717 R | 81.4% | 14.8% | 1.8% |
| 29,736 | SUMMIT | 12,121 | 6,168 | 4,601 | 1,156 | 196 | 1,567 R | 50.9% | 38.0% | 9.5% |
| 40,735 | TOOELE | 12,480 | 7,807 | 4,001 | 387 | 285 | 3,806 R | 62.6% | 32.1% | 3.1% |
| 25,224 | UINTAH | 8,397 | 6,733 | 1,387 | 132 | 145 | 5,346 R | 80.2% | 16.5% | 1.6% |
| 368,536 | UTAH | 120,256 | 98,255 | 16,445 | 2,732 | 2,824 | 81,810 R | 81.7% | 13.7% | 2.3% |
| 15,215 | WASATCH | 5,675 | 3,819 | 1,476 | 259 | 121 | 2,343 R | 67.3% | 26.0% | 4.6% |
| 90,354 | WASHINGTON | 32,461 | 25,481 | 5,465 | 714 | 801 | 20,016 R | 78.5% | 16.8% | 2.2% |
| 2,509 | WAYNE | 1,225 | 953 | 202 | 58 | 12 | 751 R | 77.8% | 16.5% | 4.7% |
| 196,533 | WEBER | 62,742 | 39,254 | 19,890 | 2,371 | 1,227 | 19,364 R | 62.6% | 31.7% | 3.8% |
| 2,233,169 | TOTAL | 770,754 | 515,096 | 203,053 | 35,850 | 16,755 | 312,043 R | 66.8% | 26.3% | 4.7% |

# UTAH

## PRESIDENT 1996

| 1995 Census Pop. Est. | County | Total Vote | Republican | Democratic | Reform (Perot) | Other | Rep.-Dem. Plurality | Percentage of Total Vote | | |
|---|---|---|---|---|---|---|---|---|---|---|
| | | | | | | | | Rep. | Dem. | Reform |
| 5,383 | BEAVER | 2,094 | 1,164 | 687 | 217 | 26 | 477 R | 55.6% | 32.8% | 10.4% |
| 39,590 | BOX ELDER | 13,365 | 8,373 | 3,170 | 1,578 | 244 | 5,203 R | 62.6% | 23.7% | 11.8% |
| 77,298 | CACHE | 26,394 | 16,832 | 6,595 | 2,399 | 568 | 10,237 R | 63.8% | 25.0% | 9.1% |
| 20,653 | CARBON | 7,582 | 2,343 | 4,172 | 952 | 115 | 1,829 D | 30.9% | 55.0% | 12.6% |
| 770 | DAGGETT | 426 | 237 | 131 | 55 | 3 | 106 R | 55.6% | 30.8% | 12.9% |
| 215,382 | DAVIS | 70,981 | 42,768 | 19,301 | 7,495 | 1,417 | 23,467 R | 60.3% | 27.2% | 10.6% |
| 13,799 | DUCHESNE | 4,159 | 2,648 | 892 | 566 | 53 | 1,756 R | 63.7% | 21.4% | 13.6% |
| 10,638 | EMERY | 4,122 | 2,033 | 1,371 | 663 | 55 | 662 R | 49.3% | 33.3% | 16.1% |
| 4,092 | GARFIELD | 1,847 | 1,330 | 283 | 222 | 12 | 1,047 R | 72.0% | 15.3% | 12.0% |
| 7,824 | GRAND | 3,251 | 1,384 | 1,199 | 432 | 236 | 185 R | 42.6% | 36.9% | 13.3% |
| 25,921 | IRON | 9,391 | 6,550 | 1,887 | 716 | 238 | 4,663 R | 69.7% | 20.1% | 7.6% |
| 6,675 | JUAB | 2,626 | 1,290 | 928 | 353 | 55 | 362 R | 49.1% | 35.3% | 13.4% |
| 6,000 | KANE | 2,316 | 1,682 | 304 | 290 | 40 | 1,378 R | 72.6% | 13.1% | 12.5% |
| 12,157 | MILLARD | 4,236 | 2,681 | 945 | 505 | 105 | 1,736 R | 63.3% | 22.3% | 11.9% |
| 6,592 | MORGAN | 2,908 | 1,659 | 859 | 337 | 53 | 800 R | 57.0% | 29.5% | 11.6% |
| 1,419 | PIUTE | 717 | 475 | 176 | 59 | 7 | 299 R | 66.2% | 24.5% | 8.2% |
| 1,831 | RICH | 796 | 523 | 179 | 88 | 6 | 344 R | 65.7% | 22.5% | 11.1% |
| 808,383 | SALT LAKE | 281,177 | 127,951 | 117,951 | 27,620 | 7,655 | 10,000 R | 45.5% | 41.9% | 9.8% |
| 13,917 | SAN JUAN | 4,165 | 2,139 | 1,675 | 271 | 80 | 464 R | 51.4% | 40.2% | 6.5% |
| 19,340 | SANPETE | 6,177 | 3,631 | 1,568 | 801 | 177 | 2,063 R | 58.8% | 25.4% | 13.0% |
| 17,166 | SEVIER | 6,127 | 4,031 | 1,327 | 670 | 99 | 2,704 R | 65.8% | 21.7% | 10.9% |
| 23,292 | SUMMIT | 9,319 | 3,867 | 4,177 | 971 | 304 | 310 D | 41.5% | 44.8% | 10.4% |
| 29,263 | TOOELE | 9,312 | 3,881 | 3,992 | 1,244 | 195 | 111 D | 41.7% | 42.9% | 13.4% |
| 25,004 | UINTAH | 7,464 | 4,743 | 1,714 | 899 | 108 | 3,029 R | 63.5% | 23.0% | 12.0% |
| 298,789 | UTAH | 98,031 | 69,653 | 18,291 | 8,106 | 1,981 | 51,362 R | 71.1% | 18.7% | 8.3% |
| 11,757 | WASATCH | 4,242 | 2,222 | 1,374 | 558 | 88 | 848 R | 52.4% | 32.4% | 13.2% |
| 70,610 | WASHINGTON | 25,020 | 17,637 | 4,816 | 2,069 | 498 | 12,821 R | 70.5% | 19.2% | 8.3% |
| 2,305 | WAYNE | 1,142 | 741 | 265 | 121 | 15 | 476 R | 64.9% | 23.2% | 10.6% |
| 175,558 | WEBER | 56,242 | 27,443 | 21,404 | 6,204 | 1,191 | 6,039 R | 48.8% | 38.1% | 11.0% |
| 1,951,408 | TOTAL | 665,629 | 361,911 | 221,633 | 66,461 | 15,624 | 140,278 R | 54.4% | 33.3% | 10.0% |

# UTAH

## PRESIDENT 1992

| 1990 Census Population | County | Total Vote | Republican | Democratic | Perot | Other | Plurality | Percentage Total Vote | | |
|---|---|---|---|---|---|---|---|---|---|---|
| | | | | | | | | Rep. | Dem. | Perot |
| 4,765 | BEAVER | 2,111 | 1,040 | 668 | 330 | 73 | 372 R | 49.3% | 31.6% | 15.6% |
| 36,485 | BOX ELDER | 15,555 | 7,712 | 2,186 | 4,507 | 1,150 | 3,205 R | 49.6% | 14.1% | 29.0% |
| 70,183 | CACHE | 30,725 | 15,971 | 4,973 | 8,032 | 1,749 | 7,939 R | 52.0% | 16.2% | 26.1% |
| 20,228 | CARBON | 8,817 | 2,038 | 4,480 | 2,002 | 297 | 2,442 D | 23.1% | 50.8% | 22.7% |
| 690 | DAGGETT | 442 | 172 | 122 | 117 | 31 | 50 R | 38.9% | 27.6% | 26.5% |
| 187,941 | DAVIS | 81,350 | 39,087 | 14,924 | 24,105 | 3,234 | 14,982 R | 48.0% | 18.3% | 29.6% |
| 12,645 | DUCHESNE | 4,565 | 1,983 | 772 | 1,229 | 581 | 754 R | 43.4% | 16.9% | 26.9% |
| 10,332 | EMERY | 4,510 | 1,643 | 1,349 | 1,138 | 380 | 294 R | 36.4% | 29.9% | 25.2% |
| 3,980 | GARFIELD | 1,983 | 1,235 | 309 | 355 | 84 | 880 R | 62.3% | 15.6% | 17.9% |
| 6,620 | GRAND | 3,342 | 1,100 | 1,160 | 991 | 91 | 60 D | 32.9% | 34.7% | 29.7% |
| 20,789 | IRON | 9,378 | 5,616 | 1,537 | 1,693 | 532 | 3,923 R | 59.9% | 16.4% | 18.1% |
| 5,817 | JUAB | 2,895 | 1,237 | 823 | 616 | 219 | 414 R | 42.7% | 28.4% | 21.3% |
| 5,169 | KANE | 2,172 | 1,241 | 295 | 534 | 102 | 707 R | 57.1% | 13.6% | 24.6% |
| 11,333 | MILLARD | 4,770 | 2,496 | 742 | 1,064 | 468 | 1,432 R | 52.3% | 15.6% | 22.3% |
| 5,528 | MORGAN | 2,940 | 1,339 | 520 | 851 | 230 | 488 R | 45.5% | 17.7% | 28.9% |
| 1,277 | PIUTE | 753 | 429 | 169 | 146 | 9 | 260 R | 57.0% | 22.4% | 19.4% |
| 1,725 | RICH | 876 | 525 | 154 | 187 | 10 | 338 R | 59.9% | 17.6% | 21.3% |
| 725,956 | SALT LAKE | 318,661 | 117,247 | 100,082 | 91,968 | 9,364 | 17,165 R | 36.8% | 31.4% | 28.9% |
| 12,621 | SAN JUAN | 4,335 | 2,004 | 1,639 | 576 | 116 | 365 R | 46.2% | 37.8% | 13.3% |
| 16,259 | SANPETE | 6,685 | 2,995 | 1,302 | 1,742 | 646 | 1,253 R | 44.8% | 19.5% | 26.1% |
| 15,431 | SEVIER | 6,258 | 3,160 | 1,039 | 1,671 | 388 | 1,489 R | 50.5% | 16.6% | 26.7% |
| 15,518 | SUMMIT | 9,399 | 3,133 | 3,013 | 3,060 | 193 | 73 R | 33.3% | 32.1% | 32.6% |
| 26,601 | TOOELE | 10,271 | 3,676 | 3,270 | 3,011 | 314 | 406 R | 35.8% | 31.8% | 29.3% |
| 22,211 | UINTAH | 7,774 | 3,505 | 1,374 | 2,250 | 645 | 1,255 R | 45.1% | 17.7% | 28.9% |
| 263,590 | UTAH | 108,178 | 61,398 | 14,090 | 24,558 | 8,132 | 36,840 R | 56.8% | 13.0% | 22.7% |
| 10,089 | WASATCH | 4,336 | 1,822 | 1,042 | 1,234 | 238 | 588 R | 42.0% | 24.0% | 28.5% |
| 48,560 | WASHINGTON | 21,476 | 11,310 | 3,364 | 4,623 | 2,179 | 6,687 R | 52.7% | 15.7% | 21.5% |
| 2,177 | WAYNE | 1,225 | 706 | 236 | 251 | 32 | 455 R | 57.6% | 19.3% | 20.5% |
| 158,330 | WEBER | 68,216 | 26,812 | 17,795 | 20,559 | 3,050 | 6,253 R | 39.3% | 26.1% | 30.1% |
| 1,722,850 | TOTAL | 743,999 | 322,632 | 183,429 | 203,400 | 34,538 | 119,232 R | 43.4% | 24.7% | 27.3% |

# UTAH

## PRESIDENT 1988

| 1980 Census Population | County | Total Vote | Republican | Democratic | Other | Rep.-Dem. Plurality | Percentage | | | |
| --- | --- | --- | --- | --- | --- | --- | --- | --- | --- | --- |
| | | | | | | | Total Vote | | Major Vote | |
| | | | | | | | Rep. | Dem. | Rep. | Dem. |
| 4,378 | BEAVER | 2,112 | 1,286 | 816 | 10 | 470 R | 60.9% | 38.6% | 61.2% | 38.8% |
| 33,222 | BOX ELDER | 15,461 | 12,585 | 2,736 | 140 | 9,849 R | 81.4% | 17.7% | 82.1% | 17.9% |
| 57,176 | CACHE | 27,963 | 21,766 | 5,871 | 326 | 15,895 R | 77.8% | 21.0% | 78.8% | 21.2% |
| 22,179 | CARBON | 8,603 | 3,019 | 5,521 | 63 | 2,502 D | 35.1% | 64.2% | 35.4% | 64.6% |
| 769 | DAGGETT | 412 | 272 | 132 | 8 | 140 R | 66.0% | 32.0% | 67.3% | 32.7% |
| 146,540 | DAVIS | 68,384 | 50,469 | 16,868 | 1,047 | 33,601 R | 73.8% | 24.7% | 74.9% | 25.1% |
| 12,565 | DUCHESNE | 4,403 | 3,118 | 1,227 | 58 | 1,891 R | 70.8% | 27.9% | 71.8% | 28.2% |
| 11,451 | EMERY | 4,144 | 2,322 | 1,788 | 34 | 534 R | 56.0% | 43.1% | 56.5% | 43.5% |
| 3,673 | GARFIELD | 1,855 | 1,470 | 370 | 15 | 1,100 R | 79.2% | 19.9% | 79.9% | 20.1% |
| 8,241 | GRAND | 3,248 | 1,895 | 1,287 | 66 | 608 R | 58.3% | 39.6% | 59.6% | 40.4% |
| 17,349 | IRON | 7,868 | 6,038 | 1,736 | 94 | 4,302 R | 76.7% | 22.1% | 77.7% | 22.3% |
| 5,530 | JUAB | 2,523 | 1,505 | 974 | 44 | 531 R | 59.7% | 38.6% | 60.7% | 39.3% |
| 4,024 | KANE | 2,255 | 1,788 | 398 | 69 | 1,390 R | 79.3% | 17.6% | 81.8% | 18.2% |
| 8,970 | MILLARD | 4,710 | 3,515 | 1,124 | 71 | 2,391 R | 74.6% | 23.9% | 75.8% | 24.2% |
| 4,917 | MORGAN | 2,567 | 1,889 | 647 | 31 | 1,242 R | 73.6% | 25.2% | 74.5% | 25.5% |
| 1,329 | PIUTE | 687 | 476 | 206 | 5 | 270 R | 69.3% | 30.0% | 69.8% | 30.2% |
| 2,100 | RICH | 860 | 621 | 234 | 5 | 387 R | 72.2% | 27.2% | 72.6% | 27.4% |
| 619,066 | SALT LAKE | 276,903 | 163,557 | 107,453 | 5,893 | 56,104 R | 59.1% | 38.8% | 60.4% | 39.6% |
| 12,253 | SAN JUAN | 3,837 | 2,377 | 1,407 | 53 | 970 R | 61.9% | 36.7% | 62.8% | 37.2% |
| 14,620 | SANPETE | 6,517 | 4,579 | 1,822 | 116 | 2,757 R | 70.3% | 28.0% | 71.5% | 28.5% |
| 14,727 | SEVIER | 6,221 | 4,747 | 1,403 | 71 | 3,344 R | 76.3% | 22.6% | 77.2% | 22.8% |
| 10,198 | SUMMIT | 6,503 | 3,881 | 2,536 | 86 | 1,345 R | 59.7% | 39.0% | 60.5% | 39.5% |
| 26,033 | TOOELE | 9,804 | 5,539 | 4,166 | 99 | 1,373 R | 56.5% | 42.5% | 57.1% | 42.9% |
| 20,506 | UINTAH | 7,218 | 5,341 | 1,799 | 78 | 3,542 R | 74.0% | 24.9% | 74.8% | 25.2% |
| 218,106 | UTAH | 88,227 | 68,134 | 18,533 | 1,560 | 49,601 R | 77.2% | 21.0% | 78.6% | 21.4% |
| 8,523 | WASATCH | 3,997 | 2,487 | 1,451 | 59 | 1,036 R | 62.2% | 36.3% | 63.2% | 36.8% |
| 26,065 | WASHINGTON | 16,565 | 13,306 | 3,054 | 205 | 10,252 R | 80.3% | 18.4% | 81.3% | 18.7% |
| 1,911 | WAYNE | 1,143 | 784 | 353 | 6 | 431 R | 68.6% | 30.9% | 69.0% | 31.0% |
| 144,616 | WEBER | 62,018 | 39,676 | 21,431 | 911 | 18,245 R | 64.0% | 34.6% | 64.9% | 35.1% |
| 1,461,037 | TOTAL | 647,008 | 428,442 | 207,343 | 11,223 | 221,099 R | 66.2% | 32.0% | 67.4% | 32.6% |

958

# UTAH

## PRESIDENT 1984

| 1980 Census Population | County | Total Vote | Republican | Democratic | Other | Rep.-Dem. Plurality | | Percentage | | | |
|---|---|---|---|---|---|---|---|---|---|---|---|
| | | | | | | | | Total Vote | | Major Vote | |
| | | | | | | | | Rep. | Dem. | Rep. | Dem. |
| 4,378 | BEAVER | 2,231 | 1,516 | 708 | 7 | 808 | R | 68.0% | 31.7% | 68.2% | 31.8% |
| 33,222 | BOX ELDER | 15,283 | 13,243 | 1,983 | 57 | 11,260 | R | 86.7% | 13.0% | 87.0% | 13.0% |
| 57,176 | CACHE | 26,442 | 22,127 | 4,123 | 192 | 18,004 | R | 83.7% | 15.6% | 84.3% | 15.7% |
| 22,179 | CARBON | 8,818 | 4,393 | 4,357 | 68 | 36 | R | 49.8% | 49.4% | 50.2% | 49.8% |
| 769 | DAGGETT | 525 | 296 | 227 | 2 | 69 | R | 56.4% | 43.2% | 56.6% | 43.4% |
| 146,540 | DAVIS | 62,102 | 49,863 | 11,727 | 512 | 38,136 | R | 80.3% | 18.9% | 81.0% | 19.0% |
| 12,565 | DUCHESNE | 5,210 | 4,437 | 746 | 27 | 3,691 | R | 85.2% | 14.3% | 85.6% | 14.4% |
| 11,451 | EMERY | 4,439 | 3,081 | 1,326 | 32 | 1,755 | R | 69.4% | 29.9% | 69.9% | 30.1% |
| 3,673 | GARFIELD | 1,935 | 1,609 | 315 | 11 | 1,294 | R | 83.2% | 16.3% | 83.6% | 16.4% |
| 8,241 | GRAND | 3,367 | 2,463 | 876 | 28 | 1,587 | R | 73.2% | 26.0% | 73.8% | 26.2% |
| 17,349 | IRON | 8,251 | 6,856 | 1,342 | 53 | 5,514 | R | 83.1% | 16.3% | 83.6% | 16.4% |
| 5,530 | JUAB | 2,829 | 1,902 | 917 | 10 | 985 | R | 67.2% | 32.4% | 67.5% | 32.5% |
| 4,024 | KANE | 2,009 | 1,710 | 294 | 5 | 1,416 | R | 85.1% | 14.6% | 85.3% | 14.7% |
| 8,970 | MILLARD | 5,563 | 4,345 | 1,192 | 26 | 3,153 | R | 78.1% | 21.4% | 78.5% | 21.5% |
| 4,917 | MORGAN | 2,430 | 1,934 | 481 | 15 | 1,453 | R | 79.6% | 19.8% | 80.1% | 19.9% |
| 1,329 | PIUTE | 757 | 606 | 151 | | 455 | R | 80.1% | 19.9% | 80.1% | 19.9% |
| 2,100 | RICH | 931 | 797 | 131 | 3 | 666 | R | 85.6% | 14.1% | 85.9% | 14.1% |
| 619,066 | SALT LAKE | 264,926 | 183,536 | 78,488 | 2,902 | 105,048 | R | 69.3% | 29.6% | 70.0% | 30.0% |
| 12,253 | SAN JUAN | 3,758 | 2,598 | 1,145 | 15 | 1,453 | R | 69.1% | 30.5% | 69.4% | 30.6% |
| 14,620 | SANPETE | 6,777 | 5,507 | 1,227 | 43 | 4,280 | R | 81.3% | 18.1% | 81.8% | 18.2% |
| 14,727 | SEVIER | 6,870 | 5,736 | 1,072 | 62 | 4,664 | R | 83.5% | 15.6% | 84.3% | 15.7% |
| 10,198 | SUMMIT | 5,701 | 4,093 | 1,539 | 69 | 2,554 | R | 71.8% | 27.0% | 72.7% | 27.3% |
| 26,033 | TOOELE | 10,130 | 6,478 | 3,584 | 68 | 2,894 | R | 63.9% | 35.4% | 64.4% | 35.6% |
| 20,506 | UINTAH | 8,574 | 7,337 | 1,186 | 51 | 6,151 | R | 85.6% | 13.8% | 86.1% | 13.9% |
| 218,106 | UTAH | 87,504 | 72,284 | 14,801 | 419 | 57,483 | R | 82.6% | 16.9% | 83.0% | 17.0% |
| 8,523 | WASATCH | 3,824 | 2,789 | 1,015 | 20 | 1,774 | R | 72.9% | 26.5% | 73.3% | 26.7% |
| 26,065 | WASHINGTON | 13,977 | 12,049 | 1,846 | 82 | 10,203 | R | 86.2% | 13.2% | 86.7% | 13.3% |
| 1,911 | WAYNE | 1,159 | 930 | 224 | 5 | 706 | R | 80.2% | 19.3% | 80.6% | 19.4% |
| 144,616 | WEBER | 63,334 | 44,590 | 18,346 | 398 | 26,244 | R | 70.4% | 29.0% | 70.8% | 29.2% |
| 1,461,037 | TOTAL | 629,656 | 469,105 | 155,369 | 5,182 | 313,736 | R | 74.5% | 24.7% | 75.1% | 24.9% |

# UTAH

## PRESIDENT 1980

| 1980 Census Population | County | Total Vote | Republican | Democratic | Other | Rep.-Dem. Plurality | Percentage | | | |
|---|---|---|---|---|---|---|---|---|---|---|
| | | | | | | | Total Vote | | Major Vote | |
| | | | | | | | Rep. | Dem. | Rep. | Dem. |
| 4,378 | BEAVER | 2,157 | 1,477 | 621 | 59 | 856 R | 68.5% | 28.8% | 70.4% | 29.6% |
| 33,222 | BOX ELDER | 15,111 | 12,500 | 2,142 | 469 | 10,358 R | 82.7% | 14.2% | 85.4% | 14.6% |
| 57,176 | CACHE | 25,735 | 20,251 | 3,639 | 1,845 | 16,612 R | 78.7% | 14.1% | 84.8% | 15.2% |
| 22,179 | CARBON | 9,063 | 4,320 | 4,317 | 426 | 3 R | 47.7% | 47.6% | 50.0% | 50.0% |
| 769 | DAGGETT | 415 | 290 | 109 | 16 | 181 R | 69.9% | 26.3% | 72.7% | 27.3% |
| 146,540 | DAVIS | 57,859 | 45,695 | 9,065 | 3,099 | 36,630 R | 79.0% | 15.7% | 83.4% | 16.6% |
| 12,565 | DUCHESNE | 4,819 | 3,827 | 854 | 138 | 2,973 R | 79.4% | 17.7% | 81.8% | 18.2% |
| 11,451 | EMERY | 4,579 | 3,076 | 1,315 | 188 | 1,761 R | 67.2% | 28.7% | 70.1% | 29.9% |
| 3,673 | GARFIELD | 2,015 | 1,578 | 375 | 62 | 1,203 R | 78.3% | 18.6% | 80.8% | 19.2% |
| 8,241 | GRAND | 3,354 | 2,362 | 703 | 289 | 1,659 R | 70.4% | 21.0% | 77.1% | 22.9% |
| 17,349 | IRON | 7,804 | 6,207 | 1,242 | 355 | 4,965 R | 79.5% | 15.9% | 83.3% | 16.7% |
| 5,530 | JUAB | 2,701 | 1,872 | 720 | 109 | 1,152 R | 69.3% | 26.7% | 72.2% | 27.8% |
| 4,024 | KANE | 1,834 | 1,492 | 256 | 86 | 1,236 R | 81.4% | 14.0% | 85.4% | 14.6% |
| 8,970 | MILLARD | 4,537 | 3,620 | 795 | 122 | 2,825 R | 79.8% | 17.5% | 82.0% | 18.0% |
| 4,917 | MORGAN | 2,435 | 1,985 | 373 | 77 | 1,612 R | 81.5% | 15.3% | 84.2% | 15.8% |
| 1,329 | PIUTE | 719 | 551 | 157 | 11 | 394 R | 76.6% | 21.8% | 77.8% | 22.2% |
| 2,100 | RICH | 939 | 762 | 143 | 34 | 619 R | 81.2% | 15.2% | 84.2% | 15.8% |
| 619,066 | SALT LAKE | 252,835 | 169,411 | 58,472 | 24,952 | 110,939 R | 67.0% | 23.1% | 74.3% | 25.7% |
| 12,253 | SAN JUAN | 3,650 | 2,774 | 763 | 113 | 2,011 R | 76.0% | 20.9% | 78.4% | 21.6% |
| 14,620 | SANPETE | 6,614 | 5,143 | 1,260 | 211 | 3,883 R | 77.8% | 19.1% | 80.3% | 19.7% |
| 14,727 | SEVIER | 6,949 | 5,614 | 1,112 | 223 | 4,502 R | 80.8% | 16.0% | 83.5% | 16.5% |
| 10,198 | SUMMIT | 5,093 | 3,330 | 1,184 | 579 | 2,146 R | 65.4% | 23.2% | 73.8% | 26.2% |
| 26,033 | TOOELE | 9,712 | 6,024 | 3,132 | 556 | 2,892 R | 62.0% | 32.2% | 65.8% | 34.2% |
| 20,506 | UINTAH | 7,332 | 6,045 | 1,049 | 238 | 4,996 R | 82.4% | 14.3% | 85.2% | 14.8% |
| 218,106 | UTAH | 86,121 | 71,859 | 12,166 | 2,096 | 59,693 R | 83.4% | 14.1% | 85.5% | 14.5% |
| 8,523 | WASATCH | 3,946 | 2,799 | 994 | 153 | 1,805 R | 70.9% | 25.2% | 73.8% | 26.2% |
| 26,065 | WASHINGTON | 12,197 | 10,181 | 1,678 | 338 | 8,503 R | 83.5% | 13.8% | 85.9% | 14.1% |
| 1,911 | WAYNE | 1,098 | 835 | 226 | 37 | 609 R | 76.0% | 20.6% | 78.7% | 21.3% |
| 144,616 | WEBER | 62,599 | 43,807 | 15,404 | 3,388 | 28,403 R | 70.0% | 24.6% | 74.0% | 26.0% |
| 1,461,037 | TOTAL | 604,222 | 439,687 | 124,266 | 40,269 | 315,421 R | 72.8% | 20.6% | 78.0% | 22.0% |

# UTAH

## PRESIDENT 1976

| 1970 Census Population | County | Total Vote | Republican | Democratic | Other | Rep.-Dem. Plurality | Percentage | | | |
|---|---|---|---|---|---|---|---|---|---|---|
| | | | | | | | Total Vote | | Major Vote | |
| | | | | | | | Rep. | Dem. | Rep. | Dem. |
| 3,800 | BEAVER | 2,076 | 1,088 | 963 | 25 | 125 R | 52.4% | 46.4% | 53.0% | 47.0% |
| 28,129 | BOX ELDER | 13,501 | 9,319 | 3,353 | 829 | 5,966 R | 69.0% | 24.8% | 73.5% | 26.5% |
| 42,331 | CACHE | 23,194 | 16,636 | 5,430 | 1,128 | 11,206 R | 71.7% | 23.4% | 75.4% | 24.6% |
| 15,647 | CARBON | 8,683 | 3,360 | 5,157 | 166 | 1,797 D | 38.7% | 59.4% | 39.5% | 60.5% |
| 666 | DAGGETT | 365 | 217 | 131 | 17 | 86 R | 59.5% | 35.9% | 62.4% | 37.6% |
| 99,028 | DAVIS | 47,097 | 31,216 | 14,084 | 1,797 | 17,132 R | 66.3% | 29.9% | 68.9% | 31.1% |
| 7,299 | DUCHESNE | 3,982 | 2,619 | 1,110 | 253 | 1,509 R | 65.8% | 27.9% | 70.2% | 29.8% |
| 5,137 | EMERY | 3,643 | 1,717 | 1,771 | 155 | 54 D | 47.1% | 48.6% | 49.2% | 50.8% |
| 3,157 | GARFIELD | 1,776 | 1,163 | 539 | 74 | 624 R | 65.5% | 30.3% | 68.3% | 31.7% |
| 6,688 | GRAND | 2,855 | 1,781 | 931 | 143 | 850 R | 62.4% | 32.6% | 65.7% | 34.3% |
| 12,177 | IRON | 6,833 | 4,757 | 1,700 | 376 | 3,057 R | 69.6% | 24.9% | 73.7% | 26.3% |
| 4,574 | JUAB | 2,501 | 1,290 | 1,091 | 120 | 199 R | 51.6% | 43.6% | 54.2% | 45.8% |
| 2,421 | KANE | 1,509 | 1,094 | 330 | 85 | 764 R | 72.5% | 21.9% | 76.8% | 23.2% |
| 6,988 | MILLARD | 3,963 | 2,484 | 1,224 | 255 | 1,260 R | 62.7% | 30.9% | 67.0% | 33.0% |
| 3,983 | MORGAN | 2,154 | 1,356 | 701 | 97 | 655 R | 63.0% | 32.5% | 65.9% | 34.1% |
| 1,164 | PIUTE | 675 | 377 | 265 | 33 | 112 R | 55.9% | 39.3% | 58.7% | 41.3% |
| 1,615 | RICH | 806 | 541 | 248 | 17 | 293 R | 67.1% | 30.8% | 68.6% | 31.4% |
| 458,607 | SALT LAKE | 238,777 | 144,100 | 86,659 | 8,018 | 57,441 R | 60.3% | 36.3% | 62.4% | 37.6% |
| 9,606 | SAN JUAN | 3,222 | 1,856 | 1,182 | 184 | 674 R | 57.6% | 36.7% | 61.1% | 38.9% |
| 10,976 | SANPETE | 5,935 | 3,683 | 1,925 | 327 | 1,758 R | 62.1% | 32.4% | 65.7% | 34.3% |
| 10,103 | SEVIER | 5,650 | 3,686 | 1,564 | 400 | 2,122 R | 65.2% | 27.7% | 70.2% | 29.8% |
| 5,879 | SUMMIT | 3,763 | 2,316 | 1,282 | 165 | 1,034 R | 61.5% | 34.1% | 64.4% | 35.6% |
| 21,545 | TOOELE | 9,251 | 4,657 | 4,371 | 223 | 286 R | 50.3% | 47.2% | 51.6% | 48.4% |
| 12,684 | UINTAH | 5,807 | 4,017 | 1,342 | 448 | 2,675 R | 69.2% | 23.1% | 75.0% | 25.0% |
| 137,776 | UTAH | 70,993 | 49,328 | 18,327 | 3,338 | 31,001 R | 69.5% | 25.8% | 72.9% | 27.1% |
| 5,863 | WASATCH | 3,150 | 1,940 | 1,092 | 118 | 848 R | 61.6% | 34.7% | 64.0% | 36.0% |
| 13,669 | WASHINGTON | 8,414 | 5,944 | 1,893 | 577 | 4,051 R | 70.6% | 22.5% | 75.8% | 24.2% |
| 1,483 | WAYNE | 939 | 555 | 334 | 50 | 221 R | 59.1% | 35.6% | 62.4% | 37.6% |
| 126,278 | WEBER | 59,684 | 34,811 | 23,111 | 1,762 | 11,700 R | 58.3% | 38.7% | 60.1% | 39.9% |
| 1,059,273 | TOTAL | 541,198 | 337,908 | 182,110 | 21,180 | 155,798 R | 62.4% | 33.6% | 65.0% | 35.0% |

# UTAH

## PRESIDENT 1972

| 1970 Census Population | County | Total Vote | Republican | Democratic | Other | Rep.-Dem. Plurality | Percentage | | | |
|---|---|---|---|---|---|---|---|---|---|---|
| | | | | | | | Total Vote | | Major Vote | |
| | | | | | | | Rep. | Dem. | Rep. | Dem. |
| 3,800 | BEAVER | 2,053 | 1,332 | 682 | 39 | 650 R | 64.9% | 33.2% | 66.1% | 33.9% |
| 28,129 | BOX ELDER | 12,794 | 9,880 | 2,134 | 780 | 7,746 R | 77.2% | 16.7% | 82.2% | 17.8% |
| 42,331 | CACHE | 21,525 | 16,538 | 4,018 | 969 | 12,520 R | 76.8% | 18.7% | 80.5% | 19.5% |
| 15,647 | CARBON | 7,438 | 3,956 | 3,335 | 147 | 621 R | 53.2% | 44.8% | 54.3% | 45.7% |
| 666 | DAGGETT | 280 | 204 | 50 | 26 | 154 R | 72.9% | 17.9% | 80.3% | 19.7% |
| 99,028 | DAVIS | 40,911 | 29,706 | 7,954 | 3,251 | 21,752 R | 72.6% | 19.4% | 78.9% | 21.1% |
| 7,299 | DUCHESNE | 3,097 | 2,183 | 629 | 285 | 1,554 R | 70.5% | 20.3% | 77.6% | 22.4% |
| 5,137 | EMERY | 2,550 | 1,666 | 769 | 115 | 897 R | 65.3% | 30.2% | 68.4% | 31.6% |
| 3,157 | GARFIELD | 1,603 | 1,290 | 242 | 71 | 1,048 R | 80.5% | 15.1% | 84.2% | 15.8% |
| 6,688 | GRAND | 2,546 | 1,837 | 560 | 149 | 1,277 R | 72.2% | 22.0% | 76.6% | 23.4% |
| 12,177 | IRON | 6,648 | 5,085 | 1,098 | 465 | 3,987 R | 76.5% | 16.5% | 82.2% | 17.8% |
| 4,574 | JUAB | 2,429 | 1,629 | 691 | 109 | 938 R | 67.1% | 28.4% | 70.2% | 29.8% |
| 2,421 | KANE | 1,454 | 1,146 | 218 | 90 | 928 R | 78.8% | 15.0% | 84.0% | 16.0% |
| 6,988 | MILLARD | 3,815 | 2,689 | 777 | 349 | 1,912 R | 70.5% | 20.4% | 77.6% | 22.4% |
| 3,983 | MORGAN | 2,036 | 1,456 | 363 | 217 | 1,093 R | 71.5% | 17.8% | 80.0% | 20.0% |
| 1,164 | PIUTE | 603 | 475 | 102 | 26 | 373 R | 78.8% | 16.9% | 82.3% | 17.7% |
| 1,615 | RICH | 759 | 604 | 120 | 35 | 484 R | 79.6% | 15.8% | 83.4% | 16.6% |
| 458,607 | SALT LAKE | 209,666 | 132,066 | 68,489 | 9,111 | 63,577 R | 63.0% | 32.7% | 65.9% | 34.1% |
| 9,606 | SAN JUAN | 2,773 | 1,893 | 677 | 203 | 1,216 R | 68.3% | 24.4% | 73.7% | 26.3% |
| 10,976 | SANPETE | 5,652 | 3,995 | 1,220 | 437 | 2,775 R | 70.7% | 21.6% | 76.6% | 23.4% |
| 10,103 | SEVIER | 5,071 | 3,700 | 820 | 551 | 2,880 R | 73.0% | 16.2% | 81.9% | 18.1% |
| 5,879 | SUMMIT | 3,158 | 2,209 | 836 | 113 | 1,373 R | 69.9% | 26.5% | 72.5% | 27.5% |
| 21,545 | TOOELE | 8,545 | 5,641 | 2,621 | 283 | 3,020 R | 66.0% | 30.7% | 68.3% | 31.7% |
| 12,684 | UINTAH | 5,868 | 4,712 | 716 | 440 | 3,996 R | 80.3% | 12.2% | 86.8% | 13.2% |
| 137,776 | UTAH | 59,460 | 42,179 | 10,828 | 6,453 | 31,351 R | 70.9% | 18.2% | 79.6% | 20.4% |
| 5,863 | WASATCH | 2,914 | 2,046 | 693 | 175 | 1,353 R | 70.2% | 23.8% | 74.7% | 25.3% |
| 13,669 | WASHINGTON | 6,662 | 5,176 | 956 | 530 | 4,220 R | 77.7% | 14.4% | 84.4% | 15.6% |
| 1,483 | WAYNE | 832 | 597 | 183 | 52 | 414 R | 71.8% | 22.0% | 76.5% | 23.5% |
| 126,278 | WEBER | 55,334 | 37,753 | 14,503 | 3,078 | 23,250 R | 68.2% | 26.2% | 72.2% | 27.8% |
| 1,059,273 | TOTAL | 478,476 | 323,643 | 126,284 | 28,549 | 197,359 R | 67.6% | 26.4% | 71.9% | 28.1% |

# UTAH

## PRESIDENT 1968

| 1960 Census Population | County | Total Vote | Republican | Democratic | AIP | Other | Plurality | Percentage Total Vote | | |
|---|---|---|---|---|---|---|---|---|---|---|
| | | | | | | | | Rep. | Dem. | AIP |
| 4,331 | BEAVER | 1,944 | 989 | 795 | 158 | 2 | 194 R | 50.9% | 40.9% | 8.1% |
| 25,061 | BOX ELDER | 11,688 | 7,680 | 3,093 | 907 | 8 | 4,587 R | 65.7% | 26.5% | 7.8% |
| 35,788 | CACHE | 17,303 | 11,906 | 4,327 | 1,050 | 20 | 7,579 R | 68.8% | 25.0% | 6.1% |
| 21,135 | CARBON | 7,239 | 2,618 | 4,344 | 271 | 6 | 1,726 D | 36.2% | 60.0% | 3.7% |
| 1,164 | DAGGETT | 291 | 152 | 97 | 42 | | 55 R | 52.2% | 33.3% | 14.4% |
| 64,760 | DAVIS | 34,087 | 20,658 | 10,624 | 2,787 | 18 | 10,034 R | 60.6% | 31.2% | 8.2% |
| 7,179 | DUCHESNE | 2,834 | 1,733 | 858 | 243 | | 875 R | 61.2% | 30.3% | 8.6% |
| 5,546 | EMERY | 2,403 | 1,223 | 1,019 | 161 | | 204 R | 50.9% | 42.4% | 6.7% |
| 3,577 | GARFIELD | 1,487 | 1,033 | 314 | 139 | 1 | 719 R | 69.5% | 21.1% | 9.3% |
| 6,345 | GRAND | 2,357 | 1,435 | 707 | 215 | | 728 R | 60.9% | 30.0% | 9.1% |
| 10,795 | IRON | 5,011 | 3,337 | 1,157 | 514 | 3 | 2,180 R | 66.6% | 23.1% | 10.3% |
| 4,597 | JUAB | 2,226 | 1,201 | 907 | 118 | | 294 R | 54.0% | 40.7% | 5.3% |
| 2,667 | KANE | 1,135 | 814 | 147 | 174 | | 640 R | 71.7% | 13.0% | 15.3% |
| 7,866 | MILLARD | 3,509 | 2,318 | 971 | 220 | | 1,347 R | 66.1% | 27.7% | 6.3% |
| 2,837 | MORGAN | 1,703 | 1,020 | 551 | 130 | 2 | 469 R | 59.9% | 32.4% | 7.6% |
| 1,436 | PIUTE | 638 | 411 | 167 | 60 | | 244 R | 64.4% | 26.2% | 9.4% |
| 1,685 | RICH | 747 | 525 | 183 | 39 | | 342 R | 70.3% | 24.5% | 5.2% |
| 383,035 | SALT LAKE | 188,663 | 101,942 | 77,247 | 9,323 | 151 | 24,695 R | 54.0% | 40.9% | 4.9% |
| 9,040 | SAN JUAN | 2,335 | 1,393 | 680 | 262 | | 713 R | 59.7% | 29.1% | 11.2% |
| 11,053 | SANPETE | 5,312 | 3,304 | 1,696 | 307 | 5 | 1,608 R | 62.2% | 31.9% | 5.8% |
| 10,565 | SEVIER | 4,744 | 3,190 | 1,167 | 384 | 3 | 2,023 R | 67.2% | 24.6% | 8.1% |
| 5,673 | SUMMIT | 2,857 | 1,782 | 961 | 113 | 1 | 821 R | 62.4% | 33.6% | 4.0% |
| 17,868 | TOOELE | 8,267 | 3,422 | 4,250 | 592 | 3 | 828 D | 41.4% | 51.4% | 7.2% |
| 11,582 | UINTAH | 4,622 | 3,034 | 1,145 | 437 | 6 | 1,889 R | 65.6% | 24.8% | 9.5% |
| 106,991 | UTAH | 49,528 | 29,226 | 16,629 | 3,666 | 7 | 12,597 R | 59.0% | 33.6% | 7.4% |
| 5,308 | WASATCH | 2,643 | 1,611 | 941 | 86 | 5 | 670 R | 61.0% | 35.6% | 3.3% |
| 10,271 | WASHINGTON | 5,000 | 3,226 | 975 | 796 | 3 | 2,251 R | 64.5% | 19.5% | 15.9% |
| 1,728 | WAYNE | 813 | 511 | 248 | 54 | | 263 R | 62.9% | 30.5% | 6.6% |
| 110,744 | WEBER | 51,182 | 27,034 | 20,465 | 3,658 | 25 | 6,569 R | 52.8% | 40.0% | 7.1% |
| 890,627 | TOTAL | 422,568 | 238,728 | 156,665 | 26,906 | 269 | 82,063 R | 56.5% | 37.1% | 6.4% |

# UTAH

## PRESIDENT 1964

| 1960 Census Population | County | Total Vote | Republican | Democratic | Other | Rep.-Dem. Plurality | Percentage | | | |
|---|---|---|---|---|---|---|---|---|---|---|
| | | | | | | | Total Vote | | Major Vote | |
| | | | | | | | Rep. | Dem. | Rep. | Dem. |
| 4,331 | BEAVER | 1,981 | 792 | 1,189 | | 397 D | 40.0% | 60.0% | 40.0% | 60.0% |
| 25,061 | BOX ELDER | 11,964 | 6,851 | 5,113 | | 1,738 R | 57.3% | 42.7% | 57.3% | 42.7% |
| 35,788 | CACHE | 15,953 | 9,326 | 6,627 | | 2,699 R | 58.5% | 41.5% | 58.5% | 41.5% |
| 21,135 | CARBON | 7,802 | 2,130 | 5,672 | | 3,542 D | 27.3% | 72.7% | 27.3% | 72.7% |
| 1,164 | DAGGETT | 282 | 112 | 170 | | 58 D | 39.7% | 60.3% | 39.7% | 60.3% |
| 64,760 | DAVIS | 28,654 | 14,477 | 14,177 | | 300 R | 50.5% | 49.5% | 50.5% | 49.5% |
| 7,179 | DUCHESNE | 2,571 | 1,251 | 1,320 | | 69 D | 48.7% | 51.3% | 48.7% | 51.3% |
| 5,546 | EMERY | 2,537 | 1,103 | 1,434 | | 331 D | 43.5% | 56.5% | 43.5% | 56.5% |
| 3,577 | GARFIELD | 1,479 | 821 | 658 | | 163 R | 55.5% | 44.5% | 55.5% | 44.5% |
| 6,345 | GRAND | 2,275 | 1,130 | 1,145 | | 15 D | 49.7% | 50.3% | 49.7% | 50.3% |
| 10,795 | IRON | 4,575 | 2,522 | 2,053 | | 469 R | 55.1% | 44.9% | 55.1% | 44.9% |
| 4,597 | JUAB | 2,245 | 926 | 1,319 | | 393 D | 41.2% | 58.8% | 41.2% | 58.8% |
| 2,667 | KANE | 1,124 | 784 | 340 | | 444 R | 69.8% | 30.2% | 69.8% | 30.2% |
| 7,866 | MILLARD | 3,435 | 1,973 | 1,462 | | 511 R | 57.4% | 42.6% | 57.4% | 42.6% |
| 2,837 | MORGAN | 1,407 | 572 | 835 | | 263 D | 40.7% | 59.3% | 40.7% | 59.3% |
| 1,436 | PIUTE | 634 | 361 | 273 | | 88 R | 56.9% | 43.1% | 56.9% | 43.1% |
| 1,685 | RICH | 761 | 435 | 326 | | 109 R | 57.2% | 42.8% | 57.2% | 42.8% |
| 383,035 | SALT LAKE | 182,044 | 78,118 | 103,926 | | 25,808 D | 42.9% | 57.1% | 42.9% | 57.1% |
| 9,040 | SAN JUAN | 2,364 | 1,371 | 993 | | 378 R | 58.0% | 42.0% | 58.0% | 42.0% |
| 11,053 | SANPETE | 5,167 | 2,620 | 2,547 | | 73 R | 50.7% | 49.3% | 50.7% | 49.3% |
| 10,565 | SEVIER | 4,565 | 2,617 | 1,948 | | 669 R | 57.3% | 42.7% | 57.3% | 42.7% |
| 5,673 | SUMMIT | 2,832 | 1,335 | 1,497 | | 162 D | 47.1% | 52.9% | 47.1% | 52.9% |
| 17,868 | TOOELE | 7,750 | 2,511 | 5,239 | | 2,728 D | 32.4% | 67.6% | 32.4% | 67.6% |
| 11,582 | UINTAH | 4,579 | 2,437 | 2,142 | | 295 R | 53.2% | 46.8% | 53.2% | 46.8% |
| 106,991 | UTAH | 44,848 | 20,912 | 23,936 | | 3,024 D | 46.6% | 53.4% | 46.6% | 53.4% |
| 5,308 | WASATCH | 2,578 | 1,158 | 1,420 | | 262 D | 44.9% | 55.1% | 44.9% | 55.1% |
| 10,271 | WASHINGTON | 4,323 | 2,534 | 1,789 | | 745 R | 58.6% | 41.4% | 58.6% | 41.4% |
| 1,728 | WAYNE | 812 | 400 | 412 | | 12 D | 49.3% | 50.7% | 49.3% | 50.7% |
| 110,744 | WEBER | 49,872 | 20,206 | 29,666 | | 9,460 D | 40.5% | 59.5% | 40.5% | 59.5% |
| 890,627 | TOTAL | 401,413 | 181,785 | 219,628 | | 37,843 D | 45.3% | 54.7% | 45.3% | 54.7% |

# UTAH

## PRESIDENT 1960

| 1960 Census Population | County | Total Vote | Republican | Democratic | Other | Rep.-Dem. Plurality | Percentage | | | |
|---|---|---|---|---|---|---|---|---|---|---|
| | | | | | | | Total Vote | | Major Vote | |
| | | | | | | | Rep. | Dem. | Rep. | Dem. |
| 4,331 | BEAVER | 2,127 | 971 | 1,156 | | 185 D | 45.7% | 54.3% | 45.7% | 54.3% |
| 25,061 | BOX ELDER | 10,428 | 6,594 | 3,831 | 3 | 2,763 R | 63.2% | 36.7% | 63.3% | 36.7% |
| 35,788 | CACHE | 15,198 | 10,281 | 4,917 | | 5,364 R | 67.6% | 32.4% | 67.6% | 32.4% |
| 21,135 | CARBON | 9,006 | 2,953 | 6,039 | 14 | 3,086 D | 32.8% | 67.1% | 32.8% | 67.2% |
| 1,164 | DAGGETT | 436 | 196 | 239 | 1 | 43 D | 45.0% | 54.8% | 45.1% | 54.9% |
| 64,760 | DAVIS | 24,034 | 13,782 | 10,244 | 8 | 3,538 R | 57.3% | 42.6% | 57.4% | 42.6% |
| 7,179 | DUCHESNE | 2,713 | 1,546 | 1,166 | 1 | 380 R | 57.0% | 43.0% | 57.0% | 43.0% |
| 5,546 | EMERY | 2,521 | 1,283 | 1,238 | | 45 R | 50.9% | 49.1% | 50.9% | 49.1% |
| 3,577 | GARFIELD | 1,554 | 1,083 | 471 | | 612 R | 69.7% | 30.3% | 69.7% | 30.3% |
| 6,345 | GRAND | 1,935 | 1,130 | 805 | | 325 R | 58.4% | 41.6% | 58.4% | 41.6% |
| 10,795 | IRON | 4,818 | 3,079 | 1,738 | 1 | 1,341 R | 63.9% | 36.1% | 63.9% | 36.1% |
| 4,597 | JUAB | 2,360 | 1,202 | 1,158 | | 44 R | 50.9% | 49.1% | 50.9% | 49.1% |
| 2,667 | KANE | 1,089 | 876 | 213 | | 663 R | 80.4% | 19.6% | 80.4% | 19.6% |
| 7,866 | MILLARD | 3,676 | 2,248 | 1,425 | 3 | 823 R | 61.2% | 38.8% | 61.2% | 38.8% |
| 2,837 | MORGAN | 1,398 | 775 | 622 | 1 | 153 R | 55.4% | 44.5% | 55.5% | 44.5% |
| 1,436 | PIUTE | 700 | 453 | 247 | | 206 R | 64.7% | 35.3% | 64.7% | 35.3% |
| 1,685 | RICH | 802 | 511 | 291 | | 220 R | 63.7% | 36.3% | 63.7% | 36.3% |
| 383,035 | SALT LAKE | 166,713 | 90,845 | 75,868 | | 14,977 R | 54.5% | 45.5% | 54.5% | 45.5% |
| 9,040 | SAN JUAN | 2,245 | 1,408 | 837 | | 571 R | 62.7% | 37.3% | 62.7% | 37.3% |
| 11,053 | SANPETE | 5,505 | 3,322 | 2,180 | 3 | 1,142 R | 60.3% | 39.6% | 60.4% | 39.6% |
| 10,565 | SEVIER | 4,857 | 3,166 | 1,690 | 1 | 1,476 R | 65.2% | 34.8% | 65.2% | 34.8% |
| 5,673 | SUMMIT | 2,824 | 1,607 | 1,217 | | 390 R | 56.9% | 43.1% | 56.9% | 43.1% |
| 17,868 | TOOELE | 6,688 | 3,016 | 3,665 | 7 | 649 D | 45.1% | 54.8% | 45.1% | 54.9% |
| 11,582 | UINTAH | 4,262 | 2,882 | 1,380 | | 1,502 R | 67.6% | 32.4% | 67.6% | 32.4% |
| 106,991 | UTAH | 42,708 | 23,057 | 19,626 | 25 | 3,431 R | 54.0% | 46.0% | 54.0% | 46.0% |
| 5,308 | WASATCH | 2,547 | 1,480 | 1,066 | 1 | 414 R | 58.1% | 41.9% | 58.1% | 41.9% |
| 10,271 | WASHINGTON | 4,174 | 2,876 | 1,298 | | 1,578 R | 68.9% | 31.1% | 68.9% | 31.1% |
| 1,728 | WAYNE | 828 | 446 | 382 | | 64 R | 53.9% | 46.1% | 53.9% | 46.1% |
| 110,744 | WEBER | 46,563 | 22,293 | 24,239 | 31 | 1,946 D | 47.9% | 52.1% | 47.9% | 52.1% |
| 890,627 | TOTAL | 374,709 | 205,361 | 169,248 | 100 | 36,113 R | 54.8% | 45.2% | 54.8% | 45.2% |

# UTAH

## ELECTION NOTES

**2004**    Other vote was 11,305 Unaffiliated (Ralph Nader); 6,841 Constitution (Michael Peroutka); 3,375 Libertarian (Michael Badnarik); 946 Personal Choice (Charles Jay); 393 Socialist Workers (James Harris); 39 write-in (David Cobb); 2 write-in (Lawrence Topham); 1 write-in (Joe Schriner); 1 write-in (John Joseph Kennedy).

**2000**    Other vote was 9,319 Reform (Buchanan); 3,616 Libertarian (Browne); 2,709 Independent American (Phillips); 763 Natural Law (Hagelin); 186 Socialist Workers (Harris); 161 Unaffiliated (Youngkeit); 1 write-in (Kunzler).

**1996**    Other vote was 4,615 Green (Nader); 4,129 Libertarian (Browne); 2,601 Taxpayers (Phillips); 1,290 Independent American (Templin); 1,101 Independent (Crane); 1,085 Natural Law (Hagelin); 298 Workers World (Moorehead); 235 Socialist Workers (Harris); 111 Prohibition (Dodge); 159 scattered write-in.

**1992**    Other vote was 28,602 Gritz (Populist); 1,900 Marrou (Libertarian); 1,319 Hagelin (Natural Law); 1,089 LaRouche (Independent for Economic Recovery); 414 Fulani (New Alliance); 393 Phillips (Taxpayers); 292 Smith (American); 200 Warren (Socialist Workers); 177 Daniels (Campaign for a New Tomorrow); 151 Brisben (Socialist); 1 scattered write-in.

**1988**    Other vote was 7,473 Paul (Libertarian); 2,158 Dennis (American); 455 Fulani (New Alliance); 427 LaRouche (National Economic Recovery); 372 Youngkeit (Independent); 209 Warren (Socialist Workers); 129 Kenoyer (Socialist).

**1984**    Other vote was 2,447 Bergland (Libertarian); 1,345 Dennis (American); 844 Johnson (Citizens); 220 Serrette (Independent Alliance); 184 Hall (Communist); 142 Mason (Socialist Workers).

**1980**    Other vote was 30,284 Anderson (Independent); 7,226 Clark (Libertarian); 1,009 Commoner (Independent); 965 Greaves (American); 522 Rarick (Independent American); 139 Hall (Independent); 124 DeBerry (Socialist Workers). Early unamended canvass gave the Libertarian state-wide total vote as 7,156.

**1976**    Other vote was 13,284 Anderson (American); 3,907 McCarthy (Independent); 2,438 MacBride (Libertarian); 1,162 Maddox (Concerned Citizens); 268 Camejo (Independent); 121 Hall (Independent). Early unamended canvass gave the American state-wide total vote as 13,304.

**1972**    Other vote was Schmitz (American Independent).

**1968**    Wallace on the ballot as American Independent. Other vote was 180 no candidate indicated for President but Gonzales for Vice-President (Peace and Freedom); 89 Halstead (Socialist Workers). Early unamended canvass incorrectly listed 54 Socialist Workers votes for San Juan county which should have been listed as cast in Salt Lake county.

**1964**    An early uncorrected canvass report gave the Republican (Goldwater) vote as 180,682.

**1960**    Other vote was Dobbs (Socialist Workers). An error of a single vote in the Republican (Nixon) vote in Juab county has been corrected.

# VERMONT

## POPULAR VOTE FOR PRESIDENT 1920 TO 2004

| Year | Total Vote | Republican Vote | Republican Candidate | Democratic Vote | Democratic Candidate | Other Vote | Plurality | Percentage Total Vote Rep. | Dem. | Major Vote Rep. | Dem. |
|---|---|---|---|---|---|---|---|---|---|---|---|
| 2004 | 312,309 | 121,180 | Bush, George W. | 184,067 | Kerry, John | 7,062 | 62,887 D | 38.8% | 58.9% | 39.7% | 60.3% |
| 2000 ** | 294,308 | 119,775 | Bush, George W. | 149,022 | Gore, Al | 25,511 | 29,247 D | 40.7% | 50.6% | 44.6% | 55.4% |
| 1996 ** | 258,449 | 80,352 | Dole, Bob | 137,894 | Clinton, Bill | 40,203 | 57,542 D | 31.1% | 53.4% | 36.8% | 63.2% |
| 1992 ** | 289,701 | 88,122 | Bush, George | 133,592 | Clinton, Bill | 67,987 | 45,470 D | 30.4% | 46.1% | 39.7% | 60.3% |
| 1988 | 243,328 | 124,331 | Bush, George | 115,775 | Dukakis, Michael S. | 3,222 | 8,556 R | 51.1% | 47.6% | 51.8% | 48.2% |
| 1984 | 234,561 | 135,865 | Reagan, Ronald | 95,730 | Mondale, Walter F. | 2,966 | 40,135 R | 57.9% | 40.8% | 58.7% | 41.3% |
| 1980 ** | 213,299 | 94,628 | Reagan, Ronald | 81,952 | Carter, Jimmy | 36,719 | 12,676 R | 44.4% | 38.4% | 53.6% | 46.4% |
| 1976 | 187,765 | 102,085 | Ford, Gerald R. | 80,954 | Carter, Jimmy | 4,726 | 21,131 R | 54.4% | 43.1% | 55.8% | 44.2% |
| 1972 | 186,947 | 117,149 | Nixon, Richard M. | 68,174 | McGovern, George S. | 1,624 | 48,975 R | 62.7% | 36.5% | 63.2% | 36.8% |
| 1968 | 161,404 | 85,142 | Nixon, Richard M. | 70,255 | Humphrey, Hubert H. | 6,007 | 14,887 R | 52.8% | 43.5% | 54.8% | 45.2% |
| 1964 | 163,089 | 54,942 | Goldwater, Barry M. | 108,127 | Johnson, Lyndon B. | 20 | 53,185 D | 33.7% | 66.3% | 33.7% | 66.3% |
| 1960 | 167,324 | 98,131 | Nixon, Richard M. | 69,186 | Kennedy, John F. | 7 | 28,945 R | 58.6% | 41.3% | 58.6% | 41.4% |
| 1956 | 152,978 | 110,390 | Eisenhower, Dwight D. | 42,549 | Stevenson, Adlai E. | 39 | 67,841 R | 72.2% | 27.8% | 72.2% | 27.8% |
| 1952 | 153,557 | 109,717 | Eisenhower, Dwight D. | 43,355 | Stevenson, Adlai E. | 485 | 66,362 R | 71.5% | 28.2% | 71.7% | 28.3% |
| 1948 | 123,382 | 75,926 | Dewey, Thomas E. | 45,557 | Truman, Harry S. | 1,899 | 30,369 R | 61.5% | 36.9% | 62.5% | 37.5% |
| 1944 | 125,361 | 71,527 | Dewey, Thomas E. | 53,820 | Roosevelt, Franklin D. | 14 | 17,707 R | 57.1% | 42.9% | 57.1% | 42.9% |
| 1940 | 143,062 | 78,371 | Willkie, Wendell | 64,269 | Roosevelt, Franklin D. | 422 | 14,102 R | 54.8% | 44.9% | 54.9% | 45.1% |
| 1936 | 143,689 | 81,023 | Landon, Alfred M. | 62,124 | Roosevelt, Franklin D. | 542 | 18,899 R | 56.4% | 43.2% | 56.6% | 43.4% |
| 1932 | 136,980 | 78,984 | Hoover, Herbert C. | 56,266 | Roosevelt, Franklin D. | 1,730 | 22,718 R | 57.7% | 41.1% | 58.4% | 41.6% |
| 1928 | 135,191 | 90,404 | Hoover, Herbert C. | 44,440 | Smith, Alfred E. | 347 | 45,964 R | 66.9% | 32.9% | 67.0% | 33.0% |
| 1924 | 102,917 | 80,498 | Coolidge, Calvin | 16,124 | Davis, John W. | 6,295 | 64,374 R | 78.2% | 15.7% | 83.3% | 16.7% |
| 1920 | 89,961 | 68,212 | Harding, Warren G. | 20,919 | Cox, James M. | 830 | 47,293 R | 75.8% | 23.3% | 76.5% | 23.5% |

In 2000 the other vote column includes 20,374 votes cast for Green (Nader). In 1996 the other vote column includes 31,024 votes cast for Perot. In 1992 the other vote column includes 65,991 votes cast for Perot. In 1980 the other column includes 31,761 votes for Independent (Anderson).

## ELECTORAL COLLEGE VOTE 1920 TO 2004

| Year | Total | Republican | Democratic | Other |
|---|---|---|---|---|
| 2004 | 3 | | 3 | |
| 2000 | 3 | | 3 | |
| 1996 | 3 | | 3 | |
| 1992 | 3 | | 3 | |
| 1988 | 3 | 3 | | |
| 1984 | 3 | 3 | | |
| 1980 | 3 | 3 | | |
| 1976 | 3 | 3 | | |
| 1972 | 3 | 3 | | |
| 1968 | 3 | 3 | | |
| 1964 | 3 | | 3 | |
| 1960 | 3 | 3 | | |
| 1956 | 3 | 3 | | |
| 1952 | 3 | 3 | | |
| 1948 | 3 | 3 | | |
| 1944 | 3 | 3 | | |
| 1940 | 3 | 3 | | |
| 1936 | 3 | 3 | | |
| 1932 | 3 | 3 | | |
| 1928 | 4 | 4 | | |
| 1924 | 4 | 4 | | |
| 1920 | 4 | 4 | | |

# VERMONT

# VERMONT

## PRESIDENT 2004

| 2000 Census Population | County | Total Vote | Republican | Democratic | Other | Rep.-Dem. Plurality | Percentage | | | |
|---|---|---|---|---|---|---|---|---|---|---|
| | | | | | | | Total Vote | | Major Vote | |
| | | | | | | | Rep. | Dem. | Rep. | Dem. |
| 35,974 | ADDISON | 18,579 | 7,077 | 11,147 | 355 | 4,070 D | 38.1% | 60.0% | 38.8% | 61.2% |
| 36,994 | BENNINGTON | 19,065 | 7,616 | 11,069 | 380 | 3,453 D | 39.9% | 58.1% | 40.8% | 59.2% |
| 29,702 | CALEDONIA | 14,211 | 6,765 | 7,106 | 340 | 341 D | 47.6% | 50.0% | 48.8% | 51.2% |
| 146,571 | CHITTENDEN | 77,696 | 26,422 | 49,369 | 1,905 | 22,947 D | 34.0% | 63.5% | 34.9% | 65.1% |
| 6,459 | ESSEX | 2,937 | 1,591 | 1,276 | 70 | 315 R | 54.2% | 43.4% | 55.5% | 44.5% |
| 45,417 | FRANKLIN | 19,920 | 8,936 | 10,598 | 386 | 1,662 D | 44.9% | 53.2% | 45.7% | 54.3% |
| 6,901 | GRAND ISLE | 4,077 | 1,754 | 2,246 | 77 | 492 D | 43.0% | 55.1% | 43.9% | 56.2% |
| 23,233 | LAMOILLE | 12,181 | 4,260 | 7,636 | 285 | 3,376 D | 35.0% | 62.7% | 35.8% | 64.2% |
| 28,226 | ORANGE | 14,895 | 6,421 | 8,159 | 315 | 1,738 D | 43.1% | 54.8% | 44.0% | 56.0% |
| 26,277 | ORLEANS | 12,242 | 5,666 | 6,330 | 246 | 664 D | 46.3% | 51.7% | 47.2% | 52.8% |
| 63,400 | RUTLAND | 30,975 | 14,440 | 15,904 | 631 | 1,464 D | 46.6% | 51.3% | 47.6% | 52.4% |
| 58,039 | WASHINGTON | 31,448 | 11,461 | 19,177 | 810 | 7,716 D | 36.4% | 61.0% | 37.4% | 62.6% |
| 44,216 | WINDHAM | 23,316 | 7,280 | 15,489 | 547 | 8,209 D | 31.2% | 66.4% | 32.0% | 68.0% |
| 57,418 | WINDSOR | 30,767 | 11,491 | 18,561 | 715 | 7,070 D | 37.3% | 60.3% | 38.2% | 61.8% |
| 608,827 | TOTAL | 312,309 | 121,180 | 184,067 | 7,062 | 62,887 D | 38.8% | 58.9% | 39.7% | 60.3% |

# VERMONT

## PRESIDENT 2000

| 2000 Census Population | County | Total Vote | Republican | Democratic | Green (Nader) | Other | Rep.-Dem. Plurality | Percentage of Total Vote | | |
|---|---|---|---|---|---|---|---|---|---|---|
| | | | | | | | | Rep. | Dem. | Green |
| 35,974 | ADDISON | 17,427 | 6,953 | 8,936 | 1,207 | 331 | 1,983 D | 39.9% | 51.3% | 6.9% |
| 36,994 | BENNINGTON | 17,677 | 7,284 | 9,021 | 1,112 | 260 | 1,737 D | 41.2% | 51.0% | 6.3% |
| 29,702 | CALEDONIA | 13,641 | 6,746 | 5,859 | 771 | 265 | 887 R | 49.5% | 43.0% | 5.7% |
| 146,571 | CHITTENDEN | 72,017 | 26,105 | 39,156 | 5,769 | 987 | 13,051 D | 36.2% | 54.4% | 8.0% |
| 6,459 | ESSEX | 2,892 | 1,564 | 1,129 | 133 | 66 | 435 R | 54.1% | 39.0% | 4.6% |
| 45,417 | FRANKLIN | 19,194 | 8,395 | 9,514 | 823 | 462 | 1,119 D | 43.7% | 49.6% | 4.3% |
| 6,901 | GRAND ISLE | 3,638 | 1,550 | 1,835 | 174 | 79 | 285 D | 42.6% | 50.4% | 4.8% |
| 23,233 | LAMOILLE | 11,246 | 4,456 | 5,676 | 878 | 236 | 1,220 D | 39.6% | 50.5% | 7.8% |
| 28,226 | ORANGE | 14,695 | 6,858 | 6,694 | 888 | 255 | 164 R | 46.7% | 45.6% | 6.0% |
| 26,277 | ORLEANS | 12,132 | 5,799 | 5,472 | 564 | 297 | 327 R | 47.8% | 45.1% | 4.6% |
| 63,400 | RUTLAND | 29,362 | 13,546 | 13,990 | 1,355 | 471 | 444 D | 46.1% | 47.6% | 4.6% |
| 58,039 | WASHINGTON | 29,749 | 11,448 | 15,281 | 2,433 | 587 | 3,833 D | 38.5% | 51.4% | 8.2% |
| 44,216 | WINDHAM | 21,491 | 7,358 | 11,319 | 2,475 | 339 | 3,961 D | 34.2% | 52.7% | 11.5% |
| 57,418 | WINDSOR | 29,147 | 11,713 | 15,140 | 1,792 | 502 | 3,427 D | 40.2% | 51.9% | 6.1% |
| 608,827 | TOTAL | 294,308 | 119,775 | 149,022 | 20,374 | 5,137 | 29,247 D | 40.7% | 50.6% | 6.9% |

# VERMONT

## PRESIDENT 1996

| 1995 Census Pop. Est. | County | Total Vote | Republican | Democratic | Reform (Perot) | Other | Rep.-Dem. Plurality | Percentage of Total Vote | | |
|---|---|---|---|---|---|---|---|---|---|---|
| | | | | | | | | Rep. | Dem. | Reform |
| 34,811 | ADDISON | 15,453 | 4,798 | 8,164 | 1,808 | 683 | 3,366 D | 31.0% | 52.8% | 11.7% |
| 36,276 | BENNINGTON | 16,152 | 5,229 | 8,139 | 2,278 | 506 | 2,910 D | 32.4% | 50.4% | 14.1% |
| 28,564 | CALEDONIA | 11,799 | 4,089 | 5,593 | 1,782 | 335 | 1,504 D | 34.7% | 47.4% | 15.1% |
| 139,041 | CHITTENDEN | 63,860 | 19,020 | 36,299 | 6,180 | 2,361 | 17,279 D | 29.8% | 56.8% | 9.7% |
| 6,570 | ESSEX | 2,449 | 819 | 1,120 | 442 | 68 | 301 D | 33.4% | 45.7% | 18.0% |
| 43,250 | FRANKLIN | 16,206 | 4,617 | 8,790 | 2,488 | 311 | 4,173 D | 28.5% | 54.2% | 15.4% |
| 5,884 | GRAND ISLE | 3,041 | 958 | 1,555 | 441 | 87 | 597 D | 31.5% | 51.1% | 14.5% |
| 21,150 | LAMOILLE | 9,186 | 2,705 | 4,997 | 1,216 | 268 | 2,292 D | 29.4% | 54.4% | 13.2% |
| 27,361 | ORANGE | 12,266 | 4,043 | 6,107 | 1,597 | 519 | 2,064 D | 33.0% | 49.8% | 13.0% |
| 24,970 | ORLEANS | 9,986 | 3,114 | 5,137 | 1,508 | 227 | 2,023 D | 31.2% | 51.4% | 15.1% |
| 62,732 | RUTLAND | 27,229 | 9,934 | 13,230 | 3,408 | 657 | 3,296 D | 36.5% | 48.6% | 12.5% |
| 56,367 | WASHINGTON | 25,884 | 7,750 | 14,267 | 2,788 | 1,079 | 6,517 D | 29.9% | 55.1% | 10.8% |
| 42,757 | WINDHAM | 18,915 | 5,261 | 10,426 | 2,033 | 1,195 | 5,165 D | 27.8% | 55.1% | 10.7% |
| 55,038 | WINDSOR | 26,023 | 8,015 | 14,070 | 3,055 | 883 | 6,055 D | 30.8% | 54.1% | 11.7% |
| 584,771 | TOTAL | 258,449 | 80,352 | 137,894 | 31,024 | 9,179 | 57,542 D | 31.1% | 53.4% | 12.0% |

# VERMONT

## PRESIDENT 1992

| 1990 Census Population | County | Total Vote | Republican | Democratic | Perot | Other | Plurality | Percentage Total Vote | | |
|---|---|---|---|---|---|---|---|---|---|---|
| | | | | | | | | Rep. | Dem. | Perot |
| 32,953 | ADDISON | 17,026 | 5,034 | 8,092 | 3,777 | 123 | 3,058 D | 29.6% | 47.5% | 22.2% |
| 35,845 | BENNINGTON | 18,216 | 5,895 | 8,178 | 4,023 | 120 | 2,283 D | 32.4% | 44.9% | 22.1% |
| 27,846 | CALEDONIA | 13,062 | 4,571 | 4,948 | 3,458 | 85 | 377 D | 35.0% | 37.9% | 26.5% |
| 131,761 | CHITTENDEN | 70,121 | 19,093 | 35,314 | 15,202 | 512 | 16,221 D | 27.2% | 50.4% | 21.7% |
| 6,405 | ESSEX | 2,996 | 1,038 | 1,092 | 845 | 21 | 54 D | 34.6% | 36.4% | 28.2% |
| 39,980 | FRANKLIN | 18,751 | 5,484 | 8,004 | 5,146 | 117 | 2,520 D | 29.2% | 42.7% | 27.4% |
| 5,318 | GRAND ISLE | 3,379 | 1,012 | 1,444 | 893 | 30 | 432 D | 29.9% | 42.7% | 26.4% |
| 19,735 | LAMOILLE | 10,142 | 2,936 | 4,459 | 2,674 | 73 | 1,523 D | 28.9% | 44.0% | 26.4% |
| 26,149 | ORANGE | 13,410 | 4,249 | 5,774 | 3,283 | 104 | 1,525 D | 31.7% | 43.1% | 24.5% |
| 24,053 | ORLEANS | 11,513 | 3,572 | 4,721 | 3,135 | 85 | 1,149 D | 31.0% | 41.0% | 27.2% |
| 62,142 | RUTLAND | 31,144 | 10,963 | 12,829 | 7,190 | 162 | 1,866 D | 35.2% | 41.2% | 23.1% |
| 54,928 | WASHINGTON | 29,338 | 9,424 | 13,452 | 6,274 | 188 | 4,028 D | 32.1% | 45.9% | 21.4% |
| 41,588 | WINDHAM | 21,411 | 5,816 | 11,414 | 4,014 | 167 | 5,598 D | 27.2% | 53.3% | 18.7% |
| 54,055 | WINDSOR | 29,192 | 9,035 | 13,871 | 6,077 | 209 | 4,836 D | 31.0% | 47.5% | 20.8% |
| 562,758 | TOTAL | 289,701 | 88,122 | 133,592 | 65,991 | 1,996 | 45,470 D | 30.4% | 46.1% | 22.8% |

# VERMONT

## PRESIDENT 1988

| 1980 Census Population | County | Total Vote | Republican | Democratic | Other | Rep.-Dem. Plurality | Percentage | | | |
|---|---|---|---|---|---|---|---|---|---|---|
| | | | | | | | Total Vote | | Major Vote | |
| | | | | | | | Rep. | Dem. | Rep. | Dem. |
| 29,406 | ADDISON | 13,791 | 6,773 | 6,791 | 227 | 18 D | 49.1% | 49.2% | 49.9% | 50.1% |
| 33,345 | BENNINGTON | 15,725 | 8,387 | 7,174 | 164 | 1,213 R | 53.3% | 45.6% | 53.9% | 46.1% |
| 25,808 | CALEDONIA | 11,312 | 6,915 | 4,251 | 146 | 2,664 R | 61.1% | 37.6% | 61.9% | 38.1% |
| 115,534 | CHITTENDEN | 57,346 | 27,380 | 29,185 | 781 | 1,805 D | 47.7% | 50.9% | 48.4% | 51.6% |
| 6,313 | ESSEX | 2,391 | 1,535 | 837 | 19 | 698 R | 64.2% | 35.0% | 64.7% | 35.3% |
| 34,788 | FRANKLIN | 14,834 | 7,293 | 7,372 | 169 | 79 D | 49.2% | 49.7% | 49.7% | 50.3% |
| 4,613 | GRAND ISLE | 2,728 | 1,316 | 1,369 | 43 | 53 D | 48.2% | 50.2% | 49.0% | 51.0% |
| 16,767 | LAMOILLE | 8,133 | 4,433 | 3,561 | 139 | 872 R | 54.5% | 43.8% | 55.5% | 44.5% |
| 22,739 | ORANGE | 11,318 | 6,151 | 4,977 | 190 | 1,174 R | 54.3% | 44.0% | 55.3% | 44.7% |
| 23,440 | ORLEANS | 9,611 | 5,257 | 4,224 | 130 | 1,033 R | 54.7% | 43.9% | 55.4% | 44.6% |
| 58,347 | RUTLAND | 26,260 | 14,482 | 11,496 | 282 | 2,986 R | 55.1% | 43.8% | 55.7% | 44.3% |
| 52,393 | WASHINGTON | 26,294 | 13,253 | 12,690 | 351 | 563 R | 50.4% | 48.3% | 51.1% | 48.9% |
| 36,933 | WINDHAM | 18,654 | 8,572 | 9,839 | 243 | 1,267 D | 46.0% | 52.7% | 46.6% | 53.4% |
| 51,030 | WINDSOR | 24,930 | 12,584 | 12,009 | 337 | 575 R | 50.5% | 48.2% | 51.2% | 48.8% |
| 511,456 | TOTAL | 243,328 | 124,331 | 115,775 | 3,222 | 8,556 R | 51.1% | 47.6% | 51.8% | 48.2% |

# VERMONT

## PRESIDENT 1984

| 1980 Census Population | County | Total Vote | Republican | Democratic | Other | Rep.-Dem. Plurality | Percentage | | | |
|---|---|---|---|---|---|---|---|---|---|---|
| | | | | | | | Total Vote | | Major Vote | |
| | | | | | | | Rep. | Dem. | Rep. | Dem. |
| 29,406 | ADDISON | 13,030 | 7,589 | 5,299 | 142 | 2,290 R | 58.2% | 40.7% | 58.9% | 41.1% |
| 33,345 | BENNINGTON | 15,304 | 9,035 | 6,039 | 230 | 2,996 R | 59.0% | 39.5% | 59.9% | 40.1% |
| 25,808 | CALEDONIA | 10,614 | 7,249 | 3,223 | 142 | 4,026 R | 68.3% | 30.4% | 69.2% | 30.8% |
| 115,534 | CHITTENDEN | 55,869 | 30,217 | 24,830 | 822 | 5,387 R | 54.1% | 44.4% | 54.9% | 45.1% |
| 6,313 | ESSEX | 2,349 | 1,632 | 693 | 24 | 939 R | 69.5% | 29.5% | 70.2% | 29.8% |
| 34,788 | FRANKLIN | 14,574 | 8,683 | 5,755 | 136 | 2,928 R | 59.6% | 39.5% | 60.1% | 39.9% |
| 4,613 | GRAND ISLE | 2,551 | 1,537 | 980 | 34 | 557 R | 60.3% | 38.4% | 61.1% | 38.9% |
| 16,767 | LAMOILLE | 7,528 | 4,674 | 2,746 | 108 | 1,928 R | 62.1% | 36.5% | 63.0% | 37.0% |
| 22,739 | ORANGE | 10,645 | 6,407 | 4,088 | 150 | 2,319 R | 60.2% | 38.4% | 61.0% | 39.0% |
| 23,440 | ORLEANS | 9,395 | 5,966 | 3,294 | 135 | 2,672 R | 63.5% | 35.1% | 64.4% | 35.6% |
| 58,347 | RUTLAND | 24,991 | 15,236 | 9,545 | 210 | 5,691 R | 61.0% | 38.2% | 61.5% | 38.5% |
| 52,393 | WASHINGTON | 25,168 | 13,706 | 11,163 | 299 | 2,543 R | 54.5% | 44.4% | 55.1% | 44.9% |
| 36,933 | WINDHAM | 18,283 | 9,880 | 8,206 | 197 | 1,674 R | 54.0% | 44.9% | 54.6% | 45.4% |
| 51,030 | WINDSOR | 24,260 | 14,054 | 9,869 | 337 | 4,185 R | 57.9% | 40.7% | 58.7% | 41.3% |
| 511,456 | TOTAL | 234,561 | 135,865 | 95,730 | 2,966 | 40,135 R | 57.9% | 40.8% | 58.7% | 41.3% |

# VERMONT

## PRESIDENT 1980

| | | | | | | | Percentage | | | |
| | | | | | | | Total Vote | | Major Vote | |
| 1980 Census Population | County | Total Vote | Republican | Democratic | Other | Rep.-Dem. Plurality | Rep. | Dem. | Rep. | Dem. |
|---|---|---|---|---|---|---|---|---|---|---|
| 29,406 | ADDISON | 11,630 | 5,216 | 4,351 | 2,063 | 865 R | 44.8% | 37.4% | 54.5% | 45.5% |
| 33,345 | BENNINGTON | 13,721 | 6,091 | 5,361 | 2,269 | 730 R | 44.4% | 39.1% | 53.2% | 46.8% |
| 25,808 | CALEDONIA | 10,523 | 5,986 | 3,284 | 1,253 | 2,702 R | 56.9% | 31.2% | 64.6% | 35.4% |
| 115,534 | CHITTENDEN | 47,003 | 18,310 | 19,027 | 9,666 | 717 D | 39.0% | 40.5% | 49.0% | 51.0% |
| 6,313 | ESSEX | 2,340 | 1,305 | 799 | 236 | 506 R | 55.8% | 34.1% | 62.0% | 38.0% |
| 34,788 | FRANKLIN | 13,445 | 5,998 | 5,914 | 1,533 | 84 R | 44.6% | 44.0% | 50.4% | 49.6% |
| 4,613 | GRAND ISLE | 2,240 | 947 | 999 | 294 | 52 D | 42.3% | 44.6% | 48.7% | 51.3% |
| 16,767 | LAMOILLE | 6,890 | 3,228 | 2,414 | 1,248 | 814 R | 46.9% | 35.0% | 57.2% | 42.8% |
| 22,739 | ORANGE | 9,402 | 4,656 | 3,079 | 1,667 | 1,577 R | 49.5% | 32.7% | 60.2% | 39.8% |
| 23,440 | ORLEANS | 9,217 | 4,503 | 3,671 | 1,043 | 832 R | 48.9% | 39.8% | 55.1% | 44.9% |
| 58,347 | RUTLAND | 24,236 | 11,142 | 9,597 | 3,497 | 1,545 R | 46.0% | 39.6% | 53.7% | 46.3% |
| 52,393 | WASHINGTON | 23,151 | 9,714 | 9,559 | 3,878 | 155 R | 42.0% | 41.3% | 50.4% | 49.6% |
| 36,933 | WINDHAM | 16,598 | 7,062 | 5,830 | 3,706 | 1,232 R | 42.5% | 35.1% | 54.8% | 45.2% |
| 51,030 | WINDSOR | 22,903 | 10,470 | 8,067 | 4,366 | 2,403 R | 45.7% | 35.2% | 56.5% | 43.5% |
| 511,456 | TOTAL | 213,299 | 94,628 | 81,952 | 36,719 | 12,676 R | 44.4% | 38.4% | 53.6% | 46.4% |

# VERMONT

## PRESIDENT 1976

| | | | | | | | Percentage | | | |
| | | | | | | | Total Vote | | Major Vote | |
| 1970 Census Population | County | Total Vote | Republican | Democratic | Other | Rep.-Dem. Plurality | Rep. | Dem. | Rep. | Dem. |
|---|---|---|---|---|---|---|---|---|---|---|
| 24,266 | ADDISON | 10,129 | 5,726 | 4,164 | 239 | 1,562 R | 56.5% | 41.1% | 57.9% | 42.1% |
| 29,282 | BENNINGTON | 12,387 | 6,712 | 5,443 | 232 | 1,269 R | 54.2% | 43.9% | 55.2% | 44.8% |
| 22,789 | CALEDONIA | 9,193 | 5,488 | 3,511 | 194 | 1,977 R | 59.7% | 38.2% | 61.0% | 39.0% |
| 99,131 | CHITTENDEN | 41,348 | 22,013 | 17,992 | 1,343 | 4,021 R | 53.2% | 43.5% | 55.0% | 45.0% |
| 5,416 | ESSEX | 2,188 | 1,161 | 1,002 | 25 | 159 R | 53.1% | 45.8% | 53.7% | 46.3% |
| 31,282 | FRANKLIN | 11,977 | 6,190 | 5,610 | 177 | 580 R | 51.7% | 46.8% | 52.5% | 47.5% |
| 3,574 | GRAND ISLE | 1,908 | 1,004 | 866 | 38 | 138 R | 52.6% | 45.4% | 53.7% | 46.3% |
| 13,309 | LAMOILLE | 5,740 | 3,535 | 2,016 | 189 | 1,519 R | 61.6% | 35.1% | 63.7% | 36.3% |
| 17,676 | ORANGE | 8,132 | 4,768 | 3,171 | 193 | 1,597 R | 58.6% | 39.0% | 60.1% | 39.9% |
| 20,153 | ORLEANS | 7,772 | 4,075 | 3,561 | 136 | 514 R | 52.4% | 45.8% | 53.4% | 46.6% |
| 52,637 | RUTLAND | 21,724 | 11,565 | 9,778 | 381 | 1,787 R | 53.2% | 45.0% | 54.2% | 45.8% |
| 47,659 | WASHINGTON | 20,254 | 10,919 | 8,764 | 571 | 2,155 R | 53.9% | 43.3% | 55.5% | 44.5% |
| 33,476 | WINDHAM | 15,223 | 7,928 | 6,794 | 501 | 1,134 R | 52.1% | 44.6% | 53.9% | 46.1% |
| 44,082 | WINDSOR | 19,691 | 11,001 | 8,282 | 408 | 2,719 R | 55.9% | 42.1% | 57.1% | 42.9% |
| 444,732 | TOTAL | 187,765 | 102,085 | 80,954 | 4,726 | 21,131 R | 54.4% | 43.1% | 55.8% | 44.2% |

# VERMONT

## PRESIDENT 1972

| 1970 Census Population | County | Total Vote | Republican | Democratic | Other | Rep.-Dem. Plurality | Percentage | | | |
|---|---|---|---|---|---|---|---|---|---|---|
| | | | | | | | Total Vote | | Major Vote | |
| | | | | | | | Rep. | Dem. | Rep. | Dem. |
| 24,266 | ADDISON | 9,800 | 6,467 | 3,262 | 71 | 3,205 R | 66.0% | 33.3% | 66.5% | 33.5% |
| 29,282 | BENNINGTON | 12,453 | 7,542 | 4,804 | 107 | 2,738 R | 60.6% | 38.6% | 61.1% | 38.9% |
| 22,789 | CALEDONIA | 9,939 | 6,762 | 3,094 | 83 | 3,668 R | 68.0% | 31.1% | 68.6% | 31.4% |
| 99,131 | CHITTENDEN | 39,704 | 23,063 | 16,163 | 478 | 6,900 R | 58.1% | 40.7% | 58.8% | 41.2% |
| 5,416 | ESSEX | 2,110 | 1,441 | 655 | 14 | 786 R | 68.3% | 31.0% | 68.8% | 31.3% |
| 31,282 | FRANKLIN | 12,065 | 8,109 | 3,898 | 58 | 4,211 R | 67.2% | 32.3% | 67.5% | 32.5% |
| 3,574 | GRAND ISLE | 2,018 | 1,259 | 743 | 16 | 516 R | 62.4% | 36.8% | 62.9% | 37.1% |
| 13,309 | LAMOILLE | 5,935 | 4,164 | 1,659 | 112 | 2,505 R | 70.2% | 28.0% | 71.5% | 28.5% |
| 17,676 | ORANGE | 7,797 | 5,389 | 2,332 | 76 | 3,057 R | 69.1% | 29.9% | 69.8% | 30.2% |
| 20,153 | ORLEANS | 7,762 | 4,906 | 2,793 | 63 | 2,113 R | 63.2% | 36.0% | 63.7% | 36.3% |
| 52,637 | RUTLAND | 22,563 | 14,143 | 8,261 | 159 | 5,882 R | 62.7% | 36.6% | 63.1% | 36.9% |
| 47,659 | WASHINGTON | 20,169 | 12,421 | 7,596 | 152 | 4,825 R | 61.6% | 37.7% | 62.1% | 37.9% |
| 33,476 | WINDHAM | 15,100 | 9,062 | 5,925 | 113 | 3,137 R | 60.0% | 39.2% | 60.5% | 39.5% |
| 44,082 | WINDSOR | 19,532 | 12,421 | 6,989 | 122 | 5,432 R | 63.6% | 35.8% | 64.0% | 36.0% |
| 444,732 | TOTAL | 186,947 | 117,149 | 68,174 | 1,624 | 48,975 R | 62.7% | 36.5% | 63.2% | 36.8% |

# VERMONT

## PRESIDENT 1968

| 1960 Census Population | County | Total Vote | Republican | Democratic | AIP | Other | Plurality | Percentage Total Vote | | |
|---|---|---|---|---|---|---|---|---|---|---|
| | | | | | | | | Rep. | Dem. | AIP |
| 20,076 | ADDISON | 8,228 | 5,006 | 2,914 | 278 | 30 | 2,092 R | 60.8% | 35.4% | 3.4% |
| 25,088 | BENNINGTON | 11,416 | 5,967 | 4,966 | 401 | 82 | 1,001 R | 52.3% | 43.5% | 3.5% |
| 22,786 | CALEDONIA | 8,485 | 4,996 | 3,201 | 250 | 38 | 1,795 R | 58.9% | 37.7% | 2.9% |
| 74,425 | CHITTENDEN | 32,250 | 14,621 | 16,420 | 1,000 | 209 | 1,799 D | 45.3% | 50.9% | 3.1% |
| 6,083 | ESSEX | 2,025 | 1,009 | 952 | 57 | 7 | 57 R | 49.8% | 47.0% | 2.8% |
| 29,474 | FRANKLIN | 11,681 | 5,218 | 6,027 | 398 | 38 | 809 D | 44.7% | 51.6% | 3.4% |
| 2,927 | GRAND ISLE | 1,559 | 754 | 730 | 73 | 2 | 24 R | 48.4% | 46.8% | 4.7% |
| 11,027 | LAMOILLE | 4,358 | 2,965 | 1,239 | 140 | 14 | 1,726 R | 68.0% | 28.4% | 3.2% |
| 16,014 | ORANGE | 6,250 | 4,135 | 1,879 | 200 | 36 | 2,256 R | 66.2% | 30.1% | 3.2% |
| 20,143 | ORLEANS | 7,118 | 4,055 | 2,762 | 269 | 32 | 1,293 R | 57.0% | 38.8% | 3.8% |
| 46,719 | RUTLAND | 20,127 | 10,318 | 9,000 | 699 | 110 | 1,318 R | 51.3% | 44.7% | 3.5% |
| 42,860 | WASHINGTON | 17,839 | 9,387 | 7,826 | 497 | 129 | 1,561 R | 52.6% | 43.9% | 2.8% |
| 29,776 | WINDHAM | 12,721 | 6,916 | 5,353 | 374 | 78 | 1,563 R | 54.4% | 42.1% | 2.9% |
| 42,483 | WINDSOR | 17,347 | 9,795 | 6,986 | 468 | 98 | 2,809 R | 56.5% | 40.3% | 2.7% |
| 389,881 | TOTAL | 161,404 | 85,142 | 70,255 | 5,104 | 903 | 14,887 R | 52.8% | 43.5% | 3.2% |

# VERMONT

## PRESIDENT 1964

| 1960 Census Population | County | Total Vote | Republican | Democratic | Other | Rep.-Dem. Plurality | Percentage | | | |
|---|---|---|---|---|---|---|---|---|---|---|
| | | | | | | | Total Vote | | Major Vote | |
| | | | | | | | Rep. | Dem. | Rep. | Dem. |
| 20,076 | ADDISON | 8,258 | 3,500 | 4,758 | | 1,258 D | 42.4% | 57.6% | 42.4% | 57.6% |
| 25,088 | BENNINGTON | 11,254 | 3,895 | 7,359 | | 3,464 D | 34.6% | 65.4% | 34.6% | 65.4% |
| 22,786 | CALEDONIA | 8,990 | 3,258 | 5,732 | | 2,474 D | 36.2% | 63.8% | 36.2% | 63.8% |
| 74,425 | CHITTENDEN | 30,867 | 9,050 | 21,817 | | 12,767 D | 29.3% | 70.7% | 29.3% | 70.7% |
| 6,083 | ESSEX | 2,423 | 750 | 1,673 | | 923 D | 31.0% | 69.0% | 31.0% | 69.0% |
| 29,474 | FRANKLIN | 12,086 | 3,261 | 8,823 | 2 | 5,562 D | 27.0% | 73.0% | 27.0% | 73.0% |
| 2,927 | GRAND ISLE | 1,503 | 506 | 996 | 1 | 490 D | 33.7% | 66.3% | 33.7% | 66.3% |
| 11,027 | LAMOILLE | 4,412 | 2,036 | 2,376 | | 340 D | 46.1% | 53.9% | 46.1% | 53.9% |
| 16,014 | ORANGE | 6,642 | 2,723 | 3,918 | 1 | 1,195 D | 41.0% | 59.0% | 41.0% | 59.0% |
| 20,143 | ORLEANS | 7,907 | 3,009 | 4,898 | | 1,889 D | 38.1% | 61.9% | 38.1% | 61.9% |
| 46,719 | RUTLAND | 20,406 | 7,165 | 13,241 | | 6,076 D | 35.1% | 64.9% | 35.1% | 64.9% |
| 42,860 | WASHINGTON | 17,763 | 5,750 | 12,002 | 11 | 6,252 D | 32.4% | 67.6% | 32.4% | 67.6% |
| 29,776 | WINDHAM | 12,555 | 4,180 | 8,371 | 4 | 4,191 D | 33.3% | 66.7% | 33.3% | 66.7% |
| 42,483 | WINDSOR | 18,023 | 5,859 | 12,163 | 1 | 6,304 D | 32.5% | 67.5% | 32.5% | 67.5% |
| 389,881 | TOTAL | 163,089 | 54,942 | 108,127 | 20 | 53,185 D | 33.7% | 66.3% | 33.7% | 66.3% |

# VERMONT

## PRESIDENT 1960

| 1960 Census Population | County | Total Vote | Republican | Democratic | Other | Rep.-Dem. Plurality | Percentage | | | |
|---|---|---|---|---|---|---|---|---|---|---|
| | | | | | | | Total Vote | | Major Vote | |
| | | | | | | | Rep. | Dem. | Rep. | Dem. |
| 20,076 | ADDISON | 8,489 | 5,520 | 2,969 | | 2,551 R | 65.0% | 35.0% | 65.0% | 35.0% |
| 25,088 | BENNINGTON | 11,602 | 7,099 | 4,502 | 1 | 2,597 R | 61.2% | 38.8% | 61.2% | 38.8% |
| 22,786 | CALEDONIA | 9,597 | 6,688 | 2,909 | | 3,779 R | 69.7% | 30.3% | 69.7% | 30.3% |
| 74,425 | CHITTENDEN | 30,031 | 13,072 | 16,959 | | 3,887 D | 43.5% | 56.5% | 43.5% | 56.5% |
| 6,083 | ESSEX | 2,502 | 1,439 | 1,063 | | 376 R | 57.5% | 42.5% | 57.5% | 42.5% |
| 29,474 | FRANKLIN | 12,472 | 5,444 | 7,028 | | 1,584 D | 43.6% | 56.4% | 43.6% | 56.4% |
| 2,927 | GRAND ISLE | 1,617 | 798 | 819 | | 21 D | 49.4% | 50.6% | 49.4% | 50.6% |
| 11,027 | LAMOILLE | 4,304 | 3,272 | 1,032 | | 2,240 R | 76.0% | 24.0% | 76.0% | 24.0% |
| 16,014 | ORANGE | 6,944 | 5,363 | 1,581 | | 3,782 R | 77.2% | 22.8% | 77.2% | 22.8% |
| 20,143 | ORLEANS | 8,381 | 5,027 | 3,354 | | 1,673 R | 60.0% | 40.0% | 60.0% | 40.0% |
| 46,719 | RUTLAND | 21,412 | 12,166 | 9,246 | | 2,920 R | 56.8% | 43.2% | 56.8% | 43.2% |
| 42,860 | WASHINGTON | 17,578 | 10,458 | 7,116 | 4 | 3,342 R | 59.5% | 40.5% | 59.5% | 40.5% |
| 29,776 | WINDHAM | 13,486 | 9,128 | 4,358 | | 4,770 R | 67.7% | 32.3% | 67.7% | 32.3% |
| 42,483 | WINDSOR | 18,909 | 12,657 | 6,250 | 2 | 6,407 R | 66.9% | 33.1% | 66.9% | 33.1% |
| 389,881 | TOTAL | 167,324 | 98,131 | 69,186 | 7 | 28,945 R | 58.6% | 41.3% | 58.6% | 41.4% |

# VERMONT

## ELECTION NOTES

**2004**   Other vote was 4,494 Independent (Ralph Nader); 1,102 Libertarian (Michael Badnarik); 265 Liberty Union (John Parker); 244 Socialist Workers (Roger Calero); 957 write-in.

**2000**   Other vote was 2,192 Reform (Buchanan); 1,044 Vermont Grassroots (Lane); 784 Libertarian (Browne); 219 Natural Law (Hagelin); 161 Liberty Union (McReynolds); 153 Constitution (Phillips); 70 Socialist Workers (Harris); 514 scattered write-in. Nader was listed on the ballot as Progressive/Green.

**1996**   Other vote was 5,585 Green (Nader); 1,183 Libertarian (Browne); 498 Natural Law (Hagelin); 480 Grassroots (Peron); 382 Taxpayers (Phillips); 292 Liberty Union (Hollis); 199 Socialist Workers (Harris); 560 scattered write-in.

**1992**   Other vote was 501 Marrou (Libertarian); 429 Fulani (Liberty Union and New Alliance); 315 Hagelin (Natural Law); 124 Phillips (Taxpayers); 82 Warren (Socialist Workers); 57 LaRouche (Freedom for LaRouche); 488 scattered write-in.

**1988**   Other vote was 1,000 Paul (Libertarian); 275 LaRouche (Independent); 205 Fulani (New Alliance); 189 Duke (Populist); 164 Lewin (Peace and Freedom); 142 Kenoyer (Liberty Union); 113 Warren (Socialist Workers); 1,134 scattered write-in.

**1984**   Other vote was 1,002 Bergland (Libertarian); 423 LaRouche (Independent); 323 Serrette (Liberty Union); 264 Johnson (Citizens); 127 Mason (Socialist Workers); 115 Hall (Communist); 712 scattered write-in.

**1980**   Other vote was 31,761 Anderson (Independent); 2,316 Commoner (Citizens); 1,900 Clark (Libertarian); 136 McReynolds (Liberty Union); 118 Hall (Communist); 75 DeBerry (Socialist Workers); 413 scattered write-in.

**1976**   Other vote was 4,001 McCarthy (McCarthy '76); 430 Camejo (Socialist Workers); 196 LaRouche (U.S. Labor); 99 scattered write-in. The Democratic candidate was also the Independent Vermonters nominee and 991 of his votes were received as the IV candidate. Early unamended canvass gave the Rutland county vote as 9,867 Republican; 7,440 Democratic/Independent Vermonters; the canvass was amended to correct an undercount in the votes from Rutland City.

**1972**   Other vote was 1,010 Spock (Liberty Union); 296 Jenness (Socialist Workers); 318 scattered write-in.

**1968**   Wallace on the ballot as George Wallace party.  Other vote was 579 no Presidential candidate indicated (New Party); 295 Halstead (Socialist Workers); 29 scattered write-in.

**1964**   Other vote was scattered write-in.

**1960**   Other vote was scattered write-in.

# VIRGINIA

## POPULAR VOTE FOR PRESIDENT 1920 TO 2004

| Year | Total Vote | Republican | | Democratic | | Other Vote | Plurality | Percentage | | | |
|------|-----------|------|-----------|------|-----------|------|-----------|------|------|------|------|
| | | | | | | | | Total Vote | | Major Vote | |
| | | Vote | Candidate | Vote | Candidate | | | Rep. | Dem. | Rep. | Dem. |
| 2004 | 3,198,367 | 1,716,959 | Bush, George W. | 1,454,742 | Kerry, John | 26,666 | 262,217 R | 53.7% | 45.5% | 54.1% | 45.9% |
| 2000 ** | 2,739,447 | 1,437,490 | Bush, George W. | 1,217,290 | Gore, Al | 84,667 | 220,200 R | 52.5% | 44.4% | 54.1% | 45.9% |
| 1996 ** | 2,416,642 | 1,138,350 | Dole, Bob | 1,091,060 | Clinton, Bill | 187,232 | 47,290 R | 47.1% | 45.1% | 51.1% | 48.9% |
| 1992 ** | 2,558,665 | 1,150,517 | Bush, George | 1,038,650 | Clinton, Bill | 369,498 | 111,867 R | 45.0% | 40.6% | 52.6% | 47.4% |
| 1988 | 2,191,609 | 1,309,162 | Bush, George | 859,799 | Dukakis, Michael S. | 22,648 | 449,363 R | 59.7% | 39.2% | 60.4% | 39.6% |
| 1984 | 2,146,635 | 1,337,078 | Reagan, Ronald | 796,250 | Mondale, Walter F. | 13,307 | 540,828 R | 62.3% | 37.1% | 62.7% | 37.3% |
| 1980** | 1,866,032 | 989,609 | Reagan, Ronald | 752,174 | Carter, Jimmy | 124,249 | 237,435 R | 53.0% | 40.3% | 56.8% | 43.2% |
| 1976 | 1,697,094 | 836,554 | Ford, Gerald R. | 813,896 | Carter, Jimmy | 46,644 | 22,658 R | 49.3% | 48.0% | 50.7% | 49.3% |
| 1972 | 1,457,019 | 988,493 | Nixon, Richard M. | 438,887 | McGovern, George S. | 29,639 | 549,606 R | 67.8% | 30.1% | 69.3% | 30.7% |
| 1968 ** | 1,361,491 | 590,319 | Nixon, Richard M. | 442,387 | Humphrey, Hubert H. | 328,785 | 147,932 R | 43.4% | 32.5% | 57.2% | 42.8% |
| 1964 | 1,042,267 | 481,334 | Goldwater, Barry M. | 558,038 | Johnson, Lyndon B. | 2,895 | 76,704 D | 46.2% | 53.5% | 46.3% | 53.7% |
| 1960 | 771,449 | 404,521 | Nixon, Richard M. | 362,327 | Kennedy, John F. | 4,601 | 42,194 R | 52.4% | 47.0% | 52.8% | 47.2% |
| 1956 | 697,978 | 386,459 | Eisenhower, Dwight D. | 267,760 | Stevenson, Adlai E. | 43,759 | 118,699 R | 55.4% | 38.4% | 59.1% | 40.9% |
| 1952 | 619,689 | 349,037 | Eisenhower, Dwight D. | 268,677 | Stevenson, Adlai E. | 1,975 | 80,360 R | 56.3% | 43.4% | 56.5% | 43.5% |
| 1948 | 419,256 | 172,070 | Dewey, Thomas E. | 200,786 | Truman, Harry S. | 46,400 | 28,716 D | 41.0% | 47.9% | 46.1% | 53.9% |
| 1944 | 388,485 | 145,243 | Dewey, Thomas E. | 242,276 | Roosevelt, Franklin D. | 966 | 97,033 D | 37.4% | 62.4% | 37.5% | 62.5% |
| 1940 | 346,608 | 109,363 | Willkie, Wendell | 235,961 | Roosevelt, Franklin D. | 1,284 | 126,598 D | 31.6% | 68.1% | 31.7% | 68.3% |
| 1936 | 334,590 | 98,336 | Landon, Alfred M. | 234,980 | Roosevelt, Franklin D. | 1,274 | 136,644 D | 29.4% | 70.2% | 29.5% | 70.5% |
| 1932 | 297,942 | 89,637 | Hoover, Herbert C. | 203,979 | Roosevelt, Franklin D. | 4,326 | 114,342 D | 30.1% | 68.5% | 30.5% | 69.5% |
| 1928 | 305,364 | 164,609 | Hoover, Herbert C. | 140,146 | Smith, Alfred E. | 609 | 24,463 R | 53.9% | 45.9% | 54.0% | 46.0% |
| 1924 | 223,603 | 73,328 | Coolidge, Calvin | 139,717 | Davis, John W. | 10,558 | 66,389 D | 32.8% | 62.5% | 34.4% | 65.6% |
| 1920 | 231,000 | 87,456 | Harding, Warren G. | 141,670 | Cox, James M. | 1,874 | 54,214 D | 37.9% | 61.3% | 38.2% | 61.8% |

In 2000 the other vote column includes 59,398 votes cast for Green (Nader). In 1996 the other vote column includes 159,861 votes cast for Perot. In 1992 the other vote column includes 348,639 votes cast for Perot. In 1980 the other column includes 95,418 votes for Independent (Anderson). In 1968 other vote was 321,833 American Independent (Wallace); 4,671 Socialist Labor; 1,680 Peace and Freedom and 601 Prohibition.

## ELECTORAL COLLEGE VOTE 1920 TO 2004

| Year | Total | Republican | Democratic | Other |
|------|-------|-----------|-----------|-------|
| 2004 | 13 | 13 | | |
| 2000 | 13 | 13 | | |
| 1996 | 13 | 13 | | |
| 1992 | 13 | 13 | | |
| 1988 | 12 | 12 | | |
| 1984 | 12 | 12 | | |
| 1980 | 12 | 12 | | |
| 1976 | 12 | 12 | | |
| 1972 ** | 12 | 11 | | 1 HOSPERS |
| 1968 | 12 | 12 | | |
| 1964 | 12 | | 12 | |
| 1960 | 12 | 12 | | |
| 1956 | 12 | 12 | | |
| 1952 | 12 | 12 | | |
| 1948 | 11 | | 11 | |
| 1944 | 11 | | 11 | |
| 1940 | 11 | | 11 | |
| 1936 | 11 | | 11 | |
| 1932 | 11 | | 11 | |
| 1928 | 12 | 12 | — | |
| 1924 | 12 | | 12 | |
| 1920 | 12 | | 12 | |

In 1972 one of the twelve Republican electors voted in the Electoral College for John Hospers and Theodora Nathan, the Libertarian candidates, rather than for the national Republican candidates.

# VIRGINIA

# VIRGINIA

## PRESIDENT 2004

| 2000 Census Population | County | Total Vote | Republican | Democratic | Other | Rep.-Dem. Plurality | Percentage Total Vote Rep. | Dem. | Major Vote Rep. | Dem. |
|---|---|---|---|---|---|---|---|---|---|---|
| 38,305 | ACCOMACK | 13,356 | 7,726 | 5,518 | 112 | 2,208 R | 57.8% | 41.3% | 58.3% | 41.7% |
| 79,236 | ALBEMARLE | 43,726 | 21,189 | 22,088 | 449 | 899 D | 48.5% | 50.5% | 49.0% | 51.0% |
| 17,215 | ALLEGHANY | 7,195 | 3,962 | 3,203 | 30 | 759 R | 55.1% | 44.5% | 55.3% | 44.7% |
| 11,400 | AMELIA | 5,397 | 3,499 | 1,862 | 36 | 1,637 R | 64.8% | 34.5% | 65.3% | 34.7% |
| 31,894 | AMHERST | 12,695 | 7,758 | 4,866 | 71 | 2,892 R | 61.1% | 38.3% | 61.5% | 38.5% |
| 13,705 | APPOMATTOX | 6,655 | 4,366 | 2,191 | 98 | 2,175 R | 65.6% | 32.9% | 66.6% | 33.4% |
| 189,453 | ARLINGTON | 94,650 | 29,635 | 63,987 | 1,028 | 34,352 D | 31.3% | 67.6% | 31.7% | 68.3% |
| 65,615 | AUGUSTA | 29,704 | 22,100 | 7,019 | 585 | 15,081 R | 74.4% | 23.6% | 75.9% | 24.1% |
| 5,048 | BATH | 2,282 | 1,432 | 828 | 22 | 604 R | 62.8% | 36.3% | 63.4% | 36.6% |
| 60,371 | BEDFORD COUNTY | 31,404 | 21,925 | 9,102 | 377 | 12,823 R | 69.8% | 29.0% | 70.7% | 29.3% |
| 6,871 | BLAND | 2,865 | 1,962 | 846 | 57 | 1,116 R | 68.5% | 29.5% | 69.9% | 30.1% |
| 30,496 | BOTETOURT | 15,797 | 10,865 | 4,801 | 131 | 6,064 R | 68.8% | 30.4% | 69.4% | 30.6% |
| 18,419 | BRUNSWICK | 6,926 | 2,852 | 4,062 | 12 | 1,210 D | 41.2% | 58.6% | 41.2% | 58.8% |
| 26,978 | BUCHANAN | 9,829 | 4,507 | 5,275 | 47 | 768 D | 45.9% | 53.7% | 46.1% | 53.9% |
| 15,623 | BUCKINGHAM | 6,027 | 3,185 | 2,789 | 53 | 396 R | 52.8% | 46.3% | 53.3% | 46.7% |
| 51,078 | CAMPBELL | 22,997 | 15,891 | 6,862 | 244 | 9,029 R | 69.1% | 29.8% | 69.8% | 30.2% |
| 22,121 | CAROLINE | 9,954 | 4,999 | 4,878 | 77 | 121 R | 50.2% | 49.0% | 50.6% | 49.4% |
| 29,245 | CARROLL | 12,128 | 8,173 | 3,888 | 67 | 4,285 R | 67.4% | 32.1% | 67.8% | 32.2% |
| 6,926 | CHARLES CITY | 3,439 | 1,254 | 2,155 | 30 | 901 D | 36.5% | 62.7% | 36.8% | 63.2% |
| 12,472 | CHARLOTTE | 5,438 | 3,166 | 2,223 | 49 | 943 R | 58.2% | 40.9% | 58.7% | 41.3% |
| 259,903 | CHESTERFIELD | 133,814 | 83,745 | 49,346 | 723 | 34,399 R | 62.6% | 36.9% | 62.9% | 37.1% |
| 12,652 | CLARKE | 6,505 | 3,741 | 2,699 | 65 | 1,042 R | 57.5% | 41.5% | 58.1% | 41.9% |
| 5,091 | CRAIG | 2,621 | 1,706 | 901 | 14 | 805 R | 65.1% | 34.4% | 65.4% | 34.6% |
| 34,262 | CULPEPER | 15,605 | 10,026 | 5,476 | 103 | 4,550 R | 64.2% | 35.1% | 64.7% | 35.3% |
| 9,017 | CUMBERLAND | 4,126 | 2,377 | 1,721 | 28 | 656 R | 57.6% | 41.7% | 58.0% | 42.0% |
| 16,395 | DICKENSON | 7,406 | 3,591 | 3,761 | 54 | 170 D | 48.5% | 50.8% | 48.8% | 51.2% |
| 24,533 | DINWIDDIE | 10,839 | 6,193 | 4,569 | 77 | 1,624 R | 57.1% | 42.2% | 57.5% | 42.5% |
| 9,989 | ESSEX | 4,344 | 2,304 | 2,007 | 33 | 297 R | 53.0% | 46.2% | 53.4% | 46.6% |
| 969,749 | FAIRFAX COUNTY | 461,379 | 211,980 | 245,671 | 3,728 | 33,691 D | 45.9% | 53.2% | 46.3% | 53.7% |
| 55,139 | FAUQUIER | 29,915 | 19,011 | 10,712 | 192 | 8,299 R | 63.6% | 35.8% | 64.0% | 36.0% |
| 13,874 | FLOYD | 6,734 | 4,162 | 2,488 | 84 | 1,674 R | 61.8% | 36.9% | 62.6% | 37.4% |
| 20,047 | FLUVANNA | 10,957 | 6,458 | 4,415 | 84 | 2,043 R | 58.9% | 40.3% | 59.4% | 40.6% |
| 47,286 | FRANKLIN COUNTY | 22,223 | 14,048 | 8,002 | 173 | 6,046 R | 63.2% | 36.0% | 63.7% | 36.3% |
| 59,209 | FREDERICK | 28,540 | 19,386 | 8,853 | 301 | 10,533 R | 67.9% | 31.0% | 68.6% | 31.4% |
| 16,657 | GILES | 7,498 | 4,320 | 3,047 | 131 | 1,273 R | 57.6% | 40.6% | 58.6% | 41.4% |
| 34,780 | GLOUCESTER | 16,333 | 11,084 | 5,105 | 144 | 5,979 R | 67.9% | 31.3% | 68.5% | 31.5% |
| 16,863 | GOOCHLAND | 10,338 | 6,668 | 3,583 | 87 | 3,085 R | 64.5% | 34.7% | 65.0% | 35.0% |
| 17,917 | GRAYSON | 7,137 | 4,655 | 2,430 | 52 | 2,225 R | 65.2% | 34.0% | 65.7% | 34.3% |
| 15,244 | GREENE | 6,939 | 4,570 | 2,240 | 129 | 2,330 R | 65.9% | 32.3% | 67.1% | 32.9% |
| 11,560 | GREENSVILLE | 4,258 | 1,732 | 2,514 | 12 | 782 D | 40.7% | 59.0% | 40.8% | 59.2% |
| 37,355 | HALIFAX | 14,656 | 8,363 | 6,220 | 73 | 2,143 R | 57.1% | 42.4% | 57.3% | 42.7% |
| 86,320 | HANOVER | 49,611 | 35,404 | 13,941 | 266 | 21,463 R | 71.4% | 28.1% | 71.7% | 28.3% |
| 262,300 | HENRICO | 133,418 | 71,809 | 60,864 | 745 | 10,945 R | 53.8% | 45.6% | 54.1% | 45.9% |
| 57,930 | HENRY | 23,458 | 13,358 | 9,851 | 249 | 3,507 R | 56.9% | 42.0% | 57.6% | 42.4% |
| 2,536 | HIGHLAND | 1,520 | 982 | 522 | 16 | 460 R | 64.6% | 34.3% | 65.3% | 34.7% |
| 29,728 | ISLE OF WIGHT | 15,871 | 9,929 | 5,871 | 71 | 4,058 R | 62.6% | 37.0% | 62.8% | 37.2% |
| 48,102 | JAMES CITY | 31,090 | 18,949 | 11,934 | 207 | 7,015 R | 60.9% | 38.4% | 61.4% | 38.6% |
| 6,630 | KING AND QUEEN | 3,286 | 1,737 | 1,506 | 43 | 231 R | 52.9% | 45.8% | 53.6% | 46.4% |
| 16,803 | KING GEORGE | 7,921 | 5,124 | 2,739 | 58 | 2,385 R | 64.7% | 34.6% | 65.2% | 34.8% |
| 13,146 | KING WILLIAM | 6,872 | 4,397 | 2,436 | 39 | 1,961 R | 64.0% | 35.4% | 64.3% | 35.7% |
| 11,567 | LANCASTER | 6,230 | 3,724 | 2,477 | 29 | 1,247 R | 59.8% | 39.8% | 60.1% | 39.9% |
| 23,589 | LEE | 9,770 | 5,664 | 4,005 | 101 | 1,659 R | 58.0% | 41.0% | 58.6% | 41.4% |
| 169,599 | LOUDOUN | 108,430 | 60,382 | 47,271 | 777 | 13,111 R | 55.7% | 43.6% | 56.1% | 43.9% |
| 25,627 | LOUISA | 12,035 | 7,083 | 4,844 | 108 | 2,239 R | 58.9% | 40.2% | 59.4% | 40.6% |
| 13,146 | LUNENBURG | 5,245 | 2,858 | 2,362 | 25 | 496 R | 54.5% | 45.0% | 54.8% | 45.2% |
| 12,520 | MADISON | 5,772 | 3,556 | 2,176 | 40 | 1,380 R | 61.6% | 37.7% | 62.0% | 38.0% |
| 9,207 | MATHEWS | 5,129 | 3,497 | 1,589 | 43 | 1,908 R | 68.2% | 31.0% | 68.8% | 31.2% |
| 32,380 | MECKLENBURG | 12,780 | 7,319 | 5,293 | 168 | 2,026 R | 57.3% | 41.4% | 58.0% | 42.0% |
| 9,932 | MIDDLESEX | 5,377 | 3,336 | 1,914 | 127 | 1,422 R | 62.0% | 35.6% | 63.5% | 36.5% |
| 83,629 | MONTGOMERY | 31,515 | 17,070 | 14,128 | 317 | 2,942 R | 54.2% | 44.8% | 54.7% | 45.3% |

# VIRGINIA

## PRESIDENT 2004

| 2000 Census Population | County | Total Vote | Republican | Democratic | Other | Rep.-Dem. Plurality | | Percentage | | | |
|---|---|---|---|---|---|---|---|---|---|---|---|
| | | | | | | | | Total Vote | | Major Vote | |
| | | | | | | | | Rep. | Dem. | Rep. | Dem. |
| 14,445 | NELSON | 7,139 | 3,539 | 3,543 | 57 | 4 | D | 49.6% | 49.6% | 50.0% | 50.0% |
| 13,462 | NEW KENT | 7,946 | 5,414 | 2,443 | 89 | 2,971 | R | 68.1% | 30.7% | 68.9% | 31.1% |
| 13,093 | NORTHAMPTON | 5,499 | 2,669 | 2,775 | 55 | 106 | D | 48.5% | 50.5% | 49.0% | 51.0% |
| 12,259 | NORTHUMBERLAND | 6,409 | 3,832 | 2,548 | 29 | 1,284 | R | 59.8% | 39.8% | 60.1% | 39.9% |
| 15,725 | NOTTOWAY | 6,030 | 3,303 | 2,635 | 92 | 668 | R | 54.8% | 43.7% | 55.6% | 44.4% |
| 25,881 | ORANGE | 12,928 | 7,749 | 5,015 | 164 | 2,734 | R | 59.9% | 38.8% | 60.7% | 39.3% |
| 23,177 | PAGE | 9,603 | 6,221 | 3,324 | 58 | 2,897 | R | 64.8% | 34.6% | 65.2% | 34.8% |
| 19,407 | PATRICK | 8,215 | 5,507 | 2,572 | 136 | 2,935 | R | 67.0% | 31.3% | 68.2% | 31.8% |
| 61,745 | PITTSYLVANIA | 27,417 | 17,673 | 9,274 | 470 | 8,399 | R | 64.5% | 33.8% | 65.6% | 34.4% |
| 22,377 | POWHATAN | 12,163 | 8,955 | 3,112 | 96 | 5,843 | R | 73.6% | 25.6% | 74.2% | 25.8% |
| 19,720 | PRINCE EDWARD | 7,316 | 3,571 | 3,632 | 113 | 61 | D | 48.8% | 49.6% | 49.6% | 50.4% |
| 33,047 | PRINCE GEORGE | 13,254 | 8,131 | 5,066 | 57 | 3,065 | R | 61.3% | 38.2% | 61.6% | 38.4% |
| 280,813 | PRINCE WILLIAM | 132,063 | 69,776 | 61,271 | 1,016 | 8,505 | R | 52.8% | 46.4% | 53.2% | 46.8% |
| 35,127 | PULASKI | 14,251 | 8,769 | 5,310 | 172 | 3,459 | R | 61.5% | 37.3% | 62.3% | 37.7% |
| 6,983 | RAPPAHANNOCK | 4,050 | 2,172 | 1,837 | 41 | 335 | R | 53.6% | 45.4% | 54.2% | 45.8% |
| 8,809 | RICHMOND COUNTY | 3,361 | 2,082 | 1,243 | 36 | 839 | R | 61.9% | 37.0% | 62.6% | 37.4% |
| 85,778 | ROANOKE COUNTY | 46,973 | 30,596 | 16,082 | 295 | 14,514 | R | 65.1% | 34.2% | 65.5% | 34.5% |
| 20,808 | ROCKBRIDGE | 9,181 | 5,412 | 3,627 | 142 | 1,785 | R | 58.9% | 39.5% | 59.9% | 40.1% |
| 67,725 | ROCKINGHAM | 29,216 | 21,737 | 7,273 | 206 | 14,464 | R | 74.4% | 24.9% | 74.9% | 25.1% |
| 30,308 | RUSSELL | 11,423 | 6,077 | 5,167 | 179 | 910 | R | 53.2% | 45.2% | 54.0% | 46.0% |
| 23,403 | SCOTT | 9,967 | 6,479 | 3,324 | 164 | 3,155 | R | 65.0% | 33.4% | 66.1% | 33.9% |
| 35,075 | SHENANDOAH | 17,146 | 11,820 | 5,186 | 140 | 6,634 | R | 68.9% | 30.2% | 69.5% | 30.5% |
| 33,081 | SMYTH | 12,319 | 7,906 | 4,143 | 270 | 3,763 | R | 64.2% | 33.6% | 65.6% | 34.4% |
| 17,482 | SOUTHAMPTON | 7,492 | 4,018 | 3,431 | 43 | 587 | R | 53.6% | 45.8% | 53.9% | 46.1% |
| 90,395 | SPOTSYLVANIA | 45,445 | 28,527 | 16,623 | 295 | 11,904 | R | 62.8% | 36.6% | 63.2% | 36.8% |
| 92,446 | STAFFORD | 45,986 | 28,500 | 17,208 | 278 | 11,292 | R | 62.0% | 37.4% | 62.4% | 37.6% |
| 6,829 | SURRY | 3,522 | 1,543 | 1,954 | 25 | 411 | D | 43.8% | 55.5% | 44.1% | 55.9% |
| 12,504 | SUSSEX | 4,345 | 1,890 | 2,420 | 35 | 530 | D | 43.5% | 55.7% | 43.9% | 56.1% |
| 44,598 | TAZEWELL | 17,480 | 10,039 | 7,184 | 257 | 2,855 | R | 57.4% | 41.1% | 58.3% | 41.7% |
| 31,584 | WARREN | 14,068 | 8,600 | 5,241 | 227 | 3,359 | R | 61.1% | 37.3% | 62.1% | 37.9% |
| 51,103 | WASHINGTON | 22,514 | 14,749 | 7,339 | 426 | 7,410 | R | 65.5% | 32.6% | 66.8% | 33.2% |
| 16,718 | WESTMORELAND | 6,848 | 3,433 | 3,370 | 45 | 63 | R | 50.1% | 49.2% | 50.5% | 49.5% |
| 40,123 | WISE | 14,312 | 8,330 | 5,802 | 180 | 2,528 | R | 58.2% | 40.5% | 58.9% | 41.1% |
| 27,599 | WYTHE | 11,554 | 7,911 | 3,581 | 62 | 4,330 | R | 68.5% | 31.0% | 68.8% | 31.2% |
| 56,297 | YORK | 29,880 | 19,396 | 10,276 | 208 | 9,120 | R | 64.9% | 34.4% | 65.4% | 34.6% |
| | **City/Town** | | | | | | | | | | |
| 128,283 | ALEXANDRIA | 61,515 | 19,844 | 41,116 | 555 | 21,272 | D | 32.3% | 66.8% | 32.6% | 67.4% |
| 6,299 | BEDFORD CITY | 2,542 | 1,472 | 1,042 | 28 | 430 | R | 57.9% | 41.0% | 58.6% | 41.4% |
| 17,367 | BRISTOL | 6,724 | 4,275 | 2,400 | 49 | 1,875 | R | 63.6% | 35.7% | 64.0% | 36.0% |
| 6,349 | BUENA VISTA | 2,389 | 1,417 | 936 | 36 | 481 | R | 59.3% | 39.2% | 60.2% | 39.8% |
| 45,049 | CHARLOTTESVILLE | 15,450 | 4,172 | 11,088 | 190 | 6,916 | D | 27.0% | 71.8% | 27.3% | 72.7% |
| 199,184 | CHESAPEAKE | 91,541 | 52,283 | 38,744 | 514 | 13,539 | R | 57.1% | 42.3% | 57.4% | 42.6% |
| 16,897 | COLONIAL HEIGHTS | 8,231 | 6,129 | 2,061 | 41 | 4,068 | R | 74.5% | 25.0% | 74.8% | 25.2% |
| 6,303 | COVINGTON | 2,301 | 1,104 | 1,179 | 18 | 75 | D | 48.0% | 51.2% | 48.4% | 51.6% |
| 48,411 | DANVILLE | 19,112 | 9,399 | 9,436 | 277 | 37 | D | 49.2% | 49.4% | 49.9% | 50.1% |
| 5,665 | EMPORIA | 2,221 | 970 | 1,247 | 4 | 277 | D | 43.7% | 56.1% | 43.8% | 56.2% |
| 21,498 | FAIRFAX CITY | 10,546 | 5,045 | 5,395 | 106 | 350 | D | 47.8% | 51.2% | 48.3% | 51.7% |
| 10,377 | FALLS CHURCH | 6,098 | 2,074 | 3,944 | 80 | 1,870 | D | 34.0% | 64.7% | 34.5% | 65.5% |
| 8,346 | FRANKLIN CITY | 3,536 | 1,613 | 1,910 | 13 | 297 | D | 45.6% | 54.0% | 45.8% | 54.2% |
| 19,279 | FREDERICKSBURG | 7,542 | 3,390 | 4,085 | 67 | 695 | D | 44.9% | 54.2% | 45.4% | 54.6% |
| 6,837 | GALAX | 2,335 | 1,336 | 987 | 12 | 349 | R | 57.2% | 42.3% | 57.5% | 42.5% |
| 146,437 | HAMPTON | 55,741 | 23,399 | 32,016 | 326 | 8,617 | D | 42.0% | 57.4% | 42.2% | 57.8% |
| 40,468 | HARRISONBURG | 11,030 | 6,165 | 4,726 | 139 | 1,439 | R | 55.9% | 42.8% | 56.6% | 43.4% |
| 22,354 | HOPEWELL | 7,936 | 4,251 | 3,573 | 112 | 678 | R | 53.6% | 45.0% | 54.3% | 45.7% |
| 6,867 | LEXINGTON | 2,349 | 982 | 1,340 | 27 | 358 | D | 41.8% | 57.0% | 42.3% | 57.7% |
| 65,269 | LYNCHBURG | 26,340 | 14,400 | 11,727 | 213 | 2,673 | R | 54.7% | 44.5% | 55.1% | 44.9% |

# VIRGINIA

## PRESIDENT 2004

| 2000 Census Population | City/Town | Total Vote | Republican | Democratic | Other | Rep.-Dem. Plurality | Percentage | | | |
|---|---|---|---|---|---|---|---|---|---|---|
| | | | | | | | Total Vote | | Major Vote | |
| | | | | | | | Rep. | Dem. | Rep. | Dem. |
| 35,135 | MANASSAS | 12,903 | 7,257 | 5,562 | 84 | 1,695 R | 56.2% | 43.1% | 56.6% | 43.4% |
| 10,290 | MANASSAS PARK | 3,332 | 1,807 | 1,498 | 27 | 309 R | 54.2% | 45.0% | 54.7% | 45.3% |
| 15,416 | MARTINSVILLE | 5,603 | 2,538 | 3,036 | 29 | 498 D | 45.3% | 54.2% | 45.5% | 54.5% |
| 180,150 | NEWPORT NEWS | 67,952 | 32,208 | 35,319 | 425 | 3,111 D | 47.4% | 52.0% | 47.7% | 52.3% |
| 234,403 | NORFOLK | 70,570 | 26,401 | 43,518 | 651 | 17,117 D | 37.4% | 61.7% | 37.8% | 62.2% |
| 3,904 | NORTON | 1,504 | 768 | 725 | 11 | 43 R | 51.1% | 48.2% | 51.4% | 48.6% |
| 33,740 | PETERSBURG | 11,949 | 2,238 | 9,682 | 29 | 7,444 D | 18.7% | 81.0% | 18.8% | 81.2% |
| 11,566 | POQUOSON | 6,480 | 5,004 | 1,424 | 52 | 3,580 R | 77.2% | 22.0% | 77.8% | 22.2% |
| 100,565 | PORTSMOUTH | 39,534 | 15,212 | 24,112 | 210 | 8,900 D | 38.5% | 61.0% | 38.7% | 61.3% |
| 15,859 | RADFORD | 4,845 | 2,564 | 2,244 | 37 | 320 R | 52.9% | 46.3% | 53.3% | 46.7% |
| 197,790 | RICHMOND CITY | 74,325 | 21,637 | 52,167 | 521 | 30,530 D | 29.1% | 70.2% | 29.3% | 70.7% |
| 94,911 | ROANOKE CITY | 36,000 | 16,661 | 18,862 | 477 | 2,201 D | 46.3% | 52.4% | 46.9% | 53.1% |
| 24,747 | SALEM | 11,484 | 7,115 | 4,254 | 115 | 2,861 R | 62.0% | 37.0% | 62.6% | 37.4% |
| 23,853 | STAUNTON | 9,629 | 5,805 | 3,756 | 68 | 2,049 R | 60.3% | 39.0% | 60.7% | 39.3% |
| 63,677 | SUFFOLK | 32,189 | 16,763 | 15,233 | 193 | 1,530 R | 52.1% | 47.3% | 52.4% | 47.6% |
| 425,257 | VIRGINIA BEACH | 175,687 | 103,752 | 70,666 | 1,269 | 33,086 R | 59.1% | 40.2% | 59.5% | 40.5% |
| 19,520 | WAYNESBORO | 7,963 | 5,092 | 2,792 | 79 | 2,300 R | 63.9% | 35.1% | 64.6% | 35.4% |
| 11,998 | WILLIAMSBURG | 4,320 | 2,064 | 2,216 | 40 | 152 D | 47.8% | 51.3% | 48.2% | 51.8% |
| 23,585 | WINCHESTER | 9,343 | 5,283 | 3,967 | 93 | 1,316 R | 56.5% | 42.5% | 57.1% | 42.9% |
| 7,078,515 | TOTAL | 3,198,367 | 1,716,959 | 1,454,742 | 26,666 | 262,217 R | 53.7% | 45.5% | 54.1% | 45.9% |

# VIRGINIA

## PRESIDENT 2000

| 2000 Census Population | County | Total Vote | Republican | Democratic | Green (Nader) | Other | Rep.-Dem. Plurality | Percentage of Total Vote | | |
|---|---|---|---|---|---|---|---|---|---|---|
| | | | | | | | | Rep. | Dem. | Green |
| 38,305 | ACCOMACK | 11,925 | 6,352 | 5,092 | 220 | 261 | 1,260 R | 53.3% | 42.7% | 1.8% |
| 79,236 | ALBEMARLE | 36,846 | 18,291 | 16,255 | 2,043 | 257 | 2,036 R | 49.6% | 44.1% | 5.5% |
| 12,926 | ALLEGHANY | 5,123 | 2,808 | 2,214 | 62 | 39 | 594 R | 54.8% | 43.2% | 1.2% |
| 11,400 | AMELIA | 4,788 | 2,947 | 1,754 | 40 | 47 | 1,193 R | 61.5% | 36.6% | 0.8% |
| 31,894 | AMHERST | 11,712 | 6,660 | 4,812 | 135 | 105 | 1,848 R | 56.9% | 41.1% | 1.2% |
| 13,705 | APPOMATTOX | 5,927 | 3,654 | 2,132 | 62 | 79 | 1,522 R | 61.7% | 36.0% | 1.0% |
| 189,453 | ARLINGTON | 83,559 | 28,555 | 50,260 | 3,952 | 792 | 21,705 D | 34.2% | 60.1% | 4.7% |
| 65,615 | AUGUSTA | 25,271 | 17,744 | 6,643 | 527 | 357 | 11,101 R | 70.2% | 26.3% | 2.1% |
| 5,048 | BATH | 2,210 | 1,311 | 822 | 35 | 42 | 489 R | 59.3% | 37.2% | 1.6% |
| 60,371 | BEDFORD COUNTY | 26,149 | 17,224 | 8,160 | 376 | 389 | 9,064 R | 65.9% | 31.2% | 1.4% |
| 6,871 | BLAND | 2,688 | 1,759 | 851 | 42 | 36 | 908 R | 65.4% | 31.7% | 1.6% |
| 30,496 | BOTETOURT | 13,840 | 8,867 | 4,627 | 207 | 139 | 4,240 R | 64.1% | 33.4% | 1.5% |
| 18,419 | BRUNSWICK | 5,997 | 2,561 | 3,387 | 28 | 21 | 826 D | 42.7% | 56.5% | 0.5% |
| 26,978 | BUCHANAN | 9,856 | 3,867 | 5,745 | 65 | 179 | 1,878 D | 39.2% | 58.3% | 0.7% |
| 15,623 | BUCKINGHAM | 5,454 | 2,738 | 2,561 | 96 | 59 | 177 R | 50.2% | 47.0% | 1.8% |
| 51,078 | CAMPBELL | 20,327 | 13,162 | 6,659 | 236 | 270 | 6,503 R | 64.8% | 32.8% | 1.2% |
| 22,121 | CAROLINE | 8,351 | 3,873 | 4,314 | 102 | 62 | 441 D | 46.4% | 51.7% | 1.2% |
| 29,245 | CARROLL | 11,001 | 7,142 | 3,638 | 126 | 95 | 3,504 R | 64.9% | 33.1% | 1.1% |
| 6,926 | CHARLES CITY | 3,066 | 1,023 | 1,981 | 31 | 31 | 958 D | 33.4% | 64.6% | 1.0% |
| 12,472 | CHARLOTTE | 4,994 | 2,855 | 2,017 | 43 | 79 | 838 R | 57.2% | 40.4% | 0.9% |
| 259,903 | CHESTERFIELD | 110,951 | 69,924 | 38,638 | 1,646 | 743 | 31,286 R | 63.0% | 34.8% | 1.5% |
| 12,652 | CLARKE | 5,284 | 2,883 | 2,166 | 195 | 40 | 717 R | 54.6% | 41.0% | 3.7% |
| 5,091 | CRAIG | 2,493 | 1,580 | 851 | 39 | 23 | 729 R | 63.4% | 34.1% | 1.6% |
| 34,262 | CULPEPER | 12,244 | 7,440 | 4,364 | 253 | 187 | 3,076 R | 60.8% | 35.6% | 2.1% |
| 9,017 | CUMBERLAND | 3,507 | 1,974 | 1,405 | 35 | 93 | 569 R | 56.3% | 40.1% | 1.0% |
| 16,395 | DICKENSON | 7,226 | 3,122 | 3,951 | 85 | 68 | 829 D | 43.2% | 54.7% | 1.2% |
| 24,533 | DINWIDDIE | 9,136 | 4,959 | 4,001 | 74 | 102 | 958 R | 54.3% | 43.8% | 0.8% |
| 9,989 | ESSEX | 3,831 | 1,995 | 1,750 | 59 | 27 | 245 R | 52.1% | 45.7% | 1.5% |
| 969,749 | FAIRFAX COUNTY | 413,775 | 202,181 | 196,501 | 12,201 | 2,892 | 5,680 R | 48.9% | 47.5% | 2.9% |
| 55,139 | FAUQUIER | 23,481 | 14,456 | 8,296 | 570 | 159 | 6,160 R | 61.6% | 35.3% | 2.4% |
| 13,874 | FLOYD | 5,739 | 3,423 | 1,957 | 244 | 115 | 1,466 R | 59.6% | 34.1% | 4.3% |
| 20,047 | FLUVANNA | 8,706 | 4,962 | 3,431 | 252 | 61 | 1,531 R | 57.0% | 39.4% | 2.9% |
| 47,286 | FRANKLIN COUNTY | 18,829 | 11,225 | 7,145 | 303 | 156 | 4,080 R | 59.6% | 37.9% | 1.6% |
| 59,209 | FREDERICK | 22,392 | 14,574 | 7,158 | 483 | 177 | 7,416 R | 65.1% | 32.0% | 2.2% |
| 16,657 | GILES | 6,820 | 3,574 | 3,004 | 137 | 105 | 570 R | 52.4% | 44.0% | 2.0% |
| 34,780 | GLOUCESTER | 13,699 | 8,718 | 4,553 | 225 | 203 | 4,165 R | 63.6% | 33.2% | 1.6% |
| 16,863 | GOOCHLAND | 8,777 | 5,378 | 3,197 | 139 | 63 | 2,181 R | 61.3% | 36.4% | 1.6% |
| 17,917 | GRAYSON | 6,852 | 4,236 | 2,467 | 102 | 47 | 1,769 R | 61.8% | 36.0% | 1.5% |
| 15,244 | GREENE | 5,412 | 3,375 | 1,774 | 194 | 69 | 1,601 R | 62.4% | 32.8% | 3.6% |
| 11,560 | GREENSVILLE | 3,906 | 1,565 | 2,314 | 13 | 14 | 749 D | 40.1% | 59.2% | 0.3% |
| 37,355 | HALIFAX | 14,072 | 7,732 | 5,963 | 110 | 267 | 1,769 R | 54.9% | 42.4% | 0.8% |
| 86,320 | HANOVER | 41,585 | 28,614 | 12,044 | 711 | 216 | 16,570 R | 68.8% | 29.0% | 1.7% |
| 262,300 | HENRICO | 114,252 | 62,887 | 48,645 | 1,893 | 827 | 14,242 R | 55.0% | 42.6% | 1.7% |
| 57,930 | HENRY | 21,463 | 11,870 | 8,898 | 234 | 461 | 2,972 R | 55.3% | 41.5% | 1.1% |
| 2,536 | HIGHLAND | 1,437 | 942 | 453 | 32 | 10 | 489 R | 65.6% | 31.5% | 2.2% |
| 29,728 | ISLE OF WIGHT | 12,950 | 7,587 | 5,162 | 123 | 78 | 2,425 R | 58.6% | 39.9% | 0.9% |
| 48,102 | JAMES CITY | 24,492 | 14,628 | 9,090 | 639 | 135 | 5,538 R | 59.7% | 37.1% | 2.6% |
| 6,630 | KING AND QUEEN | 2,859 | 1,423 | 1,387 | 33 | 16 | 36 R | 49.8% | 48.5% | 1.2% |
| 16,803 | KING GEORGE | 5,852 | 3,590 | 2,070 | 132 | 60 | 1,520 R | 61.3% | 35.4% | 2.3% |
| 13,146 | KING WILLIAM | 5,769 | 3,547 | 2,125 | 74 | 23 | 1,422 R | 61.5% | 36.8% | 1.3% |
| 11,567 | LANCASTER | 5,455 | 3,411 | 1,937 | 88 | 19 | 1,474 R | 62.5% | 35.5% | 1.6% |
| 23,589 | LEE | 8,748 | 4,551 | 4,031 | 79 | 87 | 520 R | 52.0% | 46.1% | 0.9% |
| 169,599 | LOUDOUN | 75,653 | 42,453 | 30,938 | 1,665 | 597 | 11,515 R | 56.1% | 40.9% | 2.2% |
| 25,627 | LOUISA | 10,096 | 5,461 | 4,309 | 222 | 104 | 1,152 R | 54.1% | 42.7% | 2.2% |
| 13,146 | LUNENBURG | 4,591 | 2,510 | 2,026 | 33 | 22 | 484 R | 54.7% | 44.1% | 0.7% |
| 12,520 | MADISON | 5,027 | 2,940 | 1,844 | 148 | 95 | 1,096 R | 58.5% | 36.7% | 2.9% |
| 9,207 | MATHEWS | 4,609 | 2,951 | 1,499 | 88 | 71 | 1,452 R | 64.0% | 32.5% | 1.9% |
| 32,380 | MECKLENBURG | 11,654 | 6,600 | 4,797 | 104 | 153 | 1,803 R | 56.6% | 41.2% | 0.9% |
| 9,932 | MIDDLESEX | 4,689 | 2,844 | 1,671 | 84 | 90 | 1,173 R | 60.7% | 35.6% | 1.8% |
| 83,629 | MONTGOMERY | 27,160 | 13,991 | 11,720 | 1,222 | 227 | 2,271 R | 51.5% | 43.2% | 4.5% |

# VIRGINIA

## PRESIDENT 2000

| 2000 Census Population | County | Total Vote | Republican | Democratic | Green (Nader) | Other | Rep.-Dem. Plurality | Percentage of Total Vote | | |
|---|---|---|---|---|---|---|---|---|---|---|
| | | | | | | | | Rep. | Dem. | Green |
| 14,445 | NELSON | 6,145 | 2,913 | 2,907 | 273 | 52 | 6 R | 47.4% | 47.3% | 4.4% |
| 13,462 | NEW KENT | 6,114 | 3,934 | 2,055 | 81 | 44 | 1,879 R | 64.3% | 33.6% | 1.3% |
| 13,093 | NORTHAMPTON | 4,892 | 2,299 | 2,340 | 108 | 145 | 41 D | 47.0% | 47.8% | 2.2% |
| 12,259 | NORTHUMBERLAND | 5,605 | 3,362 | 2,118 | 97 | 28 | 1,244 R | 60.0% | 37.8% | 1.7% |
| 15,725 | NOTTOWAY | 5,492 | 2,870 | 2,460 | 46 | 116 | 410 R | 52.3% | 44.8% | 0.8% |
| 25,881 | ORANGE | 10,483 | 5,991 | 4,126 | 236 | 130 | 1,865 R | 57.1% | 39.4% | 2.3% |
| 23,177 | PAGE | 7,996 | 5,089 | 2,726 | 143 | 38 | 2,363 R | 63.6% | 34.1% | 1.8% |
| 19,407 | PATRICK | 7,385 | 4,901 | 2,254 | 101 | 129 | 2,647 R | 66.4% | 30.5% | 1.4% |
| 61,745 | PITTSYLVANIA | 24,255 | 15,760 | 7,834 | 207 | 454 | 7,926 R | 65.0% | 32.3% | 0.9% |
| 22,377 | POWHATAN | 9,711 | 6,820 | 2,708 | 122 | 61 | 4,112 R | 70.2% | 27.9% | 1.3% |
| 19,720 | PRINCE EDWARD | 6,363 | 3,214 | 2,922 | 115 | 112 | 292 R | 50.5% | 45.9% | 1.8% |
| 33,047 | PRINCE GEORGE | 10,900 | 6,579 | 4,182 | 97 | 42 | 2,397 R | 60.4% | 38.4% | 0.9% |
| 280,813 | PRINCE WILLIAM | 100,511 | 52,788 | 44,745 | 1,927 | 1,051 | 8,043 R | 52.5% | 44.5% | 1.9% |
| 35,127 | PULASKI | 12,697 | 7,089 | 5,255 | 207 | 146 | 1,834 R | 55.8% | 41.4% | 1.6% |
| 6,983 | RAPPAHANNOCK | 3,513 | 1,850 | 1,462 | 161 | 40 | 388 R | 52.7% | 41.6% | 4.6% |
| 8,809 | RICHMOND COUNTY | 2,949 | 1,784 | 1,076 | 44 | 45 | 708 R | 60.5% | 36.5% | 1.5% |
| 85,778 | ROANOKE COUNTY | 42,817 | 25,740 | 16,141 | 681 | 255 | 9,599 R | 60.1% | 37.7% | 1.6% |
| 20,808 | ROCKBRIDGE | 7,827 | 4,522 | 2,953 | 248 | 104 | 1,569 R | 57.8% | 37.7% | 3.2% |
| 67,725 | ROCKINGHAM | 23,994 | 17,482 | 5,834 | 539 | 139 | 11,648 R | 72.9% | 24.3% | 2.2% |
| 30,308 | RUSSELL | 10,792 | 5,065 | 5,442 | 102 | 183 | 377 D | 46.9% | 50.4% | 0.9% |
| 23,403 | SCOTT | 9,335 | 5,535 | 3,552 | 85 | 163 | 1,983 R | 59.3% | 38.1% | 0.9% |
| 35,075 | SHENANDOAH | 14,452 | 9,636 | 4,420 | 294 | 102 | 5,216 R | 66.7% | 30.6% | 2.0% |
| 33,081 | SMYTH | 11,740 | 6,580 | 4,836 | 131 | 193 | 1,744 R | 56.0% | 41.2% | 1.1% |
| 17,482 | SOUTHAMPTON | 6,714 | 3,293 | 3,359 | 44 | 18 | 66 D | 49.0% | 50.0% | 0.7% |
| 90,395 | SPOTSYLVANIA | 35,021 | 20,739 | 13,455 | 586 | 241 | 7,284 R | 59.2% | 38.4% | 1.7% |
| 92,446 | STAFFORD | 34,246 | 20,731 | 12,596 | 657 | 262 | 8,135 R | 60.5% | 36.8% | 1.9% |
| 6,829 | SURRY | 3,230 | 1,313 | 1,845 | 29 | 43 | 532 D | 40.7% | 57.1% | 0.9% |
| 12,504 | SUSSEX | 3,906 | 1,745 | 2,006 | 41 | 114 | 261 D | 44.7% | 51.4% | 1.0% |
| 44,598 | TAZEWELL | 16,344 | 8,655 | 7,227 | 162 | 300 | 1,428 R | 53.0% | 44.2% | 1.0% |
| 31,584 | WARREN | 11,166 | 6,335 | 4,313 | 260 | 258 | 2,022 R | 56.7% | 38.6% | 2.3% |
| 51,103 | WASHINGTON | 20,222 | 12,064 | 7,549 | 288 | 321 | 4,515 R | 59.7% | 37.3% | 1.4% |
| 16,718 | WESTMORELAND | 6,026 | 2,932 | 2,922 | 88 | 84 | 10 R | 48.7% | 48.5% | 1.5% |
| 40,123 | WISE | 13,310 | 6,504 | 6,412 | 160 | 234 | 92 R | 48.9% | 48.2% | 1.2% |
| 27,599 | WYTHE | 10,225 | 6,539 | 3,462 | 132 | 92 | 3,077 R | 64.0% | 33.9% | 1.3% |
| 56,297 | YORK | 24,583 | 15,312 | 8,622 | 480 | 169 | 6,690 R | 62.3% | 35.1% | 2.0% |
| | **City/Town** | | | | | | | | | |
| 128,283 | ALEXANDRIA | 55,199 | 19,043 | 33,633 | 2,094 | 429 | 14,590 D | 34.5% | 60.9% | 3.8% |
| 6,299 | BEDFORD CITY | 2,441 | 1,269 | 1,078 | 38 | 56 | 191 R | 52.0% | 44.2% | 1.6% |
| 17,367 | BRISTOL | 6,279 | 3,495 | 2,646 | 89 | 49 | 849 R | 55.7% | 42.1% | 1.4% |
| 6,349 | BUENA VISTA | 1,975 | 980 | 941 | 27 | 27 | 39 R | 49.6% | 47.6% | 1.4% |
| 45,049 | CHARLOTTESVILLE | 13,224 | 4,034 | 7,762 | 1,196 | 232 | 3,728 D | 30.5% | 58.7% | 9.0% |
| 199,184 | CHESAPEAKE | 74,585 | 39,684 | 33,578 | 732 | 591 | 6,106 R | 53.2% | 45.0% | 1.0% |
| 4,289 | CLIFTON FORGE | 1,532 | 613 | 868 | 25 | 26 | 255 D | 40.0% | 56.7% | 1.6% |
| 16,897 | COLONIAL HEIGHTS | 7,782 | 5,519 | 2,100 | 123 | 40 | 3,419 R | 70.9% | 27.0% | 1.6% |
| 6,303 | COVINGTON | 2,214 | 966 | 1,168 | 24 | 56 | 202 D | 43.6% | 52.8% | 1.1% |
| 48,411 | DANVILLE | 18,307 | 9,427 | 8,221 | 168 | 491 | 1,206 R | 51.5% | 44.9% | 0.9% |
| 5,665 | EMPORIA | 2,080 | 938 | 1,116 | 17 | 9 | 178 D | 45.1% | 53.7% | 0.8% |
| 21,498 | FAIRFAX CITY | 9,556 | 4,762 | 4,361 | 352 | 81 | 401 R | 49.8% | 45.6% | 3.7% |
| 10,377 | FALLS CHURCH | 5,593 | 2,131 | 3,109 | 285 | 68 | 978 D | 38.1% | 55.6% | 5.1% |
| 8,346 | FRANKLIN CITY | 3,191 | 1,393 | 1,763 | 25 | 10 | 370 D | 43.7% | 55.2% | 0.8% |
| 19,279 | FREDERICKSBURG | 6,681 | 2,935 | 3,360 | 326 | 60 | 425 D | 43.9% | 50.3% | 4.9% |
| 6,837 | GALAX | 2,213 | 1,160 | 996 | 42 | 15 | 164 R | 52.4% | 45.0% | 1.9% |
| 146,437 | HAMPTON | 47,887 | 19,561 | 27,490 | 563 | 273 | 7,929 D | 40.8% | 57.4% | 1.2% |
| 40,468 | HARRISONBURG | 9,958 | 5,741 | 3,482 | 641 | 94 | 2,259 R | 57.7% | 35.0% | 6.4% |
| 22,354 | HOPEWELL | 6,978 | 3,749 | 3,024 | 73 | 132 | 725 R | 53.7% | 43.3% | 1.0% |
| 6,867 | LEXINGTON | 2,140 | 957 | 1,048 | 103 | 32 | 91 D | 44.7% | 49.0% | 4.8% |

# VIRGINIA

## PRESIDENT 2000

| 2000 Census Population | City/Town | Total Vote | Republican | Democratic | Green (Nader) | Other | Rep.-Dem. Plurality | Percentage of Total Vote | | |
|---|---|---|---|---|---|---|---|---|---|---|
| | | | | | | | | Rep. | Dem. | Green |
| 65,269 | LYNCHBURG | 23,506 | 12,518 | 10,374 | 441 | 173 | 2,144 R | 53.3% | 44.1% | 1.9% |
| 35,135 | MANASSAS | 12,410 | 6,752 | 5,262 | 230 | 166 | 1,490 R | 54.4% | 42.4% | 1.9% |
| 10,290 | MANASSAS PARK | 2,580 | 1,460 | 1,048 | 51 | 21 | 412 R | 56.6% | 40.6% | 2.0% |
| 15,416 | MARTINSVILLE | 5,694 | 2,560 | 3,048 | 59 | 27 | 488 D | 45.0% | 53.5% | 1.0% |
| 180,150 | NEWPORT NEWS | 57,825 | 27,006 | 29,779 | 722 | 318 | 2,773 D | 46.7% | 51.5% | 1.2% |
| 234,403 | NORFOLK | 61,946 | 21,920 | 38,221 | 1,153 | 652 | 16,301 D | 35.4% | 61.7% | 1.9% |
| 3,904 | NORTON | 1,530 | 639 | 867 | 20 | 4 | 228 D | 41.8% | 56.7% | 1.3% |
| 33,740 | PETERSBURG | 11,062 | 2,109 | 8,751 | 117 | 85 | 6,642 D | 19.1% | 79.1% | 1.1% |
| 11,566 | POQUOSON | 5,861 | 4,271 | 1,448 | 93 | 49 | 2,823 R | 72.9% | 24.7% | 1.6% |
| 100,565 | PORTSMOUTH | 35,455 | 12,628 | 22,286 | 348 | 193 | 9,658 D | 35.6% | 62.9% | 1.0% |
| 15,859 | RADFORD | 4,448 | 2,190 | 2,063 | 172 | 23 | 127 R | 49.2% | 46.4% | 3.9% |
| 197,790 | RICHMOND CITY | 65,926 | 20,265 | 42,717 | 2,425 | 519 | 22,452 D | 30.7% | 64.8% | 3.7% |
| 94,911 | ROANOKE CITY | 33,442 | 14,630 | 17,920 | 603 | 289 | 3,290 D | 43.7% | 53.6% | 1.8% |
| 24,747 | SALEM | 10,770 | 6,188 | 4,348 | 181 | 53 | 1,840 R | 57.5% | 40.4% | 1.7% |
| 23,853 | STAUNTON | 8,514 | 4,878 | 3,324 | 278 | 34 | 1,554 R | 57.3% | 39.0% | 3.3% |
| 63,677 | SUFFOLK | 24,661 | 11,836 | 12,471 | 199 | 155 | 635 D | 48.0% | 50.6% | 0.8% |
| 425,257 | VIRGINIA BEACH | 149,771 | 83,674 | 62,268 | 2,370 | 1,459 | 21,406 R | 55.9% | 41.6% | 1.6% |
| 19,520 | WAYNESBORO | 7,102 | 4,084 | 2,737 | 233 | 48 | 1,347 R | 57.5% | 38.5% | 3.3% |
| 11,998 | WILLIAMSBURG | 3,725 | 1,777 | 1,724 | 188 | 36 | 53 R | 47.7% | 46.3% | 5.0% |
| 23,585 | WINCHESTER | 7,886 | 4,314 | 3,318 | 209 | 45 | 996 R | 54.7% | 42.1% | 2.7% |
| 7,078,515 | TOTAL | 2,739,447 | 1,437,490 | 1,217,290 | 59,398 | 25,269 | 220,200 R | 52.5% | 44.4% | 2.2% |

# VIRGINIA

## PRESIDENT 1996

| 1995 Census Pop. Est. | County | Total Vote | Republican | Democratic | Reform (Perot) | Other | Rep.-Dem. Plurality | Rep. | Dem. | Reform |
|---|---|---|---|---|---|---|---|---|---|---|
| 32,266 | ACCOMACK | 11,654 | 5,013 | 5,220 | 1,218 | 203 | 207 D | 43.0% | 44.8% | 10.5% |
| 73,203 | ALBEMARLE | 31,228 | 15,243 | 14,089 | 1,533 | 363 | 1,154 R | 48.8% | 45.1% | 4.9% |
| 12,604 | ALLEGHANY | 5,074 | 2,015 | 2,398 | 607 | 54 | 383 D | 39.7% | 47.3% | 12.0% |
| 9,670 | AMELIA | 4,144 | 2,119 | 1,625 | 323 | 77 | 494 R | 51.1% | 39.2% | 7.8% |
| 29,770 | AMHERST | 10,924 | 5,094 | 4,864 | 835 | 131 | 230 R | 46.6% | 44.5% | 7.6% |
| 12,777 | APPOMATTOX | 5,477 | 2,625 | 2,239 | 510 | 103 | 386 R | 47.9% | 40.9% | 9.3% |
| 172,660 | ARLINGTON | 75,376 | 26,106 | 45,573 | 2,782 | 915 | 19,467 D | 34.6% | 60.5% | 3.7% |
| 59,510 | AUGUSTA | 22,102 | 13,458 | 5,965 | 1,916 | 763 | 7,493 R | 60.9% | 27.0% | 8.7% |
| 4,870 | BATH | 2,051 | 847 | 922 | 247 | 35 | 75 D | 41.3% | 45.0% | 12.0% |
| 52,335 | BEDFORD COUNTY | 22,109 | 11,955 | 7,786 | 1,976 | 392 | 4,169 R | 54.1% | 35.2% | 8.9% |
| 6,783 | BLAND | 2,537 | 1,167 | 939 | 385 | 46 | 228 R | 46.0% | 37.0% | 15.2% |
| 27,279 | BOTETOURT | 12,380 | 6,404 | 4,576 | 1,138 | 262 | 1,828 R | 51.7% | 37.0% | 9.2% |
| 16,465 | BRUNSWICK | 5,918 | 2,059 | 3,442 | 340 | 77 | 1,383 D | 34.8% | 58.2% | 5.7% |
| 30,430 | BUCHANAN | 10,332 | 2,785 | 6,551 | 858 | 138 | 3,766 D | 27.0% | 63.4% | 8.3% |
| 13,316 | BUCKINGHAM | 4,850 | 1,974 | 2,374 | 392 | 110 | 400 D | 40.7% | 48.9% | 8.1% |
| 48,918 | CAMPBELL | 18,902 | 10,273 | 6,788 | 1,505 | 336 | 3,485 R | 54.3% | 35.9% | 8.0% |
| 21,079 | CAROLINE | 7,285 | 2,816 | 3,897 | 521 | 51 | 1,081 D | 38.7% | 53.5% | 7.2% |
| 27,634 | CARROLL | 9,969 | 5,088 | 3,611 | 1,158 | 112 | 1,477 R | 51.0% | 36.2% | 11.6% |
| 6,733 | CHARLES CITY | 2,787 | 729 | 1,842 | 178 | 38 | 1,113 D | 26.2% | 66.1% | 6.4% |
| 12,188 | CHARLOTTE | 4,614 | 2,103 | 2,007 | 431 | 73 | 96 R | 45.6% | 43.5% | 9.3% |
| 239,659 | CHESTERFIELD | 93,305 | 56,650 | 30,220 | 6,004 | 431 | 26,430 R | 60.7% | 32.4% | 6.4% |
| 12,390 | CLARKE | 4,569 | 2,201 | 1,906 | 379 | 83 | 295 R | 48.2% | 41.7% | 8.3% |
| 4,821 | CRAIG | 2,159 | 979 | 895 | 262 | 23 | 84 R | 45.3% | 41.5% | 12.1% |
| 30,528 | CULPEPER | 10,553 | 5,688 | 3,907 | 787 | 171 | 1,781 R | 53.9% | 37.0% | 7.5% |
| 7,737 | CUMBERLAND | 3,190 | 1,544 | 1,303 | 275 | 68 | 241 R | 48.4% | 40.8% | 8.6% |
| 17,586 | DICKENSON | 6,868 | 2,229 | 3,913 | 660 | 66 | 1,684 D | 32.5% | 57.0% | 9.6% |
| 22,944 | DINWIDDIE | 8,166 | 3,503 | 3,871 | 666 | 126 | 368 D | 42.9% | 47.4% | 8.2% |
| 9,251 | ESSEX | 3,533 | 1,627 | 1,668 | 188 | 50 | 41 D | 46.1% | 47.2% | 5.3% |
| 887,205 | FAIRFAX COUNTY | 365,263 | 176,033 | 170,150 | 16,134 | 2,946 | 5,883 R | 48.2% | 46.6% | 4.4% |
| 51,473 | FAUQUIER | 19,258 | 11,063 | 6,759 | 1,287 | 149 | 4,304 R | 57.4% | 35.1% | 6.7% |
| 12,642 | FLOYD | 4,939 | 2,374 | 1,909 | 545 | 111 | 465 R | 48.1% | 38.7% | 11.0% |
| 16,058 | FLUVANNA | 6,663 | 3,442 | 2,676 | 457 | 88 | 766 R | 51.7% | 40.2% | 6.9% |
| 42,856 | FRANKLIN COUNTY | 16,987 | 7,382 | 7,300 | 2,015 | 290 | 82 R | 43.5% | 43.0% | 11.9% |
| 51,549 | FREDERICK | 18,412 | 10,608 | 5,976 | 1,599 | 229 | 4,632 R | 57.6% | 32.5% | 8.7% |
| 16,374 | GILES | 6,726 | 2,566 | 3,196 | 841 | 123 | 630 D | 38.2% | 47.5% | 12.5% |
| 33,421 | GLOUCESTER | 12,593 | 6,447 | 4,710 | 1,266 | 170 | 1,737 R | 51.2% | 37.4% | 10.1% |
| 16,138 | GOOCHLAND | 7,425 | 4,119 | 2,784 | 424 | 98 | 1,335 R | 55.5% | 37.5% | 5.7% |
| 16,380 | GRAYSON | 6,403 | 3,004 | 2,661 | 675 | 63 | 343 R | 46.9% | 41.6% | 10.5% |
| 12,660 | GREENE | 4,252 | 2,351 | 1,440 | 346 | 115 | 911 R | 55.3% | 33.9% | 8.1% |
| 10,967 | GREENSVILLE | 3,843 | 1,176 | 2,381 | 263 | 23 | 1,205 D | 30.6% | 62.0% | 6.8% |
| 30,317 | HALIFAX | 13,226 | 6,490 | 5,599 | 876 | 261 | 891 R | 49.1% | 42.3% | 6.6% |
| 74,641 | HANOVER | 34,724 | 22,086 | 9,880 | 2,447 | 311 | 12,206 R | 63.6% | 28.5% | 7.0% |
| 232,799 | HENRICO | 101,992 | 54,430 | 41,121 | 5,920 | 521 | 13,309 R | 53.4% | 40.3% | 5.8% |
| 56,585 | HENRY | 20,874 | 9,110 | 9,061 | 2,370 | 333 | 49 R | 43.6% | 43.4% | 11.4% |
| 2,575 | HIGHLAND | 1,221 | 631 | 446 | 134 | 10 | 185 R | 51.7% | 36.5% | 11.0% |
| 27,769 | ISLE OF WIGHT | 11,369 | 5,416 | 4,952 | 893 | 108 | 464 R | 47.6% | 43.6% | 7.9% |
| 40,489 | JAMES CITY | 18,586 | 10,120 | 7,247 | 1,116 | 103 | 2,873 R | 54.4% | 39.0% | 6.0% |
| 6,441 | KING AND QUEEN | 2,756 | 1,073 | 1,393 | 213 | 77 | 320 D | 38.9% | 50.5% | 7.7% |
| 16,463 | KING GEORGE | 4,843 | 2,597 | 1,875 | 341 | 30 | 722 R | 53.6% | 38.7% | 7.0% |
| 12,244 | KING WILLIAM | 4,469 | 2,346 | 1,765 | 339 | 19 | 581 R | 52.5% | 39.5% | 7.6% |
| 11,161 | LANCASTER | 4,893 | 2,709 | 1,844 | 324 | 16 | 865 R | 55.4% | 37.7% | 6.6% |
| 24,411 | LEE | 8,604 | 3,225 | 4,444 | 822 | 113 | 1,219 D | 37.5% | 51.7% | 9.6% |
| 115,870 | LOUDOUN | 49,330 | 25,715 | 19,942 | 3,082 | 591 | 5,773 R | 52.1% | 40.4% | 6.2% |
| 22,887 | LOUISA | 8,323 | 3,768 | 3,761 | 693 | 101 | 7 R | 45.3% | 45.2% | 8.3% |
| 11,155 | LUNENBURG | 4,460 | 2,063 | 1,995 | 299 | 103 | 68 R | 46.3% | 44.7% | 6.7% |
| 12,252 | MADISON | 4,510 | 2,296 | 1,734 | 360 | 120 | 562 R | 50.9% | 38.4% | 8.0% |
| 8,947 | MATHEWS | 4,260 | 2,206 | 1,602 | 403 | 49 | 604 R | 51.8% | 37.6% | 9.5% |
| 30,760 | MECKLENBURG | 10,278 | 4,933 | 4,408 | 789 | 148 | 525 R | 48.0% | 42.9% | 7.7% |
| 9,327 | MIDDLESEX | 4,297 | 2,141 | 1,704 | 350 | 102 | 437 R | 49.8% | 39.7% | 8.1% |
| 75,756 | MONTGOMERY | 24,298 | 10,517 | 10,867 | 2,594 | 320 | 350 D | 43.3% | 44.7% | 10.7% |

984

# VIRGINIA

## PRESIDENT 1996

| 1995 Census Pop. Est. | County | Total Vote | Republican | Democratic | Reform (Perot) | Other | Rep.-Dem. Plurality | | Percentage of Total Vote | | |
|---|---|---|---|---|---|---|---|---|---|---|---|
| | | | | | | | | | Rep. | Dem. | Reform |
| 13,357 | NELSON | 5,264 | 1,988 | 2,782 | 411 | 83 | 794 | D | 37.8% | 52.8% | 7.8% |
| 11,679 | NEW KENT | 5,267 | 2,852 | 1,859 | 520 | 36 | 993 | R | 54.1% | 35.3% | 9.9% |
| 13,013 | NORTHAMPTON | 4,948 | 1,763 | 2,569 | 522 | 94 | 806 | D | 35.6% | 51.9% | 10.5% |
| 11,122 | NORTHUMBERLAND | 5,028 | 2,605 | 1,957 | 375 | 91 | 648 | R | 51.8% | 38.9% | 7.5% |
| 15,160 | NOTTOWAY | 5,214 | 2,416 | 2,327 | 346 | 125 | 89 | R | 46.3% | 44.6% | 6.6% |
| 23,763 | ORANGE | 8,908 | 4,435 | 3,590 | 750 | 133 | 845 | R | 49.8% | 40.3% | 8.4% |
| 22,718 | PAGE | 7,479 | 3,876 | 2,868 | 640 | 95 | 1,008 | R | 51.8% | 38.3% | 8.6% |
| 17,762 | PATRICK | 6,771 | 3,547 | 2,301 | 719 | 204 | 1,246 | R | 52.4% | 34.0% | 10.6% |
| 56,101 | PITTSYLVANIA | 21,714 | 12,127 | 7,681 | 1,469 | 437 | 4,446 | R | 55.8% | 35.4% | 6.8% |
| 18,905 | POWHATAN | 7,643 | 4,679 | 2,254 | 626 | 84 | 2,425 | R | 61.2% | 29.5% | 8.2% |
| 18,752 | PRINCE EDWARD | 5,678 | 2,530 | 2,678 | 403 | 67 | 148 | D | 44.6% | 47.2% | 7.1% |
| 28,383 | PRINCE GEORGE | 9,507 | 5,216 | 3,498 | 698 | 95 | 1,718 | R | 54.9% | 36.8% | 7.3% |
| 245,184 | PRINCE WILLIAM | 78,443 | 39,292 | 33,462 | 4,881 | 808 | 5,830 | R | 50.1% | 42.7% | 6.2% |
| 34,426 | PULASKI | 12,304 | 5,387 | 5,333 | 1,399 | 185 | 54 | R | 43.8% | 43.3% | 11.4% |
| 7,117 | RAPPAHANNOCK | 3,181 | 1,505 | 1,405 | 213 | 58 | 100 | R | 47.3% | 44.2% | 6.7% |
| 8,247 | RICHMOND COUNTY | 2,797 | 1,424 | 1,101 | 201 | 71 | 323 | R | 50.9% | 39.4% | 7.2% |
| 81,717 | ROANOKE COUNTY | 39,421 | 20,700 | 15,387 | 2,934 | 400 | 5,313 | R | 52.5% | 39.0% | 7.4% |
| 19,116 | ROCKBRIDGE | 7,279 | 3,274 | 3,116 | 760 | 129 | 158 | R | 45.0% | 42.8% | 10.4% |
| 61,894 | ROCKINGHAM | 21,707 | 14,035 | 5,867 | 1,318 | 487 | 8,168 | R | 64.7% | 27.0% | 6.1% |
| 29,261 | RUSSELL | 10,128 | 3,706 | 5,437 | 862 | 123 | 1,731 | D | 36.6% | 53.7% | 8.5% |
| 23,197 | SCOTT | 8,573 | 4,086 | 3,449 | 798 | 240 | 637 | R | 47.7% | 40.2% | 9.3% |
| 33,423 | SHENANDOAH | 13,280 | 7,440 | 4,224 | 1,353 | 263 | 3,216 | R | 56.0% | 31.8% | 10.2% |
| 33,231 | SMYTH | 11,619 | 4,966 | 4,990 | 1,407 | 256 | 24 | D | 42.7% | 42.9% | 12.1% |
| 17,313 | SOUTHAMPTON | 6,715 | 2,275 | 3,454 | 564 | 422 | 1,179 | D | 33.9% | 51.4% | 8.4% |
| 71,981 | SPOTSYLVANIA | 26,197 | 13,786 | 10,342 | 1,860 | 209 | 3,444 | R | 52.6% | 39.5% | 7.1% |
| 80,107 | STAFFORD | 26,089 | 14,098 | 9,902 | 1,856 | 233 | 4,196 | R | 54.0% | 38.0% | 7.1% |
| 6,388 | SURRY | 2,938 | 944 | 1,753 | 181 | 60 | 809 | D | 32.1% | 59.7% | 6.2% |
| 10,078 | SUSSEX | 3,792 | 1,378 | 2,089 | 256 | 69 | 711 | D | 36.3% | 55.1% | 6.8% |
| 47,146 | TAZEWELL | 15,440 | 6,131 | 7,500 | 1,554 | 255 | 1,369 | D | 39.7% | 48.6% | 10.1% |
| 29,264 | WARREN | 9,652 | 4,657 | 3,814 | 904 | 277 | 843 | R | 48.2% | 39.5% | 9.4% |
| 48,347 | WASHINGTON | 18,169 | 9,098 | 6,939 | 1,654 | 478 | 2,159 | R | 50.1% | 38.2% | 9.1% |
| 16,464 | WESTMORELAND | 5,788 | 2,333 | 2,949 | 427 | 79 | 616 | D | 40.3% | 51.0% | 7.4% |
| 39,925 | WISE | 13,092 | 4,660 | 6,712 | 1,478 | 242 | 2,052 | D | 35.6% | 51.3% | 11.3% |
| 26,350 | WYTHE | 8,549 | 4,274 | 3,275 | 955 | 45 | 999 | R | 50.0% | 38.3% | 11.2% |
| 54,108 | YORK | 20,738 | 11,396 | 7,731 | 1,469 | 142 | 3,665 | R | 55.0% | 37.3% | 7.1% |
| | **City** | | | | | | | | | | |
| 115,609 | ALEXANDRIA | 45,399 | 15,554 | 27,968 | 1,472 | 405 | 12,414 | D | 34.3% | 61.6% | 3.2% |
| 6,479 | BEDFORD CITY | 2,311 | 990 | 1,065 | 212 | 44 | 75 | D | 42.8% | 46.1% | 9.2% |
| 17,918 | BRISTOL | 6,026 | 2,983 | 2,586 | 429 | 28 | 397 | R | 49.5% | 42.9% | 7.1% |
| 6,405 | BUENA VISTA | 2,057 | 713 | 1,090 | 216 | 38 | 377 | D | 34.7% | 53.0% | 10.5% |
| 40,227 | CHARLOTTESVILLE | 12,789 | 4,091 | 7,916 | 565 | 217 | 3,825 | D | 32.0% | 61.9% | 4.4% |
| 187,998 | CHESAPEAKE | 62,686 | 29,251 | 28,713 | 4,456 | 266 | 538 | R | 46.7% | 45.8% | 7.1% |
| 4,460 | CLIFTON FORGE | 1,641 | 486 | 974 | 147 | 34 | 488 | D | 29.6% | 59.4% | 9.0% |
| 16,951 | COLONIAL HEIGHTS | 6,953 | 4,632 | 1,782 | 518 | 21 | 2,850 | R | 66.6% | 25.6% | 7.5% |
| 6,787 | COVINGTON | 2,453 | 763 | 1,394 | 255 | 41 | 631 | D | 31.1% | 56.8% | 10.4% |
| 53,789 | DANVILLE | 18,519 | 9,254 | 8,168 | 762 | 335 | 1,086 | R | 50.0% | 44.1% | 4.1% |
| 5,835 | EMPORIA | 2,054 | 835 | 1,103 | 98 | 18 | 268 | D | 40.7% | 53.7% | 4.8% |
| 20,637 | FAIRFAX CITY | 8,745 | 4,319 | 3,909 | 422 | 95 | 410 | R | 49.4% | 44.7% | 4.8% |
| 9,617 | FALLS CHURCH | 4,284 | 1,644 | 2,375 | 202 | 63 | 731 | D | 38.4% | 55.4% | 4.7% |
| 8,407 | FRANKLIN CITY | 3,385 | 1,200 | 1,962 | 201 | 22 | 762 | D | 35.5% | 58.0% | 5.9% |
| 21,953 | FREDERICKSBURG | 6,164 | 2,579 | 3,215 | 300 | 70 | 636 | D | 41.8% | 52.2% | 4.9% |
| 6,632 | GALAX | 2,181 | 910 | 1,033 | 221 | 17 | 123 | D | 41.7% | 47.4% | 10.1% |
| 139,181 | HAMPTON | 44,507 | 16,596 | 24,493 | 2,783 | 635 | 7,897 | D | 37.3% | 55.0% | 6.3% |
| 33,158 | HARRISONBURG | 8,937 | 4,945 | 3,346 | 434 | 212 | 1,599 | R | 55.3% | 37.4% | 4.9% |
| 22,548 | HOPEWELL | 7,062 | 3,493 | 2,868 | 550 | 151 | 625 | R | 49.5% | 40.6% | 7.8% |
| 7,206 | LEXINGTON | 2,045 | 850 | 1,059 | 112 | 24 | 209 | D | 41.6% | 51.8% | 5.5% |

# VIRGINIA

## PRESIDENT 1996

| 1995 Census Pop. Est. | City | Total Vote | Republican | Democratic | Reform (Perot) | Other | Rep.-Dem. Plurality | Percentage of Total Vote | | |
|---|---|---|---|---|---|---|---|---|---|---|
| | | | | | | | | Rep. | Dem. | Reform |
| 66,710 | LYNCHBURG | 23,012 | 11,441 | 10,281 | 1,155 | 135 | 1,160 R | 49.7% | 44.7% | 5.0% |
| 32,657 | MANASSAS | 10,960 | 5,799 | 4,378 | 670 | 113 | 1,421 R | 52.9% | 39.9% | 6.1% |
| 7,417 | MANASSAS PARK | 1,838 | 916 | 748 | 151 | 23 | 168 R | 49.8% | 40.7% | 8.2% |
| 15,924 | MARTINSVILLE | 5,842 | 2,446 | 2,941 | 387 | 68 | 495 D | 41.9% | 50.3% | 6.6% |
| 179,794 | NEWPORT NEWS | 54,288 | 23,072 | 27,678 | 3,090 | 448 | 4,606 D | 42.5% | 51.0% | 5.7% |
| 237,570 | NORFOLK | 60,124 | 18,693 | 37,655 | 3,435 | 341 | 18,962 D | 31.1% | 62.6% | 5.7% |
| 4,335 | NORTON | 1,382 | 416 | 802 | 138 | 26 | 386 D | 30.1% | 58.0% | 10.0% |
| 37,782 | PETERSBURG | 10,890 | 2,261 | 8,105 | 423 | 101 | 5,844 D | 20.8% | 74.4% | 3.9% |
| 11,727 | POQUOSON | 5,276 | 3,422 | 1,409 | 400 | 45 | 2,013 R | 64.9% | 26.7% | 7.6% |
| 102,735 | PORTSMOUTH | 35,409 | 10,686 | 22,150 | 2,238 | 335 | 11,464 D | 30.2% | 62.6% | 6.3% |
| 16,212 | RADFORD | 4,283 | 1,742 | 2,113 | 381 | 47 | 371 D | 40.7% | 49.3% | 8.9% |
| 198,273 | RICHMOND CITY | 67,078 | 20,993 | 42,273 | 2,762 | 1,050 | 21,280 D | 31.3% | 63.0% | 4.1% |
| 95,701 | ROANOKE CITY | 32,016 | 12,283 | 17,282 | 2,169 | 282 | 4,999 D | 38.4% | 54.0% | 6.8% |
| 24,198 | SALEM | 10,079 | 4,936 | 4,282 | 796 | 65 | 654 R | 49.0% | 42.5% | 7.9% |
| 24,796 | STAUNTON | 8,435 | 4,526 | 3,162 | 605 | 142 | 1,364 R | 53.7% | 37.5% | 7.2% |
| 56,787 | SUFFOLK | 20,754 | 8,572 | 10,827 | 1,266 | 89 | 2,255 D | 41.3% | 52.2% | 6.1% |
| 431,000 | VIRGINIA BEACH | 125,943 | 63,741 | 52,142 | 9,328 | 732 | 11,599 R | 50.6% | 41.4% | 7.4% |
| 18,926 | WAYNESBORO | 6,576 | 3,466 | 2,398 | 462 | 250 | 1,068 R | 52.7% | 36.5% | 7.0% |
| 12,646 | WILLIAMSBURG | 3,592 | 1,560 | 1,820 | 162 | 50 | 260 D | 43.4% | 50.7% | 4.5% |
| 23,237 | WINCHESTER | 7,222 | 3,681 | 3,027 | 434 | 80 | 654 R | 51.0% | 41.9% | 6.0% |
| 6,618,358 | TOTAL | 2,416,642 | 1,138,350 | 1,091,060 | 159,861 | 27,371 | 47,290 R | 47.1% | 45.1% | 6.6% |

# VIRGINIA

## PRESIDENT 1992

| 1990 Census Pop. Est. | County | Total Vote | Republican | Democratic | Perot | Other | Plurality | Percentage Total Vote | | |
|---|---|---|---|---|---|---|---|---|---|---|
| | | | | | | | | Rep. | Dem. | Perot |
| 31,703 | ACCOMACK | 13,125 | 5,666 | 4,950 | 2,304 | 205 | 716 R | 43.2% | 37.7% | 17.6% |
| 68,040 | ALBEMARLE | 31,804 | 13,894 | 13,886 | 3,855 | 169 | 8 R | 43.7% | 43.7% | 12.1% |
| 13,176 | ALLEGHANY | 5,657 | 2,294 | 2,396 | 926 | 41 | 102 D | 40.6% | 42.4% | 16.4% |
| 8,787 | AMELIA | 4,224 | 2,062 | 1,534 | 574 | 54 | 528 R | 48.8% | 36.3% | 13.6% |
| 28,578 | AMHERST | 10,908 | 5,482 | 4,101 | 1,268 | 57 | 1,381 R | 50.3% | 37.6% | 11.6% |
| 12,298 | APPOMATTOX | 5,620 | 2,830 | 1,919 | 801 | 70 | 911 R | 50.4% | 34.1% | 14.3% |
| 170,936 | ARLINGTON | 82,584 | 26,376 | 47,756 | 7,992 | 460 | 21,380 D | 31.9% | 57.8% | 9.7% |
| 54,677 | AUGUSTA | 21,866 | 12,896 | 5,190 | 3,397 | 383 | 7,706 R | 59.0% | 23.7% | 15.5% |
| 4,799 | BATH | 2,330 | 1,075 | 855 | 354 | 46 | 220 R | 46.1% | 36.7% | 15.2% |
| 45,656 | BEDFORD COUNTY | 20,756 | 10,496 | 6,792 | 3,251 | 217 | 3,704 R | 50.6% | 32.7% | 15.7% |
| 6,514 | BLAND | 2,832 | 1,368 | 1,001 | 408 | 55 | 367 R | 48.3% | 35.3% | 14.4% |
| 24,992 | BOTETOURT | 12,209 | 5,904 | 4,349 | 1,819 | 137 | 1,555 R | 48.4% | 35.6% | 14.9% |
| 15,987 | BRUNSWICK | 6,718 | 2,480 | 3,687 | 479 | 72 | 1,207 D | 36.9% | 54.9% | 7.1% |
| 31,333 | BUCHANAN | 11,704 | 3,297 | 7,405 | 815 | 187 | 4,108 D | 28.2% | 63.3% | 7.0% |
| 12,873 | BUCKINGHAM | 5,103 | 2,368 | 2,193 | 459 | 83 | 175 R | 46.4% | 43.0% | 9.0% |
| 47,572 | CAMPBELL | 19,757 | 10,931 | 5,999 | 2,553 | 274 | 4,932 R | 55.3% | 30.4% | 12.9% |
| 19,217 | CAROLINE | 7,753 | 2,947 | 3,770 | 965 | 71 | 823 D | 38.0% | 48.6% | 12.4% |
| 26,594 | CARROLL | 10,915 | 5,664 | 3,790 | 1,388 | 73 | 1,874 R | 51.9% | 34.7% | 12.7% |
| 6,282 | CHARLES CITY | 3,014 | 729 | 2,010 | 251 | 24 | 1,281 D | 24.2% | 66.7% | 8.3% |
| 11,688 | CHARLOTTE | 5,111 | 2,293 | 2,098 | 640 | 80 | 195 R | 44.9% | 41.0% | 12.5% |
| 209,274 | CHESTERFIELD | 101,933 | 56,626 | 28,028 | 16,898 | 381 | 28,598 R | 55.6% | 27.5% | 16.6% |
| 12,101 | CLARKE | 4,648 | 1,994 | 1,811 | 802 | 41 | 183 R | 42.9% | 39.0% | 17.3% |
| 4,372 | CRAIG | 2,297 | 1,008 | 965 | 304 | 20 | 43 R | 43.9% | 42.0% | 13.2% |
| 27,791 | CULPEPER | 10,466 | 5,226 | 3,444 | 1,640 | 156 | 1,782 R | 49.9% | 32.9% | 15.7% |
| 7,825 | CUMBERLAND | 3,384 | 1,643 | 1,284 | 372 | 85 | 359 R | 48.6% | 37.9% | 11.0% |
| 17,620 | DICKENSON | 8,143 | 2,574 | 4,839 | 660 | 70 | 2,265 D | 31.6% | 59.4% | 8.1% |
| 20,960 | DINWIDDIE | 8,597 | 3,648 | 3,624 | 1,198 | 127 | 24 R | 42.4% | 42.2% | 13.9% |
| 8,689 | ESSEX | 3,904 | 1,897 | 1,583 | 382 | 42 | 314 R | 48.6% | 40.5% | 9.8% |
| 818,584 | FAIRFAX COUNTY | 385,218 | 170,488 | 160,186 | 53,012 | 1,532 | 10,302 R | 44.3% | 41.6% | 13.8% |
| 48,741 | FAUQUIER | 20,759 | 10,497 | 6,600 | 3,464 | 198 | 3,897 R | 50.6% | 31.8% | 16.7% |
| 12,005 | FLOYD | 5,316 | 2,575 | 2,026 | 672 | 43 | 549 R | 48.4% | 38.1% | 12.6% |
| 12,429 | FLUVANNA | 5,852 | 2,811 | 2,134 | 871 | 36 | 677 R | 48.0% | 36.5% | 14.9% |
| 39,549 | FRANKLIN COUNTY | 15,701 | 6,724 | 6,590 | 2,232 | 155 | 134 R | 42.8% | 42.0% | 14.2% |
| 45,723 | FREDERICK | 17,468 | 9,425 | 4,942 | 2,981 | 120 | 4,483 R | 54.0% | 28.3% | 17.1% |
| 16,366 | GILES | 7,632 | 3,023 | 3,346 | 1,142 | 121 | 323 D | 39.6% | 43.8% | 15.0% |
| 30,131 | GLOUCESTER | 13,345 | 6,461 | 4,058 | 2,640 | 186 | 2,403 R | 48.4% | 30.4% | 19.8% |
| 14,163 | GOOCHLAND | 7,479 | 3,834 | 2,589 | 994 | 62 | 1,245 R | 51.3% | 34.6% | 13.3% |
| 16,278 | GRAYSON | 6,939 | 3,378 | 2,615 | 860 | 86 | 763 R | 48.7% | 37.7% | 12.4% |
| 10,297 | GREENE | 4,331 | 2,265 | 1,353 | 627 | 86 | 912 R | 52.3% | 31.2% | 14.5% |
| 8,853 | GREENSVILLE | 3,986 | 1,335 | 2,237 | 360 | 54 | 902 D | 33.5% | 56.1% | 9.0% |
| 29,033 | HALIFAX | 11,262 | 5,199 | 4,752 | 1,140 | 171 | 447 R | 46.2% | 42.2% | 10.1% |
| 63,306 | HANOVER | 34,261 | 20,336 | 8,021 | 5,674 | 230 | 12,315 R | 59.4% | 23.4% | 16.6% |
| 217,881 | HENRICO | 108,868 | 56,910 | 36,807 | 14,720 | 431 | 20,103 R | 52.3% | 33.8% | 13.5% |
| 56,942 | HENRY | 21,825 | 9,005 | 9,296 | 3,212 | 312 | 291 D | 41.3% | 42.6% | 14.7% |
| 2,635 | HIGHLAND | 1,400 | 686 | 494 | 212 | 8 | 192 R | 49.0% | 35.3% | 15.1% |
| 25,053 | ISLE OF WIGHT | 11,387 | 5,370 | 4,380 | 1,536 | 101 | 990 R | 47.2% | 38.5% | 13.5% |
| 34,859 | JAMES CITY | 18,221 | 8,781 | 6,536 | 2,675 | 229 | 2,245 R | 48.2% | 35.9% | 14.7% |
| 6,289 | KING AND QUEEN | 2,917 | 1,206 | 1,363 | 323 | 25 | 157 D | 41.3% | 46.7% | 11.1% |
| 13,527 | KING GEORGE | 5,324 | 2,570 | 1,811 | 918 | 25 | 759 R | 48.3% | 34.0% | 17.2% |
| 10,913 | KING WILLIAM | 5,230 | 2,591 | 1,822 | 758 | 59 | 769 R | 49.5% | 34.8% | 14.5% |
| 10,896 | LANCASTER | 5,528 | 2,841 | 1,812 | 739 | 136 | 1,029 R | 51.4% | 32.8% | 13.4% |
| 24,496 | LEE | 9,796 | 3,504 | 5,215 | 1,002 | 75 | 1,711 D | 35.8% | 53.2% | 10.2% |
| 86,129 | LOUDOUN | 41,574 | 19,290 | 14,462 | 7,391 | 431 | 4,828 R | 46.4% | 34.8% | 17.8% |
| 20,325 | LOUISA | 8,307 | 3,461 | 3,399 | 1,381 | 66 | 62 R | 41.7% | 40.9% | 16.6% |
| 11,419 | LUNENBURG | 4,912 | 2,227 | 2,082 | 505 | 98 | 145 R | 45.3% | 42.4% | 10.3% |
| 11,949 | MADISON | 4,779 | 2,341 | 1,700 | 653 | 85 | 641 R | 49.0% | 35.6% | 13.7% |
| 8,348 | MATHEWS | 4,525 | 2,179 | 1,402 | 884 | 60 | 777 R | 48.2% | 31.0% | 19.5% |
| 29,241 | MECKLENBURG | 10,970 | 5,401 | 4,273 | 1,128 | 168 | 1,128 R | 49.2% | 39.0% | 10.3% |
| 8,653 | MIDDLESEX | 4,685 | 2,224 | 1,597 | 768 | 96 | 627 R | 47.5% | 34.1% | 16.4% |
| 73,913 | MONTGOMERY | 24,935 | 10,606 | 10,658 | 3,449 | 222 | 52 D | 42.5% | 42.7% | 13.8% |

986

# VIRGINIA

## PRESIDENT 1992

| 1990 Census Pop. Est. | County | Total Vote | Republican | Democratic | Perot | Other | Plurality | Percentage Total Vote | | |
|---|---|---|---|---|---|---|---|---|---|---|
| | | | | | | | | Rep. | Dem. | Perot |
| 12,778 | NELSON | 5,538 | 2,159 | 2,586 | 748 | 45 | 427 D | 39.0% | 46.7% | 13.5% |
| 10,445 | NEW KENT | 5,483 | 2,708 | 1,738 | 1,017 | 20 | 970 R | 49.4% | 31.7% | 18.5% |
| 13,061 | NORTHAMPTON | 5,618 | 2,088 | 2,568 | 844 | 118 | 480 D | 37.2% | 45.7% | 15.0% |
| 10,524 | NORTHUMBERLAND | 5,334 | 2,667 | 1,862 | 729 | 76 | 805 R | 50.0% | 34.9% | 13.7% |
| 14,993 | NOTTOWAY | 5,743 | 2,610 | 2,411 | 606 | 116 | 199 R | 45.4% | 42.0% | 10.6% |
| 21,421 | ORANGE | 8,966 | 4,092 | 3,348 | 1,425 | 101 | 744 R | 45.6% | 37.3% | 15.9% |
| 21,690 | PAGE | 8,460 | 4,203 | 3,010 | 1,163 | 84 | 1,193 R | 49.7% | 35.6% | 13.7% |
| 17,473 | PATRICK | 7,189 | 3,521 | 2,465 | 1,026 | 177 | 1,056 R | 49.0% | 34.3% | 14.3% |
| 55,655 | PITTSYLVANIA | 21,894 | 11,467 | 7,675 | 2,296 | 456 | 3,792 R | 52.4% | 35.1% | 10.5% |
| 15,328 | POWHATAN | 7,086 | 3,832 | 1,950 | 1,232 | 72 | 1,882 R | 54.1% | 27.5% | 17.4% |
| 17,320 | PRINCE EDWARD | 6,383 | 2,858 | 2,775 | 635 | 115 | 83 R | 44.8% | 43.5% | 9.9% |
| 27,394 | PRINCE GEORGE | 9,412 | 4,799 | 3,087 | 1,459 | 67 | 1,712 R | 51.0% | 32.8% | 15.5% |
| 215,686 | PRINCE WILLIAM | 75,680 | 35,432 | 26,486 | 13,190 | 572 | 8,946 R | 46.8% | 35.0% | 17.4% |
| 34,496 | PULASKI | 13,987 | 6,148 | 5,633 | 2,066 | 140 | 515 R | 44.0% | 40.3% | 14.8% |
| 6,622 | RAPPAHANNOCK | 3,181 | 1,410 | 1,273 | 487 | 11 | 137 R | 44.3% | 40.0% | 15.3% |
| 7,273 | RICHMOND COUNTY | 3,050 | 1,609 | 1,034 | 366 | 41 | 575 R | 52.8% | 33.9% | 12.0% |
| 79,332 | ROANOKE COUNTY | 41,080 | 20,667 | 14,704 | 5,477 | 232 | 5,963 R | 50.3% | 35.8% | 13.3% |
| 18,350 | ROCKBRIDGE | 7,503 | 3,228 | 2,908 | 1,254 | 113 | 320 R | 43.0% | 38.8% | 16.7% |
| 57,482 | ROCKINGHAM | 21,493 | 13,016 | 5,407 | 2,839 | 231 | 7,609 R | 60.6% | 25.2% | 13.2% |
| 28,667 | RUSSELL | 11,484 | 3,891 | 6,480 | 958 | 155 | 2,589 D | 33.9% | 56.4% | 8.3% |
| 23,204 | SCOTT | 9,690 | 4,515 | 3,979 | 957 | 239 | 536 R | 46.6% | 41.1% | 9.9% |
| 31,636 | SHENANDOAH | 13,896 | 7,746 | 3,956 | 2,063 | 131 | 3,790 R | 55.7% | 28.5% | 14.8% |
| 32,370 | SMYTH | 12,931 | 6,128 | 4,924 | 1,618 | 261 | 1,204 R | 47.4% | 38.1% | 12.5% |
| 17,550 | SOUTHAMPTON | 6,874 | 2,844 | 3,199 | 754 | 77 | 355 D | 41.4% | 46.5% | 11.0% |
| 57,403 | SPOTSYLVANIA | 24,014 | 11,829 | 8,133 | 3,918 | 134 | 3,696 R | 49.3% | 33.9% | 16.3% |
| 61,236 | STAFFORD | 24,871 | 12,528 | 7,718 | 4,481 | 144 | 4,810 R | 50.4% | 31.0% | 18.0% |
| 6,145 | SURRY | 3,275 | 1,046 | 1,823 | 364 | 42 | 777 D | 31.9% | 55.7% | 11.1% |
| 10,248 | SUSSEX | 4,253 | 1,527 | 2,193 | 446 | 87 | 666 D | 35.9% | 51.6% | 10.5% |
| 45,960 | TAZEWELL | 17,056 | 6,375 | 8,586 | 1,872 | 223 | 2,211 D | 37.4% | 50.3% | 11.0% |
| 26,142 | WARREN | 9,676 | 4,319 | 3,554 | 1,650 | 153 | 765 R | 44.6% | 36.7% | 17.1% |
| 45,887 | WASHINGTON | 18,995 | 9,150 | 7,269 | 2,288 | 288 | 1,881 R | 48.2% | 38.3% | 12.0% |
| 15,480 | WESTMORELAND | 6,223 | 2,554 | 2,758 | 818 | 93 | 204 D | 41.0% | 44.3% | 13.1% |
| 39,573 | WISE | 14,857 | 5,144 | 7,681 | 1,835 | 197 | 2,537 D | 34.6% | 51.7% | 12.4% |
| 25,466 | WYTHE | 10,492 | 5,121 | 3,616 | 1,557 | 198 | 1,505 R | 48.8% | 34.5% | 14.8% |
| 42,422 | YORK | 19,966 | 10,197 | 6,218 | 3,426 | 125 | 3,979 R | 51.1% | 31.1% | 17.2% |
| | **City** | | | | | | | | | |
| 67,596 | ALEXANDRIA | 52,675 | 16,700 | 30,784 | 4,934 | 257 | 14,084 D | 31.7% | 58.4% | 9.4% |
| 6,073 | BEDFORD CITY | 2,409 | 1,091 | 963 | 313 | 42 | 128 R | 45.3% | 40.0% | 13.0% |
| 18,426 | BRISTOL | 7,462 | 3,616 | 2,948 | 851 | 47 | 668 R | 48.5% | 39.5% | 11.4% |
| 6,406 | BUENA VISTA | 2,200 | 849 | 1,023 | 291 | 37 | 174 D | 38.6% | 46.5% | 13.2% |
| 40,341 | CHARLOTTESVILLE | 14,899 | 4,705 | 8,685 | 1,397 | 112 | 3,980 D | 31.6% | 58.3% | 9.4% |
| 151,976 | CHESAPEAKE | 61,868 | 28,909 | 23,495 | 9,237 | 227 | 5,414 R | 46.7% | 38.0% | 14.9% |
| 4,679 | CLIFTON FORGE | 1,873 | 632 | 958 | 251 | 32 | 326 D | 33.7% | 51.1% | 13.4% |
| 16,064 | COLONIAL HEIGHTS | 8,400 | 5,298 | 1,721 | 1,312 | 69 | 3,577 R | 63.1% | 20.5% | 15.6% |
| 6,991 | COVINGTON | 2,869 | 995 | 1,442 | 402 | 30 | 447 D | 34.7% | 50.3% | 14.0% |
| 53,056 | DANVILLE | 19,661 | 9,584 | 8,134 | 1,679 | 264 | 1,450 R | 48.7% | 41.4% | 8.5% |
| 5,306 | EMPORIA | 2,319 | 1,094 | 1,048 | 157 | 20 | 46 R | 47.2% | 45.2% | 6.8% |
| 19,622 | FAIRFAX CITY | 9,693 | 4,333 | 3,884 | 1,439 | 37 | 449 R | 44.7% | 40.1% | 14.8% |
| 9,578 | FALLS CHURCH | 5,404 | 1,912 | 2,864 | 599 | 29 | 952 D | 35.4% | 53.0% | 11.1% |
| 7,864 | FRANKLIN CITY | 3,339 | 1,347 | 1,696 | 272 | 24 | 349 D | 40.3% | 50.8% | 8.1% |
| 19,027 | FREDERICKSBURG | 6,879 | 2,819 | 3,266 | 738 | 56 | 447 D | 41.0% | 47.5% | 10.7% |
| 6,670 | GALAX | 2,344 | 1,087 | 957 | 276 | 24 | 130 R | 46.4% | 40.8% | 11.8% |
| 133,793 | HAMPTON | 49,878 | 19,219 | 23,395 | 6,581 | 683 | 4,176 D | 38.5% | 46.9% | 13.2% |
| 30,707 | HARRISONBURG | 9,632 | 4,935 | 3,414 | 1,162 | 121 | 1,521 R | 51.2% | 35.4% | 12.1% |
| 23,101 | HOPEWELL | 8,042 | 3,818 | 2,863 | 1,227 | 134 | 955 R | 47.5% | 35.6% | 15.3% |
| 6,959 | LEXINGTON | 2,277 | 894 | 1,128 | 228 | 27 | 234 D | 39.3% | 49.5% | 10.0% |

# VIRGINIA

## PRESIDENT 1992

| 1990 Census Pop. Est. | County | Total Vote | Republican | Democratic | Perot | Other | Plurality | | Percentage Total Vote | | |
|---|---|---|---|---|---|---|---|---|---|---|---|
| | | | | | | | | | Rep. | Dem. | Perot |
| 66,049 | LYNCHBURG | 24,969 | 12,518 | 9,587 | 2,545 | 319 | 2,931 | R | 50.1% | 38.4% | 10.2% |
| 27,957 | MANASSAS | 11,154 | 5,453 | 3,647 | 1,971 | 83 | 1,806 | R | 48.9% | 32.7% | 17.7% |
| 6,734 | MANASSAS PARK | 1,720 | 792 | 567 | 356 | 5 | 225 | R | 46.0% | 33.0% | 20.7% |
| 16,162 | MARTINSVILLE | 6,617 | 2,690 | 3,073 | 748 | 106 | 383 | D | 40.7% | 46.4% | 11.3% |
| 170,045 | NEWPORT NEWS | 61,091 | 26,779 | 25,743 | 8,217 | 352 | 1,036 | R | 43.8% | 42.1% | 13.5% |
| 261,229 | NORFOLK | 69,027 | 22,362 | 37,602 | 8,732 | 331 | 15,240 | D | 32.4% | 54.5% | 12.7% |
| 4,247 | NORTON | 1,548 | 472 | 871 | 182 | 23 | 399 | D | 30.5% | 56.3% | 11.8% |
| 38,386 | PETERSBURG | 12,717 | 3,125 | 8,671 | 834 | 87 | 5,546 | D | 24.6% | 68.2% | 6.6% |
| 11,005 | POQUOSON | 5,437 | 3,354 | 1,086 | 960 | 37 | 2,268 | R | 61.7% | 20.0% | 17.7% |
| 103,907 | PORTSMOUTH | 37,599 | 12,575 | 20,416 | 4,360 | 248 | 7,841 | D | 33.4% | 54.3% | 11.6% |
| 15,940 | RADFORD | 4,785 | 1,996 | 2,183 | 582 | 24 | 187 | D | 41.7% | 45.6% | 12.2% |
| 203,056 | RICHMOND CITY | 79,735 | 24,341 | 47,642 | 6,992 | 760 | 23,301 | D | 30.5% | 59.8% | 8.8% |
| 96,397 | ROANOKE CITY | 35,181 | 13,443 | 17,724 | 3,753 | 261 | 4,281 | D | 38.2% | 50.4% | 10.7% |
| 23,756 | SALEM | 10,669 | 5,143 | 4,028 | 1,430 | 68 | 1,115 | R | 48.2% | 37.8% | 13.4% |
| 6,997 | SOUTH BOSTON | 2,757 | 1,435 | 1,051 | 252 | 19 | 384 | R | 52.0% | 38.1% | 9.1% |
| 24,461 | STAUNTON | 9,232 | 4,989 | 2,851 | 1,146 | 246 | 2,138 | R | 54.0% | 30.9% | 12.4% |
| 52,141 | SUFFOLK | 20,223 | 8,697 | 9,196 | 2,150 | 180 | 499 | D | 43.0% | 45.5% | 10.6% |
| 393,069 | VIRGINIA BEACH | 137,785 | 68,936 | 44,294 | 24,087 | 468 | 24,642 | R | 50.0% | 32.1% | 17.5% |
| 18,549 | WAYNESBORO | 7,149 | 3,758 | 2,302 | 961 | 128 | 1,456 | R | 52.6% | 32.2% | 13.4% |
| 11,530 | WILLIAMSBURG | 3,719 | 1,349 | 1,856 | 445 | 69 | 507 | D | 36.3% | 49.9% | 12.0% |
| 21,947 | WINCHESTER | 7,701 | 3,833 | 2,768 | 1,048 | 52 | 1,065 | R | 49.8% | 35.9% | 13.6% |
| 6,187,358 | TOTAL | 2,558,665 | 1,150,517 | 1,038,650 | 348,639 | 20,859 | 111,867 | R | 45.0% | 40.6% | 13.6% |

# VIRGINIA

## PRESIDENT 1988

| 1980 Census Population | County | Total Vote | Republican | Democratic | Other | Rep.-Dem. Plurality | Percentage | | | |
|---|---|---|---|---|---|---|---|---|---|---|
| | | | | | | | Total Vote | | Major Vote | |
| | | | | | | | Rep. | Dem. | Rep. | Dem. |
| 31,268 | ACCOMACK | 11,542 | 6,926 | 4,443 | 173 | 2,483 R | 60.0% | 38.5% | 60.9% | 39.1% |
| 55,783 | ALBEMARLE | 25,753 | 15,117 | 10,363 | 273 | 4,754 R | 58.7% | 40.2% | 59.3% | 40.7% |
| 14,333 | ALLEGHANY | 4,926 | 2,555 | 2,316 | 55 | 239 R | 51.9% | 47.0% | 52.5% | 47.5% |
| 8,405 | AMELIA | 3,594 | 2,187 | 1,359 | 48 | 828 R | 60.9% | 37.8% | 61.7% | 38.3% |
| 29,122 | AMHERST | 10,151 | 6,507 | 3,567 | 77 | 2,940 R | 64.1% | 35.1% | 64.6% | 35.4% |
| 11,971 | APPOMATTOX | 5,040 | 3,205 | 1,740 | 95 | 1,465 R | 63.6% | 34.5% | 64.8% | 35.2% |
| 152,599 | ARLINGTON | 75,365 | 34,191 | 40,314 | 860 | 6,123 D | 45.4% | 53.5% | 45.9% | 54.1% |
| 53,732 | AUGUSTA | 17,634 | 13,251 | 4,170 | 213 | 9,081 R | 75.1% | 23.6% | 76.1% | 23.9% |
| 5,860 | BATH | 2,167 | 1,273 | 881 | 13 | 392 R | 58.7% | 40.7% | 59.1% | 40.9% |
| 34,927 | BEDFORD COUNTY | 16,382 | 10,702 | 5,406 | 274 | 5,296 R | 65.3% | 33.0% | 66.4% | 33.6% |
| 6,349 | BLAND | 2,546 | 1,556 | 937 | 53 | 619 R | 61.1% | 36.8% | 62.4% | 37.6% |
| 23,270 | BOTETOURT | 9,591 | 5,687 | 3,763 | 141 | 1,924 R | 59.3% | 39.2% | 60.2% | 39.8% |
| 15,632 | BRUNSWICK | 5,884 | 2,742 | 3,070 | 72 | 328 D | 46.6% | 52.2% | 47.2% | 52.8% |
| 37,989 | BUCHANAN | 10,965 | 3,912 | 6,935 | 118 | 3,023 D | 35.7% | 63.2% | 36.1% | 63.9% |
| 11,751 | BUCKINGHAM | 4,471 | 2,481 | 1,941 | 49 | 540 R | 55.5% | 43.4% | 56.1% | 43.9% |
| 45,424 | CAMPBELL | 17,533 | 12,713 | 4,574 | 246 | 8,139 R | 72.5% | 26.1% | 73.5% | 26.5% |
| 17,904 | CAROLINE | 6,292 | 3,065 | 3,186 | 41 | 121 D | 48.7% | 50.6% | 49.0% | 51.0% |
| 27,270 | CARROLL | 9,637 | 6,377 | 3,190 | 70 | 3,187 R | 66.2% | 33.1% | 66.7% | 33.3% |
| 6,692 | CHARLES CITY | 2,700 | 826 | 1,839 | 35 | 1,013 D | 30.6% | 68.1% | 31.0% | 69.0% |
| 12,266 | CHARLOTTE | 4,699 | 2,699 | 1,923 | 77 | 776 R | 57.4% | 40.9% | 58.4% | 41.6% |
| 141,372 | CHESTERFIELD | 78,083 | 58,828 | 18,723 | 532 | 40,105 R | 75.3% | 24.0% | 75.9% | 24.1% |
| 9,965 | CLARKE | 4,020 | 2,502 | 1,478 | 40 | 1,024 R | 62.2% | 36.8% | 62.9% | 37.1% |
| 3,948 | CRAIG | 2,005 | 1,112 | 864 | 29 | 248 R | 55.5% | 43.1% | 56.3% | 43.7% |
| 22,620 | CULPEPER | 8,599 | 5,896 | 2,555 | 148 | 3,341 R | 68.6% | 29.7% | 69.8% | 30.2% |
| 7,881 | CUMBERLAND | 3,159 | 1,978 | 1,132 | 49 | 846 R | 62.6% | 35.8% | 63.6% | 36.4% |
| 19,806 | DICKENSON | 7,604 | 3,091 | 4,461 | 52 | 1,370 D | 40.6% | 58.7% | 40.9% | 59.1% |
| 22,602 | DINWIDDIE | 7,659 | 4,165 | 3,405 | 89 | 760 R | 54.4% | 44.5% | 55.0% | 45.0% |
| 8,864 | ESSEX | 3,365 | 2,038 | 1,294 | 33 | 744 R | 60.6% | 38.5% | 61.2% | 38.8% |
| 596,901 | FAIRFAX COUNTY | 328,365 | 200,641 | 125,711 | 2,013 | 74,930 R | 61.1% | 38.3% | 61.5% | 38.5% |
| 35,889 | FAUQUIER | 16,796 | 11,733 | 4,837 | 226 | 6,896 R | 69.9% | 28.8% | 70.8% | 29.2% |
| 11,563 | FLOYD | 4,735 | 2,921 | 1,727 | 87 | 1,194 R | 61.7% | 36.5% | 62.8% | 37.2% |
| 10,244 | FLUVANNA | 4,059 | 2,447 | 1,562 | 50 | 885 R | 60.3% | 38.5% | 61.0% | 39.0% |
| 35,740 | FRANKLIN COUNTY | 13,261 | 7,391 | 5,734 | 136 | 1,657 R | 55.7% | 43.2% | 56.3% | 43.7% |
| 34,150 | FREDERICK | 13,717 | 9,921 | 3,707 | 89 | 6,214 R | 72.3% | 27.0% | 72.8% | 27.2% |
| 17,810 | GILES | 6,648 | 3,490 | 3,042 | 116 | 448 R | 52.5% | 45.8% | 53.4% | 46.6% |
| 20,107 | GLOUCESTER | 11,181 | 7,646 | 3,372 | 163 | 4,274 R | 68.4% | 30.2% | 69.4% | 30.6% |
| 11,761 | GOOCHLAND | 6,013 | 3,765 | 2,209 | 39 | 1,556 R | 62.6% | 36.7% | 63.0% | 37.0% |
| 16,579 | GRAYSON | 6,451 | 3,968 | 2,441 | 42 | 1,527 R | 61.5% | 37.8% | 61.9% | 38.1% |
| 7,625 | GREENE | 3,224 | 2,234 | 899 | 91 | 1,335 R | 69.3% | 27.9% | 71.3% | 28.7% |
| 10,903 | GREENSVILLE | 3,733 | 1,610 | 2,083 | 40 | 473 D | 43.1% | 55.8% | 43.6% | 56.4% |
| 30,599 | HALIFAX | 10,124 | 5,671 | 4,282 | 171 | 1,389 R | 56.0% | 42.3% | 57.0% | 43.0% |
| 50,398 | HANOVER | 26,718 | 20,570 | 5,985 | 163 | 14,585 R | 77.0% | 22.4% | 77.5% | 22.5% |
| 180,735 | HENRICO | 89,887 | 62,284 | 26,980 | 623 | 35,304 R | 69.3% | 30.0% | 69.8% | 30.2% |
| 57,654 | HENRY | 18,729 | 10,871 | 7,536 | 322 | 3,335 R | 58.0% | 40.2% | 59.1% | 40.9% |
| 2,937 | HIGHLAND | 1,286 | 807 | 456 | 23 | 351 R | 62.8% | 35.5% | 63.9% | 36.1% |
| 21,603 | ISLE OF WIGHT | 9,621 | 5,779 | 3,747 | 95 | 2,032 R | 60.1% | 38.9% | 60.7% | 39.3% |
| 22,763 | JAMES CITY | 13,773 | 8,945 | 4,642 | 186 | 4,303 R | 64.9% | 33.7% | 65.8% | 34.2% |
| 5,968 | KING AND QUEEN | 2,727 | 1,376 | 1,309 | 42 | 67 R | 50.5% | 48.0% | 51.2% | 48.8% |
| 10,543 | KING GEORGE | 4,146 | 2,587 | 1,519 | 40 | 1,068 R | 62.4% | 36.6% | 63.0% | 37.0% |
| 9,334 | KING WILLIAM | 4,349 | 2,735 | 1,561 | 53 | 1,174 R | 62.9% | 35.9% | 63.7% | 36.3% |
| 10,129 | LANCASTER | 5,043 | 3,380 | 1,551 | 112 | 1,829 R | 67.0% | 30.8% | 68.5% | 31.5% |
| 25,956 | LEE | 9,045 | 4,080 | 4,906 | 59 | 826 D | 45.1% | 54.2% | 45.4% | 54.6% |
| 57,427 | LOUDOUN | 30,862 | 20,448 | 10,101 | 313 | 10,347 R | 66.3% | 32.7% | 66.9% | 33.1% |
| 17,825 | LOUISA | 6,702 | 3,831 | 2,789 | 82 | 1,042 R | 57.2% | 41.6% | 57.9% | 42.1% |
| 12,124 | LUNENBURG | 4,496 | 2,530 | 1,870 | 96 | 660 R | 56.3% | 41.6% | 57.5% | 42.5% |
| 10,232 | MADISON | 4,026 | 2,501 | 1,427 | 98 | 1,074 R | 62.1% | 35.4% | 63.7% | 36.3% |
| 7,995 | MATHEWS | 4,076 | 2,752 | 1,235 | 89 | 1,517 R | 67.5% | 30.3% | 69.0% | 31.0% |
| 29,444 | MECKLENBURG | 9,278 | 5,887 | 3,275 | 116 | 2,612 R | 63.5% | 35.3% | 64.3% | 35.7% |
| 7,719 | MIDDLESEX | 4,018 | 2,571 | 1,361 | 86 | 1,210 R | 64.0% | 33.9% | 65.4% | 34.6% |
| 63,516 | MONTGOMERY | 21,444 | 12,326 | 8,909 | 209 | 3,417 R | 57.5% | 41.5% | 58.0% | 42.0% |

# VIRGINIA

## PRESIDENT 1988

| 1980 Census Population | County | Total Vote | Republican | Democratic | Other | Rep.-Dem. Plurality | Percentage | | | |
|---|---|---|---|---|---|---|---|---|---|---|
| | | | | | | | Total Vote | | Major Vote | |
| | | | | | | | Rep. | Dem. | Rep. | Dem. |
| 12,204 | NELSON | 4,849 | 2,502 | 2,272 | 75 | 230 R | 51.6% | 46.9% | 52.4% | 47.6% |
| 8,781 | NEW KENT | 4,384 | 2,917 | 1,427 | 40 | 1,490 R | 66.5% | 32.6% | 67.2% | 32.8% |
| 14,625 | NORTHAMPTON | 4,927 | 2,562 | 2,242 | 123 | 320 R | 52.0% | 45.5% | 53.3% | 46.7% |
| 9,828 | NORTHUMBERLAND | 4,581 | 2,984 | 1,506 | 91 | 1,478 R | 65.1% | 32.9% | 66.5% | 33.5% |
| 14,666 | NOTTOWAY | 5,509 | 3,161 | 2,217 | 131 | 944 R | 57.4% | 40.2% | 58.8% | 41.2% |
| 18,063 | ORANGE | 7,015 | 4,319 | 2,592 | 104 | 1,727 R | 61.6% | 36.9% | 62.5% | 37.5% |
| 19,401 | PAGE | 7,575 | 5,013 | 2,499 | 63 | 2,514 R | 66.2% | 33.0% | 66.7% | 33.3% |
| 17,647 | PATRICK | 6,229 | 3,990 | 2,093 | 146 | 1,897 R | 64.1% | 33.6% | 65.6% | 34.4% |
| 66,147 | PITTSYLVANIA | 19,201 | 12,229 | 6,612 | 360 | 5,617 R | 63.7% | 34.4% | 64.9% | 35.1% |
| 13,062 | POWHATAN | 5,541 | 4,040 | 1,467 | 34 | 2,573 R | 72.9% | 26.5% | 73.4% | 26.6% |
| 16,456 | PRINCE EDWARD | 5,720 | 3,147 | 2,434 | 139 | 713 R | 55.0% | 42.6% | 56.4% | 43.6% |
| 25,733 | PRINCE GEORGE | 7,515 | 4,982 | 2,469 | 64 | 2,513 R | 66.3% | 32.9% | 66.9% | 33.1% |
| 144,703 | PRINCE WILLIAM | 59,453 | 39,654 | 19,198 | 601 | 20,456 R | 66.7% | 32.3% | 67.4% | 32.6% |
| 35,229 | PULASKI | 11,719 | 6,844 | 4,686 | 189 | 2,158 R | 58.4% | 40.0% | 59.4% | 40.6% |
| 6,093 | RAPPAHANNOCK | 2,686 | 1,657 | 1,003 | 26 | 654 R | 61.7% | 37.3% | 62.3% | 37.7% |
| 6,952 | RICHMOND COUNTY | 2,811 | 1,862 | 924 | 25 | 938 R | 66.2% | 32.9% | 66.8% | 33.2% |
| 72,945 | ROANOKE COUNTY | 35,157 | 22,011 | 12,938 | 208 | 9,073 R | 62.6% | 36.8% | 63.0% | 37.0% |
| 17,911 | ROCKBRIDGE | 6,062 | 3,541 | 2,412 | 109 | 1,129 R | 58.4% | 39.8% | 59.5% | 40.5% |
| 57,038 | ROCKINGHAM | 18,241 | 13,241 | 4,716 | 284 | 8,525 R | 72.6% | 25.9% | 73.7% | 26.3% |
| 31,761 | RUSSELL | 10,753 | 4,374 | 6,222 | 157 | 1,848 D | 40.7% | 57.9% | 41.3% | 58.7% |
| 25,068 | SCOTT | 8,785 | 4,986 | 3,616 | 183 | 1,370 R | 56.8% | 41.2% | 58.0% | 42.0% |
| 27,559 | SHENANDOAH | 12,004 | 8,612 | 3,276 | 116 | 5,336 R | 71.7% | 27.3% | 72.4% | 27.6% |
| 33,366 | SMYTH | 11,727 | 7,446 | 3,989 | 292 | 3,457 R | 63.5% | 34.0% | 65.1% | 34.9% |
| 18,731 | SOUTHAMPTON | 6,493 | 3,439 | 3,000 | 54 | 439 R | 53.0% | 46.2% | 53.4% | 46.6% |
| 34,435 | SPOTSYLVANIA | 16,593 | 10,978 | 5,486 | 129 | 5,492 R | 66.2% | 33.1% | 66.7% | 33.3% |
| 40,470 | STAFFORD | 17,712 | 12,234 | 5,380 | 98 | 6,854 R | 69.1% | 30.4% | 69.5% | 30.5% |
| 6,046 | SURRY | 2,899 | 1,246 | 1,602 | 51 | 356 D | 43.0% | 55.3% | 43.8% | 56.3% |
| 10,874 | SUSSEX | 3,896 | 1,822 | 1,958 | 116 | 136 D | 46.8% | 50.3% | 48.2% | 51.8% |
| 50,511 | TAZEWELL | 15,453 | 7,165 | 8,098 | 190 | 933 D | 46.4% | 52.4% | 46.9% | 53.1% |
| 21,200 | WARREN | 7,598 | 4,700 | 2,769 | 129 | 1,931 R | 61.9% | 36.4% | 62.9% | 37.1% |
| 46,487 | WASHINGTON | 16,899 | 10,722 | 5,819 | 358 | 4,903 R | 63.4% | 34.4% | 64.8% | 35.2% |
| 14,041 | WESTMORELAND | 5,370 | 2,974 | 2,311 | 85 | 663 R | 55.4% | 43.0% | 56.3% | 43.7% |
| 43,863 | WISE | 13,386 | 6,189 | 7,017 | 180 | 828 D | 46.2% | 52.4% | 46.9% | 53.1% |
| 25,522 | WYTHE | 9,225 | 5,827 | 3,201 | 197 | 2,626 R | 63.2% | 34.7% | 64.5% | 35.5% |
| 35,463 | YORK | 15,871 | 11,103 | 4,639 | 129 | 6,464 R | 70.0% | 29.2% | 70.5% | 29.5% |
| | City | | | | | | | | | |
| 103,217 | ALEXANDRIA | 45,804 | 20,913 | 24,358 | 533 | 3,445 D | 45.7% | 53.2% | 46.2% | 53.8% |
| 5,991 | BEDFORD CITY | 2,328 | 1,322 | 960 | 46 | 362 R | 56.8% | 41.2% | 57.9% | 42.1% |
| 19,042 | BRISTOL | 6,895 | 4,407 | 2,446 | 42 | 1,961 R | 63.9% | 35.5% | 64.3% | 35.7% |
| 6,717 | BUENA VISTA | 1,999 | 1,121 | 828 | 50 | 293 R | 56.1% | 41.4% | 57.5% | 42.5% |
| 39,916 | CHARLOTTESVILLE | 13,652 | 5,817 | 7,671 | 164 | 1,854 D | 42.6% | 56.2% | 43.1% | 56.9% |
| 114,486 | CHESAPEAKE | 48,855 | 29,738 | 18,828 | 289 | 10,910 R | 60.9% | 38.5% | 61.2% | 38.8% |
| 5,046 | CLIFTON FORGE | 1,739 | 759 | 961 | 19 | 202 D | 43.6% | 55.3% | 44.1% | 55.9% |
| 16,509 | COLONIAL HEIGHTS | 7,638 | 6,001 | 1,581 | 56 | 4,420 R | 78.6% | 20.7% | 79.1% | 20.9% |
| 9,063 | COVINGTON | 2,915 | 1,274 | 1,567 | 74 | 293 D | 43.7% | 53.8% | 44.8% | 55.2% |
| 45,642 | DANVILLE | 19,874 | 12,221 | 7,353 | 300 | 4,868 R | 61.5% | 37.0% | 62.4% | 37.6% |
| 4,840 | EMPORIA | 2,277 | 1,289 | 977 | 11 | 312 R | 56.6% | 42.9% | 56.9% | 43.1% |
| 19,390 | FAIRFAX CITY | 9,101 | 5,576 | 3,430 | 95 | 2,146 R | 61.3% | 37.7% | 61.9% | 38.1% |
| 9,515 | FALLS CHURCH | 4,989 | 2,470 | 2,484 | 35 | 14 D | 49.5% | 49.8% | 49.9% | 50.1% |
| 7,308 | FRANKLIN CITY | 3,210 | 1,557 | 1,630 | 23 | 73 D | 48.5% | 50.8% | 48.9% | 51.1% |
| 15,322 | FREDERICKSBURG | 6,154 | 3,401 | 2,683 | 70 | 718 R | 55.3% | 43.6% | 55.9% | 44.1% |
| 6,524 | GALAX | 2,200 | 1,278 | 907 | 15 | 371 R | 58.1% | 41.2% | 58.5% | 41.5% |
| 122,617 | HAMPTON | 43,818 | 24,034 | 19,106 | 678 | 4,928 R | 54.8% | 43.6% | 55.7% | 44.3% |
| 19,671 | HARRISONBURG | 8,288 | 5,376 | 2,799 | 113 | 2,577 R | 64.9% | 33.8% | 65.8% | 34.2% |
| 23,397 | HOPEWELL | 7,360 | 4,672 | 2,566 | 122 | 2,106 R | 63.5% | 34.9% | 64.5% | 35.5% |
| 7,292 | LEXINGTON | 2,024 | 994 | 997 | 33 | 3 D | 49.1% | 49.3% | 49.9% | 50.1% |

# VIRGINIA

## PRESIDENT 1988

| 1980 Census Population | City | Total Vote | Republican | Democratic | Other | Rep.-Dem. Plurality | Percentage Total Vote Rep. | Dem. | Major Vote Rep. | Dem. |
|---|---|---|---|---|---|---|---|---|---|---|
| 66,743 | LYNCHBURG | 23,926 | 15,323 | 8,279 | 324 | 7,044 R | 64.0% | 34.6% | 64.9% | 35.1% |
| 15,438 | MANASSAS | 8,719 | 5,980 | 2,658 | 81 | 3,322 R | 68.6% | 30.5% | 69.2% | 30.8% |
| 6,524 | MANASSAS PARK | 1,446 | 993 | 434 | 19 | 559 R | 68.7% | 30.0% | 69.6% | 30.4% |
| 18,149 | MARTINSVILLE | 6,264 | 3,360 | 2,794 | 110 | 566 R | 53.6% | 44.6% | 54.6% | 45.4% |
| 144,903 | NEWPORT NEWS | 54,395 | 32,570 | 21,413 | 412 | 11,157 R | 59.9% | 39.4% | 60.3% | 39.7% |
| 266,979 | NORFOLK | 68,891 | 30,538 | 37,778 | 575 | 7,240 D | 44.3% | 54.8% | 44.7% | 55.3% |
| 4,757 | NORTON | 1,423 | 608 | 795 | 20 | 187 D | 42.7% | 55.9% | 43.3% | 56.7% |
| 41,055 | PETERSBURG | 12,591 | 4,231 | 8,177 | 183 | 3,946 D | 33.6% | 64.9% | 34.1% | 65.9% |
| 8,726 | POQUOSON | 4,751 | 3,840 | 877 | 34 | 2,963 R | 80.8% | 18.5% | 81.4% | 18.6% |
| 104,577 | PORTSMOUTH | 36,059 | 16,087 | 19,698 | 274 | 3,611 D | 44.6% | 54.6% | 45.0% | 55.0% |
| 13,225 | RADFORD | 4,365 | 2,481 | 1,855 | 29 | 626 R | 56.8% | 42.5% | 57.2% | 42.8% |
| 219,214 | RICHMOND CITY | 74,736 | 31,586 | 42,155 | 995 | 10,569 D | 42.3% | 56.4% | 42.8% | 57.2% |
| 100,220 | ROANOKE CITY | 32,813 | 15,389 | 17,185 | 239 | 1,796 D | 46.9% | 52.4% | 47.2% | 52.8% |
| 23,958 | SALEM | 9,527 | 5,694 | 3,760 | 73 | 1,934 R | 59.8% | 39.5% | 60.2% | 39.8% |
| 7,093 | SOUTH BOSTON | 2,645 | 1,694 | 936 | 15 | 758 R | 64.0% | 35.4% | 64.4% | 35.6% |
| 21,857 | STAUNTON | 8,334 | 5,775 | 2,457 | 102 | 3,318 R | 69.3% | 29.5% | 70.2% | 29.8% |
| 47,621 | SUFFOLK | 17,950 | 9,742 | 8,080 | 128 | 1,662 R | 54.3% | 45.0% | 54.7% | 45.3% |
| 262,199 | VIRGINIA BEACH | 111,018 | 76,481 | 33,780 | 757 | 42,701 R | 68.9% | 30.4% | 69.4% | 30.6% |
| 15,329 | WAYNESBORO | 6,799 | 4,672 | 2,038 | 89 | 2,634 R | 68.7% | 30.0% | 69.6% | 30.4% |
| 9,870 | WILLIAMSBURG | 3,237 | 1,648 | 1,534 | 55 | 114 R | 50.9% | 47.4% | 51.8% | 48.2% |
| 20,217 | WINCHESTER | 6,862 | 4,497 | 2,300 | 65 | 2,197 R | 65.5% | 33.5% | 66.2% | 33.8% |
| 5,346,818 | TOTAL | 2,191,609 | 1,309,162 | 859,799 | 22,648 | 449,363 R | 59.7% | 39.2% | 60.4% | 39.6% |

# VIRGINIA

## PRESIDENT 1984

| 1980 Census Population | County | Total Vote | Republican | Democratic | Other | Rep.-Dem. Plurality | | Percentage | | | |
|---|---|---|---|---|---|---|---|---|---|---|---|
| | | | | | | | | Total Vote | | Major Vote | |
| | | | | | | | | Rep. | Dem. | Rep. | Dem. |
| 31,268 | ACCOMACK | 12,466 | 8,047 | 4,355 | 64 | 3,692 | R | 64.6% | 34.9% | 64.9% | 35.1% |
| 55,783 | ALBEMARLE | 22,530 | 14,455 | 7,982 | 93 | 6,473 | R | 64.2% | 35.4% | 64.4% | 35.6% |
| 14,333 | ALLEGHANY | 5,037 | 3,067 | 1,932 | 38 | 1,135 | R | 60.9% | 38.4% | 61.4% | 38.6% |
| 8,405 | AMELIA | 3,804 | 2,336 | 1,432 | 36 | 904 | R | 61.4% | 37.6% | 62.0% | 38.0% |
| 29,122 | AMHERST | 10,530 | 7,004 | 3,409 | 117 | 3,595 | R | 66.5% | 32.4% | 67.3% | 32.7% |
| 11,971 | APPOMATTOX | 4,932 | 3,386 | 1,498 | 48 | 1,888 | R | 68.7% | 30.4% | 69.3% | 30.7% |
| 152,599 | ARLINGTON | 72,242 | 34,848 | 37,031 | 363 | 2,183 | D | 48.2% | 51.3% | 48.5% | 51.5% |
| 53,732 | AUGUSTA | 19,323 | 15,308 | 3,899 | 116 | 11,409 | R | 79.2% | 20.2% | 79.7% | 20.3% |
| 5,860 | BATH | 2,175 | 1,434 | 727 | 14 | 707 | R | 65.9% | 33.4% | 66.4% | 33.6% |
| 34,927 | BEDFORD COUNTY | 15,217 | 10,371 | 4,754 | 92 | 5,617 | R | 68.2% | 31.2% | 68.6% | 31.4% |
| 6,349 | BLAND | 2,693 | 1,812 | 867 | 14 | 945 | R | 67.3% | 32.2% | 67.6% | 32.4% |
| 23,270 | BOTETOURT | 9,289 | 5,959 | 3,243 | 87 | 2,716 | R | 64.2% | 34.9% | 64.8% | 35.2% |
| 15,632 | BRUNSWICK | 6,073 | 2,950 | 3,040 | 83 | 90 | D | 48.6% | 50.1% | 49.2% | 50.8% |
| 37,989 | BUCHANAN | 13,053 | 5,053 | 7,828 | 172 | 2,775 | D | 38.7% | 60.0% | 39.2% | 60.8% |
| 11,751 | BUCKINGHAM | 4,580 | 2,627 | 1,879 | 74 | 748 | R | 57.4% | 41.0% | 58.3% | 41.7% |
| 45,424 | CAMPBELL | 17,924 | 13,388 | 4,380 | 156 | 9,008 | R | 74.7% | 24.4% | 75.3% | 24.7% |
| 17,904 | CAROLINE | 6,138 | 2,949 | 3,111 | 78 | 162 | D | 48.0% | 50.7% | 48.7% | 51.3% |
| 27,270 | CARROLL | 10,042 | 7,056 | 2,914 | 72 | 4,142 | R | 70.3% | 29.0% | 70.8% | 29.2% |
| 6,692 | CHARLES CITY | 2,584 | 776 | 1,776 | 32 | 1,000 | D | 30.0% | 68.7% | 30.4% | 69.6% |
| 12,266 | CHARLOTTE | 4,856 | 2,999 | 1,811 | 46 | 1,188 | R | 61.8% | 37.3% | 62.3% | 37.7% |
| 141,372 | CHESTERFIELD | 68,811 | 54,896 | 13,739 | 176 | 41,157 | R | 79.8% | 20.0% | 80.0% | 20.0% |
| 9,965 | CLARKE | 3,763 | 2,529 | 1,215 | 19 | 1,314 | R | 67.2% | 32.3% | 67.5% | 32.5% |
| 3,948 | CRAIG | 2,033 | 1,173 | 845 | 15 | 328 | R | 57.7% | 41.6% | 58.1% | 41.9% |
| 22,620 | CULPEPER | 7,926 | 5,596 | 2,255 | 75 | 3,341 | R | 70.6% | 28.5% | 71.3% | 28.7% |
| 7,881 | CUMBERLAND | 3,329 | 2,027 | 1,237 | 65 | 790 | R | 60.9% | 37.2% | 62.1% | 37.9% |
| 19,806 | DICKENSON | 8,844 | 3,921 | 4,848 | 75 | 927 | D | 44.3% | 54.8% | 44.7% | 55.3% |
| 22,602 | DINWIDDIE | 8,114 | 4,547 | 3,485 | 82 | 1,062 | R | 56.0% | 43.0% | 56.6% | 43.4% |
| 8,864 | ESSEX | 3,440 | 2,120 | 1,300 | 20 | 820 | R | 61.6% | 37.8% | 62.0% | 38.0% |
| 596,901 | FAIRFAX COUNTY | 291,298 | 183,181 | 107,295 | 822 | 75,886 | R | 62.9% | 36.8% | 63.1% | 36.9% |
| 35,889 | FAUQUIER | 14,451 | 10,319 | 4,056 | 76 | 6,263 | R | 71.4% | 28.1% | 71.8% | 28.2% |
| 11,563 | FLOYD | 5,069 | 3,431 | 1,599 | 39 | 1,832 | R | 67.7% | 31.5% | 68.2% | 31.8% |
| 10,244 | FLUVANNA | 3,612 | 2,247 | 1,332 | 33 | 915 | R | 62.2% | 36.9% | 62.8% | 37.2% |
| 35,740 | FRANKLIN COUNTY | 12,762 | 7,684 | 4,903 | 175 | 2,781 | R | 60.2% | 38.4% | 61.0% | 39.0% |
| 34,150 | FREDERICK | 12,267 | 9,542 | 2,671 | 54 | 6,871 | R | 77.8% | 21.8% | 78.1% | 21.9% |
| 17,810 | GILES | 7,460 | 4,340 | 3,047 | 73 | 1,293 | R | 58.2% | 40.8% | 58.8% | 41.2% |
| 20,107 | GLOUCESTER | 10,025 | 7,109 | 2,830 | 86 | 4,279 | R | 70.9% | 28.2% | 71.5% | 28.5% |
| 11,761 | GOOCHLAND | 5,617 | 3,404 | 2,178 | 35 | 1,226 | R | 60.6% | 38.8% | 61.0% | 39.0% |
| 16,579 | GRAYSON | 6,890 | 4,508 | 2,319 | 63 | 2,189 | R | 65.4% | 33.7% | 66.0% | 34.0% |
| 7,625 | GREENE | 3,000 | 2,216 | 760 | 24 | 1,456 | R | 73.9% | 25.3% | 74.5% | 25.5% |
| 10,903 | GREENSVILLE | 4,772 | 2,304 | 2,352 | 116 | 48 | D | 48.3% | 49.3% | 49.5% | 50.5% |
| 30,599 | HALIFAX | 11,103 | 6,726 | 4,231 | 146 | 2,495 | R | 60.6% | 38.1% | 61.4% | 38.6% |
| 50,398 | HANOVER | 23,718 | 18,800 | 4,831 | 87 | 13,969 | R | 79.3% | 20.4% | 79.6% | 20.4% |
| 180,735 | HENRICO | 85,448 | 63,864 | 21,336 | 248 | 42,528 | R | 74.7% | 25.0% | 75.0% | 25.0% |
| 57,654 | HENRY | 19,906 | 12,693 | 6,976 | 237 | 5,717 | R | 63.8% | 35.0% | 64.5% | 35.5% |
| 2,937 | HIGHLAND | 1,406 | 997 | 398 | 11 | 599 | R | 70.9% | 28.3% | 71.5% | 28.5% |
| 21,603 | ISLE OF WIGHT | 9,412 | 5,664 | 3,650 | 98 | 2,014 | R | 60.2% | 38.8% | 60.8% | 39.2% |
| 22,763 | JAMES CITY | 10,677 | 7,104 | 3,486 | 87 | 3,618 | R | 66.5% | 32.6% | 67.1% | 32.9% |
| 5,968 | KING AND QUEEN | 2,664 | 1,449 | 1,201 | 14 | 248 | R | 54.4% | 45.1% | 54.7% | 45.3% |
| 10,543 | KING GEORGE | 3,841 | 2,356 | 1,450 | 35 | 906 | R | 61.3% | 37.8% | 61.9% | 38.1% |
| 9,334 | KING WILLIAM | 4,284 | 2,803 | 1,448 | 33 | 1,355 | R | 65.4% | 33.8% | 65.9% | 34.1% |
| 10,129 | LANCASTER | 5,044 | 3,416 | 1,559 | 69 | 1,857 | R | 67.7% | 30.9% | 68.7% | 31.3% |
| 25,956 | LEE | 10,554 | 5,365 | 5,085 | 104 | 280 | R | 50.8% | 48.2% | 51.3% | 48.7% |
| 57,427 | LOUDOUN | 26,128 | 17,765 | 8,227 | 136 | 9,538 | R | 68.0% | 31.5% | 68.3% | 31.7% |
| 17,825 | LOUISA | 6,543 | 3,789 | 2,703 | 51 | 1,086 | R | 57.9% | 41.3% | 58.4% | 41.6% |
| 12,124 | LUNENBURG | 4,526 | 2,713 | 1,754 | 59 | 959 | R | 59.9% | 38.8% | 60.7% | 39.3% |
| 10,232 | MADISON | 4,055 | 2,723 | 1,302 | 30 | 1,421 | R | 67.2% | 32.1% | 67.7% | 32.3% |
| 7,995 | MATHEWS | 4,005 | 2,868 | 1,106 | 31 | 1,762 | R | 71.6% | 27.6% | 72.2% | 27.8% |
| 29,444 | MECKLENBURG | 10,316 | 6,777 | 3,438 | 101 | 3,339 | R | 65.7% | 33.3% | 66.3% | 33.7% |
| 7,719 | MIDDLESEX | 3,885 | 2,612 | 1,206 | 67 | 1,406 | R | 67.2% | 31.0% | 68.4% | 31.6% |
| 63,516 | MONTGOMERY | 19,765 | 12,428 | 7,202 | 135 | 5,226 | R | 62.9% | 36.4% | 63.3% | 36.7% |

# VIRGINIA

## PRESIDENT 1984

| 1980 Census Population | County | Total Vote | Republican | Democratic | Other | Rep.-Dem. Plurality | Percentage Total Vote Rep. | Dem. | Major Vote Rep. | Dem. |
|---|---|---|---|---|---|---|---|---|---|---|
| 12,204 | NELSON | 4,853 | 2,777 | 2,021 | 55 | 756 R | 57.2% | 41.6% | 57.9% | 42.1% |
| 8,781 | NEW KENT | 3,899 | 2,679 | 1,204 | 16 | 1,475 R | 68.7% | 30.9% | 69.0% | 31.0% |
| 14,625 | NORTHAMPTON | 5,207 | 2,906 | 2,226 | 75 | 680 R | 55.8% | 42.8% | 56.6% | 43.4% |
| 9,828 | NORTHUMBERLAND | 4,628 | 3,166 | 1,407 | 55 | 1,759 R | 68.4% | 30.4% | 69.2% | 30.8% |
| 14,666 | NOTTOWAY | 5,793 | 3,418 | 2,296 | 79 | 1,122 R | 59.0% | 39.6% | 59.8% | 40.2% |
| 18,063 | ORANGE | 6,821 | 4,483 | 2,285 | 53 | 2,198 R | 65.7% | 33.5% | 66.2% | 33.8% |
| 19,401 | PAGE | 7,519 | 5,021 | 2,437 | 61 | 2,584 R | 66.8% | 32.4% | 67.3% | 32.7% |
| 17,647 | PATRICK | 6,674 | 4,703 | 1,908 | 63 | 2,795 R | 70.5% | 28.6% | 71.1% | 28.9% |
| 66,147 | PITTSYLVANIA | 23,824 | 15,743 | 7,791 | 290 | 7,952 R | 66.1% | 32.7% | 66.9% | 33.1% |
| 13,062 | POWHATAN | 5,327 | 3,921 | 1,381 | 25 | 2,540 R | 73.6% | 25.9% | 74.0% | 26.0% |
| 16,456 | PRINCE EDWARD | 6,156 | 3,454 | 2,589 | 113 | 865 R | 56.1% | 42.1% | 57.2% | 42.8% |
| 25,733 | PRINCE GEORGE | 7,178 | 4,999 | 2,136 | 43 | 2,863 R | 69.6% | 29.8% | 70.1% | 29.9% |
| 144,703 | PRINCE WILLIAM | 50,803 | 34,992 | 15,631 | 180 | 19,361 R | 68.9% | 30.8% | 69.1% | 30.9% |
| 35,229 | PULASKI | 12,699 | 8,242 | 4,364 | 93 | 3,878 R | 64.9% | 34.4% | 65.4% | 34.6% |
| 6,093 | RAPPAHANNOCK | 2,707 | 1,696 | 999 | 12 | 697 R | 62.7% | 36.9% | 62.9% | 37.1% |
| 6,952 | RICHMOND COUNTY | 2,730 | 1,869 | 830 | 31 | 1,039 R | 68.5% | 30.4% | 69.2% | 30.8% |
| 72,945 | ROANOKE COUNTY | 34,054 | 23,348 | 10,569 | 137 | 12,779 R | 68.6% | 31.0% | 68.8% | 31.2% |
| 17,911 | ROCKBRIDGE | 6,194 | 4,067 | 2,098 | 29 | 1,969 R | 65.7% | 33.9% | 66.0% | 34.0% |
| 57,038 | ROCKINGHAM | 17,807 | 13,480 | 4,220 | 107 | 9,260 R | 75.7% | 23.7% | 76.2% | 23.8% |
| 31,761 | RUSSELL | 12,599 | 5,738 | 6,760 | 101 | 1,022 D | 45.5% | 53.7% | 45.9% | 54.1% |
| 25,068 | SCOTT | 9,821 | 5,804 | 3,904 | 113 | 1,900 R | 59.1% | 39.8% | 59.8% | 40.2% |
| 27,559 | SHENANDOAH | 11,900 | 9,048 | 2,771 | 81 | 6,277 R | 76.0% | 23.3% | 76.6% | 23.4% |
| 33,366 | SMYTH | 12,811 | 8,593 | 4,102 | 116 | 4,491 R | 67.1% | 32.0% | 67.7% | 32.3% |
| 18,731 | SOUTHAMPTON | 8,051 | 4,669 | 3,300 | 82 | 1,369 R | 58.0% | 41.0% | 58.6% | 41.4% |
| 34,435 | SPOTSYLVANIA | 12,297 | 8,207 | 4,012 | 78 | 4,195 R | 66.7% | 32.6% | 67.2% | 32.8% |
| 40,470 | STAFFORD | 14,782 | 10,293 | 4,429 | 60 | 5,864 R | 69.6% | 30.0% | 69.9% | 30.1% |
| 6,046 | SURRY | 3,370 | 1,462 | 1,875 | 33 | 413 D | 43.4% | 55.6% | 43.8% | 56.2% |
| 10,874 | SUSSEX | 4,731 | 2,183 | 2,408 | 140 | 225 D | 46.1% | 50.9% | 47.5% | 52.5% |
| 50,511 | TAZEWELL | 17,896 | 9,645 | 8,014 | 237 | 1,631 R | 53.9% | 44.8% | 54.6% | 45.4% |
| 21,200 | WARREN | 7,631 | 5,016 | 2,551 | 64 | 2,465 R | 65.7% | 33.4% | 66.3% | 33.7% |
| 46,487 | WASHINGTON | 17,826 | 12,132 | 5,573 | 121 | 6,559 R | 68.1% | 31.3% | 68.5% | 31.5% |
| 14,041 | WESTMORELAND | 5,663 | 3,219 | 2,363 | 81 | 856 R | 56.8% | 41.7% | 57.7% | 42.3% |
| 43,863 | WISE | 15,399 | 7,909 | 7,303 | 187 | 606 R | 51.4% | 47.4% | 52.0% | 48.0% |
| 25,522 | WYTHE | 9,866 | 6,773 | 2,996 | 97 | 3,777 R | 68.6% | 30.4% | 69.3% | 30.7% |
| 35,463 | YORK | 14,337 | 10,214 | 4,063 | 60 | 6,151 R | 71.2% | 28.3% | 71.5% | 28.5% |
| | **City** | | | | | | | | | |
| 103,217 | ALEXANDRIA | 45,253 | 21,166 | 23,552 | 535 | 2,386 D | 46.8% | 52.0% | 47.3% | 52.7% |
| 5,991 | BEDFORD CITY | 2,573 | 1,553 | 997 | 23 | 556 R | 60.4% | 38.7% | 60.9% | 39.1% |
| 19,042 | BRISTOL | 7,468 | 5,012 | 2,429 | 27 | 2,583 R | 67.1% | 32.5% | 67.4% | 32.6% |
| 6,717 | BUENA VISTA | 2,073 | 1,335 | 724 | 14 | 611 R | 64.4% | 34.9% | 64.8% | 35.2% |
| 39,916 | CHARLOTTESVILLE | 14,306 | 6,947 | 7,317 | 42 | 370 D | 48.6% | 51.1% | 48.7% | 51.3% |
| 114,486 | CHESAPEAKE | 44,684 | 27,542 | 16,740 | 402 | 10,802 R | 61.6% | 37.5% | 62.2% | 37.8% |
| 5,046 | CLIFTON FORGE | 1,876 | 965 | 896 | 15 | 69 R | 51.4% | 47.8% | 51.9% | 48.1% |
| 16,509 | COLONIAL HEIGHTS | 7,630 | 6,387 | 1,218 | 25 | 5,169 R | 83.7% | 16.0% | 84.0% | 16.0% |
| 9,063 | COVINGTON | 3,162 | 1,722 | 1,391 | 49 | 331 R | 54.5% | 44.0% | 55.3% | 44.7% |
| 45,642 | DANVILLE | 18,161 | 12,141 | 5,846 | 174 | 6,295 R | 66.9% | 32.2% | 67.5% | 32.5% |
| 4,840 | EMPORIA | 2,078 | 1,252 | 807 | 19 | 445 R | 60.3% | 38.8% | 60.8% | 39.2% |
| 19,390 | FAIRFAX CITY | 9,538 | 6,234 | 3,263 | 41 | 2,971 R | 65.4% | 34.2% | 65.6% | 34.4% |
| 9,515 | FALLS CHURCH | 5,101 | 2,684 | 2,398 | 19 | 286 R | 52.6% | 47.0% | 52.8% | 47.2% |
| 7,308 | FRANKLIN CITY | 3,130 | 1,561 | 1,537 | 32 | 24 R | 49.9% | 49.1% | 50.4% | 49.6% |
| 15,322 | FREDERICKSBURG | 5,973 | 3,500 | 2,439 | 34 | 1,061 R | 58.6% | 40.8% | 58.9% | 41.1% |
| 6,524 | GALAX | 2,375 | 1,548 | 814 | 13 | 734 R | 65.2% | 34.3% | 65.5% | 34.5% |
| 122,617 | HAMPTON | 44,068 | 25,537 | 18,180 | 351 | 7,357 R | 57.9% | 41.3% | 58.4% | 41.6% |
| 19,671 | HARRISONBURG | 7,661 | 5,221 | 2,384 | 56 | 2,837 R | 68.2% | 31.1% | 68.7% | 31.3% |
| 23,397 | HOPEWELL | 8,292 | 5,661 | 2,564 | 67 | 3,097 R | 68.3% | 30.9% | 68.8% | 31.2% |
| 7,292 | LEXINGTON | 2,163 | 1,197 | 946 | 20 | 251 R | 55.3% | 43.7% | 55.9% | 44.1% |

# VIRGINIA

## PRESIDENT 1984

| 1980 Census Population | City | Total Vote | Republican | Democratic | Other | Rep.-Dem. Plurality | | Percentage | | | |
|---|---|---|---|---|---|---|---|---|---|---|---|
| | | | | | | | | Total Vote | | Major Vote | |
| | | | | | | | | Rep. | Dem. | Rep. | Dem. |
| 66,743 | LYNCHBURG | 26,772 | 18,047 | 8,542 | 183 | 9,505 | R | 67.4% | 31.9% | 67.9% | 32.1% |
| 15,438 | MANASSAS | 6,466 | 4,613 | 1,824 | 29 | 2,789 | R | 71.3% | 28.2% | 71.7% | 28.3% |
| 6,524 | MANASSAS PARK | 1,355 | 975 | 375 | 5 | 600 | R | 72.0% | 27.7% | 72.2% | 27.8% |
| 18,149 | MARTINSVILLE | 7,254 | 4,234 | 2,942 | 78 | 1,292 | R | 58.4% | 40.6% | 59.0% | 41.0% |
| 144,903 | NEWPORT NEWS | 55,698 | 33,614 | 21,834 | 250 | 11,780 | R | 60.4% | 39.2% | 60.6% | 39.4% |
| 266,979 | NORFOLK | 75,516 | 36,360 | 38,913 | 243 | 2,553 | D | 48.1% | 51.5% | 48.3% | 51.7% |
| 4,757 | NORTON | 1,668 | 806 | 842 | 20 | 36 | D | 48.3% | 50.5% | 48.9% | 51.1% |
| 41,055 | PETERSBURG | 15,074 | 5,753 | 9,248 | 73 | 3,495 | D | 38.2% | 61.4% | 38.4% | 61.6% |
| 8,726 | POQUOSON | 4,328 | 3,667 | 647 | 14 | 3,020 | R | 84.7% | 14.9% | 85.0% | 15.0% |
| 104,577 | PORTSMOUTH | 40,801 | 18,940 | 21,623 | 238 | 2,683 | D | 46.4% | 53.0% | 46.7% | 53.3% |
| 13,225 | RADFORD | 4,669 | 2,855 | 1,781 | 33 | 1,074 | R | 61.1% | 38.1% | 61.6% | 38.4% |
| 219,214 | RICHMOND CITY | 88,628 | 38,754 | 49,408 | 466 | 10,654 | D | 43.7% | 55.7% | 44.0% | 56.0% |
| 100,220 | ROANOKE CITY | 36,492 | 19,008 | 17,300 | 184 | 1,708 | R | 52.1% | 47.4% | 52.4% | 47.6% |
| 23,958 | SALEM | 9,810 | 6,419 | 3,347 | 44 | 3,072 | R | 65.4% | 34.1% | 65.7% | 34.3% |
| 7,093 | SOUTH BOSTON | 2,893 | 1,899 | 974 | 20 | 925 | R | 65.6% | 33.7% | 66.1% | 33.9% |
| 21,857 | STAUNTON | 8,196 | 6,137 | 2,012 | 47 | 4,125 | R | 74.9% | 24.5% | 75.3% | 24.7% |
| 47,621 | SUFFOLK | 19,119 | 10,128 | 8,842 | 149 | 1,286 | R | 53.0% | 46.2% | 53.4% | 46.6% |
| 262,199 | VIRGINIA BEACH | 97,594 | 72,571 | 24,703 | 320 | 47,868 | R | 74.4% | 25.3% | 74.6% | 25.4% |
| 15,329 | WAYNESBORO | 6,079 | 4,465 | 1,579 | 35 | 2,886 | R | 73.4% | 26.0% | 73.9% | 26.1% |
| 9,870 | WILLIAMSBURG | 3,402 | 1,913 | 1,469 | 20 | 444 | R | 56.2% | 43.2% | 56.6% | 43.4% |
| 20,217 | WINCHESTER | 7,152 | 5,055 | 2,064 | 33 | 2,991 | R | 70.7% | 28.9% | 71.0% | 29.0% |
| 5,346,818 | TOTAL | 2,146,635 | 1,337,078 | 796,250 | 13,307 | 540,828 | R | 62.3% | 37.1% | 62.7% | 37.3% |

# VIRGINIA

## PRESIDENT 1980

| 1980 Census Population | County | Total Vote | Republican | Democratic | Other | Rep.-Dem. Plurality | Percentage Total Vote Rep. | Dem. | Percentage Major Vote Rep. | Dem. |
|---|---|---|---|---|---|---|---|---|---|---|
| 31,268 | ACCOMACK | 10,698 | 5,371 | 4,872 | 455 | 499 R | 50.2% | 45.5% | 52.4% | 47.6% |
| 55,783 | ALBEMARLE | 19,582 | 10,424 | 7,293 | 1,865 | 3,131 R | 53.2% | 37.2% | 58.8% | 41.2% |
| 14,333 | ALLEGHANY | 4,756 | 2,185 | 2,411 | 160 | 226 D | 45.9% | 50.7% | 47.5% | 52.5% |
| 8,405 | AMELIA | 3,701 | 1,969 | 1,643 | 89 | 326 R | 53.2% | 44.4% | 54.5% | 45.5% |
| 29,122 | AMHERST | 8,840 | 5,088 | 3,476 | 276 | 1,612 R | 57.6% | 39.3% | 59.4% | 40.6% |
| 11,971 | APPOMATTOX | 4,217 | 2,548 | 1,492 | 177 | 1,056 R | 60.4% | 35.4% | 63.1% | 36.9% |
| 152,599 | ARLINGTON | 66,861 | 30,854 | 26,502 | 9,505 | 4,352 R | 46.1% | 39.6% | 53.8% | 46.2% |
| 53,732 | AUGUSTA | 17,120 | 11,011 | 5,202 | 907 | 5,809 R | 64.3% | 30.4% | 67.9% | 32.1% |
| 5,860 | BATH | 2,007 | 921 | 999 | 87 | 78 D | 45.9% | 49.8% | 48.0% | 52.0% |
| 34,927 | BEDFORD COUNTY | 11,840 | 6,608 | 4,721 | 511 | 1,887 R | 55.8% | 39.9% | 58.3% | 41.7% |
| 6,349 | BLAND | 2,345 | 1,278 | 1,002 | 65 | 276 R | 54.5% | 42.7% | 56.1% | 43.9% |
| 23,270 | BOTETOURT | 8,602 | 4,408 | 3,698 | 496 | 710 R | 51.2% | 43.0% | 54.4% | 45.6% |
| 15,632 | BRUNSWICK | 5,864 | 2,310 | 3,430 | 124 | 1,120 D | 39.4% | 58.5% | 40.2% | 59.8% |
| 37,989 | BUCHANAN | 10,629 | 4,554 | 5,768 | 307 | 1,214 D | 42.8% | 54.3% | 44.1% | 55.9% |
| 11,751 | BUCKINGHAM | 3,923 | 1,864 | 1,933 | 126 | 69 D | 47.5% | 49.3% | 49.1% | 50.9% |
| 45,424 | CAMPBELL | 14,721 | 9,592 | 4,473 | 656 | 5,119 R | 65.2% | 30.4% | 68.2% | 31.8% |
| 17,904 | CAROLINE | 5,154 | 2,071 | 2,924 | 159 | 853 D | 40.2% | 56.7% | 41.5% | 58.5% |
| 27,270 | CARROLL | 9,634 | 5,905 | 3,437 | 292 | 2,468 R | 61.3% | 35.7% | 63.2% | 36.8% |
| 6,692 | CHARLES CITY | 2,131 | 506 | 1,564 | 61 | 1,058 D | 23.7% | 73.4% | 24.4% | 75.6% |
| 12,266 | CHARLOTTE | 4,530 | 2,322 | 2,108 | 100 | 214 R | 51.3% | 46.5% | 52.4% | 47.6% |
| 141,372 | CHESTERFIELD | 53,613 | 37,908 | 13,060 | 2,645 | 24,848 R | 70.7% | 24.4% | 74.4% | 25.6% |
| 9,965 | CLARKE | 3,266 | 1,876 | 1,156 | 234 | 720 R | 57.4% | 35.4% | 61.9% | 38.1% |
| 3,948 | CRAIG | 1,779 | 768 | 946 | 65 | 178 D | 43.2% | 53.2% | 44.8% | 55.2% |
| 22,620 | CULPEPER | 7,255 | 4,312 | 2,519 | 424 | 1,793 R | 59.4% | 34.7% | 63.1% | 36.9% |
| 7,881 | CUMBERLAND | 3,024 | 1,515 | 1,355 | 154 | 160 R | 50.1% | 44.8% | 52.8% | 47.2% |
| 19,806 | DICKENSON | 7,995 | 3,687 | 4,177 | 131 | 490 D | 46.1% | 52.2% | 46.9% | 53.1% |
| 22,602 | DINWIDDIE | 7,018 | 3,369 | 3,475 | 174 | 106 D | 48.0% | 49.5% | 49.2% | 50.8% |
| 8,864 | ESSEX | 2,987 | 1,581 | 1,280 | 126 | 301 R | 52.9% | 42.9% | 55.3% | 44.7% |
| 596,901 | FAIRFAX COUNTY | 239,705 | 137,620 | 73,734 | 28,351 | 63,886 R | 57.4% | 30.8% | 65.1% | 34.9% |
| 35,889 | FAUQUIER | 11,670 | 6,782 | 4,119 | 769 | 2,663 R | 58.1% | 35.3% | 62.2% | 37.8% |
| 11,563 | FLOYD | 4,323 | 2,447 | 1,642 | 234 | 805 R | 56.6% | 38.0% | 59.8% | 40.2% |
| 10,244 | FLUVANNA | 3,184 | 1,605 | 1,424 | 155 | 181 R | 50.4% | 44.7% | 53.0% | 47.0% |
| 35,740 | FRANKLIN COUNTY | 11,090 | 4,993 | 5,685 | 412 | 692 D | 45.0% | 51.3% | 46.8% | 53.2% |
| 34,150 | FREDERICK | 10,787 | 7,293 | 2,948 | 546 | 4,345 R | 67.6% | 27.3% | 71.2% | 28.8% |
| 17,810 | GILES | 6,940 | 2,978 | 3,627 | 335 | 649 D | 42.9% | 52.3% | 45.1% | 54.9% |
| 20,107 | GLOUCESTER | 7,897 | 4,261 | 3,138 | 498 | 1,123 R | 54.0% | 39.7% | 57.6% | 42.4% |
| 11,761 | GOOCHLAND | 4,877 | 2,423 | 2,290 | 164 | 133 R | 49.7% | 47.0% | 51.4% | 48.6% |
| 16,579 | GRAYSON | 6,547 | 3,494 | 2,875 | 178 | 619 R | 53.4% | 43.9% | 54.9% | 45.1% |
| 7,625 | GREENE | 2,811 | 1,702 | 925 | 184 | 777 R | 60.5% | 32.9% | 64.8% | 35.2% |
| 10,903 | GREENSVILLE | 3,800 | 1,583 | 2,142 | 75 | 559 D | 41.7% | 56.4% | 42.5% | 57.5% |
| 30,599 | HALIFAX | 9,836 | 5,088 | 4,528 | 220 | 560 R | 51.7% | 46.0% | 52.9% | 47.1% |
| 50,398 | HANOVER | 20,368 | 14,262 | 5,383 | 723 | 8,879 R | 70.0% | 26.4% | 72.6% | 27.4% |
| 180,735 | HENRICO | 75,551 | 50,505 | 21,023 | 4,023 | 29,482 R | 66.8% | 27.8% | 70.6% | 29.4% |
| 57,654 | HENRY | 17,783 | 8,258 | 8,800 | 725 | 542 D | 46.4% | 49.5% | 48.4% | 51.6% |
| 2,937 | HIGHLAND | 1,278 | 751 | 487 | 40 | 264 R | 58.8% | 38.1% | 60.7% | 39.3% |
| 21,603 | ISLE OF WIGHT | 7,784 | 3,526 | 3,951 | 307 | 425 D | 45.3% | 50.8% | 47.2% | 52.8% |
| 22,763 | JAMES CITY | 8,048 | 4,289 | 3,068 | 691 | 1,221 R | 53.3% | 38.1% | 58.3% | 41.7% |
| 5,968 | KING AND QUEEN | 2,150 | 949 | 1,128 | 73 | 179 D | 44.1% | 52.5% | 45.7% | 54.3% |
| 10,543 | KING GEORGE | 3,332 | 1,784 | 1,318 | 230 | 466 R | 53.5% | 39.6% | 57.5% | 42.5% |
| 9,334 | KING WILLIAM | 3,601 | 2,036 | 1,446 | 119 | 590 R | 56.5% | 40.2% | 58.5% | 41.5% |
| 10,129 | LANCASTER | 4,557 | 2,780 | 1,567 | 210 | 1,213 R | 61.0% | 34.4% | 64.0% | 36.0% |
| 25,956 | LEE | 9,377 | 4,417 | 4,758 | 202 | 341 D | 47.1% | 50.7% | 48.1% | 51.9% |
| 57,427 | LOUDOUN | 20,492 | 12,076 | 6,694 | 1,722 | 5,382 R | 58.9% | 32.7% | 64.3% | 35.7% |
| 17,825 | LOUISA | 5,706 | 2,633 | 2,809 | 264 | 176 D | 46.1% | 49.2% | 48.4% | 51.6% |
| 12,124 | LUNENBURG | 4,136 | 2,045 | 1,958 | 133 | 87 R | 49.4% | 47.3% | 51.1% | 48.9% |
| 10,232 | MADISON | 3,521 | 1,959 | 1,351 | 211 | 608 R | 55.6% | 38.4% | 59.2% | 40.8% |
| 7,995 | MATHEWS | 3,716 | 2,204 | 1,300 | 212 | 904 R | 59.3% | 35.0% | 62.9% | 37.1% |
| 29,444 | MECKLENBURG | 8,913 | 4,853 | 3,790 | 270 | 1,063 R | 54.4% | 42.5% | 56.1% | 43.9% |
| 7,719 | MIDDLESEX | 3,344 | 1,810 | 1,395 | 139 | 415 R | 54.1% | 41.7% | 56.5% | 43.5% |
| 63,516 | MONTGOMERY | 17,344 | 8,222 | 7,455 | 1,667 | 767 R | 47.4% | 43.0% | 52.4% | 47.6% |

# VIRGINIA

## PRESIDENT 1980

| 1980 Census Population | County | Total Vote | Republican | Democratic | Other | Rep.-Dem. Plurality | Percentage Total Vote Rep. | Dem. | Major Vote Rep. | Dem. |
|---|---|---|---|---|---|---|---|---|---|---|
| 12,204 | NELSON | 4,496 | 1,866 | 2,410 | 220 | 544 D | 41.5% | 53.6% | 43.6% | 56.4% |
| 8,781 | NEW KENT | 3,035 | 1,739 | 1,204 | 92 | 535 R | 57.3% | 39.7% | 59.1% | 40.9% |
| 14,625 | NORTHAMPTON | 4,743 | 2,165 | 2,363 | 215 | 198 D | 45.6% | 49.8% | 47.8% | 52.2% |
| 9,828 | NORTHUMBERLAND | 4,330 | 2,598 | 1,551 | 181 | 1,047 R | 60.0% | 35.8% | 62.6% | 37.4% |
| 14,666 | NOTTOWAY | 5,611 | 2,813 | 2,593 | 205 | 220 R | 50.1% | 46.2% | 52.0% | 48.0% |
| 18,063 | ORANGE | 6,158 | 3,381 | 2,420 | 357 | 961 R | 54.9% | 39.3% | 58.3% | 41.7% |
| 19,401 | PAGE | 7,138 | 4,297 | 2,607 | 234 | 1,690 R | 60.2% | 36.5% | 62.2% | 37.8% |
| 17,647 | PATRICK | 6,123 | 3,436 | 2,382 | 305 | 1,054 R | 56.1% | 38.9% | 59.1% | 40.9% |
| 66,147 | PITTSYLVANIA | 20,280 | 12,022 | 7,653 | 605 | 4,369 R | 59.3% | 37.7% | 61.1% | 38.9% |
| 13,062 | POWHATAN | 4,570 | 2,933 | 1,484 | 153 | 1,449 R | 64.2% | 32.5% | 66.4% | 33.6% |
| 16,456 | PRINCE EDWARD | 5,598 | 2,774 | 2,553 | 271 | 221 R | 49.6% | 45.6% | 52.1% | 47.9% |
| 25,733 | PRINCE GEORGE | 5,888 | 3,389 | 2,310 | 189 | 1,079 R | 57.6% | 39.2% | 59.5% | 40.5% |
| 144,703 | PRINCE WILLIAM | 39,119 | 23,061 | 12,787 | 3,271 | 10,274 R | 59.0% | 32.7% | 64.3% | 35.7% |
| 35,229 | PULASKI | 12,040 | 5,747 | 5,769 | 524 | 22 D | 47.7% | 47.9% | 49.9% | 50.1% |
| 6,093 | RAPPAHANNOCK | 2,367 | 1,179 | 1,055 | 133 | 124 R | 49.8% | 44.6% | 52.8% | 47.2% |
| 6,952 | RICHMOND COUNTY | 2,495 | 1,567 | 854 | 74 | 713 R | 62.8% | 34.2% | 64.7% | 35.3% |
| 72,945 | ROANOKE COUNTY | 30,814 | 17,182 | 12,114 | 1,518 | 5,068 R | 55.8% | 39.3% | 58.6% | 41.4% |
| 17,911 | ROCKBRIDGE | 5,677 | 2,784 | 2,475 | 418 | 309 R | 49.0% | 43.6% | 52.9% | 47.1% |
| 57,038 | ROCKINGHAM | 17,859 | 11,397 | 5,294 | 1,168 | 6,103 R | 63.8% | 29.6% | 68.3% | 31.7% |
| 31,761 | RUSSELL | 10,874 | 4,778 | 5,764 | 332 | 986 D | 43.9% | 53.0% | 45.3% | 54.7% |
| 25,068 | SCOTT | 9,387 | 4,744 | 4,314 | 329 | 430 R | 50.5% | 46.0% | 52.4% | 47.6% |
| 27,559 | SHENANDOAH | 11,203 | 7,517 | 3,137 | 549 | 4,380 R | 67.1% | 28.0% | 70.6% | 29.4% |
| 33,366 | SMYTH | 11,861 | 6,033 | 5,335 | 493 | 698 R | 50.9% | 45.0% | 53.1% | 46.9% |
| 18,731 | SOUTHAMPTON | 6,587 | 2,997 | 3,347 | 243 | 350 D | 45.5% | 50.8% | 47.2% | 52.8% |
| 34,435 | SPOTSYLVANIA | 10,005 | 5,385 | 4,039 | 581 | 1,346 R | 53.8% | 40.4% | 57.1% | 42.9% |
| 40,470 | STAFFORD | 12,075 | 7,106 | 4,211 | 758 | 2,895 R | 58.8% | 34.9% | 62.8% | 37.2% |
| 6,046 | SURRY | 2,821 | 962 | 1,756 | 103 | 794 D | 34.1% | 62.2% | 35.4% | 64.6% |
| 10,874 | SUSSEX | 4,273 | 1,664 | 2,447 | 162 | 783 D | 38.9% | 57.3% | 40.5% | 59.5% |
| 50,511 | TAZEWELL | 14,425 | 7,021 | 7,003 | 401 | 18 R | 48.7% | 48.5% | 50.1% | 49.9% |
| 21,200 | WARREN | 6,920 | 3,861 | 2,597 | 462 | 1,264 R | 55.8% | 37.5% | 59.8% | 40.2% |
| 46,487 | WASHINGTON | 15,597 | 8,402 | 6,390 | 805 | 2,012 R | 53.9% | 41.0% | 56.8% | 43.2% |
| 14,041 | WESTMORELAND | 4,989 | 2,510 | 2,271 | 208 | 239 R | 50.3% | 45.5% | 52.5% | 47.5% |
| 43,863 | WISE | 13,141 | 5,767 | 6,779 | 595 | 1,012 D | 43.9% | 51.6% | 46.0% | 54.0% |
| 25,522 | WYTHE | 8,766 | 4,758 | 3,677 | 331 | 1,081 R | 54.3% | 41.9% | 56.4% | 43.6% |
| 35,463 | YORK | 12,133 | 6,744 | 4,532 | 857 | 2,212 R | 55.6% | 37.4% | 59.8% | 40.2% |
| | City | | | | | | | | | |
| 103,217 | ALEXANDRIA | 40,388 | 17,865 | 17,134 | 5,389 | 731 R | 44.2% | 42.4% | 51.0% | 49.0% |
| 5,991 | BEDFORD CITY | 2,423 | 1,145 | 1,149 | 129 | 4 D | 47.3% | 47.4% | 49.9% | 50.1% |
| 19,042 | BRISTOL | 6,515 | 3,432 | 2,889 | 194 | 543 R | 52.7% | 44.3% | 54.3% | 45.7% |
| 6,717 | BUENA VISTA | 2,089 | 942 | 1,031 | 116 | 89 D | 45.1% | 49.4% | 47.7% | 52.3% |
| 39,916 | CHARLOTTESVILLE | 14,562 | 5,907 | 6,866 | 1,789 | 959 D | 40.6% | 47.2% | 46.2% | 53.8% |
| 114,486 | CHESAPEAKE | 36,904 | 17,888 | 17,155 | 1,861 | 733 R | 48.5% | 46.5% | 51.0% | 49.0% |
| 5,046 | CLIFTON FORGE | 1,825 | 716 | 1,012 | 97 | 296 D | 39.2% | 55.5% | 41.4% | 58.6% |
| 16,509 | COLONIAL HEIGHTS | 7,063 | 5,012 | 1,692 | 359 | 3,320 R | 71.0% | 24.0% | 74.8% | 25.2% |
| 9,063 | COVINGTON | 3,150 | 1,187 | 1,813 | 150 | 626 D | 37.7% | 57.6% | 39.6% | 60.4% |
| 45,642 | DANVILLE | 17,362 | 10,665 | 6,138 | 559 | 4,527 R | 61.4% | 35.4% | 63.5% | 36.5% |
| 4,840 | EMPORIA | 1,902 | 988 | 855 | 59 | 133 R | 51.9% | 45.0% | 53.6% | 46.4% |
| 19,390 | FAIRFAX CITY | 8,004 | 4,475 | 2,614 | 915 | 1,861 R | 55.9% | 32.7% | 63.1% | 36.9% |
| 9,515 | FALLS CHURCH | 4,758 | 2,485 | 1,703 | 570 | 782 R | 52.2% | 35.8% | 59.3% | 40.7% |
| 7,308 | FRANKLIN CITY | 2,456 | 1,045 | 1,324 | 87 | 279 D | 42.5% | 53.9% | 44.1% | 55.9% |
| 15,322 | FREDERICKSBURG | 4,968 | 2,502 | 2,174 | 292 | 328 R | 50.4% | 43.8% | 53.5% | 46.5% |
| 6,524 | GALAX | 2,293 | 1,188 | 1,061 | 44 | 127 R | 51.8% | 46.3% | 52.8% | 47.2% |
| 122,617 | HAMPTON | 37,765 | 17,023 | 18,517 | 2,225 | 1,494 D | 45.1% | 49.0% | 47.9% | 52.1% |
| 19,671 | HARRISONBURG | 5,796 | 3,388 | 1,896 | 512 | 1,492 R | 58.5% | 32.7% | 64.1% | 35.9% |
| 23,397 | HOPEWELL | 7,872 | 4,423 | 3,102 | 347 | 1,321 R | 56.2% | 39.4% | 58.8% | 41.2% |
| 7,292 | LEXINGTON | 2,083 | 956 | 963 | 164 | 7 D | 45.9% | 46.2% | 49.8% | 50.2% |

# VIRGINIA

## PRESIDENT 1980

| 1980 Census Population | City | Total Vote | Republican | Democratic | Other | Rep.-Dem. Plurality | Percentage | | | |
|---|---|---|---|---|---|---|---|---|---|---|
| | | | | | | | Total Vote | | Major Vote | |
| | | | | | | | Rep. | Dem. | Rep. | Dem. |
| 66,743 | LYNCHBURG | 24,417 | 15,245 | 7,783 | 1,389 | 7,462 R | 62.4% | 31.9% | 66.2% | 33.8% |
| 15,438 | MANASSAS | 4,952 | 3,009 | 1,565 | 378 | 1,444 R | 60.8% | 31.6% | 65.8% | 34.2% |
| 6,524 | MANASSAS PARK | 1,254 | 729 | 447 | 78 | 282 R | 58.1% | 35.6% | 62.0% | 38.0% |
| 18,149 | MARTINSVILLE | 7,032 | 3,433 | 3,337 | 262 | 96 R | 48.8% | 47.5% | 50.7% | 49.3% |
| 144,903 | NEWPORT NEWS | 46,982 | 22,423 | 22,066 | 2,493 | 357 R | 47.7% | 47.0% | 50.4% | 49.6% |
| 266,979 | NORFOLK | 67,200 | 27,506 | 35,118 | 4,576 | 7,612 D | 40.9% | 52.3% | 43.9% | 56.1% |
| 4,757 | NORTON | 1,400 | 572 | 762 | 66 | 190 D | 40.9% | 54.4% | 42.9% | 57.1% |
| 41,055 | PETERSBURG | 13,277 | 5,001 | 7,931 | 345 | 2,930 D | 37.7% | 59.7% | 38.7% | 61.3% |
| 8,726 | POQUOSON | 3,399 | 2,338 | 877 | 184 | 1,461 R | 68.8% | 25.8% | 72.7% | 27.3% |
| 104,577 | PORTSMOUTH | 35,949 | 13,660 | 20,900 | 1,389 | 7,240 D | 38.0% | 58.1% | 39.5% | 60.5% |
| 13,225 | RADFORD | 4,463 | 1,964 | 2,225 | 274 | 261 D | 44.0% | 49.9% | 46.9% | 53.1% |
| 219,214 | RICHMOND CITY | 87,106 | 34,629 | 47,975 | 4,502 | 13,346 D | 39.8% | 55.1% | 41.9% | 58.1% |
| 100,220 | ROANOKE CITY | 34,946 | 15,164 | 18,139 | 1,643 | 2,975 D | 43.4% | 51.9% | 45.5% | 54.5% |
| 23,958 | SALEM | 9,389 | 4,862 | 4,091 | 436 | 771 R | 51.8% | 43.6% | 54.3% | 45.7% |
| 7,093 | SOUTH BOSTON | 2,649 | 1,615 | 971 | 63 | 644 R | 61.0% | 36.7% | 62.5% | 37.5% |
| 21,857 | STAUNTON | 7,927 | 4,819 | 2,658 | 450 | 2,161 R | 60.8% | 33.5% | 64.5% | 35.5% |
| 47,621 | SUFFOLK | 16,765 | 7,179 | 9,064 | 522 | 1,885 D | 42.8% | 54.1% | 44.2% | 55.8% |
| 262,199 | VIRGINIA BEACH | 79,235 | 47,936 | 24,895 | 6,404 | 23,041 R | 60.5% | 31.4% | 65.8% | 34.2% |
| 15,329 | WAYNESBORO | 5,978 | 3,697 | 1,926 | 355 | 1,771 R | 61.8% | 32.2% | 65.7% | 34.3% |
| 9,870 | WILLIAMSBURG | 2,953 | 1,344 | 1,199 | 410 | 145 R | 45.5% | 40.6% | 52.9% | 47.1% |
| 20,217 | WINCHESTER | 6,623 | 4,240 | 2,006 | 377 | 2,234 R | 64.0% | 30.3% | 67.9% | 32.1% |
| 5,346,818 | TOTAL | 1,866,032 | 989,609 | 752,174 | 124,249 | 237,435 R | 53.0% | 40.3% | 56.8% | 43.2% |

# VIRGINIA

## PRESIDENT 1976

| 1970 Census Population | County | Total Vote | Republican | Democratic | Other | Rep.-Dem. Plurality | Percentage Total Vote Rep. | Dem. | Major Vote Rep. | Dem. |
|---|---|---|---|---|---|---|---|---|---|---|
| 29,004 | ACCOMACK | 9,536 | 4,494 | 4,807 | 235 | 313 D | 47.1% | 50.4% | 48.3% | 51.7% |
| 37,780 | ALBEMARLE | 16,632 | 9,084 | 7,310 | 238 | 1,774 R | 54.6% | 44.0% | 55.4% | 44.6% |
| 12,461 | ALLEGHANY | 4,265 | 1,756 | 2,462 | 47 | 706 D | 41.2% | 57.7% | 41.6% | 58.4% |
| 7,592 | AMELIA | 3,458 | 1,634 | 1,715 | 109 | 81 D | 47.3% | 49.6% | 48.8% | 51.2% |
| 26,072 | AMHERST | 7,776 | 3,956 | 3,675 | 145 | 281 R | 50.9% | 47.3% | 51.8% | 48.2% |
| 9,784 | APPOMATTOX | 3,863 | 1,964 | 1,702 | 197 | 262 R | 50.8% | 44.1% | 53.6% | 46.4% |
| 174,284 | ARLINGTON | 64,599 | 30,972 | 32,536 | 1,091 | 1,564 D | 47.9% | 50.4% | 48.8% | 51.2% |
| 44,220 | AUGUSTA | 14,692 | 8,452 | 5,626 | 614 | 2,826 R | 57.5% | 38.3% | 60.0% | 40.0% |
| 5,192 | BATH | 1,932 | 888 | 1,029 | 15 | 141 D | 46.0% | 53.3% | 46.3% | 53.7% |
| 26,728 | BEDFORD COUNTY | 9,246 | 4,189 | 4,766 | 291 | 577 D | 45.3% | 51.5% | 46.8% | 53.2% |
| 5,423 | BLAND | 2,017 | 1,047 | 961 | 9 | 86 R | 51.9% | 47.6% | 52.1% | 47.9% |
| 18,193 | BOTETOURT | 7,573 | 3,343 | 4,021 | 209 | 678 D | 44.1% | 53.1% | 45.4% | 54.6% |
| 16,172 | BRUNSWICK | 5,668 | 2,387 | 3,071 | 210 | 684 D | 42.1% | 54.2% | 43.7% | 56.3% |
| 32,071 | BUCHANAN | 10,728 | 3,850 | 5,791 | 1,087 | 1,941 D | 35.9% | 54.0% | 39.9% | 60.1% |
| 10,597 | BUCKINGHAM | 3,758 | 1,487 | 2,179 | 92 | 692 D | 39.6% | 58.0% | 40.6% | 59.4% |
| 43,319 | CAMPBELL | 12,245 | 7,442 | 4,354 | 449 | 3,088 R | 60.8% | 35.6% | 63.1% | 36.9% |
| 13,925 | CAROLINE | 4,796 | 1,648 | 3,064 | 84 | 1,416 D | 34.4% | 63.9% | 35.0% | 65.0% |
| 23,092 | CARROLL | 8,968 | 4,820 | 4,010 | 138 | 810 R | 53.7% | 44.7% | 54.6% | 45.4% |
| 6,158 | CHARLES CITY | 1,951 | 439 | 1,455 | 57 | 1,016 D | 22.5% | 74.6% | 23.2% | 76.8% |
| 11,551 | CHARLOTTE | 4,394 | 2,023 | 2,312 | 59 | 289 D | 46.0% | 52.6% | 46.7% | 53.3% |
| 76,855 | CHESTERFIELD | 42,436 | 27,812 | 14,126 | 498 | 13,686 R | 65.5% | 33.3% | 66.3% | 33.7% |
| 8,102 | CLARKE | 2,794 | 1,440 | 1,276 | 78 | 164 R | 51.5% | 45.7% | 53.0% | 47.0% |
| 3,524 | CRAIG | 1,667 | 546 | 1,103 | 18 | 557 D | 32.8% | 66.2% | 33.1% | 66.9% |
| 18,218 | CULPEPER | 6,696 | 3,659 | 2,892 | 145 | 767 R | 54.6% | 43.2% | 55.9% | 44.1% |
| 6,179 | CUMBERLAND | 2,757 | 1,284 | 1,302 | 171 | 18 D | 46.6% | 47.2% | 49.7% | 50.3% |
| 16,077 | DICKENSON | 8,209 | 3,471 | 4,583 | 155 | 1,112 D | 42.3% | 55.8% | 43.1% | 56.9% |
| 25,046 | DINWIDDIE | 6,473 | 2,413 | 3,873 | 187 | 1,460 D | 37.3% | 59.8% | 38.4% | 61.6% |
| 7,099 | ESSEX | 2,730 | 1,380 | 1,306 | 44 | 74 R | 50.5% | 47.8% | 51.4% | 48.6% |
| 455,021 | FAIRFAX COUNTY | 205,957 | 110,424 | 92,037 | 3,496 | 18,387 R | 53.6% | 44.7% | 54.5% | 45.5% |
| 26,375 | FAUQUIER | 9,111 | 4,715 | 4,002 | 394 | 713 R | 51.8% | 43.9% | 54.1% | 45.9% |
| 9,775 | FLOYD | 3,925 | 2,071 | 1,728 | 126 | 343 R | 52.8% | 44.0% | 54.5% | 45.5% |
| 7,621 | FLUVANNA | 2,770 | 1,296 | 1,415 | 59 | 119 D | 46.8% | 51.1% | 47.8% | 52.2% |
| 26,858 | FRANKLIN COUNTY | 10,199 | 3,532 | 6,439 | 228 | 2,907 D | 34.6% | 63.1% | 35.4% | 64.6% |
| 28,893 | FREDERICK | 8,672 | 5,162 | 3,389 | 121 | 1,773 R | 59.5% | 39.1% | 60.4% | 39.6% |
| 16,741 | GILES | 6,739 | 2,731 | 3,779 | 229 | 1,048 D | 40.5% | 56.1% | 42.0% | 58.0% |
| 14,059 | GLOUCESTER | 6,404 | 3,025 | 3,156 | 223 | 131 D | 47.2% | 49.3% | 48.9% | 51.1% |
| 10,069 | GOOCHLAND | 4,455 | 2,104 | 2,259 | 92 | 155 D | 47.2% | 50.7% | 48.2% | 51.8% |
| 15,439 | GRAYSON | 6,251 | 3,021 | 3,146 | 84 | 125 D | 48.3% | 50.3% | 49.0% | 51.0% |
| 5,248 | GREENE | 2,130 | 1,095 | 895 | 140 | 200 R | 51.4% | 42.0% | 55.0% | 45.0% |
| 9,604 | GREENSVILLE | 3,646 | 1,137 | 2,413 | 96 | 1,276 D | 31.2% | 66.2% | 32.0% | 68.0% |
| 30,076 | HALIFAX | 8,697 | 4,045 | 4,352 | 300 | 307 D | 46.5% | 50.0% | 48.2% | 51.8% |
| 37,479 | HANOVER | 17,859 | 11,559 | 6,069 | 231 | 5,490 R | 64.7% | 34.0% | 65.6% | 34.4% |
| 154,364 | HENRICO | 68,981 | 45,405 | 21,729 | 1,847 | 23,676 R | 65.8% | 31.5% | 67.6% | 32.4% |
| 50,901 | HENRY | 16,024 | 5,612 | 9,680 | 732 | 4,068 D | 35.0% | 60.4% | 36.7% | 63.3% |
| 2,529 | HIGHLAND | 1,132 | 629 | 493 | 10 | 136 R | 55.6% | 43.6% | 56.1% | 43.9% |
| 18,285 | ISLE OF WIGHT | 7,009 | 2,718 | 4,145 | 146 | 1,427 D | 38.8% | 59.1% | 39.6% | 60.4% |
| 17,853 | JAMES CITY | 6,454 | 3,186 | 3,000 | 268 | 186 R | 49.4% | 46.5% | 51.5% | 48.5% |
| 5,491 | KING AND QUEEN | 1,992 | 778 | 1,111 | 103 | 333 D | 39.1% | 55.8% | 41.2% | 58.8% |
| 8,039 | KING GEORGE | 2,958 | 1,383 | 1,513 | 62 | 130 D | 46.8% | 51.1% | 47.8% | 52.2% |
| 7,497 | KING WILLIAM | 3,156 | 1,597 | 1,501 | 58 | 96 R | 50.6% | 47.6% | 51.5% | 48.5% |
| 9,126 | LANCASTER | 4,074 | 2,381 | 1,581 | 112 | 800 R | 58.4% | 38.8% | 60.1% | 39.9% |
| 20,321 | LEE | 10,284 | 4,679 | 5,415 | 190 | 736 D | 45.5% | 52.7% | 46.4% | 53.6% |
| 37,150 | LOUDOUN | 17,748 | 9,192 | 7,995 | 561 | 1,197 R | 51.8% | 45.0% | 53.5% | 46.5% |
| 14,004 | LOUISA | 5,135 | 2,151 | 2,857 | 127 | 706 D | 41.9% | 55.6% | 43.0% | 57.0% |
| 11,687 | LUNENBURG | 3,652 | 1,816 | 1,739 | 97 | 77 R | 49.7% | 47.6% | 51.1% | 48.9% |
| 8,638 | MADISON | 3,228 | 1,710 | 1,466 | 52 | 244 R | 53.0% | 45.4% | 53.8% | 46.2% |
| 7,168 | MATHEWS | 3,303 | 1,908 | 1,309 | 86 | 599 R | 57.8% | 39.6% | 59.3% | 40.7% |
| 29,426 | MECKLENBURG | 8,769 | 4,423 | 4,076 | 270 | 347 R | 50.4% | 46.5% | 52.0% | 48.0% |
| 6,295 | MIDDLESEX | 3,039 | 1,608 | 1,312 | 119 | 296 R | 52.9% | 43.2% | 55.1% | 44.9% |
| 47,157 | MONTGOMERY | 15,742 | 7,971 | 7,539 | 232 | 432 R | 50.6% | 47.9% | 51.4% | 48.6% |

# VIRGINIA

## PRESIDENT 1976

| 1970 Census Population | County | Total Vote | Republican | Democratic | Other | Rep.-Dem. Plurality | Percentage Total Vote Rep. | Dem. | Major Vote Rep. | Dem. |
|---|---|---|---|---|---|---|---|---|---|---|
| 11,702 | NELSON | 4,027 | 1,516 | 2,426 | 85 | 910 D | 37.6% | 60.2% | 38.5% | 61.5% |
| 5,300 | NEW KENT | 2,644 | 1,259 | 1,338 | 47 | 79 D | 47.6% | 50.6% | 48.5% | 51.5% |
| 14,442 | NORTHAMPTON | 4,735 | 2,043 | 2,459 | 233 | 416 D | 43.1% | 51.9% | 45.4% | 54.6% |
| 9,239 | NORTHUMBERLAND | 4,126 | 2,167 | 1,814 | 145 | 353 R | 52.5% | 44.0% | 54.4% | 45.6% |
| 14,260 | NOTTOWAY | 5,222 | 2,486 | 2,558 | 178 | 72 D | 47.6% | 49.0% | 49.3% | 50.7% |
| 13,792 | ORANGE | 5,161 | 2,549 | 2,309 | 303 | 240 R | 49.4% | 44.7% | 52.5% | 47.5% |
| 16,581 | PAGE | 7,337 | 3,780 | 3,401 | 156 | 379 R | 51.5% | 46.4% | 52.6% | 47.4% |
| 15,282 | PATRICK | 5,377 | 2,349 | 2,740 | 288 | 391 D | 43.7% | 51.0% | 46.2% | 53.8% |
| 58,789 | PITTSYLVANIA | 17,913 | 9,173 | 7,929 | 811 | 1,244 R | 51.2% | 44.3% | 53.6% | 46.4% |
| 7,696 | POWHATAN | 3,636 | 2,010 | 1,528 | 98 | 482 R | 55.3% | 42.0% | 56.8% | 43.2% |
| 14,379 | PRINCE EDWARD | 5,429 | 2,734 | 2,448 | 247 | 286 R | 50.4% | 45.1% | 52.8% | 47.2% |
| 29,092 | PRINCE GEORGE | 4,960 | 2,254 | 2,630 | 76 | 376 D | 45.4% | 53.0% | 46.2% | 53.8% |
| 95,094 | PRINCE WILLIAM | 31,524 | 15,446 | 15,215 | 863 | 231 R | 49.0% | 48.3% | 50.4% | 49.6% |
| 29,564 | PULASKI | 10,624 | 4,764 | 5,546 | 314 | 782 D | 44.8% | 52.2% | 46.2% | 53.8% |
| 5,199 | RAPPAHANNOCK | 1,981 | 881 | 1,071 | 29 | 190 D | 44.5% | 54.1% | 45.1% | 54.9% |
| 5,841 | RICHMOND COUNTY | 2,288 | 1,391 | 864 | 33 | 527 R | 60.8% | 37.8% | 61.7% | 38.3% |
| 67,339 | ROANOKE COUNTY | 26,948 | 13,587 | 13,120 | 241 | 467 R | 50.4% | 48.7% | 50.9% | 49.1% |
| 16,637 | ROCKBRIDGE | 4,940 | 2,157 | 2,525 | 258 | 368 D | 43.7% | 51.1% | 46.1% | 53.9% |
| 47,890 | ROCKINGHAM | 15,789 | 9,768 | 5,349 | 672 | 4,419 R | 61.9% | 33.9% | 64.6% | 35.4% |
| 24,533 | RUSSELL | 10,667 | 4,287 | 6,014 | 366 | 1,727 D | 40.2% | 56.4% | 41.6% | 58.4% |
| 24,376 | SCOTT | 9,494 | 4,313 | 4,496 | 685 | 183 D | 45.4% | 47.4% | 49.0% | 51.0% |
| 22,852 | SHENANDOAH | 9,830 | 6,296 | 3,364 | 170 | 2,932 R | 64.0% | 34.2% | 65.2% | 34.8% |
| 31,349 | SMYTH | 10,641 | 5,032 | 5,246 | 363 | 214 D | 47.3% | 49.3% | 49.0% | 51.0% |
| 18,582 | SOUTHAMPTON | 5,889 | 2,366 | 3,399 | 124 | 1,033 D | 40.2% | 57.7% | 41.0% | 59.0% |
| 16,424 | SPOTSYLVANIA | 7,560 | 3,210 | 4,210 | 140 | 1,000 D | 42.5% | 55.7% | 43.3% | 56.7% |
| 24,587 | STAFFORD | 9,502 | 4,451 | 4,900 | 151 | 449 D | 46.8% | 51.6% | 47.6% | 52.4% |
| 5,882 | SURRY | 2,833 | 929 | 1,829 | 75 | 900 D | 32.8% | 64.6% | 33.7% | 66.3% |
| 11,464 | SUSSEX | 4,094 | 1,360 | 2,497 | 237 | 1,137 D | 33.2% | 61.0% | 35.3% | 64.7% |
| 39,816 | TAZEWELL | 13,439 | 5,565 | 7,565 | 309 | 2,000 D | 41.4% | 56.3% | 42.4% | 57.6% |
| 15,301 | WARREN | 6,517 | 2,985 | 3,221 | 311 | 236 D | 45.8% | 49.4% | 48.1% | 51.9% |
| 40,835 | WASHINGTON | 14,015 | 6,865 | 6,547 | 603 | 318 R | 49.0% | 46.7% | 51.2% | 48.8% |
| 12,142 | WESTMORELAND | 4,568 | 1,909 | 2,355 | 304 | 446 D | 41.8% | 51.6% | 44.8% | 55.2% |
| 35,947 | WISE | 13,351 | 5,691 | 7,134 | 526 | 1,443 D | 42.6% | 53.4% | 44.4% | 55.6% |
| 22,139 | WYTHE | 8,241 | 4,231 | 3,578 | 432 | 653 R | 51.3% | 43.4% | 54.2% | 45.8% |
| 27,762 | YORK | 10,451 | 5,603 | 4,736 | 112 | 867 R | 53.6% | 45.3% | 54.2% | 45.8% |
| | **City** | | | | | | | | | |
| 110,938 | ALEXANDRIA | 37,910 | 16,880 | 19,858 | 1,172 | 2,978 D | 44.5% | 52.4% | 45.9% | 54.1% |
| 6,011 | BEDFORD CITY | 2,294 | 1,043 | 1,122 | 129 | 79 D | 45.5% | 48.9% | 48.2% | 51.8% |
| 14,857 | BRISTOL | 6,361 | 2,943 | 3,343 | 75 | 400 D | 46.3% | 52.6% | 46.8% | 53.2% |
| 6,425 | BUENA VISTA | 1,853 | 771 | 993 | 89 | 222 D | 41.6% | 53.6% | 43.7% | 56.3% |
| 38,880 | CHARLOTTESVILLE | 13,869 | 6,673 | 6,846 | 350 | 173 D | 48.1% | 49.4% | 49.4% | 50.6% |
| 89,580 | CHESAPEAKE | 32,157 | 12,851 | 17,651 | 1,655 | 4,800 D | 40.0% | 54.9% | 42.1% | 57.9% |
| 5,501 | CLIFTON FORGE | 1,893 | 770 | 993 | 130 | 223 D | 40.7% | 52.5% | 43.7% | 56.3% |
| 15,097 | COLONIAL HEIGHTS | 6,934 | 4,291 | 2,409 | 234 | 1,882 R | 61.9% | 34.7% | 64.0% | 36.0% |
| 10,060 | COVINGTON | 3,165 | 1,173 | 1,820 | 172 | 647 D | 37.1% | 57.5% | 39.2% | 60.8% |
| 46,391 | DANVILLE | 17,212 | 10,235 | 6,425 | 552 | 3,810 R | 59.5% | 37.3% | 61.4% | 38.6% |
| 5,300 | EMPORIA | 2,020 | 1,055 | 899 | 66 | 156 R | 52.2% | 44.5% | 54.0% | 46.0% |
| 21,970 | FAIRFAX CITY | 7,823 | 4,174 | 3,464 | 185 | 710 R | 53.4% | 44.3% | 54.6% | 45.4% |
| 10,772 | FALLS CHURCH | 4,588 | 2,323 | 2,202 | 63 | 121 R | 50.6% | 48.0% | 51.3% | 48.7% |
| 6,880 | FRANKLIN CITY | 2,290 | 1,127 | 1,116 | 47 | 11 R | 49.2% | 48.7% | 50.2% | 49.8% |
| 14,450 | FREDERICKSBURG | 5,150 | 2,527 | 2,550 | 73 | 23 D | 49.1% | 49.5% | 49.8% | 50.2% |
| 6,278 | GALAX | 2,370 | 1,128 | 1,218 | 24 | 90 D | 47.6% | 51.4% | 48.1% | 51.9% |
| 120,779 | HAMPTON | 36,048 | 15,021 | 19,202 | 1,825 | 4,181 D | 41.7% | 53.3% | 43.9% | 56.1% |
| 14,605 | HARRISONBURG | 5,358 | 3,376 | 1,803 | 179 | 1,573 R | 63.0% | 33.7% | 65.2% | 34.8% |
| 23,471 | HOPEWELL | 7,807 | 3,764 | 3,691 | 352 | 73 R | 48.2% | 47.3% | 50.5% | 49.5% |
| 7,597 | LEXINGTON | 2,035 | 1,027 | 945 | 63 | 82 R | 50.5% | 46.4% | 52.1% | 47.9% |

# VIRGINIA

## PRESIDENT 1976

| 1970 Census Population | City | Total Vote | Republican | Democratic | Other | Rep.-Dem. Plurality | Percentage | | | |
|---|---|---|---|---|---|---|---|---|---|---|
| | | | | | | | Total Vote | | Major Vote | |
| | | | | | | | Rep. | Dem. | Rep. | Dem. |
| 54,083 | LYNCHBURG | 23,804 | 14,564 | 8,227 | 1,013 | 6,337 R | 61.2% | 34.6% | 63.9% | 36.1% |
| 9,164 | MANASSAS | 3,737 | 1,992 | 1,646 | 99 | 346 R | 53.3% | 44.0% | 54.8% | 45.2% |
| 6,844 | MANASSAS PARK | 1,189 | 444 | 709 | 36 | 265 D | 37.3% | 59.6% | 38.5% | 61.5% |
| 19,653 | MARTINSVILLE | 6,935 | 3,147 | 3,491 | 297 | 344 D | 45.4% | 50.3% | 47.4% | 52.6% |
| 138,177 | NEWPORT NEWS | 44,492 | 20,914 | 23,058 | 520 | 2,144 D | 47.0% | 51.8% | 47.6% | 52.4% |
| 307,951 | NORFOLK | 70,402 | 28,099 | 39,295 | 3,008 | 11,196 D | 39.9% | 55.8% | 41.7% | 58.3% |
| 4,001 | NORTON | 1,430 | 577 | 811 | 42 | 234 D | 40.3% | 56.7% | 41.6% | 58.4% |
| 36,103 | PETERSBURG | 13,082 | 5,041 | 7,852 | 189 | 2,811 D | 38.5% | 60.0% | 39.1% | 60.9% |
| 5,441 | POQUOSON | 2,640 | 1,461 | 1,140 | 39 | 321 R | 55.3% | 43.2% | 56.2% | 43.8% |
| 110,963 | PORTSMOUTH | 36,246 | 12,872 | 22,837 | 537 | 9,965 D | 35.5% | 63.0% | 36.0% | 64.0% |
| 11,596 | RADFORD | 4,122 | 1,844 | 2,240 | 38 | 396 D | 44.7% | 54.3% | 45.2% | 54.8% |
| 249,621 | RICHMOND CITY | 83,110 | 37,176 | 44,687 | 1,247 | 7,511 D | 44.7% | 53.8% | 45.4% | 54.6% |
| 92,115 | ROANOKE CITY | 35,949 | 14,738 | 20,696 | 515 | 5,958 D | 41.0% | 57.6% | 41.6% | 58.4% |
| 21,982 | SALEM | 8,690 | 4,196 | 4,404 | 90 | 208 D | 48.3% | 50.7% | 48.8% | 51.2% |
| 6,889 | SOUTH BOSTON | 2,438 | 1,389 | 1,001 | 48 | 388 R | 57.0% | 41.1% | 58.1% | 41.9% |
| 24,504 | STAUNTON | 7,863 | 4,681 | 2,951 | 231 | 1,730 R | 59.5% | 37.5% | 61.3% | 38.7% |
| 45,024 | SUFFOLK | 15,609 | 6,066 | 9,246 | 297 | 3,180 D | 38.9% | 59.2% | 39.6% | 60.4% |
| 172,106 | VIRGINIA BEACH | 63,518 | 34,593 | 25,824 | 3,101 | 8,769 R | 54.5% | 40.7% | 57.3% | 42.7% |
| 16,707 | WAYNESBORO | 5,915 | 3,528 | 2,209 | 178 | 1,319 R | 59.6% | 37.3% | 61.5% | 38.5% |
| 9,069 | WILLIAMSBURG | 3,195 | 1,654 | 1,468 | 73 | 186 R | 51.8% | 45.9% | 53.0% | 47.0% |
| 14,643 | WINCHESTER | 6,484 | 4,075 | 2,346 | 63 | 1,729 R | 62.8% | 36.2% | 63.5% | 36.5% |
| 4,648,494 | TOTAL | 1,697,094 | 836,554 | 813,896 | 46,644 | 22,658 R | 49.3% | 48.0% | 50.7% | 49.3% |

# VIRGINIA

## PRESIDENT 1972

| 1970 Census Population | County | Total Vote | Republican | Democratic | Other | Rep.-Dem. Plurality | Percentage Total Vote | | Percentage Major Vote | |
|---|---|---|---|---|---|---|---|---|---|---|
| | | | | | | | Rep. | Dem. | Rep. | Dem. |
| 29,004 | ACCOMACK | 9,026 | 6,496 | 2,406 | 124 | 4,090 R | 72.0% | 26.7% | 73.0% | 27.0% |
| 37,780 | ALBEMARLE | 12,951 | 8,447 | 4,303 | 201 | 4,144 R | 65.2% | 33.2% | 66.3% | 33.7% |
| 12,461 | ALLEGHANY | 3,830 | 2,584 | 1,069 | 177 | 1,515 R | 67.5% | 27.9% | 70.7% | 29.3% |
| 7,592 | AMELIA | 2,471 | 1,606 | 778 | 87 | 828 R | 65.0% | 31.5% | 67.4% | 32.6% |
| 26,072 | AMHERST | 6,639 | 4,909 | 1,512 | 218 | 3,397 R | 73.9% | 22.8% | 76.5% | 23.5% |
| 9,784 | APPOMATTOX | 3,565 | 2,788 | 684 | 93 | 2,104 R | 78.2% | 19.2% | 80.3% | 19.7% |
| 174,284 | ARLINGTON | 66,383 | 39,406 | 25,877 | 1,100 | 13,529 R | 59.4% | 39.0% | 60.4% | 39.6% |
| 44,220 | AUGUSTA | 11,181 | 9,106 | 1,766 | 309 | 7,340 R | 81.4% | 15.8% | 83.8% | 16.2% |
| 5,192 | BATH | 1,636 | 1,127 | 462 | 47 | 665 R | 68.9% | 28.2% | 70.9% | 29.1% |
| 26,728 | BEDFORD COUNTY | 7,199 | 5,286 | 1,501 | 412 | 3,785 R | 73.4% | 20.9% | 77.9% | 22.1% |
| 5,423 | BLAND | 1,914 | 1,352 | 527 | 35 | 825 R | 70.6% | 27.5% | 72.0% | 28.0% |
| 18,193 | BOTETOURT | 5,481 | 3,806 | 1,519 | 156 | 2,287 R | 69.4% | 27.7% | 71.5% | 28.5% |
| 16,172 | BRUNSWICK | 5,281 | 3,072 | 2,130 | 79 | 942 R | 58.2% | 40.3% | 59.1% | 40.9% |
| 32,071 | BUCHANAN | 8,554 | 4,801 | 3,566 | 187 | 1,235 R | 56.1% | 41.7% | 57.4% | 42.6% |
| 10,597 | BUCKINGHAM | 3,352 | 2,107 | 1,186 | 59 | 921 R | 62.9% | 35.4% | 64.0% | 36.0% |
| 43,319 | CAMPBELL | 14,157 | 11,676 | 2,055 | 426 | 9,621 R | 82.5% | 14.5% | 85.0% | 15.0% |
| 13,925 | CAROLINE | 3,951 | 2,086 | 1,814 | 51 | 272 R | 52.8% | 45.9% | 53.5% | 46.5% |
| 23,092 | CARROLL | 6,989 | 5,247 | 1,583 | 159 | 3,664 R | 75.1% | 22.6% | 76.8% | 23.2% |
| 6,158 | CHARLES CITY | 1,735 | 535 | 1,177 | 23 | 642 D | 30.8% | 67.8% | 31.3% | 68.8% |
| 11,551 | CHARLOTTE | 3,777 | 2,501 | 1,182 | 94 | 1,319 R | 66.2% | 31.3% | 67.9% | 32.1% |
| 76,855 | CHESTERFIELD | 29,253 | 24,934 | 3,823 | 496 | 21,111 R | 85.2% | 13.1% | 86.7% | 13.3% |
| 8,102 | CLARKE | 2,627 | 1,816 | 715 | 96 | 1,101 R | 69.1% | 27.2% | 71.8% | 28.2% |
| 3,524 | CRAIG | 1,220 | 774 | 425 | 21 | 349 R | 63.4% | 34.8% | 64.6% | 35.4% |
| 18,218 | CULPEPER | 5,092 | 3,707 | 1,316 | 69 | 2,391 R | 72.8% | 25.8% | 73.8% | 26.2% |
| 6,179 | CUMBERLAND | 2,374 | 1,371 | 969 | 34 | 402 R | 57.8% | 40.8% | 58.6% | 41.4% |
| 16,077 | DICKENSON | 6,462 | 3,633 | 2,711 | 118 | 922 R | 56.2% | 42.0% | 57.3% | 42.7% |
| 25,046 | DINWIDDIE | 5,305 | 3,314 | 1,901 | 90 | 1,413 R | 62.5% | 35.8% | 63.5% | 36.5% |
| 7,099 | ESSEX | 2,368 | 1,482 | 808 | 78 | 674 R | 62.6% | 34.1% | 64.7% | 35.3% |
| 455,021 | FAIRFAX COUNTY | 169,246 | 112,135 | 54,844 | 2,267 | 57,291 R | 66.3% | 32.4% | 67.2% | 32.8% |
| 26,375 | FAUQUIER | 6,873 | 4,654 | 2,039 | 180 | 2,615 R | 67.7% | 29.7% | 69.5% | 30.5% |
| 9,775 | FLOYD | 3,211 | 2,444 | 708 | 59 | 1,736 R | 76.1% | 22.0% | 77.5% | 22.5% |
| 7,621 | FLUVANNA | 2,137 | 1,438 | 637 | 62 | 801 R | 67.3% | 29.8% | 69.3% | 30.7% |
| 26,858 | FRANKLIN COUNTY | 7,110 | 4,674 | 2,273 | 163 | 2,401 R | 65.7% | 32.0% | 67.3% | 32.7% |
| 28,893 | FREDERICK | 7,139 | 5,367 | 1,604 | 168 | 3,763 R | 75.2% | 22.5% | 77.0% | 23.0% |
| 16,741 | GILES | 5,706 | 3,671 | 1,869 | 166 | 1,802 R | 64.3% | 32.8% | 66.3% | 33.7% |
| 14,059 | GLOUCESTER | 5,064 | 3,642 | 1,292 | 130 | 2,350 R | 71.9% | 25.5% | 73.8% | 26.2% |
| 10,069 | GOOCHLAND | 3,488 | 2,127 | 1,254 | 107 | 873 R | 61.0% | 36.0% | 62.9% | 37.1% |
| 15,439 | GRAYSON | 5,283 | 3,565 | 1,603 | 115 | 1,962 R | 67.5% | 30.3% | 69.0% | 31.0% |
| 5,248 | GREENE | 1,544 | 1,208 | 318 | 18 | 890 R | 78.2% | 20.6% | 79.2% | 20.8% |
| 9,604 | GREENSVILLE | 2,869 | 1,608 | 1,197 | 64 | 411 R | 56.0% | 41.7% | 57.3% | 42.7% |
| 30,076 | HALIFAX | 7,959 | 5,469 | 2,384 | 106 | 3,085 R | 68.7% | 30.0% | 69.6% | 30.4% |
| 37,479 | HANOVER | 13,663 | 11,095 | 2,200 | 368 | 8,895 R | 81.2% | 16.1% | 83.5% | 16.5% |
| 154,364 | HENRICO | 61,904 | 52,536 | 8,420 | 948 | 44,116 R | 84.9% | 13.6% | 86.2% | 13.8% |
| 50,901 | HENRY | 12,024 | 7,556 | 4,042 | 426 | 3,514 R | 62.8% | 33.6% | 65.1% | 34.9% |
| 2,529 | HIGHLAND | 997 | 774 | 206 | 17 | 568 R | 77.6% | 20.7% | 79.0% | 21.0% |
| 18,285 | ISLE OF WIGHT | 5,998 | 3,555 | 2,305 | 138 | 1,250 R | 59.3% | 38.4% | 60.7% | 39.3% |
| 17,853 | JAMES CITY | 5,441 | 3,372 | 1,992 | 77 | 1,380 R | 62.0% | 36.6% | 62.9% | 37.1% |
| 5,491 | KING AND QUEEN | 1,772 | 1,033 | 708 | 31 | 325 R | 58.3% | 40.0% | 59.3% | 40.7% |
| 8,039 | KING GEORGE | 2,391 | 1,675 | 658 | 58 | 1,017 R | 70.1% | 27.5% | 71.8% | 28.2% |
| 7,497 | KING WILLIAM | 2,660 | 1,839 | 797 | 24 | 1,042 R | 69.1% | 30.0% | 69.8% | 30.2% |
| 9,126 | LANCASTER | 3,745 | 2,683 | 1,009 | 53 | 1,674 R | 71.6% | 26.9% | 72.7% | 27.3% |
| 20,321 | LEE | 7,945 | 4,957 | 2,825 | 163 | 2,132 R | 62.4% | 35.6% | 63.7% | 36.3% |
| 37,150 | LOUDOUN | 13,557 | 9,417 | 3,941 | 199 | 5,476 R | 69.5% | 29.1% | 70.5% | 29.5% |
| 14,004 | LOUISA | 4,005 | 2,545 | 1,338 | 122 | 1,207 R | 63.5% | 33.4% | 65.5% | 34.5% |
| 11,687 | LUNENBURG | 3,564 | 2,464 | 1,044 | 56 | 1,420 R | 69.1% | 29.3% | 70.2% | 29.8% |
| 8,638 | MADISON | 2,539 | 1,864 | 639 | 36 | 1,225 R | 73.4% | 25.2% | 74.5% | 25.5% |
| 7,168 | MATHEWS | 2,987 | 2,164 | 730 | 93 | 1,434 R | 72.4% | 24.4% | 74.8% | 25.2% |
| 29,426 | MECKLENBURG | 9,309 | 6,381 | 2,804 | 124 | 3,577 R | 68.5% | 30.1% | 69.5% | 30.5% |
| 6,295 | MIDDLESEX | 2,449 | 1,697 | 724 | 28 | 973 R | 69.3% | 29.6% | 70.1% | 29.9% |
| 47,157 | MONTGOMERY | 13,248 | 9,348 | 3,692 | 208 | 5,656 R | 70.6% | 27.9% | 71.7% | 28.3% |

# VIRGINIA

## PRESIDENT 1972

| 1970 Census Population | County | Total Vote | Republican | Democratic | Other | Rep.-Dem. Plurality | Percentage Total Vote Rep. | Total Vote Dem. | Major Vote Rep. | Major Vote Dem. |
|---|---|---|---|---|---|---|---|---|---|---|
| 11,702 | NELSON | 3,191 | 2,145 | 954 | 92 | 1,191 R | 67.2% | 29.9% | 69.2% | 30.8% |
| 5,300 | NEW KENT | 2,029 | 1,370 | 633 | 26 | 737 R | 67.5% | 31.2% | 68.4% | 31.6% |
| 14,442 | NORTHAMPTON | 3,893 | 2,587 | 1,246 | 60 | 1,341 R | 66.5% | 32.0% | 67.5% | 32.5% |
| 9,239 | NORTHUMBERLAND | 3,258 | 2,332 | 884 | 42 | 1,448 R | 71.6% | 27.1% | 72.5% | 27.5% |
| 14,260 | NOTTOWAY | 4,367 | 2,979 | 1,308 | 80 | 1,671 R | 68.2% | 30.0% | 69.5% | 30.5% |
| 13,792 | ORANGE | 3,869 | 2,758 | 1,032 | 79 | 1,726 R | 71.3% | 26.7% | 72.8% | 27.2% |
| 16,581 | PAGE | 5,980 | 4,326 | 1,585 | 69 | 2,741 R | 72.3% | 26.5% | 73.2% | 26.8% |
| 15,282 | PATRICK | 4,023 | 2,951 | 942 | 130 | 2,009 R | 73.4% | 23.4% | 75.8% | 24.2% |
| 58,789 | PITTSYLVANIA | 16,737 | 12,108 | 4,429 | 200 | 7,679 R | 72.3% | 26.5% | 73.2% | 26.8% |
| 7,696 | POWHATAN | 2,636 | 1,751 | 810 | 75 | 941 R | 66.4% | 30.7% | 68.4% | 31.6% |
| 14,379 | PRINCE EDWARD | 4,850 | 3,199 | 1,585 | 66 | 1,614 R | 66.0% | 32.7% | 66.9% | 33.1% |
| 29,092 | PRINCE GEORGE | 3,552 | 2,405 | 1,084 | 63 | 1,321 R | 67.7% | 30.5% | 68.9% | 31.1% |
| 111,102 | PRINCE WILLIAM | 27,884 | 20,149 | 7,266 | 469 | 12,883 R | 72.3% | 26.1% | 73.5% | 26.5% |
| 29,564 | PULASKI | 8,722 | 6,281 | 2,311 | 130 | 3,970 R | 72.0% | 26.5% | 73.1% | 26.9% |
| 5,199 | RAPPAHANNOCK | 1,547 | 1,055 | 471 | 21 | 584 R | 68.2% | 30.4% | 69.1% | 30.9% |
| 5,841 | RICHMOND COUNTY | 2,018 | 1,565 | 435 | 18 | 1,130 R | 77.6% | 21.6% | 78.3% | 21.8% |
| 67,339 | ROANOKE COUNTY | 25,778 | 19,920 | 5,318 | 540 | 14,602 R | 77.3% | 20.6% | 78.9% | 21.1% |
| 16,637 | ROCKBRIDGE | 4,051 | 3,009 | 956 | 86 | 2,053 R | 74.3% | 23.6% | 75.9% | 24.1% |
| 47,890 | ROCKINGHAM | 12,275 | 10,025 | 2,026 | 224 | 7,999 R | 81.7% | 16.5% | 83.2% | 16.8% |
| 24,533 | RUSSELL | 8,502 | 5,010 | 3,367 | 125 | 1,643 R | 58.9% | 39.6% | 59.8% | 40.2% |
| 24,376 | SCOTT | 7,744 | 5,125 | 2,474 | 145 | 2,651 R | 66.2% | 31.9% | 67.4% | 32.6% |
| 22,852 | SHENANDOAH | 8,644 | 7,128 | 1,422 | 94 | 5,706 R | 82.5% | 16.5% | 83.4% | 16.6% |
| 31,349 | SMYTH | 8,868 | 6,409 | 2,280 | 179 | 4,129 R | 72.3% | 25.7% | 73.8% | 26.2% |
| 18,582 | SOUTHAMPTON | 4,807 | 3,225 | 1,498 | 84 | 1,727 R | 67.1% | 31.2% | 68.3% | 31.7% |
| 16,424 | SPOTSYLVANIA | 5,442 | 3,577 | 1,775 | 90 | 1,802 R | 65.7% | 32.6% | 66.8% | 33.2% |
| 24,587 | STAFFORD | 7,214 | 5,222 | 1,901 | 91 | 3,321 R | 72.4% | 26.4% | 73.3% | 26.7% |
| 5,882 | SURRY | 2,117 | 1,067 | 988 | 62 | 79 R | 50.4% | 46.7% | 51.9% | 48.1% |
| 11,464 | SUSSEX | 3,855 | 2,120 | 1,645 | 90 | 475 R | 55.0% | 42.7% | 56.3% | 43.7% |
| 39,816 | TAZEWELL | 10,667 | 7,233 | 3,181 | 253 | 4,052 R | 67.8% | 29.8% | 69.5% | 30.5% |
| 15,301 | WARREN | 5,357 | 3,718 | 1,508 | 131 | 2,210 R | 69.4% | 28.2% | 71.1% | 28.9% |
| 40,835 | WASHINGTON | 12,111 | 8,805 | 3,028 | 278 | 5,777 R | 72.7% | 25.0% | 74.4% | 25.6% |
| 12,142 | WESTMORELAND | 3,532 | 2,331 | 1,113 | 88 | 1,218 R | 66.0% | 31.5% | 67.7% | 32.3% |
| 35,947 | WISE | 11,242 | 6,739 | 4,402 | 101 | 2,337 R | 59.9% | 39.2% | 60.5% | 39.5% |
| 22,139 | WYTHE | 6,156 | 4,553 | 1,431 | 172 | 3,122 R | 74.0% | 23.2% | 76.1% | 23.9% |
| 33,203 | YORK | 10,341 | 7,745 | 2,302 | 294 | 5,443 R | 74.9% | 22.3% | 77.1% | 22.9% |
| | **City** | | | | | | | | | |
| 110,938 | ALEXANDRIA | 36,169 | 20,235 | 15,409 | 525 | 4,826 R | 55.9% | 42.6% | 56.8% | 43.2% |
| 6,011 | BEDFORD CITY | 2,063 | 1,407 | 529 | 127 | 878 R | 68.2% | 25.6% | 72.7% | 27.3% |
| 14,857 | BRISTOL | 3,893 | 2,665 | 1,157 | 71 | 1,508 R | 68.5% | 29.7% | 69.7% | 30.3% |
| 6,425 | BUENA VISTA | 1,409 | 990 | 373 | 46 | 617 R | 70.3% | 26.5% | 72.6% | 27.4% |
| 38,880 | CHARLOTTESVILLE | 13,353 | 7,935 | 5,240 | 178 | 2,695 R | 59.4% | 39.2% | 60.2% | 39.8% |
| 89,580 | CHESAPEAKE | 26,080 | 17,722 | 7,289 | 1,069 | 10,433 R | 68.0% | 27.9% | 70.9% | 29.1% |
| 5,501 | CLIFTON FORGE | 1,784 | 1,127 | 575 | 82 | 552 R | 63.2% | 32.2% | 66.2% | 33.8% |
| 15,097 | COLONIAL HEIGHTS | 6,028 | 5,304 | 541 | 183 | 4,763 R | 88.0% | 9.0% | 90.7% | 9.3% |
| 10,060 | COVINGTON | 2,998 | 1,910 | 948 | 140 | 962 R | 63.7% | 31.6% | 66.8% | 33.2% |
| 46,391 | DANVILLE | 16,916 | 12,463 | 4,148 | 305 | 8,315 R | 73.7% | 24.5% | 75.0% | 25.0% |
| 5,300 | EMPORIA | 1,947 | 1,340 | 565 | 42 | 775 R | 68.8% | 29.0% | 70.3% | 29.7% |
| 21,970 | FAIRFAX CITY | 7,475 | 5,063 | 2,274 | 138 | 2,789 R | 67.7% | 30.4% | 69.0% | 31.0% |
| 10,772 | FALLS CHURCH | 4,943 | 2,967 | 1,895 | 81 | 1,072 R | 60.0% | 38.3% | 61.0% | 39.0% |
| 6,880 | FRANKLIN CITY | 2,179 | 1,416 | 738 | 25 | 678 R | 65.0% | 33.9% | 65.7% | 34.3% |
| 14,450 | FREDERICKSBURG | 4,976 | 3,211 | 1,702 | 63 | 1,509 R | 64.5% | 34.2% | 65.4% | 34.6% |
| 6,278 | GALAX | 2,061 | 1,497 | 524 | 40 | 973 R | 72.6% | 25.4% | 74.1% | 25.9% |
| 120,779 | HAMPTON | 33,435 | 21,897 | 10,648 | 890 | 11,249 R | 65.5% | 31.8% | 67.3% | 32.7% |
| 14,605 | HARRISONBURG | 4,693 | 3,626 | 992 | 75 | 2,634 R | 77.3% | 21.1% | 78.5% | 21.5% |
| 23,471 | HOPEWELL | 6,891 | 5,229 | 1,485 | 177 | 3,744 R | 75.9% | 21.5% | 77.9% | 22.1% |
| 7,597 | LEXINGTON | 2,070 | 1,345 | 695 | 30 | 650 R | 65.0% | 33.6% | 65.9% | 34.1% |

# VIRGINIA

## PRESIDENT 1972

| 1970 Census Population | City | Total Vote | Republican | Democratic | Other | Rep.-Dem. Plurality | Percentage | | | |
|---|---|---|---|---|---|---|---|---|---|---|
| | | | | | | | Total Vote | | Major Vote | |
| | | | | | | | Rep. | Dem. | Rep. | Dem. |
| 54,083 | LYNCHBURG | 17,890 | 13,259 | 4,208 | 423 | 9,051 R | 74.1% | 23.5% | 75.9% | 24.1% |
| 19,653 | MARTINSVILLE | 6,326 | 3,879 | 2,292 | 155 | 1,587 R | 61.3% | 36.2% | 62.9% | 37.1% |
| 35,166 | NANSEMOND CITY | 9,966 | 5,767 | 3,929 | 270 | 1,838 R | 57.9% | 39.4% | 59.5% | 40.5% |
| 138,177 | NEWPORT NEWS | 40,312 | 27,169 | 12,233 | 910 | 14,936 R | 67.4% | 30.3% | 69.0% | 31.0% |
| 307,951 | NORFOLK | 66,217 | 38,385 | 25,737 | 2,095 | 12,648 R | 58.0% | 38.9% | 59.9% | 40.1% |
| 4,001 | NORTON | 1,313 | 823 | 463 | 27 | 360 R | 62.7% | 35.3% | 64.0% | 36.0% |
| 36,103 | PETERSBURG | 12,053 | 6,710 | 5,156 | 187 | 1,554 R | 55.7% | 42.8% | 56.5% | 43.5% |
| 110,963 | PORTSMOUTH | 34,350 | 20,090 | 13,124 | 1,136 | 6,966 R | 58.5% | 38.2% | 60.5% | 39.5% |
| 11,596 | RADFORD | 3,752 | 2,577 | 1,121 | 54 | 1,456 R | 68.7% | 29.9% | 69.7% | 30.3% |
| 249,621 | RICHMOND CITY | 80,302 | 46,244 | 33,055 | 1,003 | 13,189 R | 57.6% | 41.2% | 58.3% | 41.7% |
| 92,115 | ROANOKE CITY | 28,671 | 18,541 | 9,498 | 632 | 9,043 R | 64.7% | 33.1% | 66.1% | 33.9% |
| 21,982 | SALEM | 7,553 | 5,649 | 1,744 | 160 | 3,905 R | 74.8% | 23.1% | 76.4% | 23.6% |
| 6,889 | SOUTH BOSTON | 2,605 | 1,865 | 709 | 31 | 1,156 R | 71.6% | 27.2% | 72.5% | 27.5% |
| 24,504 | STAUNTON | 7,068 | 5,531 | 1,416 | 121 | 4,115 R | 78.3% | 20.0% | 79.6% | 20.4% |
| 9,858 | SUFFOLK | 3,073 | 2,137 | 898 | 38 | 1,239 R | 69.5% | 29.2% | 70.4% | 29.6% |
| 172,106 | VIRGINIA BEACH | 49,733 | 38,074 | 10,373 | 1,286 | 27,701 R | 76.6% | 20.9% | 78.6% | 21.4% |
| 16,707 | WAYNESBORO | 5,354 | 4,163 | 1,061 | 130 | 3,102 R | 77.8% | 19.8% | 79.7% | 20.3% |
| 9,069 | WILLIAMSBURG | 3,108 | 1,786 | 1,274 | 48 | 512 R | 57.5% | 41.0% | 58.4% | 41.6% |
| 14,643 | WINCHESTER | 6,151 | 4,647 | 1,418 | 86 | 3,229 R | 75.5% | 23.1% | 76.6% | 23.4% |
| 4,648,494 | TOTAL | 1,457,019 | 988,493 | 438,887 | 29,639 | 549,606 R | 67.8% | 30.1% | 69.3% | 30.7% |

# VIRGINIA

## PRESIDENT 1968

| 1960 Census Population | County | Total Vote | Republican | Democratic | AIP | Other | Plurality | Percentage Total Vote Rep. | Dem. | AIP |
|---|---|---|---|---|---|---|---|---|---|---|
| 30,635 | ACCOMACK | 9,181 | 3,231 | 2,467 | 3,460 | 23 | 229 A | 35.2% | 26.9% | 37.7% |
| 30,969 | ALBEMARLE | 8,441 | 4,512 | 2,255 | 1,657 | 17 | 2,257 R | 53.5% | 26.7% | 19.6% |
| 12,128 | ALLEGHANY | 3,793 | 1,649 | 988 | 1,153 | 3 | 496 R | 43.5% | 26.0% | 30.4% |
| 7,815 | AMELIA | 2,528 | 857 | 830 | 832 | 9 | 25 R | 33.9% | 32.8% | 32.9% |
| 22,953 | AMHERST | 6,674 | 2,656 | 1,543 | 2,449 | 26 | 207 R | 39.8% | 23.1% | 36.7% |
| 9,148 | APPOMATTOX | 4,037 | 1,753 | 756 | 1,512 | 16 | 241 R | 43.4% | 18.7% | 37.5% |
| 163,401 | ARLINGTON | 61,326 | 28,163 | 26,107 | 6,746 | 310 | 2,056 R | 45.9% | 42.6% | 11.0% |
| 37,363 | AUGUSTA | 10,900 | 6,313 | 2,028 | 2,483 | 76 | 3,830 R | 57.9% | 18.6% | 22.8% |
| 5,335 | BATH | 1,897 | 872 | 494 | 529 | 2 | 343 R | 46.0% | 26.0% | 27.9% |
| 25,107 | BEDFORD COUNTY | 7,840 | 2,807 | 1,574 | 3,316 | 143 | 509 A | 35.8% | 20.1% | 42.3% |
| 5,982 | BLAND | 1,862 | 938 | 560 | 361 | 3 | 378 R | 50.4% | 30.1% | 19.4% |
| 16,715 | BOTETOURT | 5,140 | 2,598 | 1,272 | 1,267 | 3 | 1,326 R | 50.5% | 24.7% | 24.6% |
| 17,779 | BRUNSWICK | 5,147 | 1,139 | 1,910 | 2,088 | 10 | 178 A | 22.1% | 37.1% | 40.6% |
| 36,724 | BUCHANAN | 9,816 | 3,699 | 5,003 | 1,067 | 47 | 1,304 D | 37.7% | 51.0% | 10.9% |
| 10,877 | BUCKINGHAM | 3,204 | 1,027 | 984 | 1,185 | 8 | 158 A | 32.1% | 30.7% | 37.0% |
| 32,958 | CAMPBELL | 12,811 | 5,731 | 1,996 | 4,425 | 659 | 1,306 R | 44.7% | 15.6% | 34.5% |
| 12,725 | CAROLINE | 4,426 | 1,162 | 2,165 | 1,084 | 15 | 1,003 D | 26.3% | 48.9% | 24.5% |
| 23,178 | CARROLL | 7,651 | 4,909 | 1,773 | 958 | 11 | 3,136 R | 64.2% | 23.2% | 12.5% |
| 5,492 | CHARLES CITY | 1,960 | 320 | 1,457 | 176 | 7 | 1,137 D | 16.3% | 74.3% | 9.0% |
| 13,368 | CHARLOTTE | 4,265 | 1,042 | 1,045 | 2,163 | 15 | 1,118 A | 24.4% | 24.5% | 50.7% |
| 71,197 | CHESTERFIELD | 39,292 | 22,015 | 5,715 | 11,504 | 58 | 10,511 R | 56.0% | 14.5% | 29.3% |
| 7,942 | CLARKE | 2,644 | 1,127 | 768 | 742 | 7 | 359 R | 42.6% | 29.0% | 28.1% |
| 3,356 | CRAIG | 1,258 | 581 | 419 | 256 | 2 | 162 R | 46.2% | 33.3% | 20.3% |
| 15,088 | CULPEPER | 4,694 | 2,229 | 1,239 | 1,217 | 9 | 990 R | 47.5% | 26.4% | 25.9% |
| 6,360 | CUMBERLAND | 2,432 | 844 | 978 | 602 | 8 | 134 D | 34.7% | 40.2% | 24.8% |
| 20,211 | DICKENSON | 7,415 | 3,412 | 3,355 | 639 | 9 | 57 R | 46.0% | 45.2% | 8.6% |
| 22,183 | DINWIDDIE | 5,257 | 1,451 | 1,551 | 2,245 | 10 | 694 A | 27.6% | 29.5% | 42.7% |
| 6,690 | ESSEX | 2,164 | 791 | 897 | 468 | 8 | 106 D | 36.6% | 41.5% | 21.6% |
| 261,417 | FAIRFAX COUNTY | 117,319 | 57,462 | 44,796 | 14,805 | 256 | 12,666 R | 49.0% | 38.2% | 12.6% |
| 24,066 | FAUQUIER | 6,501 | 2,845 | 2,099 | 1,536 | 21 | 746 R | 43.8% | 32.3% | 23.6% |
| 10,462 | FLOYD | 3,537 | 2,275 | 715 | 537 | 10 | 1,560 R | 64.3% | 20.2% | 15.2% |
| 7,227 | FLUVANNA | 2,145 | 913 | 569 | 660 | 3 | 253 R | 42.6% | 26.5% | 30.8% |
| 25,925 | FRANKLIN COUNTY | 8,308 | 3,036 | 2,025 | 3,219 | 28 | 183 A | 36.5% | 24.4% | 38.7% |
| 21,941 | FREDERICK | 7,454 | 3,696 | 1,612 | 2,137 | 9 | 1,559 R | 49.6% | 21.6% | 28.7% |
| 17,219 | GILES | 6,277 | 2,722 | 2,045 | 1,372 | 138 | 677 R | 43.4% | 32.6% | 21.9% |
| 11,919 | GLOUCESTER | 4,364 | 1,619 | 1,210 | 1,526 | 9 | 93 R | 37.1% | 27.7% | 35.0% |
| 9,206 | GOOCHLAND | 3,461 | 1,216 | 1,389 | 836 | 20 | 173 D | 35.1% | 40.1% | 24.2% |
| 17,390 | GRAYSON | 6,587 | 3,563 | 1,926 | 1,090 | 8 | 1,637 R | 54.1% | 29.2% | 16.5% |
| 4,715 | GREENE | 1,549 | 856 | 255 | 433 | 5 | 423 R | 55.3% | 16.5% | 28.0% |
| 10,620 | GREENSVILLE | 3,165 | 529 | 1,367 | 1,256 | 13 | 111 D | 16.7% | 43.2% | 39.7% |
| 33,637 | HALIFAX | 9,102 | 2,634 | 2,199 | 4,235 | 34 | 1,601 A | 28.9% | 24.2% | 46.5% |
| 27,550 | HANOVER | 10,847 | 5,425 | 2,079 | 3,330 | 13 | 2,095 R | 50.0% | 19.2% | 30.7% |
| 117,339 | HENRICO | 54,726 | 34,212 | 8,600 | 11,868 | 46 | 22,344 R | 62.5% | 15.7% | 21.7% |
| 40,335 | HENRY | 15,224 | 3,946 | 4,175 | 6,802 | 301 | 2,627 A | 25.9% | 27.4% | 44.7% |
| 3,221 | HIGHLAND | 1,069 | 619 | 284 | 166 | | 335 R | 57.9% | 26.6% | 15.5% |
| 17,164 | ISLE OF WIGHT | 5,635 | 1,312 | 1,977 | 2,328 | 18 | 351 A | 23.3% | 35.1% | 41.3% |
| 11,539 | JAMES CITY | 4,065 | 1,443 | 1,521 | 1,083 | 18 | 78 D | 35.5% | 37.4% | 26.6% |
| 5,889 | KING AND QUEEN | 2,073 | 568 | 882 | 614 | 9 | 268 D | 27.4% | 42.5% | 29.6% |
| 7,243 | KING GEORGE | 2,195 | 829 | 730 | 632 | 4 | 99 R | 37.8% | 33.3% | 28.8% |
| 7,563 | KING WILLIAM | 2,431 | 1,046 | 764 | 615 | 6 | 282 R | 43.0% | 31.4% | 25.3% |
| 9,174 | LANCASTER | 3,650 | 1,640 | 1,134 | 876 | | 506 R | 44.9% | 31.1% | 24.0% |
| 25,824 | LEE | 9,399 | 4,450 | 4,105 | 827 | 17 | 345 R | 47.3% | 43.7% | 8.8% |
| 24,549 | LOUDOUN | 9,970 | 4,577 | 3,262 | 2,117 | 14 | 1,315 R | 45.9% | 32.7% | 21.2% |
| 12,959 | LOUISA | 3,964 | 1,510 | 1,290 | 1,149 | 15 | 220 R | 38.1% | 32.5% | 29.0% |
| 12,523 | LUNENBURG | 4,012 | 1,181 | 1,180 | 1,630 | 21 | 449 A | 29.4% | 29.4% | 40.6% |
| 8,187 | MADISON | 2,439 | 1,188 | 478 | 763 | 10 | 425 R | 48.7% | 19.6% | 31.3% |
| 7,121 | MATHEWS | 2,777 | 1,309 | 691 | 773 | 4 | 536 R | 47.1% | 24.9% | 27.8% |
| 31,428 | MECKLENBURG | 9,478 | 2,750 | 2,667 | 4,022 | 39 | 1,272 A | 29.0% | 28.1% | 42.4% |
| 6,319 | MIDDLESEX | 2,042 | 809 | 575 | 655 | 3 | 154 R | 39.6% | 28.2% | 32.1% |
| 32,923 | MONTGOMERY | 11,547 | 7,098 | 2,700 | 1,712 | 37 | 4,398 R | 61.5% | 23.4% | 14.8% |

# VIRGINIA

## PRESIDENT 1968

| 1960 Census Population | County | Total Vote | Republican | Democratic | AIP | Other | Plurality | Rep. | Dem. | AIP |
|---:|---|---:|---:|---:|---:|---:|---:|---:|---:|---:|
| 31,366 | NANSEMOND COUNTY | 10,033 | 2,101 | 4,174 | 3,723 | 35 | 451 D | 20.9% | 41.6% | 37.1% |
| 12,752 | NELSON | 3,426 | 1,130 | 1,120 | 1,163 | 13 | 33 A | 33.0% | 32.7% | 33.9% |
| 4,504 | NEW KENT | 1,904 | 526 | 765 | 609 | 4 | 156 D | 27.6% | 40.2% | 32.0% |
| 16,966 | NORTHAMPTON | 3,974 | 1,410 | 1,418 | 1,129 | 17 | 8 D | 35.5% | 35.7% | 28.4% |
| 10,185 | NORTHUMBERLAND | 3,492 | 1,438 | 1,077 | 968 | 9 | 361 R | 41.2% | 30.8% | 27.7% |
| 15,141 | NOTTOWAY | 4,830 | 1,614 | 1,529 | 1,673 | 14 | 59 A | 33.4% | 31.7% | 34.6% |
| 12,900 | ORANGE | 3,661 | 1,727 | 879 | 1,050 | 5 | 677 R | 47.2% | 24.0% | 28.7% |
| 15,572 | PAGE | 6,800 | 3,667 | 2,125 | 995 | 13 | 1,542 R | 53.9% | 31.3% | 14.6% |
| 15,282 | PATRICK | 5,275 | 2,187 | 1,105 | 1,974 | 9 | 213 R | 41.5% | 20.9% | 37.4% |
| 58,296 | PITTSYLVANIA | 19,890 | 5,096 | 5,427 | 9,302 | 65 | 3,875 A | 25.6% | 27.3% | 46.8% |
| 6,747 | POWHATAN | 2,663 | 722 | 1,004 | 929 | 8 | 75 D | 27.1% | 37.7% | 34.9% |
| 14,121 | PRINCE EDWARD | 4,666 | 1,857 | 1,567 | 1,224 | 18 | 290 R | 39.8% | 33.6% | 26.2% |
| 20,270 | PRINCE GEORGE | 4,761 | 1,559 | 1,272 | 1,920 | 10 | 361 A | 32.7% | 26.7% | 40.3% |
| 50,164 | PRINCE WILLIAM | 18,686 | 7,944 | 5,566 | 5,160 | 16 | 2,378 R | 42.5% | 29.8% | 27.6% |
| 27,258 | PULASKI | 8,265 | 4,409 | 2,497 | 1,346 | 13 | 1,912 R | 53.3% | 30.2% | 16.3% |
| 5,368 | RAPPAHANNOCK | 1,363 | 594 | 394 | 372 | 3 | 200 R | 43.6% | 28.9% | 27.3% |
| 6,375 | RICHMOND COUNTY | 2,069 | 1,011 | 490 | 563 | 5 | 448 R | 48.9% | 23.7% | 27.2% |
| 45,635 | ROANOKE COUNTY | 21,124 | 12,439 | 3,902 | 4,745 | 38 | 7,694 R | 58.9% | 18.5% | 22.5% |
| 16,502 | ROCKBRIDGE | 4,014 | 2,280 | 845 | 885 | 4 | 1,395 R | 56.8% | 21.1% | 22.0% |
| 40,485 | ROCKINGHAM | 11,715 | 7,779 | 2,111 | 1,817 | 8 | 5,668 R | 66.4% | 18.0% | 15.5% |
| 26,290 | RUSSELL | 8,872 | 3,858 | 3,554 | 1,369 | 91 | 304 R | 43.5% | 40.1% | 15.4% |
| 25,813 | SCOTT | 9,984 | 5,345 | 3,144 | 1,474 | 21 | 2,201 R | 53.5% | 31.5% | 14.8% |
| 21,825 | SHENANDOAH | 8,681 | 5,461 | 1,654 | 1,561 | 5 | 3,807 R | 62.9% | 19.1% | 18.0% |
| 31,066 | SMYTH | 9,751 | 5,297 | 2,631 | 1,808 | 15 | 2,666 R | 54.3% | 27.0% | 18.5% |
| 19,931 | SOUTHAMPTON | 5,262 | 1,376 | 1,803 | 2,070 | 13 | 267 A | 26.1% | 34.3% | 39.3% |
| 13,819 | SPOTSYLVANIA | 4,926 | 1,675 | 1,647 | 1,589 | 15 | 28 R | 34.0% | 33.4% | 32.3% |
| 16,876 | STAFFORD | 6,482 | 2,572 | 1,698 | 2,197 | 15 | 375 R | 39.7% | 26.2% | 33.9% |
| 6,220 | SURRY | 2,366 | 523 | 1,126 | 708 | 9 | 418 D | 22.1% | 47.6% | 29.9% |
| 12,411 | SUSSEX | 3,794 | 1,105 | 1,541 | 1,135 | 13 | 406 D | 29.1% | 40.6% | 29.9% |
| 44,791 | TAZEWELL | 11,338 | 4,434 | 4,734 | 2,023 | 147 | 300 D | 39.1% | 41.8% | 17.8% |
| 14,655 | WARREN | 5,296 | 2,297 | 1,513 | 1,479 | 7 | 784 R | 43.4% | 28.6% | 27.9% |
| 38,076 | WASHINGTON | 13,029 | 6,665 | 3,243 | 3,092 | 29 | 3,422 R | 51.2% | 24.9% | 23.7% |
| 11,042 | WESTMORELAND | 3,506 | 1,402 | 1,156 | 943 | 5 | 246 R | 40.0% | 33.0% | 26.9% |
| 43,579 | WISE | 12,606 | 5,004 | 5,942 | 1,635 | 25 | 938 D | 39.7% | 47.1% | 13.0% |
| 21,975 | WYTHE | 6,963 | 3,638 | 1,765 | 1,377 | 183 | 1,873 R | 52.2% | 25.3% | 19.8% |
| 21,583 | YORK | 9,088 | 3,356 | 2,370 | 3,330 | 32 | 26 R | 36.9% | 26.1% | 36.6% |
| | City | | | | | | | | | |
| 91,023 | ALEXANDRIA | 31,816 | 13,265 | 14,351 | 4,131 | 69 | 1,086 D | 41.7% | 45.1% | 13.0% |
| 5,921 | BEDFORD CITY | 2,380 | 1,047 | 569 | 679 | 85 | 368 R | 44.0% | 23.9% | 28.5% |
| 17,144 | BRISTOL | 4,377 | 1,930 | 1,531 | 911 | 5 | 399 R | 44.1% | 35.0% | 20.8% |
| 6,300 | BUENA VISTA | 1,660 | 814 | 387 | 456 | 3 | 358 R | 49.0% | 23.3% | 27.5% |
| 29,427 | CHARLOTTESVILLE | 11,335 | 5,601 | 3,831 | 1,781 | 122 | 1,770 R | 49.4% | 33.8% | 15.7% |
| 73,647 | CHESAPEAKE | 24,760 | 6,234 | 6,843 | 11,084 | 599 | 4,241 A | 25.2% | 27.6% | 44.8% |
| 5,268 | CLIFTON FORGE | 2,122 | 925 | 734 | 462 | 1 | 191 R | 43.6% | 34.6% | 21.8% |
| 9,587 | COLONIAL HEIGHTS | 5,413 | 2,650 | 650 | 2,106 | 7 | 544 R | 49.0% | 12.0% | 38.9% |
| 11,062 | COVINGTON | 3,595 | 1,551 | 1,195 | 846 | 3 | 356 R | 43.1% | 33.2% | 23.5% |
| 5,535 | DANVILLE | 2,191 | 812 | 657 | 716 | 6 | 96 R | 37.1% | 30.0% | 32.7% |
| 46,577 | EMPORIA | 16,874 | 6,796 | 4,495 | 5,391 | 192 | 1,405 R | 40.3% | 26.6% | 31.9% |
| 13,585 | FAIRFAX CITY | 6,084 | 2,963 | 2,153 | 959 | 9 | 810 R | 48.7% | 35.4% | 15.8% |
| 10,192 | FALLS CHURCH | 4,382 | 2,005 | 1,860 | 504 | 13 | 145 R | 45.8% | 42.4% | 11.5% |
| 7,264 | FRANKLIN CITY | 2,256 | 951 | 792 | 511 | 2 | 159 R | 42.2% | 35.1% | 22.7% |
| 13,639 | FREDERICKSBURG | 5,068 | 2,142 | 2,036 | 878 | 12 | 106 R | 42.3% | 40.2% | 17.3% |
| 5,254 | GALAX | 2,309 | 1,257 | 748 | 304 | | 509 R | 54.4% | 32.4% | 13.2% |
| 89,258 | HAMPTON | 32,606 | 10,532 | 11,308 | 10,690 | 76 | 618 D | 32.3% | 34.7% | 32.8% |
| 11,916 | HARRISONBURG | 4,352 | 2,859 | 1,036 | 453 | 4 | 1,823 R | 65.7% | 23.8% | 10.4% |
| 17,895 | HOPEWELL | 6,743 | 2,942 | 1,568 | 2,092 | 141 | 850 R | 43.6% | 23.3% | 31.0% |
| 7,537 | LEXINGTON | 2,085 | 1,170 | 734 | 177 | 4 | 436 R | 56.1% | 35.2% | 8.5% |

# VIRGINIA

## PRESIDENT 1968

| 1960 Census Population | City | Total Vote | Republican | Democratic | AIP | Other | Plurality | Percentage Total Vote | | |
|---|---|---|---|---|---|---|---|---|---|---|
| | | | | | | | | Rep. | Dem. | AIP |
| 54,790 | LYNCHBURG | 18,299 | 9,943 | 4,305 | 3,649 | 402 | 5,638 R | 54.3% | 23.5% | 19.9% |
| 18,798 | MARTINSVILLE | 7,276 | 2,618 | 2,727 | 1,856 | 75 | 109 D | 36.0% | 37.5% | 25.5% |
| 113,662 | NEWPORT NEWS | 37,069 | 12,774 | 13,370 | 10,763 | 162 | 596 D | 34.5% | 36.1% | 29.0% |
| 304,869 | NORFOLK | 65,829 | 22,302 | 28,477 | 14,500 | 550 | 6,175 D | 33.9% | 43.3% | 22.0% |
| 4,996 | NORTON | 1,267 | 495 | 555 | 215 | 2 | 60 D | 39.1% | 43.8% | 17.0% |
| 36,750 | PETERSBURG | 11,169 | 3,478 | 5,519 | 2,158 | 14 | 2,041 D | 31.1% | 49.4% | 19.3% |
| 114,773 | PORTSMOUTH | 37,381 | 9,402 | 15,734 | 12,127 | 118 | 3,607 D | 25.2% | 42.1% | 32.4% |
| 9,371 | RADFORD | 3,749 | 2,077 | 1,206 | 461 | 5 | 871 R | 55.4% | 32.2% | 12.3% |
| 219,958 | RICHMOND CITY | 66,668 | 26,380 | 32,857 | 7,325 | 106 | 6,477 D | 39.6% | 49.3% | 11.0% |
| 97,110 | ROANOKE CITY | 30,008 | 15,368 | 9,281 | 5,269 | 90 | 6,087 R | 51.2% | 30.9% | 17.6% |
| 16,058 | SALEM | 6,846 | 3,955 | 1,369 | 1,507 | 15 | 2,448 R | 57.8% | 20.0% | 22.0% |
| 5,974 | SOUTH BOSTON | 2,587 | 1,298 | 620 | 662 | 7 | 636 R | 50.2% | 24.0% | 25.6% |
| 22,232 | STAUNTON | 7,221 | 4,434 | 1,729 | 1,054 | 4 | 2,705 R | 61.4% | 23.9% | 14.6% |
| 12,609 | SUFFOLK | 3,365 | 1,277 | 1,044 | 1,039 | 5 | 233 R | 37.9% | 31.0% | 30.9% |
| 85,218 | VIRGINIA BEACH | 37,742 | 16,316 | 10,101 | 10,962 | 363 | 5,354 R | 43.2% | 26.8% | 29.0% |
| 15,694 | WAYNESBORO | 5,378 | 3,301 | 1,446 | 613 | 18 | 1,855 R | 61.4% | 26.9% | 11.4% |
| 6,832 | WILLIAMSBURG | 2,474 | 1,156 | 991 | 247 | 80 | 165 R | 46.7% | 40.1% | 10.0% |
| 15,110 | WINCHESTER | 4,833 | 2,695 | 1,360 | 770 | 8 | 1,335 R | 55.8% | 28.1% | 15.9% |
| 3,966,949 | TOTAL | 1,361,491 | 590,319 | 442,387 | 321,833 | 6,952 | 147,932 R | 43.4% | 32.5% | 23.6% |

# VIRGINIA

## PRESIDENT 1964

| 1960 Census Population | County | Total Vote | Republican | Democratic | Other | Rep.-Dem. Plurality | Percentage | | | |
|---|---|---|---|---|---|---|---|---|---|---|
| | | | | | | | Total Vote | | Major Vote | |
| | | | | | | | Rep. | Dem. | Rep. | Dem. |
| 30,635 | ACCOMACK | 6,683 | 3,145 | 3,528 | 10 | 383 D | 47.1% | 52.8% | 47.1% | 52.9% |
| 30,969 | ALBEMARLE | 6,315 | 3,251 | 3,062 | 2 | 189 R | 51.5% | 48.5% | 51.5% | 48.5% |
| 12,128 | ALLEGHANY | 2,685 | 1,104 | 1,580 | 1 | 476 D | 41.1% | 58.8% | 41.1% | 58.9% |
| 7,815 | AMELIA | 2,239 | 1,348 | 884 | 7 | 464 R | 60.2% | 39.5% | 60.4% | 39.6% |
| 22,953 | AMHERST | 5,410 | 2,675 | 2,730 | 5 | 55 D | 49.4% | 50.5% | 49.5% | 50.5% |
| 9,148 | APPOMATTOX | 3,791 | 2,444 | 1,339 | 8 | 1,105 R | 64.5% | 35.3% | 64.6% | 35.4% |
| 163,401 | ARLINGTON | 54,363 | 20,485 | 33,567 | 311 | 13,082 D | 37.7% | 61.7% | 37.9% | 62.1% |
| 37,363 | AUGUSTA | 8,372 | 4,327 | 4,039 | 6 | 288 R | 51.7% | 48.2% | 51.7% | 48.3% |
| 5,335 | BATH | 1,286 | 516 | 770 | | 254 D | 40.1% | 59.9% | 40.1% | 59.9% |
| 31,028 | BEDFORD COUNTY | 7,914 | 3,806 | 4,076 | 32 | 270 D | 48.1% | 51.5% | 48.3% | 51.7% |
| 5,982 | BLAND | 1,570 | 717 | 851 | 2 | 134 D | 45.7% | 54.2% | 45.7% | 54.3% |
| 16,715 | BOTETOURT | 4,476 | 2,098 | 2,377 | 1 | 279 D | 46.9% | 53.1% | 46.9% | 53.1% |
| 17,779 | BRUNSWICK | 4,446 | 2,560 | 1,883 | 3 | 677 R | 57.6% | 42.4% | 57.6% | 42.4% |
| 36,724 | BUCHANAN | 7,124 | 2,349 | 4,756 | 19 | 2,407 D | 33.0% | 66.8% | 33.1% | 66.9% |
| 10,877 | BUCKINGHAM | 2,733 | 1,547 | 1,182 | 4 | 365 R | 56.6% | 43.2% | 56.7% | 43.3% |
| 32,958 | CAMPBELL | 9,145 | 5,713 | 3,401 | 31 | 2,312 R | 62.5% | 37.2% | 62.7% | 37.3% |
| 12,725 | CAROLINE | 3,243 | 1,166 | 2,064 | 13 | 898 D | 36.0% | 63.6% | 36.1% | 63.9% |
| 23,178 | CARROLL | 6,146 | 3,617 | 2,517 | 12 | 1,100 R | 58.9% | 41.0% | 59.0% | 41.0% |
| 5,492 | CHARLES CITY | 1,348 | 323 | 1,023 | 2 | 700 D | 24.0% | 75.9% | 24.0% | 76.0% |
| 13,368 | CHARLOTTE | 3,178 | 1,974 | 1,191 | 13 | 783 R | 62.1% | 37.5% | 62.4% | 37.6% |
| 71,197 | CHESTERFIELD | 25,871 | 17,486 | 8,376 | 9 | 9,110 R | 67.6% | 32.4% | 67.6% | 32.4% |
| 7,942 | CLARKE | 2,206 | 1,068 | 1,136 | 2 | 68 D | 48.4% | 51.5% | 48.5% | 51.5% |
| 3,356 | CRAIG | 1,244 | 477 | 767 | | 290 D | 38.3% | 61.7% | 38.3% | 61.7% |
| 15,088 | CULPEPER | 3,665 | 1,775 | 1,886 | 4 | 111 D | 48.4% | 51.5% | 48.5% | 51.5% |
| 6,360 | CUMBERLAND | 1,977 | 1,099 | 871 | 7 | 228 R | 55.6% | 44.1% | 55.8% | 44.2% |
| 20,211 | DICKENSON | 5,639 | 2,143 | 3,485 | 11 | 1,342 D | 38.0% | 61.8% | 38.1% | 61.9% |
| 22,183 | DINWIDDIE | 4,285 | 2,096 | 2,182 | 7 | 86 D | 48.9% | 50.9% | 49.0% | 51.0% |
| 6,690 | ESSEX | 1,550 | 789 | 760 | 1 | 29 R | 50.9% | 49.0% | 50.9% | 49.1% |
| 261,417 | FAIRFAX COUNTY | 79,517 | 30,755 | 48,680 | 82 | 17,925 D | 38.7% | 61.2% | 38.7% | 61.3% |
| 24,066 | FAUQUIER | 5,613 | 2,101 | 3,506 | 6 | 1,405 D | 37.4% | 62.5% | 37.5% | 62.5% |
| 10,462 | FLOYD | 2,985 | 1,836 | 1,144 | 5 | 692 R | 61.5% | 38.3% | 61.6% | 38.4% |
| 7,227 | FLUVANNA | 1,834 | 823 | 1,008 | 3 | 185 D | 44.9% | 55.0% | 44.9% | 55.1% |
| 25,925 | FRANKLIN COUNTY | 5,737 | 2,279 | 3,447 | 11 | 1,168 D | 39.7% | 60.1% | 39.8% | 60.2% |
| 21,941 | FREDERICK | 5,474 | 2,585 | 2,880 | 9 | 295 D | 47.2% | 52.6% | 47.3% | 52.7% |
| 17,219 | GILES | 5,167 | 1,952 | 3,133 | 82 | 1,181 D | 37.8% | 60.6% | 38.4% | 61.6% |
| 11,919 | GLOUCESTER | 3,583 | 1,631 | 1,949 | 3 | 318 D | 45.5% | 54.4% | 45.6% | 54.4% |
| 9,206 | GOOCHLAND | 2,697 | 1,241 | 1,452 | 4 | 211 D | 46.0% | 53.8% | 46.1% | 53.9% |
| 17,390 | GRAYSON | 6,352 | 3,105 | 3,238 | 9 | 133 D | 48.9% | 51.0% | 49.0% | 51.0% |
| 4,715 | GREENE | 1,104 | 641 | 460 | 3 | 181 R | 58.1% | 41.7% | 58.2% | 41.8% |
| 16,155 | GREENSVILLE | 4,519 | 2,245 | 2,262 | 12 | 17 D | 49.7% | 50.1% | 49.8% | 50.2% |
| 33,637 | HALIFAX | 6,144 | 3,928 | 2,198 | 18 | 1,730 R | 63.9% | 35.8% | 64.1% | 35.9% |
| 27,550 | HANOVER | 7,751 | 4,879 | 2,864 | 8 | 2,015 R | 62.9% | 37.0% | 63.0% | 37.0% |
| 117,339 | HENRICO | 42,082 | 29,286 | 12,779 | 17 | 16,507 R | 69.6% | 30.4% | 69.6% | 30.4% |
| 40,335 | HENRY | 8,184 | 2,844 | 5,295 | 45 | 2,451 D | 34.8% | 64.7% | 34.9% | 65.1% |
| 3,221 | HIGHLAND | 989 | 511 | 476 | 2 | 35 R | 51.7% | 48.1% | 51.8% | 48.2% |
| 17,164 | ISLE OF WIGHT | 4,399 | 1,737 | 2,656 | 6 | 919 D | 39.5% | 60.4% | 39.5% | 60.5% |
| 11,539 | JAMES CITY | 2,839 | 1,092 | 1,744 | 3 | 652 D | 38.5% | 61.4% | 38.5% | 61.5% |
| 5,889 | KING AND QUEEN | 1,489 | 699 | 786 | 4 | 87 D | 46.9% | 52.8% | 47.1% | 52.9% |
| 7,243 | KING GEORGE | 1,729 | 644 | 1,085 | | 441 D | 37.2% | 62.8% | 37.2% | 62.8% |
| 7,563 | KING WILLIAM | 1,975 | 1,065 | 904 | 6 | 161 R | 53.9% | 45.8% | 54.1% | 45.9% |
| 9,174 | LANCASTER | 2,920 | 1,663 | 1,245 | 3 | 418 R | 57.0% | 42.6% | 57.2% | 42.8% |
| 25,824 | LEE | 8,619 | 3,463 | 5,151 | 12 | 1,688 D | 40.2% | 59.8% | 40.2% | 59.8% |
| 24,549 | LOUDOUN | 6,875 | 2,594 | 4,278 | 5 | 1,684 D | 37.7% | 62.2% | 37.7% | 62.3% |
| 12,959 | LOUISA | 3,102 | 1,369 | 1,731 | 3 | 362 D | 44.1% | 55.8% | 44.2% | 55.8% |
| 12,523 | LUNENBURG | 2,976 | 1,847 | 1,128 | 2 | 719 R | 62.1% | 37.9% | 62.1% | 37.9% |
| 8,187 | MADISON | 1,922 | 1,060 | 862 | 1 | 198 R | 55.2% | 44.8% | 55.2% | 44.8% |
| 7,121 | MATHEWS | 2,299 | 1,149 | 1,137 | | 12 R | 50.0% | 49.5% | 50.3% | 49.7% |
| 31,428 | MECKLENBURG | 8,217 | 4,976 | 3,238 | 13 | 1,738 R | 60.6% | 39.4% | 60.6% | 39.4% |
| 6,319 | MIDDLESEX | 2,005 | 1,019 | 973 | 3 | 46 R | 50.8% | 48.5% | 51.2% | 48.8% |
| 32,923 | MONTGOMERY | 8,482 | 4,604 | 3,872 | 13 | 732 R | 54.3% | 45.6% | 54.3% | 45.7% |

# VIRGINIA

## PRESIDENT 1964

| 1960 Census Population | County | Total Vote | Republican | Democratic | Other | Rep.-Dem. Plurality | Percentage | | | |
|---|---|---|---|---|---|---|---|---|---|---|
| | | | | | | | Total Vote | | Major Vote | |
| | | | | | | | Rep. | Dem. | Rep. | Dem. |
| 31,366 | NANSEMOND COUNTY | 7,398 | 2,590 | 4804 | 21 | 2,214 D | 35.0% | 64.9% | 35.0% | 65.0% |
| 12,752 | NELSON | 2,532 | 893 | 1,635 | 6 | 742 D | 35.3% | 64.6% | 35.3% | 64.7% |
| 4,504 | NEW KENT | 1,362 | 677 | 684 | 4 | 7 D | 49.7% | 50.2% | 49.7% | 50.3% |
| 16,966 | NORTHAMPTON | 3,109 | 1,586 | 1,516 | 1 | 70 R | 51.0% | 48.8% | 51.1% | 48.9% |
| 10,185 | NORTHUMBERLAND | 2,419 | 1,423 | 988 | 7 | 435 R | 58.8% | 40.8% | 59.0% | 41.0% |
| 15,141 | NOTTOWAY | 4,495 | 2,353 | 2,138 | 8 | 215 R | 52.3% | 47.6% | 52.4% | 47.6% |
| 12,900 | ORANGE | 3,112 | 1,595 | 1,508 | 4 | 87 R | 51.3% | 48.5% | 51.4% | 48.6% |
| 15,572 | PAGE | 5,412 | 2,804 | 2,606 | 9 | 198 R | 51.8% | 48.2% | 51.8% | 48.2% |
| 15,282 | PATRICK | 3,799 | 1,468 | 2,306 | 2 | 838 D | 38.6% | 60.7% | 38.9% | 61.1% |
| 58,296 | PITTSYLVANIA | 12,349 | 7,120 | 5,228 | 25 | 1,892 R | 57.7% | 42.3% | 57.7% | 42.3% |
| 6,747 | POWHATAN | 2,158 | 1,182 | 969 | 1 | 213 R | 54.8% | 44.9% | 55.0% | 45.0% |
| 14,121 | PRINCE EDWARD | 4,060 | 2,545 | 1,512 | 7 | 1,033 R | 62.7% | 37.2% | 62.7% | 37.3% |
| 20,270 | PRINCE GEORGE | 3,301 | 1,790 | 1,502 | 3 | 288 R | 54.2% | 45.5% | 54.4% | 45.6% |
| 50,164 | PRINCE WILLIAM | 8,959 | 3,343 | 5,611 | 9 | 2,268 D | 37.3% | 62.6% | 37.3% | 62.7% |
| 27,258 | PULASKI | 6,724 | 3,101 | 3,620 | 5 | 519 D | 46.1% | 53.8% | 46.1% | 53.9% |
| 5,368 | RAPPAHANNOCK | 1,127 | 449 | 675 | 3 | 226 D | 39.8% | 59.9% | 39.9% | 60.1% |
| 6,375 | RICHMOND COUNTY | 1,551 | 901 | 636 | 3 | 265 R | 58.1% | 41.0% | 58.6% | 41.4% |
| 61,693 | ROANOKE COUNTY | 19,529 | 10,714 | 8,808 | 14 | 1,906 R | 54.9% | 45.1% | 54.9% | 45.1% |
| 24,039 | ROCKBRIDGE | 4,802 | 2,200 | 2,599 | 7 | 399 D | 45.8% | 54.1% | 45.8% | 54.2% |
| 40,485 | ROCKINGHAM | 8,385 | 4,155 | 4,205 | 3 | 50 D | 49.6% | 50.1% | 49.7% | 50.3% |
| 26,290 | RUSSELL | 7,358 | 3,012 | 4,330 | 25 | 1,318 D | 40.9% | 58.8% | 41.0% | 59.0% |
| 25,813 | SCOTT | 9,256 | 4,533 | 4,720 | 16 | 187 D | 49.0% | 51.0% | 49.0% | 51.0% |
| 21,825 | SHENANDOAH | 7,174 | 3,981 | 3,184 | 3 | 797 R | 55.5% | 44.4% | 55.6% | 44.4% |
| 31,066 | SMYTH | 7,947 | 3,830 | 4,113 | 9 | 283 D | 48.2% | 51.8% | 48.2% | 51.8% |
| 19,931 | SOUTHAMPTON | 4,095 | 1,520 | 2,566 | 4 | 1,046 D | 37.1% | 62.7% | 37.2% | 62.8% |
| 13,819 | SPOTSYLVANIA | 3,365 | 1,261 | 2,097 | 9 | 836 D | 37.5% | 62.3% | 37.6% | 62.4% |
| 16,876 | STAFFORD | 4,362 | 1,888 | 2,469 | 7 | 581 D | 43.3% | 56.6% | 43.3% | 56.7% |
| 6,220 | SURRY | 2,139 | 1,004 | 1,131 | 5 | 127 D | 46.9% | 52.9% | 47.0% | 53.0% |
| 12,411 | SUSSEX | 2,876 | 1,537 | 1,234 | 4 | 303 R | 53.4% | 42.9% | 55.5% | 44.5% |
| 44,791 | TAZEWELL | 9,322 | 3,231 | 6,081 | 105 | 2,850 D | 34.7% | 65.2% | 34.7% | 65.3% |
| 14,655 | WARREN | 4,390 | 1,886 | 2,494 | 10 | 608 D | 43.0% | 56.8% | 43.1% | 56.9% |
| 38,076 | WASHINGTON | 9,222 | 4,146 | 5,070 | 10 | 924 D | 45.0% | 55.0% | 45.0% | 55.0% |
| 11,042 | WESTMORELAND | 2,503 | 1,181 | 1,312 | 6 | 131 D | 47.2% | 52.4% | 47.4% | 52.6% |
| 43,579 | WISE | 10,555 | 3,309 | 7,220 | 10 | 3,911 D | 31.4% | 68.4% | 31.4% | 68.6% |
| 21,975 | WYTHE | 5,849 | 2,958 | 2,879 | 26 | 79 R | 50.6% | 49.2% | 50.7% | 49.3% |
| 21,583 | YORK | 6,377 | 2,992 | 3,385 | 12 | 393 D | 46.9% | 53.1% | 46.9% | 53.1% |
| | City | | | | | | | | | |
| 91,023 | ALEXANDRIA | 25,683 | 8,825 | 16,828 | 30 | 8,003 D | 34.4% | 65.5% | 34.4% | 65.6% |
| 17,144 | BRISTOL | 3,723 | 1,289 | 2,429 | 5 | 1,140 D | 34.6% | 65.2% | 34.7% | 65.3% |
| 6,300 | BUENA VISTA | 1,153 | 459 | 691 | 3 | 232 D | 39.8% | 59.9% | 39.9% | 60.1% |
| 29,427 | CHARLOTTESVILLE | 9,704 | 4,415 | 5,205 | 84 | 790 D | 45.5% | 53.6% | 45.9% | 54.1% |
| 73,647 | CHESAPEAKE | 18,621 | 9,038 | 9,532 | 51 | 494 D | 48.5% | 51.2% | 48.7% | 51.3% |
| 5,268 | CLIFTON FORGE | 2,102 | 850 | 1,252 | | 402 D | 40.4% | 59.6% | 40.4% | 59.6% |
| 9,587 | COLONIAL HEIGHTS | 3,620 | 2,420 | 1,198 | 2 | 1,222 R | 66.9% | 33.1% | 66.9% | 33.1% |
| 11,062 | COVINGTON | 3,206 | 1,149 | 2,055 | 2 | 906 D | 35.8% | 64.1% | 35.9% | 64.1% |
| 46,577 | DANVILLE | 12,724 | 7,900 | 4,539 | 285 | 3,361 R | 62.1% | 35.7% | 63.5% | 36.5% |
| 13,585 | FAIRFAX CITY | 4,766 | 1,924 | 2,835 | 7 | 911 D | 40.4% | 59.5% | 40.4% | 59.6% |
| 10,192 | FALLS CHURCH | 3,707 | 1,329 | 2,371 | 7 | 1,042 D | 35.9% | 64.0% | 35.9% | 64.1% |
| 7,264 | FRANKLIN CITY | 2,041 | 783 | 1,257 | 1 | 474 D | 38.4% | 61.6% | 38.4% | 61.6% |
| 13,639 | FREDERICKSBURG | 3,928 | 1,511 | 2,410 | 7 | 899 D | 38.5% | 61.4% | 38.5% | 61.5% |
| 5,254 | GALAX | 1,416 | 697 | 717 | 2 | 20 D | 49.2% | 50.6% | 49.3% | 50.7% |
| 89,258 | HAMPTON | 22,288 | 8,731 | 13,542 | 15 | 4,811 D | 39.2% | 60.8% | 39.2% | 60.8% |
| 11,916 | HARRISONBURG | 3,590 | 1,820 | 1,765 | 5 | 55 R | 50.7% | 49.2% | 50.8% | 49.2% |
| 17,895 | HOPEWELL | 5,691 | 3,183 | 2,498 | 10 | 685 R | 55.9% | 43.9% | 56.0% | 44.0% |
| 54,790 | LYNCHBURG | 16,834 | 10,044 | 6,758 | 32 | 3,286 R | 59.7% | 40.1% | 59.8% | 40.2% |
| 18,798 | MARTINSVILLE | 4,824 | 1,805 | 2,943 | 76 | 1,138 D | 37.4% | 61.0% | 38.0% | 62.0% |
| 113,662 | NEWPORT NEWS | 25,894 | 10,584 | 15,296 | 14 | 4,712 D | 40.9% | 59.1% | 40.9% | 59.1% |

# VIRGINIA

## PRESIDENT 1964

| 1960 Census Population | City | Total Vote | Republican | Democratic | Other | Rep.-Dem. Plurality | Percentage | | | |
|---|---|---|---|---|---|---|---|---|---|---|
| | | | | | | | Total Vote | | Major Vote | |
| | | | | | | | Rep. | Dem. | Rep. | Dem. |
| 304,869 | NORFOLK | 51,546 | 18,429 | 32,388 | 729 | 13,959 D | 35.8% | 62.8% | 36.3% | 63.7% |
| 4,996 | NORTON | 1,196 | 372 | 824 | | 452 D | 31.1% | 68.9% | 31.1% | 68.9% |
| 36,750 | PETERSBURG | 7,775 | 3,253 | 4,521 | 1 | 1,268 D | 41.8% | 58.1% | 41.8% | 58.2% |
| 114,773 | PORTSMOUTH | 24,544 | 8,420 | 16,073 | 51 | 7,653 D | 34.3% | 65.5% | 34.4% | 65.6% |
| 9,371 | RADFORD | 3,358 | 1,505 | 1,850 | 3 | 345 D | 44.8% | 55.1% | 44.9% | 55.1% |
| 219,958 | RICHMOND CITY | 62,890 | 27,196 | 35,662 | 32 | 8,466 D | 43.2% | 56.7% | 43.3% | 56.7% |
| 97,110 | ROANOKE CITY | 28,496 | 13,164 | 15,314 | 18 | 2,150 D | 46.2% | 53.7% | 46.2% | 53.8% |
| 5,974 | SOUTH BOSTON | 1,843 | 1,206 | 636 | 1 | 570 R | 65.4% | 34.5% | 65.5% | 34.5% |
| 22,232 | STAUNTON | 5,680 | 2,969 | 2,705 | 6 | 264 R | 52.3% | 47.6% | 52.3% | 47.7% |
| 12,609 | SUFFOLK | 3,044 | 1,463 | 1,579 | 2 | 116 D | 48.1% | 51.9% | 48.1% | 51.9% |
| 85,218 | VIRGINIA BEACH | 23,442 | 10,529 | 12,892 | 21 | 2,363 D | 44.9% | 55.0% | 45.0% | 55.0% |
| 15,694 | WAYNESBORO | 4,531 | 2,107 | 2,369 | 55 | 262 D | 46.5% | 52.3% | 47.1% | 52.9% |
| 6,832 | WILLIAMSBURG | 2,093 | 906 | 1,171 | 16 | 265 D | 43.3% | 55.9% | 43.6% | 56.4% |
| 15,110 | WINCHESTER | 4,437 | 2,180 | 2,254 | 3 | 74 D | 49.1% | 50.8% | 49.2% | 50.8% |
| 3,966,949 | TOTAL | 1,042,267 | 481,334 | 558,038 | 2,895 | 76,704 D | 46.2% | 53.5% | 46.3% | 53.7% |

# VIRGINIA

## PRESIDENT 1960

| 1960 Census Population | County | Total Vote | Republican | Democratic | Other | Rep.-Dem. Plurality | Percentage Total Vote Rep. | Dem. | Major Vote Rep. | Dem. |
|---|---|---|---|---|---|---|---|---|---|---|
| 30,635 | ACCOMACK | 5,581 | 2,676 | 2,884 | 21 | 208 D | 47.9% | 51.7% | 48.1% | 51.9% |
| 30,969 | ALBEMARLE | 5,272 | 3,135 | 2,102 | 35 | 1,033 R | 59.5% | 39.9% | 59.9% | 40.1% |
| 12,128 | ALLEGHANY | 2,488 | 1,214 | 1,265 | 9 | 51 D | 48.8% | 50.8% | 49.0% | 51.0% |
| 7,815 | AMELIA | 1,524 | 784 | 708 | 32 | 76 R | 51.4% | 46.5% | 52.5% | 47.5% |
| 22,953 | AMHERST | 3,747 | 1,455 | 2,280 | 12 | 825 D | 38.8% | 60.8% | 39.0% | 61.0% |
| 9,148 | APPOMATTOX | 2,208 | 951 | 1,240 | 17 | 289 D | 43.1% | 56.2% | 43.4% | 56.6% |
| 163,401 | ARLINGTON | 45,977 | 23,632 | 22,095 | 250 | 1,537 R | 51.4% | 48.1% | 51.7% | 48.3% |
| 37,363 | AUGUSTA | 5,989 | 4,034 | 1,914 | 41 | 2,120 R | 67.4% | 32.0% | 67.8% | 32.2% |
| 5,335 | BATH | 1,277 | 646 | 629 | 2 | 17 R | 50.6% | 49.3% | 50.7% | 49.3% |
| 31,028 | BEDFORD COUNTY | 6,081 | 2,911 | 3,150 | 20 | 239 D | 47.9% | 51.8% | 48.0% | 52.0% |
| 5,982 | BLAND | 1,671 | 848 | 822 | 1 | 26 R | 50.7% | 49.2% | 50.8% | 49.2% |
| 16,715 | BOTETOURT | 3,802 | 2,159 | 1,621 | 22 | 538 R | 56.8% | 42.6% | 57.1% | 42.9% |
| 17,779 | BRUNSWICK | 2,932 | 926 | 1,942 | 64 | 1,016 D | 31.6% | 66.2% | 32.3% | 67.7% |
| 36,724 | BUCHANAN | 6,099 | 2,370 | 3,706 | 23 | 1,336 D | 38.9% | 60.8% | 39.0% | 61.0% |
| 10,877 | BUCKINGHAM | 1,724 | 765 | 947 | 12 | 182 D | 44.4% | 54.9% | 44.7% | 55.3% |
| 32,958 | CAMPBELL | 5,970 | 2,903 | 3,030 | 37 | 127 D | 48.6% | 50.8% | 48.9% | 51.1% |
| 12,725 | CAROLINE | 2,367 | 864 | 1,483 | 20 | 619 D | 36.5% | 62.7% | 36.8% | 63.2% |
| 23,178 | CARROLL | 5,589 | 3,705 | 1,873 | 11 | 1,832 R | 66.3% | 33.5% | 66.4% | 33.6% |
| 5,492 | CHARLES CITY | 964 | 337 | 623 | 4 | 286 D | 35.0% | 64.6% | 35.1% | 64.9% |
| 13,368 | CHARLOTTE | 2,635 | 867 | 1,735 | 33 | 868 D | 32.9% | 65.8% | 33.3% | 66.7% |
| 71,197 | CHESTERFIELD | 15,859 | 9,787 | 5,982 | 90 | 3,805 R | 61.7% | 37.7% | 62.1% | 37.9% |
| 7,942 | CLARKE | 1,736 | 804 | 923 | 9 | 119 D | 46.3% | 53.2% | 46.6% | 53.4% |
| 3,356 | CRAIG | 967 | 433 | 534 | | 101 D | 44.8% | 55.2% | 44.8% | 55.2% |
| 15,088 | CULPEPER | 2,971 | 1,630 | 1,332 | 9 | 298 R | 54.9% | 44.8% | 55.0% | 45.0% |
| 6,360 | CUMBERLAND | 1,262 | 691 | 559 | 12 | 132 R | 54.8% | 44.3% | 55.3% | 44.7% |
| 20,211 | DICKENSON | 4,960 | 2,203 | 2,756 | 1 | 553 D | 44.4% | 55.6% | 44.4% | 55.6% |
| 22,183 | DINWIDDIE | 2,686 | 935 | 1,714 | 37 | 779 D | 34.8% | 63.8% | 35.3% | 64.7% |
| 6,690 | ESSEX | 1,117 | 606 | 509 | 2 | 97 R | 54.3% | 45.6% | 54.3% | 45.7% |
| 275,002 | FAIRFAX COUNTY | 54,219 | 28,006 | 26,064 | 149 | 1,942 R | 51.7% | 48.1% | 51.8% | 48.2% |
| 24,066 | FAUQUIER | 4,094 | 2,123 | 1,958 | 13 | 165 R | 51.9% | 47.8% | 52.0% | 48.0% |
| 10,462 | FLOYD | 2,759 | 1,933 | 817 | 9 | 1,116 R | 70.1% | 29.6% | 70.3% | 29.7% |
| 7,227 | FLUVANNA | 1,390 | 763 | 614 | 13 | 149 R | 54.9% | 44.2% | 55.4% | 44.6% |
| 25,925 | FRANKLIN COUNTY | 5,016 | 2,080 | 2,924 | 12 | 844 D | 41.5% | 58.3% | 41.6% | 58.4% |
| 21,941 | FREDERICK | 3,835 | 2,061 | 1,757 | 17 | 304 R | 53.7% | 45.8% | 54.0% | 46.0% |
| 17,219 | GILES | 4,327 | 2,030 | 2,214 | 83 | 184 D | 46.9% | 51.2% | 47.8% | 52.2% |
| 11,919 | GLOUCESTER | 2,620 | 1,310 | 1,297 | 13 | 13 R | 50.0% | 49.5% | 50.2% | 49.8% |
| 9,206 | GOOCHLAND | 1,749 | 851 | 862 | 36 | 11 D | 48.7% | 49.3% | 49.7% | 50.3% |
| 17,390 | GRAYSON | 6,638 | 3,893 | 2,738 | 7 | 1,155 R | 58.6% | 41.2% | 58.7% | 41.3% |
| 4,715 | GREENE | 892 | 573 | 314 | 5 | 259 R | 64.2% | 35.2% | 64.6% | 35.4% |
| 16,155 | GREENSVILLE | 2,766 | 1,057 | 1,676 | 33 | 619 D | 38.2% | 60.6% | 38.7% | 61.3% |
| 33,637 | HALIFAX | 4,508 | 1,784 | 2,676 | 48 | 892 D | 39.6% | 59.4% | 40.0% | 60.0% |
| 27,550 | HANOVER | 5,085 | 3,020 | 2,023 | 42 | 997 R | 59.4% | 39.8% | 59.9% | 40.1% |
| 117,339 | HENRICO | 29,235 | 19,446 | 9,626 | 163 | 9,820 R | 66.5% | 32.9% | 66.9% | 33.1% |
| 40,335 | HENRY | 5,643 | 2,323 | 3,306 | 14 | 983 D | 41.2% | 58.6% | 41.3% | 58.7% |
| 3,221 | HIGHLAND | 932 | 527 | 401 | 4 | 126 R | 56.5% | 43.0% | 56.8% | 43.2% |
| 17,164 | ISLE OF WIGHT | 3,177 | 1,141 | 2,020 | 16 | 879 D | 35.9% | 63.6% | 36.1% | 63.9% |
| 11,539 | JAMES CITY | 1,729 | 873 | 845 | 11 | 28 R | 50.5% | 48.9% | 50.8% | 49.2% |
| 5,889 | KING AND QUEEN | 983 | 432 | 536 | 15 | 104 D | 43.9% | 54.5% | 44.6% | 55.4% |
| 7,243 | KING GEORGE | 1,410 | 685 | 717 | 8 | 32 D | 48.6% | 50.9% | 48.9% | 51.1% |
| 7,563 | KING WILLIAM | 1,549 | 793 | 745 | 11 | 48 R | 51.2% | 48.1% | 51.6% | 48.4% |
| 9,174 | LANCASTER | 2,250 | 1,340 | 895 | 15 | 445 R | 59.6% | 39.8% | 60.0% | 40.0% |
| 25,824 | LEE | 7,265 | 3,363 | 3,867 | 35 | 504 D | 46.3% | 53.2% | 46.5% | 53.5% |
| 24,549 | LOUDOUN | 4,954 | 2,526 | 2,399 | 29 | 127 R | 51.0% | 48.4% | 51.3% | 48.7% |
| 12,959 | LOUISA | 2,458 | 1,170 | 1,244 | 44 | 74 D | 47.6% | 50.6% | 48.5% | 51.5% |
| 12,523 | LUNENBURG | 2,379 | 838 | 1,451 | 90 | 613 D | 35.2% | 61.0% | 36.6% | 63.4% |
| 8,187 | MADISON | 1,653 | 998 | 636 | 19 | 362 R | 60.4% | 38.5% | 61.1% | 38.9% |
| 7,121 | MATHEWS | 1,754 | 1,069 | 682 | 3 | 387 R | 60.9% | 38.9% | 61.1% | 38.9% |
| 31,428 | MECKLENBURG | 4,534 | 1,936 | 2,533 | 65 | 597 D | 42.7% | 55.9% | 43.3% | 56.7% |
| 6,319 | MIDDLESEX | 1,402 | 823 | 574 | 5 | 249 R | 58.7% | 40.9% | 58.9% | 41.1% |
| 32,923 | MONTGOMERY | 6,445 | 4,270 | 2,157 | 18 | 2,113 R | 66.3% | 33.5% | 66.4% | 33.6% |

# VIRGINIA

## PRESIDENT 1960

| 1960 Census Population | County | Total Vote | Republican | Democratic | Other | Rep.-Dem. Plurality | Percentage Total Vote Rep. | Dem. | Major Vote Rep. | Dem. |
|---|---|---|---|---|---|---|---|---|---|---|
| 31,366 | NANSEMOND COUNTY | 5,323 | 1,346 | 3944 | 33 | 2,598 D | 25.3% | 74.1% | 25.4% | 74.6% |
| 12,752 | NELSON | 2,268 | 775 | 1,480 | 13 | 705 D | 34.2% | 65.3% | 34.4% | 65.6% |
| 4,504 | NEW KENT | 1,018 | 526 | 481 | 11 | 45 R | 51.7% | 47.2% | 52.2% | 47.8% |
| 51612 | NORFOLK COUNTY | 8,936 | 3769 | 5101 | 66 | 1,332 D | 42.2% | 57.1% | 42.5% | 57.5% |
| 16,966 | NORTHAMPTON | 2,392 | 995 | 1,387 | 10 | 392 D | 41.6% | 58.0% | 41.8% | 58.2% |
| 10,185 | NORTHUMBERLAND | 2,211 | 1,340 | 858 | 13 | 482 R | 60.6% | 38.8% | 61.0% | 39.0% |
| 15,141 | NOTTOWAY | 3,286 | 1,319 | 1,882 | 85 | 563 D | 40.1% | 57.3% | 41.2% | 58.8% |
| 12,900 | ORANGE | 2,603 | 1,413 | 1,108 | 82 | 305 R | 54.3% | 42.6% | 56.0% | 44.0% |
| 15,572 | PAGE | 4,331 | 2,708 | 1,608 | 15 | 1,100 R | 62.5% | 37.1% | 62.7% | 37.3% |
| 15,282 | PATRICK | 3,028 | 1,362 | 1,655 | 11 | 293 D | 45.0% | 54.7% | 45.1% | 54.9% |
| 58,296 | PITTSYLVANIA | 7,954 | 3,788 | 4,089 | 77 | 301 D | 47.6% | 51.4% | 48.1% | 51.9% |
| 6,747 | POWHATAN | 1,328 | 779 | 528 | 21 | 251 R | 58.7% | 39.8% | 59.6% | 40.4% |
| 14,121 | PRINCE EDWARD | 3,214 | 1,721 | 1,459 | 34 | 262 R | 53.5% | 45.4% | 54.1% | 45.9% |
| 20,270 | PRINCE GEORGE | 1,725 | 727 | 983 | 15 | 256 D | 42.1% | 57.0% | 42.5% | 57.5% |
| 50,164 | PRINCE WILLIAM | 5,639 | 2,624 | 2,987 | 28 | 363 D | 46.5% | 53.0% | 46.8% | 53.2% |
| 76,124 | PRINCESS ANNE | 10,843 | 4844 | 5954 | 45 | 1,110 D | 44.7% | 54.9% | 44.9% | 55.1% |
| 27,258 | PULASKI | 5,207 | 3,059 | 2,104 | 44 | 955 R | 58.7% | 40.4% | 59.2% | 40.8% |
| 5,368 | RAPPAHANNOCK | 975 | 426 | 544 | 5 | 118 D | 43.7% | 55.8% | 43.9% | 56.1% |
| 6,375 | RICHMOND COUNTY | 1,233 | 801 | 425 | 7 | 376 R | 65.0% | 34.5% | 65.3% | 34.7% |
| 61,693 | ROANOKE COUNTY | 13,532 | 9,109 | 4,384 | 39 | 4,725 R | 67.3% | 32.4% | 67.5% | 32.5% |
| 24,039 | ROCKBRIDGE | 3,585 | 2,170 | 1,405 | 10 | 765 R | 60.5% | 39.2% | 60.7% | 39.3% |
| 40,485 | ROCKINGHAM | 6,872 | 4,829 | 2,026 | 17 | 2,803 R | 70.3% | 29.5% | 70.4% | 29.6% |
| 26,290 | RUSSELL | 6,554 | 3,044 | 3,496 | 14 | 452 D | 46.4% | 53.3% | 46.5% | 53.5% |
| 25,813 | SCOTT | 8,744 | 4,936 | 3,789 | 19 | 1,147 R | 56.5% | 43.3% | 56.6% | 43.4% |
| 21,825 | SHENANDOAH | 6,199 | 4,144 | 2,053 | 2 | 2,091 R | 66.8% | 33.1% | 66.9% | 33.1% |
| 31,066 | SMYTH | 7,138 | 4,256 | 2,864 | 18 | 1,392 R | 59.6% | 40.1% | 59.8% | 40.2% |
| 27,195 | SOUTHAMPTON | 4,125 | 1,263 | 2,804 | 58 | 1,541 D | 30.6% | 68.0% | 31.1% | 68.9% |
| 13,819 | SPOTSYLVANIA | 2,799 | 1,288 | 1,482 | 29 | 194 D | 46.0% | 52.9% | 46.5% | 53.5% |
| 16,876 | STAFFORD | 2,965 | 1,447 | 1,494 | 24 | 47 D | 48.8% | 50.4% | 49.2% | 50.8% |
| 6,220 | SURRY | 1,443 | 397 | 1,003 | 43 | 606 D | 27.5% | 69.5% | 28.4% | 71.6% |
| 12,411 | SUSSEX | 1,993 | 713 | 1,253 | 27 | 540 D | 35.8% | 62.9% | 36.3% | 63.7% |
| 44,791 | TAZEWELL | 7,574 | 3,139 | 4,416 | 19 | 1,277 D | 41.4% | 58.3% | 41.5% | 58.5% |
| 14,655 | WARREN | 3,720 | 1,842 | 1,850 | 28 | 8 D | 49.5% | 49.7% | 49.9% | 50.1% |
| 38,076 | WASHINGTON | 8,347 | 4,473 | 3,833 | 41 | 640 R | 53.6% | 45.9% | 53.9% | 46.1% |
| 11,042 | WESTMORELAND | 2,219 | 1,176 | 1,034 | 9 | 142 R | 53.0% | 46.6% | 53.2% | 46.8% |
| 43,579 | WISE | 9,716 | 3,876 | 5,822 | 18 | 1,946 D | 39.9% | 59.9% | 40.0% | 60.0% |
| 21,975 | WYTHE | 4,993 | 2,871 | 2,075 | 47 | 796 R | 57.5% | 41.6% | 58.0% | 42.0% |
| 21,583 | YORK | 3,795 | 2,085 | 1,691 | 19 | 394 R | 54.9% | 44.6% | 55.2% | 44.8% |
| | **City** | | | | | | | | | |
| 91,023 | ALEXANDRIA | 18,551 | 8,826 | 9,662 | 63 | 836 D | 47.6% | 52.1% | 47.7% | 52.3% |
| 17,144 | BRISTOL | 3,299 | 1,728 | 1,561 | 10 | 167 R | 52.4% | 47.3% | 52.5% | 47.5% |
| 6,300 | BUENA VISTA | 918 | 487 | 427 | 4 | 60 R | 53.1% | 46.5% | 53.3% | 46.7% |
| 29,427 | CHARLOTTESVILLE | 6,628 | 3,651 | 2,894 | 83 | 757 R | 55.1% | 43.7% | 55.8% | 44.2% |
| 5,268 | CLIFTON FORGE | 1,663 | 885 | 771 | 7 | 114 R | 53.2% | 46.4% | 53.4% | 46.6% |
| 9,587 | COLONIAL HEIGHTS | 2,581 | 1,372 | 1,198 | 11 | 174 R | 53.2% | 46.4% | 53.4% | 46.6% |
| 11,062 | COVINGTON | 3,001 | 1,436 | 1,558 | 7 | 122 D | 47.9% | 51.9% | 48.0% | 52.0% |
| 46,577 | DANVILLE | 7,794 | 4,966 | 2,611 | 217 | 2,355 R | 63.7% | 33.5% | 65.5% | 34.5% |
| 10,192 | FALLS CHURCH | 3,165 | 1,525 | 1,629 | 11 | 104 D | 48.2% | 51.5% | 48.4% | 51.6% |
| 13,639 | FREDERICKSBURG | 2,915 | 1,566 | 1,326 | 23 | 240 R | 53.7% | 45.5% | 54.1% | 45.9% |
| 5,254 | GALAX | 1,377 | 867 | 508 | 2 | 359 R | 63.0% | 36.9% | 63.1% | 36.9% |
| 89,258 | HAMPTON | 14,808 | 7,623 | 7,133 | 52 | 490 R | 51.5% | 48.2% | 51.7% | 48.3% |
| 11,916 | HARRISONBURG | 3,015 | 2,172 | 836 | 7 | 1,336 R | 72.0% | 27.7% | 72.2% | 27.8% |
| 17,895 | HOPEWELL | 3,999 | 2,169 | 1,805 | 25 | 364 R | 54.2% | 45.1% | 54.6% | 45.4% |
| 54,790 | LYNCHBURG | 12,256 | 7,271 | 4,961 | 24 | 2,310 R | 59.3% | 40.5% | 59.4% | 40.6% |
| 18,798 | MARTINSVILLE | 3,517 | 1,729 | 1,699 | 89 | 30 R | 49.2% | 48.3% | 50.4% | 49.6% |
| 113,662 | NEWPORT NEWS | 18,855 | 10,098 | 8,678 | 79 | 1,420 R | 53.6% | 46.0% | 53.8% | 46.2% |
| 305,872 | NORFOLK | 39,473 | 17,174 | 22,037 | 262 | 4,863 D | 43.5% | 55.8% | 43.8% | 56.2% |
| 4,996 | NORTON | 1,076 | 549 | 526 | 1 | 23 R | 51.0% | 48.9% | 51.1% | 48.9% |
| 36,750 | PETERSBURG | 5,803 | 2,820 | 2,950 | 33 | 130 D | 48.6% | 50.8% | 48.9% | 51.1% |

# VIRGINIA

## PRESIDENT 1960

| 1960 Census Population | City | Total Vote | Republican | Democratic | Other | Rep.-Dem. Plurality | Percentage | | | |
|---|---|---|---|---|---|---|---|---|---|---|
| | | | | | | | Total Vote | | Major Vote | |
| | | | | | | | Rep. | Dem. | Rep. | Dem. |
| 114,773 | PORTSMOUTH | 16,980 | 6,900 | 9,902 | 178 | 3,002 D | 40.6% | 58.3% | 41.1% | 58.9% |
| 9,371 | RADFORD | 2,912 | 1,663 | 1,240 | 9 | 423 R | 57.1% | 42.6% | 57.3% | 42.7% |
| 219,958 | RICHMOND CITY | 45,205 | 27,307 | 17,642 | 256 | 9,665 R | 60.4% | 39.0% | 60.8% | 39.2% |
| 97,110 | ROANOKE CITY | 24,453 | 15,229 | 9,175 | 49 | 6,054 R | 62.3% | 37.5% | 62.4% | 37.6% |
| 5,974 | SOUTH BOSTON | 1,287 | 807 | 477 | 3 | 330 R | 62.7% | 37.1% | 62.9% | 37.1% |
| 22,035 | SOUTH NORFOLK | 3,521 | 1341 | 2155 | 25 | 814 D | 38.1% | 61.2% | 38.4% | 61.6% |
| 22,232 | STAUNTON | 4,032 | 2,789 | 1,233 | 10 | 1,556 R | 69.2% | 30.6% | 69.3% | 30.7% |
| 12,609 | SUFFOLK | 2,834 | 1,406 | 1,419 | 9 | 13 D | 49.6% | 50.1% | 49.8% | 50.2% |
| 8,091 | VIRGINIA BEACH | 2,321 | 986 | 1,301 | 34 | 315 D | 42.5% | 56.1% | 43.1% | 56.9% |
| 15,694 | WAYNESBORO | 3,513 | 2,444 | 1,047 | 22 | 1,397 R | 69.6% | 29.8% | 70.0% | 30.0% |
| 6,832 | WILLIAMSBURG | 1,220 | 721 | 486 | 13 | 235 R | 59.1% | 39.8% | 59.7% | 40.3% |
| 15,110 | WINCHESTER | 3,545 | 2,326 | 1,203 | 16 | 1,123 R | 65.6% | 33.9% | 65.9% | 34.1% |
| 3,966,949 | TOTAL | 771,449 | 404,521 | 362,327 | 4,601 | 42,194 R | 52.4% | 47.0% | 52.8% | 47.2% |

# VIRGINIA

Under Virginia's local government system a number of urban areas are organized as cities independent of county authority. The number of these cities is subject to change and their boundaries alter from year to year. There were 32 independent cities voting in the 1960 election, 34 in 1964, 38 in 1968, 39 in 1972, 41 in the 1976 through 1992 elections, and 40 in the 1996 and 2000 elections. Only the cities and counties that voted in each Presidential election are carried in the tables. Before the 1964 election Fairfax city was created from part of Fairfax county, Franklin city was created from part of Southampton county and Norfolk county and South Norfolk city were combined to form the new Chesapeake city. Before the 1968 election Princess Ann county and Virginia Beach city merged and became the new Virginia Beach city, Emporia city was created from part of Greensville county, Lexington city was created from part of Rockbridge county and Salem city was created from part of Roanoke county. Before the 1972 election the independent city of Nansemond was created from Nansemond county. Before the 1976 election Nansemond city and Suffolk city merged and became the new Suffolk city, Manassas and Manassas Park cities were created from parts of Prince William county and Poquoson city was created from part of York county.

## ELECTION NOTES

**2004**   Other vote was 11,032 Libertarian (Michael Badnarik); 10,161 Constitution (Michael Peroutka); 2,393 write-in (Ralph Nader); 104 write-in (David Cobb); 23 write-in (Walter F. Brown); 1 write-in (Joseph Spence); 2,952 scattered write-in.

**2000**   Other vote was 15,198 Libertarian (Browne); 5,455 Reform (Buchanan); 1,809 Constitution (Phillips); 171 write-in (Hagelin); 2,636 scattered write-in.

**1996**   Other vote was 13,687 Taxpayers (Phillips); 9,174 Libertarian (Browne); 4,510 Natural Law (Hagelin).

**1992**   Other vote was 11,937 LaRouche (Independent); 5,730 Marrou (Libertarian); 3,192 Fulani (Independent).

**1988**   Other vote was 14,312 Fulani (Independent); 8,336 Paul (Libertarian).

**1984**   Other vote was LaRouche (Independent).

**1980**   Other vote was 95,418 Anderson (Independent); 14,024 Commoner (Independent); 12,821 Clark (Libertarian); 1,986 DeBerry (Independent).

**1976**   Other vote was 17,802 Camejo (Socialist Workers); 16,686 Anderson (American); 7,508 LaRouche (U.S. Labor); 4,648 MacBride (Libertarian).

**1972**   Other vote was 19,721 Schmitz (American); 9,918 Fisher (Socialist Labor).

**1968**   Wallace on the ballot as American Independent. Other vote was 4,671 Blomen (Socialist Labor); 1,680 Gregory (Peace and Freedom); 601 Munn (Prohibition). The county-by-county table and the statewide vote for Wallace include 1,561 American Independent votes cast in Shenandoah county not reported on state canvass.

**1964**   Other vote was Hass (Socialist Labor).

**1960**   Other vote was 4,204 Coiner (Virginia Conservative); 397 Hass (Socialist Labor).

# WASHINGTON

## POPULAR VOTE FOR PRESIDENT 1920 TO 2004

| Year | Total Vote | Republican Vote | Candidate | Democratic Vote | Candidate | Other Vote | Plurality | Total Vote Rep. | Dem. | Major Vote Rep. | Dem. |
|------|-----------|-----------------|-----------|-----------------|-----------|------------|-----------|------|------|------|------|
| 2004 | 2,859,084 | 1,304,894 | Bush, George W. | 1,510,201 | Kerry, John | 43,989 | 205,307 D | 45.6% | 52.8% | 46.4% | 53.6% |
| 2000 ** | 2,487,433 | 1,108,864 | Bush, George W. | 1,247,652 | Gore, Al | 130,917 | 138,788 D | 44.6% | 50.2% | 47.1% | 52.9% |
| 1996 ** | 2,253,837 | 840,712 | Dole, Bob | 1,123,323 | Clinton, Bill | 289,802 | 282,611 D | 37.3% | 49.8% | 42.8% | 57.2% |
| 1992 ** | 2,288,230 | 731,234 | Bush, George | 993,037 | Clinton, Bill | 563,959 | 261,803 D | 32.0% | 43.4% | 42.4% | 57.6% |
| 1988 | 1,865,253 | 903,835 | Bush, George | 933,516 | Dukakis, Michael S. | 27,902 | 29,681 D | 48.5% | 50.0% | 49.2% | 50.8% |
| 1984 | 1,883,910 | 1,051,670 | Reagan, Ronald | 807,352 | Mondale, Walter F. | 24,888 | 244,318 R | 55.8% | 42.9% | 56.6% | 43.4% |
| 1980** | 1,742,394 | 865,244 | Reagan, Ronald | 650,193 | Carter, Jimmy | 226,957 | 215,051 R | 49.7% | 37.3% | 57.1% | 42.9% |
| 1976 | 1,555,534 | 777,732 | Ford, Gerald R. | 717,323 | Carter, Jimmy | 60,479 | 60,409 R | 50.0% | 46.1% | 52.0% | 48.0% |
| 1972 | 1,470,847 | 837,135 | Nixon, Richard M. | 568,334 | McGovern, George S. | 65,378 | 268,801 R | 56.9% | 38.6% | 59.6% | 40.4% |
| 1968 | 1,304,281 | 588,510 | Nixon, Richard M. | 616,037 | Humphrey, Hubert H. | 99,734 | 27,527 D | 45.1% | 47.2% | 48.9% | 51.1% |
| 1964 | 1,258,556 | 470,366 | Goldwater, Barry M. | 779,881 | Johnson, Lyndon B. | 8,309 | 309,515 D | 37.4% | 62.0% | 37.6% | 62.4% |
| 1960 | 1,241,572 | 629,273 | Nixon, Richard M. | 599,298 | Kennedy, John F. | 13,001 | 29,975 R | 50.7% | 48.3% | 51.2% | 48.8% |
| 1956 | 1,150,889 | 620,430 | Eisenhower, Dwight D. | 523,002 | Stevenson, Adlai E. | 7,457 | 97,428 R | 53.9% | 45.4% | 54.3% | 45.7% |
| 1952 | 1,102,708 | 599,107 | Eisenhower, Dwight D. | 492,845 | Stevenson, Adlai E. | 10,756 | 106,262 R | 54.3% | 44.7% | 54.9% | 45.1% |
| 1948 | 905,058 | 386,314 | Dewey, Thomas E. | 476,165 | Truman, Harry S. | 42,579 | 89,851 D | 42.7% | 52.6% | 44.8% | 55.2% |
| 1944 | 856,328 | 361,689 | Dewey, Thomas E. | 486,774 | Roosevelt, Franklin D. | 7,865 | 125,085 D | 42.2% | 56.8% | 42.6% | 57.4% |
| 1940 | 793,833 | 322,123 | Willkie, Wendell | 462,145 | Roosevelt, Franklin D. | 9,565 | 140,022 D | 40.6% | 58.2% | 41.1% | 58.9% |
| 1936 | 692,338 | 206,892 | Landon, Alfred M. | 459,579 | Roosevelt, Franklin D. | 25,867 | 252,687 D | 29.9% | 66.4% | 31.0% | 69.0% |
| 1932 | 614,814 | 208,645 | Hoover, Herbert C. | 353,260 | Roosevelt, Franklin D. | 52,909 | 144,615 D | 33.9% | 57.5% | 37.1% | 62.9% |
| 1928 | 500,840 | 335,844 | Hoover, Herbert C. | 156,772 | Smith, Alfred E. | 8,224 | 179,072 R | 67.1% | 31.3% | 68.2% | 31.8% |
| 1924 ** | 421,549 | 220,224 | Coolidge, Calvin | 42,842 | Davis, John W. | 158,483 | 69,497 R | 52.2% | 10.2% | 83.7% | 16.3% |
| 1920 ** | 398,715 | 223,137 | Harding, Warren G. | 84,298 | Cox, James M. | 91,280 | 138,839 R | 56.0% | 21.1% | 72.6% | 27.4% |

In 2000 the other vote column includes 103,002 votes cast for Green (Nader). In 1996 the other vote column includes 201,003 votes cast for Perot. In 1992 the other vote column includes 541,780 votes cast for Perot. In 1980 the other column includes 185,073 votes for Independent (Anderson). In 1924, the other vote was 150,727 Progressive; 5,991 American; 1,004 Socialist Labor and 761 Communist. In 1920 the other vote was 77,246 Farmer-Labor; 8,913 Socialist; 3,800 Prohibition; and 1,321 Socialist Labor.

## ELECTORAL COLLEGE VOTE 1920 TO 2004

| Year | Total | Republican | Democratic | Other |
|------|-------|-----------|-----------|-------|
| 2004 | 11 | | 11 | |
| 2000 | 11 | | 11 | |
| 1996 | 11 | | 11 | |
| 1992 | 11 | | 11 | |
| 1988 | 10 | | 10 | |
| 1984 | 10 | 10 | | |
| 1980 | 9 | 9 | | |
| 1976 ** | 9 | 8 | | 1 REAGAN |
| 1972 | 9 | 9 | | |
| 1968 | 9 | | 9 | |
| 1964 | 9 | | 9 | |
| 1960 | 9 | 9 | | |
| 1956 | 9 | 9 | | |
| 1952 | 9 | 9 | | |
| 1948 | 8 | — | 8 | |
| 1944 | 8 | — | 8 | |
| 1940 | 8 | — | 8 | |
| 1936 | 8 | — | 8 | |
| 1932 | 8 | — | 8 | |
| 1928 | 7 | 7 | | |
| 1924 | 7 | 7 | | |
| 1920 | 7 | 7 | | |

In 1976 one of the nine Republican electors voted in the Electoral College for Ronald Reagan and Bob Dole rather than for the national Republican candidates.

# WASHINGTON

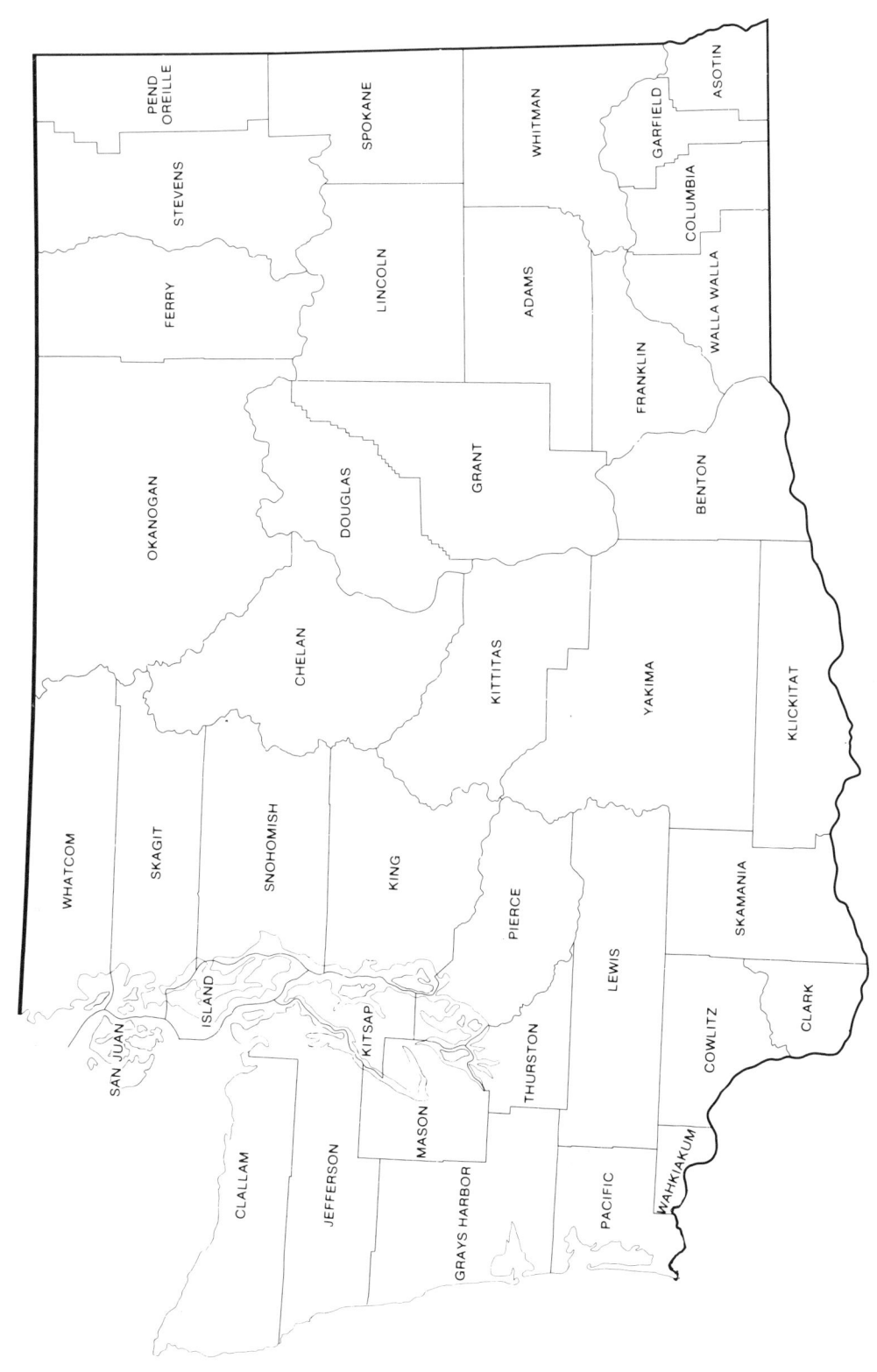

# WASHINGTON

## PRESIDENT 2004

| 2000 Census Population | County | Total Vote | Republican | Democratic | Other | Rep.-Dem. Plurality | Percentage | | | |
|---|---|---|---|---|---|---|---|---|---|---|
| | | | | | | | Total Vote | | Major Vote | |
| | | | | | | | Rep. | Dem. | Rep. | Dem. |
| 16,428 | ADAMS | 5,127 | 3,751 | 1,315 | 61 | 2,436 R | 73.2% | 25.6% | 74.0% | 26.0% |
| 20,551 | ASOTIN | 8,786 | 5,320 | 3,319 | 147 | 2,001 R | 60.6% | 37.8% | 61.6% | 38.4% |
| 142,475 | BENTON | 66,886 | 44,350 | 21,549 | 987 | 22,801 R | 66.3% | 32.2% | 67.3% | 32.7% |
| 66,616 | CHELAN | 29,396 | 18,482 | 10,471 | 443 | 8,011 R | 62.9% | 35.6% | 63.8% | 36.2% |
| 64,525 | CLALLAM | 36,766 | 18,871 | 17,049 | 846 | 1,822 R | 51.3% | 46.4% | 52.5% | 47.5% |
| 345,238 | CLARK | 170,439 | 88,646 | 79,538 | 2,255 | 9,108 R | 52.0% | 46.7% | 52.7% | 47.3% |
| 4,064 | COLUMBIA | 2,107 | 1,470 | 605 | 32 | 865 R | 69.8% | 28.7% | 70.8% | 29.2% |
| 92,948 | COWLITZ | 42,473 | 20,217 | 21,589 | 667 | 1,372 D | 47.6% | 50.8% | 48.4% | 51.6% |
| 32,603 | DOUGLAS | 13,372 | 8,900 | 4,306 | 166 | 4,594 R | 66.6% | 32.2% | 67.4% | 32.6% |
| 7,260 | FERRY | 3,341 | 2,019 | 1,201 | 121 | 818 R | 60.4% | 35.9% | 62.7% | 37.3% |
| 49,347 | FRANKLIN | 16,159 | 10,757 | 5,188 | 214 | 5,569 R | 66.6% | 32.1% | 67.5% | 32.5% |
| 2,397 | GARFIELD | 1,320 | 935 | 365 | 20 | 570 R | 70.8% | 27.7% | 71.9% | 28.1% |
| 74,698 | GRANT | 25,995 | 17,799 | 7,779 | 417 | 10,020 R | 68.5% | 29.9% | 69.6% | 30.4% |
| 67,194 | GRAYS HARBOR | 27,953 | 12,871 | 14,583 | 499 | 1,712 D | 46.0% | 52.2% | 46.9% | 53.1% |
| 71,558 | ISLAND | 38,559 | 19,754 | 18,216 | 589 | 1,538 R | 51.2% | 47.2% | 52.0% | 48.0% |
| 25,953 | JEFFERSON | 18,616 | 6,650 | 11,610 | 356 | 4,960 D | 35.7% | 62.4% | 36.4% | 63.6% |
| 1,737,034 | KING | 893,534 | 301,043 | 580,378 | 12,113 | 279,335 D | 33.7% | 65.0% | 34.2% | 65.8% |
| 231,969 | KITSAP | 118,453 | 55,608 | 60,796 | 2,049 | 5,188 D | 46.9% | 51.3% | 47.8% | 52.2% |
| 33,362 | KITTITAS | 16,084 | 9,052 | 6,731 | 301 | 2,321 R | 56.3% | 41.8% | 57.4% | 42.6% |
| 19,161 | KLICKITAT | 9,237 | 5,016 | 4,036 | 185 | 980 R | 54.3% | 43.7% | 55.4% | 44.6% |
| 68,600 | LEWIS | 32,428 | 21,042 | 10,726 | 660 | 10,316 R | 64.9% | 33.1% | 66.2% | 33.8% |
| 10,184 | LINCOLN | 5,811 | 4,015 | 1,706 | 90 | 2,309 R | 69.1% | 29.4% | 70.2% | 29.8% |
| 49,405 | MASON | 25,394 | 11,987 | 12,894 | 513 | 907 D | 47.2% | 50.8% | 48.2% | 51.8% |
| 39,564 | OKANOGAN | 16,342 | 9,636 | 6,309 | 397 | 3,327 R | 59.0% | 38.6% | 60.4% | 39.6% |
| 20,984 | PACIFIC | 10,431 | 4,634 | 5,570 | 227 | 936 D | 44.4% | 53.4% | 45.4% | 54.6% |
| 11,732 | PEND OREILLE | 6,198 | 3,693 | 2,310 | 195 | 1,383 R | 59.6% | 37.3% | 61.5% | 38.5% |
| 700,820 | PIERCE | 313,331 | 150,783 | 158,231 | 4,317 | 7,448 D | 48.1% | 50.5% | 48.8% | 51.2% |
| 14,077 | SAN JUAN | 10,088 | 3,290 | 6,589 | 209 | 3,299 D | 32.6% | 65.3% | 33.3% | 66.7% |
| 102,979 | SKAGIT | 52,230 | 26,139 | 25,131 | 960 | 1,008 R | 50.0% | 48.1% | 51.0% | 49.0% |
| 9,872 | SKAMANIA | 5,159 | 2,695 | 2,374 | 90 | 321 R | 52.2% | 46.0% | 53.2% | 46.8% |
| 606,024 | SNOHOMISH | 294,997 | 134,317 | 156,468 | 4,212 | 22,151 D | 45.5% | 53.0% | 46.2% | 53.8% |
| 417,939 | SPOKANE | 202,587 | 111,606 | 87,490 | 3,491 | 24,116 R | 55.1% | 43.2% | 56.1% | 43.9% |
| 40,066 | STEVENS | 20,340 | 13,015 | 6,822 | 503 | 6,193 R | 64.0% | 33.5% | 65.6% | 34.4% |
| 207,355 | THURSTON | 112,789 | 47,992 | 62,650 | 2,147 | 14,658 D | 42.6% | 55.5% | 43.4% | 56.6% |
| 3,824 | WAHKIAKUM | 2,235 | 1,171 | 1,021 | 43 | 150 R | 52.4% | 45.7% | 53.4% | 46.6% |
| 55,180 | WALLA WALLA | 22,925 | 14,323 | 8,257 | 345 | 6,066 R | 62.5% | 36.0% | 63.4% | 36.6% |
| 166,814 | WHATCOM | 90,394 | 40,296 | 48,268 | 1,830 | 7,972 D | 44.6% | 53.4% | 45.5% | 54.5% |
| 40,740 | WHITMAN | 18,012 | 9,397 | 8,287 | 328 | 1,110 R | 52.2% | 46.0% | 53.1% | 46.9% |
| 222,581 | YAKIMA | 72,790 | 43,352 | 28,474 | 964 | 14,878 R | 59.6% | 39.1% | 60.4% | 39.6% |
| 5,894,121 | TOTAL | 2,859,084 | 1,304,894 | 1,510,201 | 43,989 | 205,307 D | 45.6% | 52.8% | 46.4% | 53.6% |

# WASHINGTON

## PRESIDENT 2000

| 2000 Census Population | County | Total Vote | Republican | Democratic | Green (Nader) | Other | Rep.-Dem. Plurality | Percentage of Total Vote | | |
|---|---|---|---|---|---|---|---|---|---|---|
| | | | | | | | | Rep. | Dem. | Green |
| 16,428 | ADAMS | 4,974 | 3,440 | 1,406 | 85 | 43 | 2,034 R | 69.2% | 28.3% | 1.7% |
| 20,551 | ASOTIN | 7,985 | 4,909 | 2,736 | 215 | 125 | 2,173 R | 61.5% | 34.3% | 2.7% |
| 142,475 | BENTON | 59,779 | 38,367 | 19,512 | 1,102 | 798 | 18,855 R | 64.2% | 32.6% | 1.8% |
| 66,616 | CHELAN | 26,517 | 16,980 | 8,412 | 850 | 275 | 8,568 R | 64.0% | 31.7% | 3.2% |
| 64,525 | CLALLAM | 32,232 | 16,251 | 13,779 | 1,603 | 599 | 2,472 R | 50.4% | 42.7% | 5.0% |
| 345,238 | CLARK | 135,544 | 67,219 | 61,767 | 5,140 | 1,418 | 5,452 R | 49.6% | 45.6% | 3.8% |
| 4,064 | COLUMBIA | 2,107 | 1,523 | 515 | 45 | 24 | 1,008 R | 72.3% | 24.4% | 2.1% |
| 92,948 | COWLITZ | 36,962 | 16,873 | 18,233 | 1,429 | 427 | 1,360 D | 45.6% | 49.3% | 3.9% |
| 32,603 | DOUGLAS | 12,855 | 8,512 | 3,822 | 339 | 182 | 4,690 R | 66.2% | 29.7% | 2.6% |
| 7,260 | FERRY | 3,038 | 1,896 | 932 | 117 | 93 | 964 R | 62.4% | 30.7% | 3.9% |
| 49,347 | FRANKLIN | 13,614 | 8,594 | 4,653 | 210 | 157 | 3,941 R | 63.1% | 34.2% | 1.5% |
| 2,397 | GARFIELD | 1,329 | 982 | 300 | 35 | 12 | 682 R | 73.9% | 22.6% | 2.6% |
| 74,698 | GRANT | 23,798 | 15,830 | 7,073 | 528 | 367 | 8,757 R | 66.5% | 29.7% | 2.2% |
| 67,194 | GRAYS HARBOR | 25,972 | 11,225 | 13,304 | 1,059 | 384 | 2,079 D | 43.2% | 51.2% | 4.1% |
| 71,558 | ISLAND | 33,004 | 16,408 | 14,778 | 1,484 | 334 | 1,630 R | 49.7% | 44.8% | 4.5% |
| 25,953 | JEFFERSON | 15,833 | 6,095 | 8,281 | 1,241 | 216 | 2,186 D | 38.5% | 52.3% | 7.8% |
| 1,737,034 | KING | 794,196 | 273,171 | 476,700 | 37,383 | 6,942 | 203,529 D | 34.4% | 60.0% | 4.7% |
| 231,969 | KITSAP | 102,596 | 46,427 | 50,302 | 4,607 | 1,260 | 3,875 D | 45.3% | 49.0% | 4.5% |
| 33,362 | KITTITAS | 14,086 | 7,727 | 5,516 | 644 | 199 | 2,211 R | 54.9% | 39.2% | 4.6% |
| 19,161 | KLICKITAT | 8,159 | 4,557 | 3,062 | 396 | 144 | 1,495 R | 55.9% | 37.5% | 4.9% |
| 68,600 | LEWIS | 29,986 | 18,565 | 9,891 | 980 | 550 | 8,674 R | 61.9% | 33.0% | 3.3% |
| 10,184 | LINCOLN | 5,197 | 3,546 | 1,417 | 160 | 74 | 2,129 R | 68.2% | 27.3% | 3.1% |
| 49,405 | MASON | 22,480 | 10,257 | 10,876 | 1,029 | 318 | 619 D | 45.6% | 48.4% | 4.6% |
| 39,564 | OKANOGAN | 14,798 | 9,384 | 4,335 | 722 | 357 | 5,049 R | 63.4% | 29.3% | 4.9% |
| 20,984 | PACIFIC | 9,519 | 4,042 | 4,895 | 447 | 135 | 853 D | 42.5% | 51.4% | 4.7% |
| 11,732 | PEND OREILLE | 5,438 | 3,076 | 1,973 | 234 | 155 | 1,103 R | 56.6% | 36.3% | 4.3% |
| 700,820 | PIERCE | 268,427 | 118,431 | 138,249 | 8,749 | 2,998 | 19,818 D | 44.1% | 51.5% | 3.3% |
| 14,077 | SAN JUAN | 8,407 | 3,005 | 4,426 | 875 | 101 | 1,421 D | 35.7% | 52.6% | 10.4% |
| 102,979 | SKAGIT | 45,221 | 22,163 | 20,432 | 2,070 | 556 | 1,731 R | 49.0% | 45.2% | 4.6% |
| 9,872 | SKAMANIA | 4,249 | 2,151 | 1,753 | 252 | 93 | 398 R | 50.6% | 41.3% | 5.9% |
| 606,024 | SNOHOMISH | 250,967 | 109,615 | 129,612 | 9,023 | 2,717 | 19,997 D | 43.7% | 51.6% | 3.6% |
| 417,939 | SPOKANE | 172,112 | 89,299 | 74,604 | 6,250 | 1,959 | 14,695 R | 51.9% | 43.3% | 3.6% |
| 40,066 | STEVENS | 17,999 | 11,299 | 5,560 | 700 | 440 | 5,739 R | 62.8% | 30.9% | 3.9% |
| 207,355 | THURSTON | 97,422 | 39,924 | 50,467 | 5,792 | 1,239 | 10,543 D | 41.0% | 51.8% | 5.9% |
| 3,824 | WAHKIAKUM | 1,973 | 1,033 | 803 | 97 | 40 | 230 R | 52.4% | 40.7% | 4.9% |
| 55,180 | WALLA WALLA | 21,365 | 13,304 | 7,188 | 624 | 249 | 6,116 R | 62.3% | 33.6% | 2.9% |
| 166,814 | WHATCOM | 73,757 | 34,287 | 34,033 | 4,502 | 935 | 254 R | 46.5% | 46.1% | 6.1% |
| 40,740 | WHITMAN | 16,237 | 9,003 | 6,509 | 530 | 195 | 2,494 R | 55.4% | 40.1% | 3.3% |
| 222,581 | YAKIMA | 67,299 | 39,494 | 25,546 | 1,454 | 805 | 13,948 R | 58.7% | 38.0% | 2.2% |
| 5,894,121 | TOTAL | 2,487,433 | 1,108,864 | 1,247,652 | 103,002 | 27,915 | 138,788 D | 44.6% | 50.2% | 4.1% |

# WASHINGTON

## PRESIDENT 1996

| 1995 Census Pop. Est. | County | Total Vote | Republican | Democratic | Reform (Perot) | Other | Rep.-Dem. Plurality | Percentage of Total Vote | | |
|---|---|---|---|---|---|---|---|---|---|---|
| | | | | | | | | Rep. | Dem. | Reform |
| 15,150 | ADAMS | 4,614 | 2,356 | 1,740 | 448 | 70 | 616 R | 51.1% | 37.7% | 9.7% |
| 20,252 | ASOTIN | 7,311 | 2,860 | 3,349 | 936 | 166 | 489 D | 39.1% | 45.8% | 12.8% |
| 133,070 | BENTON | 53,803 | 26,664 | 20,783 | 5,311 | 1,045 | 5,881 R | 49.6% | 38.6% | 9.9% |
| 57,854 | CHELAN | 23,870 | 12,363 | 8,595 | 2,332 | 580 | 3,768 R | 51.8% | 36.0% | 9.8% |
| 62,504 | CLALLAM | 29,516 | 12,432 | 12,585 | 3,187 | 1,312 | 153 D | 42.1% | 42.6% | 10.8% |
| 292,272 | CLARK | 112,730 | 46,794 | 52,254 | 9,663 | 4,019 | 5,460 D | 41.5% | 46.4% | 8.6% |
| 4,219 | COLUMBIA | 1,955 | 948 | 743 | 228 | 36 | 205 R | 48.5% | 38.0% | 11.7% |
| 88,904 | COWLITZ | 33,515 | 11,221 | 18,054 | 3,441 | 799 | 6,833 D | 33.5% | 53.9% | 10.3% |
| 31,054 | DOUGLAS | 10,925 | 5,682 | 3,913 | 1,132 | 198 | 1,769 R | 52.0% | 35.8% | 10.4% |
| 7,140 | FERRY | 2,817 | 1,091 | 1,197 | 408 | 121 | 106 D | 38.7% | 42.5% | 14.5% |
| 44,459 | FRANKLIN | 12,096 | 5,946 | 4,961 | 992 | 197 | 985 R | 49.2% | 41.0% | 8.2% |
| 2,297 | GARFIELD | 1,255 | 623 | 497 | 117 | 18 | 126 R | 49.6% | 39.6% | 9.3% |
| 64,493 | GRANT | 21,866 | 10,895 | 8,065 | 2,496 | 410 | 2,830 R | 49.8% | 36.9% | 11.4% |
| 67,221 | GRAYS HARBOR | 26,250 | 7,635 | 14,082 | 3,757 | 776 | 6,447 D | 29.1% | 53.6% | 14.3% |
| 68,682 | ISLAND | 28,464 | 12,387 | 12,157 | 2,787 | 1,133 | 230 R | 43.5% | 42.7% | 9.8% |
| 25,028 | JEFFERSON | 14,119 | 4,607 | 7,145 | 1,385 | 982 | 2,538 D | 32.6% | 50.6% | 9.8% |
| 1,595,243 | KING | 741,104 | 232,811 | 417,846 | 51,309 | 39,138 | 185,035 D | 31.4% | 56.4% | 6.9% |
| 226,720 | KITSAP | 91,487 | 35,304 | 44,167 | 8,769 | 3,247 | 8,863 D | 38.6% | 48.3% | 9.6% |
| 30,158 | KITTITAS | 12,564 | 5,224 | 5,707 | 1,214 | 419 | 483 D | 41.6% | 45.4% | 9.7% |
| 18,231 | KLICKITAT | 7,052 | 2,662 | 3,214 | 875 | 301 | 552 D | 37.7% | 45.6% | 12.4% |
| 65,921 | LEWIS | 27,644 | 13,238 | 10,331 | 3,373 | 702 | 2,907 R | 47.9% | 37.4% | 12.2% |
| 9,510 | LINCOLN | 5,033 | 2,587 | 1,806 | 518 | 122 | 781 R | 51.4% | 35.9% | 10.3% |
| 47,127 | MASON | 20,750 | 7,149 | 10,088 | 2,816 | 697 | 2,939 D | 34.5% | 48.6% | 13.6% |
| 36,628 | OKANOGAN | 13,075 | 5,890 | 4,810 | 1,797 | 578 | 1,080 R | 45.0% | 36.8% | 13.7% |
| 20,807 | PACIFIC | 9,111 | 2,598 | 5,095 | 1,131 | 287 | 2,497 D | 28.5% | 55.9% | 12.4% |
| 10,749 | PEND OREILLE | 4,996 | 2,012 | 2,126 | 709 | 149 | 114 D | 40.3% | 42.6% | 14.2% |
| 648,994 | PIERCE | 239,073 | 89,295 | 120,893 | 22,051 | 6,834 | 31,598 D | 37.4% | 50.6% | 9.2% |
| 11,783 | SAN JUAN | 7,354 | 2,523 | 3,663 | 508 | 660 | 1,140 D | 34.3% | 49.8% | 6.9% |
| 94,023 | SKAGIT | 41,118 | 16,397 | 18,295 | 4,818 | 1,608 | 1,898 D | 39.9% | 44.5% | 11.7% |
| 9,098 | SKAMANIA | 3,789 | 1,387 | 1,724 | 450 | 228 | 337 D | 36.6% | 45.5% | 11.9% |
| 533,526 | SNOHOMISH | 220,960 | 81,885 | 109,624 | 22,731 | 6,720 | 27,739 D | 37.1% | 49.6% | 10.3% |
| 401,205 | SPOKANE | 159,232 | 66,628 | 71,727 | 16,532 | 4,345 | 5,099 D | 41.8% | 45.0% | 10.4% |
| 37,608 | STEVENS | 16,022 | 7,524 | 5,591 | 2,158 | 749 | 1,933 R | 47.0% | 34.9% | 13.5% |
| 191,974 | THURSTON | 87,280 | 29,835 | 45,522 | 7,622 | 4,301 | 15,687 D | 34.2% | 52.2% | 8.7% |
| 3,710 | WAHKIAKUM | 1,836 | 619 | 924 | 215 | 78 | 305 D | 33.7% | 50.3% | 11.7% |
| 52,982 | WALLA WALLA | 19,486 | 9,085 | 8,038 | 1,894 | 469 | 1,047 R | 46.6% | 41.3% | 9.7% |
| 148,929 | WHATCOM | 64,510 | 27,153 | 29,074 | 4,854 | 3,429 | 1,921 D | 42.1% | 45.1% | 7.5% |
| 39,380 | WHITMAN | 15,895 | 6,734 | 7,262 | 1,315 | 584 | 528 D | 42.4% | 45.7% | 8.3% |
| 212,035 | YAKIMA | 59,360 | 27,668 | 25,676 | 4,724 | 1,292 | 1,992 R | 46.6% | 43.3% | 8.0% |
| 5,430,940 | TOTAL | 2,253,837 | 840,712 | 1,123,323 | 201,003 | 88,799 | 282,611 D | 37.3% | 49.8% | 8.9% |

# WASHINGTON

## PRESIDENT 1992

| 1990 Census Population | County | Total Vote | Republican | Democratic | Perot | Other | Plurality | | Percentage Total Vote Rep. | Dem. | Perot |
|---|---|---|---|---|---|---|---|---|---|---|---|
| 13,603 | ADAMS | 4,585 | 2,087 | 1,449 | 1,010 | 39 | 638 | R | 45.5% | 31.6% | 22.0% |
| 17,605 | ASOTIN | 7,596 | 2,425 | 3,239 | 1,849 | 83 | 814 | D | 31.9% | 42.6% | 24.3% |
| 112,560 | BENTON | 52,602 | 22,883 | 16,459 | 12,878 | 382 | 6,424 | R | 43.5% | 31.3% | 24.5% |
| 52,250 | CHELAN | 23,476 | 10,716 | 7,860 | 4,606 | 294 | 2,856 | R | 45.6% | 33.5% | 19.6% |
| 56,464 | CLALLAM | 28,673 | 9,765 | 10,820 | 7,775 | 313 | 1,055 | D | 34.1% | 37.7% | 27.1% |
| 238,053 | CLARK | 106,536 | 36,906 | 42,648 | 26,163 | 819 | 5,742 | D | 34.6% | 40.0% | 24.6% |
| 4,024 | COLUMBIA | 1,914 | 761 | 668 | 466 | 19 | 93 | R | 39.8% | 34.9% | 24.3% |
| 82,119 | COWLITZ | 34,529 | 10,000 | 15,052 | 9,246 | 231 | 5,052 | D | 29.0% | 43.6% | 26.8% |
| 26,205 | DOUGLAS | 11,048 | 4,920 | 3,731 | 2,315 | 82 | 1,189 | R | 44.5% | 33.8% | 21.0% |
| 6,295 | FERRY | 2,557 | 773 | 963 | 762 | 59 | 190 | D | 30.2% | 37.7% | 29.8% |
| 37,473 | FRANKLIN | 10,937 | 4,486 | 3,743 | 2,597 | 111 | 743 | R | 41.0% | 34.2% | 23.7% |
| 2,248 | GARFIELD | 1,321 | 620 | 473 | 222 | 6 | 147 | R | 46.9% | 35.8% | 16.8% |
| 54,758 | GRANT | 21,921 | 9,503 | 7,278 | 4,898 | 242 | 2,225 | R | 43.4% | 33.2% | 22.3% |
| 64,175 | GRAYS HARBOR | 27,238 | 6,904 | 12,599 | 7,460 | 275 | 5,139 | D | 25.3% | 46.3% | 27.4% |
| 60,195 | ISLAND | 27,168 | 9,526 | 9,555 | 7,889 | 198 | 29 | D | 35.1% | 35.2% | 29.0% |
| 20,146 | JEFFERSON | 12,942 | 3,467 | 6,148 | 3,168 | 159 | 2,681 | D | 26.8% | 47.5% | 24.5% |
| 1,507,319 | KING | 778,593 | 212,986 | 391,050 | 167,216 | 7,341 | 178,064 | D | 27.4% | 50.2% | 21.5% |
| 189,731 | KITSAP | 88,568 | 29,340 | 34,442 | 23,873 | 913 | 5,102 | D | 33.1% | 38.9% | 27.0% |
| 26,725 | KITTITAS | 12,385 | 4,078 | 5,432 | 2,778 | 97 | 1,354 | D | 32.9% | 43.9% | 22.4% |
| 16,616 | KLICKITAT | 6,849 | 2,085 | 2,758 | 1,938 | 68 | 673 | D | 30.4% | 40.3% | 28.3% |
| 59,358 | LEWIS | 27,168 | 12,316 | 7,810 | 6,684 | 358 | 4,506 | R | 45.3% | 28.7% | 24.6% |
| 8,864 | LINCOLN | 4,937 | 2,152 | 1,653 | 1,098 | 34 | 499 | R | 43.6% | 33.5% | 22.2% |
| 38,341 | MASON | 19,626 | 5,776 | 8,076 | 5,577 | 197 | 2,300 | D | 29.4% | 41.1% | 28.4% |
| 33,350 | OKANOGAN | 13,033 | 4,265 | 5,015 | 3,541 | 212 | 750 | D | 32.7% | 38.5% | 27.2% |
| 18,882 | PACIFIC | 9,252 | 2,243 | 4,587 | 2,351 | 71 | 2,236 | D | 24.2% | 49.6% | 25.4% |
| 8,915 | PEND OREILLE | 4,716 | 1,528 | 1,798 | 1,340 | 50 | 270 | D | 32.4% | 38.1% | 28.4% |
| 586,203 | PIERCE | 241,149 | 77,410 | 102,243 | 59,523 | 1,973 | 24,833 | D | 32.1% | 42.4% | 24.7% |
| 10,035 | SAN JUAN | 7,117 | 1,901 | 3,353 | 1,776 | 87 | 1,452 | D | 26.7% | 47.1% | 25.0% |
| 79,555 | SKAGIT | 40,728 | 13,388 | 15,936 | 10,973 | 431 | 2,548 | D | 32.9% | 39.1% | 26.9% |
| 8,289 | SKAMANIA | 3,680 | 1,102 | 1,474 | 1,050 | 54 | 372 | D | 29.9% | 40.1% | 28.5% |
| 465,642 | SNOHOMISH | 225,430 | 69,137 | 88,643 | 65,838 | 1,812 | 19,506 | D | 30.7% | 39.3% | 29.2% |
| 361,364 | SPOKANE | 169,132 | 59,984 | 69,526 | 38,251 | 1,371 | 9,542 | D | 35.5% | 41.1% | 22.6% |
| 30,948 | STEVENS | 14,787 | 5,706 | 4,960 | 3,769 | 352 | 746 | R | 38.6% | 33.5% | 25.5% |
| 161,238 | THURSTON | 84,569 | 25,643 | 38,293 | 19,551 | 1,082 | 12,650 | D | 30.3% | 45.3% | 23.1% |
| 3,327 | WAHKIAKUM | 1,796 | 488 | 696 | 584 | 28 | 112 | D | 27.2% | 38.8% | 32.5% |
| 48,439 | WALLA WALLA | 19,881 | 7,894 | 7,325 | 4,507 | 155 | 569 | R | 39.7% | 36.8% | 22.7% |
| 127,780 | WHATCOM | 63,679 | 23,801 | 26,619 | 12,455 | 804 | 2,818 | D | 37.4% | 41.8% | 19.6% |
| 38,775 | WHITMAN | 17,478 | 6,428 | 7,637 | 3,220 | 193 | 1,209 | D | 36.8% | 43.7% | 18.4% |
| 188,823 | YAKIMA | 57,969 | 25,841 | 21,026 | 10,583 | 519 | 4,815 | R | 44.6% | 36.3% | 18.3% |
| 4,866,692 | TOTAL | 2,288,230 | 731,234 | 993,037 | 541,780 | 22,179 | 261,803 | D | 32.0% | 43.4% | 23.7% |

# WASHINGTON

## PRESIDENT 1988

| 1980 Census Population | County | Total Vote | Republican | Democratic | Other | Rep.-Dem. Plurality | Percentage Total Vote Rep. | Dem. | Major Vote Rep. | Dem. |
|---|---|---|---|---|---|---|---|---|---|---|
| 13,267 | ADAMS | 4,288 | 2,612 | 1,612 | 64 | 1,000 R | 60.9% | 37.6% | 61.8% | 38.2% |
| 16,823 | ASOTIN | 6,384 | 2,874 | 3,422 | 88 | 548 D | 45.0% | 53.6% | 45.6% | 54.4% |
| 109,444 | BENTON | 44,016 | 28,688 | 14,817 | 511 | 13,871 R | 65.2% | 33.7% | 65.9% | 34.1% |
| 45,061 | CHELAN | 20,065 | 11,601 | 8,183 | 281 | 3,418 R | 57.8% | 40.8% | 58.6% | 41.4% |
| 51,648 | CLALLAM | 22,794 | 11,200 | 11,123 | 471 | 77 R | 49.1% | 48.8% | 50.2% | 49.8% |
| 192,227 | CLARK | 78,306 | 37,285 | 40,021 | 1,000 | 2,736 D | 47.6% | 51.1% | 48.2% | 51.8% |
| 4,057 | COLUMBIA | 1,944 | 1,172 | 730 | 42 | 442 R | 60.3% | 37.6% | 61.6% | 38.4% |
| 79,548 | COWLITZ | 28,465 | 12,009 | 16,090 | 366 | 4,081 D | 42.2% | 56.5% | 42.7% | 57.3% |
| 22,144 | DOUGLAS | 9,247 | 5,378 | 3,760 | 109 | 1,618 R | 58.2% | 40.7% | 58.9% | 41.1% |
| 5,811 | FERRY | 2,021 | 972 | 972 | 77 | | 48.1% | 48.1% | 50.0% | 50.0% |
| 35,025 | FRANKLIN | 11,452 | 6,488 | 4,772 | 192 | 1,716 R | 56.7% | 41.7% | 57.6% | 42.4% |
| 2,468 | GARFIELD | 1,319 | 714 | 593 | 12 | 121 R | 54.1% | 45.0% | 54.6% | 45.4% |
| 48,522 | GRANT | 18,799 | 10,859 | 7,564 | 376 | 3,295 R | 57.8% | 40.2% | 58.9% | 41.1% |
| 66,314 | GRAYS HARBOR | 23,391 | 8,860 | 14,097 | 434 | 5,237 D | 37.9% | 60.3% | 38.6% | 61.4% |
| 44,048 | ISLAND | 21,353 | 12,552 | 8,510 | 291 | 4,042 R | 58.8% | 39.9% | 59.6% | 40.4% |
| 15,965 | JEFFERSON | 9,636 | 4,184 | 5,270 | 182 | 1,086 D | 43.4% | 54.7% | 44.3% | 55.7% |
| 1,269,749 | KING | 648,957 | 290,574 | 349,663 | 8,720 | 59,089 D | 44.8% | 53.9% | 45.4% | 54.6% |
| 147,152 | KITSAP | 69,649 | 34,743 | 33,748 | 1,158 | 995 R | 49.9% | 48.5% | 50.7% | 49.3% |
| 24,877 | KITTITAS | 10,496 | 5,048 | 5,318 | 130 | 270 D | 48.1% | 50.7% | 48.7% | 51.3% |
| 15,822 | KLICKITAT | 6,086 | 2,920 | 2,991 | 175 | 71 D | 48.0% | 49.1% | 49.4% | 50.6% |
| 56,025 | LEWIS | 23,238 | 14,184 | 8,629 | 425 | 5,555 R | 61.0% | 37.1% | 62.2% | 37.8% |
| 9,604 | LINCOLN | 4,645 | 2,689 | 1,884 | 72 | 805 R | 57.9% | 40.6% | 58.8% | 41.2% |
| 31,184 | MASON | 15,545 | 7,426 | 7,826 | 293 | 400 D | 47.8% | 50.3% | 48.7% | 51.3% |
| 30,639 | OKANOGAN | 11,740 | 5,856 | 5,630 | 254 | 226 R | 49.9% | 48.0% | 51.0% | 49.0% |
| 17,237 | PACIFIC | 8,200 | 3,073 | 5,017 | 110 | 1,944 D | 37.5% | 61.2% | 38.0% | 62.0% |
| 8,580 | PEND OREILLE | 3,794 | 1,802 | 1,925 | 67 | 123 D | 47.5% | 50.7% | 48.3% | 51.7% |
| 485,643 | PIERCE | 194,473 | 94,167 | 96,688 | 3,618 | 2,521 D | 48.4% | 49.7% | 49.3% | 50.7% |
| 7,838 | SAN JUAN | 5,814 | 2,660 | 3,008 | 146 | 348 D | 45.8% | 51.7% | 46.9% | 53.1% |
| 64,138 | SKAGIT | 32,401 | 16,550 | 15,159 | 692 | 1,391 R | 51.1% | 46.8% | 52.2% | 47.8% |
| 7,919 | SKAMANIA | 3,162 | 1,356 | 1,748 | 58 | 392 D | 42.9% | 55.3% | 43.7% | 56.3% |
| 337,720 | SNOHOMISH | 167,165 | 84,158 | 80,694 | 2,313 | 3,464 R | 50.3% | 48.3% | 51.1% | 48.9% |
| 341,835 | SPOKANE | 139,150 | 68,787 | 68,520 | 1,843 | 267 R | 49.4% | 49.2% | 50.1% | 49.9% |
| 28,979 | STEVENS | 11,962 | 6,576 | 5,068 | 318 | 1,508 R | 55.0% | 42.4% | 56.5% | 43.5% |
| 124,264 | THURSTON | 66,930 | 31,980 | 33,860 | 1,090 | 1,880 D | 47.8% | 50.6% | 48.6% | 51.4% |
| 3,832 | WAHKIAKUM | 1,626 | 629 | 961 | 36 | 332 D | 38.7% | 59.1% | 39.6% | 60.4% |
| 47,435 | WALLA WALLA | 17,403 | 9,683 | 7,448 | 272 | 2,235 R | 55.6% | 42.8% | 56.5% | 43.5% |
| 106,701 | WHATCOM | 50,094 | 23,820 | 25,571 | 703 | 1,751 D | 47.6% | 51.0% | 48.2% | 51.8% |
| 40,103 | WHITMAN | 15,333 | 7,680 | 7,403 | 250 | 277 R | 50.1% | 48.3% | 50.9% | 49.1% |
| 172,508 | YAKIMA | 53,910 | 30,026 | 23,221 | 663 | 6,805 R | 55.7% | 43.1% | 56.4% | 43.6% |
| 4,132,156 | TOTAL | 1,865,253 | 903,835 | 933,516 | 27,902 | 29,681 D | 48.5% | 50.0% | 49.2% | 50.8% |

# WASHINGTON

## PRESIDENT 1984

| 1980 Census Population | County | Total Vote | Republican | Democratic | Other | Rep.-Dem. Plurality | Percentage | | | |
|---|---|---|---|---|---|---|---|---|---|---|
| | | | | | | | Total Vote | | Major Vote | |
| | | | | | | | Rep. | Dem. | Rep. | Dem. |
| 13,267 | ADAMS | 4,809 | 3,449 | 1,311 | 49 | 2,138 R | 71.7% | 27.3% | 72.5% | 27.5% |
| 16,823 | ASOTIN | 7,021 | 3,876 | 3,042 | 103 | 834 R | 55.2% | 43.3% | 56.0% | 44.0% |
| 109,444 | BENTON | 46,631 | 32,307 | 13,784 | 540 | 18,523 R | 69.3% | 29.6% | 70.1% | 29.9% |
| 45,061 | CHELAN | 20,994 | 13,667 | 6,978 | 349 | 6,689 R | 65.1% | 33.2% | 66.2% | 33.8% |
| 51,648 | CLALLAM | 23,735 | 13,605 | 9,701 | 429 | 3,904 R | 57.3% | 40.9% | 58.4% | 41.6% |
| 192,227 | CLARK | 76,957 | 40,681 | 35,248 | 1,028 | 5,433 R | 52.9% | 45.8% | 53.6% | 46.4% |
| 4,057 | COLUMBIA | 2,095 | 1,404 | 673 | 18 | 731 R | 67.0% | 32.1% | 67.6% | 32.4% |
| 79,548 | COWLITZ | 30,968 | 14,858 | 15,361 | 749 | 503 D | 48.0% | 49.6% | 49.2% | 50.8% |
| 22,144 | DOUGLAS | 9,698 | 6,443 | 3,127 | 128 | 3,316 R | 66.4% | 32.2% | 67.3% | 32.7% |
| 5,811 | FERRY | 2,210 | 1,232 | 935 | 43 | 297 R | 55.7% | 42.3% | 56.9% | 43.1% |
| 35,025 | FRANKLIN | 12,268 | 7,724 | 4,328 | 216 | 3,396 R | 63.0% | 35.3% | 64.1% | 35.9% |
| 2,468 | GARFIELD | 1,428 | 913 | 493 | 22 | 420 R | 63.9% | 34.5% | 64.9% | 35.1% |
| 48,522 | GRANT | 19,584 | 12,888 | 6,298 | 398 | 6,590 R | 65.8% | 32.2% | 67.2% | 32.8% |
| 66,314 | GRAYS HARBOR | 25,671 | 11,286 | 14,050 | 335 | 2,764 D | 44.0% | 54.7% | 44.5% | 55.5% |
| 44,048 | ISLAND | 20,616 | 13,548 | 6,850 | 218 | 6,698 R | 65.7% | 33.2% | 66.4% | 33.6% |
| 15,965 | JEFFERSON | 9,334 | 4,543 | 4,602 | 189 | 59 D | 48.7% | 49.3% | 49.7% | 50.3% |
| 1,269,749 | KING | 639,261 | 332,987 | 298,620 | 7,654 | 34,367 R | 52.1% | 46.7% | 52.7% | 47.3% |
| 147,152 | KITSAP | 66,713 | 36,101 | 29,681 | 931 | 6,420 R | 54.1% | 44.5% | 54.9% | 45.1% |
| 24,877 | KITTITAS | 11,531 | 6,580 | 4,830 | 121 | 1,750 R | 57.1% | 41.9% | 57.7% | 42.3% |
| 15,822 | KLICKITAT | 6,757 | 3,910 | 2,712 | 135 | 1,198 R | 57.9% | 40.1% | 59.0% | 41.0% |
| 56,025 | LEWIS | 23,931 | 15,846 | 7,634 | 451 | 8,212 R | 66.2% | 31.9% | 67.5% | 32.5% |
| 9,604 | LINCOLN | 5,193 | 3,474 | 1,671 | 48 | 1,803 R | 66.9% | 32.2% | 67.5% | 32.5% |
| 31,184 | MASON | 15,650 | 8,410 | 7,007 | 233 | 1,403 R | 53.7% | 44.8% | 54.6% | 45.4% |
| 30,639 | OKANOGAN | 13,059 | 7,476 | 5,330 | 253 | 2,146 R | 57.2% | 40.8% | 58.4% | 41.6% |
| 17,237 | PACIFIC | 8,421 | 3,613 | 4,679 | 129 | 1,066 D | 42.9% | 55.6% | 43.6% | 56.4% |
| 8,580 | PEND OREILLE | 4,075 | 2,374 | 1,655 | 46 | 719 R | 58.3% | 40.6% | 58.9% | 41.1% |
| 485,643 | PIERCE | 195,108 | 112,877 | 79,498 | 2,733 | 33,379 R | 57.9% | 40.7% | 58.7% | 41.3% |
| 7,838 | SAN JUAN | 5,526 | 2,900 | 2,514 | 112 | 386 R | 52.5% | 45.5% | 53.6% | 46.4% |
| 64,138 | SKAGIT | 33,326 | 18,840 | 13,947 | 539 | 4,893 R | 56.5% | 41.9% | 57.5% | 42.5% |
| 7,919 | SKAMANIA | 3,339 | 1,736 | 1,552 | 51 | 184 R | 52.0% | 46.5% | 52.8% | 47.2% |
| 337,720 | SNOHOMISH | 158,995 | 90,362 | 66,728 | 1,905 | 23,634 R | 56.8% | 42.0% | 57.5% | 42.5% |
| 341,835 | SPOKANE | 149,336 | 88,043 | 59,620 | 1,673 | 28,423 R | 59.0% | 39.9% | 59.6% | 40.4% |
| 28,979 | STEVENS | 12,771 | 8,211 | 4,304 | 256 | 3,907 R | 64.3% | 33.7% | 65.6% | 34.4% |
| 124,264 | THURSTON | 62,045 | 34,442 | 26,840 | 763 | 7,602 R | 55.5% | 43.3% | 56.2% | 43.8% |
| 3,832 | WAHKIAKUM | 1,739 | 776 | 930 | 33 | 154 D | 44.6% | 53.5% | 45.5% | 54.5% |
| 47,435 | WALLA WALLA | 19,398 | 12,361 | 6,804 | 233 | 5,557 R | 63.7% | 35.1% | 64.5% | 35.5% |
| 106,701 | WHATCOM | 50,686 | 27,228 | 22,670 | 788 | 4,558 R | 53.7% | 44.7% | 54.6% | 45.4% |
| 40,103 | WHITMAN | 16,849 | 10,021 | 6,621 | 207 | 3,400 R | 59.5% | 39.3% | 60.2% | 39.8% |
| 172,508 | YAKIMA | 66,182 | 40,678 | 24,724 | 780 | 15,954 R | 61.5% | 37.4% | 62.2% | 37.8% |
| 4,132,156 | TOTAL | 1,883,910 | 1,051,670 | 807,352 | 24,888 | 244,318 R | 55.8% | 42.9% | 56.6% | 43.4% |

# WASHINGTON

## PRESIDENT 1980

| 1980 Census Population | County | Total Vote | Republican | Democratic | Other | Rep.-Dem. Plurality | Percentage | | | |
|---|---|---|---|---|---|---|---|---|---|---|
| | | | | | | | Total Vote | | Major Vote | |
| | | | | | | | Rep. | Dem. | Rep. | Dem. |
| 13,267 | ADAMS | 4,776 | 3,248 | 1,223 | 305 | 2,025 R | 68.0% | 25.6% | 72.6% | 27.4% |
| 16,823 | ASOTIN | 6,659 | 3,275 | 2,724 | 660 | 551 R | 49.2% | 40.9% | 54.6% | 45.4% |
| 109,444 | BENTON | 44,413 | 28,728 | 11,561 | 4,124 | 17,167 R | 64.7% | 26.0% | 71.3% | 28.7% |
| 45,061 | CHELAN | 19,850 | 11,299 | 6,483 | 2,068 | 4,816 R | 56.9% | 32.7% | 63.5% | 36.5% |
| 51,648 | CLALLAM | 22,296 | 11,515 | 8,029 | 2,752 | 3,486 R | 51.6% | 36.0% | 58.9% | 41.1% |
| 192,227 | CLARK | 72,075 | 33,223 | 30,584 | 8,268 | 2,639 R | 46.1% | 42.4% | 52.1% | 47.9% |
| 4,057 | COLUMBIA | 2,086 | 1,349 | 587 | 150 | 762 R | 64.7% | 28.1% | 69.7% | 30.3% |
| 79,548 | COWLITZ | 28,639 | 13,154 | 12,560 | 2,925 | 594 R | 45.9% | 43.9% | 51.2% | 48.8% |
| 22,144 | DOUGLAS | 8,709 | 5,171 | 2,833 | 705 | 2,338 R | 59.4% | 32.5% | 64.6% | 35.4% |
| 5,811 | FERRY | 2,100 | 1,108 | 802 | 190 | 306 R | 52.8% | 38.2% | 58.0% | 42.0% |
| 35,025 | FRANKLIN | 11,961 | 7,327 | 3,719 | 915 | 3,608 R | 61.3% | 31.1% | 66.3% | 33.7% |
| 2,468 | GARFIELD | 1,519 | 875 | 509 | 135 | 366 R | 57.6% | 33.5% | 63.2% | 36.8% |
| 48,522 | GRANT | 18,196 | 11,152 | 5,673 | 1,371 | 5,479 R | 61.3% | 31.2% | 66.3% | 33.7% |
| 66,314 | GRAYS HARBOR | 25,444 | 10,226 | 11,290 | 3,928 | 1,064 D | 40.2% | 44.4% | 47.5% | 52.5% |
| 44,048 | ISLAND | 18,559 | 10,926 | 5,422 | 2,211 | 5,504 R | 58.9% | 29.2% | 66.8% | 33.2% |
| 15,965 | JEFFERSON | 8,170 | 3,645 | 3,279 | 1,246 | 366 R | 44.6% | 40.1% | 52.6% | 47.4% |
| 1,269,749 | KING | 600,157 | 272,567 | 235,046 | 92,544 | 37,521 R | 45.4% | 39.2% | 53.7% | 46.3% |
| 147,152 | KITSAP | 60,296 | 29,420 | 20,893 | 9,983 | 8,527 R | 48.8% | 34.7% | 58.5% | 41.5% |
| 24,877 | KITTITAS | 10,748 | 5,359 | 4,075 | 1,314 | 1,284 R | 49.9% | 37.9% | 56.8% | 43.2% |
| 15,822 | KLICKITAT | 6,284 | 3,113 | 2,596 | 575 | 517 R | 49.5% | 41.3% | 54.5% | 45.5% |
| 56,025 | LEWIS | 22,749 | 13,636 | 6,962 | 2,151 | 6,674 R | 59.9% | 30.6% | 66.2% | 33.8% |
| 9,604 | LINCOLN | 5,337 | 3,324 | 1,597 | 416 | 1,727 R | 62.3% | 29.9% | 67.5% | 32.5% |
| 31,184 | MASON | 13,737 | 6,745 | 5,241 | 1,751 | 1,504 R | 49.1% | 38.2% | 56.3% | 43.7% |
| 30,639 | OKANOGAN | 12,493 | 6,460 | 4,634 | 1,399 | 1,826 R | 51.7% | 37.1% | 58.2% | 41.8% |
| 17,237 | PACIFIC | 8,012 | 3,132 | 3,727 | 1,153 | 595 D | 39.1% | 46.5% | 45.7% | 54.3% |
| 8,580 | PEND OREILLE | 3,835 | 2,136 | 1,399 | 300 | 737 R | 55.7% | 36.5% | 60.4% | 39.6% |
| 485,643 | PIERCE | 176,511 | 90,247 | 64,444 | 21,820 | 25,803 R | 51.1% | 36.5% | 58.3% | 41.7% |
| 7,838 | SAN JUAN | 5,031 | 2,363 | 1,666 | 1,002 | 697 R | 47.0% | 33.1% | 58.6% | 41.4% |
| 64,138 | SKAGIT | 30,623 | 15,520 | 11,299 | 3,804 | 4,221 R | 50.7% | 36.9% | 57.9% | 42.1% |
| 7,919 | SKAMANIA | 3,095 | 1,416 | 1,373 | 306 | 43 R | 45.8% | 44.4% | 50.8% | 49.2% |
| 337,720 | SNOHOMISH | 135,907 | 66,153 | 52,003 | 17,751 | 14,150 R | 48.7% | 38.3% | 56.0% | 44.0% |
| 341,835 | SPOKANE | 140,685 | 78,096 | 49,263 | 13,326 | 28,833 R | 55.5% | 35.0% | 61.3% | 38.7% |
| 28,979 | STEVENS | 11,530 | 7,094 | 3,584 | 852 | 3,510 R | 61.5% | 31.1% | 66.4% | 33.6% |
| 124,264 | THURSTON | 54,823 | 26,369 | 20,508 | 7,946 | 5,861 R | 48.1% | 37.4% | 56.3% | 43.7% |
| 3,832 | WAHKIAKUM | 1,778 | 828 | 751 | 199 | 77 R | 46.6% | 42.2% | 52.4% | 47.6% |
| 47,435 | WALLA WALLA | 18,977 | 11,223 | 5,825 | 1,929 | 5,398 R | 59.1% | 30.7% | 65.8% | 34.2% |
| 106,701 | WHATCOM | 46,057 | 21,371 | 18,430 | 6,256 | 2,941 R | 46.4% | 40.0% | 53.7% | 46.3% |
| 40,103 | WHITMAN | 17,024 | 8,636 | 5,726 | 2,662 | 2,910 R | 50.7% | 33.6% | 60.1% | 39.9% |
| 172,508 | YAKIMA | 61,253 | 33,815 | 21,873 | 5,565 | 11,942 R | 55.2% | 35.7% | 60.7% | 39.3% |
| 4,132,156 | TOTAL | 1,742,394 | 865,244 | 650,193 | 226,957 | 215,051 R | 49.7% | 37.3% | 57.1% | 42.9% |

# WASHINGTON

## PRESIDENT 1976

| 1970 Census Population | County | Total Vote | Republican | Democratic | Other | Rep.-Dem. Plurality | Percentage | | | |
|---|---|---|---|---|---|---|---|---|---|---|
| | | | | | | | Total Vote | | Major Vote | |
| | | | | | | | Rep. | Dem. | Rep. | Dem. |
| 12,014 | ADAMS | 4,773 | 2,795 | 1,790 | 188 | 1,005 R | 58.6% | 37.5% | 61.0% | 39.0% |
| 13,799 | ASOTIN | 5,828 | 2,752 | 2,898 | 178 | 146 D | 47.2% | 49.7% | 48.7% | 51.3% |
| 67,540 | BENTON | 34,611 | 22,135 | 11,306 | 1,170 | 10,829 R | 64.0% | 32.7% | 66.2% | 33.8% |
| 41,355 | CHELAN | 18,692 | 10,492 | 7,623 | 577 | 2,869 R | 56.1% | 40.8% | 57.9% | 42.1% |
| 34,770 | CLALLAM | 18,386 | 9,132 | 8,268 | 986 | 864 R | 49.7% | 45.0% | 52.5% | 47.5% |
| 128,454 | CLARK | 61,201 | 27,938 | 31,080 | 2,183 | 3,142 D | 45.6% | 50.8% | 47.3% | 52.7% |
| 4,439 | COLUMBIA | 2,034 | 1,153 | 829 | 52 | 324 R | 56.7% | 40.8% | 58.2% | 41.8% |
| 68,616 | COWLITZ | 28,406 | 12,531 | 14,958 | 917 | 2,427 D | 44.1% | 52.7% | 45.6% | 54.4% |
| 16,787 | DOUGLAS | 8,564 | 4,547 | 3,809 | 208 | 738 R | 53.1% | 44.5% | 54.4% | 45.6% |
| 3,655 | FERRY | 1,692 | 776 | 814 | 102 | 38 D | 45.9% | 48.1% | 48.8% | 51.2% |
| 25,816 | FRANKLIN | 10,403 | 5,671 | 4,369 | 363 | 1,302 R | 54.5% | 42.0% | 56.5% | 43.5% |
| 2,911 | GARFIELD | 1,560 | 892 | 616 | 52 | 276 R | 57.2% | 39.5% | 59.2% | 40.8% |
| 41,881 | GRANT | 17,721 | 9,192 | 7,777 | 752 | 1,415 R | 51.9% | 43.9% | 54.2% | 45.8% |
| 59,553 | GRAYS HARBOR | 23,893 | 9,464 | 13,478 | 951 | 4,014 D | 39.6% | 56.4% | 41.3% | 58.7% |
| 27,011 | ISLAND | 14,104 | 7,804 | 5,859 | 441 | 1,945 R | 55.3% | 41.5% | 57.1% | 42.9% |
| 10,661 | JEFFERSON | 6,092 | 2,794 | 2,913 | 385 | 119 D | 45.9% | 47.8% | 49.0% | 51.0% |
| 1,156,633 | KING | 550,119 | 279,382 | 248,743 | 21,994 | 30,639 R | 50.8% | 45.2% | 52.9% | 47.1% |
| 101,732 | KITSAP | 50,750 | 23,124 | 25,701 | 1,925 | 2,577 D | 45.6% | 50.6% | 47.4% | 52.6% |
| 25,039 | KITTITAS | 10,017 | 4,765 | 4,858 | 394 | 93 D | 47.6% | 48.5% | 49.5% | 50.5% |
| 12,138 | KLICKITAT | 5,719 | 2,573 | 2,890 | 256 | 317 D | 45.0% | 50.5% | 47.1% | 52.9% |
| 45,467 | LEWIS | 21,167 | 10,933 | 9,026 | 1,208 | 1,907 R | 51.7% | 42.6% | 54.8% | 45.2% |
| 9,572 | LINCOLN | 5,081 | 2,925 | 1,978 | 178 | 947 R | 57.6% | 38.9% | 59.7% | 40.3% |
| 20,918 | MASON | 11,291 | 4,758 | 6,060 | 473 | 1,302 D | 42.1% | 53.7% | 44.0% | 56.0% |
| 25,867 | OKANOGAN | 11,595 | 5,455 | 5,543 | 597 | 88 D | 47.0% | 47.8% | 49.6% | 50.4% |
| 15,796 | PACIFIC | 7,350 | 2,781 | 4,278 | 291 | 1,497 D | 37.8% | 58.2% | 39.4% | 60.6% |
| 6,025 | PEND OREILLE | 3,170 | 1,516 | 1,533 | 121 | 17 D | 47.8% | 48.4% | 49.7% | 50.3% |
| 411,027 | PIERCE | 159,148 | 74,668 | 78,238 | 6,242 | 3,570 D | 46.9% | 49.2% | 48.8% | 51.2% |
| 3,856 | SAN JUAN | 3,722 | 1,998 | 1,467 | 257 | 531 R | 53.7% | 39.4% | 57.7% | 42.3% |
| 52,381 | SKAGIT | 26,837 | 13,060 | 12,718 | 1,059 | 342 R | 48.7% | 47.4% | 50.7% | 49.3% |
| 5,845 | SKAMANIA | 2,652 | 1,102 | 1,436 | 114 | 334 D | 41.6% | 54.1% | 43.4% | 56.6% |
| 265,236 | SNOHOMISH | 115,488 | 55,375 | 55,623 | 4,490 | 248 D | 47.9% | 48.2% | 49.9% | 50.1% |
| 287,487 | SPOKANE | 127,954 | 68,290 | 55,660 | 4,004 | 12,630 R | 53.4% | 43.5% | 55.1% | 44.9% |
| 17,405 | STEVENS | 9,109 | 4,719 | 3,824 | 566 | 895 R | 51.8% | 42.0% | 55.2% | 44.8% |
| 76,894 | THURSTON | 44,056 | 21,000 | 21,247 | 1,809 | 247 D | 47.7% | 48.2% | 49.7% | 50.3% |
| 3,592 | WAHKIAKUM | 1,710 | 704 | 942 | 64 | 238 D | 41.2% | 55.1% | 42.8% | 57.2% |
| 42,176 | WALLA WALLA | 18,400 | 10,883 | 7,012 | 505 | 3,871 R | 59.1% | 38.1% | 60.8% | 39.2% |
| 81,950 | WHATCOM | 41,679 | 20,007 | 19,739 | 1,933 | 268 R | 48.0% | 47.4% | 50.3% | 49.7% |
| 37,900 | WHITMAN | 15,068 | 8,168 | 6,197 | 703 | 1,971 R | 54.2% | 41.1% | 56.9% | 43.1% |
| 144,971 | YAKIMA | 55,492 | 29,478 | 24,223 | 1,791 | 5,255 R | 53.1% | 43.7% | 54.9% | 45.1% |
| 3,409,169 | TOTAL | 1,555,534 | 777,732 | 717,323 | 60,479 | 60,409 R | 50.0% | 46.1% | 52.0% | 48.0% |

# WASHINGTON

## PRESIDENT 1972

| 1970 Census Population | County | Total Vote | Republican | Democratic | Other | Rep.-Dem. Plurality | Percentage Total Vote Rep. | Dem. | Major Vote Rep. | Dem. |
|---|---|---|---|---|---|---|---|---|---|---|
| 12,014 | ADAMS | 4,519 | 3,083 | 1,110 | 326 | 1,973 R | 68.2% | 24.6% | 73.5% | 26.5% |
| 13,799 | ASOTIN | 5,780 | 2,911 | 2,559 | 310 | 352 R | 50.4% | 44.3% | 53.2% | 46.8% |
| 67,540 | BENTON | 30,346 | 18,517 | 9,824 | 2,005 | 8,693 R | 61.0% | 32.4% | 65.3% | 34.7% |
| 41,355 | CHELAN | 17,413 | 10,470 | 5,889 | 1,054 | 4,581 R | 60.1% | 33.8% | 64.0% | 36.0% |
| 34,770 | CLALLAM | 16,089 | 9,372 | 5,620 | 1,097 | 3,752 R | 58.3% | 34.9% | 62.5% | 37.5% |
| 128,454 | CLARK | 58,569 | 28,775 | 27,179 | 2,615 | 1,596 R | 49.1% | 46.4% | 51.4% | 48.6% |
| 4,439 | COLUMBIA | 2,080 | 1,445 | 533 | 102 | 912 R | 69.5% | 25.6% | 73.1% | 26.9% |
| 68,616 | COWLITZ | 28,182 | 14,431 | 12,682 | 1,069 | 1,749 R | 51.2% | 45.0% | 53.2% | 46.8% |
| 16,787 | DOUGLAS | 7,481 | 4,512 | 2,420 | 549 | 2,092 R | 60.3% | 32.3% | 65.1% | 34.9% |
| 3,655 | FERRY | 1,527 | 815 | 560 | 152 | 255 R | 53.4% | 36.7% | 59.3% | 40.7% |
| 25,816 | FRANKLIN | 10,523 | 5,972 | 3,867 | 684 | 2,105 R | 56.8% | 36.7% | 60.7% | 39.3% |
| 2,911 | GARFIELD | 1,534 | 1,004 | 481 | 49 | 523 R | 65.4% | 31.4% | 67.6% | 32.4% |
| 41,881 | GRANT | 15,814 | 9,370 | 5,487 | 957 | 3,883 R | 59.3% | 34.7% | 63.1% | 36.9% |
| 59,553 | GRAYS HARBOR | 23,745 | 10,839 | 11,786 | 1,120 | 947 D | 45.6% | 49.6% | 47.9% | 52.1% |
| 27,011 | ISLAND | 11,003 | 7,495 | 3,149 | 359 | 4,346 R | 68.1% | 28.6% | 70.4% | 29.6% |
| 10,661 | JEFFERSON | 5,179 | 2,770 | 2,096 | 313 | 674 R | 53.5% | 40.5% | 56.9% | 43.1% |
| 1,156,633 | KING | 529,694 | 298,707 | 212,509 | 18,478 | 86,198 R | 56.4% | 40.1% | 58.4% | 41.6% |
| 101,732 | KITSAP | 45,446 | 25,831 | 17,011 | 2,604 | 8,820 R | 56.8% | 37.4% | 60.3% | 39.7% |
| 25,039 | KITTITAS | 10,126 | 5,464 | 4,299 | 363 | 1,165 R | 54.0% | 42.5% | 56.0% | 44.0% |
| 12,138 | KLICKITAT | 5,648 | 3,061 | 2,293 | 294 | 768 R | 54.2% | 40.6% | 57.2% | 42.8% |
| 45,467 | LEWIS | 20,585 | 12,071 | 6,946 | 1,568 | 5,125 R | 58.6% | 33.7% | 63.5% | 36.5% |
| 9,572 | LINCOLN | 5,275 | 3,647 | 1,453 | 175 | 2,194 R | 69.1% | 27.5% | 71.5% | 28.5% |
| 20,918 | MASON | 9,177 | 4,873 | 3,907 | 397 | 966 R | 53.1% | 42.6% | 55.5% | 44.5% |
| 25,867 | OKANOGAN | 10,334 | 5,796 | 3,835 | 703 | 1,961 R | 56.1% | 37.1% | 60.2% | 39.8% |
| 15,796 | PACIFIC | 7,166 | 3,349 | 3,585 | 232 | 236 D | 46.7% | 50.0% | 48.3% | 51.7% |
| 6,025 | PEND OREILLE | 2,931 | 1,746 | 1,071 | 114 | 675 R | 59.6% | 36.5% | 62.0% | 38.0% |
| 411,027 | PIERCE | 148,065 | 84,265 | 56,933 | 6,867 | 27,332 R | 56.9% | 38.5% | 59.7% | 40.3% |
| 3,856 | SAN JUAN | 2,795 | 1,786 | 906 | 103 | 880 R | 63.9% | 32.4% | 66.3% | 33.7% |
| 52,381 | SKAGIT | 24,448 | 14,212 | 9,233 | 1,003 | 4,979 R | 58.1% | 37.8% | 60.6% | 39.4% |
| 5,845 | SKAMANIA | 2,645 | 1,288 | 1,153 | 204 | 135 R | 48.7% | 43.6% | 52.8% | 47.2% |
| 265,236 | SNOHOMISH | 104,821 | 60,032 | 39,471 | 5,318 | 20,561 R | 57.3% | 37.7% | 60.3% | 39.7% |
| 287,487 | SPOKANE | 125,185 | 74,320 | 44,337 | 6,528 | 29,983 R | 59.4% | 35.4% | 62.6% | 37.4% |
| 17,405 | STEVENS | 7,899 | 4,839 | 2,390 | 670 | 2,449 R | 61.3% | 30.3% | 66.9% | 33.1% |
| 76,894 | THURSTON | 38,792 | 22,297 | 14,596 | 1,899 | 7,701 R | 57.5% | 37.6% | 60.4% | 39.6% |
| 3,592 | WAHKIAKUM | 1,726 | 818 | 796 | 112 | 22 R | 47.4% | 46.1% | 50.7% | 49.3% |
| 42,176 | WALLA WALLA | 18,533 | 12,579 | 5,364 | 590 | 7,215 R | 67.9% | 28.9% | 70.1% | 29.9% |
| 81,950 | WHATCOM | 38,801 | 22,585 | 15,027 | 1,189 | 7,558 R | 58.2% | 38.7% | 60.0% | 40.0% |
| 37,900 | WHITMAN | 16,266 | 9,548 | 6,248 | 470 | 3,300 R | 58.7% | 38.4% | 60.4% | 39.6% |
| 144,971 | YAKIMA | 54,705 | 32,240 | 19,729 | 2,736 | 12,511 R | 58.9% | 36.1% | 62.0% | 38.0% |
| 3,409,169 | TOTAL | 1,470,847 | 837,135 | 568,334 | 65,378 | 268,801 R | 56.9% | 38.6% | 59.6% | 40.4% |

# WASHINGTON

## PRESIDENT 1968

| 1960 Census Population | County | Total Vote | Republican | Democratic | AIP | Other | Plurality | Percentage Total Vote Rep. | Dem. | AIP |
|---|---|---|---|---|---|---|---|---|---|---|
| 9,929 | ADAMS | 4,141 | 2,572 | 1,270 | 299 | | 1,302 R | 62.1% | 30.7% | 7.2% |
| 12,909 | ASOTIN | 5,434 | 2,307 | 2,693 | 433 | 1 | 386 D | 42.5% | 49.6% | 8.0% |
| 62,070 | BENTON | 28,579 | 14,659 | 10,878 | 3,024 | 18 | 3,781 R | 51.3% | 38.1% | 10.6% |
| 40,744 | CHELAN | 17,230 | 9,093 | 6,787 | 1,324 | 26 | 2,306 R | 52.8% | 39.4% | 7.7% |
| 30,022 | CLALLAM | 14,234 | 5,921 | 7,030 | 1,248 | 35 | 1,109 D | 41.6% | 49.4% | 8.8% |
| 93,809 | CLARK | 44,474 | 18,858 | 23,046 | 2,514 | 56 | 4,188 D | 42.4% | 51.8% | 5.7% |
| 4,569 | COLUMBIA | 2,152 | 1,221 | 754 | 175 | 2 | 467 R | 56.7% | 35.0% | 8.1% |
| 57,801 | COWLITZ | 25,750 | 10,842 | 13,363 | 1,507 | 38 | 2,521 D | 42.1% | 51.9% | 5.9% |
| 14,890 | DOUGLAS | 6,665 | 3,234 | 2,764 | 663 | 4 | 470 R | 48.5% | 41.5% | 9.9% |
| 3,889 | FERRY | 1,387 | 608 | 596 | 182 | 1 | 12 R | 43.8% | 43.0% | 13.1% |
| 23,342 | FRANKLIN | 9,575 | 4,234 | 4,038 | 1,299 | 4 | 196 R | 44.2% | 42.2% | 13.6% |
| 2,976 | GARFIELD | 1,586 | 841 | 602 | 143 | | 239 R | 53.0% | 38.0% | 9.0% |
| 46,477 | GRANT | 14,367 | 7,007 | 5,773 | 1,574 | 13 | 1,234 R | 48.8% | 40.2% | 11.0% |
| 54,465 | GRAYS HARBOR | 22,684 | 7,720 | 13,480 | 1,426 | 58 | 5,760 D | 34.0% | 59.4% | 6.3% |
| 19,638 | ISLAND | 8,000 | 4,077 | 3,238 | 677 | 8 | 839 R | 51.0% | 40.5% | 8.5% |
| 9,639 | JEFFERSON | 4,505 | 1,827 | 2,251 | 407 | 20 | 424 D | 40.6% | 50.0% | 9.0% |
| 935,014 | KING | 474,935 | 218,457 | 223,469 | 31,450 | 1,559 | 5,012 D | 46.0% | 47.1% | 6.6% |
| 84,176 | KITSAP | 39,815 | 14,520 | 22,273 | 2,986 | 36 | 7,753 D | 36.5% | 55.9% | 7.5% |
| 20,467 | KITTITAS | 8,729 | 4,212 | 3,921 | 579 | 17 | 291 R | 48.3% | 44.9% | 6.6% |
| 13,455 | KLICKITAT | 5,173 | 2,355 | 2,454 | 357 | 7 | 99 D | 45.5% | 47.4% | 6.9% |
| 41,858 | LEWIS | 18,668 | 8,779 | 8,444 | 1,428 | 17 | 335 R | 47.0% | 45.2% | 7.6% |
| 10,919 | LINCOLN | 5,053 | 2,994 | 1,721 | 337 | 1 | 1,273 R | 59.3% | 34.1% | 6.7% |
| 16,251 | MASON | 8,590 | 3,397 | 4,540 | 638 | 15 | 1,143 D | 39.5% | 52.9% | 7.4% |
| 25,520 | OKANOGAN | 9,935 | 4,490 | 4,379 | 1,064 | 2 | 111 R | 45.2% | 44.1% | 10.7% |
| 14,674 | PACIFIC | 6,605 | 2,491 | 3,740 | 364 | 10 | 1,249 D | 37.7% | 56.6% | 5.5% |
| 6,914 | PEND OREILLE | 2,714 | 1,117 | 1,350 | 245 | 2 | 233 D | 41.2% | 49.7% | 9.0% |
| 321,590 | PIERCE | 135,718 | 51,436 | 72,670 | 11,391 | 221 | 21,234 D | 37.9% | 53.5% | 8.4% |
| 2,872 | SAN JUAN | 1,963 | 1,164 | 685 | 108 | 6 | 479 R | 59.3% | 34.9% | 5.5% |
| 51,350 | SKAGIT | 22,594 | 10,354 | 10,529 | 1,667 | 44 | 175 D | 45.8% | 46.6% | 7.4% |
| 5,207 | SKAMANIA | 2,380 | 968 | 1,221 | 189 | 2 | 253 D | 40.7% | 51.3% | 7.9% |
| 172,199 | SNOHOMISH | 87,424 | 36,252 | 44,019 | 7,005 | 148 | 7,767 D | 41.5% | 50.4% | 8.0% |
| 278,333 | SPOKANE | 110,594 | 52,650 | 49,423 | 8,420 | 101 | 3,227 R | 47.6% | 44.7% | 7.6% |
| 17,884 | STEVENS | 7,345 | 3,435 | 2,948 | 957 | 5 | 487 R | 46.8% | 40.1% | 13.0% |
| 55,049 | THURSTON | 30,499 | 13,742 | 14,228 | 2,493 | 36 | 486 D | 45.1% | 46.7% | 8.2% |
| 3,426 | WAHKIAKUM | 1,675 | 641 | 899 | 131 | 4 | 258 D | 38.3% | 53.7% | 7.8% |
| 42,195 | WALLA WALLA | 16,923 | 10,042 | 5,841 | 1,028 | 12 | 4,201 R | 59.3% | 34.5% | 6.1% |
| 70,317 | WHATCOM | 31,199 | 14,695 | 14,003 | 2,387 | 114 | 692 R | 47.1% | 44.9% | 7.7% |
| 31,263 | WHITMAN | 13,789 | 7,810 | 5,218 | 710 | 51 | 2,592 R | 56.6% | 37.8% | 5.1% |
| 145,112 | YAKIMA | 51,198 | 27,488 | 19,499 | 4,161 | 50 | 7,989 R | 53.7% | 38.1% | 8.1% |
| 2,853,214 | TOTAL | 1,304,281 | 588,510 | 616,037 | 96,990 | 2,744 | 27,527 D | 45.1% | 47.2% | 7.4% |

# WASHINGTON

## PRESIDENT 1964

| 1960 Census Population | County | Total Vote | Republican | Democratic | Other | Rep.-Dem. Plurality | Percentage | | | |
|---|---|---|---|---|---|---|---|---|---|---|
| | | | | | | | Total Vote | | Major Vote | |
| | | | | | | | Rep. | Dem. | Rep. | Dem. |
| 9,929 | ADAMS | 4,273 | 2,241 | 2,027 | 5 | 214 R | 52.4% | 47.4% | 52.5% | 47.5% |
| 12,909 | ASOTIN | 5,436 | 1,777 | 3,657 | 2 | 1,880 D | 32.7% | 67.3% | 32.7% | 67.3% |
| 62,070 | BENTON | 28,372 | 11,708 | 16,650 | 14 | 4,942 D | 41.3% | 58.7% | 41.3% | 58.7% |
| 40,744 | CHELAN | 17,822 | 7,406 | 10,295 | 121 | 2,889 D | 41.6% | 57.8% | 41.8% | 58.2% |
| 30,022 | CLALLAM | 13,455 | 4,175 | 9,265 | 15 | 5,090 D | 31.0% | 68.9% | 31.1% | 68.9% |
| 93,809 | CLARK | 41,790 | 12,300 | 29,341 | 149 | 17,041 D | 29.4% | 70.2% | 29.5% | 70.5% |
| 4,569 | COLUMBIA | 2,187 | 1,048 | 1,138 | 1 | 90 D | 47.9% | 52.0% | 47.9% | 52.1% |
| 57,801 | COWLITZ | 24,501 | 6,708 | 17,605 | 188 | 10,897 D | 27.4% | 71.9% | 27.6% | 72.4% |
| 14,890 | DOUGLAS | 6,376 | 2,643 | 3,728 | 5 | 1,085 D | 41.5% | 58.5% | 41.5% | 58.5% |
| 3,889 | FERRY | 1,459 | 526 | 931 | 2 | 405 D | 36.1% | 63.8% | 36.1% | 63.9% |
| 23,342 | FRANKLIN | 10,058 | 3,615 | 6,375 | 68 | 2,760 D | 35.9% | 63.4% | 36.2% | 63.8% |
| 2,976 | GARFIELD | 1,532 | 751 | 781 | | 30 D | 49.0% | 51.0% | 49.0% | 51.0% |
| 46,477 | GRANT | 14,427 | 6,065 | 8,352 | 10 | 2,287 D | 42.0% | 57.9% | 42.1% | 57.9% |
| 54,465 | GRAYS HARBOR | 23,027 | 5,744 | 17,145 | 138 | 11,401 D | 24.9% | 74.5% | 25.1% | 74.9% |
| 19,638 | ISLAND | 6,999 | 3,044 | 3,946 | 9 | 902 D | 43.5% | 56.4% | 43.5% | 56.5% |
| 9,639 | JEFFERSON | 4,456 | 1,432 | 3,012 | 12 | 1,580 D | 32.1% | 67.6% | 32.2% | 67.8% |
| 935,014 | KING | 450,640 | 177,598 | 268,216 | 4,826 | 90,618 D | 39.4% | 59.5% | 39.8% | 60.2% |
| 84,176 | KITSAP | 37,714 | 10,702 | 26,904 | 108 | 16,202 D | 28.4% | 71.3% | 28.5% | 71.5% |
| 20,467 | KITTITAS | 8,592 | 3,200 | 5,383 | 9 | 2,183 D | 37.2% | 62.7% | 37.3% | 62.7% |
| 13,455 | KLICKITAT | 5,674 | 1,850 | 3,819 | 5 | 1,969 D | 32.6% | 67.3% | 32.6% | 67.4% |
| 41,858 | LEWIS | 19,022 | 6,933 | 12,070 | 19 | 5,137 D | 36.4% | 63.5% | 36.5% | 63.5% |
| 10,919 | LINCOLN | 5,213 | 2,911 | 2,299 | 3 | 612 R | 55.8% | 44.1% | 55.9% | 44.1% |
| 16,251 | MASON | 8,071 | 2,549 | 5,514 | 8 | 2,965 D | 31.6% | 68.3% | 31.6% | 68.4% |
| 25,520 | OKANOGAN | 10,495 | 3,931 | 6,554 | 10 | 2,623 D | 37.5% | 62.4% | 37.5% | 62.5% |
| 14,674 | PACIFIC | 6,860 | 1,789 | 5,056 | 15 | 3,267 D | 26.1% | 73.7% | 26.1% | 73.9% |
| 6,914 | PEND OREILLE | 2,965 | 985 | 1,978 | 2 | 993 D | 33.2% | 66.7% | 33.2% | 66.8% |
| 321,590 | PIERCE | 125,973 | 40,164 | 84,566 | 1,243 | 44,402 D | 31.9% | 67.1% | 32.2% | 67.8% |
| 2,872 | SAN JUAN | 1,750 | 839 | 906 | 5 | 67 D | 47.9% | 51.8% | 48.1% | 51.9% |
| 51,350 | SKAGIT | 22,510 | 8,138 | 14,344 | 28 | 6,206 D | 36.2% | 63.7% | 36.2% | 63.8% |
| 5,207 | SKAMANIA | 2,414 | 653 | 1,758 | 3 | 1,105 D | 27.1% | 72.8% | 27.1% | 72.9% |
| 172,199 | SNOHOMISH | 81,405 | 25,902 | 55,013 | 490 | 29,111 D | 31.8% | 67.6% | 32.0% | 68.0% |
| 278,333 | SPOKANE | 111,581 | 49,387 | 62,092 | 102 | 12,705 D | 44.3% | 55.6% | 44.3% | 55.7% |
| 17,884 | STEVENS | 7,578 | 3,302 | 4,266 | 10 | 964 D | 43.6% | 56.3% | 43.6% | 56.4% |
| 55,049 | THURSTON | 27,021 | 9,351 | 17,578 | 92 | 8,227 D | 34.6% | 65.1% | 34.7% | 65.3% |
| 3,426 | WAHKIAKUM | 1,624 | 446 | 1,175 | 3 | 729 D | 27.5% | 72.4% | 27.5% | 72.5% |
| 42,195 | WALLA WALLA | 17,594 | 8,102 | 9,481 | 11 | 1,379 D | 46.0% | 53.9% | 46.1% | 53.9% |
| 70,317 | WHATCOM | 31,422 | 10,900 | 20,297 | 225 | 9,397 D | 34.7% | 64.6% | 34.9% | 65.1% |
| 31,263 | WHITMAN | 13,538 | 6,765 | 6,760 | 13 | 5 R | 50.0% | 49.9% | 50.0% | 50.0% |
| 145,112 | YAKIMA | 52,730 | 22,786 | 29,604 | 340 | 6,818 D | 43.2% | 56.1% | 43.5% | 56.5% |
| 2,853,214 | TOTAL | 1,258,556 | 470,366 | 779,881 | 8,309 | 309,515 D | 37.4% | 62.0% | 37.6% | 62.4% |

# WASHINGTON

## PRESIDENT 1960

| 1960 Census Population | County | Total Vote | Republican | Democratic | Other | Rep.-Dem. Plurality | Percentage Total Vote Rep. | Total Vote Dem. | Major Vote Rep. | Major Vote Dem. |
|---|---|---|---|---|---|---|---|---|---|---|
| 9,929 | ADAMS | 4,216 | 2,479 | 1,732 | 5 | 747 R | 58.8% | 41.1% | 58.9% | 41.1% |
| 12,909 | ASOTIN | 5,739 | 2,640 | 3,093 | 6 | 453 D | 46.0% | 53.9% | 46.0% | 54.0% |
| 62,070 | BENTON | 26,344 | 13,797 | 12,518 | 29 | 1,279 R | 52.4% | 47.5% | 52.4% | 47.6% |
| 40,744 | CHELAN | 18,214 | 9,854 | 8,177 | 183 | 1,677 R | 54.1% | 44.9% | 54.7% | 45.3% |
| 30,022 | CLALLAM | 13,080 | 6,227 | 6,801 | 52 | 574 D | 47.6% | 52.0% | 47.8% | 52.2% |
| 93,809 | CLARK | 40,868 | 20,080 | 20,771 | 17 | 691 D | 49.1% | 50.8% | 49.2% | 50.8% |
| 4,569 | COLUMBIA | 2,094 | 1,301 | 793 | | 508 R | 62.1% | 37.9% | 62.1% | 37.9% |
| 57,801 | COWLITZ | 24,310 | 12,103 | 12,054 | 153 | 49 R | 49.8% | 49.6% | 50.1% | 49.9% |
| 14,890 | DOUGLAS | 6,346 | 3,241 | 3,087 | 18 | 154 R | 51.1% | 48.6% | 51.2% | 48.8% |
| 3,889 | FERRY | 1,546 | 623 | 921 | 2 | 298 D | 40.3% | 59.6% | 40.3% | 59.7% |
| 23,342 | FRANKLIN | 9,409 | 4,201 | 5,156 | 52 | 955 D | 44.6% | 54.8% | 44.9% | 55.1% |
| 2,976 | GARFIELD | 1,607 | 914 | 690 | 3 | 224 R | 56.9% | 42.9% | 57.0% | 43.0% |
| 46,477 | GRANT | 15,005 | 7,568 | 7,400 | 37 | 168 R | 50.4% | 49.3% | 50.6% | 49.4% |
| 54,465 | GRAYS HARBOR | 24,006 | 10,067 | 13,773 | 166 | 3,706 D | 41.9% | 57.4% | 42.2% | 57.8% |
| 19,638 | ISLAND | 6,094 | 3,596 | 2,470 | 28 | 1,126 R | 59.0% | 40.5% | 59.3% | 40.7% |
| 9,639 | JEFFERSON | 4,307 | 2,103 | 2,197 | 7 | 94 D | 48.8% | 51.0% | 48.9% | 51.1% |
| 935,014 | KING | 440,810 | 224,150 | 208,756 | 7,904 | 15,394 R | 50.8% | 47.4% | 51.8% | 48.2% |
| 84,176 | KITSAP | 37,302 | 17,459 | 19,662 | 181 | 2,203 D | 46.8% | 52.7% | 47.0% | 53.0% |
| 20,467 | KITTITAS | 8,953 | 4,640 | 4,303 | 10 | 337 R | 51.8% | 48.1% | 51.9% | 48.1% |
| 13,455 | KLICKITAT | 5,595 | 2,836 | 2,744 | 15 | 92 R | 50.7% | 49.0% | 50.8% | 49.2% |
| 41,858 | LEWIS | 19,480 | 11,012 | 8,411 | 57 | 2,601 R | 56.5% | 43.2% | 56.7% | 43.3% |
| 10,919 | LINCOLN | 5,464 | 3,211 | 2,248 | 5 | 963 R | 58.8% | 41.1% | 58.8% | 41.2% |
| 16,251 | MASON | 7,902 | 3,703 | 4,183 | 16 | 480 D | 46.9% | 52.9% | 47.0% | 53.0% |
| 25,520 | OKANOGAN | 10,698 | 5,169 | 5,507 | 22 | 338 D | 48.3% | 51.5% | 48.4% | 51.6% |
| 14,674 | PACIFIC | 7,090 | 3,224 | 3,837 | 29 | 613 D | 45.5% | 54.1% | 45.7% | 54.3% |
| 6,914 | PEND OREILLE | 2,953 | 1,305 | 1,641 | 7 | 336 D | 44.2% | 55.6% | 44.3% | 55.7% |
| 321,590 | PIERCE | 123,475 | 57,188 | 64,292 | 1,995 | 7,104 D | 46.3% | 52.1% | 47.1% | 52.9% |
| 2,872 | SAN JUAN | 1,740 | 1,112 | 624 | 4 | 488 R | 63.9% | 35.9% | 64.1% | 35.9% |
| 51,350 | SKAGIT | 23,220 | 12,168 | 11,003 | 49 | 1,165 R | 52.4% | 47.4% | 52.5% | 47.5% |
| 5,207 | SKAMANIA | 2,306 | 1,032 | 1,269 | 5 | 237 D | 44.8% | 55.0% | 44.9% | 55.1% |
| 172,199 | SNOHOMISH | 73,163 | 33,731 | 38,793 | 639 | 5,062 D | 46.1% | 53.0% | 46.5% | 53.5% |
| 278,333 | SPOKANE | 115,369 | 59,557 | 55,553 | 259 | 4,004 R | 51.6% | 48.2% | 51.7% | 48.3% |
| 17,884 | STEVENS | 7,955 | 4,076 | 3,861 | 18 | 215 R | 51.2% | 48.5% | 51.4% | 48.6% |
| 55,049 | THURSTON | 25,606 | 13,921 | 11,620 | 65 | 2,301 R | 54.4% | 45.4% | 54.5% | 45.5% |
| 3,426 | WAHKIAKUM | 1,722 | 796 | 923 | 3 | 127 D | 46.2% | 53.6% | 46.3% | 53.7% |
| 42,195 | WALLA WALLA | 18,519 | 11,786 | 6,721 | 12 | 5,065 R | 63.6% | 36.3% | 63.7% | 36.3% |
| 70,317 | WHATCOM | 31,526 | 16,651 | 14,298 | 577 | 2,353 R | 52.8% | 45.4% | 53.8% | 46.2% |
| 31,263 | WHITMAN | 13,544 | 8,069 | 5,458 | 17 | 2,611 R | 59.6% | 40.3% | 59.7% | 40.3% |
| 145,112 | YAKIMA | 53,995 | 31,683 | 21,958 | 354 | 9,725 R | 58.7% | 40.7% | 59.1% | 40.9% |
| 2,853,214 | TOTAL | 1,241,572 | 629,273 | 599,298 | 13,001 | 29,975 R | 50.7% | 48.3% | 51.2% | 48.8% |

# WASHINGTON

## ELECTION NOTES

**2004**   Other vote was 23,283 Independent (Ralph Nader); 11,955 Libertarian (Michael Badnarik); 3,922 Constitution (Michael Peroutka); 2,974 Green (David Cobb); 1,077 Workers World (John Parker); 547 Socialist Workers (James Harris); 231 Socialist Equality (Bill Van Auken).

**2000**   Other vote was 13,135 Libertarian (Browne); 7,171 Freedom (Buchanan); 2,927 Natural Law (Hagelin); 1,989 Constitutiton (Phillips); 1,729 Workers World (Moorehead); 660 Socialist (McReynolds); 304 Socialist Workers (Harris).

**1996**   Other vote was 60,322 Independent (Nader); 12,522 Libertarian (Browne); 6,076 Natural Law (Hagelin); 4,578 Taxpayers (Phillips); 2,374 Independent (Collins); 2,189 Workers World (Moorehead); 738 Socialist Workers (Harris).

**1992**   Other vote was 7,533 Marrou (Libertarian); 4,854 Gritz (Populist); 2,456 Hagelin (Natural Law); 2,354 Phillips (Taxpayers); 1,776 Fulani (New Alliance); 1,171 Daniels (Independent); 855 LaRouche (Independent); 515 Warren (Socialist Workers); 665 scattered write-in. The total of the other vote column includes the 665 write-in votes not available by county.

**1988**   Other vote was 17,240 Paul (Libertarian); 4,412 LaRouche (Independent); 3,520 Fulani (New Alliance); 1,440 Holmes (Workers World); 1,290 Warren (Socialist Workers).

**1984**   Other vote was 8,844 Bergland (Libertarian); 5,724 Richards (Populist); 4,712 LaRouche (Independent); 1,891 Johnson (Citizens); 1,654 Serrette (New Alliance); 814 Hall (Communist); 641 Holmes (Workers World); 608 Mason (Socialist Workers). The Democratic vote in King county and the Democratic state-wide total vote have been adjusted to correct a 9,000 vote undercount in King county.

**1980**   Other vote was 185,073 Anderson (Independent); 29,213 Clark (Libertarian); 9,403 Commoner (Citizens); 1,137 DeBerry (Socialist Workers); 956 McReynolds (Socialist); 834 Hall (Communist); 341 Griswold (Workers World).

**1976**   Other vote was 36,986 McCarthy (Independent); 8,585 Maddox (American Independent); 5,046 Anderson (American Constitution); 5,042 MacBride (Libertarian); 1,124 Wright (Bicentennial Reality); 905 Camejo (Socialist Workers); 903 LaRouche (U.S. Labor); 817 Hall (Communist); 713 Levin (Socialist Labor); 358 Zeidler (Socialist).

**1972**   Other vote was 58,906 Schmitz (Independent); 2,644 Spock (People's); 1,537 Hospers (Libertarian); 1,102 Fisher (Socialist Labor); 623 Jenness (Socialist Workers); 566 Hall (Communist).

**1968**   Wallace on the ballot as American. Other vote was 1,609 Cleaver (Peace and Freedom); 488 Blomen (Socialist Labor); 377 Mitchell (Free Ballot); 270 Halstead (Socialist Workers).

**1964**   Other vote was 7,772 Hass (Socialist Labor); 537 DeBerry (Socialist Workers).

**1960**   Other vote was 10,895 Hass (Socialist Labor); 1,401 Curtis (Constitution); 705 Dobbs (Socialist Workers).

# WEST VIRGINIA

## POPULAR VOTE FOR PRESIDENT 1920 TO 2004

| Year | Total Vote | Republican | | Democratic | | Other Vote | Plurality | Percentage | | | |
|------|-----------|------|-----------|------|-----------|-----------|-----------|------|------|------|------|
| | | | | | | | | Total Vote | | Major Vote | |
| | | Vote | Candidate | Vote | Candidate | | | Rep. | Dem. | Rep. | Dem. |
| 2004 | 755,887 | 423,778 | Bush, George W. | 326,541 | Kerry, John | 5,568 | 97,237 R | 56.1% | 43.2% | 56.5% | 43.5% |
| 2000 ** | 648,124 | 336,475 | Bush, George W. | 295,497 | Gore, Al | 16,152 | 40,978 R | 51.9% | 45.6% | 53.2% | 46.8% |
| 1996 ** | 636,459 | 233,946 | Dole, Bob | 327,812 | Clinton, Bill | 74,701 | 93,866 D | 36.8% | 51.5% | 41.6% | 58.4% |
| 1992 ** | 683,762 | 241,974 | Bush, George | 331,001 | Clinton, Bill | 110,787 | 89,027 D | 35.4% | 48.4% | 42.2% | 57.8% |
| 1988 | 653,311 | 310,065 | Bush, George | 341,016 | Dukakis, Michael S. | 2,230 | 30,951 D | 47.5% | 52.2% | 47.6% | 52.4% |
| 1984 | 735,742 | 405,483 | Reagan, Ronald | 328,125 | Mondale, Walter F. | 2,134 | 77,358 R | 55.1% | 44.6% | 55.3% | 44.7% |
| 1980 ** | 737,715 | 334,206 | Reagan, Ronald | 367,462 | Carter, Jimmy | 36,047 | 33,256 D | 45.3% | 49.8% | 47.6% | 52.4% |
| 1976 | 750,964 | 314,760 | Ford, Gerald R. | 435,914 | Carter, Jimmy | 290 | 121,154 D | 41.9% | 58.0% | 41.9% | 58.1% |
| 1972 | 762,399 | 484,964 | Nixon, Richard M. | 277,435 | McGovern, George S. | | 207,529 R | 63.6% | 36.4% | 63.6% | 36.4% |
| 1968 | 754,206 | 307,555 | Nixon, Richard M. | 374,091 | Humphrey, Hubert H. | 72,560 | 66,536 D | 40.8% | 49.6% | 45.1% | 54.9% |
| 1964 | 792,040 | 253,953 | Goldwater, Barry M. | 538,087 | Johnson, Lyndon B. | | 284,134 D | 32.1% | 67.9% | 32.1% | 67.9% |
| 1960 | 837,781 | 395,995 | Nixon, Richard M. | 441,786 | Kennedy, John F. | | 45,791 D | 47.3% | 52.7% | 47.3% | 52.7% |
| 1956 | 830,831 | 449,297 | Eisenhower, Dwight D. | 381,534 | Stevenson, Adlai E. | | 67,763 R | 54.1% | 45.9% | 54.1% | 45.9% |
| 1952 | 873,548 | 419,970 | Eisenhower, Dwight D. | 453,578 | Stevenson, Adlai E. | | 33,608 D | 48.1% | 51.9% | 48.1% | 51.9% |
| 1948 | 748,750 | 316,251 | Dewey, Thomas E. | 429,188 | Truman, Harry S. | 3,311 | 112,937 D | 42.2% | 57.3% | 42.4% | 57.6% |
| 1944 | 715,596 | 322,819 | Dewey, Thomas E. | 392,777 | Roosevelt, Franklin D. | | 69,958 D | 45.1% | 54.9% | 45.1% | 54.9% |
| 1940 | 868,076 | 372,414 | Willkie, Wendell | 495,662 | Roosevelt, Franklin D. | | 123,248 D | 42.9% | 57.1% | 42.9% | 57.1% |
| 1936 | 829,945 | 325,358 | Landon, Alfred M. | 502,582 | Roosevelt, Franklin D. | 2,005 | 177,224 D | 39.2% | 60.6% | 39.3% | 60.7% |
| 1932 | 743,774 | 330,731 | Hoover, Herbert C. | 405,124 | Roosevelt, Franklin D. | 7,919 | 74,393 D | 44.5% | 54.5% | 44.9% | 55.1% |
| 1928 | 642,752 | 375,551 | Hoover, Herbert C. | 263,784 | Smith, Alfred E. | 3,417 | 111,767 R | 58.4% | 41.0% | 58.7% | 41.3% |
| 1924 | 583,662 | 288,635 | Coolidge, Calvin | 257,232 | Davis, John W. | 37,795 | 31,403 R | 49.5% | 44.1% | 52.9% | 47.1% |
| 1920 | 509,936 | 282,007 | Harding, Warren G. | 220,785 | Cox, James M. | 7,144 | 61,222 R | 55.3% | 43.3% | 56.1% | 43.9% |

In 2000 the other vote column includes 10,680 votes cast for Green (Nader). In 1996 the other vote column includes 71,639 votes cast for Perot. In 1992 the other vote column includes 108,829 votes cast for Perot. In 1980 the other column includes 31,691 votes for Independent (Anderson).

## ELECTORAL COLLEGE VOTE 1920 TO 2004

| Year | Total | Republican | Democratic | Other |
|------|-------|-----------|-----------|-------|
| 2004 | 5 | 5 | | |
| 2000 | 5 | 5 | | |
| 1996 | 5 | | 5 | |
| 1992 | 5 | | 5 | |
| 1988 ** | 6 | | 5 | 1 BENTSEN |
| 1984 | 6 | 6 | | |
| 1980 | 6 | | 6 | |
| 1976 | 6 | | 6 | |
| 1972 | 6 | 6 | | |
| 1968 | 7 | | 7 | |
| 1964 | 7 | | 7 | |
| 1960 | 8 | | 8 | |
| 1956 | 8 | 8 | | |
| 1952 | 8 | | 8 | |
| 1948 | 8 | | 8 | |
| 1944 | 8 | | 8 | |
| 1940 | 8 | | 8 | |
| 1936 | 8 | | 8 | |
| 1932 | 8 | | 8 | |
| 1928 | 8 | 8 | | |
| 1924 | 8 | 8 | | |
| 1920 | 8 | 8 | | |

In 1988 one of the six Democratic electors voted in the Electoral College for Lloyd Bentsen for President and Michael S. Dukakis for Vice-President.

# WEST VIRGINIA

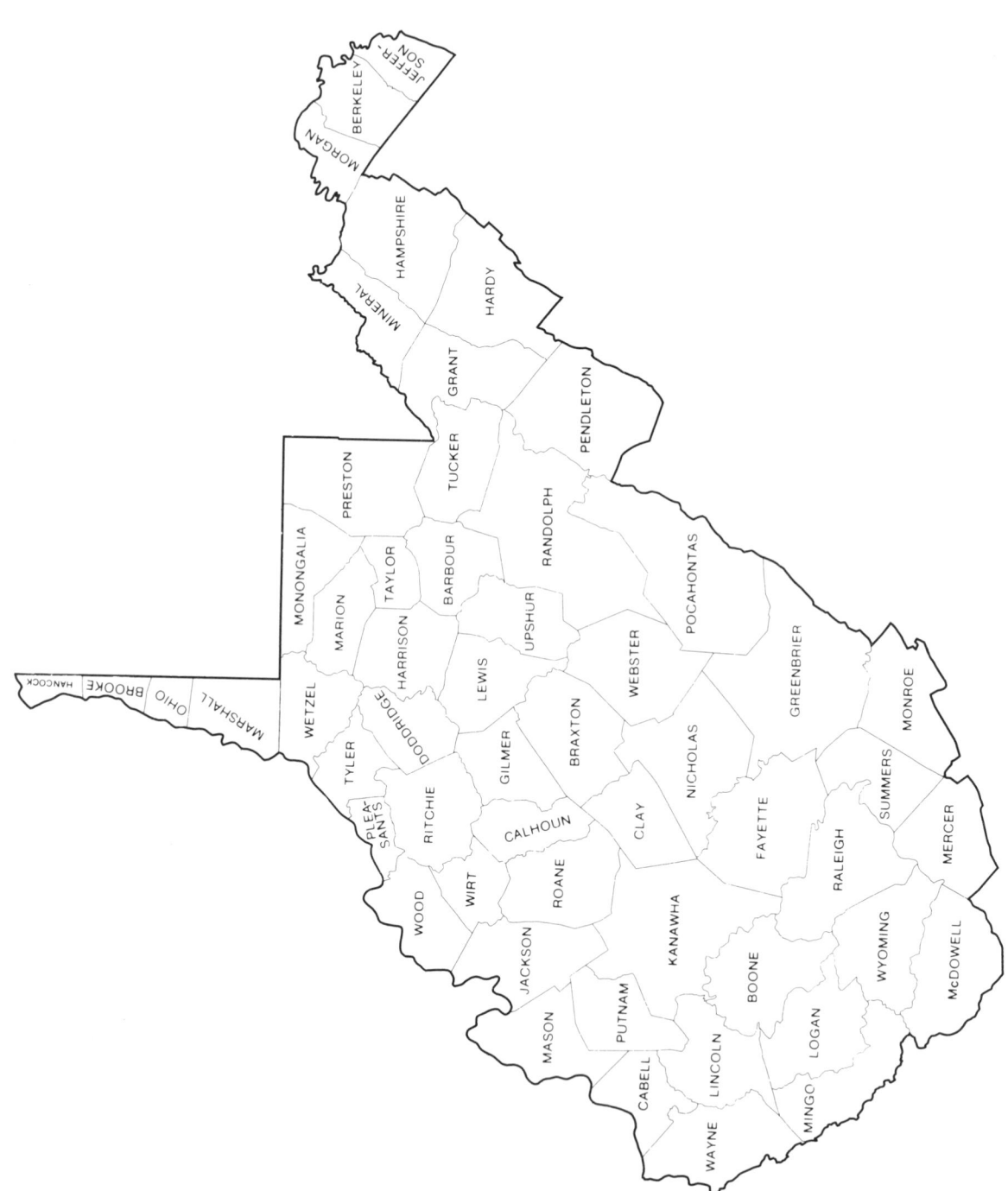

# WEST VIRGINIA

## PRESIDENT 2004

| 2000 Census Population | County | Total Vote | Republican | Democratic | Other | Rep.-Dem. Plurality | Percentage | | | |
|---|---|---|---|---|---|---|---|---|---|---|
| | | | | | | | Total Vote | | Major Vote | |
| | | | | | | | Rep. | Dem. | Rep. | Dem. |
| 15,557 | BARBOUR | 6,655 | 4,004 | 2,610 | 41 | 1,394 R | 60.2% | 39.2% | 60.5% | 39.5% |
| 75,905 | BERKELEY | 33,785 | 21,293 | 12,244 | 248 | 9,049 R | 63.0% | 36.2% | 63.5% | 36.5% |
| 25,535 | BOONE | 10,198 | 4,207 | 5,933 | 58 | 1,726 D | 41.3% | 58.2% | 41.5% | 58.5% |
| 14,702 | BRAXTON | 6,051 | 2,986 | 3,035 | 30 | 49 D | 49.3% | 50.2% | 49.6% | 50.4% |
| 25,447 | BROOKE | 10,773 | 5,189 | 5,493 | 91 | 304 D | 48.2% | 51.0% | 48.6% | 51.4% |
| 96,784 | CABELL | 37,950 | 21,035 | 16,583 | 332 | 4,452 R | 55.4% | 43.7% | 55.9% | 44.1% |
| 7,582 | CALHOUN | 2,889 | 1,588 | 1,266 | 35 | 322 R | 55.0% | 43.8% | 55.6% | 44.4% |
| 10,330 | CLAY | 4,072 | 2,198 | 1,835 | 39 | 363 R | 54.0% | 45.1% | 54.5% | 45.5% |
| 7,403 | DODDRIDGE | 3,179 | 2,362 | 800 | 17 | 1,562 R | 74.3% | 25.2% | 74.7% | 25.3% |
| 47,579 | FAYETTE | 16,967 | 7,881 | 8,971 | 115 | 1,090 D | 46.4% | 52.9% | 46.8% | 53.2% |
| 7,160 | GILMER | 2,852 | 1,665 | 1,159 | 28 | 506 R | 58.4% | 40.6% | 59.0% | 41.0% |
| 11,299 | GRANT | 5,047 | 4,063 | 963 | 21 | 3,100 R | 80.5% | 19.1% | 80.8% | 19.2% |
| 34,453 | GREENBRIER | 14,553 | 8,358 | 6,084 | 111 | 2,274 R | 57.4% | 41.8% | 57.9% | 42.1% |
| 20,203 | HAMPSHIRE | 7,996 | 5,489 | 2,455 | 52 | 3,034 R | 68.6% | 30.7% | 69.1% | 30.9% |
| 32,667 | HANCOCK | 14,321 | 7,298 | 6,906 | 117 | 392 R | 51.0% | 48.2% | 51.4% | 48.6% |
| 12,669 | HARDY | 5,276 | 3,635 | 1,617 | 24 | 2,018 R | 68.9% | 30.6% | 69.2% | 30.8% |
| 68,652 | HARRISON | 30,588 | 17,111 | 13,238 | 239 | 3,873 R | 55.9% | 43.3% | 56.4% | 43.6% |
| 28,000 | JACKSON | 13,158 | 7,686 | 5,384 | 88 | 2,302 R | 58.4% | 40.9% | 58.8% | 41.2% |
| 42,190 | JEFFERSON | 19,993 | 10,539 | 9,301 | 153 | 1,238 R | 52.7% | 46.5% | 53.1% | 46.9% |
| 200,073 | KANAWHA | 87,928 | 44,430 | 43,010 | 488 | 1,420 R | 50.5% | 48.9% | 50.8% | 49.2% |
| 16,919 | LEWIS | 6,999 | 4,445 | 2,475 | 79 | 1,970 R | 63.5% | 35.4% | 64.2% | 35.8% |
| 22,108 | LINCOLN | 8,312 | 4,102 | 4,048 | 162 | 54 R | 49.4% | 48.7% | 50.3% | 49.7% |
| 37,710 | LOGAN | 14,987 | 7,047 | 7,877 | 63 | 830 D | 47.0% | 52.6% | 47.2% | 52.8% |
| 27,329 | MCDOWELL | 7,299 | 2,762 | 4,501 | 36 | 1,739 D | 37.8% | 61.7% | 38.0% | 62.0% |
| 56,598 | MARION | 25,194 | 12,150 | 12,771 | 273 | 621 D | 48.2% | 50.7% | 48.8% | 51.2% |
| 35,519 | MARSHALL | 15,072 | 8,516 | 6,435 | 121 | 2,081 R | 56.5% | 42.7% | 57.0% | 43.0% |
| 25,957 | MASON | 11,990 | 6,487 | 5,408 | 95 | 1,079 R | 54.1% | 45.1% | 54.5% | 45.5% |
| 62,980 | MERCER | 22,379 | 13,057 | 9,178 | 144 | 3,879 R | 58.3% | 41.0% | 58.7% | 41.3% |
| 27,078 | MINERAL | 11,461 | 7,854 | 3,518 | 89 | 4,336 R | 68.5% | 30.7% | 69.1% | 30.9% |
| 28,253 | MINGO | 10,655 | 4,612 | 5,983 | 60 | 1,371 D | 43.3% | 56.2% | 43.5% | 56.5% |
| 81,866 | MONONGALIA | 34,306 | 17,670 | 16,313 | 323 | 1,357 R | 51.5% | 47.6% | 52.0% | 48.0% |
| 14,583 | MONROE | 5,951 | 3,590 | 2,311 | 50 | 1,279 R | 60.3% | 38.8% | 60.8% | 39.2% |
| 14,943 | MORGAN | 6,847 | 4,511 | 2,272 | 64 | 2,239 R | 65.9% | 33.2% | 66.5% | 33.5% |
| 26,562 | NICHOLAS | 10,351 | 5,485 | 4,788 | 78 | 697 R | 53.0% | 46.3% | 53.4% | 46.6% |
| 47,427 | OHIO | 20,392 | 11,694 | 8,543 | 155 | 3,151 R | 57.3% | 41.9% | 57.8% | 42.2% |
| 8,196 | PENDLETON | 3,544 | 2,146 | 1,381 | 17 | 765 R | 60.6% | 39.0% | 60.8% | 39.2% |
| 7,514 | PLEASANTS | 3,435 | 2,061 | 1,349 | 25 | 712 R | 60.0% | 39.3% | 60.4% | 39.6% |
| 9,131 | POCAHONTAS | 3,918 | 2,295 | 1,573 | 50 | 722 R | 58.6% | 40.1% | 59.3% | 40.7% |
| 29,334 | PRESTON | 11,929 | 7,855 | 3,963 | 111 | 3,892 R | 65.8% | 33.2% | 66.5% | 33.5% |
| 51,589 | PUTNAM | 25,151 | 15,716 | 9,301 | 134 | 6,415 R | 62.5% | 37.0% | 62.8% | 37.2% |
| 79,220 | RALEIGH | 30,525 | 18,519 | 11,815 | 191 | 6,704 R | 60.7% | 38.7% | 61.1% | 38.9% |
| 28,262 | RANDOLPH | 11,490 | 6,512 | 4,892 | 86 | 1,620 R | 56.7% | 42.6% | 57.1% | 42.9% |
| 10,343 | RITCHIE | 4,196 | 3,086 | 1,070 | 40 | 2,016 R | 73.5% | 25.5% | 74.3% | 25.7% |
| 15,446 | ROANE | 6,100 | 3,440 | 2,612 | 48 | 828 R | 56.4% | 42.8% | 56.8% | 43.2% |
| 12,999 | SUMMERS | 5,524 | 2,978 | 2,504 | 42 | 474 R | 53.9% | 45.3% | 54.3% | 45.7% |
| 16,089 | TAYLOR | 6,551 | 3,893 | 2,617 | 41 | 1,276 R | 59.4% | 39.9% | 59.8% | 40.2% |
| 7,321 | TUCKER | 3,600 | 2,179 | 1,400 | 21 | 779 R | 60.5% | 38.9% | 60.9% | 39.1% |
| 9,592 | TYLER | 4,245 | 2,798 | 1,401 | 46 | 1,397 R | 65.9% | 33.0% | 66.6% | 33.4% |
| 23,404 | UPSHUR | 9,293 | 6,191 | 3,034 | 68 | 3,157 R | 66.6% | 32.6% | 67.1% | 32.9% |
| 42,903 | WAYNE | 18,609 | 10,070 | 8,411 | 128 | 1,659 R | 54.1% | 45.2% | 54.5% | 45.5% |
| 9,719 | WEBSTER | 3,714 | 1,724 | 1,965 | 25 | 241 D | 46.4% | 52.9% | 46.7% | 53.3% |
| 17,693 | WETZEL | 7,038 | 3,656 | 3,330 | 52 | 326 R | 51.9% | 47.3% | 52.3% | 47.7% |
| 5,873 | WIRT | 2,654 | 1,727 | 896 | 31 | 831 R | 65.1% | 33.8% | 65.8% | 34.2% |
| 87,986 | WOOD | 39,227 | 24,948 | 14,025 | 254 | 10,923 R | 63.6% | 35.8% | 64.0% | 36.0% |
| 25,708 | WYOMING | 8,718 | 4,985 | 3,694 | 39 | 1,291 R | 57.2% | 42.4% | 57.4% | 42.6% |
| 1,808,344 | TOTAL | 755,887 | 423,778 | 326,541 | 5,568 | 97,237 R | 56.1% | 43.2% | 56.5% | 43.5% |

# WEST VIRGINIA

## PRESIDENT 2000

| 2000 Census Population | County | Total Vote | Republican | Democratic | Green (Nader) | Other | Rep.-Dem. Plurality | Percentage of Total Vote | | |
|---|---|---|---|---|---|---|---|---|---|---|
| | | | | | | | | Rep. | Dem. | Green |
| 15,557 | BARBOUR | 6,051 | 3,411 | 2,503 | 89 | 48 | 908 R | 56.4% | 41.4% | 1.5% |
| 75,905 | BERKELEY | 23,010 | 13,619 | 8,797 | 414 | 180 | 4,822 R | 59.2% | 38.2% | 1.8% |
| 25,535 | BOONE | 9,141 | 3,353 | 5,656 | 84 | 48 | 2,303 D | 36.7% | 61.9% | 0.9% |
| 14,702 | BRAXTON | 5,328 | 2,529 | 2,719 | 47 | 33 | 190 D | 47.5% | 51.0% | 0.9% |
| 25,447 | BROOKE | 9,405 | 4,195 | 4,678 | 228 | 304 | 483 D | 44.6% | 49.7% | 2.4% |
| 96,784 | CABELL | 32,216 | 16,440 | 14,896 | 605 | 275 | 1,544 R | 51.0% | 46.2% | 1.9% |
| 7,582 | CALHOUN | 2,615 | 1,425 | 1,112 | 63 | 15 | 313 R | 54.5% | 42.5% | 2.4% |
| 10,330 | CLAY | 3,582 | 1,887 | 1,617 | 50 | 28 | 270 R | 52.7% | 45.1% | 1.4% |
| 7,403 | DODDRIDGE | 2,816 | 1,955 | 773 | 68 | 20 | 1,182 R | 69.4% | 27.5% | 2.4% |
| 47,579 | FAYETTE | 14,619 | 5,897 | 8,371 | 239 | 112 | 2,474 D | 40.3% | 57.3% | 1.6% |
| 7,160 | GILMER | 2,740 | 1,560 | 1,092 | 66 | 22 | 468 R | 56.9% | 39.9% | 2.4% |
| 11,299 | GRANT | 4,534 | 3,571 | 891 | 39 | 33 | 2,680 R | 78.8% | 19.7% | 0.9% |
| 34,453 | GREENBRIER | 12,808 | 6,866 | 5,627 | 235 | 80 | 1,239 R | 53.6% | 43.9% | 1.8% |
| 20,203 | HAMPSHIRE | 6,097 | 3,879 | 2,069 | 97 | 52 | 1,810 R | 63.6% | 33.9% | 1.6% |
| 32,667 | HANCOCK | 13,472 | 6,458 | 6,249 | 329 | 436 | 209 R | 47.9% | 46.4% | 2.4% |
| 12,669 | HARDY | 4,514 | 2,816 | 1,621 | 44 | 33 | 1,195 R | 62.4% | 35.9% | 1.0% |
| 68,652 | HARRISON | 26,578 | 12,948 | 13,009 | 427 | 194 | 61 D | 48.7% | 48.9% | 1.6% |
| 28,000 | JACKSON | 11,518 | 6,341 | 4,937 | 166 | 74 | 1,404 R | 55.1% | 42.9% | 1.4% |
| 42,190 | JEFFERSON | 14,378 | 7,045 | 6,860 | 359 | 114 | 185 R | 49.0% | 47.7% | 2.5% |
| 200,073 | KANAWHA | 76,670 | 36,809 | 38,524 | 948 | 389 | 1,715 D | 48.0% | 50.2% | 1.2% |
| 16,919 | LEWIS | 6,134 | 3,606 | 2,355 | 114 | 59 | 1,251 R | 58.8% | 38.4% | 1.9% |
| 22,108 | LINCOLN | 7,464 | 3,389 | 3,939 | 84 | 52 | 550 D | 45.4% | 52.8% | 1.1% |
| 37,710 | LOGAN | 14,439 | 5,334 | 8,927 | 88 | 90 | 3,593 D | 36.9% | 61.8% | 0.6% |
| 27,329 | MCDOWELL | 7,303 | 2,348 | 4,845 | 67 | 43 | 2,497 D | 32.2% | 66.3% | 0.9% |
| 56,598 | MARION | 22,873 | 9,972 | 12,315 | 418 | 168 | 2,343 D | 43.6% | 53.8% | 1.8% |
| 35,519 | MARSHALL | 13,498 | 6,859 | 6,000 | 316 | 323 | 859 R | 50.8% | 44.5% | 2.3% |
| 25,957 | MASON | 11,223 | 5,972 | 4,963 | 195 | 93 | 1,009 R | 53.2% | 44.2% | 1.7% |
| 62,980 | MERCER | 18,875 | 10,206 | 8,347 | 227 | 95 | 1,859 R | 54.1% | 44.2% | 1.2% |
| 27,078 | MINERAL | 9,782 | 6,180 | 3,341 | 186 | 75 | 2,839 R | 63.2% | 34.2% | 1.9% |
| 28,253 | MINGO | 10,043 | 3,866 | 6,049 | 74 | 54 | 2,183 D | 38.5% | 60.2% | 0.7% |
| 81,866 | MONONGALIA | 27,367 | 13,595 | 12,603 | 942 | 227 | 992 R | 49.7% | 46.1% | 3.4% |
| 14,583 | MONROE | 5,139 | 2,940 | 2,094 | 78 | 27 | 846 R | 57.2% | 40.7% | 1.5% |
| 14,943 | MORGAN | 5,772 | 3,639 | 1,939 | 148 | 46 | 1,700 R | 63.0% | 33.6% | 2.6% |
| 26,562 | NICHOLAS | 8,579 | 4,359 | 4,059 | 111 | 50 | 300 R | 50.8% | 47.3% | 1.3% |
| 47,427 | OHIO | 17,964 | 9,607 | 7,653 | 390 | 314 | 1,954 R | 53.5% | 42.6% | 2.2% |
| 8,196 | PENDLETON | 3,221 | 1,996 | 1,172 | 37 | 16 | 824 R | 62.0% | 36.4% | 1.1% |
| 7,514 | PLEASANTS | 3,208 | 1,884 | 1,267 | 26 | 31 | 617 R | 58.7% | 39.5% | 0.8% |
| 9,131 | POCAHONTAS | 3,467 | 1,970 | 1,392 | 69 | 36 | 578 R | 56.8% | 40.1% | 2.0% |
| 29,334 | PRESTON | 10,439 | 6,607 | 3,515 | 209 | 108 | 3,092 R | 63.3% | 33.7% | 2.0% |
| 51,589 | PUTNAM | 20,426 | 12,173 | 7,891 | 251 | 111 | 4,282 R | 59.6% | 38.6% | 1.2% |
| 79,220 | RALEIGH | 24,061 | 12,587 | 11,047 | 299 | 128 | 1,540 R | 52.3% | 45.9% | 1.2% |
| 28,262 | RANDOLPH | 9,542 | 5,248 | 4,028 | 199 | 67 | 1,220 R | 55.0% | 42.2% | 2.1% |
| 10,343 | RITCHIE | 3,812 | 2,717 | 1,024 | 47 | 24 | 1,693 R | 71.3% | 26.9% | 1.2% |
| 15,446 | ROANE | 5,625 | 3,172 | 2,332 | 95 | 26 | 840 R | 56.4% | 41.5% | 1.7% |
| 12,999 | SUMMERS | 4,713 | 2,304 | 2,299 | 81 | 29 | 5 R | 48.9% | 48.8% | 1.7% |
| 16,089 | TAYLOR | 5,712 | 3,124 | 2,473 | 82 | 33 | 651 R | 54.7% | 43.3% | 1.4% |
| 7,321 | TUCKER | 3,346 | 1,935 | 1,319 | 50 | 42 | 616 R | 57.8% | 39.4% | 1.5% |
| 9,592 | TYLER | 3,928 | 2,582 | 1,214 | 80 | 52 | 1,368 R | 65.7% | 30.9% | 2.0% |
| 23,404 | UPSHUR | 8,123 | 5,165 | 2,770 | 130 | 58 | 2,395 R | 63.6% | 34.1% | 1.6% |
| 42,903 | WAYNE | 16,241 | 7,993 | 7,940 | 182 | 126 | 53 R | 49.2% | 48.9% | 1.1% |
| 9,719 | WEBSTER | 3,308 | 1,484 | 1,764 | 35 | 25 | 280 D | 44.9% | 53.3% | 1.1% |
| 17,693 | WETZEL | 6,288 | 3,239 | 2,849 | 104 | 96 | 390 R | 51.5% | 45.3% | 1.7% |
| 5,873 | WIRT | 2,382 | 1,518 | 818 | 21 | 25 | 700 R | 63.7% | 34.3% | 0.9% |
| 87,986 | WOOD | 33,857 | 20,428 | 12,664 | 582 | 183 | 7,764 R | 60.3% | 37.4% | 1.7% |
| 25,708 | WYOMING | 7,878 | 3,473 | 4,289 | 66 | 50 | 816 D | 44.1% | 54.4% | 0.8% |
| 1,808,344 | TOTAL | 648,124 | 336,475 | 295,497 | 10,680 | 5,472 | 40,978 R | 51.9% | 45.6% | 1.6% |

# WEST VIRGINIA

## PRESIDENT 1996

| 1995 Census Pop. Est. | County | Total Vote | Republican | Democratic | Reform (Perot) | Other | Rep.-Dem. Plurality | Percentage of Total Vote | | |
|---|---|---|---|---|---|---|---|---|---|---|
| | | | | | | | | Rep. | Dem. | Reform |
| 16,229 | BARBOUR | 6,047 | 2,155 | 3,076 | 784 | 32 | 921 D | 35.6% | 50.9% | 13.0% |
| 66,572 | BERKELEY | 20,576 | 9,859 | 8,321 | 2,291 | 105 | 1,538 R | 47.9% | 40.4% | 11.1% |
| 26,291 | BOONE | 8,922 | 1,917 | 6,048 | 927 | 30 | 4,131 D | 21.5% | 67.8% | 10.4% |
| 13,401 | BRAXTON | 4,996 | 1,441 | 3,001 | 527 | 27 | 1,560 D | 28.8% | 60.1% | 10.5% |
| 26,866 | BROOKE | 9,500 | 2,741 | 5,338 | 1,375 | 46 | 2,597 D | 28.9% | 56.2% | 14.5% |
| 96,837 | CABELL | 32,560 | 13,179 | 16,277 | 2,968 | 136 | 3,098 D | 40.5% | 50.0% | 9.1% |
| 7,918 | CALHOUN | 2,725 | 1,000 | 1,402 | 307 | 16 | 402 D | 36.7% | 51.4% | 11.3% |
| 10,380 | CLAY | 3,577 | 1,137 | 2,074 | 355 | 11 | 937 D | 31.8% | 58.0% | 9.9% |
| 7,409 | DODDRIDGE | 2,595 | 1,335 | 865 | 382 | 13 | 470 R | 51.4% | 33.3% | 14.7% |
| 48,655 | FAYETTE | 14,758 | 3,669 | 9,471 | 1,552 | 66 | 5,802 D | 24.9% | 64.2% | 10.5% |
| 7,359 | GILMER | 2,649 | 933 | 1,390 | 316 | 10 | 457 D | 35.2% | 52.5% | 11.9% |
| 11,059 | GRANT | 4,297 | 2,599 | 1,206 | 481 | 11 | 1,393 R | 60.5% | 28.1% | 11.2% |
| 35,556 | GREENBRIER | 12,194 | 4,434 | 6,286 | 1,418 | 56 | 1,852 D | 36.4% | 51.5% | 11.6% |
| 18,381 | HAMPSHIRE | 5,781 | 2,814 | 2,335 | 605 | 27 | 479 R | 48.7% | 40.4% | 10.5% |
| 34,734 | HANCOCK | 14,020 | 4,268 | 7,521 | 2,158 | 73 | 3,253 D | 30.4% | 53.6% | 15.4% |
| 11,642 | HARDY | 4,259 | 1,895 | 1,911 | 438 | 15 | 16 D | 44.5% | 44.9% | 10.3% |
| 70,931 | HARRISON | 26,843 | 8,857 | 14,746 | 3,135 | 105 | 5,889 D | 33.0% | 54.9% | 11.7% |
| 27,200 | JACKSON | 10,447 | 4,235 | 4,882 | 1,295 | 35 | 647 D | 40.5% | 46.7% | 12.4% |
| 39,477 | JEFFERSON | 13,068 | 5,287 | 6,361 | 1,307 | 113 | 1,074 D | 40.5% | 48.7% | 10.0% |
| 206,195 | KANAWHA | 76,495 | 29,311 | 40,357 | 6,412 | 415 | 11,046 D | 38.3% | 52.8% | 8.4% |
| 17,629 | LEWIS | 6,173 | 2,285 | 2,868 | 974 | 46 | 583 D | 37.0% | 46.5% | 15.8% |
| 22,167 | LINCOLN | 8,235 | 2,530 | 4,994 | 696 | 15 | 2,464 D | 30.7% | 60.6% | 8.5% |
| 42,451 | LOGAN | 15,056 | 2,627 | 10,840 | 1,532 | 57 | 8,213 D | 17.4% | 72.0% | 10.2% |
| 32,662 | MCDOWELL | 8,208 | 1,550 | 5,989 | 655 | 14 | 4,439 D | 18.9% | 73.0% | 8.0% |
| 58,063 | MARION | 22,107 | 6,160 | 12,994 | 2,881 | 72 | 6,834 D | 27.9% | 58.8% | 13.0% |
| 37,105 | MARSHALL | 13,785 | 4,460 | 7,045 | 2,202 | 78 | 2,585 D | 32.4% | 51.1% | 16.0% |
| 25,638 | MASON | 10,433 | 3,581 | 5,284 | 1,533 | 35 | 1,703 D | 34.3% | 50.6% | 14.7% |
| 64,889 | MERCER | 18,700 | 7,768 | 8,721 | 2,141 | 70 | 953 D | 41.5% | 46.6% | 11.4% |
| 27,321 | MINERAL | 9,076 | 4,380 | 3,487 | 1,170 | 39 | 893 R | 48.3% | 38.4% | 12.9% |
| 33,646 | MINGO | 10,875 | 2,229 | 7,584 | 1,020 | 42 | 5,355 D | 20.5% | 69.7% | 9.4% |
| 78,060 | MONONGALIA | 26,820 | 10,189 | 13,406 | 3,040 | 185 | 3,217 D | 38.0% | 50.0% | 11.3% |
| 12,977 | MONROE | 5,092 | 2,131 | 2,382 | 559 | 20 | 251 D | 41.8% | 46.8% | 11.0% |
| 13,182 | MORGAN | 5,080 | 2,599 | 1,929 | 513 | 39 | 670 R | 51.2% | 38.0% | 10.1% |
| 27,622 | NICHOLAS | 8,536 | 2,649 | 4,769 | 1,071 | 47 | 2,120 D | 31.0% | 55.9% | 12.5% |
| 49,865 | OHIO | 18,206 | 7,267 | 8,781 | 2,065 | 93 | 1,514 D | 39.9% | 48.2% | 11.3% |
| 8,128 | PENDLETON | 3,308 | 1,431 | 1,591 | 276 | 10 | 160 D | 43.3% | 48.1% | 8.3% |
| 7,525 | PLEASANTS | 3,171 | 1,265 | 1,478 | 416 | 12 | 213 D | 39.9% | 46.6% | 13.1% |
| 8,962 | POCAHONTAS | 3,481 | 1,242 | 1,796 | 426 | 17 | 554 D | 35.7% | 51.6% | 12.2% |
| 29,847 | PRESTON | 10,306 | 4,257 | 4,237 | 1,760 | 52 | 20 R | 41.3% | 41.1% | 17.1% |
| 48,944 | PUTNAM | 18,809 | 8,803 | 8,029 | 1,901 | 76 | 774 R | 46.8% | 42.7% | 10.1% |
| 78,656 | RALEIGH | 23,622 | 8,628 | 12,547 | 2,355 | 92 | 3,919 D | 36.5% | 53.1% | 10.0% |
| 28,939 | RANDOLPH | 10,089 | 3,348 | 5,469 | 1,184 | 88 | 2,121 D | 33.2% | 54.2% | 11.7% |
| 10,154 | RITCHIE | 3,831 | 1,906 | 1,385 | 522 | 18 | 521 R | 49.8% | 36.2% | 13.6% |
| 15,389 | ROANE | 5,280 | 2,069 | 2,572 | 622 | 17 | 503 D | 39.2% | 48.7% | 11.8% |
| 14,050 | SUMMERS | 4,363 | 1,505 | 2,397 | 438 | 23 | 892 D | 34.5% | 54.9% | 10.0% |
| 15,335 | TAYLOR | 5,533 | 1,977 | 2,692 | 844 | 20 | 715 D | 35.7% | 48.7% | 15.3% |
| 7,783 | TUCKER | 3,312 | 1,217 | 1,649 | 424 | 22 | 432 D | 36.7% | 49.8% | 12.8% |
| 10,160 | TYLER | 2,780 | 734 | 1,459 | 563 | 24 | 725 D | 26.4% | 52.5% | 20.3% |
| 23,891 | UPSHUR | 7,447 | 3,325 | 3,052 | 1,031 | 39 | 273 R | 44.6% | 41.0% | 13.8% |
| 42,669 | WAYNE | 15,476 | 5,492 | 8,300 | 1,633 | 51 | 2,808 D | 35.5% | 53.6% | 10.6% |
| 10,409 | WEBSTER | 3,331 | 654 | 2,292 | 369 | 16 | 1,638 D | 19.6% | 68.8% | 11.1% |
| 18,909 | WETZEL | 6,277 | 2,037 | 3,209 | 1,004 | 27 | 1,172 D | 32.5% | 51.1% | 16.0% |
| 5,513 | WIRT | 2,131 | 928 | 906 | 280 | 17 | 22 R | 43.5% | 42.5% | 13.1% |
| 88,295 | WOOD | 32,672 | 15,502 | 13,261 | 3,694 | 215 | 2,241 R | 47.4% | 40.6% | 11.3% |
| 28,213 | WYOMING | 8,549 | 2,155 | 5,550 | 812 | 32 | 3,395 D | 25.2% | 64.9% | 9.5% |
| 1,828,140 | TOTAL | 636,459 | 233,946 | 327,812 | 71,639 | 3,062 | 93,866 D | 36.8% | 51.5% | 11.3% |

# WEST VIRGINIA

## PRESIDENT 1992

| 1990 Census Population | County | Total Vote | Republican | Democratic | Perot | Other | Plurality | Percentage Total Vote | | |
|---|---|---|---|---|---|---|---|---|---|---|
| | | | | | | | | Rep. | Dem. | Perot |
| 15,699 | BARBOUR | 6,954 | 2,322 | 3,467 | 1,153 | 12 | 1,145 D | 33.4% | 49.9% | 16.6% |
| 59,253 | BERKELEY | 20,029 | 9,134 | 7,159 | 3,645 | 91 | 1,975 R | 45.6% | 35.7% | 18.2% |
| 25,870 | BOONE | 9,658 | 2,021 | 6,576 | 1,037 | 24 | 4,555 D | 20.9% | 68.1% | 10.7% |
| 12,998 | BRAXTON | 5,765 | 1,535 | 3,396 | 823 | 11 | 1,861 D | 26.6% | 58.9% | 14.3% |
| 26,992 | BROOKE | 10,415 | 2,582 | 5,693 | 2,103 | 37 | 3,111 D | 24.8% | 54.7% | 20.2% |
| 96,827 | CABELL | 33,725 | 13,203 | 15,111 | 5,311 | 100 | 1,908 D | 39.1% | 44.8% | 15.7% |
| 7,885 | CALHOUN | 3,268 | 1,095 | 1,627 | 537 | 9 | 532 D | 33.5% | 49.8% | 16.4% |
| 9,983 | CLAY | 3,657 | 1,255 | 1,928 | 462 | 12 | 673 D | 34.3% | 52.7% | 12.6% |
| 6,994 | DODDRIDGE | 2,992 | 1,500 | 968 | 515 | 9 | 532 R | 50.1% | 32.4% | 17.2% |
| 47,952 | FAYETTE | 15,608 | 3,991 | 9,574 | 2,002 | 41 | 5,583 D | 25.6% | 61.3% | 12.8% |
| 7,669 | GILMER | 3,154 | 1,085 | 1,576 | 484 | 9 | 491 D | 34.4% | 50.0% | 15.3% |
| 10,428 | GRANT | 4,298 | 2,762 | 1,011 | 519 | 6 | 1,751 R | 64.3% | 23.5% | 12.1% |
| 34,693 | GREENBRIER | 12,187 | 4,442 | 5,784 | 1,898 | 63 | 1,342 D | 36.4% | 47.5% | 15.6% |
| 16,498 | HAMPSHIRE | 6,171 | 2,767 | 2,365 | 1,022 | 17 | 402 R | 44.8% | 38.3% | 16.6% |
| 35,233 | HANCOCK | 15,046 | 3,897 | 7,830 | 3,267 | 52 | 3,933 D | 25.9% | 52.0% | 21.7% |
| 10,977 | HARDY | 4,671 | 2,144 | 1,917 | 602 | 8 | 227 R | 45.9% | 41.0% | 12.9% |
| 69,371 | HARRISON | 30,341 | 9,687 | 15,480 | 5,131 | 43 | 5,793 D | 31.9% | 51.0% | 16.9% |
| 25,938 | JACKSON | 11,229 | 4,192 | 5,102 | 1,908 | 27 | 910 D | 37.3% | 45.4% | 17.0% |
| 35,926 | JEFFERSON | 12,189 | 4,656 | 5,363 | 2,114 | 56 | 707 D | 38.2% | 44.0% | 17.3% |
| 207,619 | KANAWHA | 81,683 | 31,358 | 38,315 | 11,778 | 232 | 6,957 D | 38.4% | 46.9% | 14.4% |
| 17,223 | LEWIS | 6,563 | 2,413 | 2,931 | 1,197 | 22 | 518 D | 36.8% | 44.7% | 18.2% |
| 21,382 | LINCOLN | 7,984 | 2,637 | 4,502 | 787 | 58 | 1,865 D | 33.0% | 56.4% | 9.9% |
| 43,032 | LOGAN | 16,297 | 3,336 | 11,095 | 1,835 | 31 | 7,759 D | 20.5% | 68.1% | 11.3% |
| 35,233 | MCDOWELL | 9,781 | 1,941 | 7,019 | 803 | 18 | 5,078 D | 19.8% | 71.8% | 8.2% |
| 57,249 | MARION | 25,194 | 6,380 | 14,042 | 4,736 | 36 | 7,662 D | 25.3% | 55.7% | 18.8% |
| 37,356 | MARSHALL | 15,219 | 4,463 | 7,298 | 3,402 | 56 | 2,835 D | 29.3% | 48.0% | 22.4% |
| 25,178 | MASON | 11,200 | 3,808 | 5,331 | 2,045 | 16 | 1,523 D | 34.0% | 47.6% | 18.3% |
| 64,980 | MERCER | 20,290 | 7,888 | 9,511 | 2,817 | 74 | 1,623 D | 38.9% | 46.9% | 13.9% |
| 26,697 | MINERAL | 10,728 | 4,837 | 3,992 | 1,884 | 15 | 845 R | 45.1% | 37.2% | 17.6% |
| 33,739 | MINGO | 10,873 | 2,584 | 7,342 | 915 | 32 | 4,758 D | 23.8% | 67.5% | 8.4% |
| 75,509 | MONONGALIA | 28,634 | 9,831 | 14,142 | 4,576 | 85 | 4,311 D | 34.3% | 49.4% | 16.0% |
| 12,406 | MONROE | 5,420 | 2,311 | 2,418 | 685 | 6 | 107 D | 42.6% | 44.6% | 12.6% |
| 12,128 | MORGAN | 5,346 | 2,585 | 1,854 | 886 | 21 | 731 R | 48.4% | 34.7% | 16.6% |
| 26,775 | NICHOLAS | 9,531 | 2,959 | 5,042 | 1,495 | 35 | 2,083 D | 31.0% | 52.9% | 15.7% |
| 50,871 | OHIO | 20,633 | 7,421 | 9,522 | 3,632 | 58 | 2,101 D | 36.0% | 46.1% | 17.6% |
| 8,054 | PENDLETON | 3,583 | 1,589 | 1,626 | 362 | 6 | 37 D | 44.3% | 45.4% | 10.1% |
| 7,546 | PLEASANTS | 3,376 | 1,248 | 1,387 | 731 | 10 | 139 D | 37.0% | 41.1% | 21.7% |
| 9,008 | POCAHONTAS | 3,781 | 1,401 | 1,741 | 627 | 12 | 340 D | 37.1% | 46.0% | 16.6% |
| 29,037 | PRESTON | 10,495 | 4,429 | 3,933 | 2,109 | 24 | 496 R | 42.2% | 37.5% | 20.1% |
| 42,835 | PUTNAM | 17,428 | 7,653 | 6,817 | 2,910 | 48 | 836 R | 43.9% | 39.1% | 16.7% |
| 76,819 | RALEIGH | 25,214 | 8,700 | 13,171 | 3,247 | 96 | 4,471 D | 34.5% | 52.2% | 12.9% |
| 27,803 | RANDOLPH | 10,222 | 3,496 | 5,097 | 1,582 | 47 | 1,601 D | 34.2% | 49.9% | 15.5% |
| 10,233 | RITCHIE | 4,416 | 2,184 | 1,474 | 745 | 13 | 710 R | 49.5% | 33.4% | 16.9% |
| 15,120 | ROANE | 5,857 | 2,207 | 2,607 | 1,009 | 34 | 400 D | 37.7% | 44.5% | 17.2% |
| 14,204 | SUMMERS | 4,882 | 1,652 | 2,650 | 565 | 15 | 998 D | 33.8% | 54.3% | 11.6% |
| 15,144 | TAYLOR | 6,117 | 2,022 | 2,843 | 1,242 | 10 | 821 D | 33.1% | 46.5% | 20.3% |
| 7,728 | TUCKER | 3,625 | 1,261 | 1,805 | 550 | 9 | 544 D | 34.8% | 49.8% | 15.2% |
| 9,796 | TYLER | 4,203 | 1,593 | 1,587 | 1,013 | 10 | 6 R | 37.9% | 37.8% | 24.1% |
| 22,867 | UPSHUR | 8,253 | 3,505 | 3,161 | 1,558 | 29 | 344 R | 42.5% | 38.3% | 18.9% |
| 41,636 | WAYNE | 16,347 | 5,729 | 8,392 | 2,199 | 27 | 2,663 D | 35.0% | 51.3% | 13.5% |
| 10,729 | WEBSTER | 3,576 | 811 | 2,320 | 436 | 9 | 1,509 D | 22.7% | 64.9% | 12.2% |
| 19,258 | WETZEL | 7,597 | 2,271 | 3,753 | 1,550 | 23 | 1,482 D | 29.9% | 49.4% | 20.4% |
| 5,192 | WIRT | 2,382 | 939 | 1,043 | 394 | 6 | 104 D | 39.4% | 43.8% | 16.5% |
| 86,915 | WOOD | 36,068 | 15,441 | 13,529 | 6,998 | 100 | 1,912 R | 42.8% | 37.5% | 19.4% |
| 28,990 | WYOMING | 9,607 | 2,821 | 5,782 | 996 | 8 | 2,961 D | 29.4% | 60.2% | 10.4% |
| 1,793,477 | TOTAL | 683,762 | 241,974 | 331,001 | 108,829 | 1,358 | 89,027 D | 35.4% | 48.4% | 15.9% |

# WEST VIRGINIA

## PRESIDENT 1988

| 1980 Census Population | County | Total Vote | Republican | Democratic | Other | Rep.-Dem. Plurality | Percentage Total Vote Rep. | Percentage Total Vote Dem. | Percentage Major Vote Rep. | Percentage Major Vote Dem. |
|---|---|---|---|---|---|---|---|---|---|---|
| 16,639 | BARBOUR | 6,261 | 3,023 | 3,221 | 17 | 198 D | 48.3% | 51.4% | 48.4% | 51.6% |
| 46,775 | BERKELEY | 17,135 | 10,761 | 6,313 | 61 | 4,448 R | 62.8% | 36.8% | 63.0% | 37.0% |
| 30,447 | BOONE | 9,345 | 2,786 | 6,539 | 20 | 3,753 D | 29.8% | 70.0% | 29.9% | 70.1% |
| 13,894 | BRAXTON | 5,423 | 2,024 | 3,377 | 22 | 1,353 D | 37.3% | 62.3% | 37.5% | 62.5% |
| 31,117 | BROOKE | 10,306 | 4,006 | 6,258 | 42 | 2,252 D | 38.9% | 60.7% | 39.0% | 61.0% |
| 106,835 | CABELL | 32,662 | 17,197 | 15,368 | 97 | 1,829 R | 52.7% | 47.1% | 52.8% | 47.2% |
| 8,250 | CALHOUN | 3,057 | 1,395 | 1,644 | 18 | 249 D | 45.6% | 53.8% | 45.9% | 54.1% |
| 11,265 | CLAY | 3,811 | 1,536 | 2,263 | 12 | 727 D | 40.3% | 59.4% | 40.4% | 59.6% |
| 7,433 | DODDRIDGE | 2,847 | 1,880 | 955 | 12 | 925 R | 66.0% | 33.5% | 66.3% | 33.7% |
| 57,863 | FAYETTE | 16,205 | 5,143 | 11,009 | 53 | 5,866 D | 31.7% | 67.9% | 31.8% | 68.2% |
| 8,334 | GILMER | 3,064 | 1,387 | 1,661 | 16 | 274 D | 45.3% | 54.2% | 45.5% | 54.5% |
| 10,210 | GRANT | 4,130 | 3,215 | 893 | 22 | 2,322 R | 77.8% | 21.6% | 78.3% | 21.7% |
| 37,665 | GREENBRIER | 11,521 | 5,395 | 6,091 | 35 | 696 D | 46.8% | 52.9% | 47.0% | 53.0% |
| 14,867 | HAMPSHIRE | 5,363 | 3,253 | 2,085 | 25 | 1,168 R | 60.7% | 38.9% | 60.9% | 39.1% |
| 40,418 | HANCOCK | 14,280 | 5,882 | 8,338 | 60 | 2,456 D | 41.2% | 58.4% | 41.4% | 58.6% |
| 10,030 | HARDY | 4,288 | 2,581 | 1,689 | 18 | 892 R | 60.2% | 39.4% | 60.4% | 39.6% |
| 77,710 | HARRISON | 30,418 | 13,364 | 17,005 | 49 | 3,641 D | 43.9% | 55.9% | 44.0% | 56.0% |
| 25,794 | JACKSON | 10,291 | 5,696 | 4,573 | 22 | 1,123 R | 55.3% | 44.4% | 55.5% | 44.5% |
| 30,302 | JEFFERSON | 9,726 | 5,349 | 4,334 | 43 | 1,015 R | 55.0% | 44.6% | 55.2% | 44.8% |
| 231,414 | KANAWHA | 79,542 | 38,140 | 41,144 | 258 | 3,004 D | 47.9% | 51.7% | 48.1% | 51.9% |
| 18,813 | LEWIS | 6,908 | 3,602 | 3,272 | 34 | 330 R | 52.1% | 47.4% | 52.4% | 47.6% |
| 23,675 | LINCOLN | 8,529 | 3,457 | 5,049 | 23 | 1,592 D | 40.5% | 59.2% | 40.6% | 59.4% |
| 50,679 | LOGAN | 15,608 | 4,244 | 11,317 | 47 | 7,073 D | 27.2% | 72.5% | 27.3% | 72.7% |
| 49,899 | MCDOWELL | 9,714 | 2,463 | 7,204 | 47 | 4,741 D | 25.4% | 74.2% | 25.5% | 74.5% |
| 65,789 | MARION | 23,742 | 9,229 | 14,441 | 72 | 5,212 D | 38.9% | 60.8% | 39.0% | 61.0% |
| 41,608 | MARSHALL | 14,779 | 6,793 | 7,903 | 83 | 1,110 D | 46.0% | 53.5% | 46.2% | 53.8% |
| 27,045 | MASON | 10,825 | 5,332 | 5,468 | 25 | 136 D | 49.3% | 50.5% | 49.4% | 50.6% |
| 73,942 | MERCER | 20,430 | 10,221 | 10,152 | 57 | 69 R | 50.0% | 49.7% | 50.2% | 49.8% |
| 27,234 | MINERAL | 10,111 | 6,015 | 4,059 | 37 | 1,956 R | 59.5% | 40.1% | 59.7% | 40.3% |
| 37,336 | MINGO | 10,350 | 2,896 | 7,429 | 25 | 4,533 D | 28.0% | 71.8% | 28.0% | 72.0% |
| 75,024 | MONONGALIA | 26,338 | 12,091 | 14,178 | 69 | 2,087 D | 45.9% | 53.8% | 46.0% | 54.0% |
| 12,873 | MONROE | 5,168 | 2,719 | 2,427 | 22 | 292 D | 52.6% | 47.0% | 52.8% | 47.2% |
| 10,711 | MORGAN | 4,564 | 3,002 | 1,545 | 17 | 1,457 R | 65.8% | 33.9% | 66.0% | 34.0% |
| 28,126 | NICHOLAS | 8,936 | 3,731 | 5,173 | 32 | 1,442 D | 41.8% | 57.9% | 41.9% | 58.1% |
| 61,389 | OHIO | 20,578 | 10,341 | 10,121 | 116 | 220 R | 50.3% | 49.2% | 50.5% | 49.5% |
| 7,910 | PENDLETON | 3,503 | 1,901 | 1,595 | 7 | 306 R | 54.3% | 45.5% | 54.4% | 45.6% |
| 8,236 | PLEASANTS | 3,187 | 1,761 | 1,421 | 5 | 340 R | 55.3% | 44.6% | 55.3% | 44.7% |
| 9,919 | POCAHONTAS | 3,852 | 1,876 | 1,958 | 18 | 82 D | 48.7% | 50.8% | 48.9% | 51.1% |
| 30,460 | PRESTON | 10,196 | 5,804 | 4,357 | 35 | 1,447 R | 56.9% | 42.7% | 57.1% | 42.9% |
| 38,181 | PUTNAM | 14,841 | 8,163 | 6,640 | 38 | 1,523 R | 55.0% | 44.7% | 55.1% | 44.9% |
| 86,821 | RALEIGH | 24,782 | 10,395 | 14,302 | 85 | 3,907 D | 41.9% | 57.7% | 42.1% | 57.9% |
| 28,734 | RANDOLPH | 10,017 | 4,746 | 5,233 | 38 | 487 D | 47.4% | 52.2% | 47.6% | 52.4% |
| 11,442 | RITCHIE | 4,338 | 2,874 | 1,446 | 18 | 1,428 R | 66.3% | 33.3% | 66.5% | 33.5% |
| 15,952 | ROANE | 5,332 | 2,861 | 2,447 | 24 | 414 R | 53.7% | 45.9% | 53.9% | 46.1% |
| 15,875 | SUMMERS | 5,314 | 2,231 | 3,072 | 11 | 841 D | 42.0% | 57.8% | 42.1% | 57.9% |
| 16,584 | TAYLOR | 5,694 | 2,816 | 2,852 | 26 | 36 D | 49.5% | 50.1% | 49.7% | 50.3% |
| 8,675 | TUCKER | 3,577 | 1,699 | 1,869 | 9 | 170 D | 47.5% | 52.3% | 47.6% | 52.4% |
| 11,320 | TYLER | 3,874 | 2,365 | 1,501 | 8 | 864 R | 61.0% | 38.7% | 61.2% | 38.8% |
| 23,427 | UPSHUR | 7,894 | 4,813 | 3,065 | 16 | 1,748 R | 61.0% | 38.8% | 61.1% | 38.9% |
| 46,021 | WAYNE | 15,775 | 7,123 | 8,621 | 31 | 1,498 D | 45.2% | 54.6% | 45.2% | 54.8% |
| 12,245 | WEBSTER | 3,217 | 1,016 | 2,185 | 16 | 1,169 D | 31.6% | 67.9% | 31.7% | 68.3% |
| 21,874 | WETZEL | 7,350 | 3,381 | 3,928 | 41 | 547 D | 46.0% | 53.4% | 46.3% | 53.7% |
| 4,922 | WIRT | 2,066 | 1,125 | 929 | 12 | 196 R | 54.5% | 45.0% | 54.8% | 45.2% |
| 93,648 | WOOD | 32,563 | 19,450 | 12,959 | 154 | 6,491 R | 59.7% | 39.8% | 60.0% | 40.0% |
| 35,993 | WYOMING | 9,684 | 3,516 | 6,138 | 30 | 2,622 D | 36.3% | 63.4% | 36.4% | 63.6% |
| 1,949,644 | TOTAL | 653,311 | 310,065 | 341,016 | 2,230 | 30,951 D | 47.5% | 52.2% | 47.6% | 52.4% |

# WEST VIRGINIA

## PRESIDENT 1984

| 1980 Census Population | County | Total Vote | Republican | Democratic | Other | Rep.-Dem. Plurality | Percentage Total Vote Rep. | Dem. | Major Vote Rep. | Dem. |
|---|---|---|---|---|---|---|---|---|---|---|
| 16,639 | BARBOUR | 6,995 | 3,877 | 3,108 | 10 | 769 R | 55.4% | 44.4% | 55.5% | 44.5% |
| 46,775 | BERKELEY | 19,092 | 12,887 | 6,181 | 24 | 6,706 R | 67.5% | 32.4% | 67.6% | 32.4% |
| 30,447 | BOONE | 11,821 | 4,656 | 7,121 | 44 | 2,465 D | 39.4% | 60.2% | 39.5% | 60.5% |
| 13,894 | BRAXTON | 6,265 | 2,902 | 3,350 | 13 | 448 D | 46.3% | 53.5% | 46.4% | 53.6% |
| 31,117 | BROOKE | 11,498 | 4,819 | 6,636 | 43 | 1,817 D | 41.9% | 57.7% | 42.1% | 57.9% |
| 106,835 | CABELL | 37,445 | 21,815 | 15,513 | 117 | 6,302 R | 58.3% | 41.4% | 58.4% | 41.6% |
| 8,250 | CALHOUN | 3,276 | 1,765 | 1,473 | 38 | 292 R | 53.9% | 45.0% | 54.5% | 45.5% |
| 11,265 | CLAY | 3,796 | 1,667 | 2,117 | 12 | 450 D | 43.9% | 55.8% | 44.1% | 55.9% |
| 7,433 | DODDRIDGE | 3,195 | 2,343 | 836 | 16 | 1,507 R | 73.3% | 26.2% | 73.7% | 26.3% |
| 57,863 | FAYETTE | 19,086 | 7,360 | 11,650 | 76 | 4,290 D | 38.6% | 61.0% | 38.7% | 61.3% |
| 8,334 | GILMER | 3,452 | 1,953 | 1,494 | 5 | 459 R | 56.6% | 43.3% | 56.7% | 43.3% |
| 10,210 | GRANT | 4,554 | 3,715 | 828 | 11 | 2,887 R | 81.6% | 18.2% | 81.8% | 18.2% |
| 37,665 | GREENBRIER | 12,974 | 7,337 | 5,599 | 38 | 1,738 R | 56.6% | 43.2% | 56.7% | 43.3% |
| 14,867 | HAMPSHIRE | 6,187 | 4,065 | 2,102 | 20 | 1,963 R | 65.7% | 34.0% | 65.9% | 34.1% |
| 40,418 | HANCOCK | 16,124 | 7,326 | 8,708 | 90 | 1,382 D | 45.4% | 54.0% | 45.7% | 54.3% |
| 10,030 | HARDY | 4,587 | 2,938 | 1,641 | 8 | 1,297 R | 64.1% | 35.8% | 64.2% | 35.8% |
| 77,710 | HARRISON | 34,437 | 19,400 | 14,969 | 68 | 4,431 R | 56.3% | 43.5% | 56.4% | 43.6% |
| 25,794 | JACKSON | 11,310 | 7,117 | 4,147 | 46 | 2,970 R | 62.9% | 36.7% | 63.2% | 36.8% |
| 30,302 | JEFFERSON | 10,134 | 5,884 | 4,216 | 34 | 1,668 R | 58.1% | 41.6% | 58.3% | 41.7% |
| 231,414 | KANAWHA | 89,542 | 51,499 | 37,832 | 211 | 13,667 R | 57.5% | 42.3% | 57.6% | 42.4% |
| 18,813 | LEWIS | 8,031 | 5,297 | 2,693 | 41 | 2,604 R | 66.0% | 33.5% | 66.3% | 33.7% |
| 23,675 | LINCOLN | 9,902 | 4,405 | 5,467 | 30 | 1,062 D | 44.5% | 55.2% | 44.6% | 55.4% |
| 50,679 | LOGAN | 17,382 | 6,425 | 10,892 | 65 | 4,467 D | 37.0% | 62.7% | 37.1% | 62.9% |
| 49,899 | MCDOWELL | 12,883 | 4,284 | 8,546 | 53 | 4,262 D | 33.3% | 66.3% | 33.4% | 66.6% |
| 65,789 | MARION | 27,020 | 13,106 | 13,833 | 81 | 727 D | 48.5% | 51.2% | 48.7% | 51.3% |
| 41,608 | MARSHALL | 16,616 | 8,615 | 7,947 | 54 | 668 R | 51.8% | 47.8% | 52.0% | 48.0% |
| 27,045 | MASON | 12,393 | 6,648 | 5,701 | 44 | 947 R | 53.6% | 46.0% | 53.8% | 46.2% |
| 73,942 | MERCER | 23,155 | 13,910 | 9,164 | 81 | 4,746 R | 60.1% | 39.6% | 60.3% | 39.7% |
| 27,234 | MINERAL | 11,138 | 7,291 | 3,832 | 15 | 3,459 R | 65.5% | 34.4% | 65.5% | 34.5% |
| 37,336 | MINGO | 12,726 | 4,275 | 8,434 | 17 | 4,159 D | 33.6% | 66.3% | 33.6% | 66.4% |
| 75,024 | MONONGALIA | 28,274 | 14,972 | 13,236 | 66 | 1,736 R | 53.0% | 46.8% | 53.1% | 46.9% |
| 12,873 | MONROE | 5,954 | 3,612 | 2,333 | 9 | 1,279 R | 60.7% | 39.2% | 60.8% | 39.2% |
| 10,711 | MORGAN | 4,932 | 3,469 | 1,457 | 6 | 2,012 R | 70.3% | 29.5% | 70.4% | 29.6% |
| 28,126 | NICHOLAS | 9,273 | 4,656 | 4,588 | 29 | 68 R | 50.2% | 49.5% | 50.4% | 49.6% |
| 61,389 | OHIO | 23,662 | 13,447 | 10,163 | 52 | 3,284 R | 56.8% | 43.0% | 57.0% | 43.0% |
| 7,910 | PENDLETON | 3,518 | 2,047 | 1,464 | 7 | 583 R | 58.2% | 41.6% | 58.3% | 41.7% |
| 8,236 | PLEASANTS | 3,725 | 2,255 | 1,458 | 12 | 797 R | 60.5% | 39.1% | 60.7% | 39.3% |
| 9,919 | POCAHONTAS | 4,386 | 2,479 | 1,903 | 4 | 576 R | 56.5% | 43.4% | 56.6% | 43.4% |
| 30,460 | PRESTON | 11,031 | 6,955 | 4,054 | 22 | 2,901 R | 63.0% | 36.8% | 63.2% | 36.8% |
| 38,181 | PUTNAM | 14,492 | 9,238 | 5,208 | 46 | 4,030 R | 63.7% | 35.9% | 63.9% | 36.1% |
| 86,821 | RALEIGH | 29,122 | 14,571 | 14,442 | 109 | 129 R | 50.0% | 49.6% | 50.2% | 49.8% |
| 28,734 | RANDOLPH | 10,964 | 6,100 | 4,839 | 25 | 1,261 R | 55.6% | 44.1% | 55.8% | 44.2% |
| 11,442 | RITCHIE | 4,609 | 3,355 | 1,231 | 23 | 2,124 R | 72.8% | 26.7% | 73.2% | 26.8% |
| 15,952 | ROANE | 6,240 | 3,751 | 2,468 | 21 | 1,283 R | 60.1% | 39.6% | 60.3% | 39.7% |
| 15,875 | SUMMERS | 5,659 | 2,975 | 2,670 | 14 | 305 R | 52.6% | 47.2% | 52.7% | 47.3% |
| 16,584 | TAYLOR | 6,765 | 4,007 | 2,754 | 4 | 1,253 R | 59.2% | 40.7% | 59.3% | 40.7% |
| 8,675 | TUCKER | 4,014 | 2,240 | 1,766 | 8 | 474 R | 55.8% | 44.0% | 55.9% | 44.1% |
| 11,320 | TYLER | 4,575 | 3,170 | 1,395 | 10 | 1,775 R | 69.3% | 30.5% | 69.4% | 30.6% |
| 23,427 | UPSHUR | 8,466 | 5,951 | 2,468 | 47 | 3,483 R | 70.3% | 29.2% | 70.7% | 29.3% |
| 46,021 | WAYNE | 17,236 | 8,811 | 8,378 | 47 | 433 R | 51.1% | 48.6% | 51.3% | 48.7% |
| 12,245 | WEBSTER | 3,926 | 1,565 | 2,355 | 6 | 790 D | 39.9% | 60.0% | 39.9% | 60.1% |
| 21,874 | WETZEL | 8,207 | 4,626 | 3,549 | 32 | 1,077 R | 56.4% | 43.2% | 56.6% | 43.4% |
| 4,922 | WIRT | 2,322 | 1,450 | 868 | 4 | 582 R | 62.4% | 37.4% | 62.6% | 37.4% |
| 93,648 | WOOD | 36,279 | 24,821 | 11,357 | 101 | 13,464 R | 68.4% | 31.3% | 68.6% | 31.4% |
| 35,993 | WYOMING | 11,095 | 5,379 | 5,691 | 25 | 312 D | 48.5% | 51.3% | 48.6% | 51.4% |
| 1,949,644 | TOTAL | 735,742 | 405,483 | 328,125 | 2,134 | 77,358 R | 55.1% | 44.6% | 55.3% | 44.7% |

# WEST VIRGINIA

## PRESIDENT 1980

| 1980 Census Population | County | Total Vote | Republican | Democratic | Other | Rep.-Dem. Plurality | Percentage |  |  |  |
|---|---|---|---|---|---|---|---|---|---|---|
|  |  |  |  |  |  |  | Total Vote |  | Major Vote |  |
|  |  |  |  |  |  |  | Rep. | Dem. | Rep. | Dem. |
| 16,639 | BARBOUR | 7,086 | 3,311 | 3,451 | 324 | 140 D | 46.7% | 48.7% | 49.0% | 51.0% |
| 46,775 | BERKELEY | 17,454 | 9,955 | 6,783 | 716 | 3,172 R | 57.0% | 38.9% | 59.5% | 40.5% |
| 30,447 | BOONE | 12,000 | 4,164 | 7,515 | 321 | 3,351 D | 34.7% | 62.6% | 35.7% | 64.3% |
| 13,894 | BRAXTON | 6,408 | 2,403 | 3,795 | 210 | 1,392 D | 37.5% | 59.2% | 38.8% | 61.2% |
| 31,117 | BROOKE | 11,795 | 4,622 | 6,430 | 743 | 1,808 D | 39.2% | 54.5% | 41.8% | 58.2% |
| 106,835 | CABELL | 39,588 | 19,482 | 17,732 | 2,374 | 1,750 R | 49.2% | 44.8% | 52.4% | 47.6% |
| 8,250 | CALHOUN | 3,441 | 1,606 | 1,717 | 118 | 111 D | 46.7% | 49.9% | 48.3% | 51.7% |
| 11,265 | CLAY | 3,762 | 1,452 | 2,185 | 125 | 733 D | 38.6% | 58.1% | 39.9% | 60.1% |
| 7,433 | DODDRIDGE | 3,051 | 1,888 | 1,043 | 120 | 845 R | 61.9% | 34.2% | 64.4% | 35.6% |
| 57,863 | FAYETTE | 19,774 | 5,784 | 13,175 | 815 | 7,391 D | 29.3% | 66.6% | 30.5% | 69.5% |
| 8,334 | GILMER | 3,486 | 1,452 | 1,854 | 180 | 402 D | 41.7% | 53.2% | 43.9% | 56.1% |
| 10,210 | GRANT | 4,591 | 3,452 | 1,041 | 98 | 2,411 R | 75.2% | 22.7% | 76.8% | 23.2% |
| 37,665 | GREENBRIER | 14,004 | 6,221 | 7,128 | 655 | 907 D | 44.4% | 50.9% | 46.6% | 53.4% |
| 14,867 | HAMPSHIRE | 5,585 | 2,879 | 2,522 | 184 | 357 R | 51.5% | 45.2% | 53.3% | 46.7% |
| 40,418 | HANCOCK | 16,475 | 6,610 | 8,784 | 1,081 | 2,174 D | 40.1% | 53.3% | 42.9% | 57.1% |
| 10,030 | HARDY | 4,499 | 2,329 | 2,050 | 120 | 279 R | 51.8% | 45.6% | 53.2% | 46.8% |
| 77,710 | HARRISON | 34,602 | 14,251 | 18,813 | 1,538 | 4,562 D | 41.2% | 54.4% | 43.1% | 56.9% |
| 25,794 | JACKSON | 10,581 | 6,041 | 4,120 | 420 | 1,921 R | 57.1% | 38.9% | 59.5% | 40.5% |
| 30,302 | JEFFERSON | 9,818 | 4,454 | 4,679 | 685 | 225 D | 45.4% | 47.7% | 48.8% | 51.2% |
| 231,414 | KANAWHA | 91,760 | 42,604 | 42,829 | 6,327 | 225 D | 46.4% | 46.7% | 49.9% | 50.1% |
| 18,813 | LEWIS | 7,611 | 3,747 | 3,455 | 409 | 292 R | 49.2% | 45.4% | 52.0% | 48.0% |
| 23,675 | LINCOLN | 9,490 | 4,009 | 5,317 | 164 | 1,308 D | 42.2% | 56.0% | 43.0% | 57.0% |
| 50,679 | LOGAN | 17,428 | 4,945 | 12,024 | 459 | 7,079 D | 28.4% | 69.0% | 29.1% | 70.9% |
| 49,899 | MCDOWELL | 13,943 | 3,862 | 9,822 | 259 | 5,960 D | 27.7% | 70.4% | 28.2% | 71.8% |
| 65,789 | MARION | 26,471 | 10,952 | 14,189 | 1,330 | 3,237 D | 41.4% | 53.6% | 43.6% | 56.4% |
| 41,608 | MARSHALL | 15,916 | 7,252 | 7,832 | 832 | 580 D | 45.6% | 49.2% | 48.1% | 51.9% |
| 27,045 | MASON | 12,108 | 6,040 | 5,683 | 385 | 357 R | 49.9% | 46.9% | 51.5% | 48.5% |
| 73,942 | MERCER | 24,741 | 12,273 | 11,804 | 664 | 469 R | 49.6% | 47.7% | 51.0% | 49.0% |
| 27,234 | MINERAL | 11,274 | 6,125 | 4,671 | 478 | 1,454 R | 54.3% | 41.4% | 56.7% | 43.3% |
| 37,336 | MINGO | 13,280 | 3,716 | 9,328 | 236 | 5,612 D | 28.0% | 70.2% | 28.5% | 71.5% |
| 75,024 | MONONGALIA | 27,826 | 11,972 | 12,883 | 2,971 | 911 D | 43.0% | 46.3% | 48.2% | 51.8% |
| 12,873 | MONROE | 6,072 | 2,999 | 2,877 | 196 | 122 R | 49.4% | 47.4% | 51.0% | 49.0% |
| 10,711 | MORGAN | 4,627 | 2,833 | 1,594 | 200 | 1,239 R | 61.2% | 34.4% | 64.0% | 36.0% |
| 28,126 | NICHOLAS | 9,516 | 3,885 | 5,265 | 366 | 1,380 D | 40.8% | 55.3% | 42.5% | 57.5% |
| 61,389 | OHIO | 23,873 | 11,414 | 10,973 | 1,486 | 441 R | 47.8% | 46.0% | 51.0% | 49.0% |
| 7,910 | PENDLETON | 3,504 | 1,677 | 1,724 | 103 | 47 D | 47.9% | 49.2% | 49.3% | 50.7% |
| 8,236 | PLEASANTS | 3,447 | 1,852 | 1,494 | 101 | 358 R | 53.7% | 43.3% | 55.3% | 44.7% |
| 9,919 | POCAHONTAS | 4,355 | 2,011 | 2,170 | 174 | 159 D | 46.2% | 49.8% | 48.1% | 51.9% |
| 30,460 | PRESTON | 10,746 | 5,828 | 4,317 | 601 | 1,511 R | 54.2% | 40.2% | 57.4% | 42.6% |
| 38,181 | PUTNAM | 14,686 | 7,561 | 6,409 | 716 | 1,152 R | 51.5% | 43.6% | 54.1% | 45.9% |
| 86,821 | RALEIGH | 28,831 | 10,713 | 16,955 | 1,163 | 6,242 D | 37.2% | 58.8% | 38.7% | 61.3% |
| 28,734 | RANDOLPH | 10,921 | 4,374 | 5,937 | 610 | 1,563 D | 40.1% | 54.4% | 42.4% | 57.6% |
| 11,442 | RITCHIE | 4,691 | 3,081 | 1,450 | 160 | 1,631 R | 65.7% | 30.9% | 68.0% | 32.0% |
| 15,952 | ROANE | 5,953 | 3,219 | 2,498 | 236 | 721 R | 54.1% | 42.0% | 56.3% | 43.7% |
| 15,875 | SUMMERS | 5,797 | 2,456 | 3,114 | 227 | 658 D | 42.4% | 53.7% | 44.1% | 55.9% |
| 16,584 | TAYLOR | 6,487 | 3,010 | 3,216 | 261 | 206 D | 46.4% | 49.6% | 48.3% | 51.7% |
| 8,675 | TUCKER | 3,855 | 1,798 | 1,862 | 195 | 64 D | 46.6% | 48.3% | 49.1% | 50.9% |
| 11,320 | TYLER | 4,382 | 2,707 | 1,482 | 193 | 1,225 R | 61.8% | 33.8% | 64.6% | 35.4% |
| 23,427 | UPSHUR | 8,099 | 4,751 | 2,867 | 481 | 1,884 R | 58.7% | 35.4% | 62.4% | 37.6% |
| 46,021 | WAYNE | 16,719 | 7,541 | 8,687 | 491 | 1,146 D | 45.1% | 52.0% | 46.5% | 53.5% |
| 12,245 | WEBSTER | 3,974 | 1,262 | 2,578 | 134 | 1,316 D | 31.8% | 64.9% | 32.9% | 67.1% |
| 21,874 | WETZEL | 8,015 | 3,588 | 4,035 | 392 | 447 D | 44.8% | 50.3% | 47.1% | 52.9% |
| 4,922 | WIRT | 2,293 | 1,176 | 1,058 | 59 | 118 R | 51.3% | 46.1% | 52.6% | 47.4% |
| 93,648 | WOOD | 35,512 | 20,080 | 13,622 | 1,810 | 6,458 R | 56.5% | 38.4% | 59.6% | 40.4% |
| 35,993 | WYOMING | 11,512 | 4,537 | 6,624 | 351 | 2,087 D | 39.4% | 57.5% | 40.7% | 59.3% |
| 1,949,644 | TOTAL | 737,715 | 334,206 | 367,462 | 36,047 | 33,256 D | 45.3% | 49.8% | 47.6% | 52.4% |

# WEST VIRGINIA

## PRESIDENT 1976

| 1970 Census Population | County | Total Vote | Republican | Democratic | Other | Rep.-Dem. Plurality | Percentage | | | |
|---|---|---|---|---|---|---|---|---|---|---|
| | | | | | | | Total Vote | | Major Vote | |
| | | | | | | | Rep. | Dem. | Rep. | Dem. |
| 14,030 | BARBOUR | 6,882 | 3,235 | 3,647 | | 412 D | 47.0% | 53.0% | 47.0% | 53.0% |
| 36,356 | BERKELEY | 17,151 | 8,935 | 8,216 | | 719 R | 52.1% | 47.9% | 52.1% | 47.9% |
| 25,118 | BOONE | 11,604 | 3,072 | 8,528 | 4 | 5,456 D | 26.5% | 73.5% | 26.5% | 73.5% |
| 12,666 | BRAXTON | 5,928 | 1,913 | 4,012 | 3 | 2,099 D | 32.3% | 67.7% | 32.3% | 67.7% |
| 29,685 | BROOKE | 13,007 | 4,792 | 8,197 | 18 | 3,405 D | 36.8% | 63.0% | 36.9% | 63.1% |
| 106,918 | CABELL | 40,455 | 19,644 | 20,811 | | 1,167 D | 48.6% | 51.4% | 48.6% | 51.4% |
| 7,046 | CALHOUN | 3,457 | 1,283 | 2,173 | 1 | 890 D | 37.1% | 62.9% | 37.1% | 62.9% |
| 9,330 | CLAY | 3,944 | 1,282 | 2,662 | | 1,380 D | 32.5% | 67.5% | 32.5% | 67.5% |
| 6,389 | DODDRIDGE | 3,049 | 1,804 | 1,245 | | 559 R | 59.2% | 40.8% | 59.2% | 40.8% |
| 49,332 | FAYETTE | 20,955 | 5,459 | 15,496 | | 10,037 D | 26.1% | 73.9% | 26.1% | 73.9% |
| 7,782 | GILMER | 3,616 | 1,371 | 2,245 | | 874 D | 37.9% | 62.1% | 37.9% | 62.1% |
| 8,607 | GRANT | 4,302 | 2,976 | 1,323 | 3 | 1,653 R | 69.2% | 30.8% | 69.2% | 30.8% |
| 32,090 | GREENBRIER | 14,153 | 5,862 | 8,291 | | 2,429 D | 41.4% | 58.6% | 41.4% | 58.6% |
| 11,710 | HAMPSHIRE | 5,201 | 2,097 | 3,104 | | 1,007 D | 40.3% | 59.7% | 40.3% | 59.7% |
| 39,749 | HANCOCK | 17,398 | 6,771 | 10,627 | | 3,856 D | 38.9% | 61.1% | 38.9% | 61.1% |
| 8,855 | HARDY | 4,851 | 1,858 | 2,993 | | 1,135 D | 38.3% | 61.7% | 38.3% | 61.7% |
| 73,028 | HARRISON | 36,687 | 15,172 | 21,467 | 48 | 6,295 D | 41.4% | 58.5% | 41.4% | 58.6% |
| 20,903 | JACKSON | 10,694 | 5,360 | 5,334 | | 26 R | 50.1% | 49.9% | 50.1% | 49.9% |
| 21,280 | JEFFERSON | 9,030 | 3,864 | 5,166 | | 1,302 D | 42.8% | 57.2% | 42.8% | 57.2% |
| 229,515 | KANAWHA | 95,991 | 42,213 | 53,602 | 176 | 11,389 D | 44.0% | 55.8% | 44.1% | 55.9% |
| 17,847 | LEWIS | 7,696 | 3,736 | 3,960 | | 224 D | 48.5% | 51.5% | 48.5% | 51.5% |
| 18,912 | LINCOLN | 8,257 | 2,997 | 5,260 | | 2,263 D | 36.3% | 63.7% | 36.3% | 63.7% |
| 46,269 | LOGAN | 17,143 | 4,021 | 13,122 | | 9,101 D | 23.5% | 76.5% | 23.5% | 76.5% |
| 50,666 | MCDOWELL | 14,688 | 4,107 | 10,557 | 24 | 6,450 D | 28.0% | 71.9% | 28.0% | 72.0% |
| 61,356 | MARION | 28,191 | 10,391 | 17,800 | | 7,409 D | 36.9% | 63.1% | 36.9% | 63.1% |
| 37,598 | MARSHALL | 15,346 | 6,705 | 8,641 | | 1,936 D | 43.7% | 56.3% | 43.7% | 56.3% |
| 24,306 | MASON | 11,974 | 5,205 | 6,769 | | 1,564 D | 43.5% | 56.5% | 43.5% | 56.5% |
| 63,206 | MERCER | 25,552 | 10,791 | 14,761 | | 3,970 D | 42.2% | 57.8% | 42.2% | 57.8% |
| 23,109 | MINERAL | 11,028 | 5,130 | 5,898 | | 768 D | 46.5% | 53.5% | 46.5% | 53.5% |
| 32,780 | MINGO | 11,666 | 3,010 | 8,655 | 1 | 5,645 D | 25.8% | 74.2% | 25.8% | 74.2% |
| 63,714 | MONONGALIA | 27,990 | 11,827 | 16,163 | | 4,336 D | 42.3% | 57.7% | 42.3% | 57.7% |
| 11,272 | MONROE | 6,047 | 2,750 | 3,297 | | 547 D | 45.5% | 54.5% | 45.5% | 54.5% |
| 8,547 | MORGAN | 4,298 | 2,369 | 1,929 | | 440 R | 55.1% | 44.9% | 55.1% | 44.9% |
| 22,552 | NICHOLAS | 9,697 | 3,462 | 6,235 | | 2,773 D | 35.7% | 64.3% | 35.7% | 64.3% |
| 64,197 | OHIO | 24,293 | 12,476 | 11,817 | | 659 R | 51.4% | 48.6% | 51.4% | 48.6% |
| 7,031 | PENDLETON | 3,658 | 1,554 | 2,104 | | 550 D | 42.5% | 57.5% | 42.5% | 57.5% |
| 7,274 | PLEASANTS | 3,307 | 1,608 | 1,699 | | 91 D | 48.6% | 51.4% | 48.6% | 51.4% |
| 8,870 | POCAHONTAS | 4,075 | 1,740 | 2,330 | 5 | 590 D | 42.7% | 57.2% | 42.8% | 57.2% |
| 25,455 | PRESTON | 11,314 | 5,719 | 5,595 | | 124 R | 50.5% | 49.5% | 50.5% | 49.5% |
| 27,625 | PUTNAM | 14,560 | 6,334 | 8,226 | | 1,892 D | 43.5% | 56.5% | 43.5% | 56.5% |
| 70,080 | RALEIGH | 30,405 | 10,637 | 19,768 | | 9,131 D | 35.0% | 65.0% | 35.0% | 65.0% |
| 24,596 | RANDOLPH | 12,087 | 4,822 | 7,265 | | 2,443 D | 39.9% | 60.1% | 39.9% | 60.1% |
| 10,145 | RITCHIE | 4,815 | 2,874 | 1,941 | | 933 R | 59.7% | 40.3% | 59.7% | 40.3% |
| 14,111 | ROANE | 6,736 | 3,216 | 3,519 | 1 | 303 D | 47.7% | 52.2% | 47.8% | 52.2% |
| 13,213 | SUMMERS | 6,197 | 2,254 | 3,943 | | 1,689 D | 36.4% | 63.6% | 36.4% | 63.6% |
| 13,878 | TAYLOR | 6,796 | 2,891 | 3,905 | | 1,014 D | 42.5% | 57.5% | 42.5% | 57.5% |
| 7,447 | TUCKER | 3,719 | 1,396 | 2,323 | | 927 D | 37.5% | 62.5% | 37.5% | 62.5% |
| 9,929 | TYLER | 4,331 | 2,514 | 1,817 | | 697 R | 58.0% | 42.0% | 58.0% | 42.0% |
| 19,092 | UPSHUR | 8,302 | 4,789 | 3,513 | | 1,276 R | 57.7% | 42.3% | 57.7% | 42.3% |
| 37,581 | WAYNE | 15,967 | 6,009 | 9,958 | | 3,949 D | 37.6% | 62.4% | 37.6% | 62.4% |
| 9,809 | WEBSTER | 3,908 | 971 | 2,931 | 6 | 1,960 D | 24.8% | 75.0% | 24.9% | 75.1% |
| 20,314 | WETZEL | 8,835 | 3,793 | 5,042 | | 1,249 D | 42.9% | 57.1% | 42.9% | 57.1% |
| 4,154 | WIRT | 2,213 | 1,031 | 1,182 | | 151 D | 46.6% | 53.4% | 46.6% | 53.4% |
| 86,818 | WOOD | 35,457 | 18,382 | 17,075 | | 1,307 R | 51.8% | 48.2% | 51.8% | 48.2% |
| 30,095 | WYOMING | 12,061 | 4,286 | 7,775 | | 3,489 D | 35.5% | 64.5% | 35.5% | 64.5% |
| 1,744,237 | TOTAL | 750,964 | 314,760 | 435,914 | 290 | 121,154 D | 41.9% | 58.0% | 41.9% | 58.1% |

# WEST VIRGINIA

## PRESIDENT 1972

| 1970 Census Population | County | Total Vote | Republican | Democratic | Other | Rep.-Dem. Plurality | Percentage Total Vote Rep. | Dem. | Major Vote Rep. | Dem. |
|---|---|---|---|---|---|---|---|---|---|---|
| 14,030 | BARBOUR | 6,690 | 4,432 | 2,258 | | 2,174 R | 66.2% | 33.8% | 66.2% | 33.8% |
| 36,356 | BERKELEY | 15,477 | 10,954 | 4,523 | | 6,431 R | 70.8% | 29.2% | 70.8% | 29.2% |
| 25,118 | BOONE | 11,327 | 5,985 | 5,342 | | 643 R | 52.8% | 47.2% | 52.8% | 47.2% |
| 12,666 | BRAXTON | 5,926 | 3,155 | 2,771 | | 384 R | 53.2% | 46.8% | 53.2% | 46.8% |
| 29,685 | BROOKE | 12,770 | 7,544 | 5,226 | | 2,318 R | 59.1% | 40.9% | 59.1% | 40.9% |
| 106,918 | CABELL | 43,894 | 29,582 | 14,312 | | 15,270 R | 67.4% | 32.6% | 67.4% | 32.6% |
| 7,046 | CALHOUN | 3,520 | 1,992 | 1,528 | | 464 R | 56.6% | 43.4% | 56.6% | 43.4% |
| 9,330 | CLAY | 3,998 | 2,168 | 1,830 | | 338 R | 54.2% | 45.8% | 54.2% | 45.8% |
| 6,389 | DODDRIDGE | 2,929 | 2,284 | 645 | | 1,639 R | 78.0% | 22.0% | 78.0% | 22.0% |
| 49,332 | FAYETTE | 21,842 | 11,876 | 9,966 | | 1,910 R | 54.4% | 45.6% | 54.4% | 45.6% |
| 7,782 | GILMER | 3,415 | 2,056 | 1,359 | | 697 R | 60.2% | 39.8% | 60.2% | 39.8% |
| 8,607 | GRANT | 4,170 | 3,556 | 614 | | 2,942 R | 85.3% | 14.7% | 85.3% | 14.7% |
| 32,090 | GREENBRIER | 13,250 | 8,827 | 4,423 | | 4,404 R | 66.6% | 33.4% | 66.6% | 33.4% |
| 11,710 | HAMPSHIRE | 4,721 | 3,084 | 1,637 | | 1,447 R | 65.3% | 34.7% | 65.3% | 34.7% |
| 39,749 | HANCOCK | 17,361 | 10,634 | 6,727 | | 3,907 R | 61.3% | 38.7% | 61.3% | 38.7% |
| 8,855 | HARDY | 4,119 | 2,609 | 1,510 | | 1,099 R | 63.3% | 36.7% | 63.3% | 36.7% |
| 73,028 | HARRISON | 35,106 | 22,196 | 12,910 | | 9,286 R | 63.2% | 36.8% | 63.2% | 36.8% |
| 20,903 | JACKSON | 10,233 | 7,226 | 3,007 | | 4,219 R | 70.6% | 29.4% | 70.6% | 29.4% |
| 21,280 | JEFFERSON | 7,604 | 4,822 | 2,782 | | 2,040 R | 63.4% | 36.6% | 63.4% | 36.6% |
| 229,515 | KANAWHA | 103,053 | 65,021 | 38,032 | | 26,989 R | 63.1% | 36.9% | 63.1% | 36.9% |
| 17,847 | LEWIS | 7,840 | 5,778 | 2,062 | | 3,716 R | 73.7% | 26.3% | 73.7% | 26.3% |
| 18,912 | LINCOLN | 8,549 | 4,673 | 3,876 | | 797 R | 54.7% | 45.3% | 54.7% | 45.3% |
| 46,269 | LOGAN | 19,578 | 9,533 | 10,045 | | 512 D | 48.7% | 51.3% | 48.7% | 51.3% |
| 50,666 | MCDOWELL | 15,753 | 8,942 | 6,811 | | 2,131 R | 56.8% | 43.2% | 56.8% | 43.2% |
| 61,356 | MARION | 27,959 | 16,095 | 11,864 | | 4,231 R | 57.6% | 42.4% | 57.6% | 42.4% |
| 37,598 | MARSHALL | 17,344 | 10,966 | 6,378 | | 4,588 R | 63.2% | 36.8% | 63.2% | 36.8% |
| 24,306 | MASON | 11,137 | 7,129 | 4,008 | | 3,121 R | 64.0% | 36.0% | 64.0% | 36.0% |
| 63,206 | MERCER | 25,672 | 17,846 | 7,826 | | 10,020 R | 69.5% | 30.5% | 69.5% | 30.5% |
| 23,109 | MINERAL | 10,433 | 7,157 | 3,276 | | 3,881 R | 68.6% | 31.4% | 68.6% | 31.4% |
| 32,780 | MINGO | 13,069 | 7,484 | 5,585 | | 1,899 R | 57.3% | 42.7% | 57.3% | 42.7% |
| 63,714 | MONONGALIA | 27,479 | 16,758 | 10,721 | | 6,037 R | 61.0% | 39.0% | 61.0% | 39.0% |
| 11,272 | MONROE | 5,830 | 3,716 | 2,114 | | 1,602 R | 63.7% | 36.3% | 63.7% | 36.3% |
| 8,547 | MORGAN | 4,132 | 3,014 | 1,118 | | 1,896 R | 72.9% | 27.1% | 72.9% | 27.1% |
| 22,552 | NICHOLAS | 9,535 | 5,907 | 3,628 | | 2,279 R | 62.0% | 38.0% | 62.0% | 38.0% |
| 64,197 | OHIO | 28,926 | 18,435 | 10,491 | | 7,944 R | 63.7% | 36.3% | 63.7% | 36.3% |
| 7,031 | PENDLETON | 3,455 | 2,207 | 1,248 | | 959 R | 63.9% | 36.1% | 63.9% | 36.1% |
| 7,274 | PLEASANTS | 3,232 | 2,025 | 1,207 | | 818 R | 62.7% | 37.3% | 62.7% | 37.3% |
| 8,870 | POCAHONTAS | 4,026 | 2,391 | 1,635 | | 756 R | 59.4% | 40.6% | 59.4% | 40.6% |
| 25,455 | PRESTON | 10,784 | 7,807 | 2,977 | | 4,830 R | 72.4% | 27.6% | 72.4% | 27.6% |
| 27,625 | PUTNAM | 13,036 | 8,265 | 4,771 | | 3,494 R | 63.4% | 36.6% | 63.4% | 36.6% |
| 70,080 | RALEIGH | 29,736 | 19,150 | 10,586 | | 8,564 R | 64.4% | 35.6% | 64.4% | 35.6% |
| 24,596 | RANDOLPH | 10,732 | 6,923 | 3,809 | | 3,114 R | 64.5% | 35.5% | 64.5% | 35.5% |
| 10,145 | RITCHIE | 4,625 | 3,635 | 990 | | 2,645 R | 78.6% | 21.4% | 78.6% | 21.4% |
| 14,111 | ROANE | 6,639 | 4,253 | 2,386 | | 1,867 R | 64.1% | 35.9% | 64.1% | 35.9% |
| 13,213 | SUMMERS | 6,413 | 3,895 | 2,518 | | 1,377 R | 60.7% | 39.3% | 60.7% | 39.3% |
| 13,878 | TAYLOR | 6,470 | 4,385 | 2,085 | | 2,300 R | 67.8% | 32.2% | 67.8% | 32.2% |
| 7,447 | TUCKER | 3,620 | 2,163 | 1,457 | | 706 R | 59.8% | 40.2% | 59.8% | 40.2% |
| 9,929 | TYLER | 4,487 | 3,362 | 1,125 | | 2,237 R | 74.9% | 25.1% | 74.9% | 25.1% |
| 19,092 | UPSHUR | 8,244 | 6,449 | 1,795 | | 4,654 R | 78.2% | 21.8% | 78.2% | 21.8% |
| 37,581 | WAYNE | 16,026 | 9,775 | 6,251 | | 3,524 R | 61.0% | 39.0% | 61.0% | 39.0% |
| 9,809 | WEBSTER | 4,183 | 2,114 | 2,069 | | 45 R | 50.5% | 49.5% | 50.5% | 49.5% |
| 20,314 | WETZEL | 9,322 | 6,046 | 3,276 | | 2,770 R | 64.9% | 35.1% | 64.9% | 35.1% |
| 4,154 | WIRT | 2,133 | 1,442 | 691 | | 751 R | 67.6% | 32.4% | 67.6% | 32.4% |
| 86,818 | WOOD | 38,201 | 27,315 | 10,886 | | 16,429 R | 71.5% | 28.5% | 71.5% | 28.5% |
| 30,095 | WYOMING | 12,394 | 7,926 | 4,468 | | 3,458 R | 64.0% | 36.0% | 64.0% | 36.0% |
| 1,744,237 | TOTAL | 762,399 | 484,964 | 277,435 | | 207,529 R | 63.6% | 36.4% | 63.6% | 36.4% |

# WEST VIRGINIA

## PRESIDENT 1968

| 1960 Census Population | County | Total Vote | Republican | Democratic | AIP | Other | Plurality | Percentage Total Vote | | |
|---|---|---|---|---|---|---|---|---|---|---|
| | | | | | | | | Rep. | Dem. | AIP |
| 15,474 | BARBOUR | 6,781 | 3,206 | 3,210 | 365 | | 4 D | 47.3% | 47.3% | 5.4% |
| 33,791 | BERKELEY | 14,473 | 7,223 | 4,929 | 2,321 | | 2,294 R | 49.9% | 34.1% | 16.0% |
| 28,764 | BOONE | 10,287 | 2,970 | 6,391 | 926 | | 3,421 D | 28.9% | 62.1% | 9.0% |
| 15,152 | BRAXTON | 6,050 | 2,441 | 3,268 | 341 | | 827 D | 40.3% | 54.0% | 5.6% |
| 28,940 | BROOKE | 13,141 | 4,191 | 7,506 | 1,444 | | 3,315 D | 31.9% | 57.1% | 11.0% |
| 108,202 | CABELL | 43,102 | 19,418 | 19,018 | 4,666 | | 400 R | 45.1% | 44.1% | 10.8% |
| 7,948 | CALHOUN | 3,612 | 1,612 | 1,682 | 318 | | 70 D | 44.6% | 46.6% | 8.8% |
| 11,942 | CLAY | 3,739 | 1,474 | 1,916 | 349 | | 442 D | 39.4% | 51.2% | 9.3% |
| 6,970 | DODDRIDGE | 2,851 | 1,861 | 844 | 146 | | 1,017 R | 65.3% | 29.6% | 5.1% |
| 61,731 | FAYETTE | 21,723 | 5,246 | 14,546 | 1,931 | | 9,300 D | 24.1% | 67.0% | 8.9% |
| 8,050 | GILMER | 3,197 | 1,401 | 1,582 | 214 | | 181 D | 43.8% | 49.5% | 6.7% |
| 8,304 | GRANT | 3,978 | 2,936 | 786 | 256 | | 2,150 R | 73.8% | 19.8% | 6.4% |
| 34,446 | GREENBRIER | 13,599 | 5,559 | 6,318 | 1,722 | | 759 D | 40.9% | 46.5% | 12.7% |
| 11,705 | HAMPSHIRE | 4,444 | 1,959 | 1,791 | 694 | | 168 R | 44.1% | 40.3% | 15.6% |
| 39,615 | HANCOCK | 18,831 | 6,181 | 10,174 | 2,476 | | 3,993 D | 32.8% | 54.0% | 13.1% |
| 9,308 | HARDY | 4,025 | 1,768 | 1,767 | 490 | | 1 R | 43.9% | 43.9% | 12.2% |
| 77,856 | HARRISON | 34,809 | 13,703 | 18,872 | 2,234 | | 5,169 D | 39.4% | 54.2% | 6.4% |
| 18,541 | JACKSON | 9,582 | 5,173 | 3,462 | 947 | | 1,711 R | 54.0% | 36.1% | 9.9% |
| 18,665 | JEFFERSON | 6,929 | 2,718 | 3,129 | 1,082 | | 411 D | 39.2% | 45.2% | 15.6% |
| 252,925 | KANAWHA | 99,886 | 41,712 | 46,650 | 11,524 | | 4,938 D | 41.8% | 46.7% | 11.5% |
| 19,711 | LEWIS | 7,835 | 4,027 | 3,168 | 640 | | 859 R | 51.4% | 40.4% | 8.2% |
| 20,267 | LINCOLN | 8,631 | 3,662 | 4,386 | 583 | | 724 D | 42.4% | 50.8% | 6.8% |
| 61,570 | LOGAN | 20,301 | 4,754 | 13,686 | 1,861 | | 8,932 D | 23.4% | 67.4% | 9.2% |
| 71,359 | MCDOWELL | 18,937 | 4,020 | 12,842 | 2,075 | | 8,822 D | 21.2% | 67.8% | 11.0% |
| 63,717 | MARION | 29,261 | 10,177 | 17,246 | 1,838 | | 7,069 D | 34.8% | 58.9% | 6.3% |
| 38,041 | MARSHALL | 17,080 | 7,252 | 8,449 | 1,379 | | 1,197 D | 42.5% | 49.5% | 8.1% |
| 24,459 | MASON | 10,636 | 5,208 | 4,549 | 879 | | 659 R | 49.0% | 42.8% | 8.3% |
| 68,206 | MERCER | 26,087 | 9,985 | 12,739 | 3,363 | | 2,754 D | 38.3% | 48.8% | 12.9% |
| 22,354 | MINERAL | 10,043 | 4,545 | 4,225 | 1,273 | | 320 R | 45.3% | 42.1% | 12.7% |
| 39,742 | MINGO | 13,798 | 3,988 | 8,677 | 1,133 | | 4,689 D | 28.9% | 62.9% | 8.2% |
| 55,617 | MONONGALIA | 23,945 | 9,261 | 13,128 | 1,556 | | 3,867 D | 38.7% | 54.8% | 6.5% |
| 11,584 | MONROE | 5,890 | 2,925 | 2,412 | 553 | | 513 R | 49.7% | 41.0% | 9.4% |
| 8,376 | MORGAN | 3,720 | 2,244 | 1,015 | 461 | | 1,229 R | 60.3% | 27.3% | 12.4% |
| 25,414 | NICHOLAS | 9,377 | 3,678 | 4,858 | 841 | | 1,180 D | 39.2% | 51.8% | 9.0% |
| 68,437 | OHIO | 30,263 | 13,073 | 15,026 | 2,164 | | 1,953 D | 43.2% | 49.7% | 7.2% |
| 8,093 | PENDLETON | 3,628 | 1,687 | 1,643 | 298 | | 44 R | 46.5% | 45.3% | 8.2% |
| 7,124 | PLEASANTS | 3,260 | 1,534 | 1,522 | 204 | | 12 R | 47.1% | 46.7% | 6.3% |
| 10,136 | POCAHONTAS | 4,434 | 2,040 | 1,948 | 446 | | 92 R | 46.0% | 43.9% | 10.1% |
| 27,233 | PRESTON | 10,217 | 5,636 | 4,020 | 561 | | 1,616 R | 55.2% | 39.3% | 5.5% |
| 23,561 | PUTNAM | 11,601 | 5,252 | 5,009 | 1,340 | | 243 R | 45.3% | 43.2% | 11.6% |
| 77,826 | RALEIGH | 29,506 | 8,775 | 17,744 | 2,987 | | 8,969 D | 29.7% | 60.1% | 10.1% |
| 26,349 | RANDOLPH | 10,967 | 4,508 | 5,562 | 897 | | 1,054 D | 41.1% | 50.7% | 8.2% |
| 10,877 | RITCHIE | 4,671 | 3,106 | 1,281 | 284 | | 1,825 R | 66.5% | 27.4% | 6.1% |
| 15,720 | ROANE | 6,914 | 3,851 | 2,639 | 424 | | 1,212 R | 55.7% | 38.2% | 6.1% |
| 15,640 | SUMMERS | 6,675 | 2,305 | 3,521 | 849 | | 1,216 D | 34.5% | 52.7% | 12.7% |
| 15,010 | TAYLOR | 6,431 | 3,012 | 2,953 | 466 | | 59 R | 46.8% | 45.9% | 7.2% |
| 7,750 | TUCKER | 3,601 | 1,511 | 1,758 | 332 | | 247 D | 42.0% | 48.8% | 9.2% |
| 10,026 | TYLER | 4,534 | 2,897 | 1,324 | 313 | | 1,573 R | 63.9% | 29.2% | 6.9% |
| 18,292 | UPSHUR | 7,311 | 4,565 | 2,319 | 427 | | 2,246 R | 62.4% | 31.7% | 5.8% |
| 38,977 | WAYNE | 16,319 | 6,004 | 8,227 | 2,088 | | 2,223 D | 36.8% | 50.4% | 12.8% |
| 13,719 | WEBSTER | 4,107 | 1,241 | 2,582 | 284 | | 1,341 D | 30.2% | 62.9% | 6.9% |
| 19,347 | WETZEL | 8,949 | 4,122 | 4,038 | 789 | | 84 R | 46.1% | 45.1% | 8.8% |
| 4,391 | WIRT | 2,011 | 1,051 | 820 | 140 | | 231 R | 52.3% | 40.8% | 7.0% |
| 78,331 | WOOD | 36,632 | 18,960 | 14,293 | 3,379 | | 4,667 R | 51.8% | 39.0% | 9.2% |
| 34,836 | WYOMING | 11,595 | 3,947 | 6,641 | 1,007 | | 2,694 D | 34.0% | 57.3% | 8.7% |
| 1,860,421 | TOTAL | 754,206 | 307,555 | 374,091 | 72,560 | | 66,536 D | 40.8% | 49.6% | 9.6% |

# WEST VIRGINIA

## PRESIDENT 1964

| 1960 Census Population | County | Total Vote | Republican | Democratic | Other | Rep.-Dem. Plurality | Percentage | | | |
|---|---|---|---|---|---|---|---|---|---|---|
| | | | | | | | Total Vote | | Major Vote | |
| | | | | | | | Rep. | Dem. | Rep. | Dem. |
| 15,474 | BARBOUR | 7,291 | 2,533 | 4,758 | | 2,225 D | 34.7% | 65.3% | 34.7% | 65.3% |
| 33,791 | BERKELEY | 14,085 | 5,457 | 8,628 | | 3,171 D | 38.7% | 61.3% | 38.7% | 61.3% |
| 28,764 | BOONE | 11,076 | 2,467 | 8,609 | | 6,142 D | 22.3% | 77.7% | 22.3% | 77.7% |
| 15,152 | BRAXTON | 6,654 | 1,867 | 4,787 | | 2,920 D | 28.1% | 71.9% | 28.1% | 71.9% |
| 28,940 | BROOKE | 13,198 | 3,364 | 9,834 | | 6,470 D | 25.5% | 74.5% | 25.5% | 74.5% |
| 108,202 | CABELL | 45,394 | 16,957 | 28,437 | | 11,480 D | 37.4% | 62.6% | 37.4% | 62.6% |
| 7,948 | CALHOUN | 3,901 | 1,275 | 2,626 | | 1,351 D | 32.7% | 67.3% | 32.7% | 67.3% |
| 11,942 | CLAY | 4,548 | 1,366 | 3,182 | | 1,816 D | 30.0% | 70.0% | 30.0% | 70.0% |
| 6,970 | DODDRIDGE | 3,168 | 1,581 | 1,587 | | 6 D | 49.9% | 50.1% | 49.9% | 50.1% |
| 61,731 | FAYETTE | 24,041 | 4,051 | 19,990 | | 15,939 D | 16.9% | 83.1% | 16.9% | 83.1% |
| 8,050 | GILMER | 3,948 | 1,116 | 2,832 | | 1,716 D | 28.3% | 71.7% | 28.3% | 71.7% |
| 8,304 | GRANT | 3,958 | 2,464 | 1,494 | | 970 R | 62.3% | 37.7% | 62.3% | 37.7% |
| 34,446 | GREENBRIER | 14,661 | 4,549 | 10,112 | | 5,563 D | 31.0% | 69.0% | 31.0% | 69.0% |
| 11,705 | HAMPSHIRE | 4,854 | 1,473 | 3,381 | | 1,908 D | 30.3% | 69.7% | 30.3% | 69.7% |
| 39,615 | HANCOCK | 19,010 | 5,009 | 14,001 | | 8,992 D | 26.3% | 73.7% | 26.3% | 73.7% |
| 9,308 | HARDY | 4,304 | 1,308 | 2,996 | | 1,688 D | 30.4% | 69.6% | 30.4% | 69.6% |
| 77,856 | HARRISON | 35,669 | 9,986 | 25,683 | | 15,697 D | 28.0% | 72.0% | 28.0% | 72.0% |
| 18,541 | JACKSON | 9,381 | 4,359 | 5,022 | | 663 D | 46.5% | 53.5% | 46.5% | 53.5% |
| 18,665 | JEFFERSON | 6,793 | 1,901 | 4,892 | | 2,991 D | 28.0% | 72.0% | 28.0% | 72.0% |
| 252,925 | KANAWHA | 108,894 | 38,383 | 70,511 | | 32,128 D | 35.2% | 64.8% | 35.2% | 64.8% |
| 19,711 | LEWIS | 8,227 | 2,979 | 5,248 | | 2,269 D | 36.2% | 63.8% | 36.2% | 63.8% |
| 20,267 | LINCOLN | 9,288 | 3,436 | 5,852 | | 2,416 D | 37.0% | 63.0% | 37.0% | 63.0% |
| 61,570 | LOGAN | 20,775 | 3,776 | 16,999 | | 13,223 D | 18.2% | 81.8% | 18.2% | 81.8% |
| 71,359 | MCDOWELL | 21,730 | 3,684 | 18,046 | | 14,362 D | 17.0% | 83.0% | 17.0% | 83.0% |
| 63,717 | MARION | 29,754 | 7,707 | 22,047 | | 14,340 D | 25.9% | 74.1% | 25.9% | 74.1% |
| 38,041 | MARSHALL | 17,932 | 6,175 | 11,757 | | 5,582 D | 34.4% | 65.6% | 34.4% | 65.6% |
| 24,459 | MASON | 10,978 | 4,467 | 6,511 | | 2,044 D | 40.7% | 59.3% | 40.7% | 59.3% |
| 68,206 | MERCER | 27,203 | 8,905 | 18,298 | | 9,393 D | 32.7% | 67.3% | 32.7% | 67.3% |
| 22,354 | MINERAL | 10,145 | 3,801 | 6,344 | | 2,543 D | 37.5% | 62.5% | 37.5% | 62.5% |
| 39,742 | MINGO | 15,420 | 3,154 | 12,266 | | 9,112 D | 20.5% | 79.5% | 20.5% | 79.5% |
| 55,617 | MONONGALIA | 23,831 | 6,473 | 17,358 | | 10,885 D | 27.2% | 72.8% | 27.2% | 72.8% |
| 11,584 | MONROE | 5,752 | 2,385 | 3,367 | | 982 D | 41.5% | 58.5% | 41.5% | 58.5% |
| 8,376 | MORGAN | 3,686 | 1,866 | 1,820 | | 46 R | 50.6% | 49.4% | 50.6% | 49.4% |
| 25,414 | NICHOLAS | 9,506 | 2,628 | 6,878 | | 4,250 D | 27.6% | 72.4% | 27.6% | 72.4% |
| 68,437 | OHIO | 33,184 | 12,006 | 21,178 | | 9,172 D | 36.2% | 63.8% | 36.2% | 63.8% |
| 8,093 | PENDLETON | 3,794 | 1,296 | 2,498 | | 1,202 D | 34.2% | 65.8% | 34.2% | 65.8% |
| 7,124 | PLEASANTS | 3,626 | 1,339 | 2,287 | | 948 D | 36.9% | 63.1% | 36.9% | 63.1% |
| 10,136 | POCAHONTAS | 5,033 | 1,716 | 3,317 | | 1,601 D | 34.1% | 65.9% | 34.1% | 65.9% |
| 27,233 | PRESTON | 10,279 | 4,015 | 6,264 | | 2,249 D | 39.1% | 60.9% | 39.1% | 60.9% |
| 23,561 | PUTNAM | 11,075 | 4,165 | 6,910 | | 2,745 D | 37.6% | 62.4% | 37.6% | 62.4% |
| 77,826 | RALEIGH | 30,558 | 6,952 | 23,606 | | 16,654 D | 22.8% | 77.2% | 22.8% | 77.2% |
| 26,349 | RANDOLPH | 10,996 | 2,984 | 8,012 | | 5,028 D | 27.1% | 72.9% | 27.1% | 72.9% |
| 10,877 | RITCHIE | 4,961 | 2,717 | 2,244 | | 473 R | 54.8% | 45.2% | 54.8% | 45.2% |
| 15,720 | ROANE | 7,271 | 3,451 | 3,820 | | 369 D | 47.5% | 52.5% | 47.5% | 52.5% |
| 15,640 | SUMMERS | 6,999 | 1,962 | 5,037 | | 3,075 D | 28.0% | 72.0% | 28.0% | 72.0% |
| 15,010 | TAYLOR | 6,734 | 2,292 | 4,442 | | 2,150 D | 34.0% | 66.0% | 34.0% | 66.0% |
| 7,750 | TUCKER | 3,978 | 1,314 | 2,664 | | 1,350 D | 33.0% | 67.0% | 33.0% | 67.0% |
| 10,026 | TYLER | 4,797 | 2,522 | 2,275 | | 247 R | 52.6% | 47.4% | 52.6% | 47.4% |
| 18,292 | UPSHUR | 7,380 | 3,606 | 3,774 | | 168 D | 48.9% | 51.1% | 48.9% | 51.1% |
| 38,977 | WAYNE | 16,918 | 5,340 | 11,578 | | 6,238 D | 31.6% | 68.4% | 31.6% | 68.4% |
| 13,719 | WEBSTER | 4,691 | 936 | 3,755 | | 2,819 D | 20.0% | 80.0% | 20.0% | 80.0% |
| 19,347 | WETZEL | 9,454 | 3,215 | 6,239 | | 3,024 D | 34.0% | 66.0% | 34.0% | 66.0% |
| 4,391 | WIRT | 2,185 | 899 | 1,286 | | 387 D | 41.1% | 58.9% | 41.1% | 58.9% |
| 78,331 | WOOD | 36,507 | 14,947 | 21,560 | | 6,613 D | 40.9% | 59.1% | 40.9% | 59.1% |
| 34,836 | WYOMING | 12,565 | 3,377 | 9,188 | | 5,811 D | 26.9% | 73.1% | 26.9% | 73.1% |
| 1,860,421 | TOTAL | 792,040 | 253,953 | 538,087 | | 284,134 D | 32.1% | 67.9% | 32.1% | 67.9% |

# WEST VIRGINIA

## PRESIDENT 1960

| 1960 Census Population | County | Total Vote | Republican | Democratic | Other | Rep.-Dem. Plurality | Percentage | | | |
|---|---|---|---|---|---|---|---|---|---|---|
| | | | | | | | Total Vote | | Major Vote | |
| | | | | | | | Rep. | Dem. | Rep. | Dem. |
| 15,474 | BARBOUR | 7,824 | 4,006 | 3,818 | | 188 R | 51.2% | 48.8% | 51.2% | 48.8% |
| 33,791 | BERKELEY | 15,441 | 8,369 | 7,072 | | 1,297 R | 54.2% | 45.8% | 54.2% | 45.8% |
| 28,764 | BOONE | 12,162 | 4,104 | 8,058 | | 3,954 D | 33.7% | 66.3% | 33.7% | 66.3% |
| 15,152 | BRAXTON | 7,162 | 2,977 | 4,185 | | 1,208 D | 41.6% | 58.4% | 41.6% | 58.4% |
| 28,940 | BROOKE | 13,592 | 5,754 | 7,838 | | 2,084 D | 42.3% | 57.7% | 42.3% | 57.7% |
| 108,202 | CABELL | 47,899 | 26,988 | 20,911 | | 6,077 R | 56.3% | 43.7% | 56.3% | 43.7% |
| 7,948 | CALHOUN | 3,921 | 1,946 | 1,975 | | 29 D | 49.6% | 50.4% | 49.6% | 50.4% |
| 11,942 | CLAY | 5,265 | 2,406 | 2,859 | | 453 D | 45.7% | 54.3% | 45.7% | 54.3% |
| 6,970 | DODDRIDGE | 3,455 | 2,402 | 1,053 | | 1,349 R | 69.5% | 30.5% | 69.5% | 30.5% |
| 61,731 | FAYETTE | 25,646 | 7,537 | 18,109 | | 10,572 D | 29.4% | 70.6% | 29.4% | 70.6% |
| 8,050 | GILMER | 3,521 | 1,446 | 2,075 | | 629 D | 41.1% | 58.9% | 41.1% | 58.9% |
| 8,304 | GRANT | 4,241 | 3,333 | 908 | | 2,425 R | 78.6% | 21.4% | 78.6% | 21.4% |
| 34,446 | GREENBRIER | 14,976 | 6,633 | 8,343 | | 1,710 D | 44.3% | 55.7% | 44.3% | 55.7% |
| 11,705 | HAMPSHIRE | 5,390 | 2,541 | 2,849 | | 308 D | 47.1% | 52.9% | 47.1% | 52.9% |
| 39,615 | HANCOCK | 19,207 | 8,031 | 11,176 | | 3,145 D | 41.8% | 58.2% | 41.8% | 58.2% |
| 9,308 | HARDY | 4,507 | 2,042 | 2,465 | | 423 D | 45.3% | 54.7% | 45.3% | 54.7% |
| 77,856 | HARRISON | 39,105 | 18,378 | 20,727 | | 2,349 D | 47.0% | 53.0% | 47.0% | 53.0% |
| 18,541 | JACKSON | 9,150 | 5,535 | 3,615 | | 1,920 R | 60.5% | 39.5% | 60.5% | 39.5% |
| 18,665 | JEFFERSON | 7,239 | 2,887 | 4,352 | | 1,465 D | 39.9% | 60.1% | 39.9% | 60.1% |
| 252,925 | KANAWHA | 111,614 | 57,130 | 54,484 | | 2,646 R | 51.2% | 48.8% | 51.2% | 48.8% |
| 19,711 | LEWIS | 8,806 | 5,157 | 3,649 | | 1,508 R | 58.6% | 41.4% | 58.6% | 41.4% |
| 20,267 | LINCOLN | 9,602 | 4,579 | 5,023 | | 444 D | 47.7% | 52.3% | 47.7% | 52.3% |
| 61,570 | LOGAN | 24,196 | 7,836 | 16,360 | | 8,524 D | 32.4% | 67.6% | 32.4% | 67.6% |
| 71,359 | MCDOWELL | 26,056 | 6,555 | 19,501 | | 12,946 D | 25.2% | 74.8% | 25.2% | 74.8% |
| 63,717 | MARION | 32,041 | 14,138 | 17,903 | | 3,765 D | 44.1% | 55.9% | 44.1% | 55.9% |
| 38,041 | MARSHALL | 18,344 | 9,147 | 9,197 | | 50 D | 49.9% | 50.1% | 49.9% | 50.1% |
| 24,459 | MASON | 10,946 | 6,424 | 4,522 | | 1,902 R | 58.7% | 41.3% | 58.7% | 41.3% |
| 68,206 | MERCER | 29,008 | 11,719 | 17,289 | | 5,570 D | 40.4% | 59.6% | 40.4% | 59.6% |
| 22,354 | MINERAL | 10,463 | 6,299 | 4,164 | | 2,135 R | 60.2% | 39.8% | 60.2% | 39.8% |
| 39,742 | MINGO | 16,162 | 4,903 | 11,259 | | 6,356 D | 30.3% | 69.7% | 30.3% | 69.7% |
| 55,617 | MONONGALIA | 24,626 | 11,523 | 13,103 | | 1,580 D | 46.8% | 53.2% | 46.8% | 53.2% |
| 11,584 | MONROE | 6,049 | 3,139 | 2,910 | | 229 R | 51.9% | 48.1% | 51.9% | 48.1% |
| 8,376 | MORGAN | 4,121 | 2,752 | 1,369 | | 1,383 R | 66.8% | 33.2% | 66.8% | 33.2% |
| 25,414 | NICHOLAS | 10,071 | 4,297 | 5,774 | | 1,477 D | 42.7% | 57.3% | 42.7% | 57.3% |
| 68,437 | OHIO | 35,790 | 17,367 | 18,423 | | 1,056 D | 48.5% | 51.5% | 48.5% | 51.5% |
| 8,093 | PENDLETON | 3,987 | 1,930 | 2,057 | | 127 D | 48.4% | 51.6% | 48.4% | 51.6% |
| 7,124 | PLEASANTS | 3,724 | 1,982 | 1,742 | | 240 R | 53.2% | 46.8% | 53.2% | 46.8% |
| 10,136 | POCAHONTAS | 5,291 | 2,469 | 2,822 | | 353 D | 46.7% | 53.3% | 46.7% | 53.3% |
| 27,233 | PRESTON | 11,129 | 6,908 | 4,221 | | 2,687 R | 62.1% | 37.9% | 62.1% | 37.9% |
| 23,561 | PUTNAM | 10,670 | 5,702 | 4,968 | | 734 R | 53.4% | 46.6% | 53.4% | 46.6% |
| 77,826 | RALEIGH | 32,536 | 12,088 | 20,448 | | 8,360 D | 37.2% | 62.8% | 37.2% | 62.8% |
| 26,349 | RANDOLPH | 12,007 | 5,018 | 6,989 | | 1,971 D | 41.8% | 58.2% | 41.8% | 58.2% |
| 10,877 | RITCHIE | 5,563 | 3,972 | 1,591 | | 2,381 R | 71.4% | 28.6% | 71.4% | 28.6% |
| 15,720 | ROANE | 7,723 | 4,443 | 3,280 | | 1,163 R | 57.5% | 42.5% | 57.5% | 42.5% |
| 15,640 | SUMMERS | 7,759 | 3,137 | 4,622 | | 1,485 D | 40.4% | 59.6% | 40.4% | 59.6% |
| 15,010 | TAYLOR | 7,481 | 3,992 | 3,489 | | 503 R | 53.4% | 46.6% | 53.4% | 46.6% |
| 7,750 | TUCKER | 3,977 | 1,887 | 2,090 | | 203 D | 47.4% | 52.6% | 47.4% | 52.6% |
| 10,026 | TYLER | 5,095 | 3,537 | 1,558 | | 1,979 R | 69.4% | 30.6% | 69.4% | 30.6% |
| 18,292 | UPSHUR | 7,713 | 5,123 | 2,590 | | 2,533 R | 66.4% | 33.6% | 66.4% | 33.6% |
| 38,977 | WAYNE | 17,268 | 8,128 | 9,140 | | 1,012 D | 47.1% | 52.9% | 47.1% | 52.9% |
| 13,719 | WEBSTER | 5,168 | 1,689 | 3,479 | | 1,790 D | 32.7% | 67.3% | 32.7% | 67.3% |
| 19,347 | WETZEL | 9,487 | 5,149 | 4,338 | | 811 R | 54.3% | 45.7% | 54.3% | 45.7% |
| 4,391 | WIRT | 2,392 | 1,347 | 1,045 | | 302 R | 56.3% | 43.7% | 56.3% | 43.7% |
| 78,331 | WOOD | 37,527 | 22,131 | 15,396 | | 6,735 R | 59.0% | 41.0% | 59.0% | 41.0% |
| 34,836 | WYOMING | 13,686 | 5,083 | 8,603 | | 3,520 D | 37.1% | 62.9% | 37.1% | 62.9% |
| 1,860,421 | TOTAL | 837,781 | 395,995 | 441,786 | | 45,791 D | 47.3% | 52.7% | 47.3% | 52.7% |

# WEST VIRGINIA

## ELECTION NOTES

**2004** Other vote was 4,063 Independent (Ralph Nader); 1,405 Libertarian (Michael Badnarik); 82 write-in (Michael Peroutka); 13 write-in (John Kennedy); 5 write-in (David Cobb).

**2000** Other vote was 3,169 Reform (Buchanan); 1,912 Libertarian (Browne); 367 Natural Law (Hagelin); 23 write-in (Phillips); 1 write-in (Strickland).

**1996** Other vote was 3,062 Libertarian (Browne).

**1992** Other vote was 1,873 Marrou (Libertarian); 34 Gritz (write-in); 6 Fulani (write-in); 6 Warren (write-in); 2 Hagelin (write-in); 2 Phillips (write-in); 35 scattered write-in.

**1988** Other vote was Fulani (New Alliance).

**1984** Other vote was 996 Richards (Populist); 645 Mason (Socialist Workers); 493 Serrette (Alliance). Early un-amended canvass gave the Democratic vote in Jackson county as 4,179.

**1980** Other vote was 31,691 Anderson (Independent); 4,356 Clark (Libertarian).

**1976** Other vote was 113 McCarthy (write-in); 17 Anderson (write-in); 16 MacBride (write-in); 12 Maddox (write-in); 5 Hall (write-in); 2 Camejo (write-in); 125 scattered write-in. Early unamended canvass gave the Republican state-wide total vote as 314,726 and the Democratic state-wide total vote as 435,864; both the Republican and Democratic votes were amended in Wood county.

**1972**

**1968** Wallace on the ballot as American.

**1964**

**1960**

# WISCONSIN

## POPULAR VOTE FOR PRESIDENT 1920 TO 2004

| Year | Total Vote | Republican | | Democratic | | Other Vote | Plurality | Percentage | | | |
|---|---|---|---|---|---|---|---|---|---|---|---|
| | | | | | | | | Total Vote | | Major Vote | |
| | | Vote | Candidate | Vote | Candidate | | | Rep. | Dem. | Rep. | Dem. |
| 2004 | 2,997,007 | 1,478,120 | Bush, George W. | 1,489,504 | Kerry, John | 29,383 | 11,384 D | 49.3% | 49.7% | 49.8% | 50.2% |
| 2000 ** | 2,598,607 | 1,237,279 | Bush, George W. | 1,242,987 | Gore, Al | 118,341 | 5,708 D | 47.6% | 47.8% | 49.9% | 50.1% |
| 1996 ** | 2,196,169 | 845,029 | Dole, Bob | 1,071,971 | Clinton, Bill | 279,169 | 226,942 D | 38.5% | 48.8% | 44.1% | 55.9% |
| 1992 ** | 2,531,114 | 930,855 | Bush, George | 1,041,066 | Clinton, Bill | 559,193 | 110,211 D | 36.8% | 41.1% | 47.2% | 52.8% |
| 1988 | 2,191,608 | 1,047,499 | Bush, George | 1,126,794 | Dukakis, Michael S. | 17,315 | 79,295 D | 47.8% | 51.4% | 48.2% | 51.8% |
| 1984 | 2,211,689 | 1,198,584 | Reagan, Ronald | 995,740 | Mondale, Walter F. | 17,365 | 202,844 R | 54.2% | 45.0% | 54.6% | 45.4% |
| 1980 ** | 2,273,221 | 1,088,845 | Reagan, Ronald | 981,584 | Carter, Jimmy | 202,792 | 107,261 R | 47.9% | 43.2% | 52.6% | 47.4% |
| 1976 | 2,104,175 | 1,004,987 | Ford, Gerald R. | 1,040,232 | Carter, Jimmy | 58,956 | 35,245 D | 47.8% | 49.4% | 49.1% | 50.9% |
| 1972 | 1,852,890 | 989,430 | Nixon, Richard M. | 810,174 | McGovern, George S. | 53,286 | 179,256 R | 53.4% | 43.7% | 55.0% | 45.0% |
| 1968 | 1,691,538 | 809,997 | Nixon, Richard M. | 748,804 | Humphrey, Hubert H. | 132,737 | 61,193 R | 47.9% | 44.3% | 52.0% | 48.0% |
| 1964 | 1,691,815 | 638,495 | Goldwater, Barry M. | 1,050,424 | Johnson, Lyndon B. | 2,896 | 411,929 D | 37.7% | 62.1% | 37.8% | 62.2% |
| 1960 | 1,729,082 | 895,175 | Nixon, Richard M. | 830,805 | Kennedy, John F. | 3,102 | 64,370 R | 51.8% | 48.0% | 51.9% | 48.1% |
| 1956 | 1,550,558 | 954,844 | Eisenhower, Dwight D. | 586,768 | Stevenson, Adlai E. | 8,946 | 368,076 R | 61.6% | 37.8% | 61.9% | 38.1% |
| 1952 | 1,607,370 | 979,744 | Eisenhower, Dwight D. | 622,175 | Stevenson, Adlai E. | 5,451 | 357,569 R | 61.0% | 38.7% | 61.2% | 38.8% |
| 1948 | 1,276,800 | 590,959 | Dewey, Thomas E. | 647,310 | Truman, Harry S. | 38,531 | 56,351 D | 46.3% | 50.7% | 47.7% | 52.3% |
| 1944 | 1,339,152 | 674,532 | Dewey, Thomas E. | 650,413 | Roosevelt, Franklin D. | 14,207 | 24,119 R | 50.4% | 48.6% | 50.9% | 49.1% |
| 1940 | 1,405,522 | 679,206 | Willkie, Wendell | 704,821 | Roosevelt, Franklin D. | 21,495 | 25,615 D | 48.3% | 50.1% | 49.1% | 50.9% |
| 1936 | 1,258,560 | 380,828 | Landon, Alfred M. | 802,984 | Roosevelt, Franklin D. | 74,748 | 422,156 D | 30.3% | 63.8% | 32.2% | 67.8% |
| 1932 | 1,114,814 | 347,741 | Hoover, Herbert C. | 707,410 | Roosevelt, Franklin D. | 59,663 | 359,669 D | 31.2% | 63.5% | 33.0% | 67.0% |
| 1928 | 1,016,831 | 544,205 | Hoover, Herbert C. | 450,259 | Smith, Alfred E. | 22,367 | 93,946 R | 53.5% | 44.3% | 54.7% | 45.3% |
| 1924 ** | 840,827 | 311,614 | Coolidge, Calvin | 68,115 | Davis, John W. | 461,098 | 142,064 P | 37.1% | 8.1% | 82.1% | 17.9% |
| 1920 | 701,281 | 498,576 | Harding, Warren G. | 113,422 | Cox, James M. | 89,283 | 385,154 R | 71.1% | 16.2% | 81.5% | 18.5% |

In 2000 the other vote column includes 94,070 votes cast for Green (Nader). In 1996 the other vote column includes 227,339 votes cast for Perot. In 1992 the other vote column includes 544,479 votes cast for Perot. In 1980 the other column includes 160,657 votes for Independent (Anderson). In 1924 the other vote was 453,678 Progressive; 3,773 Communist; 2,918 Prohibition; 458 Socialist Labor; and 271 Commonwealth Land.

## ELECTORAL COLLEGE VOTE 1920 TO 2004

| Year | Total | Republican | Democratic | Other |
|---|---|---|---|---|
| 2004 | 10 | | 10 | |
| 2000 | 11 | | 11 | |
| 1996 | 11 | | 11 | |
| 1992 | 11 | | 11 | |
| 1988 | 11 | | 11 | |
| 1984 | 11 | 11 | | |
| 1980 | 11 | 11 | | |
| 1976 | 11 | | 11 | |
| 1972 | 11 | 11 | | |
| 1968 | 12 | 12 | | |
| 1964 | 12 | | 12 | |
| 1960 | 12 | 12 | | |
| 1956 | 12 | 12 | | |
| 1952 | 12 | 12 | | |
| 1948 | 12 | | 12 | |
| 1944 | 12 | 12 | | |
| 1940 | 12 | | 12 | |
| 1936 | 12 | | 12 | |
| 1932 | 12 | | 12 | |
| 1928 | 13 | 13 | | |
| 1924 | 13 | | | 13 PROGRESSIVE |
| 1920 | 13 | 13 | | |

# WISCONSIN

# WISCONSIN

## PRESIDENT 2004

| 2000 Census Population | County | Total Vote | Republican | Democratic | Other | Rep.-Dem. Plurality | Percentage | | | |
|---|---|---|---|---|---|---|---|---|---|---|
| | | | | | | | Total Vote | | Major Vote | |
| | | | | | | | Rep. | Dem. | Rep. | Dem. |
| 18,643 | ADAMS | 10,456 | 4,890 | 5,447 | 119 | 557 D | 46.8% | 52.1% | 47.3% | 52.7% |
| 16,866 | ASHLAND | 9,199 | 3,313 | 5,805 | 81 | 2,492 D | 36.0% | 63.1% | 36.3% | 63.7% |
| 44,963 | BARRON | 23,937 | 12,030 | 11,696 | 211 | 334 R | 50.3% | 48.9% | 50.7% | 49.3% |
| 15,013 | BAYFIELD | 9,699 | 3,754 | 5,845 | 100 | 2,091 D | 38.7% | 60.3% | 39.1% | 60.9% |
| 226,778 | BROWN | 123,294 | 67,173 | 54,935 | 1,186 | 12,238 R | 54.5% | 44.6% | 55.0% | 45.0% |
| 13,804 | BUFFALO | 7,591 | 3,502 | 3,998 | 91 | 496 D | 46.1% | 52.7% | 46.7% | 53.3% |
| 15,674 | BURNETT | 9,321 | 4,743 | 4,499 | 79 | 244 R | 50.9% | 48.3% | 51.3% | 48.7% |
| 40,631 | CALUMET | 25,276 | 14,721 | 10,290 | 265 | 4,431 R | 58.2% | 40.7% | 58.9% | 41.1% |
| 55,195 | CHIPPEWA | 30,524 | 15,450 | 14,751 | 323 | 699 R | 50.6% | 48.3% | 51.2% | 48.8% |
| 33,557 | CLARK | 15,125 | 7,966 | 6,966 | 193 | 1,000 R | 52.7% | 46.1% | 53.3% | 46.7% |
| 52,468 | COLUMBIA | 29,555 | 14,956 | 14,300 | 299 | 656 R | 50.6% | 48.4% | 51.1% | 48.9% |
| 17,243 | CRAWFORD | 8,459 | 3,680 | 4,656 | 123 | 976 D | 43.5% | 55.0% | 44.1% | 55.9% |
| 426,526 | DANE | 274,249 | 90,369 | 181,052 | 2,828 | 90,683 D | 33.0% | 66.0% | 33.3% | 66.7% |
| 85,897 | DODGE | 44,336 | 27,201 | 16,690 | 445 | 10,511 R | 61.4% | 37.6% | 62.0% | 38.0% |
| 27,961 | DOOR | 17,491 | 8,910 | 8,367 | 214 | 543 R | 50.9% | 47.8% | 51.6% | 48.4% |
| 43,287 | DOUGLAS | 25,187 | 8,448 | 16,537 | 202 | 8,089 D | 33.5% | 65.7% | 33.8% | 66.2% |
| 39,858 | DUNN | 23,172 | 10,879 | 12,039 | 254 | 1,160 D | 46.9% | 52.0% | 47.5% | 52.5% |
| 93,142 | EAU CLAIRE | 55,437 | 24,653 | 30,068 | 716 | 5,415 D | 44.5% | 54.2% | 45.1% | 54.9% |
| 5,088 | FLORENCE | 2,724 | 1,703 | 993 | 28 | 710 R | 62.5% | 36.5% | 63.2% | 36.8% |
| 97,296 | FOND DU LAC | 53,036 | 33,291 | 19,216 | 529 | 14,075 R | 62.8% | 36.2% | 63.4% | 36.6% |
| 10,024 | FOREST | 5,153 | 2,608 | 2,509 | 36 | 99 R | 50.6% | 48.7% | 51.0% | 49.0% |
| 49,597 | GRANT | 25,264 | 12,208 | 12,864 | 192 | 656 D | 48.3% | 50.9% | 48.7% | 51.3% |
| 33,647 | GREEN | 18,248 | 8,497 | 9,575 | 176 | 1,078 D | 46.6% | 52.5% | 47.0% | 53.0% |
| 19,105 | GREEN LAKE | 10,178 | 6,472 | 3,605 | 101 | 2,867 R | 63.6% | 35.4% | 64.2% | 35.8% |
| 22,780 | IOWA | 12,542 | 5,348 | 7,122 | 72 | 1,774 D | 42.6% | 56.8% | 42.9% | 57.1% |
| 6,861 | IRON | 3,879 | 1,884 | 1,956 | 39 | 72 D | 48.6% | 50.4% | 49.1% | 50.9% |
| 19,100 | JACKSON | 9,726 | 4,387 | 5,249 | 90 | 862 D | 45.1% | 54.0% | 45.5% | 54.5% |
| 74,021 | JEFFERSON | 42,115 | 23,776 | 17,925 | 414 | 5,851 R | 56.5% | 42.6% | 57.0% | 43.0% |
| 24,316 | JUNEAU | 12,379 | 6,473 | 5,734 | 172 | 739 R | 52.3% | 46.3% | 53.0% | 47.0% |
| 149,577 | KENOSHA | 76,428 | 35,587 | 40,107 | 734 | 4,520 D | 46.6% | 52.5% | 47.0% | 53.0% |
| 20,187 | KEWAUNEE | 11,273 | 5,970 | 5,175 | 128 | 795 R | 53.0% | 45.9% | 53.6% | 46.4% |
| 107,120 | LA CROSSE | 62,136 | 28,289 | 33,170 | 677 | 4,881 D | 45.5% | 53.4% | 46.0% | 54.0% |
| 16,137 | LAFAYETTE | 8,388 | 3,929 | 4,402 | 57 | 473 D | 46.8% | 52.5% | 47.2% | 52.8% |
| 20,740 | LANGLADE | 11,074 | 6,235 | 4,751 | 88 | 1,484 R | 56.3% | 42.9% | 56.8% | 43.2% |
| 29,641 | LINCOLN | 15,700 | 8,024 | 7,484 | 192 | 540 R | 51.1% | 47.7% | 51.7% | 48.3% |
| 82,887 | MANITOWOC | 44,160 | 23,027 | 20,652 | 481 | 2,375 R | 52.1% | 46.8% | 52.7% | 47.3% |
| 125,834 | MARATHON | 68,059 | 36,394 | 30,899 | 766 | 5,495 R | 53.5% | 45.4% | 54.1% | 45.9% |
| 43,384 | MARINETTE | 22,270 | 11,866 | 10,190 | 214 | 1,676 R | 53.3% | 45.8% | 53.8% | 46.2% |
| 15,832 | MARQUETTE | 8,477 | 4,604 | 3,785 | 88 | 819 R | 54.3% | 44.7% | 54.9% | 45.1% |
| 4,562 | MENOMINEE | 1,710 | 288 | 1,412 | 10 | 1,124 D | 16.8% | 82.6% | 16.9% | 83.1% |
| 940,164 | MILWAUKEE | 482,236 | 180,287 | 297,653 | 4,296 | 117,366 D | 37.4% | 61.7% | 37.7% | 62.3% |
| 40,899 | MONROE | 19,554 | 10,375 | 8,973 | 206 | 1,402 R | 53.1% | 45.9% | 53.6% | 46.4% |
| 35,634 | OCONTO | 19,794 | 11,043 | 8,534 | 217 | 2,509 R | 55.8% | 43.1% | 56.4% | 43.6% |
| 36,776 | ONEIDA | 22,039 | 11,351 | 10,464 | 224 | 887 R | 51.5% | 47.5% | 52.0% | 48.0% |
| 160,971 | OUTAGAMIE | 90,050 | 48,903 | 40,169 | 978 | 8,734 R | 54.3% | 44.6% | 54.9% | 45.1% |
| 82,317 | OZAUKEE | 53,032 | 34,904 | 17,714 | 414 | 17,190 R | 65.8% | 33.4% | 66.3% | 33.7% |
| 7,213 | PEPIN | 4,066 | 1,853 | 2,181 | 32 | 328 D | 45.6% | 53.6% | 45.9% | 54.1% |
| 36,804 | PIERCE | 21,876 | 10,437 | 11,176 | 263 | 739 D | 47.7% | 51.1% | 48.3% | 51.7% |
| 41,319 | POLK | 23,503 | 12,095 | 11,173 | 235 | 922 R | 51.5% | 47.5% | 52.0% | 48.0% |
| 67,182 | PORTAGE | 38,961 | 16,546 | 21,861 | 554 | 5,315 D | 42.5% | 56.1% | 43.1% | 56.9% |
| 15,822 | PRICE | 8,763 | 4,312 | 4,349 | 102 | 37 D | 49.2% | 49.6% | 49.8% | 50.2% |
| 188,831 | RACINE | 101,569 | 52,456 | 48,229 | 884 | 4,227 R | 51.6% | 47.5% | 52.1% | 47.9% |
| 17,924 | RICHLAND | 9,420 | 4,836 | 4,501 | 83 | 335 R | 51.3% | 47.8% | 51.8% | 48.2% |
| 152,307 | ROCK | 80,479 | 33,151 | 46,598 | 730 | 13,447 D | 41.2% | 57.9% | 41.6% | 58.4% |
| 15,347 | RUSK | 7,927 | 3,985 | 3,820 | 122 | 165 R | 50.3% | 48.2% | 51.1% | 48.9% |
| 63,155 | ST. CROIX | 41,835 | 22,679 | 18,784 | 372 | 3,895 R | 54.2% | 44.9% | 54.7% | 45.3% |
| 55,225 | SAUK | 30,417 | 14,415 | 15,708 | 294 | 1,293 D | 47.4% | 51.6% | 47.9% | 52.1% |
| 16,196 | SAWYER | 9,453 | 4,951 | 4,411 | 91 | 540 R | 52.4% | 46.7% | 52.9% | 47.1% |
| 40,664 | SHAWANO | 20,999 | 12,150 | 8,657 | 192 | 3,493 R | 57.9% | 41.2% | 58.4% | 41.6% |
| 112,646 | SHEBOYGAN | 62,625 | 34,458 | 27,608 | 559 | 6,850 R | 55.0% | 44.1% | 55.5% | 44.5% |

# WISCONSIN

## PRESIDENT 2004

| 2000 Census Population | County | Total Vote | Republican | Democratic | Other | Rep.-Dem. Plurality | Percentage | | | |
|---|---|---|---|---|---|---|---|---|---|---|
| | | | | | | | Total Vote | | Major Vote | |
| | | | | | | | Rep. | Dem. | Rep. | Dem. |
| 19,680 | TAYLOR | 9,543 | 5,582 | 3,829 | 132 | 1,753 R | 58.5% | 40.1% | 59.3% | 40.7% |
| 27,010 | TREMPEALEAU | 14,062 | 5,878 | 8,075 | 109 | 2,197 D | 41.8% | 57.4% | 42.1% | 57.9% |
| 28,056 | VERNON | 14,845 | 6,774 | 7,924 | 147 | 1,150 D | 45.6% | 53.4% | 46.1% | 53.9% |
| 21,033 | VILAS | 14,002 | 8,155 | 5,713 | 134 | 2,442 R | 58.2% | 40.8% | 58.8% | 41.2% |
| 93,759 | WALWORTH | 48,446 | 28,754 | 19,177 | 515 | 9,577 R | 59.4% | 39.6% | 60.0% | 40.0% |
| 16,036 | WASHBURN | 9,567 | 4,762 | 4,705 | 100 | 57 R | 49.8% | 49.2% | 50.3% | 49.7% |
| 117,493 | WASHINGTON | 72,467 | 50,641 | 21,234 | 592 | 29,407 R | 69.9% | 29.3% | 70.5% | 29.5% |
| 360,767 | WAUKESHA | 230,363 | 154,926 | 73,626 | 1,811 | 81,300 R | 67.3% | 32.0% | 67.8% | 32.2% |
| 51,731 | WAUPACA | 26,974 | 15,941 | 10,792 | 241 | 5,149 R | 59.1% | 40.0% | 59.6% | 40.4% |
| 23,154 | WAUSHARA | 12,246 | 6,888 | 5,257 | 101 | 1,631 R | 56.2% | 42.9% | 56.7% | 43.3% |
| 156,763 | WINNEBAGO | 88,596 | 46,542 | 40,943 | 1,111 | 5,599 R | 52.5% | 46.2% | 53.2% | 46.8% |
| 75,555 | WOOD | 40,071 | 20,592 | 18,950 | 529 | 1,642 R | 51.4% | 47.3% | 52.1% | 47.9% |
| 5,363,675 | TOTAL | 2,997,007 | 1,478,120 | 1,489,504 | 29,383 | 11,384 D | 49.3% | 49.7% | 49.8% | 50.2% |

# WISCONSIN

## PRESIDENT 2000

| 2000 Census Population | County | Total Vote | Republican | Democratic | Green (Nader) | Other | Rep.-Dem. Plurality | | Percentage of Total Vote | | |
|---|---|---|---|---|---|---|---|---|---|---|---|
| | | | | | | | | | Rep. | Dem. | Green |
| 18,643 | ADAMS | 9,116 | 3,920 | 4,826 | 217 | 153 | 906 | D | 43.0% | 52.9% | 2.4% |
| 16,866 | ASHLAND | 7,890 | 3,038 | 4,356 | 440 | 56 | 1,318 | D | 38.5% | 55.2% | 5.6% |
| 44,963 | BARRON | 19,904 | 9,848 | 8,928 | 1,009 | 119 | 920 | R | 49.5% | 44.9% | 5.1% |
| 15,013 | BAYFIELD | 8,259 | 3,266 | 4,427 | 511 | 55 | 1,161 | D | 39.5% | 53.6% | 6.2% |
| 226,778 | BROWN | 107,769 | 54,258 | 49,096 | 3,311 | 1,104 | 5,162 | R | 50.3% | 45.6% | 3.1% |
| 13,804 | BUFFALO | 6,641 | 3,038 | 3,237 | 316 | 50 | 199 | D | 45.7% | 48.7% | 4.8% |
| 15,674 | BURNETT | 8,151 | 3,967 | 3,626 | 499 | 59 | 341 | R | 48.7% | 44.5% | 6.1% |
| 40,631 | CALUMET | 19,947 | 10,837 | 8,202 | 658 | 250 | 2,635 | R | 54.3% | 41.1% | 3.3% |
| 55,195 | CHIPPEWA | 26,173 | 12,835 | 12,102 | 973 | 263 | 733 | R | 49.0% | 46.2% | 3.7% |
| 33,557 | CLARK | 14,149 | 7,461 | 5,931 | 521 | 236 | 1,530 | R | 52.7% | 41.9% | 3.7% |
| 52,468 | COLUMBIA | 25,587 | 11,987 | 12,636 | 790 | 174 | 649 | D | 46.8% | 49.4% | 3.1% |
| 17,243 | CRAWFORD | 7,394 | 3,024 | 4,005 | 309 | 56 | 981 | D | 40.9% | 54.2% | 4.2% |
| 426,526 | DANE | 232,739 | 75,790 | 142,317 | 13,030 | 1,602 | 66,527 | D | 32.6% | 61.1% | 5.6% |
| 85,897 | DODGE | 37,701 | 21,684 | 14,580 | 1,098 | 339 | 7,104 | R | 57.5% | 38.7% | 2.9% |
| 27,961 | DOOR | 15,220 | 7,810 | 6,560 | 709 | 141 | 1,250 | R | 51.3% | 43.1% | 4.7% |
| 43,287 | DOUGLAS | 21,706 | 6,930 | 13,593 | 975 | 208 | 6,663 | D | 31.9% | 62.6% | 4.5% |
| 39,858 | DUNN | 19,330 | 8,911 | 9,172 | 1,109 | 138 | 261 | D | 46.1% | 47.4% | 5.7% |
| 93,142 | EAU CLAIRE | 47,875 | 20,921 | 24,078 | 2,461 | 415 | 3,157 | D | 43.7% | 50.3% | 5.1% |
| 5,088 | FLORENCE | 2,405 | 1,528 | 816 | 48 | 13 | 712 | R | 63.5% | 33.9% | 2.0% |
| 97,296 | FOND DU LAC | 46,589 | 26,548 | 18,181 | 1,389 | 471 | 8,367 | R | 57.0% | 39.0% | 3.0% |
| 10,024 | FOREST | 4,716 | 2,404 | 2,158 | 126 | 28 | 246 | R | 51.0% | 45.8% | 2.7% |
| 49,597 | GRANT | 21,956 | 10,240 | 10,691 | 858 | 167 | 451 | D | 46.6% | 48.7% | 3.9% |
| 33,647 | GREEN | 15,276 | 6,790 | 7,863 | 493 | 130 | 1,073 | D | 44.4% | 51.5% | 3.2% |
| 19,105 | GREEN LAKE | 9,107 | 5,451 | 3,301 | 282 | 73 | 2,150 | R | 59.9% | 36.2% | 3.1% |
| 22,780 | IOWA | 10,541 | 4,221 | 5,842 | 429 | 49 | 1,621 | D | 40.0% | 55.4% | 4.1% |
| 6,861 | IRON | 3,507 | 1,734 | 1,620 | 134 | 19 | 114 | R | 49.4% | 46.2% | 3.8% |
| 19,100 | JACKSON | 8,417 | 3,670 | 4,380 | 290 | 77 | 710 | D | 43.6% | 52.0% | 3.4% |
| 74,021 | JEFFERSON | 36,099 | 19,204 | 15,203 | 1,361 | 331 | 4,001 | R | 53.2% | 42.1% | 3.8% |
| 24,316 | JUNEAU | 10,218 | 4,910 | 4,813 | 297 | 198 | 97 | R | 48.1% | 47.1% | 2.9% |
| 149,577 | KENOSHA | 63,709 | 28,891 | 32,429 | 1,852 | 537 | 3,538 | D | 45.3% | 50.9% | 2.9% |
| 20,187 | KEWAUNEE | 10,084 | 4,883 | 4,670 | 388 | 143 | 213 | R | 48.4% | 46.3% | 3.8% |
| 107,120 | LA CROSSE | 55,559 | 24,327 | 28,455 | 2,272 | 505 | 4,128 | D | 43.8% | 51.2% | 4.1% |
| 16,137 | LAFAYETTE | 7,263 | 3,336 | 3,710 | 185 | 32 | 374 | D | 45.9% | 51.1% | 2.5% |
| 20,740 | LANGLADE | 9,721 | 5,125 | 4,199 | 261 | 136 | 926 | R | 52.7% | 43.2% | 2.7% |
| 29,641 | LINCOLN | 14,239 | 6,727 | 6,664 | 509 | 339 | 63 | R | 47.2% | 46.8% | 3.6% |
| 82,887 | MANITOWOC | 38,824 | 19,358 | 17,667 | 1,301 | 498 | 1,691 | R | 49.9% | 45.5% | 3.4% |
| 125,834 | MARATHON | 58,374 | 28,883 | 26,546 | 2,021 | 924 | 2,337 | R | 49.5% | 45.5% | 3.5% |
| 43,384 | MARINETTE | 19,921 | 10,535 | 8,676 | 504 | 206 | 1,859 | R | 52.9% | 43.6% | 2.5% |
| 15,832 | MARQUETTE | 7,194 | 3,522 | 3,437 | 195 | 40 | 85 | R | 49.0% | 47.8% | 2.7% |
| 4,562 | MENOMINEE | 1,233 | 225 | 949 | 47 | 12 | 724 | D | 18.2% | 77.0% | 3.8% |
| 940,164 | MILWAUKEE | 433,537 | 163,491 | 252,329 | 13,953 | 3,764 | 88,838 | D | 37.7% | 58.2% | 3.2% |
| 40,899 | MONROE | 16,335 | 8,217 | 7,460 | 489 | 169 | 757 | R | 50.3% | 45.7% | 3.0% |
| 35,634 | OCONTO | 16,596 | 8,706 | 7,260 | 437 | 193 | 1,446 | R | 52.5% | 43.7% | 2.6% |
| 36,776 | ONEIDA | 18,891 | 9,512 | 8,339 | 805 | 235 | 1,173 | R | 50.4% | 44.1% | 4.3% |
| 160,971 | OUTAGAMIE | 75,742 | 39,460 | 32,735 | 2,583 | 964 | 6,725 | R | 52.1% | 43.2% | 3.4% |
| 82,317 | OZAUKEE | 47,751 | 31,155 | 15,030 | 1,235 | 331 | 16,125 | R | 65.2% | 31.5% | 2.6% |
| 7,213 | PEPIN | 3,664 | 1,631 | 1,854 | 152 | 27 | 223 | D | 44.5% | 50.6% | 4.1% |
| 36,804 | PIERCE | 17,962 | 8,169 | 8,559 | 1,076 | 158 | 390 | D | 45.5% | 47.7% | 6.0% |
| 41,319 | POLK | 19,762 | 9,557 | 8,961 | 1,084 | 160 | 596 | R | 48.4% | 45.3% | 5.5% |
| 67,182 | PORTAGE | 33,760 | 13,214 | 17,942 | 2,143 | 461 | 4,728 | D | 39.1% | 53.1% | 6.3% |
| 15,822 | PRICE | 7,930 | 4,136 | 3,413 | 313 | 68 | 723 | R | 52.2% | 43.0% | 3.9% |
| 188,831 | RACINE | 88,865 | 44,014 | 41,563 | 2,436 | 852 | 2,451 | R | 49.5% | 46.8% | 2.7% |
| 17,924 | RICHLAND | 8,293 | 3,994 | 3,837 | 388 | 74 | 157 | R | 48.2% | 46.3% | 4.7% |
| 152,307 | ROCK | 70,404 | 27,467 | 40,472 | 1,980 | 485 | 13,005 | D | 39.0% | 57.5% | 2.8% |
| 15,347 | RUSK | 7,366 | 3,758 | 3,161 | 346 | 101 | 597 | R | 51.0% | 42.9% | 4.7% |
| 63,155 | ST. CROIX | 29,954 | 15,240 | 13,077 | 1,369 | 268 | 2,163 | R | 50.9% | 43.7% | 4.6% |
| 55,225 | SAUK | 25,653 | 11,586 | 13,035 | 858 | 174 | 1,449 | D | 45.2% | 50.8% | 3.3% |
| 16,196 | SAWYER | 7,767 | 3,972 | 3,333 | 398 | 64 | 639 | R | 51.1% | 42.9% | 5.1% |
| 40,664 | SHAWANO | 17,603 | 9,548 | 7,335 | 532 | 188 | 2,213 | R | 54.2% | 41.7% | 3.0% |
| 112,646 | SHEBOYGAN | 55,201 | 29,648 | 23,569 | 1,487 | 497 | 6,079 | R | 53.7% | 42.7% | 2.7% |

# WISCONSIN

## PRESIDENT 2000

| 2000 Census Population | County | Total Vote | Republican | Democratic | Green (Nader) | Other | Rep.-Dem. Plurality | Percentage of Total Vote | | |
|---|---|---|---|---|---|---|---|---|---|---|
| | | | | | | | | Rep. | Dem. | Green |
| 19,680 | TAYLOR | 8,992 | 5,278 | 3,254 | 318 | 142 | 2,024 R | 58.7% | 36.2% | 3.5% |
| 27,010 | TREMPEALEAU | 12,168 | 5,002 | 6,678 | 409 | 79 | 1,676 D | 41.1% | 54.9% | 3.4% |
| 28,056 | VERNON | 13,044 | 5,684 | 6,577 | 676 | 107 | 893 D | 43.6% | 50.4% | 5.2% |
| 21,033 | VILAS | 12,322 | 6,958 | 4,706 | 557 | 101 | 2,252 R | 56.5% | 38.2% | 4.5% |
| 93,759 | WALWORTH | 40,458 | 22,982 | 15,492 | 1,582 | 402 | 7,490 R | 56.8% | 38.3% | 3.9% |
| 16,036 | WASHBURN | 8,045 | 3,912 | 3,695 | 380 | 58 | 217 R | 48.6% | 45.9% | 4.7% |
| 117,493 | WASHINGTON | 61,412 | 41,162 | 18,115 | 1,563 | 572 | 23,047 R | 67.0% | 29.5% | 2.5% |
| 360,767 | WAUKESHA | 203,734 | 133,105 | 64,319 | 4,864 | 1,446 | 68,786 R | 65.3% | 31.6% | 2.4% |
| 51,731 | WAUPACA | 22,804 | 12,980 | 8,787 | 822 | 215 | 4,193 R | 56.9% | 38.5% | 3.6% |
| 23,154 | WAUSHARA | 10,248 | 5,571 | 4,239 | 310 | 128 | 1,332 R | 54.4% | 41.4% | 3.0% |
| 156,763 | WINNEBAGO | 76,080 | 38,330 | 33,983 | 2,963 | 804 | 4,347 R | 50.4% | 44.7% | 3.9% |
| 75,555 | WOOD | 35,761 | 17,803 | 15,936 | 1,384 | 638 | 1,867 R | 49.8% | 44.6% | 3.9% |
| 5,363,675 | TOTAL | 2,598,607 | 1,237,279 | 1,242,987 | 94,070 | 24,271 | 5,708 D | 47.6% | 47.8% | 3.6% |

# WISCONSIN

## PRESIDENT 1996

| 1995 Census Pop. Est. | County | Total Vote | Republican | Democratic | Reform (Perot) | Other | Rep.-Dem. Plurality | Percentage of Total Vote | | |
|---|---|---|---|---|---|---|---|---|---|---|
| | | | | | | | | Rep. | Dem. | Reform |
| 17,422 | ADAMS | 7,824 | 2,450 | 4,119 | 1,122 | 133 | 1,669 D | 31.3% | 52.6% | 14.3% |
| 16,446 | ASHLAND | 6,798 | 1,863 | 3,808 | 861 | 266 | 1,945 D | 27.4% | 56.0% | 12.7% |
| 42,785 | BARRON | 17,191 | 6,158 | 8,025 | 2,692 | 316 | 1,867 D | 35.8% | 46.7% | 15.7% |
| 14,955 | BAYFIELD | 7,340 | 2,250 | 3,895 | 899 | 296 | 1,645 D | 30.7% | 53.1% | 12.2% |
| 210,303 | BROWN | 90,837 | 38,563 | 42,823 | 8,036 | 1,415 | 4,260 D | 42.5% | 47.1% | 8.8% |
| 13,980 | BUFFALO | 5,557 | 1,800 | 2,681 | 972 | 104 | 881 D | 32.4% | 48.2% | 17.5% |
| 14,164 | BURNETT | 7,169 | 2,452 | 3,625 | 962 | 130 | 1,173 D | 34.2% | 50.6% | 13.4% |
| 37,369 | CALUMET | 16,299 | 7,049 | 6,940 | 2,112 | 198 | 109 R | 43.2% | 42.6% | 13.0% |
| 54,175 | CHIPPEWA | 21,131 | 7,520 | 9,647 | 3,567 | 397 | 2,127 D | 35.6% | 45.7% | 16.9% |
| 32,660 | CLARK | 12,861 | 4,622 | 5,540 | 2,486 | 213 | 918 D | 35.9% | 43.1% | 19.3% |
| 49,113 | COLUMBIA | 21,521 | 8,377 | 10,336 | 2,377 | 431 | 1,959 D | 38.9% | 48.0% | 11.0% |
| 16,552 | CRAWFORD | 7,060 | 2,149 | 3,658 | 1,060 | 193 | 1,509 D | 30.4% | 51.8% | 15.0% |
| 393,296 | DANE | 192,302 | 59,487 | 109,347 | 12,436 | 11,032 | 49,860 D | 30.9% | 56.9% | 6.5% |
| 79,375 | DODGE | 29,422 | 12,890 | 12,625 | 3,322 | 585 | 265 R | 43.8% | 42.9% | 11.3% |
| 26,836 | DOOR | 12,251 | 4,948 | 5,590 | 1,475 | 238 | 642 D | 40.4% | 45.6% | 12.0% |
| 42,777 | DOUGLAS | 18,591 | 5,167 | 10,976 | 2,001 | 447 | 5,809 D | 27.8% | 59.0% | 10.8% |
| 38,392 | DUNN | 15,415 | 4,917 | 7,536 | 2,555 | 407 | 2,619 D | 31.9% | 48.9% | 16.6% |
| 88,488 | EAU CLAIRE | 40,390 | 13,900 | 20,298 | 5,160 | 1,032 | 6,398 D | 34.4% | 50.3% | 12.8% |
| 5,256 | FLORENCE | 2,142 | 927 | 869 | 316 | 30 | 58 R | 43.3% | 40.6% | 14.8% |
| 93,347 | FOND DU LAC | 36,931 | 16,488 | 15,542 | 4,204 | 697 | 946 R | 44.6% | 42.1% | 11.4% |
| 9,361 | FOREST | 3,965 | 1,166 | 2,092 | 678 | 29 | 926 D | 29.4% | 52.8% | 17.1% |
| 49,432 | GRANT | 19,215 | 7,021 | 9,203 | 2,648 | 343 | 2,182 D | 36.5% | 47.9% | 13.8% |
| 32,492 | GREEN | 12,616 | 4,697 | 6,136 | 1,534 | 249 | 1,439 D | 37.2% | 48.6% | 12.2% |
| 19,326 | GREEN LAKE | 7,882 | 3,565 | 3,152 | 1,025 | 140 | 413 R | 45.2% | 40.0% | 13.0% |
| 21,701 | IOWA | 8,916 | 2,866 | 4,690 | 1,071 | 289 | 1,824 D | 32.1% | 52.6% | 12.0% |
| 6,443 | IRON | 3,531 | 1,260 | 1,725 | 469 | 77 | 465 D | 35.7% | 48.9% | 13.3% |
| 17,233 | JACKSON | 7,279 | 2,262 | 3,705 | 1,163 | 149 | 1,443 D | 31.1% | 50.9% | 16.0% |
| 73,001 | JEFFERSON | 29,774 | 12,681 | 13,188 | 3,177 | 728 | 507 D | 42.6% | 44.3% | 10.7% |
| 23,528 | JUNEAU | 9,182 | 3,226 | 4,331 | 1,393 | 232 | 1,105 D | 35.1% | 47.2% | 15.2% |
| 139,938 | KENOSHA | 53,717 | 18,296 | 27,964 | 6,507 | 950 | 9,668 D | 34.1% | 52.1% | 12.1% |
| 19,448 | KEWAUNEE | 9,046 | 3,431 | 4,311 | 1,161 | 143 | 880 D | 37.9% | 47.7% | 12.8% |
| 101,709 | LA CROSSE | 46,001 | 16,482 | 23,647 | 4,844 | 1,028 | 7,165 D | 35.8% | 51.4% | 10.5% |
| 16,544 | LAFAYETTE | 6,460 | 2,172 | 3,261 | 944 | 83 | 1,089 D | 33.6% | 50.5% | 14.6% |
| 20,478 | LANGLADE | 8,631 | 3,206 | 4,074 | 1,249 | 102 | 868 D | 37.1% | 47.2% | 14.5% |
| 28,921 | LINCOLN | 12,246 | 4,076 | 6,166 | 1,800 | 204 | 2,090 D | 33.3% | 50.4% | 14.7% |
| 82,507 | MANITOWOC | 34,444 | 13,239 | 16,750 | 3,941 | 514 | 3,511 D | 38.4% | 48.6% | 11.4% |
| 120,776 | MARATHON | 51,449 | 19,874 | 24,012 | 6,749 | 814 | 4,138 D | 38.6% | 46.7% | 13.1% |
| 42,273 | MARINETTE | 18,216 | 7,231 | 8,413 | 2,367 | 205 | 1,182 D | 39.7% | 46.2% | 13.0% |
| 14,045 | MARQUETTE | 6,119 | 2,208 | 2,859 | 915 | 137 | 651 D | 36.1% | 46.7% | 15.0% |
| 4,601 | MENOMINEE | 1,350 | 230 | 992 | 107 | 21 | 762 D | 17.0% | 73.5% | 7.9% |
| 931,242 | MILWAUKEE | 371,380 | 119,407 | 216,620 | 26,027 | 9,326 | 97,213 D | 32.2% | 58.3% | 7.0% |
| 38,776 | MONROE | 14,600 | 5,299 | 6,924 | 2,081 | 296 | 1,625 D | 36.3% | 47.4% | 14.3% |
| 32,298 | OCONTO | 13,885 | 5,389 | 6,723 | 1,655 | 118 | 1,334 D | 38.8% | 48.4% | 11.9% |
| 34,816 | ONEIDA | 16,917 | 6,339 | 7,619 | 2,604 | 355 | 1,280 D | 37.5% | 45.0% | 15.4% |
| 149,313 | OUTAGAMIE | 64,889 | 27,758 | 28,815 | 7,235 | 1,081 | 1,057 D | 42.8% | 44.4% | 11.1% |
| 79,111 | OZAUKEE | 38,961 | 22,078 | 13,269 | 2,774 | 840 | 8,809 R | 56.7% | 34.1% | 7.1% |
| 7,151 | PEPIN | 3,093 | 1,007 | 1,585 | 456 | 45 | 578 D | 32.6% | 51.2% | 14.7% |
| 34,724 | PIERCE | 15,000 | 4,599 | 7,970 | 2,074 | 357 | 3,371 D | 30.7% | 53.1% | 13.8% |
| 37,289 | POLK | 16,413 | 5,387 | 8,334 | 2,369 | 323 | 2,947 D | 32.8% | 50.8% | 14.4% |
| 64,704 | PORTAGE | 29,928 | 9,631 | 15,901 | 3,410 | 986 | 6,270 D | 32.2% | 53.1% | 11.4% |
| 15,950 | PRICE | 7,390 | 2,545 | 3,523 | 1,218 | 104 | 978 D | 34.4% | 47.7% | 16.5% |
| 182,892 | RACINE | 77,568 | 30,107 | 38,567 | 7,611 | 1,283 | 8,460 D | 38.8% | 49.7% | 9.8% |
| 17,895 | RICHLAND | 7,222 | 2,642 | 3,502 | 901 | 177 | 860 D | 36.6% | 48.5% | 12.5% |
| 148,349 | ROCK | 60,320 | 20,096 | 32,450 | 6,800 | 974 | 12,354 D | 33.3% | 53.8% | 11.3% |
| 15,345 | RUSK | 6,643 | 2,219 | 2,941 | 1,331 | 152 | 722 D | 33.4% | 44.3% | 20.0% |
| 54,851 | ST. CROIX | 23,213 | 8,253 | 11,384 | 3,180 | 396 | 3,131 D | 35.6% | 49.0% | 13.7% |
| 51,310 | SAUK | 20,285 | 7,448 | 9,889 | 2,448 | 500 | 2,441 D | 36.7% | 48.8% | 12.1% |
| 15,664 | SAWYER | 6,475 | 2,603 | 2,773 | 962 | 137 | 170 D | 40.2% | 42.8% | 14.9% |
| 38,442 | SHAWANO | 15,500 | 6,396 | 6,850 | 2,071 | 183 | 454 D | 41.3% | 44.2% | 13.4% |
| 108,326 | SHEBOYGAN | 47,003 | 20,067 | 22,022 | 4,157 | 757 | 1,955 D | 42.7% | 46.9% | 8.8% |

# WISCONSIN

## PRESIDENT 1996

| 1995 Census Pop. Est. | County | Total Vote | Republican | Democratic | Reform (Perot) | Other | Rep.-Dem. Plurality | Percentage of Total Vote | | |
|---|---|---|---|---|---|---|---|---|---|---|
| | | | | | | | | Rep. | Dem. | Reform |
| 19,234 | TAYLOR | 7,932 | 3,108 | 3,253 | 1,457 | 114 | 145 D | 39.2% | 41.0% | 18.4% |
| 25,835 | TREMPEALEAU | 10,794 | 3,035 | 5,848 | 1,688 | 223 | 2,813 D | 28.1% | 54.2% | 15.6% |
| 27,116 | VERNON | 11,226 | 3,796 | 5,572 | 1,523 | 335 | 1,776 D | 33.8% | 49.6% | 13.6% |
| 20,416 | VILAS | 10,445 | 4,496 | 4,226 | 1,548 | 175 | 270 R | 43.0% | 40.5% | 14.8% |
| 82,045 | WALWORTH | 32,961 | 15,099 | 13,283 | 3,729 | 850 | 1,816 R | 45.8% | 40.3% | 11.3% |
| 14,982 | WASHBURN | 6,996 | 2,703 | 3,231 | 920 | 142 | 528 D | 38.6% | 46.2% | 13.2% |
| 109,632 | WASHINGTON | 48,767 | 25,829 | 17,154 | 4,786 | 998 | 8,675 R | 53.0% | 35.2% | 9.8% |
| 337,954 | WAUKESHA | 165,472 | 91,729 | 57,354 | 13,109 | 3,280 | 34,375 R | 55.4% | 34.7% | 7.9% |
| 49,156 | WAUPACA | 19,243 | 8,679 | 7,800 | 2,464 | 300 | 879 R | 45.1% | 40.5% | 12.8% |
| 21,018 | WAUSHARA | 8,830 | 3,573 | 3,824 | 1,264 | 169 | 251 D | 40.5% | 43.3% | 14.3% |
| 149,391 | WINNEBAGO | 65,247 | 27,880 | 29,564 | 6,531 | 1,272 | 1,684 D | 42.7% | 45.3% | 10.0% |
| 76,196 | WOOD | 32,500 | 12,666 | 14,650 | 4,599 | 585 | 1,984 D | 39.0% | 45.1% | 14.2% |
| 5,122,871 | TOTAL | 2,196,169 | 845,029 | 1,071,971 | 227,339 | 51,830 | 226,942 D | 38.5% | 48.8% | 10.4% |

# WISCONSIN

## PRESIDENT 1992

| 1990 Census Population | County | Total Vote | Republican | Democratic | Perot | Other | Plurality | Percentage Total Vote | | |
|---|---|---|---|---|---|---|---|---|---|---|
| | | | | | | | | Rep. | Dem. | Perot |
| 15,682 | ADAMS | 8,048 | 2,465 | 3,539 | 2,003 | 41 | 1,074 D | 30.6% | 44.0% | 24.9% |
| 16,307 | ASHLAND | 8,393 | 2,372 | 4,213 | 1,746 | 62 | 1,841 D | 28.3% | 50.2% | 20.8% |
| 40,750 | BARRON | 20,230 | 6,572 | 8,063 | 5,479 | 116 | 1,491 D | 32.5% | 39.9% | 27.1% |
| 14,008 | BAYFIELD | 8,112 | 2,393 | 3,873 | 1,786 | 60 | 1,480 D | 29.5% | 47.7% | 22.0% |
| 194,594 | BROWN | 102,701 | 42,352 | 37,513 | 22,395 | 441 | 4,839 R | 41.2% | 36.5% | 21.8% |
| 13,584 | BUFFALO | 6,950 | 2,029 | 2,996 | 1,889 | 36 | 967 D | 29.2% | 43.1% | 27.2% |
| 13,084 | BURNETT | 7,436 | 2,340 | 3,172 | 1,855 | 69 | 832 D | 31.5% | 42.7% | 24.9% |
| 34,291 | CALUMET | 18,401 | 7,541 | 5,701 | 5,055 | 104 | 1,840 R | 41.0% | 31.0% | 27.5% |
| 52,360 | CHIPPEWA | 25,230 | 8,215 | 10,487 | 6,408 | 120 | 2,272 D | 32.6% | 41.6% | 25.4% |
| 31,647 | CLARK | 14,885 | 4,977 | 5,540 | 4,284 | 84 | 563 D | 33.4% | 37.2% | 28.8% |
| 45,088 | COLUMBIA | 23,984 | 9,099 | 9,348 | 5,439 | 98 | 249 D | 37.9% | 39.0% | 22.7% |
| 15,940 | CRAWFORD | 7,812 | 2,390 | 3,540 | 1,797 | 85 | 1,150 D | 30.6% | 45.3% | 23.0% |
| 367,085 | DANE | 210,122 | 61,957 | 114,724 | 31,874 | 1,567 | 52,767 D | 29.5% | 54.6% | 15.2% |
| 76,559 | DODGE | 35,709 | 14,971 | 11,438 | 9,136 | 164 | 3,533 R | 41.9% | 32.0% | 25.6% |
| 25,690 | DOOR | 13,777 | 5,468 | 4,735 | 3,506 | 68 | 733 R | 39.7% | 34.4% | 25.4% |
| 41,758 | DOUGLAS | 22,253 | 5,679 | 12,319 | 4,150 | 105 | 6,640 D | 25.5% | 55.4% | 18.6% |
| 35,909 | DUNN | 18,218 | 5,283 | 7,965 | 4,809 | 161 | 2,682 D | 29.0% | 43.7% | 26.4% |
| 85,183 | EAU CLAIRE | 47,076 | 15,915 | 21,221 | 9,783 | 157 | 5,306 D | 33.8% | 45.1% | 20.8% |
| 4,590 | FLORENCE | 2,646 | 942 | 978 | 719 | 7 | 36 D | 35.6% | 37.0% | 27.2% |
| 90,083 | FOND DU LAC | 44,506 | 19,785 | 13,757 | 10,660 | 304 | 6,028 R | 44.5% | 30.9% | 24.0% |
| 8,776 | FOREST | 4,368 | 1,393 | 1,904 | 1,062 | 9 | 511 D | 31.9% | 43.6% | 24.3% |
| 49,264 | GRANT | 23,157 | 7,678 | 8,914 | 6,405 | 160 | 1,236 D | 33.2% | 38.5% | 27.7% |
| 30,339 | GREEN | 14,183 | 4,887 | 5,467 | 3,735 | 94 | 580 D | 34.5% | 38.5% | 26.3% |
| 18,651 | GREEN LAKE | 9,540 | 3,897 | 2,772 | 2,827 | 44 | 1,070 R | 40.8% | 29.1% | 29.6% |
| 20,150 | IOWA | 10,151 | 3,288 | 4,467 | 2,341 | 55 | 1,179 D | 32.4% | 44.0% | 23.1% |
| 6,153 | IRON | 3,891 | 1,273 | 1,762 | 835 | 21 | 489 D | 32.7% | 45.3% | 21.5% |
| 16,588 | JACKSON | 8,418 | 2,644 | 3,681 | 2,040 | 53 | 1,037 D | 31.4% | 43.7% | 24.2% |
| 67,783 | JEFFERSON | 32,802 | 13,072 | 11,593 | 7,960 | 177 | 1,479 R | 39.9% | 35.3% | 24.3% |
| 21,650 | JUNEAU | 10,993 | 4,051 | 4,177 | 2,670 | 95 | 126 D | 36.9% | 38.0% | 24.3% |
| 128,181 | KENOSHA | 61,837 | 19,854 | 27,341 | 14,232 | 410 | 7,487 D | 32.1% | 44.2% | 23.0% |
| 18,878 | KEWAUNEE | 10,377 | 3,570 | 4,050 | 2,700 | 57 | 480 D | 34.4% | 39.0% | 26.0% |
| 97,904 | LA CROSSE | 52,273 | 18,891 | 22,838 | 10,224 | 320 | 3,947 D | 36.1% | 43.7% | 19.6% |
| 16,076 | LAFAYETTE | 7,859 | 2,582 | 3,143 | 2,079 | 55 | 561 D | 32.9% | 40.0% | 26.5% |
| 19,505 | LANGLADE | 10,042 | 3,890 | 3,630 | 2,444 | 78 | 260 R | 38.7% | 36.1% | 24.3% |
| 26,993 | LINCOLN | 13,304 | 4,321 | 5,297 | 3,605 | 81 | 976 D | 32.5% | 39.8% | 27.1% |
| 80,421 | MANITOWOC | 41,268 | 14,008 | 15,903 | 11,179 | 178 | 1,895 D | 33.9% | 38.5% | 27.1% |
| 115,400 | MARATHON | 57,378 | 20,948 | 21,482 | 14,600 | 348 | 534 D | 36.5% | 37.4% | 25.4% |
| 40,548 | MARINETTE | 21,093 | 7,984 | 7,626 | 5,412 | 71 | 358 R | 37.9% | 36.2% | 25.7% |
| 12,321 | MARQUETTE | 6,720 | 2,322 | 2,533 | 1,818 | 47 | 211 D | 34.6% | 37.7% | 27.1% |
| 3,890 | MENOMINEE | 1,160 | 244 | 691 | 221 | 4 | 447 D | 21.0% | 59.6% | 19.1% |
| 959,275 | MILWAUKEE | 465,496 | 151,314 | 235,521 | 76,039 | 2,622 | 84,207 D | 32.5% | 50.6% | 16.3% |
| 36,633 | MONROE | 16,805 | 6,118 | 6,427 | 4,183 | 77 | 309 D | 36.4% | 38.2% | 24.9% |
| 30,226 | OCONTO | 16,073 | 5,720 | 5,898 | 4,405 | 50 | 178 D | 35.6% | 36.7% | 27.4% |
| 31,679 | ONEIDA | 18,714 | 6,725 | 7,160 | 4,782 | 47 | 435 D | 35.9% | 38.3% | 25.6% |
| 140,510 | OUTAGAMIE | 72,911 | 30,370 | 23,735 | 18,479 | 327 | 6,635 R | 41.7% | 32.6% | 25.3% |
| 72,831 | OZAUKEE | 42,910 | 22,805 | 11,879 | 8,002 | 224 | 10,926 R | 53.1% | 27.7% | 18.6% |
| 7,107 | PEPIN | 3,572 | 1,098 | 1,673 | 781 | 20 | 575 D | 30.7% | 46.8% | 21.9% |
| 32,765 | PIERCE | 17,272 | 4,844 | 7,824 | 4,492 | 112 | 2,980 D | 28.0% | 45.3% | 26.0% |
| 34,773 | POLK | 18,071 | 5,446 | 7,746 | 4,753 | 126 | 2,300 D | 30.1% | 42.9% | 26.3% |
| 61,405 | PORTAGE | 33,716 | 10,914 | 15,553 | 7,083 | 166 | 4,639 D | 32.4% | 46.1% | 21.0% |
| 15,600 | PRICE | 8,550 | 2,654 | 3,575 | 2,286 | 35 | 921 D | 31.0% | 41.8% | 26.7% |
| 175,034 | RACINE | 87,819 | 32,310 | 34,875 | 20,227 | 407 | 2,565 D | 36.8% | 39.7% | 23.0% |
| 17,521 | RICHLAND | 8,540 | 3,144 | 3,458 | 1,899 | 39 | 314 D | 36.8% | 40.5% | 22.2% |
| 139,510 | ROCK | 69,025 | 21,942 | 31,154 | 15,700 | 229 | 9,212 D | 31.8% | 45.1% | 22.7% |
| 15,079 | RUSK | 7,967 | 2,430 | 3,376 | 2,085 | 76 | 946 D | 30.5% | 42.4% | 26.2% |
| 50,251 | ST. CROIX | 25,676 | 8,114 | 10,281 | 7,125 | 156 | 2,167 D | 31.6% | 40.0% | 27.7% |
| 46,975 | SAUK | 23,422 | 8,886 | 9,128 | 5,280 | 128 | 242 D | 37.9% | 39.0% | 22.5% |
| 14,181 | SAWYER | 7,365 | 2,658 | 2,796 | 1,861 | 50 | 138 D | 36.1% | 38.0% | 25.3% |
| 37,157 | SHAWANO | 17,952 | 7,253 | 6,062 | 4,540 | 97 | 1,191 R | 40.4% | 33.8% | 25.3% |
| 103,877 | SHEBOYGAN | 54,559 | 22,526 | 20,568 | 11,295 | 170 | 1,958 R | 41.3% | 37.7% | 20.7% |

# WISCONSIN

## PRESIDENT 1992

| 1990 Census Population | County | Total Vote | Republican | Democratic | Perot | Other | Plurality | Rep. | Dem. | Perot |
|---|---|---|---|---|---|---|---|---|---|---|
| 18,901 | TAYLOR | 9,359 | 3,415 | 3,305 | 2,590 | 49 | 110 R | 36.5% | 35.3% | 27.7% |
| 25,263 | TREMPEALEAU | 13,012 | 3,577 | 6,218 | 3,160 | 57 | 2,641 D | 27.5% | 47.8% | 24.3% |
| 25,617 | VERNON | 12,716 | 4,072 | 5,673 | 2,890 | 81 | 1,601 D | 32.0% | 44.6% | 22.7% |
| 17,707 | VILAS | 11,262 | 4,616 | 3,764 | 2,827 | 55 | 852 R | 41.0% | 33.4% | 25.1% |
| 75,000 | WALWORTH | 36,796 | 15,727 | 11,825 | 9,029 | 215 | 3,902 R | 42.7% | 32.1% | 24.5% |
| 13,772 | WASHBURN | 7,686 | 2,586 | 3,080 | 1,978 | 42 | 494 D | 33.6% | 40.1% | 25.7% |
| 95,328 | WASHINGTON | 50,073 | 22,739 | 13,339 | 13,045 | 950 | 9,400 R | 45.4% | 26.6% | 26.1% |
| 304,715 | WAUKESHA | 179,182 | 91,461 | 50,270 | 36,622 | 829 | 41,191 R | 51.0% | 28.1% | 20.4% |
| 46,104 | WAUPACA | 23,159 | 10,252 | 6,666 | 6,088 | 153 | 3,586 R | 44.3% | 28.8% | 26.3% |
| 19,385 | WAUSHARA | 10,329 | 4,045 | 3,402 | 2,829 | 53 | 643 R | 39.2% | 32.9% | 27.4% |
| 140,320 | WINNEBAGO | 77,386 | 33,709 | 27,234 | 16,140 | 303 | 6,475 R | 43.6% | 35.2% | 20.9% |
| 73,605 | WOOD | 36,436 | 13,843 | 13,208 | 8,822 | 563 | 635 R | 38.0% | 36.2% | 24.2% |
| 4,891,769 | TOTAL | 2,531,114 | 930,855 | 1,041,066 | 544,479 | 14,714 | 110,211 D | 36.8% | 41.1% | 21.5% |

# WISCONSIN

## PRESIDENT 1988

| 1980 Census Population | County | Total Vote | Republican | Democratic | Other | Rep.-Dem. Plurality | Percentage | | | |
|---|---|---|---|---|---|---|---|---|---|---|
| | | | | | | | Total Vote | | Major Vote | |
| | | | | | | | Rep. | Dem. | Rep. | Dem. |
| 13,457 | ADAMS | 6,883 | 3,258 | 3,598 | 27 | 340 D | 47.3% | 52.3% | 47.5% | 52.5% |
| 16,783 | ASHLAND | 7,489 | 2,926 | 4,526 | 37 | 1,600 D | 39.1% | 60.4% | 39.3% | 60.7% |
| 38,730 | BARRON | 17,579 | 8,527 | 8,951 | 101 | 424 D | 48.5% | 50.9% | 48.8% | 51.2% |
| 13,822 | BAYFIELD | 7,471 | 3,095 | 4,323 | 53 | 1,228 D | 41.4% | 57.9% | 41.7% | 58.3% |
| 175,280 | BROWN | 85,953 | 43,625 | 41,788 | 540 | 1,837 R | 50.8% | 48.6% | 51.1% | 48.9% |
| 14,309 | BUFFALO | 6,322 | 2,783 | 3,481 | 58 | 698 D | 44.0% | 55.1% | 44.4% | 55.6% |
| 12,340 | BURNETT | 6,483 | 2,884 | 3,537 | 62 | 653 D | 44.5% | 54.6% | 44.9% | 55.1% |
| 30,867 | CALUMET | 14,712 | 8,107 | 6,481 | 124 | 1,626 R | 55.1% | 44.1% | 55.6% | 44.4% |
| 52,127 | CHIPPEWA | 21,367 | 9,757 | 11,447 | 163 | 1,690 D | 45.7% | 53.6% | 46.0% | 54.0% |
| 32,910 | CLARK | 13,058 | 6,296 | 6,642 | 120 | 346 D | 48.2% | 50.9% | 48.7% | 51.3% |
| 43,222 | COLUMBIA | 19,766 | 10,475 | 9,132 | 159 | 1,343 R | 53.0% | 46.2% | 53.4% | 46.6% |
| 16,556 | CRAWFORD | 6,912 | 3,238 | 3,608 | 66 | 370 D | 46.8% | 52.2% | 47.3% | 52.7% |
| 323,545 | DANE | 176,158 | 69,143 | 105,414 | 1,601 | 36,271 D | 39.3% | 59.8% | 39.6% | 60.4% |
| 75,064 | DODGE | 29,950 | 17,003 | 12,663 | 284 | 4,340 R | 56.8% | 42.3% | 57.3% | 42.7% |
| 25,029 | DOOR | 12,430 | 6,907 | 5,425 | 98 | 1,482 R | 55.6% | 43.6% | 56.0% | 44.0% |
| 44,421 | DOUGLAS | 20,468 | 6,440 | 13,907 | 121 | 7,467 D | 31.5% | 67.9% | 31.7% | 68.3% |
| 34,314 | DUNN | 16,625 | 7,273 | 9,205 | 147 | 1,932 D | 43.7% | 55.4% | 44.1% | 55.9% |
| 78,805 | EAU CLAIRE | 39,023 | 17,664 | 21,150 | 209 | 3,486 D | 45.3% | 54.2% | 45.5% | 54.5% |
| 4,172 | FLORENCE | 2,147 | 1,106 | 1,018 | 23 | 88 R | 51.5% | 47.4% | 52.1% | 47.9% |
| 88,964 | FOND DU LAC | 38,193 | 21,985 | 15,887 | 321 | 6,098 R | 57.6% | 41.6% | 58.1% | 41.9% |
| 9,044 | FOREST | 4,013 | 1,845 | 2,142 | 26 | 297 D | 46.0% | 53.4% | 46.3% | 53.7% |
| 51,736 | GRANT | 19,620 | 10,049 | 9,421 | 150 | 628 D | 51.2% | 48.0% | 51.6% | 48.4% |
| 30,012 | GREEN | 11,908 | 6,636 | 5,153 | 119 | 1,483 R | 55.7% | 43.3% | 56.3% | 43.7% |
| 18,370 | GREEN LAKE | 8,299 | 5,205 | 3,033 | 61 | 2,172 R | 62.7% | 36.5% | 63.2% | 36.8% |
| 19,802 | IOWA | 8,575 | 4,240 | 4,268 | 67 | 28 D | 49.4% | 49.8% | 49.8% | 50.2% |
| 6,730 | IRON | 3,717 | 1,599 | 2,090 | 28 | 491 D | 43.0% | 56.2% | 43.3% | 56.7% |
| 16,831 | JACKSON | 7,523 | 3,555 | 3,924 | 44 | 369 D | 47.3% | 52.2% | 47.5% | 52.5% |
| 66,152 | JEFFERSON | 26,361 | 14,309 | 11,816 | 236 | 2,493 R | 54.3% | 44.8% | 54.8% | 45.2% |
| 21,039 | JUNEAU | 8,667 | 4,869 | 3,734 | 64 | 1,135 R | 56.2% | 43.1% | 56.6% | 43.4% |
| 123,137 | KENOSHA | 52,149 | 21,661 | 30,089 | 399 | 8,428 D | 41.5% | 57.7% | 41.9% | 58.1% |
| 19,539 | KEWAUNEE | 9,191 | 4,330 | 4,786 | 75 | 456 D | 47.1% | 52.1% | 47.5% | 52.5% |
| 91,056 | LA CROSSE | 44,111 | 21,548 | 22,204 | 359 | 656 D | 48.8% | 50.3% | 49.3% | 50.7% |
| 17,412 | LAFAYETTE | 7,235 | 3,665 | 3,521 | 49 | 144 R | 50.7% | 48.7% | 51.0% | 49.0% |
| 19,978 | LANGLADE | 9,201 | 4,884 | 4,254 | 63 | 630 R | 53.1% | 46.2% | 53.4% | 46.6% |
| 26,555 | LINCOLN | 11,185 | 5,257 | 5,819 | 109 | 562 D | 47.0% | 52.0% | 47.5% | 52.5% |
| 82,918 | MANITOWOC | 36,025 | 16,020 | 19,680 | 325 | 3,660 D | 44.5% | 54.6% | 44.9% | 55.1% |
| 111,270 | MARATHON | 49,543 | 24,482 | 24,658 | 403 | 176 D | 49.4% | 49.8% | 49.8% | 50.2% |
| 39,314 | MARINETTE | 17,791 | 9,637 | 8,030 | 124 | 1,607 R | 54.2% | 45.1% | 54.5% | 45.5% |
| 11,672 | MARQUETTE | 5,573 | 3,059 | 2,463 | 51 | 596 R | 54.9% | 44.2% | 55.4% | 44.6% |
| 3,373 | MENOMINEE | 1,422 | 381 | 1,028 | 13 | 647 D | 26.8% | 72.3% | 27.0% | 73.0% |
| 964,988 | MILWAUKEE | 440,296 | 168,363 | 268,287 | 3,646 | 99,924 D | 38.2% | 60.9% | 38.6% | 61.4% |
| 35,074 | MONROE | 13,591 | 7,073 | 6,437 | 81 | 636 R | 52.0% | 47.4% | 52.4% | 47.6% |
| 28,947 | OCONTO | 13,733 | 7,084 | 6,549 | 100 | 535 R | 51.6% | 47.7% | 52.0% | 48.0% |
| 31,216 | ONEIDA | 15,670 | 8,130 | 7,414 | 126 | 716 R | 51.9% | 47.3% | 52.3% | 47.7% |
| 128,799 | OUTAGAMIE | 61,304 | 33,113 | 27,771 | 420 | 5,342 R | 54.0% | 45.3% | 54.4% | 45.6% |
| 66,981 | OZAUKEE | 35,852 | 22,899 | 12,661 | 292 | 10,238 R | 63.9% | 35.3% | 64.4% | 35.6% |
| 7,477 | PEPIN | 3,255 | 1,311 | 1,906 | 38 | 595 D | 40.3% | 58.6% | 40.8% | 59.2% |
| 31,149 | PIERCE | 14,831 | 6,045 | 8,659 | 127 | 2,614 D | 40.8% | 58.4% | 41.1% | 58.9% |
| 32,351 | POLK | 16,022 | 6,866 | 8,981 | 175 | 2,115 D | 42.9% | 56.1% | 43.3% | 56.7% |
| 57,420 | PORTAGE | 28,542 | 12,057 | 16,317 | 168 | 4,260 D | 42.2% | 57.2% | 42.5% | 57.5% |
| 15,788 | PRICE | 7,516 | 3,450 | 3,987 | 79 | 537 D | 45.9% | 53.0% | 46.4% | 53.6% |
| 173,132 | RACINE | 76,631 | 36,342 | 39,631 | 658 | 3,289 D | 47.4% | 51.7% | 47.8% | 52.2% |
| 17,476 | RICHLAND | 7,718 | 4,026 | 3,643 | 49 | 383 R | 52.2% | 47.2% | 52.5% | 47.5% |
| 139,420 | ROCK | 58,227 | 28,178 | 29,576 | 473 | 1,398 D | 48.4% | 50.8% | 48.8% | 51.2% |
| 15,589 | RUSK | 7,017 | 3,063 | 3,888 | 66 | 825 D | 43.7% | 55.4% | 44.1% | 55.9% |
| 43,262 | ST. CROIX | 21,549 | 9,960 | 11,392 | 197 | 1,432 D | 46.2% | 52.9% | 46.6% | 53.4% |
| 43,469 | SAUK | 18,699 | 10,225 | 8,324 | 150 | 1,901 R | 54.7% | 44.5% | 55.1% | 44.9% |
| 12,843 | SAWYER | 6,545 | 3,260 | 3,231 | 54 | 29 R | 49.8% | 49.4% | 50.2% | 49.8% |
| 35,928 | SHAWANO | 15,162 | 8,362 | 6,587 | 213 | 1,775 R | 55.2% | 43.4% | 55.9% | 44.1% |
| 100,935 | SHEBOYGAN | 47,234 | 23,471 | 23,429 | 334 | 42 R | 49.7% | 49.6% | 50.0% | 50.0% |

# WISCONSIN

## PRESIDENT 1988

| 1980 Census Population | County | Total Vote | Republican | Democratic | Other | Rep.-Dem. Plurality | Percentage | | | |
|---|---|---|---|---|---|---|---|---|---|---|
| | | | | | | | Total Vote | | Major Vote | |
| | | | | | | | Rep. | Dem. | Rep. | Dem. |
| 18,817 | TAYLOR | 8,113 | 4,254 | 3,785 | 74 | 469 R | 52.4% | 46.7% | 52.9% | 47.1% |
| 26,158 | TREMPEALEAU | 11,183 | 4,902 | 6,212 | 69 | 1,310 D | 43.8% | 55.5% | 44.1% | 55.9% |
| 25,642 | VERNON | 11,102 | 5,226 | 5,754 | 122 | 528 D | 47.1% | 51.8% | 47.6% | 52.4% |
| 16,535 | VILAS | 9,730 | 5,842 | 3,781 | 107 | 2,061 R | 60.0% | 38.9% | 60.7% | 39.3% |
| 71,507 | WALWORTH | 30,711 | 18,259 | 12,203 | 249 | 6,056 R | 59.5% | 39.7% | 59.9% | 40.1% |
| 13,174 | WASHBURN | 6,521 | 3,074 | 3,393 | 54 | 319 D | 47.1% | 52.0% | 47.5% | 52.5% |
| 84,848 | WASHINGTON | 40,575 | 24,328 | 15,907 | 340 | 8,421 R | 60.0% | 39.2% | 60.5% | 39.5% |
| 280,326 | WAUKESHA | 148,935 | 90,467 | 57,598 | 870 | 32,869 R | 60.7% | 38.7% | 61.1% | 38.9% |
| 42,831 | WAUPACA | 18,784 | 11,559 | 7,078 | 147 | 4,481 R | 61.5% | 37.7% | 62.0% | 38.0% |
| 18,526 | WAUSHARA | 8,567 | 4,953 | 3,535 | 79 | 1,418 R | 57.8% | 41.3% | 58.4% | 41.6% |
| 131,703 | WINNEBAGO | 64,039 | 35,085 | 28,508 | 446 | 6,577 R | 54.8% | 44.5% | 55.2% | 44.8% |
| 72,799 | WOOD | 32,856 | 16,549 | 16,074 | 233 | 475 R | 50.4% | 48.9% | 50.7% | 49.3% |
| 4,705,767 | TOTAL | 2,191,608 | 1,047,499 | 1,126,794 | 17,315 | 79,295 D | 47.8% | 51.4% | 48.2% | 51.8% |

# WISCONSIN

## PRESIDENT 1984

| 1980 Census Population | County | Total Vote | Republican | Democratic | Other | Rep.-Dem. Plurality | Percentage | | | |
|---|---|---|---|---|---|---|---|---|---|---|
| | | | | | | | Total Vote | | Major Vote | |
| | | | | | | | Rep. | Dem. | Rep. | Dem. |
| 13,457 | ADAMS | 6,413 | 3,644 | 2,713 | 56 | 931 R | 56.8% | 42.3% | 57.3% | 42.7% |
| 16,783 | ASHLAND | 8,271 | 3,517 | 4,680 | 74 | 1,163 D | 42.5% | 56.6% | 42.9% | 57.1% |
| 38,730 | BARRON | 17,784 | 9,587 | 8,060 | 137 | 1,527 R | 53.9% | 45.3% | 54.3% | 45.7% |
| 13,822 | BAYFIELD | 7,567 | 3,474 | 4,034 | 59 | 560 D | 45.9% | 53.3% | 46.3% | 53.7% |
| 175,280 | BROWN | 81,976 | 51,186 | 30,208 | 582 | 20,978 R | 62.4% | 36.8% | 62.9% | 37.1% |
| 14,309 | BUFFALO | 6,308 | 3,325 | 2,921 | 62 | 404 R | 52.7% | 46.3% | 53.2% | 46.8% |
| 12,340 | BURNETT | 6,918 | 3,528 | 3,328 | 62 | 200 R | 51.0% | 48.1% | 51.5% | 48.5% |
| 30,867 | CALUMET | 13,898 | 8,969 | 4,735 | 194 | 4,234 R | 64.5% | 34.1% | 65.4% | 34.6% |
| 52,127 | CHIPPEWA | 21,350 | 10,983 | 10,200 | 167 | 783 R | 51.4% | 47.8% | 51.8% | 48.2% |
| 32,910 | CLARK | 13,918 | 8,098 | 5,647 | 173 | 2,451 R | 58.2% | 40.6% | 58.9% | 41.1% |
| 43,222 | COLUMBIA | 19,941 | 11,658 | 8,124 | 159 | 3,534 R | 58.5% | 40.7% | 58.9% | 41.1% |
| 16,556 | CRAWFORD | 7,906 | 4,411 | 3,435 | 60 | 976 R | 55.8% | 43.4% | 56.2% | 43.8% |
| 323,545 | DANE | 169,978 | 74,009 | 94,638 | 1,331 | 20,629 D | 43.5% | 55.7% | 43.9% | 56.1% |
| 75,064 | DODGE | 31,758 | 20,455 | 11,052 | 251 | 9,403 R | 64.4% | 34.8% | 64.9% | 35.1% |
| 25,029 | DOOR | 12,270 | 8,264 | 3,915 | 91 | 4,349 R | 67.4% | 31.9% | 67.9% | 32.1% |
| 44,421 | DOUGLAS | 21,467 | 7,066 | 14,290 | 111 | 7,224 D | 32.9% | 66.6% | 33.1% | 66.9% |
| 34,314 | DUNN | 16,364 | 8,472 | 7,709 | 183 | 763 R | 51.8% | 47.1% | 52.4% | 47.6% |
| 78,805 | EAU CLAIRE | 39,931 | 20,394 | 19,344 | 193 | 1,050 R | 51.1% | 48.4% | 51.3% | 48.7% |
| 4,172 | FLORENCE | 2,115 | 1,227 | 870 | 18 | 357 R | 58.0% | 41.1% | 58.5% | 41.5% |
| 88,964 | FOND DU LAC | 40,361 | 26,067 | 13,982 | 312 | 12,085 R | 64.6% | 34.6% | 65.1% | 34.9% |
| 9,044 | FOREST | 4,546 | 2,296 | 2,213 | 37 | 83 R | 50.5% | 48.7% | 50.9% | 49.1% |
| 51,736 | GRANT | 21,471 | 13,427 | 7,890 | 154 | 5,537 R | 62.5% | 36.7% | 63.0% | 37.0% |
| 30,012 | GREEN | 12,299 | 7,826 | 4,367 | 106 | 3,459 R | 63.6% | 35.5% | 64.2% | 35.8% |
| 18,370 | GREEN LAKE | 8,721 | 6,198 | 2,441 | 82 | 3,757 R | 71.1% | 28.0% | 71.7% | 28.3% |
| 19,802 | IOWA | 8,902 | 4,982 | 3,842 | 78 | 1,140 R | 56.0% | 43.2% | 56.5% | 43.5% |
| 6,730 | IRON | 3,653 | 1,667 | 1,967 | 19 | 300 D | 45.6% | 53.8% | 45.9% | 54.1% |
| 16,831 | JACKSON | 7,856 | 4,383 | 3,427 | 46 | 956 R | 55.8% | 43.6% | 56.1% | 43.9% |
| 66,152 | JEFFERSON | 28,783 | 17,779 | 10,788 | 216 | 6,991 R | 61.8% | 37.5% | 62.2% | 37.8% |
| 21,039 | JUNEAU | 8,855 | 5,627 | 3,151 | 77 | 2,476 R | 63.5% | 35.6% | 64.1% | 35.9% |
| 123,137 | KENOSHA | 55,697 | 26,112 | 29,233 | 352 | 3,121 D | 46.9% | 52.5% | 47.2% | 52.8% |
| 19,539 | KEWAUNEE | 9,213 | 5,705 | 3,444 | 64 | 2,261 R | 61.9% | 37.4% | 62.4% | 37.6% |
| 91,056 | LA CROSSE | 43,765 | 25,717 | 17,787 | 261 | 7,930 R | 58.8% | 40.6% | 59.1% | 40.9% |
| 17,412 | LAFAYETTE | 7,592 | 4,582 | 2,959 | 51 | 1,623 R | 60.4% | 39.0% | 60.8% | 39.2% |
| 19,978 | LANGLADE | 9,582 | 5,828 | 3,675 | 79 | 2,153 R | 60.8% | 38.4% | 61.3% | 38.7% |
| 26,555 | LINCOLN | 12,134 | 6,681 | 5,352 | 101 | 1,329 R | 55.1% | 44.1% | 55.5% | 44.5% |
| 82,918 | MANITOWOC | 37,390 | 19,635 | 17,249 | 506 | 2,386 R | 52.5% | 46.1% | 53.2% | 46.8% |
| 111,270 | MARATHON | 48,672 | 27,077 | 20,126 | 1,469 | 6,951 R | 55.6% | 41.4% | 57.4% | 42.6% |
| 39,314 | MARINETTE | 18,365 | 11,439 | 6,798 | 128 | 4,641 R | 62.3% | 37.0% | 62.7% | 37.3% |
| 11,672 | MARQUETTE | 5,512 | 3,404 | 2,031 | 77 | 1,373 R | 61.8% | 36.8% | 62.6% | 37.4% |
| 3,373 | MENOMINEE | 1,231 | 392 | 832 | 7 | 440 D | 31.8% | 67.6% | 32.0% | 68.0% |
| 964,988 | MILWAUKEE | 458,042 | 196,259 | 259,134 | 2,649 | 62,875 D | 42.8% | 56.6% | 43.1% | 56.9% |
| 35,074 | MONROE | 13,884 | 8,225 | 5,564 | 95 | 2,661 R | 59.2% | 40.1% | 59.6% | 40.4% |
| 28,947 | OCONTO | 14,140 | 8,713 | 5,288 | 139 | 3,425 R | 61.6% | 37.4% | 62.2% | 37.8% |
| 31,216 | ONEIDA | 16,384 | 9,782 | 6,416 | 186 | 3,366 R | 59.7% | 39.2% | 60.4% | 39.6% |
| 128,799 | OUTAGAMIE | 56,971 | 36,765 | 19,789 | 417 | 16,976 R | 64.5% | 34.7% | 65.0% | 35.0% |
| 66,981 | OZAUKEE | 34,892 | 23,896 | 10,763 | 233 | 13,133 R | 68.5% | 30.8% | 68.9% | 31.1% |
| 7,477 | PEPIN | 3,203 | 1,555 | 1,629 | 19 | 74 D | 48.5% | 50.9% | 48.8% | 51.2% |
| 31,149 | PIERCE | 15,022 | 7,611 | 7,285 | 126 | 326 R | 50.7% | 48.5% | 51.1% | 48.9% |
| 32,351 | POLK | 16,263 | 8,101 | 8,033 | 129 | 68 R | 49.8% | 49.4% | 50.2% | 49.8% |
| 57,420 | PORTAGE | 28,192 | 13,603 | 14,399 | 190 | 796 D | 48.3% | 51.1% | 48.6% | 51.4% |
| 15,788 | PRICE | 7,856 | 4,286 | 3,479 | 91 | 807 R | 54.6% | 44.3% | 55.2% | 44.8% |
| 173,132 | RACINE | 79,654 | 42,085 | 36,953 | 616 | 5,132 R | 52.8% | 46.4% | 53.2% | 46.8% |
| 17,476 | RICHLAND | 7,760 | 4,857 | 2,844 | 59 | 2,013 R | 62.6% | 36.6% | 63.1% | 36.9% |
| 139,420 | ROCK | 59,329 | 32,483 | 26,430 | 416 | 6,053 R | 54.8% | 44.5% | 55.1% | 44.9% |
| 15,589 | RUSK | 7,985 | 4,061 | 3,843 | 81 | 218 R | 50.9% | 48.1% | 51.4% | 48.6% |
| 43,262 | ST. CROIX | 21,644 | 11,365 | 10,126 | 153 | 1,239 R | 52.5% | 46.8% | 52.9% | 47.1% |
| 43,469 | SAUK | 18,310 | 11,067 | 7,157 | 86 | 3,910 R | 60.4% | 39.1% | 60.7% | 39.3% |
| 12,843 | SAWYER | 6,971 | 3,911 | 2,981 | 79 | 930 R | 56.1% | 42.8% | 56.7% | 43.3% |
| 35,928 | SHAWANO | 16,235 | 10,635 | 5,469 | 131 | 5,166 R | 65.5% | 33.7% | 66.0% | 34.0% |
| 100,935 | SHEBOYGAN | 47,876 | 26,343 | 21,111 | 422 | 5,232 R | 55.0% | 44.1% | 55.5% | 44.5% |

# WISCONSIN

## PRESIDENT 1984

| 1980 Census Population | County | Total Vote | Republican | Democratic | Other | Rep.-Dem. Plurality | Percentage | | | |
|---|---|---|---|---|---|---|---|---|---|---|
| | | | | | | | Total Vote | | Major Vote | |
| | | | | | | | Rep. | Dem. | Rep. | Dem. |
| 18,817 | TAYLOR | 8,276 | 4,918 | 3,271 | 87 | 1,647 R | 59.4% | 39.5% | 60.1% | 39.9% |
| 26,158 | TREMPEALEAU | 11,522 | 6,007 | 5,405 | 110 | 602 R | 52.1% | 46.9% | 52.6% | 47.4% |
| 25,642 | VERNON | 11,608 | 6,468 | 5,051 | 89 | 1,417 R | 55.7% | 43.5% | 56.2% | 43.8% |
| 16,535 | VILAS | 9,024 | 5,963 | 2,940 | 121 | 3,023 R | 66.1% | 32.6% | 67.0% | 33.0% |
| 71,507 | WALWORTH | 30,715 | 20,590 | 9,876 | 249 | 10,714 R | 67.0% | 32.2% | 67.6% | 32.4% |
| 13,174 | WASHBURN | 7,078 | 3,847 | 3,188 | 43 | 659 R | 54.4% | 45.0% | 54.7% | 45.3% |
| 84,848 | WASHINGTON | 38,572 | 25,278 | 12,966 | 328 | 12,312 R | 65.5% | 33.6% | 66.1% | 33.9% |
| 280,326 | WAUKESHA | 140,663 | 92,415 | 47,308 | 940 | 45,107 R | 65.7% | 33.6% | 66.1% | 33.9% |
| 42,831 | WAUPACA | 19,184 | 13,097 | 5,894 | 193 | 7,203 R | 68.3% | 30.7% | 69.0% | 31.0% |
| 18,526 | WAUSHARA | 8,636 | 5,768 | 2,782 | 86 | 2,986 R | 66.8% | 32.2% | 67.5% | 32.5% |
| 131,703 | WINNEBAGO | 62,183 | 39,014 | 22,791 | 378 | 16,223 R | 62.7% | 36.7% | 63.1% | 36.9% |
| 72,799 | WOOD | 32,882 | 20,525 | 12,118 | 239 | 8,407 R | 62.4% | 36.9% | 62.9% | 37.1% |
| 4,705,767 | TOTAL | 2,211,689 | 1,198,584 | 995,740 | 17,365 | 202,844 R | 54.2% | 45.0% | 54.6% | 45.4% |

# WISCONSIN

## PRESIDENT 1980

| 1980 Census Population | County | Total Vote | Republican | Democratic | Other | Rep.-Dem. Plurality | Percentage Total Vote Rep. | Dem. | Major Vote Rep. | Dem. |
|---|---|---|---|---|---|---|---|---|---|---|
| 13,457 | ADAMS | 6,527 | 3,304 | 2,773 | 450 | 531 R | 50.6% | 42.5% | 54.4% | 45.6% |
| 16,783 | ASHLAND | 8,685 | 3,262 | 4,469 | 954 | 1,207 D | 37.6% | 51.5% | 42.2% | 57.8% |
| 38,730 | BARRON | 18,698 | 8,791 | 8,654 | 1,253 | 137 R | 47.0% | 46.3% | 50.4% | 49.6% |
| 13,822 | BAYFIELD | 7,802 | 3,278 | 3,705 | 819 | 427 D | 42.0% | 47.5% | 46.9% | 53.1% |
| 175,280 | BROWN | 82,997 | 47,067 | 29,796 | 6,134 | 17,271 R | 56.7% | 35.9% | 61.2% | 38.8% |
| 14,309 | BUFFALO | 7,428 | 3,569 | 3,276 | 583 | 293 R | 48.0% | 44.1% | 52.1% | 47.9% |
| 12,340 | BURNETT | 6,757 | 3,027 | 3,200 | 530 | 173 D | 44.8% | 47.4% | 48.6% | 51.4% |
| 30,867 | CALUMET | 14,321 | 7,885 | 5,036 | 1,400 | 2,849 R | 55.1% | 35.2% | 61.0% | 39.0% |
| 52,127 | CHIPPEWA | 21,921 | 10,531 | 9,836 | 1,554 | 695 R | 48.0% | 44.9% | 51.7% | 48.3% |
| 32,910 | CLARK | 15,039 | 7,921 | 6,091 | 1,027 | 1,830 R | 52.7% | 40.5% | 56.5% | 43.5% |
| 43,222 | COLUMBIA | 21,031 | 10,478 | 8,715 | 1,838 | 1,763 R | 49.8% | 41.4% | 54.6% | 45.4% |
| 16,556 | CRAWFORD | 7,861 | 3,934 | 3,392 | 535 | 542 R | 50.0% | 43.1% | 53.7% | 46.3% |
| 323,545 | DANE | 168,563 | 57,545 | 85,609 | 25,409 | 28,064 D | 34.1% | 50.8% | 40.2% | 59.8% |
| 75,064 | DODGE | 33,682 | 19,435 | 11,966 | 2,281 | 7,469 R | 57.7% | 35.5% | 61.9% | 38.1% |
| 25,029 | DOOR | 13,006 | 7,170 | 4,961 | 875 | 2,209 R | 55.1% | 38.1% | 59.1% | 40.9% |
| 44,421 | DOUGLAS | 21,219 | 7,258 | 11,703 | 2,258 | 4,445 D | 34.2% | 55.2% | 38.3% | 61.7% |
| 34,314 | DUNN | 17,095 | 7,428 | 7,743 | 1,924 | 315 D | 43.5% | 45.3% | 49.0% | 51.0% |
| 78,805 | EAU CLAIRE | 38,943 | 17,304 | 17,602 | 4,037 | 298 D | 44.4% | 45.2% | 49.6% | 50.4% |
| 4,172 | FLORENCE | 2,261 | 1,187 | 943 | 131 | 244 R | 52.5% | 41.7% | 55.7% | 44.3% |
| 88,964 | FOND DU LAC | 42,497 | 24,196 | 15,293 | 3,008 | 8,903 R | 56.9% | 36.0% | 61.3% | 38.7% |
| 9,044 | FOREST | 4,680 | 2,070 | 2,402 | 208 | 332 D | 44.2% | 51.3% | 46.3% | 53.7% |
| 51,736 | GRANT | 23,830 | 13,298 | 8,406 | 2,126 | 4,892 R | 55.8% | 35.3% | 61.3% | 38.7% |
| 30,012 | GREEN | 14,296 | 7,714 | 5,336 | 1,246 | 2,378 R | 54.0% | 37.3% | 59.1% | 40.9% |
| 18,370 | GREEN LAKE | 9,262 | 5,868 | 2,851 | 543 | 3,017 R | 63.4% | 30.8% | 67.3% | 32.7% |
| 19,802 | IOWA | 9,001 | 4,068 | 4,154 | 779 | 86 D | 45.2% | 46.2% | 49.5% | 50.5% |
| 6,730 | IRON | 4,021 | 1,811 | 1,941 | 269 | 130 D | 45.0% | 48.3% | 48.3% | 51.7% |
| 16,831 | JACKSON | 8,524 | 4,327 | 3,629 | 568 | 698 R | 50.8% | 42.6% | 54.4% | 45.6% |
| 66,152 | JEFFERSON | 30,016 | 16,174 | 11,335 | 2,507 | 4,839 R | 53.9% | 37.8% | 58.8% | 41.2% |
| 21,039 | JUNEAU | 10,146 | 5,591 | 3,884 | 671 | 1,707 R | 55.1% | 38.3% | 59.0% | 41.0% |
| 123,137 | KENOSHA | 55,893 | 24,481 | 26,738 | 4,674 | 2,257 D | 43.8% | 47.8% | 47.8% | 52.2% |
| 19,539 | KEWAUNEE | 9,794 | 5,577 | 3,706 | 511 | 1,871 R | 56.9% | 37.8% | 60.1% | 39.9% |
| 91,056 | LA CROSSE | 45,293 | 23,427 | 17,304 | 4,562 | 6,123 R | 51.7% | 38.2% | 57.5% | 42.5% |
| 17,412 | LAFAYETTE | 8,597 | 4,421 | 3,598 | 578 | 823 R | 51.4% | 41.9% | 55.1% | 44.9% |
| 19,978 | LANGLADE | 9,883 | 4,866 | 4,498 | 519 | 368 R | 49.2% | 45.5% | 52.0% | 48.0% |
| 26,555 | LINCOLN | 12,755 | 6,473 | 5,438 | 844 | 1,035 R | 50.7% | 42.6% | 54.3% | 45.7% |
| 82,918 | MANITOWOC | 38,754 | 18,591 | 17,330 | 2,833 | 1,261 R | 48.0% | 44.7% | 51.8% | 48.2% |
| 111,270 | MARATHON | 53,549 | 25,868 | 23,281 | 4,400 | 2,587 R | 48.3% | 43.5% | 52.6% | 47.4% |
| 39,314 | MARINETTE | 19,182 | 10,444 | 7,718 | 1,020 | 2,726 R | 54.4% | 40.2% | 57.5% | 42.5% |
| 11,672 | MARQUETTE | 5,789 | 3,166 | 2,180 | 443 | 986 R | 54.7% | 37.7% | 59.2% | 40.8% |
| 3,373 | MENOMINEE | 936 | 302 | 544 | 90 | 242 D | 32.3% | 58.1% | 35.7% | 64.3% |
| 964,988 | MILWAUKEE | 464,160 | 183,450 | 240,174 | 40,536 | 56,724 D | 39.5% | 51.7% | 43.3% | 56.7% |
| 35,074 | MONROE | 15,689 | 8,136 | 6,521 | 1,032 | 1,615 R | 51.9% | 41.6% | 55.5% | 44.5% |
| 28,947 | OCONTO | 14,314 | 8,292 | 5,352 | 670 | 2,940 R | 57.9% | 37.4% | 60.8% | 39.2% |
| 31,216 | ONEIDA | 16,867 | 8,602 | 7,008 | 1,257 | 1,594 R | 51.0% | 41.5% | 55.1% | 44.9% |
| 128,799 | OUTAGAMIE | 59,456 | 31,500 | 21,284 | 6,672 | 10,216 R | 53.0% | 35.8% | 59.7% | 40.3% |
| 66,981 | OZAUKEE | 35,040 | 21,371 | 10,779 | 2,890 | 10,592 R | 61.0% | 30.8% | 66.5% | 33.5% |
| 7,477 | PEPIN | 3,473 | 1,541 | 1,673 | 259 | 132 D | 44.4% | 48.2% | 47.9% | 52.1% |
| 31,149 | PIERCE | 15,662 | 6,209 | 7,312 | 2,141 | 1,103 D | 39.6% | 46.7% | 45.9% | 54.1% |
| 32,351 | POLK | 16,313 | 7,207 | 7,607 | 1,499 | 400 D | 44.2% | 46.6% | 48.6% | 51.4% |
| 57,420 | PORTAGE | 30,708 | 10,465 | 16,443 | 3,800 | 5,978 D | 34.1% | 53.5% | 38.9% | 61.1% |
| 15,788 | PRICE | 8,172 | 4,028 | 3,595 | 549 | 433 R | 49.3% | 44.0% | 52.8% | 47.2% |
| 173,132 | RACINE | 79,775 | 39,683 | 33,565 | 6,527 | 6,118 R | 49.7% | 42.1% | 54.2% | 45.8% |
| 17,476 | RICHLAND | 8,594 | 4,601 | 3,413 | 580 | 1,188 R | 53.5% | 39.7% | 57.4% | 42.6% |
| 139,420 | ROCK | 61,218 | 30,960 | 24,740 | 5,518 | 6,220 R | 50.6% | 40.4% | 55.6% | 44.4% |
| 15,589 | RUSK | 7,800 | 3,704 | 3,584 | 512 | 120 R | 47.5% | 45.9% | 50.8% | 49.2% |
| 43,262 | ST. CROIX | 21,792 | 9,265 | 10,203 | 2,324 | 938 D | 42.5% | 46.8% | 47.6% | 52.4% |
| 43,469 | SAUK | 20,208 | 9,992 | 8,456 | 1,760 | 1,536 R | 49.4% | 41.8% | 54.2% | 45.8% |
| 12,843 | SAWYER | 7,089 | 3,548 | 3,065 | 476 | 483 R | 50.0% | 43.2% | 53.7% | 46.3% |
| 35,928 | SHAWANO | 16,283 | 9,922 | 5,410 | 951 | 4,512 R | 60.9% | 33.2% | 64.7% | 35.3% |
| 100,935 | SHEBOYGAN | 48,600 | 23,036 | 20,974 | 4,590 | 2,062 R | 47.4% | 43.2% | 52.3% | 47.7% |

# WISCONSIN

## PRESIDENT 1980

| 1980 Census Population | County | Total Vote | Republican | Democratic | Other | Rep.-Dem. Plurality | Percentage | | | |
|---|---|---|---|---|---|---|---|---|---|---|
| | | | | | | | Total Vote | | Major Vote | |
| | | | | | | | Rep. | Dem. | Rep. | Dem. |
| 18,817 | TAYLOR | 8,972 | 4,596 | 3,739 | 637 | 857 R | 51.2% | 41.7% | 55.1% | 44.9% |
| 26,158 | TREMPEALEAU | 12,133 | 5,992 | 5,390 | 751 | 602 R | 49.4% | 44.4% | 52.6% | 47.4% |
| 25,642 | VERNON | 12,774 | 6,528 | 5,501 | 745 | 1,027 R | 51.1% | 43.1% | 54.3% | 45.7% |
| 16,535 | VILAS | 9,932 | 6,034 | 3,293 | 605 | 2,741 R | 60.8% | 33.2% | 64.7% | 35.3% |
| 71,507 | WALWORTH | 33,730 | 19,194 | 11,344 | 3,192 | 7,850 R | 56.9% | 33.6% | 62.9% | 37.1% |
| 13,174 | WASHBURN | 6,887 | 3,193 | 3,172 | 522 | 21 R | 46.4% | 46.1% | 50.2% | 49.8% |
| 84,848 | WASHINGTON | 39,493 | 23,213 | 12,944 | 3,336 | 10,269 R | 58.8% | 32.8% | 64.2% | 35.8% |
| 280,326 | WAUKESHA | 139,236 | 81,059 | 46,612 | 11,565 | 34,447 R | 58.2% | 33.5% | 63.5% | 36.5% |
| 42,831 | WAUPACA | 20,397 | 12,568 | 6,401 | 1,428 | 6,167 R | 61.6% | 31.4% | 66.3% | 33.7% |
| 18,526 | WAUSHARA | 9,077 | 5,576 | 2,987 | 514 | 2,589 R | 61.4% | 32.9% | 65.1% | 34.9% |
| 131,703 | WINNEBAGO | 64,360 | 34,286 | 24,203 | 5,871 | 10,083 R | 53.3% | 37.6% | 58.6% | 41.4% |
| 72,799 | WOOD | 34,483 | 17,987 | 13,804 | 2,692 | 4,183 R | 52.2% | 40.0% | 56.6% | 43.4% |
| 4,705,767 | TOTAL | 2,273,221 | 1,088,845 | 981,584 | 202,792 | 107,261 R | 47.9% | 43.2% | 52.6% | 47.4% |

# WISCONSIN

## PRESIDENT 1976

| 1970 Census Population | County | Total Vote | Republican | Democratic | Other | Rep.-Dem. Plurality | Percentage | | | |
|---|---|---|---|---|---|---|---|---|---|---|
| | | | | | | | Total Vote | | Major Vote | |
| | | | | | | | Rep. | Dem. | Rep. | Dem. |
| 9,234 | ADAMS | 5,594 | 2,377 | 3,089 | 128 | 712 D | 42.5% | 55.2% | 43.5% | 56.5% |
| 16,743 | ASHLAND | 7,961 | 3,045 | 4,688 | 228 | 1,643 D | 38.2% | 58.9% | 39.4% | 60.6% |
| 33,955 | BARRON | 16,406 | 7,393 | 8,678 | 335 | 1,285 D | 45.1% | 52.9% | 46.0% | 54.0% |
| 11,683 | BAYFIELD | 6,706 | 2,624 | 3,885 | 197 | 1,261 D | 39.1% | 57.9% | 40.3% | 59.7% |
| 158,244 | BROWN | 72,318 | 36,571 | 33,572 | 2,175 | 2,999 R | 50.6% | 46.4% | 52.1% | 47.9% |
| 13,743 | BUFFALO | 6,441 | 2,844 | 3,448 | 149 | 604 D | 44.2% | 53.5% | 45.2% | 54.8% |
| 9,276 | BURNETT | 6,469 | 2,573 | 3,720 | 176 | 1,147 D | 39.8% | 57.5% | 40.9% | 59.1% |
| 27,604 | CALUMET | 13,157 | 6,589 | 6,241 | 327 | 348 R | 50.1% | 47.4% | 51.4% | 48.6% |
| 47,717 | CHIPPEWA | 20,155 | 8,137 | 11,538 | 480 | 3,401 D | 40.4% | 57.2% | 41.4% | 58.6% |
| 30,361 | CLARK | 13,784 | 6,095 | 7,238 | 451 | 1,143 D | 44.2% | 52.5% | 45.7% | 54.3% |
| 40,150 | COLUMBIA | 19,933 | 10,075 | 9,457 | 401 | 618 R | 50.5% | 47.4% | 51.6% | 48.4% |
| 15,252 | CRAWFORD | 7,226 | 3,393 | 3,629 | 204 | 236 D | 47.0% | 50.2% | 48.3% | 51.7% |
| 290,272 | DANE | 152,756 | 63,466 | 82,321 | 6,969 | 18,855 D | 41.5% | 53.9% | 43.5% | 56.5% |
| 69,004 | DODGE | 31,674 | 17,335 | 13,643 | 696 | 3,692 R | 54.7% | 43.1% | 56.0% | 44.0% |
| 20,106 | DOOR | 11,420 | 6,557 | 4,553 | 310 | 2,004 R | 57.4% | 39.9% | 59.0% | 41.0% |
| 44,657 | DOUGLAS | 20,989 | 6,999 | 13,478 | 512 | 6,479 D | 33.3% | 64.2% | 34.2% | 65.8% |
| 29,154 | DUNN | 15,040 | 6,751 | 7,882 | 407 | 1,131 D | 44.9% | 52.4% | 46.1% | 53.9% |
| 67,219 | EAU CLAIRE | 35,386 | 16,388 | 18,263 | 735 | 1,875 D | 46.3% | 51.6% | 47.3% | 52.7% |
| 3,298 | FLORENCE | 1,925 | 922 | 965 | 38 | 43 D | 47.9% | 50.1% | 48.9% | 51.1% |
| 84,567 | FOND DU LAC | 39,895 | 22,226 | 16,571 | 1,098 | 5,655 R | 55.7% | 41.5% | 57.3% | 42.7% |
| 7,691 | FOREST | 4,245 | 1,604 | 2,574 | 67 | 970 D | 37.8% | 60.6% | 38.4% | 61.6% |
| 48,398 | GRANT | 22,220 | 12,016 | 9,639 | 565 | 2,377 R | 54.1% | 43.4% | 55.5% | 44.5% |
| 26,714 | GREEN | 13,076 | 7,085 | 5,632 | 359 | 1,453 R | 54.2% | 43.1% | 55.7% | 44.3% |
| 16,878 | GREEN LAKE | 8,612 | 5,020 | 3,411 | 181 | 1,609 R | 58.3% | 39.6% | 59.5% | 40.5% |
| 19,306 | IOWA | 8,685 | 4,195 | 4,252 | 238 | 57 D | 48.3% | 49.0% | 49.7% | 50.3% |
| 6,533 | IRON | 3,805 | 1,340 | 2,399 | 66 | 1,059 D | 35.2% | 63.0% | 35.8% | 64.2% |
| 15,325 | JACKSON | 7,276 | 3,406 | 3,735 | 135 | 329 D | 46.8% | 51.3% | 47.7% | 52.3% |
| 60,060 | JEFFERSON | 28,876 | 15,528 | 12,577 | 771 | 2,951 R | 53.8% | 43.6% | 55.2% | 44.8% |
| 18,455 | JUNEAU | 9,087 | 4,242 | 4,512 | 333 | 270 D | 46.7% | 49.7% | 48.5% | 51.5% |
| 117,917 | KENOSHA | 51,338 | 22,349 | 27,585 | 1,404 | 5,236 D | 43.5% | 53.7% | 44.8% | 55.2% |
| 18,961 | KEWAUNEE | 9,322 | 4,447 | 4,607 | 268 | 160 D | 47.7% | 49.4% | 49.1% | 50.9% |
| 80,468 | LA CROSSE | 41,704 | 24,188 | 16,674 | 842 | 7,514 R | 58.0% | 40.0% | 59.2% | 40.8% |
| 17,456 | LAFAYETTE | 8,195 | 4,131 | 3,839 | 225 | 292 R | 50.4% | 46.8% | 51.8% | 48.2% |
| 19,220 | LANGLADE | 8,936 | 4,630 | 4,134 | 172 | 496 R | 51.8% | 46.3% | 52.8% | 47.2% |
| 23,499 | LINCOLN | 11,738 | 5,672 | 5,800 | 266 | 128 D | 48.3% | 49.4% | 49.4% | 50.6% |
| 82,294 | MANITOWOC | 36,798 | 16,039 | 19,819 | 940 | 3,780 D | 43.6% | 53.9% | 44.7% | 55.3% |
| 97,457 | MARATHON | 48,054 | 21,898 | 24,934 | 1,222 | 3,036 D | 45.6% | 51.9% | 46.8% | 53.2% |
| 35,810 | MARINETTE | 17,439 | 8,591 | 8,482 | 366 | 109 R | 49.3% | 48.6% | 50.3% | 49.7% |
| 8,865 | MARQUETTE | 5,217 | 2,607 | 2,516 | 94 | 91 R | 50.0% | 48.2% | 50.9% | 49.1% |
| 2,607 | MENOMINEE | 1,122 | 324 | 766 | 32 | 442 D | 28.9% | 68.3% | 29.7% | 70.3% |
| 1,054,262 | MILWAUKEE | 456,545 | 192,008 | 249,739 | 14,798 | 57,731 D | 42.1% | 54.7% | 43.5% | 56.5% |
| 31,610 | MONROE | 13,998 | 7,242 | 6,465 | 291 | 777 R | 51.7% | 46.2% | 52.8% | 47.2% |
| 25,553 | OCONTO | 13,048 | 6,232 | 6,541 | 275 | 309 D | 47.8% | 50.1% | 48.8% | 51.2% |
| 24,427 | ONEIDA | 14,947 | 7,347 | 7,216 | 384 | 131 R | 49.2% | 48.3% | 50.4% | 49.6% |
| 119,356 | OUTAGAMIE | 52,568 | 28,363 | 23,079 | 1,126 | 5,284 R | 54.0% | 43.9% | 55.1% | 44.9% |
| 54,421 | OZAUKEE | 31,961 | 19,817 | 11,271 | 873 | 8,546 R | 62.0% | 35.3% | 63.7% | 36.3% |
| 7,319 | PEPIN | 3,338 | 1,312 | 1,955 | 71 | 643 D | 39.3% | 58.6% | 40.2% | 59.8% |
| 26,652 | PIERCE | 14,112 | 5,676 | 8,039 | 397 | 2,363 D | 40.2% | 57.0% | 41.4% | 58.6% |
| 26,666 | POLK | 14,924 | 6,159 | 8,485 | 280 | 2,326 D | 41.3% | 56.9% | 42.1% | 57.9% |
| 47,541 | PORTAGE | 26,269 | 9,520 | 15,912 | 837 | 6,392 D | 36.2% | 60.6% | 37.4% | 62.6% |
| 14,520 | PRICE | 7,428 | 3,204 | 4,028 | 196 | 824 D | 43.1% | 54.2% | 44.3% | 55.7% |
| 170,838 | RACINE | 75,787 | 37,088 | 36,740 | 1,959 | 348 R | 48.9% | 48.5% | 50.2% | 49.8% |
| 17,079 | RICHLAND | 8,258 | 4,466 | 3,634 | 158 | 832 R | 54.1% | 44.0% | 55.1% | 44.9% |
| 131,970 | ROCK | 57,860 | 28,325 | 28,048 | 1,487 | 277 R | 49.0% | 48.5% | 50.2% | 49.8% |
| 14,238 | RUSK | 6,989 | 2,724 | 4,050 | 215 | 1,326 D | 39.0% | 57.9% | 40.2% | 59.8% |
| 34,354 | ST. CROIX | 18,715 | 7,685 | 10,601 | 429 | 2,916 D | 41.1% | 56.6% | 42.0% | 58.0% |
| 39,057 | SAUK | 19,220 | 9,577 | 9,204 | 439 | 373 R | 49.8% | 47.9% | 51.0% | 49.0% |
| 9,670 | SAWYER | 5,918 | 2,720 | 3,055 | 143 | 335 D | 46.0% | 51.6% | 47.1% | 52.9% |
| 32,650 | SHAWANO | 15,584 | 8,505 | 6,751 | 328 | 1,754 R | 54.6% | 43.3% | 55.7% | 44.3% |
| 96,660 | SHEBOYGAN | 47,413 | 22,332 | 24,226 | 855 | 1,894 D | 47.1% | 51.1% | 48.0% | 52.0% |

# WISCONSIN

## PRESIDENT 1976

| 1970 Census Population | County | Total Vote | Republican | Democratic | Other | Rep.-Dem. Plurality | Percentage | | | |
|---|---|---|---|---|---|---|---|---|---|---|
| | | | | | | | Total Vote | | Major Vote | |
| | | | | | | | Rep. | Dem. | Rep. | Dem. |
| 16,958 | TAYLOR | 7,921 | 3,591 | 4,101 | 229 | 510 D | 45.3% | 51.8% | 46.7% | 53.3% |
| 23,344 | TREMPEALEAU | 11,740 | 5,341 | 6,218 | 181 | 877 D | 45.5% | 53.0% | 46.2% | 53.8% |
| 24,557 | VERNON | 11,914 | 6,132 | 5,534 | 248 | 598 R | 51.5% | 46.4% | 52.6% | 47.4% |
| 10,958 | VILAS | 8,350 | 4,929 | 3,209 | 212 | 1,720 R | 59.0% | 38.4% | 60.6% | 39.4% |
| 63,444 | WALWORTH | 31,365 | 18,091 | 12,418 | 856 | 5,673 R | 57.7% | 39.6% | 59.3% | 40.7% |
| 10,601 | WASHBURN | 6,467 | 2,787 | 3,503 | 177 | 716 D | 43.1% | 54.2% | 44.3% | 55.7% |
| 63,839 | WASHINGTON | 34,120 | 18,798 | 14,422 | 900 | 4,376 R | 55.1% | 42.3% | 56.6% | 43.4% |
| 231,365 | WAUKESHA | 121,133 | 70,418 | 47,487 | 3,228 | 22,931 R | 58.1% | 39.2% | 59.7% | 40.3% |
| 37,780 | WAUPACA | 18,086 | 10,849 | 6,857 | 380 | 3,992 R | 60.0% | 37.9% | 61.3% | 38.7% |
| 14,795 | WAUSHARA | 8,098 | 4,449 | 3,485 | 164 | 964 R | 54.9% | 43.0% | 56.1% | 43.9% |
| 129,934 | WINNEBAGO | 58,127 | 32,149 | 24,485 | 1,493 | 7,664 R | 55.3% | 42.1% | 56.8% | 43.2% |
| 65,362 | WOOD | 30,992 | 15,479 | 14,728 | 785 | 751 R | 49.9% | 47.5% | 51.2% | 48.8% |
| 4,417,933 | TOTAL | 2,104,175 | 1,004,987 | 1,040,232 | 58,956 | 35,245 D | 47.8% | 49.4% | 49.1% | 50.9% |

# WISCONSIN

## PRESIDENT 1972

| 1970 Census Population | County | Total Vote | Republican | Democratic | Other | Rep.-Dem. Plurality | Percentage | | | |
|---|---|---|---|---|---|---|---|---|---|---|
| | | | | | | | Total Vote | | Major Vote | |
| | | | | | | | Rep. | Dem. | Rep. | Dem. |
| 9,234 | ADAMS | 4,137 | 2,200 | 1,833 | 104 | 367 R | 53.2% | 44.3% | 54.5% | 45.5% |
| 16,743 | ASHLAND | 7,414 | 3,478 | 3,771 | 165 | 293 D | 46.9% | 50.9% | 48.0% | 52.0% |
| 33,955 | BARRON | 14,055 | 8,418 | 5,376 | 261 | 3,042 R | 59.9% | 38.2% | 61.0% | 39.0% |
| 11,683 | BAYFIELD | 5,879 | 3,045 | 2,736 | 98 | 309 R | 51.8% | 46.5% | 52.7% | 47.3% |
| 158,244 | BROWN | 65,675 | 37,101 | 26,511 | 2,063 | 10,590 R | 56.5% | 40.4% | 58.3% | 41.7% |
| 13,743 | BUFFALO | 5,672 | 3,079 | 2,461 | 132 | 618 R | 54.3% | 43.4% | 55.6% | 44.4% |
| 9,276 | BURNETT | 5,466 | 2,972 | 2,389 | 105 | 583 R | 54.4% | 43.7% | 55.4% | 44.6% |
| 27,604 | CALUMET | 11,542 | 6,446 | 4,804 | 292 | 1,642 R | 55.8% | 41.6% | 57.3% | 42.7% |
| 47,717 | CHIPPEWA | 17,123 | 8,451 | 8,210 | 462 | 241 R | 49.4% | 47.9% | 50.7% | 49.3% |
| 30,361 | CLARK | 12,641 | 7,138 | 4,617 | 886 | 2,521 R | 56.5% | 36.5% | 60.7% | 39.3% |
| 40,150 | COLUMBIA | 17,447 | 10,122 | 7,083 | 242 | 3,039 R | 58.0% | 40.6% | 58.8% | 41.2% |
| 15,252 | CRAWFORD | 6,315 | 3,705 | 2,487 | 123 | 1,218 R | 58.7% | 39.4% | 59.8% | 40.2% |
| 290,272 | DANE | 137,177 | 56,020 | 79,567 | 1,590 | 23,547 D | 40.8% | 58.0% | 41.3% | 58.7% |
| 69,004 | DODGE | 27,737 | 17,068 | 9,898 | 771 | 7,170 R | 61.5% | 35.7% | 63.3% | 36.7% |
| 20,106 | DOOR | 10,121 | 6,503 | 3,430 | 188 | 3,073 R | 64.3% | 33.9% | 65.5% | 34.5% |
| 44,657 | DOUGLAS | 19,771 | 8,419 | 11,054 | 298 | 2,635 D | 42.6% | 55.9% | 43.2% | 56.8% |
| 29,154 | DUNN | 12,565 | 6,660 | 5,681 | 224 | 979 R | 53.0% | 45.2% | 54.0% | 46.0% |
| 67,219 | EAU CLAIRE | 30,971 | 15,883 | 14,300 | 788 | 1,583 R | 51.3% | 46.2% | 52.6% | 47.4% |
| 3,298 | FLORENCE | 1,796 | 971 | 757 | 68 | 214 R | 54.1% | 42.1% | 56.2% | 43.8% |
| 84,567 | FOND DU LAC | 34,470 | 21,007 | 12,050 | 1,413 | 8,957 R | 60.9% | 35.0% | 63.5% | 36.5% |
| 7,691 | FOREST | 3,729 | 1,856 | 1,678 | 195 | 178 R | 49.8% | 45.0% | 52.5% | 47.5% |
| 48,398 | GRANT | 19,061 | 11,873 | 6,915 | 273 | 4,958 R | 62.3% | 36.3% | 63.2% | 36.8% |
| 26,714 | GREEN | 11,222 | 7,422 | 3,634 | 166 | 3,788 R | 66.1% | 32.4% | 67.1% | 32.9% |
| 16,878 | GREEN LAKE | 7,457 | 5,046 | 2,174 | 237 | 2,872 R | 67.7% | 29.2% | 69.9% | 30.1% |
| 19,306 | IOWA | 7,626 | 4,387 | 3,131 | 108 | 1,256 R | 57.5% | 41.1% | 58.4% | 41.6% |
| 6,533 | IRON | 3,451 | 1,723 | 1,648 | 80 | 75 R | 49.9% | 47.8% | 51.1% | 48.9% |
| 15,325 | JACKSON | 6,476 | 3,937 | 2,445 | 94 | 1,492 R | 60.8% | 37.8% | 61.7% | 38.3% |
| 60,060 | JEFFERSON | 24,648 | 14,621 | 9,303 | 724 | 5,318 R | 59.3% | 37.7% | 61.1% | 38.9% |
| 18,455 | JUNEAU | 8,030 | 4,833 | 2,943 | 254 | 1,890 R | 60.2% | 36.7% | 62.2% | 37.8% |
| 117,917 | KENOSHA | 44,576 | 24,041 | 19,441 | 1,094 | 4,600 R | 53.9% | 43.6% | 55.3% | 44.7% |
| 18,961 | KEWAUNEE | 8,403 | 4,802 | 3,360 | 241 | 1,442 R | 57.1% | 40.0% | 58.8% | 41.2% |
| 80,468 | LA CROSSE | 34,746 | 21,992 | 12,152 | 602 | 9,840 R | 63.3% | 35.0% | 64.4% | 35.6% |
| 17,456 | LAFAYETTE | 7,786 | 4,898 | 2,804 | 84 | 2,094 R | 62.9% | 36.0% | 63.6% | 36.4% |
| 19,220 | LANGLADE | 7,629 | 4,368 | 3,011 | 250 | 1,357 R | 57.3% | 39.5% | 59.2% | 40.8% |
| 23,499 | LINCOLN | 10,840 | 6,206 | 4,175 | 459 | 2,031 R | 57.3% | 38.5% | 59.8% | 40.2% |
| 82,294 | MANITOWOC | 34,237 | 16,599 | 16,489 | 1,149 | 110 R | 48.5% | 48.2% | 50.2% | 49.8% |
| 97,457 | MARATHON | 41,872 | 21,454 | 18,500 | 1,918 | 2,954 R | 51.2% | 44.2% | 53.7% | 46.3% |
| 35,810 | MARINETTE | 15,238 | 8,740 | 5,900 | 598 | 2,840 R | 57.4% | 38.7% | 59.7% | 40.3% |
| 8,865 | MARQUETTE | 4,289 | 2,682 | 1,537 | 70 | 1,145 R | 62.5% | 35.8% | 63.6% | 36.4% |
| 2,607 | MENOMINEE | 976 | 355 | 608 | 13 | 253 D | 36.4% | 62.3% | 36.9% | 63.1% |
| 1,054,262 | MILWAUKEE | 416,977 | 191,874 | 210,802 | 14,301 | 18,928 D | 46.0% | 50.6% | 47.6% | 52.4% |
| 31,610 | MONROE | 11,436 | 7,625 | 3,640 | 171 | 3,985 R | 66.7% | 31.8% | 67.7% | 32.3% |
| 25,553 | OCONTO | 10,965 | 6,511 | 4,041 | 413 | 2,470 R | 59.4% | 36.9% | 61.7% | 38.3% |
| 24,427 | ONEIDA | 11,577 | 6,811 | 4,262 | 504 | 2,549 R | 58.8% | 36.8% | 61.5% | 38.5% |
| 119,356 | OUTAGAMIE | 46,044 | 27,533 | 17,447 | 1,064 | 10,086 R | 59.8% | 37.9% | 61.2% | 38.8% |
| 54,421 | OZAUKEE | 25,466 | 15,759 | 8,503 | 1,204 | 7,256 R | 61.9% | 33.4% | 65.0% | 35.0% |
| 7,319 | PEPIN | 2,963 | 1,458 | 1,409 | 96 | 49 R | 49.2% | 47.6% | 50.9% | 49.1% |
| 26,652 | PIERCE | 11,716 | 5,899 | 5,611 | 206 | 288 R | 50.3% | 47.9% | 51.3% | 48.7% |
| 26,666 | POLK | 12,533 | 6,567 | 5,738 | 228 | 829 R | 52.4% | 45.8% | 53.4% | 46.6% |
| 47,541 | PORTAGE | 23,341 | 9,346 | 13,564 | 431 | 4,218 D | 40.0% | 58.1% | 40.8% | 59.2% |
| 14,520 | PRICE | 6,792 | 3,694 | 2,831 | 267 | 863 R | 54.4% | 41.7% | 56.6% | 43.4% |
| 170,838 | RACINE | 68,236 | 38,490 | 27,778 | 1,968 | 10,712 R | 56.4% | 40.7% | 58.1% | 41.9% |
| 17,079 | RICHLAND | 7,654 | 5,062 | 2,492 | 100 | 2,570 R | 66.1% | 32.6% | 67.0% | 33.0% |
| 131,970 | ROCK | 52,319 | 30,361 | 21,033 | 925 | 9,328 R | 58.0% | 40.2% | 59.1% | 40.9% |
| 14,238 | RUSK | 6,279 | 3,007 | 3,075 | 197 | 68 D | 47.9% | 49.0% | 49.4% | 50.6% |
| 34,354 | ST. CROIX | 16,291 | 8,553 | 7,488 | 250 | 1,065 R | 52.5% | 46.0% | 53.3% | 46.7% |
| 39,057 | SAUK | 17,522 | 10,285 | 6,980 | 257 | 3,305 R | 58.7% | 39.8% | 59.6% | 40.4% |
| 9,670 | SAWYER | 4,928 | 3,081 | 1,765 | 82 | 1,316 R | 62.5% | 35.8% | 63.6% | 36.4% |
| 32,650 | SHAWANO | 13,154 | 8,807 | 3,940 | 407 | 4,867 R | 67.0% | 30.0% | 69.1% | 30.9% |
| 96,660 | SHEBOYGAN | 43,537 | 21,500 | 21,114 | 923 | 386 R | 49.4% | 48.5% | 50.5% | 49.5% |

# WISCONSIN

## PRESIDENT 1972

| 1970 Census Population | County | Total Vote | Republican | Democratic | Other | Rep.-Dem. Plurality | Percentage | | | |
|---|---|---|---|---|---|---|---|---|---|---|
| | | | | | | | Total Vote | | Major Vote | |
| | | | | | | | Rep. | Dem. | Rep. | Dem. |
| 16,958 | TAYLOR | 7,398 | 4,125 | 2,934 | 339 | 1,191 R | 55.8% | 39.7% | 58.4% | 41.6% |
| 23,344 | TREMPEALEAU | 10,095 | 5,723 | 4,232 | 140 | 1,491 R | 56.7% | 41.9% | 57.5% | 42.5% |
| 24,557 | VERNON | 10,403 | 6,836 | 3,407 | 160 | 3,429 R | 65.7% | 32.8% | 66.7% | 33.3% |
| 10,958 | VILAS | 6,708 | 4,422 | 1,907 | 379 | 2,515 R | 65.9% | 28.4% | 69.9% | 30.1% |
| 63,444 | WALWORTH | 27,023 | 17,823 | 8,598 | 602 | 9,225 R | 66.0% | 31.8% | 67.5% | 32.5% |
| 10,601 | WASHBURN | 5,665 | 3,220 | 2,336 | 109 | 884 R | 56.8% | 41.2% | 58.0% | 42.0% |
| 63,839 | WASHINGTON | 27,024 | 15,338 | 10,434 | 1,252 | 4,904 R | 56.8% | 38.6% | 59.5% | 40.5% |
| 231,365 | WAUKESHA | 97,622 | 59,399 | 34,573 | 3,650 | 24,826 R | 60.8% | 35.4% | 63.2% | 36.8% |
| 37,780 | WAUPACA | 15,755 | 11,040 | 4,418 | 297 | 6,622 R | 70.1% | 28.0% | 71.4% | 28.6% |
| 14,795 | WAUSHARA | 6,739 | 4,466 | 2,094 | 179 | 2,372 R | 66.3% | 31.1% | 68.1% | 31.9% |
| 129,934 | WINNEBAGO | 51,482 | 29,488 | 20,450 | 1,544 | 9,038 R | 57.3% | 39.7% | 59.0% | 41.0% |
| 65,362 | WOOD | 26,980 | 14,806 | 10,415 | 1,759 | 4,391 R | 54.9% | 38.6% | 58.7% | 41.3% |
| 4,417,933 | TOTAL | 1,852,890 | 989,430 | 810,174 | 53,286 | 179,256 R | 53.4% | 43.7% | 55.0% | 45.0% |

# WISCONSIN

## PRESIDENT 1968

| 1960 Census Population | County | Total Vote | Republican | Democratic | AIP | Other | Plurality | Percentage Total Vote | | |
|---|---|---|---|---|---|---|---|---|---|---|
| | | | | | | | | Rep. | Dem. | AIP |
| 7,566 | ADAMS | 3,774 | 1,691 | 1,614 | 461 | 8 | 77 R | 44.8% | 42.8% | 12.2% |
| 17,375 | ASHLAND | 7,155 | 2,557 | 4,147 | 401 | 50 | 1,590 D | 35.7% | 58.0% | 5.6% |
| 34,270 | BARRON | 13,589 | 7,526 | 5,183 | 867 | 13 | 2,343 R | 55.4% | 38.1% | 6.4% |
| 11,910 | BAYFIELD | 5,703 | 2,333 | 3,036 | 323 | 11 | 703 D | 40.9% | 53.2% | 5.7% |
| 125,082 | BROWN | 56,165 | 30,133 | 21,615 | 4,341 | 76 | 8,518 R | 53.7% | 38.5% | 7.7% |
| 14,202 | BUFFALO | 5,520 | 2,992 | 2,112 | 413 | 3 | 880 R | 54.2% | 38.3% | 7.5% |
| 9,214 | BURNETT | 4,488 | 2,056 | 2,010 | 414 | 8 | 46 R | 45.8% | 44.8% | 9.2% |
| 22,268 | CALUMET | 10,209 | 5,792 | 3,609 | 792 | 16 | 2,183 R | 56.7% | 35.4% | 7.8% |
| 45,096 | CHIPPEWA | 16,407 | 7,772 | 7,335 | 1,282 | 18 | 437 R | 47.4% | 44.7% | 7.8% |
| 31,527 | CLARK | 12,358 | 6,325 | 4,601 | 1,398 | 34 | 1,724 R | 51.2% | 37.2% | 11.3% |
| 36,708 | COLUMBIA | 16,447 | 8,633 | 6,698 | 1,067 | 49 | 1,935 R | 52.5% | 40.7% | 6.5% |
| 16,351 | CRAWFORD | 6,135 | 3,316 | 2,391 | 419 | 9 | 925 R | 54.1% | 39.0% | 6.8% |
| 222,095 | DANE | 104,904 | 39,917 | 59,951 | 3,771 | 1,265 | 20,034 D | 38.1% | 57.1% | 3.6% |
| 63,170 | DODGE | 25,763 | 14,909 | 8,948 | 1,875 | 31 | 5,961 R | 57.9% | 34.7% | 7.3% |
| 20,685 | DOOR | 8,924 | 5,647 | 2,728 | 535 | 14 | 2,919 R | 63.3% | 30.6% | 6.0% |
| 45,008 | DOUGLAS | 19,131 | 5,656 | 12,506 | 930 | 39 | 6,850 D | 29.6% | 65.4% | 4.9% |
| 26,156 | DUNN | 10,530 | 5,415 | 4,392 | 709 | 14 | 1,023 R | 51.4% | 41.7% | 6.7% |
| 58,300 | EAU CLAIRE | 25,299 | 11,799 | 12,302 | 1,169 | 29 | 503 D | 46.6% | 48.6% | 4.6% |
| 3,437 | FLORENCE | 1,699 | 821 | 718 | 157 | 3 | 103 R | 48.3% | 42.3% | 9.2% |
| 75,085 | FOND DU LAC | 32,743 | 18,184 | 12,563 | 1,934 | 62 | 5,621 R | 55.5% | 38.4% | 5.9% |
| 7,542 | FOREST | 3,149 | 1,264 | 1,470 | 412 | 3 | 206 D | 40.1% | 46.7% | 13.1% |
| 44,419 | GRANT | 17,264 | 10,789 | 5,414 | 1,054 | 7 | 5,375 R | 62.5% | 31.4% | 6.1% |
| 25,851 | GREEN | 10,664 | 6,502 | 3,501 | 641 | 20 | 3,001 R | 61.0% | 32.8% | 6.0% |
| 15,418 | GREEN LAKE | 7,687 | 4,893 | 2,299 | 488 | 7 | 2,594 R | 63.7% | 29.9% | 6.3% |
| 19,631 | IOWA | 7,422 | 4,005 | 2,897 | 509 | 11 | 1,108 R | 54.0% | 39.0% | 6.9% |
| 7,830 | IRON | 3,319 | 1,137 | 1,913 | 262 | 7 | 776 D | 34.3% | 57.6% | 7.9% |
| 15,151 | JACKSON | 6,002 | 3,172 | 2,293 | 529 | 8 | 879 R | 52.8% | 38.2% | 8.8% |
| 50,094 | JEFFERSON | 22,726 | 12,478 | 8,716 | 1,470 | 62 | 3,762 R | 54.9% | 38.4% | 6.5% |
| 17,490 | JUNEAU | 7,148 | 3,828 | 2,595 | 712 | 13 | 1,233 R | 53.6% | 36.3% | 10.0% |
| 100,615 | KENOSHA | 42,158 | 17,089 | 21,427 | 3,548 | 94 | 4,338 D | 40.5% | 50.8% | 8.4% |
| 18,282 | KEWAUNEE | 7,804 | 4,467 | 2,622 | 703 | 12 | 1,845 R | 57.2% | 33.6% | 9.0% |
| 72,465 | LA CROSSE | 31,280 | 17,433 | 11,570 | 2,214 | 63 | 5,863 R | 55.7% | 37.0% | 7.1% |
| 18,142 | LAFAYETTE | 7,425 | 4,084 | 2,853 | 470 | 18 | 1,231 R | 55.0% | 38.4% | 6.3% |
| 19,916 | LANGLADE | 7,513 | 3,712 | 3,064 | 718 | 19 | 648 R | 49.4% | 40.8% | 9.6% |
| 22,338 | LINCOLN | 9,330 | 4,793 | 3,858 | 670 | 9 | 935 R | 51.4% | 41.4% | 7.2% |
| 75,215 | MANITOWOC | 30,680 | 13,562 | 15,298 | 1,790 | 30 | 1,736 D | 44.2% | 49.9% | 5.8% |
| 88,874 | MARATHON | 38,115 | 16,907 | 18,063 | 3,051 | 94 | 1,156 D | 44.4% | 47.4% | 8.0% |
| 34,660 | MARINETTE | 14,797 | 7,134 | 6,415 | 1,223 | 25 | 719 R | 48.2% | 43.4% | 8.3% |
| 8,516 | MARQUETTE | 3,882 | 2,374 | 1,228 | 279 | 1 | 1,146 R | 61.2% | 31.6% | 7.2% |
| 2,606 | MENOMINEE | 740 | 179 | 531 | 30 | | 352 D | 24.2% | 71.8% | 4.1% |
| 1,036,041 | MILWAUKEE | 402,575 | 160,022 | 206,027 | 35,056 | 1,470 | 46,005 D | 39.7% | 51.2% | 8.7% |
| 31,241 | MONROE | 12,024 | 6,938 | 4,012 | 1,056 | 18 | 2,926 R | 57.7% | 33.4% | 8.8% |
| 24,849 | OCONTO | 10,569 | 5,680 | 3,737 | 1,141 | 11 | 1,943 R | 53.7% | 35.4% | 10.8% |
| 22,112 | ONEIDA | 10,467 | 5,077 | 4,435 | 941 | 14 | 642 R | 48.5% | 42.4% | 9.0% |
| 101,794 | OUTAGAMIE | 42,327 | 25,080 | 14,224 | 2,956 | 67 | 10,856 R | 59.3% | 33.6% | 7.0% |
| 38,441 | OZAUKEE | 20,942 | 12,155 | 7,246 | 1,505 | 36 | 4,909 R | 58.0% | 34.6% | 7.2% |
| 7,332 | PEPIN | 2,989 | 1,493 | 1,263 | 231 | 2 | 230 R | 49.9% | 42.3% | 7.7% |
| 22,503 | PIERCE | 10,240 | 4,990 | 4,783 | 453 | 14 | 207 R | 48.7% | 46.7% | 4.4% |
| 24,968 | POLK | 11,442 | 5,583 | 5,179 | 656 | 24 | 404 R | 48.8% | 45.3% | 5.7% |
| 36,964 | PORTAGE | 17,158 | 6,180 | 10,014 | 900 | 64 | 3,834 D | 36.0% | 58.4% | 5.2% |
| 14,370 | PRICE | 6,528 | 3,096 | 2,794 | 621 | 17 | 302 R | 47.4% | 42.8% | 9.5% |
| 141,781 | RACINE | 62,639 | 28,028 | 27,045 | 7,457 | 109 | 983 R | 44.7% | 43.2% | 11.9% |
| 17,684 | RICHLAND | 6,929 | 4,141 | 2,288 | 485 | 15 | 1,853 R | 59.8% | 33.0% | 7.0% |
| 113,913 | ROCK | 49,551 | 25,229 | 20,567 | 3,655 | 100 | 4,662 R | 50.9% | 41.5% | 7.4% |
| 14,794 | RUSK | 5,963 | 2,666 | 2,559 | 726 | 12 | 107 R | 44.7% | 42.9% | 12.2% |
| 29,164 | ST. CROIX | 14,157 | 6,595 | 6,807 | 735 | 20 | 212 D | 46.6% | 48.1% | 5.2% |
| 36,179 | SAUK | 16,078 | 8,608 | 6,406 | 1,019 | 45 | 2,202 R | 53.5% | 39.8% | 6.3% |
| 9,475 | SAWYER | 4,745 | 2,475 | 1,830 | 435 | 5 | 645 R | 52.2% | 38.6% | 9.2% |
| 32,006 | SHAWANO | 13,245 | 8,444 | 3,602 | 1,181 | 18 | 4,842 R | 63.8% | 27.2% | 8.9% |
| 86,484 | SHEBOYGAN | 39,634 | 17,764 | 20,170 | 1,592 | 108 | 2,406 D | 44.8% | 50.9% | 4.0% |

# WISCONSIN

## PRESIDENT 1968

| 1960 Census Population | County | Total Vote | Republican | Democratic | AIP | Other | Plurality | Percentage Total Vote | | |
|---|---|---|---|---|---|---|---|---|---|---|
| | | | | | | | | Rep. | Dem. | AIP |
| 17,843 | TAYLOR | 6,923 | 3,043 | 2,910 | 959 | 11 | 133 R | 44.0% | 42.0% | 13.9% |
| 23,377 | TREMPEALEAU | 9,593 | 4,861 | 3,971 | 747 | 14 | 890 R | 50.7% | 41.4% | 7.8% |
| 25,663 | VERNON | 10,560 | 5,824 | 3,666 | 1,062 | 8 | 2,158 R | 55.2% | 34.7% | 10.1% |
| 9,332 | VILAS | 5,748 | 3,339 | 1,798 | 598 | 13 | 1,541 R | 58.1% | 31.3% | 10.4% |
| 52,368 | WALWORTH | 24,328 | 15,040 | 7,505 | 1,755 | 28 | 7,535 R | 61.8% | 30.8% | 7.2% |
| 10,301 | WASHBURN | 5,092 | 2,425 | 2,273 | 384 | 10 | 152 R | 47.6% | 44.6% | 7.5% |
| 46,119 | WASHINGTON | 22,661 | 12,439 | 8,104 | 2,065 | 53 | 4,335 R | 54.9% | 35.8% | 9.1% |
| 158,249 | WAUKESHA | 86,585 | 47,557 | 31,947 | 6,921 | 160 | 15,610 R | 54.9% | 36.9% | 8.0% |
| 35,340 | WAUPACA | 15,807 | 10,606 | 3,978 | 1,206 | 17 | 6,628 R | 67.1% | 25.2% | 7.6% |
| 13,497 | WAUSHARA | 6,407 | 4,187 | 1,652 | 566 | 2 | 2,535 R | 65.4% | 25.8% | 8.8% |
| 107,928 | WINNEBAGO | 47,139 | 25,361 | 18,605 | 3,045 | 128 | 6,756 R | 53.8% | 39.5% | 6.5% |
| 59,105 | WOOD | 24,445 | 11,795 | 10,921 | 1,695 | 34 | 874 R | 48.3% | 44.7% | 6.9% |
| 3,951,777 | TOTAL | 1,691,538 | 809,997 | 748,804 | 127,835 | 4,902 | 61,193 R | 47.9% | 44.3% | 7.6% |

# WISCONSIN

## PRESIDENT 1964

| 1960 Census Population | County | Total Vote | Republican | Democratic | Other | Rep.-Dem. Plurality | Percentage | | | |
|---|---|---|---|---|---|---|---|---|---|---|
| | | | | | | | Total Vote | | Major Vote | |
| | | | | | | | Rep. | Dem. | Rep. | Dem. |
| 7,566 | ADAMS | 3,489 | 1,219 | 2,262 | 8 | 1,043 D | 34.9% | 64.8% | 35.0% | 65.0% |
| 17,375 | ASHLAND | 7,591 | 2,198 | 5,383 | 10 | 3,185 D | 29.0% | 70.9% | 29.0% | 71.0% |
| 34,270 | BARRON | 14,056 | 5,701 | 8,332 | 23 | 2,631 D | 40.6% | 59.3% | 40.6% | 59.4% |
| 11,910 | BAYFIELD | 5,777 | 1,886 | 3,875 | 16 | 1,989 D | 32.6% | 67.1% | 32.7% | 67.3% |
| 125,082 | BROWN | 52,064 | 21,134 | 30,851 | 79 | 9,717 D | 40.6% | 59.3% | 40.7% | 59.3% |
| 14,202 | BUFFALO | 5,759 | 2,091 | 3,663 | 5 | 1,572 D | 36.3% | 63.6% | 36.3% | 63.7% |
| 9,214 | BURNETT | 4,463 | 1,536 | 2,921 | 6 | 1,385 D | 34.4% | 65.4% | 34.5% | 65.5% |
| 22,268 | CALUMET | 9,274 | 3,905 | 5,356 | 13 | 1,451 D | 42.1% | 57.8% | 42.2% | 57.8% |
| 45,096 | CHIPPEWA | 17,214 | 6,277 | 10,911 | 26 | 4,634 D | 36.5% | 63.4% | 36.5% | 63.5% |
| 31,527 | CLARK | 12,704 | 4,897 | 7,781 | 26 | 2,884 D | 38.5% | 61.2% | 38.6% | 61.4% |
| 36,708 | COLUMBIA | 16,370 | 6,253 | 10,093 | 24 | 3,840 D | 38.2% | 61.7% | 38.3% | 61.7% |
| 16,351 | CRAWFORD | 6,663 | 2,726 | 3,930 | 7 | 1,204 D | 40.9% | 59.0% | 41.0% | 59.0% |
| 222,095 | DANE | 95,426 | 27,124 | 68,118 | 184 | 40,994 D | 28.4% | 71.4% | 28.5% | 71.5% |
| 63,170 | DODGE | 26,308 | 10,772 | 15,497 | 39 | 4,725 D | 40.9% | 58.9% | 41.0% | 59.0% |
| 20,685 | DOOR | 8,714 | 4,289 | 4,416 | 9 | 127 D | 49.2% | 50.7% | 49.3% | 50.7% |
| 45,008 | DOUGLAS | 19,839 | 4,579 | 15,237 | 23 | 10,658 D | 23.1% | 76.8% | 23.1% | 76.9% |
| 26,156 | DUNN | 10,458 | 3,964 | 6,475 | 19 | 2,511 D | 37.9% | 61.9% | 38.0% | 62.0% |
| 58,300 | EAU CLAIRE | 24,521 | 8,700 | 15,775 | 46 | 7,075 D | 35.5% | 64.3% | 35.5% | 64.5% |
| 3,437 | FLORENCE | 1,627 | 596 | 1,029 | 2 | 433 D | 36.6% | 63.2% | 36.7% | 63.3% |
| 75,085 | FOND DU LAC | 30,778 | 12,708 | 18,040 | 30 | 5,332 D | 41.3% | 58.6% | 41.3% | 58.7% |
| 7,542 | FOREST | 3,552 | 1,069 | 2,479 | 4 | 1,410 D | 30.1% | 69.8% | 30.1% | 69.9% |
| 44,419 | GRANT | 17,211 | 7,872 | 9,309 | 30 | 1,437 D | 45.7% | 54.1% | 45.8% | 54.2% |
| 25,851 | GREEN | 10,929 | 5,364 | 5,548 | 17 | 184 D | 49.1% | 50.8% | 49.2% | 50.8% |
| 15,418 | GREEN LAKE | 7,768 | 3,871 | 3,893 | 4 | 22 D | 49.8% | 50.1% | 49.9% | 50.1% |
| 19,631 | IOWA | 7,907 | 3,275 | 4,620 | 12 | 1,345 D | 41.4% | 58.4% | 41.5% | 58.5% |
| 7,830 | IRON | 3,480 | 963 | 2,514 | 3 | 1,551 D | 27.7% | 72.2% | 27.7% | 72.3% |
| 15,151 | JACKSON | 6,357 | 2,532 | 3,818 | 7 | 1,286 D | 39.8% | 60.1% | 39.9% | 60.1% |
| 50,094 | JEFFERSON | 22,084 | 8,741 | 13,295 | 48 | 4,554 D | 39.6% | 60.2% | 39.7% | 60.3% |
| 17,490 | JUNEAU | 7,567 | 2,976 | 4,583 | 8 | 1,607 D | 39.3% | 60.6% | 39.4% | 60.6% |
| 100,615 | KENOSHA | 45,356 | 14,764 | 30,522 | 70 | 15,758 D | 32.6% | 67.3% | 32.6% | 67.4% |
| 18,282 | KEWAUNEE | 7,780 | 2,980 | 4,792 | 8 | 1,812 D | 38.3% | 61.6% | 38.3% | 61.7% |
| 72,465 | LA CROSSE | 29,803 | 13,135 | 16,625 | 43 | 3,490 D | 44.1% | 55.8% | 44.1% | 55.9% |
| 18,142 | LAFAYETTE | 7,671 | 3,194 | 4,471 | 6 | 1,277 D | 41.6% | 58.3% | 41.7% | 58.3% |
| 19,916 | LANGLADE | 8,081 | 2,994 | 5,077 | 10 | 2,083 D | 37.0% | 62.8% | 37.1% | 62.9% |
| 22,338 | LINCOLN | 9,796 | 3,894 | 5,883 | 19 | 1,989 D | 39.8% | 60.1% | 39.8% | 60.2% |
| 75,215 | MANITOWOC | 31,815 | 9,849 | 21,927 | 39 | 12,078 D | 31.0% | 68.9% | 31.0% | 69.0% |
| 88,874 | MARATHON | 37,426 | 12,766 | 24,603 | 57 | 11,837 D | 34.1% | 65.7% | 34.2% | 65.8% |
| 34,660 | MARINETTE | 15,013 | 5,332 | 9,657 | 24 | 4,325 D | 35.5% | 64.3% | 35.6% | 64.4% |
| 8,516 | MARQUETTE | 3,816 | 1,881 | 1,927 | 8 | 46 D | 49.3% | 50.5% | 49.4% | 50.6% |
| 2,606 | MENOMINEE | 726 | 78 | 647 | 1 | 569 D | 10.7% | 89.1% | 10.8% | 89.2% |
| 1,036,041 | MILWAUKEE | 439,459 | 149,962 | 288,577 | 920 | 138,615 D | 34.1% | 65.7% | 34.2% | 65.8% |
| 31,241 | MONROE | 11,524 | 5,126 | 6,385 | 13 | 1,259 D | 44.5% | 55.4% | 44.5% | 55.5% |
| 24,849 | OCONTO | 10,795 | 4,420 | 6,360 | 15 | 1,940 D | 40.9% | 58.9% | 41.0% | 59.0% |
| 22,112 | ONEIDA | 10,355 | 3,909 | 6,431 | 15 | 2,522 D | 37.7% | 62.1% | 37.8% | 62.2% |
| 101,794 | OUTAGAMIE | 40,198 | 18,595 | 21,556 | 47 | 2,961 D | 46.3% | 53.6% | 46.3% | 53.7% |
| 38,441 | OZAUKEE | 18,123 | 8,581 | 9,517 | 25 | 936 D | 47.3% | 52.5% | 47.4% | 52.6% |
| 7,332 | PEPIN | 3,229 | 1,069 | 2,154 | 6 | 1,085 D | 33.1% | 66.7% | 33.2% | 66.8% |
| 22,503 | PIERCE | 9,666 | 3,291 | 6,351 | 24 | 3,060 D | 34.0% | 65.7% | 34.1% | 65.9% |
| 24,968 | POLK | 11,003 | 3,754 | 7,215 | 34 | 3,461 D | 34.1% | 65.6% | 34.2% | 65.8% |
| 36,964 | PORTAGE | 16,498 | 4,579 | 11,887 | 32 | 7,308 D | 27.8% | 72.1% | 27.8% | 72.2% |
| 14,370 | PRICE | 6,705 | 2,406 | 4,289 | 10 | 1,883 D | 35.9% | 64.0% | 35.9% | 64.1% |
| 141,781 | RACINE | 59,306 | 21,434 | 37,785 | 87 | 16,351 D | 36.1% | 63.7% | 36.2% | 63.8% |
| 17,684 | RICHLAND | 7,548 | 3,224 | 4,315 | 9 | 1,091 D | 42.7% | 57.2% | 42.8% | 57.2% |
| 113,913 | ROCK | 48,684 | 20,372 | 28,257 | 55 | 7,885 D | 41.8% | 58.0% | 41.9% | 58.1% |
| 14,794 | RUSK | 6,405 | 2,214 | 4,176 | 15 | 1,962 D | 34.6% | 65.2% | 34.6% | 65.4% |
| 29,164 | ST. CROIX | 13,458 | 4,565 | 8,864 | 29 | 4,299 D | 33.9% | 65.9% | 34.0% | 66.0% |
| 36,179 | SAUK | 15,656 | 6,345 | 9,288 | 23 | 2,943 D | 40.5% | 59.3% | 40.6% | 59.4% |
| 9,475 | SAWYER | 4,613 | 2,012 | 2,591 | 10 | 579 D | 43.6% | 56.2% | 43.7% | 56.3% |
| 32,006 | SHAWANO | 13,105 | 6,519 | 6,560 | 26 | 41 D | 49.7% | 50.1% | 49.8% | 50.2% |
| 86,484 | SHEBOYGAN | 39,445 | 12,968 | 26,410 | 67 | 13,442 D | 32.9% | 67.0% | 32.9% | 67.1% |

# WISCONSIN

## PRESIDENT 1964

| 1960 Census Population | County | Total Vote | Republican | Democratic | Other | Rep.-Dem. Plurality | Percentage Total Vote | | Major Vote | |
|---|---|---|---|---|---|---|---|---|---|---|
| | | | | | | | Rep. | Dem. | Rep. | Dem. |
| 17,843 | TAYLOR | 6,898 | 2,261 | 4,624 | 13 | 2,363 D | 32.8% | 67.0% | 32.8% | 67.2% |
| 23,377 | TREMPEALEAU | 9,589 | 3,264 | 6,320 | 5 | 3,056 D | 34.0% | 65.9% | 34.1% | 65.9% |
| 25,663 | VERNON | 10,898 | 4,640 | 6,242 | 16 | 1,602 D | 42.6% | 57.3% | 42.6% | 57.4% |
| 9,332 | VILAS | 5,679 | 2,827 | 2,841 | 11 | 14 D | 49.8% | 50.0% | 49.9% | 50.1% |
| 52,368 | WALWORTH | 24,009 | 12,225 | 11,746 | 38 | 479 R | 50.9% | 48.9% | 51.0% | 49.0% |
| 10,301 | WASHBURN | 5,062 | 1,865 | 3,181 | 16 | 1,316 D | 36.8% | 62.8% | 37.0% | 63.0% |
| 46,119 | WASHINGTON | 20,791 | 9,191 | 11,563 | 37 | 2,372 D | 44.2% | 55.6% | 44.3% | 55.7% |
| 158,249 | WAUKESHA | 75,429 | 35,502 | 39,796 | 131 | 4,294 D | 47.1% | 52.8% | 47.1% | 52.9% |
| 35,340 | WAUPACA | 15,389 | 8,381 | 6,990 | 18 | 1,391 R | 54.5% | 45.4% | 54.5% | 45.5% |
| 13,497 | WAUSHARA | 6,441 | 3,437 | 3,004 | | 433 R | 53.4% | 46.6% | 53.4% | 46.6% |
| 107,928 | WINNEBAGO | 44,835 | 21,084 | 23,636 | 115 | 2,552 D | 47.0% | 52.7% | 47.1% | 52.9% |
| 59,105 | WOOD | 23,787 | 8,388 | 15,378 | 21 | 6,990 D | 35.3% | 64.6% | 35.3% | 64.7% |
| 3,951,777 | TOTAL | 1,691,815 | 638,495 | 1,050,424 | 2,896 | 411,929 D | 37.7% | 62.1% | 37.8% | 62.2% |

# WISCONSIN

## PRESIDENT 1960

| 1960 Census Population | County | Total Vote | Republican | Democratic | Other | Rep.-Dem. Plurality | Percentage Total Vote Rep. | Dem. | Major Vote Rep. | Dem. |
|---|---|---|---|---|---|---|---|---|---|---|
| 7,566 | ADAMS | 3,674 | 2,109 | 1,551 | 14 | 558 R | 57.4% | 42.2% | 57.6% | 42.4% |
| 17,375 | ASHLAND | 8,127 | 3,470 | 4,644 | 13 | 1,174 D | 42.7% | 57.1% | 42.8% | 57.2% |
| 34,270 | BARRON | 15,145 | 8,640 | 6,464 | 41 | 2,176 R | 57.0% | 42.7% | 57.2% | 42.8% |
| 11,910 | BAYFIELD | 6,060 | 2,841 | 3,196 | 23 | 355 D | 46.9% | 52.7% | 47.1% | 52.9% |
| 125,082 | BROWN | 52,952 | 26,329 | 26,577 | 46 | 248 D | 49.7% | 50.2% | 49.8% | 50.2% |
| 14,202 | BUFFALO | 6,256 | 3,464 | 2,790 | 2 | 674 R | 55.4% | 44.6% | 55.4% | 44.6% |
| 9,214 | BURNETT | 4,596 | 2,483 | 2,095 | 18 | 388 R | 54.0% | 45.6% | 54.2% | 45.8% |
| 22,268 | CALUMET | 9,486 | 5,166 | 4,312 | 8 | 854 R | 54.5% | 45.5% | 54.5% | 45.5% |
| 45,096 | CHIPPEWA | 18,511 | 8,690 | 9,793 | 28 | 1,103 D | 46.9% | 52.9% | 47.0% | 53.0% |
| 31,527 | CLARK | 13,343 | 7,368 | 5,934 | 41 | 1,434 R | 55.2% | 44.5% | 55.4% | 44.6% |
| 36,708 | COLUMBIA | 16,873 | 10,282 | 6,576 | 15 | 3,706 R | 60.9% | 39.0% | 61.0% | 39.0% |
| 16,351 | CRAWFORD | 7,071 | 3,719 | 3,342 | 10 | 377 R | 52.6% | 47.3% | 52.7% | 47.3% |
| 222,095 | DANE | 90,502 | 43,245 | 47,045 | 212 | 3,800 D | 47.8% | 52.0% | 47.9% | 52.1% |
| 63,170 | DODGE | 27,295 | 17,152 | 10,113 | 30 | 7,039 R | 62.8% | 37.1% | 62.9% | 37.1% |
| 20,685 | DOOR | 9,414 | 5,790 | 3,610 | 14 | 2,180 R | 61.5% | 38.3% | 61.6% | 38.4% |
| 45,008 | DOUGLAS | 21,270 | 8,307 | 12,910 | 53 | 4,603 D | 39.1% | 60.7% | 39.2% | 60.8% |
| 26,156 | DUNN | 11,239 | 6,723 | 4,487 | 29 | 2,236 R | 59.8% | 39.9% | 60.0% | 40.0% |
| 58,300 | EAU CLAIRE | 25,704 | 14,427 | 11,240 | 37 | 3,187 R | 56.1% | 43.7% | 56.2% | 43.8% |
| 3,437 | FLORENCE | 1,791 | 928 | 858 | 5 | 70 R | 51.8% | 47.9% | 52.0% | 48.0% |
| 75,085 | FOND DU LAC | 32,688 | 19,498 | 13,132 | 58 | 6,366 R | 59.6% | 40.2% | 59.8% | 40.2% |
| 7,542 | FOREST | 3,514 | 1,653 | 1,851 | 10 | 198 D | 47.0% | 52.7% | 47.2% | 52.8% |
| 44,419 | GRANT | 19,258 | 11,564 | 7,678 | 16 | 3,886 R | 60.0% | 39.9% | 60.1% | 39.9% |
| 25,851 | GREEN | 11,711 | 7,939 | 3,766 | 6 | 4,173 R | 67.8% | 32.2% | 67.8% | 32.2% |
| 15,418 | GREEN LAKE | 7,893 | 5,110 | 2,776 | 7 | 2,334 R | 64.7% | 35.2% | 64.8% | 35.2% |
| 19,631 | IOWA | 8,694 | 5,143 | 3,547 | 4 | 1,596 R | 59.2% | 40.8% | 59.2% | 40.8% |
| 7,830 | IRON | 4,170 | 1,290 | 2,873 | 7 | 1,583 D | 30.9% | 68.9% | 31.0% | 69.0% |
| 15,151 | JACKSON | 6,813 | 3,950 | 2,849 | 14 | 1,101 R | 58.0% | 41.8% | 58.1% | 41.9% |
| 50,094 | JEFFERSON | 22,929 | 14,133 | 8,757 | 39 | 5,376 R | 61.6% | 38.2% | 61.7% | 38.3% |
| 17,490 | JUNEAU | 8,246 | 4,997 | 3,238 | 11 | 1,759 R | 60.6% | 39.3% | 60.7% | 39.3% |
| 100,615 | KENOSHA | 43,011 | 19,969 | 22,956 | 86 | 2,987 D | 46.4% | 53.4% | 46.5% | 53.5% |
| 18,282 | KEWAUNEE | 8,213 | 3,950 | 4,256 | 7 | 306 D | 48.1% | 51.8% | 48.1% | 51.9% |
| 72,465 | LA CROSSE | 32,665 | 18,319 | 14,310 | 36 | 4,009 R | 56.1% | 43.8% | 56.1% | 43.9% |
| 18,142 | LAFAYETTE | 8,330 | 4,715 | 3,607 | 8 | 1,108 R | 56.6% | 43.3% | 56.7% | 43.3% |
| 19,916 | LANGLADE | 8,655 | 4,614 | 4,025 | 16 | 589 R | 53.3% | 46.5% | 53.4% | 46.6% |
| 22,338 | LINCOLN | 10,089 | 6,147 | 3,909 | 33 | 2,238 R | 60.9% | 38.7% | 61.1% | 38.9% |
| 75,215 | MANITOWOC | 32,080 | 14,622 | 17,423 | 35 | 2,801 D | 45.6% | 54.3% | 45.6% | 54.4% |
| 88,874 | MARATHON | 40,025 | 21,880 | 18,145 | | 3,735 R | 54.7% | 45.3% | 54.7% | 45.3% |
| 34,660 | MARINETTE | 15,630 | 8,205 | 7,408 | 17 | 797 R | 52.5% | 47.4% | 52.6% | 47.4% |
| 8,516 | MARQUETTE | 4,203 | 2,947 | 1,249 | 7 | 1,698 R | 70.1% | 29.7% | 70.2% | 29.8% |
| | MENOMINEE | — | — | — | — | — | — | — | — | — |
| 1,036,041 | MILWAUKEE | 445,807 | 187,067 | 257,707 | 1,033 | 70,640 D | 42.0% | 57.8% | 42.1% | 57.9% |
| 31,241 | MONROE | 12,587 | 7,410 | 5,161 | 16 | 2,249 R | 58.9% | 41.0% | 58.9% | 41.1% |
| 25,110 | OCONTO | 11,283 | 6,223 | 5,045 | 15 | 1,178 R | 55.2% | 44.7% | 55.2% | 44.8% |
| 22,112 | ONEIDA | 10,666 | 5,676 | 4,974 | 16 | 702 R | 53.2% | 46.6% | 53.3% | 46.7% |
| 101,794 | OUTAGAMIE | 41,522 | 24,146 | 17,287 | 89 | 6,859 R | 58.2% | 41.6% | 58.3% | 41.7% |
| 38,441 | OZAUKEE | 17,657 | 10,401 | 7,228 | 28 | 3,173 R | 58.9% | 40.9% | 59.0% | 41.0% |
| 7,332 | PEPIN | 3,380 | 1,612 | 1,763 | 5 | 151 D | 47.7% | 52.2% | 47.8% | 52.2% |
| 22,503 | PIERCE | 9,958 | 5,632 | 4,317 | 9 | 1,315 R | 56.6% | 43.4% | 56.6% | 43.4% |
| 24,968 | POLK | 11,565 | 6,387 | 5,148 | 30 | 1,239 R | 55.2% | 44.5% | 55.4% | 44.6% |
| 36,964 | PORTAGE | 16,972 | 6,436 | 10,516 | 20 | 4,080 D | 37.9% | 62.0% | 38.0% | 62.0% |
| 14,370 | PRICE | 6,957 | 3,555 | 3,382 | 20 | 173 R | 51.1% | 48.6% | 51.2% | 48.8% |
| 141,781 | RACINE | 60,294 | 29,562 | 30,596 | 136 | 1,034 D | 49.0% | 50.7% | 49.1% | 50.9% |
| 17,684 | RICHLAND | 8,229 | 5,253 | 2,965 | 11 | 2,288 R | 63.8% | 36.0% | 63.9% | 36.1% |
| 113,913 | ROCK | 48,945 | 29,675 | 19,194 | 76 | 10,481 R | 60.6% | 39.2% | 60.7% | 39.3% |
| 14,794 | RUSK | 6,803 | 3,094 | 3,692 | 17 | 598 D | 45.5% | 54.3% | 45.6% | 54.4% |
| 29,164 | ST. CROIX | 13,478 | 7,113 | 6,341 | 24 | 772 R | 52.8% | 47.0% | 52.9% | 47.1% |
| 36,179 | SAUK | 16,867 | 10,403 | 6,441 | 23 | 3,962 R | 61.7% | 38.2% | 61.8% | 38.2% |
| 9,475 | SAWYER | 5,036 | 2,699 | 2,325 | 12 | 374 R | 53.6% | 46.2% | 53.7% | 46.3% |
| 34,351 | SHAWANO | 14,489 | 9,734 | 4,734 | 21 | 5,000 R | 67.2% | 32.7% | 67.3% | 32.7% |
| 86,484 | SHEBOYGAN | 40,221 | 21,676 | 18,425 | 120 | 3,251 R | 53.9% | 45.8% | 54.1% | 45.9% |

# WISCONSIN

## PRESIDENT 1960

| 1960 Census Population | County | Total Vote | Republican | Democratic | Other | Rep.-Dem. Plurality | Percentage | | | |
|---|---|---|---|---|---|---|---|---|---|---|
| | | | | | | | Total Vote | | Major Vote | |
| | | | | | | | Rep. | Dem. | Rep. | Dem. |
| 17,843 | TAYLOR | 7,237 | 3,447 | 3,768 | 22 | 321 D | 47.6% | 52.1% | 47.8% | 52.2% |
| 23,377 | TREMPEALEAU | 10,781 | 5,539 | 5,223 | 19 | 316 R | 51.4% | 48.4% | 51.5% | 48.5% |
| 25,663 | VERNON | 11,760 | 6,909 | 4,836 | 15 | 2,073 R | 58.8% | 41.1% | 58.8% | 41.2% |
| 9,332 | VILAS | 5,460 | 3,508 | 1,942 | 10 | 1,566 R | 64.2% | 35.6% | 64.4% | 35.6% |
| 52,368 | WALWORTH | 24,401 | 16,395 | 7,986 | 20 | 8,409 R | 67.2% | 32.7% | 67.2% | 32.8% |
| 10,301 | WASHBURN | 5,261 | 2,848 | 2,398 | 15 | 450 R | 54.1% | 45.6% | 54.3% | 45.7% |
| 46,119 | WASHINGTON | 19,991 | 11,452 | 8,523 | 16 | 2,929 R | 57.3% | 42.6% | 57.3% | 42.7% |
| 158,249 | WAUKESHA | 68,419 | 39,380 | 28,963 | 76 | 10,417 R | 57.6% | 42.3% | 57.6% | 42.4% |
| 35,340 | WAUPACA | 16,867 | 12,247 | 4,606 | 14 | 7,641 R | 72.6% | 27.3% | 72.7% | 27.3% |
| 13,497 | WAUSHARA | 6,799 | 4,906 | 1,888 | 5 | 3,018 R | 72.2% | 27.8% | 72.2% | 27.8% |
| 107,928 | WINNEBAGO | 46,334 | 28,598 | 17,656 | 80 | 10,942 R | 61.7% | 38.1% | 61.8% | 38.2% |
| 59,105 | WOOD | 24,930 | 14,414 | 10,483 | 33 | 3,931 R | 57.8% | 42.0% | 57.9% | 42.1% |
| 3,951,777 | TOTAL | 1,729,082 | 895,175 | 830,805 | 3,102 | 64,370 R | 51.8% | 48.0% | 51.9% | 48.1% |

# WISCONSIN

Menominee county was created prior to the 1964 election from parts of Oconto and Shawano counties.

## ELECTION NOTES

2004    Other vote was 16,390 Independent (Ralph Nader); 6,464 Libertarian (Michael Badnarik); 2,661 Wisconsin Green (David Cobb); 471 Independent (Walter F. Brown); 411 Independent (James Harris); 2,986 write-in.

2000    Other vote 11,471 Reform (Buchanan); 6,640 Libertarian (Browne); 2,042 Constitution (Phillips); 1,063 Workers World (Moorehead); 853 Reform (Hagelin); 306 Socialist Workers (Harris); 1,896 scattered write-in.

1996    Other vote was 28,723 Independent (Nader); 8,811 Taxpayers (Phillips); 7,929 Libertarian (Browne); 1,379 Independent (Hagelin); 1,333 Independent (Moorehead); 848 Independent (Hollis); 483 Independent (Harris); 2,324 scattered write-in.

1992    Other vote was 2,877 Marrou (Libertarian); 2,311 Gritz (America First); 1,883 Daniels (Labor-Farm); 1,772 Phillips (Taxpayers); 1,211 Brisben (Socialist); 1,070 Hagelin (Natural Law); 654 Fulani (New Alliance); 633 LaRouche (Independent for Economic Recovery); 405 Hem (Third Party); 390 Warren (Socialist Workers); 547 Herer (Grassroots); 961 scattered write-in.

1988    Other vote was 5,157 Paul (Libertarian); 3,056 Duke (Populist); 2,574 Warren (Socialist Workers); 2,302 LaRouche (National Economic Recovery); 1,953 Fulani (New Alliance); 2,273 scattered write-in.

1984    Other vote was 4,883 Bergland (Libertarian); 3,864 Richards (Constitution); 3,791 LaRouche (Independent); 1,456 Johnson (Citizens); 1,006 Serrette (Independent Alliance); 619 Holmes (Workers World); 596 Hall (Communist); 444 Mason (Socialist Workers); 706 scattered write-in.

1980    Other vote was 160,657 Anderson (Independent); 29,135 Clark (Libertarian); 7,767 Commoner (Citizens); 1,519 Rarick (Constitution); 808 McReynolds (Socialist); 772 Hall (Communist); 414 Griswold (Workers World); 383 DeBerry (Socialist Workers); 1,337 scattered write-in.

1976    Other vote was 34,943 McCarthy (Independent); 8,552 Maddox (American); 4,298 Zeidler (Democratic Socialist); 3,814 MacBride (Libertarian); 1,691 Camejo (Socialist Workers); 943 Wright (People's); 749 Hall (Communist); 738 LaRouche (U.S. Labor); 389 Levin (Socialist Labor); 2,839 scattered write-in.

1972    Other vote was 47,525 Schmitz (American); 2,701 Spock (People's); 998 Fisher (Socialist Labor); 663 Hall (Communist); 506 Reed (Socialist Workers); 893 scattered write-in.

1968    Wallace on the ballot as Independent. Other vote was 1,338 Blomen (Socialist Labor); 1,222 Halstead (Socialist Workers); 2,342 scattered write-in.

1964    Other vote was 1,692 DeBerry (Socialist Workers); 1,204 Hass (Socialist Labor).

1960    Other vote was 1,792 Dobbs (Socialist Workers); 1,310 Hass (Socialist Labor).

# WYOMING

## POPULAR VOTE FOR PRESIDENT 1920 TO 2004

| | | Republican | | Democratic | | Other | | Percentage | | | |
| | | | | | | | | Total Vote | | Major Vote | |
| Year | Total Vote | Vote | Candidate | Vote | Candidate | Vote | Plurality | Rep. | Dem. | Rep. | Dem. |
|---|---|---|---|---|---|---|---|---|---|---|---|
| 2004 | 243,428 | 167,629 | Bush, George W. | 70,776 | Kerry, John | 5,023 | 96,853 R | 68.9% | 29.1% | 70.3% | 29.7% |
| 2000 ** | 218,351 | 147,947 | Bush, George W. | 60,481 | Gore, Al | 9,923 | 87,466 R | 67.8% | 27.7% | 71.0% | 29.0% |
| 1996 ** | 211,571 | 105,388 | Dole, Bob | 77,934 | Clinton, Bill | 28,249 | 27,454 R | 49.8% | 36.8% | 57.5% | 42.5% |
| 1992 ** | 200,598 | 79,347 | Bush, George | 68,160 | Clinton, Bill | 53,091 | 11,187 R | 39.6% | 34.0% | 53.8% | 46.2% |
| 1988 | 176,551 | 106,867 | Bush, George | 67,113 | Dukakis, Michael S. | 2,571 | 39,754 R | 60.5% | 38.0% | 61.4% | 38.6% |
| 1984 | 188,968 | 133,241 | Reagan, Ronald | 53,370 | Mondale, Walter F. | 2,357 | 79,871 R | 70.5% | 28.2% | 71.4% | 28.6% |
| 1980 ** | 176,713 | 110,700 | Reagan, Ronald | 49,427 | Carter, Jimmy | 16,586 | 61,273 R | 62.6% | 28.0% | 69.1% | 30.9% |
| 1976 | 156,343 | 92,717 | Ford, Gerald R. | 62,239 | Carter, Jimmy | 1,387 | 30,478 R | 59.3% | 39.8% | 59.8% | 40.2% |
| 1972 | 145,570 | 100,464 | Nixon, Richard M. | 44,358 | McGovern, George S. | 748 | 56,106 R | 69.0% | 30.5% | 69.4% | 30.6% |
| 1968 | 127,205 | 70,927 | Nixon, Richard M. | 45,173 | Humphrey, Hubert H. | 11,105 | 25,754 R | 55.8% | 35.5% | 61.1% | 38.9% |
| 1964 | 142,716 | 61,998 | Goldwater, Barry M. | 80,718 | Johnson, Lyndon B. | | 18,720 D | 43.4% | 56.6% | 43.4% | 56.6% |
| 1960 | 140,782 | 77,451 | Nixon, Richard M. | 63,331 | Kennedy, John F. | | 14,120 R | 55.0% | 45.0% | 55.0% | 45.0% |
| 1956 | 124,127 | 74,573 | Eisenhower, Dwight D. | 49,554 | Stevenson, Adlai E. | | 25,019 R | 60.1% | 39.9% | 60.1% | 39.9% |
| 1952 | 129,253 | 81,049 | Eisenhower, Dwight D. | 47,934 | Stevenson, Adlai E. | 270 | 33,115 R | 62.7% | 37.1% | 62.8% | 37.2% |
| 1948 | 101,425 | 47,947 | Dewey, Thomas E. | 52,354 | Truman, Harry S. | 1,124 | 4,407 D | 47.3% | 51.6% | 47.8% | 52.2% |
| 1944 | 101,340 | 51,921 | Dewey, Thomas E. | 49,419 | Roosevelt, Franklin D. | | 2,502 R | 51.2% | 48.8% | 51.2% | 48.8% |
| 1940 | 112,240 | 52,633 | Willkie, Wendell | 59,287 | Roosevelt, Franklin D. | 320 | 6,654 D | 46.9% | 52.8% | 47.0% | 53.0% |
| 1936 | 103,382 | 38,739 | Landon, Alfred M. | 62,624 | Roosevelt, Franklin D. | 2,019 | 23,885 D | 37.5% | 60.6% | 38.2% | 61.8% |
| 1932 | 96,962 | 39,583 | Hoover, Herbert C. | 54,370 | Roosevelt, Franklin D. | 3,009 | 14,787 D | 40.8% | 56.1% | 42.1% | 57.9% |
| 1928 | 82,835 | 52,748 | Hoover, Herbert C. | 29,299 | Smith, Alfred E. | 788 | 23,449 R | 63.7% | 35.4% | 64.3% | 35.7% |
| 1924 ** | 79,900 | 41,858 | Coolidge, Calvin | 12,868 | Davis, John W. | 25,174 | 16,684 R | 52.4% | 16.1% | 76.5% | 23.5% |
| 1920 | 56,253 | 35,091 | Harding, Warren G. | 17,429 | Cox, James M. | 3,733 | 17,662 R | 62.4% | 31.0% | 66.8% | 33.2% |

In 2000 the other vote column includes 4,625 votes cast for Green (Nader). In 1996 the other vote column includes 25,928 votes cast for Perot. In 1992 the other vote column includes 51,263 votes cast for Perot. In 1980 the other column includes 12,072 votes for Independent (Anderson). In 1924 the other vote was Progressive.

## ELECTORAL COLLEGE VOTE 1920 TO 2004

| Year | Total | Republican | Democratic | Other |
|---|---|---|---|---|
| 2004 | 3 | 3 | | |
| 2000 | 3 | 3 | | |
| 1996 | 3 | 3 | | |
| 1992 | 3 | 3 | | |
| 1988 | 3 | 3 | | |
| 1984 | 3 | 3 | | |
| 1980 | 3 | 3 | | |
| 1976 | 3 | 3 | | |
| 1972 | 3 | 3 | | |
| 1968 | 3 | 3 | | |
| 1964 | 3 | | 3 | |
| 1960 | 3 | 3 | | |
| 1956 | 3 | 3 | | |
| 1952 | 3 | 3 | | |
| 1948 | 3 | | 3 | |
| 1944 | 3 | 3 | | |
| 1940 | 3 | | 3 | |
| 1936 | 3 | | 3 | |
| 1932 | 3 | | 3 | |
| 1928 | 3 | 3 | | |
| 1924 | 3 | 3 | | |
| 1920 | 3 | 3 | | |

# WYOMING

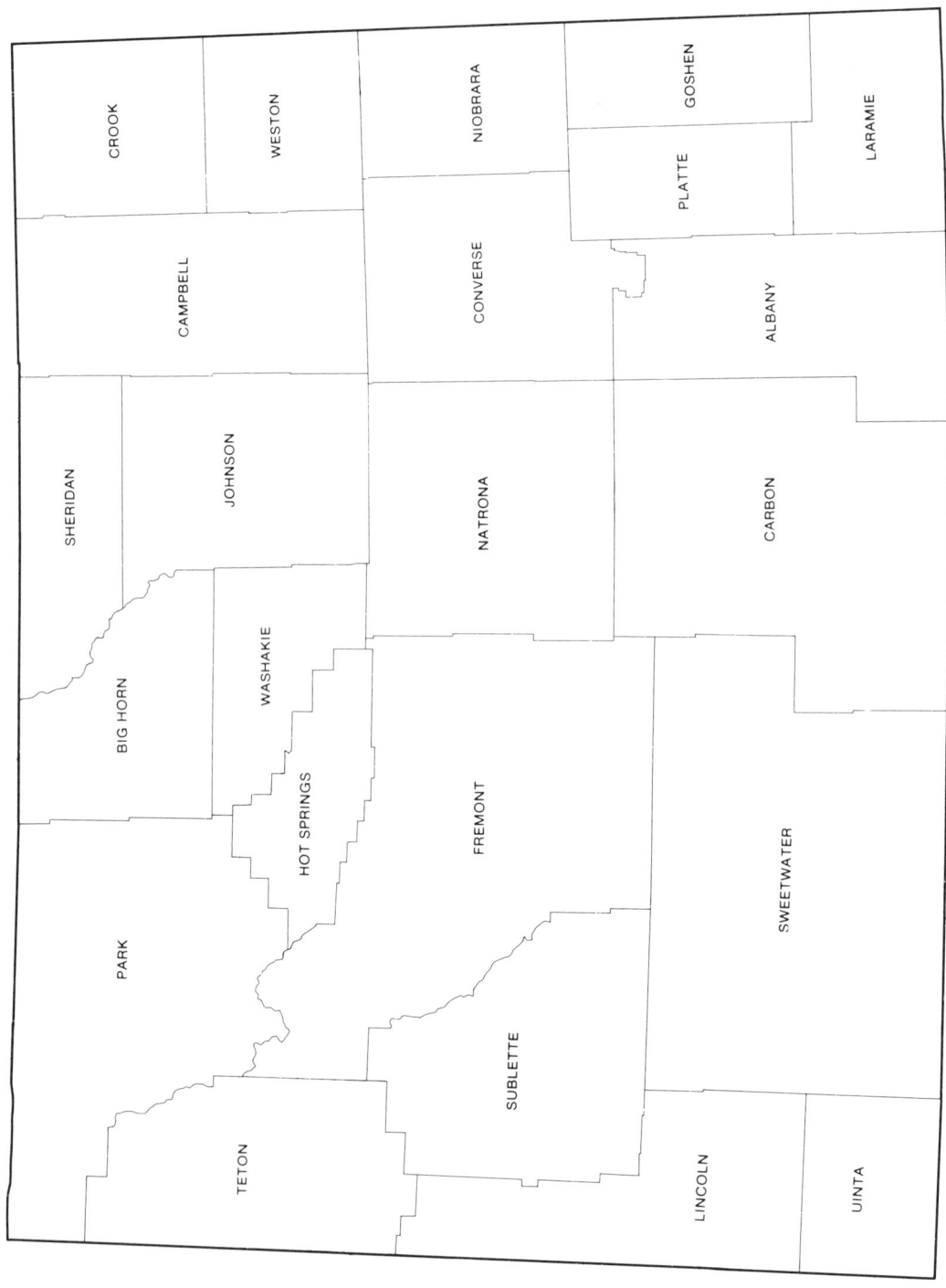

# WYOMING

## PRESIDENT 2004

| 2000 Census Population | County | Total Vote | Republican | Democratic | Other | Rep.-Dem. Plurality | Percentage | | | |
|---|---|---|---|---|---|---|---|---|---|---|
| | | | | | | | Total Vote | | Major Vote | |
| | | | | | | | Rep. | Dem. | Rep. | Dem. |
| 32,014 | ALBANY | 16,624 | 9,006 | 7,117 | 501 | 1,889 R | 54.2% | 42.8% | 55.9% | 44.1% |
| 11,461 | BIG HORN | 5,283 | 4,232 | 960 | 91 | 3,272 R | 80.1% | 18.2% | 81.5% | 18.5% |
| 33,698 | CAMPBELL | 15,099 | 12,415 | 2,464 | 220 | 9,951 R | 82.2% | 16.3% | 83.4% | 16.6% |
| 15,639 | CARBON | 7,077 | 4,758 | 2,158 | 161 | 2,600 R | 67.2% | 30.5% | 68.8% | 31.2% |
| 12,052 | CONVERSE | 5,725 | 4,447 | 1,184 | 94 | 3,263 R | 77.7% | 20.7% | 79.0% | 21.0% |
| 5,887 | CROOK | 3,396 | 2,836 | 501 | 59 | 2,335 R | 83.5% | 14.8% | 85.0% | 15.0% |
| 35,804 | FREMONT | 17,096 | 11,429 | 5,338 | 329 | 6,091 R | 66.9% | 31.2% | 68.2% | 31.8% |
| 12,538 | GOSHEN | 5,779 | 4,114 | 1,566 | 99 | 2,548 R | 71.2% | 27.1% | 72.4% | 27.6% |
| 4,882 | HOT SPRINGS | 2,480 | 1,812 | 623 | 45 | 1,189 R | 73.1% | 25.1% | 74.4% | 25.6% |
| 7,075 | JOHNSON | 3,991 | 3,231 | 676 | 84 | 2,555 R | 81.0% | 16.9% | 82.7% | 17.3% |
| 81,607 | LARAMIE | 39,879 | 25,951 | 13,171 | 757 | 12,780 R | 65.1% | 33.0% | 66.3% | 33.7% |
| 14,573 | LINCOLN | 7,914 | 6,423 | 1,364 | 127 | 5,059 R | 81.2% | 17.2% | 82.5% | 17.5% |
| 66,533 | NATRONA | 32,068 | 21,512 | 9,863 | 693 | 11,649 R | 67.1% | 30.8% | 68.6% | 31.4% |
| 2,407 | NIOBRARA | 1,314 | 1,064 | 230 | 20 | 834 R | 81.0% | 17.5% | 82.2% | 17.8% |
| 25,786 | PARK | 14,231 | 10,917 | 3,007 | 307 | 7,910 R | 76.7% | 21.1% | 78.4% | 21.6% |
| 8,807 | PLATTE | 4,574 | 3,149 | 1,328 | 97 | 1,821 R | 68.8% | 29.0% | 70.3% | 29.7% |
| 26,560 | SHERIDAN | 14,029 | 9,689 | 4,066 | 274 | 5,623 R | 69.1% | 29.0% | 70.4% | 29.6% |
| 5,920 | SUBLETTE | 3,651 | 2,847 | 730 | 74 | 2,117 R | 78.0% | 20.0% | 79.6% | 20.4% |
| 37,613 | SWEETWATER | 16,272 | 10,653 | 5,208 | 411 | 5,445 R | 65.5% | 32.0% | 67.2% | 32.8% |
| 18,251 | TETON | 11,359 | 5,124 | 5,972 | 263 | 848 D | 45.1% | 52.6% | 46.2% | 53.8% |
| 19,742 | UINTA | 8,081 | 6,081 | 1,815 | 185 | 4,266 R | 75.3% | 22.5% | 77.0% | 23.0% |
| 8,289 | WASHAKIE | 4,114 | 3,200 | 855 | 59 | 2,345 R | 77.8% | 20.8% | 78.9% | 21.1% |
| 6,644 | WESTON | 3,392 | 2,739 | 580 | 73 | 2,159 R | 80.7% | 17.1% | 82.5% | 17.5% |
| 493,782 | TOTAL | 243,428 | 167,629 | 70,776 | 5,023 | 96,853 R | 68.9% | 29.1% | 70.3% | 29.7% |

# WYOMING

## PRESIDENT 2000

| 2000 Census Population | County | Total Vote | Republican | Democratic | Green (Nader) | Other | Rep.-Dem. Plurality | Percentage of Total Vote | | |
|---|---|---|---|---|---|---|---|---|---|---|
| | | | | | | | | Rep. | Dem. | Green |
| 32,014 | ALBANY | 14,151 | 7,814 | 5,069 | 988 | 280 | 2,745 R | 55.2% | 35.8% | 7.0% |
| 11,461 | BIG HORN | 4,918 | 3,720 | 1,004 | 40 | 154 | 2,716 R | 75.6% | 20.4% | 0.8% |
| 33,698 | CAMPBELL | 12,540 | 10,203 | 1,967 | 86 | 284 | 8,236 R | 81.4% | 15.7% | 0.7% |
| 15,639 | CARBON | 6,968 | 4,498 | 2,206 | 105 | 159 | 2,292 R | 64.6% | 31.7% | 1.5% |
| 12,052 | CONVERSE | 5,175 | 3,919 | 1,076 | 32 | 148 | 2,843 R | 75.7% | 20.8% | 0.6% |
| 5,887 | CROOK | 2,738 | 2,289 | 361 | 32 | 56 | 1,928 R | 83.6% | 13.2% | 1.2% |
| 35,804 | FREMONT | 15,444 | 10,560 | 4,172 | 304 | 408 | 6,388 R | 68.4% | 27.0% | 2.0% |
| 12,538 | GOSHEN | 5,520 | 3,922 | 1,439 | 27 | 132 | 2,483 R | 71.1% | 26.1% | 0.5% |
| 4,882 | HOT SPRINGS | 2,352 | 1,733 | 544 | 13 | 62 | 1,189 R | 73.7% | 23.1% | 0.6% |
| 7,075 | JOHNSON | 3,550 | 2,886 | 555 | 33 | 76 | 2,331 R | 81.3% | 15.6% | 0.9% |
| 81,607 | LARAMIE | 35,323 | 21,797 | 12,162 | 608 | 756 | 9,635 R | 61.7% | 34.4% | 1.7% |
| 14,573 | LINCOLN | 6,845 | 5,415 | 1,184 | 83 | 163 | 4,231 R | 79.1% | 17.3% | 1.2% |
| 66,533 | NATRONA | 28,388 | 18,439 | 8,646 | 590 | 713 | 9,793 R | 65.0% | 30.5% | 2.1% |
| 2,407 | NIOBRARA | 1,127 | 888 | 190 | 16 | 33 | 698 R | 78.8% | 16.9% | 1.4% |
| 25,786 | PARK | 12,836 | 9,884 | 2,424 | 227 | 301 | 7,460 R | 77.0% | 18.9% | 1.8% |
| 8,807 | PLATTE | 4,373 | 2,925 | 1,249 | 69 | 130 | 1,676 R | 66.9% | 28.6% | 1.6% |
| 26,560 | SHERIDAN | 12,236 | 8,424 | 3,330 | 208 | 274 | 5,094 R | 68.8% | 27.2% | 1.7% |
| 5,920 | SUBLETTE | 3,216 | 2,624 | 458 | 47 | 87 | 2,166 R | 81.6% | 14.2% | 1.5% |
| 37,613 | SWEETWATER | 15,691 | 9,425 | 5,521 | 222 | 523 | 3,904 R | 60.1% | 35.2% | 1.4% |
| 18,251 | TETON | 10,431 | 5,454 | 4,019 | 764 | 194 | 1,435 R | 52.3% | 38.5% | 7.3% |
| 19,742 | UINTA | 7,418 | 5,469 | 1,650 | 76 | 223 | 3,819 R | 73.7% | 22.2% | 1.0% |
| 8,289 | WASHAKIE | 4,051 | 3,138 | 806 | 29 | 78 | 2,332 R | 77.5% | 19.9% | 0.7% |
| 6,644 | WESTON | 3,060 | 2,521 | 449 | 26 | 64 | 2,072 R | 82.4% | 14.7% | 0.8% |
| 493,782 | TOTAL | 218,351 | 147,947 | 60,481 | 4,625 | 5,298 | 87,466 R | 67.8% | 27.7% | 2.1% |

Note: The votes cast for Nader were write-ins.

# WYOMING

## PRESIDENT 1996

| 1995 Census Pop. Est. | County | Total Vote | Republican | Democratic | Reform (Perot) | Other | Rep.-Dem. Plurality | Percentage of Total Vote | | |
|---|---|---|---|---|---|---|---|---|---|---|
| | | | | | | | | Rep. | Dem. | Reform |
| 30,980 | ALBANY | 13,936 | 5,967 | 6,399 | 1,333 | 237 | 432 D | 42.8% | 45.9% | 9.6% |
| 11,110 | BIG HORN | 4,839 | 2,821 | 1,438 | 545 | 35 | 1,383 R | 58.3% | 29.7% | 11.3% |
| 31,668 | CAMPBELL | 11,889 | 6,382 | 3,468 | 1,954 | 85 | 2,914 R | 53.7% | 29.2% | 16.4% |
| 16,110 | CARBON | 6,517 | 2,930 | 2,690 | 855 | 42 | 240 R | 45.0% | 41.3% | 13.1% |
| 11,965 | CONVERSE | 4,911 | 2,702 | 1,520 | 639 | 50 | 1,182 R | 55.0% | 31.0% | 13.0% |
| 5,656 | CROOK | 2,787 | 1,698 | 651 | 394 | 44 | 1,047 R | 60.9% | 23.4% | 14.1% |
| 35,710 | FREMONT | 15,024 | 7,554 | 5,445 | 1,840 | 185 | 2,109 R | 50.3% | 36.2% | 12.2% |
| 12,627 | GOSHEN | 5,513 | 2,989 | 1,923 | 547 | 54 | 1,066 R | 54.2% | 34.9% | 9.9% |
| 4,567 | HOT SPRINGS | 2,436 | 1,348 | 779 | 287 | 22 | 569 R | 55.3% | 32.0% | 11.8% |
| 6,644 | JOHNSON | 3,309 | 2,071 | 815 | 378 | 45 | 1,256 R | 62.6% | 24.6% | 11.4% |
| 78,444 | LARAMIE | 33,869 | 16,924 | 13,676 | 2,958 | 311 | 3,248 R | 50.0% | 40.4% | 8.7% |
| 13,918 | LINCOLN | 6,536 | 3,764 | 1,803 | 906 | 63 | 1,961 R | 57.6% | 27.6% | 13.9% |
| 64,025 | NATRONA | 28,215 | 13,182 | 11,240 | 3,524 | 269 | 1,942 R | 46.7% | 39.8% | 12.5% |
| 2,618 | NIOBRARA | 1,305 | 757 | 325 | 209 | 14 | 432 R | 58.0% | 24.9% | 16.0% |
| 25,534 | PARK | 12,098 | 7,430 | 3,240 | 1,318 | 110 | 4,190 R | 61.4% | 26.8% | 10.9% |
| 8,343 | PLATTE | 4,408 | 2,155 | 1,631 | 579 | 43 | 524 R | 48.9% | 37.0% | 13.1% |
| 25,088 | SHERIDAN | 12,046 | 5,892 | 4,594 | 1,414 | 146 | 1,298 R | 48.9% | 38.1% | 11.7% |
| 5,507 | SUBLETTE | 2,943 | 1,829 | 677 | 401 | 36 | 1,152 R | 62.1% | 23.0% | 13.6% |
| 40,976 | SWEETWATER | 15,634 | 5,591 | 7,088 | 2,792 | 163 | 1,497 D | 35.8% | 45.3% | 17.9% |
| 13,444 | TETON | 8,998 | 3,918 | 4,042 | 839 | 199 | 124 D | 43.5% | 44.9% | 9.3% |
| 20,087 | UINTA | 7,218 | 3,471 | 2,414 | 1,242 | 91 | 1,057 R | 48.1% | 33.4% | 17.2% |
| 8,657 | WASHAKIE | 3,966 | 2,250 | 1,205 | 470 | 41 | 1,045 R | 56.7% | 30.4% | 11.9% |
| 6,506 | WESTON | 3,174 | 1,763 | 871 | 504 | 36 | 892 R | 55.5% | 27.4% | 15.9% |
| 480,184 | TOTAL | 211,571 | 105,388 | 77,934 | 25,928 | 2,321 | 27,454 R | 49.8% | 36.8% | 12.3% |

# WYOMING

## PRESIDENT 1992

| 1990 Census Population | County | Total Vote | Republican | Democratic | Perot | Other | Plurality | Percentage Total Vote | | |
|---|---|---|---|---|---|---|---|---|---|---|
| | | | | | | | | Rep. | Dem. | Perot |
| 30,797 | ALBANY | 12,867 | 4,176 | 5,713 | 2,862 | 116 | 1,537 D | 32.5% | 44.4% | 22.2% |
| 10,525 | BIG HORN | 4,762 | 2,216 | 1,216 | 1,236 | 94 | 980 R | 46.5% | 25.5% | 26.0% |
| 29,370 | CAMPBELL | 11,219 | 5,315 | 2,709 | 3,133 | 62 | 2,182 R | 47.4% | 24.1% | 27.9% |
| 16,659 | CARBON | 6,678 | 2,320 | 2,737 | 1,579 | 42 | 417 D | 34.7% | 41.0% | 23.6% |
| 11,128 | CONVERSE | 4,751 | 2,159 | 1,307 | 1,260 | 25 | 852 R | 45.4% | 27.5% | 26.5% |
| 5,294 | CROOK | 2,683 | 1,377 | 568 | 718 | 20 | 659 R | 51.3% | 21.2% | 26.8% |
| 33,662 | FREMONT | 13,894 | 5,387 | 4,765 | 3,594 | 148 | 622 R | 38.8% | 34.3% | 25.9% |
| 12,373 | GOSHEN | 5,318 | 2,395 | 1,754 | 1,144 | 25 | 641 R | 45.0% | 33.0% | 21.5% |
| 4,809 | HOT SPRINGS | 2,399 | 978 | 740 | 652 | 29 | 238 R | 40.8% | 30.8% | 27.2% |
| 6,145 | JOHNSON | 3,146 | 1,614 | 656 | 844 | 32 | 770 R | 51.3% | 20.9% | 26.8% |
| 73,142 | LARAMIE | 31,855 | 12,890 | 12,177 | 6,607 | 181 | 713 R | 40.5% | 38.2% | 20.7% |
| 12,625 | LINCOLN | 5,757 | 2,595 | 1,430 | 1,495 | 237 | 1,100 R | 45.1% | 24.8% | 26.0% |
| 61,226 | NATRONA | 27,400 | 9,717 | 9,817 | 7,647 | 219 | 100 D | 35.5% | 35.8% | 27.9% |
| 2,499 | NIOBRARA | 1,299 | 635 | 298 | 355 | 11 | 280 R | 48.9% | 22.9% | 27.3% |
| 23,178 | PARK | 11,209 | 5,218 | 2,771 | 3,145 | 75 | 2,073 R | 46.6% | 24.7% | 28.1% |
| 8,145 | PLATTE | 4,051 | 1,668 | 1,398 | 956 | 29 | 270 R | 41.2% | 34.5% | 23.6% |
| 23,562 | SHERIDAN | 11,559 | 4,303 | 4,139 | 3,035 | 82 | 164 R | 37.2% | 35.8% | 26.3% |
| 4,843 | SUBLETTE | 2,573 | 1,168 | 536 | 828 | 41 | 340 R | 45.4% | 20.8% | 32.2% |
| 38,823 | SWEETWATER | 14,891 | 4,476 | 6,417 | 3,879 | 119 | 1,941 D | 30.1% | 43.1% | 26.0% |
| 11,172 | TETON | 8,382 | 2,854 | 3,120 | 2,340 | 68 | 266 D | 34.0% | 37.2% | 27.9% |
| 18,705 | UINTA | 6,896 | 2,701 | 2,047 | 2,041 | 107 | 654 R | 39.2% | 29.7% | 29.6% |
| 8,388 | WASHAKIE | 3,982 | 1,720 | 1,118 | 1,084 | 60 | 602 R | 43.2% | 28.1% | 27.2% |
| 6,518 | WESTON | 3,027 | 1,465 | 727 | 829 | 6 | 636 R | 48.4% | 24.0% | 27.4% |
| 453,588 | TOTAL | 200,598 | 79,347 | 68,160 | 51,263 | 1,828 | 11,187 R | 39.6% | 34.0% | 25.6% |

# WYOMING

## PRESIDENT 1988

| 1980 Census Population | County | Total Vote | Republican | Democratic | Other | Rep.-Dem. Plurality | Percentage | | | |
|---|---|---|---|---|---|---|---|---|---|---|
| | | | | | | | Total Vote | | Major Vote | |
| | | | | | | | Rep. | Dem. | Rep. | Dem. |
| 29,062 | ALBANY | 11,335 | 5,653 | 5,486 | 196 | 167 R | 49.9% | 48.4% | 50.7% | 49.3% |
| 11,896 | BIG HORN | 4,780 | 3,258 | 1,469 | 53 | 1,789 R | 68.2% | 30.7% | 68.9% | 31.1% |
| 24,367 | CAMPBELL | 9,112 | 6,702 | 2,288 | 122 | 4,414 R | 73.6% | 25.1% | 74.5% | 25.5% |
| 21,896 | CARBON | 5,989 | 3,336 | 2,555 | 98 | 781 R | 55.7% | 42.7% | 56.6% | 43.4% |
| 14,069 | CONVERSE | 4,215 | 2,885 | 1,301 | 29 | 1,584 R | 68.4% | 30.9% | 68.9% | 31.1% |
| 5,308 | CROOK | 2,540 | 1,939 | 553 | 48 | 1,386 R | 76.3% | 21.8% | 77.8% | 22.2% |
| 38,992 | FREEMONT | 12,889 | 7,681 | 5,020 | 188 | 2,661 R | 59.6% | 38.9% | 60.5% | 39.5% |
| 12,040 | GOSHEN | 5,005 | 3,075 | 1,875 | 55 | 1,200 R | 61.4% | 37.5% | 62.1% | 37.9% |
| 5,710 | HOT SPRINGS | 2,324 | 1,490 | 800 | 34 | 690 R | 64.1% | 34.4% | 65.1% | 34.9% |
| 6,700 | JOHNSON | 2,858 | 2,081 | 707 | 70 | 1,374 R | 72.8% | 24.7% | 74.6% | 25.4% |
| 68,649 | LARAMIE | 27,770 | 15,561 | 11,851 | 358 | 3,710 R | 56.0% | 42.7% | 56.8% | 43.2% |
| 12,177 | LINCOLN | 4,897 | 3,237 | 1,592 | 68 | 1,645 R | 66.1% | 32.5% | 67.0% | 33.0% |
| 71,856 | NATRONA | 23,487 | 14,005 | 9,148 | 334 | 4,857 R | 59.6% | 38.9% | 60.5% | 39.5% |
| 2,924 | NIOBRARA | 1,191 | 825 | 354 | 12 | 471 R | 69.3% | 29.7% | 70.0% | 30.0% |
| 21,639 | PARK | 9,702 | 6,884 | 2,646 | 172 | 4,238 R | 71.0% | 27.3% | 72.2% | 27.8% |
| 11,975 | PLATTE | 3,808 | 2,253 | 1,482 | 73 | 771 R | 59.2% | 38.9% | 60.3% | 39.7% |
| 25,048 | SHERIDAN | 10,778 | 5,980 | 4,655 | 143 | 1,325 R | 55.5% | 43.2% | 56.2% | 43.8% |
| 4,548 | SUBLETTE | 2,247 | 1,636 | 576 | 35 | 1,060 R | 72.8% | 25.6% | 74.0% | 26.0% |
| 41,723 | SWEETWATER | 13,705 | 6,780 | 6,720 | 205 | 60 R | 49.5% | 49.0% | 50.2% | 49.8% |
| 9,355 | TETON | 5,926 | 3,616 | 2,217 | 93 | 1,399 R | 61.0% | 37.4% | 62.0% | 38.0% |
| 13,021 | UINTA | 5,501 | 3,464 | 1,922 | 115 | 1,542 R | 63.0% | 34.9% | 64.3% | 35.7% |
| 9,496 | WASHAKIE | 3,768 | 2,538 | 1,197 | 33 | 1,341 R | 67.4% | 31.8% | 68.0% | 32.0% |
| 7,106 | WESTON | 2,724 | 1,988 | 699 | 37 | 1,289 R | 73.0% | 25.7% | 74.0% | 26.0% |
| 469,557 | TOTAL | 176,551 | 106,867 | 67,113 | 2,571 | 39,754 R | 60.5% | 38.0% | 61.4% | 38.6% |

# WYOMING

## PRESIDENT 1984

| 1980 Census Population | County | Total Vote | Republican | Democratic | Other | Rep.-Dem. Plurality | Percentage | | | |
|---|---|---|---|---|---|---|---|---|---|---|
| | | | | | | | Total Vote | | Major Vote | |
| | | | | | | | Rep. | Dem. | Rep. | Dem. |
| 29,062 | ALBANY | 12,346 | 7,452 | 4,708 | 186 | 2,744 R | 60.4% | 38.1% | 61.3% | 38.7% |
| 11,896 | BIG HORN | 5,253 | 4,019 | 1,175 | 59 | 2,844 R | 76.5% | 22.4% | 77.4% | 22.6% |
| 24,367 | CAMPBELL | 9,995 | 8,387 | 1,525 | 83 | 6,862 R | 83.9% | 15.3% | 84.6% | 15.4% |
| 21,896 | CARBON | 6,952 | 4,557 | 2,295 | 100 | 2,262 R | 65.5% | 33.0% | 66.5% | 33.5% |
| 14,069 | CONVERSE | 4,523 | 3,542 | 929 | 52 | 2,613 R | 78.3% | 20.5% | 79.2% | 20.8% |
| 5,308 | CROOK | 2,754 | 2,286 | 450 | 18 | 1,836 R | 83.0% | 16.3% | 83.6% | 16.4% |
| 38,992 | FREMONT | 13,999 | 9,885 | 3,969 | 145 | 5,916 R | 70.6% | 28.4% | 71.4% | 28.6% |
| 12,040 | GOSHEN | 5,184 | 3,776 | 1,364 | 44 | 2,412 R | 72.8% | 26.3% | 73.5% | 26.5% |
| 5,710 | HOT SPRINGS | 2,646 | 1,943 | 672 | 31 | 1,271 R | 73.4% | 25.4% | 74.3% | 25.7% |
| 6,700 | JOHNSON | 3,241 | 2,634 | 558 | 49 | 2,076 R | 81.3% | 17.2% | 82.5% | 17.5% |
| 68,649 | LARAMIE | 29,799 | 19,348 | 10,110 | 341 | 9,238 R | 64.9% | 33.9% | 65.7% | 34.3% |
| 12,177 | LINCOLN | 4,921 | 3,854 | 1,021 | 46 | 2,833 R | 78.3% | 20.7% | 79.1% | 20.9% |
| 71,856 | NATRONA | 26,464 | 18,488 | 7,598 | 378 | 10,890 R | 69.9% | 28.7% | 70.9% | 29.1% |
| 2,924 | NIOBRARA | 1,359 | 1,098 | 239 | 22 | 859 R | 80.8% | 17.6% | 82.1% | 17.9% |
| 21,639 | PARK | 10,095 | 7,994 | 1,965 | 136 | 6,029 R | 79.2% | 19.5% | 80.3% | 19.7% |
| 11,975 | PLATTE | 4,120 | 2,813 | 1,232 | 75 | 1,581 R | 68.3% | 29.9% | 69.5% | 30.5% |
| 25,048 | SHERIDAN | 11,279 | 7,460 | 3,648 | 171 | 3,812 R | 66.1% | 32.3% | 67.2% | 32.8% |
| 4,548 | SUBLETTE | 2,396 | 1,976 | 389 | 31 | 1,587 R | 82.5% | 16.2% | 83.6% | 16.4% |
| 41,723 | SWEETWATER | 13,712 | 8,308 | 5,230 | 174 | 3,078 R | 60.6% | 38.1% | 61.4% | 38.6% |
| 9,355 | TETON | 5,139 | 3,487 | 1,565 | 87 | 1,922 R | 67.9% | 30.5% | 69.0% | 31.0% |
| 13,021 | UINTA | 5,411 | 4,075 | 1,276 | 60 | 2,799 R | 75.3% | 23.6% | 76.2% | 23.8% |
| 9,496 | WASHAKIE | 4,253 | 3,245 | 970 | 38 | 2,275 R | 76.3% | 22.8% | 77.0% | 23.0% |
| 7,106 | WESTON | 3,127 | 2,614 | 482 | 31 | 2,132 R | 83.6% | 15.4% | 84.4% | 15.6% |
| 469,557 | TOTAL | 188,968 | 133,241 | 53,370 | 2,357 | 79,871 R | 70.5% | 28.2% | 71.4% | 28.6% |

# WYOMING

### PRESIDENT 1980

| 1980 Census Population | County | Total Vote | Republican | Democratic | Other | Rep.-Dem. Plurality | Percentage | | | |
|---|---|---|---|---|---|---|---|---|---|---|
| | | | | | | | Total Vote | | Major Vote | |
| | | | | | | | Rep. | Dem. | Rep. | Dem. |
| 29,062 | ALBANY | 11,527 | 5,830 | 3,772 | 1,925 | 2,058 R | 50.6% | 32.7% | 60.7% | 39.3% |
| 11,896 | BIG HORN | 5,223 | 3,709 | 1,212 | 302 | 2,497 R | 71.0% | 23.2% | 75.4% | 24.6% |
| 24,367 | CAMPBELL | 7,669 | 5,613 | 1,400 | 656 | 4,213 R | 73.2% | 18.3% | 80.0% | 20.0% |
| 21,896 | CARBON | 7,283 | 4,337 | 2,272 | 674 | 2,065 R | 59.5% | 31.2% | 65.6% | 34.4% |
| 14,069 | CONVERSE | 4,229 | 2,987 | 922 | 320 | 2,065 R | 70.6% | 21.8% | 76.4% | 23.6% |
| 5,308 | CROOK | 2,416 | 1,909 | 413 | 94 | 1,496 R | 79.0% | 17.1% | 82.2% | 17.8% |
| 38,992 | FREEMONT | 13,403 | 9,077 | 3,307 | 1,019 | 5,770 R | 67.7% | 24.7% | 73.3% | 26.7% |
| 12,040 | GOSHEN | 5,315 | 3,572 | 1,373 | 370 | 2,199 R | 67.2% | 25.8% | 72.2% | 27.8% |
| 5,710 | HOT SPRINGS | 2,555 | 1,602 | 745 | 208 | 857 R | 62.7% | 29.2% | 68.3% | 31.7% |
| 6,700 | JOHNSON | 3,148 | 2,291 | 635 | 222 | 1,656 R | 72.8% | 20.2% | 78.3% | 21.7% |
| 68,649 | LARAMIE | 27,713 | 15,361 | 9,512 | 2,840 | 5,849 R | 55.4% | 34.3% | 61.8% | 38.2% |
| 12,177 | LINCOLN | 4,694 | 3,412 | 1,063 | 219 | 2,349 R | 72.7% | 22.6% | 76.2% | 23.8% |
| 71,856 | NATRONA | 26,672 | 16,801 | 7,111 | 2,760 | 9,690 R | 63.0% | 26.7% | 70.3% | 29.7% |
| 2,924 | NIOBRARA | 1,412 | 1,075 | 270 | 67 | 805 R | 76.1% | 19.1% | 79.9% | 20.1% |
| 21,639 | PARK | 8,811 | 6,435 | 1,718 | 658 | 4,717 R | 73.0% | 19.5% | 78.9% | 21.1% |
| 11,975 | PLATTE | 4,618 | 2,642 | 1,555 | 421 | 1,087 R | 57.2% | 33.7% | 62.9% | 37.1% |
| 25,048 | SHERIDAN | 9,646 | 5,649 | 3,034 | 963 | 2,615 R | 58.6% | 31.5% | 65.1% | 34.9% |
| 4,548 | SUBLETTE | 2,082 | 1,538 | 357 | 187 | 1,181 R | 73.9% | 17.1% | 81.2% | 18.8% |
| 41,723 | SWEETWATER | 12,067 | 6,265 | 4,728 | 1,074 | 1,537 R | 51.9% | 39.2% | 57.0% | 43.0% |
| 9,355 | TETON | 5,212 | 3,004 | 1,361 | 847 | 1,643 R | 57.6% | 26.1% | 68.8% | 31.2% |
| 13,021 | UINTA | 4,151 | 2,738 | 1,138 | 275 | 1,600 R | 66.0% | 27.4% | 70.6% | 29.4% |
| 9,496 | WASHAKIE | 3,897 | 2,634 | 945 | 318 | 1,689 R | 67.6% | 24.2% | 73.6% | 26.4% |
| 7,106 | WESTON | 2,970 | 2,219 | 584 | 167 | 1,635 R | 74.7% | 19.7% | 79.2% | 20.8% |
| 469,557 | TOTAL | 176,713 | 110,700 | 49,427 | 16,586 | 61,273 R | 62.6% | 28.0% | 69.1% | 30.9% |

# WYOMING

### PRESIDENT 1976

| 1970 Census Population | County | Total Vote | Republican | Democratic | Other | Rep.-Dem. Plurality | Percentage | | | |
|---|---|---|---|---|---|---|---|---|---|---|
| | | | | | | | Total Vote | | Major Vote | |
| | | | | | | | Rep. | Dem. | Rep. | Dem. |
| 26,431 | ALBANY | 11,622 | 6,734 | 4,663 | 225 | 2,071 R | 57.9% | 40.1% | 59.1% | 40.9% |
| 10,202 | BIG HORN | 4,747 | 3,117 | 1,618 | 12 | 1,499 R | 65.7% | 34.1% | 65.8% | 34.2% |
| 12,957 | CAMPBELL | 4,995 | 3,306 | 1,620 | 69 | 1,686 R | 66.2% | 32.4% | 67.1% | 32.9% |
| 13,354 | CARBON | 6,584 | 3,556 | 3,010 | 18 | 546 R | 54.0% | 45.7% | 54.2% | 45.8% |
| 5,938 | CONVERSE | 3,347 | 2,188 | 1,150 | 9 | 1,038 R | 65.4% | 34.4% | 65.5% | 34.5% |
| 4,535 | CROOK | 2,139 | 1,438 | 653 | 48 | 785 R | 67.2% | 30.5% | 68.8% | 31.2% |
| 28,352 | FREEMONT | 11,063 | 6,584 | 4,423 | 56 | 2,161 R | 59.5% | 40.0% | 59.8% | 40.2% |
| 10,885 | GOSHEN | 5,038 | 2,764 | 2,262 | 12 | 502 R | 54.9% | 44.9% | 55.0% | 45.0% |
| 4,952 | HOT SPRINGS | 2,379 | 1,413 | 958 | 8 | 455 R | 59.4% | 40.3% | 59.6% | 40.4% |
| 5,587 | JOHNSON | 2,866 | 2,042 | 797 | 27 | 1,245 R | 71.2% | 27.8% | 71.9% | 28.1% |
| 56,360 | LARAMIE | 26,294 | 14,061 | 12,040 | 193 | 2,021 R | 53.5% | 45.8% | 53.9% | 46.1% |
| 8,640 | LINCOLN | 4,044 | 2,464 | 1,555 | 25 | 909 R | 60.9% | 38.5% | 61.3% | 38.7% |
| 51,264 | NATRONA | 22,621 | 13,761 | 8,640 | 220 | 5,121 R | 60.8% | 38.2% | 61.4% | 38.6% |
| 2,924 | NIOBRARA | 1,477 | 1,042 | 427 | 8 | 615 R | 70.5% | 28.9% | 70.9% | 29.1% |
| 17,752 | PARK | 8,602 | 5,878 | 2,656 | 68 | 3,222 R | 68.3% | 30.9% | 68.9% | 31.1% |
| 6,486 | PLATTE | 3,450 | 1,844 | 1,593 | 13 | 251 R | 53.4% | 46.2% | 53.7% | 46.3% |
| 17,852 | SHERIDAN | 8,652 | 5,382 | 3,206 | 64 | 2,176 R | 62.2% | 37.1% | 62.7% | 37.3% |
| 3,755 | SUBLETTE | 1,826 | 1,284 | 528 | 14 | 756 R | 70.3% | 28.9% | 70.9% | 29.1% |
| 18,391 | SWEETWATER | 10,574 | 4,937 | 5,575 | 62 | 638 D | 46.7% | 52.7% | 47.0% | 53.0% |
| 4,823 | TETON | 3,957 | 2,667 | 1,204 | 86 | 1,463 R | 67.4% | 30.4% | 68.9% | 31.1% |
| 7,100 | UINTA | 3,811 | 2,124 | 1,559 | 128 | 565 R | 55.7% | 40.9% | 57.7% | 42.3% |
| 7,569 | WASHAKIE | 3,541 | 2,361 | 1,168 | 12 | 1,193 R | 66.7% | 33.0% | 66.9% | 33.1% |
| 6,307 | WESTON | 2,714 | 1,770 | 934 | 10 | 836 R | 65.2% | 34.4% | 65.5% | 34.5% |
| 332,416 | TOTAL | 156,343 | 92,717 | 62,239 | 1,387 | 30,478 R | 59.3% | 39.8% | 59.8% | 40.2% |

# WYOMING

## PRESIDENT 1972

| 1970 Census Population | County | Total Vote | Republican | Democratic | Other | Rep.-Dem. Plurality | Percentage | | | |
|---|---|---|---|---|---|---|---|---|---|---|
| | | | | | | | Total Vote | | Major Vote | |
| | | | | | | | Rep. | Dem. | Rep. | Dem. |
| 26,431 | ALBANY | 11,917 | 7,021 | 4,873 | 23 | 2,148 R | 58.9% | 40.9% | 59.0% | 41.0% |
| 10,202 | BIG HORN | 4,300 | 3,244 | 1,049 | 7 | 2,195 R | 75.4% | 24.4% | 75.6% | 24.4% |
| 12,957 | CAMPBELL | 3,755 | 2,953 | 783 | 19 | 2,170 R | 78.6% | 20.9% | 79.0% | 21.0% |
| 13,354 | CARBON | 6,339 | 4,037 | 2,292 | 10 | 1,745 R | 63.7% | 36.2% | 63.8% | 36.2% |
| 5,938 | CONVERSE | 3,000 | 2,312 | 682 | 6 | 1,630 R | 77.1% | 22.7% | 77.2% | 22.8% |
| 4,535 | CROOK | 2,110 | 1,760 | 339 | 11 | 1,421 R | 83.4% | 16.1% | 83.8% | 16.2% |
| 28,352 | FREEMONT | 10,647 | 7,359 | 3,248 | 40 | 4,111 R | 69.1% | 30.5% | 69.4% | 30.6% |
| 10,885 | GOSHEN | 5,164 | 3,629 | 1,515 | 20 | 2,114 R | 70.3% | 29.3% | 70.5% | 29.5% |
| 4,952 | HOT SPRINGS | 2,367 | 1,678 | 689 | | 989 R | 70.9% | 29.1% | 70.9% | 29.1% |
| 5,587 | JOHNSON | 2,650 | 2,203 | 436 | 11 | 1,767 R | 83.1% | 16.5% | 83.5% | 16.5% |
| 56,360 | LARAMIE | 22,855 | 15,010 | 7,791 | 54 | 7,219 R | 65.7% | 34.1% | 65.8% | 34.2% |
| 8,640 | LINCOLN | 3,666 | 2,459 | 969 | 238 | 1,490 R | 67.1% | 26.4% | 71.7% | 28.3% |
| 51,264 | NATRONA | 22,200 | 15,649 | 6,514 | 37 | 9,135 R | 70.5% | 29.3% | 70.6% | 29.4% |
| 2,924 | NIOBRARA | 1,537 | 1,245 | 289 | 3 | 956 R | 81.0% | 18.8% | 81.2% | 18.8% |
| 17,752 | PARK | 7,875 | 5,890 | 1,950 | 35 | 3,940 R | 74.8% | 24.8% | 75.1% | 24.9% |
| 6,486 | PLATTE | 3,127 | 2,200 | 925 | 2 | 1,275 R | 70.4% | 29.6% | 70.4% | 29.6% |
| 17,852 | SHERIDAN | 9,318 | 6,432 | 2,874 | 12 | 3,558 R | 69.0% | 30.8% | 69.1% | 30.9% |
| 3,755 | SUBLETTE | 1,653 | 1,348 | 304 | 1 | 1,044 R | 81.5% | 18.4% | 81.6% | 18.4% |
| 18,391 | SWEETWATER | 8,915 | 5,175 | 3,713 | 27 | 1,462 R | 58.0% | 41.6% | 58.2% | 41.8% |
| 4,823 | TETON | 3,116 | 2,182 | 810 | 124 | 1,372 R | 70.0% | 26.0% | 72.9% | 27.1% |
| 7,100 | UINTA | 3,000 | 2,011 | 968 | 21 | 1,043 R | 67.0% | 32.3% | 67.5% | 32.5% |
| 7,569 | WASHAKIE | 3,430 | 2,604 | 825 | 1 | 1,779 R | 75.9% | 24.1% | 75.9% | 24.1% |
| 6,307 | WESTON | 2,629 | 2,063 | 520 | 46 | 1,543 R | 78.5% | 19.8% | 79.9% | 20.1% |
| 332,416 | TOTAL | 145,570 | 100,464 | 44,358 | 748 | 56,106 R | 69.0% | 30.5% | 69.4% | 30.6% |

# WYOMING

## PRESIDENT 1968

| 1960 Census Population | County | Total Vote | Republican | Democratic | AIP | Other | Plurality | Percentage Total Vote | | |
|---|---|---|---|---|---|---|---|---|---|---|
| | | | | | | | | Rep. | Dem. | AIP |
| 21,290 | ALBANY | 9,079 | 4,422 | 4,079 | 578 | | 343 R | 48.7% | 44.9% | 6.4% |
| 11,898 | BIG HORN | 4,325 | 2,771 | 1,201 | 353 | | 1,570 R | 64.1% | 27.8% | 8.2% |
| 5,861 | CAMPBELL | 2,541 | 1,694 | 558 | 289 | | 1,136 R | 66.7% | 22.0% | 11.4% |
| 14,937 | CARBON | 5,656 | 2,532 | 2,725 | 399 | | 193 D | 44.8% | 48.2% | 7.1% |
| 6,366 | CONVERSE | 2,382 | 1,658 | 492 | 232 | | 1,166 R | 69.6% | 20.7% | 9.7% |
| 4,691 | CROOK | 1,733 | 1,240 | 318 | 175 | | 922 R | 71.6% | 18.3% | 10.1% |
| 26,168 | FREEMONT | 9,398 | 5,417 | 3,093 | 888 | | 2,324 R | 57.6% | 32.9% | 9.4% |
| 11,941 | GOSHEN | 4,716 | 2,719 | 1,529 | 468 | | 1,190 R | 57.7% | 32.4% | 9.9% |
| 6,365 | HOT SPRINGS | 2,144 | 1,273 | 705 | 166 | | 568 R | 59.4% | 32.9% | 7.7% |
| 5,475 | JOHNSON | 2,352 | 1,737 | 398 | 217 | | 1,339 R | 73.9% | 16.9% | 9.2% |
| 60,149 | LARAMIE | 20,992 | 9,824 | 9,519 | 1,649 | | 305 R | 46.8% | 45.3% | 7.9% |
| 9,018 | LINCOLN | 3,561 | 2,030 | 1,246 | 285 | | 784 R | 57.0% | 35.0% | 8.0% |
| 49,623 | NATRONA | 18,674 | 10,679 | 5,900 | 2,095 | | 4,779 R | 57.2% | 31.6% | 11.2% |
| 3,750 | NIOBRARA | 1,490 | 1,136 | 250 | 104 | | 886 R | 76.2% | 16.8% | 7.0% |
| 16,874 | PARK | 7,134 | 4,677 | 1,852 | 605 | | 2,825 R | 65.6% | 26.0% | 8.5% |
| 7,195 | PLATTE | 2,967 | 1,613 | 1,035 | 319 | | 578 R | 54.4% | 34.9% | 10.8% |
| 18,989 | SHERIDAN | 8,434 | 5,163 | 2,659 | 612 | | 2,504 R | 61.2% | 31.5% | 7.3% |
| 3,778 | SUBLETTE | 1,688 | 1,152 | 310 | 226 | | 842 R | 68.2% | 18.4% | 13.4% |
| 17,920 | SWEETWATER | 7,449 | 2,726 | 4,086 | 637 | | 1,360 D | 36.6% | 54.9% | 8.6% |
| 3,062 | TETON | 2,049 | 1,419 | 461 | 169 | | 958 R | 69.3% | 22.5% | 8.2% |
| 7,484 | UINTA | 2,884 | 1,510 | 1,199 | 175 | | 311 R | 52.4% | 41.6% | 6.1% |
| 8,883 | WASHAKIE | 3,184 | 2,038 | 948 | 198 | | 1,090 R | 64.0% | 29.8% | 6.2% |
| 7,929 | WESTON | 2,373 | 1,497 | 610 | 266 | | 887 R | 63.1% | 25.7% | 11.2% |
| 330,066 | TOTAL | 127,205 | 70,927 | 45,173 | 11,105 | | 25,754 R | 55.8% | 35.5% | 8.7% |

# WYOMING

## PRESIDENT 1964

| 1960 Census Population | County | Total Vote | Republican | Democratic | Other | Rep.-Dem. Plurality | Percentage Total Vote Rep. | Dem. | Major Vote Rep. | Dem. |
|---|---|---|---|---|---|---|---|---|---|---|
| 21,290 | ALBANY | 8,942 | 2,923 | 6,019 | | 3,096 D | 32.7% | 67.3% | 32.7% | 67.3% |
| 11,898 | BIG HORN | 5,358 | 2,668 | 2,690 | | 22 D | 49.8% | 50.2% | 49.8% | 50.2% |
| 5,861 | CAMPBELL | 2,802 | 1,606 | 1,196 | | 410 R | 57.3% | 42.7% | 57.3% | 42.7% |
| 14,937 | CARBON | 6,482 | 2,160 | 4,322 | | 2,162 D | 33.3% | 66.7% | 33.3% | 66.7% |
| 6,366 | CONVERSE | 2,809 | 1,559 | 1,250 | | 309 R | 55.5% | 44.5% | 55.5% | 44.5% |
| 4,691 | CROOK | 1,994 | 1,214 | 780 | | 434 R | 60.9% | 39.1% | 60.9% | 39.1% |
| 26,168 | FREEMONT | 10,794 | 4,809 | 5,985 | | 1,176 D | 44.6% | 55.4% | 44.6% | 55.4% |
| 11,941 | GOSHEN | 5,353 | 2,604 | 2,749 | | 145 D | 48.6% | 51.4% | 48.6% | 51.4% |
| 6,365 | HOT SPRINGS | 2,608 | 1,228 | 1,380 | | 152 D | 47.1% | 52.9% | 47.1% | 52.9% |
| 5,475 | JOHNSON | 2,492 | 1,640 | 852 | | 788 R | 65.8% | 34.2% | 65.8% | 34.2% |
| 60,149 | LARAMIE | 24,622 | 8,563 | 16,059 | | 7,496 D | 34.8% | 65.2% | 34.8% | 65.2% |
| 9,018 | LINCOLN | 4,084 | 1,811 | 2,273 | | 462 D | 44.3% | 55.7% | 44.3% | 55.7% |
| 49,623 | NATRONA | 21,302 | 10,135 | 11,167 | | 1,032 D | 47.6% | 52.4% | 47.6% | 52.4% |
| 3,750 | NIOBRARA | 1,965 | 1,122 | 843 | | 279 R | 57.1% | 42.9% | 57.1% | 42.9% |
| 16,874 | PARK | 7,443 | 3,698 | 3,745 | | 47 D | 49.7% | 50.3% | 49.7% | 50.3% |
| 7,195 | PLATTE | 3,360 | 1,470 | 1,890 | | 420 D | 43.8% | 56.3% | 43.8% | 56.3% |
| 18,989 | SHERIDAN | 9,238 | 4,491 | 4,747 | | 256 D | 48.6% | 51.4% | 48.6% | 51.4% |
| 3,778 | SUBLETTE | 1,691 | 900 | 791 | | 109 R | 53.2% | 46.8% | 53.2% | 46.8% |
| 17,920 | SWEETWATER | 7,913 | 1,944 | 5,969 | | 4,025 D | 24.6% | 75.4% | 24.6% | 75.4% |
| 3,062 | TETON | 2,049 | 1,081 | 968 | | 113 R | 52.8% | 47.2% | 52.8% | 47.2% |
| 7,484 | UINTA | 3,115 | 1,186 | 1,929 | | 743 D | 38.1% | 61.9% | 38.1% | 61.9% |
| 8,883 | WASHAKIE | 3,408 | 1,713 | 1,695 | | 18 R | 50.3% | 49.7% | 50.3% | 49.7% |
| 7,929 | WESTON | 2,892 | 1,473 | 1,419 | | 54 R | 50.9% | 49.1% | 50.9% | 49.1% |
| 330,066 | TOTAL | 142,716 | 61,998 | 80,718 | | 18,720 D | 43.4% | 56.6% | 43.4% | 56.6% |

# WYOMING

## PRESIDENT 1960

| 1960 Census Population | County | Total Vote | Republican | Democratic | Other | Rep.-Dem. Plurality | Percentage Total Vote Rep. | Dem. | Major Vote Rep. | Dem. |
|---|---|---|---|---|---|---|---|---|---|---|
| 21,290 | ALBANY | 8,638 | 4,356 | 4,282 | | 74 R | 50.4% | 49.6% | 50.4% | 49.6% |
| 11,898 | BIG HORN | 5,493 | 3,449 | 2,044 | | 1,405 R | 62.8% | 37.2% | 62.8% | 37.2% |
| 5,861 | CAMPBELL | 2,436 | 1,575 | 861 | | 714 R | 64.7% | 35.3% | 64.7% | 35.3% |
| 14,937 | CARBON | 6,975 | 3,147 | 3,828 | | 681 D | 45.1% | 54.9% | 45.1% | 54.9% |
| 6,366 | CONVERSE | 2,859 | 1,933 | 926 | | 1,007 R | 67.6% | 32.4% | 67.6% | 32.4% |
| 4,691 | CROOK | 2,110 | 1,537 | 573 | | 964 R | 72.8% | 27.2% | 72.8% | 27.2% |
| 26,168 | FREEMONT | 9,986 | 5,738 | 4,248 | | 1,490 R | 57.5% | 42.5% | 57.5% | 42.5% |
| 11,941 | GOSHEN | 5,592 | 3,178 | 2,414 | | 764 R | 56.8% | 43.2% | 56.8% | 43.2% |
| 6,365 | HOT SPRINGS | 2,803 | 1,659 | 1,144 | | 515 R | 59.2% | 40.8% | 59.2% | 40.8% |
| 5,475 | JOHNSON | 2,604 | 1,806 | 798 | | 1,008 R | 69.4% | 30.6% | 69.4% | 30.6% |
| 60,149 | LARAMIE | 23,723 | 11,637 | 12,086 | | 449 D | 49.1% | 50.9% | 49.1% | 50.9% |
| 9,018 | LINCOLN | 3,958 | 2,010 | 1,948 | | 62 R | 50.8% | 49.2% | 50.8% | 49.2% |
| 49,623 | NATRONA | 20,811 | 11,809 | 9,002 | | 2,807 R | 56.7% | 43.3% | 56.7% | 43.3% |
| 3,750 | NIOBRARA | 1,930 | 1,362 | 568 | | 794 R | 70.6% | 29.4% | 70.6% | 29.4% |
| 16,874 | PARK | 7,006 | 4,510 | 2,496 | | 2,014 R | 64.4% | 35.6% | 64.4% | 35.6% |
| 7,195 | PLATTE | 3,329 | 1,771 | 1,558 | | 213 R | 53.2% | 46.8% | 53.2% | 46.8% |
| 18,989 | SHERIDAN | 9,476 | 5,690 | 3,786 | | 1,904 R | 60.0% | 40.0% | 60.0% | 40.0% |
| 3,778 | SUBLETTE | 1,624 | 978 | 646 | | 332 R | 60.2% | 39.8% | 60.2% | 39.8% |
| 17,920 | SWEETWATER | 7,943 | 2,545 | 5,398 | | 2,853 D | 32.0% | 68.0% | 32.0% | 68.0% |
| 3,062 | TETON | 1,741 | 1,158 | 583 | | 575 R | 66.5% | 33.5% | 66.5% | 33.5% |
| 7,484 | UINTA | 3,206 | 1,606 | 1,600 | | 6 R | 50.1% | 49.9% | 50.1% | 49.9% |
| 8,883 | WASHAKIE | 3,595 | 2,254 | 1,341 | | 913 R | 62.7% | 37.3% | 62.7% | 37.3% |
| 7,929 | WESTON | 2,944 | 1,743 | 1,201 | | 542 R | 59.2% | 40.8% | 59.2% | 40.8% |
| 330,066 | TOTAL | 140,782 | 77,451 | 63,331 | | 14,120 R | 55.0% | 45.0% | 55.0% | 45.0% |

# WYOMING

The total of the population column for each census includes persons living in Yellowstone National Park and not under jurisdiction of any county.

## ELECTION NOTES

**2004**    Other vote was 2,741 Independent (Ralph Nader); 1,171 Libertarian (Michael Badnarik); 631 Independent (Michael Peroutka); 480 write-in.

**2000**    Other vote was 2,724 Reform (Buchanan); 1,443 Libertarian (Browne); 720 Independent (Phillips); 411 Natural Law (Hagelin). The write-in vote for Nader was tallied at Nader's request, and was not included in the certified returns.

**1996**    Other vote was 1,739 Libertarian (Browne); 582 Natural Law (Hagelin).

**1992**    Other vote was 844 Marrou (Libertarian); 569 Gritz (write-in); 270 Fulani (Independent); 11 Hagelin (write-in); 7 Phillips (write-in); 127 scattered write-in.

**1988**    Other vote was 2,026 Paul (Libertarian); 545 Fulani (New Alliance).

**1984**    Other vote was Bergland (Libertarian).

**1980**    Other vote was 12,072 Anderson (Independent); 4,514 Clark (Independent).

**1976**    Other vote was 624 McCarthy (write-in); 290 Anderson (write-in); 89 MacBride (write-in); 30 Maddox (write-in); 354 scattered write-in.

**1972**    Other vote was Schmitz (write-in).

**1968**    Wallace on the ballot as Independent.

**1964**

**1960**    Early uncorrected returns gave the Nixon (Republican) vote in Albany county as 4,456 and the Nixon statewide vote was corrected twice, once from 77,551 and again from 76,551.

# DISTRICT OF COLUMBIA

## POPULAR VOTE FOR PRESIDENT 1964 TO 2004

| Year | Total Vote | Republican | | Democratic | | Other Vote | Plurality | Percentage | | | |
| | | Vote | Candidate | Vote | Candidate | | | Total Vote | | Major Vote | |
| | | | | | | | | Rep. | Dem. | Rep. | Dem. |
|------|-----------|-------|-----------|-------|-----------|-----------|-----------|------|------|------|------|
| 2004 | 227,586 | 21,256 | Bush, George W. | 202,970 | Kerry, John | 3,360 | 181,714 D | 9.3% | 89.2% | 9.5% | 90.5% |
| 2000** | 201,894 | 18,073 | Bush, George W. | 171,923 | Gore, Al | 11,898 | 153,850 D | 9.0% | 85.2% | 9.5% | 90.5% |
| 1996** | 185,726 | 17,339 | Dole, Bob | 158,220 | Clinton, Bill | 10,167 | 140,881 D | 9.3% | 85.2% | 9.9% | 90.1% |
| 1992** | 227,572 | 20,698 | Bush, George | 192,619 | Clinton, Bill | 14,255 | 171,921 D | 9.1% | 84.6% | 9.7% | 90.3% |
| 1988 | 192,877 | 27,590 | Bush, George | 159,407 | Dukakis, Michael S. | 5,880 | 131,817 D | 14.3% | 82.6% | 14.8% | 85.2% |
| 1984 | 211,288 | 29,009 | Reagan, Ronald | 180,408 | Mondale, Walter F. | 1,871 | 151,399 D | 13.7% | 85.4% | 13.9% | 86.1% |
| 1980** | 175,237 | 23,545 | Reagan, Ronald | 131,113 | Carter, Jimmy | 20,579 | 107,568 D | 13.4% | 74.8% | 15.2% | 84.8% |
| 1976 | 168,830 | 27,873 | Ford, Gerald R. | 137,818 | Carter, Jimmy | 3,139 | 109,945 D | 16.5% | 81.6% | 16.8% | 83.2% |
| 1972 | 163,421 | 35,226 | Nixon, Richard M. | 127,627 | McGovern, George S. | 568 | 92,401 D | 21.6% | 78.1% | 21.6% | 78.4% |
| 1968 | 170,578 | 31,012 | Nixon, Richard M. | 139,566 | Humphrey, Hubert H. | | 108,554 D | 18.2% | 81.8% | 18.2% | 81.8% |
| 1964** | 198,597 | 28,801 | Goldwater, Barry M. | 169,796 | Johnson, Lyndon B. | | 140,995 D | 14.5% | 85.5% | 14.5% | 85.5% |

In 2000 the other vote column includes 10,576 votes cast for Green (Nader). In 1996 the other vote column includes 3,611 votes cast for Perot. In 1992 the other vote column includes 9,681 votes cast for Perot. In 1980 the other column includes 16,337 votes for Independent (Anderson). Under the 23rd Amendment to the Constitution, the District of Columbia became entitled to choose Electors beginning with the 1964 election.

## ELECTORAL COLLEGE VOTE 1964 TO 2004

| Year | Total | Republican | Democratic | Other |
|------|-------|-----------|-----------|-------|
| 2004 | 3 | | 3 | |
| 2000 | 3 | | 2 | 1 |
| 1996 | 3 | | 3 | |
| 1992 | 3 | | 3 | |
| 1988 | 3 | | 3 | |
| 1984 | 3 | | 3 | |
| 1980 | 3 | | 3 | |
| 1976 | 3 | | 3 | |
| 1972 | 3 | | 3 | |
| 1968 | 3 | | 3 | |
| 1964 | 3 | | 3 | |

# DISTRICT OF COLUMBIA

## PRESIDENT 2004

| 2000 Census Population | Ward | Total Vote | Republican | Democratic | Other | Rep.-Dem. Plurality | Percentage | | | |
|---|---|---|---|---|---|---|---|---|---|---|
| | | | | | | | Total Vote | | Major Vote | |
| | | | | | | | Rep. | Dem. | Rep. | Dem. |
| 73,364 | Ward 1 | 26,096 | 1,751 | 23,727 | 618 | 21,976 D | 6.7% | 90.9% | 6.9% | 93.1% |
| 68,869 | Ward 2 | 24,933 | 3,713 | 20,691 | 529 | 16,978 D | 14.9% | 83.0% | 15.2% | 84.8% |
| 73,718 | Ward 3 | 35,993 | 6,953 | 28,358 | 682 | 21,405 D | 19.3% | 78.8% | 19.7% | 80.3% |
| 74,092 | Ward 4 | 32,849 | 2,156 | 30,341 | 352 | 28,185 D | 6.6% | 92.4% | 6.6% | 93.4% |
| 72,527 | Ward 5 | 29,177 | 1,520 | 27,348 | 309 | 25,828 D | 5.2% | 93.7% | 5.3% | 94.7% |
| 68,035 | Ward 6 | 29,531 | 3,339 | 25,654 | 538 | 22,315 D | 11.3% | 86.9% | 11.5% | 88.5% |
| 70,540 | Ward 7 | 27,112 | 1,006 | 25,914 | 192 | 24,908 D | 3.7% | 95.6% | 3.7% | 96.3% |
| 70,914 | Ward 8 | 20,683 | 689 | 19,872 | 122 | 19,183 D | 3.3% | 96.1% | 3.4% | 96.6% |
| | Federal Ballots | 1,212 | 129 | 1,065 | 18 | 936 D | 10.6% | 87.9% | 10.8% | 89.2% |
| 572,059 | TOTAL | 227,586 | 21,256 | 202,970 | 3,360 | 181,714 D | 9.3% | 89.2% | 9.5% | 90.5% |

Note: Federal ballots were for president only, were basically cast as absentee votes, and were not attributed to any particular ward.

# DISTRICT OF COLUMBIA

## PRESIDENT 2000

| 2000 Census Population | Ward | Total Vote | Republican | Democratic | Green (Nader) | Other | Rep.-Dem. Plurality | Percentage of Total Vote | | |
|---|---|---|---|---|---|---|---|---|---|---|
| | | | | | | | | Rep. | Dem. | Green |
| 80,014 | Ward 1 | 24,981 | 1,707 | 20,526 | 2,542 | 206 | 18,819 D | 6.8% | 82.2% | 10.2% |
| 82,845 | Ward 2 | 27,063 | 4,070 | 20,638 | 2,091 | 264 | 16,568 D | 15.0% | 76.3% | 7.7% |
| 79,566 | Ward 3 | 35,191 | 7,508 | 24,451 | 2,922 | 310 | 16,943 D | 21.3% | 69.5% | 8.3% |
| 71,393 | Ward 4 | 28,497 | 1,037 | 26,553 | 787 | 120 | 25,516 D | 3.6% | 93.2% | 2.8% |
| 65,548 | Ward 5 | 24,553 | 785 | 23,136 | 519 | 113 | 22,351 D | 3.2% | 94.2% | 2.1% |
| 65,457 | Ward 6 | 25,239 | 2,202 | 21,477 | 1,371 | 189 | 19,275 D | 8.7% | 85.1% | 5.4% |
| 64,704 | Ward 7 | 22,136 | 477 | 21,361 | 228 | 70 | 20,884 D | 2.2% | 96.5% | 1.0% |
| 61,537 | Ward 8 | 13,920 | 251 | 13,524 | 95 | 50 | 13,273 D | 1.8% | 97.2% | 0.7% |
| | Federal Ballots | 314 | 36 | 257 | 21 | | 221 D | 11.5% | 81.8% | 6.7% |
| 572,059 | TOTAL | 201,894 | 18,073 | 171,923 | 10,576 | 1,322 | 153,850 D | 9.0% | 85.2% | 5.2% |

Note: The ward populations provided by the District of Columbia total 571,059. The official Census Bureau 2000 population for the district is 572,059.

# DISTRICT OF COLUMBIA

## PRESIDENT 1996

| Ward | Total Vote | Republican | Democratic | Reform (Perot) | Other | Rep.-Dem. Plurality | Percentage of Total Vote | | |
|---|---|---|---|---|---|---|---|---|---|
| | | | | | | | Rep. | Dem. | Reform |
| Ward 1 | 21,450 | 1,503 | 18,121 | 426 | 1,400 | 16,618 D | 7.0% | 84.5% | 2.0% |
| Ward 2 | 23,666 | 3,888 | 17,987 | 610 | 1,181 | 14,099 D | 16.4% | 76.0% | 2.6% |
| Ward 3 | 32,287 | 7,671 | 21,975 | 817 | 1,824 | 14,304 D | 23.8% | 68.1% | 2.5% |
| Ward 4 | 27,148 | 980 | 25,121 | 479 | 568 | 24,141 D | 3.6% | 92.5% | 1.8% |
| Ward 5 | 23,318 | 744 | 21,760 | 394 | 420 | 21,016 D | 3.2% | 93.3% | 1.7% |
| Ward 6 | 22,767 | 1,822 | 19,694 | 438 | 813 | 17,872 D | 8.0% | 86.5% | 1.9% |
| Ward 7 | 21,584 | 488 | 20,599 | 284 | 213 | 20,111 D | 2.3% | 95.4% | 1.3% |
| Ward 8 | 13,158 | 210 | 12,661 | 161 | 126 | 12,451 D | 1.6% | 96.2% | 1.2% |
| FEDERAL BALLOTS | 348 | 33 | 302 | 2 | 11 | 269 D | 9.5% | 86.8% | 0.6% |
| TOTAL | 185,726 | 17,339 | 158,220 | 3,611 | 6,556 | 140,881 D | 9.3% | 85.2% | 1.9% |

# DISTRICT OF COLUMBIA

## PRESIDENT 1992

| 1990 Census Population | Ward | Total Vote | Republican | Democratic | Perot | Other | Plurality | Percentage Total Vote | | |
|---|---|---|---|---|---|---|---|---|---|---|
| | | | | | | | | Rep. | Dem. | Perot |
| 79,641 | WARD 1 | 26,488 | 1,892 | 22,832 | 1,112 | 652 | 20,940 D | 7.1% | 86.2% | 4.2% |
| 78,743 | WARD 2 | 28,512 | 4,157 | 22,143 | 1,692 | 520 | 17,986 D | 14.6% | 77.7% | 5.9% |
| 77,774 | WARD 3 | 38,007 | 8,001 | 26,906 | 2,606 | 494 | 18,905 D | 21.1% | 70.8% | 6.9% |
| 78,425 | WARD 4 | 32,932 | 1,650 | 29,457 | 1,068 | 757 | 27,807 D | 5.0% | 89.4% | 3.2% |
| 75,054 | WARD 5 | 29,034 | 1,352 | 26,243 | 814 | 625 | 24,891 D | 4.7% | 90.4% | 2.8% |
| 72,273 | WARD 6 | 28,360 | 2,115 | 24,329 | 1,294 | 622 | 22,214 D | 7.5% | 85.8% | 4.6% |
| 72,769 | WARD 7 | 26,985 | 924 | 24,882 | 638 | 541 | 23,958 D | 3.4% | 92.2% | 2.4% |
| 72,221 | WARD 8 | 16,819 | 546 | 15,484 | 431 | 358 | 14,938 D | 3.2% | 92.1% | 2.6% |
| | FEDERAL BALLOTS | 435 | 61 | 343 | 26 | 5 | 282 D | 14.0% | 78.9% | 6.0% |
| 606,900 | TOTAL | 227,572 | 20,698 | 192,619 | 9,681 | 4,574 | 171,921 D | 9.1% | 84.6% | 4.3% |

# DISTRICT OF COLUMBIA

## PRESIDENT 1988

| 1980 Census Population | Ward | Total Vote | Republican | Democratic | Other | Rep.-Dem. Plurality | Percentage | | | |
|---|---|---|---|---|---|---|---|---|---|---|
| | | | | | | | Total Vote | | Major Vote | |
| | | | | | | | Rep. | Dem. | Rep. | Dem. |
| 78,700 | WARD 1 | 21,827 | 2,563 | 18,523 | 741 | 15,960 D | 11.7% | 84.9% | 12.2% | 87.8% |
| 81,400 | WARD 2 | 24,135 | 5,231 | 18,270 | 634 | 13,039 D | 21.7% | 75.7% | 22.3% | 77.7% |
| 77,800 | WARD 3 | 35,655 | 11,696 | 23,402 | 557 | 11,706 D | 32.8% | 65.6% | 33.3% | 66.7% |
| 81,900 | WARD 4 | 29,022 | 2,116 | 25,763 | 1,143 | 23,647 D | 7.3% | 88.8% | 7.6% | 92.4% |
| 82,600 | WARD 5 | 24,855 | 1,432 | 22,532 | 891 | 21,100 D | 5.8% | 90.7% | 6.0% | 94.0% |
| 75,700 | WARD 6 | 23,233 | 2,727 | 19,779 | 727 | 17,052 D | 11.7% | 85.1% | 12.1% | 87.9% |
| 82,400 | WARD 7 | 21,592 | 1,108 | 19,689 | 795 | 18,581 D | 5.1% | 91.2% | 5.3% | 94.7% |
| 77,900 | WARD 8 | 11,921 | 526 | 11,009 | 386 | 10,483 D | 4.4% | 92.3% | 4.6% | 95.4% |
| | FEDERAL BALLOTS | 637 | 191 | 440 | 6 | 249 D | 30.0% | 69.1% | 30.3% | 69.7% |
| 638,400 | TOTAL | 192,877 | 27,590 | 159,407 | 5,880 | 131,817 D | 14.3% | 82.6% | 14.8% | 85.2% |

# DISTRICT OF COLUMBIA

## PRESIDENT 1984

| 1980 Census Population | Ward | Total Vote | Republican | Democratic | Other | Rep.-Dem. Plurality | Percentage | | | |
|---|---|---|---|---|---|---|---|---|---|---|
| | | | | | | | Total Vote | | Major Vote | |
| | | | | | | | Rep. | Dem. | Rep. | Dem. |
| 78,700 | WARD 1 | 23,501 | 2,550 | 20,638 | 313 | 18,088 D | 10.9% | 87.8% | 11.0% | 89.0% |
| 81,400 | WARD 2 | 25,393 | 5,435 | 19,677 | 281 | 14,242 D | 21.4% | 77.5% | 21.6% | 78.4% |
| 77,800 | WARD 3 | 35,047 | 12,496 | 22,234 | 317 | 9,738 D | 35.7% | 63.4% | 36.0% | 64.0% |
| 81,900 | WARD 4 | 32,084 | 2,264 | 29,551 | 269 | 27,287 D | 7.1% | 92.1% | 7.1% | 92.9% |
| 82,600 | WARD 5 | 28,112 | 1,523 | 26,394 | 195 | 24,871 D | 5.4% | 93.9% | 5.5% | 94.5% |
| 75,700 | WARD 6 | 25,239 | 2,589 | 22,415 | 235 | 19,826 D | 10.3% | 88.8% | 10.4% | 89.6% |
| 82,400 | WARD 7 | 25,195 | 1,303 | 23,734 | 158 | 22,431 D | 5.2% | 94.2% | 5.2% | 94.8% |
| 77,900 | WARD 8 | 16,101 | 628 | 15,377 | 96 | 14,749 D | 3.9% | 95.5% | 3.9% | 96.1% |
| | FEDERAL BALLOTS | 616 | 221 | 388 | 7 | 167 D | 35.9% | 63.0% | 36.3% | 63.7% |
| 638,400 | TOTAL | 211,288 | 29,009 | 180,408 | 1,871 | 151,399 D | 13.7% | 85.4% | 13.9% | 86.1% |

# DISTRICT OF COLUMBIA

## PRESIDENT 1980

| 1980 Census Population | Ward | Total Vote | Republican | Democratic | Other | Rep.-Dem. Plurality | Percentage | | | |
|---|---|---|---|---|---|---|---|---|---|---|
| | | | | | | | Total Vote | | Major Vote | |
| | | | | | | | Rep. | Dem. | Rep. | Dem. |
| 78,700 | WARD 1 | 18,804 | 1,870 | 14,060 | 2,874 | 12,190 D | 9.9% | 74.8% | 11.7% | 88.3% |
| 81,400 | WARD 2 | 20,194 | 3,409 | 13,156 | 3,629 | 9,747 D | 16.9% | 65.1% | 20.6% | 79.4% |
| 77,800 | WARD 3 | 35,759 | 12,654 | 15,258 | 7,847 | 2,604 D | 35.4% | 42.7% | 45.3% | 54.7% |
| 81,900 | WARD 4 | 27,273 | 1,734 | 23,993 | 1,546 | 22,259 D | 6.4% | 88.0% | 6.7% | 93.3% |
| 82,600 | WARD 5 | 22,562 | 1,040 | 20,497 | 1,025 | 19,457 D | 4.6% | 90.8% | 4.8% | 95.2% |
| 75,700 | WARD 6 | 19,064 | 1,550 | 15,022 | 2,492 | 13,472 D | 8.1% | 78.8% | 9.4% | 90.6% |
| 82,400 | WARD 7 | 20,857 | 935 | 19,138 | 784 | 18,203 D | 4.5% | 91.8% | 4.7% | 95.3% |
| 77,900 | WARD 8 | 10,622 | 336 | 9,918 | 368 | 9,582 D | 3.2% | 93.4% | 3.3% | 96.7% |
| | FEDERAL BALLOTS | 102 | 17 | 71 | 14 | 54 D | 16.7% | 69.6% | 19.3% | 80.7% |
| 638,400 | TOTAL | 175,237 | 23,545 | 131,113 | 20,579 | 107,568 D | 13.4% | 74.8% | 15.2% | 84.8% |

# DISTRICT OF COLUMBIA

## PRESIDENT 1976

| 1970 Census Population | Ward | Total Vote | Republican | Democratic | Other | Rep.-Dem. Plurality | Percentage | | | |
|---|---|---|---|---|---|---|---|---|---|---|
| | | | | | | | Total Vote | | Major Vote | |
| | | | | | | | Rep. | Dem. | Rep. | Dem. |
| 94,215 | WARD 1 | 16,577 | 2,064 | 13,982 | 531 | 11,918 D | 12.5% | 84.3% | 12.9% | 87.1% |
| 94,076 | WARD 2 | 19,245 | 4,019 | 14,638 | 588 | 10,619 D | 20.9% | 76.1% | 21.5% | 78.5% |
| 94,719 | WARD 3 | 35,729 | 15,184 | 19,583 | 962 | 4,399 D | 42.5% | 54.8% | 43.7% | 56.3% |
| 94,193 | WARD 4 | 26,785 | 2,064 | 24,432 | 289 | 22,368 D | 7.7% | 91.2% | 7.8% | 92.2% |
| 94,679 | WARD 5 | 21,503 | 1,365 | 19,932 | 206 | 18,567 D | 6.3% | 92.7% | 6.4% | 93.6% |
| 95,192 | WARD 6 | 16,947 | 1,575 | 15,032 | 340 | 13,457 D | 9.3% | 88.7% | 9.5% | 90.5% |
| 95,019 | WARD 7 | 20,641 | 1,136 | 19,372 | 133 | 18,236 D | 5.5% | 93.9% | 5.5% | 94.5% |
| 94,417 | WARD 8 | 11,403 | 466 | 10,847 | 90 | 10,381 D | 4.1% | 95.1% | 4.1% | 95.9% |
| 756,510 | TOTAL | 168,830 | 27,873 | 137,818 | 3,139 | 109,945 D | 16.5% | 81.6% | 16.8% | 83.2% |

# DISTRICT OF COLUMBIA

## PRESIDENT 1972

| 1970 Census Population | Ward | Total Vote | Republican | Democratic | Other | Rep.-Dem. Plurality | Percentage | | | |
|---|---|---|---|---|---|---|---|---|---|---|
| | | | | | | | Total Vote | | Major Vote | |
| | | | | | | | Rep. | Dem. | Rep. | Dem. |
| 94,215 | WARD 1 | 16,944 | 2,994 | 13,860 | 90 | 10,866 D | 17.7% | 81.8% | 17.8% | 82.2% |
| 94,076 | WARD 2 | 19,080 | 4,985 | 13,999 | 96 | 9,014 D | 26.1% | 73.4% | 26.3% | 73.7% |
| 94,719 | WARD 3 | 36,994 | 18,269 | 18,608 | 117 | 339 D | 49.4% | 50.3% | 49.5% | 50.5% |
| 94,193 | WARD 4 | 25,547 | 3,106 | 22,366 | 75 | 19,260 D | 12.2% | 87.5% | 12.2% | 87.8% |
| 94,679 | WARD 5 | 19,392 | 1,830 | 17,507 | 55 | 15,677 D | 9.4% | 90.3% | 9.5% | 90.5% |
| 95,192 | WARD 6 | 16,020 | 1,686 | 14,278 | 56 | 12,592 D | 10.5% | 89.1% | 10.6% | 89.4% |
| 95,019 | WARD 7 | 18,418 | 1,641 | 16,730 | 47 | 15,089 D | 8.9% | 90.8% | 8.9% | 91.1% |
| 94,417 | WARD 8 | 11,026 | 715 | 10,279 | 32 | 9,564 D | 6.5% | 93.2% | 6.5% | 93.5% |
| 756,510 | TOTAL | 163,421 | 35,226 | 127,627 | 568 | 92,401 D | 21.6% | 78.1% | 21.6% | 78.4% |

# DISTRICT OF COLUMBIA

## PRESIDENT 1968

| 1960 Census Population | Ward | Total Vote | Republican | Democratic | AIP | Other | Plurality | Percentage Total Vote | | |
|---|---|---|---|---|---|---|---|---|---|---|
| | | | | | | | | Rep. | Dem. | AIP |
| | WARD 1 | 14,563 | 1,692 | 12,871 | | | 11,179 D | 11.6% | 88.4% | |
| | WARD 2 | 13,604 | 3,031 | 10,573 | | | 7,542 D | 22.3% | 77.7% | |
| | WARD 3 | 37,151 | 17,169 | 19,982 | | | 2,813 D | 46.2% | 53.8% | |
| | WARD 4 | 26,082 | 2,568 | 23,514 | | | 20,946 D | 9.8% | 90.2% | |
| | WARD 5 | 22,489 | 1,209 | 21,280 | | | 20,071 D | 5.4% | 94.6% | |
| | WARD 6 | 14,046 | 1,217 | 12,829 | | | 11,612 D | 8.7% | 91.3% | |
| | WARD 7 | 21,997 | 1,626 | 20,371 | | | 18,745 D | 7.4% | 92.6% | |
| | WARD 8 | 15,187 | 995 | 14,192 | | | 13,197 D | 6.6% | 93.4% | |
| | FEDERAL BALLOTS | 5,459 | 1,505 | 3,954 | | | 2,449 D | 27.6% | 72.4% | |
| 763,956 | TOTAL | 170,578 | 31,012 | 139,566 | | | 108,554 D | 18.2% | 81.8% | |

# DISTRICT OF COLUMBIA

## ELECTION NOTES

**2004**    Other vote was 1,485 Independent (Ralph Nader); 737 D.C. Statehood Green (David Cobb); 502 Libertarian (Michael Badnarik); 130 Socialist Workers (James Harris); 506 write-in.

**2000**    Other vote was 669 Libertarian (Browne); 114 Socialist Workers (Harris); 539 scattered write-in.

**1996**    Other vote was 4,780 Green (Nader); 588 Libertarian (Browne); 283 Natural Law (Hagelin); 257 Socialist Workers (Harris); 648 scattered write-in.

**1992**    Other vote was 1,459 Fulani (New Alliance); 1,186 Daniels (Independent); 467 Marrou (Libertarian); 260 LaRouche (Independent); 230 Hagelin (Natural Law); 191 Brisben (Socialist); 105 Warren (Socialist Workers); 676 scattered write-in.

**1988**    Other vote was 2,901 Fulani (New Alliance); 554 Paul (Libertarian); 236 Martin (Third World Assembly); 208 Winn (Workers League); 163 LaRouche (Independent); 142 Kenoyer (Socialist); 123 Warren (Socialist Workers); 1,553 scattered write-in.

**1984**    Other vote was 279 Bergland (Libertarian); 257 Hall (Communist); 165 Serrette (Independent); 127 LaRouche (Independent); 127 Mason (Socialist Workers); 107 Holmes (Workers World); 809 scattered write-in.

**1980**    Other vote was 16,337 Anderson (Independent); 1,840 Commoner (Citizens); 1,114 Clark (Libertarian); 371 Hall (Communist); 173 DeBerry (Socialist Workers); 52 Griswold (Workers World); 692 scattered write-in. Early unamended canvass gave the vote as 23,313 Republican; 130,231 Democratic; 16,131 Anderson (Independent); 1,826 Citizens; 1,104 Libertarian; 369 Communist; 690 scattered write-in.

**1976**    Other vote was 545 Camejo (Socialist Workers); 274 MacBride (Libertarian); 219 Hall (Communist); 157 LaRouche (U.S. Labor); 1,944 scattered write-in.

**1972**    Other vote was 316 Reed (Socialist Workers); 252 Hall (Communist).

**1968**

**1964**    Under the 23rd Amendment to the Constitution, the District of Columbia in 1964 was entitled for the first time to choose three Electors. There is no table included for the 1964 election because it was held without ward divisions; returns were reported only by precinct. The total votes cast for the candidates by party are included in the summary table at the beginning of the District of Columbia chapter.

# 2004 PRESIDENTIAL PRIMARIES

In 2004, 37 states and the District of Columbia held presidential primaries, in which at least one of the parties held contests where voters balloted directly for candidates or for a statewide slate of delegates that was pledged to a candidate. The total of primaries includes Democratic party-run contests in South Carolina and Utah, but does not include similar events in Michigan and New Mexico that were designated as caucuses by the Democratic state parties. The Democratic presidential primary in the District of Columbia that kicked off the 2004 primary season was a nonbinding event and was not involved in the selection of delegates. States that are not listed did not hold a presidential primary of any kind in 2004.

The list below, alphabetical by state, gives primary vote totals for all candidates that were listed on the ballot in at least one primary. The tables on pages 1092 to1094 give a chronological summary of the primary votes for those candidates in Republican and Democratic parties who received at least 200,000 votes nationwide.

Republican candidates on the ballot in at least one primary were: Blake Ashby, Richard P. Bosa, John Buchanan, George W. Bush, Michael Callis, George Gostigian, Robert Edward Haines, Mark "Dick" Harnes, Millie Howard, "Tom" Laughlin, Cornelius E. O'Connor, John Donald Rigazio, "Jim" Taylor, and Bill Wyatt.

Democratic candidates on the ballot in at least one primary were: George H. Ballard III, William Barchilon, Dianne Barker, Katherine Bateman, Keith Brand, Carol Moseley Braun, Harry W. Braun III, Ray Caplette, Willie Felix Carter, Jeanne Chebib, Wesley Clark, Randy Crow, Howard Dean, Gerry Dokka, John Edwards, Richard A. Gephardt, Mildred Glover, Vincent S. Hamm, Arthur H. Jackson Jr., John Kerry, Caroline Pettinato Killeen, Dennis J. Kucinich, Lyndon H. LaRouche Jr., R. Randy Lee, Joseph I. Lieberman, Robert H. Linnell, "Bill" McGaughey, Huda Muhammad, Edward Thomas O'Donnell Jr., Fern Penna, Al Sharpton, Vermin Supreme, Leonard Dennis Talbow, Evelyn Vitullo, Florence Walker, Lucian Wojciechowski, and Bill Wyatt.

## ALABAMA JUNE 1

Republican    187,038 Bush; 14,449 Uncommitted.

Democratic    164,021 Kerry; 38,223 Uncommitted; 9,076 Kucinich; 7,254 LaRouche.

## ARIZONA FEBRUARY 3

Republican    No presidential primary.

Democratic    101,809 Kerry; 63,256 Clark; 33,555 Dean; 16,596 Edwards; 15,906 Lieberman; 3,896 Kucinich; 1,177 Sharpton; 755 Gephardt; 325 Moseley Braun; 295 LaRouche; 257 Barker; 233 Wyatt; 225 Brand; 208 Penna; 136 Barchilon; 119 Muhammad; 117 Vitullo; 77 Caplette.

## ARKANSAS MAY 18

Republican    37,234 Bush; 1,129 Uncommitted.

Democratic    177,754 Kerry; 61,800 Uncommitted; 13,766 Kucinich; 13,528 LaRouche.

## CALIFORNIA MARCH 2

Republican    2,216,047 Bush; 95 Warrick (write-in); 90 Wyatt (write-in); 56 Ashby (write-in); 22 Barton (write-in); 17 Holtz (write-in); 12 Bosa (write-in); 12 Castellano (write-in).

Democratic    2,002,539 Kerry; 614,441 Edwards; 144,954 Kucinich; 130,892 Dean; 59,326 Sharpton; 52,780 Lieberman; 51,084 Clark; 24,501 Moseley Braun; 19,139 Gephardt; 7,953 LaRouche; 6 Dunmar (write-in); 4 Alexander-Pace (write-in); 4 Nigro (write-in); 3 Giacomuzzi (write-in); 3 Penna (write-in). A total of 3,107,629 votes were cast in the Democratic primary, 2,900,256 by registered Democratic voters and 207,353 votes by registered Unaffiliated voters. The two categories were tallied separately but combined into an overall vote, which also includes 20 write-in votes.

# 2004 PRESIDENTIAL PRIMARIES

## CONNECTICUT MARCH 2

Republican    No presidential primary. Bush unopposed.

Democratic    75,860 Kerry; 30,844 Edwards; 6,705 Lieberman; 5,166 Dean; 4,133 Kucinich; 3,312 Sharpton; 1,546 Clark; 1,467 LaRouche; 990 Uncommitted.

## DELAWARE FEBRUARY 3

Republican    No presidential primary.

Democratic    16,787 Kerry; 3,706 Lieberman; 3,674 Edwards; 3,462 Dean; 3,165 Clark; 1,888 Sharpton; 344 Kucinich; 187 Gephardt; 78 LaRouche.

## DISTRICT OF COLUMBIA JANUARY 13

Republican    No presidential primary.

Democratic    18,132 Dean; 14,639 Sharpton; 4,924 Moseley Braun; 3,481 Kucinich; 522 LaRouche; 257 Walker; 241 Jackson; 149 Supreme; 85 Braun; 46 Chebib; 40 Wojciechowski.

## FLORIDA MARCH 9

Republican    No presidential primary. Bush unopposed.

Democratic    581,672 Kerry; 75,703 Edwards; 21,031 Sharpton; 20,834 Dean; 17,198 Kucinich; 14,287 Lieberman; 10,226 Clark; 6,789 Moseley Braun; 6,022 Gephardt.

## GEORGIA MARCH 2

Republican    161,374 Bush.

Democratic    293,265 Kerry; 259,386 Edwards; 39,129 Sharpton; 11,322 Dean; 7,701 Kucinich; 5,666 Lieberman; 4,247 Clark; 3,747 Moseley Braun; 2,350 Gephardt.

## IDAHO MAY 25

Republican    110,800 Bush; 12,993 None of the Names Shown; 15 Warrick (write-in).

Democratic    25,921 Kerry; 2,479 None of the Names Shown; 1,568 Kucinich; 927 Sharpton; 590 LaRouche.

## ILLINOIS MARCH 16

Republican    583,575 Bush.

Democratic    873,230 Kerry; 131,966 Edwards; 53,249 Moseley Braun; 47,343 Dean; 36,123 Sharpton; 28,083 Kucinich; 24,354 Lieberman; 19,304 Clark; 3,863 LaRouche.

## INDIANA MAY 4

Republican    469,528 Bush.

Democratic    231,047 Kerry; 35,651 Edwards; 21,482 Dean; 17,437 Clark; 7,003 Kucinich; 4,591 LaRouche.

# 2004 PRESIDENTIAL PRIMARIES

## KENTUCKY MAY 18

Republican   108,603 Bush; 8,776 Uncommitted.

Democratic   138,175 Kerry; 33,403 Edwards; 21,199 Uncommitted; 11,062 Lieberman; 8,222 Dean; 6,519 Clark; 5,022 Sharpton; 4,508 Kucinich; 1,806 LaRouche.

## LOUISIANA MARCH 9

Republican   69,205 Bush; 2,805 Wyatt.

Democratic   112,639 Kerry; 26,074 Edwards; 7,948 Dean; 7,091 Clark; 3,161 McGaughey; 2,411 Kucinich; 2,329 LaRouche.

## MARYLAND MARCH 2

Republican   151,943 Bush.

Democratic   286,955 Kerry; 123,006 Edwards; 21,810 Sharpton; 12,461 Dean; 8,693 Kucinich; 8,527 Uncommitted; 5,245 Lieberman; 4,230 Clark; 4,039 Glover; 2,809 Moseley Braun; 2,146 Gephardt; 1,555 LaRouche.

## MASSACHUSETTS MARCH 2

Republican   62,773 Bush; 6,050 No Preference; 267 Kerry (write-in); 75 McCain (write-in); 63 Nader (write-in); 50 Edwards (write-in); 1,376 scattered write-in.

Democratic   440,964 Kerry; 108,051 Edwards; 25,198 Kucinich; 17,076 Dean; 6,123 Sharpton; 5,432 Lieberman; 4,451 No Preference; 3,109 Clark; 1,455 Gephardt; 1,019 Moseley Braun; 970 LaRouche; 168 Nader (write-in); 155 Robinson-Leon; 91 Bush (write-in); 34 H.R. Clinton (write-in); 892 scattered write-in.

## MISSISSIPPI MARCH 9

Republican   No presidential primary.

Democratic   59,815 Kerry; 5,582 Edwards; 3,933 Sharpton; 1,997 Dean; 1,878 Clark; 1,370 Uncommitted; 768 Kucinich; 716 Lieberman; 239 LaRouche.

## MISSOURI FEBRUARY 3

Republican   117,007 Bush; 3,830 Uncommitted; 1,268 Wyatt; 981 Ashby.

Democratic   211,745 Kerry; 103,088 Edwards; 36,288 Dean; 18,340 Clark; 14,727 Lieberman; 14,308 Sharpton; 8,281 Gephardt; 4,875 Kucinich; 4,311 Uncommitted; 1,088 Moseley Braun; 953 LaRouche; 335 Penna.

## MONTANA JUNE 8

Republican   106,407 Bush; 6,340 No Preference; 1 Warrick (write-in).

Democratic   63,611 Kerry; 9,686 Kucinich; 8,516 Edwards; 6,899 No Preference; 4,081 Clark; 750 LaRouche.

## NEBRASKA MAY 11

Republican   121,355 Bush.

Democratic   52,479 Kerry; 10,031 Edwards; 5,400 Dean; 1,490 Kucinich; 1,367 Sharpton; 805 LaRouche.

# 2004 PRESIDENTIAL PRIMARIES

## NEW HAMPSHIRE JANUARY 27

Republican
53,962 Bush; 2,819 Kerry (write-in); 1,789 Dean (write-in); 1,407 Clark (write-in); 1,088 Edwards (write-in); 914 Lieberman (write-in); 841 Bosa; 836 Buchanan; 803 Rigazio; 579 Haines; 388 Callis; 264 Ashby; 239 Howard; 154 Laughlin; 153 Wyatt; 124 Taylor; 87 Harnes; 77 O'Connor; 52 Gostigian; 38 Kucinich (write-in); 15 Sharpton (write-in); 6 Moseley Braun (write-in); 5 LaRouche (write-in); 4 Gephardt (write-in); 3 Bateman (write-in); 1 Carter (write-in); 1 Linnell (write-in); 1 O'Donnell (write-in); 1 Penna (write-in); 973 scattered write-in.

Democratic
84,377 Kerry; 57,761 Dean; 27,314 Clark; 26,487 Edwards; 18,911 Lieberman; 3,114 Kucinich; 419 Gephardt; 347 Sharpton; 257 Bush (write-in); 90 LaRouche; 86 Carter; 81 Moseley Braun; 79 O'Donnell; 68 Bateman; 60 Crow; 58 Hamm; 49 Linnell; 42 Dokka; 31 Killeen; 15 Lee; 13 Braun; 11 Glover; 8 Penna; 8 Talbow; 5 Rigazio (write-in); 2 Ashby (write-in); 2 Buchanan (write-in); 92 scattered write-in.

## NEW JERSEY JUNE 8

Republican
141,752 Bush.

Democratic
198,213 Kerry; 9,251 Kucinich; 4,514 LaRouche; 2,826 Ballard.

## NEW MEXICO JUNE 6

Republican
49,165 Bush.

Democratic
No presidential primary.

## NEW YORK MARCH 2

Republican
No presidential primary. Bush unopposed.

Democratic
437,754 Kerry; 143,960 Edwards; 57,456 Sharpton; 36,680 Kucinich; 20,471 Dean; 9,314 Lieberman; 3,954 Gephardt; 3,517 Clark; 2,527 LaRouche.

## OHIO MARCH 2

Republican
793,833 Bush.

Democratic
632,599 Kerry; 416,106 Edwards; 110,067 Kucinich; 30,983 Dean; 14,676 Lieberman; 12,577 Clark; 4,018 LaRouche. The Democratic presidential vote was compiled by the Ohio secretary of state by congressional district. *America Votes* aggregated the results into statewide totals for each candidate.

## OKLAHOMA FEBRUARY 3

Republican
59,577 Bush; 6,621 Wyatt.

Democratic
90,526 Clark; 89,310 Edwards; 81,073 Kerry; 19,680 Lieberman; 12,734 Dean; 3,939 Sharpton; 2,544 Kucinich; 1,890 Gephardt; 689 LaRouche.

## OREGON MAY 18

Republican
293,806 Bush; 15,700 scattered write-in.

Democratic
289,804 Kerry; 60,019 Kucinich; 8,571 LaRouche; 10,150 scattered write-in.

# 2004 PRESIDENTIAL PRIMARIES

## PENNSYLVANIA APRIL 27

Republican   861,555 Bush.

Democratic   585,683 Kerry; 79,799 Dean; 76,762 Edwards; 30,110 Kucinich; 17,528 LaRouche.

## RHODE ISLAND MARCH 2

Republican   2,152 Bush; 314 Uncommitted; 15 Kerry (write-in); 12 McCain (write-in); 6 Nader (write-in); 5 Edwards (write-in); 31 scattered write-in.

Democratic   25,466 Kerry; 6,635 Edwards; 1,425 Dean; 1,054 Kucinich; 415 Uncommitted; 303 Lieberman; 237 Clark; 63 LaRouche; 52 H.R. Clinton (write-in); 38 Sharpton (write-in); 10 Bush (write-in); 9 Nader (write-in); 52 scattered write-in.

## SOUTH CAROLINA FEBRUARY 3

Republican   No presidential primary.

Democratic   132,660 Edwards; 87,620 Kerry; 28,495 Sharpton; 21,218 Clark; 13,984 Dean; 7,101 Lieberman; 1,344 Kucinich; 828 Gephardt; 593 Moseley Braun.

## SOUTH DAKOTA JUNE 1

Republican   No presidential primary. Bush unopposed.

Democratic   69,473 Kerry; 5,105 Uncommitted; 4,838 Dean; 2,943 LaRouche; 2,046 Kucinich.

## TENNESSEE FEBRUARY 10

Republican   94,557 Bush; 4,504 Uncommitted.

Democratic   151,527 Kerry; 97,914 Edwards; 85,315 Clark; 16,128 Dean; 6,107 Sharpton; 3,213 Lieberman; 2,727 Uncommitted; 2,490 Moseley Braun; 2,279 Kucinich; 1,402 Gephardt; 283 LaRouche.

## TEXAS MARCH 9

Republican   635,948 Bush; 51,667 Uncommitted.

Democratic   563,237 Kerry; 120,413 Edwards; 40,035 Dean; 31,020 Sharpton; 25,245 Lieberman; 18,437 Clark; 15,475 Kucinich; 12,160 Gephardt; 6,871 LaRouche; 6,338 Crow.

## UTAH FEBRUARY 24

Republican   No presidential primary.

Democratic   19,232 Kerry; 10,384 Edwards; 2,590 Kucinich; 1,335 Dean; 489 Clark; 402 Lieberman; 298 Uncommitted; 124 Gephardt.

## VERMONT MARCH 2

Republican   25,415 Bush; 874 scattered write-in.

Democratic   44,393 Dean; 26,171 Kerry; 5,113 Edwards (write-in); 3,396 Kucinich; 2,749 Clark; 386 LaRouche; 673 scattered write-in.

# 2004 PRESIDENTIAL PRIMARIES

## VIRGINIA FEBRUARY 10

Republican    No presidential primary.

Democratic    204,142 Kerry; 105,504 Edwards; 36,572 Clark; 27,637 Dean; 12,864 Sharpton; 5,016 Kucinich; 2,866 Lieberman; 1,042 LaRouche; 580 Gephardt.

## WEST VIRGINIA MAY 11

Republican    111,109 Bush.

Democratic    175,065 Kerry; 33,950 Edwards; 13,881 Lieberman; 10,576 Dean; 9,170 Clark; 6,114 Kucinich; 4,083 LaRouche.

## WISCONSIN FEBRUARY 17

Republican    158,933 Bush; 1,184 Uninstructed Delegation; 311 scattered write-in.

Democratic    328,358 Kerry; 284,163 Edwards; 150,845 Dean; 27,353 Kucinich; 14,701 Sharpton; 12,713 Clark; 3,929 Lieberman; 1,637 LaRouche; 1,590 Moseley Braun; 1,263 Gephardt; 1,146 Uninstructed Delegation; 666 scattered write-in.

# 2004 REPUBLICAN PRESIDENTIAL PRIMARIES

| Date | State | Total Vote | Bush | Other |
|---|---|---|---|---|
| Jan. 27 | New Hampshire | 67,624 | 53,962<br>**79.8%** | 13,662<br>**20.2%** |
| Feb. 3 | Missouri | 123,086 | 117,007<br>**95.1%** | 6,079<br>**4.9%** |
| Feb. 3 | Oklahoma | 66,198 | 59,577<br>**90.0%** | 6,621<br>**10.0%** |
| Feb. 10 | Tennessee | 99,061 | 94,557<br>**95.5%** | 4,504<br>**4.5%** |
| Feb. 17 | Wisconsin | 160,428 | 158,933<br>**99.1%** | 1,495<br>**0.9%** |
| March 2 | California | 2,216,351 | 2,216,047<br>**100.0%** | 304 |
| March 2 | Georgia | 161,374 | 161,374<br>**100.0%** | |
| March 2 | Maryland | 151,943 | 151,943<br>**100.0%** | |
| March 2 | Massachusetts | 70,654 | 62,773<br>**88.8%** | 7,881<br>**11.2%** |
| March 2 | Ohio | 793,833 | 793,833<br>**100.0%** | |
| March 2 | Rhode Island | 2,535 | 2,152<br>**84.9%** | 383<br>**15.1%** |
| March 2 | Vermont | 26,289 | 25,415<br>**96.7%** | 874<br>**3.3%** |
| March 9 | Louisiana | 72,010 | 69,205<br>**96.1%** | 2,805<br>**3.9%** |
| March 9 | Texas | 687,615 | 635,948<br>**92.5%** | 51,667<br>**7.5%** |
| March 16 | Illinois | 583,575 | 583,575<br>**100.0%** | |
| April 27 | Pennsylvania | 861,555 | 861,555<br>**100.0%** | |
| May 4 | Indiana | 469,528 | 469,528<br>**100.0%** | |
| May 11 | Nebraska | 121,355 | 121,355<br>**100.0%** | |
| May 11 | West Virginia | 111,109 | 111,109<br>**100.0%** | |
| May 18 | Arkansas | 38,363 | 37,234<br>**97.1%** | 1,129<br>**2.9%** |
| May 18 | Kentucky | 117,379 | 108,603<br>**92.5%** | 8,776<br>**7.5%** |
| May 18 | Oregon | 309,506 | 293,806<br>**94.9%** | 15,700<br>**5.1%** |
| May 25 | Idaho | 123,808 | 110,800<br>**89.5%** | 13,008<br>**10.5%** |
| June 1 | Alabama | 201,487 | 187,038<br>**92.8%** | 14,449<br>**7.2%** |
| June 1 | New Mexico | 49,165 | 49,165<br>**100.0%** | |
| June 8 | Montana | 112,748 | 106,407<br>**94.4%** | 6,341<br>**5.6%** |
| June 8 | New Jersey | 141,752 | 141,752<br>**100.0%** | |
| | Total | 7,940,331 | 7,784,653<br>**98.0%** | 155,678<br>**2.0%** |

Notes: Other vote for entries that were on the ballot in at least one primary: 111,236 Uncommitted; 10,937 Wyatt; 1,301 Ashby; 853 Bosa; 836 Buchanan; 803 Rigazio; 579 Haines; 388 Callis; 239 Howard; 154 Laughlin; 124 Taylor; 87 Harnes; 77 O'Connor; 52 Gostigian; 28,012 scattered write-in.

The Uncommitted total includes votes cast on the following ballot lines: Uncommitted, None of the Names Shown, No Preference, and Uninstructed Delegation.

# 2004 DEMOCRATIC PRESIDENTIAL PRIMARIES

| Date | State | Total Vote | Clark | Dean | Edwards | Kerry | Kucinich | Lieberman | Sharpton | Other |
|---|---|---|---|---|---|---|---|---|---|---|
| Jan. 13 | District of Columbia | 42,516 | | 18,132 | | | 3,481 | | 14,639 | 6,264 |
| | | | | 42.6% | | | 8.2% | | 34.4% | 14.7% |
| Jan. 27 | New Hampshire | 219,787 | 27,314 | 57,761 | 26,487 | 84,377 | 3,114 | 18,911 | 347 | 1,476 |
| | | | 12.4% | 26.3% | 12.1% | 38.4% | 1.4% | 8.6% | 0.2% | 0.7% |
| Feb. 3 | Arizona | 238,942 | 63,256 | 33,555 | 16,596 | 101,809 | 3,896 | 15,906 | 1,177 | 2,747 |
| | | | 26.5% | 14.0% | 6.9% | 42.6% | 1.6% | 6.7% | 0.5% | 1.1% |
| Feb. 3 | Delaware | 33,291 | 3,165 | 3,462 | 3,674 | 16,787 | 344 | 3,706 | 1,888 | 265 |
| | | | 9.5% | 10.4% | 11.0% | 50.4% | 1.0% | 11.1% | 5.7% | 0.8% |
| Feb. 3 | Missouri | 418,339 | 18,340 | 36,288 | 103,088 | 211,745 | 4,875 | 14,727 | 14,308 | 14,968 |
| | | | 4.4% | 8.7% | 24.6% | 50.6% | 1.2% | 3.5% | 3.4% | 3.6% |
| Feb. 3 | Oklahoma | 302,385 | 90,526 | 12,734 | 89,310 | 81,073 | 2,544 | 19,680 | 3,939 | 2,579 |
| | | | 29.9% | 4.2% | 29.5% | 26.8% | 0.8% | 6.5% | 1.3% | 0.9% |
| Feb. 3 | South Carolina | 293,843 | 21,218 | 13,984 | 132,660 | 87,620 | 1,344 | 7,101 | 28,495 | 1,421 |
| | | | 7.2% | 4.8% | 45.1% | 29.8% | 0.5% | 2.4% | 9.7% | 0.5% |
| Feb. 10 | Tennessee | 369,385 | 85,315 | 16,128 | 97,914 | 151,527 | 2,279 | 3,213 | 6,107 | 6,902 |
| | | | 23.1% | 4.4% | 26.5% | 41.0% | 0.6% | 0.9% | 1.7% | 1.9% |
| Feb. 10 | Virginia | 396,223 | 36,572 | 27,637 | 105,504 | 204,142 | 5,016 | 2,866 | 12,864 | 1,622 |
| | | | 9.2% | 7.0% | 26.6% | 51.5% | 1.3% | 0.7% | 3.2% | 0.4% |
| Feb. 17 | Wisconsin | 828,364 | 12,713 | 150,845 | 284,163 | 328,358 | 27,353 | 3,929 | 14,701 | 6,302 |
| | | | 1.5% | 18.2% | 34.3% | 39.6% | 3.3% | 0.5% | 1.8% | 0.8% |
| Feb. 24 | Utah | 34,854 | 489 | 1,335 | 10,384 | 19,232 | 2,590 | 402 | | 422 |
| | | | 1.4% | 3.8% | 29.8% | 55.2% | 7.4% | 1.2% | | 1.2% |
| March 2 | California | 3,107,629 | 51,084 | 130,892 | 614,441 | 2,002,539 | 144,954 | 52,780 | 59,326 | 51,613 |
| | | | 1.6% | 4.2% | 19.8% | 64.4% | 4.7% | 1.7% | 1.9% | 1.7% |
| March 2 | Connecticut | 130,023 | 1,546 | 5,166 | 30,844 | 75,860 | 4,133 | 6,705 | 3,312 | 2,457 |
| | | | 1.2% | 4.0% | 23.7% | 58.3% | 3.2% | 5.2% | 2.5% | 1.9% |
| March 2 | Georgia | 626,813 | 4,247 | 11,322 | 259,386 | 293,265 | 7,701 | 5,666 | 39,129 | 6,097 |
| | | | 0.7% | 1.8% | 41.4% | 46.8% | 1.2% | 0.9% | 6.2% | 1.0% |
| March 2 | Maryland | 481,476 | 4,230 | 12,461 | 123,006 | 286,955 | 8,693 | 5,245 | 21,810 | 19,076 |
| | | | 0.9% | 2.6% | 25.5% | 59.6% | 1.8% | 1.1% | 4.5% | 4.0% |
| March 2 | Massachusetts | 615,188 | 3,109 | 17,076 | 108,051 | 440,964 | 25,198 | 5,432 | 6,123 | 9,235 |
| | | | 0.5% | 2.8% | 17.6% | 71.7% | 4.1% | 0.9% | 1.0% | 1.5% |
| March 2 | New York | 715,633 | 3,517 | 20,471 | 143,960 | 437,754 | 36,680 | 9,314 | 57,456 | 6,481 |
| | | | 0.5% | 2.9% | 20.1% | 61.2% | 5.1% | 1.3% | 8.0% | 0.9% |
| March 2 | Ohio | 1,221,026 | 12,577 | 30,983 | 416,106 | 632,599 | 110,067 | 14,676 | | 4,018 |
| | | | 1.0% | 2.5% | 34.1% | 51.8% | 9.0% | 1.2% | | 0.3% |
| March 2 | Rhode Island | 35,759 | 237 | 1,425 | 6,635 | 25,466 | 1,054 | 303 | 38 | 601 |
| | | | 0.7% | 4.0% | 18.6% | 71.2% | 2.9% | 0.8% | 0.1% | 1.7% |
| March 2 | Vermont | 82,881 | 2,749 | 44,393 | 5,113 | 26,171 | 3,396 | | | 1,059 |
| | | | 3.3% | 53.6% | 6.2% | 31.6% | 4.1% | | | 1.3% |
| March 9 | Florida | 753,762 | 10,226 | 20,834 | 75,703 | 581,672 | 17,198 | 14,287 | 21,031 | 12,811 |
| | | | 1.4% | 2.8% | 10.0% | 77.2% | 2.3% | 1.9% | 2.8% | 1.7% |
| March 9 | Louisiana | 161,653 | 7,091 | 7,948 | 26,074 | 112,639 | 2,411 | | | 5,490 |
| | | | 4.4% | 4.9% | 16.1% | 69.7% | 1.5% | | | 3.4% |
| March 9 | Mississippi | 76,298 | 1,878 | 1,997 | 5,582 | 59,815 | 768 | 716 | 3,933 | 1,609 |
| | | | 2.5% | 2.6% | 7.3% | 78.4% | 1.0% | 0.9% | 5.2% | 2.1% |
| March 9 | Texas | 839,231 | 18,437 | 40,035 | 120,413 | 563,237 | 15,475 | 25,245 | 31,020 | 25,369 |
| | | | 2.2% | 4.8% | 14.3% | 67.1% | 1.8% | 3.0% | 3.7% | 3.0% |
| March 16 | Illinois | 1,217,515 | 19,304 | 47,343 | 131,966 | 873,230 | 28,083 | 24,354 | 36,123 | 57,112 |
| | | | 1.6% | 3.9% | 10.8% | 71.7% | 2.3% | 2.0% | 3.0% | 4.7% |
| April 27 | Pennsylvania | 789,882 | | 79,799 | 76,762 | 585,683 | 30,110 | | | 17,528 |
| | | | | 10.1% | 9.7% | 74.1% | 3.8% | | | 2.2% |
| May 4 | Indiana | 317,211 | 17,437 | 21,482 | 35,651 | 231,047 | 7,003 | | | 4,591 |
| | | | 5.5% | 6.8% | 11.2% | 72.8% | 2.2% | | | 1.4% |
| May 11 | Nebraska | 71,572 | | 5,400 | 10,031 | 52,479 | 1,490 | | 1,367 | 805 |
| | | | | 7.5% | 14.0% | 73.3% | 2.1% | | 1.9% | 1.1% |
| May 11 | West Virginia | 252,839 | 9,170 | 10,576 | 33,950 | 175,065 | 6,114 | 13,881 | | 4,083 |
| | | | 3.6% | 4.2% | 13.4% | 69.2% | 2.4% | 5.5% | | 1.6% |
| May 18 | Arkansas | 266,848 | | | | 177,754 | 13,766 | | | 75,328 |
| | | | | | | 66.6% | 5.2% | | | 28.2% |

# 2004 DEMOCRATIC PRESIDENTIAL PRIMARIES

| Date | | State | Total Vote | Clark | Dean | Edwards | Kerry | Kucinich | Lieberman | Sharpton | Other |
|---|---|---|---|---|---|---|---|---|---|---|---|
| May | 18 | Kentucky | 229,916 | 6,519 2.8% | 8,222 3.6% | 33,403 14.5% | 138,175 60.1% | 4,508 2.0% | 11,062 4.8% | 5,022 2.2% | 23,005 10.0% |
| May | 18 | Oregon | 368,544 | | | | 289,804 78.6% | 60,019 16.3% | | | 18,721 5.1% |
| May | 25 | Idaho | 31,485 | | | | 25,921 82.3% | 1,568 5.0% | | 927 2.9% | 3,069 9.7% |
| June | 1 | Alabama | 218,574 | | | | 164,021 75.0% | 9,076 4.2% | | | 45,477 20.8% |
| June | 1 | South Dakota | 84,405 | | 4,838 5.7% | | 69,473 82.3% | 2,046 2.4% | | | 8,048 9.5% |
| June | 8 | Montana | 93,543 | 4,081 4.4% | | 8,516 9.1% | 63,611 68.0% | 9,686 10.4% | | | 7,649 8.2% |
| June | 8 | New Jersey | 214,804 | | | | 198,213 92.3% | 9,251 4.3% | | | 7,340 3.4% |
| | | TOTAL | 16,182,439 | 536,347 3.3% | 894,524 5.5% | 3,135,373 19.4% | 9,870,082 61.0% | 617,284 3.8% | 280,107 1.7% | 385,082 2.4% | 463,640 2.9% |

Notes: The votes cast for Edwards in Vermont and Sharpton in Rhode Island were write-ins.

Candidates that received at least 200,000 votes in the Democratic primaries are included in the table above. Other vote for entries that were on the ballot in at least one primary: 159,940 Uncommitted; 104,793 LaRouche; 103,205 Moseley Braun; 62,955 Gephardt; 6,398 Crow; 4,050 Glover; 3,161 McGaughey; 2,826 Ballard; 554 Penna; 257 Barker; 257 Walker; 241 Jackson; 233 Wyatt; 225 Brand; 149 Supreme; 136 Barchilon; 119 Muhammad; 117 Vitullo; 98 Braun; 86 Carter; 79 O'Donnell; 77 Caplette; 68 Bateman; 58 Hamm; 49 Linnell; 46 Chebib; 42 Dokka; 40 Wojciechowski; 31 Killeen; 15 Lee; 8 Talbow; 13,327 scattered write-in.

The Uncommitted total includes votes cast on the following ballot lines: Uncommitted, None of the Names Shown, No Preference, and Uninstructed Delegation.

# 2000 PRESIDENTIAL PRIMARIES

In 2000 42 states and the District of Columbia held presidential primaries, in which at least one of the parties held contests where voters balloted directly for candidates or for a statewide slate of delegates that was pledged to a candidate. In addition, there was a Republican primary in New York where delegates were elected on a congressional district basis.

The list below, alphabetical by state, lists primary vote totals for all candidates. The tables on pages 1101 and 1103 give a chronological list of the primary votes for those candidates in the Democratic and Republican parties who received at least 100,000 votes nationwide.

Republican candidates on the ballot in at least one state were: James Attia, Gary Bauer, Samuel H. Berry Jr., George W. Bush, Kenneth A. Capalbo, Steve Forbes, Mark "Dick" Harnes, Orrin G. Hatch, Lawrence L. Hornung, Alan Keyes, Andy Martin, John McCain, John R. McGrath, Timothy Lee Mosby, Tom Oyler, Richard C. Peet, Chuck See, Charles Bass Urban, Dorian Yeager, and James T. Zanon.

Democratic candidates on the ballot in at least one state were: Bill Bradley, Charles Buckley, Willie F. Carter, Thomas Coos, Randolph "Randy" W. Crow, John B. Eaton, Al Gore, Mark Greenstein, Vincent S. Hamm, Heather Harder, Lyndon H. LaRouche Jr., Angus Wheeler McDonald, Nathaniel Thomas Mullins, Edward T. O'Donnell Jr., Jeffrey B. Peters, Pat Price, Michael Skok, and Jim Taylor.

## ALABAMA JUNE 6

Republican    171,077 Bush; 23,394 Keyes; 8,608 Uncommitted.

Democratic    214,541 Gore; 48,521 Uncommitted; 15,456 LaRouche.

## ARIZONA

Republican    193,708 McCain; 115,115 Bush; 11,500 Keyes; 1,211 Forbes; 637 Hatch; 239 McGrath; 177 Bauer;
(February 22)    54 Zanon; 28 See.

Democratic    67,582 Gore; 16,383 Bradley; 1,439 No Preference; 1,358 Harder.
(March 11)

## ARKANSAS MAY 23

Republican    35,759 Bush; 8,814 Keyes.

Democratic    193,750 Gore; 53,150 LaRouche.

## CALIFORNIA MARCH 7

Republican    1,725,162 Bush; 988,706 McCain; 112,747 Keyes; 8,449 Forbes; 6,860 Bauer; 5,997 Hatch.

Democratic    2,155,321 Gore; 482,882 Bradley; 15,911 LaRouche.

## COLORADO MARCH 10

Republican    116,897 Bush; 48,996 McCain; 11,871 Keyes; 1,197 Forbes; 1,190 Bauer; 504 Hatch.

Democratic    63,384 Gore; 20,663 Bradley; 3,867 Non-committed; 821 LaRouche.

# 2000 PRESIDENTIAL PRIMARIES

## CONNECTICUT MARCH 7

Republican     87,176 McCain; 82,881 Bush; 5,913 Keyes; 1,242 Forbes; 1,222 Uncommitted; 373 Bauer; 178 Hatch.

Democratic     98,312 Gore; 73,589 Bradley; 5,400 Uncommitted.

## DELAWARE

Republican     15,250 Bush; 7,638 McCain; 5,883 Forbes; 1,148 Keyes; 120 Bauer; 21 Hatch.
(February 8)

Democratic     6,377 Gore; 4,476 Bradley; 288 LaRouche.
(February 5)

## FLORIDA MARCH 14

Republican     516,263 Bush; 139,465 McCain; 32,354 Keyes; 6,553 Forbes; 3,496 Bauer; 1,372 Hatch.

Democratic     451,718 Gore; 100,277 Bradley.

## GEORGIA MARCH 7

Republican     430,480 Bush; 179,046 McCain; 29,640 Keyes; 1,962 Bauer; 1,647 Forbes; 413 Hatch.

Democratic     238,396 Gore; 46,035 Bradley.

## IDAHO MAY 23

Republican     116,385 Bush; 30,263 Keyes; 11,798 None of the Names Shown.

Democratic     27,025 Gore; 5,722 None of the Names Shown; 2,941 LaRouche.

## ILLINOIS MARCH 21

Republican     496,685 Bush; 158,768 McCain; 66,066 Keyes; 10,334 Forbes; 5,068 Bauer.

Democratic     682,932 Gore; 115,320 Bradley; 11,415 LaRouche.

## INDIANA MAY 2

Republican     330,095 Bush; 76,569 McCain.

Democratic     219,604 Gore; 64,339 Bradley; 9,229 LaRouche.

## KENTUCKY MAY 23

Republican     75,783 Bush; 5,780 McCain; 4,337 Keyes; 2,408 Bauer; 1,829 Uncommitted; 1,186 Forbes.

Democratic     156,966 Gore; 32,340 Bradley; 26,046 Uncommitted; 4,927 LaRouche.

## LOUISIANA MARCH 14

Republican     86,038 Bush; 9,165 McCain; 5,900 Keyes; 1,041 Forbes; 768 Bauer.

Democratic     114,942 Gore; 31,385 Bradley; 6,127 LaRouche; 5,097 Crow.

# 2000 PRESIDENTIAL PRIMARIES

## MAINE MARCH 7

Republican 49,308 Bush; 42,510 McCain; 2,989 Keyes; 1,038 Uncommitted; 455 Forbes; 324 Bauer.

Democratic 34,725 Gore; 26,520 Bradley; 2,634 Uncommitted; 208 LaRouche; 192 Epstein.

## MARYLAND MARCH 7

Republican 211,439 Bush; 135,981 McCain; 25,020 Keyes; 1,678 Forbes; 1,328 Bauer; 588 Hatch.

Democratic 341,630 Gore; 144,387 Bradley; 16,935 Uncommitted; 4,510 LaRouche.

## MASSACHUSETTS MARCH 7

Republican 324,708 McCain; 159,534 Bush; 12,630 Keyes; 1,744 Bauer; 1,407 Forbes; 1,292 No Preference; 262 Hatch; 374 Write-in.

Democratic 341,586 Gore; 212,452 Bradley; 11,281 No Preference; 2,135 LaRouche; 2,620 Write-in.

## MICHIGAN FEBRUARY 22

Republican 650,805 McCain; 549,665 Bush; 59,032 Keyes; 8,714 Uncommitted; 4,894 Forbes; 2,733 Bauer; 905 Hatch; 22 Schriner (Write-in).

Democratic 31,655 Uncommitted; 13,195 LaRouche.

## MISSISSIPPI MARCH 14

Republican 101,042 Bush; 6,478 Keyes; 6,263 McCain; 588 Forbes; 475 Bauer; 133 Hatch.

Democratic 79,408 Gore; 7,621 Bradley; 1,573 LaRouche.

## MISSOURI MARCH 7

Republican 275,366 Bush; 167,831 McCain; 27,282 Keyes; 2,044 Forbes; 1,345 Uncommitted; 1,038 Bauer; 363 Hatch; 94 Hornung.

Democratic 171,562 Gore; 89,092 Bradley; 3,364 Uncommitted; 906 LaRouche; 565 Price.

## MONTANA JUNE 6

Republican 88,194 Bush; 20,822 Keyes; 4,655 No Preference; 2 John McCain (Write-in).

Democratic 68,420 Gore; 19,447 No Preference.

## NEBRASKA MAY 9

Republican 145,176 Bush; 28,065 McCain; 12,073 Keyes; 444 Write-in.

Democratic 73,639 Gore; 27,884 Bradley; 3,191 LaRouche; 557 Write-in.

# 2000 PRESIDENTIAL PRIMARIES

## NEW HAMPSHIRE FEBRUARY 1

Republican    115,606 McCain; 72,330 Bush; 30,166 Forbes; 15,179 Keyes; 1,640 Bauer; 163 Hatch; 98 Yeager; 81 Martin; 61 Berry; 51 Capalbo; 41 Mosby; 34 Harnes; 23 Peet; 14 Oyler; 2,719 Write-in.

Democratic    76,897 Gore; 70,502 Bradley; 322 Buckley; 192 Harder; 156 Peters; 134 Eaton; 124 LaRouche; 87 Taylor; 75 Greenstein; 35 Mullins; 35 O'Donnell; 30 Carter; 29 Crow; 22 Hamm; 19 Koos; 18 Skok; 5,962 Write-in.

## NEW JERSEY JUNE 6

Republican    201,209 Bush; 39,601 Keyes.

Democratic    358,951 Gore; 19,321 LaRouche.

## NEW MEXICO JUNE 6

Republican    62,161 Bush; 7,619 McCain; 4,850 Keyes; 600 Uncommitted delegates.

Democratic    98,715 Gore; 27,204 Bradley; 3,298 Uncommitted delegates; 3,063 LaRouche.

## NEW YORK MARCH 7

Republican    Voting by congressional districts for delegates.

Democratic    639,417 Gore; 326,038 Bradley; 9,008 LaRouche.

## NORTH CAROLINA MAY 2

Republican    253,485 Bush; 35,018 McCain; 25,320 Keyes; 5,383 No Preference; 3,311 Gary Bauer.

Democratic    383,696 Gore; 99,796 Bradley; 49,905 No Preference; 11,525 LaRouche.

## OHIO MARCH 7

Republican    810,369 Bush; 516,790 McCain; 55,266 Keyes; 8,934 Forbes; 6,169 Bauer.

Democratic    720,311 Gore; 241,688 Bradley; 16,513 LaRouche.

## OKLAHOMA MARCH 14

Republican    98,781 Bush; 12,973 McCain; 11,595 Keyes; 1,066 Forbes; 394 Bauer.

Democratic    92,654 Gore; 34,311 Bradley; 7,885 LaRouche.

## OREGON MAY 16

Republican    292,522 Bush; 46,764 Keyes; 10,545 Write-in.

Democratic    300,922 Gore; 38,521 LaRouche; 15,151 Write-in.

# 2000 PRESIDENTIAL PRIMARIES

## PENNSYLVANIA APRIL 4

Republican    472,398 Bush; 145,719 McCain; 16,162 Forbes; 8,806 Bauer; 7,100 Keyes (write-in); 1,624 Write-in.

Democratic    525,306 Gore; 146,797 Bradley; 32,047 LaRouche; 3,840 Write-in.

## RHODE ISLAND MARCH 7

Republican    21,754 McCain; 13,170 Bush; 923 Keyes; 114 Uncommitted; 89 Forbes; 35 Bauer; 35 Hatch; 23 Write-in.

Democratic    26,801 Gore; 19,000 Bradley; 844 Uncommitted; 199 LaRouche; 235 Write-in.

## SOUTH CAROLINA FEBRUARY 19

Republican    305,998 Bush; 239,964 McCain; 25,996 Keyes; 618 Bauer; 449 Forbes; 76 Hatch.

Democratic    No presidential primary.

## SOUTH DAKOTA JUNE 6

Republican    35,418 Bush; 6,228 McCain; 3,478 Keyes; 155 Attia.

Democratic    No Democratic primary.

## TENNESSEE MARCH 14

Republican    193,166 Bush; 36,436 McCain; 16,916 Keyes; 1,623 Uncommitted; 1,305 Bauer; 1,018 Forbes; 252 Hatch; 75 Write-in.

Democratic    198,264 Gore; 11,323 Bradley; 4,407 Uncommitted; 1,031 LaRouche; 178 Write-in.

## TEXAS MARCH 14

Republican    986,416 Bush; 80,082 McCain; 43,518 Keyes; 9,570 Uncommitted; 2,865 Forbes; 2,189 Bauer; 1,324 Hatch; 793 Urban.

Democratic    631,428 Gore; 128,564 Bradley; 26,898 LaRouche.

## UTAH MARCH 10

Republican    57,617 Bush; 19,367 Keyes; 12,784 McCain; 859 Forbes; 426 Bauer.

Democratic    12,527 Gore; 3,160 Bradley.

## VERMONT MARCH 7

Republican    49,045 McCain; 28,741 Bush; 2,164 Keyes; 616 Forbes; 293 Bauer; 496 Write-in.

Democratic    26,774 Gore; 21,629 Bradley; 355 LaRouche; 525 Write-in.

1100

# 2000 PRESIDENTIAL PRIMARIES

**VIRGINIA FEBRUARY 29**

Republican     350,588 Bush; 291,488 McCain; 20,356 Keyes; 852 Bauer; 809 Forbes.

Democratic     No Democratic primary.

**WASHINGTON FEBRUARY 29**

Republican     284,053 Bush; 191,101 McCain; 11,753 Keyes; 1,749 Forbes; 1,469 Bauer; 1,023 Hatch.

Democratic     202,456 Gore; 93,375 Bradley; 1,170 LaRouche.

**WEST VIRGINIA MAY 9**

Republican     87,050 Bush; 14,121 McCain; 5,210 Keyes; 1,733 Forbes; 1,290 Bauer.

Democratic     182,403 Gore; 46,710 Bradley; 19,374 McDonald; 4,823 LaRouche.

**WISCONSIN APRIL 4**

Republican     343,292 Bush; 89,684 McCain; 48,919 Keyes; 5,505 Forbes; 3,452 Uninstructed Delegation; 1,813 Bauer; 1,712 Hatch; 1,392 Write-in.

Democratic     328,682 Gore; 32,560 Bradley; 4,105 Uninstructed Delegation; 3,743 LaRouche; 2,106 Write-in.

**DISTRICT OF COLUMBIA  MAY 2**

Republican     1,771 Bush; 593 McCain; 69 Write-in.

Democratic     18,621 Gore; 796 LaRouche.

# 2000 REPUBLICAN PREFERENCE PRIMARIES

| Date | | State | Total Vote | Bush | Forbes | Keyes | McCain | Other |
|------|---|-------|-----------|------|--------|-------|--------|-------|
| Feb. | 1 | New Hampshire | 238,206 | 72,330 | 30,166 | 15,179 | 115,606 | 4,925 |
| | | | | 30.4% | 12.7% | 6.4% | 48.5% | 2.1% |
| Feb. | 8 | Delaware | 30,060 | 15,250 | 5,883 | 1,148 | 7,638 | 141 |
| | | | | 50.7% | 19.6% | 3.8% | 25.4% | 0.5% |
| Feb. | 19 | South Carolina | 573,101 | 305,998 | 449 | 25,996 | 239,964 | 694 |
| | | | | 53.4% | 0.1% | 4.5% | 41.9% | 0.1% |
| Feb. | 22 | Arizona | 322,669 | 115,115 | 1,211 | 11,500 | 193,708 | 1,135 |
| | | | | 35.7% | 0.4% | 3.6% | 60.0% | 0.4% |
| Feb. | 22 | Michigan | 1,276,770 | 549,665 | 4,894 | 59,032 | 650,805 | 12,374 |
| | | | | 43.1% | 0.4% | 4.6% | 51.0% | 1.0% |
| Feb. | 29 | Virginia | 664,093 | 350,588 | 809 | 20,356 | 291,488 | 852 |
| | | | | 52.8% | 0.1% | 3.1% | 43.9% | 0.1% |
| Feb. | 29 | Washington | 491,148 | 284,053 | 1,749 | 11,753 | 191,101 | 2,492 |
| | | | | 57.8% | 0.4% | 2.4% | 38.9% | 0.5% |
| March | 7 | California | 2,847,921 | 1,725,162 | 8,449 | 112,747 | 988,706 | 12,857 |
| | | | | 60.6% | 0.3% | 4.0% | 34.7% | 0.5% |
| | 7 | Connecticut | 178,985 | 82,881 | 1,242 | 5,913 | 87,176 | 1,773 |
| | | | | 46.3% | 0.7% | 3.3% | 48.7% | 1.0% |
| | 7 | Georgia | 643,188 | 430,480 | 1,647 | 29,640 | 179,046 | 2,375 |
| | | | | 66.9% | 0.3% | 4.6% | 27.8% | 0.4% |
| | 7 | Maine | 96,624 | 49,308 | 455 | 2,989 | 42,510 | 1,362 |
| | | | | 51.0% | 0.5% | 3.1% | 44.0% | 1.4% |
| | 7 | Maryland | 376,034 | 211,439 | 1,678 | 25,020 | 135,981 | 1,916 |
| | | | | 56.2% | 0.4% | 6.7% | 36.2% | 0.5% |
| | 7 | Massachusetts | 501,951 | 159,534 | 1,407 | 12,630 | 324,708 | 3,672 |
| | | | | 31.8% | 0.3% | 2.5% | 64.7% | 0.7% |
| | 7 | Missouri | 475,363 | 275,366 | 2,044 | 27,282 | 167,831 | 2,840 |
| | | | | 57.9% | 0.4% | 5.7% | 35.3% | 0.6% |
| | 7 | New York | See *America Votes 24*, page 326 | | | | | |
| | 7 | Ohio | 1,397,528 | 810,369 | 8,934 | 55,266 | 516,790 | 6,169 |
| | | | | 58.0% | 0.6% | 4.0% | 37.0% | 0.4% |
| | 7 | Rhode Island | 36,143 | 13,170 | 89 | 923 | 21,754 | 207 |
| | | | | 36.4% | 0.2% | 2.6% | 60.2% | 0.6% |
| | 7 | Vermont | 81,355 | 28,741 | 616 | 2,164 | 49,045 | 789 |
| | | | | 35.3% | 0.8% | 2.7% | 60.3% | 1.0% |
| | 10 | Colorado | 180,655 | 116,897 | 1,197 | 11,871 | 48,996 | 1,694 |
| | | | | 64.7% | 0.7% | 6.6% | 27.1% | 0.9% |
| | 10 | Utah | 91,053 | 57,617 | 859 | 19,367 | 12,784 | 426 |
| | | | | 63.3% | 0.9% | 21.3% | 14.0% | 0.5% |
| | 14 | Florida | 699,503 | 516,263 | 6,553 | 32,354 | 139,465 | 4,868 |
| | | | | 73.8% | 0.9% | 4.6% | 19.9% | 0.7% |
| | 14 | Louisiana | 102,912 | 86,038 | 1,041 | 5,900 | 9,165 | 768 |
| | | | | 83.6% | 1.0% | 5.7% | 8.9% | 0.7% |
| | 14 | Mississippi | 114,979 | 101,042 | 588 | 6,478 | 6,263 | 608 |
| | | | | 87.9% | 0.5% | 5.6% | 5.4% | 0.5% |
| | 14 | Oklahoma | 124,809 | 98,781 | 1,066 | 11,595 | 12,973 | 394 |
| | | | | 79.1% | 0.9% | 9.3% | 10.4% | 0.3% |
| | 14 | Tennessee | 250,791 | 193,166 | 1,018 | 16,916 | 36,436 | 3,255 |
| | | | | 77.0% | 0.4% | 6.7% | 14.5% | 1.3% |
| | 14 | Texas | 1,126,757 | 986,416 | — | 43,518 | 80,082 | 16,741 |
| | | | | 87.5% | — | 3.9% | 7.1% | 1.5% |
| | 21 | Illinois | 736,921 | 496,685 | 10,334 | 66,066 | 158,768 | 5,068 |
| | | | | 67.4% | 1.4% | 9.0% | 21.5% | 0.7% |
| April | 4 | Pennsylvania | 651,809 | 472,398 | 16,162 | 7,100 | 145,719 | 10,430 |
| | | | | 72.5% | 2.5% | 1.1% | 22.4% | 1.6% |
| | 4 | Wisconsin | 495,769 | 343,292 | 5,505 | 48,919 | 89,684 | 8,369 |
| | | | | 69.2% | 1.1% | 9.9% | 18.1% | 1.7% |

# 2000 REPUBLICAN PREFERENCE PRIMARIES

| Date | | State | Total Vote | Bush | Forbes | Keyes | McCain | Other |
|------|---|-------|-----------:|-----:|-------:|------:|-------:|------:|
| May | 2 | District of Columbia | 2,433 | 1,771 | | | 593 | 69 |
| | | | | 72.8% | — | — | 24.4% | 2.8% |
| | 2 | Indiana | 406,664 | 330,095 | — | — | 76,569 | — |
| | | | | 81.2% | — | — | 18.8% | — |
| | 2 | North Carolina | 322,517 | 253,485 | — | 25,320 | 35,018 | 8,694 |
| | | | | 78.6% | — | 7.9% | 10.9% | 2.7% |
| May | 9 | Nebraska | 185,758 | 145,176 | — | 12,073 | 28,065 | 444 |
| | | | | 78.2% | — | 6.5% | 15.1% | 0.2% |
| | 9 | West Virginia | 109,404 | 87,050 | 1,733 | 5,210 | 14,121 | 1,290 |
| | | | | 79.6% | 1.6% | 4.8% | 12.9% | 1.2% |
| May | 16 | Oregon | 349,831 | 292,522 | 10,545 | 46,764 | — | — |
| | | | | 83.6% | 3.0% | 13.4% | — | — |
| May | 23 | Arkansas | 44,573 | 35,759 | — | 8,814 | — | — |
| | | | | 80.2% | — | 19.8% | — | — |
| | 23 | Idaho | 158,446 | 116,385 | — | 30,263 | — | 11,798 |
| | | | | 73.5% | — | 19.1% | — | 7.4% |
| | 23 | Kentucky | 91,323 | 75,783 | 1,186 | 4,337 | 5,780 | 4,237 |
| | | | | 83.0% | 1.3% | 4.7% | 6.3% | 4.6% |
| June | 6 | Alabama | 203,079 | 171,077 | — | 23,394 | — | 8,608 |
| | | | | 84.2% | — | 11.5% | — | 4.2% |
| | 6 | Montana | 113,673 | 88,194 | — | 20,822 | 2 | 4,655 |
| | | | | 77.6% | — | 18.3% | — | 4.1% |
| | 6 | New Jersey | 240,810 | 201,209 | — | 39,601 | — | — |
| | | | | 83.6% | — | 16.4% | — | — |
| | 6 | New Mexico | 75,230 | 62,161 | — | 4,850 | 7,619 | 600 |
| | | | | 82.6% | — | 6.4% | 10.1% | 0.8% |
| | 6 | South Dakota | 45,279 | 35,418 | — | 3,478 | 6,228 | 155 |
| | | | | 78.2% | — | 7.7% | 13.8% | 0.3% |
| | | | 17,156,117 | 10,844,129 | 129,509 | 914,548 | 5,118,187 | 149,744 |

# 2000 DEMOCRATIC PREFERENCE PRIMARIES

| Date | State | Total Vote | Bradley | Gore | LaRouche | Other |
|------|-------|-----------|---------|------|----------|-------|
| Feb. 1 | New Hampshire | 154,639 | 70,502 | 76,897 | 124 | 7,116 |
| | | | 45.6% | 49.7% | 0.1% | 4.6% |
| Feb. 5 | Delaware | 11,141 | 4,476 | 6,377 | 288 | — |
| | | | 40.2% | 57.2% | 2.6% | — |
| Feb. 22 | Michigan | 44,850 | — | — | 13,195 | 31,655 |
| | | | — | — | 29.4% | 70.6% |
| Feb. 29 | Washington | 297,001 | 93,375 | 202,456 | 1,170 | — |
| | | | 31.4% | 68.2% | 0.4% | — |
| March 7 | California | 2,654,114 | 482,882 | 2,155,321 | 15,911 | — |
| | | | 18.2% | 81.2% | 0.6% | — |
| 7 | Connecticut | 177,301 | 73,589 | 98,312 | — | 5,400 |
| | | | 41.5% | 55.4% | — | 3.0% |
| 7 | Georgia | 284,431 | 46,035 | 238,396 | — | — |
| | | | 16.2% | 83.8% | — | — |
| 7 | Maine | 64,279 | 26,520 | 34,725 | 208 | 2,826 |
| | | | 41.3% | 54.0% | 0.3% | 4.4% |
| 7 | Maryland | 507,462 | 144,387 | 341,630 | 4,510 | 16,935 |
| | | | 28.5% | 67.3% | 0.9% | 3.3% |
| 7 | Massachusetts | 570,074 | 212,452 | 341,586 | 2,135 | 13,901 |
| | | | 37.3% | 59.9% | 0.4% | 2.4% |
| 7 | Missouri | 265,489 | 89,092 | 171,562 | 906 | 3,929 |
| | | | 33.6% | 64.6% | 0.3% | 1.5% |
| 7 | New York | 974,463 | 326,038 | 639,417 | 9,008 | — |
| | | | 33.5% | 65.6% | 0.9% | — |
| 7 | Ohio | 978,512 | 241,688 | 720,311 | 16,513 | — |
| | | | 24.7% | 73.6% | 1.7% | — |
| 7 | Rhode Island | 47,079 | 19,000 | 26,801 | 199 | 1,079 |
| | | | 40.4% | 56.9% | 0.4% | 2.3% |
| 7 | Vermont | 49,283 | 21,629 | 26,774 | 355 | 525 |
| | | | 43.9% | 54.3% | 0.7% | 1.1% |
| 10 | Colorado | 88,735 | 20,663 | 63,384 | 821 | 3,867 |
| | | | 23.3% | 71.4% | 0.9% | 4.4% |
| 10 | Utah | 15,687 | 3,160 | 12,527 | — | — |
| | | | 20.1% | 79.9% | — | — |
| 11 | Arizona | 86,762 | 16,383 | 67,582 | — | 2,797 |
| | | | 18.9% | 77.9% | — | 3.2% |
| 14 | Florida | 551,995 | 100,277 | 451,718 | — | — |
| | | | 18.2% | 81.8% | — | — |
| 14 | Louisiana | 157,551 | 31,385 | 114,942 | 6,127 | 5,097 |
| | | | 19.9% | 73.0% | 3.9% | 3.2% |
| 14 | Mississippi | 88,602 | 7,621 | 79,408 | 1,573 | — |
| | | | 8.6% | 89.6% | 1.8% | — |
| 14 | Oklahoma | 134,850 | 34,311 | 92,654 | 7,885 | — |
| | | | 25.4% | 68.7% | 5.8% | — |
| 14 | Tennessee | 215,203 | 11,323 | 198,264 | 1,031 | 4,585 |
| | | | 5.3% | 92.1% | 0.5% | 2.1% |
| 14 | Texas | 786,890 | 128,564 | 631,428 | 26,898 | — |
| | | | 16.3% | 80.2% | 3.4% | — |
| 21 | Illinois | 809,667 | 115,320 | 682,932 | 11,415 | — |
| | | | 14.2% | 84.3% | 1.4% | — |
| April 4 | Pennsylvania | 707,990 | 146,797 | 525,306 | 32,047 | 3,840 |
| | | | 20.7% | 74.2% | 4.5% | 0.5% |
| 4 | Wisconsin | 371,196 | 32,560 | 328,682 | 3,743 | 6,211 |
| | | | 8.8% | 88.5% | 1.0% | 1.7% |
| May 2 | District of Columbia | 19,417 | — | 18,621 | 796 | — |
| | | | — | 95.9% | 4.1% | — |
| 2 | Indiana | 293,172 | 64,339 | 219,604 | 9,229 | — |
| | | | 21.9% | 74.9% | 3.1% | — |

# 2000 DEMOCRATIC PREFERENCE PRIMARIES

| Date | | State | Total Vote | Bradley | Gore | LaRouche | Other |
|---|---|---|---|---|---|---|---|
| | 2 | North Carolina | 544,922 | 99,796 | 383,696 | 11,525 | 49,905 |
| | | | | 18.3% | 70.4% | 2.1% | 9.2% |
| May | 9 | Nebraska | 105,271 | 27,884 | 73,639 | 3,191 | 557 |
| | | | | 26.5% | 70.0% | 3.0% | 0.5% |
| | 9 | West Virginia | 253,310 | 46,710 | 182,403 | 4,823 | 19,374 |
| | | | | 18.4% | 72.0% | 1.9% | 7.6% |
| May | 16 | Oregon | 354,594 | — | 300,922 | 38,521 | 15,151 |
| | | | | — | 84.9% | 10.9% | 4.3% |
| May | 23 | Arkansas | 246,900 | — | 193,750 | 53,150 | — |
| | | | | — | 78.5% | 21.5% | — |
| | 23 | Idaho | 35,688 | — | 27,025 | 2,941 | 5,722 |
| | | | | — | 75.7% | 8.2% | 16.0% |
| | 23 | Kentucky | 220,279 | 32,340 | 156,966 | 4,927 | 26,046 |
| | | | | 14.7% | 71.3% | 2.2% | 11.8% |
| June | 6 | Alabama | 278,527 | — | 214,541 | 15,465 | 48,521 |
| | | | | — | 77.0% | 5.6% | 17.4% |
| | 6 | Montana | 87,867 | — | 68,420 | — | 19,447 |
| | | | | — | 77.9% | — | 22.1% |
| | 6 | New Jersey | 378,272 | — | 358,951 | 19,321 | — |
| | | | | — | 94.9% | 5.1% | — |
| | 6 | New Mexico | 132,280 | 27,204 | 98,715 | 3,063 | 3,298 |
| | | | | 20.6% | 74.6% | 2.3% | 2.5% |
| | | | 14,045,745 | 2,798,302 | 10,626,645 | 323,014 | 297,784 |

# 1996 PRESIDENTIAL PRIMARIES

In 1996, 40 states and the District of Columbia held presidential primaries, in which at least one of the parties held contests where voters balloted directly for candidates or for a statewide slate of delegates that was pledged to a candidate. In addition, there was a Republican primary in New York where delegates were elected on a congressional district basis.

The chronological tables, included at the end of this section, give the major-party primary vote in each state for those candidates who received at least 100,000 votes nationwide.

Republican candidates on the ballot in at least one state were C.A. Aldrich, Lamar Alexander, Richard P. Bosa, Patrick J. Buchanan, Billy Joe Clegg, Charles E. Collins, Bob Dole, Robert K. Dornan, Georgiana H. Doerschuck, Susan Ducey, William James Flanagan, Malcolm S. "Steve" Forbes Jr., Russell J. Fornwalt, Doug Fricke, Phil Gramm, Kenneth Hewitt, Charles Holden, John B. Hurd, Ann Jennings, Paul Jensen, Alan Keyes, Mary "France" Le Tulle, Michael Stephen Levinson, Richard G. Lugar, Isabell Masters, Gerald J. McManus, Hilary Michael Milko, Hubert David Patty, Joann V. Pharr, Tennie Rogers, Richard D. Skillen, Clyde Staggs and Maurice "Morry" Taylor.

Democratic candidates on the ballot in at least one state were Willie Felix Carter, Sal Casamassima, Carmen C. Chimento, Vernon Clemenson, Bill Clinton, Bruce C. Daniels, Michael E. Dass, Robert F. Drucker, James D. Griffin, Ted L. Gunderson, Vincent S. Hamm, Heather Anne Harder, Fred Hudson, Caroline P. Killeen, Lyndon H. LaRouche Jr., Frank Legas, Elvena E. Lloyd-Duffie, Stephen Michael, David Pauling, Pat Paulsen, Roland Riemers, John Safran, Ronald W. Spangler, Osie Thorpe and Ben J. Tomeo.

The tables reflect changes in the primary vote in Arkansas and Indiana that were verified after publication of U.S. Primary Elections 1995-1996 in the summer of 1997.

## ALABAMA JUNE 4

Republican   160,097 Dole; 33,409 Buchanan; 11,073 Uncommitted; 7,354 Keyes.

Democratic   243,588 Clinton; 45,764 Uncommitted; 12,686 LaRouche.

## ARIZONA FEBRUARY 27

Republican   115,962 Forbes; 102,980 Dole; 95,742 Buchanan; 24,765 Alexander; 2,790 Keyes; 2,064 Lugar; 857 Gramm; 735 Dornan; 539 Ducey; 304 Jennings; 148 Taylor; 125 Pharr; 104 Hewitt; 99 Jensen; 64 Fricke; 59 Levinson; 55 Patty; 38 Holden; 33 Staggs; 19 Aldrich.

Democratic   No presidential primary held.

## ARKANSAS MAY 21

Republican   32,687 Dole; 10,084 Buchanan; 43 Uncommitted.

Democratic   236,547 Clinton; 30,416 Uncommitted; 20,401 LaRouche; 13,025 Lloyd-Duffie.

## CALIFORNIA MARCH 26

Republican   1,619,931 Dole; 450,695 Buchanan; 183,367 Forbes; 93,577 Keyes; 44,130 Alexander; 23,215 Dornan; 15,232 Gramm; 14,801 Lugar; 5,778 Taylor; 1,586 scattered write-in.

Democratic   2,342,185 Clinton; 173,953 LaRouche; 6,924 scattered write-in.

## COLORADO MARCH 5

Republican   108,123 Dole; 53,376 Buchanan; 51,592 Forbes; 24,184 Alexander; 9,052 Keyes; 1,603 Lugar.

Democratic   48,454 Clinton; 5,981 LaRouche; 92 scattered write-in.

# 1996 PRESIDENTIAL PRIMARIES

**CONNECTICUT MARCH 5**

Republican    70,998 Dole; 26,253 Forbes; 19,664 Buchanan; 6,985 Alexander; 2,209 Keyes; 1,699 Uncommitted; 1,495 Lugar; 430 Taylor; 401 Dornan; 284 Gramm.

Democratic    No presidential primary held.

**DELAWARE FEBRUARY 24**

Republican    10,709 Forbes; 8,909 Dole; 6,118 Buchanan; 4,375 Alexander; 1,729 Keyes; 717 Lugar; 216 Gramm.

Democratic    9,694 Clinton; 1,046 LaRouche.

**FLORIDA MARCH 12**

Republican    511,377 Dole; 181,768 Forbes; 162,770 Buchanan; 16,631 Keyes; 14,142 Alexander; 4,465 Dornan; 3,236 Lugar; 2,994 Gramm; 1,133 Taylor.

Democratic    No presidential primary held.

**GEORGIA MARCH 5**

Republican    226,732 Dole; 162,627 Buchanan; 75,855 Alexander; 71,276 Forbes; 17,538 Keyes; 1,971 Lugar; 1,095 Gramm; 1,005 Dornan; 661 Collins; 307 Taylor.

Democratic    95,103 Clinton.

**IDAHO MAY 28**

Republican    74,011 Dole; 26,461 Buchanan; 12,339 "None of the Names Shown;" 5,904 Keyes.

Democratic    35,277 Clinton; 4,951 "None of the Names Shown."

**ILLINOIS MARCH 19**

Republican    532,467 Dole; 186,177 Buchanan; 39,906 Forbes; 30,052 Keyes; 12,585 Alexander; 8,286 Lugar; 6,696 Gramm; 2,189 Taylor; 6 write-in.

Democratic    770,001 Clinton; 16,045 Lloyd-Duffie; 14,624 LaRouche; 6 write-in.

**INDIANA MAY 7**

Republican    365,568 Dole; 100,166 Buchanan; 50,780 Forbes.

Democratic    329,462 Clinton.

**KENTUCKY MAY 28**

Republican    76,669 Dole; 8,526 Buchanan; 4,793 Uncommitted; 3,822 Keyes; 3,400 Forbes; 3,272 Alexander; 2,235 Lugar; 1,122 Gramm.

Democratic    211,667 Clinton; 44,028 Uncommitted; 20,324 LaRouche.

# 1996 PRESIDENTIAL PRIMARIES

**LOUISIANA MARCH 12**

Republican     37,170 Dole; 25,757 Buchanan; 10,265 Forbes; 2,464 Keyes; 1,642 Alexander; 491 Taylor.

Democratic     124,931 Clinton; 18,150 LaRouche; 11,620 Lloyd-Duffie.

**MAINE MARCH 5**

Republican     31,147 Dole; 16,478 Buchanan; 9,991 Forbes; 4,450 Alexander; 1,934 Lugar; 1,741 Uncommitted; 1,229 Keyes; 163 Gramm; 147 Taylor.

Democratic     23,879 Clinton; 2,433 Uncommitted; 715 LaRouche.

**MARYLAND MARCH 5**

Republican     135,522 Dole; 53,585 Buchanan; 32,207 Forbes; 14,061 Alexander; 13,718 Keyes; 2,872 Lugar; 1,174 Gramm; 757 Dornan; 350 Taylor.

Democratic     247,492 Clinton; 33,417 Uncommitted; 12,920 LaRouche.

**MASSACHUSETTS MARCH 5**

Republican     135,946 Dole; 71,688 Buchanan; 39,605 Forbes; 21,456 Alexander; 5,224 Keyes; 4,743 Lugar; 3,303 No Preference; 673 Gramm; 544 Dornan; 433 Taylor; 1,218 scattered write-in.

Democratic     135,360 Clinton; 12,623 No Preference; 5,212 LaRouche; 2,275 scattered write-in.

**MICHIGAN MARCH 19**

Republican     265,425 Dole; 177,562 Buchanan; 26,610 Forbes; 23,109 Uncommitted; 15,995 Keyes; 7,631 Alexander; 2,175 Lugar; 1,755 Gramm; 1,723 Dornan; 1,018 Taylor; 1,158 scattered write-in.

Democratic     123,640 Uncommitted; 19,110 scattered write-in.

**MISSISSIPPI MARCH 12**

Republican     91,639 Dole; 39,324 Buchanan; 12,119 Forbes; 2,907 Keyes; 2,781 Alexander; 2,123 Dornan; 475 Gramm; 297 Clegg; 141 Lugar; 84 Taylor; 35 Rogers.

Democratic     86,716 Clinton; 7,072 LaRouche.

**MONTANA JUNE 4**

Republican     72,176 Dole; 28,581 Buchanan; 8,533 No Preference; 8,456 Forbes.

Democratic     82,549 Clinton; 9,176 No Preference.

**NEBRASKA MAY 14**

Republican     129,131 Dole; 17,741 Buchanan; 10,612 Forbes; 5,132 Keyes; 4,423 Alexander; 1,127 Lugar; 847 Dornan; 460 Taylor; 1,118 scattered write-in.

Democratic     81,854 Clinton; 10,228 LaRouche; 2,094 scattered write-in.

# 1996 PRESIDENTIAL PRIMARIES

## NEVADA MARCH 26

Republican        72,932 Dole; 27,063 Forbes; 21,321 Buchanan; 12,026 "None of These Candidates;" 3,289 Alexander; 1,999 Keyes; 745 Gramm; 464 Lugar; 305 Collins; 290 Le Tulle; 109 Milko; 94 Taylor.

Democratic        No presidential primary held.

## NEW HAMPSHIRE FEBRUARY 20

Republican        56,874 Buchanan; 54,738 Dole; 47,148 Alexander; 25,505 Forbes; 10,838 Lugar; 5,572 Keyes; 2,944 Taylor; 752 Gramm; 529 Dornan; 216 Bosa; 154 Doerschuck; 151 Ducey; 118 Clegg; 80 Skillen; 48 Flanagan; 42 Collins; 37 Fornwalt; 35 Levinson; 26 Hurd; 20 McManus; 17 Patty; 12 Rogers; 3,082 scattered write-in.

Democratic        76,797 Clinton; 1,007 Paulsen; 656 Chimento; 433 LaRouche; 391 Killeen; 369 Harder; 312 Daniels; 307 Griffin; 94 Michael; 85 Carter; 81 Drucker; 74 Pauling; 72 Hamm; 70 Gunderson; 63 Legas; 62 Spangler; 57 Dass; 50 Thorpe; 47 Tomeo; 45 Casamassima; 42 Safran; 10,448 scattered write-in.

## NEW JERSEY JUNE 4

Republican        180,412 Dole; 23,789 Buchanan; 14,611 Keyes.

Democratic        254,004 Clinton; 12,736 LaRouche.

## NEW MEXICO JUNE 4

Republican        53,300 Dole; 5,679 Buchanan; 3,987 Forbes; 2,676 Alexander; 2,265 Keyes; 1,301 Uncommitted Delegates; 865 Dornan; 391 Taylor.

Democratic        109,595 Clinton; 11,767 Uncommitted Delegates.

## NEW YORK MARCH 7

Republican        No presidential preference vote. Vote for delegates: 599,748 Dole delegates; 325,211 Forbes delegates; 163,365 Buchanan delegates. The data represents the sum of the votes cast for delegates by congressional district pledged to the candidates indicated. Only Dole and Forbes ran delegates in all thirty-one congressional districts.

Democratic        No presidential primary held.

## NORTH CAROLINA MAY 7

Republican        202,863 Dole; 37,126 Buchanan; 11,759 Keyes; 11,588 Forbes; 10,918 No Preference; 7,400 Alexander; 2,558 Lugar.

Democratic        461,434 Clinton; 69,790 No Preference; 40,936 LaRouche.

## NORTH DAKOTA FEBRUARY 27

Republican        26,832 Dole; 12,455 Forbes; 11,653 Buchanan; 5,997 Gramm; 4,008 Alexander; 2,030 Keyes; 559 Lugar; 200 Taylor.

Democratic        651 Riemers; 549 LaRouche; 384 Clemenson.

# 1996 PRESIDENTIAL PRIMARIES

**OHIO MARCH 19**

Republican    640,954 Dole; 208,012 Buchanan; 58,131 Forbes; 27,197 Keyes; 19,530 Alexander; 9,598 Lugar.

Democratic    713,153 Clinton; 63,377 LaRouche.

**OKLAHOMA MARCH 12**

Republican    156,829 Dole; 56,949 Buchanan; 37,213 Forbes; 6,306 Keyes; 3,436 Alexander; 1,490 Gramm; 1,052 Masters; 538 Lugar; 451 Collins; 278 Taylor.

Democratic    279,454 Clinton; 46,392 LaRouche; 40,758 Lloyd-Duffie.

**OREGON MARCH 12**

Republican    206,938 Dole; 86,987 Buchanan; 54,121 Forbes; 28,332 Alexander; 14,340 Keyes; 4,971 Lugar; 2,117 Gramm; 1,872 Dornan; 1,344 Taylor; 6,492 scattered write-in.

Democratic    349,871 Clinton; 19,307 scattered write-in.

**PENNSYLVANIA APRIL 23**

Republican    435,031 Dole; 123,011 Buchanan; 55,018 Forbes; 40,025 Keyes; 31,119 Lugar.

Democratic    666,486 Clinton; 57,583 LaRouche.

**RHODE ISLAND MARCH 5**

Republican    9,664 Dole; 2,859 Alexander; 1,252 Uncommitted; 487 Lugar; 165 Taylor; 582 scattered write-in.

Democratic    7,825 Clinton; 535 Uncommitted; 392 LaRouche; 28 scattered write-in.

**SOUTH CAROLINA MARCH 2**

Republican    124,904 Dole; 80,824 Buchanan; 35,039 Forbes; 28,647 Alexander; 5,752 Keyes; 1,017 Lugar; 467 Gramm; 91 Taylor.

Democratic    No presidential primary held.

**SOUTH DAKOTA FEBRUARY 27**

Republican    30,918 Dole; 19,780 Buchanan; 8,831 Forbes; 6,037 Alexander; 2,378 Keyes; 677 Uncommitted; 387 Gramm; 162 Taylor.

Democratic    No presidential primary held.

**TENNESSEE MARCH 12**

Republican    148,063 Dole; 72,928 Buchanan; 32,742 Alexander; 22,171 Forbes; 7,661 Keyes; 3,078 Uncommitted; 898 Dornan; 688 Gramm; 531 Lugar; 210 Taylor; 416 scattered write-in.

Democratic    122,538 Clinton; 15,144 Uncommitted; 115 scattered write-in.

# 1996 PRESIDENTIAL PRIMARIES

## TEXAS MARCH 12

Republican    567,164 Dole; 217,974 Buchanan; 130,938 Forbes; 41,746 Keyes; 19,507 Uncommitted; 18,745 Alexander; 18,629 Gramm; 2,266 Lugar; 1,093 Ducey; 650 Le Tulle; 633 Collins; 458 Taylor.

Democratic    796,041 Clinton; 32,232 Hudson; 28,772 Harder; 28,137 LaRouche; 15,550 Gunderson; 10,876 Lloyd-Duffie; 9,648 Casamassima.

## VERMONT MARCH 5

Republican    23,419 Dole; 9,730 Buchanan; 9,066 Forbes; 7,881 Lugar; 6,145 Alexander; 291 Gramm; 257 Taylor; 1,324 scattered write-in.

Democratic    29,763 Clinton; 699 LaRouche; 376 scattered write-in.

## WASHINGTON MARCH 26

Republican    76,155 Dole; 25,247 Buchanan; 10,339 Forbes; 5,610 Keyes; 1,600 Alexander; 630 Gramm; 587 Lugar; 516 Dornan.

Democratic    97,495 Clinton; 1,451 LaRouche.

All-Party    In addition to the Democratic and Republican ballots, there was a non-binding, all-party ballot, with votes cast as follows: 227,120 Clinton; 125,154 Dole; 44,027 Buchanan; 28,618 Forbes; 6,631 Keyes; 5,181 Alexander; 3,160 LaRouche; 2,009 Lugar; 1,665 Gramm; 1,054 Dornan.

## WEST VIRGINIA MAY 14

Republican    87,534 Dole; 20,928 Buchanan; 6,222 Forbes; 4,822 Keyes; 3,773 Alexander; 2,391 Gramm; 1,082 Lugar; 702 Taylor.

Democratic    257,087 Clinton; 40,034 LaRouche.

## WISCONSIN MARCH 19

Republican    301,628 Dole; 194,733 Buchanan; 32,205 Forbes; 18,028 Keyes; 11,213 Alexander; 7,504 Uninstructed Delegation; 3,215 Lugar; 2,682 Gramm; 1,645 Dornan; 916 Taylor; 2,806 scattered write-in.

Democratic    347,629 Clinton; 7,005 Uninstructed Delegation; 1,534 scattered write-in.

## DISTRICT OF COLUMBIA MAY 7

Republican    2,256 Dole; 381 Uncommitted; 283 Buchanan; 67 scattered write-in.

Democratic    20,568 Clinton; 391 LaRouche.

# 1996 REPUBLICAN PREFERENCE PRIMARIES

| Date | State | Total Vote | Alexander | Buchanan | Dole | Forbes | Keyes | Lugar | Other |
|---|---|---|---|---|---|---|---|---|---|
| Feb. 20 | New Hampshire | 208,938 | 47,148 | 56,874 | 54,738 | 25,505 | 5,572 | 10,838 | 8,263 |
| | | | 22.6% | 27.2% | 26.2% | 12.2% | 2.7% | 5.2% | 4.0% |
| Feb. 24 | Delaware | 32,773 | 4,375 | 6,118 | 8,909 | 10,709 | 1,729 | 717 | 216 |
| | | | 13.3% | 18.7% | 27.2% | 32.7% | 5.3% | 2.2% | 0.7% |
| Feb. 27 | Arizona | 347,482 | 24,765 | 95,742 | 102,980 | 115,962 | 2,790 | 2,064 | 3,179 |
| | | | 7.1% | 27.6% | 29.6% | 33.4% | 0.8% | 0.6% | 0.9% |
| Feb. 27 | North Dakota | 63,734 | 4,008 | 11,653 | 26,832 | 12,455 | 2,030 | 559 | 6,197 |
| | | | 6.3% | 18.3% | 42.1% | 19.5% | 3.2% | 0.9% | 9.7% |
| Feb. 27 | South Dakota | 69,170 | 6,037 | 19,780 | 30,918 | 8,831 | 2,378 | — | 1,226 |
| | | | 8.7% | 28.6% | 44.7% | 12.8% | 3.4% | — | 1.8% |
| March 2 | South Carolina | 276,741 | 28,647 | 80,824 | 124,904 | 35,039 | 5,752 | 1,017 | 558 |
| | | | 10.4% | 29.2% | 45.1% | 12.7% | 2.1% | 0.4% | 0.2% |
| 5 | Colorado | 247,930 | 24,184 | 53,376 | 108,123 | 51,592 | 9,052 | 1,603 | — |
| | | | 9.8% | 21.5% | 43.6% | 20.8% | 3.7% | 0.6% | — |
| 5 | Connecticut | 130,418 | 6,985 | 19,664 | 70,998 | 26,253 | 2,209 | 1,495 | 2,814 |
| | | | 5.4% | 15.1% | 54.4% | 20.1% | 1.7% | 1.1% | 2.2% |
| 5 | Georgia | 559,067 | 75,855 | 162,627 | 226,732 | 71,276 | 17,538 | 1,971 | 3,068 |
| | | | 13.6% | 29.1% | 40.6% | 12.7% | 3.1% | 0.4% | 0.5% |
| 5 | Maine | 67,280 | 4,450 | 16,478 | 31,147 | 9,991 | 1,229 | 1,934 | 2,051 |
| | | | 6.6% | 24.5% | 46.3% | 14.8% | 1.8% | 2.9% | 3.0% |
| 5 | Maryland | 254,246 | 14,061 | 53,585 | 135,522 | 32,207 | 13,718 | 2,872 | 2,281 |
| | | | 5.5% | 21.1% | 53.3% | 12.7% | 5.4% | 1.1% | 0.9% |
| 5 | Massachusetts | 284,833 | 21,456 | 71,688 | 135,946 | 39,605 | 5,224 | 4,743 | 6,171 |
| | | | 7.5% | 25.2% | 47.7% | 13.9% | 1.8% | 1.7% | 2.2% |
| 5 | Rhode Island | 15,009 | 2,859 | 387 | 9,664 | 128 | 31 | 487 | 1,453 |
| | | | 19.0% | 2.6% | 64.4% | 0.9% | 0.2% | 3.2% | 9.7% |
| 5 | Vermont | 58,113 | 6,145 | 9,730 | 23,419 | 9,066 | — | 7,881 | 1,872 |
| | | | 10.6% | 16.7% | 40.3% | 15.6% | — | 13.6% | 3.2% |
| 12 | Florida | 898,516 | 14,142 | 162,770 | 511,377 | 181,768 | 16,631 | 3,236 | 8,592 |
| | | | 1.6% | 18.1% | 56.9% | 20.2% | 1.9% | 0.4% | 1.0% |
| 12 | Louisiana | 77,789 | 1,642 | 25,757 | 37,170 | 10,265 | 2,464 | — | 491 |
| | | | 2.1% | 33.1% | 47.8% | 13.2% | 3.2% | — | 0.6% |
| 12 | Mississippi | 151,925 | 2,781 | 39,324 | 91,639 | 12,119 | 2,907 | 141 | 3,014 |
| | | | 1.8% | 25.9% | 60.3% | 8.0% | 1.9% | 0.1% | 2.0% |
| 12 | Oklahoma | 264,542 | 3,436 | 56,949 | 156,829 | 37,213 | 6,306 | 538 | 3,271 |
| | | | 1.3% | 21.5% | 59.3% | 14.1% | 2.4% | 0.2% | 1.2% |
| 12 | Oregon | 407,514 | 28,332 | 86,987 | 206,938 | 54,121 | 14,340 | 4,971 | 11,825 |
| | | | 7.0% | 21.3% | 50.8% | 13.3% | 3.5% | 1.2% | 2.9% |
| 12 | Tennessee | 289,386 | 32,742 | 72,928 | 148,063 | 22,171 | 7,661 | 531 | 5,290 |
| | | | 11.3% | 25.2% | 51.2% | 7.7% | 2.6% | 0.2% | 1.8% |
| 12 | Texas | 1,019,803 | 18,745 | 217,974 | 567,164 | 130,938 | 41,746 | 2,266 | 40,970 |
| | | | 1.8% | 21.4% | 55.6% | 12.8% | 4.1% | 0.2% | 4.0% |
| 19 | Illinois | 818,364 | 12,585 | 186,177 | 532,467 | 39,906 | 30,052 | 8,286 | 8,891 |
| | | | 1.5% | 22.7% | 65.1% | 4.9% | 3.7% | 1.0% | 1.1% |
| 19 | Michigan | 524,161 | 7,631 | 177,562 | 265,425 | 26,610 | 15,995 | 2,175 | 28,763 |
| | | | 1.5% | 33.9% | 50.6% | 5.1% | 3.1% | 0.4% | 5.5% |
| 19 | Ohio | 963,422 | 19,530 | 208,012 | 640,954 | 58,131 | 27,197 | 9,598 | — |
| | | | 2.0% | 21.6% | 66.5% | 6.0% | 2.8% | 1.0% | — |
| 19 | Wisconsin | 576,575 | 11,213 | 194,733 | 301,628 | 32,205 | 18,028 | 3,215 | 15,553 |
| | | | 1.9% | 33.8% | 52.3% | 5.6% | 3.1% | 0.6% | 2.7% |
| 26 | California | 2,452,312 | 44,130 | 450,695 | 1,619,931 | 183,367 | 93,577 | 14,801 | 45,811 |
| | | | 1.8% | 18.4% | 66.1% | 7.5% | 3.8% | 0.6% | 1.9% |
| 26 | Nevada | 140,637 | 3,289 | 21,321 | 72,932 | 27,063 | 1,999 | 464 | 13,569 |
| | | | 2.3% | 15.2% | 51.9% | 19.2% | 1.4% | 0.3% | 9.6% |
| 26 | Washington | 120,684 | 1,600 | 25,247 | 76,155 | 10,339 | 5,610 | 587 | 1,146 |
| | | | 1.3% | 20.9% | 63.1% | 8.6% | 4.6% | 0.5% | 0.9% |

# 1996 REPUBLICAN PREFERENCE PRIMARIES

| Date | State | Total Vote | Alexander | Buchanan | Dole | Forbes | Keyes | Lugar | Other |
|------|-------|-----------|-----------|----------|------|--------|-------|-------|-------|
| April 23 | Pennsylvania | 684,204 | — | 123,011 | 435,031 | 55,018 | 40,025 | 31,119 | — |
| | | | — | 18.0% | 63.6% | 8.0% | 5.8% | 4.5% | — |
| May 7 | District of Columbia | 2,987 | — | 283 | 2,256 | — | — | — | 448 |
| | | | — | 9.5% | 75.5% | — | — | — | 15.0% |
| 7 | Indiana | 516,514 | — | 100,166 | 365,568 | 50,780 | — | — | — |
| | | | — | 19.4% | 70.8% | 9.8% | — | — | — |
| 7 | North Carolina | 284,212 | 7,400 | 37,126 | 202,863 | 11,588 | 11,759 | 2,558 | 10,918 |
| | | | 2.6% | 13.1% | 71.4% | 4.1% | 4.1% | 0.9% | 3.8% |
| 14 | Nebraska | 170,591 | 4,423 | 17,741 | 129,131 | 10,612 | 5,132 | 1,127 | 2,425 |
| | | | 2.6% | 10.4% | 75.7% | 6.2% | 3.0% | 0.7% | 1.4% |
| 14 | West Virginia | 127,454 | 3,773 | 20,928 | 87,534 | 6,222 | 4,822 | 1,082 | 3,093 |
| | | | 3.0% | 16.4% | 68.7% | 4.9% | 3.8% | 0.8% | 2.4% |
| 21 | Arkansas | 42,814 | — | 10,084 | 32,687 | — | — | — | 43 |
| | | | — | 23.6% | 76.3% | — | — | — | 0.1% |
| 28 | Idaho | 118,715 | — | 26,461 | 74,011 | — | 5,904 | — | 12,339 |
| | | | — | 22.3% | 62.3% | — | 5.0% | — | 10.4% |
| 28 | Kentucky | 103,839 | 3,272 | 8,526 | 76,669 | 3,400 | 3,822 | 2,235 | 5,915 |
| | | | 3.2% | 8.2% | 73.8% | 3.3% | 3.7% | 2.2% | 5.7% |
| June 4 | Alabama | 211,933 | — | 33,409 | 160,097 | — | 7,354 | — | 11,073 |
| | | | — | 15.8% | 75.5% | — | 3.5% | — | 5.2% |
| 4 | Montana | 117,746 | — | 28,581 | 72,176 | 8,456 | — | — | 8,533 |
| | | | — | 24.3% | 61.3% | 7.2% | — | — | 7.2% |
| 4 | New Jersey | 218,812 | — | 23,789 | 180,412 | — | 14,611 | — | — |
| | | | — | 10.9% | 82.5% | — | 6.7% | — | — |
| 4 | New Mexico | 70,464 | 2,676 | 5,679 | 53,300 | 3,987 | 2,265 | — | 2,557 |
| | | | 3.8% | 8.1% | 75.6% | 5.7% | 3.2% | — | 3.6% |
| | TOTAL | 13,991,649 | 494,317 | 3,020,746 | 8,191,239 | 1,424,898 | 449,459 | 127,111 | 283,879 |
| | | | 3.5% | 21.6% | 58.5% | 10.2% | 3.2% | 0.9% | 2.0% |

Candidates on the ballot in at least one state were C.A. Aldrich, Lamar Alexander, Richard P. Bosa, Patrick J. Buchanan, Billy Joe Clegg, Charles E. Collins, Bob Dole, Robert K. Dornan, Georgiana H. Doerschuck, Susan Ducey, William James Flanagan, Malcolm S. "Steve" Forbes Jr., Russell J. Fornwalt, Doug Fricke, Phil Gramm, Kenneth Hewitt, Charles Holden, John B. Hurd, Ann Jennings, Paul Jensen, Alan Keyes, Mary "France" Le Tulle, Michael Stephen Levinson, Richard G. Lugar, Isabell Masters, Gerald J. McManus, Hilary Michael Milko, Hubert David Patty, Joann V. Pharr, Tennie Rogers, Richard D. Skillen, Clyde Staggs and Maurice "Morry" Taylor.

The Uncommitted total below includes votes cast on the following ballot lines: Uncommitted, Uninstructed, No Preference, "None of These Candidates" and "None of the Names Shown."

Other vote includes 123,277 Uncommitted; 70,003 Gramm; 42,141 Dornan; 21,180 Taylor; 2,092 Collins; 1,783 Ducey; 1,052 Masters; 940 Le Tulle; 415 Clegg; 304 Jennings; 216 Bosa; 154 Doerschuck; 125 Pharr; 109 Milko; 104 Hewitt; 99 Jensen; 94 Levinson; 80 Skillen; 72 Patty; 64 Fricke; 48 Flanagan; 47 Rogers; 38 Holden; 37 Fornwalt; 33 Staggs; 26 Hurd; 20 McManus; 19 Aldrich and 19,307 scattered write-ins.

# 1996 DEMOCRATIC PREFERENCE PRIMARIES

| Date | | State | Total Vote | Clinton | LaRouche | Uncommitted | Other |
|------|---|-------|-----------|---------|----------|-------------|-------|
| Feb. | 20 | New Hampshire | 91,562 | 76,797 | 433 | — | 14,332 |
| | | | | 83.9% | 0.5% | — | 15.7% |
| | 24 | Delaware | 10,740 | 9,694 | 1,046 | — | — |
| | | | | 90.3% | 9.7% | — | — |
| | 27 | North Dakota | 1,584 | — | 549 | — | 1,035 |
| | | | | — | 34.7% | — | 65.3% |
| March | 5 | Colorado | 54,527 | 48,454 | 5,981 | — | 92 |
| | | | | 88.9% | 11.0% | — | 0.2% |
| | 5 | Georgia | 95,103 | 95,103 | — | — | — |
| | | | | 100.0% | — | — | — |
| | 5 | Maine | 27,027 | 23,879 | 715 | 2,433 | — |
| | | | | 88.4% | 2.6% | 9.0% | — |
| | 5 | Maryland | 293,829 | 247,492 | 12,920 | 33,417 | — |
| | | | | 84.2% | 4.4% | 11.4% | — |
| | 5 | Massachusetts | 155,470 | 135,360 | 5,212 | 12,623 | 2,275 |
| | | | | 87.1% | 3.4% | 8.1% | 1.5% |
| | 5 | Rhode Island | 8,780 | 7,825 | 392 | 535 | 28 |
| | | | | 89.1% | 4.5% | 6.1% | 0.3% |
| | 5 | Vermont | 30,838 | 29,763 | 699 | — | 376 |
| | | | | 96.5% | 2.3% | — | 1.2% |
| | 12 | Louisiana | 154,701 | 124,931 | 18,150 | — | 11,620 |
| | | | | 80.8% | 11.7% | — | 7.5% |
| | 12 | Mississippi | 93,788 | 86,716 | 7,072 | — | — |
| | | | | 92.5% | 7.5% | — | — |
| | 12 | Oklahoma | 366,604 | 279,454 | 46,392 | — | 40,758 |
| | | | | 76.2% | 12.7% | — | 11.1% |
| | 12 | Oregon | 369,178 | 349,871 | — | — | 19,307 |
| | | | | 94.8% | — | — | 5.2% |
| | 12 | Tennessee | 137,797 | 122,538 | — | 15,144 | 115 |
| | | | | 88.9% | — | 11.0% | 0.1% |
| | 12 | Texas | 921,256 | 796,041 | 28,137 | — | 97,078 |
| | | | | 86.4% | 3.1% | — | 10.5% |
| | 19 | Illinois | 800,676 | 770,001 | 14,624 | — | 16,051 |
| | | | | 96.2% | 1.8% | — | 2.0% |
| | 19 | Michigan | 142,750 | — | — | 123,640 | 19,110 |
| | | | | — | — | 86.6% | 13.4% |
| | 19 | Ohio | 776,530 | 713,153 | 63,377 | — | — |
| | | | | 91.8% | 8.2% | — | — |
| | 19 | Wisconsin | 356,168 | 347,629 | — | 7,005 | 1,534 |
| | | | | 97.6% | — | 2.0% | 0.4% |
| | 26 | California | 2,523,062 | 2,342,185 | 173,953 | — | 6,924 |
| | | | | 92.8% | 6.9% | — | 0.3% |
| | 26 | Washington | 98,946 | 97,495 | 1,451 | — | — |
| | | | | 98.5% | 1.5% | — | — |
| April | 23 | Pennsylvania | 724,069 | 666,486 | 57,583 | — | — |
| | | | | 92.0% | 8.0% | — | — |
| May | 7 | District of Columbia | 20,959 | 20,568 | 391 | — | — |
| | | | | 98.1% | 1.9% | — | — |
| | 7 | Indiana | 329,462 | 329,462 | — | — | — |
| | | | | 100.0% | — | — | — |
| | 7 | North Carolina | 572,160 | 461,434 | 40,936 | 69,790 | — |
| | | | | 80.6% | 7.2% | 12.2% | — |
| | 14 | Nebraska | 94,176 | 81,854 | 10,228 | — | 2,094 |
| | | | | 86.9% | 10.9% | — | 2.2% |
| | 14 | West Virginia | 297,121 | 257,087 | 40,034 | — | — |
| | | | | 86.5% | 13.5% | — | — |
| | 21 | Arkansas | 300,389 | 236,547 | 20,401 | 30,416 | 13,025 |
| | | | | 78.7% | 6.8% | 10.1% | 4.3% |

# 1996 DEMOCRATIC PREFERENCE PRIMARIES

| Date | | State | Total Vote | Clinton | LaRouche | Uncommitted | Other |
|------|---|-------|-----------|---------|----------|-------------|-------|
| | 28 | Idaho | 40,228 | 35,277 | — | 4,951 | — |
| | | | | 87.7% | — | 12.3% | — |
| | 28 | Kentucky | 276,019 | 211,667 | 20,324 | 44,028 | — |
| | | | | 76.7% | 7.4% | 16.0% | — |
| June | 4 | Alabama | 302,038 | 243,588 | 12,686 | 45,764 | — |
| | | | | 80.6% | 4.2% | 15.2% | — |
| | 4 | Montana | 91,725 | 82,549 | — | 9,176 | — |
| | | | | 90.0% | — | 10.0% | — |
| | 4 | New Jersey | 266,740 | 254,004 | 12,736 | — | — |
| | | | | 95.2% | 4.8% | — | — |
| | 4 | New Mexico | 121,362 | 109,595 | — | 11,767 | — |
| | | | | 90.3% | — | 9.7% | — |
| | | TOTAL | 10,947,364 | 9,694,499 | 596,422 | 410,689 | 245,754 |
| | | | | 88.6% | 5.4% | 3.8% | 2.2% |

Candidates on the ballot in at least one state were Willie Felix Carter, Sal Casamassima, Carmen C. Chimento, Vernon Clemenson, Bill Clinton, Bruce C. Daniels, Michael E. Dass, Robert F. Drucker, James D. Griffin, Ted L. Gunderson, Vincent S. Hamm, Heather Anne Harder, Fred Hudson, Caroline P. Killeen, Lyndon H. LaRouche Jr., Frank Legas, Elvena E. Lloyd-Duffie, Stephen Michael, David Pauling, Pat Paulsen, Roland Riemers, John Safran, Ronald W. Spangler, Osie Thorpe and Ben J. Tomeo.

The Uncommitted column above includes votes cast on the following ballot lines: Uncommitted, Uninstructed, No Preference and "None of the Names Shown."

Other vote includes 92,324 Lloyd-Duffie; 32,232 Hudson; 29,147 Harder; 15,712 Gunderson; 9,693 Casamassima; 1,317 Paulsen; 656 Chimento; 651 Riemers; 391 Killeen; 384 Clemenson; 312 Daniels; 307 Griffin; 94 Michael; 85 Carter; 81 Drucker; 74 Pauling; 72 Hamm; 72 Spangler; 63 Legas; 57 Dass; 50 Thorpe; 47 Tomeo; 42 Safran and 61,891 scattered write-ins.

# 1992 PRESIDENTIAL PRIMARIES

In 1992 thirty-eight states and the District of Columbia held Presidential primaries, though there was no Republican preference vote in New York.

In some states balloting was for delegate slates pledged to specific Presidential candidates or uncommitted; in others, electors indicated a personal preference as to their party's nominee.

The state-by-state Republican and Democratic tables, included at the end of this section, detail in chronological order the vote for major candidates in each party. An asterisk in the table indicates votes written-in for a candidate not on the ballot.

Republican candidates on the ballot in at least one state were Sharon Anderson, Jack J. H. Beemont, Norm Bertasavage, Richard P. Bosa, Emmanuel L. Branch, Patrick J. Buchanan, George Bush, Billy Joe Clegg, Paul B. Conley, Paul C. Daugherty, Georgiana H. Doerschuck, Charles R. Doty, David E. Duke, Oscar A. Erickson, Thomas S. Fabish, Jack Fellure, Maurice Horton, Paul S. Jensen, F. Dean Johnson, Stephen A. Koczak, Vincent A. Latchford, James P. Lennane, Michael S. Levinson, Isabell Masters, John D. Merwin, Stephen D. Michael, Beatrice J. Mooney, Hubert D. Patty, Pat Paulsen, Richard F. Reber, Tennie Rogers, Conrad A. Ryden, Terrance R. Scott, Philip P. Skow, Harold E. Stassen, Jack Trinsey, George A. Zimmermann.

Democratic candidates on the ballot in at least one state were Lawrence A. Agran, Nathan J. Averick, George H. Ballard, John A. Barnes, Don Beamgard, George W. Benns, Frank J. Bona, Edmund G. Brown Jr.,Stephen Burke, John P. Cahill, Bill Clinton, Bob Cunningham, Dean A. Curtis, Barry J. Deutsch, Susan C. Fey, Paul Fisher, Lenora B. Fulani, James B. Gay, Robert F. Hanson, Tom Harkin, Gary Hauptli, Tod H. Hawks, Jim Hayes, Karl J. Hegger, Rufus T. Higginbotham, Gilbert H. Holmes, William Horrigan, Bob Kerrey, Caroline P. Killeen, Ron Kovic, William P. Kreml, Lyndon H. LaRouche, Tom Laughlin, Patrick J. Mahoney, Jeffrey F. Marsh, J. Louis McAlpine, Eugene J. McCarthy, Angus W. McDonald, Fanny R. Z. Monyek, Ralph Nader, Chris Norton, Edward T. O'Donnell, William D. Pawley, Mary Jane Rachner, John D. Rigazio, Ray Rollinson, Cyril E. Sagan, Stephen H. Schwartz, Tom Shiekman, Ralph Spelbring, John J. Staradumsky, Louis Stokes, Leonard D. Talbow, Curly Thornton, Paul E. Tsongas, Raymond J. Vanskiver, L. Douglas Wilder, Charles Woods.

## ALABAMA JUNE 2

Republican   122,703 Bush; 29,830 Uncommitted; 12,588 Buchanan.

Democratic   307,621 Clinton; 90,863 Uncommitted; 30,626 Brown; 15,247 Woods; 6,542 LaRouche.

## ARKANSAS MAY 26

Republican   45,590 Bush; 6,551 Buchanan.

Democratic   342,017 Clinton; 90,710 Uncommitted; 55,234 Brown; 14,656 LaRouche.

## CALIFORNIA JUNE 2

Republican   1,587,369 Bush; 568,892 Buchanan; 203 scattered write-in.

Democratic   1,359,112 Clinton; 1,150,460 Brown; 212,522 Tsongas; 60,635 McCarthy; 33,935 Kerrey; 24,784 Agran; 21,971 LaRouche; 190 scattered write-in.

## COLORADO MARCH 3

Republican   132,100 Bush; 58,753 Buchanan; 1,592 Zimmermann; 1,332 Jensen; 719 Scott; 659 Koczak; 535 Rogers.

Democratic   69,073 Brown; 64,470 Clinton; 61,360 Tsongas; 29,572 Kerrey; 5,866 Harkin; 5,356 Noncommitted; 1,051 Woods; 672 Agran; 532 Burke; 488 McCarthy; 328 LaRouche; 279 Hayes; 202 Talbow; 165 Hawks; 76 Shiekman; 59 Marsh; 48 McAlpine; 46 Rollinson.

# 1992 PRESIDENTIAL PRIMARIES

**CONNECTICUT MARCH 24**

Republican   66,356 Bush; 21,815 Buchanan; 9,008 Uncommitted; 2,294 Duke.

Democratic   64,472 Brown; 61,698 Clinton; 33,811 Tsongas; 5,430 Uncommitted; 2,688 Agran; 1,919 Harkin; 1,169 Kerrey; 1,036 McCarthy; 896 LaRouche.

**FLORIDA MARCH 10**

Republican   608,077 Bush; 285,386 Buchanan.

Democratic   570,566 Clinton; 388,124 Tsongas; 139,569 Brown; 13,587 Harkin; 12,011 Kerrey.

**GEORGIA MARCH 3**

Republican   291,905 Bush; 162,085 Buchanan.

Democratic   259,907 Clinton; 109,148 Tsongas; 36,808 Brown; 22,033 Kerrey; 17,256 Uncommitted; 9,479 Harkin.

**IDAHO MAY 26**

Republican   73,297 Bush; 27,038 "None of the Names Shown"; 15,167 Buchanan.

Democratic   27,004 Clinton; 16,029 "None of the Names Shown"; 9,212 Brown; 2,011 LaRouche; 868 Agran.

**ILLINOIS MARCH 17**

Republican   634,588 Bush; 186,915 Buchanan; 9,637 Horton.

Democratic   776,829 Clinton; 387,891 Tsongas; 220,346 Brown; 67,612 Uncommitted; 30,710 Harkin; 10,916 Kerrey; 6,599 LaRouche; 3,227 Agran.

**INDIANA MAY 5**

Republican   374,666 Bush; 92,949 Buchanan.

Democratic   301,905 Clinton; 102,379 Brown; 58,215 Tsongas; 14,350 Kerrey.

**KANSAS APRIL 7**

Republican   132,131 Bush; 35,450 "None of the Names Shown"; 31,494 Buchanan; 5,105 Paulsen; 3,837 Duke; 1,303 Masters; 1,105 Skow; 766 Zimmermann; 735 Beemont; 417 Doty; 262 Koczak; 236 Daugherty; 164 Fellure; 85 Rogers; 62 Patty; 44 Fabish.

Democratic   82,145 Clinton; 24,413 Tsongas; 22,159 "None of the Names Shown"; 20,811 Brown; 2,215 Kerrey; 1,303 Hauptli; 1,119 Woods; 1,009 Beamgard; 940 Harkin; 892 Barnes; 765 Hawks; 631 LaRouche; 537 Spelbring; 510 Vanskiver; 364 Pawley; 160 Marsh; 147 Agran; 131 McAlpine.

**KENTUCKY MAY 26**

Republican   75,371 Bush; 25,748 Uncommitted.

Democratic   207,804 Clinton; 103,590 Uncommitted; 30,709 Brown; 18,097 Tsongas; 7,136 Harkin; 3,242 Kerrey.

# 1992 PRESIDENTIAL PRIMARIES

**LOUISIANA MARCH 10**

Republican   83,744 Bush; 36,525 Buchanan; 11,955 Duke; 1,186 Paulsen; 1,111 Rogers; 474 Zimmermann; 114 Fabish.

Democratic   267,002 Clinton; 42,508 Tsongas; 25,480 Brown; 15,129 McCarthy; 8,989 Woods; 4,294 Burke; 4,033 Harkin; 3,511 Agran; 3,082 LaRouche; 2,984 Kerrey; 2,120 Marsh; 1,857 Laughlin; 1,469 Hawks; 1,069 Rollinson; 870 McAlpine.

**MARYLAND MARCH 3**

Republican   168,374 Bush; 71,647 Buchanan.

Democratic   230,490 Tsongas; 189,905 Clinton; 46,500 Brown; 36,155 Uncommitted; 32,899 Harkin; 27,035 Kerrey; 4,259 LaRouche.

**MASSACHUSETTS MARCH 10**

Republican   176,868 Bush; 74,797 Buchanan; 10,132 No Preference; 5,557 Duke; 2,347 scattered write-in.

Democratic   526,297 Tsongas; 115,746 Brown; 86,817 Clinton; 32,881 Nader; 12,198 No Preference; 5,409 Kerrey; 3,764 Harkin; 3,127 McCarthy; 2,224 Agran; 2,167 LaRouche; 2,255 scattered write-in.

**MICHIGAN MARCH 17**

Republican   301,948 Bush; 112,122 Buchanan; 23,809 Uncommitted; 10,688 Duke; 566 scattered write-in.

Democratic   297,280 Clinton; 151,400 Brown; 97,017 Tsongas; 27,836 Uncommitted; 6,265 Harkin; 3,219 Kerrey; 2,049 LaRouche; 906 scattered write-in.

**MINNESOTA APRIL 7**

Republican   84,841 Bush; 32,094 Buchanan; 4,098 Uncommitted; 4,074 Stassen; 300 Anderson; 196 Mooney; 135 Zimmermann; 61 Rogers; 3,558 Ross Perot (write-in); 3,399 scattered write-in.

Democratic   63,584 Clinton; 62,474 Brown; 43,588 Tsongas; 11,366 Uncommitted; 4,077 Harkin; 3,704 McCarthy; 1,191 Kerrey; 1,042 Agran; 990 Woods; 620 Rachner; 532 LaRouche; 348 Burke; 183 McAlpine; 111 Hawks; 106 Marsh; 105 Averick; 4,250 Ross Perot (write-in); 5,899 scattered write-in.

**MISSISSIPPI MARCH 10**

Republican   111,794 Bush; 25,891 Buchanan; 16,426 Duke; 408 Clegg; 189 Rogers.

Democratic   139,893 Clinton; 18,396 Brown; 15,538 Tsongas; 11,796 Uncommitted; 2,509 Harkin; 1,660 Kerrey; 1,394 LaRouche; 171 scattered write-in.

**MONTANA JUNE 2**

Republican   65,176 Bush; 15,098 No Preference; 10,701 Buchanan.

Democratic   54,989 Clinton; 28,164 No Preference; 21,704 Brown; 12,614 Tsongas.

# 1992 PRESIDENTIAL PRIMARIES

**NEBRASKA MAY 12**

Republican 156,346 Bush; 25,847 Buchanan; 2,808 Duke; 1,313 Zimmermann; 751 Rogers; 5,033 scattered write-in.

Democratic 68,562 Clinton; 31,673 Brown; 24,714 Uncommitted; 10,707 Tsongas; 4,239 Harkin; 1,520 McCarthy; 1,148 LaRouche; 485 Woods; 280 Agran; 7,259 scattered write-in.

**NEW HAMPSHIRE FEBRUARY 18**

Republican 92,233 Bush; 65,087 Buchanan; 1,684 Lennane; 600 Paulsen; 349 Bosa; 223 Merwin; 206 Stassen; 115 Conley; 110 Clegg; 57 Doerschuck; 53 Daugherty; 44 Levinson; 36 Fellure; 32 Latchford; 31 Patty; 31 Zimmermann; 29 Koczak; 25 Fabish; 24 Johnson; 23 Bertasavage; 22 Trinsey; 20 Rogers; 20 Ryden; 16 Erickson; 14 Reber; 13,081 scattered write-in.

Democratic 55,638 Tsongas; 41,522 Clinton; 18,575 Kerrey; 17,057 Harkin; 13,654 Brown; 3,251 Laughlin; 2,862 Woods; 402 Fulani; 332 Agran; 303 Mahoney; 211 McCarthy; 186 Rigazio; 125 Thornton; 115 LaRouche; 103 Wilder; 93 Killeen; 83 Cahill; 82 Fisher; 65 Bona; 61 Hegger; 53 Horrigan; 43 Curtis; 39 Burke; 39 Holmes; 36 Kovic; 31 Higginbotham; 31 Norton; 29 Monyek; 28 Gay; 26 Deutsch; 26 Sagan; 24 O'Donnell; 23 Shiekman; 17 Schwartz; 11 Benns; 7 Averick; 12,636 scattered write-in.

**NEW JERSEY JUNE 2**

Republican 240,535 Bush; 46,432 Buchanan; 23,303 Ross Perot (write-in).

Democratic 243,741 Clinton; 79,877 Brown; 45,191 Tsongas; 12,478 Ross Perot (write-in); 7,799 LaRouche; 2,067 Ballard; 1,473 Hanson.

**NEW MEXICO JUNE 2**

Republican 55,522 Bush; 23,574 Uncommitted; 7,871 Buchanan.

Democratic 95,933 Clinton; 35,269 Uncommitted; 30,705 Brown; 11,315 Tsongas; 3,233 Harkin; 2,573 Agran; 2,415 LaRouche.

**NEW YORK APRIL 7**

Republican No Presidential preference vote held.

Democratic 412,349 Clinton; 288,330 Tsongas; 264,278 Brown; 11,535 Harkin; 11,147 Kerrey; 10,733 Agran; 9,354 McCarthy.

**NORTH CAROLINA MAY 5**

Republican 200,387 Bush; 55,420 Buchanan; 27,764 No Preference.

Democratic 443,498 Clinton; 106,697 No Preference; 71,984 Brown; 57,589 Tsongas; 6,216 Kerrey; 5,891 Harkin.

**NORTH DAKOTA JUNE 9**

Republican 39,863 Bush; 4,093 Paulsen; 3,852 Ross Perot (write-in).

Democratic 9,516 Ross Perot (write-in); 7,003 LaRouche; 6,641 Woods; 4,866 Shiekman; 4,760 Clinton (write-in).

# 1992 PRESIDENTIAL PRIMARIES

**OHIO JUNE 2**

Republican   716,766 Bush; 143,687 Buchanan.

Democratic   638,347 Clinton; 197,449 Brown; 110,773 Tsongas; 29,983 Stokes; 25,395 Harkin; 22,976 Kerrey; 17,412 LaRouche.

**OKLAHOMA MARCH 10**

Republican   151,612 Bush; 57,933 Buchanan; 5,672 Duke; 1,830 Masters; 674 Rogers.

Democratic   293,266 Clinton; 69,624 Brown; 16,828 Woods; 14,015 Harkin; 13,252 Kerrey; 6,474 LaRouche; 2,670 McAlpine.

**OREGON MAY 19**

Republican   203,957 Bush; 57,730 Buchanan; 6,667 Duke; 35,805 scattered write-in.

Democratic   159,802 Clinton; 110,494 Brown; 37,139 Tsongas; 6,714 McCarthy; 3,096 LaRouche; 1,895 Woods; 1,652 Agran; 33,540 scattered write-in.

**PENNSYLVANIA APRIL 28**

Republican   774,865 Bush; 233,912 Buchanan.

Democratic   715,031 Clinton; 325,543 Brown; 161,572 Tsongas; 21,534 LaRouche; 21,013 Harkin; 20,802 Kerrey.

**RHODE ISLAND MARCH 10**

Republican   9,853 Bush; 4,967 Buchanan; 444 Uncommitted; 326 Duke; 46 scattered write-in.

Democratic   26,825 Tsongas; 10,762 Clinton; 9,541 Brown; 703 Uncommitted; 469 Kerrey; 408 Woods; 319 Harkin; 308 Fey; 300 LaRouche; 235 McCarthy; 168 Staradumsky; 94 Laughlin; 91 Rollinson; 79 Agran; 52 Thornton; 48 Burke; 307 scattered write-in.

**SOUTH CAROLINA MARCH 7**

Republican   99,558 Bush; 38,247 Buchanan; 10,553 Duke; 482 Daugherty.

Democratic   73,221 Clinton; 21,338 Tsongas; 7,657 Harkin; 6,961 Brown; 3,640 Uncommitted; 1,369 Cunningham; 854 Woods; 566 Kerrey; 336 Kreml; 268 McDonald; 204 LaRouche.

**SOUTH DAKOTA FEBRUARY 25**

Republican   30,964 Bush; 13,707 Uncommitted.

Democratic   23,892 Kerrey; 15,023 Harkin; 11,375 Clinton; 5,729 Tsongas; 2,300 Brown; 606 Agran; 441 LaRouche; 137 Wilder.

**TENNESSEE MARCH 10**

Republican   178,219 Bush; 54,585 Buchanan; 7,709 Duke; 5,022 Uncommitted; 118 scattered write-in.

Democratic   214,485 Clinton; 61,717 Tsongas; 25,560 Brown; 12,551 Uncommitted; 2,099 Harkin; 1,638 Kerrey; 432 scattered write-in.

# 1992 PRESIDENTIAL PRIMARIES

## TEXAS MARCH 10

Republican   556,280 Bush; 190,572 Buchanan; 27,936 Uncommitted; 20,255 Duke; 1,349 Zimmermann; 754 Rogers.

Democratic   972,151 Clinton; 285,191 Tsongas; 118,923 Brown; 30,092 Woods; 20,298 Kerrey; 19,617 Harkin; 12,220 LaRouche; 7,876 Benns; 7,674 Higginbotham; 4,924 Hawks; 4,009 McAlpine.

## WASHINGTON MAY 19

Republican   86,839 Bush; 25,423 Ross Perot (write-in); 13,273 Buchanan; 2,619 Michael; 1,501 Duke.

Democratic   62,171 Clinton; 34,111 Brown; 28,311 Ross Perot (write-in); 18,981 Tsongas; 1,858 Harkin; 1,489 Kerrey; 1,060 LaRouche.

## WEST VIRGINIA MAY 12

Republican   99,994 Bush; 18,067 Buchanan; 6,096 Fellure.

Democratic   227,815 Clinton; 36,505 Brown; 21,271 Tsongas; 9,632 McDonald; 3,152 Kerrey; 3,141 LaRouche; 2,774 Harkin; 1,487 Woods; 1,089 Spelbring.

## WISCONSIN APRIL 7

Republican   364,507 Bush; 78,516 Buchanan; 12,867 Duke; 8,725 Uninstructed; 3,819 Stassen; 1,013 Branch; 12,801 scattered write-in.

Democratic   287,356 Clinton; 266,207 Brown; 168,619 Tsongas; 15,487 Uninstructed; 6,525 McCarthy; 5,395 Harkin; 3,193 Agran; 3,120 LaRouche; 3,044 Kerrey; 13,650 scattered write-in.

## DISTRICT OF COLUMBIA MAY 5

Republican   4,265 Bush; 970 Buchanan.

Democratic   45,716 Clinton; 6,452 Tsongas; 5,292 Uncommitted; 4,444 Brown.

# 1992 REPUBLICAN PREFERENCE PRIMARIES

| Date | | State | Total Vote | Buchanan | Bush | Duke | Uncommitted | Other |
|---|---|---|---|---|---|---|---|---|
| Feb. | 18 | New Hampshire | 174,165 | 65,087 | 92,233 | — | — | 16,845 |
| | | | | 37.4% | 53.0% | — | — | 9.7% |
| | 25 | South Dakota | 44,671 | — | 30,964 | — | 13,707 | — |
| | | | | — | 69.3% | — | 30.7% | — |
| March | 3 | Colorado | 195,690 | 58,753 | 132,100 | — | — | 4,837 |
| | | | | 30.0% | 67.5% | — | — | 2.5% |
| | 3 | Georgia | 453,990 | 162,085 | 291,905 | — | — | — |
| | | | | 35.7% | 64.3% | — | — | — |
| | 3 | Maryland | 240,021 | 71,647 | 168,374 | — | — | — |
| | | | | 29.9% | 70.1% | — | — | — |
| | 7 | South Carolina | 148,840 | 38,247 | 99,558 | 10,553 | — | 482 |
| | | | | 25.7% | 66.9% | 7.1% | — | 0.3% |
| | 10 | Florida | 893,463 | 285,386 | 608,077 | — | — | — |
| | | | | 31.9% | 68.1% | — | — | — |
| | 10 | Louisiana | 135,109 | 36,525 | 83,744 | 11,955 | — | 2,885 |
| | | | | 27.0% | 62.0% | 8.8% | — | 2.1% |
| | 10 | Massachusetts | 269,701 | 74,797 | 176,868 | 5,557 | 10,132 | 2,347 |
| | | | | 27.7% | 65.6% | 2.1% | 3.8% | 0.9% |
| | 10 | Mississippi | 154,708 | 25,891 | 111,794 | 16,426 | — | 597 |
| | | | | 16.7% | 72.3% | 10.6% | — | 0.4% |
| | 10 | Oklahoma | 217,721 | 57,933 | 151,612 | 5,672 | — | 2,504 |
| | | | | 26.6% | 69.6% | 2.6% | — | 1.2% |
| | 10 | Rhode Island | 15,636 | 4,967 | 9,853 | 326 | 444 | 46 |
| | | | | 31.8% | 63.0% | 2.1% | 2.8% | 0.3 |
| | 10 | Tennessee | 245,653 | 54,585 | 178,219 | 7,709 | 5,022 | 118 |
| | | | | 22.2% | 72.5% | 3.1% | 2.0% | 0.0% |
| | 10 | Texas | 797,146 | 190,572 | 556,280 | 20,255 | 27,936 | 2,103 |
| | | | | 23.9% | 69.8% | 2.5% | 3.5% | 0.3% |
| | 17 | Illinois | 831,140 | 186,915 | 634,588 | — | — | 9,637 |
| | | | | 22.5% | 76.4% | — | — | 1.2% |
| | 17 | Michigan | 449,133 | 112,122 | 301,948 | 10,688 | 23,809 | 566 |
| | | | | 25.0% | 67.2% | 2.4% | 5.3% | 0.1% |
| | 24 | Connecticut | 99,473 | 21,815 | 66,356 | 2,294 | 9,008 | — |
| | | | | 21.9% | 66.7% | 2.3% | 9.1% | — |
| April | 7 | Kansas | 213,196 | 31,494 | 132,131 | 3,837 | 35,450 | 10,284 |
| | | | | 14.8% | 62.0% | 1.8% | 16.6% | 4.8% |
| | 7 | Minnesota | 132,756 | 32,094 | 84,841 | — | 4,098 | 11,723 |
| | | | | 24.2% | 63.9% | — | 3.1% | 8.8% |
| | 7 | New York | No Presidential Preference Vote Held | | | | | |
| | 7 | Wisconsin | 482,248 | 78,516 | 364,507 | 12,867 | 8,725 | 17,633 |
| | | | | 16.3% | 75.6% | 2.7% | 1.8% | 3.7% |
| | 28 | Pennsylvania | 1,008,777 | 233,912 | 774,865 | — | — | — |
| | | | | 23.2% | 76.8% | — | — | — |
| May | 5 | Dist. of Col. | 5,235 | 970 | 4,265 | — | — | — |
| | | | | 18.5% | 81.5% | — | — | — |
| | 5 | Indiana | 467,615 | 92,949 | 374,666 | — | — | — |
| | | | | 19.9% | 80.1% | — | — | — |
| | 5 | North Carolina | 283,571 | 55,420 | 200,387 | — | 27,764 | — |
| | | | | 19.5% | 70.7% | — | 9.8% | — |
| | 12 | Nebraska | 192,098 | 25,847 | 156,346 | 2,808 | — | 7,097 |
| | | | | 13.5% | 81.4% | 1.5% | — | 3.7% |
| | 12 | West Virginia | 124,157 | 18,067 | 99,994 | — | — | 6,096 |
| | | | | 14.6% | 80.5% | — | — | 4.9% |
| | 19 | Oregon | 304,159 | 57,730 | 203,957 | 6,667 | — | 35,805 |
| | | | | 19.0% | 67.1% | 2.2% | — | 11.8% |
| | 19 | Washington | 129,655 | 13,273 | 86,839 | 1,501 | — | 28,042 |
| | | | | 10.2% | 67.0% | 1.2% | — | 21.6% |

# 1992 REPUBLICAN PREFERENCE PRIMARIES

| Date | | State | Total Vote | Buchanan | Bush | Duke | Uncommitted | Other |
|---|---|---|---|---|---|---|---|---|
| | 26 | Arkansas | 52,141 | 6,551 | 45,590 | — | — | — |
| | | | | 12.6% | 87.4% | — | — | — |
| | 26 | Idaho | 115,502 | 15,167 | 73,297 | — | 27,038 | — |
| | | | | 13.1% | 63.5% | — | 23.4% | — |
| | 26 | Kentucky | 101,119 | — | 75,371 | — | 25,748 | — |
| | | | | — | 74.5% | — | 25.5% | — |
| June | 2 | Alabama | 165,121 | 12,588 | 122,703 | — | 29,830 | — |
| | | | | 7.6% | 74.3% | — | 18.1% | — |
| | 2 | California | 2,156,464 | 568,892 | 1,587,369 | — | — | 203 |
| | | | | 26.4% | 73.6% | — | — | 0.0% |
| | 2 | Montana | 90,975 | 10,701 | 65,176 | — | 15,098 | — |
| | | | | 11.8% | 71.6% | — | 16.6% | — |
| | 2 | New Jersey | 310,270 | 46,432 | 240,535 | — | — | 23,303 |
| | | | | 15.0% | 77.5% | — | — | 7.5% |
| | 2 | New Mexico | 86,967 | 7,871 | 55,522 | — | 23,574 | — |
| | | | | 9.1% | 63.8% | — | 27.1% | — |
| | 2 | Ohio | 860,453 | 143,687 | 716,766 | — | — | — |
| | | | | 16.7% | 83.3% | — | — | — |
| | 9 | North Dakota | 47,808 | — | 39,863 | — | — | 7,945 |
| | | | | — | 83.4% | — | — | 16.6% |
| | | TOTAL | 12,696,547 | 2,899,488 | 9,199,463 | 119,115 | 287,383 | 191,098 |
| | | | | 22.8% | 72.5% | 0.9% | 2.3% | 1.5% |

The Uncommitted column above includes votes cast on the following ballot lines: Uncommitted, No Preference, Uninstructed and "None of the Names Shown".

Other vote includes 56,136 Perot (write-in); 10,984 Paulsen; 9,637 Horton; 8,099 Stassen; 6,296 Fellure; 5,660 Zimmermann; 4,180 Rogers; 3,133 Masters; 2,619 Michael; 1,684 Lennane; 1,332 Jensen; 1,105 Skow; 1,013 Branch; 950 Koczak; 771 Daugherty; 735 Beemont; 719 Scott; 518 Clegg; 417 Doty; 349 Bosa; 300 Anderson; 223 Merwin; 196 Mooney; 183 Fabish; 115 Conley; 93 Patty; 57 Doerschuck; 44 Levinson; 32 Latchford; 24 Johnson; 23 Bertasavage; 22 Trinsey; 20 Ryden; 16 Erickson; 14 Reber and 73,399 scattered write-ins.

# 1992 DEMOCRATIC PREFERENCE PRIMARIES

| Date | State | Total Vote | Brown | Clinton | Harkin | Kerrey | Tsongas | Uncommitted | Other |
|---|---|---|---|---|---|---|---|---|---|
| Feb. 18 | New Hampshire | 167,819 | 13,654 | 41,522 | 17,057 | 18,575 | 55,638 | — | 21,373 |
| | | | 8.1% | 24.7% | 10.2% | 11.1% | 33.2% | — | 12.7% |
| 25 | South Dakota | 59,503 | 2,300 | 11,375 | 15,023 | 23,892 | 5,729 | — | 1,184 |
| | | | 3.9% | 19.1% | 25.2% | 40.2% | 9.6% | — | 2.0% |
| March 3 | Colorado | 239,643 | 69,073 | 64,470 | 5,866 | 29,572 | 61,360 | 5,356 | 3,946 |
| | | | 28.8% | 26.9% | 2.4% | 12.3% | 25.6% | 2.2% | 1.6% |
| 3 | Georgia | 454,631 | 36,808 | 259,907 | 9,479 | 22,033 | 109,148 | 17,256 | — |
| | | | 8.1% | 57.2% | 2.1% | 4.8% | 24.0% | 3.8% | — |
| 3 | Maryland | 567,243 | 46,500 | 189,905 | 32,899 | 27,035 | 230,490 | 36,155 | 4,259 |
| | | | 8.2% | 33.5% | 5.8% | 4.8% | 40.6% | 6.4% | 0.8% |
| 7 | South Carolina | 116,414 | 6,961 | 73,221 | 7,657 | 566 | 21,338 | 3,640 | 3,031 |
| | | | 6.0% | 62.9% | 6.6% | 0.5% | 18.3% | 3.1% | 2.6% |
| 10 | Florida | 1,123,857 | 139,569 | 570,566 | 13,587 | 12,011 | 388,124 | — | — |
| | | | 12.4% | 50.8% | 1.2% | 1.1% | 34.5% | — | — |
| 10 | Louisiana | 384,397 | 25,480 | 267,002 | 4,033 | 2,984 | 42,508 | — | 42,390 |
| | | | 6.6% | 69.5% | 1.0% | 0.8% | 11.1% | — | 11.0% |
| 10 | Massachusetts | 792,885 | 115,746 | 86,817 | 3,764 | 5,409 | 526,297 | 12,198 | 42,654 |
| | | | 14.6% | 10.9% | 0.5% | 0.7% | 66.4% | 1.5% | 5.4% |
| 10 | Mississippi | 191,357 | 18,396 | 139,893 | 2,509 | 1,660 | 15,538 | 11,796 | 1,565 |
| | | | 9.6% | 73.1% | 1.3% | 0.9% | 8.1% | 6.2% | 0.8% |
| 10 | Oklahoma | 416,129 | 69,624 | 293,266 | 14,015 | 13,252 | — | — | 25,972 |
| | | | 16.7% | 70.5% | 3.4% | 3.2% | — | — | 6.2% |
| 10 | Rhode Island | 50,709 | 9,541 | 10,762 | 319 | 469 | 26,825 | 703 | 2,090 |
| | | | 18.8% | 21.2% | 0.6% | 0.9% | 52.9% | 1.4% | 4.1% |
| 10 | Tennessee | 318,482 | 25,560 | 214,485 | 2,099 | 1,638 | 61,717 | 12,551 | 432 |
| | | | 8.0% | 67.3% | 0.7% | 0.5% | 19.4% | 3.9% | 0.1% |
| 10 | Texas | 1,482,975 | 118,923 | 972,151 | 19,617 | 20,298 | 285,191 | — | 66,795 |
| | | | 8.0% | 65.6% | 1.3% | 1.4% | 19.2% | — | 4.5% |
| 17 | Illinois | 1,504,130 | 220,346 | 776,829 | 30,710 | 10,916 | 387,891 | 67,612 | 9,826 |
| | | | 14.6% | 51.6% | 2.0% | 0.7% | 25.8% | 4.5% | 0.7% |
| 17 | Michigan | 585,972 | 151,400 | 297,280 | 6,265 | 3,219 | 97,017 | 27,836 | 2,955 |
| | | | 25.8% | 50.7% | 1.1% | 0.5% | 16.6% | 4.8% | 0.5% |
| 24 | Connecticut | 173,119 | 64,472 | 61,698 | 1,919 | 1,169 | 33,811 | 5,430 | 4,620 |
| | | | 37.2% | 35.6% | 1.1% | 0.7% | 19.5% | 3.1% | 2.7% |
| April 7 | Kansas | 160,251 | 20,811 | 82,145 | 940 | 2,215 | 24,413 | 22,159 | 7,568 |
| | | | 13.0% | 51.3% | 0.6% | 1.4% | 15.2% | 13.8% | 4.7% |
| 7 | Minnesota | 204,170 | 62,474 | 63,584 | 4,077 | 1,191 | 43,588 | 11,366 | 17,890 |
| | | | 30.6% | 31.1% | 2.0% | 0.6% | 21.3% | 5.6% | 8.8% |
| 7 | New York | 1,007,726 | 264,278 | 412,349 | 11,535 | 11,147 | 288,330 | — | 20,087 |
| | | | 26.2% | 40.9% | 1.1% | 1.1% | 28.6% | — | 2.0% |
| 7 | Wisconsin | 772,596 | 266,207 | 287,356 | 5,395 | 3,044 | 168,619 | 15,487 | 26,488 |
| | | | 34.5% | 37.2% | 0.7% | 0.4% | 21.8% | 2.0% | 3.4% |
| 28 | Pennsylvania | 1,265,495 | 325,543 | 715,031 | 21,013 | 20,802 | 161,572 | — | 21,534 |
| | | | 25.7% | 56.5% | 1.7% | 1.6% | 12.8% | — | 1.7% |
| May 5 | Dist. of Col. | 61,904 | 4,444 | 45,716 | — | — | 6,452 | 5,292 | — |
| | | | 7.2% | 73.8% | — | — | 10.4% | 8.5% | — |
| 5 | Indiana | 476,849 | 102,379 | 301,905 | — | 14,350 | 58,215 | — | — |
| | | | 21.5% | 63.3% | — | 3.0% | 12.2% | — | — |
| 5 | North Carolina | 691,875 | 71,984 | 443,498 | 5,891 | 6,216 | 57,589 | 106,697 | — |
| | | | 10.4% | 64.1% | 0.9% | 0.9% | 8.3% | 15.4% | — |
| 12 | Nebraska | 150,587 | 31,673 | 68,562 | 4,239 | — | 10,707 | 24,714 | 10,692 |
| | | | 21.0% | 45.5% | 2.8% | — | 7.1% | 16.4% | 7.1% |
| 12 | West Virginia | 306,866 | 36,505 | 227,815 | 2,774 | 3,152 | 21,271 | — | 15,349 |
| | | | 11.9% | 74.2% | 0.9% | 1.0% | 6.9% | — | 5.0% |
| 19 | Oregon | 354,332 | 110,494 | 159,802 | — | — | 37,139 | — | 46,897 |
| | | | 31.2% | 45.1% | — | — | 10.5% | — | 13.2% |
| 19 | Washington | 147,981 | 34,111 | 62,171 | 1,858 | 1,489 | 18,981 | — | 29,371 |
| | | | 23.1% | 42.0% | 1.3% | 1.0% | 12.8% | — | 19.8% |

# 1992 DEMOCRATIC PREFERENCE PRIMARIES

| Date | State | Total Vote | Brown | Clinton | Harkin | Kerrey | Tsongas | Uncommitted | Other |
|---|---|---|---|---|---|---|---|---|---|
| 26 | Arkansas | 502,617 | 55,234 | 342,017 | - | — | — | 90,710 | 14,656 |
| | | | 11.0% | 68.0% | — | — | — | 18.0% | 2.9% |
| 26 | Idaho | 55,124 | 9,212 | 27,004 | — | — | — | 16,029 | 2,879 |
| | | | 16.7% | 49.0% | — | — | — | 29.1% | 5.2% |
| 26 | Kentucky | 370,578 | 30,709 | 207,804 | 7,136 | 3,242 | 18,097 | 103,590 | — |
| | | | 8.3% | 56.1% | 1.9% | 0.9% | 4.9% | 28.0% | — |
| June 2 | Alabama | 450,899 | 30,626 | 307,621 | — | — | — | 90,863 | 21,789 |
| | | | 6.8% | 68.2% | — | — | — | 20.2% | 4.8% |
| 2 | California | 2,863,609 | 1,150,460 | 1,359,112 | — | 33,935 | 212,522 | — | 107,580 |
| | | | 40.2% | 47.5% | — | 1.2% | 7.4% | — | 3.8% |
| 2 | Montana | 117,471 | 21,704 | 54,989 | — | — | 12,614 | 28,164 | — |
| | | | 18.5% | 46.8% | — | — | 10.7% | 24.0% | — |
| 2 | New Jersey | 392,626 | 79,877 | 243,741 | — | — | 45,191 | — | 23,817 |
| | | | 20.3% | 62.1% | — | — | 11.5% | — | 6.1% |
| 2 | New Mexico | 181,443 | 30,705 | 95,933 | 3,233 | — | 11,315 | 35,269 | 4,988 |
| | | | 16.9% | 52.9% | 1.8% | — | 6.2% | 19.4% | 2.7% |
| 2 | Ohio | 1,042,335 | 197,449 | 638,347 | 25,395 | 22,976 | 110,773 | — | 47,395 |
| | | | 18.9% | 61.2% | 2.4% | 2.2% | 10.6% | — | 4.5% |
| 9 | North Dakota | 32,786 | — | 4,760 | — | — | — | — | 28,026 |
| | | | — | 14.5% | — | — | — | — | 85.5% |
| | TOTAL | 20,239,385 | 4,071,232 | 10,482,411 | 280,304 | 318,457 | 3,656,010 | 750,873 | 680,098 |
| | | | 20.1% | 51.8% | 1.4% | 1.6% | 18.1% | 3.7% | 3.4% |

The Uncommitted column above includes votes cast on the following ballot lines: Uncommitted, Noncommitted, No Preference, Uninstructed and "None of the Names Shown".

Other vote includes 154,599 LaRouche; 108,678 McCarthy; 88,948 Woods; 58,611 Agran; 54,755 Perot (write-ins); 32,881 Nader; 29,983 Stokes; 9,900 McDonald; 7,911 McAlpine; 7,887 Benns; 7,705 Higginbotham; 7,434 Hawks; 5,261 Burke; 5,202 Laughlin; 4,965 Shiekman; 2,445 Marsh; 2,067 Ballard; 1,626 Spelbring; 1,473 Hanson; 1,369 Cunningham; 1,303 Hauptli; 1,206 Rollinson; 1,009 Beamgard; 892 Barnes; 620 Rachner; 510 Vanskiver; 402 Fulani; 364 Pawley; 336 Kreml; 308 Fey; 303 Mahoney; 279 Hayes; 240 Wilder; 202 Talbow; 186 Rigazio; 177 Thornton; 168 Staradumsky; 112 Averick; 93 Killeen; 83 Cahill; 82 Fisher; 65 Bona; 61 Hegger; 53 Horrigan; 43 Curtis; 39 Holmes; 36 Kovic; 31 Norton; 29 Monyek; 28 Gay; 26 Deutsch; 26 Sagan; 24 O'Donnell; 17 Schwartz and 77,045 scattered write-ins.

# 1988 PRESIDENTIAL PRIMARIES

In 1988 thirty-six states and the District of Columbia held Presidential primaries though there was no Republican voting in New York and no Democratic voting in South Carolina.

In some states balloting was for delegate slates pledged to specific Presidential candidates or uncommitted; in others, electors indicated a personal preference as to their party's nominee

The state-by-state Republican and Democratic tables, included at the end of this section, detail in chronological order the vote for major candidates in each party. An asterisk in the table indicates votes written-in for a candidate not on the ballot.

Republican candidates on the ballot in at least one state were George Bush, Paul B. Conley; Robert Dole, Robert F. Drucker; Pierre duPont; Alexander M. Haig, William Horrigan, Jack F. Kemp, Michael S. Levinson, Isabell Masters, Mary Jane Rachner, Pat Robertson and Harold E. Stassen.

Democratic candidates on the ballot in at least one state were Frank Ahern, Douglas Applegate, Bruce Babbitt, Norbert G. Dennerll, Florenzo DiDonato, Charles R. Doty, Michael S. Dukakis, David E. Duke, William J. duPont, Richard A. Gephardt, Albert Gore, Jr., Gary W. Hart, Jesse L. Jackson, Richard B. Kay, William King, Claude R. Kirk, Stephen A. Koczak, Lyndon H. LaRouche, Stanley Lock, Angus W. McDonald, William A. Marra, Anthony R. Martin-Trigona, Edward T. O'Donnell, Conrad W. Roy, Cyril E. Sagan, Paul Simon, Frank L. Thomas, Osie Thorp, James A. Traficant, A. A. VanPetten, Jennifer Alden Wesner, W. A Williams and Irwin Zucker.

## ALABAMA MARCH 8

Republican   137,807 Bush; 34,733 Dole; 29,772 Robertson; 10,557 Kemp; 392 duPont; 300 Haig.

Democratic   176,764 Jackson; 151,739 Gore; 31,306 Dukakis; 30,214 Gephardt; 7,530 Hart; 3,063 Simon; 2,410 Babbitt; 1,771 Uncommitted; 845 LaRouche.

## ARKANSAS MARCH 8

Republican   32,114 Bush, 17,667 Dole; 12,918 Robertson; 3,499 Kemp; 1,402 Uncommitted; 359 duPont; 346 Haig.

Democratic   185,758 Gore; 94,103 Dukakis; 85,003 Jackson; 59,711 Gephardt; 35,553 Uncommitted; 18,630 Hart; 9,020 Simon; 4,805 Duke; 2,614 Babbitt; 2,347 LaRouche.

## CALIFORNIA JUNE 7

Republican   1,856,273 Bush; 289,220 Dole; 94,779 Robertson; 115 scattered write-in.

Democratic   1,910,808 Dukakis; 1,102,093 Jackson; 56,645 Gore; 43,771 Simon; 25,417 LaRouche.

## CONNECTICUT MARCH 29

Republican   73,501 Bush; 21,005 Dole; 3,281 Kemp; 3,193 Uncommitted; 3,191 Robertson.

Democratic   140,291 Dukakis; 68,372 Jackson; 18,501 Gore; 5,761 Hart; 3,140 Simon; 2,370 Babbitt; 1,951 Uncommitted; 1,009 Gephardt.

## FLORIDA MARCH 8

Republican   559,820 Bush; 191,197 Dole; 95,826 Robertson; 41,795 Kemp; 6,726 duPont; 5,858 Haig.

Democratic   521,041 Dukakis; 254,912 Jackson; 182,861 Gephardt; 161,165 Gore; 79,088 Undecided; 36,315 Hart; 27,620 Simon; 10,296 Babbitt.

# 1988 PRESIDENTIAL PRIMARIES

## GEORGIA MARCH 8

Republican 215,516 Bush; 94,749 Dole; 65,163 Robertson; 23,409 Kemp; 1,309 duPont; 782 Haig.

Democratic 247,831 Jackson; 201,490 Gore; 97,179 Dukakis; 41,489 Gephardt; 15,852 Hart; 8,388 Simon; 7,276 Uncommitted; 3,247 Babbitt.

## IDAHO MAY 24

Republican 55,464 Bush; 6,935 "None of the Names Shown"; 5,876 Robertson.

Democratic 37,696 Dukakis; 8,066 Jackson; 2,308 "None of the Names Shown"; 1,891 Gore; 1,409 Simon.

## ILLINOIS MARCH 15

Republican 469,151 Bush; 309,253 Dole; 59,087 Robertson; 12,687 Kemp; 4,653 duPont; 3,806 Haig.

Democratic 635,219 Simon; 484,233 Jackson; 245,289 Dukakis; 77,265 Gore; 35,108 Gephardt; 12,769 Hart; 6,094 LaRouche; 4,953 Babbitt.

## INDIANA MAY 3

Republican 351,829 Bush; 42,878 Dole; 28,712 Robertson; 14,236 Kemp.

Democratic 449,495 Dukakis; 145,021 Jackson; 21,865 Gore; 16,777 Gephardt; 12,550 Simon.

## KENTUCKY MARCH 8

Republican 72,020 Bush; 27,868 Dole; 13,526 Robertson; 4,020 Kemp; 2,245 Uncommitted; 844 Stassen; 457 duPont; 422 Haig.

Democratic 145,988 Gore; 59,433 Dukakis; 49,667 Jackson; 28,982 Gephardt; 11,798 Hart; 10,465 Uncommitted; 9,393 Simon; 1,290 Babbitt; 681 LaRouche; 537 Martin-Trigona; 487 Kay.

## LOUISIANA MARCH 8

Republican 83,687 Bush; 26,295 Robertson; 25,626 Dole; 7,722 Kemp; 853 duPont; 598 Haig.

Democratic 221,532 Jackson; 174,974 Gore; 95,667 Dukakis; 66,434 Gephardt; 26,442 Hart; 23,390 Duke; 5,155 Simon; 3,701 Ahern; 3,076 Babbitt; 1,681 LaRouche; 1,575 Dennerll; 823 Kay.

## MARYLAND MARCH 8

Republican 107,026 Bush; 64,987 Dole; 12,860 Robertson; 11,909 Kemp; 2,551 duPont; 1,421 Haig.

Democratic 242,479 Dukakis; 152,642 Jackson; 46,063 Gore; 42,059 Gephardt; 16,513 Simon; 14,948 Uncommitted; 9,732 Hart; 4,750 Babbitt; 2,149 LaRouche.

## MASSACHUSETTS MARCH 8

Republican 141,113 Bush; 63,392 Dole; 16,791 Kemp; 10,891 Robertson; 3,522 duPont; 3,416 No Preference; 1,705 Haig; 351 scattered write-in.

Democratic 418,256 Dukakis; 133,141 Jackson; 72,944 Gephardt; 31,631 Gore; 26,176 Simon; 11,866 No Preference; 10,837 Hart; 4,222 Babbitt; 1,971 DiDonato; 998 LaRouche; 1,405 scattered write-in.

# 1988 PRESIDENTIAL PRIMARIES

**MISSISSIPPI MARCH 8**

Republican    104,814 Bush; 26,855 Dole; 21,378 Robertson; 5,479 Kemp.

Democratic    160,651 Jackson; 120,364 Gore; 29,941 Dukakis; 19,693 Gephardt; 13,934 Hart; 9,384 Uncommitted; 2,118 Simon; 2,037 Babbitt; 1,295 LaRouche. Data given are for the amended returns.

**MISSOURI MARCH 8**

Republican    168,812 Bush; 164,394 Dole; 44,705 Robertson; 14,180 Kemp; 5,563 Uncommitted; 1,788 duPont; 858 Haig.

Democratic    305,287 Gephardt; 106,386 Jackson; 61,303 Dukakis; 21,433 Simon; 14,549 Gore; 7,607 Hart; 6,635 Uncommitted; 1,760 Duke; 1,377 Babbitt; 664 LaRouche; 372 Kay; 241 Koczak; 191 Dennerll.

**MONTANA JUNE 7**

Republican    63,098 Bush; 16,762 Dole; 6,520 No Preference.

Democratic    83,684 Dukakis; 26,908 Jackson; 4,083 No Preference; 3,369 Gephardt; 2,261 Gore; 1,566 Simon.

**NEBRASKA MAY 10**

Republican    138,784 Bush; 45,572 Dole; 10,334 Robertson; 8,423 Kemp; 936 scattered write-in.

Democratic    106,334 Dukakis; 43,380 Jackson; 4,948 Gephardt; 4,763 Uncommitted; 4,220 Hart; 2,519 Gore; 2,104 Simon; 416 LaRouche; 324 scattered write-in.

**NEW HAMPSHIRE FEBRUARY 16**

Republican    59,290 Bush; 44,797 Dole; 20,114 Kemp; 15,885 Pierre duPont; 14,775 Robertson; 481 Haig; 130 Stassen; 107 Conley; 107 Rachner; 83 Drucker; 76 Horrigan; 43 Levinson; 1,756 scattered write-in.

Democratic    44,112 Dukakis; 24,513 Gephardt; 21,094 Simon; 9,615 Jackson; 8,400 Gore; 5,644 Babbitt; 4,888 Hart; 1,349 William J. duPont; 264 Duke; 188 LaRouche; 142 Marra; 122 Roy; 84 DiDonato; 61 Martin-Trigona; 47 Koczak; 36 King; 33 O'Donnell; 33 Sagan; 28 Thomas; 25 Kirk; 22 Zucker; 18 Dennerll; 16 Thorpe; 10 VanPetten; 9 Lock; 2,759 scattered write-in.

**NEW JERSEY JUNE 7**

Republican    241,033 Bush.

Democratic    414,829 Dukakis; 213,705 Jackson; 18,062 Gore; 2,621 LaRouche; 2,594 Marra; 2,491 Duke.

**NEW MEXICO JUNE 7**

Republican    69,359 Bush; 9,305 Dole; 5,350 Robertson; 2,569 Uncommitted; 2,161 Haig.

Democratic    114,968 Dukakis; 52,988 Jackson; 6,898 Hart; 4,747 Gore; 3,275 Uncommitted; 2,913 Babbitt; 2,821 Simon.

**NEW YORK APRIL 19**

Republican    No Presidential primary held.

Democratic    801,457 Dukakis; 585,076 Jackson; 157,559 Gore; 17,011 Simon; 10,258 Uncommitted; 2,672 Gephardt; 1,153 LaRouche.

# 1988 PRESIDENTIAL PRIMARIES

**NORTH CAROLINA MARCH 8**

Republican   124,260 Bush; 107,032 Dole; 26,861 Robertson; 11,361 Kemp; 2,797 No Preference; 944 duPont; 546 Haig.

Democratic   235,669 Gore; 224,177 Jackson; 137,993 Dukakis; 37,553 Gephardt; 16,381 Hart; 16,337 No Preference; 8,032 Simon; 3,816 Babbitt.

**NORTH DAKOTA JUNE 14**

Republican   37,062 Bush; 2,372 Rachner.

Democratic   No candidate names appeared on the ballot; tallied write-in votes were 2,890 Dukakis; 515 Jackson.

**OHIO MAY 3**

Republican   643,907 Bush slate; 94,650 Dole slate; 56,347 Robertson slate. The data given are for the statewide at-large slates pledged to the candidates indicated.

Democratic   869,792 Dukakis slates; 378,866 Jackson slates; 29,931 Gore slates; 29,912 Traficant slates; 28,414 Hart slates; 25,068 Applegate slates; 15,524 Simon slates; 6,065 LaRouche slates. The data given are the sum of the votes cast for delegate slates by congressional district pledged to the candidates indicated. Only Dukakis and Gore had delegate slates in all twenty-one districts.

**OKLAHOMA MARCH 8**

Republican   78,224 Bush; 73,016 Dole; 44,067 Robertson; 11,439 Kemp; 938 duPont; 715 Haig; 539 Masters.

Democratic   162,584 Gore; 82,596 Gephardt; 66,278 Dukakis; 52,417 Jackson; 14,336 Hart; 6,901 Simon; 2,388 Duke; 1,601 Babbitt; 1,078 LaRouche; 1,068 Koczak; 1,005 Doty; 475 Dennerll.

**OREGON MAY 17**

Republican   199,938 Bush; 49,128 Dole; 21,212 Robertson; 4,208 scattered write-in.

Democratic   221,048 Dukakis; 148,207 Jackson; 6,772 Gephardt; 5,445 Gore; 4,757 Simon; 1,562 LaRouche; 1,141 scattered write-in.

**PENNSYLVANIA APRIL 26**

Republican   687,323 Bush; 103,763 Dole; 79,463 Robertson.

Democratic   1,002,480 Dukakis; 411,260 Jackson; 44,542 Gore; 20,473 Hart; 9,692 Simon; 7,546 Wesner; 7,254 Gephardt; 4,443 LaRouche.

**RHODE ISLAND MARCH 8**

Republican   10,401 Bush; 3,628 Dole; 911 Robertson; 792 Kemp; 174 Uncommitted; 80 duPont; 49 Haig.

Democratic   34,211 Dukakis; 7,445 Jackson; 2,028 Gephardt; 1,939 Gore; 1,395 Simon; 809 Uncommitted; 733 Hart; 469 Babbitt.

**SOUTH CAROLINA MARCH 5**

Republican   94,738 Bush; 40,265 Dole; 37,261 Robertson; 22,431 Kemp; 316 duPont; 177 Haig; 104 Stassen.

Democratic   No Presidential primary held.

# 1988 PRESIDENTIAL PRIMARIES

**SOUTH DAKOTA FEBRUARY 23**

Republican   51,599 Dole slate; 18,310 Robertson slate; 17,404 Bush slate; 4,290 Kemp slate; 1,226 Uncommitted slate; 576 duPont slate.

Democratic   31,184 Gephardt; 22,349 Dukakis; 5,993 Gore; 3,992 Simon; 3,875 Hart; 3,867 Jackson; 346 Babbitt.

**TENNESSEE MARCH 8**

Republican   152,515 Bush; 55,027 Dole; 32,015 Robertson; 10,911 Kemp; 2,340 Uncommitted; 777 Haig; 646 duPont; 21 scattered write-in.

Democratic   416,861 Gore; 119,248 Jackson; 19,348 Dukakis; 8,470 Gephardt; 4,706 Hart; 3,032 Uncommitted; 2,647 Simon; 1,946 Babbitt; 56 scattered write-in.

**TEXAS MARCH 8**

Republican   648,178 Bush; 155,449 Robertson; 140,795 Dole; 50,586 Kemp; 12,563 Uncommitted; 4,245 duPont; 3,140 Haig.

Democratic   579,713 Dukakis; 433,335 Jackson; 357,764 Gore; 240,158 Gephardt; 82,199 Hart; 34,499 Simmon; 11,618 Babbitt; 9,013 LaRouche; 8,808 Duke; 6,238 Williams; 3,700 Dennerll.

**VERMONT MARCH 1**

Republican   23,565 Bush; 18,655 Dole; 2,452 Robertson; 1,877 Kemp; 808 duPont; 324 Haig; 151 scattered write-in.

Democratic   28,353 Dukakis; 13,044 Jackson; 3,910 Gephardt; 2,620 Simon; 2,055 Hart; 809 scattered write-in.

**VIRGINIA MARCH 8**

Republican   124,738 Bush; 60,921 Dole; 32,173 Robertson; 10,809 Kemp; 3,675 Uncommitted; 1,229 duPont; 597 Haig.

Democratic   164,709 Jackson; 81,419 Gore; 80,183 Dukakis; 15,935 Gephardt; 7,045 Simon; 6,266 Hart; 6,142 Uncommitted; 2,454 Babbitt; 746 LaRouche.

**WEST VIRGINIA MAY 10**

Republican   110,705 Bush; 15,600 Dole; 10,417 Robertson; 3,820 Kemp; 1,604 Stassen; 994 Conley.

Democratic   254,289 Dukakis; 45,788 Jackson; 11,573 Gore; 9,284 Hart; 6,130 Gephardt; 3,604 McDonald; 2,280 Simon; 1,978 Babbitt; 1,482 LaRouche; 1,383 Duke; 1,339 Dennerll; 967 Traficant.

**WISCONSIN APRIL 5**

Republican   295,295 Bush; 28,460 Dole; 24,798 Robertson; 4,915 Kemp; 2,372 Uninstructed delegation; 1,554 Haig; 1,504 duPont; 396 scattered write-in.

Democratic   483,172 Dukakis; 285,995 Jackson; 176,712 Gore; 48,419 Simon; 7,996 Gephardt; 7,068 Hart; 2,554 Uninstructed delegation; 2,353 Babbitt; 513 scattered write-in.

**DISTRICT OF COLUMBIA MAY 3**

Republican   5,890 Bush; 469 Dole; 268 Robertson; 93 scattered write-in.

Democratic   68,840 Jackson; 15,415 Dukakis; 769 Simon; 648 Gore; 300 Gephardt; 80 Thorpe.

# 1988 REPUBLICAN PREFERENCE PRIMARIES

| Date | | State | Total Vote | Bush | Dole | Kemp | Robertson | Uncommitted | Other |
|------|---|-------|-----------|------|------|------|-----------|-------------|-------|
| March | 16 | New Hampshire | 157,644 | 59,290 | 44,797 | 20,114 | 14,775 | — | 18,668 |
| | | | | 37.6% | 28.4% | 12.8% | 9.4% | — | 11.8% |
| | 23 | South Dakota | 93,405 | 17,404 | 51,599 | 4,290 | 18,310 | 1,226 | 576 |
| | | | | 18.6% | 55.2% | 4.6% | 19.6% | 1.3% | 0.6% |
| March | 1 | Vermont | 47,832 | 23,565 | 18,655 | 1,877 | 2,452 | — | 1,283 |
| | | | | 49.3% | 39.0% | 3.9% | 5.1% | — | 2.7% |
| | 5 | South Carolina | 195,292 | 94,738 | 40,265 | 22,431 | 37,261 | — | 597 |
| | | | | 48.5% | 20.6% | 11.5% | 19.1% | — | 0.3% |
| | 8 | Alabama | 213,561 | 137,807 | 34,733 | 10,557 | 29,772 | — | 692 |
| | | | | 64.5% | 16.3% | 4.9% | 13.9% | — | 0.3% |
| | 8 | Arkansas | 68,305 | 32,114 | 17,667 | 3,499 | 12,918 | 1,402 | 705 |
| | | | | 47.0% | 25.9% | 5.1% | 18.9% | 2.1% | 1.0% |
| | 8 | Florida | 901,222 | 559,820 | 191,197 | 41,795 | 95,826 | — | 12,584 |
| | | | | 62.1% | 21.2% | 4.6% | 10.6% | — | 1.4% |
| | 8 | Georgia | 400,928 | 215,516 | 94,749 | 23,409 | 65,163 | — | 2,091 |
| | | | | 53.8% | 23.6% | 5.8% | 16.3% | — | 0.5% |
| | 8 | Kentucky | 121,402 | 72,020 | 27,868 | 4,020 | 13,526 | 2,245 | 1,723 |
| | | | | 59.3% | 23.0% | 3.3% | 11.1% | 1.8% | 1.4% |
| | 8 | Louisiana | 144,781 | 83,687 | 25,626 | 7,722 | 26,295 | — | 1,451 |
| | | | | 57.8% | 17.7% | 5.3% | 18.2% | — | 1.0% |
| | 8 | Maryland | 200,754 | 107,026 | 64,987 | 11,909 | 12,860 | — | 3,972 |
| | | | | 53.3% | 32.4% | 5.9% | 6.4% | — | 2.0% |
| | 8 | Massachusetts | 241,181 | 141,113 | 63,392 | 16,791 | 10,891 | 3,416 | 5,578 |
| | | | | 58.5% | 26.3% | 7.0% | 4.5% | 1.4% | 2.3% |
| | 8 | Mississippi | 158,526 | 104,814 | 26,855 | 5,479 | 21,378 | — | — |
| | | | | 66.1% | 16.9% | 3.5% | 13.5% | — | — |
| | 8 | Missouri | 400,300 | 168,812 | 164,394 | 14,180 | 44,705 | 5,563 | 2,646 |
| | | | | 42.2% | 41.1% | 3.5% | 11.2% | 1.4% | 0.7% |
| | 8 | North Carolina | 273,801 | 124,260 | 107,032 | 11,361 | 26,861 | 2,797 | 1,490 |
| | | | | 45.4% | 39.1% | 4.1% | 9.8% | 1.0% | 0.5% |
| | 8 | Oklahoma | 208,938 | 78,224 | 73,016 | 11,439 | 44,067 | — | 2,192 |
| | | | | 37.4% | 34.9% | 5.5% | 21.1% | — | 1.0% |
| | 8 | Rhode Island | 16,035 | 10,401 | 3,628 | 792 | 911 | 174 | 129 |
| | | | | 64.9% | 22.6% | 4.9% | 5.7% | 1.1% | 0.8% |
| | 8 | Tennessee | 254,252 | 152,515 | 55,027 | 10,911 | 32,015 | 2,340 | 1,444 |
| | | | | 60.0% | 21.6% | 4.3% | 12.6% | 0.9% | 0.6% |
| | 8 | Texas | 1,014,956 | 648,178 | 140,795 | 50,586 | 155,449 | 12,563 | 7,385 |
| | | | | 63.9% | 13.9% | 5.0% | 15.3% | 1.2% | 0.7% |
| | 8 | Virginia | 234,142 | 124,738 | 60,921 | 10,809 | 32,173 | 3,675 | 1,826 |
| | | | | 53.3% | 26.0% | 4.6% | 13.7% | 1.6% | 0.8% |
| | 15 | Illinois | 858,637 | 469,151 | 309,253 | 12,687 | 59,087 | — | 8,459 |
| | | | | 54.6% | 36.0% | 1.5% | 6.9% | — | 1.0% |
| | 29 | Connecticut | 104,171 | 73,501 | 21,005 | 3,281 | 3,191 | 3,193 | — |
| | | | | 70.6% | 20.2% | 3.1% | 3.1% | 3.1% | — |
| April | 5 | Wisconsin | 359,294 | 295,295 | 28,460 | 4,915 | 24,798 | 2,372 | 3,454 |
| | | | | 82.2% | 7.9% | 1.4% | 6.9% | 0.7% | 1.0% |
| | 19 | New York | No Presidential Preference Vote Held | | | | | | |
| | 26 | Pennsylvania | 870,549 | 687,323 | 103,763 | — | 79,463 | — | — |
| | | | | 79.0% | 11.9% | — | 9.1% | — | — |
| May | 3 | Indiana | 437,655 | 351,829 | 42,878 | 14,236 | 28,712 | — | — |
| | | | | 80.4% | 9.8% | 3.3% | 6.6% | — | — |
| | 3 | Ohio | 794,904 | 643,907 | 94,650 | — | 56,347 | — | — |
| | | | | 81.0% | 11.9% | — | 7.1% | — | — |
| | 3 | Dist. of Col. | 6,720 | 5,890 | 469 | — | 268 | — | 93 |
| | | | | 87.6% | 7.0% | — | 4.0% | — | 1.4% |
| | 10 | Nebraska | 204,049 | 138,784 | 45,572 | 8,423 | 10,334 | — | 936 |
| | | | | 68.0% | 22.3% | 4.1% | 5.1% | — | 0.5% |

# 1988 REPUBLICAN PREFERENCE PRIMARIES

| Date | | State | Total Vote | Bush | Dole | Kemp | Robertson | Uncommitted | Other |
|---|---|---|---|---|---|---|---|---|---|
| | 10 | West Virginia | 143,140 | 110,705 | 15,600 | 3,820 | 10,417 | — | 2,598 |
| | | | | 77.3% | 10.9% | 2.7% | 7.3% | — | 1.8% |
| | 17 | Oregon | 274,486 | 199,938 | 49,128 | — | 21,212 | — | 4,208 |
| | | | | 72.8% | 17.9% | — | 7.7% | — | 1.5% |
| | 24 | Idaho | 68,275 | 55,464 | — | — | 5,876 | 6,935 | — |
| | | | | 81.2% | — | — | 8.6% | 10.2% | — |
| June | 7 | California | 2,240,387 | 1,856,273 | 289,220 | — | 94,779 | — | 115 |
| | | | | 82.9% | 12.9% | — | 4.2% | — | 0.0% |
| | 7 | Montana | 86,380 | 63,098 | 16,762 | — | — | 6,520 | — |
| | | | | 73.0% | 19.4% | — | — | 7.5% | — |
| | 7 | New Jersey | 241,033 | 241,033 | — | — | — | — | — |
| | | | | 100.0% | — | — | — | — | — |
| | 7 | New Mexico | 88,744 | 69,359 | 9,305 | — | 5,350 | 2,569 | 2,161 |
| | | | | 78.2% | 10.5% | — | 6.0% | 2.9% | 2.4% |
| | 14 | North Dakota | 39,434 | 37,062 | — | — | — | — | 2,372 |
| | | | | 94.0% | — | — | — | — | 6.0% |
| | | Total | 12,165,115 | 8,254,654 | 2,333,268 | 331,333 | 1,097,442 | 56,990 | 91,428 |
| | | | | 67.9% | 19.2% | 2.7% | 9.0% | 0.5% | 0.8% |

Candidates on the ballot in at least one state were George Bush, Paul B. Conley, Robert Dole, Robert F. Drucker, Pierre duPont, Alexander M. Haig, William Horrigan, Jack F. Kemp, Michael S. Levinson, Isabell Masters, Mary Jane Rachner, Pat Robertson and Harold E. Stassen.

The Uncommitted column above includes votes cast on the following ballot lines: Uncommitted, No Preference, Uninstructed and "None of the Names Shown".

Other vote includes 49,781 duPont; 26,617 Haig; 2,682 Stassen; 2,479 Rachner; 1,101 Conley; 539 Masters; 83 Drucker; 76 Horrigan; 43 Levinson and 8,027 scattered write-ins.

# 1988 DEMOCRATIC PREFERENCE PRIMARIES

| Date | State | Total Vote | Dukakis | Gephardt | Gore | Hart | Jackson | Simon | Other |
|---|---|---|---|---|---|---|---|---|---|
| Feb. 16 | New Hampshire | 123,512 | 44,112 | 24,513 | 8,400 | 4,888 | 9,615 | 21,094 | 10,890 |
| | | | 35.7% | 19.8% | 6.8% | 4.0% | 7.8% | 17.1% | 8.8% |
| 23 | South Dakota | 71,606 | 22,349 | 31,184 | 5,993 | 3,875 | 3,867 | 3,992 | 346 |
| | | | 31.2% | 43.5% | 8.4% | 5.4% | 5.4% | 5.6% | 0.5% |
| March 1 | Vermont | 50,791 | 28,353 | 3,910 | — | 2,055 | 13,044 | 2,620 | 809 |
| | | | 55.8% | 7.7% | — | 4.0% | 25.7% | 5.2% | 1.6% |
| 5 | South Carolina | No Presidential Preference Vote Held | | | | | | | |
| 8 | Alabama | 405,642 | 31,306 | 30,214 | 151,739 | 7,530 | 176,764 | 3,063 | 5,026 |
| | | | 7.7% | 7.4% | 37.4% | 1.9% | 43.6% | 0.8% | 1.2% |
| 8 | Arkansas | 497,544 | 94,103 | 59,711 | 185,758 | 18,630 | 85,003 | 9,020 | 45,319 |
| | | | 18.9% | 12.0% | 37.3% | 3.7% | 17.1% | 1.8% | 9.1% |
| 8 | Florida | 1,273,298 | 521,041 | 182,861 | 161,165 | 36,315 | 254,912 | 27,620 | 89,384 |
| | | | 40.9% | 14.4% | 12.7% | 2.9% | 20.0% | 2.2% | 7.0% |
| 8 | Georgia | 622,752 | 97,179 | 41,489 | 201,490 | 15,852 | 247,831 | 8,388 | 10,523 |
| | | | 15.6% | 6.7% | 32.4% | 2.5% | 39.8% | 1.3% | 1.7% |
| 8 | Kentucky | 318,721 | 59,433 | 28,982 | 145,988 | 11,798 | 49,667 | 9,393 | 13,460 |
| | | | 18.6% | 9.1% | 45.8% | 3.7% | 15.6% | 2.9% | 4.2% |
| 8 | Louisiana | 624,450 | 95,667 | 66,434 | 174,974 | 26,442 | 221,532 | 5,155 | 34,246 |
| | | | 15.3% | 10.6% | 28.0% | 4.2% | 35.5% | 0.8% | 5.5% |
| 8 | Maryland | 531,335 | 242,479 | 42,059 | 46,063 | 9,732 | 152,642 | 16,513 | 21,847 |
| | | | 45.6% | 7.9% | 8.7% | 1.8% | 28.7% | 3.1% | 4.1% |
| 8 | Massachusetts | 713,447 | 418,256 | 72,944 | 31,631 | 10,837 | 133,141 | 26,176 | 20,462 |
| | | | 58.6% | 10.2% | 4.4% | 1.5% | 18.7% | 3.7% | 2.9% |
| 8 | Mississippi | 359,417 | 29,941 | 19,693 | 120,364 | 13,934 | 160,651 | 2,118 | 12,716 |
| | | | 8.3% | 5.5% | 33.5% | 3.9% | 44.7% | 0.6% | 3.5% |
| 8 | Missouri | 527,805 | 61,303 | 305,287 | 14,549 | 7,607 | 106,386 | 21,433 | 11,240 |
| | | | 11.6% | 57.8% | 2.8% | 1.4% | 20.2% | 4.1% | 2.1% |
| 8 | North Carolina | 679,958 | 137,993 | 37,553 | 235,669 | 16,381 | 224,177 | 8,032 | 20,153 |
| | | | 20.3% | 5.5% | 34.7% | 2.4% | 33.0% | 1.2% | 3.0% |
| 8 | Oklahoma | 392,727 | 66,278 | 82,596 | 162,584 | 14,336 | 52,417 | 6,901 | 7,615 |
| | | | 16.9% | 21.0% | 41.4% | 3.7% | 13.3% | 1.8% | 1.9% |
| 8 | Rhode Island | 49,029 | 34,211 | 2,028 | 1,939 | 733 | 7,445 | 1,395 | 1,278 |
| | | | 69.8% | 4.1% | 4.0% | 1.5% | 15.2% | 2.8% | 2.6% |
| 8 | Tennessee | 576,314 | 19,348 | 8,470 | 416,861 | 4,706 | 119,248 | 2,647 | 5,034 |
| | | | 3.4% | 1.5% | 72.3% | 0.8% | 20.7% | 0.5% | 0.9% |
| 8 | Texas | 1,767,045 | 579,713 | 240,158 | 357,764 | 82,199 | 433,335 | 34,499 | 39,377 |
| | | | 32.8% | 13.6% | 20.2% | 4.7% | 24.5% | 2.0% | 2.2% |
| 8 | Virginia | 364,899 | 80,183 | 15,935 | 81,419 | 6,266 | 164,709 | 7,045 | 9,342 |
| | | | 22.0% | 4.4% | 22.3% | 1.7% | 45.1% | 1.9% | 2.6% |
| 15 | Illinois | 1,500,930 | 245,289 | 35,108 | 77,265 | 12,769 | 484,233 | 635,219 | 11,047 |
| | | | 16.3% | 2.3% | 5.1% | 0.9% | 32.3% | 42.3% | 0.7% |
| 29 | Connecticut | 241,395 | 140,291 | 1,009 | 18,501 | 5,761 | 68,372 | 3,140 | 4,321 |
| | | | 58.1% | 0.4% | 7.7% | 2.4% | 28.3% | 1.3% | 1.8% |
| April 5 | Wisconsin | 1,014,782 | 483,172 | 7,996 | 176,712 | 7,068 | 285,995 | 48,419 | 5,420 |
| | | | 47.6% | 0.8% | 17.4% | 0.7% | 28.2% | 4.8% | 0.5% |
| 19 | New York | 1,575,186 | 801,457 | 2,672 | 157,559 | — | 585,076 | 17,011 | 11,411 |
| | | | 50.9% | 0.2% | 10.0% | — | 37.1% | 1.1% | 0.7% |
| 26 | Pennsylvania | 1,507,690 | 1,002,480 | 7,254 | 44,542 | 20,473 | 411,260 | 9,692 | 11,989 |
| | | | 66.5% | 0.5% | 3.0% | 1.4% | 27.3% | 0.6% | 0.8% |
| May 3 | Indiana | 645,708 | 449,495 | 16,777 | 21,865 | — | 145,021 | 12,550 | — |
| | | | 69.6% | 2.6% | 3.4% | — | 22.5% | 1.9% | — |
| 3 | Ohio | 1,383,572 | 869,792 | — | 29,931 | 28,414 | 378,866 | 15,524 | 61,045 |
| | | | 62.9% | — | 2.2% | 2.1% | 27.4% | 1.1% | 4.4% |
| 3 | Dist. of Col. | 86,052 | 15,415 | 300 | 648 | — | 68,840 | 769 | 80 |
| | | | 17.9% | 0.3% | 0.8% | — | 80.0% | 0.9% | 0.1% |
| 10 | Nebraska | 169,008 | 106,334 | 4,948 | 2,519 | 4,220 | 43,380 | 2,104 | 5,503 |
| | | | 62.9% | 2.9% | 1.5% | 2.5% | 25.7% | 1.2% | 3.3% |

# 1988 DEMOCRATIC PREFERENCE PRIMARIES

| Date | State | Total Vote | Dukakis | Gephardt | Gore | Hart | Jackson | Simon | Other |
|---|---|---|---|---|---|---|---|---|---|
| 10 | West Virginia | 340,097 | 254,289 | 6,130 | 11,573 | 9,284 | 45,788 | 2,280 | 10,753 |
| | | | 74.8% | 1.8% | 3.4% | 2.7% | 13.5% | 0.7% | 3.2% |
| 17 | Oregon | 388,932 | 221,048 | 6,772 | 5,445 | — | 148,207 | 4,757 | 2,703 |
| | | | 56.8% | 1.7% | 1.4% | — | 38.1% | 1.2% | 0.7% |
| 24 | Idaho | 51,370 | 37,696 | — | 1,891 | — | 8,066 | 1,409 | 2,308 |
| | | | 73.4% | — | 3.7% | — | 15.7% | 2.7% | 4.5% |
| June 7 | California | 3,138,734 | 1,910,808 | — | 56,645 | — | 1,102,093 | 43,771 | 25,417 |
| | | | 60.9% | — | 1.8% | — | 35.1% | 1.4% | 0.8% |
| 7 | Montana | 121,871 | 83,684 | 3,369 | 2,261 | — | 26,908 | 1,566 | 4,083 |
| | | | 68.7% | 2.8% | 1.9% | — | 22.1% | 1.3% | 3.4% |
| 7 | New Jersey | 654,302 | 414,829 | — | 18,062 | — | 213,705 | — | 7,706 |
| | | | 63.4% | — | 2.8% | — | 32.7% | — | 1.2% |
| 7 | New Mexico | 188,610 | 114,968 | — | 4,747 | 6,898 | 52,988 | 2,821 | 6,188 |
| | | | 61.0% | — | 2.5% | 3.7% | 28.1% | 1.5% | 3.3% |
| 14 | North Dakota | 3,405 | 2,890 | — | — | — | 515 | — | — |
| | | | 84.9% | — | — | — | 15.1% | — | — |
| | Total | 22,961,936 | 9,817,185 | 1,388,356 | 3,134,516 | 389,003 | 6,685,699 | 1,018,136 | 529,041 |
| | | | 42.8% | 6.0% | 13.7% | 1.7% | 29.1% | 4.4% | 2.3% |

Candidates on the ballot in at least one state were Frank Ahern, Douglas Applegate, Bruce Babbitt, Norbert G. Dennerll, Florenzo DiDonato, Charles R. Doty, Michael S. Dukakis, David E. Duke, William J. duPont, Richard A. Gephardt, Albert Gore, Jr., Gary W. Hart, Jesse L. Jackson, Richard B. Kay, William King, Claude R. Kirk, Stephen A. Koczak, Lyndon H. LaRouche, Stanley Lock, Angus W. McDonald William A. Marra, Anthony R. Martin-Trigona, Edward T. O'Donnell, Conrad W. Roy, Cyril E. Sagan, Paul Simon, Frank L. Thomas, Osie Thorpe, James A. Traficant, A. A. VanPetten, Jennifer Alden Wesner, W. A. Williams and Irwin Zucker.

Other vote includes 116,262 Uncommitted; 79,088 Undecided; 77,780 Babbitt; 70,938 LaRouche; 45,289 Duke; 32,286 No Preference; 30,879 Traficant; 25,068 Applegate; 7,298 Dennerll; 7,546 Wesner; 6,238 Williams; 3,701 Ahern; 3,604 McDonald; 2,736 Marra; 2,554 Uninstructed; 2,308 "None of the Names Shown"; 2,055 DiDonato; 1,682 Kay; 1,356 Koczak; 1,349 duPont; 1,005 Doty; 598 Martin-Trigona; 122 Roy; 96 Thorpe; 36 King; 33 O'Donnell; 33 Sagan; 28 Thomas; 25 Kirk; 22 Zucker; 10 VanPetter; 9 Lock and 7,007 scattered write-ins.

# 1984 PRESIDENTIAL PRIMARIES

In 1984 twenty-nine states and the District of Columbia held Presidential primaries though there was no Republican voting in Alabama, Connecticut, New York, North Carolina or South Dakota, and no Democratic voting in Texas.

In some states balloting was for delegate slates pledged to specific Presidential candidates or uncommitted; in others, electors indicated a personal preference as to their party's nominee. The votes listed in California for the Democratic primary are the sum of the highest delegate vote for each candidate in each of the state's forty-five Congressional Districts.

The state-by-state Republican and Democratic tables, included at the end of this section, detail in chronological order the vote for major candidates in each party. An asterisk in the table indicates votes written-in for a candidate not on the ballot.

Republican candidates on the ballot in at least one state were Gary R. Arnold, Benjamin Fernandez, David M. Kelley, Ronald Reagan, Harold E. Stassen.

Democratic candidates on the ballot in at least one state were Reubin Askew, Hugh G. Bagley, Martin J. Beckman, Bob Brewster, Walter R. Buchanan, Raymond J. Caplette, Roy J. Clendenan, Alan Cranston, John H. Glenn, Robert K. Griser, Gary W. Hart, Ernest F. Hollings, Jesse L. Jackson, Richard B. Kay, William King, Claude R. Kirk, Stephen A. Koczak, William P. Kreml, Lyndon H. LaRouche, George S. McGovern, Walter F. Mondale, Edward T. O'Donnell, Chester M. Rudnicki, Cyril E. Sagan, Alfred Timinski, Betty J. Williams, Gerald Willis.

## ALABAMA MARCH 13

Republican  No Presidential primary held.

Democratic  148,165 Mondale; 89,286 Glenn; 88,465 Hart; 83,787 Jackson; 6,153 Willis; 4,759 Hollings; 4,464 Uncommitted; 1,827 Askew; 1,377 Cranston.

## CALIFORNIA JUNE 5

Republican  1,874,897 Reagan; 78 scattered write-in.

Democratic  1,155,499 Hart; 1,049,342 Mondale; 546,693 Jackson; 96,770 Glenn; 69,926 McGovern; 52,647 LaRouche; 26 scattered write-in.

## CONNECTICUT MARCH 27

Republican  No Presidential primary held.

Democratic  116,286 Hart; 64,230 Mondale; 26,395 Jackson; 6,098 Askew; 2,426 McGovern; 2,283 Hollings; 1,973 Uncommitted; 955 Glenn; 196 Cranston.

## FLORIDA MARCH 13

Republican  344,150 Reagan.

Democratic  463,799 Hart; 394,350 Mondale; 144,263 Jackson; 128,209 Glenn; 26,258 Askew; 17,614 McGovern; 3,115 Hollings; 2,097 Cranston; 1,328 Kay; 1,157 Koczak.

# 1984 PRESIDENTIAL PRIMARIES

**GEORGIA MARCH 13**

Republican  50,793 Reagan.

Democratic  208,588 Mondale; 186,903 Hart; 143,730 Jackson; 122,744 Glenn; 11,321 McGovern; 3,800 Hollings; 3,068 Uncommitted; 1,804 Willis; 1,660 Askew; 923 Cranston.

**IDAHO MAY 22**

Republican  97,450 Reagan; 8,237 "None of the Names Shown".

Democratic  31,737 Hart; 16,460 Mondale; 3,104 Jackson; 2,225 "None of the Names Shown"; 1,196 LaRouche.

**ILLINOIS MARCH 20**

Republican  594,742 Reagan; 336 scattered write-in.

Democratic  670,951 Mondale; 584,579 Hart; 348,843 Jackson; 25,336 McGovern; 19,800 Glenn; 4,797 Williams; 2,786 Cranston; 2,182 Askew; 151 scattered write-in.

**INDIANA MAY 8**

Republican  428,559 Reagan.

Democratic  299,491 Hart; 293,413 Mondale; 98,190 Jackson; 16,046 Glenn; 9,815 Brewster.

**LOUISIANA MAY 5**

Republican  14,964 Reagan; 1,723 Uncommitted.

Democratic  136,707 Jackson; 79,593 Hart; 71,162 Mondale; 19,409 Uncommitted; 4,970 LaRouche; 3,158 McGovern; 1,924 Griser; 1,344 Kay; 543 Koczak.

**MARYLAND MAY 8**

Republican  73,663 Reagan.

Democratic  215,222 Mondale; 129,387 Jackson; 123,365 Hart; 15,807 Uncommitted; 7,836 LaRouche; 5,796 McGovern; 6,238 Glenn; 1,768 Cranston; 1,467 Hollings.

**MASSACHUSETTS MARCH 13**

Republican  58,996 Reagan; 5,005 No Preference; 1,936 scattered write-in.

Democratic  245,943 Hart; 160,893 Mondale; 134,341 McGovern; 45,456 Glenn; 31,824 Jackson; 5,080 No Preference; 1,394 Askew; 1,203 Hollings; 853 Cranston; 3,975 scattered write-in.

**MONTANA JUNE 5**

Republican  66,432 Reagan; 5,378 No Preference; 77 scattered write-in.

Democratic  28,385 No Preference; 3,080 Hart (write-in); 2,026 Mondale (write-in); 388 Jackson (write-in); 335 scattered write-in.

# 1984 PRESIDENTIAL PRIMARIES

**NEBRASKA MAY 15**

Republican   145,245 Reagan; 1,403 scattered write-in.

Democratic   86,582 Hart; 39,635 Mondale; 13,495 Jackson; 4,631 Uncommitted; 1,561 McGovern; 1,227 La-Rouche; 538 Cranston; 450 Hollings; 736 scattered write-in.

**NEW HAMPSHIRE FEBRUARY 28**

Republican   65,033 Reagan; 1,543 Stassen; 360 Kelley; 252 Arnold; 202 Fernandez; 8,180 scattered write-in.

Democratic   37,702 Hart; 28,173 Mondale; 12,088 Glenn; 5,311 Jackson; 5,217 McGovern; 3,583 Hollings; 2,136 Cranston; 1,025 Askew; 155 Koczak; 132 Buchanan; 127 Beckman; 74 O'Donnell; 50 Willis; 34 King; 27 Kay; 25 Kreml; 24 Bagley; 24 Kirk; 21 Rudnicki; 20 Clendenan; 20 Sagan; 19 Caplette; 5,144 scattered write-in.

**NEW JERSEY JUNE 5**

Republican   240,054 Reagan.

Democratic   305,516 Mondale; 200,948 Hart; 159,788 Jackson; 10,309 LaRouche.

**NEW MEXICO JUNE 5**

Republican   40,805 Reagan; 2,189 Uncommitted.

Democratic   87,610 Hart; 67,675 Mondale; 22,168 Jackson; 5,143 McGovern; 3,330 LaRouche; 1,477 Uncommitted.

**NEW YORK APRIL 3**

Republican   No Presidential primary held.

Democratic   621,581 Mondale; 380,564 Hart; 355,541 Jackson; 15,941 Glenn; 6,815 Cranston; 4,547 McGovern; 2,877 Askew; 84 scattered.

**NORTH CAROLINA MAY 8**

Republican   No Presidential primary held.

Democratic   342,324 Mondale; 289,877 Hart; 243,945 Jackson; 44,232 No Preference; 17,659 Glenn; 10,149 McGovern; 8,318 Hollings; 3,144 Askew; 1,209 Cranston.

**NORTH DAKOTA JUNE 12**

Republican   44,109 Reagan.

Democratic   28,603 Hart; 4,018 LaRouche; 934 Mondale (write-in).

**OHIO MAY 8**

Republican   658,169 Reagan.

Democratic   608,528 Hart; 583,595 Mondale; 237,133 Jackson; 8,991 McGovern; 4,653 Cranston; 4,336 La-Rouche.

# 1984 PRESIDENTIAL PRIMARIES

**OREGON MAY 15**

Republican  238,594 Reagan; 4,752 scattered write-in.

Democratic  233,638 Hart; 110,374 Mondale; 37,106 Jackson; 10,831 Glenn; 5,943 LaRouche; 1,787 scattered write-in.

**PENNSYLVANIA APRIL 10**

Republican  616,916 Reagan; 4,290 scattered write-in.

Democratic  747,267 Mondale; 551,335 Hart; 264,463 Jackson; 22,829 Cranston; 22,605 Glenn; 19,180 La-Rouche; 13,139 McGovern; 6,090 Griser; 5,071 Askew; 2,972 Hollings; 1,343 scattered write-in.

**RHODE ISLAND MARCH 13**

Republican  2,028 Reagan; 207 Uncommitted.

Democratic  20,011 Hart; 15,338 Mondale; 3,875 Jackson; 2,249 Glenn; 2,146 McGovern; 439 Uncommitted; 273 Cranston; 96 Askew; 84 Hollings.

**SOUTH DAKOTA JUNE 5**

Republican  No Presidential primary held.

Democratic  26,641 Hart; 20,495 Mondale; 2,738 Jackson; 1,383 LaRouche; 1,304 Uncommitted.

**TENNESSEE MAY 1**

Republican  75,367 Reagan; 7,546 Uncommitted; 8 scattered write-in.

Democratic  132,201 Mondale; 93,710 Hart; 81,418 Jackson; 6,682 Uncommitted; 4,198 Glenn; 3,824 McGovern; 30 scattered write-in.

**TEXAS MAY 5**

Republican  308,713 Reagan; 11,126 Uncommitted.

Democratic  No Presidential primary held.

**VERMONT MARCH 6**

Republican  33,218 Reagan; 425 scattered write-in.

Democratic  51,873 Hart; 14,834 Mondale; 5,761 Jackson; 444 Askew; 1,147 scattered write-in.

**WEST VIRGINIA JUNE 5**

Republican  125,790 Reagan; 11,206 Stassen.

Democratic  198,776 Mondale; 137,866 Hart; 24,697 Jackson; 7,274 LaRouche; 632 Timinski.

# 1984 PRESIDENTIAL PRIMARIES

**WISCONSIN APRIL 3**

Republican   280,608 "Ronald Reagan Yes"; 14,047 "Ronald Reagan No"; 158 scattered write-in.

Democratic   282,435 Hart; 261,374 Mondale; 62,524 Jackson; 10,166 McGovern; 7,036 "None of the Names Shown"; 6,398 Glenn; 2,984 Cranston; 1,650 Hollings; 683 Askew; 518 scattered write-in.

**DISTRICT OF COLUMBIA MAY 1**

Republican   5,692 Reagan.

Democratic   69,106 Jackson; 26,320 Mondale; 7,305 Hart.

# 1984 REPUBLICAN PREFERENCE PRIMARIES

| Date | | State | Total Vote | Reagan | Other |
|------|---|-------|-----------|--------|-------|
| Feb. | 28 | New Hampshire | 75,570 | 65,033<br>**86.1%** | 10,537<br>**13.9%** |
| March | 6 | Vermont | 33,643 | 33,218<br>**98.7%** | 425<br>**1.3%** |
| | 13 | Alabama | No Presidential Preference<br>Vote Held | | |
| | 13 | Florida | 344,150 | 344,150<br>**100.0%** | —<br>— |
| | 13 | Georgia | 50,793 | 50,793<br>**100.0%** | —<br>— |
| | 13 | Massachusetts | 65,937 | 58,996<br>**89.5%** | 6,941<br>**10.5%** |
| | 13 | Rhode Island | 2,235 | 2,028<br>**90.7%** | 207<br>**9.3%** |
| | 20 | Illinois | 595,078 | 594,742<br>**99.9%** | 336<br>**0.1%** |
| | 27 | Connecticut | No Presidential Preference<br>Vote Held | | |
| April | 3 | New York | No Presidential Preference<br>Vote Held | | |
| | 3 | Wisconsin | 294,813 | 280,608<br>**95.2%** | 14,205<br>**4.8%** |
| | 10 | Pennsylvania | 621,206 | 616,916<br>**99.3%** | 4,290<br>**0.7%** |
| May | 1 | Dist. of Col. | 5,692 | 5,692<br>**100.0%** | —<br>— |
| | 1 | Tennessee | 82,921 | 75,367<br>**90.9%** | 7,554<br>**9.1%** |
| | 5 | Louisiana | 16,687 | 14,964<br>**89.7%** | 1,723<br>**10.3%** |
| | 5 | Texas | 319,839 | 308,713<br>**96.5%** | 11,126<br>**3.5%** |
| | 8 | Indiana | 428,559 | 428,559<br>**100.0%** | —<br>— |
| | 8 | Maryland | 73,663 | 73,663<br>**100.0%** | —<br>— |
| | 8 | North Carolina | No Presidential Preference<br>Vote Held | | |
| | 8 | Ohio | 658,169 | 658,169<br>**100.0%** | —<br>— |
| | 15 | Nebraska | 146,648 | 145,245<br>**99.0%** | 1,403<br>**1.0%** |
| | 15 | Oregon | 243,346 | 238,594<br>**98.0%** | 4,752<br>**2.0%** |
| | 22 | Idaho | 105,687 | 97,450<br>**92.2%** | 8,237<br>**7.8%** |
| June | 5 | California | 1,874,975 | 1,874,897<br>**100.0%** | 78<br>— |
| | 5 | Montana | 71,887 | 66,432<br>**92.4%** | 5,455<br>**7.6%** |
| | 5 | New Jersey | 240,054 | 240,054<br>**100.0%** | —<br>— |
| | 5 | New Mexico | 42,994 | 40,805<br>**94.9%** | 2,189<br>**5.1%** |
| | 5 | South Dakota | No Presidential Preference<br>Vote Held | | |

# 1984 REPUBLICAN PREFERENCE PRIMARIES

| Date | State | Total Vote | Reagan | Other |
|------|-------|-----------|--------|-------|
| 5 | West Virginia | 136,996 | 125,790 | 11,206 |
| | | | **91.8%** | **8.2%** |
| 12 | North Dakota | 44,109 | 44,109 | — |
| | | | **100.0%** | — |
| | Total | 6,575,651 | 6,484,987 | 90,664 |
| | | | **98.6%** | **1.4%** |

Candidates on the ballot in at least one state were Gary R. Arnold, Benjamin Fernandez, David M. Kelley, Ronald Reagan, Harold E. Stassen.

Other vote includes 22,791 Uncommitted; 14,047 "Ronald Reagan No", 12,749 Stassen; 10,383 No Preference; 8,237 "None of the Names Shown"; 360 Kelley; 252 Arnold; 202 Fernandez and 21,643 scattered write-ins.

# 1984 DEMOCRATIC PREFERENCE PRIMARIES

| Date | | State | Total Vote | Glenn | Hart | Jackson | McGovern | Mondale | Other |
|------|---|-------|-----------|-------|------|---------|----------|---------|-------|
| Feb. | 28 | New Hampshire | 101,131 | 12,088 | 37,702 | 5,311 | 5,217 | 28,173 | 12,640 |
| | | | | 12.0% | 37.3% | 5.3% | 5.2% | 27.9% | 12.5% |
| March | 6 | Vermont | 74,059 | — | 51,873 | 5,761 | — | 14,834 | 1,591 |
| | | | | — | 70.0% | 7.8% | — | 20.0% | 2.1% |
| | 13 | Alabama | 428,283 | 89,286 | 88,465 | 83,787 | — | 148,165 | 18,580 |
| | | | | 20.8% | 20.7% | 19.6% | — | 34.6% | 4.3% |
| | 13 | Florida | 1,182,190 | 128,209 | 463,799 | 144,263 | 17,614 | 394,350 | 33,955 |
| | | | | 10.8% | 39.2% | 12.2% | 1.5% | 33.4% | 2.9% |
| | 13 | Georgia | 684,541 | 122,744 | 186,903 | 143,730 | 11,321 | 208,588 | 11,255 |
| | | | | 17.9% | 27.3% | 21.0% | 1.7% | 30.5% | 1.6% |
| | 13 | Massachusetts | 630,962 | 45,456 | 245,943 | 31,824 | 134,341 | 160,893 | 12,505 |
| | | | | 7.2% | 39.0% | 5.0% | 21.3% | 25.5% | 2.0% |
| | 13 | Rhode Island | 44,511 | 2,249 | 20,011 | 3,875 | 2,146 | 15,338 | 892 |
| | | | | 5.1% | 45.0% | 8.7% | 4.8% | 34.5% | 2.0% |
| | 20 | Illinois | 1,659,425 | 19,800 | 584,579 | 348,843 | 25,336 | 670,951 | 9,916 |
| | | | | 1.2% | 35.2% | 21.0% | 1.5% | 40.4% | 0.6% |
| | 27 | Connecticut | 220,842 | 955 | 116,286 | 26,395 | 2,426 | 64,230 | 10,550 |
| | | | | 0.4% | 52.7% | 12.0% | 1.1% | 29.1% | 4.8% |
| April | 3 | New York | 1,387,950 | 15,941 | 380,564 | 355,541 | 4,547 | 621,581 | 9,776 |
| | | | | 1.1% | 27.4% | 25.6% | 0.3% | 44.8% | 0.7% |
| | 3 | Wisconsin | 635,768 | 6,398 | 282,435 | 62,524 | 10,166 | 261,374 | 12,871 |
| | | | | 1.0% | 44.4% | 9.8% | 1.6% | 41.1% | 2.0% |
| | 10 | Pennsylvania | 1,656,294 | 22,605 | 551,335 | 264,463 | 13,139 | 747,267 | 57,485 |
| | | | | 1.4% | 33.3% | 16.0% | 0.8% | 45.1% | 3.5% |
| May | 1 | Dist. of Col. | 102,731 | — | 7,305 | 69,106 | — | 26,320 | — |
| | | | | — | 7.1% | 67.3% | — | 25.6% | — |
| | 1 | Tennessee | 322,063 | 4,198 | 93,710 | 81,418 | 3,824 | 132,201 | 6,712 |
| | | | | 1.3% | 29.1% | 25.3% | 1.2% | 41.0% | 2.1% |
| | 5 | Louisiana | 318,810 | — | 79,593 | 136,707 | 3,158 | 71,162 | 28,190 |
| | | | | — | 25.0% | 42.9% | 1.0% | 22.3% | 8.8% |
| | 5 | Texas | No Presidential Preference Vote Held | | | | | | |
| | 8 | Indiana | 716,955 | 16,046 | 299,491 | 98,190 | — | 293,413 | 9,815 |
| | | | | 2.2% | 41.8% | 13.7% | — | 40.9% | 1.4% |
| | 8 | Maryland | 506,886 | 6,238 | 123,365 | 129,387 | 5,796 | 215,222 | 26,878 |
| | | | | 1.2% | 24.3% | 25.5% | 1.1% | 42.5% | 5.3% |
| | 8 | North Carolina | 960,857 | 17,659 | 289,877 | 243,945 | 10,149 | 342,324 | 56,903 |
| | | | | 1.8% | 30.2% | 25.4% | 1.1% | 35.6% | 5.9% |
| | 8 | Ohio | 1,447,236 | — | 608,528 | 237,133 | 8,991 | 583,595 | 8,989 |
| | | | | — | 42.0% | 16.4% | 0.6% | 40.3% | 0.6% |
| | 15 | Nebraska | 148,855 | — | 86,582 | 13,495 | 1,561 | 39,635 | 7,582 |
| | | | | — | 58.2% | 9.1% | 1.0% | 26.6% | 5.1% |
| | 15 | Oregon | 399,679 | 10,831 | 233,638 | 37,106 | — | 110,374 | 7,730 |
| | | | | 2.7% | 58.5% | 9.3% | — | 27.6% | 1.9% |
| | 22 | Idaho | 54,722 | — | 31,737 | 3,104 | — | 16,460 | 3,421 |
| | | | | — | 58.0% | 5.7% | — | 30.1% | 6.3% |
| June | 5 | California | 2,970,903 | 96,770 | 1,155,499 | 546,693 | 69,926 | 1,049,342 | 52,673 |
| | | | | 3.3% | 38.9% | 18.4% | 2.4% | 35.3% | 1.8% |
| | 5 | Montana | 34,214 | — | 3,080 | 388 | — | 2,026 | 28,720 |
| | | | | — | 9.0% | 1.1% | — | 5.9% | 83.9% |
| | 5 | New Jersey | 676,561 | — | 200,948 | 159,788 | — | 305,516 | 10,309 |
| | | | | — | 29.7% | 23.6% | — | 45.2% | 1.5% |
| | 5 | New Mexico | 187,403 | — | 87,610 | 22,168 | 5,143 | 67,675 | 4,807 |
| | | | | — | 46.7% | 11.8% | 2.7% | 36.1% | 2.6% |
| | 5 | South Dakota | 52,561 | — | 26,641 | 2,738 | — | 20,495 | 2,687 |
| | | | | — | 50.7% | 5.2% | — | 39.0% | 5.1% |

# 1984 DEMOCRATIC PREFERENCE PRIMARIES

| Date | State | Total Vote | Glenn | Hart | Jackson | McGovern | Mondale | Other |
|------|-------|-----------|-------|------|---------|----------|---------|-------|
| 5 | West Virginia | 369,245 | — | 137,866 | 24,697 | — | 198,776 | 7,906 |
|  |  |  | — | 37.3% | 6.7% | — | 53.8% | 2.1% |
| 12 | North Dakota | 33,555 | — | 28,603 | — | — | 934 | 4,018 |
|  |  |  | — | 85.2% | — | — | 2.8% | 12.0% |
|  | Total | 18,009,192 | 617,473 | 6,503,968 | 3,282,380 | 334,801 | 6,811,214 | 459,356 |
|  |  |  | 3.4% | 36.1% | 18.2% | 1.9% | 37.8% | 2.6% |

Candidates on the ballot in at least one state were Reubin Askew, Hugh G. Bagley, Martin J. Beckman, Bob Brewster, Walter R. Buchanan, Raymond J. Caplette, Roy J. Clendenan, Alan Cranston, John H. Glenn, Robert K. Griser, Gary W. Hart, Ernest F. Hollings, Jesse L. Jackson, Richard B. Kay, William King, Claude R. Kirk, Stephen A. Koczak, William P. Kreml, Lyndon H. LaRouche, George S. McGovern, Walter F. Mondale, Edward T. O'Donnell, Chester M. Rudnicki, Cyril E. Sagan, Alfred Timinski, Betty J. Williams and Gerald Willis.

Other vote includes 123,649 LaRouche; 77,697 No Preference; 59,254 Uncommitted; 52,759 Askew; 51,437 Cranston; 33,684 Hollings; 9,815 Brewster; 9,261 "None of the Names Shown"; 8,014 Griser; 7,957 Willis; 4,847 Williams; 2,699 Kay; 1,855 Koczak; 632 Timinski; 132 Buchanan; 127 Beckman; 74 O'Donnell; 34 King; 25 Kreml; 24 Bagley; 24 Kirk; 21 Rudnick; 20 Clendenan; 20 Sagan; 19 Caplette; 15,276 scattered write-ins.

# 1980 PRESIDENTIAL PRIMARIES

In 1980 thirty-five states and the District of Columbia held Presidential primaries. In some states balloting was for delegate slates pledged to specific Presidential candidates or uncommitted; in others, electors indicated a personal preference as to their party's nominee. In New York, Democrats had a Presidential preference, but Republicans held primaries for the selection of delegates only, without indication of Presidential preference. In Mississippi, Republicans elected delegates by congressional district pledged to candidates and the vote given is the sum of the CD slates. In Arkansas, the Republicans did not hold a primary although Democrats did. In South Carolina, the Democrats did not hold a primary but Republicans did. The vote in Ohio is for at-large delegates pledged to specific candidates and elected as a group.

The state-by-state Republican and Democratic tables, included at the end of this section, detail in chronological order the vote for major candidates in each party. An asterisk in the table indicates votes written-in for a candidate not on the ballot.

Republican candidates on the ballot in at least one state were John B. Anderson, Donald Badgley, Howard H. Baker,Jr., Nick Belluso, George Bush, William E. Carlson, Alvin G. Carris, John B. Connally, Philip M. Crane, Robert Dole, Benjamin Fernandez, Alvin J. Jacobson, V. A. Kelley, C. Leon Pickett, Ronald Reagan, Harold E. Stassen, R. W. Yeager.

Democratic candidates on the ballot in at least one state were Frank Ahern, Edmund G. Brown, Jr., Jimmy Carter, Cliff Finch, Richard B. Kay, Edward M. Kennedy, Lyndon H. LaRouche, Bob Maddox, William L. Nuckols, Don Reaux, Ray Rollinson.

## ALABAMA MARCH 11

Republican    147,352 Reagan; 54,730 Bush; 5,099 Crane; 1,963 Baker; 1,077 Connally; 544 Stassen; 447 Dole; 141 Belluso.

Democratic    193,734 Carter; 31,382 Kennedy; 9,529 Brown; 1,670 Uncommitted; 609 Nuckols; 540 Maddox.

## ARKANSAS MAY 27

Republican    No Presidential primary held.

Democratic    269,375 Carter; 80,904 Uncommitted; 78,542 Kennedy; 19,469 Finch.

## CALIFORNIA JUNE 3

Republican    2,057,923 Reagan; 349,315 Anderson; 125,113 Bush; 21,465 Crane; 10,242 Fernandez; 14 scattered write-in.

Democratic    1,507,142 Kennedy slate; 1,266,276 Carter slate; 382,759 Unpledged slate; 135,962 Brown slate; 71,779 LaRouche slate; 51 scattered write-in.

## CONNECTICUT MARCH 15

Republican    70,367 Bush; 61,735 Reagan; 40,354 Anderson; 4,256 Uncommitted; 2,446 Baker; 1,887 Crane; 598 Connally; 333 Dole; 308 Fernandez.

Democratic    98,662 Kennedy; 87,207 Carter; 13,403 Uncommitted; 5,617 LaRouche; 5,386 Brown.

## FLORIDA MARCH 11

Republican    345,699 Reagan; 185,996 Bush; 56,636 Anderson; 12,000 Crane; 6,345 Baker; 4,958 Connally; 1,377 Stassen; 1,086 Dole; 898 Fernandez.

Democratic    666,321 Carter; 254,727 Kennedy; 104,321 No Preference; 53,474 Brown; 19,160 Kay.

# 1980 PRESIDENTIAL PRIMARIES

**GEORGIA MARCH 11**

Republican   146,500 Reagan; 25,293 Bush; 16,853 Anderson; 6,308 Crane; 2,388 Connally; 1,571 Baker; 809 Fernandez; 249 Dole; 200 Stassen.

Democratic   338,772 Carter; 32,315 Kennedy; 7,255 Brown; 3,707 Uncommitted; 1,378 Finch; 840 Kay; 513 LaRouche.

**IDAHO MAY 27**

Republican   111,868 Reagan; 13,130 Anderson; 5,416 Bush; 3,441 Uncommitted; 1,024 Crane.

Democratic   31,383 Carter; 11,087 Kennedy; 5,934 Uncommitted; 2,078 Brown.

**ILLINOIS MARCH 18**

Republican   547,355 Reagan; 415,193 Anderson; 124,057 Bush; 24,865 Crane; 7,051 Baker; 4,548 Connally; 3,757 Kelley; 1,843 Dole; 1,412 scattered write-in.

Democratic   780,787 Carter; 359,875 Kennedy; 39,168 Brown; 19,192 LaRouche; 2,045 scattered write-in.

**INDIANA MAY 6**

Republican   419,016 Reagan; 92,955 Bush; 56,342 Anderson.

Democratic   398,949 Carter; 190,492 Kennedy.

**KANSAS APRIL 1**

Republican   179,739 Reagan; 51,924 Anderson; 35,838 Bush; 3,603 Baker; 2,067 Connally; 1,650 Fernandez; 1,367 Crane; 1,063 Yeager; 483 Carris; 383 Stassen; 311 Carlson; 244 Badgley; 6,726 "None of the Names Shown".

Democratic   109,807 Carter; 61,318 Kennedy; 9,434 Brown; 632 Maddox; 629 Finch; 571 Ahern; 364 Rollinson; 11,163 "None of the Names Shown".

**KENTUCKY MAY 27**

Republican   78,072 Reagan; 6,861 Bush; 4,791 Anderson; 3,084 Uncommitted; 1,223 Stassen; 764 Fernandez.

Democratic   160,819 Carter; 55,167 Kennedy; 19,219 Uncommitted; 2,609 Kay; 2,517 Finch.

**LOUISIANA APRIL 5**

Republican   31,212 Reagan; 7,818 Bush; 2,221 Uncommitted; 155 Belluso; 126 Stassen; 84 Fernandez; 67 Pickett.

Democratic   199,956 Carter; 80,797 Kennedy; 41,614 Uncommitted; 16,774 Brown; 11,153 Finch; 3,362 Kay; 2,830 Maddox; 2,255 Reaux.

**MARYLAND MAY 13**

Republican   80,557 Reagan; 68,389 Bush; 16,244 Anderson; 2,113 Crane.

Democratic   226,528 Carter; 181,091 Kennedy; 45,879 Uncommitted; 14,313 Brown; 4,891 Finch; 4,388 LaRouche.

# 1980 PRESIDENTIAL PRIMARIES

### MASSACHUSETTS MARCH 4

Republican   124,365 Bush; 122,987 Anderson; 115,334 Reagan; 19,366 Baker; 4,714 Connally; 4,669 Crane; 2,243 No Preference; 577 Dole; 374 Fernandez; 218 Stassen; 5,979 scattered write-in.

Democratic   590,393 Kennedy; 260,401 Carter; 31,498 Brown; 19,663 No Preference; 5,368 scattered write-in.

### MICHIGAN MAY 20

Republican   341,998 Bush; 189,184 Reagan; 48,947 Anderson; 10,265 Uncommitted; 2,248 Fernandez; 1,938 Stassen; 596 scattered write-in.

Democratic   36,385 Uncommitted; 23,043 Brown; 8,948 LaRouche; 10,048 scattered write-in.

### MISSISSIPPI JUNE 3

Republican   23,028 Reagan slate; 2,105 Bush slate; 618 Unslated (CD's 3 and 4 only).

Democratic   No Presidential primary held.

### MONTANA JUNE 3

Republican   68,744 Reagan; 7,665 Bush; 3,014 No Preference.

Democratic   66,922 Carter; 47,671 Kennedy; 15,466 No Preference.

### NEBRASKA MAY 13

Republican   155,995 Reagan; 31,380 Bush; 11,879 Anderson; 1,420 Dole; 1,062 Crane; 799 Stassen; 400 Fernandez; 2,268 scattered write-in.

Democratic   72,120 Carter; 57,826 Kennedy; 16,041 Uncommitted; 5,478 Brown; 1,169 LaRouche; 1,247 scattered write-in.

### NEVADA MAY 27

Republican   39,352 Reagan; 3,078 Bush; 4,965 "None of These Candidates".

Democratic   25,159 Carter; 19,296 Kennedy; 22,493 "None of These Candidates".

### NEW HAMPSHIRE FEBRUARY 26

Republican   72,983 Reagan; 33,443 Bush; 18,943 Baker; 14,458 Anderson; 2,618 Crane; 2,239 Connally; 597 Dole; 1,876 scattered write-in.

Democratic   52,692 Carter; 41,745 Kennedy; 10,743 Brown; 2,326 LaRouche; 566 Kay; 3,858 scattered write-in.

### NEW JERSEY JUNE 3

Republican   225,959 Reagan; 47,447 Bush; 4,571 Stassen.

Democratic   315,109 Kennedy; 212,387 Carter; 19,499 Uncommitted; 13,913 LaRouche.

1146

# 1980 PRESIDENTIAL PRIMARIES

**NEW MEXICO JUNE 3**

Republican  37,982 Reagan; 7,171 Anderson; 5,892 Bush; 4,412 Crane; 1,795 Fernandez; 1,347 Uncommitted; 947 Stassen.

Democratic  73,721 Kennedy; 66,621 Carter; 9,734 Uncommitted; 4,798 LaRouche; 4,490 Finch.

**NEW YORK MARCH 25**

Republican  No Presidential primary was held. Delegates were elected, but without indication of Presidential preference.

Democratic  582,757 Kennedy; 406,305 Carter.

**NORTH CAROLINA MAY 6**

Republican  113,854 Reagan; 36,631 Bush; 8,542 Anderson; 4,538 No Preference; 2,543 Baker; 1,107 Connally; 629 Dole; 547 Crane.

Democratic  516,778 Carter; 130,684 Kennedy; 68,380 No Preference; 21,420 Brown.

**OHIO JUNE 3**

Republican  692,288 Reagan; 164,485 Bush.

Democratic  605,744 Carter; 523,874 Kennedy; 35,268 LaRouche; 21,524 Kay.

**OREGON MAY 20**

Republican  170,449 Reagan; 109,210 Bush; 32,118 Anderson; 2,324 Crane; 1,265 scattered write-in.

Democratic  208,693 Carter; 114,651 Kennedy; 34,409 Brown; 10,569 scattered write-in.

**PENNSYLVANIA APRIL 22**

Republican  626,759 Bush; 527,916 Reagan; 30,846 Baker; 26,890 Anderson (write-in); 10,656 Connally; 6,767 Stassen; 4,357 Jacobson; 2,521 Fernandez; 4,699 scattered write-in.

Democratic  736,854 Kennedy; 732,332 Carter; 93,865 No Preference; 37,669 Brown; 12,831 scattered write-in.

**RHODE ISLAND JUNE 3**

Republican  3,839 Reagan; 993 Bush; 348 Uncommitted; 107 Stassen; 48 Fernandez.

Democratic  26,179 Kennedy; 9,907 Carter; 1,160 LaRouche; 771 Uncommitted; 310 Brown.

**SOUTH CAROLINA MARCH 8**

Republican  79,549 Reagan; 43,113 Connally; 21,569 Bush; 773 Baker; 171 Fernandez; 150 Stassen; 117 Dole; 59 Belluso.

Democratic  No Presidential primary was held.

**SOUTH DAKOTA JUNE 3**

Republican  72,861 Reagan slate; 5,366 No Preference slate; 3,691 Bush slate; 987 Stassen slate.

Democratic  33,418 Kennedy slate; 31,251 Carter slate; 4,094 Uncommitted slate (in CD 1 only).

# 1980 PRESIDENTIAL PRIMARIES

## TENNESSEE MAY 6

Republican   144,625 Reagan; 35,274 Bush; 8,722 Anderson; 4,976 Uncommitted; 1,574 Crane; 39 scattered write-in.

Democratic   221,658 Carter; 53,258 Kennedy; 11,515 Uncommitted; 5,612 Brown; 1,663 Finch; 925 LaRouche; 49 scattered write-in.

## TEXAS MAY 3

Republican   268,798 Reagan; 249,819 Bush; 8,152 Uncommitted.

Democratic   770,390 Carter; 314,129 Kennedy; 257,250 Uncommitted; 35,585 Brown.

## VERMONT MARCH 4

Republican   19,720 Reagan; 19,030 Anderson; 14,226 Bush; 8,055 Baker; 1,238 Crane; 884 Connally; 105 Stassen; 2,353 scattered write-in.

Democratic   29,015 Carter; 10,135 Kennedy; 553 scattered write-in.

## WEST VIRGINIA JUNE 3

Republican   115,407 Reagan; 19,509 Bush; 3,100 Stassen.

Democratic   197,687 Carter; 120,247 Kennedy.

## WISCONSIN APRIL 1

Republican   364,898 Reagan; 276,164 Bush; 248,623 Anderson; 3,298 Baker; 2,951 Crane; 2,312 Connally; 1,051 Fernandez; 1,010 Stassen; 2,595 "None of the Names Shown"; 4,951 scattered write-in.

Democratic   353,662 Carter; 189,520 Kennedy; 74,496 Brown; 6,896 LaRouche; 1,842 Finch; 2,694 "None of the Names Shown"; 509 scattered write-in.

## DISTRICT OF COLUMBIA MAY 6

Republican   4,973 Bush; 2,025 Anderson; 270 Crane; 201 Stassen; 60 Fernandez.

Democratic   39,561 Kennedy; 23,697 Carter; 892 LaRouche.

# 1980 REPUBLICAN PREFERENCE PRIMARIES

| Date | State | Total Vote | Anderson | Baker | Bush | Connally | Crane | Reagan | Other |
|---|---|---|---|---|---|---|---|---|---|
| Feb. 26 | New Hampshire | 147,157 | 14,458 | 18,943 | 33,443 | 2,239 | 2,618 | 72,983 | 2,473 |
| March 4 | Massachusetts | 400,826 | 122,987 | 19,366 | 124,365 | 4,714 | 4,669 | 115,334 | 9,391 |
| 4 | Vermont | 65,611 | 19,030 | 8,055 | 14,226 | 884 | 1,238 | 19,720 | 2458 |
| 8 | South Carolina | 145,501 | — | 773 | 21,569 | 43,113 | — | 79,549 | 497 |
| 11 | Alabama | 211,353 | — | 1,963 | 54,730 | 1,077 | 5,099 | 147,352 | 1,132 |
| 11 | Florida | 614,995 | 56,636 | 6,345 | 185,996 | 4,958 | 12,000 | 345,699 | 3,361 |
| 11 | Georgia | 200,171 | 16,853 | 1,571 | 25,293 | 2,388 | 6,308 | 146,500 | 1,258 |
| 18 | Illinois | 1,130,081 | 415,193 | 7,051 | 124,057 | 4,548 | 24,865 | 547,355 | 7,012 |
| 25 | Connecticut | 182,284 | 40,354 | 2,446 | 70,367 | 598 | 1,887 | 61,735 | 4,897 |
| 25 | New York | No Primary Held | | | | | | | |
| April 1 | Kansas | 285,398 | 51,924 | 3,603 | 35,838 | 2,067 | 1,367 | 179,739 | 10,860 |
| 2 | Wisconsin | 907,853 | 248,623 | 3,298 | 276,164 | 2,312 | 2,951 | 364,898 | 9,607 |
| 5 | Louisiana | 41,683 | — | — | 7,818 | — | — | 31,212 | 2,653 |
| 22 | Pennsylvania | 1,241,411 | 26,890 | 30,846 | 626,759 | 10,656 | — | 527,916 | 18,344 |
| May 3 | Texas | 526,769 | — | — | 249,819 | — | — | 268,798 | 8,152 |
| 6 | Indiana | 568,313 | 56,342 | — | 92,955 | — | — | 419,016 | |
| 6 | North Carolina | 168,391 | 8,542 | 2,543 | 36,631 | 1,107 | 547 | 113,854 | 5,167 |
| 6 | Tennessee | 195,210 | 8,722 | — | 35,274 | — | 1,574 | 144,625 | 5,015 |
| 6 | District of Columbia | 7,529 | 2,025 | — | 4,973 | — | 270 | — | 261 |
| 13 | Maryland | 167,303 | 16,244 | — | 68,389 | — | 2,113 | 80,557 | |
| 13 | Nebraska | 205,203 | 11,879 | — | 31,380 | — | 1,062 | 155,995 | 4,887 |
| 20 | Michigan | 595,176 | 48,947 | — | 341,998 | — | — | 189,184 | 15,047 |
| 20 | Oregon | 315,366 | 32,118 | — | 109,210 | — | 2,324 | 170,449 | 1,265 |
| 27 | Arkansas | No Primary Held | | | | | | | |
| 27 | Idaho | 134,879 | 13,130 | 5,416 | — | — | 1,024 | 111,868 | 3,441 |
| 27 | Kentucky | 94,795 | 4,791 | — | 6,861 | — | — | 78,072 | 5,071 |
| 27 | Nevada | 47,395 | — | — | 3,078 | — | — | 39,352 | 4,965 |
| June 3 | California | 2,564,072 | 349,315 | — | 125,113 | — | 21,465 | 2,057,923 | 10,256 |
| 3 | Mississippi | 25,751 | — | — | 2,105 | — | — | 23,028 | 618 |
| 3 | Montana | 79,423 | — | — | 7,665 | — | — | 68,744 | 3,014 |
| 3 | New Jersey | 277,977 | — | — | 47,447 | — | — | 225,959 | 4,571 |
| 3 | New Mexico | 59,546 | 7,171 | — | 5,892 | — | 4,412 | 37,982 | 4,089 |
| 3 | Ohio | 856,773 | — | — | 164,485 | — | — | 692,288 | |
| 3 | Rhode Island | 5,335 | — | — | 993 | — | — | 3,839 | 503 |
| 3 | South Dakota | 82,905 | — | — | 3,691 | — | — | 72,861 | 6,353 |
| 3 | West Virginia | 138,016 | — | — | 19,509 | — | — | 115,407 | 3,100 |
| | | 12,690,451 | 1,572,174 | 112,219 | 2,958,093 | 80,661 | 97,793 | 7,709,793 | 159,718 |

Other vote includes 38,708 Uncommitted; 24,753 Stassen; 23,423 Fernandez; 15,161 No Preference; 9,321 "None of the Names Shown"; 7298 Dole; 4965 "None of These Candidates"; 4,357 Jacobson; 3,757 Kelley; 1,063 Yeager; 483 Carris; 355 Befluso; 311 Carlson 24; 244 Badgley; 67 Pickett; 25,452 scattered.

# 1980 DEMOCRATIC PREFERENCE PRIMARIES

| Date | | State | Total Vote | Carter | Edward M. Kennedy | Brown | LaRouche | Other |
|------|---|-------|-----------:|-------:|------------------:|------:|---------:|------:|
| February | 26 | New Hampshire | 111,930 | 52,692 | 41,745 | 10,743 | 2,326 | 4,424 |
| March | 4 | Massachusetts | 907,323 | 260,401 | 590,393 | 31,498 | — | 25,031 |
| | 4 | Vermont | 39,703 | 29,015 | 10,135 | — | — | 553 |
| | 8 | South Carolina | No Primary Held | — | — | — | — | — |
| | 11 | Alabama | 237,464 | 193,734 | 31,382 | 9,529 | — | 2,819 |
| | 11 | Florida | 1,098,003 | 666,321 | 254,727 | 53,474 | — | 123,481 |
| | 11 | Georgia | 384,780 | 338,772 | 32,315 | 7,255 | 513 | 5,925 |
| | 18 | Illinois | 1,201,067 | 780,787 | 359,875 | 39,168 | 19,192 | 2,045 |
| | 25 | Connecticut | 210,275 | 87,207 | 98,662 | 5,386 | 5,617 | 13,403 |
| | 25 | New York | 989,062 | 406,305 | 582,757 | — | | |
| April | 1 | Kansas | 193,918 | 109,807 | 61,318 | 9,434 | — | 13,359 |
| | 1 | Wisconsin | 629,619 | 353,662 | 189,520 | 74,496 | 6,896 | 5,045 |
| | 5 | Louisiana | 358,741 | 199,956 | 80,797 | 16,774 | — | 61,214 |
| | 22 | Pennsylvania | 1,613,551 | 732,332 | 736,854 | 37,669 | — | 106,696 |
| May | 3 | Texas | 1,377,354 | 770,390 | 314,129 | 35,585 | — | 257,250 |
| | 6 | Indiana | 589,441 | 398,949 | 190,492 | — | — | — |
| | 6 | North Carolina | 737,262 | 516,778 | 130,684 | 21,420 | — | 68,380 |
| | 6 | Tennessee | 294,680 | 221,658 | 53,258 | 5,612 | 925 | 13,227 |
| | 6 | District of Columbia | 64,150 | 23,697 | 39,561 | — | 892 | — |
| | 13 | Maryland | 477,090 | 226,528 | 181,091 | 14,313 | 4,388 | 50,770 |
| | 13 | Nebraska | 153,881 | 72,120 | 57,826 | 5,478 | 1,169 | 17,288 |
| | 20 | Michigan | 78,424 | — | — | 23,043 | 8,948 | 46,433 |
| | 20 | Oregon | 368,322 | 208,693 | 114,651 | 34,409 | — | 10,569 |
| | 27 | Arkansas | 448,290 | 269,375 | 78,542 | — | — | 100,373 |
| | 27 | Idaho | 50,482 | 31,383 | 11,087 | 2,078 | — | 5,934 |
| | 27 | Kentucky | 240,331 | 160,819 | 55,167 | — | — | 24,345 |
| | 27 | Nevada | 66,948 | 25,159 | 19,296 | — | — | 22,493 |
| June | 3 | California | 3,363,969 | 1,266,276 | 1,507,142 | 135,962 | 71,779 | 382,810 |
| | 3 | Mississippi | No Primary Held | — | — | — | — | — |
| | 3 | Montana | 130,059 | 66,922 | 47,671 | — | — | 15,466 |
| | 3 | New Jersey | 560,908 | 212,387 | 315,109 | — | 13,913 | 19,499 |
| | 3 | New Mexico | 159,364 | 66,621 | 73,721 | — | 4,798 | 14,224 |
| | 3 | Ohio | 1,186,410 | 605,744 | 523,874 | — | 35,268 | 21,524 |
| | 3 | Rhode Island | 38,327 | 9,907 | 26,179 | 310 | 1,160 | 771 |
| | 3 | South Dakota | 68,763 | 31,251 | 33,418 | — | — | 4,094 |
| | 3 | West Virginia | 317,934 | 197,687 | 120,247 | — | — | — |
| | | Total | 18,747,825 | 9,593,335 | 6,963,625 | 573,636 | 177,784 | 1,439,445 |
| | | | | 51.2% | 37.1% | 3.1% | 0.9% | 7.7% |

Other vote includes 950,378 Uncommitted; 301,695 No Preference; 48,061 Kay; 48,032 Finch; 22,493 "None of These Candidates"; 13,857 "None of the Names Shown"; 4,002 Maddox; 2,255 Reaux; 609 Nuckols; 571 Ahern; 364 Rollinson; 47,128 scattered write-in.

# 1976 PRESIDENTIAL PRIMARIES

In 1976 twenty-six states and the District of Columbia held Presidential primaries though there was no Republican voting in the District of Columbia. Alabama, New York and Texas elected delegates to the national party conventions, but none of these states provided for a specific expression of Presidential preference by the voter.

In some states balloting was for delegate slates pledged to specific Presidential candidates or uncommitted; in others, electors indicated a personal preference as to their party's nominee. In Ohio, the vote used is for at-large delegates pledged to specific candidates and elected as a group. In several states which held a preference vote and a delegate vote, the preference vote is used.

The state-by-state Republican and Democratic tables, included at the end of this section, detail in chronologicasl order the vote for major candidates in each party. As asterisk in the table indicates votes written-in for a candidate not on the ballot.

Republican candidates on the ballot in at least one state were Lar Daly, Gerald R. Ford; Tommy Klein and Ronald Reagan.

Democratic candidates on the ballot in at least one state were Frank Ahern, Stanley N. Arnold, Birch Bayh, Lloyd Bentsen; Arthur O. Blessitt, Frank Bona, Edmund G. Brown, Jr., Robert C. Byrd, Jimmy Carter, Frank Chruch, Billy Joe Clegg, Gertrude W. Donahey, Abram Eisenman, John S. Gonas, Jesse Gray, Fred R. Harris, Hubert H. Humphrey, Henry M. Jackson, Robert L. Kelleher, Edward M. Kennedy, Rick Loewenherz, Frank Lomento, Floyd L. Lunger, Ellen McCormack, Fifi Rockefeller, George Roden, Ray Rollinson, Terry Sanford, Bernard B. Schechter, Milton Shapp, R. Sargent Shriver, Morris K. Udall and George C. Wallace.

## ARKANSAS MAY 25

Republican   20,628 Reagan; 11,430 Ford; 483 Uncommitted.

Democratic   314,306 Carter; 83,005 Wallace; 57,152 Uncommitted; 37,783 Udall; 9,554 Jackson. Original uncorrected canvass gave the Uncommitted vote as 57,067.

## CALIFORNIA JUNE 8

Republican   1,604,836 Reagan; 845,655 Ford; 20 scattered write-in.

Democratic   2,013,210 Brown slate; 697,092 Carter slate; 250,581 Church slate; 171,501 Udall slate; 102,292 Wallace slate; 78,595 Uncommitted slate; 38,634 Jackson slate; 29,242 McCormack slate; 16,920 Harris slate; 11,419 Bayh slate; 215 scattered write-in.

## FLORIDA MARCH 9

Republican   321,982 Ford; 287,837 Reagan.

Democratic   448,844 Carter; 396,820 Wallace; 310,944 Jackson; 37,626 No Preference; 32,198 Shapp; 27,235 Udall; 8,750 Bayh; 7,889 Blessitt; 7,595 McCormack; 7,084 Shriver; 5,397 Harris; 5,042 Byrd; 4,906 Church.

## GEORGIA MAY 4

Republican   128,671 Reagan; 59,801 Ford.

Democratic   419,272 Carter; 57,594 Wallace; 9,755 Udall; 3,628 Byrd; 3,358 Jackson; 2,477 Church; 1,487 Ahern; 1,378 Shriver; 824 Bayh; 699 Harris; 635 McCormack; 351 Eisenman; 277 Bentsen; 263 Bona; 181 Shapp; 153 Roden; 139 Kelleher.

# 1976 PRESIDENTIAL PRIMARIES

## IDAHO MAY 25

Republican  66,743 Reagan; 22,323 Ford; 727 Uncommitted.

Democratic  58,570 Church; 8,818 Carter; 1,700 Humphrey; 1,453 Brown (write-in); 1,115 Wallace; 981 Udall; 964 Uncommitted; 485 Jackson; 319 Harris.

## ILLINOIS MARCH 16

Republican  456,750 Ford; 311,295 Reagan; 7,582 Daly; 266 scattered write-in.

Democratic  630,915 Carter; 361,798 Wallace; 214,024 Shriver; 98,862 Harris; 6,315 scattered write-in.

## INDIANA MAY 4

Republican  323,779 Reagan; 307,513 Ford.

Democratic  417,480 Carter; 93,121 Wallace; 72,080 Jackson; 31,708 McCormack.

## KENTUCKY MAY 25

Republican  67,976 Ford; 62,683 Reagan; 1,781 Uncommitted; 1,088 Klein.

Democratic  181,690 Carter; 51,540 Wallace; 33,262 Udall; 17,061 McCormack; 11,962 Uncommitted; 8,186 Jackson; 2,305 Rockefeller.

## MARYLAND MAY 18

Republican  96,291 Ford; 69,680 Reagan.

Democratic  286,672 Brown; 219,404 Carter; 32,790 Udall; 24,176 Wallace; 13,956 Jackson; 7,907 McCormack; 6,841 Harris.

## MASSACHUSETTS MARCH 2

Republican  115,375 Ford; 63,555 Reagan; 6,000 No Preference; 3,519 scattered write-in.

Democratic  164,393 Jackson; 130,440 Udall; 123,112 Wallace; 101,948 Carter; 55,701 Harris; 53,252 Shriver; 34,963 Bayh; 25,772 McCormack; 21,693 Shapp; 9,804 No Preference; 7,851 Humphrey (write-in); 1,623 Kennedy (write-in); 1,603 Kelleher; 364 Bentsen; 351 Sanford; 2,951 scattered write-in.

## MICHIGAN MAY 18

Republican  690,180 Ford; 364,052 Reagan; 8,473 Uncommitted; 109 scattered write-in.

Democratic  307,559 Carter; 305,134 Udall; 49,204 Wallace; 15,853 Uncommitted; 10,332 Jackson; 7,623 McCormack; 5,738 Shriver; 4,081 Harris; 3,142 scattered write-in.

## MONTANA JUNE 1

Republican  56,683 Reagan; 31,100 Ford; 1,996 No Preference.

Democratic  63,448 Church; 26,329 Carter; 6,708 Udall; 3,820 No Preference; 3,680 Wallace; 2,856 Jackson.

# 1976 PRESIDENTIAL PRIMARIES

**NEBRASKA MAY 11**

Republican   113,493 Reagan; 94,542 Ford; 379 scattered write-in.

Democratic   67,297 Church; 65,833 Carter; 12,685 Humphrey; 7,199 Kennedy; 6,033 McCormack; 5,567 Wallace; 4,688 Udall; 2,642 Jackson; 811 Harris; 407 Bayh; 384 Shriver; 1,467 scattered write-in.

**NEVADA MAY 25**

Republican   31,637 Reagan; 13,747 Ford; 2,365 "None of These Candidates".

Democratic   39,671 Brown; 17,567 Carter; 6,778 Church; 4,603 "None of These Candidates"; 2,490 Wallace; 2,237 Udall; 1,896 Jackson.

**NEW HAMPSHIRE FEBRUARY 24**

Republican   55,156 Ford; 53,569 Reagan; 2,949 scattered write-in.

Democratic   23,373 Carter; 18,710 Udall; 12,510 Bayh; 8,863 Harris; 6,743 Shriver; 4,596 Humphrey (write-in); 1,857 Jackson (write-in); 1,061 Wallace (write-in); 1,007 McCormack; 828 Blessitt; 371 Arnold; 174 Clegg; 173 Schechter; 135 Bona; 87 Kelleher; 53 Sanford; 49 Lowewenherz; 1,791 scattered write-in.

**NEW JERSEY JUNE 8**

Republican   242,122 Ford.

Democratic   210,655 Carter; 49,034 Church; 31,820 Jackson; 31,183 Wallace; 21,774 McCormack; 3,935 Lunger; 3,574 Gray; 3,555 Lomento; 3,021 Rollinson; 2,288 Gonas.

**NORTH CAROLINA MARCH 23**

Republican   101,468 Reagan; 88,897 Ford; 3,362 No Preference.

Democratic   324,437 Carter; 210,166 Wallace; 25,749 Jackson; 22,850 No Preference; 14,032 Udall; 5,923 Harris; 1,675 Bentsen.

**OHIO JUNE 8**

Republican   516,111 Ford; 419,646 Reagan.

Democratic   593,130 Carter; 240,342 Udall; 157,884 Chruch; 63,953 Wallace; 43,661 Donahey; 35,404 Jackson.

**OREGON MAY 25**

Republican   150,181 Ford; 136,691 Reagan; 11,663 scattered write-in.

Democratic   145,394 Church; 115,310 Carter; 106,812 Brown (write-in); 22,488 Humphrey; 11,747 Udall; 10,983 Kennedy; 5,797 Wallace; 5,298 Jackson; 3,753 McCormack; 1,344 Harris; 743 Bayh; 2,963 scattered write-in.

**PENNSYLVANIA APRIL 27**

Republican   733,472 Ford; 40,510 Reagan (write-in); 22,678 scattered write-in.

Democratic   511,905 Carter; 340,340 Jackson; 259,166 Udall; 155,902 Wallace; 38,800 McCormack; 32,947 Shapp; 15,320 Bayh; 13,067 Harris; 12,563 Humphrey (write-in); 5,032 scattered write-in.

# 1976 PRESIDENTIAL PRIMARIES

**RHODE ISLAND JUNE 1**

Republican   9,365 Ford; 4,480 Reagan; 507 Uncommitted.

Democratic   19,035 Uncommitted; 18,237 Carter; 16,423 Church; 2,543 Udall; 2,468 McCormack; 756 Jackson; 507 Wallace; 247 Bayh; 132 Shapp.

**SOUTH DAKOTA JUNE 1**

Republican   43,068 Reagan slate; 36,976 Ford slate; 4,033 No Preference slate.

Democratic   24,186 Carter slate; 19,510 Udall slate; 7,871 No Preference slate; 4,561 McCormack slate; 1,412 Wallace slate; 573 Harris slate; 558 Jackson slate.

**TENNESSEE MAY 25**

Republican   120,685 Ford; 118,997 Reagan; 2,756 Uncommitted; 97 scattered write-in.

Democratic   259,243 Carter; 36,495 Wallace; 12,420 Udall; 8,026 Church; 6,148 Uncommitted; 5,672 Jackson; 1,782 McCormack; 1,628 Harris; 1,556 Brown (write-in); 507 Shapp; 109 Humphrey (write-in); 492 scattered write-in.

**VERMONT MARCH 2**

Republican   27,014 Ford; 4,892 Reagan (write-in); 251 scattered write-in.

Democratic   16,335 Carter; 10,699 Shriver; 4,893 Harris; 3,324 McCormack; 3,463 scattered write-in.

**WEST VIRGINIA MAY 11**

Republican   88,386 Ford; 67,306 Reagan.

Democratic   331,639 Byrd; 40,938 Wallace.

**WISCONSIN APRIL 6**

Republican   326,869 Ford; 262,126 Reagan; 2,234 "None of the Names Shown"; 583 scattered write-in.

Democratic   271,220 Carter; 263,771 Udall; 92,460 Wallace; 47,605 Jackson; 26,982 McCormack; 8,185 Harris; 7,154 "None of the Names Shown"; 5,097 Shriver; 1,730 Bentsen; 1,255 Bayh; 596 Shapp; 14,473 scattered write-in.

**DISTRICT OF COLUMBIA MAY 4**

Republican   Ford unopposed; no primary election held.

Democratic   10,521 Carter; 10,149 Uncommitted (Fauntroy slate); 6,999 Udall; 5,161 Uncommitted (Washington slate); 461 Harris.

# 1976 REPUBLICAN PREFERENCE PRIMARIES

| Date | | State | Total Vote | Ford | Reagan | Other |
|---|---|---|---|---|---|---|
| February | 24 | New Hampshire | 111,674 | 55,156 | 53,569 | 2,949 |
| March | 2 | Massachusetts | 188,449 | 115,375 | 63,555 | 9,519 |
| | 2 | Vermont | 32,157 | 27,014 | 4,892 * | 251 |
| | 9 | Florida | 609,819 | 321,982 | 287,837 | — |
| | 16 | Illinois | 775,893 | 456,750 | 311,295 | 7,848 |
| | 23 | North Carolina | 193,727 | 88,897 | 101,468 | 3,362 |
| April | 6 | Wisconsin | 591,812 | 326,869 | 262,126 | 2,817 |
| | 27 | Pennsylvania | 796,660 | 733,472 | 40,510 * | 22,678 |
| May | 4 | District of Columbia | No Primary Held | — | — | — |
| | 4 | Georgia | 188,472 | 59,801 | 128,671 | — |
| | 4 | Indiana | 631,292 | 307,513 | 323,779 | — |
| | 11 | Nebraska | 208,414 | 94,542 | 113,493 | 379 |
| | 11 | West Virginia | 155,692 | 88,386 | 67,306 | — |
| | 18 | Maryland | 165,971 | 96,291 | 69,680 | — |
| | 18 | Michigan | 1,062,814 | 690,180 | 364,052 | 8,582 |
| | 25 | Arkansas | 32,541 | 11,430 | 20,628 | 483 |
| | 25 | Idaho | 89,793 | 22,323 | 66,743 | 727 |
| | 25 | Kentucky | 133,528 | 67,976 | 62,683 | 2,869 |
| | 25 | Nevada | 47,749 | 13,747 | 31,637 | 2,365 |
| | 25 | Oregon | 298,535 | 150,181 | 136,691 | 11,663 |
| | 25 | Tennessee | 242,535 | 120,685 | 118,997 | 2,853 |
| June | 1 | Montana | 89,779 | 31,100 | 56,683 | 1,996 |
| | 1 | Rhode Island | 14,352 | 9,365 | 4,480 | 507 |
| | 1 | South Dakota | 84,077 | 36,976 | 43,068 | 4,033 |
| | 8 | California | 2,450,511 | 845,655 | 1,604,836 | 20 |
| | 8 | New Jersey | 242,122 | 242,122 | — | — |
| | 8 | Ohio | 935,757 | 516,111 | 419,646 | — |
| | | Total | 10,374,125 | 5,529,899 | 4,758,325 | 85,901 |
| | | | | 53.3% | 45.9% | 0.8% |

An asterisk (*) indicates write-in. Other vote includes 7,582 Daly; 1,088 Klein; 42,514 scattered write-in; 15,391 No Preference; 14,727 Uncommitted; 2,365 "None of These Candidates"; 2,234 "None of the Names Shown".

# 1976 DEMOCRATIC PREFERENCE PRIMARIES

| Date | | State | Total Vote | Carter | Brown | Wallace | Udall | Henry M. Jackson | Church | Other |
|---|---|---|---|---|---|---|---|---|---|---|
| February | 24 | New Hampshire | 82,381 | 23,373 | — | 1,061* | 18,710 | 1,857* | — | 37,380 |
| March | 2 | Massachusetts | 735,821 | 101,948 | — | 123,112 | 130,440 | 164,393 | — | 215,928 |
| | 2 | Vermont | 38,714 | 16,335 | — | — | — | — | — | 22,379 |
| | 9 | Florida | 1,300,330 | 448,844 | — | 396,820 | 27,235 | 310,944 | 4,906 | 111,581 |
| | 16 | Illinois | 1,311,914 | 630,915 | — | 361,798 | — | — | — | 319,201 |
| | 23 | North Carolina | 604,832 | 324,437 | — | 210,166 | 14,032 | 25,749 | — | 30,448 |
| April | 6 | Wisconsin | 740,528 | 271,220 | — | 92,460 | 263,771 | 47,605 | — | 65,472 |
| | 27 | Pennsylvania | 1,385,042 | 511,905 | — | 155,902 | 259,166 | 340,340 | — | 117,729 |
| May | 4 | District of Columbia | 33,291 | 10,521 | — | — | 6,999 | — | — | 15,771 |
| | 4 | Georgia | 502,471 | 419,272 | — | 57,594 | 9,755 | 3,358 | 2,477 | 10,015 |
| | 4 | Indiana | 614,389 | 417,480 | — | 93,121 | — | 72,080 | — | 31,708 |
| | 11 | Nebraska | 175,013 | 65,833 | — | 5,567 | 4,688 | 2,642 | 67,297 | 28,986 |
| | 11 | West Virginia | 372,577 | — | — | 40,938 | — | — | — | 331,639 |
| | 18 | Maryland | 591,746 | 219,404 | 286,672 | 24,176 | 32,790 | 13,956 | — | 14,748 |
| | 18 | Michigan | 708,666 | 307,559 | — | 49,204 | 305,134 | 10,332 | — | 36,437 |
| | 25 | Arkansas | 501,800 | 314,306 | — | 83,005 | 37,783 | 9,554 | — | 57,152 |
| | 25 | Idaho | 74,405 | 8,818 | 1,453* | 1,115 | 981 | 485 | 58,570 | 2,983 |
| | 25 | Kentucky | 306,006 | 181,690 | — | 51,540 | 33,262 | 8,186 | — | 31,328 |
| | 25 | Nevada | 75,242 | 17,567 | 39,671 | 2,490 | 2,237 | 1,896 | 6,778 | 4,603 |
| | 25 | Oregon | 432,632 | 115,310 | 106,812* | 5,797 | 11,747 | 5,298 | 145,394 | 42,274 |
| | 25 | Tennessee | 334,078 | 259,243 | 1,556* | 36,495 | 12,420 | 5,672 | 8,026 | 10,666 |
| June | 1 | Montana | 106,841 | 26,329 | — | 3,680 | 6,708 | 2,856 | 63,448 | 3,820 |
| | 1 | Rhode Island | 60,348 | 18,237 | — | 507 | 2,543 | 756 | 16,423 | 21,882 |
| | 1 | South Dakota | 58,671 | 24,186 | — | 1,412 | 19,510 | 558 | — | 13,005 |
| | 8 | California | 3,409,701 | 697,092 | 2,013,210 | 102,292 | 171,501 | 38,634 | 250,581 | 136,391 |
| | 8 | New Jersey | 360,839 | 210,655 | — | 31,183 | — | 31,820 | 49,034 | 38,147 |
| | 8 | Ohio | 1,134,374 | 593,130 | — | 63,953 | 240,342 | 35,404 | 157,884 | 43,661 |
| | | Total | 16,052,652 | 6,235,609 | 2,449,374 | 1,995,388 | 1,611,754 | 1,134,375 | 830,818 | 1,795,334 |
| | | | | 38.8% | 15.3% | 12.4% | 10.0% | 7.1% | 5.2% | 11.2% |

An asterisk (*) indicates write-in. Other vote includes 340,309 Byrd; 304,399 Shriver; 238,027 McCormack; 234,568 Harris; 88,254 Shapp; 86,438 Bayh; 61,992 Humphrey; 43,661 Donahey; 19,805 Kennedy; 8,717 Blessitt; 4,046 Bentsen; 3,935 Lunger; 3,574 Gray; 3,555 Lomento; 3,021 Rollinson; 2,305 Rockefeller; 2,288 Gonas; 1,829 Kelleher; 1,487 Ahern; 404 Sanford; 398 Bona; 371 Arnold; 351 Eisenman; 174 Clegg; 173 Schechter; 153 Roden; 49 Lowewenherz; 205,019 Uncommitted; 81,971 No Preference; 42,304 scattered write-in; 7,154 "None of the Names Shown"; 4,603 "None of These Candidates."

# 1972 PRESIDENTIAL PRIMARIES

In 1972 twenty states and the District of Columbia held Presidential primaries though there was no Republican voting in the District of Columbia. In some states balloting was for delegate slates pledged to a specific Presidential candidate or uncommitted; in others, electors indicated a personal preference as to their party's nominee. In Ohio candidates ran at-large statewide blocks of delegates and the vote given is for the highest vote winner in each of the blocks.

The state-by-state Republican and Democratic tables, included at the end of this section, detail in chronological order the vote for major candidates in each party. An asterisk in the table indicates votes written-in for a candidate not on the ballot.

Republican candidates on the ballot in at least one state were John M. Ashbrook, Paul N. McCloskey, Richard M. Nixon and Patrick Paulsen.

Democratic candidates on the ballot in at least one state were Shirley Chisholm, Edward T. Coll; Walter E. Fauntroy, R. Vance Hartke, Hubert H. Humphrey, Henry M. Jackson, Edward M. Kennedy, John V. Lindsay, Eugene J. McCarthy, George S. McGovern, Wilbur D. Mills, Patsy Mink, Edmund S. Muskie, Terry Sanford, George C. Wallace and Samuel W. Yorty.

## CALIFORNIA JUNE 6

Republican   2,058,825 Nixon slate; 224,922 Ashbrook slate; 175 scattered write-in.

Democratic   1,550,652 McGovern slate; 1,375,064 Humphrey slate; 268,551 Wallace (write-in); 157,435 Chisholm slate; 72,701 Muskie slate; 50,745 Yorty slate; 34,203 McCarthy slate; 28,901 Jackson slate; 26,246 Lindsay slate; 20 scattered write-in.

## FLORIDA MARCH 14

Republican   360,278 Nixon; 36,617 Ashbrook; 17,312 McCloskey.

Democratic   526,651 Wallace; 234,658 Humphrey; 170,156 Jackson; 112,523 Muskie; 82,386 Lindsay; 78,232 McGovern; 43,989 Chisholm; 5,847 McCarthy; 4,539 Mills; 3,009 Hartke; 2,564 Yorty.

## ILLINOIS MARCH 21

Republican   No candidate names appeared on the ballot and all votes were write-in as follows: 32,550 Nixon; 170 Ashbrook; 47 McCloskey; 802 scattered write-in.

Democratic   766,914 Muskie; 444,260 McCarthy; 7,017 Wallace (write-in); 3,687 McGovern (write-in); 1,476 Humphrey (write-in); 777 Chisholm (write-in); 442 Jackson (write-in); 242 Kennedy (write-in); 118 Lindsay (write-in); 211 scattered write-in.

## INDIANA MAY 2

Republican   417,069 Nixon.

Democratic   354,244 Humphrey; 309,495 Wallace; 87,719 Muskie.

## MARYLAND MAY 16

Republican   99,308 Nixon; 9,223 McCloskey; 6,718 Ashbrook.

Democratic   219,687 Wallace; 151,981 Humphrey; 126,978 McGovern; 17,728 Jackson; 13,584 Yorty; 13,363 Muskie; 12,602 Chisholm; 4,776 Mills; 4,691 McCarthy; 2,168 Lindsay; 573 Mink.

# 1972 PRESIDENTIAL PRIMARIES

**MASSACHUSETTS APRIL 25**

Republican   99,150 Nixon; 16,435 McCloskey; 4,864 Ashbrook; 1,690 scattered write-in.

Democratic   325,673 McGovern; 131,709 Muskie; 48,929 Humphrey; 45,807 Wallace; 22,398 Chisholm; 19,441 Mills; 8,736 McCarthy; 8,499 Jackson; 2,348 Kennedy (write-in); 2,107 Lindsay; 874 Hartke; 646 Yorty; 589 Coll; 760 scattered write-in.

**MICHIGAN MAY 16**

Republican   321,652 Nixon; 9,691 McCloskey; 5,370 Uncommitted; 30 scattered write-in.

Democratic   809,239 Wallace; 425,694 McGovern; 249,798 Humphrey; 44,090 Chisholm; 38,701 Muskie; 10,700 Uncommitted; 6,938 Jackson; 2,862 Hartke; 51 scattered write-in.

**NEBRASKA MAY 9**

Republican   179,464 Nixon; 9,011 McCloskey; 4,996 Ashbrook; 801 scattered write-in.

Democratic   79,309 McGovern; 65,968 Humphrey; 23,912 Wallace; 6,886 Muskie; 5,276 Jackson; 3,459 Yorty; 3,194 McCarthy; 1,763 Chisholm; 1,244 Lindsay; 377 Mills; 293 Kennedy (write-in); 249 Hartke; 207 scattered write-in.

**NEW HAMPSHIRE MARCH 7**

Republican   79,239 Nixon; 23,190 McCloskey; 11,362 Ashbrook; 1,211 Paulsen; 2,206 scattered write-in.

Democratic   41,235 Muskie; 33,007 McGovern; 5,401 Yorty; 3,563 Mills (write-in); 2,417 Hartke; 954 Kennedy (write-in); 348 Humphrey (write-in); 280 Coll; 197 Jackson (write-in); 175 Wallace (write-in); 1,277 scattered write-in.

**NEW JERSEY JUNE 6**

Republican   215,719 Unpledged at-large delegates.

Democratic   51,433 Chisholm; 25,401 Sanford.

**NEW MEXICO JUNE 6**

Republican   49,067 Nixon; 3,367 McCloskey; 3,035 None of the Names Shown.

Democratic   51,011 McGovern; 44,843 Wallace; 39,768 Humphrey; 6,411 Muskie; 4,236 Jackson; 3,819 None of the Names Shown; 3,205 Chisholm.

**NORTH CAROLINA MAY 6**

Republican   159,167 Nixon; 8,732 McCloskey.

Democratic   413,518 Wallace; 306,014 Sanford; 61,723 Chisholm; 30,739 Muskie; 9,416 Jackson.

**OHIO MAY 2**

Republican   692,828 Nixon.

Democratic   499,680 Humphrey; 480,320 McGovern; 107,806 Muskie; 98,498 Jackson; 26,026 McCarthy.

# 1972 PRESIDENTIAL PRIMARIES

**OREGON MAY 23**

Republican   231,151 Nixon; 29,365 McCloskey; 16,696 Ashbrook; 4,798 scattered write-in.

Democratic   205,328 McGovern; 81,868 Wallace; 51,163 Humphrey; 22,042 Jackson; 12,673 Kennedy; 10,244 Muskie; 8,943 McCarthy; 6,500 Mink; 5,082 Lindsay; 2,975 Chisholm; 1,208 Mills; 618 scattered write-in.

**PENNSYLVANIA APRIL 25**

Republican   No candidate names appeared on the ballot and all votes were write-in as follows: 153,886 Nixon; 30,915 scattered write-in. The write-in votes were cast mostly for the Democratic candidates including 20,472 for Wallace.

Democratic   481,900 Humphrey; 292,437 Wallace; 280,861 McGovern; 279,983 Muskie; 38,767 Jackson; 306 Chisholm (write-in); 585 scattered write-in.

**RHODE ISLAND MAY 23**

Republican   4,953 Nixon; 337 McCloskey; 175 Ashbrook; 146 Uncommitted.

Democratic   15,603 McGovern; 7,838 Muskie; 7,701 Humphrey; 5,802 Wallace; 490 Uncommitted; 245 McCarthy; 138 Jackson; 41 Mills; 6 Yorty.

**SOUTH DAKOTA JUNE 6**

Republican   52,820 Nixon slate.

Democratic   28,017 McGovern slate.

**TENNESSEE MAY 4**

Republican   109,696 Nixon; 2,419 Ashbrook; 2,370 McCloskey; 4 scattered write-in.

Democratic   335,858 Wallace; 78,350 Humphrey; 35,551 McGovern; 18,809 Chisholm; 9,634 Muskie; 5,896 Jackson; 2,543 Mills; 2,267 McCarthy; 1,621 Hartke; 1,476 Lindsay; 692 Yorty; 24 scattered write-in.

**WEST VIRGINIA MAY 9**

Republican   95,813 Unpledged at-large delegates.

Democratic   246,596 Humphrey; 121,888 Wallace.

**WISCONSIN APRIL 4**

Republican   277,601 Nixon; 3,651 McCloskey; 2,604 Ashbrook; 2,315 None of the Names Shown; 273 scattered write-in.

Democratic   333,528 McGovern; 248,676 Wallace; 233,748 Humphrey; 115,811 Muskie; 88,068 Jackson; 75,579 Lindsay; 15,543 McCarthy; 9,198 Chisholm; 2,450 None of the Names Shown; 2,349 Yorty; 1,213 Mink; 913 Mills; 766 Hartke; 183 Kennedy (write-in); 559 scattered write-in.

**DISTRICT OF COLUMBIA MAY 2**

Republican   No primary held; no slates entered.

Democratic   21,217 Fauntroy slate; 8,343 Uncommitted slate.

# 1972 REPUBLICAN PREFERENCE PRIMARIES

| Date | | State | Total Vote | Nixon | Ashbrook | McCloskey | Other |
|------|---|-------|-----------|-------|----------|-----------|-------|
| March | 7 | New Hampshire | 117,208 | 79,239 | 11,362 | 23,190 | 3,417 |
| | 14 | Florida | 414,207 | 360,278 | 36,617 | 17,312 | — |
| | 21 | Illinois | 33,569 | 32,550 * | 170 * | 47 * | 802 |
| April | 4 | Wisconsin | 286,444 | 277,601 | 2,604 | 3,651 | 2,588 |
| | 25 | Massachusetts | 122,139 | 99,150 | 4,864 | 16,435 | 1,690 |
| | 25 | Pennsylvania | 184,801 | 153,886 * | — | — | 30,915 |
| May | 2 | District of Columbia | No Primary Held | — | — | — | — |
| | 2 | Indiana | 417,069 | 417,069 | — | — | — |
| | 2 | Ohio | 692,828 | 692,828 | — | — | — |
| | 4 | Tennessee | 114,489 | 109,696 | 2,419 | 2,370 | 4 |
| | 6 | North Carolina | 167,899 | 159,167 | — | 8,732 | — |
| | 9 | Nebraska | 194,272 | 179,464 | 4,996 | 9,011 | 801 |
| | 9 | West Virginia | 95,813 | — | — | — | 95,813 |
| | 16 | Maryland | 115,249 | 99,308 | 6,718 | 9,223 | — |
| | 16 | Michigan | 336,743 | 321,652 | — | 9,691 | 5,400 |
| | 23 | Rhode Island | 5,611 | 4,953 | 175 | 337 | 146 |
| | 23 | Oregon | 282,010 | 231,151 | 16,696 | 29,365 | 4,798 |
| June | 6 | California | 2,283,922 | 2,058,825 | 224,922 | — | 175 |
| | 6 | New Jersey | 215,719 | — | — | — | 215,719 |
| | 6 | New Mexico | 55,469 | 49,067 | — | 3,367 | 3,035 |
| | 6 | South Dakota | 52,820 | 52,820 | — | — | — |
| | | Total | 6,188,281 | 5,378,704 | 311,543 | 132,731 | 365,303 |
| | | | | 86.9% | 5.0% | 2.1% | 5.9% |

An asterisk (*) indicates write-in. Other vote includes 317,048 Uncommitted; 5,350 None of These Names; 1,211 Paulsen; 41,694 scattered write-in.

# 1972 DEMOCRATIC PREFERENCE PRIMARIES

| Date | | State | Total Vote | Humphrey | McGovern | Wallace | Muskie | McCarthy | Henry M. Jackson | Other |
|---|---|---|---|---|---|---|---|---|---|---|
| March | 7 | New Hampshire | 88,854 | 348 * | 33,007 | 175 * | 41,235 | — | 197 * | 13,892 |
| | 14 | Florida | 1,264,554 | 234,658 | 78,232 | 526,651 | 112,523 | 5,847 | 170,156 | 136,487 |
| | 21 | Illinois | 1,225,144 | 1,476 * | 3,687 * | 7,017 * | 766,914 | 444,260 | 442 * | 1,348 |
| April | 4 | Wisconsin | 1,128,584 | 233,748 | 333,528 | 248,676 | 115,811 | 15,543 | 88,068 | 93,210 |
| | 25 | Massachusetts | 618,516 | 48,929 | 325,673 | 45,807 | 131,709 | 8,736 | 8,499 | 49,163 |
| | 25 | Pennsylvania | 1,374,839 | 481,900 | 280,861 | 292,437 | 279,983 | — | 38,767 | 891 |
| May | 2 | District of Columbia | 29,560 | — | — | — | — | — | — | 29,560 |
| | 2 | Indiana | 751,458 | 354,244 | — | 309,495 | 87,719 | — | — | — |
| | 2 | Ohio | 1,212,330 | 499,680 | 480,320 | | 107,806 | 26,026 | 98,498 | — |
| | 4 | Tennessee | 492,721 | 78,350 | 35,551 | 335,858 | 9,634 | 2,267 | 5,896 | 25,165 |
| | 6 | North Carolina | 821,410 | — | — | 413,518 | 30,739 | — | 9,416 | 367,737 |
| | 9 | Nebraska | 192,137 | 65,968 | 79,309 | 23,912 | 6,886 | 3,194 | 5,276 | 7,592 |
| | 9 | West Virginia | 368,484 | 246,596 | — | 121,888 | — | — | — | — |
| | 16 | Maryland | 568,131 | 151,981 | 126,978 | 219,687 | 13,363 | 4,691 | 17,728 | 33,703 |
| | 16 | Michigan | 1,588,073 | 249,798 | 425,694 | 809,239 | 38,701 | — | 6,938 | 57,703 |
| | 23 | Rhode Island | 37,864 | 7,701 | 15,603 | 5,802 | 7,838 | 245 | 138 | 537 |
| | 23 | Oregon | 408,644 | 51,163 | 205,328 | 81,868 | 10,244 | 8,943 | 22,042 | 29,056 |
| June | 6 | California | 3,564,518 | 1,375,064 | 1,550,652 | 268,551 * | 72,701 | 34,203 | 28,901 | 234,446 |
| | 6 | New Jersey | 76,834 | — | — | — | — | — | — | 76,834 |
| | 6 | New Mexico | 153,293 | 39,768 | 51,011 | 44,843 | 6,411 | — | 4,236 | 7,024 |
| | 6 | South Dakota | 28,017 | — | 28,017 | — | — | — | — | — |
| | | Total | 15,993,965 | 4,121,372 | 4,053,451 | 3,755,424 | 1,840,217 | 553,955 | 505,198 | 1,164,348 |
| | | | | 25.8% | 25.3% | 23.5% | 11.5% | 3.5% | 3.2% | 7.3% |

An asterisk (*) indicates write-in. Other vote includes 430,703 Chisholm; 331,415 Sanford; 196,406 Lindsay; 79,446 Yorty; 37,401 Mills; 21,217 Fauntroy; 19,533 Uncommitted; 16,693 Kennedy; 11,798 Hartke; 8,286 Mink; 6,269 None of the Names Shown; 869 Coll; 4,312 scattered write-in.

# 1968 PRESIDENTIAL PRIMARIES

In 1968 fourteen states and the District of Columbia held Presidential primaries. In some states balloting was for delegate slates pledged to specific Presidential candidates or uncommitted; in others, electors indicated a personal preference as to their party's nominee.

The state-by-state Republican and Democratic tables, included at the end of this section, detail in chronological order the vote for major candidates in each party. An asterisk in the table indicates votes written-in for a candidate not on the ballot.

Republican candidates who were on the ballot in at least one state or who received substantial write-in votes were Elmer W. Coy, Don DuMont, William E. Evans, Herbert F. Hoover, Americus Liberator, Richard M. Nixon, Ronald Reagan, James A. Rhodes, Nelson A. Rockefeller, George W. Romney, Raymond P. Shafer, Harold E. Stassen, Willis E. Stone, John A. Volpe and David Watumull.

Democratic candidates who were on the ballot in at least one state or who received substantial write-in votes were Roger D. Branigin, John G. Crommelin, Jacob J. Gordon, Hubert H. Humphrey, Lyndon B. Johnson, Edward M. Kennedy, Robert F. Kennedy, Richard E. Lee, Eugene J. McCarthy, George A. Smathers, George C. Wallace and Stephen M. Young.

## CALIFORNIA JUNE 4

Republican   1,525,091 Reagan slate.

Democratic   1,472,166 Robert F. Kennedy slate; 1,329,301 McCarthy slate; 380,286 No Preference slate.

## FLORIDA MAY 28

Republican   51,509 No Preference slate.

Democratic   236,242 Smathers slate; 147,216 McCarthy slate; 128,899 No Preference slate.

## ILLINOIS JUNE 11

Republican   No candidate names appeared on the ballot and all votes were write-in as follows: 17,490 Nixon; 2,165 Rockefeller; 1,601 Reagan; 1,147 scattered write-in.

Democratic   No candidate names appeared on the ballot and all votes were write-in as follows: 4,646 McCarthy; 4,052 Edward M. Kennedy; 2,059 Humphrey; 1,281 scattered write-in.

## INDIANA MAY 7

Republican   508,362 Nixon.

Democratic   328,118 Robert F. Kennedy; 238,700 Branigin; 209,695 McCarthy.

## MASSACHUSETTS APRIL 30

Republican   31,964 Rockefeller (write-in); 31,465 Volpe; 27,447 Nixon (write-in); 1,770 Reagan (write-in); 13,875 scattered write-in.

Democratic   122,697 McCarthy; 68,604 Robert F. Kennedy (write-in); 44,156 Humphrey (write-in); 6,890 Johnson (write-in); 1,688 Wallace (write-in); 4,868 scattered write-in.

## NEBRASKA MAY 14

Republican   140,336 Nixon; 42,703 Reagan; 10,225 Rockefeller (write-in); 2,638 Stassen; 1,302 Liberator; 3,272 scattered write-in.

Democratic   84,102 Robert F. Kennedy; 50,655 McCarthy; 12,087 Humphrey (write-in); 9,187 Johnson; 1,298 Wallace (write-in); 5,282 scattered write-in.

# 1968 PRESIDENTIAL PRIMARIES

## NEW HAMPSHIRE MARCH 12

Republican   80,666 Nixon; 11,241 Rockefeller (write-in); 1,743 Romney; 527 Stone; 429 Stassen; 247 Hoover; 161 Watumull; 151 Evans; 73 Coy; 39 DuMont; 8,661 scattered write-in.

Democratic   27,520 Johnson (write-in); 23,263 McCarthy; 186 Crommelin; 170 Lee; 77 Gordon; 4,248 scattered write-in.

## NEW JERSEY JUNE 4

Republican   No candidate names appeared on the ballot and all votes were write-in as follows: 71,809 Nixon; 11,530 Rockefeller; 2,737 Reagan; 2,516 scattered write-in.

Democratic   No candidate names appeared on the ballot and all votes were write-in as follows: 9,906 McCarthy; 8,603 Robert F. Kennedy; 5,578 Humphrey; 1,399 Wallace; 1,960 scattered write-in.

## OHIO MAY 7

Republican   614,492 Rhodes slate.

Democratic   549,140 Young slate.

## OREGON MAY 28

Republican   203,037 Nixon; 63,707 Reagan; 36,305 Rockefeller (write-in); 9,110 scattered write-in.

Democratic   163,990 McCarthy; 141,631 Robert F. Kennedy; 45,174 Johnson; 12,421 Humphrey (write-in); 957 Wallace (write-in); 8,897 scattered write-in.

## PENNSYLVANIA APRIL 23

Republican   No candidate names appeared on the ballot and all votes were write-in as follows: 171,815 Nixon; 52,915 Rockefeller; 7,934 Reagan; 1,223 Shafer; 53,686 scattered write-in.

Democratic   428,259 McCarthy; 65,430 Robert F. Kennedy (write-in); 51,998 Humphrey (write-in); 24,147 Wallace (write-in); 21,265 Johnson (write-in); 5,990 scattered write-in.

## SOUTH DAKOTA JUNE 4

Republican   68,113 Nixon slate.

Democratic   31,826 Robert F. Kennedy slate; 19,316 Johnson slate; 13,145 McCarthy slate.

## WEST VIRGINIA MAY 14

Republican   81,039 Unpledged at-large delegates.

Democratic   149,282 Unpledged at-large delegates.

## WISCONSIN APRIL 2

Republican   390,368 Nixon; 50,727 Reagan; 28,531 Stassen; 7,995 Rockefeller (write-in); 6,763 No Preference; 2,087 Romney (write-in); 3,382 scattered write-in.

Democratic   412,160 McCarthy; 253,696 Johnson; 46,507 Robert F. Kennedy (write-in); 11,861 No Preference; 4,031 Wallace (write-in); 3,605 Humphrey (write-in); 1,142 scattered write-in.

# 1968 PRESIDENTIAL PRIMARIES

**DISTRICT OF COLUMBIA MAY 7**

Republican  12,102 pledged delegate slate (Prior the primary, the D. C. Republican organization had decided that of its nine delegates to the National convention six would be pledged to Nixon and 3 pledged to Rockefeller); 1,328 unpledged delegate slate.

Democratic  57,555 Robert F. Kennedy slate; 32,309 Humphrey slate; 2,250 Independent Humphrey slate.

# 1968 REPUBLICAN PREFERENCE PRIMARIES

| Date | | State | Total Vote | Reagan | Nixon | Rhodes | Rockefeller | Uncommitted | Other |
|------|---|-------|-----------|--------|-------|--------|-------------|-------------|-------|
| March | 12 | New Hampshire | 103,938 | — | 80,666 | — | 11,241 * | — | 12,031 |
| April | 2 | Wisconsin | 489,853 | 50,727 | 390,368 | — | 7,995 * | 6,763 | 34,000 |
| | 23 | Pennsylvania | 287,573 | 7,934 * | 171,815 * | — | 52,915 * | — | 54,909 |
| | 30 | Massachusetts | 106,521 | 1,770 * | 27,447 * | — | 31,964 * | — | 45,340 |
| May | 7 | District of Columbia | 13,430 | — | — | — | — | 1,328 | 12,102 |
| | 7 | Indiana | 508,362 | — | 508,362 | — | — | — | — |
| | 7 | Ohio | 614,492 | — | — | 614,492 | — | — | — |
| | 14 | Nebraska | 200,476 | 42,703 | 140,336 | — | 10,225 * | — | 7,212 |
| | 14 | West Virginia | 81,039 | — | — | — | — | 81,039 | — |
| | 28 | Florida | 51,509 | — | — | — | — | 51,509 | — |
| | 28 | Oregon | 312,159 | 63,707 | 203,037 | — | 36,305 * | — | 9,110 |
| June | 4 | California | 1,525,091 | 1,525,091 | — | — | — | — | — |
| | 4 | New Jersey | 88,592 | 2,737 * | 71,809 * | — | 11,530 * | — | 2,516 |
| | 4 | South Dakota | 68,113 | — | 68,113 | — | — | — | — |
| | 11 | Illinois | 22,403 | 1,601 * | 17,490 * | — | 2,165 * | — | 1,147 |
| | | Total | 4,473,551 | 1,696,270 | 1,679,443 | 614,492 | 164,340 | 140,639 | 178,367 |
| | | | | 37.9% | 37.5% | 13.7% | 3.7% | 3.1% | 4.0% |

As asterisk (*) indicates write-in votes. Other vote includes 31,598 Stassen; 31,465 Volpe; 12,102 DC split delegation; 3,830 Romney; 1,302 Liberator; 1,223 Shafer; 527 Stone; 247 Hoover; 161 Watumull; 151 Evans; 73 Coy; 39 DuMont; 95,649 scattered write-in.

# 1968 DEMOCRATIC PREFERENCE PRIMARIES

| Date | | State | Total Vote | McCarthy | Robert F. Kennedy | Johnson | Humphrey | Uncommitted | Other |
|------|---|-------|-----------|----------|------------------|---------|----------|-------------|-------|
| March | 12 | New Hampshire | 55,464 | 23,263 | — | 27,520 * | — | — | 4,681 |
| April | 2 | Wisconsin | 733,002 | 412,160 | 46,507 * | 253,696 | 3,605 * | 11,861 | 5,173 |
| | 23 | Pennsylvania | 597,089 | 428,259 | 65,430 * | 21,265 * | 51,998 * | — | 30,137 |
| | 30 | Massachusetts | 248,903 | 122,697 | 68,604 * | 6,890 * | 44,156 * | — | 6,556 |
| May | 7 | District of Columbia | 92,114 | — | 57,555 | — | 34,559 | — | — |
| | 7 | Indiana | 776,513 | 209,695 | 328,118 | — | — | — | 238,700 |
| | 7 | Ohio | 549,140 | — | — | — | — | — | 549,140 |
| | 14 | Nebraska | 162,611 | 50,655 | 84,102 | 9,187 * | 12,087 * | — | 6,580 |
| | 14 | West Virginia | 149,282 | — | — | — | — | 149,282 | — |
| | 28 | Florida | 512,357 | 147,216 | — | — | — | 128,899 | 236,242 |
| | 28 | Oregon | 373,070 | 163,990 | 141,631 | 45,174 | 12,421 * | — | 9,854 |
| June | 4 | California | 3,181,753 | 1,329,301 | 1,472,166 | — | — | 380,286 | — |
| | 4 | New Jersey | 27,446 | 9906 * | 8603 * | — | 5578 * | — | 3359 |
| | 4 | South Dakota | 64,287 | 13,145 | 31,826 | 19,316 | — | — | — |
| | 11 | Illinois | 12,038 | 4,646 * | — | — | 2,059 * | — | 5,333 |
| | | Total | 7,535,069 | 2,914,933 | 2,304,542 | 383,048 | 166,463 | 670,328 | 1,095,755 |
| | | | | 38.7% | 30.6% | 5.1% | 2.2% | 8.9% | 14.5% |

An asterisk (*) indicates write-in. Other vote includes 549,140 Young; 238,700 Branigin; 236,242 Smathers; 33,520 Wallace; 4,052 Edward M. Kennedy; 186 Crommelin; 170 Lee; 77 Gordon; 33,668 scattered write-in.

# 1964 PRESIDENTIAL PRIMARIES

In 1964 sixteen states and the District of Columbia held Presidential primaries though there was no Republican voting in the District of Columbia and no Democratic voting in Texas.

In some states balloting was for delegate slates pledged to specific Presidential candidates or uncommitted; in others, electors indicated a personal preference as to their party's nominee.

The state-by-state Republican and Democratic tables, included at the end of this section, detail in chronological order the vote for major candidates in each party. An asterisk in the table indicates votes written-in for a candidate not on the ballot.

Republican candidates on the ballot in at least one state were Frank R. Beckwith, John W. Byrnes, Robert E. Ennis, Joseph G. Ettl, Barry M. Goldwater, Norman LePage, Henry Cabot Lodge, Richard M. Nixon, James A. Rhodes, Nelson A. Rockefeller, William W. Scranton, Margaret Chase Smith, Harold E. Stassen and John W. Steffey.

Democratic candidates on the ballot in at least one state were Daniel B. Brewster, Lar Daly, Andrew J. Easter, Lyndon B. Johnson, John H. Latham, Albert S. Porter, John W. Reynolds, Fay T. Carpenter Swain, George C. Wallace and Matthew E. Welsh.

## CALIFORNIA JUNE 2

Republican   1,120,403 Goldwater slate; 1,052,053 Rockefeller slate.

Democratic   1,693,813 No Preference slate (Edmund G. Brown, Sr., chairman); 798,431 No Preference slate (Samuel W. Yorty, chairman).

## FLORIDA MAY 26

Republican   58,179 No Preference slate; 42,525 Goldwater slate.

Democratic   393,339 Johnson slate.

## ILLINOIS APRIL 14

Republican   512,840 Goldwater; 209,521 Smith; 68,122 Lodge; 30,313 Nixon; 2,048 Rockefeller (write-in); 1,842 Scranton (write-in); 465 Romney (write-in); 2,640 scattered write-in.

Democratic   No candidate names appeared on the ballot and all votes were write-in as follows: 82,027 Johnson; 3,761 Wallace; 2,894 Robert F. Kennedy; 841 scattered write-in.

## INDIANA MAY 5

Republican   267,935 Goldwater; 107,157 Stassen; 17,884 Beckwith; 6,704 Ettl.

Democratic   376,023 Welsh; 172,646 Wallace; 15,160 Daly; 8,067 Latham; 7,140 Swain.

## MARYLAND MAY 19

Republican   57,004 Uninstructed delegation; 22,135 Steffey; 18,859 Ennis.

Democratic   267,106 Brewster; 214,849 Wallace; 12,377 Uninstructed delegation; 8,275 Easter.

# 1964 PRESIDENTIAL PRIMARIES

**MASSACHUSETTS APRIL 28**

Republican    No candidate names appeared on the ballot and all votes were write-in as follows: 70,809 Henry Cabot Lodge; 9,338 Goldwater; 5,460 Nixon; 2,454 Rockefeller; 1,709 Scranton; 426 Smith; 365 George C. Lodge; 262 Romney; 1,311 scattered write-in.

Democratic    No candidate names appeared on the ballot and all votes were write-in as follows: 61,035 Johnson; 15,870 Robert F. Kennedy; 1,259 Edward M. Kennedy; 565 Wallace; 452 Stevenson; 323 Humphrey; 3,705 scattered write-in.

**NEBRASKA MAY 12**

Republican    68,050 Goldwater; 43,613 Nixon (write-in); 22,622 Lodge (write-in); 2,333 Rockefeller (write-in); 578 Scranton (write-in); 1,326 scattered write-in.

Democratic    No candidate names appeared on the ballot and all votes were write-in as follows: 54,713 Johnson; 1,099 Robert F. Kennedy; 1,067 Wallace; 3,391 scattered write-in.

**NEW HAMPSHIRE MARCH 10**

Republican    33,007 Lodge (write-in); 20,692 Goldwater; 19,504 Rockefeller; 15,587 Nixon (write-in); 2,120 Smith; 1,373 Stassen; 105 Scranton (write-in); 82 LePage; 383 scattered write-in.

Democratic    No candidate names appeared on the ballot and all votes were write-in as follows: 29,317 Johnson; 487 Robert F. Kennedy; 973 scattered write-in.

**NEW JERSEY APRIL 21**

Republican    No candidate names appeared on the ballot and all votes were write-in as follows: 7,896 Lodge; 5,309 Goldwater; 4,179 Nixon; 633 Scranton; 612 Rockefeller; 304 scattered write-in.

Democratic    No candidate names appeared on the ballot and all votes were write-in as follows: 4,863 Johnson; 491 Wallace; 431 Robert F. Kennedy; 124 scattered write-in.

**OHIO MAY 5**

Republican    615,754 Rhodes statewide delegate slate.

Democratic    493,619 Porter statewide delegate slate.

**OREGON MAY 15**

Republican    94,190 Rockefeller; 79,169 Lodge; 50,105 Goldwater; 48,274 Nixon; 8,087 Smith; 4,509 Scranton; 1,152 scattered write-in.

Democratic    272,099 Johnson; 1,365 Wallace (write-in).

**PENNSYLVANIA APRIL 28**

Republican    No candidate names appeared on the ballot and all votes were write-in as follows: 235,222 Scranton; 92,712 Lodge; 44,396 Nixon; 38,669 Goldwater; 9,123 Rockefeller; 32,746 scattered write-in.

Democratic    No candidate names appeared on the ballot and all votes were write-in as follows: 209,606 Johnson; 12,104 Wallace; 12,029 Robert F. Kennedy; 19,489 scattered write-in.

# 1964 PRESIDENTIAL PRIMARIES

**SOUTH DAKOTA JUNE 2**

Republican  57,653 No Preference slate; 27,076 Goldwater slate.

Democratic  28,142 No Preference slate.

**TEXAS MAY 2**

Republican  104,137 Goldwater; 12,324 Lodge (write-in); 6,207 Rockefeller; 5,390 Nixon (write-in); 5,273 Stassen; 4,816 Smith; 803 Scranton (write-in); 373 scattered write-in.

Democratic  No primary held.

**WEST VIRGINIA MAY 12**

Republican  115,680 Rockefeller.

Democratic  131,432 Unpledged at-large delegates.

**WISCONSIN APRIL 7**

Republican  299,612 Byrnes slate; 816 Unpledged delegate.

Democratic  522,405 Reynolds slate; 266,136 Wallace slate.

**DISTRICT OF COLUMBIA MAY 5**

Republican  No primary held.

Democratic  41,095 Unpledged delegate slate.

# 1964 REPUBLICAN PREFERENCE PRIMARIES

| Date | | State | Total Vote | Goldwater | Rockefeller | Rhodes | Lodge | Byrnes | Other |
|------|------|-------|-----------|-----------|-------------|--------|-------|--------|-------|
| March | 10 | New Hampshire | 92,853 | 20,692 | 19,504 | — | 33,007 * | — | 19,650 |
| April | 7 | Wisconsin | 300,428 | — | — | — | — | 299,612 | 816 |
| | 14 | Illinois | 827,791 | 512,840 | 2,048 * | — | 68,122 * | — | 244,781 |
| | 21 | New Jersey | 18,933 | 5,309 | 612 * | — | 7,896 * | — | 5,116 |
| | 28 | Massachusetts | 92,134 | 9,338 * | 2,454 * | — | 70,809 * | — | 9,533 |
| | 28 | Pennsylvania | 452,868 | 38,669 * | 9,123 * | — | 92,712 * | — | 312,364 |
| May | 2 | Texas | 139,323 | 104,137 | 6,207 | — | 12,324 * | — | 16,655 |
| | 5 | District of Columbia | No Primary Held | — | — | — | — | — | — |
| | 5 | Indiana | 399,680 | 267,935 | — | — | — | — | 131,745 |
| | 5 | Ohio | 615,754 | — | — | 615,754 | — | — | — |
| | 12 | Nebraska | 138,522 | 68,050 | 2,333 * | — | 22,622 * | — | 45,517 |
| | 12 | West Virginia | 115,680 | — | 115,680 | — | — | — | — |
| | 15 | Oregon | 285,486 | 50,105 | 94,190 | — | 79,169 | — | 62,022 |
| | 19 | Maryland | 97,998 | — | — | — | — | — | 97,998 |
| | 26 | Florida | 100,704 | 42,525 | — | — | — | — | 58,179 |
| June | 2 | California | 2,172,456 | 1,120,403 | 1,052,053 | — | — | — | — |
| | 2 | South Dakota | 84,729 | 27,076 | — | — | — | — | 57,653 |
| | | Total | 5,935,339 | 2,267,079 | 1,304,204 | 615,754 | 386,661 | 299,612 | 1,062,029 |
| | | | | 38.2% | 22.0% | 10.4% | 6.5% | 5.0% | 17.9% |

An asterisk (*) indicates write-in votes. Other vote includes 245,451 Scranton; 224,970 Smith; 197,212 Nixon; 173,652 Uncommitted; 113,803 Stassen; 22,135 Steffey; 18,859 Ennis; 17,884 Beckwith; 6,704 Ettl; 727 Romney; 365 George C. Lodge; 82 LePage; 40,185 scattered write-in.

# 1964 DEMOCRATIC PREFERENCE PRIMARIES

| Date | | State | Total Vote | Johnson | Wallace | Reynolds | Porter | Welsh | Uncommitted | Other |
|------|---|-------|-----------|---------|---------|----------|--------|-------|-------------|-------|
| March | 10 | New Hampshire | 30,777 | 29,317 * | — | — | — | — | — | 1,460 |
| April | 7 | Wisconsin | 788,541 | — | 266,136 | 522,405 | — | — | — | — |
| | 14 | Illinois | 89,523 | 82,027 * | 3,761 * | — | — | — | — | 3,735 |
| | 21 | New Jersey | 5,909 | 4,863 * | 491 * | — | — | — | — | 555 |
| | 28 | Massachusetts | 83,209 | 61,035 * | 565 * | — | — | — | — | 21,609 |
| | 28 | Pennsylvania | 253,228 | 209,606 * | 12,104 * | — | — | — | — | 31,518 |
| May | 2 | Texas | No Primary Held | — | — | — | — | — | — | — |
| | 5 | District of Columbia | 41,095 | — | — | — | — | — | 41,095 | — |
| | 5 | Indiana | 579,036 | — | 172,646 | — | — | 376,023 | — | 30,367 |
| | 5 | Ohio | 493,619 | — | — | — | 493,619 | — | — | — |
| | 12 | Nebraska | 61,270 | 54,713 * | 1,067 * | — | — | — | — | 5,490 |
| | 12 | West Virginia | 131,432 | — | — | — | — | — | 131,432 | — |
| | 15 | Oregon | 273,464 | 272,099 | 1,365 * | — | — | — | — | — |
| | 19 | Maryland | 502,607 | — | 214,849 | — | — | — | 12,377 | 275,381 |
| | 26 | Florida | 393,339 | 393,339 | — | — | — | — | — | — |
| June | 2 | California | 2,492,244 | — | — | — | — | — | 2,492,244 | — |
| | 2 | South Dakota | 28,142 | — | — | — | — | — | 28,142 | — |
| | | Total | 6,247,435 | 1,106,999 | 672,984 | 522,405 | 493,619 | 376,023 | 2,705,290 | 370,115 |
| | | | | 17.7% | 10.8% | 8.4% | 7.9% | 6.0% | 43.3% | 5.9% |

An asterisk (*) indicates write-in votes. Other vote includes 267,106 Brewster; 15,160 Daly; 33,810 Robert F. Kennedy; 8,156 Scranton; 8,275 Easter; 8,067 Swain; 1,259 Edward M. Kennedy; 452 Stevenson; 323 Humphrey; and 27,507 scattered write-in.

# 1960 PRESIDENTIAL PRIMARIES

In 1960 fifteen states and the District of Columbia held Presidential primaries though there was no Republican voting in Maryland.

In some states balloting was for delegate slates pledged to specific Presidential candidates or uncommitted; in others, electors indicated a personal preference as to their party's nominee.

The state-by-state Republican and Democratic tables, included at the end of this section, detail in chronological order the vote for major candidates in each party. An asterisk in the table indicates votes written-in for a candidate not on the ballot.

Republican candidates on the ballot in at least one state were Frank R. Beckwith and Richard M. Nixon.

Democratic candidates on the ballot in at least one state were Edmund G. Brown, Sr., Lar Daly, Michael V. DiSalle, Andrew J. Easter, Paul C. Fisher, Hubert H. Humphrey, Lyndon B. Johnson, John F. Kennedy, John H. Latham, George H. McLain, Wayne L. Morse, George A. Smathers and Stuart Symington.

## CALIFORNIA JUNE 5

Republican   1,517,652 Nixon.

Democratic   1,354,031 Brown slate; 646,387 McLain slate.

## FLORIDA MAY 24

Republican   51,036 Nixon slate.

Democratic   322,235 Smathers slate.

## ILLINOIS APRIL 12

Republican   782,849 Nixon; 442 scattered write-in.

Democratic   No candidate names appeared on the ballot and all votes were write-in as follows: 34,332 Kennedy; 8,029 Adlai E.Stevenson; 5,744 Symington; 4,283 Humphrey; 442 Johnson; 337 scattered write-in.

## INDIANA MAY 3

Republican   408,408 Nixon; 19,677 Beckwith.

Democratic   353,832 Kennedy; 42,084 Latham; 40,853 Daly.

## MARYLAND MAY 17

Republican   No primary held; no candidates entered.

Democratic   201,769 Kennedy; 49,420 Morse; 7,536 Daly; 3,881 Easter; 24,350 uninstructed delegation.

## MASSACHUSETTS APRIL 26

Republican   No candidate names appeared on the ballot and all votes were write-in as follows: 53,164 Nixon; 4,068 Nelson Rockefeller; 373 Henry Cabot Lodge; 221 Barry Goldwater; 172 Dwight D. Eisenhower; 3,847 scattered write-in.

Democratic   No candidate names appeared on the ballot and all votes were write-in as follows: 91,607 Kennedy; 4,684 Adlai E. Stevenson; 794 Humphrey; 443 Symington; 268 Johnson; 1,367 scattered write-in.

# 1960 PRESIDENTIAL PRIMARIES

**NEBRASKA MAY 10**

Republican  No candidate names appeared on the ballot and all votes were write-in as follows: 74,356 Nixon; 2,028 Rockefeller; 1,068 Goldwater; 1,805 scattered write-in.

Democratic  80,408 Kennedy; 4,083 Symington (write-in); 3,202 Humphrey (write-in); 1,368 Stevenson (write-in); 962 Johnson (write-in); 669 scattered write-in.

**NEW HAMPSHIRE MARCH 8**

Republican  65,204 Nixon; 2,745 Rockefeller (write-in); 5,082 scattered write-in.

Democratic  43,372 Kennedy; 6,853 Fisher; 674 scattered write-in.

**NEW JERSEY APRIL 19**

Republican  304,766, Unpledged at-large delegates.

Democratic  217,608, Unpledged at-large delegates.

**OHIO MAY 3**

Republican  504,072 Nixon slate.

Democratic  315,312 DiSalle slate.

**OREGON MAY 20**

Republican  211,276 Nixon; 9,307 Rockefeller (write-in); 1,571 Goldwater (write-in); 4,879 scattered write-in.

Democratic  146,332 Kennedy; 91,715 Morse; 16,319 Humphrey; 12,496 Symington; 11,101 Johnson; 7,924 Stevenson (write-in); 1,210 scattered write-in.

**PENNSYLVANIA APRIL 26**

Republican  968,538 Nixon; 12,491 Rockefeller (write-in); 286 Goldwater (write-in); 5,516 scattered write-in.

Democratic  No candidate names appeared on the ballot and all votes were write-in as follows: 183,073 Kennedy; 29,660 Stevenson; 13,860 Humphrey; 6,791 Symington; 2,918 Johnson; 20,511 scattered write-in.

**SOUTH DAKOTA JUNE 7**

Republican  48,461 No Preference slate.

Democratic  24,773 Humphrey slate.

**WEST VIRGINIA MAY 10**

Republican  123,756 Unpledged at-large delegates.

Democratic  236,510 Kennedy; 152,187 Humphrey.

# 1960 PRESIDENTIAL PRIMARIES

**WISCONSIN APRIL 5**

Republican  339,383 Nixon slate.

Democratic  476,024 Kennedy slate; 366,753 Humphrey slate.

**DISTRICT OF COLUMBIA MAY 3**

Republican  9,468 Unpledged delegate slate.

Democratic  8,239 Humphrey; 6,127 Morse.

# 1960 REPUBLICAN PREFERENCE PRIMARIES

| Date | | State | Total Vote | Nixon | Rockefeller | Goldwater | Uncommitted | Other |
|------|---|-------|-----------|-------|-------------|-----------|-------------|-------|
| March | 8 | New Hampshire | 73,031 | 65,204 | 2,745 * | — | — | 5,082 |
| April | 5 | Wisconsin | 339,383 | 339,383 | — | — | — | — |
| | 12 | Illinois | 783,291 | 782,849 | — | — | — | 442 |
| | 19 | New Jersey | 304,766 | — | — | — | 304,766 | — |
| | 26 | Massachusetts | 61,845 | 53,164 * | 4,068 * | 221 * | — | 4,392 |
| | 26 | Pennsylvania | 986,831 | 968,538 | 12,491 * | 286 * | — | 5,516 |
| May | 3 | District of Columbia | 9,468 | — | — | — | 9,468 | — |
| | 3 | Indiana | 428,085 | 408,408 | — | — | — | 19,677 |
| | 3 | Ohio | 504,072 | 504,072 | — | — | — | — |
| | 10 | Nebraska | 79,257 | 74,356 * | 2,028 * | 1,068 * | — | 1,805 |
| | 10 | West Virginia | 123,756 | — | — | — | 123,756 | — |
| | 17 | Maryland | No Primary Held | — | — | — | — | — |
| | 20 | Oregon | 227,033 | 211,276 | 9,307 * | 1,571 * | — | 4,879 |
| | 24 | Florida | 51,036 | 51,036 | — | — | — | — |
| June | 7 | California | 1,517,652 | 1,517,652 | — | — | — | — |
| | 7 | South Dakota | 48,461 | — | — | — | 48,461 | — |
| | | Total | 5,537,967 | 4,975,938 | 30,639 | 3,146 | 486,451 | 41,793 |
| | | | | 89.9% | 0.6% | 0.1% | 8.8% | 0.8% |

An asterisk (*) indicates write-in votes. Other vote includes 19,677 Beckwith; 373 Lodge; 172 Eisenhower; 21,571 scattered write-in.

# 1960 DEMOCRATIC PREFERENCE PRIMARIES

| Date | | State | Total Vote | John F. Kennedy | Brown | McLain | Humphrey | Uncommitted | Other |
|------|---|-------|-----------|-----------------|-------|--------|----------|-------------|-------|
| March | 8 | New Hampshire | 50,899 | 43,372 | — | — | — | — | 7,527 |
| April | 5 | Wisconsin | 842,777 | 476,024 | — | — | 366,753 | — | — |
| | 12 | Illinois | 53,167 | 34,332 * | — | — | 4,283 | — | 14,552 |
| | 19 | New Jersey | 217,608 | — | — | — | — | 217,608 | — |
| | 26 | Massachusetts | 99,163 | 91,607 | — | — | 794 | — | 6,762 |
| | 26 | Pennsylvania | 256,813 | 183,073 * | — | — | 13,860 * | — | 59,880 |
| May | 3 | District of Columbia | 14,366 | — | — | — | 8,239 | — | 6,127 |
| | 3 | Indiana | 436,769 | 353,832 | — | — | — | — | 82,937 |
| | 3 | Ohio | 315,312 | — | — | — | — | — | 315,312 |
| | 10 | Nebraska | 90,692 | 80,408 | — | — | 3,202 * | — | 7,082 |
| | 10 | West Virginia | 388,697 | 236,510 | — | — | 152,187 | — | — |
| | 17 | Maryland | 286,956 | 201,769 | — | — | — | 24,350 | 60,837 |
| | 20 | Oregon | 287,097 | 146,332 | — | — | 16,319 * | — | 124,446 |
| | 24 | Florida | 322,235 | — | — | — | — | — | 322,235 |
| June | 7 | California | 2,000,418 | — | 1,354,031 | 646,387 | — | — | — |
| | 7 | South Dakota | 24,773 | — | — | — | 24,773 | — | — |
| | | Total | 5,687,742 | 1,847,259 | 1,354,031 | 646,387 | 590,410 | 241,958 | 1,007,697 |
| | | | | 32.5% | 23.8% | 11.4% | 10.4% | 4.3% | 17.7% |

An asterisk (*) indicates write-in votes. Other vote includes 322,235 Smathers; 315,312 DiSalle; 147,262 Morse; 51,665 Stevenson; 48,389 Daly; 42,084 Latham; 29,557 Symington; 15,691 Johnson; 6,853 Fisher; 3,881 Easter; 24,768 scattered write-in.